A CHARLTON STANDARD C

HOCKEY CARDS

THIRTEENTH EDITION

published under agreement by

TRAJAN
PUBLISHING CORPORATION

Paul Winkler, Publisher
ST. CATHARINES, ONTARIO

The Charlton Press

W. K. Cross, Publisher
NORTH YORK, ONTARIO ❖ PALM HARBOR, FLORIDA

COVER PHOTO

Hockey Hall of Fame

Canadian Cataloguing in Publication Data

The National Library of Canada has catalogued this publication as follows:

Hockey cards (Toronto, Ont.)
Hockey cards.

Annual.
13th ed.-
Continues: Charlton standard catalogue of hockey cards, ISSN 1188-7737
ISSN 1704-5746
ISBN 0-8896 8-283-6 (13th edition)

1. Hockey cards--Catalogs.

GV847.C5 769'.49796962 C2002-904889-3

Printed in Canada
in the Province of Ontario

TRAJAN PUBLISHING CORPORATION

Editorial Office
103 Lakeshore Road, Suite 202
St. Catharines, Ontario L2N 2T6
Tel: (905) 646-7744 1-800-408-0352
Fax: (905) 646-0995
Web site: www.trajan.ca
E-mail: office@trajan.ca

The Charlton Press

Editorial Office
P.O. Box 820, Station Willowdale B
North York, Ontario M2K 2R1 Canada
Tel: (416) 488-1418 1-800-442-6042
Fax: (416) 488-4656 1-800-442-1542
Web site: www.charltonpress.com
E-mail: chpress@charltonpress.com

EDITORIAL

Editor	Richard Scott
Production Co-ordinator	Jim Szeplaki
Production Team	Sylvie Tremblay
	Mary-Anne Leftley
Advertising Sales	Paolo Del Rio
Publisher	Paul Winkler

ACKNOWLEDGEMENTS

The Charlton Press and Trajan Publishing Corporation wish to thank all of those who have helped and assisted with *The Charlton Standard Catalogue of Hockey Cards.*

The editor would first like to thank his wife Lisa, his family and all Trajan families. He would also like to acknowledge all past *Canadian Sports/Sportscard Collector* editors, *Canadian Sports Collector* associate editor Paolo Del Rio, correspondent Jon Waldman, and the following institutional contributors: Cartes, Timbres, Monnaies Ste-Foy; Fleer Trading Cards; In The Game; Jogo; Pacific Trading Cards; The Topps Company; The Upper Deck Company; the National Hockey League; the National Hockey League Players' Association; the Professional Hockey Players' Association; and the Hockey Hall of Fame.

www.SportsCollector.ca/eTrends.html

AC Card & Comics (Vancouver, BC)
Belushi's Hobbies (Surrey, BC)
Gem Mint Collectibles (Richmond, BC)
John's Collectibles & Cards (Steveston, BC)
Maxx Sports Collectibles (Comox, BC)
Mostly Music (Port Coquitlam, BC)
MVP Sports (Victoria, BC)
Pastime Sports & Games (Langley, BC)
Sports Card Alley (Nanaimo, BC)
All-Star Sports Collectibles (Edmonton, AB)
Chow's Variety (Fort McMurray, AB)
Delta Sports Cards (Edmonton, AB)
Dick's Collectibles (Calgary, AB)
George's II (Sherwood Park, AB)
Harvey's Collectors Corner (Calgary, AB)
Jim's Sports Cards & Collectables (Fort McMurray, AB)
Ultimate Sportscards (Edmonton, AB)
Wayne's Sports Cards (Edmonton, AB)
West's Sports Cards (Edmonton, AB)
AJW Sports Cards (Saskatoon, SK)
Kard Sharks (Regina, SK)
Tramp's (Prince Albert, SK)
Right Way Sports (Winnipeg, MB)
Superstars Sports Collectables (Winnipeg, MB)
Allstar Cards, Comics & Collectables (Brantford, ON)
Dave's Sports Collectibles (Woodstock, ON)
Definitely Dennis (Hanover, ON)
Fresher Sports Cards (London, ON)
Helou Sportscards & Collectibles (Windsor, ON)
J.R. Sports Cards (Elliot Lake, ON)
Kitchener Coin Shop (Kitchener, ON)
Little Shop of Heroes (Listowel, ON)
Lookin' for Heroes (Kitchener, ON)
Martin Sports Cards (Guelph, ON)
MVP Sportscards (Orillia, ON)
Penalty Box, The (Waterloo, ON)
Puck Stops Here, The (Collingwood, ON)
Simcoe Coin & Card (Barrie, ON)
Ultimate Sportscards (North Bay, ON)
A.J. Sports Cards (Toronto, ON)
A.K. Comics & Cards (Agincourt, ON)
Action Coin & Card (Toronto, ON)
Cardboard Memories Inc. (Brampton, ON)
Collector's Edge (Hamilton, ON)
Combination Sports Cards (Hamilton, ON)
Comic Connection (Hamilton, ON)
Fastball Sportscards (Toronto, ON)
Hockey Heaven (King City, ON)
Legends of the Game (Toronto, ON)
M&L Sportscards (Niagara Falls, ON)
Major Leagues (Burlington, ON)
Sliders House of Cards Inc. (Courtice, ON)
Superstars Sports Cards and Collectibles (Hamilton, ON)
Entertainment Ink (Orléans, ON)
Game Breakers Sportscards (Ottawa, ON)
Gananoque All Sports & Collectibles (Gananoque, ON)
Jim's Sports Cards (Ottawa, ON)
Quinte Card Shop (Belleville, ON)
Silver Maple Collectables (Gananoque, ON)
L'ami du collectionneur (Québec, QC)
Cart-o-folie (Sherbrooke, QC)
Coin de la carte sportive (Gatineau, QC)
Collecto Sports (Drummondville, QC)
Mordus de la carte (Joliette, QC)
Raxan Collectibles (Kirkland, QC)
Castlevania Sportscards (Miramichi, NB)
Coin Cabinet, The (Moncton, NB)
Diggers Sports Cards (Sydney, NS)
Strictly Singles (Halifax, NS)
Maverick Sport Collectables (St. John's, NL)

TABLE OF CONTENTS

VINTAGE ISSUES: 1879 - 1943 — 1
Hockey's oldest collectibles from the earliest trade and advertising cards to the first group of BeeHive photos.

ORIGINAL SIX: 1943 - 68 — 23
After World War II and before the 1967-68 NHL expansion, hockey's best players competed in a six-team league.

OPC YEARS: 1968 - 90 — 47
O-Pee-Chee and Topps ruled the post-NHL expansion hockey-card era from 1968 to 1990.

BOOM YEARS: 1990 - 97 — 117
From the entry of three new card companies in 1990-91 to the dawn of the memorabilia cards in 1996-97.

MODERN ISSUES: 1997 - 2003 — 289
The newest era is led by the four fully-licensed card companies, In The Game, Pacific, Topps, and Upper Deck.

NHL TEAM ISSUES — 603
From Anaheim to Winnipeg, everything from club-issued to sponsor-issued team sets.

WHA MINOR, WORLD TEAMS — 627
Sets from the American League, the defunct International League, and other minor-pro leagues.

JUNIOR & COLLEGE TEAM ISSUES — 649
Junior and college team sets, including teams from Canada's WHL, the OHL, and the QMJHL.

INDEX OF PLAYERS — 664
A full index cross-referencing every player in the eight preceeding chapters.

FROM the EDITOR

Welcome to the 13th edition of *A Charlton Standard Catalogue Hockey Cards*. It has been quite the year in the hockey-card market with more than 40 new mainstream brands released over the course of the 2002-03 season. Fourteen of those sets were first-time brands on the hockey-card market.

In this new edition of *A Charlton Standard Catalogue Hockey Cards*, you will find checklists for every one of those 2002-03 hockey-card sets. You will also find checklists for many NHL, minor league, and junior team-issued sets, both from this past season and previous sets.

This book has checklists and price listings for thousands of different card sets. We provide a check-box for each card (and each parallel) so that you can mark off the cards you have or need. All standard league sets are sorted chronologically through 2002-03 while team-issued sets are listed alphabetically in one of three different chapters (NHL, WHA/Minor/World leagues, Junior/College leagues).

We identify teams for individual players and mark all goalies throughout the book. Rookie card collectors will find rookie cards marked "RC" with the line highlighted in bold text. Starting with last year's edition, we also identify autographed cards (✍) and game-used memorabilia cards (✂). When the informations is available, we also add the colour of the jersey swatch.

This year, we have added the autograph and memorabilia symbols to the alphabetical player index. This will help you identify quickly which players have jersey and autographed cards.

We have also added hundreds of new photos to this edition, both from the new 2002-03 season as well as past seasons. For the 1950s and 1960s, we have shown some of the original packaging and advertising pieces for those hockey collectible products.

The most significant change to the old stuff is the year identified with the V356 World Wide Gum hockey-card set. While the set has long been identified as a 1936-37 series, it is now recognized as a 1937-38 series. This change of year affected the rookie-card status of some cards in the V356 set as well as the 1937-38 O-Pee-Chee series (see page 15).

As always, this book would not be possible without the collector, dealer, and industry input that we receive every day. To all those that provide checklists, set information, pricing notes, and special collecting stories, your contributions are always welcome.

From all of us at The Charlton Press and The Trajan Publishing Corporation, please enjoy this book and enjoy collecting.

Cheers,

Richard

CHECKLISTS

CHAPTER ONE
Vintage Issues 1879 To 1943

1879 - 1896 Anonymous Advertising Cards 2
1900 - 1917 Miscellaneous postcards, etc. 2
1908 American Tobacco Co. Flannels 2
1909 - 10 Murad Cigarettes 3
1910 Imperial Tobacco Silks 3
1910 - 11 Imperial Tobacco C56 3
1910 - 11 Sweet Caporal Postacards 3
1910 - 11 Murad Rochester College Card 3
1911 - 12 Imperial Tobacco C55 3
1912 - 13 Imperial Tobacco C57 3
1912 - 13 Richmond Cigarettes 4
1912 - 15 Murad Silks 4
1914 Winter Sports 4
1919 - 1930 Miscellaneous postcards, etc. 4
1919 Vancouver Millionaires 4
1920s Patience Playing Cardss 4
1923 - 24 Crescent Selkirks 4
1923 - 24 Paulins Candy 4
1923 Willard's Chocolates 5
1923 - 24 William Paterson 5
1924 - 25 Champ's Cigarettes 5
1924 - 25 Maple Crispette 5
1924 - 25 Crescent Selkirks 5
1924 - 25 Crescent Falcons 5
1924 - 25 Holland Creameries 5
1924 - 25 William Paterson 5
1925 - 27 Anonymous Issue 8
1925 Dominion Chocolate 8
1926 Dominion Chocolate 8
1927 World of Sport 8
1927 - 28 La Presse 8
1927 - 28 La Patrie 8
1928 World in Pictures 8
1928 - 29 La Presse 8
1928 - 29 Paulins Candy 8
1929 Sports & Games in Many Lands 9
1929 - 30 La Presse 9
1930s A&BC Chewing Gum 9
1930 - 31 La Presse 9
1931 - 32 La Presse 9
1932 - 1942 Miscellaneous postcards, etc. 9
1932 Reemsta Olympia 9
1932 - 33 CCM Grey Border Photos 9
1932 - 33 O'Keefe Coasters 9
1933 Goudey Sport Kings 9
1933 - 34 Boston Garden Magazine Photos 9
1933 - 34 Canadian Chewing Gum 9
1933 - 34 CCM Brown Border Photos 10
1933 - 34 Hamilton Gum 10
1933 - 34 O-Pee-Chee Series A 10
1933 - 34 O-Pee-Chee Series B 10
1933 - 34 V129 10
1933 - 34 World Wide Gum Ice Kings 10
1933 - 35 Diamond Match Silver Series 12
1934 - 35 CCM Green Border Photos 12
1934 - 35 Sweet Caporal Photos 12
1935 J.A. Pattreiouex Ltd. Sporting Events And Stars 12
1935 - 36 Amalgamated Press 12
1935 - 36 CCM Blue Border Photos 12
1935 - 36 O-Pee-Chee Series C 12
1935 - 40 Canada Starch Crown Brand 12
1936 Ronfranck 13
1936 Weitere Werke 13
1936 - 37 O-Pee-Chee Series D 13
1936 - 39 Diamond Match Tan Matchbooks 13
1937 British Sporting Personalities 14
1937 - 38 O-Pee-Chee Series E 14
1937 - 38 World Wide Gum 14
1938 - 39 La Presse Photos 16
1938 - 39 Quaker Oats 16
1939 - 40 O-Pee-Chee 16
1940 - 41 O-Pee-Chee 16
1934 - 43 BeeHive Photos (Group 1) 18

CHAPTER TWO
Original Six Era 1944 To 1968

1945 - 64 BeeHive Photos (Group 2) 24
1940s Hockey 25
1943 - 47 Parade Sportive Photos 25
1945 - 46 Kellogg's All-Wheat 25
1945 - 46 La Presse Photos 25
1945 - 54 Quaker Oats Photos 25
1948 - 52 Exhibits 26
1948 - 59 W. Paterson Long Fellows 26
1948 (C.) Maurice Richard Playing Cards 26
1949 Carreras Ltd. Cigarettes 27
1951 Berk Ross 27
1951 - 52 Bas Du Fleuve 27
1951 - 52 Cleveland Barons 27
1951 - 52 Lac St. Jean 27
1951 - 52 La Patrie Photos 27
1951 - 52 Laval Dairy QHL 27
1951 - 52 Parkhurst 27
1952 Royal Stars of Hockey 28
1952 - 53 Anonymous OHL 28
1952 - 53 Bas Du Fleuve 28
1952 - 53 La Patrie Photos 29
1952 - 53 Laval Dairy QHL Update 29
1952 - 53 Parkhurst 29
1952 - 53 St. Lawrence Sales 29
1953 - 54 La Patrie Photos 30
1953 - 54 Parkhurst 30
1954 Weekend Photos 30
1954 - 55 Parkhurst 30
1954 - 55 Topps 30
1954 - 55 Toronto Star Photos 31
1955 Weekend Photos 31
1955 - 56 Nabisco 31
1955 - 56 Parkhurst 31
1955 - 56 Quaker Oats 31
1955 - 56 Toronto Star Photos 31
1956 Adventure Gum 31
1956 - 57 Toronto Star Photos 31
1957 - 58 Parkhurst 31
1957 - 58 Topps 31
1957 - 58 Toronto Star Photos 32
1958 - 59 Parkhurst 32
1958 - 59 Topps 32
1958 - 59 Toronto Star Photos 32
1958 - 59 Weekend Photos 32
1959 - 60 Parkhurst 32
1959 - 60 Topps 33
1959 - 60 Toronto Star Photos 33
1959 - 60 Weekend Photos 33
1959 - 60 Whitby Dunlops 33
1960 - 61 Cleveland Barons 33
1960 - 61 Parkhurst 33
1960 - 61 Shirriff 33
1960 - 61 Topps 34
1960 - 61 Toronto Star Photos 34
1960 - 61 Weekend Photos 34
1960 - 61 Wonder Bread Wrapper Issue 34
1960 - 61 York Peanut Butter 34
1960 - 61 York Peanut Butter Glasses 34
1961 - 62 Parkhurst 34
1961 - 62 Shirriff & Salada 35
1961 - 62 Topps 35
1961 - 62 Toronto Star Photos 35
1961 - 62 Weekend Photos 35
1961 - 62 York Peanut Butter Yellow Backs 35
1962 - 63 H.M. Cowan Ceramic Tiles 36
1962 - 63 El Producto Disks 36
1962 - 63 Parkhurst 36
1962 - 63 Shirriff Metal Wheels 36

1962 - 63 Topps 36
1962 - 63 Toronto Star Photos 37
1962 - 63 Weekend Photos 37
1962 - 63 York Peanut Butter Iron-On Transfers 37
1963 - 64 Parkhurst 37
1963 - 64 Québec Aces 37
1963 - 64 Topps 38
1963 - 64 Toronto Stars In Action 38
1963 - 64 Toronto Star Photos 38
1963 - 64 Weekend Photos 38
1963 - 64 York Peanut Butter White Backs 38
1963 - 65 Chex Photos 38
1964 - 65 Coca-Cola Caps 39
1964 - 65 Sprite Caps 39
1964 - 65 Topps 39
1964 - 65 Toronto Star 40
1964 - 65 Toronto Star Photos 40
1964 - 67 Eaton's Gordie Howe 40
1965 - 66 Coca-Cola 40
1964 - 65 Cocal-Cola How To Play Booklets 41
1965 - 66 Hellas 41
1965 - 66 Québec Aces 41
1965 - 66 Topps 41
1965 - 66 Toronto Star Photos 42
1965 - 66 Weekend Photos 42
1966 - 67 Champion 42
1966 - 67 Post Hockey Tips 42
1966 - 67 Topps 43
1966 - 67 Topps USA Test Set 43
1966 - 67 Weekend Photos 43
1967 - 68 Post 43
1967 - 68 Post Cereal Flip Books 43
1967 - 68 Topps 43
1967 - 68 York Peanut Butter Disks 44
1964 - 67 BeeHive Photos (Group 3) 44

CHAPTER THREE
O-Pee-Chee Years 1968 - 1990

1968 - 69 Bauer Photos 48
1968 - 69 O-Pee-Chee 48
1968 - 69 Post Marbles 48
1968 - 69 Shirriff 48
1968 - 69 Topps 49
1969 - 70 O-Pee-Chee 49
1969 - 70 Mästar Serien 50
1969 - 70 Soviet Stars 51
1969 - 70 Topps 51
1970 - 71 Colgate Stamps 53
1970 - 71 Dad's Cookies 53
1970 - 71 Eddie Sargent Stickers 53
1970 - 71 Esso Power Players 54
1970 - 71 Kuvajulkaisut 55
1970 - 71 O-Pee-Chee 56
1970 - 71 Post Shooters 57
1970 - 71 Soviet Stars Postcards 57
1970 - 71 Topps 57
1971 Kellogg's Iron On Transfers 57
1971 - 72 Bazooka Panels 57
1971 - 72 Colgate Hockey Heads 57
1971 - 72 Eddie Sargent Stickers 58
1971 - 72 Frito-Lay 58
1971 - 72 O-Pee-Chee 58
1971 - 72 O-Pee-Chee Posters 59
1971 - 72 Pro Star Promotions 59
1971 - 72 Soviet Stars Postcards 59
1971 - 72 Topps 59
1971 - 72 Sun Photos 60
1971 - 72 Williams (Suomi) 61
1972 Hellas MM - Jenkki 62
1972 Panda MM - Toronto 62
1972 Scotia Bank Postcard Issue 62
1972 Semic Stickers 62
1972 - 73 Dimanche / Dernière Photos 63
1972 - 73 Eddie Sargent Stickers 63
1972 - 73 Letraset Action Transfers 64
1972 - 73 O-Pee-Chee 64
1972 - 73 Post Action Transfers 65
1972 - 73 Topps 65
1972 - 73 Williams (Suomi) 66
1973 - 74 Dimanche / Dernière Photos 67
1973 - 74 Mac's Milk 67
1973 - 74 Nabisco Sugar Daddy Pro Faces 67
1973 - 74 O-Pee-Chee 67
1973 - 74 O-Pee-Chee WHA Posters 68
1973 - 74 Quaker Oats 68
1973 - 74 Soviet Champions Postcards 68
1973 - 74 Soviet Stars Postcards 68
1973 - 74 Topps 68
1973 - 74 Williams (Suomi) 69
1974 Hellas MM - Jenkki 70
1974 Scotia Bank Go Canada Postcard 70
1974 Stop Action Hockey Play 70
1974 Semic Stickers 70
1974 - 75 Lipton Soup 71
1974 - 75 Loblaws Action Players 71
1974 - 75 Nabisco Sugar Daddy All-Stars 72
1974 - 75 O-Pee-Chee 72
1974 - 75 O-Pee-Chee WHA 73
1974 - 75 Soviet Stars Postcards 73
1974 - 75 Topps 73
1975 - 76 Hockey Heroes Stand Ups 74
1975 - 76 O-Pee-Chee 74
1975 - 76 O-Pee-Chee WHA 75
1975 - 76 Popsicle 75
1975 - 76 Topps 75
1976 - 77 Dimanche / Dernière Photos 76
1976 - 77 Hockey Digest Blow-In 76
1976 - 77 O-Pee-Chee 76
1976 - 77 O-Pee-Chee WHA 78
1976 - 77 Popsicle 78
1976 - 77 Topps 78
1977 - 78 Coca-Cola Minis 79
1977 - 78 Dimanche / Dernière Photos 79
1977 - 78 Hockey Digest Blow-In 79
1977 - 78 O-Pee-Chee & Topps 79
1977 - 78 O-Pee-Chee WHA 80
1977 - 79 Sportscaster Cards 80
1978 - 79 Dimanche / Dernière Photos 81
1978 - 79 O-Pee-Chee & Topps 81
1978 - 79 SM-Liiga 82
1979 Panini Stickers 82
1979 Soviet National Team Photo Card 83
1979 - 80 Dimanche / Dernière Photos 83
1979 - 80 O-Pee-Chee & Topps 83
1979 - 80 Soviet Stars 84
1980 U.S.A. Olympic Mini-Pics 84
1980 U.S.S.R. Olympic Mini-Pics 84
1980 - 81 Dimanche / Dernière Photos 86
1980 - 81 Mallasjuoma 86
1980 - 81 O-Pee-Chee & Topps 86
1980 - 81 O-Pee-Chee Super Photos 87
1980 - 81 Pepsi Caps 87
1981 - 82 Dimanche / Dernière Photos 88
1981 - 82 O-Pee-Chee 88
1981 - 82 O-Pee-Chee Stickers 89
1981 - 82 Post Stars In Action 90
1981 - 82 TCMA 90
1981 - 82 Topps 90
1982 Mallasjuoma Mm 90
1982 Semic Stickers 90
1982 Skopbank 91
1982 Valio 91
1982 - 83 Dimanche / Dernière Photos 91
1982 - 83 McDonald's Stickers 91
1982 - 83 Neilson's Wayne Gretzy 91
1982 - 83 O-Pee-Chee 91
1982 - 83 O-Pee-Chee / Topps Stickers 92
1982 - 83 Post 93
1982 - 83 Stater Mint Hockey Dollars 93
1983 Canadian Junior Team Postcards 93
1983 Hockey Hall Of Fame Postcards 94
1983 & 87 Hockey Hall Of Fame Cards 94
1983 - 84 Dimanche / Dernière Photos 95
1983 - 84 Esso 95
1983 - 84 Funmate Puffy Stickers 95
1983 - 84 O-Pee-Chee 95
1983 - 84 O-Pee-Chee / Topps Stickers 96
1983 - 84 Souhaits Renaissance Keychains 97
1983 - 84 Soviet Stars 98
1983 - 84 Stater Mint Hockey Dollars 98
1983 - 84 Vachon 98
1984 - 85 Islander News Bryan Trottier 98
1984 - 85 Kellogg's Disks 98
1984 - 85 Kelowna Wings & WHL Graduates 98
1984 - 85 O-Pee-Chee 99
1984 - 85 O-Pee-Chee Stickers 100
1984 - 85 7-Eleven Disks 100
1984 - 85 Topps 101
1985 - 86 O-Pee-Chee & Topps 101
1985 - 86 O-Pee-Chee Stickers 102
1985 - 86 7-Eleven Superstars 102
1986 - 87 Kraft Sports / Posters 103
1986 - 87 O-Pee-Chee & Topps 103
1986 - 87 O-Pee-Chee Stickers 104
1987 Pepsi / Burger King
Super Jeu De Puissance 104
1987 - 88 O-Pee-Chee & Topps 104
1987 - 88 O-Pee-Chee Hockey Leaders 105
1987 - 88 O-Pee-Chee Stickers 105
1987 - 88 Panini Stickers 106
1987 - 88 Soviet Stars 107
1988 Soviet National Team / Olympics 107
1988 - 89 Esso All-Star Stickers 107
1988 - 89 Frito-Lay Stickers 107
1988 - 89 O-Pee-Chee & Topps 108
1988 - 89 O-Pee-Chee NHL Stars 108
1988 - 89 O-Pee-Chee Stickers 109
1988 - 89 Panini Stickers 109
1988 - 89 ProCards Team Sets 110
1989 Pelimiehen Passi 111
1989 Semic Stickers 111
1989 - 90 Action Packed Promos 112
1989 - 90 Kraft 112
1989 - 90 O-Pee-Chee & Topps 112
1989 - 90 O-Pee-Chee Stickers 113
1989 - 90 Panini 114
1989 - 90 ProCards Team Sets 114
1989 - 90 Semic Elitserien 115
1989 - 90 7th Inning Sketch OHL 116
1989 - 90 Soviet Stars 116
1990 7th Inning Sketch Memorial Cup 116

CHAPTER FOUR
The Boom Years 1990 - 1997

1990 - 91 Bowman 118
1990 - 91 Canadian Olympic Team 118
1990 - 91 Jyvas Hyva 118
1990 - 91 Kraft 118
1990 - 91 O-Pee-Chee / Topps 119
1990 - 91 O-Pee-Chee Premier 120
1990 - 91 Panini Stickers 120
1990 - 91 Panini Team Sticker Panels 121
1990 - 91 Pro Set 121
1990 - 91 Pro Set Player of the Month 122
1990 - 91 ProCards Team Sets 122
1990 - 91 Score 123
1990 - 91 Score Hot Cards 123
1990 - 91 Score Young Superstars 124
1990 - 91 Semic Elisterien Stickers 124
1990 - 91 7th Inning Sketch LHJMQ 124
1990 - 91 7th Inning Sketch OHL 124
1990 - 91 7th Inning Sketch WHL 125
1990 - 91 Sports Illustrated For Kids 125
1990 - 91 Tim Horton 125
1990 - 91 Upper Deck 125
1990 - 91 Upper Deck – Buybacks 127
1991 C55 Reprints 127
1991 Canada Cup - J.L. Productions 127
1991 Ivan Fiodorov Sport Unites Hearts 127
1991 Pro Set NHL Awards 127
1991 Semic Stickers 127
1991 7th Inning Sketch Memorial Cup 127
1991 - 92 Air Canada SJHL 128
1991 - 92 Arena Draft Picks 128
1991 - 92 Avant Garde BCJHL 128
1991 - 92 Bowman 128
1991 - 92 Canadian Olympic Team 129
1991 - 92 Classic Draft Picks 129
1991 - 92 Classic 4-Sport 129
1991 - 92 Future Trends '72 Hockey Canada 129
1991 - 92 Gillette 129
1991 - 92 Jyvas Hyva 129
1991 - 92 Kellogg's - Score 130
1991 - 92 Kraft 130
1991 - 92 McDonald's - Upper Deck 130
1991 - 92 O-Pee-Chee / Topps 130
1991 - 92 O-Pee-Chee Premier 131
1991 - 92 Panini Stickers 131
1991 - 92 Parkhurst 132
1991 - 92 Pinnacle 133
1991 - 92 Pro Set 133
1991 - 92 Pro Set Platinum 134
1991 - 92 ProCards Team Sets 134
1991 - 92 Puck - Pro Set 135
1991 - 92 Red Ace 136
1991 - 92 Score 136
1991 - 92 Semic Elitserien Stickers 137
1991 - 92 7th Inning Sketch LHJMQ 138
1991 - 92 7th Inning Sketch OHL 138
1991 - 92 7th Inning Sketch WHL 139
1991 - 92 Sports Illustrated For Kids 139
1991 - 92 Star Pics 139
1991 - 92 Topps Stadium Club 139
1991 - 92 Tri-Globe From Russia with Puck 140
1991 - 92 Tri-Globe Magnificent Five 140
1991 - 92 Ultimate Draft Picks 140
1991 - 92 Ultimate Original Six 140
1991 - 92 Upper Deck 140
1991 - 92 Upper Deck – Buybacks 142
1991 - 92 Upper Deck World Jr. Tournament 142
1992 Canadian Winter Olympians 142
1992 National Game 143
1992 Québec International Pee-Wee 143
1992 Semic Stickers 145
1992 7th Inning Sketch Award Winners 145
1992 Topps Stadium Club Members Only 146
1992 - 93 All-World 146
1992 - 93 American Licorice Sour Punch Caps 146
1992 - 93 BCJHL 146
1992 - 93 Bowman 146
1992 - 93 Bowman 146
1992 - 93 Canadian Olympic Team 147
1992 - 93 Canadian Card News 147
1992 - 93 CSC Premium Sheet 147
1992 - 93 Classic Draft Picks 147
1992 - 93 Classic 4-Sport 147
1992 - 93 Classic Pro Prospects 148
1992 - 93 Durivage / Diana - Panini Stickers 148
1992 - 93 Fleer Ultra 148
1992 - 93 Fleer Ultra The Collection 149
1992 - 93 Future Trends Canada Cup '76 149
1992 - 93 High Five Preview 150
1992 - 93 High Five – Buyback 150
1992 - 93 High Liner Centennial Series 150
1992 - 93 Humpty Dumpty 150
1992 - 93 Jyvas Hyva 150
1992 - 93 Kellogg's All-Star Posters 150
1992 - 93 Kellogg's Mini Posters 150
1992 - 93 Kellogg's Trophies 150
1992 - 93 Kraft 150
1992 - 93 Legends of Hockey 151
1992 - 93 Mario Bun 151
1992 - 93 McDonald's Upper Deck 151
1992 - 93 McDonald's Transfers 151
1992 - 93 MPS Photographics SJHL 151
1992 - 93 O-Pee-Chee 151
1992 - 93 Panini Action Freaks 152
1992 - 93 O-Pee-Chee Premier 152
1992 - 93 Panini Stickers 152
1992 - 93 Parkhurst 152
1992 - 93 Pinnacle 154
1992 - 93 Pinnacle Road to the NHL 155
1992 - 93 Pro Set 155

1992 - 93 Red Ace 155
1992 - 93 Score 156
1992 - 93 Score Young Superstars 157
1992 - 93 Seasons Action Player Patches 157
1992 - 93 Semic Elitserien Stickers 157
1992 - 93 Semic Nordisk 157
1992 - 93 Sport Flash 158
1992 - 93 Sports Illustrated For Kids 158
1992 - 93 Topps 158
1992 - 93 Topps Stadium Club 159
1992 - 93 Topps Stadium Club Members Only 160
1992 - 93 Upper Deck 160
1992 - 93 Upper Deck – Buybacks 162
1992 - 93 Upper Deck Locker All-Star 162
1992 - 93 Zellers Masters of Hockey 163
1993 Koululainen 163
1993 Québec International Pee-Wee 163
1993 Semic Stickers 165
1993 Upper Deck World Cup of Soccer 165
1993 - 94 Action Packed 166
1993 - 94 Canadian Olympic Team 166
1993 - 94 Classic 166
1993 - 94 Classic 4-Sport 166
1993 - 94 Classic Images 4-Sport 166
1993 - 94 Classic Pro Prospects 166
1993 - 94 Coca-Cola POGs 167
1993 - 94 Donruss 167
1993 - 94 Durivage / Diana - Score 169
1993 - 94 EA Sports 169
1993 - 94 Fax Pax World of Sport 169
1993 - 94 Fleer Ultra 169
1993 - 94 Global Telecommunications 171
1993 - 94 High Liner Greatest Goalies 171
1993 - 94 Hockey Wit 171
1993 - 94 Jyvas Hyva 171
1993 - 94 Kraft 172
1993 - 94 Leaf 172
1993 - 94 Legends of Hockey 173
1993 - 94 McDonald's - Upper Deck 173
1993 - 94 Panini Sticker 174
1993 - 94 Parkhurst 174
1993 - 94 Parkhurst Missing Link '56-57 176
1993 - 94 Pinnacle 176
1993 - 94 Power Play 178
1993 - 94 Premier 179
1993 - 94 Score 181
1993 - 94 Seasons Action Patches 182
1993 - 94 Sisu 182
1993 - 94 Slapshot 183
1993 - 94 Sports Illustrated For Kids 183
1993 - 94 Starting Lineup 183
1993 - 94 Titrex / Power Play 184
1993 - 94 Topps Stadium Club 184
1993 - 94 Topps Stadium Club Members Only 186
1993 - 94 Upper Deck 186
1993 - 94 Upper Deck – Buybacks 188
1993 - 94 Upper Deck Be A Player 188
1993 - 94 Upper Deck Be A Player / Roots 188
1993 - 94 Zellers Masters of Hockey 188
1994 Koululainen 188
1994 Panini Olympic Stickers 188
1994 Québec International Pee Wee 188
1994 Pinnacle -Toronto At The Expo 191
1994 Semic 191
1994 Sportflics 192
1994 Topps Finest Bronze 192
1994 Upper Deck World Cup of Soccer 192
1994 - 95 Action Packed 192
1994 - 95 APS 192
1994 - 95 Assets 192
1994 - 95 Be A Player Magazine Cards 192
1994 - 95 Classic 193
1994 - 95 Classic Draft Day 193
1994 - 95 Classic 4-Sport 193
1994 - 95 Classic Images 194
1994 - 95 Classic Images 4-Sport 194
1994 - 95 DEL 194
1994 - 95 Donruss 195
1994 - 95 Flair 195
1994 - 95 Fleer 196
1994 - 95 Fleer Ultra 197
1994 - 95 Incomnet Phonecards 198
1994 - 95 Kraft 198
1994 - 95 Kraft Jumbo Masks 199
1994 - 95 Leaf 199
1994 - 95 Leaf Elit Set 200
1994 - 95 Leaf Limited 201
1994 - 95 Legends of Hockey 201
1994 - 95 McDonald's / Upper Deck 201
1994 - 95 Panini Stickers 202
1994 - 95 Parkhurst 202
1994 - 95 Pawrkhurst SE 203
1994 - 95 Parkie Tall Boys '64-65 204
1994 - 95 Pinnacle 204
1994 - 95 POG 206
1994 - 95 POG Western Power Team 207
1994 - 95 Post 207
1994 - 95 Premier 207
1994 - 95 Score 208
1994 - 95 Select 209
1994 - 95 Signature Rookies 210
1994 - 95 Signature Rookies Auto-Phonex 210
1994 - 95 Signature Rookies Gold Standard 211
1994 - 95 Signature Rookies Miracle On Ice 211
1994 - 95 Signature Rookies Tetrad 211
1994 - 95 Sisu 211
1994 - 95 Slapshot 212
1994 - 95 Slapshot Memorial Cup 212
1994 - 95 SP 213
1994 - 95 SP – Buybacks 213
1994 - 95 Sports Illustrated For Kids 213
1994 - 95 Starting Lineup 213
1994 - 95 Topps Finest 214
1994 - 95 Topps Stadium Club 215
1994 - 95 Topps Stadium Club Members Only 216
1994 - 95 Upper Deck 216
1994 - 95 Upper Deck – Buybacks 218
1994 - 95 Upper Deck Be A Player 218
1994 - 95 Upper Deck World Junior Alumni 218
1994 - 95 Zellers Master of Hockey 219
1995 Globe 219
1995 Hartwall Karjala 220
1995 Koululainen 220
1995 Leaf Latkaliiga 220
1995 Panini World Championships Stickers 220
1995 Parkhurst Phonecards 221
1995 Parkhurst Phonecards 221
1995 Québec Pee-Wee 221
1995 Semic 223
1995 Suomen All-Star 223
1995 Suomen Beckett All-Stars 223
1995 Topps Finest Bronze 223
1995 - 96 APS 223
1995 - 96 Bicycle Sports Aces 224
1995 - 96 Bowman 224
1995 - 96 Classic 224
1995 - 96 Classic Assets 225
1995 - 96 Classic Clear Assets 225
1995 - 96 Classic 5-Sport 225
1995 - 96 Classic Visions 226
1995 - 96 Classic Visions Signings 226
1995 - 96 DEL 226
1995 - 96 Donruss 226
1995 - 96 Donruss Elite 228
1995 - 96 Edge Ice 228
1995 - 96 Fleer Metal 229
1995 - 96 Fleer Ultra 230
1995 - 96 Future Legends 231
1995 - 96 Hoyle Eastern Conference 232
1995 - 96 Hoyle Western Conference 232
1995 - 96 Kellogg's - Donruss 232
1995 - 96 Kellogg's Pop-Ups 232
1995 - 96 Kraft 232
1995 - 96 Leaf 232
1995 - 96 Leaf Elit Set 233
1995 - 96 Leaf Limited 234
1995 - 96 Legends of Hockey 234
1995 - 96 McDonald's - Pinnacle UC3 234
1995 - 96 McDonald's Muppet Mania 235
1995 - 96 NHL-NHLPA / Cool Trade 235
1995 - 96 NHL-NHLPA / Fanfest 235
1995 - 96 Panini Sticker 235
1995 - 96 Parkhurst 235
1995 - 97 Parkhurst 24 kt. Gold 237
1995 - 96 Parkie Revolution '66-67 237
1995 - 96 Pinnacle 238
1995 - 96 Pinnacle FANtasy 239
1995 - 96 Pinnacle Summit 239
1995 - 96 Pinnacle Zenith 239
1995 - 96 Playoff One-on-One Challenge 240
1995 - 96 POGs 241
1995 - 96 Pro Magnet 241
1995 - 96 Pro Stamps 242
1995 - 96 Radio City Postcards 242
1995 - 96 Score 242
1995 - 96 Select Certified Edition 243
1995 - 96 Signature Rookies Draft Day 244
1995 - 96 Signature Rookies Tetrad 244
1995 - 96 Signature Rookies Tetrad Autobilia 244
1995 - 96 Sisu 244
1995 - 96 Sisu Limited 244
1995 - 96 SkyBox Emotion 245
1995 - 96 SkyBox Impact 246
1995 - 96 SkyMint 246
1995 - 96 Slapshot 246
1995 - 96 SP 247
1995 - 96 SP – Buybacks 248
1995 - 96 Sports Illustrated For Kids 248
1995 - 96 Starting Lineup 248
1995 - 96 Starting Lineup Canadian Legends 248
1995 - 96 Starting Lineup Timeless Legends 248
1995 - 96 Super Sticker 248
1995 - 96 Topps 249
1995 - 96 Topps Finest 250
1995 - 96 Topps Stadium Club 251
1995 - 96 Topps Stadium Club Members Only 252
1995 - 96 Topps Super Skills 252
1995 - 96 Upper Deck 252
1995 - 96 Upper Deck – Buybacks 254
1995 - 96 Upper Deck All-Star Predictor 254
1995 - 96 Upper Deck Be A Player 255
1995 - 96 Upper Deck Collector's Choice 256
1995 - 96 Upper Deck Elitserien 257
1995 - 96 Upper Deck / Post 257
1995 - 96 Upper Deck Record Collection 257
1995 - 96 Zellers Masters of Hockey 258
1996 Super Mario 258
1996 Québec International Pee-Wee 258
1996 Topps Finest Bronze 260
1996 Wien 260
1996 - 97 All-Sport PPF 260
1996 - 97 APS 260
1996 - 97 Autograph Collection 261
1996 - 97 Bicycle Sports / Aces 261
1996 - 97 DEL 262
1996 - 97 Donruss 262
1996 - 97 Donruss Canadian Ice 263
1996 - 97 Donruss Elite 264
1996 - 97 DS Stickers 264
1996 - 97 Duracell 265
1996 - 97 Flair 265
1996 - 97 Fleer 266
1996 - 97 Fleer Picks 266
1996 - 97 Fleer Ultra 267
1996 - 97 Got-Um / Greats Medallions 268
1996 - 97 Kellogg's 268
1996 - 97 Kraft 268
1996 - 97 Kraft Flex Magnets 268
1996 - 97 Leaf 268
1996 - 97 Leaf Limited 269
1996 - 97 Leaf Preferred 270
1996 - 97 Legends of Hockey 270
1996 - 97 Maggers 270
1996 - 97 McDonald's 271
1996 - 97 Metal Universe 271
1996 - 97 Panini Stickers 271
1996 - 97 Pinnacle 272
1996 - 97 Pinnacle Be A Player 273
1996 - 97 Pinnacle Fantasy 275
1996 - 97 Pinnacle Lemieux Moments 275
1996 - 97 Pinnacle Lemieux 600 Goals 275
1996 - 97 Pinnacle Mint Collection 275
1996 - 97 Pinnacle Summit 275
1996 - 97 Pinnacle Zenith 276
1996 - 97 Playoff One on One Challenge 277
1996 - 97 Score 277
1996 - 97 Select Certified Edition 279
1996 - 97 Score Board 7-Eleven Phonecard 279
1996 - 97 Sisu 279
1996 - 97 SkyBox Impact 280
1996 - 97 SP 281
1996 - 97 SP – Buybacks 281
1996 - 97 SP^{X} 281
1996 - 97 Sports Illustrated For Kids 282
1996 - 97 Starting Lineup 282
1996 - 97 Starting Lineup Timeless Legends 282
1996 - 97 Team Out! 282
1996 - 97 Topps Picks 282
1996 - 97 Upper Deck 283
1996 - 97 Upper Deck – Buybacks 284
1996 - 97 Upper Deck All-Star YCTG 284
1996 - 97 Upper Deck Black Diamond 284
1996 - 97 Upper Deck Collector's Choice 285
1996 - 97 Upper Deck Ice 286
1996 - 97 Upper Deck Post 287
1996 - 97 Visions 287
1996 - 97 Visions Signings 287
1997 Québec International Pee Wee 287

CHAPTER FIVE

Modern Issues 1997 - 2004

1997 Bowman 290
1997 - 98 APS 290
1997 - 98 Autographed Collection 291
1997 - 98 Bell Phonecards 291
1997 - 98 Bicycle Sports Aces 291
1997 - 98 Donruss 291
1997 - 98 Donruss Canadian Ice 292
1997 - 98 Donruss Elite 293
1997 - 98 Donruss Preferred 294
1997 - 98 Donruss Priority 295
1997 - 98 Donruss Studio 296
1997 - 98 DS 297
1997 - 98 DS Stickers 297
1997 - 98 Esso Olympic Heroes 298
1997 - 98 Eurotel 299
1997 - 98 Game of Her Life 299
1997 - 98 General Mills 299
1997 - 98 Hockey-Box 299
1997 - 98 Kraft 299
1997 - 98 Leaf 299
1997 - 98 Leaf International 300
1997 - 98 Limited 301
1997 - 98 McDonald's 301
1997 - 98 Omega 302
1997 - 98 Pacific Crown Collection 303
1997 - 98 Pacific Crown Royale 306
1997 - 98 Pacific Dynagon 307
1997 - 98 Pacific Invincible 309
1997 - 98 Pacific Paramount 310
1997 - 98 Pacific Revolution 312
1997 - 98 Panini Stickers 313
1997 - 98 Pinnacle 313
1997 - 98 Pinnacle Be A Player 314
1997 - 98 Pinnacle BeeHives 316
1997 - 98 Pinnacle CBC Sports 316
1997 - 98 Pinnacle Certified 316
1997 - 98 Pinnacle Epix 317
1997 - 98 Pinnacle Inside 318
1997 - 98 Pinnacle Mint Collection 319
1997 - 98 Pinnacle Totally Certified 319
1997 - 98 Pinnacle Uncut 320

1997 - 98 Pinnacle Post 320
1997 - 98 Score 320
1997 - 98 Score Team Sets 321
1997 - 98 SP Authentic 322
1997 - 98 SP Authentic – Buybacks 322
1997 - 98 SP^X 323
1997 - 98 SLU Canadian Legends 323
1997 - 98 Starting Lineup 323
1997 - 98 Upper Deck 323
1997 - 98 Upper Deck – Buybacks 325
1997 - 98 Upper Deck Black Diamond 325
1997 - 98 Upper Deck Collector's Choice 326
1997 - 98 Upper Deck Diamond Vision 327
1997 - 98 Upper Deck Coll. Choice Elitserien 328
1997 - 98 Upper Deck Ice 329
1997 - 98 Upper Deck Willie O'Ree Promo 329
1997 - 98 Valu-net 329
1997 - 98 Visions Signings 329
1997 - 98 Zenith 329
1998 Bonaparte 330
1998 Bonaparte Pexeso 330
1998 McDonald's Nagano 330
1998 Québec International Pee Wee 330
1998 Zatkovy Pasta 333
1998 Bowman 333
1998 Bowman Chrome 334
1998 - 99 Aurora 334
1998 - 99 Be A Player 336
1998 - 99 Bicycle Sports / Aces 338
1998 - 99 Bowman's Best 338
1998 - 99 Cardset 339
1998 - 99 Collection Souvenir 340
1998 - 99 DEL 340
1998 - 99 Donruss 341
1998 - 99 DS 341
1998 - 99 Dynagon Ice 342
1998 - 99 EBK Sports / ECHL All-Stars 343
1998 - 99 EBK Sports / IHL All-Stars 343
1998 - 99 Kraft / Post Collection 343
1998 - 99 McDonald's 343
1998 - 99 Mir 343
1998 - 99 NHC 344
1998 - 99 NHL/NHLPA Power Play 344
1998 - 99 O-Pee-Chee Chrome 344
1998 - 99 OFS 344
1998 - 99 Omega 346
1998 - 99 Pacific 347
1998 - 99 Pacific Crown Royale 349
1998 - 99 Pacific Paramount 350
1998 - 99 Pacific Revolution 351
1998 - 99 Panini Photocards 352
1998 - 99 Panini Stickers 353
1998 - 99 SP Authentic 353
1998 - 99 SP Authentic – Buybacks 354
1998 - 99 SP^X Finite 354
1998 - 99 SP^X Prospects 355
1998 - 99 Starting Lineup 356
1998 - 99 Starting Lineup Canadian Legends 356
1998 - 99 Topps & O-Pee-Chee Chrome 356
1998 - 99 Topps Finest 357
1998 - 99 Topps Gold Label 358
1998 - 99 Topps Pearson Award 359
1998 - 99 Topps Wendy's 359
1998 - 99 UD Choice 359
1998 - 99 UD^3 361
1998 - 99 Upper Deck & UD Gold Reserve 361
1998 - 99 Upper Deck – Buybacks 363
1998 - 99 Upper Deck Black Diamond 363
1998 - 99 Upper Deck Elitserien 364
1998 - 99 Upper Deck Gold Reserve 365
1998 - 99 Upper Deck Gretzky Retirement 365
1998 - 99 Upper Deck MVP 365
1998 - 99 Upper Deck MVP – Buybacks 366
1999 Québec International Pee Wee 366
1999 Upper Deck Year of the Great One 368
1999 Bowman 368
1999 - 00 Aurora 369
1999 - 00 Be A Player Memorabilia 370
1999 - 00 Canada Post 372
1999 - 00 Bicycle Sports / Aces 372
1999 - 00 Cardset 372
1999 - 00 Challenger Energy Bar 373
1999 - 00 Choice AHL All-Stars 373
1999 - 00 Crown Royale 373
1999 - 00 DS 374
1999 - 00 Dynagon Ice 375
1999 - 00 Eishockey News 376
1999 - 00 HoloGrFX 377
1999 - 00 Kraft 377
1999 - 00 McDonald's For the Record 378
1999 - 00 McDonald's 378
1999 - 00 Millennium Signature 378
1999 - 00 Mir 380
1999 - 00 NHC 381
1999 - 00 NHL-NHLPA / 2T0R0NT0 FANtasy 381
1999 - 00 NHL-NHLPA / Power Play 381
1999 - 00 OFS 382
1999 - 00 Omega 383
1999 - 00 Pacific 385
1999 - 00 Pacific Paramount 388
1999 - 00 Panini Stickers 390
1999 - 00 Post The Great One 391
1999 - 00 Post Great Moments 391
1999 - 00 Prism 391
1999 - 00 Revolution 392
1999 - 00 Score 393
1999 - 00 Sobey's 394
1999 - 00 SP Authentic 394
1999 - 00 SP Authentic – Buybacks 395
1999 - 00 SP^X 395
1999 - 00 Stadium Club 396
1999 - 00 Starting Lineup 397
1999 - 00 Topps & O-Pee-Chee 397
1999 - 00 Topps Chrome & OPC Chrome 399
1999 - 00 Topps Gold Label 400
1999 - 00 Topps Premier Plus 401
1999 - 00 Ultimate Victory 402
1999 - 00 Ultimate Victory – Buybacks 403
1999 - 00 Upper Deck 403
1999 - 00 Upper Deck – Buybacks 405
1999 - 00 Upper Deck Black Diamond 405
1999 - 00 Upper Deck Century Legends 406
1999 - 00 UD Century Legends– Buybacks 406
1999 - 00 Upper Deck Elitserien 406
1999 - 00 Upper Deck Gold Reserve 407
1999 - 00 UDGold Reserve - Buybacks 408
1999 - 00 Upper Deck Gretzky Exclusive 408
1999 - 00 Upper Deck Living Legend 409
1999 - 00 Upper Deck MVP 409
1999 - 00 Upper Deck MVP Stanley Cup 411
1999 - 00 UDMVP Stanley Cup – Buybacks 412
1999 - 00 Upper Deck Ovation 412
1999 - 00 Upper Deck Ovation – Buybacks 413
1999 - 00 Upper Deck PowerDeck 413
1999 - 00 Upper Deck Prospects 413
1999 - 00 Upper Deck Retro 414
1999 - 00 Upper Deck Retro – Buybacks 415
1999 - 00 Victory 415
1999 - 00 Wayne Gretzky Hockey 416
1999 - 00 W. Gretzky Hockey – Buybacks 417
2000 CSAS Signature Series 417
2000 Gatorade Stickers 417
2000 UD A Piece of History 500 Goal Club 417
2000 UD Gretzky Master Collection 417
2000 - 01 Alfabilder 417
2000 - 01 Aurora 417
2000 - 01 Be A Player All-Star Fantasy 418
2000 - 01 Be A Player Memorabilia 418
2000 - 01 Cardset 422
2000 - 01 Crown Royale 423
2000 - 01 Crown Royale Calder Collection 424
2000 - 01 Crown Royale Gold Rookies 424
2000 - 01 DS 424
2000 - 01 Kraft 425
2000 - 01 Kudos 425
2000 - 01 McDonald's 425
2000 - 01 Mir 426
2000 - 01 Mir Fetisov Farewell 427
2000 - 01 Nortel Networks 427
2000 - 01 O-Pee-Chee 427
2000 - 01 OFS 427
2000 - 01 Pacific 428
2000 - 01 Pacific Paramount 430
2000 - 01 Panini Sticker 432
2000 - 01 Parkhurst 433
2000 - 01 Premier Plus 433
2000 - 01 Private Stock 434
2000 - 01 Private Stock Titanium 436
2000 - 01 Private Stock Titanium Draft Day 439
2000 - 01 Revolution 439
2000 - 01 Signature Series 440
2000 - 01 SP Authentic 443
2000 - 01 SP Authentic – Buybacks 444
2000 - 01 SP Game-Used Edition 444
2000 - 01 SP Game-Used Edition – Buybacks 445
2000 - 01 SP^X 445
2000 - 01 Stadion 446
2000 - 01 Stadium Club 446
2000 - 01 Starting Lineup 447
2000 - 01 Starting Lineup Classic Doubles 447
2000 - 01 Topps & O-Pee-Chee 447
2000 - 01 Topps Chrome 449
2000 - 01 Topps Gold Label 450
2000 - 01 Topps Heritage 452
2000 - 01 Topps Heritage All-Star Fantasy 453
2000 - 01 Topps Heritage Sportscard Expo 453
2000 - 01 Topps Stars 453
2000 - 01 UD Heroes 454
2000 - 01 UD Reserve 454
2000 - 01 Ultimate Memorabilia 455
2000 - 01 Upper Deck 457
2000 - 01 Upper Deck All-Star Fantasy 460
2000 - 01 Upper Deck – Buybacks 460
2000 - 01 Upper Deck Black Diamond 460
2000 - 01 UD Black Diamond – Buybacks 460
2000 - 01 Upper Deck DEL 460
2000 - 01 Upper Deck E-Card 461
2000 - 01 Upper Deck Elitserien 461
2000 - 01 Upper Deck Great Futures 462
2000 - 01 Upper Deck Ice 462
2000 - 01 Upper Deck Legends 463
2000 - 01 Upper Deck Legends – Buybacks 464
2000 - 01 Upper Deck MVP 464
2000 - 01 Upper Deck Pearson Award 465
2000 - 01 Upper Deck Pros & Prospects 465
2000 - 01 Upper Deck Prospects 466
2000 - 01 Upper Deck Return to Excellence 467
2000 - 01 Upper Deck Rookie Update 467
2000 - 01 Upper Deck Vintage 467
2000 - 01 Vanguard 468
2000 - 01 Victory 469
2001 UD Prospects Game Used Edition 470
2001 - 02 Adrenaline 471
2001 - 02 All-Star Game History 472
2001 - 02 AGF 472
2001 - 02 Atomic 472
2001 - 02 Be A Player Draft Day 2001 474
2001 - 02 Be A Player Memorabilia 474
2001 - 02 Be A Player Update 477
2001 - 02 Between The Pipes 477
2001 - 02 Blizzak 479
2001 - 02 Bowman 479
2001 - 02 Crown Royale 480
2001 - 02 DS 481
2001 - 02 EA Sports / Upper Deck 482
2001 - 02 eTopps 482
2001 - 02 Fleer Greats of the Game 482
2001 - 02 Fleer All-Star Fantasy 482
2001 - 02 Fleer Legacy 483
2001 - 02 Fleer Ultra 483
2001 - 02 Heads Up 483
2001 - 02 McDonald's 484
2001 - 02 Nextel All-Stars 485
2001 - 02 O-Pee-Chee 485
2001 - 02 OFS 485
2001 - 02 Pacific 486
2001 - 02 Pacific / Calder Collection 489
2001 - 02 Pacific / Entry Draft 489
2001 - 02 Pacific / High Voltage 489
2001 - 02 Pacific / Collectors' International 489
2001 - 02 Pacific / Montréal Sport Collectibles 489
2001 - 02 Pacific / National 489
2001 - 02 Pacific / Rookie Collection 489
2001 - 02 Parkhurst 489
2001 - 02 Private Stock 492
2001 - 02 Private Stock Titanium 494
2001 - 02 Private Stock Titanium Draft Day 496
2001 - 02 Signature Series 496
2001 - 02 SP Authentic 499
2001 - 02 SP Game Used Edition 500
2001 - 02 SP^X 502
2001 - 02 SP^X Rookie 503
2001 - 02 Stadium Club 503
2001 - 02 Topps & O-Pee-Chee 505
2001 - 02 Topps All-Star Game 507
2001 - 02 Topps Chrome 507
2001 - 02 Topps Heritage 507
2001 - 02 Topps Reserve 508
2001 - 02 Topps / O-Pee-Chee Archives 509
2001 - 02 UD PlayMakers Limited 510
2001 - 02 Ultimate Memorabilia 511
2001 - 02 Upper Deck 514
2001 - 02 Upper Deck All-Star Fantasy 517
2001 - 02 Upper Deck Challenge for the Cup 517
2001 - 02 Upper Deck Collector's Club 518
2001 - 02 Upper Deck DEL 518
2001 - 02 Upper Deck Honor Roll 519
2001 - 02 Upper Deck Ice 520
2001 - 02 Upper Deck Legends 521
2001 - 02 Upper Deck Mask Collection 522
2001 - 02 Upper Deck MVP 523
2001 - 02 Upper Deck / 23rd National 525
2001 - 02 Upper Deck Pearson Award 525
2001 - 02 Upper Deck Premier Collection 525
2001 - 02 Upper Deck Stanley Cup Champs 525
2001 - 02 Upper Deck Top Shelf 526
2001 - 02 Upper Deck Vintage 527
2001 - 02 Vanguard 528
2001 - 02 Victory 529
2001 - 02 Waving the Flag 530
2002 - 03 AGF 530
2002 - 03 Atomic 530
2002 - 03 BAP All-Star Edition 532
2002 - 03 Be A Player Draft Florida 2001 533
2002 - 03 Be A Player Draft Toronto 2002 533
2002 - 03 Be A Player Memorabilia 533
2002 - 03 Between the Pipes 536
2002 - 03 Bowman 538
2002 - 03 Calder 539
2002 - 03 Canada Post 540
2002 - 03 Canadian Museum of Civilization 540
2002 - 03 Cardset 540
2002 - 03 Choice Top Prospects 541
2002 - 03 Crown Royale 541
2002 - 03 eTopps 542
2002 - 03 Exclusive 542
2002 - 03 First Edition 544
2002 - 03 Fleer Throwbacks 546
2002 - 03 Heads Up 547
2002 - 03 In The Game-Used 548
2002 - 03 McDonald's 551
2002 - 03 Mike's Restaurant Trio Théo 551
2002 - 03 Pacific 552
2002 - 03 Pacific Complete 553
2002 - 03 Pacific Trading Cards All-Star 555
2002 - 03 Pacific / Les Gardiens 555
2002 - 03 Pacific / Montréal Collections 555
2002 - 03 Pacific / Toronto Spring Expo 555

2002 - 03 Parkhurst 555
2002 - 03 Parkhurst Retro 558
2002 - 03 Private Stock Reserve 559
2002 - 03 Private Stock Titanium 561
2002 - 03 Quest for the Cup 562
2002 - 03 Russian Future Stars 563
2002 - 03 Signature Series 563
2002 - 03 Slam Card 565
2002 - 03 SP Authentic 566
2002 - 03 SP Game-Used Edition 567
2002 - 03 Sports Vault 569
2002 - 03 SP^{X} 570
2002 - 03 SP^{X} Rookie 571
2002 - 03 Stadium Club 572
2002 - 03 Starz 572
2002 - 03 Topps & O-Pee-Chee 573
2002 - 03 Topps Chrome 575
2002 - 03 Topps Heritage 575
2002 - 03 Topps Limited 576
2002 - 03 Topps Total 577
2002 - 03 UD Superstars 579
2002 - 03 Ultimate Memorabilia 579
2002 - 03 Upper Deck 583
2002 - 03 Upper Deck Artistic Impressions 586
2002 - 03 Upper Deck Classic Portraits 588
2002 - 03 Upper Deck Foundations 590
2002 - 03 Upper Deck Honor Roll 591
2002 - 03 Upper Deck Mask Collection 592
2002 - 03 Upper Deck MVP 593
2002 - 03 Upper Deck Piece of History 594
2002 - 03 Upper Deck Premier Collection 595
2002 - 03 Upper Deck Rookie Update 596
2002 - 03 Upper Deck Top Shelf 598
2002 - 03 Upper Deck Vintage 599
2002 - 03 Vanguard 600
2002 - 03 Victory 601

CHAPTER SIX

NHL Team Sets

Anaheim Mighty Ducks 604
Atlanta Flames 604
Atlanta Thrashers 604
Boston Bruins 604
Buffalo Sabres 605
Calgary Flames 606
California Golden Seals 606
Carolina Hurricanes 660
Chicago Blackhawks 607
Colorado Avalanche 607
Colorado Rockies 607
Columbus Blue Jackets 608
Dallas Stars 608
Detroit Red Wings 608
Edmonton Oilers 608
Florida Panthers 610
Hartford Whalers 610
Los Angeles Kings 611
Minnesota North Stars 611
Minnesota Wild 612
Montréal Canadiens 612
Nashville Predators 615
New Jersey Devils 615
New York Islanders 615
New York Rangers 616
Ottawa Senators 616
Philadelphia Flyers 616
Phoenix Coyotes 617
Pittsburgh Penguins 617
Québec Nordiques 618
St. Louis Blues 620
San Jose Sharks 620
Tampa Bay Lightning 620
Toronto Maple Leafs 621
Vancouver Canucks 622
Washington Capitals 624
Winnipeg Jets 625

CHAPTER SEVEN

WHA Team Sets

Cincinnati Stingers 628
Cleveland Crusaders 628
Houston Aeros 628
Los Angeles Sharks 628
Minnesota Fighting Saints 628
New England Whalers 628
Ottawa Nationals 628
Phoenix Roadrunners 628
Québec Nordiques 628
San Diego Mariners 628
Vancouver Blazers 628
Winnipeg Jets 628

Minor League Team Sets

Adirondack Red Wings 629
Albany River Rats 629
Anchorage Aces 629
Asheville Smoke 629
Atlanta Knights 629
Austin Ice Bats 629
Baltimore Skipjacks 629
BC Icemen 630
Binghampton Rangers 630
Birmingham Bulls 630
Cape Breton Oilers 630
Carolina Monarchs 630
Central Texas Stampede 630
Charlotte Checkers 630
Chicago Wolves 630
Cincinnati Cyclones 631
Cincinnati Mighty Ducks 631
Cleveland Barons 631
Cleveland Lumberjacks 631
Colorado Gold Kings 632
Columbus Checkers 632
Dayton Bombers 632
Dayton Ice Bandits 632
Des Moines Buccaneers 632
Detroit Vipers 632
Erie Panthers 632
Flint Generals 632
Flint Spirits 633
Florida Everblades 633
Fort Wayne Komets 633
Fort Worth Brahmas 633
Fredericton Canadiens 633
Fredericton Express 634
Grand Rapids Griffins 634
Greensboro Generals 634
Greensboro Monarchs 634
Halifax Citadels 634
Hamilton Bulldogs 634
Hamilton Canucks 634
Hampton Roads Admirals 635
Hartford Wolf Pack 635
Hershey Bears 635
Houston Aeros 636
Humberside Hawks 636
Huntington Blizzard 636
Indianapolis Checkers 636
Indianapolis Ice 636
Johnstown Chiefs 637
Kalamazoo Wings 637
Kansas City Blades 637
Kentucky Thoroughblades 637
Knoxville Cherokees 637
Las Vegas Thunder 637
Long Beach Ice Dogs 638
Louisiana Ice Gators 638
Louisville Panthers 638
Lowell Lock Monsters 638
Manchester Monarchs 638
Manitoba Moose 638
Michigan K-Wings 639
Milwaukee Admirals 639
Minnesota Moose 639
Mississippi Sea Wolves 639
Missouri Riverotters 640
Mobile Mysticks 640
Moncton Alpines 640
Moncton Golden Flames 640
Moncton Hawks 640
Muskegon Fury 640
Nashville Knights 640
New Haven Beast 640
New Haven Nighthawks 640
Newmarket Saints 640
New Mexico Scorpions 640
New Orleans Brass 641
Norflok Admirals 641
Nova Scotia Oilers 641
Nova Scotia Voyageurs 641
Odessa Jackalopes 641
Oklahoma City Blazers 641
Orlando Solar Bears 641
Pensacola Ice Pilots 641
Peoria Rivermen 641
Philadelphia Phantoms 642
Phoenix Mustangs 642
Phoenix Roadrunners 642
Portland Pirates 642
Providence Bruins 642
Quad City Mallards 634
Québec Aces 643
Québec Citadelles 643
Raleigh Icecaps 643
Richmond Renegades 643
Roanoke Express 643
Rochester Americans 644
Rockford Icehogs 644
Saginaw Gears 644
Saint John Flames 644
St. John's Maple Leafs 644
Salt Lake Golden Eagles 645
San Angelo Outlaws 645
San Diego Gulls 645
Sheffield Steelers 645
Sherbrooke Canadiens 645
Sioux City Musketeers 645
Springfield Falcons 645
Springfield Indians 645
Syracuse Crunch 646
Tallahassee Tiger Sharks 646
Thunder Bay Senators 646
Toledo Storm 646
Topeka Scarecrows 646
Utah Grizzlies 646
Wheeling Thunderbirds 647
Whitby Dunlops 647
Wichita Thunder 647
Wilkes-Barre / Scranton Penguins 647
Worcester Icecats 647

World Team Sets

Belfast Giants 647
Cardiff Devils 647
Coventry Blaze 647
Dundee Texol Stars 647
Guildford Flames 647
London Knights 648
Magnitogorsk Metalliburg 648
Manchester Storm 648
Moscow Dynamo 648
Nottingham Panthers 648
Peterborough Phantoms 648
Sheffield Steelers 648
Zug Swiss 648

CHAPTER EIGHT

Junior & College Team Issues

U. Arizona Icecatsx 650
Baie-Comeau Drakkar 650
Barrie Colts 650
Belleville Bulls 650
Brampton Battalions 650
Brandon Wheat Kings 650
Brantford Alexanders 651
Brockville Braves 651
Calgary Hitmen 651
Cape Breton Screaming Eagles 651
Chicoutimi Saguenéens 651
Clarkson Golden Knights 651
Cornwall Royals 651
Drummondville Voltigeurs 651
Ferris State Bulldogs 651
Guelph Storm 651
Halifax Moosehead 652
Hamilton Fincups 652
Hull Olympiques 652
Kamloops Blazers 653
Kelowna Rockets 653
Kelowna Wings 653
Kingston Canadians 653
Kingston Frontenacs 654
Kitchener Rangers 654
Lake Superior State Lakers 655
Lethbridge Hurricanes 655
London Knights 655
Maine Black Bears 655
Medicine Hat Tigers 655
Michigan State Spartans 655
Michigan Tech Huskies 656
Minnesota Golden Gophers 656
Minn.-Duluth Bulldogs 656
Mississauga IceDogs 656
Moncton Wildcats 656
Montréal Juniors 656
Moose Jaw Warriors 656
Nanaimo Clippers 657
Niagara Falls Thunder 657
North Bay Centennials 657
Northern Michigan Wildcats 657
Oshawa Generals 657
Ottawa 67's 658
Owen Sound Attack 658
Owen Sound Platers 658
Peterborough Petes 658
Plymouth Whalers 658
Portland Winter Hawks 658
Prince Albert Raiders 658
Prince George Cougars 659
Québec Remparts 659
Rayside-Balfour Jr. Canadians 659
Red Deer Rebels 659
Regina Pats 659
Richelieu Riverains 660
Rimouski Océanic 660
Rouyn-Noranda Huskies 660
Saskatoon Blades 660
Sault Ste. Marie Greyhounds 661
Seattle Thunderbirds 661
Shawinigan Cataractes 661
Sherbrooke Castors 661
Spokane Chiefs 662
Sudbury Wolves 662
Swift Current Broncos 662
Tacoma Rockets 663
Toronto St. Mike's Majors 663
Tri-City Americans 663
Val d'Or Foreurs 663
Vancouver Giants 663
Victoria Cougars 663
Victoriaville Tigres 663
W. Michigan Broncos 663
Windsor Spitfires 663

Topps Heritage named CSC's 2002-03 Set of the Year

When it came down to it, there were four sets that made a run for *Canadian Sports Collector*'s annual Hockey Set of the Year. Topps Heritage was the winner, but it won by a hair over O-Pee-Chee/Topps, Upper Deck and SP Authentic.

This marked the second time in three years that Topps Heritage has been named *Canadian Sports Collector*'s Hockey Set of the Year. It had previously been named Hockey Set of the Year in 2000-01, the year it made its debut and brought bubble gum back into the packs.

The Topps Heritage line relies on the design and concept of past Topps hockey card sets. In 2000-01, it borrowed the design and concept from the 1954-55 Topps series, the very first Topps hockey card set. In 2001-02, when it finished seventh in the year-end ranking, it borrowed the 1957-58 Topps series, the second Topps hockey set.

This past year, the Topps Company decided to skip ahead and grab the design from the 1966-67 series. The 1966-67 series is well remembered for its use of a television frame for the card-front border. It is very popular thanks to the inclusion of the Bobby Orr rookie card.

Even without the inclusion of Bobby Orr in the new series, the 2002-03 edition was a hit. The Topps Company could not use Orr because Orr has an exclusive arrangement with the Upper Deck Company. Instead, the Topps Company decided to commemorate members of the 1966-67 Toronto Maple Leafs team, the last Maple Leafs team to win the Stanley Cup.

Said collector Derek Eng of Toronto, ON, "there were better looking sets, but Topps Heritage had a classic design, strong player selection, (lots of) autographed and memorabilia inserts, and a set you could build without breaking the bank. (You got) all that and a stick of gum in every pack."

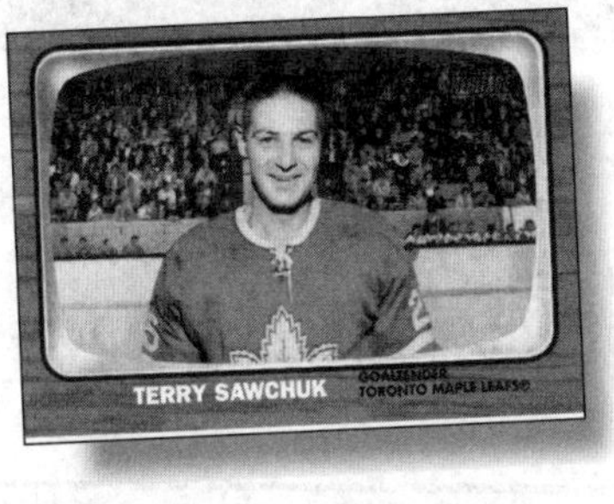

Says *Canadian Sports Collector* correspondent Jon Waldman, "Topps Heritage, like it was in 2000-01, was the dominant set of the year. By the All-Star break, there were very few packs left on dealer shelves, as collectors busted packs like crazy. Every card, from the short prints to inserts, were winners. No one was left dissapointed after breaking open their packs."

The 2002-03 Topps Heritage series included a 130-card shell set plus 25 short-printed rookies and 25 "high numbers" veteran short prints. There was even a 100-card Chrome parallel (cards 1-100) and a 10-card light woodgrain parallel (skip-numbered).

The Best of 2002-03

The series included a seven-card reprint set of '66-67 Maple Leafs along with seven relic variations and five autographed variations. Other relic inserts were Calder Cloth, Crease Piece and Great Skates. The lone other insert was the Real One Ceritifed Autograph insert.

Behind Topps Heritage, the second, third and fourth place spots were identical to the previous season. This was not too surprising since the scoring from sports collector stores places a premium on winning votes within your particular class (see *Canadian Sports Collector*'s September 2003 issue).

Since 2001-02, *Canadian Sports Collector* has surveyed stores across Canada. As stores vote for only one set in each of five different classes, some potential second- or third-best sets may not receive as many votes simply because it is stuck in a very competitive category. In essence, the better you are against your peers, the better you are in the overall score.

O-Pee-Chee (second overall, Best Entry Level), Upper Deck (third overall, Best Premium), and SP Authentic (fourth overall, Best High End) have all won their categories in back-to-back years.

Sports collector stores made their votes between June 30 and July 8. The stores voted for five class winners (one point each) and one overall best set (three extra points).

Collectors and readers, meanwhile, made their picks through July 15. They voted for a Set of the Year (two points) and provided individual marks out of 10 for each set that they collected or purchased (1.0 to 0.1 points). Both store votes and collector votes were then combined to determine *Canadian Sports Collector*'s Set of the Year.

Topps Heritage finished a close second in its category in the store vote, but overtook its Premium Brand peer Upper Deck in the collector vote.

As *CSC* did last year, the top 16 sets are ranked from the overall Set of the Year scores (see "Sweet Sixteen" below). Their scores are a percentage of the entire score.

Eleven of the 2002-03 Sweet Sixteen sets also finished in the Sweet Sixteen for 2001-02. Only one veteran brand (SP^X) jumped into the top group. Four other brands were first-year brands in hockey (Topps Total, Upper Deck Classic Portraits, Parkhurst Retro, and In The Game-Used).

SP Authentic had the highest score from all of the store votes followed by O-Pee-Chee in second and Upper Deck in third. Topps Heritage had the highest score from the collector votes followed by McDonald's in second and O-Pee-Chee in third.

Sweet Sixteen

'02-03 Brand	SCORE	'01-2
1. Topps Heritage	6.96%	7
2. O-Pee-Chee/Topps	6.59%	2
3. Upper Deck	6.40%	3
4. SP Authentic	6.01%	4
5. Upper Deck Mask Collection	4.36%	6
6. Bowman	4.08%	1
7. Private Stock Reserve	3.50%	16
8. SP^X	3.43%	NR
9. Signature Series	3.12%	13
10. McDonald's	3.11%	9
11. Topps Total	3.10%	FY
12. Between the Pipes	2.82%	5
13. Upper Deck Classic Portraits	2.65%	FY
14. Atomic	2.58%	11
15. Parkhurst Retro	2.41%	FY
16. In The Game-Used	2.34%	FY

CHAPTER ONE

VINTAGE ISSUES 1879 TO 1943

1879-1890

HD-5 - "Eishockey"

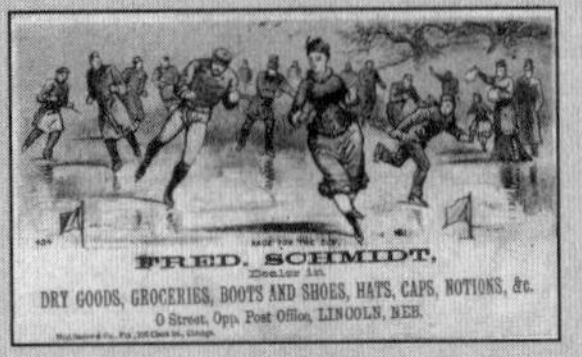

H-820 - Bufford Litho

1880 Bufford Litho

1880 Bensdorf Trade Card

1884 Cibils Trade Card

1888 Atlantic & Pacific Tea Co.

1890 F. Mayer Boot & Shoe Co.

1879 - 1896 POSTCARDS, STOCK AND ADVERTISEMENT CARDS

These cards feature various designs and are printed on different card stocks.In some cases, the card back was left blank for an advertisement.

1879 (ACC # HD-5) VG EX EX-MT
☐ 4 Eishockey (2 13/16" x 4 7/16", colourized print, white card stock) 65 125 275

1879 - 82 (ACC # H-820) VG EX EX-MT
☐ Bufford Litho / 431 Hockey on the Ice (2 11/16" x 4 1/2", pastel colourized print, beige border) 70 140 300
☐ Bufford Litho / 434 Race for the Cup (2 11/16" x 4 1/2", pastel colourized print, beige border) 35 70 150

1880 (ACC # HD-2E) VG EX EX-MT
☐ Great Match Game of Polo, Cottage City vs. Providence (2 1/2" x 4", pastel colourized print, beige border) 35 70 150

1880 (ACC # HD-5) VG EX EX-MT
☐ Bufford Litho / 903 Child with field hockey stick (2 11/16" x 4 5/16", colourized print, white card stock) 35 70 150

1880 (ACC # HD-5) VG EX EX-MT
☐ Bensdorf / Three children playing ice hockey (3 1/2" x 5 3/8", colourized print, white border, postcard back) 35 70 150

1884 (ACC # HD-5) VG EX EX-MT
☐ Cibils / Le jeu du Hockey (2 13/16" x 4 5/16", colourized print, white card stock) 70 140 300

1888 (ACC # HD-820) VG EX EX-MT
◆ An example of this card, deemed to be in "very good to excellent condition despite the presence of a few miniscule pinholes," recently closed at $275 U.S. ($316 with the buyer's premium) in the May 17, 2002 Lelands Vintage Sports Auction. This closing amount translates to about $425 Cdn. This particular card was dated July 7, 1988 and had an advertisement for A&P Bakery Powder on the back of the card.
☐ Bufford / The Great Atlantic & Pacific Tea Company (3 3/8" x 5 1/8", colourized print, yellow border) 70 140 300

1890 (ACC # HP-3H) VG EX EX-MT
☐ F. Mayer Boot & Shoe Co. / Children on ice (3 1/4" x 5 1/2", colourized print, white card stock) 35 70 150

1896 WARWICK BROS & RUTTER VG EX EX-MT
☐ Warwick Bro's & Rutter / 3247 New Liskeard's hockey team (5 9/16" x 3 5/8", black & white photo, brown & white back) 60 125 225

1900 - 1917 POSTCARDS, STOCK AND ADVERTISEMENT CARDS

These cards feature various designs and are printed on different card stocks.In some cases, the card back was left blank for an advertisement.

1900 ÉMILE PÉCAUD VG EX EX-MT
☐ Émile Pécaud / Le hockey sur la glace (5 9/16" x 3 5/8", black & white, white border, postcard-format card back) 15 30 60

1900 GOTTMANN (ACC # HD-8F) VG EX EX-MT
This card was part of a 12-card set that was available from Gottmann & Kretchner by mailing in 10¢ U.S. in stamps.
☐ Gottmann & Kretchmer / January Birthday Horoscope (2 1/2" x 5 1/8", colour,blue and white back) 25 50 100

1902 BREFKORT VG EX EX-MT
☐ Brefkort / Stockholm Idrottsparken (3 3/8" x 5 1/2", colour, white border, postcard-format card back) 15 30 60

1902 HAMILTON KINGS (ACC # T-7) VG EX EX-MT
There are several cards in this series, each depicting a lady in a different sports activity.
☐ Hamilton Kings Cards / Turkish Trophies (5 15/16" x 8", black & blue with white print, beige stock, blank back) 100 200 400

1902 RAPHAEL VG EX EX-MT
There is also a version with "ice-crystal" glued to the card surface area below the players.
☐ Raphael Tuck & Sons / 2624 Hockey (3 9/16" x 5 1/2", colour, postcard-format card back) 20 40 80

1905 MONTRÉAL IMPORT VG EX EX-MT
☐ Montréal Import / 308 Hockey is a winter game, very healthful & full of exercise (3 5/8" x 5 7/16", colour cartoon, postcard-format card back) 15 30 60

1905 NATIONAL ART VG EX EX-MT
☐ National Art / 39 Female skater with hockey stick (3 1/2" x 5 3/8", colour, postcard-format card back) 15 30 60

1905 -06 VELVO VG EX EX-MT
☐ Velvo/ Grand mère hockey club (3 1/4" x 5 3/8", black & white, postcard-format card back) 50 100 225

1906 CHOCOLAT MEURISSE (ACC #HD-5) VG EX EX-MT
☐ 1 Hockey Serie 1 (1-6) (2 3/4" x 4 1/4", colour, blank back for ad.) 60 120 275

1906 MARGARINE BELGICA (ACC #HD-5) VG EX EX-MT
☐ Margarine Belgica (2 3/4" x 4 1/4", colour, blank back for ad.) 60 120 275

1906 MONTRÉAL IMPORT (ACC # PC-745) VG EX EX-MT
☐ Montréal Import / 261 McGill hockey (3 1/2" x 5 3/8", black & white, postcard-format card back) 50 100 200

1906 OTTAWA SILVER SEVEN VG EX EX-MT
◆ A postmarked (1908) and framed example of this card recently closed at $345 U.S. ($396 with the buyer's premium) in theMay 17, 2002 Lelands Vintage Sports Auction. This closing amount translates to about $535 Cdn.
☐ Ottawa Silver Seven, Holders of the Stanley Cup

1907 MONTRÉAL IMPORT (ACC # PC-745) VG EX EX-MT
☐ Montréal Import Canadian Sports Series / Hockey match (3 3/8" x 5 7/16", black & white, postcard-format card back) 20 40 80

1907 - 08 NORTHERN HARDWARE VG EX EX-MT
☐ Northern Hardware Co. (5 1/2" x 3 11/16", black & white front and back) 30 60 120

1908 VOUGS VG EX EX-MT
☐ Vougs / Les sports d'hiver a Luchon (3 1/2" x 5 7/16", black & white, postcard-format card back) 12 25 50

1909 ANONYMOUS VG EX EX-MT
☐ Hockey scene (3 9/16" x 5 7/16", blue pastel colour print, white border, postcard-format card back) 12 25 50

1911 STEDMAN BROS. VG EX EX-MT
☐ Stedman Bros. / A popular Canadian winter sport (3 9/16" x 5 1/2", colour postcard-format card back) 12 25 50

1912 - 13 CALUMET VG EX EX-MT
☐ AZO / Calumet hockey club of Laurium (5 5/16" x 3 9/16", black & white, sepia &white back) 25 50 100

1912 - 13 A.R. CLARKE & CO. VG EX EX-MT
☐ AZO / Riverdale Manufacturers (5 9/16" x 3 7/16", black & white, sepia &white back) 25 50 100

1913 QUÉBEC BULLDOGS VG EX EX-MT
☐ Montiminy / Québec Bulldogs Champions (black & white)

1916 CHRISTMAS FROM A FRIEND VG EX EX-MT
☐ Christmas thought from a friend / C-216 Two boys play hockey (colour, postcard-format card back) 15 30 60

1917 ANONYMOUS VG EX EX-MT
☐ Playing hockey with square puck (3 1/2" x 5 1/2" colour, postcard-format card back) 12 25 50

1908 AMERICAN TOBACCO CO.

These college flannels were issued with 11 different sports: baseball, basketball, fencing, football, hockey, hurdles, rowing, shotput, swimming, tennis, and track. The imprint varies with each cigarette brand. Other flannels may exist.

The regular flannels (pictured) measure 3 1/8" x 5 3/8" and have a fringe. The larger flannels measure 5 1/2" x 8 1/2".

SMALLER (ACC # B-33) VG EX EX-MT
Common flannel 35 65 125

☐ Amherst	☐ Army	☐ Brown
☐ Bucknell	☐ California	☐ Chicago
☐ Colgate	☐ Colorado	☐ Columbia
☐ Cornell	☐ Dartmouth	☐ Harvard
☐ Johns Hopkins	☐ Knox	☐ Michigan
☐ Navy	☐ Oregon	☐ Pennsylvania
☐ Princeton	☐ Rutgers	☐ St. Louis
☐ Stanford	☐ Syracuse	☐ Trinity
☐ Tufts	☐ Utah	☐ Vermont
☐ Williams	☐ Wisconsin	☐ Yale

LARGER (ACC # B-16-2) VG EX EX-MT
☐ Oregon 40 80 160

1879-1890

1900 Gottmann & Kretchmer

1902 Turkish Trophies

1905 Montréal Import

1906 Chocolat Meurisse

1907 Montréal Import

1907 - 08 Northern Hardware

1912 - 13 Calumet Hockey Club

1909 - 1910 MURAD CIGARETTES

This card was part of a six series, 25-card college set. It is the only hockey card in the series. The card measures 2 1/8" x 2 11/16".

The card has a colour photo on the front, and is black & white on the back. Of the six different series, the first two (of which Rochester was included) were reprinted with a slight graphic change.

1909 - 10 MURAD (ACC # T-51)	VG	EX	EX-MT
☐ Rochester	15	30	60
☐ Rochester 2nd edition	15	30	60

1910 IMPERIAL TOBACCO SILKS

This multi-sport silk series was issued in 10 different colours. There are only two hockey silks. White silks may appear beige. Pricing is the same for each colour variation.Each blank-back silk measures 1 3/4" x 3 1/8".ACC # SC-12

			VG	EX	EX-MT
Hockey silk			10	20	40
☐ Black	☐ Dark Blue	☐ Light Blue			
☐ Brown	☐ Green	☐ Purple			
☐ Red	☐ Dark Red	☐ White			
☐ Yellow					
Montréal AAA			15	25	50
☐ Black	☐ Dark Blue	☐ Light Blue			
☐ Brown	☐ Green	☐ Purple			
☐ Red	☐ Dark Red	☐ White			
☐ Yellow					

1910 - 11 IMPERIAL TOBACCO C56

All these cards are considered rookie cards. Cards are numbered on the upper left corner. The player's name and team appear on the bottom border. The name of the series, Hockey Series, appears on the back with a picture of two inverted crossed hockey sticks with a puck below them. Each card measures 1 1/2" x 2 1/2".

Complete Set (36 cards):	5,500	7,000	12,000
ACC # C56	VG	EX	EX-MT
☐ 1 Frank Patrick, Renfrew RC	300	450	850
☐ 2 Percy Lesueur (G), Ottawa RC	200	300	400
☐ 3 Gordon Roberts, Ottawa RC	150	225	300
☐ 4 Barney Holden, Sha. RC	90	135	180
☐ 5 Frank Glass, Mont.WRC	90	135	180
☐ 6 Edgar Dey, Hab. RC	90	135	180
☐ 7 Marty Walsh, Cobalt RC	150	225	300
☐ 8 Art Ross, Hab. RC	500	750	1,000
☐ 9 Angus Campbell, Cobalt RC	150	215	285
☐ 10 Harry Hyland, Mont.WRC	170	245	325
☐ 11 Herb Clarke, Cobalt RC	90	135	180
☐ 12 Art Ross, Hab. RC	500	750	1,000
☐ 13 Ed Decarie, Mont. RC	90	135	180
☐ 14 Tommy Dunderdale, Sha. RC	200	300	400
☐ 15 Fred Taylor, Renfrew RC	500	750	1,000
☐ 16 Joe Cattarinich (G), Mont. RC	125	190	250
☐ 17 Bruce Stuart, Ottawa RC	170	250	350
☐ 18 Nick Bawlf, Hab. RC	90	135	180
☐ 19 J. Jones, Cobalt (G)RC	125	190	250
☐ 20 Ernest Russell, Mont.WRC	200	300	400
☐ 21 Jack Laviolette, Mont. RC	170	245	325
☐ 22 Riley Hern (G), Mont.WRC	170	245	325
☐ 23 Didier Pitre, Mont. RC	170	245	325
☐ 24 George Poulin, Mont. RC	90	135	180
☐ 25 Art Bernier, Mont. RC	90	135	180
☐ 26 Lester Patrick, Renfrew RC	400	600	800
☐ 27 Fred Lake, Ottawa RC	90	135	180
☐ 28 Paddy Moran (G), Hab. RC	220	325	425
☐ 29 C. Toms, Cobalt RC	90	135	180
☐ 30 Ernie Johnson, Mont.WRC	200	300	400
☐ 31 Horace Gaul, Hab. RC	90	135	180
☐ 32 Harold McNamara, Cobalt RC	90	135	180
☐ 33 Jack Marshall, Mont.WRC	150	225	300
☐ 34 Bruce Ridpath, Ottawa RC	90	135	180
☐ 35 Jack Marshall, Sha. RC	150	225	300
☐ 36 Edouard Lalonde, Renfrew RC	450	750	1,500
Salesman sample	VG	EX	EX-MT
☐ 37 Newsy Lalonde salesman sample			

1910 - 11 SWEET CAPORAL POSTCARDS

These blank-back postcard-size cards were printed in England and issued in 50-count boxes of Sweet Caporal "Flat" cigarettes. Each card measures 2 7/8" x 4 5/8". The photos from this series were used as a template for the drawings of the small Imperial Tobacco cards from the following season.

Black & White Postcard	VG	EX	EX-MT
☐ 1 Paddy Moran (G), Québec	350	550	1,000
☐ 2 Joe Hall, Québec	300	450	600
☐ 3 Barney Holden, Québec	160	230	300
☐ 4 Joe Malone, Québec	500	760	1,000
☐ 5 Ed Oatman, Québec	160	230	300
☐ 6 Tommy Dunderdale, Québec	300	450	600
☐ 7 Ken Mallen, Québec	160	230	300
☐ 8 Jack McDonald, Québec	160	230	300
☐ 9 Fred Lake, Ottawa	160	230	300
☐ 10 Albert Kerr, Ottawa	160	230	300
☐ 11 Marty Walsh, Ottawa	240	370	475
☐ 12 Hamby Shore, Ottawa	160	230	300
☐ 13 Alex Currie, Ottawa	160	230	300
☐ 14 Bruce Ridpath, Ottawa	160	230	300
☐ 15 Bruce Stuart, Ottawa	240	370	475
☐ 16 Percy Lesueur (G), Ottawa	300	450	600
☐ 17 Jack Darragh, Ottawa	240	370	475
☐ 18 Steve Vair, Renfrew	160	230	300
☐ 19 Don Smith, Renfrew	160	230	300
☐ 20 Fred (Cyclone) Taylor, Renfrew	650	950	1,250
☐ 21 Bert Lindsay (G), Renfrew	160	230	300
☐ 22 Larry Gilmour, Renfrew	240	370	475
☐ 23 Bobby Rowe, Renfrew	160	230	300
☐ 24 Sprague Cleghorn, Renfrew	380	575	750
☐ 25 Odie Cleghorn, Renfrew	230	340	450
☐ 26 Skene Ronan, Renfrew	160	230	300
☐ 27 Walter Smaill, Mont.W.	300	450	600
☐ 28 Ernie Johnson, Mont.W.	250	385	500
☐ 29 Jack Marshall, Mont.W.	240	370	475
☐ 30 Harry Hyland, Mont.W.	240	370	475
☐ 31 Art Ross, Mont.W.	800	1,200	1,600
☐ 32 Riley Hern (G), Mont.W.	240	370	475
☐ 33 Gordon Roberts, Mont.W.	240	370	475
☐ 34 Frank Glass, Mont.W.	160	230	300
☐ 35 Ernest Russell, Mont.W.	250	375	500
☐ 36 James Gardiner, Mont.W.	240	370	475
☐ 37 Art Bernier, Mont.	160	230	300
☐ 38 Georges Vézina (G), Mont.	3,200	4,750	6,500
☐ 39 Henri Dellaire, Mont.	160	230	300
☐ 40 R. Power, Mont.	160	230	300
☐ 41 Didier Pitre, Mont.	240	370	475
☐ 42 Edouard Lalonde, Mont.	800	1,200	1,600
☐ 43 Eugene Payan, Mont.	160	230	300
☐ 44 George Poulin, Mont.	160	230	300
☐ 45 Jack Laviolette, Mont.	340	500	950

1910 - 11 MURAD ROCHESTER COLLEGE CARD

This multi-sport college series were issued as a premium in exchange for 15 picture coupons from Murad Cigarettes. The only hockey card is Rochester. This card measures 8" x 5". On a black & white back, the card reads "Murad Picture Dept., Drawer S. Jersey City. This offer expires June 30th, 1911."

1910 - 11 MURAD (ACC # T-6)	VG	EX	EX-MT
☐ Rochester	100	200	400

1911 - 12 IMPERIAL TOBACCO C55

Players in the 1911-12 set are exact duplicates of those on the 1910-11 postcard issue. The player photos appear to form the models for the drawings used on this set. The colour portrait is framed by two hockey sticks. Both the front and back of the card are numbered. Each card measures 1 1/2" x 2 1/2".

Please note that the complete-set price only includes one of the two Smaill variations.

◆ A 45-card set graded "Poor to VG" recently closed at $1,611 U.S. ($1,852 with the buyer's premium) in the May 17, 2002 Lelands Vintage Sports Auction. This closing amount comes to about $2,500 Cdn. In this particular set, the Vézina and Lalonde cards each graded G-VG, the Ross card graded Fair-Good, the Malone and Moran cards each graded Poor, and the Taylor card graded Fair.

Complete Set (45 cards):	6,250	9,500	12,500
ACC # C55	VG	EX	EX-MT
☐ 1 Paddy Moran (G), Québec	200	300	550
☐ 2 Joe Hall, Québec RC	165	250	325
☐ 3 Barney Holden, Québec	85	130	170
☐ 4 Joe Malone, Québec RC	350	525	700
☐ 5 Ed Oatman, Québec RC	85	130	170
☐ 6 Tommy Dunderdale, Québec	170	255	340
☐ 7 Ken Mallen, Québec RC	85	130	170
☐ 8 Jack McDonald, Québec RC	85	130	170
☐ 9 Fred Lake, Ottawa	85	130	170
☐ 10 Albert Kerr, Ottawa RC	85	130	170
☐ 11 Marty Walsh, Ottawa	140	210	275
☐ 12 Hamby Shore, Ottawa RC	85	130	170
☐ 13 Alex Currie, Ottawa RC	85	130	170
☐ 14 Bruce Ridpath, Ottawa	85	130	170
☐ 15 Bruce Stuart, Ottawa	150	225	300
☐ 16 Percy Lesueur (G), Ottawa	165	245	325
☐ 17 Jack Darragh, Ottawa RC	140	210	275
☐ 18 Steve Vair, Renfrew RC	85	130	170
☐ 19 Don Smith, Renfrew RC	85	130	170
☐ 20 Fred (Cyclone) Taylor, Renfrew	425	625	850
☐ 21 Bert Lindsay (G), Renfrew RC	115	175	225
☐ 22 Larry Gilmour, Renfrew RC	140	210	275
☐ 23 Bobby Rowe, Renfrew RC	85	130	170
☐ 24 S. Cleghorn, Renfrew RC	215	320	425
☐ 25 Odie Cleghorn, Renfrew RC	125	190	250
☐ 26 Skene Ronan, Renfrew RC	85	130	170
☐ 27 W. Smaill, Mont.W RC (with stick)	190	285	375
☐ 27 W. Smaill, Mont.W RC (without Stick)	190	285	375
☐ 28 Ernie Johnson, Mont.W	150	225	300
☐ 29 Jack Marshall, Mont.W	140	210	275
☐ 30 Harry Hyland, Mont.W	150	230	300
☐ 31 Art Ross, Mont.W	500	750	1,000
☐ 32 Riley Hern (G), Mont.W	150	230	300
☐ 33 Gordon Roberts, Mont.W	140	210	275
☐ 34 Frank Glass, Mont.W	85	130	170
☐ 35 Ernest Russell, Mont.W	150	225	300
☐ 36 James Gardiner, Mont.W RC	150	210	275
☐ 37 Art Bernier, Mont.	85	130	170
☐ 38 Geo. Vézina (G), Mont. RC	2,250	3,400	4,700
☐ 39 Henri Dellaire, Mont.	85	130	170
☐ 40 R. Power, Mont. RC	85	130	170
☐ 41 Didier Pitre, Mont.	150	210	300
☐ 42 Edouard Lalonde, Mont.	500	750	1,000
☐ 43 Eugene Payan, Mont. RC	85	130	170
☐ 44 George Poulin, Mont.	85	130	170
☐ 45 Jack Laviolette, Mont.	200	300	550

1912 - 13 IMPERIAL TOBACCO C57

The card number is found on the back to the right of the phrase, "Series of 50". The same crossed hockey sticks and puck design over the series' name "Hockey Series", is found on the C56 series, suggesting that the same producer issued the C56 and C57 issues. Each card measures 1 1/2" x 2 1/2".

Complete Set (50 cards):	10,000	14,000	18,000
ACC # C57	VG	EX	EX-MT
☐ 1 Georges Vézina (G), Mont.	1,800	2,400	5,000
☐ 2 Harry Broadbent, Ottawa RC	250	375	500
☐ 3 Clint Benedict (G), Ottawa RC	325	485	650
☐ 4 A. Atchinson, NE RC	150	230	300
☐ 5 Tommy Dunderdale, Québec	235	345	450
☐ 6 Art Bernier, Mont.W	150	230	300
☐ 7 Henri Dellaire, Mont.	150	230	300
☐ 8 George Poulin, Mont.	150	230	300
☐ 9 Eugene Payan, Mont.	150	230	300
☐ 10-Steve Vair, Renfrew	150	230	300
☐ 11 Bobby Rowe, Renfrew	150	230	300

The first hockey card sets: C56, C55, C57

The C55 series was the first to be catalogued by Jefferson Burdick (American Card Catalogue), but we've since come to understand that the C56 series was in fact produced a year earlier. From that first series, there is a number-37 salesman card of Newsy Lalonde. Salesmen would have taken this card to various retail stores to promote the product and to explain how they could sell more tobacco with the help of this card inside the package.

C55 Vézina

Today, we can look back and see that every significant Hall of Fame honoured member from that time period is included in one of those three sets. The top star is Georges Vézina (C55) and his card is one of the most valuable hockey cards ever.

The toughest series is by far the C57 set, but it is also the least collected. The toughest series to find in premium condition is the C56 set because it has been handled the most. The toughest card to find in nice condition is the Vézina C57 card (#1) with the best known example in EX-EX+ condition. The next toughest is the C56 card (#36) of Newsy Lalonde.

– Brian Wentz, BMW Sportscards, Madison, WI, USA.

		VG	EX	EX-MT
□	12 Don Smith, Renfrew	150	230	300
□	13 Bert Lindsay (G), Renfrew	175	265	350
□	14 Skene Ronan, Ottawa	150	230	300
□	15 Sprague Cleghorn, Renfrew	275	400	550
□	16 Joe Hall, Québec	260	370	475
□	17 Jack McDonald, Québec	150	230	300
□	18 Paddy Moran (G), Québec	235	345	450
□	19 Harry Hyland, Mont.W	225	325	425
□	20 Art Ross, Mont.W	700	1,000	1,400
□	21 Frank Glass, Mont.W	150	230	300
□	22 Walter Smaill, Mont.W	150	230	300
□	23 Gordon Roberts, Mont.W	225	325	425
□	24 James Gardiner, Mont.W	225	325	425
□	25 Ernie Johnson, Mont.W	225	325	425
□	26 Ernest Russell, Mont.W	225	325	425
□	27 Percy Lesueur (G), Ottawa	235	445	450
□	28 Bruce Ridpath, Ottawa	150	230	300
□	29 Jack Darragh, Ottawa	225	325	425
□	30 Hamby Shore, Ottawa	150	230	300
□	31 Fred Lake, Ottawa	150	230	300
□	32 Alex Currie, Ottawa	150	230	300
□	33 Albert Kerr, Ottawa	150	230	300
□	**34 Eddie Gerard, NE RC**	**225**	**325**	**425**
□	**35 Carl Kendall RC**	**150**	**230**	**300**
□	**36 Jack Fournier RC**	**150**	**230**	**300**
□	**37 Goldie Prodgers, Victoria RC**	**150**	**230**	**300**
□	**38 Jack Marks, Québec RC**	**150**	**230**	**300**
□	**39 G. Broughton (G), Mont.W RC**	**175**	**265**	**350**
□	**40 Arthur Boyce (G), Mont.W RC**	**175**	**265**	**350**
□	41 Lester Patrick	425	615	800
□	**42 Joe Dennison RC**	**150**	**230**	**300**
□	43 Fred (Cyclone) Taylor	600	900	1,200
□	44 Edouard Lalonde, Mont.	600	900	1,200
□	45 Didier Pitre, Mont.	225	325	425
□	46 Jack Laviolette, Mont.	225	325	425
□	47 Ed Oatman, Victoria	150	230	300
□	48 Joe Malone, Québec	400	600	800
□	49 Marty Walsh, Ottawa	225	325	425
□	50 Odie Cleghorn, Mont.	150	225	450

1912 - 13 RICHMOND CIGARETTES

The only hockey silk in this series is Rochester. The silk measures 3 15/16" x 5 1/2". It features a multi-coloured print on white silk.The back is blank. The imprint on the silk is "Richmond Straight Cut Cigarettes, Factory No. 25, 2nd Dist., Va.

RICHMOND (ACC # S-23)	VG	EX	EX-MT
□ Rochester	75	125	250

1912 - 15 MURAD SILKS

These college silks were issued with 10 different sport scenes: baseball pitcher, baseball hitter, football, golf, hammer, throwing, ice hockey, hurdles, rowing, running, and putting the shot. These silks are found with or without an impressed floral design and paper-backing sheet.

The larger silks (pictured) measure 5" x 7". The smaller silks measure 3 1/2" x 5 1/2".

Complete hockey set (25 large silks)	**1,200**	**2,500**	**4,500**
Complete hockey set (25 small silks)	**675**	**1,350**	**2,700**
LARGER (ACC # S-21)	**VG**	**EX**	**EX-MT**
Common large silk	70	125	250

□ Annapolis	□ Brown	□ California
□ Chicago	□ Colorado	□ Columbia
□ Cornell	□ Dartmouth	□ Georgetown
□ Harvard	□ Illinois	□ Michigan
□ Minnesota	□ Missouri	□ Ohio
□ Pennsylvania	□ Princeton	□ Purdue
□ Stanford	□ Syracuse	□ Texas
□ West Point	□ Wisconsin	□ Virginia
□ Yale		

SMALLER (ACC # S-22)	**VG**	**EX**	**EX-MT**
Common smaller silk	35	75	150

□ Annapolis	□ Brown	□ California
□ Chicago	□ Colorado	□ Columbia
□ Cornell	□ Dartmouth	□ Georgetown
□ Harvard	□ Illinois	□ Michigan
□ Minnesota	□ Missouri	□ Ohio
□ Pennsylvania	□ Princeton	□ Purdue
□ Stanford	□ Syracuse	□ Texas
□ West Point	□ Wisconsin	□ Virginia
□ Yale		

1914 WINTER SPORTS

There is only one hockey card in the set. The card measures 1 3/8" x 2 5/8".

Imperial Tobacco / Lambert & Butler	**VG**	**EX**	**EX-MT**
□ 23 Hockey on the Ice	10	20	40

1919 - 1930 POSTCARDS, STOCK AND ADVERTISEMENT CARDS

These cards feature various designs and are printed on different card stocks.In some cases, the card back was left blank for an advertisement.

	VG	EX	EX-MT
1919 VICTORIA RIVERS	**VG**	**EX**	**EX-MT**
□ Victoria Rivers (3 7/16" x 5 3/16", black & white, postcard-format card back)	35	70	150
□ Victoria Rivers at train station (3 7/16" x 5 3/16", black & white, postcard-format card back)	45	85	175
1920 BREFKORT	**VG**	**EX**	**EX-MT**
□ Brefkort / Gelukkig Nieuujaar (3 1/2" x 5 3/8" colour, postcard-format card back)	12	25	50
1923 NICOLAS SARONY	**VG**	**EX**	**EX-MT**
There are 15 cards in this set. Larger-size versions also exist.			
□ Nicolas Sarony / 14 Roman soldier playing hockey (2 1/2" x 3", black & white, postcard-format card back)	12	25	50
1924 ANONYMOUS FRANCE	**VG**	**EX**	**EX-MT**
□ 74 Chamonix, match de hockey (3 1/2" x 5 7/16", black & white, postcard-format card back)	12	25	50
1925 FSM WINTERSPORT	**VG**	**EX**	**EX-MT**
□ FSM / Wintersport XII,4 Eishockey (2 7/16" x 4 1/16", colour)	40	80	160
1925 HOSPODARSKE	**VG**	**EX**	**EX-MT**
□ Ve prosěch Hospodárské pomoci / goalie (3 9/16" x 5 9/16", colour, postcard-format card back)	12	25	50
1925 VERLAG A. RUEGG	**VG**	**EX**	**EX-MT**
□ Verlag A. Ruegg / hockey game cartoon (3 1/2" x 5 3/8", colour, postcard-format card back)	12	25	50
1928 RORNFRANCK OLYMPIA	**VG**	**EX**	**EX-MT**
□ Rornfranck / Olympia Amsterdam, Serie 14 Bild 5, Der Towart (G) (colour)	30	60	150
1930 CAMPBELL'S SOUP	**VG**	**EX**	**EX-MT**
□ Campbell's Soup / I'm always sure to be a winner (2 3/16" x 6 3/4", colour)	35	65	125

1919 VANCOUVER MILLIONAIRES

These black & white postcards measure 3 1/8" x 5 1/2".

	VG	EX	EX-MT
Complete Set (18 cards):	**1,200**	**2,500**	**4,500**
Photo Postcards	**VG**	**EX**	**EX-MT**
□ Lloyd Cook	65	95	125
□ Art Duncan	65	95	125
□ Smokey Harris	65	95	125
□ Alex Irvin	65	95	125
□ Hughie Lehman (G)	90	135	175
□ Duncan (Mickey) MacKay	65	95	125
□ Barney Stanley	150	225	300
□ Fred (Cyclone) Taylor	250	375	500
□ C. Uksila	65	95	125
Caricature Postcards	**VG**	**EX**	**EX-MT**
□ Lloyd Cook	65	95	125
□ Art Duncan	65	95	125
□ Smokey Harris	65	95	125
□ Alex Irvin	65	95	125
□ Hughie Lehman (G)	90	135	175
□ Duncan (Mickey) MacKay	65	95	125
□ Barney Stanley	150	225	300
□ Fred (Cyclone) Taylor	250	375	500
□ C. Uksila	65	95	125

1920S PATIENCE PLAYING CARDS

This deck of playing cards was issued in the 1920s.

Complete deck (52 cards)	**40**	**75**	**150**
Playing Cards	**VG**	**EX**	**EX-MT**
Common card	3	5	10

□ A of Clubs	□ 2 of Clubs	□ 3 of Clubs
□ 4 of Clubs	□ 5 of Clubs	□ 6 of Clubs
□ 7 of Clubs	□ 8 of Clubs	□ 9 of Clubs
□ 10 of Clubs	□ J of Clubs	□ Q of Clubs
□ K of Clubs	□ A of Diamonds	□ 2 of Diamonds
□ 3 of Diamonds	□ 4 of Diamonds	□ 5 of Diamonds
□ 6 of Diamonds	□ 7 of Diamonds	□ 8 of Diamonds
□ 9 of Diamonds	□ 10 of Diamonds	□ J of Diamonds
□ Q of Diamonds	□ K of Diamonds	□ A of Hearts
□ 2 of Hearts	□ 3 of Hearts	□ 4 of Hearts
□ 5 of Hearts	□ 6 of Hearts	□ 7 of Hearts
□ 8 of Hearts	□ 9 of Hearts	□ 10 of Hearts
□ J of Hearts	□ Q of Hearts	□ K of Hearts
□ A of Spades	□ 2 of Spades	□ 3 of Spades
□ 4 of Spades	□ 5 of Spades	□ 6 of Spades
□ 7 of Spades	□ 8 of Spades	□ 9 of Spades
□ 10 of Spades	□ J of Spades	□ Q of Spades
□ K of Spades		

1923 - 24 CRESCENT SELKIRKS

These black & white cards measure 1 9/16" x 2 3/8" and depict members of the Selkirks hockey team. The shell set price does not include card #6.

		VG	EX	EX-MT
Shell Set (13 cards):		**600**	**900**	**1,400**
Crescent Ice Cream		**VG**	**EX**	**EX-MT**
□	1 Cliff O'Meara	50	75	125
□	2 Leo Benard	50	75	100
□	3 Pete Speirs	50	75	100
□	4 Howard Brandow	50	75	100
□	5 George Clark	50	75	100
□	6 (redemption)			
□	7 Cecil Browne	50	75	100
□	8 Jack Connelly	50	75	100
□	9 Chuck Gardner (G)	150	225	350
□	10 Ward Turvey	50	75	100
□	11 Connie Johanneson	50	75	100
□	12 Frank Woodall	50	75	100
□	13 Harold McMunn	50	75	100
□	14 Connie Neil	50	75	125

1923 - 24 PAULINS CANDY

These black & white cards measure 1 3/8" x 2 3/4" and depict players of the Western Canadian Hockey League. A prize was awarded to collectors that completed the 90-card set (either a hockey stick or a box of chocolates).

		VG	EX	EX-MT
Complete Set (70 cards):		**4,500**	**7,000**	**10,000**
ACC # V128		**VG**	**EX**	**EX-MT**
□	1 Bill Borland	80	125	250
□	2 Pete Speirs	70	100	140
□	3 Jack Hughes	70	100	140
□	4 Errol Gillis	70	100	140
□	5 Cecil Browne	70	100	140
□	6 W. Roberts	70	100	140
□	7 Howard Brandow	70	100	140
□	8 Fred Comfort	70	100	140
□	9 Cliff O'Meara	70	100	140
□	10 Leo Benard	70	100	140
□	11 Lloyd Harvey	70	100	140
□	12 Bobby Connors	70	100	140
□	13 Daddy Dalman	70	100	140
□	14 Dub Mackie	70	100	140
□	15 Lorne Chabot (G)	175	225	375
□	16 Phat Wilson	100	150	200
□	17 Wilf L'Heureux	70	100	140
□	18 Danny Cox	90	135	175
□	19 Bill Brydge	90	135	175
□	20 Alex Gray	70	100	140
□	21 Albert Pudas	70	100	140
□	22 Dick Irvin, Sr.	250	375	500
□	23 Puss Traub	70	100	140
□	24 Red McCusker (G)	75	115	150
□	25 Jack Asseltine	70	100	140
□	26 Duke Dutkowski	75	115	150
□	27 Charlie McVeigh	90	135	175
□	28 George Hay	175	265	350
□	29 Amby Moran	70	100	140
□	30 Barney Stanley	175	265	350
□	31 Art Gagne	75	135	150
□	32 Louis Berlinquette	90	135	175
□	33 P.C. Stevens	70	100	140
□	34 W.D. Elmer	70	100	140
□	35 Bill Cook	275	425	550
□	36 Leo Reise	90	135	175
□	37 Curly Headley	100	150	200
□	38 Edouard (Newsy) Lalonde	325	475	675
□	39 George Hainsworth (G)	325	475	675
□	40 Laurie Scott	70	100	140
□	41 Joe Simpson	190	275	375
□	42 Bob Trapp	70	100	140
□	43 Joe McCormick	70	100	140
□	44 Ty Arbour	75	115	150
□	45 Duke Keats	70	100	140
□	46 Hal Winkler	70	100	140
□	47 Johnny Sheppard	90	135	175
□	48 Crutchy Morrison	70	100	140
□	49 Spunk Sparrow	70	100	140
□	50 Percy McGregor	70	100	140
□	51 Harry Tuckwell	70	100	140
□	52 Chubby Scott	70	100	140
□	53 Scotty Fraser	70	100	140
□	54 Bob Davis	70	100	140
□	55 Clucker White	70	100	140
□	56 Bob Armstrong	70	100	140
□	57 Doc Langtry	70	100	140

1919 - 1930

1925 FSM Wintersport

1930 Campbell's Soup

☐ 58 Darb Sommers	70	100	140
☐ 59 Frank Hacquoil	70	100	140
☐ 60 Stan Evans	70	100	140
☐ 61 Ed Oatman	70	100	140
☐ 62 Red Dutton	190	275	375
☐ 63 Herb Gardiner	165	250	325
☐ 64 Bernie Morris	70	100	140
☐ 65 Bobbie Benson	70	100	140
☐ 66 Ernie Anderson	70	100	140
☐ 67 Cully Wilson	75	135	140
☐ 68 Charlie Reid (G)	75	115	140
☐ 69 Harry Oliver	225	335	450
☐ 70 Rusty Crawford	120	150	300

1923 WILLARD'S CHOCOLATES

This 56-card multi-sport set features only four hockey players. The set was made in the United States and inserted in Willard's Sports Nut Bar. It is uncertain whether a Canadian version was produced. Cards measure 1 3/8" x 3 7/8".

ACC # V122	VG	EX	EX-MT
☐ 43 Harry Watson, Canada	140	225	350
☐ 45 Ernie Collett (G), Canada	75	115	200
☐ 47 Hooley Smith, Canada	165	250	375
☐ 52 Dunc Munro, Canada	100	150	250

1923 - 24 WILLIAM PATERSON

This set is very similar to the subsequent V145-2 set except for its sepia (dark brown) colour and size. Cards measure 2" x 3 1/4". Card #25 (Bert Corbeau) is scarce and is not included in the set price.

Shell Set (39 cards):	8,000	12,500	20,000
ACC # V145-1	VG	EX	EX-MT
☐ 1 Eddie Gerard, Otta.	180	260	450
☐ **2 Frank Nighbor, Otta. RC**	300	450	650
☐ **3 King Clancy, Otta. RC**	1,200	1,800	2,600
☐ 4 Jack Darragh, Otta.	175	265	350
☐ **5 Harry Helman, Otta. RC**	100	150	200
☐ **6 George Boucher, Otta. RC**	175	265	350
☐ 7 Clint Benedict (G), Otta.	240	360	475
☐ **8 Lionel Hitchman, Otta. RC**	140	210	275
☐ 9 Harry Broadbent, Otta.	190	285	375
☐ **10 Cy Denneny, Otta. RC**	250	375	500
☐ 11 Sprague Cleghorn, Mont.	215	325	425
☐ **12 Sylvio Mantha, Mont. RC**	190	285	375
☐ 13 Joe Malone, Mont.	265	400	525
☐ **14 Aurèle Joliat, Mont. RC**	1,000	1,500	2,000
☐ **15 Howie Morenz, Mont. RC**	3,000	4,400	6,000
☐ **16 Billy Boucher, Mont. RC**	100	150	200
☐ **17 Billy Couture, Mont. RC**	100	150	200
☐ 18 Odie Cleghorn, Mont.	140	210	275
☐ 19 Georges Vézina (G), Mont.	1,000	1,500	2,000
☐ **20 Amos Arbour, Toro. RC**	100	150	200
☐ **21 Lloyd Andrews, Toro. RC**	100	150	200
☐ **22 Billy Stuart, Toro. RC**	100	150	200
☐ **23 Cecil (Babe) Dye, Toro. RC**	240	360	475
☐ **24 Jack J. Adams, Toro. RC**	240	360	475
☐ **25 Bert Corbeau, Toro. RC**			
☐ **26 Reg Noble, Toro. RC**	175	265	350
☐ **27 Stan Jackson, Toro. RC**	100	150	200
☐ **28 John Roach (G), Toro. RC**	150	230	300
☐ **29 Vernon Forbes (G), Ham. RC**	100	150	200
☐ **30 Wilf (Shorty) Green, Ham. RC**	175	265	350
☐ **31 Redvers (Red) Green, Ham. RC**	100	150	200
☐ 32 Goldie Prodgers, Ham.	100	150	200
☐ **33 Leo Reise, Sr., Ham. RC**	100	150	200
☐ **34 Ken Randall, Ham. RC**	100	150	200
☐ **35 Billy Burch, Ham RC**	175	265	350
☐ **36 Jesse Spring, Ham RC**	100	150	200
☐ **37 Edmond Bouchard, Ham RC**	100	150	200
☐ **38 Mickey Roach, Ham RC**	100	150	200
☐ **39 Charles Fraser, Ham RC**	100	150	200
☐ **40 Corbett Denneny, Ham RC**	200	250	450

1924 - 25 CHAMP'S CIGARETTES

The sepia-toned cards contain a short biography on the card back. Cards measure 1 1/2" x 2 1/2".

Complete Set (60 cards):	9,000	13,500	20,000
ACC # C144	VG	EX	EX-MT
☐ **Carson Cooper, Bost. RC**	115	170	225
☐ **Hec Fowler (G), Bost. RC**	115	170	225
☐ **Curley Headley, Bost. RC**	115	170	225
☐ **James Herberts, Bost. RC**	115	170	225
☐ **Herb Mitchell, Bost. RC**	115	170	225
☐ **George Redding, Bost. RC**	115	170	225
☐ **Werner Schnarr, Bost. RC**	115	170	225
☐ **Alfred Skinner, Bost. RC**	115	170	225
☐ Edmond Bouchard, Ham.	115	170	225
☐ Billy Burch, Ham.	200	300	400
☐ Vernon Forbes (G), Ham.	115	170	225
☐ Redvers (Red) Green, Ham.	115	170	225
☐ Wilf (Shorty) Green, Ham.	175	265	350
☐ **Charlie Langlois, Ham. RC**	115	170	225
☐ **Alex McKinnon, Ham. RC**	115	170	225
☐ Goldie Prodgers, Ham.	115	170	225
☐ Ken Randall, Ham.	115	170	225
☐ Mickey Roach, Ham.	115	170	225
☐ Jesse Spring, Ham.	115	170	225
☐ Billy Boucher, Mont.	115	170	225
☐ Odie Cleghorn, Mont.	135	250	265
☐ Sprague Cleghorn, Mont.	215	320	425
☐ Billy Couture, Mont.	115	170	225
☐ Aurèle Joliat, Mont.	850	1,275	1,700
☐ Sylvio Mantha, Mont.	190	285	375
☐ Howie Morenz, Mont.	2,000	3,000	4,000
☐ Georges Vézina (G), Mont.	900	1,300	1,800
☐ Clint Benedict (G), Mont.M	250	375	500
☐ **Louis Berlinquette, Mont.M RC**	115	170	225
☐ Harry Broadbent, Mont.M	200	300	400
☐ **Jim Cain, Mont.M RC**	115	170	225
☐ **George Carroll, Mont.M RC**	115	170	225
☐ **Chuck Dinsmore, Mont.M RC**	115	170	225
☐ **Fred Lowrey, Mont.M RC**	115	170	225
☐ **Dunc Munro, Mont.M RC**	115	170	225
☐ **Gerry Munro, Mtl M RC**	115	170	225
☐ **Sam Rothschild, Mtl M RC**	115	170	225
☐ **Ganton Scott, Mont.M RC**	115	170	225
☐ **Robert Boucher, Otta. RC**	115	170	225
☐ **Spiff (Earl) Campbell, Otta. RC**	115	170	225
☐ Francis (King) Clancy, Otta.	900	1,350	1,800
☐ **Alex Connell (G), Otta. RC**	225	375	450
☐ Cy Denneny, Otta.	240	360	475
☐ **Frank Finnigan, Otta. RC**	175	265	350
☐ Lionel Hitchman, Otta.	135	200	265
☐ Frank Nighbor, Otta.	250	375	500
☐ **Hooley Smith, Otta. RC**	240	360	475
☐ Jack Adams, Toro.	275	425	575
☐ Lloyd Andrews, Toro.	115	170	225
☐ Bert Corbeau, Toro.	115	170	225
☐ **Hap Day, Toro. RC**	250	375	500
☐ Babe Dye, Toro.	215	320	425
☐ **Albert Holway, Toro. RC**	115	170	225
☐ **Stan Jackson, Toro. RC**	115	170	225
☐ **Bert McCaffrey, Toro. RC**	115	170	225
☐ Reg Noble, Toro.	190	285	375
☐ **Mickey O'Leary, Toro. RC**	115	170	225
☐ John Roach (G), Toro.	135	200	265
☐ **Chris Speyers, Toro. RC**	115	170	225
☐ The Stanley Cup	225	500	750

1924 - 25 MAPLE CRISPETTE

These black & white cards measure 1 3/8" x 2 3/8". Card #15 (Sprague Cleghorn) is rare or scarce and is not included in the set price.

Shell Set (29 cards):	5,200	7,500	12,000
ACC # V130	VG	EX	EX-MT
☐ **1 Dunc Munro, Mont.M RC**	170	200	425
☐ 2 Clint Benedict (G), Mont.M	250	375	500
☐ **3 Hec Fowler (G), Bost. RC**	125	190	250
☐ **4 Fern Headley, Bost. RC**	115	170	225
☐ **5 Alf Skinner, Bost. RC**	115	170	225
☐ **6 Lloyd Cook, Bost. RC**	115	170	225
☐ **7 Smokey Harris, Bost. RC**	115	170	225
☐ **8 James Herberts, Bost. RC**	115	170	225
☐ **9 Carson Cooper, Bost. RC**	115	170	225
☐ 10 Redvers (Red) Green, Ham.	115	170	225
☐ 11 Billy Boucher, Mont.	115	170	225
☐ 12 Howie Morenz, Mont.	1,750	2,600	3,500
☐ 13 Georges Vézina (G), Mont.	1,000	1,500	2,000
☐ 14 Aurèle Joliat, Mont.	800	1,250	1,700
☐ 15 Sprague Cleghorn, Mont.			
☐ **16 Jim Cain, Mont.M RC**	115	170	225
☐ **17 Chuck Dinsmore, Mont.M RC**	115	170	225
☐ 18 Harry Broadbent, Mont.M	200	300	400
☐ **19 Sam Rothschild, Mont.M RC**	115	170	225
☐ **20 George Carroll, Mont.M RC**	115	170	225
☐ 21 Billy Burch, Ham.	175	265	350
☐ 22 Wilf (Shorty) Green, Ham.	175	265	350
☐ 23 Mickey Roach, Ham.	115	170	225
☐ 24 Ken Randall, Ham.	115	170	225
☐ 25 Vernon Forbes (G), Ham.	125	190	250
☐ **26 Charlie Langlois, Ham. RC**	115	170	225
☐ 27 Edouard Lalonde, Mont.	400	600	800
☐ **28 Fred Lowrey, Mont.M RC**	115	170	225
☐ **29 Ganton Scott, Mont.M RC**	115	170	225
☐ **30 Louis Berlinquette, Mont.M RC**	135	200	425

1924 - 25 CRESCENT SELKIRKS

These sepia cards measure 1 9/16" x 2 3/8" and depict members of the Selkirks hockey team. The shell set price does not include card #7.

Shell Set (13 cards):	600	800	1,200
Complete Set (14 cards):	900	1,200	1,800
Crescent Ice Cream	VG	EX	EX-MT
☐ 1 Howard Brandow	50	75	125
☐ 2 Jack Hughes	50	75	100
☐ 3 Tony Baril	50	75	100
☐ 4 Bill Bowman	50	75	100
☐ 5 W. Roberts	50	75	100
☐ 6 Cecil Browne	350	500	700
☐ 7 Errol Gillis	50	75	100
☐ 8 Selkirks Team	115	179	225
☐ 9 Fred Comfort	50	75	100
☐ 10 Cliff O'Meara	50	75	100
☐ 11 Leo Benard	50	75	100
☐ 12 Pete Speirs	50	75	100
☐ 13 Peter Meurer	50	75	100
☐ 14 Billy Borland	50	75	125

1924 - 25 CRESCENT FALCONS

These sepia cards measure 1 9/16" x 2 3/8" and depict members of the Falcons hockey team. The shell set price does not include card #6.

Shell Set (13 cards):	1,500	2,000	3,000
Crescent Ice Cream	VG	EX	EX-MT
☐ 1 Bill Cockburn	150	225	400
☐ 2 Wally Byron	150	225	300
☐ 3 Wally Fridfinnson	150	225	300
☐ 4 Murray Murdoch	150	225	300
☐ 5 Oliver Redpath	150	225	300
☐ 7 Ward McVey	150	225	300
☐ 8 Tote Mitchell	150	225	300
☐ 9 Lorne Carrol	150	225	300
☐ 10Tony Wise	150	225	300
☐ 11 Johnny Myres	150	225	300
☐ 12 Gordon McKenzie	150	225	300
☐ 13 Harry Neil	150	225	300
☐ 14 Blake Watson	150	225	400

1924 - 25 HOLLAND CREAMERIES

These black & white cards measure 1 1/2" x 2 7/8" and depict members of the Western Hockey League.

Complete Set (10 cards):	750	1,100	1,600
Holland Creameries	VG	EX	EX-MT
☐ 1 Wally Fridfinnson	80	125	200
☐ 2 Harold McMunn	80	125	200
☐ 3 Art Somers	80	125	200
☐ 4 Frank Woodall	80	125	200
☐ 5 Frank Fredrickson	150	225	400
☐ 6 R.J. Benson	80	125	200
☐ 7 Harry Neil	80	125	200
☐ 8 Wally Byron	80	125	200
☐ 9 Connie Neil	300	450	800
☐ 10 J. Austman	80	125	200

1924 - 25 WILLIAM PATERSON

The cards are slightly smaller than the otherwise very similar V145-1 series and have a greenish-black tone. The cards measure 1 1/16" x 3 1/4". Card no. 3, Francis (King) Clancy, is the only card numbered the same as in the V145-1 series.

Complete Set (60 cards):	8,000	12,500	18,000
ACC # V145-2	VG	EX	EX-MT
☐ **1 Joe Ironstone (G), Otta. RC**	115	175	335
☐ 2 George Boucher, Otta.	125	190	250
☐ 3 Francis (King) Clancy, Otta.	850	1,350	1,800
☐ 4 Lionel Hitchman, Otta.	120	180	235
☐ **5 Hooley Smith, Otta. RC**	225	340	450
☐ 6 Frank Nighbor, Otta.	240	350	475
☐ 7 C. Denneny, Otta., Err (Dennenay)	225	340	450
☐ **8 Spiff Campbell, Otta. RC**	95	135	190
☐ **9 Frank Finnigan, Otta. RC**	125	190	250
☐ **10 Alex Connell (G), Otta. RC**	200	300	400
☐ 11 Vernon Forbes (G), Ham.	95	145	190
☐ 12 Ken Randall, Ham.	95	145	190
☐ 13 Billy Burch, Ham.	165	250	325
☐ 14 Wilf (Shorty) Green, Ham.	165	250	325
☐ 15 Redvers (Red) Green, Ham,	95	145	190
☐ **16 Alex McKinnon, Ham. RC**	95	145	190
☐ **17 Charlie Langlois, Ham. RC**	95	145	190
☐ 18 Mickey Roach, Ham.	95	145	190
☐ 19 Edmond Bouchard, Ham.	95	145	190
☐ 20 Jesse Spring, Error, Ham.	95	145	190
☐ **21 Carson Cooper, Bost. RC**	95	145	190
☐ **22 Smokey Harris, Bost. RC**	95	145	190
☐ **23 Fern Headley, Bost. RC**	95	145	190
☐ **24 Bill Cook, Bost. RC**	275	415	550
☐ **25 James Herberts, Bost. RC**	95	145	190
☐ **26 Werner Schnarr, Bost. RC**	95	145	190
☐ **27 Alf Skinner, Bost. RC**	95	145	190
☐ **28 George Redding, Bost. RC**	95	145	190
☐ **29 Herb Mitchell, Bost. RC**	95	145	190
☐ **30 Hec Fowler (G), Bost. RC**	115	170	225
☐ 31 Billy Stuart, Bost.	95	145	190
☐ 32 Clint Benedict (G), Mont.M	215	320	425
☐ **33 Gerry Munro, Mont.M RC**	95	145	190
☐ **34 Dunc Munro, Mont.M RC**	125	185	250
☐ 35 Jim Cain, Mont.M	95	145	190
☐ **36 Fred Lowrey, Mont.M RC**	95	145	190
☐ **37 Sam Rothschild,, Mont.M RC**	95	145	190
☐ **38 Ganton Scott, Mont.M RC**	95	145	190
☐ 39 Harry Broadbent, Mont.M	190	285	375
☐ **40 Chuck Dinsmore, Mont.M RC**	95	145	190
☐ **41 Louis Berlinquette, Mont.M RC**	95	145	190
☐ **42 George Carroll, Mont.M RC**	95	145	190
☐ 43 Georges Vézina (G), Mont.	850	1,250	1,700
☐ 44 Billy Couture, Mont.	95	145	190
☐ 45 Odie Cleghorn, Mont.	125	190	250
☐ 46 Billy Boucher, Mont.	95	145	190
☐ 47 Howie Morenz, Mont.	1,600	2,400	3,200
☐ 48 Aurèle Joliat, Mont.	700	1,100	1,500
☐ 49 Sprague Cleghorn, Mont.	200	300	400
☐ **50 Billy Mantha, Mont. RC**	95	145	190
☐ 51 Reg Noble, Toro.	175	265	350
☐ 52 John Roach (G), Toro.	125	190	250
☐ 53 Jack Adams, Toro.	225	340	450
☐ 54 Babe Dye, Toro	200	300	400
☐ **55 Reg Reid, Toro. RC**	95	145	190
☐ **56 Albert Holway, Toro. RC**	95	145	190

	VG	EX	EX-MT
57 Bert McCaffery, Toro. RC	**95**	**145**	**190**
58 Bert Corbeau, Toro.	125	185	250
59 Lloyd Andrews, Toro.	95	145	190
60 Stan Jackson, Toro.	120	180	335

1925 - 27 ANONYMOUS ISSUES

The black & white cards measure 1 3/8" x 2 3/8". It has become evident that more than two different anonymous sets were issued during this time period. Previously designated as "with borders" and "without borders", additional cards have surfaced with numbers that do not correspond to prior checklists. Until further information is available, all these cards will be grouped together. Cards without borders are designated with an "NB".

Anonymous	VG	EX	EX-MT
1 Billy Boucher, Mont.	200	300	550
1 George Hainsworth, Mont.	575	800	1,200
2 Billy Boucher, Mont.	285	395	500
2 Billy Coutu, Mont.	225	315	400
3 Sylvio Mantha, Mont.	285	395	500
3 Georges Vézina (G), Mont.	850	1,200	1,600
4 Sylvio Mantha, Mont.	300	425	550
4 Roland Paulhus, Mont.	110	155	200
4 Roland Paulhus, Mont.	110	155	200
5 Alphonse Lacroix (G), Mont.	125	185	250
6 Albert Leduc, Mont., Error	50	100	200
7 W. Larochelle, Mont., Error (Victor)	140	195	250
7 Wildor Larochelle (NB), Mont.	140	195	250
8 Aurèle Joliat, Mont.	750	1,000	1,400
9 Howie Morenz, Mont.	2,800	3,600	4,800
10 Hector Lepiné, Mont.	110	155	200
11 Alphonse Lacroix (G), Mont.	125	185	250
11 Amby Moran (G), Mont.	125	185	250
12 Art Gagné, Mont.	125	190	250
12 Herb Rheaume (NB) (G), Mont.	125	185	250
13 Pit Lépine, Mont.	250	350	450
14 Bill Holmes, Mont.	110	155	200
15 Léo Dandurand, Director, Mont.	285	395	500
16 Alex Connell (G), Otta.	325	465	600
16 Frank Nighbor, Otta.	325	465	600
17 Francis (King) Clancy, Otta.	1,000	1,400	1,800
17 Cy Denneny, Otta.	285	395	500
18 Francis (King) Clancy (NB), Otta.	1,000	1,400	1,800
19 Billy Boucher, Otta.	140	195	250
19 Hec Kilrea, Otta. RC	**110**	**155**	**200**
20 Hec Kilrea, Otta. RC	**110**	**155**	**200**
21 Hooley Smith, Otta.	325	415	600
22 Alex Smith, Otta. RC	**140**	**195**	**250**
22 Alex Smith (NB), Otta.	140	195	250
25 Ed Gorman, Otta.	110	155	200
28 Alex Connell (G), Otta.	300	425	550
31 Sprague Cleghorn, Bost.	325	465	600
31 Carson Cooper, Bost.	110	155	200
32 Carson Cooper, Bost.	110	155	200
36 Hugo Harrington, Bost.	110	155	200
38 Herb Mitchell, Bost.	110	155	200
39 Herb Mitchell (NB), Bost.	125	185	250
39 Charles Stewart (G), Bost.	110	155	200
40 Red Stuart, Bost.	110	155	200
41 Lloyd Cook, Bost.	110	155	200
41 Sprague Cleghorn (NB), Bost. (Mont.)	285	395	500
42 Billy Coutu, Mont.	225	315	400
42 Billy Coutu, Mont.	100	200	400
91 Dutch Cain (NB), Bost.	135	190	250
46 Odie Cleghorn, Pitt.P	150	215	275
46 Odie Cleghorn (NB), Pitt.P	150	215	275
46 Odie Cleghorn (NB), Mont.	150	215	275
47 Louis Berlinquette, Pitt.P (Toro.)	110	155	200
47 Roy Worters, Pitt.P	450	625	800
48 Hib (Hibbert) Milks, Pitt.P	110	155	200
52 Hib (Hibbert) Milks (NB), Pitt.P	110	155	200
57 Odie Cleghorn, Pitt.P	150	215	275
61 Pete Bellefeuille, Toro. StP	175	250	350
76 Charlie Langlois, NYAm.	65	125	250
77 Jake Forbes (G), NYAm.	100	200	400
79 Billy Burch, NYAm.	225	300	400
62 Gerry Munro, Mont.M	110	155	200
64 Bert Corbeau, Mont.M	135	195	250
76 Charlie Langlois, Mont.M	110	155	200
77 Jake Forbes, Mont.M	110	155	200
79 Billie Burch, Mont.M	225	315	400
82 Joe Simpson, Mt. M	225	315	400
82 Joe Simpson, NYAm.	150	200	400
91 Dutch Cain, Mont.M	135	195	250
91 Dunc Munro, Mont.M	150	215	275
92 Dunc Munro (NB), Mont.M	150	215	275
92 Nels Stewart, Mont.M RC	**425**	**615**	**800**
95 Clint Benedict (G), Mont.M	350	500	650
96 Reg Noble, Mont.M	215	295	375
97 Nels Stewart, Mont.M	425	615	800
100 Sam Rothschild, Mont.M Err (Rotchild)	110	155	200
121 Harry Holmes (G), Detr.C	225	315	400
127 Clem Loughlin, Detr.C	110	155	200
129 Johnny Sheppard, Detr.C	110	155	200
136 Gord Fraser, Chic.	110	155	200
138 Dick Irvin, Chic.	350	525	700

1925 DOMINION CHOCOLATE

This 120-card multi-sport set features only 32 hockey cards. The black & white cards measure 1 1/4" x 2 7/8". A 120-card set in EX-MT may sell at $10,000.00.

Dominion Chocolate	VG	EX	EX-MT
13 Granite Club, Olympic Champs	115	170	225
28 North Toronto, O.H.A.	90	135	175
35 Peterborough, O.H.A.	90	135	175
49 Owen Sound Jrs., O.H.A.	90	135	175
55 E.J. Collett, Granite	70	100	140
56 Hughie J. Fox, Granite	70	100	140
57 Dunc Munro, Granite	90	135	175
58 M. Rutherford, Granite	75	100	150
59 Beattie Ramsay, Granite	75	100	150
60 Bert McCaffery, Toro.	75	100	150
61 Soo Greyhounds	90	135	175
68 J.P. Aggatts	70	100	140
69 Hooley Smith, Granite	150	225	300
70 J. Cameron (G), Granite	90	135	175
81 William Fraser, Nova Scotia	75	100	150
82 Vernon Forbes (G), Hamilton	90	135	175
83 Wilf (Shorty) Green, Hamilton	135	200	265
84 Redvers (Red) Green, Hamilton	75	100	150
86 Jack Langtry	75	100	150
89 Billy Coutu, Mont.	75	100	150
92 J. Hughes	75	100	150
95 Edouard Lalonde	275	375	550
101 Bill Brydge, Port Arthur	75	100	150
103 Cecil Browne, Selkirk	75	100	150
106 J.C. "Red" Porter, Toro.	75	100	150
112 North Bay Hockey Team	90	135	175
113 Ross Somerville, Toro. Univ.	75	100	150
114 Harry Watson, Granite	150	225	300
117 Odie Cleghorn, Error (Ogie)	90	135	175
118 Lionel Conacher, Toro.	300	450	600
119 Aurèle Joliat, Mont.	450	640	900
120 Georges Vézina (G), Mont.	600	750	1,400

1926 DOMINION CHOCOLATE

This 60-card set features Canadian athletes from several different sports. This set had a premium tab along the bottom of the card. There were two series of this set, both of which are identical except the second set was printed on a lighter weight stock. Only the 11 hockey cards are listed here. The black & white cards measure 1 1/16" x 2 3/8". A 120-card set in EX-MT may sell at $10,000.

Dominion Chocolate	VG	EX	EX-MT
11 Alex Gray, Toronto	75	115	150
12 Duncan B. Munro, Toronto	100	150	200
17 Gerald Green, Toronto	75	115	150
18 Ernie Williams, Toronto	75	115	150
23 Douglas Young, Toronto	75	115	150
24 A. Gauthier, Toronto	75	115	150
25 Don Cameron, Québec	75	115	150
26 George Clarke	75	115	150
27 "Steve" Rice, Toronto	75	115	150
28 "Ken" Doraty, Regina	125	185	250
29 "Bud" Fisher (G), Toronto	90	135	175

1927 WORLD OF SPORT

This 50-card set features but one hockey card. The black & white cards measure 1 7/16" x 2 5/8".

Imperial Tobacco / Lambert & Butler	VG	EX	EX-MT
9 Montréal Victorias	60	80	120

1927 - 28 LA PRESSE

These photos, cut from the Montréal newspaper, measure 10" x 16 1/2".

La Presse photo	VG	EX	EX-MT
Dec. 10 Howie Morenz, Mont.	250	350	475
Dec. 17 Aurèle Joliat, Mont.	170	250	335
Dec. 24 Sylvio Mantha, Mont.	70	100	140
Dec. 31 Pit Lépine, Mont.	45	65	85
Jan. 7 George Hainsworth (G), Mont.	80	120	160
Jan. 14 Art Gagné, Mont.	45	65	85
Jan. 21 Herb Gardiner, Mont.	65	95	125
Jan. 28 Albert Leduc, Mont.	45	65	85
Feb. 4 Wildor Larochelle, Mont.	45	65	85
Feb. 11 Léonard Gaudreault, Mont.	45	65	85
Feb. 18 Gizzy Hart, Mont.	45	65	85
Feb. 25 Charles Langlois, Mont.	45	65	85
Mar. 3 Georges Vézina (G), Mont.	225	350	450
Mar. 31 Cattarinich/ Hart/ Dandurand / Letourmeau	65	95	125
Apr. 7 Eddie Shore, Bost.	175	250	350
Apr. 14 Lionel Conacher, NYAm.	100	150	200
Apr. 21 Red Porter, Toro. Grad.	45	65	85
Apr. 28 George Patterson, Mont.	45	65	85

1927 - 28 LA PATRIE

These photos measure 8 1/2" x 11".

La Patrie photo	VG	EX	EX-MT
1 Sylvio Mantha	70	100	135
2 Art Gagné	30	50	65
3 Léo Lafrance	30	50	65
4 Aurèle Joliat	175	260	350
5 Pit Lepine	40	65	90
6 Gizzy Hart	30	50	65
7 Wildor Larochelle	30	50	65
8 George Hainsworth (G)	90	135	175
9 Herb Gardiner	50	75	100
10 Albert LeDuc	40	65	90
11 Marty Burke	40	65	90
12 Charlie Langlois	30	50	65
13 Léo Gaudreault	40	70	90
14 Howie Morenz	250	375	500
15 Cecil M. Hart	40	70	90
16 Léo Dandurand	40	65	90
17 Edouard Lalonde	100	150	200
18 Didier Pitre	40	65	90
19 Jack Laviolette	50	75	100
20 George Patterson	30	50	65
21 Georges Vézina (G)	225	335	450

1928 WORLD IN PICTURES

Other cards may exist in this series. Cards measure 1 9/16" x 2 1/4".

Salem Zigarettenfabrik Dresden	VG	EX	EX-MT
2 Canada	35	70	140

1928 - 29 LA PRESSE

These photos, cut from the Montréal newspaper, measure 10" x 16 1/2".

La Presse photo	VG	EX	EX-MT
Dec. 15 Martin Burke, Mont.	60	90	120
Dec. 22 Nels Stewart, Mont.M	85	130	170
Jan. 5 Babe Siebert, Mont.M	70	100	140
Jan. 12 Happy Day, Toro.	65	95	130
Jan. 19 Clint Benedict (G), Mont.M	80	120	160
Jan. 26 Red Dutton, Mont.M	65	100	130
Feb. 2 Jimmy Ward, Mont.M	45	65	85
Feb. 9 Bill Phillips, Mont.M	45	65	85
Feb. 16 Frank Boucher, NYRa.	75	115	150
Feb. 23 Lucien Brunet, Local League	45	65	85
Mar. 2 George Boucher, Otta.	65	95	130
Mar. 16 Armand Mondou, Mont.	45	65	85
Mar. 23 Bun Cook, NYRa.	70	100	140
Apr. 6 Georges Mantha, Mont.	45	65	90

1928 - 29 PAULINS CANDY

These black & white cards measure 1 3/8" x 2 5/8". The players on cards 51, 53, 72, 75, 82, 84, 85, 86, and 90 have not yet been identified.

	VG	EX	EX-MT
Complete Set (90 cards):	2,250	3,500	4,700
Paulins Candy			
1 U. of Manitoba Girls Team	80	120	200
2 Elgin Hockey Team	65	95	125
3 Brandon Schools Boy Champions	65	95	125
4 Port Arthur Hockey Team	65	95	125
5 Enderby Hockey Team	65	95	125
6 Humbolt H.S. Hockey Team	65	95	125
7 Regina Collegiate Hockey Team	65	95	125
8 Weyburn Beavers	65	95	125
9 Moose Jaw College Jr. Team	65	95	125
10 M.A.C. Junior Hockey	65	95	125
11 Vermilion Agricultural School	65	95	125
12 Rovers, Cranbrook	65	95	125
13 Empire School, Moose Jaw	65	95	125
14 Arts Senior Hockey	65	95	125
15 Juvenile Varsity Hockey	65	95	125
16 St. Peter's College Hockey	65	95	125
17 Arts Girls Hockey Team	65	95	125
18 Swan River Hockey Team	65	95	125
19 UMSU Junior Hockey Team	65	95	125
20 Champion College Hockey Team	65	95	125
21 Drinkwater Hockey Team	65	95	125
22 Elks Hockey Team, Biggar, Sask.	65	95	125
23 South Calgary High School	65	95	125
24 Meota Hockey	65	95	125
25 Chartered Accountants	65	95	125
26 Nutana Collegiate Hockey Team	65	95	125
27 MacLeod Hockey Team	65	95	125
28 Arts Junior Hockey	65	95	125
29 Fort William Juniors	65	95	125
30 Swan Lake Hockey Team	65	95	125
31 Dauphin Hockey Team	65	95	125
32 Mount Royal Hockey Team	65	95	125
33 Port Arthur W. End Junior Hockey	65	95	125
34 Hanna Hockey Club	65	95	125
35 Vermilion Junior Hockey	65	95	125
36 Smithers Hockey Team	65	95	125
37 Lloydminster High School	65	95	125
38 Winnipeg Rangers	65	95	125
39 Delisle Intermediate Hockey	65	95	125
40 Moose Jaw College Senior Hockey	65	95	125
41 Art Bonneyman	65	95	125
42 Jimmy Graham	65	95	125

		VG	EX	EX-MT
☐	43 Pat O'Hunter	65	95	125
☐	44 Leo Moret	65	95	125
☐	45 Blondie McLennen	65	95	125
☐	46 Red Beattie	65	95	125
☐	47 Frank Peters	65	95	125
☐	48 Lloyd McIntyre	65	95	125
☐	49 Art Somers	65	95	125
☐	50 Ikey Morrison	65	95	125
☐	51 Calgary Jimmies	65	95	125
☐	52 Don Cummings	65	95	125
☐	53 Calgary Jimmies	65	95	125
☐	54 P. Gerlitz	65	95	125
☐	55 A. Kay	65	95	125
☐	56 Paul Runge	65	95	125
☐	57 J. Gerlitz	65	95	125
☐	58 H. Gerlitz	65	95	125
☐	59 C. Biles	65	95	125
☐	60 Jimmy Evans	65	95	125
☐	61 Ira Stuart	65	95	125
☐	62 Berg Irving	65	95	125
☐	63 Cecil Browne	65	95	125
☐	64 Nick Wasnie	65	95	125
☐	65 Gordon Teal	65	95	125
☐	66 Jack Hughes	65	95	125
☐	67 D. Yeatman	65	95	125
☐	68 Connie Johanneson	65	95	125
☐	69 S. Walters	65	95	125
☐	70 Harold McMunn	65	95	125
☐	71 Smokey Harris	65	95	125
☐	72 Calgary Jimmies	65	95	125
☐	73 Burney Morris	65	95	125
☐	74 J. Fowler	65	95	125
☐	75 Calgary Jimmies	65	95	125
☐	76 Pete Speirs	65	95	125
☐	77 Bill Borland	65	95	125
☐	78 Cliff O'Meara	65	95	125
☐	79 F. Porteous	65	95	125
☐	80 W. Brooks	65	95	125
☐	81 Everett McGowan	65	95	125
☐	82 Calgary Jimmies	65	95	125
☐	83 George Dame	65	95	125
☐	84 Calgary Jimmies	65	95	125
☐	85 Calgary Jimmies	65	95	125
☐	86 Calgary Jimmies	65	95	125
☐	87 Heck Fowler	65	95	125
☐	88 Jimmy Hoyle	65	95	125
☐	89 Chuck Gardiner (G)	140	210	275
☐	90 Calgary Jimmies	65	95	175

1929 SPORTS & GAMES IN MANY LANDS

This 25-card set features only one hockey card. These black & white cards measure 1 5/8" x 2 5/16". There is both a "Issued by Edwards, Ringer & Bigg" variation and a "W.A. & A.C. Churchman" variation.

Imperial Tobacco		VG	EX	EX-MT
☐ ☐	3 Ice-Hockey, Canada	20	30	40

1929 - 30 LA PRESSE

These photos, cut from the Montréal newspaper, measure 10" x 16 1/2".

La Presse photo		VG	EX	EX-MT
☐	Nov. 30 Gordon Fraser, Mont.	45	65	85
☐	Dec. 7 Bert McCaffrey, Mont.	45	65	85
☐	Dec. 28 Hec Kilrea, Otta.	45	65	85
☐	Jan. 4 Andy Blair, Toro.	45	65	85
☐	Jan. 11 Francis (King) Clancy, Otta.	125	185	250
☐	Jan. 18 John Ross Roach (G), Toro.	60	90	115
☐	Jan. 25 Leo Bourgeault, NYRa.	45	65	85
☐	Feb. 1 Ray Belanger, Club Champtre	45	65	85
☐	Feb. 8 Lionel Hitchman, Bost.	60	90	115
☐	Feb. 15 Joe Primeau, Toro.	75	115	150
☐	Feb. 22 Dutch Gainor, Bost.	45	65	85
☐	Mar. 1 Tiny Thompson (G), Bost.	80	120	160
☐	Mar. 8 Gus Rivers, Mont.	45	65	85
☐	Mar. 29 Hooley Smith, Mont.	65	100	130
☐	Apr. 5 Flat Walsh, Mont.M	45	65	85
☐	Apr. 26 Montréal Canadiens Team	75	115	15

c.1930 A. & B.C. CHEWING GUM

This multi-sport set features only five hockey players. These black & white cards measure 1 13/16" x 3".

A & BC Chewing Gum		VG	EX	EX-MT
☐	37 Sonny Rost, Wembley Lions	7.50	15	30
☐	39 Ray Gariepy (G), Wembley Lions	10	20	40
☐	40 George Beach, Wembley Lions	7.50	15	30
☐	41 Lefty Wilmot, Wembley Lions	7.50	15	30
☐	76 Tony Licari, Harringay	7.50	15	30

1930 - 31 LA PRESSE

These photos, cut from the Montréal newspaper, measure 10" x 16 1/2".

La Presse photo		VG	EX	EX-MT
☐	Dec. 13 Earl Miller, Chic.	45	65	85
☐	Dec. 20 Johnny Gagnon, Mont.	45	65	85
☐	Dec. 27 Art Sommers, Chic.	45	65	85
☐	Jan. 3 Johnny Gottselig, Chic.	50	75	100
☐	Jan. 17 Johnny Gallagher, Mont.M	45	65	85
☐	Jan. 24 Earl Roche, Mont.M	45	65	85
☐	Jan. 31 Jack McVicar, Mont.M	45	65	85
☐	Feb. 7 Dave Kerr (G), Mont.M	60	90	120
☐	Feb. 14 Desse Roche, Mont.M	45	65	85
☐	Feb. 21 Paul Hayes, Mont.M	45	65	85
☐	Feb. 28 Al Huggins, Mont.M	45	65	85
☐	Mar. 7 Red Horner, Toro.	65	100	130
☐	Mar. 21 Harvey Jackson, Toro.	75	115	150
☐	Mar. 28 Charlie Conacher, Toro.	90	135	175
☐	Apr. 4 Ralph Saint Germain, McGill	45	65	85
☐	Apr. 11 Ebbie Goodfellow, Falcons	65	100	130

1931 - 32 LA PRESSE

These photos, cut from the Montréal newspaper, measure 10" x 16 1/2".

La Presse photo		VG	EX	EX-MT
☐	Dec. 19 Normie Himes, NYAm.	45	65	85
☐	Dec. 26 Rosario (Lolo) Couture, Chic.	45	65	85
☐	Jan. 2 George Owen, Bost.	45	65	85
☐	Jan. 9 Chuck Gardiner (G), Chic.	70	100	140
☐	Jan. 16 Tommy Cook, Chic.	45	65	85
☐	Mar. 12 Frank Finnigan	55	80	110
☐	Mar. 19 William Cockburn, Winn.	45	65	85
☐	Apr. 16 Arthur Alexandre, Mont.	45	65	85

1932 - 1942 POSTCARDS, STOCK AND ADVERTISEMENT CARDS

These cards feature various designs and are printed on different card stocks.In some cases, the card back was left blank for an advertisement.

1932 SANELLA		VG	EX	EX-MT
☐	Sanella Postfach / Canada (2 3/4" x 4 1/8", colour)	40	80	175

1932-33 RANGERS POSTCARD VG EX EX-MT

◆ An example of this card recently closed at $360 U.S. ($414 with the buyer's premium) in the May 7, 2002 Classic Collectibles Auction. This closing amount translates to about $555 Cdn.

☐ New York Rangers (black & white)

1935 TORONTO TOURIST CONVENTION		VG	EX	EX-MT
☐	Toronto Tourist Convention / Maple Leafs (3 1/2" x 5 3/8",colour)	15	30	65

1938 - 39 DEFOE PHOTOGRAPHIC		VG	EX	EX-MT
☐	Defoe Photographic / Brighton Penguins (3 3/16" x 5 3/8", black & white)	15	30	65

1932 REEMSTA OLYMPIA

1932 WEITERE WERKE / REEMSTA		VG	EX	EX-MT
☐	Weitere Werke/ 188 Germany vs. Poland (3 1/8" x 4 11/16",black & white)	25	50	100
☐	Weitere Werke/ 191 Canada vs. USA (4 3/4" x 6 11/16",colour)	80	160	325

1932 - 33 C.C.M. GREY BORDER

This series of photos was issued over a four year period starting in 1932-33. Different border designs were utilized depending on the type of photo. The black & white photos measure 11 1/4" x 8 7/8".

Grey-border Photo		VG	EX	EX-MT
☐	New York Rangers	50	75	100
☐	Toronto Maple Leafs	60	90	120
☐	Allan Cup: Moncton	30	40	55
☐	Memorial Cup: Newmarket	30	40	55

1932 - 33 TORONTO MAPLE LEAFS O'KEEFE COASTERS

Thecoasters measure 3" in diametre.

Coaster		VG	EX	EX-MT
☐	1 Lorne Chabot (G)	175	275	425
☐	2 Red Horner	190	285	375
☐	3 Alex Levinsky	115	175	230
☐	4 Hap Day	215	325	425
☐	5 Andy Blair	115	175	230
☐	6 Ace Bailey	275	400	550
☐	7 Francis (King) Clancy	475	700	950
☐	8 Baldy Cotton	115	175	230
☐	9 Charlie Conacher	325	500	650
☐	10 Joe Primeau	240	360	475
☐	11 Harvey Jackson	300	450	600
☐	12 Frank Finnagan	175	265	350
☐	13 Bill Thomas			
☐	14 Bob Gracie	115	175	230
☐	15 Ken Doraty			
☐	16 Harry Darragh	115	175	230
☐	17 Ben Grant	115	175	230
☐	18 Fred Robertson	115	175	230
☐	19 Conn Smythe			
☐	20 Dick Irvin			

1933 GOUDEY SPORT KINGS

This 48-card set features 18 different sports. Listed and priced here are the hockey cards from the set. Each card measures 2 3/8" x 2 7/8".

Goudey		VG	EX	EX-MT
☐	19 Eddie Shore	450	675	900
☐	24 Howie Morenz	600	900	1,200
☐	29 Ace Bailey	300	450	600
☐	30 Ivan (Ching) Johnson	250	375	500

1933 - 34 BOSTON GARDEN HOCKEY MAGAZINE PHOTOS

We have little information on this set and its sponsor. More singles exist. Each photo measures 8" x 10".

Boston Garden Photos		VG	EX	EX-MT
☐	Marty Barry	25	35	50
☐	Red Beattie	25	35	50
☐	Art Chapman	25	35	50
☐	Dit Clapper	50	75	100
☐	Pinkie Davie	25	35	50
☐	Walter Gailbraith	25	35	50
☐	Bob Gracie	25	35	50
☐	Lionel Hitchman	40	60	75
☐	Joseph Lamb	25	35	50
☐	Harry Oliver	50	75	100
☐	Vic Ripley	25	35	50
☐	Art Ross	90	135	175
☐	Eddie Shore	175	265	350
☐	Alex Smith	25	35	50
☐	Nels Stewart	65	100	125
☐	Tiny Thompson (G)	75	115	150

1933 - 34 CANADIAN CHEWING GUM

These black & white cards measure 2 1/2" x 3 1/4". A premium tab attached to the bottom of the card displays a large single letter in the middle. Cards with the tabs removed are worth 50% less.

		VG	EX	EX-MT
Complete Set (50 cards):		5,500	8,000	12,000
ACC # V252		VG	EX	EX-MT
☐	**Clarence Abel, Chic. RC**	150	225	300
☐	**Larry Aurie, Detr. RC**	115	170	225
☐	**Ace Bailey, Toro. RC**	265	400	525
☐	**Helge Bostrom, Chic. RC**	75	115	150
☐	**Bill Brydge, NYAm. RC**	75	115	150
☐	**Glenn Brydson, Mont.M RC**	75	115	150
☐	**Marty Burke, Mont. RC**	75	115	150
☐	**Gerry Carson, Mont. RC**	75	115	150
☐	**Lorne Chabot (G), Mont. RC**	150	225	300
☐	Francis (King) Clancy, Toro.	600	900	1,200
☐	**Dit Clapper, Bost. RC**	215	320	425
☐	**Charlie Conacher, Toro. RC**	425	640	850
☐	**Lionel Conacher, Chic. RC**	275	415	550
☐	Alex Connell (G), Otta.	165	245	325
☐	**Bun Cook, NYRa. RC**	175	265	350
☐	**Danny Cox, Otta. RC**	75	115	150
☐	Hap Day, Toro.	165	245	325
☐	**Cecil Dillon, NYRa. RC**	100	150	200
☐	**Lorne Duguid, Mont.M RC**	75	115	150
☐	**Duke Dutkowski, NYAm. RC**	75	115	150
☐	**Red Dutton, NYAm. RC**	175	265	350
☐	**Hap Emms, Detr. RC**	90	135	175
☐	Frank Finnigan, Otta.	100	150	200
☐	**Chuck Gardiner (G), Chic. RC**	175	265	350
☐	**Ebbie Goodfellow, Detr. RC**	165	245	325
☐	**Johnny Gottselig, Chic. RC**	90	135	175
☐	**Bob Gracie, Bost. RC**	75	115	150
☐	**Geo. Hainsworth (G), Toro. RC**	225	335	450
☐	**Ott Heller, NYRa. RC**	75	115	150
☐	**Normie Himes, NYAm. RC**	75	115	150

☐ Red Horner, Toro. RC	165	245	325
☐ Harvey Jackson, Toro. RC	225	335	450
☐ Walt Jackson, NYAm. RC	75	115	150
☐ Aurèle Joliat, Mont.	450	675	900
☐ Dave Kerr (G), Mont.M RC	125	190	250
☐ Pit Lépine, Mont. RC	75	115	150
☐ Georges Mantha, Mont. RC	75	115	150
☐ Howie Morenz, Mont.	1,200	1,750	2,400
☐ Murray Murdoch, NYRa. RC	75	115	150
☐ Baldy Northcott, Mont.M RC	100	150	200
☐ John Roach (G), Detr.	125	190	250
☐ Johnny Sheppard, Bost. RC	75	115	150
☐ Babe Siebert, NYRa. RC	190	280	375
☐ Alex Smith, Bost.	75	115	150
☐ John Sorrell, Detr. RC	75	115	150
☐ Nels Stewart, Bost.	350	525	700
☐ Dave Trottier, Mont.M RC	75	115	150
☐ Bill Touhey, Otta. RC	75	115	150
☐ Jimmy Ward, Mont.M RC	75	115	150
☐ Nick Wasnie, Mont. RC	75	115	150

1933 - 34 C.C.M. BROWN BORDER

This series of photos was issued over a four year period starting in 1932-33. Different border designs were utilized depending on the type of photo. The black & white photos measure 11 1/4" x 8 7/8".

Brown-border Photo	VG	EX	EX-MT
☐ Boston Bruins	50	75	100
☐ Chicago Blackhawks	70	100	140
☐ Detroit Red Wings	50	75	100
☐ Montréal Canadiens	65	95	125
☐ Montréal Maroons	55	85	110
☐ New York Americans	50	75	100
☐ New York Rangers	50	75	100
☐ Toronto Maple Leafs	60	90	120
☐ 1934 All-Star Game	100	150	200
☐ Allan Cup: Moncton	30	40	55
☐ Cam-Am: Providence	30	40	55
☐ Memorial Cup: St. Mike's	30	40	55

1933 - 34 HAMILTON GUM

These black & white cards measure 2 3/8" x 3". It is doubtful that missing numbers exist.

Complete Set (21 cards):	3,800	5,700	8,000
ACC # V288	VG	EX	EX-MT
☐ 1 Nick Wasnie, Mont. RC	100	150	275
☐ 2 Joe Primeau, Toro. RC	225	335	450
☐ 3 Marty Burke, Mont. RC	75	115	150
☐ 7 Bill Thoms, Toro. RC	100	150	200
☐ 8 Howie Morenz, Mont.	1,250	1,850	2,500
☐ 9 Andy Blair, Toro. RC	75	115	150
☐ 11 Ace Bailey, Toro. RC	265	400	525
☐ 14 Wildor Larochelle, Mont. RC	75	115	150
☐ 17 Francis (King) Clancy, Toro.	550	825	1,100
☐ 18 Sylvio Mantha, Mont.	175	265	350
☐ 21 Red Horner, Toro. RC	165	245	325
☐ 23 Pit Lépine, Mont. RC	75	115	150
☐ 27 Aurèle Joliat, Mont.	450	675	900
☐ 29 Harvey Jackson, Toro. RC	225	335	450
☐ 30 Lorne Chabot (G), Mont. RC	150	225	300
☐ 33 Hap Day, Toro.	165	245	325
☐ 36 Alex Levinsky, Toro. RC	75	115	150
☐ 39 Baldy Cotton, Toro. RC	90	135	180
☐ 42 Ebbie Goodfellow, Detr. RC	165	245	325
☐ 44 Larry Aurie, Detr. RC	115	175	225
☐ 49 Charlie Conacher, Toro. RC	500	850	1,200

1933 - 34 O-PEE-CHEE V304A

The black & white cards measure 2 5/16" x 3 9/16".

Complete Set (48 cards):	6,000	9,000	12,000
ACC # V304A	VG	EX	EX-MT
☐ 1 Danny Cox, Otta. RC	100	150	275
☐ 2 Joe Lamb, Bost. RC	70	100	140
☐ 3 Eddie Shore, Bost. RC	1,000	1,450	1,900
☐ 4 Ken Doraty, Toro. RC	85	125	165
☐ 5 Lionel Hitchman, Bost.	90	135	175
☐ 6 Nels Stewart, Bost. RC	350	525	700
☐ 7 Walter Galbraith, Otta. RC	70	100	140
☐ 8 Dit Clapper, Bost. RC	215	325	425
☐ 9 Harry Oliver, Bost. RC	150	225	300
☐ 10 Red Horner, Toro. RC	150	225	300
☐ 11 Alex Levinsky, Toro. RC	70	100	140
☐ 12 Joe Primeau, Toro. RC	225	335	450
☐ 13 Ace Bailey, Toro. RC	250	375	500
☐ 14 George Patterson, NYAm. RC	70	100	140
☐ 15 Geo. Hainsworth (G), Toro. RC	190	285	375
☐ 16 Ott Heller, NYRa. RC	70	100	140
☐ 17 Art Somers, NYRa. RC	70	100	140
☐ 18 Lorne Chabot (G), Mont. RC	140	210	275
☐ 19 Johnny Gagnon, Mont. RC	70	100	140
☐ 20 Alfred Lepine, Mont. RC	70	100	140
☐ 21 Wildor Larochelle, Mont. RC	70	100	140
☐ 22 Georges Mantha, Mont. RC	70	100	140
☐ 23 Howie Morenz, Mont.	1,250	1,800	2,400
☐ 24 Syd Howe, Otta. RC	190	285	375
☐ 25 Frank Finnigan, Otta.	95	145	190
☐ 26 Bill Touhey, Otta. RC	70	100	140
☐ 27 Cooney Weiland, Otta. RC	165	245	325
☐ 28 Leo Bourgeault, Otta. RC	70	100	140
☐ 29 Normie Himes, NYAm. RC	70	100	140
☐ 30 Johnny Sheppard, Bost. RC	70	100	140
☐ 31 Francis (King) Clancy, Toro.	600	900	1,200
☐ 32 Hap Day, Toro.	140	210	275
☐ 33 Harvey Jackson, Toro. RC	225	335	450
☐ 34 Charlie Conacher, Toro. RC	550	850	1,100
☐ 35 Baldy Cotton, Toro. RC	85	125	165
☐ 36 Butch Keeling, NYRa. RC	70	100	140
☐ 37 Murray Murdoch, NYRa. RC	70	100	140
☐ 38 Bill Cook, NYRa.	200	300	400
☐ 39 I. (Ching) Johnson, NYRa. RC	240	360	475
☐ 40 Hap Emms, Detr. RC	85	125	165
☐ 41 Bert McInenly, Detr.F RC	70	100	140
☐ 42 John Sorrell, Detr.F RC	70	100	140
☐ 43 Bill Phillips, NYAm. RC	70	100	140
☐ 44 Charley McVeigh, NYAm. RC	70	100	140
☐ 45 Roy Worters (G), NYAm. RC	225	340	450
☐ 46 Albert Leduc, Mont. RC	70	100	140
☐ 47 Nick Wasnie, Mont. RC	70	100	140
☐ 48 Armand Mondou, Mont. RC	100	150	275

1933 - 34 O-PEE-CHEE V304B

The black & white cards measure 2 5/16" x 2 7/16". A Hockey Star Picture Album was issued to hold the 72 cards of Series A and B. Each page was cut to hold six cards. An album in VG condition sells for $150.

Complete Set (24 cards):	2,000	3,000	5,000
ACC # V304B	VG	EX	EX-MT
☐ 49 Babe Siebert, NYRa.	175	265	450
☐ 50 Aurèle Joliat, Mont.	500	700	950
☐ 51 Larry Aurie, Detr. RC, Err (Laurie)	120	175	235
☐ 52 Ebbie Goodfellow, Detr.	150	225	300
☐ 53 John Roach (G), Detr.	125	190	250
☐ 54 Bill Beveridge (G), Otta. RC	85	125	165
☐ 55 Earle Robinson, Mont.M RC	70	100	140
☐ 56 Jimmy Ward, Mont.M	70	100	140
☐ 57 Archie Wilcox, Mont.M RC	70	100	140
☐ 58 Lorne Duguid, Mont.M	70	100	140
☐ 59 Dave Kerr (G), Mont.M	125	190	250
☐ 60 Baldy Northcott, Mont.M	95	145	190
☐ 61 Cy Wentworth, Mont.M RC	70	100	140
☐ 62 Dave Trottier, Mont.M	70	100	140
☐ 63 Wally Kilrea, Mont.M RC	70	100	140
☐ 64 Glenn Brydson, Mont.M	70	100	140
☐ 65 Vernon Ayers, Mont.M RC	70	100	140
☐ 66 Robert Gracie, Bost.	70	100	140
☐ 67 Vic Ripley, Bost. RC	70	100	140
☐ 68 Tiny Thompson (G), Bost. RC	200	300	400
☐ 69 Hooley Smith, Mont.M	70	100	140
☐ 70 Andy Blair, Toro.	70	100	140
☐ 71 Cecil Dillon, NYRa.	110	165	215
☐ 72 Fred (Bun) Cook, NYRa.	160	240	425

1933 - 34 V129

The sepia-tone cards measure 1 5/8" x 2 7/8". Card 39 (Harry Oliver) is scarce and is not included in the shell set price.

Shell Set (49 cards):	8,000	12,000	16,000
ACC # V129	VG	EX	EX-MT
☐ 1 Red Horner, Toro. RC	200	325	600
☐ 2 Hap Day, Toro.	215	320	425
☐ 3 Ace Bailey, Toro. RC	325	440	650
☐ 4 Buzz Boll, Toro. RC	100	150	200
☐ 5 Charlie Conacher, Toro. RC	700	1,000	1,300
☐ 6 Harvey Jackson, Toro. RC	275	415	550
☐ 7 Joe Primeau, Toro. RC	275	400	550
☐ 8 Francis (King) Clancy, Toro.	800	1,100	1,500
☐ 9 Alex Levinsky, Toro. RC	100	150	200
☐ 10 Bill Thoms, Toro. RC	140	210	275
☐ 11 Andy Blair, Toro. RC	100	150	200
☐ 12 Baldy Cotton, Toro. RC	120	180	235
☐ 13 George Hainsworth (G), Toro.	300	450	600
☐ 14 Ken Doraty, Toro. RC	120	180	235
☐ 15 Fred Robertson, Bost. RC	100	150	200
☐ 16 Charlie Sands, Bost. RC	100	150	200
☐ 17 Hec Kilrea, Bost.	100	150	200
☐ 18 John Roach (G), Bost.	175	265	350
☐ 19 Larry Aurie, Bost. RC	150	225	300
☐ 20 Ebbie Goodfellow, Bost. RC	215	320	425
☐ 21 Normie Himes, NYAm. RC	100	150	200
☐ 22 Bill Brydge, NYAm. RC	100	150	200
☐ 23 Red Dutton, NYAm.	215	320	425
☐ 24 Cooney Weiland, Otta. RC	225	340	450
☐ 25 Bill Beveridge (G), Otta. RC	125	180	235
☐ 26 Frank Finnigan, Otta.	135	200	265
☐ 27 Albert Leduc, Mont. RC	100	150	200
☐ 28 Babe Siebert, NYRa. RC, Err (Seibert)	240	360	475
☐ 29 Murray Murdoch, NYRa.	100	150	200
☐ 30 Butch Keeling, NYRa. RC	100	150	200
☐ 31 Bill Cook, NYRa.	275	415	550
☐ 32 Cecil Dillon, NYRa. RC	140	210	275
☐ 33 Ching Johnson, NYRa. RC	275	415	550
☐ 34 Ott Heller, NYRa. RC	100	150	200
☐ 35 Red Beattie, Bost., Error (Beatty)	100	150	200
☐ 36 Dit Clapper, Bost. RC	275	415	550
☐ 37 Eddie Shore, Bost. RC	1,400	2,000	2,700
☐ 38 Marty Barry, Bost. RC	215	320	425
☐ 39 Harry Oliver, Bost.			
☐ 40 Bob Gracie, Bost. RC	100	150	200
☐ 41 Howie Morenz, Mont.	1,600	2,400	3,200
☐ 42 Pit Lepine, Mont. RC	100	150	200
☐ 43 Johnny Gagnon, Mont. RC	100	150	200
☐ 44 Armand Mondou, Mont. RC	100	150	200
☐ 45 Lorne Chabot (G), Mont.	200	300	400
☐ 46 Bun Cook, NYRa. RC	215	320	425
☐ 47 Alex Smith	100	150	200
☐ 48 Danny Cox, Otta. RC	100	150	200
☐ 49 Baldy Northcott, Mont.M RC	140	210	275
☐ 50 Paul Thompson, NYRa. RC	175	265	500

1933 - 34 WORLD WIDE GUM

The black & white cards measure 2 3/8" x 2 7/8".

Complete Set (72 cards):	8,000	12,000	16,000
ACC # V357	VG	EX	EX-MT
☐ 1 Dit Clapper, Bost. RC	200	400	600
☐ 2 Bill Brydge, NYAm. RC	75	115	150
☐ 3 Aurèle Joliat, Mont.	500	750	1,000
☐ 4 Andy Blair, Toro. RC	75	115	150
☐ 5 Earl Robinson, Mont.M RC	75	115	150
☐ 6 Paul Haynes, Mont.M RC	75	115	150
☐ 7 Ron Martin, NYAm. RC	75	115	150
☐ 8 B. Siebert, NYRa. RC, Err (Seibert)	190	285	375
☐ 9 Archie Wilcox, Mont.M RC	75	115	150
☐ 10 Hap Day, Toro.	150	225	300
☐ 11 Roy Worters (G), NYAm. RC	240	360	475
☐ 12 Nels Stewart, Bost. RC	350	525	700
☐ 13 Francis (King) Clancy, Toro.	600	900	1,200
☐ 14 Marty Burke, Mont. RC	75	115	150
☐ 15 Cecil Dillon, NYRa. RC	100	150	200
☐ 16 Red Horner, Toro. RC	165	245	325
☐ 17 Armand Mondou, Mont. RC	75	115	150
☐ 18 Paul Raymond, Mont. RC	75	115	150
☐ 19 Dave Kerr (G), Mont.M RC	125	185	250
☐ 20 Butch Keeling, NYRa. RC	75	115	150
☐ 21 Johnny Gagnon, Mont. RC	75	115	150
☐ 22 Ace Bailey, Toro. RC	300	450	600
☐ 23 Harry Oliver, Bost.	165	245	325
☐ 24 Gerry Carson, Mont. RC	75	115	150
☐ 25 Red Dutton, NYAm.	175	265	350
☐ 26 Georges Mantha, Mont. RC	75	115	150
☐ 27 Marty Barry, Bost. RC	165	245	325
☐ 28 Wildor Larochelle, Mont. RC	75	115	150
☐ 29 Red Beattie, Bost.	75	115	150
☐ 30 Bill Cook, NYRa.	225	335	450
☐ 31 Hooley Smith, Mont.M	150	225	300
☐ 32 Art Chapman, Bost. RC	75	115	150
☐ 33 Baldy Cotton, Toro. RC	90	135	180
☐ 34 Lionel Hitchman, Bost.	100	150	200
☐ 35 George Patterson, NYAm. RC	75	115	150
☐ 36 Howie Morenz, Mont.	1,200	1,800	2,400
☐ 37 Jimmy Ward, Mont.M RC	75	45	150
☐ 38 Charley McVeigh, NYAm. RC	75	45	150
☐ 39 G. Brydson, Mont.M, RC, Error	75	45	150
☐ 40 Joe Primeau, Toro. RC	225	335	450
☐ 41 Joe Lamb, Bost. RC	75	115	150
☐ 42 Sylvio Mantha, Mont.	175	265	350
☐ 43 Cy Wentworth, Mont.M RC	100	150	200
☐ 44 Normie Himes, NYAm. RC	75	115	150
☐ 45 Doug Brennan, NYRa. RC	75	115	150
☐ 46 Pit Lepine, Mont. RC	75	115	150
☐ 47 Alex Levinsky, Toro. RC	75	115	150
☐ 48 Baldy Northcott, Mont.M RC	125	185	250
☐ 49 Ken Doraty, NYAm. RC	115	175	225
☐ 50 Bill Thoms, Toro. RC	125	185	250
☐ 51 Vern Ayers, Mont.M RC	100	150	200
☐ 52 Lorne Duguid, Mont.M RC	100	150	200
☐ 53 Wally Kilrea, Mont.M RC	100	150	200
☐ 54 Vic Ripley, Bost. RC	100	150	200
☐ 55 Hap Emms, Detr. RC	125	185	250
☐ 56 Duke Dutkowski, NYRa. RC	100	150	200
☐ 57 Tiny Thompson (G), Bost. RC	275	415	550
☐ 58 Charlie Sands, Toro. RC	100	150	200
☐ 59 Larry Aurie, Detr. RC	150	225	300
☐ 60 Bill Beveridge (G), Otta. RC	125	185	250
☐ 61 Bill MacKenzie, Mont. RC	100	150	200
☐ 62 Earl Roche, Otta. RC	100	150	200
☐ 63 Bob Gracie, Bost. RC	100	150	200
☐ 64 Hec Kilrea, Detr.	100	150	200
☐ 65 Cooney Weiland, Otta. RC	250	375	450
☐ 66 Fred (Bun) Cook, NYRa. RC	175	265	350
☐ 67 John Roach (G), Detr.	190	280	375
☐ 68 Murray Murdock, NYRa.	100	150	200
☐ 69 Danny Cox, Otta. RC	100	150	200
☐ 70 Desse Roche, Mont.M RC	100	150	200
☐ 71 Lorne Chabot (G), Mont.	200	300	400
☐ 72 Syd Howe, Otta. RC	200	300	600

1933 - 34 ICE KINGS PREMIUM

The following six cards are write-in offers from the Ice Kings wrappers. Each card measures 7" x 9".

Redemption Set (6 cards):	2,000	3,200	5,000
Redemption card	VG	EX	EX-MT
☐ 1 Francis (King) Clancy, Toro.	800	1,175	1,600
☐ 2 Hap Day, Toro.	175	265	350
☐ 3 Aurèle Joliat, Mont.	700	1,000	1,350
☐ 4 Howie Morenz, Mont.	1,650	2,450	3,200
☐ 5 Al Shields, Otta.	100	150	200
☐ 6 Hooley Smith, Mont.M	175	265	350

1933 - 35 DIAMOND MATCH SILVER

This first issue has a silver finish with green and black stripes running vertically on the left side of the cover. The book cover has a player's portrait with the back giving the player's resume. The back cover is black on green. Each book measures 1 1/16" x 4 1/2".

Complete Set (60 cards):	1,200	1,600	2,200
Diamond Match Co.	**VG**	**EX**	**EX-MT**
☐ Clarence Abel, Chic.	15	22	30
☐ Marty Barry, Bost.	20	30	40
☐ Jack Beattie, Bost.	15	22	30
☐ Frank Boucher, NYRa.	25	35	50
☐ Doug Brennan, NYRa.	15	22	30
☐ Bill Brydge, NYRa.	15	22	30
☐ Eddie Burke, NYRa.	15	22	30
☐ Marty Burke, Mont.	15	22	30
☐ Gerry Carson, Mont.	15	22	30
☐ Lorne Chabot (G), Mont.	25	35	50
☐ Art Chapman, Bost.	15	22	30
☐ Dit Clapper, Bost.	35	50	65
☐ Lional Conacher, Chic.	35	50	65
☐ Hugh (Red) Conn, NYAm.	15	22	30
☐ Bill Cook, NYRa.	30	45	60
☐ Fred (Bun) Cook, NYRa.	25	35	50
☐ Tom Cook, Chic.	15	22	30
☐ Rosario (Lolo) Couture, Chic.	15	22	30
☐ Bob Davie, Bost.	15	22	30
☐ Cecil Dillon, NYRa.	15	22	30
☐ Duke Dutkowski, NYAm.	15	22	30
☐ Red Dutton, NYAm.	25	35	50
☐ Johnny Gagnon, Mont.	15	22	30
☐ Chuck Gardiner (G), Chic.	30	45	60
☐ John Gottselig, Chic.	15	22	30
☐ Bob Gracie, Bost.	15	22	30
☐ Lloyd Gross, NYAm.	15	22	30
☐ Otto Heller, NYRa.	15	22	30
☐ Normie Himes, NYAm.	15	22	30
☐ Lional Hitchman, Bost.	25	35	50
☐ Walter (Red) Jackson, NYAm.	15	22	30
☐ Roger Jenkins, Chic.	15	22	30
☐ Aurèle Joliat, Mont.	50	75	100
☐ Butch (Melville) Keeling, Chic.	15	22	30
☐ William Kendall, Chic.	15	22	30
☐ Lloyd Klein, NYAm.	15	22	30
☐ Joe Lamb, Bost.	15	22	30
☐ Wildor Larochelle, Mont.	15	22	30
☐ Pit Lépine, Mont.	15	22	30
☐ Jack Leswick, Chic.	15	22	30
☐ Georges Mantha, Mont.	20	30	40
☐ Sylvio Mantha, Mont.	25	35	50
☐ Mush March, Chic.	15	22	30
☐ Ron Martin, NYAm.	15	22	30
☐ Charley McVeigh, NYAm.	15	22	30
☐ Howie Morenz, Mont.	300	425	550
☐ John Murray Murdoch, NYRa.	15	22	30
☐ Harry Oliver, Bost.	25	35	50
☐ George Patterson, NYAm.	15	22	30
☐ Hal Picketts, NYAm.	15	22	30
☐ Vic Ripley, Bost.	15	22	30
☐ Doc Romnes, Chic.	15	22	30
☐ Johnny Sheppard, Bost.	15	22	30
☐ Eddie Shore, Bost.	125	175	250
☐ Art Somers, NYRa.	15	22	30
☐ Chris Speyers, NYAm.	15	22	30
☐ Nels Stewart, Bost.	35	50	65
☐ Tiny Thompson (G), Bost.	30	45	60
☐ Louis Trudel, Chic.	15	22	30
☐ Roy Worters (G), NYAm.	30	45	60

1934 - 35 C.C.M. GREEN BORDER

This series of photos was issued over a four year period starting in 1932-33. Different border designs were utilized depending on the type of photo. The black & white photos measure 11 1/4" x 8 7/8".

Green-border Photo	VG	EX	EX-MT
☐ Boston Bruins	50	75	100
☐ Montréal Marrons	55	85	110
☐ Toronto Maple Leafs	55	85	110
☐ Allan Cup: Halifax	30	40	55
☐ Cam-Am: Boston Cubs	30	40	55
☐ Memorial Cup: Winnipeg	30	40	55
☐ AW: Frank Boucher (HOF)	65	90	115
☐ AW: Lorne Chabot (G)	45	70	90
☐ AW: Charlie Conacher	65	100	130
☐ Foster Hewitt (HOF)	45	70	90

1934 - 35 SWEET CAPORAL

These photos were inserts in the Montréal Forum game programs. A photo was inserted in the home game programs of the Canadiens and the Maroons. Each photo measures 6 7/8" x 9 1/2".

Complete Set (48 photos):	4,200	5,500	7,000
Sweet Caporal Cigarettes	**VG**	**EX**	**EX-MT**
☐ Eddie Shore, Bost.	450	550	700
☐ Babe Siebert, Bost.	135	165	200
☐ Nels Stewart, Bost.	235	290	350
☐ Tiny Thompson (G), Bost.	150	190	250
☐ Lorne Chabot (G), Chic.	90	110	150
☐ Mush March, Chic.	80	100	125
☐ Howie Morenz, Chic.	600	750	1,200
☐ Larry Aurie, Detr.	80	100	135
☐ Ebbie Goodfellow, Detr.	115	145	175
☐ Herbie Lewis, Detr.	65	85	135
☐ Ralph Weiland, Detr.	135	165	200
☐ Gerry Carson, Error (Jerry), Mont.	65	85	135
☐ Nels Crutchfield, Mont.	65	85	135
☐ Wilf Cude (G), Mont.	80	100	150
☐ Roger Jenkins, Mont.	65	85	125
☐ Aurèle Joliat, Mont.	365	450	600
☐ Joe Lamb, Mont.	65	85	135
☐ Wildor Larochelle, Mont., Error (Victor)	65	85	135
☐ Pit Lépine, Mont.	65	85	135
☐ Georges Mantha, Mont.	65	85	130
☐ Sylvio Mantha, Mont.	115	145	200
☐ Jack McGill, Mont.	65	85	135
☐ Armand Mondou, Mont.	65	85	135
☐ Paul Raymond, Mont.	65	85	135
☐ Jack Riley, Mont.	65	85	135
☐ Russ Blinco, Mont.M	65	85	135
☐ Herbert Cain, Mont.M	80	100	125
☐ Lionel Conacher, Mont.M	200	250	350
☐ Alex Connell (G), Mont.M	115	145	200
☐ Stewart Evans, Mont.M	65	85	135
☐ Dutch Gainor, Mont.M	65	85	135
☐ Paul Haynes, Mont.M	65	85	135
☐ Gus Marker, Mont.M	65	85	135
☐ Baldy Northcott, Mont.M	80	100	125
☐ Earle Robinson, Mont.M	65	85	135
☐ Hooley Smith, Mont.M	115	150	200
☐ Dave Trottier, Mont.M	65	85	135
☐ Jimmy Ward, Mont.M	65	85	135
☐ Cy Wentworth, Mont.M	80	100	125
☐ Bill Cook, NYRa.	165	210	275
☐ Fred (Bun) Cook, NYRa.	115	150	200
☐ Ivan (Ching) Johnson, NYRa.	115	150	200
☐ Dave Kerr (G), NYRa.	90	115	140
☐ Francis (King) Clancy, Toro.	365	450	600
☐ Charlie Conacher, Toro.	325	415	600
☐ Red Horner, Toro.	115	145	200
☐ Harvey Jackson, Toro.	150	190	250
☐ Joe Primeau, Toro.	165	210	300

1935 J.A. PATTREIOUEX LTD. SPORTING EVENTS AND STARS

This 96-card set features only two hockey cards. Each black & white card measures 2" x 3".

Sr. Service, Jr. Service, Illingworth	VG	EX	EX-MT
☐ 31 Ice Skating (Monarchs)	10	20	40
☐ 89 G. A. Johnson, Manchester	10	20	40

1935 - 36 AMALGAMATED PRESS

These postcards were issued as premiums to the magazines The Champion and The Triumph. Each postcard measures 4" x 6".

The Champion Set (10 postcards):	1,000	1,600	2,300
The Triumph Set (10 postcards):	**800**	**1,200**	**1,700**
The Champion	**VG**	**EX**	**EX-MT**
☐ Marty Barry, Bost.	75	115	150
☐ Francis (King) Clancy, Toro.	300	450	600
☐ Charlie Conacher, Toro.	225	340	450
☐ Fred (Bun) Cook, NYRa.	125	185	250
☐ Bill Cook, NYRa.	165	250	325
☐ Aurèle Joliat, Mont.	275	400	550
☐ Reg Kelly, Toro.	75	115	150
☐ Mush March, Chic.	75	115	150
☐ Sweeney Schriner, NYAm.	125	185	250
☐ Hooley Smith, Mont.	125	185	250
The Triumph	**VG**	**EX**	**EX-MT**
☐ Lionel Conacher, Mont.	200	300	400
☐ Harvey Jackson, Toro.	150	225	300
☐ Ivan (Ching) Johnson, NYRa.	125	185	250
☐ Herbie Lewis, Detr.	75	115	150
☐ Sylvio Mantha, Mont.	100	150	200
☐ Nick Metz, Toro.	75	115	150
☐ Baldy Northcott, Mont.M	75	115	150
☐ Eddie Shore, Bost.	325	500	650
☐ Paul Thomson, Chic.	75	115	150
☐ Roy Worters (G), NYAm.	125	185	250

1935 - 36 C.C.M. BLUE BORDER

This series of photos was issued over a four year period starting in 1932-33. Different border designs were utilized depending on the type of photo. The black & white photos measure 11 1/4" x 8 7/8".

Blue-border Photo	VG	EX	EX-MT
☐ Allan Cup: Kimberley	30	40	55
☐ Can-Am: Philadelphia	30	40	55
☐ Int'l League: Detroit	30	40	55
☐ Memorial Cup: W. Toronto	30	40	55

1935 - 36 O-PEE-CHEE SERIES "C"

This series shows the player's surname on the face of the card and may or may not show the initial of the player's first name. These cards measure 2 3/8" x 2 7/8".

Complete Set (24 cards):	1,800	2,500	4,500
ACC # V304C	**VG**	**EX**	**EX-MT**
☐ **73 Wilf Cude (G), Mont. RC**	**150**	**200**	**350**
☐ **74 Jack McGill, Mont. RC**	**70**	**100**	**140**
☐ **75 Russ Blinco, Mont.M RC**	**70**	**100**	**140**
☐ 76 Hooley Smith, Mont.M	140	210	275
☐ **77 Herbert Cain, Mont.M RC**	**90**	**135**	**175**
☐ **78 Gus Marker, Mont.M RC**	**70**	**100**	**140**
☐ **79 Lynn Patrick, NYRa. RC**	**200**	**300**	**400**
☐ 80 Johnny Gottselig, Chic.	90	135	175
☐ 81 Marty Barry, Detr.	150	225	300
☐ 82 Sylvio Mantha, Mont.	140	210	275
☐ **83 Bill Hollett, Toro. RC**	**70**	**100**	**140**
☐ **84 Nick Metz, Toro. RC**	**90**	**135**	**175**
☐ 85 Bill Thoms, Toro.	90	135	175
☐ 86 Hec Kilrea, Detr.	70	100	140
☐ **87 Reg Kelly, Toro. RC**	**70**	**100**	**140**
☐ **88 Art Jackson, Toro. RC**	**70**	**100**	**140**
☐ **89 Al Shields, Mont.M RC**	**70**	**100**	**140**
☐ 90 Buzz Boll, Toro.	70	100	140
☐ **91 Jean Pusie, Mont. RC**	**70**	**100**	**140**
☐ **92 Roger Jenkins, Bost. RC**	**70**	**100**	**140**
☐ **93 Art Coulter, Chic. RC**	**150**	**225**	**300**
☐ 94 Art Chapman, NYAm.	90	135	175
☐ 95 Paul Haynes, Mont.	70	100	140
☐ **96 Leroy Goldsworthy, Mont. RC**	**125**	**175**	**300**

1935 - 40 CANADA STARCH CROWN BRAND

The photos issued by Canada Starch are all Rice or Rice Copyrighted from the Rice Studios of Montréal. Player photos measure 4 1/2" x 7 3/4" (or 6 3/4" x 8 3/4" with mat). Team photos measure 9 1/2" x 4 3/4" (or 10 3/4" x 6 1/2" with mat).

Rice Photo	VG	EX	EX-MT
☐ 49 Montréal Maroons 1936-37	20	40	75
☐ 50 Montréal Les Canadiens 1936-37	20	40	75
☐ 51 Baldy Northcott, Mont.M	15	30	60
☐ 52 Dave Trottier, Mont.M	12	25	50
☐ 53 Russ Blinco, Mont.M	12	25	50
☐ 54 Earle Robinson, Mont.M	12	25	50
☐ 55 Bob Gracie, Mont.M	12	25	50
☐ 56 Gus Marker, Mont.M	12	25	50
☐ 57 Howie Morenz, Mont.M	85	175	300
☐ 58 Johnny Gagnon, Mont.M	12	25	50
☐ 59 Wilf Cude (G), Mont.M	15	30	60
☐ 60 Georges Mantha, Mtl M	12	25	50
☐ 61 Paul Haynes, Mont.M	12	25	50
☐ 62 Marty Barry, Detr.	18	35	70
☐ 63 Pete Kelly, Detr.	12	25	50
☐ 64 Dave Kerr (G)	18	35	65
☐ 65 Roy Worters (G)	20	40	80
☐ 66 Ace Bailey, Toro.	40	80	150
☐ 67 Art Lesieur	12	25	50
☐ 68 Frank Boucher, NYRa.	20	40	75
☐ 69 Marty Burke, Chic.	12	25	50
☐ 70 Alex Levinsky	12	25	50
☐ 71 The Maple Leaf Team of "Father Levesque's Pee Wee Hockey Club"	75	150	300
☐ 72 Six Stars of "Father Levesque's Pee Wee Hockey Club"	75	150	300
☐ 76 The "Canadien" team of "Father Levesque's Pee Wee Hockey Club"	75	150	300
☐ 77 Stewart Evans, Mont.M	12	25	50
☐ 78 Herbert Cain	15	30	60
☐ 79 Carl Voss, Mont.M	20	40	75
☐ 80 Roger Jenkins	12	25	50
☐ 81 Jack McGill	12	25	50
☐ 82 Mush March	15	30	60
☐ 106 Montréal Maroons 1937-38	25	50	100
☐ 107 Montréal Les Canadiens 1937-38	25	50	100
☐ 108 Toe Blake	30	60	120
☐ 109 Joffre Desilets	15	30	60
☐ 110 Babe Siebert	25	50	100
☐ 111 Francis (King) Clancy	225	450	800
☐ 112 Aurèle Joliat, Error	75	135	250
☐ 113 Walt Buswell	15	30	60
☐ 114 Bill MacKenzie	15	30	60
☐ 115 Pit Lépine	15	30	60
☐ 116 Red Goupille	15	30	60
☐ 117 Rod Lorraine	15	30	60
☐ 118 Polly Drouin	15	30	60
☐ 119 Cy Wentworth	18	35	70
☐ 120 Al Shields	15	30	60
☐ 121 Jimmy Ward	15	30	60
☐ 122 Bill Beveridge (G)	18	35	70
☐ 123 Gerry Shannon	15	30	60
☐ 124 Des Smith	15	30	60
☐ 125 Armand Mondou	15	30	60
☐ 151 Montréal Canadiens 1938-39	35	70	135
☐ 152 Herbert Cain	20	40	80

		VG	EX	EX-MT
☐	153 Bob Gracie	18	35	70
☐	154 Jimmy Ward	18	35	70
☐	155 Stewart Evans	18	35	70
☐	156 Louis Trudel	18	35	70
☐	157 Cy Wentworth	22	45	85
☐	195 Marty Barry	25	50	100
☐	196 Earl Robinson	18	35	70
☐	197 Ray Getliffe	18	35	70
☐	198 Charlie Sands	20	40	80
☐	199 Claude Bourque (G)	18	35	70
☐	200 Douglas Young	18	35	70
☐	201 Montréal Les Canadiens 1939-40	35	70	135
☐	1936-37 Montréal Maroons	25	50	100
☐	1935-36 Montréal Canadiens	25	50	100
☐	1936 Canadian Olympic Team	22	45	90

1936 RONFRANCK

	1936 Olympia	VG	EX	EX-MT
☐	Serie 8, Bild 5, Great Britain (colour)	15	30	65

1936 WEITERE WERKE

These black & white cards measure 2 3/4" x 4 1/8". Other singles exist.

	1936 Olympia	VG	EX	EX-MT
☐	Gruppe 53, Bild 35, Canada in action	20	40	85
☐	Gruppe 54, Bild 33, Cdn. vs. Austria	20	40	85
☐	Gruppe 54, Bild 36, Canada	20	40	85
☐	Gruppe 54, Bild 39, T. Homma (G)	40	75	150
☐	Gruppe 56, Bild 34, Canada vs. USA	20	40	85

1936 - 37 O-PEE-CHEE

These die-cut black & white cards measure 2 3/8" x 3". The cards in the fourth series are die-cut, allowing the cards to be folded so they could stand on end. The cards are black and white with a drawing of a mock game in the background. These cards show only the player's surname on the face of the card. This is the most valuable set of the series because the cards are very difficult to find unpopped.

	Complete Set (36 cards):	8,000	11,000	16,000
	ACC # V304D	VG	EX	EX-MT
☐	**97 Turk Broda (G), Toro. RC**	475	750	1,500
☐	**98 Sweeney Schriner, NYAm. RC**	275	375	475
☐	**99 Jack Shill, Toro. RC**	110	155	200
☐	**100 Bob Davidson, Toro. RC**	150	200	250
☐	**101 Syl Apps, Sr., Toro. RC**	475	650	850
☐	102 Lionel Conacher, Mont.M	400	500	700
☐	**103 Jimmy Fowler, Toro. RC**	110	155	200
☐	**104 Allan Murray, NYAm. RC**	110	155	200
☐	**105 Neil Colville, NYRa. RC**	275	375	475
☐	**106 Paul Runge, Mont.M RC**	110	155	200
☐	**107 Mike Karakas (G), Chic. RC**	150	200	250
☐	**108 John Gallagher, NYAm. RC**	110	155	200
☐	**109 Alex Shibicky, NYRa. RC**	110	155	200
☐	110 Herbert Cain, Mont.M	150	200	250
☐	111 Bill MacKenzie, Mont.	110	155	200
☐	**112 Hal Jackson, Chic. RC**	110	155	200
☐	**113 Art Wiebe, Chic. RC, Error (Weibe)**	110	155	200
☐	**114 Joffre Desilets, Mont. RC**	110	155	200
☐	115 Earle Robinson, Mont.M	110	155	200
☐	116 Cy Wentworth, Mont.M	150	215	300
☐	117 Ebbie Goodfellow, Detr.	235	330	425
☐	118 Eddie Shore, Bost.	1,200	1,600	2,200
☐	119 Buzz Boll, Toro.	110	155	200
☐	120 Wilf Cude (G), Mont.	150	200	250
☐	121 Howie Morenz, Mont.	1,700	2,250	3,000
☐	122 Red Horner, Toro.	235	330	450
☐	123 Charlie Conacher, Toro.	550	775	1,000
☐	124 Harvey Jackson, Toro.	300	425	600
☐	125 Francis (King) Clancy, Toro.	650	925	1,300
☐	126 Dave Trottier, Mont.M	110	155	200
☐	127 Russ Blinco, Mont.M	110	155	200
☐	128 Lynn Patrick, NYRa.	285	395	500
☐	129 Aurèle Joliat, Mont.	600	850	1,200
☐	130 Baldy Northcott, Mont.M	150	215	275
☐	131 Larry Aurie, Detr.	175	235	300
☐	132 Hooley Smith, Mont.M	200	300	550

1936 - 39 DIAMOND MATCH TAN

The design of the book was modified with the cover being redesigned and its colour changing to tan. This basic design continued until the end of the issue in 1939. The issue can be broken down into six different types issued over the years from 1934 to 1939. Each book measures 1 1/16" x 4 1/2".

TYPE 1

At the top of the résumé (back) is the player's name and the name of the team or the player's position. The imprint "The Diamond Match Co. N.Y.C." is on one line. Joe Starke's matchbook is considered rare.

	Complete Set (70 books):	750	1,100	1,600
	Diamond Match Co.	VG	EX	EX-MT
☐	Andy Aitkenhead (G), NYRa.	10	15	20
☐	Vern Ayres, St. Louis Eagles	10	15	20
☐	Bill Beveridge (G), St. Louis Eagles	12	18	25
☐	Ralph Bowman, St. Louis Eagles	10	15	20
☐	Bill Brydge, NYAm.	10	15	20
☐	Glenn Brydson, St. Louis Eagles	10	15	20
☐	Eddie Burke, NYAm.	10	15	20
☐	Marty Burke, Chic.	10	15	20
☐	Lorne Carr, NYAm.	10	15	20
☐	Gerry Carson, Mont.	10	15	20
☐	Lorne Chabot (G), Chic.	20	30	40
☐	Art Chapman, NYAm.	10	15	20
☐	Hugh (Red) Conn, NYAm.	10	15	20
☐	Bert Connolly, NYRa.	10	15	20
☐	Bun (Fred) Cook, NYRa.	20	30	40
☐	Tom Cook, Chic.	10	15	20
☐	Art Coulter, Chic.	10	15	20
☐	Rosario (Lolo) Couture, Chic.	10	15	20
☐	Bill Cowley, St. Louis Eagles	20	30	40
☐	Wilf Cude (G), Mont.	12	18	25
☐	Red Dutton, NYAm.	20	30	40
☐	Frank Finnigan, St. Louis Eagles	15	22	30
☐	Irvin Frew, St. Louis Eagles	10	15	20
☐	Leroy Goldsworthy, Chic.	10	15	20
☐	Johnny Gottselig, Chic.	10	15	20
☐	Bob Gracie, NYAm.	10	15	20
☐	Otto Heller, NYRa.	10	15	20
☐	Normie Himes, NYAm.	10	15	20
☐	Syd Howe, St. Louis Eagles	20	30	40
☐	Roger Jenkins, Mont.	10	15	20
☐	Ivan (Ching) Johnson, NYRa.	25	35	50
☐	Aurèle Joliat, Mont.	40	55	75
☐	Max Kaminsky, St. Louis Eagles	10	15	20
☐	Butch (Melville) Keeling, Chic.	10	15	20
☐	William Kendall, Chic.	10	15	20
☐	Lloyd Klein, NYAm.	10	15	20
☐	Joe Lamb, Mont.	10	15	20
☐	Wildor Larochelle, Mont.	10	15	20
☐	Pit Lépine, Mont.	10	15	20
☐	Norman Locking, Chic.	10	15	20
☐	Georges Mantha, Mont.	15	22	30
☐	Sylvio Mantha, Mont.	20	30	40
☐	Mush March, Chic.	10	15	20
☐	Charley Mason, NYRa.	10	15	20
☐	Donnie McFayden, Chic.	10	15	20
☐	Jack McGill, Mont.	10	15	20
☐	Charley McVeigh, NYAm.	10	15	20
☐	Armand Mondou, Mont.	10	15	20
☐	Howie Morenz, Chic.	175	265	350
☐	John Murray Murdoch, NYRa.	10	15	20
☐	Allan Murray, NYAm.	10	15	20
☐	Harry Oliver, NYAm.	20	30	40
☐	Jean Pusie, Bost.	10	15	20
☐	Paul Raymond, Mont.	10	15	20
☐	Jack Riley, Mont.	10	15	20
☐	Vic Ripley, St. Louis Eagles	10	15	20
☐	Desse Roche, St. Louis Eagles	10	15	20
☐	Earl Roche, St. Louis Eagles	10	15	20
☐	Doc Romnes, Chic.	10	15	20
☐	Sweeney Schriner, NYAm.	25	35	45
☐	Earl Seibert, NYRa.	20	30	40
☐	Gerry Shannon, St. Louis Eagles	10	15	20
☐	Alex Smith, NYAm.	10	15	20
☐	Joe Starke, Chic.			
☐	Nels Stewart, Bost.	25	35	50
☐	Paul Thompson, Chic.	10	15	20
☐	Louis Trudel, Chic.	10	15	20
☐	Carl Voss, St. Louis Eagles	15	22	30
☐	Art Wiebe, Chic.	10	15	20
☐	Roy Worters (G), NYAm.	25	35	50

TYPE 2

The team name, or team position has been removed from the top of the résumé. The imprint is still on one line as in Type 1.

These matchbooks have the same colours, and design and are the same size as the Type 1 Diamond Matchbooks.

Irving Jaffes' and Harold Starr's matchbooks are considered rare.

	Complete Set (65 books):	750	1,100	1,600
	Diamond Match Co.	VG	EX	EX-MT
☐	Tom Anderson, NYAm.	10	15	20
☐	Vern Ayres, NYRa.	10	15	20
☐	Frank Boucher, NYRa.	20	30	40
☐	Frank Boucher, NYRa.	20	30	40
☐	Bill Brydge, NYAm.	10	15	20
☐	Marty Burke, Mont.	10	15	20
☐	Lorne Carr, NYAm.	10	15	20
☐	Lorne Chabot (G), NYAm.	20	30	40
☐	Art Chapman, NYAm.	10	15	20
☐	Bert Connolly, NYRa.	10	15	20
☐	Bill Cook, NYRa.	25	35	50
☐	Bill Cook, NYRa.	25	35	50
☐	Bun (Fred) Cook, NYRa.	20	30	40
☐	Tom Cook, Chic.	10	15	20
☐	Art Coulter, Chic.	10	15	20
☐	Rosario (Lolo) Couture, Mont.	10	15	20
☐	Wilf Cude (G), Mont.	12	18	25
☐	Cecil Dillon, NYRa.	10	15	20
☐	Cecil Dillon, NYRa.	10	15	20
☐	Red Dutton, NYAm.	20	30	40
☐	Hap Emms, NYAm.	15	22	30
☐	Irvin Frew, Mont.	10	15	20
☐	Johnny Gagnon, Mont.	10	15	20
☐	Leroy Goldsworthy, Mont.	10	15	20
☐	Johnny Gottselig, Chic.	10	15	20
☐	William Paul Haynes, Mont.	10	15	20
☐	Otto Heller, NYRa.	10	15	20
☐	Irving Jaffes	Very Rare		
☐	Joe Jerwa, NYAm.	10	15	20
☐	Ivan (Ching) Johnson, NYRa.	25	35	50
☐	Aurèle Joliat, Mont.	40	55	75
☐	Butch (Melville) Keeling, NYRa.	10	15	20
☐	William Kendall, Chic.	10	15	20
☐	Dave Kerr (G), NYRa.	15	22	30
☐	Lloyd Klein, NYAm.	10	15	20
☐	Wildor Larochelle, Mont.	10	15	20
☐	Pit Lepine, Mont.	10	15	20
☐	Art Lesieur, Mont.	10	15	20
☐	Alex Levinsky, NYRa.	10	15	20
☐	Alex Levinsky, NYRa.	10	15	20
☐	Norman Locking, Chic.	10	15	20
☐	Georges Mantha, Mont.	15	22	30
☐	Sylvio Mantha, Mont.	20	30	40
☐	Mush March, Chic.	10	15	20
☐	Charley Mason, NYRa.	10	15	20
☐	Donnie McFaydon, Chic.	10	15	20
☐	Jack McGill, Mont.	10	15	20
☐	Armand Mondou, Mont.	10	15	20
☐	Howie Morenz, Chic.	175	265	350
☐	John Murray Murdoch, NYRa.	10	15	20
☐	Allan Murray, NYAm.	10	15	20
☐	Harry Oliver, NYAm.	20	30	40
☐	Adelard Ouellette, Chic.	10	15	20
☐	Lynn Patrick, NYRa.	25	35	50
☐	Lynn Patrick, NYRa.	25	35	50
☐	Paul Runge, Mont.	10	15	20
☐	Sweeney Schriner, NYAm.	20	30	40
☐	Art Somers, NYRa.	10	15	20
☐	Harold Starr, NYRa.	Very Rare		
☐	Nels Stewart, NYAm.	25	35	50
☐	Paul Thompson, Chic.	10	15	20
☐	Louis Trudel, Chic.	10	15	20
☐	Carl Voss, NYAm.	15	22	30
☐	Art Wiebe, Chic.	10	15	20
☐	Roy Worters (G), NYAm.	25	35	50

TYPE 3

The imprint is now on two lines and reads "Made in the U.S.A./ Diamond Match Co. N.Y.C."

These matchbooks have the same colours and design and are the same size as the Type 1 Diamond Matchbooks.

Harold Starr's matchbook is considered rare.

	Complete Set (60 books):	700	1,000	1,500
	Diamond Match Co.	VG	EX	EX-MT
☐	Tom Anderson, NYAm.	10	15	20
☐	Vern Ayres, NYRa.	10	15	20
☐	Frank Boucher, NYRa.	20	30	40
☐	Bill Brydge, NYAm.	10	15	20
☐	Marty Burke, Chic.	10	15	20
☐	Walt Buswell, Mont.	10	15	20
☐	Lorne Carr, NYAm.	10	15	20
☐	Lorne Chabot (G), NYAm.	20	30	40
☐	Art Chapman, NYAm.	10	15	20
☐	Bert Connolly, NYRa.	10	15	20
☐	Bill Cook, NYRa.	25	35	50
☐	Bun (Fred) Cook, NYRa.	20	30	40
☐	Tom Cook, Chic.	10	15	20
☐	Art Coulter, Chic.	10	15	20
☐	Rosario (Lolo) Couture, Mont.	10	15	20
☐	Wilf Cude (G), Mont.	12	18	25
☐	Cecil Dillon, NYRa.	10	15	20
☐	Red Dutton, NYAm.	20	30	40
☐	Hap Emms, NYAm.	15	22	30
☐	Irvin Frew, Mont.	10	15	20
☐	Johnny Gagnon, Mont.	10	15	20
☐	Leroy Goldsworthy, Mont.	10	15	20
☐	Johnny Gottselig, Chic.	10	15	20
☐	Paul Haynes, Mont.	10	15	20
☐	Otto Heller, NYRa.	10	15	20
☐	Joe Jerwa, NYAm.	10	15	20
☐	Ivan (Ching) Johnson, NYRa.	25	35	50
☐	Aurèle Joliat, Mont.	40	55	75
☐	Mike Karakas (G), Chic.	12	18	25
☐	Butch (Melville) Keeling, NYRa.	10	15	20
☐	Dave Kerr (G), NYRa.	15	22	30
☐	Lloyd Klein, NYAm.	10	15	20
☐	Wildoer Larochelle, Mont.	10	15	20
☐	Pit Lepine, Mont.	10	15	20
☐	Art Lesieur, Mont.	10	15	20
☐	Alex Levinsky, Chic.	10	15	20
☐	Norman Locking, Chic.	10	15	20
☐	Georges Mantha, Mont.	15	22	30
☐	Sylvio Mantha, Mont.	20	30	40
☐	Mush March, Chic.	10	15	20
☐	Charlie Mason, NYRa.	10	15	20
☐	Charlie Mason, NYRa.	10	15	20
☐	Donnie McFayden, Chic.	10	15	20

Jack McGill, Mont.	10	15	20
Armand Mondou, Mont.	10	15	20
Howie Morenz, Chic.	175	265	350
John Murray Murdoch, NYRa.	10	15	20
Allan Murray, NYAm.	10	15	20
Harry Oliver, NYAm.	20	30	40
Adelard Ouellette, Chic.	10	15	20
Lynn Patrick, NYRa.	25	35	50
Paul Runge, Mont.	10	15	20
Sweeney Schriner, NYAm.	20	30	40
Harold Starr, NYRa.			
Nels Stewart, NYA	25	35	50
Paul Thompson, Chic.	10	15	20
Louis Trudel, Chic.	10	15	20
Carl Voss, NYAm.	15	22	30
Art Wiebe, Chic.	10	15	20
Roy Worters (G), NYAm.	25	35	50

TYPE 4

The imprint is again on two lines and reads "Made in the U.S.A./ Diamond Match Co. N.Y.C." The team name reappears below the player's name but above the resumé on the back of the book. These matchbooks have the same colours and design and are the same size as the Type 1 Diamond Matchbooks.

Complete Set (15 books):	120	185	235
Diamond Match Co.	**VG**	**EX**	**EX-MT**
Andy Blair, Chic.	10	15	20
Glenn Brydson, Chic.	10	15	20
Marty Burke, Chic.	10	15	20
Tom Cook, Chic.	10	15	20
Johnny Gottselig, Chic.	10	15	20
Hal Jackson, Chic.	10	15	20
Mike Karakas (G), Chic.	12	18	25
Wildor Larochelle, Chic.	10	15	20
Alex Levinsky, Chic.	10	15	20
Clem Loughlin, Chic.	10	15	20

Mush March, Chic.	10	15	20
Earl Seibert, Chic.	20	30	40
Paul Thompson, Chic.	10	15	20
Louis Trudel, Chic.	10	15	20
Art Wiebe, Chic.	10	15	20

TYPE 5

The imprint is again on two lines and reads "Made in the U.S.A./ Diamond Match Co. N.Y.C." On the back, above the résumé, the team name again disappears as does the "Chicago" of the Chicago Blackhawks on the front cover. The tan background colour covers the complete book with the striker pad being overlaid on the tan. These matchbooks have the same colours and design and are the same size as the Type 1 Diamond Matchbooks.

Complete Set (14 books):	120	185	235
Diamond Match Co.	**VG**	**EX**	**EX-MT**
Glenn Brydson, Chic.	10	15	20
Marty Burke, Chic.	10	15	20
Tom Cook, Chic.	10	15	20
Cully Dahlstrom, Chic.	10	15	20
Johnny Gottselig, Chic.	10	15	20
Vic Heyliger, Chic.	10	15	20
Mike Karakas (G), Chic.	12	18	25
Alex Levinsky, Chic.	10	15	20
Mush March, Chic.	10	15	20
Earl Seibert, Chic.	20	30	40
Bill Stewart, Manager, Chic.	10	15	20
Paul Thompson, Chic.	10	15	20
Louis Trudel, Chic.	10	15	20
Art Wiebe, Chic.	10	15	20

TYPE 6

The imprint is again on two lines and reads "Made in the U.S.A./ Diamond Match Co. N.Y.C."

This variety differs from Type 5 only in the background colour on which the striker is overlaid. This area is a dark brown or black giving the appearance that the tip is black instead of tan. These matchbooks have the same colours and design and are the same size as the Type 1 Diamond Matchbooks.

Complete Set (14 books):	120	185	235
Diamond Match Co.	**VG**	**EX**	**EX-MT**
Glenn Brydson, Chic.	10	15	20
Marty Burke, Chic.	10	15	20
Tom Cook, Chic.	10	15	20
Cully Dahlstrom, Chic.	10	15	20
Johnny Gottselig, Chic.	10	15	20
Vic Heyliger, Chic.	10	15	20
Mike Karakas (G), Chic.	12	18	25
Alex Levinsky, Chic.	10	15	20
Mush March, Chic.	10	15	20
Earl Seibert, Chic.	20	30	40
Bill Stewart, Manager, Chic.	10	15	20
Paul Thompson, Chic.	10	15	20
Louis Trudel, Chic.	10	15	20
Art Wiebe, Chic.	10	15	20

1937 BRITISH SPORTING PERSONALITIES

This 48-card set features only two hockey cards. Each black & white card measures 2" x 3".

Imperial Tobacco	VG	EX	EX-MT
36 L. Bates, Wembley Lions	10	20	45
37 Joe Beaton, Richmond Hawks	10	20	45

1937 - 38 O-PEE-CHEE

Cards can be found with either purple or blue borders. Each card measures 2 3/8" x 3 7/8".

Complete Set (48 cards):	4,000	5,500	8,000
ACC # V304E	**VG**	**EX**	**EX-MT**
133 Turk Broda (G), Toro.	275	400	700
134 Red Horner, Toro.	125	190	250
135 Jimmy Fowler, Toro.	60	90	115
136 Bob Davidson, Toro.	65	100	130
137 Reg Hamilton, Toro. RC	**60**	**90**	**115**
138 Charlie Conacher, Toro.	300	450	600
139 Harvey Jackson, Toro.	200	275	350
140 Buzz Boll, Toro.	60	90	115
141 Syl Apps, Sr., Toro.	200	300	400
142 Gordie Drillon, Toro. RC	**250**	**350**	**450**
143 Bill Thoms, Toro.	90	140	185
144 Nick Metz, Toro.	70	100	140
145 Reg Kelly, Toro.	60	90	115
146 Murray Armstrong, Toro. RC	**60**	**90**	**115**
147 Murph Chamberlain, Toro. RC	**60**	**90**	**115**
148 Des Smith, Mont.M RC	**60**	**90**	**115**
149 Wilf Cude (G), Mont.	70	100	140
150 Babe Siebert	125	190	250
151 Bill MacKenzie, Mont., Error (McKenzie)	60	90	115
152 Aurèle Joliat, Mont.	300	450	600
153 Georges Mantha, Mont.	60	90	115
154 Johnny Gagnon, Mont.	60	90	115
155 Paul Haynes, Mont.	60	90	115
156 Joffre Desilets, Mont.	60	90	115
157 George Brown, Mont. RC	**60**	**90**	**115**
158 Polly Drouin, Mont. RC	**60**	**90**	**115**
159 Pit Lépine, Mont.	60	90	115
160 Toe Blake, Mont. RC	**525**	**775**	**1,000**
161 Bill Beveridge (G), Mont.M	70	100	140
162 Al Shields, Mont.M	60	90	115
163 Cy Wentworth, Mont.M	65	100	130
164 Stewart Evans, Mont.M RC	**60**	**90**	**115**
165 Earle Robinson, Mont.M	60	90	115
166 Baldy Northcott, Mont.M	90	135	175
167 Paul Runge, Mont.M	60	90	115
168 Dave Trottier, Mont.M	60	90	115
169 Russ Blinco, Mont.M	60	90	115
170 Jimmy Ward, Mont.M	60	90	115
171 Bob Gracie, Mont.M	60	90	115
172 Herbert Cain, Mont.M	85	125	165
173 Gus Marker, Mont.M	60	90	115
174 Walt Buswell, Mont. RC	**60**	**90**	**115**
175 Carl Voss, Mont.M RC	**100**	**150**	**200**
176 Rod Lorraine, Mont. RC, Err (Lorrain)	**60**	**90**	**115**
177 Armand Mondou, Mont.	60	90	115
178 Red Goupille, Mont. RC	**60**	**90**	**115**
179 Gerry Shannon, Mont. RC, Err (Jerry)	**60**	**90**	**115**
180 Tom Cook, Mont. RC	**100**	**150**	**275**

1937 - 38 WORLD WIDE GUM

These cards measure 2 3/8" x 2 7/8".

Complete Set (135 cards):	14,000	20,000	30,000
ACC # V304D	**VG**	**EX**	**EX-MT**
1 Charlie Conacher, Toro.	500	800	1,400
2 Jimmy Ward, Mont.M	90	135	175
3 Babe Siebert, Mont.	215	320	425
4 Marty Barry, Detr.	190	285	375
5 Eddie Shore, Bost.	1,000	1,500	2,000
6 Paul Thompson, Chic.	140	210	275
7 Roy Worters (G), NYAm.	240	360	475
8 Red Horner, Toro.	200	300	400
9 Wilf Cude (G), Mont.	115	170	225
10 Lionel Conacher, Mont.M	265	395	525
11 Ebbie Goodfellow, Detr.	200	300	400
12 Tiny Thompson (G), Bost.	215	320	425
13 Mush March, Chic. RC	**125**	**190**	**250**
14 Red Dutton, NYAm.	200	300	400
15 Butch Keeling, NYRa.	90	135	175
16 Frank Boucher, NYRa.	200	300	400
17 Tommy Gorman, Mgr., Mont.M	90	135	175
18 Howie Morenz, NYRa.	1,500	2,150	3,000
19 Cy Wentworth, Mont.M	115	170	225
20 Hooley Smith, Bost.	190	285	375
21 Ivan (Ching) Johnson, NYRa.	225	340	450
22 Baldy Northcott	125	190	250
23 Syl Apps, Sr., Toro.	500	700	950
24 Hec Kilrea, Toro.	90	135	175
25 John Sorrell, Detr.	90	135	175
26 Lorne Carr, NYAm. RC	**100**	**150**	**200**
27 Charlie Sands, Bost.	90	135	175
28 Nick Metz, Toro.	100	150	200
29 Francis (King) Clancy, Toro.	600	900	1,200
30 Russ Blinco, Mont.M	90	135	175
31 Pete Martin RC	**90**	**135**	**175**
32 Walt Buswell, Mont. RC	**90**	**135**	**175**
33 Paul Haynes, Mont.	90	135	175
34 Wildor Larochelle, Chic.	90	135	175
35 Baldy Cotton, Toro.	115	170	225
36 Dit Clapper, Bost.	225	340	450
37 Joe Lamb, NYAm.	90	135	175
38 Bob Gracie, Mont.M	90	135	175
39 Jack Shill, Toro.	90	135	175
40 Buzz Boll, Toro.	90	135	175
41 John Gallagher, NYAm.	90	135	175
42 Art Chapman, NYAm.	100	150	200
43 Tom Cook, Chic. RC	**90**	**135**	**175**
44 Bill MacKenzie, Mont.	90	135	175
45 Georges Mantha, Mont.	90	135	175
46 Herbert Cain, Mont.M	120	180	235
47 Mud Bruneteau, Detr.	110	165	215
48 Bob Davidson, Toro.	100	150	200
49 Douglas Young, Detr. RC	**90**	**135**	**175**
50 Polly Drouin, Mont. RC	**90**	**135**	**175**
51 Harvey Jackson, Toro.	250	375	500
52 Hap Day, Toro.	190	285	375
53 Dave Kerr (G)	150	225	300
54 Allan Murray, NYAm.	90	135	175
55 Johnny Gottselig, Chic.	120	180	235
56 Andy Blair, Chic.	90	135	175
57 Lynn Patrick, NYRa.	225	340	450
58 Sweeney Schriner, NYAm.	**200**	**300**	**400**
59 Hap Emms, NYAm.	115	170	225
60 Al Shields, NYAm.	90	135	175
61 Alex Levinsky, Toro.	90	135	175
62 Bill Hollett, Bost.	90	135	175
63 Peggy O'Neil, Bost.	90	135	175
64 Herbie Lewis, Detr.	200	300	400
65 Aurèle Joliat, Mont.	550	850	1,100
66 Carl Voss, Mont.M RC	**165**	**245**	**325**
67 Stewart Evans, Mont.M RC	**90**	**135**	**175**
68 Fred (Bun) Cook, Bost.	190	285	375
69 Cooney Weiland, Bost.	190	285	375
70 Dave Trottier, Mont.M	90	135	175
71 Louis Trudel, Chic.	90	135	175
72 Marty Burke, Chic.	90	135	175
73 Leroy Goldsworthy, Bost.	90	135	175
74 Norman Smith (G), Detr.	100	150	200
75 Syd Howe, Detr.	200	300	400
76 Gord Pettinger, Detr.	90	135	175
77 Jack McGill, Mont.	90	135	175
78 Pit Lepine, Mont.	90	135	175
79 Sammy McManus, Bost.	90	135	175
80 Phil Watson, NYRa.	125	190	250
81 Paul Runge, Mont.M	90	135	175
82 Bill Beveridge (G), Mont.M	115	170	225
83 Johnny Gagnon, Mont.	90	135	175
84 Bucko McDonald, Detr.	90	135	175
85 Earle Robinson, Mont.M	90	135	175
86 Reg (Regis) Kelly, Toro.	90	135	175
87 Ott Heller, NYRa.	90	135	175
88 Murray Murdock, NYRa.	90	135	175
89 Mac Colville, NYRa.	90	135	175
90 Alex Shibicky, NYRa.	90	135	175
91 Neil Colville, NYRa.	200	300	400
92 Normie Himes, NYAm.	90	135	175
93 Charley McVeigh, NYAm.	90	135	175
94 Lester Patrick, Coach, NYRa.	240	360	475
95 Conn Smythe, Mgr., Toro.	275	415	550
96 Art Ross, Coach, Bost.	225	340	450
97 Cecil M. Hart, Coach, Mont.	165	250	325
98 Dutch Gainor, Mont.M	90	135	175
99 Jack J. Adams, Coach, Detr.	200	300	400
100 Howie Morenz, Jr., Mascot, Mont.	250	375	500
101 Buster Mundy RC	**90**	**135**	**175**
102 Johnny Wing RC	**90**	**135**	**175**
103 Maurice Croghan, Mont.M	90	135	175
104 Pete Jotkus RC	**90**	**135**	**175**
105 Doug MacQuisten RC	**90**	**135**	**175**
106 Lester Brennan RC, LC	**90**	**135**	**175**
107 Jack O'Connell RC	**90**	**135**	**175**
108 Ray Malenfant RC	**90**	**135**	**175**
109 Ken Murray, Mont. RC	**90**	**135**	**175**
110 Frank Stangle RC	**90**	**135**	**175**
111 Dave Neville RC	**90**	**135**	**175**
112 Claude Burke RC	**90**	**135**	**175**
113 Herman Murray RC	**90**	**135**	**175**
114 Buddy O'Connor RC	**200**	**300**	**400**
115 Albert Perreault RC	**90**	**135**	**175**

Vintage Sports

by Richard Scott

New year for old World Wide Gum cards

Collector Stephen Laroche made a significant discovery on the old V356 World Wide Gum hockey cards. You see, this series has always been listed as a 1936-37 series, but Laroche's purchase of a Bill Stewart card led him to believe otherwise.

Laroche found on the back of the Stewart card text about Stewart's employment as referee-in-chief for the 1936-37 season and how he became "manager of the Black Hawks at the close of the 1936-37 season." Such a card could not have been produced earlier than the end of the 1936-37 season or, more likely, the beginning of the 1937-38 season.

Laroche suddenly had a project at hand. He went out and found other cards in the series and double-checked the backs. In early July, he presented his proof in an article at his *SLAM! Collectibles* Web site.

Roy Worters' card said "he retired from hockey this Fall" (he retired after the 1936-37 season). Ebbie Goodfellow's card said the Red Wings won the '37 Stanley Cup. Doug Young's card referred to him breaking a leg and missing the '37 playoffs.

Laroche's discovery has led us to changing the year of the series in both this magazine and the annual *Hockey Cards (A Charlton Standard Catalogue).* The series is now known as the 1937-38 World Wide Gum series.

Of course, for those keeping track of rookie cards from the 1930s, you will have to go back and replace some of the cards in your collection. For starters, there are 11 cards that are no longer deemed rookie cards in the V356 World Wide Gum series: 23 Syl Apps; 39 Jack Shill; 41 John Gallagher; 48 Bob Davidson; 54 Al Murray; 58 Sweeney Schriner; 81 Paul Runge; 90 Alex Shibicky; 91 Neil Colville; 123 Mike Karakas; and 124 Art Wiebe. The lone rookie cards for those 11 players are included in the 1936-37 O-Pee-Chee series.

Secondly, there are now five new rookie cards in the 1937-38 O-Pee-Chee series: 158 Polly Drouin; 164 Stewart Evans; 174 Walter Buswell; 175 Carl Voss; and 180 Tommy Cook.

The 1937-38 World Wide Gum set is a 135-card series of NHL and junior players. It was the biggest hockey card set of the time (in terms of cards in the set) and the largest until the 1968-69 O-Pee-Chee series (217 cards). Cards in this series measure 60.3 mm x 73 mm (2-3/8" by 2-7/8").

Other hockey-card sets from the 1930s and early 1940s are 1933-34 Canadian Gum, 1933-34 Hamilton Gum, 1933-34 O-Pee-Chee (Series A and Series B), 1933-34 World Wide Gum, 1933-34 anonymous (noted as V129), 1935-36 O-Pee-Chee (Series C), 1936-37 O-Pee-Chee (Series D), 1937-38 O-Pee-Chee (Series E), 1939-40 O-Pee-Chee, and 1940-41 O-Pee-Chee. There are also several multi-sport Olympic series from the 1930s that were issued in Europe (ie: Weitere Werke in Germany).

RETRO GAMEPLAY

I'm hoping you can provide me some information of a mail-in premium game from O-Pee-Chee which I bought last year. I was told that to receive this game, you would need to send in a 1937-38 wax wrapper to the O-Pee-Chee company. Is this correct? Do you have any additional information on this game? Is there a price guide which list, such items and what is the value of this item? Is there a price guide for wax wrappers? I really hope you can help me. – Dennis Scandella

Hi Dennis. If you like old hockey wax and pack premiums, the book you have to read is the Hockey Wax Pack Collector's Price Guide. *Written by Bobby Burrell and Roger Cunha, it includes more than 350 photos over a 60-year time period.*

Shortly after they went to print on this book, Burrell says they learned some new information regarding the O-Pee-Chee premiums from the 1930s. First, the orange and blue game that they showed on page 38 is not from the 1936-37 set, but from an earlier year. It is either from the 1933-34 Series B wrapper or the 1935-36 Series C wrapper. Burrell has not seen a wrapper for 1935-36 O-Pee-Chee Series C, so for now he believes the game to be from 1933-34 Series B (there was no game premium on the 1933-34 Series A wrappers).

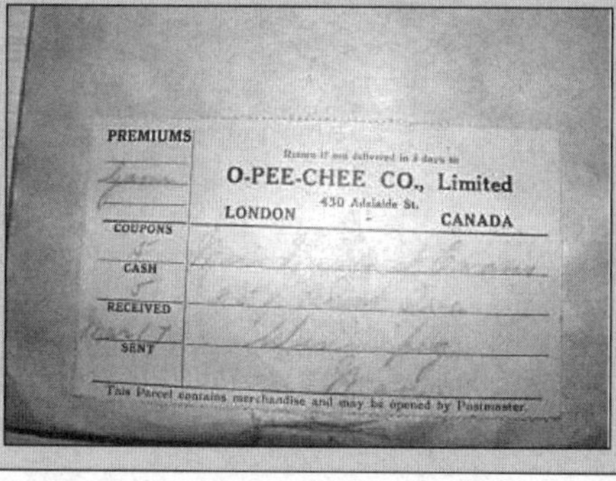

Now, if you are still following me, the image in the bottom left corner of this page is the 1936-37 premium. As per your follow-up e-mail, we know this because of the March 1937 date on the envelope in which the red and blue game was mailed.

At last, your yellow and blue game in question should indeed be from the 1937-38 O-Pee-Chee series. Along with the difference in colours, the 1937-38 O-Pee-Chee series includes images of players.

Thanks for your letter and thanks to Mr. Burrell for his new information. It's always great to learn new things about an old hobby.

116 Johnny Taugher RC	90	135	175
117 Rene Boudreau RC	90	135	175
118 Kenny McKinnon (G), RC	90	135	175
119 Alex Bolduc RC	90	135	175
120 Jimmy Keiller RC	90	135	175
121 Lloyd McIntyre RC	90	135	175
122 Emile Fortin RC	90	135	175
123 Mike Karakas	110	170	215
124 Art Wiebe, Chic.	90	135	175
125 Louis Denis RC	90	135	175
126 Stan Pratt RC	90	135	175
127 Jules Cholette RC, LC	90	135	175
128 Jimmy Muir RC	90	135	175
129 Pete Morin RC	90	135	175
130 Jimmy Heffernan RC	90	135	175
131 Morris Bastien RC	90	135	175
132 Tuffy Griffiths RC	90	135	175
133 John Mahaffy RC	90	135	175
134 Truman Donnelly RC	90	135	175
135 Bill Stewart RC	125	170	350

1938 - 39 LA PRESSE

These photos, cut from the Montréal newspaper, measure 10" x 16 1/2".

La Presse photo	VG	EX	EX-MT
Feb. 11 Montréal Team	75	115	150

1938 - 39 QUAKER OATS

These photosmeasure 6 1/4" x 7 1/2".

Complete Set (30 photos):	750	1,200	1,600
Quaker Oats	VG	EX	EX-MT
Toe Blake, Mont.	95	145	185
Walt Buswell, Mont.	25	35	50
Herbert Cain, Mont.	30	45	60
Wilf Cude (G), Mont.	30	45	60
Polly Drouin, Mont.	25	35	50
Stewart Evans, Mont.	25	35	50
Johnny Gagnon, Mont.	25	35	50
Bob Gracie, Mont.	25	35	50
Paul Haynes, Mont.	25	35	50
Rod Lorraine, Mont.	25	35	50
Georges Mantha, Mont.	25	35	50
Babe Siebert, Mont.	45	70	90
Jimmy Ward, Mont.	25	35	50
Cy Wentworth, Mont.	30	45	60
Syl Apps, Sr., Toro.	75	120	150
Buzz Boll, Toro.	25	35	50
Turk Broda (G), Toro.	80	120	160
Murph Chamberlain, Toro.	25	35	50
Bob Davidson, Toro.	30	45	60
Gordie Drillon, Toro.	45	70	90
Jimmy Fowler, Toro.	25	35	50
Reg Hamilton, Toro.	25	35	50
Red Horner, Toro.	40	60	80
Harvey Jackson, Toro.	55	85	110
Bingo Kampman, Toro.	25	35	50
Reg Kelly, Toro.	25	35	50
Nick Metz, Toro.	30	45	60
George Parsons, Toro.	25	35	50
Bill Thoms, Toro.	30	45	60
Foster Hewitt	50	75	100

1939 - 40 O-PEE-CHEE

These black & white cards have blank backs and are larger than the previous issues of the '30s. The player's name, team and position are shown beneath the photo with the card number to the right. Each card measures 5" x 7".

Complete Set (100 cards):	3,500	6,000	9,000
ACC # V301-1	VG	EX	EX-MT
1 Reg Hamilton, Toro.	35	55	110
2 Turk Broda (G), Toro.	150	210	325
3 Bingo Kampman, Toro. RC	25	45	60
4 Gordie Drillon, Toro.	50	80	135
5 Bob Davidson, Toro.	25	55	85
6 Syl Apps, Sr., Toro.	100	140	225
7 Pete Langelle, Toro. RC	25	45	60
8 Don Metz, Toro. RC	25	45	60
9 Reg Kelly, Toro.	25	45	60
10 Red Horner, Toro.	50	75	125
11 W. Stanowski, Toro. RC, Error (Stanowsky)	35	55	75
12 Murph Chamberlain, Toro.	25	45	60
13 Bucko McDonald, Toro.	25	45	60
14 Sweeny Schriner, Toro.	60	90	140
15 Billy Taylor, Toro. RC	35	60	80
16 Gus Marker, Toro.	25	45	60
17 Hooley Smith, NYAm.	50	75	125
18 Art Chapman, NYAm.	25	70	85
19 Murray Armstrong, NYAm.	25	45	60
20 Harvey Jackson, NYAm.	75	110	175
21 Buzz Boll, NYAm.	25	45	60
22 Red Goupille, Mont.	25	45	60
23 Rod Lorraine, Mont.	25	45	60
24 Polly Drouin, Mont.	25	45	60
25 Johnny Gagnon, Mont.	25	45	60
26 Georges Mantha, Mont.	25	45	60
27 Armand Mondou, Mont.	25	45	60
28 Claude Bourque (G), Mont. RC	25	45	60
29 Ray Getliffe, Mont. RC	25	45	60
30 Cy Wentworth, Mont.	35	55	75
31 Paul Haynes, Mont.	25	45	60
32 Walt Buswell, Mont.	25	45	60
33 Ott Heller, NYRa.	25	45	60
34 Art Coulter, NYRa.	45	70	115
35 Clint Smith, NYRa. RC	50	75	130
36 Lynn Patrick, NYRa.	50	75	125
37 Dave Kerr (G), NYRa.	40	60	100
38 Murray Patrick, NYRa. RC	25	45	60
39 Neil Colville, NYRa.	50	75	130
40 Jack Portland, Bost. RC	25	45	60
41 Bill Hollett, Bost.	25	45	60
42 Herbert Cain, Bost.	40	60	90
43 Mud Bruneteau, Detr. RC	35	55	75
44 Joffre Desilets, Chic.	25	45	60
45 Mush March, Chic.	35	55	75
46 C. Dahlstrom, Chic. RC, Err. (Dalhstrom)	25	45	60
47 Mike Karakas (G), Chic.	25	55	70
48 Bill Thoms, Chic.	40	60	85
49 Art Wiebe, Chic.	25	15	60
50 Johnny Gottselig, Chic.	35	55	75
51 Nick Metz, Toro.	25	55	70
52 Jack Church, Toro. RC	25	45	60
53 Red Heron, Toro. RC	25	45	60
54 Hank Goldup, Toro. RC	25	45	60
55 Jimmy Fowler, Toro.	25	45	60
56 Charlie Sands, Mont.	25	45	60
57 Marty Barry, Mont.	45	80	125
58 Doug Young, Mont. RC	25	45	60
59 Charlie Conacher, NYAm.	125	165	275
60 John Sorrell, NYAm.	25	45	60
61 Tom Anderson, NYAm. RC	30	65	85
62 Lorne Carr, NYAm.	35	60	80
63 Earl Robertson (G), NYAm. RC	25	45	60
64 Wilf Field, NYAm. RC	25	45	60
65 Jimmy Orlando, Detr. RC	25	45	60
66 Ebbie Goodfellow, Detr.	45	80	120
67 Jack Keating, Detr. RC	25	45	60
68 Sid Abel, Detr. RC	130	200	325
69 Gus Giesebrecht, Detr. RC	25	45	60
70 Don Deacon, Detr. RC	25	45	60
71 Hec Kilrea, Detr.	25	45	60
72 Syd Howe, Detr.	50	75	125
73 Eddie Wares, Detr. RC	25	45	60
74 Carl Liscombe, Detr. RC	25	45	60
75 Tiny Thompson (G), Detr.	60	90	150
76 Earl Seibert, Chic.	60	90	150
77 Des Smith, Chic.	25	45	60
78 Les Cunningham, Chic. RC	25	45	60
79 George Allen, Chic. RC	25	45	60
80 Bill Carse, Chic. RC	25	45	60
81 Bill MacKenzie, Chic.	25	45	60
82 Ab DeMarco, Chic. RC	25	45	60
83 Phil Watson, Chic. RC	40	60	90
84 Alf Pike, NYRa. RC	25	45	60
85 Babe Pratt, NYRa. RC	70	100	160
86 Bryan Hextall, Sr., NYRa. RC	80	125	200
87 Kilby MacDonald, NYRa. RC	25	45	60
88 Alex Shibicky, NYRa.	25	45	60
89 Dutch Hiller, NYRa. RC	30	65	85
90 Mac Colville, NYRa. RC	25	45	60
91 Roy Conacher, Bost. RC	40	60	100
92 Cooney Weiland, Bost.	50	75	125
93 Art Jackson	25	45	60
94 Woodie Dumart, Bost. RC	60	90	150
95 Dit Clapper, Bost.	100	150	225
96 Mel Hill, Bost. RC	25	45	60
97 Frank Brimsek (G), Bost. RC	160	240	400
98 Bill Cowley, Bost. RC	120	180	300
99 Bobby Bauer, Bost. RC	45	70	115
100 Eddie Shore, Bost.	300	400	700

1940 - 41 O-PEE-CHEE

This set continues the sequential numbering from the V301-1 issue and follows the same format except for the sepia-toned photos. Each card measures 5" x 7".

Complete Set (50 cards):	2,200	3,500	5,500
ACC # V301-1	VG	EX	EX-MT
101 Toe Blake, Mont.	150	225	350
102 Charlie Sands	30	50	65
103 Wally Stanowski, Toro.	35	55	75
104 Jack E. Adams, Mont. RC	30	50	65
105 Johnny Mowers (G) RC	30	50	65
106 John Quilty RC	30	50	65
107 Billy Taylor, Toro.	35	55	75
108 Turk Broda (G), Toro.	125	170	300
109 Bingo Kampman, Toro.	30	50	65
110 Gordie Drillon	50	75	120
111 Don Metz, Toro.	30	50	65
112 Paul Haynes	30	50	65
113 Gus Marker, Toro.	30	50	65
114 Alex Singbush, Mont. RC	30	50	65
115 Alex Motter RC	30	50	65
116 Ken Reardon, Mont. RC	75	110	175
117 Pete Langelle, Toro.	30	50	65
118 Syl Apps, Toro.	100	140	225
119 Reg Hamilton, Toro.	30	50	65
120 Red Goupille, Mont.	30	50	65
121 Joe Benoit RC	30	50	65
122 Sweeny Schriner, Toro.	50	75	120
123 Joe Carveth, Detr. RC	35	55	75
124 Jack Stewart RC	60	90	150
125 Elmer Lach, Mont. RC	130	200	325
126 Jack Schewchuk RC	45	70	110
127 Norman Larson RC	45	70	110
128 Don Grosso RC	45	70	110
129 Les Douglas, Detr. RC	45	70	110
130 Turk Broda (G), Toro.	200	275	450
131 Max Bentley, Chic. RC	140	210	350
132 Milt Schmidt, Bost. RC	200	300	500
133 Nick Metz, Toro.	50	75	120
134 John Crawford, Bost. RC	50	75	120
135 Bill Benson RC	45	70	110
136 Lynn Patrick, NYRa.	70	110	175
137 Cully Dahlstrom, Chic.	45	70	110
138 Mud Bruneteau, Detr.	50	75	120
139 Dave Kerr (G)	55	85	135
140 Red Heron	45	70	110
141 Nick Metz, Toro.	55	80	120
142 Ott Heller, NYR	45	70	110
143 Philip Hergesheimer RC	45	70	110
144 Tony DeMeres RC	45	70	110
145 Arch Wilder, Detr. RC	45	70	110
146 Syl Apps, Sr., Toro.	120	180	300
147 Ray Getliffe	50	75	110
148 Lex Chisholm, Toro. RC	50	75	110
149 Eddie Wiseman RC	50	75	110
150 Paul Goodman (G), Chic. RC	55	80	150

1934 - 43 BEEHIVE PHOTOS

The first group of BeeHive photos were issued between 1934 and 1943. There are three main styles used on these photos: facsimile signature names, block signature names and script signature names. Photos measure 4 1/4" x 6 3/4" (matted photos measure 5 1/2" x 8").

Group One • Boston Bruins	EX	EX-MT
Bobby Bauer	10	15
Red Beattie	12	20
Yank Boyd	100	150
Frank Brimsek (G)	15	25
Dit Clapper	12	20
Roy Conacher	10	15
Fred (Bun) Cook	13	22
Cowboy Cowley	12	20
Johnny Crawford (#19)	10	15
Woody Dumart	15	25
Don Gallinger	90	150
Ray Getliffe	10	15
Bep Guidolin	75	110
Red Hamill	18	28
Melvin Hill	12	20
Alex Motter	22	35
Peggy O'Neill	12	20
Charles Sands	12	20
Jack Schmidt	130	200
Milt Schmidt	12	20
Jack Shewchuk	12	20
Eddie Shore	40	60
Tiny Thompson (G)	20	30
Cooney Weiland	12	20
Group One • Chicago Blackhawks	**EX**	**EX-MT**
George Allen	20	30
Doug Bentley	18	28
Max Bentley, Error (Doug Bentley)	18	28
Glenn Brydson	75	125
Marty Burke	15	25
Bill Carse	11	18
Bob Carse	11	18
Lorne Chabot (G)	25	40
Johnny Chad	22	35
Les Cunningham	20	30
Cully Dahlstrom	12	20
Goldy Goldsworthy	20	30
Paul Goodman (G)	22	35
Johnnie Gottselig	15	25
Phil Hergesheimer	12	20
Wingy Johnston	100	155
Alex Kaleta	20	30
Mike Karakas (G)	13	22
Alex Levinsky	22	35
Sam LoPresti (G)	30	50
Dave Mackay	1,000	1,600
Mush March	12	20
John Mariucci	28	45
Joe Matte	90	150
Red Mitchell	90	145
Pete Palangio	50	80
Joe Papike	75	120
Fido Purpur	110	175
Doc Romnes	30	50
Earl Seibert	12	20
Paul Thompson	15	25
Louis Trudel	22	35
Audley Tuten	100	150
Art Wiebe	12	20
Group One • Detroit Red Wings	**EX**	**EX-MT**
Sid Abel	20	35
Larry Aurie	10	15
Martin J. Barry	12	20
Ralph Bowman	13	22
Adam Brown	80	135
Conny Brown	50	80
Jerry Brown	750	1,200
Modere Bruneteau	10	15
Eddie Bush	180	300
Joe Carveth	11	18
Les Douglas	25	40

□ Gus Geisebrecht	10	15
□ Ebbie Goodfellow	12	20
□ Don Grosso	10	15
□ Sydney H. Howe	13	22
□ Bill Jennings	45	75
□ Jack Keating	15	28
□ Pete Kelly	13	22
□ Hec Kilrea	10	15
□ Ken Kilrea	12	20
□ Wally Kilrea	10	15
□ Herbert A. Lewis	12	20
□ Carl Liscombe	10	15
□ Doug McCaig	75	125
□ Wilfred McDonald (On ice)	100	175
□ Wilfred McDonald (Dressing room)	100	175
□ Pat McReavy	45	75
□ Johnny Mowers	13	22
□ Jimmy Orlando	10	15
□ Gordon Pettinger	15	25
□ Johnny Sherf	22	35
□ Norman E. Smith (G)	20	30
□ Johnnie Sorrell	18	28
□ Jack Stewart	18	28
□ Carl Voss	70	100
□ Eddie Wares	12	20
□ Archie Wilder	15	25
□ Douglas Young	15	25

Group One • Montréal Canadiens	EX	EX-MT
□ Jack Adams	15	25
□ Marty Barry	600	900
□ Joe Benoît	11	18
□ Paul Bibeault (G)	35	60
□ Toe Blake	20	30
□ Emile Bouchard	25	40
□ Claude Bourque (G)	28	45
□ George Allan Brown	80	125
□ Walter Buswell	25	40
□ Murph Chamberlain	30	50
□ Wilf Cude (G)	22	35
□ Bunny Dame	35	60
□ Tony Demers	11	18
□ Joffre Desilets	11	18
□ Gordon Drillon	950	1,400
□ Polly Drouin	12	20
□ Johnny Gagnon	10	15
□ Bert Gardiner (G)	18	28
□ Ray Getliffe	40	65
□ Cliff Goupille	12	20
□ Tony Graboski	11	18
□ Paul Haynes	10	15
□ Gerry Heffernan	90	150
□ Roger Jenkins	40	70
□ Aurèle Joliat	25	40
□ Elmer Lach (On ice)	22	35
□ Léo Lamoureaux	80	135
□ Pit Lépine	10	15
□ Rod Lorraine	18	28
□ Georges Mantha	10	15
□ Sylvio Mantha	13	22
□ Armand Mondou	10	15
□ Howie Morenz	575	750
□ Pete Morin	100	175
□ Buddy O'Connor	90	150
□ Jack Portland	10	15
□ John Quilty	15	25
□ Ken Reardon	28	45
□ Terry Reardon	70	115
□ Maurice Richard (On ice)	450	750
□ Earle Robinson	400	650
□ Charlie Sands	40	65
□ Babe Siebert	20	30
□ Alex Singbush	45	75
□ Bill Summerhill	175	250
□ Louis Trudel	40	70
□ Cy Wentworth	5,000	8,000
□ Doug Young	50	80

Group One • Montréal Maroons	EX	EX-MT
□ Bill Beveridge (G)	35	55
□ Russ Blinco	28	45
□ Herb Cain	25	40
□ Jerry Carson	120	200
□ Alex Connell (G)	40	70
□ Tommy Cook	25	40
□ Stew Evans	25	40
□ Bob Gracie	25	40
□ Max Kaminsky	200	275
□ Bill MacKenzie	70	120
□ Gus Marker	300	375
□ Baldy Northcott	28	45
□ Earle Robinson	25	40
□ Paul Runge	120	200
□ Jerry Shannon	150	225
□ Des Smith	25	40
□ Hooley Smith	25	40
□ Dave Trottier	75	125
□ Jimmy Ward	25	40
□ Cy Wentworth	25	40

Group One • New York Americans	EX	EX-MT
□ Squee Allen	50	75
□ Tommy Anderson	25	40
□ Bill Benson	30	50
□ Lorne Carr	25	40
□ Art Chapman	25	40
□ Red Dutton	28	45
□ Pat Egan	25	40
□ Hap Emms	50	80
□ Wilf Field	25	40
□ Johnny Gallagher	25	40
□ Joe Jerwa	35	55
□ Dede Klein	60	90
□ Joe Krol	1,400	2,400
□ Joe Lamb	55	85
□ Norm Larson, Err (Ralph Wycherly)	30	50
□ Hazen McAndrew	2,100	3,000
□ Ken Mosdell	425	675
□ Al Murray	25	40
□ Johnny O'Flaherty	40	70
□ Chuck Rayner (G)	150	200
□ Earl Robertson (G)	28	45
□ Dave Schriner	25	40
□ Allen Shields	90	150
□ Pete Slobodian	45	75
□ Nels Stewart	35	55
□ Alfred Thurier	90	150
□ Harry Watson	225	300
□ Eddie Wiseman	25	40
□ Roy Worters	40	70
□ Ralph Wycherly, Err. (Norm Larson)	45	75

Group One • New York Rangers	EX	EX-MT
□ Frank Boucher	22	35
□ Norman Burns	70	110
□ Mac Colville	11	18
□ Neil Colville	12	20
□ Bill Cook	15	25
□ Joe Cooper	11	18
□ Art Coulter	12	20
□ Gord Davidson	45	75
□ Cecil Dillon	10	15
□ Jim Franks	130	200
□ Red Garrett	85	150
□ Eberhardt Heller	10	15
□ Jim Henry (G) (Vertical)	75	125
□ Jim Henry (G) (Horizontal)	40	70
□ Bryan Hextall	15	25
□ Dutch Hiller	10	15
□ Ivan W. Johnson	13	22
□ Bill Juzda	13	22
□ Melville Keeling	11	18
□ David A. Kerr (G)	13	22
□ Bobby Kirk	70	100
□ Bob Kirkpatrick	55	85
□ Kilby MacDonald	11	18
□ Larry Molyneaux	20	30
□ John Murray Murdoch	15	25
□ Vic Myles	110	175
□ Lynn Patrick	13	22
□ Murray Patrick	10	15
□ Alf Pike	10	15
□ Babe Pratt	15	25
□ Alex Shibicky	10	15
□ Clint Smith	13	22
□ Norman Tustin	65	110
□ Grant Warwick	13	22
□ Phil Watson	10	15

Group One • Toronto Maple Leafs	EX	EX-MT
□ Syl Apps (On ice)	13	22
□ Murray Armstrong	11	18
□ Andy Blair	10	15
□ Buzz Boll	10	15
□ George Boothman	125	200
□ Turk Broda (G)	15	25
□ Lorne Carr	40	70
□ Murph Chamberlain	10	15
□ Lex Chisholm	12	20
□ Jack Church	10	15
□ Francis (King) Clancy	28	45
□ Charlie Conacher	18	28
□ Robert Copp	40	60
□ Harold Cotton	11	18
□ Bob Davidson	10	15
□ Happy Day	12	20
□ Ernie Dickens	110	175
□ Gord Drillon	12	20
□ Frank Finnigan	15	25
□ Jack Forsey	125	200
□ Jimmie Fowler	10	15
□ Bob Goldham	140	225
□ Hank Goldup	10	15
□ George Hainsworth (G)	28	45
□ Reg Hamilton	10	15
□ Red Heron	11	18
□ Melvin Hill	190	250
□ William Hollett	11	18
□ Red Horner	10	20
□ Art Jackson	11	18
□ Harvey Jackson	13	22
□ Rudolph Kampman	10	15
□ Reg Kelly	10	15
□ Bill Kendall	50	80
□ Hec Kilrea	40	60
□ Pete Langelle	12	20
□ Bucko McDonald	12	20
□ Normie Mann	12	20
□ Normie Mann (Script over stick)	115	185
□ Gus Marker	10	15
□ Johnny McCreedy	28	45
□ Jack McLean	60	100
□ Don Metz	11	18
□ Nick Metz	10	15
□ George Parsons	13	22
□ Norman "Bud" Poile	125	200
□ Walter "Babe" Pratt	225	325
□ Joe Primeau	18	30
□ Doc Romnes	35	60
□ Dave Schriner	22	35
□ Jack Shill	15	25
□ Walter Stanowsky	11	18
□ Phil Stein (G)	25	40
□ Gaye Stewart (Home)	300	400
□ Gaye Stewart (Away)	155	250
□ Billy Taylor	10	15
□ Rhys Thompson	450	750
□ Bill Thoms	10	15
□ 1944-45 Team Picture	250	350

Group One • Miscellaneous	EX	EX-MT
□ 1937 Winnipeg Monarchs	120	200
□ Foster Hewitt	55	90
□ Wes McKnight	65	110

Group One • Trophies / Dated on back	EX	EX-MT
□ Allan Cup	55	85
□ Byng Trophy	55	85
□ Calder Trophy	55	85
□ Hart Trophy	55	85
□ Memorial Cup	55	85
□ Prince of Wales Trophy (Unverifiable)		
□ Stanley Cup	60	100
□ Georges Vezina Trophy	55	85

Group One • Trophies / Blank backs	EX	EX-MT
□ Allan Cup	90	150
□ Byng Trophy	90	150
□ Calder Trophy	90	150
□ Hart Trophy	90	150
□ Memorial Cup	110	175
□ Prince of Wales Trophy Stanley Cup	250	325
□ (Horizontal Script) Stanley Cup	115	185
□ (Diagonal Script) Stanley Cup	210	275
□ Vezina Trophy	90	150

DAMON ALLEN

GRETZKY
99

1975 TOPPS
#620 GARY CARTER
7.5
NM+
1975 Rookie Catchers-Outfielders

Looking for something?

ST. LAWRENCE STARCH COMPANY BEEHIVE PHOTOS

BY THE CHARLTON PRESS

PLANT OF

ST. LAWRENCE STARCH COMPANY LIMITED

PORT CREDIT, ONT.

The photos were produced by the St. Lawrence Starch Company of Port Credit, Ontario. They were obtained by sending complete labels from St. Lawrence Starch products to the company. The name BeeHive became associated with the photos because the majority of labels submitted were from BeeHive Corn Syrup. Collectors were allowed to select the photo of their choice from player lists published each year. Because of this, photos of the favourite players are easier to find. Photos of the less popular players are the hardest to find and are valued higher due to their scarcity. The issuing of these player lists, however, still did not guarantee photo distribution. Some player's names appeared on the lists, but their actual photos remain unconfirmed.

The mat colours the photos were mounted on vary and may be beige, red, or blue. All photographs are unnumbered and are listed alphabetically by team and then by player name. In some cases a number of photographic variations of the same player exist. These variations are included in the listings with brief descriptions indicating the major identifying feature.

The photos are divided into three groups according to their autographs. The information below will help the collector identify the different groups and assign photos to the right era. Over the years, the method used to print the player's name on the photo varied. The groupings below are not 100% fool proof but will prove extremely helpful to collectors.

BEEHIVE VARIATIONS

One of the interesting aspects of the BeeHive series is the many variations that exist and it seems that more are found each year. We have divided the variations into four major categories. Many of the players have more than one photo issued. Variations of the BeeHive photos were also offered in the form of dress pins and tie clips. The photo was reduced in size and usually cropped around the player's head or upper body. The portrait was then enclosed under a clear plastic shield and included as part of the pin or clip. These are considerably more scarce than the photos and may have only been available to the public for a short period of time. A complete checklist for these does not exist though several dozen different examples have surfaced. We are looking for further information.

UNIFORM VARIATIONS
- "A" on sweater
- Away, light uniform
- Home, dark uniform
- "C" on sweater
- Helmet
- No helmet
- Number on sleeve
- No number on sleeve
- Plain sleeve

PHOTOGRAPH VARIATIONS
- White background
- Light background
- Dark background
- White border around photo
- Action shot
- Posed on ice
- Posed in dressing room
- Portrait pose
- Full length pose
- Horizontal photo
- Vertical photo
- Negative reversed
- BeeHive promotion

NAME VARIATIONS
- White script
- Black script
- Name away from skate
- Name near skate
- Name overlaps stick
- Name overlaps skate
- Name printed diagonally
- Name parallel to bottom

STICK VARIATIONS
- Blade of stick visible
- Blade of stick not visible

1934 TO 1943 GROUP I

Facsimile Autograph

Block Letter Autograph

Script Letter Autograph
White Type (upper)
Black Type (lower)

1944 TO 1963 GROUP II

1944 - 1945
Facsimile Autograph

Script Letter Autograph
Thin Type — Thick Type

UNIFORM VARIATIONS

HELMET

NUMBER ON SLEEVE

AWAY, LIGHT UNIFORM

NO HELMET

NO NUMBER ON SLEEVE

HOME, DARK UNIFORM

PHOTOGRAPH VARIATIONS

Action shot

Posed on ice

Posed in dressing room

NAME VARIATIONS AND STICK VARIATIONS

Name overlaps stick

Blade of stick visible

Blade of stick not visible

Taking care of your cards and determining a grade

BY THE CHARLTON PRESS

CARD CARE

In order to ensure the continued appreciation in value of your cards, you must keep card handling to a minimum. It is highly recommended that you obtain suitable storage containers to preserve the condition of your cards. Items such as sleeves, boxes, and binder sheets are commercially available in specific sizes in which to safely store your prized collectibles.

Card sleeves are handy for displaying single cards. Sleeves are made of various materials, ranging from pliable polypropylene and polyethylene, to a stiffer mylar, to hard acrylic and Plexiglass.

Specially designed cardboard boxes enable you to store hundreds of cards and also facilitate transportation or storage. Try to use boxes with flat bottoms since boxes with interior bottom flaps can damage your cards. Since some cardboard boxes may contain an element of acid, you may wish to insert your cards into individual sleeves before placing them in boxes. As an added precaution, take care not to place your valuable cards at either end of the box.

Plastic three-ring binder sheets with pockets are a popular means of holding and displaying cards. Make certain that the pockets will hold your cards snugly but not tightly, as some sheets are designed to hold a specific size of card. Sheets made of polyvinyl chloride (PVC) are less flexible and more transparent, but contain certain oils which may, after long periods of time, damage your cards. PVC may be detected by its customary vinyl odour, whereas polypropylene and polyethylene are odourless.

Needless to say, mint condition cards do not have foreign substances applied to them. Adding glue, tape, protective coating, or writing, removing tabs, applying elastic bands to stacks of cards or using photograph corners to store cards in a scrap album are all taboo.

Extreme environmental conditions will, in time, adversely affect the condition of your cards. Prolonged direct sunlight will remove the gloss from cards and fade their colours. High humidity or extreme changes in humidity will result in gradual deterioration and warping, while excessive heat will increase the rate of decomposition.

It's not necessary to handle cards with gloves or tongs, just be aware of the adverse affects of mishandling and take a realistic approach to preserving the condition of your cards.

CARD GRADING

Grading any collectible item is always a subjective decision, but grading is the most important characteristic the collector must understand, for condition determines the price category.

THE CONDITION OF THE CARD MUST BE DETERMINED BEFORE A CARD CAN BE PRICED

The main criteria for judging the condition of a card are centering, corner wear, creases, alterations, and surface wear.

CENTERING

A card in Mint condition must have perfect centering from top to bottom and from left to right. A card's centering is refered to in percentages: perfectly centred is 50/50, slightly off-centred may be 45/55 and badly off-centred may be 30/70 or 20/80.

CORNER WEAR

A card in Mint condition must have four perfect and sharp corners. A card with corner wear may have slightly frayed, dented or rounded corners.

PRINTING DEFECTS

A card in Mint condition must have no printing defects. A card with printing defects may have poor photo quality, missing gloss or foil, a wrong back or an out of focus picture.

SURFACE WEAR

A card in Mint condition must have no surface wear. A card with surface wear may have been exposed to creasing, wax or gum stains, ink marks, water drops, discolouration or mishandling.

CONDITION GUIDE

MINT • A virtually perfect card, looks as if it just came out of the pack. A MT card may have one of the following very minor defects: a very slight knick on one corner, minor printing flaw, or slight discolouration. Centering must be 60/40 or better. **MT** cards from 1990-91 to present are valued at 100% of the listed price (unless otherwise noted); cards from 1970-71 to 1989-90 are valued at 110-125%; cards from 1969-70 and older are valued at 150-250%.

NEAR-MINT MINT • A card that looks Mint at first glance, but upon closer inspection, may have up to two of the following minor defects: very slight knick on one or two corners, minor printing flaws, or slight discolouration. Centering must be 70/30 or better. **NM-MT** cards from 1990-91 to present are valued at 80-90% of the listed price (unless otherwise noted); cards from 1970-71 to 1989-90 at 100-110%; cards from 1969-70 and older at 110-150%.

NEAR-MINT • A card with a few minor defects: very slight fraying at corners, minor printing flaws, or slight discolouration. Centering must be 75/25 or better. **NM** cards from 1990-91 to present are valued at 50-75% (unless otherwise noted); 1970-71 to 1989-90 at 75-90%; 1969-70 and older at 100-110%.

EXCELLENT-MINT • A card with a several minor defects (very slight fraying at corners, minor printing flaws, or slight discolouration) or a major defect (3-4 slightly-rounded corners, slight wax stain, or light scratches). Centering must be 80/20 or better. **EX-MT** cards from 1990-91 to present are valued at 50% of the listed price; 1970-71 to 1989-90 at 60-75%; 1969-70 and older at 70-90%.

VERY GOOD • A card with some noticeable wear or mishandling. This grade permits rounded corners, more obvious discolouration, and/or slight creasing. Centering must be 90/10 or better. **VG** cards are valued at 20-25% of the listed price.

GOOD-FAIR • An abused card. This grade permits heavier creasing, more serious printing imperfections, obvious wear on edges and/or corners, wax or gum stains, or scuffing on the reverse. **GD-FR** cards are valued at 5-10% of the listed price.

CHAPTER TWO

ORIGINAL SIX 1944 TO 1968

1945 - 64 BEEHIVE PHOTOS

The second group of BeeHive photos were issued between 1945 and 1964. Photos measure 4 1/4" x 6 3/4" (5 1/2" x 8" with the mat). Photographs were updated starting with the Toronto Maple Leafs team of 1944-45. These photos were issued with the player's facsimile autograph. A team photo of the 1944-45 Stanley Cup champions was also issued. After 1945 the Maple Leaf photos were issued with a new large-size script for the players' names which is now characteristic of Group Two. New photos with the new script were gradually added year by year until 1948, when the complete series was available. In some cases, although a player's name may appear on the company photo list, proof of actual photo distribution remains unconfirmed.

Group Two • Boston Bruins	EX	EX-MT
☐ Bob Armstrong	5	8
☐ Pete Babando	30	50
☐ Ray Barry	40	70
☐ Gus Bodnar	50	85
☐ Leo Boivin	7	12
☐ Frank Brimsek (White background)	18	30
☐ Johnny Bucyk	8	13
☐ Charlie Burns	5	8
☐ Jack Caffery	35	60
☐ Real Chevrefils	5	8
☐ Wayne Connelly	12	20
☐ Wayne Connelly (Script over skate)	40	70
☐ Murray Costello	18	28
☐ Johnny Crawford (#6)	12	20
☐ Dave Creighton (White background)	7	12
☐ Dave Creighton (Dark background)	40	70
☐ Norm DeFelice		
☐ Woody Dumart	10	16
☐ Pat Eagan	22	35
☐ Lorne Ferguson	7	12
☐ Fernie Flaman	9	15
☐ Fern Flaman	6	10
☐ Bruce Gamble (G)	9	15
☐ Cal Gardner	9	15
☐ Ray Gariepy	12	20
☐ Jack Gelineau (G)	11	18
☐ Jean-Guy Gendron	5	8
☐ Warren Godfrey (A on jersey)	9	15
☐ Warren Godfrey (#25, W under skate)	35	60
☐ Warren Godfrey (#25, W left of skate)	70	120
☐ Ed Harrison	5	8
☐ Don Head (G)	7	12
☐ Andy Hebenton	13	22
☐ Murray Henderson	9	15
☐ Jim Henry (G)	20	30
☐ Larry Hillman	25	40
☐ Pete Horeck	9	15
☐ Rudy Horvath	5	8
☐ Tom Johnson	7	12
☐ Ed Johnston (G)	9	15
☐ Joe Klukay	150	250
☐ Ed Kryznowski	9	15
☐ Orland Kurtenbach	25	40
☐ Léo Labine	5	8
☐ Hal Laycoe	5	8
☐ Harry Lumley (G)	11	18
☐ Pentti Lund		
☐ Fleming Mackell	5	8
☐ Phil Maloney	12	20
☐ Frank Martin	12	20
☐ Jack McIntyre	9	15
☐ Don McKenney	5	8
☐ Richard Meissner	5	8
☐ Doug Mohns	5	8
☐ Murray Oliver	5	8
☐ Willy O'Ree	11	18
☐ John Peirson	8	13
☐ Johnny Peirson	80	135
☐ C. Pennington (Script away from skate)	13	22
☐ C. Pennington (Script near skate)	60	95
☐ Bob Perreault (G)	18	28
☐ Bob Perreault (G) (Script overlaps skate)	60	100
☐ Jim Peters	11	18
☐ Dean Prentice	7	12
☐ Andre Pronovost	5	8
☐ Bill Quackenbush	8	13
☐ Larry Regan	28	45
☐ Earl Reibel	30	50
☐ Paul Ronty	7	12
☐ Ed Sandford	5	8
☐ Terry Sawchuk	100	175
☐ Don Simmons (G)	6	10
☐ Don Simmons (G), Err. (Norm Defelice)	150	250
☐ Ken Smith	8	13
☐ P. Stapleton (Script away from skate)	13	22
☐ P. Stapleton (Script near skate)	55	85
☐ Vic Stasiuk	5	8
☐ George Sullivan	13	22
☐ Jerry Toppazzini	5	8
☐ Zellio Toppazzini	11	18
☐ Grant Warwick	20	30
☐ Tom Williams	5	8

Group Two • Chicago Blackhawks	EX	EX-MT
☐ Al Arbour	8	13
☐ Pete Babando	11	18
☐ Earl Balfour	5	8
☐ Murray Balfour	5	8
☐ Jim Bedard	12	20
☐ Doug Bentley	12	20
☐ Gus Bodnar	7	12
☐ Frank Brimsek (G)	30	50
☐ Adam Brown	15	25
☐ Hank Ciesla	22	35
☐ Jim Conacher	7	12
☐ Pete Conacher	6	10
☐ Roy Conacher	5	8
☐ Joe Conn	40	70
☐ Murray Costello	90	150
☐ Gerry Couture	11	18
☐ Al Dewsbury	7	12
☐ Ernie Dickens	7	12
☐ Jack Evans	5	8
☐ Reg Fleming	5	8
☐ Lee Fogolin	7	12
☐ Bill Gadsby	7	12
☐ George Gee	15	25
☐ Bob Goldham	12	20
☐ Bep Guidolin	7	12
☐ Glenn Hall (G)	9	15
☐ Murray Hall	20	30
☐ Red Hamill	18	28
☐ Bill Hay	5	8
☐ Jim Henry (G)	28	45
☐ Wayne Hillman	15	25
☐ Bronco Horvath	9	15
☐ Fred Hucul	12	20
☐ Bobby Hull (#16)	20	30
☐ Bobby Hull (#9)	175	250
☐ Lou Jankowski	20	30
☐ Forbes Kennedy	45	70
☐ Ted Lindsay	11	18
☐ Eddie Litzenberger	6	10
☐ Harry Lumley (G)	30	50
☐ Len Lunde	45	75
☐ Len Lunde (Script over stick)	12	20
☐ Pat Lundy	11	18
☐ Al MacNeil (Script over stick and skate)	30	50
☐ Al MacNeil (Script over stick)	13	22
☐ Chico Maki	9	15
☐ Chico Maki (Script over stick)	80	125
☐ Doug McCaig	15	25
☐ Ab McDonald	5	8
☐ Jim McFadden	25	40
☐ Jerry Melnyk	6	10
☐ Stan Mikita	9	15
☐ Gus Mortson	5	8
☐ Bill Mosienko	9	15
☐ Ron Murphy	5	8
☐ Ralph Nattrass	13	22
☐ Eric Nesterenko	5	8
☐ Bert Olmstead	13	22
☐ Jim Peters	28	45
☐ Pierre Pilote	7	12
☐ Metro Prystai	7	12
☐ Clare Raglan	20	30
☐ Al Rollins (G) (Vertical)	110	175
☐ Al Rollins (G) (Horizontal)	25	40
☐ Tod Sloan	5	8
☐ Dollard St. Laurent	5	8
☐ Gaye Stewart	12	20
☐ Jack Stewart	22	35
☐ Bob Turner	35	55
☐ Bob Turner (Script over stick)	15	25
☐ Elmer Vasko	5	8
☐ Ken Wharram	5	8
☐ Larry Wilson	11	18
☐ Howie Young	12	20

Group Two • Detroit Red Wings	EX	EX-MT
☐ Syd Abel (C on jersey)	11	18
☐ Al Arbour	25	40
☐ Pete Babando	13	22
☐ Doug Barkley (Partial blade)	35	55
☐ Doug Barkley (No blade)	9	15
☐ Hank Bassen (G)	7	12
☐ Steve Black	20	30
☐ Marcel Bonin	9	15
☐ John Bucyk	40	70
☐ Jim Conacher	110	175
☐ Jerry Couture	7	12
☐ Billy Dea	15	25
☐ Alex Delvecchio	7	12
☐ Bill Delvecchio	9	15
☐ Bill Dineen	5	8
☐ Jim Enio	35	60
☐ Alex Faulkner	12	20
☐ Lee Fogolin	9	15
☐ Val Fonteyne	5	8
☐ Bill Gadsby (Name low)	7	12
☐ Bill Gadsby (Name high)	13	22
☐ Fern Gauthier (As Jerry Couture)	300	450
☐ Fern Gauthier	22	35
☐ George Gee	9	15
☐ Fred Glover	6	10
☐ Howie Glover	6	10
☐ Warren Godfrey	5	8
☐ Peter Goegan	5	8
☐ Bob Goldham	8	13
☐ Glenn Hall (G)	50	85
☐ Larry Hillman	35	60
☐ Pete Horeck	28	40
☐ Gordie Howe (Home jersey)	22	35
☐ Gordie Howe (Away jersey)	30	50
☐ Ron Ingram	18	28
☐ Larry Jeffrey	20	30
☐ Allan Johnson	5	8
☐ Red Kelly	7	12
☐ Forbes Kennedy	6	10
☐ Léo Labine	6	10
☐ Tony Leswick	6	10
☐ Ted Lindsay	8	13
☐ Ed Litzenberger	30	40
☐ Harry Lumley (G)	12	20
☐ Len Lunde	5	8
☐ Parker MacDonald	5	8
☐ Bruce MacGregor	5	8
☐ Clare Martin	12	20
☐ Jimmy McFadden	11	18
☐ Max McNab	12	20
☐ Gerry Melnyk	6	10
☐ Don Morrison	15	25
☐ Rod Morrison	30	50
☐ Gerry Odrowski	6	10
☐ Murray Oliver	7	12
☐ Martin Pavelich	5	8
☐ Jimmy Peters	30	50
☐ Bud Poile	75	125
☐ Andre Pronovost	7	12
☐ Marcel Pronovost	6	10
☐ Metro Prystai	5	8
☐ Bill Quackenbush (A)	35	60
☐ Earl Reibel	5	8
☐ Leo Reise	5	8
☐ Terry Sawchuk (G) (Blade)	12	20
☐ Terry Sawchuk (G) (No blade)	28	45
☐ Glen Skov	5	8
☐ Floyd Smith	7	12
☐ Vic Stasiuk (Home jersey with blade)	15	25
☐ Vic Stasiuk (Home jersey/ no blade)	30	50
☐ Vic Stasiuk (Away jersey)	5	8
☐ Gaye Stewart	20	30
☐ Jack Stewart	25	40
☐ Norm Ullman	7	12
☐ Johnny Wilson	5	8
☐ Ben Woit	5	8
☐ Howie Young	9	15
☐ Larry Zeidel	20	30

Group Two • Montréal Canadiens	EX	EX-MT
☐ Ralph Backstrom	5	8
☐ Dave Balon	7	12
☐ Jean Béliveau	12	20
☐ Red Berenson (White script)	20	30
☐ Red Berenson (Black script)	225	300
☐ Marcel Bonin	5	8
☐ Emile (Butch) Bouchard	7	12
☐ Tod Campeau	75	125
☐ Joe Carveth	11	18
☐ Murph Chamberlain	30	50
☐ Doc Couture	40	70
☐ Floyd Curry	5	8
☐ Ian Cushenan	9	15
☐ Lorne Davis	9	15
☐ Eddie Dorohoy	15	25
☐ Gilles Dubé	40	60
☐ Bill Durnan (G)	25	40
☐ Norman Dussault	13	22
☐ John Ferguson	8	13
☐ Bobby Fillion	9	15
☐ Lou Fontinato	6	10
☐ Dick Gamble	9	15
☐ Bernard Geoffrion	8	13
☐ Phil Goyette	5	8
☐ Léo Gravelle	13	22
☐ John Hanna	50	85
☐ Glen Harmon	8	13
☐ Terry Harper	6	10
☐ Doug Harvey	8	13
☐ Bill Hicke	5	8
☐ Charlie Hodge (G) (Black script)	9	15
☐ Charlie Hodge (G) (White script)	50	80
☐ Tom Johnson	7	12
☐ Vern Kaiser	28	45
☐ Frank King	40	65
☐ Elmer Lach (White background)	7	12
☐ Albert Langlois	5	8
☐ Jacques Laperriere	8	13
☐ Hal Laycoe	7	12
☐ Jack Leclair	5	8
☐ Roger Leger	9	15
☐ Eddie Litzenberger	40	60
☐ Ross Lowe	35	60
☐ Al MacNeil	7	12
☐ Bud MacPherson	5	8
☐ Cesare Maniago (G)	12	20
☐ Don Marshall	5	8
☐ Paul Masnick	5	8
☐ Eddie Mazur	11	18
☐ John McCormack	7	12
☐ Alvin McDonald	6	10
☐ Callum MacKay	7	12
☐ Gerry McNeil (G)	9	15
☐ Paul Meger	9	15
☐ Dick Moore	7	12
☐ Ken Mosdell	8	13
☐ Bert Olmstead	7	12
☐ Gerry Plamondon	12	20
☐ Jacques Plante (G)	18	28
☐ André Pronovost	5	8
☐ Claude Provost	5	8
☐ Kenny Reardon	18	28
☐ Billy Reay	5	8
☐ Henri Richard	11	18
☐ Maurice Richard (White background)	22	35
☐ Rip Riopelle	22	35
☐ George Robertson	70	110
☐ Bob Rousseau	5	8
☐ Dollard St. Laurent	5	8
☐ Jean Guy Talbot	5	8
☐ Gilles Tremblay (Dark background)	5	8
☐ Gilles Tremblay (Light background)	275	375
☐ J.C. Tremblay (Dark background)	5	8
☐ J.C. Tremblay (Light background)	325	450
☐ Bob Turner	5	8
☐ Grant Warwick	25	40
☐ Gump Worsley (G)	12	20

Group Two • Ne wYork Rangers	EX	EX-MT
☐ Clint Albright	9	15
☐ Dave Balon (Name high)	12	20
☐ Dave Balon (Name low)	7	12
☐ Andy Bathgate (Home jersey)	7	12
☐ Andy Bathgate (Away jersey)	11	18
☐ Max Bentley	35	55
☐ Johnny Bower (G)	40	70
☐ Hy Buller	9	15
☐ Larry Cahan (Home jersey)	7	12
☐ Larry Cahan (Away, script over both skates)	12	20
☐ Larry Cahan (Away, script over right skate)	130	200
☐ Bob Chrystal	18	28
☐ Brian Cullen	6	10
☐ Ian Cushenan	7	12
☐ Billy Dea	22	35
☐ Frank Eddolls	5	8
☐ Pat Egan	22	35
☐ Jack Evans (Name parallel)	5	8
☐ Jack Evans (Name diagonal)	28	45
☐ Duncan Fisher	9	15
☐ Lou Fontinato	5	8
☐ Bill Gadsby	6	10
☐ Guy Gendron	5	8
☐ Rod Gilbert	9	15

☐ Howie Glover	50	75
☐ Jack Gordon (Unverifiable)		
☐ Phil Goyette	6	10
☐ Aldo Guidolin	22	35
☐ Vic Hadfield	6	10
☐ Ted Hampson	5	8
☐ Doug Harvey	9	15
☐ Andy Hebenton	6	10
☐ Camille Henry	5	8
☐ Wally Hergesheimer	5	8
☐ Ike Hildebrand	20	30
☐ Bronco Horvath	9	15
☐ Harry Howell	6	10
☐ Earl Ingarfield (Name near stick)	11	18
☐ Earl Ingarfield (Name away from stick)	5	8
☐ Bing Juckes	20	30
☐ Alex Kaleta	7	12
☐ Steve Kraftcheck	20	30
☐ Ed Kullman	7	12
☐ Gus Kyle	7	12
☐ Gordon Labossière	40	60
☐ Albert Langlois	5	8
☐ Edgar Laprade	7	12
☐ Tony Leswick	5	8
☐ Danny Lewicki	5	8
☐ Pentti Lund	8	13
☐ Don Marshall	12	20
☐ Jack McCartan (G)	9	15
☐ Bill McDonagh	12	20
☐ Don McKenney	11	18
☐ Jack McLeod	9	15
☐ Nick Mickoski	5	8
☐ Bill Moe	8	13
☐ Ron Murphy	5	8
☐ Buddy O'Connor	8	13
☐ Marcel Paille (G)	80	125
☐ Jacques Plante (G)	70	110
☐ Bud Poile	20	30
☐ Larry Popein	5	8
☐ Dean Prentice (Home)	5	8
☐ Dean Prentice (Away, name high)	8	13
☐ Dean Prentice (Away, name low)	13	22
☐ Don Raleigh	7	12
☐ Jean Ratelle	25	40
☐ Jean Ratelle, Err. (John)	55	85
☐ Chuck Rayner (G)	18	28
☐ Leo Reise	8	13
☐ Paul Ronty	7	12
☐ Ken Schinkel	5	8
☐ Eddie Shack	12	20
☐ Fred Shero	15	25
☐ Reggie Sinclair	18	28
☐ Ed Slowinski	7	12
☐ Allan Stanley	7	12
☐ Wally Stanowski	8	13
☐ Red Sullivan	5	8
☐ Gump Worsley (G)	9	15

Group Two • Toronto Maple Leafs	EX	EX-MT
☐ Gary Aldcorn	9	15
☐ Syl Apps (Posed near boards)	95	150
☐ Al Arbour	6	10
☐ George Armstrong	6	10
☐ George Armstrong (Cap., dark background)	12	20
☐ George Armstrong (Cap., light background)	200	300
☐ Bob Bailey	22	35
☐ Earl Balfour	11	18
☐ Bill Barilko	15	25
☐ Andy Bathgate	40	65
☐ Bob Baun	5	8
☐ Max Bentley	18	28
☐ Jack Bionda	100	175
☐ Garth Boesch	7	12
☐ Leo Boivin	8	13
☐ Hugh Bolton	5	8
☐ Johnny Bower (G)	11	18
☐ Carl Brewer	5	8
☐ Turk Broda (G)	11	18
☐ Larry Cahan	9	15
☐ Ray Ceresino	40	65
☐ Ed Chadwick (G)	6	10
☐ Pete Conacher	55	90
☐ Les Costello	30	50
☐ Dave Creighton	12	20
☐ Barry Cullen	11	18
☐ Barry Cullen, Err. (Brian Cullen)	35	60
☐ Brian Cullen	5	8
☐ Bob Dawes	20	30
☐ Kent Douglas	6	10
☐ Dick Duff	5	8
☐ Garry Edmundson	6	10
☐ Gerry Ehman	5	8
☐ Bill Ezinicki	8	13
☐ Fern Flaman	35	55
☐ Cal Gardner	9	15
☐ Ted Hampson	7	12
☐ Gord Hannigan	9	15
☐ Billy Harris	5	8
☐ Bob Hassard	35	60
☐ Larry Hillman	5	8
☐ Tim Horton	11	18
☐ Bronco Horvath	11	18
☐ Ron Hurst	90	150
☐ Gerry James	22	35
☐ Bill Juzda	9	15
☐ Red Kelly	7	12
☐ Red Kelly (Wearing helmet)	22	35
☐ Ted Kennedy	8	13
☐ Dave Keon	9	15
☐ Joe Klukay	5	8
☐ Steve Kraftcheck	20	30
☐ Danny Lewicki	11	18
☐ Ed Litzenberger	6	10
☐ Harry Lumley (G)	12	20
☐ Vic Lynn	7	12
☐ Fleming McKell	7	12
☐ John MacMillan	6	10
☐ Al MacNeil	9	15
☐ Frank Mahovlich	11	18
☐ Phil Maloney	140	225
☐ Cesare Maniago (G)	9	15
☐ Frank Mathers	22	35
☐ Johnny McCormack	40	65
☐ Parker McDonald	15	25
☐ Don McKenney	22	35
☐ Howie Meeker	7	12
☐ Don Metz - Older photo	225	300
☐ Nick Metz - Older photo	175	250
☐ Rudy Migay	5	8
☐ Jim Mikol	7	12
☐ Jim Morrison	5	8
☐ Gus Mortson	5	8
☐ Eric Nesterenko	7	13
☐ Bob Nevin	5	8
☐ Mike Nykoluk	30	50
☐ Bert Olmstead	7	12
☐ Bob Pulford	7	12
☐ Marc Reaume	9	15
☐ Larry Regan	6	10
☐ Dave Reid	130	200
☐ Al Rollins (G)	20	30
☐ Eddie Shack (Dark background)	9	15
☐ Eddie Shack (Light background)	275	350
☐ Don Simmons (G)	8	13
☐ Tod Sloan	5	8
☐ Sid Smith	5	8
☐ Bob Solinger	35	60
☐ Allan Stanley, Error (Alan)	8	13
☐ Allan Stanley	12	20
☐ Wally Stanowski	280	400
☐ Ron Stewart	5	8
☐ Harry Taylor	25	40
☐ Jim Thomson	5	8
☐ Ray Timgren	6	10
☐ Harry Watson	6	10
☐ John Wilson	6	10
☐ 1962-63 Team Picture	450	600

Group Two • Trophies / four white borders	EX	EX-MT
☐ Byng Trophy	300	425
☐ Calder Memorial Trophy	300	425
☐ Hart Trophy	300	425
☐ James Norris Trophy	300	425
☐ Prince of Wales Trophy	300	425
☐ Art Ross Trophy	300	425
☐ Stanley Cup	300	425
☐ Georges Vezina Trophy	300	425

Group Two • Trophies / bottom white borders	EX	EX-MT
☐ Byng Trophy	80	140
☐ Calder Memorial Trophy	80	140
☐ Hart Trophy	80	140
☐ James Norris Trophy	80	140
☐ Prince of Wales Trophy	80	140
☐ Art Ross Trophy	80	140
☐ Stanley Cup	80	140
☐ Georges Vezina Trophy	80	140

1940s HOCKEY

It is uncertain which year these cards were issued, as players from both the 1930s and 1940s are represented. Goalie Gordie Bell, for instance, played his lone season with the Maple Leafs in 1945-46. Cards measure 5/8" x 7/8". They are similar in design to the R423 baseball series.

Hockey	VG	EX	EX-MT
☐ Gordie Bell (G), Toro.			
☐ Jerry Couture, Detr.			
☐ Cecil Dillon, NYRa.			
☐ Happy Emms, Bost.			
☐ Bill Ezinicki, Toro.			
☐ Chuck Gardiner (G), Chic.			
☐ Mike Karakas (G), Chic.			
☐ Ted Kennedy, Toro.			
☐ Sam LoPresti (G), Chic.			
☐ Nick Metz, Toro.			
☐ Johnny Mowers (G), Detr.			
☐ Doug Stevenson (G), Chic.			
☐ Nels Stewart			

1943 - 47 PARADE SPORTIVE

Issued on semi-glossy paper stock, these items were available at a nominal cost from three radio stations that aired the Parade Sportive show during the 1943 to 1947 era. Most photos are black and white but blue, brown, green and red tints have been seen. Sizes vary from 4 3/4" x 8 3/8" to 6 3/4" x 10". Variations of the same poses are plentiful. Different sizes, tints, script, etc., exist. No variation of a specific pose is scarce or valuable. Other athletes and sports were included but this listing is limited to hockey. It is possible that three different sets, one for each of the three radio stations, exist.

Parade Sportive • Boston Bruins	EX	EX-MT
☐ Bauer/Schmidt/Dumart	9	18
☐ Frank Brimsek (G)	8	15
☐ Bill Cowley	7	13
☐ Armand Gaudreault	4	7
☐ Jean Gladu	4	7
☐ Jean Gladu	4	7

Parade Sportive • Chicago Blackhawks	EX	EX-MT
☐ Mike Karakas (G)	5	9
☐ B. Mosienko/ M. Bentley/ D. Bentley	9	18

Parade Sportive • Detroit Red Wings	EX	EX-MT
☐ Eddie Bruneteau	4	7
☐ Modere Bruneteau	4	7
☐ Harry Lumley	9	18

Parade Sportive • New York Rangers	EX	EX-MT
☐ Edgar Laprade	5	10
☐ Phil Watson	5	9

Parade Sportive • Toronto Maple Leafs	EX	EX-MT
☐ Baz Bastien (G)	5	9
☐ Turk Broda (G)	9	18
☐ Gaye Stewart	4	7

Parade Sportive • Minor Leagues	EX	EX-MT
☐ Lionel Bouvrette (G)	5	9
☐ Denys Casavant	4	7
☐ Connie Dion (G)	5	9
☐ Jim Henry	6	12
☐ Ernie Laforce	4	7
☐ Jean Marois (G)	5	9
☐ Gerry McNeil (G)	6	12
☐ Robert Pepin	4	7
☐ Gerry Plamondon	4	7

Parade Sportive • Montréal Canadiens	EX	EX-MT
☐ 1943 - 44 Team Photo	9	18
☐ 1944 - 45 Team Photo	9	18
☐ 1945 - 46 Team Photo	9	18
☐ 1946 - 47 Team Photo	9	18
☐ George Allen	4	7
☐ Joe Benoît	4	7
☐ Paul Bibeault (G)	5	9
☐ Toe Blake	7	13
☐ Emile (Butch) Bouchard	5	10
☐ Jean-Claude Campeau	4	7
☐ Bob Carse	4	7
☐ Joe Carveth	4	7
☐ Murph Chamberlain	4	7
☐ Floyd Curry	4	7
☐ Tony Demers	4	7
☐ Bill Durnan (G)	8	15
☐ Norm Dussault	4	7
☐ Frank Eddolls	4	7
☐ Bob Fillion	4	7
☐ Johnny Gagnon	4	7
☐ Gagnon/ Joliat/ Howie Morenz	18	35
☐ Fern Gauthier	4	7
☐ Gauthier/ O'Connor/ Hiller	8	15
☐ Léo Gravelle	4	7
☐ Glen Harmon	4	7
☐ Doug Harvey	9	18
☐ Heffernan/ O'Connor/ Morin	8	15
☐ Dutch Hiller	4	7
☐ Rosario Joanette	4	7
☐ Elmer Lach	8	15
☐ Léo Lamoreaux	4	7
☐ Bouchard/ Lamoureux/ Durnan	8	15
☐ Hal Laycoe	4	7
☐ Roger Legér	4	7
☐ Jacques Locas	4	7
☐ Fern Majeau	4	7
☐ Georges Mantha	4	7
☐ Mike McMahon	4	7
☐ Kenny Mosdell	4	7
☐ Buddy O'Connor	7	13
☐ Jim Peters	4	7
☐ John Quilty	4	7
☐ Paul Raymond	4	7
☐ Ken Reardon	5	10
☐ Billy Reay	5	9
☐ Maurice Richard	35	65
☐ Howard Riopellie	4	7

1945 - 46 KELLOGG'S ALL-WHEAT

Other hockey singles do exist in this multi-sport set. Cards measure 2 1/2" x 1 3/4".

All-Wheat	VG	EX	EX-MT
☐ 1 Body Shift	5	10	15

1945 - 46 LA PRESSE PHOTOS

This colour newspaper photo measures 10" x 16 1/2".

La Presse	VG	EX	EX-MT
☐ Feb. 16 Maurice Richard, Mont.	150	225	300

1945 - 54 QUAKER OATS PHOTOS

These black & white photos measure 8" x 10".

Complete Set: (202 photos):	**3,000**	**5,000**
Common Player:	**7**	**12**

Quaker Oats • Montréal Canadiens	EX	EX-MT
☐ George Allen	7	12
☐ Jean Béliveau	90	150
☐ Joe Benoît (Black & white)	7	12
☐ Joe Benoît (Blue tint)	20	35
☐ Toe Blake (Autograph above skates)	75	125
☐ Toe Blake (Autograph below skates)	12	20
☐ Toe Blake (Retouched photo)	18	30
☐ E. Bouchard (Still, skates visible)	9	15
☐ E. Bouchard (Still, skates cropped)	9	15
☐ E. Bouchard (Action)	9	15
☐ Tod Campeau	20	35
☐ Bob Carse	12	20
☐ Joe Carveth	12	20
☐ Murph Chamberlain (Still, blue tint)	28	45
☐ Murph Chamberlain (Still, side view)	12	20
☐ Murph Chamberlain		

	(Still, side view, skates cropped)	12	20
□	Gerry Couture	18	30
□	Floyd Curry (Still)	55	90
□	Floyd Curry (Action)	7	12
□	Eddie Dorohoy	12	20
□	Bill Durnan (G) (Still, stick cropped)	15	25
□	Bill Durnan (G) (Action)	20	35
□	Bill Durnan (G) (Still, blue tint)	65	115
□	B. Durnan (G) (Still, handle touches border)	20	35
□	Norm Dussault (Portrait)	7	12
□	Norm Dussault (Action)	12	20
□	Frank Eddolls	7	12
□	Bob Fillion (Still on ice)	18	30
□	Bob Fillion (Still on ice, larger image)	12	20
□	Bob Fillion (Still on ice, background airbrushed)	12	20
□	Bob Fillion (Action)	7	12
□	Dick Gamble	12	20
□	Bernie Geoffrion	15	25
□	Léo Gravelle (Still, home uniform)	7	12
□	Léo Gravelle (Still, away uniform)	20	35
□	Léo Gravelle (Action)	7	12
□	Glen Harmon (Still, with puck)	12	20
□	Glen Harmon (Still, no puck)	7	12
□	Glen Harmon (Action)	10	18
□	Doug Harvey (Still)	13	22
□	Doug Harvey (Action)	18	30
□	Dutch Hiller	12	20
□	Bert Hirschfeld	12	20
□	Tom Johnson	12	20
□	Vern Kaiser	12	20
□	Elmer Lach (Still, stick cropped)	10	18
□	Elmer Lach (Still, stick in corner)	10	18
□	Elmer Lach (Still, stick near corner)	40	65
□	Elmer Lach (Action)	15	25
□	Leo Lamoureux (Still, entire blade)	10	18
□	Leo Lamoureux (Still, blade cropped)	7	12
□	Hal Laycoe (Action)	12	20
□	Hal Laycoe (Portrait)	80	135
□	Roger Léger (Still, light background)	7	12
□	Roger Léger (Still, dark background)	7	12
□	Roger Léger (Action)	20	35
□	Jacques Locas	7	12
□	Ross Lowe	10	18
□	Calum MacKay	7	12
□	Murdo MacKay	7	12
□	Paul Masnick	7	12
□	John McCormack (Horizontal)	28	45
□	John McCormack (Vertical)	35	60
□	Mike McMahon	40	65
□	Gerry McNeil (G)	18	30
□	Bud MacPherson	12	20
□	Paul Meger	12	20
□	Dickie Moore	18	28
□	Kenny Mosdell (Still, small image)	12	20
□	Kenny Mosdell (Still, large image)	15	25
□	K. Mosdell (Still, large image, auto cropped)	15	25
□	Kenny Mosdell (Action)	12	20
□	Buddy O'Connor (Still, with blade)	20	35
□	Buddy O'Connor (Still, blade cropped)	7	12
□	Bert Olmstead	12	20
□	Jim Peters (Still, stick touching border)	7	12
□	Jim Peters (Still, stick away from border)	7	12
□	Jim Peters (Still, small image)	7	12
□	Gerry Plamondon	7	12
□	John Quilty	15	25
□	Ken Reardon (Still, small image)	15	25
□	Ken Reardon (Stil, large image)	12	20
□	Ken Reardon (Still, large higher image)	15	25
□	Ken Reardon (Action)	12	20
□	Billy Reay (Still, blade on border)	7	12
□	Billy Reay (Stil, blade away from border)	7	12
□	Billy Reay (Action)	9	15
□	Billy Reay (Small image)	30	50
□	Maurice Richard (Still)	75	125
□	Maurice Richard (Full autograph)	28	45
n	Maurice Richard (Autograph cropped)	25	40
n	Maurice Richard (Action)	18	30
□	Howard Riopelle (Still)	7	12
□	Howard Riopelle (Action)	7	12
□	George Robertson	20	35
□	Dollard St. Laurent	35	60
□	Grant Warwick	60	100

	Quaker Oats • Toronto Maple Leafs	**EX**	**EX-MT**
□	1947-48-49 Team Picture	55	90
□	Syl Apps, Sr. (Still, auto. C.J.S. Apps)	18	30
□	Syl Apps, Sr. (Still, auto. Syl Apps)	12	20
□	Syl Apps, Sr. (With Stanley Cup)	65	110
□	George Armstrong	12	20
□	Doug Baldwin	50	80
□	Bill Barilko (Home uniform)	20	35
□	Bill Barilko (Home, higher image)	20	35
□	Bill Barilko (Away uniform)	20	35
□	Baz Bastien (G)	80	135
□	Gordie Bell (G)	80	135
□	Max Bentley (Home uniform)	12	20
□	Max Bentley (Away uniform)	12	20
□	Max Bentley (In front of locker)	200	325
□	Gus Bodnar	18	28
□	Garth Boesch (Home, closed "B" in auto.)	9	15
□	Garth Boesch (Home, open "B" in auto.)	9	15
□	Garth Boesch (Away)	28	45
□	Léo Boivin	18	30
□	Hugh Bolton	7	12
□	Turk Broda (G) (Splits, auto. W.E. Broda)	20	35
□	Turk Broda (G) (Splits, auto. Turk Broda)	20	35
□	Turk Broda (G) (Action)	20	35
□	Lorne Carr	15	25
□	Les Costello	15	25
□	Bob Davidson	15	25
□	Bill Ezinicki (Still, auto. William Ezinicki)	10	18
□	Bill Ezinicki (Still, auto., larger image)	7	12
□	Bill Ezinicki (Still, auto. Bill Ezinicki)	7	12
□	Bill Ezinicki (Action)	10	18
□	Fern Flaman	12	20
□	Cal Gardner (Home uniform)	7	12
□	Cal Gardner (Away uniform)	7	12
□	Bob Goldham (Sweeping "G" auto.)	7	12
□	Bob Goldham (Normal "G" auto.)	7	12
□	Bob Goldham (Blade cropped)	15	25
□	Gord Hannigan	15	25
□	Bob Hassard	25	40
□	Mel Hill	35	60
□	Tim Horton	40	70
□	Bill Juzda (Home uniform)	7	12
□	Bill Juzda (Away uniform)	7	12
□	Ted Kennedy (Home, blade cropped)	25	40
□	T. Kennedy (Home, blade touching border)	18	30
□	Ted Kennedy ("C" on uniform)	12	20
□	Ted Kennedy (With Stanley Cup)	75	125
□	Ted Kennedy (Away uniform)	12	20
□	Joe Klukay (Home uniform)	7	12
□	Joe Klukay (Away uniform)	7	12
□	Danny Lewicki	10	18
□	Harry Lumley (G)	30	50
□	Vic Lynn (Home small image)	9	15
□	Vic Lynn (Home large image)	15	25
□	Vic Lynn (Away uniform)	9	15
□	Fleming Mackell (Home uniform)	7	12
□	Fleming Mackell (Away uniform)	7	12
□	Phil Maloney	35	55
□	Frank Mathers	22	35
□	Frank McCool (G)	80	135
□	John McCormack	15	25
□	Howie Meeker (Home uniform)	9	15
□	Howie Meeker (Home uniform, larger image)	9	15
□	Howie Meeker (Away uniform)	12	20
□	Don Metz (Still, small image)	7	12
□	Don Metz (Still, large image)	10	18
□	Don Metz (Blue tint)	30	50
□	Nick Metz (Still, large image)	10	18
□	N. Metz (Still, large image, stick retouched)	10	18
□	Nick Metz (Blue tint)	15	25
□	Rudy Migay	25	40
□	Elwyn Morris	30	50
□	Jim Morrison	7	12
□	Gus Mortson (Home uniform)	7	12
□	Gus Mortson (Away uniform)	7	12
□	Eric Nesterenko	35	55
□	Bud Poile	15	25
□	Babe Pratt	50	85
□	Al Rollins (G)	15	25
□	Sweeny Schriner	28	45
□	Tod Sloan (Home uniform)	18	30
□	Tod Sloan (Away uniform)	7	12
□	Sid Smith (Home uniform)	10	18
□	Sid Smith (Away uniform)	7	12
□	Bob Solinger	18	30
□	Wally Stanowski (Full blade)	20	35
□	Wally Stanowski (Blade cropped)	13	22
□	Gaye Stewart (Black & white)	7	12
□	Gaye Stewart (Blue tint)	35	60
□	Ron Stewart	35	60
□	Harry Taylor	7	12
□	W.J. Taylor	25	40
□	Cy Thomas	18	30
□	Jim Thomson (Home blade cropped)	15	25
□	Jim Thomson (Home blade touching border)	7	12
□	Jim Thomson (Away uniform)	7	12
□	Jim Thomson (Blue tint)	25	40
□	Ray Timgren (Home uniform)	7	12
□	Ray Timgren (Away uniform)	7	12
□	Harry Watson (Home uniform)	12	20
□	Harry Watson (Higher image)	12	20
□	Harry Watson (Away uniform)	12	20
□	Gardner, Watson, Meeker Attack McNeil	140	235
□	Gardner Coming In On Harvey	140	235
□	Juzda And Rollins Stop Curry	140	235
□	McNeil Saves On Gardner	140	235

1948 - 52 EXHIBITS

These oversized black and white cards feature a full-bleed design on heavy cardboard stock. The player's name is imprinted near the bottom. These black & white cards measure 3 1/4" x 5 1/4".

	Exhibits	**EX**	**EX-MT**
□	Reggie Abbott, Mont.	5	10
□	Sid Abel, Detr.	12	25
□	Bill Barilko, Toro.	25	50
□	Jean Béliveau, Mont.	50	10
□	Jean Béliveau, Québec	70	140
□	Doug Bentley, Chi.	12	25
□	Max Bentley, Chi.	15	30
□	Toe Blake, Mont.	25	50
□	Butch Bouchard, Mont.	10	20
□	Turk Broda (G), Toro.	30	60
□	Roy Conacher, Chi.	10	20
□	Floyd Curry, Toro.	5	10
□	Bob Fillion, Mont.	5	10
□	Dick Gamble, Mont.	5	10
□	Cal Gardner, Toro.	8	15
□	Jack Gelineau, Bost.	5	10
□	Bernie Geoffrion, Mont.	25	50
□	Doug Harvey, Mont.	30	60
□	Gordie Howe, Detr.	75	150
□	Tom Johnson, Mont.	10	20
□	Bill Juzda, Toro.	5	10
□	Ted Kennedy, Toro.	18	35
□	Joe Klukay, Toro.	5	10
□	Elmer Lach, Mont.	20	40
□	Hal Laycoe, Mont.	5	10
□	Ted Lindsay, Detr.	25	45
□	Jacques Locas, Mont.	5	10
□	Harry Lumley (G), Detr.	20	40
□	Fleming Mackell, Toro.	5	10
□	Bud MacPherson, Mont.	5	10
□	Paul Maznick, Mont.	5	10
□	Gerry McNeil (G), Mont.	15	30
□	Howie Meeker, Toro.	20	40
□	Paul Meger, Mont.	5	10
□	Dickie Moore, Mont.	18	35
□	Gus Mortson, Toro.	5	10
□	Ken Mosdell, Mont.	5	10
□	Bert Olmstead, Mont.	10	20
□	Chuck Rayner, NYRa.	15	30
□	Ken Reardon, Mont.	10	20
□	Billy Reay, Mont.	8	15
□	Maurice Richard, Mont.	60	120
□	Maurice Richard, Mont. (Stairs in background)	60	120
□	Al Rollins (G), Toro.	10	20
□	Paul Ronty, Bost.	5	10
□	Sid Smith, Toro.	5	10
□	Tod Sloan, Toro.	5	10
□	Dollard St. Laurent, Mont.	5	10
□	Jim Thomson, Toro.	5	10
□	Ray Timgren, Toro.	5	10
□	Grant Warwick, Mont.	5	10
□	Bost. vs. Mont.	10	20
□	Chic. vs. Mont.	10	20
□	Chic. vs. Mont. (Bernie Geoffrion)	25	50
□	Chic. vs. Mont.: Montréal scores	10	20
□	Detr. vs. NYRa. (Gordie Howe)	50	100
□	Detr. vs. Mont.	10	20
□	Detr. vs. Mont. (Terry Sawchuk)	30	60
□	Detr. vs. Mont.	10	20
□	Mont. vs. Bost.	10	20
□	Mont. vs. Toro. (Maurice Richard)	30	60
□	NYRa. vs. Mont. (Maurice Richard)	30	60
□	NYRa. vs. Mont.	10	20
□	NYRa. vs. Mont. (M. Richard/ Lach/ Rayner)	50	100
□	Toro. vs. Mont.	10	20

1948 - 59 W. PATERSON LONG FELLOWS

A free box of chocolates was awarded to anyone who could spell the name of an NHL player using the letters on these cards. According to the card back, there is a card for each letter in the alphabet. These cards measure 1 3/4" x 3 9/16".

	ACC # V19	**EX**	**EX-MT**
□	C Flip shot	12	25
□	D Face-off	12	25
□	G Goal crease	12	25
□	H Back-checking	12	25
□	I Break away	12	25
□	K Blocking	12	25
□	L Cutting the angle	12	25
□	M Stadium in NHL	12	25
□	N Tip-in	12	25
□	P Slapshot	12	25
□	R NHL Uniforms, Chi.	20	50
□	T NHL Uniforms, NYRa.	20	50
□	W NHL Uniforms, Toro.	20	50
□	X NHL Uniforms, Mont.	20	50
□	Y Memorial Cup	20	40

c1948 RICHARD PLAYING CARDS

Maurice Richard appears on the back of each of these playing cards.

Complete Deck (54 cards):	**200**	**400**
Maurice Richard	**EX**	**EX-MT**
Common card	8	15

□ A of Clubs	□ 2 of Clubs	□ 3 of Clubs
□ 4 of Clubs	□ 5 of Clubs	□ 6 of Clubs
□ 7 of Clubs	□ 8 of Clubs	□ 9 of Clubs
□ 10 of Clubs	□ J of Clubs	□ Q of Clubs
□ K of Clubs	□ A of Diamonds	□ 2 of Diamonds
□ 3 of Diamonds	□ 4 of Diamonds	□ 5 of Diamonds
□ 6 of Diamonds	□ 7 of Diamonds	□ 8 of Diamonds
□ 9 of Diamonds	□ 10 of Diamonds	□ J of Diamonds
□ Q of Diamonds	□ K of Diamonds	□ A of Hearts
□ 2 of Hearts	□ 3 of Hearts	□ 4 of Hearts
□ 5 of Hearts	□ 6 of Hearts	□ 7 of Hearts
□ 8 of Hearts	□ 9 of Hearts	□ 10 of Hearts
□ J of Hearts	□ Q of Hearts	□ K of Hearts
□ A of Spades	□ 2 of Spades	□ 3 of Spades
□ 4 of Spades	□ 5 of Spades	□ 6 of Spades
□ 7 of Spades	□ 8 of Spades	□ 9 of Spades
□ 10 of Spades	□ J of Spades	□ Q of Spades
□ K of Spades	□ Joker	□ Joker

1949 CARRERAS LTD. CIGARETTES

There are 50 cards in this multi-sport set. Each card measures 1 1/2" x 2 11/16".

	Turf Cigarettes	**EX**	**EX-MT**
□	37 Duke Campbell	20	40
□	44 Les Anning, Wembley Lions	20	40

1951 BERK ROSS

This 72-card multi-sport set was issued in two-card panels. Each cut card measures 2 1/16" x 2 1/2".

Hit Parade of Champions	EX	EX-MT
Sid Abel, Detr.	60	115
Jack Stewart, Detr.	45	85
1-17 Bill Durnan (G), Mont.	65	125
1-18 Bill Quackenbush, Bost.	45	85

1951 - 52 BAS DU FLEUVE

Complete Set (58 cards):	350	750
Bas du Fleuve	**EX**	**EX-MT**
1 Gordon Poirier	9	25
2 Denis Brodeur	40	80
3 Conrad Poitras	7	16
4 Clement Tremblay	7	16
5 Raymond Leduc	7	16
6 Jacques Armstrong	7	16
7 Joe Schmidt	7	16
8 Gilles Laroche	7	16
9 Frank Pearce	7	16
10 Wayne Stephenson	7	16
11 Guy Lapointe	7	16
12 Guy Delisle	7	16
13 Ossie Carnegie	7	16
14 Gilbert Girouard	7	16
15 Jean-Paul Vandal	7	16
16 Guy Lalonde	7	16
17 Roland Bilodeau	7	16
18 Gaetan Laliberté	7	16
19 Maurice Benoît	7	16
20 Thomas McDougall	7	16
21 Roger Guay	7	16
22 Bob Brault	7	16
23 Edouard Theberge	7	16
24 Paul Lessard	7	16
25 Lucien Gilbert	7	16
26 Réal Lafrenière	7	16
27 Rénald Limoges	7	16
28 Roger Ste. Marie	7	16
29 Arthur Leyte	7	16
30 Magella Laforest	7	16
31 Bill Leblanc	7	16
32 Pius Gaudet	7	16
33 Jean-Roch Bellavance	7	16
34 Gérard Lachance	7	16
35 Marcel St. Pierre	7	16
36 Pierre Brillant	7	16
37 Paul Provost	7	16
38 Maurice Lamirande	7	16
39 Roger Hayfield	7	16
40 Normand Bellavance	7	16
41 Marcel Houde	7	16
42 Dan Janelle	7	16
43 Roland Rossignol	7	16
44 Roger Gagné	7	16
45 Jacques Monette	7	16
46 Bernie Bernaquez	7	16
47 Paul Gagnon	7	16
48 Jean-Marie Fillion	7	16
49 Bert Scullion	7	16
50 Don Bellringer	7	16
51 Frank Cote	7	16
52 Eddy Bolan	7	16
53 Maurice Parr	7	16
54 Many McIntyre	7	16
55 Roger Jodoin	7	16
56 Mario Senecal	7	16
57 Denis Fillion	7	16
58 Marcel Fillion	9	25

1951 - 52 CLEVELAND BARONS

Photo Size: 6" x 9"

Complete Set (20 photos):	90	200
Bob Bailey	4	8
Johnny Bower (G)	35	70
Joe Carveth	4	8
Ray Ceresino	4	8
Bob Chrystal	4	8
Bun Cook	8	15
Paul Gladu	4	8
Jack Gordon	4	8
Ike Hildebrand	4	8
Joe Lund	4	8
Eddie Olson	4	8
Fern Perreault	4	8
Jerry Reid	4	8
Ed Reigle	4	8
Phil Samis	4	8
Ken Schultz	4	8
Fred Shero	12	25
Fred Thurier	4	8
Tom Williams	6	12
Steve Wochy	4	8

1951 - 52 LAC ST-JEAN

These blank-back cards measure 1 3/4" x 2 1/2". Regional stars do sell at a premium.

Complete Set (59 cards):	300	650
Common Player	8	16

Lac St-Jean • Jonquière	
1 Eddy Daoust	2 Guy Gareau
3 Gilles Desrosiers	4 Robert Desbiens
5 James Hayes	6 Paul Gagnon
7 Gerry Perreault	8 Marcel Dufour
9 Armand Bourdon	10 Jean-Marc Pichette
11 Gerry Gagnon	12 Jules Racette
13 Real Marcotte	14 Gerry Theberge
15 Rene Harvey	
Lac St-Jean • Dolbeau	
16 Joseph Lacoursiere	17 Fernand Benaquez
18 Andre Boisvert	19 Claude Chretien
20 Nobert Clark	21 Sylvio Lambert
22 Lucien Roy	23 Gerard Audet
24 Jacques Lalancette	25 Maurice St. Jean
26 Camille Lupien	27 Rodrigue Pelchat
28 Conrad L'Heureux	29 Paul Tremblay
30 Robert Vincent	
Lac St-Jean • Alma	
31 Charles Lamirande	32 Léon Gaudreault
33 Maurice Thiffault	34 Marc-Aurele Tremblay
35 René Pronovost	36 Victor Corbin
37 Tiny Tamminen	38 Guildor Levesque
39 Gaston Lamirande	40 Guy Gervais
41 Rayner Makila	42 Jules Tremblay
43 Roland Girard	44 Germain Bergeron
Lac St-Jean • Pt. Alfred	
45 Paul Duchesne	46 Roger Beaudoin
47 Georges Archibal	48 Claude Basque
49 Roger Sarda	50 Edgar Gendron
51 Gaston Labossiere	52 Roland Clantara
53 Florian Gravel	54 Jean-Guy Thompson
55 Yvan Fortin	56 Yves Laporte
57 Claude Germain	58 Gerry Brunet
59 Maurice Courteau	

1951 - 52 LA PATRIE

Prices are for photos with three stripes down right side intact. These newspaper photos measure 11" x 15 1/2".

La Patrie	EX	EX-MT
Dec. 2 Maurice Richard, Mont.	120	200
Dec. 9 Emile Bouchard, Mont.	50	75
Dec. 16 Elmer Lach, Mont.	60	100
Dec. 23 Gerry McNeil, Mont.	55	85
Dec. 31 Bernie Geoffrion, Mont.	80	125
Jan. 6 Doug Harvey, Mont.	80	125
Jan. 15 Jean Béliveau, Québec Aces	90	150
Jan. 20 Kenny Mosdell, Mont.	50	75
Jan. 27 Dick Gamble, Mont.	30	50
Feb. 3 Paul Meger	30	50
Feb. 10 Billy Reay, Mont.	45	70
Feb. 17 Floyd Curry, Mont.	35	60
Feb. 24 Dollard St. Laurent, Mont.	35	60
Mar. 2 Jean Guy Talbot, Trois Rivières	30	50
Mar. 9 Dickie Moore, Mont.	60	100
Mar. 16 Bert Olmstead, Mont.	50	75
Mar. 23 André Corriveau, Valleyfield	25	40
Mar. 30 Marcel Pelletier, Les Saguénéens	25	40
Apr. 8 Tom Johnson, Mont.	50	75
Apr. 13 Bud MacPherson, Mont.	25	40
Apr. 20 John McCormack, Mont.	30	50

1951 - 52 LAVAL DAIRY QHL

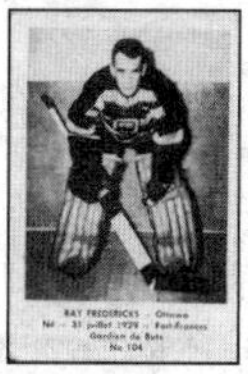

"Herb Carnegie, he was probably the greatest black player at that time. He was a great player. When I saw his cards, I looked him up and found out that he was a super player, someone that should have been in the National Hockey League." – Winston Hart, Winnie's Cards, Nova Scotia.

These black & white blank-back cards measure 1 3/4" x 2 1/2".

Complete Set (109 cards):	850	1,700
Québec Senior League	**EX**	**EX-MT**
1 Jean Béliveau, Québec	250	600
2 Jean Marois (G), Québec	8	15
3 Joe Crozier, Québec	12	20
4 Jack Gélineau (G), Québec	8	15
5 Murdo McKay, Québec	6	13
6 Arthur Leyte, Québec	6	13
7 W. Leblanc, Québec	6	13
8 Robert Hayes, Québec	6	13
9 Yogi Kraiger, Québec	6	13
10 Frank King, Québec	6	13
11 Ludger Tremblay, Québec	6	13
12 Jackie Leclair, Québec	13	22
13 Martial Pruneau, Québec	6	13
14 Armand Gaudreault, Québec	6	13
15 Marcel Bonin, Québec	20	30
16 Herbie Carnegie, Québec	75	150
17 Claude Robert, Québec	6	13
18 Phil Renaud, Québec	6	13
19 Roland Hebert, Chicoutimi	6	13
20 Donat Deschesne, Chicoutimi	6	13
21 Jacques Gagnon, Chicoutimi	6	13
22 Normand Dussault, Chicoutimi	6	13
23 Stan Smrke, Chicoutimi	11	18
24 Louis Smrke, Chicoutimi	6	13
25 Floyd Crawford, Chicoutimi	6	13
26 Germain Leger, Chicoutimi	6	13
27 Delphis Franche, Chicoutimi	6	13
28 Dick Wray, Chicoutimi	6	13
29 Guildor Levesque, Chicoutimi	6	13
30 Georges Roy, Chicoutimi	6	13
31 J.P. Lamirande, Chicoutimi	6	13
32 Gerard Glaude, Chicoutimi	6	13
33 Marcel Pelletier, Chicoutimi	6	13
34 Pete Tkachuck, Chicoutimi	6	13
35 Sherman White, Chicoutimi	6	13
36 Jimmy Moore, Chicoutimi	6	13
37 Punch Imlach, Québec	50	90
38 Alex Sandalax, Sherbrooke	6	13
39 William Kyle, Sherbrooke	6	13
40 Kenneth Biggs, Sherbrooke	6	13
41 Peter Wright, Sherbrooke	6	13
42 René Pépin, Sherbrooke	6	13
43 Jean-Claude (Tod) Campeau, Sherbrooke	11	18
44 John Smith, Sherbrooke	6	13
45 Thomas McDougall, Sherbrooke	6	13
46 Jos Lépine, Sherbrooke	6	13
47 Guy Labrie, Sherbrooke	6	13
48 Roger Bessette, Sherbrooke	6	13
49 Yvan Dugre, Sherbrooke	6	13
50 James Planche, Sherbrooke	6	13
51 Nils Tremblay, Sherbrooke	6	13
52 Bill McDonagh, Shawinigan Falls	6	13
53 Georges Ouellet, Shawinigan Falls	6	13
54 Billy Arcand, Shawinigan Falls	6	13
55 Johnny Mahaffy, Shawinigan Falls	6	13
56 Bucky Buchanan, Shawinigan Falls	6	13
57 Al Miller (G), Shawinigan Falls	6	13
58 Don Penniston, Shawinigan Falls	6	13
59 Spike Laliberte, Shawinigan Falls	6	13
60 Ernie Oakley, Shawinigan Falls	6	13
61 Jack Bownass, Shawinigan Falls	11	18
62 Ted Hodgson, Shawinigan Falls	6	13
63 Lyall Wiseman, Shawinigan Falls	6	13
64 Erwin Grosse, Shawinigan Falls	6	13
65 Mel Read, Shawinigan Falls	6	13
66 Lloyd Henchberger, Shawinigan Falls	6	13
67 Jack Taylor, Shawinigan Falls	6	13
68 Marcel Bessette, Valleyfield	6	13
69 Jack Schmidt, Valleyfield	6	13
70 Paul Saindon, Valleyfield	6	13
71 J.P. Bisaillon, Valleyfield	6	13
72 Eddie Redmond, Valleyfield	6	13
73 Larry Kwong, Valleyfield	11	18
74 Andre Corriveau, Valleyfield	10	16
75 Kitoute Joanette, Valleyfield	6	13
76 Toe Blake, Valleyfield	70	120
77 Georges Bougie, Valleyfield	6	13
78 Jack Irvine, Valleyfield	6	13
79 Paul Larivée, Valleyfield	6	13
80 Paul Leclerc, Valleyfield	6	13
81 Bertrand Bourassa, Valleyfield	6	13
82 Jacques Deslauriers, Valleyfield	6	13
83 Bingo Ernst, Valleyfield	6	13
84 Gaston Gervais, Valleyfield	6	13
85 Gerry Plamondon, Royal de Montréal	12	20
86 Glen Harmon, Royal de Montréal	15	30
87 Bob Friday, Royal de Montréal	6	13
88 Rolland Rousseau, Royal de Montréal	6	13
89 Billy Goold, Royal de Montréal	6	13
90 Lloyd Finkbeiner, Royal de Montréal	6	13
91 Clifford Malone, Royal de Montréal	6	13
92 Jacques Plante (G), Royal de Montréal	300	500
93 Gerard Desaulniers, Royal de Montréal	6	13
94 Arthur Rose, Royal de Montréal	6	13
95 Jacques Locas, Royal de Montréal	6	13
96 Walter Clune, Royal de Montréal	6	13
97 Louis Denis, Royal de Montréal	6	13
98 Fernand Perreault, Royal de Montréal	6	13
99 Douglas McNeil, Royal de Montréal	6	13
100 Les Douglas, Royal de Montréal	10	18
101 Howard Riopelle, Ottawa	10	18
102 Vic Grigg, Ottawa	6	13
103 Bobby Roberts, Ottawa	6	13
104 Legs Fraser, Ottawa	6	13
105 Butch Stahan, Ottawa	6	13
106 Fritz Frazer, Ottawa	6	13
107 Bill Robinson, Ottawa	6	13
108 Eddie Emberg, Ottawa	6	13
109 Leo Gravelle, Ottawa	6	28

1951 - 52 PARKHURST

"Bill Barilko's card actually shows the game-winning goal that won the Cup in the 1951 season. He was then killed in a plane crash and his body was only found 11 years later in Northern Ontario. The Maple Leafs didn't win the Cup until (the year) his body was found (1962). It is a very interesting story behind the card, so it (the card) is very sought after." – Kevin Lawr, Niagara Collectibles, St. Catharines, Ontario.

"The 1951-52 Parkies set is (the set) that started it all. I think their popularity among older collectors reflects that historic status. Younger collectors are fascinated by those cards when they see them at shows, but it's the 45-and-older hobbyists who are seriously dedicated to acquiring them. That's the age group that saw a lot of these guys play the game, so there is a connection. I literally can't keep (these cards) in stock." – Gerry Chartrand, Gerry's Sports Cards, Montréal, Québec.

These black & white blank-back cards measure 1 3/4" x 2 1/2". It is very difficult to find these cards in high grades.

Complete Set (105 cards): 9,500 16,000

◆ A complete set in NM to NM-MT closed at $12,245.20 U.S. (approx. $16,500 Cdn.) in a May 2003 Leland's auction.

Common Player:	40	70
Parkhurst	**EX**	**EX-MT**
1 Elmer Lach, Mont.	275	550
2 Paul Meger, Mont. RC	40	70
3 Emile (Butch) Bouchard, Mont.	75	140
4 Maurice Richard, Mont. RC	1,500	2,800
5 Bert Olmstead, Mont. RC	80	140
6 Bud MacPherson, Mont. RC	40	70
7 Tom Johnson, Mont. RC	60	110
8 Paul Masnick, Mont. RC	40	70
9 Calum MacKay, Mont. RC	40	70
10 Doug Harvey, Mont. RC	500	800
11 Kenny Mosdell, Mont. RC	40	70
12 Floyd Curry, Mont. RC	40	70
13 Billy Reay, Mont. RC	50	80
14 Bernie Geoffrion, Mont. RC	450	700
15 Gerry McNeil (G), Mont. RC	225	350
16 Dick Gamble, Mont. RC	40	70
17 Gerald Couture, Mont. RC	40	70
18 Ross Lowe, Mont. RC	40	70
19 Jim Henry (G), Bost. RC	100	175
20 Vic Lynn, Bost. RC	40	70
21 Walter Kyle, Bost. RC	40	70
22 Ed Sandford, Bost. RC	40	70

☐ 23 John Henderson, Bost. RC	40	70
☐ 24 Robert Fisher, Bost. RC	40	70
☐ 25 Hal Laycoe, Bost. RC	40	70
☐ 26 Bill Quackenbush, Bost. RC	110	175
☐ 27 George Sullivan, Bost. RC	40	70
☐ 28 Woody Dumart, Bost.	70	110
☐ 29 Milt Schmidt, Bost.	100	175
☐ 30 Adam Brown, Bost. RC	40	70
☐ 31 Pentti Lund, Bost. RC	40	70
☐ 32 Ray Barry, Bost. RC	40	70
☐ 33 Kryznowski, Err. (Kryzanowski), Bost. RC	40	70
☐ 34 Johnny Peirson, Bost. RC	40	70
☐ 35 Lorne Ferguson, Bost. RC	40	70
☐ 36 Clare Raglan, Bost. RC	40	70
☐ 37 Bill Gadsby, Chic. RC	80	125
☐ 38 Al Dewsbury, Chic. RC	40	70
☐ 39 George Martin, Chic. RC	40	70
☐ 40 Gus Bodnar, Chic. RC	40	70
☐ 41 Jim Peters, Chic.	40	70
☐ 42 Bep Guidolin, Chic. RC	40	70
☐ 43 George Gee, Chic. RC	40	70
☐ 44 Jim McFadden, Chic. RC	60	85
☐ 45 Fred Hucul, Chic. RC	40	70
☐ 46 Lidio Fogolin, Chic. RC	40	70
☐ 47 Harry Lumley (G), Chic. RC	150	225
☐ 48 Doug Bentley, Chic. RC	80	125
☐ 49 Bill Mosienko, Chic. RC	80	110
☐ 50 Roy Conacher, Chic.	50	85
☐ 51 Pete Babando, Chic. RC	40	70
☐ 52 Bill Barilko, Toro. (The Winning Goal)	400	600
☐ 53 Jack Stewart, Chic.	45	80
☐ 54 Marty Pavelich, Chic. RC	40	70
☐ 55 Red Kelly, Detr. RC	230	375
☐ 56 Ted Lindsay, Detr. RC	230	375
☐ 57 Glen Skov, Detr. RC	40	70
☐ 58 Benny Woit, Detr. RC	40	70
☐ 59 Tony Leswick, Detr. RC	40	70
☐ 60 Fred Glover, Detr. RC	40	70
☐ 61 Terry Sawchuk (G), Detr. RC	1,000	1,700
☐ 62 Vic Stasiuk, Detr. RC	45	70
☐ 63 Alex Delvecchio, Detr. RC	300	450
☐ 64 Sid Abel, Detr.	70	110
☐ 65 Metro Prystai, Detr. RC	40	60
☐ 66 Gordie Howe, Detr. RC	2,400	4,300
☐ 67 Bob Goldham, Detr. RC	45	70
☐ 68 Marcel Pronovost, Detr. RC	70	110
☐ 69 Leo Reise, Detr. RC	40	70
☐ 70 Harry Watson, Toro. RC	75	110
☐ 71 Danny Lewicki, Toro. RC	40	70
☐ 72 Howie Meeker, Toro. RC	125	200
☐ 73 Gus Mortson, Toro. RC	40	70
☐ 74 Joe Klukay, Toro. RC	40	70
☐ 75 Turk Broda (G), Toro.	175	275
☐ 76 Al Rollins (G), Toro. RC	90	150
☐ 77 Bill Juzda, Toro. RC	40	70
☐ 78 Ray Timgren, Toro. RC	40	70
☐ 79 Hugh Bolton, Toro. RC	40	70
☐ 80 Fern Flaman, Toro. RC	70	110
☐ 81 Max Bentley, Toro.	70	110
☐ 82 Jim Thomson, Toro. RC	40	70
☐ 83 Fleming Mackell, Toro.	40	70
☐ 84 Sid Smith, Toro. RC	50	80
☐ 85 Cal Gardner, Toro. RC	40	70
☐ 86 Ted Kennedy, Toro. RC	150	250
☐ 87 Tod Sloan, Toro. RC	40	70
☐ 88 Bob Solinger, Toro. RC	40	70
☐ 89 Frank Eddolls, Toro. RC	40	70
☐ 90 Jack Evans, NYRa. RC	40	70
☐ 91 Hyman Buller, NYRa. RC	40	70
☐ 92 Stephen Kraftcheck, NYRa. RC	40	70
☐ 93 Don Raleigh, NYRa. RC	40	70
☐ 94 Allan Stanley, NYRa. RC	125	200
☐ 95 Paul Ronty, NYRa. RC	40	70
☐ 96 Edgar LaPrade, NYRa. RC	70	110
☐ 97 Nick Mickoski, NYRa. RC	40	70
☐ 98 Jackie McLeod, NYRa. RC	40	70
☐ 99 Gaye Stewart, NYRa. RC	40	70
☐ 100 Wally Hergesheimer, NYRa. RC	40	70
☐ 101 Eddie Kullman, NYRa. RC	40	70
☐ 102 Eddie Slowinski, NYRa. RC	40	70
☐ 103 Reg Sinclair, NYRa. RC	40	70
☐ 104 Chuck Rayner (G), NYRa. RC	110	175
☐ 105 Jim Conacher, NYRa. RC	130	275

1952 ROYAL STARS OF HOCKEY

These blank-back cards measure 2 5/8" x 3 1/4" once they are cut from the back of Royal Desserts packages.

Complete Set (8 cards):	**4,000**	**6,500**
Album:	**75**	**150**
Royal Desserts	**EX**	**EX-MT**
☐ 1 Tony Leswick, Detr.	175	300

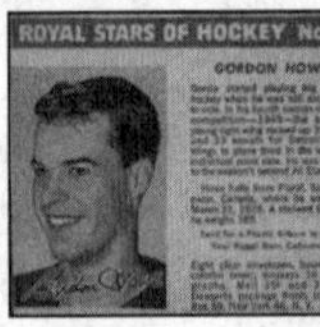

☐ 2 Chuck Rayner (G), NYRa.	375	650
☐ 3 Edgar Laprade, NYRa.	250	450
☐ 4 Sid Abel, Detr.	425	750
☐ 5 Ted Lindsay, Detr.	500	900
☐ 6 Leo Reise, Detr.	175	300
☐ 7 Red Kelly, Detr.	425	750
☐ 8 Gordie Howe, Detr.	2,500	4,500

1952 - 53 ANONYMOUS OHL

These cards measure 2" x 3". Regional stars do sell at a premium.

Complete Set (182 cards):	**1,800**	**2,700**
Ontario Hockey	**EX**	**EX-MT**
☐ 1 Dennis Riggin (G), Windsor	9	25
☐ 2 Joe Zorica, Windsor	9	15
☐ 3 Larry Hillman, Windsor	22	35
☐ 4 Edward Reid, Windsor	9	15
☐ 5 Al Arbour, Windsor	55	90
☐ 6 Marlin McAlendin, Windsor	9	15
☐ 7 Ross Graham, Windsor	9	15
☐ 8 Cumming Burton, Windsor	9	15
☐ 9 Ed Palamar, Windsor	9	15
☐ 10 Elmer Skov, Windsor	9	15
☐ 11 Eddie Louttit, Windsor	9	15
☐ 12 Gerry Price, Windsor	9	15
☐ 13 Lou Dietrich, Windsor	9	15
☐ 14 Gaston Marcotte, Windsor	9	15
☐ 15 Bob Brown, Windsor	9	15
☐ 16 Archie Burton, Windsor	9	15
☐ 17 Marven Edwards (G), St. Catharines	15	25
☐ 18 Norman Defelice (G), St. Catharines	13	22
☐ 19 Pete Kamula, St. Catharines	9	15
☐ 20 Charles Marshall, St. Catharines	9	15
☐ 21 Alex Leslie, St. Catharines	9	15
☐ 22 Minpy Roberts, St. Catharines	9	15
☐ 23 Danny Poliziani, St. Catharines	9	15
☐ 24 Allen Kellog, St. Catharines	9	15
☐ 25 Brian Cullen, St. Catharines	18	28
☐ 26 Ken Schinkel, St. Catharines	20	30
☐ 27 W. Hass, St. Catharines	9	15
☐ 28 Don Nash, St. Catharines	9	15
☐ 29 Robert Maxwell, St. Catharines	9	15
☐ 30 Eddie Mateka, St. Catharines	9	15
☐ 31 Joe Kastelic, St. Catharines	9	15
☐ 32 Hank Ciesla, St. Catharines	12	20
☐ 33 Hugh Barlow, St. Catharines	9	15
☐ 34 Claude Roy (G), St. Catharines	9	15
☐ 35 Jean-Guy Gamache, Trois-Rivières	9	15
☐ 36 Leon Michelin, Trois-Rivières	9	15
☐ 37 Gerard Bergeron, Trois-Rivières	9	15
☐ 38 Herve Lalonde, Trois-Rivières	9	15
☐ 39 J.M. Cossette, Trois-Rivières	9	15
☐ 40 Jean-Guy Gendron, Trois-Rivières	22	35
☐ 41 Camille Bedard, Trois-Rivières	9	15
☐ 42 Alfred Soucy, Trois-Rivières	9	15
☐ 43 Jean Leclerc, Trois-Rivières	9	15
☐ 44 Raymond St. Cyr, Trois-Rivières	9	15
☐ 45 Lester Lahaye, Trois-Rivières	9	15
☐ 46 Yvan Houle, Trois-Rivières	9	15
☐ 47 Louis Desrosiers, Trois-Rivières	9	15
☐ 48 Douglas Lessor, Guelph	9	15
☐ 49 Irvin Scott, Guelph	9	15
☐ 50 Danny Blair, Guelph	9	15
☐ 51 Jim Connelly, Guelph	9	15
☐ 52 William Chalmers, Guelph	9	15
☐ 53 Frank Bettiol, Guelph	9	15
☐ 54 James Holmes, Guelph	9	15
☐ 55 Birley Dimme, Guelph	9	15
☐ 56 Donald Beattie, Guelph	9	15
☐ 57 Terrance Chattington, Guelph	9	15
☐ 58 Bruce Wallace, Guelph	9	15
☐ 59 William McCreary, Guelph	15	25
☐ 60 Fred Brady, Guelph	9	15
☐ 61 Ronald Murphy, Guelph	22	35
☐ 62 Lavi Purola, Guelph	9	15
☐ 63 George Whyte, Guelph	9	15
☐ 64 Marcel Paille (G), Citadels	20	30
☐ 65 Maurice Collins, Citadels	9	15
☐ 66 Gerard Houle, Citadels	9	15
☐ 67 Gilles Laperrière, Citadels	9	15
☐ 68 Robert Chevalier, Citadels	9	15
☐ 69 Bertrand Lepage, Citadels	9	15
☐ 70 Michel Labadie, Citadels	9	15
☐ 71 Gabriel Alain, Citadels	9	15
☐ 72 Jean-Jacques Pichette, Citadels	9	15
☐ 73 Camille Henry, Citadels	28	45
☐ 74 Jean-Guy Gignac, Citadels	9	15
☐ 75 Leo Amadio, Citadels	9	15
☐ 76 Gilles Thibault, Citadels	9	15
☐ 77 Gaston Pelletier, Citadels	9	15
☐ 78 Adolph Kukulowicz, Citadels	9	15
☐ 79 Roland Leclerc, Citadels	9	15
☐ 80 Phil Watson, Citadels	30	45
☐ 81 Raymond Cyr, Citadels	9	15
☐ 82 Jacques Marcotte, Citadels	9	15
☐ 83 Floyd Hillman, Oshawa	9	15
☐ 84 Bob Attersley, Oshawa	9	15
☐ 85 Harry Sinden, Oshawa	50	75
☐ 86 Stan Parker, Err. (Owhaha), Oshawa	9	15
☐ 87 Bob Mader, Oshawa	9	15
☐ 88 Roger Maisonneuve, Oshawa	9	15
☐ 89 Phil Chapman, Oshawa	9	15
☐ 90 Don McIntosh, Oshawa	9	15
☐ 91 Jack Armstrong, Oshawa	9	15
☐ 92 Carlo Montemurro, Oshawa	9	15
☐ 93 Ken Courtney (G), Oshawa	9	15
☐ 94 Bill Stewart, Oshawa	9	15
☐ 95 Gerald Casey, Oshawa	9	15
☐ 96 Fred Etcher, Oshawa	9	15
☐ 97 Orrin Carver, Barrie	9	15
☐ 98 Ralph Willis, Barrie	9	15
☐ 99 Kenneth Robertson, Barrie	9	15
☐ 100 Don Cherry, Barrie	180	325
☐ 101 Fred Pletsch, Barrie	9	15
☐ 102 Larry Thibault, Barrie	9	15
☐ 103 James Robertson, Barrie	9	15
☐ 104 Orval Tessier, Barrie	13	22
☐ 105 Jack Higgins, Barrie	9	15
☐ 106 Robert White, Barrie	9	15
☐ 107 Doug Mohns, Barrie	35	60
☐ 108 William Sexton, Barrie	9	15
☐ 109 John Martan, Barrie	9	15
☐ 110 Tony Poeta, Barrie	9	15
☐ 111 Don McKenney, Barrie	25	40
☐ 112 Bill Harrington, Barrie	9	15
☐ 113 Allen Teal, Barrie	9	15
☐ 114 John Ford, Kitchener	9	15
☐ 115 Ken Collins, Kitchener	9	15
☐ 116 Marc Boileau, Kitchener	9	15
☐ 117 Doug Vaughan, Kitchener	9	15
☐ 118 Gilles Boisvert, Kitchener	9	15
☐ 119 Buddy Horne, Kitchener	9	15
☐ 120 Graham Joyce, Kitchener	9	15
☐ 121 Gary Collins, Kitchener	9	15
☐ 122 Roy Greenan, Kitchener	9	15
☐ 123 Beryl Klynck, Kitchener	9	15
☐ 124 Grieg Hicks, Kitchener	9	15
☐ 125 Jack Novak, Kitchener	9	15
☐ 126 Ken Tennant, Kitchener	9	15
☐ 127 Glen Cressman, Kitchener	9	15
☐ 128 Curly Davies, Coach / Manager, Kitchener	9	15
☐ 129 Charlie Hodge (G), Jr. Canadiens	55	85
☐ 130 Bob McCord, Jr. Canadiens	13	22
☐ 131 Gordie Hollingworth, Jr. Canadiens	9	15
☐ 132 Ronald Pilon, Jr. Canadiens	9	15
☐ 133 Brian MacKay, Jr. Canadiens	9	15
☐ 134 Yvon Chasle, Jr. Canadiens	9	15
☐ 135 Denis Boucher, Jr. Canadiens	12	20
☐ 136 Claude Boileau, Jr. Canadiens	9	15
☐ 137 Claude Vinet, Jr. Canadiens	9	15
☐ 138 Claude Provost, Jr. Canadiens	35	55
☐ 139 Henri Richard, Jr. Canadiens	250	375
☐ 140 Les Lilley, Jr. Canadiens	9	15
☐ 141 Phil Goyette, Jr. Canadiens	28	45
☐ 142 Guy Rousseau, Jr. Canadiens	9	15
☐ 143 Paul Knox, St. Michael's	9	15
☐ 144 Bill Lee, St. Michael's	9	15
☐ 145 Ted Topazzini, St. Michael's	9	15
☐ 146 Marc Reaume, St. Michael's	13	22
☐ 147 Bill Dineen, St. Michael's	22	35
☐ 148 Ed Plata, St. Michael's	9	15
☐ 149 Noel Price, St. Michael's	18	28
☐ 150 Mike Ratchford, St. Michael's	9	15
☐ 151 Jim Logan, St. Michael's	9	15
☐ 152 Art Clune, St. Michael's	9	15
☐ 153 Jerry MacNamara, St. Michael's	12	20
☐ 154 Jack Caffery, St. Michael's	13	22
☐ 155 Less Duff, St. Michael's	9	15
☐ 156 Murray Costello, St. Michael's	12	20
☐ 157 Ed Chadwick (G), St. Michael's	35	60
☐ 158 Mike Desilets, Royal	9	15
☐ 159 Ross Watson, Royal	9	15
☐ 160 Roger Landry, Royal	9	15
☐ 161 Terry O'Connor, Royal	9	15
☐ 162 Ovila Gagnon, Royal	9	15
☐ 163 Dave Broadbelt, Royal	9	15
☐ 164 Sandy Monrisson, Royal	9	15
☐ 165 John MacGillvray, Royal	9	15
☐ 166 Claude Beaupré, Royal	9	15
☐ 167 Eddie Eustache, Royal	9	15
☐ 168 Stan Rodek, Royal	9	15
☐ 169 Maurice Mantha, Galt	9	15
☐ 170 Hector Lalonde, Galt	9	15
☐ 171 Bob Wilson, Galt	9	15
☐ 172 Frank Bonello, Galt	9	15
☐ 173 Peter Kowalchuck, Galt	9	15
☐ 174 Les Binkley (G), Galt	28	45
☐ 175 John Muckler, Galt	30	50
☐ 176 Ken Wharram, Galt	28	45
☐ 177 John Sleaver, Galt	9	15
☐ 178 Ralph Markarian, Galt	9	15
☐ 179 Ken McMeekin, Galt	9	15
☐ 180 Ron Boomer, Galt	9	15
☐ 181 Kenneth Crawford, Galt	9	15
☐ 182 Jim McBurney, Galt	9	25

1952 - 53 BAS DU FLEUVE

Regional stars do sell at a premium.

Complete Set (65 cards):	**350**	**750**
Common Player:	**8**	**15**
Bas du Fleuve	**EX**	**EX-MT**
☐ 1 Roger Gagner	10	20
☐ 2 Martial Pruneau	8	15
☐ 3 Fernand Gladu	8	15
☐ 4 Joseph Lacoursière	8	15
☐ 5 Maurice Lamirande	8	15
☐ 6 Denis Smith	8	15
☐ 7 Real Jacques	8	15
☐ 8 Roland Landry	8	15
☐ 9 Dan Janelle	8	15
☐ 10 Pete Gaudette	8	15
☐ 11 Normand Bellavance	8	15
☐ 12 Roger Hayfield	8	15
☐ 13 Bill Leblanc	8	15
☐ 14 Victor Corbin	8	15
☐ 15 Gerard Lachance	8	15
☐ 16 Guy Labrie	8	15
☐ 17 Denis Brodeur (G)	20	40
☐ 18 Gerard Paquin	8	15
☐ 19 Irene St-Hilaire	8	15
☐ 20 Guy Gervais	8	15
☐ 21 Marcel Benoît	8	15
☐ 22 Roger Dumas	8	15
☐ 23 Gaston Gervais	8	15
☐ 24 Maurice St. Jean	8	15
☐ 25 Frank Pearce	8	15
☐ 26 Fernand Bernaquez	8	15
☐ 27 Henri-Paul Gagnon	8	15
☐ 28 Jean-Jacques Pichette	8	15
☐ 29 Jim Hayes	8	15
☐ 30 Fernand Rancourt	8	15
☐ 31 Nils Tremblay	8	15
☐ 32 Clement Tremblay	8	15
☐ 33 Jacques Lalancette	8	15
☐ 34 Marcel Fillion	8	15
☐ 35 Jacques Monette	8	15
☐ 36 Frank Côté	8	15
☐ 37 Bernie Lemonde	8	15
☐ 38 Guildor Lévesque	8	15
☐ 39 Hector Legris	8	15
☐ 40 Jacques Gagnon	8	15
☐ 41 Donat Deschesnes	8	15
☐ 42 Bertrand LePage	8	15
☐ 43 Paul Lavoie	8	15
☐ 44 Denis Filion	10	20
☐ 45 Floyd Crawford	8	15
☐ 46 Paul Duchesne	8	15
☐ 47 René Pronovost	8	15
☐ 48 Roger Jodoin	8	15
☐ 49 Mario Senecal	8	15

☐ 50 Garry Plamondon	10	20
☐ 51 Marcel Paille	10	20
☐ 52 Rene Pepin	8	15
☐ 53 Gilles Desrosiers	8	15
☐ 54 Edgard Gendron	8	15
☐ 55 Ronald Limoges	8	15
☐ 56 Roland Bilodeau	8	15
☐ 57 Leon Bouchard	8	15
☐ 58 Bob Leger	8	15
☐ 59 Conrad L'Heureux	8	15
☐ 60 Raymond Leduc	8	15
☐ 61 Bob Brault	8	15
☐ 62 Roger Ste. Marie	8	15
☐ 63 Real Lafreniere	8	15
☐ 64 Lucien Gilbert	8	15
☐ 65 Louis Desrosiers	10	20

1952 - 53 LA PATRIE

These colour newspaper photos measure 11" x 15 1/2".

La Patrie	EX	EX-MT
☐ Jan. 11 Roger Léger, RHC.	30	50
☐ Jan. 18 Henri Richard, Mont.	100	175
☐ Jan. 25 Camille Henry, Québec	30	50
☐ Feb. 1 Jean Paul Lamirande, Chicoutimi	20	30
☐ Feb. 8 Eddie Litzenberger, RHC.	30	50
☐ Feb. 1 Skippy Burchell, RHC.	25	40
☐ Mar. 1 Herbie Carnegie, Québec Aces	75	100
☐ Mar. 8 Jean Marois, Québec	25	40
☐ Mar. 15 Don Raleigh, NYRa.	30	50
☐ Mar. 22 Wally Hergesheimer, NYRa.	30	50
☐ Mar. 29 Tod Campeau, Sherbrooke Saints	25	40
☐ Apr. 5 Guy Rousseau, Jr. Canadiens	20	30

1952 - 53 LAVAL DAIRY QHL UPDATE

These black & white, blank-back cards measure 1 3/4" x 2 1/2". They were believed to be issued during the 1952-53 season, updating new players and trades that took place between the teams. Short prints are marked with an asterisk (*).

Complete Set (66 cards):	**600**	**1,300**
Québec Senior League	**EX**	**EX-MT**
☐ 4 Jack Gélineau, Québec (*)	15	35
☐ 7 Al Miller, Québec	7	16
☐ 8 Walter Pawlyshyn, Québec	7	16
☐ 9 Yogi Kraiger, Québec (*)	15	35
☐ 10 Al Baccari, Québec	7	16
☐ 12 Denis Smith, Québec	7	16
☐ 13 Pierre Brillant, Québec	7	16
☐ 14 Frank Mario, Québec	7	16
☐ 15 Danny Nixon, Québec	7	16
☐ 25 Leon Bouchard, Québec	7	16
☐ 26 Pete Taillefer, Chicoutimi	7	16
☐ 29 Bucky Buchanen, Chicoutimi	7	16
☐ 36 Marius Groleau, Chicoutimi	7	16
☐ 38 Fernand Perreault, Chicoutimi	7	16
☐ 39 Robert Drainville, Sherbrooke	7	16
☐ 40 Ronnie Matthews, Sherbrooke	7	16
☐ 44 Roger Roberge, Sherbrooke	7	16
☐ 46 Pete Wywrot, Sherbrooke	7	16
☐ 50 Gilles Dubé, Sherbrooke	7	16
☐ 51 Nils Tremblay, Sherbrooke (*)	15	35
☐ 52 Bob Pepin, Sherbrooke	7	16
☐ 53 Dewar Thompson, Sherbrooke	7	16
☐ 55 Irene St. Hilaire, Sherbrooke	7	16
☐ 56 Martial Pruneau, Sherbrooke	7	16
☐ 57 Jacques Locas, Sherbrooke	7	16
☐ 59 Nelson Podolsky, Shawinigan Falls	7	16
☐ 60 Bert Giesebrecht, Shawinigan Falls	7	16
☐ 61 Steve Brklacich, Shawinigan Falls	7	16
☐ 65 Jack Hamilton, Shawinigan Falls	7	16
☐ 66 Dave Gatherum, Shawinigan Falls	7	16
☐ 67 Jean-Marie Plante, Shawinigan Falls	7	16
☐ 68 Gordie Haworth, Valleyfield	7	16
☐ 69 Jack Schmidt, Valleyfield (*)	15	35
☐ 70 Bruce Cline, Valleyfield	10	22
☐ 72 Phil Vitale, Valleyfield	7	16
☐ 81 Carl Smelle, Valleyfield	7	16
☐ 84 Tom Smelle, Valleyfield	7	16
☐ 85 Gerry Plamondon, Royals	7	22
☐ 86 Glen Harmon, Royals	15	30
☐ 89 Frank Bathgate, Shawinigan Falls	7	16
☐ 90 Bernie Lemonde, Shawinigan Falls	7	16
☐ 92 Jacques Plante (G), Royals	250	575
☐ 93 Gerard Desaulniers, Royals	7	16
☐ 94 Jean-Claude Lebrun, Shawinigan Falls	7	16
☐ 95 Bob Leger, Shawinigan Falls	7	22
☐ 96 Walter Clune, Royals	7	16
☐ 97 Louis Denis, Royals	7	16
☐ 98 Jackie Leclair, Ottawa	11	25
☐ 99 John Arundel, Ottawa	7	16
☐ 100 Leslie Douglas, Ottawa	7	16
☐ 103 Bobby Robertson, Ottawa	7	16
☐ 104 Ray Fredericks (G), Ottawa	7	16
☐ 106 Emil Dagenais, Ottawa	7	16
☐ 108 Al Kuntz, Ottawa	7	16
☐ 110 Red Johnson, Ottawa	7	16
☐ 111 John O'Flaherty, Ottawa	7	16
☐ 112 Jack Giesebrecht, Ottawa	7	16
☐ 113 Bill Richardson, Ottawa	7	16
☐ 114 Bep Guidolin, Ottawa	15	35
☐ 115 Roger Bedard, Shawinigan Falls	7	16
☐ 116 Renald Lacroix, Valleyfield	7	16
☐ 117 Gordie Hudson, Québec	7	16
☐ 118 Dick Wray, Shawinigan Falls	7	16
☐ 119 Ronnie Hurst, Ottawa	10	22
☐ 120 Eddie Joss, Shawinigan Falls	7	16
☐ 121 Lyall Wiseman, Québec	7	25

1952 - 53 PARKHURST

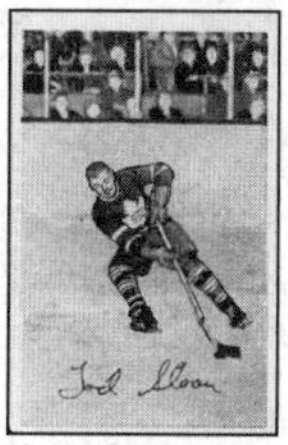

These cards measure 1 15/16" x 2 15/16". The card backs feature player stats for the 1951-52 season.

"I love some of the stories that go with the early Parkhurst series. They (the original Parkhurst manufacturers) actually die-cut sheets of '51-52 Parkhurst into the shape of a wrapper to package the '52-53 cards. Some of these sheets are still in existence." – Baron Bedesky, In The Game (current manufacturers of the Parkhurst brand), Toronto, Ontario.

"There was an album with this set. It was something (into which) you put the corners of the cards. We'd put them in the little slots and take them out, so they would get damaged. As a kid, I hated that (they would get damaged), so I would just used a shoe box with a separator." – Ronald Carrier, JR Sports Cards, Elliot Lake, Ontario.

Complete Set (105 cards):	**5,400**	**9,000**
Common Player:	**30**	**45**
Album:	**70**	**130**
Parkhurst	**EX**	**EX-MT**
☐ 1 Maurice Richard, Mont.	950	1,850
☐ 2 Billy Reay, Mont.	30	45
☐ 3 Bernie Geoffrion, Mont., Err. (Gioffrion)	170	300
☐ 4 Paul Meger, Mont.	30	45
☐ 5 Dick Gamble, Mont.	30	45
☐ 6 Elmer Lach, Mont.	60	100
☐ 7 Floyd Curry, Mont.	30	45
☐ 8 Kenny Mosdell, Mont.	30	45
☐ 9 Tom Johnson, Mont.	35	70
☐ **10 Dickie Moore, Mont. RC**	**190**	**325**
☐ 11 Bud MacPherson, Mont.	30	45
☐ 12 Gerry McNeil (G), Mont.	65	125
☐ 13 Emile (Butch) Bouchard, Mont.	40	75
☐ 14 Doug Harvey, Mont.	170	325
☐ **15 John McCormack, Mont. RC**	**30**	**45**
☐ 16 Pete Babando, Chic.	30	45
☐ 17 Al Dewsbury, Chic.	30	45
☐ 18 Eddie Kullman, NYRa.	30	45
☐ 19 Eddie Slowinski, NYRa.	30	45
☐ 20 Wally Hergesheimer, NYRa.	30	45
☐ 21 Allan Stanley, NYRa.	55	110
☐ 22 Chuck Rayner (G), NYRa.	45	80
☐ 23 Stephen Kraftcheck, NYRa.	30	45
☐ 24 Paul Ronty, NYRa.	30	45
☐ 25 Gaye Stewart, NYRa.	30	45
☐ 26 Fred Hucul, Chic.	30	45
☐ 27 Bill Mosienko, Chic.	35	70
☐ **28 Jim Morrison, Toro. RC**	**30**	**45**
☐ 29 Ed Kryznowski, Chic., Err. (Krysanowski)	30	45
☐ 30 Cal Gardner, Chic.	30	45
☐ 31 Al Rollins (G), Chic.	40	75
☐ **32 Enio Sclisizzi, Chic. RC**	**30**	**45**
☐ **33 Pete Conacher, Chic. RC**	**30**	**45**
☐ **34 Léo Boivin, Toro. RC**	**50**	**100**
☐ 35 Jim Peters, Chic.	30	45
☐ 36 George Gee, Chic.	30	45
☐ 37 Gus Bodnar, Chic.	30	45
☐ 38 Jim McFadden, Chic.	30	45
☐ 39 Gus Mortson, Chic.	30	45
☐ 40 Fred Glover, Chic.	30	45
☐ 41 Gerry Couture, Chic.	30	45
☐ 42 Howie Meeker, Toro.	55	100
☐ 43 Jim Thomson, Toro.	30	45
☐ 44 Ted Kennedy, Toro.	70	130
☐ 45 Sid Smith, Toro.	30	50
☐ 46 Harry Watson, Toro.	30	65
☐ 47 Fern Flaman, Toro.	35	65
☐ 48 Tod Sloan, Toro.	30	45
☐ 49 Leo Reise, NYRa.	30	45
☐ 50 Bob Solinger, Toro.	30	45
☐ **51 George Armstrong, Toro. RC**	**135**	**250**
☐ **52 Dollard St. Laurent, Mont. RC**	**30**	**45**
☐ 53 Alex Delvecchio, Detr.	110	200
☐ **54 Gordon Hannigan, Toro. RC**	**30**	**45**
☐ 55 Lidio Fogolin, Chic.	30	45
☐ 56 Bill Gadsby, Chic.	35	70
☐ **57 Herb Dickenson, NYRa. RC**	**30**	**45**
☐ **58 Tim Horton, Toro. RC**	**500**	**900**
☐ 59 Harry Lumley (G), Toro.	65	125
☐ 60 Metro Prystai, Detr.	30	45
☐ 61 Marcel Pronovost, Detr.	35	65
☐ 62 Benny Woit, Detr.	30	45
☐ 63 Glen Skov, Detr.	30	45
☐ 64 Bob Goldham, Detr.	30	50
☐ 65 Tony Leswick, Detr.	30	45
☐ 66 Marty Pavelich, Detr.	30	45
☐ 67 Red Kelly, Detr.	100	175
☐ 68 Bill Quackenbush, Bost.	35	65
☐ 69 Ed Sandford, Bost.	30	45
☐ 70 Milt Schmidt, Bost.	50	90
☐ 71 Hal Laycoe, Bost.	30	45
☐ 72 Woody Dumart, Bost.	35	55
☐ **73 Zellio Toppazzini, Bost. RC**	**30**	**45**
☐ 74 Jim Henry (G), Bost.	40	75
☐ 75 Joe Klukay, Bost.	30	45
☐ **76 Dave Creighton, Bost. RC**	**30**	**50**
☐ **77 Jack McIntyre, Bost. RC**	**30**	**45**
☐ 78 Johnny Peirson, Bost.	30	45
☐ 79 George Sullivan, Bost.	30	45
☐ **80 Real Chevrefils, Bost. RC**	**30**	**45**
☐ **81 Léo Labine, Bost. RC**	**30**	**45**
☐ 82 Fleming Mackell, Bost.	30	45
☐ 83 Pentti Lund, Bost.	30	45
☐ **84 Bob Armstrong, Bost. RC**	**30**	**45**
☐ **85 Warren Godfrey, Bost. RC**	**30**	**45**
☐ 86 Terry Sawchuk (G), Detr.	375	750
☐ 87 Ted Lindsay, Detr.	110	200
☐ 88 Gordie Howe, Detr.	900	1,600

◆ In 2002, a graded SGC-88 copy of card 88 Gordie Howe sold for $3,260 U.S. (approx. $5,000 Cdn.).

☐ **89 Johnny Wilson, Detr. RC**	**30**	**45**
☐ 90 Vic Stasiuk, Detr.	30	50
☐ **91 Larry Zeidel, Detr. RC**	**30**	**45**
☐ **92 Larry Wilson, Detr. RC**	**30**	**45**
☐ 93 Bert Olmstead, Mont.	35	70
☐ **94 Ron Stewart, Toro. RC**	**35**	**65**
☐ 95 Max Bentley, Toro.	35	65
☐ **96 Rudy Migay, Toro. RC**	**30**	**45**
☐ **97 Jack Stoddard, NYRa. RC**	**30**	**45**
☐ 98 Hyman Buller, NYRa.	30	45
☐ 99 Don Raleigh, NYRa.	30	45
☐ 100 Edgar Laprade, NYRa.	35	65
☐ 101 Nick Mickoski, NYRa.	30	45
☐ 102 Jackie McLeod, NYRa.	30	45
☐ 103 Jim Conacher, NYRa.	30	45
☐ 104 Reg Sinclair, Detr.	30	45
☐ **105 Bob Hassard, Toro. RC**	**50**	**110**

1952 - 53 ST. LAWRENCE SALES

These black & white cards measure 1 3/4" x 2 3/4"

Complete Set (107 cards):	**1,000**	**1,800**
St. Lawrence	**EX**	**EX-MT**
☐ 1 Jacques Plante (G), Royals	150	425
☐ 2 Glenn Harmon, Royals	9	25
☐ 3 Jimmy Moore, Royals	9	16
☐ 4 Gerry Desaulniers, Royals	9	16
☐ 5 Les Douglas, Royals	12	20
☐ 6 Fred Burchell, Royals	9	16
☐ 7 Eddie Litzenberger, Royals	30	50
☐ 8 Rollie Rousseau, Royals	9	16
☐ 9 Roger Leger, Royals	9	16
☐ 10 Phil Samis, Royals	9	16
☐ 11 Paul Masnick, Royals	9	16
☐ 12 Walter Clune, Royals	9	16
☐ 13 Louis Denis, Royals	9	16
☐ 14 Gerry Plamondon, Royals	12	20
☐ 15 Cliff Malone, Royals	9	16
☐ 16 Pete Morin, Royals	9	16
☐ 17 Jackie Schmidt, Valleyfield	11	18
☐ 17 Aldo Guidolin, Valleyfield	15	25
☐ 18 Paul Leclerc, Valleyfield	9	16
☐ 19 Larry Kwong, Valleyfield	9	16
☐ 20 Rosario Joanette, Valleyfield	9	16
☐ 21 Tom Smelle, Valleyfield	9	16
☐ 22 Gordie Haworth, Valleyfield	9	16
☐ 23 Bruce Cline, Valleyfield	9	16
☐ 24 Andre Corriveau, Valleyfield	9	16
☐ 25 Jacques Deslauriers, Valleyfield	9	16
☐ 26 Bingo Ernst, Valleyfield	9	16
☐ 27 Jacques Chartrand, Valleyfield	9	16
☐ 28 Phil Vitale, Valleyfield	9	16
☐ 29 Renald Lacroix, Valleyfield	9	16
☐ 30 J.P. Bisaillon, Valleyfield	9	16
☐ 31 Jack Irvine, Valleyfield	9	16
☐ 32 Georges Bougie, Valleyfield	9	16
☐ 33 Paul Larivee, Valleyfield	9	16
☐ 34 Carl Smelle, Valleyfield	9	16
☐ 35 Walter Pawlyschyn, Québec	9	16
☐ 36 Jean Marois, Québec	9	16
☐ 37 Jack Gelineau, Québec	9	16
☐ 38 Danny Nixon, Québec	9	16
☐ 39 Jean Béliveau, Québec	180	350
☐ 40 Phil Renaud, Québec	9	16
☐ 41 Leon Bouchard, Québec	9	16
☐ 42 Dennis Smith, Québec	9	16
☐ 43 Jos Crozier, Québec	12	20
☐ 44 Al Bacari, Québec	9	16
☐ 45 Murdo MacKay, Québec	9	16
☐ 46 Gordie Hudson, Québec	9	16
☐ 47 Claude Robert, Québec	9	16
☐ 48 Yogi Kraiger, Québec	9	16
☐ 49 Ludger Tremblay, Québec	9	16
☐ 50 Pierre Brillant, Québec	9	16
☐ 51 Frank Mario, Québec	9	16
☐ 52 Cooper Leyth, Québec	9	16
☐ 53 Herbie Carnegie, Québec	65	130
☐ 54 Punch Imlach, Québec	45	75
☐ 55 Howard Riopelle, Ottawa	9	16
☐ 56 Ken Laufman, Ottawa	9	16
☐ 57 Jackie Leclair, Ottawa	15	25
☐ 58 Bill Robinson, Ottawa	9	16
☐ 59 George Ford, Ottawa	9	16
☐ 60 Bill Johnson, Ottawa	9	16
☐ 61 Leo Gravelle, Ottawa	9	16
☐ 62 Jack Giesbrecht, Ottawa	9	16
☐ 63 John Arundel, Ottawa	9	16
☐ 64 Vic Gregg, Ottawa	9	16
☐ 65 Bep Guidolin, Ottawa	15	25
☐ 66 Al Kuntz, Ottawa	9	16
☐ 67 Emile Dagenais, Ottawa	9	16
☐ 68 Bill Richardson, Ottawa	9	16
☐ 69 Bob Robertson, Ottawa	9	16
☐ 70 Ray Fredericks, Ottawa	9	16
☐ 71 James O'Flaherty, Ottawa	9	16
☐ 72 Butch Stahan, Ottawa	9	16
☐ 73 Roger Roberge, Sherbrooke	9	16
☐ 74 Guy Labrie, Sherbrooke	9	16
☐ 75 Gilles Dubé, Sherbrooke	9	16
☐ 76 Pete Wywrot, Sherbrooke	9	16
☐ 77 Tod Campeau, Sherbrooke	12	20
☐ 78 Roger Bessette, Sherbrooke	9	16
☐ 79 Martial Pruneau, Sherbrooke	9	16
☐ 80 Nils Tremblay, Sherbrooke	9	16
☐ 81 Jacques Locas, Sherbrooke	9	16
☐ 82 René Pépin, Sherbrooke	9	16
☐ 83 Bob Pepin, Sherbrooke	9	16
☐ 84 Tom McDougal, Sherbrooke	9	16
☐ 85 Pete Wright, Sherbrooke	9	16
☐ 86 Ronnie Mathews, Sherbrooke	9	16
☐ 87 Irene St. Hilaire, Sherbrooke	9	16
☐ 88 Dewar Thompson, Sherbrooke	9	16
☐ 89 Bob Dainville, Sherbrooke	9	16
☐ 90 Marcel Pelletier, Chicoutimi	9	16
☐ 91 Delphis Franche, Chicoutimi	9	16
☐ 92 Georges Roy, Chicoutimi	9	16
☐ 93 Andy McCallum, Chicoutimi	9	16
☐ 94 Lou Smrke, Chicoutimi	9	16
☐ 95 J.P. Lamirande, Chicoutimi	9	16
☐ 96 Normand Dussault, Chicoutimi	9	16
☐ 97 Stan Smrke, Chicoutimi	12	20
☐ 98 Jack Bownass, Chicoutimi	12	20
☐ 99 Billy Arcand, Shawinigan Falls	9	16
☐ 100 Lyall Wiseman, Shawinigan Falls	9	16
☐ 101 Jack Hamilton, Shawinigan Falls	9	16
☐ 102 Bob Leger, Shawinigan Falls	9	16
☐ 103 Larry Regan, Shawinigan Falls	20	30
☐ 104 Erwin Grosse, Shawinigan Falls	9	16
☐ 105 Roger Bedard, Shawinigan Falls	9	16

		EX	EX-MT
□	106 Ted Hodgson, Shawinigan Falls	9	16
□	107 Dave Gatherum, Shawinigan Falls	9	25

1953 - 54 LA PATRIE PHOTOS

Prices are for photos with three stripes down right side intact. These colour newspaper photos measure 11" x 15 1/2".

	La Patrie	EX	EX-MT
□	Nov. 29 Sherman White,Chicoutimi	30	50
□	Dec. 13 Claude Provost, Mont.	25	40
□	Dec. 20 Gaetan Dessureault, Mont.	20	30
□	Dec. 27 Del Topoll, Frontenac Que.	20	30
□	Jan. 3 Claude Pronovost, RHC.	25	40
□	Jan. 10 Herve Lalonde, Trois Rivières	20	30
□	Jan. 17 Guy Rousseau, Frontenac Que.	20	30
□	Jan. 24 Jean Guy Gendron, Trois Rivières	25	40
□	Jan. 31 Claude Dufour, Trois Rivières	20	30
□	Feb. 7 Jacques Marcotte, Frontenac Que.	20	30
□	Feb. 14 Calum Mackay, Mont.	30	50

1953 - 54 PARKHURST

The card stock used for this set ages very poorly, the white face portion turning an uneven light brown across the card face. Beware of cards that do not have this discolouration. It would be unnatural for it not to appear. Cards measure 2 1/2" x 3/58".

		EX	EX-MT
	Complete Set (100 cards):	**3,750**	**6,200**
	Common Player:	**25**	**40**
	Parkies Album:	**60**	**110**

	Parkhurst	EX	EX-MT
□	1 Harry Lumley (G), Toro.	160	350
□	2 Sid Smith, Toro.	25	40
□	3 Gord Hannigan, Toro.	25	40
□	4 Bob Hassard, Toro. LC	25	40
□	5 Tod Sloan, Toro.	25	40
□	6 Léo Boivin, Toro.	28	45
□	7 Ted Kennedy, Toro.	55	85
□	8 Jim Thomson, Toro.	25	40
□	9 Ron Stewart, Toro.	25	40
□	**10 Eric Nesterenko, Toro. RC**	**50**	**80**
□	11 George Armstrong, Toro.	80	125
□	12 Harry Watson, Toro.	25	40
□	13 Tim Horton, Toro.	240	375
□	14 Fern Flaman, Toro.	30	50
□	15 Jim Morrison, Toro.	25	40
□	16 Bob Solinger, Toro. LC	25	40
□	17 Rudy Migay, Toro.	25	40
□	18 Dick Gamble, Mont.	25	40
□	19 Bert Olmstead, Mont.	30	50
□	**20 Eddie Mazur, Mont. RC**	**25**	**40**
□	21 Paul Meger, Mont.	25	40
□	22 Bud MacPherson, Mont.	25	40
□	23 Dollard St. Laurent, Mont.	25	40
□	24 Maurice Richard, Mont.	390	750
□	25 Gerry McNeil (G), Mont.	65	100
□	26 Doug Harvey, Mont.	150	250
□	**27 Jean Béliveau, Mont. RC**	**550**	**925**
□	28 Dickie Moore, Mont.	90	150
□	29 Bernie Geoffrion, Mont.	135	225
□	30 Lach & Richard, Mont.	165	275
□	31 Elmer Lach, Mont. LC	40	70
□	32 Emile (Butch) Bouchard, Mont.	30	50
□	33 Kenny Mosdell, Mont.	25	40
□	34 John McCormack, Mont.	25	40
□	35 Floyd Curry, Mont.	25	40
□	**36 Earl Reibel, Mont. RC, Detr.**	**25**	**40**
□	37 Al Arbour, Mont., Err. (Bill Dineen)	40	70
□	38 Bill Dineen, Mont., Err. (Al Arbour)	75	125
□	39 Vic Stasiuk, Mont.	25	40
□	40 Red Kelly, Mont.	65	110
□	41 Marcel Pronovost, Mont.	30	50
□	42 Metro Prystai, Mont.	25	40
□	43 Tony Leswick, Mont.	25	40
□	44 Marty Pavelich, Mont.	25	40
□	45 Benny Woit, Mont.	25	40
□	46 Terry Sawchuk (G), Mont.	275	475
□	47 Alex Delvecchio, Mont.	75	125
□	48 Glen Skov, Mont.	25	40
□	49 Bob Goldham, Mont.	25	40
□	50 Gordie Howe, Mont.	550	925
□	51 Johnny Wilson, Mont.	25	40
□	52 Ted Lindsay, Mont.	65	110
□	**53 Gump Worsley (G), NYRa. RC**	**310**	**500**
□	54 Jack Evans, NYRa.	25	40
□	55 Max Bentley, NYRa. LC	30	50
□	**56 Andy Bathgate, NYRa. RC**	**110**	**175**
□	**57 Harry Howell, NYRa. RC**	**110**	**175**
□	58 Hyman Buller, NYRa. LC	25	40
□	59 Chuck Rayner (G), NYRa. LC	35	55
□	60 Jack Stoddard, NYRa. LC	25	40
□	61 Eddie Kullman, NYRa. LC	25	40
□	62 Nick Mickoski, NYRa.	25	40
□	63 Paul Ronty, NYRa.	25	40
□	64 Allan Stanley, NYRa.	45	75
□	65 Leo Reise, NYRa.	25	40
□	**66 Aldo Guidolin, NYRa. RC/LC**	**35**	**60**
□	67 Wally Hergesheimer, NYRa.	25	40
□	68 Don Raleigh, NYRa.	25	40
□	69 Jim Peters, Chic. LC	25	40
□	70 Pete Conacher, Chic.	25	40
□	71 Fred Hucul, Chic. LC	25	40
□	72 Lidio Fogolin, Chic.	25	40
□	73 Larry Zeidel, Chic.	25	40
□	74 Larry Wilson, Chic.	25	40
□	75 Gus Bodnar, Chic.	25	40
□	76 Bill Gadsby, Chic.	30	50
□	77 Jim McFadden, Chic. LC	25	40
□	78 Al Dewsbury, Chic.	25	40
□	79 Clare Raglan, Chic. LC	25	40
□	80 Bill Mosienko, Chic.	35	55
□	81 Gus Mortson, Chic.	25	40
□	82 Al Rollins (G), Chic.	30	50
□	83 George Gee, Chic.	25	40
□	84 Gerald Couture, Chic. LC	25	40
□	85 Dave Creighton, Bost.	25	40
□	86 Jim Henry (G), Bost.	30	50
□	87 Hal Laycoe, Bost.	25	40
□	88 Johnny Peirson, Bost., Err. (Pierson)	25	40
□	89 Real Chevrefils, Bost.	25	40
□	90 Ed Sandford, Bost.	25	40
□	91 F. Mackell, Bost. (w/ biography on back)	30	50
□	91 F.Mackell, Bost. (w/o biography on back)	30	50
□	92 Milt Schmidt, Bost.	45	70
□	93 Léo Labine, Bost.	25	40
□	94 Joe Klukay, Bost.	25	40
□	95 Warren Godfrey, Bost.	25	40
□	96 Woody Dumart, Bost. LC	30	55
□	**97 Frank Martin, Bost. RC**	**25**	**40**
□	**98 Jerry Toppazzini, Bost. RC**	**25**	**40**
□	99 Cal Gardner, Bost.	25	40
□	100 Bill Quackenbush, Bost.	55	110

1954 WEEKEND PHOTOS

These newsprint colour photos measure 5 1/2" x 6 1/2".These photos appeared in the Star Weekend Magazine between 1954 and 1967 to help boost sales. No photos appeared during 1964-65. Pictures within intact magazines valued at about 50% more.

	Toronto Star	EX	EX-MT
□	V4,n2 Gordie Howe, Detr.	30	50
□	V4,n3 Maurice Richard, Mont.	30	50
□	V4,n4 Ted Kennedy, Toro.	12	20
□	V4,n5 Red Kelly. Detr.	9	16
□	V4,n6 Elmer Lach, Mont.	12	20
□	V4,n7 Gus Mortson, Chic.	7	12
□	V4,n8 Ted Lindsay, Detr.	12	20
□	V4,n9 Milt Schmidt, Bost.	12	20
□	V4,n10 Ed Sandford, Bost.	7	12
□	V4,n11 Wally Hergesheimer, NYRa.	7	12
□	V4,n13 Butch Bouchard, Mont.	9	16

1954 - 55 PARKHURST

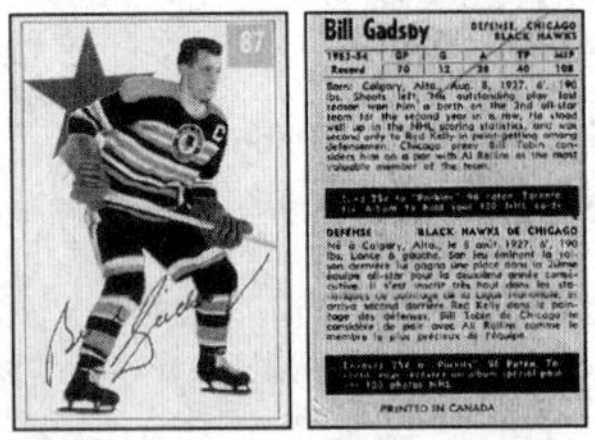

"Lucky Premium" versions parallel cards 1-88. Pricing for both versions is the same. Cards measure 2 1/2" x 3 5/8".

		EX	EX-MT
	Complete Set (100 cards):	**3,600**	**5,800**
	Common Player:	**20**	**30**
	Parkies Album:	**60**	**110**

	Parkhurst	EX	EX-MT
□ □	1 Gerry McNeil (G), Mont.	60	125
□ □	2 Dickie Moore, Mont.	60	100
□ □	3 Jean Béliveau, Mont.	300	475
□ □	4 Eddie Mazur, Mont. LC	20	30
□ □	5 Bert Olmstead, Mont.	30	50
□ □	6 Emile (Butch) Bouchard, Mont.	25	40
□ □	7 Maurice Richard, Mont.	330	600
□ □	8 Bernie Geoffrion, Mont.	90	150
□ □	9 John McCormack, Mont. LC	20	30
□ □	10 Tom Johnson, Mont.	30	45
□ □	11 Calum MacKay, Mont.	20	30
□ □	12 Kenny Mosdell, Mont.	20	30
□ □	13 Paul Masnick, Mont. LC	20	30
□ □	14 Doug Harvey, Mont.	90	150
□ □	15 Floyd Curry, Mont.	20	30
□ □	16 Harry Lumley (G), Toro.	40	65
□ □	17 Harry Watson, Toro. LC	20	30
□ □	18 Jim Morrison, Toro.	20	30
□ □	19 Eric Nesterenko, Toro.	20	30
□ □	20 Fernie Flaman, Toro.	25	40
□ □	21 Rudy Migay, Toro.	20	30
□ □	22 Sid Smith, Toro.	20	30
□ □	23 Ron Stewart, Toro.	20	30
□ □	24 George Armstrong, Toro.	65	100
□ □	**25 Earl Balfour, Toro. RC**	**20**	**30**
□ □	26 Léo Boivin, Toro.	20	30
□ □	27 Gord Hannigan, Toro. LC	20	30
□ □	**28 Bob Bailey, Toro. RC**	**15**	**30**
□ □	29 Ted Kennedy, Toro.	40	65
□ □	30 Tod Sloan, Toro.	20	30
□ □	31 Tim Horton, Toro.	180	300
□ □	32 Jim Thomson, Toro., Err. (Thompson)	20	30
□ □	33 Terry Sawchuk (G), Detr.	210	325

◆ A graded PSA-8 copy of this card recently closed at $330 U.S. ($379 U.S. with the buyer's premium) in the May 17, 2002 Lelands Vintage Sports Auction. That closing amount is approximately $510 Cdn.

		EX	EX-MT
□ □	34 Marcel Pronovost, Detr.	30	45
□ □	35 Metro Prystai, Detr. LC	20	30
□ □	36 Alex Delvecchio, Detr.	65	100
□ □	37 Earl Reibel, Detr.	20	30
□ □	38 Benny Woit, Detr. LC	20	30
□ □	39 Bob Goldham, Detr. LC	20	30
□ □	40 Glen Skov, Detr.	20	30
□ □	41 Gordie Howe, Detr.	450	750
□ □	42 Red Kelly, Detr.	55	85
□ □	43 Marty Pavelich, Detr. LC	20	30
□ □	44 Johnny Wilson, Detr.	20	30
□ □	45 Tony Leswick, Detr. LC	20	30
□ □	46 Ted Lindsay, Detr.	55	85
□ □	**47 Keith Allen, Detr. RC/LC**	**25**	**50**
□ □	**48 Bill Dineen, Detr. RC**	**20**	**30**
□ □	49 Jim Henry (G), Bost. LC	25	40
□ □	50 Fleming Mackell, Bost.	20	30
□ □	51 Bill Quackenbush, Bost. LC	25	40
□ □	52 Hal Laycoe, Bost. LC	20	30
□ □	53 Cal Gardner, Bost. LC	20	30
□ □	54 Joe Klukay, Bost.	20	30
□ □	55 Bob Armstrong, Bost.	20	30
□ □	56 Warren Godfrey, Bost.	20	30
□ □	**57 Doug Mohns, Bost. RC**	**30**	**50**
□ □	58 Dave Creighton, Bost.	20	30
□ □	59 Milt Schmidt, Bost. LC	30	45
□ □	60 Johnny Peirson, Bost. LC	20	30
□ □	61 Léo Labine, Bost.	20	30
□ □	62 Gus Bodnar, Bost. LC	20	30
□ □	63 Real Chevrefils, Bost.	20	30
□ □	64 Ed Sandford, Bost. LC	20	30
□ □	**65 Johnny Bower (G), NYRa. RC, Err. (Bowers)**	**275**	**475**

◆ A graded PSA-8 copy of this rookie card recently closed at $439 U.S. ($504 U.S. with the buyer's premium) in the May 17, 2002 Lelands Vintage Sports Auction. That closing amount is approximately $680 Cdn.

		EX	EX-MT
□ □	**66 Paul Ronty, NYRa. LC**	**20**	**30**
□ □	67 Leo Reise, NYRa. LC	20	30
□ □	68 Don Raleigh, NYRa. LC	20	30
□ □	**69 Bob Chrystal, NYRa. RC/LC**	**20**	**40**
□ □	70 Harry Howell, NYRa.	60	85
□ □	71 Wally Hergesheimer, NYRa.	20	30
□ □	72 Jack Evans, NYRa.	20	30
□ □	**73 Camille Henry, NYRa. RC**	**30**	**45**
□ □	**74 Dean Prentice, NYRa. RC**	**30**	**45**
□ □	75 Nick Mickoski, NYRa.	20	30
□ □	**76 Ron Murphy, NYRa. RC**	**20**	**30**
□ □	77 Al Rollins (G), Chic. LC	25	40
□ □	78 Al Dewsbury, Chic. LC	20	30
□ □	**79 Lou Jankowski, Chic. RC/LC**	**25**	**40**
□ □	80 George Gee, Chic. LC	20	30
□ □	81 Gus Mortson, Chic.	20	30
□ □	**82 Fred Saskamoose, Chic. RC/LC**	**45**	**75**
□ □	**83 Ike Hildebrand, Chic. RC/LC**	**25**	**40**
□ □	84 Lidio Fogolin, Chic. LC	20	30
□ □	85 Larry Wilson, Chic. LC	20	30
□ □	86 Pete Conacher, Chic.	20	30
□ □	87 Bill Gadsby, Chic.	30	45
□ □	88 Jack McIntyre, Chic.	20	30
□	89 Busher Curry Goes Up-And-Over	20	30
□	90 Delvecchio Finds Leaf Defense Hard...	30	45
□	91 The Battle of the All-Stars	30	45
□	92 Lum Stops Howe With Help of Stewart's Stick	90	150
□	93 Netminder's Nightmare	20	30
□	94 Meger Goes Down And Under	20	30
□	95 Harvey Takes a Nose-Dive	40	70
□	96 Terry Boots Out Teeder's Blast	65	110
□	97 Dutch Reibel Tests Habs' Rookie "Mr. Zero"	100	150
□	98 Plante Protects Against Slippery Sloan	100	150
□	99 Placid Plante Foils Tireless Teeder	100	150
□	100 Sawchuk Stops Boom Boom	100	200

1954 - 55 TOPPS

Cards measure 2 5/8" x 3 3/4".

		EX	EX-MT
	Complete Set (60 cards):	**4,000**	**6,200**
	Common Player:	**30**	**50**

	Topps	EX	EX-MT
□	1 Dick Gamble, Chic. LC	85	180
□	**2 Bob Chrystal, NYRa. RC/LC**	**30**	**50**
□	3 Harry Howell, NYRa.	90	140
□	4 Johnny Wilson, Detr.	30	50
□	5 Red Kelly, Detr.	110	180
□	6 Real Chevrefils, Bost.	30	50
□	7 Bob Armstrong, Bost.	30	50
□	8 Gordie Howe, Detr.	1,600	2,600

◆ A graded PSA-9 copy of the Gordie Howe card closed at $10,101 U.S. (approx. $13,650 Cdn.) in a May 11-18, 2003 Internet auction at eBay.

		EX	EX-MT
□	9 Benny Woit, Detr. LC	30	50
□	10 Gump Worsley (G), NYRa.	180	290
□	11 Andy Bathgate, NYRa.	90	140
□	**12 Bucky Hollingworth, Chic. RC/LC**	**35**	**55**
□	13 Ray Timgren, Chic. LC	30	50
□	14 Jack Evans, NYRa.	30	50
□	15 Paul Ronty, NYRa. LC	30	50
□	16 Glen Skov, Detr.	30	50
□	17 Gus Mortson, Chic.	30	50
□	**18 Doug Mohns, Bost. RC**	**75**	**125**
□	19 Léo Labine, Bost.	30	50
□	20 Bill Gadsby, Chic.	60	90
□	21 Jerry Toppazzini, Chic.	30	50
□	22 Wally Hergesheimer, NYRa.	30	50
□	23 Danny Lewicki, NYRa.	30	50
□	24 Metro Prystai, Chic. LC	30	50
□	25 Fern Flaman, Bost.	45	75
□	26 Al Rollins (G), Chic. LC	60	90
□	27 Marcel Pronovost, Detr.	45	75
□	**28 Lou Jankowski, Chic. RC/LC**	**35**	**55**
□	29 Nick Mickoski, NYRa.	30	50
□	30 Frank Martin, Chic. LC	30	50
□	31 Lorne Ferguson, Bost.	30	50
□	**32 Camille Henry, NYRa. RC**	**45**	**75**
□	33 Pete Conacher, Chic.	30	50
□	34 Marty Pavelich, Detr. LC	30	50
□	**35 Don McKenney, Bost. RC**	**35**	**65**
□	36 Fleming Mackell, Bost.	30	50
□	37 Jim Henry (G), Bost. LC	45	75
□	38 Hal Laycoe, Bost. LC	30	50
□	39 Alex Delvecchio, Detr.	110	180
□	40 Larry Wilson, Chic. LC	30	50
□	41 Allan Stanley, NYRa.	75	125
□	**42 Red Sullivan, Chic. RC**	**30**	**50**
□	43 Jack McIntyre, Chic.	30	50
□	**44 Ivan Irwin, NYRa. RC/LC**	**35**	**55**
□	45 Tony Leswick, Detr. LC	30	50
□	46 Bob Goldham, Detr. LC	35	60
□	47 Cal Gardner, Bost. LC	30	50
□	48 Ed Sandford, Bost. LC	30	50
□	49 Bill Quackenbush, Bost. LC	50	85
□	50 Warren Godfrey, Bost.	30	50
□	51 Ted Lindsay, Detr.	110	175
□	52 Earl Reibel, Detr.	30	50
□	53 Don Raleigh, NYRa. LC	30	50
□	54 Bill Mosienko, Chic. LC	55	85

55 Larry Popein, NYRa. RC	**30**	**50**
56 Edgar Laprade, NYRa. LC	35	60
57 Bill Dineen, Detr.	30	50
58 Terry Sawchuk (G), Detr.	600	900
59 Marcel Bonin, Detr. RC	**30**	**50**
60 Milt Schmidt, Bost. LC	120	250

1954 - 55 TORONTO STAR PHOTOS

Other singles exist.

Toronto Star	EX	EX-MT
Mar. 26 Toronto Maple Leafs Team Photo	15	25
Apr. 2 Montreal and Detroit (Double page)	20	30

1955 WEEKEND PHOTOS

These newsprint colour photos measure 5 1/2" x 6 1/2". These photos appeared in the Weekend Magazine between 1954 and 1967 to help boost sales.

Toronto Star	EX	EX-MT
V5,n2 Harry Lumley (G), Toro.	12	20
V5 n3 Fleming Mackell, Bost.	7	12
V5,n4 Bernie Geoffrion, Mont.	18	30
V5,n5 Danny Lewicki, NYRa.	7	12
V5,n6 Harry Watson, Chic.	10	18
V5,n7 Ken Mosdel, Mont.	7	12
V5,n8 Earl Reibel, Detr.	7	12
V5,n9 Bill Quackenbush, Bost.	9	16
V5,n10 Bill Gadsby, NYRa.	9	16
V5,n11 Jimmy Thomson, Toro.	7	12

1955 - 56 NABISCO

These cards measure 1 15/16" x 2 7/8". Other singles exist.

Shredded Wheat / ACC # FC-26-3	EX	EX-MT
62 Ted Reeve, Stick Handling	12	20

1955 - 56 PARKHURST

These cards measure 2 1/2" x 3 9/16".

Complete Set (79 cards):	**3,300**	**5,400**
Common Player:	**20**	**30**
Parkhurst	**EX**	**EX-MT**
1 Harry Lumley (G), Toro. LC	220	425
2 Sid Smith, Toro.	15	25
3 Tim Horton, Toro.	175	300
4 George Armstrong, Toro.	60	95
5 Ron Stewart, Toro.	15	25
6 Joe Klukay, Toro. LC	15	25
7 Marc Reaume, Toro. RC	**15**	**25**
8 Jim Morrison, Toro.	15	25
9 Parker MacDonald, Toro. RC	**15**	**25**
10 Tod Sloan, Toro.	15	25
11 Jim Thomson, Toro.	15	25
12 Rudy Migay, Toro.	15	25
13 Brian Cullen, Toro. RC	**15**	**25**
14 Hugh Bolton, Toro.	15	25
15 Eric Nesterenko, Toro.	15	25
16 Larry Cahan, Toro. RC	**15**	**25**
17 Willie Marshall, Toro. RC	**15**	**25**
18 Dick Duff, Toro. RC	**60**	**95**
19 Jack Caffery, Toro. RC	**15**	**25**
20 Billy Harris, Toro. RC	**25**	**40**
21 Lorne Chabot (G), Toro.	22	35
22 Harvey Jackson, Toro.	40	65
23 Turk Broda (G), Toro.	75	125
24 Joe Primeau, Toro.	30	45
25 Gordie Drillon, Toro.	22	35
26 Charlie Conacher, Toro.	30	45
27 Sweeney Schriner, Toro.	22	35
28 Syl Apps Sr., Toro.	30	45
29 Ted Kennedy, Toro.	40	65
30 Ace Bailey, Toro.	45	75
31 Babe Pratt, Toro.	25	40
32 Harold Cotton, Toro.	22	35
33 Francis (King) Clancy, Toro., Coach	75	125
34 Hap Day, Toro., Manager	22	35
35 Don Marshall, Mont. RC	**30**	**50**
36 Jackie LeClair, Mont. RC/LC	**20**	**30**
37 Maurice Richard, Mont.	325	500
38 Dickie Moore, Mont.	65	100
39 Kenny Mosdell, Mont. LC	15	25
40 Floyd Curry, Mont.	15	25
41 Calum MacKay, Mont. LC	15	25
42 Bert Olmstead, Mont.	25	40
43 Bernie Geoffrion, Mont.	95	175

◆ A graded PSA-9 copy of this card recently closed at $399 U.S. ($458 U.S. with the buyer's premium) in the May 17, 2002 Lelands Vintage Sports Auction. That closing amount is approximately $615 Cdn.

44 Jean Béliveau, Mont.	225	350
45 Doug Harvey, Mont.	90	150
46 Emile (Butch) Bouchard, Mont. LC	25	40
47 Bud MacPherson, Mont. LC	15	25
48 Dollard St. Laurent, Mont.	15	25
49 Tom Johnson, Mont.	30	45
50 Jacques Plante (G), Mont. RC	**700**	**1,100**
51 Paul Meger, Mont. LC	15	25
52 Gerry McNeil (G), Mont. LC	35	55
53 Jean-Guy Talbot, Mont. RC	**30**	**45**
54 Bob Turner, Mont. RC	**15**	**25**
55 Edouard Lalonde, Mont.	40	65
56 Georges Vézina (G), Mont.	90	145
57 Howie Morenz, Mont.	75	125
58 Aurèle Joliat, Mont.	45	75
59 George Hainsworth (G), Mont.	45	75
60 Sylvio Mantha, Mont.	25	40
61 Albert Leduc, Mont.	22	35
62 Babe Siebert, Mont., Err. (Seibert)	25	40
63 Bill Durnan (G), Mont.	45	75
64 Ken Reardon, Mont.	35	55
65 Johnny Gagnon, Mont.	22	35
66 Billy Reay, Mont.	22	35
67 Toe Blake, Coach, Mont.	40	65
68 Frank Selke, Manager, Mont.	30	45
69 Hugh Beats Hodge	25	40
70 Lum Stops Boom-Boom	45	75
71 Plante Is Protected	60	100
72 Rocket Roars Through	60	100
73 Richard Tests Lumley	65	110
74 Béliveau Bats Puck	55	85
75 Leaf Speedster Attack	60	100
76 Curry Scores Again	25	40
77 Jammed On The Boards	60	100
78 The Montréal Forum	185	325
79 Maple Leaf Gardens	200	350

1955 - 56 PARKIE / QUAKER OATS

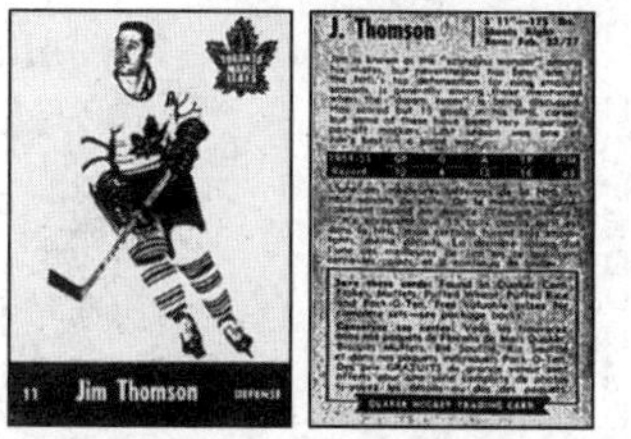

These cards measure 2 1/2" x 3 9/16". Quaker Oats issued a set virtually identical to the Parkhurst set of the same year. The only difference is the distinctive green backs. A Quaker Oats advertisement is in place of the Did You Know tip on the back of the card. Short prints are marked with an asterisk (*).

Parkhurst Quaker Oats	EX	EX-MT
1 Harry Lumley (G), Toro. LC (*)		
2 Sid Smith, Toro.	50	100
3 Tim Horton, Toro.	500	1,00
4 George Armstrong, Toro.	125	250
5 Ron Stewart, Toro.	50	100
6 Joe Klukay, Toro. LC	50	100
7 Marc Reaume, Toro. RC	**50**	**100**
8 Jim Morrison, Toro.	50	100
9 Parker MacDonald, Toro. RC	**50**	**100**
10 Tod Sloan, Toro.	50	100
11 Jim Thomson, Toro.	50	100
12 Rudy Migay, Toro.	50	100
13 Brian Cullen, Toro. RC	**50**	**100**
14 Hugh Bolton, Toro.	50	100
15 Eric Nesterenko, Toro.	50	100
16 Larry Cahan, Toro. RC	**50**	**100**
17 Willie Marshall, Toro. RC	**50**	**100**
18 Dick Duff, Toro. RC	**115**	**225**
19 Jack Caffery, Toro. RC	**50**	**100**
20 Billy Harris, Toro. RC	**80**	**160**
21 Lorne Chabot (G), Toro.	75	150
22 Harvey Jackson, Toro.	75	150
23 Turk Broda (G), Toro.	140	275
24 Joe Primeau, Toro.	75	150
25 Gordie Drillon, Toro.	75	150
26 Charlie Conacher, Toro.	75	150
27 Sweeny Schriner, Toro.	75	150
28 Syl Apps, Sr., Toro.	75	150
29 Ted Kennedy, Toro.	90	175
30 Ace Bailey, Toro.	100	200
31 Babe Pratt, Toro.	65	125
32 Baldy Cotton, Toro.	65	125
33 Francis (King) Clancy, Coach, Toro. (*)		
34 Hap Day, Manager, Toro.	65	125
35 Don Marshall, Mont. RC	**75**	**150**
36 Jackie Leclair, Mont. RC/LC	**50**	**100**
37 Maurice Richard, Mont. (*)		
38 Dickie Moore, Mont.	125	250
39 Kenny Mosdell, Mont. LC	50	100
40 Floyd Curry, Mont.	50	100
41 Calum MacKay, Mont. LC	50	100
42 Bert Olmstead, Mont.	75	150
43 Bernie Geoffrion, Mont.	225	450
44 Jean Béliveau, Mont.	600	1,200
45 Doug Harvey, Mont.	190	375
46 Emile (Butch) Bouchard, Mont. LC	50	100
47 Bud MacPherson, Mont. LC	50	100
48 Dollard St. Laurent, Mont.	50	100
49 Tom Johnson, Mont.	75	150
50 Jacques Plante (G), Mont. RC	**1,750**	**3,500**
51 Paul Meger, Mont.	50	100
52 Gerry McNeil (G), Mont. LC	100	200
53 Jean-Guy Talbot, Mont. RC	**90**	**175**
54 Bob Turner, Mont. RC	**50**	**100**
55 Edouard Lalonde, Mont.	100	200
56 Georges Vézina (G), Mont.	190	375
57 Howie Morenz, Mont.	215	425
58 Aurèle Joliat, Mont.	100	200
59 George Hainsworth (G), Mont.	125	250
60 Sylvio Mantha, Mont.	75	150
61 Albert Leduc, Mont.	75	150
62 Babe Siebert, Mont., Err. (Seibert)	75	150
63 Bill Durnan (G), Mont. RC/LC	**100**	**200**
64 Ken Reardon, Mont.	75	150
65 Johnny Gagnon, Mont.	75	150
66 Billy Reay, Mont.	75	150
67 Toe Blake, Coach, Mont.	85	175
68 Frank Selke, Manager, Mont.	75	150
69 Hugh Beats Hodge	75	150
70 Lum Stops Boom-Boom	125	250
71 Plante Is Protected	215	425
72 Rocket Roars Through	215	425
73 Richard Tests Lumley	215	425
74 Béliveau Bats Puck	150	300
75 Leaf Speedster Attack	215	425
76 Curry Scores Again	75	150
77 Jammed On The Boards	175	350
78 The Montréal Forum	500	1,000
79 Maple Leaf Gardens	550	1,200

1955 - 56 TORONTO STAR PHOTOS

This is a colour newspaper photo.

Toronto Star	EX	EX-MT
Dec. 10 Toronto Team Photo	15	25
Feb. 25 Kitchener-Waterloo Olympic Team	9	15
Mar. 10 Chicago Team Photo	15	25
Mar. 24 NY Rangers Team Photo	15	25

1956 ADVENTURE GUM

This standard-size card is the only hockey image in the 100-card set.

ACC # R749	EX	EX-MT
63 Gordie Howe/ Chuck Rayner (G)	90	150

1956 - 57 TORONTO STAR PHOTOS

This is a colour newspaper photo.

Toronto Star	EX	EX-MT
Jan. 5 Montréal Team Photo	15.00	25.00

1957 - 58 PARKHURST

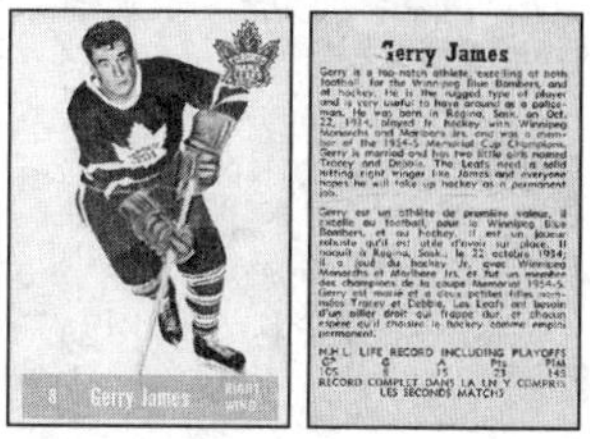

These cards measure 2 7/16" x 3 5/8".

Complete Set (50 cards):	**2,300**	**3,600**
Montréal Canadiens	**EX**	**EX-MT**
1 Doug Harvey, Mont.	160	300
2 Bernie Geoffrion, Mont.	90	150
3 Jean Béliveau, Mont.	250	350
4 Henri Richard, Mont. RC	**450**	**725**

◆ A graded PSA-8 copy of this card recently closed at $707 U.S. ($813 U.S. with the buyer's premium) in the May 17, 2002 Lelands Vintage Sports Auction. That closing amount is approximately $1,100 Cdn.

5 Maurice Richard, Mont.	325	525
6 Tom Johnson, Mont.	22	35
7 André Pronovost, Mont. RC	**15**	**25**
8 Don Marshall, Mont.	22	35
9 Jean-Guy Talbot, Mont.	15	25
10 Dollard St. Laurent, Mont.	15	25
11 Phil Goyette, Mont. RC	**30**	**45**
12 Claude Provost, Mont. RC	**30**	**50**
13 Bob Turner, Mont.	15	25
14 Dickie Moore, Mont.	45	75
15 Jacques Plante (G), Mont.	310	500

◆ A graded PSA-9 copy of this card recently closed at $1,072 U.S. ($1,232 U.S. with the buyer's premium) in the May 17, 2002 Lelands Vintage Sports Auction. That closing amount is approximately $1,660 Cdn.

16 Toe Blake, Coach, Mont.	30	50
17 Charlie Hodge (G), Mont. RC	**65**	**110**
18 Marcel Bonin, Mont.	15	25
19 Bert Olmstead, Mont.	22	35
20 Floyd Curry, Mont. LC	15	25
21 Canadiens on Guard	30	50
22 Barry Cullen Scores	20	30
23 Puck and Sticks High	30	50
24 Geoffrion Sidesteps Chadwick	35	55
25 Olmstead Beats Chadwick	30	50
Toronto Maple Leafs	**EX**	**EX-MT**
1 George Armstrong, Toro.	65	100
2 Ed Chadwick (G), Toro. RC	**85**	**140**
3 Dick Duff, Toro.	40	65
4 Bob Pulford, Toro. RC	**75**	**125**
5 Tod Sloan, Toro.	30	45
6 Rudy Migay, Toro. LC	15	25
7 Ron Stewart, Toro.	15	25
8 Gerry James, Toro. RC	**22**	**35**
9 Brian Cullen, Toro.	15	25
10 Sid Smith, Toro. LC	15	25
11 Jim Morrison, Toro.	15	25
12 Marc Réaume, Toro.	15	25
13 Hugh Bolton, Toro. LC	15	25
14 Pete Conacher, Toro. LC	15	25
15 Billy Harris, Toro.	15	25
16 Mike Nykoluk, Toro. RC/LC	**20**	**30**
17 Frank Mahovlich, Toro. RC	**375**	**600**
18 Kenny Girard, Toro. RC/LC	**20**	**30**
19 Al MacNeil, Toro. RC, Err. (McNeil)	**15**	**25**
20 Bob Baun, Toro. RC	**80**	**140**
21 Barry Cullen, Toro. RC	**15**	**25**
22 Tim Horton, Toro.	145	250
23 Gary Collins, Toro. RC/LC	**20**	**30**
24 Gary Aldcorn, Toro. RC	**15**	**25**
25 Billy Reay, Coach, Toro.	30	50

1957 - 58 TOPPS

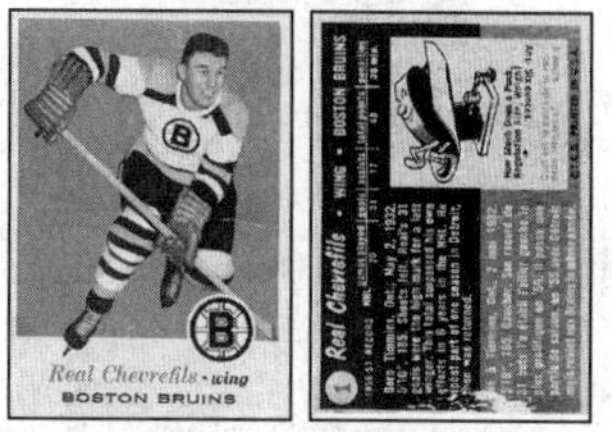

These cards measure the standard 2 1/2" x 3 1/2".

Complete Set (66 cards):	**1,750**	**2,800**

Topps	EX	EX-MT
□ 1 Real Chevrefils, Bost. LC	30	65
□ **2 Jack Bionda, Bost. RC/LC**	**20**	**30**
□ 3 Bob Armstrong, Bost.	15	25
□ 4 Fern Flaman, Bost.	20	35
□ 5 Jerry Toppazzini, Bost.	15	25
□ **6 Larry Regan, Bost. RC**	**15**	**25**
□ **7 Bronco Horvath, Bost. RC**	**18**	**28**
□ 8 Jack Caffery, Bost. LC	15	25
□ 9 Léo Labine, Bost.	15	25
□ **10 John Bucyk, Bost. RC**	**200**	**300**
□ 11 Vic Stasiuk, Bost.	15	25
□ 12 Doug Mohns, Bost.	18	28
□ 13 Don McKenney, Bost.	18	28
□ **14 Don Simmons (G), Bost. RC**	**20**	**35**
□ 15 Allan Stanley, Bost.	25	45
□ 16 Fleming Mackell, Bost.	15	25
□ **17 Larry Hillman, Bost. RC**	**18**	**28**
□ 18 Léo Boivin, Bost.	18	28
□ 19 Bob Bailey, Chic. LC	15	25
□ **20 Glenn Hall (G), Chic. RC**	**300**	**475**
□ 21 Ted Lindsay, Chic.	40	65
□ **22 Pierre Pilote, Chic. RC**	**115**	**175**
□ 23 Jim Thomson, Chic. LC	15	25
□ 24 Eric Nesterenko, Chic.	18	28
□ 25 Gus Mortson, Chic.	15	25
□ **26 Ed Litzenberger, Chic. RC**	**20**	**30**
□ **27 Elmer Vasko, Chic. RC**	**25**	**40**
□ 28 Jack McIntyre, Chic.	15	25
□ 29 Ron Murphy, Chic.	15	25
□ 30 Glen Skov, Chic.	15	25
□ **31 Hec Lalande, Chic. RC/LC**	**20**	**30**
□ 32 Nick Mickoski, Chic.	15	25
□ 33 Wally Hergesheimer, Chic. LC	15	25
□ 34 Alex Delvecchio, Detr.	40	65
□ 35 Terry Sawchuk (G), Detr., Err. (Sawchuck)	135	245
□ **36 Guyle Fielder, Detr. RC/LC**	**20**	**30**
□ **37 Tom McCarthy, Detr. RC/LC**	**20**	**30**
□ 38 Al Arbour, Detr.	35	55
□ **39 Billy Dea, Detr. RC**	**15**	**25**
□ 40 Lorne Ferguson, Detr.	15	25
□ 41 Warren Godfrey, Detr.	15	25
□ 42 Gordie Howe, Detr.	350	600
□ 43 Marcel Pronovost, Detr.	18	28
□ **44 Billy McNeill, Detr. RC**	**18**	**28**
□ 45 Earl Reibel, Detr.	15	25
□ **46 Norm Ullman, Detr. RC**	**165**	**275**
□ 47 Johnny Wilson, Detr.	15	25
□ 48 Red Kelly, Detr.	40	65
□ 49 Bill Dineen, Detr. LC	15	25
□ **50 Forbes Kennedy, Detr. RC**	**18**	**28**
□ 51 Harry Howell, NYRa.	30	50
□ **52 Jean-Guy Gendron, NYRa. RC**	**18**	**28**
□ 53 Gump Worsley (G), NYRa.	90	150
□ 54 Larry Popein, NYRa.	15	25
□ 55 Jack Evans, NYRa.	15	25
□ 56 Red Sullivan, NYRa.	15	25
□ **57 Gerry Foley, NYRa. RC/LC**	**20**	**30**
□ **58 Andy Hebenton, NYRa. RC**	**15**	**25**
□ 59 Larry Cahan, NYRa.	15	25
□ 60 Andy Bathgate, NYRa.	30	50
□ 61 Danny Lewicki, NYRa.	15	25
□ 62 Dean Prentice, NYRa.	18	28
□ 63 Camille Henry, NYRa.	18	28
□ **64 Louie Fontinato, NYRa. RC**	**30**	**50**
□ 65 Bill Gadsby, NYRa.	25	40
□ 66 Dave Creighton, NYRa.	30	55

1957 - 58 TORONTO STAR PHOTOS

These are colour newspaper photos.

Toronto Star	EX	EX-MT
□ Nov. 2 E. Chadwick (G)/ T. Horton	20	30
□ Nov. 9 S. Smith/ B. Pulford	9	15
□ Nov. 16 D. Duff/ J. Morrison	7	12
□ Nov. 23 G. Mortson/ J. Thompson	7	12
□ Nov. 30 T. Lindsay/ E. Nesterenko	12	20
□ Dec. 7 Toronto Maple Leafs Team Photo	15	25
□ Dec. 14 M. Richard/ H. Richard	30	55
□ Dec. 21 B. Geoffrion/ D. Harvey	22	35
□ Dec. 28 A. Hebenton/ L. Worsley (G)	18	28
□ Jan. 4 Montréal Canadiens Team Photo	15	25
□ Jan. 11 F. Flaman/ D. Simmons (G)	11	18
□ Jan. 18 B. Gadsby/ C. Henry	9	15
□ Jan. 25 D. McKenney/ R. Chevrefils	7	12
□ Feb. 1 G. Howe/ R. Kelly	30	55
□ Feb. 8 Detroit Red Wings Team Photo	15	25
□ Feb. 15 J. Plante/ J. Béliveau	30	55
□ Feb. 22 New York Rangers Team Photo	15	25
□ Mar. 1 Whitby Dunlops Team Photo	9	15
□ Mar. 8 A. Delvecchio/ T. Sawchuk (G)	30	55
□ Mar. 15 G. Armstrong/ B. Cullen	10	18
□ Mar. 22 R. Stewart/ F. Mahovlich	20	30

1958 - 59 PARKHURST

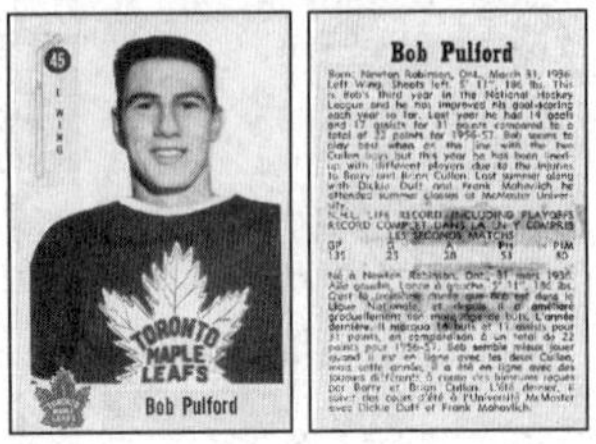

"For some reason, I remember the gum was so nice, so sweet that year. The cards themselves were very clean, a white background with a stick on one side and the player name at the bottom... I used to buy them in a restaurant." – Dave Pike, Dave's Sports Collectibles, Woodstock, Ontario.

These cards measure 2 7/16" x 3 5/8".

Complete Set (50 cards):	1,500	2,600
Parkhurst	EX	EX-MT
□ 1 Pulford Comes Close	50	85
□ 2 Henri Richard, Mont.	175	275
□ 3 André Pronovost, Mont.	15	25
□ 4 Billy Harris, Toro.	15	25
□ **5 Al Langlois, Mont. RC**	**15**	**25**
□ **6 Noel Price, Toro. RC**	**15**	**25**
□ 7 Armstrong Breaks Through	25	40
□ 8 Dickie Moore, Mont.	35	55
□ 9 Toe Blake, Coach, Mont.	25	40
□ 10 Tom Johnson, Mont.	20	30
□ 11 An Object of Interest	40	70
□ 12 Ed Chadwick (G), Toro.	30	50
□ **13 Bob Nevin, Toro. RC**	**25**	**40**
□ 14 Ron Stewart, Toro.	15	25
□ 15 Bob Baun, Toro.	30	50
□ **16 Ralph Backstrom, Mont. RC**	**40**	**65**
□ 17 Charlie Hodge (G), Mont.	30	50
□ 18 Gary Aldcorn, Toro.	15	25
□ 19 Willie Marshall, Toro. LC	15	25
□ 20 Marc Reaume, Toro.	15	25
□ 21 All Eyes On The Puck	45	70
□ 22 Jacques Plante (G), Mont.	225	350
□ 23 Allan Stanley, Toro., Err. (Alan/Allen)	25	40
□ **24 Ian Cushenan, Mont. RC**	**15**	**25**
□ 25 Billy Reay, Coach, Toro.	15	25
□ 26 Plante Catches A Shot	45	70
□ 27 Bert Olmstead, Toro.	20	30
□ 28 Bernie Geoffrion, Mont.	65	100
□ 29 Dick Duff, Toro.	15	25
□ **30 Ab McDonald, Mont. RC**	**15**	**25**
□ 31 Barry Cullen, Toro.	15	25
□ 32 Marcel Bonin, Mont.	15	25
□ 33 Frank Mahovlich, Toro.	150	250
□ 34 Jean Béliveau, Mont.	140	225
□ 35 Canadiens on Guard	45	70
□ 36 Barry Cullen Shoots	15	25
□ 37 Stephen Kraftcheck, Toro.	15	25
□ 38 Maurice Richard, Mont.	275	425
□ 39 Action Around the Net	45	70
□ 40 Bob Turner, Mont.	15	25
□ 41 Jean-Guy Talbot, Mont.	15	25
□ 42 Tim Horton, Toro.	120	180
□ 43 Claude Provost, Mont.	15	25
□ 44 Don Marshall, Mont.	15	25
□ 45 Bob Pulford, Toro.	30	45
□ 46 Johnny Bower (G), Toro., Err. (Bowers)	125	200
□ 47 Phil Goyette, Mont.	15	25
□ 48 George Armstrong, Toro.	30	50
□ 49 Doug Harvey, Mont.	60	100
□ 50 Brian Cullen, Toro.	25	50

1958 - 59 TOPPS

These cards measure the standard 2 1/2" x 3 1/2".

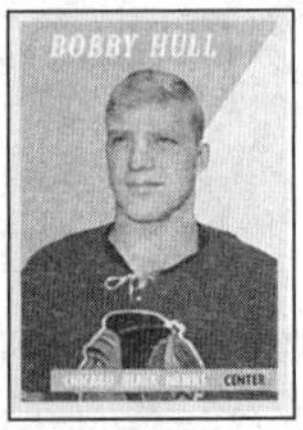

Complete Set (66 cards):	3,750	6,000
Topps	EX	EX-NM
□ 1 Bob Armstrong, Bost.	25	50
□ 2 Terry Sawchuk (G), Detr.	150	250
□ 3 Glen Skov, Chic.	15	25
□ 4 Léo Labine, Bost.	15	25
□ 5 Dollard St. Laurent, Chic.	15	25
□ 6 Danny Lewicki, Chic. LC	15	25
□ **7 John Hanna, NYRa. RC**	**15**	**25**
□ 8 Gordie Howe, Detr., Err. (Gordy)	400	650
□ 9 Vic Stasiuk, Bost.	15	25
□ 10 Larry Regan, Bost.	15	25
□ 11 Forbes Kennedy, Detr.	15	25
□ 12 Elmer Vasko, Chic.	15	25
□ 13 Glenn Hall (G), Chic.	130	200
□ **14 Kenny Wharram, Chic. RC**	**25**	**35**
□ **15 Len Lunde, Detr. RC**	**15**	**25**
□ 16 Ed Litzenberger, Chic.	18	28
□ **17 Norm Johnson, Bost. RC/LC**	**20**	**30**
□ **18 Earl Ingarfield, NYRa. RC**	**15**	**25**
□ **19 Les Colwill, NYRa. RC/LC**	**20**	**30**
□ 20 Léo Boivin, Bost.	18	28
□ 21 Andy Bathgate, NYRa.	30	45
□ 22 Johnny Wilson, Detr.	15	25
□ 23 Larry Cahan, NYRa.	15	25
□ 24 Marcel Pronovost, Detr.	18	28
□ 25 Larry Hillman, Bost.	15	25
□ **26 Jim Bartlett, NYRa. RC**	**15**	**25**
□ 27 Nick Mickoski, Detr.	15	25
□ 28 Larry Popein, NYRa.	15	25
□ 29 Fleming Mackell, Bost.	15	25
□ **30 Eddie Shack, NYRa. RC**	**190**	**300**
□ 31 Jack Evans, Chic.	15	25
□ 32 Dean Prentice, NYRa.	15	25
□ **33 Claude Laforge, Detr. RC**	**15**	**25**
□ 34 Bill Gadsby, NYRa.	20	35
□ 35 Bronco Horvath, Bost.	15	25
□ 36 Pierre Pilote, Chic.	55	85
□ 37 Earl Balfour, Chic.	15	25
□ 38 Gus Mortson, Detr. LC	15	25
□ 39 Gump Worsley (G), NYRa.	60	100
□ 40 John Bucyk, Bost.	80	135
□ 41 Louie Fontinato, NYRa.	15	25
□ 42 Tod Sloan, Chic.	15	25
□ **43 Charlie Burns, Detr. RC**	**18**	**28**
□ 44 Don Simmons (G), Bost.	18	28
□ 45 Jerry Toppazzini, Bost., Err. (Toppazini)	15	25
□ 46 Andy Hebenton, NYRa.	15	25
□ **47 Peter Goegan, Detr. RC, Err. (Geogan)**	**12**	**20**
□ 48 George Sullivan, NYRa.	15	25
□ **49 Hank Ciesla, NYRa. RC**	**15**	**25**
□ 50 Doug Mohns, Bost.	18	28
□ 51 Jean-Guy Gendron, Bost.	15	25
□ 52 Alex Delvecchio, Detr.	35	55
□ 53 Eric Nesterenko, Chic.	18	28
□ 54 Camille Henry, NYRa.	15	25
□ 55 Lorne Ferguson, Chic. LC	15	25
□ 56 Fern Flaman, Bost.	20	35
□ 57 Earl Reibel, Bost. LC	15	25
□ 58 Warren Godfrey, Detr.	15	25
□ 59 Ron Murphy, Chic.	15	25
□ 60 Harry Howell, NYRa.	30	45
□ 61 Red Kelly, Detr.	35	50
□ 62 Don McKenney, Bost.	15	25
□ 63 Ted Lindsay, Chic.	30	50
□ 64 Al Arbour, Chic.	25	40
□ 65 Norm Ullman, Detr.	75	125
□ **66 Bobby Hull, Chic. RC**	**1,900**	**3,800**

1958 - 59 TORONTO STAR PHOTOS

These are colour newspaper photos.

Toronto Star	EX	EX-MT
□ Nov. 29 Armstrong/ Olmstead/ F. Mahovlich	22	35
□ Dec. 6 D. Duff/ B. Harris/ R. Stewart	7	12
□ Dec. 13 G. Howe/ N. Ullman/ A. Delvecchio	35	60
□ Dec. 20 Montréal Canadiens Team Photo	15	25
□ Dec. 27 K. Wharram/ D. Lewicki/ T. Lindsay	12	20
□ Jan. 3 H. Richard/ M. Richard	30	50
□ Jan. 10 E. Litzenberger/ T. Sloan/ L. Ferguson	7	12
□ Jan. 17 Boston Bruins Team Photo	15	25
□ Jan. 24 Minor Hockey Picture of Boys on Ice	7	12
□ Jan. 31 D. Moore/ J. Béliveau/ A. McDonald	20	30
□ Feb. 7 New York Rangers Team Photo	15	25
□ Feb. 14 Flaman/ Simmons (G)/ Morrison	11	18
□ Feb. 21 Detroit Red Wings Team Photo	15	25
□ Feb. 28 A. Bathgate/ L. Popein/ D. Prentice	9	15
□ Mar. 7 Toronto Maple Leafs Team Photo	15	25
□ Mar. 14 Belleville McFarlands Cdn Hky Champ.	13	22
□ Mar. 21 J.G. Talbot/ T. Johnson/ B. Turner	9	15

(Right) An opened 1959-60 Parkie wrapper with a stick of gum.

1958 - 59 WEEKEND PHOTOS

These colour newspaper photos measure 5 1/2" x 6 1/2".

Toronto Star	EX	EX-NM
□ V6 Dickie Moore, Mont.	12	20
□ V6 Glenn Hall (G), Chic.	20	30
□ V6 Frank Mahovlich, Toro.	20	30
□ V6 Henri Richard, Mont.	13	22
□ V6 Camille Henry, NYRa.	7	12
□ V6 Marcel Pronovost , Detr.	9	15
□ V6 Eddie Litzenberger, Chic.	7	12
□ V6 Bob Pulford, Toro.	9	15
□ V6 Andy Bathgate, NYRa.	9	15
□ V6 Fern Flaman, Bost.	9	15
□ V6 Doug Harvey, Mont.	15	25
□ V6 Vic Stasiuk, Bost.	7	12
□ V6 Alex Delvecchio, Detr.	12	20

1959 - 60 PARKHURST

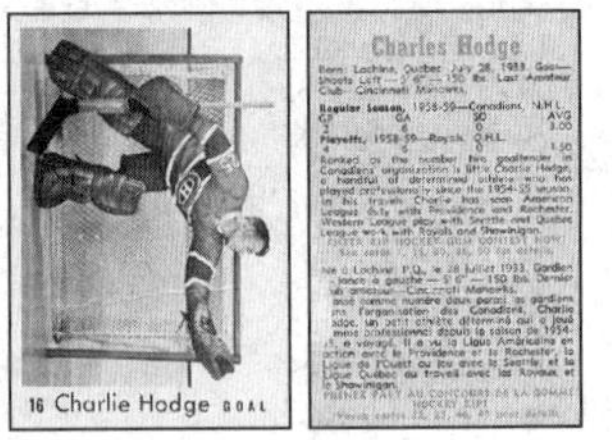

These cards measure 2 7/16" x 3 5/8"

Complete Set (50 cards):	1,100	1,900
Parkhurst	EX	EX-NM
□ 1 Canadiens On Guard	65	125
□ 2 Maurice Richard, Mont.	225	350
□ **3 Carl Brewer, Toro. RC**	**40**	**60**
□ 4 Phil Goyette, Mont.	15	25
□ 5 Ed Chadwick (G), Toro. LC	25	35
□ 6 Jean Béliveau, Mont.	90	150
□ 7 George Armstrong, Toro.	25	40
□ 8 Doug Harvey, Mont.	55	85
□ 9 Billy Harris, Toro.	15	25
□ 10 Tom Johnson, Mont.	18	28
□ 11 Marc Reaume, Toro.	15	25
□ 12 Marcel Bonin, Mont.	15	25
□ 13 Johnny Wilson, Toro.	15	25
□ 14 Dickie Moore, Mont.	30	45
□ 15 Punch Imlach, Mgr. & Coach, Toro.	30	50
□ 16 Charlie Hodge (G), Mont.	18	28
□ 17 Larry Regan, Toro.	15	25
□ 18 Claude Provost, Mont.	15	25
□ **19 Gerry Ehman, Toro. RC**	**13**	**25**
□ 20 Ab McDonald, Mont.	15	25
□ 21 Bob Baun, Toro.	25	40
□ 22 Ken Reardon, Vice President, Mont.	18	28
□ 23 Tim Horton, Toro.	75	125
□ 24 Frank Mahovlich, Toro.	95	150
□ 25 Bower In Action	35	55
□ 26 Ron Stewart, Toro.	15	25
□ 27 Toe Blake, Coach, Mont.	20	35
□ 28 Bob Pulford, Toro.	20	35
□ 29 Ralph Backstrom, Mont.	15	25
□ 30 Action Around The Net	18	28
□ **31 Bill Hicke, Mont. RC**	**15**	**25**
□ 32 Johnny Bower (G), Toro.	75	125
□ 33 Bernie Geoffrion, Mont.	60	85
□ **34 Ted Hampson, Toro. RC**	**15**	**25**
□ 35 André Pronovost, Mont.	15	25
□ 36 Stafford Smythe, Chairman, Toro.	15	25
□ 37 Don Marshall, Mont.	15	25
□ 38 Dick Duff, Toro.	15	25

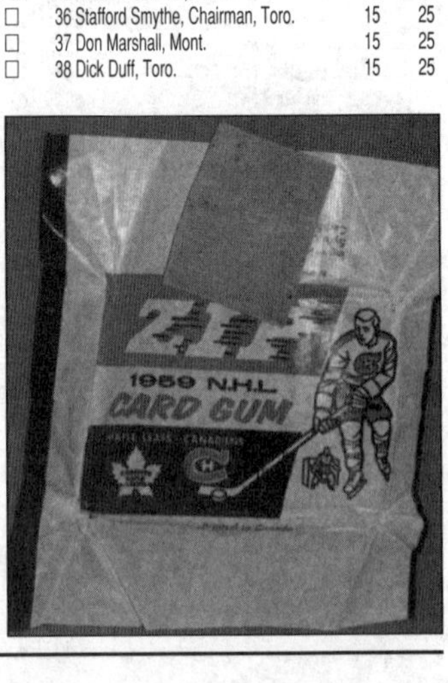

39 Henri Richard, Mont.	90	150
40 Bert Olmstead, Toro.	18	28
41 Jacques Plante (G), Mont.	170	275
42 Noel Price, Toro.	15	25
43 Bob Turner, Mont.	15	25
44 Allan Stanley, Toro.	20	35
45 Al Langlois, Mont.	15	25
46 Officials Intervene	15	25
47 Frank Selke, Managing Director, Mont.	**18**	**28**
48 Gary Edmundson, Toro. RC	**15**	**25**
49 Jean-Guy Talbot, Mont.	15	25
50 King Clancy, AGM, Toro.	55	100

1959 - 60 TOPPS

These cards measure the standard 2 1/2" x 3 1/2".

Complete Set (66 cards):	1,750	2,800
Topps	**EX**	**EX-NM**
1 Eric Nesterenko, Chic.	25	50
2 Pierre Pilote, Chic.	35	55
3 Elmer Vasko, Chic.	15	25
4 Peter Goegan, Detr.	15	25
5 Louie Fontinato, NYRa.	15	25
6 Ted Lindsay, Chic.	25	45
7 Léo Labine, Bost.	15	25
8 Alex Delvecchio, Detr., Err. (Wing)	30	45
9 Don McKenney, Bost., Err. (Mckenny)	15	25
10 Earl Ingarfield, NYRa.	15	25
11 Don Simmons (G), Bost.	15	25
12 Glen Skov, Chic. LC	15	25
13 Tod Sloan, Chic.	15	25
14 Vic Stasiuk, Bost.	15	25
15 Gump Worsley (G), NYRa.	55	90
16 Andy Hebenton, NYRa.	15	25
17 Dean Prentice, NYRa.	15	25
18 Oops! Pardon My Stick! Strickly Accidental!	10	18
19 Fleming Mackell, Bost. LC	15	25
20 Harry Howell, NYRa.	25	40
21 Larry Popein, NYRa. LC	15	25
22 Len Lunde, Detr.	15	25
23 John Bucyk, Bost.	55	85
24 Jean-Guy Gendron, Bost.	15	25
25 Barry Cullen, Detr., Err. (Brian's résumé)	15	25
26 Léo Boivin, Bost.	15	25
27 Warren Godfrey, Detr.	15	25
28 Hall/ Henry (Action)	30	45
29 Fern Flaman, Bost.	15	25
30 Jack Evans, Chic.	15	25
31 John Hanna, NYRa. LC	15	25
32 Glenn Hall (G), Chic.	80	125
33 Murray Balfour, Chic. RC	**15**	**25**
34 Andy Bathgate, NYRa.	25	40
35 Al Arbour, Chic.	20	35
36 Jim Morrison, Detr.	15	25
37 Nick Mickoski, Bost. LC	15	25
38 Jerry Toppazzini, Bost.	15	25
39 Bob Armstrong, Bost.	15	25
40 Charlie Burns, Bost., Err. (Charley)	15	25
41 Billy McNeill, Detr.	15	25
42 Terry Sawchuk (G), Detr.	110	175
43 Dollard St. Laurent, Chic.	15	25
44 Marcel Pronovost, Detr.	15	25
45 Norm Ullman, Detr.	55	85
46 Camille Henry, NYRa.	15	25
47 Bobby Hull, Chic., Error (Center)	450	700
48 Howe/ Evans (Action)	75	120
49 Lou Marcon, Detr. RC/LC	**20**	**30**
50 Earl Balfour, Chic.	15	25
51 Jim Bartlett, NYRa. LC	15	25
52 Forbes Kennedy, Detr.	15	25
53 Mickoski/ Hanna (Action)	10	18
54 N. Johnson / Worsley (G) (Action)	25	40
55 Brian Cullen, NYRa. LC	15	25
56 Bronco Horvath, Bost.	15	25
57 Eddie Shack, NYRa.	75	120
58 Doug Mohns, Bost.	15	25
59 George Sullivan, NYRa.	15	25
60 Pilote/ Mackell (Action)	10	18
61 Ed Litzenberger, Chic.	15	25
62 Bill Gadsby, NYRa.	25	35
63 Gordie Howe, Detr.	325	525
64 Claude LaForge, Detr.	15	25
65 Red Kelly, Detr.	25	40
66 Ron Murphy, Chic.	25	50

1959 - 60 TORONTO STAR PHOTOS

These are colour newspaper photos.

Toronto Star	EX	EX-MT
Dec. 15 Harry Lumley (G), Bost.	12	20
Dec. 26 Bert Olmstead, Toro.	9	15
Jan. 2 Henri Richard, Mont.	13	22
Jan. 9 Gordie Howe, Detr.	30	50
Jan. 16 Johnny Bower (G), Toro.	15	25
Jan. 23 Red Sullivan, NYRa.	7	12
Jan. 30 Tod Sloan, Chic.	7	12
Feb. 6 Bob Armstrong, Bost.	7	12
Feb. 13 Jacques Plante (G), Mont.	25	40
Feb. 20 Tom Johnson, Mont.	9	15
Feb. 27 Glenn Hall (G), Chic.	20	30
Mar. 5 Bill Gadsby, NYRa.	9	15

1959 - 60 WEEKEND PHOTOS

These colour newspaper photos measure 5 1/2" x 6 1/2".

Toronto Star	EX	EX-NM
V7 Tom Johnson, Mont.	9	15
V7 Dick Duff , Toro.	7	12
V7 Norm Ullman, Detr.	11	18
V7 Jacques Plante (G), Mont.	28	45
V7 Bobby Hull, Chic.	28	45
V7 Bronco Horvath, Bost.	7	12
V7 Andy Hebenton, NYRa.	7	12
V7 Léo Boivin, Bost.	9	15
V7 Terry Sawchuk (G), Detr.	28	45
V7 Billy Harris, Toro.	7	12
V7 Tod Sloan, Chic.	7	12
V7 Ralph Backstrom, Mont.	7	12
V7 Red Sullivan, NYRa.	7	12
V7 Carl Brewer, Toro.	7	12

1959 - 60 WHITBY DUNLOPS

- 10-♣ Dunlops
- 10-♦ Dunlops
- 10-♥ Dunlops
- 10-♠ Dunlops
- 2-♣ Roy Edwards
- 2-♦ Jack MacKenzie
- 2-♥ Wally Brakin
- 2-♠ Senior B Trophy
- 3-♣ G. Samolenko
- 3-♦ Wren Blair
- 3-♥ Ted O'Connor
- 3-♠ Doug Williams
- 4-♣ Jack Donlevy
- 4-♦ Ed Redmond
- 4-♥ Sandy Air
- 4-♠ Bob Hersketh
- 5-♣ Eishocky
- 5-♦Bob Attersley
- 5-♥ G. Gosselin
- 5-♠ Harry Sinden
- 6-♣ Stan Waylett
- 6-♦ Tom O'Connor
- 6-♥ Alf Treen
- 6-♠ J.P. Lamirande
- 7-♣ Charlie Burns
- 7-♦ Don McBeth
- 7-♥ John Henderson
- 7-♠ Fred Etcher
- 8-♣ Frank Bonello
- 8-♦ Bill Hannah
- 8-♥ Gord Myles
- 8-♠ Sid Smith
- 9-♣ Bus Gagnon
- 9-♦ Allan Cup
- 9-♥ Connie Broden
- 9-♠ International Cup
- A-♣ Statistics
- A-♦ Statistics
- A-♥ Statistics
- A-♠ Statistics
- J-♣ Jack
- J-♦ Jack
- J-♥ Jack
- J-♠ Jack
- Joker
- Joker
- K-♣ King
- K-♦ King
- K-♥ King
- K-♠ King
- Q-♣ Queen
- Q-♦ Queen
- Q-♥ Queen
- Q-♠ Queen

1960 - 61 CLEVELAND BARONS

Card Size: 5 3/8" x 6 3/4"

Complete Set (20 photos):	75	150
Ron Attwell	4	8
Les Binkley (G)	6	12
Bill Dineen	4	8
John Ferguson	12	25
Cal Gardner	4	8
Fred Glover	4	8
Jack Godron	4	8
Aldo Guidolin	4	8
Greg Hicks	4	8
Wayne Larkin	4	8
Moe Mantha	4	8
Gil Mayer	4	8
Eddie Mazur	4	8
Jim Mikol	4	8
Bill Needham	4	8
Cal Stearns	4	8
Bill Sutherland	4	8
Tom Williams	6	12
Team Photo	6	12

1960 - 61 PARKHURST

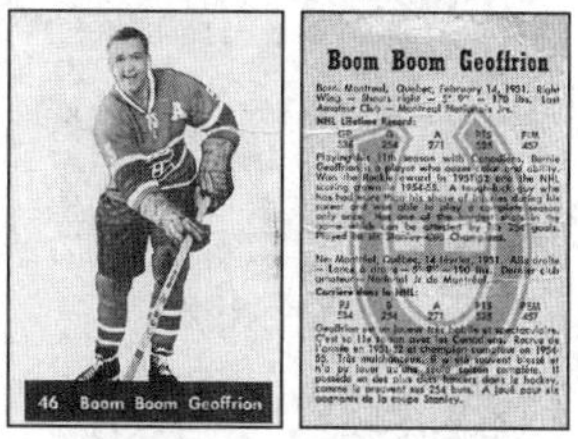

These cards measure 2 7/16" x 3 5/8".

Complete Set (61 cards):	1,500	2,500
Parkhurst	**EX**	**EX-NM**
1 Tim Horton, Toro.	100	200
2 Frank Mahovlich, Toro.	85	135
3 Johnny Bower (G), Toro.	60	90
4 Bert Olmstead, Toro.	15	25
5 Gary Edmundson, Toro. LC	12	20
6 Ron Stewart, Toro.	12	20
7 Gerry James, Toro. LC	12	20
8 Gerry Ehman, Toro.	12	20
9 Red Kelly, Toro.	25	40
10 Dave Creighton, Toro. LC	12	20
11 Bob Baun, Toro.	15	25
12 Dick Duff, Toro.	12	20
13 Larry Regan, Toro. LC	12	20
14 Johnny Wilson, Toro. LC	12	20
15 Billy Harris, Toro.	12	20
16 Allan Stanley, Toro.	20	35
17 George Armstrong, Toro.	25	35
18 Carl Brewer, Toro.	15	25
19 Bob Pulford, Toro.	20	35
20 Gordie Howe, Detr.	260	400
21 Val Fonteyne, Detr. RC	**12**	**20**
22 Murray Oliver, Detr. RC	**25**	**35**
23 Sid Abel, Coach, Detr.	15	25
24 Jack McIntyre, Detr. LC	12	20
25 Marc Réaume, Detr.	12	20
26 Norm Ullman, Detr.	40	60
27 Brian S. Smith, Detr. RC/LC	**15**	**25**
28 Gerry Melnyk, Detr. RC, Err. (Jerry)	**12**	**20**
29 Marcel Pronovost, Detr.	15	25
30 Warren Godfrey, Detr.	12	20
31 Terry Sawchuk (G), Detr.	110	175
32 Barry Cullen, Detr. LC	12	20
33 Gary Aldcorn, Detr. LC	12	20
34 Peter Goegan, Detr.	12	20
35 Len Lunde, Detr.	12	20
36 Alex Delvecchio, Detr.	25	40
37 John McKenzie, Detr. RC	**25**	**40**
38 Dickie Moore, Mont.	25	40
39 Al Langlois, Mont.	12	20
40 Bill Hicke, Mont.	12	20
41 Ralph Backstrom, Mont.	12	20
42 Don Marshall, Mont.	12	20
43 Bob Turner, Mont.	12	20
44 Tom Johnson, Mont.	15	25
45 Maurice Richard, Mont. LC	185	300
46 Bernie Geoffrion, Mont.	45	70
47 Henri Richard, Mont.	80	125
48 Doug Harvey, Mont.	35	65
49 Jean Béliveau, Mont.	75	125
50 Phil Goyette, Mont.	12	20
51 Marcel Bonin, Mont.	12	20
52 Jean-Guy Talbot, Mont.	12	20
53 Jacques Plante (G), Mont.	140	250
54 Claude Provost, Mont.	12	20
55 André Pronovost, Mont.	12	20
56 Hicke/ Backstrom/ McDonald	15	25
57 Marshall/ Henri Richard/ Moore	35	60
58 Provost/ Goyette/ Pronovost	15	25
59 Geoffrion/ Béliveau/ Marshall	60	100
60 Ab McDonald, Mont.	12	20
61 Jim Morrison, Detr.	70	135

1960 - 61 SHIRRIFF

These wheels measure 1 9/16" in diameter.

Complete Set (120 wheels):	325	600
Common Player:	2	4
Shirriff	**EX**	**EX-NM**
1 Johnny Bower (G), Toro.	10	17
2 Dick Duff, Toro.	2	4
3 Carl Brewer, Toro.	2	4
4 Red Kelly, Toro.	6	12
5 Tim Horton, Toro.	13	22
6 Allan Stanley, Toro.	3	6
7 Bob Baun, Toro.	2	4
8 Billy Harris, Toro.	2	4
9 George Armstrong, Toro.	5	9
10 Ron Stewart, Toro.	2	4
11 Bert Olmstead, Toro.	3	6
12 Frank Mahovlich, Toro.	11	20
13 Bob Pulford, Toro.	5	7
14 Garry Edmundson, Toro.	2	4
15 Johnny Wilson, Toro.	2	4
16 Larry Regan, Toro.	2	4
17 Gerry James, Toro.	2	4
18 Rudy Migay, Toro.	2	4
19 Gerry Ehman, Toro.	2	4
20 Punch Imlach, Coach, Toro.	3	6
21 Jacques Plante (G), Mont.	17	28
22 Dickie Moore, Mont.	6	12
23 Don Marshall, Mont.	2	4
24 Al Langlois, Mont.	2	4
25 Tom Johnson, Mont.	3	6
26 Doug Harvey, Mont.	8	15
27 Phil Goyette, Mont.	2	4
28 Bernie Geoffrion, Mont.	9	17
29 Marcel Bonin, Mont.	2	4
30 Jean Béliveau, Mont.	15	28
31 Ralph Backstrom, Mont.	2	4
32 André Pronovost, Mont.	2	4
33 Claude Provost, Mont.	2	4
34 Henri Richard, Mont.	11	17
35 Jean-Guy Talbot, Mont.	2	4
36 J.C. Tremblay, Mont.	3	6
37 Bob Turner, Mont.	2	4
38 Bill Hicke, Mont.	2	4
39 Charlie Hodge (G), Mont.	3	6
40 Toe Blake, Coach, Mont.	5	7
41 Terry Sawchuk (G), Detr.	17	28
42 Gordie Howe, Detr.	40	70
43 John McKenzie, Detr.	2	4
44 Alex Delvecchio, Detr.	8	15
45 Norm Ullman, Detr.	6	12
46 Jack McIntyre, Detr.	2	4
47 Barry Cullen, Detr.	2	4
48 Val Fonteyne, Detr.	2	4

☐	49 Warren Godfrey, Detr.	2	4
☐	50 Peter Goegan, Detr.	2	4
☐	51 Gerry Melnyk, Detr., Err. (Jerry)	2	4
☐	52 Marc Reaume, Detr.	2	4
☐	53 Gary Aldcorn, Detr.	2	4
☐	54 Len Lunde, Detr.	2	4
☐	55 Murray Oliver, Detr.	2	4
☐	56 Marcel Pronovost, Detr.	3	6
☐	57 Howie Glover, Detr.	2	4
☐	58 Gerry Odrowski, Detr.	2	4
☐	59 Parker MacDonald, Detr.	2	4
☐	60 Sid Abel, Coach, Detr.	3	6
☐	61 Glenn Hall (G), Chic.	11	20
☐	62 Ed Litzenberger, Chic.	2	4
☐	63 Bobby Hull, Chic.	30	50
☐	64 Tod Sloan, Chic.	2	4
☐	65 Murray Balfour, Chic.	2	4
☐	66 Pierre Pilote, Chic.	3	6
☐	67 Al Arbour, Chic.	3	6
☐	68 Earl Balfour, Chic.	2	4
☐	69 Eric Nesterenko, Chic.	2	4
☐	70 Kenny Wharram, Chic.	2	4
☐	71 Stan Mikita, Chic.	13	22
☐	72 Ab McDonald, Chic.	2	4
☐	73 Elmer Vasko, Chic.	2	4
☐	74 Dollard St. Laurent, Chic.	2	4
☐	75 Ron Murphy, Chic.	2	4
☐	76 Jack Evans, Chic.	2	4
☐	77 Billy Hay, Chic.	2	4
☐	78 Reggie Fleming, Chic.	2	4
☐	79 Cecil Hoekstra, Chic.	2	4
☐	80 Tommy Ivan, Coach, Chic.	2	4
☐	81 Jack McCartan (G), NYRa.	3	6
☐	82 Red Sullivan, NYRa.	2	4
☐	83 Camille Henry, NYRa.	2	4
☐	84 Larry Popein, NYRa.	2	4
☐	85 John Hanna, NYRa.	2	4
☐	86 Harry Howell, NYRa.	3	6
☐	87 Eddie Shack, NYRa.	6	10
☐	88 Irv Spencer, NYRa.	2	4
☐	89 Andy Bathgate, NYRa.	5	9
☐	90 Bill Gadsby, NYRa.	3	6
☐	91 Andy Hebenton, NYRa.	2	4
☐	92 Earl Ingarfield, NYRa.	2	4
☐	93 Don Johns, NYRa.	2	4
☐	94 Dave Balon, NYRa.	2	4
☐	95 Jim Morrison, NYRa.	2	4
☐	96 Ken Schinkel, NYRa.	2	4
☐	97 Louie Fontinato, NYRa.	2	4
☐	98 Ted Hampson, NYRa.	2	4
☐	99 Brian Cullen, NYRa.	2	4
☐	100 Alf Pike, Coach, NYRa.	2	4
☐	101 Don Simmons (G), Bost.	3	6
☐	102 Fern Flaman, Bost.	3	6
☐	103 Vic Stasiuk, Bost.	2	4
☐	104 John Bucyk, Bost.	9	15
☐	105 Bronco Horvath, Bost.	2	4
☐	106 Doug Mohns, Bost.	7	14
☐	107 Léo Boivin, Bost.	3	6
☐	108 Don McKenney, Bost.	2	4
☐	109 John-Guy Gendron, Bost.	2	4
☐	110 Jerry Toppazzini, Bost.	2	4
☐	111 Dick Meissner, Bost.	2	4
☐	112 Aut Erickson, Bost.	2	4
☐	113 Jim Bartlett, Bost.	2	4
☐	114 Orval Tessier, Bost.	2	4
☐	115 Billy Carter, Bost.	2	4
☐	116 Dallas Smith, Bost.	2	4
☐	117 Léo Labine, Bost.	2	4
☐	118 Bob Armstrong, Bost.	2	4
☐	119 Bruce Gamble (G), Bost.	3	6
☐	120 Milt Schmidt, Coach, Bost.	7	14

1960 - 61 TOPPS

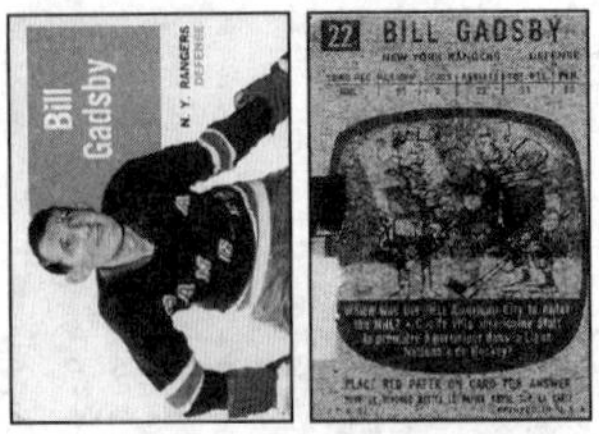

These cards measure the standard 2 1/2" x 3 1/2".

Complete Set (66 cards):		**1,750**	**2,800**
Topps		**EX**	**EX-NM**
☐	1 Lester Patrick, All-Time Great	50	100

◆ A graded PSA-9 copy of this card recently closed at $484 U.S. ($555 U.S. with the buyer's premium) in the May 17, 2002 Lelands Vintage Sports Auction. That closing amount is approximately $750 Cdn.

☐	2 Paddy Moran (G), All-Time Great	18	30
☐	3 Joe Malone, All-Time Great	25	45
☐	4 Ernest (Moose) Johnson, All-Time Great	13	22
☐	5 Nels Stewart, All-Time Great	20	35
☐	**6 Billy Hay, Chic. RC**	**10**	**17**
☐	7 Eddie Shack, NYRa.	60	100
☐	8 Cy Denneny, All-Time Great	13	22
☐	9 Jim Morrison, NYRa.	10	17
☐	10 Bill Cook, All-Time Great	13	22
☐	11 John Bucyk, Bost.	40	60
☐	12 Murray Balfour, Chic.	10	17
☐	13 Léo Labine, Bost.	10	17
☐	**14 Stan Mikita, Chic. RC**	**325**	**550**
☐	15 George Hay, All-Time Great	13	22
☐	16 Red Dutton, All-Time Great	13	22
☐	17 Richard (Dickie) Boon, All-Time Great	13	22
☐	18 George Sullivan, NYRa.	10	17
☐	19 Georges Vézina (G), All-Time Great	50	80
☐	20 Eddie Shore, All-Time Great	45	70
☐	21 Ed Litzenberger, Chic.	10	17
☐	22 Bill Gadsby, NYRa.	13	22
☐	23 Elmer Vasko, Chic.	10	17
☐	24 Charlie Burns, Bost.	10	17
☐	25 Glenn Hall (G), Chic.	60	100
☐	26 Dit Clapper, All-Time Great	20	30
☐	27 Art Ross, All-Time Great	40	60
☐	28 Jerry Toppazzini, Bost.	10	17
☐	29 Frank Boucher, All-Time Great	13	22
☐	30 Jack Evans, Chic.	10	17
☐	31 Jean Guy Gendron, Bost.	10	17
☐	32 Chuck Gardiner (G), All-Time Great	20	35
☐	33 Ab McDonald, Chic.	10	17
☐	34 F. Frederickson, All-Time Great, Err. (Fredrickson)	13	22
☐	35 Frank Nighbor, All-Time Great	20	35
☐	36 Gump Worsley (G), NYRa.	45	70
☐	37 Dean Prentice, NYRa.	10	17
☐	38 Hugh Lehman (G), All-Time Great	13	22
☐	**39 Jack McCartan (G), NYRa. RC/LC**	**20**	**30**
☐	40 Don McKenney, Bost., Err. (Mckenny)	10	17
☐	41 Ron Murphy, Chic.	10	17
☐	42 Andy Hebenton, NYRa.	10	17
☐	43 Don Simmons (G), Bost.	13	22
☐	44 Herb Gardiner, All-Time Great	13	22
☐	45 Andy Bathgate, NYRa.	18	30
☐	46 Fred (Cyclone) Taylor, All-Time Great	30	50
☐	47 King Clancy, All-Time Great	40	60
☐	48 Edouard (Newsy) Lalonde, All-Time Great	30	45
☐	49 Harry Howell, NYRa.	20	30
☐	**50 Ken Schinkel, NYRa. RC**	**10**	**17**
☐	51 Tod Sloan, Chic. LC	10	17
☐	52 Doug Mohns, Bost.	10	17
☐	53 Camille Henry, NYRa.	10	17
☐	54 Bronco Horvath, Bost.	10	17
☐	55 Tiny Thompson (G), All-Time Great	30	45
☐	56 Bob Armstrong, Bost.	10	17
☐	57 Fern Flaman, Bost. LC	13	22
☐	58 Bobby Hull, Chic.	375	575
☐	59 Howie Morenz, All-Time Great	50	75
☐	60 Dick Irvin, All-Time Great	25	40
☐	61 Louie Fontinato, NYRa. LC	10	17
☐	62 Léo Boivin, Bost.	13	22
☐	63 Francis (Moose) Goheen, All-Time Great	13	22
☐	64 Al Arbour, Chic.	20	30
☐	65 Pierre Pilote, Chic.	25	40
☐	66 Vic Stasiuk, Bost.	30	50

1960 - 61 TORONTO STAR PHOTOS

These are colour newspaper photos.

Toronto Star		**EX**	**EX-MT**
☐	Dec. 10 Bobby Hull, Chic.	25	40
☐	Dec. 17 Frank Mahovlich, Toro.	20	30
☐	Dec. 24 Terry Sawchuk (G) Detr.	25	40
☐	Jan. 7 Elmer Vasko, Chic.	7	12
☐	Jan. 14 Andy Bathgate, NYRa.	11	18
☐	Jan. 28 Ralph Backstrom, Mont.	7	12
☐	Feb. 4 Fern Flaman, Bost.	9	15
☐	Feb. 11 Allan Stanley, Toro.	9	15
☐	Feb. 18 Gump Worsley (G), NYRa.	18	28
☐	Mar. 4 Marcel Pronovost, Detr.	9	15
☐	Mar. 11 Don Marshall, Mont.	7	12

1960 - 61 WEEKEND PHOTOS

These colour newspaper photos measure 5 1/2" x 6 1/2".

Toronto Star		**EX**	**EX-NM**
☐	V8 Gordie Howe, Detr.	30	50
☐	V8 Jean Béliveau, Mont.	20	30
☐	V8 George Armstrong, Toro.	11	18
☐	V8 Billy Hay, Chic.	7	12
☐	V8 Lou Fontinato, NYRa.	7	12
☐	V8 Jerry Toppazzini, Bost.	7	12
☐	V8 Bernie Geoffrion, Mont.	15	25
☐	V8 Red Kelly, Toro.	12	20
☐	V8 John Bucyk, Bost.	11	18
☐	V8 Dean Prentice, NYRa.	7	12
☐	V8 Pierre Pilote, Chic.	9	15
☐	V8 Ron Stewart, Toro.	7	12
☐	V8 Don Marshall, Mont.	7	12

1960 - 61 WONDER BREAD

These blank-back square cards came enclosed two per loaf of Wonder Bread. The cards measure 2 3/4" x 2 3/4".

Complete Set (4 cards):		**300**	**500**
Wonder Bread		**EX**	**EX-NM**
☐	Gordie Howe, Detr.	170	275
☐	Bobby Hull, Chic.	90	150
☐	Dave Keon, Toro.	45	75
☐	Maurice Richard, Mont.	125	200

PREMIUM PHOTOS

These premium photos could be redeemed by sending in 25¢ plus five wrappers. The black & white 5" x 7" photos are printed on heavier stock that the smaller cards.

Complete Set (4 cards):		**400**	**650**
Wonder Bread		**EX**	**EX-NM**
☐	Gordie Howe, Detr.	200	350
☐	Bobby Hull, Chic.	125	225
☐	Dave Keon, Toro.	60	100
☐	Maurice Richard, Mont.	150	250

1960 - 61 YORK PEANUT BUTTER

These black & white blank-back photos measure 5" x 7".

Complete Set (37 cards):		**1,500**	**2,500**
Montréal Canadiens		**EX**	**EX-NM**
☐	Ralph Backstrom	35	60
☐	Jean Béliveau	130	225
☐	Marcel Bonin	35	60
☐	Jean-Guy Gendron	35	60
☐	Bernie Geoffrion	80	140
☐	Phil Goyette	35	60
☐	Doug Harvey	75	130
☐	Bill Hicke	35	60
☐	Charlie Hodge (G)	50	75
☐	Tom Johnson	55	85
☐	Al Langlois	35	60
☐	Don Marshall	35	60
☐	Dickie Moore	60	95
☐	Jacques Plante (G)	175	275
☐	Claude Provost	50	75
☐	Henri Richard	70	120
☐	Jean-Guy Talbot	35	60
☐	Gilles Tremblay	35	60
☐	Bob Turner	35	60
Toronto Maple Leafs		**EX**	**EX-NM**
☐	George Armstrong	60	95
☐	Bob Baun	50	75
☐	Johnny Bower (G)	80	130
☐	Carl Brewer	35	60
☐	Dick Duff	50	75
☐	Billy Harris	35	60
☐	Larry Hillman	35	60
☐	Tim Horton	110	200
☐	Red Kelly	60	100
☐	Dave Keon	80	130
☐	Frank Mahovlich	85	160
☐	Bob Nevin	35	60
☐	Bert Olmstead	55	85
☐	Bob Pulford	55	90
☐	Larry Regan	35	60
☐	Eddie Shack	60	100
☐	Allan Stanley	55	85
☐	Ron Stewart	35	60

1960 - 61 YORK PEANUT BUTTER GLASSES

Other glasses likely exist. The Red Wings and Canadiens glasses measure 4 3/4" high while the Maple Leafs glasses measure 4 1/2" high.

Peanut Butter Glass		**EX**	**EX-NM**
☐	Alex Delvecchio, Detr.	90	150
☐	Gordie Howe, Detr.	200	325
☐	Terry Sawchuk (G), Detr.	200	325
☐	Jean Béliveau, Mont.	60	100
☐	Marcel Bonin, Mont.	30	50
☐	Bernie Geoffrion, Mont.	60	100
☐	Doug Harvey, Mont.	75	125
☐	Tom Johnson, Mont.	30	50
☐	Albert Langlois, Mont.	30	50
☐	Don Marshall, Mont.	30	50
☐	Dickie Moore, Mont.	55	90
☐	Jacques Plante (G), Mont.	200	325
☐	Henri Richard, Mont.	50	75
☐	Gilles Tremblay, Mont.	30	50
☐	George Armstrong, Toro.	50	90
☐	Johnny Bower (G), Toro.	75	125
☐	Carl Brewer, Toro.	30	50
☐	Dick Duff, Toro.	30	50
☐	Tim Horton, Toro.	90	150
☐	Red Kelly, Toro.	50	90
☐	Dave Keon, Toro.	65	110
☐	Frank Mahovlich, Toro.	90	150
☐	Bert Olmstead, Toro.	50	75
☐	Allan Stanley, Toro.	50	75
☐	Billy Harris, Toro.	50	75

1961 - 62 PARKHURST

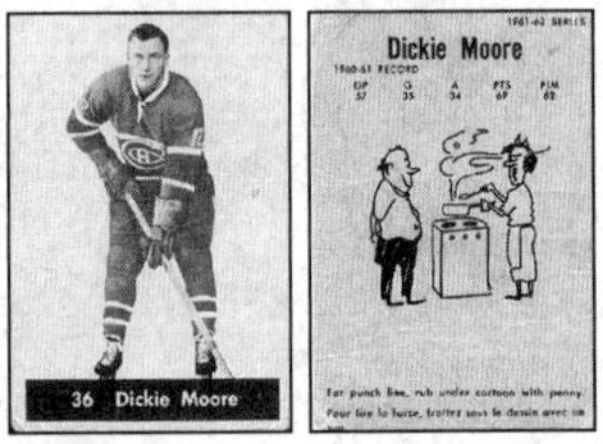

"These hockey cards were available at corner stores.I got into it slowly, but I put together the set. I liked hockey and someone else at school had some cards. I had seen his cards so that's how I got into collecting." – John Rioux, R & S Sportscards, Ottawa, Ontario.

These cards measure 2 7/16" x 3 5/8".

Complete Set (51 cards):		**1,150**	**1,900**
Parkhurst		**EX**	**EX-MT**
☐	1 Tim Horton, Toro.	100	185
☐	2 Frank Mahovlich, Toro.	65	105
☐	3 Johnny Bower (G), Toro.	50	80
☐	4 Bert Olmstead, Toro.	13	22
☐	**5 Dave Keon, Toro. RC**	**185**	**325**
☐	6 Ron Stewart, Toro.	12	20
☐	7 Eddie Shack, Toro.	60	95
☐	8 Bob Pulford, Toro.	20	30
☐	9 Red Kelly, Toro.	22	35
☐	10 Bob Nevin, Toro.	12	20
☐	11 Bob Baun, Toro.	12	20
☐	12 Dick Duff, Toro.	12	20
☐	**13 Larry Keenan, Toro. RC**	**12**	**20**
☐	14 Larry Hillman, Toro.	12	20
☐	15 Billy Harris, Toro.	12	20
☐	16 Allan Stanley, Toro.	17	30
☐	17 George Armstrong, Toro.	20	30
☐	18 Carl Brewer, Toro.	12	20
☐	**19 Howie Glover, Detr. RC**	**12**	**20**
☐	20 Gordie Howe, Detr.	225	350
☐	21 Val Fonteyne, Detr.	12	20
☐	**22 Al Johnson, Detr. RC/LC**	**15**	**25**
☐	23 Peter Goegan, Detr.	12	20
☐	24 Len Lunde, Detr.	12	20
☐	25 Alex Delvecchio, Detr.	25	35
☐	26 Norm Ullman, Detr.	35	55
☐	27 Bill Gadsby, Detr.	13	22
☐	28 Ed Litzenberger, Detr.	12	20
☐	29 Marcel Pronovost, Detr.	13	22
☐	30 Warren Godfrey, Detr.	12	20
☐	31 Terry Sawchuk (G), Detr.	95	150
☐	32 Vic Stasiuk, Detr.	12	20
☐	33 Léo Labine, Detr.	12	20
☐	34 John McKenzie, Detr.	13	22
☐	35 Bernie Geoffrion, Mont.	40	65
☐	36 Dickie Moore, Mont.	18	30
☐	37 Al Langlois, Mont.	12	20
☐	38 Bill Hicke, Mont.	12	20
☐	39 Ralph Backstrom, Mont.	12	20
☐	40 Don Marshall, Mont.	12	20

☐	41 Bob Turner, Mont.	12	20
☐	42 Tom Johnson, Mont.	13	22
☐	43 Henri Richard, Mont.	60	95
☐	**44 Wayne Connelly, Mont. RC, Err. (Connolly)**	**13**	**22**
☐	45 Jean Béliveau, Mont.	60	100
☐	46 Phil Goyette, Mont.	12	20
☐	47 Marcel Bonin, Mont.	12	20
☐	48 Jean-Guy Talbot, Mont.	12	20
☐	49 Jacques Plante (G), Mont.	125	200
☐	50 Claude Provost, Mont.	12	20
☐	51 André Pronovost, Mont.	30	55

1961 - 62 SHIRRIFF & SALADA

These wheels measure 1 7/8" in diameter. Prices are identical for both the Shirriff and Salada versions.

Complete Set (120 wheels):		**250**	**425**
Common Player:		**2**	**4**
Common Shield (all six teams available):		**50**	**80**
Shirriff		**EX**	**EX-NM**
☐☐	1 Cliff Pennington, Bost.	2	4
☐☐	2 Dallas Smith, Bost.	2	4
☐☐	3 André Pronovost, Bost.	2	4
☐☐	4 Charlie Burns, Bost.	2	4
☐☐	5 Léo Boivin, Bost.	3	6
☐☐	6 Don McKenney, Bost.	2	4
☐☐	7 John Bucyk, Bost.	6	11
☐☐	8 Murray Oliver, Bost.	2	4
☐☐	9 Jerry Toppazzini, Bost.	2	4
☐☐	10 Doug Mohns, Bost.	2	4
☐☐	11 Don Head (G), Bost.	2	4
☐☐	12 Bob Armstrong, Bost.	2	4
☐☐	13 Pat Stapleton, Bost.	2.75	4
☐☐	14 Orland Kurtenbach, Bost.	2	4
☐☐	15 Dick Meissner, Bost.	2	4
☐☐	16 Ted Green, Bost.	2.75	4
☐☐	17 Tom Williams, Bost.	2	4
☐☐	18 Aut Erickson, Bost.	2	4
☐☐	19 Phil Watson, Coach, Bost.	3	5
☐☐	20 Ed Chadwick (G), Bost.	2	4
☐☐	21 Wayne Hillman, Chic.	12	20
☐☐	22 Stan Mikita, Chic.	8	13
☐☐	23 Eric Nesterenko, Chic.	2	4
☐☐	24 Reggie Fleming, Chic.	2	4
☐☐	25 Bobby Hull, Chic.	17	25
☐☐	26 Elmer Vasko, Chic.	2	4
☐☐	27 Pierre Pilote, Chic.	3	6
☐☐	28 Chico Maki, Chic.	2	4
☐☐	29 Glenn Hall (G), Chic.	9	15
☐☐	30 Murray Balfour, Chic.	2	4
☐☐	31 Bronco Horvath, Chic.	2	4
☐☐	32 Kenny Wharram, Chic.	2	4
☐☐	33 Ab McDonald, Chic.	2	4
☐☐	34 Billy Hay, Chic.	2	4
☐☐	35 Dollard St. Laurent, Chic.	2	4
☐☐	36 Ron Murphy, Chic.	2	4
☐☐	37 Bob Turner, Chic.	2	4
☐☐	38 Gerry Melnyk, Chic., Error (Jerry)	2	4
☐☐	39 Jack Evans, Chic.	2	4
☐☐	40 Rudy Pilous, Coach, Chic.	3	6
☐☐	41 Johnny Bower (G), Toro.	8	13
☐☐	42 Allan Stanley, Toro.	3	6
☐☐	43 Frank Mahovlich, Toro.	9	15
☐☐	44 Tim Horton, Toro.	10	15
☐☐	45 Carl Brewer, Toro.	2	4
☐☐	46 Bob Pulford, Toro.	4	6
☐☐	47 Bob Nevin, Toro.	2	4
☐☐	48 Eddie Shack, Toro.	5	8
☐☐	49 Red Kelly, Toro.	5	9
☐☐	50 Bob Baun, Toro.	2	4
☐☐	51 George Armstrong, Toro.	4	7
☐☐	52 Bert Olmstead, Toro.	3	6
☐☐	53 Dick Duff, Toro.	2	4
☐☐	54 Billy Harris, Toro.	2	4
☐☐	55 Larry Keenan, Toro.	2	4
☐☐	56 John MacMillan, Toro.	2	4
☐☐	57 Punch Imlach, Coach, Toro.	3.25	5
☐☐	58 Dave Keon, Toro.	8	12
☐☐	59 Larry Hillman, Toro.	2	4
☐☐	60 Al Arbour, Toro.	3	6
☐☐	61 Sid Abel, Coach, Detr.	3	5
☐☐	62 Warren Godfrey, Detr.	2	4
☐☐	63 Vic Stasiuk, Detr.	2	4
☐☐	64 Léo Labine, Detr.	2	4
☐☐	65 Howie Glover, Detr.	2	4
☐☐	66 Gordie Howe, Detr.	26	40
☐☐	67 Val Fonteyne, Detr.	2	4
☐☐	68 Marcel Pronovost, Detr.	3	6
☐☐	69 Parker MacDonald, Detr.	2	4
☐☐	70 Alex Delvecchio, Detr.	6	10
☐☐	71 Ed Litzenberger, Detr.	2	4
☐☐	72 Al Johnson, Detr.	2	4
☐☐	73 Bruce MacGregor, Detr.	2	4
☐☐	74 Howie Young, Detr.	2	4
☐☐	75 Peter Goegan, Detr.	2	4
☐☐	76 Norm Ullman, Detr.	5	9
☐☐	77 Terry Sawchuk (G), Detr.	13	20
☐☐	78 Gerry Odrowski, Detr.	2	4
☐☐	79 Bill Gadsby, Detr.	3	6
☐☐	80 Hank Bassen (G), Detr.	2	4
☐☐	81 Doug Harvey, Coach, NYRa.	6	11
☐☐	82 Earl Ingarfield, NYRa.	2	4
☐☐	83 Pat Hannigan, NYRa.	2	4
☐☐	84 Dean Prentice, NYRa.	2	4
☐☐	85 Gump Worsley (G), NYRa.	8	14
☐☐	86 Irv Spencer, NYRa.	2	4
☐☐	87 Camille Henry, NYRa.	2	4
☐☐	88 Andy Bathgate, NYRa.	4	7
☐☐	89 Harry Howell, NYRa.	3	6
☐☐	90 Andy Hebenton, NYRa.	2	4
☐☐	91 Red Sullivan, NYRa.	2	4
☐☐	92 Ted Hampson, NYRa.	2	4
☐☐	93 Jean-Guy Gendron, NYRa.	2	4
☐☐	94 Al Langlois, NYRa.	2	4
☐☐	95 Larry Cahan, NYRa.	2	4
☐☐	96 Bob Cunningham, NYRa.	2	4
☐☐	97 Vic Hadfield, NYRa.	2.75	4
☐☐	98 Jean Ratelle, NYRa.	7	12
☐☐	99 Ken Schinkel, NYRa.	2	4
☐☐	100 Johnny Wilson, NYRa.	2	4
☐☐	101 Toe Blake, Coach, Mont.	4	6
☐☐	102 Jean Béliveau, Mont.	12	20
☐☐	103 Don Marshall, Mont.	2	4
☐☐	104 Bernie Geoffrion, Mont.	8	13
☐☐	105 Claude Provost, Mont.	2	4
☐☐	106 Tom Johnson, Mont.	3	6
☐☐	107 Dickie Moore, Mont.	6	10
☐☐	108 Bill Hicke, Mont.	2	4
☐☐	109 Jean-Guy Talbot, Mont.	2	4
☐☐	110 Henri Richard, Mont.	6	13
☐☐	111 Louie Fontinato, Mont.	2	4
☐☐	112 Gilles Tremblay, Mont.	2	4
☐☐	113 Jacques Plante (G), Mont.	12	20
☐☐	114 Ralph Backstrom, Mont.	2	4
☐☐	115 Marcel Bonin, Mont.	2	4
☐☐	116 Phil Goyette, Mont.	2	4
☐☐	117 Bobby Rousseau, Mont.	2	4
☐☐	118 J.C. Tremblay, Mont.	2	4
☐☐	119 Al MacNeil, Mont.	2	4
☐☐	120 Jean Gauthier, Mont.	2	4

1961 - 62 TOPPS

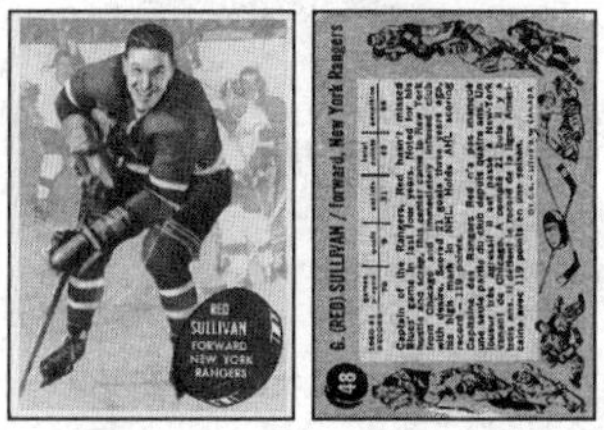

These cards measure the standard 2 1/2" x 3 1/2".

Complete Set (66 cards):		**1,350**	**2,200**
Topps		**EX**	**EX-NM**
☐	1 Phil Watson, Coach, Bost.	20	40
☐	**2 Ted Green, Bost. RC**	**30**	**50**
☐	3 Earl Balfour, Bost. LC	9	15
☐	**4 Dallas Smith, Bost. RC**	**25**	**35**
☐	5 André Pronovost, Bost.	9	15
☐	**6 Dick Meissner, Bost. RC**	**9**	**15**
☐	7 Léo Boivin, Bost.	12	20
☐	8 John Bucyk, Bost.	35	50
☐	9 Jerry Toppazzini, Bost.	9	15
☐	10 Doug Mohns, Bost.	9	15
☐	11 Charlie Burns, Bost.	9	15
☐	12 Don McKenney, Bost.	9	15
☐	13 Bob Armstrong, Bost. LC	9	15
☐	14 Murray Oliver, Bost.	9	15
☐	**15 Orland Kurtenbach, Bost. RC**	**13**	**22**
☐	**16 Terry Gray, Bost. RC**	**9**	**15**
☐	**17 Don Head (G), Bost. RC/LC**	**15**	**25**
☐	**18 Pat Stapleton, Bost. RC**	**25**	**35**
☐	**19 Cliff Pennington, Bost. RC**	**9**	**15**
☐	20 1961 Boston Bruins	40	60
☐	21 Balfour / Flaman (Action)	9	15
☐	22 Bathgate / Hall (Action)	25	35
☐	23 Rudy Pilous, Coach, Chic.	20	30
☐	24 Pierre Pilote, Chic.	20	30
☐	25 Elmer Vasko, Chic.	9	15
☐	**26 Reggie Fleming, Chic. RC**	**12**	**20**
☐	27 Ab McDonald, Chic.	9	15
☐	28 Eric Nesterenko, Chic.	9	15
☐	29 Bobby Hull, Chic.	275	425
☐	30 Kenny Wharram, Chic.	9	15
☐	31 Dollard St.Laurent, Chic.	9	15
☐	32 Glenn Hall (G), Chic.	40	75
☐	33 Murray Balfour, Chic.	9	15
☐	34 Ron Murphy, Chic.	9	15
☐	35 Red Hay, Chic.	9	15
☐	36 Stan Mikita, Chic.	150	250
☐	**37 Denis DeJordy (G), Chic. RC**	**25**	**40**
☐	**38 Wayne Hillman, Chic. RC**	**9**	**15**
☐	**39 Rino Robazza, Chic. RC/LC**	**12**	**20**
☐	40 Bronco Horvath, Chic.	9	15
☐	41 Bob Turner, Chic.	9	15
☐	42 1961 Chicago Blackhawks	40	60
☐	43 Wharran (Action)	9	15
☐	44 Dollard St. Laurent/ Hall (Action)	20	35
☐	45 Doug Harvey, NYRa.	30	50
☐	46 Al Langlois, NYRa.	9	15
☐	**47 Irv Spencer, NYRa. RC**	**9**	**15**
☐	48 Red Sullivan, NYRa.	9	15
☐	49 Earl Ingarfield, NYRa.	9	15
☐	50 Gump Worsley (G), NYRa.	35	55
☐	51 Harry Howell, NYRa.	20	30
☐	52 Larry Cahan, NYRa.	9	15
☐	53 Andy Bathgate, NYRa.	20	30
☐	54 Dean Prentice, NYRa.	9	15
☐	55 Andy Hebenton, NYRa.	9	15
☐	56 Camille Henry, NYRa.	9	15
☐	57 Jean Guy Gendron, NYRa.	9	15
☐	**58 Pat Hannigan, NYRa. RC**	**9**	**15**
☐	59 Ted Hampson, NYRa.	9	15
☐	**60 Jean Ratelle, NYRa. RC**	**100**	**175**
☐	**61 Al LeBrun, NYRa. RC**	**9**	**15**
☐	**62 Rod Gilbert, NYRa. RC**	**100**	**175**
☐	63 1961 New York Rangers	35	60
☐	64 Meissner / Worsley (Action)	20	35
☐	65 Worsley (Action)	20	35
☐	66 Checklist (1 - 66)	200	425

STAMPS

These blank-back stamps were issued in pairs. Separated stamps measure 1 3/8" x 1 7/8". Pricing below is for separated stamps.

Insert Set (52 stamps):		**1,000**	**1,800**
Boston Bruins		**EX**	**EX-NM**
☐	Léo Boivin	15	25
☐	John Bucyk	30	50
☐	Charlie Burns	13	25
☐	Don McKenney	13	25
☐	Doug Mohns	13	25
☐	Murray Oliver	13	25
☐	André Pronovost	13	25
☐	Dallas Smith	20	30
New York Rangers		**EX**	**EX-NM**
☐	Andy Bathgate	18	30
☐	Doug Harvey	35	55
☐	Andy Hebenton	13	25
☐	Camille Henry	13	25
☐	Harry Howell	15	25
☐	Al Langlois	13	25
☐	Dean Prentice	13	25
☐	Gump Worsley (G)	35	55
Chicago Blackhawks		**EX**	**EX-NM**
☐	Murray Balfour	13	25
☐	Jack Evans	13	25
☐	Glenn Hall (G)	45	75
☐	Billy Hay	13	25
☐	Bronco Horvath	13	25
☐	Bobby Hull	150	250
☐	Stan Mikita	90	150
☐	Ron Murphy	13	25
☐	Pierre Pilote	15	25
☐	Elmer Vasko	13	25
All-Time Greats		**EX**	**EX-NM**
☐	Richard Boon	15	25
☐	Frank Boucher	15	25
☐	Francis (King) Clancy	30	50
☐	Dit Clapper	20	35
☐	Spague Cleghorn	18	30
☐	Alex Connell (G)	15	25
☐	Bill Cook	15	25
☐	Cy Denneny	15	25
☐	Frank Frederickson	13	25
☐	Chuck Gardiner (G)	18	30
☐	Herb Gardiner	13	25
☐	Eddie Gerard	13	25
☐	Frank (Moose) Goheen	13	25
☐	George Hay	15	25
☐	Dick Irvin	25	40
☐	Ernest (Moose) Johnson	13	25
☐	Edouard (Newsy) Lalonde	20	35
☐	Hugh Lehman	13	25
☐	Joe Malone	35	55
☐	Paddy Moran (G)	18	30
☐	Howie Morenz	75	125
☐	Frank Nighbor	15	25
☐	Art Ross	40	65
☐	Nels Stewart	25	40
☐	Fred (Cyclone) Taylor	35	55
☐	Georges Vézina (G)	60	100

1961 - 62 TORONTO STAR PHOTOS

These are colour newspaper photos.

Toronto Star		**EX**	**EX-MT**
☐	Jan. 6 Elmer Vasko, Chic.	7	12
☐	Jan. 13 Gump Worsley (G), NYRa.	18	28
☐	Jan. 20 Don McKenney, Bost.	7	12
☐	Jan. 27 Eddie Shack, Toro.	12	20
☐	Feb. 3 Claude Provost, Mont.	7	12
☐	Feb. 10 Gordie Howe, Detr.	30	50
☐	Feb. 17 Glenn Hall (G), Chic.	20	30
☐	Feb. 24 Doug Harvey, NYRa.	15	25
☐	Mar. 3 Jacques Plante (G), Mont.	25	40
☐	Mar. 10 Carl Brewer, Toro.	7	12
☐	Mar. 17 Dave Keon, Toro.	13	22
☐	Mar. 24 Bill Gadsby, NYRa.	9	15

1961 - 62 WEEKEND PHOTOS

These colour newspaper photos measure 5 1/2" x 6 1/2".

Toronto Star		**EX**	**EX-NM**
☐	V9 Claude Provost, Mont.	7	12
☐	V9 Elmer Vasko, Chic.	7	12
☐	V9 Dave Keon, Toro.	13	22
☐	V9 Warren Godfrey, Detr.	7	12
☐	V9 Gump Worsley (G), NYRa.	18	28
☐	V9 Doug Mohns, Bost.	7	12
☐	V9 Marcel Bonin, Mont.	7	12
☐	V9 Allan Stanley, Toro.	9	15
☐	V9 Johnny Bower (G), Toro.	15	25
☐	V9 Stan Mikita, Chic.	20	30
☐	V9 Don McKenney, Bost.	7	12
☐	V9 Doug Harvey, NYRa.	15	25
☐	V9 Jean Guy Talbot, Mont.	7	12

1961 - 62 YORK YELLOW BACKS

These cards measure the standard 2 1/2" x 3 1/2".

Complete Set (42 cards):		**350**	**600**
Album:		**30**	**60**
York Peanut Butter		**EX**	**EX-NM**
☐	1 Bob Baun, Toro.	11	22
☐	2 Dick Duff, Toro.	7	12
☐	3 Frank Mahovlich, Toro.	22	45
☐	4 Gilles Tremblay, Mont.	7	12
☐	5 Dickie Moore, Mont.	13	22
☐	6 Don Marshall, Mont.	7	12
☐	7 Tim Horton, Toro.	22	45
☐	8 Johnny Bower (G), Toro.	18	28
☐	9 Allan Stanley, Toro.	12	20
☐	10 Jean Béliveau, Mont.	28	45
☐	11 Tom Johnson, Mont.	12	20
☐	12 Jean-Guy Talbot, Mont.	7	12
☐	13 Carl Brewer, Toro.	7	12
☐	14 Bob Pulford, Toro.	13	22
☐	15 Billy Harris, Toro.	7	12
☐	16 Bill Hicke, Mont.	7	12
☐	17 Claude Provost, Mont.	9	15
☐	18 Henri Richard, Mont.	18	28

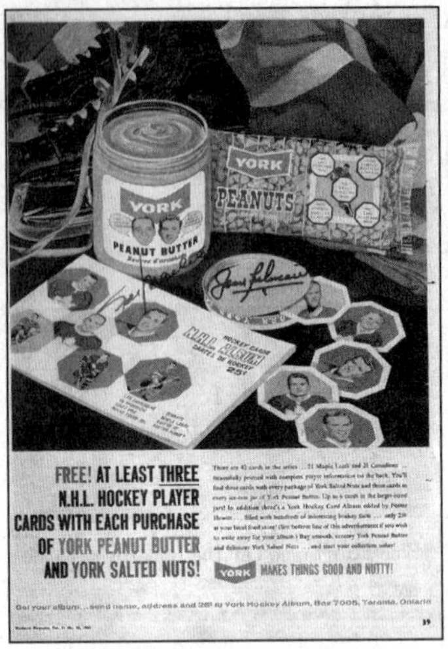

(Left) An advertisement for the 1961-62 York series, placed in Weekend magazine.

19 Bert Olmstead, Toro.	12	20
20 Ron Stewart, Toro.	7	12
21 Red Kelly, Toro.	15	25
22 Toe Blake, Coach, Mont.	13	22
23 Jacques Plante (G), Mont.	35	60
24 Ralph Backstrom, Mont.	7	12
25 Eddie Shack, Toro.	13	22
26 Bob Nevin, Toro.	7	12
27 Dave Keon, Toro.	22	45
28 Bernie Geoffrion, Mont.	18	28
29 Marcel Bonin, Mont.	7	12
30 Phil Goyette, Mont.	7	12
31 Larry Hillman, Toro.	7	12
32 Larry Keenan, Toro.	7	12
33 Al Arbour, Toro.	12	20
34 J.C. Tremblay, Mont.	9	15
35 Bobby Rousseau, Mont.	7	12
36 Al MacNeil, Mont.	7	12
37 George Armstrong, Toro.	13	22
38 Punch Imlach, Manager & Coach, Toro.	12	20
39 Francis (King) Clancy, Toro.	15	25
40 Louie Fontinato, Mont.	7	12
41 Césare Maniago (G), Mont.	9	15
42 Jean Gauthier, Mont.	8	16

1962 - 63 H.M. COWAN CERAMIC TILES

These tiles were manufactured, at least in part, in Hamilton, Ontario. The packaging indicates the tiles came from England. It was reported that this series was never officially licensed.

H.M. Cowan — **EX EX-NM**

- Sid Abel
- Al Arbour, Toro.
- George Armstrong, Toro.
- Ralph Backstrom, Mont.
- Murray Balfour, Chic.
- Dave Balon, NYRa.
- Doug Barkley, Detr.
- Andy Bathgate, NYRa.
- Bobby Baun, Toro.
- Red Berenson, Mont.
- Léo Boivin, Bost.
- Johnny Bower (G), Toro.
- Carl Brewer, Toro.
- Johnny Bucyk, Bost.
- Charlie Burns, Bost.
- Larry Cahan, NYRa.
- Wayne Connelly, Bost.
- Alex Delvecchio, Detr.
- Jack Evans, Chic.
- Alex Faulkner, Detr.
- Reggie Fleming, Chic.
- Val Fonteyne, Detr.
- Lou Fontinato, Mont.
- Bill Gadsby, Detr.
- Jean Gauthier, Mont.
- Guy Gendron, Bost.
- Bernie Geoffrion, Mont.
- Warren Godfrey, Bost.
- Phil Goyette, Mont.
- Ted Green, Bost.
- Vic Hadfield, NYRa.
- Glenn Hall (G), Chic.
- Ted Hampson, NYRa.
- Billy Harris, Toro.
- Doug Harvey, NYRa.
- Bill Hay, Chic.
- Andy Hebenton, NYRa.
- Bill Hicke, Mont.
- Wayne Hicks, Bost.
- Wayne Hillman, Chic.
- Tim Horton, Toro.
- Bronco Horvath, NYRa.
- Gordie Howe, Detr.
- Harry Howell, NYRa.
- Bobby Hull, Chic.
- Punch Imlach, Toro.
- Earl Ingarfield, NYRa.
- Tom Johnson, Mont.
- Red Kelly, Toro.
- Dave Keon, Toro.
- Al Langlois, NYRa.
- Eddie Litzenberger, Toro.
- Len Lunde, Chic.
- Parker MacDonald, Detr.
- Bruce MacGregor, Detr.
- John MacMillan, Toro.
- Al MacNeil, Chic.
- Frank Mahovlich, Toro.
- Chico Maki, Chic.
- Césare Maniago (G), Mont.
- Don Marshall, Mont.
- Ab McDonald, Chic.
- Don McKenney, Bost.
- Stan Mikita, Chic.
- Doug Mohns, Bost.
- Dickie Moore, Mont.
- Ron Murphy, Chic.
- Eric Nesterenko, Chic.
- Bob Nevin, Toro.
- Murray Oliver, Bost.
- Muzz Patrick, Bost.
- Cliff Pennington, Bost.
- Bob Perreault (G), Bost.
- Pierre Pilote, Chic.
- Jacques Plante (G), Mont.
- Dean Prentice, NYRa.
- Andre Pronovost, Bost.
- Marcel Pronovost, Detr.
- Claude Provost, Mont.
- Bob Pulford, Toro.
- Jean Ratelle, NYRa.
- Henri Richard, Mont.
- Dennis Riggin (G), Detr.
- Bobby Rousseau, Mont.
- Terry Sawchuk (G), Detr.
- Eddie Shack, Toro.
- Floyd Smith, Detr.
- Irv Spencer, Bost.
- Allan Stanley, Toro.
- Pat Stapleton, Bost.
- Vic Stasiuk, Detr.
- Ron Stewart, Toro.
- Jean Guy Talbot, Mont.
- Jerry Toppazzini, Bost.
- Gilles Tremblay, Mont.
- J.C. Tremblay, Mont.
- Bob Turner, Chic.
- Norm Ullman, Detr.
- Elmer Vasko, Chic.
- Ken Wharram, Chic.
- Tommy Williams, Bost.
- Gump Worsley (G), NYRa.
- Howie Young, Detr.

1962 - 63 EL PRODUCTO

These disks measure 3" in diameter. They were issued as a six-disk panel.

Complete Set (6 disks):	**150**	**300**
El Producto	**EX**	**EX-NM**
Jean Béliveau, Mont.	45	70
Gordie Howe, Detr.	65	110
Dave Keon, Toro.	28	45
Glenn Hall (G), Chic.	30	50
Henri Richard, Mont.	28	45
Frank Mahovlich, Toro.	30	50

1962 - 63 PARKHURST

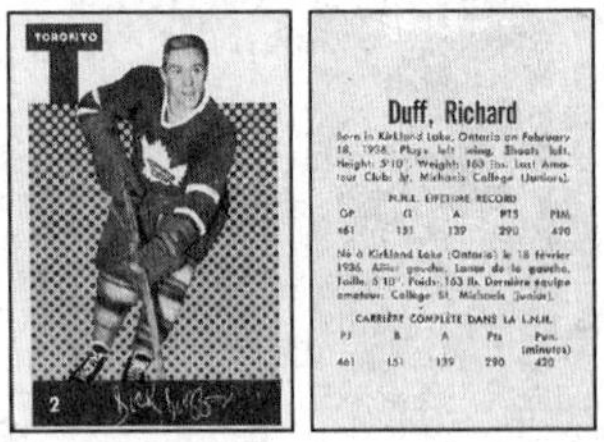

These cards measure 2 7/16" x 3 5/8".

Complete Set (56 cards):	**1,350**	**2,200**
Parkhurst	**EX**	**EX-NM**
1 Billy Harris, Toro.	30	55
2 Dick Duff, Toro.	10	18
3 Bob Baun, Toro.	10	18
4 Frank Mahovlich, Toro.	60	95
5 Red Kelly, Toro.	20	30
6 Ron Stewart, Toro.	10	18
7 Tim Horton, Toro.	70	110
8 Carl Brewer, Toro.	10	18
9 Allan Stanley, Toro.	15	25
10 Bob Nevin, Toro.	10	18
11 Bob Pulford, Toro.	15	25
12 Ed Litzenberger, Toro.	10	18
13 George Armstrong, Toro.	13	22
14 Eddie Shack, Toro.	45	70
15 Dave Keon, Toro.	80	125
16 Johnny Bower (G), Toro.	40	60
18 Larry Hillman, Toro.	10	18
18 Frank Mahovlich, Toro.	60	95
19 Hank Bassen (G), Detr. RC	**12**	**20**
20 Gerry Odrowski, Detr. RC	**10**	**18**
21 Norm Ullman, Detr.	25	45
22 Vic Stasiuk, Detr.	10	18
23 Bruce MacGregor, Detr. RC	**10**	**18**
24 Claude Laforge, Detr. LC	10	18
25 Bill Gadsby, Detr.	12	20
26 Léo Labine, Detr. LC	10	18
27 Val Fonteyne, Detr.	10	18
28 Howie Glover, Detr. LC	10	18
29 Marc Boileau, Detr. RC/LC	**12**	**20**
30 Gordie Howe, Detr.	200	325
31 Gordie Howe, Detr.	200	325
32 Alex Delvecchio, Detr.	20	30
33 Marcel Pronovost, Detr.	12	20
34 Sid Abel, Coach, Detr.	12	20
35 Len Lunde, Detr.	10	18
36 Warren Godfrey, Detr. LC	10	18
37 Phil Goyette, Mont.	10	18
38 Henri Richard, Mont.	55	85
39 Jean Béliveau, Mont.	65	100
40 Bill Hicke, Mont.	10	18
41 Claude Provost, Mont.	10	18
42 Dickie Moore, Mont. LC	15	25
43 Don Marshall, Mont.	10	18
44 Ralph Backstrom, Mont.	10	18
45 Marcel Bonin, Mont. LC	10	18
46 Gilles Tremblay, Mont. RC	**22**	**45**
47 Bobby Rousseau, Mont. RC	**20**	**30**
48 Bernie Geoffrion, Mont.	40	60
49 Jacques Plante (G), Mont.	90	150
50 Tom Johnson, Mont.	12	20
51 Jean-Guy Talbot, Mont.	10	18
52 Louie Fontinato, Mont. LC	10	18
53 Bernie Geoffrion, Mont.	40	60
54 J.C. Tremblay, Mont. RC	**50**	**80**
Checklist Card	300	475
Zip Card	160	275

1962 - 63 SHIRRIFF

These metal wheels measure 1 1/2" in diameter.

Complete Set (60 wheels):	**250**	**400**
Common Player:	**3**	**5**
Shirriff	**EX**	**EX-NM**
1 Johnny Bower (G), Toro.	8	14
2 Allan Stanley, Toro.	4	7
3 Frank Mahovlich, Toro.	12	18
4 Tim Horton, Toro.	12	20
5 Carl Brewer, Toro.	3	5
6 Bob Pulford, Toro.	5	8
7 Bob Nevin, Toro.	3	5
8 Eddie Shack, Toro.	6	10
9 Red Kelly, Toro.	6	10
10 George Armstrong, Toro.	5	8
11 Bert Olmstead, Toro.	4	7
12 Dick Duff, Toro.	3	5
13 Billy Harris, Toro.	3	5
14 John MacMillan, Toro.	3	5
15 Punch Imlach, Coach, Toro.	4	7
16 Dave Keon, Toro.	8	13
18 Larry Hillman, Toro.	3	5
18 Ed Litzenberger, Toro.	3	5
19 Bob Baun, Toro.	3	5
20 Al Arbour, Toro.	4	7
21 Ron Stewart, Toro.	3	5
22 Don Simmons (G), Toro.	3	6
23 Louie Fontinato, Mont.	3	5
24 Gilles Tremblay, Mont.	3	5
25 Jacques Plante (G), Mont.	16	25
26 Ralph Backstrom, Mont.	3	5
27 Marcel Bonin, Mont.	3	5
28 Phil Goyette, Mont.	3	5
29 Bobby Rousseau, Mont.	3	5
30 J.C. Tremblay, Mont.	3	6
31 Toe Blake, Coach, Mont.	5	8
32 Jean Béliveau, Mont.	16	25
33 Don Marshall, Mont.	3	5
34 Bernie Geoffrion, Mont.	9	15
35 Claude Provost, Mont.	3	5
36 Tom Johnson, Mont.	4	7
37 Dickie Moore, Mont.	6	10
38 Bill Hicke, Mont.	3	6
39 Jean-Guy Talbot, Mont.	3	5
40 Al MacNeil, Mont.	3	5
41 Henri Richard, Mont.	7	13
42 Red Berenson, Mont.	3	5
43 AS: Jacques Plante (G)	11	18
44 AS: Jean-Guy Talbot	3	5
45 AS: Doug Harvey	6	11
46 AS: Stan Mikita	8	14
47 AS: Bobby Hull	20	30
48 AS: Andy Bathgate	5	8
49 AS: Glenn Hall (G)	9	15
50 AS: Pierre Pilote	5	8
51 AS: Carl Brewer	3	5
52 AS: Dave Keon	7	12
53 AS: Frank Mahovlich	9	14
54 AS: Gordie Howe	32	55
55 AW: Dave Keon, Toro.	7	12
56 AW: Bobby Rousseau, Mont.	3	5
57 AW: Bobby Hull, Chic.	20	30
58 AW: Jacques Plante (G), Mont.	11	20
59 AW: Jacques Plante (G), Mont.	11	20
60 AW: Doug Harvey, NYR	8	13

1962 - 63 TOPPS

These blue-border cards measure the standard 2 1/2" x 3 1/2".

Complete Set (66 cards):	**1,100**	**1,800**
Topps	**EX**	**EX-NM**
1 Phil Watson, Coach, Bost.	12	45
2 Robert (Miche) Perreault (G), Bost. RC/LC	**15**	**25**
3 Bruce Gamble (G), Bost. RC	**13**	**22**
4 Warren Godfrey, Bost. LC	9	16
5 Léo Boivin, Bost.	12	20
6 Doug Mohns, Bost.	9	16
7 Ted Green, Bost.	9	16

		EX	EX-NM
☐	8 Pat Stapleton, Bost.	9	16
☐	9 Dallas Smith, Bost.	9	16
☐	10 Don McKenney, Bost.	9	16
☐	11 John Bucyk, Bost.	30	45
☐	12 Murray Oliver, Bost.	9	16
☐	13 Jerry Toppazzini, Bost.	9	16
☐	14 Cliff Pennington, Bost. LC	9	16
☐	15 Charlie Burns, Bost.	9	16
☐	16 Jean-Guy Gendron, Bost.	9	16
☐	17 Irv Spencer, Bost. LC	9	16
☐	18 Wayne Connelly, Bost.	9	16
☐	19 André Pronovost, Bost.	9	16
☐	20 Terry Gray, Bost.	9	16
☐	**21 Tom Williams, Bost. RC**	**10**	**20**
☐	22 Boston Bruins	30	55
☐	23 Rudy Pilous, Coach, Chic.	12	20
☐	24 Glenn Hall (G), Chic.	45	70
☐	25 Denis DeJordy (G), Chic.	12	20
☐	26 Jack Evans, Chic. LC	9	16
☐	27 Elmer Vasko, Chic.	9	16
☐	28 Pierre Pilote, Chic.	20	30
☐	29 Bob Turner, Chic.	9	16
☐	30 Dollard St. Laurent, Chic. LC	9	16
☐	31 Wayne Hillman, Chic.	9	16
☐	32 Al MacNeil, Chic.	9	16
☐	33 Bobby Hull, Chic.	275	425
☐	34 Stan Mikita, Chic.	110	175
☐	35 Red Hay, Chic.	9	16
☐	36 Murray Balfour, Chic.	9	16
☐	**37 Chico Maki, Chic. RC**	**20**	**30**
☐	38 Ab McDonald, Chic., Error (MacDonald)	9	16
☐	39 Kenny Wharram, Chic.	9	16
☐	40 Ron Murphy, Chic.	9	16
☐	41 Eric Nesterenko, Chic.	9	16
☐	42 Reggie Fleming, Chic.	9	16
☐	**43 Murray Hall, Chic. RC**	**10**	**20**
☐	44 Chicago Blackhawks	30	50
☐	45 Gump Worsley (G), NYRa.	30	45
☐	46 Harry Howell, NYRa.	20	30
☐	47 Al Langlois, NYRa.	9	16
☐	48 Larry Cahan, NYRa.	9	16
☐	**49 Jim Neilson, NYRa. RC**	**20**	**30**
☐	50 Al LeBrun, NYRa. LC	9	16
☐	51 Earl Ingarfield, NYRa.	9	16
☐	52 Andy Bathgate, NYRa.	20	30
☐	53 Dean Prentice, NYRa.	9	16
☐	54 Andy Hebenton, NYRa.	9	16
☐	55 Ted Hampson, NYRa.	9	16
☐	**56 Dave Balon, NYRa. RC**	**10**	**20**
☐	57 Bert Olmstead, NYRa. LC	12	20
☐	58 Jean Ratelle, NYRa.	40	65
☐	59 Rod Gilbert, NYRa.	40	65
☐	**60 Vic Hadfield, NYRa. RC**	**30**	**50**
☐	61 Frank Paice, Trainer, NYRa.	9	16
☐	62 Camille Henry, NYRa.	9	16
☐	63 Bronco Horvath, NYRa. LC	9	16
☐	64 Pat Hannigan, NYRa. LC, Error (Hanningan)	9	16
☐	65 New York Rangers	30	50
☐	66 Checklist (1 - 66)	175	350

HOCKEY DOLLARS

The paper-stock dollars came folded one per pack. Each bill measures 4 1/8" x 1 3/4".

	Complete Set (24 bills):	**750**	**1,300**
	Topps	**EX**	**EX-NM**
☐	Léo Boivin, Bost.	30	45
☐	John Bucyk, Bost.	40	65
☐	Warren Godfrey, Bost.	20	30
☐	Ted Green, Bost.	22	45
☐	Don McKenney, Bost.	22	45
☐	Doug Mohns, Bost.	22	45
☐	Murray Oliver, Bost.	20	30
☐	Jerry Toppazzini, Bost.	20	30
☐	Reggie Fleming, Chic.	20	30
☐	Glenn Hall (G), Chic.	50	85
☐	Billy Hay, Chic.	22	45
☐	Bobby Hull, Chic.	150	250
☐	Ab McDonald, Chic., Error (MacDonald)	20	30
☐	Stan Mikita, Chic.	70	125
☐	Pierre Pilote, Chic.	35	60
☐	Elmer Vasko, Chic.	20	30
☐	Dave Balon, NYRa.	20	30
☐	Andy Bathgate, NYRa.	35	60
☐	Andy Hebenton, NYRa.	20	30
☐	Harry Howell, NYRa.	25	45
☐	Earl Ingarfield, NYRa.	22	45
☐	Al Langlois, NYRa.	22	45
☐	Dean Prentice, NYRa.	22	45
☐	Gump Worsley (G), NYRa.	40	70

1962 - 63 TORONTO STAR PHOTOS

These are colour newspaper photos.

	Toronto Star	**EX**	**EX-MT**
☐	Dec. 8 Ron Stewart, Toro.	7	12
☐	Dec. 15 Bob Perreault (G), Bost. (2 Pages)	9	15
☐	Dec. 22 Dean Prentice, NYRa.	7	12
☐	Dec. 29 Terry Sawchuk (G), Detr. (2 Pages)	25	45
☐	Dec. 29 Bobby Hull, Chic.	25	45
☐	Jan. 5 Louie Fontinato, Mont. (2 Pages)	7	12
☐	Jan. 12 Frank Mahovlich, Toro.	20	35
☐	Jan. 19 Bill Hay, Chic.	7	12
☐	Jan. 26 Charlie Burns, Bost.	7	12
☐	Feb. 2 Rod Gilbert, NYRa.	12	20
☐	Feb. 9 Henri Richard, Mont.	15	25
☐	Feb. 16 Camille Henry, NYRa.	7	12
☐	Feb. 23 Léo Boivin, Bost.	9	15
☐	Mar. 2 Dickie Moore, Mont.	12	20
☐	Mar. 9 Parker MacDonald, Detr.	7	12
☐	Mar. 16 Kenny Wharram, Chic.	7	12
☐	Mar. 23 Kent Douglas, Toro.	7	12

1962 - 63 WEEKEND PHOTOS

These colour newspaper photos measure 5 1/2" x 6 1/2".

	Toronto Star	**EX**	**EX-NM**
☐	V10 Frank Mahovlich, Toro.	20	30
☐	V10 Gilles Tremblay, Mont.	7	12
☐	V10 Ab McDonald, Chic.	7	12
☐	V10 Alex Delvecchio, Detr.	12	20
☐	V10 Earl Ingarfield, NYRa.	7	12
☐	V10 Tim Horton, Toro.	22	45
☐	V10 Glenn Hall (G), Chic.	20	30
☐	V10 Murray Oliver, Bost.	7	12
☐	V10 Marcel Pronovost, Detr.	9	15
☐	V10 Henri Richard, Mont.	13	22
☐	V10 Andy Bathgate, NYRa.	11	18

1962 - 63 YORK PEANUT BUTTER IRON-ON TRANSFERS

These transfers were inserted into jars of York peanut butter and packages of salted peanuts. Each transfer measures 2 3/16" x 4 5/16".

	Complete Set (36 transfers):	**1,500**	**2,500**
	York	**EX**	**EX-NM**
☐	1 Johnny Bower (G), Toro.	50	85
☐	2 Jacques Plante (G), Mont.	110	200
☐	3 Tim Horton, Toro.	65	110
☐	4 Jean-Guy Talbot, Mont.	25	40
☐	5 Carl Brewer, Toro.	25	40
☐	6 J.C. Tremblay, Mont.	30	50
☐	7 Dick Duff, Mont.	25	40
☐	8 Jean Béliveau, Mont.	75	125
☐	9 Dave Keon, Toro.	45	75
☐	10 Henri Richard, Mont.	50	85
☐	11 Frank Mahovlich, Toro.	50	85
☐	12 Bernie Geoffrion, Mont.	50	80
☐	13 Kent Douglas, Toro.	25	40
☐	14 Claude Provost, Mont.	30	50
☐	15 Bob Pulford, Toro.	35	60
☐	16 Ralph Backstrom, Mont.	25	40
☐	17 George Armstrong, Toro.	40	70
☐	18 Bobby Rousseau, Mont.	25	40
☐	19 Gordie Howe, Detr.	190	365
☐	20 Red Kelly,Toro.	45	75
☐	21 Alex Delvecchio, Detr.	45	75
☐	22 Dickie Moore, Mont.	40	70
☐	23 Marcel Pronovost, Mont.	35	55
☐	24 Doug Barkley, Detr.	25	40
☐	25 Terry Sawchuk (G), Detr.	85	140
☐	26 Billy Harris, Toro.	25	40
☐	27 Parker MacDonald, Detr.	25	40
☐	28 Don Marshall, Mont.	25	40
☐	29 Norm Ullman, Toro.	50	75
☐	30 André Pronovost, Mont.	25	40
☐	30 Vic Stasiuk, Detr.	25	40
☐	31 Bill Gadsby, Detr.	35	55
☐	32 Eddie Shack, Toro.	45	75
☐	33 Larry Jeffrey, Detr.	25	40
☐	34 Gilles Tremblay, Mont.	25	40
☐	35 Howie Young, Detr.	25	40
☐	36 Bruce MacGregor, Detr.	25	50

1963 - 64 PARKHURST

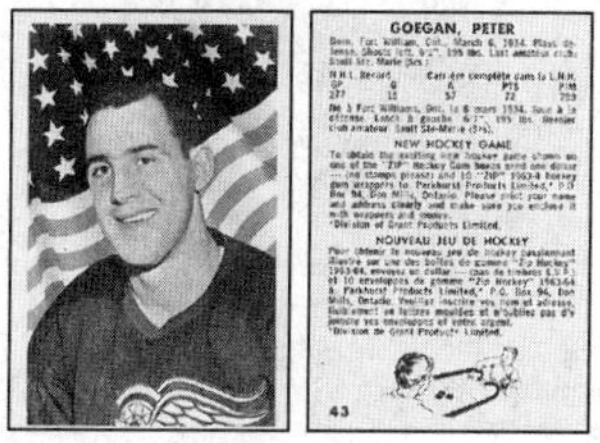

"These cards have a flag in the background. The Detroit players had the United States flag while the Canadian team players had a Union Jack. The '63-64 set is a classic set. It has the nicest Gordie Howe card as well as so many other cards that look so nice. It was the last year I collected cards for awhile. When you got a little older (as a teenager), you get into other things." – Jerry Semaka, J.J.'s Sportscards, Courtenay, British Columbia.

These cards measure 2 7/16" x 3 5/8".

	Complete Set (99 cards):	**1,650**	**2,900**
	Parkhurst	**EX**	**EX-MT**
☐	1 Allan Stanley, Toro.	25	55
☐	2 Don Simmons (G), Toro.	12	20
☐	3 Red Kelly, Toro.	18	30
☐	4 Dick Duff, Toro.	10	17
☐	5 Johnny Bower (G), Toro.	35	60
☐	6 Ed Litzenberger, Toro. LC	10	17
☐	**7 Kent Douglas, Toro. RC**	**10**	**20**
☐	8 Carl Brewer, Toro.	10	17
☐	9 Eddie Shack, Toro.	35	60
☐	10 Bob Nevin, Toro.	10	17
☐	11 Billy Harris, Toro.	10	17
☐	12 Bob Pulford, Toro.	12	20
☐	13 George Armstrong, Toro.	13	25
☐	14 Ron Stewart, Toro.	10	17
☐	**15 John MacMillan, Toro. RC/LC**	**15**	**25**
☐	16 Tim Horton, Toro.	60	110
☐	17 Frank Mahovlich, Toro.	60	100
☐	18 Bob Baun, Toro.	10	17
☐	19 Punch Imlach, G.M. & Coach, Toro.	15	25
☐	20 Francis (King) Clancy, A.G.M., Toro.	22	45
☐	21 Gilles Tremblay, Mont.	10	17
☐	22 Jean-Guy Talbot, Mont.	10	17
☐	23 Henri Richard, Mont.	50	75
☐	24 Ralph Backstrom, Mont.	10	17
☐	25 Bill Hicke, Mont.	10	17
☐	**26 Red Berenson, Mont. RC**	**30**	**50**
☐	**27 Jacques Laperrière, Mont. RC**	**35**	**55**
☐	**28 Jean Gauthier, Mont. RC/LC**	**12**	**20**
☐	29 Bernie Geoffrion, Mont.	30	50
☐	30 Jean Béliveau, Mont.	50	90
☐	31 J.C. Tremblay, Mont.	13	25
☐	**32 Terry Harper, Mont. RC**	**22**	**45**
☐	**33 John Ferguson Sr., Mont. RC**	**60**	**100**
☐	34 Toe Blake, Coach, Mont.	13	25
☐	35 Bobby Rousseau, Mont.	10	17
☐	36 Claude Provost, Mont.	10	17
☐	37 Marc Réaume, Mont.	10	17
☐	38 Dave Balon, Mont.	10	17
☐	39 Gump Worsley (G), Mont.	30	50
☐	**40 Césare Maniago (G), Mont. RC**	**40**	**65**
☐	41 Bruce MacGregor, Detr.	10	17
☐	**42 Alex Faulkner, Detr. RC/LC**	**50**	**80**
☐	43 Peter Goegan, Detr. LC	10	17
☐	44 Parker MacDonald, Detr.	10	17
☐	45 André Pronovost, Detr. LC	10	17
☐	46 Marcel Pronovost, Detr.	12	20
☐	**47 Bob Dillabough, Detr. RC**	**10**	**20**
☐	**48 Larry Jeffrey, Detr. RC**	**10**	**20**
☐	49 Ian Cushenan, Detr. LC	10	17
☐	50 Alex Delvecchio, Detr.	20	30
☐	51 Hank Ciesla, Detr. LC	10	17
☐	52 Norm Ullman, Detr.	25	40
☐	53 Terry Sawchuk (G), Detr.	90	150
☐	**54 Ron Ingram, Detr. RC/LC**	**12**	**20**
☐	55 Gordie Howe, Detr.	320	525
☐	56 Billy McNeill, Detr. LC	10	17
☐	**57 Floyd Smith, Detr. RC**	**12**	**22**
☐	58 Vic Stasiuk, Detr. LC	10	17
☐	59 Bill Gadsby, Detr.	12	20
☐	**60 Doug Barkley, Detr. RC**	**10**	**20**
☐	61 Allan Stanley, Toro.	13	22
☐	62 Don Simmons (G), Toro.	12	20
☐	63 Red Kelly, Toro.	18	28
☐	64 Dick Duff, Toro.	10	17
☐	65 Johnny Bower (G), Toro.	35	60
☐	66 Ed Litzenberger, Toro. LC	10	17
☐	**67 Kent Douglas, Toro. RC**	**10**	**20**
☐	68 Carl Brewer, Toro.	10	17
☐	69 Eddie Shack, Toro.	35	60
☐	70 Bob Nevin, Toro.	10	17
☐	71 Billy Harris, Toro.	10	17
☐	72 Bob Pulford, Toro.	12	22
☐	73 George Armstrong, Toro.	13	22
☐	74 Ron Stewart, Toro.	10	17
☐	75 Dave Keon, Toro.	55	85
☐	76 Tim Horton, Toro.	60	100
☐	77 Frank Mahovlich, Toro.	60	100
☐	78 Bob Baun, Toro.	10	17
☐	79 Punch Imlach, G.M. & Coach, Toro.	15	25
☐	80 Gilles Tremblay, Mont.	10	17
☐	81 Jean-Guy Talbot, Mont.	10	17
☐	82 Henri Richard, Mont.	50	75
☐	83 Ralph Backstrom, Mont.	10	17
☐	84 Bill Hicke, Mont.	10	17
☐	**85 Red Berenson, Mont. RC**	**30**	**50**
☐	**86 Jacques Laperrière, Mont. RC**	**35**	**55**
☐	**87 Jean Gauthier, Mont. RC/LC**	**15**	**25**
☐	88 Bernie Geoffrion, Mont.	30	50
☐	89 Jean Béliveau, Mont.	50	85
☐	90 J.C. Tremblay, Mont.	13	25
☐	**91 Terry Harper, Mont. RC**	**22**	**45**
☐	**92 John Ferguson, Mont. RC**	**60**	**100**
☐	93 Toe Blake, Coach, Mont.	13	25
☐	94 Bobby Rousseau, Mont.	10	17
☐	95 Claude Provost, Mont.	10	17
☐	96 Marc Réaume, Mont.	10	17
☐	97 Dave Balon, Mont.	10	17
☐	98 Gump Worsley (G), Mont.	30	50
☐	**99 Césare Maniago (G), Mont. RC**	**100**	**200**

1963 - 64 QUÉBEC ACES

Card Size: 3 1/2" x 5 1/2"

	Set (22 photos):	**90**	**175**
☐	Don Blackburn	3	6
☐	Skippy Burchell	3	6
☐	Billy Carter	3	6
☐	Floyd Curry	6	12
☐	Bill Dineen	5	10
☐	Wayne Freitag	3	6
☐	Jean Gauthier	3	6
☐	Terry Gray	3	6
☐	John Hanna	3	6
☐	Doug Harvey	20	40
☐	Wayne Hicks	3	6
☐	Charlie Hodge (G)	8	15
☐	Charlie Hodge (G)	8	15
☐	Ed Hoekstra	3	6
☐	Frank Martin	3	6
☐	Jim Morrison	3	6
☐	Cleveland Mortson	3	6

Gerry O'Drowski	3	6
Rino Robazza	3	6
Léon Rochefort	3	6
Bill Sutherland	3	6
Gump Worsley (G)	20	40

1963 - 64 TOPPS

These cards measure the standard 2 1/2" x 3 1/2".

Complete Set (66 cards):	850	1,400
Topps	**EX**	**EX-NM**
1 Milt Schmidt, Coach, Bost.	12	45
2 Ed Johnston (G), Bost. RC	**30**	**50**
3 Doug Mohns, Bost.	8	15
4 Tom Johnson, Bost.	11	18
5 Léo Boivin, Bost.	11	18
6 Bob McCord, Bost. RC	**8**	**15**
7 Ted Green, Bost.	8	15
8 Ed Westfall, Bost. RC	**22**	**45**
9 Charlie Burns, Bost.	8	15
10 Murray Oliver, Bost.	8	15
11 John Bucyk, Bost.	22	45
12 Tom Williams, Bost.	8	15
13 Dean Prentice, Bost.	8	15
14 Bobby Leiter, Bost. RC	**8**	**15**
15 Andy Hebenton, Bost. LC	8	15
16 Jean-Guy Gendron, Bost.	8	15
17 Wayne Rivers, Bost. RC	**9**	**14**
18 Jerry Toppazzini, Bost. LC	8	15
19 Forbes Kennedy, Bost.	8	15
20 Orland Kurtenbach, Bost.	8	15
21 Boston Bruins Team Picture	30	45
22 Billy Reay, Coach, Chic.	8	15
23 Glenn Hall (G), Chic.	35	55
24 Denis DeJordy (G), Chic.	11	18
25 Pierre Pilote, Chic.	15	25
26 Elmer Vasko, Chic.	8	15
27 Wayne Hillman, Chic.	8	15
28 Al MacNeil, Chic.	8	15
29 Howie Young, Chic. RC	**11**	**18**
30 Ed Van Impe, Chic. RC	**11**	**18**
31 Reggie Fleming, Chic.	8	15
32 Bob Turner, Chic. LC	8	15
33 Bobby Hull, Chic.	200	325
34 Red Hay, Chic.	8	15
35 Murray Balfour, Chic.	8	15
36 Stan Mikita, Chic.	70	120
37 Ab McDonald, Chic., Error (MacDonald)	8	15
38 Kenny Wharram, Chic.	8	15
39 Eric Nesterenko, Chic.	8	15
40 Ron Murphy, Chic.	8	15
41 Chico Maki, Chic.	8	15
42 John McKenzie, Chic.	8	15
43 Chicago Blackhawks, Team Picture	30	45
44 Red Sullivan, NYRa.	8	40
45 Jacques Plante (G), NYRa.	100	160
46 Gilles Villemure (G), NYRa. RC	**25**	**40**
47 Doug Harvey, NYRa. LC	25	40
48 Harry Howell, NYRa.	15	25
49 Al Langlois, NYRa.	8	15
50 Jim Neilson, NYRa.	8	15
51 Larry Cahan, NYRa.	8	15
52 Andy Bathgate, NYRa.	15	25
53 Don McKenney, NYRa.	8	15
54 Vic Hadfield, NYRa.	11	18
55 Earl Ingarfield, NYRa.	8	15
56 Camille Henry, NYRa.	8	15
57 Rod Gilbert, NYRa.	30	45
58 Phil Goyette, NYRa.	8	15
59 Don Marshall, NYRa.	8	15
60 Dick Meissner, NYRa. LC	8	15
61 Val Fonteyne, NYRa.	8	15
62 Ken Schinkel, NYRa.	8	15
63 Jean Ratelle, NYRa.	30	45
64 Don Johns, NYRa. RC/LC	**8**	**15**
65 New York Rangers, Team Picture	30	45
66 Checklist (1 - 66)	135	275

1963 - 64 TORONTO STAR STARS IN ACTION

These colour photos measure 4 3/4" x 6 11/16".

Complete Set (42 cards):	250	400
Toronto Star	**EX**	**EX-NM**
Léo Boivin, Bost. (xcx: Andy Hebenton)	4	9
John Bucyk, Bost. (xcx: Johnny Bower)	6	12
Jean-Guy Gendron, Bost.	3	6
Glenn Hall (G), Chic.	7	15
Billy Hay, Chic.	3	6
Bobby Hull, Chic.	20	40
Stan Mikita, Chic.	9	18
Eric Nesterenko, Chic.	3	6
Elmer Vasko, Chic.	3	6
Ken Wharram, Chic. (xcx: Tom Johnson)	3	6
Alex Delvecchio, Detr., Error (Alec)	6	12
Bill Gadsby, Detr.	4	9
Gordie Howe, Detr.	35	65
Parker MacDonald, Detr.	3	6
Marcel Pronovost, Detr., Error (Provost), (xcx: D. Duff)	4	9
Terry Sawchuk (G), Detr.	12	2
Norm Ullman, Detr.	6	12
Jean Béliveau, Mont.	11	22
Bernie Geoffrion, Mont.	9	18
Dickie Moore, Mont. (xcx: Jean-Guy Talbot)	6	12
Claude Provost, Mont.	4	8
Henri Richard, Mont.	9	18
Jean-Guy Talbot, Mont.	3	6
Gilles Tremblay, Mont.	3	6
J.C. Tremblay, Mont.	4	8
Andy Bathgate, NYRa.	5	10
Doug Harvey, NYRa. (xcx: Floyd Smith)	7	15
Camille Henry, NYRa.	3	6
George Armstrong, Toro. (xcx: Bobby Hull)	7	15
Bob Baun, Toro.	4	8
John Bower (G), Toro.	7	15
Carl Brewer, Toro. (xcx: Bob Beckett)	3	6
Kent Douglas, Toro.	3	6
Dick Duff, Toro.	3	6
Tim Horton, Toro. (xcx: Parker MacDonald)	9	18
Red Kelly, Toro.	6	12
Dave Keon, Toro.	7	15
Frank Mahovlich, Toro.	9	18
Bob Pulford, Toro.	5	10
Eddie Shack, Toro.	6	12
Allan Stanley, Toro.	4	9
Ron Stewart, Toro.	3	6

1963 - 64 TORONTO STAR PHOTOS

These are colour newspaper photos.

Toronto Star	EX	EX-MT
Dec. 7 John Bucyk, Bost.	12	20
Dec. 14 Bob Pulford, Toro.	11	18
Dec. 21 Stan Mikita, Chic.	20	30
Dec. 28 Henri Richard, Mont.	13	22
Jan. 4 Bobby Hull, Chic.	22	45
Jan. 11 Bobby Rousseau, Mont.	7	12
Jan. 18 Tim Horton, Toro.	20	35
Jan. 25 Andy Bathgate, NYRa.	11	18
Feb. 1 Bob Baun, Toro.	7	12
Feb. 8 Glenn Hall (G), Chic.	20	30
Feb. 15 Alan Stanley, Toro.	9	15
Feb. 22 Vic Hadfield, NYRa.	9	15
Feb. 29 Kenny Wharram, Chic.	7	12
Mar. 7 Gordie Howe, Detr.	30	55
Mar. 14 Charlie Hodge (G), Mont.	9	15
Mar. 21 Marcel Pronovost, Detr.	9	15
Mar. 28 George Armstrong, Toro.	11	18
Apr. 4 Jean Béliveau, Mont.	20	30

1963 - 64 WEEKEND PHOTOS

These colour newspaper photos measure 5 1/2" x 6 1/2".

Toronto Star	EX	EX-NM
V11 Bobby Rousseau, Mont.	7	12
V11 Bob Pulford, Toro.	11	18
V11 Parker MacDonald, Detr.	7	12
V11 Jacques Plante (G), NYRa.	25	40
V11 Kenny Wharram, Chic.	7	12
V11 Tom Williams, Bost.	7	12
V11 Gordie Howe, Detr.	30	50
V11 Dave Balon, Mont.	7	12
V11 Phil Goyette, NYRa.	7	12
V11 Carl Brewer, Toro.	7	12
V11 Terry Sawchuk (G), Detr.	25	40
V11 Bobby Hull, Chic.	25	40
V11 John Ferguson, Mont.	9	15

1963 - 64 YORK PEANUT BUTTER WHITE BACKS

These cards measure 2 1/2" in diameter.

Complete Set (54 cards):	500	850
Album:	**30**	**60**
York	**EX**	**EX-NM**
1 Tim Horton, Toro.	22	45
2 Johnny Bower (G), Toro.	15	25
3 Ron Stewart, Toro.	7	12
4 Eddie Shack, Toro.	13	22
5 Frank Mahovlich, Toro.	22	45
6 Dave Keon, Toro.	18	30
7 Bob Baun, Toro.	9	15
8 Bob Nevin, Toro.	7	12
9 Dick Duff, Toro.	7	12
10 Billy Harris, Toro.	7	12
11 Larry Hillman, Toro.	7	12
12 Red Kelly, Toro.	13	22
13 Kent Douglas, Toro.	7	12
14 Allan Stanley, Toro.	11	18
15 Don Simmons (G), Toro.	9	15
16 George Armstrong, Toro.	13	22
17 Carl Brewer, Toro.	7	12
18 Bob Pulford, Toro.	12	20
19 Henri Richard, Mont.	18	28
20 Bernie Geoffrion, Mont.	18	28
21 Gilles Tremblay, Mont.	7	12
22 Gump Worsley (G), Mont.	18	28
23 Jean-Guy Talbot, Mont.	7	12
24 J.C. Tremblay, Mont.	9	15
25 Bobby Rousseau, Mont.	7	12
26 Jean Béliveau, Mont.	28	45
27 Ralph Backstrom, Mont.	7	12
28 Claude Provost, Mont.	9	15
29 Jean Gauthier, Mont.	7	12
30 Bill Hicke, Mont.	7	12
31 Terry Harper, Mont.	7	12
32 Marc Réaume, Mont.	7	12
33 Dave Balon, Mont.	7	12
34 Jacques Laperrière, Mont.	13	22
35 John Ferguson, Mont.	9	15
36 Red Berenson, Mont.	7	12
37 Terry Sawchuk (G), Detr.	35	60
38 Marcel Pronovost, Detr.	11	18
39 Bill Gadsby, Detr.	11	18
40 Parker MacDonald, Detr.	7	12
41 Larry Jeffrey, Detr.	7	12
42 Floyd Smith, Detr.	7	12
43 André Pronovost, Detr.	7	12
44 Art Stratton, Detr.	7	12
45 Gordie Howe, Detr.	75	125
46 Doug Barkley, Detr.	7	12
47 Norm Ullman, Detr.	13	22
48 Eddie Joyal, Detr.	7	12
49 Alex Faulkner, Detr.	9	15
50 Alex Delvecchio, Detr.	15	25
51 Bruce MacGregor, Detr.	7	12
52 Ted Hampson, Detr.	7	12
53 Peter Goegan, Detr.	7	12
54 Ron Ingram, Detr.	7	15

(Left) A wax wrapper from the 1963-64 Topps hockey series.

(Right) An advertisement for the 1963-65 Chex series, placed in Weekend magazine.

1963 - 65 CHEX PHOTOS

These cards measure 5 1/16" x 7". There were two printings of this set. One is believed to have been issued in 1963-64 and the other in 1964-65. The colouring between the two printings varies slightly, with the second printing having more of a reddish tint.

Complete Set (59 cards):	1,100	1,900
Chicago Blackhawks	**EX**	**EX-NM**
Denis DeJordy	110	175
Phil Esposito	75	125
Glenn Hall (G)	45	70
Billy Hay	12	20
Wayne Hillman	12	20
Bobby Hull	90	150
Chico Maki	12	20
Stan Mikita	40	70
Pierre Pilote	22	45
Elmer Vasko	12	20
Ken Wharram	12	20
Detroit Red Wings	**EX**	**EX-NM**
Alex Delvecchio	28	45
Bill Gadsby	22	45
Paul Henderson	28	45
Gordie Howe	125	200
Parker MacDonald	12	20
Bruce MacGregor	12	20
Pit Martin	12	20
Marcel Pronovost	22	45
Norm Ullman	28	45
Montréal Canadiens	**EX**	**EX-NM**
Ralph Backstrom	12	20
Dave Balon	12	20
Jean Béliveau (Front view)	65	110
Jean Béliveau (Side view)	65	110
Red Berenson	12	20
Toe Blake, Coach	25	40
John Ferguson	15	25
Jean Gauthier	12	20
Bernie Geoffrion	35	55
Terry Harper	12	20

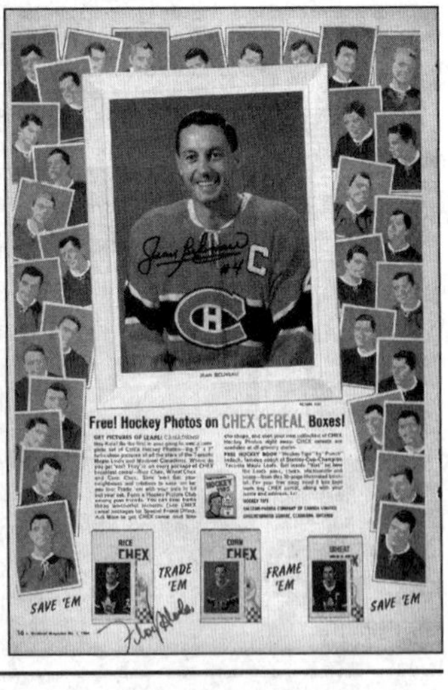

□	Bill Hicke	12	20
□	Charlie Hodge (G)	18	28
□	Jacques Laperrière	28	45
□	Claude Provost	15	25
□	Marc Reaume	12	20
□	Henri Richard	35	55
□	Bobby Rousseau	12	20
□	Bobby Rousseau (Bob Rousseau on card)	50	80
□	Jean Guy Talbot	12	20
□	Gilles Tremblay	12	20
□	J.C. Tremblay	15	25
□	Gump Worsley (G)	35	60

	Toronto Maple Leafs	EX	EX-NM
□	George Armstrong	28	45
□	Bob Baun	15	25
□	Johnny Bower (G)	35	60
□	Kent Douglas	12	20
□	Dick Duff	15	25
□	Billy Harris	12	20
□	Tim Horton	55	90
□	Punch Imlach, Coach	22	45
□	Red Kelly	28	45
□	Dave Keon	30	50
□	Ed Litzenberger	12	20
□	John MacMillan	12	20
□	Frank Mahovlich	45	75
□	Bob Nevin	12	20
□	Bob Pulford	25	40
□	Eddie Shack	28	45
□	Don Simmons (G)	15	25
□	Allan Stanley	22	45
□	Ron Stewart	12	20

1964 - 65 COCA-COLA BOTTLE CAPS

These caps measure 1 1/8" in diameter. They came on the top of Coca-Cola bottles and are similar to those found on Sprite bottles.

Complete Set (108 caps):	**350**	**600**
Plastic Display Rink:	**150**	**275**
Common Player:	**3**	**5**

	Coca-Cola • Boston Bruins	EX	EX-NM
□	Murray Balfour	3	5
□	Léo Boivin	5	8
□	John Bucyk	7	12
□	Gary Dornhoefer	3	5
□	Reggie Fleming	3	5
□	Ted Green	3	5
□	Tom Johnson	5	8
□	Eddie Johnston (G)	4	7
□	Forbes Kennedy	3	5
□	Orland Kurtenbach	3	5
□	Bobby Leiter	3	5
□	Bob McCord	3	5
□	Ab McDonald	3	5
□	Murray Oliver	3	5
□	Dean Prentice	3	5
□	Ron Schock	3	5
□	Ed Westfall	3	5
□	Tom Williams	3	5

	Coca-Cola • Chicago Blackhawks	EX	EX-NM
□	John Brenneman	3	5
□	Denis DeJordy (G)	4	7
□	Phil Esposito	22	45
□	Glenn Hall (G)	13	22
□	Billy Hay	3	5
□	Wayne Hillman	3	5
□	Bobby Hull	20	35
□	Al MacNeil	3	5
□	Chico Maki	3	5
□	John McKenzie	3	5
□	Stan Mikita	11	18
□	Doug Mohns	3	5
□	Eric Nesterenko	3	5
□	Pierre Pilote	5	8
□	Doug Robinson	3	5
□	Fred Stanfield	3	5
□	Elmer Vasko	3	5
□	Kenny Wharram	3	5

	Ccca-Cola • Detroit Red Wings	EX	EX-NM
□	Doug Barkley	3	5
□	Gary Bergman	3	5
□	Roger Crozier (G)	5	8
□	Alex Delvecchio (#10)	9	12
□	Bill Gadsby	5	8
□	Paul Henderson	5	8
□	Gordie Howe (#9)	30	45
□	Larry Jeffrey	3	5
□	Eddie Joyal	3	5
□	Al Langlois	3	5
□	Ted Lindsay	7	12
□	Parker MacDonald	3	5
□	Bruce MacGregor	3	5
□	Pit Martin	3	5
□	Ron Murphy	3	5
□	Marcel Pronovost	5	8
□	Floyd Smith	3	5
□	Norm Ullman	7	12

	Coca-Cola • Montréal Canadiens	EX	EX-NM
□	Ralph Backstrom	3	5
□	Dave Balon	3	5
□	Jean Béliveau	15	25
□	Yvan Cournoyer	10	18
□	John Ferguson	4	7
□	Terry Harper	3	5
□	Ted Harris	3	5
□	Bill Hicke	3	5
□	Charlie Hodge (G)	5	8
□	Jacques Laperrière	5	8
□	Claude Larose	3	5
□	Claude Provost	4	7
□	Henri Richard	9	15
□	Jim Roberts	3	5
□	Bobby Rousseau	4	7
□	Jean-Guy Talbot	3	5
□	Gilles Tremblay	3	5
□	J.C. Tremblay	4	7

	Coca-Cola • New York Rangers	EX	EX-NM
□	Lou Angotti	3	5
□	Arnie Brown	3	5
□	Dick Duff	3	5
□	Val Fonteyne	4	7
□	Rod Gilbert	7	12
□	Phil Goyette	3	5
□	Vic Hadfield	4	7
□	Camille Henry	3	5
□	Harry Howell	5	8
□	Earl Ingarfield	3	5
□	Don Johns	3	5
□	Don Marshall	3	5
□	Jim Mikol	3	5
□	Jim Neilson	3	5
□	Bob Nevin	3	5
□	Marcel Paille (G)	4	7
□	Jacques Plante (G)	15	25
□	Rod Seiling	3	5

	Coca-Cola • Toronto Maple Leafs	EX	EX-NM
□	George Armstrong	6	10
□	Andy Bathgate (#9)	6	10
□	Bob Baun	4	7
□	Johnny Bower (G)	10	18
□	Carl Brewer	3	5
□	Kent Douglas	3	5
□	Ron Ellis	4	7
□	Tim Horton	13	22
□	Red Kelly	6	11
□	Dave Keon	9	15
□	Frank Mahovlich	13	22
□	Don McKenney	3	5
□	Dickie Moore	6	11
□	Bob Pulford	6	10
□	Terry Sawchuk (G)	15	25
□	Eddie Shack	5	9
□	Allan Stanley	5	8
□	Ron Stewart	3	5

(Left) An advertisement for the 1964-65 Coke series, placed in Weekend magazine.

1964 - 65 SPRITE BOTTLE CAPS

These caps measure 1 1/8" in diameter. They came on the top of Sprite bottles and are similar to those found on Coca-Cola bottles.

Complete Set (108 caps):	**1,200**	**2,500**
Common Player:	**10**	**15**

	Sprite • Boston Bruins	EX	EX-NM
□	Murray Balfour	10	15
□	Léo Boivin	15	25
□	John Bucyk	20	30
□	Gary Dornhoefer	10	15
□	Reggie Fleming	10	15
□	Ted Green	10	15
□	Tom Johnson	15	25
□	Eddie Johnston (G)	12	20
□	Forbes Kennedy	10	15
□	Orland Kurtenbach	10	15
□	Bobby Leiter	10	15
□	Bob McCord	10	15
□	Ab McDonald	10	15
□	Murray Oliver	10	15
□	Dean Prentice	10	15
□	Ron Schock	10	15
□	Ed Westfall	10	15
□	Tom Williams	10	15

	Sprite • Chicago Blackhawks	EX	EX-NM
□	John Brenneman	10	15
□	Denis DeJordy (G)	12	20
□	Phil Esposito	100	150
□	Glenn Hall (G)	50	100
□	Billy Hay	10	15
□	Wayne Hillman	10	15
□	Bobby Hull	100	180
□	Al MacNeil	10	15
□	Chico Maki	10	15
□	John McKenzie	10	15
□	Stan Mikita	35	60
□	Doug Mohns	10	15
□	Eric Nesterenko	10	15
□	Pierre Pilote	15	25
□	Doug Robinson	10	15
□	Fred Stanfield	10	15
□	Elmer Vasko	10	15
□	Kenny Wharram	10	15

	Sprite • Detroit Red Wings	EX	EX-NM
□	Doug Barkley	10	15
□	Gary Bergman	10	15
□	Roger Crozier (G)	15	25
□	Alex Delvecchio (#10)	20	30
□	Bill Gadsby	15	25
□	Paul Henderson	15	25
□	Gordie Howe (#9)	150	250
□	Larry Jeffrey	10	15
□	Eddie Joyal	10	15
□	Al Langlois	10	15
□	Ted Lindsay	20	30
□	Parker MacDonald	10	15
□	Bruce MacGregor	10	15
□	Pit Martin	10	15
□	Ron Murphy	10	15
□	Marcel Pronovost	15	25
□	Floyd Smith	10	15
□	Norm Ullman	20	30

	Sprite • Montréal Canadiens	EX	EX-NM
□	Ralph Backstrom	10	15
□	Dave Balon	10	15
□	Jean Béliveau	100	180
□	Yvan Cournoyer	40	75
□	John Ferguson	12	20
□	Terry Harper	10	15
□	Ted Harris	10	15
□	Bill Hicke	10	15
□	Charlie Hodge (G)	15	25
□	Jacques Laperrière	15	25
□	Claude Larose	10	15
□	Claude Provost	12	20
□	Henri Richard	35	60
□	Jim Roberts	10	15
□	Bobby Rousseau	12	20
□	Jean-Guy Talbot	10	15
□	Gilles Tremblay	10	15
□	J.C. Tremblay	12	20

	Sprite • New York Rangers	EX	EX-NM
□	Lou Angotti	10	15
□	Arnie Brown	10	15
□	Dick Duff	10	15
□	Val Fonteyne	12	20
□	Rod Gilbert	20	30
□	Phil Goyette	10	15
□	Vic Hadfield	12	20
□	Camille Henry	10	15
□	Harry Howell	15	25
□	Earl Ingarfield	10	15
□	Don Johns	10	15
□	Don Marshall	10	15
□	Jim Mikol	10	15
□	Jim Neilson	10	15
□	Bob Nevin	10	15
□	Marcel Paille (G)	12	20
□	Jacques Plante (G)	80	150
□	Rod Seiling	10	15

	Sprite • Toronto Maple Leafs	EX	EX-NM
□	George Armstrong	20	30
□	Andy Bathgate (#9)	20	30
□	Bob Baun	12	20
□	Johnny Bower (G)	40	75
□	Carl Brewer	10	15
□	Kent Douglas	10	15
□	Ron Ellis	12	20
□	Tim Horton	45	80
□	Red Kelly	20	30
□	Dave Keon	35	60
□	Frank Mahovlich	60	100
□	Don McKenney	10	15
□	Dickie Moore	20	30
□	Bob Pulford	20	30
□	Terry Sawchuk (G)	80	150
□	Eddie Shack	15	25
□	Allan Stanley	15	25
□	Ron Stewart	10	15

1964 - 65 TOPPS

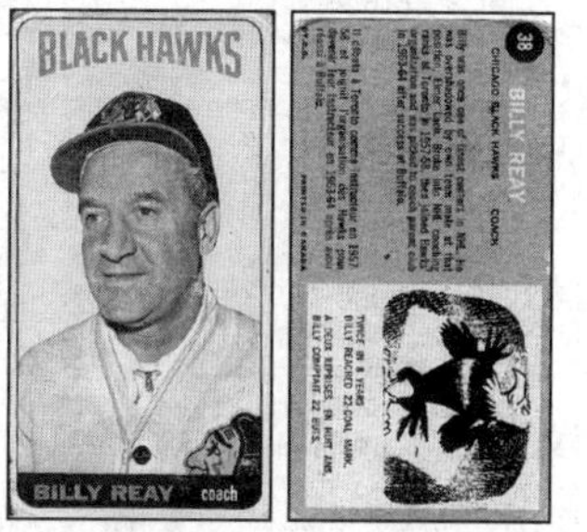

These tall-boy cards measure 2 1/2" x 4 11/16". Short-print cards are marked with an asterisk (*).

Series One Set (55 cards):	**1,200**	**2,100**
Series Two Set (55 cards):	**3,200**	**6,200**

	Topps Series One	EX	EX-NM
□	**1 Pit Martin, Detr. RC**	**50**	**120**

◆ A graded PSA-9 copy of this card recently closed at $1,139 U.S. ($1,309 U.S. with the buyer's premium) in the May 17, 2002 Lelands Vintage Sports Auction. That closing amount is approximately $1,765 Cdn.

□	2 Gilles Tremblay, Mont.	13	25
□	3 Terry Harper, Mont.	15	25
□	4 John Ferguson, Mont.	30	50
□	5 Elmer Vasko, Chic.	13	25
□	6 Terry Sawchuk (G), Toro.	80	125
□	7 Billy Hay, Chic.	13	25
□	**8 Gary Bergman, Detr. RC**	**20**	**30**
□	9 Doug Barkley, Detr.	13	25
□	10 Bob McCord, Bost.	13	25
□	11 Parker MacDonald, Detr.	13	25
□	12 Glenn Hall (G), Chic.	50	80
□	13 Al Langlois, Detr.	13	25
□	14 Camille Henry, NYRa.	13	25
□	15 Norm Ullman, Detr.	25	40
□	16 Ab McDonald, Bost.	13	25
□	17 Charlie Hodge (G), Mont.	20	30
□	18 Orland Kurtenbach, Bost.	13	25
□	19 Dean Prentice, Bost.	13	25
□	20 Bobby Hull, Chic.	275	425
□	21 Ed Johnston (G), Bost.	20	30
□	22 Denis DeJordy (G), Chic.	20	30
□	23 Claude Provost, Mont.	13	25
□	24 Rod Gilbert, NYRa.	30	50
□	25 Doug Mohns, Chic.	13	25
□	26 Al MacNeil, Chic.	13	25
□	27 Billy Harris, Toro.	13	25

☐ 28 Kenny Wharram, Chic.	13	25
☐ 29 Red Sullivan, NYRa. LC	13	25
☐ 30 John McKenzie, Chic.	13	25
☐ 31 Stan Mikita, Chic.	70	125
☐ 32 Ted Green, Bost.	13	25
☐ 33 Jean Béliveau, Mont.	90	150
☐ **34 Arnie Brown, NYRa. RC**	**13**	**25**
☐ 35 Reggie Fleming, Bost.	13	25
☐ **36 Jim Mikol, NYRa. RC/LC**	**13**	**25**
☐ 37 Dave Balon, Mont.	13	25
☐ 38 Billy Reay, Coach, Chic.	13	25
☐ 39 Marcel Pronovost, Detr.	20	30
☐ 40 Johnny Bower (G), Toro.	45	70
☐ 41 Wayne Hillman, Chic.	13	25
☐ 42 Floyd Smith, Detr.	13	25
☐ 43 Toe Blake, Coach, Mont.	22	45
☐ 44 Red Kelly, Toro.	22	45
☐ 45 Punch Imlach, Coach, Toro.	20	30
☐ 46 Dick Duff, NYRa.	13	25
☐ **47 Roger Crozier (G), Detr. RC**	**50**	**80**
☐ 48 Henri Richard, Mont.	55	85
☐ 49 Larry Jeffrey, Detr.	13	25
☐ 50 Léo Boivin, Bost.	20	30
☐ 51 Ed Westfall, Bost.	13	25
☐ 52 Jean-Guy Talbot, Mont.	13	25
☐ 53 Jacques Laperrière, Mont.	22	45
☐ 54 Checklist 1 (1 - 54)	250	400
☐ 55 Checklist 2 (55 - 110)	350	575
Topps Series Two	**EX**	**EX-NM**
☐ 56 Ron Murphy, Detr.	50	80
☐ 57 Bob Baun, Toro.	40	65
☐ 58 Tom Williams, Bost. (*)	130	215
☐ 59 Pierre Pilote, Chic. (*)	140	325
☐ 60 Bob Pulford, Toro.	40	65
☐ 61 Red Berenson, Mont.	35	55
☐ 62 Vic Hadfield, NYRa.	35	55
☐ 63 Bobby Leiter, Bost.	35	55
☐ **64 Jim Pappin, Toro. RC**	**40**	**65**
☐ 65 Earl Ingarfield, NYRa.	35	55
☐ **66 Lou Angotti, NYRa. RC**	**35**	**55**
☐ **67 Rod Seiling, NYRa. RC**	**35**	**55**
☐ 68 Jacques Plante (G), NYRa.	120	200
☐ 69 George Armstrong, Toro.	50	80
☐ 70 Milt Schmidt, Coach, Bost.	40	65
☐ 71 Eddie Shack, Toro.	75	125
☐ **72 Gary Dornhoefer, Bost. RC (*)**	**165**	**265**
☐ 73 Chico Maki, Chic. (*)	130	215
☐ 74 Gilles Villemure (G), NYRa. (*)	165	265
☐ 75 Carl Brewer, Toro.	35	55
☐ 76 Bruce MacGregor, Detr.	35	55
☐ 77 Bob Nevin, NYRa.	35	55
☐ 78 Ralph Backstrom, Mont.	35	55
☐ 79 Murray Oliver, Bost.	35	55
☐ 80 Bobby Rousseau, Mont. (*)	130	215
☐ 81 Don McKenney, Toro.	35	55
☐ 82 Ted Lindsay, Detr. LC	55	90
☐ 83 Harry Howell, NYRa.	45	75
☐ **84 Doug Robinson, Chic. RC**	**35**	**55**
☐ 85 Frank Mahovlich, Toro.	110	165
☐ 86 Andy Bathgate, Toro.	45	75
☐ 87 Phil Goyette, NYRa.	35	55
☐ 88 J.C. Tremblay, Mont.	40	65
☐ 89 Gordie Howe, Detr.	350	550
☐ 90 Murray Balfour, Bost. LC	35	55
☐ 91 Eric Nesterenko, Chic. (*)	130	215
☐ **92 Marcel Paille (G), NYRa. RC/LC (*)**	**200**	**350**
☐ 93 Sid Abel, Coach, Detr.	35	55
☐ 94 Dave Keon, Toro.	65	110
☐ 95 Alex Delvecchio, Detr.	55	90
☐ 96 Bill Gadsby, Detr.	40	65
☐ 97 Don Marshall, NYRa.	35	55
☐ 98 Bill Hicke, Mont. (*)	130	215
☐ 99 Ron Stewart, Toro.	35	55
☐ 100 John Bucyk, Bost.	60	100
☐ 101 Tom Johnson, Bost.	40	65
☐ 102 Tim Horton, Toro.	110	165
☐ 103 Jim Neilson, NYRa.	35	55
☐ 104 Allan Stanley, Toro.	30	65
☐ 105 AS: Tim Horton, Toro. (*)	235	400
☐ 106 AS: Stan Mikita, Chic. (*)	220	375
☐ 107 AS: Bobby Hull, Chic.	150	250
☐ 108 AS: Kenny Wharram, Chic.	35	55
☐ 109 AS: Pierre Pilote, Chic.	50	80
☐ 110 AS: Glenn Hall (G), Chic.	75	175

1964 - 65 TORONTO STAR

These blank-back colour cards measure 4 1/8" x 5 1/8".

Complete Set (48 cards):	**250**	**375**
Album:	**25**	**50**
Toronto Star	**EX**	**EX-NM**
☐ 1 Léo Boivin, Bost.	4	9
☐ 2 Ted Green, Bost.	3	6
☐ 3 Tom Johnson, Bost.	4	9
☐ 4 Forbes Kennedy, Bost.	3	6
☐ 5 Orland Kurtenbach, Bost.	3	6
☐ 6 Wayne Rivers, Bost.	3	6
☐ 7 Glenn Hall (G), Chic.	7	15
☐ 8 Billy Hay, Chic.	3	6
☐ 9 Wayne Hillman, Chic.	3	6
☐ 10 Bobby Hull, Chic.	18	35
☐ 11 Al MacNeil, Chic.	3	6
☐ 12 Chico Maki, Chic.	3	6
☐ 13 John McKenzie, Chic.	3	6
☐ 14 Stan Mikita, Chic.	7	15
☐ 15 Pierre Pilote, Chic.	4	9
☐ 16 Elmer Vasko, Chic.	3	6
☐ 17 Alex Delvecchio, Detr.	6	12
☐ 18 Paul Henderson, Detr.	5	10
☐ 19 Gordie Howe, Detr.	30	55
☐ 20 Larry Jeffrey, Detr.	3	6
☐ 21 Parker MacDonald, Detr.	3	6
☐ 22 Marcel Pronovost, Detr., Error (Provost)	4	9
☐ 23 Floyd Smith, Detr.	3	6
☐ 24 Norm Ullman, Detr.	6	12
☐ 25 Dave Balon, Mont.	3	6
☐ 26 Jean Béliveau, Mont.	11	22
☐ 27 Red Berenson, Mont.	3	6
☐ 28 Charlie Hodge (G), Mont.	4	9
☐ 29 Jacques Laperrière, Mont.	6	12
☐ 30 Claude Provost, Mont.	3	6
☐ 31 Henri Richard, Mont.	7	15
☐ 32 J.C. Tremblay, Mont.	3	6
☐ 33 Rod Gilbert, NYRa.	6	12
☐ 34 Harry Howell, NYRa.	4	9
☐ 35 Jim Neilson, NYRa.	3	6
☐ 36 Jacques Plante (G), NYRa.	13	25
☐ 37 Andy Bathgate, Toro.	5	10
☐ 38 Bob Baun, Toro.	3	6
☐ 39 Carl Brewer, Toro.	3	6
☐ 40 Billy Harris, Toro.	3	6
☐ 41 Tim Horton, Toro.	9	18
☐ 42 Dave Keon, Toro.	7	15
☐ 43 Frank Mahovlich, Toro.	9	18
☐ 44 Don McKenney, Toro.	3	6
☐ 45 Jim Pappin, Toro.	3	6
☐ 46 Bob Pulford, Toro.	5	10
☐ 47 Allan Stanley, Toro.	4	9
☐ 48 Ron Stewart, Toro.	3	6

(Left) An advertisement for the 1964-65 Toronto Star hockey series.

1964 - 65 TORONTO STAR PHOTOS

These are colour newspaper photos.

Toronto Star	**EX**	**EX-MT**
☐ Dec. 5 Stan Mikita, Chic.	20	30
☐ Dec. 12 Bobby Hull, Chic.	25	40
☐ Dec. 19 Tim Horton, Toro.	20	30
☐ Dec. 26 Jean Béliveau, Mont.	20	30
☐ Jan. 2 Bob Pulford, Toro.	11	18
☐ Jan. 9 Dean Prentice, NYRa.	7	12
☐ Jan. 16 Ron Ellis, Toro.	7	12
☐ Jan. 23 Rod Gilbert, NYRa.	12	20
☐ Jan. 30 Jacques Laperrière, Mont.	11	18
☐ Feb. 6 Terry Sawchuk (G), Toro.	25	40
☐ Feb. 20 Charlie Hodge (G), Mont.	9	15
☐ Feb. 27 Vic Hadfield, NYRa.	7	12
☐ Mar. 6 Frank Mahovlich, Toro.	20	30
☐ Mar. 13 Glenn Hall (G), Chic.	20	30
☐ Mar. 20 Ken Wharram, Chic.	7	12
☐ Mar. 27 Norm Ullman, Detr.	12	20

1964 - 67 EATON'S SPORTS ADVISER

These cards were issued by Eaton's between 1964 and 1967 as promotional cards for their Truline Sports Equipment. During the summer months Howe toured Canada appearing at the Eaton stores to promote this line of equipment. Each card measures 3 1/2" x 5 1/2".

Sports Adviser • Gordie Howe	**EX**	**EX-NM**
☐ 1 Gordie Howe 1964-65 All-Star Uniform	35	65
☐ 2 Gordie Howe 1965-66 Action Pose	35	65
☐ 3 Gordie Howe 1966-67 Standing Pose	35	65

1965 - 66 COCA-COLA

These perforated cards measure 2 3/4" x 3 1/2". Complete player stats appear on the card back. Cards were issued in team panels. A complete set of six attached team panels sells for $600-800. Attached team sets sell as follows (EX-NM): Bruins $100; Blackhawks $200; Red Wings $150; Canadiens $130; Rangers $100; Maple Leafs $175.

Complete Set (108 cards):	**225**	**400**
Album:	**65**	**125**
Coca-Cola • Boston Bruins	**EX**	**EX-NM**
☐ Barry Ashbee	3	5
☐ Don Awrey	1	2
☐ Léo Boivin	3	5
☐ John Bucyk	5	8
☐ Gerry Cheevers (G)	15	25
☐ Bob Dillabough	1	2
☐ Reggie Fleming	1	2
☐ Ted Green	1	2
☐ Forbes Kennedy	1	2
☐ Al Langlois	1	2
☐ Parker MacDonald	1	2
☐ Murray Oliver	1	2
☐ Bernie Parent (G)	17	28
☐ Dean Prentice	1	2
☐ Ron Stewart	1	2
☐ Ed Westfall	1	2
☐ Tom Williams	1	2
☐ Bob Woytowich	1	2
Coca-Cola • Chicago Blackhawks	**EX**	**EX-NM**
☐ Dave Dryden (G)	2	4
☐ Phil Esposito	25	40
☐ Glenn Hall (G)	10	18
☐ Billy Hay	1	2
☐ Ken Hodge	2	4
☐ Bobby Hull	30	50
☐ Dennis Hull	3	6
☐ Doug Jarrett	1	2
☐ Al MacNeil	1	2
☐ Chico Maki	1	2
☐ Stan Mikita	9	15
☐ Doug Mohns	1	2
☐ Eric Nesterenko	1	2
☐ Pierre Pilote	3.25	5
☐ Matt Ravlich	1	2
☐ Fred Stanfield	1	2
☐ Elmer Vasko	1	2
☐ Kenny Wharram	1	2
Coca-Cola • Detroit Red Wings	**EX**	**EX-NM**
☐ Doug Barkley	1	2
☐ Hank Bassen (G)	2	4
☐ Andy Bathgate	3	6
☐ Gary Bergman	1	2
☐ Roger Crozier (G)	3	6
☐ Alex Delvecchio	6	10
☐ Val Fonteyne	1	2
☐ Bill Gadsby	3.25	5
☐ Warren Godfrey	1	2
☐ Billy Harris	1	2
☐ Paul Henderson	4	7
☐ Gordie Howe	45	70
☐ Bruce MacGregor	1	2
☐ Bert Marshall	1	2
☐ Ab McDonald	1	2
☐ Ron Murphy	1	2
☐ Floyd Smith	1	2
☐ Norm Ullman	5	8
Coca-Cola • Montréal Canadiens	**EX**	**EX-NM**
☐ Ralph Backstrom	1	2
☐ Jean Béliveau	15	25
☐ Yvan Cournoyer	9	14
☐ Dick Duff	1	2
☐ John Ferguson	2	4
☐ Terry Harper	1	2
☐ Ted Harris	1	2
☐ Charlie Hodge (G)	2	4
☐ Jacques Laperrière	3.25	5
☐ Claude Larose	1	2
☐ Claude Provost	2	4
☐ Henri Richard	8	13
☐ Jim Roberts	1	2
☐ Bobby Rousseau	1	2
☐ Jean-Guy Talbot	1	2
☐ Gilles Tremblay	1	2
☐ J.C. Tremblay	2	4
☐ Gump Worsley (G)	10	16
Coca-Cola • New York Rangers	**EX**	**EX-NM**
☐ Arnie Brown	1	2
☐ Ed Giacomin (G)	15	25
☐ Rod Gilbert	5	8
☐ Phil Goyette	1	2
☐ Vic Hadfield	2	4
☐ Bill Hicke	1	2
☐ Wayne Hillman	1	2
☐ Harry Howell	3.25	5
☐ Earl Ingarfield	1	2
☐ Don Marshall	1	2
☐ John McKenzie	1	2
☐ Mike McMahon	1	2
☐ Jim Neilson	1	2
☐ Bob Nevin	1	2
☐ Garry Peters	1	2
☐ Jean Ratelle	5	8
☐ Doug Robinson	1	2
☐ Don Simmons (G)	2	4
Coca-Cola • Toronto Maple Leafs	**EX**	**EX-NM**
☐ George Armstrong	3	6
☐ Bob Baun	2	4
☐ Johnny Bower (G)	8	14
☐ Kent Douglas	1	2
☐ Ron Ellis	2	4
☐ Tim Horton	12	20
☐ Red Kelly	4	7
☐ Dave Keon	7	12
☐ Orland Kurtenbach	1	2
☐ Frank Mahovlich	12	20
☐ Bob Pulford	3	6
☐ Marcel Pronovost	3.25	5
☐ Terry Sawchuk (G)	18	28
☐ Brit Selby	1	2
☐ Eddie Shack	4	7
☐ Allan Stanley	3.25	5
☐ Pete Stemkowski	1	2
☐ Mike Walton	1	2

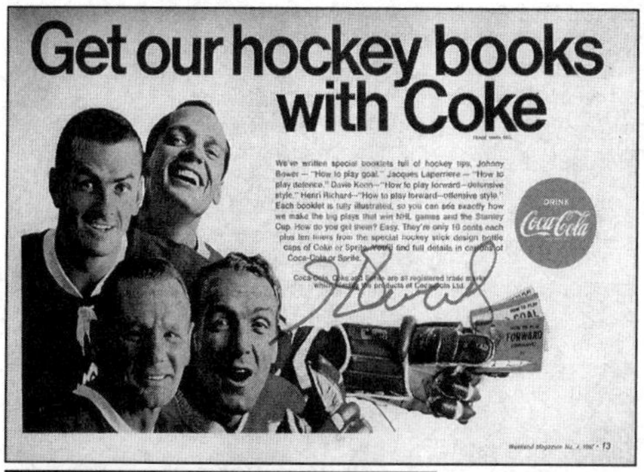

(Left) An advertisement for the 1964-65 Coke series, placed in Weekend magazine.

1964 - 65 COCA-COLA HOW TO PLAY BOOKLETS

This is a 32-page instructional booklet called "How to Play". The booklet measures 4 5/16" x 3 15/16".

	Coca-Cola • English	**EX**	**EX-NM**
☐	A Johnny Bower, Toro. (Goal)	40	60
☐	B David Keon, Toro. (Forward)	30	50
☐	C Jacques Laperrière, Mont. (Defense)	18	30
☐	D Henri Richard, Mont. (Foward)	30	50
	Coca-Cola • Français	**EX**	**EX-NM**
☐	W Johnny Bower, Toro. (Goal)	40	80
☐	X David Keon, Toro. (Forward)	30	70
☐	Y Jacques Laperrière, Mont. (Defense)	18	40
☐	Z Henri Richard, Mont. (Foward)	30	70

1965 - 66 HELLAS

These colour cards measure 2 1/8" x 3 1/2". The cards were issued by Hellas (Leaf) in Finland.

Complete Set (160 cards):

	Hellas / Leaf	**EX**	**EX-NM**
☐	1 Lasse Kiili, Turun Palloseura		
☐	2 Ilkka Mesikammen, Turun Palloseura		
☐	3 Jorma Laapas, Turun Palloseura		
☐	4 Esko Reijonen, Turun Palloseura		
☐	5 Juhani IsoEskeli, Turun Palloseura		
☐	6 Pertti Nieminen, Turun Palloseura		
☐	7 Kari Aro, Turun Palloseura		
☐	8 Juhani Wahlsten, Turun Palloseura		
☐	9 Rauno Heinonen, Turun Palloseura		
☐	10 Kalevi Leppanen, Turun Palloseura		
☐	11 Pertti Karelius, Turun Palloseura		
☐	12 Pekka Olkkonen, Turun Palloseura		
☐	13 Kari Sillanpaa, Turun Palloseura		
☐	14 Jarmo Rantanen, Turun Palloseura		
☐	15 Heikki Heimo, Turun Palloseura		
☐	16 Jorma Valtonen, Turun Palloseura		
☐	17 Risto Kaitala, Rauman Lukko		
☐	18 Kalevi Virkku, Rauman Lukko		
☐	19 Helkko Stenvall, Rauman Lukko		
☐	20 Teppo Rastio, Rauman Lukko		
☐	21 Seppo Vainio, Rauman Lukko		
☐	22 Pentti Jokinen, Rauman Lukko		
☐	23 Matti Kelnonen, Rauman Lukko		
☐	24 Matti Koivunen, Rauman Lukko		
☐	25 Esa Isaksson, Rauman Lukko		
☐	26 Juhani Jylha, Rauman Lukko		
☐	27 Pentti Rautalin, Rauman Lukko		
☐	28 Simo Sainio, Rauman Lukko		
☐	29 Hannu Torma, Rauman Lukko		
☐	30 Olli Malmivuori, Rauman Lukko		
☐	31 Matti Saurio, Rauman Lukko		
☐	32 Mikko Erholm, Rauman Lukko		
☐	33 Anto Virtanen, Porin Karhut		
☐	34 Juha Rantasila, Porin Karhut		
☐	35 Jaakko Honkanen, Porin Karhut		
☐	36 Antti Heikkila, Porin Karhut		
☐	37 Lasse Heikkila, Porin Karhut		
☐	38 VeliPekka Ketola, Porin Karhut		
☐	39 Keijo Koistinen, Porin Karhut		
☐	40 Mikko Myllyniemi, Porin Karhut		
☐	41 Matti Salmi, Porin Karhut		
☐	42 Tuomo Pirskanen, Porin Karhut		
☐	43 Matti Jansson, Porin Karhut		
☐	44 Erkki Saine, Porin Karhut		
☐	45 Erkki Harju, Porin Karhut		
☐	46 Kaj Matalamaki, Porin Karhut		
☐	47 Seppo Nystrom, Porin Karhut		
☐	48 Timo Jussila, Porin Karhut		
☐	49 Jorma Rikala, HJK		
☐	50 Tapio Raunio, HJK		
☐	51 Pekka Korjakoff, HJK		
☐	52 Jorma Borgstrom, HJK		
☐	53 Jorma Kyntola, HJK		
☐	54 Jyrki Malmio, HJK		
☐	55 Aarno Hiekkaranta, HJK		
☐	56 Kalevi Salo, HJK		
☐	57 Martti Kuokkanen, HJK		
☐	58 Seppo Ikola, HJK		
☐	59 Hannu Kyllastinen, HJK		
☐	60 Pentti Katainen, HJK		
☐	61 Harri Linnonmaa, HJK		
☐	62 Kyosti Wall, HJK		
☐	63 Kari Kinnunen, HJK		
☐	64 Martti Kallionpaa, HJK		
☐	65 Pekka Kuusisto, RU38 Pori		
☐	66 Johannes Karttunen, RU38 Pori		
☐	67 Heikki Veravainen, RU38 Pori		
☐	68 Pentti Riitahaara, RU38 Pori		
☐	69 Lauri Lehtonen, RU38 Pori		
☐	70 Matti Harju, RU38 Pori		
☐	71 Pertti Kontto, RU38 Pori		
☐	72 Timo Makela, RU38 Pori		
☐	73 Tapio Rautalammi, RU38 Pori		
☐	74 Kimmo Kivela, RU38 Pori		
☐	75 Raimo Maattanen, RU38 Pori		
☐	76 Kari Rajala, RU38 Pori		
☐	77 Tapani Suominen, RU38 Pori		
☐	78 Heimo Tervo, RU38 Pori		
☐	79 Raimo Kilpio, RU38 Pori		
☐	80 Matti Lampainen, RU38 Pori		
☐	81 Raimo Helppolainen, Saimaan		
☐	82 Esko Nenonen, Saimaan		
☐	83 Lalli Partinen, Saimaan		
☐	84 Leo Haakana, Saimaan		
☐	85 Hannu Lemander, Saimaan		
☐	86 Leevi Ryhanen, Saimaan		
☐	87 Yrjo Hakala, Saimaan		
☐	88 Pauli Hyvari, Saimaan		
☐	89 Jorma Hietanen, Saimaan		
☐	90 Juhani Pyyhtia, Saimaan		
☐	91 Timo Vaatamoinen, Saimaan		
☐	92 Heikki Juselius, Saimaan		
☐	93 Pentti Hyvari, Saimaan		
☐	94 Antti Ravi, Saimaan		
☐	95 Markku Eiskonen, Saimaan		
☐	96 Martti Sinkkonen, Saimaan		
☐	97 Tapio Majaniemi, Tampereen		
☐	98 Matti Reunamaki, Tampereen		
☐	99 Rauno Heinonen, Tampereen		
☐	100 Rauno Lehtio, Tampereen		
☐	101 Risto Lehtio, Tampereen		
☐	102 Juhani Tammi, Tampereen		
☐	103 Matti Kautto, Tampereen		
☐	104 Pekka Lehtolainen, Tampereen		
☐	105 Markku Pulli, Tampereen		
☐	106 Eero Holopainen, Tampereen		
☐	107 Aaro Nurminen, Tampereen		
☐	108 Kalevi Pulli, Tampereen		
☐	109 Jorma Suokko, Tampereen		
☐	110 Erkki Suokko, Tampereen		
☐	111 Heino Pulli, Tampereen		
☐	112 Seppo Nikkila, Tampereen		
☐	113 Pentti Pynnonen, Ilves		
☐	114 Lasse Oksanen, Ilves		
☐	115 Olli Wirzenius, Ilves		
☐	116 Pentti Uotila, Ilves		
☐	117 Jaakko Jaskari, Ilves		
☐	118 Markku Hakanen, Ilves		
☐	119 Ilkka Halme, Ilves		
☐	120 Pekka Alfors, Ilves		
☐	121 Tauno Niemi, Ilves		
☐	122 Erkan Nasib, Ilves		
☐	123 Veikko Ukkonen, Ilves		
☐	124 Jarmo Wasama, Ilves		
☐	125 Juhani Lahtinen, Ilves		
☐	126 Jorma Peltonen, Ilves		
☐	127 Kari Palooja, Ilves		
☐	128 Reijo Hakanen, Ilves		
☐	129 Esko Kaonpaa, HIFK		
☐	130 Kimmo Heino, HIFK		
☐	131 Jaakko Siren, HIFK		
☐	132 Seppo Naukkarinen, HIFK		
☐	133 Rainer Kolehmainen, HIFK		
☐	134 Henrik Granholm, HIFK		
☐	135 Erkki Partanen, HIFK		
☐	136 Heikki Jarn, HIFK		
☐	137 Jerry Sullivan, HIFK		
☐	138 Jaakko Marttinen, HIFK		
☐	139 Ulf Lindholm, HIFK		
☐	140 Pentti Lindegren, HIFK		
☐	141 Pentti Kotkas, HIFK		
☐	142 Pekka Perttula, HIFK		
☐	143 Esko Rekomaa, HIFK		
☐	144 Christer Thun, HIFK		
☐	145 Matti Kaski, Tappara		
☐	146 Pekka Marjamaki, Tappara		
☐	147 Antti Virtanen, Tappara		
☐	148 Matti Peltonen, Tappara		
☐	149 Reijo Ojanen, Tappara		
☐	150 Timo Ahlqvist, Tappara		
☐	151 Seppo Makinen, Tappara		
☐	152 Jouni Seistamo, Tappara		
☐	153 Harri Harvala, Tappara		
☐	154 Kari Makinen, Tappara		
☐	155 Heikki Koskimies, Tappara		
☐	156 Timo Jussila, Tappara		
☐	157 Pertti Ansakorpi, Tappara		
☐	158 Hannu Elo, Tappara		
☐	159 Mikko Holopainen, Tappara		
☐	160 Kalevi Numminen, Tappara		

1965 - 66 QUÉBEC ACES

Card Size: 3 1/2" x 5 1/2"

	Set (18 cards):	**60**	**120**
☐	Gilles Banville (G)	4	8
☐	Gary Bauman (G)	4	8
☐	Don Blackburn	3	6
☐	Jean-Guy Gendron	3	6
☐	Bernie Geoffrion	15	30
☐	Terry Gray	3	6
☐	John Hanna	3	6
☐	Wayne Hicks	3	6
☐	Ed Hoekstra	3	6
☐	Don Johns	3	6
☐	Gordon Labossière	3	6
☐	Yvon Lacoste	3	6
☐	Jimmy Morrison	3	6
☐	Cleveland Mortson	3	6
☐	Simon Nolet	4	8
☐	Noel Price	3	6
☐	Rino Robazza	3	6
☐	Bill Sutherland	3	6

1965 - 66 TOPPS

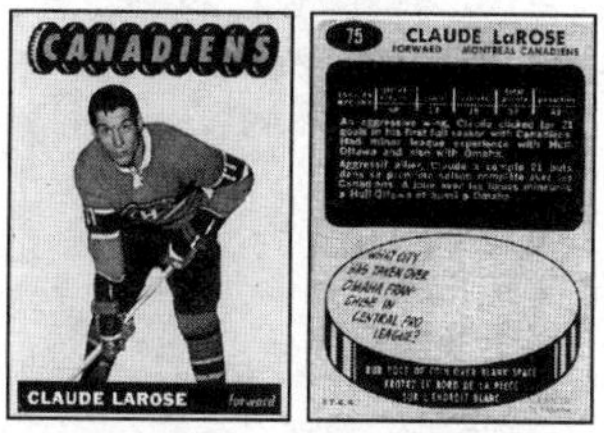

"The design has the little pucks (along the top). The best card in the set is the Cournoyer rookie. The '65-66 set was probably at that time what I had the most of. We'd use the cards for trading and flipping on the school grounds. The point of trading was to get your favourite team. My team had Mahovlich, Keon, Shack, Armstrong." – Fred LaCroix, Fresher Sports Cards, London, Ontario.

These cards measure the standard 2 1/2" x 3 1/2".

	Complete Set (128 cards):	**2,200**	**3,500**
	Common Player:	**6**	**11**
	Topps	**EX**	**EX-NM**
☐	1 Toe Blake, Coach, Mont.	12	40
☐	2 Gump Worsley (G), Mont.	22	45
☐	3 Jacques Laperrière, Mont.	12	20
☐	4 Jean-Guy Talbot, Mont.	6	11
☐	**5 Ted Harris, Mont. RC**	**6**	**11**
☐	6 Jean Béliveau, Mont.	40	70
☐	7 Dick Duff, Mont.	6	11
☐	8 Claude Provost, Mont.	6	11
☐	9 Red Berenson, Mont.	6	11
☐	10 John Ferguson, Mont.	9	15
☐	11 Punch Imlach, Coach, Toro.	9	15
☐	12 Terry Sawchuk (G), Toro.	55	85
☐	13 Bob Baun, Toro.	9	15
☐	14 Kent Douglas, Toro.	6	11
☐	15 Red Kelly, Toro.	12	20
☐	16 Jim Pappin, Toro.	6	11
☐	17 Dave Keon, Toro.	35	60
☐	18 Bob Pulford, Toro.	9	15
☐	19 George Armstrong, Toro.	11	18
☐	20 Orland Kurtenbach, Toro.	6	11
☐	**21 Ed Giacomin (G), NYRa. RC**	**110**	**175**
☐	22 Harry Howell, NYRa.	9	15
☐	23 Rod Seiling, NYRa.	6	11
☐	**24 Mike McMahon, NYRa. RC**	**6**	**14**
☐	25 Jean Ratelle, NYRa.	20	30
☐	26 Doug Robinson, NYRa.	6	11
☐	27 Vic Hadfield, NYRa.	6	11
☐	**28 Garry Peters, NYRa. RC, Error (Gary)**	**6**	**14**
☐	29 Don Marshall, NYRa.	6	11
☐	30 Bill Hicke, NYRa.	6	11
☐	**31 Gerry Cheevers (G), Bost. RC**	**110**	**175**
☐	32 Léo Boivin, Bost.	9	15
☐	33 Al Langlois, Bost. LC	6	11
☐	34 Murray Oliver, Bost.	6	11
☐	35 Tom Williams, Bost.	6	11
☐	**36 Ron Schock, Bost. RC**	**6**	**14**
☐	37 Ed Westfall, Bost.	6	11
☐	38 Gary Dornhoefer, Bost.	6	11
☐	39 Bob Dillabough, Bost.	6	11
☐	**40 Poul Popiel, Bost. RC, Error (Paul)**	**6**	**14**
☐	41 Sid Abel, Coach, Detr.	9	15
☐	42 Roger Crozier (G), Detr.	12	20
☐	43 Doug Barkley, Detr. LC	6	11
☐	44 Bill Gadsby, Detr. LC	9	15
☐	**45 Bryan Watson, Detr. RC**	**12**	**20**
☐	46 Bob McCord, Detr.	6	11
☐	47 Alex Delvecchio, Detr.	12	20
☐	48 Andy Bathgate, Detr.	9	15
☐	49 Norm Ullman, Detr.	13	22
☐	50 Ab McDonald, Detr.	6	11
☐	**51 Paul Henderson, Detr. RC**	**40**	**75**
☐	52 Pit Martin, Detr.	6	11
☐	53 Billy Harris, Detr.	6	11
☐	54 Billy Reay, Coach, Chic.	6	11
☐	55 Glenn Hall (G), Chic.	25	40
☐	56 Pierre Pilote, Chic.	9	15
☐	57 Al MacNeil, Chic.	6	11
☐	58 Camille Henry, Chic.	6	11
☐	59 Bobby Hull, Chic.	145	235
☐	60 Stan Mikita, Chic.	60	90
☐	61 Kenny Wharram, Chic.	6	11
☐	62 Billy Hay, Chic. LC	6	11
☐	**63 Fred Stanfield, Chic. RC**	**9**	**18**
☐	**64 Dennis Hull, Chic. RC**	**22**	**45**

Card	EX	EX-MT
65 Ken Hodge, Chic. RC	**22**	**45**
66 Checklist (1 - 66)	180	300
67 Charlie Hodge (G), Mont.	9	15
68 Terry Harper, Mont.	6	11
69 J.C. Tremblay, Mont.	9	15
70 Bobby Rousseau, Mont.	6	11
71 Henri Richard, Mont.	30	50
72 Dave Balon, Mont.	6	11
73 Ralph Backstrom, Mont.	6	11
74 Jim Roberts, Mont. RC	**9**	**18**
75 Claude Larose, Mont. RC	**6**	**14**
76 Yvan Cournoyer, Mont. RC, Error (Yvon)	**80**	**130**
77 Johnny Bower (G), Toro.	18	30
78 Carl Brewer, Toro.	6	11
79 Tim Horton, Toro.	35	55
80 Marcel Pronovost, Toro.	9	15
81 Frank Mahovlich, Toro.	30	50
82 Ron Ellis, Toro. RC	**25**	**40**
83 Larry Jeffrey, Toro.	6	11
84 Pete Stemkowski, Toro. RC	**9**	**18**
85 Eddie Joyal, Toro. RC	**6**	**14**
86 Mike Walton, Toro. RC	**9**	**18**
87 Red Sullivan, NYRa. LC	6	11
88 Don Simmons (G), NYRa. LC	9	15
89 Jim Neilson, NYRa.	6	11
90 Arnie Brown, NYRa.	6	11
91 Rod Gilbert, NYRa.	20	30
92 Phil Goyette, NYRa.	6	11
93 Bob Nevin, NYRa.	6	11
94 John McKenzie, NYRa.	6	11
95 Ted Taylor, NYRa. RC	**6**	**14**
96 Milt Schmidt, Coach, Bost.	9	15
97 Ed Johnston (G), Bost.	9	15
98 Ted Green, Bost.	6	11
99 Don Awrey, Bost. RC	**9**	**18**
100 Bob Woytowich, Bost. RC	**6**	**14**
101 John Bucyk, Bost.	15	25
102 Dean Prentice, Bost.	6	11
103 Ron Stewart, Bost.	6	11
104 Reggie Fleming, Bost.	6	11
105 Parker MacDonald, Bost.	6	11
106 Hank Bassen (G), Detr.	9	11
107 Gary Bergman, Detr.	6	11
108 Gordie Howe, Detr.	110	175
109 Floyd Smith, Detr.	6	11
110 Bruce MacGregor, Detr.	6	11
111 Ron Murphy, Detr.	6	11
112 Don McKenney, Detr. LC	6	11
113 Denis DeJordy (G), Chic.	6	11
114 Elmer Vasko, Chic.	6	11
115 Matt Ravlich, Chic. RC	**6**	**14**
116 Phil Esposito, Chic. RC	**250**	**425**
117 Chico Maki, Chic.	6	11
118 Doug Mohns, Chic.	6	11
119 Eric Nesterenko, Chic.	6	11
120 Pat Stapleton, Chic.	6	11
121 Checklist (67 - 121)	180	300
122 Gordie Howe, (600 Goals)	275	450
123 Toronto Maple Leafs	60	100
124 Chicago Blackhawks	55	90
125 Detroit Red Wings	55	90
126 Montréal Canadiens	60	100
127 New York Rangers	55	90
128 Boston Bruins	110	240

1965 - 66 TORONTO STAR PHOTOS

These are colour newspaper photos.

Toronto Star	EX	EX-MT
Dec. 18 Marcel Pronovost, Toro.	11	18
Dec. 25 Henri Richard, Mont.	13	22
Jan. 1 Norm Ullman, Detr.	12	20
Jan. 8 Frank Mahovlich, Toro.	20	30
Jan. 15 Ed Giacomin (G), NYRa.	20	30
Jan. 22 Jean Béliveau, Mont.	20	30
Jan. 29 Doug Mohns, Chic.	7	12
Feb. 5 Eddie Shack, Toro.	12	20
Feb. 12 Claude Provost, Mont.	9	15
Feb. 19 Ted Green, Bost.	7	12
Feb. 26 Tim Horton, Toro.	20	30
Mar. 5 Jacques Lapierrère, Mont.	11	18
Mar. 12 Bill Hay, Chic.	7	12
Mar. 19 Dave Keon, Toro.	13	22
Mar. 26 J. C. Tremblay, Mont.	9	15
Apr. 2 Bob Baun, Toro.	9	15

1965 - 66 WEEKEND PHOTOS

These newsprint colour photos measure 5 1/2" x 6 1/2". These back-to-back photos appeared in the Star Weekend Magazine.

Toronto Star	EX	EX-MT
Glenn Hall (G), Chic./ J. Laperrière, Mont.	20	25
Pierre Pilote, Chic./ Gordie Howe, Detr.	35	60
Stan Mikita, Chic./ Bobby Hull, Chic.	30	50

1966 - 67 CHAMPION

These cards measure 2 1/8" x 3 1/8". They were issued by the chewing-gum factory Champion in Finland.

Complete Set (220 cards):

Champion EX EX-NM

1 Jukka Haapala, Rauman Lukko
2 Simo Saimo, Rauman Lukko
3 Hannu Torma, Rauman Lukko
4 Jukka Savunen, Rauman Lukko
5 Tenho Lotila, Rauman Lukko
6 Tapani Koskimaki, Rauman Lukko
7 Matti Saurio, Rauman Lukko
8 Risto Kaitala, Rauman Lukko
9 Raimo Tiainen, Rauman Lukko
10 Esa Isaksson, Rauman Lukko
11 Pentti Rautalin, Rauman Lukko
12 Helkko Stenvall, Rauman Lukko
13 Teppo Rastio, Rauman Lukko
14 Jorma Vehmanen, Rauman Lukko
15 Raimo Kilpio, RU38 Pori
16 Veikko Ukkonen, RU38 Pori
17 Lauri Lehtonen, RU38 Pori
18 Heikki Veravainen, RU38 Pori
19 Pentti Riitahaara, RU38 Pori
20 Pekka Kuusisto, RU38 Pori
21 Tapio Rautalammi, RU38 Pori
22 Raimo Tuli, RU38 Pori
23 Matti Paivinen, RU38 Pori
24 Matti Harju, RU38 Pori
25 Kari Sillanpaa, RU38 Pori
26 Matti Keinonen, RU38 Pori
27 Pekka Lahti, RU38 Pori
28 Johannes Karttunen, RU38 Pori
29 Sakari Isomaki, RU38 Pori
30 Samu Leikko, RU38 Pori
31 Tapani Suominen, RU38 Pori
32 Esa Vesslin, Porin Karhut
33 Pekka Jalava, Porin Karhut
34 Pertti Makela, Porin Karhut
35 Juha Rantasila, Porin Karhut
36 Jukka Haanpaa, Porin Karhut
37 Teuvo Helenius, Porin Karhut
38 Anto Virtanen, Porin Karhut
39 Kimmo Nokikuru, Porin Karhut
40 Jaakko Honkanen, Porin Karhut
41 Seppo Nystrom, Porin Karhut
42 Tuomo Pirskainen, Porin Karhut
43 Matti Jansson, Porin Karhut
44 Alpo Suhonen, Porin Karhut
45 Matti Varpela, Porin Karhut
46 Kaj Matalamaki, Porin Karhut
47 Antti Heikkila, Porin Karhut
48 Jaakko Jaskari, Porin Karhut
49 Jouko Ojansuu, Porin Karhut
50 Mikko Myllyniemi, Porin Karhut
51 VeliPekka Ketola, Porin Karhut
52 Matti Salmi, Porin Karhut
53 Pentti Vihanto, Turun Taverit
54 Hannu Luojola, Turun Taverit
55 Seppo Parikka, Turun Taverit
56 Martti Salonen, Turun Taverit
57 Risto Forss, Turun Taverit
58 Hannu Niittoaho, Turun Taverit
59 Kari Johansson, Turun Taverit
60 Henry Leppa, Turun Taverit
61 Jarmo Rantanen, Turun Taverit
62 Kari Torkkel, Turun Taverit
63 Seppo Vikstrom, Turun Taverit
64 Veijo Saarinen, Turun Taverit
65 Pekka Lahtela, Turun Taverit
66 Risto Vainio, Turun Taverit
67 Reijo Paksal, Turun Taverit
68 Erkan Nasib, Turun Taverit
69 Matti Breilin, Turun Taverit
70 Voitto Soini, Turun Taverit
71 Urpo Ylonen, Turun Taverit
72 Rauno Heinonen, Turun Palloseura
73 Heikki Heino, Turun Palloseura
74 Lasse Kiili, Turun Palloseura
75 Ilkka Mesikammen, Turun Palloseura
76 Timo Nummelin, Turun Palloseura
77 Pertti Kuismanen, Turun Palloseura
78 Juhani Wahlsten, Turun Palloseura
79 Rauli Ottila, Turun Palloseura
80 Pertti Karelius, Turun Palloseura
81 Teuvo Andelmin, Turun Palloseura
82 Kari Varjanen, Turun Palloseura
83 Kalevi Leppanen, Turun Palloseura
84 Juhani IsoEskeli, Turun Palloseura
85 Hannu Koivunen, Turun Palloseura
86 Yrjo Hakala, Saimaan
87 Kari Ruontimo, Saimaan
88 Raimo Lohko, Saimaan
89 Markku Eiskonen, Saimaan
90 Hannu Lemander, Saimaan
91 Timo Vaatamoinen, Saimaan
92 Pekka Moisio, Saimaan
93 Martti Makia, Saimaan
94 Risto Heinvirta, Saimaan
95 Taisto Jahma, Saimaan
96 Veikko Makia, Saimaan
97 Raimo Helppolainen, Saimaan
98 Lalli Partinen, Saimaan
99 Keijo Sinkkonen, Saimaan
100 Antti Ravi, Saimaan
101 Martti Sinkkonen, Saimaan
102 Heikki Juselius, Saimaan
103 Timo Rantala, Lahden Reipas
104 Heikki Mikkola, Lahden Reipas
105 Jaakko Siren, Lahden Reipas
106 Matti Korhonen, Lahden Reipas
107 Erkki Mononen, Lahden Reipas
108 Pertti Valkonen, Lahden Reipas
109 Ilpo Koskela, Lahden Reipas
110 Bengt Wilenius, Lahden Reipas
111 Hannu Lindberg, Lahden Reipas
112 Kristen Bertell, Lahden Reipas
113 Veikko Kuusisto, Lahden Reipas
114 Tapio Majaniemi, Lahden Reipas
115 Leo Vankka, Lahden Reipas
116 Pentti Harju, Lahden Reipas
117 Ari Myllymaki, Lahden Reipas
118 Matti Koskinen, Lahden Reipas
119 Pentti Andersson, Lahden Reipas
120 Pertti Heikkinen, Lahden Reipas
121 Pekka Peltoniemi, Lahden Reipas
122 Jouko Jarvinen, Lahden Reipas
123 Matti Vartiainen, Lahden Reipas
124 Esko Reijonen, Sapko
125 Erkki Rasanen, Sapko
126 Timo Viskari, Sapko
127 Raimo Turkulainen, Sapko
128 Paavo Tirkkonen, Sapko
129 Orvo Paatero, Sapko
130 Juhani Leirivaara, Sapko
131 Jyrki Turunen, Sapko
132 Timo Tuomainen, Sapko
133 Pentti Karkkainen, Sapko
134 Jussi Piuhola, Sapko
135 Pentti Pihlapuro, Sapko
136 Pentti Pennanen, Sapko
137 Esa Viskari, Sapko
138 Timo Luostarinen, Sapko
139 Seppo Iivonen, Sapko
140 Risto Alho, Sapko
141 Esko Kiuru, Sapko
142 Jaakko Hovinheimo, Sapko
143 Jaakko Koikkalainen, Sapko
144 Juhani Sodervik, Sapko
145 Seppo Makinen, Tappara
146 Teuvo Peltola, Tappara
147 Antti Alenius, Tappara
148 Kalevi Numminen, Tappara
149 Esko Kaonpaa, Tappara
150 Lauri Salomaa, Tappara
151 Risto Pirttiaho, Tappara
152 Antti Leppanen, Tappara
153 Kari Makinen, Tappara
154 Jorma Oksala, Tappara
155 Pekka Marjamaki, Tappara
156 Jouni Seistamo, Tappara
157 Pertti Ansakorpi, Tappara
158 Erkki Jarkko, Tappara
159 Juhani Peltola, Tappara
160 Erkki Mannikko, Tappara
161 Keijo Mannisto, Tappara
162 Matti Peltonen, Tappara
163 Hannu Heikkonen, Tappara
164 Pentti Hyytiainen, Tappara
165 Antti Virtanen, Tappara
166 Seppo Nurmi, Tampereen
167 Matti Reunamaki, Tampereen
168 Mikko Raikkonen, Tampereen
169 Esko Rantanen, Tampereen
170 Eero Holopainen, Tampereen
171 Juhani Ruohonen, Tampereen
172 Veikko Savolainen, Tampereen
173 Heikki Sivonen, Tampereen
174 Markku Pulli, Tampereen
175 Pekka Uitus, Tampereen
176 Heikki Keinonen, Tampereen
177 Jorma Saarikorpi, Tampereen
178 Rauno Lehtio, Tampereen
179 Kalevi Toivonen, Tampereen
180 Jorma Vilen, Tampereen
181 Pentti Kuusinen, Tampereen
182 Olavi Haapalainen, Tampereen
183 Seppo Nikkila, Tampereen
184 Jorma Suokko, Tampereen
185 Heino Pulli, Tampereen
186 Risto Lehtio, Tampereen
187 Pekka Lehtolainen, Tampereen
188 Timo Hirsimaki, Ilves
189 Kari Palooja, Ilves
190 Pekka Leimu, Ilves
191 Ali Saadetin, Ilves
192 Erkki Jarvinen, Ilves
193 Markku Hakanen, Ilves
194 Jorma Kallio, Ilves
195 Vaino Kolkka, Ilves
196 Timo Saari, Ilves
197 Jorma Peltonen, Ilves
198 Pentti Pynnonen, Ilves
199 Pentti Uotila, Ilves
200 Timo Lahtinen, Ilves
201 Juhani Lahtinen, Ilves
202 Reijo Hakanen, Ilves
203 Lasse Oksanen, Ilves
204 Juhani Aromaki, Ilves
205 Jukka Alkula, Hermes Kokkola
206 Pekka Olkkonen, Hermes Kokkola
207 Tapani Salo, Hermes Kokkola
208 Vesa Kartsalo, Hermes Kokkola
209 Antti Komsi, Hermes Kokkola
210 Asko Sallamaa, Hermes Kokkola
211 Juhani Tarkiainen, Hermes Kokkola
212 Antero Hakala, Hermes Kokkola
213 Ulf Slotte, Hermes Kokkola
214 Raimo Savolainen, Hermes Kokkola
215 Matias Savolainen, Hermes Kokkola
216 Risto Savolainen, Hermes Kokkola
217 Keijo Makinen, Hermes Kokkola
218 Tapio Makinen, Hermes Kokkola
219 Ossi Peltoniemi, Hermes Kokkola
220 Matti Valikangas, Hermes Kokkola

1966 - 67 POST HOCKEY TIPS

These 6" x 9 1/4" blank-back cards were issued on the backs of Post cereal boxes. Two different photos for each player were issued. The smaller cards measure 2 5/8" x 2 5/8".

Complete Set (18 large cards):	**150**	**300**
Complete Set (9 small cards):	**60**	**100**
Post Cereal Box Backs	**EX**	**EX-NM**
1 AS: Glenn Hall (G), Chic.	15	25
2 AS: Tim Horton, Toro.	15	25
3 AS: Gordie Howe, Detr.	28	45
4 AS: Harry Howell, NYRa.	9	15
5 AS: Dave Keon, Toro.	12	20
6 AS: Frank Mahovlich, Toro.	15	25
7 AS: Stan Mikita, Chic.	15	25
8 AS: Bob Nevin, NYRa.	6	10
9 AS: Murray Oliver, Bost.	6	10
10 AS: Pierre Pilote, Chic.	9	15
11 AS: Bob Pulford, Toro.	11	18
12 AS: Norm Ullman, Detr.	11	18

□	13 Jacques Laperrière, Mont.	9	15
□	14 Henri Richard, Mont.	12	20
□	15 Bobby Rousseau, Mont.	6	10
□	16 Gilles Tremblay, Mont.	6	10
□	17 J.C. Tremblay, Mont.	7	12
□	18 Gump Worsley (G), Mont.	13	22

Post Cereal Small Cards		EX	EX-NM
□	1 AS: Glenn Hall (G), Chic.	12	20
□	2 AS: Gordie Howe, Detr.	20	30
□	3 AS: Dave Keon, Toro.	9	15
□	4 AS: Frank Mahovlich, Toro.	11	18
□	5 AS: Bob Nevin, NYRa.	5	7
□	6 AS: Bob Pulford, Toro.	7	12
□	7 Bobby Rousseau, Mont.	5	7
□	8 J.C. Tremblay, Mont.	6	10
□	9 Gump Worsley (G), Mont.	11	18

1966 - 67 TOPPS

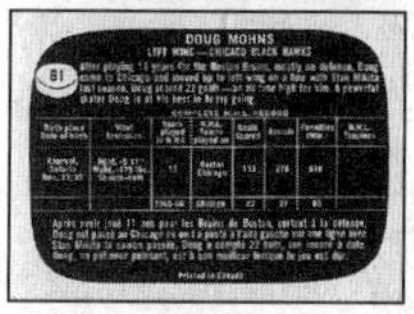

"There is a love-hate relationship with that 1966-67 set. The problem with that set is it is a one-card set. A lot of people build that set without the Bobby Orr. A lot of other people will go out and get the Bobby Orr first and then go out and build the rest of the set." – Gerry Chartrand, Gerry's Sports Cards, Montréal, Québec.

These cards measure the standard 2 1/2" x 3 1/2".

Complete Set (132 cards):		**3,600**	**5,200**
Common Player:		**7**	**12**
Topps		**EX**	**EX-NM**
□	1 Toe Blake, Coach, Mont.	12	40
□	2 Gump Worsley (G), Mont.	20	30
□	3 Jean-Guy Talbot, Mont.	7	12
□	4 Gilles Tremblay, Mont.	7	12
□	5 J.C. Tremblay, Mont.	7	12
□	6 Jim Roberts, Mont.	7	12
□	7 Bobby Rousseau, Mont.	7	12
□	8 Henri Richard, Mont.	25	40
□	9 Claude Provost, Mont.	7	12
□	10 Claude Larose, Mont.	7	12
□	11 Punch Imlach, Coach, Toro.	9	15
□	12 Johnny Bower (G), Toro.	18	30
□	13 Terry Sawchuk (G), Toro.	40	70
□	14 Mike Walton, Toro.	7	12
□	15 Pete Stemkowski, Toro.	7	12
□	16 Allan Stanley, Toro.	9	15
□	17 Eddie Shack, Toro.	22	40
□	**18 Brit Selby, Toro. RC**	**8**	**15**
□	19 Bob Pulford, Toro.	9	15
□	20 Marcel Pronovost, Toro.	9	15
□	21 Emile Francis, Coach, NYRa.	20	30
□	22 Rod Seiling, NYRa.	7	12
□	23 Ed Giacomin (G), NYRa.	35	60
□	24 Don Marshall, NYRa.	7	12
□	25 Orland Kurtenbach, NYRa.	7	12
□	26 Rod Gilbert, NYRa.	18	28
□	27 Bob Nevin, NYRa.	7	12
□	28 Phil Goyette, NYRa.	7	12
□	29 Jean Ratelle, NYRa.	18	28
□	30 Earl Ingarfield, NYRa.	7	12
□	31 Harry Sinden, Coach, Bost.	30	50
□	32 Ed Westfall, Bost.	7	12
□	**33 Joe Watson, Bost. RC**	**8**	**15**
□	34 Bob Woytowich, Bost.	7	12
□	**35 Bobby Orr, Bost. RC**	**2,000**	**3,500**
□	**36 Gilles Marotte, Bost. RC**	**8**	**15**
□	37 Ted Green, Bost.	7	12
□	38 Tom Williams, Bost.	7	12
□	39 John Bucyk, Bost.	13	22
□	40 Wayne Connelly, Bost.	7	12
□	41 Pit Martin, Bost.	7	12
□	42 Sid Abel, Coach, Detr.	9	15
□	43 Roger Crozier (G), Detr.	12	20
□	44 Andy Bathgate, Detr.	9	15
□	45 Dean Prentice, Detr.	7	12
□	46 Paul Henderson, Detr.	12	20
□	47 Gary Bergman, Detr.	7	12
□	48 Bryan Watson, Detr.	7	12
□	**49 Bob Wall, Detr. RC**	**8**	**15**
□	50 Léo Boivin, Detr.	9	15
□	**51 Bert Marshall, Detr. RC**	**8**	**15**
□	52 Norm Ullman, Detr.	12	20
□	53 Billy Reay, Coach, Chic.	7	12
□	54 Glenn Hall (G), Chic.	22	45
□	**55 Wally Boyer, Chic. RC**	**8**	**15**
□	56 Fred Stanfield, Chic.	7	12
□	57 Pat Stapleton, Chic.	7	12
□	58 Matt Ravlich, Chic.	7	12
□	59 Pierre Pilote, Chic.	9	15
□	60 Eric Nesterenko, Chic.	7	12
□	61 Doug Mohns, Chic.	7	12
□	62 Stan Mikita, Chic.	40	70
□	63 Phil Esposito, Chic.	85	140
□	64 Bobby Hull, Scoring Leader	55	90
□	65 AW: Hodge & Worsley	22	45
□	66 Checklist 1 (1 - 66)	180	300
□	67 Jacques Laperrière, Mont.	12	20
□	68 Terry Harper, Mont.	7	12
□	69 Ted Harris, Mont.	7	12
□	70 John Ferguson, Mont.	7	12
□	71 Dick Duff, Mont.	7	12
□	72 Yvan Cournoyer, Mont.	35	60
□	73 Jean Béliveau, Mont.	35	60
□	74 Dave Balon, Mont.	7	12
□	75 Ralph Backstrom, Mont.	7	12
□	76 Jim Pappin, Toro.	7	12
□	77 Frank Mahovlich, Toro.	25	40
□	78 Dave Keon, Toro.	22	45
□	79 Red Kelly, Toro. LC	12	20
□	80 Tim Horton, Toro.	30	50
□	81 Ron Ellis, Toro.	9	15
□	82 Kent Douglas, Toro.	7	12
□	83 Bob Baun, Toro.	7	12
□	84 George Armstrong, Toro.	9	15
□	85 Bernie Geoffrion, NYRa.	22	45
□	86 Vic Hadfield, NYRa.	7	12
□	87 Wayne Hillman, NYRa.	7	12
□	88 Jim Neilson, NYRa.	7	12
□	89 Al MacNeil, NYRa. LC	7	12
□	90 Arnie Brown, NYRa.	7	12
□	91 Harry Howell, NYRa.	9	15
□	92 Red Berenson, NYRa.	7	12
□	93 Reggie Fleming, NYRa.	7	12
□	94 Ron Stewart, Bost.	7	12
□	95 Murray Oliver, Bost.	7	12
□	96 Ron Murphy, Bost.	7	12
□	97 John McKenzie, Bost.	7	12
□	98 Bob Dillabough, Bost.	7	12
□	99 Ed Johnston (G), Bost.	9	15
□	100 Ron Schock, Bost.	7	12
□	101 Dallas Smith, Bost.	7	12
□	102 Alex Delvecchio, Detr.	12	20
□	**103 Pete Mahovlich, Detr. RC**	**25**	**40**
□	104 Bruce MacGregor, Detr.	7	12
□	105 Murray Hall, Detr.	7	12
□	106 Floyd Smith, Detr.	7	12
□	107 Hank Bassen (G), Detr. LC	9	15
□	108 Val Fonteyne, Detr.	7	12
□	109 Gordie Howe, Detr.	150	235
□	110 Chico Maki, Chic.	7	12
□	**111 Doug Jarrett, Chic. RC**	**8**	**15**
□	112 Bobby Hull, Chic.	100	170
□	113 Dennis Hull, Chic.	9	15
□	114 Ken Hodge, Chic.	9	15
□	115 Denis DeJordy (G), Chic.	9	15
□	116 Lou Angotti, Chic.	7	12
□	117 Kenny Wharram, Chic.	7	12
□	118 Montréal Canadiens	20	30
□	119 Detroit Red Wings	20	30
□	120 Checklist 2 (67 - 132)	180	300
□	121 AS: Gordie Howe, Detr.	75	125
□	122 AS: Jacques Laperrière, Mont.	9	15
□	123 AS: Pierre Pilote, Chic.	9	15
□	124 AS: Stan Mikita, Chic.	25	40
□	125 AS: Bobby Hull, Chic. (/b: G. Howe)	55	90
□	126 AS: Glenn Hall (G), Chic.	13	22
□	127 AS: Jean Béliveau, Mont.	20	30
□	128 AS: Allan Stanley, Toro.	9	15
□	129 AS: Pat Stapleton, Chic.	7	12
□	130 AS: Gump Worsley (G), Mont. (/b: B. Orr)	15	25
□	131 AS: Frank Mahovlich, Mont.	15	25
□	132 AS: Bobby Rousseau, Mont.	12	40

1966 - 67 TOPPS USA TEST

"The test set Orr is extremely rare, but we've had a few of them over the years. I'd say it's probably at least 20 times harder to find cards from the test set than the regular issue." – Harvey Goldfarb, A.J. Sports Cards, Toronto, Ontario.

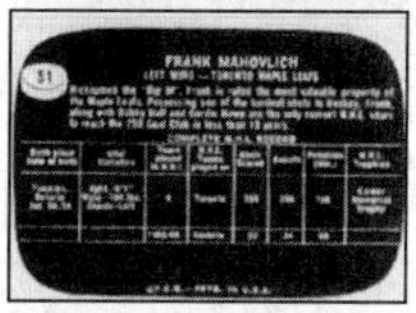

These cards measure the standard 2 1/2" x 3 1/2". Thought to be a market test, this issue is very tough to find because of its limited distribution. The card format is very similar to that of the regular 1966-67 Topps series, except the card backs are printed in English only. The wood grain border, which simulates a television screen, is a lighter shade than the regular issue.

Complete Set (66 cards):		**8,000**	**14,000**
Topps Test		**EX**	**EX-NM**
□	1 Dennis Hull, Chic.	50	100
□	2 Gump Worsley (G), Mont.	90	150
□	3 Dallas Smith, Bost.	40	65
□	4 Gilles Tremblay, Mont.	40	65
□	5 J.C. Tremblay, Mont.	45	70
□	6 Ralph Backstrom, Mont.	40	65
□	7 Bobby Rousseau, Mont.	40	65
□	8 Henri Richard, Mont.	100	175
□	9 Claude Provost, Mont.	45	70
□	10 Red Berenson, NYRa.	40	65
□	11 Punch Imlach, Coach, Toro.	45	75
□	12 Johnny Bower (G), Toro.	80	135
□	13 Yvan Cournoyer, Mont.	180	300
□	14 Mike Walton. Toro.	40	65
□	15 Pete Stemkowski, Toro.	40	65
□	16 Allan Stanley, Toro.	45	75
□	17 George Armstrong, Toro.	50	85
□	18 Harry Howell, NYRa.	45	75
□	19 Vic Hadfield, NYRa.	40	65
□	20 Marcel Pronovost, Toro.	45	75
□	21 Pete Mahovlich, Detr.	45	75
□	22 Rod Seiling, NYRa.	40	65
□	23 Gordie Howe, Detr.	700	1,200
□	24 Don Marshall, NYRa.	40	65
□	25 Orland Kurtenbach, NYRa.	40	65
□	26 Rod Gilbert, NYR	85	140
□	27 Bob Nevin, NYRa.	40	65
□	28 Phil Goyette, NYRa.	40	65
□	29 Jean Ratelle, NYRa.	85	140
□	30 Dave Keon, Toro.	110	175
□	31 Jean Béliveau, Mont.	200	350
□	32 Ed Westfall, Bost.	40	65
□	33 Ron Murphy, Bost.	40	65
□	34 Wayne Hillman, NYRa.	40	65
□	35 Bobby Orr, Bost.	7,000	12,000
□	36 Bernie Geoffrion, NYRa.	110	175
□	37 Ted Green, Bost.	40	65
□	38 Tom Williams, Bost.	40	65
□	39 John Bucyk, Bost.	65	110
□	40 Bobby Hull, Chic.	500	850
□	41 Ted Harris, Mont.	40	65
□	42 Red Kelly, Toro. LC	60	100
□	43 Roger Crozier (G), Detr.	60	100
□	44 Kenny Wharram, Chic.	40	65
□	45 Dean Prentice, Detr.	40	65
□	46 Paul Henderson, Detr.	60	100
□	47 Gary Bergman, Detr.	40	65
□	48 Arnie Brown, NYRa.	40	65
□	49 Jim Pappin, Toro.	40	65
□	50 Denis DeJordy (G), Chic.	45	75
□	51 Frank Mahovlich, Mont.	125	200
□	52 Norm Ullman, Detr.	60	100
□	53 Chico Maki, Chic.	40	65
□	54 Reggie Fleming, NYRa.	40	65
□	55 Jim Neilson, NYRa.	40	65
□	56 Bruce MacGregor, Detr.	40	65
□	57 Pat Stapleton, Chic.	45	70
□	58 Matt Ravlich, Chic.	40	65
□	59 Pierre Pilote, Chic.	45	75
□	60 Eric Nesterenko, Chic.	40	65
□	61 Doug Mohns, Chic.	40	65
□	62 Stan Mikita, Chic.	225	350
□	63 Alex Delvecchio, Detr.	75	125
□	64 Ed Johnston (G), Bost.	45	75
□	65 John Ferguson, Sr., Mont.	40	75
□	66 John McKenzie, Bost.	50	100

1966 - 67 WEEKEND PHOTOS

These newsprint colour photos measure 5 1/2" x 6 1/2".

Toronto Star		**EX**	**EX-MT**
□	101 Frank Mahovlich, Toro.	20	30
□	102 Bobby Rousseau, Mont.	7	12
□	103 Pat Stapleton, Chic.	9	15
□	104 Roger Crozier (G), Detr.	11	18
□	105 Don Marshall, NYRa.	7	12
□	106 Terry Sawchuk (G), Toro.	25	40
□	107 Jean Béliveau, Mont.	20	30
□	108 Doug Mohns, Chic.	7	12
□	109 Bob Nevin, NYRa.	7	12
□	110 Pit Martin, Bost.	7	12
□	111 Allan Stanley, Toro.	11	18
□	112 Harry Howell, NYRa.	11	18
1966 - 67 ALL-STAR TEAM			
□	101 Ed Giacomin/ Ken Wharram	20	30
□	102 Harry Howell/ Pierre Pilote	12	20
□	103 Bobby Hull/ Stan Mikita	25	40

1967 - 68 POST

These 6 1/8" x 7 1/8" blank-back cards were issued on the backs of Post cereal boxes. Two different photos for each player were issued.

Complete Set (12 large cards):		**150**	**300**
Post Cereal Box Backs		**EX**	**EX-NM**
□	Gordie Howe, Detr. (With net)	25	40
□	Gordie Howe, Detr. (Without net)	25	40
□	Harry Howell, NYRa. (Passing)	9	15
□	Harry Howell, NYRa. (Blocking shot)	9	15
□	Jacques Laperrière, Mont. (With net)	9	15
□	Jacques Laperrière, Mont. (Without net)	9	15
□	Stan Mikita, Chic.	15	25
□	Stan Mikita, Chic.	15	25
□	Bobby Orr, Bost. (Still)	30	50
□	Bobby Orr, Bost. (Action)	30	50
□	Henri Richard, Mont. (Puck in skates)	12	20
□	Henri Richard, Mont.	12	20

1967 - 68 POST CEREAL FLIP BOOKS

Each "Hockey Tips" book shows one Maple Leafs' player and one Canadiens' player. The booklets measure 1 1/4" x 2 3/4".

Complete Set (12 booklets):		**125**	**250**
Post Cereal		**EX**	**EX-NM**
□	1 Johnny Bower (G)/ Gump Worsley (G)	20	40
□	2 Johnny Bower (G)/ Rogatien Vachon (G)	18	30
□	3 Tim Horton/ Gilles Tremblay, Err. (J.C.)	18	30
□	4 Marcel Pronovost/ Jacques Laperrière	12	20
□	5 Frank Mahovlich/ Henri Richard	25	40
□	6 Dave Keon/ Dick Duff	18	30
□	7 Jim Pappin/ Jean Béliveau	25	40
□	8 Ron Ellis/ Jean Béliveau	25	40
□	9 George Armstrong/ Gilles Tremblay	13	22
□	10 Pete Stemkowski/ J.C. Tremblay	9	15
□	11 Bob Pulford/ Ralph Backstrom	12	20
□	12 Larry Hillman/ Bobby Rousseau	9	15

1967 - 68 TOPPS

"This set brings me back to my youth. It has different colour backgrounds with drawings of people in the stands. The key players include Bobby Orr second year, Gordie Howe, and Bobby Hull." – Alan Pearson, Raxan Collectibles, Montréal, Québec.

These cards measure the standard 2 1/2" x 3 1/2".

Complete Set (132 cards):		**2,300**	**3,600**
Common Player:		**6**	**10**
Topps		**EX**	**EX-NM**
□	1 Gump Worsley (G), Mont.	25	55
□	2 Dick Duff, Mont.	6	10
□	**3 Jacques Lemaire, Mont. RC**	**50**	**80**
□	4 Claude Larose, Mont.	6	10
□	5 Gilles Tremblay, Mont.	6	10

□	6 Terry Harper, Mont.	6	10
□	7 Jacques Laperrière, Mont.	9	15
□	**8 Garry Monahan, Mont. RC**	**6**	**12**
□	**9 Carol Vadnais, Mont. RC**	**8**	**15**
□	10 Ted Harris, Mont.	6	10
□	11 Dave Keon, Toro.	15	25
□	12 Pete Stemkowski, Toro.	6	10
□	13 Allan Stanley, Toro.	7	10
□	14 Ron Ellis, Toro.	6	10
□	15 Mike Walton, Toro.	6	10
□	16 Tim Horton, Toro.	25	40
□	**17 Brian Conacher, Toro. RC**	**6**	**12**
□	18 Bruce Gamble (G), Toro.	7	13
□	19 Bob Pulford, Toro.	7	13
□	**20 Duane Rupp, Toro. RC**	**6**	**12**
□	21 Larry Jeffrey, NYRa.	6	10
□	22 Wayne Hillman, NYRa.	6	10
□	23 Don Marshall, NYRa.	6	10
□	24 Red Berenson, NYRa.	6	10
□	25 Phil Goyette, NYRa.	6	10
□	26 Camille Henry, NYRa.	6	10
□	27 Rod Seiling, NYRa.	6	10
□	28 Bob Nevin, NYRa.	6	10
□	29 Bernie Geoffrion, NYRa. LC	18	28
□	30 Reggie Fleming, NYRa.	6	10
□	31 Jean Ratelle, NYRa.	13	22
□	32 Phil Esposito, Bost.	55	95
□	**33 Derek Sanderson, Bost. RC**	**65**	**110**
□	34 Eddie Shack, Bost.	18	30
□	**35 Ross Lonsberry, Bost. RC**	**6**	**12**
□	36 Fred Stanfield, Bost.	6	10
□	37 Don Awrey, Bost., Error (Skip Krake)	6	10
□	**38 Glen Sather, Bost. RC**	**25**	**40**
□	39 John McKenzie, Bost.	6	10
□	40 Tom Williams, Bost.	6	10
□	41 Dallas Smith, Bost.	6	10
□	42 John Bucyk, Bost.	12	20
□	43 Gordie Howe, Detr.	125	200
□	**44 Gary Jarrett, Detr. RC**	**6**	**12**
□	45 Bert Marshall, Detr.	6	10
□	46 Dean Prentice, Detr.	6	10
□	47 Gary Bergman, Detr.	6	10
□	48 Roger Crozier (G), Detr.	9	15
□	49 Howie Young, Detr.	6	10
□	**50 Doug Roberts, Detr. RC**	**6**	**12**
□	51 Alex Delvecchio, Detr.	11	18
□	52 Floyd Smith, Detr.	6	10
□	**53 Doug Shelton, Chic. RC/LC**	**6**	**12**
□	**54 Gerry Goyer, Chic. RC/LC**	**6**	**12**
□	**55 Wayne Maki, Chic. RC**	**6**	**12**
□	56 Dennis Hull, Chic.	7	13
□	**57 Dave Dryden (G), Chic. RC**	**12**	**20**
□	**58 Paul Terbenche, Chic. RC**	**5**	**12**
□	59 Gilles Marotte, Chic.	6	10
□	60 Eric Nesterenko, Chic.	6	10
□	61 Pat Stapleton, Chic.	6	10
□	62 Pierre Pilote, Chic.	7	13
□	63 Doug Mohns, Chic.	6	10
□	64 AW: Stan Mikita, Chic.	25	40
□	65 AW: Hall & DeJordy, Chic.	15	25
□	66 Checklist 1 (1 - 66)	175	275
□	67 Ralph Backstrom, Mont.	6	10
□	68 Bobby Rousseau, Mont.	6	10
□	69 John Ferguson, Mont.	6	10
□	70 Yvan Cournoyer, Mont.	22	45
□	71 Claude Provost, Mont.	6	10
□	72 Henri Richard, Mont.	18	28
□	73 J.C. Tremblay, Mont.	6	10
□	74 Jean Béliveau, Mont.	25	45
□	**75 Rogatien Vachon (G), Mont. RC**	**55**	**95**
□	76 Johnny Bower (G), Toro.	13	22
□	**77 Wayne Carleton, Toro. RC**	**6**	**12**
□	78 Jim Pappin, Toro.	6	10
□	79 Frank Mahovlich, Toro.	25	35
□	80 Larry Hillman, Toro.	6	10
□	81 Marcel Pronovost, Toro.	7	13
□	82 Murray Oliver, Toro.	6	10
□	83 George Armstrong, Toro.	7	13
□	84 Harry Howell, NYRa.	7	13
□	85 Ed Giacomin (G), NYRa.	25	45
□	86 Gilles Villemure (G), NYRa.	7	13
□	87 Orland Kurtenbach, NYRa.	6	10
□	88 Vic Hadfield, NYRa.	6	10
□	89 Arnie Brown, NYRa.	6	10
□	90 Rod Gilbert, NYRa.	13	22
□	91 Jim Neilson, NYRa.	6	10
□	92 Bobby Orr, Bost.	475	800
□	93 Skip Krake, Bost., Error (Don Awrey)	6	10
□	94 Ted Green, Bost.	6	10
□	95 Ed Westfall, Bost.	6	10
□	96 Ed Johnston (G), Bost.	7	13
□	**97 Gary Doak, Bost. RC**	**8**	**15**
□	98 Ken Hodge, Bost.	6	10
□	99 Gerry Cheevers (G), Bost.	35	55
□	100 Ron Murphy, Bost.	6	10
□	101 Norm Ullman, Detr.	11	18
□	102 Bruce MacGregor, Detr.	6	10
□	103 Paul Henderson, Detr.	9	15
□	104 Jean Guy Talbot, Detr.	6	10
□	**105 Bart Crashley, Detr. RC**	**6**	**12**
□	**106 Roy Edwards (G), Detr. RC**	**8**	**15**
□	**107 Jim Watson, Detr. RC**	**6**	**12**
□	108 Ted Hampson, Detr.	6	10
□	**109 Bill Orban, Chic. RC/LC**	**6**	**12**
□	**110 Jeff Powis, Chic. RC/LC**	**6**	**12**
□	111 Chico Maki, Chic.	6	10
□	112 Doug Jarrett, Chic.	6	10
□	113 Bobby Hull, Chic.	90	140
□	114 Stan Mikita, Chic.	35	60
□	115 Denis DeJordy (G), Chic.	7	13
□	116 Pit Martin, Chic.	6	10
□	117 Kenny Wharram, Chic.	6	10
□	118 AW: Bobby Orr, Bost.	225	375
□	119 AW: Harry Howell, NYRa.	7	12
□	120 Checklist 2 (67 - 132)	210	325
□	121 AS: Harry Howell, NYRa.	7	12
□	122 AS: Pierre Pilote, Chic.	7	12
□	123 AS: Ed Giacomin (G), NYRa.	15	25
□	124 AS: Bobby Hull, Chic.	55	90
□	125 AS: Kenny Wharram, Chic.	6	10
□	126 AS: Stan Mikita, Chic.	20	30
□	127 AS: Tim Horton, Toro.	15	25
□	128 AS: Bobby Orr, Bost.	225	375
□	129 AS: Glenn Hall (G), Chic.	15	25
□	130 AS: Don Marshall, NYRa.	6	10
□	131 AS: Gordie Howe, Detr.	70	115
□	132 AS: Norm Ullman, Detr.	10	25

1967 - 68 YORK PEANUT BUTTER

The first 12 cards in this series are unnumbered. Eachcard measures 2 7/8" x 2 7/8".

	Complete Set (36 cards):	**350**	**550**
	York Peanut Butter	**EX**	**EX-NM**
□	B. Conacher/ A. Stanley/ L. Rochefort	9	15
□	T. Harper/ G. Worsley (G)/ M. Walton	13	22
□	T. Horton/ G. Armstrong/ J. Béliveau	28	45
□	D. Keon/ G. Armstrong/ C. Provost	13	22
□	J. Laperrière/ R. Vachon (G)/ B. Pulford	13	22
□	B. Pulford/ B. Conacher/ C. Provost	11	18
□	B. Pulford/ J. Pappin/ T. Harper	9	15
□	P. Stemkowski/ J. Pappin/ T. Harris	7	13
□	J.C. Tremblay/ R. Vachon (G)/ P. Stemkowski	9	15
□	R. Vachon (G)/ R. Backstrom/ B. Pulford	12	20
□	R. Vachon (G)/ J. Laperrière/ M. Walton	12	20
□	M. Walton/ P. Stemkowski/ J.C. Tremblay	7	13
□	13 D. Keon/ M. Walton/ J.C. Tremblay	11	18
□	14 P. Stemkowski/ R. Backstrom	7	13
□	15 R. Vachon (G)/ B. Pulford	11	18
□	16 J. Bower (G)/ R. Ellis/ J. Ferguson, Sr.	11	18
□	17 R. Ellis/ G. Worsley (G)	11	18
□	18 G. Worsley (G)/ J. Laperrière/ F. Mahovlich	22	45
□	19 J.C. Tremblay/ D. Keon	11	18
□	20 C. Provost/ F. Mahovlich	13	22
□	21 J. Ferguson, Sr./ T. Horton	13	22
□	22 G. Worsley (G)/ R. Ellis	11	18
□	23 J. Bower (G)/ M. Walton/ J. Béliveau	18	28
□	24 J.C. Tremblay/ G. Worsley (G)/ B. Pulford	15	25
□	25 T. Horton/ J. Bower (G)/ J. Béliveau	25	40
□	26 A. Stanley/ J. Bower (G)/ D. Duff	15	25
□	27 R. Backstrom/ J. Bower (G)	11	18
□	28 Y. Cournoyer/ J. Béliveau/ F. Mahovlich	30	50
□	29 J. Bower (G)/ L. Hillman/ Y. Cournoyer	15	25
□	30 J. Bower (G)/ Y. Cournoyer	15	25
□	31 T. Horton/ R. Vachon (G)	15	25
□	32 J. Pappin/ B. Pulford/ R. Vachon (G)	11	18
□	33 T. Harper/ B. Rousseau/ M. Pronovost	9	15
□	34 J. Bower (G)/ M. Pronovost/ R. Backstrom	12	20
□	35 F. Mahovlich/ G. Worsley (G)	18	28
□	36 C. Provost/ J. Bower (G)	12	20

1964 - 67 BEEHIVE PHOTOS

The third group of BeeHive photos were issued between 1964 and 1967. These blank-back photos measure 5 1/2" x 8". All of these BeeHive photos feature a wood grain border. The players' names appear inscribed in a name plate at the bottom centre of the border. Other singles may exist.

	BeeHive • Boston Bruins	**EX**	**EX-NM**
□	Murray Balfour	20	30
□	Léo Boivin	9	15
□	Johnny Bucyk	9	15
□	Wayne Connelly	100	160
□	Bob Dillabough	7	12
□	Gary Dornhoefer	9	15
□	Reg Fleming	7	12
□	Guy Gendron	80	130
□	Warren Godfrey	250	350
□	Ted Green	7	12
□	Andy Hebenton	100	160
□	Tom Johnson	11	18
□	Ed Johnston (G)	9	15
□	Forbes Kennedy	7	12
□	Orland Kurtenbach	25	40
□	Bob Leiter	9	15
□	Parker MacDonald	9	15
□	Bob McCord	9	15
□	Ab McDonald	18	30
□	Murray Oliver	7	12
□	Bernie Parent (G)	45	75
□	Cliff Pennington	190	250
□	Bob Perreault (G)	300	400
□	Dean Prentice	7	12
□	Ron Schock, Err. (Shock)	7	12
□	Pat Stapleton	40	65
□	Ron Stewart	9	15
□	Ed Westfall	7	12
□	Tom Williams	7	12
	BeeHive • Chicago Blackhawks	**EX**	**EX-NM**
□	Lou Angotti	7	12
□	Wally Boyer	10	18
□	Dennis Dejordy (G)	9	15
□	Dave Dryden (G)	11	18
□	Phil Esposito (With blade)	22	45
□	Phil Esposito (Blade cropped)	11	18
□	Glenn Hall (G), Err. (Glen)	12	20
□	Murray Hall	225	300
□	Bill Hay	7	12
□	Camille Henry	12	20
□	Wayne Hillman	90	160
□	Ken Hodge	7	12
□	Bobby Hull (Home)	200	275
□	Bobby Hull (Home, reversed negative)	625	850
□	Bobby Hull (Away jersey with blade)	13	22
□	Bobby Hull (Away jersey, no blade)	13	22
□	Bobby Hull (Promotion picture)	13	22
□	Bobby Hull (Home jersey, portrait)	600	800
□	Dennis Hull	7	12
□	Doug Jarrett	7	12
□	Len Lunde	10	18
□	Al MacNeil	7	12
□	Chico Maki (Full length pose)	60	100
□	Chico Maki (Portrait)	7	12
□	Johnny McKenzie	9	15
□	Stan Mikita	11	18
□	Doug Mohns	7	12
□	Eric Nesterenko (Dark background)	7	12
□	Eric Nesterenko (Light background)	200	275
□	Pierre Pilote (Home jersey)	200	275
□	Pierre Pilote (Away jersey)	9	15
□	Matt Ravlich	7	12
□	Fred Stanfield	80	135
□	Fred Stanfield (Reversed negative)	100	170
□	Pat Stapleton	7	12
□	Bob Turner	275	400
□	Ed Van Impe	10	18
□	Elmer Vasko	7	12
□	Ken Wharram	7	12
	BeeHive • Detroit Red Wings	**EX**	**EX-NM**
□	Doug Barkley	7	12
□	Hank Bassen (G)	11	18
□	Andy Bathgate	9	15
□	Gary Bergman	7	12
□	Léo Boivin	9	15
□	Roger Crozier (G)	9	15
□	Alex Delvecchio (Home)	11	18
□	Alex Delvecchio (Away)	250	350
□	Alex Faulkner	325	450
□	Val Fonteyne	7	12
□	Bill Gadsby	9	15
□	Warren Godfrey	18	28
□	Pete Goegan	18	28
□	Murray Hall	9	15
□	Ted Hampson	7	12
□	Billy Harris	18	30
□	Paul Henderson	9	15
□	Gordie Howe	22	35
□	Gordie Howe (C on jersey)	250	350
□	Ron Ingram	250	350
□	Larry Jeffrey (Home)	50	90
□	Larry Jeffrey (Away)	40	70
□	Eddie Joyal	15	25
□	Eddie Joyal (Reversed negative)	160	225
□	Albert Langlois	10	18
□	Ted Lindsay	10	18
□	Parker MacDonald	7	12
□	Bruce MacGregor (Home jersey)	7	12
□	Bruce MacGregor (Away jersey)	50	85
□	Pete Mahovlich	9	15
□	Bert Marshall	7	12
□	Pit Martin	7	12
□	Ab McDonald	7	12
□	Ron Murphy	9	15
□	Dean Prentice	7	12
□	Andre Pronovost	12	20
□	Floyd Smith (Away jersey)	100	170
□	Floyd Smith (Home jersey)	7	12
□	Floyd Smith (Home jersey, reversed negative)	190	250
□	Norm Ullman	9	15
□	Bob Wall	7	12
	BeeHive • Montréal Canadiens	**EX**	**EX-NM**
□	Ralph Backstrom	7	12
□	Dave Balon	7	12
□	Jean Béliveau	13	22
□	Red Berenson	10	18
□	Yvan Cournoyer	9	15
□	Dick Duff	7	12
□	John Ferguson	7	12
□	John Hanna	150	225
□	Terry Harper (Dark background)	7	12
□	Terry Harper (Light background)	240	325
□	Ted Harris	7	12
□	Bill Hicke	25	40
□	Charlie Hodge (G)	9	15
□	Jacques Laperriere	9	15
□	Claude Larose	7	12
□	Claude Larose (Reversed negative)	350	500
□	Claude Provost	7	12
□	Henri Richard	13	22
□	Maurice Richard	40	60
□	Jim Roberts	7	12
□	Bobby Rousseau	7	12
□	Jean Guy Talbot	7	12
□	Gilles Tremblay (#21)	7	12
□	Gilles Tremblay (#24)	75	125
□	J.C. Tremblay	7	12
□	Gump Worsley (G)	11	18
	BeeHive • New York Rangers	**EX**	**EX-NM**
□	Lou Angotti	7	12
□	Arnie Brown	7	12
□	Larry Cahan	325	450
□	Reg Fleming	7	12
□	Bernie Geoffrion	10	18
□	Ed Giacomin (G)	11	18
□	Rod Gilbert	10	18
□	Phil Goyette	7	12
□	Vic Hadfield	7	12

☐ Camille Henry	125	200
☐ Bill Hicke	7	12
☐ Wayne Hillman	7	12
☐ Harry Howell	9	15
☐ Earl Ingarfield	7	12
☐ Orland Kurtenbach	10	18
☐ Gordon Labossière	100	150
☐ Al MacNeil	10	18
☐ Cesare Maniago (G)	10	18
☐ Don Marshall	7	12
☐ Jim Neilson	7	12
☐ Bob Nevin	7	12
☐ Marcel Paille	30	55
☐ Jacques Plante (G)	50	85
☐ Jean Ratelle	15	25
☐ Rod Seiling	7	12
BeeHive • Toronto Maple Leafs	**EX**	**EX-NM**
☐ George Armstrong	9	15
☐ Andy Bathgate (A)	10	18
☐ Bobby Baun (No number)	9	15
☐ Bobby Baun (#21)	70	120
☐ Johnny Bower (G) (No number)	18	28
☐ Johnny Bower (G) (#1)	100	175
☐ Wally Boyer	20	30
☐ John Brenneman	10	18
☐ Carl Brewer	13	22
☐ Turk Broda (G)	20	30
☐ Brian Conacher	7	12
☐ Kent Douglas	7	12
☐ Ron Ellis	7	12
☐ Bruce Gamble (G)	9	15
☐ Billy Harris (No number)	175	250
☐ Billy Harris (#15)	50	80
☐ Larry Hillman	13	22
☐ Tim Horton (No number)	13	22
☐ Tim Horton (#7)	85	140
☐ Bronco Horvath	175	250
☐ Larry Jeffrey	18	28
☐ Eddie Joyal	30	50
☐ Red Kelly	9	15
☐ Ted Kennedy (C)	13	20
☐ Dave Keon (No number)	13	22
☐ Dave Keon (#14)	90	150
☐ Orland Kurtenbach	11	18
☐ Ed Litzenberger	30	45
☐ Frank Mahovlich (No number)	13	22
☐ Frank Mahovlich (#27)	110	175
☐ Don McKenney (Larger image)	11	18
☐ Don McKenney (Smaller image)	60	100
☐ Dickie Moore	11	18
☐ Jim Pappin	7	12
☐ Marcel Pronovost (Blade)	9	15
☐ Marcel Pronovost (No blade)	13	22
☐ Bob Pulford (No number)	11	18
☐ Bob Pulford (#20)	65	110
☐ Terry Sawchuk (G)	18	28
☐ Brit Selby	7	12
☐ Eddie Shack	11	18
☐ Don Simmons (G)	20	35
☐ Allan Stanley	9	15
☐ Peter Stemkowski	7	12
☐ Ron Stewart (No number)	50	85
☐ Ron Stewart (#12)	175	250
☐ Mike Walton	25	40
BeeHive • Trophies / Miscellaneous	**EX**	**EX-NM**
☐ Bernie Geoffrion (Québec coach)	35	55
☐ Byng Trophy	85	150
☐ Calder Memorial Trophy	85	150
☐ Hart Trophy	85	150
☐ Prince of Wales Trophy	85	150
☐ J. Norris Memorial Trophy	85	150
☐ Art Ross Trophy	85	150
☐ Stanley Cup	85	150
☐ Vezina Trophy	85	150

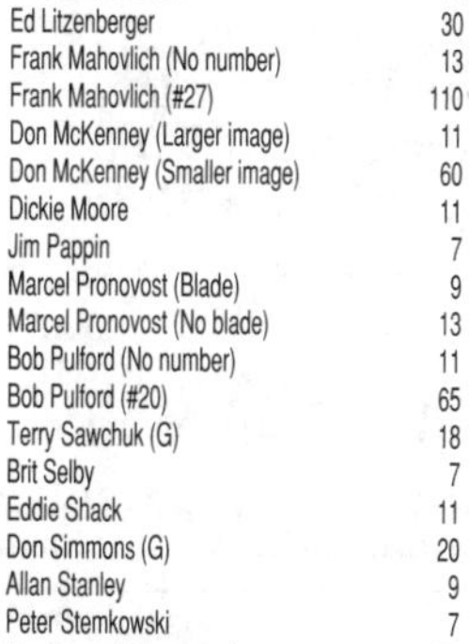

CHRISTMAS CARDS

Montréal Canadiens Christmas

☐ 1970 Solid red with Canadiens logo (Meilleurs Voeux in red, Season's Greetings in blue). Single fold, 8 1/4" x 5 1/2".
☐ 1970 Christmas tree and Canadiens logo (green holly leaf interior). Double fold, 4 1/4" x 5 1/2".
☐ 1970s Canadiens logo and Stanley Cup (blank interior). Double fold, 4 1/4" x 5 1/2".
☐ 1977 Canadiens logo on white backgroud (Meilleurs Voeux in red, Season's Greetings in blue, player autographs). Single fold, 6 1/2" x 5".
☐ 1978 Canadiens logo on red backgroud (Meilleurs Voeux in red, Season's Greetings in blue, player autographs, Bob Gainey autograph in top left corner). Single fold, 6 1/2" x 5".
☐ 1979 Canadiens logo on red backgroud (Meilleurs Voeux in red, Season's Greetings in blue, player autographs, Denis Herron autograph in top left corner). Single fold, 6 1/2" x 5".
☐ 1980 Canadiens logo on white backgroud (Meilleurs Voeux and Season's Greetings in blue, art of kids playing in yard). Single fold, 6 1/2" x 5".
☐ 1981 Canadiens logo on red backgroud (Meilleurs Voeux in red, Season's Greetings in blue, stamped team name). Single fold, 6 1/2" x 5".
☐ 1982 Canadiens logo on red backgroud (Meilleurs Voeux and Season's Greetings in blue). Single fold, 6 1/2" x 5".
☐ 1983 Thin-white border, night scene at rink, boy shoveling under the lights (Meilleurs Voeux and Season's Greetings in blue, Club de Hockey Canadien in black). Double fold, 6 1/2" x 4 1/4".
☐ 1984 Art montage for Canadiens 75th anniversary by Lapensée (Meilleurs Voeux and Season's Greetings in grey, black & white legend at top). Single fold, 9 1/4" x 6 1/4".
☐ 1985 Art of young boy at tree, just opened present of Canadiens jersey, art by Lapensée (Meilleurs Voeux and Season's Greetings in black). Single fold, 7 3/4" x 6 1/4".
☐ 1986 Ultimate Victory by Lapensée (Meilleurs Voeux and Season's Greetings in grey). Single fold, 8 3/4" x 6 1/4".
☐ 1987 Art of father tying up his son's skates, boys in background playing on the pond, art by Lapensée (Meilleurs Voeux and Season's Greetings in grey). Single fold, 7" x 6".
☐ 1988 Salmon-colour border, art of kids playing ball hockey on the street, art by Lapensée (Salmon colour insert with greetings in English and French). Single fold, 7" x 5 1/4".
☐ 1989 Night scene outside Forum, fans arriving for the game, art by Lapensée (Meilleurs Voeux and Season's Greetings in grey). Single fold, 7 1/4" x 5 1/4".
☐ 1990 Kids descending staircase with hockey gear, art by Lapensée (Meilleurs Voeux and Season's Greetings in black). Single fold, 7 1/4" x 5 1/4".
☐ 1991 Kids playing in outdoor rink, evening snow storm, door to rink is open (Meilleurs Voeux and Season's Greetings in black). Single fold, 7 1/4" x 5 1/4".
☐ 1992 100 years of history, 23 Stanley Cups, art by Lapensée, white border (Meilleurs Voeux and Season's Greetings in black, black & white legend at top). Single fold, 8 3/4" x 6 1/4".
☐ 1993 Art of Canadiens 24th Stanley Cup victory, art by Lapensée (Meilleurs Voeux and Season's Greetings in black, black & white legend at top). Single fold, 8 3/4" x 6 1/4".
☐ 1994 Under the tree, Canadiens jersey, skates and other toys, art by Lapensée (Meilleurs Voeux and Season's Greetings in black). Single fold, 5" x 7".
☐ 1995 Forver Proud, montage of events at the Forum, art by Lapensée (Meilleurs Voeux and Season's Greetings in black, black & white legend at top). Single fold, 8 1/2" x 5 3/4".
☐ 1996 Four kids and the dog playing ball hockey on the street at night, art by Del Signore (Joyeyse fêtes and Season's Greetings in black, Canadiens logo). Single fold, 7" x 5 1/4".
☐ 1997 Temps d'arrêt by Lapensée, kids in Canadiens jerseys plowing an outdoor rink in a snow fall (Meilleurs Voeux and Season's Greetings in black, autographs). Single fold, 7 1/4" x 5".
☐ 1998 Sur le lac by Archambault, seven kids playing hockey, two kids and a dog watching (Meilleurs Voeux and Season's Greetings in black, autographs). Single fold, 7 1/4" x 5".
☐ 1999 White border, official team photo (Interior blank, legend of players on back). Single fold, 7 1/4" x 5".
☐ 2000 Canadiens puck on blue ice, white line trailing behind in the shape of a Christmas tree (Meilleurs Voeux and Season's Greetings in white, Green autograph tree, Canadiens logo in blue). Single fold, 5" x 5". CD-ROM included inside card.
☐ 2001 Close-up painting of the Canadiens jersey (Espoir paix santé and hope, peace and health on left page, message on rigt page). Single fold, 6 1/2" x 6 1/2".

Montréal Canadiens • Miscellaneous Christmas

☐ 1997 Cartoon of three Canadiens dancing the Can Can in a chorus line (Happy hockey days on the ice, by Hallmark). Single fold, 7" x 5".
☐ 1998 Cartoon of two Canadiens on the floor in front of the hearth, playing table hockey (Happy hockey days on the ice, by Hallmark). Single fold, 7" x 5".
☐ Large puck with Canadiens logo flying out of a table-hockey game (Crowd scene cameo at left, Hope your day's right ON GOAL! at right). Single fold, 5" x 7".

Montréal Canadiens • Toe Blake Christmas

☐ 1955 Blake arriving in Montréal from Valleyfield, Braves pulling sleigh. Card, 5" x 4".
☐ 1956 Blake plugging in Christmas tree, Best Wishes from the Old Lamplighter. Card, 5" x 4".
☐ 1957 Santa with Stanley Cup and Toe in front of the fireplace Just leave it in my stocking again Santa). Card, 5" x 4".
☐ 1960 Team photo with six trophies (Season's Greeting, Meilleurs Souhaits). 5 1/2" x 4 1/2".
☐ 1961 Blake on Santa's knee, Hawk with Stanley Cup, We just loaned it for a year! (Merry Christma and a Happy New Year). Single fold, 6 1/4" x 5".
☐ 1962 Blake leading Canadiens carolers, Santa in background, You better be Good... (Meilleur Souhaits pour un Joyeux Noël et une Bonne et Heureux Année). Single fold, 6 1/4" x 5".
☐ 1963 Santa Blake removing beard, sleigh with a load of trophies in background (Merry Christmas and a Happy New Year). Single fold, 6 1/4" x 5".
☐ 1964 Blake in front of fireplace, looking at four trophies, Santa on roof with Stanley Cup (Meilleurs Souhaits pour un Joyeux Noël et une Bonne et Heureuse Année). Single fold, 6 1/4" x 5".
☐ 1966 Blake whispering to Santa Claus, YES/same as last year (Meilleurs Souhaits pour un Joyeux Noël et une Bonne Heureuse Année). Single fold, 6 1/4" x 5".
☐ 1967 Blake meets the press, Santa in back with Stanley Cup #7, I hope you get the message (With Best Wishes for a Merry Christmas and a Happy New Year). Single fold, 6 1/4" x 5".

Montréal Canadiens • Jacques Plante Christmas

☐ Plante in uniform hugging Stanley Cup, message and three bells at right. Card, 5" x 4".
☐ Plante in sports jacket with Vézina Trophy, message and three bells at right. Card, 5 1/2" x 4 1/4".

Montréal Canadiens • Sam Pollock Christmas

☐ 1966 Santa emptying a bag of pucks on the ice, reindeer & sleigh in the background (Santa with the goal all boraded up, Lorne & Charlie tags on top of net). Double fold, 7 1/4" x 6".
☐ 1967 Santa starting down chimney (Joyeux Noël and Merry Christmas, 12 team stockings on fireplace, Santa with Stanley Cup). Double fold, 7 1/2" x 6".
☐ 1968 Jean Béliveau receiving new Forum from construction Santa Claus (Joyeux Noël and Merry Christmas, Canadian Arena Company & Canadien). Double fold, 7 1/2" x 6".

Montréal Canadiens • Molson Breweries Christmas

☐ 1977 Vignette of farmhouse at night, TV antenna on chimney (Family watching game on TV, Canadiens jersey on wall, Jerry Trudel message in French). Double fold, 8" x 6 1/2".
☐ 1977 Players in civies around tree, opening presents, Molson O'Keefe (Autographs and Molson O'Keefe logo on back). Card, 10" x 6 3/4".

Toronto Maple Leafs Christmas

☐ View of winter country, view of game, and Greeting from the Gondola in red and black. (Foster Hewitt & message on right, Perce Lesueur & message on right, Imperial on back). Double fold, 6" x 9".
☐ 1967 Pale blue logo, Season's Greetings from Maple Leaf Gardens in blue. (Marlboros team photo on left, Maple Leafs team photo on right, both ID'ed). Single fold, 7" x 5 3/4".
☐ 1970 Santa dragging his bag, greetings from Garden and Maple Leafs, Maple Leafs logo on Santa (Autographs on left, team photo on right). Single fold, 7" x 5 1/2".
☐ 1972 Dark blue with white border, Season's Greetings in white (Pale logo and autographs on left, small head shots of the Maple Leafs on a pale blue background). Single fold,6 1/2" x 8 1/2".
☐ 1973 Dark blue background, colour picture of Maple Leaf Gardens with white border, Season's Greetings in white (Autographs on left, team photo on right). Single fold, 8 1/2" x 5 3/4".
☐ 1974 White background, colour picture of Maple Leaf Gardens with blue border, Season's Greetings in green (Autographs on left, team photo on right). Single fold, 8 1/2" x 5 3/4".
☐ 1975 White background, colour picture of Maple Leaf Gardens with blue border, Season's Greetings in green (autographs on left, team photo on right). Single fold, 8 1/2" x 5 3/4".
☐ 1976 Art of Ian Turnbull, Börje Salming, Darryl Sittle, and Lanny McDonald, Season's Greetings in red, 50th Anniversary (autographs on left with 50th Anniversary logo, team photo on right). Single fold, 5 3/4" x 8 1/2".
☐ 1977 Art of current Maple Leafs stars and Ballard, Season's Greetings 1977 in red (Autographs on left, team photo on right, legend on back). Single fold, 5 3/4" x 8 1/4".
☐ 1978 Embossed white logo, Season's Greetings in red, Maple Leafs 1978/79 in blue (legend on left, team photo on right, autographs on back). Single fold, 8 1/2" x 5 1/2".
☐ 1979 Two Christmas trees with nine bodies in front, holes die-cut so players heads show (Autographs on top, team photo at bottom, legend on back). Single fold, 8 1/4" x 6".
☐ 1980 Rudolph with three players under him, all blue except Rudy's nose (Autographs on left, team photo on right, legend on back). Single fold, 8 1/2" x 6".
☐ 1981 Montage of events at MLG for its 50th anniversary (Autographs at left, photo on right, legend on back, Holoday Greeting inwhite). Single fold, 5 3/4" x 8 1/2".
☐ 1982 Scoreboard with Ballard driving sleigh, Christmas decor & Seasons Greetings (Autographs on left, Maple Leafs team photo on the right, legend on back). Single fold, 8 1/2" x 5 3/4".
☐ 1983 Thin vertical blue lines, white logo, Season's Greeting in red (Autographs on left, team photo on right, legend on back). Single fold, 8 1/2" x 5 1/2".
☐ 1984 Dark blue background, logo at top, Season's Greetings in white at bottom right (Autographs on left, team photo on right, legend on back). Single fold, 8 1/2" x 5 1/2".
☐ 1985 Lone boy on rink in a circular shape, cameo on white background (Message and legend on left, team photo on right). Single fold, 8 1/2" x 5 1/2".
☐ 1986 Young boy with newly opened jersey in front on fireplace (Photo at top, message and legend at bottom). Single fold, 5 1/2" x 8 1/2".
☐ 1987 Ballard as Santa with his dog and a young fan in Maple Leafs jersey, tree in background (Photo at top, message and legend at bottom). Single fold, 5 1/2" x 8 1/2".
☐ 1988 Art of father with his boy & girl at frozen pond, snowing & house in background (Photo at top, message and legend at bottom). Single fold, 8 1/2" x 5 1/2".
☐ 1989 Pale blue border with snow flakes, boy in Maple Leafs toque looking up at City Hall, stick in hand (Season's Greetings, team photo, legend across both pages, on pale blue background). Single fold, 5 1/2" x 8 1/2".
☐ 1990 Art of young Maple Leafs fan preparing for the arrival of Santa Claus, fireplace and snack for Santa (Message in red, Maple Leafs logo and sign-off in blue). Single fold, 8 1/2" x 5 1/2".
☐ 1991 Blue background, wreath made of Maple Leafs logos, red bow & Season's Greetings in green (message and logo in blue). Single fold, 7 1/4" x 5 1/4".
☐ 1992 Art of snowman in Maple Leafs jersey, snow flakes falling, Season's Greetings in green (Maple Leafs team photo at top, autographs and sign off at the bottom). Single fold, 8 1/4" x 5 1/4".
☐ 1993 Toronto stocking hanging on the fireplace, canes & presents inside, bugle and roaring fire (team photo and autographs). Single fold, 5 1/4" x 8 1/4".
☐ 1994.
☐ 1995 Stick blade and holly, Season's Greetings and team logo in dark blue (stick across card, autographs at left, team photo on right). Single fold, 8 1/4" x 5 1/4".
☐ 1996 Box of blue & white Christmas balls, faint photo image on each one (Leaf team photo in vintage jerseys, message & logo balls in blue). Single fold, 8 1/4" x 5 1/4".
☐ 1997 Polar bear in Maple Leafs jersey, hanging stocking on net, Season's Greeting in white (Pale blue border with snow, message, logo & sign-off in dark blue). Single fold, 8 1/4" x 5 1/4".
☐ 1998 Aerial night view of Maple Leaf Gardens all lit up, lots of snow around building (Home for the Holidays 1931-1998 in gold, Maple Leafs logo in dark blue). Single fold, 8" x 5".
☐ 1999 Crystal ball on puck, Air Canada Centre inside ball, sprigs and holly at base (Black autographs of Maple Leafs, Maple Leafs logo, ACC logo & Raptors logo, message in black). Single fold, 5 1/4" x 5 1/4".
☐ 2000 Photo of Mats & Tina Sundin in fancy cameo, sprig and holly under frame (Photos of Curtis & Nancy Joseph, Dmitry & Oksana Yushkevich, Steve & Lori Thomas, Yanic & July Perreault). Single fold, 5 3/4" x 8 1/2".
☐ 2001 Art of Joseph and Sundin visiting rink with many young players (May all of your holiday wishes come true in grey, 75th anniversary logo in blue). Single fold, 8" x 5 3/4".

Toronto Maple Leafs

• Miscellaneous Christmas

☐ Cartoon of Maple Leafs around hot stove, warming up, Maple Leafs logo in right corner (Warm wishes for a Great Season!, by Hallmark). Single fold, 7" x 4 3/4".
☐ Cartoon of Maple Leafs being examined by doctors, guy in background fleeing, Maple Leafs logo in right corner (Wishing you a happy, healthy Holiday Season!, by Hallmark). Single fold, 7" x 4 3/4".

Collector's Marketplace

CHAPTER THREE

THE O-PEE-CHEE YEARS 1968 TO 1990

1968 - 69 BAUER PHOTOS

These colour blank-back photos measure 8" x 10".

Complete Set (22 photos):	225	450
Bauer	**EX**	**EX-NM**
Andy Bathgate, Pitt.	18.00	35.00
Gary Bergman, Detr.	10.00	20.00
Charlie Burns, Pitt.	10.00	20.00
Ray Cullen, Minn.	10.00	20.00
Gary Dornhoefer, Phil.	10.00	20.00
Kent Douglas, Toro.	10.00	20.00
Tim Ecclestone, SLou.	10.00	20.00
Bill Flett, LosA.	10.00	20.00
Ed Giacomin (G), NYRa.	25.00	50.00
Ted Harris, Mont.	10.00	20.00
Paul Henderson, Toro.	15.00	30.00
Ken Hodge, Bost.	10.00	20.00
Harry Howell, NYRa.	15.00	30.00
Earl Ingarfield, Pitt.	10.00	20.00
Gilles Marotte, Chic.	10.00	20.00
Mike McMahon, Minn.	10.00	20.00
Doug Mohns, Chic.	10.00	20.00
Bobby Orr, Bost.	100.00	200.00
Claude Provost, Mont.	13.00	25.00
Gary Sabourin, SLou.	10.00	20.00
Brian Smith, Detr.	10.00	20.00
Bob Woytowich, Minn.	10.00	20.00

1968 - 69 O-PEE-CHEE

"This is the first set that I remember that was real to me – the first one in which I was old enough. I remember my dad would buy us two packs of cards so we would sit in the back of the car quietly while we drove to our aunts or uncles or some place. You would be set until you got there. We did a lot of travelling." – Cliff Goff, Ganaoque All Sports, Gananoque, Ontario.

These cards measure the standard 2 1/2" x 3 1/2".

Complete Set (217 cards):	1,250	2,500
Common Player:	**3.50**	**7.00**
O-Pee-Chee	**EX**	**EX-NM**
1 Doug Harvey, SLou.	18.00	50.00
2 Bobby Orr, Bost.	225.00	425.00
3 Don Awrey, Bost., Error (Skip Krake)	3.50	7.00
4 Ted Green, Bost.	3.50	7.00
5 John Bucyk, Bost.	6.50	13.00
6 Derek Sanderson, Bost.	25.00	45.00
7 Phil Esposito, Bost.	28.00	55.00
8 Ken Hodge, Bost.	3.50	7.00
9 John McKenzie, Bost.	3.50	7.00
10 Fred Stanfield, Bost.	3.50	7.00
11 Tom Williams, Bost.	3.50	7.00
12 Denis DeJordy (G), Chic.	5.00	10.00
13 Doug Jarrett, Chic.	3.50	7.00
14 Gilles Marotte, Chic.	3.50	7.00
15 Pat Stapleton, Chic.	3.50	7.00
16 Bobby Hull, Chic.	55.00	110.00
17 Chico Maki, Chic.	3.50	7.00
18 Pit Martin, Chic.	3.50	7.00
19 Doug Mohns, Chic.	3.50	7.00
20 John Ferguson, Mont.	5.00	10.00
21 Jim Pappin, Chic.	3.50	7.00
22 Kenny Wharram, Chic.	3.50	7.00
23 Roger Crozier (G), Detr.	5.00	10.00
24 Bob Baun, Detr.	3.50	7.00
25 Gary Bergman, Detr.	3.50	7.00
26 Kent Douglas, Detr.	3.50	7.00
27 Ron Harris, Detr. RC	**5.00**	**10.00**
28 Alex Delvecchio, Detr.	6.50	13.00
29 Gordie Howe, Detr.	80.00	150.00
30 Bruce MacGregor, Detr.	3.50	7.00
31 Frank Mahovlich, Detr.	13.00	25.00
32 Dean Prentice, Detr.	3.50	7.00
33 Pete Stemkowski, Detr.	3.50	7.00
34 Terry Sawchuk (G), Detr.	30.00	60.00
35 Larry Cahan, LosA.	3.50	7.00
36 Real Lemieux, LosA. RC	**5.00**	**10.00**
37 Bill White, LosA. RC	**5.00**	**10.00**
38 Gord Labossiere, LosA. RC	**5.00**	**10.00**
39 Ted Irvine, LosA. RC	**5.00**	**10.00**
40 Eddie Joyal, LosA.	3.50	7.00
41 Dale Rolfe, LosA. RC	**5.00**	**10.00**
42 Lowell MacDonald, LosA. RC	**5.00**	**10.00**
43 Skip Krake, LosA., Error (Don Awrey)	3.50	7.00
44 Terry Gray, LosA.	3.50	7.00
45 Césare Maniago (G), Minn.	5.00	10.00
46 Mike McMahon, Minn.	3.50	7.00
47 Wayne Hillman, Minn.	3.50	7.00
48 Larry Hillman, Mont.	3.50	7.00
49 Bob Woytowich, Minn.	3.50	7.00
50 Wayne Connelly, Minn.	3.50	7.00
51 Claude Larose, Minn.	3.50	7.00
52 Danny Grant, Minn. RC	**6.00**	**12.00**
53 André Boudrias, Minn. RC	**5.00**	**10.00**
54 Ray Cullen, Minn. RC	**5.00**	**10.00**
55 Parker MacDonald, Minn., Error, (/b: Jacques) (LC)	3.50	7.00
56 Lorne Worsley (G), Mont.	10.00	20.00
57 Terry Harper, Mont.	3.50	7.00
58 Jacques Laperrière, Mont.	5.00	10.00
59 J.C. Tremblay, Mont.	5.00	10.00
60 Ralph Backstrom, Mont.	3.50	7.00
61 Checklist 1	115.00	225.00
62 Yvan Cournoyer, Mont.	13.00	25.00
63 Jacques Lemaire, Mont.	15.00	30.00
64 Mickey Redmond, Mont. RC	**25.00**	**45.00**
65 Bobby Rousseau, Mont.	3.50	7.00
66 Gilles Tremblay, Mont.	3.50	7.00
67 Ed Giacomin (G), NYRa.	13.00	25.00
68 Arnie Brown, NYRa.	3.50	7.00
69 Harry Howell, NYRa.	5.00	10.00
70 Al Hamilton, NYRa. RC	**5.00**	**10.00**
71 Rod Seiling, NYRa.	3.50	7.00
72 Rod Gilbert, NYRa.	6.50	13.00
73 Phil Goyette, NYRa.	3.50	7.00
74 Larry Jeffrey, NYRa.	3.50	7.00
75 Don Marshall, NYRa.	3.50	7.00
76 Bob Nevin, NYRa.	3.50	7.00
77 Jean Ratelle, NYRa.	6.50	13.00
78 Charlie Hodge (G), Oakl.	5.00	10.00
79 Bert Marshall, Oakl.	3.50	7.00
80 Billy Harris, Oakl.	3.50	7.00
81 Carol Vadnais, Oakl.	3.50	7.00
82 Howie Young, Chic.	3.50	7.00
83 John Brenneman, Oakl. RC	**5.00**	**10.00**
84 Gerry Ehman, Oakl.	3.50	7.00
85 Ted Hampson, Oakl.	3.50	7.00
86 Bill Hicke, Oakl.	3.50	7.00
87 Gary Jarrett, Oakl.	3.50	7.00
88 Doug Roberts, Oakl.	3.50	7.00
89 Bernie Parent (G), Phil. RC	**75.00**	**150.00**
90 Joe Watson, Phil.	3.50	7.00
91 Ed Van Impe, Phil.	3.50	7.00
92 Larry Zeidel, Phil.	3.50	7.00
93 John Miszuk, Phil. RC	**5.00**	**10.00**
94 Gary Dornhoefer, Phil.	3.50	7.00
95 Leon Rochefort, Phil. RC	**5.00**	**10.00**
96 Brit Selby, Phil.	3.50	7.00
97 Forbes Kennedy, Phil.	3.50	7.00
98 Ed Hoekstra, Phil. RC	**5.00**	**10.00**
99 Garry Peters, Phil.	3.50	7.00
100 Les Binkley (G), Pitt. RC	**9.00**	**18.00**
101 Leo Boivin, Pitt.	5.00	10.00
102 Earl Ingarfield, Pitt.	3.50	7.00
103 Lou Angotti, Pitt.	3.50	7.00
104 Andy Bathgate, Pitt.	5.00	10.00
105 Wally Boyer, Pitt.	3.50	7.00
106 Ken Schinkel, Pitt.	3.50	7.00
107 Ab McDonald, SLou.	3.50	7.00
108 Charlie Burns, Pitt.	3.50	7.00
109 Val Fonteyne, Pitt.	3.50	7.00
110 Noel Price, Pitt.	3.50	7.00
111 Glenn Hall (G), SLou.	13.00	25.00
112 Bob Plager, SLou. RC	**6.50**	**13.00**
113 Jim Roberts, SLou.	3.50	7.00
114 Red Berenson, SLou.	3.50	7.00
115 Larry Keenan, SLou.	3.50	7.00
116 Camille Henry, SLou.	3.50	7.00
117 Gary Sabourin, SLou. RC	**5.00**	**10.00**
118 Ron Schock, SLou.	3.50	7.00
119 Gary Veneruzzo, SLou. RC	**5.00**	**10.00**
120 Gerry Melnyk, SLou.	3.50	7.00
121 Checklist 2	120.00	235.00
122 Johnny Bower (G), Toro.	8.00	16.00
123 Tim Horton, Toro.	14.00	28.00
124 Pierre Pilote, Toro.	5.00	10.00
125 Marcel Pronovost, Toro.	5.00	10.00
126 Ron Ellis, Toro.	5.00	10.00
127 Paul Henderson, Toro.	5.00	10.00
128 Al Arbour, SLou.	5.00	10.00
129 Bob Pulford, Toro.	5.00	10.00
130 Floyd Smith, Toro.	3.50	7.00
131 Norm Ullman, Toro.	6.50	13.00
132 Mike Walton, Toro.	3.50	7.00
133 Eddie Johnston (G), Bost.	5.00	10.00
134 Glen Sather, Bost.	7.00	14.00
135 Ed Westfall, Bost.	3.50	7.00
136 Dallas Smith, Bost.	3.50	7.00
137 Eddie Shack, Bost.	9.00	18.00
138 Gary Doak, Bost.	3.50	7.00
139 Ron Murphy, Bost.	3.50	7.00
140 Gerry Cheevers (G), Bost.	14.00	28.00
141 Bob Falkenberg, Detr. RC	**5.00**	**10.00**
142 Garry Unger, Detr. RC	**13.00**	**25.00**
143 Pete Mahovlich, Detr.	3.50	7.00
144 Roy Edwards (G), Detr.	5.00	10.00
145 Gary Bauman (G), Minn. RC	**5.00**	**10.00**
146 Bob McCord, Minn.	3.50	7.00
147 Elmer Vasko, Minn.	3.50	7.00
148 Bill Goldsworthy, Minn. RC	**7.50**	**15.00**
149 Jean-Paul Parise, Minn. RC	**5.00**	**10.00**
150 Dave Dryden (G), Chic.	5.00	10.00
151 Howie Young, Chic.	3.50	7.00
152 Matt Ravlich, Chic.	3.50	7.00
153 Dennis Hull, Chic.	3.50	7.00
154 Eric Nesterenko, Chic.	3.50	7.00
155 Stan Mikita, Chic.	20.00	40.00
156 Bob Wall, LosA.	3.50	7.00
157 Dave Amadio, LosA. RC	**5.00**	**10.00**
158 Howie Hughes, LosA. RC	**5.00**	**10.00**
159 Bill Flett, LosA. RC	**5.00**	**10.00**
160 Doug Robinson, LosA.	3.50	7.00
161 Dick Duff, Minn.	3.50	7.00
162 Ted Harris, Mont.	3.50	7.00
163 Claude Provost, Mont.	3.50	7.00
164 Rogatien Vachon (G), Mont.	25.00	45.00
165 Henri Richard, Mont.	13.00	25.00
166 Jean Béliveau, Mont.	15.00	30.00
167 Reggie Fleming, NYRa.	3.50	7.00
168 Ron Stewart, NYRa.	3.50	7.00
169 Dave Balon, NYRa.	3.50	7.00
170 Orland Kurtenbach, NYRa.	3.50	7.00
171 Vic Hadfield, NYRa.	3.50	7.00
172 Jim Neilson, NYRa.	3.50	7.00
173 Bryan Watson, Oakl.	3.50	7.00
174 George Swarbrick, Oakl. RC	**5.00**	**10.00**
175 Joe Szura, Oakl. RC	**5.00**	**10.00**
176 Gary Smith (G), Oakl. RC	**8.00**	**16.00**
177 Barclay Plager, SLou. RC, Error (Bob Plager)	**5.00**	**10.00**
178 Tim Ecclestone, SLou. RC	**5.00**	**10.00**
179 Jean Guy Talbot, SLou.	3.50	7.00
180 Ab McDonald, SLou.	3.50	7.00
181 Jacques Plante (G), SLou.	30.00	60.00
182 Bill E. McCreary, SLou. RC	**5.00**	**10.00**
183 Allan Stanley, Phil., Error (/b: Alan)	5.00	10.00
184 André Lacroix, Phil. RC	**7.50**	**15.00**
185 Jean Guy Gendron, Phil.	3.50	7.00
186 Jim Johnson, Phil. RC	**5.00**	**10.00**
187 Simon Nolet, Phil. RC	**5.00**	**10.00**
188 Joe Daley (G), Pitt. RC	**6.50**	**13.00**
189 John Arbour, Pitt. RC	**5.00**	**10.00**
190 Billy Dea, Pitt.	3.50	7.00
191 Bob Dillabough, Pitt.	3.50	7.00
192 Bob Woytowich, Pitt.	3.50	7.00
Keith McCreary, Pitt. RC, Error (no #)	**15.00**	**30.00**
193 Keith McCreary, Pitt. RC, Corrected	**5.00**	**10.00**
194 Murray Oliver, Toro.	3.50	7.00
195 Larry Mickey, Toro. RC	**5.00**	**10.00**
196 Bill Sutherland, Toro. RC	**5.00**	**10.00**
197 Bruce Gamble (G), Toro.	5.00	10.00
198 Dave Keon, Toro.	7.00	14.00
199 AS: Gump Worsley (G), Mont.	6.00	12.00
200 AS: Bobby Orr, Bost.	100.00	200.00
201 AS: Tim Horton, Toro.	9.00	18.00
202 AS: Stan Mikita, Chic.	13.00	25.00
203 AS: Gordie Howe, Detr.	45.00	85.00
204 AS: Bobby Hull, Chic.	35.00	65.00
205 AS: Ed Giacomin (G), NYRa.	9.00	18.00
206 AS: J.C. Tremblay, Mont.	3.00	6.00
207 AS: Jim Neilson, NYRa.	3.00	6.00
208 AS: Phil Esposito, Bost.	20.00	30.00
209 AS: Rod Gilbert, NYRa.	5.00	10.00
210 AS: John Bucyk, Bost.	5.00	10.00
211 AW: Stan Mikita, Chic.	13.00	25.00
212 AW: G. Worsley (G)/ R. Vachon (G)	13.00	25.00
213 AW: Derek Sanderson, Bost.	25.00	45.00
214 AW: Bobby Orr, Bost.	100.00	200.00
215 AW: Glenn Hall, Chic.	7.50	15.00
216 AW: Claude Provost, Mont.	7.00	20.00
O-Pee-Chee Special	**EX**	**EX-NM**
Gordie Howe, Detr. (700th Goal)	50.00	100.00

PUCK PUSH-OUTS

These cards measure the standard 2 1/2" x 3 1/2".

Complete Set (21 stickers):	200	400
O-Pee-Chee	**EX**	**EX-NM**
1 Stan Mikita, Chic.	13.00	22.00
2 Frank Mahovlich, Detr.	9.00	18.00
3 Bobby Hull, Chic.	35.00	60.00
4 Bobby Orr, Bost.	60.00	100.00
5 Phil Esposito, Bost.	13.00	22.00
6 Gump Worsley (G), Mont.	9.00	18.00
7 Jean Béliveau, Mont.	15.00	30.00
8 Elmer Vasko, Minn.	3.00	6.00
9 Rod Gilbert, NYRa.	5.00	10.00
10 Roger Crozier (G), Detr.	4.00	8.00
11 Lou Angotti, Pitt.	3.00	6.00
12 Charlie Hodge (G), Oak.	4.00	8.00
13 Glenn Hall (G), SLou., Error (Glen)	9.00	18.00
14 Doug Harvey, SLou.	7.50	15.00
15 Jacques Plante (G), SLou.	20.00	35.00
16 Allan Stanley, Phil.	5.00	10.00
17 Johnny Bower (G), Toro.	6.00	12.00
18 Tim Horton, Toro.	13.00	25.00
19 Dave Keon, Toro.	6.00	12.00
20 Terry Sawchuk (G), Detr.	14.00	28.00
21 Henri Richard, Mont.	7.50	15.00

1968 - 69 POST MARBLES

A white plastic rink-shaped game board was available. The Montréal and Toronto team logos and the Post logo was dispalyed on the rink, and the wording was bilingual. There were perforations on the rink and in the penalty box to hold the marbles.

Complete Set (30 marbles):	150.00	325.00
Plastic Display Rink (30" x 18"):	**125**	**250**
Post Cereal	**EX**	**EX-NM**
Ralph Backstrom, Mont.	5.00	10.00
Jean Béliveau, Mont.	20.00	40.00
Yvan Cournoyer, Mont.	9.00	18.00
John Ferguson, Mont.	6.00	12.00
Terry Harper, Mont.	5.00	10.00
Ted Harris, Mont.	5.00	10.00
Jacques Laperrière, Mont.	6.50	13.00
Jacques Lemaire, Mont.	10.00	18.00
Henri Richard, Mont.	11.00	22.00
Bobby Rousseau, Mont.	5.00	10.00
Serge Savard, Mont.	7.50	15.00
Gilles Tremblay, Mont.	5.00	10.00
J.C. Tremblay, Mont.	6.00	12.00
Rogatien Vachon (G), Mont.	11.00	18.00
Gump Worsley (G), Mont.	12.00	25.00
Johnny Bower (G), Toro.	10.00	20.00
Wayne Carleton, Toro.	5.00	10.00
Ron Ellis, Toro.	6.00	12.00
Bruce Gamble (G), Toro.	6.00	12.00
Paul Henderson, Toro.	7.50	15.00
Tim Horton, Toro.	20.00	35.00
Dave Keon, Toro.	10.00	18.00
Murray Oliver, Toro.	5.00	10.00
Mike Pelyk, Toro.	5.00	10.00
Pierre Pilote, Toro.	6.50	13.00
Marcel Pronovost, Toro.	6.50	13.00
Bob Pulford, Toro.	7.50	15.00
Floyd Smith, Toro.	5.00	10.00
Norm Ullman, Toro.	7.50	15.00
Mike Walton, Toro.	5.00	10.00

1968 - 69 SHIRRIFF

"The series includes players from all 12 teams and the checklist goes deep into the rosters for each team. The colours are unique, distinguished by the team. This is the hardest set to put together of the four Shirriff hockey sets. The short prints are short like none other that was produced. The only problem is there is only a small group who are collecting this set." – Brad Norris-Jones, MVP Sports Collectibles, Victoria, British Columbia.

Each wheel measures 1 3/8". Some caps were short-issued and are marked with an asterisk (*).

Complete Set (176 wheels): **4.000** **6,500**

	EX	EX-NM
Plastic Display Rink (30" x 18"):	**4.50**	**6.50**
Shirriff • Boston Bruins	**EX**	**EX-NM**
☐ 1 Eddie Shack	9.00	15.00
☐ 2 Ed Westfall	4.00	6.50
☐ 3 Don Awrey	4.00	6.50
☐ 4 Gerry Cheevers (G)	13.00	25.00
☐ 5 Bobby Orr	115.00	185.00
☐ 6 John Bucyk	11.00	18.00
☐ 7 Derek Sanderson	11.00	18.00
☐ 8 Phil Esposito	22.00	35.00
☐ 9 Fred Stanfield	4.00	6.50
☐ 10 Ken Hodge	4.00	6.50
☐ 11 John McKenzie	4.00	6.50
☐ 12 Ted Green	4.00	6.50
☐ 13 Dallas Smith (*)	75.00	125.00
☐ 14 Gary Doak (*)	75.00	125.00
☐ 15 Glen Sather (*)	90.00	150.00
☐ 16 Tom Williams (*)	75.00	125.00
Shirriff • Chicago Blackhawks	**EX**	**EX-NM**
☐ 1 Bobby Hull	40.00	65.00
☐ 2 Pat Stapleton	4.00	6.50
☐ 3 Wayne Maki	4.00	6.50
☐ 4 Denis DeJordy (G)	5.00	8.00
☐ 5 Kenny Wharram	4.00	6.50
☐ 6 Pit Martin	4.00	6.50
☐ 7 Chico Maki	4.00	6.50
☐ 8 Doug Mohns	4.00	6.50
☐ 9 Stan Mikita	15.00	25.00
☐ 10 Doug Jarrett	4.00	6.50
☐ 11 Dennis Hull (Small portrait)	110.00	175.00
☐ 11 Dennis Hull (Large portrait)	22.00	35.00
☐ 12 Matt Ravlich	4.00	6.50
☐ 13 Dave Dryden (G) (*)	75.00	125.00
☐ 14 Eric Nesterenko (*)	75.00	125.00
☐ 15 Gilles Marotte (*)	75.00	125.00
☐ 16 Jim Pappin (*)	75.00	125.00
Shirriff • Detroit Red Wings	**EX**	**EX-NM**
☐ 1 Gary Bergman	4.00	6.50
☐ 2 Roger Crozier (G)	7.00	12.00
☐ 3 Pete Mahovlich	4.00	6.50
☐ 4 Alex Delvecchio	12.00	20.00
☐ 5 Dean Prentice	4.00	6.50
☐ 6 Kent Douglas	4.00	6.50
☐ 7 Roy Edwards (G)	5.00	8.00
☐ 8 Bruce MacGregor	4.00	6.50
☐ 9 Garry Unger	6.00	10.00
☐ 10 Pete Stemkowski	4.00	6.50
☐ 11 Gordie Howe	80.00	130.00
☐ 12 Frank Mahovlich	18.00	30.00
☐ 13 Bob Baun (*)	75.00	125.00
☐ 14 Brian Conacher (*)	75.00	125.00
☐ 15 Jimmy Watson (*)	75.00	125.00
☐ 16 Nick Libett (*)	75.00	125.00
Shirriff • Los Angeles Kings	**EX**	**EX-NM**
☐ 1 Real Lemieux	4.00	6.50
☐ 2 Ted Irvine	4.00	6.50
☐ 3 Bob Wall	4.00	6.50
☐ 4 Bill White	4.00	6.50
☐ 5 Gord Labossiere	4.00	6.50
☐ 6 Eddie Joyal	4.00	6.50
☐ 7 Lowell MacDonald	4.00	6.50
☐ 8 Bill Flett	4.00	6.50
☐ 9 Wayne Rutledge (G)	5.00	8.00
☐ 10 Dave Amadio	4.00	6.50
☐ 11 Skip Krake (*)	55.00	85.00
☐ 12 Doug Robinson (*)	55.00	85.00
Shirriff • Minnesota North Stars	**EX**	**EX-NM**
☐ 1 Wayne Connelly	4.00	6.50
☐ 2 Bob Woytowich	4.00	6.50
☐ 3 André Boudrias	4.00	6.50
☐ 4 Bill Goldsworthy	4.00	6.50
☐ 5 Cesare Maniago (G)	5.00	8.00
☐ 6 Milan Marcetta	4.00	6.50
☐ 7 Bill Collins	35.00	60.00
☐ 7 Claude Larose (*)	80.00	150.00
☐ 8 Parker MacDonald	80.00	135.00
☐ 9 Ray Cullen	4.00	6.50
☐ 10 Mike McMahon	4.00	6.50
☐ 11 Bob McCord (*)	55.00	90.00
☐ 12 Larry Hillman (*)	55.00	90.00
Shirriff • Montréal Canadiens	**EX**	**EX-NM**
☐ 1 Gump Worsley (G)	14.00	25.00
☐ 2 Rogatien Vachon (G)	8.00	15.00
☐ 3 Ted Harris	4.00	6.50
☐ 4 Jacques Laperrière	8.00	15.00
☐ 5 J.C. Tremblay	6.00	10.00
☐ 6 Jean Béliveau	35.00	55.00
☐ 7 Gilles Tremblay	4.00	6.50
☐ 8 Ralph Backstrom	4.00	6.50
☐ 9 Bobby Rousseau	4.00	6.50
☐ 10 John Ferguson	6.00	10.00
☐ 11 Dick Duff	4.00	6.50
☐ 12 Terry Harper	4.00	6.50
☐ 13 Yvan Cournoyer	13.00	22.00
☐ 14 Jacques Lemaire	13.00	22.00
☐ 15 Henri Richard	12.00	20.00
☐ 16 Claude Provost (*)	100.00	165.00
☐ 17 Serge Savard (*)	135.00	225.00
☐ 18 Mickey Redmond (*)	120.00	200.00
Shirriff • New York Rangers	**EX**	**EX-NM**
☐ 1 Rod Seiling	4.00	6.50
☐ 2 Jean Ratelle	11.00	20.00
☐ 3 Ed Giacomin (G)	15.00	25.00
☐ 4 Reggie Fleming	4.00	6.50
☐ 5 Phil Goyette	4.00	6.50
☐ 6 Arnie Brown	4.00	6.50
☐ 7 Don Marshall	4.00	6.50
☐ 8 Orland Kurtenbach	4.00	6.50
☐ 9 Bob Nevin	4.00	6.50
☐ 10 Rod Gilbert	11.00	20.00
☐ 11 Harry Howell	9.00	15.00
☐ 12 Jim Neilson	4.00	6.50
☐ 13 Vic Hadfield (*)	100.00	185.00
☐ 14 Larry Jeffrey (*)	350.00	600.00
☐ 15 Dave Balon (*)	90.00	150.00
☐ 16 Ron Stewart (*)	90.00	150.00
Shirriff • Oakland Seals	**EX**	**EX-NM**
☐ 1 Gerry Ehman	4.00	6.50
☐ 2 John Brenneman	4.00	6.50
☐ 3 Ted Hampson	4.00	6.50
☐ 4 Billy Harris	4.00	6.50
☐ 5 George Swarbrick	345.00	60.00
☐ 5 Carol Vadnais (*)	425.00	700.00
☐ 6 Gary Smith (G)	5.00	8.00
☐ 7 Charlie Hodge (G)	6.00	10.00
☐ 8 Bert Marshall	4.00	6.50
☐ 9 Bill Hicke	4.00	6.50
☐ 10 Tracy Pratt	4.00	6.50
☐ 11 Gary Jarrett (*)	425.00	700.00
☐ 12 Howie Young (*)	500.00	800.00
Shirriff • Philadelphia Flyers	**EX**	**EX-NM**
☐ 1 Bernie Parent (G)	20.00	30.00
☐ 2 John Miszuk	4.00	6.50
☐ 3 Ed Hoekstra	35.00	60.00
☐ 3 Allan Stanley	100.00	170.00
☐ 4 Gary Dornhoefer	6.00	10.00
☐ 5 Doug Favell (G)	5.00	8.00
☐ 6 André Lacroix	4.00	6.50
☐ 7 Brit Selby	4.00	6.50
☐ 8 Don Blackburn	4.00	6.50
☐ 9 Leon Rochefort	4.00	6.50
☐ 10 Forbes Kennedy	4.00	6.50
☐ 11 Claude Laforge (*)	75.00	120.00
☐ 12 Pat Hannigan (*)	75.00	120.00
Shirriff • Pittsburgh Penguins	**EX**	**EX-NM**
☐ 1 Ken Schinkel	4.00	6.50
☐ 2 Earl Ingarfield	4.00	6.50
☐ 3 Val Fonteyne	4.00	6.50
☐ 4 Noel Price	4.00	6.50
☐ 5 Andy Bathgate	9.00	15.00
☐ 6 Les Binkley (G)	5.00	8.00
☐ 7 Leo Boivin	7.00	15.00
☐ 8 Paul Andréa	4.00	6.50
☐ 9 Dunc McCallum	4.00	6.50
☐ 10 Keith McCreary	4.00	6.50
☐ 11 Lou Angotti (*)	60.00	100.00
☐ 12 Wally Boyer (*)	60.00	100.00
Shirriff • St. Louis Blues	**EX**	**EX-NM**
☐ 1 Ron Schock	4.00	6.50
☐ 2 Bob Plager	6.00	10.00
☐ 3 Al Arbour	9.00	15.00
☐ 4 Red Berenson	4.00	6.50
☐ 5 Glenn Hall (G)	20.00	30.00
☐ 6 Jim Roberts	4.00	6.50
☐ 7 Noel Picard	4.00	6.50
☐ 8 Barclay Plager	6.00	10.00
☐ 9 Larry Keenan	4.00	6.50
☐ 10 Terry Crisp	7.00	12.00
☐ 11 Gary Sabourin (*)	75.00	120.00
☐ 12 Ab McDonald (*)	75.00	120.00
Shirriff • Toronto Maple Leafs	**EX**	**EX-NM**
☐ 1 George Armstrong	9.00	15.00
☐ 2 Wayne Carleton	4.00	6.50
☐ 3 Paul Henderson	7.00	12.00
☐ 4 Bob Pulford	7.00	12.00
☐ 5 Mike Walton	4.00	6.50
☐ 6 Johnny Bower (G)	12.00	20.00
☐ 7 Ron Ellis	4.00	6.50
☐ 8 Mike Pelyk	4.00	6.50
☐ 9 Murray Oliver	4.00	6.50
☐ 10 Norm Ullman	9.00	15.00
☐ 11 Dave Keon	12.00	20.00
☐ 12 Floyd Smith	4.00	6.50
☐ 13 Marcel Pronovost	7.00	12.00
☐ 14 Tim Horton	20.00	30.00
☐ 15 Bruce Gamble (G)	6.00	10.00
☐ 16 Jim McKenny (*)	75.00	125.00
☐ 17 Mike Byers (*)	75.00	125.00
☐ 18 Pierre Pilote (*)	100.00	175.00

1968 - 69 TOPPS

These cards measure the standard 2 1/2" x 3 1/2".

	EX	EX-NM
Complete Set (132 cards):	**375.00**	**750.00**
Common Player:	**2.50**	**5.00**
Topps	**EX**	**EX-NM**
☐ 1 Gerry Cheevers (G), Bost.	10.00	30.00
☐ 2 Bobby Orr, Bost.	125.00	250.00
☐ 3 Don Awrey, Bost., Error (Skip Krake)	2.50	5.00
☐ 4 Ted Green, Bost.	2.50	5.00
☐ 5 John Bucyk, Bost.	4.50	8.50
☐ 6 Derek Sanderson, Bost.	15.00	30.00
☐ 7 Phil Esposito, Bost.	20.00	40.00
☐ 8 Ken Hodge, Bost.	2.50	5.00
☐ 9 John McKenzie, Bost.	2.50	5.00
☐ 10 Fred Stanfield, Bost.	2.50	5.00
☐ 11 Tom Williams, Bost.	2.50	5.00
☐ 12 Denis DeJordy (G), Chic.	4.00	8.00
☐ 13 Doug Jarrett, Chic.	2.50	5.00
☐ 14 Gilles Marotte, Chic.	2.50	5.00
☐ 15 Pat Stapleton, Chic.	2.50	5.00
☐ 16 Bobby Hull, Chic.	35.00	70.00
☐ 17 Chico Maki, Chic.	2.50	5.00
☐ 18 Pit Martin, Chic.	2.50	5.00
☐ 19 Doug Mohns, Chic.	2.50	5.00
☐ 20 Stan Mikita, Chic.	11.00	22.00
☐ 21 Jim Pappin, Chic.	2.50	5.00
☐ 22 Kenny Wharram, Chic.	2.50	5.00
☐ 23 Roger Crozier (G), Detr.	4.00	8.00
☐ 24 Bob Baun, Detr.	2.50	5.00
☐ 25 Gary Bergman, Detr.	2.50	5.00
☐ 26 Kent Douglas, Detr.	2.50	5.00
☐ **27 Ron Harris, Detr. RC**	**4.00**	**8.00**
☐ 28 Alex Delvecchio, Detr.	4.50	8.50
☐ 29 Gordie Howe, Detr.	50.00	100.00
☐ 30 Bruce MacGregor, Detr.	2.50	5.00
☐ 31 Frank Mahovlich, Detr.	7.00	14.00
☐ 32 Dean Prentice, Detr.	2.50	5.00
☐ 33 Pete Stemkowski, Detr.	2.50	5.00
☐ 34 Terry Sawchuk (G), LosA.	25.00	50.00
☐ 35 Larry Cahan, LosA.	2.50	5.00
☐ **36 Real Lemieux, LosA. RC**	**4.00**	**8.00**
☐ **37 Bill White, LosA. RC**	**4.00**	**8.00**
☐ **38 Gord Labossiere, LosA. RC**	**4.00**	**8.00**
☐ **39 Ted Irvine, LosA. RC**	**4.00**	**8.00**
☐ 40 Eddie Joyal, LosA.	2.50	5.00
☐ **41 Dale Rolfe, LosA. RC**	**4.00**	**8.00**
☐ **42 Lowell MacDonald, LosA. RC**	**4.00**	**8.00**
☐ 43 Skip Krake, LosA., Error (Don Awrey)	2.50	5.00
☐ 44 Terry Gray, LosA.	2.50	5.00
☐ 45 Césare Maniago (G), Minn.	4.00	8.00
☐ 46 Mike McMahon, Minn.	2.50	5.00
☐ 47 Wayne Hillman, Minn.	2.50	5.00
☐ 48 Larry Hillman, Minn.	2.50	5.00
☐ 49 Bob Woytowich, Minn.	2.50	5.00
☐ 50 Wayne Connelly, Minn.	2.50	5.00
☐ 51 Claude Larose, Minn.	2.50	5.00
☐ **52 Danny Grant, Minn. RC**	**4.00**	**8.00**
☐ **53 André Boudrias, Minn. RC**	**4.00**	**8.00**
☐ **54 Ray Cullen, Minn. RC**	**4.00**	**8.00**
☐ 55 Parker MacDonald, Minn.	2.50	5.00
☐ 56 Gump Worsley (G), Mont.	6.50	13.00
☐ 57 Terry Harper, Mont.	2.50	5.00
☐ 58 Jacques Laperrière, Mont.	4.00	8.00
☐ 59 J.C. Tremblay, Mont.	2.50	5.00
☐ 60 Ralph Backstrom, Mont.	2.50	5.00
☐ 61 Jean Béliveau, Mont.	10.00	20.00
☐ 62 Yvan Cournoyer, Mont.	6.50	13.00
☐ 63 Jacques Lemaire, Mont.	8.00	16.00
☐ 64 Henri Richard, Mont.	7.50	15.00
☐ 65 Bobby Rousseau, Mont.	2.50	5.00
☐ 66 Gilles Tremblay, Mont.	2.50	5.00
☐ 67 Ed Giacomin (G), NYRa.	8.00	16.00
☐ 68 Arnie Brown, NYRa.	2.50	5.00
☐ 69 Harry Howell, NYRa.	4.00	8.00
☐ 70 Jim Neilson, NYRa.	2.50	5.00
☐ 71 Rod Seiling, NYRa.	2.50	5.00
☐ 72 Rod Gilbert, NYRa.	4.50	9.00
☐ 73 Phil Goyette, NYRa.	2.50	5.00
☐ 74 Vic Hadfield, NYRa.	2.50	5.00
☐ 75 Don Marshall, NYRa.	2.50	5.00
☐ 76 Bob Nevin, NYRa.	2.50	5.00
☐ 77 Jean Ratelle, NYRa.	4.50	9.00
☐ 78 Charlie Hodge (G), Oakl.	4.00	8.00
☐ 79 Bert Marshall, Oakl.	2.50	5.00
☐ 80 Billy Harris, Oakl.	2.50	5.00
☐ 81 Carol Vadnais, Oakl.	2.50	5.00
☐ 82 Howie Young, Oakl.	2.50	5.00
☐ **83 John Brenneman, Oakl. RC**	**4.00**	**8.00**
☐ 84 Gerry Ehman, Oakl.	2.50	5.00
☐ 85 Ted Hampson, Oakl.	2.50	5.00
☐ 86 Bill Hicke, Oakl.	2.50	5.00
☐ 87 Gary Jarrett, Oakl.	2.50	5.00
☐ 88 Doug Roberts, Oakl.	2.50	5.00
☐ **89 Bernie Parent (G), Phil. RC**	**45.00**	**90.00**
☐ 90 Joe Watson, Phil.	2.50	5.00
☐ 91 Ed Van Impe, Phil.	2.50	5.00
☐ 92 Larry Zeidel, Phil.	2.50	5.00
☐ **93 John Miszuk, Phil. RC**	**4.00**	**8.00**
☐ 94 Gary Dornhoefer, Phil.	2.50	5.00
☐ **95 Leon Rochefort, Phil. RC**	**4.00**	**8.00**
☐ 96 Brit Selby, Phil.	2.50	5.00
☐ 97 Forbes Kennedy, Phil.	2.50	5.00
☐ **98 Ed Hoekstra, Phil. RC**	**4.00**	**8.00**
☐ 99 Garry Peters, Phil.	2.50	5.00
☐ **100 Les Binkley (G), Pitt. RC**	**5.00**	**10.00**
☐ 101 Léo Boivin, Pitt.	4.00	8.00
☐ 102 Earl Ingarfield, Pitt.	2.50	5.00
☐ 103 Lou Angotti, Pitt.	2.50	5.00
☐ 104 Andy Bathgate, Pitt.	4.00	8.00
☐ 105 Wally Boyer, Pitt.	2.50	5.00
☐ 106 Ken Schinkel, Pitt.	2.50	5.00
☐ 107 Ab McDonald, Pitt.	2.50	5.00
☐ 108 Charlie Burns, Pitt.	2.50	5.00
☐ 109 Val Fonteyne, Pitt.	2.50	5.00
☐ 110 Noel Price, Pitt.	2.50	5.00
☐ 111 Glenn Hall (G), SLou.	7.00	14.00
☐ **112 Bob Plager, SLou. RC**	**4.50**	**8.50**
☐ 113 Jim Roberts, SLou.	2.50	5.00
☐ 114 Red Berenson, SLou.	2.50	5.00
☐ 115 Larry Keenan, SLou.	2.50	5.00
☐ 116 Camille Henry, SLou.	2.50	5.00
☐ **117 Gary Sabourin, SLou. RC**	**4.00**	**8.00**
☐ 118 Ron Schock, SLou.	2.50	5.00
☐ **119 Gary Veneruzzo, SLou. RC**	**4.00**	**8.00**
☐ 120 Gerry Melnyk, SLou.	2.50	5.00
☐ 121 Checklist (1 - 132)	60.00	115.00
☐ 122 Johnny Bower (G), Toro.	6.00	12.00
☐ 123 Tim Horton, Toro.	8.00	16.00
☐ 124 Pierre Pilote, Toro.	4.00	8.00
☐ 125 Marcel Pronovost, Toro.	4.00	8.00
☐ 126 Ron Ellis, Toro.	2.50	5.00
☐ 127 Paul Henderson, Toro.	4.00	8.00
☐ 128 Dave Keon, Toro.	5.00	10.00
☐ 129 Bob Pulford, Toro.	4.00	8.00
☐ 130 Floyd Smith, Toro.	2.50	5.00
☐ 131 Norm Ullman, Toro.	5.00	10.00
☐ 132 Mike Walton, Toro.	3.00	8.50

1969 - 70 O-PEE-CHEE

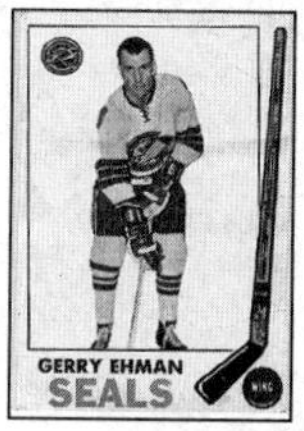

"The 1969-70 series was issued in two series. I missed out on Series One, so my first hockey cards were from Series Two, even though I had started with 1969 baseball. So I didn't really know about the stamps from Series One even though I saw some of my friends with them. Meanwhile, I had the Four-In-One inserts that came with the albums in Series Two. At the time, I found the albums kind of annoying and often threw them out, but I still separated the (mini) cards from the Four-In-One inserts." – Baron Bedesky, In The Game, Toronto, ON.

These cards measure the standard 2 1/2" x 3 1/2". The backs to cards 206, 208, 209, 210, 212, 213, 218, 225, 226, 230, and 231 form a Bobby Orr puzzle. The backs to cards 205, 207, 211, 214, 215, 216, 217, 220, 221, 222, 223, 224, 227, 228, and 229, meanwhile, form a Phil Esposito puzzle.

	EX	EX-NM
Complete Set (231 cards):	**1,100**	**2,200**
Common Player:	**3.00**	**6.00**
O-Pee-Chee	**EX**	**EX-NM**
☐ 1 Gump Worsley (G), Mont.	12.00	35.00
☐ 2 Ted Harris, Mont.	3.00	6.00
☐ 3 Jacques Laperrière, Mont.	4.00	8.00
☐ **4 Serge Savard, Mont. RC**	**20.00**	**40.00**
☐ 5 J. C. Tremblay, Mont.	3.00	6.00
☐ 6 Yvan Cournoyer, Mont.	7.50	15.00
☐ 7 John Ferguson, Mont.	3.00	6.00
☐ 8 Jacques Lemaire, Mont.	9.00	18.00
☐ 9 Bobby Rousseau, Mont.	3.00	6.00
☐ 10 Jean Béliveau, Mont.	13.00	26.00
☐ 11 Dick Duff, Mont.	3.00	6.00

☐	12 Glenn Hall (G), SLou.	7.50	15.00
☐	13 Bob Plager, SLou.	3.00	6.00
☐	**14 Ron C. Anderson, SLou. RC**	**4.00**	**8.00**
☐	15 Jean-Guy Talbot, SLou.	3.00	6.00
☐	16 André Boudrias, SLou.	3.00	6.00
☐	17 Camille Henry, SLou.	3.00	6.00
☐	18 Ab McDonald, SLou.	3.00	6.00
☐	19 Gary Sabourin, SLou.	3.00	6.00
☐	20 Red Berenson, SLou.	3.00	6.00
☐	21 Phil Goyette, SLou.	3.00	6.00
☐	22 Gerry Cheevers (G), Bost.	10.00	20.00
☐	23 Ted Green, Bost.	3.00	6.00
☐	24 Bobby Orr, Bost.	130.00	250.00
☐	25 Dallas Smith, Bost.	3.00	6.00
☐	26 John Bucyk, Bost.	5.00	10.00
☐	27 Ken Hodge, Bost.	3.00	6.00
☐	28 John McKenzie, Bost.	3.00	6.00
☐	29 Ed Westfall, Bost.	3.00	6.00
☐	30 Phil Esposito, Bost.	20.00	40.00
☐	31 Checklist 2 (133 - 231)	90.00	175.00
☐	32 Fred Stanfield, Bost.	3.00	6.00
☐	33 Ed Giacomin (G), NYRa.	10.00	20.00
☐	34 Arnie Brown, NYRa.	3.00	6.00
☐	35 Jim Neilson, NYRa.	3.00	6.00
☐	36 Rod Seiling, NYRa.	3.00	6.00
☐	37 Rod Gilbert, NYRa.	5.00	10.00
☐	38 Vic Hadfield, NYRa.	3.00	6.00
☐	39 Don Marshall, NYRa.	3.00	6.00
☐	40 Bob Nevin, NYRa.	3.00	6.00
☐	41 Ron Stewart, NYRa.	3.00	6.00
☐	42 Jean Ratelle, NYRa.	5.00	10.00
☐	**43 Walt Tkaczuk, NYRa. RC**	**6.00**	**12.00**
☐	44 Bruce Gamble (G), Toro.	4.00	8.00
☐	**45 Jim Dorey, Toro. RC**	**4.00**	**8.00**
☐	46 Ron Ellis, Toro.	3.00	6.00
☐	47 Paul Henderson, Toro.	4.00	8.00
☐	48 Brit Selby, Toro.	3.00	6.00
☐	49 Floyd Smith, Toro.	3.00	6.00
☐	50 Mike Walton, Toro.	3.00	6.00
☐	51 Dave Keon, Toro.	5.00	10.00
☐	52 Murray Oliver, Toro.	3.00	6.00
☐	53 Bob Pulford, Toro.	4.00	8.00
☐	54 Norm Ullman, Toro.	5.00	10.00
☐	55 Roger Crozier (G), Detr.	4.00	8.00
☐	56 Roy Edwards (G), Detr.	4.00	8.00
☐	57 Bob Baun, Detr.	3.00	6.00
☐	58 Gary Bergman, Detr.	3.00	6.00
☐	59 Carl Brewer, Detr.	3.00	6.00
☐	60 Wayne Connelly, Detr.	3.00	6.00
☐	61 Gordie Howe, Detr.	65.00	125.00
☐	62 Frank Mahovlich, Detr.	9.00	18.00
☐	63 Bruce MacGregor, Detr.	3.00	6.00
☐	64 Ron Harris, Detr.	3.00	6.00
☐	65 Pete Stemkowski, Detr.	3.00	6.00
☐	66 Denis DeJordy (G), Chic.	4.00	8.00
☐	67 Doug Jarrett, Chic.	3.00	6.00
☐	68 Gilles Marotte, Chic.	3.00	6.00
☐	69 Pat Stapleton, Chic.	3.00	6.00
☐	70 Bobby Hull, Chic.	40.00	80.00
☐	71 Dennis Hull, Chic.	3.00	6.00
☐	72 Doug Mohns, Chic.	3.00	6.00
☐	**73 Howie Menard, Chic. RC**	**4.00**	**8.00**
☐	74 Kenny Wharram, Chic.	3.00	6.00
☐	75 Pit Martin, Chic.	3.00	6.00
☐	76 Stan Mikita, Chic.	15.00	30.00
☐	77 Charlie Hodge (G), Cali.	4.00	8.00
☐	78 Gary Smith (G), Cali.	4.00	8.00
☐	79 Harry Howell, Cali.	4.00	8.00
☐	80 Bert Marshall, Cali.	3.00	6.00
☐	81 Doug Roberts, Cali.	3.00	6.00
☐	82 Carol Vadnais, Cali.	3.00	6.00
☐	83 Gerry Ehman, Cali.	3.00	6.00
☐	**84 Brian Perry, Cali. RC**	**4.00**	**8.00**
☐	85 Gary Jarrett, Cali.	3.00	6.00
☐	86 Ted Hampson, Cali.	3.00	6.00
☐	87 Earl Ingarfield, Cali.	3.00	6.00
☐	**88 Doug Favell (G), Phil. RC**	**9.00**	**18.00**
☐	89 Bernie Parent (G), Phil.	28.00	55.00
☐	90 Larry Hillman, Phil.	3.00	6.00
☐	91 Wayne Hillman, Phil.	3.00	6.00
☐	92 Ed Van Impe, Phil.	3.00	6.00
☐	93 Joe Watson, Phil.	3.00	6.00
☐	94 Gary Dornhoefer, Phil.	3.00	6.00
☐	95 Reggie Fleming, Phil.	3.00	6.00
☐	**96 Ralph MacSweyn, Phil. RC**	**4.00**	**8.00**
☐	97 Jim Johnson, Phil.	3.00	6.00
☐	98 André Lacroix, Phil.	3.00	6.00
☐	**99 Gerry Desjardins (G), LosA. RC**	**7.00**	**14.00**
☐	100 Dale Rolfe, LosA.	3.00	6.00
☐	101 Bill White, LosA.	3.00	6.00
☐	102 Bill Flett, LosA.	3.00	6.00
☐	103 Ted Irvine, LosA.	3.00	6.00
☐	104 Ross Lonsberry, LosA.	3.00	6.00
☐	105 Leon Rochefort, LosA.	3.00	6.00
☐	**106 Brian Campbell, LosA. RC**	**4.00**	**8.00**
☐	**107 Dennis Hextall, LosA. RC**	**4.00**	**8.00**
☐	108 Eddie Joyal, LosA.	3.00	6.00
☐	109 Gord Labossiere, LosA.	3.00	6.00
☐	110 Les Binkley (G), Pitt.	4.00	8.00
☐	**111 Tracy Pratt, Pitt. RC**	**4.00**	**8.00**
☐	112 Bryan Watson, Pitt.	3.00	6.00
☐	**113 Bob Blackburn, Pitt. RC**	**4.00**	**8.00**
☐	114 Keith McCreary, Pitt.	3.00	6.00
☐	115 Dean Prentice, Pitt.	3.00	6.00
☐	116 Glen Sather, Pitt.	5.00	10.00
☐	117 Ken Schinkel, Pitt.	3.00	6.00
☐	118 Wally Boyer, Pitt.	3.00	6.00
☐	119 Val Fonteyne, Pitt.	3.00	6.00
☐	120 Ron Schock, Pitt.	3.00	6.00
☐	121 César Maniago (G), Minn.	4.00	8.00
☐	122 Leo Boivin, Minn.	4.00	8.00
☐	123 Bob McCord, Minn.	3.00	6.00
☐	124 John Miszuk, Minn.	3.00	6.00
☐	125 Danny Grant, Minn.	3.00	6.00
☐	**126 Bill Collins, Minn. RC**	**4.00**	**8.00**
☐	127 J. P. Parise, Minn.	3.00	6.00
☐	128 Tom Williams, Minn.	3.00	6.00
☐	129 Charlie Burns, Minn.	3.00	6.00
☐	130 Ray Cullen, Minn.	3.00	6.00
☐	**131 Danny O'Shea, Minn. RC**	**4.00**	**8.00**
☐	132 Checklist 1 (1 - 132)	120.00	235.00
☐	133 Jim Pappin, Chic.	3.00	6.00
☐	134 Lou Angotti, Chic.	3.00	6.00
☐	**135 Terry Caffery, Chic. RC**	**4.00**	**8.00**
☐	136 Eric Nesterenko, Chic.	3.00	6.00
☐	137 Chico Maki, Chic.	3.00	6.00
☐	**138 Tony Esposito (G), Chic. RC**	**90.00**	**180.00**
☐	139 Eddie Shack, LosA.	7.00	14.00
☐	140 Bob Wall, LosA.	3.00	6.00
☐	**141 Skip Krake, LosA. RC**	**4.00**	**8.00**
☐	142 Howie Hughes, LosA.	3.00	6.00
☐	**143 Jimmy Peters, LosA. RC**	**4.00**	**8.00**
☐	**144 Brent Hughes, LosA. RC**	**4.00**	**8.00**
☐	145 Bill Hicke, Cali.	3.00	6.00
☐	**146 Norm Ferguson, Cali. RC**	**4.00**	**8.00**
☐	**147 Dick Mattiussi, Cali. RC**	**4.00**	**8.00**
☐	**148 Mike Laughton, Cali. RC**	**4.00**	**8.00**
☐	**149 Gene Ubriaco, Cali. RC**	**4.00**	**8.00**
☐	150 Bob Dillabough, Cali.	3.00	6.00
☐	151 Bob Woytowich, Pitt.	3.00	6.00
☐	152 Joe Daley (G), Pitt.	4.00	8.00
☐	153 Duane Rupp, Pitt.	3.00	6.00
☐	**154 Bryan Hextall, Jr., Pitt. RC**	**5.00**	**10.00**
☐	**155 Jean Pronovost, Pitt. RC**	**4.50**	**9.00**
☐	156 Jim Morrison, Pitt.	3.00	6.00
☐	157 Alex Delvecchio, Detr.	5.50	11.00
☐	158 Poul Popiel, Detr.	3.00	6.00
☐	159 Garry Unger, Detr.	4.50	9.00
☐	160 Garry Monahan, Detr.	3.00	6.00
☐	161 Matt Ravlich, Detr.	3.00	6.00
☐	**162 Nick Libett, Detr. RC, Error (Libbett)**	**4.00**	**8.00**
☐	163 Henri Richard, Mont.	7.50	15.00
☐	164 Terry Harper, Mont.	3.00	6.00
☐	165 Rogatien Vachon (G), Mont.	10.00	20.00
☐	166 Ralph Backstrom, Mont.	3.00	6.00
☐	167 Claude Provost, Mont.	3.00	6.00
☐	168 Gilles Tremblay, Mont.	3.00	6.00
☐	169 Jean-Guy Gendron, Phil.	3.00	6.00
☐	**170 Earl Heiskala, Phil. RC**	**4.00**	**8.00**
☐	171 Garry Peters, Phil.	3.00	6.00
☐	172 Bill Sutherland, Phil.	3.00	6.00
☐	**173 Dick Cherry, Phil. RC**	**4.00**	**8.00**
☐	174 Jim Roberts, SLou.	3.00	6.00
☐	**175 Noel Picard, SLou. RC**	**4.00**	**8.00**
☐	**176 Barclay Plager, SLou. RC**	**4.00**	**8.00**
☐	**177 Frank St. Marseille, SLou. RC**	**4.00**	**8.00**
☐	178 Al Arbour, SLou.	5.00	10.00
☐	179 Tim Ecclestone, SLou.	3.00	6.00
☐	180 Jacques Plante (G), SLou.	25.00	50.00
☐	181 Billy McCreary, SLou.	3.00	6.00
☐	182 Tim Horton, Toro.	11.00	22.00
☐	**183 Rick Ley, Toro. RC**	**4.00**	**8.00**
☐	184 Wayne Carleton, Toro.	3.00	6.00
☐	**185 Marv Edwards (G), Toro. RC**	**5.00**	**10.00**
☐	**186 Pat Quinn, Toro. RC**	**10.00**	**20.00**
☐	187 Johnny Bower (G), Toro.	6.50	13.00
☐	188 Orland Kurtenbach, NYRa.	3.00	6.00
☐	189 Terry Sawchuk (G), NYRa.	25.00	50.00
☐	190 Real Lemieux, NYRa.	3.00	6.00
☐	191 Dave Balon, NYRa.	3.00	6.00
☐	192 Al Hamilton, NYRa.	3.00	6.00
☐	Gordie Howe, Error (no#)	90.00	175.00
☐	193 Gordie Howe, Corrected	90.00	175.00
☐	194 Claude Larose, Minn.	3.00	6.00
☐	195 Bill Goldsworthy, Minn.	3.00	6.00
☐	**196 Bob Barlow, Minn. RC**	**4.00**	**8.00**
☐	**197 Ken Broderick (G), Minn. RC**	**4.00**	**8.00**
☐	**198 Lou Nanne, Minn. RC**	**4.00**	**8.00**
☐	**199 Tom Polonic, Minn. RC**	**4.00**	**8.00**
☐	200 Eddie Johnston (G), Bost.	4.00	8.00
☐	201 Derek Sanderson, Bost.	15.00	30.00
☐	202 Gary Doak, Bost.	3.00	6.00
☐	203 Don Awrey, Bost.	3.00	6.00
☐	204 Ron Murphy, Bost.	3.00	6.00
☐	205 AW: Phil Esposito, Bost., Error (#214)	13.00	25.00
☐	205 AW: Phil Esposito, Bost., Corrected	13.00	25.00
☐	206 AW: Alex Delvecchio	4.00	8.00
☐	207 AW: J. Plante (G)/ G. Hall (G)	28.00	55.00
☐	208 J. Plante (G)/ G. Hall (G)/ D. Grant	4.00	8.00
☐	209 AW: Bobby Orr, Bost.	45.00	85.00
☐	210 AW: Serge Savard, Mont.	6.00	12.00
☐	211 AS: Glenn Hall (G), SLou.	7.50	15.00
☐	212 AS: Bobby Orr, Bost.	45.00	85.00
☐	213 AS: Tim Horton, Toro.	9.00	18.00
☐	214 AS: Phil Esposito, Bost.	13.00	25.00
☐	215 AS: Gordie Howe, Detr.	30.00	60.00
☐	216 AS: Bobby Hull, Chic.	25.00	45.00
☐	217 AS: Ed Giacomin (G), NYRa.	7.50	15.00
☐	218 AS: Ted Green, Bost.	3.00	6.00
☐	219 AS: Ted Harris, Mont.	3.00	6.00
☐	220 AS: Jean Béliveau, Mont.	9.00	18.00
☐	221 AS: Yvan Cournoyer, Mont.	4.50	9.00
☐	222 AS: Frank Mahovlich, Detr.	5.00	10.00
☐	223 The Art Ross Trophy	4.00	8.00
☐	224 The Hart Memorial Trophy	4.00	8.00
☐	225 The Lady Byng Trophy	4.00	8.00
☐	226 The Vezina Trophy	4.50	9.00
☐	227 The Calder Memorial Trophy	4.00	8.00
☐	228 The James Norris Memorial Trophy	4.00	8.00
☐	229 The Conn Smythe Trophy	4.00	8.00
☐	230 The Prince of Wales Trophy	4.00	8.00
☐	231 The Stanley Cup	35.00	70.00

STAMPS

These stamps measure 2 1/2" x 1 1/4". The stamps are meant to be applied to the backs of the following cards: 6, 10, 12, 20, 24, 27, 30, 33, 37, 42, 51, 54, 61, 62, 70, 76, 82, 86, 89, 98, 99, 108, 110, 114, 125, 130.

Series One Insert Set (25 stamps):		85.00	130.00
O-Pee-Chee		**EX**	**EX-NM**
☐	Jean Béliveau, Mont.	7.50	15.00
☐	Red Berenson, SLou.	1.75	3.50
☐	Les Binkley (G), Pitt.	2.50	5.00
☐	Yvan Cournoyer, Mont.	5.00	10.00
☐	Ray Cullen, Minn.	1.75	3.50
☐	Gerry Desjardins (G), LosA.	2.50	5.00
☐	Phil Esposito, Bost.	7.50	15.00
☐	Ed Giacomin (G), NYRa.	5.00	10.00
☐	Rod Gilbert, NYRa.	4.00	8.00
☐	Danny Grant, Minn.	1.75	3.50
☐	Glenn Hall (G), SLou.	6.00	12.00
☐	Ted Hampson, Cali.	1.75	3.50
☐	Ken Hodge Bost.	1.75	3.50
☐	Gordie Howe, Detr.	20.00	40.00
☐	Bobby Hull, Chic.	11.00	22.00
☐	Eddie Joyal, LosA.	1.75	3.50
☐	Dave Keon, Toro.	5.00	10.00
☐	André Lacroix, Phil.	1.75	3.50
☐	Frank Mahovlich, Detr.	6.00	12.00
☐	Keith McCreary, Pitt.	1.75	3.50
☐	Stan Mikita, Chic.	6.0	12.00
☐	Bobby Orr, Bost.	25.00	50.00
☐	Bernie Parent (G), Phil.	6.00	12.00
☐	Jean Ratelle, NYRa.	4.00	8.00
☐	Norm Ullman, Toro.	3.50	7.00
☐	Carol Vadnais, Cali.	1.75	3.50

MINI CARDS

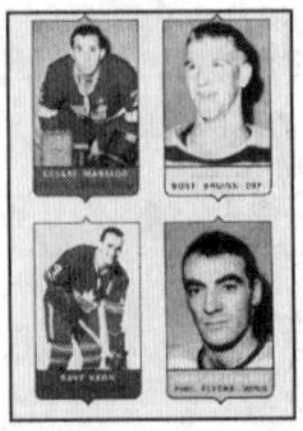

These cards measure the standard 2 1/2" x 3 1/2".

Series Two Insert Set (18 cards):		450	900
O-Pee-Chee		**EX**	**EX-NM**
☐	Bob Baun, Detr./ Ken Schinkel, Pitt.; Tim Horton, Toro./ Bernie Parent (G), Phil.	35.00	70.00
☐	Les Binkley (G), Pitt./ Ken Hodge, Bost./ Reggie Fleming, Phil./ Jacques Laperrière, Mont.	18.00	35.00
☐	Y. Cournoyer, Mont./ J. Neilson, NYRa./ Gary Sabourin, SLou./ John Miszuk, Minn.	20.00	40.00
☐	Bruce Gamble (G), Toro./ Vadnais, Oakl./ Frank Mahovlich, Detr./ Larry Hillman, Phil.	25.00	45.00
☐	Giacomin (G), NYRa./ Béliveau, Mont./ Eddie Joyal, LosA./ Léo Boivin, Minn.	40.00	80.00
☐	Phil Goyette, SLou./ Doug Jarrett, Chic./ Ted Green, Bost./ Bill Hicke, Oakl.	18.00	35.00
☐	Ted Hampson, Oakl./ Carl Brewer, Detr., Denis DeJordy (G), Chic./ Leon Rochefort, LosA.	18.00	35.00
☐	Charlie Hodge (G), Oakl./ Quinn, Toro./ Derek Sanderson, Bost./ Duane Rupp, Pitt.	25.00	50.00
☐	Earl Ingarfield, Oakl./ Jim Roberts, SLou./ Gump Worsley (G), Mont./ Bobby Hull, Chic.	55.00	110.00
☐	André Lacroix, Phil./ Bob Wall, LosA./ Serge Savard, Mont./ Roger Crozier (G), Detr.	18.00	35.00
☐	C. Maniago (G), Mont./ B. Orr, Bost./ Dave Keon, Toro./ Jean-Guy Gendron, Phil.	115.00	225.00
☐	McCreary, Pitt./ Claude Larose, Minn./ Rod Gilbert, NYRa./ Gerry Cheevers (G), Bost.	28.00	55.00
☐	Stan Mikita, Chic./ Al Arbour, SLou./ Rod Seiling, NYRa./ Ron Schock, Pitt.	25.00	50.00
☐	Doug Mohns, Chic./ Bob Woytowich, Pitt./ Gordie Howe, Detr./ Gerry Desjardins (G), LosA.	90.00	175.00
☐	Nevin, NYRa./ Plante (G), SLou./ Mike Walton, Toro./ Ray Cullen, Minn.	30.00	60.00
☐	Bob Pulford, Toro./ Henri Richard, Mont./ Red Berenson, SLou./ Eddie Shack, LosA.	35.00	65.00
☐	Pat Stapleton, Chic./ Danny Grant, Minn./ Bert Marshall, Oakl./ Jean Ratelle, NYRa.	20.00	40.00
☐	Ed Van Impe, Phil./ Dale Rolfe, LosA./ Alex Delvecchio, Detr./ Phil Esposito, Bost.	40.00	75.00

MINI-CARD ALBUMS

Series Two Insert Set (12 booklets):		45.00	85.00
O-Pee-Chee		**EX**	**EX-NM**
☐	Boston Bruins	5.00	10.00
☐	Chicago Blackhawks	5.00	10.00
☐	Detroit Red Wings	5.00	10.00
☐	Los Angeles Kings	5.00	10.00
☐	Minnesota North Stars	5.00	10.00

☐	Montréal Canadiens	5.00	10.00
☐	New York Rangers	5.00	10.00
☐	Oakland Seals	5.00	10.00
☐	Philadelphia Flyers	5.00	10.00
☐	Pittsburgh Penguins	5.00	10.00
☐	St. Louis Blues	5.00	10.00
☐	Toronto Maple Leafs	5.00	10.00

1969 - 70 MÄSTAR SERIEN

These cards measure 2 3/8" x 3 5/16".

Complete Set (50 cards):		100.00	200.00
Mästar Serien		**EX**	**EX-NM**
☐	1 Vladimir Dzurila (G), CSR.	2.50	5.00
☐	2 Jozef Golonka	.50	1.00
☐	3 Jiri Holik	2.00	4.00
☐	4 Vaclav Nedomansky, CSR.	2.00	4.00
☐	5 Vaclav Nedomansky, CSR.	2.00	4.00
☐	6 Jaroslav Holik	2.00	4.00
☐	7 Jozef Golonka	.50	1.00
☐	8 Vaclav Nedomansky, CSR.	2.00	4.00
☐	9 Vladimir Bednar	1.00	2.00
☐	10 Jan Havel	.50	1.00
☐	11 Jan Hrbaty	.50	1.00
☐	12 Jan Suchy	.50	1.00
☐	13 Lasse Oksane	.50	1.00
☐	14 Urpo Ylonen	1.00	2.00
☐	15 Michael Curran	.50	1.00
☐	16 Gary Begg	.50	1.00
☐	17 Carl Lackey, USA.	.50	1.00
☐	18 Terry O'Malley	.50	1.00
☐	19 Gary Gamuicci	.50	1.00
☐	20 Seppo Lindstrom	.50	1.00
☐	21 U.S.S.R. Nationals	2.00	4.00

☐ 22 Victor Pujkov, USSR	.50	1.00
☐ 23 Alexander Ragulin, USSR	.75	1.50
☐ 24 Gerry Pinder	1.00	2.00
☐ 25 Fran Huck	.75	1.50
☐ 26 Ken Dryden (G), Cdn.	75.00	150.00
☐ 27 Viktor Zinger, USSR	.50	1.00
☐ 28 Vladimir Petrov, USSR	4.00	8.00
☐ 29 I.Romishevsky/ V. Zinger	.50	1.00
☐ 30 Valeri Kharlamov, USSR	10.00	20.00
☐ 31 Alexander Ragulin, USSR	1.00	2.00
☐ 32 Ab DeMarco	.75	1.50
☐ 33 Morris Mott	.75	1.50
☐ 34 Fran Huck	.75	1.50
☐ 35 Vyacheslav Starsinov	.50	1.00
☐ 36 L.G. Nilsson/ R.Bourbonnais	.50	1.00
☐ 37 S-G Johansson, Swe. (XCX: K. Dryden)	5.00	10.00
☐ 38 Leif Holmqvist (G), Swe.	2.00	4.00
☐ 39 Hakan Nygren, Swe.	.50	1.00
☐ 40 Tord Lundström, Swe.	.50	1.00
☐ 41 Ulf Sterner, Swe.	1.50	3.00
☐ 42 Lars-Eik Sjoberg, Swe.	1.50	3.00
☐ 43 Kjell-Rune Milton, Swe.	.50	1.00
☐ 44 Leif Holmqvist (G), Swe.	2.00	4.00
☐ 45 Stefan Karlsson, Swe.	.50	1.00
☐ 46 Lennart Svedberg, Swe.	.50	1.00
☐ 47 Tord Lundström, Swe.	.50	1.00
☐ 48 Ulf Sterner, Swe.	2.00	4.00
☐ 49 Tord Lundström, Swe.	.50	1.00
☐ 50 Lennart Svedberg, Swe.	.50	1.00

1969 - 70 SOVIET STARS

These postcards measure 3 1/2" x 6".

Complete Set (26 postcards and folder):	**75.00**	**150.00**
Soviet Stars	**EX**	**EX-NM**
☐ Victor Zinger (G)	3.50	7.00

☐ Vitaly Davydov	2.50	5.00
☐ Vladimir Lutchenko	2.50	5.00
☐ Victor Kuzkin	2.50	5.00
☐ Alexander Ragulin	7.50	15.00
☐ Igor Romishevsky	2.50	5.00
☐ Boris Mikhailov	10.00	20.00
☐ Vyacheslav Starshinov	2.50	5.00
☐ Evgeny Zimin	2.50	5.00
☐ Alexander Maltsev	5.00	10.00
☐ Anatoli Firsov	2.50	5.00
☐ Evgeny Paladiev	2.50	5.00
☐ Alexander Yakushev	10.00	20.00
☐ Vladimir Petrov	5.00	10.00
☐ Valeri Kharlamov	15.00	30.00
☐ Vladimir Vikulov	2.50	5.00
☐ Vladimir Yursinov	2.50	5.00
☐ Victor Pushkov	2.50	5.00
☐ A. Czepnishev	2.50	5.00
☐ A. Tapasov	2.50	5.00
☐ U.S.S.R. vs. Sweden	4.00	8.00
☐ U.S.S.R. vs. Sweden	4.00	8.00
☐ U.S.S.R. vs. Sweden	4.00	8.00
☐ U.S.S.R. vs. Finland, Sweden	4.00	8.00
☐ U.S.S.R. vs. Canada, Sweden	7.50	15.00
☐ Team Photo	7.50	15.00

1969 - 70 TOPPS

These cards measure the standard 2 1/2" x 3 1/2".

Complete Set (132 cards):	**300.00**	**575.00**
Common Player:	**1.75**	**3.50**
Topps	**EX**	**EX-NM**
☐ 1 Gump Worsley (G), Mont.	7.50	22.00
☐ 2 Ted Harris, Mont.	1.75	3.50
☐ 3 Jacques Laperrière, Mont.	2.50	5.00
☐ **4 Serge Savard, Mont. RC**	**13.00**	**25.00**
☐ 5 J.C. Tremblay, Mont.	1.75	3.50
☐ 6 Yvan Cournoyer, Mont.	5.00	10.00
☐ 7 John Ferguson, Mont.	1.75	3.50
☐ 8 Jacques Lemaire, Mont.	6.00	12.00
☐ 9 Bobby Rousseau, Mont.	1.75	3.50
☐ 10 Jean Béliveau, Mont.	9.00	18.00
☐ 11 Henri Richard, Mont.	6.00	10.00
☐ 12 Glenn Hall (G), SLou.	5.50	11.00
☐ 13 Bob Plager, SLou.	1.75	3.50
☐ 14 Jim Roberts, SLou.	1.75	3.50
☐ 15 Jean-Guy Talbot, SLou.	1.75	3.50
☐ 16 André Boudrias, SLou.	1.75	3.50
☐ 17 Camille Henry, SLou.	1.75	3.50
☐ 18 Ab McDonald, SLou.	1.75	3.50
☐ 19 Gary Sabourin, SLou.	1.75	3.50
☐ 20 Red Berenson, SLou.	1.75	3.50
☐ 21 Phil Goyette, SLou.	1.75	3.50
☐ 22 Gerry Cheevers (G), Bost.	7.00	14.00
☐ 23 Ted Green, Bost.	1.75	3.50
☐ 24 Bobby Orr, Bost.	75.00	150.00
☐ 25 Dallas Smith, Bost.	1.75	3.50
☐ 26 John Bucyk, Bost.	3.50	7.00
☐ 27 Ken Hodge, Bost.	1.75	3.50
☐ 28 John McKenzie, Bost.	1.75	3.50
☐ 29 Ed Westfall, Bost.	1.75	3.50
☐ 30 Phil Esposito, Bost.	14.00	28.00
☐ 31 Derek Sanderson, Bost.	9.00	18.00
☐ 32 Fred Stanfield, Bost.	1.75	3.50
☐ 33 Ed Giacomin (G), NYRa.	7.00	14.00
☐ 34 Arnie Brown, NYRa.	1.75	3.50
☐ 35 Jim Neilson, NYRa.	1.75	3.50
☐ 36 Rod Seiling, NYRa.	1.75	3.50
☐ 37 Rod Gilbert, NYRa.	3.50	7.00
☐ 38 Vic Hadfield, NYRa.	1.75	3.50
☐ 39 Don Marshall, NYRa.	1.75	3.50
☐ 40 Bob Nevin, NYRa.	1.75	3.50
☐ 41 Ron Stewart, NYRa.	1.75	3.50
☐ 42 Jean Ratelle, NYRa.	3.50	7.00
☐ **43 Walt Tkaczuk, NYRa. RC**	**3.25**	**6.50**
☐ 44 Bruce Gamble (G), Toro.	2.50	5.00
☐ 45 Tim Horton, Toro.	6.50	13.00
☐ 46 Ron Ellis, Toro.	1.75	3.50
☐ 47 Paul Henderson, Toro.	2.50	5.00
☐ 48 Brit Selby, Toro.	1.75	3.50
☐ 49 Floyd Smith, Toro.	1.75	3.50
☐ 50 Mike Walton, Toro.	1.75	3.50
☐ 51 Dave Keon, Toro.	3.50	7.00
☐ 52 Murray Oliver, Toro.	1.00	3.00
☐ 53 Bob Pulford, Toro.	2.50	5.00
☐ 54 Norm Ullman, Toro.	3.50	7.00
☐ 55 Roger Crozier (G), Detr.	2.50	5.00
☐ 56 Roy Edwards (G), Detr.	2.50	5.00
☐ 57 Bob Baun, Detr.	1.75	3.50
☐ 58 Gary Bergman, Detr.	1.75	3.50
☐ 59 Carl Brewer, Detr.	1.75	3.50
☐ 60 Wayne Connelly, Detr.	1.75	3.50
☐ 61 Gordie Howe, Detr.	35.00	65.00
☐ 62 Frank Mahovlich, Detr.	6.00	12.00
☐ 63 Bruce MacGregor, Detr.	1.75	3.50
☐ 64 Alex Delvecchio, Detr.	3.50	7.00
☐ 65 Pete Stemkowski, Detr.	1.75	3.50
☐ 66 Denis DeJordy (G), Chic.	2.50	5.00
☐ 67 Doug Jarrett, Chic.	1.75	3.50
☐ 68 Gilles Marotte, Chic.	1.75	3.50
☐ 69 Pat Stapleton, Chic.	1.75	3.50
☐ 70 Bobby Hull, Chic.	25.00	50.00
☐ 71 Dennis Hull, Chic.	1.75	3.50
☐ 72 Doug Mohns, Chic.	1.75	3.50
☐ 73 Jim Pappin, Chic.	1.75	3.50
☐ 74 Kenny Wharram, Chic.	1.75	3.50
☐ 75 Pit Martin, Chic.	1.75	3.50
☐ 76 Stan Mikita, Chic.	9.00	18.00
☐ 77 Charlie Hodge (G), Oakl.	2.50	5.00
☐ 78 Gary Smith (G), Oakl.	2.50	5.00
☐ 79 Harry Howell, Oakl.	2.50	5.00
☐ 80 Bert Marshall, Oakl.	1.75	3.50
☐ 81 Doug Roberts, Oakl.	1.75	3.50
☐ 82 Carol Vadnais, Oakl.	1.75	3.50
☐ 83 Gerry Ehman, Oakl.	1.75	3.50
☐ 84 Bill Hicke, Oakl.	1.75	3.50
☐ 85 Gary Jarrett, Oakl.	1.75	3.50
☐ 86 Ted Hampson, Oakl.	1.75	3.50
☐ 87 Earl Ingarfield, Oakl.	1.75	3.50
☐ **88 Doug Favell (G), Phil. RC**	**5.00**	**10.00**
☐ 89 Bernie Parent (G), Phil.	20.00	35.00
☐ 90 Larry Hillman, Phil.	1.75	3.50
☐ 91 Wayne Hillman, Phil.	1.75	3.50
☐ 92 Ed Van Impe, Phil.	1.75	3.50
☐ 93 Joe Watson, Phil.	1.75	3.50
☐ 94 Gary Dornhoefer, Phil.	1.75	3.50
☐ 95 Reggie Fleming, Phil.	1.75	3.50
☐ 96 Jean-Guy Gendron, Phil.	1.75	3.50
☐ 97 Jim Johnson, Phil.	1.75	3.50
☐ 98 André Lacroix, Phil.	1.75	3.50
☐ **99 Gerry Desjardins (G), LosA. RC**	**5.00**	**10.00**
☐ 100 Dale Rolfe, LosA.	1.75	3.50
☐ 101 Bill White, LosA.	1.75	3.50
☐ 102 Bill Flett, LosA.	1.75	3.50
☐ 103 Ted Irvine, LosA.	1.75	3.50
☐ 104 Ross Lonsberry, LosA.	1.75	3.50
☐ 105 Leon Rochefort, LosA.	1.75	3.50
☐ 106 Eddie Shack, LosA.	5.00	10.00
☐ **107 Dennis Hextall, LosA. RC**	**2.50**	**5.00**
☐ 108 Eddie Joyal, LosA.	1.75	3.50
☐ 109 Gord Labossiere, LosA.	1.75	3.50
☐ 110 Les Binkley (G), Pitt.	2.50	5.00
☐ **111 Tracy Pratt, Pitt. RC**	**2.50**	**5.00**
☐ 112 Bryan Watson, Pitt.	1.75	3.50
☐ 113 Bob Woytowich, Pitt.	1.75	3.50
☐ 114 Keith McCreary, Pitt.	1.75	3.50
☐ 115 Dean Prentice, Pitt.	1.75	3.50
☐ 116 Glen Sather, Pitt.	2.50	5.00
☐ 117 Ken Schinkel, Pitt.	1.75	3.50
☐ 118 Wally Boyer, Pitt.	1.75	3.50
☐ 119 Val Fonteyne, Pitt.	1.75	3.50
☐ 120 Ron Schock, Pitt.	1.75	3.50
☐ 121 Césare Maniago (G), Minn.	2.50	5.00
☐ 122 Leo Boivin, Minn.	2.50	5.00
☐ 123 Bob McCord, Minn.	1.75	3.50
☐ 124 John Miszuk, Minn.	1.75	3.50
☐ 125 Danny Grant, Minn.	1.75	3.50
☐ 126 Claude Larose, Minn.	1.75	3.50
☐ 127 Jean Paul Parise, Minn.	1.75	3.50
☐ 128 Tom Williams, Minn.	1.75	3.50
☐ 129 Charlie Burns, Minn.	1.75	3.50
☐ 130 Ray Cullen, Minn.	1.75	3.50
☐ **131 Danny O'Shea, Minn. RC**	**2.50**	**5.00**
☐ 132 Checklist (1 - 132)	45.00	90.00

Canadian Marketplace

NORTHWEST TERRITORIES

Tiger Sport Card Collectables
YK Mall, 49 Franklin Ave.
Yellowknife, NT X1A 2N2
(867) 920-7174

BRITISH COLUMBIA

AC Card & Comics
1792 Renfrew Street
Vancouver, BC V5M 3H8
(604) 255-1158

Belushi's Hobbies
10225 King George Hwy
Surrey, BC V3T 2W1
(604) 588-1115

Fascination Street
334 S Birch Ave.
100 Mile House, BC
V0K 2E0
(250) 395-1133

Gem Mint Collectibles
8060 Westminster Hwy
Richmond, BC V6X 1A6
(604) 279-1833
#108-370 East Broadway
Vancouver, BC V5T 4G5
(604) 877-1198

Great Canadian Collectibles
2802 St. Johns St.
Port Moody, BC V3H 2C1

J.J.'s Sportscards
204- 307 5th St.
Courtenay, BC V9N 1J9
(250) 338-5009

John's Collectibles & Cards
Unit 110, 3760 Moncton St.
Steveston, BC V7E 3A6
(604) 275-5530

Maxx Sports Collectibles
221 Church St.
Comox, BC
(250) 339-9720

Mostly Music
2646 Shaughnessy St.
Port Coquitlam, BC
V3C 3G6
(604) 552-8055

M.V.P Sports Collectibles
807 Fort St.
Victoria, BC V8W 1H6
(250) 380-1958

Pastime Sports & Games
20364 Fraser Hwy
Langley, BC V3A 4G1
(604) 530-5507

Sonny's Collectables
Skeena Mall
#275-4741 Lakelse Ave.
Terrace, BC
(250) 638-7788
1-800-716-7784

Wiser's Wide World of Collectibles
Unit B2, 9640 - 201 St.
Langley, BC V1M 3E8

ALBERTA

Aldo's
95 Carry Dr. Plazza SE
Medicine Hat, AB T1B 3N6
(403) 527-9770

All Star Sports Cards & Collectables
Capilano Mall, 5004 98 Ave.,
Edmonton, AB S6A 0A1
(780) 465-3771

Chow's Varieties
10014 Franklin Ave.
Fort McMurry, AB T9H 2K6
(780) 743-2056

Collectors Books & Cards
615 Centre St. SW.
Calgary, AB T2G 2C6
(403) 265-3455

Delta Sports Cards
#406 West Mount Shopping Centre N.W.
Edmonton, AB T5M 3L7
(780) 455-4044

Dick's Collectables
Deer Valley Shopping Centre
36-1221 Canyon Meadows Dr. S.E.
Calgary, AB T2J 2P9
(403) 278-5380

Frost Inc.
#10-3220 5th Ave., NE
Calgary, AB T2A 5N1
(403) 248-9033

George's II
4-52 Brentwood Blvd.
Sherwood Park, AB T8A 2H6
(780) 467-1621

Harvey's Collectors Corner
901 64th Ave. N.E.
Calgary, AB T2E 7P4
(403) 275-4006

Jim's Cards & Collectables
207-8706 Franklin Ave.
Fort McMurray, AB T9H 2J6
(780) 791-5511

Maple Leaf Sports
1043 40th Ave. N.W.
Calgary, AB T2K 0G2
(403) 338-0668

Premier Sportscards
215 Banff Ave.
Sundance Mall
Banff, AB T1L 1A7
(403) 762-9474

Ultimate Sportscards
213 6th Ave. S.E.
Medicine Hat, AB T1A 7G4
(403) 526-2579

Wayne's Sportscards
17034 - 90th Ave.
Edmonton, AB T5T 1L6
(780) 483-3177

West's Sports Cards
27818 - 118 Ave.
Edmonton, AB T5B 0R4
(780) 477-2102

SASKATCHEWAN

AJW Sports Cards
300 Confederation Dr.
Saskatoon, SK S7L 4R6
(306) 384-3838

BJ's Collectors Centre
1954 Angus St.
Regina, SK S4T 1Z6
(306) 757-8285

Collectors Paradise Gallery and Custom Framing
1652 Albert St.
Regina, SK S4P 2S6
(306) 525-5004

Kard Sharks
1235 Broad St.
Regina, SK S4R 1Y2
(306) 721-2888

Prairie Sportex, Inc.
115 3rd Avenue South
Saskatoon, SK S7K 1L7
(306) 665-8373

T.N.T. Sportscards
236 Main St., Box 3759,
Humboldt, SK S0K 2A0
(306) 682-5510

Tramp's (PA)
1127 Central Ave.,
Prince Albert, SK S6V 4V7
(306) 764-3816

MANITOBA

Cancentral Card & Supply
Unit 1-1381 Erin Street
Winnipeg, MB R3E 2S7
(204) 775-9631

Joe's Sports Cards & Collectibles
960 Queens Ave.
Brandon, MB R7A 1L7
(204) 729-9388

Joe Daley's Sportscards
666 St. James St.
Winnipeg, MB R3G 3J6
(204) 783-8430

Right Way Sports Inc.
1103 Corydon Ave.
Winnipeg, MB R3M 0X3
(204) 453-4545

Skylake Sports Cards
23-845 Dakota St.
Suite 266
Winnipeg, MB R2M 5M3

Superstar Sports Collectibles
1885 C Portage Ave.
Winnipeg, MB R3J 0H3
(204) 831-9001

ONTARIO WEST

California Crazee Wear
125 Bruce St.
Sault Ste. Marie, ON P6A 2X6
1-800-465-9444

Collectors Corner
137 Christina St. N.
Sarnia, ON N7T 5T8
(519) 344-7416

Collector Headquarter
210 N. Archibald St.
Thunder Bay, ON P7C 3Y1
(807) 623-8201

Dave's Sports Collectibles
567 Dundas St.
Woodstock, ON N4F 1C6
(519) 421-3448

Fresher Sports Cards
639 Southdale Rd.
London, ON N6E 3M2
(519) 649-6116

Four Seasons
293 Bay, Sault Ste. Marie, ON
P6A 1X3
(705) 945-9679

Game City
1367 Grand Marais W.
Windsor, ON N9E 1E2
(519) 969-2831
3747 Tercumseh Rd. E.
Windsor, ON N8W 1H8
(519) 945-0325

Great Canadian Card Co.
1410 Lasalle Blvd.
Sudbury, ON P3A 1Z6
(705) 566-5093

Helou Sportscards & Collectibles
474 University Ave. W.
Windsor, ON N9A 5P8
(519) 258-2189

J R Sports Cards
1 Newfoundland
Walk Plaza
Elliot Lake, ON P5A 1Z5
(705) 849-5494

Kitchener Coin Shop
29 Scott St.
Kitchener, ON N2H 2P8
(519) 742-9181

Little Shop of Heroes
160 Wallace Ave. S.
Listowel, ON N4W 1X9
(519) 291-2281

Lookin For Heroes
93 Ontario St. S
Kitchener, ON N2G 1X5
(519) 570-4361

Martin Sports Cards
20 Dovercliffe Rd.,
Guelph, ON N1G 2V4
(519) 836-3061

MVP Sportscards
51 West St. North
Orillia, ON L3V 5C1
(705) 327-7891

Overtime Sports
16-1101 Arthur St. W.
Thunder Bay, ON P7E 5S5
(807) 577-6995

Pete's Collectibles
1712 Dundas St. E.
London, ON
(519) 457-2983

Prospect's Sportscard Company
110 Anne Street South Unit 22,
Barrie, ON L4N 5J3
(705) 737-5725

RJ Newton Inc.
22 Covent Market Place
London, ON N6A 1E2
(519) 433-0061

Roarrr Store (Hamilton Tiger-Cats)
2 King St. W., Jackson Square
Hamilton, ON L8P 1A1
(905) 527-1508

Roarrr Store (Hamilton Tiger-Cats)
1227 Barton St. E., Centre Mall
Hamilton, ON L8H 2V4
(905) 312-0574

Simcoe Coin & Card
202-400 Bayfield St.
Barrie, ON L4M 5A1
(705) 727-0273

Ultimate Sportscards
380 Fisher St.
North Bay, ON P1B 2E1
(705) 474-7975

Wings n' Things
295 Landcaster St. W.
Kitchener, ON N2H 4V4
(519) 741-0762

Zoep's Pro Sports
155 Main St. S.
Kenora, ON P9N 1T1
(807) 468-9030

ONTARIO CENTRAL

Action Coin & Card
230 Sheppard Ave. W.
Suite #200 (2nd floor)
Toronto, ON M2N 1N1
(416) 222-6227

A.J. Sports Cards
300 Towers Rd. Unit #1,
Woodbridge, ON L4L 5Z9
(905) 265-7700

A.K Comic & Cards
Agincourt Mall
3850 Sheppard Ave. E.
Agincourt, ON M1J 3L4
(416) 292-0954

All-Star Cards & Comics
16640 Yonge St. Unit #2
Newmarket, ON L3X 2N8
(905) 895-9990

Coin Hut
897 King St. E
Hamilton, ON L8M 1B5
(905) 547-2128

Coins Unlimited
150 Thorold Rd.
Welland, ON L3C 3V4
(905) 788-0376

Collector's Edge
640 Mohawk W.
Hamilton, ON
(905) 575-4563

Comic Book Connection
44 Centre N.
Brampton, ON L6V 1S8
(905) 459-2665

Comic Connection
895 King St. W.
Hamilton, ON L8S 1K5
(905) 522-2357

401 Convenience
401 Yonge St.
Toronto, ON M5B 1S9
(416) 599-6446

Bruno's Collectors Nook
3259 Lakeshore Blvd. West
Toronto, ON M8V 1M2
(416) 252-8262

Fastball Sports Collectibles
624 Yonge St.
Toronto, ON M4Y 1Z8
(416) 323-0403

Frank Leardi
PO Box 361, Stn. N T
Toronto, ON M6B 4A3
(416) 781-3170

Frozen Pond
3232 Steeles, Ave. W #12,
Concord, ON L4K 4C8
(905) 760-8404

Go For It Sportscards
743 Lakeshore E.
Mississauga, ON L5E 1C6
(905) 891-1817

Heinz's Toronto Discount Hockey Card Shop
3130 Dundas St. W.
Toronto, ON M6P 2A1
(416) 762-3049

Image Collections
181 Queen St.
Streetsville, ON L5M 1L2
(905) 542-8307

Jersey Source, The
1070 Main W.,
Hamilton, ON L8S 1B4
(905) 842-0252

KD Sports
357 Canon St. E.
Hamilton, ON L8L 2C1
(905) 522-1119

Legends of the Game
322A King St. W.
Toronto, ON M5V 1J2
(416) 971-8848

Magic Realms
511 New
Burlington, ON L7L 1V2
(905) 681-6382

Major Leagues
1450 Headon Rd. Unit 7
Burlington, ON L7M3Z5
800-410-4517

M&L Sportscards
7174A Drummond Rd.
Niagara Falls, ON L2G 4P6
(905) 371-3010

Niagara Sports Cards
76 Merritt St.
St. Catharines, ON
L2T 1J5
(905) 227-4627

Overtime Sportscards
Applewood Village Plaza
1077 N Service Rd., Unit 15
Mississauga, ON L4Y 1A6
(905) 949-2727

Quick Pick
1603 Clarkson Rd., Unit 4
Mississauga, ON L5J 2X1
(905) 822-7763

Red Nails II
1700 Wilson Ave.
North York, ON M3L 1B2
(416) 242-7899

Sliders House of Cards
2 Glenabby Dr.
Courtice, ON L1E 1C1
(905) 436-6944

Superstars S C and Collectibles
856 Lawrence Rd.
Hamilton, ON L8K 2A2
(905) 544-2510

Tally's Sportscards & Collectibles
661 Upper James (Mountain Plaza),
Hamilton, ON L9C 5R8
(905) 318-7000

Westend Sportstop
240 Leighland Ave. Oakville, ON, L6H 3H6
(905) 526-0336

ONTARIO EAST

Card Collectors Corner
143 Pembroke St. W.
Suite #11,
Pembroke, ON K8A 5M9
(613) 735-3849

Cirella Variety & Trophies
1024-D Victoria
Petawawa, ON K8H 2E3
(613) 687-4923

Entertainment Ink
157-110 Place d"Orléans Dr.
Orléans, ON K1C 2L9
(613) 841-5531

Game Breakers Sports Cards
780 Baseline Rd.
Ottawa, ON K2C 3V8
(613) 228-9554

Gananoque All Sports & Collectibles
174 King St. E
Gananoque, ON K7G 1K5
(613) 382-5752

Jim's Sports Cards
409 McArthur Rd.
Ottawa, ON K1K 1G7
(613) 741-6383

Peever & Son Sportscards
1206 Bank Street (Suite A)
Ottawa, ON

Pit Stop, The
Kingslake Plaza, Division St.
Kingston, ON
(613) 542-1903

Quinte Card Shop
200 North Front St. #4
Belleville, ON K8P 3C2
(613) 968-2855

Touch Down Trading Inc.
1564 Carling Ave.
Ottawa, ON K1Z 7M4
(613) 798-8199

QUÉBEC

L'Ami du collectionneur
2485, boul Ste-Anne
Quebec, QC G1J 1Y4
(418) 666-4942

Cartes champions
5553 Leger Blvd.
Montréal N., QC H1J 1K4
(514) 955-4120

Cart-o-folie
9, rue Parc
Sherbrooke, QC J1G 1E6
(819) 346-7117

Cartomania
82, Principale
Cheneville, QC J0V 1E0
(819) 428-7053

Coin de la carte sportive
246, boul. Maisonneuve
Hull, QC, J8X 3N8
819-770-4103

Collecto Sports
8-750 boul. René-Lévesque,
Drummondville, QC
J2C 7N7
1-877-377-9595

Épicerie Windsor
210, rue Cartier
Rouyn, QC J9X 1S8
(819) 762-4813

International Sports Souvenirs
3090 Coderre,
Saint Hubert, QC J9X 1S8
(450) 658-5353

KSKS
375 Robin,
Beaconfield, QC H9W 1R9
(514) 630-4821

Les Mordus de la carte
545 de Lanaudière
Joliette, QC J6E 3M2
(450) 759-2362

Le Père Vincent
194, rue Champlain
St-Jn-Richeli, QC J3B 6V6
(450) 346-5757

Raxan Collectibles
2892 St-Charles Blvd.
Kirkland, QC H9H 3B6
(514) 426-0987

Sport Collect
55, rue Grand-Île
Valleyfield, QC J6S 3M1
(450) 371-0400

NEW BRUNSWICK

Castlevania Sportscards
310 Pleasant St.
Miramichi, NB E1V 3Y9
(506) 622-1936

Coin Cabinet, The
118 Cameron St.
Moncton, NB E1C 5Y6
(506) 857-9403

Coin Cabinet, The
154 Waterloo St.
Saint John, NB E2L 3R1
(506) 642-2646

Rolly's Cards & Collectibles
720 Coverdale Rd., Riverview Mall
Riverview, NB E1V 3L8
(506) 387-4880

NOVA SCOTIA

Diggers Sports Cards
455 Price St.
Sydney, NS B1P 5L3
(902) 562-3412

Hobby Stop, The
130 Starrs Rd.,
Yarmouth NS B5A 4E3
(902) 742-1300

Platinum Promotions
31 Lake Dr.,
Bedford, NS B4A 1J1
(902) 835-1347

Strictly Singles
6245 Almon St.
Halifax, NS B3L 1V1
(902) 455-2132
1-800-880-2132

NEWFOUNDLAND

Maverick Sport Collectables
250 Water St.
St. John's, NF A1C 1B7
(709) 738-2888

USA

BMW Cards
555 D'Onofrio Dr. Ste. 101
Madison, WI 53719
(608) 833-5515

Sports International
PO Box 16687
Jackson, MS 39236 USA
(601) 366-1115

WHOLESALERS

BRITISH COLUMBIA

Mint Cards Ltd.
4584 Dawson St.
Burnaby, BC V5C 4C1
(604) 294-9511

ALBERTA

Dynamic Distribution
3431 12th St. NE
Calgary, AB T2E 6S6
(403) 291-9331

ONTARIO

Everest Wholesale Sportscards
1367 Osprey Drive, Unit #3
Ancaster, ON L9G 4V5
(905) 304-9155

Grosnor Sportscards
C-100 Brydon Drive
Etobicoke, ON M9W 4N9
(416) 744-3344

Grosnor Sportscards
370 Monarch Ave. #21-22
Ajax, ON L1S 3W5
(905) 428-7225

MVP Trading
340 Woodlawn Rd. West #6
Guelph, ON N1H 7V8
(519) 827-1989

Prince Wholesalers
700-780 Baker Rd. Unit #732
North York, ON M2H 3B4
(416) 492-1280

NEW BRUNSWICK

D & M Sportscards Ltd.
281 Collishaw St. Unit D
Moncton, NB E1C 9R1
(506) 852-3244

SPORTS STORES

If you don't see your name, call Paolo Del Rio at 613-834-2562 or e-mail pdelrio@trajan.ca for a FREE store listing

1970 - 71 COLGATE STAMPS

Sheets of 31 stamps were offered as premiums with various size tubes of toothpaste. Stamps measure 1" x 1 1/4".

	EX	EX-NM
Complete Set (93 cards):	65.00	125.00
Colgate	**EX**	**EX-NM**
☐ 1 Walt McKechnie, Minn.	.50	1.00
☐ 2 Bob Pulford, LosA.	1.25	2.50
☐ 3 Mike Walton, Toro.	.50	1.00
☐ 4 Alex Delvecchio, Detr.	1.75	3.50
☐ 5 Tom Williams, Minn.	.50	1.00
☐ 6 Derek Sanderson, Bost.	2.25	4.50
☐ 7 Garry Unger, Detr.	.50	1.00
☐ 8 Lou Angotti, Chic.	.50	1.00
☐ 9 Ted Hampson, Cgy.	.50	1.00
☐ 10 Phil Goyette, Buff.	.50	1.00
☐ 11 Juha Widing, LosA.	.50	1.00
☐ 12 Norm Ullman, Toro.	1.75	3.50
☐ 13 Garry Monahan, Toro.	.50	1.00
☐ 14 Henri Richard, Mont.	2.50	5.00
☐ 15 Ray Cullen, Vanc.	.50	1.00
☐ 16 Danny O'Shea, Chic.	.50	1.00
☐ 17 Marc Tardif, Mont.	.50	1.00
☐ 18 Jude Drouin, Minn.	.50	1.00
☐ 19 Charlie Burns, Minn.	.50	1.00
☐ 20 Gerry Meehan, Buff.	.50	1.00
☐ 21 Ralph Backstrom, Mont.	.50	1.00
☐ 22 Frank St. Marseille, SLou.	.50	1.00
☐ 23 Orland Kurtenbach, Vanc.	.50	1.00
☐ 24 Red Berenson, SLou.	.50	1.00
☐ 25 Jean Ratelle, NYls.	1.75	3.50
☐ 26 Syl Apps, Pitt.	.50	1.00
☐ 27 Don Marshall, Buff.	.50	1.00
☐ 28 Gilbert Perreault, Buff.	5.00	10.00
☐ 29 André Lacroix, Phil.	.50	1.00
☐ 30 Jacques Lemaire, Mont.	1.75	3.50
☐ 31 Pit Martin, Chic.	.50	1.00
☐ 32 Dennis Hull, Chic.	.50	1.00
☐ 33 Dave Balon, NYls.	.50	1.00
☐ 34 Keith McCreary, Pitt.	.50	1.00
☐ 35 Bobby Rousseau, Minn.	.50	1.00
☐ 36 Danny Grant, Minn.	.50	1.00
☐ 37 Brit Selby, SLou.	.50	1.00
☐ 38 Bob Nevin, NYls.	.50	1.00
☐ 39 Rosaire Paiement, Vanc.	.50	1.00
☐ 40 Gary Dornhoefer, Phil.	.50	1.00
☐ 41 Eddie Shack, LosA.	1.25	2.50
☐ 42 Ron Schock, Pitt.	.50	1.00
☐ 43 Jim Pappin, Chic.	.50	1.00
☐ 44 Mickey Redmond, Mont.	1.00	2.00
☐ 45 Vic Hadfield, NYls.	.50	1.00
☐ 46 John Bucyk, Bost.	1.75	3.50
☐ 47 Gordie Howe, Detr.	20.00	40.00
☐ 48 Ron C. Anderson, Buff.	.50	1.00
☐ 49 Gary Jarrett, Cali.	.50	1.00
☐ 50 Jean Pronovost, Pitt.	.50	1.00
☐ 51 Simon Nolet, Phil.	.50	1.00
☐ 52 Bill Goldsworthy, Minn.	.50	1.00
☐ 53 Rod Gilbert, NYls.	1.75	3.50
☐ 54 Ron Ellis, Toro.	.50	1.00
☐ 55 Mike Byers, LosA.	.50	1.00
☐ 56 Norm Ferguson, Cali.	.50	1.00
☐ 57 Gary Sabourin, SLou.	.50	1.00
☐ 58 Tim Ecclestone, SLou.	.50	1.00
☐ 59 John McKenzie, Bost.	.50	1.00
☐ 60 Yvan Cournoyer, Mont.	1.75	3.50
☐ 61 Ken Schinkel, Pitt.	.50	1.00
☐ 62 Ken Hodge., Bost.	.50	1.00
☐ 63 Césare Maniago (G), Minn.	.75	1.50
☐ 64 J.C. Tremblay, Mont.	.75	1.50
☐ 65 Gilles Marotte, LosA.	.50	1.00
☐ 66 Bob Baun, Toro.	.50	1.00
☐ 67 Gerry Desjardins (G), Chic.	.75	1.50
☐ 68 Charlie Hodge (G), Vanc.	1.00	2.00
☐ 69 Matt Ravlich, LosA.	.50	1.00
☐ 70 Ed Giacomin (G), NYls.	2.25	4.50
☐ 71 Gerry Cheevers (G), Bost.	2.50	5.00
☐ 72 Pat Quinn, Vanc.	1.00	2.00
☐ 73 Gary Bergman, Detr.	.50	1.00
☐ 74 Serge Savard, Mont.	1.00	2.00
☐ 75 Les Binkley (G), Pitt.	.75	1.50
☐ 76 Arnie Brown, NYls.	.50	1.00
☐ 77 Pat Stapleton, Chic.	.50	1.00
☐ 78 Ed Van Impe, Phil.	.50	1.00
☐ 79 Jim Dorey, Toro.	.50	1.00
☐ 80 Dave Dryden (G), Buff.	.75	1.50
☐ 81 Dale Tallon, Vanc.	.50	1.00
☐ 82 Bruce Gamble (G), Toro.	.75	1.50
☐ 83 Roger Crozier (G), Buff.	1.00	2.00
☐ 84 Denis DeJordy (G), LosA.	.75	1.50
☐ 85 Rogatien Vachon (G), Mont.	1.25	2.50
☐ 86 Carol Vadnais, Cali.	.50	1.00
☐ 87 Bobby Orr, Bost.	30.00	60.00
☐ 88 Noel Picard, SLou.	.50	1.00
☐ 89 Gilles Villemure (G), NYls.	.75	1.50
☐ 90 Gary Smith (G), Cali.	.75	1.50
☐ 91 Doug Favell (G), Phil.	.75	1.50
☐ 92 Ernie Wakely (G), SLou.	.75	1.50
☐ 93 Bernie Parent (G), Phil.	4.00	8.00

1970 - 71 DAD'S COOKIES

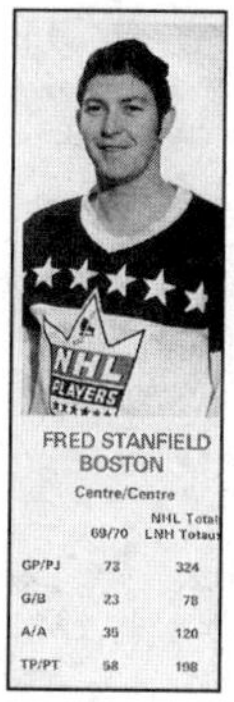

These cards measure 1 7/8" x 5 3/8".

	EX	EX-NM
Complete Set (144 cards):	100.00	200.00
Dad's Cookies • Boston Bruins	**EX**	**EX-NM**
☐ Don Awrey	.50	1.00
☐ John Bucyk	1.75	3.50
☐ Gerry Cheevers (G)	2.75	5.50
☐ Phil Esposito	5.00	10.00
☐ Ted Green	.50	1.00
☐ Ken Hodge	.50	1.00
☐ Eddie Johnston	.75	1.50
☐ John McKenzie	.50	1.00
☐ Bobby Orr	33.00	65.00
☐ Derek Sanderson	2.50	5.00
☐ Fred Stanfield	.50	1.00
Dad's Cookies • Buffalo Sabres	**EX**	**EX-NM**
☐ Roger Crozier (G)	1.00	2.00
☐ Dick Duff	.50	1.00
☐ Reggie Fleming	.50	1.00
☐ Phil Goyette	.50	1.00
☐ Al Hamilton	.50	1.00
☐ Skip Krake	.50	1.00
☐ Don Marshall	.50	1.00
☐ Mike McMahon	.50	1.00
☐ Gilbert Perreault	5.00	10.00
☐ Tracy Pratt	.50	1.00
☐ Eddie Shack	1.75	3.50
☐ Floyd Smith	.50	1.00
Dad's Cookies • California Golden Seals	**EX**	**EX-NM**
☐ Gerry Ehman	.50	1.00
☐ Norm Ferguson	.50	1.00
☐ Ted Hampson	.50	1.00
☐ Bill Hicke	.50	1.00
☐ Harry Howell	1.25	2.50
☐ Earl Ingarfield	.50	1.00
☐ Gary Jarrett	.50	1.00
☐ Bert Marshall	.50	1.00
☐ Wayne Muloin	.50	1.00
☐ Carol Vadnais	.50	1.00
Dad's Cookies • Chicago Blackhawks	**EX**	**EX-NM**
☐ Lou Angotti	.50	1.00
☐ Tony Esposito (G)	5.00	10.00
☐ Bobby Hull	12.00	25.00
☐ Dennis Hull	.50	1.00
☐ Doug Jarrett	.50	1.00
☐ Keith Magnuson	.50	1.00
☐ Chico Maki	.50	1.00
☐ Pit Martin	.50	1.00
☐ Stan Mikita	3.25	6.50
☐ Doug Mohns	.50	1.00
☐ Pat Stapleton	.50	1.00
Dad's Cookies • Detroit Red Wings	**EX**	**EX-NM**
☐ Gary Bergman	.50	1.00
☐ Wayne Connelly	.50	1.00
☐ Alex Delvecchio	1.75	3.50
☐ Roy Edwards (G)	.75	1.50
☐ Gordie Howe	20.00	40.00
☐ Bruce MacGregor	.50	1.00
☐ Frank Mahovlich	4.00	7.50
☐ Dale Rolfe	.50	1.00
☐ Garry Unger	.50	1.00
☐ Tom Webster	.50	1.00
Dad's Cookies • Los Angeles Kings	**EX**	**EX-NM**
☐ Larry Cahan	.50	1.00
☐ Denis DeJordy (G)	.75	1.50
☐ Bill Flett	.50	1.00
☐ Gilles Marotte	.50	1.00
☐ Larry Mickey	.50	1.00
☐ Bob Pulford	1.50	3.00
☐ Matt Ravlich	.50	1.00
☐ Juha Widing	.50	1.00
Dad's Cookies • Minnesota North Stars	**EX**	**EX-NM**
☐ Charlie Burns	.50	1.00
☐ Bill Goldsworthy	.50	1.00
☐ Danny Grant	.50	1.00
☐ Ted Harris	.50	1.00
☐ Murray Oliver	.50	1.00
☐ Danny O'Shea	.50	1.00
☐ Jean Paul Parise	.50	1.00
☐ Bobby Rousseau	.50	1.00
☐ Tom Williams	.50	1.00
☐ Gump Worsley (G)	3.25	6.50
Dad's Cookies • Montréal Canadiens	**EX**	**EX-NM**
☐ Jean Béliveau	5.00	10.00
☐ Yvan Cournoyer	2.25	4.50
☐ John Ferguson	.75	1.50
☐ Terry Harper	.50	1.00
☐ Jacques Laperrière	1.25	2.50
☐ Jacques Lemaire	2.50	5.00
☐ Mickey Redmond	1.25	2.25
☐ Henri Richard	3.00	6.00
☐ Serge Savard	1.50	3.00
☐ J.C. Tremblay	.50	1.00
☐ Rogatien Vachon (G)	1.50	3.00
Dad's Cookies • New York Rangers	**EX**	**EX-NM**
☐ Arnie Brown	.50	1.00
☐ Ed Giacomin (G)	2.75	5.50
☐ Rod Gilbert	1.75	3.50
☐ Vic Hadfield	.50	1.00
☐ Jim Neilson	.50	1.00
☐ Bob Nevin	.50	1.00
☐ Brad Park	3.00	6.00
☐ Jean Ratelle	1.75	3.50
☐ Rod Seiling	.50	1.00
☐ Walt Tkaczuk	.50	1.00
Dad's Cookies • Philadelphia Flyers	**EX**	**EX-NM**
☐ Bobby Clarke	6.50	12.00
☐ Gary Dornhoefer	.50	1.00
☐ Doug Favell (G)	.75	1.50
☐ Jean-Guy Gendron	.50	1.00
☐ Larry Hillman	.50	1.00
☐ Wayne Hillman	.50	1.00
☐ André Lacroix	.75	1.50
☐ Bernie Parent (G)	4.00	7.50
☐ Ed Van Impe	.50	1.00
☐ Joe Watson	.50	1.00
Dad's Cookies • Pittsburgh Penguins	**EX**	**EX-NM**
☐ Les Binkley (G)	.75	1.50
☐ Wally Boyer	.50	1.00
☐ Bryan Hextall	.50	1.00
☐ Keith McCreary	.50	1.00
☐ Dean Prentice	.50	1.00
☐ Jean Pronovost	.50	1.00
☐ Glen Sather	1.75	3.25
☐ Ken Schinkel	.50	1.00
☐ Bryan Watson	.50	1.00
☐ Bob Woytowich	.50	1.00
Dad's Cookies • St. Louis Blues	**EX**	**EX-NM**
☐ Red Berenson	.50	1.00
☐ Tim Ecclestone	.50	1.00
☐ Ab McDonald	.50	1.00
☐ Noel Picard	.50	1.00
☐ Barclay Plager	.50	1.00
☐ Jim Roberts	.50	1.00
☐ Gary Sabourin	.50	1.00
☐ Brit Selby	.50	1.00
☐ Frank St. Marseille	.50	1.00
☐ Bob Wall	.50	1.00
Dad's Cookies • Toronto Maple Leafs	**EX**	**EX-NM**
☐ Bob Baun	.50	1.00
☐ Ron Ellis	.50	1.00
☐ Bruce Gamble (G)	.75	1.50
☐ Paul Henderson	1.25	2.50
☐ Dave Keon	2.25	4.50
☐ Rick Ley	.50	1.00
☐ Jim McKenny	.50	1.00
☐ Mike Pelyk	.50	1.00
☐ Jacques Plante (G)	7.50	15.00
☐ Norm Ullman	2.00	4.00
☐ Mike Walton	.50	1.00
Dad's Cookies • Vancouver Canucks	**EX**	**EX-NM**
☐ André Boudrias	.50	1.00
☐ Ray Cullen	.50	1.00
☐ Bob Dillabough	.50	1.00
☐ Gary Doak	.50	1.00
☐ Charlie Hodge (G)	1.00	2.00
☐ Orland Kurtenbach	.50	1.00
☐ Rosaire Paiement	.50	1.00
☐ Pat Quinn	.50	1.00
☐ Dale Tallon	.50	1.00
☐ Jim Wiste	.50	1.00

1970 - 71 EDDIE SARGENT STICKERS

These blank-back stickers measure 1 7/8" x 2 1/2".

	EX	EX-NM
Complete Set (224 stickers):	350.00	700.00
Album:	40.00	80.00

Eddie Sargent	**EX**	**EX-NM**
☐ 1 Bobby Orr, Bost.	60.00	110.00
☐ 2 Don Awrey, Bost.	.75	1.50
☐ 3 Derek Sanderson, Bost.	3.00	6.00
☐ 4 Ted Green, Bost.	.75	1.50
☐ 5 Ed Johnston (G), Bost.	1.00	2.00
☐ 6 Wayne Carleton, Bost.	.75	1.50
☐ 7 Ed. Westfall, Bost.	.75	1.50
☐ 8 John Bucyk, Bost.	3.00	6.00
☐ 9 John McKenzie, Bost.	.75	1.50
☐ 10 Ken Hodge, Bost.	.75	1.50
☐ 11 Rick Smith, Bost.	.75	1.50
☐ 12 Fred Stanfield, Bost.	.75	1.50
☐ 13 Garnet Bailey, Bost.	.75	1.50
☐ 14 Phil Esposito, Bost.	9.00	18.00
☐ 15 Gerry Cheevers (G), Bost.	4.50	9.00
☐ 16 Dallas Smith, Bost.	.75	1.50
☐ 17 Joe Daley (G), Buff.	1.00	2.00
☐ 18 Ron Anderson, Buff.	.75	1.50
☐ 19 Tracy Pratt, Buff.	.75	1.50
☐ 20 Gerry Meehan, Buff.	.75	1.50
☐ 21 Reg Fleming, Buff.	.75	1.50
☐ 22 Allan Hamilton, Buff.	.75	1.50
☐ 23 Gilbert Perreault, Buff.	7.50	15.00
☐ 24 Skip Krake, Buff.	.75	1.50
☐ 25 Kevin O'Shea, Buff.	.75	1.50
☐ 26 Roger Crozier (G), Buff.	1.25	2.50
☐ 27 Bill Inglis, Buff.	.75	1.50
☐ 28 Mike McMahon, Buff.	.75	1.50
☐ 29 Cliff Shmautz, Buff.	.75	1.50
☐ 30 Floyd Smith, Buff.	.75	1.50
☐ 31 Randy Wyrozub, Buff.	.75	1.50
☐ 32 Jim Watson, Buff.	.75	1.50
☐ 33 Tony Esposito (G), Chic.	10.00	20.00
☐ 34 Doug Jarrett, Chic.	.75	1.50
☐ 35 Keith Magnuson, Chic.	.75	1.50
☐ 36 Dennis Hull, Chic.	.75	1.50
☐ 37 Cliff Koroll, Chic.	.75	1.50
☐ 38 Eric Nesterenko, Chic.	.75	1.50
☐ 39 Pit Martin, Chic.	.75	1.50
☐ 40 Lou Angotti, Chic.	.75	1.50
☐ 41 Jim Pappin, Chic.	.75	1.50
☐ 42 Gerry Pinder, Chic.	.75	1.50
☐ 43 Bobby Hull, Chic.	20.00	40.00
☐ 44 Pat Stapleton, Chic.	.75	1.50
☐ 45 Gerry Desjardins (G), Chic.	1.00	2.00
☐ 46 Chico Maki, Chic.	.75	1.50
☐ 47 Doug Mohns, Chic.	.75	1.50
☐ 48 Stan Mikita, Chic.	7.50	15.00
☐ 49 Gary Bergman, Detr.	.75	1.50
☐ 50 Pete Stemkowski, Detr.	.75	1.50
☐ 51 Bruce MacGregor, Detr.	.75	1.50
☐ 52 Ron Harris, Detr.	.75	1.50
☐ 53 Billy Dea, Detr.	.75	1.50
☐ 54 Wayne Connelly, Detr.	.75	1.50
☐ 55 Dale Rolfe, Detr.	.75	1.50
☐ 56 Gordie Howe, Detr.	45.00	80.00
☐ 57 Tom Webster, Detr.	.75	1.50
☐ 58 Al Karlander, Detr.	.75	1.50
☐ 59 Alex Delvecchio, Detr.	3.00	6.00
☐ 60 Nick Libett, Detr.	.75	1.50
☐ 61 Garry Unger, Detr.	.75	1.50
☐ 62 Roy Edwards (G), Detr.	1.00	2.00
☐ 63 Frank Mahovlich, Detr.	6.00	12.00
☐ 64 Bob Baun, Detr.	.75	1.50
☐ 65 Dick Duff, LosA.	.75	1.50
☐ 66 Ross Lonsberry, LosA.	.75	1.50
☐ 67 Ed Joyal, LosA.	.75	1.50
☐ 68 Dale Hoganson, LosA.	.75	1.50
☐ 69 Ed Shack, LosA.	3.00	6.00
☐ 70 Réal Lemieux, LosA.	.75	1.50
☐ 71 Matt Ravlich, LosA.	.75	1.50
☐ 72 Bob Pulford, LosA.	2.00	4.00
☐ 73 Denis Dejordy (G), LosA.	1.00	2.00
☐ 74 Larry Mickey, LosA.	.75	1.50
☐ 75 Bill Flett, LosA.	.75	1.50
☐ 76 Juha Widing, LosA.	.75	1.50
☐ 77 Jim Peters, LosA.	.75	1.50
☐ 78 Gilles Marotte, LosA.	.75	1.50
☐ 79 Larry Cahan, LosA.	.75	1.50
☐ 80 Howie Hughes, LosA.	.75	1.50
☐ 81 Césare Maniago (G), Minn.	1.00	2.00
☐ 82 Ted Harris, Minn.	.75	1.50
☐ 83 Tom Williams, Minn.	.75	1.50
☐ 84 Gump Worsley (G), Minn.	4.50	9.00
☐ 85 Tom Reid, Minn.	.75	1.50
☐ 86 Murray Oliver, Minn.	.75	1.50
☐ 87 Charlie Burns, Minn.	.75	1.50
☐ 88 Jude Drouin, Minn.	.75	1.50

89 Walt McKechnie, Minn.	.75	1.50
90 Danny O'Shea, Minn.	.75	1.50
91 Barry Gibbs, Minn.	.75	1.50
92 Danny Grant, Minn.	.75	1.50
93 Bob Barlow, Minn.	.75	1.50
94 Jean Paul Parise, Minn.	.75	1.50
95 Bill Goldsworthy, Minn.	.75	1.50
96 Bob Rousseau, Minn.	.75	1.50
97 Jacques Laperrière, Mont.	2.00	4.00
98 Henri Richard, Mont.	4.00	8.00
99 J.C. Tremblay, Mont.	1.00	2.00
100 Rogatien Vachon (G), Mont.	3.00	6.00
101 Claude Larose, Mont.	.75	1.50
102 Peter Mahovlich, Mont.	.75	1.50
103 Jacques Lemaire, Mont.	4.00	8.00
104 Bill Collins, Mont.	.75	1.50
105 Guy Lapointe, Mont.	2.00	4.00
106 Mickey Redmond, Mont.	1.25	2.50
107 Larry Pleau, Mont.	.75	1.50
108 Jean Béliveau, Mont.	10.00	20.00
109 Yvan Cournoyer, Mont.	4.00	8.00
110 Serge Savard, Mont.	3.00	6.00
111 Terry Harper, Mont.	.75	1.50
112 Phil Myre (G), Mont.	1.00	2.00
113 Syl Apps, NYRa.	.75	1.50
114 Ted Irvine, NYRa.	.75	1.50
115 Ed Giacomin (G), NYRa.	4.00	8.00
116 Arnie Brown, NYRa.	.75	1.50
117 Walt Tkaczuk, NYRa.	1.00	2.00
118 Jean Ratelle, NYRa.	3.00	6.00
119 Dave Balon, NYRa.	.75	1.50
120 Ron Stewart, NYRa.	.75	1.50
121 Jim Neilson, NYRa.	.75	1.50
122 Rod Gilbert, NYRa.	3.00	6.00
123 Bill Fairbairn, NYRa.	.75	1.50
124 Brad Park, NYRa.	6.00	12.00
125 Tim Horton, NYRa.	6.00	12.00
126 Vic Hadfield, NYRa.	.75	1.50
127 Bob Nevin, NYRa.	.75	1.50
128 Rod Seiling, NYRa.	.75	1.50
129 Gary Smith (G), Cali.	1.00	2.00
130 Carol Vadnais, Cali.	.75	1.50
131 Bert Marshall, Cali.	.75	1.50
132 Earl Ingarfield, Cali.	.75	1.50
133 Dennis Hextall, Cali.	.75	1.50
134 Harry Howell, Cali.	2.00	4.00
135 Wayne Muloin, Cali.	.75	1.50
136 Mike Laughton, Cali.	.75	1.50
137 Ted Hampson, Cali.	.75	1.50
138 Doug Roberts, Cali.	.75	1.50
139 Dick Mattiussi, Cali.	.75	1.50
140 Gary Jarrett, Cali.	.75	1.50
141 Gary Croteau, Cali.	.75	1.50
142 Norm Ferguson, Cali.	.75	1.50
143 Bill Hicke, Cali.	.75	1.50
144 Gerry Ehman, Cali.	.75	1.50
145 Ralph MacSweyn, Phil.	.75	1.50
146 Bernie Parent (G), Phil.	6.00	12.00
147 Brent Hughes, Phil.	.75	1.50
148 Bob Clarke, Phil.	10.00	20.00
149 Gary Dornhoefer, Phil.	.75	1.50
150 Simon Nolet, Phil.	.75	1.50
151 Garry Peters, Phil.	.75	1.50
152 Doug Favell (G), Phil.	1.00	2.00
153 Jim Johnson, Phil.	.75	1.50
154 André Lacroix, Phil.	.75	1.50
155 Larry Hale, Phil.	.75	1.50
156 Joe Watson, Phil.	.75	1.50
157 Jean-Guy Gendron, Phil.	.75	1.50
158 Larry Hillman, Phil.	.75	1.50
159 Ed Van Impe, Phil.	.75	1.50
160 Wayne Hillman, Phil.	.75	1.50
161 Al Smith (G), Pitt.	1.00	2.00
162 Jean Pronovost, Pitt.	1.00	2.00
163 Bob Woytowich, Pitt.	.75	1.50
164 Bryan Watson, Pitt.	.75	1.50
165 Dean Prentice, Pitt.	.75	1.50
166 Duane Rupp, Pitt.	.75	1.50
167 Glen Sather, Pitt.	1.50	3.00
168 Keith McCreary, Pitt.	.75	1.50
169 Jim Morrison, Pitt.	.75	1.50
170 Ron Schock, Pitt.	.75	1.50
171 Wally Boyer, Pitt.	.75	1.50
172 Nick Harbaruk, Pitt.	.75	1.50
173 Andy Bathgate, Pitt.	2.50	5.00
174 Ken Schinkel, Pitt.	.75	1.50
175 Les Binkley (G), Pitt.	1.00	2.00
176 Val Fonteyne, Pitt.	.75	1.50
177 Red Berenson, SLou.	.75	1.50
178 Ab McDonald, SLou.	.75	1.50
179 Jim Roberts, SLou.	.75	1.50
180 Frank St. Marseille, SLou.	.75	1.50
181 Ernie Wakely (G), SLou.	.75	1.50
182 Terry Crisp, SLou.	1.00	2.00
183 Bob Plager, SLou.	.75	1.50
184 Barclay Plager, SLou.	.75	1.50
185 Christian Bordeleau, SLou.	.75	1.50
186 Gary Sabourin, SLou.	.75	1.50
187 Bill Plager, SLou.	.75	1.50
188 Tim Ecclestone, SLou.	.75	1.50
189 Jean-Guy Talbot, SLou.	.75	1.50
190 Noel Picard, SLou.	.75	1.50
191 Bob Wall, SLou.	.75	1.50
192 Jim Lorentz, SLou.	.75	1.50
193 Bruce Gamble (G), Toro.	1.00	2.00
194 Jim Harrison, Toro.	.75	1.50
195 Paul Henderson, Toro.	1.25	2.50
196 Brian Glennie, Toro.	.75	1.50
197 Jim Dorey, Toro.	.75	1.50
198 Rick Ley, Toro.	.75	1.50
199 Jacques Plante (G), Toro.	11.00	22.00
200 Ron Ellis, Toro.	1.00	2.00
201 Jim McKenny, Toro.	.75	1.50
202 Brit Selby, Toro.	.75	1.50
203 Mike Pelyk, Toro.	.75	1.50
204 Norm Ullman, Toro.	3.00	6.00
205 Bill MacMillan, Toro.	.75	1.50
206 Mike Walton, Toro.	.75	1.50
207 Garry Monahan, Toro.	.75	1.50
208 Dave Keon, Toro.	3.00	6.00
209 Pat Quinn, Vanc.	1.50	3.00
210 Wayne Maki, Vanc.	.75	1.50
211 Charlie Hodge (G), Vanc.	1.00	2.00
212 Orland Kurtenbach, Vanc.	.75	1.50
213 Poul Popiel, Vanc.	.75	1.50
214 Danny Johnson, Vanc.	.75	1.50
215 Dale Tallon, Vanc.	.75	1.50
216 Ray Cullen, Vanc.	.75	1.50
217 Bob Dillabough, Vanc.	.75	1.50
218 Gary Doak, Vanc.	.75	1.50
219 André Boudrias, Vanc.	.75	1.50
220 Rosaire Paiement, Vanc.	.75	1.50
221 Darryl Sly, Vanc.	.75	1.50
222 George Gardner (G), Vanc.	1.00	2.00
223 Jim Wiste, Vanc.	.75	1.50
224 Murray Hall, Vanc.	.75	1.50

1970 - 71 ESSO POWER PLAYERS

These cards measure 1 1/2" x 2 1/8".

Complete Set (252 stickers):	**90.00**	**160.00**
Common Player:	**.25**	**.50**
Hardcover Album:	**30.00**	**60.00**
Soft Cover Album:	**15.00**	**30.00**

Esso Power Players • Boston Bruins	EX	EX-NM
Don Awrey	.25	.50
Garnet Bailey	.25	.50
John Bucyk	1.25	2.50
Wayne Carleton	.25	.50
Wayne Cashman	.50	1.00
Gerry Cheevers (G)	1.50	3.00
Phil Esposito	3.00	6.00
Ted Green	.25	.50
Ken Hodge	.25	.50
Eddie Johnston (G)	.50	1.00
Don Marcotte	.25	.50
John McKenzie	.25	.50
Bobby Orr	18.00	35.00
Derek Sanderson	1.50	3.00
Dallas Smith	.25	.50
Rick Smith	.25	.50
Fred Stanfield	.25	.50
Ed Westfall	.25	.50

Esso Power Players • Buffalo Sabres	EX	EX-NM
Ron C. Anderson	.25	.50
Paul Andrea	.25	.50
Steve Atkinson	.25	.50
Doug Barrie	.25	.50
Roger Crozier (G)	.50	1.00
Reggie Fleming	.25	.50
Phil Goyette	.25	.50
Al Hamilton	.25	.50
Larry Keenan	.25	.50
Skip Krake	.25	.50
Don Marshall	.25	.50
Gerry Meehan	.25	.50
Gilbert Perreault	2.00	4.00
Tracy Pratt	.25	.50
Cliff Schmautz	.25	.50
Eddie Shack	1.25	2.50
Floyd Smith	.25	.50
Jimmy Watson	.25	.50

Esso Power Players • California Seals	EX	EX-NM
Gary Croteau	.25	.50
Gerry Ehman	.25	.50
Tony Featherstone	.25	.50
Ted Hampson	.25	.50
Joe Hardy	.25	.50
Dennis Hextall	.25	.50
Bill Hicke	.25	.50
Ernie Hicke	.25	.50
Harry Howell	.75	1.50
Earl Ingarfield	.25	.50
Gary Jarrett	.25	.50
Dick Mattiussi	.25	.50
Wayne Muloin	.25	.50
Doug Roberts	.25	.50
Gary Smith (G)	.50	1.00
Bob Sneddon (G)	.50	1.00
Ron Stackhouse	.25	.50
Carol Vadnais	.25	.50

Esso Power Players • Chicago Blackhawks	EX	EX-NM
Lou Angotti	.25	.50
Bryan Campbell	.25	.50
Gerry Desjardins (G)	.250	1.00
Tony Esposito (G)	2.50	5.00
Bobby Hull	8.00	15.00
Dennis Hull	.50	1.00
Doug Jarrett	.25	.50
Cliff Koroll	.25	.50
Keith Magnuson, Err. (Magnusson)	.25	.50
Chico Maki	.25	.50
Pit Martin	.25	.50
Stan Mikita	2.00	4.00
Doug Mohns	.25	.50
Eric Nesterenko	.25	.50
Jim Pappin	.25	.50
Gerry Pinder	.25	.50
Pat Stapleton	.25	.50
Bill White	.25	.50

Esso Power Players • Detroit Red Wings	EX	EX-NM
Gary Bergman	.25	.50
Larry Brown	.25	.50
Wayne Connelly	.25	.50
Billy Dea	.25	.50
Alex Delvecchio	1.25	2.50
Roy Edwards (G)	.50	1.00
Ron Harris	.25	.50
Gordie Howe	12.00	25.00
Al Karlander	.25	.50
Serge Lajeunesse	.25	.50
Nick Libett	.25	.50
Don Luce	.25	.50
Bruce MacGregor	.25	.50
Frank Mahovlich	2.00	4.00
Dale Rolfe	.25	.50
Jim Rutherford (G)	.75	1.50
Garry Unger	.50	1.00
Tom Webster	.25	.50

Esso Power Players • Los Angeles Kings	EX	EX-NM
Bob Berry	.25	.50
Mike Byers	.25	.50
Larry Cahan	.25	.50
Paul Curtis	.25	.50
Denis DeJordy (G)	.50	1.00
Bill Flett	.25	.50
Dale Hoganson	.25	.50
Eddie Joyal	.25	.50
Gord Labossière	.25	.50
Ross Lonsberry	.25	.50
Gilles Marotte	.25	.50
Larry Mickey	.25	.50
Jack Norris (G)	.50	1.00
Noel Price	.25	.50
Bob Pulford	.75	1.50
Matt Ravlich	.25	.50
Doug Robinson	.25	.50
Juha Widing	.25	.50

Esso Power Players • Minnesota North Stars	EX	EX-NM
Fred Barrett	.25	.50
Charlie Burns	.25	.50
Barry Gibbs	.25	.50
Bill Goldsworthy	.25	.50
Danny Grant	.25	.50
Ted Harris	.25	.50
Fred (Buster) Harvey	.25	.50
Danny Lawson	.25	.50
Césare Maniago (G)	.50	1.00
Walt McKechnie	.25	.50
Lou Nanne	.25	.50
Murray Oliver	.25	.50
Danny O'Shea	.25	.50
Jean Paul Parise	.25	.50
Tom Reid	.25	.50
Bobby Rousseau	.25	.50
Tom Williams	.25	.50
Gump Worsley (G)	1.75	3.50

Esso Power Players • Montréal Canadiens	EX	EX-NM
Jean Béliveau	5.00	10.00
Bill Collins	.25	.50
Yvan Cournoyer	1.25	2.25
John Ferguson	.50	1.00
Terry Harper	.25	.50
Fran Huck	.25	.50
Guy Lapointe	.75	1.50
Jacques Laperrière	.75	1.50
Claude Larose	.25	.50
Jacques Lemaire	1.25	2.50
Pete Mahovlich	.25	.50
Phil Myre (G)	.50	1.00
Mickey Redmond	.50	1.00
Henri Richard	1.50	3.00
Serge Savard	1.00	1.75
Marc Tardif	.25	.50
J.C. Tremblay	.50	1.00
Rogatien Vachon (G)	1.25	2.50

Esso Power Players • New York Rangers	EX	EX-NM
Dave Balon	.25	.50
Arnie Brown	.25	.50
Jack Egers	.25	.50
Bill Fairbairn	.25	.50
Ed Giacomin (G)	1.50	3.00
Rod Gilbert	1.00	2.00
Vic Hadfield	.25	.50
Tim Horton	2.00	4.00
Ted Irvine	.25	.50
Jim Neilson	.25	.50
Bob Nevin	.25	.50
Brad Park	2.00	4.00
Jean Ratelle	1.00	2.00
Rod Seiling	.25	.50
Pete Stemkowski	.25	.50
Ron Stewart	.25	.50
Walt Tkaczuk	.25	.50
Gilles Villemure (G)	.50	1.00

Esso Power Players • Philadelphia Flyers	EX	EX-NM
Barry Ashbee	.25	.50
Serge Bernier	.25	.50
Bobby Clarke	3.50	7.00
Gary Dornhoefer	.25	.50
Doug Favell (G)	.50	1.00
Jean-Guy Gendron	.25	.50
Larry Hale	.25	.50
Earl Heiskala	.25	.50
Larry Hillman	.25	.50
Wayne Hillman	.25	.50
Jim Johnson	.25	.50
Bob Kelly	.25	.50
André Lacroix	.50	1.00
Lew Morrison	.25	.50
Bernie Parent (G)	1.75	3.50
Garry Peters	.25	.50
Ed Van Impe	.25	.50
Joe Watson	.25	.50

Esso Power Players • Pittsburgh Penguins	EX	EX-NM
Andy Bathgate	1.00	2.00
Les Binkley (G)	.50	1.00
Bob Blackburn	.25	.50
Wally Boyer	.25	.50
Nick Harbaruk	.25	.50
Bryan Hextall	.25	.50
Dunc McCallum	.25	.50
Keith McCreary	.25	.50
Jim Morrison	.25	.50
Dean Prentice	.25	.50
Jean Pronovost	.25	.50
Duane Rupp	.25	.50
Glen Sather	.75	1.50
Ken Schinkel	.25	.50
Ron Schock	.25	.50
Al Smith (G)	.50	1.00
Bryan Watson	.25	.50
Bob Woytowich	.25	.50

Esso Power Players • St. Louis Blues	EX	EX-NM
Red Berenson	.25	.50
Chris Bordeleau	.25	.50
Terry Crisp	.75	1.50
Tim Ecclestone	.25	.50
Glenn Hall (G)	2.00	4.00
Jim Lorentz	.25	.50
Bill E. McCreary	.25	.50
Ab McDonald	.25	.50
George Morrison	.25	.50
Noel Picard	.25	.50
Barclay Plager	.25	.50
Bob Plager	.25	.50
Jim Roberts	.25	.50
Gary Sabourin	.25	.50
Brit Selby	.25	.50
Frank St. Marseille	.25	.50
Ernie Wakely (G)	.50	1.00
Bob Wall	.25	.50

Esso Power Players • Toronto Maple Leafs	EX	EX-NM
Bob Baun	.25	.50
Jim Dorey	.25	.50
Ron Ellis	.25	.50
Bruce Gamble (G)	.50	1.00
Brian Glennie	.25	.50
Jim Harrison	.25	.50
Paul Henderson	1.50	3.00
Dave Keon	1.50	3.00
Rick Ley	.25	.50

☐ Billy MacMillan	.25	.50
☐ Jim McKenny	.25	.50
☐ Garry Monahan	.25	.50
☐ Mike Pelyk	.25	.50
☐ Jacques Plante (G)	3.00	6.00
☐ Darryl Sittler	4.00	8.00
☐ Guy Trottier	.25	.50
☐ Norm Ullman	1.25	2.50
☐ Mike Walton	.25	.50
Esso Power Players • Vancouver Canucks	**EX**	**EX-NM**
☐ André Boudrias	.25	.50
☐ Mike Corrigan	.25	.50
☐ Ray Cullen	.25	.50
☐ Gary Doak	.25	.50
☐ Murray Hall	.25	.50
☐ Charlie Hodge (G)	.50	1.00
☐ Danny Johnson	.25	.50
☐ Orland Kurtenbach	.25	.50
☐ Len Lunde	.25	.50
☐ Wayne Maki	.25	.50
☐ Rosaire Paiement	.25	.50
☐ Poul Popiel	.25	.50
☐ Pat Quinn	.75	1.50
☐ Marc Réaume	.25	.50
☐ Darryl Sly	.25	.50
☐ Dale Tallon	.25	.50
☐ Barry Wilkins	.25	.50
☐ Dunc Wilson (G)	.50	1.00

1970 - 71 KUVAJULKAISUT

These cards measure the standard 1 7/8" x 2 1/2".

Complete Set (384 cards):

Album:

Kuvajulkaisut **EX EX-NM**

☐ 1 Vitali Davydov, USSR
☐ 2 Anatoli Firsov, USSR
☐ 3 Valeri Kharlamov, USSR
☐ 4 Alexander Yakushev, USSR
☐ 5 Viktor Konovalenko, USSR
☐ 6 Vladimir Lutchenko, USSR
☐ 7 Aleksandr Maltsev, USSR
☐ 8 Boris Mikhailov, USSR
☐ 9 Jevgeni Mishakov, USSR
☐ 10 Valeri Nikitin, USSR
☐ 11 Vladimir Petrov, USSR
☐ 12 Evgeni Paladiev, USSR
☐ 13 Viktor Polupanov, USSR
☐ 14 Alexandr Ragulin, USSR
☐ 15 Igor Romishevski, USSR
☐ 16 Vladimir Shadrin, USSR
☐ 17 Vyatjeslav Starsinov, USSR
☐ 18 Vladislav Tretiak (G), USSR
☐ 19 Valeri Vasiliev, USSR
☐ 20 Vladimir Vikulov, USSR
☐ 21 Tommy Abrahamsson, Swe.
☐ 22 Gunnar Backman, Swe.
☐ 23 Arne Carlsson, Swe.
☐ 24 Anders Hagstrom, Swe.
☐ 25 Anders Hedberg, Swe.
☐ 26 Leif Holmqvist (G), Swe.
☐ 27 Nils Johansson, Swe.
☐ 28 Stig-Goran Johansson, Swe.
☐ 29 Stefan Karlsson, Swe.
☐ 30 Hans Lindberg, Swe.
☐ 31 Tord Lundstrom, Swe.
☐ 32 Kjell-Rune Milton, Swe.
☐ 33 Lars-Goran Nilsson, Swe.
☐ 34 Anders Nordin, Swe.
☐ 35 Roger Olsson, Swe.
☐ 36 Bjorn Palmqvist, Swe.
☐ 37 Lars-Erik Sjoberg, Swe.
☐ 38 Ulf Sterner, Swe.
☐ 39 Lennart Svedberg, Swe.
☐ 40 Hakan Wickberg, Swe.
☐ 41 Vladimir Bednar, CSR.
☐ 42 Josef Cerny, CSR.
☐ 43 Vladimir Dzurilla, CSR.
☐ 44 Richard Farda, CSR.
☐ 45 Julius Haas, CSR.
☐ 46 Ivan Hlinka, CSR.
☐ 47 Jaroslav Holik, CSR.
☐ 48 Jiri Holik, CSR.
☐ 49 Josef Horesovsky, CSR.
☐ 50 Jan Hrbaty, CSR.
☐ 51 Jiri Kochta, CSR.
☐ 52 Miroslav Lacky, CSR.
☐ 53 Oldrich Machac, CSR.
☐ 54 Vladislav Martinec, CSR.
☐ 55 Vaclav Nedomansky, CSR.
☐ 56 Frantisek Pospisil, CSR.
☐ 57 Stanislav Pryl, CSR.
☐ 58 Frantisek Sevcik, CSR.
☐ 59 Jan Suchy, CSR.
☐ 60 Lubomir Ujvary, CSR.
☐ 61 Matti Keinonen, Fin.
☐ 62 VeliPekka Ketola, Fin.
☐ 63 Vaino Kolkka, Fin.
☐ 64 Ilpo Koskela, Fin.
☐ 65 Pekka Leimu, Fin.
☐ 66 Seppo Lindstrom, Fin.
☐ 67 Harri Linnonmaa, Fin.
☐ 68 Pekka Marjamaki, Fin.
☐ 69 Lauri Mononen, Fin.
☐ 70 Matti Murto, Fin.
☐ 71 Lasse Oksanen, Fin.
☐ 72 Lalli Partinen, Fin.
☐ 73 Esa Peltonen, Fin.
☐ 74 Jorma Peltonen, Fin.
☐ 75 Juha Rantasila, Fin.
☐ 76 Heikki Riihiranta, Fin.
☐ 77 Juhani Tamminen, Fin.
☐ 78 Jorma Valtonen, Fin.
☐ 79 Jorma Vehmanen, Fin.
☐ 80 Urpo Ylonen, Fin.
☐ 81 Rolf Bielas, DDR.
☐ 82 Frank Braun, DDR.
☐ 83 Dieter Dewitz, DDR.
☐ 84 Lothar Fuchs, DDR.
☐ 85 Bernd Hiller, DDR.
☐ 86 Klaus Hirche, DDR.
☐ 87 Reinhard Karger, DDR.
☐ 88 Bernd Karrenbauer, DDR.
☐ 89 Hartmut Nickel, DDR.
☐ 90 Rudiger Noack, DDR.
☐ 91 Helmut Novy, DDR.
☐ 92 Rainer Patschinski, DDR.
☐ 93 Dietmar Peters, DDR.
☐ 94 Wolfgang Plotka, DDR.
☐ 95 Peter Prusa, DDR.
☐ 96 Dieter Purschel, DDR.
☐ 97 Wilfried Rohrbach, DDR.
☐ 98 Dieter Rohl, DDR.
☐ 99 Peter Slapke, DDR.
☐ 100 Joachim Ziesche, DDR.
☐ 101 Juhani Bostrom, HIFK
☐ 102 Henrik Granholm, HIFK
☐ 103 Matti Harju, HIFK
☐ 104 Kimmo Heino, HIFK
☐ 105 Esa Isaksson, HIFK
☐ 106 Juhani Jylha, HIFK
☐ 107 Heikki Jarn, HIFK
☐ 108 Mauri Kaukokari, HIFK
☐ 109 Vaino Kolkka, HIFK
☐ 110 Harri Linnonmaa, HIFK
☐ 111 Matti Murto, HIFK
☐ 112 Lalli Partinen, HIFK
☐ 113 Juha Rantasila, HIFK
☐ 114 Heikki Riihiranta, HIFK
☐ 115 Jorma Rikala, HIFK
☐ 116 Jorma Thusberg, HIFK
☐ 117 Matti Vaisanen, HIFK
☐ 118 Sakari Ahlberg, Ilves
☐ 119 Jorma Aro, Ilves
☐ 120 Esko Eriksson, Ilves
☐ 121 Markku Hakanen, Ilves
☐ 122 Matti Hakanen, Ilves
☐ 123 Reijo Hakanen, Ilves
☐ 124 Pentti Hartin, Ilves
☐ 125 Timo Hirsimaki, Ilves
☐ 126 Jorma Kallio, Ilves
☐ 127 Pekka Kuusisto, Ilves
☐ 128 Juhani Lahtinen, Ilves
☐ 129 Timo Lahtinen, Ilves
☐ 130 Pekka Leimu, Ilves
☐ 131 Jukka Mattila, Ilves
☐ 132 Esko Makinen, Ilves
☐ 133 Lasse Oksanen, Ilves
☐ 134 Kari Palooja, Ilves
☐ 135 Jorma Peltonen, Ilves
☐ 136 Ali Saadetdin, Ilves
☐ 137 Timo Saari, Ilves
☐ 138 Heikki Hurme, Turun Toverit
☐ 139 Matti Jakonen, Turun Toverit
☐ 140 Kari Johansson, Turun Toverit
☐ 141 Keijo Jarvinen, Turun Toverit
☐ 142 Reijo Leppanen, Turun Toverit
☐ 143 Seppo Lindstrom, Turun Toverit
☐ 144 Hannu Luojola, Turun Toverit
☐ 145 Hannu Niittoaho, Turun Toverit
☐ 146 Reijo Paksal, Turun Toverit
☐ 147 Seppo Parikka, Turun Toverit
☐ 148 Jarmo Rantanen, Turun Toverit
☐ 149 Martti Salonen, Turun Toverit
☐ 150 Voitto Soini, Turun Toverit
☐ 151 Kari Torkkel, Turun Toverit
☐ 152 Risto Vainio, Turun Toverit
☐ 153 Pertti Vihanto, Turun Toverit
☐ 154 Urpo Ylonen, Turun Toverit
☐ 155 Rauno Heinonen, Turun Palloseura
☐ 156 Lauri Jamsen, Turun Palloseura
☐ 157 Lasse Kiili, Turun Palloseura
☐ 158 Hannu Koivunen, Turun Palloseura
☐ 159 Jarmo Koivunen, Turun Palloseura
☐ 160 Pertti Kuismanen, Turun Palloseura
☐ 161 Pekka Lahtela, Turun Palloseura
☐ 162 Harry Luoto, Turun Palloseura
☐ 163 Jaakko Marttinen, Turun Palloseura
☐ 164 Timo Nummelin, Turun Palloseura
☐ 165 Rauli Ottila, Turun Palloseura
☐ 166 Matti Rautee, Turun Palloseura
☐ 167 Pekka Rautee, Turun Palloseura
☐ 168 Jouni Samuli, Turun Palloseura
☐ 169 Rauli Tammelin, Turun Palloseura
☐ 170 Juhani Tamminen, Turun Palloseura
☐ 171 Kari Varjanne, Turun Palloseura
☐ 172 Pertti Ahokas, Jokerit
☐ 173 Pertti Hiirros, Jokerit
☐ 174 Eero Holopainen, Jokerit
☐ 175 VeliPekka Ketola, Jokerit
☐ 176 Kari Kinnunen, Jokerit
☐ 177 Ilpo Koskela, Jokerit
☐ 178 Osmo Kuusisto, Jokerit
☐ 179 Timo Kyntola, Jokerit
☐ 180 Henry Leppa, Jokerit
☐ 181 Erkki Mononen, Jokerit
☐ 182 Lauri Mononen, Jokerit
☐ 183 Pertti Nurmi, Jokerit
☐ 184 Antti Perttula, Jokerit
☐ 185 Seppo Peraoja, Jokerit
☐ 186 Timo Relas, Jokerit
☐ 187 Alpo Suhonen, Jokerit
☐ 188 Timo Turunen, Jokerit
☐ 189 Tapio Flinck, Assat
☐ 190 Jaakko Honkanen, Assat
☐ 191 Antti Heikkila, Assat
☐ 192 Matti Jansson, Assat
☐ 193 Esa Kari, Assat
☐ 194 Raimo Kilpio, Assat
☐ 195 Tapio Koskinen, Assat
☐ 196 Kaj Matalamaki, Assat
☐ 197 Ilkka Mesikammen, Assat
☐ 198 Pertti Makela, Assat
☐ 199 Jaakko Nurminen, Assat
☐ 200 Pekka Rautakallio, Assat
☐ 201 Tapio Rautalammi, Assat
☐ 202 Markku Riihimaki, Assat
☐ 203 Matti Salmi, Assat
☐ 204 KariPekka Toivonen, Assat
☐ 205 Jorma Valtonen, Assat
☐ 206 Anto Virtanen, Assat
☐ 207 Erkki Vakiparta, Assat
☐ 208 Pertti Ansakorpi, Tappara
☐ 209 Pertti Koivulahti, Tappara
☐ 210 Ilpo Kuisma, Tappara
☐ 211 Harri Lappalainen, Tappara
☐ 212 Pekka Marjamaki, Tappara
☐ 213 Mikko Mynttinen, Tappara
☐ 214 Kari Makinen, Tappara
☐ 215 Pekka Makinen, Tappara
☐ 216 Seppo Makinen, Tappara
☐ 217 Keijo Mannisto, Tappara
☐ 218 Jorma Oksala, Tappara
☐ 219 Matti Peltonen, Tappara
☐ 220 Tuomo Rautiainen, Tappara
☐ 221 Lauri Salomaa, Tappara
☐ 222 Risto Seesvuori, Tappara
☐ 223 Jorma Siitarinen, Tappara
☐ 224 Teemu Sistonen, Tappara
☐ 225 Lasse Aaltonen, Rauman Lukko
☐ 226 Mikko Erholm, Rauman Lukko
☐ 227 Jukka Haapala, Rauman Lukko
☐ 228 Veikko Ihalainen, Rauman Lukko
☐ 229 Matti Keinonen, Rauman Lukko
☐ 230 Tapani Koskimaki, Rauman Lukko
☐ 231 Arto Laine, Rauman Lukko
☐ 232 Hannu Lunden, Rauman Lukko
☐ 233 Pentti Rautalin, Rauman Lukko
☐ 234 Paavo Riekkinen, Rauman Lukko
☐ 235 Kai Rosvall, Rauman Lukko
☐ 236 Matti Saurio, Rauman Lukko
☐ 237 Jukka Savunen, Rauman Lukko
☐ 238 Hannu Siivonen, Rauman Lukko
☐ 239 Helkko Stenvall, Rauman Lukko
☐ 240 Jorma Vehmanen, Rauman Lukko
☐ 241 Hannu Haapalainen, Tampereen
☐ 242 Timo Jarvinen, Tampereen
☐ 243 Heikki Keinonen, Tampereen
☐ 244 Heimo Keinonen, Tampereen
☐ 245 Rauno Lehtio, Tampereen
☐ 246 Tapio Nummela, Tampereen
☐ 247 Seppo Nurmi, Tampereen
☐ 248 Markku Pulli, Tampereen
☐ 249 Esko Rantanen, Tampereen
☐ 250 Juhani Ruohonen, Tampereen
☐ 251 Mikko Raikkonen, Tampereen
☐ 252 Jorma Saarikorpi, Tampereen
☐ 253 Veikko Savolainen, Tampereen
☐ 254 Leo Seppanen, Tampereen
☐ 255 Pertti Sihvonen, Tampereen
☐ 256 Pekka Uitus, Tampereen
☐ 257 Jorma Vilen, Tampereen
☐ 258 Tapio Virhimo, Tampereen
☐ 259 Jaakko Koikkalainen, Sapko
☐ 260 Jorma Muikku, Sapko
☐ 261 Ossi Oksala, Sapko
☐ 262 Pekka Parikka, Sapko
☐ 263 Pentti Pennanen, Sapko
☐ 264 Jussi Piuhola, Sapko
☐ 265 Seppo Repo, Sapko
☐ 266 Erkki Rasanen, Sapko
☐ 267 Juhani Sodervik, Sapko
☐ 268 Heikki Tirkkonen, Sapko
☐ 269 Paavo Tirkkonen, Sapko
☐ 270 Timo Tuomainen, Sapko
☐ 271 Raimo Turkulainen, Sapko
☐ 272 Jyrki Turunen, Sapko
☐ 273 Martti Turunen, Sapko
☐ 274 Timo Viskari, Sapko
☐ 275 Antero Vaatamoinen, Sapko
☐ 276 Juhani Aaltonen, HJK.
☐ 277 Matti Ahvenharju, HJK.
☐ 278 Hannu Auvinen, HJK.
☐ 279 Jorma Borgstrom, HJK.
☐ 280 Seppo Laakkio, HJK.
☐ 281 Jarmo Laukkanen, HJK.
☐ 282 Hannu Lindberg, HJK.
☐ 283 Reijo Myyrylainen, HJK.
☐ 284 Raimo Maattanen, HJK.
☐ 285 Esa Peltonen, HJK.
☐ 286 Keijo Puhakka, HJK.
☐ 287 Antti Ravi, HJK.
☐ 288 Erkki Suni, HJK.
☐ 289 Henrik Wahl, HJK.
☐ 290 Stig Wetzell, HJK.
☐ 291 Olli Viilma, HJK.
☐ 292 Esa Willberg, HJK.
☐ 293 Kauko Fomin, Kiekko 67
☐ 294 Risto Forss, Kiekko 67
☐ 295 Rauno Karlsson, Kiekko 67
☐ 296 Jarmo Kiprusoff, Kiekko 67
☐ 297 Matti Koivunen, Kiekko 67
☐ 298 Timo Kokkonen, Kiekko 67
☐ 299 Timo Lehtonen, Kiekko 67
☐ 300 Kalevi Leppanen, Kiekko 67
☐ 301 Hans Martin, Kiekko 67
☐ 302 Timo Nurminen, Kiekko 67
☐ 303 Jari Rosberg, Kiekko 67
☐ 304 Veijo Saarinen, Kiekko 67
☐ 305 Simo Suoknuuti, Kiekko 67
☐ 306 Veikko Suominen, Kiekko 67
☐ 307 Seppo Wikstrom, Kiekko 67
☐ 308 JuhaPekka Aho, Ilves Jrs.
☐ 309 Seppo Aro, Ilves Jrs.
☐ 310 Kari Jokinen, Ilves Jrs.
☐ 311 Pekka Karhunen, Ilves Jrs.
☐ 312 Pertti Kettunen, Ilves Jrs.
☐ 313 Lauri Kosonen, Ilves Jrs.
☐ 314 Jyrki Kahonen, Ilves Jrs.
☐ 315 Marko Lepaus, Ilves Jrs.
☐ 316 Matti Lisko, Ilves Jrs.
☐ 317 Marko Niemi, Ilves Jrs.
☐ 318 Hannu Pohja, Ilves Jrs.
☐ 319 Jarmo Ronkainen, Ilves Jrs.
☐ 320 Mikko Silvasti, Ilves Jrs.
☐ 321 Jari Suokas, Ilves Jrs.
☐ 322 Kimmo Turunen, Ilves Jrs.
☐ 323 Jari Viitala, Ilves Jrs.
☐ 324 Mikko Vilonen, Ilves Jrs.
☐ 325 Jaakko Virtanen, Ilves Jrs.
☐ 326 Jarmo Viteli, Ilves Jrs.
☐ 327 Kari Anttila, Assat Pori Jrs.
☐ 328 Harri Hiltunen, Assat Pori Jrs.
☐ 329 Arto Javanainen, Assat Pori Jrs.
☐ 330 Tapio Jylhasaari, Assat Pori Jrs.
☐ 331 Jorma Korkeamaki, Assat Pori Jrs.
☐ 332 Kari Koskinen, Assat Pori Jrs.
☐ 333 Martti Lunden, Assat Pori Jrs.
☐ 334 Petri Niskanen, Assat Pori Jrs.
☐ 335 Jari Nystrom, Assat Pori Jrs.
☐ 336 Ari Peltola, Assat Pori Jrs.
☐ 337 Jari Peltonen, Assat Pori Jrs.
☐ 338 Petri Salminen, Assat Pori Jrs.
☐ 339 Juha Salo, Assat Pori Jrs.
☐ 340 Esa Salosensaari, Assat Pori Jrs.
☐ 341 Rauli Siimes, Assat Pori Jrs.
☐ 342 Esa Suvanto, Assat Pori Jrs.
☐ 343 Jukka Tuli, Assat Pori Jrs.
☐ 344 Jukka Virtanen, Assat Pori Jrs.
☐ 345 Pertti Vaisanen, Assat Pori Jrs.
☐ 346 Timo Hyrsky, Turun P. Jrs.
☐ 347 Jorma Jokinen, Turun P. Jrs.

☐ 338 Jari Kokkola, Turun P. Jrs.
☐ 349 Pentti Kuosmanen, Turun P. Jrs.
☐ 350 Pekka Laukkanen, Turun P. Jrs.
☐ 351 Tom Lund, Turun P. Jrs.
☐ 352 Jouni Niemela, Turun P. Jrs.
☐ 353 Kari Rantanen, Turun P. Jrs.
☐ 354 Pekka Reimola, Turun P. Jrs.
☐ 355 Teijo Salminen, Turun P. Jrs.
☐ 356 VeliMatti Tammi, Turun P. Jrs.
☐ 357 Juha Tamminen, Turun P. Jrs.
☐ 358 Risto Vaihinen, Turun P. Jrs.
☐ 359 Antti Vanne, Turun P. Jrs.
☐ 360 Ari Vanne, Turun P. Jrs.
☐ 361 Hannu Vehmanen, Turun P. Jrs.
☐ 362 Heikki Virta, Turun P. Jrs.
☐ 363 Hannu Virtanen, Turun P. Jrs.
☐ 364 Jyrki Valimaki, Turun P. Jrs.
☐ 365 Pekka Anttila, Oulun Jrs.
☐ 366 Jouni Honkanen, Oulun Jrs.
☐ 367 Kari Jalonen, Oulun Jrs.
☐ 368 Ari Kaikkonen, Oulun Jrs.
☐ 369 Timo Kajula, Oulun Jrs.
☐ 370 Jorma Kinnunen, Oulun Jrs.
☐ 371 Esa Kontio, Oulun Jrs.
☐ 372 Tapio Kuiri, Oulun Jrs.
☐ 373 Pekka Kyllonen, Oulun Jrs.
☐ 374 Ari Mustaniemi, Oulun Jrs.
☐ 375 Jukka Pajala, Oulun Jrs.
☐ 376 Pentti Perhomaa, Oulun Jrs.
☐ 377 Reijo Raatesalmi, Oulun Jrs.
☐ 378 Markku Ruotsalainen, Oulun Jrs.
☐ 379 Reijo Ruotsalainen, Oulun Jrs.
☐ 380 Jarmo Tauriainen, Oulun Jrs.
☐ 381 Ari Timosaari, Oulun Jrs.
☐ 382 Pekka Tuomisto, Oulun Jrs.
☐ 383 Timo Vahanen, Oulun Jrs.
☐ 384 Sakari Valiharju, Oulun Jrs.

1970 - 71 O-PEE-CHEE

"I remember the spotlights and those silly background colours. Anybody who collected that set remembers the backgrounds. I remember the Park and Perreault cards were important. I loved Park and I remember the hype around Perreault. I had been collecting Batman cards, but when I couldn't get them anymore, I switched to the '70 O-Pee-Chee baseball and the '70-71 O-Pee-Chee hockey." – Everett Shade, Right Way Sports, Winnipeg, Manitoba.

These cards measure the standard 2 1/2" x 3 1/2".

Complete Set (264 cards):	**950**	**1,900**
Common Player:	**2.50**	**5.00**
O-Pee-Chee	**EX**	**NM-MT**
☐ 1 Gerry Cheevers (G), Bost.	10.00	30.00
☐ 2 John Bucyk, Bost.	4.00	8.00
☐ 3 Bobby Orr, Bost.	80.00	165.00
☐ 4 Don Awrey, Bost.	2.50	5.00
☐ 5 Fred Stanfield, Bost.	2.50	5.00
☐ 6 John McKenzie, Bost.	2.50	5.00
☐ **7 Wayne Cashman, Bost. RC**	**8.00**	**16.00**
☐ 8 Ken Hodge, Bost.	2.50	5.00
☐ 9 Wayne Carleton, Bost.	2.50	5.00
☐ **10 Garnet Bailey, Bost. RC**	**5.00**	**10.00**
☐ 11 Phil Esposito, Bost.	15.00	30.00
☐ 12 Lou Angotti, Chic.	2.50	5.00
☐ 13 Jim Pappin, Chic.	2.50	5.00
☐ 14 Dennis Hull, Chic.	2.50	5.00
☐ 15 Bobby Hull, Chic.	28.00	55.00
☐ 16 Doug Mohns, Chic.	2.50	5.00
☐ 17 Pat Stapleton, Chic.	2.50	5.00
☐ 18 Pit Martin, Chic.	2.50	5.00
☐ 19 Eric Nesterenko, Chic.	2.50	5.00
☐ 20 Stan Mikita, Chic.	12.00	25.00
☐ 21 Roy Edwards (G), Detr.	3.50	7.00
☐ 22 Frank Mahovlich, Detr.	7.50	15.00
☐ 23 Ron Harris, Detr.	2.50	5.00
☐ 24 Checklist	90.00	175.00
☐ 25 Pete Stemkowski, Detr.	2.50	5.00
☐ 26 Garry Unger, Detr.	2.50	5.00
☐ 27 Bruce MacGregor, Detr.	2.50	5.00
☐ 28 Larry Jeffrey, Detr.	2.50	5.00
☐ 29 Gordie Howe, Detr.	50.00	95.00
☐ 30 Billy Dea, Detr.	2.50	5.00
☐ 31 Denis DeJordy (G), LosA.	3.50	7.00
☐ 32 Matt Ravlich, LosA.	2.50	5.00
☐ 33 Dave Amadio, LosA.	2.50	5.00
☐ 34 Gilles Marotte, LosA.	2.50	5.00
☐ 35 Eddie Shack, LosA.	6.00	12.00
☐ 36 Bob Pulford, LosA.	3.50	7.00
☐ 37 Ross Lonsberry, LosA.	2.50	5.00
☐ 38 Gord Labossiere, LosA.	2.50	5.00
☐ 39 Eddie Joyal, LosA.	2.50	5.00
☐ 40 Gump Worsley (G), Minn.	7.00	14.00
☐ 41 Bob McCord, Minn.	2.50	5.00
☐ 42 Leo Boivin, Minn.	3.50	7.00
☐ **43 Tom Reid, Minn. RC**	**4.00**	**8.00**
☐ 44 Charlie Burns, Minn.	2.50	5.00
☐ 45 Bob Barlow, Minn.	2.50	5.00
☐ 46 Bill Goldsworthy, Minn.	2.50	5.00
☐ 47 Danny Grant, Minn.	2.50	5.00
☐ **48 Norm Beaudin, Minn. RC**	**4.00**	**8.00**
☐ 49 Rogatien Vachon (G), Mont.	6.50	12.00
☐ 50 Yvan Cournoyer, Mont.	6.00	12.00
☐ 51 Serge Savard, Mont.	6.00	12.00
☐ 52 Jacques Laperrière, Mont.	3.50	7.00
☐ 53 Terry Harper, Mont.	2.50	5.00
☐ 54 Ralph Backstrom, Mont.	2.50	5.00
☐ 55 Jean Béliveau, Mont.	10.00	20.00
☐ 56 Claude Larose, Mont.	2.50	5.00
☐ 57 Jacques Lemaire, Mont.	6.00	12.00
☐ 58 Pete Mahovlich, Mont.	2.50	5.00
☐ 59 Tim Horton, NYRa.	9.00	18.00
☐ 60 Bob Nevin, NYRa.	2.50	5.00
☐ 61 Dave Balon, NYRa.	2.50	5.00
☐ 62 Vic Hadfield, NYRa.	2.50	5.00
☐ 63 Rod Gilbert, NYRa.	5.00	10.00
☐ 64 Ron Stewart, NYRa.	2.50	5.00
☐ 65 Ted Irvine, NYRa.	2.50	5.00
☐ 66 Arnie Brown, NYRa.	2.50	5.00
☐ **67 Brad Park, NYRa. RC**	**30.00**	**60.00**
☐ 68 Ed Giacomin (G), NYRa.	7.00	14.00
☐ 69 Gary Smith (G), Cali.	3.50	7.00
☐ 70 Carol Vadnais, Cali.	2.50	5.00
☐ 71 Doug Roberts, Cali.	2.50	5.00
☐ 72 Harry Howell, Cali.	3.50	7.00
☐ 73 Joe Szura, Cali.	2.50	5.00
☐ 74 Mike Laughton, Cali.	2.50	5.00
☐ 75 Gary Jarrett, Cali.	2.50	5.00
☐ 76 Bill Hicke, Cali.	2.50	5.00
☐ **77 Paul Andrea, Phil. RC**	**4.00**	**8.00**
☐ 78 Bernie Parent (G), Phil.	18.00	35.00
☐ 79 Joe Watson, Phil.	2.50	5.00
☐ 80 Ed Van Impe, Phil.	2.50	5.00
☐ 81 Larry Hillman, Phil.	2.50	5.00
☐ 82 George Swarbrick, Phil.	2.50	5.00
☐ 83 Bill Sutherland, SLou.	2.50	5.00
☐ 84 André Lacroix, Pitt.	2.50	5.00
☐ 85 Gary Dornhoefer, Pitt.	2.50	5.00
☐ 86 Jean Guy Gendron, Pitt.	2.50	5.00
☐ **87 Al Smith (G), Pitt. RC**	**4.00**	**8.00**
☐ 88 Bob Woytowich, Pitt.	2.50	5.00
☐ 89 Duane Rupp, Pitt.	2.50	5.00
☐ 90 Jim Morrison, Pitt.	2.50	5.00
☐ 91 Ron Schock, Pitt.	2.50	5.00
☐ 92 Ken Schinkel, Pitt.	2.50	5.00
☐ 93 Keith McCreary, Pitt.	2.50	5.00
☐ 94 Bryan Hextall, Pitt.	2.50	5.00
☐ **95 Wayne Hicks, Jr., Pitt. RC**	**4.00**	**8.00**
☐ 96 Gary Sabourin, SLou.	2.50	5.00
☐ **97 Ernie Wakely (G), SLou. RC**	**4.00**	**8.00**
☐ 98 Bob Wall, SLou.	2.50	5.00
☐ 99 Barclay Plage, SLou.	2.50	5.00
☐ 100 Jean-Guy Talbot, SLou.	2.50	5.00
☐ 101 Gary Veneruzzo, SLou.	2.50	5.00
☐ 102 Tim Ecclestone, SLou.	2.50	5.00
☐ 103 Red Berenson, SLou.	2.50	5.00
☐ 104 Larry Keenan, SLou.	2.50	5.00
☐ 105 Bruce Gamble (G), Toro.	3.50	7.00
☐ 106 Jim Dorey, Toro.	2.50	5.00
☐ **107 Mike Pelyk, Toro. RC**	**4.00**	**8.00**
☐ 108 Rick Ley, Toro.	2.50	5.00
☐ 109 Mike Walton, Toro.	2.50	5.00
☐ 110 Norm Ullman, Toro.	4.00	8.00
☐ 111 Brit Selby, SLou. (Traded to)	3.50	7.00
☐ 111 Brit Selby, SLou. (No Trade)	18.00	35.00
☐ 112 Garry Monahan, Toro.	2.50	5.00
☐ 113 George Armstrong, Toro.	3.50	7.00
☐ 114 Gary Doak, Vanc.	2.50	5.00
☐ **115 Darryl Sly, Vanc. RC**	**4.00**	**8.00**
☐ 116 Wayne Maki, Vanc.	2.50	5.00
☐ 117 Orland Kurtenbach, Vanc.	2.50	5.00
☐ 118 Murray Hall, Vanc.	2.50	5.00
☐ 119 Marc Reaume, Vanc.	2.50	5.00
☐ 120 Pat Quinn, Vanc.	3.50	7.00
☐ 121 André Boudrias, Vanc.	2.50	5.00
☐ 122 Poul Popiel, Vanc.	2.50	5.00
☐ 123 Paul Terbenche, Buff.	2.50	5.00
☐ 124 Howie Menard, Buff.	2.50	5.00
☐ **125 Gerry Meehan, Buff. RC**	**4.00**	**8.00**
☐ 126 Skip Krake, Buff.	2.50	5.00
☐ 127 Phil Goyette, Buff.	2.50	5.00
☐ 128 Reggie Fleming, Buff.	2.50	5.00
☐ 129 Don Marshall, Buff.	2.50	5.00
☐ **130 Bill Inglis, Buff. RC**	**4.00**	**8.00**
☐ **131 Gilbert Perreault, Buff. RC**	**60.00**	**120.00**
☐ 132 Checklist 2	90.00	175.00
☐ 133 Eddie Johnston (G), Bost.	3.50	7.00
☐ 134 Ted Green, Bost.	2.50	5.00
☐ **135 Rick Smith, Bost. RC**	**4.00**	**8.00**
☐ 136 Derek Sanderson, Bost.	9.00	18.00
☐ 137 Dallas Smith, Bost.	2.50	5.00
☐ **138 Don Marcotte, Bost. RC**	**4.00**	**8.00**
☐ 139 Ed Westfall, Bost.	2.50	5.00
☐ 140 Floyd Smith, Buff.	2.50	5.00
☐ **141 Randy Wyrozub, Buff. RC**	**4.00**	**8.00**
☐ **142 Cliff Schmautz, Buff. RC**	**4.00**	**8.00**
☐ 143 Mike McMahon, Buff.	2.50	5.00
☐ 144 Jim Watson, Buff.	2.50	5.00
☐ 145 Roger Crozier (G), Buff.	3.50	7.00
☐ 146 Tracy Pratt, Buff.	2.50	5.00
☐ **147 Cliff Koroll, Chic. RC**	**4.00**	**8.00**
☐ **148 Gerry Pinder, Chic. RC**	**4.00**	**8.00**
☐ 149 Chico Maki, Chic.	2.50	5.00
☐ 150 Doug Jarrett, Chic.	2.50	5.00
☐ **151 Keith Magnuson, Chic. RC**	**5.00**	**10.00**
☐ 152 Gerry Desjardins (G), Chic.	3.50	7.00
☐ 153 Tony Esposito (G), Chic.	35.00	65.00
☐ 154 Gary Bergman, Detr.	2.50	5.00
☐ **155 Tom Webster, Detr. RC**	**4.00**	**8.00**
☐ 156 Dale Rolfe, Detr.	2.50	5.00
☐ 157 Alex Delvecchio, Detr.	5.00	10.00
☐ 158 Nick Libett, Detr.	2.50	5.00
☐ 159 Wayne Connelly, Detr.	2.50	5.00
☐ **160 Mike Byers, LosA. RC**	**4.00**	**8.00**
☐ 161 Bill Flett, LosA.	2.50	5.00
☐ 162 Larry Mickey, LosA.	2.50	5.00
☐ 163 Noel Price, LosA.	2.50	5.00
☐ 164 Larry Cahan, LosA.	2.50	5.00
☐ **165 Jack Norris (G), LosA. RC**	**4.00**	**8.00**
☐ 166 Ted Harris, Minn.	2.50	5.00
☐ 167 Murray Oliver, Minn.	2.50	5.00
☐ 168 J.P. Parise, Minn.	2.50	5.00
☐ 169 Tom Williams, Minn.	2.50	5.00
☐ 170 Bobby Rousseau, Minn.	2.50	5.00
☐ **171 Jude Drouin, Minn. RC**	**4.00**	**8.00**
☐ **172 Walt McKechnie, Minn. RC**	**4.00**	**8.00**
☐ 173 Césare Maniago (G), Minn.	3.50	7.00
☐ **174 Réjean Houle, Mont. RC**	**6.00**	**12.00**
☐ 175 Mickey Redmond, Mont. (Traded to)	4.50	8.50
☐ 175 Mickey Redmond, Mont. (No trade)	7.00	14.00
☐ 176 Henri Richard, Mont.	6.00	12.00
☐ **177 Guy Lapointe, Mont. RC**	**12.00**	**25.00**
☐ 178 J.C. Tremblay, Mont.	2.50	5.00
☐ **179 Marc Tardif, Mont. RC**	**5.00**	**10.00**
☐ 180 Walt Tkaczuk, NYRa.	2.50	5.00
☐ 181 Jean Ratelle, NYRa.	4.00	8.00
☐ 182 Pete Stemkowski, NYRa.	2.50	5.00
☐ 183 Gilles Villemure (G), NYRa.	3.50	7.00
☐ 184 Rod Seiling, NYRa.	2.50	5.00
☐ 185 Jim Neilson, NYRa.	2.50	5.00
☐ 186 Dennis Hextall, Cali.	2.50	5.00
☐ 187 Gerry Ehman, Cali.	2.50	5.00
☐ 188 Bert Marshall, Cali.	2.50	5.00
☐ **189 Gary Croteau, Cali. RC**	**4.00**	**8.00**
☐ 190 Ted Hampson, Cali.	2.50	5.00
☐ 191 Earl Ingarfield, Cali.	2.50	5.00
☐ 192 Dick Mattiussi, Cali.	2.50	5.00
☐ 193 Earl Heiskala, Phil.	2.50	5.00
☐ 194 Simon Nolet, Phil.	2.50	5.00
☐ **195 Bobby Clarke, Phil. RC**	**85.00**	**170.00**
☐ 196 Garry Peters, Phil.	2.50	5.00
☐ **197 Lew Morrison, Phil. RC**	**4.00**	**8.00**
☐ 198 Wayne Hillman, Phil.	2.50	5.00
☐ 199 Doug Favell (G), Phil.	3.50	7.00
☐ 200 Les Binkley (G), Pitt.	3.50	7.00
☐ 201 Dean Prentice, Pitt.	2.50	5.00
☐ 202 Jean Pronovost, Pitt.	2.50	5.00
☐ 203 Wally Boyer, Pitt.	2.50	5.00
☐ 204 Bryan Watson, Pitt.	2.50	5.00
☐ 205 Glen Sather, Pitt.	3.50	7.00
☐ 206 Lowell MacDonald, Pitt.	2.50	5.00
☐ 207 Andy Bathgate, Pitt.	3.50	7.00
☐ 208 Val Fonteyne, Pitt.	2.50	5.00
☐ **209 Jim Lorentz, SLou. RC**	**4.00**	**8.00**
☐ 210 Glenn Hall (G), SLou.	6.50	12.00
☐ 211 Bob Plager, SLou.	2.50	5.00
☐ 212 Noel Picard, SLou.	2.50	5.00
☐ 213 Jim Roberts, SLou.	2.50	5.00
☐ 214 Frank St. Marseille, SLou.	2.50	5.00
☐ 215 Ab McDonald, SLou.	2.50	5.00
☐ **216 Brian Glennie, Toro. RC**	**4.00**	**8.00**
☐ 217 Paul Henderson, Toro.	3.50	7.00
☐ **218 Darryl Sittler, Toro. RC**	**70.00**	**135.00**
☐ 219 Dave Keon, Toro.	4.00	8.00
☐ **220 Jim Harrison, Toro. RC**	**4.00**	**8.00**
☐ 221 Ron Ellis, Toro.	2.50	5.00
☐ 222 Jacques Plante (G), Toro.	18.00	35.00
☐ 223 Bob Baun, Toro.	2.50	5.00
☐ **224 George Gardner (G), Vanc. RC**	**5.00**	**10.00**
☐ **225 Dale Tallon, Vanc. RC**	**4.00**	**8.00**
☐ **226 Rosaire Paiement, Vanc. RC**	**4.00**	**8.00**
☐ **227 Mike Corrigan, Vanc. RC**	**4.00**	**8.00**
☐ 228 Ray Cullen, Vanc.	2.50	5.00
☐ 229 Charlie Hodge (G), Vanc.	3.50	7.00
☐ 230 Len Lunde, Vanc.	2.50	5.00
☐ 231 Terry Sawchuk (G)	35.00	65.00
☐ 232 Bruins: Stanley Cup Champions	8.00	16.00
☐ 233 Hodge, Esposito, Cashman	12.00	25.00
☐ 234 AS: Tony Esposito (G), Chic.	15.00	30.00
☐ 235 AS: Bobby Hull, Chic.	14.00	28.00
☐ 236 AS: Bobby Orr, Bost.	35.00	70.00
☐ 237 AS: Phil Esposito, Bost.	9.00	18.00
☐ 238 AS: Gordie Howe, Detr.	25.00	45.00
☐ 239 AS: Brad Park, NYRa.	12.00	24.00
☐ 240 AS: Stan Mikita, Chic.	6.50	12.00
☐ 241 AS: John McKenzie, Bost.	2.50	5.00
☐ 242 AS: Frank Mahovlich, Detr.	3.75	7.50
☐ 243 AS: Carl Brewer, Detr.	2.50	5.00
☐ 244 AS: Ed Giacomin (G), NYRa.	4.50	9.00
☐ 245 AS: J. Laperrière, Mont.,		
Err. (Perreault Rookie)	3.50	7.00
☐ 245 Jacques Laperrière, Mont.	3.50	7.00
☐ 246 AW: Bobby Orr	35.00	70.00
☐ 247 AW: Tony Esposito	15.00	30.00
☐ 248 AW: Bobby Orr, Err. (no overprint)	35.00	70.00
☐ 248 AW: Bobby Orr, Corrected	35.00	70.00
☐ 249 AW: Bobby Orr	35.00	70.00
☐ 250 AW: Tony Esposito	15.00	30.00
☐ 251 AW: Phil Goyette	3.50	7.00
☐ 252 AW: Bobby Orr	35.00	70.00
☐ 253 AW: Pit Martin	3.50	7.00
☐ 254 The Stanley Cup	10.00	20.00
☐ 255 The Prince of Wales Trophy	3.50	7.00
☐ 256 The Conn Smythe Trophy	3.50	7.00
☐ 257 The James Norris Memorial Trophy	3.50	7.00
☐ 258 The Calder Memorial Trophy	3.50	7.00
☐ 259 The Vezina Trophy	3.50	7.00
☐ 260 The Lady Byng Trophy	3.50	7.00
☐ 261 The Hart Memorial Trophy	3.50	7.00
☐ 262 The Art Ross Trophy	3.50	7.00
☐ 263 The Clarence S. Campbell Bowl	3.50	7.00
☐ 264 John Ferguson	6.00	15.00

DECKLE EDGE

These black & white inserts measure 2 1/4" x 3 1/4".

Insert Set (48 cards):	**175.00**	**375.00**
O-Pee-Chee	**EX**	**NM-MT**
☐ 1 Pat Quinn, Vanc.	2.50	7.50
☐ 2 Eddie Shack, LosA.	4.00	7.50
☐ 3 Eddie Joyal, LosA.	2.00	4.00
☐ 4 Bobby Orr, Bost.	50.00	100.00
☐ 5 Derek Sanderson, Bost.	5.00	10.00
☐ 6 Phil Esposito, Bost.	10.00	20.00
☐ 7 Fred Stanfield, Bost.	2.00	4.00
☐ 8 Bob Woytowich, Pitt.	2.00	4.00
☐ 9 Ron Schock, Pitt.	2.00	4.00
☐ 10 Les Binkley (G), Pitt.	3.00	6.00
☐ 11 Roger Crozier (G), Buff.	4.00	7.50
☐ 12 Reggie Fleming, Buff.	2.00	4.00
☐ 13 Charlie Burns, Minn.	2.00	4.00
☐ 14 Bobby Rousseau, Minn.	2.00	4.00
☐ 15 Leo Boivin, Minn.	4.00	7.50
☐ 16 Garry Unger, Detr.	3.00	6.00
☐ 17 Frank Mahovlich, Detr.	7.50	15.00
☐ 18 Gordie Howe, Detr.	45.00	75.00
☐ 19 Jacques Lemaire, Mont.	6.00	12.00
☐ 20 Jacques Laperrière, Mont.	4.00	7.50
☐ 21 Jean Béliveau, Mont.	11.00	22.00
☐ 22 Rogatien Vachon (G), Mont.	4.00	7.50
☐ 23 Yvan Cournoyer, Mont.	5.00	10.00
☐ 24 Henri Richard, Mont.	6.00	12.00
☐ 25 Red Berenson, SLou.	2.00	4.00
☐ 26 Frank St. Marseille, SLou.	2.00	4.00
☐ 27 Glenn Hall (G), SLou.	7.50	15.00
☐ 28 Gary Sabourin, SLou.	2.00	4.00
☐ 29 Doug Mohns, Chic.	2.00	4.00
☐ 30 Bobby Hull, Chic.	25.00	50.00
☐ 31 Ray Cullen, Vanc.	2.00	4.00
☐ 32 Tony Esposito (G), Chic.	12.00	25.00
☐ 33 Gary Dornhoefer, Phil.	2.00	4.00
☐ 34 Ed Van Impe, Phil.	2.00	4.00
☐ 35 Doug Favell (G), Phil.	3.00	6.00
☐ 36 Carol Vadnais, Cali.	2.00	4.00
☐ 37 Harry Howell, Cali.	4.00	7.50
☐ 38 Bill Hicke, Cali.	2.00	4.00
☐ 39 Rod Gilbert, NYRa.	4.50	8.50
☐ 40 Jean Ratelle, NYRa.	4.50	8.50
☐ 41 Walt Tkaczuk, NYRa.	2.00	4.00
☐ 42 Ed Giacomin (G), NYRa.	5.00	10.00

	EX	NM
43 Brad Park, NYRa.	6.00	12.00
44 Bruce Gamble (G), Toro.	3.00	6.00
45 Orland Kurtenbach, Vanc.	2.00	4.00
46 Ron Ellis, Toro.	2.00	4.00
47 Dave Keon, Toro.	4.50	8.50
48 Norm Ullman, Toro.	4.50	8.50

O-PEE-CHEE STICKER STAMPS

Insert Set (33 cards):	**165.00**	**350.00**
O-Pee-Chee	**EX**	**NM-MT**
Jean Béliveau	15.00	30.00
Red Berenson	2.50	5.00
Wayne Carleton	2.50	5.00
Tim Ecclestone	2.50	5.00
Ron Ellis	2.50	5.00
Phil Esposito	15.00	30.00
Tony Esposito (G)	15.00	30.00
Bill Flett	2.50	5.00
Ed Giacomin (G)	6.00	12.00
Rod Gilbert	5.00	10.00
Danny Grant	2.50	5.00
Bill Hicke	2.50	5.00
Gordie Howe	40.00	75.00
Bobby Hull	25.00	45.00
Earl Ingarfield	2.50	5.00
Eddie Joyal	2.50	5.00
Dave Keon	5.00	10.00
André Lacroix	2.50	5.00
Jacques Laperrière	4.00	7.50
Jacques Lemaire	7.00	14.00
Frank Mahovlich	9.00	18.00
Keith McCreary	2.50	5.00
Stan Mikita	8.00	16.00
Bobby Orr	45.00	90.00
Jean Paul Parise	2.50	5.00
Jean Ratelle	5.00	10.00
Derek Sanderson	4.00	7.50
Frank St. Marseille	2.50	5.00
Ron Schock	2.50	5.00
Garry Unger	4.00	7.50
Carol Vadnais	2.50	5.00
Ed Van Impe	2.50	5.00
Bob Woytowich	2.50	5.00

1970 - 71 POST SHOOTERS

These flat plastic hockey-figures were pulled from cereal boxes and were intended for use as part of a game. Each figure came with a sheet of stickers meant to be applied to the figure. Each figure measure 4 1/2" high.

Complete Set (16 shooters):	**140.00**	**275.00**
Post Cereal	**EX**	**EX-NM**
Johnny Bucyk, NHLPA	11.00	22.00
Ron Ellis, NHLPA	7.50	15.00
Ed Giacomin (G), NHLPA	12.00	25.00
Paul Henderson, NHLPA	9.00	18.00
Ken Hodge, NHLPA	7.50	15.00
Dennis Hull, NHLPA	7.50	15.00
Orland Kurtenbach, NHLPA	7.50	15.00
Jacques Laperriere, NHLPA	10.00	20.00
Jacques Lemaire, NHLPA	11.00	22.00
Frank Mahovlich, NHLPA	12.00	25.00
Peter Mahovlich, NHLPA	7.50	15.00
Bobby Orr, NHLPA	50.00	100.00
Jacques Plante (G), NHLPA	20.00	40.00
Jean Ratelle, NHLPA	11.00	22.00
Dale Tallon, NHLPA	7.50	15.00
J.C. Tremblay, NHLPA	9.00	18.00

1970 - 71 SOVIET STARS

These postcards measure 3 1/2" x 5 3/4".

Complete Set (27 postcards and folder):	**100.00**	**225.00**
Soviet Stars	**EX**	**NM**
Victor Konovalenko (G)	3.50	7.00
Valery Davydov	2.50	5.00
Vladimir Lutchenko	2.50	5.00
Valeri Nikitin	2.50	5.00
Alexander Ragulin	6.00	12.00
Igor Romishevsky	2.50	5.00
Evgeny Paladiev	2.50	5.00
Vyacheslav Starshinov	2.50	5.00
Viktor Polupanov	2.50	5.00
Alexander Maltsev	4.00	8.00
Anatoli Firsov	2.50	5.00
Evgeny Mishakov	2.50	5.00
Boris Mikhailov	7.50	15.00
Valery Vasiliev	5.00	10.00
Alexander Yakushev	7.50	15.00
Vladimir Petrov	4.00	8.00
Valery Kharlamov	15.00	30.00
Vladimir Vikulov	2.50	5.00
Vladimir Shadrin	2.50	5.00
Vladislav Tretiak (G)	50.00	90.00
A. Czepnishev	2.50	5.00
A. Tapasov	2.50	5.00
Team Photo	10.00	20.00
U.S.S.R. vs. C.S.S.R.	4.00	8.00
U.S.S.R. vs. Finland	4.00	8.00
Team Photo	10.00	20.00
Airport shot	4.00	8.00

1970 - 71 TOPPS

These cards measure the standard 2 1/2" x 3 1/2" size.

Complete Set (132 cards):	**250.00**	**500.00**
Common Player:	**1.25**	**2.25**
Topps	**EX**	**NM-MT**
1 Gerry Cheevers (G), Bost.	7.50	22.00
2 John Bucyk, Bost.	2.50	5.00
3 Bobby Orr, Bost.	50.00	100.00
4 Don Awrey, Bost.	1.25	2.25
5 Fred Stanfield, Bost.	1.25	2.25
6 John McKenzie, Bost.	1.25	2.25
7 Wayne Cashman, Bost. RC	**5.50**	**11.00**
8 Ken Hodge, Bost.	1.25	2.25
9 Wayne Carleton, Bost.	1.25	2.25
10 Garnet Bailey, Bost. RC	**2.00**	**4.00**
11 Phil Esposito, Bost.	12.00	24.00
12 Lou Angotti, Chic.	1.25	2.25
13 Jim Pappin, Chic.	1.25	2.25
14 Dennis Hull, Chic.	1.25	2.25
15 Bobby Hull, Chic.	22.00	45.00
16 Doug Mohns, Chic.	1.25	2.25
17 Pat Stapleton, Chic.	1.25	2.25
18 Pit Martin, Chic.	1.25	2.25
19 Eric Nesterenko, Chic.	1.25	2.25
20 Stan Mikita, Chic.	7.50	15.00
21 Roy Edwards (G), Detr.	1.75	3.50
22 Frank Mahovlich, Detr.	4.50	9.00
23 Ron Harris, Detr.	1.25	2.25
24 Bob Baun, Buff.	1.25	2.25
25 Pete Stemkowski, Detr.	1.25	2.25
26 Garry Unger, Detr.	1.75	3.50
27 Bruce MacGregor, Detr.	1.25	2.25
28 Larry Jeffrey, Detr.	1.25	2.25
29 Gordie Howe, Detr.	35.00	65.00
30 Billy Dea, Detr.	1.25	2.25
31 Denis DeJordy (G), LosA.	1.75	3.50
32 Matt Ravlich, LosA.	1.25	2.25
33 Dave Amadio, LosA.	1.25	2.25
34 Gilles Marotte, LosA.	1.25	2.25
35 Eddie Shack, LosA.	3.50	7.00
36 Bob Pulford, LosA.	1.75	3.50
37 Ross Lonsberry, LosA.	1.25	2.25
38 Gord Labossiere, LosA.	1.25	2.25
39 Eddie Joyal, LosA.	1.25	2.25
40 Gump Worsley (G), Minn.	4.00	8.00
41 Bob McCord, Minn.	1.25	2.25
42 Léo Boivin, Minn.	1.75	3.50
43 Tom Reid, Minn. RC	**2.00**	**4.00**
44 Charlie Burns, Minn.	1.25	2.25
45 Bob Barlow, Minn.	1.25	2.25
46 Bill Goldsworthy, Minn.	1.25	2.25
47 Danny Grant, Minn.	1.25	2.25
48 Norm Beaudin, Minn. RC	**2.00**	**4.00**
49 Rogatien Vachon (G), Mont.	4.00	7.50
50 Yvan Cournoyer, Mont.	3.50	7.00
51 Serge Savard, Mont.	4.50	8.50
52 Jacques Laperrière, Mont.	1.75	3.50
53 Terry Harper, Mont.	1.25	2.25
54 Ralph Backstrom, Mont.	1.25	2.25
55 Jean Béliveau, Mont.	7.50	15.00
56 Claude Larose, Mont., Err. (LaRose)	1.25	2.25
57 Jacques Lemaire, Mont.	4.00	8.00
58 Pete Mahovlich, Mont.	1.25	2.25
59 Tim Horton, NYRa.	6.00	12.00
60 Bob Nevin, NYRa.	1.25	2.25
61 Dave Balon, NYRa.	1.25	2.25
62 Vic Hadfield, NYRa.	1.25	2.25
63 Rod Gilbert, NYRa.	3.00	6.00
64 Ron Stewart, NYRa.	1.25	2.25
65 Ted Irvine, NYRa.	1.25	2.25
66 Arnie Brown, NYRa.	1.25	2.25
67 Brad Park, NYRa. RC	**15.00**	**30.00**
68 Ed Giacomin (G), NYRa.	4.50	9.00
69 Gary Smith (G), Cali.	1.75	3.50
70 Carol Vadnais, Cali.	1.25	2.25
71 Doug Roberts, Cali.	1.25	2.25
72 Harry Howell, Cali.	1.75	3.50
73 Joe Szura, Cali.	1.25	2.25
74 Mike Laughton, Cali.	1.25	2.25
75 Gary Jarrett, Cali.	1.25	2.25
76 Bill Hicke, Cali.	1.25	2.25
77 Paul Andrea, Buff. RC	**2.00**	**4.00**
78 Bernie Parent (G), Phil.	10.00	20.00
79 Joe Watson, Phil.	1.25	2.25
80 Ed Van Impe, Phil.	1.25	2.25
81 Larry Hillman, Phil.	1.25	2.25
82 George Swarbrick, Phil.	1.25	2.25
83 Bill Sutherland, SLou.	1.25	2.25
84 André Lacroix, Phil.	1.25	2.25
85 Gary Dornhoefer, Phil.	1.25	2.25
86 Jean-Guy Gendron, Phil.	1.25	2.25
87 Al Smith (G), Pitt. RC	**1.75**	**3.50**
88 Bob Woytowich, Pitt.	1.25	2.25
89 Duane Rupp, Pitt.	1.25	2.25
90 Jim Morrison, Pitt.	1.25	2.25
91 Ron Schock, Pitt.	1.25	2.25
92 Ken Schinkel, Pitt.	1.25	2.25
93 Keith McCreary, Pitt.	1.25	2.25
94 Bryan Hextall, Pitt.	1.25	2.25
95 Wayne Hicks, Jr., Pitt. RC	**2.00**	**4.00**
96 Gary Sabourin, SLou.	1.25	2.25
97 Ernie Wakely (G), SLou. RC	**1.75**	**3.50**
98 Bob Wall, SLou.	1.25	2.25
99 Barclay Plager, SLou.	1.25	2.25
100 Jean-Guy Talbot, SLou.	1.25	2.25
101 Gary Veneruzzo, SLou.	1.25	2.25
102 Tim Ecclestone, SLou.	1.25	2.25
103 Red Berenson, SLou.	1.25	2.25
104 Larry Keenan, SLou.	1.25	2.25
105 Bruce Gamble (G), Toro.	1.75	3.50
106 Jim Dorey, Toro.	1.25	2.25
107 Mike Pelyk, Toro. RC	**2.00**	**4.00**
108 Rick Ley, Toro.	1.25	2.25
109 Mike Walton, Toro.	1.25	2.25
110 Norm Ullman, Toro.	2.50	5.00
111 Brit Selby, SLou.	1.25	2.25
112 Garry Monahan, Toro.	1.25	2.25
113 George Armstrong,Toro.	1.75	3.50
114 Gary Doak, Vanc.	1.25	2.25
115 Darryl Sly, Vanc. RC	**2.00**	**4.00**
116 Wayne Maki, Vanc.	1.25	2.25
117 Orland Kurtenbach, Vanc.	1.25	2.25
118 Murray Hall, Vanc.	1.25	2.25
119 Marc Réaume, Vanc.	1.25	2.25
120 Pat Quinn, Vanc.	3.00	7.00
121 André Boudrias, Vanc.	1.25	2.25
122 Poul Popiel, Buff., Err. (Paul)	1.25	2.25
123 Paul Terbenche, Buff.	1.25	2.25
124 Howie Menard, Buff.	1.25	2.25
125 Gerry Meehan, Buff. RC	**1.75**	**3.50**
126 Skip Krake, Buff.	1.25	2.25
127 Phil Goyette, Buff.	1.25	2.25
128 Reggie Fleming, Buff.	1.25	2.25
129 Don Marshall, Buff.	1.25	2.25
130 Bill Inglis, Buff. RC	**2.00**	**4.00**
131 Gilbert Perreault, Buff. RC	**30.00**	**60.00**
132 Checklist (1 - 132)	50.00	100.00

1971 KELLOGG'S IRON-ON TRANSFERS

These transfers measure 8 1/2" x 6 1/2".

Complete Set (6 transfers):	**150.00**	**300.00**
Kellogg's	**EX**	**NM**
Ron Ellis, Toro.	18.00	35.00
Phil Esposito, Bost.	45.00	90.00
Rod Gilbert, NYRa.	25.00	50.00
Bobby Hull, Chic.	65.00	130.00
Frank Mahovlich, Toro.	30.00	60.00
Stan Mikita, Chic.	35.00	70.00

1971 - 72 BAZOOKA PANELS

Issued in 12 panels of three cards each, one panel was included on the bottom of each Bazooka Bubble Gum box. The designs are identical to 1971-72 O-Pee-Chee and Topps regular issues. The cut cards measure the standard 2 1/2" x 3 1/2" size.

Complete Set (36 cards):	**1,500**	**3,000**
Panel 1 - 3:	**275**	**550**
Panel 4 - 6:	**600**	**1,200**
Panel 7 - 9:	**165**	**325**
Panel 10 - 12:	**190**	**375**
Panel 13- 15:	**140**	**275**
Panel 16 - 18:	**125**	**250**
Panel 19 - 21:	**100**	**200**
Panel 22 - 24:	**80**	**175**
Panel 25 - 27:	**80**	**175**
Panel 28 - 30:	**300**	**600**
Panel 31 - 33:	**80**	**175**
Panel 34 - 36:	**1,150**	**2,300**
Topps	**EX**	**EX-NM**
1 Phil Esposito, Bost.	140.00	275.00
2 Frank Mahovlich, Mont.	90.00	175.00
3 Ed Van Impe, Phil.	20.00	40.00
4 Bobby Hull, Chic.	300.00	600.00
5 Henri Richard, Mont.	70.00	135.00
6 Gilbert Perreault, Buff.	115.00	225.00
7 Alex Delvecchio, Detr.	65.00	125.00
8 Denis DeJordy (G), LosA.	25.00	50.00
9 Ted Harris, Minn.	20.00	40.00
10 Gilles Villemure (G), NYRa.	25.00	50.00
11 Dave Keon, Toro.	65.00	125.00
12 Derek Sanderson, Bost.	50.00	100.00
13 Orland Kurtenbach, Vanc.	20.00	40.00
14 Bob Nevin, Minn.	20.00	40.00
15 Yvan Cournoyer, Mont.	65.00	125.00
16 André Boudrias, Vanc.	20.00	40.00
17 Frank St. Marseille, SLou.	20.00	40.00
18 Norm Ullman, Toro.	50.00	100.00
19 Garry Unger, SLou.	30.00	60.00
20 Pierre Bouchard, Mont.	20.00	40.00
21 Roy Edwards (G), LosA.	25.00	50.00
22 Ralph Backstrom, LosA.	20.00	40.00
23 Guy Trottier, Toro.	20.00	40.00
24 Serge Bernier, Phil.	20.00	40.00
25 Bert Marshall, Cali.	20.00	40.00
26 Wayne Hillman, Phil.	20.00	40.00
27 Tim Ecclestone, Detr.	20.00	40.00
28 Walt McKechnie, Cali.	20.00	40.00
29 Tony Esposito (G), Chic.	165.00	325.00
30 Rod Gilbert, NYRa.	50.00	100.00
31 Walt Tkaczuk, NYRa.	20.00	40.00
32 Roger Crozier (G), Detr.	30.00	60.00
33 Ken Schinkel, Pitt.	20.00	40.00
34 Ron Ellis, Toro.	20.00	40.00
35 Stan Mikita, Chic.	100.00	200.00
36 Bobby Orr, Bost.	750.00	1500.00

1971 - 72 COLGATE HOCKEY HEADS

Short prints are marked with an asterisk (*). These plastic heads measure 1 1/4" high.

Complete Set (16 heads):	**80.00**	**160.000**
Colgate	**EX**	**NM**
Yvan Cournoyer, Mont.	4.25	8.50
Marcel Dionne, Detr.	10.00	20.00

☐	Ken Dryden (G), Mont.	9.00	18.00
☐	Paul Henderson, Toro.	3.50	7.00
☐	Guy Lafleur, Mont.	9.00	18.00
☐	Frank Mahovlich, Mont.	7.50	15.00
☐	Richard Martin, Buff. (*)	12.00	25.00
☐	Bobby Orr, Bost.	14.00	28.00
☐	Brad Park, NYIs. (*)	15.00	30.00
☐	Jacques Plante (G), Toro.	7.00	12.00
☐	Jean Ratelle, NYIs.	4.25	8.50
☐	Derek Sanderson, Bost.	5.00	10.00
☐	Dale Tallon, Vanc.	2.00	4.00
☐	Walter Tkaczuk, NYIs.	2.00	4.00
☐	Norn Ullman, Toro., Error (Ullmann)	9.00	18.00
☐	Norm Ullman, Toro., Corrected	8.00	15.00
☐	Garry Unger, SLou.	2.00	4.00

1971 - 72 EDDIE SARGENT STICKERS

These stickers were issued in a 7 3/4" x 9 3/4" sheet with 14 players and two series stickers per sheet. Each sheet contains one player from each of the 14 teams in the NHL during that season. These stickers measure 1 7/8" x 2 1/2".

Complete Set (224 stickers):		**240.00**	**475.00**
Common Player:		**.50**	**1.00**
Album:		**30.00**	**75.00**
Eddie Sargent		**EX**	**NM**
☐	1 Fred Stanfield, Bost.	.50	1.00
☐	2 Ed Westfall, Bost.	.50	1.00
☐	3 John McKenzie, Bost.	.50	1.00
☐	4 Derek Sanderson, Bost.	2.50	5.00
☐	5 Rick Smith, Bost.	.50	1.00
☐	6 Ted Green, Bost.	.50	1.00
☐	7 Phil Esposito, Bost.	6.50	12.00
☐	8 Ken Hodge, Bost.	.50	1.00
☐	9 John Bucyk, Bost.	3.25	6.50
☐	10 Bobby Orr, Bost.	45.00	85.00
☐	11 Dallas Smith, Bost.	.50	1.00
☐	12 Mike Walton, Bost.	.50	1.00
☐	13 Don Awrey, Bost.	.50	1.00
☐	14 Wayne Cashman, Bost.	.50	1.00
☐	15 Ed Johnston (G), Bost.	.75	1.50
☐	16 Gerry Cheevers (G), Bost.	3.50	7.00
☐	17 Gerry Meehan, Buff.	.50	1.00
☐	18 Ron C. Anderson, Buff.	.50	1.00
☐	19 Gilbert Perreault, Buff.	4.50	9.00
☐	20 Eddie Shack, Buff.	2.50	5.00
☐	21 Jim Watson, Buff.	.50	1.00
☐	22 Kevin O'Shea, Buff.	.50	1.00
☐	23 Al Hamilton, Buff.	.50	1.00
☐	24 Dick Duff, Buff.	.50	1.00
☐	25 Tracy Pratt, Buff.	.50	1.00
☐	26 Don Luce, Buff.	.50	1.00
☐	27 Roger Crozier (G), Buff.	1.00	2.00
☐	28 Doug Barrie, Buff.	.50	1.00
☐	29 Mike Robitaille, Buff.	.50	1.00
☐	30 Phil Goyette, Buff.	.50	1.00
☐	31 Larry Keenan, Buff.	.50	1.00
☐	32 Dave Dryden (G), Buff.	.75	1.50
☐	33 Stan Mikita, Chic.	4.50	9.00
☐	34 Bobby Hull, Chic.	18.00	35.00
☐	35 Cliff Koroll, Chic.	.50	1.00
☐	36 Chico Maki, Chic.	.50	1.00
☐	37 Danny O'Shea, Chic.	.50	1.00
☐	38 Lou Angotti, Chic.	.50	1.00
☐	39 André Lacroix, Chic.	.50	1.00
☐	40 Jim Pappin, Chic.	.50	1.00
☐	41 Doug Jarrett, Chic.	.50	1.00
☐	42 Pit Martin, Chic.	.50	1.00
☐	43 Gary Smith (G), Chic.	.75	1.50
☐	44 Tony Esposito (G), Chic.	6.50	12.00
☐	45 Pat Stapleton, Chic.	.50	1.00
☐	46 Dennis Hull, Chic.	.50	1.00
☐	47 Bill White, Chic.	.50	1.00
☐	48 Keith Magnasun, Chic.	.50	1.00
☐	49 Bill Collins, Detr.	.50	1.00
☐	50 Bob Wall, Detr.	.50	1.00
☐	51 Red Berenson, Detr.	.50	1.00
☐	52 Mickey Redmond, Detr.	.75	1.50
☐	53 Nick Libett, Detr.	.50	1.00
☐	54 Gary Bergman, Detr.	.50	1.00
☐	55 Alex Delvecchio, Detr.	2.25	4.50
☐	56 Tim Ecclestone, Detr.	.50	1.00
☐	57 Arnie Brown, Detr.	.50	1.00
☐	58 Ron Harris, Detr.	.50	1.00
☐	59 Ab McDonald, Detr.	.50	1.00
☐	60 Guy Charron, Detr.	.50	1.00
☐	61 Al Smith (G), Detr.	.75	1.50
☐	62 Joe Daley (G), Detr.	.75	1.50
☐	63 Leon Rochefort, Detr.	.50	1.00
☐	64 Ron Stackhouse, Detr.	.50	1.00
☐	65 Juha Widing, LosA.	.50	1.00
☐	66 Bob Pulford, LosA.	1.50	3.00
☐	67 Bill Flett, LosA.	.50	1.00
☐	68 Rogatien Vachon (G), LosA.	2.00	4.00
☐	69 Ross Lonsberry, LosA.	.50	1.00
☐	70 Gilles Marotte, LosA.	.50	1.00
☐	71 Harry Howell, LosA.	1.50	3.00
☐	72 Réal Lemieux, LosA.	.50	1.00
☐	73 Butch Goring, LosA.	.50	1.00
☐	74 Ed Joyal, LosA.	.50	1.00
☐	75 Larry Hillman, LosA.	.50	1.00
☐	76 Lucien Grenier, LosA.	.50	1.00
☐	77 Paul Curtis, LosA.	.50	1.00
☐	78 Jim Stanfield, LosA.	.50	1.00
☐	79 Ralph Backstrom, LosA.	.50	1.00
☐	80 Mike Byers, LosA.	.50	1.00
☐	81 Tom Reid, Minn.	.50	1.00
☐	82 Jude Drouin, Minn.	.50	1.00
☐	83 Jean Paul Parise, Minn.	.50	1.00
☐	84 Doug Mohns, Minn.	.50	1.00
☐	85 Danny Grant, Minn.	.50	1.00
☐	86 Bill Goldsworthy, Minn.	.50	1.00
☐	87 Charlie Burns, Minn.	.50	1.00
☐	88 Murray Oliver, Minn.	.50	1.00
☐	89 Dean Prentice, Minn.	.50	1.00
☐	90 Bob Nevin, Minn.	.50	1.00
☐	91 Ted Harris, Minn.	.50	1.00
☐	92 Césare Maniago (G), Minn.	.75	1.50
☐	93 Lou Nanne, Minn.	.50	1.00
☐	94 Ted Hampson, Minn.	.50	1.00
☐	95 Barry Gibbs, Minn.	.50	1.00
☐	96 Gump Worsley (G), Minn.	3.50	7.00
☐	97 J.C. Tremblay, Mont.	.50	1.00
☐	98 Guy Lapointe, Mont.	1.50	3.00
☐	99 Peter Mahovlich, Mont.	.50	1.00
☐	100 Larry Pleau, Mont.	.50	1.00
☐	101 Phil Myre (G), Mont.	.75	1.50
☐	102 Yvan Cournoyer, Mont.	2.75	5.50
☐	103 Henri Richard, Mont.	3.50	7.00
☐	104 Frank Mahovlich, Mont.	4.00	8.00
☐	105 Jacques Lemaire, Mont.	2.50	5.00
☐	106 Claude Larose, Mont.	.50	1.00
☐	107 Terry Harper, Mont.	.50	1.00
☐	108 Jacques Laperrière, Mont.	1.50	3.00
☐	109 Phil Roberto, Mont.	.50	1.00
☐	110 Serge Savard, Mont.	1.75	3.50
☐	111 Pierre Bouchard, Mont.	.50	1.00
☐	112 Marc Tardif, Mont.	.50	1.00
☐	113 Rod Gilbert, NYRa.	2.25	4.50
☐	114 Jean Ratelle, NYRa.	2.25	4.50
☐	115 Peter Stemkowski, NYRa.	.50	1.00
☐	116 Brad Park, NYRa.	3.50	7.00
☐	117 Bobby Rousseau, NYRa.	.50	1.00
☐	118 Dale Rolfe, NYRa.	.50	1.00
☐	119 Rod Seiling, NYRa.	.50	1.00
☐	120 Walt Tkachuk, NYRa.	.50	1.00
☐	121 Vic Hadfield, NYRa.	.50	1.00
☐	122 Jim Neilson, NYRa.	.50	1.00
☐	123 Bill Fairbairn, NYRa.	.50	1.00
☐	124 Bruce MacGregor, NYRa.	.50	1.00
☐	125 Dave Balon, NYRa.	.50	1.00
☐	126 Ted Irvine, NYRa.	.50	1.00
☐	127 Gilles Villemure (G), NYRa.	.75	1.50
☐	128 Ed Giacomin (G), NYRa.	3.25	6.50
☐	129 Walt McKechnie, Cali.	.50	1.00
☐	130 Tommy Williams, Cali.	.50	1.00
☐	131 Wayne Carleton, Cali.	.50	1.00
☐	132 Gerry Pinder, Cali.	.50	1.00
☐	133 Gary Croteau, Cali.	.50	1.00
☐	134 Bert Marshall, Cali.	.50	1.00
☐	135 Tom Webster, Cali.	.50	1.00
☐	136 Norm Ferguson, Cali.	.50	1.00
☐	137 Carol Vadnais, Cali.	.50	1.00
☐	138 Gary Jarrett, Cali.	.50	1.00
☐	139 Ernest Hicke, Cali.	.50	1.00
☐	140 Paul Shmyr, Cali.	.50	1.00
☐	141 Marshall Johnston, Cali.	.50	1.00
☐	142 Don O'Donoghue, Cali.	.50	1.00
☐	143 Joey Johnston, Cali.	.50	1.00
☐	144 Dick Redmond, Cali.	.50	1.00
☐	145 Jim Johnson, Phil.	.50	1.00
☐	146 Wayne Hillman, Phil.	.50	1.00
☐	147 Brent Hughes, Phil.	.50	1.00
☐	148 Simon Nolet, Phil.	.50	1.00
☐	149 Larry Mickey, Phil.	.50	1.00
☐	150 Ed Van Impe, Phil.	.50	1.00
☐	151 Gary Dornhoffer, Phil.	.50	1.00
☐	152 Bob Clarke, Phil.	7.50	15.00
☐	153 Jean-Guy Gendron, Phil.	.50	1.00
☐	154 Larry Hale, Phil.	.50	1.00
☐	155 Serge Bernier, Phil.	.50	1.00
☐	156 Doug Favel (G), Phil.	.75	1.50
☐	157 Bob Kelly, Phil.	.50	1.00
☐	158 Joe Watson, Phil.	.50	1.00
☐	159 Larry Brown, Phil.	.50	1.00
☐	160 Bruce Gamble (G), Phil.	.75	1.50
☐	161 Syl Apps, Pitt.	.50	1.00
☐	162 Ken Schinkel, Pitt.	.50	1.00
☐	163 Val Fonteyne, Pitt.	.50	1.00
☐	164 Bryan Watson, Pitt.	.50	1.00
☐	165 Bob Woytowich, Pitt.	.50	1.00
☐	166 Les Binkley (G), Pitt.	.75	1.50
☐	167 Roy Edwards (G), Pitt.	.75	1.50
☐	168 Jean Pronovost, Pitt.	.50	1.00
☐	169 Tim Horton, Pitt.	4.50	9.00
☐	170 Ron Schock, Pitt.	.50	1.00
☐	171 Nick Harbaruk, Pitt.	.50	1.00
☐	172 Greg Polis, Pitt.	.50	1.00
☐	173 Bryan Hextall, Pitt.	.50	1.00
☐	174 Keith McCreary, Pitt.	.50	1.00
☐	175 Bill Hicke, Pitt.	.50	1.00
☐	176 Jim Rutherford (G), Pitt.	.75	1.50
☐	177 Gary Sabourin, SLou.	.50	1.00
☐	178 Garry Unger, SLou.	.50	1.00
☐	179 Terry Crisp, SLou.	1.00	2.00
☐	180 Noel Picard, SLou.	.50	1.00
☐	181 Jim Roberts, SLou.	.50	1.00
☐	182 Barclay Plager, SLou.	.50	1.00
☐	183 Brit Selby, SLou.	.50	1.00
☐	184 Frank St. Marseille, SLou.	.50	1.00
☐	185 Ernie Wakley (G), SLou.	.75	1.50
☐	186 Wayne Connelly, SLou.	.50	1.00
☐	187 Christain Bordeleau, SLou.	.50	1.00
☐	188 Bill Sutherland, SLou.	.50	1.00
☐	189 Bob Plager, SLou.	.50	1.00
☐	190 Bill Plager, SLou.	.50	1.00
☐	191 George Morrison, SLou.	.50	1.00
☐	192 Jim Lorentz, SLou.	.50	1.00
☐	193 Norn Ullman, Toro.	3.00	6.00
☐	194 Jim McKenny, Toro.	.50	1.00
☐	195 Rick Ley, Toro.	.50	1.00
☐	196 Bob Baun, Toro.	.50	1.00
☐	197 Mike Pelyk, Toro.	.50	1.00
☐	198 Bill MacMillan, Toro.	.50	1.00
☐	199 Garry Monahan, Toro.	.50	1.00
☐	200 Paul Henderson, Toro.	1.00	2.00
☐	201 Jim Dorey, Toro.	.50	1.00
☐	202 Jim Harrison, Toro.	.50	1.00
☐	203 Ron Ellis, Toro.	.50	1.00
☐	204 Darryl Sittler, Toro.	3.50	7.00
☐	205 Bernie Parent. (G), Toro.	2.75	5.50
☐	206 Dave Keon, Toro.	2.75	5.50
☐	207 Brad Selwood, Toro.	.50	1.00
☐	208 Don Marshall, Toro.	.50	1.00
☐	209 Dale Tallon, Vanc.	.50	1.00
☐	210 Danny Johnson, Vanc.	.50	1.00
☐	211 Murray Hall, Vanc.	.50	1.00
☐	212 Poul Popiel, Vanc.	.50	1.00
☐	213 George Gardner (G), Vanc.	.75	1.50
☐	214 Gary Doak, Vanc.	.50	1.00
☐	215 André Boudrais, Vanc.	.50	1.00
☐	216 Orland Kurtenbach, Vanc.	.50	1.00
☐	217 Wayne Maki, Vanc.	.50	1.00
☐	218 Rosaire Paiement, Vanc.	.50	1.00
☐	219 Pat Quinn, Vanc.	1.00	2.00
☐	220 Fred Speck, Vanc.	.50	1.00
☐	221 Barry Wilkins, Vanc.	.50	1.00
☐	222 Dunc Wilson (G), Vanc.	.75	1.50
☐	223 Ted Taylor, Vanc.	.50	1.00
☐	224 Mike Corrigan, Vanc.	.50	1.00

1971 - 72 FRITO-LAY

These paper cards measure 2" x 3". They were folded twice before being inserted into packages of Frito Lay products.

Complete Set (10 cards):		**50.00**	**110.00**
Frito Lay		**EX**	**NM**
☐	Bobby Baun, Toro.	3.75	7.50
☐	Yvan Cournoyer, Mont.	6.50	12.00
☐	Ken Dryden (G), Mont.	20.00	40.00
☐	Ron Ellis, Toro.	3.00	6.00
☐	Paul Henderson, Toro.	4.50	9.00
☐	Frank Mahovlich, Mont.	7.50	15.00
☐	Jacques Plante, (G), Toro.	11.00	22.00
☐	Henri Richard, Mont.	6.00	12.00
☐	J.C. Tremblay, Mont.	3.75	7.50
☐	Norm Ullman, Toro.	5.50	11.00

1971 - 72 O-PEE-CHEE

"A lot of people are chasing the older sets from the 1980s and before. That 1971-72 set seems to be really popular. The two checklists (in the set) are ridiculously tough. The set has a nice cross section of players. It is from that period of time that even if the collector didn't see them play, they know the players. The set also has a classic design that everybody seems to like." – Mike Drandzyk, Kitchener Coin Shop, Kitchener, ON.

These cards measure the standard 2 1/2" x 3 1/2" size.

Complete Set (264 cards):		**1,100**	**2,100**
Common Player:		**2.00**	**4.50**
O-Pee-Chee		**EX**	**NM-MT**
☐	1 Poul Popiel, Vanc.	3.00	9.00
☐	**2 Pierre Bouchard, Mont. RC**	**3.00**	**6.00**
☐	3 Don Awrey, Bost.	2.00	4.50
☐	**4 Paul Curtis, LosA. RC**	**3.00**	**6.00**
☐	**5 Guy Trottier, Toro. RC**	**3.00**	**6.00**
☐	**6 Paul Shmyr, Cali. RC**	**3.00**	**6.00**
☐	7 Fred Stanfield, Bost.	2.00	4.50
☐	**8 Mike Robitaille, Buff. RC**	**3.00**	**6.00**
☐	9 Vic Hadfield, NYRa.	2.00	4.50
☐	10 Jim Harrison, Toro.	2.00	4.50
☐	11 Bill White, Chic.	2.00	4.50
☐	12 André Boudrias, Vanc.	2.00	4.50
☐	13 Gary Sabourin, SLou.	2.00	4.50
☐	14 Arnie Brown, Detr.	2.00	4.50
☐	15 Yvan Cournoyer, Mont.	4.50	9.00
☐	16 Bryan Hextall, Pitt.	2.00	4.50
☐	17 Gary Croteau, Cali.	2.00	4.50
☐	18 Gilles Villemure (G), NYRa.	3.00	6.00
☐	**19 Serge Bernier, Phil. RC**	**3.00**	**6.00**
☐	20 Phil Esposito, Bost.	12.00	25.00
☐	21 Tom Reid, Minn.	2.00	4.50
☐	**22 Doug Barrie, Buff. RC**	**3.00**	**6.00**
☐	23 Eddie Joyal, LosA.	2.00	4.50
☐	**24 Dunc Wilson (G), Vanc. RC**	**3.00**	**6.00**
☐	25 Pat Stapleton, Chic.	2.00	4.50
☐	26 Garry Unger, SLou., Err. (Gary)	2.00	4.50
☐	27 Al Smith (G), Detr.	3.00	6.00
☐	28 Bob Woytowich, Pitt.	2.00	4.50
☐	29 Marc Tardif, Mont., Err. (Tardiff)	2.00	4.50
☐	30 Norm Ullman, Toro.	3.50	7.00
☐	31 Tom Williams, Cali.	2.00	4.50
☐	32 Ted Harris, Minn.	2.00	4.50
☐	33 André Lacroix, Phil.	2.00	4.50
☐	34 Mike Byers, LosA.	2.00	4.50
☐	35 John Bucyk, Bos	3.50	7.00
☐	36 Roger Crozier (G), Buff.	3.00	6.00
☐	37 Alex Delvecchio, Detr.	3.50	7.00
☐	38 Frank St. Marseille, SLou.	2.00	4.50
☐	39 Pit Martin, Chic.	2.00	4.50
☐	40 Brad Park, NYRa.	10.00	20.00
☐	**41 Greg Polis, Pitt. RC**	**3.00**	**6.00**
☐	42 Orland Kurtenbach, Vanc.	2.00	4.50
☐	**43 Jim McKenny, Toro. RC**	**3.00**	**6.00**
☐	44 Bob Nevin, Minn.	2.00	4.50
☐	**45 Ken Dryden (G), Mont. RC**	**175.00**	**375.00**
☐	46 Carol Vadnais, Cali.	2.00	4.50
☐	47 Bill Flett, LosA.	2.00	4.50
☐	48 Jim Johnson, Phil.	2.00	4.50
☐	49 Al Hamilton, Buff.	2.00	4.50
☐	50 Bobby Hull, Chic.	25.00	50.00
☐	**51 Chris Bordeleau, SLou. RC**	**3.00**	**6.00**
☐	52 Tim Ecclestone, Detr.	2.00	4.50
☐	53 Rod Seiling, NYRa.	2.00	4.50
☐	54 Gerry Cheevers (G), Bost.	5.50	11.00
☐	55 Bill Goldsworthy, Minn.	2.00	4.50
☐	56 Ron Schock, Pitt.	2.00	4.50
☐	57 Jim Dorey, Toro.	2.00	4.50
☐	58 Wayne Maki, Vanc.	2.00	4.50
☐	59 Terry Harper, Mont.	2.00	4.50
☐	60 Gilbert Perreault, Buff.	18.00	35.00
☐	**61 Ernie Hicke, Cali. RC**	**3.00**	**6.00**
☐	62 Wayne Hillman, Phil.	2.00	4.50
☐	63 Denis DeJordy (G), LosA.	3.00	6.00
☐	64 Ken Schinkel, Pitt.	2.00	4.50
☐	65 Derek Sanderson, Bost.	6.00	12.00
☐	66 Barclay Plager, SLou.	2.00	4.50
☐	67 Paul Henderson, Toro.	3.00	6.00
☐	68 Jude Drouin, Minn.	2.00	4.50
☐	69 Keith Magnuson, Chic.	2.00	4.50
☐	70 Ron Harris, Detr.	2.00	4.50
☐	71 Jacques Lemaire, Mont.	4.00	8.00
☐	72 Doug Favell (G), Phil.	3.00	6.00
☐	73 Bert Marshall, Cali.	2.00	4.50
☐	74 Ted Irvine, NYRa.	2.00	4.50
☐	75 Walt Tkaczuk, NYRa.	2.00	4.50
☐	**76 Bob Berry, LosA. RC**	**3.00**	**6.00**
☐	**77 Syl Apps, Jr., Pitt. RC**	**3.00**	**6.00**
☐	78 Tom Webster, Detr.	2.00	4.50
☐	79 Danny Grant, Minn.	2.00	4.50
☐	80 Dave Keon, Toro.	3.25	6.50
☐	81 Ernie Wakely (G), SLou.	3.00	6.00
☐	82 John McKenzie, Bost.	2.00	4.50
☐	**83 Ron Stackhouse, Cali. RC**	**3.00**	**6.00**
☐	84 Pete Mahovlich, Mont.	2.00	4.50

85 Dennis Hull, Chic.	2.00	4.50
86 Juha Widing, LosA. RC	**3.00**	**6.00**
87 Gary Doak, Vanc.	2.00	4.50
88 Phil Goyette, Buff.	2.00	4.50
89 Lew Morrison, Phil.	2.00	4.50
90 Ab DeMarco, NYRa. RC	**3.00**	**6.00**
91 Red Berenson, Detr.	2.00	4.50
92 Mike Pelyk, Toro.	2.00	4.50
93 Gary Jarrett, Cali.	2.00	4.50
94 Bob Pulford, LosA.	3.00	6.00
95 Danny Johnson, Vanc. RC	**3.00**	**6.00**
96 Eddie Shack, Buff.	4.25	8.50
97 Jean Ratelle, NYRa.	3.50	7.00
98 Jim Pappin, Chic.	2.00	4.50
99 Roy Edwards (G), Pitt.	3.00	6.00
100 Bobby Orr, Bost.	60.00	120.00
101 Ted Hampson, Minn.	2.00	4.50
102 Mickey Redmond, Detr.	3.25	6.50
103 Bob Plager, SLou.	2.00	4.50
104 Barry Ashbee, Phil. RC	**3.00**	**6.00**
105 Frank Mahovlich, Mont.	5.50	11.00
106 Dick Redmond, Cali. RC	**3.00**	**6.00**
107 Tracy Pratt, Buff.	2.00	4.50
108 Ralph Backstrom, LosA.	2.00	4.50
109 Murray Hall, Vanc.	2.00	4.50
110 Tony Esposito (G), Chic.	25.00	50.00
111 Checklist 1 (1 - 132)	350.00	700.00
112 Jim Neilson, NYRa.	2.00	4.50
113 Ron Ellis, Toro.	2.00	4.50
114 Bobby Clarke, Phil.	35.00	70.00
115 Ken Hodge, Bost.	2.00	4.50
116 Jim Roberts, SLou.	2.00	4.50
117 Césare Maniago (G), Minn.	3.00	6.00
118 Jean Pronovost, Pitt.	2.00	4.50
119 Gary Bergman, Detr.	2.00	4.50
120 Henri Richard, Mont.	4.25	8.50
121 Ross Lonsberry, LosA.	2.00	4.50
122 Pat Quinn, Vanc.	3.00	6.00
123 Rod Gilbert, NYRa.	3.50	7.00
124 Walt McKechnie, Cali.	2.00	4.50
125 Stan Mikita, Chic.	9.00	18.00
126 Ed Van Impe, Phil.	2.00	4.50
127 Terry Crisp, SLou. RC	**7.00**	**14.00**
128 Fred Barrett, Minn. RC	**3.00**	**6.00**
129 Wayne Cashman, Bost.	2.00	4.50
130 J.C. Tremblay, Mont.	2.00	4.50
131 Bernie Parent (G), Toro.	11.00	22.00
132 Bryan Watson, Pitt.	2.00	4.50
133 Marcel Dionne, Detr. RC	**125.00**	**250.00**
134 Ab McDonald, Detr.	2.00	4.50
135 Leon Rochefort, Detr.	2.00	4.50
136 Serge Lajeunesse, Detr. RC	**3.00**	**6.00**
137 Joe Daley (G), Detr.	3.00	6.00
138 Brian Conacher, Detr.	2.00	4.50
139 Bill Collins, Detr.	2.00	4.50
140 Nick Libett, Detr.	2.00	4.50
141 Bill Sutherland, Detr.	2.00	4.50
142 Bill Hicke, Detr.	2.00	4.50
143 Serge Savard, Mont.	3.50	7.00
144 Jacques Laperrière, Mont.	3.00	6.00
145 Guy Lapointe, Mont.	4.00	7.50
146 Claude Larose, Mont., Err. (La Rose)	2.00	4.50
147 Réjean Houle, Mont.	3.00	6.00
148 Guy Lafleur, Mont. RC, Err. (LaFleur)	**132.00**	**285.00**
149 Dale Hoganson, Mont. RC	**3.00**	**6.00**
150 Al McDonough, LosA. RC	**3.00**	**6.00**
151 Gilles Marotte, LosA.	2.00	4.50
152 Butch Goring, LosA. RC	**6.50**	**12.00**
153 Harry Howell, LosA.	3.00	6.00
154 Real Lemieux, LosA.	2.00	4.50
155 Gary Edwards (G), LosA. RC	**3.00**	**6.00**
156 Rogatien Vachon (G), LosA.	4.50	9.00
157 Mike Corrigan, LosA.	2.00	4.50
158 Floyd Smith, Buff.	2.00	4.50
159 Dave Dryden (G), Buff.	3.00	6.00
160 Gerry Meehan, Buff.	2.00	4.50
161 Rick Martin, Buff. RC	**10.00**	**20.00**
162 Steve Atkinson, Buff. RC	**3.00**	**6.00**
163 Ron C. Anderson, Buff.	2.00	4.50
164 Dick Duff, Buff.	2.00	4.50
165 Jim Watson, Buff.	2.00	4.50
166 Don Luce, Buff. RC	**3.00**	**6.00**
167 Larry Mickey, Buff.	2.00	4.50
168 Larry Hillman, Buff.	2.00	4.50
169 Ed Westfall, Bost.	2.00	4.50
170 Dallas Smith, Bost.	2.00	4.50
171 Mike Walton, Bost.	2.00	4.50
172 Eddie Johnston (G), Bost.	3.00	6.00
173 Ted Green, Bost.	2.00	4.50
174 Rick Smith, Bost.	2.00	4.50
175 Reggie Leach, Bost. RC	**9.00**	**18.00**
176 Don Marcotte, Bost.	2.00	4.50
177 Bobby Sheehan, Cali. RC	**3.00**	**6.00**
178 Wayne Carleton, Cali.	2.00	4.50
179 Norm Ferguson, Cali.	2.00	4.50
180 Don O'Donoghue, Cali. RC	**3.00**	**6.00**
181 Gary Kurt (G), Cali. RC	**3.00**	**6.00**
182 Joey Johnston, Cali. RC	**3.00**	**6.00**
183 Stan Gilbertson, Cali. RC	**3.00**	**6.00**
184 Craig Patrick, Cali. RC	**6.00**	**12.00**
185 Gerry Pinder, Cali.	2.00	4.50
186 Tim Horton, Pitt.	6.50	12.00
187 Darryl Edestrand, Pitt. RC	**3.00**	**6.00**
188 Keith McCreary, Pitt.	2.00	4.50
189 Val Fonteyne, Pitt.	2.00	4.50
190 Sheldon Kannegiesser, Pitt. RC	**3.00**	**6.00**
191 Nick Harbaruk, Pitt. RC	**3.00**	**6.00**
192 Les Binkley (G), Pitt.	3.00	6.00
193 Darryl Sittler, Toro.	25.00	50.00
194 Rick Ley, Toro.	2.00	4.50
195 Jacques Plante (G), Toro.	15.00	30.00
196 Bobby Baun, Toro.	2.00	4.50
197 Brian Glennie, Toro.	2.00	4.50
198 Brian Spencer, Toro. RC	**5.00**	**10.00**
199 Don Marshall, Toro.	2.00	4.50
200 Denis Dupère, Toro. RC	**3.00**	**6.00**
201 Bruce Gamble (G), Phil.	3.00	6.00
202 Gary Dornhoefer, Phil.	2.00	4.50
203 Bob Kelly, Phil. RC	**3.00**	**6.00**
204 Jean-Guy Gendron, Phil.	2.00	4.50
205 Brent Hughes, Phil.	2.00	4.50
206 Simon Nolet, Phil.	2.00	4.50
207 Rick MacLeish, Phil. RC	**9.00**	**18.00**
208 Doug Jarrett, Chic.	2.00	4.50
209 Cliff Koroll, Chic.	2.00	4.50
210 Chico Maki, Chic.	2.00	4.50
211 Danny O'Shea, Chic.	2.00	4.50
212 Lou Angotti, Chic.	2.00	4.50
213 Eric Nesterenko, Chic.	2.00	4.50
214 Bryan Campbell, Chic.	2.00	4.50
215 Bill Fairbairn, NYRa. RC	**3.00**	**6.00**
216 Bruce MacGregor, NYRa.	2.00	4.50
217 Pete Stemkowski, NYRa.	2.00	4.50
218 Bobby Rousseau, NYRa.	2.00	4.50
219 Dale Rolfe, NYRa.	2.00	4.50
220 Ed Giacomin (G), NYRa.	5.50	11.00
221 Glen Sather, NYRa.	3.00	6.00
222 Carl Brewer, SLou.	2.00	4.50
223 George Morrison, SLou. RC	**3.00**	**6.00**
224 Noel Picard, SLou.	2.00	4.50
225 Pete McDuffe (G), SLou. RC, Err. (Defence)	**3.00**	**6.00**
226 Brit Selby, SLou.	2.00	4.50
227 Jim Lorentz, SLou.	2.00	4.50
228 Phil Roberto, SLou. RC	**3.00**	**6.00**
229 Dave Balon, Vanc.	2.00	4.50
230 Barry Wilkins, Vanc. RC	**3.00**	**6.00**
231 Dennis Kearns, Vanc. RC	**3.00**	**6.00**
232 Jocelyn Guevremont, Vanc. RC	**3.00**	**6.00**
233 Rosaire Paiement, Vanc.	2.00	4.50
234 Dale Tallon, Vanc.	2.00	4.50
235 George Gardner (G), Vanc.	3.00	6.00
236 Ron Stewart, Vanc.	2.00	4.50
237 Wayne Connelly, Vanc.	2.00	4.50
238 Charlie Burns, Minn.	2.00	4.50
239 Murray Oliver, Minn.	2.00	4.50
240 Lou Nanne, Minn.	2.00	4.50
241 Gump Worsley (G), Minn.	5.50	11.00
242 Doug Mohns, Minn.	2.00	4.50
243 J.P. Parise, Minn.	2.00	4.50
244 Dennis Hextall, Minn.	2.00	4.50
245 AW: Bobby Orr, Bost.	35.00	65.00
246 AW: Gilbert Perreault, Buff.	10.00	20.00
247 AW: Phil Esposito, Bost.	7.50	15.00
248 AW: E. Giacomin/ G. Villemure, NYRa.	4.00	8.00
249 AW: John Bucyk Bost.	3.00	6.00
250 AS: Ed Giacomin (G), NYRa.	3.25	6.50
251 AS: Bobby Orr, Bost.	35.00	65.00
252 AS: J.C. Tremblay, Mont.	2.00	4.50
253 AS: Phil Esposito, Bost.	7.50	15.00
254 AS: Ken Hodge, Sr., Bost.	2.00	4.50
255 AS: John Bucyk, Bost.	3.00	6.00
256 AS: Jacques Plante (G), Toro., Err. (63 shutouts)	6.00	12.00
257 AS: Brad Park, NYRa.	6.00	12.00
258 AS: Pat Stapleton, Chic.	9.00	18.00
259 AS: Dave Keon, Toro.	3.00	6.00
260 AS: Yvan Cournoyer, Mont.	3.00	6.00
261 AS: Bobby Hull, Chic.	15.00	30.00
262 Gordie Howe, Mr. Hockey	65.00	125.00
263 Jean Béliveau, Le Gros Bill	35.00	70.00
264 Checklist 2 (133 - 264)	75.00	225.00

BOOKLETS

These booklets measure the standard 2 1/2" x 3 1/2" size.

Insert Set (24 booklets):	**70.00**	**140.00**
O-Pee-Chee	**EX**	**NM-MT**
1 Bobby Hull, Chic.	6.00	18.00
2 Phil Esposito, Bost.	4.50	8.50
3 Dale Tallon, Vanc.	1.50	3.00
4 Jacques Plante (G), Toro.	6.00	12.00
5 Roger Crozier (G), Buff.	2.50	5.00
6 Henri Richard, Mont.	4.00	8.00
7 Ed Giacomin (G), NYRa.	4.00	8.00
8 Gilbert Perreault, Buff.	4.00	8.00
9 Greg Polis, Pitt.	1.50	3.00
10 Bobby Clarke, Phil.	4.50	9.00
11 Danny Grant, Minn.	1.50	3.00
12 Alex Delvecchio, Detr.	2.50	5.00
13 Tony Esposito (G), Chic.	4.50	8.50
14 Garry Unger, SLou.	2.00	4.00
15 Frank St. Marseille, SLou.	1.50	3.00
16 Dave Keon, Toro.	3.00	6.00
17 Ken Dryden (G), Mont.	12.00	25.00
18 Rod Gilbert, NYRa.	3.25	6.50
19 Juha Widing, LosA.	1.50	3.00
20 Orland Kurtenbach, Vanc.	1.50	3.00
21 Jude Drouin, Minn.	1.50	3.00
22 Gary Smith (G), Cali.	2.00	4.00
23 Gordie Howe, Detr.	15.00	30.00
24 Bobby Orr, Bost.	22.00	38.00

1971 - 72 O-PEE-CHEE POSTERS

These posters measure 9 15/16" x 17 7/8".

Complete Set (24 posters):	**9.00**	**18.00**
O-Pee-Chee	**EX**	**NM**
1 Bobby Orr, Bost.	110.00	220.00
2 Bob Pulford, LosA.	12.00	25.00
3 Dave Keon, Toro.	18.00	35.00
4 Yvan Cournoyer, Mont.	18.00	35.00
5 Dale Tallon, Vanc.	9.00	18.00
6 Richard Martin, Buff.	11.00	22.00
7 Rod Gilbert, NYRa.	15.00	30.00
8 Tony Esposito (G), Chic.	30.00	60.00
9 Bobby Hull, Chic.	45.00	90.00
10 Red Berenson, Detr.	9.00	18.00
11 Norm Ullman, Toro.	15.00	30.00
12 Orland Kurtenbach, Vanc.	9.00	18.00
13 Guy Lafleur, Mont.	75.00	140.00
14 Gilbert Perreault, Buff.	25.00	45.00
15 Jacques Plante (G), Toro.	28.00	55.00
16 Bruce Gamble (G), Phil.	11.00	22.00
17 Walt McKechnie, Cali.	9.00	18.00
18 Tim Horton, Pitt.	25.00	50.00
19 Jean Ratelle, NYRa.	15.00	30.00
20 Garry Unger, SLou.	11.00	22.00
21 Phil Esposito, Bost.	30.00	60.00
22 Ken Dryden (G), Mont.	65.00	125.00
23 Gump Worsley (G), Minn.	25.00	45.00
24 Club de Hockey Canadien 1970-71	25.00	50.00

1971 - 72 PRO STAR PROMOTIONS

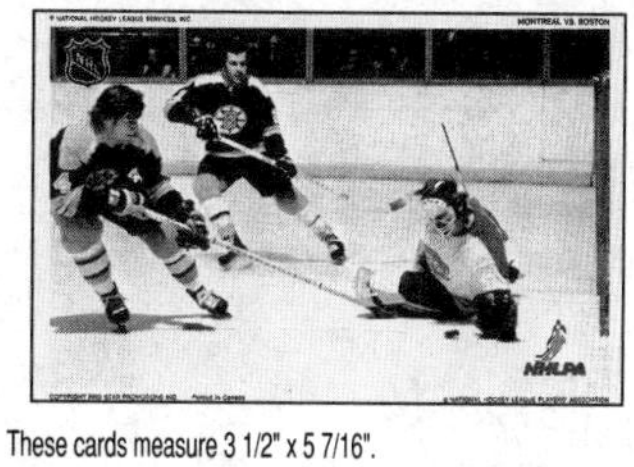

These cards measure 3 1/2" x 5 7/16".

Pro Star Promotions	**EX**	**NM-MT**
Bost./ NYRa.: R. Gilbert/ P. Esposito	10.00	20.00
Bost./ NYRa.: Rousseau/ Seiling/ B. Orr	25.00	50.00
Bost./ Toro.: B. Orr/ J. McKenny/ etc.	30.00	60.00
Bost./ Mont.: Cournoyer/ F. Mahovlich/ Orr	25.00	50.00
Bost./ Minn.: J. Bucyk/ etc.	7.50	15.00
Mont./ Bost.: Orr/ D. Marcotte/ K. Dryden	35.00	70.00
Mont./ NYRa.: R. Seiling/ F. Mahovlich	15.00	30.00
Mont./ Detr.: G. Bergman/ K. Dryden	20.00	40.00
Mont./ Minn.: K. Dryden/ J. Roberts/ etc.	20.00	40.00
Mont./ Detr.: S. Savard/ K. Dryden/ etc.	25.00	45.00
Mont./ Minn.: Y. Cournoyer/ etc.	10.00	20.00
Mont./ NYRa.: Lapointe/ E. Giacomin/ etc.	10.00	20.00
Mont./ NYRa.: Seiling/ Giacomin/ Cournoyer	10.00	20.00
Mont./ NYRa.: Neilson/ H. Richard/ Villemure	7.50	15.00
Mont./ NYRa.: P. Mahovlich/ Giacomin/ etc.	7.50	15.00
Mont./ NYRa.: H. Richard/ [NYR-5, NYR-30]	7.50	15.00
NYRa./ Chic.: R. Gilbert/ [NYR-5, CHI-10]	7.50	15.00
Vanc./ Atla.: [ATL-1, ATL-24, VAN-5]	7.50	15.00
Vanc./ Atla.: [ATL1, ATL-4, VAN-25]	7.50	15.00
Vanc./ NYRa.: [VAN-1, NYR-18, VAN-2]	7.50	15.00
Vanc./ Mont.: [VAN-6, VAN-2]	7.50	15.00
Vanc./ Mont.: [VAN-14, MTL-14, VAN-1]	7.50	15.00

1971 - 72 SOVIET STARS

These postcards measure the standard 4 1/8" x 5 3/4".

Complete Set (25 cards and folder):	**75.00**	**150.00**
Soviet Stars	**EX**	**NM**
Victor Konovalenko (G)	3.50	7.00
Valery Davydov	2.50	5.00
Vladimir Lutchenko	2.50	5.00
Viktor Kuzkin	2.50	5.00
Alexander Ragulin	5.00	10.00
Igor Romishevsky	2.50	5.00
Gennady Tsycakov	2.50	5.00
Vyacheslav Starshinov	2.50	5.00
Evgney Zimin	2.50	5.00
Alexander Maltsev	4.00	8.00
Anatoli Firsov	2.50	5.00
Evgeny Mishakov	2.50	5.00
Boris Mikhailov	6.00	12.00
Yuri Liapkin	2.50	5.00
Alexander Martiniuk	2.50	5.00
Vladimir Petrov	4.00	8.00
Valery Kharlamov	9.00	18.00
Vladimir Vikulov	2.50	5.00
Vladimir Shadrin	2.50	5.00
Vladislav Tretiak (G)	15.00	30.00
Team Photo	6.00	12.00
A. Czepnishev	2.50	5.00
A. Tapasov	2.50	5.00
U.S.S.R. vs. Finland	4.00	8.00
U.S.S.R. in action	4.00	8.00

1971 - 72 TOPPS

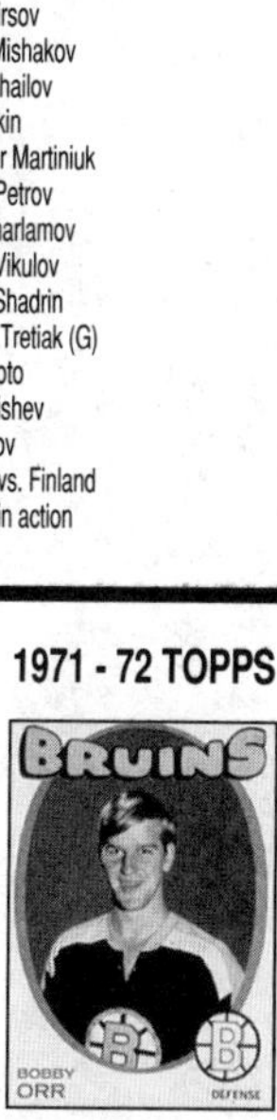

These cards measure the standard 2 1/2" x 3 1/2" size.

Complete Set (176 cards): **200.00** **400.00**

◆ A set, including 14 graded cards, closed at $611.18 U.S. (approx. $825 Cdn.) in the May 2003 Leland's auction.

Common Player:	**1.00**	**2.00**
Topps	**EX**	**NM-MT**
1 LL: P. Esposito/ J. Bucyk/ B. Hull	8.50	25.00
2 LL: B. Orr/ P. Esposito/ J. Bucyk	9.00	18.00
3 LL: P. Esposito/ B. Orr/ J. Bucyk	9.00	18.00
4 LL: T. Esposito/ E. Johnston/ G. Cheevers/ E. Giacomin	6.50	12.00
5 LL: E. Giacomin/ T. Esposito/ C. Maniago	4.50	8.50
6 LL: J. Plante/ E. Giacomin/ T. Esposito	8.00	16.00
7 Fred Stanfield, Bost.	1.00	2.00

8 Mike Robitaille, Buff. RC	**2.00**	**4.00**
9 Vic Hadfield, NYRa.	1.00	2.00
10 Jacques Plante (G), Toro.	10.00	20.00
11 Bill White, Chic.	1.00	2.00
12 André Boudrias, Vanc.	1.00	2.00
13 Jim Lorentz, SLou.	1.00	2.00
14 Arnie Brown, Detr.	1.00	2.00
15 Yvan Cournoyer, Mont.	2.75	6.00
16 Bryan Hextall, Jr., Pitt.	1.00	2.00
17 Gary Croteau, Cali.	1.00	2.00
18 Gilles Villemure (G), NYRa.	1.50	3.00
19 Serge Bernier, Phil. RC	**2.00**	**4.00**
20 Phil Esposito, Bost.	9.00	18.00
21 Charlie Burns, Minn.	1.00	2.00
22 Doug Barrie, Buff. RC	**2.00**	**4.00**
23 Eddie Joyal, LosA.	1.00	2.00
24 Rosaire Paiement, Vanc.	1.00	2.00
25 Pat Stapleton, Chic.	1.00	2.00
26 Garry Unger, SLou.	1.50	3.00
27 Al Smith (G), Detr.	1.50	3.00
28 Bob Woytowich, Pitt.	1.00	2.00
29 Marc Tardif, Mont.	1.00	2.00
30 Norm Ullman, Toro.	2.00	4.50
31 Tom Williams, Cali.	1.00	2.00
32 Ted Harris, Minn.	1.00	2.00
33 André Lacroix, Phil.	1.00	2.00
34 Mike Byers, LosA.	1.00	2.00
35 John Bucyk, Bost.	2.25	5.00
36 Roger Crozier (G), Buff.	1.75	3.50
37 Alex Delvecchio, Detr.	2.50	5.00
38 Frank St. Marseille, SLou.	1.00	2.00
39 Pit Martin, Chic.	1.00	2.00
40 Brad Park, NYRa.	6.00	12.00
41 Greg Polis, Pitt. RC	**2.00**	**4.00**
42 Orland Kurtenbach, Vanc.	1.00	2.00
43 Jim McKenny, Toro. RC	**1.50**	**3.00**
44 Bob Nevin, Minn.	1.00	2.00
45 Ken Dryden (G), Mont. RC	**80.00**	**160.00**
46 Carol Vadnais, Cali.	1.00	2.00
47 Bill Flett, LosA.	1.00	2.00
48 Jim Johnson, Phil.	1.00	2.00
49 Allan Hamilton, Buff.	1.00	2.00
50 Bobby Hull, Chic.	15.00	30.00
51 Chris Bordeleau, SLou. RC	**2.00**	**4.00**
52 Tim Ecclestone, Detr.	1.00	2.00
53 Rod Seiling, NYRa.	1.00	2.00
54 Gerry Cheevers (G), Bost.	3.25	6.50
55 Bill Goldsworthy, Minn.	1.00	2.00
56 Ron Schock, Pitt.	1.00	2.00
57 Jim Dorey, Toro.	1.00	2.00
58 Wayne Maki, Vanc.	1.00	2.00
59 Terry Harper, Mont.	1.00	2.00
60 Gilbert Perreault, Buff.	11.00	22.00
61 Ernie Hicke, Cali. RC	**2.00**	**4.00**
62 Wayne Hillman, Phil.	1.00	2.00
63 Denis DeJordy (G), LosA.	1.50	3.00
64 Ken Schinkel, Pitt.	1.00	2.00
65 Derek Sanderson, Bost.	3.50	7.00
66 Barclay Plager, SLou.	1.00	2.00
67 Paul Henderson, Toro.	1.50	3.00
68 Jude Drouin, Minn.	1.00	2.00
69 Keith Magnuson, Chic.	1.00	2.00
70 Gordie Howe, Detr.	35.00	65.00
71 Jacques Lemaire, Mont.	2.75	5.50
72 Doug Favell (G), Phil.	1.50	3.00
73 Bert Marshall, Cali.	1.00	2.00
74 Gerry Meehan, Buff.	1.00	2.00
75 Walt Tkaczuk, NYRa.	1.00	2.00
76 Bob Berry, LosA. RC	**2.00**	**4.00**
77 Syl Apps, Pitt. RC	**2.00**	**4.00**
78 Tom Webster, Detr.	1.00	2.00
79 Danny Grant, Minn.	1.00	2.00
80 Dave Keon, Toro.	2.00	4.50
81 Ernie Wakely (G), SLou.	1.50	3.00
82 John McKenzie, Bost.	1.00	2.00
83 Doug Roberts, Cali.	1.00	2.00
84 Peter Mahovlich, Mont.	1.00	2.00
85 Dennis Hull, Chic.	1.00	2.00
86 Juha Widing, LosA. RC	**2.00**	**4.00**
87 Gary Doak, Vanc.	1.00	2.00
88 Phil Goyette, Buff.	1.00	2.00
89 Gary Dornhoefer, Phil.	1.00	2.00
90 Ed Giacomin (G), NYRa.	4.00	8.00
91 Red Berenson, Detr.	1.00	2.00
92 Mike Pelyk, Toro.	1.00	2.00
93 Gary Jarrett, Cali.	1.00	2.00
94 Bob Pulford, LosA.	1.75	3.50
95 Dale Tallon, Vanc.	1.00	2.00
96 Eddie Shack, Buff.	2.75	5.50
97 Jean Ratelle, NYRa.	2.50	5.00
98 Jim Pappin, Chic.	1.00	2.00
99 Roy Edwards (G), Pitt.	1.50	3.00
100 Bobby Orr, Bost.	35.00	60.00
101 Ted Hampson, Minn.	1.00	2.00
102 Mickey Redmond, Detr.	2.00	4.50
103 Bob Plager, SLou.	1.00	2.00
104 Bruce Gamble (G), Phil.	1.50	3.00
105 Frank Mahovlich, Mont.	3.50	7.00
106 Tony Featherstone, Cali. RC	**2.00**	**4.00**
107 Tracy Pratt, Buff.	1.00	2.00
108 Ralph Backstrom, LosA.	1.00	2.00
109 Murray Hall, Vanc.	1.00	2.00
110 Tony Esposito (G), Chic.	14.00	28.00
111 Checklist (1 - 132)	40.00	80.00
112 Jim Neilson, NYRa.	1.00	2.00
113 Ron Ellis, Toro.	1.00	2.00
114 Bobby Clarke, Phil.	20.00	40.00
115 Ken Hodge, Bost.	1.00	2.00
116 Jim Roberts, SLou.	1.00	2.00
117 Césare Maniago (G), Minn.	1.50	3.00
118 Jean Pronovost, Pitt.	1.50	3.00
119 Gary Bergman, Detr.	1.00	2.00
120 Henri Richard, Mont.	3.00	6.00
121 Ross Lonsberry, LosA.	1.00	2.00
122 Pat Quinn, Vanc.	1.50	3.00
123 Rod Gilbert, NYRa.	2.50	5.00
124 Gary Smith (G), Cali.	1.50	3.00
125 Stan Mikita, Chic.	6.00	12.00
126 Ed Van Impe, Phil.	1.00	2.00
127 Wayne Connelly, SLou.	1.00	2.00
128 Dennis Hextall, Minn.	1.00	2.00
129 Wayne Cashman, Bost.	1.50	3.00
130 J.C. Tremblay, Mont.	1.00	2.00
131 Bernie Parent (G), Toro.	6.50	12.00
132 Dunc McCallum, Pitt. RC	**2.25**	**6.50**

1971 - 72 SUN PHOTOS

This series was also issued in the Vancouver area with the Columbian logo replacing the Sun logo, and in Moncton, NB, with Les Etoiles, De la LNH en Action Presentees Le Progrès l'évangéline. These photos measure 5 1/4" x 7".

Complete Set (294 photos):	**250.00**	**550.00**
Album:	**20.00**	**40.00**
Common Player:	**.75**	**1.50**

Sun Photos	**EX**	**NM**
Scott Young	1.00	2.00

Sun Photos • Boston Bruins	**EX**	**NM**
Bruins Team Crest	1.25	2.50
Don Awrey	.75	1.50
Garnet Bailey	.75	1.50
Ivan Boldirev	.75	1.50
John Bucyk	2.50	5.00
Wayne Cashman	.75	1.50
Gerry Cheevers (G)	3.25	6.50
Phil Esposito	6.00	12.00
Ted Green	.75	1.50
Ken Hodge	.75	1.50
Eddie Johnston (G)	1.00	2.00
Reggie Leach	.75	1.50
Don Marcotte	.75	1.50
John McKenzie	.75	1.50
Bobby Orr	25.00	50.00
Derek Sanderson	3.00	6.00
Dallas Smith	.75	1.50
Rick Smith	.75	1.50
Fred Stanfield	.75	1.50
Mike Walton	.75	1.50
Ed Westfall	.75	1.50

Sun Photos • Buffalo Sabres	**EX**	**NM**
Sabres Team Crest	1.25	2.50
Doug Barrie	.75	1.50
Roger Crozier (G)	1.50	3.00
Dave Dryden (G)	1.00	2.00
Dick Duff	.75	1.50
Phil Goyette	.75	1.50
Al Hamilton	.75	1.50
Larry Keenan	.75	1.50
Danny Lawson	.75	1.50
Don Luce	.75	1.50
Richard Martin	1.25	2.50
Ray McKay	.75	1.50
Gerry Meehan	.75	1.50
Kevin O'Shea	.75	1.50
Gilbert Perreault	4.50	9.00
Tracy Pratt	.75	1.50
Mike Robitaille	.75	1.50
Eddie Shack	2.50	5.00
Jimmy Watson	.75	1.50
Rod Zaine	.75	1.50

Sun Photos • California Golden Seals	**EX**	**NM**
California Team Crest	1.25	2.50
Wayne Carleton	.75	1.50
Lyle Carter (G)	1.00	2.00
Gary Croteau	.75	1.50
Norm Ferguson	.75	1.50
Stan Gilbertson	.75	1.50
Ernie Hicke	.75	1.50
Gary Jarrett	.75	1.50
Joey Johnston	.75	1.50
Marshall Johnston	.75	1.50
Bert Marshall	.75	1.50
Walt McKechnie	.75	1.50
Don O'Donoghue	.75	1.50
Gerry Pinder	.75	1.50
Dick Redmond	.75	1.50
Bobby Sheehan	.75	1.50
Paul Shmyr	.75	1.50
Ron Stackhouse	2.50	5.00
Carol Vadnais	.75	1.50
Tom Williams	.75	1.50

Sun Photos • Chicago Blackhawks	**EX**	**NM**
Chicago Team Crest	1.25	2.50
Lou Angotti	.75	1.50
Bryan Campbell	.75	1.50
Tony Esposito (G)	6.00	12.00
Bobby Hull	18.00	35.00
Dennis Hull	.75	1.50
Doug Jarrett	.75	1.50
Jerry Korab	.75	1.50
Cliff Koroll	.75	1.50
Daryl Maggs	.75	1.50
Keith Magnuson	.75	1.50
Chico Maki	.75	1.50
Dan Maloney	.75	1.50
Pit Martin	.75	1.50
Stan Mikita	4.50	9.00
Eric Nesterenko	.75	1.50
Danny O'Shea	.75	1.50
Jim Pappin	.75	1.50
Gary Smith (G)	1.00	2.00
Pat Stapleton	.75	1.50
Bill White	.75	1.50

Sun Photos • Detroit Red Wings	**EX**	**NM**
Detroit Team Crest	1.25	2.50
Red Berenson	.75	1.50
Gary Bergman	.75	1.50
Arnie Brown	.75	1.50
Guy Charron	.75	1.50
Bill Collins	.75	1.50
Brian Conacher	.75	1.50
Joe Daley (G)	1.00	2.00
Alex Delvecchio	2.50	5.00
Marcel Dionne	6.00	12.00
Tim Ecclestone	.75	1.50
Ron Harris	.75	1.50
Gerry Hart	.75	1.50
Gordie Howe	25.00	45.00
Al Karlander	.75	1.50
Nick Libett	.75	1.50
Ab McDonald	.75	1.50
Jim Niekamp	.75	1.50
Mickey Redmond	1.25	2.50
Leon Rochefort	.75	1.50
Al Smith (G)	1.00	2.00

Sun Photos • Los Angeles Kings	**EX**	**NM**
Kings Team Crest	1.25	2.50
Ralph Backstrom	.75	1.50
Robert Perry	.75	1.50
Mike Byers	.75	1.50
Larry Cahan	.75	1.50
Paul Curtis	.75	1.50
Denis DeJordy (G)	1.00	2.00
Gary Edwards (G)	1.00	2.00
Bill Flett	.75	1.50
Butch Goring	.75	1.50
Lucien Grenier	.75	1.50
Larry Hillman	.75	1.50
Dale Hoganson	.75	1.50
Harry Howell	1.50	3.00
Eddie Joyal	.75	1.50
Real Lemieux	.75	1.50
Ross Lonsberry	.75	1.50
Al McDonough	.75	1.50
Jean Potvin	.75	1.50
Bob Pulford	1.75	3.50
Juha Widing	.75	1.50

Sun Photos • Minnesota North Stars	**EX**	**NM**
Minnesota Team Crest	1.25	2.50
Fred Barrett	.75	1.50
Charlie Burns	.75	1.50
Jude Drouin	.75	1.50
Barry Gibbs	.75	1.50
Gilles Gilbert (G)	1.00	2.00
Bill Goldsworthy	.75	1.50
Danny Grant	.75	1.50
Ted Hampson	.75	1.50
Ted Harris	.75	1.50
Buster (Fred) Harvey	.75	1.50
Césare Maniago (G)	1.00	2.00
Doug Mohns	.75	1.50
Lou Nanne	.75	1.50
Bob Nevin	.75	1.50
Dennis O'Brien	.75	1.50
Murray Oliver	.75	1.50
Jean Paul Parise	.75	1.50
Dean Prentice	.75	1.50
Tom Reid	.75	1.50
Gump Worsley (G)	3.25	6.50

Sun Photos • Montréal Canadiens	**EX**	**NM**
Montréal Team Crest	1.25	2.50
Pierre Bouchard	.75	1.50
Yvan Cournoyer	2.50	5.00
Ken Dryden (G)	15.00	30.00
Terry Harper	.75	1.50
Réjean Houle	1.00	2.00
Guy Lafleur	12.00	25.00
Jacques Laperrière	1.25	2.50
Guy Lapointe	1.50	3.00
Claude Larose	.75	1.50
Jacques Lemaire	2.50	5.00
Frank Mahovlich	4.50	9.00
Pete Mahovlich	.75	1.50
Phil Myre (G)	1.00	2.00
Larry Pleau	.75	1.50
Henri Richard	4.00	8.00
Phil Roberto	.75	1.50
Serge Savard	1.50	3.00
Marc Tardif	.75	1.50
J.C. Tremblay	.75	1.50
Rogatien Vachon (G)	2.00	4.00

Sun Photos • New York Rangers	**EX**	**NM**
Rangers Team Crest	1.25	2.50
Dave Balon	.75	1.50
Ab DeMarco	.75	1.50
Jack Egers	.75	1.50
Bill Fairbairn	.75	1.50
Ed Giacomin (G)	3.25	6.50
Rod Gilbert	2.50	5.00
Vic Hadfield	.75	1.50
Ted Irvine	.75	1.50
Bruce MacGregor	.75	1.50
Jim Neilson	.75	1.50
Brad Park	3.50	7.00
Jean Ratelle	2.50	5.00
Dale Rolfe	.75	1.50
Bobby Rousseau	.75	1.50
Glen Sather	1.50	3.00
Rod Seiling	.75	1.50
Pete Stemkowski	.75	1.50
Walt Tkaczuk	.75	1.50
Gilles Villemure (G)	1.00	2.00

Sun Photos • Philadelphia Flyers	**EX**	**NM**
Flyers Team Crest	1.25	2.50
Barry Ashbee	.75	1.50
Serge Bernier	.75	1.50
Larry Brown	.75	1.50
Bobby Clarke	7.50	15.00
Gary Dornhoefer	.75	1.50
Doug Favell (G)	1.00	2.00
Bruce Gamble (G)	1.00	2.00
Jean-Guy Gendron	.75	1.50
Larry Hale	.75	1.50
Wayne Hillman	.75	1.50
Brent Hughes	.75	1.50
Jim Johnson	.75	1.50
Bob Kelly	.75	1.50
André Lacroix	1.00	2.00
Bill Lesuk	.75	1.50
Rick MacLeish	1.00	2.00
Larry Mickey	.75	1.50
Simon Nolet	.75	1.50
Pierre Plante	.75	1.50
Ed Van Impe	.75	1.50
Joe Watson	.75	1.50

Sun Photos • Pittsburgh Penguins	**EX**	**NM**
Penguins Team Crest	1.25	2.50
Syl Apps	.75	1.50
Les Binkley (G)	1.00	2.00
Wally Boyer	.75	1.50
Darryl Edestrand	.75	1.50
Roy Edwards (G)	1.00	2.00
Nick Harbaruk	.75	1.50
Bryan Hextall	.75	1.50
Bill Hicke	.75	1.50
Tim Horton	4.50	9.00
Sheldon Kannegiesser	.75	1.50
Bobby Leiter	.75	1.50
Keith McCreary	.75	1.50
Joe Noris	.75	1.50
Greg Polis	.75	1.50
Jean Pronovost	.75	1.50
Rene Robert	.75	1.50
Duane Rupp	.75	1.50
Ken Schinkel	.75	1.50
Ron Schock	.75	1.50

□□□	Bryan Watson	.75	1.50
□□□	Bob Woytowich	.75	1.50
Sun Photos • St. Louis Blues		**EX**	**NM**
□□□	Blues Team Crest	1.25	2.50
□□□	Al Arbour	1.00	2.00
□□□	John Arbour	.75	1.50
□□□	Chris Bordeleau	.75	1.50
□□□	Carl Brewer	.75	1.50
□□□	Gene Carr	.75	1.50
□□□	Wayne Connelly	.75	1.50
□□□	Terry Crisp	1.00	2.00
□□□	Jim Lorentz	.75	1.50
□□□	Pete McDuffe (G)	1.00	2.00
□□□	George Morrison	.75	1.50
□□□	Michel Parizeau	.75	1.50
□□□	Noel Picard	.75	1.50
□□□	Barclay Plager	1.00	2.00
□□□	Bob Plager	.75	1.50
□□□	Jim Roberts	.75	1.50
□□□	Gary Sabourin	.75	1.50
□□□	Jim Shires	.75	1.50
□□□	Frank St. Marseille	.75	1.50
□□□	Bill Sutherland	.75	1.50
□□□	Garry Unger	1.00	2.00
□□□	Ernie Wakely (G)	1.00	2.00
Sun Photos • Toronto Maple Leafs		**EX**	**NM**
□□□	Toronto Team Crest	1.25	2.50
□□□	Bobby Baun	.75	1.50
□□□	Jim Dorey	.75	1.50
□□□	Denis Dupère	.75	1.50
□□□	Ron Ellis	.75	1.50
□□□	Brian Glennie	.75	1.50
□□□	Jim Harrison	.75	1.50
□□□	Paul Henderson	1.25	2.50
□□□	Dave Keon	2.50	5.00
□□□	Rick Ley	.75	1.50
□□□	Billy MacMillan	.75	1.50
□□□	Don Marshall	.75	1.50
□□□	Jim McKenny	.75	1.50
□□□	Garry Monahan	.75	1.50
□□□	Bernie Parent (G)	5.00	10.00
□□□	Mike Pelyk	.75	1.50
□□□	Jacques Plante (G)	7.50	15.00
□□□	Brad Selwood	.75	1.50
□□□	Darryl Sittler	5.00	10.00
□□□	Brian Spencer	.75	1.50
□□□	Guy Trottier	.75	1.50
□□□	Norm Ullman	2.50	5.00
Sun Photos • Vancouver Canucks		**EX**	**NM**
□□□	Canucks Team Crest	1.25	2.50
□□□	André Boudrias	.75	1.50
□□□	George Gardner (G)	1.00	2.00
□□□	Jocelyn Guevremont	.75	1.50
□□□	Murray Hall	.75	1.50
□□□	Danny Johnson	.75	1.50
□□□	Dennis Kearns	.75	1.50
□□□	Orland Kurtenbach	.75	1.50
□□□	Bobby Lalonde	.75	1.50
□□□	Wayne Maki	.75	1.50
□□□	Rosaire Paiement	.75	1.50
□□□	Poul Popeil	.75	1.50
□□□	Pat Quinn	1.00	2.00
□□□	John Schella	.75	1.50
□□□	Bobby Schmautz	.75	1.50
□□□	Fred Speck	.75	1.50
□□□	Dale Tallon	.75	1.50
□□□	Ron Ward	.75	1.50
□□□	Barry Wilkins	.75	1.50
□□□	Dunc Wilson (G)	1.00	2.00

1971 - 72 WILLIAMS (SUOMI)

These stickers measure 1 7/8" x 2 9/16".

Complete Set (384 stickers):

Williams EX NM

□ 1 Vitaly Davydov, USSR
□ 2 Anatoli Firsov, USSR
□ 3 Valeri Kharlamov, USSR
□ 4 Viktor Konovalenko (G), USSR
□ 5 Viktor Kuzkin, USSR
□ 6 Yuri Liapkin, USSR
□ 7 Vladimir Lutchenko, USSR
□ 8 Alexander Maltsev, USSR
□ 9 Alexander Martiniuk, USSR
□ 10 Boris Mikhailov, USSR
□ 11 Evgeni Mishakov, USSR
□ 12 Vladimir Petrov, USSR
□ 13 Alexander Ragulin, USSR
□ 14 Igor Romishevski, USSR
□ 15 Vladimir Shadrin, USSR
□ 16 Viatjeslav Starshinov, USSR
□ 17 Vladislav Tretiak (G), USSR
□ 18 Gennady Tsicankov, USSR
□ 19 Vladimir Vikulov, USSR
□ 20 Evgeni Zimin, USSR
□ 21 Bedrich Brunschk, CSR.
□ 22 Jiri Bubla, CSR.
□ 23 Josef Cerny, CSR.
□ 24 Richard Farda, CSR.
□ 25 Jan Havel, CSR.
□ 26 Ivan Hlinka, CSR.
□ 27 Jiri Holecek, CSR.
□ 28 Jiri Holik, CSR.
□ 29 Josef Horesovsky, CSR.
□ 30 Jiri Kochta, CSR.
□ 31 Oldrich Machac, CSR.
□ 32 Vladimir Martinec, CSR.
□ 33 Vaclav Nedomansky, CSR.
□ 34 Eduard Novak, CSR.
□ 35 Frantisek Panchartek, CSR.
□ 36 Frantisek Pospisil, CSR.
□ 37 Marcel Sakac, CSR.
□ 38 Bohuslav Stastny, CSR.
□ 39 Jan Suchy, CSR.
□ 40 Christer Abrahamsson, Swe.
□ 41 Thommy Abrahamsson, Swe.
□ 42 Thommie Bergman, Swe.
□ 43 Arne Carlsson, Swe.
□ 44 Inge Hammarstrom, Swe.
□ 45 Anders Hedberg, Swe.
□ 46 Leif Holmqvist (G), Swe.
□ 47 Stig-Goran Johansson, Swe.
□ 48 Stefan Karlsson, Swe.
□ 49 Hans Lindberg, Swe.
□ 50 Tord Lundstrom, Swe.
□ 51 William Lofqvist, Swe.
□ 52 Kjell-Rune Milton, Swe.
□ 53 LarsGoran Nilsson, Swe.
□ 54 Bert-Ola Nordlander, Swe.
□ 55 Hakan Nygren, Swe.
□ 56 Bjorn Palmqvist, Swe.
□ 57 Hakan Pettersson, Swe.
□ 58 Ulf Sterner, Swe.
□ 59 Lennart Svedberg, Swe.
□ 60 Hakan Wickberg, Swe.
□ 61 Esa Isaksson, Fin.
□ 62 Heikki Jarn, Fin.
□ 63 Veli-Pekka Ketola, Fin.
□ 64 Ilpo Koskela, Fin.
□ 65 Seppo Lindstrom, Fin.
□ 66 Harri Linnonmaa, Fin.
□ 67 Hannu Luojola, Fin.
□ 68 Pekka Marjamaki, Fin.
□ 69 Erkki Mononen, Fin.
□ 70 Lauri Mononen, Fin.
□ 71 Matti Murto, Fin.
□ 72 Lasse Oksanen, Fin.
□ 73 Esa Peltonen, Fin.
□ 74 Seppo Repo, Fin.
□ 75 Tommi Salmelainen, Fin.
□ 76 Juhani Tamminen, Fin.
□ 77 Jorma Valtonen, Fin.
□ 78 Jorma Vehmanen, Fin.
□ 79 Urpo Ylonen, Fin.
□ 80 Jouko Oystila, Fin.
□ 81 Tapio Flinck, Assat Pori
□ 82 Antti Heikkila, Assat Pori
□ 83 Reijo Heinonen, Assat Pori
□ 84 Jaakko Honkanen, Assat Pori
□ 85 Veli-Pekka Ketola, Assat Pori
□ 86 Raimo Kilpio, Assat Pori
□ 87 Tapio Koskinen, Assat Pori
□ 88 Kaj Matalamaki, Assat Pori
□ 89 Pertti Makela, Assat Pori
□ 90 Pekka Rautakallio, Assat Pori
□ 91 Markku Riihimaki, Assat Pori
□ 92 Matti Salmi, Assat Pori
□ 93 Jorma Valtonen, Assat Pori
□ 94 Anto Virtanen, Assat Pori
□ 95 Erkki Vakiparta, Assat Pori
□ 96 Pertti Ahokas, Jokerit
□ 97 Pertti Arvaja, Jokerit
□ 98 Olli Hietanen, Jokerit
□ 99 Pentti Hiiros, Jokerit
□ 100 Eero Holopainen, Jokerit
□ 101 Kari Kinnunen, Jokerit
□ 102 Ilpo Koskela, Jokerit
□ 103 Timo Kyntola, Jokerit
□ 104 Henry Leppa, Jokerit
□ 105 Erkki Mononen, Jokerit
□ 106 Pertti Nurmi, Jokerit
□ 107 Timo Relas, Jokerit
□ 108 Timo Sutinen, Jokerit
□ 109 Timo Turunen, Jokerit
□ 110 Jouko Oystila, Jokerit
□ 111 Juhani Bostrom, HIFK
□ 112 Kimmo Heino, HIFK
□ 113 Esa Isaksson, HIFK
□ 114 Juhani Jylha, HIFK
□ 115 Heikki Jarn, HIFK
□ 116 Mauri Kaukokari, HIFK
□ 117 Vaino Kolkka, HIFK
□ 118 Harri Linnonmaa, HIFK
□ 119 Jaakko Marttinen, HIFK
□ 120 Matti Murto, HIFK
□ 121 Lalli Partinen, HIFK
□ 122 Juha Rantasila, HIFK
□ 123 Heikki Riihiranta, HIFK
□ 124 Jorma Rikala, HIFK
□ 125 Tommi Salmelainen, HIFK
□ 126 Jorma Thusberg, HIFK
□ 127 Matti Vaisanen, HIFK
□ 128 Jukka Alkula, Tappara
□ 129 Pertti Ansakorpi, Tappara
□ 130 Keijo Jarvinen, Tappara
□ 131 Pertti Koivulahti, Tappara
□ 132 Ilpo Kuisma, Tappara
□ 133 Vesa Lehtoranta, Tappara
□ 134 Antti Leppanen, Tappara
□ 135 Pekka Marjamaki, Tappara
□ 136 Mikko Mynttinen, Tappara
□ 137 Pekka Makinen, Tappara
□ 138 Seppo Makinen, Tappara
□ 139 Keijo Mannisto, Tappara
□ 140 Antti Perttula, Tappara
□ 141 Tuomo Rautiainen, Tappara
□ 142 Juhani Saarelainen, Tappara
□ 143 Jorma Saarikorpi, Tappara
□ 144 Risto Seesvuori, Tappara
□ 145 Jorma Siitarinen, Tappara
□ 146 Raimo Suoniemi, Tappara
□ 147 Juhani Aaltonen, HJK
□ 148 Matti Ahvenharju, HJK.
□ 149 Hannu Auvinen, HJK.
□ 150 Jorma Borgstrom, HJK.
□ 151 Martti Immonen, HJK.
□ 152 Matti Keinonen, HJK.
□ 153 Seppo Laakkio, HJK.
□ 154 Timo Lahtinen, HJK.
□ 155 Esa Peltonen, HJK.
□ 156 Keijo Puhakka, HJK.
□ 157 Antti Ravi, HJK.
□ 158 Timo Saari, HJK.
□ 159 Esa Siren, HJK.
□ 160 Erkki Suni, HJK.
□ 161 Seppo Suoraniemi, HJK.
□ 162 Juhani Tamminen, HJK.
□ 163 Jorma Vehmanen, HJK.
□ 164 Stig Wetzell, HJK.
□ 165 Olli Viilma, HJK.
□ 166 Leo Aikas, HJK.
□ 167 Sakari Ahlberg, Ilves
□ 168 Seppo Ahokainen, Ilves
□ 169 Jorma Aro, Ilves
□ 170 Esko Eriksson, Ilves
□ 171 Markku Hakanen, Ilves
□ 172 Matti Hakanen, Ilves
□ 173 Reijo Hakanen, Ilves
□ 174 Martti Helle, Ilves
□ 175 Timo Hirsimaki, Ilves
□ 176 Jorma Kallio, Ilves
□ 177 Esko Kaonpaa, Ilves
□ 178 Pentti Koskela, Ilves
□ 179 Pekka Kuusisto, Ilves
□ 180 Pekka Leimu, Ilves
□ 181 Jukka Mattila, Ilves
□ 182 Lasse Oksanen, Ilves
□ 183 Kari Palooja, Ilves
□ 184 Jorma Peltonen, Ilves
□ 185 Tuomo Sillman, Ilves
□ 186 Jaakko Siren, Ilves
□ 187 Veikko Suominen, Ilves
□ 188 Matti Jakonen, Turun Toverit
□ 189 Kari Johansson, Turun Toverit
□ 190 Arto Kaunonen, Turun Toverit
□ 191 Timo Kokkonen, Turun Toverit
□ 192 Reijo Leppanen, Turun Toverit
□ 193 Seppo Lindstrom, Turun Toverit
□ 194 Hannu Luojola, Turun Toverit
□ 195 Hannu Niittoaho, Turun Toverit
□ 196 Reijo Paksal, Turun Toverit
□ 197 Seppo Parikka, Turun Toverit
□ 198 Jarmo Rantanen, Turun Toverit
□ 199 Veijo Saarinen, Turun Toverit
□ 200 Martti Salonen, Turun Toverit
□ 201 Voitto Soini, Turun Toverit
□ 202 Kari Torkkel, Turun Toverit
□ 203 Risto Vainio, Turun Toverit
□ 204 Pentti Vihanto, Turun Toverit
□ 205 Seppo Wikstrom, Turun Toverit
□ 206 Urpo Ylonen, Turun Toverit
□ 207 Hannu Haapalainen, Koovee
□ 208 JukkaPekka Jarvenpaa, Koovee
□ 209 Timo Jarvinen, Koovee
□ 210 Heikki Keinonen, Koovee
□ 211 Heimo Keinonen, Koovee
□ 212 Rauno Lehtio, Koovee
□ 213 Markku Moisio, Koovee
□ 214 Seppo Nurmi, Koovee
□ 215 Esko Rantanen, Koovee
□ 216 Juhani Ruohonen, Koovee
□ 217 Mikko Raikkonen, Koovee
□ 218 Lauri Salomaa, Koovee
□ 219 Veikko Savolainen, Koovee
□ 220 Leo Seppanen, Koovee
□ 221 Pekka Uitus, Koovee
□ 222 Jorma Vilen, Koovee
□ 223 Tapio Virhimo, Koovee
□ 224 Kauko Fomin, Turun Palloseura
□ 225 Heikki Hurme, Turun Palloseura
□ 226 Eero Juntunen, Turun Palloseura
□ 227 Lauri Jamsen, Turun Palloseura
□ 228 Lasse Kiili, Turun Palloseura
□ 229 Hannu Koivunen, Turun Palloseura
□ 230 Jarmo Koivunen, Turun Palloseura
□ 231 Pekka Lahtela, Turun Palloseura
□ 232 Ilkka Mesikammen, Turun Palloseura
□ 233 Timo Nummelin, Turun Palloseura
□ 234 Rauli Ottila, Turun Palloseura
□ 235 Matti Rautee, Turun Palloseura
□ 236 Pekka Rautee, Turun Palloseura
□ 237 Jari Rosberg, Turun Palloseura
□ 238 Jouni Samuli, Turun Palloseura
□ 239 Harry Silver, Turun Palloseura
□ 240 Rauli Tammelin, Turun Palloseura
□ 241 Bengt Wilenius, Turun Palloseura
□ 242 Mikko Erholm, Rauman Lukko
□ 243 Veikko Ihalainen, Rauman Lukko
□ 244 Heikki Kauhanen, Rauman Lukko
□ 245 Tapani Koskimaki, Rauman Lukko
□ 246 Antti Laine, Rauman Lukko
□ 247 Arto Laine, Rauman Lukko
□ 248 Timo Lehtorinne, Rauman Lukko
□ 249 Hannu Lunden, Rauman Lukko
□ 250 Teppo Rastio, Rauman Lukko
□ 251 Pentti Rautalin, Rauman Lukko
□ 252 Kai Rosvall, Rauman Lukko
□ 253 Ilkka Saarikko, Rauman Lukko
□ 254 Jari Sarronlahti, Rauman Lukko
□ 255 Matti Saurio, Rauman Lukko
□ 256 Hannu Siivonen, Rauman Lukko
□ 257 Erkki Sundelin, Rauman Lukko
□ 258 Simo Suoknuuti, Rauman Lukko
□ 259 Martti Haapala, Joensuun
□ 260 Yrjo Hakulinen, Joensuun
□ 261 Pentti Hirvonen, Joensuun
□ 262 Antero Honkanen, Joensuun
□ 263 Pekka Lavikainen, Joensuun
□ 264 Pentti Lavikainen, Joensuun
□ 265 Pertti Martikainen, Joensuun
□ 266 Pentti Matikainen, Joensuun
□ 267 Seppo Nevalainen, Joensuun
□ 268 Tapio Pohtinen, Joensuun
□ 269 Kari Puustinen, Joensuun
□ 270 Markku Rouhiainen, Joensuun
□ 271 Jarmo Sahlman, Joensuun
□ 272 Seppo Saros, Joensuun
□ 273 Juha Silvennoinen, Joensuun
□ 274 Unto Turpeinen, Joensuun
□ 275 Kari Viitalahti, Joensuun
□ 276 Erkki Airaksinen, Karhukissat
□ 277 Kauko Alkunen, Karhukissat
□ 278 Jarmo Gummerus, Karhukissat
□ 279 Bjorn Herbert, Karhukissat
□ 280 Jarmo Jaakkola, Karhukissat
□ 281 Hannu Kapanen, Karhukissat
□ 282 Matti Koskinen, Karhukissat
□ 283 Martti Kuokkanen, Karhukissat
□ 284 Juhani Laine, Karhukissat
□ 285 Heikki Leppik, Karhukissat
□ 286 Juhani Langstrom, Karhukissat
□ 287 Osmo Lotjonen, Karhukissat
□ 288 Lauri Mononen, Karhukissat
□ 289 Christer Nordblad, Karhukissat
□ 290 Juha Poikolainen, Karhukissat
□ 291 Kimmo Rantanen, Karhukissat
□ 292 Seppo Repo, Karhukissat
□ 293 Ilpo Ruokosalmi, Karhukissat
□ 294 Arto Siissala, Karhukissat
□ 295 Bo Sjostedt, Karhukissat
□ 296 Pentti Viitanen, Karhukissat
□ 297 Pekka Arbelius, Oulun Jrs.
□ 298 Olli Enqvist, Oulun Jrs.
□ 299 Hannu Hiltunen, Oulun Jrs.
□ 300 Paavo Holopainen, Oulun Jrs.
□ 301 Juha Huikari, Oulun Jrs.
□ 302 Ari Jalonen, Oulun Jrs.
□ 303 Kari Jalonen, Oulun Jrs.
□ 304 Ari Kaikkonen, Oulun Jrs.
□ 305 Ari Kalmokoski, Oulun Jrs.
□ 306 Arto Lehtinen, Oulun Jrs.
□ 307 Markku Narhi, Oulun Jrs.
□ 308 Ilkka Okkonen, Oulun Jrs.
□ 309 Matti Perhonmaa, Oulun Jrs.
□ 310 JuhaPekka Porvari, Oulun Jrs.
□ 311 Arto Ruotanen, Oulun Jrs.
□ 312 Reijo Ruotsalainen, Oulun Jrs.
□ 313 Matti Ruutti, Oulun Jrs.
□ 314 Pertti Raisanen, Oulun Jrs.
□ 315 Ari Timosaari, Oulun Jrs.

☐ 316 Janne Oro, Oulun Jrs.
☐ 317 Anssi Eronen, Sapko Jrs.
☐ 318 Seppo Hirvonen, Sapko Jrs.
☐ 319 Jari Hannu Hamalainen, Sapko Jrs.
☐ 320 Jari Pekka Hamalainen, Sapko Jrs.
☐ 321 Timo Harkonen, Sapko Jrs.
☐ 322 Jouko Ikonen, Sapko Jrs.
☐ 323 Lasse Kaiponen, Sapko Jrs.
☐ 324 Jyri Kemppinen, Sapko Jrs.
☐ 325 Jouni Kostiainen, Sapko Jrs.
☐ 326 Kai Kulhoranta, Sapko Jrs.
☐ 327 Olli Lemola, Sapko Jrs.
☐ 328 Jari Lopponen, Sapko Jrs.
☐ 329 Pasi Makkonen, Sapko Jrs.
☐ 330 Vesa Massinen, Sapko Jrs.
☐ 331 Timo Minkkila, Sapko Jrs.
☐ 332 Petri Pellinen, Sapko Jrs.
☐ 333 Juha Rasanen, Sapko Jrs.
☐ 334 Pasi Sallinen, Sapko Jrs.
☐ 335 Kauko Tamminen, Sapko Jrs.
☐ 336 Olli Teijonmaa, Sapko Jrs.
☐ 337 Ismo Tolvanen, Sapko Jrs.
☐ 338 Timo Vaahtoluoto, Sapko Jrs.
☐ 339 Kari Heikkila, Ilves, Jrs.
☐ 340 Pekka Helander, Ilves, Jrs.
☐ 341 Jari Hirsimaki, Ilves, Jrs.
☐ 342 Jari Huotari, Ilves, Jrs.
☐ 343 Ilkka Huura, Ilves, Jrs.
☐ 344 Tero Juojarvi, Ilves, Jrs.
☐ 345 Jari Jarvinen, Ilves, Jrs.
☐ 346 Mika Laine, Ilves, Jrs.
☐ 347 Marko Lepaus, Ilves, Jrs.
☐ 338 Pertti Lundberg, Ilves, Jrs.
☐ 349 Tino Minetti, Ilves, Jrs.
☐ 350 Jarmo Partanen, Ilves, Jrs.
☐ 351 OlliPekka Perala, Ilves, Jrs.
☐ 352 Ari Ruuska, Ilves, Jrs.
☐ 353 Kai Saario, Ilves, Jrs.
☐ 354 Olli-Pekka Turunen, Ilves, Jrs.
☐ 355 VeliMatti Uusimaa, Ilves, Jrs.
☐ 356 Mauri Viita, Ilves, Jrs.
☐ 357 Timo Virtanen, Ilves, Jrs.
☐ 358 Jarmo Viteli, Ilves, Jrs.
☐ 359 Petri Viteli, Ilves, Jrs.
☐ 360 Ari Havukainen, Rauman Jrs.
☐ 361 Ismo Heinonen, Rauman Jrs.
☐ 362 Riku Hoyden, Rauman Jrs.
☐ 363 Jari Jokinen, Rauman Jrs.
☐ 364 Timo Joutsenvuori, Rauman Jrs.
☐ 365 Jyrki Jantti, Rauman Jrs.
☐ 366 Kimmo Jantti, Rauman Jrs.
☐ 367 Toni Ketola, Rauman Jrs.
☐ 368 Juha Korhonen, Rauman Jrs.
☐ 369 Ari Laine, Rauman Jrs.
☐ 370 Kari Lainio, Rauman Jrs.
☐ 371 Juha Makinen, Rauman Jrs.
☐ 372 Reima Numminen, Rauman Jrs.
☐ 373 Mika Pirila, Rauman Jrs.
☐ 374 Kai Pulli, Rauman Jrs.
☐ 375 Tero Tommila, Rauman Jrs.
☐ 376 Harri Tuohimaa, Rauman Jrs.
☐ 377 Pasi Tuohimaa, Rauman Jrs.
☐ 378 Ari Veijalainen, Rauman Jrs.
☐ 379 Jean Béliveau, Mont.
☐ 380 Phil Esposito, Bost.
☐ 381 Tony Esposito (G), Chic.
☐ 382 Gordie Howe, Detr.
☐ 383 Bobby Hull, Chic.
☐ 384 Bobby Orr, Bost.

1972 HELLAS MM - JENKKI

These cards measure 2 1/8" x 3 1/8".
Complete Set (99 cards):

Hellas EX NM

☐ 1 Seppo Ahokainen, Fin.
☐ 2 VeliPekka Ketola, Fin.
☐ 3 Henry Leppa, Fin.
☐ 4 Harri Linnonmaa, Fin.
☐ 5 Pekka Marjamaki, Fin.
☐ 6 Lauri Mononen, Fin.
☐ 7 Matti Murto, Fin.
☐ 8 Timo Nummelin, Fin.
☐ 9 Lasse Oksanen, Fin.
☐ 10 Esa Peltonen, Fin.
☐ 11 Pekka Rautakallio, Fin.
☐ 12 Seppo Repo, Fin.
☐ 13 Heikki Riihiranta, Fin.
☐ 14 Tommi Salmelainen, Fin.
☐ 15 Leo Seppanen, Fin.
☐ 16 Juhani Tamminen, Fin.
☐ 17 Timo Turunen, Fin.
☐ 18 Pertti Valkeapaa, Fin.
☐ 19 Jorma Valtonen, Fin.
☐ 20 Jouko Oystila, Fin.
☐ 21 Timo Saari, Fin.
☐ 22 Seppo Suoraniemi, Fin.
☐ 23 Leif Holmqvist (G), Swe.
☐ 24 Thommy Abrahamsson, Swe.
☐ 25 Thommie Bergman, Swe.
☐ 26 Stig Ostling, Swe.
☐ 27 Lars Sjoberg, Swe.
☐ 28 Carl Sundquist, Swe.
☐ 29 Bjorn Johansson, Swe.
☐ 30 Tord Lundstrom, Swe.
☐ 31 Stig-Goran Johansson, Swe.
☐ 32 Stefan Karlsson, Swe.
☐ 33 Lars-Goran Nilsson, Swe.
☐ 34 Stig Larsson, Swe.
☐ 35 Mats Lindh, Swe.
☐ 36 Bjorn Palmqvist, Swe.
☐ 37 Inge Hammarstrom, Swe.
☐ 38 Anders Hedberg, Swe.
☐ 39 Kurt Larsson, Swe.
☐ 40 Hakan Pettersson, Swe.
☐ 41 Hakan Wickberg, Swe.
☐ 42 Borje Salming, Swe.
☐ 43 Franz Funk, BRD.
☐ 44 Otto Schneitberger, BRD.
☐ 45 Josef Volk, BRD.
☐ 46 Rudolph Thanner, BRD.
☐ 47 Paul Langner, BRD.
☐ 48 Harald Kadow, BRD.
☐ 49 Anton Pohl, BRD.
☐ 50 KarlHeine Egger, BRD.
☐ 51 Lorenz Funk, BRD.
☐ 52 Alois Schloder, BRD.
☐ 53 Gustav Hanig, BRD.
☐ 54 Philip Reiner, BRD.
☐ 55 Bernd Kuhn, BRD.
☐ 56 Johann Eimansberger, BRD.
☐ 57 Rainer Makatsch, BRD.
☐ 58 Michael Eibl, BRD.
☐ 59 Hans Schichtl, BRD.
☐ 60 Anton Hoffher, BRD.
☐ 61 Vladimir Sepovalov, USSR
☐ 62 Aleksandr Gusev, USSR
☐ 63 Vladimir Lutchenko, USSR
☐ 64 Viktor Kuzkin, USSR
☐ 65 Aleksandr Ragulin, USSR
☐ 66 Igor Romishevski, USSR
☐ 67 Gennadi Tsigankov, USSR
☐ 68 Valeri Vasiliev, USSR
☐ 69 Yuri Blinov, USSR
☐ 70 Alexander Maltsev, USSR
☐ 71 Evgeny Mishakov, USSR
☐ 72 Boris Mikhailov, USSR
☐ 73 Vjatseslav Anisin, USSR
☐ 74 Alexander Yakhailov, USSR
☐ 75 Vladimir Petrov, USSR
☐ 76 Valeri Kharlamov, USSR
☐ 77 Vladimir Vikulov, USSR
☐ 78 Vladimir Shadrin, USSR
☐ 79 Vladislav Tretiak (G), USSR
☐ 80 Vladimir Dzurilla, CSR.
☐ 81 Jiri Holecek, CSR.
☐ 82 Josef Horesovsky, CSR.
☐ 83 Oldrich Machac, CSR.
☐ 84 Jaroslav Holik, CSR.
☐ 85 Rudolf Tajhnar, CSR.
☐ 86 Frantisek Pospisil, CSR.
☐ 87 Jiri Kochta, CSR.
☐ 88 Jan Klapac, CSR.
☐ 89 Vladimir Martinec, CSR.
☐ 90 Richard Farda, CSR.
☐ 91 Bohuslav Stastny, CSR.
☐ 92 Vaclav Nedomansky, CSR.
☐ 93 Julius Haas, CSR.
☐ 94 Josef Palecek, CSR.
☐ 95 Jiri Bubla, CSR.
☐ 96 Milan Kuzela, CSR.
☐ 97 Vladimir Bednar, CSR.
☐ 98 Jiri Holik, CSR.
☐ 99 Ivan Hlinka, CSR.

1972 PANDA MM - TORONTO

These cards measure 2 1/8" x 3 1/8".
Complete Set (112 cards):

Panda EX NM

☐ Juhani Bostrom, HIFK Helsinki
☐ Gary Engberg, HIFK Helsinki
☐ Kimmo Heino, HIFK Helsinki
☐ Mauri Kaukokari, HIFK Helsinki

☐ Vaino Kolkka, HIFK Helsinki
☐ Harri Linnonmaa, HIFK Helsinki
☐ Jaakko Marttinen, HIFK Helsinki
☐ Matti Murto, HIFK Helsinki
☐ Lalli Partinen, HIFK Helsinki
☐ Juha Rantasila, HIFK Helsinki
☐ Heikki Riihiranta, HIFK Helsinki
☐ Jorma Rikala, HIFK Helsinki
☐ Tommi Salmelainen, HIFK Helsinki
☐ Jorma Thusberg, HIFK Helsinki
☐ Jorma Virtanen, HIFK Helsinki
☐ Matti Vaisanen, HIFK Helsinki
☐ Sakari Ahlberg, Ilves Tampere
☐ Jorma Aro, Ilves Tampere
☐ Esko Eriksson, Ilves Tampere
☐ Markku Hakanen, Ilves Tampere
☐ Matti Hakanen, Ilves Tampere
☐ Reijo Hakanen, Ilves Tampere
☐ Timo Hirsimaki, Ilves Tampere
☐ Jorma Kallio, Ilves Tampere
☐ Esko Kaonpaa, Ilves Tampere
☐ Pentti Koskela, Ilves Tampere
☐ Pekka Kuusisto, Ilves Tampere
☐ Pekka Leimu, Ilves Tampere
☐ Lasse Oksanen, Ilves Tampere
☐ Kari Palooja, Ilves Tampere
☐ Jorma Peltonen, Ilves Tampere
☐ Veikko Suominen, Ilves Tampere
☐ Tapio Flinck, Ässät Pori
☐ Pentti Hakamaki, Ässät Pori
☐ Antti Heikkila, Ässät Pori
☐ Reijo Heinonen, Ässät Pori
☐ Jaakko Honkanen, Ässät Pori
☐ VeliPekka Ketola, Ässät Pori
☐ Raimo Kilpio, Ässät Pori
☐ Tapio Koskinen, Ässät Pori
☐ Kaj Matalamaki, Ässät Pori
☐ Pekka Rautakallio, Ässät Pori
☐ Matti Salmi, Ässät Pori
☐ KariPekka Toivonen, Ässät Pori
☐ Jorma Valtonen, Ässät Pori
☐ Anto Virtanen, Ässät Pori
☐ Erkki Vakiparta, Ässät Pori
☐ Vitaly Davydov, Soviet Union
☐ Anatoli Firsov, Soviet Union
☐ Valery Kharlamov, Soviet Union
☐ Victor Konovalenko (G), Soviet Union
☐ Victor Kuzkin, Soviet Union
☐ Yuri Liapkin, Soviet Union
☐ Vladimir Lutchenko, Soviet Union
☐ Alexander Maltsev, Soviet Union
☐ Alexander Martiniuk, Soviet Union
☐ Boris Mikhailov, Soviet Union
☐ Alexander Ragulin, Soviet Union
☐ Igor Romishevskyi, Soviet Union
☐ Vladimir Shadrin, Soviet Union
☐ Viacheslav Starshinov, Soviet Union
☐ Vladislav Tretiak (G), Soviet Union
☐ Evgenyi Zimin, Soviet Union
☐ Christer Abrahamsson, Sweden
☐ Tommy Abrahamsson, Sweden
☐ Arne Carlsson, Sweden
☐ Inge Hammarstrom, Sweden
☐ Leif Holmqvist (G), Sweden
☐ Stig-Goran Johansson, Sweden
☐ Stefan Karlsson, Sweden
☐ Hans Lindberg, Sweden
☐ Tord Lundstrom, Sweden
☐ Lars-Göran Nilsson, Sweden
☐ Bert-Ola Nordlander, Sweden
☐ Hakan Nygren, Sweden
☐ Bjorn Palmqvist, Sweden
☐ Ulf Sterner, Sweden
☐ Lennart Svedberg, Sweden
☐ Hakan Wickberg, Sweden
☐ Josef Cerny, Czechoslovakia
☐ Richard Farda, Czechoslovakia
☐ Ivan Hlinka, Czechoslovakia
☐ Jiri Holecek, Czechoslovakia
☐ Jiri Holik, Czechoslovakia
☐ Josef Horesovsky, Czechoslovakia
☐ Milan Kuzela, Czechoslovakia
☐ Oldrich Machac, Czechoslovakia
☐ Vladimir Martinec, Czechoslovakia
☐ Vladimir Nadrachal, Czechoslovakia
☐ Vaclav Nedomansky, Czechoslovakia
☐ Frantisek Panchartek, Czechoslovakia
☐ Frantisek Pospisil, Czechoslovakia
☐ Marcel Sakac, Czechoslovakia
☐ Bohuslav Stastny, Czechoslovakia
☐ Rudolf Tajcnar, Czechoslovakia
☐ Esa Isaksson, Finland
☐ Heikki Jarn, Finland
☐ VeliPekka Ketola, Finland
☐ Ilpo Koskela, Finland
☐ Seppo Lindstrom, Finland
☐ Harri Linnonmaa, Finland
☐ Pekka Marjamaki, Finland
☐ Erkki Mononen, Finland
☐ Lauri Mononen, Finland
☐ Matti Murto, Finland
☐ Lasse Oksanen, Finland
☐ Esa Peltonen, Finland
☐ Seppo Repo, Finland
☐ Tommi Salmelainen, Finland
☐ Jorma Valtonen, Finland
☐ Urpo Ylonen, Finland
☐ Jouko Oystila, Finland

1972 SCOTIA BANK POSTCARD

This postcard measures 5 13/16" x 3 15/16".

Scotia Bank	**EX**	**NM**
☐ Go Canada	6.00	12.00

1972 SEMIC STICKERS

These stickers measure 1 7/8" x 2 9/16". There are two versions: a Finland (Jââkiekko/Olympia-MM72) and a Sweden (ISHOCKEY/OS-VM72) version.

Complete Set (233 stickers):	**225.00**	**450.00**
Common Player:	**.35**	**.75**
Semic Stickers	**EX**	**NM**
☐ ☐ 1 Viktor Konovalenko (G), USSR	.35	.75
☐ ☐ 2 Vitali Davydov, USSR	.35	.75
☐ ☐ 3 Vladimir Lutchenko, USSR	.35	.75
☐ ☐ 4 Viktor Kuzkin, USSR	.35	.75
☐ ☐ 5 Aleksandr Ragulin, USSR	1.25	2.50
☐ ☐ 6 Igor Romishevski, USSR	.35	.75
☐ ☐ 7 Gennadi Tsycankov, USSR	.35	.75
☐ ☐ 8 Vjatsjeslav Starsinov, USSR	.35	.75
☐ ☐ 9 Jevgeni Zimin, USSR	.35	.75
☐ ☐ 10 Alexander Maltsev, USSR	2.25	4.50
☐ ☐ 11 Anatoli Firsov, USSR	1.00	2.00
☐ ☐ 12 Evgeny Mishakov, USSR	.35	.75
☐ ☐ 13 Boris Mikhailov, USSR	2.50	5.00
☐ ☐ 14 Yuri Liapkin, USSR	.35	.75
☐ ☐ 15 Alexander Martiniuk, USSR	.35	.75
☐ ☐ 16 Vladimir Petrov, USSR	1.50	3.00
☐ ☐ 17 Valeri Harlamov, USSR	6.00	12.00
☐ ☐ 18 Vladimir Vikulov, USSR	.35	.75
☐ ☐ 19 Vladimir Shadrin, USSR	.35	.75
☐ ☐ 20 Vladislav Tretiak (G), USSR	11.00	22.00
☐ ☐ 21 Marcel Sakac, CSR.	.35	.75
☐ ☐ 22 Jiri Holecek, CSR.	1.00	2.00
☐ ☐ 23 Josef Horesovsky, CSR.	.35	.75
☐ ☐ 24 Oldrich Machac, CSR.	.35	.75
☐ ☐ 25 Rudolf Tajcnar, CSR.	.35	.75
☐ ☐ 26 Frantisek Panchartek, CSR.	.35	.75
☐ ☐ 27 Frantisek Pospisil, CSR.	.35	.75
☐ ☐ 28 Jiri Kochta, CSR.	.35	.75
☐ ☐ 29 Jan Havel, CSR.	.35	.75
☐ ☐ 30 Vladimir Martinec, CSR.	.35	.75
☐ ☐ 31 Richard Farda, CSR.	.35	.75
☐ ☐ 32 Bohuslav Stastny, CSR.	.35	.75
☐ ☐ 33 Vaclav Nedomansky, CSR.	1.25	2.50
☐ ☐ 34 Josef Cerny, CSR.	.35	.75
☐ ☐ 35 Bedrich Brunchlik, CSR.	.35	.75
☐ ☐ 36 Jan Suchy, CSR.	.35	.75
☐ ☐ 37 Eduard Novak, CSR.	.35	.75
☐ ☐ 38 Jiri Bubla, CSR.	1.00	2.00

☐☐ 39 Jiri Holik, CSR.	.35	.75
☐☐ 40 Ivan Hlinka, CSR.	1.00	2.00
☐☐ 41 Vladimir Bednar, CSR.	.35	.75
☐☐ 42 Leif Holmqvist (G), Swe.	.35	.75
☐☐ 43 Christer Abrahamsson, Swe.	1.00	2.00
☐☐ 44 Christer Andersson, Swe.	.35	.75
☐☐ 45 Lars-Erik Sjöberg, Swe.	1.25	2.50
☐☐ 46 Lennart Svedberg, Swe.	.35	.75
☐☐ 47 Stig-Göran Johansson, Swe.	.35	.75
☐☐ 48 Bert-Ola Nordlander, Swe.	.35	.75
☐☐ 49 Thommy Abrahamsson, Swe.	1.00	2.00
☐☐ 50 Arne Carlsson, Swe.	.35	.75
☐☐ 51 Stefan Karlsson, Swe.	.35	.75
☐☐ 52 Håkan Wickberg, Swe.	.35	.75
☐☐ 53 Håkan Nygren, Swe.	.35	.75
☐☐ 54 Lars-Göran Nilsson, Swe.	.35	.75
☐☐ 55 Thommie Bergman, Swe.	1.50	3.00
☐☐ 56 Ulf Sterner, Swe.	.35	.75
☐☐ 57 Hans Lindberg, Swe.	.35	.75
☐☐ 58 Tord Lundström, Swe.	.35	.75
☐☐ 60 Björn Palmqvist, Swe.	.35	.75
☐☐ 61 Inge Hammarström, Swe.	2.00	4.00
☐☐ 62 Kjell-Rune Milton, Swe.	.35	.75
☐☐ 63 Kjell Brus, Swe.	.35	.75
☐☐ 64 Kenneth Ekman, Swe.	.35	.75
☐☐ 65 Bengt-Göran Karlsson, Swe.	.35	.75
☐☐ 66 Håkan Pettersson, Swe.	.35	.75
☐☐ 67 Dan Labraaten, Swe.	1.00	2.00
☐☐ 68 Dan Söderström, Swe.	.35	.75
☐☐ 69 Anders Hedberg, Swe.	4.00	8.00
☐☐ 70 Ake Söderberg, Swe.	.35	.75
☐☐ 71 Urpo Ylönen, Fin.	.35	.75
☐☐ 72 Ilpo Koskela, Fin.	.35	.75
☐☐ 73 Seppo Lindström, Fin.	.35	.75
☐☐ 74 Hannu Luojola, Fin.	.35	.75
☐☐ 75 Pekka Marjamäki, Fin.	.35	.75
☐☐ 76 Jouko Öystilä, Fin.	.35	.75
☐☐ 77 Heikki Järn, Fin.	.35	.75
☐☐ 78 Esa Isaksson, Fin.	.35	.75
☐☐ 79 Veli-Pekka Ketola, Fin.	1.25	2.50
☐☐ 80 Harri Linnonmtaa, Fin.	.35	.75
☐☐ 81 Erkki Mononen, Fin.	.35	.75
☐☐ 82 Lauri Mononen, Fin.	.35	.75
☐☐ 83 Matti Murto, Fin.	.35	.75
☐☐ 84 Lasse Oksanen, Fin.	.35	.75
☐☐ 85 Esa Peltonen, Fin.	.35	.75
☐☐ 86 Seppo Repo, Fin.	.35	.75
☐☐ 87 Tommi Salmelainen, Fin.	.35	.75
☐☐ 88 Juhani Tamminen, Fin.	.35	.75
☐☐ 89 Jorma Vehmanen, Fin.	.35	.75
☐☐ 90 Jorma Valtonen, Fin.	.35	.75
☐☐ 91 Matti Keinonen, Fin.	.35	.75
☐☐ 92 Juha Rantasila, Fin.	.35	.75
☐☐ 93 Toni Kehle, BRD.	.35	.75
☐☐ 94 Josef Schramm, BRD.	.35	.75
☐☐ 95 Walter Stadler, BRD.	.35	.75
☐☐ 96 Josef Völk, BRD.	.35	.75
☐☐ 97 Hans Schichtl, BRD.	.35	.75
☐☐ 98 Erwin Riedmeier, BRD.	.35	.75
☐☐ 99 Werner Modes, BRD.	.35	.75
☐☐ 100 Johan Eimansberger, BRD.	.35	.75
☐☐ 101 Heinz Egger, BRD.	.35	.75
☐☐ 102 Lorentz Funk, BRD.	.35	.75
☐☐ 103 Klaus Ego, BRD.	.35	.75
☐☐ 104 Anton Hofherr, BRD.	.35	.75
☐☐ 105 Otto Schneitberger, BRD.	.35	.75
☐☐ 106 Heinz Weisenbach, BRD.	.35	.75
☐☐ 107 Alois Schloder, BRD.	.35	.75
☐☐ 108 Gustav Hanig, BRD.	.35	.75
☐☐ 109 Rainer Philipp, BRD.	.35	.75
☐☐ 110 Bernd Kuhn, BRD.	.35	.75
☐☐ 111 Paul Langner, BRD.	.35	.75
☐☐ 112 Franz Hofherr, BRD.	.35	.75
☐☐ 113 Reinhold Bauer, BRD.	.35	.75
☐☐ 114 Johann Rotkirch, BRD.	.35	.75
☐☐ 115 Walter Köberle, BRD.	.35	.75
☐☐ 116 Rainer Makatsch, BRD.	.35	.75
☐☐ 117 Carl Wetzel, USA.	.35	.75
☐☐ 118 Mike Curran, USA.	.35	.75
☐☐ 119 Jim McElmury, USA.	.75	1.50
☐☐ 120 Bruce Riutta, USA.	.35	.75
☐☐ 121 Tom Mellor, USA.	.35	.75
☐☐ 122 Don Ross, USA.	.35	.75
☐☐ 123 Gary Gambucci, USA.	.35	.75
☐☐ 124 Keith Christiansen, USA.	.35	.75
☐☐ 125 Len Lilyholm, USA.	.35	.75
☐☐ 126 Henry Boucha, USA.	1.00	2.00
☐☐ 127 Craig Falkman, USA.	.35	.75
☐☐ 128 Tim Sheehy, USA.	.35	.75
☐☐ 129 Kevin Ahearn, USA.	.35	.75
☐☐ 130 Craig Patrick, USA.	1.75	3.50
☐☐ 131 Pete Fichuk, USA.	.35	.75
☐☐ 132 George Konik, USA.	.35	.75
☐☐ 133 Dick McGlynn, USA.	.35	.75
☐☐ 134 Dick Toomey, USA.	.35	.75
☐☐ 135 Paul Schilling, USA.	.35	.75
☐☐ 136 Bob Lindberg, USA.	.35	.75
☐☐ 137 Dick Tomasoni, USA.	.35	.75
☐☐ 138 Nando Mathieu, Sui.	.35	.75
☐☐ 139 Francis Reinhard, Sui.	.35	.75
☐☐ 140 Gaston Furrer, Sui.	.35	.75
☐☐ 141 Bruno Wittwer, Sui.	.35	.75
☐☐ 142 André Berra, Sui.	.35	.75
☐☐ 143 Hens Keller, Sui.	.35	.75
☐☐ 144 Peter Luthi, Sui.	.35	.75
☐☐ 145 Peter Aeschlimann, Sui.	.35	.75
☐☐ 146 Werner Kuenzi, Sui.	.35	.75
☐☐ 147 Tony Neininger, Sui.	.35	.75
☐☐ 148 Jacques Pousaz, Sui.	.35	.75
☐☐ 149 Roger Chappot, Sui.	.35	.75
☐☐ 150 Charly Henzen, Sui.	.35	.75
☐☐ 151 Paul Probst, Sui.	.35	.75
☐☐ 152 Guy Duboi, Sui.	.35	.75
☐☐ 153 Rene Sgualdo, Sui.	.35	.75
☐☐ 154 Rene Hueguenin, Sui.	.35	.75
☐☐ 155 Gaston Pelletier, Sui.	.35	.75
☐☐ 156 Beat Kaufmann, Sui.	.35	.75
☐☐ 157 Alfio Molina, Sui.	.35	.75
☐☐ 158 Gerald Rigolet, Sui.	.35	.75
☐☐ 159 Harald Jones, Sui.	.35	.75
☐☐ 160 Gilbert Mathieu, Sui.	.35	.75
☐☐ 161 Michel Turler, Sui.	.35	.75
☐☐ 162 Reto Taillens , Sui.	.35	.75
☐☐ 163 Norm Ullman	1.75	3.50
☐☐ 164 Dave Keon	2.50	5.00
☐☐ 165 Roger Crozier (G)	1.25	2.50
☐☐ 166 Ron Ellis	1.00	2.00
☐☐ 167 Paul Henderson	1.75	3.50
☐☐ 168 Jim Dorey	.75	1.50
☐☐ 169 Jacques Plante (G)	10.00	20.00
☐☐ 170 Jean-Guy Gendron	.75	1.50
☐☐ 171 Gary Smith (G)	1.25	2.50
☐☐ 172 Dennis Hextall	.75	1.50
☐☐ 173 Norm Ferguson	.75	1.50
☐☐ 174 Simon Nolet	.75	1.50
☐☐ 175 Bernie Parent (G)	5.00	10.00
☐☐ 176 Ted Hampson	.75	1.50
☐☐ 177 Earl Ingarfield	.75	1.50
☐☐ 178 Larry Hillman	.75	1.50
☐☐ 179 Gary Dornhoefer	.75	1.50
☐☐ 180 Gary Croteau	.75	1.50
☐☐ 181 Carol Vadnais	.75	1.50
☐☐ 182 Jim Roberts	.75	1.50
☐☐ 183 Red Berenson	.75	1.50
☐☐ 184 Phil Esposito	6.00	12.00
☐☐ 185 John McKenzie	.75	1.50
☐☐ 186 Barclay Plager	.75	1.50
☐☐ 187 Glenn Hall (G)	7.50	15.00
☐☐ 188 Gerry Cheevers (G)	4.00	8.00
☐☐ 189 Jim McKenny	.75	1.50
☐☐ 190 Gordie Howe	25.00	50.00
☐☐ 191 Garry Unger	.75	1.50
☐☐ 192 Roy Edwards (G)	1.25	2.50
☐☐ 193 Alex Delvecchio	2.00	4.00
☐☐ 194 Brad Park	2.50	5.00
☐☐ 195 Frank Mahovlich	5.00	10.00
☐☐ 196 Phil Goyette	.75	1.50
☐☐ 197 Don Marshall	.75	1.50
☐☐ 198 Henri Richard	3.00	6.00
☐☐ 199 Claude Larose	.75	1.50
☐☐ 200 Bobby Rousseau	.75	1.50
☐☐ 201 Lorne Worsley (G)	4.00	8.00
☐☐ 202 Gilles Marotte	.75	1.50
☐☐ 203 Bob Pulford	1.50	3.00
☐☐ 204 Yvan Cournoyer	2.50	5.00
☐☐ 205 Eddie Joyal	.75	1.50
☐☐ 206 Ross Lonsberry	.75	1.50
☐☐ 207 Jean Béliveau	9.00	18.00
☐☐ 208 Jacques Lemaire	2.50	5.00
☐☐ 209 Orland Kurtenbach	.75	1.50
☐☐ 210 André Boudrias	.75	1.50
☐☐ 211 Jim Nielson	.75	1.50
☐☐ 212 Walt Tkaczuk	.75	1.50
☐☐ 213 Ed Giacomin (G)	4.50	9.00
☐☐ 214 Jean Ratelle	2.50	5.00
☐☐ 215 Les Binkley (G)	1.25	2.50
☐☐ 216 Jean Pronovost	.75	1.50
☐☐ 217 Bryan Watson	.75	1.50
☐☐ 218 Dean Prentice	.75	1.50
☐☐ 219 Jean-Paul Parise	.75	1.50
☐☐ 220 Bill Goldworthy	.75	1.50
☐☐ 221 Wayne Maki	.75	1.50
☐☐ 222 Dale Tallon	.75	1.50
☐☐ 223 Bobby Orr	30.00	60.00
☐☐ 224 Pit Martin	.75	1.50
☐☐ 225 Jacques Laperrière	1.50	3.00
☐☐ 226 Bill Flett	.75	1.50
☐☐ 227 Stan Mikita	5.00	10.00
☐☐ 228 Bobby Hull	12.00	25.00
☐☐ 229 Larry Pleau	.75	1.50
☐☐ 230 Keith Magnuson	.75	1.50
☐☐ 231 Tony Esposito (G), Chic.	6.00	12.00
☐☐ 232 Rogatien Vachon (G)	1.75	3.50
☐☐ 233 Mickey Redmond	1.25	2.50

1972 - 73 DERNIÈRE PHOTOS

This multi-sport series of photos were inserted in Dernière magazine from 1972 through 1984. Three holes were punched on the left side to allow for storage in a binder. The series featured Montréal Canadiens players. These photos measure 8" x 10".

Dernière	**EX**	**NM**
☐ 15OCT Ken Dryden (G)	10.00	20.00
☐ 22OCT Frank Mahovlich	6.00	12.00
☐ 29OCT Guy Lapointe	3.00	6.00
☐ 5NOV Serge Savard	3.00	6.00
☐ 12NOV Jacques Lemaire	4.00	8.00
☐ 19NOV Pierre Bouchard	1.50	3.00
☐ 26 NOV Henri Richard	4.00	8.00
☐ 3DEC Guy Lafleur	6.00	12.00
☐ 10DEC Jacques Laperrière	3.00	6.00
☐ 17DEC Marc Tardif	1.50	3.00
☐ 24DEC Scotty Bowman, Coach	3.00	6.00
☐ 31DEC Pete Mahovlich	1.50	3.00
☐ 7JAN Michel Plasse (G)	2.50	5.00
☐ 14JAN Chuck Lefley	1.50	3.00
☐ 21JAN Claude Larose	1.50	3.00
☐ 28JAN Jim Roberts	1.50	3.00
☐ 4FEB Bob Murdoch	1.50	3.00
☐ 11FEB Chuck Arnason	1.50	3.00
☐ 18FEB Murray Wilson	1.50	3.00
☐ 25FEB Wayne Thomas (G)	2.50	5.00
☐ 4MAR Dale Hoganson	1.50	3.00
☐ 11MAR Larry Robinson	5.00	10.00
☐ 18MAR Réjean Houle	2.50	5.00
☐ 25MAR Steve Shutt	4.00	8.00
☐ 1APR Yvan Cournoyer	4.00	8.00
☐ 8APR Jean Béliveau	6.00	12.00
Dernière • Unknown dates	**EX**	**NM**
☐ Marcel Dionne	5.00	10.00
☐ Réal Cloutier	1.50	3.00
☐ Pierre Larouche	2.50	5.00
☐ Richard Martin	2.50	5.00
☐ Gilbert Perreault	4.00	8.00
☐ Jean Pronovost	1.50	3.00
☐ Dan Bouchard	2.50	5.00
☐ Christian Bordeleau	1.50	3.00

1972 - 73 EDDIE SARGENT STICKERS

Issued one sheet per NHL team, the 16 stamp sheets had 14 players plus two series number stickers. Two different covered albums were available. These stickers measure 1 7/8" x 2 1/2".

Complete Set (224 stickers):	**140.00**	**275.00**
Album (Paul Henderson):	**25.00**	**50.00**
Album (Bobby Orr):	**40.00**	**75.00**
Album (Richard Martin):	**30.00**	**75.00**
Common Player:	**.25**	**.50**
Eddie Sargent	**EX**	**NM**
☐ 1 Lucien Grenier, Atla.	.25	.50
☐ 2 Phil Myre (G), Atla.	.25	.50
☐ 3 Ernie Hicke, Atla.	.25	.50
☐ 4 Keith McCreary, Atla.	.25	.50
☐ 5 Billy MacMillan, Atla.	.25	.50
☐ 6 Pat Quinn, Atla.	.50	1.00
☐ 7 Bill Plager, Atla.	.25	.50
☐ 8 Noel Price, Atla.	.25	.50
☐ 9 Bobby Leiter, Atla.	.25	.50
☐ 10 Randy Manery, Atla.	.25	.50
☐ 11 Bob Paradise, Atla.	.25	.50
☐ 12 Larry Romanchych, Atla.	.25	.50
☐ 13 Lew Morrison, Atla.	.25	.50
☐ 14 Dan Bouchard (G), Atla.	.50	1.00
☐ 15 Fred Stanfield, Bost.	.25	.50
☐ 16 John Bucyk, Bost.	1.75	3.50
☐ 17 Bobby Orr, Bost.	18.00	35.00
☐ 18 Wayne Cashman, Bost.	.25	.50
☐ 19 Dallas Smith, Bost.	.25	.50
☐ 20 Eddie Johnston (G), Bost.	.50	1.00
☐ 21 Phil Esposito, Bost.	4.00	8.00
☐ 22 Ken Hodge, Sr., Bost.	.25	.50
☐ 23 Don Awrey, Bost.	.25	.50
☐ 24 Mike Walton, Bost.	.25	.50
☐ 25 Carol Vadnais, Bost.	.25	.50
☐ 26 Doug Roberts, Bost.	.25	.50
☐ 27 Don Marcotte, Bost.	.25	.50
☐ 28 Garnet Bailey, Bost.	.25	.50
☐ 29 Gerry Meehan, Buff.	.25	.50
☐ 30 Tracy Pratt, Buff.	.25	.50
☐ 31 Gilbert Perreault, Buff.	2.25	4.50
☐ 32 Roger Crozier (G), Buff.	.50	1.00
☐ 33 Don Luce, Buff.	.25	.50
☐ 34 Dave Dryden (G), Buff.	.50	1.00
☐ 35 Richard Martin, Buff.	.50	1.00
☐ 36 Jim Lorentz, Buff.	.25	.50
☐ 37 Tim Horton, Buff.	3.00	6.00
☐ 38 Craig Ramsey, Buff.	.50	1.00
☐ 39 Larry Hillman, Buff.	.25	.50
☐ 40 Steve Atkinson, Buff.	.25	.50
☐ 41 Jim Schoenfeld, Buff.	.60	1.25
☐ 42 René Robert, Buff.	.25	.50
☐ 43 Walt McKechnie, Cali.	.25	.50
☐ 44 Marshall Johnston, Cali.	.25	.50
☐ 45 Joey Johnston, Cali.	.25	.50
☐ 46 Dick Redmond, Cali.	.25	.50
☐ 47 Bert Marshall, Cali.	.25	.50
☐ 48 Gary Croteau, Cali.	.25	.50
☐ 49 Marv Edwards (G), Cali.	.50	1.00
☐ 50 Gilles Meloche (G), Cali.	.50	1.00
☐ 51 Ivan Boldirev, Cali.	.25	.50
☐ 52 Stan Gilbertson, Cali.	.25	.50
☐ 53 Pete Laframboise, Cali.	.25	.50
☐ 54 Reggie Leach, Cali.	.25	.50
☐ 55 Craig Patrick, Cali.	.25	.50
☐ 56 Bob Stewart, Cali.	.25	.50
☐ 57 Keith Magnuson, Chic.	.25	.50
☐ 58 Doug Jarrett., Chic.	.25	.50
☐ 59 Cliff Koroll, Chic.	.25	.50
☐ 60 Chico Maki, Chic.	.25	.50
☐ 61 Gary Smith (G), Chic.	.50	1.00
☐ 62 Bill White, Chic.	.25	.50
☐ 63 Stan Mikita, Chic.	3.50	7.00
☐ 64 Jim Pappin, Chic.	.25	.50
☐ 65 Lou Angotti, Chic.	.25	.50
☐ 66 Tony Esposito (G), Chic.	4.00	8.00
☐ 67 Dennis Hull, Chic.	.25	.50
☐ 68 Pit Martin, Chic.	.25	.50
☐ 69 Pat Stapleton, Chic.	.25	.50
☐ 70 Dan Maloney, Chic.	.25	.50
☐ 71 Bill Collins, Detr.	.25	.50
☐ 72 Arnie Brown, Detr.	.25	.50
☐ 73 Red Berenson, Detr.	.25	.50
☐ 74 Mickey Redmond, Detr.	.50	1.00
☐ 75 Nick Libett, Detr.	.25	.50
☐ 76 Alex Delvecchio, Detr.	1.50	3.00
☐ 77 Ron Stackhouse, Detr.	.25	.50
☐ 78 Tim Ecclestone, Detr.	.25	.50
☐ 79 Gary Bergman, Detr.	.25	.50
☐ 80 Guy Charron, Detr.	.25	.50
☐ 81 Leon Rochefort, Detr.	.25	.50
☐ 82 Larry Johnston, Detr.	.25	.50
☐ 83 Andy Brown (G), Detr.	.50	1.00
☐ 84 Henry Boucha, Detr.	.25	.50
☐ 85 Paul Curtis, LosA.	.25	.50
☐ 86 Jim Stanfield, LosA.	.25	.50
☐ 87 Rogatien Vachon (G), LosA.	1.00	2.00
☐ 88 Ralph Backstrom, LosA.	.25	.50
☐ 89 Gilles Marotte, LosA.	.25	.50
☐ 90 Harry Howell, LosA.	.75	1.50
☐ 91 Réal Lemieux, LosA.	.25	.50
☐ 92 Butch Goring, LosA.	.25	.50
☐ 93 Juha Widing, LosA.	.25	.50
☐ 94 Mike Corrigan, LosA.	.25	.50
☐ 95 Larry Brown, LosA.	.25	.50
☐ 96 Terry Harper, LosA.	.25	.50
☐ 97 Serge Bernier, LosA.	.25	.50
☐ 98 Bob Berry, LosA.	.25	.50
☐ 99 Tom Reid, Minn.	.25	.50
☐ 100 Jude Drouin, Minn.	.25	.50
☐ 101 Jean Paul Parise, Minn.	.25	.50
☐ 102 Doug Mohns, Minn.	.25	.50
☐ 103 Danny Grant, Minn.	.25	.50
☐ 104 Bill Goldsworthy, Minn.	.25	.50
☐ 105 Gump Worsley (G), Minn.	2.50	5.00
☐ 106 Charlie Burns, Minn.	.25	.50
☐ 107 Murray Oliver, Minn.	.25	.50
☐ 108 Barry Gibbs, Minn.	.25	.50
☐ 109 Ted Harris, Minn.	.25	.50
☐ 110 Césare Maniago (G), Minn.	.50	1.00
☐ 111 Lou Nanne, Minn.	.25	.50
☐ 112 Bob Nevin, Minn.	.25	.50
☐ 113 Guy Lapointe, Mont.	.50	1.00
☐ 114 Pete Mahovlich, Mont.	.25	.50

☐	115 Jacques Lemaire, Mont.	1.50	3.00
☐	116 Pierre Bouchard, Mont.	.25	.50
☐	117 Yvan Cournoyer, Mont.	1.75	3.25
☐	118 Marc Tardif, Mont.	.25	.50
☐	119 Henri Richard, Mont.	2.00	4.00
☐	120 Frank Mahovlich, Mont.	3.00	6.00
☐	121 Jacques Laperrière, Mont.	.75	1.50
☐	122 Claude Larose, Mont.	.25	.50
☐	123 Serge Savard, Mont.	1.00	2.00
☐	124 Ken Dryden (G), Mont.	11.00	22.00
☐	125 Réjean Houle, Mont.	.50	1.00
☐	126 Jim Roberts, Mont.	.25	.50
☐	127 Ed Westfall, NYIs.	.25	.50
☐	128 Terry Crisp, NYIs.	.25	.50
☐	129 Gerry Desjardins (G), NYIs.	.50	1.00
☐	130 Denis DeJordy (G), NYIs., Error (Dennis)	.50	1.00
☐	131 Billy Harris, NYIs.	.25	.50
☐	132 Brian Spencer, NYIs.	.25	.50
☐	133 Germain Gagnon, NYIs.	.25	.50
☐	134 Dave Hudson, NYIs.	.25	.50
☐	135 Lorne Henning, NYIs.	.25	.50
☐	136 Brian Marchinko, NYIs.	.25	.50
☐	137 Tom Miller, NYIs.	.25	.50
☐	138 Gerry Hart, NYIs.	.25	.50
☐	139 Bryan Lefley, NYIs.	.25	.50
☐	140 Jim Mair, NYIs.	.25	.50
☐	141 Rod Gilbert, NYRa.	1.50	3.00
☐	142 Jean Ratelle, NYRa.	1.50	3.00
☐	143 Pete Stemkowski, NYRa.	.25	.50
☐	144 Brad Park, NYRa.	1.75	3.50
☐	145 Bobby Rousseau, NYRa.	.25	.50
☐	146 Dale Rolfe, NYRa.	.25	.50
☐	147 Ed Giacomin (G), NYRa.	1.75	3.50
☐	148 Rod Seiling, NYRa.	.25	.50
☐	149 Walt Tkaczuk, NYRa.	.25	.50
☐	150 Bill Fairbairn, NYRa.	.25	.50
☐	151 Vic Hadfield, NYRa.	.25	.50
☐	152 Ted Irvine, NYRa.	.25	.50
☐	153 Bruce MacGregor, NYRa.	.25	.50
☐	154 Jim Neilson, NYRa.	.25	.50
☐	155 Brent Hughes, Phil.	.25	.50
☐	156 Wayne Hillman, Phil.	.25	.50
☐	157 Doug Favell (G), Phil.	.50	1.00
☐	158 Simon Nolet, Phil.	.25	.50
☐	159 Joe Watson, Phil.	.25	.50
☐	160 Ed Van Impe, Phil.	.25	.50
☐	161 Gary Dornhoefer, Phil.	.25	.50
☐	162 Bobby Clarke, Phil.	4.00	8.00
☐	163 Bob Kelly, Phil.	.25	.50
☐	164 Bill Flett, Phil.	.25	.50
☐	165 Rick Foley, Phil.	.25	.50
☐	166 Ross Lonsberry, Phil.	.25	.50
☐	167 Rick MacLeish, Phil.	.50	1.00
☐	168 Bill Clement, Phil.	.25	.50
☐	169 Syl Apps, Jr., Pitt.	.25	.50
☐	170 Ken Schinkel, Pitt.	.25	.50
☐	171 Nick Harbaruk, Pitt.	.25	.50
☐	172 Bryan Watson, Pitt.	.25	.50
☐	173 Bryan Hextall, Pitt.	.25	.50
☐	174 Roy Edwards (G), Pitt.	.50	1.00
☐	175 Jim Rutherford (G), Pitt.	.50	1.00
☐	176 Jean Pronovost, Pitt.	.25	.50
☐	177 Rick Kessell, Pitt.	.25	.50
☐	178 Greg Polis, Pitt.	.25	.50
☐	179 Ron Schock, Pitt.	.25	.50
☐	180 Duane Rupp, Pitt.	.25	.50
☐	181 Darryl Edestrand, Pitt.	.25	.50
☐	182 Dave Burrows, Pitt.	.25	.50
☐	183 Gary Sabourin, SLou.	.25	.50
☐	184 Garry Unger, SLou.	.50	1.00
☐	185 Noel Picard, SLou.	.25	.50
☐	186 Bob Plager, SLou.	.25	.50
☐	187 Barclay Plager, SLou.	.25	.50
☐	188 Frank St. Marseille, SLou.	.25	.50
☐	189 Danny O'Shea, SLou.	.25	.50
☐	190 Kevin O'Shea, SLou.	.25	.50
☐	191 Wayne Stephenson (G), SLou.	.50	1.00
☐	192 Chris Evans, SLou.	.25	.50
☐	193 Jacques Caron (G), SLou.	.50	1.00
☐	194 André Dupont, SLou.	.25	.50
☐	195 Mike Murphy, SLou.	.25	.50
☐	196 Jack Egers, SLou.	.25	.50
☐	197 Norm Ullman, Toro.	1.50	3.00
☐	198 Jim McKenny, Toro.	.25	.50
☐	199 Bob Baun, Toro.	.25	.50
☐	200 Mike Pelyk, Toro.	.25	.50
☐	201 Ron Ellis, Toro.	.25	.50
☐	202 Garry Monahan, Toro.	.25	.50
☐	203 Paul Henderson, Toro.	1.25	2.50
☐	204 Darryl Sittler, Toro.	2.25	4.50
☐	205 Brian Glennie, Toro.	.25	.50
☐	206 Dave Keon, Toro.	1.50	3.00
☐	207 Jacques Plante (G), Toro.	4.00	8.00
☐	208 Pierre Jarry, Toro.	.25	.50
☐	209 Rick Kehoe, Toro.	.50	1.00
☐	210 Denis Dupère, Toro.	.25	.50
☐	211 Dale Tallon, Vanc.	.25	.50
☐	212 Murray Hall, Vanc.	.25	.50
☐	213 Dunc Wilson (G), Vanc.	.50	1.00
☐	214 André Boudrias, Vanc.	.25	.50
☐	215 Orland Kurtenbach, Vanc.	.25	.50
☐	216 Wayne Maki, Vanc.	.25	.50
☐	217 Barry Wilkins, Vanc.	.25	.50
☐	218 Richard Lemieux, Vanc.	.25	.50
☐	219 Bobby Schmautz, Vanc.	.25	.50
☐	220 Dave Balon, Vanc.	.25	.50
☐	221 Bobby Lalonde, Vanc.	.25	.50
☐	222 Jocelyn Guevremont, Vanc.	.25	.50
☐	223 Gregg Boddy, Vanc.	.25	.50
☐	224 Dennis Kearns, Vanc.	.25	.50

1972 - 73 LETRASET TRANSFERS

Issued in booklet form, the action transfers could be used on any part of the action rink illustrated in the booklet. These transfers measure 4 7/8" x 2 3/8".

	Complete Set (24 transfers):	**150.00**	**325.00**
	Letraset	**EX**	**NM**
☐	1 Vachon (G)/ Keon/ Marotte	9.00	18.00
☐	2 Ken Dryden (G)/ Maki/ Laperrière	20.00	40.00
☐	3 Dornhoefer/ Crozier (G)/ Pratt	5.00	10.00
☐	4 Tkaczuk/ Worsley (G)/ Hadfield	7.50	15.00
☐	5 Dallas Smith/ Orr/ McKechnie	25.00	50.00
☐	6 Ab MacDonald/ Sabourin/ Unger	5.00	10.00
☐	7 Rutherford/ Kurtenbach/ Woytowich	5.00	10.00
☐	8 Cheevers (G)/ Frank Mahovlich/ Awrey	15.00	30.00
☐	9 Ecclestone/ Baun/ Plante (G)	12.00	25.00
☐	10 Mikita/ Giacomin (G)/ Pappn	12.00	25.00
☐	11 Favell (G)/ Grant/ Van Impe	5.00	10.00
☐	12 Wakley/ Barclay Plager/ Croteau	5.00	10.00
☐	13 Hextall/ Tony Esposito (G)/ Stapleton	10.00	20.00
☐	14 Ratelle/ Gilbert /Jim Roberts	10.00	20.00
☐	15 Lemaire/ Henri Richard/ Cournoyer	12.00	25.00
☐	16 Gardiner/ Dennis Hull/ Angotti	5.00	10.00
☐	17 Ed Johnston/ Ullman/ Orr	30.00	60.00
☐	18 Meloche/ Carleton/ Redmond	5.00	10.00
☐	19 Al Smith/ Bergman/ Gilbertson	5.00	10.00
☐	20 Dunc Wilson (G)/ Park/ Tallon	7.50	15.00
☐	21 Drouin/ Favell (G)/ Ashbee	5.00	10.00
☐	22 Ellis/ Ken Dryden (G)/ Henderson	20.00	40.00
☐	23 Gary Edwards (G)/ Pronovost/ Schock	5.00	10.00
☐	24 Maniago (G)/ Chris Bordeleau/ Harris	5.00	10.00

1972 - 73 O-PEE-CHEE

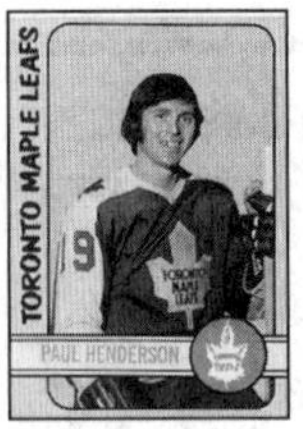

"The ('72-73) set is a historical set. It is jam packed with rookie cards. The WHA cards in the high numbers are pretty tough to find. There were also three different inserts: the player crests (you would push them out and they were stickers), the Team Canada cards, and the team emblems." – Ted Krieg, Comic Connection, Hamilton, Ontario.

These cards measure the standard 2 1/2" x 3 1/2" size. Card 208 does not exist.

	Complete Set (340 cards):	**800**	**1,600**
	Common Player (1-209):	**1.25**	**2.50**
	Common Player (210-289):	**2.50**	**5.00**
	Common Player (290-342):	**5.50**	**11.00**
	O-Pee-Chee	**EX**	**NM-MT**
☐	1 John Bucyk, Bost.	3.50	10.00
☐	**2 René Robert, Buff. RC**	**3.00**	**6.00**
☐	3 Gary Croteau, Cali.	1.25	2.50
☐	4 Pat Stapleton, Chic.	1.25	2.50
☐	5 Ron Harris, Atla.	1.25	2.50
☐	6 Checklist 1 (1 - 110)	35.00	65.00
☐	7 1971 - 72 Playoffs: Game 1 at Boston	1.75	3.50
☐	8 Marcel Dionne, Detr.	18.00	35.00
☐	9 Bob Berry, LosA.	1.25	2.50
☐	10 Lou Nanne, Minn.	1.25	2.50
☐	11 Marc Tardif, Mont.	1.25	2.50
☐	12 Jean Ratelle, NYRa.	3.00	6.00
☐	**13 Craig Cameron, NYIs. RC**	**2.00**	**4.00**
☐	14 Bobby Clarke, Phil.	20.00	40.00
☐	**15 Jim Rutherford (G), Pitt. RC**	**5.50**	**11.00**
☐	**16 André Dupont, SLou. RC**	**2.00**	**4.00**
☐	17 Mike Pelyk, Toro.	1.25	2.50
☐	18 Dunc Wilson (G), Vanc.	1.75	3.50
☐	19 Checklist, Error	30.00	60.00
☐	20 1971 - 72 Playoffs: Game 2 at Boston	1.75	3.50
☐	21 Dallas Smith, Bost.	1.25	2.50
☐	22 Gerry Meehan, Buff.	1.25	2.50
☐	23 Rick Smith, Cali., Err. (GP=265)	1.25	2.50
☐	24 Pit Martin, Chic.	1.25	2.50
☐	25 Keith McCreary, Atla.	1.25	2.50
☐	26 Alex Delvecchio, Detr.	2.75	5.50
☐	27 Gilles Marotte, LosA.	1.25	2.50
☐	28 Gump Worsley (G), Minn.	3.25	6.50
☐	29 Yvan Cournoyer, Mont.	3.00	6.00
☐	30 1971 - 72 Playoffs: Game 3 at New York	1.75	3.50
☐	31 Vic Hadfield, NYRa.	1.25	2.50
☐	**32 Tom Miller, NYIs. RC**	**2.00**	**4.00**
☐	33 Ed Van Impe, Phil.	1.25	2.50
☐	34 Greg Polis, Pitt.	1.25	2.50
☐	35 Barclay Plager, SLou.	1.25	2.50
☐	36 Ron Ellis, Toro.	1.25	2.50
☐	37 Jocelyn Guevremont, Vanc.	1.25	2.50
☐	38 1971 - 72 NHL Playoffs: Game 4 at New York	1.75	3.50
☐	39 Carol Vadnais, Bost.	1.25	2.50
☐	40 Steve Atkinson, Buff.	1.25	2.50
☐	**41 Ivan Boldirev, Cali. RC**	**4.00**	**8.00**
☐	42 Jim Pappin, Chic.	1.25	2.50
☐	**43 Phil Myre (G), Atla. RC**	**5.00**	**10.00**
☐	44 Yvan Cournoyer (Action)	2.00	4.00
☐	45 Nick Libett, Detr.	1.25	2.50
☐	46 Juha Widing, LosA.	1.25	2.50
☐	47 Jude Drouin, Minn.	1.25	2.50
☐	48 Jean Ratelle (Action), Err. (Defence)	3.00	6.00
☐	48 Jean Ratelle (Action), Corrected	2.00	4.00
☐	49 Ken Hodge, Sr., Bost.	1.25	2.50
☐	50 Roger Crozier (G), Buff.	1.75	3.50
☐	51 Reggie Leach, Cali.	2.50	5.00
☐	52 Dennis Hull, Chic.	1.25	2.50
☐	**53 Larry Hale, Atla. RC**	**2.00**	**4.00**
☐	54 1971 - 72 Playoffs: Game 5 at Boston	1.75	3.50
☐	55 Tim Ecclestone, Detr.	1.25	2.50
☐	56 Butch Goring, LosA.	2.50	5.00
☐	57 Danny Grant, Minn.	1.25	2.50
☐	58 Bobby Orr (Action)	25.00	50.00
☐	59 Guy Lafleur, Mont.	30.00	60.00
☐	60 Jim Neilson, NYRa.	1.25	2.50
☐	61 Brian Spencer, NYIs.	1.25	2.50
☐	62 Joe Watson, Phil.	1.25	2.50
☐	63 1971 - 72 Playoffs: Game 6 at New York	1.75	3.50
☐	64 Jean Pronovost, Pitt.	1.25	2.50
☐	65 Frank St. Marseille, SLou.	1.25	2.50
☐	66 Bob Baun, Toro.	1.25	2.50
☐	67 Poul Popiel, Vanc.	1.25	2.50
☐	68 Wayne Cashman, Bost.	1.25	2.50
☐	69 Tracy Pratt, Buff.	1.25	2.50
☐	70 Stan Gilbertson, Cali.	1.25	2.50
☐	71 Keith Magnuson, Chic.	1.25	2.50
☐	72 Ernie Hicke, Atla.	1.25	2.50
☐	73 Gary Doak, Detr.	1.25	2.50
☐	74 Mike Corrigan, LosA.	1.25	2.50
☐	75 Doug Mohns, Minn.	1.25	2.50
☐	76 Phil Esposito (Action)	4.50	9.00
☐	77 Jacques Lemaire, Mont.	3.00	6.00
☐	78 Pete Stemkowski, NYRa.	1.25	2.50
☐	**79 Bill Mikkelson, NYIs. RC**	**2.00**	**4.00**
☐	**80 Rick Foley, Phil. RC**	**2.00**	**4.00**
☐	81 Ron Schock, Pitt.	1.25	2.50
☐	82 Phil Roberto, SLou.	1.25	2.50
☐	83 Jim McKenny, Toro.	1.25	2.50
☐	84 Wayne Maki, Vanc.	1.25	2.50
☐	85 Brad Park (Action), Err. (Centre)	4.00	8.00
☐	85 Brad Park (Action), Corrected	2.50	5.00
☐	86 Guy Lapointe, Mont.	2.50	5.00
☐	87 Bill Fairbairn, NYRa.	1.25	2.50
☐	88 Terry Crisp, NYIs.	2.00	4.00
☐	89 Doug Favell (G), Phil.	1.75	3.50
☐	90 Bryan Watson, Pitt.	1.25	2.50
☐	91 Gary Sabourin, SLou.	1.25	2.50
☐	92 Jacques Plante (G), Toro.	12.00	25.00
☐	93 André Boudrias, Vanc.	1.25	2.50
☐	94 Mike Walton, Bost.	1.25	2.50
☐	95 Don Luce, Buff.	1.25	2.50
☐	96 Joey Johnston, Cali.	1.25	2.50
☐	97 Doug Jarrett, Chic.	1.25	2.50
☐	**98 Billy MacMillan, Atla. RC**	**2.00**	**4.00**
☐	99 Mickey Redmond, Detr.	1.75	3.50
☐	100 R. Vachon (G), LosA., Err. (Ragatien)	3.50	7.00
☐	**101 Barry Gibbs, Minn. RC**	**2.00**	**4.00**
☐	102 Frank Mahovlich, Mont.	3.00	6.00
☐	103 Bruce MacGregor, NYRa.	1.25	2.50
☐	104 Ed Westfall, NYIs.	1.25	2.50
☐	105 Rick MacLeish, Phil.	3.00	6.00
☐	106 Nick Harbaruk, Pitt.	1.25	2.50
☐	**107 Jack Egers, SLou. RC**	**2.00**	**4.00**
☐	108 Dave Keon, Toro.	2.50	5.00
☐	109 Barry Wilkins, Vanc.	1.25	2.50
☐	110 Walt Tkaczuk (Action)	1.25	2.50
☐	111 Phil Esposito, Bost.	9.00	18.00
☐	**112 Gilles Meloche (G), Cali. RC**	**6.00**	**12.00**
☐	113 Gary Edwards (G), LosA.	1.75	3.50
☐	114 Brad Park, NYRa.	7.00	14.00
☐	115 Syl Apps, Pitt.	1.25	2.50
☐	116 Jim Lorentz, Buff.	1.25	2.50
☐	117 Gary Smith (G), Chic.	1.75	3.50
☐	118 Ted Harris, Minn.	1.25	2.50
☐	119 Gerry Desjardins (G), NYIs.	1.75	3.50
☐	120 Garry Unger, SLou.	1.25	2.50
☐	121 Dale Tallon, Vanc.	1.25	2.50
☐	**122 William Plager, Atla. RC**	**2.00**	**4.00**
☐	123 Red Berenson, Detr.	1.25	2.50
☐	124 Pete Mahovlich, Mont.	1.25	2.50
☐	125 Simon Nolet, Phil.	1.25	2.50
☐	126 Paul Henderson, Toro.	1.75	3.50
☐	127 AW: Bobby Orr, Bost.	2.00	4.00
☐	128 NHL Action: Montréal vs. Toronto	2.50	5.00
☐	129 Bobby Orr, Bost.	45.00	90.00
☐	130 Bert Marshall, Cali.	1.25	2.50
☐	131 Ralph Backstrom, LosA.	1.25	2.50
☐	132 Gilles Villemure (G), NYRa.	1.75	3.50
☐	**133 Dave Burrows, Pitt. RC**	**2.00**	**4.00**
☐	134 AW: Ken Dryden, Mont.	2.00	4.00
☐	135 NHL Action: Boston vs. Toronto	1.25	2.50
☐	136 Gilbert Perreault, Buff.	9.00	18.00
☐	137 Tony Esposito (G), Chic.	12.00	25.00
☐	138 César Maniago (G), Minn.	1.75	3.50
☐	**139 Gerry Hart, NYIs. RC**	**2.00**	**4.00**
☐	**140 Jacques Caron (G), SLou. RC**	**2.00**	**4.00**
☐	141 Orland Kurtenbach, Vanc.	1.25	2.50
☐	142 AW: Bobby Orr, Bost.	2.00	4.00
☐	143 Lew Morrison, Atla.	1.25	2.50
☐	144 Arnie Brown, NYIs.	1.25	2.50
☐	145 Ken Dryden (G), Mont.	35.00	65.00
☐	146 Gary Dornhoefer, Phil.	1.25	2.50
☐	147 Norm Ullman, Toro.	2.50	5.00
☐	148 AW: Phil Esposito, Bost.	2.00	4.00
☐	149 NHL Action: Vancouver vs. Toronto	1.25	2.50
☐	150 Fred Stanfield, Bost.	1.25	2.50
☐	151 Dick Redmond, Cali.	1.25	2.50
☐	152 Serge Bernier, LosA.	1.25	2.50
☐	153 Rod Gilbert, NYRa.	3.00	6.00
☐	154 Duane Rupp, Pitt.	1.25	2.50
☐	155 AW: T. Esposito/ G. Smith	2.00	4.00
☐	156 NHL Action: Chicago vs. Toronto	2.75	5.50
☐	157 Rick Martin, Buff.	3.25	6.50
☐	158 Bill White, Chic.	1.25	2.50
☐	159 Bill Goldsworthy, Minn.	1.25	2.50
☐	**160 Jack Lynch, Pitt. RC**	**2.00**	**4.00**
☐	161 Bob Plager, SLou.	1.25	2.50
☐	162 Dave Balon, Vanc., Err. (Ballon)	1.25	2.50
☐	163 Noel Price, Atla.	1.25	2.50
☐	164 Gary Bergman, Detr.	1.25	2.50
☐	165 Pierre Bouchard, Mont.	1.25	2.50
☐	166 Ross Lonsberry, Phil.	1.25	2.50
☐	167 Denis Dupère, Toro.	1.25	2.50
☐	168 AW: Jean Ratelle, NYRa.	2.00	4.00
☐	169 NHL Action: Boston vs. Toronto	1.25	2.50
☐	170 Don Awrey, Bost.	1.25	2.50
☐	**171 Marshall Johnston, Cali. RC**	**2.00**	**4.00**
☐	172 Terry Harper, LosA.	1.25	2.50
☐	173 Ed Giacomin (G), NYRa.	4.00	7.50
☐	174 Bryan Hextall, Pitt.	1.25	2.50
☐	175 AW: Bobby Orr, Bost.	2.00	4.00
☐	176 Larry Hillman, Buff.	1.25	2.50
☐	177 Stan Mikita, Chic.	5.50	11.00
☐	178 Charlie Burns, Minn.	1.25	2.50
☐	**179 Brian Marchinko, NYIs. RC**	**2.00**	**4.00**
☐	180 Noel Picard, SLou.	1.25	2.50
☐	**181 Bobby Schmautz, Vanc. RC**	**2.00**	**4.00**
☐	182 NHL Action: Buffalo vs. Toronto	1.75	3.50
☐	183 Pat Quinn, Atla.	1.25	2.50
☐	184 Denis DeJordy (G), Detr.	1.75	3.50
☐	185 Serge Savard, Mont.	2.00	4.00
☐	186 NHL Action: Pittsburgh vs. Toronto	1.75	3.50
☐	187 Bill Flett, Phil.	1.25	2.50
☐	188 Darryl Sittler, Toro.	15.00	30.00
☐	189 NHL Action: Minnesota vs. Toronto	2.00	4.00
☐	190 Checklist	45.00	85.00
☐	191 Garnet Bailey, Bost.	1.25	2.50
☐	192 Walt McKechnie, Cali.	1.25	2.50
☐	193 Harry Howell, LosA.	1.25	2.50
☐	194 Rod Seiling, NYRa.	1.25	2.50
☐	195 Darryl Edestrand, Pitt.	1.25	2.50
☐	196 NHL Action: Chicago vs. Toronto	6.00	12.00
☐	197 Tim Horton, Buff.	5.00	10.00
☐	198 Chico Maki, Chic.	1.25	2.50
☐	199 J.P. Parise, Minn.	1.25	2.50
☐	**200 Germaine Gagnon, NYIs. RC**	**2.00**	**4.00**
☐	201 Danny O'Shea, SLou.	1.25	2.50
☐	**202 Richard Lemieux, Vanc. RC**	**2.00**	**4.00**
☐	**203 Dan Bouchard (G), Atla. RC**	**6.00**	**12.00**
☐	204 Léon Rochefort, Detr.	1.25	2.50
☐	205 Jacques Laperrière, Mont.	1.25	2.50
☐	206 Barry Ashbee, Phil.	1.25	2.50
☐	207 Garry Monahan, Toro.	1.25	2.50
☐	209 NHL Action: Toronto vs. Chicago	2.50	5.00

☐ 210 Réjean Houle, Mont. 4.00 7.50
☐ **211 Dave Hudson, NYIs. RC 4.00 8.00**
☐ 212 Ted Irvine, NYRa. 2.50 5.00
☐ **213 Don Saleski, Phil. RC 4.00 8.00**
☐ 214 Lowell MacDonald, Pitt. 2.50 5.00
☐ **215 Mike Murphy, SLou. RC 4.00 8.00**
☐ 216 Brian Glennie, Toro. 2.50 5.00
☐ **217 Bobby Lalonde, Vanc. RC 4.00 8.00**
☐ **218 Bobby Leiter, Atla. RC 4.00 8.00**
☐ 219 Don Marcotte, Bost. 2.50 5.00
☐ **220 Jim Schoenfeld, Buff. RC 8.00 16.00**
☐ 221 Craig Patrick, Cali. 4.00 7.50
☐ 222 Cliff Koroll, Chic. 2.50 5.00
☐ **223 Guy Charron, Detr. RC 4.00 8.00**
☐ 224 Jimmy Peters, LosA. 2.50 5.00
☐ 225 Dennis Hextall, Minn. 2.50 5.00
☐ 226 AS: Tony Esposito (G), Chic. 9.00 18.00
☐ 227 AS: B. Orr, Bost./ B. Park, NYRa. 25.00 50.00
☐ 228 AS: Bobby Hull, Chic. 18.00 35.00
☐ 229 AS: Rod Gilbert, NYRa. 4.00 7.50
☐ 230 AS: Phil Esposito, Bost. 6.00 12.00
☐ 231 Claude Larose, Mont., Err. (La Rose) 2.50 5.00
☐ **232 Jim Mair, NYIs. RC 4.00 8.00**
☐ 233 Bobby Rousseau, NYRa. 2.50 5.00
☐ 234 Brent Hughes, SLou. 2.50 5.00
☐ 235 Al McDonough, Pitt. 2.50 5.00
☐ **236 Chris Evans, SLou. RC 4.00 8.00**
☐ **237 Pierre Jarry, Toro. RC 4.00 8.00**
☐ **238 Don Tannahill, Vanc. RC 4.00 8.00**
☐ **239 Rey Comeau, Atla. RC 4.00 8.00**
☐ 240 Gregg Sheppard, Bost. RC, Err. (Greg) 2.50 5.00
☐ 241 Dave Dryden (G), Buff. 4.00 7.50
☐ **242 Ed McAneeley, Cali. RC 4.00 8.00**
☐ 243 Lou Angotti, Chic. 2.50 5.00
☐ **244 Len Fontaine, Detr. RC 4.00 8.00**
☐ **245 Bill Lesuk, LosA. RC 4.00 8.00**
☐ 246 Fred (Buster) Harvey, Minn. 2.50 5.00
☐ 247 AS: Ken Dryden (G), Mont. 18.00 35.00
☐ 248 AS: Bill White, Chic. 2.50 5.00
☐ 249 AS: Pat Stapleton, Chic. 2.50 5.00
☐ 250 AS: V. Hadfield/ J. Ratelle/ Y. Cournoyer 4.50 8.50
☐ 251 Henri Richard, Mont. 4.50 8.50
☐ **252 Bryan Lefley, NYIs. RC 4.00 8.00**
☐ 253 Stanley Cup: Boston Bruins 9.00 18.00
☐ **254 Steve Vickers, NYRa. RC 4.00 8.00**
☐ 255 Wayne Hillman, Phil. 2.50 5.00
☐ 256 Ken Schinkel, Pitt., Err. (Shinkel) 2.50 5.00
☐ **257 Kevin O'Shea, SLou. RC 4.00 8.00**
☐ **258 Ron Low, Toro. (G) RC 8.00 16.00**
☐ **259 Don Lever, Vanc. RC 4.00 8.00**
☐ **260 Randy Manery, Atla. RC 4.00 8.00**
☐ 261 Eddie Johnston (G), Bost. 4.00 7.50
☐ **262 Craig Ramsay, Buff. RC 4.00 8.00**
☐ **263 Pete Laframboise, Cali. RC 4.00 8.00**
☐ **264 Dan Maloney, Chic. RC 4.00 8.00**
☐ 265 Bill Collins, Detr. 2.50 5.00
☐ 266 Paul Curtis, LosA. 2.50 5.00
☐ 267 Bob Nevin, Minn. 2.50 5.00
☐ 268 LL: B. Watson/ K. Magnuson/ G. Dornhoefer4.00 7.50
☐ 269 Jim Roberts, Mont. 2.50 5.00
☐ **270 Brian Lavender, NYIs. RC 4.00 8.00**
☐ 271 Dale Rolfe, NYRa. 2.50 5.00
☐ 272 LL: P. Esposito/ V. Hadfield/ B. Hull 12.00 25.00
☐ **273 Michel Belhumeur (G), Phil. RC 4.00 8.00**
☐ 274 Eddie Shack, Pitt. 4.00 7.50
☐ **275 Wayne Stephenson (G), SLou. RC 4.50 9.00**
☐ 276 Stanley Cup Champions: Boston Bruins 5.00 10.00
☐ **277 Rick Kehoe, Toro. RC 4.50 8.50**
☐ 278 Gerry O'Flaherty, Vanc. RC, Err. (Jerry) 2.50 5.00
☐ **279 Jacques Richard, Atla. RC 4.00 8.00**
☐ 280 LL: P. Esposito/ B. Orr/ J. Ratelle 18.00 35.00
☐ **281 Nick Beverley, Bost. RC 4.00 8.00**
☐ **282 Larry Carriere, Buff. RC 4.00 8.00**
☐ 283 LL: B. Orr/ P. Esposito/ J. Ratelle 18.00 35.00
☐ 284 Rick Smith, Cali. 2.50 5.00
☐ **285 Jerry Korab, Chic. RC 4.00 8.00**
☐ 286 LL: T. Esposito/ Villemure/ Worsley 7.00 14.00
☐ 287 Ron Stackhouse, Detr. 2.50 5.00
☐ **288 Barry Long, LosA. RC 4.00 8.00**
☐ 289 Dean Prentice, Minn. 2.50 5.00
☐ 290 Norm Beaudin, Winnipeg 5.50 11.00
☐ **291 Mike Amodeo, Ottawa RC 8.00 15.00**
☐ 292 Jim Harrison, Alberta. 5.50 11.00
☐ 293 J.C. Tremblay, Québec 7.50 15.00
☐ 294 Murray Hall, Houston 5.50 11.00
☐ 295 Bart Crashley, Los Angeles 5.50 11.00
☐ 296 Wayne Connelly, Minnesota 5.50 11.00
☐ 297 Bobby Sheehan, New York 5.50 11.00
☐ **298 Ron C. Anderson, Chicago RC 8.00 15.00**
☐ 299 Chris Bordeleau, Winnipeg 5.50 11.00
☐ 300 Les Binkley (G), Ottawa 7.50 15.00
☐ **301 Ron Walters, Alberta RC 8.00 15.00**
☐ 302 Jean-Guy Gendron, Québec 5.50 11.00
☐ 303 Gord Labossiere, Houston 5.50 11.00
☐ 304 Gerry Odrowski, Los Angeles 5.50 11.00
☐ 305 Mike McMahon, Minnesota 5.50 11.00
☐ 306 Gary Kurt (G), New York 7.50 15.00
☐ 307 Larry Cahan, Chicago 5.50 11.00
☐ 308 Wally Boyer, Winnipeg 5.50 11.00
☐ **309 Bob Charlebois, Ottawa RC 8.00 15.00**
☐ 310 Bob Falkenberg, Alberta 5.50 11.00
☐ **311 Jean Payette, Quebec RC 8.00 15.00**
☐ 312 Ted Taylor, Houston 5.50 11.00
☐ 313 Joe Szura, Los Angeles 5.50 11.00
☐ 314 George Morrison, Minnesota 5.50 11.00
☐ 315 Wayne Rivers, New York 5.50 11.00
☐ 316 Reggie Fleming, Chicago 5.50 11.00
☐ **317 Larry Hornung, Winnipeg RC 8.00 15.00**
☐ **318 Ron Climie, Ottawa RC 8.00 15.00**
☐ 319 Val Fonteyne, Alberta 5.50 11.00
☐ **320 Michel Archambault, Québec RC 10.00 20.00**
☐ 321 Ab McDonald, Winnipeg 5.50 11.00
☐ **322 Bob Leduc, Ottawa RC 8.00 15.00**
☐ 323 Bob Wall, Alberta 5.50 11.00
☐ **324 Alain Caron, Québec RC 8.00 15.00**
☐ 325 Bob Woytowich, Winnipeg 5.50 11.00
☐ 326 Guy Trottier, Ottawa 5.50 11.00
☐ 327 Bill Hicke, Alberta 5.50 11.00
☐ **328 Guy Dufour, Québec RC 8.00 15.00**
☐ **329 Wayne Rutledge, Houston (G) RC 7.50 15.00**
☐ 330 Gary Veneruzzo, Los Angeles 5.50 11.00
☐ **331 Fred Speck, Minnesota RC 8.00 15.00**
☐ **332 Ron Ward, New York RC 8.00 15.00**
☐ 333 Rosaire Paiement, Chicago 5.50 11.00
☐ 334 Checklist 3, Err. (210 - 341) 50.00 100.00
☐ 334 Checklist 3, Corrected 45.00 90.00
☐ **335 Michel Parizeau, Quebec RC 8.00 15.00**
☐ 336 Bobby Hull, Winnipeg 35.00 65.00
☐ 337 Wayne Carleton, Ottawa, Err. (Carlton) 5.50 11.00
☐ 338 John McKenzie, Philadelphia 5.50 11.00
☐ 339 Jim Dorey, New England 5.50 11.00
☐ 340 Gerry Cheevers (G), Cleveland 20.00 40.00
☐ 341 Gerry Pinder, Cleveland 10.00 30.00

PLAYER CREST

Series 1 Insert Set (22 stickers): 65.00 130.00
O-Pee-Chee EX NM-MT
☐ 1 Pat Quinn, Atla. 3.00 6.00
☐ 2 Phil Esposito, Bost. 6.50 12.00
☐ 3 Bobby Orr, Bost. 30.00 55.00
☐ 4 Richard Martin, Buff. 3.00 6.00
☐ 5 Stan Mikita, Chic. 6.00 12.00
☐ 6 Bill White, Chic. 2.00 4.00
☐ 7 Red Berenson, Detr. 2.00 4.00
☐ 8 Gary Bergman, Detr. 2.00 4.00
☐ 9 Gary Edwards (G), LosA. 3.00 6.00
☐ 10 Bill Goldsworthy, Minn. 2.00 4.00
☐ 11 Jacques Laperrière, Mont. 4.00 8.00
☐ 12 Ken Dryden (G), Mont. 15.00 30.00
☐ 13 Ed Westfall, NYIs. 2.00 4.00
☐ 14 Walt Tkaczuk, NYRa. 2.00 4.00
☐ 15 Brad Park, NYRa. 5.00 10.00
☐ 16 Doug Favell (G), Phil. 3.00 6.00
☐ 17 Eddie Shack, Pitt. 3.50 7.00
☐ 18 Jacques Caron (G), SLou. 3.00 6.00
☐ 19 Paul Henderson, Toro. 3.00 6.00
☐ 20 Jim Harrison, Atla. 2.00 4.00
☐ 21 Dale Tallon, Vanc. 2.00 4.00
☐ 22 Orland Kurtenbach, Vanc. 2.00 4.00

TEAM CANADA

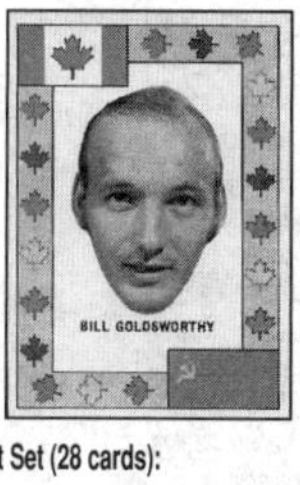

Series Two Insert Set (28 cards): 125.00 235.00
O-Pee-Chee EX NM-MT
☐ Don Awrey 2.50 5.00
☐ Red Berenson 2.50 5.00
☐ Gary Bergman 2.50 5.00
☐ Wayne Cashman 3.50 7.00
☐ Bobby Clarke 10.00 20.00
☐ Yvan Cournoyer 6.50 12.00
☐ Ken Dryden (G) 22.00 45.00
☐ Ron Ellis 2.50 5.00
☐ Phil Esposito 15.00 30.00
☐ Tony Esposito (G) 12.00 25.00
☐ Rod Gilbert 5.00 10.00
☐ Bill Goldsworthy 2.50 5.00
☐ Vic Hadfield 2.50 5.00
☐ Paul Henderson 15.00 30.00
☐ Dennis Hull 2.50 5.00
☐ Guy Lapointe 4.00 8.00
☐ Frank Mahovlich 9.00 18.00
☐ Pete Mahovlich 2.50 5.00
☐ Stan Mikita 9.00 18.00
☐ Jean Paul Parise 2.50 5.00
☐ Brad Park 6.50 12.00
☐ Gilbert Perreault 6.00 12.00
☐ Jean Ratelle 5.00 10.00
☐ Mickey Redmond 3.00 6.00
☐ Serge Savard 4.00 8.00
☐ Rod Seiling 2.50 5.00
☐ Pat Stapleton 2.50 5.00
☐ Bill White 2.50 5.00

TEAM EMBLEMS

These stickers differ from the 1973-74 stickers in that they do not have the application instructions on the face of the sticker.

Series Three Insert Set (30 stickers): 85.00 185.00
O-Pee-Chee EX NM-MT
☐ NHL Logo 2.00 4.00
☐ Atlanta Flames 5.00 10.00
☐ Boston Bruins 2.00 4.00
☐ Buffalo Sabres 2.00 4.00
☐ California Golden Seals 2.00 4.00
☐ Chicago Blackhawks 2.00 4.00
☐ Detroit Red Wings 2.00 4.00
☐ Los Angeles Kings 2.00 4.00
☐ Minnesota North Stars 2.00 4.00
☐ Montréal Canadiens 3.00 6.00
☐ New York Islanders 5.00 10.00
☐ New York Rangers 2.00 4.00
☐ Philadelphia Flyers 2.00 4.00
☐ Pittsburgh Penguins 2.00 4.00
☐ St. Louis Blues 2.00 4.00
☐ Toronto Maple Leafs 3.00 6.00
☐ Vancouver Canucks 2.00 4.00
☐ WHA Logo 7.50 15.00
☐ Chicago Cougars 7.50 15.00
☐ Cleveland Crusaders 7.50 15.00
☐ Edmonton Oilers 7.50 15.00
☐ Houston Aeros 7.50 15.00
☐ Los Angeles Sharks 7.50 15.00
☐ Minnesota Fighting Saints 7.50 15.00
☐ New England Whalers 7.50 15.00
☐ New York Raiders 7.50 15.00
☐ Ottawa Nationals 7.50 15.00
☐ Philadelphia Blazers 7.50 15.00
☐ Québec Nordiques 9.00 18.00
☐ Winnipeg Jets 9.00 18.00

1972 - 73 POST ACTION TRANSFERS

These transfers measure 4 7/8" x 2 5/8". Each number has the prefix PR 146.

Complete Set (12 transfers): 140.00 275.00
Letraset EX NM
☐ 1 Defense: G. Unger/ B. Orr 50.00 75.00
☐ 2 In the corner: R. Berenson/ D. Tallon 12.00 20.00
☐ 3 Face off: G. Dornhoefer/ W. Cashman 12.00 20.00
☐ 4 Power save: McKenny/ Giacomin (G) 20.00 30.00
☐ 5 Power play goal: P. Quinn/ K. Magnuson 12.00 25.00
☐ 6 Break away: P. Shmyr/ R. Seiling 12.00 20.00
☐ 7 Slapshot: D. Grant/ J. Plante 15.00 30.00
☐ 8 Rebound: S. Apps/ S. Savard 15.00 30.00
☐ 9 Wrist shot: G. Worsley (G)/ G. Bergman 20.00 30.00
☐ 10 Last minute: R. Crozier (G)/ E. Westfall 15.00 25.00
☐ 11 Goalmouth scramble : D. Hull/ Kurtenbach12.00 20.00
☐ 12 Chest save: R. Vachon (G)/ Cournoyer 22.00 35.00

1972 - 73 TOPPS

These cards measure the standard 2 1/2" x 3 1/2".
Complete Set (176 cards): 200.00 400.00

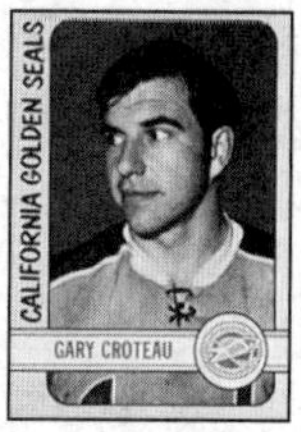

Common Player: .65 1.25
Topps EX NM-MT
☐ 1 Boston Bruins 2.50 7.00
☐ 2 Game 1 at Boston 1.00 2.00
☐ 3 Game 2 at Boston 1.00 2.00
☐ 4 Game 3 at New York 1.00 2.00
☐ 5 Game 4 at New York 1.00 2.00
☐ 6 Game 5 at Boston 1.00 2.00
☐ 7 Game 6 at New York 1.00 2.00
☐ 8 Stanley Cup Trophy 3.00 6.00
☐ 9 Ed Van Impe, Phil. .65 1.25
☐ 10 Yvan Cournoyer, Mont. 1.75 3.25
☐ 11 Syl Apps, Jr., Pitt. .65 1.25
☐ **12 Bill Plager, SLou. (Atla.) RC 1.00 2.00**
☐ 13 Ed Johnston (G), Bost. 1.00 2.00
☐ 14 Walt Tkaczuk, NYRa. .65 1.25
☐ 15 Dale Tallon, Vanc. .65 1.25
☐ 16 Gerry Meehan, Buff. .65 1.25
☐ 17 Reggie Leach, Cali. 1.25 2.50
☐ 18 Marcel Dionne, Detr. 10.00 20.00
☐ **19 André Dupont, NYIs. (SLou.) RC 1.00 2.00**
☐ 20 Tony Esposito (G), Chic. 8.00 16.00
☐ 21 Bob Berry, LosA. .65 1.25
☐ **22 Craig Cameron, NYIs. RC 1.00 2.00**
☐ 23 Ted Harris, Minn. .65 1.25
☐ 24 Jacques Plante (G), Toro. 7.00 14.00
☐ 25 Jacques Lemaire, Mont. 1.50 3.00
☐ 26 Simon Nolet, Phil. .65 1.25
☐ 27 Keith McCreary, Pitt. (Atla.) .65 1.25
☐ 28 Duane Rupp, Pitt. .65 1.25
☐ 29 Wayne Cashman, Bost. 1.00 2.00
☐ 30 Brad Park, NYRa. 4.00 8.00
☐ 31 Roger Crozier (G), Buff. 1.25 2.50
☐ 32 Wayne Maki, Vanc. .65 1.25
☐ 33 Tim Ecclestone, Detr. .65 1.25
☐ 34 Rick Smith, Cali. .65 1.25
☐ 35 Garry Unger, SLou. .65 1.25
☐ 36 Serge Bernier, LosA. .65 1.25
☐ 37 Brian Glennie, Toro. .65 1.25
☐ 38 Gerry Desjardins (G), Cali. (NYIs.) 1.00 2.50
☐ 39 Danny Grant, Minn. .65 1.25
☐ 40 Bill White, Chic. .65 1.25
☐ 41 Gary Dornhoefer, Phil. .65 1.25
☐ 42 Pete Mahovlich, Mont. .65 1.25
☐ 43 Greg Polis, Pitt. .65 1.25
☐ **44 Larry Hale, Phil. (Atla.) RC 1.00 2.00**
☐ 45 Dallas Smith, Bost. .65 1.25
☐ 46 Orland Kurtenbach, Vanc. .65 1.25
☐ 47 Steve Atkinson, Buff. .65 1.25
☐ 48 Joey Johnston, Cali. .65 1.25
☐ 49 Gary Bergman, Detr. .65 1.25
☐ 50 Jean Ratelle, NYRa. 2.00 4.00
☐ 51 Rogatien Vachon (G), LosA. 1.75 3.25
☐ 52 Phil Roberto, Mont. (SLou.) .65 1.25
☐ 53 Brian Spencer, Toro. (NYIs.) .65 1.25
☐ 54 Jim McKenny, Toro. .65 1.25
☐ 55 Gump Worsley (G), Minn. 2.25 4.50
☐ 56 Stan Mikita, Chic. 3.25 6.50
☐ 57 Guy Lapointe, Mont. 1.25 2.50
☐ 58 Lew Morrison, Phil. (Atla.) .65 1.25
☐ 59 Ron Schock, Pitt. .65 1.25
☐ 60 John Bucyk, Bost. 1.75 3.50
☐ 61 LL: P. Esposito/ V. Hadfield/ B. Hull 6.00 12.00
☐ 62 LL: B. Orr/ P. Esposito/ J. Ratelle 8.00 16.00
☐ 63 LL: P. Esposito/ B. Orr/ J. Ratelle 8.00 16.00
☐ 64 LL: T. Esposito/ G. Villemure/ G. Worsley 4.50 8.50
☐ 65 LL: B. Watson/ K. Magnuson/ G. Dornhoefer1.00 2.00
☐ 66 Jim Neilson, NYRa. .65 1.25
☐ 67 Nick Libett, Detr. .65 1.25
☐ 68 Jim Lorentz, SLou. (Buff.) .65 1.25
☐ **69 Gilles Meloche (G), Cali. RC 3.75 7.50**
☐ 70 Pat Stapleton, Chic. .65 1.25
☐ 71 Frank St. Marseille, SLou. .65 1.25
☐ 72 Butch Goring, LosA. 1.50 3.00
☐ 73 Paul Henderson, Toro. 1.00 2.00
☐ 74 Doug Favell (G), Phil. 1.00 2.00
☐ 75 Jocelyn Guevremont, Vanc. .65 1.25
☐ **76 Tom Miller, Buff. (NYIs.) RC 1.00 2.00**
☐ **77 Billy MacMillan, Toro. (Atla.) RC 1.00 2.00**
☐ 78 Doug Mohns, Minn. .65 1.25
☐ 79 Guy Lafleur, Mont. 18.00 35.00
☐ 80 Rod Gilbert, NYRa. 1.50 3.00
☐ 81 Gary Doak, Detr. .65 1.25
☐ **82 Dave Burrows, Pitt. RC 1.00 2.00**
☐ 83 Gary Croteau, Cali. .65 1.25
☐ 84 Tracy Pratt, Buff. .65 1.25
☐ 85 Carol Vadnais, Cali. (Bost.) .65 1.25
☐ **86 Jacques Caron (G), SLou. RC 2.00 4.00**

□	87 Keith Magnuson, Chic.	.65	1.25
□	88 Dave Keon, Toro.	1.50	3.00
□	89 Mike Corrigan, Vanc. (LosA.)	.65	1.25
□	90 Bobby Clarke, Phil.	10.00	20.00
□	91 Dunc Wilson (G), Vanc.	1.00	2.00
□	**92 Gerry Hart, Detr. (NYIs.) RC**	**1.00**	**2.00**
□	93 Lou Nanne, Minn.	.65	1.25
□	94 Checklist (1-176)	20.00	40.00
□	95 Red Berenson, Detr.	.65	1.25
□	96 Bob Plager, SLou.	.65	1.25
□	**97 Jim Rutherford (G), Detr. (Pitt.) RC**	**3.25**	**6.50**
□	**98 Rick Foley, Phil. RC**	**1.00**	**2.00**
□	99 Pit Martin, Chic.	.65	1.25
□	100 Bobby Orr, Bost.	22.00	45.00
□	101 Stan Gilbertson, Cali.	.65	1.25
□	102 Barry Wilkins, Vanc.	.65	1.25
□	103 Terry Crisp, SLou. (NYIs.)	.65	1.25
□	104 Césare Maniago (G), Minn.	1.00	2.00
□	105 Marc Tardif, Mont.	.65	1.25
□	106 Don Luce, Buff.	.65	1.25
□	107 Mike Pelyk, Toro.	.65	1.25
□	108 Juha Widing, LosA.	.65	1.25
□	**109 Phil Myre (G), Mont. (Atla.) RC**	**2.00**	**4.00**
□	110 Vic Hadfield, NYRa.	.65	1.25
□	111 Arnie Brown, Detr.	.65	1.25
□	112 Ross Lonsberry, Phil.	.65	1.25
□	113 Dick Redmond, Cali.	.65	1.25
□	114 Gary Smith (G), Chic.	1.00	2.00
□	115 Bill Goldsworthy, Minn.	.65	1.25
□	116 Bryan Watson, Pitt.	.65	1.25
□	117 Dave Balon, Vanc.	.65	1.25
□	**118 Bill Mikkelson, LosA. (NYIs.) RC**	**1.00**	**2.00**
□	119 Terry Harper, Mont.	.65	1.25
□	120 Gilbert Perreault, Buff.	4.50	8.50
□	121 Tony Esposito (G), Chic.	4.00	8.00
□	122 Bobby Orr, Bost.	15.00	30.00
□	123 Brad Park, NYRa.	2.00	4.00
□	124 Phil Esposito, Bost.	3.00	6.00
□	125 Rod Gilbert, NYRa.	1.50	3.00
□	126 Bobby Hull, Chic.	10.00	20.00
□	127 Ken Dryden (G), Mont.	9.00	17.00
□	128 Bill White, Chic.	.65	1.25
□	129 Pat Stapleton, Chic.	.65	1.25
□	130 Jean Ratelle, NYRa.	1.25	2.50
□	131 Yvan Cournoyer, Mont.	1.25	2.50
□	132 Vic Hadfield, NYRa.	.65	1.25
□	133 Ralph Backstrom, LosA.	.65	1.25
□	134 Bob Baun, Toro.	.65	1.25
□	135 Fred Stanfield, Bost.	.65	1.25
□	136 Barclay Plager, SLou.	.65	1.25
□	137 Gilles Villemure (G), NYRa.	1.00	2.00
□	138 Ron Harris, Detr. (Atla.)	.65	1.25
□	139 Bill Flett, Phil.	.65	1.25
□	140 Frank Mahovlich, Mont.	3.00	6.00
□	141 Alex Delvecchio, Detr.	1.50	3.00
□	142 Poul Popiel, Vanc.	.65	1.25
□	143 Jean Pronovost, Pitt.	.65	1.25
□	144 Denis DeJordy (G), LosA. (NYIs.)	1.00	2.00
□	145 Rick Martin, Buff.	2.00	4.00
□	**146 Ivan Boldirev, Cali. RC**	**2.00**	**4.00**
□	**147 Jack Egers, SLou. RC**	**1.00**	**2.00**
□	148 Jim Pappin, Chic.	.65	1.25
□	149 Rod Seiling, NYRa.	.65	1.25
□	150 Phil Esposito, Bost.	6.00	12.00
□	151 Gary Edwards (G), LosA.	1.00	2.00
□	152 Ron Ellis, Toro.	.65	1.25
□	153 Jude Drouin, Minn.	.65	1.25
□	154 Ernie Hicke, Cali. (Atla.)	.65	1.25
□	155 Mickey Redmond, Detr.	1.00	2.00
□	156 Joe Watson, Phil.	.65	1.25
□	157 Bryan Hextall, Jr., Pitt.	.65	1.25
□	158 André Boudrias, Vanc.	.65	1.25
□	159 Ed Westfall, NYIs.	.65	1.25
□	160 Ken Dryden (G), Mont.	28.00	50.00
□	**161 Rene Robert, Pitt. (Buff.) RC**	**1.75**	**3.25**
□	162 Bert Marshall, Cali.	.65	1.25
□	163 Gary Sabourin, SLou.	.65	1.25
□	164 Dennis Hull, Chic.	.65	1.25
□	165 Ed Giacomin (G), NYRa.	1.75	3.50
□	166 Ken Hodge, Bost.	.65	1.25
□	167 Gilles Marotte, LosA.	.65	1.25
□	168 Norm Ullman, Toro.	1.25	2.50
□	**169 Barry Gibbs, Minn. RC**	**1.00**	**2.00**
□	170 AW: Phil Esposito	1.25	2.50
□	171 AW: Bobby Orr	1.50	3.00
□	172 AW: Bobby Orr	1.50	3.00
□	173 AW: Tony Esposito, Gary Smith	1.25	2.50
□	174 AW: Ken Dryden	1.50	3.00
□	175 AW: Jean Ratelle	1.25	2.50
□	176 AW: Bobby Orr	1.50	4.50

1972 - 73 WILLIAMS (SUOMI)

These stickers measure 1 7/8" x 2 1/4".

Complete Set (360 stickers):

Williams EX NM

□ 1 Vladimir Bednar, CSR.
□ 2 Jiri Bubla, CSR.

□ 3 Vladimir Dzurilla, CSR.
□ 4 Richard Farda, CSR.
□ 5 Julius Haas, CSR.
□ 6 Ivan Hlinka, CSR.
□ 7 Jiri Holecek, CSR.
□ 8 Jaroslav Holik, CSR.
□ 9 Jiri Holik, CSR.
□ 10 Josef Horesovsky, CSR.
□ 11 Jan Klapac, CSR.
□ 12 Jiri Kochta, CSR.
□ 13 Milan Kuzela, CSR.
□ 14 Oldrich Machac, CSR.
□ 15 Vladimir Martinec, CSR.
□ 16 Vaclav Nedomansky, CSR.
□ 17 Josef Palecek, CSR.
□ 18 Frantisek Pospisil, CSR.
□ 19 Bohuslav Stastny, CSR.
□ 20 Rudolf Tajcnar, CSR.
□ 21 Vyatcheslav Anisin, USSR
□ 22 Yuri Blinov, USSR
□ 23 Alexander Gusev, USSR
□ 24 Valeri Kharlamov, USSR
□ 25 Alexander Yakushev, USSR
□ 26 Viktor Kuzkin, USSR
□ 27 Vladimir Lutshenko, USSR
□ 28 Alexander Maltsev, USSR
□ 29 Boris Mikhailov, USSR
□ 30 Evgeny Mishakov, USSR
□ 31 Vladimir Petrov, USSR
□ 32 Alexander Ragulin, USSR
□ 33 Igor Romishevski, USSR
□ 34 Vladimir Shadrin, USSR
□ 35 Vladimir Shepovalov, USSR
□ 36 Vjatsjeslav Soloduhin, USSR
□ 37 Vladimir Tretiak, USSR
□ 38 Gennady Tsicankov, USSR
□ 39 Valeri Vasiliev, USSR
□ 40 Vladimir Vikulov, USSR
□ 41 Christer Abrahamsson, Swe.
□ 42 Thommy Abrahamsson, Swe.
□ 43 Thommie Bergman, Swe.
□ 44 Inge Hammarstrom, Swe.
□ 45 Anders Hedberg, Swe.
□ 46 Leif Holmqvist (G), Swe.
□ 47 Bjorn Johansson, Swe.
□ 48 Stig-Goran Johansson, Swe.
□ 49 Stefan Karlsson, Swe.
□ 50 Stig Larsson, Swe.
□ 51 Mats Lind, Swe.
□ 52 Tord Lundstrom, Swe.
□ 53 Lars-Göran Nilsson, Swe.
□ 54 Bjorn Palmqvist, Swe.
□ 55 Hakan Pettersson, Swe.
□ 56 Borje Salming, Swe.
□ 57 Lars-Erik Sjoberg, Swe.
□ 58 Carl Sundqvist, Swe.
□ 59 Hakan Wickberg, Swe.
□ 60 Stig Ostling, Swe.
□ 61 Seppo Ahokainen, Fin.
□ 62 Matti Keinonen, Fin.
□ 63 Veli-Pekka Ketola, Fin.
□ 64 Harri Linnonmaa, Fin.
□ 65 Pekka Marjamaki, Fin.
□ 66 Lauri Mononen, Fin.
□ 67 Matti Murto, Fin.
□ 68 Timo Nummelin, Fin.
□ 69 Lasse Oksanen, Fin.
□ 70 Esa Peltonen, Fin.
□ 71 Juha Rantasila, Fin.
□ 72 Pekka Rautakallio, Fin.
□ 73 Seppo Repo, Fin.
□ 74 Heikki Riihiranta, Fin.
□ 75 Juhani Tamminen, Fin.
□ 76 Timo Turunen, Fin.
□ 77 Pertti Valkeapaa, Fin.
□ 78 Jorma Valtonen, Fin.
□ 79 Stig Wetzell, Fin.
□ 80 Jouko Oystila, Fin.
□ 81 Juhani Bostrom, HIFK
□ 82 Kimmo Heino, HIFK
□ 83 Pentti Karlsson, HIFK
□ 84 Mauri Kaukokari, HIFK
□ 85 Jarmo Koivunen, HIFK
□ 86 Heikki Kojola, HIFK
□ 87 Vaino Kolkka, HIFK
□ 88 Harri Linnonmaa, HIFK
□ 89 Jaakko Marttinen, HIFK
□ 90 Matti Murto, HIFK
□ 91 Lalli Partinen, HIFK
□ 92 Juha Rantasila, HIFK
□ 93 Heikki Riihiranta, HIFK
□ 94 Jorma Rikala, HIFK
□ 95 Henry Saleva, HIFK
□ 96 Tommi Salmelainen, HIFK
□ 97 Jorma Thusberg, HIFK
□ 98 Jorma Virtanen, HIFK
□ 99 Matti Vaisanen, HIFK
□ 100 Juhani Aaltonen, HJK
□ 101 Jorma Immonen, HJK
□ 102 Martti Immonen, HJK
□ 103 Heikki Jarn, HJK
□ 104 Matti Keinonen, HJK
□ 105 Seppo Laakkio, HJK
□ 106 Timo Lahtinen, HJK
□ 107 Esa Peltonen, HJK
□ 108 Keijo Puhakka, HJK
□ 109 Seppo Railio, HJK
□ 110 Antti Ravi, HJK
□ 111 Timo Saari, HJK
□ 112 Esa Siren, HJK
□ 113 Seppo Suoraniemi, HJK
□ 114 Juhani Tamminen, HJK
□ 115 Jorma Vehmanen, HJK
□ 116 Stig Wetzell, HJK
□ 117 Leo Aikas, HJK
□ 118 Sakari Ahlberg, Ilves
□ 119 Seppo Ahokainen, Ilves
□ 120 Jorma Aro, Ilves
□ 121 Esko Eriksson, Ilves
□ 122 Markku Hakanen, Ilves
□ 123 Timo Hirsimaki, Ilves
□ 124 Jorma Kallio, Ilves
□ 125 Esko Kaonpaa, Ilves
□ 126 Pentti Koskela, Ilves
□ 127 Pekka Kuusisto, Ilves
□ 128 Pekka Leimu, Ilves
□ 129 Len Lunde, Ilves
□ 130 Jukka Mattila, Ilves
□ 131 Lasse Oksanen, Ilves
□ 132 Hannu Palmu, Ilves
□ 133 Kari Palooja, Ilves
□ 134 Jorma Peltonen, Ilves
□ 135 Tuomo Sillman, Ilves
□ 136 Veikko Suominen, Ilves
□ 137 Pertti Ahokas, Jokerit
□ 138 Pertti Arvaja, Jokerit
□ 139 Christer Bergenheim, Jokerit
□ 140 Jorma Borgstrom, Jokerit
□ 141 Olli Hietanen, Jokerit
□ 142 Pentti Hiiros, Jokerit
□ 143 Eero Holopainen, Jokerit
□ 144 Kari Kinnunen, Jokerit
□ 145 Keijo Koivunen, Jokerit
□ 146 Ilpo Koskela, Jokerit
□ 147 Timo Kyntola, Jokerit
□ 148 Henry Leppa, Jokerit
□ 149 Erkki Mononen, Jokerit
□ 150 Pertti Nurmi, Jokerit
□ 151 Tero Raty, Jokerit
□ 152 Timo Sutinen, Jokerit
□ 153 Timo Turunen, Jokerit
□ 154 Jouko Oystila, Jokerit
□ 155 Hannu Haapalainen, Koovee
□ 156 Olavi Haapalainen, Koovee
□ 157 JukkaPekka Jarvenpaa, Koovee
□ 158 Heimo Keinonen, Koovee
□ 159 Markku Moisio, Koovee
□ 160 Heikki Nurmi, Koovee
□ 161 Seppo Nurmi, Koovee
□ 162 Oiva Oijennus, Koovee
□ 163 Reino Pulkkinen, Koovee
□ 164 Esko Rantanen, Koovee
□ 165 Juhani Ruohonen, Koovee
□ 166 Mikko Raikkonen, Koovee
□ 167 Lauri Salomaa, Koovee
□ 168 Leo Seppanen, Koovee
□ 169 Pekka Uitus, Koovee
□ 170 Jorma Vilen, Koovee
□ 171 Tapio Virhimo, Koovee
□ 172 Leo Haakana, Saipa
□ 173 Seppo Hyvonen, Saipa
□ 174 Heikki Juselius, Saipa
□ 175 Hannu Lemander, Saipa
□ 176 Kyosti Lahde, Saipa
□ 177 Ari Mikkola, Saipa
□ 178 Martti Makia, Saipa
□ 179 Martti Narinen, Saipa
□ 180 Pekka Nieminen, Saipa
□ 181 Teijo Rasanen, Saipa
□ 182 Timo Sartiala, Saipa
□ 183 Pekka Sartjarvi, Saipa
□ 184 Keijo Sinkkonen, Saipa
□ 185 Martti Sinkkonen, Saipa
□ 186 Arto Summanen, Saipa
□ 187 Erkki Suni, Saipa
□ 188 Seppo Urpalainen, Saipa
□ 189 Matti Vaatamoinen, Saipa
□ 190 Timo Vaatamoinen, Saipa
□ 191 Jukka Alkula, Tappara
□ 192 Pertti Ansakorpi, Tappara
□ 193 Keijo Jarvinen, Tappara
□ 194 Pertti Koivulahti, Tappara
□ 195 Ilpo Kuisma, Tappara
□ 196 Vesa Lehtoranta, Tappara
□ 197 Antti Leppanen, Tappara
□ 198 Pekka Marjamaki, Tappara
□ 199 Mikko Mynttinen, Tappara
□ 200 Pekka Makinen, Tappara
□ 201 Seppo Makinen, Tappara
□ 202 Antti Perttula, Tappara
□ 203 Tuomo Rautiainen, Tappara
□ 204 Jorma Saarikorpi, Tappara
□ 205 Jorma Siitarinen, Tappara
□ 206 Raimo Suoniemi, Tappara
□ 207 Pertti Valkeapaa, Tappara
□ 208 Kari Horkko, Turun Palloseura
□ 209 Eero Juntunen, Turun Palloseura
□ 210 Lauri Jamsen, Turun Palloseura
□ 211 Kari Kauppila, Turun Palloseura
□ 212 Lasse Kiili, Turun Palloseura
□ 213 Olli Kokkonen, Turun Palloseura
□ 214 Pekka Lahtela, Turun Palloseura
□ 215 Robert Lamoureux, Turun Palloseura
□ 216 Ilkka Mesikammen, Turun Palloseura
□ 217 Timo Nummelin, Turun Palloseura
□ 218 Rauli Ottila, Turun Palloseura
□ 219 Matti Rautee, Turun Palloseura
□ 220 Pekka Rautee, Turun Palloseura
□ 221 Jari Rosberg, Turun Palloseura
□ 222 Jouni Samuli, Turun Palloseura
□ 223 Harri Silver, Turun Palloseura
□ 224 Rauli Tammelin, Turun Palloseura
□ 225 Bengt Wilenius, Turun Palloseura
□ 226 Pertti Hasanen, Turun Toverit
□ 227 Kari Johansson, Turun Toverit
□ 228 Arto Kaunonen, Turun Toverit
□ 229 Timo Kokkonen, Turun Toverit
□ 230 Reijo Leppanen, Turun Toverit
□ 231 Seppo Lindstrom, Turun Toverit
□ 232 Hannu Luojola, Turun Toverit
□ 233 Hannu Niittoaho, Turun Toverit
□ 234 Reijo Paksal, Turun Toverit
□ 235 Seppo Parikka, Turun Toverit
□ 236 Jarmo Rantanen, Turun Toverit
□ 237 Kari Salonen, Turun Toverit
□ 238 Tapani Sura, Turun Toverit
□ 239 Kari Torkkel, Turun Toverit
□ 240 Risto Vainio, Turun Toverit
□ 241 Pentti Vihanto, Turun Toverit
□ 242 Seppo Wikstrom, Turun Toverit
□ 243 Urpo Ylonen, Turun Toverit
□ 244 Tapio Flinck, Assat Pori
□ 245 Antti Heikkila, Assat Pori
□ 246 Reijo Heinonen, Assat Pori
□ 247 Jaakko Honkanen, Assat Pori
□ 248 VeliPekka Ketola, Assat Pori
□ 249 Raimo Kilpio, Assat Pori
□ 250 Tapio Koskinen, Assat Pori
□ 251 Jarkko Levonen, Assat Pori
□ 252 Kaj Matalamaki, Assat Pori
□ 253 Pertti Makela, Assat Pori
□ 254 Hannu Pulkkinen, Assat Pori
□ 255 Pekka Rautakallio, Assat Pori
□ 256 Markku Riihimaki, Assat Pori
□ 257 Matti Salmi, Assat Pori
□ 258 Jorma Valtonen, Assat Pori
□ 259 Anto Virtanen, Assat Pori
□ 260 Erkki Vakiparta, Assat Pori
□ 261 Martti Jarkko, Tappara Jrs.
□ 262 Torsti Jarvenpaa, Tappara Jrs.
□ 263 Tapio Kallio, Tappara Jrs.
□ 264 Jussi Kiansten, Tappara Jrs.
□ 265 Kimmo Korpela, Tappara Jrs.
□ 266 Jarmo Kuisma, Tappara Jrs.
□ 267 Antero Lehtonen, Tappara Jrs.
□ 268 Mikko Leinonen, Tappara Jrs.
□ 269 Tuomas Leinonen, Tappara Jrs.
□ 270 Lasse Litma, Tappara Jrs.
□ 271 Seppo Makinen, Tappara Jrs.
□ 272 Heikki Niemi, Tappara Jrs.
□ 273 Reijo Narvanen, Tappara Jrs.
□ 274 Kalevi Paakkonen, Tappara Jrs.
□ 275 Reijo Rossi, Tappara Jrs.
□ 276 Seppo Sevon, Tappara Jrs.
□ 277 Jorma Siren, Tappara Jrs.
□ 278 Risto Sirkkola, Tappara Jrs.
□ 279 Risto Hevonkorpi, Koovee Jrs.
□ 280 Veijo Hukkanen, Koovee Jrs.
□ 281 Timo Hytti, Koovee Jrs.
□ 282 Kalle Impola, Koovee Jrs.
□ 283 Pertti Jarvenpaa, Koovee Jrs.
□ 284 Rauno Jarvinen, Koovee Jrs.
□ 285 Antti Kaivola, Koovee Jrs.
□ 286 Jorma Karvonen, Koovee Jrs.
□ 287 Pekka Karvonen, Koovee Jrs.
□ 288 Seppo Kettunen, Koovee Jrs.

☐ 289 Kari Niemi, Koovee Jrs.
☐ 290 Timo Niiniviita, Koovee Jrs.
☐ 291 Jari Nurminen, Koovee Jrs.
☐ 292 Pentti Poussu, Koovee Jrs.
☐ 293 Matti Rautiainen, Koovee Jrs.
☐ 294 Vesa Ronkainen, Koovee Jrs.
☐ 295 Mauri Salminen, Koovee Jrs.
☐ 296 Kari Silius, Koovee Jrs.
☐ 297 Kimmo Turtiainen, Koovee Jrs.
☐ 298 Juha Wikman, Koovee Jrs.
☐ 299 JuhaPekka Aho, Ilves Jrs.
☐ 300 Matti Estola, Ilves Jrs.
☐ 301 Markku Heinonen, Ilves Jrs.
☐ 302 Mauri Heinonen, Ilves Jrs.
☐ 303 Jukka Hirsimaki, Ilves Jrs.
☐ 304 Jarmo Huhtala, Ilves Jrs.
☐ 305 Harri Huotari, Ilves Jrs.
☐ 306 Kari Jarvinen, Ilves Jrs.
☐ 307 Jari Kaarela, Ilves Jrs.
☐ 308 Kai Lehto, Ilves Jrs.
☐ 309 Jari Leppanen, Ilves Jrs.
☐ 310 Jarmo Lilius, Ilves Jrs.
☐ 311 Markus Mattsson, Ilves Jrs.
☐ 312 Jari Niinimaki, Ilves Jrs.
☐ 313 Hannu Oksanenx, Ilves Jrs.
☐ 314 Sakari Pehu, Ilves Jrs.
☐ 315 Mika Rajala, Ilves Jrs.
☐ 316 Risto Siltanen, Ilves Jrs.
☐ 317 Jarmo Siro, Ilves Jrs.
☐ 318 Jukka Siro, Ilves Jrs.
☐ 319 Jari Uusikartano, Ilves Jrs.
☐ 320 Seppo Vartiainen, Ilves Jrs.
☐ 321 Mika Weissman, Ilves Jrs.
☐ 322 Seppo Aro, Ilves Jrs.
☐ 323 Jari Huotari, Ilves Jrs.
☐ 324 Ilkka Huura, Ilves Jrs.
☐ 325 Jari Hytti, Ilves Jrs.
☐ 326 Jarmo Jamalainen, Ilves Jrs.
☐ 327 Jari Jokinen, Ilves Jrs.
☐ 328 Tero Juojarvi, Ilves Jrs.
☐ 329 Jari Jarvinen, Ilves Jrs.
☐ 330 Lauri Kosonen, Ilves Jrs.
☐ 331 Aki Laakso, Ilves Jrs.
☐ 332 Ismo Laine, Ilves Jrs.
☐ 333 Matti Lisko, Ilves Jrs.
☐ 334 Dale Lunde, Ilves Jrs.
☐ 335 Markku Pirkkalaniem, Ilves Jrs.
☐ 336 Rauno Saarnio, Ilves Jrs.
☐ 337 Jukka Silander, Ilves Jrs.
☐ 338 Olli-Pekka Turunen, Ilves Jrs.
☐ 339 Mauri Unkila, Ilves Jrs.
☐ 340 Jarmo Viteli, Ilves Jrs.
☐ 341 Jukka Ahonen, Ilves Jrs.
☐ 342 Jari Hallila, Ilves Jrs.
☐ 343 Jari Helle, Ilves Jrs.
☐ 344 Jari Hirsimaki, Ilves Jrs.
☐ 345 Petri Jokinen, Ilves Jrs.
☐ 346 Kari Jarvinen, Ilves Jrs.
☐ 347 Arto Laine, Ilves Jrs.
☐ 348 Ari Leinonen, Ilves Jrs.
☐ 349 Jukka Oksanen, Ilves Jrs.
☐ 350 Sten Pakarinen, Ilves Jrs.
☐ 351 Jyrki Seppa, Ilves Jrs.
☐ 352 Jari Simola, Ilves Jrs.
☐ 353 Olli Sarkilahti, Ilves Jrs.
☐ 354 KariPekka Tarko, Ilves Jrs.
☐ 355 Timo Toivonen, Ilves Jrs.
☐ 356 VeliMatti Uusimaa, Ilves Jrs.
☐ 357 Risto Viljanen, Ilves Jrs.
☐ 358 Timo Virtanen, Ilves Jrs.
☐ 359 Teppo Valimaki, Ilves Jrs.
☐ 360 Juha Yrjola, Ilves Jrs.

1973 - 74 DERNIÈRE PHOTOS

This multi-sport series of photos were inserted in Dernière magazine from 1972 through 1984. Three holes were punched on the left side to allow for storage in a binder. The series featured Montréal Canadiens players. These photos measure 8" x 10".

Dernière	EX	NM
☐ 18NOV Henri Richard	3.50	7.00
☐ 25NOV Guy Lapointe	3.00	6.00
☐ 2DEC Chuck Lefley	1.50	3.00
☐ 9DEC Yvan Cournoyer	3.50	7.00
☐ 16DEC Guy Lafleur	6.00	12.00
☐ 23DEC Pierre Bouchard	1.50	3.00
☐ 30DEC Wayne Thomas (G)	2.50	5.00
☐ 6JAN Jacques Laperrière	3.00	6.00
☐ 13JAN Serge Savard	3.00	6.00
☐ 20JAN Frank Mahovlich	5.00	10.00
☐ 27JAN Claude Larose	1.50	3.00
☐ 3FEB Michel Plasse (G)	2.50	5.00
☐ 10FEB Michel Larocque (G)	2.50	5.00
☐ 17FEB Pete Mahovlich	1.50	3.00
☐ 24FEB Steve Shutt	3.00	6.00
☐ 3MAR Jim Roberts	1.50	3.00
☐ 10MAR Bob Gainey	3.50	7.00
☐ 17MAR Murray Wilson	1.50	3.00
☐ 24MAR Larry Robinson	4.00	8.00
☐ 31MAR Yvon Lambert	1.50	3.00
☐ 7APR Jacques Lemaire	3.50	7.00

1973 - 74 MAC'S MILK

These disks measure 3".

Complete Set (30 disks):	**80.00**	**160.00**
Mac's Milk	**EX**	**NM**
☐ Gary Bergman, Detr.	1.75	3.50
☐ John Bucyk, Bost.	3.50	7.00
☐ Wayne Cashman, Bost.	2.50	5.00
☐ Bobby Clarke, Phi.	6.00	12.00
☐ Yvan Cournoyer, Mont.	4.00	8.00
☐ Ron Ellis, Toro.	1.75	3.50
☐ Rod Gilbert, NYRa.	3.50	7.00
☐ Brian Glennie, Toro.	1.75	3.50
☐ Paul Henderson, Toro.	3.00	6.00
☐ Eddie Johnston (G), Toro.	2.50	5.00
☐ Rick Kehoe, Toro.	1.75	3.50
☐ Orland Kurtenbach, Vanc.	1.75	3.50
☐ Guy Lapointe, Mont.	3.00	6.00
☐ Jacques Lemaire, Mont.	4.00	8.00
☐ Frank Mahovlich, Mont.	6.00	12.00
☐ Pete Mahovlich, Mont.	1.75	3.50
☐ Richard Martin, Buff.	2.50	5.00
☐ Jim McKenny, Toro.	1.75	3.50
☐ Bobby Orr, Bost.	25.00	45.00
☐ Jean Paul Parise, Minn.	1.75	3.50
☐ Brad Park, NYRa.	4.00	8.00
☐ Jacques Plante (G), Toro.	9.00	18.00
☐ Jean Ratelle, NYR	3.50	7.00
☐ Mickey Redmond, Detr.	2.50	5.00
☐ Serge Savard, Mont.	3.00	6.00
☐ Darryl Sittler, Toro.	6.00	12.00
☐ Pat Stapleton, Chic.	1.75	3.50
☐ Dale Tallon, Chic.	1.75	3.50
☐ Norm Ullman, Toro.	3.50	7.00
☐ Bill White, Chic.	1.75	3.50

1973 - 74 NABISCO SUGAR DADDY

These stickers measure 1 1/16" x 2 3/4". This 25 sticker set features players from four different sports. Other singles exist. An 18 x 24 wall poster was also available.

Complete Set (264 cards):	**950**	**1,900**
Common Player:	**2.50**	**5.00**
O-Pee-Chee	**EX**	**NM**
☐ 11 Phil Esposito	7.50	15.00
☐ 12 Dennis Hull	4.00	7.50
☐ 13 Reg Fleming	2.50	5.00
☐ 14 Garry Unger	2.50	5.00
☐ 15 Derek Sanderson	5.00	10.00
☐ 16 Jerry Korab	2.50	5.00
☐ 22 Mickey Redmond	4.00	7.50

1973 - 74 O-PEE-CHEE

"I put a hole punch in the top corner of each of my ('73-74) cards. I had a paper route at the time and I think I was practising with my hole punch. The cards themselves have a weird design, they were so very different with their red and green colours. I remember the Bobby Orr card – he looks like he is slipping." – George Kumagai, Major Leagues, Burlington, Ontario.

This set was produced from two different card stocks; one light beige and the other grey. Cards 1 to 132 have a red border while cards 133 to 264 were printed with a green border. These cards measure the standard 2 1/2" x 3 1/2".

Complete Set (264 cards):	**300.00**	**600.00**
Common Player:	**1.00**	**2.00**
O-Pee-Chee	**EX**	**NM-MT**
☐ 1 Alex Delvecchio, Detr.	2.50	7.50
☐ 2 Gilles Meloche, Cali. (G)	1.50	3.00
☐ 3 Phil Roberto, SLou.	1.00	2.00
☐ 4 Orland Kurtenbach, Vanc.	1.00	2.00
☐ 5 Gilles Marotte, LosA.	1.00	2.00
☐ 6 Stan Mikita, Chic.	5.00	10.00
☐ 7 Paul Henderson, Toro.	1.50	3.00
☐ 8 Gregg Sheppard, Bost., Err. (Greg)	1.00	2.00
☐ 9 Rod Seiling, NYRa.	1.00	2.00
☐ 10 Red Berenson, Detr.	1.00	2.00
☐ 11 Jean Pronovost, Pitt.	1.00	2.00
☐ 12 Dick Redmond, Chic.	1.00	2.00
☐ 13 Keith McCreary, Atla.	1.00	2.00
☐ 14 Bryan Watson, Pitt.	1.00	2.00
☐ 15 Garry Unger, SLou.	1.00	2.00
☐ **16 Neil Komadoski, LosA. RC**	**2.00**	**4.00**
☐ 17 Marcel Dionne, Detr.	12.00	25.00
☐ 18 Ernie Hicke, NYIs.	1.00	2.00
☐ 19 André Boudrias, Vanc.	1.00	2.00
☐ 20 AS: Bill Flett, Phil.	1.50	3.00
☐ 21 Marshall Johnston, Cali.	1.00	2.00
☐ 22 Gerry Meehan, Buff.	1.00	2.00
☐ 23 Eddie Johnston (G), Toro.	1.50	3.00
☐ 24 Serge Savard, Mont.	1.75	3.50
☐ 25 Walt Tkaczuk, NYRa.	1.00	2.00
☐ 26 Ken Hodge, Bost.	1.00	2.00
☐ 27 Norm Ullman, Toro.	2.50	5.00
☐ 28 Cliff Koroll, Chic.	1.00	2.00
☐ 29 Rey Comeau, Alt.	1.00	2.00
☐ 30 AS: Bobby Orr, Bost.	40.00	70.00
☐ 31 Wayne Stephenson (G), SLou.	1.50	3.00
☐ 32 Dan Maloney, LosA.	1.00	2.00
☐ **33 Henry Boucha, Detr. RC**	**2.00**	**4.00**
☐ 34 Gerry Hart, NYIs.	1.00	2.00
☐ 35 Bobby Schmautz, Vanc.	1.00	2.00
☐ 36 Ross Lonsberry, Phil.	1.00	2.00
☐ 37 Ted McAneeley, Cali.	1.00	2.00
☐ 38 Don Luce, Buff.	1.00	2.00
☐ 39 Jim McKenny, Toro.	1.00	2.00
☐ 40 Jacques Laperrière, Mont.	1.75	3.50
☐ 41 Bill Fairbairn, NYRa.	1.00	2.00
☐ 42 Craig Cameron, NYIs.	1.00	2.00
☐ 43 Bryan Hextall, Jr., Pitt.	1.00	2.00
☐ **44 Chuck Lefley, Mont. RC**	**2.00**	**4.00**
☐ 45 Dan Bouchard (G), Atla.	1.50	3.00
☐ 46 J.P. Parise, Minn.	1.00	2.00
☐ 47 Barclay Plager, SLou.	1.00	2.00
☐ 48 Mike Corrigan, LosA.	1.00	2.00
☐ 49 Nick Libett, Detr.	1.00	2.00
☐ 50 AS: Bobby Clarke, Phil.	14.00	28.00
☐ 51 Bert Marshall, NYIs.	1.00	2.00
☐ 52 Craig Patrick, Cali.	1.50	3.00
☐ 53 Richard Lemieux, Vanc.	1.00	2.00
☐ 54 Tracy Pratt, Buff.	1.00	2.00
☐ 55 Ron Ellis, Toro.	1.00	2.00
☐ 56 Jacques Lemaire, Mont.	2.50	5.00
☐ 57 Steve Vickers, NYRa.	1.00	2.00
☐ 58 Carol Vadnais, Bost.	1.00	2.00
☐ 59 Jim Rutherford (G), Pitt.	1.50	3.00
☐ 60 Rick Kehoe, Toro.	1.00	2.00
☐ 61 Pat Quinn, Atla.	1.00	2.00
☐ 62 Bill Goldsworthy, Minn.	1.00	2.00
☐ 63 Dave Dryden (G), Buff.	1.50	3.00
☐ 64 Rogatien Vachon (G), LosA.	3.00	6.00
☐ 65 Gary Bergman, Detr.	1.00	2.00
☐ 66 Bernie Parent (G), Phil.	6.00	12.00
☐ 67 Ed Westfall, NYIs.	1.00	2.00
☐ 68 Ivan Boldirev, Cali.	1.00	2.00
☐ 69 Don Tannahill, Vanc.	1.00	2.00
☐ 70 Gilbert Perreault, Buff.	7.50	15.00
☐ 71 Mike Pelyk, Toro.	1.00	2.00
☐ 72 Guy Lafleur, Mont.	20.00	40.00
☐ 73 Pit Martin, Chic.	1.00	2.00
☐ **74 Gilles Gilbert (G), Bost. RC**	**4.50**	**9.00**
☐ 75 Jim Lorentz, Buff.	1.00	2.00
☐ 76 Syl Apps, Jr., Pitt.	1.00	2.00
☐ 77 Phil Myre (G), Atla.	1.50	3.00
☐ 78 AS: Bill White, Chic.	1.50	3.00
☐ 79 Jack Egers, SLou.	1.00	2.00
☐ 80 Terry Harper, LosA.	1.00	2.00
☐ **81 Bill Barber, Phil. RC**	**12.00**	**25.00**
☐ 82 Roy Edwards (G), Detr.	1.50	3.00
☐ 83 Brian Spencer, NYIs.	1.00	2.00
☐ 84 Reggie Leach, Cali.	1.00	2.00
☐ 85 Wayne Cashman, Bost.	1.00	2.00
☐ 86 Jim Schoenfeld, Buff.	2.25	4.50
☐ 87 Henri Richard, Mont.	3.50	7.00
☐ **88 Dennis O'Brien, Minn. RC**	**2.00**	**4.00**
☐ 89 Al McDonough, Pitt.	1.00	2.00
☐ 90 AS: Tony Esposito (G), Chic.	9.00	18.00
☐ 91 Joe Watson, Phil.	1.00	2.00
☐ 92 Atlanta Flames	2.75	5.50
☐ 93 Boston Bruins	2.75	5.50
☐ 94 Buffalo Sabres	2.75	5.50
☐ 95 California Golden Seals	2.75	5.50
☐ 96 Chicago Blackhawks	2.75	5.50
☐ 97 Detroit Red Wings	2.75	5.50
☐ 98 Los Angeles Kings	2.75	5.50
☐ 99 Minnesota North Stars	2.75	5.50
☐ 100 Montréal Canadiens	2.75	5.50
☐ 101 New York Islanders	2.75	5.50
☐ 102 New York Rangers	2.75	5.50
☐ 103 Philadelphia Flyers	2.75	5.50
☐ 104 Pittsburgh Penguins	2.75	5.50
☐ 105 St. Louis Blues	2.75	5.50
☐ 106 Toronto Maple Leafs	2.75	5.50
☐ 107 Vancouver Canucks	2.75	5.50
☐ 108 Vic Hadfield, NYRa.	1.00	2.00
☐ 109 Tom Reid, Minn.	1.00	2.00
☐ **110 Hilliard Graves, Cali. RC**	**2.00**	**4.00**
☐ 111 Don Lever, Vanc.	1.00	2.00
☐ 112 Jim Pappin, Chic.	1.00	2.00
☐ 113 André Dupont, Phil.	1.00	2.00
☐ 114 AS: Guy Lapointe, Mont.	2.00	4.00
☐ 115 Dennis Hextall, Minn.	1.00	2.00
☐ 116 Checklist 1 (1 - 132)	30.00	55.00
☐ 117 Bobby Leiter, Atla.	1.00	2.00
☐ 118 Ab DeMarco, SLou.	1.00	2.00
☐ 119 Gilles Villemure (G), NYRa.	1.50	3.00
☐ 120 AS: Phil Esposito, Bost.	6.00	12.00
☐ 121 Mike Robitaille, Buff.	1.00	2.00
☐ 122 Réal Lemieux, LosA.	1.00	2.00
☐ 123 Jim Neilson, NYRa.	1.00	2.00
☐ **124 Steve Durbano, SLou. RC**	**1.50**	**3.00**
☐ 125 Jude Drouin, Minn.	1.00	2.00
☐ 126 Gary Smith (G), Vanc.	1.50	3.00
☐ 127 Césare Maniago (G), Minn.	1.50	3.00
☐ 128 Lowell MacDonald, Pitt.	1.00	2.00
☐ 129 Checklist, Error	30.00	55.00
☐ **130 Billy Harris, NYIs. RC**	**2.00**	**4.00**
☐ 131 Randy Manery, Atla.	1.00	2.00
☐ 132 Darryl Sittler, Toro.	11.00	22.00
☐ 133 LL: P. Esposito, Bost./ R. MacLeish, Phil.	2.50	5.00
☐ 134 LL: P. Esposito, Bost./ B. Clarke, Phil.	4.50	9.00
☐ 135 LL: P. Esposito, Bost./ B. Clarke, Phil.	4.50	9.00
☐ 136 LL: K. Dryden, Mont./ T. Esposito, Chic.	7.50	15.00
☐ 137 LL: J. Schoenfeld, Buff./ D. Schultz, Phil.	2.00	4.00
☐ 138 LL: P. Esposito, Bost./ R. MacLeish, Phil.	2.50	5.00
☐ 139 René Robert, Buff.	1.00	2.00
☐ 140 Dave Burrows, Pitt.	1.00	2.00
☐ 141 Jean Ratelle, NYRa.	2.50	5.00
☐ **142 Billy Smith (G), NYIs. RC**	**25.00**	**60.00**
☐ 143 Jocelyn Guevremont, Vanc.	1.00	2.00
☐ 144 Tim Ecclestone, Toro.	1.00	2.00
☐ 145 AS: Frank Mahovlich, Mont.	4.00	7.50
☐ 146 Rick MacLeish, Phil.	1.50	3.00
☐ 147 John Bucyk, Bost.	2.50	5.00
☐ 148 Bob Plager, SLou.	1.00	2.00
☐ **149 Curt Bennett, Atla. RC**	**2.00**	**4.00**
☐ 150 Dave Keon, Toro.	2.50	5.00
☐ 151 Keith Magnuson, Chic.	1.00	2.00
☐ 152 Walt McKechnie, Cali.	1.00	2.00
☐ 153 Roger Crozier (G), Buff.	1.50	3.00
☐ 154 Ted Harris, Detr.	1.00	2.00
☐ 155 Butch Goring, LosA.	1.00	2.00
☐ 156 Rod Gilbert, NYRa.	2.50	5.00
☐ 157 Yvan Cournoyer, Mont.	2.50	5.00
☐ 158 Doug Favell (G), Toro.	1.50	3.00
☐ 159 Juha Widing, LosA.	1.00	2.00
☐ 160 Ed Giacomin (G), NYRa.	2.75	5.50
☐ 161 Germaine Gagnon, NYIs.	1.00	2.00
☐ 162 Dennis Kearns, Vanc.	1.00	2.00
☐ 163 Bill Collins, Detr.	1.00	2.00
☐ 164 Pete Mahovlich, Mont.	1.00	2.00
☐ 165 Brad Park, NYRa.	4.00	8.00
☐ **166 Dave Schultz, Phil. RC**	**7.00**	**15.00**
☐ 167 Dallas Smith, Bost.	1.00	2.00
☐ 168 Gary Sabourin, SLou.	1.00	2.00
☐ 169 Jacques Richard, Atla.	1.00	2.00
☐ 170 Brian Glennie, Toro.	1.00	2.00
☐ 171 AS: Dennis Hull, Chic.	1.50	3.00
☐ 172 Joey Johnston, Cali.	1.00	2.00
☐ 173 Rick Martin, Buff.	1.50	3.00
☐ 174 AS: Barry Gibbs, Minn.	1.50	3.00
☐ 175 Bob Berry, LosA.	1.00	2.00
☐ 176 Greg Polis, Pitt.	1.00	2.00
☐ 177 Dale Rolfe, NYRa.	1.00	2.00
☐ 178 Gerry Desjardins (G), NYIs.	1.50	3.00
☐ 179 Bobby Lalonde, Vanc.	1.00	2.00
☐ 180 AS: Mickey Redmond, Detr.	1.50	3.00
☐ 181 Jim Roberts, Mont.	1.00	2.00
☐ 182 Gary Dornhoefer, Phil.	1.00	2.00
☐ 183 Derek Sanderson, Bost.	3.25	6.50
☐ 184 Brent Hughes, Detr.	1.00	2.00
☐ **185 Larry Romanchych, Atla. RC**	**2.00**	**4.00**

☐	186 Pierre Jarry, Detr.	1.00	2.00
☐	187 Doug Jarrett, Chic.	1.00	2.00
☐	**188 Bob Stewart, Cali. RC**	**2.00**	**4.00**
☐	189 Tim Horton, Buff.	4.50	8.50
☐	190 Fred (Buster) Harvey, Minn.	1.00	2.00
☐	191 Canadiens vs. Sabres	1.50	3.00
☐	192 Flyers vs. North Stars	1.50	3.00
☐	193 Blackhawks vs. Blues	1.50	3.00
☐	194 Rangers vs. Bruins	1.50	3.00
☐	195 Canadiens vs. Flyers	1.50	3.00
☐	196 Blackhawks vs. Rangers	1.50	3.00
☐	197 Canadiens vs Blackhawks	1.75	3.50
☐	198 Stanley Cup Champs: Canadiens	2.50	5.00
☐	199 Gary Edwards (G), LosA.	1.50	3.00
☐	200 Ron Schock, Pitt.	1.00	2.00
☐	201 Bruce MacGregor, NYRa.	1.00	2.00
☐	**202 Bob Nystrom, NYIs. RC**	**5.00**	**10.00**
☐	203 Jerry Korab, Vanc.	1.00	2.00
☐	**204 Thommie Bergman, Detr. RC**	**2.00**	**4.00**
☐	205 Bill Lesuk, LosA.	1.00	2.00
☐	206 Ed Van Impe, Phil.	1.00	2.00
☐	207 Doug Roberts, Detr.	1.00	2.00
☐	208 Chris Evans, SLou.	1.00	2.00
☐	**209 Lynn Powis, Chic. RC**	**2.00**	**4.00**
☐	210 Denis Dupère, Toro.	1.00	2.00
☐	211 Dale Tallon, Chic.	1.00	2.00
☐	212 Stan Gilbertson, Cali.	1.00	2.00
☐	213 Craig Ramsay, Buff.	1.00	2.00
☐	214 Danny Grant, Minn.	1.00	2.00
☐	**215 Doug Volmar, LosA. RC**	**2.00**	**4.00**
☐	216 Darryl Edestrand, Bost.	1.00	2.00
☐	217 Pete Stemkowski, NYRa.	1.00	2.00
☐	**218 Lorne Henning, NYIs. RC**	**2.00**	**4.00**
☐	**219 Bryan McSheffrey, Vanc. RC**	**2.00**	**4.00**
☐	220 Guy Charron, Detr.	1.00	2.00
☐	**221 Wayne Thomas (G), Mont. RC**	**3.00**	**6.00**
☐	222 Simon Nolet, Phil.	1.00	2.00
☐	**223 Fred O'Donnell, Bost. RC**	**2.00**	**4.00**
☐	224 Lou Angotti, SLou.	1.00	2.00
☐	225 Arnie Brown, Atla.	1.00	2.00
☐	226 Garry Monahan, Toro.	1.00	2.00
☐	227 Chico Maki, Chic.	1.00	2.00
☐	228 Gary Croteau, Cali.	1.00	2.00
☐	229 Paul Terbenche, Buff.	1.00	2.00
☐	230 Gump Worsley (G), Minn.	2.75	5.50
☐	231 Jimmy Peters, LosA.	1.00	2.00
☐	232 Jack Lynch, Pitt.	1.00	2.00
☐	233 Bobby Rousseau, NYRa.	1.00	2.00
☐	234 Dave Hudson, NYIs.	1.00	2.00
☐	235 Gregg Boddy, Vanc. RC, Err. (Greg)	1.00	2.00
☐	236 Ron Stackhouse, Detr.	1.00	2.00
☐	**237 Larry Robinson, Mont. RC**	**40.00**	**75.00**
☐	**238 Bobby Taylor (G), Phil. RC**	**1.50**	**3.00**
☐	239 Nick Beverley, Pitt.	1.00	2.00
☐	240 Don Awrey, SLou.	1.00	2.00
☐	241 Doug Mohns, Atla.	1.00	2.00
☐	242 Eddie Shack, Toro.	2.00	4.00
☐	**243 Phil Russell, Chic. RC**	**1.50**	**3.00**
☐	244 Pete Laframboise, Cali.	1.00	2.00
☐	245 Steve Atkinson, Buff.	1.00	2.00
☐	246 Lou Nanne, Minn.	1.00	2.00
☐	**247 Yvon Labre, Pitt. RC**	**2.00**	**4.00**
☐	248 Ted Irvine, NYRa.	1.00	2.00
☐	249 Tom Miller, NYIs.	1.00	2.00
☐	250 Gerry O'Flaherty, Vanc.	1.00	2.00
☐	**251 Larry Johnston, Detr. RC**	**2.00**	**4.00**
☐	**252 Michel Plasse (G), Mont. RC**	**3.00**	**6.00**
☐	253 Bob Kelly, Phil.	1.00	2.00
☐	**254 Terry O'Reilly, Bost. RC**	**6.00**	**12.00**
☐	**255 Pierre Plante, SLou. RC**	**2.00**	**4.00**
☐	256 Noel Price, Atla.	1.00	2.00
☐	257 Dunc Wilson (G), Toro.	1.50	3.00
☐	**258 J.P. Bordeleau, Chic. RC**	**2.00**	**4.00**
☐	**259 Terry Murray, Cali. RC**	**2.00**	**4.00**
☐	260 Larry Carriere, Buff.	1.00	2.00
☐	261 Pierre Bouchard, Mont.	1.00	2.00
☐	262 Frank St. Marseille, LosA.	1.00	2.00
☐	263 Checklist	28.00	55.00
☐	264 Fred Barrett, Minn.	1.50	4.50

TEAM LOGO

Insert Set (17 cards):		**25.00**	**50.00**
O-Pee-Chee		**EX**	**NM-MT**
☐	1 NHL Logo	2.00	4.00
☐	2 Atlanta Flames	2.00	4.00
☐	3 Boston Bruins	2.00	4.00
☐	4 Buffalo Sabres	2.00	4.00
☐	5 California Golden Seals	2.00	4.00
☐	6 Chicago Blackhawks	2.00	4.00
☐	7 Detroit Red Wings	2.00	4.00
☐	8 Los Angeles Kings	2.00	4.00
☐	9 Minnesota North Stars	2.00	4.00
☐	10 Montréal Canadiens	2.00	4.00
☐	11 New York Islanders	2.00	4.00
☐	12 New York Rangers	2.00	4.00
☐	13 Philadelphia Flyers	2.00	4.00
☐	14 Pittsburgh Penguins	2.00	4.00
☐	15 St. Louis Blues	2.00	4.00
☐	16 Toronto Maple Leafs	2.00	4.00
☐	17 Vancouver Canucks	2.00	4.00

TEAM RINGS

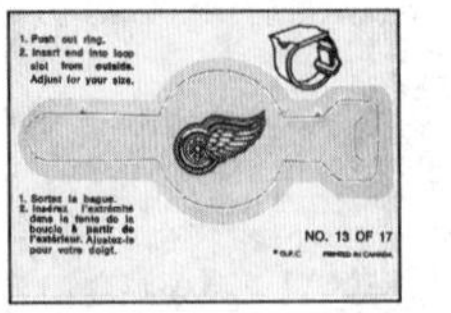

Insert Set (17 cards):		**35.00**	**70.00**
O-Pee-Chee		**EX**	**NM-MT**
☐	1 Vancouver Canucks	3.00	6.00
☐	2 Montréal Canadiens	3.00	6.00
☐	3 Toronto Maple Leafs	3.00	6.00
☐	4 NHL Logo	3.00	6.00
☐	5 Minnesota North Stars	3.00	6.00
☐	6 New York Rangers	3.00	6.00
☐	7 California Golden Seals	3.00	6.00
☐	8 Pittsburgh Penguins	3.00	6.00
☐	9 Philadelphia Flyers	3.00	6.00
☐	10 Chicago Blackhawks	3.00	6.00
☐	11 Boston Bruins	3.00	6.00
☐	12 Los Angeles Kings	3.00	6.00
☐	13 Detroit Red Wings	3.00	6.00
☐	14 St. Louis Blues	3.00	6.00
☐	15 Buffalo Sabres	3.00	6.00
☐	16 Atlanta Flames	3.00	6.00
☐	17 New York Islanders	3.00	6.00

1973 - 74 OPC WHA POSTERS

These posters measure 7 1/2" x 12 1/2".

Complete Set (20 posters):		**50.00**	**110.00**
O-Pee-Chee		**EX**	**NM**
☐	1 Al Smith (G), New England	2.50	5.00
☐	2 J.C. Tremblay, Québec	2.50	5.00
☐	3 Guy Dufour, Québec	1.50	3.00
☐	4 Pat Stapleton, Chicago	1.50	3.00
☐	5 Rosaire Paiement, Chicago	1.50	3.00
☐	6 Gerry Cheevers (G), Cleveland	4.50	9.00
☐	7 Gerry Pinder, Cleveland	1.50	3.00
☐	8 Wayne Carleton, Toronto	1.50	3.00
☐	9 Bob LeDuc, Toronto	1.50	3.00
☐	10 André Lacroix, New Jersey	2.50	5.00
☐	11 Jim Harrison, Edmonton	1.50	3.00
☐	12 Ron Climie, Edmonton	1.50	3.00
☐	13 Gordie Howe, Houston	15.00	30.00
☐	14 Marty, Gordie and Mark Howe	15.00	30.00
☐	15 Mike Walton, Minnesota	1.50	3.00
☐	16 Bobby Hull, Winnipeg	11.00	22.00
☐	17 Chris Bordeleau, Winnipeg	1.50	3.00
☐	18 Claude St. Sauveur, Vancouver	1.50	3.00
☐	19 Bryan Campbell, Vancouver, Err. (Brian)	1.50	3.00
☐	20 Marc Tardif, Los Angeles	3.00	5.00

1973 - 74 QUAKER OATS

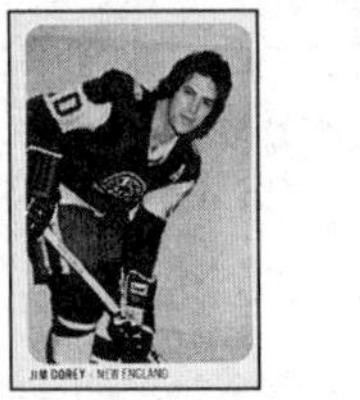

This series was issued in five-card panels in Quaker Oats products. The cut cards measure 2 1/4" x 3 1/4".

Complete Set (59 cards):		**125.00**	**250.00**
Panel 1-5:		**20.00**	**35.00**
Panel 6-10:		**30.00**	**60.00**
Panel 11-15:		**18.00**	**35.00**
Panel 16-20:		**20.00**	**40.00**
Panel 21-25:		**20.00**	**40.00**
Panel 26-30:		**25.00**	**40.00**
Panel 31-35:		**18.00**	**35.00**
Panel 36-40:		**18.00**	**35.00**
Panel 41-45:		**18.00**	**35.00**
Panel 46-50:		**65.00**	**125.00**
Quaker Oats		**EX**	**NM**
☐	1 Jim Wiste, Cleveland	3.50	7.00
☐	2 Al Smith (G), New England	3.50	7.00
☐	3 Rosaire Paiement, Calgary	2.50	5.00
☐	4 Ted Hampson, Minnesota	2.50	5.00
☐	5 Gavin Kirk, Toronto	2.50	5.00
☐	6 André Lacroix, New York	3.50	7.00
☐	7 John Schella, Houston	2.50	5.00
☐	8 Gerry Cheevers (G), Cleveland	10.00	20.00
☐	9 Norm Beaudin, Winnipeg	2.50	5.00
☐	10 Jim Harrison, Alberta	2.50	5.00
☐	11 Gerry Pinder, Cleveland	2.50	5.00
☐	12 Bob Sicinski, Calgary	2.50	5.00
☐	13 Bryan Campbell, Vancouver	2.50	5.00
☐	14 Murray Hall, Houston	2.50	5.00
☐	15 Chris Bordeleau, Winnipeg	2.50	5.00
☐	16 Al Hamilton, Alberta	3.50	7.00
☐	17 Jim McLeod (G), Chicago (New York)	2.50	5.00
☐	18 Larry Pleau, New England	2.50	5.00
☐	19 Larry Lund, Houston	2.50	5.00
☐	20 Bobby Sheehan, New York	2.50	5.00
☐	21 Jan Popiel, Calgary	2.50	5.00
☐	22 André Gaudette, Québec	2.50	5.00
☐	23 Bob Charlebois, New England	2.50	5.00
☐	24 Gene Peacosh, New York	2.50	5.00
☐	25 Rick Ley, New England	4.00	8.00
☐	26 Larry Hornung, Winnipeg	2.50	5.00
☐	27 Gary Jarrett, Cleveland	2.50	5.00
☐	28 Ted Taylor, Houston	2.50	5.00
☐	29 Pete Donnelly (G), New York (Vancouver)	3.50	7.00
☐	30 J.C. Tremblay, Québec	3.50	7.00
☐	31 Jim Cardiff, Vancouver	2.50	5.00
☐	32 Gary Veneruzzo, Los Angeles	2.50	5.00
☐	33 John French, New England	2.50	5.00
☐	34 Ron Ward, New York (Vancouver)	2.50	5.00
☐	35 Wayne Connelly, Minnesota	2.50	5.00
☐	36 Ron Buchanan, Cleveland	2.50	5.00
☐	37 Ken Block, New York	2.50	5.00
☐	38 Alain Caron, Québec	2.50	5.00
☐	39 Brit Selby, New England (Toronto)	2.50	5.00
☐	40 Guy Trottier, Toronto	2.50	5.00
☐	41 Ernie Wakely (G), Winnipeg	3.50	7.00
☐	42 J.P. LeBlanc, Los Angeles	2.50	5.00
☐	43 Michel Parizeau, Québec	2.50	5.00
☐	44 Wayne Rivers, New York	2.50	5.00
☐	45 Reggie Fleming, Calgary	2.50	5.00
☐	46 Don Herriman, Vancouver (New York)	2.50	5.00
☐	47 Jim Dorey, New England	2.50	5.00
☐	48 Danny Lawson, Vancouver	2.50	5.00
☐	49 Dick Paradise, Minnesota	2.50	5.00
☐	50 Bobby Hull, Winnipeg	25.00	60.00

1973 - 74 SOVIET CHAMPIONS

These postcards measure 8 1/2" x 3 1/2".

Complete Set (17 postcards and folder):		**90.00**	**175.00**
Soviet Champions		**EX**	**NM**
☐	1 World Champions	6.00	12.00
☐	2 USSR Champions/ Goalie Mask	6.00	12.00
☐	3 Sweden/ Boris Mikhailov vs. Sweden	6.00	12.00
☐	4 USSR vs. CSSR/ CSSR	4.00	8.00
☐	5 USSR vs. Finland/ USSR vs. Sweden	4.00	8.00
☐	6 USSR vs. CSSR/ Tretiak and USSR	10.00	20.00
☐	7 USSR/ Alexander Yakushev	6.00	12.00
☐	8 A.Ragulin vs. Sweden/ Sweden vs. USSR	5.00	10.00
☐	9 Sweden/ Alexander Yakushev/ USSR	6.00	12.00
☐	10 A.Yakushev/ G. Tsycankov and Ragulin	7.50	15.00
☐	11 V. Tretiak/ V. Petrov/ USSR	10.00	20.00
☐	12 V. Kharlamov and USSR/ CSSR (G)	7.50	15.00
☐	13 V. Treitiak and V. Vasiliev/ USSR	10.00	20.00
☐	14 Kharlamov and Mikhailov/ Mikhailov	7.50	15.00
☐	15 Mikhailov, Tretiak and USSR/ USSR flag	10.00	20.00
☐	16 V. Tretiak and USSR/ World Champions	10.00	20.00
☐	17 Autographed Sticks/ European Champs	4.00	8.00

1973 - 74 SOVIET STARS

These postcards measure 5 3/4" x 4 1/16".

Complete Set (25 postcards and folder):		**65.00**	**130.00**
Soviet Stars		**EX**	**NM**
☐	1 Team Photo	5.00	10.00
☐	2 Vladislav Tretiak (G)	12.00	25.00
☐	3 Alexander Sidelnikov	2.50	3.00
☐	4 Alexander Gusov	2.50	5.00
☐	5 Valery Vasiliev	2.50	5.00
☐	6 Boris Mikhailov	5.00	10.00
☐	7 Vladimir Petrov	4.00	8.00
☐	8 Valery Kharlamov	7.50	15.00
☐	9 V. Kharlamov/ B. Mikhailov/ V. Petrov	10.00	20.00
☐	10 Vladimir Lutchenko	2.50	5.00
☐	11 Gennedy Tsycakov	2.50	5.00
☐	12 Alexander Regulin	4.00	8.00
☐	13 Alexander Volchkov	2.50	5.00
☐	14 Vyacheslav Anisin	2.50	5.00
☐	15 Yuri Lebedev	2.50	5.00
☐	16 Alexander Bodunov	2.50	5.00
☐	17 Alexander Martyniuk	2.50	5.00
☐	18 Vladimir Shadrin	2.50	5.00
☐	19 Alexander Yakushev	7.50	15.00
☐	20 Alexander Maltsev	4.00	8.00
☐	21 Evgeny Paladiev	2.50	5.00
☐	22 Yuri Liapkin	2.50	5.00
☐	23 Vsevold Bobrov, Boris Kulagin	2.50	5.00
☐	24 Boris Mikhailov	5.00	10.00
☐	25 Viktor Kuzkin and opponent	2.50	5.00

1973 - 74 TOPPS

There are two colour variations for each card: red or blue for cards 1-99 and green or yellow for cards 100-198.

Complete Set (198 cards):		**125.00**	**250.00**
Common Player:		**.50**	**1.00**
Topps		**EX**	**NM-MT**
☐ ☐	1 LL: P. Esposito/ R. MacLeish	2.50	7.50
☐ ☐	2 LL: P. Esposito/ B. Clarke	3.25	6.50
☐ ☐	3 LL: P. Esposito/ B. Clarke	3.25	6.50
☐ ☐	4 LL: K. Dryden/ T. Esposito	5.00	10.00
☐ ☐	5 LL: J. Schoenfeld/ D. Schultz	1.25	2.50
☐ ☐	6 LL: P. Esposito/ R. MacLeish	2.00	4.00
☐ ☐	7 Paul Henderson, Toro.	.75	1.50
☐ ☐	8 Gregg Sheppard, Bost., Err. (Greg)	.50	1.00
☐ ☐	9 Rod Seiling, NYRa.	.50	1.00
☐ ☐	10 Ken Dryden (G), Mont.	30.00	60.00
☐ ☐	11 Jean Pronovost, Pitt.	.50	1.00
☐ ☐	12 Dick Redmond, Chic.	.50	1.00
☐ ☐	13 Keith McCreary, Atla.	.50	1.00
☐ ☐	14 Ted Harris, Minn.	.50	1.00
☐ ☐	15 Garry Unger, SLou.	.50	1.00
☐ ☐	**16 Neil Komadoski, LosA. RC**	**1.00**	**2.00**
☐ ☐	17 Marcel Dionne, Detr.	7.50	15.00
☐ ☐	18 Ernie Hicke, NYIs.	.50	1.00
☐ ☐	19 André Boudrias, Vanc.	.50	1.00
☐ ☐	20 AS: Bill Flett, Phil.	.50	1.00
☐ ☐	21 Marshall Johnston, Cali.	.50	1.00
☐ ☐	22 Gerry Meehan, Buff.	.50	1.00
☐ ☐	23 Ed Johnston (G), Toro.	.75	1.50
☐ ☐	24 Serge Savard, Mont.	1.00	1.75
☐ ☐	25 Walt Tkaczuk, NYRa.	.50	1.00
☐ ☐	26 John Bucyk, Bost.	1.25	2.50
☐ ☐	27 Dave Burrows, Pitt.	.50	1.00
☐ ☐	28 Cliff Koroll, Chic.	.50	1.00
☐ ☐	29 Rey Comeau, Atla.	.50	1.00
☐ ☐	30 AS: Barry Gibbs, Minn.	.50	1.00

□□	31 Wayne Stephenson (G), SLou.	.75	1.50
□□	32 Dan Maloney, LosA.	.50	1.00
□□	**33 Henry Boucha, Detr. RC**	**1.00**	**2.00**
□□	34 Gerry Hart, NYIs.	.50	1.00
□□	35 Bobby Schmautz, Vanc.	.50	1.00
□□	36 Ross Lonsberry, Phil.	.50	1.00
□□	37 Ted McAneeley, Cali.	.50	1.00
□□	38 Don Luce, Buff.	.50	1.00
□□	39 Jim McKenny, Toro.	.50	1.00
□□	40 AS: Frank Mahovlich, Mont.	2.50	5.00
□□	41 Bill Fairbairn, NYRa.	.50	1.00
□□	42 Dallas Smith, Bost.	.50	1.00
□□	43 Bryan Hextall, Pitt.	.50	1.00
□□	44 Keith Magnuson, Chic.	.50	1.00
□□	45 Dan Bouchard (G), Atla.	.75	1.50
□□	46 Jean Paul Parise, Minn.	.50	1.00
□□	47 Barclay Plager, SLou.	.50	1.00
□□	48 Mike Corrigan, LosA.	.50	1.00
□□	49 Nick Libett, Detr.	.50	1.00
□□	50 AS: Bobby Clarke, Phil.	6.50	12.00
□□	51 Bert Marshall, NYIs.	.50	1.00
□□	52 Craig Patrick, Cali.	.50	1.00
□□	53 Richard Lemieux, Vanc.	.50	1.00
□□	54 Tracy Pratt, Buff.	.50	1.00
□□	55 Ron Ellis, Toro.	.50	1.00
□□	56 Jacques Lemaire, Mont.	1.25	2.50
□□	57 Steve Vickers, NYRa.	.50	1.00
□□	58 Carol Vadnais, Bost.	.50	1.00
□□	59 Jim Rutherford (G), Pitt.	.75	1.50
□□	60 AS: Dennis Hull, Chic.	.50	1.00
□□	61 Pat Quinn, SLou.	.50	1.00
□□	62 Bill Goldsworthy, Minn.	.50	1.00
□□	**63 Frank Huck, SLou. RC**	**1.00**	**2.00**
□□	64 Rogatien Vachon (G), LosA.	1.50	2.75
□□	65 Gary Bergman, Detr.	.50	1.00
□□	66 Bernie Parent (G), Phil.	3.50	7.00
□□	67 Ed Westfall, NYIs.	.50	1.00
□□	68 Ivan Boldirev, Cali.	.50	1.00
□□	69 Don Tannahill, Vanc.	.50	1.00
□□	70 Gilbert Perreault, Buff.	4.00	8.00
□□	71 Mike Pelyk, Toro.	.50	1.00
□□	72 Guy Lafleur, Mont.	10.00	20.00
□□	73 Jean Ratelle, NYRa.	1.00	1.75
□□	**74 Gilles Gilbert (G), Bost. RC**	**2.00**	**4.00**
□□	75 Greg Polis, Pitt.	.50	1.00
□□	76 Doug Jarrett, Chic.	.50	1.00
□□	77 Phil Myre (G), Atla.	.75	1.50
□□	78 Buster Harvey, Minn.	.50	1.00
□□	79 Jack Egers, SLou.	.50	1.00
□□	80 Terry Harper, LosA.	.50	1.00
□□	**81 Bill Barber, Phil. RC**	**7.50**	**15.00**
□□	82 Roy Edwards (G), Detr.	.75	1.50
□□	83 Brian Spencer, NYI	.50	1.00
□□	84 Reggie Leach, Cali.	.50	1.00
□□	85 Dave Keon, Toro.	1.50	3.00
□□	86 Jim Schoenfeld, Buff.	1.50	2.75
□□	87 Henri Richard, Mont.	1.50	3.00
□□	88 Rod Gilbert, NYRa.	1.00	1.75
□□	89 Don Marcotte, Bost.	.50	1.00
□□	90 AS: Tony Esposito (G), Chic.	4.50	9.00
□□	91 Joe Watson, Phil.	.50	1.00
□□	92 Atlanta Flames	1.25	2.50
□□	93 Boston Bruins	1.25	2.50
□□	94 Buffalo Sabres	1.25	2.50
□□	95 California Golden Seals	1.25	2.50
□□	96 Chicago Blackhawks	1.25	2.50
□□	97 Detroit Red Wings	1.25	2.50
□□	98 Los Angeles Kings	1.25	2.50
□□	99 Minnesota North Stars	1.25	2.50
□□	100 Montréal Canadiens	1.25	2.50
□□	101 New York Islanders	1.25	2.50
□□	102 New York Rangers	1.25	2.50
□□	103 Philadelphia Flyers	1.25	2.50
□□	104 Pittsburgh Penguins	1.25	2.50
□□	105 St. Louis Blues	1.25	2.50
□□	106 Toronto Maple Leafs	1.25	2.50
□□	107 Vancouver Canucks	1.25	2.50
□□	108 Roger Crozier (G), Buff.	1.00	1.75
□□	109 Tom Reid, Minn.	.50	1.00
□□	**110 Hilliard Graves, Cali. RC**	**1.00**	**2.00**
□□	111 Don Lever, Vanc.	.50	1.00
□□	112 Jim Pappin, Chic.	.50	1.00
□□	113 Ron Schock, Pitt.	.50	1.00
□□	114 Gerry Desjardins (G), NYIs.	.75	1.50
□□	115 Yvan Cournoyer, Mont.	1.25	2.50
□□	116 Checklist (1 - 198)	14.00	28.00
□□	117 Bobby Leiter, Atla.	.50	1.00
□□	118 Ab DeMarco, SLou.	.50	1.00
□□	119 Doug Favell (G), Toro.	.75	1.50
□□	120 AS: Phil Esposito, Bost.	4.50	8.50
□□	121 Mike Robitaille, Buff.	.50	1.00
□□	122 Réal Lemieux, LosA.	.50	1.00
□□	123 Jim Neilson, NYRa.	.50	1.00
□□	124 Tim Ecclestone, Detr.	.50	1.00
□□	125 Jude Drouin, Minn.	.50	1.00
□□	126 Gary Smith (G), Vanc.	.75	1.50
□□	127 Walt McKechnie, Cali.	.50	1.00
□□	128 Lowell MacDonald, Pitt.	.50	1.00
□□	129 Dale Tallon, Chic.	.50	1.00
□□	**130 Billy Harris, NYIs. RC**	**1.00**	**2.00**
□□	131 Randy Manery, Atla.	.50	1.00
□□	132 Darryl Sittler, Toro.	4.00	7.50
□□	133 Ken Hodge, Bost.	.50	1.00
□□	134 Bob Plager, SLou.	.50	1.00
□□	135 Rick MacLeish, Phil.	1.50	3.00
□□	136 Dennis Hextall, Minn.	.50	1.00
□□	137 Jacques Laperrière, Mont.	1.00	1.75
□□	138 Butch Goring, LosA.	.75	1.50
□□	139 René Robert, Buff.	.50	1.00
□□	140 Ed Giacomin (G), NYRa.	1.75	3.25
□□	141 Alex Delvecchio, Detr.	1.25	2.25
□□	142 Jocelyn Guevremont, Vanc.	.50	1.00
□□	143 Joey Johnston, Cali.	.50	1.00
□□	144 Bryan Watson, Pitt.	.50	1.00
□□	145 Stan Mikita, Chic.	3.50	7.00
□□	146 Césare Maniago (G), Minn.	.75	1.50
□□	147 Craig Cameron, NYIs.	.50	1.00
□□	148 Norm Ullman,Toro.	1.00	1.75
□□	**149 Dave Schultz, Phil. RC**	**6.00**	**12.00**
□□	150 AS: Bobby Orr, Bost.	18.00	35.00
□□	151 Phil Roberto, SLou.	.50	1.00
□□	**152 Curt Bennett, Atla. RC**	**1.00**	**2.00**
□□	153 Gilles Villemure (G), NYRa.	.75	1.50
□□	**154 Chuck Lefley, Mont. RC**	**1.00**	**2.00**
□□	155 Rick Martin, Buff.	1.00	2.00
□□	156 Juha Widing, LosA.	.50	1.00
□□	157 Orland Kurtenbach, Vanc.	.50	1.00
□□	158 Bill Collins, Detr.	.50	1.00
□□	**159 Bob Stewart, Cali. RC**	**1.00**	**2.00**
□□	160 Syl Apps, Pitt.	.50	1.00
□□	161 Danny Grant, Minn.	.50	1.00
□□	**162 Billy Smith (G), NYIs. RC**	**15.00**	**30.00**
□□	163 Brian Glennie, Toro.	.50	1.00
□□	164 Pit Martin, Chic.	.50	1.00
□□	165 Brad Park, NYRa.	2.50	5.00
□□	166 Wayne Cashman, Bost.	.75	1.50
□□	167 Gary Dornhoefer, Phil.	.50	1.00
□□	**168 Steve Durbano, Cali. RC**	**2.00**	**4.00**
□□	169 Jacques Richard, Atla.	.50	1.00
□□	170 AS: Guy Lapointe, Mont.	1.50	3.00
□□	171 Jim Lorentz, Buff.	.50	1.00
□□	172 Bob Berry, LosA.	.50	1.00
□□	173 Dennis Kearns, Vanc.	.50	1.00
□□	174 Red Berenson, Detr.	.50	1.00
□□	175 Gilles Meloche (G), Cali.	.75	1.50
□□	176 Al McDonough, Pitt.	.50	1.00
□□	**177 Dennis O'Brien, Minn. RC**	**1.00**	**2.00**
□□	178 Germaine Gagnon, NYIs.	.50	1.00
□□	179 Rick Kehoe, Toro.	.50	1.00
□□	180 AS: Bill White, Chic.	.50	1.00
□□	181 Vic Hadfield, NYRa.	.50	1.00
□□	182 Derek Sanderson, Bost.	1.75	3.50
□□	183 André Dupont, Phil.	.50	1.00
□□	184 Gary Sabourin, SLou.	.50	1.00
□□	**185 Larry Romanchych, Atla. RC**	**1.00**	**2.00**
□□	186 Pete Mahovlich, Mont.	.50	1.00
□□	187 Dave Dryden (G), Buff.	.75	1.50
□□	188 Gilles Marotte, LosA.	.50	1.00
□□	189 Bobby Lalonde, Vanc.	.50	1.00
□□	190 AS: Mickey Redmond, Detr.	.75	1.50
□□	191 Playoffs: Canadiens vs. Sabres	1.00	2.00
□□	192 Playoffs: Flyers vs. North Stars	1.00	2.00
□□	193 Playoffs: Blackhawks vs. Blues	1.00	2.00
□□	194 Playoffs: Rangers vs. Bruins	1.00	2.00
□□	195 Playoffs: Canadiens vs. Flyers	1.00	2.00
□□	196 Playoffs: Blackhawks vs. Rangers	1.00	2.00
□□	197 Playoffs: Canadiens vs. Blackhawks	1.00	2.00
□□	198 Stanley Cup Champions : Canadiens	2.00	4.00

1973 - 74 WILLIAMS (SUOMI)

These stickers measure 1 1/2" x 1 7/8".

Complete Set (324 stickers):

Williams	**EX**	**NM**
□ 1 Vyatsjeslav Anisin, USSR		
□ 2 Alexander Bodunov, USSR		
□ 3 Alexander Gusev, USSR		
□ 4 Valeri Kharlamov, USSR		
□ 5 Alexander Yakushev, USSR		
□ 6 Juri Lebedev, USSR		
□ 7 Yuri Liapkin, USSR		
□ 8 Vladimir Lutchenko, USSR		
□ 9 Alexander Maltsev, USSR		
□ 10 Alexander Martiniuk, USSR		
□ 11 Boris Mikhailov, USSR		
□ 12 Evgeni Paladiev, USSR		
□ 13 Vladimir Petrov, USSR		
□ 14 Alexander Ragulin, USSR		
□ 15 Vladimir Shadrin, USSR		
□ 16 Alexander Sidelnikov, USSR		
□ 17 Vladislav Tretiak (G), USSR		
□ 18 Gennadi Bycankov, USSR		
□ 19 Valeri Vasiliev, USSR		
□ 20 Vladimir Vikulov, USSR		
□ 21 Alexander Volchkov, USSR		
□ 22 Christer Abrahamsson, Swe.		
□ 23 Thommy Abrahamsson, Swe.		
□ 24 Roland Bond, Swe.		
□ 25 Arne Carlsson, Swe.		
□ 26 Inge Hammarstrom, Swe.		
□ 27 Anders Hedberg, Swe.		
□ 28 Bjorn Johansson, Swe.		
□ 29 Stefan Karlsson, Swe.		
□ 30 Curt Larsson, Swe.		
□ 31 Tord Lundstrom, Swe.		
□ 32 William Lofqvist, Swe.		
□ 33 Ulf Nilsson, Swe.		
□ 34 Borje Salming, Swe.		
□ 35 LarsErik Sjoberg, Swe.		
□ 36 Ulf Sterner, Swe.		
□ 37 KarlJohan Sundqvist, Swe.		
□ 38 Dan Soderstrom, Swe.		
□ 39 Hakan Wickberg, Swe.		
□ 40 Kjell-Arne Wicktstrom, Swe.		
□ 41 Dick Yderstrom, Swe.		
□ 42 Mats Ahlberg, Swe.		
□ 43 Peter Adamik, CSR.		
□ 44 Jiri Bubla, CSR.		
□ 45 Jiri Crha, CSR.		
□ 46 Richard Farda, CSR.		
□ 47 Ivan Hlinka, CSR.		
□ 48 Jiri Holecek, CSR.		
□ 49 Jaroslav Holik, CSR.		
□ 50 Jiri Holik, CSR.		
□ 51 Josef Horesovsky, CSR.		
□ 52 Jan Klapac, CSR.		
□ 53 Jiri Kochta, CSR.		
□ 54 Milan Kuzela, CSR.		
□ 55 Oldrich Machac, CSR.		
□ 56 Vladimir Martinec, CSR.		
□ 57 Vaclav Nedomansky, CSR.		
□ 58 Jiri Novak, CSR.		
□ 59 Josef Palecek, CSR.		
□ 60 Frantisek Pospisil, CSR.		
□ 61 Bohuslav Stastny, CSR.		
□ 62 Karel Vohralik, CSR.		
□ 63 Seppo Ahokainen, Fin.		
□ 64 Matti Keinonen, Fin.		
□ 65 Veli-Pekka Ketola, Fin.		
□ 66 Ilpo Koskela, Fin.		
□ 67 Ilpo Kuisma, Fin.		
□ 68 Pekka Kuusisto, Fin.		
□ 69 Henry Leppa, Fin.		
□ 70 Antti Leppanen, Fin.		
□ 71 Seppo Lindstrom, Fin.		
□ 72 Lauri Mononen, Fin.		
□ 73 Timo Nummelin, Fin.		
□ 74 Lalli Partinen, Fin.		
□ 75 Esa Peltonen, Fin.		
□ 76 Pekka Rautakallio, Fin.		
□ 77 Seppo Repo, Fin.		
□ 78 Heikki Riihiranta, Fin.		
□ 79 Timo Sutinen, Fin.		
□ 80 Juhani Tamminen, Fin.		
□ 81 Timo Turunen, Fin.		
□ 82 Jorma Valtonen, Fin.		
□ 83 Jorma Vehmanen, Fin.		
□ 84 Jouko Oystila, Fin.		
□ 85 Josef Batkiewicz, Pol.		
□ 86 Krzysztof Bialynicki, Pol.		
□ 87 Stefan Chowaniec, Pol.		
□ 88 Ludwik Czachovski, Pol.		
□ 89 Andrzej Czczepaniec, Pol.		
□ 90 Stanislav Fryzlewicz, Pol.		
□ 91 Robert Goralczyk, Pol.		
□ 92 Mieczyslaw Jaskiersk, Pol.		
□ 93 Tadeusz Kacik, Pol.		
□ 94 Adam Kopczynski, Pol.		
□ 95 Valery Kosyl, Pol.		
□ 96 Tadeusz Obloj, Pol.		
□ 97 Jerzy Potz, Pol.		
□ 98 Andrzej Slowakiewicz, Pol.		
□ 99 Josef Slowakiewicz, Pol.		
□ 100 Jan Szeja, Pol.		
□ 101 Leszek Tokarz, Pol.		
□ 102 Wieslav Tokarz, Pol.		
□ 103 Henryk Vojtynek, Pol.		
□ 104 Walenty Zietara, Pol.		
□ 105 Pertti Arvaja, Jokerit		
□ 106 Olli J. Hietanen, Jokerit		
□ 107 Olli T. Hietanen, Jokerit		
□ 108 Pentti Hiiros, Jokerit		
□ 109 Eero Holopainen, Jokerit		
□ 110 Kari Kinnunen, Jokerit		
□ 111 Ilpo Koskela, Jokerit		
□ 112 Timo Kyntola, Jokerit		
□ 113 Henry Leppa, Jokerit		
□ 114 Jan Lindberg, Jokerit		
□ 115 Lauri Mononen, Jokerit		
□ 116 Mika Rajala, Jokerit		
□ 117 Pertti Nurmi, Jokerit		
□ 118 Jyrki Seivo, Jokerit		
□ 119 Jorma Siitarinen, Jokerit		
□ 120 Seppo Suoraniemi, Jokerit		
□ 121 Timo Sutinen, Jokerit		
□ 122 Timo Turunen, Jokerit		
□ 123 Jorma Valtonen, Jokerit		
□ 124 Seppo Vartiainen, Jokerit		
□ 125 Jouko Oystila, Jokerit		
□ 126 Juhani Bostrom, HIFK		
□ 127 Matti Hagman, HIFK		
□ 128 Kimmo Heino, HIFK		
□ 129 Jorma Immonen, HIFK		
□ 130 Pentti Karlsson, HIFK		
□ 131 Mauri Kaukokari, HIFK		
□ 132 Jarmo Koivunen, HIFK		
□ 133 Vaino Kolkka, HIFK		
□ 134 Harri Linnonmaa, HIFK		
□ 135 Jaakko Marttinen, HIFK		
□ 136 Matti Murto, HIFK		
□ 137 Lalli Partinen, HIFK		
□ 138 Esa Peltonen, HIFK		
□ 139 Juha Rantasila, HIFK		
□ 140 Heikki Riihiranta, HIFK		
□ 141 Jorma Rikala, HIFK		
□ 142 Tommi Salmelainen, HIFK		
□ 143 Henry Saleva, HIFK		
□ 144 Juhani Tamminen, HIFK		
□ 145 Jorma Thusberg, HIFK		
□ 146 Jorma Virtanen, HIFK		
□ 147 Matti Vaisanen, HIFK		
□ 148 Stig Wetzell, HIFK		
□ 149 Jukka Alkula, Tappara		
□ 150 Pertti Ansakorpi, Tappara		
□ 151 Hannu Haapalainen, Tappara		
□ 152 Martti Jarkko, Tappara		
□ 153 Keijo Jarvinen, Tappara		
□ 154 Pertti Koivulahti, Tappara		
□ 155 Ilpo Kuisma, Tappara		
□ 156 Antero Lehtonen, Tappara		
□ 157 Antti Leppanen, Tappara		
□ 158 Lasse Litma, Tappara		
□ 159 Pekka Marjamaki, Tappara		
□ 160 Mikko Mynttinen, Tappara		
□ 161 Pekka Makinen, Tappara		
□ 162 Seppo I. Makinen, Tappara		
□ 163 Seppo S. Makinen, Tappara		
□ 164 Keijo Mannisto, Tappara		
□ 165 Antti Perttula, Tappara		
□ 166 Tuomo Rautiainen, Tappara		
□ 167 Jorma Saarikorpi, Tappara		
□ 168 Juha Silvennoinen, Tappara		
□ 169 Jorma Siren, Tappara		
□ 170 Raimo Suoniemi, Tappara		
□ 171 Pertti Valkeapaa, Tappara		
□ 172 Sakari Ahlberg, Ilves		
□ 173 Seppo Ahokainen, Ilves		
□ 174 Jorma Aro, Ilves		
□ 175 Esko Eriksson, Ilves		
□ 176 Markku Hakanen, Ilves		
□ 177 Reijo Hakanen, Ilves		
□ 178 Martti Helle, Ilves		
□ 179 Erkki Jarvinen, Ilves		
□ 180 Jorma Kallio, Ilves		
□ 181 Erkki Kesalainen, Ilves		
□ 182 Pekka Kuusisto, Ilves		
□ 183 Pekka Leimu, Ilves		
□ 184 Jukka Mattila, Ilves		
□ 185 Esko Makinen, Ilves		
□ 186 Lasse Oksanen, Ilves		
□ 187 Kari Palooja, Ilves		
□ 188 Jorma Peltonen, Ilves		
□ 189 Pekka Rampa, Ilves		
□ 190 Heikki Salminen, Ilves		
□ 191 Tuomo Sillman, Ilves		
□ 192 Veikko Suominen, Ilves		
□ 193 Tapio Virhimo, Ilves		
□ 194 Juhani Aaltonen, HJK		
□ 195 Bjorn Herbert, HJK		
□ 196 Hannu Kapanen, HJK		
□ 197 Matti Keinonen, HJK		
□ 198 Lasse Kiili, HJK		
□ 199 Matti Koskinen, HJK		
□ 200 Martti Kuokkanen, HJK		
□ 201 Urpo Kuukauppi, HJK		
□ 202 Seppo Laakkio, HJK		
□ 203 Timo Lahtinen, HJK		
□ 204 Juhani Laine, HJK		
□ 205 Heikki Leppik, HJK		
□ 206 Osmo Lotjonen, HJK		
□ 207 Kyosti Majava, HJK		
□ 208 Keijo Puhakka, HJK		
□ 209 Antti Ravi, HJK		
□ 210 Seppo Repo, HJK		
□ 211 Timo Saari, HJK		
□ 212 Arto Siissala, HJK		
□ 213 Jorma Vehmanen, HJK		
□ 214 Pentti Viitanen, HJK		
□ 215 Leo Aikas, HJK		
□ 216 Raine Heinonen, Koovee		

☐ 217 Vladimir Jursinov, Koovee
☐ 218 JukkaPekka Jarvenpaa, Koovee
☐ 219 Pertti Jarvenpaa, Koovee
☐ 220 Heimo Keinonen, Koovee
☐ 221 Seppo Kettunen, Koovee
☐ 222 Veikko Kirveskoski, Koovee
☐ 223 Reijo Laksola, Koovee
☐ 224 Raimo Majapuro, Koovee
☐ 225 Markku Moisio, Koovee
☐ 226 Heikki Nurmi, Koovee
☐ 227 Seppo Nurmi, Koovee
☐ 228 Oiva Oijennus, Koovee
☐ 229 Esko Rantanen, Koovee
☐ 230 Matti Rautiainen, Koovee
☐ 231 Juhani Ruohonen, Koovee
☐ 232 Mikko Raikkonen, Koovee
☐ 233 Lauri Salomaa, Koovee
☐ 234 Veikko Savolainen, Koovee
☐ 235 Leo Seppanen, Koovee
☐ 236 Veikko Seppanen, Koovee
☐ 237 Pekka Uitus, Koovee
☐ 238 Kari Viitalahti, Koovee
☐ 239 Jorma Vilen, Koovee
☐ 240 Asko Ahonen, Assat Pori
☐ 241 Tapio Flinck, Assat Pori
☐ 242 Matti Hakanen, Assat Pori
☐ 243 Antti Heikkila, Assat Pori
☐ 244 Reijo Heinonen, Assat Pori
☐ 245 Jaakko Honkanen, Assat Pori
☐ 246 Jari Kaski, Assat Pori
☐ 247 VeliPekka Ketola, Assat Pori
☐ 248 Raimo Kilpio, Assat Pori
☐ 249 Tapio Koskinen, Assat Pori
☐ 250 Jarkko Levonen, Assat Pori
☐ 251 Kaj Matalamaki, Assat Pori
☐ 252 Pertti Makela, Assat Pori
☐ 253 Jaakko Niemi, Assat Pori
☐ 254 Hannu Pulkkinen, Assat Pori
☐ 255 Pekka Rautakallio, Assat Pori
☐ 256 Markku Riihimaki, Assat Pori
☐ 257 Anto Virtanen, Assat Pori
☐ 258 Erkki Vakiparta, Assat Pori
☐ 259 Pertti Hasanen, Turun Toverit
☐ 260 Rainer Holmroos, Turun Toverit
☐ 261 Kari Johansson, Turun Toverit
☐ 262 Arto Kaunonen, Turun Toverit
☐ 263 Timo Kokkonen, Turun Toverit
☐ 264 Reijo Leppanen, Turun Toverit
☐ 265 Seppo Lindstrom, Turun Toverit
☐ 266 Hannu Luojola, Turun Toverit
☐ 267 Hannu Niittoaho, Turun Toverit
☐ 268 Reijo Paksal, Turun Toverit
☐ 269 Seppo Parikka, Turun Toverit
☐ 270 Jarmo Rantanen, Turun Toverit
☐ 271 Kari Hyokki, Turun Toverit
☐ 272 Kari Salonen, Turun Toverit
☐ 273 Tapani Sura, Turun Toverit
☐ 274 Kari Torkkel, Turun Toverit
☐ 275 Risto Vainio, Turun Toverit
☐ 276 Pentti Vihanto, Turun Toverit
☐ 277 Urpo Ylonen, Turun Toverit
☐ 278 Lars Ellfolk, Turun Palloseura
☐ 279 Kari Horkko, Turun Palloseura
☐ 280 Hannu Jortikka, Turun Palloseura
☐ 281 Eero Juntunen, Turun Palloseura
☐ 282 Lauri Jamsen, Turun Palloseura
☐ 283 Jari Kapanen, Turun Palloseura
☐ 284 Kari Kauppila, Turun Palloseura
☐ 285 Matti Kauppila, Turun Palloseura
☐ 286 Jukka Koskilahti, Turun Palloseura
☐ 287 Jukka Koivu, Turun Palloseura
☐ 288 Ilkka Laaksonen, Turun Palloseura
☐ 289 Robert Lamoureux, Turun Palloseura
☐ 290 Hannu Lunden, Turun Palloseura
☐ 291 Ilkka Mesikammen, Turun Palloseura
☐ 292 Timo Nummelin, Turun Palloseura
☐ 293 Timo Nurminen, Turun Palloseura
☐ 294 Rauli Ottila, Turun Palloseura
☐ 295 Matti Rautee, Turun Palloseura
☐ 296 Pekka Rautee, Turun Palloseura
☐ 297 Jari Rosberg, Turun Palloseura
☐ 298 Tarmo Saarni, Turun Palloseura
☐ 299 Asko Salminen, Turun Palloseura
☐ 300 Jouni Samuli, Turun Palloseura
☐ 301 Rauli Tammelin, Turun Palloseura
☐ 302 Veijo Wahlsten, Turun Palloseura
☐ 303 Bengt Wilenius, Turun Palloseura
☐ 304 Denis Bavaudin, Rauman Lukko
☐ 305 Mikko Erholm, Rauman Lukko
☐ 306 Matti Forss, Rauman Lukko
☐ 307 Esa Hakkarainen, Rauman Lukko
☐ 308 Veikko Ihalainen, Rauman Lukko
☐ 309 Esa Isaksson, Rauman Lukko
☐ 310 Juhani Jylha, Rauman Lukko
☐ 311 Heikki Kauhanen, Rauman Lukko
☐ 312 Jari Laiho, Rauman Lukko
☐ 313 Arto Laine, Rauman Lukko
☐ 314 Jouni Peltonen, Rauman Lukko
☐ 315 Jouni Rinne, Rauman Lukko
☐ 316 Kai Rosvall, Rauman Lukko
☐ 317 Seppo Santala, Rauman Lukko
☐ 318 Jari Sarronlahti, Rauman Lukko
☐ 319 Matti Saurio, Rauman Lukko
☐ 320 Ari Sjoman, Rauman Lukko
☐ 321 Erkki Sundelin, Rauman Lukko
☐ 322 Ismo Villa, Rauman Lukko
☐ 323 Mikko Ylaja, Rauman Lukko
☐ 324 Veijo Ylonen, Rauman Lukko

1974 HELLAS MM - JENKKI

These cards measure 2 1/8" x 3 1/8".
Complete Set (120 cards):

Hellas EX NM

☐ 1 Sakari Ahlberg, Fin.
☐ 2 Seppo Ahokainen, Fin.
☐ 3 Jukka Alkula, Fin.
☐ 4 Jorma Aro, Fin.
☐ 5 Hannu Haapalainen, Fin.
☐ 6 VeliPekka Ketola, Fin.
☐ 7 Tapio Koskinen, Fin.
☐ 8 Henry Leppa, Fin.
☐ 9 Antti Leppanen, Fin.
☐ 10 Reijo Leppanen, Fin.
☐ 11 Pekka Marjamaki, Fin.
☐ 12 Matti Murto, Fin.
☐ 13 Esa Peltonen, Fin.
☐ 14 Pekka Rautakallio, Fin.
☐ 15 Leo Seppanen, Fin.
☐ 16 Juha Silvennoinen, Fin.
☐ 17 Raimo Suoniemi, Fin.
☐ 18 Seppo Suoraniemi, Fin.
☐ 19 Timo Sutinen, Fin.
☐ 20 Juhani Tamminen, Fin.
☐ 21 Pertti Valkeapaa, Fin.
☐ 22 Christer Abrahamsson, Swe.
☐ 23 Thommie Bergman, Swe.
☐ 24 Roland Bond, Swe.
☐ 25 Anders Hedberg, Swe.
☐ 26 Bjorn Johansson, Swe.
☐ 27 Stefan Karlsson, Swe.
☐ 28 Mats Lind, Swe.
☐ 29 Tord Lundstrom, Swe.
☐ 30 William Lofqvist, Swe.
☐ 31 Ulf Nilsson, Swe.
☐ 32 Bjorn Palmqvist, Swe.
☐ 33 Hakan Pettersson, Swe.
☐ 34 LarsErik Sjoberg, Swe.
☐ 35 Ulf Sterner, Swe.
☐ 36 KarlJohan Sundqvist, Swe.
☐ 37 Hakan Wickberg, Swe.
☐ 38 KjellArne Wickstrom, Swe.
☐ 39 Dick Yderstrom, Swe.
☐ 40 Mats Ahlberg, Swe.
☐ 41 Stig Ostling, Swe.
☐ 42 Vjatseslav Anisin, USSR
☐ 43 Aleksandr Bodunov, USSR
☐ 44 Aleksandr Gusev, USSR
☐ 45 Valeri Kharlamov, USSR
☐ 46 Alexander Yakushev, USSR
☐ 47 Yuri Liapkin, USSR
☐ 48 Vladimir Lutshenko, USSR
☐ 49 Alexander Maltsev, USSR
☐ 50 Alexander Martiniuk, USSR
☐ 51 Boris Mikhailov, USSR
☐ 52 Evgeny Paladiev, USSR
☐ 53 Vladimir Petrov, USSR
☐ 54 Alexander Ragulin, USSR
☐ 55 Vladimir Shadrin, USSR
☐ 56 Alexander Sidelnikov, USSR
☐ 57 Vladimir Tretiak, USSR
☐ 58 Gennadi Tsicankov, USSR
☐ 59 Valeri Vasiliev, USSR
☐ 60 Vladimir Vikulov, USSR
☐ 61 Alexander Voltshkov, USSR
☐ 62 Julij Blinov, USSR
☐ 63 Vladimir Sepovalov, USSR
☐ 64 Josef Horesovsky, CSR.
☐ 65 Peter Adamik, CSR.
☐ 66 Vladimir Bednar, CSR.
☐ 67 Jiri Bubla, CSR.
☐ 68 Richard Farda, CSR.
☐ 69 Julius Haas, CSR.
☐ 70 Ivan Hlinka, CSR.
☐ 71 Jiri Holecek, CSR.
☐ 72 Jaroslav Holik, CSR.
☐ 73 Jiri Holik, CSR.
☐ 74 Jan Klapac, CSR.
☐ 75 Jiri Kochta, CSR.
☐ 76 Milan Kuzela, CSR.
☐ 77 Oldrich Machac, CSR.
☐ 78 Vladimir Martinec, CSR.
☐ 79 Vaclav Nedomansky, CSR.
☐ 80 Josef Palecek, CSR.
☐ 81 Frantisek Pospisil, CSR.
☐ 82 Bohuslav Stastny, CSR.
☐ 83 Rudolf Tajcnar, CSR.
☐ 84 Karel Vohralik, CSR.
☐ 85 Jerzy Potz, Pol.
☐ 86 Andrzej Slowakiewicz, Pol.
☐ 87 Josef Slowakiewicz, Pol.
☐ 88 Leszek Tokarz, Pol.
☐ 89 Wieslav Tokarz, Pol.
☐ 90 Henryk Vojtynek, Pol.
☐ 91 Walenty Zietara, Pol.
☐ 92 Josef Batkiewicz, Pol.
☐ 93 Stefan Chowaniec, Pol.
☐ 94 Ludvik Czachovski, Pol.
☐ 95 Andrzej Czczepaniec, Pol.
☐ 96 Robert Goralczyk, Pol.
☐ 97 Mieczyslaw Jaskierski, Pol.
☐ 98 Tadeusz Kacik, Pol.
☐ 99 Adam Kopczynski, Pol.
☐ 100 Valery Kosyl, Pol.
☐ 101 Tadeusz Obloj, Pol.
☐ 102 Joachim Stasche, DDR.
☐ 103 Roland Peters, DDR.
☐ 104 Dietmar Peters, DDR.
☐ 105 Bernd Karrenbauer, DDR.
☐ 106 Peter Prusa, DDR.
☐ 107 Rainer Patschinski, DDR.
☐ 108 Hartmut Nickel, DDR.
☐ 109 Dieter Dewitz, DDR.
☐ 110 Harald Felber, DDR.
☐ 111 Joachim Hurbanek, DDR.
☐ 112 Wolfgang Fischer, DDR.
☐ 113 Frank Braun, DDR.
☐ 114 Dieter Huscfo, DDR.
☐ 115 Ruediger Hoack, DDR.
☐ 116 Dieter Simon, DDR.
☐ 117 Hartwig Schur, DDR.
☐ 118 Jochen Philip, DDR.
☐ 119 Rolf Bielas, DDR.
☐ 120 Peter Slapke, DDR.

1974 SCOTIA BANK GO CANADA

This postcard measures 3 1/2" x 5 3/4".

Scotia Bank	EX	NM
☐ Go Canada	5.00	10.00

1974 STOP ACTION HOCKEY PLAY

These cards measure 3 1/2" x 5 1/2" and feature a black & white photo.

Stop Action Play	EX	NM
☐ Howie Meeker / Kick Three Times	5.00	10.00
☐ Howie Meeker / Russian Exercise	5.00	10.00
☐ Howie Meeker / Skating Hips Down	5.00	10.00

1974 SEMIC STICKERS

Complete Set (100 stickers):	50.00	100.00

Common Player:	.35	.75
Semic	**EX**	**NM**
☐ 1 Christer Abrahamsson, Swe.	1.00	2.00
☐ 2 William Löfqvist, Swe.	.35	.75
☐ 3 Arne Carlsson, Swe.	.35	.75
☐ 4 Lars-Erik Sjöberg, Swe.	1.25	2.50
☐ 5 Björn Johansson, Swe.	.35	.75
☐ 6 Thommy Abrahamsson, Swe.	1.00	2.00
☐ 7 Karl-Johan Sundqvist, Swe.	.35	.75
☐ 8 Ulf Nilsson, Swe.	3.00	6.00
☐ 9 Håkan Wickberg, Swe.	.35	.75
☐ 10 Dan Söderström, Swe.	.35	.75
☐ 11 Mats Åhlberg, Swe.	.35	.75
☐ 12 Anders Hedberg, Swe.	3.00	6.00
☐ 13 Dick Yderström, Swe.	.35	.75
☐ 14 Stefan Karlssonn, Swe.	.35	.75
☐ 15 Roland Bond, Swe.	.35	.75
☐ 16 Kjell-Rune Milton, Swe.	.35	.75
☐ 17 Willy Lindström, Swe.	2.00	4.00
☐ 18 Mats Waltin, Swe.	.35	.75
☐ 19 Lars-Göran Nilsson, Swe.	.35	.75
☐ 20 Björn Palmqvist, Swe.	.35	.75
☐ 21 Stig-Göran Johansson, Swe.	.35	.75
☐ 22 Bo Berggren, Swe.	.35	.75
☐ 23 Dan Labraaten, Swe.	1.00	2.00
☐ 24 Curt Larsson, Swe.	.35	.75
☐ 25 Mats Lindh, Swe.	.35	.75
☐ 26 Vladislav Tretiak, USSR	9.00	18.00
☐ 27 Alexander Ragulin, USSR	1.25	2.50
☐ 28 Vladimir Lutchenko, USSR	.35	.75
☐ 29 Gennadij Tsycankov, USSR	.35	.75
☐ 30 Alexander Gusev, USSR	.35	.75
☐ 31 Evgeny Poladiev, USSR	.35	.75
☐ 32 Yuri Liapkin, USSR	.35	.75
☐ 33 Boris Mikhailov, USSR	2.50	5.00
☐ 34 Valeri Kharlamov, USSR	4.50	9.00
☐ 35 Vladimir Petrov, USSR	1.75	3.50
☐ 36 Alexander Maltsev, USSR	2.50	5.00
☐ 37 Vladimir Sjadrin, USSR	.35	.75
☐ 38 Alexander Yakushev, USSR	3.50	7.00
☐ 39 Alexander Martiniuk, USSR	.35	.75
☐ 40 Yuri Lebedev, USSR	.35	.75
☐ 41 Alexander Bodunov, USSR	.35	.75
☐ 42 Anatoli Firsov, USSR	1.00	2.00
☐ 43 Vitali Davydov, USSR	.35	.75
☐ 44 Vjateslav Starsjinov, USSR	.35	.75
☐ 45 Viktor Kuzkin, USSR	.35	.75
☐ 46 Igor Romitjevskij, USSR	.35	.75
☐ 47 Evgeny Zimin, USSR	.35	.75
☐ 48 Evgeny Mishakov, USSR	.35	.75
☐ 49 Vladimir Vikulov, USSR	.35	.75
☐ 50 Viktor Konovalenko, USSR	.35	.75
☐ 51 Jiri Holecek, CSR.	1.00	2.00
☐ 52 Frantisek Pospjsil, CSR.	.35	.75
☐ 53 Jiri Bubla, CSR.	1.00	2.00
☐ 54 Josef Horesovs, CSR.	.35	.75
☐ 55 Oldrich Machac, CSR.	.35	.75
☐ 56 Vladimir Martinec, CSR.	.35	.75
☐ 57 Vaclav Nedomansky, CSR.	1.00	2.00
☐ 58 Jiri Kochta, CSR.	.35	.75
☐ 59 Milan Novy, CSR.	1.50	3.00
☐ 60 Jaroslav Holik, CSR.	.35	.75
☐ 61 Jiri Holik, CSR.	.35	.75
☐ 62 Jiri Klapac, CSR.	.35	.75
☐ 63 Richard Farda, CSR.	.35	.75
☐ 64 Bohuslav Stastny, CSR.	.35	.75
☐ 65 Jiri Novak, CSR.	.35	.75
☐ 66 Ivan Hlinka, CSR.	1.00	2.00
☐ 67 Jan Suchy, CSR.	.35	.75
☐ 68 Vladimir Bednar, CSR.	.35	.75
☐ 69 Rudolf Tajcnar, CSR.	.35	.75
☐ 70 Josef Cerny, CSR.	.35	.75
☐ 71 Jan Haveln, CSR.	.35	.75
☐ 72 Marcel Sakac, CSR.	.35	.75
☐ 73 Frantisek Pancharek, CSR.	.35	.75
☐ 74 Bedrich Brunchk, CSR.	.35	.75
☐ 75 Edvard Novak, CSR.	.35	.75
☐ 76 Jorma Valtonen, Fin.	.35	.75
☐ 77 Seppo Lindström, Fin.	.35	.75
☐ 78 Pekka Marjamäki, Fin.	.35	.75
☐ 79 Pekka Rautakallio, Fin.	1.00	2.00
☐ 80 Heikki Riihiranta, Fin.	1.00	2.00
☐ 81 Seppo Suoraniemi, Fin.	.35	.75
☐ 82 Jouko Öystilä, Fin.	.35	.75
☐ 83 Veli-Pekka Ketola, Fin.	1.25	2.50
☐ 84 Henry Leppä, Fin.	.35	.75
☐ 85 Harri Linnonmaa, Fin.	.35	.75
☐ 86 Matti Murto, Fin.	.35	.75
☐ 87 Lasse Oksanen, Fin.	.35	.75
☐ 88 Esa Peltonen, Fin.	.35	.75

☐	89 Seppo Repo, Fin.	.35	.75
☐	90 Raimo Suoniemi, Fin.	.35	.75
☐	91 Time Sutinen, Fin.	.35	.75
☐	92 Juhani Tamminen, Fin.	.35	.75
☐	93 Leo Seppanen, Fin.	.35	.75
☐	94 Hannu Haapalainen, Fin.	.35	.75
☐	95 Pertti Valkeapää, Fin.	.35	.75
☐	96 Sakari Ahlberg, Fin.	.35	.75
☐	97 Antti Leppänen, Fin.	.35	.75
☐	98 Kalevi Numminen, Fin.	.35	.75
☐	99 Lauri Mononen, Fin.	.35	.75
☐	100 Ilpo Koskela , Fin.	.35	.75

1974 - 75 LIPTON SOUP

This series was originally issued in two-card panels. The cut cards measure 2 1/4" x 3 3/8".

Complete Set (50 cards): **300.00**

	Lipton Soup	**NM**
☐	1 Norm Ullman, Toro.	12.00
☐	2 Gilbert Perreault, Buff.	12.00
☐	3 Darryl Sittler, Toro.	12.00
☐	4 Jean Paul Parise, Minn.	4.00
☐	5 Garry Unger, SLou.	4.00
☐	6 Ron Ellis, Toro.	4.00
☐	7 Rogatien Vachon (G), LosA.	8.00
☐	8 Bobby Orr, Bost.	55.00
☐	9 Wayne Cashman, Bost.	4.00
☐	10 Brad Park, NYRa.	10.00
☐	11 Serge Savard, Mont.	8.50
☐	12 Walt Tkaczuk, NYRa.	4.00
☐	13 Yvan Cournoyer, Mont.	10.00
☐	14 André Boudrias, Vanc.	4.00
☐	15 Gary Smith (G), Vanc.	5.00
☐	16 Guy Lapointe, Mont.	8.50
☐	17 Dennis Hull, Chic.	4.00
☐	18 Bernie Parent (G), Phil.	12.00
☐	19 Ken Dryden (G), Mont.	35.00
☐	20 Rick MacLeish, Phil.	5.00
☐	21 Bobby Clarke, Phil.	14.00
☐	22 Dale Tallon, Chic.	4.00
☐	23 Jim McKenny, Toro.	4.00
☐	24 René Robert, Buff.	4.00
☐	25 Red Berenson, Detr.	4.00
☐	26 Ed Giacomin (G), NYRa.	12.00
☐	27 Césare Maniago (G), Minn.	5.00
☐	28 Ken Hodge, Bost.	4.00
☐	29 Gregg Sheppard, Bost.	4.00
☐	30 Dave Schultz, Phil.	8.00
☐	31 Bill Barber, Phil.	12.00
☐	32 Henry Boucha, Detr.	4.00
☐	33 Richard Martin, Buff.	6.00
☐	34 Steve Vickers, NYRa.	4.00
☐	35 Billy Harris, NYIs.	4.00
☐	36 Jim Pappin, Chic., Err. (Papin)	4.00
☐	37 Pit Martin, Chic.	4.00
☐	38 Jacques Lemaire, Mont.	10.00
☐	39 Pete Mahovlich, Mont.	4.00
☐	40 Rod Gilbert, NYRa.	10.00
☐	41 Borje Salming, Toro., Horizontal picture	12.00
☐	41 Borje Salming, Toro., Vertical picture	12.00
☐	42 Pete Stemkowski, NYRa.	4.00
☐	43 Ron Schock, Pitt.	4.00
☐	44 Dan Bouchard (G), Atla.	5.00
☐	45 Tony Esposito (G), Chic.	15.00
☐	46 Craig Patrick, Cali.	4.00
☐	47 Ed Westfall, NYIs.	4.00
☐	48 Jocelyn Guevremont, Vanc.	4.00
☐	49 Syl Apps, Pitt.	4.00
☐	50 Dave Keon, Toro.	12.00

1974 - 75 LOBLAWS ACTION PLAYERS

These stickers measure 1 11/16" x 2 1/4".

Complete Set (324 cards): **250.00**

Album: **35.00**

Common Player: **.50**

	Action Players • Atlanta Flames	**NM**
☐	Curt Bennett	.50
☐	Dan Bouchard (G)	1.00
☐	Arnie Brown	.50
☐	Jerry Byers	.50
☐	Rey Comeau	.50
☐	Fred (Buster) Harvey	.50
☐	Bobby Leiter	.50
☐	Jean Lemieux	.50
☐	Tom Lysiak	.50
☐	Randy Manery	.50
☐	Keith McCreary	.50
☐	Bob Murray	.50
☐	Phil Myre (G)	1.00
☐	Noel Price	.50
☐	Pat Quinn	1.00
☐	Jacques Richard	.50
☐	Larry Romanchych	.50
☐	Eric Vail	.50

	Action Players • Boston Bruins	**NM**
☐	Ross Brooks (G)	1.00
☐	John Bucyk	1.75
☐	Wayne Cashman	.50
☐	Darryl Edestrand	.50
☐	Phil Esposito	4.00
☐	Dave Forbes	.50
☐	Gilles Gilbert (G)	1.00
☐	Ken Hodge	.50
☐	Don Marcotte	.50
☐	Walt McKechnie	.50
☐	Terry O'Reilly	.50
☐	Bobby Orr	22.00
☐	André Savard	.50
☐	Bobby Schmautz	.50
☐	Gregg Sheppard	.50
☐	Al Sims	.50
☐	Dallas Smith	.50
☐	Carol Vadnais	.50

	Action Players • Buffalo Sabres	**NM**
☐	Gary Bromley (G)	1.00
☐	Larry Carrière	.50
☐	Roger Crozier (G)	1.00
☐	Rick Dudley	1.00
☐	Lee Fogolin	.50
☐	Norm Gratton	.50
☐	Jerry Korab	.50
☐	Jim Lorentz	.50
☐	Don Luce	.50
☐	Richard Martin	1.00
☐	Gerry Meehan	.50
☐	Larry Mickey	.50
☐	Gilbert Perreault	4.00
☐	Craig Ramsay	.50
☐	René Robert	.50
☐	Mike Robitaille	.50
☐	Jim Schoenfeld	.50
☐	Brian Spencer	.50

	Action Players • California Golden Seals	**NM**
☐	Bruce Affleck	.50
☐	Mike Christie	.50
☐	Len Frig	.50
☐	Stan Gilbertson	.50
☐	Rick Hampton	.50
☐	David Hrechosy	.50
☐	Ron Huston	.50
☐	Joseph Johnston	.50
☐	Wayne King	.50
☐	Al MacAdam	.50
☐	Ted McAneely	.50
☐	Gilles Meloche (G)	1.00
☐	Jim Neilson	.50
☐	Larry Patey	.50
☐	Craig Patrick	1.00
☐	Bob Stewart	.50
☐	Stan Weir	.50
☐	Larry Wright	.50

	Action Players • Chicago Blackhawks	**NM**
☐	Ivan Boldirev	.50
☐	J.P. Bordeleau	.50
☐	Tony Esposito (G)	4.00
☐	Germain Gagnon	.50
☐	Dennis Hull	.50
☐	Doug Jarrett	.50
☐	Cliff Koroll	.50
☐	Keith Magnuson	.50
☐	Chico Maki	.50
☐	John Marks	.50
☐	Pit Martin	.50
☐	Stan Mikita	3.50
☐	Jim Pappin	.50
☐	Dick Redmond	.50
☐	Darcy Rota	.50
☐	Phil Russell	.50
☐	Dale Tallon	.50
☐	Bill White	.50

	Action Players • Detroit Red Wings	**NM**
☐	Red Berenson	.50
☐	Thommie Bergman	.50
☐	Guy Charron	.50
☐	Marcel Dionne	5.00
☐	Danny Grant	.50
☐	Doug Grant (G)	1.00
☐	Jean Hamel	.50
☐	Bill Hogaboam	.50
☐	Pierre Jarry	.50
☐	Nick Libett	.50
☐	Bill Lochead	.50
☐	Jack Lynch	.50
☐	Hank Nowak	.50
☐	Nelson Pyatt	.50
☐	Mickey Redmond	1.00
☐	Doug Roberts	.50
☐	Jim Rutherford (G)	1.00
☐	Bryan Watson	.50

	Action Players • Kansas City Scouts	**NM**
☐	Robin Burns	.50
☐	Gary Coalter	.50
☐	Gary Croteau	.50
☐	Chris Evans	.50
☐	Ed Gilbert	.50
☐	Doug Horbul	.50
☐	Dave Hudson	.50
☐	Brent Hughes	.50
☐	Bryan Lefley	.50
☐	Richard Lemieux	.50
☐	Pete McDuffe (G)	1.00
☐	Simon Nolet	.50
☐	Dennis Patterson	.50
☐	Michel Plasse (G)	1.00
☐	Lynn Powis	.50
☐	Randy Rota	.50
☐	Ted Snell	.50
☐	John Wright	.50

	Action Players • Los Angeles Kings	**NM**
☐	Bob Berry	.50
☐	Gene Carr	.50
☐	Mike Corrigan	.50
☐	Gary Edwards (G)	1.00
☐	Butch Goring	.50
☐	Terry Harper	.50
☐	Dave Hutchison	.50
☐	Sheldon Kannegiesser	.50
☐	Neil Komadoski	.50
☐	Don Kozak	.50
☐	Dan Maloney	.50
☐	Bob Murdoch	.50
☐	Mike Murphy	1.00
☐	Bob Nevin	.50
☐	Frank St. Marseille	.50
☐	Rogatien Vachon (G)	2.00
☐	Juha Widing	.50
☐	Tom Williams	.50

	Action Players • Minnesota North Stars	**NM**
☐	Chris Ahrens	.50
☐	Fred Barrett	.50
☐	Gary Bergman	.50
☐	Henry Boucha	.50
☐	Jude Drouin	.50
☐	Blake Dunlop	.50
☐	Barry Gibbs	.50
☐	Bill Goldsworthy	.50
☐	Dennis Hextall	.50
☐	Césare Maniago (G)	1.00
☐	Don Martineau	.50
☐	Lou Nanne	.50
☐	Dennis O'Brien	.50
☐	Murray Oliver	.50
☐	Jean Paul Parise	.50
☐	Tom Reid	.50
☐	Fern Rivard (G)	1.00
☐	Fred Stanfield	.50

	Action Players • Montréal Canadiens	**NM**
☐	Pierre Bouchard	.50
☐	Yvan Cournoyer	3.00
☐	Ken Dryden (G)	10.00
☐	Guy Lafleur	10.00
☐	Yvon Lambert	.50
☐	Jacques Laperrière	1.50
☐	Guy Lapointe	1.50
☐	Michel Larocque (G)	1.00
☐	Claude Larose	.50
☐	Chuck Lefley	.50
☐	Jacques Lemaire	2.00
☐	Pete Mahovlich	.50
☐	Henri Richard	3.00
☐	Jim Roberts	.50
☐	Larry Robinson	4.00
☐	Serge Savard	1.50
☐	Steve Shutt	3.00
☐	Murray Wilson	.50

	Action Players • New York Islanders	**NM**
☐	Craig Cameron	.50
☐	Clark Gillies	1.50
☐	Billy Harris	.50
☐	Gerry Hart	.50
☐	Lorne Henning	.50
☐	Ernie Hicke	.50
☐	Garry Howatt	.50
☐	Dave Lewis	.50
☐	Billy MacMillan	.50
☐	Bert Marshall	.50
☐	Bob Nystrom	.50
☐	Denis Potvin	9.00
☐	Jean Potvin	.50
☐	Glenn Resch (G)	2.50
☐	Doug Rombough	.50
☐	Billy Smith (G)	4.00
☐	Ralph Stewart	.50
☐	Ed Westfall	.50

	Action Players • New York Rangers	**NM**
☐	Jerry Butler	.50
☐	Bill Fairbairn	.50
☐	Ed Giacomin (G)	2.50
☐	Rod Gilbert	2.50
☐	Ron Harris	.50
☐	Ted Irvine	.50
☐	Gilles Marotte	.50
☐	Brad Park	2.75
☐	Greg Polis	.50
☐	Jean Ratelle	2.50
☐	Dale Rolfe	.50
☐	Bobby Rousseau	.50
☐	Derek Sanderson	2.50
☐	Rod Seiling	.50
☐	Pete Stemkowski	.50
☐	Walt Tkaczuk	.50
☐	Steve Vickers	.50
☐	Gilles Villemure (G)	1.00

	Action Players • Philadelphia Flyers	**NM**
☐	Bill Barber	2.25
☐	Tom Bladon	.50
☐	Bobby Clarke	7.00
☐	Bill Clement	.50
☐	Terry Crisp	.50
☐	Gary Dornhoefer	.50
☐	André Dupont	.50
☐	Bob Kelly	.50
☐	Orest Kindrachuk	.50
☐	Reggie Leach	.50
☐	Ross Lonsberry	.50
☐	Rick MacLeish	1.00
☐	Bernie Parent (G)	4.00
☐	Don Saleski	.50
☐	Dave Schultz	1.00
☐	Ed Van Impe	.50
☐	Jimmy Watson	.50
☐	Joe Watson	.50

	Action Players • Pittsburgh Penguins	**NM**
☐	Syl Apps	.50
☐	Chuck Arnason	.50
☐	Wayne Bianchin	.50
☐	Dave Burrows	.50
☐	Nelson Debenedet	.50
☐	Ab DeMarco	.50
☐	Steve Durbano	1.00
☐	Vic Hadfield	.50
☐	Denis Herron	1.00
☐	Bob Johnson (G)	1.00
☐	Rick Kehoe	.50
☐	Bob Kelly	.50
☐	Bobby Lalonde	.50
☐	Lowell MacDonald	.50
☐	Bob Paradise	.50
☐	Jean Pronovost	.50
☐	Ron Schock	.50
☐	Ron Stackhouse	.50

	Action Players • St. Louis Blues	**NM**
☐	Don Awrey	.50
☐	Ace Bailey	.50
☐	Bill Collins	.50
☐	John Davidson (G)	2.50
☐	Dave Gardner	.50
☐	Bob Gassoff	.50
☐	Larry Giroux	.50
☐	Eddie Johnston (G)	1.00
☐	Wayne Merrick	.50
☐	Brian Ogilvie	.50
☐	Barclay Plager	.50
☐	Bob Plager	.50
☐	Pierre Plante	.50
☐	Phil Roberto	.50
☐	Larry Sacharuk	.50
☐	Floyd Thomson	.50
☐	Garry Unger	.50
☐	Rick Wilson	.50

	Action Players • Toronto Maple Leafs	**NM**
☐	Willie Brossart	.50
☐	Tim Ecclestone	.50
☐	Ron Ellis	.50
☐	Doug Favell (G)	1.00
☐	Bill Flett	.50
☐	Brian Glennie	.50
☐	Inge Hammarstrom	.50
☐	Dave Keon	2.00
☐	Lanny McDonald	5.00
☐	Jim McKenny	.50
☐	Bob Neely	.50
☐	Gary Sabourin	.50
☐	Borje Salming	3.00

Darryl Sittler	4.00
Errol Thompson	.50
Ian Turnbull	.50
Norm Ullman	1.75
Dunc Wilson (G)	1.00
Action Players • Vancouver Canucks	**NM**
Gregg Boddy	.50
Paulin Bordeleau	.50
André Boudrias	.50
Bob Dailey	.50
Dave Dunn	.50
John Gould	.50
Jocelyn Guevremont	.50
Dennis Kearns	.50
Don Lever	.50
Ken Lockett (G)	1.00
Bryan McSheffrey	.50
Chris Oddleifson	.50
Gerry O'Flaherty	.50
Tracy Pratt	.50
Gary Smith (G)	1.00
Dennis Ververgaert	.50
Jim Wiley	.50
Barry Wilkins	.50
Action Players • Washington Capitals	**NM**
Ron H. Anderson	.50
Steve Atkinson	.50
Mike Bloom	.50
Gord Brooks	.50
Bob Collyard	.50
Jack Egers	.50
Lawrence Fullan	.50
Bob Gryp	.50
Jim Hrycuik	.50
Greg Joly	.50
Dave Kryskow	.50
Peter Laframboise	.50
Ron Low (G)	1.00
Joe Lundrigan	.50
Mike Marson	.50
Bill Mikkelson	.50
Doug Mohns	.50
Lew Morrison	.50

LOBLAWS UPDATE

Update Set (45 stickers):	**65.00**
Action Players	**NM**
Barry Gibbs, Atla.	1.50
Hank Nowak, Buff.	1.50
Jocelyn Guevremont, Buff.	1.50
Fred Stanfield, Buff.	1.50
Bryan McSheffrey, Buff.	1.50
Dave Gardner, Cali.	1.50
Morris Mott, Cali.	1.50
Gary Simmons, Cali.	3.00
Dave Kryskow, Detr.	1.50
Ted Snell, Detr.	1.50
Gary Bergman, Detr.	1.50
Phil Roberto, Detr.	1.50
Walt McKechnie, Detr.	1.50
Guy Charron, Kans.	1.50
Denis Herron, Kans.	3.00
J.G. Lagace, Kans.	1.50
Doug Rombough, Minn.	1.50
Ernie Hicke, Minn.	1.50
Craig Cameron, Minn.	1.50
John Flesch, Minn.	1.50
Norm Gratton, Minn.	1.50
Don Awrey, Mont.	1.50
Wayne Thomas, Mont.	3.00
J.P. Parise, NYIs.	1.50
Jude Drouin, NYIs.	1.50
Dave Fortier, NYIs.	1.50
Rick Middleton, NYRa.	10.00
Barry Wilkins, Pitt.	1.50
Lew Morrison, Pitt.	1.50
Michel Plasse, Pitt.	3.00
Craig Patrick, SLou.	3.00
Chris Evans, SLou.	1.50
Chuck Lefley, SLou.	1.50
Claude Larose, SLou.	1.50
Red Berenson, SLou.	1.50
Dave Dunn, Toro.	1.50
Rod Seiling, Toro.	1.50
George Ferguson, Toro.	1.50
Gerry Meehan, Vanc.	1.50
Mike Robitaille, Vanc.	1.50
Ab DeMarco, Vanc.	1.50
Garry Monahan, Vanc.	1.50
Jack Lynch, Wash.	1.50
Ron Lalonde, Wash.	1.50
Willie Brossart, Wash.	1.50

1974 - 75 NABISCO SUGAR DADDY

These cards measure 1 1/16" x 2 3/4". This 25 sticker set features players from four different sports. Other hockey singles exist. A 10 x 15 wall poster was also available.

Nabisco	**NM**
11 Phil Esposito	15.00
13 Brad Park	10.00
14 Tom Lysiak	5.00
15 Bernie Parent (G)	15.00
16 Mickey Redmond	7.50
22 Don Awrey	5.00

1974 - 75 O-PEE-CHEE

"There are no super rookies like Guy Lafleur or Ken Dryden, but there are a ton of rookie cards in the set. There are also the coach cards of Scotty Bowman, Don Cherry, Fred Shero, and others. There is good colour on the images, so overall, it is a nice looking set. The cardstock also seems to survive better than the other sets from the 1970s." – Brian Vanclief, Great Canadian Card Company, Sudbury, Ontario.

These cards measure the standard 2 1/2" x 3 1/2".

Complete Set (396 cards):	**600.00**
Common Player:	**1.50**
O-Pee-Chee	**NM-MT**
1 LL: P. Esposito/ B. Goldsworthy	7.50
2 LL: B. Orr/ D. Hextall	10.00
3 LL: P. Esposito/ B. Clarke	7.50
4 LL: D. Favel (G)/ B. Parent (G)	3.00
5 LL: B. Watson/ D. Schultz	2.50
6 LL: M. Redmond/ R. MacLeish	2.50
7 Gary Bromley (G), Buff. RC	**3.00**
8 Bill Barber, Phil.	10.00
9 Emile Francis, Coach, NYRa.	2.50
10 Gilles Gilbert (G), Bost.	2.50
11 John Davidson (G), SLou. RC	**20.00**
12 Ron Ellis, Toro.	1.50
13 Syl Apps, Pitt.	1.50
14 TL: J. Richard/ T. Lysiak/ K. McCreary	2.50
15 Dan Bouchard (G), Atla.	3.00
16 Ivan Boldirev, Chic.	1.50
17 Gary Coalter, Kans. RC	**2.50**
18 Bob Berry, LosA.	1.50
19 Red Berenson, Detr.	1.50
20 Stan Mikita, Chic.	9.00
21 Fred Shero, Coach, Phil. RC	**10.00**
22 Gary Smith (G), Vanc.	2.50
23 Bill Mikkelson, Wash.	1.50
24 Jacques Lemaire, Mont., Err. (Buff.)	4.00
25 Gilbert Perreault, Buff.	10.00
26 Césare Maniago (G), Minn.	2.50
27 Bobby Schmautz, Bost.	1.50
28 TL: P. Esposito/ B. Orr/ J. Bucyk	15.00
29 Steve Vickers, NYRa.	1.50
30 Lowell MacDonald, Pitt.	1.50
31 Fred Stanfield, Minn.	1.50
32 Ed Westfall, NYIs.	1.50
33 Curt Bennett, Atla.	1.50
34 Bep Guidolin, Coach, Kans.	1.50
35 Cliff Koroll, Chic.	1.50
36 Gary Croteau, Kans.	1.50
37 Mike Corrigan, LosA.	1.50
38 Henry Boucha, Detr.	1.50
39 Ron Low (G), Wash.	2.50
40 Darryl Sittler, Toro.	15.00
41 Tracy Pratt, Vanc.	1.50
42 TL: R. Martin/ R. Robert	2.50
43 Larry Carrière, Buff.	1.50
44 Gary Dornhoefer, Phil.	1.50
45 Denis Herron (G), Pitt. RC	**5.00**
46 Doug Favell (G), Toro.	2.50
47 Dave Gardner, SLou. RC	**2.50**
48 Morris Mott, Cali. RC	**2.50**
49 Marc Boileau, Coach, Pitt.	1.50
50 Brad Park, NYRa.	6.00
51 Bobby Leiter, Atla.	1.50
52 Tom Reid, Minn.	1.50
53 Serge Savard, Mont.	3.00
54 Checklist 1	45.00
55 Terry Harper, LosA.	1.50
56 TL: J. Johnston/ W. McKechnie	2.50
57 Guy Charron, Detr.	1.50
58 Pit Martin, Chic.	1.50
59 Chris Evans, Kans.	1.50
60 Bernie Parent (G), Phil.	7.00
61 Jim Lorentz, Buff.	1.50
62 Dave Kryskow, Wash. RC	**2.50**
63 Lou Angotti, SLou.	1.50
64 Bill Flett, Toro.	1.50
65 Vic Hadfield, Pitt.	1.50
66 Wayne Merrick, SLou. RC	**2.50**
67 André Dupont, Phil.	1.50
68 Tom Lysiak, Atla. RC	**4.00**
69 TL: J. Pappin/ S. Mikita/ J.P. Bordeleau	2.50
70 Guy Lapointe, Mont.	4.00
71 Gerry O'Flaherty, Vanc.	1.50
72 Marcel Dionne, Detr.	15.00
73 Butch Deadmarsh, Kans. RC	**2.50**
74 Butch Goring, LosA.	1.50
75 Keith Magnuson, Chic.	1.50
76 Red Kelly, Coach, Toro.	2.50
77 Pete Stemkowski, NYRa.	1.50
78 Jim Roberts, Mont.	1.50
79 Don Luce, Buff.	1.50
80 Don Awrey, SLou.	1.50
81 Rick Kehoe, Toro.	1.50
82 Billy Smith (G), NYIs.	15.00
83 J.P. Parise, Minn.	1.50
84 TL: M. Redmond/ M. Dionne/ B. Hogaboam	2.50
85 Ed Van Impe, Phil.	1.50
86 Randy Manery, Atla.	1.50
87 Barclay Plager, SLou.	1.50
88 Inge Hammarstrom, Toro. RC	**4.00**
89 Ab DeMarco, Pitt.	1.50
90 Bill White, Chic.	1.50
91 Al Arbour, Coach, NYIs.	2.50
92 Bob Stewart, Cali.	1.50
93 Jack Egers, Wash.	1.50
94 Don Lever, Vanc.	1.50
95 Reggie Leach, Phil.	1.50
96 Dennis O'Brien, Minn.	1.50
97 Pete Mahovlich, Mont.	1.50
98 TL: B. Goring/ F. St. Marseille/ D. Kozak	2.50
99 Gerry Meehan, Buff.	1.50
100 Bobby Orr, Bost.	50.00
101 Jean Potvin, NYIs. RC	**2.50**
102 Rod Seiling, NYRa.	1.50
103 Keith McCreary, Atla.	1.50
104 Phil Maloney, Coach, Vanc.	1.50
105 Denis Dupère, Wash.	1.50
106 Steve Durbano, Pitt.	1.50
107 Bob Plager, SLou., Err. (Barclay Plager)	1.50
108 Chris Oddleifson, Vanc. RC	**2.50**
109 Jim Neilson, Cali.	1.50
110 Jean Pronovost, Pitt.	1.50
111 Don Kozak, LosA. RC	**2.50**
112 TL: B. Goldsworthy/ D. Hextall/ D. Grant	6.00
113 Jim Pappin, Chic.	1.50
114 Richard Lemieux, Kans.	1.50
115 Dennis Hextall, Minn.	1.50
116 Bill Hogaboam, Detr. RC	**2.50**
117 TL: Ververgaert/ Schmautz/ Boudrias/ Tannahill	2.50
118 Jim Anderson, Coach, Wash.	1.50
119 Walt Tkaczuk, NYRa.	1.50
120 Mickey Redmond, Detr.	2.50
121 Jim Schoenfeld, Buff.	1.50
122 Jocelyn Guevremont, Vanc.	1.50
123 Bob Nystrom, NYIs.	2.50
124 TL: Y. Cournoyer/ F. Mahovlich/ C. Larose	3.50
125 Lew Morrison, Wash.	1.50
126 Terry Murray, Cali.	1.50
127 AS: Rick Martin, Buff.	2.50
128 AS: Ken Hodge, Sr., Bost.	1.50
129 AS: Phil Esposito, Bost.	5.00
130 AS: Bobby Orr, Bost.	24.00
131 AS: Brad Park, NYRa.	3.50
132 AS: Gilles Gilbert (G), Bost.	2.50
133 AS: Lowell MacDonald, Pitt.	1.50
134 AS: Bill Goldsworthy, Minn.	1.50
135 AS: Bobby Clarke, Phil.	9.00
136 AS: Bill White, Chic.	1.50
137 AS: Dave Burrows, Pitt.	1.50
138 AS: Bernie Parent (G), Phil.	4.00
139 Jacques Richard, Atla.	1.50
140 Yvan Cournoyer, Mont.	4.25
141 TL: R. Gilbert/ B. Park	3.75
142 René Robert, Buff.	1.50
143 J. Bob Kelly, Pitt. RC	**2.50**
144 Ross Lonsberry, Phil.	1.50
145 Jean Ratelle, NYRa.	3.00
146 Dallas Smith, Bost.	1.50
147 Bernie Geoffrion, Coach, Atla.	4.25
148 Ted McAneeley, Cali.	1.50
149 Pierre Plante, SLou.	1.50
150 Dennis Hull, Chic.	1.50
151 Dave Keon, Toro.	3.00
152 Dave Dunn, Vanc. RC	**2.50**
153 Michel Belhumeur (G), Wash.	2.50
154 TL: B. Clarke/ D. Schultz	5.00
155 Ken Dryden (G), Mont.	35.00
156 John Wright, Kans. RC	**2.50**
157 Larry Romanchych, Atla.	1.50
158 Ralph Stewart, NYIs. RC	**2.50**
159 Mike Robitaille, Buff.	1.50
160 Ed Giacomin (G), NYRa.	3.50
161 Don Cherry, Coach, Bost. RC	**60.00**
162 Checklist 2 (133 - 264)	45.00
163 Rick MacLeish, Phil.	2.50
164 Greg Polis, SLou.	1.50
165 Carol Vadnais, Bost.	1.50
166 Pete Laframboise, Wash.	1.50
167 Ron Schock, Pitt.	1.50
168 Lanny McDonald, Toro. RC	**35.00**
169 Kansas City Scouts Emblem	2.50
170 Tony Esposito (G), Chic.	12.00
171 Pierre Jarry, Detr.	1.50
172 Dan Maloney, LosA.	1.50
173 Pete McDuffe (G), Kans.	2.50
174 Danny Grant, Minn.	1.50
175 John Stewart, Cali. RC	**2.50**
176 Floyd Smith, Buff.	1.50
177 Bert Marshall, NYIs.	1.50
178 Chuck Lefley, Mont., Err. (Pierre Bouchard)	1.50
179 Gilles Villemure (G), NYRa.	2.50
180 Börje Salming, Toro. RC	**30.00**
181 Doug Mohns, Wash.	1.50
182 Barry Wilkins, Vanc.	1.50
183 TL: L. MacDonald/ Syl Apps	2.50
184 Gregg Sheppard, Bost.	1.50
185 Joey Johnston, Cali.	1.50
186 Dick Redmond, Chic.	1.50
187 Simon Nolet, Kans.	1.50
188 Ron Stackhouse, Pitt.	1.50
189 Marshall Johnston, Coach, Cali.	1.50
190 Rick Martin, Buff.	2.50
191 André Boudrias, Vanc.	1.50
192 Steve Atkinson, Wash.	1.50
193 Nick Libett, Detr.	1.50
194 Bob J. Murdoch, LosA. RC	**2.50**
195 Denis Potvin, NYIs. RC	**55.00**
196 Dave Schultz, Phil.	4.25
197 TL: G. Unger/ P. Plante	2.50
198 Jim McKenny, Toro.	1.50
199 Gerry Hart, NYIs.	1.50
200 Phil Esposito, Bost.	10.00
201 Rod Gilbert, NYRa.	3.00
202 Jacques Laperrière, Mont.	2.50
203 Barry Gibbs, Minn.	1.50
204 Billy Reay, Coach, Chic.	1.50
205 Gilles Meloche (G), Cali.	2.50
206 Wayne Cashman, Bost.	1.50
207 Dennis Ververgaert, Vanc. RC	**2.50**
208 Phil Roberto, SLou.	1.50
209 Playoffs: Flyers vs. Flames	2.50
210 Playoffs: Rangers vs. Canadiens	2.50
211 Playoffs: Bruins vs. Maple Leafs	2.50
212 Playoffs: Blackhawks vs. Kings	2.50
213 Playoffs: Flyers vs. Rangers	2.50
214 Playoffs: Blackhawks vs. Bruins	2.50
215 Playoffs: Flyers vs. Bruins	3.00
216 Stanley Cup Champions: Philadelphia Flyers	3.00
217 Joe Watson, Phil.	1.50
218 Wayne Stephenson (G), SLou.	2.50
219 TL: D. Sittler/ N. Ullman/ P. Henderson/ D. Dupère	3.00
220 Bill Goldsworthy, Minn.	1.50
221 Don Marcotte, Bost.	1.50
222 Alex Delvecchio, Coach, Detr.	2.50
223 Stan Gilbertson, Cali.	1.50
224 Mike Murphy, LosA.	1.50
225 Jim Rutherford (G), Detr.	2.50
226 Phil Russell, Chic.	1.50
227 Lynn Powis, Kans.	1.50
228 Billy Harris, NYIs.	1.50
229 Bob Pulford, Coach, LosA.	2.50
230 Ken Hodge, Bost.	1.50
231 Bill Fairbairn, NYRa.	1.50
232 Guy Lafleur, Mont.	30.00
233 TL: B. Harris/ R. Stewart/ D. Potvn	4.00
234 Fred Barrett, Minn.	1.50
235 Rogatien Vachon (G), LosA.	4.50
236 Norm Ullman, Toro.	3.00
237 Garry Unger, SLou.	1.50
238 Jackie Gordon, Coach, Minn.	1.50
239 John Bucyk, Bost.	3.00
240 Bob Dailey, Vanc. RC	**2.50**
241 Dave Burrows, Pitt.	1.50
242 Len Frig, Cali. RC	**2.50**
243 AW: Henri Richard, Mont.	2.50
244 AW: Phil Esposito, Bost.	5.00
245 AW: John Bucyk, Bost.	2.50
246 AW: Phil Esposito, Bost.	5.00
247 AW: Boston Bruins	2.50
248 AW: Bobby Orr, Bost.	25.00
249 AW: Bernie Parent (G), Phil.	4.00
250 AW: Philadelphia Flyers	3.00
251 AW: Bernie Parent (G), Phil.	4.00
252 AW: Denis Potvin, NYIs.	12.00
253 AW: Philadelphia Flyers	2.50
254 Pierre Bouchard, Mont.	1.50
255 Jude Drouin, Minn.	1.50

☐ 256 Washington Capitals Emblem 2.50
☐ 257 Michel Plasse (G), Kans. 2.50
☐ 258 Juha Widing, LosA. 1.50
☐ 259 Bryan Watson, Detr. 1.50
☐ 260 Bobby Clarke, Phil. 15.00
☐ **261 Scotty Bowman, Coach, Mont. RC 90.00**
☐ 262 Craig Patrick, Cali. 1.50
☐ 263 Craig Cameron, NYIs. 1.50
☐ 264 Ted Irvine, NYRa. 1.50
☐ 265 Eddie Johnston (G), SLou. 2.50
☐ **266 Dave Forbes, Bost. RC 2.50**
☐ 267 Detroit Red Wings Checklist 6.00
☐ **268 Rick Dudley, Buff. RC 5.00**
☐ **269 Darcy Rota, Chic. RC 4.00**
☐ 270 Phil Myre (G), Atla. 2.50
☐ **271 Larry Brown, LosA. RC 2.50**
☐ **272 Bob Neely, Toro. RC 2.50**
☐ **273 Jerry Byers, Atla. RC 2.50**
☐ 274 Pittsburgh Penguins Checklist 6.00
☐ 275 Glenn Goldup, Mont. RC, Err. (Glen) 1.50
☐ 276 Ron Harris, NYRa. 1.50
☐ **277 Joe Lundrigan, Wash. RC 2.50**
☐ **278 Mike Christie, Cali. RC 2.50**
☐ **279 Doug Rombough, NYIs. RC 2.50**
☐ 280 Larry Robinson, Mont. 25.00
☐ 281 St. Louis Blues Checklist 6.00
☐ **282 John Marks, Chic. RC 2.50**
☐ 283 Don Saleski, Phil. 1.50
☐ **284 Rick Wilson, SLou. RC 2.50**
☐ **285 André Savard, Bost. RC 8.00**
☐ 286 Pat Quinn, Atla. 1.50
☐ 287 Los Angeles Kings Checklist 6.00
☐ **288 Norm Gratton, Buff. RC 2.50**
☐ **289 Ian Turnbull, Toro. RC 4.00**
☐ 290 Derek Sanderson, NYRa. 5.00
☐ 291 Murray Oliver, Minn. 1.50
☐ 292 Wilf Paiement, Kans. RC, Err. (Paiemont) 2.50
☐ **293 Nelson Debenedet, Pitt. RC 2.50**
☐ **294 Greg Joly, Wash. RC 2.50**
☐ 295 Terry O'Reilly, Bost. 3.00
☐ 296 Rey Comeau, Atla. 1.50
☐ **297 Michel Larocque (G), Mont. RC 6.50**
☐ 298 Floyd Thomson, SLou. RC, Err. (Thompson) 1.50
☐ **299 Jean-Guy Lagace, Pitt. RC 2.50**
☐ 300 Philadelphia Flyers Checklist 6.00
☐ **301 Al MacAdam, Cali. RC 2.50**
☐ **302 George Ferguson, Toro. RC 2.50**
☐ **303 Jimmy Watson, Phil. RC 2.50**
☐ **304 Rick Middleton, NYRa. RC 20.00**
☐ 305 Craig Ramsay, Buff. 1.50
☐ 306 Hilliard Graves, Atla. 1.50
☐ 307 New York Islanders Checklist 6.00
☐ **308 Blake Dunlop, Minn. RC 2.50**
☐ 309 J. P. Bordeleau, Chic. 1.50
☐ 310 Brian Glennie, Toro. 1.50
☐ 311 Checklist 3 (265 - 396) 45.00
☐ 312 Doug Roberts, Detr. 1.50
☐ 313 Darryl Edestrand, Bost. 1.50
☐ **314 Ron H. Anderson, Wash. RC 2.50**
☐ 315 Chicago Blackhawks Checklist 6.00
☐ **316 Steve Shutt, Mont. RC 25.00**
☐ **317 Doug Horbul, Kans. RC 2.50**
☐ **318 Bill Lochead, Detr. RC 2.50**
☐ 319 Fred (Buster) Harvey, Atla. 1.50
☐ **320 Gene Carr, LosA. RC 2.50**
☐ 321 Henri Richard, Mont. 4.50
☐ 322 Vancouver Canucks Checklist 6.00
☐ 323 Tim Ecclestone, Toro. 1.50
☐ **324 Dave Lewis, NYIs. RC 4.00**
☐ 325 Lou Nanne, Minn. 1.50
☐ 326 Bobby Rousseau, NYRa. 1.50
☐ 327 Dunc Wilson (G), Toro. 2.50
☐ 328 Brian Spencer, Buff. 1.50
☐ **329 Rick Hampton, Cali. RC 2.50**
☐ 330 Montréal Canadiens Checklist 6.00
☐ 331 Jack Lynch, Detr. 1.50
☐ 332 Garnet Bailey, SLou. 1.50
☐ **333 Al Sims, Bost. RC 4.00**
☐ **334 Orest Kindrachuk, Phil. RC 2.50**
☐ 335 Dave Hudson, Kans. 1.50
☐ **336 Bob Murray, Atla. RC 2.50**
☐ 337 Buffalo Sabres Checklist 6.00
☐ 338 Sheldon Kannegiesser, LosA. 1.50
☐ 339 Billy MacMillan, NYIs. 1.50
☐ **340 Paulin Bordeleau, Vanc. RC 4.00**
☐ 341 Dale Rolfe, NYRa. 1.50
☐ **342 Yvon Lambert, Mont. RC 6.00**
☐ **343 Bob Paradise, Pitt. RC 2.50**
☐ 344 Germain Gagnon, Chic. 1.50
☐ 345 Yvon Labre, Wash. 1.50
☐ **346 Chris Ahrens, Minn. RC 2.50**
☐ **347 Doug Grant (G), Detr. RC 2.50**
☐ **348 Blaine Stoughton, Toro. RC 4.00**
☐ 349 Gregg Boddy, Vanc., Err. (Greg) 1.50
☐ 350 Boston Bruins Checklist 6.00
☐ 351 Doug Jarrett, Chic. 1.50
☐ 352 Terry Crisp, Phil. 1.50
☐ **353 Glenn Resch (G), NYIs. RC, Err. (Glen) 25.00**
☐ 354 Jerry Korab, Buff. 1.50
☐ **355 Stan Weir, Cali. RC 2.50**
☐ 356 Noel Price, Atla. 1.50
☐ **357 Bill Clement, Phil. RC 15.00**
☐ 358 Neil Komadoski, LosA. 1.50
☐ **359 Murray Wilson, Mont. RC 2.50**
☐ 360 Dale Tallon, Chic., Err. (Talon) 1.50
☐ 361 Gary Doak, Bost. 1.50
☐ **362 Randy Rota, Kans. RC 2.50**
☐ 363 Minnesota North Stars Checklist 6.00
☐ 364 Bill Collins, SLou. 1.50
☐ 365 Thommie Bergman, Detr., Err, (Tommie) 1.50
☐ 366 Dennis Kearns, Vanc. 1.50
☐ 367 Lorne Henning, NYIs. 1.50
☐ 368 Gary Sabourin, Toro. 1.50
☐ **369 Mike Bloom, Wash. RC 2.50**
☐ 370 New York Rangers Checklist 6.00
☐ **371 Gary Simmons (G), Cali. RC 5.00**
☐ **372 Dwight Bialowas, Atla. RC 2.50**
☐ 373 Gilles Marotte, NYRa. 1.50
☐ 374 Frank St. Marseille, LosA. 1.50
☐ **375 Garry Howatt, NYIs. RC 2.50**
☐ **376 Ross Brooks (G), Bost. RC 2.50**
☐ 377 Atlanta Flames Checklist 6.00
☐ 378 Bob Nevin, LosA. 1.50
☐ **379 Lyle Moffat, Toro. RC 2.50**
☐ 380 Bob Kelly, Phil. 1.50
☐ **381 John Gould, Vanc. RC 2.50**
☐ **382 Dave Fortier, NYIs. RC 2.50**
☐ **383 Jean Hamel, Detr. RC 2.50**
☐ **384 Bert Wilson, NYRa. RC 2.50**
☐ **385 Chuck Arnason, Pitt. RC 2.50**
☐ **386 Bruce Cowick, Wash. RC 2.50**
☐ 387 Ernie Hicke, NYIs. 1.50
☐ **388 Bob Gainey, Mont. RC 40.00**
☐ **389 Vic Venasky, LosA. RC 2.50**
☐ 390 Toronto Maple Leafs Checklist 6.00
☐ **391 Eric Vail, Atla. RC 2.50**
☐ 392 Bobby Lalonde, Vanc. 1.50
☐ **393 Jerry Butler, NYRa. RC 2.50**
☐ **394 Tommy Williams, LosA. RC 2.50**
☐ 395 Chico Maki, Chic. 1.50
☐ **396 Tom Bladon, Phil. RC 6.00**

1974 - 75 O-PEE-CHEE WHA

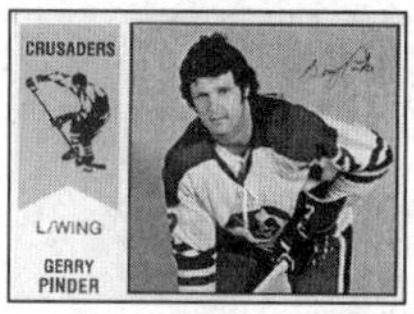

"(This) set has all the old WHA teams that are no longer around. It has a horizontal design with the picture of the player and the team banner on the left. I collected that small set. It was available at the corner stores. Key cards include Bobby Hull, the Howe family, Anders Hedberg (rookie card), and Ulf Nilsson (rookie card)." – John Oickle, The Card Stop, Charlottetown, Prince Edward Island.

These cards measure the standard 2 1/2" x 3 1/2".

Complete Set (66 cards): 250.00
Common Player: 3.00
O-Pee-Chee NM-MT

☐ 1 The Howes: Gordie, Mark, Marty, Houston 100.00
☐ 2 Bruce MacGregor, Edmonton 3.50
☐ **3 Wayne Dillon, Toronto RC 4.50**
☐ **4 Ulf Nilsson, Winnipeg RC 14.00**
☐ 5 Serge Bernier, Québec 3.50
☐ 6 Bryan Campbell, Vancouver 3.50
☐ 7 Rosaire Paiement, Chicago 3.50
☐ 8 Tom Webster, New England 3.50
☐ 9 Gerry Pinder, Cleveland 3.50
☐ 10 Mike Walton, Minnesota 3.50
☐ 11 Norm Beaudin, Winnipeg 3.50
☐ **12 Bob Whitlock, Indianapolis RC 4.50**
☐ 13 Wayne Rivers, San Diego 3.50
☐ 14 Gerry Odrowski, Phoenix 3.50
☐ 15 Ron Climie, Edmonton 3.50
☐ **16 Tom Simpson, Toronto RC 4.50**
☐ **17 Anders Hedberg, Winnipeg RC 16.00**
☐ 18 J.C. Tremblay, Québec, 5.00
☐ 19 Mike Pelyk, Vancouver 3.50
☐ 20 Dave Dryden (G), Chicago 5.00
☐ 21 Ron Ward, Cleveland. 3.50
☐ **22 Larry Lund, Houston RC 4.50**
☐ **23 Ron Buchanan, Edmonton RC 4.50**
☐ **24 Pat Hickey, Toronto RC 6.00**
☐ **25 Danny Lawson, Vancouver RC 4.50**
☐ **26 Bobby Guindon, Québec RC 4.50**
☐ **27 Gene Peacosh, San Diego RC 4.50**
☐ 28 Fran Huck, Minnesota 3.50
☐ 29 Al Hamilton, Edmonton 5.00
☐ 30 Gerry Cheevers (G), Cleveland 20.00
☐ **31 Heikki Riihiranta, Winnipeg RC 4.50**
☐ **32 Don Burgess, Vancouver RC 4.50**
☐ **33 John French, New England RC 4.50**
☐ **34 Jim Wiste, Indianapolis RC 4.50**
☐ 35 Pat Stapleton, Chicago 5.00
☐ **36 J.P. LeBlanc, Michigan RC 4.50**
☐ **37 Mike Antonovich, Minnesota RC 4.50**
☐ 38 Joe Daley (G), Winnipeg 5.00
☐ **39 Ross Perkins, Edmonton RC 4.50**
☐ 40 Frank Mahovlich, Toronto 15.00
☐ 41 Réjean Houle, Québec 5.00
☐ **42 Ron Chipperfield, Vancouver RC 4.50**
☐ 43 Marc Tardif, Michigan 5.00
☐ **44 Murray Keogan, Phoenix RC 4.50**
☐ 45 Wayne Carleton, New England 3.50
☐ **46 André Gaudette, Québec RC 4.50**
☐ 47 Ralph Backstrom, Chicago 3.50
☐ **48 Don McLeod (G), Vancouver RC 5.00**
☐ **49 Vaclav Nedomansky, Toronto RC 5.00**
☐ 50 Bobby Hull, Winnipeg 50.00
☐ **51 Rusty Patenaude, Edmonton RC 4.50**
☐ 52 Michel Parizeau, Québec 3.50
☐ 53 Checklist (1- 66) 45.00
☐ 54 Wayne Connelly, Minnesota 3.50
☐ 55 Gary Veneruzzo, Michigan 3.50
☐ **56 Dennis Sobchuk, Phoenix RC 4.50**
☐ 57 Paul Henderson, Toronto 7.50
☐ **58 Andy Brown (G), Indianapolis RC 5.00**
☐ 59 Poul Popiel, Houston 3.50
☐ 60 André Lacroix, San Diego 5.00
☐ 61 Gary Jarrett, Cleveland 3.50
☐ **62 Claude St. Sauveur, Vancouver RC 4.50**
☐ **63 Réal Cloutier, Québec RC 4.50**
☐ 64 Jacques Plante (G), Edmonton 55.00
☐ **65 Gilles Gratton (G), Toronto RC 10.00**
☐ **66 Lars-Erik Sjoberg, Winnipeg RC 10.00**

1974 - 75 SOVIET STARS

These postcards measure 8 1/4" x 3 1/2".

Complete Set (25 postcards and folder): 125.00
Soviet Stars NM

☐ 1 U.S.S.R. 8.00
☐ 2 Vladislav Tretiak (G) 20.00
☐ 3 Alexander Sidelnikov 5.00
☐ 4 Alexander Gusev 5.00
☐ 5 Valery Vasiliev 5.00
☐ 6 Vladimir Lutchenko 5.00
☐ 7 Yuri Liapkin 5.00
☐ 8 Gennady Tsycankov 5.00
☐ 9 Yuri Shatalov 5.00
☐ 10 Viktor Kuzkin 5.00
☐ 11 Boris Mikhailov 10.00
☐ 12 Vladimir Petrov 8.00
☐ 13 Valery Kharlamov 12.00
☐ 14 Alexander Maltsev 8.00
☐ 15 Vladimir Shadrin 5.00
☐ 16 Alexander Yakushev 12.00
☐ 17 Yuri Lebedev 5.00
☐ 18 Vyacheslav Anisin 5.00
☐ 19 Alexander Bodunov 5.00
☐ 20 Sergei Kapustin 5.00
☐ 21 Vladimir Repnev 5.00
☐ 22 Vsevold Bobrov 5.00
☐ 23 Boris Kulagin 5.00
☐ 24 Boris Mikhailov 8.00
☐ 25 U.S.S.R. 8.00

1974 - 75 TOPPS

These cards measure the standard 2 1/2" x 3 1/2".

Complete Set (264 cards): 275.00
Common Player: .75
Topps NM-MT

☐ 1 LL: P. Esposito/ B. Goldsworthy 4.50
☐ 2 LL: B. Orr/ D. Hextall 7.00
☐ 3 LL: P. Esposito/ B. Clarke 5.50
☐ 4 LL: D. Favell/ B. Parent 1.50
☐ 5 LL: B. Watson/ D. Schultz 1.25
☐ 6 LL: M. Redmond/ R. MacLeish 1.25
☐ **7 Gary Bromley (G), Buff. RC 1.25**
☐ 8 Bill Barber, Phil. 6.50
☐ 9 Emile Francis, Coach, NYRa. 1.50
☐ 10 Gilles Gilbert (G), Bost. 1.25
☐ **11 John Davidson (G), SLou. RC 12.00**
☐ 12 Ron Ellis, Toro. .75
☐ 13 Syl Apps, Pitt. .75
☐ 14 TL: J. Richard/ T. Lysiak/ K. McCreary 1.25
☐ 15 Dan Bouchard (G), Atla. 1.25
☐ 16 Ivan Boldirev, Chic. .75
☐ **17 Gary Coalter, Kans. RC 1.25**
☐ 18 Bob Berry, LosA. .75
☐ 19 Red Berenson, Detr. .75
☐ 20 Stan Mikita, Chic. 5.50
☐ **21 Fred Shero, Coach, Phil. RC 5.00**
☐ 22 Gary Smith (G), Vanc. 1.25
☐ 23 Bill Mikkelson .75
☐ 24 Jacques Lemaire, Mont., Err. (Sabres) 2.50
☐ 25 Gilbert Perreault, Buff. 5.50
☐ 26 Césare Maniago (G), Minn. 1.25
☐ 27 Bobby Schmautz, Bost. .75
☐ 28 TL: P. Esposito/ B. Orr/ J. Bucyk 10.00
☐ 29 Steve Vickers, NYRa. .75
☐ 30 Lowell MacDonald, Pitt. .75
☐ 31 Fred Stanfield, Minn. .75
☐ 32 Ed Westfall, NYIs. .75
☐ 33 Curt Bennett, Atla. .75
☐ 34 Bep Guidolin, Coach, Kans. .75
☐ 35 Cliff Koroll, Chic. .75
☐ 36 Gary Croteau, Kans. .75
☐ 37 Mike Corrigan, LosA. .75
☐ 38 Henry Boucha, Detr. .75
☐ 39 Ron Low (G), Wash. 1.25
☐ 40 Darryl Sittler, Toro. 7.00
☐ 41 Tracy Pratt, Vanc. .75
☐ 42 TL: R. Martin/ R. Robert 1.25
☐ 43 Larry Carrière, Buff. .75
☐ 44 Gary Dornhoefer, Phil., Error .75
☐ **45 Denis Herron (G), Ppg. RC 3.00**
☐ 46 Doug Favell (G), Toro. .75
☐ **47 Dave Gardner, SLou. RC 1.25**
☐ **48 Morris Mott, Cali. RC 1.25**
☐ 49 Marc Boileau, Coach, Pitt. .75
☐ 50 Brad Park, NYRa. 4.00
☐ 51 Bobby Leiter, Atla. .75
☐ 52 Tom Reid, Minn. .75
☐ 53 Serge Savard, Mont. 1.50
☐ 54 Checklist 1 (1 - 132) 18.00
☐ 55 Terry Harper, LosA. .75
☐ 56 TL: J. Johnston/ W. McKechnie .75
☐ 57 Guy Charron, Detr. .75
☐ 58 Pit Martin, Chic. .75
☐ 59 Chris Evans, Kans. .75
☐ 60 Bernie Parent (G), Phil. 4.00
☐ 61 Jim Lorentz, Buff. .75
☐ **62 Dave Kryskow, Wash. RC 1.25**
☐ 63 Lou Angotti, SLou. .75
☐ 64 Bill Flett, Toro. .75
☐ 65 Vic Hadfield, Pitt. .75
☐ **66 Wayne Merrick, SLou. RC 1.25**
☐ 67 André Dupont, Phil. .75
☐ **68 Tom Lysiak, Atla. RC 1.25**
☐ 69 TL: J. Pappin/ S. Mikita/ J. P. Bordelaeau 1.50
☐ 70 Guy Lapointe, Mont. 2.00
☐ 71 Gerry O'Flaherty, Vanc. .75
☐ 72 Marcel Dionne, Detr. 9.00
☐ **73 Butch Deadmarsh, Kans. RC 1.25**
☐ 74 Butch Goring, LosA. .75
☐ 75 Keith Magnuson, Chic. .75
☐ 76 Red Kelly, Coach, Toro. 1.50
☐ 77 Pete Stemkowski, NYRa. .75
☐ 78 Jim Roberts, Mont. .75
☐ 79 Don Luce, Buff. .75
☐ 80 Don Awrey, SLou. .75
☐ 81 Rick Kehoe, Toro. .75
☐ 82 Billy Smith (G), NYIs. 9.00
☐ 83 J.P. Parise, Minn. .75
☐ 84 TL: M. Redmond/ M. Dionne/ B. Hogaboam 2.00
☐ 85 Ed Van Impe, Phil. .75
☐ 86 Randy Manery, Atla. .75
☐ 87 Barclay Plager, SLou. .75
☐ **88 Inge Hammarstrom, Toro. RC 1.25**
☐ 89 Ab DeMarco, Pitt. .75
☐ 90 Bill White, Chic. .75
☐ 91 Al Arbour, Coach, NYIs. 1.50
☐ 92 Bob Stewart, Cali. .75
☐ 93 Jack Egers .75
☐ 94 Don Lever, Vanc. .75
☐ 95 Reggie Leach, Phil. .75
☐ 96 Dennis O'Brien, Minn. .75
☐ 97 Pete Mahovlich, Mont. .75
☐ 98 TL: B. Goring/ F. St. Marseille/ D. Kozak 1.25
☐ 99 Gerry Meehan, Buff. .75
☐ 100 Bobby Orr, Bost. 30.00
☐ **101 Jean Potvin, NYIs. RC 1.25**
☐ 102 Rod Seiling, NYRa. .75
☐ 103 Keith McCreary, Atla. .75
☐ 104 Phil Maloney, Coach, Vanc. .75
☐ 105 Denis Dupère .75
☐ 106 Steve Durbano, Pitt. .75
☐ 107 Bob Plager, SLou., Err. (Barclay Plager) .75

☐	**108 Chris Oddleifson, Vanc. RC**	**1.25**
☐	109 Jim Neilson, Cali.	.75
☐	110 Jean Pronovost, Pitt.	.75
☐	**111 Don Kozak, LosA. RC**	**1.25**
☐	112 TL: B. Goldsworthy/ D. Hextall/ D. Grant	1.25
☐	113 Jim Pappin, Chic.	.75
☐	114 Richard Lemieux, Kans.	.75
☐	115 Dennis Hextall, Minn.	.75
☐	**116 Bill Hogaboam, Detr. RC**	**1.25**
☐	117 TL: Ververgaert/ Schmautz/ Boudrias/ Tannahill	1.25
☐	118 Jim Anderson, Coach, Wash.	.75
☐	119 Walt Tkaczuk, NYRa.	.75
☐	120 Mickey Redmond, Detr.	1.25
☐	121 Jim Schoenfeld, Buff.	.75
☐	122 Jocelyn Guevremont, Vanc.	.75
☐	123 Bob Nystrom, NYIs.	.75
☐	124 TL: Y. Cournoyer/ F. Mahovlich/ C. Larose	3.00
☐	125 Lew Morrison, Wash.	.75
☐	126 Terry Murray, Cali.	.75
☐	127 AS: Rick Martin, Buff.	1.25
☐	128 AS: Ken Hodge, Bost.	.75
☐	129 AS: Phil Esposito, Bost.	3.00
☐	130 AS: Bobby Orr, Bost.	15.00
☐	131 AS: Brad Park, NYRa.	2.00
☐	132 AS: Gilles Gilbert (G), Bost.	1.25
☐	133 AS: Lowell MacDonald, Pitt.	.75
☐	134 AS: Bill Goldsworthy, Minn.	.75
☐	135 AS: Bobby Clarke, Phil.	6.00
☐	136 AS: Bill White, Chic.	.75
☐	137 AS: Dave Burrows, Pitt.	.75
☐	138 AS: Bernie Parent (G), Phil.	2.50
☐	139 Jacques Richard, Atla.	.75
☐	140 Yvan Cournoyer, Mont.	3.00
☐	141 TL: R. Gilbert/ B. Park	2.25
☐	142 René Robert, Buff.	.75
☐	**143 J. Bob Kelly, Pitt. RC**	**1.25**
☐	144 Ross Lonsberry, Phil.	.75
☐	145 Jean Ratelle, NYRa.	2.00
☐	146 Dallas Smith, Bost.	.75
☐	147 Bernie Geoffrion, Coach, Atla.	3.00
☐	148 Ted McAneeley, Cali.	.75
☐	149 Pierre Plante, SLou.	.75
☐	150 Dennis Hull, Chic.	.75
☐	151 Dave Keon, Toro.	2.00
☐	**152 Dave Dunn, Vanc. RC**	**1.25**
☐	153 Michel Belhumeur (G), Wash.	1.25
☐	154 TL: B. Clarke/ D. Schultz	3.00
☐	155 Ken Dryden (G), Mont.	25.00
☐	**156 John Wright, Kans. RC**	**1.25**
☐	157 Larry Romanchych, Atla.	.75
☐	**158 Ralph Stewart, NYIs. RC**	**1.25**
☐	159 Mike Robitaille, Buff.	.75
☐	160 Ed Giacomin (G), NYRa.	2.50
☐	**161 Don Cherry, Coach, Bost. RC**	**30.00**
☐	162 Checklist 2 (133 - 264)	18.00
☐	163 Rick MacLeish, Phil.	1.25
☐	164 Greg Polis, SLou.	.75
☐	165 Carol Vadnais, Bost.	.75
☐	166 Pete Laframboise, Wash.	.75
☐	167 Ron Schock, Pitt.	.75
☐	**168 Lanny McDonald, Toro. RC**	**20.00**
☐	169 Kansas City Scouts Emblem Entered NHL, 1974	1.50
☐	170 Tony Esposito (G), Chic.	6.50
☐	171 Pierre Jarry, Detr.	.75
☐	172 Dan Maloney, LosA.	.75
☐	173 Pete McDuffe (G), Kans.	1.25
☐	174 Danny Grant, Minn.	.75
☐	**175 John Stewart, Cali. RC**	**1.25**
☐	176 Floyd Smith, Buff.	.75
☐	177 Bert Marshall, NYIs.	.75
☐	178 Chuck Lefley, Mont., Err. (Pierre Bouchard)	.75
☐	179 Gilles Villemure (G), NYRa.	.75
☐	**180 Borje Salming, Toro. RC**	**15.00**
☐	181 Doug Mohns, Wash.	.75
☐	182 Barry Wilkins, Vanc.	.75
☐	183 TL: L. MacDonald/ S. Apps	1.25
☐	184 Gregg Sheppard, Bost.	.75
☐	185 Joey Johnston, Cali.	.75
☐	186 Dick Redmond, Chic.	.75
☐	187 Simon Nolet, Kans.	.75
☐	188 Ron Stackhouse, Pitt.	.75
☐	189 Marshall Johnston, Coach, Cali.	.75
☐	190 Rick Martin, Buff.	1.25
☐	191 André Boudrias, Vanc.	.75
☐	192 Steve Atkinson, Wash.	.75
☐	193 Nick Libett, Detr.	.75
☐	**194 Bob J. Murdoch, LosA. RC**	**1.25**
☐	**195 Denis Potvin, NYIs. RC**	**30.00**
☐	196 Dave Schultz, Phil.	3.00
☐	197 TL: G. Unger/ P. Plante	1.25
☐	198 Jim McKenny, Toro.	.75
☐	199 Gerry Hart, NYIs.	.75
☐	200 Phil Esposito, Bost.	5.50
☐	201 Rod Gilbert, NYRa.	2.00
☐	202 Jacques Laperrière, Mont.	.75
☐	203 Barry Gibbs, Minn.	.75
☐	204 Billy Reay, Coach, Chic.	.75
☐	205 Gilles Meloche (G), Cali.	1.25
☐	206 Wayne Cashman, Bost.	.75
☐	**207 Dennis Ververgaert, Vanc. RC**	**1.25**
☐	208 Phil Roberto, SLou.	.75
☐	209 Playoffs: Flyers vs. Flames	1.25
☐	210 Playoffs: Rangers vs. Canadiens	1.25
☐	211 Playoffs: Bruins vs. Maple Leafs	1.25
☐	212 Playoffs: Blackhawks vs. Kings	1.25
☐	213 Playoffs: Flyers vs. Rangers	1.25
☐	214 Playoffs: Blackhawks vs. Bruins	1.25
☐	215 Playoffs: Flyers vs. Bruins	1.50
☐	216 Stanley Cup Champions: Philadelphia Flyers	2.00
☐	217 Joe Watson, Phil.	.75
☐	218 Wayne Stephenson (G), SLou.	1.25
☐	219 TL: . Sittler/ Ullman/ Henderson/ Dupère	2.00
☐	220 Bill Goldsworthy, Minn.	.75
☐	221 Don Marcotte, Bost.	.75
☐	222 Alex Delvecchio, Coach, Detr.	1.50
☐	223 Stan Gilbertson, Cali.	.75
☐	224 Mike Murphy, LosA.	1.25
☐	225 Jim Rutherford (G), Detr.	1.25
☐	226 Phil Russell, Chic.	.75
☐	227 Lynn Powis, Kans.	.75
☐	228 Billy Harris, NYIs.	.75
☐	229 Bob Pulford, Coach, LosA.	1.50
☐	230 Ken Hodge, Bost.	.75
☐	231 Bill Fairbairn, NYRa.	.75
☐	232 Guy Lafleur, Mont.	20.00
☐	233 TL: B. Harris/ R. Stewart/ D. Potvin	3.00
☐	234 Fred Barrett, Minn.	.75
☐	235 Rogatien Vachon (G), LosA.	2.75
☐	236 Norm Ullman, Toro.	2.00
☐	237 Garry Unger, SLou.	.75
☐	238 Jackie Gordon, Coach, Minn.	.75
☐	239 John Bucyk, Bost.	2.00
☐	**240 Bob Dailey, Vanc. RC**	**1.25**
☐	241 Dave Burrows, Pitt.	.75
☐	**242 Len Frig, Cali. RC**	**1.25**
☐	243 AW: Henri Richard, Mont.	1.50
☐	244 AW: Phil Esposito, Bost.	3.00
☐	245 AW: John Bucyk, Bost.	1.50
☐	246 AW: Phil Esposito, Bost.	3.00
☐	247 AW: Boston Bruins	1.25
☐	248 AW: Bobby Orr, Bost.	15.00
☐	249 AW: Bernie Parent (G), Phil.	2.50
☐	250 Stanley Cup / Philadelphia Flyers	2.00
☐	251 AW: Bernie Parent (G), Phil.	2.50
☐	252 AW: Denis Potvin, NYIs.	9.00
☐	253 AW: Philadelphia Flyers	1.50
☐	254 Pierre Bouchard, Mont.	.75
☐	255 Jude Drouin, Minn.	.75
☐	256 Washington Capitals Entered NHL, 1974	.75
☐	257 Michel Plasse (G), Kans.	1.80
☐	258 Juha Widing, LosA.	.75
☐	259 Bryan Watson, Detr.	.75
☐	260 Bobby Clarke, Phil.	10.00
☐	**261 Scotty Bowman, Coach, Mont. RC**	**45.00**
☐	262 Craig Patrick, Cali.	1.25
☐	263 Craig Cameron, NYIs.	.75
☐	264 Ted Irvine, NYRa.	2.00

1975 - 76 HOCKEY HEROES

These yellow-border cardboard stand-ups measure 13 1/2" x 7 1/2" or 15 1/2" x 8 3/4".

	Complete Set (31 stand-ups):	**225.00**
	Hockey Heroes	**NM**
☐	Bill Barber, Phil.	10.00
☐	Gerry Cheevers (G), Bost.	15.00
☐	Bobby Clarke, Phil.	15.00
☐	Yvan Cournoyer, Mont.	12.00
☐	Billy Harris, NYIs.	6.00
☐	Gerry Hart, NYIs.	6.00
☐	Guy Lafleur, Mont.	20.00
☐	Reggie Leach, Phil.	6.00
☐	Jacques Lemaire, Mont.	12.00
☐	Rick MacLeish, Phil.	6.00
☐	Peter Mahovlich, Mont.	6.00
☐	Lanny McDonald, Toro.	10.00
☐	Terry O'Reilly, Bost.	6.00
☐	Bobby Orr, Bost.	50.00
☐	Bernie Parent (G), Phil.	15.00
☐	Brad Park, Bost.	10.00
☐	Denis Potvin, NYI.	12.00
☐	Jean Ratelle, Bost.	10.00
☐	Glenn Resch (G), NYIs.	7.00
☐	Doug Riseborough, Mont.	6.00
☐	Larry Robinson, Mont.	12.00
☐	Börje Salming, Toro.	10.00
☐	André Savard, Bost.	6.00
☐	Dave Schultz, Phil.	10.00
☐	Gregg Sheppard, Bost.	6.00
☐	Darryl Sittler, Toro.	12.00
☐	Wayne Thomas (G), Toro.	7.00
☐	Errol Thompson, Toro.	6.00
☐	Bryan Trottier, NYIs.	15.00
☐	Ed Westfall, NYIs.	6.00
☐	Dave Williams, Toro.	10.00

1975 - 76 O-PEE-CHEE

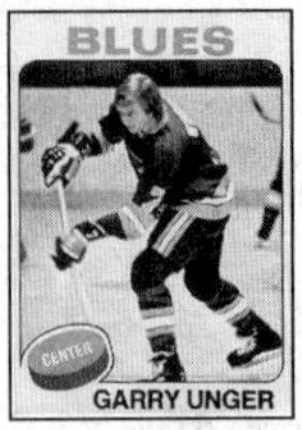

"The '75-76 doesn't have a lot to offer, but the packs are rare. There is a lot more people that want it than people that get it. There is also the grading factor that is pushing the pack price up." – Jason Martin, Martin Sports Cards, Guelph, Ontario.

These cards measure the standard 2 1/2" x 3 1/2". Checklist card number 395 was not issued, but two different checklist cards, both numbered 267, were produced.

	Complete Set (396 cards):	**400.00**
	Common Player:	**1.25**
	O-Pee-Chee	**NM-MT**
☐	1 Playoffs: Philadelphia vs. Buffalo	3.50
☐	2 Playoffs: Philadelphia vs. N.Y. Islanders	2.00
☐	3 Playoffs: Buffalo vs. Montréal	2.00
☐	4 Playoffs: N.Y. Islanders vs. Pittsburgh	2.00
☐	5 Playoffs: Montréal vs. Vancouver	2.00
☐	6 Playoffs: Buffalo vs. Chicago	2.00
☐	7 Playoffs: Philadelphia vs. Toronto	2.00
☐	8 Curt Bennett, Atla.	1.25
☐	9 John Bucyk, Bost.	3.00
☐	10 Gilbert Perreault, Buff.	7.50
☐	11 Darryl Edestrand, Bost.	1.25
☐	12 Ivan Boldirev, Chic.	1.25
☐	13 Nick Libett, Detr.	1.25
☐	**14 Jim McElmury, Kans. RC**	**2.00**
☐	15 Frank St. Marseille, LosA.	1.25
☐	16 Blake Dunlop, Minn.	1.25
☐	17 Yvon Lambert, Mont.	1.25
☐	18 Gerry Hart, NYIs.	1.25
☐	19 Steve Vickers, NYRa.	1.25
☐	20 Rick MacLeish, Phil.	1.25
☐	21 Bob Paradise, Pitt.	1.25
☐	22 Red Berenson, SLou.	1.25
☐	23 Lanny McDonald, Toro.	10.00
☐	24 Mike Robitaille, Vanc.	1.25
☐	25 Ron Low (G), Wash.	2.00
☐	26 Bryan Hextall, Detr.	1.25
☐	27 Carol Vadnais, Bost.	1.25
☐	28 Jim Lorentz, Buff.	1.25
☐	29 Gary Simmons (G), Cal.	2.00
☐	30 Stan Mikita, Chic.	6.00
☐	31 Bryan Watson, Detr.	1.25
☐	32 Guy Charron, Kans.	1.25
☐	33 Bob J. Murdoch, LosA.	1.25
☐	34 Norm Gratton, Minn.	1.25
☐	35 Ken Dryden (G), Mont.	28.00
☐	36 Jean Potvin, NYIs.	1.25
☐	37 Rick Middleton, NYRa.	5.50
☐	38 Ed Van Impe, Phil.	1.25
☐	39 Rick Kehoe, Pitt.	1.25
☐	40 Garry Unger, SLou.	1.25
☐	41 Ian Turnbull, Toro.	1.25
☐	42 Dennis Ververgaert, Vanc.	1.25
☐	**43 Mike Marson, Wash. RC**	**2.00**
☐	44 Randy Manery, Atla.	1.25
☐	45 Gilles Gilbert (G), Bost.	2.00
☐	46 René Robert, Buff.	1.25
☐	47 Bob Stewart, Cal.	1.25
☐	48 Pit Martin, Chic.	1.25
☐	49 Danny Grant, Detr.	1.25
☐	50 Pete Mahovlich, Mont.	1.25
☐	**51 Dennis Patterson, Kans. RC**	**2.00**
☐	52 Mike Murphy, LosA.	1.25
☐	53 Dennis O'Brien, Minn.	1.25
☐	54 Garry Howatt, NYIs.	1.25
☐	55 Ed Giacomin (G), NYRa. (Detr.)	3.00
☐	56 André Dupont, Phil.	1.25
☐	57 Chuck Arnason, Pitt.	1.25
☐	**58 Bob Gassoff, SLou. RC**	**2.00**
☐	59 Ron Ellis, Toro.	1.25
☐	60 André Boudrias, Vanc.	1.25
☐	61 Yvon Labre, Wash.	1.25
☐	62 Hilliard Graves, Atla.	1.25
☐	63 Wayne Cashman, Bost.	1.25
☐	**64 Danny Gare, Buff. RC**	**5.00**
☐	65 Rick Hampton, Cal.	1.25
☐	66 Darcy Rota, Chic.	1.25
☐	67 Bill Hogaboam, Detr.	1.25
☐	68 Denis Herron (G), Kans.	2.00
☐	69 Sheldon Kannegiesser, LosA.	1.25
☐	70 Yvan Cournoyer, Mont., Err. (Yvon)	3.50
☐	71 Ernie Hicke, Minn.	1.25
☐	72 Bert Marshall, NYIs.	1.25
☐	73 Derek Sanderson, NYRa. (SLou.)	5.00
☐	74 Tom Bladon, Phil.	1.25
☐	75 Ron Schock, Pitt.	1.25
☐	**76 Larry Sacharuk, SLou. (NYRa.) RC**	**2.00**
☐	77 George Ferguson, Toro.	1.25
☐	78 Ab DeMarco, Vanc.	1.25
☐	79 Tom Williams, Wash.	1.25
☐	80 Phil Roberto, Detr.	1.25
☐	81 Boston Bruins	5.00
☐	82 California Golden Seals	5.00
☐	83 Buffalo Sabres	5.00
☐	84 Chicago Blackhawks	5.00
☐	85 Atlanta Flames	5.00
☐	86 Los Angeles Kings	5.00
☐	87 Detroit Red Wings	5.00
☐	88 Kansas City Scouts	5.00
☐	89 Minnesota North Stars	5.00
☐	90 Montréal Canadiens	5.00
☐	91 Toronto Maple Leafs	5.00
☐	92 New York Islanders	5.00
☐	93 Pittsburgh Penguins	5.00
☐	94 New York Rangers	5.00
☐	95 Philadelphia Flyers	5.00
☐	96 St. Louis Blues	5.00
☐	97 Vancouver Canucks	5.00
☐	98 Washington Capitals	5.00
☐	99 Checklist 1 (1 - 110)	22.00
☐	100 Bobby Orr, Bost.	40.00
☐	101 Germain Gagnon, Chic., (Kans.)	1.25
☐	102 Phil Russell, Chic.	1.25
☐	103 Bill Lochead, Detr.	1.25
☐	**104 Robin Burns, Kans. RC**	**2.00**
☐	105 Gary Edwards (G), LosA.	2.00
☐	106 Dwight Bialowas, Minn.	1.25
☐	107 Doug Risebrough, Mont., Error (Bob Gainey)	3.50
☐	108 Dave Lewis, NYIs.	1.25
☐	109 Bill Fairbairn, NYRa.	1.25
☐	110 Ross Lonsberry, Phil.	1.25
☐	111 Ron Stackhouse, Pitt.	1.25
☐	112 Claude Larose, SLou.	1.25
☐	113 Don Luce, Buff.	1.25
☐	**114 Errol Thompson, Toro. RC**	**2.00**
☐	115 Gary Smith (G), Vanc.	2.00
☐	116 Jack Lynch, Wash.	1.25
☐	117 Jacques Richard, Atla. (Buff.)	1.25
☐	118 Dallas Smith, Bost.	1.25
☐	119 Dave Gardner, Cal.	1.25
☐	120 Mickey Redmond, Detr.	1.25
☐	121 John Marks, Chic.	1.25
☐	122 Dave Hudson, Kans.	1.25
☐	123 Bob Nevin, LosA.	1.25
☐	124 Fred Barrett, Minn.	1.25
☐	125 Gerry Desjardins (G), Buff.	2.00
☐	126 Guy Lafleur, Mont., Error (defence)	25.00
☐	127 J.P. Parise, NYIs.	1.25
☐	128 Walt Tkaczuk, NYRa.	1.25
☐	129 Gary Dornhoefer, Phil.	1.25
☐	130 Syl Apps, Pitt.	1.25
☐	131 Bob Plager, SLou.	1.25
☐	132 Stan Weir, Toro.	1.25
☐	133 Tracy Pratt, Vanc.	1.25
☐	134 Jack Egers, Wash.	1.25
☐	135 Eric Vail, Atla.	1.25
☐	136 Al Sims, Bost.	1.25
☐	**137 Larry Patey, Cal. RC**	**2.00**
☐	138 Jim Schoenfeld, Buff.	1.25
☐	139 Cliff Koroll, Chic.	1.25
☐	140 Marcel Dionne, LosA.	10.00
☐	141 Jean-Guy Lagacé, Kans.	1.25
☐	142 Juha Widing, LosA.	1.25
☐	143 Lou Nanne, Minn.	1.25
☐	144 Serge Savard, Mont.	2.50
☐	145 Glenn Resch (G), NYIs.	5.00
☐	**146 Ronald Greschner, NYRa. RC**	**3.00**
☐	147 Dave Schultz, Phil.	2.00
☐	148 Barry Wilkins, Pitt.	1.25
☐	149 Floyd Thomson, SLou.	1.25
☐	150 Darryl Sittler, Toro.	10.00
☐	151 Paulin Bordeleau, Vanc.	1.25
☐	**152 Ron Lalonde, Wash. RC**	**2.00**
☐	153 Larry Romanchych, Atla.	1.25
☐	154 Larry Carrière, Buff. (Atla.)	1.25
☐	155 André Savard, Bost.	1.25
☐	**156 Dave Hrechkosy, Cal. RC**	**2.00**
☐	157 Bill White, Chic.	1.25
☐	158 Dave Kryskow, Atla.	1.25
☐	159 Denis Dupere, Kans.	1.25
☐	160 Rogatien Vachon (G), LosA.	3.75
☐	161 Doug Rombough, Minn.	1.25
☐	162 Murray Wilson, Mont.	1.25
☐	**163 Bob Bourne, NYIs. RC**	**3.00**
☐	164 Gilles Marotte, NYRa.	1.25
☐	165 Vic Hadfield, Pitt.	1.25
☐	166 Reggie Leach, Phil.	1.25
☐	167 Jerry Butler, SLou.	1.25
☐	168 Inge Hammarstrom, Toro.	1.25
☐	169 Chris Oddleifson, Vanc.	1.25
☐	170 Greg Joly, Wash.	1.25
☐	171 Checklist 2 (111 - 220)	22.00
☐	172 Pat Quinn, Atla.	2.00
☐	173 Dave Forbes, Bost.	1.25
☐	174 Len Frig, Cal.	1.25
☐	175 Rick Martin, Buff.	1.25
☐	176 Keith Magnuson, Chic.	1.25

☐	177 Dan Maloney, Detr.	1.25
☐	178 Craig Patrick, Kans.	1.25
☐	179 Tommy Williams, LosA.	1.25
☐	180 Bill Goldsworthy, Minn.	1.25
☐	181 Steve Shutt, Mont.	7.00
☐	182 Ralph Stewart, NYIs.	1.25
☐	183 John Davidson (G), NYRa.	6.00
☐	184 Bob Kelly, Phil.	1.25
☐	185 Eddie Johnston (G), SLou.	2.00
☐	186 Dave Burrows, Pitt.	1.25
☐	187 Dave Dunn, Toro.	1.25
☐	188 Dennis Kearns, Vanc.	1.25
☐	189 Bill Clement, Wash.	3.50
☐	190 Gilles Meloche (G), Cal.	2.00
☐	191 Bobby Leiter, Atla.	1.25
☐	192 Jerry Korab, Buff.	1.25
☐	193 Joey Johnston, Chic.	1.25
☐	194 Walt McKechnie, Detr.	1.25
☐	195 Wilf Paiement, Kans.	1.25
☐	196 Bob Berry, LosA.	1.25
☐	**197 Dean Talafous, Minn. RC**	**2.00**
☐	198 Guy Lapointe, Mont.	2.00
☐	**199 Clark Gillies, NYIs. RC**	**15.00**
☐	200 Phil Esposito, Traded Bost.	10.00
☐	200 Phil Esposito, Not Traded, Bost.	7.50
☐	201 Greg Polis, NYRa.	1.25
☐	202 Jimmy Watson, Phil.	1.25
☐	**203 Gord McRae (G), Toro. RC**	**2.00**
☐	204 Lowell MacDonald, Pitt.	1.25
☐	205 Barclay Plager, SLou.	1.25
☐	206 Don Lever, Vanc.	1.25
☐	207 Bill Mikkelson, Wash.	1.25
☐	208 LL: P. Esposit/ G. Lafleur/ R. Martin	6.00
☐	209 LL: B. Orr/ B. Clarke/ P. Mahovlich	9.00
☐	210 LL: B. Orr/ P. Esposito/ M. Dionne	12.00
☐	211 LL: D. Schultz/ A. Dupont/ P. Russell	2.00
☐	212 LL: P. Esposito/ R. Martin/ D. Grant	4.00
☐	213 LL: B. Parent (G)/ R. Vachon (G)/ K. Dryden (G)	12.00
☐	214 Barry Gibbs, Atla.	1.25
☐	215 Ken Hodge, Sr., Bost.	1.25
☐	216 Jocelyn Guevremont, Buff.	1.25
☐	**217 Warren Williams, Calg. RC**	**2.00**
☐	218 Dick Redmond, Chic.	1.25
☐	219 Jim Rutherford (G), Detr.	2.00
☐	220 Simon Nolet, Kans.	1.25
☐	221 Butch Goring, LosA.	1.25
☐	222 Glen Sather, Minn.	1.25
☐	223 Mario Tremblay, Mont. RC, Err. (wrong photo)	8.00
☐	224 Jude Drouin, NYIs.	1.25
☐	225 Rod Gilbert, NYRa.	3.00
☐	226 Bill Barber, Phil.	6.00
☐	**227 Gary Inness (G), Pitt. RC**	**2.00**
☐	228 Wayne Merrick, SLou.	1.25
☐	229 Rod Seiling, Toro.	1.25
☐	230 Tom Lysiak, Atla.	1.25
☐	231 Bob Dailey, Vanc.	1.25
☐	232 Michel Belhumeur (G), Wash.	2.00
☐	**233 Bill Hajt, Buff. RC**	**2.00**
☐	234 Jim Pappin, Calg.	1.25
☐	235 Gregg Sheppard, Bost.	1.25
☐	236 Gary Bergman, Detr.	1.25
☐	237 Randy Rota, Kans.	1.25
☐	238 Neil Komadoski, LosA.	1.25
☐	239 Craig Cameron, Minn.	1.25
☐	240 Tony Esposito (G), Chic.	8.00
☐	241 Larry Robinson, Mont.	15.00
☐	242 Billy Harris, NYIs.	1.25
☐	243 Jean Ratelle, NYRa.	3.00
☐	244 Ted Irvine, SLou., Err. (Ted Harris)	1.25
☐	245 Bob Neely, Toro.	1.25
☐	246 Bobby Lalonde, Vanc.	1.25
☐	**247 Ron Jones, Wash. RC**	**2.00**
☐	248 Rey Comeau, Atla.	1.25
☐	249 Michel Plasse (G), Pitt.	2.00
☐	250 Bobby Clarke, Phil.	12.00
☐	251 Bobby Schmautz, Bost.	1.25
☐	**252 Peter McNab, Buff. RC**	**3.50**
☐	253 Al MacAdam, Calg.	1.25
☐	254 Dennis Hull, Chic.	1.25
☐	255 Terry Harper, Detr.	1.25
☐	256 Pete McDuffe (G), Kans., (Detr.)	2.00
☐	257 Jean Hamel, Detr.	1.25
☐	258 Jacques Lemaire, Mont.	3.00
☐	259 Bob Nystrom, NYIs.	1.25
☐	260 Brad Park, Traded, NYRa.	5.00
☐	260 Brad Park, Not Traded, NYRa.	4.00
☐	261 Césare Maniago (G), Minn.	2.00
☐	262 Don Saleski, Phil.	1.25
☐	263 J. Bob Kelly, Pitt.	1.25
☐	**264 Bob Hess, SLou. RC**	**2.00**
☐	265 Blaine Stoughton, Toro.	1.25
☐	266 John Gould, Vanc.	1.25
☐	267 Checklist 3 (221 - 330)	30.00
☐	267 Checklist 4 (331 - 396), Error (should be 395)	30.00
☐	268 Dan Bouchard (G), Atla.	2.00
☐	269 Don Marcotte, Bost.	1.25
☐	270 Jim Neilson, Calg.	1.25
☐	271 Craig Ramsay, Buff.	1.25
☐	**272 Grant Mulvey, Chic. RC**	**2.00**
☐	**273 Larry Giroux, Detr. RC**	**2.00**
☐	274 Richard Lemieux, Kans. (Atla.)	1.25
☐	275 Denis Potvin, NYIs.	15.00
☐	276 Don Kozak, LosA.	1.25
☐	277 Tom Reid, Minn.	1.25
☐	278 Bob Gainey, Mont.	8.50
☐	279 Nick Beverley, NYRa.	1.25
☐	280 Jean Pronovost, Pitt.	1.25
☐	281 Joe Watson, Phil.	1.25
☐	282 Chuck Lefley, SLou.	1.25
☐	283 Börje Salming, Toro.	10.00
☐	284 Garnet Bailey, Wash.	1.25
☐	285 Gregg Boddy, Vanc.	1.25
☐	286 AS: Bobby Clarke, Phil.	7.00
☐	287 AS: Denis Potvin, NYIs.	9.00
☐	288 AS: Bobby Orr, Bost.	20.00
☐	289 AS: Rick Martin, Buff.	1.25
☐	290 AS: Guy Lafleur, Mont.	10.00
☐	291 AS: Bernie Parent (G), Phil.	3.00
☐	292 AS: Phil Esposito, Bost.	4.50
☐	293 AS: Guy Lapointe, Mont.	1.25
☐	294 AS: Börje Salming, Toro.	5.00
☐	295 AS: Steve Vickers, NYRa.	1.25
☐	296 AS: René Robert, Buff.	1.25
☐	297 AS: Rogatien Vachon (G), LosA.	2.25
☐	298 Buster Harvey, Atla. (Kans.)	1.25
☐	299 Gary Sabourin, Calg.	1.25
☐	300 Bernie Parent (G), Phil.	5.50
☐	301 Terry O'Reilly, Bost.	1.25
☐	302 Ed Westfall, NYIs.	1.25
☐	303 Pete Stemkowski, NYRa.	1.25
☐	304 Pierre Bouchard, Mont.	1.25
☐	**305 Pierre Larouche, Pitt. RC**	**7.00**
☐	**306 Lee Fogolin, Buff. RC**	**4.00**
☐	307 Gerry O'Flaherty, Vanc.	1.25
☐	308 Phil Myre (G), Atla.	2.00
☐	309 Pierre Plante, SLou.	1.25
☐	310 Dennis Hextall, Minn.	1.25
☐	311 Jim McKenny, Toro.	1.25
☐	312 Vic Venasky, LosA.	1.25
☐	313 TL: E. Vail/ T. Lysiak	2.00
☐	314 TL: P. Esposito/ B. Orr	10.00
☐	315 TL: R. Martin/ R. Robert	2.00
☐	316 TL: D. Hrechkosy/ L. Patey/ S. Weir	2.00
☐	317 TL: S. Mikita/ J. Pappin	3.00
☐	318 TL: D. Grant/ M. Dionne	2.00
☐	319 TL: S. Nolet/ W. Paiement/ G. Charron	2.00
☐	320 TL: B. Nevin/ J. Widing/ B. Berry	2.00
☐	321 TL: B. Goldsworthy/ D. Hextall	2.00
☐	322 TL: G. Lafleur/ P. Mahovlich	4.00
☐	323 TL: B. Nystrom/ D. Potvin/ C. Gilles	2.50
☐	324 TL: S. Vickers/ R. Gilbert/ J. Ratelle	2.00
☐	325 TL: R. Leach/ B. Clarke	3.00
☐	326 TL: J. Pronovost/ R. Schock	2.00
☐	327 TL: G. Unger/ L. Sacharuk	2.00
☐	328 TL: D. Sittler	3.00
☐	329 TL: D. Lever/ A. Boudrias	2.00
☐	330 TL: T. Williams/ G. Bailey/ T. Williams	2.00
☐	331 Noel Price, Atla., (Retired)	1.25
☐	332 Fred Stanfield, Buff.	1.25
☐	333 Doug Jarrett, Chic. (NYRa.)	1.25
☐	334 Gary Coalter, Kans.	1.25
☐	335 Murray Oliver, Minn., (Retired)	1.25
☐	336 Dave Fortier, NYIs.	1.25
☐	337 Terry Crisp, Phil.	1.25
☐	338 Bert Wilson, SLou.	1.25
☐	**339 John Grisdale, Vanc. RC**	**2.00**
☐	340 Ken Broderick (G), Bost.	2.00
☐	**341 Frank Spring, Calg. RC**	**2.00**
☐	**342 Mike Korney, Detr. RC**	**2.00**
☐	343 Gene Carr, LosA.	1.25
☐	344 Don Awrey, Mont.	1.25
☐	345 Pat Hickey, NYRa.	1.25
☐	**346 Colin Campbell, Pitt. RC**	**6.00**
☐	347 Wayne Thomas (G), Toro.	2.00
☐	**348 Bob Gryp, Wash. RC**	**2.00**
☐	349 Bill Flett, Atla.	1.25
☐	350 Roger Crozier (G), Buff.	2.00
☐	351 Dale Tallon, Chic.	1.25
☐	352 Larry Johnston, Kans.	1.25
☐	**353 John Flesch, Minn. RC**	**2.00**
☐	354 Lorne Henning, NYIs.	1.25
☐	355 Wayne Stephenson (G), Phil.	2.00
☐	356 Rick Wilson, SLou.	1.25
☐	357 Garry Monahan, Vanc.	1.25
☐	358 Gary Doak, Bost.	1.25
☐	359 Pierre Jarry, Detr.	1.25
☐	359 Pierre Jarry, Detr. (Minn.)	1.25
☐	**360 George Pesut, Calg. RC**	**2.00**
☐	361 Mike Corrigan, LosA.	1.25
☐	362 Michel Larocque (G), Mont.	2.00
☐	363 Wayne Dillon, NYRa.	1.25
☐	364 Pete Laframboise, Pitt.	1.25
☐	365 Brian Glennie, Toro.	1.25
☐	366 Mike Christie, Calg.	1.25
☐	**367 Jean Lemieux, Atla. RC**	**2.00**
☐	368 Gary Bromley (G), Buff.	2.00
☐	369 J.P. Bordeleau, Chic.	1.25
☐	**370 Ed Gilbert, Kans. RC**	**2.00**
☐	371 Chris Ahrens, Minn.	1.25
☐	372 Billy Smith (G), NYIs.	9.00
☐	**373 Larry Goodenough, Phil. RC**	**2.00**
☐	374 Leon Rochefort, Vanc.	1.25
☐	**375 Doug Gibson, Bost. RC**	**2.00**
☐	376 Mike Bloom, Detr.	1.25
☐	377 Larry Brown, LosA.	1.25
☐	378 Jim Roberts, Mont.	1.25
☐	379 Gilles Villemure (G), NYRa. (Chic.)	2.00
☐	**380 Dennis Owchar, Pitt. RC**	**2.00**
☐	381 Doug Favell (G), Toro.	2.00
☐	382 Stan Gilbertson, Wash., Err. (Denis Dupère)	1.25
☐	**383 Ed Kea, Atla. RC**	**4.00**
☐	384 Brian Spencer, Buff.	1.25
☐	**385 Mike Veisor (G), Chic. RC**	**2.00**
☐	386 Bob Murray, Vanc.	1.25
☐	**387 André St. Laurent, NYIs. RC**	**2.00**
☐	**388 Rick Chartraw, Mont. RC**	**3.00**
☐	389 Orest Kindrachuk, Phil.	1.25
☐	**390 Dave Hutchison, LosA. RC**	**2.00**
☐	391 Glenn Goldup, Mont.	1.25
☐	**392 Jerry Holland, NYRa. RC**	**2.00**
☐	**393 Peter Sturgeon, Bost. RC**	**2.00**
☐	**394 Alain Daigle, Chic. RC**	**2.00**
☐	**396 Harold Snepsts, Vanc. RC**	**25.00**

1975 - 76 O-PEE-CHEE WHA

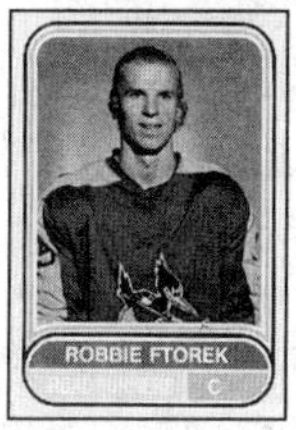

These cards measure the standard 2 1/2" x 3 1/2".

Complete Set (132 cards):		**550.00**
Common Player:		**4.50**
O-Pee-Chee		**NM-MT**
☐	1 Bobby Hull, Winnipeg	80.00
☐	2 Dale Hoganson (G), Québec	4.50
☐	3 Serge Aubry, Cincinnati RC, Err. (Aubrey)	4.50
☐	4 Ron Chipperfield, Calgary	4.50
☐	5 Paul Shmyr, Cleveland	4.50
☐	**6 Perry Miller, Winnipeg RC**	**6.00**
☐	**7 Mark Howe, Houston RC**	**50.00**
☐	**8 Mike Rogers, Edmonton RC**	**8.00**
☐	9 Byron Baltimore, Ottawa RC, Err. (Bryon)	4.50
☐	10 André Lacroix, San Diego	6.00
☐	11 Nick Harbaruk, Indianapolis	4.50
☐	**12 John Garrett (G), Minnesota RC**	**15.00**
☐	**13 Lou Nistico, Toronto RC**	**6.00**
☐	14 Rick Ley, New England	4.50
☐	**15 Veli-Pekka Ketola, Winnipeg RC**	**10.00**
☐	16 Réal Cloutier, Québec	4.50
☐	**17 Pierre Guite, Cincinnati RC**	**6.00**
☐	18 Duane Rupp, Calgary	4.50
☐	**19 Robbie Ftorek, Phoenix RC**	**20.00**
☐	20 Gerry Cheevers (G), Cleveland	20.00
☐	**21 John Schella, Houston RC**	**6.00**
☐	22 Bruce MacGregor, Edmonton	4.50
☐	23 Ralph Backstrom, Ottawa	4.50
☐	24 Gene Peacosh, San Diego	4.50
☐	**25 Pierre Roy, Québec RC**	**6.00**
☐	26 Mike Walton, Minnesota	4.50
☐	27 Vaclav Nedomansky, Toronto	4.50
☐	**28 Christer Abrahamsson (G), New England RC**	**6.00**
☐	29 Thommie Bergman, Winnipeg	4.50
☐	30 Marc Tardif, Québec	6.00
☐	31 Bryan Campbell, Cincinnati	4.50
☐	32 Don McLeod (G), Calgary	6.00
☐	33 Al McDonough, Cleveland	4.50
☐	34 Jacques Plante (G), Edmonton	55.00
☐	**35 André Hinse, Houston RC**	**6.00**
☐	36 Eddie Joyal, Edmonton	4.50
☐	**37 Ken Baird, Edmonton RC**	**6.00**
☐	38 Wayne Rivers, San Diego	4.50
☐	39 Ron Buchanan, Indianapolis	4.50
☐	40 Anders Hedberg, Winnipeg	6.00
☐	41 Rick Smith, Minnesota	4.50
☐	42 Paul Henderson, Toronto	6.00
☐	43 Wayne Carleton, New England	4.50
☐	**44 Richard Brodeur (G), Québec RC**	**20.00**
☐	**45 John Hughes, Cincinnati RC**	**6.00**
☐	**46 Larry Israelson, Calgary RC**	**6.00**
☐	47 Jim Harrison, Cleveland	4.50
☐	**48 Cam Connor, Phoenix RC**	**6.00**
☐	49 Al Hamilton, Edmonton	4.50
☐	**50 Ron Grahame (G), Houston RC**	**8.00**
☐	**51 Frank Rochon, Ottawa RC**	**6.00**
☐	52 Ron Climie, New England	4.50
☐	**53 Murray Heatley, Indianapolis RC**	**6.00**
☐	54 John Arbour, Ottawa	4.50
☐	**55 Jim Shaw, Toronto (G) RC**	**6.00**
☐	**56 Larry Pleau, New England RC**	**10.00**
☐	57 Ted Green, Winnipeg	4.50
☐	58 Rick Dudley, Cincinnati	4.50
☐	59 Butch Deadmarsh, Calgary	4.50
☐	60 Serge Bernier, Québec	4.50
☐	61 AS: Ron Grahame (G), Houston	6.00
☐	62 AS: J. C. Tremblay, Québec	6.00
☐	63 AS: Kevin Morrison, San Diego	4.50
☐	64 AS: André Lacroix, San Diego	4.50
☐	65 AS: Bobby Hull, Winnipeg	25.00
☐	66 AS: Gordie Howe, Houston	35.00
☐	67 AS: Gerry Cheevers (G), Cleveland	10.00
☐	68 AS: Poul Popiel, Houston	4.50
☐	69 AS: Barry Long, Edmonton	4.50
☐	70 AS: Serge Bernier, Québec	4.50
☐	71 AS: Marc Tardif, Québec	6.00
☐	72 AS: Anders Hedberg, Winnipeg	6.00
☐	73 Ron Ward, Cleveland	4.50
☐	**74 Michel Cormier, Phoenix RC**	**6.00**
☐	**75 Marty Howe, Houston RC**	**8.00**
☐	76 Rusty Patenaude, Edmonton	4.50
☐	77 John McKenzie, Minnesota	4.50
☐	**78 Mark Napier, Toronto RC**	**6.00**
☐	79 Henry Boucha, Minnesota	4.50
☐	**80 Kevin Morrison, San Diego RC**	**6.00**
☐	81 Tom Simpson, Toronto	4.50
☐	**82 Brad Selwood, New England RC**	**6.00**
☐	83 Ulf Nilsson, Winnipeg	6.00
☐	84 Réjean Houle, Québec	6.00
☐	85 Normand Lapointe, Clev. RC, Err. (LaPoint)	4.50
☐	86 Danny Lawson, Calgary	4.50
☐	87 Gary Jarrett, Clev., Err. (Garry)	4.50
☐	**88 Al McLeod, Phoenix RC**	**6.00**
☐	89 Gord Labossierre, Houston, Err. (Labossiere)	4.50
☐	90 Barry Long, Edmonton	4.50
☐	**91 Rick Morris, Ottawa RC**	**6.00**
☐	92 Norm Ferguson, San Diego	4.50
☐	93 Bob Whitlock, Indianapolis	4.50
☐	94 Jim Dorey, Toronto	4.50
☐	95 Tom Webster, New England	4.50
☐	**96 Gordie Gallant, Québec RC**	**6.00**
☐	97 Dave Keon, Minnesota	10.00
☐	**98 Ron Plumb, Cincinnati RC**	**6.00**
☐	**99 Rick Jodzio, Calgary RC**	**6.00**
☐	100 Gordie Howe, Houston	75.00
☐	101 Joe Daley (G), Winnipeg	6.00
☐	**102 Wayne Muloin, Cleveland RC**	**6.00**
☐	**103 Gavin Kirk, Toronto RC**	**6.00**
☐	104 Dave Dryden (G), Edmonton	6.00
☐	**105 Bob Liddington, Ottawa RC**	**6.00**
☐	106 Rosaire Paiement, New England	4.50
☐	**107 John Sheridan, Indianapolis RC**	**6.00**
☐	**108 Nick Fotiu, New England RC**	**10.00**
☐	109 Lars-Erik Sjoberg, Winnipeg, Err. (Sjoverg)	4.50
☐	110 Frank Mahovlich, Toronto	15.00
☐	111 Mike Antonovich, Minnesota	4.50
☐	112 Paul Terbenche, Calgary	4.50
☐	**113 Rich LeDuc, Cleveland RC**	**6.00**
☐	114 Jack Norris (G), Phoenix	6.00
☐	115 Dennis Sobchuk, Cincinnati	4.50
☐	116 Chris Bordeleau, Québec	4.50
☐	117 Doug Barrie, Edmonton	4.50
☐	**118 Hugh Harris, Calgary RC**	**6.00**
☐	**119 Cam Newton (G), Ottawa RC**	**6.00**
☐	120 Poul Popiel, Houston	4.50
☐	121 Fran Huck, Minnesota	4.50
☐	122 Tony Featherstone, Toronto	4.50
☐	123 Bob Woytowich, Indianapolis	4.50
☐	124 Claude St. Sauveur, Calgary, (Atla.)	4.50
☐	125 Heikki Riihiranta, Winnipeg	4.50
☐	126 Gary Kurt (G), Phoenix	6.00
☐	**127 Thommy Abrahamsson, New England RC**	**6.00**
☐	**128 Danny Gruen, Cleveland RC**	**6.00**
☐	**129 Jacques Locas, Cincinnati RC**	**6.00**
☐	130 J.C. Tremblay, Québec	6.00
☐	131 Checklist (1 - 132)	50.00
☐	132 Ernie Wakely (G), San Diego	10.00

1975 - 76 POPSICLE

Complete Set (18 cards): **35.00**
Common Team: **3.00**

☐	Atlanta Flames	☐	Boston Bruins
☐	Buffalo Sabres	☐	California Seals
☐	Chicago Blackhawks	☐	Detroit Red Wings
☐	Kansas City Scouts	☐	Los Angeles Kings
☐	Minn. North Stars	☐	Montréal Canadiens
☐	New York Islanders	☐	New York Rangers
☐	Philadelphia Flyers	☐	Pittsburgh Penguins
☐	St. Louis Blues	☐	Toronto Maple Leafs
☐	Vancouver Canucks	☐	Washington Capitals

1975 - 76 TOPPS

These cards measure the standard 2 1/2" x 3 1/2".

Complete Set (330 cards): **200.00**
Common Player: **.50**
Topps **NM-MT**

☐	1 Playoffs: Philadelphia vs. Buffalo	2.25
☐	2 Playoffs: Philadelphia vs. NY Islanders	1.00
☐	3 Playoffs: Buffalo vs. Montréal	1.00
☐	4 Playoffs: NY Islanders vs. Pittsburgh	1.00
☐	5 Playoffs: Montréal vs. Vancouver	1.00
☐	6 Playoffs: Buffalo vs. Chicago	1.00
☐	7 Playoffs: Philadelphia vs. Toronto	1.00
☐	8 Curt Bennett, Atla.	.50
☐	9 John Bucyk, Bost.	1.75
☐	10 Gilbert Perreault, Buff.	4.25
☐	11 Darryl Edestrand, Bost.	.50
☐	12 Ivan Boldirev, Chic.	.50
☐	13 Nick Libett, Detr.	.50
☐	**14 Jim McElmury, Kans. RC**	**1.00**
☐	15 Frank St. Marseille, LosA.	.50
☐	16 Blake Dunlop, Minn.	.50
☐	17 Yvon Lambert, Mont.	.50
☐	18 Gerry Hart, NYIs.	.50
☐	19 Steve Vickers, NYRa.	.50
☐	20 Rick MacLeish, Phil.	.50
☐	21 Bob Paradise, Pitt.	.50
☐	22 Red Berenson, SLou.	.50
☐	23 Lanny McDonald, Toro.	7.00
☐	24 Mike Robitaille, Vanc.	.50
☐	25 Ron Low (G), Wash.	1.00
☐	26 Bryan Hextall, Detr.	.50
☐	27 Carol Vadnais, Bost.	.50
☐	28 Jim Lorentz, Buff.	.50
☐	29 Gary Simmons (G), Calg.	1.00
☐	30 Stan Mikita, Chic.	4.25
☐	31 Bryan Watson, Detr.	.50
☐	32 Guy Charron, Kans.	.50
☐	33 Bob J. Murdoch, LosA.	.50
☐	34 Norm Gratton, Minn.	.50
☐	35 Ken Dryden (G), Mont.	20.00
☐	36 Jean Potvin, NYIs.	.50
☐	37 Rick Middleton, NYRa.	3.25
☐	38 Ed Van Impe, Phil.	.50
☐	39 Rick Kehoe, Pitt.	.50
☐	40 Garry Unger, SLou.	.50
☐	41 Ian Turnbull, Toro.	.50
☐	42 Dennis Ververgaert, Vanc.	.50
☐	**43 Mike Marson, Wash. RC**	**1.00**
☐	44 Randy Manery, Atla.	.50
☐	45 Gilles Gilbert (G), Bost.	1.00
☐	46 René Robert, Buff.	.50
☐	47 Bob Stewart, Calg.	.50
☐	48 Pit Martin, Chic.	.50
☐	49 Danny Grant, Detr.	.50
☐	50 Pete Mahovlich, Mont.	.50
☐	**51 Dennis Patterson, Kans. RC**	**1.00**
☐	52 Mike Murphy, LosA.	.50
☐	53 Dennis O'Brien, Minn.	.50
☐	54 Garry Howatt, NYIs.	.50
☐	55 Ed Giacomin (G), NYRa.	1.75
☐	56 André Dupont, Phil.	.50
☐	57 Chuck Arnason, Pitt.	.50
☐	**58 Bob Gassoff, SLou. RC**	**1.00**
☐	59 Ron Ellis, Toro.	.50
☐	60 André Boudrias, Vanc.	.50
☐	61 Yvon Labre, Wash.	.50
☐	62 Hilliard Graves, Atla.	.50
☐	63 Wayne Cashman, Bost.	.50
☐	**64 Danny Gare, Buff. RC**	**2.50**
☐	65 Rick Hampton, Calg.	.50
☐	66 Darcy Rota, Chic.	.50
☐	67 Bill Hogaboam, Detr.	.50
☐	68 Denis Herron (G), Kans.	1.00
☐	69 Sheldon Kannegiesser, LosA.	.50
☐	70 Yvan Cournoyer, Mont., Err. (Yvon)	2.25
☐	71 Ernie Hicke, Minn.	.50
☐	72 Bert Marshall, NYIs.	.50
☐	73 Derek Sanderson, NYRa.	2.75
☐	74 Tom Bladon, Phil.	.50
☐	75 Ron Schock, Pitt.	.50
☐	**76 Larry Sacharuk, SLou. RC**	**1.00**
☐	77 George Ferguson, Toro.	.50
☐	78 Ab DeMarco, Vanc.	.50
☐	79 Tom Williams, Wash.	.50
☐	80 Phil Roberto, Detr.	.50
☐	81 Boston Bruins	3.00
☐	82 California Golden Seals	3.00
☐	83 Buffalo Sabres	3.00
☐	84 Chicago Blackhawks	3.00
☐	85 Atlanta Flames	3.00
☐	86 Los Angeles Kings	3.00
☐	87 Detroit Red Wings	3.00
☐	88 Kansas City Scouts, Error	3.00
☐	89 Minnesota North Stars	3.00
☐	90 Montréal Canadiens	3.00
☐	91 Toronto Maple Leafs	3.00
☐	92 New York Islanders	3.00
☐	93 Pittsburgh Penguins	3.00
☐	94 New York Rangers	3.00
☐	95 Philadelphia Flyers	3.00
☐	96 St. Louis Blues	3.00
☐	97 Vancouver Canucks	3.00
☐	98 Washington Capitals	3.00
☐	99 Checklist 1 (1 - 110)	15.00
☐	100 Bobby Orr, Bost.	30.00
☐	101 Germaine Gagnon, Chic., Err. (Germain)	.50
☐	102 Phil Russell, Chic.	.50
☐	103 Bill Lochead, Detr.	.50
☐	**104 Robin Burns, Kans. RC**	**1.00**
☐	105 Gary Edwards (G), LosA.	1.00
☐	106 Dwight Bialowas, Minn.	.50
☐	107 Doug Risebrough, Mont., Err. (Bob Gainey)	2.50
☐	108 Dave Lewis, NYIs.	.75
☐	109 Bill Fairbairn, NYRa.	.50
☐	110 Ross Lonsberry, Phil.	.50
☐	111 Ron Stackhouse. Pitt.	.50
☐	112 Claude Larose, SLou.	.50
☐	113 Don Luce, Buff.	.50
☐	**114 Errol Thompson, Toro. RC**	**1.00**
☐	115 Gary Smith (G), Vanc.	1.00
☐	116 Jack Lynch, Wash.	.50
☐	117 Jacques Richard, Atla.	.50
☐	118 Dallas Smith, Bost.	.50
☐	119 Dave Gardner, Calg.	.50
☐	120 Mickey Redmond, Detr.	1.25
☐	121 John Marks, Chic.	.50
☐	122 Dave Hudson, Kans.	.50
☐	123 Bob Nevin, LosA.	.50
☐	124 Fred Barrett, Minn.	.50
☐	125 Gerry Desjardins (G), Buff.	1.00
☐	126 Guy Lafleur, Mont., Err. (defence)	15.00
☐	127 J.P. Parise, NYIs.	.50
☐	128 Walt Tkaczuk, NYRa.	.50
☐	129 Gary Dornhoefer, Phil.	.50
☐	130 Syl Apps, Pitt.	.50
☐	131 Bob Plager, SLou.	.50
☐	132 Stan Weir, Toro.	.50
☐	133 Tracy Pratt, Vanc.	.50
☐	134 Jack Egers, Wash.	.50
☐	135 Eric Vail, Atla.	.50
☐	136 Al Sims, Bost.	.50
☐	**137 Larry Patey, Calg. RC**	**1.00**
☐	138 Jim Schoenfeld, Buff.	.50
☐	139 Cliff Koroll, Chic.	.50
☐	140 Marcel Dionne, LosA.	7.00
☐	141 Jean-Guy Lagacé, Kans.	.50
☐	142 Juha Widing, LosA.	.50
☐	143 Lou Nanne, Minn.	.50
☐	144 Serge Savard, Mont.	1.25
☐	145 Glenn Resch (G), NYIs.	3.25
☐	**146 Ronald Greschner, NYRa. RC**	**2.25**
☐	147 Dave Schultz, Phil.	.50
☐	148 Barry Wilkins, Pitt.	.50
☐	149 Floyd Thomson, SLou.	.50
☐	150 Darryl Sittler, Toro.	5.00
☐	151 Paulin Bordeleau, Vanc.	.50
☐	**152 Ron Lalonde, Wash. RC**	**1.00**
☐	153 Larry Romanchych, Atla.	.50
☐	154 Larry Carrière, Buff.	.50
☐	155 André Savard, Bost.	.50
☐	**156 Dave Hrechkosy, Calg. RC**	**1.00**
☐	157 Bill White, Chic.	.50
☐	158 Dave Kryskow, Atla.	.50
☐	159 Denis Dupere, Kans.	.50
☐	160 Rogatien Vachon (G), LosA.	2.50
☐	161 Doug Rombough, Minn.	.50
☐	162 Murray Wilson, Mont.	.50
☐	**163 Bob Bourne, NYIs. RC**	**1.50**
☐	164 Gilles Marotte, NYRa.	.50
☐	165 Vic Hadfield, Pitt.	.50
☐	166 Reggie Leach, Phil.	.50
☐	167 Jerry Butler, SLou.	.50
☐	168 Inge Hammarstrom, Toro.	.50
☐	169 Chris Oddleifson, Vanc.	.50
☐	170 Greg Joly, Wash.	.50
☐	171 Checklist 2 (111 - 220)	15.00
☐	172 Pat Quinn, Atla.	.50
☐	173 Dave Forbes, Bost.	.50
☐	174 Len Frig, Calg.	.50
☐	175 Rick Martin, Buff.	.50
☐	176 Keith Magnuson, Chic.	.50
☐	177 Dan Maloney, Detr.	.50
☐	178 Craig Patrick, Kans.	1.00
☐	179 Tommy Williams, LosA.	.50
☐	180 Bill Goldsworthy, Minn.	.50
☐	181 Steve Shutt, Mont.	4.25
☐	182 Ralph Stewart, NYIs.	.50
☐	183 John Davidson (G), NYRa.	3.50
☐	184 Bob Kelly, Phil.	.50
☐	185 Ed Johnston (G), SLou.	1.00
☐	186 Dave Burrows, Pitt.	.50
☐	187 Dave Dunn, Toro.	.50
☐	188 Dennis Kearns, Vanc.	.50
☐	189 Bill Clement, Wash.	2.00
☐	190 Gilles Meloche (G), Calg.	1.00
☐	191 Bobby Leiter, Atla.	.50
☐	192 Jerry Korab, Buff.	.50
☐	193 Dave Johnston, Chic.	.50
☐	194 Walt McKechnie, Detr.	.50
☐	195 Wilf Paiement, Kans.	.50
☐	196 Bob Berry, LosA.	.50
☐	**197 Dean Talafous, Minn. RC**	**1.00**
☐	198 Guy Lapointe, Mont.	1.25
☐	**199 Clark Gillies, NYIs. RC**	**7.50**
☐	200 Phil Esposito, Bost.	4.25
☐	201 Greg Polis, NYRa.	.50
☐	202 Jimmy Watson, Phil.	.50
☐	**203 Gord McRae (G), Toro. RC**	**1.00**
☐	204 Lowell MacDonald, Pitt.	.50
☐	205 Barclay Plager, SLou.	.50
☐	206 Don Lever, Vanc.	.50
☐	207 Bill Mikkelson, Wash.	.50
☐	208 LL: P. Esposito/ G. Lafleur/ R. Martin	4.25
☐	209 LL: B. Orr/ B. Clarke/ P. Mahovlich	5.50
☐	210 LL: B. Orr/ P. Esposito/ M. Dionne	7.50
☐	211 LL: D. Schultz/ A. Dupont/ P. Russel	1.00
☐	212 LL: P. Esposito/ R. Martin/ D. Grant	2.25
☐	213 LL: B. Parent/ R. Vachon/ K. Dryden	7.50
☐	214 Barry Gibbs, Alt.	.50
☐	215 Ken Hodge, Bost.	.50
☐	216 Jocelyn Guevremont, Buff.	.50
☐	**217 Warren Williams, Calg. RC**	**1.00**
☐	218 Dick Redmond, Chic.	.50
☐	219 Jim Rutherford (G), Detr.	1.00
☐	220 Simon Nolet, Kans.	.50
☐	221 Butch Goring, LosA.	.50
☐	222 Glen Sather, Minn.	1.25
☐	**223 Mario Tremblay, Mont. RC**	**4.00**
☐	224 Jude Drouin, NYIs.	.50
☐	225 Rod Gilbert, NYRa.	1.75
☐	226 Bill Barber, Phil.	3.75
☐	**227 Gary Inness (G), Pitt. RC**	**1.00**
☐	228 Wayne Merrick, SLou.	.50
☐	229 Rod Seiling, Toro.	.50
☐	230 Tom Lysiak, Atla.	.50
☐	231 Bob Dailey, Vanc.	.50
☐	232 Michel Belhumeur (G), Wash.	1.00
☐	**233 Bill Hajt, Buff. RC**	**1.00**
☐	234 Jim Pappin, Calg.	.50
☐	235 Gregg Sheppard, Bost.	.50
☐	236 Gary Bergman, Detr.	.50
☐	237 Randy Rota, Kans.	.50
☐	238 Neil Komadoski, LosA.	.50
☐	239 Craig Cameron, Minn.	.50
☐	240 Tony Esposito (G), Chic.	4.50
☐	241 Larry Robinson, Mont.	8.50
☐	242 Billy Harris, NYIs.	.50
☐	243 Jean Ratelle, NYRa.	1.75
☐	244 Ted Irvine, SLou., Err. (Ted Harris)	.50
☐	245 Bob Neely, Toro.	.50
☐	246 Bobby Lalonde, Vanc.	.50
☐	**247 Ron Jones, Wash. RC**	**1.00**
☐	248 Rey Comeau, Atla.	.50
☐	249 Michel Plasse (G), Pitt.	1.00
☐	250 Bobby Clarke, Phil.	7.50
☐	251 Bobby Schmautz, Bost.	.50
☐	**252 Peter McNab, Buff. RC**	**2.50**
☐	253 Al MacAdam, Calg.	.50
☐	254 Dennis Hull, Chic.	.50
☐	255 Terry Harper, Detr.	.50
☐	256 Peter McDuffe (G), Kans.	1.00
☐	257 Jean Hamel, Detr.	.50
☐	258 Jacques Lemaire, Mont.	1.75
☐	259 Bob Nystrom, NYIs.	.50
☐	260 Brad Park, NYRa.	2.50
☐	261 Césare Maniago (G), Minn.	1.00
☐	262 Don Saleski, Phil.	.50
☐	263 J. Bob Kelly, Pitt.	.50
☐	**264 Bob Hess, SLou. RC**	**1.00**
☐	265 Blaine Stoughton, Toro.	.50
☐	266 John Gould, Vanc.	.50
☐	267 Checklist 3 (221 - 330)	15.00
☐	268 Dan Bouchard (G), Atla.	1.00
☐	269 Don Marcotte, Bost.	.50
☐	270 Jim Neilson, Calg.	.50
☐	271 Craig Ramsay, Buff.	.50
☐	**272 Grant Mulvey, Chic. RC**	**1.00**
☐	**273 Larry Giroux, Detr. RC**	**1.00**
☐	274 Richard Lemieux, Kans.	.50
☐	275 Denis Potvin, NYIs.	10.00
☐	276 Don Kozak, LosA.	.50
☐	277 Tom Reid, Minn.	.50
☐	278 Bob Gainey, Mont.	5.00
☐	279 Nick Beverley, NYRa.	.50
☐	280 Jean Pronovost, Pitt.	.50
☐	281 Joe Watson, Phil.	.50
☐	282 Chuck Lefley, SLou.	.50
☐	283 Börje Salming, Toro.	6.00
☐	284 Garnet Bailey, Wash.	.50
☐	285 Gregg Boddy, Vanc.	.50
☐	286 AS: Bobby Clarke, Phil.	4.50
☐	287 AS: Denis Potvin, NYIs.	5.00
☐	288 AS: Bobby Orr, Bost.	15.00
☐	289 AS: Rick Martin, Buff.	1.00
☐	290 AS: Guy Lafleur, Mont.	7.00
☐	291 AS: Bernie Parent (G), Phil.	2.00
☐	292 AS: Phil Esposito, Bost.	2.50
☐	293 AS: Guy Lapointe, Mont.	1.00
☐	294 AS: Börje Salming, Toro.	3.00
☐	295 AS: Steve Vickers, NYRa.	.50
☐	296 AS: René Robert, Buff.	.50
☐	297 AS: Rogatien Vachon (G), LosA.	1.50
☐	298 Buster Harvey, Atla.	.50
☐	299 Gary Sabourin, Calg.	.50
☐	300 Bernie Parent (G), Phil.	3.25
☐	301 Terry O'Reilly, Bost.	.50
☐	302 Ed Westfall, NYIs.	.50
☐	303 Pete Stemkowski, NYRa.	.50
☐	304 Pierre Bouchard, Mont.	.50
☐	**305 Pierre Larouche, Pitt. RC**	**4.25**
☐	**306 Lee Fogolin, Buff. RC**	**1.00**
☐	307 Gerry O'Flaherty, Vanc.	.50
☐	308 Phil Myre (G), Atla.	1.00
☐	309 Pierre Plante, SLou.	.50
☐	310 Dennis Hextall, Minn.	.50
☐	311 Jim McKenny, Toro.	.50
☐	312 Vic Venasky, LosA.	.50
☐	313 TL: E. Vail/ T. Lysiak	1.00
☐	314 TL: P. Esposito/ B. Orr	7.50
☐	315 TL: R. Martin/ R. Robert	1.00
☐	316 TL: D. Hrechkosy/ L. Patey/ S. Weir	1.00
☐	317 TL: S. Mikita/ J. Pappin	1.50
☐	318 TL: D. Grant/ M. Dionne	1.50
☐	319 TL: S. Nolet/ W. Paiement/ G. Charron	1.00
☐	320 TL: B. Nevin/ J. Widing/ B. Berry	1.00
☐	321 TL: B. Goldsworthy/ D. Hextall	1.00
☐	322 TL: G. Lafleur/ P. Mahovlich	2.25
☐	323 TL: B. Nystrom/ D. Potvin/ C. Gilles	2.00
☐	324 TL: R. Gilbert/ J. Ratelle/ S. Vickers	1.75
☐	325 TL: R. Leach/ B. Clarke	2.00
☐	326 TL: J. Pronovost/ R. Schock	1.00
☐	327 TL: G. Unger/ Sacharuk	1.00
☐	328 TL: D. Sittler	2.00
☐	329 TL: D. Lever/ A. Boudrias	1.00
☐	330 TL: T. Williams/ G. Bailey	1.00

1976 - 77 DERNIÈRE PHOTOS

This multi-sport series of photos were inserted in Dernière magazine from 1972 through 1984. Three holes were punched on the left side to allow for storage in a binder. The series featured Montréal Canadiens players. These photos measure 8" x 10".

Dernière		NM
☐	13MAR Réal Cloutier	3.00
☐	20MAR Rogatien Vachon (G)	7.00
☐	27MAR Bernie Parent (G)	12.00
☐	3APR Réal Cloutier	3.00
☐	10APR J.C. Tremblay	5.00
☐	17APR Serge Bernier	3.00
☐	24APR Denis Potvin	8.00

1976 - 77 HOCKEY DIGEST BLOW-IN

These blow-in cards highlighted subscription offers for the hockey publication *Hockey Digest*. Othe blow-in cards exist.

Hockey Digest		NM
☐	Dec. 76 • J7H1 Bobby Orr (Nov. 76 cover) / red	
☐	Jan. 77 • J9H2 Phil Esposito (Dec. 76 cover) / red	
☐	Feb. 77 • J9H2 Phil Esposito (Dec. 76 cover) / green	
☐	May 77 • JCH1 Steve Shutt (Apr. 77 cover) / orange	

1976 - 77 O-PEE-CHEE

These cards measure the standard 2 1/2" x 3 1/2".

Complete Set (50 cards): **1,900**
Common Player: **5.00**

O-Pee-Chee		NM-MT
☐	1 LL: R. Leach/ G. Lafleur/ P. Larouche	4.50
☐	2 LL: B. Clarke/ P. Mahovlich/ G. Lafleur/ G. Perreault/ J. Ratelle	4.00
☐	3 LL: G. Lafleur/ B. Clarke/ G. Perrault	4.00
☐	4 LL: S. Durbano/ B. Watson/ D. Schultz	1.25
☐	5 LL: P. Esposito/ G. Lafleur/ R. Martin/ P. Larouche/ D. Potvin	4.00
☐	6 LL: K. Dryden (G)/ G. Resch (G)/ M. Larocque (G)	5.00

☐ 7 Gary Doak, Bost. .75
☐ 8 Jacques Richard, Buff. .75
☐ 9 Wayne Dillon, NYRa. .75
☐ 10 Bernie Parent (G), Phil. 3.50
☐ 11 Ed Westfall, NYIs. .75
☐ 12 Dick Redmond, Chic. .75
☐ 13 Bryan Hextall, Minn. .75
☐ 14 Jean Pronovost, Pitt. .75
☐ 15 Pete Mahovlich, Mont. 1.25
☐ 16 Danny Grant, Detr. .75
☐ 17 Phil Myre (G), Atla. 1.50
☐ 18 Wayne Merrick, Clev. .75
☐ 19 Steve Durbano, Colo. .75
☐ 20 Derek Sanderson, SLou. 3.00
☐ 21 Mike Murphy, LosA. .75
☐ 22 AS: Börje Salming, Toro. 4.50
☐ 23 Mike Walton, Vanc. .75
☐ 24 Randy Manery, Atla. .75
☐ 25 Ken Hodge, NYRa. .75
☐ **26 Mel Bridgman, Phil. RC 3.00**
☐ 27 Jerry Korab, Buff. .75
☐ 28 Gilles Gratton (G), NYRa. 1.50
☐ 29 André St. Laurent, NYIs. .75
☐ 30 Yvan Cournoyer, Mont. 3.50
☐ 31 Phil Russell, Chic. .75
☐ 32 Dennis Hextall, Detr. .75
☐ 33 Lowell MacDonald, Pitt. .75
☐ 34 Dennis O'Brien, Minn. .75
☐ 35 Gerry Meehan, Wash. .75
☐ 36 Gilles Meloche (G), Calg. (Clev.) 1.50
☐ 37 Wilf Paiement, Kans. (Colo.) .75
☐ **38 Bob MacMillan, SLou. RC 1.25**
☐ 39 Ian Turnbull, Toro. .75
☐ 40 Rogatien Vachon (G), LosA. 2.00
☐ 41 Nick Beverley, NYRa. .75
☐ 42 René Robert, Buff. .75
☐ 43 André Savard, Buff. .75
☐ 44 Bob Gainey, Mont. 5.00
☐ 45 Joe Watson, Phil. .75
☐ 46 Billy Smith (G), NYIs. 6.00
☐ 47 Darcy Rota, Chic. .75
☐ **48 Rick Lapointe, Detr. RC 1.25**
☐ 49 Pierre Jarry, Minn. .75
☐ 50 Syl Apps, Pitt. .75
☐ 51 Eric Vail, Atla. .75
☐ 52 Greg Joly, Wash. .75
☐ 53 Don Lever, Vanc. .75
☐ **54 Bob L. Murdoch, Calg. (Clev.) RC 1.25**
☐ 55 Denis Herron (G), Kans. (Pitt.) 1.50
☐ 56 Mike Bloom, Detr. .75
☐ 57 Bill Fairbairn, NYRa. .75
☐ 58 Fred Stanfield, Buff. .75
☐ 59 Steve Shutt, Mont. 3.50
☐ 60 AS: Brad Park, Bost. 3.50
☐ 61 Gilles Villemure (G), Chic. 1.50
☐ 62 Bert Marshall, NYIs. .75
☐ 63 Chuck Lefley, SLou. .75
☐ 64 Simon Nolet, Colo. .75
☐ 65 RB: Reggie Leach, Phil. 1.50
☐ 66 RB: Darryl Sittler, Toro. 2.00
☐ 67 RB: Bryan Trottier, NYIs. 8.00
☐ 68 RB: Garry Unger, SLou. 1.50
☐ 69 Ron Low (G), Wash. 1.50
☐ 70 AS: Bobby Clarke, Phil. 7.00
☐ **71 Michel Bergeron, Detr. RC 1.50**
☐ 72 Ron Stackhouse, Pitt. .75
☐ 73 Bill Hogaboam, Minn. .75
☐ 74 Bob J. Murdoch, LosA. .75
☐ 75 Steve Vickers, NYRa. .75
☐ 76 Pit Martin, Chic. .75
☐ 77 Gerry Hart, NYIs. .75
☐ 78 Craig Ramsay, Buff. 1.25
☐ 79 Michel Larocque (G), Mont. 1.50
☐ 80 Jean Ratelle, Bost. 2.00
☐ 81 Don Saleski, Phil. .75
☐ 82 Bill Clement, Atla. .75
☐ 83 Dave Burrows, Pitt. .75
☐ 84 Wayne Thomas (G), Toro. 1.50
☐ 85 John Gould, Vanc. .75
☐ **86 Dennis Maruk, Calg. (Clev.) RC 4.00**
☐ 87 Ernie Hicke, Minn. .75
☐ 88 Jim Rutherford (G), Detr. 1.50
☐ 89 Dale Tallon, Chic. .75
☐ 90 Rod Gilbert, NYRa. 2.00
☐ 91 Marcel Dionne, LosA. 7.00
☐ 92 Chuck Arnason, Colo. .75
☐ 93 Jean Potvin, NYIs. .75
☐ 94 Don Luce, Buff. .75
☐ 95 John Bucyk, Bost. 2.00
☐ 96 Larry Goodenough, Phil. .75
☐ 97 Mario Tremblay, Mont. 2.00
☐ **98 Nelson Pyatt, Wash. (Colo.) RC 1.25**
☐ 99 Brian Glennie, Toro. .75
☐ 100 Tony Esposito (G), Chic. 5.00
☐ 101 Dan Maloney, Detr. .75
☐ 102 Dunc Wilson (G), Pitt. 1.50
☐ 103 Dean Talafous, Minn. .75
☐ **104 Ed Staniowski (G), SLou. RC 1.50**
☐ 105 Dallas Smith, Bost. .75
☐ 106 Jude Drouin, NYIs. .75
☐ 107 Pat Hickey, NYRa. .75
☐ 108 Jocelyn Guevremont, Buff. .75
☐ 109 Doug Risebrough, Mont. 1.00
☐ 110 AS: Reggie Leach, Phil. 1.25
☐ 111 Dan Bouchard (G), Atla. 1.50
☐ 112 Chris Oddleifson, Vanc. .75
☐ 113 Rick Hampton, Calg. (Clev.) .75
☐ 114 John Marks, Chic. .75
☐ **115 Bryan Trottier, NYIs. RC 90.00**
☐ 116 Checklist 1 (1 - 132) 15.00
☐ 117 Greg Polis, NYRa. .75
☐ 118 Peter McNab, Bost. .75
☐ 119 Jim Roberts, Mont. .75
☐ 120 Gerry Cheevers (G), Bost. 3.50
☐ 121 Rick MacLeish, Phil. .75
☐ 122 Bill Lochead, Detr. .75
☐ 123 Tom Reid, Minn. .75
☐ 124 Rick Kehoe, Pitt. 1.25
☐ 125 Keith Magnuson, Chic. .75
☐ 126 Clark Gillies, NYIs. 3.00
☐ 127 Rick Middleton, Bost. 3.50
☐ 128 Bill Hajt, Buff. .75
☐ 129 Jacques Lemaire, Mont. 2.00
☐ 130 Terry O'Reilly, Bost. .75
☐ 131 André Dupont, Phil. .75
☐ 132 Atlanta Flames 4.00
☐ 133 Bruins, Adams Division 4.00
☐ 134 Sabres, Adams Division 4.00
☐ 135 Seals, Adams Division, (Cleveland) 4.00
☐ 136 Blackhawks, Smythe Division 4.00
☐ 137 Red Wings, Norris Division 4.00
☐ 138 Scouts, Smythe Division, (Colorado) 4.00
☐ 139 Kings, Norris Division 4.00
☐ 140 North Stars, Smythe Division 4.00
☐ 141 Canadiens, Norris Division 4.00
☐ 142 Islanders, Patrick Division 4.00
☐ 143 Rangers, Patrick Division 4.00
☐ 144 Flyers, Patrick Division 4.00
☐ 145 Penguins, Norris Division 4.00
☐ 146 Blues, Smythe Division 4.00
☐ 147 Maple Leafs, Adams Division 4.00
☐ 148 Canucks, Smythe Division 4.00
☐ 149 Capitals, Norris Division 4.00
☐ 150 Dave Schultz, Phil. (LosA.) .75
☐ 151 Larry Robinson, Mont. 7.00
☐ 152 Al Smith (G), Buff. 1.50
☐ 153 Bob Nystrom, NYIs. .75
☐ 154 Ron Greschner, NYRa. 1.25
☐ 155 Gregg Sheppard, Bost. .75
☐ 156 Alain Daigle, Chic. .75
☐ 157 Ed Van Impe, Pitt. .75
☐ **158 Tim Young, Minn. RC 1.50**
☐ 159 Bryan Lefley, Colo. .75
☐ 160 Ed Giacomin (G), Detr. 3.00
☐ 161 Yvon Labre, Wash. .75
☐ 162 Jim Lorentz, Buff. .75
☐ 163 AS: Guy Lafleur, Mont. 20.00
☐ 164 Tom Bladon, Phil. .75
☐ 165 Wayne Cashman, Bost. 1.25
☐ 166 Pete Stemkowski, NYRa. .75
☐ 167 Grant Mulvey, Chic. .75
☐ **168 Yves Belanger (G), SLou. RC 1.50**
☐ 169 Bill Goldsworthy, Minn. 1.25
☐ 170 AS: Denis Potvin, NYIs. 7.00
☐ 171 Nick Libett, Detr. .75
☐ 172 Michel Plasse (G), Colo. 1.50
☐ 173 Lou Nanne, Minn. .75
☐ 174 Tom Lysiak, Atla. .75
☐ 175 Dennis Ververgaert, Vanc. .75
☐ 176 Gary Simmons (G), Clev. 1.50
☐ 177 Pierre Bouchard, Mont. .75
☐ 178 AS: Bill Barber, Phil. 3.50
☐ 179 Darryl Edestrand, Bost. .75
☐ 180 AS: Gilbert Perreault, Buff. 5.00
☐ **181 Dave Maloney, NYRa. RC 2.00**
☐ 182 J.P. Parise, NYIs. .75
☐ 183 Jim Harrison, Chic. .75
☐ **184 Pete LoPresti (G), Minn. RC 1.50**
☐ 185 Don Kozak, LosA. .75
☐ 186 Guy Charron, Kans. (Wash.) .75
☐ 187 Stan Gilbertson, Pitt. .75
☐ **188 Bill Nyrop, Mont. RC 1.25**
☐ 189 Bobby Schmautz, Bost. .75
☐ 190 Wayne Stephenson (G), Phil. 1.50
☐ 191 Brian Spencer, Buff. .75
☐ 192 Gilles Marotte, NYRa. (SLou.) .75
☐ 193 Lorne Henning, NYIs. .75
☐ 194 Bob Neely, Toro. .75
☐ 195 Dennis Hull, Chic. 1.25
☐ 196 Walt McKechnie, Detr. .75
☐ **197 Curt Ridley (G), Vanc. RC 1.50**
☐ 198 Dwight Bialowas, Minn. .75
☐ 199 Pierre Larouche, Pitt. 2.00
☐ 200 AS: Ken Dryden (G), Mont. 25.00
☐ 201 Ross Lonsberry, Phil. .75
☐ 202 Curt Bennett, Atla. .75
☐ **203 Hartland Monahan, Wash. RC 1.25**
☐ 204 John Davidson (G), NYRa. 3.50
☐ 205 Serge Savard, Mont. 2.00
☐ 206 Garry Howatt, NYIs. .75
☐ 207 Darryl Sittler, Toro. 6.00
☐ 208 J. P. Bordeleau, Chic. .75
☐ 209 Henry Boucha, Kans. (Colo.) .75
☐ 210 AS: Rick Martin, Buff. 1.25
☐ 211 Vic Venasky, LosA. .75
☐ 212 Fred (Buster) Harvey, Detr. .75
☐ 213 Bobby Orr, Chic. 35.00
☐ 214 French Connection: Martin/ Perreault/ Robert 4.00
☐ 215 LCB Line: Barber/ Clarke/ Leach 5.00
☐ 216 Long Island Lightning Co.:Gillies/ Trottier/ Harris 6.50
☐ 217 Checking Line: Gainey/ Jarvis/ Roberts 1.50
☐ 218 Bicentennial Line:MacDonald/ Apps/ Pronovost 1.50
☐ 219 Bob Kelly, Phil. .75
☐ 220 Walt Tkaczuk, NYRa. .75
☐ 221 Dave Lewis, NYIs. .75
☐ 222 Danny Gare, Buff. 1.25
☐ 223 AS: Guy Lapointe, Mont. 3.00
☐ **224 Hank Nowak, Bost. RC 1.25**
☐ 225 Stan Mikita, Chic. 5.00
☐ 226 Vic Hadfield, Pitt. .75
☐ **227 Bernie Wolfe (G), Wash. RC 1.50**
☐ 228 Bryan Watson, Detr. .75
☐ 229 Ralph Stewart, NYIs. (Vanc.) .75
☐ 230 Gerry Desjardins (G), Buff. 1.50
☐ **231 John Bednarski, NYRa. RC 1.25**
☐ 232 Yvon Lambert, Mont. .75
☐ 233 Orest Kindrachuk, Phil. .75
☐ 234 Don Marcotte, Bost. .75
☐ 235 Bill White, Chic. .75
☐ 236 Red Berenson, SLou. .75
☐ 237 Al MacAdam, Calg. (Clev.) .75
☐ **238 Rick Blight, Vanc. RC 1.25**
☐ 239 Butch Goring, LosA. 1.25
☐ 240 Césare Maniago (G), Vanc. 1.50
☐ 241 Jim Schoenfeld, Buff. 1.25
☐ 242 Cliff Koroll, Chic. .75
☐ **243 Scott Garland, Toro. RC 1.25**
☐ 244 Rick Chartraw, Mont. .75
☐ 245 Phil Esposito, NYRa. 5.00
☐ 246 Dave Forbes, Bost. .75
☐ 247 Jimmy Watson, Phil. .75
☐ 248 Ron Schock, Pitt. .75
☐ 249 Fred Barrett, Minn. .75
☐ 250 AS: Glenn Resch (G) 2.50
☐ 251 Ivan Boldirev, Chic. .75
☐ 252 Billy Harris, NYIs. .75
☐ 253 Lee Fogolin, Buff. .75
☐ 254 Murray Wilson, Mont. .75
☐ 255 Gilles Gilbert (G), Bost. 1.50
☐ 256 Gary Dornhoefer, Phil. .75
☐ 257 Carol Vadnais, NYRa. .75
☐ 258 Checklist 2 (133 - 264) 15.00
☐ 259 Errol Thompson, Toro. .75
☐ 260 Garry Unger, SLou. 1.25
☐ 261 J. Bob Kelly, Pitt. .75
☐ 262 Terry Harper, Detr. .75
☐ 263 Blake Dunlop, Minn. .75
☐ 264 1975-76 Stanley Cup Champions: Canadiens 2.00
☐ **265 Richard Mulhern, Atla. RC 1.25**
☐ 266 Gary Sabourin, Clev. .75
☐ 267 Bill McKenzie (G), Colo. RC, Err. (KcKenzie) 1.50
☐ 268 Mike Corrigan, Pitt. .75
☐ 269 Rick Smith, SLou. .75
☐ 270 Stan Weir, Toro. .75
☐ **271 Ron Sedlbauer, Vanc. RC 1.25**
☐ 272 Jean Lemieux, Wash. .75
☐ 273 Hilliard Graves, Atla. .75
☐ 274 Dave Gardner, Clev. .75
☐ 275 Tracy Pratt, Colo. .75
☐ 276 Frank St. Marseille, LosA. .75
☐ 277 Bob Hess, SLou. .75
☐ 278 Bobby Lalonde, Vanc. .75
☐ **279 Tony White, Wash. RC 1.25**
☐ 280 Rod Seiling, SLou. .75
☐ 281 Larry Romanchych, Atla. .75
☐ **282 Ralph Klassen, Clev. RC 1.25**
☐ 283 Gary Croteau, Colo. .75
☐ 284 Neil Komadoski, LosA. .75
☐ 285 Eddie Johnston (G), SLou. 1.50
☐ 286 George Ferguson, Toro. .75
☐ 287 Gerry O'Flaherty, Vanc. .75
☐ 288 Jack Lynch, Wash. .75
☐ 289 Pat Quinn, Atla. 1.50
☐ 290 Gene Carr, LosA. .75
☐ 291 Bob Stewart, Clev. .75
☐ 292 Doug Favell (G), Colo. 1.50
☐ 293 Rick Wilson, Detr. .75
☐ **294 Jack Valiquette, Toro. RC 1.25**
☐ 295 Garry Monahan, Vanc. .75
☐ 296 Michel Belhumeur (G), Atla. 1.50
☐ 297 Larry Carrière, Atla. .75
☐ **298 Fred Ahern, Clev. RC 1.25**
☐ 299 Dave Hudson, Colo. .75
☐ 300 Bob Berry, LosA. .75
☐ 301 Bob Gassoff, SLou. .75
☐ 302 Jim McKenny, Toro. .75
☐ **303 Gord Smith, Wash. RC 1.25**
☐ 304 Garnet Bailey, Wash. .75
☐ **305 Bruce Affleck, SLou. RC 1.25**
☐ **306 Doug Halward, Bost. RC 1.25**
☐ 307 Lew Morrison, Pitt. .75
☐ **308 Bob Sauvé (G), Buff. RC 4.00**
☐ 309 Bob Murray, Chic. .75
☐ 310 Claude Larose, SLou. .75
☐ 311 Don Awrey, Pitt. .75
☐ 312 Billy MacMillan, NYIs. .75
☐ **313 Doug Jarvis, Mont. RC 6.00**
☐ 314 Dennis Owchar, Pitt. .75
☐ 315 Jerry Holland, NYRa. .75
☐ **316 Guy Chouinard, Atla. RC 3.00**
☐ 317 Gary Smith (G), Minn. 1.50
☐ **318 Pat Price, NYIs. RC 1.25**
☐ 319 Tommy Williams, LosA. .75
☐ 320 Larry Patey, SLou. .75
☐ **321 Claire Alexander, Toro. RC 1.25**
☐ **322 Larry Bolonchuk, Wash. RC 1.25**
☐ **323 Bob Sirois, Wash. RC 1.25**
☐ **324 Joe Zanussi, Bost. RC 1.25**
☐ 325 Joey Johnston, Chic. .75
☐ 326 J.P. LeBlanc, Detr., Err. (LaBlanc) .75
☐ 327 Craig Cameron, Minn. .75
☐ 328 Dave Fortier, Vanc. .75
☐ 329 Ed Gilbert, Pitt. .75
☐ **330 John Van Boxmeer, Mont. RC 2.00**
☐ 331 Gary Inness (G), Phil. 1.50
☐ 332 Bill Flett, Atla. .75
☐ 333 Mike Christie, Clev. .75
☐ 334 Denis Dupere, Colo. .75
☐ 335 Sheldon Kannegiesser, LosA. .75
☐ 336 Jerry Butler, SLou. .75
☐ 337 Gord McRae (G), Toro. 1.50
☐ 338 Dennis Kearns, Vanc. .75
☐ 339 Ron Lalonde, Wash. .75
☐ 340 Jean Hamel, Detr. .75
☐ 341 Barry Gibbs, Atla. .75
☐ 342 Mike Pelyk, Toro. .75
☐ 343 Rey Comeau, Atla. .75
☐ 344 Jim Neilson, Clev. .75
☐ 345 Phil Roberto, Colo. .75
☐ 346 Dave Hutchison, LosA. .75
☐ 347 Ted Irvine, SLou. .75
☐ 348 Lanny McDonald, Toro., Err. (MacDonald) 4.00
☐ **349 Jim Moxey, Clev. RC 1.25**
☐ 350 Bob Dailey, Vanc. .75
☐ 351 Tim Ecclestone, Atla. .75
☐ 352 Len Frig, Clev. .75
☐ 353 Randy Rota, Colo. .75
☐ 354 Juha Widing, LosA. .75
☐ 355 Larry Brown, LosA. .75
☐ 356 Floyd Thomson, SLou. .75
☐ **357 Richard Nantais, Minn. RC 1.25**
☐ 358 Inge Hammarstrom, Toro. .75
☐ 359 Mike Robitaille, Vanc. .75
☐ 360 Réjean Houle, Mont. 1.25
☐ 361 Ed Kea, Atla. .75
☐ **362 Bob Girard, Clev. RC 1.25**
☐ 363 Bob Murray, Vanc. .75
☐ 364 Dave Hrechkosy, SLou. .75
☐ 365 Gary Edwards (G), LosA. 1.50
☐ 366 Harold Snepsts, Vanc. 3.50
☐ **367 Pat Boutette, Toro. RC 1.25**
☐ 368 Bob Paradise, Wash. .75
☐ 369 Bob Plager, SLou. .75
☐ **370 Tim Jacobs, Clev. RC 1.25**
☐ 371 Pierre Plante, SLou. .75
☐ 372 Colin Campbell, Colo. 1.25
☐ **373 David Williams, Toro. RC 30.00**
☐ 374 Ab DeMarco, LosA. .75
☐ **375 Mike Lampman, Wash. RC 1.25**
☐ **376 Mark Heaslip, NYRa. RC 1.25**
☐ 377 Checklist 3 (265 - 396) 15.00
☐ 378 Bert Wilson, LosA. .75
☐ 379 TL: Bennett/ Lysiak/ P. Quinn/ C. St. Sauveur 1.50
☐ 380 TL: D. Gare/ G. Perreault/ R. Martin 2.00
☐ 381 TL: J. Bucyk/ J. Ratelle/ T. O'Reilly, 2.50
☐ 382 TL: P. Martin/ D. Tallon/ P. Russell/ C. Koroll 1.50
☐ 383 TL: W. Merrick/ MacAdam/ R. Hampton/ M. Christie/ B. Murdoch 1.50
☐ 384 TL: G. Charron/ S. Durbano 1.50
☐ 385 TL: M. Bergeron/ W. McKechnie/ B. Watson 1.50
☐ 386 TL: M. Dionne/ D. Hutchison/ M. Corrigan 2.00
☐ 387 TL: B. Hogaboam/ T. Young/ D. O'Brien 1.50
☐ 388 TL: G. Lafleur/ P. Mahovlich/ D. Risebrough 2.50
☐ 389 TL: C. Gilles/ D. Potvin/ G. Howatt, 2.00
☐ 390 TL: R. Gilbert/ S. Vickers/ Vadnais/ P. Esposito 2.50
☐ 391 TL: R. Leach/ B. Clarke/ D. Schultz/ B. Barber 2.50
☐ 392 TL: P. Larouche/ S. Apps/ R. Shock 1.50
☐ 393 TL: C. Lefley/ G. Unger/ B. Gassoff 1.50
☐ 394 TL: E. Thompson/ D. Sittler/ D. Williams 2.00
☐ 395 TL: Ververgaer/ Oddleifson/ Kearns/ Snepsts 1.50
☐ 396 TL: N. Pyatt/ G. Meehan/ Y. Labre/ T. White 1.50

1976 - 77 O-PEE-CHEE WHA

These cards measure the standard 2 1/2" x 3 1/2".

Complete Set (132 cards):	**200.00**
Common Player:	**2.00**
O-Pee-Chee	**NM-MT**
☐ 1 LL: M. Tardif/ R. Cloutier/ V. Nedomansky	6.00
☐ 2 LL: J.C. Tremblay/M. Tardif/ U. Nilsson	3.00
☐ 3 LL: M. Tardif/ B. Hull/ R. Cloutier/ U. Nilsson	8.50
☐ 4 LL: C. Brackenbury/ G. Gallant	2.00
☐ 5 LL: M. Tardif/ B. Hull/ U. Nilsson	8.50
☐ 6 LL: M. Dion(G)/ J. Daley (G)/ W. Rutledge (G)	3.50
☐ 7 Barry Long, Winnipeg	2.00
☐ 8 Danny Lawson, Calgary	2.00
☐ 9 Ulf Nilsson, Winnipeg	3.50
☐ 10 Kevin Morrison, San Diego	2.00
☐ 11 Gerry Pinder, Minnesota	2.00
☐ 12 Richard Brodeur (G), Québec	6.50
☐ 13 Robbie Ftorek, Phoenix	5.00
☐ 14 Tom Webster, New England	2.00
☐ 15 Marty Howe, Houston	3.50
☐ 16 Bryan Campbell, Edmonton	2.00
☐ 17 Rick Dudley, Cincinnati	2.00
☐ **18 Jim Turkiewicz, Birmingham RC**	**3.00**
☐ 19 Rusty Patenaude, Edmonton	2.00
☐ 20 Joe Daley (G), Winnipeg	3.50
☐ 21 Gary Veneruzzo, San Diego	2.00
☐ 22 Chris Evans, Calgary	2.00
☐ 23 Mike Antonovich, Minnesota	2.00
☐ 24 Jim Dorey, Québec	2.00
☐ **25 John Gray, Houston RC**	**3.00**
☐ 26 Larry Pleau, New England	2.00
☐ 27 Poul Popiel, Houston	2.00
☐ **28 René Leclerc, Indianapolis RC**	**3.00**
☐ 29 Dennis Sobchuk, Cincinnati	2.00
☐ 30 Lars-Erik Sjoberg, Winnipeg	2.00
☐ **31 Wayne Wood (G), Birmingham RC**	**3.50**
☐ 32 Ron Chipperfield, Calgary	2.00
☐ **33 Tim Sheehy, Edmonton RC**	**3.00**
☐ 34 Brent Hughes, San Diego	2.00
☐ 35 Ron Ward, Minnesota	2.00
☐ **36 Ron Huston, Phoenix RC**	**3.00**
☐ 37 Rosaire Paiement, Indianapolis	2.00
☐ **38 Terry Ruskowski, Houston RC**	**5.00**
☐ 39 Hugh Harris, Indianapolis	2.00
☐ 40 J.C.Tremblay, Québec	3.50
☐ 41 Rich LeDuc, Cincinnati	2.00
☐ **42 Peter Sullivan, Winnipeg RC**	**3.00**
☐ **43 Jerry Rollins, Phoenix RC**	**3.00**
☐ 44 Ken Broderick (G), Edmonton	3.50
☐ **45 Pete Driscoll, Calgary RC**	**3.00**
☐ **46 Joe Noris, San Diego RC**	**3.00**
☐ 47 Al McLeod, Houston	2.00
☐ **48 Bruce Landon (G), New England RC**	**3.50**
☐ 49 Chris Bordeleau, Québec	2.00
☐ 50 Gordie Howe, Houston	50.00
☐ 51 Thommie Bergman, Winnipeg	2.00
☐ 52 Dave Keon, Minnesota	5.50
☐ 53 Butch Deadmarsh, Minnesota	2.00
☐ **54 Bryan Maxwell, Cincinnati RC**	**3.00**
☐ 55 John Garrett (G), Birmingham	3.50
☐ 56 Glen Sather, Edmonton	3.50
☐ 57 John Miszuk, Calgary	2.00
☐ 58 Heikki Riihiranta, Winnipeg	2.00
☐ **59 Richard Grenier, Québec RC**	**3.00**
☐ 60 Gene Peacosh, Indianapolis	2.00
☐ 61 AS: Joe Daley (G), Winnipeg	3.50
☐ 62 AS: J.C. Tremblay, Québec	2.00
☐ 63 AS: Lars-Erik Sjoberg, Winnipeg	2.00
☐ 64 AS: Vaclav Nedomansky, Toronto	2.00
☐ 65 AS: Bobby Hull, Winnipeg	20.00
☐ 66 AS: Anders Hedberg, Winnipeg	3.50
☐ 67 AS: Christer Abrahamsson, New England (G)	3.50
☐ 68 AS: Kevin Morrison, San Diego	2.00
☐ 69 AS: Paul Shmyr, Cleveland	2.00
☐ 70 André Lacroix, San Diego	2.00
☐ 71 AS: Gene Peacosh, San Diego	2.00
☐ 72 AS: Gordie Howe, Houston	30.00
☐ 73 Bob Nevin, Edmonton	2.00
☐ 74 Richard Lemieux, Calgary	2.00
☐ **75 Mike Ford, Calgary RC**	**3.00**
☐ 76 Real Cloutier, Québec	2.00
☐ 77 Al McDonough, Minnesota	2.00
☐ **78 Del Hall, Phoenix RC**	**3.00**
☐ 79 Thommy Abrahamsson, New England	2.00
☐ 80 André Lacroix, San Diego	3.50
☐ **81 Frank Hughes, Phoenix RC**	**3.00**
☐ **82 Reg Thomas, Indianapolis RC**	**3.00**
☐ **83 Dave Inkpen, Cincinnati RC**	**3.00**
☐ 84 Paul Henderson, Birmingham	3.50
☐ 85 Dave Dryden (G), Edmonton	3.50
☐ 86 Lynn Powis, Calgary	2.00
☐ 87 André Boudrias, Québec	2.00
☐ 88 Veli-Pekka Ketola, Winnipeg	2.00
☐ 89 Cam Connor, Houston	2.00
☐ 90 Claude St. Sauver, Calgary	2.00
☐ **91 Garry Swain, New England RC**	**3.00**
☐ 92 Ernie Wakely, San Diego (G)	3.50
☐ **93 Blair MacDonald, Indianapolis RC**	**3.00**
☐ 94 Ron Plumb, Cincinnati	2.00
☐ 95 Mark Howe, Houston	12.00
☐ **96 Peter Marrin, Birmingham RC**	**3.00**
☐ 97 Al Hamilton, Edmonton	2.00
☐ 98 Paulin Bordeleau, Québec	2.00
☐ 99 Gavin Kirk	2.00
☐ 100 Bobby Hull, Winnipeg	45.00
☐ 101 Rick Ley, New England	3.50
☐ 102 Gary Kurt (G), Phoenix	3.50
☐ 103 John McKenzie, Minnesota	2.00
☐ **104 Al Karlander, Indianapolis RC**	**3.00**
☐ 105 John French, San Diego	2.00
☐ 106 John Hughes, Cincinnati	2.00
☐ 107 Ron Grahame (G), Houston	3.50
☐ 108 Mark Napier, Birmingham	3.50
☐ 109 Serge Bernier, Québec	2.00
☐ 110 Christer Abrahamsson (G), New England	3.50
☐ 111 Frank Mahovlich, Birmingham	6.50
☐ 112 Ted Green, Winnipeg	2.00
☐ 113 Rick Jodzio, Calgary	2.00
☐ **114 Michel Dion (G), Indianapolis RC**	**5.00**
☐ **115 Rich Preston, Houston RC**	**3.00**
☐ **116 Pekka Rautakallio, Phoenix RC**	**5.00**
☐ 117 Checklist (1 - 132)	40.00
☐ 118 Marc Tardif, Québec	3.50
☐ 119 Doug Barrie, Edmonton	2.00
☐ 120 Vaclav Nedomansky, Birmingham	2.00
☐ 121 Bill Lesuk, Winnipeg	2.00
☐ 122 Wayne Connelly, Calgary	2.00
☐ 123 Pierre Guite, Cincinnati	2.00
☐ 124 Ralph Backstrom, New England	2.00
☐ 125 Anders Hedberg, Winnipeg	3.50
☐ 126 Norm Ullman, Edmonton	4.50
☐ **127 Steve Sutherland, Québec RC**	**3.00**
☐ 128 John Schella, Houston	2.00
☐ 129 Don McLeod (G), Calgary	3.50
☐ 130 Canadian O'Keefe Finals: Winnipeg wins	3.50
☐ 131 U.S. Finals: Houston wins	3.50
☐ 132 World Trophy Finals: Winnipeg wins Trophy	12.00

1976 - 77 POPSICLE

Complete Set (18 cards):	**35.00**
Common Team:	**3.00**

☐ Atlanta Flames	☐ Boston Bruins
☐ Buffalo Sabres	☐ Cleveland Barons Seals
☐ Chicago Blackhawks	☐ Detroit Red Wings
☐ Colorado Rockies	☐ Los Angeles Kings
☐ Minnesota North Stars	☐ Montréal Canadiens
☐ New York Islanders	☐ New York Rangers
☐ Philadelphia Flyers	☐ Pittsburgh Penguins
☐ St. Louis Blues	☐ Toronto Maple Leafs
☐ Vancouver Canucks	☐ Washington Capitals

1976 - 77 TOPPS

These cards measure the standard 2 1/2" x 3 1/2". Cards 102, 159, 183, and 243 are different from O-Pee-Chee checklist.

Complete Set (264 cards):	**150.00**
Common Player:	**.50**
Topps	**NM-MT**
☐ 1 LL: R. Leach/ G. Lafleur/ P. Larouche	3.25
☐ 2 LL: Clarke/ P. Mahovlich/ Lafleur/ Perreault/ Ratelle	3.00
☐ 3 LL: G. Lafleur/ B. Clarke/ G. Perreault	3.00
☐ 4 LL: Steve Durbano/ Bryan Watson/ Dave Schultz	1.00
☐ 5 LL: P. Esposito/ Lafleur/ Martin/ Larouche/ Potvin	3.00
☐ 6 LL: K. Dryden/ G. Resch/ M. Larocque	3.25
☐ 7 Gary Doak, Bost.	.50
☐ 8 Jacques Richard, Buff.	.50
☐ 9 Wayne Dillon, NYRa.	.50
☐ 10 Bernie Parent (G), Phil.	3.50
☐ 11 Ed Westfall, NYIs.	.50
☐ 12 Dick Redmond, Chic.	.50
☐ 13 Bryan Hextall, Minn.	.50
☐ 14 Jean Pronovost, Pitt.	.50
☐ 15 Pete Mahovlich, Mont.	1.00
☐ 16 Danny Grant, Detr.	.50
☐ 17 Phil Myre (G), Atla.	1.00
☐ 18 Wayne Merrick, Calg.	.50
☐ 19 Steve Durbano, Kans.	.50
☐ 20 Derek Sanderson, SLou.	2.25
☐ 21 Mike Murphy, LosA.	.50
☐ 22 Börje Salming, Toro.	3.00
☐ 23 Mike Walton, Vanc.	.50
☐ 24 Randy Manery, Atla.	.50
☐ 25 Ken Hodge, Sr., NYRa.	.50
☐ **26 Mel Bridgman, Phil. RC**	**1.50**
☐ 27 Jerry Korab, Buff.	.50
☐ 28 Gilles Gratton (G), NYRa.	1.00
☐ 29 André St. Laurent, NYIs.	.50
☐ 30 Yvan Cournoyer, Mont.	2.25
☐ 31 Phil Russell, Chic.	.50
☐ 32 Dennis Hextall, Detr.	.50
☐ 33 Lowell MacDonald, Pitt.	.50
☐ 34 Dennis O'Brien, Minn.	.50
☐ 35 Gerry Meehan, Wash.	.50
☐ 36 Gilles Meloche (G), Calg.	1.00
☐ 37 Wilf Paiement, Kans.	.50
☐ **38 Bob MacMillan, SLou. RC**	**1.00**
☐ 39 Ian Turnbull, Toro.	.50
☐ 40 Rogatien Vachon (G), LosA.	1.00
☐ 41 Nick Beverley, NYRa.	.50
☐ 42 René Robert, Buff.	.50
☐ 43 André Savard, Buff.	.50
☐ 44 Bob Gainey, Mont.	3.50
☐ 45 Joe Watson, Phil.	.50
☐ 46 Billy Smith (G), NYIs.	3.50
☐ 47 Darcy Rota, Chic.	.50
☐ **48 Rick Lapointe, Detr. RC**	**1.00**
☐ 49 Pierre Jarry, Minn.	.50
☐ 50 Syl Apps, Pitt.	.50
☐ 51 Eric Vail, Atla.	.50
☐ 52 Greg Joly, Wash.	.50
☐ 53 Don Lever, Vanc.	.50
☐ **54 Bob L. Murdoch, Calg. RC**	**1.00**
☐ 55 Denis Herron (G), Kans.	1.00
☐ 56 Mike Bloom, Detr.	.50
☐ 57 Bill Fairbairn, NYRa.	.50
☐ 58 Fred Stanfield, Buff.	.50
☐ 59 Steve Shutt, Mont.	2.25
☐ 60 Brad Park, Bost.,	2.25
☐ 61 AS: Gilles Villemure (G), Chic.	1.00
☐ 62 AS: Bert Marshall, NYIs.	.50
☐ 63 AS: Chuck Lefley, SLou.	.50
☐ 64 AS: Simon Nolet, Pitt.	.50
☐ 65 Most Goals, Playoffs: Reggie Leach, Phil.	.50
☐ 66 Most Points, Game: Darryl Sittler, Toro.	2.00
☐ 67 Most Points, Season, Rookie: Bryan Trottier, NYIs.	6.00
☐ 68 Most Consecutive Games, Lifetime: Garry Unger, SLou.	.50
☐ 69 Ron Low (G), Wash.	1.00
☐ 70 AS: Bobby Clarke, Phil.	4.50
☐ **71 Michel Bergeron, Detr. RC**	**1.00**
☐ 72 Ron Stackhouse, Pitt.	.50
☐ 73 Bill Hogaboam, Minn.	.50
☐ 74 Bob J. Murdoch, LosA.	.50
☐ 75 Steve Vickers, NYRa.	.50
☐ 76 Pit Martin, Chic.	.50
☐ 77 Gerry Hart, NYIs.	.50
☐ 78 Craig Ramsay, Buff.	1.00
☐ 79 Michel Larocque (G), Mont.	1.00
☐ 80 Jean Ratelle, Bost.	1.25
☐ 81 Don Saleski, Phil.	.50
☐ 82 Bill Clement, Atla.	.50
☐ 83 Dave Burrows, Pitt.	.50
☐ 84 Wayne Thomas (G), Toro.	1.00
☐ 85 John Gould, Vanc.	.50
☐ **86 Dennis Maruk, Calg. RC**	**2.50**
☐ 87 Ernie Hicke, Minn.	.50
☐ 88 Jim Rutherford (G), Detr.	1.00
☐ 89 Dale Tallon, Chic.	.50
☐ 90 Rod Gilbert, NYRa.	1.25
☐ 91 Marcel Dionne, LosA.	3.50
☐ 92 Chuck Arnason, Kans.	.50
☐ 93 Jean Potvin, NYIs.	.50
☐ 94 Don Luce, Buff.	.50
☐ 95 John Bucyk, Bost.	1.25
☐ 96 Larry Goodenough, Phil.	.50
☐ 97 Mario Tremblay, Mont.	.50
☐ **98 Nelson Pyatt, Wash. RC**	**1.00**
☐ 99 Brian Glennie, Toro.	.50
☐ 100 Tony Esposito (G), Chic.	3.50
☐ 101 Dan Maloney, Detr.	.50
☐ 102 Barry Wilkins, Pitt.	.50
☐ 103 Dean Talafous, Minn.	.50
☐ **104 Ed Staniowski (G), SLou. RC**	**1.00**
☐ 105 Dallas Smith, Bost.	.50
☐ 106 Jude Drouin, NYIs.	.50
☐ 107 Pat Hickey, NYRa.	.50
☐ 108 Jocelyn Guevremont, Buff.	.50
☐ 109 Doug Risebrough, Mont.	1.00
☐ 110 Reggie Leach, Phil.	.50
☐ 111 Dan Bouchard (G), Atla.	1.00
☐ 112 Chris Oddleifson, Vanc.	.50
☐ 113 Rick Hampton, Calg.	.50
☐ 114 John Marks, Chic.	.50
☐ **115 Bryan Trottier, NYIs. RC**	**60.00**
☐ 116 Checklist 1 (1 - 132)	9.00
☐ 117 Greg Polis, NYRa.	.50
☐ 118 Peter McNab, Bost.	.50
☐ 119 Jim Roberts, Mont.	.50
☐ 120 Gerry Cheevers (G), Bost.	2.25
☐ 121 Rick MacLeish, Phil.	.50
☐ 122 Bill Lochead, Detr.	.50
☐ 123 Tom Reid, Minn.	.50
☐ 124 Rick Kehoe, Pitt.	1.00
☐ 125 Keith Magnuson, Chic.	.50
☐ 126 Clark Gillies, NYIs.	1.25
☐ 127 Rick Middleton, Bost.	2.50
☐ 128 Bill Hajt, Buff.	.50
☐ 129 Jacques Lemaire, Mont.	1.25
☐ 130 Terry O'Reilly, Bost.	.50
☐ 131 André Dupont, Phil.	.50
☐ 132 CL: Flames, Patrick Division	2.25
☐ 133 CL: Bruins, Adams Division	2.25
☐ 134 CL: Sabres, Adams Division	2.25
☐ 135 CL: Seals, Adams Division	2.25
☐ 136 CL: Blackhawks, Smythe Division	2.25
☐ 137 CL: Red Wings, Norris Division	2.25
☐ 138 CL: Scouts, Smythe Division	2.25
☐ 139 CL: Kings, Norris Division	2.25
☐ 140 CL: North Stars, Smythe Division	2.25
☐ 141 CL: Canadiens, Norris Division	2.25
☐ 142 CL: Islanders, Patrick Division	2.25
☐ 143 CL: Rangers, Patrick Division	2.25
☐ 144 CL: Flyers, Patrick Division	2.25
☐ 145 CL: Penguins, Norris Division	2.25
☐ 146 CL: Blues, Smythe Division	2.25
☐ 147 CL: Maple Leafs, Adams Division	2.25
☐ 148 CL: Canucks, Smythe Division	2.25
☐ 149 CL: Capitals, Norris Division	2.25
☐ 150 Dave Schultz, Phil.	.50
☐ 151 Larry Robinson, Mont.	4.50
☐ 152 Al Smith (G), Buff.	1.00
☐ 153 Bob Nystrom, NYIs.	.50
☐ 154 Ron Greschner, NYRa.	1.00
☐ 155 Gregg Sheppard, Bost.	.50
☐ 156 Alain Daigle, Chic.	.50
☐ 157 Ed Van Impe, Pitt.	.50
☐ **158 Tim Young, Minn. RC**	**1.00**
☐ 159 Gary Bergman, Kans.	.50
☐ 160 Ed Giacomin (G), Detr.	2.00
☐ 161 Yvon Labre, Wash.	.50
☐ 162 Jim Lorentz, Buff.	.50
☐ 163 Guy Lafleur, Mont.	10.00
☐ 164 Tom Bladon, Phil.	.50
☐ 165 Wayne Cashman, Bost.	.50
☐ 166 Pete Stemkowski, NYRa.	.50
☐ 167 Grant Mulvey, Chic.	.50
☐ **168 Yves Belanger (G), SLou. RC**	**1.00**
☐ 169 Bill Goldsworthy, Minn.	.50
☐ 170 Denis Potvin, NYIs.	6.00
☐ 171 Nick Libett, Detr.	.50
☐ 172 Michel Plasse (G), Pitt.	1.00
☐ 173 Lou Nanne, Minn.	.50
☐ 174 Tom Lysiak, Atla.	.50
☐ 175 Dennis Ververgaert, Vanc.	.50
☐ 176 Gary Simmons (G), Calg.	1.00
☐ 177 Pierre Bouchard, Mont.	.50
☐ 178 Bill Barber, Phil.	2.25
☐ 179 Darryl Edestrand, Bost.	.50
☐ 180 Gilbert Perreault, Buff.	3.00
☐ **181 Dave Maloney, NYRa. RC**	**1.00**
☐ 182 J.P. Parise, NYIs.	.50
☐ 183 Bobby Sheehan, Chic.	.50
☐ **184 Pete LoPresti (G), Minn. RC**	**1.00**
☐ 185 Don Kozak, LosA.	.50
☐ 186 Guy Charron, Kans.	.50
☐ 187 Stan Gilbertson, Pitt.	.50
☐ **188 Bill Nyrop, Mont. RC**	**1.00**
☐ 189 Bobby Schmautz, Bost.	.50
☐ 190 Wayne Stephenson (G), Phil.	1.00
☐ 191 Brian Spencer, Buff.	.50
☐ 192 Gilles Marotte, NYRa.	.50
☐ 193 Lorne Henning, NYIs.	.50
☐ 194 Bob Neely, Toro.	.50
☐ 195 Dennis Hull, Chic.	1.00
☐ 196 Walt McKechnie, Detr.	.50
☐ **197 Curt Ridley (G), Vanc. RC**	**1.00**
☐ 198 Dwight Bialowas, Minn.	.50
☐ 199 Pierre Larouche, Pitt.	1.25
☐ 200 Ken Dryden (G), Mont.	15.00
☐ 201 Ross Lonsberry, Phil.	.50
☐ 202 Curt Bennett, Atla.	.50
☐ **203 Hartland Monahan, Wash. RC**	**1.00**
☐ 204 John Davidson (G), NYRa.	2.00
☐ 205 Serge Savard, Mont.	1.25
☐ 206 Garry Howatt, NYIs.	.50
☐ 207 Darryl Sittler, Toro.	3.50
☐ 208 J.P. Bordeleau, Chic.	.50
☐ 209 Henry Boucha, Kans.	.50
☐ 210 Rick Martin, Buff.	1.00

☐	211 Vic Venasky, LosA.	.50
☐	212 Fred (Buster) Harvey, Detr.	.50
☐	213 Bobby Orr, Bost.	25.00
☐	214 French Connection: Martin/ Perreault/ Robert	2.75
☐	215 LCB Line: Barber/ Clarke/ Leach	3.00
☐	216 Long Island Lightning Co.: Gillies/ Trottier/ Harris	4.00
☐	217 Checking Line: Gainey/ Jarvis/ Roberts	1.00
☐	218 Bicentennial Line: MacDonald/ Apps/ Pronovost	1.00
☐	219 Bob Kelly, Phil.	.50
☐	220 Walt Tkaczuk, NYRa.	.50
☐	221 Dave Lewis, NYIs.	1.00
☐	222 Danny Gare, Buff.	1.00
☐	223 Guy Lapointe, Mont.	2.00
☐	**224 Hank Nowak, Bost. RC**	**1.00**
☐	225 Stan Mikita, Chic.	5.00
☐	226 Vic Hadfield, Pitt.	.50
☐	**227 Bernie Wolfe (G), Wash. RC**	**1.00**
☐	228 Bryan Watson, Detr.	.50
☐	229 Ralph Stewart, NYIs.	.50
☐	230 Gerry Desjardins (G), Buff.	1.00
☐	**231 John Bednarski, NYRa. RC**	**1.00**
☐	232 Yvon Lambert, Mont.	.50
☐	233 Orest Kindrachuk, Phil.	.50
☐	234 Don Marcotte, Bost.	.50
☐	235 Bill White, Chic.	.50
☐	236 Red Berenson, SLou.	.50
☐	237 Al MacAdam, Calg.	.50
☐	**238 Rick Blight, Vanc. RC**	**1.00**
☐	239 Butch Goring, LosA.	.50
☐	240 Césare Maniago (G), Minn.	1.00
☐	241 Jim Schoenfeld, Buff.	.50
☐	242 Cliff Koroll, Chic.	.50
☐	243 Mickey Redmond, Detr.	1.00
☐	244 Rick Chartraw, Mont.	.50
☐	245 Phil Esposito, NYRa.	3.50
☐	246 Dave Forbes, Bost.	.50
☐	247 Jimmy Watson, Phil.	.50
☐	248 Ron Schock, Pitt.	.50
☐	249 Fred Barrett, Minn.	.50
☐	250 Glenn Resch (G), NYIs.	1.75
☐	251 Ivan Boldirev, Chic.	.50
☐	252 Billy Harris, NYIs.	.50
☐	253 Lee Fogolin, Buf	.50
☐	254 Murray Wilson, Mont.	.50
☐	255 Gilles Gilbert (G), Bost.	1.00
☐	256 Gary Dornhoefer, Phil.	.50
☐	257 Carol Vadnais, NYRa.	.50
☐	258 Checklist 2 (133 - 264)	9.00
☐	259 Errol Thompson, Toro.	.50
☐	260 Garry Unger, SLou.	1.00
☐	261 J. Bob Kelly, Pitt.	.50
☐	262 Terry Harper, Detr.	.50
☐	263 Blake Dunlop, Minn.	.50
☐	264 1975-76 Stanley Cup Champions: Canadiens	2.50

GLOSSY

These cards have rounded cards.

Insert Set (22 cards):		**75.00**
Topps		**NM-MT**
☐	1 Bobby Clarke, Phil.	5.00
☐	2 Brad Park, Bost.	3.50
☐	3 Tony Esposito (G), Chic.	5.00
☐	4 Marcel Dionne, LosA.	5.00
☐	5 Ken Dryden (G), Mont.	12.00
☐	6 Glenn Resch (G), NYIs.	2.50
☐	7 Phil Esposito, NYRa.	6.00
☐	8 Darryl Sittler, Toro.	4.00
☐	9 Gilbert Perreault, Buff.	4.00
☐	10 Denis Potvin, NYIs.	5.00
☐	11 Guy Lafleur, Mont.	12.00
☐	12 Bill Barber, Phil.	3.50
☐	13 Syl Apps, Jr., Pitt.	1.50
☐	14 John Bucyk, Bost.	3.50
☐	15 Bryan Trottier, NYIs.	15.00
☐	16 Dennis Hull, Chic.	1.50
☐	17 Guy Lapointe, Mont.	3.00
☐	18 Rod Gilbert, NYRa.	3.50
☐	19 Richard Martin, Buff.	1.50
☐	20 Bobby Orr, Chic.	30.00
☐	21 Reggie Leach, Phil.	1.50
☐	22 Jean Ratelle, NYRa.	3.50

1977 - 78 COCA-COLA MINIS

These cards measure 1 3/8" x 1 3/8".

Complete Set (30 cards);		**130.00**
Coca-Cola		**NM**
☐	Syl Apps, Pitt.	2.50
☐	Dave Burrows, Pitt.	2.50
☐	Bobby Clarke, Phil.	10.00
☐	Yvan Cournoyer, Mont.	6.00
☐	John Davidson (G), NYRa.	5.00
☐	Marcel Dionne, LosA.	7.50
☐	Doug Favell (G)	4.00
☐	Rod Gilbert, NYRa.	6.00
☐	Brian Glennie, Toro.	2.50
☐	Butch Goring, LosA.	2.50
☐	Lorne Henning, NYIs.	2.50
☐	Cliff Koroll, Chic.	2.50
☐	Guy Lapointe, Mont.	5.00
☐	Dave Maloney, NYRa.	2.50
☐	Pit Martin, Chic.	2.50
☐	Lou Nanne, Minn.	2.50
☐	Bobby Orr, Chic.	60.00
☐	Brad Park, Bost.	6.00
☐	Craig Ramsay, Buff.	2.50
☐	Larry Robinson, Mont.	9.00
☐	Jim Rutherford (G), Detr.	4.00
☐	Don Saleski, Phil.	2.50
☐	Steve Shutt, Mont.	6.00
☐	Darryl Sittler, Toro.	7.50
☐	Billy Smith (G), NYIs.	7.50
☐	Bob Stewart, Clev.	2.50
☐	Rogatien Vachon (G), LosA.	5.00
☐	Jimmy Watson, Phil.	2.50
☐	Joe Watson, Phil.	2.50
☐	Ed Westfall, NYIs.	2.50

1977 - 78 DERNIÈRE PHOTOS

This multi-sport series of photos were inserted in Dernière magazine from 1972 through 1984. Three holes were punched on the left side to allow for storage in a binder. The series featured Montréal Canadiens players. These photos measure 8" x 10".

Dernière		**NM**
☐	1JAN Robert Picard	3.00
☐	8JAN Lucien Deblois	3.00
☐	15JAN Michael Bossy	10.00
☐	22JAN Jean Savard	3.00
☐	29JAN Jere Gillis	3.00
☐	5FEB Maurice Richard	18.00
☐	12FEB Toe Blake, Coach	8.00
☐	19FEB Elmer Lach	10.00
☐	26FEB Jean Béliveau	12.00
☐	5MAR Floyd Curry	3.00
☐	12MAR Emile Bouchard	6.00
☐	19MAR Tom Johnson	6.00
☐	26MAR Bernard Geoffrion	10.00
☐	2APR Henri Richard	8.00
☐	9APR Dickie Moore	7.00
☐	16APR Claude Provost	3.00
☐	23APR Jean-Guy Talbot	3.00
☐	30APR Jacques Plante (G)	15.00

1977 - 78 HOCKEY DIGEST BLOW-IN

These blow-in cards highlighted subscription offers for the hockey publication *Hockey Digest*. Other blow-in cards exist.

Hockey Digest		**NM**
☐	Feb. 78 • JMH3 Glenn Resch (Jun. 77 cover) / blue	
☐	Mar. 78 • JNH3 Wayne Cashman (Feb. 78 cover) / blue	
☐	Jun. 78 • JSH3 Darryl Sittler (May 78 cover) / red	

1977 - 78 O-PEE-CHEE & TOPPS

These cards measure the standard 2 1/2" x 3 1/2". There are two versions for cards 1-264: the O-Pee-Chee card and the Topps card. The Topps card do not have the traded line that appears on the O-Pee-Chee counterparts.

Complete Set (396 cards):		**-**	**160.00**
Topps Set (264 cards):		**100.00**	**-**
Common Player:		**.35**	**.50**
Description		**Topps**	**OPC**
☐ ☐	1 LL: S. Shutt/ G. Lafleur/ M. Dionne	3.00	4.00
☐ ☐	2 LL: Lafleur/ Dionne/ Robinson/ Salming/ Young	2.00	3.00
☐ ☐	3 LL: G. Lafleur/ M. Dionne/ S. Shutt	2.00	3.75
☐ ☐	4 LL: D. Williams/ D. Polonich/ B. Gassoff	.75	1.00
☐ ☐	5 LL: L. McDonald/ P. Esposito/ T. Williams	1.25	2.00
☐ ☐	6 LL: Larocque (G)/ K.Dryden (G)/ Resch (G)	3.00	4.50
☐ ☐	7 LL: Perreault/ Shutt/ Lafleur/ MacLeish/ McNab	2.00	3.75
☐ ☐	8 LL: Dryden(G)/ Vachon (G)/ Parent (G)/ Wilson (G)	4.00	6.00
☐ ☐	9 Brian Spencer, Buff., (Pitt.)	.35	.50
☐ ☐	10 AS: Denis Potvin	2.50	4.00
☐ ☐	11 Nick Fotiu, NYRa.	.35	.50
☐ ☐	12 Bob Murray, Chic.	.75	1.00
☐ ☐	13 Pete LoPresti (G), Minn.	.75	1.00
☐ ☐	14 J. Bob Kelly, Pitt. (Chic.)	.35	.50
☐ ☐	15 Rick MacLeish, Phil.	.75	1.00
☐ ☐	16 Terry Harper, Detr.	.35	.50
☐ ☐	**17 Willi Plett, Atla. RC**	**2.00**	**3.00**
☐ ☐	18 Peter McNab, Bost.	.35	.50
☐ ☐	19 Wayne Thomas (G), Toro. (NYRa.)	.75	1.00
☐ ☐	20 Pierre Bouchard, Mont.	.35	.50
☐ ☐	21 Dennis Maruk, Clev.	.35	.50
☐ ☐	22 Mike Murphy, LosA.	.35	.50
☐ ☐	23 Césare Maniago (G), Vanc.	.75	1.00
☐ ☐	**24 Paul Gardner, Colo. RC**	**.75**	**1.00**
☐ ☐	25 Rod Gilbert, NYRa.	1.00	1.50
☐ ☐	26 Orest Kindrachuk, Phil.	.35	.50
☐ ☐	27 Bill Hajt, Buff.	.35	.50
☐ ☐	28 John Davidson (G), NYRa.	1.25	2.00
☐ ☐	29 J.P. Parise, NYIs.	.35	.50
☐ ☐	30 AS: Larry Robinson	2.50	4.00
☐ ☐	31 Yvon Labre, Wash.	.35	.50
☐ ☐	32 Walt McKechnie, Detr. (Wash.)	.35	.50
☐ ☐	33 Rick Kehoe, Pitt.	.75	1.00
☐ ☐	**34 Randy Holt, Chic. RC**	**.75**	**1.00**
☐ ☐	35 Garry Unger, SLou.	.75	1.00
☐ ☐	36 Lou Nanne, Minn.	.35	.50
☐ ☐	37 Dan Bouchard (G), Atla.	.75	1.00
☐ ☐	38 Darryl Sittler, Toro.	2.50	4.00
☐ ☐	39 Bob L. Murdoch, Clev.	.35	.50
☐ ☐	40 Jean Ratelle, Bost.	1.00	1.50
☐ ☐	41 Dave Maloney, NYRa.	.35	.50
☐ ☐	42 Danny Gare, Buff.	.75	1.00
☐ ☐	43 Jimmy Watson, Phil.	.35	.50
☐ ☐	44 Tommy Williams, LosA.	.35	.50
☐ ☐	45 Serge Savard, Mont.	1.00	1.50
☐ ☐	46 Derek Sanderson, Vanc.	1.00	1.50
☐ ☐	47 John Marks, Chic.	.35	.50
☐ ☐	**48 Al Cameron, Detr. RC**	**.75**	**1.00**
☐ ☐	49 Dean Talafous, Minn.	.35	.50
☐ ☐	50 Glenn Resch (G), NYIs.	1.00	1.50
☐ ☐	51 Ron Schock, Pitt. (Buff.)	.35	.50
☐ ☐	52 Gary Croteau, Colo.	.35	.50
☐ ☐	53 Gerry Meehan, Wash.	.35	.50
☐ ☐	54 Ed Staniowski (G), SLou.	.75	1.00
☐ ☐	55 Phil Esposito, NYRa.	2.50	4.00
☐ ☐	56 Dennis Ververgaert, Vanc.	.35	.50
☐ ☐	57 Rick Wilson, Detr.	.35	.50
☐ ☐	58 Jim Lorentz, Buff.	.35	.50
☐ ☐	59 Bobby Schmautz, Bost.	.35	.50
☐ ☐	60 AS: Guy Lapointe	1.25	2.00
☐ ☐	61 Ivan Boldirev, Chic.	.35	.50
☐ ☐	62 Bob Nystrom, NYIs.	.75	1.00
☐ ☐	63 Rick Hampton, Clev.	.35	.50
☐ ☐	64 Jack Valiquette, Toro.	.35	.50
☐ ☐	65 Bernie Parent (G), Phil.	1.50	2.50
☐ ☐	66 Dave Burrows, Pitt.	.35	.50
☐ ☐	67 Butch Goring, LosA.	.75	1.00
☐ ☐	68 Checklist 1 (1 - 132)	6.00	12.00
☐ ☐	69 Murray Wilson, Mont.	.35	.50
☐ ☐	70 Ed Giacomin (G), Detr.	1.25	2.00
☐ ☐	71 CL: Atlanta Flames	1.00	1.50
☐ ☐	72 CL: Boston Bruins	1.00	1.50
☐ ☐	73 CL: Buffalo Sabres	1.00	1.50
☐ ☐	74 CL: Chicago Blackhawks	1.00	1.50
☐ ☐	75 CL: Cleveland Barons	1.00	1.50
☐ ☐	76 CL: Colorado Rockies	1.00	1.50
☐ ☐	77 CL: Detroit Red Wings	1.00	1.50
☐ ☐	78 CL: Los Angeles Kings	1.00	1.50
☐ ☐	79 CL: Minnesota North Stars	1.00	1.50
☐ ☐	80 CL: Montréal Canadiens	1.00	1.50
☐ ☐	81 CL: New York Islanders	1.00	1.50
☐ ☐	82 CL: New York Rangers	1.00	1.50
☐ ☐	83 CL: Philadelphia Flyers	1.00	1.50
☐ ☐	84 CL: Pittsburgh Penguins	1.00	1.50
☐ ☐	85 CL: St. Louis Blues	1.00	1.50
☐ ☐	86 CL: Toronto Maple Leafs	1.00	1.50
☐ ☐	87 CL: Vancouver Canucks	1.00	1.50
☐ ☐	88 CL: Washington Capitals	1.00	1.50
☐ ☐	89 Keith Magnuson, Chic.	.35	.50
☐ ☐	90 Walt Tkaczuk, NYRa.	.35	.50
☐ ☐	91 Bill Nyrop, Mont.	.35	.50
☐ ☐	92 Michel Plasse (G), Colo.	.75	1.00
☐ ☐	93 Bob Bourne, NYIs.	.35	.50
☐ ☐	94 Lee Fogolin, Buff.	.35	.50
☐ ☐	95 Gregg Sheppard, Bost.	.35	.50
☐ ☐	96 Hartland Monahan, Wash. (LosA.)	.35	.50
☐ ☐	97 Curt Bennett, Atla.	.35	.50
☐ ☐	98 Bob Dailey, Phil.	.35	.50
☐ ☐	99 Bill Goldsworthy, NYRa.	.35	.50
☐ ☐	100 AS: Ken Dryden (G), Mont.	10.00	15.00
☐ ☐	101 Grant Mulvey, Chic.	.35	.50
☐ ☐	102 Pierre Larouche, Pitt.	.35	.50
☐ ☐	103 Nick Libett, Detr.	.35	.50
☐ ☐	104 Rick Smith, Bost.	.35	.50
☐ ☐	105 Bryan Trottier, NYIs.	10.00	20.00
☐ ☐	106 Pierre Jarry, Minn.	.35	.50
☐ ☐	107 Red Berenson, SLou.	.35	.50
☐ ☐	108 Jim Schoenfeld, Buff.	.35	.50
☐ ☐	109 Gilles Meloche (G), Clev.	.75	1.00
☐ ☐	110 AS: Lanny McDonald	1.50	2.50
☐ ☐	111 Don Lever, Vanc.	.35	.50
☐ ☐	112 Greg Polis, NYRa.	.35	.50
☐ ☐	**113 Gary Sargent, LosA. RC**	**.75**	**1.00**
☐ ☐	**114 Earl Anderson, Bost. RC**	**.75**	**1.00**
☐ ☐	115 Bobby Clarke, Phil.	2.50	4.00
☐ ☐	116 Dave Lewis, NYIs.	.75	1.00
☐ ☐	117 Darcy Rota, Chic.	.35	.50
☐ ☐	118 André Savard, Buff.	.35	.50
☐ ☐	119 Denis Herron (G), Pitt.	.75	1.00
☐ ☐	120 AS: Steve Shutt, Mont.	1.50	2.50
☐ ☐	121 Mel Bridgman, Phil.	.35	.50
☐ ☐	122 Fred (Buster) Harvey, Detr.	.35	.50
☐ ☐	**123 Rolie Eriksson, Minn. RC**	**.75**	**1.00**
☐ ☐	124 Dale Tallon, Chic.	.35	.50
☐ ☐	125 Gilles Gilbert (G), Bost.	.75	1.00
☐ ☐	126 Billy Harris, NYIs.	.35	.50
☐ ☐	127 Tom Lysiak, Atla.	.35	.50
☐ ☐	128 Jerry Korab, Buff.	.35	.50
☐ ☐	129 Bob Gainey, Mont.	2.50	4.00
☐ ☐	130 Wilf Paiement, Colo.	.35	.50
☐ ☐	131 Tom Bladon, Phil.	.35	.50
☐ ☐	132 Ernie Hicke, Minn. (LosA.)	.35	.50
☐ ☐	133 J.P. LeBlanc, Detr.	.35	.50
☐ ☐	**134 Mike Milbury, Bost. RC**	**5.00**	**8.00**
☐ ☐	135 Pit Martin, Chic. (Vanc.)	.35	.50
☐ ☐	136 Steve Vickers, NYRa.	.35	.50
☐ ☐	137 Don Awrey, Pitt. (NYRa.)	.35	.50
☐ ☐	138 Bernie Wolfe (G), Wash.	.75	1.00
☐ ☐	139 Doug Jarvis, Mont.	1.00	1.50
☐ ☐	140 AS: Börje Salming	1.50	2.50
☐ ☐	141 Bob MacMillan, SLou.	.35	.50
☐ ☐	142 Wayne Stephenson (G), Phil.	.75	1.00
☐ ☐	143 Dave Forbes, Bost. (Wash.)	.35	.50
☐ ☐	144 Jean Potvin, NYIs.	.35	.50
☐ ☐	145 Guy Charron, Wash.	.35	.50
☐ ☐	146 Cliff Koroll, Chic.	.35	.50
☐ ☐	147 Danny Grant, Detr.	.35	.50
☐ ☐	148 Bill Hogaboam, Minn.	.35	.50
☐ ☐	149 Al MacAdam, Clev.	.35	.50
☐ ☐	150 Gerry Desjardins (G), Buff.	.75	1.00
☐ ☐	151 Yvon Lambert, Mont.	.35	.50
☐ ☐	152 Rick Lapointe, Phil.	.35	.50
☐ ☐	153 Ed Westfall, NYIs.	.35	.50
☐ ☐	154 Carol Vadnais, NYRa.	.35	.50
☐ ☐	155 John Bucyk, Bost.	1.00	1.50
☐ ☐	156 J.P. Bordeleau, Chic.	.35	.50
☐ ☐	157 Ron Stackhouse, Pitt.	.35	.50
☐ ☐	**158 Glen Sharpley, Minn. RC**	**.75**	**1.00**
☐ ☐	159 Michel Bergeron, Detr. (NYIs.)	.35	.50
☐ ☐	160 AS: Rogatien Vachon (G), LosA.	1.00	1.50
☐ ☐	161 Fred Stanfield, Buff.	.35	.50
☐ ☐	162 Gerry Hart, NYIs.	.35	.50
☐ ☐	163 Mario Tremblay, Mont.	.75	1.00
☐ ☐	164 André Dupont, Phil.	.35	.50
☐ ☐	165 Don Marcotte, Bost.	.35	.50
☐ ☐	166 Wayne Dillon, NYRa.	.35	.50
☐ ☐	167 Claude Larose, SLou.	.35	.50
☐ ☐	168 Eric Vail, Atla.	.35	.50
☐ ☐	**169 Tom Edur, Colo. RC**	**.75**	**1.00**
☐ ☐	170 Tony Esposito (G), Chic.	2.50	4.00
☐ ☐	171 André St. Laurent, NYIs., (Detr.)	.35	.50
☐ ☐	172 Dan Maloney, Detr.	.35	.50
☐ ☐	173 Dennis O'Brien, Minn.	.35	.50
☐ ☐	**174 Blair Chapman, Pitt. RC**	**.75**	**1.00**
☐ ☐	175 Dennis Kearns, Vanc.	.35	.50
☐ ☐	176 Wayne Merrick, Clev.	.35	.50
☐ ☐	177 Michel Larocque (G), Mont.	.75	1.00
☐ ☐	178 Bob Kelly, Phil.	.35	.50
☐ ☐	**179 Dave Farrish, NYRa. RC**	**.75**	**1.00**
☐ ☐	180 AS: Rick Martin, Buff.	.75	1.00
☐ ☐	181 Gary Doak, Bost.	.35	.50
☐ ☐	182 Jude Drouin, NYIs.	.35	.50
☐ ☐	**183 Barry Dean, Colo. (Phil.) RC**	**.75**	**1.00**
☐ ☐	184 Gary Smith (G), Minn. (Wash.)	.75	1.00
☐ ☐	185 Reggie Leach, Phil.	.75	1.00
☐ ☐	186 Ian Turnbull, Toro.	.35	.50
☐ ☐	187 Vic Venasky, LosA.	.35	.50
☐ ☐	**188 Wayne Bianchin, Pitt. RC**	**.75**	**1.00**
☐ ☐	189 Doug Risebrough, Mont.	.35	.50
☐ ☐	190 Brad Park, Bost.	1.50	2.50
☐ ☐	191 Craig Ramsay, Buff.	.75	1.00
☐ ☐	192 Ken Hodge, NYRa.	.35	.50
☐ ☐	193 Phil Myre (G), Atla.	.75	1.00
☐ ☐	194 Garry Howatt, NYIs.	.35	.50
☐ ☐	195 Stan Mikita, Chic.	2.50	4.00
☐ ☐	196 Garnet Bailey, Wash.	.35	.50
☐ ☐	197 Dennis Hextall, Detr.	.35	.50
☐ ☐	198 Nick Beverley, Minn.	.35	.50
☐ ☐	199 Larry Patey, SLou.	.35	.50
☐ ☐	200 AS: Guy Lafleur, Mont.	10.00	15.00
☐ ☐	**201 Don Edwards (G), Buff. RC**	**3.00**	**5.00**
☐ ☐	202 Gary Dornhoefer, Phil.	.35	.50
☐	203 Bob Paradise, Pitt.	-	.50

203 Stan Gilbertson, Pitt.	.50	–
204 Alex Pirus, Minn. RC	**.75**	**1.00**
205 Pete Mahovlich, Mont.	.75	1.00
206 Bert Marshall, NYIs.	.35	.50
207 Gilles Gratton (G), NYRa.	.75	1.00
208 Alain Daigle, Chic.	.35	.50
209 Chris Oddleifson, Vanc.	.35	.50
210 AS: Gilbert Perreault, Buff.	2.50	4.00
211 Mike Palmateer (G), Toro. RC	**7.00**	**12.00**
212 Bill Lochead, Detr.	.35	.50
213 Dick Redmond, Chic., (SLou.)	.35	.50
214 RB: Guy Lafleur, Mont.	2.00	3.00
215 RB: Ian Turnbull, Toro.	.75	1.00
216 RB: Guy Lafleur, Mont.	2.00	3.00
217 RB: Steve Shutt, Mont.	1.00	1.50
218 RB: Guy Lafleur, Mont.	2.00	3.00
219 Lorne Henning, NYIs.	.35	.50
220 Terry O'Reilly, Bost.	.35	.50
221 Pat Hickey, NYRa.	.35	.50
222 René Robert, Buff.	.35	.50
223 Tim Young, Minn.	.35	.50
224 Dunc Wilson (G), Pitt.	.75	1.00
225 Dennis Hull, Chic.	.75	1.00
226 Rod Seiling, SLou.	.35	.50
227 Bill Barber, Phil.	1.50	2.50
228 Dennis Polonich, Detr. RC	**.75**	**1.00**
229 Billy Smith (G), NYIs.	2.50	4.00
230 Yvan Cournoyer, Mont.	1.25	2.00
231 Don Luce, Buff.	.35	.50
232 Mike McEwen, NYRa. RC	**.75**	**1.00**
233 Don Saleski, Phil.	.35	.50
234 Wayne Cashman, Bost.	.35	.50
235 Phil Russell, Chic.	.35	.50
236 Mike Corrigan, Pitt.	.35	.50
237 Guy Chouinard, Atla.	.35	.50
238 Steve Jensen, Minn. RC	**.75**	**1.00**
239 Jim Rutherford (G), Detr.	.75	1.00
240 AS: Marcel Dionne, LosA.	2.50	4.00
241 Réjean Houle, Mont.	.75	1.00
242 Jocelyn Guevremont, Buff.	.35	.50
243 Jim Harrison, Chic.	.35	.50
244 Don Murdoch, NYRa. RC	**.75**	**1.00**
245 Richard Green, Wash. RC	**2.00**	**3.00**
246 Rick Middleton, Bost.	1.50	2.50
247 Joe Watson, Phil.	.35	.50
248 Syl Apps, Pitt. (LosA.)	.35	.50
249 Checklist 2 (133 - 264)	6.00	12.00
250 Clark Gillies, NYIs.	.75	1.00
251 Bobby Orr, Chic.	20.00	30.00
252 Nelson Pyatt, Colo.	.35	.50
253 Gary McAdam, Buff. RC	**.75**	**1.00**
254 Jacques Lemaire, Mont.	1.00	1.50
255 Bob Girard, Clev.	–	.50
255 Bill Fairbairn, Minn.	.50	–
256 Ron Greschner, NYRa.	.35	.50
257 Ross Lonsberry, Phil.	.35	.50
258 Dave Gardner, Clev.	.35	.50
259 Rick Blight, Vanc.	.35	.50
260 Gerry Cheevers (G), Bost.	1.50	2.50
261 Jean Pronovost, Pitt.	.35	.50
262 Playoffs: Canadiens Skate Past Islanders	.75	1.00
263 Playoffs: Bruins Advance to Finals	.75	1.00
264 Canadiens Win 20th Stanley Cup	1.00	1.50

Description	OPC
265 Rick Bowness, Atla. (Det). RC	**2.00**
266 George Ferguson, Toro.	.50
267 Mike Kitchen, Colo. RC	**1.00**
268 Bob Berry, LosA.	.50
269 Greg Smith, Clev. RC	**1.00**
270 Stan Jonathan, Bost. RC	**6.00**
271 Dwight Bialowas, Minn.	.50
272 Pete Stemkowski, (LosA.)	.50
273 Greg Joly, Detr.	.50
274 Ken Houston, Atla. RC	**1.00**
275 Brian Glennie, Toro.	.50
276 Eddie Johnston (G), SLou.	1.00
277 John Grisdale, Vanc.	.50
278 Craig Patrick, Wash.	.50
279 Ken Breitenbach, Buff. RC	**1.00**
280 Fred Ahern, Calg. (Clev.)	.50
281 Jim Roberts, Mont. (SLou.)	.50
282 Harvey Bennett, Phil. RC	**1.00**
283 Ab DeMarco, LosA. (Atla.)	.50
284 Pat Boutette, Toro.	.50
285 Bob Plager, SLou.	.50
286 Hilliard Graves, Vanc.	.50
287 Gordie Lane, Wash. RC	**1.00**
288 Ron Andruff, Colo. RC	**1.00**
289 Larry Brown, LosA.	.50
290 Mike Fidler, Clev. RC	**1.00**
291 Fred Barrett, Minn.	.50
292 Bill Clement, Atla.	.50
293 Errol Thompson, Toro.	.50
294 Doug Grant (G), SLou.	1.00
295 Harold Snepsts, Vanc.	1.50
296 Rick Bragnalo, Wash. RC	**1.00**
297 Bryan Lefley, Colo.	.50
298 Gene Carr, LosA. (Pitt.)	.50
299 Bob Stewart, Clev.	.50
300 Lew Morrison, Pitt.	.50
301 Ed Kea, Atla.	.50
302 Scott Garland, Toro.	.50
303 Bill Fairbairn, NYRa. (SLou.)	.50
304 Larry Carrière, Vanc.	.50
305 Ron Low (G), Wash. (Detr.)	1.00
306 Tom Reid, Minn.	.50
307 Paul Holmgren, Phil. RC	**4.00**
308 Pat Price, NYIs.	.50
309 Kirk Bowman, Chic. RC	**1.00**
310 Bobby Simpson, Atla. RC	**1.00**
311 Ron Ellis, Toro.	.50
312 Rick Bourbonnais, SLou., Err. (Bernie Federko)	.50
313 Bobby Lalonde, (Atla.)	.50
314 Tony White, Wash.	.50
315 John Van Boxmeer, Colo.	.50
316 Don Kozak, LosA.	.50
317 Jim Neilson, NYRa. (Clev.)	.50
318 Terry Martin, Buff. RC	**1.00**
319 Barry Gibbs, Atla.	.50
320 Inge Hammarstrom, Toro. (SLou.)	.50
321 Darryl Edestrand, Bost.	.50
322 Atlanta Flames	3.00
323 Boston Bruins	3.00
324 Buffalo Sabres	3.00
325 Chicago Blackhawks	3.00
326 Cleveland Barons	3.00
327 Colorado Rockies	3.00
328 Detroit Red Wings	3.00
329 Los Angeles Kings	3.00
330 Minnesota North Stars	3.00
331 Montréal Canadiens	3.00
332 New York Islanders	3.00
333 New York Rangers	3.00
334 Philadelphia Flyers	3.00
335 Pittsburgh Penguins	3.00
336 St. Louis Blues	3.00
337 Toronto Maple Leafs	3.00
338 Vancouver Canucks	3.00
339 Washington Capitals	3.00
340 Chuck Lefley, SLou.	.50
341 Garry Monahan, Vanc.	.50
342 Bryan Watson, Wash.	.50
343 Dave Hudson, Colo.	.50
344 Neil Komadoski, LosA.	.50
345 Gary Edwards (G), LosA. (Clev.)	1.00
346 Rey Comeau, Atla.	.50
347 Bob Neely, Toro.	.50
348 Jean Hamel, Detr.	.50
349 Jerry Butler, Toro.	.50
350 Mike Walton, Vanc.	.50
351 Bob Sirois, Wash.	.50
352 Jim McElmury, Colo.	.50
353 Dave Schultz, (Pitt.)	.50
354 Doug Palazzari, SLou. RC	**1.00**
355 Dave Shand, Atla. RC	**1.00**
356 Stan Weir, Toro.	.50
357 Mike Christie, Clev.	.50
358 Floyd Thomson, SLou.	.50
359 Larry Goodenough, Phil. (Vanc.)	.50
360 Bill Riley, Wash. RC	**1.00**
361 Doug Hicks, Minn. RC	**1.00**
362 Dan Newman, NYRa. RC	**1.00**
363 Rick Chartraw, Mont.	.50
364 Tim Ecclestone, Atla.	.50
365 Don Ashby, Toro. RC	**1.00**
366 Jacques Richard, Buff.	.50
367 Yves Belanger (G), SLou.	1.00
368 Ron Sedlbauer, Vanc.	.50
369 Jack Lynch, Wash., Err. (Bill Collins)	.50
370 Doug Favell (G), Colo.	1.00
371 Bob Murdoch, LosA.	.50
372 Ralph Klassen, Clev.	.50
373 Richard Mulhern, Atla.	.50
374 Jim McKenny, Toro.	.50
375 Mike Bloom, Detr.	.50
376 Bruce Affleck, SLou.	.50
377 Gerry O'Flaherty, Vanc.	.50
378 Ron Lalonde, Wash.	.50
379 Chuck Arnason, Colo.	.50
380 Dave Hutchison, LosA.	.50
381 Checklist 3 (265 - 396)	12.00
382 John Gould, Atla.	.50
383 Dave Williams, Toro.	5.00
384 Len Frig, Clev. (SLou.)	.50
385 Pierre Plante, SLou. (Chic.)	.50
386 Ralph Stewart, Vanc.	.50
387 Gord Smith, Wash.	.50
388 Denis Dupère, Colo.	.50
389 Randy Manery, Atla. (LosA.)	.50
390 Lowell MacDonald, Pitt.	.50
391 Dennis Owchar, Pitt.	.50
392 Jimmy Roberts, Minn. RC	**1.00**
393 Mike Veisor (G), Chic.	1.00
394 Bob Hess, SLou.	.50
395 Curt Ridley (G), Vanc.	1.00
396 Mike Lampman, Wash.	1.00

GLOSSY

Insert Set (22 cards):	**15.00**
Common Player:	**.50**
O-Pee-Chee	**NM-MT**
1 Wayne Cashman, Bost.	.50
2 Gerry Cheevers (G), Bost.	1.50
3 Bobby Clarke, Phil.	2.00
4 Marcel Dionne, LosA.	2.00
5 Ken Dryden (G), Mont.	4.00
6 Clark Gillies, NYIs.	.50
7 Guy Lafleur, Mont.	4.00
8 Reggie Leach, Phil.	.50
9 Rick MacLeish, Phil.	.50
10 Dave Maloney, NYRa.	.50
11 Richard Martin, Buff.	.50
12 Don Murdoch, NYRa.	.50
13 Brad Park, Bost.	1.00
14 Gilbert Perreault, Buff.	1.25
15 Denis Potvin, NYIs.	2.00
16 Jean Ratelle, Bost.	1.00
17 Glenn Resch (G), NYIs.	.75
18 Larry Robinson, Mont.	1.00
19 Steve Shutt, Mont.	1.25
20 Darryl Sittler, Toro.	1.50
21 Rogatien Vachon (G), LosA.	1.00
22 Tim Young, Minn.	.50

1977 - 78 O-PEE-CHEE WHA

These cards measure the standard 2 1/2" x 3 1/2".

Complete Set (66 cards):	**100.00**
Common Player:	**1.00**
O-Pee-Chee	**NM-MT**
1 Gordie Howe, New England	50.00
2 Jean Bernier, Québec RC	**1.50**
3 Anders Hedberg, Winnipeg	2.00
4 Ken Broderick (G), Québec	2.00
5 Joe Noris, Birmingham	1.00
6 Blaine Stoughton, Cleveland	1.00
7 Claude St. Sauveur, Indianapolis	1.00
8 Réal Cloutier, Québec	1.00
9 Joe Daley (G), Winnipeg	2.00
10 Ron Chipperfield, Edmonton	1.00
11 Wayne Rutledge (G), Houston	2.00
12 Mark Napier, Birmingham	2.00
13 Rich LeDuc, Cincinnati	1.00
14 Don McLeod (G), Québec	2.00
15 Ulf Nilsson, Winnipeg	2.00
16 Blair MacDonald, Edmonton	1.00
17 Mike Rogers, New England	1.00
18 Gary Inness (G), Indianapolis	2.00
19 Larry Lund, Houston	1.00
20 Marc Tardif, Québec	1.00
21 Lars-Erik Sjoberg, Winnipeg	1.00
22 Bryan Campbell, Edmonton	1.00
23 John Garrett (G), Birmingham	2.00
24 Ron Plumb, Cincinnati	1.00
25 Mark Howe, New England	7.50
26 Garry Lariviere, Québec RC	**1.50**
27 Peter Sullivan, Winnipeg	1.00
28 Dave Dryden (G), Edmonton	2.00
29 Reg Thomas, Indianapolis	1.00
30 André Lacroix, Houston	2.00
31 Paul Henderson, Birmingham	3.50
32 Paulin Bordeleau, Québec	1.00
33 Juha Widing, Edmonton	1.00
34 Mike Antonovich, New England	1.00
35 Robbie Ftorek, Cincinnati	2.00
36 Rosaire Paiement, Indianapolis	1.00
37 Terry Ruskowski, Houston	1.00
38 Richard Brodeur (G), Québec	5.00
39 Willy Lindstrom, Winnipeg RC	**2.00**
40 Al Hamilton, Edmonton	1.00
41 John McKenzie, New England	1.00
42 Wayne Wood (G), Birmingham	2.00
43 Claude Larose, Cincinnati	1.00
44 J.C. Tremblay, Québec	2.00
45 Gary Bromley (G), Winnipeg	2.00
46 Ken Baird, Edmonton	1.00
47 Bobby Sheehan, Indianapolis	1.00
48 Don Larway, Houston RC	**1.50**
49 Al Smith (G), New England	2.00
50 Bobby Hull, Winnipeg	30.00
51 Peter Marrin, Birmingham	1.00
52 Norm Ferguson, Edmonton	1.00
53 Dennis Sobchuk, Cincinnati	1.00
54 Norm Dubé, Québec RC	**1.50**
55 Tom Webster, New England	1.00
56 Jim Park (G), Indianapolis RC	**2.00**
57 Dan Labraaten, Winnipeg RC	**1.50**
58 Checklist (1 - 66)	15.00
59 Paul Shmyr, Edmonton	1.00
60 Serge Bernier, Québec	1.00
61 Frank Mahovlich, Birmingham	7.00
62 Michel Dion (G), Cincinnati,	2.00
63 Poul Popiel, Houston	1.00
64 Lyle Moffat, Winnipeg	1.00
65 Marty Howe, New England	2.00
66 Don Burgess, Indianapolis	3.50

1977 - 79 SPORTSCASTER CARDS

These cards measure 4 3/4" x 6 1/4". The cards have rounded corners.

Common Player:	**4.00**
Sportscaster	**NM**
01-02 Bobby Orr	35.00
02-06 Gordie Howe	30.00
02-13 Yvan Cournoyer (The Stanley Cup)	10.00
03-19 Phil Esposito, Bost. (Sibling Rivalry)	15.00
05-09 U.S.A. vs. C.S.S.R.	4.00
05-20 Bobby Hull	20.00
06-07 Gump Worsley (G), Minn.	10.00
07-08 Team U.S.S.R. '76	8.00
07-17 Brad Park, NYRa.	8.00
10-14 Jean Béliveau	15.00
11-19 Bob Hodges (Hat Trick)	4.00
12-15 U.S.S.R. vs. C.S.S.R. (XCX-V.Petrov)	4.00
12-22 Stan Mikita	10.00
17-09 Denis Potvin	10.00
14-23 Ken Dryden (G)	25.00
15-13 Yvan Cournoyer	10.00
18-23 Garry Unger	4.00
19-15 Canada vs. C.S.S.R.	8.00
21-12 Fussen WGE (The Equipment)	4.00
27-24 National Hockey League	4.00
29-08 Phil Esposito, NYRa. (The Power Play)	10.00
31-03 Bobby Clarke (Penalty Killing)	10.00
33-03 Rod Gilbert (Lines In The Ice)	4.00
35-03 The Spengler Cup (U.S.S.R. vs. C.S.S.R.)	4.00
38-07 Guy Lafleur, Mont.	15.00
40-24 Rangers vs. Blues (XCX-Ed Giacomin)	4.00
43-04 Major and Minor Penalties	4.00
43-06 Rogatien Vachon (G)	4.00
44-03 Jaroslav Jirik	4.00
44-20 Gerry Cheevers (G)	10.00
45-13 Steve Shutt	10.00
46-14 In The Corners	4.00
46-21 Bryan Trottier	12.00
47-16 B. Trottier/ C. Gillies/ M. Bossy	15.00
47-18 Darryl Sittler	12.00
50-03 Bobby Hull (Sticks)	20.00
50-04 Facemasks	4.00
51-01 Czechoslovakia 1977	4.00
51-18 Guy Lafleur, Mont.	15.00
55-14 Jiri Holik/ Jaroslav Holik	4.00
55-23 Bobby Hull, Winnipeg	20.00
56-06 Montréal Forum	4.00
60-12 Bobby Clarke	12.00
61-03 Ed Giacomin (G) (Lingo)	10.00
62-17 Lester Patrick	4.00
63-09 The Howe Family	30.00
64-16 Pete Stemkowski (Sudden Death)	4.00
67-21 Bill Chadwick	4.00
70-06 Hall of Fame	4.00
71-12 A.Hedberg/ U. Nilsson	8.00
73-01 U.S.S.R. vs. NHL	8.00
73-11 Czechoslovakia 1976	4.00
74-17 Team U.S.S.R.	8.00
74-24 Vaclav Nedomansky	4.00
76-03 NCAA Hockey Champions	4.00
77-01 Wayne Gretzky	400.00
77-24 NHL Expansions - Oilers, Whalers	4.00
78-04 Réal Cloutier	4.00
80-18 John Davidson (G)	10.00
81-19 Jacques Lemaire	10.00
82-05 Scotty Bowman	15.00
82-23 Dave Dryden (G)	4.00
102-14 V. Kharlamov/ V. Petrov/ B. Mikhailov	12.00
103-08 Alexander Volchkov	8.00
Sportscaster • Finnish	**NM**
UK-327 Suomen Jääkiekkoilu	4.00
02-27 Tsekkoslovakia	4.00
02-39 Stanley Cup	6.00

☐	03-71 Olympiakiekkoilu 1960	4.00
☐	04-83 Bobby Orr	40.00
☐	05-105 Phil Esposito (Sibling Rivalry)	20.00
☐	05-115 Tappara 1976-77	4.00
☐	07-152 Soviet Union 1976	10.00
☐	07-168 Gordie Howe	35.00
☐	08-181 Bobby Hull	25.00
☐	12-279 MM-Kilpailut I	4.00
☐	14-335 Finnish Maajoukkue	4.00
☐	16-364 A. Leppänen/ J. Valtonen	4.00
☐	17-397 Veli-Pekka Ketola	6.00
☐	19-436 Pekka Marrjamäki	4.00
☐	19-447 MM-Kilpailut II	4.00
☐	20-469 Vaclav Nedomansky	6.00
☐	21-492 Pelaajien Varusteet	4.00
☐	23-532 Hat Trick	4.00
☐	26-673 Kharlamov/ Petrov/ Mikhailov	15.00
☐	29-692 Brad Park	10.00
☐	31-736 National Hockey League	6.00
☐	32-747 Matti Hagman	6.00
☐	33-775 Porin Ässät	4.00
☐	33-785 Jean Béliveau	20.00
☐	36-845 Lalli Partinen	4.00
☐	37-869 Phil Esposito	15.00
☐	38-891 Bobby Clarke	18.00
☐	38-895 Guy Lafleur	20.00
☐	40-937 Matti Keinonen	4.00
☐	40-945 Stanley Cup	6.00
☐	41-961 Matti Murto	4.00
☐	42-1008 Viivoja Jäässä	4.00
☐	43-1009 HIFK	4.00
☐	43-1031 C. and T. Abrahamsson	6.00
☐	45-1057 Lasse Oksanen	4.00
☐	45-1069 Jaroslav Jirik	4.00
☐	45-1075 Ilves Tampere	4.00
☐	46-1084 Juhani Tamminen	4.00
☐	47-1106 Pekka Rautakallio	6.00
☐	47-1113 Helmut Balderis	8.00
☐	47-1125 Liiga-TPS	4.00
☐	48-1145 Ken Dryden (G)	30.00
☐	48-1152 Timo Nummelin	4.00
☐	49-1174 Gerry Cheevers (G)	12.00
☐	49-1175 Esa Peltonen	4.00
☐	49-1197 Bryan Trottier	15.00
☐	50-1178 Steve Shutt	12.00
☐	50-1188 Izvestija-Turnaus	4.00
☐	50-1190 Lämäri	4.00
☐	50-1197 Rogie Vachon (G)	8.00
☐	50-1199 Teppo Rastio	4.00
☐	51-1201 Markus Mattson	6.00
☐	51-1212 Pienet and Isot Rangaistukset	4.00
☐	51-1214 Jokerit Helsinki	4.00
☐	51-1218 Jiri and Jaroslav Holik	4.00
☐	51-1224 Stan Mikita	12.00
☐	52-1230 Nurkkapeli	4.00
☐	52-1232 Garry Unger	8.00
☐	52-1235 Oulun Kärpät	4.00
☐	52-1243 Ilpo Koskela	4.00
☐	53-1265 Darryl Sittler	15.00
☐	53-1273 Antero Lehtonen	4.00
☐	54-1290 Trio Grande	20.00
☐	56-1324 Denis Potvin	12.00
☐	57-1356 Guy Lafleur	20.00
☐	57-1358 Bobby Hull	25.00
☐	57-1364 Kasvosuojukset	4.00
☐	58-1381 Bobby Hull	25.00
☐	58-1392 Yvan Cournoyer	12.00
☐	66-1566 Montréal Forum	6.00
☐	68-1623 Pete Stemkowski	6.00
☐	69-1649 Bobby Clarke	15.00
☐	70-1663 Börje Salming	10.00
☐	70-1670 Howen perhe	4.00
☐	71-1686 Alexander Yakushev	10.00
☐	71-1699 Soviet Union 1978-79	10.00
☐	72-1705 Jukka Porvari	4.00
☐	72-1716 Lester Patrick	8.00
☐	73-1730 Kanadan Jääkiekkomuseo	4.00
☐	74-1758 Eddie Giacomin	12.00
☐	74-1760 Seppo Repo	4.00
☐	75-1796 Risto Siltanen	6.00
☐	75-1800 Kalevi Numminen	4.00
☐	76-1801 Pertti Koivulahti	4.00
☐	76-1821 Mikko Leinonen	4.00
☐	77-1848 Jari Kurri	15.00
☐	78-1849 Tapio Levo	6.00
☐	78-1861 Vladislav Tretiak (G)	30.00
☐	78-1872 Kiekkoreipas	4.00
☐	79-1973 KooVee	4.00
☐	79-1896 Rauman Lukko	4.00
☐	80-1911 A. Hedberg/ U. Nilsson	10.00
☐	80-1918 Olympiakisat	4.00
☐	81-1922 NHL and Soviet Union	10.00
☐	81-1931 Tsekkoslovakia 1976-1977	4.00
☐	82-1949 Hannu Haapalainen	4.00
☐	82-1955 Markku and Yrjö Hakulinen	4.00
☐	83-1970 Reijo Leppänen	4.00
☐	83-1982 Seppo Lindström	4.00
☐	83-1983 Jiri Holecek	6.00
☐	84-2006 Kanada	10.00
☐	84-2015 Aleksandr Yakushev	10.00
☐	84-2016 Lasse Litma	4.00
☐	85-2017 Seppo Suoraniemi	4.00
☐	85-2024 Dave Dryden	8.00
☐	85-2035Jacques Lemaire	12.00
☐	86-2041 Reijo Ruotsalainen	6.00
☐	86-2064 Hannu Koskinen	4.00
☐	87-2072 Jouni Rinne	4.00
☐	87-2075 Nuorten MM-kisat	4.00
☐	88-2103 Helsingin IFK	4.00
☐	89-2127 Wayne Gretzky	500.00
☐	90-2139 Real Cloutier	6.00
☐	90-2148 Antero Kivelä	4.00
☐	90-2150 Markku Kiimalainen	4.00
☐	90-2152 Jarmo Mäkitalo	4.00
☐	90-2160 NHL and WHA	6.00
☐	90-2162 Scotty Bowman, Coach	15.00
☐	90-2165 Ismo Villa	4.00
☐	90-2169 Timo Susi	4.00
☐	103-2455 Ivan Hlinka	6.00
☐	105-2513 Soviet Union 1979	6.00
☐	107-2559 Jorma Valtonen	4.00
☐	108-2573 Henry Leppä	4.00
☐	108-2579 Ruotsi	4.00
☐	108-2583 Suomen Jäähallit	4.00
☐	108-2587 Saimaan Pallo	4.00

1978 - 79 DERNIÈRE PHOTOS

This multi-sport series of photos were inserted in Dernière magazine from 1972 through 1984. Three holes were punched on the left side to allow for storage in a binder. The series featured Montréal Canadiens players. These photos measure 8" x 10".

	Dernière	NM
☐	10DEC J.C. Tremblay	5.00
☐	17DEC Nordique Player	3.00
☐	24DEC Danny Geoffrion	3.00
☐	31DEC Paul Baxter	3.00
☐	7JAN Normand Dubé	3.00
☐	14JAN Jim Corsi (G)	5.00
☐	21JAN Jim Dorey	3.00
☐	28JAN Marc Tardiff	5.00
☐	4FEB Bob Fitchner	3.00
☐	11FEB Alain Côté	3.00
☐	18FEB Richard David	3.00
☐	25FEB Jacques Demers, Coach	5.00
☐	4MAR François Lacombe	3.00
☐	11MAR Réal Cloutier	3.00
☐	18MAR Curt Brackenbury	3.00
☐	25MAR Richard Brodeur (G)	5.00
☐	1APR Dale Hoganson	3.00
☐	8APR Wally Weir	3.00
☐	15APR Serge Bernier	3.00
☐	2APR Gary Larivière	3.00
☐	29APR Paul Baxter	3.00

1978 - 79 O-PEE-CHEE & TOPPS

"I remember opening packs of 1978-79 and pulling the Bobby Orr team Canada commemorative card #300. On the card, it said Collector's Card. That was the first time it occurred to me that cards were a collectible item. I was seven or eight at the time and all we did was chew gum and then throw around the cards. But this card actually said right on it (Collector's Card) and that is what put it into my mind (that these are collectible)." – Kevin Lawr, Niagara Collectibles, St. Catharines, ON.

These cards measure the standard 2 1/2" x 3 1/2". There are two versions for cards 1-264: the O-Pee-Chee and the Topps card. Topps cards do not have the traded line that appears on the O-Pee-Chee counterparts. O-Pee-Chee cards do not have the All-Star line that appears on the Topps counterparts.

O-Pee-Chee Set (396 cards):	–	**200.00**
Topps Set (264 cards):	85.00	–
Common Player:	**.25**	**.35**

	Description	Topps	OPC
☐ ☐	1 HL: Mike Bossy, NYIs.	5.00	9.00
☐ ☐	2 HL: Phil Esposito, NYRa.	1.50	2.00
☐ ☐	3 HL: Guy Lafleur, Mont.	1.75	2.50
☐ ☐	4 HL: Darryl Sittler, Toro.	1.00	1.50
☐ ☐	5 HL: Garry Unger, SLou.	.50	.75
☐ ☐	6 Gary Edwards (G), Minn.	.50	.75
☐ ☐	7 Rick Blight, Vanc.	.25	.35
☐ ☐	8 Larry Patey, SLou.	.25	.35
☐ ☐	9 Craig Ramsay, Buff.	.35	.50
☐ ☐	10 Bryan Trottier, NYIs.	6.00	12.00
☐ ☐	11 Don Murdoch, NYRa.	.25	.35
☐ ☐	12 Phil Russell, Chic.	.25	.35
☐ ☐	13 Doug Jarvis, Mont.	.35	.50
☐ ☐	14 Gene Carr, Atla.	.25	.35
☐ ☐	15 Bernie Parent (G), Phil.	1.25	2.50
☐ ☐	16 Perry Miller, Detr.	.25	.35
☐ ☐	**17 Kent-Erik Andersson, Minn. RC**	**.50**	**.75**
☐ ☐	18 Gregg Sheppard, Pitt.	.25	.35
☐ ☐	19 Dennis Owchar, Colo.	.25	.35
☐ ☐	20 Rogatien Vachon (G), LosA. (Detr.)	.65	1.00
☐ ☐	21 Dan Maloney, Toro.	.25	.35
☐ ☐	22 Guy Charron, Wash.	.25	.35
☐ ☐	23 Dick Redmond, Bost.	.25	.35
☐ ☐	24 Checklist 1 (1 - 132)	5.00	7.50
☐ ☐	25 Anders Hedberg, NYRa.	.25	.35
☐ ☐	26 Mel Bridgman, Phil.	.25	.35
☐ ☐	27 Lee Fogolin, Buff.	.25	.35
☐ ☐	28 Gilles Meloche (G), Minn.	.50	.75
☐ ☐	29 Garry Howatt, NYIs.	.25	.35
☐ ☐	30 Darryl Sittler, Toro.	1.50	3.00
☐ ☐	31 Curt Bennett, SLou.	.25	.35
☐ ☐	32 André St. Laurent, Detr.	.25	.35
☐ ☐	33 Blair Chapman, Pitt.	.25	.35
☐ ☐	34 Keith Magnuson, Chic.	.25	.35
☐ ☐	35 Pierre Larouche, Mont.	.25	.35
☐ ☐	36 Michael Plasse (G), Colo.	.50	.75
☐ ☐	37 Gary Sargent, Minn.	.25	.35
☐ ☐	38 Mike Walton, SLou.	.25	.35
☐ ☐	**39 Robert Picard, Wash. RC**	**.50**	**.75**
☐ ☐	40 Terry O'Reilly, Bost.	.50	.75
☐ ☐	41 Dave Farrish, NYRa.	.25	.35
☐ ☐	42 Gary McAdam, Buff.	.25	.35
☐ ☐	43 Joe Watson, Phil. (Colo.)	.25	.35
☐ ☐	44 Yves Belanger (G), Atla.	.25	.35
☐ ☐	45 Steve Jensen, Minn. (LosA.)	.25	.35
☐ ☐	46 Bob Stewart, SLou.	.25	.35
☐ ☐	47 Darcy Rota, Chic.	.25	.35
☐ ☐	48 Dennis Hextall, Detr.	.25	.35
☐ ☐	49 Bert Marshall, NYIs.	.25	.35
☐ ☐	50 Ken Dryden (G), Mont.	8.00	15.00
☐ ☐	51 Pete Mahovlich, Pitt.	.35	.50
☐ ☐	52 Dennis Ververgaert, Vanc.	.25	.35
☐ ☐	53 Inge Hammarstrom, SLou.	.25	.35
☐ ☐	54 Doug Favell (G), Colo.	.50	.75
☐ ☐	55 Steve Vickers, NYRa.	.25	.35
☐ ☐	56 Syl Apps, Jr., LosA.	.25	.35
☐ ☐	57 Errol Thompson, Detr.	.25	.35
☐ ☐	58 Don Luce, Buff.	.25	.35
☐ ☐	59 Mike Milbury, Bost.	.25	.35
☐ ☐	60 Yvan Cournoyer, Mont.	.75	1.50
☐ ☐	61 Kirk Bowman, Chic.	.25	.35
☐ ☐	62 Billy Smith (G), NYIs.	1.25	2.50
☐ ☐	63 LL: G. Lafleur/ M. Bossy/ S. Shutt	3.00	5.00
☐ ☐	64 LL: B. Trottier/ G. Lafleur/ D. Sittler	2.00	3.50
☐ ☐	65 LL: G. Lafleur/ B. Trottier/ D. Sittler	2.00	3.50
☐ ☐	66 LL: D. Schultz/ D. Williams/ D. Polonich	.50	.75
☐ ☐	67 LL: M. Bossy/ P. Esposito/ S. Shutt	2.25	4.50
☐ ☐	68 LL: Dryden (G)/ Parent (G)/ Gilbert (G)	4.50	
☐ ☐	69 LL: Lafleur/ Barber/ Sittler/ Bourne	3.50	
☐ ☐	70 LL: Parent (G)/ Dryden (G)/ Edwards (G)/ T. Esposito (G)/ M. Palmateer (G)	3.00	6.00
☐ ☐	71 Bob Kelly, Phil.	.25	.35
☐ ☐	72 Ron Stackhouse, Pitt.	.25	.35
☐ ☐	73 Wayne Dillon, NYRa.	.25	.35
☐ ☐	74 Jim Rutherford (G), Detr.	.50	.75
☐ ☐	75 Stan Mikita, Chic.	1.25	2.50
☐ ☐	76 Bob Gainey, Mont.	1.25	2.50
☐ ☐	77 Gerry Hart, NYIs.	.25	.35
☐ ☐	78 Lanny McDonald, Toro.	1.00	2.00
☐ ☐	79 Brad Park, Bost.	1.00	2.00
☐ ☐	80 Rick Martin, Buff.	.35	.50
☐ ☐	81 Bernie Wolfe (G), Wash.	.50	.75
☐ ☐	82 Bob MacMillan, Atla.	.25	.35
☐ ☐	**83 Brad Maxwell, Minn. RC**	**.50**	**.75**
☐ ☐	84 Mike Fidler, Minn.	.25	.35
☐ ☐	85 Carol Vadnais, NYRa.	.25	.35
☐ ☐	86 Don Lever, Vanc.	.25	.35
☐ ☐	87 Phil Myre (G), SLou.	.50	.75
☐ ☐	88 Paul Gardner, Colo.	.25	.35
☐ ☐	89 Bob Murray, Chic.	.25	.35
☐ ☐	90 Guy Lafleur, Mont.	6.00	12.00
☐ ☐	91 Bob J. Murdoch, LosA.	.25	.35
☐ ☐	92 Ron Ellis, Toro.	.25	.35
☐ ☐	93 Jude Drouin, NYIs.	.25	.35
☐ ☐	94 Jocelyn Guevremont, Buff.	.25	.35
☐ ☐	95 Gilles Gilbert (G), Bost.	.50	.75
☐ ☐	96 Bob Sirois, Wash.	.25	.35
☐ ☐	97 Tom Lysiak, Atla.	.25	.35
☐ ☐	98 André Dupont, Phil.	.25	.35
☐ ☐	**99 Per-Olov Brasar, Minn. RC**	**.50**	**.75**
☐ ☐	100 Phil Esposito, NYRa.	1.75	3.50
☐ ☐	101 J.P. Bordeleau, Chic.	.25	.35
☐ ☐	**102 Pierre Mondou, Mont. RC**	**1.00**	**1.50**
☐ ☐	103 Wayne Bianchin, Pitt.	.25	.35
☐ ☐	104 Dennis O'Brien, Bost.	.25	.35
☐ ☐	105 Glenn Resch (G), NYIs.	.50	.75
☐ ☐	106 Dennis Polonich, Detr.	.25	.35
☐ ☐	**107 Kris Manery, Minn. RC**	**.50**	**.75**
☐ ☐	108 Bill Hajt, Buff.	.25	.35
☐ ☐	109 Jere Gillis, Vanc. RC	.50	.75
☐ ☐	110 Garry Unger, SLou.	.35	.50
☐ ☐	111 Nick Beverley, Minn. (LosA.)	.25	.35
☐ ☐	112 Pat Hickey, NYRa.	.25	.35
☐ ☐	113 Rick Middleton, Bost.	.25	.35
☐ ☐	114 Orest Kindrachuk, Pitt.	.25	.35
☐ ☐	**115 Mike Bossy, NYIs. RC**	**50.00**	**100.00**
☐ ☐	116 Pierre Bouchard, Mont. (Retired)	.25	.35
☐ ☐	117 Alain Daigle, Chic.	.25	.35
☐ ☐	118 Terry Martin, Buff.	.25	.35
☐ ☐	119 Tom Edur, Pitt. (SLou.)	.25	.35
☐ ☐	120 Marcel Dionne, LosA.	1.75	3.50
☐ ☐	**121 Barry Beck, Colo. RC**	**1.00**	**2.00**
☐ ☐	122 Bill Lochead, Detr.	.25	.35
☐ ☐	**123 Paul Harrison (G), Toro. RC**	**.50**	**.75**
☐ ☐	124 Wayne Cashman, Bost.	.25	.35
☐ ☐	125 Rick MacLeish, Phil.	.35	.50
☐ ☐	126 Bob Bourne, NYIs.	.25	.35
☐ ☐	127 Ian Turnbull, Toro.	.25	.35
☐ ☐	128 Gerry Meehan, Wash.	.25	.35
☐ ☐	129 Eric Vail, Atla.	.25	.35
☐ ☐	130 Gilbert Perreault, Buff.	1.25	2.50
☐ ☐	131 Bob Dailey, Phil.	.25	.35
☐ ☐	**132 Dale McCourt, Detr. RC**	**.75**	**1.00**
☐ ☐	**133 John Wensink, Bost. RC**	**.50**	**.75**
☐ ☐	134 Bill Nyrop, Mont.	.25	.35
☐ ☐	135 Ivan Boldirev, Chic.	.25	.35
☐ ☐	**136 Lucien Deblois, NYRa. RC**	**.50**	**.75**
☐ ☐	137 Brian Spencer, Pitt.	.25	.35
☐ ☐	138 Tim Young, Minn.	.25	.35
☐ ☐	139 Ron Sedlbauer, Vanc.	.25	.35
☐ ☐	140 Gerry Cheevers (G), Bost.	1.00	2.00
☐ ☐	141 Dennis Maruk, Minn. (Wash.)	.25	.35
☐ ☐	142 Barry Dean, Phil.	.25	.35
☐ ☐	**143 Bernie Federko, SLou. RC**	**8.00**	**15.00**
☐ ☐	**144 Stefan Persson, NYIs. RC**	**.50**	**.75**
☐ ☐	145 Wilf Paiement, Colo.	.25	.35
☐ ☐	146 Dale Tallon, Chic. (Pitt.)	.25	.35
☐ ☐	147 Yvon Lambert, Mont.	.25	.35
☐ ☐	148 Greg Joly, Detr.	.25	.35
☐ ☐	149 Dean Talafous, Minn. (NYRa.)	.25	.35
☐ ☐	150 Don Edwards (G), Buff.	.50	.75
☐ ☐	151 Butch Goring, LosA.	.35	.50
☐ ☐	152 Tom Bladon, Pitt.	.25	.35
☐ ☐	153 Bob Nystrom, NYIs.	.25	.35
☐ ☐	154 Ron Greschner, NYRa.	.25	.35
☐ ☐	155 Jean Ratelle, Bost.	.75	1.50
☐ ☐	**156 Russ Anderson, Pitt. RC**	**.50**	**.75**
☐ ☐	157 John Marks, Chic.	.25	.35
☐ ☐	158 Michel Larocque (G), Mont.	.50	.75
☐ ☐	159 Paul Woods, Detr. RC	.50	.75
☐ ☐	160 Mike Palmateer (G), Toro.	.75	1.50
☐ ☐	161 Jim Lorentz, Buff. (Retired)	.25	.35
☐ ☐	162 Dave Lewis, NYIs.	.35	.50
☐ ☐	163 Harvey Bennett, Minn. (SLou.)	.25	.35
☐ ☐	164 Rick Smith, Bost.	.25	.35
☐ ☐	165 Reggie Leach, Phil.	.35	.50
☐ ☐	166 Wayne Thomas (G), NYRa.	.50	.75
☐ ☐	167 Dave Forbes, Wash.	.25	.35
☐ ☐	**168 Doug Wilson, Chic. RC**	**5.00**	**10.00**
☐ ☐	169 Dan Bouchard (G), Atla.	.50	.75
☐ ☐	170 Steve Shutt, Mont.	1.00	2.00
☐ ☐	**171 Mike Kaszycki, NYIs. RC**	**.50**	**.75**
☐ ☐	172 Denis Herron (G), Pitt.	.50	.75
☐ ☐	173 Rick Bowness, Detr. (SLou.)	.25	.35
☐ ☐	174 Rick Hampton, Minn. (LosA.)	.25	.35
☐ ☐	175 Glen Sharpley, Minn.	.25	.35
☐ ☐	176 Bill Barber, Phil.	1.00	2.00
☐ ☐	**177 Ron Duguay, NYRa. RC**	**2.50**	**5.00**
☐ ☐	178 Jim Schoenfeld, Buff.	.35	.50
☐ ☐	179 Pierre Plante, Chic. (NYRa.)	.25	.35
☐ ☐	180 Jacques Lemaire, Mont.	.65	1.25
☐ ☐	181 Stan Jonathan, Bost.	.25	.35
☐ ☐	182 Billy Harris, NYIs.	.25	.35
☐ ☐	183 Chris Oddleifson, Vanc.	.25	.35
☐ ☐	184 Jean Pronovost, Pitt. (Atla.)	.25	.35
☐ ☐	185 Fred Barrett, Minn.	.25	.35
☐ ☐	186 Ross Lonsberry, Pitt.	.25	.35
☐ ☐	187 Mike McEwen, NYRa.	.25	.35
☐ ☐	188 René Robert, Buff.	.25	.35
☐ ☐	189 J. Bob Kelly, Chic.	.25	.35
☐ ☐	190 Serge Savard, Mont.	.65	1.25
☐ ☐	191 Dennis Kearns, Vanc.	.25	.35
☐ ☐	192 CL: Atlanta Flames	1.00	1.50
☐ ☐	193 CL: Boston Bruins	1.00	1.50
☐ ☐	194 CL: Buffalo Sabres	1.00	1.50
☐ ☐	195 CL: Chicago Blackhawks	1.00	1.50
☐ ☐	196 CL: Colorado Rockies	1.00	1.50
☐ ☐	197 CL: Detroit Red Wings	1.00	1.50
☐ ☐	198 CL: Los Angeles Kings	1.00	1.50
☐ ☐	199 CL: Minnesota North Stars	1.00	1.50
☐ ☐	200 CL: Montréal Canadiens	1.00	1.50
☐ ☐	201 CL: New York Islanders	1.00	1.50
☐ ☐	202 CL: New York Rangers	1.00	1.50
☐ ☐	203 CL: Philadelphia Flyers	1.00	1.50
☐ ☐	204 CL: Pittsburgh Penguins	1.00	1.50
☐ ☐	205 CL: St. Louis Blues	1.00	1.50
☐ ☐	206 CL: Toronto Maple Leafs	1.00	1.50
☐ ☐	207 CL: Vancouver Canucks	1.00	1.50
☐ ☐	208 CL: Washington Capitals	1.00	1.50
☐ ☐	209 Danny Gare, Buff.	.35	.50

210 Larry Robinson, Mont.	1.25	2.50
211 John Davidson (G), NYRa.	.65	1.00
212 Peter McNab, Bost.	.25	.35
213 Rick Kehoe, Pitt.	.35	.50
214 Terry Harper, Detr.	.25	.35
215 Bobby Clarke, Phil.	1.75	3.50
216 Bryan Maxwell, Minn., Err. (Brad Maxwell)	.25	.35
217 Ted Bulley, Chic. RC	.50	.75
218 Red Berenson, SLou. (Retired)	.25	.35
219 Ron Grahame (G), Bost. (LosA.)	.50	.75
220 Clark Gillies, NYIs.	.25	.35
221 Dave Maloney, NYRa.	.25	.35
222 Derek Smith, Buff. RC	.50	.75
223 Wayne Stephenson (G), Phil.	.50	.75
224 John Van Boxmeer, Colo.	.25	.35
225 Dave Schultz, Pitt.	.25	.35
226 Reed Larson, Detr. RC	.50	.75
227 Réjean Houle, Mont.	.35	.50
228 Doug Hicks, Chic.	.25	.35
229 Mike Murphy, LosA.	.25	.35
230 Pete LoPresti (G), Minn.	.50	.75
231 Jerry Korab, Buff.	.25	.35
232 Ed Westfall, NYIs.	.25	.35
233 Greg Malone, Pitt. RC	**.50**	**.75**
234 Paul Holmgren, Phil.	.25	.35
235 Walt Tkaczuk, NYRa.	.25	.35
236 Don Marcotte, Bost.	.25	.35
237 Ron Low (G), Detr.	.50	.75
238 Rick Chartraw, Mont.	.25	.35
239 Cliff Koroll, Chic.	.25	.35
240 Börje Salming, Toro.	1.25	2.50
241 Rolie Eriksson, Vanc.	.25	.35
242 Ric Seiling, Buff. RC	.50	.75
243 Jim Bedard (G), Wash. RC	**.75**	**1.00**
244 Peter Lee, Pitt. RC	.50	.75
245 Denis Potvin, NYIs.	1.50	3.00
246 Greg Polis, NYRa.	.25	.35
247 Jimmy Watson, Phil.	.25	.35
248 Bobby Schmautz, Bost.	.25	.35
249 Doug Risebrough, Mont.	.25	.35
250 Tony Esposito (G), Chic.	1.50	3.00
251 Nick Libett, Detr.	.25	.35
252 Ron Zanussi, Minn. RC	**.50**	**.75**
253 André Savard, Buff.	.25	.35
254 Dave Burrows, Toro.	.25	.35
255 Ulf Nilsson, NYRa.	.25	.35
256 Richard Mulhern, Atla.	.25	.35
257 Don Saleski, Phil.	.25	.35
258 Wayne Merrick, NYIs.	.25	.35
259 Checklist 2 (133 - 264)	5.00	7.50
260 Guy Lapointe, Mont.	1.00	1.75
261 Grant Mulvey, Chic.	.25	.35
262 Canadiens sweep Maple Leafs	.50	.75
263 Bruins skate past the Flyers	.50	.75
264 Cup: Larry Robinson, Mont.	.75	1.25

Description	OPC
265 Bob Sauvé (G), Buff.	.75
266 Randy Manery, LosA.	.35
267 Bill Fairbairn, SLou.	.35
268 Garry Monahan, Toro.	.35
269 Colin Campbell, Pitt.	.50
270 Dan Newman, NYRa. (Mont.)	.35
271 Dwight Foster, Bost. RC	**.75**
272 Larry Carrière, Vanc. (Buff.)	.35
273 Michel Bergeron, NYIs. (Wash.)	.35
274 Scott Garland, Toro. (LosA.)	.35
275 Bill McKenzie (G), Colo.	.75
276 Garnet Bailey, Wash.	.35
277 Ed Kea, Atla.	.35
278 Dave Gardner, Clev. (LosA.)	.35
279 Bruce Affleck, SLou.	.35
280 Bruce Boudreau, Toro. RC	**.75**
281 Jean Hamel, Detr.	.35
282 Kurt Walker, Toro. (LosA.) RC	**.75**
283 Denis Dupere, Colo.	.35
284 Gordie Lane, Wash.	.35
285 Bobby Lalonde, Atla.	.35
286 Pit Martin, Vanc.	.35
287 Jean Potvin, NYIs. (Minn.)	.35
288 Jimmy Jones, Toro. RC	**.75**
289 Dave Hutchison, Toro.	.35
290 Pete Stemkowski, LosA.	.35
291 Mike Christie, Colo.	.35
292 Bill Riley, Wash.	.35
293 Rey Comeau, Atla. (Colo.)	.35
294 Jack McIlhargey, Vanc. RC	**.75**
295 Tom Younghans, Minn. RC	**.75**
296 Mario Faubert, Pitt. RC	**.75**
297 Checklist 3 (265 - 396)	7.50
298 Rob Palmer, LosA. RC	**.75**
299 Dave Hudson, Colo.	.35
300 Bobby Orr, Cdn.	45.00
301 Lorne Stamler, Toro. RC	**.75**
302 Curt Ridley (G), Vanc.	.75
303 Greg Smith, Clev. (Minn.)	.35
304 Jerry Butler, Toro.	.35
305 Gary Doak, Bost.	.35
306 Danny Grant, Detr. (LosA.)	.35
307 Mark Suzor, Colo. (Bost.) RC	**.75**
308 Rick Bragnalo, Wash.	.35
309 John Gould, Atla.	.35
310 Sheldon Kannegiesser, Vanc.	.35
311 Bobby Sheehan, Chic. (Minn.)	.35
312 Randy Carlyle, Toro. (Pitt.) RC	**5.00**
313 Lorne Henning, NYIs.	.35
314 Tommy Williams, LosA.	.35
315 Ron Andruff, Colo.	.35
316 Bryan Watson, Wash.	.35
317 Willi Plett, Atla.	.35
318 John Grisdale, Vanc.	.35
319 Brian Sutter, SLou. RC	**10.00**
320 Trevor Johansen, Toro. RC	**.75**
321 Vic Venasky, LosA.	.35
322 Rick Lapointe, Phil.	.35
323 Ron Delorme, Colo. RC	**.75**
324 Yvon Labre, Wash.	.35
325 AS: Bryan Trottier, NYIs.	6.00
326 AS: Guy Lafleur, Mont.	4.00
327 AS: Clark Gillies, NYIs.	.75
328 AS: Börje Salming, Toro.	1.00
329 AS: Larry Robinson, Mont.	1.75
330 AS: Ken Dryden (G), Mont.	9.00
331 AS: Darryl Sittler, Toro.	1.75
332 AS: Terry O'Reilly, Bost.	.75
333 AS: Steve Shutt, Mont.	1.25
334 AS: Denis Potvin, NYIs.	2.50
335 AS: Serge Savard, Mont.	.75
336 AS: Don Edwards (G), Buff.	.75

Note: cards 325-336 feature a puzzle of Ken Dryden, Larry Robinson and Wayne Cashman

337 Glenn Goldup, LosA.	.35
338 Mike Kitchen, Colo.	.35
339 Bob Girard, Wash.	.35
340 Guy Chouinard, Atla.	.35
341 Randy Holt, Chic. (Vanc.)	.35
342 Jimmy Roberts, Minn.	.35
343 Dave Logan, Chic. RC	**.75**
344 Walt McKechnie, Toro.	.35
345 Brian Glennie, Toro. (LosA.)	.35
346 Ralph Klassen, Colo.	.35
347 Gord Smith, Wash.	.35
348 Ken Houston, Atla.	.35
349 Bob Manno, Vanc. RC	**.75**
350 J.P. Parise, NYIs. (Minn.)	.35
351 Don Ashby, Toro.	.35
352 Fred Stanfield, Buff.	.35
353 David Taylor, LosA. RC	**25.00**
354 Nelson Pyatt, Colo.	.35
355 Blair Stewart, Wash. RC	**.75**
356 Dave Shand, Atla.	.35
357 Hilliard Graves, Vanc.	.35
358 Bob Hess, SLou.	.35
359 David Williams, Toro.	2.00
360 Larry Wright, Detr. RC	**.75**
361 Larry Brown, LosA.	.35
362 Gary Croteau, Colo.	.35
363 Richard Green, Wash.	.35
364 Bill Clement, Atla.	.35
365 Gerry O'Flaherty, Vanc. (Atla.)	.35
366 John Baby, Clev. (Minn.) RC	**.75**
367 Nick Fotiu, NYRa.	.35
368 Pat Price, NYIs.	.35
369 Bert Wilson, LosA.	.35
370 Bryan Lefley, Colo.	.35
371 Ron Lalonde, Wash.	.35
372 Bobby Simpson, Atla.	.35
373 Doug Grant (G), SLou.	.75
374 Pat Boutette, Toro.	.35
375 Bob Paradise, Pitt.	.35
376 Mario Tremblay, Mont.	.35
377 Darryl Edestrand, Bost. (LosA.)	.35
378 Andy Spruce, Colo. RC	**.75**
379 Jack Brownschidle, SLou. RC	**.75**
380 Harold Snepsts, Vanc.	.35
381 Al MacAdam, Clev. (Minn.)	.35
382 Neil Komadoski, LosA. (SLou.)	.35
383 Don Awrey, NYRa. (Colo.)	.35
384 Ron Schock, Pitt. (Buff.)	.35
385 Gary Simmons (G), LosA.	.75
386 Fred Ahern, Colo. (Minn.)	.35
387 Larry Bolonchuk, Wash.	.35
388 Brad Gassoff, Vanc. RC	**.75**
389 Chuck Arnason, Colo. (Minn.)	.35
390 Barry Gibbs, (SLou.)	.35
391 Jack Valiquette, Toro. (Colo.)	.35
392 Doug Halward, Bost. (LosA.)	.35
393 Hartland Monahan, LosA.	.35
394 Rod Seiling, SLou. (Atla.)	.35
395 George Ferguson, Toro. (Pitt.)	.35
396 Al Cameron, Detr.	.35

1978 - 79 SM - LIIGA

These cards measure 2" x 2 3/8".

Complete Set (240 cards):

SM-Liiga **NM**

1 Hannu Kamppuri
2 Pekka Rautakallio
3 Timo Nummelin
4 Pertti Valkeapaa
5 Risto Siltanen
6 Hannu Haapalainen
7 Markku Kiimalainen
8 Tapio Levo
9 Lasse Litma
10 Reijo Ruotsalainen
11 Jukka Porvari
12 Matti Rautiainen
13 VeliPekka Ketola
14 Antero Lehtonen
15 Martti Jarkko
16 Juhani Tamminen
17 Pertti Koivulahti
18 Kari Makkonen
19 Antero Kivela
20 VeliMatti Ruisma
21 Stig Wetzell
22 Kyosti Majava
23 Seppo Pakola
24 Reijo Laksola
25 Heikki Riihiranta
26 Raimo Hirvonen
27 Jorma Immonen
28 Terry Ball
29 Pertti Lehtonen
30 Jaakko Marttinen
31 Esa Peltonen
32 Lauri Mononen
33 Tommi Salmelainen
34 Hannu Kapanen
35 Matti Forss
36 Harri Linnonmaa
37 Matti Murto
38 Juhani Bostrom
39 Matti Hagman
40 Ilkka Sinisalo
41 Tomi Taimio
42 Ari Lahteenmaki
43 Tapio Virhimo
44 Jukka Airaksinen
45 Hannu Helander
46 Jorma Aro
47 Jouko Urvikko
48 Hannu Pulkkinen
49 Olli Pennanen
50 Ari Kankaanpera
51 Risto Siltanen
52 Jari Jarvinen
53 Sakari Ahlberg
54 Keijo Kivela
55 Lasse Oksanen
56 Risto Kankaanpera
57 Kari Jarvinen
58 Pekka Orimus
59 Jarmo Huhtala
60 Hannu Oksanen
61 Jari Viitala
62 Veikko Suominen
63 Antti Heikkila
64 Seppo Hiitela
65 Hannu Kamppuri
66 Patrik Wainio
67 Timo Blomqvist
68 Ilmo Uotila
69 Pertti Savolainen
70 Jussi Lepisto
71 Jorma Piisinen
72 Robert Barnes
73 Ari Makinen
74 David Conte
75 Juha Jyrkkio
76 Jari Kurri
77 Matti Heikkila
78 Henry Leppa
79 Pekka Kaski
80 Jari Kapanen
81 Ari Mikkola
82 Vesa Rajaniemi
83 Ari Blomqvist
84 Erkki Korhonen
85 Rainer Risku
86 Henry Saleva
87 Leo Seppanen
88 Rauli Sohlman
89 Juhani Ruohonen
90 Tuomo Martin
91 Reijo Mansikka
92 Reino Pulkkinen
93 Mauri Kultakuusi
94 Kari Saarikko
95 Kari Viitalahti
96 Barry Salovaara
97 Auvo Vaananen
98 Pauli Pyykko
99 Ari Jortikka
100 JP Jarvenpaa
101 Seppo Sevon
102 Pekka Koskela
103 Arto Jokinen
104 Timo Niinivirta
105 Matti Rautiainen
106 Pertti Jarvenpaa
107 Reima Pullinen
108 JP Vuorinen
109 Petteri Kanerva
110 Kalevi Rantanen
111 Jorma Virtanen
112 Matti Kaario
113 Frank Neal
114 Eero Mantere
115 Harri Nyman
116 Olli Saarinen
117 Jari Saarela
118 Pasi Virta
119 Dave Chalk
120 Hannu Koskinen
121 Harri Toivonen
122 Jarmo Makitalo
123 Kari Makitalo
124 Olavi Niemenranta
125 Pekka Laine
126 Markku Hakulinen
127 Pekka Nissinen
128 Yrjo Hakulinen
129 Timo Heino
130 Hannu Savolainen
131 Ari Hellgren
132 Matti Saikkonen
133 Ilpo Kukkola
134 Pentti Karlsson
135 Pekka Karjala
136 Juha Tuohimaa
137 Pekka Makinen
138 Reijo Ruotsalainen
139 Seppo Tenhunen
140 Hannu Jalonen
141 Jari Virtanen
142 Juha Huikuri
143 Veikko Torkkeli
144 Markku Kiimalainen
145 Kalevi Hongisto
146 Eero Vartiainen
147 Jouko Kamarainen
148 Kai Suikkanen
149 Ilkka Alatalo
150 Markku Perkkio
151 Jorma Torkkeli
152 Kari Jalonen
153 Hannu Siivonen
154 Kari Kaupinsalo
155 Teppo Mattsson
156 Esa Hakkarainen
157 Jouni Peltonen
158 Timo Peltonen
159 Hannu Luojola
160 Tapani Koskimaki
161 Tuomo Jormakka
162 Mika Rajala
163 Pekka Santanen
164 Jorma Vehmanen
165 Olli Tuominen
166 Hannu Kemppainen
167 Ismo Villa
168 Matti Tynkkynen
169 Jouni Rinne
170 Jari Rastio
171 Harri Tuohimaa
172 Jari Laiho
173 Juhani Wallenius
174 Pekka Strander
175 Pertti Hasanen
176 Petri Karjalainen
177 Jorma Kallio
178 Pekka Marjamaki
179 Hannu Haapalainen
180 Pertti Valkeapaa
181 Lasse Litma
182 Jukka Hirsimaki
183 Oiva Oijennus
184 Jukka Alkula
185 Timo Susi
186 Jukka Porvari
187 Erkki Lehtonen
188 Antero Lehtonen
189 Juha Silvennoinen
190 Pertti Koivulahti
191 Keijo Mannisto
192 Jorma Sevon
193 Martti Jarkko
194 Jari Lindgren
195 Tapio Kallio
196 Tero Kapynen
197 Urpo Ylonen
198 Jorma Valtonen
199 Harri Kari
200 Hannu Jortikka
201 Timo Nummelin
202 Seppo Suoraniemi
203 Ilkka Mesikammen
204 Pertti Ahokas
205 Hannu Niittoaho
206 Arto Kaunonen
207 Pekka Rautee
208 Juhani Tamminen
209 Timo Viljanen
210 Kari Kauppila
211 Bengt Wilenius
212 Reijo Leppanen
213 Rauli Tammelin
214 Jukka Koskilahti
215 Markku Haapaniemi
216 Kari Horkko
217 Kalevi Aho
218 Hakan Hjerpe
219 Antero Kivela
220 Pertti Lehti
221 Antti Heikkila
222 Tapio Flinck
223 Pekka Rautakallio
224 Jaakko Niemi
225 Tapio Levo
226 Jyrki Levonen
227 Harry Nikander
228 Arto Javanainen
229 Pekka Makela
230 Tapio Koskinen
231 Pekka Stenfors
232 Ari Peltola
233 VeliPekka Ketola
234 Erkki Vakiparta
235 Rauli Levonen
236 Martti Nenonen
237 Jouni Makitalo
238 VeliMatti Ruisma
239 Tauno Makela
240 Kari Makkonen

1979 PANINI STICKERS

These stickers measure 1 15/16" x 2 11/16". Common stickers start at 25¢ while stars and regional heroes sell at 50¢-$1.

Complete Set (400 stickers):	**65.00**
Album:	**8.00**
Common Player:	**.20**

1 Wash-Out
2 Butt-Ending
3 Delayed Penalty
4 Hooking
5 Charging
6 Misconduct
7 Holding
8 High-Sticking
9 Tripping
10 Cross-Checking
11 Elbowing
12 Off-Side
13 Icing
14 Boarding
15 Kneeing
16 Slashing
17 Roughness
18 Spearing
19 Interference
20 MA 78 PRAHA
21 CSR - USSR 6-4
22 CSR - USSR 6-4
23 USSR - CSR 3-1
24 USSR - CSR 3-1
25 USSR - CSR 3-1
26 USSR - CSR 3-1
27 CAN - SWE 3-2
28 CAN - Sweden 3-2
29 USSR - CAN 5-1
30 USSR - CAN 5-1
31 CSR - CAN 3-2
32 CSR - CAN 3-2
33 USSR - Sweden 7-1
34 USSR - Sweden 7-1
35 USA - Finland 4-3
36 USA - Finland 4-3
37 Finland - DDR 7-2
38 DDR - BRD 0-0
39 DDR - BRD 0-0
40 CSR
41 Poland
42 USSR
43 USA
44 CAN
45 Deutschland - BRD
46 Finland
47 Sweden
48 CAN Team Photo
49 CAN Team Photo
50 CAN Team Photo
51 CAN Team Photo
52 Denis Herron (G) $2
53 D. Bouchard (G) $2
54 Rick Hampton
55 Robert Picard
56 Brad Maxwell
57 David Shand
58 Dennis Kearns
59 Tom Lysiak
60 Dennis Maruk
61 Marcel Dionne $4
62 Guy Charron
63 Glen Sharpley
64 Jean Pronovost
65 Don Lever
66 Bob MacMillan
67 Wilf Paiement
68 Pat Hickey
69 Mike Murphy
70 CSR Team Photo
71 CSR Team Photo
72 CSR Team Photo
73 CSR Team Photo
74 Jiri Holecek (G)
75 Jiri Crha (G) $2
76 Jiri Bubla
77 Milan Kajkl
78 Miroslav Dvorak
79 Milan Chalupa
80 Frantisek Kaberle
81 Jan Zajicek
82 Jiri Novak
83 Ivan Hlinka
84 Peter Stastny $4
85 Milan Novy
86 Vladimir Martinec
87 Jaroslav Pouzar
88 Pavel Richter
89 Bohuslav Ebermann
90 Marian Stastny
91 Frantisek Cernick
92 Germany - BRD Photo
93 Germany BRD Photo
94 Germany - BRD Photo
95 Germany BRD Photo
96 Erich Weishaupt (G)
97 B. Engelbrecht (G)
98 Ignaz Berndaner
99 Robert Murray
100 Udo Kiessling
101 Klaus Auhuber
102 Horst Kretschmer
103 Erich Kuhnhackl
104 Martin Wild
105 Lorenz Funk
106 Martin Hinterstocker
107 Alois Schloder
108 Rainer Philipp
109 H. Hinterstocker
110 Franz Reindl

☐ 111 Walter Koberle ☐ 112 Johann Zach
☐ 113 Marcus Kuhl ☐ 114 Poland Team Photo
☐ 115 Poland Team Photo ☐ 116 Poland Team Photo
☐ 117 Poland Team Photo ☐ 118 Henryk Wojtynek (G)
☐ 119 T. Slowakiewicz (G) ☐ 120 Henryk Janiszewski
☐ 121 Henryk Gruth ☐ 122 Andrzej Slowakiewicz
☐ 123 Andrzej Iskrzycki ☐ 124 Jerzy Potz
☐ 125 Marek Marcinczak ☐ 126 Jozef Batkiewicz
☐ 127 Stefan Chowaniec ☐ 128 Andrzej Malysiak
☐ 129 Walenty Zietara ☐ 130 Henryk Pytel
☐ 131 M. Jaskierski ☐ 132 Andrzej Zabawa
☐ 133 Tadeusz Obloj ☐ 134 Jan Piecko
☐ 135 Leszek Tokarz ☐ 136 USSR Photo
☐ 137 USSR Photo ☐ 138 USSR Photo
☐ 139 USSR Photo ☐ 140 V. Tretiak (G) $8
☐ 141 V. Fetisov $6 ☐ 142 Vladimir Lutchenko
☐ 143 Vasili Pervukhin ☐ 144 Valeri Vasiliev $3
☐ 145 G. Tsycankov ☐ 146 Yuri Fedorov
☐ 147 Vladimir Petrov $3 ☐ 148 Vladimir Golikov
☐ 149 Victor Zhluktov ☐ 150 Boris Mikhailov $2
☐ 151 V. Kharlamov $5 ☐ 152 Helmut Balderis
☐ 153 Sergei Kapustin ☐ 154 Alexander Golikov
☐ 155 A. Maltsev $2 ☐ 156 Yuri Lebedev
☐ 157 Sergei Makarov $3 ☐ 158 Finland Team Photo
☐ 159 Finland Team Photo ☐ 160 Finland Team Photo
☐ 161 Finland Team Photo ☐ 162 Urpo Ylonen (G)
☐ 163 Antero Kivela (G) ☐ 164 Pekka Rautakallio
☐ 165 Timo Nummelin ☐ 166 Risto Siltanen
☐ 167 Pekka Marjamaki ☐ 168 Tapio Levo
☐ 169 Lasse Litma ☐ 170 Esa Peltonen
☐ 171 Martti Jarkko ☐ 172 Matti Hagman
☐ 173 Seppo Repo ☐ 174 Pertti Koivulahti
☐ 175 Seppo Ahokainen ☐ 176 Juhani Tamminen
☐ 177 Jukko Provari ☐ 178 Mikko Leinonen
☐ 179 Matti Rautiainen ☐ 180 Sweden Photo
☐ 181 Sweden Photo ☐ 182 Sweden Photo
☐ 183 Sweden Photo ☐ 184 Goran Hogosta (G)
☐ 185 Hardy Aström (G) ☐ 186 Stig Ostling
☐ 187 Ulf Weinstock ☐ 188 Mats Waltin
☐ 189 Stig Salming ☐ 190 Lars Zetterstrom
☐ 191 Lars Lindgren ☐ 192 Leif Holmgren
☐ 193 Roland Eriksson ☐ 194 Rolf Edberg
☐ 195 Per Olov Brasar ☐ 196 Mats Ahlberg
☐ 197 Bengt Lundholm ☐ 198 L.G. Lundberg
☐ 199 Nils Olov Olsson ☐ 200 Kent Erik Andersson
☐ 201 Thomas Gradin ☐ 202 USA Team Photo
☐ 203 USA Team Photo ☐ 204 USA Team Photo
☐ 205 USA Team Photo ☐ 206 Peter LoPresti (G)
☐ 207 Jim Warden ☐ 208 Dick Lamby
☐ 209 Craig Norwich ☐ 210 Glen Patrick
☐ 211 Patrick Westrum ☐ 212 Don Jackson
☐ 213 Mark Johnson ☐ 214 Curt Bennett
☐ 215 Dave Debol ☐ 216 Robert Collyard
☐ 217 Mike Fidler ☐ 218 Tom Younghans
☐ 219 Harvey Bennett ☐ 220 Steve Jensen
☐ 221 Jim Warner ☐ 222 Mike Eaves
☐ 223 William Gilligan ☐ 224 HOCKEY 76
☐ 225 POL - ROM 8-6 ☐ 226 POL - ROM 8-6
☐ 227 POL - ROM 8-6 ☐ 228 POL - ROM 8-6
☐ 229 POL - MAG 7-2 ☐ 230 POL - MAG 7-2
☐ 231 JAP - YUG 6 - 1 ☐ 232 JAP - YUG 6-1
☐ 233 ITA - YUG 12-3 ☐ 234 ITA - YUG 12-3
☐ 235 ROM - ITA 5-5 ☐ 236 ROM - ITA 5-5
☐ 237 POL ☐ 238 POL
☐ 239 Deutschland - DDR ☐ 240 Magyarorszag
☐ 241 Netherlands ☐ 242 Romania
☐ 243 Helvetia ☐ 244 Japan
☐ 245 Norway ☐ 246 Austria
☐ 247 Deutschland - DDR ☐ 248 Deutschland - DDR
☐ 249 Roland Herzig/ Wolfgang Kraske, DDR.
☐ 250 Dieter Simon/ Dietmar Peters, DDR.
☐ 251 Dieter Frenzel/ Joachim Lempio, DDR.
☐ 252 Reinhard Frengler/ Peter Slapke, DDR.
☐ 253 Rainer Patschinski/ Rolf Bielas, DDR.
☐ 254 Roland Peters/ Eckhard Scholz, DDR.
☐ 255 Friedhelm Bogelsack/ Joachim Stasche, DDR.
☐ 256 Helvetia ☐ 257 Helvetia
☐ 258 Edgar Grubauer/ Olivier Anken, Sui.
☐ 259 Aldo Zenhausern/ Andreas Meyer, Sui.
☐ 260 Jakob Kolliker/ Jean-Claude Locher, Sui.
☐ 261 Georg Mattli/ Giovanni Conte, Sui.
☐ 262 Renzo Holzer/ Roland Dellsperger, Sui.
☐ 263 Michael Horisberger/ Luca Rossetti, Sui.
☐ 264 Jurg Berger/ Lorenz Schmid, Sui.
☐ 265 Magyarorszag ☐ 266 Magyarorszag
☐ 267 Janos Balogh/ Andras Farkas, Hun.
☐ 268 Csaba Kovacs/ Janos Hajzer, Hun.
☐ 269 Peter Flora/ Adam Kereszty, Hun.
☐ 270 Antal Palla/ Andras Meszoly, Hun.
☐ 271 Gaspar Menyhart/ Peter Havran, Hun.
☐ 272 Janos Poth/ Albert Muhr, Hun.
☐ 273 Gyorgy Buzas/ Gyorgy Pek, Hun.
☐ 274 Netherlands ☐ 275 Netherlands
☐ 276 Harry Van Bilsen/ Henk Krikke, Ned.
☐ 277 Frank Van Soldt/ George Peternousek, Ned.
☐ 278 Patrick Kolijn/ Klaas Van Den Broek, Ned.
☐ 279 Larry Van Wieren/ Johan Toren, Ned.
☐ 280 Robert Van Onlangs/ Jerry Schaffer, Ned.
☐ 281 Jan Janssen/ John Van Der Griendt, Ned.
☐ 282 Jack De Heer/ Leo Koopmans, Ned.

☐ 283 Japan ☐ 284 Japan
☐ 285 Takeshi Iwamoto/ Minoru Misawa, Jap.
☐ 286 Norio Ito/ Kazuma Tonozaki, Jap.
☐ 287 Hiroshi Hori/ Iwao Nakayama, Jap.
☐ 288 Yasushin Tanaka/ Yoshiaki Kyoya, Jap.
☐ 289 Katsutoshi Kawamura/ Yoshio Hoshino, Jap.
☐ 290 Satoru Misawa/ Teruo Sakurai, Jap.
☐ 291 Sadaki Honma/ Tsutomu Hanzawa, Jap.
☐ 292 Norway ☐ 293 Norway
☐ 294 Tore Walberg/ Jorn Goldstein, Nor.
☐ 295 Thor Martisen/ Rune Molberg, Nor.
☐ 296 Nils Nilsen/ Jone Erevik, Nor.
☐ 297 Sven Lien/ Tom Roymark, Nor.
☐ 298 Per Erik Eriksen/ Roar Ovstedal, Nor.
☐ 299 Vidar Johansen/ Harry Haraldsen, Nor.
☐ 300 Morten Sethereng/ Kjell Thorkildsen, Nor.
☐ 301 Austria ☐ 302 Austria
☐ 303 Schilcheri/ Prohaska, Aut.
☐ 304 Pentti Hyytiainen/ Othmar Russ, Aut.
☐ 305 Silvester Staribacher/ Walter Schneider, Aut.
☐ 306 Franz Kotnauer/ Herbert Pök, Aut.
☐ 307 Alexander Sadjina/ Rudolf Konig, Aut.
☐ 308 Herbert Mortl/ Gerhard Pepeunig, Aut.
☐ 309 Werner Schilcher/ Herbert Haisza, Aut.
☐ 310 Romania ☐ 311 Romania
☐ 312 Gheorghe Hutan/ Valerian Netedu, Rom.
☐ 313 Elod Antal/ Sandor Gall, Rom.
☐ 314 Gheorghe Iustinian/ Ion Ionita, Rom.
☐ 315 Vasile Hutanu/ Alexandru Halauca, Rom.
☐ 316 Doru Tureanu/ Dimitru Axinte, Rom.
☐ 317 Zoltan Nagy/ Marian Costea, Rom.
☐ 318 Constantin Nistor/ Adrian Olenici, Rom.
☐ 319 1978 Worlds ☐ 320 DEN - NED 3-3
☐ 321 DEN - NED 3-3 ☐ 322 NED - ESP 19-0
☐ 323 NED - ESP 19-0 ☐ 324 AUT - DEN 7-4
☐ 325 AUT - DEN 7-4 ☐ 326 NED - BUL 8-0
☐ 327 CHI - DEN 3-2 ☐ 328 CHI - FRA 8-4
☐ 329 Bulgaria ☐ 330 France
☐ 331 Italy ☐ 332 Yugoslavia
☐ 333 Belgium ☐ 334 China
☐ 335 Denmark ☐ 336 Spain
☐ 337 Belgium ☐ 338 Belgium
☐ 339 Pierre Smeets/ Guy Lauwers, Bel.
☐ 340 Georges Andriaensen/ Alain Zwikel, Bel.
☐ 341 Christian Cuvelier/ Pierre Sarazin, Bel.
☐ 342 Philippe Vermeulen/ Christian Voskertian, Bel.
☐ 343 Bob Verschraegen/ Patrick Arnould, Bel.
☐ 344 Jozef Lejeune/ Pierre Langh, Bel.
☐ 345 Bulgaria ☐ 346 Bulgaria
☐ 347 Atanas Iliev/ Dimitar Lazarov, Bul.
☐ 348 Gueorgui Iliev/ Dimo Krastinov, Bul.
☐ 349 Kroum Hristov/ Nikolay Petrov, Bul.
☐ 350 Ivan Atanasov/ Milcho Nenov, Bul.
☐ 351 Atanas Todorov/ Lubomir Stoilov, Bul.
☐ 352 Kiril Guerasimov/ Marin Batchvarov, Bul.
☐ 353 China ☐ 354 China
☐ 355 Tsui Ting Wen/ Yang Yung Ke, Chic.
☐ 356 Cheng Ke/ Pien Shao Tang, Chic.
☐ 357 Wan Ta Chun/ Chang Yung Sheng, Chic.
☐ 358 Chen Hsi Kiang/ Wei Chang Shun, Chic.
☐ 359 Li Cheng Hsin/ Liu Te Hsi, Chic.
☐ 360 Hsiang Shu Ching/ Chen Sheng Wen, Chic.
☐ 361 Denmark ☐ 362 Denmark
☐ 363 Bent Hansen/ Per Holten Moller, Den.
☐ 364 Richard Andersen/ Tommy Pedersen, Den.
☐ 365 Kenneth Henriksen/ Jesper Hviid, Den.
☐ 366 Frits Nielsen/ Steen Thomsen, Den.
☐ 367 Carsten Nielsen/ Egon Kahl, Den.
☐ 368 Jens Jensen/ Sören Jerding, Den.
☐ 369 Spain ☐ 370 Spain
☐ 371 Sergio Estrada/ Josian Lizarraga, Esp.
☐ 372 Francisco Gonzalez/ Ramon Munitiz, Esp.
☐ 373 Alberto Marin/ Bievenido Aguado, Esp.
☐ 374 Toni Raventos/ Ezequiel Encinas, Esp.
☐ 375 Antonio Capillas/ Jose Sarazibar, Esp.
☐ 376 Perico Labayen/ Antonio Plaza, Esp.
☐ 377 France ☐ 378 France
☐ 379 Daniel Maric/ Pascal Del Monaco, Fra.
☐ 380 Robert Oprandi/ Bernard Combe, Fra.
☐ 381 Allard/ Le Blond, Fra.
☐ 382 Jean Vassieux/ Philippe Rey, Fra.
☐ 383 Guy Galiay/ Jean Le Blond, Fra.
☐ 384 Alain Vinard/ Louis Smaniotto, Fra.
☐ 385 Italy ☐ 386 Italy
☐ 387 Giorgio Tigliani/ Norbert Gasser, Ita.
☐ 388 Kostner/ Pasqualotto\, Ita.
☐ 389 Renato Lacedelli/ Fabio Polloni, Ita.
☐ 390 Adolf Insam/ Renato De Toni, Ita.
☐ 391 Herbert Strohmaier/ Fabrizio Kasslatter, Ita.
☐ 392 Pat De Marchi/ Mario Pugliese, Ita.
☐ 393 Yugoslavia ☐ 394 Yugoslavia
☐ 395 Marjan Zbontar/ Ivan Scap, Yug.
☐ 396 Bojan Kumar/ Tomaz Kosir, Yug.
☐ 397 Ignac Kavec/ Roman Smolej, Yug.
☐ 398 Edvard Hafner/ Tomaz Lepsa, Yug.
☐ 399 Silvo Poljansek/ Saso Kosir, Yug.
☐ 400 Petar-Igor Klemenc/ Milan Jan, Yug.

1979 SOVIET NATIONAL TEAM

This postcard measures 8 1/4" x 5 7/8".

Soviet National Team	NM
☐ 1 Team Photograph	4.00

1979 - 80 DERNIÈRE PHOTOS

This multi-sport series of photos were inserted in Dernière magazine from 1972 through 1984. Three holes were punched on the left side to allow for storage in a binder. The series featured Montréal Canadiens players. These photos measure 8" x 10".

Dernière	NM
☐ 2DEC Jean Ratelle	7.00
☐ 9DEC Guy Chouinard	3.00
☐ 16DEC Ray Bourque	15.00
☐ 23DEC Robert Picard	3.00
☐ 30DEC Carol Vadnais	3.00
☐ 6JAN Marcel Dionne	10.00
☐ 13JAN Anders Hedberg	3.00
☐ 20JAN Bobby Hull	18.00
☐ 27JAN Wilf Paiement	3.00
☐ 3FEB Guy Charron	3.00
☐ 10FEB Phil Myre (G)	5.00
☐ 17FEB René Robert	3.00
☐ 24FEB Bobby Clarke	10.00
☐ 2MAR J.P. Bordeleau	3.00
☐ 9MAR André Dupont	3.00
☐ 16MAR Brad Park	7.00
☐ 23MAR Pierre Bouchard	3.00
☐ 30MAR Börje Salming	7.00
☐ 6APR Dale McCourt	3.00
☐ 13APR Daniel Bouchard (G)	5.00

1979 - 80 O-PEE-CHEE & TOPPS

"Being a Wayne Gretzky fan, it was an automatic choice to go after the Gretzky rookie card and then the others in the set. I bought my Gretzky card through a classified ad in the Pennysaver. (The '79-80 set) is a nice set. It was the first time in six years that they went with a colour border. The set has the last playing-career cards of Bobby Hull and Gordie Howe." – Hans Tan, Game Breakers Sports Cards, Ottawa, Ontario.

There are two versions for cards 1-264: the O-Pee-Chee and the Topps card. Topps cards do not have the traded line that appears on the O-Pee-Chee counterpart. These cards measure the standard 2 1/2" x 3 1/2".

O-Pee-Chee Set (396 cards):		**1,350.00**
Topps Set (264 cards):	**650.00**	**–**
Common Player:	**.35**	**.75**
Description	**OPC**	**Topps**
☐☐ 1 LL: M. Bossy/ M. Dionne/ G. Lafleur	3.25	6.00
☐☐ 2 LL: Trottier/ Lafleur/ Dionne/ MacMillan	2.25	4.25
☐☐ 3 LL: B. Trottier/ M. Dionne/ G. Lafleur	2.25	4.25
☐☐ 4 LL: D. Williams/ R. Holt/ D. Schultz	.50	1.00
☐☐ 5 LL: Bossy/ Dionne/ McDonald/ Gardner	1.50	3.00
☐☐ 6 LL: Dryden (G)/ Resch (G)/ Parent (G)	2.25	4.50
☐☐ 7 LL: G. Lafleur/ M. Bossy/ B. Trottier/ J. Pronovost / T. Bulley	2.25	4.50
☐☐ 8 LL: K. Dryden (G)/ T. Esposito (G)/ Palmateer (G)/ M. Lessard (G)/ B. Parent (G)	3.25	6.50
☐☐ 9 Greg Malone, Pitt.	.35	.75
☐☐ 10 Rick Middleton, Bost.	.65	1.25
☐☐ 11 Greg Smith, Minn.	.35	.75
☐☐ 12 René Robert, Buff. (Colo.)	.35	.75
☐☐ 13 Doug Risebrough, Mont.	.50	1.00
☐☐ 14 Bob Kelly, Phil.	.35	.75
☐☐ 15 Walt Tkaczuk, NYRa.	.35	.75
☐☐ 16 John Marks, Chic.	.35	.75
☐☐ **17 Willie Huber, Detr. RC**	**.75**	**1.25**
☐☐ **18 Wayne Gretzky, Edmo. RC**	**600.00**	**1100.00**

◆ A graded BGS-9.5 copy of this Gretzky rookie card recently closed at $17,601 U.S. in an eBay.com auction in August 2002. The card, the first one ever to be graded gem mint, was sold by Dave and Adam's Card World of Amherst, NY.That closing amount is approximately $27,500 Cdn.

☐☐ 19 Ron Sedlbauer, Vanc.	.35	.75
☐☐ 20 AS: Glenn Resch (G), NYIs.	.65	1.25
☐☐ 21 Blair Chapman, Pitt.	.35	.75
☐☐ 22 Ron Zanussi, Minn.	.35	.75
☐☐ 23 Brad Park, Bost.	1.00	2.00
☐☐ 24 Yvon Lambert, Mont.	.35	.75
☐☐ 25 André Savard, Buff.	.35	.75
☐☐ 26 Jimmy Watson, Phil.	.35	.75
☐☐ **27 Harold Phillipoff, Chic. RC**	**.75**	**1.25**
☐☐ 28 Dan Bouchard (G), Atla.	.65	1.25
☐☐ 29 Bob Sirois, Wash.	.35	.75
☐☐ 30 Ulf Nilsson, NYRa.	.35	.75
☐☐ 31 Mike Murphy, LosA.	.35	.75
☐☐ 32 Stefan Persson, NYIs.	.35	.75
☐☐ 33 Garry Unger, SLou. (Atla.)	.35	.75
☐☐ 34 Réjean Houle, Mont.	.50	1.00
☐☐ 35 Barry Beck, NYRa.	.35	.75
☐☐ 36 Tim Young, Minn.	.35	.75
☐☐ 37 Rick Dudley, Buff.	.35	.75
☐☐ 38 Wayne Stephenson (G), Phil. (Wash.)	.65	1.25
☐☐ 39 Peter McNab, Bost.	.35	.75
☐☐ 40 AS: Börje Salming, Toro.	1.00	2.00
☐☐ 41 Tom Lysiak, Chic.	.35	.75
☐☐ **42 Don Maloney, NYRa. RC**	**.75**	**1.25**
☐☐ 43 Mike Rogers, Hart.	.35	.75
☐☐ 44 Dave Lewis, NYIs.	.50	1.00
☐☐ 45 Peter Lee, Pitt.	.35	.75
☐☐ 46 Marty Howe, Hart.	.35	.75
☐☐ 47 Serge Bernier, Québ.	.35	.75
☐☐ 48 Paul Woods, Detr.	.35	.75
☐☐ 49 Bob Sauvé (G), Buff.	.65	1.25
☐☐ 50 AS: Larry Robinson, Mont.	1.50	3.00
☐☐ **51 Tom Gorence, Phil. RC**	**.75**	**1.25**
☐☐ 52 Gary Sargent, Minn.	.35	.75
☐☐ **53 Thomas Gradin, Vanc. RC**	**1.50**	**3.00**
☐☐ 54 Dean Talafous, NYRa.	.35	.75
☐☐ 55 Bob Murray, Chic.	.35	.75
☐☐ 56 Bob Bourne, NYIs.	.35	.75
☐☐ 57 Larry Patey, SLou.	.35	.75
☐☐ 58 Ross Lonsberry, Pitt.	.35	.75
☐☐ 59 Rick Smith, Bost., Error (/b: Kinston)	.35	.75
☐☐ 60 Guy Chouinard, Atla.	.35	.75
☐☐ 61 Danny Gare, Buff.	.50	1.00
☐☐ 62 Jim Bedard (G), Wash.	.65	1.25
☐☐ 63 Dale McCourt, Detr.	.35	.75
☐☐ **64 Steve Payne, Minn. RC**	**.75**	**1.25**
☐☐ **65 Pat Hughes, Mont. (Pitt.) RC**	**.75**	**1.25**
☐☐ 66 Mike McEwen, NYRa. (Colo.)	.35	.75
☐☐ **67 Reg Kerr, Chic. RC**	**.75**	**1.25**
☐☐ 68 Walt McKechnie, Toro.	.35	.75
☐☐ 69 Michel Plasse (G), Colo.	.65	1.25
☐☐ 70 AS: Denis Potvin, NYIs.	1.50	3.00
☐☐ 71 Dave Dryden (G), Edmo.	.65	1.25
☐☐ 72 Gary McAdam, Pitt.	.35	.75
☐☐ 73 André St. Laurent, Detr. (LosA.)	.35	.75
☐☐ 74 Jerry Korab, Buff.	.35	.75
☐☐ 75 Rick MacLeish, Phil.	.35	.75
☐☐ 76 Dennis Kearns, Vanc.	.35	.75
☐☐ 77 Jean Pronovost, Atla.	.35	.75
☐☐ 78 Ron Greschner, NYRa.	.35	.75
☐☐ 79 Wayne Cashman, Bost.	.35	.75
☐☐ 80 Tony Esposito (G), Chic.	1.50	3.00
☐ 81 CL: Winnipeg Jets	–	12.00
☐ 81 Canadiens squeak past Bruins	.75	–
☐ 82 CL: Edmonton Oilers	–	15.00
☐ 81 Rangers upset Islanders in six	.75	–
☐☐ 83 Montréal vs. New York Rangers	1.00	2.00
☐☐ 84 Brian Sutter, SLou.	1.25	2.50
☐☐ 85 Gerry Cheevers (G), Bost.	1.00	2.00
☐☐ 86 Pat Hickey, NYRa. (Colo.)	.35	.75
☐☐ 87 Mike Kaszycki, NYIs.	.35	.75
☐☐ 88 Grant Mulvey, Chic.	.35	.75
☐☐ 89 Derek Smith, Buff.	.35	.75
☐☐ 90 Steve Shutt, Mont.	1.00	2.00
☐☐ 91 Robert Picard, Wash.	.35	.75
☐☐ 92 Dan Labraaten, Detr.	.35	.75
☐☐ 93 Glen Sharpley, Minn.	.35	.75
☐☐ 94 Denis Herron (G), Pitt. (Mont.)	.65	1.25
☐☐ 95 Reggie Leach, Phil.	.50	1.00
☐☐ 96 John Van Boxmeer, Colo. (Buff.)	.35	.75
☐☐ 97 Dave Williams, Toro.	.65	1.25
☐☐ 98 Butch Goring, LosA.	.50	1.00
☐☐ 99 Don Marcotte, Bost.	.35	.75
☐☐ 100 AS: Bryan Trottier, NYIs.	2.50	5.00
☐☐ 101 AS: Serge Savard, Mont.	.65	1.25
☐☐ 102 Cliff Koroll, Chic.	.35	.75
☐☐ 103 Gary Smith (G), Winn.	.65	1.25
☐☐ 104 Al MacAdam, Minn.	.35	.75
☐☐ 105 Don Edwards (G), Buff.	.65	1.25
☐☐ 106 Errol Thompson, Detr.	.35	.75
☐☐ 107 André Lacroix, Hart.	.35	.75
☐☐ 108 Marc Tardif, Québ.	.35	.75
☐☐ 109 Rick Kehoe, Pitt.	.50	1.00
☐☐ 110 John Davidson (G), NYRa.	.75	1.50
☐☐ **111 Behn Wilson, Phil. RC**	**.75**	**1.25**
☐☐ 112 Doug Jarvis, Mont.	.50	1.00
☐☐ **113 Tom Rowe, Wash. RC**	**.75**	**1.25**
☐☐ 114 Mike Milbury, Bost.	.65	1.25
☐☐ 115 Billy Harris, NYIs.	.35	.75
☐☐ **116 Greg Fox, Chic. RC**	**.75**	**1.25**
☐☐ **117 Curt Fraser, Vanc. RC**	**2.00**	**4.00**
☐☐ 118 J.P. Parise, Minn.	.35	.75
☐☐ 119 Ric Seiling, Buff.	.35	.75
☐☐ 120 Darryl Sittler, Toro.	1.25	2.50
☐☐ 121 Rick Lapointe, SLou.	.35	.75
☐☐ 122 Jim Rutherford (G), Detr.	.65	1.25
☐☐ 123 Mario Tremblay, Mont.	.35	.75
☐☐ 124 Randy Carlyle, Pitt.	.75	1.50

125 Bobby Clarke, Phil.	1.50	3.00
126 Wayne Thomas (G), NYRa.	.65	1.25
127 Ivan Boldirev, Atla.	.35	.75
128 Ted Bulley, Chic.	.35	.75
129 Dick Redmond, Bost.	.35	.75
130 AS: Clark Gillies, NYIs.	.35	.75
131 Checklist 1 (1 - 132)	6.50	12.00
132 Vaclav Nedomansky, Detr.	.35	.75
133 Richard Mulhern, LosA.	.35	.75
134 Dave Schultz, Buff.	.35	.75
135 Guy Lapointe, Mont.	.85	1.75
136 Gilles Meloche (G), Minn.	.65	1.25
137 Randy Pierce, Colo., Error (Ron Delorme)	.35	.75
138 Cam Connor, Edmo.	.35	.75
139 George Ferguson, Pitt.	.35	.75
140 AS: Bill Barber, Phil.	1.00	2.00
141 Terry Ruskowski, Chic., Error (Ruskouski)	.35	.75
142 Wayne Babych, SLou. RC	**.75**	**1.25**
143 Phil Russell, Atla.	.35	.75
144 Bobby Schmautz, Bost.	.35	.75
145 Carol Vadnais, NYRa.	.35	.75
146 John Tonelli, NYIs. RC	**3.00**	**6.00**
147 Peter Marsh, Winn. RC	**.75**	**1.25**
148 Thommie Bergman, Detr.	.35	.75
149 Rick Martin, Buff.	.50	1.00
150 AS: Ken Dryden (G), Mont.	6.00	12.00
151 Kris Manery, Minn.	.35	.75
152 Guy Charron, Wash.	.35	.75
153 Lanny McDonald, Toro.	1.00	2.00
154 Ron Stackhouse, Pitt.	.35	.75
155 Stan Mikita, Chic.	1.50	3.00
156 Paul Holmgren, Phil.	.35	.75
157 Perry Miller, Detr.	.35	.75
158 Gary Croteau, Colo.	.35	.75
159 Dave Maloney, NYRa.	.50	1.00
160 AS: Marcel Dionne, LosA.	1.50	3.00
161 RB: Mike Bossy, NYIs.	2.25	4.50
162 RB: Don Maloney, NYRa.	.35	.75
163 CL: Hartford Whalers	–	12.00
163 RB: Ulf Nilsson, NYRa.	.75	–
164 RB: Brad Park, Bost.	.65	1.25
165 RB: Bryan Trottier, NYIs.	1.00	2.00
166 Al Hill, Phil. RC	**.75**	**1.25**
167 Gary Bromley (G), Vanc.	.65	1.25
168 Don Murdoch, NYRa.	.35	.75
169 Wayne Merrick, NYIs.	.35	.75
170 Bob Gainey, Mont.	1.50	3.00
171 Jim Schoenfeld, Buff.	.50	1.00
172 Gregg Sheppard, Pitt.	.35	.75
173 Dan Bolduc, Detr. RC	**.75**	**1.25**
174 Blake Dunlop, SLou.	.35	.75
175 Gordie Howe, Hart.	18.00	35.00
176 Richard Brodeur (G), Québ. (NYIs.)	.65	1.25
177 Tom Younghans, Minn.	.35	.75
178 André Dupont, Phil.	.35	.75
179 Eddie Johnstone, NYRa. RC	**.75**	**1.25**
180 Gilbert Perreault, Buff.	1.50	3.00
181 Bob Lorimer, NYIs. RC	**.75**	**1.25**
182 John Wensink, Bost.	.35	.75
183 Lee Fogolin, Edmo.	.35	.75
184 Greg Carroll, Detr. (Hart.)	.35	.75
185 Bobby Hull, Chic. (Winn.)	14.00	28.00
186 Harold Snepsts, Vanc.	.50	1.00
187 Pete Mahovlich, Pitt. (Detr.)	.50	1.00
188 Eric Vail, Atla.	.35	.75
189 Phil Myre (G), Phil.	.50	1.00
190 Wilf Paiement, Colo.	.35	.75
191 Charlie Simmer, LosA. RC	**2.50**	**5.00**
192 Per-Olov Brasar, Minn.	.35	.75
193 Lorne Henning, NYIs.	.35	.75
194 Don Luce, Buff.	.35	.75
195 Steve Vickers, NYRa.	.35	.75
196 Bob Miller, Bost. RC	**.75**	**1.25**
197 Mike Palmateer (G), Toro.	.75	1.50
198 Nick Libett, Detr. (Pitt.)	.35	.75
199 Pat Ribble, Chic. RC	**.75**	**1.25**
200 AS: Guy Lafleur, Mont.	5.00	10.00
201 Mel Bridgman, Phil.	.35	.75
202 Morris Lukowich, Winn. RC	**.75**	**1.25**
203 Don Lever, Vanc.	.35	.75
204 Tom Bladon, Pitt.	.35	.75
205 Garry Howatt, NYIs.	.35	.75
206 Bobby Smith, Minn. RC	**4.50**	**9.00**
207 Craig Ramsay, Buff.	.50	1.00
208 Ron Duguay, NYRa.	.50	1.00
209 Gilles Gilbert (G), Bost.	.50	1.00
210 Bob MacMillan, Atla.	.35	.75
211 Pierre Mondou, Mont.	.35	.75
212 J.P. Bordeleau, Chic.	.35	.75
213 Reed Larson, Detr.	.35	.75
214 Dennis Ververgaert, Phil.	.35	.75
215 Bernie Federko, SLou.	2.00	4.00
216 Mark Howe, Hart.	1.75	3.50
217 Bob Nystrom, NYIs.	.50	1.00
218 Orest Kindrachuk, Pitt.	.35	.75
219 Mike Fidler, Minn.	.35	.75
220 Phil Esposito, NYRa.	1.50	3.00
221 Bill Hajt, Buff.	.35	.75
222 Mark Napier, Mont.	.35	.75
223 Dennis Maruk, Wash.	.35	.75
224 Dennis Polonich, Detr.	.35	.75
225 Jean Ratelle, Bost.	.50	1.00
226 Bob Dailey, Phil.	.35	.75
227 Alain Daigle, Chic.	.35	.75
228 Ian Turnbull, Toro.	.35	.75
229 Jack Valiquette, Colo.	.35	.75
230 AS: Mike Bossy, NYIs.	9.00	18.00
231 Brad Maxwell, Minn.	.35	.75
232 Dave Taylor, LosA.	2.50	5.00
233 Pierre Larouche, Mont.	.50	1.00
234 Rod Schutt, Pitt. RC	**.75**	**1.25**
235 Rogatien Vachon (G), Detr.	.75	1.50
236 Ryan Walter, Wash. RC	**1.50**	**3.00**
237 Checklist 2 (133 - 264)	6.50	12.00
238 Terry O'Reilly, Bost.	.50	1.00
239 Réal Cloutier, Québ.	.35	.75
240 Anders Hedberg, NYRa.	.65	1.25
241 Ken Linseman, Phil. RC	**2.00**	**4.00**
242 Billy Smith (G), NYIs.	1.50	3.00
243 Rick Chartraw, Mont.	.35	.75
244 CL: Atlanta Flames	1.50	3.00
245 CL: Boston Bruins	1.50	3.00
246 CL: Buffalo Sabres	1.50	3.00
247 CL: Chicago Blackhawks	1.50	3.00
248 CL: Colorado Rockies	1.50	3.00
249 CL: Detroit Red Wings	1.50	3.00
250 CL: Los Angeles Kings	1.50	3.00
251 CL: Minnesota North Stars	1.50	3.00
252 CL: Montréal Canadiens	1.50	3.00
253 CL: New York Islanders	1.50	3.00
254 CL: New York Rangers	1.50	3.00
255 CL: Philadelphia Flyers	1.50	3.00
256 CL: Pittsburgh Penguins	1.50	3.00
257 CL: St. Louis Blues	1.50	3.00
258 CL: Toronto Maple Leafs	1.50	3.00
259 CL: Vancouver Canucks	1.50	3.00
260 CL: Washington Capitals	1.50	3.00
261 CL: Québec Nordiques	–	12.00
261 Expansion teams	12.00	–
262 Jean Hamel, Detr.	.35	.75
263 Stan Jonathan, Bost.	.35	.75
264 Russ Anderson, Pitt.	.50	.75

Description	OPC
265 Gord Roberts, Hart. RC	**1.50**
266 Bill Flett, Edmo.	.75
267 Robbie Ftorek, Québ.	1.00
268 Mike Amodeo, Winn.	.75
269 Vic Venasky, LosA.	.75
270 Bob Manno, Vanc.	.75
271 Dan Maloney, Toro.	.75
272 Al Sims, Hart.	.75
273 Greg Polis, Wash.	.75
274 Doug Favell (G), Colo. (Edmo.)	1.25
275 Pierre Plante, Québ.	.75
276 Bob J. Murdoch, Atla.	.75
277 Lyle Moffat, Winn.	.75
278 Jack Brownschidle, SLou.	.75
279 Dave Keon, Hart.	1.50
280 Darryl Edestrand, LosA.	.75
281 Greg Millen (G), Pitt. RC	**7.00**
282 John Gould, Atla. (Buff.)	.75
283 Rich LeDuc, Québ.	.75
284 Ron Delorme, Colo.	.75
285 Gord Smith, Winn.	.75
286 Nick Fotiu, Hart.	.75
287 Kevin McCarthy, Phil. (Vanc.) RC	**3.00**
288 Jimmy Jones, Toro.	.75
289 Pierre Bouchard, Mont. (Wash.)	.75
290 Wayne Bianchin, Pitt. (Edmo.)	.75
291 Garry Larivière, Québ.	.75
292 Steve Jensen, LosA.	.75
293 John Garrett (G), Hart.	1.25
294 Hilliard Graves, Winn.	.75
295 Bill Clement, Atla.	.75
296 Michel Larocque (G), Mont.	.75
297 Bob Stewart, SLou.	.75
298 Doug Patey, Wash. (Edmo.) RC	**1.25**
299 Dave Farrish, Québ.	.75
300 Al Smith (G), Hart.	1.25
301 Bill Lochead, Detr. (NYRa.)	.75
302 Dave Hutchison, Toro.	.75
303 Bill Riley, Wsh (Winn.)	.75
304 Barry Gibbs, SLou. (LosA.)	.75
305 Chris Oddleifson, Vanc.	.75
306 J. Bob Kelly, Phil. (Edmo.), Error (Bob Kelly)	.75
307 Al Hangsleben, Hart. RC	**1.25**
308 Curt Brackenbury, Québ. RC	**1.25**
309 Rick Green, Wash.	.75
310 Ken Houston, Atla.	.75
311 Greg Joly, Detr.	.75
312 Bill Lesuk, Winn.	.75
313 Bill Stewart, Buff. RC	**1.25**
314 Rick Ley, Hart.	.75
315 Brett Callighen, Edmo. RC	**1.25**
316 Michel Dion (G), Québ.	1.25
317 Randy Manery, LosA.	.75
318 Barry Dean, Phil.	.75
319 Pat Boutette, Toro.	.75
320 Mark Heaslip, LosA. (Winn.)	.75
321 Dave Inkpen, Hart.	.75
322 Jere Gillis, Vanc.	.75
323 Larry Brown, LosA. (Edmo.)	.75
324 Alain Côté, Québ. RC	**1.00**
325 Gordie Lane, Wash.	.75
326 Bobby Lalonde, Atla. (Bost.)	.75
327 Ed Staniowski (G), SLou.	1.25
328 Ron Plumb, S.D. (Hart.)	.75
329 Jude Drouin, Winn.	.75
330 Rick Hampton, Clev. (LosA.)	.75
331 Stan Weir, Edmo.	.75
332 Blair Stewart, Wash. (Québ.)	.75
333 Mike Polich, Minn. RC	**1.25**
334 Jean Potvin, NYIs.	.75
335 Jordy Douglas, Hart. RC	**1.25**
336 Joel Quenneville, Toro. RC	**4.00**
337 Glen Hanlon (G), Vanc. RC	**4.00**
338 Dave Hoyda, Winn. RC	**1.25**
339 Colin Campbell, Pitt. (Edmo.)	1.00
340 John Smrke, Québ. RC	**1.25**
341 Brian Glennie, LosA.	.75
342 Don Kozak, Hart.	.75
343 Yvon Labre, Wash.	.75
344 Curt Bennett, Atla.	.75
345 Mike Christie, Colo.	.75
346 Checklist 3 (265 - 396)	12.00
347 Pat Price, NYIs. (Edmo.)	.75
348 Ron Low (G), Wash. (Québ.)	1.50
349 Mike Antonovich, Hart.	.75
350 Rolie Eriksson, Minn. (Winn.)	.75
351 Bob L. Murdoch (SLou.)	.75
352 Rob Palmer, LosA.	.75
353 Brad Gassoff, Vanc.	.75
354 Bruce Boudreau, Toro.	.75
355 Al Hamilton, Edmo.	.75
356 Blaine Stoughton, Hart.	.75
357 John Baby, Québ.	.75
358 Gary Inness (G), Wash.	1.25
359 Wayne Dillon, Winn.	.75
360 Darcy Rota, Atla.	.75
361 Brian Engblom, Mont. RC	**1.25**
362 Bill Hogaboam, Detr.	.75
363 Dave Debol, Hart. RC	**1.25**
364 Pete LoPresti (G), Minn. (Edmo.)	1.25
365 Gerry Hart, Québ.	.75
366 Syl Apps, Jr., LosA.	.75
367 Jack McIlhargey, Vanc.	.75
368 Willy Lindstrom, Winn.	.75
369 Don Laurence, Atla. (SLou.) RC	**1.25**
370 Chuck Luksa, Hart. RC	**1.25**
371 Dave Semenko, Edmo. RC	**5.00**
372 Paul Baxter, Québ. RC	**1.25**
373 Ron Ellis, Toro.	.75
374 Leif Svensson, Wash. RC	**1.25**
375 Dennis O'Brien, Minn. (Bost.)	.75
376 Glenn Goldup, LosA.	.75
377 Terry Richardson (G), Hart. RC	**1.25**
378 Peter Sullivan, Winn.	.75
379 Doug Hicks, Chic. (Edmo.)	.75
380 Jamie Hislop, Québ. RC	**1.25**
381 Jocelyn Guevremont, Buff. (NYRa.)	.75
382 Willi Plett, Atla.	.75
383 Larry Goodenough, Vanc.	.75
384 Jim Warner, Hart. RC	**1.25**
385 Rey Comeau, Colo.	.75
386 Barry Melrose, Winn. RC	**5.00**
387 Dave Hunter, Edmo. RC	**1.25**
388 Wally Weir, Québ. RC	**1.25**
389 Mario Lessard (G), LosA. RC	**1.25**
390 Ed Kea, Atla. (SLou.)	.75
391 Bob Stephenson, Hart. RC	**1.25**
392 Dennis Hextall, Wash.	.75
393 Jerry Butler, Toro.	.75
394 Dave Shand, Atla.	.75
395 Rick Blight, Vanc.	.75
396 Lars-Erik Sjoberg, Winn.	4.00

TOPPS STICKERS

These cards measure the standard 2 1/2" x 3 1/2".

Topps Insert Set (21 stickers): 18.00
Common Team: 1.25

1 Atlanta Flames	2 Boston Bruins
3 Buffalo Sabres	4 Chicago Blackhawks
5 Colorado Rockies	6 Detroit Red Wings
7 Edmonton Oilers	8 Hartford Whalers
9 Los Angeles Kings	10 Minnesota North Stars
11 Montréal Canadiens	12 New York Islanders
13 New York Rangers	14 Philadelphia Flyers
15 Pittsburgh Penguins	16 Québec Nordiques
17 St. Louis Blues	18 Toronto Maple Leafs
19 Vancouver Canucks	20 Washington Capitals
21 Winnipeg Jets	

1979 - 80 SOVIET STARS

These postcards measure 8 1/4" x 5 7/8".

Complete Set (24 cards and folder): 50.00

Soviet Stars	NM
1 Title Card: Team Photograph	3.00
2 Victor Tikhonov, Coach	3.00
3 Vladimir Yursinov, Coach	1.50
4 Vladislav Tretiak (G)	10.00
5 Alexander Pashkov (G)	3.00
6 Vladimir Lutchenko	1.50
7 Valeri Vasiliev	1.50
8 Gennady Tsycankov	1.50
9 Yuri Fedorov	1.50
10 Viacheslav Fetisov	6.00
11 Zinetula Bilylatinov	1.50
12 Vasiliy Pervukhin	1.50
13 Boris Mikhailov	3.00
14 Vladimir Petrov	3.00
15 Valeri Kharlamov	5.00
16 Alexander Maltsev	3.00
17 Sergei Kapustin	1.50
18 Yuri Lebedev	1.50
19 Viktor Zluktov	1.50
20 Helmut Balderis	3.00
21 Alexander Golikov	1.50
22 Sergei Makarov	6.00
23 Vladimir Golikov	1.50
24 Closing Ceremonies	1.50

1980 U.S.A. OLYMPIC MINI-PICS

These black & white cards measure 1 3/4" x 2 3/4".

Complete Set (16 cards):

Olympics

- 1 Jim Craig (G)
- 2 Mike Eruzione
- 3 John Harrington
- 4 Mark Johnson
- 5 Rob McClanahan
- 6 Jack O'Callahan
- 7 Phil Verchota
- 8 Bob Suter
- 9 Eric Strobel
- 10 Dave Silk
- 11 Mike Ramsey
- 12 Mark Pavelich
- 13 Steve Christoff
- 14 Dave Christian
- 15 Herb Brooks, Coach
- 16 1980 Game Scores

1980 U.S.S.R OLYMPIC MINI-PICS

These black & white cards measure 1 3/4" x 2 3/4".

Complete Set (10 cards):

Olympics

- Yuri Fedorov
- Irek Gimayev
- Alexander Golikov
- Sergei Kapustin
- V. Kovin
- Boris Mikhailov
- V. Myshikin (G)
- Vladimir Petrov
- Vladislav Tretiak (G)
- Valeri Vasiliev

Hockey

How do I know if it is real?

We often get letters and phone calls from our readers inquiring whether their Wayne Gretzky or other hot rookie card is real. As of late, the person more often than not would have bought the card in question over the Internet ("at a great price!") and ungraded. Sometimes the card they bought was graded but they still weren't sure if the card was real or not.

The first thing we always tell collectors is to take their card to a local dealer. Before anyone tells you whether the card is real or not, you should get the visual opinion from someone who works in the industry. With a card like the Wayne Gretzky rookie card, countless reprints and forgeries have been made. Many of the forgeries are pretty hard to miss, but some are getting better and better with each passing year.

Established and reputable grading companies have helped curb the anxiety of purchasing a popular rookie card through the mail or over the Internet. Collectors should be wary, however, that some "grading" companies have slabbed the forgeries as if they were real – sometimes by ignorance, sometimes with malicious intent.

Here are three reputable opinions from the Canadian market.

Rick Kressler, KSA

"One thing you should look at is the ice. The ice (on the real Gretzky RC) should be nice and white. Most of the reprints seem to have red dots (when viewed under a magnifying glass) on the ice. The yellow spot on the shoulder is a good tip – you will find the spot on Gretzky's left shoulder on the real card, but not on most reprints. Some of today's reprints do, however, have that yellow dot on the shoulder.

"You should be wary of anything that is very smooth on the front and that has sharp corners. There are real cards that have those qualities, but not many. All the black lines (part of the border) should be solid, not dotted (again, under a magnifying glass) like it is on many reprints. The skate laces on the front should consist of six or seven dots together. On the fake cards, those dots on the laces are not present. Also, the skate on the back of the real Gretzky card is usually lighter than it is on fake Gretzky cards."

Jason Martin, Martin Sports Cards

"The best rule of thumb is to not look for one particular thing. I find a lot of people that get stuck looking for the dot on the shoulder or the laces on the skates. There are all kinds of variations of Gretzky reprints. There are always new ones being made and there are always better photocopiers out there that are going to pick all those things up, so it's never good to look for one thing in particular.

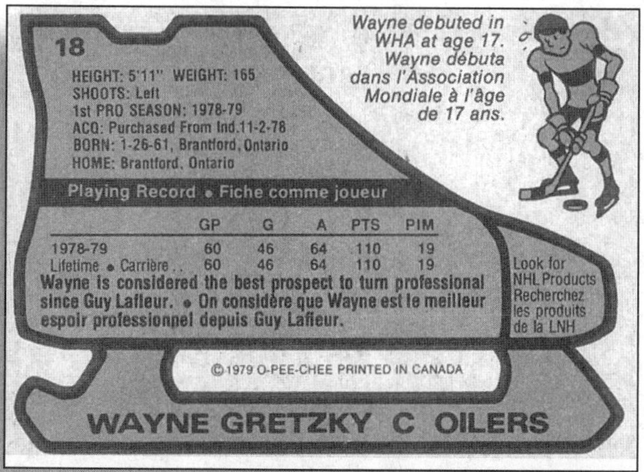

"On a whole, remember that, like any copy of anything, the reprint is not going to be as crisp or as clean as the original. Another thing to keep in mind is the sides of the card. I have never really seen a reprint where the sides of the card isn't white. But even with the sides, it would not be hard for someone to make them yellow somehow."

Wayne Gretzky's rookie card is number 18 in the 1979-80 O-Pee-Chee hockey set.

Wayne Wagner, Wayne's Sports Cards

"The real Gretzky card is not as grainy as some of the fakes. There is less to pick out in the background of many of the fake cards. The bleed of the card on all four sides should be brown-yellow or tan, not a blue colouring (which would be impossible since the original came from the inside of a bigger sheet of cards). Some reprints actually say "reprint" on the back. Reprint cards usually have much sharper corners than the original cards. With nearly all of the original Gretzky rookie cards, there is not that sharpness in the four corners, which is typical of all O-Pee-Chee cards from those days. We've seen one Gretzky rookie card come around with which you could almost shave your face. The paper stock on the original Gretzky rookie cards should be old. You can usually tell the difference in paper stocks simply by looking at a real and fake Gretzky rookie card. Many reprints have newer paper or shinier material as opposed to the 20-plus-year-old O-Pee-Chee paper which was less bright and less colourful."

1980 - 81 DERNIÈRE PHOTOS

This multi-sport series of photos were inserted in Dernière magazine from 1972 through 1984. Three holes were punched on the left side to allow for storage in a binder. The series featured Montréal Canadiens players. These photos measure 8" x 10".

	Dernière	**NM**
□	30NOV Serge Savard	6.00
□	7DEC Yvon Lambert	3.00
□	14DEC Bob Gainey	7.00
□	21DEC Réjean Houle	5.00
□	28DEC Claude Ruel, Coach	3.00
□	4JAN Doug Jarvis	3.00
□	11JAN Michel Larocque (G)	5.00
□	18JAN Pierre Larouche	3.00
□	25JAN Larry Robinson	8.00
□	1FEB Mario Tremblay	5.00
□	8FEB Guy Lapointe	6.00
□	15FEB Gaston Gingras	3.00
□	22FEB Richard / Bossy	15.00
□	1MAR Brian Engblom	3.00
□	8MAR Doug Risebrough	3.00
□	15MAR Rod Langway	6.00
□	22MAR Guy Lafleur	12.00
□	29MAR Steve Shutt	7.00
□	5APR Mark Napier	3.00
□	12APR Richard Sevigny (G)	5.00
□	119APR Chris Nilan	3.00
□	26APR Pierre Mondou	3.00
□	3MAY Keith Acton	3.00
□	10MAY Denis Herron (G)	5.00

1980 - 81 MALLASJUOMA

These cards measure 2" x 2 5/16". The labels themselves measure 3" x 3 1/2".

Complete Set (220 cards):

Mallasjuoma

□	Jukka Porvari	□	1 Stig Wetzell
□	2 Seppo Pakola	□	3 Frank Neal
□	4 Heikki Riihiranta	□	5 Esa Peltonen
□	6 T. Salmelainen	□	7 Matti Forss
□	8 Olli Ignatius	□	9 Raimo Hirvonen
□	10 Harri Linnonmaa	□	11 Jorma Immonen
□	12 Arto Sirvio	□	13 Matti Murto
□	14 Jari Kapanen	□	15 Ilkka Sinisalo
□	16 Arto Jokinen	□	17 Pertti Lehtonen
□	18 Timo Ukkola	□	19 Rainer Risku
□	20 Ari Lahteenmaki	□	21 Hannu Riihimaki
□	22 Jarmo Vuorinen	□	23 Jukka Airaksinen
□	24 Reijo Laksola	□	25 Jorma Aro
□	26 Jari Jarvinen	□	27 Jouko Urvikko
□	28 Ari Jokinen	□	29 Kari Heikkila
□	30 Auvo Vaananen	□	31 Risto Jalo
□	32 Lasse Oksanen	□	33 Lasse Tasala
□	34 Kari Jarvinen	□	35 Jarmo Lilius
□	36 Jyrki Seppa	□	37 Jorma Huhtala
□	38 Jari Viitala	□	39 Antti Heikkila
□	40 Matti Rautiainen	□	41 Pertti Jarvenpaa
□	42 Seppo Sevon	□	43 Henry Lehvonen
□	44 Tapio Virhimo	□	45 Rauli Sohlman
□	46 Martti Tuomisto	□	47 Pekka Rasanen
□	48 Aarre Kourula	□	49 Timo Saari
□	50 Arto Laine	□	51 Anssi Melametsa
□	52 VeliPekka Kinnunen	□	53 Matti Heikkila
□	54 Tony Arima	□	55 Ismo Lehkonen
□	56 Matti Virmanen	□	57 Sakari Petajaaho
□	58 Antti Lehto	□	59 Pasi Mustonen
□	60 Erkki Korhonen	□	61 Ilmo Uotila
□	62 Jussi Lepisto	□	63 Hannu Nykvist
□	64 Ari Blomqvist	□	65 Henry Leppa
□	66 Ari Makinen	□	67 Jari Vuorio
□	68 Olli Saarinen	□	69 Matti Kaario
□	70 Timo Blomqvist	□	71 Petteri Kanerva
□	72 Timo Harkanen	□	73 Keijo Koivisto
□	74 Eero Mantere	□	75 Harri Nyman
□	76 Harri Toivanen	□	77 Mika Laine
□	78 Olavi Niemenranta	□	79 Pekka Laine
□	80 Harri Haapaniemi	□	81 Juha Silvennoinen
□	82 Pekka Lumela	□	83 Yrjo Hakulinen
□	84 Tom Regnier	□	85 Richard Regnier
□	86 Jukka Holtari	□	87 Timo Heino
□	88 Hannu Koskinen	□	89 Ari Hellgren
□	90 Arto Ruotanen	□	91 Hannu Jalonen
□	92 Kari Suoraniemi	□	93 Hannu Hiltunen
□	94 Juha Tuohimaa	□	95 Pentti Perhomaa
□	96 Reijo Ruotsalainen	□	97 Seppo Tenhunen
□	98 Kari Jalonen	□	99 Markku Kiimalainen
□	100 Juha Huikari	□	101 Pekka Tuomisto
□	102 Jouni Koutuaniemi	□	103 Veikko Torkkeli
□	104 Jouko Kamarainen	□	105 Kai Suikkanen
□	106 Jorma Torkkeli	□	107 Mikko Leinonen
□	108 Ari Timosaari	□	109 Jarmo Tauriainen
□	110 Pekka Arbelius	□	111 Teppo Mattsson
□	112 Esa Hakkarainen	□	113 Jouni Peltonen
□	114 Jarmo Kuusisto	□	115 Timo Peltonen
□	116 Ari-Pekka Strander	□	117 Jorma Vehmanen
□	118 Pasi Tuohimaa	□	119 Olli Tuominen
□	120 Hannu Kemppainen	□	121 Ismo Villa
□	122 Esa Wallin	□	123 Matti Tynkkynen
□	124 Jari Rastio	□	125 Kari Kaupinsalo
□	126 Lasse Lindberg	□	127 Olli-Pekka Rajala
□	128 Harri Tuohimaa	□	129 Hannu Vierimaa
□	130 Jari Laiho	□	131 Juhani Wallenius
□	132 Jarmo Kaistakari	□	133 Jukka Peitsoma
□	134 Tuomo Martin	□	135 Keijo Taskula
□	136 Martti Immonen	□	137 Ilkka Kaarna
□	138 Pertti Ahokas	□	139 Ari Lehikoinen
□	140 Jyrki Paakkarinen	□	141 Jouko Kukko
□	142 Harri Poyhia	□	143 Pentti Matikainen
□	144 Juha Sokkanen	□	145 Antero Vaatamoinen
□	146 Pertti Heikkeri	□	147 Esko Heikkeri
□	148 Heikki Malkia	□	149 Tuomo Laukkanen
□	150 Kari Weckstrom	□	151 Seppo Urpalainen
□	152 Kari Saarikko	□	153 Tuomo Jormakka
□	154 Juha Henttonen	□	155 Lasse Schultz
□	156 Mikko Vilonen	□	157 Hannu Helander
□	158 Pertti Valkeapaa	□	159 Lasse Litma
□	160 Timo Jutila	□	161 Oiva Oijennus
□	162 Timo Susi	□	163 Jukka Porvari
□	164 Erkki Lehtonen	□	165 Esa Valioja
□	166 Pertti Koivulahti	□	167 Juha Nurmi
□	168 Hannu Kamppuri	□	169 Petri Karjalainen
□	170 Timo Penttila	□	171 Jari Lindgren
□	172 Seppo Virta	□	173 Jukka Hirsimaki
□	174 Petri Niukkanen	□	175 Seppo Ahokainen
□	176 Antero Lehtonen	□	177 Hannu Jortikka
□	178 Timo Nummelin	□	179 Seppo Suoraniemi
□	180 Pasi Virta	□	181 Kari Vaihinen
□	182 Henry Saleva	□	183 Jari Hytti
□	184 Kari Kauppila	□	185 Reijo Leppanen
□	186 Rauli Tammelin	□	187 Markku Haapaniemi
□	188 Kari Horkko	□	189 Martti Jarkko
□	190 Juhani Tamminen	□	191 Kalevi Aho
□	192 Reima Pullinen	□	193 Hakan Hjerppe
□	194 Rauno Sjoroos	□	195 Hannu Niittoaho
□	196 Jari Paavola	□	197 Petteri Lehto
□	198 Jim Bedard	□	199 Antero Kivela
□	200 Antti Heikkila	□	201 Tapio Flinck
□	202 Arto Javanainen	□	203 Jukka Virtanen
□	204 Risto Tuomi	□	205 Tapio Koskinen
□	206 Juha Jyrkkio	□	207 Ari Peltola
□	208 Tapio Levo	□	209 Veli-Pekka Ketola
□	210 Erkki Vakiparta	□	211 Simo Ketola
□	212 Rauli Levonen	□	213 Jari Nystrom
□	214 Matti Ruisma	□	215 Tauno Makela
□	216 Kari Makkonen	□	217 Harry Nikander
□	218 Pentti Rautakallio	□	219 Martti Nenonen
□	220 Kari Takko		

1980 - 81 OPEE-CHEE & TOPPS

These cards measure the standard 2 1/2" x 3 1/2". There are two versions for cards 1-264: the O-Pee-Chee and the Topps card. Topps cards do not include the traded line from the O-Pee-Chee counterparts. Topps cards also have a scratch-off surface in the bottom right corner of the card front. Topps cards without the scratch-off surface usually sell at 50-75% of the listed price (taking into account that the rest of the card is NM-MT).

	Complete Set (396 cards):	**325.00**	**600.00**
	Common Player:	**.30**	**.35**
	Desription	**Topps**	**OPC**
□ □	1 RB: Flyers go to 35 games without a loss	1.00	1.50
□ □	2 RB: Raymond Bourque, Bost.	12.00	20.00
□ □	3 RB: Wayne Gretzky, Edmo.	25.00	35.00
□ □	4 RB: Charlie Simmer, LosA.	.35	.50
□ □	5 RB: Billy Smith (G), NYIs.	.50	.75
□ □	6 Jean Ratelle, Bost.	.35	.50
□ □	7 Dave Maloney, NYRa.	.30	.35
□ □	8 Phil Myre (G), Phil.	.40	.50
□ □	**9 Ken Morrow, NYIs. RC**	**1.25**	**2.00**
□ □	10 Guy Lafleur, Mont.	5.00	7.00
□ □	**11 Bill Derlago, Toro. RC**	**.75**	**1.00**
□ □	12 Doug Wilson, Chic.	.65	1.00
□ □	13 Craig Ramsay, Buff.	.40	.50
□ □	14 Pat Boutette, Hart.	.30	.35
□ □	15 Eric Vail, Calg.	.30	.35
□ □	16 TL: Mike Foligno, Detr.	.40	.50
□ □	17 Bobby Smith, Minn.	1.00	1.50
□ □	18 Rick Kehoe, Pitt.	.40	.50
□ □	19 Joel Quenneville, Colo.	.50	.75
□ □	20 Marcel Dionne, LosA.	1.25	2.00
□ □	21 Kevin McCarthy, Vanc.	.30	.35
□ □	**22 Jim Craig (G), Bost. RC**	**3.00**	**4.00**
□ □	23 Steve Vickers, NYRa.	.30	.35
□ □	24 Ken Linseman, Phil.	.40	.50
□ □	25 Mike Bossy, NYIs.	6.00	10.00
□ □	26 Serge Savard, Mont.	.50	.75
□ □	27 TL: Grant Mulvey, Chic.	.40	.50
□ □	28 Pat Hickey, Toro.	.30	.35
□ □	29 Peter Sullivan, Winn.	.30	.35
□ □	30 Blaine Stoughton, Hart.	.30	.35
□ □	**31 Mike Liut (G), SLou. RC**	**6.00**	**8.00**
□ □	32 Blair MacDonald, Edmo.	.30	.35
□ □	33 Rick Green, Wash.	.30	.35
□ □	34 Al MacAdam, Minn.	.30	.35
□ □	35 Robbie Ftorek, Québ.	.40	.50
□ □	36 Dick Redmond, Bost.	.30	.35
□ □	37 Ron Duguay, NYRa.	.40	.50
□ □	38 TL: Danny Gare, Buff.	.40	.50
□ □	**39 Brian Propp, Phil. RC**	**3.00**	**5.00**
□ □	40 Bryan Trottier, NYIs.	2.00	3.00
□ □	41 Rich Preston, Chic.	.30	.35
□ □	42 Pierre Mondou, Mont.	.30	.35
□ □	43 Reed Larson, Detr.	.30	.35
□ □	44 George Ferguson, Pitt.	.30	.35
□ □	45 Guy Chouinard, Calg.	.30	.35
□ □	46 Billy Harris, LosA.	.30	.35
□ □	47 Gilles Meloche (G), Minn.	.40	.50
□ □	48 Blair Chapman, SLou.	.30	.35
□ □	49 TL: Mike Gartner, Wash.	6.00	8.00
□ □	50 Darryl Sittler, Toro.	1.00	1.75
□ □	51 Rick Martin, Buff.	.30	.35
□ □	52 Ivan Boldirev, Vanc.	.40	.50
□ □	**53 Craig Norwich, SLou. RC**	**.65**	**.75**
□ □	54 Dennis Polonich, Detr.	.30	.35
□ □	55 Bobby Clarke, Phil.	1.00	1.75
□ □	56 Terry O'Reilly, Bost.	.40	.50
□ □	57 Carol Vadnais, NYRa.	.30	.35
□ □	58 Bob Gainey, Mont.	1.00	1.75
□ □	59 TL: Blaine Stoughton, Hart.	.40	.50
□ □	60 Billy Smith (G), NYIs.	1.00	1.75
□ □	**61 Mike O'Connell, Chic. RC**	**1.25**	**2.00**
□ □	62 Lanny McDonald, Colo.	.75	1.25
□ □	63 Lee Fogolin, Edmo.	.30	.35
□ □	**64 Rocky Saganiuk, Toro. RC**	**.65**	**.75**
□ □	**65 Rolf Edberg, Wash. RC**	**.65**	**.75**
□ □	66 Paul Shmyr, Minn.	.30	.35
□ □	**67 Michel Goulet, Québ. RC**	**15.00**	**25.00**
□ □	68 Dan Bouchard (G), Calg.	.40	.50
□ □	**69 Mark Johnson, Pitt. RC**	**.75**	**1.00**
□ □	70 Reggie Leach, Phil.	.40	.50
□ □	71 TL: Bernie Federko, SLou.	.40	.50
□ □	72 Pete Mahovlich, Detr.	.40	.50
□ □	73 Anders Hedberg, NYRa.	.40	.50
□ □	74 Brad Park, Bost.	.75	1.25
□ □	75 Clark Gillies, NYIs.	.40	.50
□ □	76 Doug Jarvis, Mont.	.40	.50
□ □	77 John Garrett (G), Hart.	.40	.50
□ □	78 Dave Hutchison, Chic.	.30	.35
□ □	**79 John Anderson, Toro. RC**	**.75**	**1.00**
□ □	80 Gilbert Perreault, Buff.	1.00	1.75
□ □	81 AS: Marcel Dionne, LosA.	.65	1.00
□ □	82 AS: Guy Lafleur, Mont.	2.00	3.00
□ □	83 AS: Charlie Simmer, LosA.	.40	.50
□ □	84 AS: Larry Robinson, Mont.	.50	.75
□ □	85 AS: Börje Salming, Toro.	.50	.75
□ □	86 AS: Tony Esposito (G), Chic.	.65	1.00
□ □	87 AS: Wayne Gretzky, Edmo.	35.00	50.00
□ □	88 AS: Danny Gare, Buff.	.40	.50
□ □	89 AS: Steve Shutt, Mont.	.50	.75
□ □	90 AS: Barry Beck, NYRa.	.40	.50
□ □	91 AS: Mark Howe, Hart.	.40	.50
□ □	92 AS: Don Edwards (G), Buff.	.40	.50
□ □	**93 Tom McCarthy, Minn. RC**	**.65**	**.75**
□ □	94 TL: P. McNab/ R. Middleton, Bost.	.40	.50
□ □	95 Mike Palmateer (G), Wash.	.50	.75
□ □	96 Jim Schoenfeld, Buff.	.40	.50
□ □	97 Jordy Douglas, Hart.	.30	.35
□ □	**98 Keith Brown, Chic. RC**	**.75**	**1.00**
□ □	99 Dennis Ververgaert, Phil. (Wash.)	.30	.35
□ □	100 Phil Esposito, NYRa.	1.00	1.75
□ □	101 Jack Brownschidle, SLou.	.30	.35
□ □	102 Bob Nystrom, NYIs.	.40	.50
□ □	**103 Steve Christoff, Minn. RC**	**.65**	**.75**
□ □	104 Rob Palmer, LosA.	.30	.35
□ □	105 Dave Williams, Vanc.	.40	.50
□ □	106 TL: Kent Nilsson, Calg.	.40	.50
□ □	107 Morris Lukowich, Winn.	.30	.35
□ □	108 Jack Valiquette, Colo.	.30	.35
□ □	**109 Richard Dunn, Buff. RC**	**.65**	**.75**
□ □	110 Rogatien Vachon (G), Bost.	.40	.50
□ □	111 Mark Napier, Mont.	.30	.35
□ □	112 Gord Roberts, Hart.	.30	.35
□ □	113 Stan Jonathan, Bost.	.30	.35
□ □	114 Brett Callighen, Edmo.	.30	.35
□ □	115 Rick MacLeish, Phil.	.30	.35
□ □	116 Ulf Nilsson, NYRa.	.30	.35
□ □	117 TL: Rick Kehoe, Pitt.	.40	.50
□ □	118 Dan Maloney, Toro.	.30	.35
□ □	119 Terry Ruskowski, Chic.	.30	.35
□ □	120 Denis Potvin, NYIs.	1.00	1.75
□ □	121 Wayne Stephenson (G), Wash.	.40	.50
□ □	122 Rich LeDuc, Québ.	.30	.35
□ □	123 Checklist 1 (1 - 132)	6.00	8.00
□ □	124 Don Lever, Calg.	.30	.35
□ □	125 Jim Rutherford (G), Detr.	.40	.50
□ □	**126 Ray Allison, Hart. RC**	**.65**	**.75**
□ □	**127 Mike Ramsey, Buff. RC**	**3.00**	**4.00**
□ □	128 TL: Stan Smyl, Vanc.	.40	.50
□ □	**129 Al Secord, Bost. RC**	**2.00**	**3.00**
□ □	130 Denis Herron (G), Mont.	.40	.50
□ □	131 Bob Dailey, Phil.	.30	.35
□ □	132 Dean Talafous, NYRa.	.30	.35
□ □	133 Ian Turnbull, Toro.	.30	.35
□ □	134 Ron Sedlbauer, Chic.	.30	.35
□ □	135 Tom Bladon, Pitt. (Edmo.)	.30	.35
□ □	136 Bernie Federko, SLou.	1.25	2.00
□ □	137 Dave Taylor, LosA.	2.00	3.00
□ □	138 Bob Lorimer, NYIs.	.30	.35
□ □	139 TL: A. MacAdam/ S. Payne, Minn.	.40	.50
□ □	**140** Raymond Bourque, **Bost. RC**	**110.00**	**175.00**
□ □	141 Glen Hanlon (G), Vanc.	.40	.50
□ □	142 Willy Lindstrom, Winn.	.30	.35
□ □	143 Mike Rogers, Hart.	.30	.35
□ □	**144 Tony McKegney, Buff. RC**	**1.25**	**2.00**
□ □	145 Behn Wilson, Phil.	.30	.35
□ □	146 Lucien DeBlois, Colo.	.30	.35
□ □	147 Dave Burrows, Toro. (Pitt.)	.30	.35
□ □	148 Paul Woods, Detr.	.30	.35
□ □	149 TL: Phil Esposito, NYRa.	.65	1.00
□ □	150 Tony Esposito (G), Chic.	1.00	1.75
□ □	151 Pierre Larouche, Mont.	.40	.50
□ □	152 Brad Maxwell, Minn.	.30	.35
□ □	153 Stan Weir, Edmo.	.30	.35
□ □	154 Ryan Walter, Wash.	.40	.50
□ □	155 Dale Hoganson, Québ.	.30	.35
□ □	**156 Anders Kallur, NYIs. RC**	**.75**	**1.00**
□ □	**157 Paul Reinhart, Calg. RC**	**1.00**	**1.50**
□ □	158 Greg Millen (G), Pitt.	.40	.50
□ □	159 Ric Seiling, Buff.	.30	.35
□ □	160 Mark Howe, Hart.	1.25	2.00
□ □	161 LL: D. Gare/ C. Simmer/ B. Stoughton	.40	.50
□ □	162 LL: W. Gretzky/ M. Dionne/ G. Lafleur	10.00	15.00
□ □	163 LL: M. Dionne/ W. Gretzky/ G. Lafleur	10.00	15.00
□ □	164 LL: J. Mann/ D. WIlliams/ P. Holmgren	.40	.50
□ □	165 LL: Simmer/ Dionne/ Gare/ Shutt/ Sittler	.40	.50
□ □	166 LL: Sauvé (G)/ Herron (G)/ Edwards (G)	.40	.50
□ □	167 LL: D. Gare/ P. McNab/ B. Stoughton	.40	.50
□ □	168 LL: T. Esposito (G)/ G. Cheevers (G)/	1.25	2.00
□ □	**169 Perry Turnbull, SLou. RC**	**.65**	**.75**
□ □	170 Barry Beck, NYRa.	.30	.35
□ □	171 TL: Charlie Simmer, LosA.	.40	.50
□ □	172 Paul Holmgren, Phil.	.30	.35
□ □	173 Willie Huber, Detr.	.30	.35
□ □	174 Tim Young, Minn.	.30	.35
□ □	175 Gilles Gilbert (G), Detr.	.40	.50
□ □	**176 Dave Christian, Winn. RC**	**1.25**	**2.00**
□ □	**177 Lars Lindgren, Vanc. RC**	**.65**	**.75**
□ □	178 Réal Cloutier, Québ.	.30	.35
□ □	**179 Laurie Boschman, Toro. RC**	**.75**	**1.00**
□ □	180 Steve Shutt, Mont.	.75	1.25
□ □	181 Bob Murray, Chic.	.30	.35
□ □	182 TL: Wayne Gretzky, Edmo.	20.00	25.00
□ □	183 John Van Boxmeer, Buff.	.30	.35
□ □	184 Nick Fotiu, Hart.	.30	.35
□ □	185 Mike McEwen, Colo.	.30	.35
□ □	186 Greg Malone, Pitt.	.30	.35
□ □	**187 Mike Foligno, Detr. RC**	**2.00**	**3.00**
□ □	**188 Dave Langevin, NYIs. RC**	**.65**	**.75**
□ □	189 Mel Bridgman, Phil.	.30	.35
□ □	190 John Davidson (G), NYRa.	.30	.35
□ □	191 Mike Milbury, Bost.	.30	.35
□ □	192 Ron Zanussi, Minn.	.30	.35
□ □	193 TL: Darryl Sittler, Toro.	.50	.75
□ □	194 John Marks, Chic.	.30	.35
□ □	**195 Mike Gartner, Wash. RC**	**40.00**	**70.00**
□ □	196 Dave Lewis, LosA.	.40	.50
□ □	**197 Kent Nilsson, Calg. RC**	**2.50**	**4.00**
□ □	198 Rick Ley, Hart.	.30	.35
□ □	199 Derek Smith, Buff.	.30	.35
□ □	200 Bill Barber, Phil.	.75	1.25
□ □	201 Guy Lapointe, Mont.	.75	1.25

□ □	202 Vaclav Nedomansky, Detr.	.30	.35
□ □	203 Don Murdoch, Edmo.	.30	.35
□ □	204 TL: Mike Bossy, NYIs.	2.00	3.00
□ □	**205 Pierre Hamel (G), Winn. RC**	**.65**	**.75**
□ □	**206 Mike Eaves, Minn. RC**	**.65**	**.75**
□ □	207 Doug Halward, LosA.	.30	.35
□ □	**208 Stan Smyl, Vanc. RC**	**2.00**	**3.00**
□ □	**209 Mike Zuke, SLou. RC**	**.65**	**.75**
□ □	210 Börje Salming, Toro.	.75	1.25
□ □	211 Walt Tkaczuk, NYRa.	.30	.35
□ □	212 Grant Mulvey, Chic.	.30	.35
□ □	**213 Rob Ramage, Colo. RC**	**2.00**	**3.00**
□ □	214 Tom Rowe, Hart.	.30	.35
□ □	215 Don Edwards (G), Buff.	.40	.50
□ □	216 TL: G. Lafleur/ P Larouche, Mont.	1.00	1.75
□ □	217 Dan Labraaten, Detr.	.30	.35
□ □	218 Glen Sharpley, Minn.	.30	.35
□ □	219 Stefan Persson, NYIs.	.30	.35
□ □	220 Peter McNab, Bost.	.30	.35
□ □	221 Doug Hicks, Edmo.	.30	.35
□ □	**222 Bengt Gustafsson, Wash. RC**	**1.25**	**2.00**
□ □	223 Michel Dion (G), Québ.	.40	.50
□ □	224 Jimmy Watson, Phil.	.30	.35
□ □	225 Wilf Paiement, Toro.	.30	.35
□ □	226 Phil Russell, Calg.	.30	.35
□ □	227 TL: Morris Lukowich, Winn.	.40	.50
□ □	228 Ron Stackhouse, Pitt.	.30	.35
□ □	229 Ted Bulley, Chic.	.30	.35
□ □	230 Larry Robinson, Mont.	1.00	1.75
□ □	231 Don Maloney, NYRa.	.30	.35
□ □	**232 Rob McClanahan, Buff. RC**	**.75**	**1.00**
□ □	233 Al Sims, Hart.	.30	.35
□ □	234 Errol Thompson, Detr.	.30	.35
□ □	235 Glenn Resch (G), NYIs.	.40	.50
□ □	236 Bob Miller, Bost.	.30	.35
□ □	237 Gary Sargent, Minn.	.30	.35
□ □	238 TL: Réal Cloutier, Québ.	.40	.50
□ □	239 René Robert, Colo.	.30	.35
□ □	240 Charlie Simmer, LosA.	1.00	1.50
□ □	241 Thomas Gradin, Vanc.	.40	.50
□ □	**242 Rick Vaive, Toro. RC**	**2.00**	**3.00**
□ □	**243 Ron Wilson, Winn. RC**	**.65**	**.75**
□ □	244 Brian Sutter, SLou.	.65	1.00
□ □	245 Dale McCourt, Detr.	.30	.35
□ □	246 Yvon Lambert, Mont.	.30	.35
□ □	247 Tom Lysiak, Chic.	.30	.35
□ □	248 Ron Greschner, NYRa.	.30	.35
□ □	249 TL: Reggie Leach, Phil.	.40	.50
□ □	250 Wayne Gretzky, Edmo.	100.00	150.00
□ □	251 Rick Middleton, Bost.	.40	.50
□ □	252 Al Smith (G), Hart. (Colo.)	.40	.50
□ □	253 Fred Barrett, Minn.	.30	.35
□ □	254 Butch Goring, NYIs.	.40	.50
□ □	255 Robert Picard, Toro.	.30	.35
□ □	256 Marc Tardif, Québ.	.30	.35
□ □	257 Checklist 2 (133 - 264)	6.00	8.00
□ □	258 Barry Long, Detr. (Winn.)	.30	.35
□ □	259 TL: René Robert, Colo.	.40	.50
□ □	260 Danny Gare, Buff.	.40	.50
□ □	261 Réjean Houle, Mont.	.40	.50
□ □	262 Cup: Mike Bossy/ Gilbert Perreault	1.00	1.75
□ □	263 Semi-Finals: Flyers skate past North Stars	.30	.35
□ □	264 Cup: Billy Smith (G), NYIs.	.50	.75

Desription	OPC
□ 265 Bobby Lalonde, Atla. (Bost.)	.35
□ 266 Bob Sauvé (G), Buff.	.50
□ 267 Bob MacMillan, Calg.	.35
□ 268 Greg Fox, Chic.	.35
□ **269 Hardy Astrom (G), Colo. RC**	**1.00**
□ 270 Greg Joly, Detr.	.35
□ **271 Dave Lumley, Edmo. RC**	**1.00**
□ 272 Dave Keon, Hart.	.75
□ 273 Garry Unger, SLou. (LosA.)	.50
□ 274 Steve Payne, Minn.	.35
□ 275 Doug Risebrough, Mont., Error (Serge Savard)	.50
□ 276 Bob Bourne, NYIs.	.35
□ 277 Eddie Johnstone, NYRa.	.35
□ 278 Peter Lee, Pitt.	.35
□ **279 Pete Peeters (G), Phil. RC**	**6.00**
□ 280 Ron Chipperfield, Edmo. (Québ.)	.35
□ 281 Wayne Babych, SLou.	.35
□ 282 Dave Shand, Atla. (Toro.)	.35
□ 283 Jere Gillis, Vanc. (NYRa.)	.35
□ 284 Dennis Maruk, Wash.	.35
□ 285 Jude Drouin, NYIs. (Winn.)	.35
□ 286 Mike Murphy, LosA.	.35
□ 287 Curt Fraser, Vanc.	.35
□ 288 Gary McAdam, Pitt.	.35
□ **289 Mark Messier, Edmo. RC**	**175.00**
□ 290 Vic Venasky, LosA.	.35
□ 291 Per-Olov Brasar, Vanc.	.35
□ 292 Orest Kindrachuk, Pitt.	.35
□ 293 Dave Hunter, Edmo.	.35
□ 294 Steve Jensen, LosA.	.35
□ 295 Chris Oddleifson, Vanc.	.35
□ **296 Larry Playfair, Buff. RC**	**.75**
□ 297 Mario Tremblay, Mont.	.35
□ **298 Gilles Lupien, Pitt. RC**	**.75**
□ 299 Pat Price, Edmo.	.35
□ 300 Jerry Korab, Buff. (LosA.)	.35
□ 301 Darcy Rota, Atla. (Vanc.)	.35
□ 302 Don Luce, Buff.	.35
□ 303 Ken Houston, Calg.	.35
□ 304 Brian Engblom, Mont.	.35
□ 305 John Tonelli, NYIs.	2.00
□ **306 Doug Sulliman, NYRa. RC**	**.75**
□ 307 Rod Schutt, Pitt.	.35
□ **308 Norm Barnes, Phil. RC**	**.75**
□ 309 Serge Bernier, Québ.	.35
□ 310 Larry Patey, SLou.	.35
□ 311 Dave Farrish, Québ. (Toro.)	.35
□ 312 Harold Snepsts, Vanc.	.50
□ 313 Bob Sirois, Wash.	.35
□ 314 Peter Marsh, Winn.	.35
□ **315 Risto Siltanen, Edmo. RC**	**.75**
□ 316 André St. Laurent, LosA.	.35
□ **317 Craig Hartsburg, Minn. RC**	**3.00**
□ 318 Wayne Cashman, Bost.	.35
□ **319 Lindy Ruff, Buff. RC**	**4.00**
□ 320 Willi Plett, Calg.	.35
□ 321 Ron Delorme, Colo.	.35
□ **322 Gaston Gingras, Mont. RC**	**1.00**
□ 323 Gordie Lane, NYIs.	.35
□ **324 Doug Soetaert (G), NYRa. RC**	**1.00**
□ 325 Gregg Sheppard, Pitt.	.35
□ **326 Mike Busniuk, Phil. RC**	**.75**
□ 327 Jamie Hislop, Québ.	.35
□ 328 Ed Staniowski (G), SLou.	.50
□ 329 Ron Ellis, Toro.	.50
□ 330 Gary Bromley (G), Vanc.	.50
□ **331 Mark Lofthouse, Wash. RC**	**.75**
□ 332 Dave Hoyda, Winn.	.35
□ 333 Ron Low (G), Wash. (Edmo.)	.50
□ 334 Barry Gibbs, LosA.	.35
□ 335 Gary Edwards (G), Minn.	.35
□ 336 Don Marcotte, Bost.	.35
□ 337 Bill Hajt, Buff.	.35
□ **338 Brad Marsh, Calg. RC**	**4.00**
□ 339 J.P. Bordeleau, Chic.	.35
□ **340 Randy Pierce, Colo. RC**	**.75**
□ **341 Ed Mio (G), Edmo. RC**	**2.00**
□ 342 Randy Manery, LosA.	.35
□ 343 Tom Younghans, Minn.	.35
□ **344 Rod Langway, Mont. RC**	**12.00**
□ 345 Wayne Merrick, NYIs.	.35
□ **346 Steve Baker (G), NYRa. RC**	**.75**
□ 347 Pat Hughes, Pitt.	.35
□ 348 Al Hill, Phil.	.35
□ 349 Gerry Hart, Québ. (SLou.)	.35
□ 350 Richard Mulhern, Bost. (Toro.)	.35
□ 351 Jerry Butler, Toro. (Vanc.)	.35
□ 352 Guy Charron, Wash.	.35
□ **353 Jimmy Mann, Winn. RC**	**1.00**
□ **354 Brad McCrimmon, Bost. RC**	**2.00**
□ 355 Rick Dudley, Buff.	.35
□ 356 Pekka Rautakallio, Calg.	.35
□ **357 Tim Trimper, Chic. RC**	**.75**
□ 358 Mike Christie, Colo.	.35
□ **359 John Ogrodnick, Detr. RC**	**2.00**
□ 360 Dave Semenko, Edmo.	.50
□ 361 Mike Veisor (G), Chic. (Hart.)	.50
□ 362 Syl Apps, LosA.	.35
□ 363 Mike Polich, Minn.	.35
□ 364 Rick Chartraw, Mont.	.35
□ **365 Steve Tambellini, NYIs. RC**	**3.00**
□ **366 Ed Hospodar, NYRa. RC**	**1.00**
□ 367 Randy Carlyle, Pitt.	.50
□ 368 Tom Gorence Phil.	.35
□ 369 Pierre Plante, Québ.	.35
□ 370 Blake Dunlop, Phil. (SLou.)	.35
□ 371 Mike Kaszycki, NYIs. (Toro.)	.35
□ 372 Rick Blight, Vanc.	.35
□ 373 Pierre Bouchard, Wash.	.50
□ 374 Gary Doak, Bost.	.35
□ 375 André Savard, Buff.	.35
□ 376 Bill Clement, Calg.	.35
□ 377 Reg Kerr, Chic.	.35
□ 378 Walt McKechnie, Toro. (Colo.)	.35
□ **379 George Lyle, Detr. RC**	**.75**
□ 380 Colin Campbell, Edmo.	.50
□ 381 Dave Debol, Hart.	.35
□ 382 Glenn Goldup, LosA.	.35
□ 383 Kent-Erik Andersson, Minn.	.35
□ **384 Tony Currie, SLou. RC**	**.75**
□ **385 Richard Sévigny (G), Mont. RC**	**1.50**
□ 386 Garry Howatt, NYIs.	.35
□ 387 Cam Connor, NYRa.	.35
□ 388 Ross Lonsberry, Pitt.	.35
□ **389 Frank Bathe, Phil. RC**	**.75**
□ 390 John Wensink, Bost. (Québ.)	.35
□ 391 Paul Harrison (G), Toro.	.50
□ 392 Dennis Kearns, Vanc.	.35
□ 393 Pat Ribble, Atla. (Wash.)	.35
□ **394 Markus Mattsson (G), Winn. RC**	**.75**
□ 395 Chuck Lefley, SLou.	.35
□ 396 Checklist 3 (265 - 396)	12.00

TOPPS TEAM POSTERS

These blank-back photos came folded inside packs. Each poster measures 5" x 7".

Topps Insert Set (16 posters): 20.00
Individual Team: 2.00-4.00

□ 1 New York Islanders	□ 2 New York Rangers
□ 3 Philadelphia Flyers	□ 4 Boston Bruins
□ 5 Hartford Whalers	□ 6 Buffalo Sabres
□ 7 Chicago Blackhawks	□ 8 Detroit Red Wings
□ 9 Minnesota North Stars	□ 10 Toronto Maple Leafs
□ 11 Montréal Canadiens	□ 12 Colorado Rockies
□ 13 Los Angeles Kings	□ 14 Vancouver Canucks
□ 15 St. Louis Blues	□ 16 Washington Captials

1980 - 81 OPC SUPER PHOTOS

These cards measure 5" x 7".

Complete Set (24 cards): 40.00

O-Pee-Chee	**NM-MT**
□ 1 Brad Park, Bost.	3.00
□ 2 Gilbert Perreault, Buff.	3.00
□ 3 Kent Nilsson, Calg.	1.25
□ 4 Tony Esposito (G), Chic.	4.00
□ 5 Lanny McDonald, Colo.	3.00
□ 6 Pete Mahovlich, Detr.	1.25
□ 7 Wayne Gretzky, Edmo.	18.00
□ 8 Marcel Dionne, LosA.	3.50
□ 9 Bob Gainey, Mont.	3.00
□ 10 Guy Lafleur, Mont.	6.50
□ 11 Larry Robinson, Mont.	3.00
□ 12 Mike Bossy, NYIs.	6.00
□ 13 Denis Potvin, NYIs.	3.00
□ 14 Phil Esposito, NYRa.	3.50
□ 15 Anders Hedberg, NYRa.	1.25
□ 16 Bobby Clarke, Phil.	3.50
□ 17 Marc Tardif, Québ.	1.25
□ 18 Bernie Federko, SLou.	2.00
□ 19 Börje Salming, Toro.	3.00
□ 20 Darryl Sittler, Toro.	3.50
□ 21 Ian Turnbull, Toro.	1.25
□ 22 Glen Hanlon, Vanc.	2.00
□ 23 Mike Palmateer (G), Wash.	2.50
□ 24 Morris Lukowich, Winn.	1.25

1980 - 81 PEPSI CAPS

These caps measure 1 1/8" in diameter.

Complete Set (140 caps): 175.00
Common Player: 2.00
Plastic Display Holder: 60.00

Pepsi • Calgary Flames	**NM**
□ Dan Bouchard (G)	3.00
□ Guy Chouinard	2.00
□ Bill Clement	2.00
□ Randy Holt	2.00
□ Ken Houston	2.00
□ Kevin LaVallée, Error (LaValee)	2.00
□ Don Lever	2.00
□ Bob MacMillan	2.00
□ Brad Marsh	3.00
□ Bob Murdoch	2.00
□ Kent Nilsson	3.00
□ Jim Peplinski	2.00
□ Willi Plett	2.00
□ Pekka Rautakillio	2.00
□ Paul Reinhart	2.00
□ Pat Riggin (G)	3.00
□ Phil Russell	2.00
□ Brad Smith	2.00
□ Eric Vail	2.00
□ Bert Wilson	2.00
Pepsi • Edmonton Oilers	**NM**
□ Glenn Anderson	4.00
□ Curt Brackenbury	2.00
□ Brett Callighen	2.00
□ Paul Coffey	12.00
□ Lee Fogolin	2.00
□ Matti Hagman	2.00
□ John Hughes	2.00
□ Dave Hunter	2.00
□ Jari Kurri	9.00
□ Ron Low (G)	3.00
□ Kevin Lowe	3.00
□ Dave Lumley	2.00
□ Blair MacDonald	2.00
□ Mark Messier	18.00
□ Ed Mio (G)	3.00
□ Don Murdoch	2.00
□ Pat Price	2.00
□ Dave Semenko	2.00
□ Risto Siltanen	2.00
□ Stan Weir	2.00
Pepsi • Montréal Canadiens	**NM**
□ Keith Acton	2.00
□ Brian Engblom	2.00
□ Bob Gainey	3.50
□ Gaston Gingras	2.00
□ Denis Herron (G)	3.00
□ Réjean Houle	3.00
□ Doug Jarvis	3.00
□ Yvon Lambert	2.00
□ Rod Langway	3.00
□ Guy Lapointe	3.00
□ Pierre Larouche	2.00
□ Pierre Mondou	2.00
□ Mark Napier	2.00
□ Chris Nilan	2.00
□ Doug Risebrough	2.00
□ Larry Robinson	3.50
□ Serge Savard	3.00
□ Steve Shutt	3.50
□ Mario Tremblay	3.00
□ Doug Wickenheiser	2.00
Pepsi • Québec Nordiques	**NM**
□ Serge Bernier	2.00
□ Kim Clackson	2.00
□ Réal Cloutier	2.00
□ André Dupont	2.00
□ Robbie Ftorek	3.00
□ Michel Goulet	6.00
□ Jamie Hislop	2.00
□ Dale Hoganson	2.00
□ Dale Hunter	3.50
□ Pierre Lacroix	2.00
□ Garry Larivière	2.00
□ Rich Leduc	2.00
□ John Paddock	2.00
□ Michel Plasse (G)	3.00
□ Jacques Richard	2.00
□ Anton Stastny	2.00
□ Peter Stastny	6.00
□ Marc Tardif	3.00
□ Wally Weir	2.00
□ John Wensink	2.00
Pepsi • Toronto Maple Leafs	**NM**
□ John Anderson	2.00
□ Laurie Boschman	2.00
□ Jiri Crha (G)	3.00
□ Bill Derlago	2.00
□ Vitezslav Duris	2.00
□ Ron Ellis	2.00
□ Dave Farrish	2.00
□ Stewart Gavin	2.00
□ Pat Hickey	2.00
□ Dan Maloney	2.00
□ Terry Martin	2.00
□ Barry Melrose	3.00
□ Wilf Paiement	2.00
□ Robert Picard	2.00
□ Jim Rutherford (G)	3.00
□ Rocky Saganiuk	2.00
□ Börje Salming	3.00
□ Dave Shand	2.00
□ Ian Turnbull	2.00
□ Rick Vaive	2.00
Pepsi • Vancouver Canucks	**NM**
□ Brent Ashton	2.00
□ Ivan Boldirev	2.00

☐	Per-Olov Brasar	2.00
☐	Richard Brodeur (G)	3.00
☐	Jerry Butler	2.00
☐	Colin Campbell	3.00
☐	Curt Fraser	3.00
☐	Thomas Gradin	2.00
☐	Dennis Kearns	2.00
☐	Rick Lanz	2.00
☐	Lars Lindgren	2.00
☐	Dave Logan	2.00
☐	Mario Marois	2.00
☐	Kevin McCarthy	2.00
☐	Gerry Minor	2.00
☐	Darcy Rota	2.00
☐	Bobby Schmautz	2.00
☐	Stan Smyl	2.00
☐	Harold Snepsts	2.00
☐	Dave Williams	3.00
Pepsi • Winnipeg Jets		**NM**
☐	Dave Babych	2.00
☐	Al Cameron	2.00
☐	Scott Campbell	2.00
☐	Dave Christian	2.00
☐	Jude Drouin	2.00
☐	Norm Dupont	2.00
☐	Danny Geoffrion	2.00
☐	Pierre Hamel (G)	3.00
☐	Barry Legge	2.00
☐	Willy Lindstrom	2.00
☐	Barry Long	2.00
☐	Kris Manery	2.00
☐	Jimmy Mann	2.00
☐	Moe Mantha	2.00
☐	Markus Mattsson (G)	3.00
☐	Don Spring	2.00
☐	Doug Smail	2.00
☐	Anders Steen	2.00
☐	Peter Sullivan	2.00
☐	Ron Wilson	2.00

1981 - 82 DERNIÈRE PHOTOS

This multi-sport series of photos were inserted in Dernière magazine from 1972 through 1984. Three holes were punched on the left side to allow for storage in a binder. The series featured Montréal Canadiens players. These photos measure 8" x 10".

Dernière		**NM**
☐	8NOV Marc Tardif	5.00
☐	15NOV Michel Bergeron	3.00
☐	22NOV Daniel Bouchard (G)	5.00
☐	29NOV Jacques Richard	3.00
☐	6DEC Marian Stastny	3.00
☐	13DEC Michel Goulet	7.00
☐	20DEC André Dupont	3.00
☐	27DEC Robbie Ftorek	5.00
☐	3JAN Michel Plasse (G)	5.00
☐	10JAN Pierre Lacroix	3.00
☐	17JAN Dale Hoganson	3.00
☐	24JAN Mario Marois	3.00
☐	31JAN Normand Rochefort	3.00
☐	7FEB Anton Stastny	5.00
☐	14FEB Dale Hunter	5.00
☐	21FEB Dave Pichette	3.00
☐	28FEB Pierre Aubry	3.00
☐	7MAR Réal Cloutier	3.00
☐	14MAR Alain Côté	3.00
☐	21MAR Wally Weir	3.00
☐	28MAR Peter Stastny	8.00
☐	4APR Miroslav Frycer	3.00
☐	11APR Wayne Gretzky	30.00

1981 - 82 O-PEE-CHEE

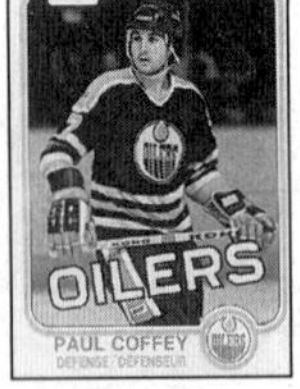

These cards measure the standard 2 1/2" x 3 1/2".

Complete Set (396 cards):		**450.00**
Common Player:		**.35**
O-Pee-Chee		**NM-MT**
☐	1 Raymond Bourque, Bost.	40.00
☐	2 Rick Middleton, Bost.	.50
☐	3 Dwight Foster, Bost. (Colo.)	.35
☐	**4 Steve Kasper, Bost. RC**	**2.00**
☐	5 Peter McNab, Bost.	.35
☐	6 Mike O'Connell, Bost.	.35
☐	7 Terry O'Reilly, Bost.	.50
☐	8 Brad Park, Bost.	1.25
☐	9 Dick Redmond, Bost.	.35
☐	10 Rogatien Vachon (G), Bost.	.50
☐	11 Wayne Cashman, Bost.	.35
☐	**12 Mike Gillis, Bost. RC**	**2.00**
☐	13 Stan Jonathan, Bost.	.35
☐	14 Don Marcotte, Bost.	.35
☐	15 Brad McCrimmon, Bost.	.75
☐	16 Mike Milbury, Bost.	.50
☐	17 Super Action: Raymond Bourque, Bost.	8.00
☐	18 Super Action: Rick Middleton, Bost.	.50
☐	19 TL: Rick Middleton, Bost.	.50
☐	20 Danny Gare, Buff. (Detr.)	.50
☐	21 Don Edwards (G), Buff.	.50
☐	22 Tony McKegney, Buff.	.35
☐	23 Bob Sauvé (G), Buff. (Detr.)	.50
☐	24 André Savard, Buff.	.35
☐	25 Derek Smith, Buff. (Detr.)	.35
☐	26 John Van Boxmeer, Buff.	.35
☐	27 Super Action: Danny Gare, Buff. (Detr.)	.35
☐	28 TL: Danny Gare, Buff.	.35
☐	29 Richard Dunn, Buff.	.35
☐	30 Gilbert Perreault, Buff.	1.75
☐	31 Craig Ramsay, Buff.	.50
☐	32 Ric Seiling, Buff.	.35
☐	33 Guy Chouinard, Calg.	.35
☐	34 Kent Nilsson, Calg.	.35
☐	35 Willi Plett, Calg.	.35
☐	36 Paul Reinhart, Calg.	.35
☐	**37 Pat Riggin (G), Calg. RC**	**2.00**
☐	38 Eric Vail, Calg. (Detr.)	.35
☐	39 Bill Clement, Calg.	.35
☐	40 Jamie Hislop, Calg.	.35
☐	41 Randy Holt, Calg. (Wash.)	.35
☐	42 Dan Labraaten, Calg.	.35
☐	**43 Kevin LaVallée, Calg. RC**	**.75**
☐	**44 Réjean Lemelin (G), Calg. RC**	**5.00**
☐	45 Don Lever, Calg. (Colo.)	.35
☐	46 Bob MacMillan, Calg. (Colo.)	.35
☐	47 Brad Marsh, Calg. (Phil.)	.35
☐	48 Bob J. Murdoch, Calg.	.35
☐	**49 Jim Peplinski, Calg. RC**	**3.00**
☐	50 Pekka Rautakallio, Calg.	.35
☐	51 Phil Russell, Calg.	.35
☐	52 Super Action: Kent Nilsson, Calg.	.35
☐	53 TL: Kent Nilsson, Calg.	.35
☐	54 Tony Esposito (G), Chic.	1.25
☐	55 Keith Brown, Chic.	.35
☐	56 Ted Bulley, Chic.	.35
☐	**57 Tim Higgins, Chic. RC**	**.75**
☐	58 Reg Kerr, Chic.	.35
☐	59 Tom Lysiak, Chic.	.35
☐	60 Grant Mulvey, Chic.	.35
☐	61 Bob Murray, Chic.	.35
☐	62 Terry Ruskowski, Chic.	.35
☐	**63 Denis Savard, Chic. RC**	**35.00**
☐	64 Glen Sharpley, Chic.	.35
☐	**65 Darryl Sutter, Chic. RC**	**3.00**
☐	66 Doug Wilson, Chic.	1.00
☐	67 Super Action: Tony Esposito (G), Chic.	.50
☐	**68 Murray Bannerman (G), Chic. RC**	**2.00**
☐	69 Greg Fox, Chic.	.35
☐	70 John Marks, Chic.	.35
☐	71 Peter Marsh, Chic.	.35
☐	72 Al Secord, Chic.	.35
☐	73 TL: Tom Lysiak, Chic.	.35
☐	74 Lucien DeBlois, Winn.	.35
☐	**75 Paul Gagné, Colo. RC**	**.75**
☐	**76 Merlin Malinowski, Colo. RC**	**.75**
☐	77 Lanny McDonald, Colo. (Calg.)	1.25
☐	78 Joel Quenneville, Colo.	.50
☐	79 Rob Ramage, Colo.	.50
☐	80 Glenn Resch (G), Colo.	.50
☐	81 Steve Tambellini, Colo.	.35
☐	82 Ron Delorme, Colo. (Vanc.)	.35
☐	83 Mike Kitchen, Colo.	.35
☐	**84 Yvon Vautour, Colo. RC**	**.75**
☐	85 TL: Lanny McDonald, Colo.	.50
☐	86 Dale McCourt, Detr. (Buff.)	.35
☐	87 Mike Foligno, Detr. (Buff.)	.35
☐	88 Gilles Gilbert (G), Detr.	.50
☐	89 Willie Huber, Detr.	.35
☐	**90 Mark Kirton, Detr. RC**	**.75**
☐	**91 Jim Korn, Detr. RC**	**.75**
☐	92 Reed Larson, Detr.	.35
☐	93 Gary McAdam, Detr. (Calg.)	.35
☐	94 Vaclav Nedomansky, Detr.	.35
☐	95 John Ogrodnick, Detr.	.50
☐	96 Super Action: Dale McCourt, Detr. (Buff.)	.35
☐	97 Jean Hamel, Detr. (Québ.)	.35
☐	**98 Glenn Hicks, Detr. (Winn.) RC**	**.75**
☐	**99 Larry Lozinski (G), Detr. RC**	**1.00**
☐	100 George Lyle, Detr. (Hart.)	.35
☐	101 Perry Miller, Detr.	.35
☐	102 Brad Maxwell, Detr. (Minn.)	.35
☐	**103 Brad Smith, Detr. RC**	**.75**
☐	104 Paul Woods, Detr.	.35
☐	105 TL: Dale McCourt, Detr.	.35
☐	106 Wayne Gretzky, Edmo.	75.00
☐	**107 Jari Kurri, Edmo. RC**	**50.00**
☐	**108 Glenn Anderson, Edmo. RC**	**12.00**
☐	109 Curt Brackenbury, Edmo.	.35
☐	110 Brett Callighen, Edmo.	.35
☐	**111 Paul Coffey, Edmo. RC**	**90.00**
☐	112 Lee Fogolin, Edmo.	.35
☐	**113 Matti Hagman, Edmo. RC**	**1.50**
☐	114 Doug Hicks, Edmo.	.35
☐	115 Dave Hunter, Edmo.	.35
☐	116 Garry Larivière, Québ. (Edmo.)	.35
☐	**117 Kevin Lowe, Edmo. RC**	**10.00**
☐	118 Mark Messier, Edmo.	45.00
☐	119 Ed Mio (G), Edmo.	.50
☐	**120 Andy Moog (G), Edmo. RC**	**30.00**
☐	121 Dave Semenko, Edmo.	.35
☐	122 Risto Siltanen, Edmo.	.35
☐	123 Garry Unger, Québ. (Edmo.)	.35
☐	124 Stan Weir, Edmo.	.35
☐	125 Super Action: Wayne Gretzky, Edmo.	30.00
☐	126 TL: Wayne Gretzky, Edmo.	10.00
☐	127 Mike Rogers, Hart. (NYRa.)	.35
☐	128 Mark Howe, Hart.	.75
☐	129 Dave Keon, Hart.	.50
☐	**130 Warren Miller, Hart. RC**	**.75**
☐	131 Al Sims, Hart. (LosA.)	.35
☐	132 Blaine Stoughton, Hart.	.35
☐	133 Rick MacLeish, Hart.	.35
☐	134 Greg Millen (G), Hart.	.50
☐	135 Super Action: Mike Rogers, Hart.	.35
☐	136 Mike Fidler, Hart.	.35
☐	137 John Garrett (G), Hart.	.50
☐	**138 Donald Nachbauer, Hart. RC**	**.75**
☐	139 Tom Rowe, Hart.	.35
☐	140 TL: Mike Rogers, Hart.	.35
☐	141 Marcel Dionne, LosA.	1.75
☐	142 Charlie Simmer, LosA.	.75
☐	143 Dave Taylor, LosA.	1.25
☐	144 Billy Harris, LosA. (Toro.)	.35
☐	145 Jerry Korab, LosA.	.35
☐	146 Mario Lessard (G), LosA.	.35
☐	147 Don Luce, Toro.	.35
☐	**148 Larry Murphy, LosA. RC**	**18.00**
☐	149 Mike Murphy, LosA.	.35
☐	150 Super Action: Marcel Dionne, LosA.	1.00
☐	151 Super Action: Charlie Simmer, LosA.	.50
☐	152 Super Action: Dave Taylor, LosA.	.50
☐	**153 Jim Fox, LosA. RC**	**2.00**
☐	154 Steve Jensen, LosA.	.35
☐	**155 Greg Terrion, LosA. RC**	**.75**
☐	156 TL: Marcel Dionne, LosA.	.75
☐	157 Bobby Smith, Minn.	1.00
☐	158 Kent-Erik Andersson, Minn.	.35
☐	**159 Don Beaupré (G), Minn. RC**	**6.00**
☐	160 Steve Christoff, Minn.	.35
☐	**161 Dino Ciccarelli, Minn. RC**	**25.00**
☐	162 Craig Hartsburg, Minn.	.50
☐	163 Al MacAdam, Minn.	.35
☐	164 Tom McCarthy, Minn.	.35
☐	165 Gilles Meloche (G), Minn.	.50
☐	166 Steve Payne, Minn.	.35
☐	167 Gord Roberts, Minn.	.35
☐	168 Greg Smith, Minn. (Detr.)	.35
☐	169 Tim Young, Minn.	.35
☐	170 Super Action: Bobby Smith, Minn.	.50
☐	171 Mike Eaves, Minn.	.35
☐	172 Mike Polich, Minn.	.35
☐	173 Tom Younghans, Minn. (NYRa.)	.35
☐	174 TL: Bobby Smith, Minn.	.50
☐	175 Brian Engblom, Mont.	.35
☐	176 Bob Gainey, Mont.	1.75
☐	177 Guy Lafleur, Mont.	5.00
☐	178 Mark Napier, Mont.	.35
☐	179 Larry Robinson, Mont.	1.75
☐	180 Steve Shutt, Mont.	1.25
☐	**181 Keith Acton, Mont. RC**	**1.50**
☐	182 Gaston Gingras, Mont.	.35
☐	183 Réjean Houle, Mont.	.50
☐	184 Doug Jarvis, Mont.	.50
☐	185 Yvon Lambert, Mont. (Buff.)	.35
☐	186 Rod Langway, Mont.	2.00
☐	187 Pierre Larouche, Mont.	.35
☐	188 Pierre Mondou, Mont.	.35
☐	189 Robert Picard, Mont.	.35
☐	190 Doug Risebrough, Mont.	.50
☐	191 Richard Sévigny (G), Mont.	.50
☐	192 Mario Tremblay, Mont.	.50
☐	**193 Doug Wickenheiser, Mont. RC**	**3.00**
☐	194 Super Action: Bob Gainey, Mont.	.50
☐	195 Super Action: Guy Lafleur, Mont.	2.00
☐	196 Super Action: Larry Robinson, Mont.	.50
☐	197 TL: Steve Shutt, Mont.	.50
☐	198 Mike Bossy, NYIs.	5.00
☐	199 Denis Potvin, NYIs.	1.75
☐	200 Bryan Trottier, NYIs.	2.50
☐	201 Bob Bourne, NYIs.	.35
☐	202 Clark Gillies, NYIs.	.75
☐	203 Butch Goring, NYIs.	.35
☐	204 Anders Kallur, NYIs.	.35
☐	205 Ken Morrow, NYIs.	.35
☐	206 Stefan Persson, NYIs.	.35
☐	207 Billy Smith (G), NYIs.	1.75
☐	208 Super Action: Mike Bossy, NYIs.	2.50
☐	209 Super Action: Denis Potvin, NYIs.	.75
☐	210 Super Action: Bryan Trottier, NYIs.	1.00
☐	**211 Duane Sutter, NYIs. RC**	**1.50**
☐	212 Gord Lane, NYIs.	.35
☐	213 Dave Langevin, NYIs.	.35
☐	214 Bob Lorimer, NYIs. (Colo.)	.35
☐	215 Mike McEwen, Colo. (NYIs.)	.35
☐	216 Wayne Merrick, NYIs.	.35
☐	217 Bob Nystrom, NYIs.	.35
☐	218 John Tonelli, NYIs.	.75
☐	219 TL: Mike Bossy, NYIs.	2.00
☐	220 Barry Beck, NYRa.	.35
☐	**221 Mike Allison, NYRa. RC**	**.75**
☐	222 John Davidson (G), NYRa.	.50
☐	223 Ron Duguay, NYRa.	.50
☐	224 Ron Greschner, NYRa.	.35
☐	225 Anders Hedberg, NYRa.	.35
☐	226 Eddie Johnstone, NYRa.	.35
☐	227 Dave Maloney, NYRa.	.35
☐	228 Don Maloney, NYRa.	.35
☐	229 Ulf Nilsson, NYRa.	.35
☐	230 Super Action: Barry Beck, NYRa.	.35
☐	231 Steve Baker (G), NYRa.	.50
☐	232 Jere Gillis, Vanc. (NYRa.)	.35
☐	233 Ed Hospodar, NYRa.	.35
☐	**234 Tom Laidlaw, NYRa. RC**	**.75**
☐	235 Dean Talafous, NYRa.	.35
☐	236 Carol Vadnais, NYRa.	.35
☐	237 TL: Anders Hedberg, NYRa.	.35
☐	238 Bill Barber, Phil.	1.25
☐	239 Behn Wilson, Phil.	.35
☐	240 Bobby Clarke, Phil.	1.75
☐	241 Bob Dailey, Phil.	.35
☐	242 Paul Holmgren, Phil.	.35
☐	243 Reggie Leach, Phil.	.35
☐	244 Ken Linseman, Phil.	.35
☐	245 Pete Peeters (G), Phil.	1.25
☐	246 Brian Propp, Phil.	1.50
☐	247 Super Action: Bill Barber, Phil.	1.25
☐	248 Mel Bridgman, Calg. (Phil.)	.35
☐	249 Mike Busniuk, Phil.	.35
☐	250 Tom Gorence, Phil.	.35
☐	**251 Tim Kerr, Phil. RC**	**4.00**
☐	**252 Rick St. Croix (G), Phil. RC**	**1.00**
☐	253 TL: Bill Barber, Phil.	.50
☐	254 Rick Kehoe, Pitt.	.50
☐	255 Pat Boutette, Pitt.	.35
☐	256 Randy Carlyle, Pitt.	.50
☐	257 Paul Gardner, Pitt.	.35
☐	258 Peter Lee, Pitt.	.35
☐	259 Rod Schutt, Pitt.	.35
☐	260 Super Action: Rick Kehoe, Pitt.	.50
☐	261 Mario Faubert, Pitt.	.35
☐	262 George Ferguson, Pitt.	.35
☐	263 Ross Lonsberry, Pitt.	.35
☐	264 Greg Malone, Pitt.	.35
☐	265 Pat Price, Québ. (Pitt.)	.35
☐	266 Ron Stackhouse, Pitt.	.35
☐	267 TL: Rick Kehoe, Pitt.	.35
☐	268 Jacques Richard, Québ.	.35
☐	**269 Peter Stastny, Québ. RC**	**20.00**
☐	270 Dan Bouchard (G), Québ.	.50
☐	**271 Kim Clackson, Québ. (Toro.) RC**	**.75**
☐	272 Alain Côté, Québ.	.35
☐	273 André Dupont, Québ.	.35
☐	274 Robbie Ftorek, Québ.	.50
☐	275 Michel Goulet, Québ.	5.00
☐	276 Dale Hoganson, Québ.	.35
☐	**277 Dale Hunter, Québ. RC**	**10.00**
☐	**278 Pierre Lacroix, Québ. RC**	**.75**
☐	**279 Mario Marois, Vanc. (Québ.) RC**	**.75**
☐	**280 Dave Pichette, Québ. RC**	**.75**
☐	281 Michel Plasse (G), Québ.	.35
☐	**282 Anton Stastny, Québ. RC**	**1.50**
☐	283 Marc Tardif, Québ.	.35
☐	284 Wally Weir, Québ.	.35
☐	285 Super Action: Jacques Richard, Québ.	.35
☐	286 Super Action: Peter Stastny, Québ.	6.00
☐	287 TL: Peter Stastny, Québ.	4.00
☐	288 Bernie Federko, SLou.	1.25
☐	289 Mike Liut (G), SLou.	2.00
☐	290 Wayne Babych, SLou.	.35
☐	291 Blair Chapman, SLou.	.35
☐	292 Tony Currie, SLou.	.35
☐	293 Blake Dunlop, SLou.	.35
☐	294 Ed Kea, SLou.	.35
☐	295 Rick Lapointe, SLou.	.35
☐	**296 Jorgen Pettersson, SLou. RC**	**.75**
☐	297 Brian Sutter, SLou.	.50
☐	298 Perry Turnbull, SLou.	.35
☐	299 Mike Zuke, SLou.	.35

- 300 Super Action: Bernie Federko, SLou. .50
- 301 Super Action: Mike Liut, SLou. 1.00
- 302 Jack Brownschidle, SLou. .35
- 303 Larry Patey, SLou. .35
- 304 TL: Bernie Federko, SLou. .50
- 305 Bill Derlago, Toro. .35
- 306 Wilf Paiement, Toro. .35
- 307 Börje Salming, Toro. 1.25
- 308 Darryl Sittler, Toro. 1.50
- 309 Ian Turnbull, Toro. (LosA.) .35
- 310 Rick Vaive, Toro. .50
- 311 Super Action: Wilf Paiement, Toro. .35
- 312 Super Action: Darryl Sittler, Toro. 1.50
- 313 John Anderson, Toro. .35
- 314 Laurie Boschman, Toro. .35
- **315 Jiri Crha (G), Toro. RC 1.50**
- **316 Vitezslav Duris, Toro. RC .75**
- 317 Dave Farrish, Toro. .35
- 318 Pat Hickey, Toro. (NYRa.) .35
- 319 Michel Larocque (G), Mont. (Toro.) .50
- 320 Dan Maloney, Toro. .35
- 321 Terry Martin, Buff. (Toro.) .35
- 322 René Robert, Toro. .35
- 323 Rocky Saganiuk, Toro. .35
- 324 Ron Sedlbauer, Chic. (Toro.) .35
- 325 Ron Zanussi, Minn. (Toro.) .35
- 326 TL: Wilf Paiement, Toro. .35
- 327 Thomas Gradin, Vanc. .35
- 328 Stan Smyl, Vanc. .50
- 329 Ivan Boldirev, Vanc. .35
- 330 Per-Olov Brasar, Vanc., Error (Brent Ashton) .35
- 331 Richard Brodeur (G), Vanc. .50
- 332 Jerry Butler, Vanc. .35
- 333 Colin Campbell, Vanc. .50
- 334 Curt Fraser, Vanc. .35
- 335 Doug Halward, Vanc. .35
- 336 Glen Hanlon (G), Vanc. .50
- 337 Dennis Kearns, Vanc. .35
- 338 Rick Lanz, Vanc., Error (Thomas Gradin) .35
- 339 Pat Ribble, Wash. .35
- 340 Blair MacDonald, Vanc. .35
- 341 Kevin McCarthy, Vanc. .35
- **342 Gerry Minor, Vanc. RC .75**
- 343 Darcy Rota, Vanc. .35
- 344 Harold Snepsts, Vanc. .50
- 345 Dave Williams, Vanc. .50
- 346 TL: Thomas Gradin, Vanc. .35
- 347 Mike Gartner, Wash. 15.00
- 348 Rick Green, Wash. .35
- 349 Bob Kelly, Wash. .35
- 350 Dennis Maruk, Wash. .35
- 351 Mike Palmateer (G), Wash. .50
- 352 Ryan Walter, Wash. .35
- 353 Bengt Gustafsson, Wash. .35
- 354 Al Hangsleben, Wash. .35
- 355 Jean Pronovost, Wash. .35
- 356 Dennis Ververgaert, Wash. .35
- 357 TL: Dennis Maruk, Wash. .35
- **358 Dave Babych, Winn. RC 2.00**
- 359 Dave Christian, Winn. .35
- 360 Super Action: Dave Christian, Winn. .35
- 361 Rick Bowness, Winn. .35
- 362 Rick Dudley, Winn. .35
- **363 Norm Dupont, Winn. RC .75**
- **364 Danny Geoffrion, Winn. RC .75**
- 365 Pierre Hamel (G), Winn. .35
- 366 Dave Hoyda, Winn., Error (Doug Lecuyer) .35
- **367 Doug Lecuyer, Winn. RC .75**
- 368 Willy Lindstrom, Winn. .35
- 369 Barry Long, Winn. .35
- 370 Morris Lukowich, Winn. .35
- 371 Kris Manery, Winn. .35
- 372 Jimmy Mann, Winn. .35
- **373 Moe Mantha, Winn. RC .75**
- 374 Markus Mattsson (G), Winn. .50
- **375 Don Spring, Winn. RC .75**
- 376 Tim Trimper, Winn. .35
- 377 Ron Wilson, Winn. .35
- 378 TL: Dave Christian, Winn. .35
- 379 Checklist 1 (1 - 132) 7.00
- 380 Checklist 2 (133 - 264) 7.00
- 381 Checklist 3 (265 - 396) 7.00
- 382 LL: Mike Bossy, NYIs. 2.00
- 383 LL: Wayne Gretzky, Edmo. 10.00
- 384 LL: Wayne Gretzky, Edmo. 10.00
- 385 LL: Dave Williams, Vanc. .50
- 386 LL: Mike Bossy, NYIs. 2.00
- 387 LL: Richard Sévigny, Mont. .50
- 388 LL: Mike Bossy, NYIs. 2.00
- 389 LL: Don Edwards/ G. Resch .50
- 390 RB: Mike Bossy, NYIs. 2.00
- 391 RB: Dionne/ Simmer/ Taylor, LosA. 3.00
- 392 RB: Wayne Gretzky, Edmo. 10.00
- 393 RB: Larry Murphy, LosA. 3.00
- 394 RB: Mike Palmateer (G), Wash. .50
- 395 RB: Peter Stastny, Québ. 4.00
- 396 Bob Manno, Toro. .50

1981 - 82 O-PEE-CHEE STICKERS

These stickers measure 2" x 2 1/2".

Complete Set (269 stickers): 50.00
Album: 5.00
Common Player: .20
O-Pee-Chee NM-MT

- 1 Foil: The Stanley Cup .35
- 2 Foil: The Stanley Cup .35
- 3 Foil: The Stanley Cup .35
- 4 Foil: The Stanley Cup .35
- 5 Foil: The Stanley Cup .35
- 6 Foil: The Stanley Cup .35
- 7 Oilers vs. Islanders .20
- 8 Oilers vs. Islanders .20
- 9 Oilers vs. Islanders .20
- 10 Oilers vs. Islanders .20

Note: Stickers 7-10 feature Trottier, Potvin, Anderson and M. Hagman

- 11 Jari Kurri, Edmo. 4.00
- 12 Pat Riggin (G) .35
- 13 Flames vs. Flyers .20
- 14 Flames vs. Flyers .20
- 15 Flames vs. Flyers .20
- 16 Flames vs. Flyers .20

Note: Stickers 13-16 feature Willi Plett and Pete Peeters

- 17 Stanley Cup Winners 1980/81 N.Y. Islanders .20
- 18 Stanley Cup Winners 1980/81 N.Y. Islanders .20
- 19 Foil: Conn Smythe, Trophy MVP - Finals .35
- 20 Butch Goring, Most Valuable Player .20
- 21 North Stars vs. Islanders .20
- 22 Steve Payne .20
- 23 North Stars vs. Islanders .20
- 24 North Stars vs. Islanders .20
- 25 North Stars vs. Islanders .20
- 26 North Stars vs. Islanders .20

Note: Stickers 23-26 feature Morrow, Ciccarelli and Langevin.

- 27 Foil: Prince of Wales Trophy .35
- 28 Foil: Prince of Wales Trophy .35
- 29 Guy Lafleur, Mont. 3.00
- 30 Bob Gainey, Mont. .50
- 31 Larry Robinson, Mont. .75
- 32 Steve Shutt, Mont. .50
- 33 Brian Engblom, Mont. .20
- 34 Doug Jarvis, Mont. .20
- 35 Yvon Lambert, Mont. .20
- 36 Mark Napier, Mont. .20
- 37 Réjean Houle, Mont. .35
- 38 Pierre Larouche, Mont. .20
- 39 Rod Langway, Mont. .35
- 40 Richard Sévigny (G), Mont. .35
- 41 Guy Lafleur, Mont. 3.00
- 42 Larry Robinson, Mont. .75
- 43 Bob Gainey, Mont. .50
- 44 Steve Shutt, Mont. .50
- 45 Rick Middleton, Bost. .35
- 46 Peter McNab, Bost. .20
- 47 Rogatien Vachon (G), Bost. .35
- 48 Brad Park, Bost. .50
- 49 Raymond Bourque, Bost. 5.00
- 50 Terry O'Reilly, Bost. .20
- 51 Steve Kasper, Bost. .20
- 52 Dwight Foster, Bost. .20
- 53 Danny Gare, Buff. .20
- 54 André Savard, Buff. .20
- 55 Don Edwards (G), Buff. .35
- 56 Bob Sauvé (G), Buff. .35
- 57 Tony McKegney, Buff. .20
- 58 John Van Boxmeer, Buff. .20
- 59 Derek Smith, Buff. .20
- 60 Gilbert Perreault, Buff. .75
- 61 Mike Rogers, Hart. .20
- 62 Mark Howe, Hart. .50
- 63 Blaine Stoughton, Hart. .20
- 64 Rick Ley, Hart. .20
- 65 Jordy Douglas, Hart. .20
- 66 Al Sims, Hart. .20
- 67 Norm Barnes, Hart. .20
- 68 John Garrett (G), Hart. .35
- 69 Peter Stastny, Québ. 2.00
- 70 Anton Stastny, Québ. .20
- 71 Jacques Richard, Québ. .20
- 72 Robbie Ftorek, Québ. .35
- 73 Dan Bouchard (G), Québ. .35
- 74 Réal Cloutier, Québ. .20
- 75 Michel Goulet, Québ. 1.50
- 76 Marc Tardif, Québ. .20
- 77 Capitals vs. Maple Leafs .20
- 78 Capitals vs. Maple Leafs .20
- 79 Capitals vs. Maple Leafs .20
- 80 Capitals vs. Maple Leafs .20
- 81 Paul Mulvey, Wash. .20
- 82 Whalers player .20
- 83 Canadiens vs. Capitals .20
- 84 Dan Bouchard (G), Québ. .35
- 85 North Stars vs. Capitals .20
- 86 North Stars vs. Capitals .20

Note: Stickers 85-86 feature Craig Hartsburg and Paul Mulvey

- 87 Bruins vs. Capitals .20
- 88 Bobby Smith, Minn. .50
- 89 Don Beaupré (G), Minn. .75
- 90 Al MacAdam, Minn. .20
- 91 Craig Hartsburg, Minn. .35
- 92 Steve Payne, Minn. .20
- 93 Gilles Meloche (G), Minn. .35
- 94 Tim Young, Minn. .20
- 95 Tom McCarthy, Minn. .20
- 96 Wilf Paiement, Toro. .20
- 97 Darryl Sittler, Toro. .50
- 98 Börje Salming, Toro. .50
- 99 Bill Derlago, Toro. .20
- 100 Ian Turnbull, Toro. .20
- 101 Rick Vaive, Toro. .50
- 102 Dan Maloney, Toro. .20
- 103 Laurie Boschman, Toro. .20
- 104 Pat Hickey, Toro. .20
- 105 Michel Larocque (G), Toro. .35
- 106 Jiri Crha (G), Toro. .35
- 107 John Anderson, Toro. .20
- 108 Bill Derlago, Toro. .20
- 109 Darryl Sittler, Toro. .50
- 110 Wilf Paiement, Toro. .20
- 111 Börje Salming, Toro. .50
- 112 Denis Savard, Chic. 2.00
- 113 Tony Esposito (G), Chic. .75
- 114 Tom Lysiak, Chic. .20
- 115 Keith Brown, Chic. .20
- 116 Glen Sharpley, Chic. .20
- 117 Terry Ruskowski, Chic. .20
- 118 Reg Kerr, Chic. .20
- 119 Bob Murray, Chic. .20
- 120 Dale McCourt, Detr. .20
- 121 John Ogrodnick, Detr. .35
- 122 Mike Foligno, Detr. .20
- 123 Gilles Gilbert (G), Detr. .35
- 124 Reed Larson, Detr. .20
- 125 Vaclav Nedomansky, Detr. .20
- 126 Willie Huber, Detr. .20
- 127 Jim Korn, Detr. .20
- 128 Bernie Federko, SLou. .50
- 129 Mike Liut (G), SLou. .75
- 130 Wayne Babych, SLou. .20
- 131 Blake Dunlop, SLou. .20
- 132 Mike Zuke, SLou. .20
- 133 Brian Sutter, SLou. .50
- 134 Rick Lapointe, SLou. .20
- 135 Jorgen Pettersson, SLou. .20
- 136 Dave Christian, Winn. .20
- 137 Dave Babych, Winn. .50
- 138 Morris Lukowich, Winn. .20
- 139 Norm Dupont, Winn. .20
- 140 Ron Wilson, Winn. .20
- 141 Danny Geoffrion, Winn. .20
- 142 Barry Long, Winn. .20
- 143 Pierre Hamel (G), Winn. .35
- 144 AS: Foil: Charlie Simmer, LosA. .35
- 145 AS: Foil: Mark Howe, Hart. .50
- 146 AS: Foil: Don Beaupré (G), Minn. .75
- 147 AS: Foil: Marcel Dionne, LosA. .75
- 148 AS: Foil: Larry Robinson, Mont. .75
- 149 AS: Foil: Dave Taylor, LosA. .35
- 150 AS: Foil: Mike Bossy, NYIs. 1.25
- 151 AS: Foil: Denis Potvin, NYIs. .75
- 152 AS: Foil: Bryan Trottier, NYIs. .75
- 153 AS: Foil: Mike Liut (G), SLou. .75
- 154 AS: Foil: Rob Ramage, Colo. .35
- 155 AS: Foil: Bill Barber, Phil. .50
- 156 Foil: Campbell Bowl .35
- 157 Foil: Campbell Bowl .35
- 158 Mike Bossy, NYIs. 1.00
- 159 Denis Potvin, NYIs. .75
- 160 Bryan Trottier, NYIs. .75
- 161 Billy Smith (G), NYIs. .50
- 162 Anders Kallur, NYIs. .20
- 163 Bob Bourne, NYIs. .20
- 164 Clark Gillies, NYIs. .20
- 165 Ken Morrow, NYIs. .20
- 166 Anders Hedberg, NYRa. .20
- 167 Ron Greschner, NYRa. .20
- 168 Barry Beck, NYRa. .20
- 169 Eddie Johnstone, NYRa. .20
- 170 Don Maloney, NYRa. .20
- 171 Ron Duguay, NYRa. .35
- 172 Ulf Nilsson, NYRa. .20
- 173 Dave Maloney, NYRa. .20
- 174 Bill Barber, Phil. .50
- 175 Behn Wilson, Phil. .20
- 176 Ken Linseman, Phil. .20
- 177 Pete Peeters (G), Phil. .35
- 178 Bobby Clarke, Phil. 1.00
- 179 Paul Holmgren, Phil. .20
- 180 Brian Propp, Phil. .50
- 181 Reggie Leach, Phil. .20
- 182 Rick Kehoe, Pitt. .20
- 183 Randy Carlyle, Pitt. .20
- 184 George Ferguson, Pitt. .20
- 185 Peter Lee, Pitt. .20
- 186 Rod Schutt, Pitt. .20
- 187 Paul Gardner, Pitt. .20
- 188 Ron Stackhouse, Pitt. .20
- 189 Mario Faubert, Pitt. .20
- 190 Mike Gartner, Wash. 3.00
- 191 Dennis Maruk, Wash. .20
- 192 Ryan Walter, Wash. .20
- 193 Rick Green, Wash. .20
- 194 Mike Palmateer (G), Wash. .35
- 195 Bob Kelly, Wash. .20
- 196 Jean Pronovost, Wash. .20
- 197 Al Hangsleben, Wash. .20
- 198 Flames vs. Capitals .20
- 199 Oilers vs. Islanders .20
- 200 Oilers vs. Islanders .20
- 201 Oilers vs. Islanders .20
- 202 Oilers vs. Islanders .20
- 203 Rangers vs. Islanders .20
- 204 Rangers vs. Islanders .20
- 205 Flyers vs. Capitals .20
- 206 Flyers vs. Capitals .20
- 207 Rangers vs. Capitals .20
- 208 Canadiens (Bob Gainey) vs. Capitals .35
- 209 Wayne Gretzky, Edmo. 15.00
- 210 Mark Messier, Edmo. 6.00
- 211 Jari Kurri, Edmo. 4.00
- 212 Brett Callighen, Edmo. .20
- 213 Matti Hagman, Edmo. .20
- 214 Risto Siltanen, Edmo. .20
- 215 Lee Fogolin, Edmo. .20
- 216 Ed Mio (G), Edmo. .35
- 217 Glenn Anderson, Edmo. 1.50
- 218 Kent Nilsson, Calg. .20
- 219 Guy Chouinard, Calg. .20
- 220 Eric Vail, Calg. .20
- 221 Pat Riggin (G), Calg. .35
- 222 Willi Plett, Calg. .20
- 223 Pekka Rautakallio, Calg. .20
- 224 Paul Reinhart, Calg. .20
- 225 Brad Marsh, Calg. .35
- 226 Phil Russell, Calg. .20
- 227 Lanny McDonald, Colo. .75
- 228 Merlin Malinowski, Colo. .20
- 229 Rob Ramage, Colo. .20
- 230 Glenn Resch (G), Colo. .35
- 231 Ron Delorme, Colo. .20
- 232 Lucien DeBlois, Colo. .20
- 233 Paul Gagné, Colo. .20
- 234 Joel Quenneville, Colo. .35
- 235 Marcel Dionne, LosA. .75
- 236 Charlie Simmer, LosA. .20
- 237 Dave Taylor, LosA. .35
- 238 Mario Lessard (G), LosA. .35
- 239 Larry Murphy, LosA. 1.50
- 240 Jerry Korab, LosA. .20
- 241 Mike Murphy, LosA. .20
- 242 Billy Harris, LosA. .20
- 243 Thomas Gradin, Vanc. .20
- 244 Per-Olov Brasar, Vanc. .20
- 245 Glen Hanlon (G), Vanc. .50
- 246 Chris Oddleifson, Vanc. .20
- 247 Dave Williams, Vanc. .35
- 248 Kevin McCarthy, Vanc. .20
- 249 Dennis Kearns, Vanc. .20
- 250 Harold Snepsts, Vanc. .20
- 251 Foil: Art Ross Trophy .35
- 252 AW: Wayne Gretzky, Edmo. 9.00
- 253 LL:Mike Bossy, NYIs. .75
- 254 Foil: Norris Trophy .35
- 255 AW: Randy Carlyle, Pitt. .20
- 256 AW: Richard Sévigny, Mont. .35
- 257 Foil: Vezina Trophy .35
- 258 AW: Denis Herron, Mont. .35
- 259 AW: Michel Larocque, Mont. .35
- 260 Foil: Lady Byng Trophy .35
- 261 AW: Rick Kehoe, Pitt. .20
- 262 Foil: Calder Trophy .35
- 263 AW: Peter Stastny, Québ. 1.25
- 264 AW: Wayne Gretzky, Edmo. 9.00
- 265 Foil: Hart Trophy .35
- 266 LL: Charlie Simmer .35
- 267 LL: Marcel Dionne .75
- 268 LL: Dave Taylor .35
- 269 LL: Bob Gainey, Mont. .50

1981 - 82 POST STARS IN ACTION

These cards measure 2 3/16" x 3 3/16".

Complete Set (28 cards):		**60.00**
Post Cereal • Promo		**NM**
☐	Darryl Sittler Promo	5.00
Post Cereal		**NM**
☐	1 Raymond Bourque, Bost.	15.00

☐	2 Gilbert Perreault, Buff.	3.00
☐	3 Denis Savard, Chic.	5.00
☐	4 Dale McCourt, Detr.	1.50
☐	5 Bobby Smith, Minn.	2.50
☐	6 Mike Bossy, NYIs.	7.00
☐	7 Bobby Clarke, Phil.	5.00
☐	8 Randy Carlyle, Pitt.	1.50
☐	9 Mike Palmateer (G), Wash.	2.50
☐	10 Dave Williams, Vanc.	1.50
☐	11 Mark Howe, Hart.	2.50
☐	12 Marcel Dionne, LosA.	3.00
☐	13 Mike Liut (G), SLou.	3.00
☐	14 Barry Beck, NYRa.	1.50
☐	15 Mark Messier, Edmo.	15.00
☐	16 Larry Robinson, Mont.	4.00
☐	17 Real Cloutier, Québ.	1.50
☐	18 Börje Salming, Toro.	3.00
☐	19 Morris Lukowich, Winn.	1.50
☐	20 Brett Callighen, Edmo.	1.50
☐	21 Rob Ramage, Colo.	1.50
☐	22 Wilf Paiement, Toro.	1.50
☐	23 Mario Tremblay, Mont.	1.50
☐	24 Robbie Ftorek, Québ.	2.50
☐	25 Stan Smyl, Vanc.	1.50
☐	26 Dave Babych, Winn.	1.50
☐	27 Willi Plett, Calg.	1.50
☐	28 Kent Nilsson, Calg.	1.50

1981 - 82 TCMA

These cards measure the standard 2 1/2" x 3 1/2".

Complete Set (13 cards):		**50.00**
TCMA		**NM-MT**
☐	1 Norm Ullman, Detr.	3.00
☐	2 Gump Worsley (G), NYRa.	6.00
☐	3 J.C. Tremblay, Mont.	1.50
☐	4 Louie Fontinato, NYRa.	1.50
☐	5 John Bucyk, Bost.	3.00
☐	6 Harry Howell, NYRa.	2.50
☐	7 Henri Richard, Mont.	5.00
☐	8 Andy Bathgate, NYRa.	2.50
☐	9 Bobby Orr, Bost.	30.00
☐	10 Frank Mahovlich, Toro.	6.00
☐	11 Jean Béliveau, Mont.	9.00
☐	12 Jacques Plante (G), Mont.	12.00
☐	13 Stan Mikita, Chic.	6.00

1981 - 82 TOPPS

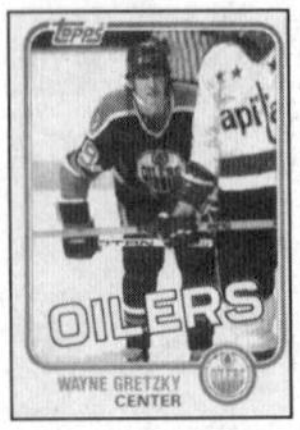

These cards measure the standard 2 1/2" x 3 1/2".

Complete Set (198 cards):		**90.00**
Common Player (1-66):		**.20**
Common Player East (67-132):		**.25**
Common Player West (67-132):		**.30**
Topps		**NM-MT**
☐	**1 Dave Babych, Winn. RC**	**1.00**
☐	2 Bill Barber, Phil.	.75
☐	3 Barry Beck, NYRa.	.20
☐	4 Mike Bossy, NYIs.	3.00
☐	5 Raymond Bourque, Bost.	5.50
☐	6 Guy Chouinard, Calg.	.20
☐	7 Dave Christian, Winn.	.20
☐	8 Bill Derlago, Toro.	.20
☐	9 Marcel Dionne, LosA.	1.00
☐	10 Brian Engblom, Mont.	.20
☐	11 Tony Esposito (G), Chic.	.50
☐	12 Bernie Federko, SLou.	.50
☐	13 Bob Gainey, Mont.	1.00
☐	14 Danny Gare, Buff.	.25
☐	15 Thomas Gradin, Vanc.	.20
☐	16 Wayne Gretzky, Edmo.	18.00
☐	17 Rick Kehoe, Pitt.	.25
☐	**18 Jari Kurri, Edmo. RC**	**9.00**
☐	19 Guy Lafleur, Mont.	2.00
☐	20 Mike Liut (G), SLou.	1.00
☐	21 Dale McCourt, Detr.	.20
☐	22 Rick Middleton, Bost.	.25
☐	23 Mark Napier, Mont.	.20
☐	24 Kent Nilsson, Calg.	.25
☐	25 Wilf Paiement, Toro.	.20
☐	26 Willi Plett, Calg.	.20
☐	27 Denis Potvin, NYIs.	1.00
☐	28 Paul Reinhart, Calg.	.20
☐	29 Jacques Richard, Québ.	.20
☐	**30 Pat Riggin (G), Calg. RC**	**.75**
☐	31 Larry Robinson, Mont.	1.00
☐	32 Mike Rogers, Hart.	.20
☐	33 Börje Salming, Toro.	.75
☐	34 Steve Shutt, Mont.	.75
☐	35 Charlie Simmer, LosA.	.25
☐	36 Darryl Sittler, Toro.	1.00
☐	37 Bobby Smith, Minn.	.25
☐	38 Stan Smyl, Vanc.	.20
☐	**39 Peter Stastny, Québ. RC**	**5.00**
☐	40 David Taylor, LosA.	.35
☐	41 Bryan Trottier, NYIs.	1.50
☐	42 Ian Turnbull, Toro.	.20
☐	43 Eric Vail, Calg.	.20
☐	44 Rick Vaive, Toro.	.25
☐	45 Behn Wilson, Phil.	.20
☐	46 TL: Rick Middleton, Bost.	.25
☐	47 TL: Danny Gare, Buff.	.25
☐	48 TL: Kent Nilsson, Calg.	.25
☐	49 TL: Tom Lysiak, Chic.	.20
☐	50 TL: Lanny McDonald, Colo.	.25
☐	51 TL: Dale McCourt, Detr.	.20
☐	52 TL: Wayne Gretzky, Edmo.	4.00
☐	53 TL: Mike Rogers, Hart.	.20
☐	54 TL: Marcel Dionne, LosA.	.35
☐	55 TL: Bobby Smith, Minn.	.25
☐	56 TL: Steve Shutt, Mont.	.25
☐	57 TL: Mike Bossy, NYIs.	1.00
☐	58 TL: Anders Hedberg, NYRa.	.20
☐	59 TL: Bill Barber, Phil.	.20
☐	60 TL: Rick Kehoe, Pitt.	.25
☐	61 TL: Peter Stastny, Québ.	1.50
☐	62 TL: Bernie Federko, SLou.	.25
☐	63 TL: Wilf Paiement, Toro.	.20
☐	64 TL: Thomas Gradin, Vanc.	.20
☐	65 TL: Dennis Maruk, Wash.	.20
☐	66 TL: Dave Christian, Winn.	.20
Topps • Eastern Distribution		**NM-MT**
☐	67 Dwight Foster, Bost.	.25
☐	**68 Steve Kasper, Bost. RC**	**1.00**
☐	69 Peter McNab, Bost.	.25
☐	70 Mike O'Connell, Bost.	.25
☐	71 Terry O'Reilly, Bost.	.35
☐	72 Brad Park, Bost.	1.00
☐	73 Dick Redmond, Bost.	.25
☐	74 Rogatien Vachon (G), Bost.	.35
☐	75 Don Edwards (G), Buff.	.25
☐	76 Tony McKegney, Buff.	.25
☐	77 Bob Sauvé (G), Buff.	.35
☐	78 André Savard, Buff.	.25
☐	79 Derek Smith, Buff.	.25
☐	80 John Van Boxmeer, Buff.	.25
☐	81 Pat Boutette, Pitt.	.25
☐	82 Mark Howe, Hart.	.50
☐	83 Dave Keon, Hart.	.35
☐	**84 Warren Miller, Hart. RC**	**.75**
☐	85 Al Sims, Hart.	.25
☐	86 Blaine Stoughton, Hart.	.25
☐	87 Bob Bourne, NYIs.	.25
☐	88 Clark Gillies, NYIs.	.25
☐	89 Butch Goring, NYIs.	.25
☐	90 Anders Kallur, NYIs.	.25
☐	91 Ken Morrow, NYIs.	.25
☐	92 Stefan Persson, NYIs.	.25
☐	93 Billy Smith (G), NYIs.	1.25
☐	**94 Mike Allison, NYRa. RC**	**.75**
☐	95 John Davidson (G), NYRa.	.35
☐	96 Ron Duguay, NYRa.	.25
☐	97 Ron Greschner, NYRa.	.25
☐	98 Anders Hedberg, NYRa.	.25
☐	99 Eddie Johnstone, NYRa.	.25
☐	100 Dave Maloney, NYRa.	.25
☐	101 Don Maloney, NYRa.	.25
☐	102 Ulf Nilsson, NYRa.	.25
☐	103 Bobby Clarke, Phil.	1.25
☐	104 Bob Dailey, Phil.	.25
☐	105 Paul Holmgren, Phil.	.25
☐	106 Reggie Leach, Phil.	.25
☐	107 Ken Linseman, Phil.	.25
☐	108 Rick MacLeish, Hart.	.25
☐	109 Pete Peeters (G), Phil.	.35
☐	110 Brian Propp, Phil.	.35
☐	111 Checklist 1 (1 - 132)	1.75
☐	112 Randy Carlyle, Pitt.	.35
☐	113 Paul Gardner, Pitt.	.25
☐	114 Peter Lee, Pitt.	.25
☐	115 Greg Millen (G), Hart.	.35
☐	116 Rod Schutt, Pitt.	.25
☐	117 Mike Gartner, Wash.	6.00
☐	118 Rick Green, Wash.	.25
☐	119 Bob Kelly, Wash.	.25
☐	120 Dennis Maruk, Wash.	.25
☐	121 Mike Palmateer (G), Wash.	.35
☐	122 Ryan Walter, Wash.	.25
☐	123 Super Action: Bill Barber, Phil.	.35
☐	124 Super Action: Barry Beck, NYRa.	.25
☐	125 Super Action: Mike Bossy, NYIs.	1.25
☐	126 Super Action: Raymond Bourque, Bost.	3.00
☐	127 Super Action: Danny Gare, Buff.	.25
☐	128 Super Action: Rick Kehoe, Pitt.	.35
☐	129 Super Action: Rick Middleton, Bost.	.35
☐	130 Super Action: Denis Potvin, NYIs.	.50
☐	131 Super Action: Mike Rogers, Hart.	.25
☐	132 Super Action: Bryan Trottier, NYIs.	.75
Topps • Western Distribution		**NM-MT**
☐	67 Keith Brown, Chic.	.30
☐	68 Ted Bulley, Chic.	.30
☐	**69 Tim Higgins, Chic. RC**	**.75**
☐	70 Reg Kerr, Chic.	.30
☐	71 Tom Lysiak, Chic.	.30
☐	72 Grant Mulvey, Chic.	.30
☐	73 Bob Murray, Chic.	.30
☐	74 Terry Ruskowski, Chic.	.30
☐	**75 Denis Savard, Chic. RC**	**15.00**
☐	76 Glen Sharpley, Chic.	.30
☐	**77 Darryl Sutter, Chic. RC**	**1.50**
☐	78 Doug Wilson, Chic.	.75
☐	79 Lucien DeBlois, Winn.	.30
☐	**80 Paul Gagné, Colo. RC**	**.75**
☐	**81 Merlin Malinowski, Colo. RC**	**.75**
☐	82 Lanny McDonald, Colo.	1.00
☐	83 Joel Quenneville, Colo.	.50
☐	84 Rob Ramage, Colo.	.50
☐	85 Glenn Resch (G), Colo.	.50
☐	86 Steve Tambellini, Colo.	.30
☐	87 Mike Foligno, Detr.	.30
☐	88 Gilles Gilbert (G), Detr.	.50
☐	89 Willie Huber, Detr.	.30
☐	**90 Mark Kirton, Detr. RC**	**.75**
☐	**91 Jim Korn, Detr. RC**	**.75**
☐	92 Reed Larson, Detr.	.30
☐	93 Gary McAdam, Detr.	.30
☐	94 Vaclav Nedomansky, Detr.	.30
☐	95 John Ogrodnick, Detr.	.30
☐	96 Billy Harris, LosA.	.30
☐	97 Jerry Korab, LosA.	.30
☐	98 Mario Lessard (G), LosA.	.50
☐	99 Don Luce, Toro.	.30
☐	**100 Larry Murphy, LosA. RC**	**8.00**
☐	101 Mike Murphy, LosA.	.30
☐	102 Kent-Erik Andersson, Minn.	.30
☐	**103 Don Beaupré (G), Minn. RC**	**3.00**
☐	104 Steve Christoff, Minn.	.30
☐	**105 Dino Ciccarelli, Minn. RC**	**12.00**
☐	106 Craig Hartsburg, Minn.	.50
☐	107 Al MacAdam, Minn.	.30
☐	108 Tom McCarthy, Minn.	.30
☐	109 Gilles Meloche (G), Minn.	.50
☐	110 Steve Payne, Minn.	.30
☐	111 Gord Roberts, Minn.	.30
☐	112 Greg Smith, Minn.	.30
☐	113 Tim Young, Minn.	.30
☐	114 Wayne Babych, SLou.	.30
☐	115 Blair Chapman, SLou.	.30
☐	116 Tony Currie, SLou.	.30
☐	117 Blake Dunlop, SLou.	.30
☐	118 Ed Kea, SLou.	.30
☐	119 Rick Lapointe, SLou.	.30
☐	120 Checklist 2	2.50
☐	**121 Jorgen Pettersson, SLou. RC**	**.75**
☐	122 Brian Sutter, SLou.	.50
☐	123 Perry Turnbull, SLou.	.30
☐	124 Mike Zuke, SLou.	.30
☐	125 Super Action: Marcel Dionne, LosA.	.75
☐	126 Super Action: Tony Esposito (G), Chic.	.75
☐	127 Super Action: Bernie Federko, SLou.	.75
☐	128 Super Action: Mike Liut (G), SLou.	.75
☐	129 Super Action: Dale McCourt, Detr.	.30
☐	130 Super Action: Charlie Simmer, LosA.	.50
☐	131 Super Action: Bobby Smith, Minn.	.50
☐	132 Super Action: Dave Taylor, LosA.	.50

1982 MALLASJUOMA

These labels measure 3" x 3 1/2".

Mallasjuoma

☐	Timo Nummelin
☐	Jukka Porvari
☐	Reijo Ruotsalainen
☐	Ilkka Sinisalo

1982 SEMIC STICKERS

These stickers measure 2 1/8" x 3".

Complete Set (162 stickers):		**55.00**
Album:		**8.00**
Common Player:		**.35**
Semic		**NM-MT**
☐	1 Peter Lindmark, Swe.	.35
☐	2 Göte Wälitalo, Swe.	.35
☐	3 Gunnar Leidborg, Swe.	.35
☐	4 Göran Lindblom, Swe.	.35
☐	5 Thomas Eriksson, Swe.	.35
☐	6 Mats Waltin, Swe.	.35
☐	7 Jan Eriksson, Swe.	.35
☐	8 Mats Thelin, Swe.	.35
☐	9 Peter Helander, Swe.	.35
☐	10 Tommy Samuelsson, Swe.	.35
☐	11 Bo Ericsson, Swe.	.35
☐	12 Peter Andersson, Swe.	.35
☐	13 Mats Näslund, Swe.	5.00
☐	14 Ulf Isaksson, Swe.	.35
☐	15 Patrik Sundström, Swe.	2.00
☐	16 Peter Sundstrom, Swe.	1.00
☐	17 Thomas Rundqvist, Swe.	.35
☐	18 Mats Ulander, Swe.	.35
☐	19 Tommy Mörth, Swe.	.35
☐	20 Ove Olsson, Swe.	.35
☐	21 Rolf Edberg, Swe.	.35
☐	22 Håkan Loob, Swe.	5.00
☐	23 Leif Holmgren, Swe.	.50
☐	24 Jan Erixon, Swe.	1.00
☐	25 Harald Luckner, Swe.	.35
☐	26 Hannu Kamppuri, Fin.	.35
☐	27 Hannu Lassila, Fin.	.35
☐	28 Kari Heikkilä, Fin.	.35
☐	29 Time Nummelin, Fin.	.35
☐	30 Pertti Lehtonen, Fin.	.35
☐	31 Raimo Hirvonen, Fin.	.35
☐	32 Seppo Suoraniemi, Fin.	.35
☐	33 Juha Huikari, Fin.	.35
☐	34 Hannu Helander, Fin.	.35
☐	35 Lasse Litma, Fin.	.35
☐	36 Håkan Hjerpe, Fin.	.35
☐	37 Kari Jalonen, Fin.	.35
☐	38 Arte Javanainen, Fin.	.35
☐	39 Jari Lindgren, Fin.	.35
☐	40 Markku Kiimalainen, Fin.	.35
☐	41 Jarmo Mäkitalo, Fin.	.35
☐	42 Jorma Seven, Fin.	.35
☐	43 Erkki Laine, Fin.	.35
☐	44 Hannu Koskinen, Fin.	.35
☐	45 Reijo Leppänen, Fin.	.35
☐	46 Pekka Arbelius, Fin.	.35
☐	47 Markku Hakulinen, Fin.	.35
☐	48 Time Susi, Fin.	.35
☐	49 Esa Peltonen, Fin.	.35
☐	50 Juhani Tamminen, Fin.	.50
☐	51 Vladislav Tretiak (G), USSR	12.00

☐ 52 Vladimir Mishkin, USSR	.35
☐ 53 Viacheslav Fetisov, USSR	4.00
☐ 54 Sergei Babinov, USSR	.35
☐ 55 Vasili Pervuchin, USSR	.35
☐ 56 Valeri Vasiliev, USSR	1.00
☐ 57 Alexie Kasatonov, USSR	1.50
☐ 58 Zinetula Biljaletdinov, USSR	.35
☐ 59 Sergei Starikov, USSR	.35
☐ 60 Sergei Makarov, USSR	3.50
☐ 61 Sergei Sjepelev, USSR	.75
☐ 62 Vladimir Krutov, USSR	2.00
☐ 63 Nikolaj Drozdetskij, USSR	.35
☐ 64 Viktor Ziluktov, USSR	.35
☐ 65 Viktor Sjalimov, USSR	.35
☐ 66 Vladimir Golikov, USSR	.35
☐ 67 Alexander Maltsev, USSR	2.00
☐ 68 Andre Khomutov, USSR	1.50
☐ 69 Sergei Svetlov, USSR	.35
☐ 70 Helmut Balderis, USSR	1.50
☐ 71 Sergei Kapustin, USSR	.35
☐ 72 Vladimir Zubkov, USSR	.35
☐ 73 Alexander Kozjevnikov, USSR	.35
☐ 74 Yuri Lebedev, USSR	.35
☐ 75 Nikolai Makarov, USSR	.35
☐ 76 Jiri Kralik, CSR.	.35
☐ 77 Karel Lang, CSR.	.35
☐ 78 Jaromir Sindel, CSR.	.35
☐ 79 Miroslav Horava, CSR.	.35
☐ 80 Milan Chalupa, CSR.	.35
☐ 81 Stanislav Hajdusek, CSR.	.35
☐ 82 Arnold Kadlec, CSR.	.35
☐ 83 Miroslav Dvorak, CSR.	.35
☐ 84 Jan Neliba, CSR.	.35
☐ 85 Petr Misek, CSR.	.35
☐ 86 Eduard Uvira, CSR.	.35
☐ 87 Milan Novy, CSR.	1.00
☐ 88 Frantisek Cerny, CSR.	.35
☐ 89 Jiri Lala, CSR.	.35
☐ 90 Jindrich Kokrment, CSR.	.35
☐ 91 Frantisek Cernik, CSR.	.35
☐ 92 Darius Rusnak, CSR.	.35
☐ 93 Dusan Pasek, CSR.	.35
☐ 94 Lubomir Penicka, CSR.	.35
☐ 95 Jaroslav Korbela, CSR.	.35
☐ 96 Peter Ihnacak, CSR.	1.00
☐ 97 Jaroslav Hrdina, CSR.	.35
☐ 98 Igor Liban, CSR.	.35
☐ 99 Peter Slaninan, CSR.	.35
☐ 100 Vincent Lukac, CSR.	.35
☐ 101 Erich Weishaupt, BRD.	.35
☐ 102 Bernhard Engelbrecht, BRD.	.35
☐ 103 Robert Murray, BRD.	.35
☐ 104 Peter Gailer, BRD.	.35
☐ 105 Udo Kiessling, BRD.	.35
☐ 106 Harold Kreis, BRD.	.35
☐ 107 Joachim Reil, BRD.	.35
☐ 108 Harald Krull, BRD.	.35
☐ 109 Ulrich Egen, BRD.	.35
☐ 110 Marcus Kuhl, BRD.	.35
☐ 111 Peter Schiller, BRD.	.35
☐ 112 Erich Kuhnhackl, BRD.	.35
☐ 113 Holger Meitinger, BRD.	.35
☐ 114 Ernst Höfner, BRD.	.35
☐ 115 Vladimir Vacatko, BRD.	.35
☐ 116 Manfred Wolf, BRD.	.35
☐ 117 Johann Mörz, BRD.	.35
☐ 118 Franz Reindl, BRD.	.35
☐ 119 Helmut Steiger, BRD.	.35
☐ 120 Georg Holzmann, BRD.	.35
☐ 121 Roy Roedeger, BRD.	.35
☐ 122 Jim Corsi, Ita.	.50
☐ 123 Nick Santa, Ita.	.35
☐ 124 GuidoTenisi, Ita.	.35
☐ 125 Erwin Kostner, Ita.	.35
☐ 126 Mike Amodeo, Ita.	.35
☐ 127 John Bellio, Ita.	.35
☐ 128 DaveTomassoni, Ita.	.35
☐ 129 Daniel Pupillo, Ita.	.35
☐ 130 Giulio Francella, Ita.	.35
☐ 131 Fabio Polloni, Ita.	.35
☐ 132 Adolf Insam, Ita.	.35
☐ 133 Patrick Dell'Jannone, Ita.	.35
☐ 134 Rick Bragnalo, Ita.	.35
☐ 135 Michael Mair, Ita.	.35
☐ 136 Alberto Di Fazio, Ita.	.35
☐ 137 Cary Farelli, Ita.	.35
☐ 138 Tom Milani, Ita.	.35
☐ 139 Martin Pavlu, Ita.	.35
☐ 140 Bob De Piero, Ita.	.35
☐ 141 Grant Goegan, Ita.	.35
☐ 142 Jerry Ciarcia, Ita.	.35
☐ 143 Börje Salming	4.00
☐ 144 Lars Lindgren	.50
☐ 145 Ulf Nilsson	2.00
☐ 146 Bengt Gustavsson	1.00
☐ 147 Kent Nilsson	3.50
☐ 148 Thomas Gradin	2.50
☐ 149 Lars Molin	.50
☐ 150 Thomas Steen, Swe.	2.50
☐ 151 Bengt Lundholm	.50
☐ 152 Jörgen Pettersson	.50
☐ 153 Jukka Porvari	.35
☐ 154 Tapio Levo	.35
☐ 155 Reijo Ruotsalainen	1.50
☐ 156 Matti Hagman	1.00
☐ 157 Risto Siltanen	1.00
☐ 158 Ilkka Sinisalo	1.00
☐ 159 Markus Mattson (G)	.50
☐ 160 Mikko Leinonen	.50
☐ 161 Pekka Rautakalli	.50
☐ 162 Veli-Pekka Ketola	1.00

1982 SKOPBANK

These sticker sheets measure 2 1/2" x 3 3/4".

- ☐ Pekka Arbelius
- ☐ Raimo Hirvonen
- ☐ Markku Kiimalainen
- ☐ Hannu Koskinen
- ☐ Reijo Leppanen
- ☐ Timo Nummelin
- ☐ Reijo Ruotsalainen
- ☐ Timo Susi
- ☐ Ari Hellgren
- ☐ Hannu Kamppuri
- ☐ Pertti Koivulahti
- ☐ Mikko Leinonen
- ☐ Tapio Levo
- ☐ Jukka Porvari
- ☐ Seppo Suoraniemi
- ☐ Juhani Tamminen

1982 VALIO

These ice cream labels measure 2 3/8" in diameter.

Valio

- ☐ Kari Eloranta
- ☐ Jari Kurri
- ☐ Tapio Levo
- ☐ Markus Mattsson
- ☐ Jukka Porvari
- ☐ Pekka Rautakallio

1982 - 83 DERNIÈRE PHOTOS

This multi-sport series of photos were inserted in Dernière magazine from 1972 through 1984. Three holes were punched on the left side to allow for storage in a binder. The series featured Montréal Canadiens players. These photos measure 8" x 10".

Dernière	NM
☐ 14NOV Raymond Bourque	10.00
☐ 21NOV Denis Savard	8.00
☐ 28NOV Serge Savard	6.00
☐ 5DEC Bryan Trottier	10.00
☐ 12DEC Wilf Paiement	3.00
☐ 19DEC Michael Bossy	10.00
☐ 26DEC Ron Duguay	3.00
☐ 2JAN Bobby Clarke	10.00
☐ 9JAN Mike Rogers	3.00
☐ 16JAN Darryl Sittler	10.00
☐ 23JAN Carol Vadnais	3.00
☐ 30JAN Mark Howe	6.00
☐ 6FEB Vladislav Tretiak (G)	20.00
☐ 13FEB Pierre Larouche	5.00
☐ 20FEB Gilbert Perreault	8.00
☐ 27FEB Gaston Gingras	3.00
☐ 6MAR Richard Brodeur (G)	5.00
☐ 13MAR Dale Hawerchuk	8.00
☐ 20MAR Pat LaFontaine	20.00
☐ 27MAR Brian Engblom	3.00
☐ 3APR Dan Daoust	3.00
☐ 10APR Doug Risebrough	3.00
☐ 17APR Rod Langway	6.00
☐ 24APR Doug Jarvis	3.00

1982 - 83 MCDONALD'S STICKERS

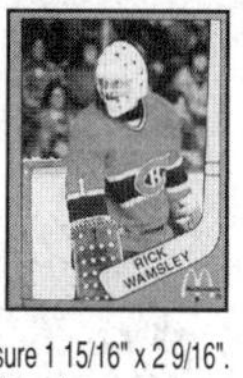

These stickers measure 1 15/16" x 2 9/16".

Complete Set (36 stickers):	**30.00**
Album:	**6.00**
McDonald's	**NM**
☐ 1 Dan Bouchard (G), Québ.	.50
☐ 2 Richard Brodeur (G), Vanc.	.50
☐ 3 Gilles Meloche (G), Minn.	.50
☐ 4 Billy Smith (G), NYIs.	1.50
☐ 5 Rick Wamsley (G), Mont.	.50
☐ 6 Mike Bossy, NYIs.	2.50
☐ 7 Dino Ciccarelli, Minn.	1.50
☐ 8 Guy Lafleur, Mont.	3.00
☐ 9 Rick Middleton, Bost.	.50
☐ 10 Marian Stastny, Québ.	.35
☐ 11 Bill Barber, Phil.	1.00
☐ 12 Bob Gainey, Mont.	1.00
☐ 13 Clark Gillies, NYIs.	.50
☐ 14 Michel Goulet, Québ.	1.00
☐ 15 Mark Messier, Edmo.	5.00
☐ 16 AS: Billy Smith (G), NYIs.	1.00
☐ 17 AS: Larry Robinson, Mont.	1.00
☐ 18 AS: Denis Potvin, NYIs.	1.00
☐ 19 AS: Michel Goulet, Québ.	1.00
☐ 20 AS: Wayne Gretzky, Edmo.	10.00
☐ 21 AS: Mike Bossy, NYIs.	1.50
☐ 22 Wayne Gretzky, Edmo.	12.00
☐ 23 Denis Savard, Chic.	1.00
☐ 24 Peter Stastny, Québ.	1.00
☐ 25 Bryan Trottier, NYIs.	1.50
☐ 26 Doug Wickenheiser, Mont.	.35
☐ 27 Barry Beck, NYRa.	.35
☐ 28 Raymond Bourque, Bost.	4.00
☐ 29 Brian Engblom, Wash.	.35
☐ 30 Craig Hartsburg, Minn.	.50
☐ 31 Mark Howe, Phil.	.50
☐ 32 Rod Langway, Wash.	.50
☐ 33 Denis Potvin, NYIs.	1.00
☐ 34 Larry Robinson, Mont.	1.00
☐ 35 Normand Rochefort, Québ.	.35
☐ 36 Doug Wilson, Chic.	.50

1982 - 83 NEILSON'S (GRETZKY)

These blue-border cards measure the standard 2 1/2" x 3 1/2".

Complete Set (50 cards):	**185.00**
Wayne Gretzky	**NM**
☐ 1 Discard Broken Stick	8.50
☐ 2 Handling the Puck	5.00
☐ 3 Offsides	5.00
☐ 4 Penalty Shot	5.00
☐ 5 Icing the Puck	5.00
☐ 6 Taping your Stick	5.00
☐ 7 Skates	5.00
☐ 8 The Helmet	5.00
☐ 9 Selecting Skates	5.00
☐ 10 Choosing a Stick (w/ G.Howe)	20.00
☐ 11 General Equipment Care	5.00
☐ 12 The Hook Check (w/ M. Dionne)	8.50
☐ 13 The Hip Check	5.00
☐ 14 Forward Skating (w/ M. Gartner)	8.00
☐ 15 Stopping	5.00
☐ 16 Sharp Turning	5.00
☐ 17 Fast Starts	5.00
☐ 18 Backward Skating	5.00
☐ 19 The Grip	5.00
☐ 20 The Wrist Shot	5.00
☐ 21 The Back Hand Shot	5.00
☐ 22 The Slap Shot	5.00
☐ 23 The Flip Shot	5.00
☐ 24 Pass Receiving	5.00
☐ 25 Faking	5.00
☐ 26 Puck Handling	5.00
☐ 27 Deflecting Shots	5.00
☐ 28 One On One	5.00
☐ 29 Keep Your Head Up	5.00
☐ 30 Passing to the Slot	5.00
☐ 31 Winning Face-Offs w/ G. Lafleur/ M. Bossy	15.00
☐ 32 Forechecking	5.00
☐ 33 Body Checking	5.00
☐ 34 Breaking Out	5.00
☐ 35 The Drop Pass	5.00
☐ 36 Backchecking (w/ P. Esposito)	12.00
☐ 37 Using the Boards	5.00
☐ 38 The Power Play	5.00
☐ 39 Passing the Puck	5.00
☐ 40 Clear the Slot	5.00
☐ 41 Leg Lifts	5.00
☐ 42 Balance Exercise	5.00
☐ 43 Leg Stretches (w/ M. Zuke)	5.00
☐ 44 Hip and Groin Stretch	5.00
☐ 45 Toe Touches (w/ M. Messier)	10.00
☐ 46 Goalie Warm Up Drill	5.00
☐ 47 Leg Exercises	5.00
☐ 48 Arm Exercises (w/ J. Stackhouse)	5.00
☐ 49 Wrist Exercises	5.00
☐ 50 Flip Pass	8.50

1982 - 83 O-PEE-CHEE

These cards measure the standard 2 1/2" x 3 1/2".

Complete Set (396 cards):	**125.00**
Common Player:	**.30**
O-Pee-Chee	**NM-MT**
☐ 1 Wayne Gretzky, Edmo.	12.00
☐ 2 Mike Bossy, NYIs.	1.50
☐ 3 Dale Hawerchuk, Winn.	5.00
☐ **4 Mikko Leinonen, NYRa. RC**	**.75**
☐ 5 Bryan Trottier, NYIs.	.75
☐ 6 TL: Rick Middleton, Bost.	.30
☐ 7 Raymond Bourque, Bost.	15.00
☐ 8 Wayne Cashman, Bost.	.30
☐ **9 Bruce Crowder, Bost. RC**	**.75**
☐ **10 Keith Crowder, Bost. RC**	**.75**
☐ **11 Tom Fergus, Bost. RC**	**.75**
☐ 12 Steve Kasper, Bost.	.30
☐ **13 Normand Léveillé, Bost. RC**	**1.25**
☐ 14 Don Marcotte, Bost.	.30
☐ 15 Rick Middleton, Bost.	.50
☐ 16 Peter McNab, Bost.	.30
☐ 17 Mike O'Connell, Bost.	.30
☐ 18 Terry O'Reilly, Bost.	.30
☐ 19 Brad Park, Bost.	1.00
☐ **20 Barry Pederson, Bost. RC**	**1.00**
☐ **21 Brad Palmer, Bost. RC**	**.75**
☐ 22 Pete Peeters (G), Bost.	.50
☐ 23 Rogatien Vachon (G), Bost.	.50
☐ 24 In Action: Raymond Bourque, Bost.	4.00
☐ 25 TL: Gilbert Perreault, Buff.	.50
☐ 26 Mike Foligno, Buff.	.30
☐ 27 Yvon Lambert, Buff.	.30
☐ 28 Dale McCourt, Buff.	.30
☐ 29 Tony McKegney, Buff.	.30
☐ 30 Gilbert Perreault, Buff.	1.50
☐ 31 Lindy Ruff, Buff.	.50
☐ 32 Mike Ramsey, Buff.	.30
☐ **33 J.F. Sauvé, Buff. RC**	**.75**
☐ 34 Bob Sauvé (G), Buff.	.50
☐ 35 Ric Seiling, Buff.	.30
☐ 36 John Van Boxmeer, Buff.	.30
☐ 37 In Action: John Van Boxmeer, Buff.	.30
☐ 38 TL: Lanny McDonald, Calg.	.50
☐ 39 Mel Bridgman, Calg.	.30
☐ 40 In Action: Mel Bridgman, Calg.	.30
☐ 41 Guy Chouinard, Calg.	.30
☐ 42 Steve Christoff, Calg.	.30
☐ **43 Denis Cyr, Calg. RC**	**.75**
☐ 44 Bill Clement, Calg.	.30
☐ 45 Rich Dunn, Calg.	.30
☐ 46 Don Edwards (G), Calg.	.50
☐ 47 Jamie Hislop, Calg.	.30
☐ **48 Steve Konroyd, Calg. RC**	**.75**
☐ 49 Kevin LaVallée, Calg.	.30
☐ 50 Réjean Lemelin (G), Calg.	.75
☐ 51 Lanny McDonald, Calg.	1.00
☐ 52 In Action: Lanny McDonald, Calg.	.50
☐ 53 Bob Murdoch, Calg.	.30
☐ 54 Kent Nilsson, Calg.	.30
☐ 55 Jim Peplinski, Calg.	.30
☐ 56 Paul Reinhart, Calg.	.30
☐ 57 Doug Risebrough, Calg.	.30
☐ 58 Phil Russell, Calg.	.30
☐ **59 Howard Walker, Calg. RC**	**.75**
☐ 60 TL: Al Secord, Chic.	.30
☐ 61 Murray Bannerman (G), Chic.	.50
☐ 62 Keith Brown, Chic.	.30
☐ **63 Doug Crossman, Chic. RC**	**.75**
☐ 64 Tony Esposito (G), Chic.	.85
☐ 65 Greg Fox, Chic.	.30
☐ 66 Tim Higgins, Chic.	.30
☐ 67 Reg Kerr, Chic.	.30
☐ 68 Tom Lysiak, Chic.	.30
☐ 69 Grant Mulvey, Chic.	.30

☐ 70 Bob Murray, Chic. .30
☐ 71 Rich Preston, Chic. .30
☐ 72 Terry Ruskowski, Chic. (LosA.) .30
☐ 73 Denis Savard, Chic. 5.00
☐ 74 Al Secord, Chic. .30
☐ 75 Glen Sharpley, Chic. .30
☐ 76 Darryl Sutter, Chic. .50
☐ 77 Doug Wilson, Chic. .75
☐ 78 In Action: Doug Wilson, Chic. .50
☐ 79 TL: John Ogrodnick, Detr. .30
☐ **80 John Barrett, Detr. RC 1.00**
☐ **81 Mike Blaisdell, Detr. RC .75**
☐ 82 Colin Campbell, Detr. .50
☐ 83 Danny Gare, Detr. .50
☐ 84 Gilles Gilbert (G), Detr. .30
☐ 85 Willie Huber, Detr. .30
☐ 86 Greg Joly, Detr. .30
☐ 87 Mark Kirton, Detr. .30
☐ 88 Reed Larson, Detr. .30
☐ 89 In Action: Reed Larson, Detr. .30
☐ 90 Reggie Leach, Detr. .30
☐ 91 Walt McKechnie, Detr. .30
☐ 92 John Ogrodnick, Detr. .30
☐ **93 Mark Osborne, Detr. RC 1.00**
☐ 94 Jim Schoenfeld, Detr. .50
☐ 95 Derek Smith, Detr. .30
☐ 96 Greg Smith, Detr. .30
☐ 97 Eric Vail, Detr. .30
☐ 98 Paul Woods, Detr. .30
☐ 99 TL: Wayne Gretzky, Edmo. 6.00
☐ 100 Glenn Anderson, Edmo. 2.50
☐ 101 Paul Coffey, Edmo. 18.00
☐ 102 In Action: Paul Coffey, Edmo. 6.00
☐ 103 Brett Callighen, Edmo. .30
☐ 104 Lee Fogolin, Edmo. .30
☐ **105 Grant Fuhr (G), Edmo. RC 40.00**
☐ 106 Wayne Gretzky, Edmo. 45.00
☐ 107 In Action: Wayne Gretzky, Edmo. 20.00
☐ 108 Matti Hagman, Edmo. .30
☐ 109 Pat Hughes, Edmo. .30
☐ 110 Dave Hunter, Edmo. .30
☐ 111 Jari Kurri, Edmo. 10.00
☐ 112 Ron Low (G), Edmo. .50
☐ 113 Kevin Lowe, Edmo. 2.00
☐ 114 Dave Lumley, Edmo. .30
☐ 115 Ken Linseman, Edmo. .30
☐ 116 Garry Larivière, Edmo. .30
☐ 117 Mark Messier, Edmo. 20.00
☐ **118 Tom Roulston, Edmo. RC .75**
☐ 119 Dave Semenko, Edmo. .30
☐ 120 Garry Unger, Edmo. .50
☐ 121 Checklist 1 (1 - 132) 4.00
☐ 122 TL: Blaine Stoughton, Hart. .30
☐ **123 Ron Francis, Hart. RC 35.00**
☐ **124 Chris Kotsopoulos, Hart. RC .75**
☐ 125 Pierre Larouche, Hart. .30
☐ 126 Greg Millen (G), Hart. .50
☐ 127 Warren Miller, Hart. .30
☐ 128 Merlin Malinowski, Hart. .30
☐ 129 Risto Siltanen, Hart. .30
☐ 130 Blaine Stoughton, Hart. .30
☐ 131 In Action: Blaine Stoughton, Hart. .30
☐ 132 Doug Sulliman, Hart. .30
☐ **133 Blake Wesley, Hart. RC .75**
☐ 134 TL: Steve Tambellini, NJer. .30
☐ **135 Brent Ashton, NJer. RC .75**
☐ **136 Aaron Broten, NJer. RC 1.25**
☐ **137 Joe Cirella, NJer. RC 1.00**
☐ 138 Dwight Foster, NJer. (Detr.) .30
☐ 139 Paul Gagné, NJer. .30
☐ 140 Garry Howatt, NJer. .30
☐ 141 Don Lever, NJer. .30
☐ 142 Bob Lorimer, NJer. .30
☐ 143 Bob MacMillan, NJer. .30
☐ **144 Rick Meagher, NJer. RC 1.25**
☐ 145 Glenn Resch (G), NJer. .50
☐ 146 In Action: Glenn Resch (G), NJer. .50
☐ 147 Steve Tambellini, NJer. .30
☐ 148 Carol Vadnais, NJer. .30
☐ 149 TL: Marcel Dionne, LosA. .65
☐ **150 Dan Bonar, LosA. RC .75**
☐ **151 Steve Bozek, LosA. RC .75**
☐ 152 Marcel Dionne, LosA. 1.50
☐ 153 In Action: Marcel Dionne, LosA. .65
☐ 154 Jim Fox, LosA. .30
☐ **155 Mark Hardy, LosA. RC .75**
☐ 156 Mario Lessard (G), LosA. .50
☐ 157 Dave Lewis, LosA. .50
☐ 158 Larry Murphy, LosA. 3.50
☐ 159 Charlie Simmer, LosA. .50
☐ **160 Doug Smith, LosA. RC .75**
☐ 161 Dave Taylor, LosA. .50
☐ 162 TL: Dino Ciccarelli, Minn. 1.50
☐ 163 Don Beaupré (G), Minn. 1.00
☐ **164 Neal Broten, Minn. RC 5.00**
☐ 165 Dino Ciccarelli, Minn. 4.50
☐ **166 Curt Giles, Minn. RC .75**
☐ 167 Craig Hartsburg, Minn. .50
☐ 168 Brad Maxwell, Minn. .30
☐ 169 Tom McCarthy, Minn. .30
☐ 170 Gilles Meloche (G), Minn. .50
☐ 171 Al MacAdam, Minn. .30
☐ 172 Steve Payne, Minn. .30
☐ 173 Willi Plett, Minn. .30
☐ 174 Gord Roberts, Minn. .30
☐ 175 Bobby Smith, Minn. .50
☐ 176 In Action: Bobby Smith, Minn. .50
☐ 177 Tim Young, Minn. .30
☐ 178 TL: Mark Napier, Mont. .30
☐ 179 Keith Acton, Mont. .30
☐ 180 In Action: Keith Acton, Mont. .30
☐ 181 Bob Gainey, Mont. 1.50
☐ 182 Gaston Gingras, Mont. .30
☐ 183 Rick Green, Mont. .30
☐ 184 Réjean Houle, Mont. .30
☐ **185 Mark Hunter, Mont. RC 1.00**
☐ 186 Guy Lafleur, Mont. 3.00
☐ 187 In Action: Guy Lafleur, Mont. 1.50
☐ 188 Pierre Mondou, Mont. .30
☐ 189 Mark Napier, Mont. .30
☐ 190 Robert Picard, Mont. .30
☐ 191 Larry Robinson, Mont. 1.50
☐ 192 Steve Shutt, Mont. 1.00
☐ 193 Mario Tremblay, Mont. .30
☐ 194 Ryan Walter, Mont. .30
☐ **195 Rick Wamsley (G), Mont. RC 2.00**
☐ 196 Doug Wickenheiser, Mont. .30
☐ 197 TL: Mike Bossy, NYIs. 1.30
☐ 198 Bob Bourne, NYIs. .30
☐ 199 Mike Bossy, NYIs. 3.00
☐ 200 Butch Goring, NYIs. .50
☐ 201 Clark Gillies, NYIs. 1.50
☐ **202 Tomas Jonsson, NYIs. RC 1.00**
☐ 203 Anders Kallur, NYIs. .30
☐ 204 Dave Langevin, NYIs. .30
☐ 205 Wayne Merrick, NYIs. .30
☐ 206 Ken Morrow, NYIs. .30
☐ 207 Mike McEwen, NYIs. .30
☐ 208 Bob Nystrom, NYIs. .30
☐ 209 Stefan Persson, NYIs. .30
☐ 210 Denis Potvin, NYIs. 1.50
☐ 211 Billy Smith (G), NYIs. 1.50
☐ 212 Duane Sutter, NYIs. .50
☐ 213 John Tonelli, NYIs. .50
☐ 214 Bryan Trottier, NYIs. 1.50
☐ 215 In Action: Bryan Trottier, NYIs. 1.00
☐ **216 Brent Sutter, NYIs. RC 3.00**
☐ 217 TL: Ron Duguay, NYRa. .30
☐ 218 Kent-Erik Andersson, Minn. (NYRa.) .30
☐ 219 Barry Beck, NYRa. .30
☐ 220 In Action: Barry Beck, NYRa. .30
☐ 221 Ron Duguay, NYRa. .30
☐ 222 Nick Fotiu, NYRa. .30
☐ 223 Robbie Ftorek, NYRa. .50
☐ 224 Ron Greschner, NYRa. .30
☐ 225 Anders Hedberg, NYRa. .50
☐ 226 Eddie Johnstone, NYRa. .30
☐ 227 Tom Laidlaw, NYRa. .30
☐ 228 Dave Maloney, NYRa. .30
☐ 229 Don Maloney, NYRa. .30
☐ 230 Ed Mio (G), NYRa. .50
☐ **231 Mark Pavelich, NYRa. RC .75**
☐ 232 Mike Rogers, NYRa. .30
☐ **233 Reijo Ruotsalainen, NYRa. RC 1.00**
☐ **234 Steve Weeks (G), NYRa. RC 1.00**
☐ 235 LL: Wayne Gretzky, Edmo. 6.00
☐ 236 LL: Paul Gardner, Pitt. .30
☐ 237 LL: Wayne Gretzky/ Michel Goulet 6.00
☐ 238 LL: Paul Baxter, Pitt. .30
☐ 239 LL: Denis Herron, Mont. .50
☐ 240 LL: Wayne Gretzky, Edmo. 6.00
☐ 241 LL: Denis Herron, Mont. .50
☐ 242 LL: Wayne Gretzky, Edmo. 6.00
☐ 243 LL: Wayne Gretzky, Edmo. 6.00
☐ 244 TL: Bill Barber, Phil. .50
☐ **245 Fred Arthur, Phil. RC .75**
☐ 246 Bill Barber, Phil. 1.00
☐ 247 In Action: Bill Barber, Phil. .50
☐ 248 Bobby Clarke, Phil. 1.50
☐ **249 Ron Flockhart, Phil. RC .75**
☐ 250 Tom Gorence, Phil. .30
☐ 251 Paul Holmgren, Phil. .30
☐ 252 Mark Howe, Phil. .50
☐ 253 Tim Kerr, Phil. .75
☐ 254 Brad Marsh, Phil. .50
☐ 255 Brad McCrimmon, Phil. 1.25
☐ 256 Brian Propp, Phil. .75
☐ 257 Darryl Sittler, Phil. 1.50
☐ 258 Rick St. Croix (G), Phil. .50
☐ 259 Jimmy Watson, Phil. .30
☐ 260 Behn Wilson, Phil. .30
☐ 261 Checklist 2 (133 - 264) 4.00
☐ 262 TL: Mike Bullard, Pitt. .50
☐ 263 Pat Boutette, Pitt. .30
☐ **264 Mike Bullard, Pitt. RC 2.00**
☐ 265 Randy Carlyle, Pitt. .30
☐ 266 In Action: Randy Carlyle, Pitt. .30
☐ 267 Michel Dion (G), Pitt. .50
☐ 268 George Ferguson, Pitt. (Minn.) .30
☐ 269 Paul Gardner, Pitt. .30
☐ 270 Denis Herron (G), Pitt. .50
☐ 271 Rick Kehoe, Pitt. .50
☐ 272 Greg Malone, Pitt. .30
☐ 273 Rick MacLeish, Pitt. .30
☐ 274 Pat Price, Pitt. .30
☐ 275 Ron Stackhouse, Pitt. .30
☐ 276 TL: Peter Stastny, Québ. 1.50
☐ **277 Pierre Aubry, Québ. RC .75**
☐ 278 Dan Bouchard (G), Québ. .50
☐ 279 Réal Cloutier, Québ. .30
☐ 280 In Action: Réal Cloutier, Québ. .30
☐ 281 Alain Côté, Québ. .30
☐ 282 André Dupont, Québ. .30
☐ 283 John Garrett (G), Québ. .50
☐ 284 Michel Goulet, Québ. 3.00
☐ 285 Dale Hunter, Québ. 2.50
☐ 286 Pierre Lacroix, Québ. .30
☐ 287 Mario Marois, Québ. .30
☐ 288 Wilf Paiement, Québ. .30
☐ 289 Dave Pichette, Québ. .30
☐ 290 Jacques Richard, Québ. .30
☐ **291 Normand Rochefort, Québ. RC .75**
☐ 292 Peter Stastny, Québ. 4.00
☐ 293 In Action: Peter Stastny, Québ. 2.00
☐ 294 Anton Stastny, Québ. .30
☐ **295 Marian Stastny, Québ. RC 1.00**
☐ 296 Marc Tardif, Québ. .30
☐ 297 Wally Weir, Québ. .30
☐ 298 TL: Brian Sutter, SLou. .50
☐ 299 Wayne Babych, SLou. .30
☐ 300 Jack Brownschidle, SLou. .30
☐ 301 Blake Dunlop, SLou. .30
☐ 302 Bernie Federko, SLou. .50
☐ 303 In Action: Bernie Federko, SLou. .50
☐ 304 Pat Hickey, SLou. .30
☐ 305 Guy Lapointe, SLou. 1.00
☐ 306 Mike Liut (G), SLou. .50
☐ **307 Joe Mullen, SLou. RC 16.00**
☐ 308 Larry Patey, SLou. .30
☐ 309 Jorgen Pettersson, SLou. .30
☐ 310 Rob Ramage, SLou. .50
☐ 311 Brian Sutter, SLou. .50
☐ 312 Perry Turnbull, SLou. .30
☐ 313 Mike Zuke, SLou. .30
☐ 314 TL: Rick Vaive, Toro. .50
☐ 315 John Anderson, Toro. .30
☐ **316 Normand Aubin, Toro. RC .75**
☐ **317 Jim Benning, Toro. RC .75**
☐ **318 Fred Boimistruck, Toro. RC .75**
☐ 319 Bill Derlago, Toro. .30
☐ 320 In Action: Bill Derlago, Toro. .30
☐ **321 Miroslav Frycer, Toro. RC .75**
☐ 322 Billy Harris, Toro. .30
☐ 323 James Korn, Toro. .30
☐ 324 Michel Larocque (G), Toro. .50
☐ 325 Bob Manno, Toro. .30
☐ 326 Dan Maloney, Toro. .30
☐ **327 Bob McGill, Toro. RC .75**
☐ 328 Barry Melrose, Toro. .30
☐ 329 Terry Martin, Toro. .30
☐ 330 René Robert, Toro. .30
☐ 331 Rocky Saganiuk, Toro. .30
☐ 332 Börje Salming, Toro. 1.00
☐ 333 Greg Terrion, LosA. (Toro.) .30
☐ **334 Vincent Tremblay (G), Toro. RC 1.00**
☐ 335 Rick Vaive, Toro. .50
☐ 336 In Action: Rick Vaive, Toro. .50
☐ 337 TL: Thomas Gradin, Vanc. .30
☐ 338 Ivan Boldirev, Vanc. .30
☐ 339 Richard Brodeur (G), Vanc. .50
☐ 340 In Action: Richard Brodeur (G), Vanc. .50
☐ 341 Tony Currie, Vanc. .30
☐ **342 Marc Crawford, Vanc. RC 3.00**
☐ 343 Curt Fraser, Vanc. .30
☐ 344 Thomas Gradin, Vanc. .30
☐ 345 In Action: Thomas Gradin, Vanc. .30
☐ 346 Ivan Hlinka, Vanc. RC, Error (Jiri Bubla) .50
☐ 347 Ron Delorme, Vanc. .30
☐ 348 Rick Lanz, Vanc. .30
☐ 349 Lars Lindgren, Vanc. .30
☐ 350 Blair MacDonald, Vanc. .30
☐ 351 Kevin McCarthy, Vanc. .30
☐ 352 Gerry Minor, Vanc. .30
☐ **353 Lars Molin, Vanc. RC 1.00**
☐ **354 Gary Lupul, Vanc. RC 1.00**
☐ 355 Darcy Rota, Vanc. .30
☐ 356 Stan Smyl, Vanc. .50
☐ 357 Harold Snepsts, Vanc. .50
☐ 358 Dave Williams, Vanc. .50
☐ 359 TL: Dennis Maruk, Wash. .30
☐ 360 Ted Bulley, Chic. (Wash.) .30
☐ **361 Bob Carpenter, Wash. RC 2.00**
☐ 362 Brian Engblom, Wash. .30
☐ 363 Mike Gartner, Wash. 6.00
☐ 364 Bengt Gustafsson, Wash. .30
☐ 365 Doug Hicks, Wash. .30
☐ 366 Ken Houston, Wash. .30
☐ 367 Doug Jarvis, Mont., (Wash.) .50
☐ 368 Rod Langway, Mont., (Wash.) .75
☐ 369 Dennis Maruk, Wash. .30
☐ 370 In Action: Dennis Maruk, Wash. .30
☐ **371 Dave Parro (G), Wash. RC 1.00**
☐ 372 Pat Riggin (G), Wash. .30
☐ **373 Chris Valentine, Wash. RC .75**
☐ 374 TL: Dale Hawerchuk, Winn. 4.00
☐ 375 Dave Babych, Winn. .50
☐ 376 In Action: Dave Babych, Winn. .50
☐ 377 Dave Christian, Winn. .30
☐ 378 Norm Dupont, Winn. .30
☐ 379 Lucien DeBlois, Winn. .30
☐ **380 Dale Hawerchuk, Winn. RC 28.00**
☐ 381 In Action: Dale Hawerchuk, Winn. 6.00
☐ **382 Craig Levie, Winn. RC .75**
☐ 383 Morris Lukowich, Winn. .30
☐ 384 Willy Lindstrom, Winn. .30
☐ **385 Bengt Lundholm, Winn. RC .75**
☐ **386 Paul MacLean, Winn. RC 1.00**
☐ 387 Bryan Maxwell, Winn. .30
☐ **388 Doug Smail, Winn. RC 1.00**
☐ 389 Doug Soetaert (G), Winn. .30
☐ 390 Serge Savard, Winn. .50
☐ **391 Thomas Steen, Winn. RC 4.00**
☐ 392 Don Spring, Winn. .30
☐ 393 Ed Staniowski (G), Winn. .30
☐ 394 Tim Trimper, Winn. .30
☐ **395 Tim Watters, Winn. RC .75**
☐ 396 Checklist 3 (265 - 396) 5.00

1982 - 83 OPC / TOPPS STICKERS

These stickers measure 1 15/16" x 2 9/16". It is rumoured that some of the Topps stickers may not have been issued.

Complete Set (263 stickers): 50.00
Album (Wayne Gretzky cover): 8.00
Common Player: .20

O-Pee-Chee NM-MT

☐ ☐ 1 Conn Smythe Trophy: Mike Bossy, NYIs. .35
☐ ☐ 2 Foil: Conn Smythe Trophy .35
☐ ☐ 3 1981/82 Stanley Cup Winners: NY Islanders .20
☐ ☐ 4 1981/82 Stanley Cup Winners: NY Islanders .20
☐ ☐ 5 Stanley Cup Finals .20
☐ ☐ 6 Stanley Cup Finals .20

Note: Stickers 5-6 feature Ken Morrow, Thomas Gradin and Billy Smith

☐ ☐ 7 Richard Brodeur (G), Vanc. .35
☐ ☐ 8 Victory .20
☐ ☐ 9 Curt Fraser, Vanc. .20
☐ ☐ 10 Billy Smith (G), NYIs. .35
☐ ☐ 11 Stanley Cup Playoffs .20
☐ ☐ 12 Stanley Cup Playoffs .20
☐ ☐ 13 Stanley Cup Playoffs .20
☐ ☐ 14 Tom Lysiak, Chic. .20
☐ ☐ 15 Peter Stastny, Québ. 1.00
☐ ☐ 16 Stanley Cup Playoffs .20
☐ ☐ 17 Stanley Cup Playoffs .20
☐ ☐ 18 Butch Goring/ Peter Stastny .35
☐ ☐ 19 Peter Stastny, Québ. 1.00
☐ ☐ 20 Marian Stastny, Québ. .20
☐ ☐ 21 Marc Tardif, Québ. .20
☐ ☐ 22 Wilf Paiement, Québ. .20
☐ ☐ 23 Réal Cloutier, Québ. .20
☐ ☐ 24 Anton Stastny, Québ. .20
☐ ☐ 25 Michel Goulet, Québ. .75
☐ ☐ 26 Dale Hunter, Québ. .50
☐ ☐ 27 Dan Bouchard (G), Québ. .35
☐ ☐ 28 Guy Lafleur, Mont. 3.00
☐ ☐ 29 Guy Lafleur (Action), Mont. 3.00
☐ ☐ 30 Mario Tremblay, Mont. .20
☐ ☐ 31 Larry Robinson, Mont. .50
☐ ☐ 32 Steve Shutt, Mont. .35
☐ ☐ 33 Steve Shutt (Action), Mont. .35
☐ ☐ 34 Rod Langway, Mont. .35
☐ ☐ 35 Pierre Mondou, Mont. .20
☐ ☐ 36 Bob Gainey, Mont. .50
☐ ☐ 37 Rick Wamsley (G), Mont. .35
☐ ☐ 38 Mark Napier, Mont. .20
☐ ☐ 39 Mark Napier (Action), Mont. .20
☐ ☐ 40 Doug Jarvis, Mont. .25
☐ ☐ 41 Denis Herron (G), Mont. .35
☐ ☐ 42 Keith Acton, Mont. .20
☐ ☐ 43 Keith Acton (Action), Mont. .20
☐ ☐ 44 Foil: Prince of Wales Trophy .20

□□ 45 Foil: Prince of Wales Trophy .20
□□ 46 Denis Potvin, NYIs. .50
□□ 47 Bryan Trottier, NYIs. .50
□□ 48 Bryan Trottier (Action), NYIs. .50
□□ 49 John Tonelli, NYIs. .20
□□ 50 Mike Bossy, NYIs. .75
□□ 51 Mike Bossy (Action), NYIs. .75
□□ 52 Duane Sutter, NYIs. .20
□□ 53 Bob Bourne, NYIs. .20
□□ 54 Clark Gillies, NYIs. .20
□□ 55 Clark Gillies (Action), NYIs. .20
□□ 56 Brent Sutter, NYIs. .20
□□ 57 Anders Kallur, NYIs. .20
□□ 58 Ken Morrow, NYIs. .20
□□ 59 Bob Nystrom, NYIs. .20
□□ 60 Billy Smith (G), NYIs. .50
□□ 61 Billy Smith (G) (Action), NYIs. .50
□□ 62 Rick Vaive, Toro. .20
□□ 63 Rick Vaive (Action), Toro. .20
□□ 64 Jim Benning, Toro. .20
□□ 65 Miroslav Frycer, Toro. .20
□□ 66 Terry Martin, Toro. .20
□□ 67 Bill Derlago, Toro. .20
□□ 68 Bill Derlago (Action), Toro. .20
□□ 69 Rocky Saganiuk, Toro. .20
□□ 70 Vincent Tremblay (G), Toro. .35
□□ 71 Bob Manno, Toro. .20
□□ 72 Dan Maloney, Toro. .20
□□ 73 John Anderson, Toro. .20
□□ 74 John Anderson (Action), Toro. .20
□□ 75 Börje Salming, Toro. .35
□□ 76 Börje Salming (Action), Toro. .35
□□ 77 Michel Larocque (G), Toro. .35
□□ 78 Rick Middleton, Bost. .35
□□ 79 Rick Middleton (Action), Bost. .35
□□ 80 Keith Crowder, Bost. .20
□□ 81 Steve Kasper, Bost. .20
□□ 82 Brad Park, Bost. .35
□□ 83 Peter McNab, Bost. .20
□□ 84 Peter McNab (Action), Bost. .20
□□ 85 Terry O'Reilly, Bost. .20
□□ 86 Raymond Bourque, Bost. 3.00
□□ 87 Raymond Bourque (Action), Bost. 3.00
□□ 88 Tom Fergus, Bost. .20
□□ 89 Mike O'Connell, Bost. .20
□□ 90 Brad McCrimmon, Bost. .20
□□ 91 Don Marcotte, Bost. .20
□□ 92 Barry Pederson, Bost. .20
□□ 93 Barry Pederson (Action), Bost. .20
□□ 94 Mark Messier, Edmo. 3.50
□□ 95 Grant Fuhr (G), Edmo. 2.50
□□ 96 Kevin Lowe, Edmo. .35
□□ 97 Wayne Gretzky, Edmo. 8.00
□□ 98 Wayne Gretzky (Action), Edmo. 8.00
□□ 99 Glenn Anderson, Edmo. .50
□□ 100 Glenn Anderson (Action), Edmo. .50
□□ 101 Dave Lumley, Edmo. .20
□□ 102 Dave Hunter, Edmo. .20
□□ 103 Matti Hagman, Edmo. .20
□□ 104 Paul Coffey, Edmo. 2.50
□□ 105 Paul Coffey (Action), Edmo. 2.50
□□ 106 Lee Fogolin, Edmo. .20
□□ 107 Ron Low (G), Edmo. .35
□□ 108 Jari Kurri, Edmo. 1.25
□□ 109 Jari Kurri (Action), Edmo. 1.25
□□ 110 Bill Barber, Phil. .35
□□ 111 Brian Propp, Phil. .20
□□ 112 Ken Linseman, Phil. .20
□□ 113 Ron Flockhart, Phil. .20
□□ 114 Darryl Sittler, Phil. .50
□□ 115 Bobby Clarke, Phil. .50
□□ 116 Paul Holmgren, Phil. .20
□□ 117 Pete Peeters (G), Pha .35
□□ 118 Gilbert Perreault, Buff. .50
□□ 119 Dale McCourt, Buff. .20
□□ 120 Mike Foligno, Buff. .20
□□ 121 John Van Boxmeer, Buff. .20
□□ 122 Tony McKegney, Buff. .20
□□ 123 Ric Seiling, Buff. .20
□□ 124 Don Edwards (G), Buff. .35
□□ 125 Yvon Lambert, Buff. .20
□□ 126 Blaine Stoughton, Hart. .20
□□ 127 Pierre Larouche, Hart. .20
□□ 128 Doug Sulliman, Hart. .20
□□ 129 Ron Francis, Hart. 5.00
□□ 130 Greg Millen (G), Hart. .35
□□ 131 Mark Howe, Hart. .35
□□ 132 Chris Kotsopoulos, Hart. .20
□□ 133 Garry Howatt, Hart. .20
□□ 134 Ron Duguay, NYRa. .20
□□ 135 Barry Beck, NYRa. .20
□□ 136 Mike Rogers, NYRa. .20
□□ 137 Don Maloney, NYRa. .20
□□ 138 Mark Pavelich, NYRa. .20
□□ 139 Eddie Johnstone, NYRa. .20
□□ 140 Dave Maloney, NYRa. .20
□□ 141 Steve Weeks (G), NYRa. .35
□□ 142 Ed Mio (G), NYRa. .35
□□ 143 Rick Kehoe, Pitt. .20
□□ 144 Randy Carlyle, Pitt. .20
□□ 145 Paul Gardner, Pitt. .20
□□ 146 Michel Dion (G), Pitt. .35
□□ 147 Rick MacLeish, Pitt. .20
□□ 148 Pat Boutette, Pitt. .20
□□ 149 Mike Bullard, Pitt. .20
□□ 150 George Ferguson, Pitt. .20
□□ 151 Dennis Maruk, Wash. .20
□□ 152 Ryan Walter, Wash. .20
□□ 153 Mike Gartner, Wash. 2.00
□□ 154 Bob Carpenter, Wash. .20
□□ 155 Chris Valentine, Wash. .20
□□ 156 Rick Green, Wash. .20
□□ 157 Bengt Gustafsson, Wash. .20
□□ 158 Dave Parro (G), Wash. .35
□□ 159 AS: Foil: Mark Messier, Edmo. 3.50
□□ 160 AS: Foil: Paul Coffey, Edmo. 3.00
□□ 161 AS: Foil: Grant Fuhr (G), Edmo. 2.50
□□ 162 AS: Foil: Wayne Gretzky, Edmo. 9.00
□□ 163 AS: Foil: Doug Wilson, Chic. .35
□□ 164 AS: Foil: Dave Taylor, LosA. .35
□□ 165 AS: Foil: Mike Bossy, NYIs. 1.25
□□ 166 AS: Foil: Raymond Bourque, Bost. 3.00
□□ 167 AS: Foil: Peter Stastny, Québ. 1.00
□□ 168 AS: Foil: Michel Dion (G), Pitt. .35
□□ 169 AS: Foil: Larry Robinson, Mont. .50
□□ 170 AS: Foil: Bill Barber, Phil. .35
□□ 171 Denis Savard, Chic. 1.00
□□ 172 Doug Wilson, Chic. .35
□□ 173 Grant Mulvey, Chic. .20
□□ 174 Tom Lysiak, Chic. .20
□□ 175 Al Secord, Chic. .20
□□ 176 Reg Kerr, Chic. .20
□□ 177 Tim Higgins, Chic. .20
□□ 178 Terry Ruskowski, Chic. .20
□□ 179 John Ogrodnick, Detr. .20
□□ 180 Reed Larson, Detr. .20
□□ 181 Bob Sauvé (G), Detr. .35
□□ 182 Mark Osborne, Detr. .20
□□ 183 Jim Schoenfeld, Detr. .20
□□ 184 Danny Gare, Detr. .20
□□ 185 Willie Huber, Detr. .20
□□ 186 Walt McKechnie, Detr. .20
□□ 187 Paul Woods, Detr. .20
□□ 188 Bobby Smith, Minn. .50
□□ 189 Dino Ciccarelli, Minn. 1.00
□□ 190 Neal Broten, Minn. .75
□□ 191 Steve Payne, Minn. .20
□□ 192 Craig Hartsburg, Minn. .20
□□ 193 Don Beaupré (G), Minn. .35
□□ 194 Steve Christoff, Minn. .20
□□ 195 Gilles Meloche (G), Minn. .35
□□ 196 Mike Liut (G), SLou. .35
□□ 197 Bernie Federko, SLou. .50
□□ 198 Brian Sutter, SLou. .50
□□ 199 Blake Dunlop, SLou. .20
□□ 200 Joe Mullen, SLou. 1.25
□□ 201 Wayne Babych, SLou. .20
□□ 202 Jorgen Pettersson, SLou. .20
□□ 203 Perry Turnbull, SLou. .20
□□ 204 Dale Hawerchuk, Winn. 3.00
□□ 205 Morris Lukowich, Winn. .20
□□ 206 Dave Christian, Winn. .20
□□ 207 Dave Babych, Winn. .20
□□ 208 Paul MacLean, Winn. .20
□□ 209 Willy Lindstrom, Winn. .20
□□ 210 Ed Staniowski (G), Winn. .35
□□ 211 Doug Soetaert (G), Winn. .35
□□ 212 Lucien DeBlois, Winn. .20
□□ 213 Mel Bridgman, Calg. .20
□□ 214 Lanny McDonald, Calg. .35
□□ 215 Guy Chouinard, Calg. .20
□□ 216 Jim Peplinski, Calg. .20
□□ 217 Kent Nilsson, Calg. .20
□□ 218 Pekka Rautakallio, Calg. .20
□□ 219 Paul Reinhart, Calg. .20
□□ 220 Kevin LaVallée, Calg. .20
□□ 221 Ken Houston, Calg. .20
□□ 222 Glenn Resch (G), Colo. .35
□□ 223 Rob Ramage, Colo. .20
□□ 224 Don Lever, Colo. .20
□□ 225 Bob MacMillan, Colo. .20
□□ 226 Steve Tambellini, Colo. .20
□□ 227 Brent Ashton, Colo. .20
□□ 228 Bob Lorimer, Colo. .20
□□ 229 Merlin Malinowski, Colo. .20
□□ 230 Marcel Dionne, LosA. .50
□□ 231 Dave Taylor, LosA. .35
□□ 232 Larry Murphy, LosA. .35
□□ 233 Steve Bozek, LosA. .20
□□ 234 Greg Terrion, LosA. .20
□□ 235 Jim Fox, LosA. .20
□□ 236 Mario Lessard (G), LosA. .35
□□ 237 Charlie Simmer, LosA. .35
□□ 238 Foil: Campbell Bowl .20
□□ 239 Foil: Campbell Bowl .20
□□ 240 Thomas Gradin, Vanc. .20
□□ 241 Ivan Boldirev, Vanc. .20
□□ 242 Stan Smyl, Vanc. .20
□□ 243 Harold Snepsts, Vanc. .20
□□ 244 Curt Fraser, Vanc. .20
□□ 245 Lars Molin, Vanc. .20
□□ 246 Kevin McCarthy, Vanc. .20
□□ 247 Richard Brodeur (G), Vanc. .35
□□ 248 Foil: Calder Trophy .20
□□ 249 AW: Dale Hawerchuk, Winn. 2.00
□□ 250 Foil: Vezina Trophy .20
□□ 251 AW: Billy Smith, NYIs. .35
□□ 252 AW: Denis Herron/ Rick Wamsley, Mont. .35
□□ 253 AW: Steve Kasper, Bost. .20
□□ 254 AW: Doug Wilson, Chic. .35
□□ 255 Foil: Norris Trophy .20
□□ 256 AW: Wayne Gretzky, Edmo. 7.00
□□ 257 AW: Wayne Gretzky, Edmo. 7.00
□□ 258 AW: Wayne Gretzky, Edmo. 7.00
□□ 259 AW: Wayne Gretzky, Edmo. 7.00
□□ 260 Foil: Hart Trophy .20
□□ 261 Foil: Art Ross Trophy .20
□□ 262 AW: Rick Middleton, Bost. .20
□□ 263 Foil: Lady Byng Trophy .20

1982 - 83 POST

These cards were issued in 16-card panel in Post cereals. Cut-out cards measure 1 5/8" x 2 1/8".

Complete Set (21 panels): 110.00

Post Cereal NM

□ Boston Bruins: 8.00
R. Bourque/ W. Cashman/ B. Crowder/ T. Fergus
M. Gillis/ S. Jonathan/ S. Kasper/ B. McCrimmon
P. McNab/ L. Melnyk/ R. Middleton/ M. Milbury
Mike O'Connell/ T. O'Reilly/ B. Park/ R. Vachon (G)

□ Buffalo Sabres: 4.00
R. Dunn/ D. Edwards (G)/ M. Foligno/ B. Hajt
Y. Lambert/ D. McCourt/ T. McKegney/ G. Perreault
L. Playfair/ C. Ramsey/ M. Ramsey/ L. Ruff
R. Seiling/ J.F. Sauvé/ A. Savard/ J. Van Boxmeer

□ Calgary Flames: 4.00
M. Bridgman/ G. Chouinard/ D. Cyr/ J. Hislop
K. Houston/ K. LaValée/ G. McAdam/ L. McDonald
B. Murdoch/ K. Nilsson/ J. Peplinski/ W. Plett
P. Rautakallio/ P. Reinhart/ P. Riggin (G)/ P. Russell

□ Chicago Blackhawks: 7.00
T. Bulley/ D. Crossman/ T. Esposito (G)/ G. Fox
B. Gardner/ T. Higgins/ D. Hutchison/ R. Kerr
T. Lysiak/ G. Mulvey/ R. Paterson/ P. Preston
T. Ruskowski/ D. Savard/ A. Secord/ D. Wilson

□ Colorado Rockies: 3.00
B. Ashton/ D. Cameron/ J. Cirella/ D. Foster
M. Kitchen/ D. Lever/ B. Lorimer/ M. Malinowski
B. MacMillan/ K. Maxwell/ J. Micheletti/B. Miller
R. Ramage/ G. Resch (G)/ S. Tambellini/ J. Wensink

□ Detroit Red Wings: 3.00
John Barrett/ Mike Blaisdell/ Danny Gare/ Willie Huber
Greg Joly/ Mark Kirton/ Reed Larson/ Walt McKechnie
V. Nedomansky/ J. Ogrodnick/ M. Osborne/ B. Sauvé (G)
J. Schoenfeld/ D. Smith/ G. Smith/ P. Woods

□ Edmonton Oilers: 30.00
G. Anderson/ B. Callighen/ P. Coffey/ L. Fogolin
G. Fuhr (G)/ W. Gretzky/ M. Hagman/ P. Hughes
D. Hunter/ J. Kurri/ G. Larivière/ K. Lowe
D. Lumley/ M. Messier/ D. Semenko/ R. Siltanen

□ Hartford Whalers: 8.00
J. Douglas/ R. Francis/ G. Howatt/ M. Howe
D. Keon/ C. Kotsopoulos/ P. Larouche/ G. Lyle
J. McIlhargey/ G. Millen (G)/ W. Miller/ D. Nachbauer
P. Shmyr/ B. Stoughton/ D. Sulliman/ B. Wesley

□ Los Angeles Kings: 5.00
S. Bozek/ R. Chartraw/ M. Dionne/ J. Fox
M. Hardy/ D. Hopkins/ S. Jensen/ J.P. Kelly
J. Korab/ M. Lessard (G)/ D. Lewis/ L. Murphy
C. Simmer/ D. Smith/ D. Taylor/ J. Wells

□ Minnesota North Stars: 4.00
K.E. Andersson/ F. Barrett/ S. Christoff/ D. Ciccarelli
C. Giles/ C. Hartsburg/ B. Maxwell/ A. MacAdam
T. McCarthy/ G. Meloche (G)/ B. Palmer/ S. Payne
G. Roberts/ G. Sargent/ B. Smith/ T. Young

□ Montréal Canadiens: 10.00
K. Acton/ B. Engblom/ B. Gainey/ M. Hunter
D. Jarvis/ G. Lafleur/ R. Langway/ C. Laughlin
P. Mondou/ M. Napier/ R. Picard/ D. Risebrough
L. Robinson/ R. Sévigny (G)/ S. Shutt/ M. Tremblay

□ New York Islanders: 10.00
M. Bossy/ B. Bourne/ C. Gillies/ B. Goring
A. Kallur/ T. Jonsson/ D. Langevin/ M. McEwen
W. Merrick/ K. Morrow/ B. Nystrom/ S. Persson
D. Potvin/ B. Smith (G)/ J. Tonelli/ B. Trottier

□ New York Rangers: 3.00
M. Allison/ B. Beck/ A. Dore/ R. Duguay
N. Fotiu/ R. Ftorek/ R. Greschner/ E. Johnstone
T. Laidlaw/ D. Maloney/ D. Maloney/ M. Pavelich
M. Rogers/ R. Ruotsalainen/ S. Weeks (G)/ S. Vickers

□ Philadelphia Flyers 6.00
F. Arthur/ R. Bailey/ B. Barber/ B. Clarke
G. Cochrane/ P. Holmgren/ T. Kerr/ R. Leach
K. Linseman/ B. Marsh/ P. Peeters (G)/ I. Sinisalo
D. Sittler/ B. Propp/ Ji. Watson/ B. Wilson

□ Pittsburgh Penguins 3.00
P. Baxter/ P. Boutette/ M. Bullard/ R. Carlyle
M. Chorney/ M. Dion (G)/ G. Ferguson/ P. Gardner
P. Graham/ R. Kehoe/ P. Lee/ G. Malone
P. Price/ D. Shedden/ G. Sheppard/ R. Stackhouse

□ Québec Nordiques: 5.00
R. Cloutier/ A. Côté/ A. Dupont/ J. Garrett (G)
J. Gillis/ M. Goulet/ Dale Hunter/ M. Marois
W. Paiement/ J. Richard/ N. Rochefort/ A. Stastny
M. Stastny/ P. Stastny/ M. Tardif/ W. Weir

□ St. Louis Blues: 4.00
W. Babych/ B. Baker/ J. Brownschidle/ M. Crombeen
B. Dunlop/ B. Federko/ E. Kea/ R. Lapointe
G. Lapointe/ M. Liut (G)/ L. Patey/ J. Pavese
J. Pettersson/ B. Sutter/ P. Turnbull/ M. Zuke

□ Toronto Maple Leafs: 4.00
J. Anderson/ N. Aubin/ J. Benning/ F. Boimistruck
B. Derlago/ M. Frycer/ S. Gavin/ M. Larocque (G)
B. Manno/ T. Martin/ B. McGill/ B. Melrose
W. Poddubny/ R. Saganiuk/ B. Salming/ R. Vaive

□ Vancouver Canucks: 3.00
I. Boldirev/ R. Brodeur (G)/ M. Crawford/ R. Delorme
C. Fraser/ T. Gradin/ D. Halward/ I. Hlinka
L. Lindgren/ G. Lupul/ K. McCarthy/ L. Molin
D. Rota/ S. Smyl/ H. Snepsts/ D. Williams

□ Washington Capitals: 4.00
B. Carpenter/ G. Currie/ G. Duchesne/ M. Gartner
B. Gould/ R. Green/ B. Gustafsson/ D. Hicks
R. Holt/ A. Jensen (G)/ D. Maruk/ T. Murray
G. Theberge/ C. Valentine/ D. Veitch/ R. Walter

□ Winnipeg Jets: 5.00
S. Arniel/ D. Babych/ D. Christian/ L. DeBlois
N. Dupont/ D. Hawerchuk/ W. Lindstrom/ B. Lundholm
M. Lukowich/ P. MacLean/ B. Maxwell/ S. Savard
D. Spring/ E. Staniowski (G)/ T. Trimper/ T. Watters

1982 - 83 STATER MINT DOLLARS

Medallions measure 1 1/4" in diameter. Each cupro-nickel coin came with a 3 x 8 3/8 perforated card. Singles sell at $3-5. Other singles may exist.

Stater Mint **Stater Mint**

□ 1 Mel Bridgman, Calg. □ 2 D. Edwards (G), Calg.
□ 3 Lanny McDonald, Calg. □ 4 Kent Nilsson, Calg.
□ 5 Jim Peplinski, Calg. □ 6 Paul Reinhart, Calg.

1983 CANADIAN JUNIOR TEAM

The regular cards in this set measure 3 9/16" x 5".

Complete Set (21 cards): 200.00

◆ A complete 21-card set closed at $110 U.S. (approx. $170) in a June 6, 2002, About Time / Barry Sloate auction.

Canadian Junior Team NM

□ Title Card 1.50
□ Dave Andreychuk 10.00
□ Joe Cirella 1.50
□ Paul Cyr 1.50
□ Dale Derkatch 1.50
□ Mike Eagles 1.50
□ Pat Flatley 2.50
□ Mario Gosselin (G) 2.50
□ Gary Leeman 2.50
□ Mario Lemieux 120.00

☐	Mark Morrison	1.50
☐	James Patrick	3.50
☐	Mike Sands (G)	2.50
☐	Gord Sherven	1.50
☐	Tony Tanti	2.50
☐	Larry Trader	1.50
☐	Sylvain Turgeon	2.50
☐	Pat Verbeek	7.00
☐	Mike Vernon (G)	12.00
☐	Steve Yzerman	80.00
☐	Canada's National Junior Team	7.00

LARGE POSTCARDS

☐	1982 Champions 9 3/4 x 7 3/16	15.00
☐	1982 Celebration 5 x 7 3/16	12.00

1983 HALL OF FAME POSTCARDS

These cards were produced by Cartophilium with artwork by Carlton McDiarmid and write-ups by Lefty Reid of the Hockey Hall of Fame. This set consists of 15 subseries of 16 players elected to the Hockey Hall of Fame. Each postcard measures 4" x 6".

Complete Set (240 cards): **450.00**
Common Player: **1.50**

	Hockey Hall of Fame	NM
☐	A1 Sid Abel	3.00
☐	A2 Harry Broadbent	3.00
☐	A3 Clarence Campbell	1.50
☐	A4 Neil Colville	1.50
☐	A5 Charlie Conacher	5.00
☐	A6 Red Dutton	1.50
☐	A7 Foster Hewitt	3.00
☐	A8 Fred Hume	1.50
☐	A9 Mickey Ion	1.50
☐	A10 Ernest (Moose) Johnson	1.50
☐	A11 Bill Mosienko	1.50
☐	A12 Maurice Richard	18.00
☐	A13 Russell (Barney) Stanley	1.50
☐	A14 Lord Stanley	1.50
☐	A15 Fred Taylor	3.00
☐	A16 Tiny Thompson (G)	3.00
☐	B1 Donald Bain	1.50
☐	B2 Hobey Baker	1.50
☐	B3 Frank Calder	1.50
☐	B4 Frank Foyston	1.50
☐	B5 James Hendy	1.50
☐	B6 Gordie Howe	18.00
☐	B7 Harry Lumley (G)	3.00
☐	B8 Reg Noble	1.50
☐	B9 Frank Patrick	1.50
☐	B10 Harvey Pulford	1.50
☐	B11 Ken Reardon	1.50
☐	B12 Joe Simpson	1.50
☐	B13 Conn Smythe	1.50
☐	B14 Red Storey	1.50
☐	B15 Lloyd Turner	1.50
☐	B16 Georges Vézina (G)	12.00
☐	C1 Jean Béliveau	12.00
☐	C2 Max Bentley	2.50
☐	C3 Francis Clancy	6.00
☐	C4 Babe Dye	1.50
☐	C5 Ebbie Goodfellow	1.50
☐	C6 Charles Hay	1.50
☐	C7 Percy Lesueur (G)	3.00
☐	C8 Tommy Lockhart	1.50
☐	C9 Jack Marshall	1.50
☐	C10 Lester Patrick	3.00
☐	C11 Bill Quackenbush	1.50
☐	C12 Frank Selke	1.50
☐	C13 Cooper Smeaton	1.50
☐	C14 Hooley Smith	1.50
☐	C15 James T. Sutherland	1.50
☐	C16 Fred Whitcroft	1.50
☐	D1 Charles Adams	1.50
☐	D2 Russell Bowie	1.50
☐	D3 Frank Frederickson	1.50
☐	D4 Billy Gilmour	1.50
☐	D5 Ivan (Ching) Johnson	3.00
☐	D6 Tom Johnson	1.50
☐	D7 Aurel Joliat	7.50
☐	D8 Duke Keats	1.50
☐	D9 Red Kelly	3.00
☐	D10 Frank McGee	1.50
☐	D11 James D. Norris	1.50
☐	D12 Philip Ross	1.50
☐	D13 Terry Sawchuk (G)	12.00
☐	D14 Babe Siebert	1.50
☐	D15 Anatoli V. Tarasov	1.50
☐	D16 Roy Worters (G)	3.00
☐	E1 T. Franklin Ahean	1.50
☐	E2 Harold Ballard	3.00
☐	E3 Billy Burch	1.50
☐	E4 Bill Chadwick	1.50
☐	E5 Sprague Cleghorn	3.00
☐	E6 Rusty Crawford	1.50
☐	E7 Alex Delvecchio	4.00
☐	E8 George Dudley	1.50
☐	E9 Ted Kennedy	5.00
☐	E10 Edouard Lalonde	4.00
☐	E11 Billy McGimsie	1.50
☐	E12 Frank Nighbor	3.00
☐	E13 Bobby Orr	20.00
☐	E14 Sen. Donat Raymond	1.50
☐	E15 Art Ross	3.00
☐	E16 Jack Walker	1.50
☐	F1 Doug Bentley	3.00
☐	F2 Walter Brown	1.50
☐	F3 Dit Clapper	3.00
☐	F4 Hap Day	1.50
☐	F5 Frank Dilio	1.50
☐	F6 Bobby Hewitson	1.50
☐	F7 Harry Howell	1.50
☐	F8 Paul Loicq	1.50
☐	F9 Sylvio Mantha	1.50
☐	F10 Jacques Plante (G)	12.00
☐	F11 George Richardson	1.50
☐	F12 Nels Stewart	3.00
☐	F13 Hod Stuart	1.50
☐	F14 Harry Trihey	1.50
☐	F15 Marty Walsh	1.50
☐	F16 Arthur Wirtz	1.50
☐	G1 Toe Blake	3.00
☐	G2 Frank Boucher	3.00
☐	G3 Turk Broda (G)	6.00
☐	G4 Harry Cameron	1.50
☐	G5 Leo Dandurand	1.50
☐	G6 Joe Hall	1.50
☐	G7 George Hay	1.50
☐	G8 William A. Hewitt	1.50
☐	G9 Bouse Hutton	1.50
☐	G10 Dick Irvin	1.50
☐	G11 Henri Richard	5.00
☐	G12 John Ross Robertson	1.50
☐	G13 Frank D. Smith	1.50
☐	G14 Allan Stanley	1.50
☐	G15 Norm Ullman	1.50
☐	G16 Harry Watson	1.50
☐	H1 Clint Benedict (G)	3.00
☐	H2 Richard Boon	1.50
☐	H3 Gordie Drillon	3.00
☐	H4 Bill Gadsby	1.50
☐	H5 Rod Gilbert	1.50
☐	H6 Francis (Moose) Goheen	1.50
☐	H7 Tommy Gorman	1.50
☐	H8 Glenn Hall (G)	7.50
☐	H9 Red Horner	1.50
☐	H10 John Kilpatrick	1.50
☐	H11 Robert LeBel	1.50
☐	H12 Howie Morenz	15.00
☐	H13 Fred Scanlan	1.50
☐	H14 Tommy Smith	1.50
☐	H15 Fred C. Waghorne	1.50
☐	H16 Cooney Weiland	1.50
☐	I1 Weston W. Adams	1.50
☐	I2 Montagu Allan	1.50
☐	I3 Frankie Brimsek (G)	4.00
☐	I4 Angus Campbell	1.50
☐	I5 Bill Cook	3.00
☐	I6 Tommy Dunderdale	1.50
☐	I7 Emile Francis	1.50
☐	I8 Chuck Gardiner (G)	3.00
☐	I9 Elmer Lach	3.00
☐	I10 Frank Mahovlich	5.00
☐	I11 Didier Pitre	1.50
☐	I12 Joe Primeau	3.00
☐	I13 Frank Rankin	1.50
☐	I14 Ernie Russell	1.50
☐	I15 W. Thayer Tutt	1.50
☐	I16 Harry Westwick	1.50
☐	J1 Jack J. Adams	1.50
☐	J2 J. Frank Ahearne	1.50
☐	J3 J.P. Bickell	1.50
☐	J4 John Bucyk	3.00
☐	J5 Art Coulter	1.50
☐	J6 Graham Drinkwater	1.50
☐	J7 George Hainsworth (G)	4.00
☐	J8 Tim Horton	7.00
☐	J9 Frederic McLaughlin	1.50
☐	J10 Dickie Moore	3.00
☐	J11 Pierre Pilote	1.50
☐	J12 Claude Robinson	1.50
☐	J13 Sweeny Schriner	1.50
☐	J14 Oliver Seibert	1.50
☐	J15 Albert Smith	1.50
☐	J16 Phat Wilson	1.50
☐	K1 Yvan Cournoyer	3.00
☐	K2 Scotty Davidson	1.50
☐	K3 Cy Denneny	3.00
☐	K4 Bill Durnan (G)	4.00
☐	K5 Wilf (Shorty) Green	1.50
☐	K6 Riley Hern (G)	3.00
☐	K7 Bryan Hextall, Sr.	1.50
☐	K8 Bill Jennings	1.50
☐	K9 Gordon W. Juckes	1.50
☐	K10 Paddy Moran (G)	3.00
☐	K11 James D. Norris	1.50
☐	K12 Harry Oliver	1.50
☐	K13 Sam Pollock	1.50
☐	K14 Marcel Pronovost	1.50
☐	K15 Jack Ruttan	1.50
☐	K16 Earl Seibert	1.50
☐	L1 Buck Boucher	1.50
☐	L2 George V. Brown	1.50
☐	L3 Arthur F. Farrell	1.50
☐	L4 Herb Gardiner	1.50
☐	L5 Si Griffis	1.50
☐	L6 Harry Holmes (G)	3.00
☐	L7 Harry Hyland	1.50
☐	L8 Tommy Ivan	1.50
☐	L9 Jack Laviolette	1.50
☐	L10 Ted Lindsay	5.00
☐	L11 Francis Nelson	1.50
☐	L12 William Northey	1.50
☐	L13 Babe Pratt	1.50
☐	L14 Chuck Rayner (G)	3.00
☐	L15 Mike Rodden	1.50
☐	L16 Milt Schmidt	3.00
☐	M1 Emile (Butch) Bouchard	1.50
☐	M2 Jack Butterfield	1.50
☐	M3 Joseph Cattarinich (G)	3.00
☐	M4 Alex Connell (G)	3.00
☐	M5 Bill Cowley	2.50
☐	M6 Chaucer Elliott	1.50
☐	M7 Jimmy Gardner	1.50
☐	M8 Bernie Geoffrion	5.00
☐	M9 Tom Hooper	1.50
☐	M10 Syd Howe	1.50
☐	M11 Harvey Jackson	3.00
☐	M12 Al Leader	1.50
☐	M13 Kevin Maxwell	1.50
☐	M14 Blair Russell	1.50
☐	M15 Bill Wirtz	1.50
☐	M16 Gump Worsley (G)	5.00
☐	N1 George Armstrong	3.00
☐	N2 Ace Bailey	4.00
☐	N3 Jack Darragh	1.50
☐	N4 Ken Dryden (G)	12.00
☐	N5 Eddie Gerard	1.50
☐	N6 Jack Gibson	1.50
☐	N7 Hugh Lehman (G)	3.00
☐	N8 Mickey MacKay	1.50
☐	N9 Joe Malone	1.50
☐	N10 Bruce A. Norris	3.00
☐	N11 J.A. O'Brien	1.50
☐	N12 Lynn Patrick	1.50
☐	N13 Tommy Phillips	1.50
☐	N14 Allan W. Pickard	1.50
☐	N15 Jack Stewart	1.50
☐	N16 Frank Udvari	1.50
☐	O1 Syl Apps	3.00
☐	O2 John Ashley	1.50
☐	O3 Marty Barry	1.50
☐	O4 Andy Bathgate	1.50
☐	O5 Johnny Bower (G)	5.00
☐	O6 Frank Buckland	1.50
☐	O7 James Dunn	1.50
☐	O8 Mike Grant	1.50
☐	O9 Doug Harvey	5.00
☐	O10 George McNamara	1.50
☐	O11 Stan Mikita	5.00
☐	O12 Sen. H. de M. Molson	1.50
☐	O13 Gordon Roberts	1.50
☐	O14 Eddie Shore	12.00
☐	O15 Bruce Stuart	1.50
☐	O16 Carl Voss	1.50

1983 & 1987 HALL OF FAME CARDS

These cards measure the standard 2 1/2" x 3 1/2". The first series was released in 1983. The second set was released in 1987 and added another 21 cards to include Hall of Fame inductees after 1983. The two sets are distinguished by the copyright year marked on the backs of the cards. The 1987 series also includes career statistics. Colour artwork interpretations were supplied by Carlton McDiarmid. Prices for the 1983 copyright and 1987 copyright are the same.

1983 Set (240 cards): **90.00**
1987 Set (261 cards): **110.00**
Common Player: **.75**

	Hockey Hall of Fame	NM-MT
☐☐	1 Maurice Richard, Mont.	9.00
☐☐	2 Sid Abel	1.50
☐☐	3 Punch Broadbent, OH.	1.50
☐☐	4 Clarence Campbell	.75
☐☐	5 Neil Colville, NYRa.	.75
☐☐	6 Charlie Conacher, Toro.	2.50
☐☐	7 Red Dutton, NYAm..	.75
☐☐	8 Foster Hewitt	1.50
☐☐	9 Mickey Ion, Referee	.75
☐☐	10 Ernest (Moose) Johnson	.75
☐☐	11 Bill Mosienko, Chic.	.75
☐☐	12 Russell (Barney) Stanley	.75
☐☐	13 Lord Stanley	.75
☐☐	14 Fred Taylor	1.50
☐☐	15 Tiny Thompson (G)	1.50
☐☐	16 Gordie Howe, Detr.	9.00
☐☐	17 Hobey Baker	.75
☐☐	18 Frank Calder	.75
☐☐	19 Jim Hendy	.75
☐☐	20 Frank Foyston, Sea.	.75
☐☐	21 Harry Lumley (G)	1.50
☐☐	22 Reg Noble, Toronto St. Pats.	.75
☐☐	23 Frank Patrick, Vanc.	.75
☐☐	24 Harvey Pulford, Ott.	.75
☐☐	25 Ken Reardon	.75
☐☐	26 Joe Simpson, NYAm.	.75
☐☐	27 Conn Smythe	.75
☐☐	28 Red Storey	.75
☐☐	29 Lloyd Turner	.75
☐☐	30 Georges Vézina (G), Mont.	5.00
☐☐	31 Jean Béliveau, Mont.	5.00
☐☐	32 Max Bentley, Toro.	1.25
☐☐	33 King Clancy, Toro.	2.50
☐☐	34 Babe Dye, Toronto St. Pats.	.75
☐☐	35 Ebbie Goodfellow, Detr.	.75
☐☐	36 Charles Hay	.75
☐☐	37 Percy Lesueur (G)	1.50
☐☐	38 Tommy Lockhart	.75
☐☐	39 Jack Marshall	.75
☐☐	40 Lester Patrick, NYRa.	1.50
☐☐	41 Frank Selke	.75
☐☐	42 Cooper Smeaton	.75
☐☐	43 Hooley Smith, Mont. Maroons	.75
☐☐	44 James T. Sutherland	.75
☐☐	45 Fred Whitcroft, Kenora	.75
☐☐	46 Terry Sawchuk (G)	6.00
☐☐	47 Charles Adams, Bost.	.75
☐☐	48 Russell Bowie	.75
☐☐	49 Frank Fredickson, Error	.75
☐☐	50 Billy Gilmour, Ott.	.75
☐☐	51 Ching Johnson, NYRa.	1.50
☐☐	52 Tom Johnson	.75
☐☐	53 Aurèle Joliat, Mont.	3.00
☐☐	54 Duke Keats, Chic.	.75
☐☐	55 Red Kelly	1.50
☐☐	56 Frank McGee	.75
☐☐	57 James D. Norris, Detr.	.75
☐☐	58 Philip Ross, Cup Trustee	.75
☐☐	59 Babe Siebert	.75
☐☐	60 Roy Worters (G), NYA.	1.50
☐☐	61 Bobby Orr, Bost.	10.00
☐☐	62 T. Franklin Ahearn	.75
☐☐	63 Harold Ballard, Toro.	1.50
☐☐	64 Billy Burch	.75
☐☐	65 Bill Chadwick	.75
☐☐	66 Sprague Cleghorn	1.50
☐☐	67 Rusty Crawford	.75

☐☐	68 George Dudley, CAHA President	.75
☐☐	69 Ted Kennedy	2.50
☐☐	70 Edouard Lalonde	2.00
☐☐	71 Billy McGimsie	.75
☐☐	72 Frank Nighbor, OH.	1.50
☐☐	73 Donat Raymond	.75
☐☐	74 Art Ross	1.50
☐☐	75 Jack Walker, Sea.	.75
☐☐	76 Jacques Plante (G)	6.00
☐☐	77 Doug Bentley	1.50
☐☐	78 Walter Brown	.75
☐☐	79 Dit Clapper	1.50
☐☐	80 Hap Day	.75
☐☐	81 Frank Dilio	.75
☐☐	82 Bobby Hewitson	.75
☐☐	83 Harry Howell	.75
☐☐	84 Sylvio Mantha	.75
☐☐	85 George Richardson	.75
☐☐	86 Nels Stewart	1.50
☐☐	87 Hod Stuart	.75
☐☐	88 Harry Trihey	.75
☐☐	89 Marty Walsh	.75
☐☐	90 Arthur Wirtz, Chic.	.75
☐☐	91 Henri Richard	2.50
☐☐	92 Toe Blake	1.50
☐☐	93 Frank Boucher	1.50
☐☐	94 Turk Broda (G)	3.00
☐☐	95 Harry Cameron	.75
☐☐	96 Leo Dandurand	.75
☐☐	97 Joe Hall	.75
☐☐	98 George Hay	.75
☐☐	99 William A. Hewitt	.75
☐☐	100 J.B. Hutton (G), Ott.	.75
☐☐	101 Dick Irvin	.75
☐☐	102 John Ross Robertson	.75
☐☐	103 Frank D. Smith, MTHL Secretary	.75
☐☐	104 Norm Ullman	.75
☐☐	105 Harry Watson	.75
☐☐	106 Howie Morenz	6.00
☐☐	107 Clint Benedict (G)	1.50
☐☐	108 Richard Boon, Mont. Wanderers	.75
☐☐	109 Gordie Drillon	1.50
☐☐	110 Bill Gadsby	.75
☐☐	111 Rod Gilbert	.75
☐☐	112 Francis (Moose) Goheen	.75
☐☐	113 Tommy Gorman	.75
☐☐	114 Glenn Hall (G)	3.00
☐☐	115 Red Horner	.75
☐☐	116 John Kilpatrick, NYRa.	.75
☐☐	117 Robert LeBel	.75
☐☐	118 Fred Scanlan	.75
☐☐	119 Fred C. Waghorne	.75
☐☐	120 Cooney Weiland	.75
☐☐	121 Frank Mahovlich	2.50
☐☐	122 Weston W. Adams Sr.	.75
☐☐	123 Montagu Allan	.75
☐☐	124 Frankie Brimsek (G)	2.00
☐☐	125 Angus Campbell	.75
☐☐	126 Bill Cook	1.50
☐☐	127 Tommy Dunderdale	.75
☐☐	128 Chuck Gardiner (G), Chic.	1.50
☐☐	129 Elmer Lach	1.50
☐☐	130 Didier Pitre	.75
☐☐	131 Joe Primeau	1.50
☐☐	132 Frank Rankin	.75
☐☐	133 Ernie Russell	.75
☐☐	134 W. Thayer Tutt	.75
☐☐	135 Harry Westwick	.75
☐☐	136 Yvan Cournoyer	1.50
☐☐	137 Scotty Davidson	.75
☐☐	138 Cy Denneny	1.50
☐☐	139 Bill Durnan (G)	2.00
☐☐	140 Wilf (Shorty) Green	.75
☐☐	141 Bryan Hextall, Sr.	.75
☐☐	142 William Jennings	.75
☐☐	143 Gordon W. Juckes	.75
☐☐	144 Paddy Moran (G)	1.50
☐☐	145 James D. Norris	.75
☐☐	146 Harry Oliver	.75
☐☐	147 Sam Pollock	.75
☐☐	148 Marcel Pronovost	.75
☐☐	149 Jack Ruttan	.75
☐☐	150 Earl Seibert	.75
☐☐	151 Ted Lindsay	2.50
☐☐	152 George V. Brown	.75
☐☐	153 Arthur Farrell	.75
☐☐	154 Herb Gardiner	.75
☐☐	155 Si Griffis, Kenora	.75
☐☐	156 Harry Holmes (G)	1.50
☐☐	157 Harry Hyland, Mont. Wanderers	.75
☐☐	158 Tommy Ivan	.75
☐☐	159 Jack Laviolette	.75
☐☐	160 Francis Nelson, OHA	.75
☐☐	161 William Northey, Mont. AAA President	.75
☐☐	162 Babe Pratt	.75
☐☐	163 Chuck Rayner (G)	1.50
☐☐	164 Mike Rodden	.75
☐☐	165 Milt Schmidt	1.50
☐☐	166 Bernie Geoffrion	2.50
☐☐	167 Jack Butterfield	.75
☐☐	168 Joseph Cattarinich (G)	1.50
☐☐	169 Alex Connell (G)	1.50
☐☐	170 Bill Cowley	1.25
☐☐	171 Chaucer Elliott	.75
☐☐	172 Jimmy Gardner, Mont. Wanderers	.75
☐☐	173 Tom Hooper, Kenora	.75
☐☐	174 Syd Howe	.75
☐☐	175 Harvey (Busher) Jackson	1.50
☐☐	176 Al Leader	.75
☐☐	177 Fred Maxwell	.75
☐☐	178 Blair Russell	.75
☐☐	179 Bill Wirtz, Chic.	.75
☐☐	180 Gump Worsley (G)	2.50
☐☐	181 John Bucyk	1.50
☐☐	182 Jack J. Adams	.75
☐☐	183 J. Frank Ahearne, IIHF	.75
☐☐	184 J.P. Bickell	.75
☐☐	185 Art Coulter	.75
☐☐	186 Graham Drinkwater	.75
☐☐	187 George Hainsworth (G)	2.00
☐☐	188 Tim Horton	3.50
☐☐	189 Frederic McLaughlin	.75
☐☐	190 Dickie Moore	1.50
☐☐	191 Pierre Pilote	.75
☐☐	192 Claude Robinson	.75
☐☐	193 Oliver Seibert	.75
☐☐	194 Alf Smith	.75
☐☐	195 Gord (Phat) Wilson	.75
☐☐	196 Ken Dryden (G), Mont.	6.00
☐☐	197 George Armstrong	1.50
☐☐	198 Ace Bailey	2.00
☐☐	199 Jack Darragh	.75
☐☐	200 Eddie Gerard	.75
☐☐	201 Jack Gibson	.75
☐☐	202 Hugh Lehman (G)	1.50
☐☐	203 Mickey MacKay	.75
☐☐	204 Joe Malone	1.50
☐☐	205 Bruce Norris	.75
☐☐	206 J.A. O'Brien	.75
☐☐	207 Lynn Patrick	.75
☐☐	208 Tom Phillips	.75
☐☐	209 Allan Pickard	.75
☐☐	210 Jack Stewart, Detr.	.75
☐☐	211 Johnny Bower (G)	2.50
☐☐	212 Syl Apps, Sr.	1.50
☐☐	213 John Ashley, Referee	.75
☐☐	214 Marty Barry	.75
☐☐	215 Andy Bathgate	.75
☐☐	216 Frank Buckland	.75
☐☐	217 James Dunn	.75
☐☐	218 Mike Grant	.75
☐☐	219 Doug Harvey	2.50
☐☐	220 George McNamara	.75
☐☐	221 Hartland Molson	.75
☐☐	222 Gordon Roberts	.75
☐☐	223 Eddie Shore	5.00
☐☐	224 Bruce Stuart	.75
☐☐	225 Carl Voss	.75
☐☐	226 Stan Mikita, Chic.	2.50
☐☐	227 Donald Bain	.75
☐☐	228 Emile (Butch) Bouchard	.75
☐☐	229 George Boucher	.75
☐☐	230 Alex Delvecchio	2.00
☐☐	231 Emile Francis	.75
☐☐	232 Riley Hern (G)	1.50
☐☐	233 Fred Hume	.75
☐☐	234 Paul Loicq	.75
☐☐	235 Bill Quackenbush	.75
☐☐	236 Sweeny Schriner	.75
☐☐	237 Tommy Smith	.75
☐☐	238 Allan Stanley	.75
☐☐	239 Anatoli Tarasov	.75
☐☐	240 Frank Udvari	.75
☐	241 Harry Sinden	.75
☐	242 Bobby Hull	6.00
☐	243 Punch Imlach, Buff.	.75
☐	244 Phil Esposito	4.00
☐	245 Jacques Lemaire, Mont.	1.50
☐	246 Bernard Marcel	.75
☐	247 Rudy Pilous, Chic.	.75
☐	248 Bert Olmstead, Mont.	.75
☐	249 Jean Ratelle, NYRa.	1.50
☐	250 Gerry Cheevers (G)	2.00
☐	251 Bill Hanley, OHA Secretary Mgr.	.75
☐	252 Léo Boivin, Bost.	.75
☐	253 Jake Milford, Vanc.	.75
☐	254 John Mariucci	.75
☐	255 Dave Keon, Toro.	2.00
☐	256 Serge Savard	1.50
☐	257 John Ziegler, NHL President	.75
☐	258 Bobby Clarke, Phil.	3.00
☐	259 Ed Giacomin (G), NYRa.	1.50
☐	260 Jacques Laperrière, Mont.	1.50
☐	261 Matt Pavelich, NHL Linesman	.75

1983 - 84 DERNIÈRE PHOTOS

This multi-sport series of photos were inserted in Dernière magazine from 1972 through 1984. Three holes were punched on the left side to allow for storage in a binder. The series featured Montréal Canadiens players. These photos measure 8" x 10".

Dernière		NM
☐	20NOV Superstar	3.00
☐	27NOV Rick Wamsley (G)	5.00
☐	4DEC Larry Robinson	8.00
☐	11DEC Guy Lafleur	12.00
☐	18DEC Mario Tremblay	5.00
☐	25DEC Mats Näslund	3.00
☐	1JAN Chris Nilan	8.00
☐	8JAN Les Canadiens	20.00
☐	15JAN Marcel Dionne	10.00
☐	22JAN Pierre Mondou	3.00
☐	29JAN Steve Shutt	7.00
☐	5FEB Bill Root	3.00

1983 - 84 ESSO

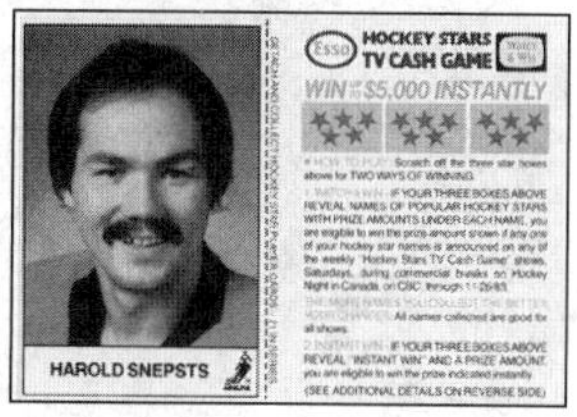

There are two versions to each card: a French version and an English version. These cut cards measure 2" x 3".

Complete Set (21 cards):		**25.00**
Esso Canada		**NM**
☐☐	Glenn Anderson, Edmo.	2.00
☐☐	John Anderson, Toro.	1.00
☐☐	Dave Babych, Winn.	1.00
☐☐	Richard Brodeur (G), Vanc.	2.00
☐☐	Paul Coffey, Edmo.	3.50
☐☐	Bill Derlago, Toro.	1.00
☐☐	Bob Gainey, Mont.	2.00
☐☐	Michel Goulet, Québ.	2.00
☐☐	Dale Hawerchuk, Winn.	3.00
☐☐	Dale Hunter, Québ.	1.50
☐☐	Morris Lukowich, Winn.	1.00
☐☐	Lanny McDonald, Calg.	2.00
☐☐	Mark Messier, Edmo.	6.00
☐☐	Jim Peplinski, Calg.	1.00
☐☐	Paul Reinhart, Calg.	1.00
☐☐	Larry Robinson, Mont.	2.00
☐☐	Stan Smyl, Vanc.	1.00
☐☐	Harold Snepsts, Vanc.	1.00
☐☐	Marc Tardif, Québ.	1.00
☐☐	Mario Tremblay, Mont.	1.00
☐☐	Rick Vaive, Toro.	1.00

1983 - 84 FUNMATE PUFFY STICKERS

These oval stickers were issued six to a panel. The individual panels measure 1 3/8" x 1 13/16".

Complete Set (25 panels):		**50.00**
Album:		**8.00**
Funmate		**NM-MT**
☐	1 D. Risebrough/ W. Gretzky/ M. Näslund/ B. Derlago/ R. Brodeur/ D. Babych	20.00
☐	2 G. Anderson/ L. Robinson/ R. Vaive/ S. Smyl/ S. Arniel/ D. Edwards	4.00
☐	3 R. Walter/ P. Ihnacak/ T. Gradin/ M. Lukowich/ K. Nilsson/ P. Coffey	3.00
☐	4 J. Anderson/ D. Williams/ B. Mullen/ S. Tambellini/ M. Messier/ G. Lafleur	5.00
☐	5 D. Rota/ D. Hawerchuk/ P. Reinhart/ J. Kurri/ M. Tremblay/ M. Palmateer (G)	4.00
☐	6 P. MacLean/ L. McDonald/ K. Linseman/ S. Shutt/ B. Salming/ K. McCarthy	4.00
☐	7 B. Pederson/ M. Foligno/ J. Fox/ D. Lever/ B. Clarke/ G. Malone	3.00
☐	8 G. Perreault/ C. Simmer/ H. Marini/ M. Howe/ R. Kehoe/ J. Schoenfeld	4.00
☐	9 L. Murphy/ P. Russell/ B. Barber/ M. Bullard/ P. Peeters (G)/ J. Van Boxmeer	4.00
☐	10 T. Levo/ D. Sittler/ P. Gardner/ R. Middleton/ R. Cloutier/ B. Nicholls	4.00
☐	11 B. Propp/ M. Dion/ R. Bourque/ D. McCourt/ M. Dionne/ B. MacMillan	5.00
☐	12 R. Carlyle/ T. O'Reilly/ P. Housley/ D. Taylor/ G. Resch (G)/ B. Wilson	3.00
☐	13 T. Esposito (G)/ R. Duguay/ P. Larouche/ N. Broten/ P. Stastny/ B. Dunlop	4.00
☐	14 W. McKechnie/ R. Siltanen/ B. Smith (G)/ A. Stastny/ M. Liut (G)/ D. Wilson	3.00
☐	15 B. Stoughton/ D. Ciccarelli/ M. Goulet/ J. Pettersson/ T. Lysiak/ B. Park	4.00
☐	16 C. Hartsburg/ M. Stastny/ R. Ramage/ A. Secord/ J. Ogrodnick/ G. Millen	2.00
☐	17 T. McKegney/ B. Sutter/ S. Larmer/ D. Gare/ M. Johnson/ B. Bellows	3.00
☐	18 B. Federko/ D. Savard/ R. Larson/ R. Francis/ D. Maruk/ D. Bouchard	4.00
☐	19 M. Bossy/ A. Hedberg/ R. Langway/ B. Smith (G)/ R. Ruotsalainen/ M. Novy	4.00
☐	20 B. Beck/ B. Carpenter/ C. Gillies/ R. McClanahan/ B. Engblom/ D. Potvin	3.00
☐	21 M. Gartner/ J. Tonelli/ W. Huber/ P. Riggin (G)/ B. Trottier/ D. Maloney	4.00
☐	Norris Division: Blackhawks/ Red Wings/ North Stars/ Blues/ Maple Leafs/ NHL	3.00
☐	Patrick Division: Devils/ Islanders/ Rangers/ Flyers/ Penguins/ Capitals	3.00
☐	Adams Division: Bruins/ Sabres/ Whalers/ Canadiens/ Nordiques/ NHL	3.00
☐	Smythe Division: Flames/ Oilers/ Kings/ Canucks/ Jets/ NHL	3.00

1983 - 84 O-PEE-CHEE

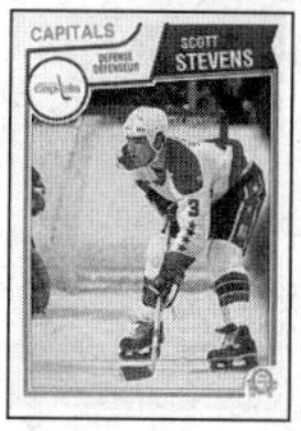

These cards measure the standard 2 1/2" x 3 1/2".

Complete Set (396 cards):		**120.00**
Common Player:		**.30**
O-Pee-Chee		**NM-MT**
☐	1 TL: Mike Bossy, NYIs.	1.00
☐	2 HL: Denis Potvin, NYIs.	.50
☐	3 Mike Bossy, NYIs.	3.50
☐	4 Bob Bourne, NYIs.	.30
☐	**5 Billy Carroll, NYIs. RC**	**.75**
☐	6 Clark Gillies, NYIs.	.50
☐	7 Butch Goring, NYIs.	.50
☐	**8 Mats Hallin, NYIs. RC**	**.75**
☐	9 Tomas Jonsson, NYIs.	.30
☐	10 Gord Lane, NYIs.	.30
☐	11 Dave Langevin, NYIs.	.50
☐	**12 Rollie Melanson (G), NYIs. RC**	**1.50**
☐	13 Ken Morrow, NYIs.	.30
☐	14 Bob Nystrom, NYIs.	.30
☐	15 Stefan Persson, NYIs.	.30
☐	16 Denis Potvin, NYIs.	1.50
☐	17 Billy Smith (G), NYIs.	1.50
☐	18 Brent Sutter, NYIs.	.50
☐	19 Duane Sutter, NYIs.	.50
☐	20 John Tonelli, NYIs.	.50
☐	21 Bryan Trottier, NYIs.	2.00
☐	22 TL: Wayne Gretzky, Edmo.	6.00
☐	23 HL: Messier & Gretzky, Edmo.	45.00
☐	24 Glenn Anderson, Edmo.	1.25
☐	25 Paul Coffey, Edmo.	12.00
☐	26 Lee Fogolin, Edmo.	.30
☐	27 Grant Fuhr (G), Edmo.	8.00
☐	**28 Randy Gregg, Edmo. RC**	**1.50**
☐	29 Wayne Gretzky, Edmo.	35.00
☐	**30 Charlie Huddy, Edmo. RC**	**2.00**
☐	31 Pat Hughes, Edmo.	.30
☐	32 Dave Hunter, Edmo.	.30
☐	**33 Don Jackson, Edmo. RC**	**.75**
☐	34 Jari Kurri, Edmo.	7.00
☐	35 Willy Lindstrom, Edmo.	.30
☐	36 Ken Linseman, Edmo.	.30
☐	37 Kevin Lowe, Edmo.	.75
☐	38 Dave Lumley, Edmo.	.30
☐	39 Mark Messier, Edmo.	15.00
☐	40 Andy Moog (G), Edmo.	5.00
☐	**41 Jaroslav Pouzar, Edmo. RC**	**.75**
☐	42 Tom Roulston, Edmo.	.30
☐	43 TL: Rick Middleton, Bost.	.50
☐	44 HL: Pete Peeters (G), Bost.	.50
☐	45 Raymond Bourque, Bost.	10.00
☐	46 Bruce Crowder, Bost.	.30

☐ 47 Keith Crowder, Bost. .30
☐ **48 Luc Dufour, Bost. RC .75**
☐ 49 Tom Fergus, Bost. .30
☐ 50 Steve Kasper, Bost. .30
☐ **51 Gord Kluzak, Bost. RC .75**
☐ **52 Mike Krushelnyski, Bost. RC 1.25**
☐ 53 Peter McNab, Bost. .30
☐ 54 Rick Middleton, Bost. .50
☐ 55 Mike Milbury, Bost. .50
☐ 56 Mike O'Connell, Bost. .30
☐ 57 Barry Pederson, Bost. .30
☐ 58 Pete Peeters (G), Bost. .50
☐ 59 Jim Schoenfeld, Bost. .50
☐ 60 TL: Tony McKegney, Buff. .30
☐ 61 HL: Bob Sauvé (G), Buff. .50
☐ 62 Réal Cloutier, Buff. .30
☐ 63 Mike Foligno, Buff. .30
☐ 64 Bill Hajt, Buff. .30
☐ **65 Phil Housley, Buff. RC 10.00**
☐ 66 Dale McCourt, Buff. (Toro.) .30
☐ 67 Gilbert Perreault, Buff. 1.50
☐ **68 Brent Peterson, Buff. RC 1.00**
☐ 69 Craig Ramsay, Buff. .50
☐ 70 Mike Ramsey, Buff. .30
☐ 71 Bob Sauvé (G), Buff. .50
☐ 72 Ric Seiling, Buff. .30
☐ 73 John Van Boxmeer, Buff. (Que) .30
☐ 74 TL: Lanny McDonald, Calg. .50
☐ 75 HL: Lanny McDonald, Calg. .50
☐ **76 Ed Beers, Calg. RC .75**
☐ 77 Steve Bozek, Calg. .30
☐ 78 Guy Chouinard, Calg. (SLou.) .30
☐ 79 Mike Eaves, Calg. .30
☐ 80 Don Edwards (G), Calg. .50
☐ **81 Kari Eloranta, Calg. RC 1.00**
☐ **82 Dave Hindmarch, Calg. RC .75**
☐ 83 Jamie Hislop, Calg. .30
☐ **84 Jim Jackson, Calg. RC .75**
☐ 85 Steve Konroyd, Calg. .30
☐ 86 Réjean Lemelin (G), Calg. .50
☐ 87 Lanny McDonald, Calg. 1.00
☐ **88 Greg Meredith, Calg. RC .75**
☐ 89 Kent Nilsson, Calg. .50
☐ 90 Jim Peplinski, Calg. .30
☐ 91 Paul Reinhart, Calg. .30
☐ 92 Doug Risebrough, Calg. .30
☐ 93 Steve Tambellini, Calg. .30
☐ **94 Mickey Volcan, Calg. RC .75**
☐ 95 TL: Al Secord, Chic. .30
☐ 96 HL: Denis Savard, Chic. 1.00
☐ 97 Murray Bannerman (G), Chic. .50
☐ 98 Keith Brown, Chic. .30
☐ 99 Tony Esposito (G), Chic. .75
☐ **100 Dave Feamster, Chic. RC .75**
☐ 101 Greg Fox, Chic. .30
☐ 102 Curt Fraser, Chic. .30
☐ **103 Bill Gardner, Chic. RC .75**
☐ 104 Tim Higgins, Chic. .30
☐ **105 Steve Larmer, Chic. RC, Error (Steve Ludzik) 14.00**
☐ **106 Steve Ludzik, Chic. RC, Error (Steve Larmer) 4.00**

Because Larmer and Ludzig's images are reversed on cards 105 and 106, they are often sold as a pair.

☐ 107 Tom Lysiak, Chic. .30
☐ 108 Bob Murray, Chic. .30
☐ **109 Rick Paterson, Chic. RC .75**
☐ 110 Rich Preston, Chic. .30
☐ 111 Denis Savard, Chic. 3.00
☐ 112 Al Secord, Chic. .30
☐ 113 Darryl Sutter, Chic. .50
☐ 114 Doug Wilson, Chic. .60
☐ 115 TL: John Ogrodnick, Detr. .30
☐ 116 HL: Corrado Micalef (G), Detr. .50
☐ 117 John Barrett, Detr. .30
☐ 118 Ivan Boldirev, Detr. .30
☐ 119 Colin Campbell, Detr. .50
☐ **120 Murray Craven, Detr. RC 1.00**
☐ 121 Ron Duguay, Detr. .30
☐ 122 Dwight Foster, Detr. .30
☐ 123 Danny Gare, Detr. .50
☐ 124 Eddie Johnstone, Detr. .30
☐ 125 Reed Larson, Detr. .30
☐ 126 Corrado Micalef (G), Detr. RC, Error (Carrado) .50
☐ 127 Ed Mio (G), Detr. .50
☐ 128 John Ogrodnick, Detr. .30
☐ 129 Brad Park, Detr. 1.00
☐ 130 Greg Smith, Detr. .30
☐ **131 Ken Solheim, Detr. (Minn.) RC .75**
☐ 132 Bob Manno, Detr. .30
☐ 133 Paul Woods .30
☐ 134 Checklist 1 (1 - 132) 4.00
☐ 135 TL: Blaine Stoughton, Hart. .30
☐ 136 HL: Blaine Stoughton, Hart. .30
☐ 137 Richie Dunn, Hart. .30
☐ 138 Ron Francis, Hart. 7.00
☐ 139 Marty Howe, Hart. .30
☐ 140 Mark Johnson, Hart. .30
☐ **141 Paul Lawless, Hart. RC .75**
☐ 142 Merlin Malinowski, Hart. (Playing in Europe) .30
☐ 143 Greg Millen (G), Hart. .50
☐ **144 Ray Neufeld, Hart. RC 1.25**
☐ 145 Joel Quenneville, Hart. .50
☐ 146 Risto Siltanen, Hart. .30
☐ 147 Blaine Stoughton, Hart. .30
☐ 148 Doug Sulliman, Hart. .30
☐ **149 Bob Sullivan, Hart. RC .75**
☐ 150 TL: Marcel Dionne, LosA. .50
☐ 151 HL: Marcel Dionne, LosA. .50
☐ 152 Marcel Dionne, LosA. 1.50
☐ **153 Daryl Evans, LosA. RC .75**
☐ 154 Jim Fox, LosA. .30
☐ 155 Mark Hardy, LosA. .30
☐ **156 Gary Laskoski (G), LosA. RC 1.00**
☐ 157 Kevin LaVallée, LosA. .30
☐ 158 Dave Lewis, LosA. (NJer.) .50
☐ 159 Larry Murphy, LosA. 2.00
☐ **160 Bernie Nicholls, LosA. RC 6.00**
☐ 161 Terry Ruskowski, LosA. .30
☐ 162 Charlie Simmer, LosA. .30
☐ 163 Dave Taylor, LosA. .60
☐ 164 TL: Dino Ciccarelli, Minn. 1.00
☐ 165 HL: Brian Bellows, Minn. 1.75
☐ 166 Don Beaupré (G), Minn. .50
☐ **167 Brian Bellows, Minn. RC 5.00**
☐ 168 Neal Broten, Minn. .75
☐ 169 Steve Christoff, Minn. (LosA.) .30
☐ 170 Dino Ciccarelli, Minn. 2.00
☐ 171 George Ferguson, Minn. .30
☐ 172 Craig Hartsburg, Minn. .50
☐ 173 Al MacAdam, Minn. .30
☐ 174 Dennis Maruk, Minn. .30
☐ 175 Brad Maxwell, Minn. .30
☐ 176 Tom McCarthy, Minn. .30
☐ 177 Gilles Meloche (G), Minn. .50
☐ 178 Steve Payne, Minn. .30
☐ 179 Willi Plett, Minn. .30
☐ 180 Gord Roberts, Minn. .30
☐ 181 Bobby Smith, Minn. (Mont.) .50
☐ 182 TL: Mark Napier, Mont. .30
☐ 183 HL: Guy Lafleur, Mont. 1.00
☐ 184 Keith Acton, Mont. (Minn.) .30
☐ **185 Guy Carbonneau, Mont. RC 10.00**
☐ **186 Gilbert Delorme, Mont. RC .75**
☐ 187 Bob Gainey, Mont. 1.00
☐ 188 Rick Green, Mont. .30
☐ 189 Guy Lafleur, Mont. 2.50
☐ **190 Craig Ludwig, Mont. RC 2.00**
☐ 191 Pierre Mondou, Mont. .30
☐ 192 Mark Napier, Mont. (Minn.) .30
☐ **193 Mats Näslund, Mont. RC, Error (wrong stats) 6.00**
☐ **194 Chris Nilan, Mont. RC 1.50**
☐ 195 Larry Robinson, Mont. 1.50
☐ **196 Bill Root, Mont. RC .75**
☐ 197 Richard Sévigny (G), Mont. .50
☐ 198 Steve Shutt, Mont. 1.00
☐ 199 Mario Tremblay, Mont. .30
☐ 200 Ryan Walter, Mont. .30
☐ 201 Rick Wamsley (G), Mont. .50
☐ 202 Doug Wickenheiser, Mont. .30
☐ 203 AW: Wayne Gretzky 6.00
☐ 204 AW: Wayne Gretzky 6.00
☐ 205 AW: Mike Bossy 1.00
☐ 206 AW: Steve Larmer 3.00
☐ 207 AW: Rod Langway .50
☐ 208 AW: Lanny McDonald .50
☐ 209 AW: Pete Peeters .50
☐ 210 RB: Mike Bossy, NYIs. 1.00
☐ 211 RB: Marcel Dionne, LosA. .50
☐ 212 RB: Wayne Gretzky, Edmo. 6.00
☐ 213 RB: Pat Hughes, Edmo. .30
☐ 214 RB: Rick Middleton, Bost. .50
☐ 215 LL: Wayne Gretzky, Edmo. 6.00
☐ 216 LL: Wayne Gretzky, Edmo. 6.00
☐ 217 LL: Wayne Gretzky, Edmo. 6.00
☐ 218 LL: Brian Propp, Phil. .30
☐ 219 LL: Paul Gardner/ Al Secord .30
☐ 220 LL: Randy Holt, Wash. .30
☐ 221 LL: Pete Peeters (G), Bost. .50
☐ 222 LL: Pete Peeters (G), Bost. .50
☐ 223 TL: Steve Tambellini, NJer. .30
☐ 224 HL: Don Lever, NJer. .30
☐ 225 Brent Ashton, NJer. (Minn.) .30
☐ 226 Mel Bridgman, NJer. .30
☐ 227 Aaron Broten, NJer. .30
☐ **228 Murray Brumwell, NJer. RC .75**
☐ 229 Garry Howatt, NJer. .30
☐ **230 Jeff Larmer, NJer. RC 1.50**
☐ 231 Don Lever, NJer. .30
☐ 232 Bob Lorimer, NJer. .30
☐ 233 Ron Low (G), NJer. .50
☐ 234 Bob MacMillan, NJer. .30
☐ **235 Hector Marini, NJer. RC .75**
☐ 236 Glenn Resch (G), NJer. .50
☐ 237 Phil Russell, NJer. .30
☐ 238 TL: Mark Pavelich, NYRa. .30
☐ 239 HL: Mark Pavelich, NYRa. .30
☐ **240 Bill Baker, NYRa. RC .75**
☐ 241 Barry Beck, NYRa. .30
☐ 242 Mike Blaisdell, NYRa. .30
☐ 243 Nick Fotiu, NYRa. .30
☐ 244 Robbie Ftorek, NYRa. .50
☐ 245 Anders Hedberg, NYRa. .50
☐ 246 Willie Huber, NYRa. .30
☐ 247 Tom Laidlaw, NYRa. .30
☐ 248 Mikko Leinonen, NYRa. .30
☐ 249 Dave Maloney, NYRa. .30
☐ 250 Don Maloney, NYRa. .30
☐ 251 Rob McClanahan, NYRa. .30
☐ 252 Mark Osborne, NYRa. .30
☐ 253 Mark Pavelich, NYRa. .30
☐ 254 Mike Rogers, NYRa. .30
☐ 255 Reijo Ruotsalainen, NYRa. .30
☐ 256 Checklist 2 (133 - 264) 4.00
☐ 257 TL: Darryl Sittler, Phil. .50
☐ 258 HL: Darryl Sittler, Phil. .50
☐ 259 Ray Allison, Phil. .30
☐ 260 Bill Barber, Phil. 1.00
☐ **261 Lindsay Carson, Phil. RC .75**
☐ 262 Bobby Clarke, Phil. 1.50
☐ 263 Doug Crossman, Phil. .30
☐ 264 Ron Flockhart, Phil. .30
☐ **265 Bob Froese (G), Phil. RC 1.50**
☐ 266 Paul Holmgren, Phil. .30
☐ 267 Mark Howe, Phil. .60
☐ **268 Pelle Lindbergh (G), Phil. RC 15.00**
☐ 269 Brad Marsh, Phil. .30
☐ 270 Brad McCrimmon, Phil. .50
☐ 271 Brian Propp, Phil. .50
☐ 272 Darryl Sittler, Phil. 1.50
☐ **273 Mark Taylor, Phil. RC .75**
☐ 274 TL: Rick Kehoe, Pitt. .30
☐ 275 HL: Paul Gardner, Pitt. .30
☐ 276 Pat Boutette, Pitt. .30
☐ 277 Mike Bullard, Pitt. .30
☐ 278 Randy Carlyle, Pitt. .30
☐ 279 Michel Dion (G), Pitt. .50
☐ 280 Paul Gardner, Pitt. .30
☐ **281 Dave Hannan, Pitt. RC 1.25**
☐ 282 Rick Kehoe, Pitt. .50
☐ **283 Randy Boyd, Pitt. RC .75**
☐ 284 Greg Malone, Pitt. (Hart.) .30
☐ **285 Doug Shedden, Pitt. RC .75**
☐ 286 André St. Laurent, Pitt. .30
☐ 287 TL: Michel Goulet, Québ. .75
☐ 288 HL: Michel Goulet, Québ. .75
☐ 289 Pierre Aubry, Québ. .30
☐ 290 Dan Bouchard (G), Québ. .50
☐ 291 Alain Côté, Québ. .30
☐ 292 Michel Goulet, Québ. 1.50
☐ 293 Dale Hunter, Québ. .75
☐ 294 Rick Lapointe, Québ. .30
☐ 295 Mario Marois, Québ. .30
☐ 296 Tony McKegney, Québ. .30
☐ **297 Randy Moller, Québ. RC .75**
☐ 298 Wilf Paiement, Québ. .30
☐ 299 Dave Pichette, Québ. .30
☐ 300 Normand Rochefort, Québ. .30
☐ **301 Louis Sleigher, Québ. RC .75**
☐ 302 Anton Stastny, Québ. .30
☐ 303 Marian Stastny, Québ. .30
☐ 304 Peter Stastny, Québ. 2.00
☐ 305 Marc Tardif, Québ. .30
☐ 306 Wally Weir, Québ. .30
☐ 307 Blake Wesley, Québ. .30
☐ 308 TL: Brian Sutter, SLou. .50
☐ 309 HL: Mike Liut (G), SLou. .50
☐ 310 Wayne Babych, SLou. .30
☐ 311 Jack Brownschidle, SLou. .30
☐ **312 Mike Crombeen, SLou. (Hart.) RC .75**
☐ **313 André Doré, SLou. RC .75**
☐ 314 Blake Dunlop, SLou. .30
☐ 315 Bernie Federko, SLou. .60
☐ 316 Mike Liut (G), SLou. .60
☐ 317 Joe Mullen, SLou. 2.50
☐ 318 Jorgen Pettersson, SLou. .30
☐ 319 Rob Ramage, SLou. .50
☐ 320 Brian Sutter, SLou. .50
☐ 321 Perry Turnbull, SLou. .30
☐ 322 Mike Zuke, SLou. (Hart.) .30
☐ 323 TL: Rick Vaive, Toro. .50
☐ 324 HL: Rick Vaive, Toro. .50
☐ 325 John Anderson, Toro. .30
☐ 326 Jim Benning, Toro. .30
☐ 327 Bill Derlago, Toro. .30
☐ **328 Dan Daoust, Toro. RC 1.25**
☐ 329 Dave Farrish, Toro. .30
☐ 330 Miroslav Frycer, Toro. .30
☐ **331 Stewart Gavin, Toro. RC .75**
☐ 332 Gaston Gingras, Toro. .30
☐ 333 Billy Harris, Toro. .30
☐ **334 Peter Ihnacak, Toro. RC 1.00**
☐ 335 Jim Korn, Toro. .30
☐ 336 Terry Martin, Toro. .30
☐ **337 Frank Nigro, Toro. RC .75**
☐ 338 Mike Palmateer (G), Toro. .50
☐ **339 Walt Poddubny, Toro. RC 1.25**
☐ 340 Rick St. Croix (G), Toro. .35
☐ 341 Börje Salming, Toro. 1.00
☐ 342 Greg Terrion, Toro. .30
☐ 343 Rick Vaive, Toro. .50
☐ 344 TL: Darcy Rota, Vanc. .30
☐ 345 HL: Darcy Rota, Vanc. .30
☐ 346 Richard Brodeur (G), Vanc. .50
☐ **347 Jiri Bubla, Vanc. RC 1.00**
☐ 348 Ron Delorme, Vanc. .30
☐ 349 John Garrett (G), Vanc. .50
☐ 350 Thomas Gradin, Vanc. .30
☐ 351 Doug Halward, Vanc. .30
☐ 352 Mark Kirton, Vanc. .30
☐ 353 Rick Lanz, Vanc. .30
☐ 354 Lars Lindgren, Vanc. (Minn.) .30
☐ 355 Gary Lupul, Vanc. .30
☐ 356 Kevin McCarthy, Vanc. .30
☐ **357 Jim Nill, Vanc. RC 1.50**
☐ 358 Darcy Rota, Vanc. .30
☐ 359 Stan Smyl, Vanc. .30
☐ 360 Harold Snepsts, Vanc. .30
☐ **361 Patrik Sundström, Vanc. RC 2.00**
☐ **362 Tony Tanti, Vanc. RC 2.00**
☐ 363 Dave Williams, Vanc. .50
☐ 364 TL: Mike Gartner, Wash. 1.00
☐ 365 HL: Rod Langway, Wash. .50
☐ 366 Bob Carpenter, Wash. .50
☐ 367 Dave Christian, Wash. .30
☐ 368 Brian Engblom, Wash. (LosA.) .30
☐ 369 Mike Gartner, Wash. 5.00
☐ 370 Bengt Gustafsson, Wash. .30
☐ 371 Ken Houston, Wash. (Minn.) .30
☐ 372 Doug Jarvis, Wash. .30
☐ **373 Al Jensen (G), Wash. RC 1.00**
☐ 374 Rod Langway, Wash. .60
☐ **375 Craig Laughlin, Wash. RC .75**
☐ **376 Scott Stevens, Wash. RC 15.00**
☐ 377 TL: Dale Hawerchuk, Winn. 1.00
☐ 378 HL: Lucien DeBlois, Winn. .30
☐ **379 Scott Arniel, Winn. RC 1.00**
☐ 380 Dave Babych, Winn. .50
☐ 381 Laurie Boschman, Winn. .30
☐ 382 Wade Campbell, Winn. .30
☐ 383 Lucien DeBlois, Winn. .30
☐ **384 Murray Eaves, Winn. RC .75**
☐ 385 Dale Hawerchuk, Winn. 6.00
☐ 386 Morris Lukowich, Winn. .30
☐ 387 Bengt Lundholm, Winn. .30
☐ 388 Paul Maclean, Winn. .30
☐ **389 Brian Mullen, Winn. RC 1.50**
☐ 390 Doug Smail, Winn. .30
☐ 391 Doug Soetaert (G), Winn. .50
☐ 392 Don Spring, Winn. .30
☐ 393 Thomas Steen, Winn. .50
☐ 394 Tim Watters, Winn. .30
☐ 395 Tim Young, Winn. .30
☐ 396 Checklist 3 (265 - 396) 4.00

1983 - 84 OPC / TOPPS STICKERS

These stickers measure 1 15/16" x 2 9/16".

Complete Set (330 stickers): 50.00
Album (Pete Peeters on the cover): 5.00
Common Player: .20

O-Pee-Chee NM-MT

☐☐ 1 Foil: Marcel Dionne, LosA. .75
☐☐ 2 Foil: Guy Lafleur, Mont. 2.00
☐☐ 3 Foil: Darryl Sittler, Phil. .50
☐☐ 4 Foil: Gilbert Perreault, Buff. .50
☐☐ 5 Bill Barber, Phil. .35
☐☐ 6 Steve Shutt, Mont. .35
☐☐ 7 Wayne Gretzky, Edmo. 7.00
☐☐ 8 Lanny McDonald, Calg. .35
☐☐ 9 Reggie Leach, Detr. .20
☐☐ 10 Mike Bossy, NYIs. .50
☐☐ 11 Rick Kehoe, Pitt. .20
☐☐ 12 Bobby Clarke, Phil. .50
☐☐ 13 Butch Goring, NYIs. .20
☐☐ 14 Rick Middleton, Bost. .35
☐☐ 15 Foil: Conn Smythe Trophy .20
☐☐ 16 AW: Billy Smith (G), NYIs., MVP .20

☐☐ 17 Lee Fogolin, Edmo. .20
☐☐ 18 Stanley Cup Finals 1.00
☐☐ 19 Stanley Cup Finals .20
☐☐ 20 Stanley Cup Finals .20
☐☐ 21 Stanley Cup Finals .20
Stickers 18-21 feature Jari Kurri shooting on Billy Smith.
☐☐ 22 Foil: Stanley Cup .20
☐☐ 23 Foil: Stanley Cup .20
☐☐ 24 Foil: Stanley Cup .20
☐☐ 25 Rick Vaive, Toro. .20
☐☐ 26 Rick Vaive, Toro. .20
☐☐ 27 Billy Harris, Toro. .20
☐☐ 28 Dan Daoust, Toro. .20
☐☐ 29 Dan Daoust, Toro. .20
☐☐ 30 John Anderson, Toro. .20
☐☐ 31 John Anderson, Toro. .20
☐☐ 32 Peter Ihnacak, Toro. .20
☐☐ 33 Börje Salming, Toro. .35
☐☐ 34 Börje Salming, Toro. .35
☐☐ 35 Bill Derlago, Toro. .20
☐☐ 36 Rick St. Croix (G), Toro. .35
☐☐ 37 Greg Terrion, Toro. .20
☐☐ 38 Miroslav Frycer, Toro. .20
☐☐ 39 Mike Palmateer (G), Toro. .35
☐☐ 40 Gaston Gingras, Toro. .20
☐☐ 41 Pete Peeters (G), Bost. .35
☐☐ 42 Pete Peeters (G), Bost. .35
☐☐ 43 Mike Krushelnyski, Bost. .20
☐☐ 44 Rick Middleton, Bost. .35
☐☐ 45 Rick Middleton, Bost. .35
☐☐ 46 Raymond Bourque, Bost. 2.00
☐☐ 47 Raymond Bourque, Bost. 2.00
☐☐ 48 Brad Park, Bost. .35
☐☐ 49 Barry Pederson, Bost. .20
☐☐ 50 Barry Pederson, Bost. .20
☐☐ 51 Peter McNab, Bost. .20
☐☐ 52 Mike O'Connell, Bost. .20
☐☐ 53 Steve Kasper, Bost. .20
☐☐ 54 Marty Howe, Bost. .20
☐☐ 55 Tom Fergus, Bost. .20
☐☐ 56 Keith Crowder, Bost. .20
☐☐ 57 Steve Shutt, Mont. .35
☐☐ 58 Guy Lafleur, Mont. 2.00
☐☐ 59 Guy Lafleur, Mont. 2.00
☐☐ 60 Larry Robinson, Mont. .35
☐☐ 61 Larry Robinson, Mont. .35
☐☐ 62 Ryan Walter, Mont. .20
☐☐ 63 Ryan Walter, Mont. .20
☐☐ 64 Mark Napier, Mont. .20
☐☐ 65 Mark Napier, Mont. .20
☐☐ 66 Bob Gainey, Mont. .35
☐☐ 67 Doug Wickenheiser, Mont. .20
☐☐ 68 Pierre Mondou, Mont. .20
☐☐ 69 Mario Tremblay, Mont. .20
☐☐ 70 Gilbert Delorme, Mont. .20
☐☐ 71 Mats Näslund, Mont. .50
☐☐ 72 Rick Wamsley (G), Mont. .25
☐☐ 73 Ken Morrow, NYIs. .20
☐☐ 74 John Tonelli, NYIs. .20
☐☐ 75 John Tonelli, NYIs. .20
☐☐ 76 Bryan Trottier, NYIs. .50
☐☐ 77 Bryan Trottier, NYIs. .50
☐☐ 78 Mike Bossy, NYIs. .50
☐☐ 79 Mike Bossy, NYIs. .50
☐☐ 80 Bob Bourne, NYIs. .20
☐☐ 81 Denis Potvin, NYIs. .50
☐☐ 82 Denis Potvin, NYIs. .50
☐☐ 83 Dave Langevin, NYIs. .20
☐☐ 84 Clark Gillies, NYIs. .20
☐☐ 85 Bob Nystrom, NYIs. .20
☐☐ 86 Billy Smith (G), NYIs. .35
☐☐ 87 Tomas Jonsson, NYIs. .20
☐☐ 88 Rollie Melanson (G), NYIs. .35
☐☐ 89 Wayne Gretzky, Edmo. 7.00
☐☐ 90 Wayne Gretzky, Edmo. 7.00
☐☐ 91 Willy Lindstrom, Edmo. .20
☐☐ 92 Glenn Anderson, Edmo. .50
☐☐ 93 Glenn Anderson, Edmo. .50
☐☐ 94 Paul Coffey, Edmo. 1.50
☐☐ 95 Paul Coffey, Edmo. 1.50
☐☐ 96 Charlie Huddy, Edmo. .20
☐☐ 97 Mark Messier, Edmo. 2.50
☐☐ 98 Mark Messier, Edmo. 2.50
☐☐ 99 Andy Moog (G), Edmo. 1.25
☐☐ 100 Lee Fogolin, Edmo. .20
☐☐ 101 Kevin Lowe, Edmo. .50
☐☐ 102 Ken Linseman, Edmo. .20
☐☐ 103 Tom Roulston, Edmo. .20
☐☐ 104 Jari Kurri, Edmo. 1.25
☐☐ 105 Darryl Sutter, Chic. .20
☐☐ 106 Denis Savard, Chic. .75
☐☐ 107 Denis Savard, Chic. .75
☐☐ 108 Steve Larmer, Chic. 1.75
☐☐ 109 Bob Murray, Chic. .20
☐☐ 110 Tom Lysiak, Chic. .20
☐☐ 111 Al Secord, Chic. .20
☐☐ 112 Doug Wilson, Chic. .35
☐☐ 113 Murray Bannerman (G), Chic. .35
☐☐ 114 Gord Roberts, Minn. .20
☐☐ 115 Tom McCarthy, Minn. .20
☐☐ 116 Bobby Smith, Minn. .35
☐☐ 117 Craig Hartsburg, Minn. .20
☐☐ 118 Dino Ciccarelli, Minn. .50
☐☐ 119 Dino Ciccarelli, Minn. .50
☐☐ 120 Neal Broten, Minn. .35
☐☐ 121 Steve Payne, Minn. .20
☐☐ 122 Don Beaupré (G), Minn. .35
☐☐ 123 Jorgen Pettersson, SLou. .20
☐☐ 124 Perry Turnbull, SLou. .20
☐☐ 125 Bernie Federko, SLou. .35
☐☐ 126 Mike Crombeen, SLou. .20
☐☐ 127 Brian Sutter, SLou. .35
☐☐ 128 Brian Sutter, SLou. .35
☐☐ 129 Mike Liut (G), SLou. .35
☐☐ 130 Rob Ramage, SLou. .20
☐☐ 131 Blake Dunlop, SLou. .20
☐☐ 132 Ivan Boldirev, Detr. .20
☐☐ 133 Dwight Foster, Detr. .20
☐☐ 134 Reed Larson, Detr. .20
☐☐ 135 Danny Gare, Detr. .20
☐☐ 136 Jim Schoenfeld, Detr. .20
☐☐ 137 John Ogrodnick, Detr. .20
☐☐ 138 John Ogrodnick, Detr. .20
☐☐ 139 Willie Huber, Detr. .20
☐☐ 140 Greg Smith, Detr. .20
☐☐ 141 Eddy Beers, Calg. .20
☐☐ 142 Brian Bellows, Minn. .75
☐☐ 143 Jiri Bubla, Vanc. .20
☐☐ 144 Daryl Evans, LosA. .20
☐☐ 145 Randy Gregg, Edmo. .20
☐☐ 146 Jim Jackson, Calg. .20
☐☐ 147 Corrado Micalef (G), Detr. .35
☐☐ 148 Brian Mullen, Winn. .20
☐☐ 149 Frank Nigro, Toro. .20
☐☐ 150 Walt Poddubny, Toro. .20
☐☐ 151 Jaroslav Pouzar, Edmo. .20
☐☐ 152 Patrik Sundstrom, Vanc. .20
☐☐ 153 Denis Savard, Chic. .75
☐☐ 154 Dave Hunter, Edmo. .20
☐☐ 155 Andy Moog (G), Edmo. 1.25
☐☐ 156 Al Secord, Chic. .20
☐☐ 157 Mark Messier, Edmo. 2.50
☐☐ 158 Glenn Anderson, Edmo. .50
☐☐ 159 Jaroslav Pouzar, Edmo. .20
☐☐ 160 AS: Al Secord, Chic. .20
☐☐ 161 AS: Wayne Gretzky, Edmo. 7.00
☐☐ 162 AS: Lanny McDonald, Calg. .35
☐☐ 163 AS: Dave Babych, Winn. .20
☐☐ 164 AS: Murray Bannerman (G), Chic. .35
☐☐ 165 AS: Doug Wilson, Chic. .35
☐☐ 166 AS: Michel Goulet, Québ. .50
☐☐ 167 AS: Peter Stastny, Québ. .50
☐☐ 168 AS: Marian Stastny, Québ. .20
☐☐ 169 AS: Denis Potvin, NYIs. .50
☐☐ 170 AS: Pete Peeters (G), Bost. .35
☐☐ 171 AS: Mark Howe, Phil. .35
☐☐ 172 Luc Dufour, Bost. .20
☐☐ 173 Raymond Bourque, Bost. 2.00
☐☐ 174 Bob Bourne, NYIs. .20
☐☐ 175 Denis Potvin, NYIs. .50
☐☐ 176 Mike Bossy, NYIs. .50
☐☐ 177 Butch Goring, NYIs. .20
☐☐ 178 Brad Park, Bost. .35
☐☐ 179 Murray Brumwell, NJer. .20
☐☐ 180 Guy Carbonneau, Mont. 1.00
☐☐ 181 Lindsay Carson, Phil. .20
☐☐ 182 Luc Dufour, Bost. .20
☐☐ 183 Bob Froese (G), Phil. .35
☐☐ 184 Mats Hallin, NYIs. .20
☐☐ 185 Gord Kluzak, Bost. .20
☐☐ 186 Jeff Larmer, NJer. .20
☐☐ 187 Milan Novy, Wash. .20
☐☐ 188 Scott Stevens, Wash. 1.75
☐☐ 189 Bob Sullivan, Hart. .20
☐☐ 190 Mark Taylor, Phil. .20
☐☐ 191 Darryl Sittler, Phil. .35
☐☐ 192 Ron Flockhart, Phil. .20
☐☐ 193 Brad McCrimmon, Phil. .20
☐☐ 194 Bill Barber, Phil. .35
☐☐ 195 Mark Howe, Phil. .35
☐☐ 196 Mark Howe, Phil. .35
☐☐ 197 Pelle Lindbergh (G), Phil. 3.50
☐☐ 198 Bobby Clarke, Phil. .50
☐☐ 199 Brian Propp, Phil. .20
☐☐ 200 Ken Houston, Wash. .20
☐☐ 201 Rod Langway, Wash. .20
☐☐ 202 Al Jensen (G), Wash. .35
☐☐ 203 Brian Engblom, Wash. .20
☐☐ 204 Dennis Maruk, Wash. .20
☐☐ 205 Dennis Maruk, Wash. .20
☐☐ 206 Bob Carpenter, Wash. .20
☐☐ 207 Mike Gartner, Wash. 1.50
☐☐ 208 Doug Jarvis, Wash. .20
☐☐ 209 Ed Mio (G), NYRa. .35
☐☐ 210 Barry Beck, NYRa. .20
☐☐ 211 Dave Maloney, NYRa. .20
☐☐ 212 Don Maloney, NYRa. .20
☐☐ 213 Mark Pavelich, NYRa. .20
☐☐ 214 Mark Pavelich, NYRa. .20
☐☐ 215 Anders Hedberg, NYRa. .20
☐☐ 216 Reijo Ruotsalainen, NYRa. .20
☐☐ 217 Mike Rogers, NYRa. .20
☐☐ 218 Don Lever, NJer. .20
☐☐ 219 Steve Tambellini, NJer. .20
☐☐ 220 Bob MacMillan, NJer. .20
☐☐ 221 Hector Marini, NJer. .20
☐☐ 222 Glenn Resch (G), NJer. .35
☐☐ 223 Glenn Resch (G), NJer. .35
☐☐ 224 Carol Vadnais, NJer. .20
☐☐ 225 Joel Quenneville, NJer. .20
☐☐ 226 Aaron Broten, NJer. .20
☐☐ 227 Randy Carlyle, Pitt. .20
☐☐ 228 Doug Shedden, Pitt. .20
☐☐ 229 Greg Malone, Pitt. .20
☐☐ 230 Paul Gardner, Pitt. .20
☐☐ 231 Rick Kehoe, Pitt. .20
☐☐ 232 Rick Kehoe, Pitt. .20
☐☐ 233 Pat Boutette, Pitt. .20
☐☐ 234 Michel Dion (G), Pitt. .35
☐☐ 235 Mike Bullard, Pitt. .20
☐☐ 236 Dale McCourt, Buff. .20
☐☐ 237 Mike Foligno, Buff. .20
☐☐ 238 Phil Housley, Buff. .75
☐☐ 239 Tony McKegney, Buff. .20
☐☐ 240 Gilbert Perreault, Buff. .35
☐☐ 241 Gilbert Perreault, Buff. .35
☐☐ 242 Bob Sauvé (G), Buff. .35
☐☐ 243 Mike Ramsey, Buff. .20
☐☐ 244 John Van Boxmeer, Buff. .20
☐☐ 245 Dan Bouchard (G), Québ. .35
☐☐ 246 Réal Cloutier, Québ. .20
☐☐ 247 Marc Tardif, Québ. .20
☐☐ 248 Randy Moller, Québ. .20
☐☐ 249 Michel Goulet, Québ. .50
☐☐ 250 Michel Goulet, Québ. .50
☐☐ 251 Marian Stastny, Québ. .20
☐☐ 252 Anton Stastny, Québ. .20
☐☐ 253 Peter Stastny, Québ. .50
☐☐ 254 Mark Johnson, Hart. .20
☐☐ 255 Ron Francis, Hart. 2.00
☐☐ 256 Doug Sulliman, Hart. .20
☐☐ 257 Risto Siltanen, Hart. .20
☐☐ 258 Blaine Stoughton, Hart. .20
☐☐ 259 Blaine Stoughton, Hart. .20
☐☐ 260 Ray Neufeld, Hart. .20
☐☐ 261 Pierre Lacroix, Hart. .20
☐☐ 262 Greg Millen (G), Hart. .35
☐☐ 263 Lanny McDonald, Calg. .35
☐☐ 264 Paul Reinhart, Calg. .20
☐☐ 265 Mel Bridgman, Calg. .20
☐☐ 266 Réjean Lemelin (G), Calg. .35
☐☐ 267 Kent Nilsson, Calg. .20
☐☐ 268 Kent Nilsson, Calg. .20
☐☐ 269 Doug Risebrough, Calg. .20
☐☐ 270 Kari Eloranta, Calg. .20
☐☐ 271 Phil Russell, Calg. .20
☐☐ 272 Darcy Rota, Vanc. .20
☐☐ 273 Thomas Gradin, Vanc. .20
☐☐ 274 Stan Smyl, Vanc. .25
☐☐ 275 John Garrett (G), Vanc. .25
☐☐ 276 Richard Brodeur (G), Vanc. .25
☐☐ 277 Richard Brodeur (G), Vanc. .25
☐☐ 278 Doug Halward, Vanc. .20
☐☐ 279 Kevin McCarthy, Vanc. .20
☐☐ 280 Rick Lanz, Vanc. .20
☐☐ 281 Morris Lukowich, Winn. .20
☐☐ 282 Dale Hawerchuk, Winn. 1.50
☐☐ 283 Paul MacLean, Winn. .20
☐☐ 284 Lucien DeBlois, Winn. .20
☐☐ 285 Dave Babych, Winn. .20
☐☐ 286 Dave Babych, Winn. .20
☐☐ 287 Doug Smail, Winn. .20
☐☐ 288 Doug Soetaert (G), Winn. .35
☐☐ 289 Thomas Steen, Winn. .20
☐☐ 290 Charlie Simmer, LosA. .20
☐☐ 291 Terry Ruskowski, LosA. .20
☐☐ 292 Bernie Nicholls, LosA. 1.00
☐☐ 293 Jim Fox, LosA. .20
☐☐ 294 Marcel Dionne, LosA. .50
☐☐ 295 Marcel Dionne, LosA. .50
☐☐ 296 Gary Laskoski (G), LosA. .35
☐☐ 297 Jerry Korab, LosA. .20
☐☐ 298 Larry Murphy, LosA. .35
☐☐ 299 Foil: Hart Trophy .20
☐☐ 300 Foil: Hart Trophy .20
☐☐ 301 AW: Wayne Gretzky, Edmo. 7.00
☐☐ 302 AW: Bobby Clarke, Phil. .50
☐☐ 303 AW: Lanny McDonald, Calg. .35
☐☐ 304 Foil: Lady Byng Trophy .20
☐☐ 305 Foil: Lady Byng Trophy .20
☐☐ 306 AW: Mike Bossy, NYIs. .50
☐☐ 307 AW: Wayne Gretzky, Edmo. 7.00
☐☐ 308 Foil: Art Ross Trophy .20
☐☐ 309 Foil: Art Ross Trophy .20
☐☐ 310 Foil: Calder Trophy .20
☐☐ 311 Foil: Calder Trophy .20
☐☐ 312 AW: Steve Larmer, Chic. 1.75
☐☐ 313 AW: Rod Langway, Wash. .20
☐☐ 314 Foil: Norris Trophy .20
☐☐ 315 Foil: Norris Trophy .20
☐☐ 316 AW: Billy Smith, NYIs. .50
☐☐ 317 AW: Rollie Melanson, NYIs. .35
☐☐ 318 AW: Pete Peeters, Bost. .35
☐☐ 319 Foil: Vezina Trophy .20
☐☐ 320 Foil: Vezina Trophy .20
☐☐ 321 Foil: Mike Bossy, NYIs. .50
☐☐ 322 Foil: Mike Bossy, NYIs. .50
☐☐ 323 Foil: Marcel Dionne, LosA. .50
☐☐ 324 Foil: Marcel Dionne, LosA. .50
☐☐ 325 Foil: Wayne Gretzky, Edmo. 7.00
☐☐ 326 Foil: Wayne Gretzky, Edmo. 7.00
☐☐ 327 Foil: Pat Hughes, Edmo. .20
☐☐ 328 Foil: Pat Hughes, Edmo. .20
☐☐ 329 Foil: Rick Middleton, Bost. .35
☐☐ 330 Foil: Rick Middleton, Bost. .35

1983 - 84 SOUHAITS RENAISSANCE KEYCHAIN CARDS

Cards are listed and priced per team. Each set of seven checkboxes signify that there are seven mini-cards to each team set. The St. Louis Blues were the only team not produced. There is a small hole punched in the top left corner of each card. Individual cards measure 1 1/4" x 2 1/8".

Complete Set (140 cards): 80.00
Team/Players NRMT-MT

☐☐☐☐☐☐☐ Boston Bruins: 8.00
Bruins/ P. Peeters (G); G. Kluzak/ R. Bourque; B. Pederson/ R. Middleton; M. O'Connell/ R. Hillier; M. Krushelnyski/ M. Milbury; T. Fergus/ L. Dufour; B. Crowder/ Title Card

☐☐☐☐☐☐☐ Buffalo Sabres: 7.00
Sabres/ J. Cloutier (G); J. Van Boxmeer/ M. Ramsey; P. Housley/ D. McCourt; T. McKegney/ C. Ramsay; G. Perreault/ A. Savard; R. Seiling/ M. Foligno; B. Peterson/ Title Card

☐☐☐☐☐☐☐ Calgary Flames: 6.00
Flames/ D. Edwards (G); P. Russell/ R. Dunn; G. Chouinard/ D. Risebrough; L. McDonald/ K. Nilsson; J. Hislop/ K. Eloranta; P. Reinhart/ J. Peplinski; M. Bridgman/ Title Card

☐☐☐☐☐☐☐ Chicago Blackhawks: 7.00
Blackhawks/ G. Fox; B. Murray/ T. Lysiak; B. Gardner/ R. Preston; D. Savard/ A. Secord; D. Crossman/ Do. Wilson; Da. Sutter/ S. Larmer; T. Esposito (G)/ Title Card

☐☐☐☐☐☐☐ Detroit Red Wings: 7.00
Red Wings/ J. Schoenfeld; C. Campbell/ G. Smith; W. Huber/ W. McKechnie; D. Gare/ D. Foster; M. Blaisdell/ M. Osborne; J. Ogrodnick/ R. Larson; C. Micalef/ Title Card

☐☐☐☐☐☐☐ Edmonton Oilers: 20.00
Oilers/ L. Fogolin; G. Anderson/ M. Messier; K. Lowe/ P. Coffey; K. Linseman/ P. Hughes; J. Kurri/ C. Huddy; D. Semenko/ A. Moog (G); W. Gretzky/ Title Card

☐☐☐☐☐☐☐ Hartford Whalers: 6.00
Whaler/ M. Volcan; P. Lacroix/ R. Siltanen; R. Francis/ R. Neufeld; C. Kotsopoulos/ M. Renaud; B. Stoughton/ D. Sulliman; B. Sullivan/ P. Larouche; G. Millen (G)/ Title Card

☐☐☐☐☐☐☐ Los Angeles Kings: 7.00
Kings/ J. Korab; L. Murphy/ D. Kennedy; M. Murphy/ B. Nicholls; C. Simmer/ D. Evans; M. Dionne/ J. Fox; M. Hardy/ D. Lewis; G. Laskoski (G)/ Title Card

☐☐☐☐☐☐☐ Minnesota North Stars: 6.00
North Stars/ C. Giles; F. Barrett/ C. Hartsburg; Brad Maxwell/ T. McCarthy; J. Douglas/ Bob. Smith; D. Ciccarelli/ B. Bellows; W. Plett/ S. Payne; D. Beaupré/ Title Card

☐☐☐☐☐☐☐ Montréal Canadiens: 10.00

Canadiens/ R. Green; G. Lafleur/ K. Acton; M. Tremblay/ L. Robinson; S. Shutt/ B. Gainey; D. Wickenheiser/ M. Näslund; G. Delorme/ M. Napier; R. Sévigny (G)/ Title Card

□□□□□□□ New Jersey Devils: 5.00
Devils/ G. Resch (G); B. Lorimer/ J. Quenneville; J. Larmer/ T. Levo; D. Lever/ B. MacMillan; S. Tambellini/ B. Ashton/ R. Meagher/ P. Gagné; M. Kitchen/ TItle Card

□□□□□□□ New York Islanders: 10.00
Islanders/ T. Jonsson; B. Trottier/ Bre. Sutter; M. Bossy/ D. Langevin; D. Potvin/ S. Persson; J. Tonelli/ Bill Smith; C. Gillies/ B. Bourne; B. Goring/ Title Card

□□□□□□□ New York Rangers: 5.00
Rangers/ G. Hanlon (G); B. Beck/ R. McClanahan; R. Duguay/ Do. Maloney; A. Hedberg/ E. Johnstone; Da. Maloney/ M. Rogers; M. Leinonen/ R. Ruotsalainen; M. Pavelich; Title Card

□□□□□□□ Philadelphia Flyers: 7.00
Flyers/ Mark Howe; D. Sittler/ G. Cochrane; I. Sinisalo/ B. Propp; B. Barber/ M. Dvorak; B. Clarke/ P. Holmgren; B. McCrimmon/ R. Flockhart; B. Froese (G)/ Title Card

□□□□□□□ Pittsburgh Penguins: 5.00
Penguins/ P. Lee; M. Dion (G)/D. Hannan; M. Bullard/ R. Carlyle; G. Malone/ D. Shedden; P. Boutette/ M. Chorney; R. Kehoe/ P. Gardner; A. St.Laurent/ Title Card

□□□□□□□ Québec Nordiques: 7.00
Nordiques/ N. Rochefort; R. Cloutier/ P. Aubry; M. Goulet/ M. Stastny; A. Stastny/ R. Moller; B. Wesley/ P. Stastny; W. Paiement/ Dale Hunter; D. Bouchard (G)/ Title Card

□□□□□□□ Toronto Maple Leafs: 6.00
Maple Leafs/ G. Nylund; G. Terrion/ W. Poddubny; J. Anderson/ G. Gingras; M. Frycer/ B. Derlago; B. Salming/ R. Vaive; D. Daoust/ T. Martin; M. Palmateer (G)/ Title Card

□□□□□□□ Vancouver Canucks: 6.00
Canucks/ D. Halward; R. Lanz/ J. Nill; I. Hlinka/ D. Williams; S. Smyl/ D. Rota; T. Gradin/ L. Molin; J. Bubla/ H. Snepsts; R. Brodeur/ Title Card

□□□□□□□ Washington Capitals: 6.00
Capitals/ R. Langway; B. Carpenter/ M. Gartner; G. Currie/ A. Haworth; B. Gustafsson/K. Houston; D. Maruk/ B. Gould; D. Jarvis/ A. Jensen (G); M. Novy/ Title Card

□□□□□□□ Winnipeg Jets: 6.00
Jets/ Bry. Maxwell; D. Hawerchuk/ S. Arniel; M. Lukowich/ D. Christian; P. MacLean/ S. Savard; L. DeBlois/ D. Spring; N. Dupont/ E. Stanowski (G); D. Babych/ Title Card

1983 - 84 SOVIET STARS

Complete Set (23 cards w/folder):	55.00
Soviet Stars	**NRMT-MT**
□ Sergei Babinov	2.00
□ Helmut Balderis	2.00
□ Zinetula Bilyaletdinov	2.00
□ Vyacheslav Bykov	5.00
□ Viacheslav Fetisov	12.00
□ Irek Gimayev	2.00
□ Sergei Kapustin	2.00
□ Alexei Kasatonov	5.00
□ Andrei Khomutov	4.00
□ Vladimir Krutov	4.00
□ Igor Larionov	12.00
□ Sergei Makarov	8.00
□ Alexander Maltsev	4.00
□ Vasili Pervukhin	2.00
□ Sergei Shepelev	2.00
□ Alexander Skvorstsov	2.00
□ Sergei Starikov	2.00
□ Viktor Tikhonov, Coach	5.00
□ Vladislav Tretiak (G)	15.00
□ Mikhail Vasiliev	2.00
□ Vladimir Yursinov	2.00
□ Viktor Zhluktov	2.00
□ Vladimir Zubkov	2.00

1983 - 84 STATER MINT DOLLARS

Each cupro-nickel coin came with a 3" x 8 3/8" perforated card. Other singles may exist. These coins measure 1 1/4" in diamatre.

Hockey Dollars	NRMT-MT
□ H1 Lanny McDonald, Calg.	5.00
□ H7 Dale Hawerchuk, Winn.	8.00
□ H8 Dave Babych, Winn.	5.00
□ H9 Morris Lukowich, Winn.	3.00
□ H10 Brian Mullen, Winn.	3.00
□ H11 Lucien DeBlois, Winn.	3.00
□ H12 Brian Hayward (G), Winn.	4.00
□ H13 Tim Watters, Winn.	3.00

□ H14 Wayne Gretzky, Edmo.	18.00
□ H15 Andy Moog (G), Edm	8.00
□ H16 Dave Hunter, Edmo.	3.00
□ H17 Ken Linseman, Edmo. (*)	25.00
□ H18 Lee Fogolin, Edmo. (*)	25.00
□ H19 Dave Semenko, Edmo.	3.00
□ H20 Mark Messier, Edmo.	10.00

1983 - 84 VACHON

This 140-card set was issued in two-card panels. A number of cards are featured on more than one panel. Cut cards measure 2 1/2" x 3 1/2". The most expensive cut singles are Wayne Gretzky at $55, Mark Messier at $20 and, Guy Lafleur at $8. Cut singles start at 50¢; a complete 140-card set sells for $150. The corrected version for card #96 (Walt Poddubny) was only issued as a single card.

Complete Set (80 panels plus 1 card):	175.00
Vachon Panel	**NM-MT**
□ 1-121 Paul Baxter, Calg./ Scott Arniel, Winn.	1.00
□ 2-122 Eddy Beers, Calg./ Dave Babych, Winn.	1.00
□ 3-123 Steve Bozek, Calg./ Laurie Boschman, Winn.	1.00
□ 4-124 Mike Eaves, Calg./ Wade Campbell, Winn.	1.00
□ 5-125 Don Edwards (G), Calg./ L. DeBlois, Winn.	1.50
□ 6-126 Kari Eloranta, Calg./ Dale Hawerchuk, Winn.	7.00
□ 7-127 D. Hindmarch, Calg./ B. Hayward (G), Winn.	1.50
□ 8-128 Jamie Hislop, Calg./ Jim Kyte, Winn.	1.00
□ 9-129 Stephen Konroyd, Calg./ M. Lukowich, Winn.	1.00
□ 10-130 R. Lemelin (G), Calg./ B. Lundholm, Winn.	1.50
□ 11-131 Hakan Loob, Calg./ Paul MacLean, Winn.	1.00
□ 12-132 Jamie Macoun, Calg./ Moe Mantha, Winn.	1.00
□ 13-133 L. McDonald, Calg./ A. McBain, Winn.	5.00
□ 14-134 Kent Nilsson, Calg./ Brian Mullen, Winn.	1.00
□ 15-135 Colin Patterson, Calg./ Robert Picard,Winn.	1.00
□ 16-136 Jim Peplinski, Calg./ Doug Smail, Winn.	1.00
□ 17-137 Paul Reinhart, Calg./ D. Soetaert (G), Winn.	1.50
□ 18-138 Doug Risebrough, Calg./ T. Steen, Winn.	1.00
□ 19-139 Steve Tambellini, Calg./ Tim Watters, Winn.	1.00
□ 20-140 Mickey Volcan, Calg./ Tim Young, Winn.	1.00
□ 21-101 G.Anderson, Edmo./ R. Brodeur (G), Vanc.	6.00
□ 22-102 Paul Coffey, Edmo./ Jiri Bubla, Vanc.	7.50
□ 23-103 Lee Fogolin, Edmo./ Garth Butcher, Vanc.	1.00
□ 24- 104 Grant Fuhr (G), Edmo./ Ron Delorme, Vanc.	6.50
□ 25- 105 Randy Gregg, Edmo./ J. Garrett (G), Vanc.	1.50
□ 26-106 Wayne Gretzky, Edmo./ Jere Gillis, Vanc.	45.00
□ 27-107 Charlie Huddy, Edmo./ Thomas Gradin, Vanc.	1.00
□ 28-108 Pat Hughes, Edmo./ Doug Halward, Vanc.	1.00
□ 29-109 Dave Hunter, Edmo./ Mark Kirton, Vanc.	1.00
□ 30-110 Don Jackson, Edmo./ Rick Lanz, Vanc.	1.00
□ 31-111 Jari Kurri, Edmo./ Gary Lupul, Vanc.	5.00
□ 32-112 W. Lindstrom, Edmo./ K. McCarthy, Vanc.	1.00
□ 33-113 Ken Linseman, Edmo./ Lars Molin, Vanc.	1.00
□ 34-114 Kevin Lowe, Edmo./ James Nill, Vanc.	3.00
□ 35-115 Dave Lumley, Edmo./ Darcy Rota, Vanc.	1.00
□ 36-116 Mark Messier, Edmo./ Stan Smyl, Vanc.	15.00
□ 37-117 Andy Moog (G), Edmo./ H. Snepsts, Vanc.	8.00
□ 38-118 J. Pouzar, Edmo./ P. Sundström, Vanc.	1.00
□ 39-119 Tom Roulston, Edmo./ Tony Tanti, Vanc.	1.00
□ 40-120 Dave Semenko, Edmo./ Dave Williams, Vanc.	1.00
□ 61-41 Bo Berglund, Québ./ Guy Carbonneau, Mont.	5.00
□ 62-42 Dan Bouchard (G), Québ./ Kent Carlson, Mont.	1.50
□ 63-43 Alain Côté, Québ./ Gilbert Delorme, Mont.	1.00
□ 64/44 Brian Ford (G), Québ./ Bob Gainey, Mont.	1.50
□ 65-45 Michel Goulet, Que/ Jean Hamel, Mont.	4.00
□ 66-46 Dale Hunter, Québ./ Mark Hunter, Mont.	2.50
□ 67-47 Mario Marois, Québ./ Guy Lafleur, Mont.	6.00
□ 68-48 Tony McKegney, Québ./ Craig Ludwig, Mont.	1.00
□ 69-49 Randy Moller, Québ./ Pierre Mondou, Mont.	1.00
□ 70-50 Wilf Paiment, Québ./ Mats Näslund, Mont.	1.00
□ 71/51 Pat Price, Québ./ Chris Nilan, Mont.	1.00
□ 72-52 N. Rochefort, Québ./ G. Paslawski, Mont.	1.00
□ 73-53 André Savard, Québ./ Larry Robinson, Mont.	3.00
□ 74-54 L. Sleigher, Québ./ R. Sévigny (G), Mont.	1.50
□ 75-55 Anton Stastny, Québ./ Steve Shutt, Mont.	3.00
□ 76-56 Marian Stastny, Québ./ Bobby Smith, Mont.	2.00
□ 77-57 Peter Stastny, Québ./ Mario Tremblay, Mont.	4.00
□ 78-58 John Van Boxmeer, Québ./ Ryan Walter, Mont.	1.00
□ 79-59 Wally Weir, Québ./ Rick Wamsley (G), Mont.	1.50
□ 80-60 B. Wesley, Québ./ D. Wickenheiser, Mont.	1.00
□ 81-36 John Anderson, Toro./ Mark Messier, Edmo.	20.00
□ 82-31 Jim Benning, Toro./ Jari Kurri, Edmo.	10.00
□ 83-22 Dan Daoust, Toro./ Paul Coffey, Edmo.	15.00
□ 84-47 Bill Derlago, Toro./ Guy Lafleur, Mont.	6.00
□ 85-53 Dave Farrish, Toro./ Larry Robinson, Mont.	3.00
□ 86-56 Miroslav Frycer, Toro./ Bobby Smith, Mont.	2.00
□ 87-57 Stewart Gavin, Toro./ Mario Tremblay, Mont.	2.00
□ 88-65 Gaston Gingras, Toro./ Michel Goulet, Québ.	4.00
□ 89-66 Billy Harris, Toro./ Dale Hunter, Québ.	2.50
□ 90-77 Peter Ihnacak, Toro./ Peter Stastny, Québ.	5.00
□ 91-67 James Korn, Toro./ Mario Marois, Québ.	1.00
□ 92-107 Terry Martin, Toro./ Thomas Gradin, Vanc.	1.00
□ 93-119 Dale McCourt, Toro./ Tony Tanti, Vanc.	1.00
□ 94-101 G. Nylund, Toro./ R. Brodeur (G), Vanc.	1.50
□ 95-13 M. Palmateer (G), Toro./ L. McDonald, Calg.	5.00
□ 96-14 W. Poddubny, Toro., Error/ K. Nilsson, Calg.	10.00
□ 97-17 Börje Salming, Toro./ Paul Reinhart, Calg.	5.00
□ 98-126 R. St. Croix (G), Toro./ D. Hawerchuck, Winn.	5.00
□ 99-122 Greg Terrion, Toro./ Dave Babych, Winn.	1.00
□ 100-125 Rick Vaive, Toro./ Lucien DeBlois, Winn.	1.00
Vachon correction	**NRMT-MT**
□ 96 Walt Poddubny, Toro.	3.00

1984 - 85 ISLANDER NEWS TROTTIER

These blue-border cards measure the standard 2 1/2" x 3 1/2".

Complete Set (33 cards):	35.00
Islander News	**NM-MT**
□ 1 Using Drugs Puts You In A Permanent Penalty Box	.50
□ 2 Say No to Drugs! (Bossy)	3.50
□ 3 Don't Drink. Don't Smoke. Don't Play With Drugs...	.50
□ 4 Don't Let Your Mind Go To Pot	.50
□ 5 Friends Don't Let Friends Drive Drunk	.50
□ 6 Enjoy Alternatives To Drugs & Booze	.50
□ 7 Help Friends Feel Good About Themselves	.50
□ 8 People Who Are Involved Don't Need Drugs	.50
□ 9 Think Before You Drink	.50
□ 10 It's Your Choice. Don't Be A Victim	.50
□ 11 Drugs...Don't...Ruin Your Life (LaFontaine)	7.00
□ 12 Living With Drugs Can Hurt	.50
□ 13 Alcohol Is The Worst Drug Of All	.50
□ 14 Drugs And School Don't Mix	.50
□ 15 Don't Be Embarrassed If You Have...Get Help	.50
□ 16 Be A Winner...Don't Play With Drugs (Trottier)	5.00
□ 17 Develop Good Habits...Not Drug Habits	.50
□ 18 Alcholol is A Drug Think Don't Drink	.50
□ 19 It May Take Five Years To Cure A Drug Addict	.50
□ 20 Grow Up Tall, Use No Drugs At All	.50
□ 21 Don't Play With Drugs...It's A Losing Game	.50
□ 22 Keep Off The Grass	.50
□ 23 Don't Be A Fool Trying To Act Cool..."Be Straight"	.50
□ 24 Even A Kid Can Become An Alcoholic	.50
□ 25 Drugs...Be Smart...Don't Start (Potvin)	3.00
□ 26 You Can't Take Your Best Shot When... (Hrudey)	2.00
□ 27 You Don't Need Drugs... (B. Smith)	2.50
□ 28 Drugs Can Cause Genetic Damage	.50
□ 29 Make The Save Of Your Life...Don't Drink	.50
□ 30 Be A Winner...Shut Out Drugs	.50
□ 31 Stopping Is Hard...Don't Start On Drugs	.50
□ 32 Starting With Drugs Can Finish Your Life (Bossy)	3.50
□ 33 Real Life Is Fun... (Potvin)	3.00

1984 - 85 KELLOGG'S DISKS

These player disks were issued in strips of six disks and the team logos individually. Both came inside a black or orange plastic puck with the NHL crest moulded on the top lid. The pucks in turn can be mounted in a display shield. The seventh and eighth panel feature Olympic athletes. An 8-panel set sells for $45. These disks have a 2 1/16" diametre.

Kellogg's	NM-MT
□ P. Coffey/ M. Tremblay/ J. Anderson D. Hawerchuk/ R. Kehoe/ B. Beck	8.00
□ B. Federko/ R. Francis/ S. Smyl M. Gartner/ D. Babych/ L. McDonald	9.00
□ P. Reinhart/ J. Kurri/ M. Goulet R. Brodeur (G)/ M. Bossy/ D. Ciccarelli	9.00
□ L. Robinson/ D. Risebrough/ P. MacLean P. Stastny/ M. Dionne/ R. Larson	8.00
□ B. Salming/ K. Lowe/ G. Lafleur R. Middleton/ G. Perreault/ Stanley Cup	10.00
□ R. Vaive/ G. Resch/ D. Sittler D. Wilson/ Dale Hunter/ T. Gradin	8.00

1984 - 85 KELOWNA WINGS & WHL GRADUATES

Complete Set (56 cards):	80.00
Kelowna / WHL grads	**NM-MT**
□ 1 Checklist	2.00
□ 2 Darcy Wakaluk (G)	2.00
□ 3 Stacey Nickel	.75
□ 4 Jeff Sharples	1.25
□ 5 Greg Zuk	.75
□ 6 Daryn Sivertson	.75
□ 7 Randy Cameron	.75
□ 8 Mark Fioretti	.75
□ 9 Ron Viglasi	.75
□ 10 Ian Herbers	.75
□ 11 Mike Wegleitner	.75
□ 12 Terry Zaporzan	.75
□ 13 Dwaine Hutton	.75
□ 14 Rod Williams	.75
□ 15 Jeff Rohlicek	.75
□ 16 Brent Gilchrist	2.50
□ 17 Rocky Dundas	.75
□ 18 Grant Delcourt	.75
□ 19 Cam Laroruk	.75
□ 20 Tony Horacek	.75
□ 21 Mark Wingerter	.75
□ 22 Mick Vukota	1.25
□ 23 Danny Gare	2.50
□ 24 Rich Sutter	1.25
□ 25 Alfie Turcotte	1.25
□ 26 Bryan Trottier	10.00
□ 27 Bill Derlago	1.25
□ 28 Stan Smyl	2.00
□ 29 Brent Sutter	2.50
□ 30 Mel Bridgman	1.25
□ 31 Paul Cyr	1.25
□ 32 Gary Lupul	1.25
□ 33 Ray Neufeld	1.25
□ 34 Brian Propp	3.00
□ 35 Bob Nystrom	2.00
□ 36 Ryan Walter	1.25
□ 37 Russ Courtnall	3.00
□ 38 Larry Playfair	1.25
□ 39 Ron Delorme	1.25
□ 40 Ron Sutter	1.25
□ 41 Bobby Clarke	10.00
□ 42 Bob Bourne	1.25
□ 43 Cam Neely	12.00
□ 44 Murray Craven	2.00
□ 45 Clark Gillies	3.00
□ 46 Ron Flockhart	1.25
□ 47 Harold Snepts	2.50
□ 48 Duane Sutter	1.25
□ 49 Garth Butcher	1.25
□ 50 Bill Hajt	1.25
□ 51 Jim Benning	1.25
□ 52 Ray Allison	1.25
□ 53 Ken Wregget (G)	4.00
□ 54 Phil Russell	1.25
□ 55 Brad McCrimmon	2.00
□ 56 Dan Hodgson	1.25

1984 - 85 O-PEE-CHEE

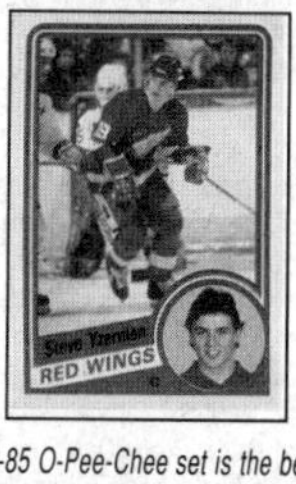

"I think the 1984-85 O-Pee-Chee set is the best of the 1980s, especially for rookies. There are so many future Hall of Fame (honoured) members: Yzerman, Chelios, Gilmour, Neely. It is a very nice looking card, with the small picture of the face and the action photo both on the front. It may not be the most expensive set from the 1980s, but it is my favourite set for sure." – Don Harada, Superstar S C and Collectibles, Hamilton, Ontario.

Complete Set (396 cards):	**300.00**
Common Player:	**.40**
O-Pee-Chee	**NM-MT**
☐ 1 Raymond Bourque, Bost.	8.00
☐ 2 Keith Crowder, Bost.	.40
☐ 3 Luc Dufour, Bost.	.40
☐ 4 Tom Fergus, Bost.	.40
☐ **5 Doug Keans (G), Bost. RC**	**1.00**
☐ 6 Gord Kluzak, Bost.	.40
☐ 7 Ken Linseman, Bost.	.40
☐ **8 Nevin Markwart, Bost. RC**	**.75**
☐ 9 Rick Middleton, Bost.	.50
☐ 10 Mike Milbury, Bost.	.40
☐ 11 Jim Nill, Bost.	.40
☐ 12 Mike O'Connell, Bost.	.40
☐ 13 Terry O'Reilly, Bost.	.50
☐ 14 Barry Pederson, Bost.	.40
☐ 15 Pete Peeters (G), Bost.	.50
☐ **16 Dave Silk, Bost. RC**	**.75**
☐ **17 Dave Andreychuk, Buff. RC**	**8.00**
☐ **18 Tom Barrasso (G), Buff. RC**	**10.00**
☐ 19 Réal Cloutier, Buff.	.40
☐ 20 Mike Foligno, Buff.	.40
☐ 21 Bill Hajt, Buff.	.40
☐ **22 Gilles Hamel, Buff. RC**	**.75**
☐ 23 Phil Housley, Buff.	1.50
☐ 24 Gilbert Perreault, Buff.	1.50
☐ 25 Brent Peterson, Buff.	.40
☐ 26 Larry Playfair, Buff.	.40
☐ 27 Craig Ramsay, Buff.	.50
☐ 28 Mike Ramsey, Buff.	.40
☐ 29 Lindy Ruff, Buff.	.50
☐ 30 Bob Sauvé (G), Buff.	.50
☐ 31 Ric Seiling, Buff.	.40
☐ 32 Murray Bannerman (G), Chic.	.50
☐ 33 Keith Brown, Chic.	.40
☐ 34 Curt Fraser, Chic.	.40
☐ 35 Bill Gardner, Chic.	.40
☐ 36 Jeff Larmer, Chic.	1.00
☐ 37 Steve Larmer, Chic.	3.00
☐ 38 Steve Ludzik, Chic.	.40
☐ 39 Tom Lysiak, Chic.	.40
☐ 40 Bob MacMillan, Chic.	.40
☐ 41 Bob Murray, Chic.	.40
☐ **42 Troy Murray, Chic. RC**	**1.25**
☐ **43 Jack O'Callahan, Chic. RC**	**.75**
☐ 44 Rick Paterson, Chic.	.40
☐ 45 Denis Savard, Chic.	1.50
☐ 46 Alan Secord, Chic.	.40
☐ 47 Darryl Sutter, Chic.	.50
☐ 48 Doug Wilson, Chic.	.50
☐ 49 John Barrett, Detr.	.40
☐ 50 Ivan Boldirev, Detr.	.40
☐ 51 Colin Campbell, Detr.	.50
☐ 52 Ron Duguay, Detr.	.40
☐ 53 Dwight Foster, Detr.	.40
☐ 54 Danny Gare, Detr.	.50
☐ 55 Eddie Johnstone, Detr.	.40
☐ **56 Kelly Kisio, Detr. RC**	**1.25**
☐ **57 Lane Lambert, Detr. RC**	**.75**
☐ 58 Reed Larson, Detr.	.40
☐ 59 Bob Manno, Detr.	.40
☐ **60 Randy Ladouceur, Detr. RC**	**1.00**
☐ 61 Ed Mio (G), Detr.	.50
☐ 62 John Ogrodnick, Detr.	.40
☐ 63 Brad Park, Detr.	1.50
☐ 64 Greg Smith, Detr.	.40
☐ **65 Greg Stefan (G), Detr. RC**	**1.50**
☐ 66 Paul Woods, Detr.	.40
☐ **67 Steve Yzerman, Detr. RC**	**160.00**
☐ **68 Bob Crawford, Hart. RC**	**.75**
☐ 69 Rich Dunn, Hart.	.40
☐ 70 Ron Francis, Hart.	5.00
☐ 71 Marty Howe, Hart.	.40
☐ 72 Mark Johnson, Hart.	.40
☐ 73 Chris Kotsopoulos, Hart.	.40
☐ 74 Greg Malone, Hart.	.40
☐ 75 Greg Millen (G), Hart.	.50
☐ 76 Ray Neufeld, Hart.	.40
☐ 77 Joel Quenneville, Hart.	.50
☐ 78 Risto Siltanen, Hart.	.40
☐ **79 Sylvain Turgeon, Hart. RC**	**1.25**
☐ 80 Mike Zuke, Hart.	.40
☐ 81 Steve Christoff, LosA.	.40
☐ 82 Marcel Dionne, LosA.	1.50
☐ 83 Brian Engblom, LosA.	.25
☐ 84 Jim Fox, LosA.	.40
☐ **85 Anders Hakansson, LosA. RC**	**.75**
☐ 86 Mark Hardy, LosA.	.40
☐ **87 Brian MacLellan, LosA. RC**	**.75**
☐ 88 Bernie Nicholls, LosA.	1.50
☐ 89 Terry Ruskowski, LosA.	.40
☐ 90 Charlie Simmer, LosA. (Bost.)	.40
☐ 91 Doug Smith, LosA.	.40
☐ 92 Dave Taylor, LosA.	.50
☐ 93 Keith Acton, Minn.	.40
☐ 94 Don Beaupré (G), Minn.	.50
☐ 95 Brian Bellows, Minn.	.75
☐ 96 Neal Broten, Minn.	.50
☐ 97 Dino Ciccarelli, Minn.	1.00
☐ 98 Craig Hartsburg, Minn.	.50
☐ **99 Tom Hirsch, Minn. RC**	**.75**
☐ 100 Paul Holmgren, Minn.	.40
☐ 101 Dennis Maruk, Minn.	.40
☐ 102 Brad Maxwell, Minn.	.40
☐ 103 Tom McCarthy, Minn.	.40
☐ 104 Gilles Meloche (G), Minn.	.50
☐ 105 Mark Napier, Minn.	.40
☐ 106 Steve Payne, Minn.	.40
☐ 107 Gord Roberts, Minn.	.40
☐ 108 Harold Snepsts, Minn.	.40
☐ 109 Mel Bridgman, NJer.	.40
☐ 110 Joe Cirella, NJer.	.40
☐ 111 Tim Higgins, NJer.	.40
☐ 112 Don Lever, NJer.	.40
☐ 113 Dave Lewis, NJer.	.40
☐ 114 Bob Lorimer, NJer.	.40
☐ 115 Ron Low (G), NJer.	.50
☐ **116 Jan Ludvig, NJer. RC**	**.75**
☐ 117 Gary McAdam, NJer.	.40
☐ 118 Rich Preston, Chic. (NJer.)	.40
☐ 119 Glenn Resch (G), NJer.	.50
☐ 120 Phil Russell, NJer.	.40
☐ **121 Pat Verbeek, NJer. RC**	**15.00**
☐ 122 Mike Bossy, NYIs.	3.00
☐ 123 Bob Bourne, NYIs.	.40
☐ **124 Patrick Flatley, NYIs. RC**	**1.50**
☐ **125 Greg Gilbert, NYIs. RC**	**3.00**
☐ 126 Clark Gillies, NYIs.	1.50
☐ 127 Butch Goring, NYIs.	.50
☐ 128 Tomas Jonsson, NYIs.	.40
☐ **129 Pat LaFontaine, NYIs. RC**	**20.00**
☐ 130 Rollie Melanson (G), NYIs.	.50
☐ 131 Ken Morrow, NYIs.	.40
☐ 132 Bob Nystrom, NYIs.	.40
☐ 133 Stefan Persson, NYIs.	.40
☐ 134 Denis Potvin, NYIs.	1.50
☐ 135 Billy Smith (G), NYIs.	1.50
☐ 136 Brent Sutter, NYIs.	.50
☐ 137 Duane Sutter, NYIs.	.40
☐ 138 John Tonelli, NYIs.	.50
☐ 139 Bryan Trottier, NYIs.	2.00
☐ 140 Barry Beck, NYRa.	.40
☐ 141 Ron Greschner, NYRa.	.40
☐ 142 Glen Hanlon (G), NYRa.	.50
☐ 143 Anders Hedberg, NYRa.	.50
☐ 144 Tom Laidlaw, NYRa.	.40
☐ 145 Pierre Larouche, NYRa.	.40
☐ 146 Dave Maloney, NYRa.	.40
☐ 147 Don Maloney, NYRa.	.40
☐ 148 Mark Osborne, NYRa.	.40
☐ 149 Larry Patey, NYRa.	.40
☐ **150 James Patrick, NYRa. RC**	**1.50**
☐ 151 Mark Pavelich, NYRa.	.40
☐ 152 Mike Rogers, NYRa.	.40
☐ 153 Reijo Ruotsalainen, NYRa.	.40
☐ 154 Blaine Stoughton, NYRa.	.40
☐ **155 Peter Sundström, NYRa. RC**	**1.00**
☐ 156 Bill Barber, Phil.	1.00
☐ 157 Doug Crossman, Phil.	.40
☐ **158 Thomas Eriksson, Phil. RC**	**.75**
☐ 159 Bob Froese (G), Phil.	.50
☐ **160 Paul Guay, Phil. RC**	**.75**
☐ 161 Mark Howe, Phil.	.50
☐ 162 Tim Kerr, Phil.	.50
☐ 163 Brad Marsh, Phil.	.50
☐ 164 Brad McCrimmon, Phil.	.50
☐ **165 Dave Poulin, Phil. RC**	**1.25**
☐ 166 Brian Propp, Phil.	.50
☐ **167 Ilkka Sinisalo, Phil. RC**	**1.00**
☐ 168 Darryl Sittler, Phil. (Detr.)	1.50
☐ **169 Rich Sutter, Phil. RC**	**1.25**
☐ **170 Ron Sutter, Phil. RC**	**1.25**
☐ 171 Pat Boutette, Pitt.	.40
☐ 172 Mike Bullard, Pitt.	.40
☐ 173 Michel Dion (G), Pitt.	.50
☐ 174 Ron Flockhart, Pitt.	.40
☐ 175 Greg Fox, Pitt.	.40
☐ 176 Denis Herron (G), Pitt.	.50
☐ 177 Rick Kehoe, Pitt.	.40
☐ 178 Kevin McCarthy, Pitt.	.40
☐ 179 Tom Roulston, Pitt.	.40
☐ 180 Mark Taylor, Pitt.	.40
☐ 181 Wayne Babych, SLou. (Pgh)	.40
☐ **182 Tim Bothwell, SLou. RC**	**1.00**
☐ 183 Kevin LaVallée, SLou.	.40
☐ 184 Bernie Federko, SLou.	1.50
☐ **185 Doug Gilmour, SLou. RC**	**40.00**
☐ **186 Terry Johnson, SLou. RC**	**.75**
☐ 187 Mike Liut (G), SLou.	.50
☐ 188 Joe Mullen, SLou.	1.50
☐ 189 Jorgen Pettersson, SLou.	.40
☐ 190 Rob Ramage, SLou.	.40
☐ **191 Dwight Schofield, SLou. RC**	**.75**
☐ 192 Brian Sutter, SLou.	.50
☐ 193 Doug Wickenheiser, SLou.	.40
☐ 194 Bob Carpenter, Wash.	.50
☐ 195 Dave Christian, Wash.	.40
☐ **196 Bob Gould, Wash. RC**	**.75**
☐ 197 Mike Gartner, Wash.	3.50
☐ 198 Bengt Gustafsson, Wash.	.40
☐ **199 Alan Haworth, Wash. RC**	**.75**
☐ 200 Doug Jarvis, Wash.	.40
☐ 201 Al Jensen (G), Wash.	.50
☐ 202 Rod Langway, Wash.	1.50
☐ 203 Craig Laughlin, Wash.	.40
☐ 204 Larry Murphy, Wash.	1.00
☐ 205 Pat Riggin (G), Wash.	.50
☐ 206 Scott Stevens, Wash.	3.00
☐ 207 AS: Michel Goulet, Québ.	.50
☐ 208 AS: Wayne Gretzky, Edmo.	6.00
☐ 209 AS: Mike Bossy, NYIs.	1.00
☐ 210 AS: Rod Langway, Wash.	.50
☐ 211 AS: Raymond Bourque, Bost.	3.00
☐ 212 AS: Tom Barrasso (G), Buff.	1.75
☐ 213 AS: Mark Messier, Edmo.	4.00
☐ 214 AS: Bryan Trottier, NYIs.	1.00
☐ 215 AS: Jari Kurri, Edmo.	2.00
☐ 216 AS: Denis Potvin, NYIs.	.75
☐ 217 AS: Paul Coffey, Edmo.	2.50
☐ 218 AS: Pat Riggin (G), Wash.	.50
☐ 219 Ed Beers, Calg.	.40
☐ 220 Steve Bozek, Calg.	.40
☐ 221 Mike Eaves, Calg.	.40
☐ 222 Don Edwards (G), Calg.	.50
☐ 223 Kari Eloranta, Calg.	.40
☐ 224 Dave Hindmarch, Calg.	.40
☐ 225 Jim Jackson, Calg.	.40
☐ 226 Steve Konroyd, Calg.	.40
☐ **227 Richard Kromm, Calg. RC**	**.75**
☐ 228 Réjean Lemelin (G), Calg.	.50
☐ **229 Håkan Loob, Calg. RC**	**3.00**
☐ **230 Jamie Macoun, Calg. RC**	**1.00**
☐ 231 Lanny McDonald, Calg.	1.50
☐ 232 Kent Nilsson, Calg.	.40
☐ 233 James Peplinski, Calg.	.40
☐ **234 Dan Quinn, Calg. RC**	**1.00**
☐ 235 Paul Reinhart, Calg.	.40
☐ 236 Doug Risebrough, Calg.	.50
☐ 237 Steve Tambellini, Calg.	.40
☐ 238 Glenn Anderson, Edmo.	.75
☐ 239 Paul Coffey, Edmo.	7.00
☐ 240 Lee Fogolin, Edmo.	.40
☐ 241 Grant Fuhr (G), Edmo.	5.00
☐ 242 Randy Gregg, Edmo.	.40
☐ 243 Wayne Gretzky, Edmo.	25.00
☐ 244 Charlie Huddy, Edmo.	.50
☐ 245 Pat Hughes, Edmo.	.40
☐ 246 Dave Hunter, Edmo.	.40
☐ 247 Don Jackson, Edmo.	.40
☐ 248 Mike Krushelnyski, Bost. (Edm.)	.40
☐ 249 Jari Kurri, Edmo.	5.00
☐ 250 Willy Lindstrom, Edmo.	.40
☐ 251 Kevin Lowe, Edmo.	.50
☐ 252 Dave Lumley, Edmo. (Hart.)	.40
☐ **253 Kevin McClelland, Edmo. RC**	**.75**
☐ 254 Mark Messier, Edmo.	10.00
☐ 255 Andy Moog (G), Edmo.	4.00
☐ 256 Jaroslav Pouzar, Edmo.	.40
☐ 257 Guy Carbonneau, Mont.	1.00
☐ **258 John Chabot, Mont. RC**	**.75**
☐ **259 Chris Chelios, Mont. RC**	**35.00**
☐ 260 Lucien DeBlois, Mont., Error (Deblois)	.40
☐ 261 Bob Gainey, Mont.	1.50
☐ 262 Rick Green, Mont.	.40
☐ 263 Jean Hamel, Mont.	.40
☐ 264 Guy Lafleur, Mont.	4.00
☐ 265 Craig Ludwig, Mont.	.50
☐ 266 Pierre Mondou, Mont.	.40
☐ 267 Mats Näslund, Mont.	.75
☐ 268 Chris Nilan, Mont.	.40
☐ **269 Steve Penney (G), Mont. RC**	**1.50**
☐ 270 Larry Robinson, Mont.	1.50
☐ 271 Bill Root, Mont. (Toro.)	.40
☐ 272 Steve Shutt, Mont.	1.00
☐ 273 Bobby Smith, Mont.	.50
☐ 274 Mario Tremblay, Mont.	.50
☐ 275 Ryan Walter, Mont.	.50
☐ **276 Bo Berglund, Québ. RC**	**.75**
☐ 277 Dan Bouchard (G), Québ.	.50
☐ 278 Alain Côté, Québ.	.40
☐ 279 André Doré, Québ. (NYRa.)	.40
☐ 280 Michel Goulet, Québ.	1.50
☐ 281 Dale Hunter, Québ.	.50
☐ 282 Mario Marois, Québ.	.40
☐ 283 Tony McKegney, Québ.	.40
☐ 284 Randy Moller, Québ.	.40
☐ 285 Wilf Paiement, Québ.	.40
☐ 286 Pat Price, Québ.	.40
☐ 287 Normand Rochefort, Québ.	.40
☐ 288 André Savard, Québ.	.40
☐ 289 Richard Sévigny (G), Québ.	.50
☐ 290 Louis Sleigher, Québ. (Bost.)	.40
☐ 291 Anton Stastny, Québ.	.40
☐ 292 Marian Stastny, Québ.	.40
☐ 293 Peter Stastny, Québ.	1.50
☐ 294 Blake Wesley, Québ.	.40
☐ 295 John Anderson, Toro.	.40
☐ 296 Jim Benning, Toro.	.40
☐ **297 Allan Bester (G), Toro. RC, Error (Alan)**	**1.50**
☐ **298 Rich Costello, Toro. RC**	**.75**
☐ 299 Dan Daoust, Toro.	.40
☐ 300 Bill Derlago, Toro.	.40
☐ 301 Dave Farrish, Toro.	.40
☐ 302 Stewart Gavin, Toro.	.40
☐ 303 Gaston Gingras, Toro.	.40
☐ 304 Jim Korn, Toro.	.40
☐ **305 Gary Leeman, Toro. RC**	**1.25**
☐ 306 Terry Martin, Toro. (Edm.)	.40
☐ **307 Gary Nylund, Toro. RC**	**.75**
☐ 308 Mike Palmateer (G), Toro.	.75
☐ 309 Walt Poddubny, Toro.	.40
☐ 310 Rick St. Croix (G), Toro.	.50
☐ 311 Börje Salming, Toro.	1.00
☐ 312 Greg Terrion, Toro.	.40
☐ 313 Rick Vaive, Toro.	.50
☐ 314 Richard Brodeur (G), Vanc.	.50
☐ 315 Jiri Bubla, Vanc.	.40
☐ 316 Ron Delorme, Vanc.	.40
☐ 317 John Garrett (G), Vanc.	.50
☐ 318 Jere Gillis, Vanc.	.40
☐ 319 Thomas Gradin, Vanc.	.40
☐ 320 Doug Halward, Vanc.	.40
☐ 321 Rick Lanz, Vanc.	.40
☐ **322 Moe Lemay, Vanc. RC**	**.75**
☐ 323 Gary Lupul, Vanc.	.40
☐ 324 Al MacAdam, Minn. (Vanc.)	.40
☐ 325 Rob McClanahan, Vanc.	.40
☐ 326 Peter McNab, Vanc.	.40
☐ **327 Cam Neely, Vanc. RC**	**30.00**
☐ 328 Darcy Rota, Vanc.	.40
☐ **329 Andy Schliebener, Vanc. RC**	**.75**
☐ 330 Stan Smyl, Vanc.	.40
☐ 331 Patrik Sundstrom, Vanc.	.40
☐ 332 Tony Tanti, Vanc.	.25
☐ 333 Scott Arniel, Winn.	.40
☐ 334 Dave Babych, Winn.	.50
☐ 335 Laurie Boschman, Winn.	.40
☐ 336 Wade Campbell, Winn.	.40
☐ 337 Randy Carlyle, Winn.	.50
☐ 338 Jordy Douglas, Winn.	.40
☐ 339 Dale Hawerchuk, Winn.	5.00
☐ 340 Morris Lukowich, Winn.	.40
☐ 341 Bengt Lundholm, Winn.	.40
☐ 342 Paul MacLean, Winn.	.40
☐ **343 Andrew McBain, Winn. RC**	**.75**
☐ 344 Brian Mullen, Winn.	.40
☐ 345 Robert Picard, Winn.	.40
☐ 346 Doug Smail, Winn.	.40
☐ 347 Doug Soetaert (G), Winn. (Mont.)	.50
☐ 348 Thomas Steen, Winn.	.40
☐ 349 Perry Turnbull, Winn.	.40
☐ 350 Tim Watters, Winn.	.40
☐ 351 Tim Young, Winn.	.40
☐ 352 TL: Rick Middleton, Bost.	.40
☐ 353 TL: Dave Andreychuk, Buff.	1.50
☐ 354 TL: Ed Beers, Calg.	.40
☐ 355 TL: Denis Savard, Chic.	.75
☐ 356 TL: John Ogrodnick, Detr.	.40
☐ 357 TL: Wayne Gretzky, Edm.	6.00
☐ 358 TL: Charlie Simmer, LosA.	.40
☐ 359 TL: Brian Bellows, Minn.	.50
☐ 360 TL: Guy Lafleur, Mont.	2.00
☐ 361 TL: Mel Bridgman, NJer.	.40
☐ 362 TL: Mike Bossy, NYIs.	.75
☐ 363 TL: Pierre Larouche, NYRa.	.40
☐ 364 TL: Tim Kerr, Phil.	.40
☐ 365 TL: Mike Bullard, Pitt.	.40
☐ 366 TL: Michel Goulet, Québ.	.50
☐ 367 TL: B. Federko/ J. Mullen, SLou.	.50
☐ 368 TL: Rick Vaive, Toro.	.40
☐ 369 TL: Tony Tanti, Vanc.	.40
☐ 370 TL: Mike Gartner, Wash.	1.00

□	371 TL: Paul MacLean, Winn.	.40
□	372 TL: Sylvain Turgeon, Hart.	.40
□	373 AW: Wayne Gretzky, Edmo.	6.00
□	374 AW: Wayne Gretzky, Edmo.	6.00
□	375 AW: Tom Barrasso, Buff.	1.75
□	376 AW: Mike Bossy, NYIs.	1.00
□	377 AW: Rod Langway, Wash.	.75
□	378 AW: Brad Park, Detr.	.75
□	379 AW: Tom Barrasso, Buff.	2.00
□	380 LL: Wayne Gretzky, Edmo.	6.00
□	381 LL: Wayne Gretzky, Edmo.	6.00
□	382 LL: Wayne Gretzky, Edmo.	6.00
□	383 LL: Wayne Gretzky, Edmo.	6.00
□	384 LL: Michel Goulet, Que	.50
□	385 LL: Steve Yzerman, Detr.	20.00

♦ A Steve Yzerman league leader card graded BGS 10 closed at $1,195.59 U.S. (approx. $1,615 Cdn.) in an April 18-25, 2003 auction at eBay.

□	386 LL: Pat Riggin, Wash.	.50
□	387 LL: Rollie Melanson, NYIs.	.50
□	388 RB: Wayne Gretzky, Edmo.	6.00
□	389 RB: Denis Potvin, NYIs.	.50
□	390 RB: Brad Park, Detr.	.50
□	391 RB: Michel Goulet, Québ.	.50
□	392 RB: Pat LaFontaine, NYIs.	5.00
□	393 RB: Dale Hawerchuk, Winn.	1.00
□	394 Checklist 1 (1 - 132)	3.00
□	395 Checklist 2 (133 -264)	3.00
□	396 Checklist 3 (264 - 396)	4.00

1984 - 85 O-PEE-CHEE STICKERS

Complete Set (270 stickers): **50.00**
Common Sticker: **.20**
Album (Wayne Gretzky cover): **8.00**

	O-Pee-Chee	**NM-MT**
□	1 Islanders vs. Oilers	.20
□	2 Islanders vs. Oilers	.20
□	3 Islanders vs. Oilers	.20
□	4 Islanders vs. Oilers	.20
□	5 Foil: Mark Messier, Edmo.	1.50
□	7 Börje Salming, Toro.	.35
□	8 Börje Salming, Toro.	.35
□	9 Dan Daoust, Toro.	.20
□	10 Dan Daoust, Toro.	.20
□	11 Rick Vaive, Toro.	.20
□	12 Rick Vaive, Toro.	.20
□	13 Dale McCourt, Toro.	.20
□	14 Bill Derlago, Toro.	.20
□	15 Gary Nylund, Toro.	.20
□	16 Gary Nylund, Toro.	.20
□	17 Jim Korn, Toro.	.20
□	18 John Anderson, Toro.	.20
□	19 Greg Terrion, Toro.	.20
□	20 Allan Bester (G), Toro.	.35
□	21 Jim Benning, Toro.	.20
□	22 Mike Palmateer (G), Toro.	.35
□	24 Denis Savard, Chic.	.50
□	25 Denis Savard, Chic.	.50
□	26 Bob Murray, Chic.	.20
□	27 Doug Wilson, Chic.	.35
□	28 Keith Brown, Chic.	.20
□	29 Steve Larmer, Chic.	1.00
□	30 Darryl Sutter, Chic.	.20
□	31 Tom Lysiak, Chic.	.20
□	32 Murray Bannerman (G), Chic.	.35
□	34 John Ogrodnick, Detr.	.20
□	35 John Ogrodnick, Detr.	.20
□	36 Reed Larson, Detr.	.20
□	37 Steve Yzerman, Detr.	15.00
□	38 Brad Park, Detr.	.35
□	39 Ivan Boldirev, Detr.	.20
□	40 Kelly Kisio, Detr.	.20
□	41 Greg Stefan (G), Detr.	.35
□	42 Ron Duguay, Detr.	.20
□	44 Brian Bellows, Minn.	.35
□	45 Brian Bellows, Minn.	.35
□	46 Neal Broten, Minn.	.20
□	47 Dino Ciccarelli, Minn.	.35
□	48 Dennis Maruk, Minn.	.20
□	49 Steve Payne, Minn.	.20
□	50 Brad Maxwell, Minn.	.20
□	51 Gilles Meloche (G), Minn.	.35
□	52 Tom McCarthy, Minn.	.20
□	54 Bernie Federko, SLou.	.35
□	55 Bernie Federko, SLou.	.35
□	56 Brian Sutter, SLou.	.35
□	57 Mike Liut (G), SLou.	.35
□	58 Doug Wickenheiser, SLou.	.20
□	59 Jorgen Pettersson, SLou.	.20
□	60 Doug Gilmour, SLou.	6.00
□	61 Joe Mullen, SLou.	.50
□	62 Rob Ramage, SLou.	.20
□	68 Glenn Resch (G), NJer.	.35
□	69 Glenn Resch (G), NJer.	.35
□	70 Don Lever, NJer.	.20
□	71 Mel Bridgman, NJer.	.20
□	72 Bob MacMillan, NJer.	.20
□	73 Pat Verbeek, NJer.	1.00
□	74 Joe Cirella, NJer.	.20
□	75 Phil Russell, NJer.	.20
□	76 Jan Ludvig, NJer.	.20
□	78 Denis Potvin, NYIs.	.35
□	79 Denis Potvin, NYIs.	.35
□	80 John Tonelli, NYIs.	.20
□	81 John Tonelli, NYIs.	.20
□	82 Mike Bossy, NYIs.	.50
□	83 Mike Bossy, NYIs.	.50
□	84 Butch Goring, NYIs.	.20
□	85 Bob Nystrom, NYIs.	.20
□	86 Bryan Trottier, NYIs.	.35
□	87 Bryan Trottier, NYIs.	.35
□	88 Brent Sutter, NYIs.	.20
□	89 Bob Bourne, NYIs.	.20
□	90 Greg Gilbert, NYIs.	.20
□	91 Billy Smith (G), NYIs.	.50
□	92 Rollie Melanson (G), NYIs.	.35
□	93 Ken Morrow, NYIs.	.20
□	95 Don Maloney, NYRa.	.20
□	96 Don Maloney, NYRa.	.20
□	97 Mark Pavelich, NYRa.	.20
□	98 Glen Hanlon (G), NYRa.	.35
□	99 Mike Rogers, NYRa.	.20
□	100 Barry Beck, NYRa.	.20
□	101 Reijo Ruotsalainen, NYRa.	.20
□	102 Anders Hedberg, NYRa.	.20
□	103 Pierre Larouche, NYRa.	.20
□	105 Tim Kerr, Phil.	.20
□	106 Tim Kerr, Phil.	.20
□	107 Ron Sutter, Phil.	.20
□	108 Darryl Sittler, Phil.	.35
□	109 Mark Howe, Phil.	.35
□	110 Dave Poulin, Phil.	.20
□	111 Rich Sutter, Phil.	.20
□	112 Brian Propp, Phil.	.20
□	113 Bob Froese (G), Phil.	.35
□	115 Ron Flockhart, Pitt.	.20
□	116 Ron Flockhart, Pitt.	.20
□	117 Rick Kehoe, Pitt.	.20
□	118 Mike Bullard, Pitt.	.20
□	119 Kevin McCarthy, Pitt.	.20
□	120 Doug Shedden, Pitt.	.20
□	121 Mark Taylor, Pitt.	.20
□	122 Denis Herron (G), Pitt.	.35
□	123 Tom Roulston, Pitt.	.20
□	125 Rod Langway, Wash.	.35
□	126 Rod Langway, Wash.	.35
□	127 Larry Murphy, Wash.	.35
□	128 Al Jensen (G), Wash.	.35
□	129 Doug Jarvis, Wash.	.20
□	130 Bengt Gustafsson, Wash.	.20
□	131 Mike Gartner, Wash.	1.00
□	132 Bob Carpenter, Wash.	.20
□	133 Dave Christian, Wash.	.20
□	134 AS: Foil: Paul Coffey, Edmo.	2.00
□	135 AS: Foil: Murray Bannerman (G), Chic.	.35
□	136 AS: Foil: Rob Ramage, SLou.	.20
□	137 AS: Foil: John Ogrodnick, Detr.	.20
□	138 AS: Foil: Wayne Gretzky, Edmo.	6.00
□	139 AS: Foil: Rick Vaive, Toro.	.20
□	140 AS: Foil: Michel Goulet, Québ.	.35
□	141 AS: Foil: Peter Stastny, Québ.	.35
□	142 AS: Foil: Rick Middleton, Bost.	.35
□	143 AS: Foil: Raymond Bourque, Bost.	2.00
□	144 AS: Foil: Pete Peeters (G), Bost.	.35
□	145 AS: Foil: Denis Potvin, NYIs.	.50
□	147 Larry Robinson, Mont.	.35
□	148 Larry Robinson, Mont.	.35
□	149 Guy Lafleur, Mont.	1.50
□	150 Guy Lafleur, Mont.	2.00
□	151 Bobby Smith, Mont.	.35
□	152 Bobby Smith, Mont.	.35
□	153 Bob Gainey, Mont.	.35
□	154 Craig Ludwig, Mont.	.20
□	155 Mats Näslund, Mont.	.20
□	156 Mats Näslund, Mont.	.20
□	157 Rick Wamsley (G), Mont.	.35
□	158 Jean Hamel, Mont.	.20
□	159 Ryan Walter, Mont.	.20
□	160 Guy Carbonneau, Mont.	.35
□	161 Mario Tremblay, Mont.	.20
□	162 Pierre Mondou, Mont.	.20
□	164 Peter Stastny, Québ.	.50
□	165 Peter Stastny, Québ.	.50
□	166 Mario Marois, Québ.	.20
□	167 Mario Marois, Québ.	.20
□	168 Michel Goulet, Québ.	1.00
□	169 Michel Goulet, Québ.	1.00
□	170 André Savard, Québ.	.20
□	171 Tony McKegney, Québ.	.20
□	172 Dan Bouchard (G), Québ.	.35
□	173 Dan Bouchard (G), Québ.	.35
□	174 Randy Moller, Québ.	.20
□	175 Wilf Paiement, Québ.	.20
□	176 Normand Rochefort, Québ.	.20
□	177 Marian Stastny, Québ.	.20
□	178 Anton Stastny, Québ.	.20
□	179 Dale Hunter, Québ.	.35
□	181 Rick Middleton, Bost.	.35
□	182 Rick Middleton, Bost.	.35
□	183 Raymond Bourque, Bost.	2.00
□	184 Pete Peeters (G), Bost.	.35
□	185 Mike O'Connell, Bost.	.20
□	186 Gord Kluzak, Bost.	.20
□	187 Barry Pederson, Bost.	.20
□	188 Mike Krushelnyski, Bost.	.20
□	189 Tom Fergus, Bost.	.20
□	191 Sylvain Turgeon, Hart.	.20
□	192 Sylvain Turgeon, Hart.	.20
□	193 Mark Johnson, Hart.	.20
□	194 Greg Malone, Hart.	.20
□	195 Mike Zuke, Hart.	.20
□	196 Ron Francis, Hart.	1.50
□	197 Bob Crawford, Hart.	.20
□	198 Greg Millen (G), Hart.	.35
□	199 Ray Neufeld, Hart.	.20
□	201 Gilbert Perreault, Buff.	.35
□	202 Gilbert Perreault, Buff.	.35
□	203 Phil Housley, Buff.	.35
□	204 Phil Housley, Buff.	.35
□	205 Tom Barrasso (G), Buff.	1.50
□	206 Tom Barrasso (G), Buff.	1.50
□	207 Larry Playfair, Buff.	.20
□	208 Bob Sauvé (G), Buff.	.35
□	209 Dave Andreychuk, Buff.	1.50
□	210 Dave Andreychuk, Buff.	1.50
□	211 Mike Ramsey, Buff.	.20
□	212 Mike Foligno, Buff.	.20
□	213 Lindy Ruff, Buff.	.20
□	214 Bill Hajt, Buff.	.20
□	215 Craig Ramsay, Buff.	.20
□	216 Ric Seiling, Buff.	.20
□	237 Lanny McDonald, Calg.	.35
□	238 Lanny McDonald, Calg.	.35
□	239 Steve Tambellini, Calg.	.20
□	240 Réjean Lemelin (G), Calg.	.35
□	241 Doug Risebrough, Calg.	.20
□	242 Hakan Loob, Calg.	.20
□	243 Eddy Beers, Calg.	.20
□	244 Mike Eaves, Calg.	.20
□	245 Kent Nilsson, Calg.	.20
□	247 Glenn Anderson, Edmo.	.50
□	248 Glenn Anderson, Edmo.	.50
□	249 Jari Kurri, Edmo.	1.25
□	250 Jari Kurri, Edmo.	1.25
□	251 Paul Coffey, Edmo.	1.50
□	252 Paul Coffey, Edmo.	1.50
□	253 Kevin Lowe, Edmo.	.35
□	254 Lee Fogolin, Edmo.	.20
□	255 Wayne Gretzky, Edmo.	5.00
□	256 Wayne Gretzky, Edmo.	4.00
□	257 Randy Gregg, Edmo.	.20
□	258 Charlie Huddy, Edmo.	.20
□	259 Grant Fuhr (G), Edmo.	1.00
□	260 Willy Lindstrom, Edmo.	.20
□	261 Mark Messier, Edmo.	2.00
□	262 Andy Moog (G), Edmo.	1.00
□	264 Marcel Dionne, LosA.	.35
□	265 Marcel Dionne, LosA.	.35
□	266 Charlie Simmer, LosA.	.20
□	267 Dave Taylor, LosA.	.35
□	268 Jim Fox, LosA.	.20
□	269 Bernie Nicholls, LosA.	.20
□	270 Terry Ruskowski, LosA.	.20
□	271 Brian Engblom, LosA.	.20
□	272 Mark Hardy, LosA.	.20
□	274 Tony Tanti, Vanc.	.20
□	275 Tony Tanti, Vanc.	.20
□	276 Rick Lanz, Vanc.	.20
□	277 Richard Brodeur (G), Vanc.	.35
□	278 Doug Halward, Vanc.	.20
□	279 Patrik Sundstrom, Vanc.	.20
□	280 Darcy Rota, Vanc.	.20
□	281 Stan Smyl, Vanc.	.20
□	282 Thomas Gradin, Vanc.	.20
□	284 Dale Hawerchuk, Winn.	1.25
□	285 Dale Hawerchuk, Winn.	1.25
□	286 Scott Arniel, Winn.	.20
□	287 Dave Babych, Winn.	.20
□	288 Laurie Boschman, Winn.	.20
□	289 Paul MacLean, Winn.	.20
□	290 Lucien DeBlois, Winn.	.20
□	291 Randy Carlyle, Winn.	.20
□	292 Thomas Steen, Winn.	.20

	O-Pee-Chee	**NM-MT**
□	6/23 Foil: Toronto Maple Leafs/ Chicago Blackhawks	.20
□	33/43 Foil: Detroit Red Wings/ Minnesota North Stars	.20
□	53/67 Foil: St. Louis Blues/ New Jersey Devils	.20
□	63/64 Foil: Wayne Gretzky/ Michel Goulet	4.00
□	65/66 Foil: Pat Riggin (G)/ Denis Potvin	.50
□	77/94 Foil: New York Islanders/ New York Rangers	.20
□	104/114 Foil: Philadelphia Flyers/ Pittburgh Penguins	.20
□	124/146 Foil: Washington Capitals/ Montréal Canadiens	.20
□	163/180 Foil: Québec Nordiques/ Boston Bruins	.20
□	190/200 Foil: Hartford Whalers/ Buffalo Sabres	.20
□	217/224 Foil: Hart Trophy/ Selke Trophy	.20
□	218/223 Foil: Vezina Trophy/ Masterton Trophy	.20
□	219/221 Foil: Jennings Trophy/ Art Ross Trophy	.20
□	220/225 Foil: Calder Trophy/ Lady Byng Trophy	.20
□	222/283 Norris Trophy/ Norris Trophy Winnipeg	.20
□	226/227 AW: Wayne Gretzky/ Tom Barrasso (G)	4.00
□	228/229 AW: Tom Barrasso (G)/ Wayne Gretzky	4.00
□	230/231 AW: Rod Langway/ Brad Park	.50
□	232/233 AW: Al Jensen (G)/ Pat Riggin (G)	.35
□	234/235 AW: Doug Jarvis/ Mike Bossy	.50
□	235/246 Foil: Calgary Flames/ Edmonton Oilers	.20
□	263/273 Foil: Los Angeles Kings/ Vancouver Canucks	.20

1984 - 85 7-ELEVEN DISKS

With the exception of the special large Gretzky disk, these disks measure 2" in diametre.

Complete Set (60 disks): **110.00**

	7-Eleven	**NRMT-MT**
□	Raymond Bourque, Bost.	7.00
□	Rick Middleton, Bost.	2.50
□	Tom Barrasso (G), Buff.	3.00
□	Gilbert Perreault, Buff.	2.50
□	Réjean Lemelin (G), Calg.	2.00
□	Lanny McDonald, Calg.	2.50
□	Paul Reinhart, Calg.	1.50
□	Doug Risebrough, Calg.	1.50
□	Denis Savard, Chic.	2.50
□	Alan Secord, Chic.	1.50
□	Dave Williams, Detr.	1.50
□	Steve Yzerman, Detr.	18.00
□	Glenn Anderson, Edmo.	2.50
□	Paul Coffey, Edmo.	6.00
□	Wayne Gretzky, Edmo	25.00
□	Charlie Huddy, Edmo.	1.50
□	Pat Hughes, Edmo.	1.50
□	Jari Kurri, Edmo.	4.00
□	Kevin Lowe, Edmo.	2.00
□	Mark Messier, Edmo.	10.00
□	Ron Francis, Hart.	5.00
□	Sylvain Turgeon, Hart.	1.50
□	Marcel Dionne, LosA.	3.00
□	Dave Taylor, LosA.	2.00
□	Brian Bellows, Minn.	2.00
□	Dino Ciccarelli, Minn.	2.50
□	Harold Snepsts, Minn.	1.50
□	Bob Gainey, Mont.	3.00
□	Larry Robinson, Mont.	3.00
□	Mel Bridgman, NJer.	1.50
□	Glenn Resch (G), NJer.	2.00
□	Mike Bossy, NYIs.	5.00
□	Bryan Trottier, NYIs.	3.00
□	Barry Beck, NYRa.	1.50
□	Don Maloney, NYRa.	1.50
□	Tim Kerr, Phil.	1.50
□	Darryl Sittler, Phil.	2.50
□	Mike Bullard, Pitt.	1.50
□	Rick Kehoe, Pitt.	1.50
□	Michel Goulet, Québ.	3.00
□	Peter Stastny, Québ.	3.50
□	Bernie Federko, SLou.	2.50
□	Rob Ramage, SLou.	1.50
□	John Anderson, Toro.	1.50
□	Bill Derlago, Toro.	1.50
□	Gary Nylund, Toro.	1.50
□	Rick Vaive, Toro.	1.50
□	Richard Brodeur (G), Vanc.	2.00
□	Gary Lupul, Vanc.	1.50
□	Darcy Rota, Vanc.	1.50
□	Stan Smyl, Vanc.	1.50
□	Tony Tanti, Vanc.	1.50
□	Mike Gartner, Wash.	4.00
□	Rod Langway, Wash.	2.50
□	Scott Arniel, Winn.	1.50

□ Dave Babych, Winn. 1.50
□ Laurie Boschman, Winn. 1.50
□ Dale Hawerchuk, Winn. 3.00
□ Paul MacLean, Winn. 1.50
□ Brian Mullen, Winn. 1.50

7-Eleven **NM-MT**

□ Wayne Gretzky, Edmo. 25.00

1984 - 85 TOPPS

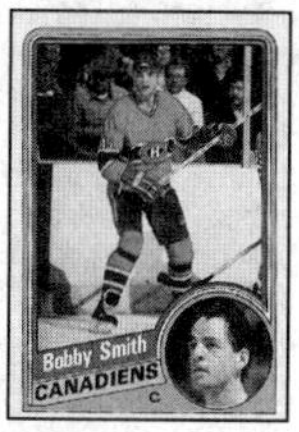

Complete Set (165 cards): **65.00**
Common Player: **.15**
Topps **NM-MT**

□ 1 Raymond Bourque, Bost. 2.00
□ 2 Keith Crowder, Bost. (*) .20
□ 3 Tom Fergus, Bost. .15
□ **4 Doug Keans (G), Bost. RC** **.50**
□ 5 Gord Kluzak, Bost. (*) .20
□ 6 Mike Krushelnyski, Bost. (*) .20
□ **7 Nevin Markwart, Bost. RC** **.35**
□ 8 Rick Middleton, Bost. .25
□ 9 Mike O'Connell, Bost. .15
□ 10 Terry O'Reilly, Bost. (*) .20
□ 11 Barry Pederson, Bost. .15
□ 12 Pete Peeters (G), Bost. .25
□ **13 Dave Andreychuk, Buff. RC (*)** **4.50**
□ **14 Tom Barrasso (G), Buff. RC** **5.00**
□ 15 Réal Cloutier, Buff. (*) .20
□ 16 Mike Foligno, Buff. .15
□ 17 Bill Hajt, Buff. (*) .20
□ 18 Phil Housley, Buff. (*) 1.50
□ 19 Gilbert Perreault, Buff. .75
□ 20 Larry Playfair, Buff. (*) .20
□ 21 Craig Ramsay, Buff. (*) .20
□ 22 Mike Ramsey, Buff. (*) .20
□ 23 Lindy Ruff, Buff. (*) .20
□ 24 Ed Beers, Calg. .15
□ 25 Réjean Lemelin (G), Calg. (*) .30
□ 26 Lanny McDonald, Calg. .50
□ 27 Murray Bannerman (G), Chic. .25
□ 28 Keith Brown, Chic. (*) .20
□ 29 Curt Fraser, Chic. .15
□ 30 Steve Larmer, Chic. 1.50
□ 31 Tom Lysiak, Chic. .15
□ 32 Bob Murray, Chic. .15
□ **33 Jack O'Callahan, Chic. RC (*)** **.35**
□ 34 Rich Preston, Chic. .15
□ 35 Denis Savard, Chic. .75
□ 36 Darryl Sutter, Chic. .25
□ 37 Doug Wilson, Chic. .25
□ 38 Ivan Boldirev, Detr. .15
□ 39 Colin Campbell, Detr. (*) .35
□ 40 Ron Duguay, Detr. (*) .20
□ 41 Dwight Foster, Detr. (*) .20
□ 42 Danny Gare, Detr. (*) .20
□ 43 Eddie Johnstone, Detr. .15
□ 44 Reed Larson, Detr. (*) .20
□ 45 Ed Mio (G), Detr. (*) .35
□ 46 John Ogrodnick, Detr. .15
□ 47 Brad Park, Detr. .50
□ **48 Greg Stefan (G), Detr. RC (*)** **.50**
□ **49 Steve Yzerman, Detr. RC** **50.00**
□ 50 Paul Coffey, Edmo. 2.50
□ 51 Wayne Gretzky, Edmo. 12.00
□ 52 Jari Kurri, Edmo. 1.00
□ **53 Bob Crawford, Hart. RC** **.35**
□ 54 Ron Francis, Hart. 2.00
□ 55 Marty Howe, Hart. .15
□ 56 Mark Johnson, Hart. (*) .20
□ 57 Greg Malone, Hart. (*) .20
□ 58 Greg Millen (G), Hart. (*) .35
□ 59 Ray Neufeld, Hart. .15
□ 60 Joel Quenneville, Hart. (*) .35
□ 61 Risto Siltanen, Hart. .15
□ **62 Sylvain Turgeon, Hart. RC** **.35**
□ 63 Mike Zuke, Hart. (*) .20
□ 64 Marcel Dionne, LosA. .35
□ 65 Brian Engblom, LosA. (*) .20
□ 66 Jim Fox, LosA. (*) .20
□ 67 Bernie Nicholls, LosA. 1.00
□ 68 Terry Ruskowski, LosA. (*) .20
□ 69 Charlie Simmer, LosA. .15
□ 70 Don Beaupré (G), Minn. .25
□ 71 Brian Bellows, Minn. .75
□ 72 Neal Broten, Minn. (*) .35
□ 73 Dino Ciccarelli, Minn. .50
□ 74 Paul Holmgren, Minn. (*) .20
□ 75 Al MacAdam, Minn. (*) .20
□ 76 Dennis Maruk, Minn. .15
□ 77 Brad Maxwell, Minn. (*) .20
□ 78 Tom McCarthy, Minn. (*) .20
□ 79 Gilles Meloche (G), Minn. (*) .35
□ 80 Steve Payne, Minn. .15
□ 81 Guy Lafleur, Mont. 2.50
□ 82 Larry Robinson, Mont. .50
□ 83 Bobby Smith, Mont. .25
□ 84 Mel Bridgman, NJer. .15
□ 85 Joe Cirella, NJer. .15
□ 86 Don Lever, NJer. .15
□ 87 Dave Lewis, NJer. .15
□ **88 Jan Ludvig, NJer. RC** **.35**
□ 89 Glenn Resch (G), NJer. .25
□ **90 Pat Verbeek, NJer. RC** **5.00**
□ 91 Mike Bossy, NYIs. 2.00
□ 92 Bob Bourne, NYIs. .15
□ **93 Greg Gilbert, NYIs. RC** **1.50**
□ 94 Clark Gillies, NYIs. (*) .35
□ 95 Butch Goring, NYIs. (*) .35
□ **96 Pat LaFontaine, NYIs. RC (*)** **10.00**
□ 97 Ken Morrow, NYIs. .15
□ 98 Bob Nystrom, NYIs. (*) .20
□ 99 Stefan Persson, NYIs. (*) .20
□ 100 Denis Potvin, NYIs. .50
□ 101 Billy Smith (G), NYIs. (*) .50
□ 102 Brent Sutter, NYIs. (*) .35
□ 103 John Tonelli, NYIs. .15
□ 104 Bryan Trottier, NYIs. .75
□ 105 Barry Beck, NYRa. .15
□ 106 Glen Hanlon (G), NYRa. (*) .35
□ 107 Anders Hedberg, NYRa. (*) .20
□ 108 Pierre Larouche, NYRa. (*) .20
□ 109 Don Maloney, NYRa. (*) .20
□ 110 Mark Osborne, NYRa. (*) .20
□ 111 Larry Patey, NYRa. .15
□ **112 James Patrick, NYRa. RC** **.75**
□ 113 Mark Pavelich, NYRa. (*) .20
□ 114 Mike Rogers, NYRa. (*) .20
□ 115 Reijo Ruotsalainen, NYRa. (*) .20
□ **116 Peter Sundström, NYRa. RC (*)** **.35**
□ 117 Rob Froese (G), Phil. .25
□ 118 Mark Howe, Phil. .35
□ 119 Tim Kerr, Phil. (*) .35
□ **120 David Poulin, Phil. RC** **1.00**
□ 121 Darryl Sittler, Phil. (*) .50
□ 122 Ron Sutter, Phil. .15
□ 123 Mike Bullard, Pitt. (*) .20
□ 124 Ron Flockhart, Pitt. (*) .20
□ 125 Rick Kehoe, Pitt. .15
□ 126 Kevin McCarthy, Pitt. (*) .20
□ 127 Mark Taylor, Pitt. .15
□ 128 Dan Bouchard (G), Québ. .25
□ 129 Michel Goulet, Québ. .50
□ 130 Peter Stastny, Québ. (*) .75
□ 131 Bernie Federko, SLou. .25
□ 132 Mike Liut (G), SLou. .25
□ 133 Joe Mullen, SLou. (*) .75
□ 134 Rob Ramage, SLou. .25
□ 135 Brian Sutter, SLou. .25
□ 136 John Anderson, Toro. (*) .20
□ 137 Dan Daoust, Toro. .15
□ 138 Rick Vaive, Toro. .25
□ 139 Darcy Rota, Vanc. (*) .20
□ 140 Stan Smyl, Vanc. (*) .20
□ 141 Tony Tanti, Vanc. .15
□ 142 Dave Christian, Wash. (*) .20
□ 143 Mike Gartner, Wash. (*) 2.00
□ 144 Bengt Gustafsson, Wash. (*) .20
□ 145 Doug Jarvis, Wash. .15
□ 146 Al Jensen (G), Wash. .25
□ 147 Rod Langway, Wash. .25
□ 148 Pat Riggin (G), Wash. (*) .25
□ 149 Scott Stevens, Wash. 2.50
□ 150 Dave Babych, Winn. .25
□ 151 Laurie Boschman, Winn. .15
□ 152 Dale Hawerchuk, Winn. 1.50
□ 153 AS: Michel Goulet, Québ. .25
□ 154 AS: Wayne Gretzky, Edmo. 3.50
□ 155 AS: Mike Bossy, NYIs. .50
□ 156 AS: Rod Langway, Wash. .25
□ 157 AS: Raymond Bourque, Bost. .75
□ 158 AS: Tom Barrasso (G), Buff. .75
□ 159 AS: Mark Messier, Edmo. 2.50
□ 160 AS: Bryan Trottier, NYIs. .25
□ 161 AS: Jari Kurri, Edmo. .60
□ 162 AS: Denis Potvin, NYIs. .50
□ 163 AS: Paul Coffey, Edmo. .75
□ 164 AS: Pat Riggin (G), Wash. .25
□ 165 Checklist (*) 3.00

1985 - 86 O-PEE-CHEE & TOPPS

There are two versions for this series: an O-Pee-Chee card (1-264) and a Topps card (1-165). Topps short prints are marked with an asterisk (*).

	Topps	OPC
O-Pee-Chee Set (264 cards):	–	**550.00**
Topps Set (165 cards):	**275.00**	–
Common Player:	**.30**	**.50**
Player	**Topps**	**OPC**
□□ 1 Lanny McDonald, Calg.	1.00	2.00
□□ 2 Mike O'Connell, Bost. (*)	.50	.50
□□ 3 Curt Fraser, Chic. (*)	.50	.50
□□ 4 Steve Penney (G), Mont.	.50	.75
□□ 5 Brian Engblom, LosA.	.30	.50
□□ 6 Ron Sutter, Phil.	.30	.50
□□ 7 Joe Mullen, SLou.	1.00	2.00
□□ 8 Rod Langway, Wash.	.50	.75
□□ **9 Mario Lemieux, Pitt. RC**	**200.00**	**400.00**

◆ A Mario Lemieux rookie card graded BGS-9.5 closed at $1,300 U.S. (approx. $1,750 Cdn.) in a May 4-11, 2003 auction at eBay.

	Topps	OPC
□□ 10 Dave Babych, Winn.	.50	.75
□□ 11 Bob Nystrom, NYIs.	.30	.50
□□ 12 Andy Moog (G), Edmo. (*)	2.75	3.50
□□ 13 Dino Ciccarelli, Minn.	1.25	1.00
□□ 14 Dwight Foster, Detr. (*)	.50	.50
□□ 15 James Patrick, NYRa. (*)	.50	.50
□□ 16 Thomas Gradin, Vanc. (*)	.50	.50
□□ 17 Mike Foligno, Buff.	.30	.50
□□ **18 Mario Gosselin (G), Québ. RC**	**.75**	**1.00**
□□ 19 Mike Zuke, Hart. (*)	.50	.50
□□ 20 John Anderson, Toro. (Québ.) (*)	.50	.50
□□ 21 Dave Pichette, NJer.	.30	.50
□□ 22 Nick Fotiu, NYRa. (*)	.50	.50
□□ 23 Tom Lysiak, Chic.	.30	.50
□□ **24 Peter Zezel, Phil. RC**	**1.25**	**2.00**
□□ 25 Denis Potvin, NYIs.	1.50	2.00
□□ 26 Bob Carpenter, Wash.	.30	.50
□□ 27 Murray Bannerman (G), Chic. (*)	.75	.75
□□ 28 Gord Roberts, Minn. (*)	.50	.50
□□ 29 Steve Yzerman, Detr.	25.00	55.00
□□ 30 Phil Russell, NJer.	.30	.50
□□ 31 Peter Stastny, Québ.	1.50	1.50
□□ 32 Craig Ramsay, Buff. (*)	.75	.75
□□ 33 Terry Ruskowski, Pitt. (*)	.50	.50
□□ **34 Kevin Dineen, Hart. RC (*)**	**4.00**	**4.00**
□□ 35 Mark Howe, Phil.	.50	.75
□□ 36 Glenn Resch (G), NJer.	.50	.75
□□ 37 Danny Gare, Detr. (*)	.75	.75
□□ **38 Doug Bodger, Pitt. RC**	**.75**	**1.00**
□□ 39 Mike Rogers, NYRa.	.30	.50
□□ 40 Raymond Bourque, Bost.	3.50	7.00
□□ 41 John Tonelli, NYIs.	.50	.75
□□ 42 Mel Bridgman, NJer.	.30	.50
□□ 43 Sylvain Turgeon, Hart. (*)	.50	.50
□□ 44 Mark Johnson, SLou.	.30	.50
□□ 45 Doug Wilson, Chic.	.50	.75
□□ 46 Mike Gartner, Wash.	2.00	3.50
□□ 47 Brent Peterson, Buff.	.30	.50
□□ 48 Paul Reinhart, Calg. (*)	.50	.50
□□ 49 Mike Krushelnyski, Edmo.	.30	.50
□□ 50 Brian Bellows, Minn.	.50	.75
□□ 51 Chris Chelios, Mont.	6.00	10.00
□□ 52 Barry Pederson, Bost. (*)	.50	.50
□□ 53 Murray Craven, Phil. (*)	.50	.50
□□ 54 Pierre Larouche, NYRa. (*)	.50	.50
□□ 55 Reed Larson, Detr.	.30	.50
□□ 56 Pat Verbeek, NJer. (*)	.75	.75
□□ 57 Randy Carlyle, Winn.	.30	.50
□□ 58 Ray Neufeld, Hart. (*)	.50	.50
□□ 59 Keith Brown, Chic. (*)	.50	.50
□□ 60 Bryan Trottier, NYIs.	1.75	2.00
□□ 61 Jim Fox, LosA. (*)	.50	.50
□□ 62 Scott Stevens, Wash.	1.00	2.00
□□ 63 Phil Housley, Buff.	.50	.75
□□ 64 Rick Middleton, Bost.	.50	.75
□□ 65 Steve Payne, Minn.	.30	.50
□□ 66 Dave Lewis, NJer.	.30	.50
□□ 67 Mike Bullard, Pitt.	.30	.50
□□ 68 Stan Smyl, Vanc. (*)	.30	.50
□□ 69 Mark Pavelich, NYRa. (*)	.50	.50
□□ 70 John Ogrodnick, Detr.	.30	.50
□□ 71 Bill Derlago, Toro. (Bost.) (*)	.50	.50
□□ 72 Brad Marsh, Phil. (*)	.50	.50
□□ 73 Denis Savard, Chic.	1.25	1.50
□□ **74 Mark Fusco, Hart. RC**	**.75**	**1.00**
□□ 75 Pete Peeters (G), Bost. (Wash.)	.50	.75
□□ 76 Doug Gilmour, SLou.	9.00	12.00
□□ 77 Mike Ramsey, Buff.	.30	.50
□□ 78 Anton Stastny, Québ. (*)	.50	.50
□□ 79 Steve Kasper, Bost. (*)	.50	.50
□□ **80 Bryan Erickson, Wash. RC (*)**	**1.00**	**1.00**
□□ 81 Clark Gillies, NYIs.	.30	.75
□□ 82 Keith Acton, Minn.	.30	.50
□□ 83 Pat Flatley, NYIs.	.30	.50
□□ **84 Kirk Muller, NJer. RC**	**4.00**	**7.00**
□□ 85 Paul Coffey, Edmo.	3.50	6.00
□□ **86 Ed Olczyk, Chic. RC**	**1.25**	**2.00**
□□ 87 Charlie Simmer, Bost.	.30	.50
□□ 88 Mike Liut (G), Hart.	.50	.75
□□ 89 Dave Maloney, Buff.	.30	.50
□□ 90 Marcel Dionne, LosA.	1.25	1.50
□□ 91 Tim Kerr, Phil.	.50	.75
□□ 92 Ivan Boldirev, Detr. (*)	.50	.50
□□ 93 Ken Morrow, NYIs. (*)	.50	.50
□□ 94 Don Maloney, NYRa. (*)	.50	.50
□□ 95 Réjean Lemelin (G), Calg.	.50	.75
□□ 96 Curt Giles, Minn.	.30	.50
□□ 97 Bob Bourne, NYIs.	.30	.50
□□ 98 Joe Cirella, NJer.	.30	.50
□□ 99 Dave Christian, Wash. (*)	.50	.50
□□ 100 Darryl Sutter, Chic.	.50	.75
□□ 101 Kelly Kisio, Detr.	.30	.50
□□ 102 Mats Näslund, Mont.	.50	.75
□□ 103 Joel Quenneville, Hart. (*)	.50	.75
□□ 104 Bernie Federko, SLou.	.50	.75
□□ 105 Tom Barrasso (G), Buff.	1.25	2.00
□□ 106 Rick Vaive, Toro.	.50	.75
□□ 107 Brent Sutter, NYIs.	.50	.75
□□ 108 Wayne Babych, SLou. (Québ.)	.30	.50
□□ 109 Dale Hawerchuk, Winn.	1.75	3.50
□□ 110 Pelle Lindbergh (G), Phil. (*)	12.00	12.00
□□ 111 Dennis Maruk, Minn. (*)	.50	.50
□□ 112 Reijo Ruotsalainen, NYRa. (*)	.50	.50
□□ 113 Tom Fergus, Bost. (Toro.) (*)	.50	.50
□□ 114 Bob Murray, Chic. (*)	.50	.50
□□ 115 Patrik Sundstrom, Vanc.	.30	.50
□□ 116 Ron Duguay, Detr. (*)	.50	.50
□□ 117 Alan Haworth, Wash. (*)	.50	.50
□□ 118 Greg Malone, Hart.	.30	.50
□□ 119 Bill Hajt, Buff.	.30	.50
□□ 120 Wayne Gretzky, Edmo.	25.00	35.00
□□ **121 Craig Redmond, LosA. RC**	**.75**	**1.00**
□□ **122 Kelly Hrudey (G), NYIs. RC**	**6.00**	**10.00**
□□ **123 Tomas Sandström, NYRa. RC**	**4.00**	**6.00**
□□ 124 Neal Broten, Minn.	.50	.75
□□ 125 Moe Mantha, Pitt. (*)	.50	.50
□□ 126 Greg Gilbert, NYIs. (*)	.50	.50
□□ **127 Bruce Driver, NJer. RC**	**1.00**	**1.50**
□□ 128 Dave Poulin, Phil.	.50	.75
□□ 129 Morris Lukowich, Bost.	.30	.50
□□ 130 Mike Bossy, NYIs.	2.00	3.00
□□ 131 Larry Playfair, Buff. (*)	.50	.50
□□ 132 Steve Larmer, Chic.	1.25	1.50
□□ 133 Doug Keans (G), Bost. (*)	.50	.75
□□ 134 Bob Manno, Detr.	.30	.50
□□ 135 Brian Sutter, SLou.	.50	.75
□□ 136 Pat Riggin (G), Wash. (Bost.)	.50	.70
□□ 137 Pat LaFontaine, NYIs.	6.00	8.00
□□ 138 Barry Beck, NYRa. (*)	.50	.50
□□ 139 Rich Preston, NJer. (*)	.50	.50
□□ 140 Ron Francis, Hart.	3.00	4.50
□□ 141 Brian Propp, Phil. (*)	.50	.50
□□ 142 Don Beaupré (G), Minn.	.50	.75
□□ 143 Dave Andreychuk, Buff. (*)	2.50	3.50
□□ 144 Ed Beers, Calg.	.30	.50
□□ 145 Paul MacLean, Winn.	.30	.50
□□ 146 Troy Murray, Chic. (*)	.50	.50
□□ 147 Larry Robinson, Mont.	1.25	2.00
□□ 148 Bernie Nicholls, LosA.	.50	.75
□□ 149 Glen Hanlon (G), NYRa. (*)	.50	.75
□□ 150 Michel Goulet, Québ.	1.25	2.00
□□ 151 Doug Jarvis, Wash. (*)	.50	.50
□□ **152 Warren Young, Pitt. (Detr.) RC**	**.75**	**1.00**
□□ 153 Tony Tanti, Vanc.	.50	.50
□□ 154 Tomas Jonsson, NYIs. (*)	.50	.50
□□ 155 Jari Kurri, Edmo.	2.50	3.50
□□ 156 Tony McKegney, Minn.	.30	.50
□□ 157 Greg Stefan (G), Detr. (*)	.75	.75
□□ 158 Brad McCrimmon, Phil. (*)	.50	.50
□□ 159 Keith Crowder, Bost. (*)	.50	.50
□□ 160 Gilbert Perreault, Buff.	.50	2.00
□□ 161 Tim Bothwell, SLou. (Hart.) (*)	.50	.50
□□ 162 Bob Crawford, Hart. (*)	.50	.50
□□ 163 Paul Gagné, NJer. (*)	.50	.50

□ □	164 Dan Daoust, Toro. (*)	.50	.50
□ □	165 Checklist 1 (1 - 132) (*)	4.00	6.00

	Player	OPC
□	**166 Tim Bernhardt (G), Toro. RC**	**1.50**
□	167 Gord Kluzak, Bost.	.50
□	168 Glenn Anderson, Edmo.	.75
□	169 Bob Gainey, Mont.	2.00
□	170 Brent Ashton, Québ.	.50
□	171 Ron Flockhart, SLou.	.50
□	172 Gary Nylund, Toro.	.50
□	173 Moe Lemay, Vanc.	.50
□	174 Bob Sauvé (G), Chic.	.75
□	175 Doug Smail, Winn.	.50
□	176 Dan Quinn, Calg.	.50
□	177 Mark Messier, Edmo.	12.00
□	**178 Jay Wells, LosA. RC**	**1.50**
□	179 Dale Hunter, Québ.	.75
□	180 Richard Brodeur (G), Vanc.	.75
□	181 Bobby Smith, Mont.	.50
□	182 Ron Greschner, NYRa.	.50
□	183 Don Edwards (G), Toro.	.75
□	184 Hakan Loob, Calg.	.50
□	**185 Dave Ellett, Winn. RC**	**1.50**
□	186 Denis Herron (G), Pitt.	.75
□	187 Charlie Huddy, Edmo.	.50
□	188 Ilkka Sinisalo, Phil.	.50
□	189 Doug Halward, Vanc.	.50
□	190 Craig Laughlin, Wash.	.50
□	**191 Carey Wilson, Calg. RC**	**1.00**
□	192 Craig Ludwig, Mont.	.50
□	193 Bob MacMillan, Chic.	.50
□	194 Mario Marois, Québ.	.50
□	195 Brian Mullen, Winn.	.50
□	196 Rob Ramage, SLou.	.50
□	197 Rick Lanz, Vanc.	.50
□	198 Miroslav Frycer, Toro.	.50
□	199 Randy Gregg, Edmo.	.50
□	200 Corrado Micalef (G), Detr.	.75
□	201 Jamie Macoun, Calg.	.50
□	**202 Bob Brooke, NYRa. RC**	**1.00**
□	203 Billy Carroll, Edmo.	.50
□	204 Brian MacLellan, LosA.	.50
□	205 Alain Côté, Québ.	.50
□	206 Thomas Steen, Winn.	.50
□	207 Grant Fuhr (G), Edmo.	4.50
□	208 Rich Sutter, Phil.	.50
□	209 Al MacAdam, Vanc.	.50
□	**210 Al Iafrate, Toro. RC**	**5.00**
□	211 Pierre Mondou, Mont.	.50
□	**212 Randy Hillier, Pitt. RC**	**1.00**
□	213 Mike Eaves, Calg.	.50
□	214 Dave Taylor, LosA.	.50
□	215 Robert Picard, Winn.	.50
□	216 Randy Ladouceur, Detr.	.50
□	217 Willy Lindstrom, Pitt.	.50
□	**218 Torrie Robertson, Hart. RC**	**1.00**
□	**219 Tom Kurvers, Mont. RC**	**1.00**
□	220 John Garrett, Vanc.	.75
□	221 Greg Millen (G), SLou.	.75
□	222 Richard Kromm, Calg.	.50
□	**223 Bob Janecyk (G), LosA. RC**	**1.00**
□	224 Brad Maxwell, Toro.	.50
□	**225 Mike McPhee, Mont. RC**	**1.50**
□	**226 Brian Hayward (G), Winn. RC**	**3.00**
□	227 Duane Sutter, NYIs.	.50
□	228 Cam Neely, Vanc.	12.00
□	229 Doug Wickenheiser, SLou.	.50
□	230 Rollie Melanson (G), Minn.	.75
□	**231 Bruce Bell, SLou. RC**	**1.00**
□	232 Harold Snepsts, Detr.	.50
□	233 Guy Carbonneau, Mont.	.75
□	234 Doug Sulliman, NJer.	.50
□	235 Lee Fogolin, Edmo.	.50
□	236 Larry Murphy, Wash.	1.50
□	**237 Al MacInnis, Calg. RC**	**40.00**
□	238 Don Lever, Buff.	.50
□	239 Kevin Lowe, Edmo.	.75
□	240 Randy Moller, Québ.	.50
□	**241 Doug Lidster, Vanc. RC**	**1.00**
□	242 Craig Hartsburg, Minn.	.75
□	243 Doug Risebrough, Calg.	.75
□	244 John Chabot, Pitt.	.50
□	245 Mario Tremblay, Mont.	.75
□	246 Dan Bouchard (G), Winn.	.75
□	247 Doug Shedden, Pitt.	.50
□	248 Börje Salming, Toro.	1.00
□	249 Aaron Broten, NJer.	.50
□	250 Jim Benning, Toro.	.50
□	251 Laurie Boschman, Winn.	.50
□	**252 George McPhee, NYRa. RC**	**3.00**
□	253 Mark Napier, Edmo.	.50
□	254 Perry Turnbull, Winn.	.50
□	**255 Warren Skorodenski (G), Chic. RC**	**1.50**
□	256 Checklist 2 (133 - 264)	6.00
□	257 LL: Wayne Gretzky, Edmo.	8.00
□	258 LL: Wayne Gretzky, Edmo.	8.00
□	259 LL: Wayne Gretzky, Edmo.	8.00
□	260 LL: Tim Kerr, Phil.	.50
□	261 LL: Jari Kurri, Edmo.	1.25
□	262 LL: Mario Lemieux, Pitt.	50.00
□	263 LL: Tom Barrasso (G), Buff.	.75
□	264 LL: Warren Skorodenski (G), Chic.	.75

OPC / TOPPS BOX BOTTOMS

These four-card 5" x 7" panels were issued on the bottom of O-Pee-Chee and Topps wax boxes. The most expensive cut-out singles are Mario Lemieux (OPC $85, Topps $75) and Wayne Gretzky (OPC $30, Topps $25). O-Pee-Chee singles start at $1.00; Topps singles start at 75¢.

	Box Bottom	Topps	OPC
	Complete Set (16 cards):	**100.00**	**130.00**
□ □	A-D Bellows/ Bourque/ Carpenter/ Chelios	8.00	12.00
□ □	E-H Dionne/ Francis/ Gretzky/ Kerr	30.00	40.00
□ □	I-L Lemieux/ Ogrodnick/ Perreault/ Resch (G)	80.00	100.00
□ □	M-P Ruotsalainen/ Bri. Sutter/ Tonelli/ Do. Wilson	3.00	5.00

TOPPS STICKER INSERTS

	Sticker	NM-MT
	Insert Set (33 stickers):	**22.00**
□	1 John Ogrodnick, Detr.	.50
□	2 Wayne Gretzky, Edmo.	12.00
□	3 Jari Kurri, Edmo.	1.50
□	4 Paul Coffey, Edmo.	2.00
□	5 Raymond Bourque, Bost.	3.00
□	6 Pelle Lindbergh (G), Phil.	4.00
□	7 John Tonelli, NYIs.	.50
□	8 Dale Hawerchuk, Winn.	1.00
□	9 Mike Bossy, NYIs.	1.50
□	10 Rod Langway, Wash.	.50
□	11 Doug Wilson, Chic.	.50
□	12 Tom Barrasso (G), Buff.	.75

□	13 Maple Leafs	□	14 Sabres
□	15 Red Wings	□	16 Penguins
□	17 Rangers	□	18 Flames
□	19 Jets	□	20 Nordiques
□	21 Blackhawks	□	22 Kings
□	23 Canadiens	□	24 Canucks
□	25 Whalers	□	26 Flyers
□	27 Devils	□	28 Blues
□	29 North Stars	□	30 Capitals
□	31 Bruins	□	32 Islanders
□	33 Oilers		

1985 - 86 O-PEE-CHEE STICKERS

These stickers measure 2 1/8" x 2 15/16".

	O-Pee-Chee	NM-MT
	Complete Set (163 stickers):	**60.00**
	Album:	**5.00**
	Common Player:	**.20**
□	1 Stanley Cup Final	.20
□	2 Stanley Cup Final	.20
□	3 Stanley Cup Final	.20
□	4 Stanley Cup Final	.20

Note: Stickers 1-4 feature Mark Messier, Don Jackson and Tim Kerr.

□	5 Wayne Gretzky, Edmo.	6.00
□	6 Rick Vaive, Toro.	.20
□	7 Bill Derlago, Toro.	.20
□	12 Börje Salming, Toro.	.35
□	21 Miroslav Frycer, Toro.	.20
□	22 Denis Savard, Chic.	.50
□	25 Doug Wilson, Chic.	.35
□	30 Steve Yzerman, Detr.	7.00
□	37 John Ogrodnick, Detr.	.20
□	38 Keith Acton, Minn.	.20
□	41 Brian Bellows, Minn.	.20
□	46 Brian Sutter, SLou.	.20
□	53 Bernie Federko, SLou.	.20
□	57 Mel Bridgman, NJer.	.20
□	64 Kirk Muller, NJer.	.50
□	65 Bryan Trottier, NYIs.	.35
□	66 Mike Bossy, NYIs.	.50
□	71 Brent Sutter, NYIs.	.20
□	80 John Tonelli, NYIs.	.20
□	81 Reijo Ruotsalainen, NYRa.	.20
□	84 Mark Pavelich, NYRa.	.20
□	89 Dave Poulin, Phil.	.20
□	96 Tim Kerr, Phil.	.20
□	97 Mario Lemieux, Pitt.	20.00
□	100 Warren Young, Pitt.	.20
□	105 Rod Langway, Wash.	.35
□	112 Bob Carpenter, Wash.	.20
□	113 Foil-AS: Rod Langway, Wash.	.50
□	114 Foil-AS: Tom Barrasso (G), Buff.	.75
□	115 Foil-AS: Raymond Bourque, Bost.	2.50
□	116 Foil-AS: John Tonelli, NYIs.	.35
□	117 Foil-AS: Brent Sutter, NYIs.	.35
□	118 Foil-AS: Mike Bossy, NYIs.	.75
□	119 Foil-AS: John Ogrodnick, Detr.	.35
□	120 Foil-AS: Wayne Gretzky, Edmo.	9.00
□	121 Foil-AS: Jari Kurri, Edmo.	1.50
□	122 Foil-AS: Doug Wilson, Chic.	.35
□	123 Foil-AS: Andy Moog (G), Edmo.	1.50
□	124 Foil-AS: Paul Coffey, Edmo.	2.00
□	125 Chris Chelios, Mont.	2.00
□	126 Steve Penney (G), Mont.	.35
□	131 Mats Näslund, Mont.	.20
□	140 Larry Robinson, Mont.	.35
□	141 Michel Goulet, Québ.	.35
□	142 Bruce Bell, Québ.	.20
□	147 Anton Stastny, Québ.	.20
□	156 Peter Stastny, Québ.	.35
□	157 Raymond Bourque, Bost.	2.00
□	160 Pete Peeters (G), Bost.	.35
□	165 Sylvain Turgeon, Hart.	.20
□	172 Ron Francis, Hart.	1.00
□	173 Phil Housley, Buff.	.35
□	174 Mike Foligno, Buff.	.20
□	179 Tom Barrasso (G), Buff.	.50
□	188 Gilbert Perreault, Buff.	.35
□	208 Kent Nilsson, Calg.	.20
□	215 Lanny McDonald, Calg.	.35
□	216 Charlie Huddy, Edmo.	.20
□	217 Paul Coffey, Edmo.	1.50
□	222 Wayne Gretzky, Edmo.	6.00
□	231 Jari Kurri, Edmo.	1.25
□	232 Bernie Nicholls, LosA.	.50
□	235 Marcel Dionne, LosA.	.35
□	240 Thomas Gradin, Vanc.	.20
□	247 Stan Smyl, Vanc.	.20
□	248 Dale Hawerchuk, Winn.	.75
□	251 Randy Carlyle, Winn.	.20

	O-Pee-Chee	NM-MT
□	8/136 R. St. Croix (G), Toro./ D. Soetaert (G), Mont.	.35
□	9/137 Tim Bernhardt (G), Toro./ Mark Hunter, Mont.	.35
□	10/138 John Anderson, Toro./ Bob Gainey, Mont.	.35
□	11/139 Dan Daoust, Toro./ Petr Svoboda, Mont.	.20
□	13/143 Al Iafrate, Toro./ Dan Bouchard (G), Québ.	1.50
□	14/144 Gary Nylund, Toro./ Mario Marois, Québ.	.20
□	15/145 Bob McGill, Toro./ Randy Moller, Québ.	.20
□	16/146 J. Benning, Toro./ Mario Gosselin (G), Québ.	.35
□	17/148 S. Gavin, Toro./ Normand Rochefort, Québ.	.20
□	18/149 Greg Terrion, Toro./ Alain Côté, Québ.	.20
□	19/150 Peter Ihnacak, Toro./ Paul Gillis, Québ.	.20
□	20/151 Russ Courtnall, Toro./ Dale Hunter, Québ.	1.00
□	23/152 Darryl Sutter, Chic./ Wilf Paiement, Québ.	.20
□	24/153 Curt Fraser, Chic./ Brent Ashton, Québ.	.20
□	26/154 Ed Olczyk, Chic./ Brad Maxwell, Québ.	.20
□	27/155 M. Bannerman (G), Chic./ J.F. Sauvé, Québ.	.35
□	28/128 Steve Larmer, Chic./ Charlie Simmer, Bost.	.75
□	29/159 Troy Murray, Chic./ Rick Middleton, Bost.	.35
□	31/161 Greg Stefan (G), Detr./ Mike O'Connell, Bost.	.35
□	32/162 Ron Duguay, Detr./ Terry O'Reilly, Bost.	.20
□	33/163 Reed Larson, Detr./ Keith Crowder, Bost.	.20
□	34/164 Ivan Boldirev, Detr./ Tom Fergus, Bost.	.20
□	35/166 Danny Gare, Detr./ Greg Malone, Hart.	.20
□	36/167 Darryl Sittler, Detr./ Bob Crawford, Hart.	.35
□	39/168 Dino Ciccarelli, Minn./ Kevin Dineen, Hart.	.50
□	40/169 Neal Broten, Minn./ Mike Liut (G), Hart.	.35
□	42/170 Steve Payne, Minn./ Joel Quenneville, Hart.	.35
□	43/171 Gord Roberts, Minn./ Ray Neufeld, Hart.	.20
□	44/175 Harold Snepsts, Minn./ Craig Ramsay, Buff.	.20
□	45/176 Tony McKegney, Minn./ Bill Hajt, Buff.	.20
□	47/177 Joe Mullen, SLou./ Dave Maloney, Buff.	.35
□	48/178 Doug Gilmour, SLou./ Brent Peterson, Buff.	2.50
□	49/180 Tim Bothwell, SLou./ Mike Ramsey, Buff.	.20
□	50/181 Mark Johnson, SLou./ Bob Sauvé (G), Buff.	.35
□	51/182 Greg Millen (G), SLou./ Ric Seiling, Buff.	.35
□	52/183 Doug Wickenheiser, SLou./ Paul Cyr, Buff.	.20
□	54/197 Foil: Wayne Gretzky, Edmo./ Vezina Trophy	4.00
□	55/203 Foil: Tom Barrasso, Buff./ Hart Trophy	.35
□	56/204 Foil: Paul Coffey, Edmo./ Calder Trophy	1.00
□	58/184 Phil Russell, NJer./ John Tucker, Buff.	.20
□	59/185 Dave Lewis, NJer./ Gilles Hamel, Buff.	.20
□	60/186 Paul Gagné, NJer./ Mal Davis, Buff.	.20
□	61/187 Glenn Resch (G), NJer./ D. Andreychuk, Buff.	.35
□	62/189 Aaron Broten, NJer./ Tom Barrasso (G), Buff.	.50
□	63/190 Dave Pichette, NJer./ Bob Sauvé (G), Buff.	.35
□	67/191 Bob Bourne, NYIs. /Paul Coffey, Edmo.	1.00
□	68/192 Clark Gillies, NYIs./ Craig Ramsay, Buff.	.20
□	69/193 Bob Nystrom, NYIs./ Pelle Lindbergh (G), Phil.	1.50
□	70/198 Denis Potvin, NYIs./ Wayne Gretzky, Edmo.	5.00
□	72/199 Duane Sutter, NYIs./ Mario Lemieux, Pitt.	10.00
□	73/200 Patrick Flatley, NYIs./ Anders Hedberg, NYRa.	.20
□	74/201 Pat LaFontaine, NYIs./ Jari Kurri, Edmo.	2.00
□	75/202 Greg Gilbert, NYIs./ Wayne Gretzky, Edmo.	5.00
□	76/209 Billy Smith (G), NYIs./ Paul Reinhart, Calg.	.35
□	77/210 Gord Lane, NYIs./ Réjean Lemelin (G), Calg.	.35
□	78/211 Tomas Jonsson, NYIs./ Al MacInnis, Calg.	4.00
□	79/212 Kelly Hrudey (G), NYIs./ Jamie Macoun, Calg.	.35
□	82/213 Barry Beck, NYRa./ Carey Wilson, Calg.	.20
□	83/214 James Patrick, NYRa./ Eddy Beers, Calg.	.20
□	85/218 Pierre Larouche, NYRa./ Lee Fogolin, Edmo.	.20
□	86/219 Mike Rogers, NYRa./ Kevin Lowe, Edmo.	.35
□	87/220 G. Hanlon (G), NYRa./ A. Moog (G), Edmo.	1.00
□	88/221 Vanbiesbrouck (G), NYRa./ Fuhr (G), Edmo.	5.00
□	90/223 Brian Propp, Phil./ Mike Krushelnyski, Edmo.	.20
□	91/224 Pelle Lindbergh (G), Phil./ Billy Carroll, Edmo.	1.50
□	92/225 Brad McCrimmon, Phil./ Randy Gregg, Edmo.	.20
□	93/226 Mark Howe, Phil./ Willy Lindstrom, Edmo.	.35
□	94/227 Peter Zezel, Phil./ Glenn Anderson, Edmo.	.35
□	95/228 Murray Craven, Phil./ Mark Messier, Edmo.	1.50
□	98/229 Moe Mantha, Pitt./ Pat Hughes, Edmo.	.20
□	99/230 Doug Bodger, Pitt./ Kevin McClelland, Edmo.	.20
□	101/233 John Chabot, Pitt./ Brian Engblom, LosA.	.20
□	102/234 Doug Shedden, Pitt./ Mark Hardy, LosA.	.20
□	103/236 Wayne Babych, Pitt./ Jim Fox, LosA.	.20
□	104/237 Mike Bullard, Pitt./ Terry Ruskowski, LosA.	.20
□	106/238 Pat Riggin (G), Wash./ Dave Taylor, LosA.	.35
□	107/239 S. Stevens, Wash./ Bob Janecyk (G), LosA.	.50
□	108/241 A. Haworth, Wash./ Patrik Sundstrom, Vanc.	.20
□	109/242 Doug Jarvis, Wash./ Al MacAdam, Vanc.	.20
□	110/243 Dave Christian, Wash./ Doug Halward, Vanc.	.20
□	111/244 Mike Gartner, Wash./ Peter McNab, Vanc.	.50
□	127/245 Chris Nilan, Mont./ Tony Tanti, Vanc.	.20
□	128/246 Ron Flockhart, Mont./ Moe Lemay, Vanc.	.20
□	129/249 Tom Kurvers, Mont./ Dave Babych, Winn.	.35
□	130/250 Craig Ludwig, Mont./ Paul MacLean, Winn.	.20
□	132/252 Bobby Smith, Mont./ Robert Picard, Winn.	.35
□	133/253 Pierre Mondou, Mont./ Thomas Steen, Winn.	.20
□	134/254 Mario Tremblay, Mont./ L. Boschman, Winn.	.20
□	135/255 Guy Carbonneau, Mont./ Doug Smail, Winn.	.35
□	194/205 Foil: Jennings Trophy/ Masterton Trophy	.20
□	195/206 Foil: Norris Trophy/ Lady Byng Trophy	.20
□	196/207 Foil: Selke Trophy/ Art Ross Trophy	.20

1985 - 86 7-ELEVEN SUPERSTARS

These plastic cards measure 2 1/8" x 3 3/8". The cards have rounded corners.

	7-Eleven	NM-MT
	Complete Set (25 cards):	**40.00**
	Album:	**5.00**
□	1 Raymond Bourque/ Rick Middleton	4.00
□	2 Tom Barrasso (G)/ Gilbert Perreault	2.50
□	3 Paul Reinhart/ Lanny McDonald	2.00
□	4 Denis Savard/ Doug Wilson	2.50
□	5 Ron Duguay/ Steve Yzerman	10.00
□	6 Paul Coffey/ Jari Kurri	4.00
□	7 Ron Francis/ Mike Liut (G)	2.50
□	8 Marcel Dionne/ Dave Taylor	2.50
□	9 Brian Bellows/ Dino Ciccarelli	2.00
□	10 Larry Robinson/ Guy Carbonneau	2.50
□	11 Mel Bridgman/ Chico Resch (G)	1.50
□	12 Mike Bossy/ Bryan Trottier	3.50
□	13 Reijo Ruotsalainen/ Barry Beck	1.00
□	14 Tim Kerr/ Mark Howe	2.00
□	15 Mario Lemieux/ Mike Bullard	25.00
□	16 Peter Stastny/ Michel Goulet	4.00
□	17 Rob Ramage/ Brian Sutter	1.50
□	18 Rick Vaive/ Börje Salming	2.50
□	19 Patrik Sundstrom/ Stan Smyl	1.50
□	20 Rod Langway/ Mike Gartner	3.00
□	21 Dale Hawerchuk/ Paul MacLean	2.50
□	22 Stanley Cup Winners	1.00
□	23 Prince of Wales; Trophy Winners	1.00
□	24 Clarence S. Campbell; Bowl Winners	1.00
□	25 Title Card: Superstar Collectors' Series	1.00

1986 - 87 KRAFT SPORTS

"You could order team sets from this series directly by writing to Kraft. I ordered Montréal and Edmonton. You could also order the large sketches. This series is very different from the Kraft sets from the 1990s. Key players include Gretzky, Messier, Coffey, Kurri, and Roy." – Brian Bell, The Coin Cabinet, Moncton, New Brunswick.

These cards measure approximately 2 1/2" x 3 5/16". The large posters measure 16" x 20". Most of the drawings were done by Jerry Hersh (42 different) and Carleton McDiarmid (30 different). An album was available which today retails for about $50.

It should be noted that numerous collectors consider the Glen Cochrane card as a rookie card.

		Thin	Thick	Poster
Complete Set (81 cards):		**80.00**	**300.00**	**550.00**
Common Player:		**.75**	**2.00**	**4.00**
Kraft Sports		**Thin**	**Thick**	**Poster**
□□□	1 Réjean Lemelin (G), Calg.	1.00	2.50	5.00
□□□	2 Hakan Loob, Calg.	.75	2.00	4.00
□□□	3 Lanny McDonald, Calg.	1.75	4.00	10.00
□□□	4 Joe Mullen, Calg.	1.25	3.00	6.00
□□□	5 Jim Peplinski, Calg.	.75	2.00	4.00
□□□	6 Paul Reinhart, Calg.	.75	2.00	4.00
□□□	7 Doug Risebrough, Calg.	.75	2.00	4.00
□□□	8 Gary Suter, Calg.	1.25	3.00	6.00
□□□	9 Mike Vernon (G), Calg.	5.00	12.00	35.00
□□□	10 Carey Wilson, Calg.	.75	2.00	4.00
□□□	11 Glenn Anderson, Edmo.	1.25	3.00	6.00
□□□	12 Paul Coffey, Edmo.	3.50	9.00	25.00
□□□	13 Grant Fuhr (G), Edmo.	2.50	6.50	15.00
□□□	14 Wayne Gretzky, Edmo.	30.00	75.00	200.00
□□□	15 Mike Krushelnyski, Edmo.	.75	2.00	4.00
□□□	16 Jari Kurri, Edmo.	2.00	5.00	12.00
□□□	17 Kevin Lowe, Edmo.	1.25	3.00	6.00
□□□	18 Mark Messier, Edmo.	7.00	18.00	50.00
□□□	19 Andy Moog (G), Edmo.	2.00	5.00	12.00
□□□	20 Mark Napier, Edmo.	.75	2.00	4.00
□□□	21 Guy Carbonneau, Mont.	1.25	3.00	6.00
□□□	22 Chris Chelios, Mont.	3.50	9.00	25.00
□□□	23 Kjell Dahlin, Mont.	.75	2.00	4.00
□□□	24 Bob Gainey, Mont.	1.50	3.50	8.00
□□□	25 Gaston Gingras, Mont.	.75	2.00	4.00
□□□	26 Rick Green, Mont.	.75	2.00	4.00
□□□	27 Brian Hayward (G), Mont.	1.00	2.50	5.00
□□□	28 Mike Lalor, Mont.	.75	2.00	4.00
□□□	29 Claude Lemieux, Mont.	3.00	7.50	15.00
□□□	30 Craig Ludwig, Mont.	.75	2.00	4.00
□□□	31 Mike McPhee, Mont.	.75	2.00	4.00
□□□	32 Sergio Momesso, Mont.	.75	2.00	4.00
□□□	33 Mats Näslund, Mont.	.75	2.00	4.00
□□□	34 Chris Nilan, Mont.	.75	2.00	4.00
□□□	35 Stéphane Richer, Mont.	1.25	3.00	6.00
□□□	36 Larry Robinson, Mont.	1.75	4.00	10.00
□□□	37 Patrick Roy (G), Mont.	18.00	50.00	135.00
□□□	38 Brian Skrudland, Mont.	.75	2.00	4.00
□□□	39 Bobby Smith, Mont.	1.25	3.00	6.00
□□□	40 Petr Svoboda, Mont.	.75	2.00	4.00
□□□	41 Ryan Walter, Mont.	.75	2.00	4.00
□□□	42 Brent Ashton, Québ.	.75	2.00	4.00
□□□	43 Alain Côté, Québ.	.75	2.00	4.00
□□□	44 Mario Gosselin (G), Québ.	1.00	2.50	5.00
□□□	45 Michel Goulet, Québ.	1.50	3.50	7.00
□□□	46 Dale Hunter, Québ.	1.25	3.00	6.00
□□□	47 Clint Malarchuk (G), Québ.	1.00	2.50	5.00
□□□	48 Randy Moller, Québ.	.75	2.00	4.00
□□□	49 Pat Price, Québ.	.75	2.00	4.00
□□□	50 Anton Stastny, Québ.	.75	2.00	4.00
□□□	51 Peter Stastny, Québ.	1.50	3.50	8.00
□□□	52 Wendel Clark, Toro.	5.00	12.00	35.00
□□□	53 Russ Courtnall, Toro.	.75	2.00	4.00
□□□	54 Dan Daoust, Toro.	.75	2.00	4.00
□□□	55 Tom Fergus, Toro.	.75	2.00	4.00
□□□	56 Gary Leeman, Toro.	.75	2.50	4.00
□□□	57 Börje Salming, Toro.	1.50	3.50	8.00
□□□	58 Greg Terrion, Toro.	.75	2.00	4.00
□□□	59 Steve Thomas, Toro.	1.25	3.00	6.00
□□□	60 Rick Vaive, Toro.	.75	2.00	4.00
□□□	61 Ken Wregget (G), Toro.	2.00	5.00	12.00
□□□	62 Richard Brodeur (G), Vanc.	1.00	2.50	5.00
□□□	63 Glen Cochrane, Vanc.	2.00	3.00	6.00
□□□	64 Doug Halward, Vanc.	.75	2.00	4.00
□□□	65 Doug Lidster, Vanc.	.75	2.00	4.00
□□□	66 Barry Pederson, Vanc.	.75	2.00	4.00
□□□	67 Brent Peterson, Vanc.	.75	2.00	4.00
□□□	68 Petri Skriko, Vanc.	.75	2.00	4.00
□□□	69 S. Smyl, Vanc., Error (Syml)	.75	2.00	4.00
□□□	70 Patrik Sundstrom, Vanc.	.75	2.00	4.00
□□□	71 Tony Tanti, Vanc.	.75	2.00	4.00
□□□	72 Laurie Boschman, Winn.	.75	2.00	4.00
□□□	73 Randy Carlyle, Winn.	.75	2.00	4.00
□□□	74 Bill Derlago, Winn.	.75	2.00	4.00
□□□	75 Dale Hawerchuk, Winn.	1.75	4.00	10.00
□□□	76 Paul MacLean, Winn.	.75	2.00	4.00
□□□	77 Mario Marois, Winn.	.75	2.00	4.00
□□□	78 Brian Mullen, Winn.	.75	2.00	4.00
□□□	79 Steve Penney (G), Winn.	1.00	2.50	5.00
□□□	80 Thomas Steen, Winn.	.75	2.00	4.00
□□□	81 Perry Turnbull, Winn.	.75	2.00	4.00

1986 - 87 O-PEE-CHEE & TOPPS

"My older brother collected that set. He has a very nice Patrick Roy rookie card which I have tried to get off him ever since. Other key cards in the set are Wendel Clark's rookie card, John Vanbiesbrouck's rookie card, and Mario Lemieux's second-year card." – Robert Collins, Ultimate Sportscards, North Bay, Ontario.

There are two versions to this series: an O-Pee-Chee (1-264) and a Topps (1-198). Topps double prints are marked with a double-asterisk (**) below.

		Topps	OPC
O-Pee-Chee Set (264 cards):		–	**325.00**
Topps Set (198 cards):		**175.00**	–
Common Player:		**.25**	**.30**
O-Pee-Chee/Topps		**Topps**	**OPC**
□□	1 Raymond Bourque, Bost.	3.00	5.00
□□	2 Pat LaFontaine, NYIs. (**)	3.00	5.00
□□	3 Wayne Gretzky, Edmo.	20.00	30.00
□□	4 Lindy Ruff, Buff.	.25	.30
□□	5 Brad McCrimmon, Phil.	.25	.30
□□	6 Dave Williams, LosA.	.25	.30
□□	7 Denis Savard, Chic. (**)	.35	.85
□□	8 Lanny McDonald, Calg.	1.00	1.50
□□	**9 J. Vanbiesbrouck (G), NYRa. RC (**)**	**18.00**	**30.00**
□□	**10 Greg Adams, NJer. RC**	**1.50**	**2.50**
□□	11 Steve Yzerman, Detr.	13.00	20.00
□□	12 Craig Hartsburg, Minn.	.35	.50
□□	13 John Anderson, Hart. (**)	.20	.35
□□	14 Bob Bourne, NYIs. (LosA.) (**)	.20	.35
□□	**15 Kjell Dahlin, Mont. RC (**)**	**.60**	**1.00**
□□	16 Dave Andreychuk, Buff.	.50	.75
□□	17 Rob Ramage, SLou. (**)	.20	.35
□□	18 Ron Greschner, NYRa. (**)	.20	.35
□□	19 Bruce Driver, NJer.	.25	.30
□□	20 Peter Stastny, Québ.	1.00	1.50
□□	21 Dave Christian, Wash.	.25	.30
□□	22 Doug Keans (G), Bost.	.35	.50
□□	**23 Scott Bjugstad, Minn. RC**	**.50**	**.75**
□□	24 Doug Bodger, Pitt. (**)	.35	.50
□□	25 Troy Murray, Chic. (**)	.20	.35
□□	26 Al Iafrate, Toro.	.35	.75
□□	27 Kelly Hrudey (G), NYIs.	.35	.75
□□	28 Doug Jarvis, Hart.	.25	.30
□□	29 Rich Sutter, Vanc.	.25	.30
□□	30 Marcel Dionne, LosA.	1.00	1.50
□□	31 Curt Fraser, Chic.	.25	.30
□□	32 Doug Lidster, Vanc.	.25	.30
□□	33 Brian MacLellan, Calg. (Minn.)	.25	.30
□□	34 Barry Pederson, Vanc.	.25	.30
□□	35 Craig Laughlin, Wash.	.25	.30
□□	36 Ilkka Sinisalo, Phil. (**)	.20	.35
□□	**37 John MacLean, NJer. RC**	**3.00**	**5.00**
□□	38 Brian Mullen, Winn.	.25	.30
□□	39 Duane Sutter, NYIs. (**)	.20	.35
□□	40 Brian Engblom, Buff. (Calg.)	.25	.30
□□	**41 Chris Cichocki, Detr. RC**	**.50**	**.75**
□□	42 Gord Roberts, Minn.	.25	.30
□□	43 Ron Francis, Hart.	2.00	3.00
□□	44 Joe Mullen, Calg.	.50	.75
□□	45 Moe Mantha, Pitt. (**)	.20	.35
□□	46 Pat Verbeek, NJer.	.35	.75
□□	**47 Clint Malarchuk (G), Québ. RC**	**.75**	**1.00**
□□	48 Bob Brooke, NYRa. (**)	.20	.35
□□	49 Darryl Sutter, Chic. (**)	.20	.35
□□	50 Stan Smyl, Vanc. (**)	.20	.35
□□	51 Greg Stefan (G), Detr.	.35	.50
□□	52 Bill Hajt, Buff. (**)	.20	.35
□□	**53 Patrick Roy (G), Mont. RC**	**150.00**	**300.00**
□□	54 Gord Kluzak, Bost.	.25	.30
□□	55 Bob Froese (G), Phil. (**)	.35	.50
□□	56 Grant Fuhr (G), Edmo.	3.00	3.00
□□	57 Mark Hunter, SLou. (**)	.20	.35
□□	**58 Dana Murzyn, Hart. RC**	**.75**	**1.00**
□□	59 Mike Gartner, Wash.	1.25	2.00
□□	60 Dennis Maruk, Minn.	.25	.30
□□	61 Rich Preston, NJer. (Chic.)	.25	.30
□□	62 Larry Robinson, Mont. (**)	.75	1.50
□□	63 Dave Taylor, LosA. (**)	.35	.50
□□	64 Bob Murray, Chic. (**)	.20	.35
□□	65 Ken Morrow, NYIs.	.20	.35
□□	**66 Mike Ridley, NYRa. RC**	**1.00**	**1.50**
□□	**67 John Tucker, Buff. RC**	**.75**	**1.00**
□□	68 Miroslav Frycer, Toro.	.20	.35
□□	69 Danny Gare, Detr. (Edm.)	.20	.35
□□	**70 Randy Burridge, Bost. RC**	**.75**	**1.00**
□□	71 Dave Poulin, Phil.	.35	.50
□□	72 Brian Sutter, SLou.	.35	.50
□□	73 Dave Babych, Hart.	.35	.50
□□	74 Dale Hawerchuk, Winn. (**)	1.00	1.75
□□	75 Brian Bellows, Minn.	.35	.50
□□	**76 Dave Pasin, Bost. RC**	**.50**	**.75**
□□	77 Pete Peeters (G), Wash. (**)	.35	.50
□□	78 Tomas Jonsson, NYIs. (**)	.20	.35
□□	79 Gilbert Perreault, Buff. (**)	.75	1.50
□□	80 Glenn Anderson, Edmo. (**)	.35	.75
□□	81 Don Maloney, NYRa.	.25	.30
□□	82 Ed Olczyk, Chic. (**)	.35	.50
□□	83 Mike Bullard, Pgh	.25	.30
□□	84 Tom Fergus, Toro.	.25	.30
□□	85 Dave Lewis, NJer. (Detr.)	.35	.50
□□	86 Brian Propp, Phil.	.35	.50
□□	87 John Ogrodnick, Detr.	.25	.30
□□	88 Kevin Dineen, Hart. (**)	.35	.50
□□	89 Don Beaupré (G), Minn.	.25	.50
□□	90 Mike Bossy, NYIs. (**)	1.50	2.50
□□	91 Tom Barrasso (G), Buff. (**)	.35	.75
□□	92 Michel Goulet, Québ. (**)	.75	1.50
□□	93 Doug Gilmour, SLou.	3.00	7.00
□□	94 Kirk Muller, NJer.	.35	.75
□□	**95 Larry Melnyk, NYRa. RC (**)**	**.50**	**.75**
□□	96 Bob Gainey, Mont. (**)	.65	1.00
□□	97 Steve Kasper, Bost.	.25	.30
□□	**98 Petr Klima, Detr. RC**	**.85**	**1.25**
□□	99 Neal Broten, Minn. (**)	.35	.50
□□	100 Al Secord, Chic. (**)	.20	.35
□□	101 Bryan Erickson, LosA. (**)	.20	.35
□□	102 Réjean Lemelin (G), Calg.	.35	.50
□□	103 Sylvain Turgeon, Hart.	.25	.30
□□	104 Bob Nystrom, NYIs.	.25	.30
□□	105 Bernie Federko, SLou.	.50	.75
□□	106 Doug Wilson, Chic. (**)	.35	.75
□□	107 Alan Haworth, Wash.	.25	.30
□□	108 Jari Kurri, Edmo.	1.50	3.00
□□	109 Ron Sutter, Phil.	.25	.30
□□	110 Reed Larson, Bost. (**)	.20	.35
□□	111 Terry Ruskowski, Pitt. (**)	.20	.35
□□	112 Mark Johnson, NJer. (**)	.20	.35
□□	113 James Patrick, NYRa.	.25	.30
□□	114 Paul MacLean, Winn.	.25	.30
□□	115 Mike Ramsey, Buff. (**)	.20	.35
□□	116 Kelly Kisio, Detr. (NYRa.)	.20	.35
□□	117 Brent Sutter, NYIs.	.35	.50
□□	118 Joel Quenneville, Hart.	.35	.50
□□	119 Curt Giles, Minn. (**)	.20	.35
□□	120 Tony Tanti, Vanc. (**)	.20	.35
□□	121 Doug Sulliman, NJer. (**)	.20	.35
□□	122 Mario Lemieux, Pitt.	40.00	60.00
□□	123 Mark Howe, Phil. (**)	.35	.50
□□	124 Bob Sauvé (G), Chic.	.25	.50
□□	125 Anton Stastny, Québ.	.20	.35
□□	126 Scott Stevens, Wash. (**)	.35	.75
□□	127 Mike Foligno, Buff.	.25	.30
□□	128 Reijo Ruotsalainen, NYRa. (**)	.20	.35
□□	129 Denis Potvin, NYIs.	1.00	1.50
□□	130 Keith Crowder, Bost.	.25	.30
□□	131 Bob Janecyk (G), LosA. (**)	.35	.50
□□	132 John Tonelli, Calg.	.25	.50
□□	133 Mike Liut (G), Hart. (**)	.35	.50
□□	134 Tim Kerr, Phil. (**)	.35	.50
□□	135 Al Jensen (G), Wash.	.35	.50
□□	136 Mel Bridgman, NJer.	.25	.30
□□	137 Paul Coffey, Edmo. (**)	2.00	4.50
□□	138 Dino Ciccarelli, Minn. (**)	.35	.85
□□	139 Steve Larmer, Chic.	.35	.75
□□	140 Mike O'Connell, Detr.	.25	.30
□□	141 Clark Gillies, NYIs. (Buff.)	.35	.50
□□	142 Phil Russell, Buff. (**)	.20	.35
□□	**143 Dirk Graham, Minn. RC (**)**	**.75**	**1.50**
□□	144 Randy Carlyle, Winn.	.25	.30
□□	145 Charlie Simmer, Bost.	.25	.30
□□	146 Ron Flockhart, SLou. (**)	.20	.35
□□	147 Tom Laidlaw, NYRa.	.25	.30
□□	**148 Dave Tippett, Hart. RC**	**.75**	**1.00**
□□	**149 Wendel Clark, Toro. RC (**)**	**15.00**	**30.00**
□□	150 Bob Carpenter, Wash. (**)	.20	.35
□□	**151 Bill Watson, Chic. RC**	**.50**	**.75**
□□	**152 Roberto Romano (G), Pitt. RC (**)**	**.75**	**1.00**
□□	153 Doug Shedden, Detr.	.25	.30
□□	154 Phil Housley, Buff.	.50	.75
□□	155 Bryan Trottier, NYIs.	1.00	1.75
□□	156 Patrik Sundstrom, Vanc. (**)	.20	.35
□□	157 Rick Middleton, Bost. (**)	.35	.50
□□	158 Glenn Resch (G), Phil.	.35	.50
□□	159 Bernie Nicholls, LosA. (**)	.75	1.00
□□	**160 Ray Ferraro, Hart. RC**	**5.50**	**8.00**
□□	161 Mats Näslund, Mont. (**)	.35	.50
□□	162 Patrick Flatley, NYIs. (**)	.20	.35
□□	163 Joe Cirella, NJer.	.25	.30
□□	164 Rod Langway, Wash. (**)	.35	.50
□□	165 Checklist 1 (1 - 132)	2.00	4.00
□□	166 Carey Wilson, Calg.	.25	.30
□□	167 Murray Craven, Phil.	.25	.30
□□	**168 Paul Gillis, Québ. RC**	**.50**	**.75**
□□	169 Börje Salming, Toro.	.50	1.00
□□	170 Perry Turnbull, Winn.	.25	.30
□□	171 Chris Chelios, Mont.	3.50	6.00
□□	172 Keith Acton, Minn.	.25	.30
□□	173 Al MacInnis, Calg.	6.00	10.00
□□	**174 Russ Courtnall, Toro. RC**	**3.00**	**5.00**
□□	175 Brad Marsh, Phil.	.25	.30
□□	176 Guy Carbonneau, Mont.	.50	.75
□□	177 Ray Neufeld, Winn.	.25	.30
□□	**178 Craig MacTavish, Edmo. RC**	**2.00**	**4.00**
□□	179 Rick Lanz, Vanc.	.25	.30
□□	180 Murray Bannerman (G), Chic.	.35	.50
□□	181 Brent Ashton, Québ.	.25	.30
□□	182 Jim Peplinski, Calg.	.25	.30
□□	183 Mark Napier, Edmo.	.25	.30
□□	184 Laurie Boschman, Winn.	.25	.30
□□	185 Larry Murphy, Wash.	.50	.75
□□	186 Mark Messier, Edmo.	4.00	7.00
□□	187 Risto Siltanen, Québ.	.25	.30
□□	188 Bobby Smith, Mont.	.35	.50
□□	**189 Gary Suter, Calg. RC**	**3.00**	**4.00**
□□	190 Peter Zezel, Phil.	.35	.50
□□	191 Rick Vaive, Toro.	.35	.50
□□	192 Dale Hunter, Québ.	.35	.50
□□	193 Mike Krushelnyski, Edmo.	.25	.30
□□	194 Scott Arniel, Winn. (Buff.)	.25	.30
□□	195 Larry Playfair, LosA.	.25	.30
□□	196 Doug Risebrough, Calg.	.35	1.50
□□	197 Kevin Lowe, Edmo.	.50	.75
□□	198 Checklist 2 (133 - 264)	2.00	4.00

		OPC
O-Pee-Chee		**OPC**
□	199 Chris Nilan, Mont.	.35
□	**200 Paul Cyr, Buff. RC**	**.75**
□	201 Ric Seiling, Detr.	.35
□	202 Doug Smith, Buff.	.35
□	203 Jamie Macoun, Calg.	.35
□	204 Dan Quinn, Calg.	.35
□	205 Paul Reinhart, Calg.	.35
□	206 Keith Brown, Chic.	.35
□	207 Jack O'Callahan, Chic.	.35
□	**208 Steve Richmond, NJer. RC**	**.75**
□	209 Warren Young, Pitt.	.35
□	210 Lee Fogolin, Edmo.	.35
□	211 Charlie Huddy, Edmo.	.35
□	212 Andy Moog (G), Edmo.	2.00
□	213 Wayne Babych, Hart.	.35
□	214 Torrie Robertson, Hart.	.35
□	215 Jim Fox, LosA.	.35
□	**216 Phil Sykes, LosA. RC**	**.75**
□	217 Jay Wells, LosA.	.35
□	218 Dave Langevin, Minn.	.35
□	219 Steve Payne, Minn.	.35
□	220 Craig Ludwig, Mont.	.35
□	221 Mike McPhee, Mont.	.50
□	222 Steve Penney (G), Winn.	.50
□	223 Mario Tremblay, Mont. (Now retired from NHL)	.50
□	224 Ryan Walter, Mont.	.50
□	**225 Alain Chevrier (G), NJer. RC**	**1.00**
□	**226 Ullie Hiemer, NJer. RC, Error (Uli)**	**.75**
□	227 Tim Higgins, Detr.	.35
□	228 Billy Smith (G), NYIs.	1.50
□	229 Richard Kromm, NYIs.	.35
□	230 Tomas Sandström, NYRa.	.50
□	**231 Jim Johnson, Pitt. RC**	**1.00**
□	232 Willy Lindstrom, Pitt.	.35
□	233 Alain Côté, Québ.	.35
□	234 Gilbert Delorme, Québ.	.35
□	235 Mario Gosselin (G), Québ.	.50
□	**236 David Shaw, Québ. RC**	**.75**
□	**237 Dave Barr, Hart. RC**	**.75**
□	238 Ed Beers, SLou.	.35
□	**239 Charlie Bourgeois, SLou. RC**	**.75**
□	240 Rick Wamsley (G), SLou.	.50
□	241 Dan Daoust, Toro.	.35

□	242 Brad Maxwell, Vanc.	.35
□	243 Gary Nylund, Chic.	.35
□	244 Greg Terrion, Toro.	.35
□	**245 Steve Thomas, Toro. RC**	**6.00**
□	246 Richard Brodeur (G), Vanc.	.50
□	**247 Joel Otto RC, Error (Moe Lemay)**	**2.50**
□	248 Doug Halward, Vanc.	.35
□	249 Moe Lemay, Error (Joel Otto)	.75
□	250 Cam Neely, Bost.	7.00
□	251 Brent Peterson, Vanc.	.35
□	**252 Petri Skriko, Vanc. RC**	**1.00**
□	**253 Greg C. Adams, Wash. RC**	**.75**
□	254 Bill Derlago, Winn.	.35
□	255 Brian Hayward (G), Mont.	.50
□	256 Doug Smail, Winn.	.35
□	257 Thomas Steen, Winn.	.35
□	258 LL: Jari Kurri, Edmo.	1.50
□	259 LL: Wayne Gretzky, Edmo.	6.50
□	260 LL: Wayne Gretzky, Edmo.	6.50
□	261 LL: Tim Kerr, Phil.	.35
□	262 LL: Kjell Dahlin, Mont.	.35
□	263 LL: Bob Froese (G), Phil.	.50
□	264 LL: Bob Froese (G), Phil.	.50

OPC / TOPPS BOX BOTTOMS

These four-card panels were issued on the bottom of O-Pee-Chee and Topps wax boxes. The most expensive cut-out singles are Mario Lemieux (OPC $25, Topps $20) and Wayne Gretzky (OPC $22, Topps $18). O-Pee-Chee singles start at $1.00; Topps singles start at 75¢. Panels measure 5" x 7" while the cut-out cards measure 2 1/2" x 3 1/2".

Complete Set (50 cards):		**50.00**	**60.00**
Panel		**Topps**	**OPC**
□ □	A-D Adams/ Bossy/ Christian/ Foligno	4.00	5.00
□ □	E-H Goulet/ Gretzky/ Kerr/ Kurri	20.00	30.00
□ □	I-L Lemieux/ McDonald/ Nicholls/ Ridley	22.00	35.00
□ □	M-P Robinson/ Savard/ Bri. Sutter/ Trottier	4.00	6.00

TOPPS STICKER INSERTS

Complete Set (33 stickers):		**25.00**
Common Team Sticker:		**.25**
Topps		**NM-MT**
□	1 AS: John Vanbiesbrouck (G), NYRa.	9.00
□	2 AS: Michel Goulet, Québ.	1.00
□	3 AS: Wayne Gretzky, Edmo.	10.00
□	4 AS: Mike Bossy, NYIs.	3.00
□	5 AS: Paul Coffey, Edmo.	1.50
□	6 AS: Mark Howe, Phil.	.50
□	7 AS: Bob Froese (G), Phil.	.50
□	8 AS: Mats Näslund, Mont.	.50
□	9 AS: Mario Lemieux, Pitt.	12.00
□	10 AS: Jari Kurri, Edmo.	1.50
□	11 AS: Raymond Bourque, Bost.	3.00
□	12 AS: Larry Robinson, Mont.	1.00

□	13 Toronto Maple Leafs	□	14 Buffalo Sabres
□	15 Detroit Red Wings	□	16 Pittsburgh Penguins
□	17 New York Rangers	□	18 Calgary Flames
□	19 Winnipeg Jets	□	20 Québec Nordiques
□	21 Chicago Blackhawks	□	22 Los Angeles Kings
□	23 Montréal Canadiens	□	24 Vancouver Canucks
□	25 Hartford Whalers	□	26 Philadelphia Flyers
□	27 New Jersey Devils	□	28 St. Louis Blues
□	29 Minn. North Stars	□	30 Washington Capitals
□	31 Boston Bruins	□	32 New York Islanders
□	33 Edmonton Oilers		

1986 - 87 O-PEE-CHEE STICKERS

These stickers measure 2 1/8" x 2 15/16".

Complete Set (167 stickers):		**50.00**
Album: (Patrick Roy on cover)		**7.00**
Common Player:		**.20**
O-Pee-Chee		**NM-MT**
□	1 Stanley Cup Finals	1.00
□	2 Stanley Cup Finals	1.00
□	3 Stanley Cup Finals	1.00
□	4 Stanley Cup Finals	1.00

Note: Stickers 1-4 feature Patrick Roy, Larry Robinson, Steve Bozek.

□	5 Foil: Patrick Roy (G), Mont.	13.00
□	8 Larry Robinson, Mont.	.35
□	11 Mats Näslund, Mont.	.35
□	12 Bob Gainey, Mont.	.35
□	13 Bobby Smith, Mont.	.35
□	18 Kjell Dahlin, Mont.	.20
□	19 Patrick Roy (G), Mont.	15.00
□	22 Michel Goulet, Québ.	.35
□	25 Brent Ashton, Québ.	.20
□	26 Peter Stastny, Québ.	.35
□	27 Anton Stastny, Québ.	.20
□	32 Dale Hunter, Québ.	.35
□	33 Clint Malarchuk (G), Québ.	.35
□	34 Raymond Bourque, Bost.	2.00
□	37 Keith Crowder, Bost.	.20
□	42 Mike Foligno, Buff.	.20
□	49 Dave Andreychuk, Buff.	.35
□	50 Dave Babych, Hart.	.20
□	53 Sylvain Turgeon, Hart.	.20
□	58 Craig Wolanin/ Scott Arniel	.20
□	59 Gilles Meloche	.20
□	60 Reijo Ruotsalainen	.20
□	61 Kirk Muller/ Bob Janecyk (G)	.35
□	62 Tom Barrasso, et al	.35
□	63 Joe Cirella, et al	.20
□	64 Doug Jarvis, et al	.20
□	65 Kirk Muller, et al	.20
□	68 Paul Coffey, Edmo.	1.50
□	71 Lee Fogolin, Edmo.	.20
□	72 Wayne Gretzky, Edmo.	6.00
□	73 Jari Kurri, Edmo.	1.25
□	78 Glenn Anderson, Edmo.	.35
□	79 Mark Messier, Edmo.	1.50
□	80 Lanny McDonald, Calg.	.35
□	83 Réjean Lemelin (G), Calg.	.35
□	88 Marcel Dionne, LosA.	.35
□	95 Bernie Nicholls, LosA.	.35
□	96 Stan Smyl, Vanc.	.20
□	99 Tony Tanti, Vanc.	.20
□	104 Dale Hawerchuk, Winn.	.50
□	111 Laurie Boschman, Winn.	.20
□	138 Rick Vaive, Toro.	.20
□	141 Wendel Clark, Toro.	2.00
□	142 Miroslav Frycer, Toro.	.20
□	143 Tom Fergus, Toro.	.20
□	148 Al Iafrate, Toro.	.35
□	149 Russ Courtnall, Toro.	.75
□	150 Denis Savard, Chic.	.35
□	153 Doug Wilson, Chic.	.35
□	158 John Ogrodnick, Detr.	.20
□	165 Greg Stefan (G), Detr.	.35
□	166 Neal Broten, Minn.	.20
□	169 Dino Ciccarelli, Minn.	.35
□	174 Bernie Federko, SLou.	.35
□	181 Mark Hunter, SLou.	.20
□	196 Greg Adams, NJer.	.20
□	203 Mel Bridgman, NJer.	.20
□	206 Pat LaFontaine, NYIs.	.50
□	209 Denis Potvin, NYIs.	.35
□	210 Duane Sutter, NYIs.	.20
□	211 Brent Sutter, NYIs.	.20
□	216 Bryan Trottier, NYIs.	.35
□	217 Mike Bossy, NYIs.	.50
□	218 John Vanbiesbrouck (G), NYRa.	3.50
□	221 Mike Ridley, NYRa.	.50
□	226 Terry Ruskowski, Pitt.	.20
□	233 Mario Lemieux, Pitt.	8.00
□	236 Bob Froese (G), Phil.	.35
□	239 Brian Propp, Phil.	.20
□	240 Tim Kerr, Phil.	.20
□	241 Dave Poulin, Phil.	.20
□	246 Mark Howe, Phil.	.35
□	247 Brad McCrimmon, Phil.	.20
□	248 Dave Christian, Wash.	.20
□	251 Mike Gartner, Wash.	.50

O-Pee-Chee		**NM-MT**
□	6/151 Chris Chelios, Mont./ Darryl Sutter, Chic.	1.00
□	7/152 Guy Carbonneau, Mont./ Bob Sauvé (G), Chic.	.35
□	9/154 Mario Tremblay, Mont./ Troy Murray, Chic.	.35
□	10/155 Tom Kurvers, Mont./ Al Secord, Chic.	.20
□	14/156 Craig Ludwig, Mont./ Ed Olczyk, Chic.	.20
□	15/157 Mike McPhee, Mont./ Steve Larmer, Chic.	.35
□	16/159 Doug Soetaert (G), Mont./ Danny Gare, Detr.	.35
□	17/160 Petr Svoboda, Mont./ Mike O'Connell, Detr.	.20
□	20/161 Alain Côté, Québ./ Steve Yzerman, Detr.	4.00
□	21/162 Mario Gosselin (G), Québ./ Petr Klima, Detr.	.35
□	23/163 J.F. Sauvé, Québ./ Kelly Kisio, Detr.	.20
□	24/164 Paul Gillis, Québ./ Doug Shedden, Detr.	.20
□	28/167 Gilbert Delorme, Québ./ Brian Bellows, Minn.	.35
□	29/168 Risto Siltanen, Québ./ Scott Bjugstad, Minn.	.20
□	30/170 Robert Picard, Québ./ Dennis Maruk, Minn.	.20
□	31/171 David Shaw, Québ./ Dirk Graham, Minn.	.20
□	35/172 Rick Middleton, Bost./ Curt Giles, Minn.	.35
□	36/173 Charlie Simmer, Bost./ Craig Hartsburg, Minn.	.35
□	38/175 Barry Pederson, Bost./ Brian Sutter, SLou.	.35
□	39/176 Reed Larson, Bost./ Ron Flockhart, SLou.	.20
□	40/177 Steve Kasper, Bost./ Doug Gilmour, SLou.	2.00
□	41/178 Pat Riggin (G), Bost./ C. Bourgeois, SLou.	.35
□	43/179 G. Perreault, Buff./ Rick Wamsley (G), SLou.	.35
□	44/180 Mike Ramsey, Buff./ Rob Ramage, SLou.	.20
□	45/186 Tom Barrasso (G), Buff./ Bob Froese (G), Phil.	.50
□	46/187 Brian Engblom, Buff./ Darren Jensen (G), Phil.	.35
□	47/188 Phil Housley, Buff./ Paul Coffey, Edmo.	1.00
□	48/189 John Tucker, Buff./ Troy Murray, Chic.	.20
□	51/190 R. Francis, Hart./ J. Vanbiesbrouck (G), NYRa.	2.00
□	52/191 Mike Liut (G), Hart./ Wayne Gretzky, Edmo.	5.00
□	54/192 John Anderson, Hart./ Gary Suter, Calg.	.20
□	55/193 Joel Quenneville, Hart./ Bob Froese (G), Phil.	.35
□	56/194 Kevin Dineen, Hart./ Mike Bossy, NYIs.	.50
□	57/195 Ray Ferraro, Hart./ Wayne Gretzky, Edmo.	5.00
□	66/197 Andy Moog (G), Edmo./ Dave Lewis, NJer.	.75
□	67/198 Grant Fuhr (G), Edmo./ Joe Cirella, NJer.	.75
□	69/199 Charlie Huddy, Edmo./ Rich Preston, NJer.	.20
□	70/200 Kevin Lowe, Edmo./ Mark Johnson, NJer.	.35
□	74/201 Mike Krushelnyski, Edmo./ Kirk Muller, NJer.	.75
□	75/202 Mark Napier, Edmo./ Pat Verbeek, NJer.	.35
□	76/204 Craig MacTavish, Edmo./ Bob Nystrom, NYIs.	.35
□	77/205 Kevin McClelland, Edmo./ Clark Gillies, NYIs.	.20
□	81/207 John Tonelli, Calg./ Patrick Flatley, NYIs.	.20
□	82/208 Joe Mullen, Calg./ Bob Bourne, NYIs.	.35
□	84/212 Jim Peplinski, Calg./ Kelly Hrudey (G), NYIs.	.35
□	85/213 Jamie Macoun, Calg./ Billy Smith (G), NYIs.	.35
□	86/214 Al MacInnis, Calg./ Tomas Jonsson, NYIs.	1.00
□	87/215 Dan Quinn, Calg./ Ken Morrow, NYIs.	.20
□	89/219 Jim Fox, LosA./ Bob Brooke, NYRa.	.20
□	90/220 Dave Taylor, LosA./ James Patrick, NYRa.	.35
□	91/222 Bob Janecyk (G), LosA./ Ron Greschner, NYRa.	.35
□	92/223 Jay Wells, LosA./ Tom Laidlaw, NYRa.	.20
□	93/224 Bryan Erikson, LosA./ Larry Melnyk, NYRa.	.20
□	94/225 D. Williams, LosA./ R. Ruotsalainen, NYRa.	.20
□	97/227 Doug Halward, Vanc./ Willy Lindstrom, Pitt.	.20
□	98/228 Richard Brodeur (G), Vanc./ Mike Bullard, Pitt.	.35
□	100/229 Brent Peterson, Vanc./ R. Romano (G), Pitt.	.35
□	101/230 Patrik Sundstrom, Vanc./ John Chabot, Pitt.	.20
□	102/231 Doug Lidster, Vanc./ Moe Mantha, Pitt.	.20
□	103/232 Petri Skriko, Vanc./ Doug Bodger, Pitt.	.20
□	105/234 Bill Derlago, Winn./ Glenn Resch (G), Phil.	.35
□	106/235 Ray Neufeld, Winn./ Brad Marsh, Phil.	.20
□	107/237 Randy Carlyle, Winn./ Doug Crossman, Phil.	.20
□	108/238 Paul MacLean, Winn./ Ilkka Sinisalo, Phil.	.20
□	109/242 Brian Mullen, Winn./ Rich Sutter, Phil.	.20
□	110/243 Thomas Steen, Winn./ Ron Sutter, Phil.	.20
□	112/126 Foil: Paul Coffey, Edmo./ Kjell Dahlin, Mont.	1.00
□	113/127 Foil: Michel Goulet, Québ./ PE Eklund, Phil.	.50
□	114/128 Foil: Vanbiesbrouck (G), NYRa./ J. Johnson, Pitt.	3.00
□	115/129 Foil: Wayne Gretzky, Edmo./ P. Klima, Detr.	5.00
□	116/130 Foil: Mark Howe, Phil./ Joel Otto, Calg.	.35
□	117/131 Foil: Mike Bossy, NYIs./ Mike Ridley, NYRa.	.50
□	118/132 Foil: J. Kurri, Edmo./ P. Roy (G), Mont.	8.00
□	119/133 Foil: R. Bourque, Bost./ David Shaw, Québ.	.35
□	120/134 Foil: Mario Lemieux, Pitt./ Gary Suter, Calg.	5.00
□	121/135 Foil: G. Fuhr (G), Edmo./ S. Thomas, Toro.	.75
□	122/182 Foil: Mats Näslund, Mont./ B. Froese (G), Phil.	.35
□	123/183 Foil: L. Robinson, Mont./ W. Gretzky, Edmo.	5.00
□	124/184 Foil: Chris Cichocki, Detr./ Mark Howe, Phil.	.35
□	125/185 Foil: Wendel Clark, Toro./ Jari Kurri, Edmo.	3.00
□	136/244 Börje Salming, Toro./ Murray Craven, Phil.	.35
□	137/245 Gary Nylund, Toro./ Peter Zezel, Phil.	.20
□	139/249 Don Edwards (G), Toro./ R. Langway, Wash.	.35
□	140/250 Steve Thomas, Toro./ Bob Carpenter, Wash.	.35
□	144/252 Marian Stastny, Toro./ Al Jensen (G), Wash.	.35
□	145/253 Brad Maxwell, Toro./ Craig Laughlin, Wash.	.20
□	146/254 Dan Daoust, Toro./ Scott Stevens, Wash.	.35
□	147/255 Greg Terrion, Toro./ Alan Haworth, Wash.	.20

1987 PEPSI / BURGER KING SUPER JEU DE PUISSANCE

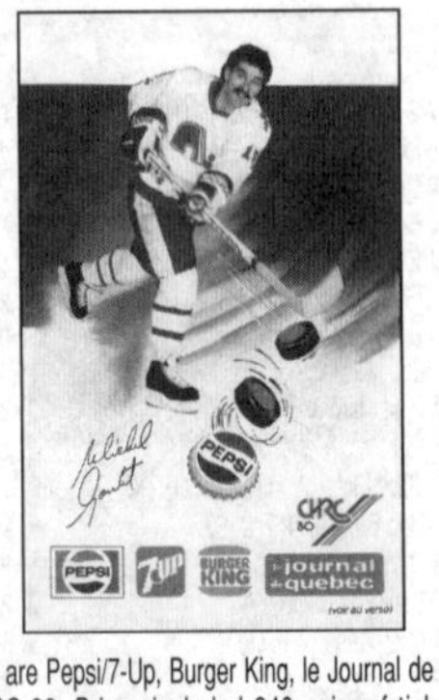

Sponsors are Pepsi/7-Up, Burger King, le Journal de Québec, and CHRC 80. Prizes included 840 pairs of tickets, 200 Nordiques' jerseys, 135 Titan hockey sticks, and millions of whoppers. This card measures 3 1/2" x 5 1/2".

□	Michel Goulet, Québ.	2.00

1987 - 88 O-PEE-CHEE & TOPPS

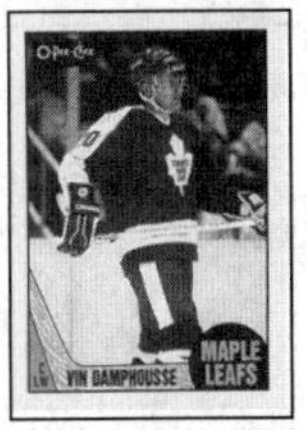

There are two versions for this series: an O-Pee-Chee (1-264) and a Topps (1-198). Topps double prints are marked with a double asterisk (**). Cards measure the standard 2 1/2" x 3 1/2".

O-Pee-Chee Set (264 cards):		**–**	**200.00**
Topps Set (198 cards):		**130.00**	**–**
Common Player:		**.20**	**.25**
Player		**Topps**	**OPC**
□ □	1 Denis Potvin, NYIs. (**)	.65	1.25
□ □	**2 Rick Tocchet, Phil. RC**	**8.00**	**10.00**
□ □	3 Dave Andreychuk, Buff.	.75	.75
□ □	4 Stan Smyl, Vanc.	.25	.35
□ □	5 Dave Babych, Hart. (**)	.25	.35
□ □	6 Pat Verbeek, NJer.	.25	.35
□ □	**7 Esa Tikkanen, Edmo. RC**	**6.00**	**8.00**
□ □	8 Mike Ridley, Wash.	.25	.35
□ □	9 Randy Carlyle, Winn., Err (Calryle)	.20	.25
□ □	**10 Greg Paslawski, SLou. RC**	**.50**	**.75**
□ □	11 Neal Broten, Minn.	.20	.35
□ □	12 Wendel Clark, Toro. (**)	3.50	7.00
□ □	**13 Bill Ranford (G), Bost. RC (**)**	**6.00**	**10.00**
□ □	14 Doug Wilson, Chic.	.20	.35
□ □	15 Mario Lemieux, Pitt.	20.00	30.00
□ □	16 Mats Näslund, Mont.	.20	.35
□ □	17 Mel Bridgman, Detr.	.20	.25
□ □	18 James Patrick, NYRa. (**)	.20	.20
□ □	19 Rollie Melanson (G), LosA.	.25	.35
□ □	20 Lanny McDonald, Calg.	.75	.75
□ □	21 Peter Stastny, Québ.	.75	1.25
□ □	22 Murray Craven, Phil.	.20	.25
□ □	**23 Ulf Samuelsson, Hart. RC (**)**	**3.50**	**7.00**
□ □	**24 M. Thelven, Bost. RC (**), Err. (Thelvin)**	**.50**	**.75**
□ □	25 Scott Stevens, Wash.	.25	.35
□ □	26 Petr Klima, Detr.	.20	.25
□ □	27 Brent Sutter, NYIs. (**)	.20	.35
□ □	28 Tomas Sandström, NYRa.	.35	.50
□ □	29 Tim Bothwell, SLou.	.20	.25
□ □	30 Bob Carpenter, LosA. (**)	.20	.25
□ □	31 Brian MacLellan, Minn. (**)	.20	.25
□ □	32 John Chabot, Pitt.	.20	.25
□ □	33 Phil Housley, Buff. (**)	.20	.35
□ □	34 Patrik Sundstrom, Vanc. (**)	.20	.20
□ □	35 Dave Ellett, Winn.	.20	.25
□ □	36 John Vanbiesbrouck (G), NYRa.	10.00	15.00
□ □	37 Dave Lewis, Detr.	.20	.25
□ □	38 Tom McCarthy, Bost. (**)	.20	.20
□ □	39 Dave Poulin, Phil.	.20	.35
□ □	40 Mike Foligno, Buff.	.20	.25
□ □	41 Gord Roberts, Minn.	.20	.25
□ □	**42 Luc Robitaille, LosA. RC**	**25.00**	**40.00**
□ □	43 Duane Sutter, NYIs.	.20	.25
□ □	44 Pete Peeters (G), Wash.	.20	.35
□ □	45 John Anderson, Hart.	.20	.25
□ □	46 Aaron Broten, NJer.	.20	.25
□ □	47 Keith Brown, Chic.	.20	.25
□ □	48 Bobby Smith, Mont.	.20	.35
□ □	49 Don Maloney, NYRa.	.20	.25
□ □	50 Mark Hunter, SLou.	.20	.25
□ □	51 Moe Mantha, Pitt.	.20	.25
□ □	52 Charlie Simmer, Bost.	.20	.25
□ □	53 Wayne Gretzky, Edmo.	18.00	25.00
□ □	54 Mark Howe, Phil.	.20	.35
□ □	55 Bob Gould, Wash.	.20	.25
□ □	56 Steve Yzerman, Detr. (**)	6.00	12.00
□ □	57 Larry Playfair, LosA.	.20	.25
□ □	58 Alain Chevrier (G), NJer.	.20	.35
□ □	59 Steve Larmer, Chic.	.35	.50
□ □	60 Bryan Trottier, NYIs.	1.00	1.75
□ □	61 Stewart Gavin, Hart. (**)	.20	.20
□ □	62 Russ Courtnall, Toro. (**)	.50	.75
□ □	63 Mike Ramsey, Buff. (**)	.20	.20
□ □	64 Bob Brooke, Minn.	.20	.25
□ □	65 Rick Wamsley (G), SLou. (**)	.20	.35
□ □	66 Ken Morrow, NYIs.	.20	.25
□ □	**67 Gerard Gallant, Detr. RC, Error (Gerald)**	**1.00**	**2.00**
□ □	**68 Kevin Hatcher, Wash. RC**	**1.25**	**2.50**
□ □	69 Cam Neely, Bost.	1.50	2.50
□ □	70 Sylvain Turgeon, Hart. (**)	.20	.20
□ □	71 Peter Zezel, Phil.	.20	.35
□ □	72 Al MacInnis, Calg.	3.00	4.00
□ □	73 Terry Ruskowski, Pitt. (**)	.20	.20
□ □	74 Troy Murray, Chic.	.20	.25
□ □	75 Jim Fox, LosA. (**)	.20	.20
□ □	76 Kelly Kisio, NYRa.	.20	.25
□ □	77 Michel Goulet, Québ. (**)	.75	1.25

□□ 78 Tom Barrasso (G), Buff. (**)	.25	.50
□□ 79 Bruce Driver, NJer. (**)	.20	.35
□□ **80 Craig Simpson, Pitt. RC (**)**	**2.00**	**3.00**
□□ 81 Dino Ciccarelli, Minn.	.25	.35
□□ 82 Gary Nylund, Chic. (**)	.20	.20
□□ 83 Bernie Federko, SLou.	.20	.35
□□ 84 John Tonelli, Calg. (**)	.20	.20
□□ 85 Brad McCrimmon, Phil. (**)	.20	.20
□□ 86 Dave Tippett, Hart. (**)	.20	.20
□□ 87 Raymond Bourque, Bost. (**)	1.75	3.50
□□ 88 Dave Christian, Wash.	.20	.25
□□ 89 Glen Hanlon (G), Detr.	.20	.35
□□ **90 Brian Curran, NYIs. RC**	**.50**	**.75**
□□ 91 Paul MacLean, Winn.	.20	.25
□□ **92 Jimmy Carson, LosA. RC**	**.85**	**1.75**
□□ 93 Willie Huber, NYRa. (Vanc.)	.20	.25
□□ 94 Brian Bellows, Minn.	.25	.35
□□ 95 Doug Jarvis, Hart. (**)	.20	.20
□□ 96 Clark Gillies, Buff.	.20	.25
□□ 97 Tony Tanti, Vanc.	.20	.25
□□ **98 Per-Erik Eklund, Phil. RC (**)**	**.75**	**1.50**
□□ 99 Paul Coffey, Edmo.	1.50	2.50
□□ 100 Brent Ashton, Detr. (**)	.20	.20
□□ 101 Mark Johnson, NJer.	.20	.25
□□ **102 Greg Johnston, Bost. RC**	**.50**	**.75**
□□ 103 Ron Flockhart, SLou.	.20	.25
□□ 104 Ed Olczyk, Chic. (Toro.)	.25	.35
□□ 105 Mike Bossy, NYIs.	2.00	2.50
□□ 106 Chris Chelios, Mont.	2.00	3.50
□□ 107 Gilles Meloche (G), Pitt.	.20	.35
□□ 108 Rod Langway, Wash.	.20	.35
□□ 109 Ray Ferraro, Hart. (**)	.35	.75
□□ 110 Ron Duguay, NYRa. (**)	.20	.20
□□ 111 Al Secord, Chic. (Toro.) (**)	.20	.20
□□ 112 Mark Messier, Edmo.	3.25	4.50
□□ 113 Ron Sutter, Phil.	.20	.25
□□ **114 Darren Veitch, Detr. RC**	**.50**	**.75**
□□ 115 Rick Middleton, Bost. (**)	.20	.35
□□ 116 Doug Sulliman, NJer.	.20	.25
□□ 117 Dennis Maruk, Minn. (**)	.20	.20
□□ 118 Dave Taylor, LosA.	.20	.35
□□ 119 Kelly Hrudey (G), NYIs.	.35	.50
□□ 120 Tom Fergus, Toro.	.20	.25
□□ **121 Christian Ruuttu, Buff. RC**	**.75**	**1.00**
□□ **122 Brian Benning, SLou. RC**	**.50**	**.75**
□□ **123 Adam Oates, Detr. RC**	**18.00**	**20.00**
□□ 124 Kevin Dineen, Hart.	.25	.35
□□ 125 Doug Bodger, Pitt. (**)	.20	.35
□□ 126 Joe Mullen, Calg.	.25	.35
□□ 127 Denis Savard, Chic.	.35	.50
□□ 128 Brad Marsh, Phil.	.20	.25
□□ 129 Marcel Dionne, NYRa. (**)	.65	1.25
□□ 130 Bryan Erickson, LosA.	.20	.25
□□ 131 Reed Larson, Bost. (**)	.20	.20
□□ 132 Don Beaupré (G), Minn.	.20	.35
□□ 133 Larry Murphy, Wash. (**)	.25	.50
□□ 134 John Ogrodnick, Québ. (**)	.20	.20
□□ 135 Greg Adams, NJer. (**)	.25	.35
□□ 136 Patrick Flatley, NYIs.	.20	.25
□□ 137 Scott Arniel, Buff.	.20	.25
□□ 138 Dana Murzyn, Hart.	.20	.25
□□ 139 Greg Adams, Wash. (**)	.20	.25
□□ 140 Bob Sauvé (G), NJer.	.20	.35
□□ 141 Mike O'Connell, Detr.	.20	.25
□□ 142 Walt Poddubny, NYRa. (**)	.20	.25
□□ 143 Paul Reinhart, Calg.	.20	.25
□□ 144 Tim Kerr, Phil. (**)	.20	.25
□□ **145 Brian Lawton, Minn. RC**	**.50**	**.75**
□□ **146 Gino Cavallini , SLou. RC**	**.50**	**.75**
□□ 147 Doug Keans (G), Bost. (**)	.20	.35
□□ 148 Jari Kurri, Edmo.	.75	1.25
□□ 149 Dale Hawerchuk, Winn.	.50	.75
□□ **150 Randy Cunneyworth, Pitt. RC**	**.65**	**1.25**
□□ 151 Jay Wells, LosA.	.20	.25
□□ 152 Mike Liut (G), Hart. (**)	.20	.35
□□ 153 Steve Konroyd, NYIs.	.20	.25
□□ 154 John Tucker, Buff.	.20	.25
□□ 155 Rick Vaive, Toro. (Chic.) (**)	.20	.35
□□ 156 Bob Murray, Chic.	.20	.25
□□ 157 Kirk Muller, NJer. (**)	.60	.75
□□ 158 Brian Propp, Phil.	.20	.35
□□ 159 Ron Greschner, NYRa.	.20	.25
□□ 160 Rob Ramage, SLou.	.20	.25
□□ 161 Craig Laughlin, Wash.	.20	.25
□□ 162 Steve Kasper, Bost. (**)	.20	.25
□□ 163 Patrick Roy (G), Mont.	35.00	50.00
□□ **164 Shawn Burr, Detr. RC (**)**	**.75**	**1.00**
□□ 165 Craig Hartsburg, Minn. (**)	.20	.35
□□ **166 Dean Evason, Hart. RC**	**.75**	**1.00**
□□ 167 Bob Bourne, LosA.	.20	.25
□□ 168 Mike Gartner, Wash.	1.00	1.50
□□ **169 Ron Hextall (G), Phil. RC**	**8.00**	**12.00**
□□ 170 Joe Cirella, NJer.	.20	.25
□□ 171 Dan Quinn, Pitt. (**)	.20	.25
□□ 172 Tony McKegney, SLou.	.20	.25
□□ 173 Pat LaFontaine, NYIs. (**)	1.00	2.00
□□ **174 Allen Pedersen, Bost. RC (**)**	**.50**	**.75**
□□ 175 Doug Gilmour, SLou.	2.50	4.00
□□ 176 Gary Suter, Calg. (**)	.20	.35
□□ 177 Barry Pederson, Vanc. (**)	.20	.25
□□ 178 Grant Fuhr (G), Edmo. (**)	1.00	2.00
□□ **179 Wayne Presley, Chic. RC**	**.50**	**.75**
□□ 180 Wilf Paiement, Pitt.	.20	.25
□□ 181 Doug Smail, Winn.	.20	.25
□□ 182 Doug Crossman, Phil. (**)	.20	.25
□□ 183 Bernie Nicholls, LosA., Error (Nichols)	.35	.50
□□ 184 Dirk Graham, Minn., Error (Dick)	.20	.25
□□ 185 Anton Stastny, Québ.	.20	.25
□□ 186 Greg Stefan (G), Detr.	.25	.35
□□ 187 Ron Francis, Hart.	1.25	2.00
□□ 188 Steve Thomas, Toro. (Chic.) (**)	.25	.75
□□ **189 Kelly Miller, Wash. RC**	**.65**	**1.25**
□□ 190 Tomas Jonsson, NYIs.	.20	.25
□□ 191 John MacLean, NJer.	.50	.75
□□ 192 Larry Robinson, Mont. (**)	.65	1.25
□□ 193 Doug Wickenheiser, SLou. (**)	.20	.25
□□ 194 Keith Crowder, Bost. (**)	.20	.25
□□ 195 Bob Froese (G), NYRa.	.25	.35
□□ 196 Jim Johnson, Pitt.	.20	.25
□□ 197 Checklist 1 (1 - 132)	1.25	2.50
□□ 198 Checklist 2 (133 - 264)	1.50	2.50

Player	**OPC**
□ 199 Glenn Anderson, Edmo.	.50
□ 200 Kevin Lowe, Edmo.	.35
□ 201 Kevin McClelland, Edmo.	.25
□ 202 Mike Krushelnyski, Edmo.	.25
□ 203 Craig MacTavish, Edmo.	.25
□ 204 Andy Moog (G), Edmo.	1.25
□ **205 Marty McSorley, Edmo. RC**	**6.00**
□ **206 Craig Muni, Edmo. RC**	**1.00**
□ 207 Charlie Huddy, Edmo.	.25
□ 208 Hakan Loob, Calg.	.25
□ 209 Jim Peplinski, Calg.	.25
□ 210 Mike Bullard, Calg.	.25
□ 211 Carey Wilson, Calg.	.20
□ 212 Joel Otto, Calg.	.35
□ **213 Neil Sheehy, Calg. RC**	**1.00**
□ 214 Jamie Macoun, Calg.	.25
□ **215 Mike Vernon (G), Calg. RC**	**15.00**
□ 216 Steve Bozek, Calg.	.25
□ **217 Daniel Berthiaume (G), Winn. RC**	**1.50**
□ 218 Gilles Hamel, Winn.	.25
□ 219 Tim Watters, Winn.	.25
□ 220 Mario Marois, Winn., Error (Marios)	.25
□ 221 Thomas Steen, Winn.	.25
□ 222 Laurie Boschman, Winn.	.25
□ **223 Steve Rooney, Winn. RC**	**.75**
□ 224 Ron Wilson, Winn.	.25
□ **225 Fredrik Olausson, Winn. RC**	**2.00**
□ **226 Jim Kyte, Winn. RC**	**1.25**
□ **227 Claude Lemieux, Mont. RC**	**15.00**
□ 228 Bob Gainey, Mont.	1.25
□ 229 Gaston Gingras, SLou.	.25
□ 230 Brian Hayward (G), Mont.	.35
□ 231 Ryan Walter, Mont.	.35
□ 232 Guy Carbonneau, Mont.	.50
□ **233 Stéphane Richer, Mont. RC**	**5.00**
□ 234 Rick Green, Mont.	.25
□ **235 Brian Skrudland, Mont. RC**	**2.00**
□ 236 Allan Bester (G), Toro.	.35
□ 237 Börje Salming, Toro.	.75
□ 238 Al Iafrate, Toro.	.25
□ 239 Rick Lanz, Toro.	.25
□ 240 Gary Leeman, Toro.	.25
□ 241 Greg Terrion, Toro.	.25
□ **242 Ken Wregget (G), Toro. RC**	**5.00**
□ **243 Vincent Damphousse, Toro. RC**	**20.00**
□ 244 Chris Kotsopoulos, Toro.	.25
□ 245 Dale Hunter, Wash.	.35
□ 246 Clint Malarchuk (G), Wash.	.35
□ 247 Paul Gillis, Québ.	.25
□ 248 Robert Picard, Québ.	.25
□ 249 Doug Shedden, Québ.	.25
□ 250 Mario Gosselin (G), Québ.	.35
□ 251 Randy Moller, Québ.	.25
□ 252 David Shaw, Québ.	.25
□ **253 Mike Eagles, Québ. RC**	**.75**
□ 254 Alain Côté, Québ.	.25
□ 255 Petri Skriko, Vanc.	.25
□ 256 Doug Lidster, Vanc.	.25
□ 257 Richard Brodeur (G), Vanc.	.35
□ 258 Rich Sutter, Vanc.	.25
□ 259 Steve Tambellini, Vanc.	.25
□ 260 Jim Benning, Vanc.	.25
□ **261 Dave Richter, Vanc. RC**	**.75**
□ **262 Michel Petit, Vanc. (NYRa.) RC**	**1.00**
□ 263 Brent Peterson, Vanc.	.25
□ **264 Jim Sandlak, Vanc. RC**	**2.00**

OPC / TOPPS BOX BOTTOMS

These four-card panels were issued on the bottom of O-Pee-Chee and Topps wax boxes. The most expensive cut-out singles are Wayne Gretzky (OPC $18, Topps $15), Steve Yzerman (OPC $10, Topps $7) and Luc Robitaille (OPC $8, Topps $6). O-Pee-Chee singles start at 75¢; Topps singles start at 50¢. Panels measure 5" x 7" while the cut cards measure the standard 2 1/2" x 3 1/2".

Complete Set (4 panels):	**30.00**	**40.00**
Box Bottom	**Topps**	**OPC**
□□ A-D Gretzky/ Kerr/ Yzerman/ Robitaille	25.00	40.00
□□ E-H Gilmour/ Bourque/ J. Mullen/ L. Murphy	5.00	8.00
□□ I-L Hawerchuk/ Francis/ Poddubny/ Näslund	2.00	4.00
□□ M-P Goulet/ Savard/ Trottier/ Courtnall	3.50	5.00

TOPPS STICKER INSERTS

Insert Set (33 stickers):	**20.00**
Common Team Sticker (13-33):	**.25**
Topps	**NRMT-MT**
□ 1 AS: Raymond Bourque, Bost.	2.50
□ 2 AS: Ron Hextall (G), Phil.	.75
□ 3 AS: Mark Howe, Phil.	.35
□ 4 AS: Jari Kurri, Edmo.	1.50
□ 5 AS: Wayne Gretzky, Edmo.	8.00
□ 6 AS: Michel Goulet, Québ.	.75
□ 7 AS: Larry Murphy, Wash.	.50
□ 8 AS: Mike Liut (G)	.35
□ 9 AS: Al MacInnis, Calg.	1.50
□ 10 AS: Tim Kerr, Phil.	.35
□ 11 AS: Mario Lemieux, Pitt.	7.00
□ 12 AS: Luc Robitaille, LosA.	3.00

□ 13 Toronto Maple Leafs	□ 14 Buffalo Sabres
□ 15 Detroit Red Wings	□ 16 Pittsburgh Penguins
□ 17 New York Rangers	□ 18 Calgary Flames
□ 19 Winnipeg Jets	□ 20 Québec Nordiques
□ 21 Chicago Blackhawks	□ 22 Los Angeles Kings
□ 23 Montréal Canadiens	□ 24 Vancouver Canucks
□ 25 Hartford Whalers	□ 26 Philadelphia Flyers
□ 27 New Jersey Devils	□ 28 St. Louis Blues
□ 29 Minn. North Stars	□ 30 Washington Capitals
□ 31 Boston Bruins	□ 32 New York Islanders
□ 33 Edmonton Oilers	

1987 - 88 O-PEE-CHEE LEADERS

These cards measure 2 1/8" x 3".

Complete Set (42 cards):	**20.00**
O-Pee-Chee	**NM-MT**
□ 1 Glenn Anderson, Edmo.	.35
□ 2 Brian Benning, SLou.	.20
□ 3 Daniel Berthiaume (G), Winn.	.50
□ 4 Raymond Bourque, Bost.	2.00
□ 5 Shawn Burr, Detr.	.20
□ 6 Jimmy Carson, LosA.	.20
□ 7 Dino Ciccarelli, Minn.	.50
□ 8 Paul Coffey, Edmo.	1.25
□ 9 Per-Erik Eklund, Phil.	.20
□ 10 Ron Francis, Hart.	1.50
□ 11 Doug Gilmour, SLou.	1.00
□ 12 Michel Goulet, Québ.	.35
□ 13 Wayne Gretzky, Edmo.	7.00
□ 14 Glen Hanlon (G), Detr.	.35
□ 15 Brian Hayward (G), Mont.	.35
□ 16 Ron Hextall (G), Phil.	1.00
□ 17 Phil Housley, Buff.	.35
□ 18 Mark Howe, Phil.	.35
□ 19 Doug Jarvis, Hart.	.20
□ 20 Tim Kerr, Phil.	.20
□ 21 Jari Kurri, Edmo.	.50
□ 22 Pat LaFontaine, NYIs.	.50
□ 23 Mario Lemieux, Pitt.	6.00
□ 24 Mike Liut (G), Hart.	.35
□ 25 Kevin Lowe, Edmo.	.35
□ 26 Al MacInnis, Calg.	1.00
□ 27 Brad McCrimmon, Phil.	.20
□ 28 Mark Messier, Edmo.	2.00
□ 29 Joe Mullen, Calg.	.50
□ 30 Craig Muni, Edmo.	.20
□ 31 Larry Murphy, Wash.	.35
□ 32 Dave Poulin, Phil.	.20
□ 33 Brian Propp, Phil.	.20
□ 34 Paul Reinhart, Calg.	.20
□ 35 Luc Robitaille, LosA.	2.50
□ 36 Patrick Roy (G), Mont.	7.00
□ 37 Christian Ruuttu, Buff.	.20
□ 38 Tomas Sandstrom, NYRa.	.35
□ 39 Denis Savard, Chic.	.35
□ 40 Petri Skriko, Vanc.	.20
□ 41 Bryan Trottier, NYIs.	.50
□ 42 Checklist	.50

1987 - 88 O-PEE-CHEE STICKERS

These stickers measure 2 1/8" x 3".

Complete Set (168 stickers):	**35.00**
Album:	**5.00**
Common Player:	**.20**
O-Pee-Chee	**NM-MT**
□ 1 Ron Hextall (G), Phil., M.V.P.	.75
□ 2 Stanley Cup Action	.20
□ 3 Stanley Cup Action	.20
□ 4 Stanley Cup Action	.20
□ 5 Stanley Cup Action	.20

Note: Stickers 2-5 feature Craig MacTavish and Grant Fuhr.

□ 6 Mats Näslund, Mont.	.25
□ 9 Chris Chelios, Mont.	1.00
□ 10 Bobby Smith, Mont.	.25
□ 13 Patrick Roy (G), Mont.	6.50
□ 16 Larry Robinson, Mont.	.25
□ 19 Claude Lemieux, Mont.	1.50
□ 24 Bernie Federko, SLou.	.25
□ 27 Doug Gilmour, SLou.	1.00
□ 32 Walt Poddubny, NYRa.	.20
□ 35 Tomas Sandstrom, NYRa.	.20
□ 36 Joe Mullen, Calg.	.25
□ 39 Paul Reinhart, Calg.	.20
□ 40 Al MacInnis, Calg.	.50
□ 43 Lanny McDonald, Calg.	.25
□ 46 Jim Peplinski, Calg.	.20
□ 49 Gary Suter, Calg.	.75
□ 54 Craig Hartsburg, Minn.	.25
□ 57 Dino Ciccarelli, Minn.	.50
□ 62 Aaron Broten, NJer.	.20
□ 65 Kirk Muller, NJer.	.20
□ 66A Face-off: Jim Sandlak, Vanc.	.20
□ 66B Face-off: Steve Kasper, Bost.	.20
□ 67 Raymond Bourque/ Brian Propp	.50
□ 68 Calgary vs Boston	.20
□ 69 Murray Craven, Phil.	.20
□ 70 Boston Bruins	.20
□ 71 New York Islanders	.20
□ 72 Alain Chevrier (G), NJer.	.25
□ 73 Patrick Roy (G)/ Mike Lalor	3.50
□ 78 Denis Savard, Chic.	.35
□ 81 Steve Larmer, Chic.	.50
□ 82 Jari Kurri, Edmo.	.75
□ 85 Grant Fuhr (G), Edmo.	.50
□ 86 Wayne Gretzky, Edmo.	5.00
□ 89 Paul Coffey, Edmo.	.75
□ 92 Mark Messier, Edmo.	1.50
□ 95 Glenn Anderson, Edmo.	.25
□ 100 Mark Howe, Phil.	.25
□ 103 Tim Kerr, Phil.	.20
□ 108 Brent Ashton, Detr.	.20
□ 111 Steve Yzerman, Detr.	2.00
□ 140 Raymond Bourque, Bost.	1.00
□ 143 Cam Neely, Bost.	.75
□ 148 Tom Barrasso (G), Buff.	.25
□ 151 Phil Housley, Buff.	.25
□ 152 Wendel Clark, Toro.	1.00
□ 155 Rick Vaive, Toro.	.20
□ 156 Russ Courtnall, Toro.	.50
□ 159 Tom Fergus, Toro.	.20
□ 162 Allan Bester (G), Toro.	.25
□ 165 Börje Salming, Toro.	.25
□ 170 Mario Lemieux, Pitt.	4.00
□ 173 Dan Quinn, Pitt.	.20
□ 188 Barry Pederson, Vanc.	.20

☐ 191 Doug Lidster, Vanc. .20
☐ 192 Petri Skriko, Vanc. .20
☐ 195 Tony Tanti, Vanc. .20
☐ 198 Stan Smyl, Vanc. .20
☐ 201 Patrik Sundstrom, Vanc. .20
☐ 206 Ron Francis, Hart. .75
☐ 209 Mike Liut (G), Hart. .25
☐ 214 Bernie Nicholls, LosA. .20
☐ 217 Luc Robitaille, LosA. 3.50
☐ 218 John Ogrodnick, Québ. .20
☐ 221 Paul Gillis, Québ. .20
☐ 222 Peter Stastny, Québ. .35
☐ 225 Michel Goulet, Québ. .35
☐ 228 Anton Stastny, Québ. .20
☐ 231 Mario Gosselin (G), Québ. .25
☐ 236 Rod Langway, Wash. .20
☐ 239 Mike Gartner, Wash. .50
☐ 244 Mike Bossy, NYIs. .50
☐ 247 Denis Potvin, NYIs. .35
☐ 252 Paul MacLean, Winn. .20
☐ 255 Dale Hawerchuk, Winn. .35

O-Pee-Chee **NM-MT**

☐ 7/146 Guy Carbonneau, Mont./ Steve Dykstra, Buff. .25
☐ 8/147 Gaston Gingras, Mont./ Dave Andreychuk, Buff. .50
☐ 11/149 Rick Green, Mont./ Mike Ramsey, Buff. .20
☐ 12/150 Bob Gainey, Mont./ Mike Foligno, Buff. .25
☐ 14/153 Kjell Dahlin, Mont./ Greg Terrion, Toro. .20
☐ 15/154 Chris Nilan, Mont./ Steve Thomas, Toro. .25
☐ 17/157 Ryan Walter, Mont./ Rick Lanz, Toro. .20
☐ 18/158 Petr Svoboda, Mont./ Miroslav Frycer, Toro. .20
☐ 20/160 Rob Ramage, SLou./ Al Iafrate, Toro. .20
☐ 21/161 Mark Hunter, SLou./ Gary Leeman, Toro. .20
☐ 22/163 Rick Wamsley (G), SLou./ Todd Gill, Toro. .25
☐ 23/164 Greg Palawski, SLou./ Ken Wregget (G), Toro. .50
☐ 25/166 Ron Flockhart, SLou./ Craig Simpson, Pitt. .20
☐ 26/167 Tim Bothwell, SLou./ Terry Ruskowski, Pitt. .20
☐ 28/168 Kelly Kisio, NYRa./ Gilles Meloche (G), Pitt. .25
☐ 29/169 Don Maloney, NYRa./ John Chabot, Pitt. .20
☐ 30/171 James Patrick, NYRa./ Moe Mantha, Pitt. .20
☐ 31/172 Willie Huber, NYRa./ Jim Johnson, Pitt. .20
☐ 33/178 Vanbiesbrouck (G), NYRa./ Bourque, Bost. 2.00
☐ 34/179 Marcel Dionne, NYRa./ Dave Poulin, Phil. .35
☐ 37/180 Mike Bullard, Calg./ Wayne Gretzky, Edmo. 4.00
☐ 38/181 Neil Sheehy, Calg./ Wayne Gretzky, Edmo. 4.00
☐ 41/182 Mike Vernon (G), Calg./ Ron Hextall (G), Phil. 2.00
☐ 42/183 Joel Otto, Calg./ Doug Jarvis, Hart. .20
☐ 44/184 Hakan Loob, Calg./ Brian Hayward (G), Mont. .25
☐ 45/185 Carey Wilson, Calg./ Patrick Roy (G), Mont. 3.00
☐ 47/186 John Tonelli, Calg./ Joe Mullen, Calg. .25
☐ 48/187 Jamie Macoun, Calg./ Luc Robitaille, LosA. 1.25
☐ 50/189 Maruk, Minn./ R. Brodeur (G), Vanc. .25
☐ 51/190 Don Beaupré (G), Minn./ Dave Richter, Vanc. .25
☐ 52/193 Neal Broten, Minn./ Rich Sutter, Vanc. .25
☐ 53/194 Brian Bellows, Minn./ Jim Sandlak, Vanc. .20
☐ 55/196 Gord Roberts, Minn./ Michel Petit, Vanc. .20
☐ 56/197 Steve Payne, Minn./ Jim Benning, Vanc. .20
☐ 58/199 Pat Verbeek, NJer./ Brent Peterson, Vanc. .20
☐ 59/200 Doug Sulliman, NJer./ Garth Butcher, Vanc. .20
☐ 60/202 Bruce Driver, NJer./ Kevin Dineen, Hart. .20
☐ 61/203 Joe Cirella, NJer./ Sylvain Turgeon, Hart. .20
☐ 63/204 Chevrier (G), NJer./ John Anderson, Hart. .25
☐ 64/205 Mark Johnson, NJer./ Ulf Samuelsson, Hart. .25
☐ 74/207 Al Secord, Chic./ Doug Jarvis, Hart. .20
☐ 75/208 Bob Sauvé (G), Chic./ Dave Babych, Hart. .25
☐ 76/210 Ed Olczyk, Chic./ Jimmy Carson, LosA. .20
☐ 77/211 Doug Wilson, Chic./ Larry Playfair, LosA. .25
☐ 79/212 Troy Murray, Chic./ Jay Wells, LosA. .20
☐ 80/213 Gary Nylund, Chic./ Melanson (G), LosA. .25
☐ 83/215 Esa Tikkanen, Edmo./ Dave Taylor, LosA. .50
☐ 84/216 Kevin Lowe, Edmo./ Jim Fox, LosA. .35
☐ 87/219 Huddy, Edmo./ Jason Lafrenière, Québ. .20
☐ 88/220 Kent Nilsson, Edmo./ Mike Hough, Québ. .20
☐ 90/223 Mike Krushelnyski, Edmo./ David Shaw, Québ. .20
☐ 91/224 Craig MacTavish, Edmo./ Bill Derlago, Québ. .20
☐ 93/226 Andy Moog (G), Edmo./ Shedden, Québ. .50
☐ 94/227 Randy Gregg, Edmo./ Basil McRae, Québ. .20
☐ 96/229 Peter Zezel, Phil./ Randy Moller, Québ. .20
☐ 97/230 Brian Propp, Phil./ Robert Picard, Québ. .20
☐ 98/232 Dave Poulin, Phil./ Larry Murphy, Wash. .25
☐ 99/233 Brad McCrimmon, Phil./ Scott Stevens, Wash. .20
☐ 101/234 Ron Hextall (G), Phil./ Mike Ridley, Wash. 1.25
☐ 102/235 Ron Sutter, Phil./ Dave Christian, Wash. .20
☐ 104/237 Petr Klima, Detr./ Bob Gould, Wash. .20
☐ 105/238 Adam Oates, Detr./ Bob Mason (G), Wash. 3.00
☐ 106/240 Gerard Gallant, Detr./ Bryan Trottier, NYIs. .25
☐ 107/241 Mike O'Connell, Detr./ Brent Sutter, NYIs. .25
☐ 109/242 Glen Hanlon (G), Detr./ Hrudey (G), NYIs. .25
☐ 110/243 Harold Snepsts, Detr./ Pat LaFontaine, NYIs. .75
☐ 112/124 Mark Howe, Phil./ Brian Benning, SLou. .25
☐ 113/125 Michel Goulet, Québ./ Shawn Burr, Detr. .25
☐ 114/126 Ron Hextall (G), Phil./ Jimmy Carson, LosA. .50
☐ 115/127 Gretzky, Edmo./ Shayne Corson, Mont. 3.50
☐ 116/128 Bourque, Bost./ Damphousse, Toro. 1.50
☐ 117/129 Jari Kurri, Edmo./ Ron Hextall (G), Phil. .50
☐ 118/130 Dino Ciccarelli, Minn./ Lafrenière, Québ. .35
☐ 119/131 Larry Murphy, Wash./ Ken Leiter, NYIs. .25
☐ 120/132 Mario Lemieux, Pitt./ A. Pedersen, Bost. 3.00
☐ 121/133 Mike Liut (G), Hart./ Luc Robitaille, LosA. 1.25
☐ 122/134 Luc Robitaille, LosA./ Christian Ruuttu, Buff. 1.25
☐ 123/135 Al MacInnis, Calg./ Jim Sandlak, Vanc. .25
☐ 136/245 Keith Crowder, Bost./ Pat Flatley, NYIs. .20
☐ 137/246 Charlie Simmer, Bost./ Ken Morrow, NYIs. .20
☐ 138/248 Rick Middleton, Bost./ Randy Carlyle, Winn. .25
☐ 139/249 Keans (G), Bost./ Berthiaume (G), Winn. .35
☐ 141/250 Tom McCarthy, Bost./ Mario Marois, Winn. .20
☐ 142/251 Reed Larson, Bost./ Dave Ellett, Winn. .20
☐ 144/253 Christian Ruuttu, Buff./ Gilles Hamel, Winn. .20
☐ 145/254 John Tucker, Buff./ Doug Smail, Winn. .20
☐ 174/176 Wayne Gretzky, Edmo./ Mark Howe, Phil. 4.00
☐ 175/177 Brian Hayward (G), Mont./ Robitaille, LosA. 1.25

1987 - 88 PANINI STICKERS

These stickers measure 2 1/8" x 2 11/16".

Complete Set (396 stickers):	**70.00**
Album (Grant Fuhr on cover):	**6.00**
Common Player:	**.20**

Panini **NM-MT**

☐ 1 Stanley Cup .20
☐ 2 Charlie Simmer (Action), Bost. .20
☐ 3 Boston Bruins Team Logo .20
☐ 4 Doug Keans (G), Bost. .35
☐ 5 Bill Ranford (G), Bost. 2.00
☐ 6 Raymond Bourque, Bost. 1.00
☐ 7 Reed Larson, Bost. .20
☐ 8 Mike Milbury, Bost. .20
☐ 9 Michael Thelven, Bost. .20
☐ 10 Cam Neely, Bost. 1.00
☐ 11 Charlie Simmer, Bost. .20
☐ 12 Rick Middleton, Bost. .35
☐ 13 Tom McCarthy, Bost. .20
☐ 14 Keith Crowder, Bost. .20
☐ 15 Steve Kasper, Bost. .20
☐ 16 Ken Linseman, Bost. .20
☐ 17 Dwight Foster, Bost. .20
☐ 18 Jay Miller, Bost. .20
☐ 19 Dave Andreychuk, Buff. .35
☐ 20 Buffalo Sabres Team Logo .20
☐ 21 Jacques Cloutier (G), Buff. .35
☐ 22 Tom Barrasso (G), Buff. .35
☐ 23 Daren Puppa (G), Buff. .75
☐ 24 Phil Housley, Buff. .35
☐ 25 Mike Ramsey, Buff. .20
☐ 26 Bill Hajt, Buff. .20
☐ 27 Dave Andreychuk, Buff. .75
☐ 28 Christian Ruuttu, Buff. .20
☐ 29 Mike Foligno, Buff. .20
☐ 30 John Tucker, Buff. .20
☐ 31 Adam Creighton, Buff. .20
☐ 32 Wilf Paiement, Buff. .20
☐ 33 Paul Cyr, Buff. .20
☐ 34 Clark Gillies, Buff. .20
☐ 35 Lindy Ruff, Buff. .20
☐ 36 Sylvain Turgeon, Hart. .35
☐ 37 Hartford Whalers Team Logo .20
☐ 38 Mike Liut (G), Hart. .35
☐ 39 Steve Weeks (G), Hart. .35
☐ 40 Dave Babych, Hart. .20
☐ 41 Ulf Samuelsson, Hart. .75
☐ 42 Dana Murzyn, Hart. .20
☐ 43 Ron Francis, Hart. .75
☐ 44 Kevin Dineen, Hart. .20
☐ 45 John Anderson, Hart. .20
☐ 46 Ray Ferraro, Hart. .20
☐ 47 Dean Evason, Hart. .20
☐ 48 Paul Lawless, Hart. .20
☐ 49 Stewart Gavin, Hart. .20
☐ 50 Sylvain Turgeon, Hart. .20
☐ 51 Dave Tippett, Hart. .20
☐ 52 Doug Jarvis, Hart. .20
☐ 53 Bob Gainey, Mont. .35
☐ 54 Montréal Canadiens Team Logo .20
☐ 55 Brian Hayward (G), Mont. .35
☐ 56 Patrick Roy (G), Mont. 5.00
☐ 57 Larry Robinson, Mont. .50
☐ 58 Chris Chelios, Mont. 1.00
☐ 59 Craig Ludwig, Mont. .20
☐ 60 Rick Green, Mont. .20
☐ 61 Mats Näslund, Mont. .35
☐ 62 Bobby Smith, Mont. .20
☐ 63 Claude Lemieux, Mont. 1.50
☐ 64 Guy Carbonneau, Mont. .35
☐ 65 Stéphane Richer, Mont. 1.00
☐ 66 Mike McPhee, Mont. .20
☐ 67 Brian Skrudland, Mont. .20
☐ 68 Chris Nilan, Mont. .20
☐ 69 Bob Gainey, Mont. .50
☐ 70 Kirk Muller, NJer. .35
☐ 71 New Jersey Devils Team Logo .20
☐ 72 Craig Billington (G), NJer. .35
☐ 73 Alain Chevrier (G), NJer. .35
☐ 74 Bruce Driver, NJer. .20
☐ 75 Joe Cirella, NJer. .20
☐ 76 Ken Daneyko, NJer. .20
☐ 77 Craig Wolanin, NJer. .20
☐ 78 Aaron Broten, NJer. .20
☐ 79 Kirk Muller, NJer. .50
☐ 80 John MacLean, NJer. .20
☐ 81 Pat Verbeek, NJer. .35
☐ 82 Doug Sulliman, NJer. .20
☐ 83 Mark Johnson, NJer. .20
☐ 84 Greg Adams, NJer. .20
☐ 85 Claude Loiselle, NJer. .20
☐ 86 Andy Brickley, NJer. .20
☐ 87 New York Islanders Action Player .20
☐ 88 New York Islanders Team Logo .20
☐ 89 Billy Smith (G), NYIs. .50
☐ 90 Kelly Hrudey (G), NYIs. .35
☐ 91 Denis Potvin, NYIs. .50
☐ 92 Tomas Jonsson, NYIs. .20
☐ 93 Ken Leiter, NYIs. .20
☐ 94 Ken Morrow, NYIs. .20
☐ 95 Brian Curran, NYIs. .20
☐ 96 Bryan Trottier, NYIs. .75
☐ 97 Mike Bossy, NYIs. .75
☐ 98 Pat LaFontaine, NYIs. 1.00
☐ 99 Brent Sutter, NYIs. .20
☐ 100 Mikko Makelä, NYIs. .20
☐ 101 Patrick Flatley, NYIs. .20
☐ 102 Duane Sutter, NYIs. .20
☐ 103 Richard Kromm, NYIs. .20
☐ 104 Ron Greschner, NYRa. .20
☐ 105 New York Rangers Team Logo .20
☐ 106 John Vanbiesbrouck (G), NYRa. 2.50
☐ 107 James Patrick, NYRa. .20
☐ 108 Ron Greschner, NYRa. .20
☐ 109 Willie Huber, NYRa. .20
☐ 110 Curt Giles, NYRa. .20
☐ 111 Larry Melnyk, NYRa. .20
☐ 112 Walt Poddubny, NYRa. .20
☐ 113 Marcel Dionne, NYRa. .50
☐ 114 Tomas Sandstrom, NYRa. .35
☐ 115 Kelly Kisio, NYRa. .20
☐ 116 Pierre Larouche, NYRa. .20
☐ 117 Don Maloney, NYRa. .20
☐ 118 Tony McKegney, NYRa. .20
☐ 119 Ron Duguay, NYRa. .20
☐ 120 Jan Erixon, NYRa. .20
☐ 121 Brad McCrimmon, Phil. .20
☐ 122 Philadelphia Flyers Team Logo .20
☐ 123 Ron Hextall (G), Phil. 1.50
☐ 124 Mark Howe, Phil. .35
☐ 125 Doug Crossman, Phil. .20
☐ 126 Brad McCrimmon, Phil. .20
☐ 127 Brad Marsh, Phil. .20
☐ 128 Tim Kerr, Phil. .20
☐ 129 Peter Zezel, Phil. .20
☐ 130 Dave Poulin, Phil. .20
☐ 131 Brian Propp, Phil. .20
☐ 132 Per-Erik Eklund, Phil. .20
☐ 133 Murray Craven, Phil. .20
☐ 134 Rick Tocchet, Phil. 1.75
☐ 135 Derrick Smith, Phil. .20
☐ 136 Ilkka Sinisalo, Phil. .20
☐ 137 Ron Sutter, Phil. .20
☐ 138 Terry Ruskowski, Pitt. .20
☐ 139 Pittsburgh Penguins Team Logo .20
☐ 140 Gilles Meloche (G), Pitt. .35
☐ 141 Doug Bodger, Pitt. .20
☐ 142 Moe Mantha, Pitt. .20
☐ 143 Jim Johnson, Pitt. .20
☐ 144 Rod Buskas, Pitt. .20
☐ 145 Randy Hillier, Pitt. .20
☐ 146 Mario Lemieux, Pitt. 5.00
☐ 147 Dan Quinn, Pitt. .20
☐ 148 Randy Cunneyworth, Pitt. .35
☐ 149 Craig Simpson, Pitt. .35
☐ 150 Terry Ruskowski, Pitt. .20
☐ 151 John Chabot, Pitt. .20
☐ 152 Bob Errey, Pitt. .20
☐ 153 Dan Frawley, Pitt. .20
☐ 154 Dave Hannan, Pitt. .20
☐ 155 Dale Hunter, Québ. .35
☐ 156 Québec Nordiques Team Logo .20
☐ 157 Mario Gosselin (G), Québ. .35
☐ 158 Clint Malarchuk (G), Québ. .35
☐ 159 Risto Siltanen, Québ. .20
☐ 160 Robert Picard, Québ. .20
☐ 161 Normand Rochefort, Québ. .20
☐ 162 Randy Moller, Québ. .20
☐ 163 Michel Goulet, Québ. .50
☐ 164 Peter Stastny, Québ. .50
☐ 165 John Ogrodnick, Québ. .20
☐ 166 Anton Stastny, Québ. .20
☐ 167 Paul Gillis, Québ. .20
☐ 168 Dale Hunter, Québ. .35
☐ 169 Alain Côté, Québ. .20
☐ 170 Mike Eagles, Québ. .20
☐ 171 Jason Lafrenière, Québ. .20
☐ 172 Greg Smith, Wash. .20
☐ 173 Washington Capitals Team Logo .20
☐ 174 Pete Peeters (G), Wash. .35
☐ 175 Bob Mason (G), Wash. .35
☐ 176 Larry Murphy, Wash. .35
☐ 177 Scott Stevens, Wash. .50
☐ 178 Rod Langway, Wash. .35
☐ 179 Kevin Hatcher, Wash. .35
☐ 180 Mike Gartner, Wash. .50
☐ 181 Mike Ridley, Wash. .20
☐ 182 Craig Laughlin, Wash. .20
☐ 183 Gaetan Duchesne, Wash. .20
☐ 184 Dave Christian, Wash. .20
☐ 185 Greg Adams, Wash. .20
☐ 186 Kelly Miller, Wash. .20
☐ 187 Alan Haworth, Wash. .20
☐ 188 Lou Franceschetti, Wash. .20
☐ 189 Stanley Cup .20
☐ 190 Stanley Cup .20
☐ 191 Ron Hextall (G), Phil. 1.00
☐ 192 Wayne Gretzky, Edmo. 6.00
☐ 193 Brian Propp, Phi. .20
☐ 194 Mark Messier, Edmo. 1.50
☐ 195 Messier Skates Through Flyers Defence 1.00
☐ 196 Messier Skates Through Flyers Defence 1.00
☐ 197 Gretzky Hoists Cup for the Third Time 3.00
☐ 198 Gretzky Hoists Cup for the Third Time 3.00
☐ 199 Gretzky Hoists Cup for the Third Time 3.00
☐ 200 Gretzky Hoists Cup for the Third Time 3.00
☐ 201 Hakan Loob, Calg. .20
☐ 202 Calgary Flames Team Logo .20
☐ 203 Mike Vernon (G), Calg. 2.00
☐ 204 Réjean Lemelin (G), Calg. .35
☐ 205 Al MacInnis, Calg. .75
☐ 206 Paul Reinhart, Calg. .20
☐ 207 Gary Suter, Calg. .35
☐ 208 Jamie Macoun, Calg. .20
☐ 209 Neil Sheehy, Calg. .20
☐ 210 Joe Mullen, Calg. .50
☐ 211 Carey Wilson, Calg. .20
☐ 212 Joel Otto, Calg. .20
☐ 213 Jim Peplinski, Calg. .20
☐ 214 Hakan Loob, Calg. .20
☐ 215 Lanny McDonald, Calg. .50
☐ 216 Tim Hunter, Calg. .20
☐ 217 Gary Roberts, Calg. 2.50
☐ 218 Murray Bannerman (G), Chic. .35
☐ 219 Chicago Blackhawks Team Logo .20
☐ 220 Bob Sauvé (G), Chic. .35
☐ 221 Murray Bannerman (G), Chic. .35
☐ 222 Doug Wilson, Chic. .35
☐ 223 Rob Murray, Chic. .20
☐ 224 Gary Nylund, Chic. .20
☐ 225 Denis Savard, Chic. .50
☐ 226 Steve Larmer, Chic. .35
☐ 227 Troy Murray, Chic. .20
☐ 228 Wayne Presley, Chic. .20
☐ 229 Al Secord, Chic. .20
☐ 230 Ed Olczyk, Chic. .20
☐ 231 Curt Fraser, Chic. .20
☐ 232 Bill Watson, Chic. .20

☐	233 Keith Brown, Chic.	.20
☐	234 Darryl Sutter, Chic.	.20
☐	235 Lee Norwood, Detr.	.20
☐	236 Detroit Red Wings Team Logo	.20
☐	237 Greg Stefan (G), Detr.	.35
☐	238 Glen Hanlon (G), Detr.	.35
☐	239 Darren Veitch, Detr.	.20
☐	240 Mike O'Connell, Detr.	.20
☐	241 Harold Snepsts, Detr.	.20
☐	242 Dave Lewis, Detr.	.20
☐	243 Steve Yzerman, Detr.	3.00
☐	244 Brent Ashton, Detr.	.20
☐	245 Gerard Gallant, Detr.	.20
☐	246 Petr Klima, Detr.	.20
☐	247 Shawn Burr, Detr.	.20
☐	248 Adam Oates, Detr.	4.00
☐	249 Mel Bridgman, Detr.	.20
☐	250 Tim Higgins, Detr.	.20
☐	251 Joey Kocur, Detr.	.20
☐	252 Mark Messier, Edmo.	1.50
☐	253 Edmonton Oilers Team Logo	.20
☐	254 Grant Fuhr (G), Edmo.	1.00
☐	255 Andy Moog (G), Edmo.	1.00
☐	256 Paul Coffey, Edmo.	1.00
☐	257 Kevin Lowe, Edmo.	.35
☐	258 Craig Muni, Edmo.	.20
☐	259 Steve Smith, Edmo.	.20
☐	260 Charlie Huddy, Edmo.	.20
☐	261 Wayne Gretzky, Edmo.	6.00
☐	262 Jari Kurri, Edmo.	.75
☐	263 Mark Messier, Edmo.	2.00
☐	264 Esa Tikkanen, Edmo.	.75
☐	265 Glenn Anderson, Edmo.	.35
☐	266 Mike Krushelnyski, Edmo.	.20
☐	267 Craig MacTavish, Edmo.	.20
☐	268 Dave Hunter, Edmo.	.20
☐	269 Los Angeles Kings Action Player	.20
☐	270 Los Angeles Kings Team Logo	.20
☐	271 Rolllie Melanson (G), LosA.	.35
☐	272 Darren Eliot (G), LosA.	.35
☐	273 Grant Ledyard, LosA.	.20
☐	274 Jay Wells, LosA.	.20
☐	275 Mark Hardy, LosA.	.20
☐	276 Dean Kennedy, LosA.	.20
☐	277 Luc Robitaille, LosA.	2.50
☐	278 Bernie Nicholls, LosA.	.50
☐	279 Jimmy Carson, LosA.	.20
☐	280 Dave Taylor, LosA.	.35
☐	281 Jim Fox, LosA.	.20
☐	282 Bryan Erickson, LosA.	.20
☐	283 Dave Williams, LosA.	.20
☐	284 Sean McKenna, LosA.	.20
☐	285 Phil Sykes, LosA.	.20
☐	286 Brian Bellows, Minn.	.20
☐	287 Minnesota North Stars Team Logo	.20
☐	288 Kari Takko (G), Minn.	.35
☐	289 Don Beaupré (G), Minn.	.35
☐	290 Craig Hartsburg, Minn.	.20
☐	291 Ron Wilson, Minn.	.20
☐	292 Frantisek Musil, Minn.	.20
☐	293 Dino Ciccarelli, Minn.	.35
☐	294 Brian MacLellan, Minn.	.20
☐	295 Dirk Graham, Minn.	.20
☐	296 Brian Bellows, Minn.	.35
☐	297 Neal Broten, Minn.	.20
☐	298 Dennis Maruk, Minn.	.20
☐	299 Keith Acton, Minn.	.20
☐	300 Brian Lawton, Minn.	.20
☐	301 Bob Brooke, Minn.	.20
☐	302 Willi Plett, Minn.	.20
☐	303 Brian Sutter, SLou.	.20
☐	304 St. Louis Blues Team Logo	.20
☐	305 Rick Wamsley (G), SLou.	.35
☐	306 Rob Ramage, SLou.	.20
☐	307 Ric Nattress, SLou.	.20
☐	308 Bruce Bell, SLou.	.20
☐	309 Charlie Bourgeois, SLou.	.20
☐	310 Jim Pavese, SLou.	.20
☐	311 Doug Gilmour, SLou.	.50
☐	312 Bernie Federko, SLou.	.20
☐	313 Mark Hunter, SLou.	.20
☐	314 Greg Paslawski, SLou.	.20
☐	315 Gino Cavallini, SLou.	.20
☐	316 Rick Meagher, SLou.	.20
☐	317 Ron Flockhart, SLou.	.20
☐	318 Doug Wickenheiser, SLou.	.20
☐	319 Jocelyn Lemieux, SLou.	.20
☐	320 Wendel Clark, Toro.	.35
☐	321 Toronto Maple Leafs Team Logo	.20
☐	322 Ken Wregget (G), Toro.	.50
☐	323 Allan Bester (G), Toro.	.35
☐	324 Todd Gill, Toro.	.20
☐	325 Al Iafrate, Toro.	.20
☐	326 Börje Salming, Toro.	.35
☐	327 Russ Courtnall, Toro.	.20
☐	328 Rick Vaive, Toro.	.20
☐	329 Steve Thomas, Toro.	.20
☐	330 Wendel Clark, Toro.	1.00
☐	331 Gary Leeman, Toro.	.20
☐	332 Tom Fergus, Toro.	.20
☐	333 Vincent Damphousse, Toro.	2.00
☐	334 Peter Ihnacak, Toro.	.20
☐	335 Brad Smith, Toro.	.20
☐	336 Miroslav Ihnacak, Toro.	.20
☐	337 Stan Smyl, Vanc.	.20
☐	338 Vancouver Canucks Team Logo	.20
☐	339 Frank Caprice (G), Vanc.	.35
☐	340 Richard Brodeur (G), Vanc.	.35
☐	341 Doug Lidster, Vanc.	.20
☐	342 Michel Petit, Vanc.	.20
☐	343 Garth Butcher, Vanc.	.20
☐	344 Dave Richter, Vanc.	.20
☐	345 Tony Tanti, Vanc.	.20
☐	346 Barry Pederson, Vanc.	.20
☐	347 Petri Skriko, Vanc.	.20
☐	348 Patrik Sundstrom, Vanc.	.20
☐	349 Stan Smyl, Vanc.	.20
☐	350 Rich Sutter, Vanc.	.20
☐	351 Steve Tambellini, Vanc.	.20
☐	352 Jim Sandlak, Vanc.	.20
☐	353 Dave Lowry, Vanc.	.20
☐	354 Paul MacLean, Winn.	.20
☐	355 Winnipeg Jets Team Logo	.20
☐	356 Daniel Berthiaume (G), Winn.	.35
☐	357 Eldon Reddick (G), Winn.	.35
☐	358 Dave Ellett, Winn.	.20
☐	359 Mario Marois, Winn.	.20
☐	360 Randy Carlyle, Winn.	.20
☐	361 Fredrick Olausson, Winn.	.20
☐	362 Jim Kyte, Winn.	.20
☐	363 Dale Hawerchuk, Winn.	.50
☐	364 Paul MacLean, Winn.	.20
☐	365 Thomas Steen, Winn.	.20
☐	366 Gilles Hamel, Winn.	.20
☐	367 Doug Smail, Winn.	.20
☐	368 Laurie Boschman, Winn.	.20
☐	369 Ray Neufeld, Winn.	.20
☐	370 Andrew McBain, Winn.	.20
☐	371 AW: Wayne Gretzky, Edmo.	5.00
☐	372 Hart Memorial Trophy	.20
☐	373 AW: Wayne Gretzky, Edmo.	5.00
☐	374 Art Ross Trophy	.20
☐	375 William M. Jennings Trophy	.20
☐	376A AW: Brian Hayward (G), Mont.	.35
☐	376B AW: Patrick Roy (G), Mont.	4.50
☐	377 Vezina Trophy	.20
☐	378 AW: Ron Hextall (G), Phil.	.75
☐	379 AW: Luc Robitaille, LosA.	2.00
☐	380 Calder Memorial Trophy	.20
☐	381 AW: Raymond Bourque, Bost.	1.00
☐	382 James Norris Memorial Trophy	.20
☐	383 Lady Byng Memorial Trophy	.20
☐	384 AW: Joe Mullen, Calg.	.35
☐	385 Frank J. Selke Trophy	.20
☐	386 AW: Dave Poulin, Phil.	.20
☐	387 AW: Doug Jarvis, Hart.	.20
☐	388 Bill Masterton Memorial Trophy	.20
☐	389 AW: Wayne Gretzky, Edmo.	5.00
☐	390 Emery Edge Award	.20
☐	391 Philadelphia Flyers Team Photo	.20
☐	392 Philadelphia Flyers Team Photo	.20
☐	393 Prince of Wales Trophy	.20
☐	394 Clarence S. Campbell Bowl	.20
☐	395 Edmonton Oilers Team Photo	2.00
☐	396 Edmonton Oilers Team Photo	2.00

1987 - 88 SOVIET STARS

Complete Set (24 cards): 45.00

	Soviet Stars	**NM-MT**
☐	Sergei Ageikin	1.00
☐	Evgeny Belosheikin	1.00
☐	Zinetula Bilyaletdinov	1.00
☐	Vyacheslav Bykov	3.00
☐	Sergei Fedorov	12.00
☐	Viacheslav Fetisov	8.00
☐	Alexei Gusarov	2.00
☐	Valeri Kamensky	5.00
☐	Yuri Khmylev	2.00

☐	Valeri Kasatonov	2.00
☐	Andrei Khomutov	1.00
☐	Vladimir Konstantinov	5.00
☐	Vladimir Krutov	2.00
☐	Igor Larionov	8.00
☐	Sergei Makarov	5.00
☐	Sergei Mylnikov (G)	1.50
☐	Vasili Pervukhin	1.00
☐	Sergei Starikov	1.00
☐	Igor Stelnov	1.00
☐	Viktor Tikhonov	3.00
☐	Viktor Tjumenev	1.00
☐	Michael Varnakov	1.00
☐	Sergei Yashin	1.00
☐	Vladimir Yursinov	1.00

1988 SOVIET NATIONAL TEAM / OLYMPIC GAMES

These cards measure 3 5/8" x 5 5/8".

Complete Set (14 cards): 35.00

	Soviet Nationals	**NM-MT**
☐	1 Sweden vs USSR, Corinta 1956	2.50
☐	2 Tregubov, Alexaudsov, Puchkov, Squaw Valley 1960	2.50
☐	3 Statshinov, Konovalenko, Ivanov, Yakushev, Innsbruck 1964	2.50
☐	4 Three Times Olympic Champions Grenoble 1968	2.50
☐	5 A. Firsov, Sapporo 1972	2.50
☐	6 Soviets vs Finland, Innsbruck 1976	2.50
☐	7 Silver Medalist, Lake Placid 1980	2.50
☐	8 Olympic Champions, Sarajevo 1984	2.50
☐	9 Soviet Coaches of Olympic Teams	2.50
☐	10 Captains of Olympic Gold Teams	4.00
☐	11 Three Time Winners of Olympic Gold Medals	2.50
☐	12 Vsevolod Bobrov, Coach, Gold Medalist	2.50
☐	13 Valeri Kharlamov, Twice Gold Medalist	4.00
☐	14 Makarov, Larionov, Krutov, Fetisov, Kasatonov, Calgary 1988	6.00

1988 - 89 ESSO ALL-STAR STICKERS

These stickers measure 2 1/8" x 3 1/4".

Complete Set (48 stickers): 15.00
Album (English): 4.00
Album (French): 4.00

	Esso All-Stars	**NM**
☐	Jean Béliveau, Mont.	1.25
☐	Mike Bossy, NYIs.	1.00
☐	Raymond Bourque, Bost.	1.00
☐	Johnny Bower (G), Toro.	.75
☐	Bobby Clarke, Phil.	.75
☐	Paul Coffey, Pitt.	.75
☐	Yvan Cournoyer, Mont.	.75
☐	Marcel Dionne, LosA.	.75
☐	Ken Dryden (G), Mont.	1.50
☐	Phil Esposito, Bost.	1.00
☐	Tony Esposito (G), Chic.	1.00
☐	Grant Fuhr (G), Edmo.	.50
☐	Clark Gillies, NYIs.	.25
☐	Michel Goulet, Québ.	.50
☐	Wayne Gretzky, Edmo.	3.00
☐	Dale Hawerchuk, Winn.	.50
☐	Ron Hextall (G), Phil.	.50
☐	Gordie Howe, Detr.	2.00
☐	Mark Howe, Phil.	.50
☐	Bobby Hull, Chic.	1.50
☐	Tim Kerr, Phil.	.25
☐	Jari Kurri, Edmo.	.75
☐	Guy Lafleur, Mont.	1.25
☐	Rod Langway, Wash.	.50
☐	Jacques Laperrière, Mont.	.50
☐	Guy Lapointe, Mont.	.50
☐	Mario Lemieux, Pitt.	2.50
☐	Frank Mahovlich, Mont.	1.00
☐	Lanny McDonald, Calg.	.75
☐	Mark Messier, Edmo.	1.00
☐	Stan Mikita, Chic.	.75
☐	Mats Näslund, Mont.	.25
☐	Bobby Orr, Bost.	2.50
☐	Brad Park, NYRa.	.75
☐	Gilbert Perreault, Buff.	.50
☐	Denis Potvin, NYIs.	.75
☐	Larry Robinson, Mont.	.75
☐	Luc Robitaille, LosA.	.75
☐	Börje Salming, Toro.	.50
☐	Denis Savard, Chic.	.50
☐	Serge Savard, Mont.	.50
☐	Steve Shutt, Mont.	.75
☐	Darryl Sittler, Toro.	.75
☐	Billy Smith (G), NYIs.	.75
☐	John Tonelli, NYIs.	.25
☐	Bryan Trottier, NYIs.	.75
☐	Norm Ullman, Toro.	.75
☐	Gump Worsley (G), Mont.	.75

1988 - 89 FRITO-LAY STICKERS

These stickers came in specially marked bags of Frito Lay potato chips. Each sticker measures 1 3/8" x 1 3/4".

Complete Set (42 sticker): 35.00
Poster: 6.00

	Frito-Lay	**NM-MT**
☐	Glenn Anderson, Edmo.	.50
☐	Tom Barrasso (G), Buff.	.50
☐	Brian Bellows, Minn.	.35
☐	Raymond Bourque, Bost.	2.00
☐	Neal Broten, Minn.	.35
☐	Sean Burke (G), NJer.	.50
☐	Wendel Clark, Toro.	.50
☐	Paul Coffey, Pitt.	1.50
☐	Kevin Dineen, Hart.	.35
☐	Marcel Dionne, NYRa.	.75
☐	Bernie Federko, SLou.	.35
☐	Michael Foligno, Buff.	.35
☐	Ron Francis, Hart.	.75
☐	Mike Gartner, Wash.	1.00
☐	Doug Gilmour, SLou.	1.25
☐	Michel Goulet, Québ.	.75
☐	Dale Hawerchuk, Winn.	.75
☐	Ron Hextall (G), Phil.	.50
☐	Pat LaFontaine, NYIs.	.75
☐	Mario Lemieux, Pitt.	7.00
☐	Al MacInnis, Calg.	.50
☐	Andrew McBain, Winn.	.35
☐	Mark Messier, Edmo.	2.50
☐	Kirk Muller, NJer.	.35
☐	Troy Murray, Chic.	.35
☐	Mats Näslund, Mont.	.35
☐	Cam Neely, Bost.	1.25
☐	Bernie Nicholls, LosA.	.35
☐	Joe Nieuwendyk, Calg.	.50
☐	Ed Olczyk, Toro.	.35
☐	James Patrick, NYRa.	.35
☐	Barry Pederson, Vanc.	.35
☐	Dave Poulin, Phil.	.35
☐	Bob Probert, Detr.	.75
☐	Stéphane Richer, Mont.	.35
☐	Luc Robitaille, LosA.	1.25
☐	Denis Savard, Chic.	.75
☐	Peter Stastny, Québ.	.75
☐	Scott Stevens, Wash.	.35
☐	Tony Tanti, Vanc.	.35
☐	Bryan Trottier, NYIs.	1.00
☐	Steve Yzerman, Detr.	4.00

1988 - 89 O-PEE-CHEE & TOPPS

"The Brett Hull rookie card is the one that stands out the most in this set. In the early 1990s, Hull was very hot and that card in particular was the card everyone was looking for. It's funny how things go. The price has dropped, but at one point it used to sell for more than $100." – Greg Zoep, Zoep's Pro Sports, Kenora, Ontario.

There are two versions for this series: an O-Pee-Chee (1-264) and a Topps (1-198). Topps double prints are marked by a double asterisk (**). Cards measure the standard 2 1/2" x 3 1/2".

	Topps	OPC
O-Pee-Chee Set (264 cards):	–	125.00
Topps Set (198 cards):	90.00	–
Common Player:	.20	.25

Player	Topps	OPC
1 Mario Lemieux, Pitt. (**)	7.00	12.00
2 Bob Joyce, Bost. RC (**)	**.50**	**.75**
3 Joel Quenneville, Hart. (**)	.20	.25
4 Tony McKegney, SLou.	.20	.25
5 Stéphane Richer, Mont. (**)	.35	.75
6 Mark Howe, Phil. (**)	.35	.75
7 Brent Sutter, NYIs. (**)	.20	.25
8 Gilles Meloche (G), Pitt. (**)	.20	.35
9 Jimmy Carson, Edmo. (**)	.20	.25
10 John MacLean, NJer.	.25	.35
11 Gary Leeman, Toro.	.20	.25
12 Gerard Gallant, Detr. (**)	.20	.25
13 Marcel Dionne, NYRa.	.75	1.25
14 Dave Christian, Wash. (**)	.20	.25
15 Gary Nylund, Chic.	.20	.25
16 Joe Nieuwendyk, Calg. RC	**6.00**	**12.00**
17 Billy Smith (G), NYIs. (**)	.65	1.25
18 Christian Ruuttu, Buff.	.20	.25
19 Randy Cunneyworth, Pitt.	.20	.25
20 Brian Lawton, Minn.	.20	.25
21 Scott Mellanby, Phil. RC (**)	**1.25**	**3.00**
22 Peter Stastny, Québ.	.75	1.25
23 Gord Kluzak, Bost.	.20	.25
24 Sylvain Turgeon, Hart.	.20	.25
25 Clint Malarchuk (G), Wash.	.20	.35
26 Denis Savard, Chic.	.35	.50
27 Craig Simpson, Edmo.	.20	.25
28 Petr Klima, Detr.	.20	.25
29 Pat Verbeek, NJer.	.20	.35
30 Moe Mantha, Minn.	.20	.25
31 Chris Nilan, NYRa.	.20	.25
32 Barry Pederson, Vanc.	.20	.25
33 Randy Burridge, Bost.	.20	.25
34 Ron Hextall (G), Phil.	.75	1.50
35 Gaston Gingras, SLou.	.20	.25
36 Kevin Dineen, Hart.	.20	.35
37 Tom Laidlaw, LosA.	.20	.25
38 Paul MacLean, Detr. (**)	.20	.25
39 John Chabot, Detr. (**)	.20	.25
40 Lindy Ruff, Buff.	.20	.25
41 Dan Quinn, Pitt. (**)	.20	.25
42 Don Beaupré (G), Minn.	.20	.35
43 Gary Suter, Calg.	.20	.35
44 Mikko Mäkelä, NYIs. RC (**)	**.65**	**1.00**
45 Mark Johnson, NJer. (**)	.20	.25
46 Dave Taylor, LosA. (**)	.20	.35
47 Ulf Dahlen, NYRa. RC	**1.00**	**1.50**
48 Jeff Sharples, Detr. RC	**.50**	**.75**
49 Chris Chelios, Mont.	1.25	2.50
50 Mike Gartner, Wash. (**)	.65	1.25
51 Darren Pang (G), Chic. RC (**)	**1.25**	**2.00**
52 Ron Francis, Hart.	1.00	1.50
53 Ken Morrow, NYIs.	.20	.25
54 Michel Goulet, Québ.	.75	1.25
55 Ray Sheppard, Buff. RC	**1.25**	**2.00**
56 Doug Gilmour, SLou. (Calg.)	1.00	2.00
57 David Shaw, NYRa. (**)	.20	.25
58 Cam Neely, Bost. (**)	.65	1.25
59 Grant Fuhr (G), Edmo. (**)	.75	1.25
60 Scott Stevens, Wash.	.25	.35
61 Bob Brooke, Minn.	.20	.25
62 Dave Hunter, Pitt. (Winn.)	.20	.25
63 Alan Kerr, NYIs. RC	**.50**	**.75**
64 Brad Marsh, Phil. (Toro.)	.20	.25
65 Dale Hawerchuk, Winn. (**)	.35	.75
66 Brett Hull, SLou. RC (**)	**25.00**	**45.00**
67 Patrik Sundstrom, NJer. (**)	.20	.25
68 Greg Stefan (G), Detr.	.20	.35
69 James Patrick, NYRa.	.20	.25
70 Dale Hunter, Wash. (**)	.20	.35
71 Al Iafrate, Toro.	.20	.35
72 Bob Carpenter, LosA.	.20	.25
73 Raymond Bourque, Bost. (**)	1.25	2.50
74 John Tucker, Buff. (**)	.20	.25
75 Carey Wilson, Hart.	.20	.25
76 Joe Mullen, Calg.	.25	.35
77 Rick Vaive, Chic.	.20	.35
78 Shawn Burr, Detr. (**)	.20	.25
79 Murray Craven, Phil.	.20	.25
80 Clark Gillies, Buff.	.20	.25
81 Bernie Federko, SLou.	.20	.35
82 Tony Tanti, Vanc.	.20	.25
83 Greg Gilbert, NYIs.	.20	.25
84 Kirk Muller, NJer.	.30	.50
85 Dave Tippett, Hart.	.20	.25
86 Kevin Hatcher, Wash. (**)	.25	.50
87 Rick Middleton, Bost. (**)	.20	.35
88 Bobby Smith, Mont.	.20	.35
89 Doug Wilson, Chic. (**)	.20	.35
90 Scott Arniel, Buff.	.20	.25
91 Brian Mullen, NYRa.	.20	.25
92 Mike O'Connell, Detr. (**)	.20	.25
93 Mark Messier, Edmo. (**)	1.50	3.50
94 Sean Burke (G), NJer. RC	**6.00**	**10.00**
95 Brian Bellows, Minn. (**)	.20	.35
96 Doug Bodger, Pitt.	.20	.25
97 Bryan Trottier, NYIs.	1.00	1.25
98 Anton Stastny, Québ.	.20	.25
99 Checklist 1	.50	.75
100 Dave Poulin, Phil. (**)	.20	.25
101 Bob Bourne, LosA. (**)	.20	.25
102 John Vanbiesbrouck (G), NYRa.	4.00	6.00
103 Allen Pedersen, Bost.	.20	.25
104 Mike Ridley, Wash.	.20	.35
105 Andrew McBain, Winn.	.20	.25
106 Troy Murray, Chic. (**)	.20	.25
107 Tom Barrasso (G), Buff.	.25	.35
108 Tomas Jonsson, NYIs.	.20	.25
109 Rob Brown, Pitt. RC	**1.00**	**1.50**
110 Hakan Loob, Calg. (**)	.20	.25
111 Ilkka Sinisalo, Phil. (**)	.20	.25
112 Dave Archibald, Minn. RC	**.50**	**.75**
113 Doug Halward, Detr.	.20	.25
114 Ray Ferraro, Hart.	.25	.35
115 Doug Brown, NJer. RC	**.65**	**1.00**
116 Patrick Roy (G), Mont. (**)	10.00	18.00
117 Greg Millen (G), SLou.	.20	.35
118 Ken Linseman, Bost.	.20	.25
119 Phil Housley, Buff. (**)	.20	.35
120 Wayne Gretzky, LosA.	30.00	25.00
121 Tomas Sandström, NYRa.	.20	.35
122 Brendan Shanahan, NJer. RC	**25.00**	**45.00**
123 Pat LaFontaine, NYIs.	.75	1.25
124 Luc Robitaille, LosA. (**)	1.50	3.50
125 Ed Olczyk, Toro. (**)	.20	.25
126 Ron Sutter, Phil.	.20	.25
127 Mike Liut (G), Hart.	.25	.35
128 Brent Ashton, Winn. (**)	.20	.25
129 Tony Hrkac, SLou. RC	**.75**	**1.25**
130 Kelly Miller, Wash.	.20	.25
131 Alan Haworth, Québ.	.20	.25
132 Dave McLlwain, Pitt. RC	**.50**	**.75**
133 Mike Ramsey, Buff.	.20	.25
134 Bob Sweeney, Bost. RC	**.50**	**.75**
135 Dirk Graham, Chic. (**)	.20	.25
136 Ulf Samuelsson, Hart.	.50	.75
137 Petri Skriko, Vanc.	.20	.25
138 Aaron Broten, NJer. (**)	.20	.25
139 Jim Fox, LosA.	.20	.25
140 Randy Wood, NYIs. RC (**)	**.50**	**.75**
141 Larry Murphy, Wash.	.50	.75
142 Daniel Berthiaume (G), Winn.	.25	.35
143 Kelly Kisio, NYRa.	.20	.25
144 Neal Broten, Minn.	.20	.35
145 Reed Larson, Bost.	.20	.25
146 Peter Zezel, Phil. (**)	.20	.25
147 Jari Kurri, Edmo.	.75	1.25
148 Jim Johnson, Pitt.	.20	.25
149 Gino Cavallini, SLou. (**)	.20	.25
150 Glen Hanlon (G), Detr. (**)	.20	.35
151 Bengt Gustafsson, Wash.	.20	.25
152 Mike Bullard, Calg. (SLou.) (**)	.20	.25
153 John Ogrodnick, NYRa.	.20	.25
154 Steve Larmer, Chic.	.35	.50
155 Kelly Hrudey (G), NYIs.	.25	.35
156 Mats Näslund, Mont.	.20	.25
157 Bruce Driver, NJer.	.20	.35
158 Randy Hillier, Pitt.	.20	.25
159 Craig Hartsburg, Minn.	.20	.35
160 Rollie Melanson (G), LosA.	.20	.35
161 Adam Oates, Detr.	3.00	5.00
162 Greg Adams, Vanc.	.20	.35
163 Dave Andreychuk, Buff.	.25	.35
164 Dave Babych, Hart.	.20	.35
165 Brian Noonan, Chic. RC	**.75**	**1.25**
166 Glen Wesley, Bost. RC	**1.25**	**2.00**
167 Dave Ellett, Winn.	.20	.35
168 Brian Propp, Phil.	.20	.25
169 Bernie Nicholls, LosA.	.20	.35
170 Walt Poddubny, NYRa. (Québ.)	.20	.25
171 Steve Konroyd, NYIs.	.20	.25
172 Doug Sulliman, NJer. (Phil.) (**)	.10	.20
173 Mario Gosselin (G), Québ.	.20	.35
174 Brian Benning, SLou.	.20	.25
175 Dino Ciccarelli, Minn.	.25	.35
176 Steve Kasper, Bost.	.20	.25
177 Rick Tocchet, Phil.	.50	1.50
178 Brad McCrimmon, Calg.	.20	.25
179 Paul Coffey, Pitt.	1.00	2.00
180 Pete Peeters (G), Wash.	.20	.35
181 Bob Probert, Detr. RC (**)	**2.50**	**5.00**
182 Steve Duchesne, LosA. RC (**)	**1.00**	**2.50**
183 Russ Courtnall, Toro.	.20	.35
184 Mike Foligno, Buff. (**)	.20	.25
185 Wayne Presley, Chic. (**)	.20	.25
186 Réjean Lemelin (G), Bost.	.20	.35
187 Mark Hunter, SLou. (Calg.)	.20	.25
188 Joe Cirella, NJer.	.20	.25
189 Glenn Anderson, Edmo. (**)	.20	.35
190 John Anderson, Hart.	.20	.25
191 Pat Flatley, NYIs.	.20	.25
192 Rod Langway, Wash.	.20	.35
193 Brian MacLellan, Minn.	.20	.25
194 Pierre Turgeon, Buff. RC	**18.00**	**25.00**
195 Brian Hayward (G), Mont.	.20	.35
196 Steve Yzerman, Detr. (**)	4.00	8.00
197 Doug Crossman, Phil.	.20	.25
198 Checklist 2	.50	.75

Player	OPC
199 Greg Adams, Wash. (Edm.)	.25
200 Laurie Boschman, Winn.	.25
201 Jeff Brown, Québ. RC	**1.00**
202 Garth Butcher, Vanc. RC	**1.00**
203 Guy Carbonneau, Mont.	.35
204 Randy Carlyle, Winn.	.25
205 Alain Côté, Québ.	.25
206 Keith Crowder, Bost.	.25
207 Vincent Damphousse, Toro.	4.00
208 Gaetan Duchesne, Québ. RC	**.75**
209 Iain Duncan, Winn. RC	.75
210 Tommy Albelin, Québ. RC	**1.50**
211 Per-Erik Eklund, Phil.	.25
212 Jan Erixon, NYRa. RC	**.75**
213 Paul Fenton, LosA. RC	**.75**
214 Tom Fergus, Toro.	.25
215 Dave Gagner, Minn. RC	**1.25**
216 Bob Gainey, Mont.	1.50
217 Stewart Gavin, Hart. (Minn.)	.25
218 Charlie Huddy, Edmo.	.25
219 Jeff Jackson, Québ. RC	**.75**
220 Uwe Krupp, Buff. RC	1.00
221 Mike Krushelnyski, Edmo. (LosA.)	.25
222 Tom Kurvers, NJer.	.25
223 Jason Lafrenière, Québ. RC	**.75**
224 Lane Lambert, Québ.	.25
225 Rick Lanz, Toro.	.25
226 Brad Lauer, NYIs. RC	**.75**
227 Claude Lemieux, Mont.	1.25
228 Doug Lidster, Vanc.	.25
229 Kevin Lowe, Edmo., Error	.35
230 Craig Ludwig, Mont.	.25
231 Al MacInnis, Calg.	2.00
232 Craig MacTavish, Edmo.	.25
233 Mario Marois, Winn., Error (Marios)	.25
234 Lanny McDonald, Calg.	1.00
235 Rick Meagher, SLou.	.25
236 Craig Muni, Edmo.	.25
237 Mike McPhee, Mont.	.25
238 Ric Nattress, Calg. RC	**.75**
239 Ray Neufeld, Winn.	.25
240 Lee Norwood, Detr. RC	**.75**
241 Mark Osborne, Toro., Error (Osbourne)	.25
242 Joel Otto, Calg.	.25
243 Jim Peplinski, Calg.	.25
244 Rob Ramage, Calg.	.25
245 Luke Richardson, Toro. RC	**1.00**
246 Larry Robinson, Mont.	1.25
247 Börje Salming, Toro.	.75
248 David Saunders, Vanc. RC	**.75**
249 Al Secord, Toro.	.25
250 Charlie Simmer, Pitt.	.25
251 Doug Smail, Winn.	.25
252 Steve Smith, Edmo. RC	**2.00**
253 Stan Smyl, Vanc.	.25
254 Thomas Steen, Winn.	.25
255 Rich Sutter, Vanc.	.25
256 Petr Svoboda, Mont. RC	**1.50**
257 Peter Taglianetti, Winn. RC	**.75**
258 Steve Tambellini, Vanc.	.25
259 Steve Thomas, Chic.	.25
260 Esa Tikkanen, Edmo.	1.00
261 Mike Vernon (G), Calg.	2.50
262 Ryan Walter, Mont.	.25
263 Doug Wickenheiser, Vanc. (NYRa.)	.25
264 Ken Wregget (G), Toro.	.50

O-PEE-CHEE & TOPPS BOX BOTTOMS

These four-card panels were found on the bottom of O-Pee-Chee and Topps wax boxes. The most expensive singles are Wayne Gretzky (OPC $10, Topps $8) and Steve Yzerman (OPC $6, Topps $4.50). O-Pee-Chee singles start at 75¢; Topps singles start at 50¢. Panels measure 5" x 7" while the cut cards measure 2 1/2" x 3 1/2".

	Topps	OPC
Complete Set (4 panels):	**15.00**	**25.00**
Box Bottoms:	**Topps**	**OPC**
A-D Francis/ Gretzky/ LaFontaine/ Bo. Smith	10.00	15.00
E-H Federko/ Muller/ Olczyk/ Savard	2.00	3.00
I-L Bourque/ Craven & Propp/ Hawerchuk/ Yzerman	6.00	10.00
M-P Andreychuk/ Gartner/ Loob/ Robitaille	3.00	4.00

TOPPS STICKER INSERTS

Complete Set (33 stickers):	**20.00**
Common Team Sticker:	**.25**
Topps	**NM-MT**
1 AS: Luc Robitaille, LosA.	.85
2 AS: Mario Lemieux, Pitt.	5.00
3 AS: Hakan Loob, Calg.	.35
4 AS: Scott Stevens, Wash.	.75
5 AS: Raymond Bourque, Bost.	1.50
6 AS: Grant Fuhr (G), Edmo.	1.00
7 AS: Michel Goulet, Québ.	.50
8 AS: Wayne Gretzky, Edmo.	7.00
9 AS: Cam Neely, Bost.	.75
10 AS: Brad McCrimmon, Phil.	.35
11 AS: Gary Suter, Calg.	.35
12 AS: Patrick Roy (G), Mont.	4.50

13 Toronto Maple Leafs	14 Buffalo Sabres
15 Detroit Red Wings	16 Pittsburgh Penguins
17 New York Rangers	18 Calgary Flames
19 Winnipeg Jets	20 Québec Nordiques
21 Chicago Blackhawks	22 Los Angeles Kings
23 Montréal Canadiens	24 Vancouver Canucks
25 Hartford Whalers	26 Philadelphia Flyers
27 New Jersey Devils	28 St. Louis Blues
29 Minn. North Stars	30 Washington Capitals
31 Boston Bruins	32 New York Islanders
33 Edmonton Oilers	

1988 - 89 OPC NHL STARS

These cards measure 2 1/8" x 3".

Complete Set (46 cards):	**20.00**
O-Pee-Chee	**NM-MT**
1 Tom Barrasso (G), Buff.	.35
2 Bob Bourne, LosA.	.20
3 Raymond Bourque, Bost.	1.50

☐ 4 Guy Carbonneau, Mont. .35
☐ 5 Jimmy Carson, Edmo. .20
☐ 6 Paul Coffey, Pitt. 1.00
☐ 7 Ulf Dahlen, NYRa. .20
☐ 8 Marcel Dionne, NYRa. 1.00
☐ 9 Grant Fuhr (G), Edmo. .50
☐ 10 Michel Goulet, Québ. .35
☐ 11 Wayne Gretzky, LosA. 7.00
☐ 12 Dale Hawerchuk, Winn. .35
☐ 13 Brian Hayward (G), Mont. .35
☐ 14 Ron Hextall (G), Phil. .50
☐ 15 Tony Hrkac, SLou. .20
☐ 16 Brett Hull, SLou. 4.00
☐ 17 Steve Larmer, Chic. .35
☐ 18 Réjean Lemelin (G), Bost. .35
☐ 19 Mario Lemieux, Pitt. 5.00
☐ 20 Mike Liut (G), Hart. .35
☐ 21 Hakan Loob, Calg. .20
☐ 22 Al MacInnis, Calg. .35
☐ 23 Paul MacLean, Winn. .20
☐ 24 Brad McCrimmon, Calg. .20
☐ 25 Mark Messier, Edmo. 2.00
☐ 26 Mats Näslund, Mont. .20
☐ 27 Cam Neely, Bost. .60
☐ 28 Bernie Nicholls, LosA. .35
☐ 29 Joe Nieuwendyk, Calg. 1.50
☐ 30 Pete Peeters (G), Wash. .35
☐ 31 Stéphane Richer, Mont. .50
☐ 32 Luc Robitaille, LosA. .50
☐ 33 Patrick Roy (G), Mont. 5.00
☐ 34 Denis Savard, Chic. .35
☐ 35 Ray Sheppard, Buff. .50
☐ 36 Craig Simpson, Edmo. .20
☐ 37 Peter Stastny, Québ. .35
☐ 38 Greg Stefan (G), Detr. .35
☐ 39 Scott Stevens, Wash. .35
☐ 40 Gary Suter, Calg. .20
☐ 41 Petr Svoboda, Mont. .20
☐ 42 John Vanbiesbrouck (G), NYRa. 1.50
☐ 43 Pat Verbeek, NJer. .20
☐ 44 Mike Vernon (G), Calg. .35
☐ 45 Carey Wilson, Hart. .20
☐ 46 Checklist .35

1988 - 89 O-PEE-CHEE STICKERS

Stickers measure 2 1/8" x 3". A series of 22 Future Stars can be found on the back of selective stickers. A 22-card set sells for $5-8.

Complete Set (152 stickers): **25.00**
Album: **5.00**
Common Player: **.20**
O-Pee-Chee **NM-MT**

☐ 1 AW: Wayne Gretzky, Edmo. 4.00
☐ 2 Oilers/ Bruins .20
☐ 3 Oilers/ Bruins .20
☐ 4 Oilers/ Bruins .20
☐ 5 Oilers/ Bruins .20

Note: Stickers 2-5 feature a puzzle with Keith Crowder, Steve Smith and Grant Fuhr.

☐ 12 Steve Larmer, Chic. .25
☐ 13 Denis Savard, Chic. .25
☐ 20 Doug Gilmour, SLou. 1.00
☐ 21 Bernie Federko, SLou. .20
☐ 22 Cam Neely, Bost. .50
☐ 23 Raymond Bourque, Bost.
(/b: Future Star #2 Doug Brown) 1.00
☐ 30 Keith Crowder/ Steve Kasper .20
☐ 31 Canadiens/ Bruins .35
☐ 32 Canadiens/ Bruins .35

Note: Stickers 31-32 feature a puzzle with Patrick Roy (G) and Bob Sweeney.

☐ 33 Blues vs Devils .20
☐ 34 Canadiens/ Bruins .25
☐ 35 Canadiens/ Bruins .25
☐ 36 Canadiens/ Bruins (/b: Future Star #8 Tony Hrkac) .25
☐ 37 Canadiens/ Bruins .25

Note: Stickers 34-37 feature a puzzle with Réjean Lemelin, Raymond Bourque, Larry Robinson and Bob Sweeney.

☐ 38 Brian Skrudland/ Raymond Bourque .35
☐ 45 Patrick Roy (G), Mont. 3.00
☐ 46 Bobby Smith, Mont. .20
☐ 49 Stéphane Richer, Mont. .20
☐ 50 Mats Näslund, Mont. .25
☐ 51 Chris Chelios, Mont. 1.00
☐ 52 Brian Hayward (G), Mont. .25
☐ 59 Tony Tanti, Vanc. .20
☐ 60 Stan Smyl, Vanc. .20
☐ 63 Doug Lidster, Vanc. (/b: Future Star #3 Rob Brown) .20
☐ 64 Petri Skriko, Vanc. .20
☐ 65 Barry Pederson, Vanc. .20
☐ 66 Greg Adams, Vanc. .20
☐ 67 Mike Gartner, Wash. .50
☐ 68 Scott Stevens, Wash.
(/b: Future Star #19 Bob Sweeney) .20
☐ 75 Kirk Muller, NJer. .20
☐ 76 Aaron Broten, NJer. .20
☐ 89 Gary Suter, Calg. .20
☐ 90 Joe Nieuwendyk, Calg.
(/b: Future Star #10 C. Janney) .75
☐ 93 Mike Bullard, Calg. .20
☐ 94 Hakan Loob, Calg. .20
☐ 95 Joe Mullen, Calg. .50
☐ 96 Brad McCrimmon, Calg. .20
☐ 103 Ron Hextall (G), Phil. .50
☐ 104 Mark Howe, Phil. .25
☐ 111 Pat LaFontaine, NYIs. .50
☐ 112 Bryan Trottier, NYIs. .25
☐ 143 Dale Hawerchuk, Winn. .35
☐ 144 Paul MacLean, Winn. .20
☐ 147 Andrew McBain, Winn.
(/b: Future Star #15 B. Noonan) .20
☐ 148 Randy Carlyle, Winn. .20
☐ 149 Daniel Berthiaume (G), Winn. .25
☐ 150 Dave Ellett, Winn. .20
☐ 157 Luc Robitaille, LosA. .75
☐ 158 Jimmy Carson, LosA.
(/b: Future Star #4 Sean Burke) 2.00
☐ 159 Randy Burridge/ Patrick Roy (G) 1.50
☐ 160 Nordiques/ Devils .20
☐ 161 Nordiques/ Devils
(/b: Future Star #18 Ray Sheppard) .20

Note: Stickers 160-161 feature Randy Moller, Claude Loiselle, Paul Gillis, Dave Maley, Clint Malarchuk, and Robert Picard.

☐ 162 A. Chevrier/ B. MacLellan/ G. Mark .20
☐ 163 Oilers/ Devils .20
☐ 164 Oilers/ Devils .20
☐ 165 Oilers/ Devils .20
☐ 166 Oilers/ Devils .20

Note: Stickers 163-166 feature Grant Fuhr, Kevin Lowe, Craig Muni, Patrik Sundstrom and Doug Sulliman.

☐ 167 C. Neely/ P. Roy (G) 1.50
☐ 174 Börje Salming, Toro. .25
☐ 175 Russ Courtnall, Toro. .20
☐ 178 Gary Leeman, Toro. .20
☐ 179 Al Secord, Toro. .20
☐ 180 Al Iafrate, Toro. .20
☐ 181 Ed Olczyk, Toro. .20
☐ 188 Michel Goulet, Québ. .35
☐ 189 Peter Stastny, Québ.
(/b: Future Star #12 Brian Leetch) 3.50
☐ 192 Jeff Brown, Québ. .35
☐ 193 Mario Gosselin (G), Québ. .25
☐ 194 Anton Stastny, Québ. .20
☐ 195 Alan Haworth, Québ. .20
☐ 202 Dino Ciccarelli, Minn
(/b: Future Star #22 Randy Wood) .35
☐ 203 Brian Bellows, Minn. .20
☐ 214 Brian Hayward/ Patrick Roy (G) 1.50
☐ 223 Grant Fuhr (G), Edmo. .50
☐ 224 Wayne Gretzky, Edmo. 4.00
☐ 227 Jari Kurri, Edmo. .50
☐ 228 Craig Simpson, Edmo. .20
☐ 229 Glenn Anderson, Edmo. .25
☐ 230 Mark Messier, Edmo. 1.00
☐ 231 Randy Cunneyworth, Pitt. .20
☐ 232 Mario Lemieux, Pitt. 3.00
☐ 239 Kelly Kisio, NYRa. .20
☐ 240 Walt Poddubny, NYRa. .20
☐ 253 Steve Yzerman, Detr. 1.50
☐ 254 Gerald Gallant, Detr.
(/b: Future Star #11 C. Johansson) .20
☐ 261 Dave Andreychuk, Buff. .35
☐ 262 Ray Sheppard, Buff. .20
☐ 263 Mike Liut (G), Hart. .25
☐ 264 Ron Francis, Hart. .50

O-Pee-Chee **NM-MT**

☐ 6/135 Doug Wilson, Chic./ Darren Pang (G), Chic. .25
☐ 7/136 Dirk Graham, Chic./ Kirk McLean (G), Vanc. .75
☐ 8/137 Darren Pang (G), Chic./ Doug Smail, Winn. .25
☐ 9/138 Rick Vaive, Chic./ Thomas Steen, Winn. .20
☐ 10/139 Troy Murray, Chic./ Laurie Boschman, Winn. .20
☐ 11/140 Brian Noonan, Chic./ Iain Duncan, Winn. .75
(/b: Future Star #13 Kirk McLean)
☐ 14/141 Mark Hunter, SLou./ Ray Neufeld, Winn. .20
☐ 15/142 Brian Sutter, SLou./ Mario Marois, Winn. .20
☐ 16/145 Brett Hull, SLou./ Jim Kyte, Winn. 3.00
(/b: Future Star #16 Darren Pang)
☐ 17/146 McKegney, SLou./ Reddick (G), Winn. .25
☐ 18/151 Benning, SLou./ Melanson (G), LosA. .25
☐ 19/152 Tony Hrkac, SLou./ Steve Duchesne, LosA. .20
☐ 24/153 Lemelin (G), Bost./ Carpenter, LosA. .25
☐ 25/154 Gord Kluzak, Bost./ Jim Fox, LosA. .20
☐ 26/155 Rick Middleton, Bost./ Dave Taylor, LosA. .25
☐ 27/156 Steve Kasper, Bost./ Bernie Nicholls, LosA. .20
☐ 28/168 Bob Sweeney, Bost./ Mark Osborne, Toro. .20
☐ 29/169 Randy Burridge, Bost./ Dan Daoust, Toro. .20
☐ 39/170 Larry Robinson, Mont./ Tom Fergus, Toro. .35
☐ 40/171 Ryan Walter, Mont./ Damphousse, Toro. .50
☐ 41/172 Guy Carbonneau, Mont./ Wendel Clark, Toro. .50
☐ 42/173 Bob Gainey, Mont./ Luke Richardson, Toro. .35
☐ 43/176 Claude Lemieux, Mont./ Rick Lanz, Toro. .20
☐ 44/177 Petr Svoboda, Mont./ Ken Wregget (G), Toro. .25
☐ 47/182 Mike McPhee, Mont./ Rochefort, Québ. .20
☐ 48/183 Craig Ludwig, Mont./ Lane Lambert, Québ. .20
☐ 53/184 Larry Melnyk, Vanc./ Tommy Albelin, Québ. .20
(/b: Future Star #1 Dave Archibald)
☐ 54/185 Garth Butcher, Vanc./ Jason Lafrenière, Québ. .20
☐ 55/186 Kirk McLean (G), Vanc./ Alain Côté, Québ. .75
☐ 56/187 Wickenheiser, Vanc./ Gaetan Duchesne, Québ. .20
☐ 57/190 Rich Sutter, Vanc./ Jeff Jackson, Québ. .20
☐ 58/191 Jim Benning, Vanc./ Mike Eagles, Québ. .20
☐ 61/196 David Saunders, Vanc./ Beaupré (G), Minn. .25
☐ 62/197 Steve Tambellini, Vanc./ MacLellan, Minn. .20
☐ 69/198 Rod Langway, Wash./ Brian Lawton, Minn. 2.00
(/b: Future Star #20 Pierre Turgeon)
☐ 70/199 Dave Christian, Wash./ Craig Hartsburg, Minn. .25
☐ 71/200 Larry Murphy, Wash./ Moe Mantha, Minn. .35
☐ 72/201 Clint Malarchuk (G), Wash./ Neal Broten, Minn. .25
☐ 73/204 Dale Hunter, Wash./ Mario Lemieux, Pitt. 2.00
☐ 74/205 Mike Ridley, Wash./ Joe Nieuwendyk, Calg. .50
(/b: Future Star #17 Jeff Sharples)
☐ 77/206 Bruce Driver, NJer./ Brad McCrimmon, Calg. .20
☐ 78/207 John MacLean, NJer./ Pete Peeters (G), Wash. .25
☐ 79/208 Joe Cirella, NJer./ Raymond Bourque, Bost. .50
☐ 80/209 Doug Brown, NJer./ Guy Carbonneau, Mont. .25
☐ 81/210 Pat Verbeek, NJer./ Mario Lemieux, Pitt. 5.00
(/b: Future Star #91 Brett Hull)
☐ 82/211 Sean Burke (G), NJer./ Mario Lemieux, Pitt. 2.00
☐ 83/212 Joel Otto, Calg./ Grant Fuhr (G), Edmo. .50
☐ 84/213 Rob Ramage, Calg./ Bob Bourne, LosA. .20
☐ 85/215 Lanny McDonald, Calg./ Mats Näslund, Mont. .50
(/b: Future Star #21 Glen Wesley)
☐ 86/216 Mike Vernon (G), Calg./ Nieuwendyk, Calg. 1.00
☐ 87/217 John Tonelli, Calg./ Craig MacTavish, Edmo. .20
☐ 88/218 Jim Peplinski, Calg./ Chris Joseph, Edmo. .20
☐ 91/219 Ric Nattress, Calg./ Kevin Lowe, Edmo. .25
☐ 92/220 Al MacInnis, Calg./ Esa Tikkanen, Edmo. .35
☐ 97/221 Brian Propp, Phil./ Charlie Huddy, Edmo. .20
☐ 98/222 Murray Craven, Phil./ Geoff Courtnall, Edmo. .20
☐ 99/225 Rick Tocchet, Phil./ Steve Smith, Edmo. .20
☐ 100/226 Doug Crossman, Phil./ Krushelnyski, Edmo. .20
☐ 101/233 Brad Marsh, Phil./ Paul Coffey, Pitt. .35
☐ 102/234 Peter Zezel, Phil./ Doug Bodger, Pitt. .20
☐ 105/235 Brent Sutter, NYIs./ Dave Hunter, Pitt. .20
☐ 106/236 Alan Kerr, NYIs./ Dan Quinn, Pitt. .20
☐ 107/237 Randy Wood, NYIs./ Rob Brown, Pitt. .20
☐ 108/238 Mikko Makelä, NYIs./ Meloche (G), Pitt. .25
(/b: Future Star #6 Iain Duncan)
☐ 109/241 Hrudey (G), NYIs./ Vanbiesbrouck (G), NYRa. 1.50
☐ 110/242 Steve Konroyd, NYIs./ Sandstrom, NYRa. .20
☐ 113/243 Gary Suter, Calg./ David Shaw, NYRa. .20
☐ 114/244 Luc Robitaille, LosA./ Marcel Dionne, NYRa. .50
☐ 115/245 Patrick Roy (G), Mont./ Chris Nilan, NYRa. 2.00
☐ 116/246 Mario Lemieux, Pitt./ James Patrick, NYRa. 2.50
☐ 117/247 Raymond Bourque, Bost./ Bob Probert, Detr. .50
☐ 118/248 Hakan Loob, Calg./ Mike O'Connell, Detr. .20
☐ 119/249 Mike Bullard, Calg./ Jeff Sharples, Detr. .20
☐ 120/250 Brad McCrimmon, Calg./ Brent Ashton, Detr. .20
☐ 121/251 Wayne Gretzky, LosA./ Petr Klima, Detr. 3.50
☐ 122/252 Grant Fuhr (G), Edmo./ Greg Stefan (G), Detr. .35
☐ 123/255 Craig Simpson, Edmo./ Phil Housley, Buff. .50
(/b: Future Star #7 Glenn Healy)
☐ 124/256 Mark Howe, Phil./ Christian Ruuttu, Buff. .25
☐ 125/257 Joe Nieuwendyk, Calg./ Mike Foligno, Buff. .75
☐ 126/258 Ray Sheppard, Buff./ Scott Arniel, Buff. .50
(/b: Future Star #5 Ulf Dahlen)
☐ 127/259 Brett Hull, SLou./ Tom Barrasso (G), Buff. 2.50
☐ 128/260 Ulf Dahlen, NYRa./ Mike Ramsey, Buff. .20
☐ 129/265 Tony Hrkac, SLou./ Ulf Samuelsson, Hart. .35
☐ 130/266 Bob Sweeney, Bost./ Carey Wilson, Hart. .20
☐ 131/267 Rob Brown, Pitt./ Dave Babych, Hart. .20
☐ 132/268 Iain Duncan, Winn./ Ray Ferraro, Hart. .20
☐ 133/269 Pierre Turgeon, Buff./ Kevin Dineen, Hart. 2.00
☐ 134/270 C. Johansson, Buff./ John Anderson, Hart. 1.50
(/b: Future Star #14 Nieuwendyk)

1988 - 89 PANINI STICKERS

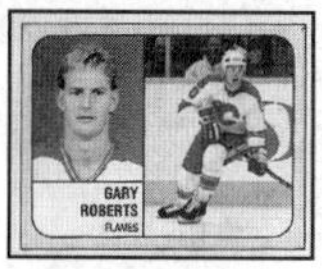

These stickers measure 2 1/8" x 2 15/16".

Complete Set (408 stickers): **40.00**
Album (Mario Lemieux on the cover): **10.00**
Common Player: **.20**

☐ 1 Road to the Cup/ Stanley Cup Draw .20
☐ 2 Calgary Flames Team Logo .20
☐ 3 Calgary Flames Uniform .20
☐ 4 Mike Vernon (G), Calg. .50
☐ 5 Al MacInnis, Calg. .25
☐ 6 Brad McCrimmon, Calg. .20
☐ 7 Gary Suter, Calg. .20
☐ 8 Mike Bullard, Calg. .20
☐ 9 Hakan Loob, Calg. .20
☐ 10 Lanny McDonald, Calg. .25
☐ 11 Joe Mullen, Calg. .25
☐ 12 Joe Nieuwendyk, Calg. 1.00
☐ 13 Joel Otto, Calg. .20
☐ 14 Jim Peplinski, Calg. .20
☐ 15 Gary Roberts, Calg. .50
☐ 16 Calgary Flames Team Photo .20
☐ 17 Calgary Flames Team Photo .20
☐ 18 Chicago Blackhawks Team Logo .20
☐ 19 Chicago Blackhawks Uniform .20
☐ 20 Bob Mason (G), Chic. .25
☐ 21 Darren Pang (G), Chic. .25
☐ 22 Rob Murray, Chic. .20
☐ 23 Gary Nylund, Chic. .20
☐ 24 Doug Wilson, Chic. .20
☐ 25 Dirk Graham, Chic. .20
☐ 26 Steve Larmer, Chic. .25
☐ 27 Troy Murray, Chic. .20
☐ 28 Brian Noonan, Chic. .25
☐ 29 Denis Savard, Chic. .35
☐ 30 Steve Thomas, Chic. .20
☐ 31 Rick Vaive, Chic. .20
☐ 32 Chicago Blackhawks Team Photo .20
☐ 33 Chicago Blackhawks Team Photo .20
☐ 34 Detroit Red Wings Team Logo .20
☐ 35 Detroit Red Wings Uniform .20
☐ 36 Glen Hanlon (G), Detr. .25
☐ 37 Greg Stefan (G), Detr. .25
☐ 38 Jeff Sharples, Detr. .20
☐ 39 Darren Veitch, Detr. .20
☐ 40 Brent Ashton, Detr. .20
☐ 41 Shawn Burr, Detr. .20
☐ 42 John Chabot, Detr. .20
☐ 43 Gerard Gallant, Detr. .20
☐ 44 Petr Klima, Detr. .20
☐ 45 Adam Oates, Detr. 1.00
☐ 46 Bob Probert, Detr. .50
☐ 47 Steve Yzerman, Detr. 2.00
☐ 48 Detroit Red Wings Team Photo .20
☐ 49 Detroit Red Wings Team Photo .20
☐ 50 Edmonton Oilers Team Logo .20
☐ 51 Edmonton Oilers Uniform .20
☐ 52 Grant Fuhr (G), Edmo. .35
☐ 53 Charlie Huddy, Edmo. .20
☐ 54 Kevin Lowe, Edmo. .20
☐ 55 Steve Smith, Edmo. .20
☐ 56 Jeff Beukeboom, Edmo. .20
☐ 57 Glenn Anderson, Edmo. .25
☐ 58 Wayne Gretzky, Edmo. 4.00
☐ 59 Jari Kurri, Edmo. .25
☐ 60 Craig MacTavish, Edmo. .20
☐ 61 Mark Messier, Edmo. 1.00
☐ 62 Craig Simpson, Edmo. .20
☐ 63 Esa Tikkanen, Edmo. .25
☐ 64 Edmonton Oilers Team Photo 1.50
☐ 65 Edmonton Oilers Team Photo 1.50
☐ 66 Los Angeles Kings Team Logo .20
☐ 67 Los Angeles Kings Uniform .20
☐ 68 Glenn Healy (G), LosA. .50
☐ 69 Rollie Melanson (G), LosA. .25
☐ 70 Steve Duchesne, LosA. .35
☐ 71 Tom Laidlaw, LosA. .20
☐ 72 Jay Wells, LosA. .20
☐ 73 Mike Allison, LosA. .20
☐ 74 Bobby Carpenter, LosA. .20
☐ 75 Jimmy Carson, LosA. .20
☐ 76 Jim Fox, LosA. .20
☐ 77 Bernie Nicholls, LosA. .35
☐ 78 Luc Robitaille, LosA. .75
☐ 79 Dave Taylor, LosA. .25
☐ 80 Los Angeles Kings Team Photo .20
☐ 81 Los Angeles Kings Team Photo .20
☐ 82 Minnesota North Stars Team Logo .20
☐ 83 Minnesota North Stars Uniform .20
☐ 84 Don Beaupré (G), Minn. .25
☐ 85 Kari Takko (G), Minn. .25
☐ 86 Craig Hartsburg, Minn. .20
☐ 87 Frantisek Musil, Minn. .20
☐ 88 Dave Archibald, Minn. .20
☐ 89 Brian Bellows, Minn. .20
☐ 90 Scott Bjugstad, Minn. .20
☐ 91 Bob Brooke, Minn. .20
☐ 92 Neal Broten, Minn. .25

	No.	Player	Price
□	93	Dino Ciccarelli, Minn.	.25
□	94	Brian Lawton, Minn.	.20
□	95	Brian MacLellan, Minn.	.20
□	96	Minnesota North Stars Team Photo	.20
□	97	Minnesota North Stars Team Photo	.20
□	98	St. Louis Blues Team Logo	.20
□	99	St. Louis Blues Uniform	.20
□	100	Greg Millen (G), SLou.	.25
□	101	Brian Benning, SLou.	.20
□	102	Gord Roberts, SLou.	.20
□	103	Gino Cavallini, SLou.	.20
□	104	Bernie Federko, SLou.	.25
□	105	Doug Gilmour, SLou.	.75
□	106	Tony Hrkac, SLou.	.20
□	107	Brett Hull, SLou.	5.00
□	108	Mark Hunter, SLou.	.20
□	109	Tony McKegney, SLou.	.20
□	110	Rick Meagher, SLou.	.20
□	111	Brian Sutter, SLou.	.20
□	112	St. Louis Blues Team Photo	.20
□	113	St. Louis Blues Team Photo	.20
□	114	Toronto Maple Leafs Team Logo	.20
□	115	Toronto Maple Leafs Uniform	.20
□	116	Allan Bester (G), Toro.	.25
□	117	Ken Wregget (G), Toro.	.35
□	118	Al Iafrate, Toro.	.20
□	119	Luke Richardson, Toro.	.20
□	120	Börje Salming, Toro.	.25
□	121	Wendel Clark, Toro.	.60
□	122	Russ Courtnall, Toro.	.20
□	123	Vincent Damphousse, Toro.	.75
□	124	Dan Daoust, Toro.	.20
□	125	Gary Leeman, Toro.	.20
□	126	Ed Olczyk, Toro.	.20
□	127	Mark Osborne, Toro.	.20
□	128	Toronto Maple Leafs Team Photo	.20
□	129	Toronto Maple Leafs Team Photo	.20
□	130	Vancouver Canucks Team Logo	.20
□	131	Vancouver Canucks Uniform	.20
□	132	Kirk McLean (G), Vanc.	.60
□	133	Jim Benning, Vanc.	.20
□	134	Garth Butcher, Vanc.	.20
□	135	Doug Lidster, Vanc.	.20
□	136	Greg Adams, Vanc.	.20
□	137	David Bruce, Vanc.	.20
□	138	Barry Pederson, Vanc.	.20
□	139	Jim Sandlak, Vanc.	.20
□	140	Petri Skriko, Vanc.	.20
□	141	Stan Smyl, Vanc.	.20
□	142	Rich Sutter, Vanc.	.20
□	143	Tony Tanti, Vanc.	.20
□	144	Vancouver Canucks Team Photo	.20
□	145	Vancouver Canucks Team Photo	.20
□	146	Winnipeg Jets Team Logo	.20
□	147	Winnipeg Jets Uniform	.20
□	148	Daniel Berthiaume (G), Winn.	.25
□	149	Randy Carlyle, Winn.	.20
□	150	Dave Ellett, Winn.	.20
□	151	Mario Marois, Winn.	.20
□	152	Peter Taglianetti, Winn.	.20
□	153	Laurie Boschman, Winn.	.20
□	154	Iain Duncan, Winn.	.20
□	155	Dale Hawerchuk, Winn.	.35
□	156	Paul MacLean, Winn.	.20
□	157	Andrew McBain, Winn.	.20
□	158	Doug Smail, Winn.	.20
□	159	Thomas Steen, Winn.	.20
□	160	Winnipeg Jets Team Photo	.20
□	161	Winnipeg Jets Team Photo	.20
□	162	Prince of Wales Trophy	.20
□	163	Washington Defeats Flyers	.20
□	164	Boston Beat Montréal	.20
□	165	Devils Skate Past the Capitals	.20
□	166	Bruins Were Victorious Over New Jersey	.20
□	167	Bruins Were Victorious Over New Jersey	.20
□	168	Calgary Too Much For Kings	.20
□	169	Clarence S. Campbell Bowl	.20
□	170	Edmonton Put Out Flames	3.00
□	171	Detroit Defeats St. Louis	.20
□	172	Oilers Overpowered Detroit	.20
□	173	Oilers Overpowered Detroit	.20
□	174	Edmonton Celebrate a Victory in Game 1	.20
□	175	Game 2, Oilers Eyed Another Victory	.20
□	176	Stanley Cup	.20
□	177	Stanley Cup	.20
□	178	Gretzky & Teammates .. in Boston	2.00
□	179	Gretzky & Teammates .. in Boston	.50
□	180	Gretzky & Teammates .. in Boston	.50
□	181	Wayne Gretzky, Edmo., M.V.P.	4.00
□	182	Conn Smythe Trophy	.20
□	183	Edmonton Oilers Celebrate	.20
□	184	Edmonton Oilers Celebrate	.20
□	185	Edmonton Oilers Celebrate	.20
□	186	Edmonton Oilers Celebrate	.20
		Note: cards 183-186 feature Geoff Courtnall.	
□	187	Calgary Flames Action	.20
□	188	Grant Fuhr (G), Edmo.	.35
□	189	New Jersey Devils Action	.20
□	190	Marcel Dionne	.25
□	191	Boston Bruins Action	.20
□	192	Washington Capitals Action	.20
□	193	Wayne Gretzky	4.00
□	194	Winnipeg Jets	.20
□	195	Boston Bruins	.20
□	196	St. Louis Blues	.20
□	197	Philadelphia Flyers vs. Washington Capitals	.20
□	198	New York Islanders	.20
□	199	Calgary Flames	.20
□	200	Pittsburgh Penguins	.20
□	201	Boston Bruins Team Logo	.20
□	202	Boston Bruins Uniform	.20
□	203	Réjean Lemelin (G), Bost.	.25
□	204	Raymond Bourque, Bost.	.50
□	205	Gord Kluzak, Bost.	.20
□	206	Michael Thelven, Bost.	.20
□	207	Glen Wesley, Bost.	.20
□	208	Randy Burridge, Bost.	.20
□	209	Keith Crowder, Bost.	.20
□	210	Steve Kasper, Bost.	.20
□	211	Ken Linseman, Bost.	.20
□	212	Jay Miller, Bost.	.20
□	213	Cam Neely, Bost.	.60
□	214	Bob Sweeney, Bost.	.20
□	215	Boston Bruins Team Photo	.20
□	216	Boston Bruins Team Photo	.20
□	217	Buffalo Sabres Team Logo	.20
□	218	Buffalo Sabres Uniform	.20
□	219	Tom Barrasso (G), Buff.	.25
□	220	Phil Housley, Buff.	.25
□	221	Calle Johansson, Buff.	.20
□	222	Mike Ramsey, Buff.	.20
□	223	Dave Andreychuk, Buff.	.50
□	224	Scott Arniel, Buff.	.20
□	225	Adam Creighton, Buff.	.20
□	226	Mike Foligno, Buff.	.20
□	227	Christian Ruuttu, Buff.	.20
□	228	Ray Sheppard, Buff.	1.00
□	229	John Tucker, Buff.	.20
□	230	Pierre Turgeon, Buff.	2.00
□	231	Buffalo Sabres Team Photo	.20
□	232	Buffalo Sabres Team Photo	.20
□	233	Hartford Whalers Team Logo	.20
□	234	Hartford Whalers Uniform	.20
□	235	Mike Liut (G), Hart.	.25
□	236	Dave Babych, Hart.	.50
□	237	Sylvain Côté, Hart.	.20
□	238	Ulf Samuelsson, Hart.	.25
□	239	John Anderson, Hart.	.20
□	240	Kevin Dineen, Hart.	.20
□	241	Ray Ferraro, Hart.	.20
□	242	Ron Francis, Hart.	.50
□	243	Paul MacDermid, Hart.	.20
□	244	Dave Tippett, Hart.	.20
□	245	Sylvain Turgeon, Hart.	.20
□	246	Carey Wilson, Hart.	.20
□	247	Hartford Whalers Team Photo	.20
□	248	Hartford Whalers Team Photo	.20
□	249	Montréal Canadiens Team Logo	.20
□	250	Montréal Canadiens Uniform	.20
□	251	Brian Hayward (G), Mont.	.25
□	252	Patrick Roy (G), Mont.	2.50
□	253	Chris Chelios, Mont.	.50
□	254	Craig Ludwig, Mont.	.20
□	255	Petr Svoboda, Mont.	.20
□	256	Guy Carbonneau, Mont.	.20
□	257	Claude Lemieux, Mont.	.20
□	258	Mike McPhee, Mont.	.20
□	259	Mats Näslund, Mont.	.20
□	260	Stéphane Richer, Mont.	.50
□	261	Bobby Smith, Mont.	.20
□	262	Ryan Walter, Mont.	.20
□	263	Montréal Canadiens Team Photo	.20
□	264	Montréal Canadiens Team Photo	.20
□	265	New Jersey Devils Team Logo	.20
□	266	New Jersey Devils Uniform	.20
□	267	Sean Burke (G), NJer.	.75
□	268	Joe Cirella, NJer.	.20
□	269	Bruce Driver, NJer.	.20
□	270	Craig Wolanin, NJer.	.20
□	271	Aaron Broten, NJer.	.20
□	272	Doug Brown, NJer.	.20
□	273	Claude Loiselle, NJer.	.20
□	274	John MacLean, NJer.	.20
□	275	Kirk Muller, NJer.	.25
□	276	Brendan Shanahan, NJer.	5.00
□	277	Patrik Sundstrom, NJer.	.20
□	278	Pat Verbeek, NJer.	.20
□	279	New Jersey Devils Team Photo	.20
□	280	New Jersey Devils Team Photo	.20
□	281	New York Islanders Team Logo	.20
□	282	New York Islanders Uniform	.20
□	283	Kelly Hrudey (G), NYIs.	.25
□	284	Steve Konroyd, NYIs.	.20
□	285	Ken Morrow, NYIs.	.20
□	286	Patrick Flatley, NYIs.	.20
□	287	Greg Gilbert, NYIs.	.20
□	288	Alan Kerr, NYIs.	.20
□	289	Derek King, NYIs.	.20
□	290	Pat LaFontaine, NYIs.	.60
□	291	Mikko Makelä, NYIs.	.20
□	292	Brent Sutter, NYIs.	.20
□	293	Bryan Trottier, NYIs.	.25
□	294	Randy Wood, NYIs.	.20
□	295	New York Islanders Team Photo	.20
□	296	New York Islanders Team Photo	.20
□	297	New York Rangers Team Logo	.20
□	298	New York Rangers Uniform	.20
□	299	Bob Froese (G), NYRa.	.25
□	300	John Vanbiesbrouck (G), NYRa.	1.00
□	301	Brian Leetch, NYRa.	2.00
□	302	Norm Maciver, NYRa.	.20
□	303	James Patrick, NYRa.	.20
□	304	Michel Petit, NYRa.	.20
□	305	Ulf Dahlen, NYRa.	.20
□	306	Jan Erixon, NYRa.	.20
□	307	Kelly Kisio, NYRa.	.20
□	308	Don Maloney, NYRa.	.20
□	309	Walt Poddubny, NYRa.	.20
□	310	Tomas Sandstrom, NYRa.	.20
□	311	New York Rangers Team Photo	.20
□	312	New York Rangers Team Photo	.20
□	313	Philadelphia Flyers Team Logo	.20
□	314	Philadelphia Flyers Uniform	.20
□	315	Ron Hextall (G), Phil.	.50
□	316	Mark Howe, Phil.	.25
□	317	Kerry Huffman, Phil.	.20
□	318	Kjell Samuelsson, Phil.	.20
□	319	Dave Brown, Phil.	.20
□	320	Murray Craven, Phil.	.20
□	321	Tim Kerr, Phil.	.20
□	322	Scott Mellanby, Phil.	.20
□	323	Dave Poulin, Phil.	.20
□	324	Brian Propp, Phil.	.20
□	325	Ilkka Sinisalo, Phil.	.20
□	326	Rick Tocchet, Phil.	.50
□	327	Philadelphia Flyers Team Photo	.20
□	328	Philadelphia Flyers Team Photo	.20
□	329	Pittsburgh Penguins Team Logo	.20
□	330	Pittsburgh Penguins Uniform	.20
□	331	Frank Pietrangelo (G), Pitt.	.25
□	332	Doug Bodger, Pitt.	.20
□	333	Paul Coffey, Pitt.	.50
□	334	Jim Johnson, Pitt.	.20
□	335	Ville Siren, Pitt.	.20
□	336	Rob Brown, Pitt.	.20
□	337	Randy Cunneyworth, Pitt.	.20
□	338	Dan Frawley, Pitt.	.20
□	339	Dave Hunter, Pitt.	.20
□	340	Mario Lemieux, Pitt.	3.00
□	341	Troy Loney, Pitt.	.20
□	342	Dan Quinn, Pitt.	.20
□	343	Pittsburgh Penguins Team Photo	.20
□	344	Pittsburgh Penguins Team Photo	.20
□	345	Québec Nordiques Team Logo	.20
□	346	Québec Nordiques Uniform	.20
□	347	Mario Gosselin (G), Québ.	.25
□	348	Tommy Albelin, Québ.	.20
□	349	Jeff Brown, Québ.	.50
□	350	Steven Finn, Québ.	.20
□	351	Randy Moller, Québ.	.20
□	352	Alain Côté, Québ.	.20
□	353	Gaetan Duchesne, Québ.	.20
□	354	Mike Eagles, Québ.	.20
□	355	Michel Goulet, Québ.	.35
□	356	Lane Lambert, Québ.	.20
□	357	Anton Stastny, Québ.	.20
□	358	Peter Stastny, Québ.	.35
□	359	Québec Nordiques Team Photo	.20
□	360	Québec Nordiques Team Photo	.20
□	361	Washington Capitals Team Logo	.20
□	362	Washington Capitals Uniform	.20
□	363	Clint Malarchuk (G), Wash.	.25
□	364	Pete Peeters (G), Wash.	.25
□	365	Kevin Hatcher, Wash.	.50
□	366	Rod Langway, Wash.	.25
□	367	Larry Murphy, Wash.	.25
□	368	Scott Stevens, Wash.	.25
□	369	Dave Christian, Wash.	.20
□	370	Mike Gartner, Wash.	.35
□	371	Bengt Gustafsson, Wash.	.20
□	372	Dale Hunter, Wash.	.25
□	373	Kelly Miller, Wash.	.20
□	374	Mike Ridley, Wash.	.20
□	375	Washington Capitals Team Photo	.20
□	376	Washington Capitals Team Photo	.20
□	377	Hockey Rink	.20
□	378	Hockey Rink	.20
□	379	Cross-checking	.20
□	380	Elbowing	.20
□	381	High-sticking	.20
□	382	Holding	.20
□	383	Hooking	.20
□	384	Interference	.20
□	385	Spearing	.20
□	386	Tripping	.20
□	387	Boarding	.20
□	388	Charging	.20
□	389	Delayed Calling of Penalty	.20
□	390	Kneeing	.20
□	391	Misconduct	.20
□	392	Roughing	.20
□	393	Slashing	.20
□	394	Unsportsmanlike Conduct	.20
□	395	Wash-out	.20
□	396	Icing	.20
□	397	Off-side	.20
□	398	Wash-out	.20
□	399	AW: Bob Bourne, Pitt.	.20
□	400	AW: Mario Lemieux, Pitt.	2.00
□	401	AW: Mario Lemieux, Pitt.	2.00
□	402	AW: Brian Hayward (G)/ Patrick Roy (G)	1.50
□	403	AW: Grant Fuhr, Edmo.	.25
□	404	AW: Joe Nieuwendyk, Calg.	.75
□	405	AW: Raymond Bourque, Bost.	.50
□	406	AW: Mats Näslund, Mont.	.20
□	407	AW: Guy Carbonneau, Mont.	.20
□	408	AW: Brad McCrimmon, Calg.	.20

1988 - 89 PROCARDS TEAM SETS

These cards have a red border. Singles start at 35¢ while regional stars start at $1.00. Each card measures the standard 2 1/2" x 3 1/2".

Complete AHL Set (348 cards): **100.00**
Complete IHL Set (119 cards): **65.00**
Common Player: **.25**

ADIRONDACK RED WINGS - AHL

Team Set (25 cards): **8.00**

	Player		Player
□	John Blum	□	Jeff Brubaker
□	Dave Casey, Trainer	□	Tim Cheveldae (G)
□	Lou Crawford	□	Bill Dineen, Coach
□	Peter Dineen	□	Rob Doyle
□	Murray Eaves	□	Brent Fedyk
□	Joe Ferras	□	Mike Gober
□	Miroslav Ihnacak	□	Dave Korol
□	Dale Krentz	□	Randy McKay
□	Glenn Merkosky	□	John Mokosak
□	Dean Morton	□	Rob Nichols
□	Tim Paris, Asst.Trainer	□	Mark Reimer (G)
□	Sam St. Laurent (G)	□	Daniel Shank
□	Dennis Smith		

BALTIMORE SKIPJACKS - AHL

Team Set (23 cards): **7.00**

	Player		Player
□	Robin Bawa	□	Tim Bergland
□	Shawn Cronin	□	Frank Dimuzio
□	Dallas Eakins	□	David Farrish
□	Chris Felix	□	Lou Franceschetti
□	Jeff Greenlaw	□	Mark Hatcher
□	Bill Houlder	□	Doug Keans (G)
□	Tyler Larter	□	J.P. Mattingly, Trainer
□	Scott McCrory	□	Mike Millar
□	Rob Murray	□	Terry Murray, Coach
□	Mike Richard	□	Steve Seftel
□	Dave Sherrid, Trainer	□	Shawn Simpson (G)

BINGHAMPTON WHALERS - AHL

Team Set (24 cards): 8.00

Player	Player
Charles Bourgeois	Chris Brant
Richard Brodeur (G)	L. Carson, Err. (Lindsy)
Gary Callaghan	Brian Chapman
Jim Culhane	Mark Dumas, Equip. Mgr
Dallas Gaume	Roger Kortko
Todd Krygier	Marc Laforge
Claude Larose, Coach	Mark Lavarre
Tom Mitchell, G.M.	David O'Brien
Mark Reeds	Dave Rowbotham
Jon Smith, Trainer	Larry Trader
Allan Tuer	Mike Vellucci
Kay Whitmore (G)	Terry Yake

CAPE BRETON OILERS - AHL

Team Set (24 cards): 7.00

Player	Player
Marlo Barbe	Darren Beals (G)
Nicholas Beaulieu	Dan Currie
Jim Ennis	Larry Floyd
Mike Glover	David Haas
John B. Hanna	Kim Issel
Fabian Joseph	Mark Lamb
Brad MacGregor	Rob MacInnis
Don Martin	Alan May
Jamie Nichols	Selmar Odelein
Daryl Reaugh (G)	Dave Roach (G)
Ron Shudra	Shaun Van Allen (B& W)
Mike Ware	Jim Wiemer

HALIFAX CITADELS - AHL

Ron Tugnutt is the most expensive player at $4-6

Team Set (23 cards): 10.00

Player	Player
Joel Baillargeon	Gerald Bzdel
D.Carpenter, Coach	Bobby Dollas
Marc Fortier	Scott Gordon (G)
Dean Hopkins	Mike Hough
Claude Julien	Darin Kimble
Jacques Mailhot	Ken McRae
Max Middendorf	Keith Miller
Mike Natyshak	Ken Quinney
Jean-Marc Richard	Jean-Marc Routhier
Jaroslav Sevcik	Brent Severyn
Scott Shaunessy	Ladislav Tresel
Ron Tugnutt (G)	

HERSHEY BEARS - AHL

Team Set (28 cards): 7.00

Player	Player
Don Biggs	B. Bucciarelli, A.. Trainer
J.J. Daigneault	Marc D'Amour (G)
David Fenyves	Mark Freer
Darryl Gilmour (G)	Jeff Harding
Warren Harper	Kent Hawley
Al Hill	Tony Horacek
Chris Jensen	Craig Kitteringham
Mark Lofthouse	F. Mathers, Pres./G.M.
K. McCarthy, A. Coach	Don Nachbaur
Gordon Paddock	John Paddock, Coach
Jocelyn Perrault (G)	Bruce Randall
Shawn Sabol	Glen Seabrooke
John Stevens	Mike Stothers
Dan Stuck, Head Trainer	Doug Yingst, Asst.G.M.

MAINE MARINERS - AHL

Team Set (22 cards): 8.00

Player	Player
Paul Beraldo	John Carter
Phil Degaetano	Scott Drevitch
Joe Flaherty	Doug Foerster, P.R.
Norm Foster (G)	Paul Guay
Greg Hawgood	Mike Jeffrey (G)
Jeff Lamb	Jean-Marc Lanthier
Darren Lowe	Carl Mokosak
Mitch Molloy	Mike Neill
Ray Podloski	Stéphane Quintal
Bruce Shoebottom	Terry Taillefer (G)
Steve Tsujiura	S. Wykoff, Brdcstr/ PR

MONCTON HAWKS - AHL

Team Set (21 cards): 7.00

Player	Player
S. Beauregard (G)	Rick Bowness, Coach
Sean Clement	Tom Draper (G)
W. Flemming, Equ. Mgr	Steven Fletcher
Todd Flichel	Guy Gosselin
Gilles Hamel	Matt Hervey
Brent Hughes	Jamie Husgen
Stuart Kulak	Guy Larose
Neil Meadmore	Len Nielson
Chris Norton	Scott Schneider
R. Snitzer, Therapist	Mike Warus
Ron Wilson	

NEW HAVEN NIGHTHAWKS - AHL

Mark Fiztpatrick is the most expensive player at $1-2.

Team Set (32 cards): 10.00

Player	Player
Ken Baumgartner	François Breault
Mario Chitaroni	Sylvain Couturier
Rick Dudley, Coach	John English
Mark Fitzpatrick (G)	Eric Germain
Dan Gratton	S. Green, Trainer
P.Hickey, Director	Brad Hyatt
Paul Kelly	Bob Kudelski
Denis Larocque	Bob Logan
S. Lombardi, Trainer	Al Loring (G)
Hubie McDonough	Chris Panek
Dave Pasin	Joe Paterson
Lyle Phair	Petr Prajsler
Tom Pratt	Steve Richmond
Phil Sykes	Tim Tookey
J. Tortorella, Asst. Coach	Gordie Walker
Brian Wilks	Darryl Williams

NEWMARKET SAINTS - AHL

Team Set (22 cards): 7.00

Player	Player
Tim Armstrong	Tim Bernhardt (G)
Brian Blad	Mike Blaisdell
Jack Capuano	Marty Dallman
Daryl Evans	Paul Gagné
Alan Hepple	Brian Hoard
Greg Hotham	Wes Jarvis
Trevor Jobe	Mark Kirton
Sean McKenna	J. Ralph (G)
Jeff Reese (G)	Bill Root
Darryl Shannon	Doug Shedden
Greg Terrion	Ken Yaremchuk

ROCHESTER AMERICANS - AHL

Team Set (24 cards): 8.00

Player	Player
Shawn Anderson	Mikael Andersson
J. Van Boxmeer, Coach	Paul Brydges
Jeff Capello	Jacques Cloutier (G)
Mike Donnelly	Richie Dunn
Mark Ferner	Jody Gage
François Guay	Jim Hofford
Jim Jackson	Kevin Kerr
Don McSween	Scott Metcalfe
Jeff Parker	Ken Priestlay
Rob Ray	Steve Smith
Grant Tkachuk	Wayne Van Dorp
Darcy Wakaluk (G)	Mascot The Moose

SHERBROOKE CANADIENS - AHL

Benoît Brunet is the most expensive player at $3-4.

Team Set (29 cards): 12.00

Player	Player
Steve Bisson	B.Boulanger, Equip. Mgr
Benoît Brunet	Rob Bryden
José Charbonneau	Ron Chyzowski
J.J. Daigneault	Martin Desjardins
Donald Dufresne	Rocky Dundas
Randy Exelby (G)	Luc Gauthier
François Gravel (G)	J. Hamel, Coach
C. Larose, Asst Coach	Stéphan Lebeau
Sylvain Lefebvre	Jocelyn Lemieux
Jyrki Lumme	Steven Martinson
Jim Nesich	Martin Nicoletti
J. Parent, Therapist	Mark Pederson
Stéphane Richer	Mario Roberge
Serge Roberge	Scott Sandelin
Marc Saumier	

SPRINGFIELD INDIANS - AHL

Jeff Hackett is the most expensive player at $3-5.

Team Set (25 cards): 10.00

Player	Player
Bill Berg	Bruce Boudreau
Stu Burnie	Shawn Byram
R. Calvanese, Equip.Mgr	Kerry Clark
Rod Dallman	Rob DiMaio
Shawn Evans	Jeff Finley
Tom Fitzgerald	Jeff Hackett (G)
Dale Henry	Richard Kromm
Hank Lammens	Duncan MacPherson
George Maneluk (G)	Todd McLellan
Chris Prior	Jim Roberts, Coach
Vern Smith	Mike Stevens
E. Tyburski, Trainer	Mike Walsh
Doug Weiss	

UTICA DEVILS - AHL

Chris Terreri is the most expensive player at $1-2.

Team Set (24 cards): 10.00

Player	Player
Robert Bill, Trainer	Craig Billington (G)
John Blessman	Neil Brady
Murray Brumwell	Anders Carlsson
Chris Cichocki	J. Croop, Trainer
Dan Delianedls (G)	Dan Dorion
Jamie Huscroft	Marc Laniel
Tim Lenardon	Jeff Madill
David Marcinyshyn	Tom McVie, Coach
S. Moon, Trainer's Asst.	Janne Ojanen
Alan Stewart	Chris Terreri (G)
Kevin Todd	John Walker
Eric Weinrich	Paul Ysebaert

INDIANAPOLIS ICE - IHL

Team Set (22 cards): 7.00

Player	Player
Dave Allison	Rick Barkovich
Brad Beck	Geoff Benic
Graeme Bonar	Rick Boyd
Scott Clements	Shane Doyle
Ron Handy	Archie Henderson
Paul Houck	Glen Johannesen
Bob Lakso	Jimmy Mann
Darwin McCutcheon	Chris McSorley
Rich Oberlin, Trainer	Alan Perry (G)
Brent Sapergia	Gary Stewart
Randy Taylor	Mark Teevens

KALAMAZOO WINGS - IHL

Team Set (21 cards): 7.00

Player	Player
Andy Akervik	Warren Babe
Darin Baker (G)	Mike Berger
Scott Bjugstad	Larry Dyck (G)
Ken Hodge	Joe Lockwood
Gary McColgan	Scott McCrady
Michael McHugh	Mitch Messier
Jarmo Myllys (G)	D'Arcy Norton
Stéphane Roy	Dave Schofield
Randy Smith	Kirk Tomlinson
Emanuel Viveiros	Neil Wilkinson
Rob Zettler	

MUSKEGON LUMBERJACKS - IHL

Mark Recchi is the most expensive player at $10-15.

Team Set (23 cards): 20.00

Player	Player
Brad Aitken	Jock Callander
Todd Charlesworth	Jeff Cooper (G)
Jeff Daniels	Greg Davies
Lee Giffin	Dave Goertz
Steve Gotaas	Scott Gruhl
Doug Hobson	Kevin MacDonald
Pat Mayer	Dave McLlwain
Dave Michayluk	Glenn Mulvenna
Jim Paek	Frank Pietrangelo (G)
Bruce Racine (G)	Mark Recchi
Troy Vollhoffer	Jeff Waver
Mitch Wilson	

PEORIA RIVERMEN - IHL

Cliff Ronning is the most expensive player at $2-3.

Team Set (28 cards): 15.00

Player	Player
Tim Bothwell	Kelly Chase
Peter Douris	Toby Ducolon
G. Eberle, Head Trainer	Glen Featherstone
Wayne Gagne	Scott Harlow
Pat Jablonski (G)	Dominic Lavoie
Dave Lowry	Shane MacEachern
Terry MacLean	Darrell May (G)
Brad McCaughey	Ed McMurray, Asst G.M.
Lyle Odelein	Scott Paluch
Rivermen 1988-1989	Skip Probst, G.M.
Sheryl Reeves, Admin.	Cliff Ronning
Darin Smith	Wayne Thomas, Coach
Dave Thomlinson	C. Thompson, Sales Mgr.
Tony Twist	Jim Vesey

SAGINAW HAWKS - IHL

Ed Belfour is the most expensive player at $15-20.

Team Set (25 cards): 35.00

Player	Player
Ed Belfour (G)	Bruce Cassidy
Chris Clifford (G)	Mario Doyon
Bill Gardner	Mark Kurzawski
Lonnie Loach	Steve Ludzik
David Mackey	Dale Marquette
Gary Moscaluk	Marty Nanne
Brian Noonan	Mark Paterson
Kent Paynter	Guy Phillips
John Reid (G)	Mike Rucinski
Warren Rychel	Everett Sanipass
Mike Stapleton	Darryl Sutter, Coach
Jari Torkki	Bill Watson
Sean Williams	

1989 PELIMIEHEN PASSI

A set of 6 stickers issued by the Finnish Ice Hockey Assosiation. A poster was also issued. We have no pricing information on this set. Each sticker measures 3 1/8" x 3 7/8".

Player	Player
Kari Eloranta	Jari Kurri
Reijo Ruotsalainen	Christian Ruuttu
Kari Takko	Esa Tikkanen

1989 SEMIC STICKERS

These stickers measure 2 1/8" x 3".

Complete Set (200 stickers): 60.00
Album: 6.00
Common Player: .20

Panini	NM-MT
1 Sweden	.20
2 Tommy Sandlin	.20
3 Peter Lindmark	.20
4 Rolf Ridderwall	.20
5 Tomas Jonsson	.35
6 Tommy Albelin	.35
7 Mats Kihlström	.20
8 Tommy Samuelsson	.20
9 Anders Eldebrink	.20
10 Fredrik Olausson	.35
11 Peter Andersson	.20
12 Thomas Eriksson	.20
13 Them Eklund	.20
14 Bo Berglund	.20
15 Thomas Steen	.50
16 Ulf Sandström	.20
17 Jonas Bergqvist	.20
18 Thomas Rundqvist	.20
19 Per-Erik Eklund	.50
20 Bengt Gustavsson	.35
21 Patrik Sundström	.35
22 Mikael Johansson	.20
23 Hakan Södergren	.20
24 Kent Nilsson	.50
25 Lars-Gunnar Pettersson	.20
26 Finland	.20
27 Pentii Matikainen	.20
28 Jukka Tammi (G)	.20
29 Sakari Lindfors	.20
30 Reijo Ruotsalainen	.35
31 Kari Eloranta	.20
32 Timo Blomqvist	.20
33 Simo Saarinen	.20
34 Hannu Virta	.20
35 Jouko Narvanmaa	.20
36 Jarmo Kuusisto	.20
37 Kari Suoraniemi	.20
38 Reijo Mikkolainen	.20
39 Raimo Helminen	.20
40 Raimo Summanen	.20
41 Mikko Mäkelä	.20
42 Kari Jalonen	.20
43 Kari Laitinen	.20
44 Petri Skriko	.20
45 Erkki Laine	.20
46 Pauli Järvinen	.20
47 Jukka Vilander	.20

48 Esa Keskinen	.35
49 Ari Vuori	.20
50 Mika Nieminen	.20
51 Canada	.35
52 Dave King	.50
53 Grant Fuhr (G)	1.50
54 Patrick Roy (G)	8.00
55 Ron Hextall (G)	.75
56 Al MacInnis	.50
57 Raymond Bourque	3.00
58 Scott Stevens	.50
59 Paul Coffey	2.00
60 Zarley Zalapski	.35
61 James Patrick	.35
62 Kevin Lowe	.50
63 Brad McCrimmon	.35
64 Mario Lemieux	8.00
65 Wayne Gretzky	12.00
66 Denis Savard	.50
67 Dale Hawerchuk	.75
68 Luc Robitaille	.75
69 Mark Messier	3.00
70 Michel Goulet	.75
71 Cam Neely	1.50
72 Steve Yzerman	5.00
73 Bernie Nicholls	.50
74 Joe Nieuwendyk	.50
75 Mike Gartner	1.50
76 Soviet Union	.35
77 Victor Tikhonov	.20
78 Evgeni Belosjejkin	.20
79 Sergei Mylnikov (G)	.20
80 Sergei Golosjumov	.20
81 Alexei Kasatonov	.35
82 Alexei Gusarov	.50
83 Andrei Smirnov	.20
84 Valeri Shiryev	.20
85 Igor Stelnov	.20
86 Vladimir Konstantinov	3.00
87 Viacheslav Fetisov	1.50
88 Sergei Yashin	.20
89 Vladimir Krutov	.50
90 Igor Larionov	1.50
91 Valeri Kamenski	2.00
92 Vyacheslav Bykov	.75
93 Andrei Khomutov	.50
94 Yuri Kmylev	.50
95 Sergei Nemchinov	.50
96 Sergei Makarov	1.00
97 Igor Jesmantoviti	.20
98 Andrei Lomakin	.35
99 Anatoli Semenov	.50
100 Alexander Tiernych	.20
101 Germany	.20
102 Xaver Unsinn	.20
103 Karl Friesen	.20
104 Josef Schlickenrieder	.20
105 Matthias Hoppe	.20
106 Andreas Niederberger	.20
107 Udo Kiessling	.20
108 Uli Hiemer	.20
109 Harold Kreis	.20
110 Manfred Schuster	.20
111 Jörg Hanft	.20
112 Ron Fischer	.20
113 Michael Heidt	.20
114 Dieter Hegen	.20
115 Gerd Truntschka	.20
116 Helmut Steiger	.20
117 Georg Franz	.20
118 Georg Holzmann	.20
119 Peter Obresa	.20
120 Berndt Truntschka	.20
121 Manfred Wolf	.20
122 Roy Roedger	.20
123 Axel Kammerer	.20
124 Peter Draisatl	.20
125 Daniel Held	.20
126 Poland	.20
127 Leszek Lejczyk	.20
128 Jerzy Mruk	.20
129 Andrzei Hanisz	.20
130 Dariusz Wieczorek	.20
131 Jacek Zamojski	.20
132 Marek Cholewa	.20
133 Henryk Gruth	.20
134 Robert SzoDinski	.20
135 Jerzy Potz	.20
136 Andrzei Swiate	.20
137 Ludvik Czapka	.20
138 Piotr Zdunek	.20
139 Jedrzej Kasperczyk	.20
140 Krzysztof Podsiadlo	.20
141 Miroslav Copija	.20
142 Krzysztof Bujar	.20
143 Janusz Adamiec	.20
144 Jasek Solinski	.20
145 Roman Steblecki	.20
146 Adam Fraszkol	.20
147 Leszek Minge	.20
148 Piotr Kwasigroch	.20
149 Ireneusz Pacula	.20
150 MM-kisatunnus	.20
151 USA	.20
152 Art Berglund	.20
153 Tom Barrasso (G)	.50
154 John Vanbiesbrouck (G)	4.00
155 Gary Suter	.35
156 Phil Housley	.35
157 Chris Chelios	2.00
158 Mike Ramsey	.35
159 Rod Langway	.50
160 Mark Howe	.50
161 Brian Leetch	5.00
162 Al Iafrate	.35
163 Jimmy Carson	.35
164 Pat LaFontaine	1.50
165 Neal Broten	.50
166 Dave Christian	.35
167 Brett Hull	4.00
168 Bob Carpenter	.35
169 Ed Olczyk	.35
170 Joe Mullen	.50
171 Bob Brooke	.35
172 Brian Lawton	.35
173 Craig Janney	.50
174 Mark Johnson	.35
175 Chris Nilan	.35
176 Czechoslovakia	.20
177 Pavel Wohl	.20
178 Dominik Hasek	5.00
179 Jaromir Sindel	.20
180 Petr Briza (G)	.35
181 Antonin Stavjana	.20
182 Bedrich Scerban	.20
183 Petr Slanina	.20
184 Frantisek Kucera	.20
185 Jergus Baca	.20
186 Leo Gudas	.20
187 Drahomir Kadlec	.20
188 Mojmir Bozik	.20
189 Petr Vlk	.20
190 Vladimir Ruzicka	.20
191 Otakar Janecky	.20
192 Jan Vodila	.20
193 Jiri Dolezal	.20
194 Rostislav Vlach	.20
195 Jiri Kucera	.20
196 Jiri Sejba	.20
197 Oldrich Valek	.20
198 Jiri Lala	.20
199 Robert Kron	.20
200 Petr Rosol	.20

1989 - 90 ACTION PACKED PROMOS

Each card measures the standard 2 1/2" x 3 1/2".

Action Packed	NM-MT
1 Wayne Gretzky, LosA.	250.00
2 Mario Lemieux, Pitt.	175.00
3 Steve Yzerman, Detr. (*)	300.00

1989 - 90 KRAFT

Cards 1 to 51 and 64 were issued on the backs of packages of Kraft Dinner, Rock-O-Rama, Spirals and Egg Noodles. Cards 52 to 63 were issued only in full cases of Kraft Dinner as six panels of two cards. Factory cut cards were also available by mail. Cut cards measure the standard 2 1/2" x 3 1/2".

Complete Set (64 cards):	**60.00**
Album:	**30.00**
Kraft Canada	**NM-MT**
1 Doug Gilmour, Calg.	1.50
2 Theoren Fleury, Calg.	2.50
3 Al MacInnis, Calg.	1.00
4 Sergei Makarov, Calg.	1.00
5 Joe Nieuwendyk, Calg.	1.00
6 Joel Otto, Calg.	.50
7 Colin Patterson, Calg.	50.00
8 Sergei Priakin, Calg.	.50
9 Paul Ranheim, Calg.	.50
10 Glenn Anderson, Edmo.	.80
11 Grant Fuhr (G), Edmo.	1.50
12 Charlie Huddy, Edmo.	.50
13 Jari Kurri, Edmo.	2.50
14 Kevin Lowe, Edmo.	.80
15 Mark Messier, Edmo.	2.50
16 Craig Simpson, Edmo.	.50
17 J. Steve Smith, Edmo.	.60
18 Esa Tikkanen, Edmo.	.50
19 Guy Carbonneau, Mont.	.80
20 Chris Chelios, Mont.	1.50
21 Shayne Corson, Mont.	.80
22 Russ Courtnall, Mont.	.60
23 Mats Näslund, Mont.	.80
24 Stéphane J.J. Richer, Mont.	.60
25 Patrick Roy (G), Mont.	6.50
26 Bobby Smith, Mont.	.80
27 Petr* Svoboda, Mont.	.60
28 Jeff R. Brown, Québ.	.50
29 Paul Gillis, Québ.	.50
30 Michel Goulet, Québ.	1.20
31 Guy Lafleur, Québ.	5.00
32 Joe Sakic, Québ.	3.00
33 Peter Stastny, Québ.	1.50
34 Wendel Clark, Toro.	1.50
35 Vincent Damphousse, Toro.	1.00
36 Gary Leeman, Toro.	.50
37 Daniel Marois, Toro.	.50
38 Ed Olczyk, Toro.	.60
39 Rob Ramage, Toro.	.60
40 Vladimir Krutov, Vanc.	.60
41 Igor Larionov, Vanc.	1.20
42 Trevor Linden, Vanc.	1.00
43 Kirk McLean (G), Vanc.	.80
44 Paul Reinhart, Vanc.	.50
45 Tony Tanti, Vanc.	.50
46 Brent Ashton, Winn.	.50
47 Randy Carlyle, Winn.	.60
48 Randy Cunneyworth, Winn.	.50
49 Dave Ellett, Winn.	.50
50 Dale Hawerchuk, Winn.	1.50
51 Fredrik Olausson, Winn.	.60
52 Raymond Bourque, NHL All-Star (Bost.)	3.00
53 Sean Burke (G), NHL All-Star (NJer.)	1.00
54 Paul Coffey, NHL All-Star (Pitt.)	2.00
55 Mario Lemieux, NHL All-Star (Pitt.)	8.00
56 Cam Neely, NHL All-Star (Bost.)	1.50
57 Rick Tocchet, NHL All-Star (Phil.)	.80
58 Steve Duchesne, NHL All-Star (LosA.)	.50
59 Wayne Gretzky, NHL All-Star (LosA.)	10.00
60 Joe Mullen, NHL All-Star (Calg.)	1.00
61 Gary Suter, NHL All-Star (Calg.)	.60
62 Mike Vernon (G), NHL All-Star (Calg.)	1.00
63 Steve Yzerman, NHL All-Star (Detr.)	5.50
64 Checklist	.50

KRAFT SLICES / ALL-STAR STICKERS

These sticker panels measure 41/2" x 2 3/4".

Complete Set (6 panels):	**20.00**
Kraft Canada	**NM**
1 P. Reinhart / M. McPhee	1.00
2 R. Tocchet / W. Gretzky	10.00
3 S. Yzerman / P. Coffey	5.50
4 R. Bourque / M. Vernon	3.00
5 M. Lemieux / J. Kurri	8.00
6 S. Burke / K. Lowe	1.00

1989 - 90 O-PEE-CHEE & TOPPS

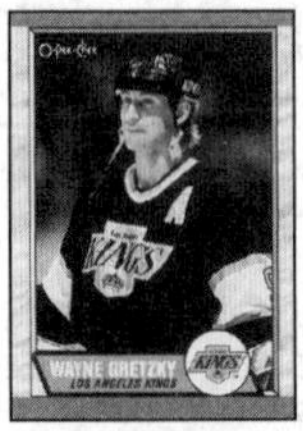

There are two versions for this series: an O-Pee-Chee (1-330) and a Topps (1-198). Topps double prints are marked by a double asterisk (**). Each card measures the standard 2 1/2" x 3 1/2".

O-Pee-Chee Set (330 cards):	**-**	**25.00**
Topps Set (198 cards):	**35.00**	**-**
Common Player:	**.20**	**.20**
Description	**Topps**	**OPC**
1 Mario Lemieux, Pitt.	4.00	2.00
2 Ulf Dahlén, NYRa.	.20	.20
3 Terry Carkner, Phil. RC	**.75**	**.50**
4 Tony McKegney, Detr.	.30	.20
5 Denis Savard, Chic.	.50	.20
6 Derek King, NYIs. RC	**.75**	**.50**
7 Lanny McDonald, Calg.	1.00	.40
8 John Tonelli, LosA.	.30	.20
9 Tom Kurvers, NJer. (Toro.)	.20	.20
10 Dave Archibald, Minn.	.20	.20
11 Peter Sidorkiewicz (G), Hart. RC	**.40**	**.30**
12 Esa Tikkanen, Edmo.	.20	.20
13 Dave Barr, Detr.	.20	.20
14 Brent Sutter, NYIs.	.30	.20
15 Cam Neely, Bost.	.70	.30
16 Calle Johansson, Wash. RC	**.75**	**.50**
17 Patrick Roy (G), Mont.	1.70	1.30
18 Dale (Digger) DeGray, LosA. RC	**.75**	**.50**
19 Phil Bourque, Pitt. RC	**.75**	**.50**
20 Kevin Dineen, Hart.	.20	.20
21 Mike Bullard, Phil.	.30	.20
22 Gary Leeman, Toro.	.20	.20
23 Greg Stefan (G), Detr.	.40	.30
24 Brian Mullen, NYRa.	.20	.20
25 Pierre Turgeon, Buff.	.30	.30
26 Bob Rouse, Wash. RC	**.75**	**.50**
27 Peter Zezel, SLou.	.20	.20
28 Jeff R. Brown, Québ.	.20	.20
29 Andy Brickley, Bost. RC	**.75**	**.50**
30 Mike Gartner, Minn.	1.00	.40
31 Darren Pang (G), Chic.	.30	.20
32 Pat Verbeek, Hart.	.40	.30
33 Petri Skriko, Vanc.	.20	.20
34 Tom Laidlaw, LosA.	.20	.20
35 Randy Wood, NYIs.	.20	.20
36 Tom Barrasso (G), Pitt.	.20	.20
37 John Tucker, Buff.	.20	.20
38 Andrew McBain, Pitt.	.20	.20
39 David Shaw, NYRa.	.20	.20
40 Réjean Lemelin (G), Bost.	.30	.20
41 Dino Ciccarelli, Wash.	.20	.20
42 Jeff Sharples, Detr.	.20	.20
43 Jari Kurri, Edmo.	1.20	.50
44 Murray Craven, Phil.	.20	.20
45 Cliff Ronning, SLou. RC	**1.00**	**.65**
46 Dave Babych, Hart.	.20	.20
47 Bernie Nicholls, LosA.	.20	.20
48 Jon Casey (G), Minn. RC	**1.00**	**.65**
49 Al MacInnis, Calg.	.50	.20
50 Bob Errey, Pitt. RC	**.75**	**.50**
51 Glen Wesley, Bost.	.20	.20
52 Dirk Graham, Chic.	.20	.20
53 Guy Carbonneau, Mont.	.40	.30
54 Tomas Sandström, NYRa. RC	**1.00**	**.65**
55 Rod Langway, Wash.	.20	.20
56 Patrik Sundström, NJer.	.20	.20
57 Michel Goulet, Québ.	.60	.20
58 Dave Taylor, LosA.	.30	.20
59 Phil Housley, Buff.	.40	.30
60 Pat LaFontaine, NYIs.	.30	.30
61 Kirk McLean (G), Vanc. RC	**1.25**	**1.00**
62 Ken Linseman, Bost.	.20	.20
63 Randy Cunneyworth, Winn.	.20	.20
63 Randy Cunneyworth, Winn. (Pitt.)	9.00	
64 Tony Hrkac, SLou.	.20	.20
65 Mark Messier, Edmo.	.60	.50
66 Carey Wilson, NYRa.	.20	.20
67 Stephen Leach, Wash. RC	**.75**	**.50**
68 Christian Ruuttu, Buff.	.20	.20
69 Dave Ellett, Winn.	.20	.20
70 Ray Ferraro, Hart.	.20	.20
71 Colin Patterson, Calg. RC	**.75**	**.50**
72 Tim Kerr, Phil.	.30	.20
73 Bob Joyce, Bost.	.20	.20
74 Doug Gilmour, Calg.	.30	.30
75 Lee Norwood, Detr.	.20	.20
76 Dale Hunter, Wash.	.40	.30
77 Jim* Johnson, Pitt.	.20	.20
78 Mike Foligno, Buff.	.30	.20
79 Al Iafrate, Toro.	.30	.20
80 Rick Tocchet, Phil.	.20	.20
81 Greg Hawgood, Bost. RC	**.75**	**.50**
82 Steve Thomas, Chic.	.30	.20
83 Steve Yzerman, Detr.	1.30	1.00
84 Mike McPhee, Mont.	.20	.20
85 David Volek, NYIs. RC	**.75**	**.50**
86 Brian Benning, SLou.	.20	.20
87 Neal Broten, Minn.	.30	.20
88 Luc Robitaille, LosA.	.50	.40
89 Trevor Linden, Vanc. RC	**2.50**	**2.00**
90 James Patrick, NYRa.	.20	.20
91 Brian Lawton, Hart.	.20	.20
92 Sean Burke (G), NJer.	.20	.20
93 Scott Stevens, Wash.	.50	.20
94 Pat Elynuik, Winn. RC	**.75**	**.50**
95 Paul Coffey, Pitt.	1.00	.40
96 Jan Erixon, NYRa.	.20	.20
97 Mike Liut (G), Hart.	.40	.30
98 Wayne Presley, Chic.	.20	.20
99 Craig Simpson, Edmo.	.20	.20
100 Kjell Samuelsson, Phil. RC	**.75**	**.50**
101 Shawn Burr, Detr.	.20	.20
102 John MacLean, NJer.	.20	.20
103 Tom Fergus, Toro.	.20	.20
104 Mike Krushelnyski, LosA.	.20	.20

☐☐ 105 Gary Nylund, NYIs. .20 .20
☐☐ 106 Dave Andreychuk, Buff. .40 .30
☐☐ 107 Bernie Federko, Detr. .40 .30
☐☐ 108 Gary Suter, Calg. .30 .20
☐☐ 109 Dave Gagner, Minn. .20 .20
☐☐ 110 Raymond Bourque, Bost. 1.50 .60
☐☐ **111 Geoff Courtnall, Wash. RC 1.00 .65**
☐☐ 112 Doug Wilson, Chic. .40 .30
☐☐ **113 Joe Sakic, Québ. RC 20.00 15.00**
☐☐ 114 John Vanbiesbrouck (G), NYRa. .50 .20
☐☐ 115 Dave Poulin, Phil. .20 .20
☐☐ 116 Rick Meagher, SLou. .20 .20
☐☐ 117 Kirk Muller, NJer. .20 .20
☐☐ 118 Mats Näslund, Mont. .40 .30
☐☐ 119 Ray Sheppard, Buff. .20 .20
☐☐ **120 Jeff Norton, NYIs. RC .75 .50**
☐☐ 121 Randy Burridge, Bost. .20 .20
☐☐ 122 Dale Hawerchuk, Winn. .30 .30
☐☐ 123 Steve Duchesne, LosA. .20 .20
☐☐ 124 John Anderson, Hart. .20 .20
☐☐ 125 Rick Vaive, Buff. .40 .30
☐☐ 126 Randy Hillier, Pitt. .20 .20
☐☐ 127 Jimmy Carson, Edmo. .20 .20
☐☐ 128 Larry Murphy, Minn. .30 .20
☐☐ 129 Paul MacLean, SLou. .20 .20
☐☐ 130 Joe Cirella, Québ. .20 .20
☐☐ 131 Kelly Miller, Wash. .20 .20
☐☐ 132 Alain Chevrier (G), Chic. .40 .30
☐☐ 133 Ed Olczyk, Toro. .30 .20
☐☐ 134 Dave Tippett, Hart. .20 .20
☐☐ 135 Bob Sweeney, Bost. .20 .20
☐☐ **136 Brian Leetch, NYRa. RC 8.00 4.00**
☐☐ 137 Greg Millen (G), SLou. .60 .20
☐☐ 138 Joe Nieuwendyk, Calg. .50 .20
☐☐ 139 Brian Propp, Phil. .30 .20
☐☐ 140 Mike Ramsey, Buff. .20 .20
☐☐ 141 Mike Allison, LosA. .20 .20
☐☐ **142 Shawn Chambers, Minn. RC .75 .50**
☐☐ 143 Peter Stastny, Québ. .30 .30
☐☐ 144 Glen Hanlon (G), Detr. .20 .20
☐☐ **145 John Cullen, Pitt. RC 1.25 .75**
☐☐ 146 Kevin Hatcher, Wash. .20 .20
☐☐ 147 Brendan Shanahan, NJer. 1.50 .60
☐☐ 148 Paul Reinhart, Vanc. .20 .20
☐☐ 149 Bryan Trottier, NYIs. 1.20 .50
☐☐ **150 Dave Manson, Chic. RC .75 .50**
☐☐ **151 Marc Habscheid, Detr. RC .75 .50**
☐☐ 152 Dan Quinn, Pitt. .20 .20
☐☐ 153 Stéphane J.J. Richer, Mont. .20 .20
☐☐ 154 Doug Bodger, Buff. .20 .20
☐☐ 155 Ron Hextall (G), Phil. .50 .20
☐☐ 156 Wayne Gretzky, LosA. 5.00 2.00
☐☐ **157 Steve Tuttle, SLou. RC .75 .50**
☐☐ 158 Charlie Huddy, Edmo. .20 .20
☐☐ 159 Dave Christian, Wash. .20 .20
☐☐ 160 Andy Moog (G), Bost. .50 .20
☐☐ **161 Tony Granato, NYRa. RC 1.50 1.00**
☐☐ **162 Sylvain Côté, Hart. RC .40 .30**
☐☐ 163 Mike Vernon (G), Calg. .50 .20
☐☐ **164 Steve Chiasson, Detr. RC .75 .50**
☐☐ 165 Mike Ridley, Wash. .20 .20
☐☐ 166 Kelly Hrudey (G), LosA. .40 .30
☐☐ 167 Bob Carpenter, Bost. .30 .20
☐☐ **168 Zarley Zalapski, Pitt. RC .75 .50**
☐☐ **169 Derek Laxdal, Toro. RC .75 .50**
☐☐ 170 Clint Malarchuk (G), Buff. .30 .20
☐☐ 171 Kelly Kisio, NYRa. .20 .20
☐☐ 172 Gerard Gallant, Detr. .20 .20
☐☐ 173 Ron Sutter, Phil. .30 .20
☐☐ 174 Chris Chelios, Mont. .70 .30
☐☐ 175 Ron Francis, Hart. .60 .20
☐☐ 176 Gino Cavallini, SLou. .20 .20
☐☐ 177 Brian Bellows, Minn. .20 .20
☐☐ 178 Greg A. Adams, Vanc. .20 .20
☐☐ 179 Steve Larmer, Chic. .50 .20
☐☐ 180 Aaron Broten, NJer. .20 .20
☐☐ 181 Brent Ashton, Winn. .20 .20
☐☐ **182 Gerald Diduck, NYIs. RC .75 .50**
☐☐ **183 Paul MacDermid, Hart. RC .75 .50**
☐☐ 184 Walt Poddubny, NJer. .20 .20
☐☐ 185 Adam Oates, SLou. .50 .20
☐☐ 186 Brett Hull, SLou. 1.20 .50
☐☐ 187 Scott Arniel, Buff. .20 .20
☐☐ 188 Bobby Smith, Mont. .40 .30
☐☐ 189 Guy Lafleur, NYRa. 2.50 1.00
☐☐ **190 Craig Janney, Bost. RC 1.00 .65**
☐☐ 191 Mark Howe, Phil. .40 .30
☐☐ 192 Grant Fuhr (G), Edmo. .30 .30
☐☐ 193 Rob (Jr.) Brown, Pitt. .20 .20
☐☐ 194 Steve Kasper, LosA. .20 .20
☐☐ 195 Pete Peeters (G), Phil. .40 .30
☐☐ 196 Joe Mullen, Calg. .50 .20
☐☐ 197 Checklist .20 .20
☐☐ 198 Checklist .20 .20

O-Pee-Chee **OPC**
☐ 199 Keith Crowder, LosA. .20
☐ **200 Daren Puppa (G), Buff. RC .75**
☐ **201 Benoit Hogue, Buff. RC .50**
☐ **202 Gary Roberts, Calg. RC 3.50**
☐ 203 Brad McCrimmon, Calg. .20
☐ 204 Rick Wamsley (G), Calg. .20
☐ 205 Joel Otto, Calg. .20
☐ 206 Jim Peplinski, Calg. .20
☐ 207 Jamie Macoun, Calg. .20
☐ 208 Brian MacLellan, Calg. .20
☐ **209 Scott Young, Hart. RC 2.00**
☐ 210 Ulf Samuelsson, Hart. .20
☐ 211 Joel Quenneville, Hart. .20
☐ 212 Tim Watters, LosA. .20
☐ 213 Curt Giles, Minn. .20
☐ 214 Stewart Gavin, Minn. .20
☐ 215 Bob Brooke, Minn. .20
☐ **216 Basil McRae, Minn. RC .50**
☐ **217 Frantisek Musil, Minn. RC .50**
☐ **218 Adam Creighton, Chic. RC .50**
☐ 219 Troy Murray, Chic. .20
☐ 220 Steve Konroyd, Chic. .20
☐ 221 Duane Sutter, Chic. .20
☐ **222 Trent Yawney, Chic. RC .50**
☐ 223 Mike O'Connell, Detr. .20
☐ 224 Jim Nill, Detr. .20
☐ 225 John Chabot, Detr. .20
☐ 226 Glenn Anderson, Edmo. .20
☐ 227 Kevin Lowe, Edmo. .20
☐ 228 J. Steve Smith, Edmo. .20
☐ 229 Randy Gregg, Edmo. .20
☐ 230 Craig MacTavish, Edmo. .20
☐ 231 Craig Muni, Edmo. .20
☐ **232 Theoren Fleury, Calg. RC 7.00**
☐ 233 Bill Ranford (G), Edmo. .20
☐ 234 Claude Lemieux, Mont. .20
☐ 235 Larry Robinson, LosA. .30
☐ 236 Craig Ludwig, Mont. .20
☐ 237 Brian Hayward (G), Mont. .20
☐ 238 Petr' Svoboda, Mont. .20
☐ 239 Russ Courtnall, Mont. .20
☐ 240 Ryan Walter, Mont. .20
☐ 241 Tommy Albelin, NJer. .20
☐ 242 Doug Brown, NJer. .20
☐ **243 Ken Daneyko, NJer. RC .75**
☐ 244 Mark Johnson, NJer. .20
☐ **245 Randy Velischek, NJer. RC .50**
☐ **246 Brad Dalgarno, NYIs. RC .50**
☐ 247 Mikko Mäkelä, NYIs. .20
☐ **248 Shayne Corson, Mont. RC 2.00**
☐ **249 Marc Bergevin, NYIs. RC .50**
☐ 250 Patrick Flatley, NYIs. .20
☐ 251 Michel Petit, NYRa. (Québ.) .20
☐ 252 Mark Hardy, NYRa. .20
☐ 253 Scott Mellanby, Phil. .20
☐ 254 Keith Acton, Phil. .20
☐ 255 Ken Wregget (G), Phil. .20
☐ **256 Gord Dineen, Pitt. RC .50**
☐ 257 Dave Hannan, Pitt. (Toro.) .20
☐ 258 Mario Gosselin (G), LosA. .20
☐ 259 Randy Moller, Québ. (NYRa.) .20
☐ 260 Mario Marois, Québ. .20
☐ 261 Robert Picard, Québ. .20
☐ **262 Marc Fortier, Québ. RC .50**
☐ **263 Ron Tugnutt (G), Québ. RC 2.00**
☐ **264 Iiro Järvi, Québ. RC .50**
☐ 265 Paul Gillis, Québ. .20
☐ **266 Mike Hough, Québ. RC .50**
☐ 267 Jim Sandlak, Vanc. .20
☐ 268 Greg Paslawski, Winn. .20
☐ **269 Paul Cavallini, SLou. RC .50**
☐ 270 Gaston Gingras, SLou. .20
☐ 271 Allan Bester (G), Toro. .20
☐ 272 Vincent Damphousse, Toro. .20
☐ **273 Daniel Marois, Toro. RC .50**
☐ 274 Mark Osborne, Toro. .20
☐ 275 Craig Laughlin, Toro. .20
☐ 276 Brad Marsh, Toro. .20
☐ 277 Dan Daoust, Toro. .20
☐ 278 Börje Salming, Detr. .40
☐ 279 Chris Kotsopoulos, Detr. .20
☐ 280 Tony Tanti, Vanc. .20
☐ 281 Barry Pederson, Vanc. .20
☐ 282 Rich Sutter, Vanc. .20
☐ 283 Stan Smyl, Vanc. .20
☐ 284 Doug Lidster, Vanc. .20
☐ 285 Steve Weeks (G), Vanc. .20
☐ 286 Harold Snepsts, Vanc. .20
☐ **287 Brian Bradley, Vanc. RC .75**
☐ 288 Larry Melnyk, Vanc. .20
☐ 289 Bob Gould, Wash. (Bost.) .20
☐ 290 Thomas Steen, Winn. .20
☐ 291 Randy Carlyle, Winn. .20
☐ **292 Hannu Järvenpää, Winn. RC .50**
☐ 293 Iain Duncan, Winn. .20
☐ 294 Doug Smail, Winn. .20
☐ 295 Jim Kyte, Pitt. .20
☐ 296 Daniel Berthiaume (G), Winn. .20
☐ 297 Peter Taglianetti, Winn. .20
☐ 298 Bruins .20
☐ 299 Sabres .20
☐ 300 Flames .20
☐ 301 Blackhawks .20
☐ 302 Red Wings .20
☐ 303 Oilers .20
☐ 304 Whalers .20
☐ 305 Kings .20
☐ 306 North Stars .20
☐ 307 Canadiens .20
☐ 308 Devils .20
☐ 309 Islanders .20
☐ 310 Rangers .20
☐ 311 Flyers .20
☐ 312 Penguins (Mario Lemieux) .80
☐ 313 Nordiques (Joe Sakic) .40
☐ 314 Blues .20
☐ 315 Maple Leafs .20
☐ 316 Canucks .20
☐ 317 Capitals .20
☐ 318 Jets .20
☐ 319 Mario Lemieux, Pitt. [Award Winner] .80
☐ 320 Wayne Gretzky, LosA. [Award Winner] 1.00
☐ 321 Brian Leetch, NYRa. [Award Winner] .80
☐ 322 Patrick Roy (G), Mont. [Award Winner] .60
☐ 323 Chris Chelios, Mont. [Award Winner] .30
☐ 324 Joe Mullen, Calg. [Award Winner] .20
☐ 325 Wayne Gretzky, LosA. [Highlight] 1.00
☐ 326 Brian Leetch, NYRa. [Highlight] [Photo is David Shaw] .60
☐ 327 Mario Lemieux, Pitt. [Highlight] .80
☐ 328 Esa Tikkanen, Edmo. [Highlight] .20
☐ 329 Flames .20
☐ 330 Checklist .20

TOPPS STICKER INSERTS

Insert Set (33 stickers): 14.00
Common Team Sticker (13-33): .20

Topps **NM-MT**
☐ 1 Chris Chelios, Mont. .70
☐ 2 Gerard Gallant, Detr. .20
☐ 3 Mario Lemieux, Pitt. 4.00
☐ 4 Al MacInnis, Calg. .50
☐ 5 Joe Mullen, Calg. .20
☐ 6 Patrick Roy (G), Mont. 3.00
☐ 7 Raymond Bourque, Bost. 1.50
☐ 8 Rob (Jr.) Brown, Pitt. .20
☐ 9 Geoff Courtnall, Wash. .20
☐ 10 Steve Duchesne, LosA. .20
☐ 11 Wayne Gretzky, LosA. 5.00
☐ 12 Mike Vernon (G), Calg. .50
☐ 13 Toronto Maple Leafs ☐ 14 Buffalo Sabres
☐ 15 Detroit Red Wings ☐ 16 Pittsburgh Penguins
☐ 17 New York Rangers ☐ 18 Calgary Flames
☐ 19 Winnpeg Jets ☐ 20 Québec Nordiques
☐ 21 Chicago Blackhawks ☐ 22 Los Angeles Kings
☐ 23 Montréal Canadiens ☐ 24 Vancouver Canucks
☐ 25 Hartford Whalers ☐ 26 Philadelphia Flyers
☐ 27 New Jersey Devils ☐ 28 St. Louis Blues
☐ 29 Minn. North Stars ☐ 30 Washington Capitals
☐ 31 Boston Bruins ☐ 32 New York Islanders
☐ 33 Edmonton Oilers

OPC / TOPPS BOX BOTTOMS

These four-card panels were found on the bottoms of O-Pee-Chee and Topps wax boxes. The most expensive cut-out singles are Wayne Gretzky (OPC $4, Topps $3) and Mario Lemieux (OPC $3, Topps $2). O-Pee-Chee singles start at 50¢; Topps singles start at 35¢. Panels measure 5" x 7" while cut cards measure 2 1/2" x 3 1/2".

Complete Set (4 panels)	**10.00**	**14.00**
Box Bottoms:	**Topps**	**OPC**
☐☐ A-D Lemieux/ Ridley/ Sandström/ Skriko	3.50	5.00
☐☐ E-H Gretzky/ Hull/ Kerr/ Näslund	4.50	6.50
☐☐ I-L Kurri/ Larmer/ Neely/ Yzerman	2.80	4.00
☐☐ M-P Dineen/ Gagner/ J. Mullen/ P. Turgeon	1.00	1.50

1989 - 90 O-PEE-CHEE STICKERS

Stickers measure 2 1/2" x 3". The most expensive singles are Wayne Gretzky ($2-3), Patrick Roy (G) ($1-2), Joe Sakic ($1-2) and Mario Lemieux ($1-2). All other singles sell between 15¢ and $1.50.

A series of 34 Future Stars and All Stars can be found on the back of selevtive stickers. A 34-card set sells for $5-8.

Complete Set (152 stickers): 25.00
Album: (Lanny McDonald) 4.00
Common Player: .20

Player/ Trophy/ Logo **Player/ Trophy/ Logo**
☐ 1 Action ☐ 2 Action [b/ FS 14]
☐ 3 Action ☐ 4 Action [b/ FS 3]
☐ 5 Al MacInnis [MVP] ☐ 6 Action
☐ 7 Action [b/ FS 15] ☐ 8 Action
☐ 9 Action ☐ 16 Denis Savard
☐ 17 Steve Larmer ☐ 22 Brett Hull
☐ 23 Peter Zezel ☐ 32 R. Bourque [b/ AS 25]
☐ 33 Cam Neely ☐ 46 Mats Näslund
☐ 47 Bo. Smith [b/ AS 30] ☐ 50 Brian Hayward
☐ 51 Stéphane Richer ☐ 56 Chris Chelios
☐ 57 Patrick Roy (G) ☐ 60 B. Pederson [b/ FS 5]
☐ 61 T. Linden [b/ AS 23] ☐ 64 Kirk McLean [b/ FS 13]
☐ 65 P. Reinhart [b/ AS 32] ☐ 70 Petri Skriko
☐ 71 Tony Tanti ☐ 80 Geoff Courtnall
☐ 81 Mike Ridley ☐ 86 Sean Burke
☐ 87 John MacLean ☐ 90 Joe Mullen
☐ 91 McCrimmon [b/ FS 11] ☐ 94 Mike Vernon
☐ 95 Al MacInnis ☐ 100 Gary Suter
☐ 101 Joe Nieuwendyk ☐ 110 Tim Kerr
☐ 111 Ron Hextall ☐ 118 Trottier [b/ FS 6]
☐ 119 Pat LaFontaine ☐ 120 Action
☐ 121 Action ☐ 122 Action
☐ 123 Action ☐ 124 Bannerman [Action]
☐ 125 Action ☐ 126 B. Joyce/ J. Cirella
☐ 127 Action ☐ 128 P. Roy [Action]
☐ 129 Action ☐ 130 Action
☐ 131 Action ☐ 132 Action
☐ 133 Action ☐ 134 Dale Hawerchuk
☐ 135 Andrew McBain ☐ 138 Brent Ashton
☐ 139 Dave Ellett ☐ 144 Thomas Steen
☐ 145 Hannu Järvenpää ☐ 154 Wayne Gretzky
☐ 155 Bernie Nicholls ☐ 168 Gary Leeman
☐ 169 Allan Bester ☐ 172 Ed Olczyk
☐ 173 Tom Fergus ☐ 178 Al Iafrate
☐ 179 Damphousse ☐ 182 Peter Stastny
☐ 183 Paul Gillis ☐ 186 Michel Goulet
☐ 187 Joe Sakic [b/ FS 9] ☐ 192 Iiro Järvi
☐ 193 Jeff R. Brown ☐ 202 Neal Broten
☐ 203 Gagner [b/ FS 8] ☐ 211 B. Hayward / P. Roy
☐ 217 Craig Simpson ☐ 218 Glenn Anderson
☐ 221 Jari Kurri ☐ 222 Jimmy Carson
☐ 227 Mark Messier ☐ 228 Grant Fuhr
☐ 237 Paul Coffey ☐ 238 Mario Lemieux
☐ 243 Brian Mullen ☐ 244 Tomas Sandström
☐ 253 Gerard Gallant ☐ 254 Steve Yzerman
☐ 261 Phil Housley ☐ 262 Pierre Turgeon
☐ 269 Ron Francis ☐ 270 Kevin Dineen

O-Pee-Chee
☐ 10/150 Pang (G)/ Duchesne [/FS]
☐ 11/151 T. Murray/ D. Taylor
☐ 12/152 D. Graham/ S. Kasper
☐ 13/153 Manson/ Krushelnyski
☐ 14/156 Do. Wilson/ Chelios [FS]
☐ 15/157 S. Thomas/ G. Gallant
☐ 18/158 P. MacLean/ M. Lemieux
☐ 19/159 P. Cavallini/ MacInnis
☐ 20/160 C. Ronning/ J. Mullen
☐ 21/161 Gingras/ Roy (G) [/FS]
☐ 24/162 B. Benning/ R. Bourque
☐ 25/163 T. Hrkac/ R. Brown
☐ 26/164 Linseman/ G. Courtnall
☐ 27/165 Wesley/ S. Duchesne
☐ 28/166 R. Burridge/ W. Gretzky
☐ 29/167 Janney/ Vernon (G)
☐ 30/170 A. Moog (G)/ D. Reid
☐ 31/171 Joyce/ Laughlin [/AS]
☐ 34/174 S. Burke (G)/ Osborne
☐ 35/175 Elynuik/ Marsh [/FS]
☐ 36/176 T. Granato/ D. Marois
☐ 37/177 B. Hogue/ D. Daoust
☐ 38/180 Janney/ Kotsopoulos
☐ 39/181 B. Leetch/ D. Laxdal
☐ 40/184 Linden/ J. Jackson [/CL]

- ☐ 41/185 J. Sakic/ Marois [/FS]
- ☐ 42/188 Sidork'cz (G)/ Mason (G)
- ☐ 43/189 D. Volek/ M. Fortier
- ☐ 44/190 S. Young/ R. Picard
- ☐ 45/191 Z. Zalapski/ S. Finn
- ☐ 48/194 Carbonneau/ G.Duchesne
- ☐ 49/195 S. Corson/ R. Moller
- ☐ 52/196 C. Lemieux/ Gartner
- ☐ 53/197 R. Courtnall/Casey (G)
- ☐ 54/198 Svoboda/ Habsch. [/AS]
- ☐ 55/199 Rob'ns'n/ Murph. [/AS]
- ☐ 58/200 B. Gainey/ B. Bellows
- ☐ 59/201 M. McPhee/ Archibald
- ☐ 62/204 Ri. Sutter/ Trophy
- ☐ 63/205 Bradley/ Trophy [/FS]
- ☐ 66/206 Nordmark/ Trophy [/FS]
- ☐ 67/207 S. Bozek/ Trophy [/FS]
- ☐ 68/208 S. Smyl/ M. Lemieux
- ☐ 69/209 D. Lidster/ Gretzky
- ☐ 72/210 G. Butcher/ Roy (G) [/AS]
- ☐ 73/212 L. Melnyk/ C. Chelios
- ☐ 74/213 Kel. Miller/ Carbonneau
- ☐ 75/214 Ciccarelli/ J. Mullen
- ☐ 76/215 S. Stevens/ Leetch[/AS]
- ☐ 77/216 Langway/ T. Kerr [/FS]
- ☐ 78/219 D. Christian/ E. Tikkanen
- ☐ 79/220 S. Leach/ C. Huddy
- ☐ 82/223 Pa. Sundström/ S. Smith
- ☐ 83/224 K. Muller/ K. Lowe
- ☐ 84/225 T. Kurvers/ Ch. Joseph
- ☐ 85/226 Poddubny/ MacTavish
- ☐ 88/229 A. Broten/ C. Muni [/FS]
- ☐ 89/230 Shanah./ Ranford (G)
- ☐ 92/231 L. McDonald/ J. Cullen
- ☐ 93/232 Wamsley (G)/ Zalaps.
- ☐ 96/233 J. Otto/ B. Errey [/FS]
- ☐ 97/234 Ji. Hrdina/ D. Quinn
- ☐ 98/235 Ga.Roberts/ Barrasso (G)
- ☐ 99/236 J. Peplinski/ R. Brown
- ☐ 102/239 Patterson/ C. Wilson [/FS]
- ☐ 103/240 D. Gilmour/ B. Leetch
- ☐ 104/241 M. Bullard/ T. Granato
- ☐ 105/242 PE. Eklund/ J. Patrick
- ☐ 106/245 B. Propp/ G. Lafleur
- ☐ 107/246 Ro.Sutter/V'b'k(G)[/AS]
- ☐ 108/247 R. Tocchet/ B. Federko
- ☐ 109/248 Mrk.Howe/ Stefan (G)
- ☐ 112/249 Mäkelä/ O'Connell [/FS]
- ☐ 113/250 D. Volek/ D. Barr
- ☐ 114/251 G. Nylund/ L. Norwood
- ☐ 115/252 Bre. Sutter/ S. Burr
- ☐ 116/255 Der. King/ C. Ruuttu
- ☐ 117/256 G. Diduck/ R. Vaive
- ☐ 136/257 I. Duncan/ D. Bodger
- ☐ 137/258 Reddick(G)/ Andrey.
- ☐ 140/259 J. Kyte/ R. Sheppard
- ☐ 141/260 D. Smail/ M. Foligno
- ☐ 142/263 P. Elynuik/ R. Sheppard
- ☐ 143/264 R. Carlyle/ S. Young
- ☐ 146/265 Taglian./ D. Babych [/FS]
- ☐ 147/266 Boschman/MacDermid
- ☐ 148/267 L. Robitaille/ M. Liut (G)
- ☐ 149/268 Hrudey (G)/ Tippett

STICKER BACKS

Player[sticker number]	Player [sticker number]
1 G. Hawgood [b/ 67-207]	2 C. Janney [b/ 35-175]
3 Bob Joyce [b/ 4]	4 B. Hogue [b/ 77-216]
5 Jiri Hrdina [b/ 60]	6 Sidorkiewicz [b/ 118]
7 S. Young [b/ 96-233]	8 Sean Burke [b/ 203]
9 David Volek [b/ 187]	10 T. Granato [b/ 10-150]
11 Brian Leetch [b/ 91]	12 G. Murphy [b/ 88-229]
13 John Cullen [b/ 64]	14 Z. Zalapski [b/ 2]
15 Iiro Järvi [b/ 7]	16 Joe Sakic [b/ 41-185]
17 Riendeau [b/ 146-265]	18 D. Marois [b/ 102-239]
19 T. Linden [b/ 112-249]	20 P. Elynuik [b/ 66-206]
21 Bob Essensa [b/ 63-205]	22 Checklist [b/ 40-184]
23 Joe Mullen [b/ 61]	24 M. Lemieux [b/ 55-199]
25 Gerard Gallant [b/ 32]	26 C. Chelios [b/ 54-198]
27 A. MacInnis [b/ 21-161]	28 P. Roy [b/ 14-156]
29 G. Courtnall [b/ 107-246]	30 W. Gretzky [b/ 47]
31 R. Brown [b/ 31-171]	32 S. Duchesne [b/ 65]
33 R. Bourque [b/ 72-210]	34 M. Vernon [b/ 76-215]

1989 - 90 PANINI

Wayne Gretzky sells at $2-3 while Patrick Roy, Joe Sakic, and Mario Lemieux each at $1-2. Other singles sell between 20¢ and $1.50. Stickers measure 1 7/8" x 3".

Complete Set (384 stickers):	**30.00**
Album:	**4.00**
Common Player:	**.20**

Player/ Trophy/ Logo	Player/ Trophy/ Logo
☐ 1 NHL Logo	☐ 2 Road to the Cup
☐ 3 Wayne Presley	☐ 4 Flames vs. Canucks
☐ 5 Kings vs Oilers	☐ 6 Flames vs. Blackhawks
☐ 7 Flames vs. Blackhawks	☐ 8 Bruins vs Sabres
☐ 9 Patrick Roy (G)	☐ 10 Flyers, Penguins
☐ 11 Rick Green	☐ 12 Tim Kerr
☐ 13 Patrick Roy (G)	☐ 14 Canadiens
☐ 15 Action	☐ 16 Patrick Roy (G)
☐ 17 Flames	☐ 18 P. Roy/ B. MacLellan
☐ 19 P.Roy (G)/ Ludwig	☐ 20 Al MacInnis
☐ 21 Flames	☐ 22 Flames
☐ 23 Flames	☐ 24 Flames
☐ 25 Stanley Cup	☐ 26 Flames
☐ 27 Joe Mullen	☐ 28 Doug Gilmour
☐ 29 Joe Nieuwendyk	☐ 30 Gary Suter
☐ 31 Flames	☐ 32 Al MacInnis
☐ 33 Brad McCrimmon	☐ 34 Mike Vernon (G)
☐ 35 Gary Roberts	☐ 36 Colin Patterson
☐ 37 Jim Peplinski	☐ 38 Jamie Macoun
☐ 39 Lanny McDonald	☐ 40 Saddledome
☐ 41 Blackhawks	☐ 42 Darren Pang (G)
☐ 43 Steve Larmer	☐ 44 Dirk Graham
☐ 45 Doug Wilson	☐ 46 Ed Belfour (G)
☐ 47 Dave Manson	☐ 48 Troy Murray
☐ 49 Denis Savard	☐ 50 Steve Thomas
☐ 51 Adam Creighton	☐ 52 Wayne Presley
☐ 53 Trent Yawney	☐ 54 Alain Chevrier (G)
☐ 55 Chicago Stadium	☐ 56 Red Wings
☐ 57 Steve Yzerman	☐ 58 Gerard Gallant
☐ 59 Greg Stefan (G)	☐ 60 Dave Barr
☐ 61 Red Wings	☐ 62 Steve Chiasson
☐ 63 Shawn Burr	☐ 64 Rick Zombo
☐ 65 Glen Hanlon (G)	☐ 66 Jeff Sharples
☐ 67 Joey Kocur	☐ 68 Lee Norwood
☐ 69 Mike O'Connell	☐ 70 Joe Louis Arena
☐ 71 Oilers	☐ 72 Jimmy Carson
☐ 73 Jari Kurri	☐ 74 Mark Messier
☐ 75 Craig Simpson	☐ 76 Keith Acton
☐ 77 Glenn Anderson	☐ 78 Craig MacTavish
☐ 79 Kevin Lowe	☐ 80 Craig Muni
☐ 81 Bill Ranford (G)	☐ 82 Charlie Huddy
☐ 83 J. Steve Smith	☐ 84 Normand Lacombe
☐ 85 Northlands Coliseum	☐ 86 Kings
☐ 87 Wayne Gretzky	☐ 88 Bernie Nicholls
☐ 89 Kelly Hrudey (G)	☐ 90 John Tonelli
☐ 91 Action	☐ 92 Steve Kasper
☐ 93 Steve Duchesne	☐ 94 Mike Krushelnyski
☐ 95 Luc Robitaille	☐ 96 Ron Duguay
☐ 97 Glenn Healy (G)	☐ 98 Dave Taylor
☐ 99 Marty McSorley	☐ 100 Western Forum
☐ 101 North Stars	☐ 102 Kari Takko (G)
☐ 103 Dave Gagner	☐ 104 Mike Gartner
☐ 105 Brian Bellows	☐ 106 Kari Takko
☐ 107 Neal Broten	☐ 108 Larry Murphy
☐ 109 Basil McRae	☐ 110 Perry Berezan
☐ 111 Shawn Chambers	☐ 112 Curt Giles
☐ 113 Stewart Gavin	☐ 114 Jon Casey (G)
☐ 115 Metro. Center	☐ 116 Blues
☐ 117 Brett Hull	☐ 118 Peter Zezel
☐ 119 Tony Hrkac	☐ 120 Vincent Riendeau
☐ 121 Blues vs. Islanders	☐ 122 Cliff Ronning
☐ 123 Gino Cavallini	☐ 124 Brian Benning
☐ 125 Rick Meagher	☐ 126 Steve Tuttle
☐ 127 Paul Cavallini	☐ 128 Tom Tilley
☐ 129 Greg Millen (G)	☐ 130 St. Louis Arena
☐ 131 Maple Leafs	☐ 132 Ed Olczyk
☐ 133 Gary Leeman	☐ 134 Vincent Damphousse
☐ 135 Tom Fergus	☐ 136 Mark Osborne
☐ 137 Daniel Marois	☐ 138 Mark Osborne
☐ 139 Allan Bester (G)	☐ 140 Al Iafrate
☐ 141 Brad Marsh	☐ 142 Luke Richardson
☐ 143 Todd Gill	☐ 144 Wendel Clark
☐ 145 Leaf Gardens	☐ 146 Canucks
☐ 147 Petri Skriko	☐ 148 Trevor Linden
☐ 149 Tony Tanti	☐ 150 Steve Weeks (G)
☐ 151 Tony Tanti	☐ 152 Brian Bradley
☐ 153 Barry Pederson	☐ 154 Greg A. Adams
☐ 155 Kirk McLean (G)	☐ 156 Jim Sandlak
☐ 157 Rich Sutter	☐ 158 Garth Butcher
☐ 159 Stan Smyl	☐ 160 Pacific Coliseum
☐ 161 Jets	☐ 162 Dale Hawerchuk
☐ 163 Thomas Steen	☐ 164 Brent Ashton
☐ 165 Pat Elynuik	☐ 166 Jets, Islanders
☐ 167 Dave Ellett	☐ 168 Randy Carlyle
☐ 169 Laurie Boschman	☐ 170 Iain Duncan
☐ 171 Doug Smail	☐ 172 Teppo Numminen
☐ 173 Bob Essensa (G)	☐ 174 Peter Taglianetti
☐ 175 Winnipeg Arena	☐ 176 Steve Duchesne
☐ 177 Luc Robitaille	☐ 178 Mike Vernon (G)
☐ 179 Wayne Gretzky	☐ 180 Kevin Lowe
☐ 181 Jari Kurri	☐ 182 Cam Neely
☐ 183 Paul Coffey	☐ 184 Mario Lemieux
☐ 185 Sean Burke (G)	☐ 186 Rob (Jr.) Brown
☐ 187 Raymond Bourque	☐ 188 Bruins
☐ 189 Greg Hawgood	☐ 190 Ken Linseman
☐ 191 Andy Moog (G)	☐ 192 Cam Neely
☐ 193 Bruins vs. Flyers	☐ 194 Andy Brickley
☐ 195 Réjean Lemelin	☐ 196 Bob Carpenter
☐ 197 Randy Burridge	☐ 198 Craig Janney
☐ 199 Bob Joyce	☐ 200 Glen Wesley
☐ 201 Raymond Bourque	☐ 202 Boston Garden
☐ 203 Sabres	☐ 204 Pierre Turgeon
☐ 205 Phil Housley	☐ 206 Rick Vaive
☐ 207 Christian Ruuttu	☐ 208 Flyers vs. Sabres
☐ 209 Doug Bodger	☐ 210 Mike Foligno
☐ 211 Ray Sheppard	☐ 212 John Tucker
☐ 213 Scott Arniel	☐ 214 Daren Puppa (G)
☐ 215 Dave Andreychuk	☐ 216 Uwe Krupp
☐ 217 Auditorium	☐ 218 Whalers
☐ 219 Kevin Dineen	☐ 220 P. Sidorkiewicz (G)
☐ 221 Ron Francis	☐ 222 Ray Ferraro
☐ 223 Dean Evason	☐ 224 Scott A. Young
☐ 225 Dave Babych	☐ 226 Dave Tippett
☐ 227 Paul MacDermid	☐ 228 Ulf Samuelsson
☐ 229 Sylvain Côté	☐ 230 Jody Hull
☐ 231 Don Maloney	☐ 232 Hartford Civic Center
☐ 233 Canadiens	☐ 234 Mats Näslund
☐ 235 Patrick Roy (G)	☐ 236 Bobby Smith
☐ 237 Chris Chelios	☐ 238 Chris Chelios
☐ 239 Stéphane Richer	☐ 240 Claude Lemieux
☐ 241 Guy Carbonneau	☐ 242 Shayne Corson
☐ 243 Mike McPhee	☐ 244 Petr Svoboda
☐ 245 Larry Robinson	☐ 246 Brian Hayward
☐ 247 Montréal Forum	☐ 248 Devils
☐ 249 John MacLean	☐ 250 Patrik Sundström
☐ 251 Kirk Muller	☐ 252 Tom Kurvers
☐ 253 Pat Conacher	☐ 254 Aaron Broten
☐ 255 Brendan Shanahan	☐ 256 Sean Burke (G)
☐ 257 Tommy Albelin	☐ 258 Ken Daneyko
☐ 259 Randy Velischek	☐ 260 Mark Johnson
☐ 261 Jim Korn	☐ 262 Byrne Arena
☐ 263 Islanders	☐ 264 Pat LaFontaine
☐ 265 Mark Fitzpatrick	☐ 266 Brent Sutter
☐ 267 David Volek	☐ 268 Flatley / Mäkelä
☐ 269 Bryan Trottier	☐ 270 Mikko Mäkelä
☐ 271 Derek King	☐ 272 Patrick Flatley
☐ 273 Jeff Norton	☐ 274 Gerald Diduck
☐ 275 Alan Kerr	☐ 276 Jeff Hackett
☐ 277 Nassau Coliseum	☐ 278 Rangers
☐ 279 Brian Leetch	☐ 280 Carey Wilson
☐ 281 Tomas Sandström	☐ 282 J. Vanbiesbrouck (G)
☐ 283 Michel Petit	☐ 284 Bob Froese (G)
☐ 285 Tony Granato	☐ 286 Brian Mullen
☐ 287 Kelly Kisio	☐ 288 Ulf Dahlén
☐ 289 James Patrick	☐ 290 John Ogrodnick
☐ 291 Michel Petit	☐ 292 Madison Garden
☐ 293 Flyers	☐ 294 Tim Kerr
☐ 295 Rick Tocchet	☐ 296 Pelle Eklund
☐ 297 Terry Carkner	☐ 298 Flyers vs. Canadiens
☐ 299 Ron Sutter	☐ 300 Mark Howe
☐ 301 Keith Acton	☐ 302 Ron Hextall (G)
☐ 303 Gord Murphy	☐ 304 Derrick Smith
☐ 305 Dave Poulin	☐ 306 Brian Propp
☐ 307 The Spectrum	☐ 308 Penguins
☐ 309 Mario Lemieux	☐ 310 Rob (Jr.) Brown
☐ 311 Paul Coffey	☐ 312 Tom Barrasso
☐ 313 Penguins Action	☐ 314 Dan Quinn
☐ 315 Bob Errey	☐ 316 John Cullen
☐ 317 Phil Bourque	☐ 318 Zarley Zalapski
☐ 319 Troy Loney	☐ 320 Jim Johnson
☐ 321 Kevin Stevens	☐ 322 Civic Arena
☐ 323 Nordiques	☐ 324 Peter Stastny
☐ 325 Jeff R. Brown	☐ 326 Michel Goulet
☐ 327 Joe Sakic	☐ 328 Mario Marois
☐ 329 Iiro Järvi	☐ 330 Paul Gillis
☐ 331 Randy Moller	☐ 332 Ron Tugnutt (G)
☐ 333 Robert Picard	☐ 334 Curtis Leschyshyn
☐ 335 Marc Fortier	☐ 336 Mario Marois
☐ 337 Le Colise	☐ 338 Capitals
☐ 339 Mike Ridley	☐ 340 Geoff Courtnall
☐ 341 Scott Stevens	☐ 342 Dino Ciccarelli
☐ 343 Tim Hunter	☐ 344 Bob Mason (G)
☐ 345 Dave Christian	☐ 346 Dale Hunter
☐ 347 Kevin Hatcher	☐ 348 Kelly Miller
☐ 349 Stephen Leach	☐ 350 Rod Langway
☐ 351 Bob Rouse	☐ 352 Capital Centre
☐ 353 Flames	☐ 354 Oilers
☐ 355 Jets	☐ 356 Maple Leafs
☐ 357 Sabres	☐ 358 Canadiens
☐ 359 Nordiques	☐ 360 Devils
☐ 361 Bruins	☐ 362 Whalers
☐ 363 Canucks	☐ 364 North Stars
☐ 365 Kings	☐ 366 Blues
☐ 367 Blackhawks	☐ 368 Red Wings
☐ 369 Penguins	☐ 370 Capitals
☐ 371 Flyers	☐ 372 Rangers
☐ 373 Islanders	☐ 374 Wayne Gretzky
☐ 375 Mario Lemieux	☐ 376 Roy / Hayward
☐ 377 Tim Kerr	☐ 378 Brian Leetch
☐ 379 Chris Chelios	☐ 380 Joe Mullen
☐ 381 Guy Carbonneau	☐ 382 Bryan Trottier
☐ 383 Patrick Roy (G)	☐ 384 Joe Mullen

1989 - 90 PROCARDS TEAM SETS

These cards have a yellow border.Singles start at 35¢; regional stars start at $1.00. Each card measures the standard 2 1/2" x 3 1/2".

Complete AHL Set (360 cards):	**90.00**
Complete IHL Set (208 cards):	**60.00**
Common Player:	**.35**

NEW HAVEN NIGHTHAWKS - AHL

Team Set (27 cards): **7.00**

Player	Player
☐ 1 Nighthawks Checklist	☐ 2 François Breault
☐ 3 Paul Kelly	☐ 4 Phil Skyes
☐ 5 Ron Scott (G)	☐ 6 Micah Aivazoff
☐ 7 Sylvain Couturier	☐ 8 Carl Repp (G)
☐ 9 Murray Brumwell	☐ 10 Todd Elik
☐ 11 Darwin Bozek	☐ 12 Eric Germain
☐ 13 Scott Young	☐ 14 Chris Kontos
☐ 15 Scot Bjugstad	☐ 16 Eric Ricard
☐ 17 Ross Wilson	☐ 18 Graham Stanley
☐ 19 Chris Panek	☐ 20 Nick Fotiu
☐ 21 René Chapdelaine	☐ 22 Gordie Walker
☐ 23 Tim Bothwell	☐ 24 Kevin MacDonald
☐ 25 Darryl Williams	☐ 26 John Van Kessel
☐ 27 Paul Brydges	

MONCTON HAWKS - AHL

Bob Essensa is the most expensive player at $2-3.

Team Set (25 cards): **8.00**

Player	Player
☐ 28 Hawks Checklist	☐ 29 Guy Larose
☐ 30 Danton Cole	☐ 31 Brent Hughes
☐ 32 Larry Bernard	☐ 33 Stu Kulak
☐ 34 Bob Essensa (G)	☐ 35 Luciano Borsato
☐ 36 Guy Gosselin	☐ 37 Todd Flichel
☐ 38 Brian Hunt	☐ 39 Neil Meadmore
☐ 40 Matt Hervey	☐ 41 Dallas Eakins
☐ 42 Brad Jones	☐ 43 Chris Norton
☐ 44 Bryan Marchment	☐ 45 Rick Tabaracci (G)
☐ 46 Grant Richison	☐ 47 Brian McReynolds
☐ 48 Tony Joseph	☐ 49 D. Farish, Coach/G.M.
☐ 50 Rob Snitzer, Trainer	☐ 51 Ron Wilson
☐ 52 Scott Schneider	

MAINE MARINERS - AHL

Don Sweeney is the most expensive player at $2-3.

Team Set (24 cards): **8.00**

Player	Player
☐ 53 Mariners Checklist	☐ 54 Dave Buda
☐ 55 Paul Beraldo	☐ 56 Lou Crawford
☐ 57 Mark Montanari	☐ 58 Don Sweeney
☐ 59 Jeff Sirkka	☐ 60 Norm Foster (G)
☐ 61 Greg Poss	☐ 62 Gord Cruickshank
☐ 63 Bruce Shoebottom	☐ 64 Mark Ziliotto
☐ 65 Ron Hoover	☐ 66 Scott Harlow
☐ 67 Mike Millar	☐ 68 Bob Beers
☐ 69 Ray Neufeld	☐ 70 Graeme Townshend

☐ 71 Billy O'Dwyer	☐ 72 Frank Caprice (G)
☐ 73 John Blum	☐ 74 Jerry Foster, Trainer
☐ 75 Sutherland/Bowness	☐ 76 Scott Drevitch

BALTIMORE SKIPJACKS - AHL

Bob Mason is the most expensive player at $2-3.

Team Set (27 cards): 8.00

Player	Player
☐ 77 Skipjacks Checklist	☐ 78 John Purves
☐ 79 Jeff Greenlaw	☐ 80 Tim Taylor
☐ 81 Alfie Turcotte	☐ 82 D. Redmond, Trainer
☐ 83 Chris Felix	☐ 84 Bobby Babcock
☐ 85 Steve Maltais	☐ 86 Mike Richard
☐ 87 Skipjacks Photo	☐ 88 Bob Mason (G)
☐ 89 Mark Ferner	☐ 90 Steve Seftel
☐ 91 Brian Tutt	☐ 92 Terry Murray, Coach
☐ 93 Jim Hrivnak (G)	☐ 94 Tyler Larter
☐ 95 Tim Bergland	☐ 96 Dennis Smith
☐ 97 Steve Hollett	☐ 98 Shawn Simpson (G)
☐ 99 Robin Bawa	☐ 100 John Druce
☐ 101 Kent Paynter	☐ 102 Alain Côté
☐ 103 J.P. Mattingly, Trainer	

NEWMARKET SAINTS - AHL

Tie Domi is the most expensive player at $3-4.

Team Set (25 cards): 8.00

Player	Player
☐ 104 Saints Checklist	☐ 105 Dean Anderson (G)
☐ 106 Wes Jarvis	☐ 107 Brian Blad
☐ 108 Derek Laxdal	☐ 109 Kent Hulst
☐ 110 Tim Bernhardt (G)	☐ 111 Brian Hoard
☐ 112 Bill Root	☐ 113 Paul Gardner, Coach
☐ 114 Tim Armstrong	☐ 115 Sean McKenna
☐ 116 Tim Bean	☐ 117 Alan Hepple
☐ 118 Greg Hotham	☐ 119 Scott Pearson
☐ 120 Peter Ihnacak	☐ 121 John McIntyre
☐ 122 Paul Gagné	☐ 123 Darren Veitch
☐ 124 Mark LaForest (G)	☐ 125 Doug Shedden
☐ 126 Bobby Reynolds	☐ 127 Tie Domi
☐ 128 Ken Hammond	

CAPE BRETON OILERS - AHL

Shaun Van Allen is the most expensive player at $2-3.

Team Set (23 cards): 8.00

Player	Player
☐ 129 Oilers Checklist	☐ 130 Wade Campbell
☐ 131 Chris Joseph	☐ 132 Mario Barbe
☐ 133 Mike Greenlay (G)	☐ 134 Peter Soberlak
☐ 135 Bruce Bell	☐ 136 Dan Currie
☐ 137 Fabian Joseph	☐ 138 Stan Drulia
☐ 139 Todd Charlesworth	☐ 140 Norm Maciver
☐ 141 David Haas	☐ 142 Tim Tisdale
☐ 143 Eldon Reddick (G)	☐ 144 Alex. Tyjnych (G)
☐ 145 Kim Issel	☐ 146 Corey Foster
☐ 147 Tomas Kapusta	☐ 148 Brian Wilks
☐ 149 John LeBlanc	☐ 150 Ivan Matulik
☐ 151 Shaun Van Allen	

HALIFAX CITADELS - AHL

Claude Lapointe is the most expensive player at $2-3.

Team Set (27 cards): 8.00

Player	Player
☐ 152 Citadels Checklist	☐ 153 Scott Gordon (G)
☐ 154 Trevor Steinburg	☐ 155 Miroslav Ihnacak
☐ 156 Jamie Baker	☐ 157 R. Ftorek, Coach
☐ 158 C.McQuaid/B.Smith	☐ 159 Mario Brunetta (G)
☐ 160 Jean-Marc Routhier	☐ 161 David Espe
☐ 162 Ken Quinney	☐ 163 Mark Vermette
☐ 164 Dean Hopkins	☐ 165 Claude Julien
☐ 166 Claude Lapointe	☐ 167 Stéphane Morin
☐ 168 Bryan Fogarty	☐ 169 Dave Pichette
☐ 170 Kevin Kaminski	☐ 171 Brent Severyn
☐ 172 Max Middendorf	☐ 173 Jean-Marc Richard
☐ 174 Gerald Bzdel	☐ 175 Ladislav Tresl
☐ 176 Jaroslav Sevcik	☐ 177 Greg Smyth
☐ 178 Joel Baillargeon	

SHERBROOKE CANADIENS - AHL

Mathieu Schneider and Andrew Cassels are the most expensive players at $2-3.

Team Set (23 cards): 10.00

Player	Player
☐ 179 Canadiens Checklist	☐ 180 André Racicot (G)
☐ 181 J.C. Bergeron (G)	☐ 182 Jim Nesich
☐ 183 Todd Richards	☐ 184 François Gravel (G)
☐ 185 Lyle Odelein	☐ 186 Benoît Brunet
☐ 187 Mario Roberge	☐ 188 Marc Saumier
☐ 189 Normand Desjardins	☐ 190 Dan Woodley
☐ 191 Andrew Cassels	☐ 192 Roy Mitchell
☐ 193 Guy Darveau	☐ 194 Ed Cristofoli
☐ 195 Stéph. JG. Richer	☐ 196 J. Parent, Therapist
☐ 197 Luc Gauthier	☐ 198 John Ferguson
☐ 199 Mathieu Schneider	☐ 200 Serge Roberge
☐ 201 Jean Hamel, Coach	

UTICA DEVILS - AHL

Craig Billington is the most expensive player at $2-3.

Team Set (27 cards): 8.00

Player	Player
☐ 202 Devils Checklist	☐ 203 Jason Simon
☐ 204 Jeff Madill	☐ 205 Kevin Todd
☐ 206 Myles O'Connor	☐ 207 Jon Morris
☐ 208 Hoffmeyer, A.Coach	☐ 209 Paul Ysebaert
☐ 210 Steve Rooney	☐ 211 Claude Vilgrain
☐ 212 Paul Guay	☐ 213 Rollie Melanson (G)
☐ 214 Tom McVie, Coach	☐ 215 Dave Marcinyshyn
☐ 216 Perry Anderson	☐ 217 Jamie Huscroft
☐ 218 Bob Woods	☐ 219 Pat Conacher
☐ 220 Jean-Marc Lanthier	☐ 221 Chris Kiene
☐ 222 Eric Weinrich	☐ 223 Fitzgerald, A Trainer
☐ 224 Craig Billington (G)	☐ 225 Jim Thomson
☐ 226 Tim Budy	☐ 227 Marc Laniel
☐ 228 Robert Bill, Trainer	

SPRINGFIELD INDIANS - AHL

Jeff Hackett is the most expensive player at $2-3.

Team Set (26 cards): 12.00

Player	Player
☐ 229 Indians Checklist	☐ 230 Mike Walsh
☐ 231 Dale Henry	☐ 232 Bill Berg
☐ 233 Hank Lammens	☐ 234 Rob DiMaio
☐ 235 Shawn Byram	☐ 236 Jeff Hackett (G)
☐ 237 Wayne McBean	☐ 238 Tim Hanley
☐ 239 Tom Fitzgerald	☐ 240 Mike Stevens
☐ 241 George Maneluk (G)	☐ 242 Brian Ewen
☐ 243 Dale Kushner	☐ 244 Shawn Evans
☐ 245 Rod Dallman	☐ 246 Mike Kelfer
☐ 247 Sean Lebrun	☐ 248 Kerry Clark
☐ 249 Ed Tyburski, Trainer	☐ 250 Derek King
☐ 251 Marc Bergevin	☐ 252 Jeff Finley
☐ 253 Jim Roberts, Coach	☐ 254 Chris Pryor

ROCHESTER AMERICANS - AHL

Donald Audette is the most expensive player at $4-6.

Team Set (28 cards): 10.00

Player	Player
☐ 255 Americans Checklist	☐ 256 Rob Ray
☐ 257 Ken Priestlay	☐ 258 Darcy Wakaluk (G)
☐ 259 Richie Dunn	☐ 260 Ken Sutton
☐ 261 T. Martin, A Coach	☐ 262 Scott Metcalfe
☐ 263 Joel Savage	☐ 264 Brad Miller
☐ 265 Donald Audette	☐ 266 Van Boxmeer, Coach
☐ 267 Mascot The Moose	☐ 268 Brian Ford (G)
☐ 269 Darcy Loewen	☐ 270 Bob Halkidis
☐ 271 Steve Ludzik	☐ 272 Steve Smith
☐ 273 François Guay	☐ 274 Mike Donnelly
☐ 275 Darrin Shannon	☐ 276 Jody Gage
☐ 277 Dave Baseggio	☐ 278 Bob Corkum
☐ 279 Jim Jackson	☐ 280 Don McSween
☐ 281 Jim Hofford	☐ 282 Scott McCrory

BINGHAMTON WHALERS - AHL

Team Set (23 cards): 7.00

Player	Player
☐ 283 Whalers Checklist	☐ 284 Raymond Saumier
☐ 285 Mike Berger	☐ 286 Corey Beaulieu
☐ 287 D. McKay, Coach	☐ 288 Blair Atcheynum
☐ 289 Al Tuer	☐ 290 Chris Lindberg
☐ 291 Daryl Reaugh (G)	☐ 292 James Black
☐ 293 Vern Smith	☐ 294 Todd Krygier
☐ 295 Bob Bodak	☐ 296 Jon Smith, Trainer
☐ 297 Michel Picard	☐ 298 Jim Culhane
☐ 299 Brian Chapman	☐ 300 Jim Ennis
☐ 301 J. Caron, Coach	☐ 302 Jim McKenzie
☐ 303 Kay Whitmore (G)	☐ 304 Terry Yake
☐ 305 Mike Moller	

ADIRONDACK RED WINGS - AHL

Sheldon Kennedy is the most expensive player at $2-3.

Team Set (24 cards): 8.00

Player	Player
☐ 306 Wings Checklist	☐ 307 Bob Wilkie
☐ 308 Chris McRae	☐ 309 Chris Kotsopoulos
☐ 310 Sumner, A Trainer	☐ 311 T. Abbott, A Trainer
☐ 312 Gordon Kruppke	☐ 313 Mike Gober
☐ 314 Al Conroy	☐ 315 Sam St. Laurent (G)
☐ 316 Dave Casey, Trainer	☐ 317 Yves Racine
☐ 318 Randy McKay	☐ 319 Dale Krentz
☐ 320 Sheldon Kennedy	☐ 321 B. Melrose, Coach
☐ 322 Dennis Holland	☐ 323 Glenn Merkosky
☐ 324 Murray Eaves	☐ 325 Mark Reimer (G)
☐ 326 Tim Cheveldae (G)	☐ 327 Peter Dineen
☐ 328 Dean Morton	☐ 329 Derek Mayer

HERSHEY BEARS - AHL

Team Set (31 cards): 9.00

Player	Player
☐ 330 Bears Checklist	☐ 331 Don Biggs
☐ 332 Scott Sandelin	☐ 333 Shaun Sabol
☐ 334 Murray Baron	☐ 335 David Fenyves
☐ 336 Glen Seabrooke	☐ 337 Mark Freer
☐ 338 Ray Allison	☐ 339 Chris Jensen
☐ 340 Ross Fitzpatrick	☐ 341 Brian Dobbin
☐ 342 Darren Rumble	☐ 343 Mike Stothers
☐ 344 Jiri Latal	☐ 345 Don Nachbaur
☐ 346 John Stevens	☐ 347 Steven Fletcher
☐ 348 Kent Hawley	☐ 349 Bill Armstrong
☐ 350 Bruce Hoffort (G)	☐ 351 Gordon Paddock
☐ 352 Marc D'Amour (G)	☐ 353 Tim Tookey
☐ 354 Reid Simpson	☐ 355 Mark Bassen
☐ 356 Rocky Trottier	☐ 357 H. Bricker, A Trainer
☐ 358 Dan Stuck, Trainer	☐ 359 Al Hill, A. Coach
☐ 360 Kevin McCarthy, Coach	

PEORIA RIVERMEN - IHL

Curtis Joseph is the most expensive player at $12-18.

Team Set (23 cards): 30.00

Player	Player
☐ 1 Rivermen Checklist	☐ 2 Darwin McPherson
☐ 3 Pat Jablonski (G)	☐ 4 Scott Paluch
☐ 5 Guy Hebert (G), Error	☐ 6 Richard Pion
☐ 7 Curtis Joseph (G)	☐ 8 Robert Dirk
☐ 9 Darin Smith	☐ 10 Terry MacLean
☐ 11 Kevin Miehm	☐ 12 Toby Ducolon
☐ 13 Mike Wolak	☐ 14 Adrien Plavsic
☐ 15 Dave Thomlinson	☐ 16 Jim Vesey
☐ 17 Michel Mongeau	☐ 18 Tom Nash, Trainer
☐ 19 David O'Brien	☐ 20 Dominic Lavoie
☐ 21 Keith Osborne	☐ 22 Rob Robinson
☐ 23 Wayne Thomas, Coach	

FLINT SPIRITS - IHL

Mike Richter is the most expensive player at $10-15. Rob Zamuner sells at $2-3.

Team Set (25 cards): 20.00

Player	Player
☐ 24 Spirits Checklist	☐ 25 Jason Lafrenière
☐ 26 Rick Knickle (G)	☐ 27 Jerry Tarrant
☐ 28 Paul Broten	☐ 29 Kevin Miller
☐ 30 James Latos	☐ 31 Daniel Lacroix
☐ 32 Dennis Vial	☐ 33 Denis Larocque
☐ 34 Mike Golden	☐ 35 Mike Hurlbut
☐ 36 Scott Brower (G)	☐ 37 Lee Giffin
☐ 38 Jeff Bloemberg	☐ 39 Simon Wheeldon
☐ 40 Rob Zamuner	☐ 41 Joe Paterson
☐ 42 Barry Chyzowski	☐ 43 Peter Laviolette
☐ 44 Corey Millen	☐ 45 Darren Lowe
☐ 46 Peter Florentino	☐ 47 Soren True
☐ 48 Mike Richter (G)	

INDIANAPOLIS ICE - IHL

Darryl Sutter is the most expensive card at $2-3.

Team Set (25 cards): 8.00

Player	Player
☐ 49 Ice Checklist	☐ 50 Sean Williams
☐ 51 Bruce Cassidy	☐ 52 Mark Kurzawski
☐ 53 Bob Bassen	☐ 54 Marty Nanne
☐ 55 Jari Torkki	☐ 56 Ryan McGill
☐ 57 Mike Peluso	☐ 58 Darryl Sutter, Coach
☐ 59 Dan Vincelette	☐ 60 Lonnie Loach
☐ 61 Mike Rucinski	☐ 62 Jim Playfair
☐ 63 Everett Sanipass	☐ 64 Dale Marquette
☐ 65 Gary Moscaluk	☐ 66 Mario Doyon
☐ 67 Ray Leblanc (G)	☐ 68 Mike Eagles
☐ 69 Warren Rychel	☐ 70 Jim Johannson
☐ 71 Cam Russell	☐ 72 Michael McNeill
☐ 73 Jim Waite (G)	

KALAMAZOO WINGS - IHL

Team Set (25 cards): 8.00

Player	Player
☐ 74 Wings Checklist	☐ 75 Kevin Schamehorn
☐ 76 Kevin Evans	☐ 77 D'Arcy Norton
☐ 78 Scott Robinson	☐ 79 Larry PePalma
☐ 80 Ed Courtenay	☐ 81 Rob Zettler
☐ 82 Dusan Pasek	☐ 83 Gary Emmons
☐ 84 Peter Lappin	☐ 85 Mario Thyer
☐ 86 Mike McHugh	☐ 87 Randy Smith
☐ 88 Link Gaetz	☐ 89 Ken Hodge
☐ 90 Pat MacLeod	☐ 91 Neil Wilkinson
☐ 92 Brett Barnett	☐ 93 Larry Dyck (G)
☐ 94 Dean Kolstad	☐ 95 Jarmo Myllys (G)
☐ 96 Paul Jerrard	☐ 97 Jean-François Quintin
☐ 98 Mitch Messier	

PHOENIX ROADRUNNERS - IHL

Team Set (23 cards): 7.00

Player	Player
☐ 99 Roadrunners CL	☐ 100 Bryant Perrier
☐ 101 Keith Gretzky	☐ 102 Don Martin
☐ 103 David Littman (G)	☐ 104 Mike Decarle
☐ 105 Grant Tkachuk	☐ 106 Richard Novak
☐ 107 Chris Luongo	☐ 108 Bruce Boudreau
☐ 109 Nick Beaulieu	☐ 110 Jeff Lamb
☐ 111 Rob Nichols	☐ 112 Gary Unger, Coach
☐ 113 Larry Floyd	☐ 114 Brent Sapergia
☐ 115 Randy Exelby (G)	☐ 116 Jim McGeough
☐ 117 Tom Karalis	☐ 118 Ken Spangler
☐ 119 Jacques Mailhot	☐ 120 S. Dineen, A Coach
☐ 121 Dave Korol	

FORT WAYNE KOMETS - IHL

Team Set (20 cards): 6.00

Player	Player
☐ 122 Komets Checklist	☐ 123 Colin Chin
☐ 124 Scott Shaunessy	☐ 125 Bob Lakso
☐ 126 Duane Joyce	☐ 127 Joe Stephan
☐ 128 Ron Shudra	☐ 129 Bob Fowler
☐ 130 Steve Bisson	☐ 131 Craig Endean
☐ 132 Carl Mokosak	☐ 133 Carey Lucyk
☐ 134 Craig Channell	☐ 135 Frédéric Chabot (G)
☐ 136 Brian Hannon	☐ 137 Keith Miller
☐ 138 Al Sims, Coach	☐ 139 S. Beauregard (G)
☐ 140 Ron Handy	☐ 141 Byron Lomow

MUSKEGON LUMBERJACKS - IHL

Team Set (23 cards): 6.00

Player	Player
☐ 142 Lumberjacks CL	☐ 143 Jamie Leach
☐ 144 Chris Clifford (G)	☐ 145 Dave Capuano
☐ 146 Jeff Daniels	☐ 147 Dave Goertz
☐ 148 Perry Ganchar	☐ 149 Mitch Wilson
☐ 150 Scott Gruhl	☐ 151 Randy Taylor
☐ 152 Bruce Racine (G)	☐ 153 Dave Michayluk
☐ 154 Richard Zemlak	☐ 155 Brad Aitken
☐ 156 Paul Stanton	☐ 157 Darren Stolk
☐ 158 Jim Paek	☐ 159 Mark Kachowski
☐ 160 Dan Frawley	☐ 161 Mike Mersch
☐ 162 Glenn Mulvenna	☐ 163 Phil Russell, A Coach
☐ 164 Blair MacDonald, Coach	

MILWAUKEE ADMIRALS - IHL

Ron Wilson is the most expensive player at $2-3.

Team Set (25 cards): 8.00

Player	Player
☐ 165 Admirals Checklist	☐ 166 Shaun Clouston
☐ 167 Steve Veilleux	☐ 168 P. George Bakovic
☐ 169 Peter Deboer	☐ 170 Ernie Vargas
☐ 171 Keith Street	☐ 172 Rob Murphy
☐ 173 David Bruce	☐ 174 Shannon Travis
☐ 175 Jeff Rohlicek	☐ 176 Jay Mazur
☐ 177 Kevan Guy	☐ 178 Troy Gamble (G)
☐ 179 Ronnie Stern	☐ 180 Jime Revenberg
☐ 181 José Charbonneau	☐ 182 Ian Kidd
☐ 183 Todd Hawkins	☐ 184 Carl Valimont
☐ 185 Jim Agnew	☐ 186 Curtis Hunt
☐ 187 Dean Cook (G)	☐ 188 Ron Wilson, A Coach
☐ 189 Ron Lapointe, Coach	

SALT LAKE GOLDEN EAGLES - IHL

Stu Grimson is the most expensive player at $2-3.

Team Set (19 cards): 6.00

Player	Player
☐ 190 Eagles Checklist	☐ 191 Brian Glynn
☐ 192 Stéphane Matteau	☐ 193 Rick Barkovich
☐ 194 Jeff Wenaas	☐ 195 Darryl Olsen
☐ 196 Rick Lessard	☐ 197 Kevin Grant
☐ 198 Rich Chernomaz	☐ 199 Stu Grimson
☐ 200 J. Hislop/ B. Francis	☐ 201 Doug Pickell
☐ 202 Chris Biotti	☐ 203 Tim Sweeney
☐ 204 Ken Sabourin	☐ 205 Randy Bucyk
☐ 206 Wayne Cowley (G)	☐ 207 Rick Hayward
☐ 208 Marc Bureau	

1989 - 90 SEMIC ELITSERIEN

The most expensive singles are Mats Sundin at $10-15 and Nicklas Lidström at $3-5. Singles start at 20¢; stars and regional favourites start at $1.00. Stickers measure 2 1/8" x 3".

Complete Set (285 stickers): 45.00

Album: 6.00

Player	Player
☐ 1 AIK	☐ 2 Ake Liljebojorn
☐ 3 Thomas Ostlund	☐ 4 Mats Thelin
☐ 5 Thomas Ahlen	☐ 6 Petri Liimatainen
☐ 7 Roger Ohman	☐ 8 Rikard Franzen
☐ 9 Stefan Claesson	☐ 10 Tommy Hedlund
☐ 11 Stefan Jansson	☐ 12 Peter Gradin
☐ 13 Thomas Gradin	☐ 14 Bo Berglund
☐ 15 Heinze Ehlers	☐ 16 Robert Burakovsky
☐ 17 Alex. Kozjevnikov	☐ 18 Peter Hammarstrom
☐ 19 Anders Gozzi	☐ 20 Thomas Bjuhr
☐ 21 Patric Englund	☐ 22 O. Nilsson
☐ 23 Mats Lindberg	☐ 24 Peter Johansson
☐ 25 Patric Kjellberg	☐ 26 Brynas IF
☐ 27 Lars Eriksson	☐ 28 Michael Sundlov

☐ 29 Per Djoos	☐ 30 Tommy Sjodin
☐ 31 Nikolai Davydkin	☐ 32 Niklas Gallstedt
☐ 33 Mikael Lindman	☐ 34 Jan-Erik Stormqvist
☐ 35 Tommy Melkersson	☐ 36 Mikael Enander
☐ 37 Anders Huuss	☐ 38 Anders Carlsson
☐ 39 Willy Lindstrom	☐ 40 Kyosti Karjalainen
☐ 41 Jan Larsson	☐ 42 Patrik Erickson
☐ 43 Joakim Persson	☐ 44 Johan Brummer
☐ 45 Peter Eriksson	☐ 46 Peter Gustafsson
☐ 47 Thomas Olund	☐ 48 Magnus Aberg
☐ 49 Djurgardens IF	☐ 50 Rolf Ridderwall
☐ 51 T. Söderström (G)	☐ 52 Thomas Eriksson
☐ 53 Arto Blomsten	☐ 54 Orvar Stambert
☐ 55 Christian Due-Boje	☐ 56 Kenneth Kennholt
☐ 57 Mats Wallin	☐ 58 Karl-Erik Lilja
☐ 59 Marcus Ragnarsson	☐ 60 Hakan Sodergren
☐ 61 Mikael Johannson	☐ 62 Jens Ohling
☐ 63 Jan Viktorsson	☐ 64 Peter Nilsson
☐ 65 Charles Berglund	☐ 66 Ken Johansson
☐ 67 Johan Garpenlov	☐ 68 Ole Andersson
☐ 69 Anders Jonsson	☐ 70 Bengt Akerblom
☐ 71 Ola Josefsson	☐ 72 Mats Sundin
☐ 73 Farjestads BK	☐ 74 Anders Bergman
☐ 75 Jorgen Ryden	☐ 76 Tommy Samuelsson
☐ 77 Fredrik Olausson	☐ 78 Peter Hasselblad
☐ 79 Jesper Duus	☐ 80 Anders Berglund
☐ 81 Mattias Andersson	☐ 82 Mattias Olsson
☐ 83 Greger Artursson	☐ 84 Jacob Karlsson
☐ 85 Thomas Rundqvist	☐ 86 Staffan Lundh
☐ 87 Jan Ingman	☐ 88 Kjell Dahlin
☐ 89 Bengt Gustafsson	☐ 90 Magnus Roupe
☐ 91 Hakan Loob	☐ 92 Mikael Holmberg
☐ 93 Daniel Rydmark	☐ 94 Lars Karlsson
☐ 95 Peter Ottosson	☐ 96 HV 71
☐ 97 Kenneth Johansson	☐ 98 Claes Heljemo
☐ 99 Lars Ivarsson	☐ 100 Arto Routanen
☐ 101 Fredrik Stillman	☐ 102 Klas Heed
☐ 103 N-G Svensson	☐ 104 Per Gustafsson
☐ 105 Tommy Fritz	☐ 106 Mats Nilsson
☐ 107 Hasse Sjoo	☐ 108 Mats Loov
☐ 109 Ove Thornberg	☐ 110 Eddy Ericsson
☐ 111 Ivan Avdejev	☐ 112 Stefan Persson
☐ 113 Rick Erdall	☐ 114 Stefan Nilsson
☐ 115 Stefan Ornskog	☐ 116 Patrik Ross
☐ 117 Stefan Falk	☐ 118 Claes Roupe
☐ 119 Peter Ekelund	☐ 120 Leksands IF
☐ 121 Peter Aslin	☐ 122 O. Sundstrom
☐ 123 Jonas Leven	☐ 124 Tomas Jonsso
☐ 125 Magnus Svensson	☐ 126 Ricard Persson
☐ 127 Per Lundell	☐ 128 Tomas Nord
☐ 129 Peter Wallin	☐ 130 Orjan Lindmark
☐ 131 Henric Bjorkman	☐ 132 Anders Pettersson
☐ 133 Per-Olaf Carlsson	☐ 134 Tomas Forslund
☐ 135 Niklas Eriksson	☐ 136 Richard Kromm
☐ 137 Jarmo Makitalo	☐ 138 Peter Lundmark
☐ 139 Ronny Reichenberg	☐ 140 Cenneth Soderlund
☐ 141 Jens Nielsen	☐ 142 Marcus Thuresson
☐ 143 Anders Broms	☐ 144 Joakim Backlund
☐ 145 Lulea HF	☐ 146 Robert Skoog
☐ 147 Tomas Javeblad	☐ 148 Lars Modig
☐ 149 J-O Mettavainio	☐ 150 Osmo Soutokorva
☐ 151 Torbjorn Lindberg	☐ 152 Timo Jutila
☐ 153 Roger Akerstrom	☐ 154 Per Ljusterdang
☐ 155 Tomas Lilja	☐ 156 Johan Stromvall
☐ 157 L-G Pettersson	☐ 158 Lars Hurtig
☐ 159 Morgan Samuelsson	☐ 160 Stefan Nilsson
☐ 161 Vesa Kangas	☐ 162 Kari Jaako
☐ 163 Juha Nurmi	☐ 164 Jens Hellgren
☐ 165 Tomas Berglund	☐ 166 Lars Edstrom
☐ 167 Petter Antti	☐ 168 MoDo HK
☐ 169 Fredrik Andersson	☐ 170 Goran Arnmark
☐ 171 Timo Blomqvist	☐ 172 Hakan Stromqvist
☐ 173 Robert Frestadius	☐ 174 Lars Jansson
☐ 175 Hans Lodin	☐ 176 Ove Pettersson
☐ 177 Tony Olofsson	☐ 178 Jorgen Eriksson
☐ 179 Ulf Sandstrom	☐ 180 Michael Hjalm
☐ 181 Urban Nordin	☐ 182 Lars Bystrom
☐ 183 Jens Ohman	☐ 184 Ulf Odmark
☐ 185 Mikael Stahl	☐ 186 Per Nilsson
☐ 187 Ingmar Strom	☐ 188 Kent Lantz
☐ 189 kent Norberg	☐ 190 Patrik Soderholm
☐ 191 Skelleftea HC	☐ 192 Sam Lindstahl
☐ 193 Dick Andersson	☐ 194 Kari Suoraniemi
☐ 195 Robert Larsson	☐ 196 Kari Yli-Maenpaa
☐ 197 Ola Stenlund	☐ 198 Tony Barthelson
☐ 199 Lars Marklund	☐ 200 Glenn Hedman
☐ 201 Dick Burlin	☐ 202 Michael Granstedt
☐ 203 Pekka Jarvela	☐ 204 Hans Hjalmar
☐ 205 Mats Lundstrom	☐ 206 Martin Pettersson
☐ 207 Johnny Forsman	☐ 208 Daniel Petteresson
☐ 209 Niklas Mannberg	☐ 210 Niklas Brannstrom
☐ 211 Jan Johansson	☐ 212 Jorgen Wannstrom
☐ 213 Leif Johansson	☐ 214 Par Mikaelsson
☐ 215 Fredrik Andersson	☐ 216 Sodertalji SK
☐ 217 Reino Sundberg	☐ 218 Jari Luoma
☐ 219 Anders Eldebrink	☐ 220 Mats Kilstrom
☐ 221 Jonas Heed	☐ 222 Hans Pettersson
☐ 223 Jan Bergman	☐ 224 Thomas Carlsson
☐ 225 Stefan Jonsson	☐ 226 Thomas Eklund
☐ 227 Ola Rosander	☐ 228 Bjorn Carlsson
☐ 229 Thomas Sjogren	☐ 230 Thomas Ljungbergh
☐ 231 Stefan Olsson	☐ 232 Reine Landsgren
☐ 233 Anders Frykbo	☐ 234 Conny Jansson
☐ 235 Peter larsson	☐ 236 Tomaz Eriksson
☐ 237 Erik Holmberg	☐ 238 Patrik Lindh
☐ 239 Vasteras IK	☐ 240 Mats Ytter (G)
☐ 241 Par Hellenberg	☐ 242 Jan Eriksson
☐ 243 Peter Popovic	☐ 244 Tore Lindgren
☐ 245 Leif Rohlin	☐ 246 Henrik Andersson
☐ 247 Nicklas Lidström	☐ 248 Jan Karlsson
☐ 249 Peter Jacobsson	☐ 250 Patrik Juhlin
☐ 251 Goran Sjoberg	☐ 252 Fredrik Nilsson
☐ 253 Stefan Hellkvist	☐ 254 Tomas Strandberg
☐ 255 Anders Berglund	☐ 256 Claes Lindblom
☐ 257 Magnus Wallin	☐ 258 Bjorn Akerblom
☐ 259 Joakim Lundholm	☐ 260 Jorgen Holmberg
☐ 261 Ronny Hansen	☐ 262 Misjat Fachrutdinov
☐ 263 Vastra Frolunda HC	☐ 264 Hakan Algotsson
☐ 265 Per Lundbergh	☐ 266 Jan Karlsson
☐ 267 Loacim Esbjors	☐ 268 Leif Carlsson
☐ 269 Stefan Axelsson	☐ 270 Peter Ekroth
☐ 271 Jorgen Palm	☐ 272 Hakan Nordin
☐ 273 Stefan Larsson	☐ 274 Mikael Andersson
☐ 275 Terho Koskela	☐ 276 Patrik Carnback
☐ 277 Serge Boisvert	☐ 278 Arto Sirvio
☐ 279 Peter Berndtsson	☐ 280 Jorgen Pettersson
☐ 281 Niklas Andersson	☐ 282 Peter Gustavsson
☐ 283 Paul Andersson	☐ 284 Mats Graesen
☐ 285 Kent Orrgren	

1989 - 90 7th INNING SKETCH OHL

The most expensive singles are Eric Lindros (card 1 is $8-10; all others are $4-5). Other expensive singles include Keith Primeau ($2-3) and Owen Nolan ($3-4). Other NHL stars sell between 25¢ and $1.50. All other singles sell between 5¢ and $1.50. These cards measure the standard 2 1/2" x 3 1/2".

Complete Set (200 cards): 45.00

Player	Player
☐ 1 Eric Lindros	☐ 2 Jarrod Skalde
☐ 3 Joe Busillo	☐ 4 Dale Craigwell
☐ 5 Clair Cornish	☐ 6 Jean-Paul Davis
☐ 7 Craig Donaldson	☐ 8 Wade Simpson
☐ 9 Mike Craig	☐ 10 Mark Deazeley
☐ 11 Scott Hollis	☐ 12 Brian Grieve
☐ 13 Dave Craievich	☐ 14 Paul O'Hagan
☐ 15 Matt Hoffman	☐ 16 Trevor McIvor
☐ 17 Cory Banika	☐ 18 Kevin Butt (G)
☐ 19 Iain Fraser	☐ 20 Bill Armstrong
☐ 21 Scott Luik	☐ 22 Brent Grieve
☐ 23 Fred Brathwaite (G)	☐ 24 Paul Holden
☐ 25 Trevor Dam	☐ 26 Chris Taylor
☐ 27 Mark Guy	☐ 28 Louie DeBrusk
☐ 29 John Battice	☐ 30 Chris Crombie
☐ 31 Sean Basilio (G)	☐ 32 Aaron Nagy
☐ 33 Greg Ryan	☐ 34 Steve Martell
☐ 35 Scott MacKayj	☐ 36 Dennis Purdie
☐ 37 Steve Boyd	☐ 38 John Tanner (G)
☐ 39 David Anderson	☐ 40 Rick Corriveau
☐ 41 Todd Hlushko	☐ 42 Doug Synishin
☐ 43 Dan LeBlanc	☐ 44 Dave Noseworthy
☐ 45 Karl Taylor	☐ 46 Jeff Hogden
☐ 47 Kelly/ Agnew, A. Co.	☐ 48 W. Maxner, Coach
☐ 49 Brett Seguin	☐ 50 Greg Walters
☐ 51 Chris Snell	☐ 52 Troy Binnie
☐ 53 Joni Lehto	☐ 54 Steve Kluczkowski
☐ 55 Ryan Kuwabara	☐ 56 Chris Simon
☐ 57 Jerrett DeFazio	☐ 58 Robert Sangster
☐ 59 Greg Clancy	☐ 60 Peter Ambroziak
☐ 61 Jeff Ricciardi	☐ 62 John East
☐ 63 Joey McTamney	☐ 64 Dan Poirier
☐ 65 Gairin Smith	☐ 66 Wade Gibson
☐ 67 Checklist (1 - 88)	☐ 68 Andrew Brodie
☐ 69 Craig Wilson	☐ 70 Peter McGlynn (G)
☐ 71 George Dourian (G)	☐ 72 Bob Berg
☐ 73 Richard Fatrola	☐ 74 Craig Fraser
☐ 75 Brent Gretzky	☐ 76 Jake Grimes
☐ 77 Darren McCarty	☐ 78 Ted Miskolczi
☐ 79 Rob Pearson	☐ 80 Gordon Pell
☐ 81 John Porco	☐ 82 Ken Rowbotham
☐ 83 Scott Thornton	☐ 84 Shawn Way
☐ 85 Steve Bancroft	☐ 86 Greg Bignell
☐ 87 Scott Boston	☐ 88 Scott Feasby
☐ 89 Derek Morin	☐ 90 Sean O'Reilly
☐ 91 Jason Skellet	☐ 92 Greg Dreveny
☐ 93 Jeff Fife	☐ 94 Rob Stopar (G)
☐ 95 J.Desrosiers, Trainer	☐ 96 Danny Flynn, Coach
☐ 97 Dr. Vaughan, Owner	☐ 98 Troy Stephens
☐ 99 Dan Brown	☐ 100 Mike Ricci
☐ 101 Brent Pope	☐ 102 Mike Dagenais
☐ 103 Scott Campbell	☐ 104 Jamie Pegg
☐ 105 Joe Hawley	☐ 106 Jason Dawe
☐ 107 Paul Mitton	☐ 108 Mike Tomlinson
☐ 109 David Lorentz	☐ 110 Dale McTavish
☐ 111 Willie McGarvey	☐ 112 Don O'Neill
☐ 113 Mark Myles	☐ 114 Chris Longo
☐ 115 Tom Hopkins	☐ 116 Jassen Cullimore
☐ 117 Geoff Ingram	☐ 118 Twohey/ Bovair,A.Co
☐ 119 Doug Searle	☐ 120 Bryan Gendron
☐ 121 Andrew Verner (G)	☐ 122 Todd Bojcun (G)
☐ 123 Dick Todd, Coach	☐ 124 G. Burnett, Coach
☐ 125 Brad May	☐ 126 David Benn
☐ 127 Brian Mueggler	☐ 128 Todd Coopman
☐ 129 Geoff Rawson	☐ 130 Keith Primeau
☐ 131 Mark Lawrence	☐ 132 Randy Hall, A. C/ GM
☐ 133 Greg Suchan	☐ 134 Ken Ruddick
☐ 135 Jason Winch	☐ 136 Paul Wolanski
☐ 137 D. Scott, Trainer	☐ 138 Steve Udvari (G)
☐ 139 Roch Belley (G)	☐ 140 Donald Pancoe
☐ 141 Bruneau, A.Trainer	☐ 142 Paul Laus
☐ 143 Mike St. John	☐ 144 John Johnson
☐ 145 Greg Allen	☐ 146 Don McConnell
☐ 147 Andy Bezeau	☐ 148 Jeff Walker
☐ 149 John Spoltore	☐ 150 Derek Switzer
☐ 151 Tyler Ertel	☐ 152 Shawn Antoski
☐ 153 Jason Corrigan	☐ 154 Derian Hatcher
☐ 155 John Vary	☐ 156 Jamie Caruso
☐ 157 Trevor Halverson	☐ 158 Robert Deschamps
☐ 159 Jeff Gardiner	☐ 160 Gary Miller
☐ 161 Shayne Antoski,	☐ 162 John Van Kessel
☐ 163 Colin Austin	☐ 164 Tom Purcell
☐ 165 Joel Morin	☐ 166 Tim Favot
☐ 167 Checklist (89 - 176)	☐ 168 Jason Beaton
☐ 169 Chris Ottmann	☐ 170 Mike Matuszek (G)
☐ 171 Rob Fournier (G)	☐ 172 Ron Bertrand (G)
☐ 173 Templeton, Coach	☐ 174 Mascot Casey Jones
☐ 175 Robert Frayn	☐ 176 C. Noel, Asst. Coach
☐ 177 AW: S. Basilio (G)	☐ 178 AW: Chris Longo
☐ 179 AW: Cory Keenan	☐ 180 AW: Owen Nolan
☐ 181 AS: Steven Rice	☐ 182 AS: S. Stevenson
☐ 183 AW: Mike Ricci	☐ 184 AW: Jason Firth
☐ 185 AW: John Slaney	☐ 186 AW: Iain Fraser
☐ 187 AW: Steven Rice	☐ 188 AW: Eric Lindros
☐ 189 AW: Keith Primeau	☐ 190 AW: Mike Ricci
☐ 191 AS: M. Torchia (G)	☐ 192 AS: Mike Torchia (G)
☐ 193 AS: Jarrod Skalde	☐ 194 AS: Paul O'Hagan
☐ 195 Eric Lindros	☐ 196 AS: Eric Lindros
☐ 197 AS: Jeff Fife (G)	☐ 198 AW: Iain Fraser
☐ 199 AS: Bill Armstrong	☐ 200 Checklist (177 - 200)

1989 - 90 SOVIET STARS

The most expensive player is Sergei Fedorov at $5-8. NHL stars sell between $2-4; all other national stars sell between $1-4. Each card measures 4 1/8" x 5 5/8".

Complete Set (24 cards with folder): 30.00

Player	Player
☐ Ilya Byakin	☐ Viacheslav Bykov
☐ Alexander Chernik	☐ Igor Dmitriev, A. Coach
☐ Sergei Fedorov	☐ Viacheslav Fetisov
☐ Alexei Gusarov	☐ Arturs Irbe (G)
☐ Valeri Kamensky	☐ Alexsei Kasatonov
☐ Sviatoslav Khalizov	☐ Yuri Khmylev
☐ Andrei Khomutov	☐ Vladimir Konstantinov
☐ Vladimir Krutov	☐ Dmitri Kvartalnov
☐ Igor Larionov	☐ Sergei Makarov
☐ Vladimir Mishkin (G)	☐ Sergei Mylnikov (G)
☐ Sergei Nemchinov	☐ Valeri Shiriaev
☐ Victor Tikhonov, Coach	☐ Sergei Yashin

1990 7TH INNING SKETCH MEMORIAL CUP

These cards have a blue border. The most expensive singles are Eric Lindros at $25-40 each. NHL stars sell between $1-5. All other singles sell between 50¢ and $2.00. Each card measures the standard 2 1/2" x 3 1/2".

Complete Set (100 cards): 150.00

Player	Player
☐ 1 Len Barrie	☐ 2 Zac Boyer
☐ 3 David Chyzowski	☐ 4 Shea Esselmont
☐ 5 Todd Esselmont	☐ 6 Phil Huber
☐ 7 Lance Johnson	☐ 8 Paul Kruse
☐ 9 Cal McGowan	☐ 10 Mike Needham
☐ 11 Brian Shantz	☐ 12 Daryl Sydor
☐ 13 Jeff Watchorn	☐ 14 Jarrett Bousquet
☐ 15 Todd Harris	☐ 16 Dean Malkoc
☐ 17 Joey Mittelsteadt	☐ 18 Scott Niedermayer
☐ 19 Clayton Young	☐ 20 Trevor Sim
☐ 21 Murray Duval	☐ 22 Steve Yule
☐ 23 Craig Bonner	☐ 24 Dale Masson (G)
☐ 25 Corey Hirsch (G)	☐ 26 Joe McDonnell, Coach
☐ 27 R. Chambers, Trainer	☐ 28 John Finnie (G)
☐ 29 Randy Pearce	☐ 30 Mark Montanari
☐ 31 Mike Torchia (G)	☐ 32 Jason York
☐ 33 Jason Firth	☐ 34 Jamie Israel
☐ 35 Richard Borgo	☐ 36 John Uniac
☐ 37 Steve Smith	☐ 38 Steven Rice
☐ 39 Gilbert Dionne	☐ 40 Cory Keenan
☐ 41 Rick Allain	☐ 42 John Copley
☐ 43 Gib Tucker	☐ 44 Chris LiPuma
☐ 45 Brad Barton	☐ 46 Rival Fullum
☐ 47 Joey St. Aubin	☐ 48 Jack Williams
☐ 49 S. Stevenson	☐ 50 P. Creamer, Coach
☐ 51 Carl Mantha	☐ 52 Julian Cameron (G)
☐ 53 Sandy McCarthy	☐ 54 Gino Odjick
☐ 55 Eric Raymond (G)	☐ 56 Carl Boudreau
☐ 57 Greg MacEachern	☐ 58 Allen Kerr
☐ 59 Patrice Brisebois	☐ 60 Eric Bissonnette
☐ 61 Martin Lapointe	☐ 62 Michel Gingras
☐ 63 Sylvain Naud	☐ 64 Patrick Caron
☐ 65 Regis Tremblay	☐ 66 François Pelletier
☐ 67 Jason Brousseau	☐ 68 Eric Dubois
☐ 69 Claude Boivin	☐ 70 Denis Chalifoux
☐ 71 Jim Bermingham	☐ 72 Daniel Arsenault
☐ 73 Normand Demers	☐ 74 Serge Anglehart
☐ 75 R. Cornacchia, Coach	☐ 76 Kevin Butt (G)
☐ 77 Fred Brathwaite (G)	☐ 78 Paul O'Hagan
☐ 79 Craig Donaldson	☐ 80 Jean-Paul Davis
☐ 81 Brian Grieve	☐ 82 Bill Armstrong
☐ 83 Wade Simpson	☐ 84 Dave Craievich, Error
☐ 85 Dale Craigwell	☐ 86 Joe Busillo
☐ 87 Cory Banika	☐ 88 Eric Lindros
☐ 89 Iain Fraser	☐ 90 Mike Craig
☐ 91 Jarrod Skalde	☐ 92 Brent Grieve
☐ 93 Scott Luik	☐ 94 Matt Hoffman
☐ 95 Trevor McIvor	☐ 96 Scott Hollis
☐ 97 Mark Deazeley	☐ 98 Clair Cornish
☐ 99 Eric Lindros	☐ 100 Checklist

CHAPTER FOUR

THE BOOM YEARS 1990 TO 1997

1990 - 91 BOWMAN

These cards have two versions: the regular issue and a Tiffany parallel.

Complete Set (264 cards): 180.00 15.00
Common Player: .50 .20

	Description	Tiff.	Bowm.
☐☐	**1 Jeremy Roenick, Chic. RC**	**15.00**	**2.00**
☐☐	2 Doug Wilson, Chic.	1.00	.20
☐☐	3 Greg Millen (G), Chic.	.50	.20
☐☐	4 Steve Thomas, Chic.	.50	.20
☐☐	5 Steve Larmer, Chic.	1.50	.20
☐☐	6 Denis Savard, Chic.	1.50	.20
☐☐	**7 Ed Belfour (G), Chic. RC**	**18.00**	**2.50**
☐☐	8 Dirk Graham, Chic.	.50	.20
☐☐	9 Adam Creighton, Chic.	.50	.20
☐☐	10 Keith Brown, Chic.	.50	.20
☐☐	**11 Jacques Cloutier (G), Chic. RC**	**3.00**	**.40**
☐☐	12 Secord, Chic. [Photo is Du. Sutter]	.50	.20
☐☐	13 Troy Murray, Chic.	.50	.20
☐☐	**14 Kelly Chase, SLou. RC**	**3.00**	**.40**
☐☐	**15 Dave Lowry, SLou. RC**	**4.50**	**.50**
☐☐	16 Adam Oates, SLou.	1.50	.20
☐☐	**17 Sergio Momesso, SLou. RC**	**1.50**	**.40**
☐☐	18 Paul MacLean, SLou.	.50	.20
☐☐	19 Peter Zezel, SLou.	.50	.20
☐☐	**20 Vincent Riendeau (G), SLou. RC**	**3.00**	**.40**
☐☐	**21 Dave Thomlinson, SLou. RC**	**1.50**	**.40**
☐☐	22 Paul Cavallini, SLou.	.50	.20
☐☐	**23 Rod Brind'Amour, SLou. RC**	**6.00**	**.50**
☐☐	24 Brett Hull, SLou.	5.50	.50
☐☐	25 Jeff R. Brown, SLou.	.50	.20
☐☐	**26 Dominic Lavoie, SLou. RC**	**1.50**	**.40**
☐☐	27 Andy Brickley, Bost.	.50	.20
☐☐	28 Bob Sweeney, Bost.	.50	.20
☐☐	29 Cam Neely, Bost.	5.50	.50
☐☐	30 Bob Carpenter, Bost.	.50	.20
☐☐	31 Raymond Bourque, Bost.	7.00	.50
☐☐	32 Réjean Lemelin (G), Bost.	.50	.20
☐☐	33 Craig Janney, Bost.	.50	.20
☐☐	**34 Bob Beers, Bost. RC**	**1.50**	**.40**
☐☐	35 Andy Moog (G), Bost.	1.50	.20
☐☐	36 Dave Poulin, Bost.	.50	.20
☐☐	37 Brian Propp, Bost.	.50	.20
☐☐	**38 John Byce, Bost. RC**	**1.50**	**.40**
☐☐	**39 John Carter, Bost. RC**	**1.50**	**.40**
☐☐	40 Dave Christian, Bost.	.50	.20
☐☐	41 Shayne Corson, Mont.	1.00	.20
☐☐	42 Chris Chelios, Mont.	3.00	.20
☐☐	43 Mike McPhee, Mont.	.50	.20
☐☐	44 Guy Carbonneau, Mont.	1.00	.20
☐☐	45 Stéphane J.J. Richer, Mont.	.50	.20
☐☐	46 Svoboda, Mont. [Photo is Chelios]	1.50	.20
☐☐	47 Russ Courtnall, Mont.	.50	.20
☐☐	**48 Sylvain Lefebvre, Mont. RC**	**3.00**	**.40**
☐☐	49 Brian Skrudland, Mont.	.50	.20
☐☐	50 Patrick Roy (G), Mont.	20.00	1.50
☐☐	51 Bobby Smith, Mont.	1.00	.20
☐☐	**52 Mathieu Schneider, Mont. RC**	**4.50**	**.50**
☐☐	**53 Stéphan Lebeau, Mont. RC**	**1.50**	**.40**
☐☐	54 Petri Skriko, Vanc.	.50	.20
☐☐	55 Jim Sandlak, Vanc.	.50	.20
☐☐	56 Doug Lidster, Vanc.	.50	.20
☐☐	57 Kirk McLean (G), Vanc.	1.00	.20
☐☐	58 Brian Bradley, Vanc.	.50	.20
☐☐	59 Greg A. Adams, Vanc.	.50	.20
☐☐	60 Paul Reinhart, Vanc.	.50	.20
☐☐	61 Trevor Linden, Vanc.	1.50	.20
☐☐	**62 Adrien Plavsic, Vanc. RC**	**1.50**	**.40**
☐☐	**63 Igor Larionov, Vanc. RC**	**10.00**	**1.50**
☐☐	64 Steve Bozek, Vanc.	.50	.20
☐☐	65 Dan Quinn, Vanc.	.50	.20
☐☐	66 Mike Liut (G), Wash.	1.00	.20
☐☐	**67 Nick Kypreos, Wash. RC**	**4.50**	**.50**
☐☐	**68 Michal Pivonka, Wash. RC**	**1.50**	**.40**
☐☐	69 Dino Ciccarelli, Wash.	1.00	.20
☐☐	70 Kevin Hatcher, Wash.	.50	.20
☐☐	71 Dale Hunter, Wash.	1.00	.20
☐☐	72 Don Beaupré (G), Wash.	.50	.20
☐☐	73 Geoff Courtnall, Wash.	.50	.20
☐☐	**74 Rob Murray, Wash. RC**	**1.50**	**.40**
☐☐	75 Calle Johansson, Wash.	.50	.20
☐☐	76 Kelly Miller, Wash.	.50	.20
☐☐	77 Mike Ridley, Wash.	.50	.20
☐☐	**78 Alan May, Wash. RC**	**1.50**	**.40**
☐☐	79 Bob Brooke, NJer.	.50	.20
☐☐	**80 Viacheslav Fetisov, NJer. RC**	**10.00**	**1.50**
☐☐	81 Sylvain Turgeon, NJer.	.50	.20
☐☐	82 Kirk Muller, NJer.	1.00	.20
☐☐	83 John MacLean, NJer.	.50	.20
☐☐	**84 Jon Morris, NJer. RC**	**1.50**	**.40**
☐☐	85 Brendan Shanahan, NJer.	5.50	.50
☐☐	86 Peter Stastny, NJer.	3.00	.20
☐☐	87 Bruce Driver, NJer.	.50	.20
☐☐	**88 Neil Brady, NJer. RC**	**1.50**	**.40**
☐☐	89 Patrik Sundström, NJer.	.50	.20
☐☐	**90 Eric Weinrich, NJer. RC**	**1.50**	**.40**
☐☐	91 Joe Nieuwendyk, Calg.	1.50	.20
☐☐	**92 Sergei Makarov, Calg. RC**	**7.00**	**1.00**
☐☐	93 Al MacInnis, Calg.	1.50	.20
☐☐	94 Mike Vernon (G), Calg.	1.50	.20
☐☐	95 Gary Roberts, Calg.	1.50	.20
☐☐	96 Doug Gilmour, Calg.	3.00	.20
☐☐	97 Joe Mullen, Calg.	1.50	.20
☐☐	98 Rick Wamsley (G), Calg.	.50	.20
☐☐	99 Joel Otto, Calg.	.50	.20
☐☐	**100 Paul Ranheim, Calg. RC**	**3.00**	**.40**
☐☐	101 Gary Suter, Calg.	.50	.20
☐☐	102 Theoren Fleury, Calg.	3.00	.20
☐☐	**103 Sergei Priakin, Calg. RC**	**1.50**	**.40**
☐☐	**104 Tony Horacek, Phil. RC**	**1.50**	**.40**
☐☐	105 Ron Hextall (G), Phil.	2.50	.20
☐☐	**106 Gord Murphy, Phil. RC**	**1.50**	**.40**
☐☐	107 Pelle Eklund, Phil.	.50	.20
☐☐	108 Rick Tocchet, Phil.	1.00	.20
☐☐	109 Murray Craven, Phil.	.50	.20
☐☐	110 Doug Sulliman, Phil.	.50	.20
☐☐	111 Kjell Samuelsson, Phil.	.50	.20
☐☐	112 Ilkka Sinisalo, Phil.	.50	.20
☐☐	113 Keith Acton, Phil.	.50	.20
☐☐	114 Mike Bullard, Phil.	.50	.20
☐☐	115 Doug Crossman, NYIs.	.50	.20
☐☐	**116 Tom Fitzgerald, NYIs. RC**	**1.50**	**.40**
☐☐	117 Don Maloney, NYIs.	.50	.20
☐☐	118 Alan Kerr, NYIs.	.50	.20
☐☐	**119 Mark Fitzpatrick (G), NYIs. RC**	**3.00**	**.40**
☐☐	**120 Hubie McDonough, NYIs. RC**	**1.50**	**.40**
☐☐	121 Randy Wood, NYIs.	.50	.20
☐☐	122 Jeff Norton, NYIs.	.50	.20
☐☐	123 Pat LaFontaine, NYIs.	3.00	.20
☐☐	124 Patrick Flatley, NYIs.	.50	.20
☐☐	**125 Joe Reekie, NYIs. RC**	**1.50**	**.40**
☐☐	126 Brent Sutter, NYIs.	.50	.20
☐☐	127 David Volek, NYIs.	.50	.20
☐☐	**128 Shawn Cronin, Winn. RC**	**1.50**	**.40**
☐☐	129 Dale Hawerchuk, Winn.	3.00	.20
☐☐	130 Brent Ashton, Winn.	.50	.20
☐☐	**131 Bob Essensa (G), Winn. RC**	**4.50**	**.50**
☐☐	132 Dave Ellett, Winn.	.50	.20
☐☐	133 Thomas Steen, Winn.	.50	.20
☐☐	134 Doug Smail, Winn.	.50	.20
☐☐	135 Fredrik Olausson, Winn.	.50	.20
☐☐	136 Dave McLlwain, Winn.	.50	.20
☐☐	137 Pat Elynuik, Winn.	.50	.20
☐☐	**138 Teppo Numminen, Winn. RC**	**6.00**	**.50**
☐☐	139 Paul Fenton, Winn.	.50	.20
☐☐	140 Tony Granato, LosA.	.50	.20
☐☐	141 Tomas Sandström, LosA.	.50	.20
☐☐	**142 Rob Blake, LosA. RC**	**10.00**	**1.50**
☐☐	143 Wayne Gretzky, LosA.	25.00	2.00
☐☐	144 Kelly Hrudey (G), LosA.	1.00	.20
☐☐	145 Mike Krushelnyski, LosA.	.50	.20
☐☐	146 Steve Duchesne, LosA.	.50	.20
☐☐	147 Steve Kasper, LosA.	.50	.20
☐☐	148 John Tonelli, LosA.	.50	.20
☐☐	149 Dave Taylor, LosA.	.50	.20
☐☐	150 Larry Robinson, LosA.	3.00	.20
☐☐	**151 Todd Elik, LosA. RC**	**1.50**	**.40**
☐☐	152 Luc Robitaille, LosA.	4.50	.20
☐☐	153 Al Iafrate, Toro.	.50	.20
☐☐	154 Allan Bester (G), Toro.	1.00	.20
☐☐	155 Gary Leeman, Toro.	.50	.20
☐☐	156 Mark Osborne, Toro.	.50	.20
☐☐	157 Tom Fergus, Toro.	.50	.20
☐☐	158 Brad Marsh, Toro.	.50	.20
☐☐	159 Wendel Clark, Toro.	4.50	.20
☐☐	160 Daniel Marois, Toro.	.50	.20
☐☐	161 Ed Olczyk, Toro.	.50	.20
☐☐	162 Rob Ramage, Toro.	.50	.20
☐☐	163 Vincent Damphousse, Toro.	3.00	.20
☐☐	**164 Lou Franceschetti, Toro. RC**	**1.50**	**.40**
☐☐	165 Paul Gillis, Québ.	.50	.20
☐☐	**166 Craig Wolanin, Québ. RC**	**1.50**	**.40**
☐☐	167 Marc Fortier, Québ.	.50	.20
☐☐	168 Tony McKegney, Québ.	.50	.20
☐☐	169 Joe Sakic, Québ.	10.00	.50
☐☐	170 Michel Petit, Québ.	.50	.20
☐☐	**171 Scott Gordon (G), Québ. RC**	**1.50**	**.40**
☐☐	172 Tony Hrkac, Québ.	.50	.20
☐☐	**173 Bryan Fogarty, Québ. RC**	**1.50**	**.40**
☐☐	174 Mike Hough, Québ.	.50	.20
☐☐	**175 Claude Loiselle, Québ. RC**	**1.50**	**.40**
☐☐	176 Ulf Dahlén, Minn.	.50	.20
☐☐	177 Larry Murphy, Minn.	.50	.20
☐☐	178 Neal Broten, Minn.	.50	.20
☐☐	**179 Don Barber, Minn. RC**	**1.50**	**.40**
☐☐	180 Shawn Chambers, Minn.	.50	.20
☐☐	**181 Clark Donatelli, Minn. RC**	**1.50**	**.40**
☐☐	182 Brian Bellows, Minn.	.50	.20
☐☐	183 Jon Casey (G), Minn.	.50	.20
☐☐	**184 Neil Wilkinson, Minn. RC**	**1.50**	**.40**
☐☐	185 Aaron Broten, Minn.	.50	.20
☐☐	186 Dave Gagner, Minn.	.50	.20
☐☐	187 Basil McRae, Minn.	.50	.20
☐☐	**188 Mike Modano, Minn. RC**	**18.00**	**2.50**
☐☐	189 Grant Fuhr (G), Edmo.	3.00	.20
☐☐	**190 Martin Gélinas, Edmo. RC**	**4.50**	**.50**
☐☐	191 Jari Kurri, Edmo.	5.50	.50
☐☐	**192 Geoff Smith, Edmo. RC**	**1.50**	**.40**
☐☐	193 Craig MacTavish, Edmo.	.50	.20
☐☐	194 Esa Tikkanen, Edmo.	.50	.20
☐☐	195 Glenn Anderson, Edmo.	1.00	.20
☐☐	**196 Joe Murphy, Edmo. RC**	**3.00**	**.40**
☐☐	197 Petr Klima, Edmo.	.50	.20
☐☐	198 Kevin Lowe, Edmo.	1.00	.20
☐☐	199 Mark Messier, Edmo.	5.50	.50
☐☐	200 J. Steve Smith, Edmo.	.50	.20
☐☐	201 Craig Simpson, Edmo.	.50	.20
☐☐	202 Rob (Jr.) Brown, Pitt.	.50	.20
☐☐	**203 Wendell Young (G), Pitt. RC**	**3.00**	**.40**
☐☐	204 Mario Lemieux, Pitt.	20.00	1.50
☐☐	205 Phil Bourque, Pitt.	.50	.20
☐☐	**206 Mark Recchi, Pitt. RC**	**7.00**	**1.00**
☐☐	207 Zarley Zalapski, Pitt.	.50	.20
☐☐	**208 Kevin Stevens, Pitt. RC**	**4.00**	**.50**
☐☐	209 Tom Barrasso (G), Pitt.	2.00	.20
☐☐	210 John Cullen, Pitt.	.50	.20
☐☐	211 Paul Coffey, Pitt.	3.00	.20
☐☐	212 Bob Errey, Pitt.	.50	.20
☐☐	213 Tony Tanti, Pitt.	.50	.20
☐☐	214 Carey Wilson, NYRa.	.50	.20
☐☐	215 B. Leetch, NYRa. [Error: Eetch]	3.00	.20
☐☐	215 Brian Leetch, NYRa.	3.00	.20
☐☐	**216 Darren Turcotte, NYRa. RC**	**3.00**	**.40**
☐☐	217 Brian Mullen, NYRa.	.50	.20
☐☐	**218 Mike Richter (G), NYRa. RC**	**9.00**	**1.00**
☐☐	**219 Troy Mallette, NYRa. RC**	**1.50**	**.40**
☐☐	220 Mike Gartner, NYRa.	4.50	.20
☐☐	221 Bernie Nicholls, NYRa.	.50	.20
☐☐	222 John Vanbiesbrouck (G), NYRa.	2.50	.20
☐☐	223 John Ogrodnick, NYRa.	.50	.20
☐☐	**224 Paul Broten, NYRa. RC**	**3.00**	**.40**
☐☐	225 James Patrick, NYRa.	.50	.20
☐☐	**226 Mark Janssens, NYRa. RC**	**1.50**	**.40**
☐☐	**227 Randy McKay, Detr. RC**	**1.50**	**.40**
☐☐	228 Marc Habscheid, Detr.	.50	.20
☐☐	229 Jimmy Carson, Detr.	.50	.20
☐☐	**230 Yves Racine, Detr. RC**	**1.50**	**.40**
☐☐	231 Dave Barr, Detr.	.50	.20
☐☐	232 Shawn Burr, Detr.	.50	.20
☐☐	233 Steve Yzerman, Detr.	15.00	1.00
☐☐	234 Steve Chiasson, Detr.	.50	.20
☐☐	**235 Daniel Shank, Detr. RC**	**1.50**	**.40**
☐☐	236 John Chabot, Detr.	.50	.20
☐☐	237 Gerard Gallant, Detr.	.50	.20
☐☐	238 Bernie Federko, Detr.	1.00	.20
☐☐	239 Phil Housley, Buff.	1.00	.20
☐☐	**240 Alexander Mogilny, Buff. RC**	**9.00**	**1.00**
☐☐	241 Pierre Turgeon, Buff.	1.50	.20
☐☐	242 Daren Puppa (G), Buff.	.50	.20
☐☐	243 Scott Arniel, Buff.	.50	.20
☐☐	244 Christian Ruuttu, Buff.	.50	.20
☐☐	245 Doug Bodger, Buff.	.50	.20
☐☐	246 Dave Andreychuk, Buff.	1.00	.20
☐☐	247 Mike Foligno, Buff.	.50	.20
☐☐	**248 Dean Kennedy, Buff. RC**	**1.50**	**.40**
☐☐	**249 Dave Snuggerud, Buff. RC**	**1.50**	**.40**
☐☐	250 Rick Vaive, Buff.	1.00	.20
☐☐	**251 Todd Krygier, Hart. RC**	**1.50**	**.40**
☐☐	**252 Adam Burt, Hart. RC**	**1.50**	**.40**
☐☐	253 Scott Young, Hart.	1.00	.20
☐☐	254 Ron Francis, Hart.	3.00	.20
☐☐	255 Peter Sidorkiewicz (G), Hart.	.50	.20
☐☐	256 Dave Babych, Hart.	.50	.20
☐☐	257 Pat Verbeek, Hart.	1.00	.20
☐☐	258 Ray Ferraro, Hart.	.50	.20
☐☐	**259 Chris Govedaris, Hart. RC**	**1.50**	**.40**
☐☐	**260 Brad Shaw, Hart. RC**	**1.50**	**.40**
☐☐	261 Kevin Dineen, Hart.	.50	.20
☐☐	262 Dean Evason, Hart.	.50	.20
☐☐	263 Checklist	.50	.20
☐☐	264 Checklist	.50	.20

HAT TRICKS

These cards have two versions: the regular issue and a Tiffany parallel.

Insert Set (22 cards): 40.00 10.00

	Description	Tiff.	Bowm.
☐☐	1 Brett Hull, SLou.	3.00	1.00
☐☐	2 Mario Lemieux, Pitt.	10.00	3.00
☐☐	3 Rob (Jr.) Brown, Pitt.	.50	.50
☐☐	4 Mark Messier, Edmo.	3.00	1.00
☐☐	5 Steve Yzerman, Detr.	9.00	2.00
☐☐	6 Vincent Damphousse, Toro.	2.00	.50
☐☐	7 Kevin Dineen, Hart.	.50	.50
☐☐	8 Mike Gartner, Minn.	3.00	.50
☐☐	9 Pat LaFontaine, NYIs.	2.00	.50
☐☐	10 Gary Leeman, Toro.	.50	.50
☐☐	11 Stéphane J.J. Richer, Mont.	.50	.50
☐☐	12 Luc Robitaille, LosA.	3.00	.50
☐☐	13 Steve Thomas, Chic.	.50	.50
☐☐	14 Rick Tocchet, Phil.	1.00	.50
☐☐	15 Dino Ciccarelli, Wash.	1.00	.50
☐☐	16 John Druce, Wash.	.50	.50
☐☐	17 Mike Gartner, NYRa.	3.00	.50
☐☐	18 Tony Granato, LosA.	.50	.50
☐☐	19 Jari Kurri, Edmo.	3.00	1.00
☐☐	20 Bernie Nicholls, NYRa.	.50	.50
☐☐	21 Tomas Sandström, LosA.	.50	.50
☐☐	22 Dave Taylor, LosA.	.50	.50

1990 - 91 CANADIAN OLYMPIC TEAM

Vladislav Tretiak is the most expensive single at $3-4. Singles start at 50¢; regional stars start at $1.00.

Imprint: Alberta Lotteries

Complete Set (23 cards): 15.00

- ☐ 1 Craig Billington (G)
- ☐ 2 Doug Dadswell (G)
- ☐ 3 Greg Andrusak
- ☐ 4 Karl Dykhuis
- ☐ 5 Gord Hynes
- ☐ 6 Ken MacArthur
- ☐ 7 Jim Paek
- ☐ 8 Brad Schlegel
- ☐ 9 Dave Archibald
- ☐ 10 Stu Barnes
- ☐ 11 Brad Bennett
- ☐ 12 Todd Brost
- ☐ 13 José Charbonneau
- ☐ 14 Jason Lafrenière
- ☐ 15 Chris Lindberg
- ☐ 16 Ken Priestlay
- ☐ 17 Stéphane Roy
- ☐ 18 Randy Smith
- ☐ 19 Todd Strueby
- ☐ 20 Vladislav Tretiak
- ☐ 21 David King
- ☐ 22 Wayne Fleming
- ☐ 23 Checklist

1990 - 91 JYVAS HYVA

A set of 12 team logo stickers issued by the Finnish biscuit factory Jvas Hyva.

Size: 1 5/8" x 4 1/4"

Complete Set (12 cards): 100.00

- ☐ HIFK Helsinki
- ☐ HPK Hameenlinna
- ☐ Jokerit Helsinki
- ☐ Hockeyreipas
- ☐ Ilves Tampere
- ☐ JyPHT
- ☐ KalPa Kuopio
- ☐ SaiPa
- ☐ TPS Turku
- ☐ Lukko Raumo
- ☐ Tappara Tampere
- ☐ Assat Pori

1990 - 91 KRAFT

Cards 1-64 were issued on the backs of Kraft Dinner, Kraft Spirals and Kraft Noodles boxes; cards 65-91 were issued on the backs of JELL-O boxes. Cards 92-112 were issued with Kraft Singles.

Cards 1-91 (box backs) have red text while cards 92-112 have blue backs.

Card Size: 2 1/2" x 3 1/2"

Imprint: KRAFT

Complete Set (112 cards): 110.00
Album: 30.00
Common Player: .50

	Description	EX-NM
☐	1 Dave Babych, Hart.	.50
☐	2 Brian Bellows, Minn.	.50
☐	3 Raymond Bourque, Bost.	3.00
☐	4 Sean Burke (G), NJer.	1.50
☐	5 Jimmy Carson, Detr.	.50
☐	6 Chris Chelios, Chic.	1.50
☐	7 Dino Ciccarelli, Wash.	.50
☐	8 Paul Coffey, Pitt.	1.50
☐	9 Geoff Courtnall, SLou.	.50
☐	10 Doug Crossman, NYIs.	.50
☐	11 Kevin Dineen, Hart.	.50
☐	12 Pat Elynuik, Winn.	.50
☐	13 Ron Francis, Hart.	1.50
☐	14 Gerard Gallant, Detr.	.50
☐	15 Wayne Gretzky, LosA.	10.00
☐	16 Dale Hawerchuk, Buff.	1.50
☐	17 Ron Hextall (G), Phil.	1.50
☐	18 Phil Housley, Winn.	.50
☐	19 Mark Howe, Phil.	.50
☐	20 Brett Hull, SLou.	2.50
☐	21 Al Iafrate, Toro.	.50
☐	22 Guy Lafleur, Québ.	5.00
☐	23 Pat LaFontaine, NYIs.	1.50
☐	24 Rod Langway, Wash.	1.00
☐	25 Igor Larionov, Vanc.	1.50
☐	26 Steve Larmer, Chic.	1.00
☐	27 Gary Leeman, Toro.	.50
☐	28 Brian Leetch, NYRa.	1.50
☐	29 Mario Lemieux, Pitt.	7.50
☐	30 Trevor Linden, Vanc.	1.00
☐	31 Mike Liut (G), Wash.	.50
☐	32 Mark Messier, Edmo.	2.50
☐	33 Al MacInnis, Calg.	1.00
☐	34 Mike Modano, Minn.	2.50
☐	35 Andy Moog (G), Bost.	1.00
☐	36 Joe Mullen, Pitt.	1.00
☐	37 Kirk Muller, NJer.	.50
☐	38 Petr Nedved, Vanc.	.50
☐	39 Cam Neely, Bost.	2.50
☐	40 Bernie Nicholls, NYRa.	.50
☐	41 Joe Nieuwendyk, Calg.	1.00
☐	42 Mats Sundin, Québ.	2.50
☐	43 Daren Puppa (G), Buff.	.50
☐	44 Rob Ramage, Toro.	.50
☐	45 Bill Ranford (G), Edmo.	1.00
☐	46 Stéphane J.J. Richer, Mont.	.50
☐	47 Larry Robinson, LosA.	1.50
☐	48 Luc Robitaille, LosA.	2.00
☐	49 Patrick Roy (G), Mont.	7.50
☐	50 Joe Sakic, Québ.	4.00

□	51 Denis Savard, Mont.	1.00
□	52 Craig Simpson, Edmo.	.50
□	53 Bobby Smith, Minn.	.50
□	54 Peter Stastny, NJer.	1.50
□	55 Thomas Steen, Winn.	.50
□	56 Scott Stevens, SLou.	1.00
□	57 Brent Sutter, NYIs.	.50
□	58 Rick Tocchet, Phil.	.50
□	59 Pierre Turgeon, Buff.	1.00
□	60 John Vanbiesbrouck (G), NYRa.	1.00
□	61 Mike Vernon (G), Calg.	1.00
□	62 Doug Wilson, Chic.	.50
□	63 Steve Yzerman, Detr.	6.00
□	64 Checklist	.50
□	65 Steve Duchesne, LosA.	.50
□	66 Brett Hull, SLou.	2.50
□	67 Wayne Gretzky, LosA.	10.00
□	68 Jari Kurri, Edmo.	2.50
□	69 Mike Gartner, NYRa.	2.00
□	70 Kirk McLean (G), Vanc.	.50
□	71 Mark Messier, Edmo.	2.50
□	72 Joe Mullen, Pitt.	1.00
□	73 Bernie Nicholls, NYRa.	.50
□	74 Joe Nieuwendyk, Calg.	1.00
□	75 Luc Robitaille, LosA.	2.00
□	76 Mike Vernon (G), Calg.	1.00
□	77 Doug Wilson, Chic.	.50
□	78 Steve Yzerman, Detr.	6.00
□	79 Joe Sakic, Québ.	4.00
□	80 Raymond Bourque, Bost.	3.00
□	81 Chris Chelios, Chic.	1.50
□	82 Paul Coffey, Pitt.	1.50
□	83 Ron Francis, Hart.	1.50
□	84 Cam Neely, Bost.	2.50
□	85 Phil Housley, Winn.	.50
□	86 Pat LaFontaine, NYIs.	1.50
□	87 Mario Lemieux, Pitt.	7.50
□	88 Kirk Muller, NJer.	.50
□	89 Stéphane J.J. Richer, Mont.	.50
□	90 Patrick Roy (G), Mont.	7.50
□	91 Pierre Turgeon, Buff.	1.00

	Team		Team
□	92 Boston Bruins	□	93 Buffalo Sabres
□	94 Calgary Flames	□	95 Chicago Blackhawks
□	96 Detroit Red Wings	□	97 Edmonton Oilers
□	98 Hartford Whalers	□	99 Los Angeles Kings
□	100 Minn. North Stars	□	101 Montréal Canadiens
□	102 New Jersey Devils	□	103 New York Islanders
□	104 New York Rangers	□	105 Philadelphia Flyers
□	106 Pitt. Penguins	□	107 Québec Nordiques
□	108 St. Louis Blues	□	109 Toronto Maple Leafs
□	110 Vanc. Canucks	□	111 Washington Capitals
□	112 Winnipeg Jets		

1990 - 91 O-PEE-CHEE / TOPPS

There are up to three versions for this series: a Topps and Topps Tiffany card (1 - 396) plus an O-Pee-Chee card (1 - 528). The Topps and O-Pee-Chee cards have the same value.

Imprint: © 1990 O-PEE-CHEE CO. LTD.

O-Pee-Chee Set (528 cards):	-	**20.00**
Topps Set (396 cards):	**240.00**	**15.00**
Common Player:	**.50**	**.20**

	Description	Tiff.	Reg.
□□□	1 Gretzky, Indianapolis [Highlight]	7.00	1.00
□□□	2 Gretzky, Edmo. [Highlight]	7.00	1.00
□□□	3 Gretzky, LosA. [Highlight]	7.00	1.00
□□□	4 Brett Hull, SLou. [Highlight]	2.50	.20
□□□	5 Jari Kurri, Edmo. [Highlight]	2.50	.20
□□□	6 Bryan Trottier, NYIs. [Highlight]	2.50	.20
□□□	**7 Jeremy Roenick, Chic. RC**	**15.00**	**2.00**
□□□	8 Brian Propp, Bost.	.50	.20
□□□	**9 Jim Hrivnak (G), Wash. RC**	**1.50**	**.40**
□□□	**10 Mick Vukota, NYIs. RC**	**1.50**	**.40**
□□□	11 Tom Kurvers, Toro.	.50	.20
□□□	12 Ulf Dahlén, Minn.	.50	.20
□□□	13 Bernie Nicholls, NYRa.	.50	.20
□□□	14 Peter Sidorkiewicz (G), Hart.	.50	.20
□□□	15 Peter Zezel, SLou. (NJer.)	.50	.20
□□□	**16 Mike Hartman, Buff. RC**	**1.50**	**.40**
□□□	17 Kings team leaders	.50	.20
□□□	18 Jim Sandlak, Vanc.	.50	.20
□□□	19 Rob (Jr.) Brown, Pitt.	.50	.20
□□□	**20 Paul Ranheim, Calg. RC**	**3.00**	**.40**
□□□	**21 Rick Zombo, Detr. RC**	**1.50**	**.40**
□□□	22 Paul Gillis, Québ.	.50	.20
□□□	23 Brian Hayward (G), Mont.	.50	.20
□□□	24 Brent Ashton, Winn.	.50	.20
□□□	**25 Mark Lamb, Edmo. RC**	**1.50**	**.40**
□□□	26 Rick Tocchet, Phil.	1.00	.20
□□□	**27 Viacheslav Fetisov, NJer. RC**	**10.00**	**1.50**
□□□	28 Denis Savard, Chic. (Mont.)	1.50	.20
□□□	29 Chris Chelios, Mont. (Chic.)	2.00	.20
□□□	**30 Janne Ojanen, NJer. RC**	**1.50**	**.40**
□□□	31 Don Maloney, NYIs.	.50	.20
□□□	32 Allan Bester (G), Toro.	.50	.20
□□□	**33 Geoff Smith, Edmo. RC**	**1.50**	**.40**
□□□	**34 Daniel Shank, Detr. RC**	**1.50**	**.40**
□□□	**35 Mikael Andersson, Hart. RC**	**1.50**	**.40**
□□□	36 Gino Cavallini, SLou.	.50	.20
□□□	**37 Rob Murphy, Vanc. RC**	**1.50**	**.40**
□□□	38 Jim Peplinski, Calg.	.50	.20
□□□	39 Laurie Boschman, Winn.	.50	.20
□□□	**40 Craig Wolanin, Québ. RC**	**1.50**	**.40**
□□□	41 Phil Bourque, Pitt.	.50	.20
□□□	**42 Alexander Mogilny, Buff. RC**	**9.00**	**1.00**
□□□	43 Raymond Bourque, Bost.	4.50	.50
□□□	44 Mike Liut (G), Wash.	1.00	.20
□□□	45 Ron Sutter, Phil.	.50	.20
□□□	**46 Bob Kudelski, LosA. RC**	**1.50**	**.40**
□□□	47 Larry Murphy, Minn.	.50	.20
□□□	**48 Darren Turcotte, NYRa. RC**	**3.00**	**.40**
□□□	**49 Paul Ysebaert, NJer. RC**	**1.50**	**.40**
□□□	50 Alan Kerr, NYIs.	.50	.20
□□□	51 Randy Carlyle, Winn.	.50	.20
□□□	52 Iiro Järvi, Québ.	.50	.20
□□□	**53 Don Barber, Minn. RC**	**1.50**	**.40**
□□□	54 Carey Wilson, Hart. [Error: Cary]	.50	.20
□□□	**55 Joey Kocur, Detr. RC**	**3.00**	**.40**
□□□	56 Steve Larmer, Chic.	1.50	.20
□□□	57 Paul Cavallini, SLou.	.50	.20
□□□	58 Shayne Corson, Mont.	1.00	.20
□□□	59 Brian Bradley, Vanc. [Team Card]	.50	.20
□□□	**60 Sergei Makarov, Calg. RC**	**7.00**	**1.00**
□□□	61 Kjell Samuelsson, Phil.	.50	.20
□□□	62 Tony Granato, LosA.	.50	.20
□□□	63 Tom Fergus, Toro.	.50	.20
□□□	**64 Martin Gélinas, Edmo. RC**	**4.50**	**.50**
□□□	65 Tom Barrasso (G), Pitt.	2.00	.20
□□□	66 Pierre Turgeon, Buff.	1.50	.20
□□□	67 Randy Cunneyworth, Hart.	.50	.20
□□□	**68 Michal Pivonka, Wash. RC**	**1.50**	**.40**
□□□	69 Cam Neely, Bost.	3.50	.50
□□□	70 Brian Bellows, Minn.	.50	.20
□□□	71 Pat Elynuik, Winn.	.50	.20
□□□	72 Doug Crossman, NYIs.	.50	.20
□□□	73 Sylvain Turgeon, NJer.	.50	.20
□□□	74 Shawn Burr, Detr.	.50	.20
□□□	75 John Vanbiesbrouck (G), NYRa.	1.50	.20
□□□	76 Steve Bozek, Vanc.	.50	.20
□□□	77 Brett Hull, SLou.	3.50	.50
□□□	78 Zarley Zalapski, Pitt.	.50	.20
□□□	79 Wendel Clark, Toro.	3.00	.20
□□□	80 B. Hoffort (G), Phil. [Team Card]	.50	.20
□□□	81 Kelly Miller, Wash.	.50	.20
□□□	**82 Mark Pederson, Mont. RC**	**1.50**	**.40**
□□□	83 Adam Creighton, Chic.	.50	.20
□□□	84 Scott Young, Hart.	1.00	.20
□□□	85 Petr Klima, Edmo.	.50	.20
□□□	86 Steve Duchesne, LosA.	.50	.20
□□□	87 Joe Nieuwendyk, Calg.	1.50	.20
□□□	88 Andy Brickley, Bost.	.50	.20
□□□	89 Phil Housley, Buff. (Winn.)	1.00	.20
□□□	90 Neal Broten, Minn.	.50	.20
□□□	91 Al Iafrate, Toro.	.50	.20
□□□	92 Steve Thomas, Chic.	.50	.20
□□□	93 Guy Carbonneau, Mont.	1.00	.20
□□□	94 Steve Chiasson, Detr.	.50	.20
□□□	**95 Mike Tomlak, Hart. RC**	**1.50**	**.40**
□□□	**96 Roger Johansson, Calg. RC**	**1.50**	**.40**
□□□	97 Randy Wood, NYIs.	.50	.20
□□□	98 Jim* Johnson, Pitt.	.50	.20
□□□	99 Bob Sweeney, Bost.	.50	.20
□□□	100 Dino Ciccarelli, Wash.	1.00	.20
□□□	101 Rangers [Team Card]	.50	.20
□□□	102 Mike Ramsey, Buff.	.50	.20
□□□	103 Kelly Hrudey (G), LosA.	1.00	.20
□□□	104 Dave Ellett, Winn.	.50	.20
□□□	105 Bob Brooke, NJer.	.50	.20
□□□	106 Greg A. Adams, Vanc.	.50	.20
□□□	107 Joe Cirella, Québ.	.50	.20
□□□	108 Jari Kurri, Edmo.	3.50	.50
□□□	109 Pete Peeters (G), Phil.	1.00	.20
□□□	110 Paul MacLean, SLou.	.50	.20
□□□	111 Doug Wilson, Chic.	1.00	.20
□□□	112 Pat Verbeek, Hart.	1.00	.20
□□□	**113 Bob Beers, Bost. RC**	**1.50**	**.40**
□□□	114 Mike O'Connell, Detr.	.50	.20
□□□	115 Brian Bradley, Vanc.	.50	.20
□□□	116 Paul Coffey, Pitt.	2.00	.20
□□□	117 Doug Brown, NJer.	.50	.20
□□□	118 Aaron Broten, Minn.	.50	.20
□□□	**119 Bob Essensa (G), Winn. RC**	**4.50**	**.50**
□□□	120 Wayne Gretzky, LosA.	25.00	2.00
□□□	121 Vincent Damphousse, Toro.	2.00	.20
□□□	122 Paul Gillis, Québ. [Team Card]	.50	.20
□□□	123 Mike Foligno, Buff.	.50	.20
□□□	124 Russ Courtnall, Mont.	.50	.20
□□□	125 Rick Meagher, SLou.	.50	.20
□□□	**126 Craig Fisher, Phil. RC**	**1.50**	**.40**
□□□	127 Al MacInnis, Calg.	1.50	.20
□□□	128 Derek King, NYIs.	.50	.20
□□□	129 Dale Hunter, Wash.	1.00	.20
□□□	130 Mark Messier, Edmo.	3.50	.50
□□□	131 James Patrick, NYRa.	.50	.20
□□□	132 Checklist	.50	.20
□□□	133 Red Wings team leaders	4.50	.50
□□□	134 Barry Pederson, Pitt.	.50	.20
□□□	135 Gary Leeman, Toro.	.50	.20
□□□	136 Doug Gilmour, Calg.	2.00	.20
□□□	137 Mike McPhee, Mont.	.50	.20
□□□	138 Bob F. Murray, Chic.	.50	.20
□□□	139 Bob Carpenter, Bost.	.50	.20
□□□	140 Sean Burke (G), NJer.	2.00	.20
□□□	141 D. Hawerchuk, Winn. (Buff.)	2.00	.20
□□□	142 Guy Lafleur, Québ.	7.00	1.00
□□□	143 Lindy Ruff, NYRa.	.50	.20
□□□	144 Whalers	.50	.20
□□□	145 Glenn Anderson, Edmo.	1.00	.20
□□□	**146 Dave Chyzowski, NYIs. RC**	**1.50**	**.40**
□□□	147 Kevin Hatcher, Wash.	.50	.20
□□□	148 Rick Vaive, Buff.	1.00	.20
□□□	149 Adam Oates, SLou.	1.50	.20
□□□	150 Garth Butcher, Vanc.	.50	.20
□□□	151 Basil McRae, Minn.	.50	.20
□□□	152 Ilkka Sinisalo, Phil. (Minn.)	.50	.20
□□□	153 Steve Kasper, LosA.	.50	.20
□□□	154 Greg Paslawski, Winn.	.50	.20
□□□	155 Brad Marsh, Toro.	.50	.20
□□□	156 Esa Tikkanen, Edmo.	.50	.20
□□□	157 Tony Tanti, Pitt.	.50	.20
□□□	158 Mario Marois, Québ.	.50	.20
□□□	**159 Sylvain Lefebvre, Mont. RC**	**3.00**	**.40**
□□□	160 Troy Murray, Chic.	.50	.20
□□□	161 Gary Roberts, Calg.	1.50	.20
□□□	162 Randy Ladouceur, Hart.	.50	.20
□□□	163 John Chabot, Detr.	.50	.20
□□□	164 Calle Johansson, Wash.	.50	.20
□□□	165 Bruins	.50	.20
□□□	166 Jeff Norton, NYIs.	.50	.20
□□□	167 Mike Krushelnyski, LosA.	.50	.20
□□□	168 Dave Gagner, Minn.	.50	.20
□□□	169 Dave Andreychuk, Buff.	1.00	.20
□□□	**170 Dave Capuano, Vanc. RC**	**1.50**	**.40**
□□□	**171 Cu. Joseph (G), SLou. RC**	**18.00**	**2.50**
□□□	172 Bruce Driver, NJer.	.50	.20
□□□	173 Scott Mellanby, Phil.	.50	.20
□□□	174 John Ogrodnick, NYRa.	.50	.20
□□□	175 Mario Lemieux, Pitt.	20.00	1.50
□□□	176 Marc Fortier, Québ.	.50	.20
□□□	**177 V. Riendeau (G), SLou. RC**	**3.00**	**.40**
□□□	178 Mark Johnson, NJer.	.50	.20
□□□	179 Dirk Graham, Chic.	.50	.20
□□□	180 Beauregard (G), Winn. [Team]	.50	.20
□□□	**181 Robb Stauber (G), LosA. RC**	**3.00**	**.40**
□□□	182 Christian Ruuttu, Buff.	.50	.20
□□□	183 Dave Tippett, Hart.	.50	.20
□□□	184 Pat LaFontaine, NYIs.	2.00	.20
□□□	185 Mark Howe, Phil.	1.00	.20
□□□	186 Stéphane J.J. Richer, Mont.	.50	.20
□□□	187 Jan Erixon, NYRa.	.50	.20
□□□	188 Neil Sheehy, Wash.	.50	.20
□□□	189 Craig MacTavish, Edmo.	.50	.20
□□□	190 Randy Burridge, Bost.	.50	.20
□□□	191 Bernie Federko, Detr.	1.00	.20
□□□	192 Shawn Chambers, Minn.	.50	.20
□□□	193 Mark Messier, Edmo. [AS]	3.50	.50
□□□	194 Luc Robitaille, LosA. [AS]	3.00	.20
□□□	195 Brett Hull, SLou. [AS]	3.50	.50
□□□	196 Raymond Bourque, Bost. [AS]	4.50	.50
□□□	197 Al MacInnis, Calg. [AS]	1.50	.20
□□□	198 Patrick Roy (G), Mont. [AS]	20.00	1.50
□□□	199 Wayne Gretzky, LosA. [AS]	25.00	2.00
□□□	200 Brian Bellows, Minn. [AS]	.50	.20
□□□	201 Cam Neely, Bost. [AS]	3.50	.50
□□□	202 Paul Coffey, Pitt. [AS]	2.00	.20
□□□	203 Doug Wilson, Chic. [AS]	1.00	.20
□□□	204 Daren Puppa (G), Buff. [AS]	.50	.20
□□□	205 Gary Suter, Calg.	.50	.20
□□□	206 Ed Olczyk, Toro.	.50	.20
□□□	207 Doug Lidster, Vanc.	.50	.20
□□□	208 John Cullen, Pitt.	.50	.20
□□□	209 Luc Robitaille, LosA.	3.00	.20
□□□	210 Tim Kerr, Phil.	.50	.20
□□□	211 Scott Stevens, Wash. (SLou.)	1.50	.20
□□□	212 Craig Janney, Bost.	.50	.20
□□□	213 Kevin Dineen, Hart.	.50	.20
□□□	**214 Jimmy Waite (G), Chic. RC**	**3.00**	**.40**
□□□	215 Benoît Hogue, Buff.	.50	.20
□□□	**216 C. Leschyshyn, Québ. RC**	**3.00**	**.40**
□□□	217 Brad Lauer, NYIs.	.50	.20
□□□	218 Joe Mullen, Calg. (NYRa.)	1.50	.20
□□□	219 Patrick Roy (G), Mont.	20.00	1.50
□□□	220 Blues team card	.50	.20
□□□	221 Brian Leetch, NYRa.	2.00	.20
□□□	222 Steve Yzerman, Detr.	9.00	1.00
□□□	**223 S. Beauregard (G), Winn. RC**	**3.00**	**.40**
□□□	224 John MacLean, NJer.	.50	.20
□□□	225 Trevor Linden, Vanc.	1.50	.20
□□□	226 Bill Ranford (G), Edmo.	1.50	.20
□□□	227 Mark Osborne, Toro.	.50	.20
□□□	228 Curt Giles, Minn.	.50	.20
□□□	229 Mikko Mäkelä, LosA.	.50	.20
□□□	230 Bob Errey, Pitt.	.50	.20
□□□	231 Jimmy Carson, Detr.	.50	.20
□□□	**232 Kay Whitmore (G), Hart. RC**	**3.00**	**.40**
□□□	233 Gary Nylund, NYIs.	.50	.20
□□□	**234 Jiri Hrdina, Calg. RC**	**3.00**	**.40**
□□□	235 S. Leach, Wash [Err.: Stephan]	.50	.20
□□□	236 Greg Hawgood, Bost.	.50	.20
□□□	**237 Jocelyn Lemieux, Chic. RC**	**1.50**	**.40**
□□□	238 Daren Puppa (G), Buff.	.50	.20
□□□	239 Kelly Kisio, NYRa.	.50	.20
□□□	240 Craig Simpson, Edmo.	.50	.20
□□□	241 Damphousse, Toro. [Team]	2.00	.20
□□□	242 Fredrik Olausson, Winn.	.50	.20
□□□	243 Ron Hextall (G), Phil.	2.00	.20
□□□	**244 Sergio Momesso, SLou. RC**	**1.50**	**.40**
□□□	245 Kirk Muller, NJer.	1.00	.20
□□□	246 Petr* Svoboda, Mont.	.50	.20
□□□	247 Daniel Berthiaume (G), Minn.	.50	.20
□□□	248 Andrew McBain, Vanc.	.50	.20
□□□	249 Jeff Jackson, Québ.	.50	.20
□□□	**250 Randy Gilhen, Pitt. RC**	**1.50**	**.40**
□□□	251 Adam Graves, Edmo. [Team]	1.50	.20
□□□	**252 Rick Bennet, NYRa. RC**	**1.50**	**.40**
□□□	253 Don Beaupré (G), Wash.	.50	.20
□□□	254 Pelle Eklund, Phil.	.50	.20
□□□	255 Greg Gilbert, Chic.	.50	.20
□□□	256 Gord** Roberts, SLou.	1.50	.20
□□□	257 Kirk McLean (G), Vanc.	1.00	.20
□□□	258 Brent Sutter, NYIs.	.50	.20
□□□	259 Brendan Shanahan, NJer.	3.50	.50
□□□	**260 Todd Krygier, Hart. RC**	**1.50**	**.40**
□□□	261 Larry Robinson, LosA.	2.00	.20
□□□	262 Sabres team card	.50	.20
□□□	263 Dave Christian, Bost.	.50	.20
□□□	264 Checklist	.50	.20
□□□	265 Jamie Macoun, Calg.	.50	.20
□□□	266 Glen Hanlon (G), Detr.	.50	.20
□□□	267 Daniel Marois, Toro.	.50	.20
□□□	268 Doug Smail, Winn.	.50	.20
□□□	269 Jon Casey (G), Minn.	.50	.20
□□□	270 Brian Skrudland, Mont.	.50	.20
□□□	271 Michel Petit, Québ.	.50	.20
□□□	272 Dan Quinn, Vanc.	.50	.20
□□□	273 Geoff Courtnall, Wash. (SLou.)	.50	.20
□□□	274 Mike Bullard, Phil.	.50	.20
□□□	275 Randy Gregg, Edmo.	.50	.20
□□□	276 Keith Brown, Chic.	.50	.20
□□□	**277 Troy Mallette, NYRa. RC**	**1.50**	**.40**
□□□	278 Steve Tuttle, SLou.	.50	.20
□□□	**279 Brad Shaw, Hart. RC**	**1.50**	**.40**
□□□	**280 Mark Recchi, Pitt. RC**	**7.00**	**1.00**
□□□	281 John Tonelli, LosA.	.50	.20
□□□	282 Doug Bodger, Buff.	.50	.20
□□□	283 Thomas Steen, Winn.	.50	.20
□□□	284 Chris Terreri (G), NJer. [Team]	1.00	.20
□□□	285 Lee Norwood, Detr.	.50	.20
□□□	286 Brian MacLellan, Calg.	.50	.20
□□□	287 Bobby Smith, Mont.	1.00	.20
□□□	**288 Robert Cimetta, Bost. RC**	**1.50**	**.40**
□□□	**289 Rob Zettler, Minn. RC**	**1.50**	**.40**
□□□	**290 David Reid, Toro. RC**	**3.00**	**.40**
□□□	291 Bryan Trottier, NYIs. (Pitt.)	3.50	.50
□□□	292 Brian Mullen, NYRa.	.50	.20
□□□	293 Paul Reinhart, Vanc.	.50	.20
□□□	294 Andy Moog (G), Bost.	1.50	.20
□□□	295 Jeff R. Brown, SLou.	.50	.20
□□□	296 Ryan Walter, Mont.	.50	.20
□□□	297 Trent Yawney, Chic.	.50	.20
□□□	**298 John Druce, Wash. RC**	**1.50**	**.40**
□□□	299 Dave McLlwain, Winn.	.50	.20
□□□	300 David Volek, NYIs.	.50	.20
□□□	301 Tomas Sandström, LosA.	.50	.20
□□□	**302 Gord Murphy, Phil. RC**	**1.50**	**.40**
□□□	**303 Lou Franceschetti, Toro. RC**	**1.50**	**.40**
□□□	304 Dana Murzyn, Calg.	.50	.20
□□□	305 North Stars team leaders	.50	.20
□□□	306 Patrik Sundström, NJer.	.50	.20
□□□	307 Kevin Lowe, Edmo.	1.00	.20
□□□	308 Dave Barr, Detr.	.50	.20
□□□	**309 Wendell Young (G), Pitt. RC**	**3.00**	**.40**
□□□	**310 Darrin Shannon, Buff. RC**	**1.50**	**.40**
□□□	311 Ron Francis, Hart.	2.00	.20
□□□	**312 Stéphane Fiset, Québ. RC**	**6.00**	**.50**
□□□	313 Paul Fenton, Winn.	.50	.20
□□□	314 Dave Taylor, LosA.	.50	.20
□□□	315 Islanders team leaders	.50	.20
□□□	316 Petri Skriko, Vanc.	.50	.20
□□□	317 Rob Ramage, Toro.	.50	.20
□□□	318 Murray Craven, Phil.	.50	.20
□□□	319 Gaétan Duchesne, Minn.	.50	.20
□□□	320 Brad McCrimmon, Calg. (Detr.)	.50	.20
□□□	321 Grant Fuhr (G), Edmo.	2.00	.20
□□□	322 Gerard Gallant, Detr.	.50	.20
□□□	323 Tommy Albelin, NJer.	.50	.20
□□□	324 Scott Arniel, Buff. (Winn.)	.50	.20
□□□	**325 Mike Keane, Mont. RC**	**3.00**	**.40**
□□□	326 Doug Smith, Pitt. [Team Card]	.50	.20
□□□	327 Mike Ridley, Wash.	.50	.20
□□□	328 Dave Babych, Hart.	.50	.20
□□□	329 Michel Goulet, Chic.	1.50	.20
□□□	**330 Mike Richter (G), NYRa. RC**	**9.00**	**1.00**
□□□	**331 Garry Galley, Bost. RC**	**1.50**	**.40**
□□□	**332 Rod Brind'Amour, SLou. RC**	**6.00**	**.50**
□□□	333 Tony McKegney, Québ.	.50	.20
□□□	334 Peter Stastny, NJer.	2.00	.20
□□□	335 Greg Millen (G), Chic.	.50	.20
□□□	336 Ray Ferraro, Hart.	.50	.20
□□□	**337 Miloslav Horava, NYRa. RC**	**1.50**	**.40**
□□□	338 Paul MacDermid, Winn.	.50	.20
□□□	**339 Craig Coxe, Vanc. RC**	**1.50**	**.40**
□□□	**340 Dave Snuggerud, Buff. RC**	**1.50**	**.40**
□□□	**341 M. Lalor, SLou. (Wash.) RC**	**1.50**	**.40**
□□□	342 Marc Habscheid, Detr.	.50	.20
□□□	343 Réjean Lemelin (G), Bost.	.50	.20
□□□	344 Charlie Huddy, Edmo.	.50	.20
□□□	345 Ken Linseman, Phil.	.50	.20
□□□	346 Canadiens team card	.50	.20
□□□	**347 Troy Loney, Pitt. RC**	**1.50**	**.40**
□□□	**348 Mike Modano, Minn. RC**	**18.00**	**2.50**
□□□	**349 Jeff Reese (G), Toro. RC**	**3.00**	**.40**
□□□	350 Patrick Flatley, NYIs.	.50	.20
□□□	351 Mike Vernon (G), Calg.	1.50	.20
□□□	**352 Todd Elik, LosA. RC**	**1.50**	**.40**
□□□	353 Rod Langway, Wash.	1.50	.20
□□□	354 Moe Mantha, Winn.	.50	.20
□□□	355 Keith Acton, Phil.	.50	.20
□□□	**356 Scott Pearson, Toro. RC**	**1.50**	**.40**
□□□	**357 Perry Berezan, Minn. RC**	**1.50**	**.40**
□□□	**358 Alexei Kasatonov, NJer. RC**	**4.50**	**.50**
□□□	**359 Igor Larionov, Vanc. RC**	**10.00**	**1.50**
□□□	**360 Kevin Stevens, Pitt. RC**	**4.00**	**.50**
□□□	**361 Yves Racine, Detr. RC**	**1.50**	**.40**
□□□	362 Dave Poulin, Bost.	.50	.20
□□□	363 Blackhawks team card	.50	.20
□□□	**364 Yvon Corriveau, Hart. RC**	**1.50**	**.40**
□□□	365 Brian Benning, LosA.	.50	.20
□□□	**366 H. McDonough, NYIs. RC**	**1.50**	**.40**
□□□	367 Ron Tugnutt (G), Québ.	1.50	.20
□□□	368 J. Steve Smith, Edmo.	.50	.20
□□□	369 Joel Otto, Calg.	.50	.20
□□□	**370 Dave Lowry, SLou. RC**	**4.50**	**.50**
□□□	371 Clint Malarchuk (G), Buff.	.50	.20
□□□	**372 M. Schneider, Mont. RC**	**4.50**	**.50**
□□□	373 Mike Gartner, NYRa.	3.00	.20
□□□	374 John Tucker, Wash. (Buff.)	.50	.20
□□□	**375 Chris Terreri (G), NJer. RC**	**3.00**	**.40**
□□□	376 Dean Evason, Hart.	.50	.20
□□□	**377 Jamie Leach, Pitt. RC**	**1.50**	**.40**
□□□	**378 J. Cloutier (G), Chic. RC**	**3.00**	**.40**
□□□	379 Glen Wesley, Bost.	.50	.20
□□□	**380 Vladimir Krutov, Vanc. RC**	**4.50**	**.50**
□□□	381 Terry Carkner, Phil.	.50	.20
□□□	**382 John* McIntyre, Toro. RC**	**1.50**	**.40**
□□□	**383 Ville Siren, Minn. RC**	**1.50**	**.40**
□□□	384 Joe Sakic, Québ.	6.00	.50
□□□	**385 T. Numminen, Winn. RC**	**6.00**	**.50**
□□□	386 Theoren Fleury, Calg.	2.00	.20
□□□	**387 G. Featherstone, SLou. RC**	**1.50**	**.40**
□□□	**388 Stéphan Lebeau, Mont. RC**	**1.50**	**.40**
□□□	389 Kevin McClelland, Detr.	.50	.20
□□□	390 Uwe Krupp, Buff.	.50	.20
□□□	**391 Mark Janssens, NYRa. RC**	**1.50**	**.40**
□□□	392 Marty McSorley, LosA.	.50	.20
□□□	**393 Vladimir Ruzicka, Edmo. RC**	**4.50**	**.50**
□□□	394 Scott Stevens, Wash. [Team]	1.50	.20
□□□	**395 M. Fitzpatrick (G), NYIs. RC**	**3.00**	**.40**
□□□	396 Checklist	.50	.20

Description	Reg.
397 Dave Manson, Chic.	.20
398 Bob Gould, Bost.	.20
399 Bill Houlder, Wash. RC	.40
400 Glenn Healy (G), NYIs. RC	.50
401 John Kordic, Toro. RC	.40
402 Stewart Gavin, Minn.	.20
403 David Shaw, NYRa.	.20
404 Ed Kastelic, Hart. RC	.40
405 Rich Sutter, SLou.	.20
406 Grant Ledyard, Buff. RC	.40
407 Steve Weeks (G), Vanc.	.20
408 Randy Hillier, Pitt.	.20
409 Rick Wamsley (G), Calg.	.20
410 Doug Houda, Detr. RC	.40
411 Ken McRae, Québ. RC	.40
412 Craig Ludwig, Mont.	.20
413 Doug Evans, Winn. RC	.40
414 Ken Baumgartner, NYIs. RC	.40
415 Ken Wregget (G), Phil.	.20
416 Eric Weinrich, NJer. RC	.40
417 Mike Allison, LosA.	.20
418 Joel Quenneville, Hart.	.20
419 Larry Melnyk, Vanc.	.20
420 Colin Patterson, Calg.	.20
421 Gerald Diduck, NYIs.	.20
422 Brent Gilchrist, Mont. RC	.40
423 Craig Muni, Edmo.	.20
424 Mike Hudson, Chic. RC	.40
425 Éric Desjardins, Mont. RC	.50
426 Walt Poddubny, NJer.	.20
427 Mike Hough, Québ.	.20
428 Luke Richardson, Toro.	.20
429 Joe Murphy, Edmo. RC	.40
430 Tim Cheveldae (G), Detr. RC	.40
431 Adam Burt, Hart. RC	.40
432 Kelly Chase, SLou. RC	.40
433 Robert Nordmark, Vanc. RC	.40
434 Tim Hunter, Calg. RC	.40
435 Peter Taglianetti, Winn.	.20
436 Alain Chevrier (G), Pitt.	.20
437 Darin Kimble, Québ. RC	.40
438 David Maley, NJer. RC	.40
439 Jim Wiemer, Bost. RC	.40
440 Nick Kypreos, Wash. RC	.50
441 Lucien DeBlois, Québ.	.20
442 Mario Gosselin (G), LosA.	.20
443 Neil Wilkinson, Minn. RC	.40
444 Mark Kumpel, Winn. RC	.40
445 Sergei Mylnikov (G), Québ. RC	.40
446 Ray Sheppard, Buff. (NYRa.)	.20
447 Ron Greschner, NYRa.	.20
448 Craig Berube, Phil. RC	.40
449 Dave Hannan, Toro.	.20
450 Jim Korn, Calg.	.20
451 Claude Lemieux, Mont.	.20
452 (Pokey) Reddick (G), Edmo. RC	.40
453 Randy Velischek, NJer.	.20
454 Chris Nilan, NYRa. (Bost.)	.20
455 Jim Benning, Vanc.	.20
456 Wayne Presley, Chic.	.20
457 Jon Morris, NJer. RC	.40
458 Clark Donatelli, Minn. RC	.40
459 Ric Nattress, Calg.	.20
460 Rob Murray, Wash. RC	.40
461 Tim Watters, LosA.	.20
462 Checklist	.20
463 Derrick Smith, Phil. RC	.40
464 Lyndon Byers, Bost. RC	.40
465 Jeff Chychrun, Phil. RC	.40
466 Duane Sutter, Chic.	.20
467 Bill Ranford (G), Edmo. [AW]	.20
468 Anatoli Semenov, Riga RC	.40
469 Konstantin Kurashov, Krylja RC	.40
470 Gord Dineen, Pitt.	.20
471 Jeff Beukeboom, Edmo. RC	.40
472 Andrei Lomakin, Riga RC	.40
473 Doug Sulliman, Phil.	.20
474 Alexander Kerch, Riga RC	.40
475 R. Bourque, NHL Awards (Bost.)	.50
476 Keith Crowder, LosA.	.20
477 Oleg Znarok, Riga RC	.40
478 Dimitri Zinovjev, Riga RC	.40
479 Igor Esmantovich, Krylja RC	.40
480 Adam Graves, Edmo. RC	1.00
481 Petr Prajsler, LosA. RC	.40
482 Sergei Yashin, Riga RC	.40
483 Jeff Bloemberg, NYRa. RC	.40
484 Yuri Strakhov, Krylja RC	.40
485 Sergei B. Makarov, Krylja RC	.40
486 R.Lemelin / A. Moog	.20
487 Sergei Zaitsev, Krylja RC	.40
488 Rick Meagher, NHL Awards (SLou.)	.20
489 Yuri Kuznetsov, Krylja RC	.40
490 Tom Chorske, Mont. RC	.40
491 Igor Akulinin, Riga RC	.40
492 Mikhail Panin, Krylja RC	.40
493 Sergei Nemchinov, Krylja RC	.50
494 V. Yursinov, Riga [Coach] RC	.40
495 Gord Kluzak, Bost.	.20
496 Sergei Skosyrev, Riga RC	.40
497 Jeff Parker, Buff. (Winn.) RC	.40
498 Tom Tilley, SLou. RC	.40
499 Alexander Smirnov, Riga RC	.40
500 Alexander Lysenko, Krylja RC	.40
501 A. Irbe (G), Riga [Error: Artur] RC	4.00
502 Alexei Frolikov, Riga RC	.40
503 S. Makarov, NHL Awards (Calg.)	.20
504 Nikolai Varjanov, Riga RC	.40
505 Allen Pedersen, Bost.	.20
506 Vladimir Shashov, Riga RC	.40
507 Tim Bergland, Wash. RC	.40
508 Gennady Lebedev, Krylja RC	.40
509 Rod Buskas, Pitt. RC	.40
510 Grant Jennings, Hart. RC	.40
511 Ulf Samuelsson, Hart.	.20
512 P. Roy (G), NHL Awards (Mont.)	1.50
513 Brett Hull, NHL Awards (SLou.)	.50
514 Dmitri Mironov, Krylja RC	.40
515 Randy Moller, NYRa.	.20
516 Kerry Huffman, Phil. RC	.40
517 Gilbert Delorme, Pitt.	.20
518 Greg C. Adams, Detr.	.20
519 Mark Messier, NHL Awards (Edmo.)	.50
520 Sheldon Kennedy, Detr. RC	.40
521 Harijs Vitolinsh, Riga RC	.40
522 W. Gretzky, NHL Awards (LosA.)	2.00
523 Dmitri Frolov, Riga RC	.40
524 Tom Laidlaw, LosA.	.20
525 Oleg Bratash (G), Krylja RC	.40
526 Kris King, NYRa. RC	.40
527 Wayne Van Dorp, Chic. RC	.40
528 Chris Dahlquist, Pitt. RC	.40

O-PEE-CHEE / CENTRAL RED ARMY

O-Pee-Chee Insert Set (22 cards): 8.00

Insert (1:1)	OPC
1R Ilya Byakin, CSKA Moscow RC	.30
2R Vladimir Malakhov, CSKA Moscow RC	.50
3R Andrei Khomutov, CSKA Moscow RC	.30
4R Valeri Kamensky, CSKA Moscow RC	1.00
5R Dmitri Motkov, CSKA Moscow RC	.30
6R Evgeny Shastin, CSKA Moscow RC	.30
7R Arturs Irbe (G), CSKA Moscow	2.00
8R Igor Chibirev, CSKA Moscow RC	.30
9R M. Mikhailovsky (G), CSKA Moscow RC	.30
10R Vyacheslav Bykov, CSKA Moscow RC	.50
11R Super Series, CSKA Moscow	.20
12R Super Series, CSKA Moscow	.20
13R Valeri Shiryev, CSKA Moscow RC	.30
14R Igor Maslennikov, CSKA Moscow RC	.30
15R Igor Malykhin, CSKA Moscow RC	.30
16R Dmitri Khristich, CSKA Moscow RC	.50
17R Viktor Tikhonov, CSKA Moscow RC	.50
18R Evgeny Davydov, CSKA Moscow RC	.30
19R Sergei Fedorov, CSKA Moscow RC	5.00
20R Pavel Kostichkin, CSKA Moscow RC	.30
21R V. Konstantinov, CSKA Moscow RC	1.00
22R Checklist	.20

TOPPS / SCORING LEADERS

These cards have two versions: the regular inserts and a Tiffany parallel.

Topps Insert Set (21 cards): 10.00 10.00

Insert (1:1)	Tiff.	TSL
1 Steve Larmer, Chic.	.50	.50
2 Brett Hull, SLou.	.50	.50
3 Cam Neely, Bost.	.50	.50
4 Stéphane J.J. Richer, Mont.	.50	.50
5 Paul Reinhart, Vanc.	.50	.50
6 Dino Ciccarelli, Wash.	.50	.50
7 Kirk Muller, NJer.	.50	.50
8 Joe Nieuwendyk, Calg.	.50	.50
9 Rick Tocchet, Phil.	.50	.50
10 Pat LaFontaine, NYIs.	.50	.50
11 Dale Hawerchuk, Winn.	.50	.50
12 Wayne Gretzky, LosA.	3.00	3.00
13 Gary Leeman, Toro.	.50	.50
14 Joe Sakic, Québ.	1.00	1.00
15 Brian Bellows, Minn.	.50	.50
16 Mark Messier, Edmo.	.50	.50
17 Mario Lemieux, Pitt.	2.00	2.00
18 John Ogrodnick, NYRa.	.50	.50
19 Steve Yzerman, Detr.	1.50	1.50
20 Pierre Turgeon, Buff.	.50	.50
21 Ron Francis, Hart.	.50	.50

BOX BOTTOMS

These four-card panels were found on the bottom of both O-Pee-Chee and Topps wax boxes. The most expensive cut-out singles are Wayne Gretzky at $3 and Mario Lemieux at $2.

Panel Size: 5" x 7"

Complete Set (16 cards): 10.00

Description	
A-D Mogilny/ Casey/ Coffey/ Gretzky	4.00
E-H Roy/ Modano/ Lemieux/ MacInnis	4.00
I-L Bourque/ Yzerman/ Turcotte/ Vernon	3.00
M-P Turgeon/ Wilson/ Beaupré/ Makarov	2.00

1990 - 91 O-PEE-CHEE PREMIER

Complete Set (132 cards): 80.00

Common Player: .25

Description	
1 Scott Arniel, Winn.	.25
2 Jergus Baca, Hart. RC	.50
3 Brian Bellows, Minn.	.25
4 Jean-Claude Bergeron (G), Mont. RC	1.00
5 Daniel Berthiaume (G), LosA.	.25
6 Rob Blake, LosA. RC	5.00
7 Peter Bondra, Wash. RC	5.00
8 Laurie Boschman, NJer.	.25
9 Raymond Bourque, Bost.	1.50
10 Aaron Broten, Québ. (Toro.)	.25
11 Greg Brown, Buff. RC	.50
12 Jimmy Carson, Detr.	.25
13 Chris Chelios, Chic.	.50
14 Dino Ciccarelli, Wash.	.25
15 Zdeno Ciger, NJer. RC	1.00
16 Paul Coffey, Pitt.	.50
17 Danton Cole, Winn. RC	.50
18 Geoff Courtnall, SLou.	.25
19 Mike Craig, Minn. RC	.50
20 John Cullen, Pitt.	.25
21 Vincent Damphousse, Toro.	.50
22 Gerald Diduck, Mont.	.25
23 Kevin Dineen, Hart.	.25
24 Pår Djoos, Detr. RC	1.00
25 Tie Domi, NYRa. RC	2.50
26 Peter Douris, Bost. RC	.50
27 Rob DiMaio, NYIs. RC	1.00
28 Pat Elynuik, Winn.	.25
29 Bob Essensa (G), Winn. RC	2.00
30 Sergei Fedorov, Detr. RC	12.00
31 Brent Fedyk, Detr. RC	.50
32 Ron Francis, Hart.	.50
33 Link Gaetz, Minn. RC	.50
34 Troy Gamble (G), Vanc. RC	1.00
35 Johan Garpenlöv, Detr. RC	.50
36 Mike Gartner, NYRa.	1.00
37 Rick Green, Detr.	.25
38 Wayne Gretzky, LosA.	5.00
39 Jeff Hackett (G), NYIs. RC	2.50
40 Dale Hawerchuk, Buff.	.50
41 Ron Hextall (G), Phil.	.50
42 Bruce Hoffort (G), Phil. RC	.50
43 Bobby Holik, Hart. RC	2.50
44 Martin Hostak, Phil. RC	.50
45 Phil Housley, Winn.	.25
46 Jody Hull, NYRa. RC	.50
47 Brett Hull, SLou.	1.00
48 Al Iafrate, Toro.	.25
49 Peter Ing (G), Toro. RC	1.00
50 Jaromir Jagr, Pitt. RC	20.00
51 Curtis Joseph (G), SLou. RC	8.00
52 Robert Kron, Vanc. RC	1.00
53 Frantisek Kucera, Chic. RC	.50
54 Dale Kushner, Phil. RC	.50
55 Guy Lafleur, Québ.	2.50
56 Pat LaFontaine, NYIs.	.50
57 Mike Lalor, Wash. RC	.50
58 Steve Larmer, Chic.	.50
59 Jiri Latal, Phil. RC	.50
60 Jamie Leach, Pitt. RC	.50
61 Brian Leetch, NYRa.	.50
62 Claude Lemieux, NJer.	.25
63 Mario Lemieux, Pitt.	3.50
64 Craig Ludwig, NYIs.	.25
65 Al MacInnis, Calg.	.50
66 Mikko Mäkelä, Buff.	.25
67 Dave Marcinyshyn, NJer. RC	.50
68 Stéphane Matteau, Calg. RC	1.00
69 Brad McCrimmon, Detr.	.25
70 Kirk McLean (G), Vanc.	.25
71 Mark Messier, Edmo.	1.00
72 Kelly Miller, Wash.	.25
73 Kevin Miller, NYRa. RC	.50
74 Mike Modano, Minn. RC	10.00
75 Alexander Mogilny, Buff. RC	5.00
76 Andy Moog (G), Bost.	.50
77 Joe Mullen, Pitt.	.50
78 Kirk Muller, NJer.	.25
79 Pat Murray, Phil. RC	.50
80 Jarmo Myllys (G), Minn. RC	1.00
81 Petr Nedved, Vanc. RC	2.50
82 Cam Neely, Bost.	1.00
83 Bernie Nicholls, NYRa.	.25
84 Joe Nieuwendyk, Calg.	.50
85 Chris Nilan, Bost.	.25
86 Owen Nolan, Québ. RC	5.00
87 B. Noonan, Chic. [Error: Vincelette]	.25
88 Adam Oates, SLou.	.50
89 Greg Parks, NYIs. RC	.50
90 Adrien Plavsic, Vanc. RC	.50
91 Keith Primeau, Detr. RC	3.50
92 Brian Propp, Minn.	.25
93 Dan Quinn, Vanc.	.25
94 Bill Ranford (G), Edmo.	.50
95 Robert Reichel, Calg. RC	2.50
96 Mike Ricci, Phil. RC	2.50
97 Steven Rice, NYRa. RC	.50
98 Stéphane J.J. Richer, Mont.	.25
99 Luc Robitaille, LosA.	1.00
100 Jeremy Roenick, Chic. RC	7.00
101 Patrick Roy (G), Mont.	3.50
102 Joe Sakic, Québ.	2.00
103 Denis Savard, Mont.	.50
104 Anatoli Semenov, Edmo. RC	.50
105 Brendan Shanahan, NJer.	1.00
106 Ray Sheppard, NYRa.	.25
107 Mike Sillinger, Detr. RC	1.00
108 Ilkka Sinisalo, Minn.	.25
109 Bobby Smith, Minn.	.25
110 Paul Stanton, Pitt. RC	.50
111 Kevin Stevens, Pitt. RC	2.00
112 Scott Stevens, SLou.	.50
113 Allan Stewart, NJer. RC	.50
114 Mats Sundin, Québ. RC	8.00
115 Brent Sutter, NYIs.	.25
116 Tim Sweeney, Calg. RC	.50
117 Peter Taglianetti, Minn.	.25
118 John Tanner (G), Québ. RC	.50
119 Dave Tippett, Wash.	.25
120 Rick Tocchet, Phil.	.25
121 Bryan Trottier, Pitt.	1.00
122 John Tucker, Buff.	.25
123 Darren Turcotte, NYRa. RC	1.00
124 Pierre Turgeon, Buff.	.50
125 Randy Velischek, Québ.	.25
126 Mike Vernon (G), Calg.	.50
127 Wes Walz, Bost. RC	2.00
128 Carey Wilson, Hart.	.25
129 Doug Wilson, Chic.	.25
130 Steve Yzerman, Detr.	3.00
131 Peter Zezel, Wash.	.25
132 Checklist	.25

1990 - 91 PANINI STICKERS

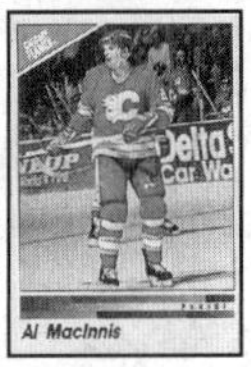

The most expensive single is Wayne Gretzky at $1-$2. All other singles sell between 20¢ and $1.00.

Sticker Size: 2 1/6" x 2 15/16"

Imprint: PANINI

Complete Set (351 stickers): 18.00

Album (Wayne Gretzky): 4.00

Panini	Panini
1 Wales Conference	2 Campbell Conference
3 Stanley Cup	4 Dave Poulin
5 Brian Propp	6 Glen Wesley
7 Bob Carpenter	8 John Carter
9 Cam Neely	10 Greg Hawgood
11 Andy Moog (G)	12 Bruins Logo
13 Réjean Lemelin (G)	14 Craig Janney
15 Bob Sweeney	16 Andy Brickley
17 Ray Bourque	18 Dave Christian
19 Dave Snuggerud	20 Christian Ruuttu
21 Phil Housley	22 Uwe Krupp
25 Martin Lapointe	26 Eric Brulé, Error
23 Rick Vaive	24 Mike Ramsey
25 Mike Foligno	26 Clint Malarchuk (G)
27 Sabres Logo	28 Pierre Turgeon
29 Dave Andreychuk	30 Scott Arniel
31 Daren Puppa (G)	32 Mike Hartman
33 Doug Bodger	34 Scott Young
35 Todd Krygier	36 Pat Verbeek
37 Dave Tippett	38 P. Sidorkiewicz (G)
39 Ron Francis	40 Dave Babych
41 Randy Ladouceur	42 Whalers Logo
43 Kevin Dineen	44 Dean Evason
45 Ray Ferraro	46 Mike Tomlak
47 Mikael Andersson	48 Brad Shaw
49 Chris Chelios	50 Petr Svoboda
51 Patrick Roy (G)	52 Bobby Smith
53 Stéphane Richer	54 Shayne Corson
55 Brian Skrudland	56 Russ Courtnall
57 Canadiens Logo	58 Guy Carbonneau
59 Sylvain Lefebvre	60 Mathieu Schneider
61 Brian Hayward (G)	62 Mats Näslund
63 Mike McPhee	64 Brendan Shanahan
65 Patrik Sundstrom	66 Mark Johnson
67 Doug Brown	68 Chris Terreri (G)
69 Bruce Driver	70 Peter Stastny
71 Sylvain Turgeon	72 Devils Logo
73 Kirk Muller	74 John MacLean
75 Viacheslav Fetisov	76 Tommy Albelin
77 Sean Burke (G)	78 Janne Ojanen
79 Randy Wood	80 Gary Nylund
81 Pat LaFontaine	82 Patrick Flatley
83 Bryan Trottier	84 Don Maloney
85 Gerald Diduck	86 Islanders Logo
87 Mark Fitzpatrick (G)	88 Glenn Healy (G)
89 Alan Kerr	90 Brent Sutter
91 Doug Crossman	92 Hubie McDonough
93 Jeff Norton	94 Kelly Kisio
95 Brian Leetch	96 Brian Mullen
97 James Patrick	98 Mike Richter (G)
99 John Ogrodnick	100 Troy Mallette
101 Mark Janssens	102 Rangers Logo
103 Mike Gartner	104 Jan Erixon
105 Carey Wilson	106 Bernie Nicholls
107 Darren Turcotte	108 Vanbiesbrouck (G)
109 Ron Sutter	110 Kjell Samuelsson
111 Ken Linseman	112 Ken Wregget (G)
113 Per-Erik Eklund	114 Terry Carkner
115 Gord Murphy	116 Murray Craven
117 Flyers Logo	118 Ron Hextall (G)
119 Mike Bullard	120 Tim Kerr
121 Rick Tocchet	122 Mark Howe
123 Ilkka Sinisalo	124 Tony Tanti
125 John Cullen	126 Zarley Zalapski
127 Wendell Young (G)	128 Rob Brown
129 Phil Bourque	130 Mark Recchi
131 Kevin Stevens	132 Penguins Logo
133 Bob Errey	134 Tom Barrasso (G)
135 Paul Coffey	136 Mario Lemieux
137 Randy Hillier	138 Troy Loney
139 Joe Sakic	140 Lucien DeBlois
141 Joe Cirella	142 Ron Tugnutt (G)
143 Paul Gillis	144 Bryan Fogarty
145 Guy Lafleur	146 Tony Hrkac
147 Nordiques Logo	148 Michel Petit
149 Tony McKegney	150 Curtis Leschyshyn
151 Claude Loiselle	152 Mario Brunetta (G)

☐ 153 Marc Fortier ☐ 154 Michal Pivonka
☐ 155 Scott Stevens ☐ 156 Kelly Miller
☐ 157 John Tucker ☐ 158 Don Beaupré (G)
☐ 159 Geoff Courtnall ☐ 160 Alan May
☐ 161 Dino Ciccarelli ☐ 162 Capitals Logo
☐ 163 Mike Ridley ☐ 164 Bob Rouse
☐ 165 Mike Liut (G) ☐ 166 Stephen Leach
☐ 167 Kevin Hatcher ☐ 168 Dale Hunter
☐ 169 Wales Trophy ☐ 170 Campbell Trophy
☐ 171 Cup Championship ☐ 172 Doug Gilmour
☐ 173 Brad McCrimmon ☐ 174 Joe Nieuwendyk
☐ 175 Mike Vernon (G) ☐ 176 Theoren Fleury
☐ 177 Gary Suter ☐ 178 Jamie Macoun
☐ 179 Gary Roberts ☐ 180 Flames Logo
☐ 181 Paul Ranheim ☐ 182 Jiri Hrdina
☐ 183 Joe Mullen ☐ 184 Sergei Makarov
☐ 185 Al MacInnis ☐ 186 Rick Wamsley (G)
☐ 187 Trent Yawney ☐ 188 Greg Millen (G)
☐ 189 Doug Wilson ☐ 190 Jocelyn Lemieux
☐ 191 Dirk Graham ☐ 192 Keith Brown
☐ 193 Adam Creighton ☐ 194 Steve Larmer
☐ 195 Blackhawks Logo ☐ 196 Greg Gilbert
☐ 197 J. Cloutier (G) ☐ 198 Denis Savard
☐ 199 Dave Manson ☐ 200 Troy Murray
☐ 201 Jeremy Roenick ☐ 202 Lee Norwood
☐ 203 Glen Hanlon (G) ☐ 204 Marc Habscheid
☐ 205 Gerard Gallant ☐ 206 Rick Zombo
☐ 207 Steve Chiasson ☐ 208 Steve Yzerman
☐ 209 Bernie Federko ☐ 210 Red Wings Logo
☐ 211 Joey Kocur ☐ 212 Tim Cheveldae (G)
☐ 213 Shawn Burr ☐ 214 Jimmy Carson
☐ 215 Mike O'Connell ☐ 216 John Chabot
☐ 217 Craig Muni ☐ 218 Bill Ranford (G)
☐ 219 Mark Messier ☐ 220 Craig MacTavish
☐ 221 Charlie Huddy ☐ 222 Jari Kurri
☐ 223 Esa Tikkanen ☐ 224 Kevin Lowe
☐ 225 Oilers Logo ☐ 226 Steve Smith
☐ 227 Glenn Anderson ☐ 228 Petr Klima
☐ 229 Craig Simpson ☐ 230 Grant Fuhr (G)
☐ 231 Randy Gregg ☐ 232 Bob Kudelski
☐ 233 Luc Robitaille ☐ 234 Marty McSorley
☐ 235 John Tonelli ☐ 236 Dave Taylor
☐ 237 Mikko Makelä ☐ 238 Steve Kasper
☐ 239 Tony Granato ☐ 240 Kings Logo
☐ 241 Steve Duchesne ☐ 242 Wayne Gretzky
☐ 243 Tomas Sandström ☐ 244 Larry Robinson
☐ 245 Mike Krushelnyski ☐ 246 Kelly Hrudey (G)
☐ 247 Aaron Broten ☐ 248 Dave Gagner
☐ 249 Basil McRae ☐ 250 Curt Giles
☐ 251 Larry Murphy ☐ 252 Shawn Chambers
☐ 253 Mike Modano ☐ 254 Jon Casey (G)
☐ 255 North Stars Logo ☐ 256 Gaetan Duchesne
☐ 257 Brian Bellows ☐ 258 Frantisek Musil
☐ 259 Don Barber ☐ 260 Stewart Gavin
☐ 261 Neal Broten ☐ 262 Brett Hull
☐ 263 Sergio Momesso ☐ 264 Peter Zezel
☐ 265 Gino Cavallini ☐ 266 Rod Brind'Amour
☐ 267 Mike Lalor ☐ 268 V. Riendeau (G)
☐ 269 Gord Roberts ☐ 270 Blues Logo
☐ 271 Paul MacLean ☐ 272 Curtis Joseph (G)
☐ 273 Rick Meagher ☐ 274 Jeff Brown
☐ 275 Adam Oates ☐ 276 Paul Cavallini
☐ 277 Brad Marsh ☐ 278 Mark Osborne
☐ 279 Gary Leeman ☐ 280 Rob Ramage
☐ 281 Jeff Reese (G) ☐ 282 Tom Fergus
☐ 283 Ed Olczyk ☐ 284 Daniel Marois
☐ 285 Maple Leafs Logo ☐ 286 Wendel Clark
☐ 287 Tom Kurvers ☐ 288 Gilles Thibaudeau
☐ 289 Lou Franceschetti ☐ 290 Al Iafrate
☐ 291 V. Damphousse ☐ 292 Stan Smyl
☐ 293 Paul Reinhart ☐ 294 Igor Larionov
☐ 295 Doug Lidster ☐ 296 Kirk McLean (G)
☐ 297 Andrew McBain ☐ 298 Petri Skriko
☐ 299 Trevor Linden ☐ 300 Canucks Logo
☐ 301 Steve Bozek ☐ 302 Brian Bradley
☐ 303 Greg Adams ☐ 304 Vladimir Krutov
☐ 305 Dan Quinn ☐ 306 Jim Sandlak
☐ 307 Teppo Numminen ☐ 308 Doug Smail
☐ 309 Greg Paslawski ☐ 310 Dave Ellett
☐ 311 Bob Essensa (G) ☐ 312 Pat Elynuik
☐ 313 Paul Fenton ☐ 314 Randy Carlyle
☐ 315 Jets Logo ☐ 316 Thomas Steen
☐ 317 Dale Hawerchuk ☐ 318 Fredrick Olausson
☐ 319 Dave McLlwain ☐ 320 Laurie Boschman
☐ 321 Brent Ashton ☐ 322 AS: Ray Bourque
☐ 323 AS: P. Roy (G) ☐ 324 AS: Paul Coffey
☐ 325 AS: Brian Propp ☐ 326 AS: Mario Lemieux
☐ 327 AS: Cam Neely ☐ 328 AS: Al MacInnis
☐ 329 AS: M. Vernon (G) ☐ 330 AS: Kevin Lowe
☐ 331 AS: Luc Robitaille ☐ 332 AS: W. Gretzky
☐ 335 Alexei Kasatonov ☐ 336 Igor Larionov
☐ 337 Vladamir Krutov ☐ 338 Alexander Mogilny
☐ 339 Viacheslav Fetisov ☐ 340 Mike Modano
☐ 341 Mark Recchi ☐ 342 Paul Ranheim
☐ 343 Rod Brind'Amour ☐ 344 Brad Shaw
☐ 345 Mike Richter (G) ☐ 346 Hart Trophy
☐ 347 Art Ross Trophy ☐ 348 Calder Trophy
☐ 349 Lady Byng Trophy ☐ 350 Norris Trophy
☐ 351 Vezina Trophy

1990 - 91 PANINI TEAM STICKER PANELS

Team panels were issued for the seven Canadian NHL teams. Each team bag contained two 16-sticker panels and one poster. Each cut-out sticker measures 2 1/8" x 2 7/8".

Panel Size: 9" x 12"
Imprint: PANINI
Complete Set (7 panels): 40.00

Teams — Panini

☐ Calgary Flames (32 stickers plus poster) 8.00
1 T. Fleury/ 2 D. Gilmour/ 3 J. Hrdina/ 4 M. Hunter/ 5 T. Hunter/ 6 Johansson/ 7 Al MacInnis/ 8 MacLellan/ 9 J. Macoun/ 10 S. Makarov/ 11 S. Matteau/ 12 D. Murzyn/ 13 R. Nattress/ 14 J. Nieuwendyk/ 15 J. Otto/ 16 C. Patterson/ 17 S. Priakin/ 18 P. Ranheim/ 19 G. Roberts/ 20 K. Sabourin/ 21 G. Suter/ 22 T. Sweeney/ 23 M. Vernon/ 24 R. Wamsley/ A-B Logo/ C-F Action/ G J. Otto & R. Johansson/ H G. Suter

☐ Edmonton Oilers (32 stickers plus poster) 10.00
1 G. Anderson/ 2 J. Beukeboom/ 3 D. Brown/ 4 K. Buchberger/ 5 M. Gelinas/ 6 A. Graves/ 7 C. Huddy/ 8 C. Joseph/ 9 P. Klima/ 10 M. Lamb/ 11 K. Linseman/ 12 K. Lowe/ 13 C. MacTavish/ 14 M. Messier/ 15 C. Muni/ 16 J. Murphy/ 17 B. Ranford/ 18 E. Reddick/ 19 A. Semenov/ 20 C. Simpson/ 21 G. Smith/ 22 S. Smith/ 23 E. Tikkanen/ 24 Action/ A-B Logo/ C-F Action/ G M. Messier/ H Action

☐ Montréal Canadiens (32 stickers plus poster) 10.00
1 J.C. Bergeron/ 2 G. Carbonneau/ 3 A. Cassels/ 4 T. Chorske/ 5 S. Corson/ 6 R. Courtnall/ 7 J.J. Daigneault/ 8 E. Desjardins/ 9 G. Diduck/ 10 D. Dufresne/ 11 T. Ewen/ 12 B. Gilchrist/ 13 M. Keane/ 14 S. Lebeau/ 15 S. Lefebvre/ 16 M. McPhee/ 17 M. Pederson/ 18 S. Richer/ 19 P. Roy/ 20 D. Savard/ 21 M. Schneider/ 22 B. Skrudland/ 23 P. Svoboda/ 24 R. Walter/ A-B Logo/ C-F Action/ G P. Roy/ H Action

☐ Québec Nordiques (32 stickers plus poster) 10.00
1 J. Cirella/ 2 D. Doré/ 3 S. Finn/ 4 B. Fogarty/ 5 M. Fortier/ 6 P. Gillis/ 7 S. Gordon/ 8 S. Guerard/ 9 M. Hough/ 10 T. Hrkac/ 11 D. Kimble/ 12 G. Lafleur/ 13 C. Leschyshyn/ 14 C. Loiselle/ 15 T. McKegney/ 16 K. McRae/ 17 O. Nolan/ 18 J. Sakic/ 19 E. Sanipass/ 20 M. Sundin/ 21 J. Tanner/ 22 R. Tugnutt/ 23 R. Velischek/ 24 C. Wolanin/ A-B Logo/ C-F Action/ G G. Lafleur/ H M. Sundin

☐ Toronto Maple Leafs (32 stickers plus poster) 8.00
1 D. Berehowsky/ 2 A. Bester/ 3 W. Clark/ 4 B. Curran/ 5 V. Damphousse/ 6 L. Franceschetti/ 7 T. Gill/ 8 D. Hannan/ 9 A. Iafrate/ 10 P. Ing/ 11 T. Kurvers/ 12 G. Leeman/ 13 K. Maguire/ 14 D. Marois/ 15 B. Marsh/ 16 J. McIntyre/ 17 E. Olczyk/ 18 M. Osborne/ 19 S. Pearson/ 20 R. Ramage/ 21 J. Reese/ 22 D. Reid/ 23 L. Richardson/ 24 Action/ A-B Logo/ C-F Action/ G Iafrate & Wregget/H Leeman & Kordic

☐ Vancouver Canucks (32 stickers plus poster) 8.00
1 J. Agnew/ 2 G. Adams/ 3 S. Bozek/ 4 B. Bradley/ 5 G. Butcher/ 6 D. Capuano/ 7 C. Coxe/ 8 T. Gamble/ 9 K. Guy/ 10 R.Kron/ 11 I. Larionov/ 12 D. Lidster/ 13 T. Linden/ 14 J. Lumme/ 15 A. McBain/ 16 R. Murphy/ 17 P. Nedved/ 18 R. Nordmark/ 19 A. Plavsic/ 20 D. Quinn/ 21 J. Sandlak/ 22 P. Skriko/ 23 S. Smyl/ 24 R. Stern/ A-B Logo/ C-F Action/ G K. McLean/ H T. Linden

☐ Winnipeg Jets (32 stickers plus poster) 8.00
1 S. Arniel/ 2 B. Ashton/ 3 S. Beauregard/ 4 R. Carlyle/ 5 D. Cole/ 6 S. Cronin/ 7 G. Donnelly/ 8 K. Draper/ 9 D. Ellett/ 10 P. Elynuik/ 11 D. Evans/ 12 P. Fenton/ 13 P. Housley/ 14 M. Kumpel/ 15 P. MacDermid/ 16 M. Mantha/ 17 D. McLlwain/ 18 T. Numminen/ 19 F. Olausson/ 20 G. Paslawski/ 21 D. Smail/ 22 T. Steen/ 23 P. Sykes/ 24 R. Tabaracci/ A-B Logo/ C-F Action/ G P. Fenton/ H P. Housley

1990 - 91 PRO SET

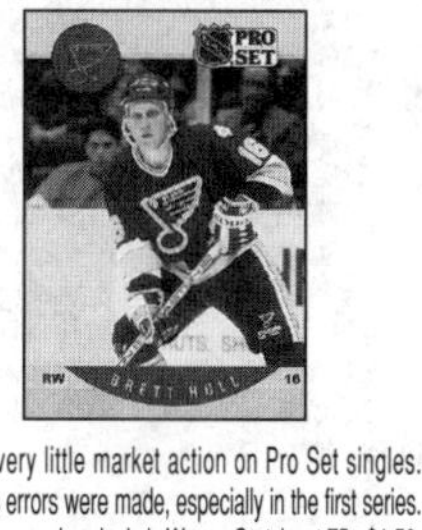

There is very little market action on Pro Set singles. Numerous errors were made, especially in the first series. The most expensive single is Wayne Gretzky at 75¢-$1.50. All other singles sell between 5¢ and $1.00. Regular player cards are organized alphabetically by team (Boston through Winnipeg) in each series.

Imprint: Pro Set NHL & NHLPA 1990
Complete Set (705 cards): 15.00

Promo — Promo
☐ 1 Brett Hull 4.00

Pro Set — Pro Set
☐ 1 R. Bourque (Borque) ☐ 1 R. Bourque
☐ 2 R. Burridge ☐ 3 L. Byers RC
☐ 4 B. Carpenter, Err. ☐ 5 J. Carter RC
☐ 6 D. Christian, Err. ☐ 7 G. Galley RC (Gary)
☐ 7 G. Galley RC ☐ 8 C. Janney
☐ 9 R. Lemelin (G), Err. ☐ 10 A. Moog (G), Err.
☐ 11 C. Neely, Err. ☐ 12 A. Pedersen
☐ 13 D. Poulin, Err. ☐ 14 B. Propp, Err.
☐ 15 B. Sweeney ☐ 16 G. Wesley
☐ 17 Dave Andreychuk (Photo on back Scott Arniel)
☐ 17 Dave Andreychuk (Traded line)
☐ 17 Dave Andreychuk (Photo on back Andreychuk)
☐ 18 Scott Arniel (Photo on back Dave Andreychuk)
☐ 18 Scott Arniel (Photo on back Arniel)
☐ 19 D. Bodger ☐ 20 M. Foligno
☐ 21 P. Housley ☐ 21 P. Housley (Traded)
☐ 22 D. Kennedy RC, Err. ☐ 23 U. Krupp
☐ 24 G. Ledyard RC ☐ 25 Malarchuk (G), Err.
☐ 26 A. Mogilny RC ☐ 27 D. Puppa (G), Err.
☐ 28 M. Ramsey ☐ 29 C. Ruuttu, Err.
☐ 30 D. Snuggerud RC ☐ 31 P. Turgeon
☐ 32 R. Vaive, Err. ☐ 33 Theoren Fleury
☐ 34 D. Gilmour ☐ 35 Al MacInnis, Err.
☐ 36 B. MacLellan ☐ 37 J. Macoun, Err.
☐ 38 S. Makarov RC ☐ 39 McCrimmon, [Uni. #]
☐ 39 McCrimmon (Traded) ☐ 40 J. Mullen
☐ 40 J. Mullen (Traded) ☐ 41 D. Murzyn
☐ 42 Nieuwendyk (Niewendyk)
☐ 42 Nieuwendyk, Corr. ☐ 43 J. Otto, Cgy.
☐ 44 Ranheim RC, Err. ☐ 45 G. Roberts
☐ 46 G. Suter ☐ 47 M. Vernon (G)
☐ 48 Wamsley (G), Err. ☐ 49 Keith Brown
☐ 50 A. Creighton ☐ 51 Dirk Graham, Err.
☐ 52 Konroyd, [White/ red] ☐ 53 S. Larmer, Err.
☐ 53 S. Larmer ☐ 54 Manson, [b/ Konroyd]
☐ 54 D. Manson ☐ 55 B. McGill
☐ 56 G. Millen (G) ☐ 57 Murray, [White/ red]
☐ 57 T. Murray, Corr. ☐ 58 J. Roenick RC
☐ 59 D. Savard ☐ 59 D. Savard (Traded)
☐ 60 Secord (/b: Alan) ☐ 60 Al Secord
☐ 61 Du. Sutter (RW) ☐ 61 Du. Sutter (Retired)
☐ 62 S. Thomas ☐ 63 . Wilson, [White/ red]
☐ 63 D. Wilson, Corr. ☐ 64 T. Yawney
☐ 65 D. Barr ☐ 66 S. Burr, [w/o résumé]
☐ 66 S. Burr, Corr. ☐ 67 J. Carson
☐ 68 J. Chabot ☐ 69 S. Chiasson
☐ 70 B. Federko, Err. ☐ 71 Gerard Gallant
☐ 72 G. Hanlon (G) ☐ 73 J. Kocur RC
☐ 74 Lee Norwood ☐ 75 M. O'Connel, Err.
☐ 76 B. Probert ☐ 77 T. Robertson
☐ 78 D. Shank RC ☐ 79 S. Yzerman
☐ 80 R. Zombo RC ☐ 81 G. Anderson
☐ 82 G. Fuhr (G)
☐ 83 M. Gélinas RC (Photo on back Joe Murphy)
☐ 84 A. Graves RC, Err. ☐ 85 C. Huddy, Err.
☐ 86 P. Klima, Err. ☐ 87 J. Kurri
☐ 87 J. Kurri (Milan) ☐ 88 M. Lamb RC
☐ 89 K. Lowe, Err. ☐ 90 C. MacTavish
☐ 91 M. Messier ☐ 92 C. Muni
☐ 93 J. Murphy RC ☐ 94 B. Ranford (G)
☐ 95 C. Simpson, Err. ☐ 96 S. Smith, Err.
☐ 97 E. Tikkanen ☐ 98 M. Andersson RC
☐ 99 D. Babych, Err. ☐ 100 Corriveau RC, Err.
☐ 101 Cunneyworth, Err. ☐ 102 K. Dineen
☐ 103 D. Evason ☐ 104 R. Ferraro
☐ 105 R. Francis ☐ 106 G. Jennings RC
☐ 107 T. Krygier RC ☐ 108 RA. Ladouceur
☐ 109 U. Samuelsson ☐ 110 B. Shaw RC
☐ 111 D. Tippett, Err. ☐ 112 P. Verbeek
☐ 113 S. Young ☐ 114 B. Benning, Err.
☐ 115 S. Duchesne, Err. ☐ 116 T. Elik RC
☐ 117 T. Granato, Err. ☐ 118 W. Gretzky
☐ 119 K. Hrudey (G) ☐ 120 S. Kasper
☐ 121 M. Krushelnyski (No position)
☐ 121 M. Krushelnyski (Position listed)
☐ 122 Kudelski RC, Err. ☐ 123 T. Laidlaw
☐ 124 M. McSorley ☐ 125 L. Robinson
☐ 126 L. Robitaille, Err. ☐ 127 T. Sandström, Err.
☐ 128 D. Taylor ☐ 129 Tonelli (Tonnelli)
☐ 129 J. Tonelli, Corr.
☐ 130 Brian Bellows (Photo on back Dave Gagner)
☐ 130 Brian Bellows (Photo on back Bellows)
☐ 131 A. Broten, Err. ☐ 132 N. Broten
☐ 133 J. Casey (G), Err. ☐ 134 S. Chambers, Err.
☐ 135 S. Churla RC ☐ 136 U. Dahlén, Err.
☐ 137 G. Duchesne ☐ 138 D. Gagner
☐ 139 S. Gavin ☐ 140 Curt Giles
☐ 141 B. McRae ☐ 142 M. Modano RC
☐ 143 L. Murphy ☐ 144 V. Siren RC
☐ 145 M. Tinordi RC ☐ 146 G. Carbonneau, Err.
☐ 147 C. Chelios ☐ 147 C. Chelios (Traded)
☐ 148 S. Corson ☐ 149 Russ Courtnall, Err.
☐ 150 B. Hayward (G) ☐ 151 M. Keane RC
☐ 152 S. Lebeau RC ☐ 153 C. Lemieux, Err.
☐ 154 C. Ludwig ☐ 155 M. McPhee
☐ 156 Stéphane Richer ☐ 157 P. Roy (G)
☐ 158 M. Schneider RC ☐ 159 B. Skrudland
☐ 160 Bobby Smith, Err. ☐ 161 P. Svoboda
☐ 162 Tommy Albelin ☐ 163 D. Brown, Err.
☐ 164 Sean Burke (G) ☐ 165 Ken Daneyko
☐ 166 Bruce Driver
☐ 167 V. Fetisov RC (Spelled Vlacheslav on front)
☐ 167 V. Fetisov RC ("L" on Vlacheslav whited out)
☐ 167 V. Fetisov RC (Viacheslav)
☐ 168 M. Johnson ☐ 169 Kasatonov RC, Err.
☐ 170 J. MacLean, Err.
☐ 171 D. Maley RC (Reversed negative)
☐ 171 D. Maley RC (Corrected image)
☐ 172 Kirk Muller ☐ 173 Janne Ojanen RC
☐ 174 B. Shanahan
☐ 175 P. Stastny (Photo Patrik Sundström)
☐ 176 P. Sundström (Photo Peter Stastny)
☐ 175 P. Stastny, Corr. ☐ 176 Sundstrom, Corr.
☐ 177 Sylvain Turgeon ☐ 178 K. Baumgartner RC
☐ 179 D. Crossman, Err. ☐ 180 Gerald Diduck
☐ 181 Fitzpatrick (G) RC ☐ 182 P. Flatley, Err.
☐ 183 Healy RC (G) [Glen] ☐ 184 Alan Kerr
☐ 185 Derek King ☐ 186 P. LaFontaine
☐ 187 Don Maloney ☐ 188 McDonough RC Err.
☐ 189 J. Norton, Err. ☐ 190 G. Nylund
☐ 191 Brent Sutter ☐ 192 Bryan Trottier, Err.
☐ 193 D. Volek, Err. ☐ 194 RA. Wood
☐ 195 Jan Erixon ☐ 196 M. Gartner, Err.
☐ 197 R. Greschner
☐ 198 M. Horava RC (Miroslav)
☐ 198 Miloslav Horava RC
☐ 199 M. Janssens RC ☐ 200 K. Kisio
☐ 201 B. Leetch ☐ 202 RA. Moller
☐ 203 B. Mullen ☐ 204 B. Nicholls, Err.
☐ 205 C. Nilan ☐ 205 C. Nilan (Traded)
☐ 206 J. Ogrodnick ☐ 207 J. Patrick
☐ 208 Turcotte RC, Err. ☐ 209 V'b'sbrouck (G), Err.
☐ 210 Carey Wilson ☐ 211 M. Bullard
☐ 212 T. Carkner ☐ 213 J. Chychrun RC
☐ 214 M. Craven ☐ 215 P. Eklund, Err.
☐ 216 R. Hextall (G), Err. ☐ 217 M. Howe
☐ 218 T. Kerr ☐ 219 Ken Linseman, Err.
☐ 220 S. Mellanby ☐ 221 GorD. Murphy RC
☐ 222 K. Samuelsson, Err. ☐ 223 Ilkka Sinisalo
☐ 224 R. Sutter ☐ 225 R. Tocchet
☐ 226 Ken Wregget (G) ☐ 227 T. Barrasso (G)
☐ 228 Bourque (Borque) ☐ 228 P. Bourque, Corr.
☐ 229 R. Brown, Err. ☐ 230 A. Chevrier (G), Err.
☐ 231 P. Coffey, Err. ☐ 232 J. Cullen
☐ 233 G. Dineen, Err. ☐ 234 B. Errey
☐ 235 Jim Johnson, Err. ☐ 236 M. Lemieux, Err.
☐ 237 T. Loney RC ☐ 238 Barry Pederson, Err.
☐ 239 M. Recchi RC ☐ 240 K. Stevens RC, Err.
☐ 241 T. Tanti, Err. ☐ 242 Z. Zalapski, Err.
☐ 243 J. Cirella ☐ 244 L. DeBlois, Err.
☐ 245 Fortier, Err. (Mark) ☐ 245 Marc Fortier
☐ 246 P. Gillis ☐ 247 M. Hough
☐ 248 T. Hrkac, Err. ☐ 249 J. Jackson
☐ 250 G. Lafleur ☐ 251 C. Leschyshyn RC
☐ 252 C. Loiselle RC ☐ 253 M. Marois
☐ 254 T. McKegney, Err. ☐ 255 Ken McRae RC
☐ 256 Petit, Err. (Uni. #) ☐ 256 Michel Petit, Corr.
☐ 257 J. Sakic, Err. ☐ 258 R. Tugnutt (G)
☐ 259 B'Amour RC, Err. ☐ 260 J. Brown, Err.
☐ 261 Gino Cavallini, Err. ☐ 262 P. Cavallini
☐ 263 Brett Hull ☐ 264 M. Lalor RC, Err.
☐ 265 D. Lowry RC ☐ 266 P. MacLean
☐ 267 R. Meagher ☐ 268 Momesso RC, Err.
☐ 269 A. Oates ☐ 270 V. Riendeau (G) RC
☐ 271 G. Roberts ☐ 272 R. Sutter, Err.
☐ 273 S. Tuttle ☐ 274 P. Zezel, Err.
☐ 275 Bester (G) (Alan) ☐ 275 Bester (G) (Allan)
☐ 276 W. Clark ☐ 277 B. Curran, Err.
☐ 278 V. Damphousse ☐ 279 T. Fergus
☐ 280 Franceschetti RC ☐ 281 Al Iafrate
☐ 282 T. Kurvers, Err. ☐ 283 G. Leeman
☐ 284 D. Marois ☐ 285 B. Marsh
☐ 286 Ed Olczyk, Err. ☐ 287 M. Osborne
☐ 288 R. Ramage ☐ 289 Luke Richardson
☐ 290 Th'deau RC, Err. ☐ 291 G. Adams, Err.
☐ 292 Jim Benning ☐ 293 S. Bozek
☐ 294 B. Bradley ☐ 295 G. Butcher
☐ 296 V. Krutov RC ☐ 297 I. Larionov RC, Err.
☐ 298 D. Lidster ☐ 299 T. Linden
☐ 300 Lumme RC, Err.
☐ 301 A. McBain (Photo on back is Jim Sandlak)
☐ 301 A. McBain, Corr. ☐ 302 K. McLean (G),Err.
☐ 303 D. Quinn, Err. ☐ 304 P. Reinhart, Err.
☐ 305 Jim Sandlak ☐ 306 Petri Skriko
☐ 307 D. Beaupré (G) ☐ 308 Dino Ciccarelli
☐ 309 Geoff Courtnall, Err. ☐ 310 J. Druce RC
☐ 311 K. Hatcher ☐ 312 Dale Hunter, Err.
☐ 313 C. Johansson, Err. ☐ 314 Rod Langway
☐ 315 Stephen Leach ☐ 316 M. Liut (G), Err.
☐ 317 Alan May RC ☐ 318 K. Miller, Err.
☐ 319 M. Pivonka RC, Err. ☐ 320 Ridley, [/b: point.s.]
☐ 320 M. Ridley, Corr. ☐ 321 S. Stevens, Err.
☐ 322 J. Tucker, Err. ☐ 323 Brent Ashton
☐ 324 Laurie Boschman ☐ 325 R. Carlyle
☐ 326 D. Ellett ☐ 327 P. Elynuik
☐ 328 Essensa (G) RC ☐ 329 P. Fenton, Err.
☐ 330 Dale Hawerchuk ☐ 330 Hawerchuk [Traded]
☐ 331 P. MacDermid ☐ 332 Moe Mantha
☐ 333 McLlwain, Err. ☐ 334 T. Numminen RC
☐ 335 Olausson (Fred) ☐ 335 Olausson (Fredrik)
☐ 336 G. Paslawski, Err. ☐ 337 AS Al MacInnis
☐ 338 AS Vernon (G), Err. ☐ 339 AS K. Lowe
☐ 340 AS W. Gretzky ☐ 341 AS L. Robitaille Err.
☐ 342 AS Brett Hull ☐ 343 AS J. Mullen
☐ 344 AS Nieuwendyk Err. ☐ 345 AS S. Larmer
☐ 346 AS D. Wilson, Err. ☐ 347 AS S. Yzerman
☐ 348 AS J. Kurri (Milan) ☐ 348 AS J. Kurri (Edmo.)
☐ 349 AS M. Messier ☐ 350 AS Duchesne, Err.
☐ 351 AS M. Gartner, Err. ☐ 352 AS B. Nicholls
☐ 353 AS P. Cavallini ☐ 354 AS Al Iafrate
☐ 355 AS K. McLean (G) ☐ 356 AS T. Steen, [Smail]
☐ 357 AS R. Bourque ☐ 358 AS C. Neely
☐ 359 AS P. Roy (G) ☐ 360 AS B. Propp, Err.
☐ 361 AS P. Coffey, Err. ☐ 362 AS M. Lemieux
☐ 363 AS D. Andreychuk ☐ 364 AS P. Housley
☐ 365 AS D. Puppa (G) ☐ 366 AS P. Turgeon
☐ 367 AS R. Francis ☐ 368 AS C. Chelios
☐ 369 AS S. Corson, Err. ☐ 369 AS S. Corson, Corr.
☐ 370 AS S. Richer ☐ 371 AS Kirk Muller
☐ 372 AS P. LaFontaine ☐ 373 AS B. Leetch
☐ 374 AS R. Tocchet ☐ 375 AS J. Sakic
☐ 376 AS K. Hatcher ☐ 377 Adams Trophy
☐ 378 Byng Trophy ☐ 379 Calder Trophy
☐ 380 Clancy Trophy ☐ 381 Hart Trophy
☐ 382 Jennings Trophy ☐ 383 Masterton Trophy
☐ 384 Norris Trophy ☐ 385 Patrick Trophy
☐ Patrick Trophy/ Ceglarski (no card number)
☐ 386 Pearson Award ☐ 387 Presidents' Trophy
☐ 388 Art Ross Trophy ☐ 389 Selke Trophy
☐ 390 Smythe Trophy ☐ 391 Vézina Trophy
☐ 392 Campbell Bowl ☐ 393 Wales Trophy
☐ 394 LL: W. Gretzky ☐ 395 LL: Brett Hull, Err.
☐ 396 LL: S. Makarov ☐ 397 LL: M. Messier
☐ 398 LL: M. Richter (G) ☐ 399 LL: P. Roy (G)
☐ 400 LL: D. Turcotte ☐ 401 Owen Nolan RC
☐ 402 P. Nedved RC ☐ 403 P. Esposito, Bost.
☐ 404 Darryl Sittler, Toro. ☐ 405 Stan Mikita, Chic.
☐ 406 A. Brickley ☐ 407 P. Douris RC
☐ 408 Nevin Markwart ☐ 409 C. Nilan
☐ 410 S. Quintal RC ☐ 411 Shoebottom RC
☐ 412 D. Sweeney RC ☐ 413 J. Wiemer RC
☐ 414 M. Hartman RC ☐ 415 Dale Hawerchuk
☐ 416 Benoît Hogue ☐ 417 B. Houlder RC
☐ 418 Mikko Makelä ☐ 419 R. Ray RC
☐ 420 J. Tucker ☐ 421 Jiri Hrdina RC
☐ 422 M. Hunter, Cgy. ☐ 423 T. Hunter RC
☐ 424 R. Johansson RC ☐ 425 Frantisek Musil
☐ 426 Ric Nattress ☐ 427 C. Chelios
☐ 428 J. Cloutier (G) RC ☐ 429 G. Gilbert
☐ 430 Michel Goulet, Err. ☐ 431 M. Hudson RC
☐ 432 J. Lemieux RC ☐ 433 B. Noonan
☐ 434 W. Presley ☐ 435 Brent Fedyk RC
☐ 436 R. Green ☐ 437 Marc Habscheid
☐ 438 B. McCrimmon ☐ 439 J. Beukeboom RC
☐ 440 D. Brown RC ☐ 441 K. Buchberger RC
☐ 442 G. Hawgood ☐ 443 C. Joseph RC
☐ 444 Ken Linseman ☐ 445 E. Reddick (G) RC
☐ 446 Geoff Smith RC ☐ 447 A. Burt RC
☐ 448 Sylvain Côté ☐ 449 P. Cyr RC
☐ 450 Ed Kastelic RC ☐ 451 P. Sidorkiewicz (G)
☐ 452 M. Tomlak RC ☐ 453 Carey Wilson
☐ 454 D. Berthiaume (G) ☐ 455 S. Bjugstad
☐ 456 Rod Buskas RC ☐ 457 J. McIntyre RC
☐ 458 T. Watters ☐ 459 P. Berezan RC
☐ 460 B. Propp ☐ 461 Ilkka Sinisalo
☐ 462 D. Smail ☐ 463 Bobby Smith
☐ 464 C. Dahlquist ☐ 465 Neil Wilkinson RC
☐ 466 J.J. Daigneault RC ☐ 467 E. Desjardins RC
☐ 468 Gerald Diduck ☐ 469 D. Dufresne RC
☐ 470 T. Ewen RC (Photo on back is Éric Desjardins)
☐ 470 T. Ewen RC, Corr. ☐ 471 Brent Gilchrist RC
☐ 472 S. Lefebvre RC ☐ 473 D. Savard
☐ 474 Sylvain Turgeon ☐ 475 Ryan Walter
☐ 476 Laurie Boschman ☐ 477 P. Conacher RC
☐ 478 C. Lemieux ☐ 479 Walt Poddubny
☐ 480 Stewart RC (Alan) ☐ 481 C. Terreri (G) RC
☐ 482 B. Dalgarno ☐ 483 D. Chyzowski RC

☐ 484 C. Ludwig ☐ 485 W. McBean RC
☐ 486 R. Pilon RC ☐ 487 J. Reekie RC
☐ 488 Mick Vukota RC ☐ 489 M. Hardy
☐ 490 Jody Hull RC ☐ 491 Kris King RC
☐ 492 T. Mallette RC ☐ 493 K. Miller RC
☐ 494 N. Rochefort ☐ 495 D. Shaw
☐ 496 R. Sheppard ☐ 497 Keith Acton
☐ 498 C. Berube RC ☐ 499 T. Horacek RC
☐ 500 N. Lacombe RC ☐ 501 Jiri Latal RC
☐ 502 Pete Peeters (G) ☐ 503 DerR. Smith RC
☐ 504 Jay Caufield RC ☐ 505 P. Taglianetti
☐ 506 RA. Gilhen RC ☐ 507 R. Hillier
☐ 508 J. Mullen ☐ 509 Pietrangelo (G) RC
☐ 510 G. Roberts ☐ 511 Bryan Trottier
☐ 512 W. Young (G) RC ☐ 513 S. Anderson RC
☐ 514 Steven Finn RC ☐ 515 Bryan Fogarty RC
☐ 516 M. Hough, Err. ☐ 517 Darin Kimble RC
☐ 518 RA. Velischek ☐ 519 C. Wolanin RC
☐ 520 B. Bassen RC ☐ 521 Geoff Courtnall
☐ 522 R. Dirk RC ☐ 523 G. Featherstone RC
☐ 524 M. Marois ☐ 525 Herb Raglan RC
☐ 526 Cliff Ronning ☐ 527 Harold Snepsts
☐ 528 S. Stevens ☐ 529 R. Wilson
☐ 530 A. Broten ☐ 531 L. DeBlois
☐ 532 D. Ellett ☐ 533Fenton (inverted TM)
☐ 533 P. Fenton, Corr. ☐ 534 T. Gill RC
☐ 535 D. Hannan ☐ 536 J. Kordic RC
☐ 537 M. Krushelnyski ☐ 538 K. Maguire RC
☐ 539 Michel Petit ☐ 540 J. Reese (G) RC
☐ 541 D. Reid RC ☐ 542 D. Shedden
☐ 543 D. Capuano RC ☐ 544 C. Coxe RC
☐ 545 Kevan G. RC ☐ 546 R. Murphy RC
☐ 547 R. Nordmark RC ☐ 548 Stan Smyl
☐ 549 R. Stern RC ☐ 550 T. Bergland RC
☐ 551 Nick Kypreos RC ☐ 552 M. Lalor RC
☐ 553 R. Murray RC ☐ 554 B. Rouse
☐ 555 D. Tippett ☐ 556 P. Zezel
☐ 557 S. Arniel ☐ 558 D. Barber RC
☐ 559 S. Cronin RC ☐ 560 G. Donnelly RC
☐ 561 D. Evans RC ☐ 562 P. Housley
☐ 563 Ed Olczyk ☐ 564 M. Osborne
☐ 565 Thomas Steen ☐ 566 Boston Bruins
☐ 567 Buffalo Sabres ☐ 568 CalG. Flames
☐ 569 Chic. Blackhawks ☐ 570 Detroit Red Wings
☐ 571 Edmonton Oilers ☐ 572 Hartford Whalers
☐ 573 LosA. Kings, Err. ☐ 573 LosA. Kings, Corr.
☐ 574 Minn. North Stars ☐ 575 Montréal Canadiens
☐ 576 New Jersey Devils ☐ 577 New York Islanders
☐ 578 New York Rangers ☐ 579 Philadelphia Flyers
☐ 580 Pitt. Penguins ☐ 581 Québec Nordiques
☐ 582 St. Louis Blues ☐ 583 Toronto Maple Leafs
☐ 584 Vanc. Canucks ☐ 585 Washington Capitals
☐ 586 Winnipeg Jets ☐ 587 Ken Hodge RC
☐ 588 V. Ruzicka RC ☐ 589 Wes Walz RC
☐ 590 G. Brown RC ☐ 591 B. Miller RC
☐ 592 Darrin Shannon RC ☐ 593 S. Matteau RC
☐ 594 S. Priakin RC ☐ 595 R. Reichel RC
☐ 596 Ken Sabourin RC ☐ 597 T. Sweeney RC
☐ 598 E. Belfour (G) RC ☐ 599 F. Kucera RC
☐ 600 M. McNeill RC ☐ 601 M. Peluso RC
☐ 602 Cheveldae (G) RC ☐ 603 Per Djoos RC
☐ 604 S. Fedorov RC ☐ 605 J. Garpenlov RC
☐ 606 Keith Primeau RC ☐ 607 P. Ysebaert RC
☐ 608 A. Semenov RC ☐ 609 Bobby Holik RC
☐ 610 Whitmore (G) RC ☐ 611 R. Blake RC
☐ 612 F. Breault RC ☐ 613 M. Craig RC
☐ 614 Bergeron (G) RC ☐ 615 A. Cassels RC
☐ 616 T. Chorske RC ☐ 617 Lyle Odelein RC
☐ 618 M. Pederson RC ☐ 619 Zdeno Ciger RC
☐ 620 T. Crowder RC ☐ 621 J. Morris RC
☐ 622 Eric WeinR. RC ☐ 623 D. Marcinyshyn RC
☐ 624 J. Hackett (G) RC ☐ 625 R. DiMaio RC
☐ 626 Steven Rice RC ☐ 627 M. Richter (G) RC
☐ 628 Dennis Vial RC ☐ 629 Martin Hostak RC
☐ 630 P. Murray RC ☐ 631 M. Ricci RC
☐ 632 Jaromir Jagr RC ☐ 633 P. Stanton RC
☐ 634 Gordon (G) RC ☐ 635 Owen Nolan RC
☐ 636 Mats Sundin RC ☐ 637 J. Tanner (G) RC
☐ 638 C. Joseph (G) RC ☐ 639 P. Ing (G) RC
☐ 640 S. Thornton RC ☐ 641 T. Gamble (G) RC
☐ 642 R. Kron RC ☐ 643 P. Nedved
☐ 644 Adrien Plavsic RC ☐ 645 P. Bondra RC
☐ 646 J. Hrivnak (G) RC ☐ 647 M. Tatarinov RC
☐ 648 B'regard (G) RC Er. ☐ 649 R. Tabaracci (G) RC
☐ 650 M. Bossy ☐ 651 Bobby Clarke
☐ 652 Alex Delvecchio ☐ 653 Marcel Dionne
☐ 654 Gordie Howe ☐ 655 Stan Mikita
☐ 656 D. Potvin ☐ 657 Bobby Clarke
☐ 658 Alex Delvecchio ☐ 659 T. Esposito (G)
☐ 660 Gordie Howe ☐ 661 M. Milbury
☐ 662 R. Dudley ☐ 663 D. Risebrough
☐ 664 Bryan Murray RC ☐ 665 J. Muckler RC
☐ 666 R. Ley ☐ 667 T. Webster
☐ 668 B. Gainey ☐ 669 P. Burns RC
☐ 670 J. Cunniff RC ☐ 671 Al Arbour
☐ 672 R. Neilson RC ☐ 673 P. Holmgren
☐ 674 B. Johnson RC ☐ 675 D. Chambers RC
☐ 676 Br. Sutter ☐ 677 T. Watt RC
☐ 678 B. McCammon ☐ 679 T. Murray
☐ 680 B. J. Murdoch ☐ 681 R. Asselstine RC
☐ 682 W. Bonney RC ☐ 683 K. Collins RC
☐ 684 P. Dapuzzo RC ☐ 685 R. Finn RC
☐ 686 K. Fraser RC ☐ 687 Gérard Gauthier RC
☐ 688 T. Gregson RC ☐ 689 B. Hodges RC
☐ 690 R. Hoggarth RC ☐ 691 D. Koharski RC
☐ 692 D. Marouelli RC ☐ 693 D. McCourt RC
☐ 694 B. McCreary RC ☐ 695 D. Morel RC
☐ 696 J. Pateman RC ☐ 697 R. Scapinello RC
☐ 698 R. Shick RC ☐ 699 P. Shick RC
☐ 700 L. Stickle RC ☐ 701 van Hellemond RC
☐ 702 M. Vines RC ☐ 703 HL: W. Gretzky
☐ 704 M. Messier w/ Cup ☐ 705 The Puck

Hologram (#/5,000) **Promo**
☐ Stanley Cup Hologram 65.00

1990 - 91 PRO SET PLAYER OF THE MONTH

These cards were issued each month to honour the player selected Pro Set Player of the Month. October 1990 and March 1991 player cards were not issued.

Complete Set (4 cards): 25.00

Description	PotM
☐ Pete Peeters, Phil.	3.00
☐ PM1 Tom Barrasso (G), Pitt.	4.00
☐ PM2 Wayne Gretzky, LosA.	20.00
☐ PM3 Brett Hull, SLou.	5.00

1990 - 91 PROCARDS

Imprint: © 1990 ProCards, Inc.
Complete Set (629 cards): 140.00
Common Player: .25

BINGHAMPTON RANGERS - AHL

Rob Zamuner is the most expensive single at $3.00.
Team Set (25 cards): 8.00
ProCards **ProCards**
☐ 1 Rob Zamuner ☐ 2 Todd Charlesworth
☐ 3 Bob Bodak ☐ 4 Len Hachborn
☐ 5 Peter Fiorentino ☐ 6 Kord Cernich
☐ 7 Daniel Lacroix ☐ 8 Joe Paterson
☐ 9 Sam St. Laurent (G) ☐ 10 Jeff Bloemberg
☐ 11 Mike Golden ☐ 12 Mike Hurlbut
☐ 13 Mark Laforest (G) ☐ 14 Chris Cichocki
☐ 15 J. Paddock, Coach ☐ 16 Peter Laviolette
☐ 17 Martin Bergeron ☐ 18 Rudy Poeschek
☐ 19 Eric Germain ☐ 20 Al Hill, A. Coach
☐ 21 Ric Bennett ☐ 22 Tie Domi
☐ 23 Ross Fitzpatrick ☐ 24 Brian McReynolds
☐ 25 Rangers Checklist

HERSHEY BEARS - AHL

Team Set (28 cards): 8.00
ProCards **ProCards**
☐ 26 Mike Eaves, Coach ☐ 27 Lance Pitlick
☐ 28 Dale Kushner ☐ 29 Reid Simpson
☐ 30 Craig Fisher ☐ 31 Dominic Roussel (G)
☐ 32 David Fenyves ☐ 33 Brian Dobbin
☐ 34 Darren Rumble ☐ 35 Murray Baron
☐ 36 Bruce Hoffort (G) ☐ 37 Steve Beadle
☐ 38 Chris Jensen ☐ 39 Mike Stothers
☐ 40 Kent Hawley ☐ 41 Scott Sandelin
☐ 42 Guy Phillips ☐ 43 Mark Bassen
☐ 44 Steve Scheifele ☐ 45 Bill Armstrong
☐ 46 Shaun Sabol ☐ 47 Mark Freer
☐ 48 Claude Boivin ☐ 49 Len Barrie
☐ 50 Bill Armstrong ☐ 51 Tim Tookey
☐ 52 H. Bricker, A Coach ☐ 53 Bears Checklist

FREDERICTON CANADIENS - AHL

Team Set (22 cards): 8.00
ProCards **ProCards**
☐ 54 Alain Côté ☐ 55 Luc Gauthier
☐ 56 Eric Charron ☐ 57 Mario Roberge
☐ 58 Tom Sagissor ☐ 59 Brent Bobyck
☐ 60 John Ferguson ☐ 61 Jim Nesich
☐ 62 Gilbert Dionne ☐ 63 Herbert Hohenberger
☐ 64 Dan Woodley ☐ 65 Roy Mitchell
☐ 66 Fréderic Chabot (G) ☐ 67 André Racicot (G)
☐ 68 Paul DiPietro ☐ 69 Norman Desjardins
☐ 70 Martin St. Amour ☐ 71 Jessie Belanger
☐ 72 Ed Cristofoli ☐ 73 Patrick Lebeau
☐ 74 P. Bordeleau, Coach ☐ 75 Canadiens Checklist

PEORIA RIVERMEN - IHL

Guy Hebert is the most expensive player at $2-3.
Team Set (24 cards): 10.00
ProCards **ProCards**
☐ 76 Keith Osborne ☐ 77 Richard Pion
☐ 78 Alain Raymond (G) ☐ 79 Rob Robinson
☐ 80 Andy Rymsha ☐ 81 Randy Skarda
☐ 82 Dave Thomlinson ☐ 83 Tom Tilley
☐ 84 Steve Tuttle ☐ 85 Tony Twist
☐ 86 David Bruce ☐ 87 Kelly Chase
☐ 88 Nelson Emerson ☐ 89 Guy Hebert (G)
☐ 90 Tony Hejna ☐ 91 Michel Mongeau
☐ 92 David O'Brien ☐ 93 Kevin Miehm
☐ 94 Darwin McPherson ☐ 95 Dominic Lavoie
☐ 96 Yves Heroux ☐ 97 Pat Jablonski (G)
☐ 98 Bob Plager, Coach ☐ 99 Rivermen Checklist

KALAMAZOO WINGS - IHL

Team Set (24 cards): 8.00
ProCards **ProCards**
☐ 99 Jayson More ☐ 100 Kevin Evans
☐ 101 Warren Babe ☐ 102 Mitch Messier
☐ 103 John Blue (G) ☐ 104 Larry Dyck (G)
☐ 105 Duane Joyce ☐ 106 Kari Takko (G)
☐ 107 Brett Barnett ☐ 108 Pat MacLeod
☐ 109 Peter Lappin ☐ 110 Link Gaetz
☐ 111 Larry DePalma ☐ 112 Steve Gotaas
☐ 113 Mike McHugh ☐ 114 Dan Keczmer
☐ 115 Jackson Penney ☐ 116 Ed Courtenay
☐ 117 J-F Quintin ☐ 118 Scott Robinson
☐ 119 Mario Thyer ☐ 120 Enrico Ciccone
☐ 121 Constantine/Marks ☐ 122 Wings Checklist

MAINE MARINERS - AHL

Team Set (23 cards): 8.00
ProCards **ProCards**
☐ 123 Shayne Stevenson ☐ 124 Jeff Lazaro
☐ 125 Matt Delguidice (G) ☐ 126 Ron Hoover
☐ 127 John Mokosak ☐ 128 John Blum
☐ 129 Mike Parson (G) ☐ 130 Bruce Shoebottom
☐ 131 Dave Donnelly ☐ 132 Ralph Barahona
☐ 133 G. Townshend ☐ 134 Ken Hodge
☐ 135 Norm Foster (G) ☐ 136 Greg Poss
☐ 137 Brad James ☐ 138 Lou Crawford
☐ 139 Rick Allain ☐ 140 Bob Beers
☐ 141 Ken Hammond ☐ 142 Mark Montanari
☐ 143 R. Bowness, Coach ☐ 144 Gould Player/Coach
☐ 145 Mariners Checklist

NEWMARKET SAINTS - AHL

Damian Rhodes is the most expensive player at $1-2.
Team Set (25 cards): 8.00
ProCards **ProCards**
☐ 146 Mike Stevens ☐ 147 Greg Walters
☐ 148 Mike Moes ☐ 149 Kent Hulst
☐ 150 Len Esau ☐ 151 Darryl Shannon
☐ 152 Bobby Reynolds ☐ 153 Derek Langille
☐ 154 Jeff Serowik ☐ 155 Darren Veitch
☐ 156 Joe Sacco ☐ 157 Alan Hepple
☐ 158 Doug Shedden ☐ 159 Steve Bancroft
☐ 160 Greg Johnston ☐ 161 Trevor Jobe
☐ 162 Bill Root ☐ 163 Tim Bean
☐ 164 Brian Blad ☐ 165 Robert Horyna (G)
☐ 166 Dean Anderson (G) ☐ 167 Damian Rhodes (G)
☐ 168 Mike Millar ☐ 169 Mike Jackson
☐ 170 Saints Checklist

SPRINGFIELD INDIANS - AHL

Team Set (24 cards): 8.00
ProCards **ProCards**
☐ 171 Cal Brown ☐ 172 Michel Picard
☐ 173 Cam Brauer ☐ 174 Jim Burke
☐ 175 Jim McKenzie ☐ 176 Mike Tomlak
☐ 177 Ross McKay (G) ☐ 178 Blair Atcheynum
☐ 179 Chris Tancill ☐ 180 Mark Greig
☐ 181 Joe Day ☐ 182 Jim Roberts, Coach
☐ 183 Emanuel Viveiros ☐ 184 Daryl Reaugh (G)
☐ 185 Tommie Eriksen ☐ 186 Terry Yake
☐ 187 Chris Govedaris ☐ 188 Chris Bright
☐ 189 John Stevens ☐ 190 Brian Chapman
☐ 191 James Black ☐ 192 Scott Daniels
☐ 193 Kelly Ens ☐ 194 Indians Checklist

BALTIMORE SKIPJACKS - AHL

Team Set (25 cards): 8.00
ProCards **ProCards**
☐ 195 Ken Lovsin ☐ 196 Kent Paynter
☐ 197 Jim Mathieson ☐ 198 Bob Mendel
☐ 199 Reggie Savage ☐ 200 Alfie Turcotte
☐ 201 Victor Gervais ☐ 202 Todd Hlushko
☐ 203 Steve Seftel ☐ 204 Thomas Sjogren
☐ 205 Steve Maltais ☐ 206 Bob Joyce
☐ 207 Tyler Larter ☐ 208 Mark Ferner
☐ 209 Bobby Babcock ☐ 210 Jeff Greenlaw
☐ 211 Tim Taylor ☐ 212 John Purves
☐ 213 Chris Felix ☐ 214 Jiri Vykoukal
☐ 215 Sh. Simpson (G) ☐ 216 Jim Hrivnak (G)
☐ 217 Laird, Coach/G.M. ☐ 218 Barry Trotz, ACoach
☐ 219 Skipjacks Checklist

CAPE BRETON OILERS - AHL

Team Set (23 cards): 8.00
ProCards **ProCards**
☐ 220 David Haas ☐ 221 Wade Campbell
☐ 222 Dan Currie ☐ 223 Shaun Van Allen
☐ 224 Norm Maciver ☐ 225 Mike Greenlay (G)
☐ 226 Peter Soberlak ☐ 227 Tim Tisdale
☐ 228 Marlo Barbe ☐ 229 Shjon Podein
☐ 230 Trevor Sim ☐ 231 Corey Foster
☐ 232 Mike Ware ☐ 233 Marc LaForge
☐ 234 Bruce Bell ☐ 235 Tomas Kapusta
☐ 236 A. Tyjnych (G) ☐ 237 Tomas Srsen
☐ 238 Collin Bauer ☐ 239 François Leroux
☐ 240 MacAdam, Coach ☐ 241 Ferguson, A Coach
☐ 242 Oilers Checklist

MONCTON HAWKS - AHL

Team Set (24 cards): 8.00
ProCards **ProCards**
☐ 243 Tony Joseph ☐ 244 Brent Hughes
☐ 245 Larry Bernard ☐ 246 Simon Wheeldon
☐ 247 Todd Filchel ☐ 248 Craig Duncanson
☐ 249 Iain Duncan ☐ 250 Bryan Marchment
☐ 251 Matt Hervey ☐ 252 Chris Norton
☐ 253 Dallas Eakins ☐ 254 Peter Hankinson
☐ 255 Grant Richison ☐ 256 Lee Davidson
☐ 257 Denis Larocque ☐ 258 Scott Levins
☐ 259 Guy Larose ☐ 260 Scott Schneider
☐ 261 Sergei Kharin ☐ 262 Mascot The Hawk
☐ 263 Farrish, Coach/G.M. ☐ 264 Hawks Checklist
☐ 343 Rick Tabaracci (G) ☐ 344 Mike O'Neill (G)

ROCHESTER AMERICANS - AHL

Donald Audette is the most expensive player at $1-2.
Team Set (31 cards): 8.00
ProCards **ProCards**
☐ 265 Kevin Haller ☐ 266 Joel Savage
☐ 267 Scott Metcalfe ☐ 268 Ian Boyce
☐ 269 David Littman (G) ☐ 270 Dave Baseggio
☐ 271 Ken Sutton ☐ 272 Brad Miller
☐ 273 Bill Houlder ☐ 274 Dan Frawley
☐ 275 Scott McCrory ☐ 276 Steve Ludzik
☐ 277 Rob Ray ☐ 278 Darrin Shannon
☐ 279 Dale Degray ☐ 280 Bob Corkum
☐ 281 Grant Tkachuk ☐ 282 Kevin Kerr
☐ 283 Mitch Molloy ☐ 284 Darcy Loewen
☐ 285 Jody Gage ☐ 286 Jiri Sejba
☐ 287 Steve Smith ☐ 288 Darcy Wakaluk (G)
☐ 289 Donald Audette ☐ 290 Don McSween
☐ 291 Francois Guay ☐ 292 T. Martin, A Coach
☐ 293 Don Lever, Coach ☐ 294 Mascot The Moose
☐ 295 Americans Checklist

SAN DIEGO GULLS - IHL

Team Set (26 cards): 8.00
ProCards **ProCards**
☐ 296 O'Connell, Coach ☐ 297 Paul Marshall
☐ 298 Darin Bannister ☐ 299 Rob Nichols
☐ 300 Simmer, A. Coach ☐ 301 Bob Jones
☐ 302 Scott Brower (G) ☐ 303 Taylor Hall
☐ 304 Carl Mokosak ☐ 305 Glen Hanlon (G)
☐ 306 Peter Dineen ☐ 307 Mike Sullivan
☐ 308 Steven Martinson ☐ 309 Dave Korol
☐ 310 Darren Lowe ☐ 311 Mark Reimer (G)
☐ 312 Mike Gober ☐ 313 Al Tuer
☐ 314 Dean Morton ☐ 315 Jim McGeough
☐ 316 Clark Donatelli ☐ 317 Steven Dykstra
☐ 318 Brent Sapergia ☐ 319 Larry Floyd
☐ 320 D'Arcy Norton ☐ 321 Gulls Checklist

MILWAUKEE ADMIRALS - IHL

Team Set (21 cards): 8.00
ProCards **ProCards**
☐ 322 Garry Valk ☐ 323 Ian Kidd
☐ 324 Todd Hawkins ☐ 325 Carl Valimont
☐ 326 Peter DeBoer ☐ 327 C. Fraser, A Coach
☐ 328 David Mackey ☐ 329 Jim Benning
☐ 330 P. George Bakovic ☐ 331 Steve Weeks (G)
☐ 332 Steve Veilleux ☐ 333 Shaun Clouston
☐ 334 Gino Odjick ☐ 335 Mike Murphy, Coach
☐ 336 Cam Brown ☐ 337 Patrice Lefebvre
☐ 338 Eric Murano ☐ 339 Jim Revenberg
☐ 340 Don Gibson ☐ 341 Steve McKichan (G)
☐ 342 Admirals Checklist

PHOENIX ROADRUNNERS - IHL

Team Set (25 cards): 8.00
ProCards **ProCards**
☐ 345 Rick Hayward ☐ 346 Sean Whyte
☐ 347 Petr Prajsler ☐ 348 John Van Kessel
☐ 349 Mario Gosselin (G) ☐ 350 Kyosti Karjalainen
☐ 351 Mikael Lindholm ☐ 352 David Goverde (G)
☐ 353 Graham Stanley ☐ 354 Stéphane Richer
☐ 355 Brian Lawton ☐ 356 Jérôme Béchard
☐ 357 Jeff Rohlicek ☐ 358 Steve Jaques
☐ 359 Chris Kontos ☐ 360 Sylvain Couturier
☐ 361 Peter Sentner ☐ 362 Steve Graves
☐ 263 Daryn McBride ☐ 364 Steve Rooney
☐ 365 Mickey Volcan ☐ 366 Kevin MacDonald
☐ 367 Backstrom, Coach ☐ 368 Unger, Asst Coach
☐ 369 Roadrunners Checklist

MUSKEGON LUMBERJACKS - IHL

Team Set (23 cards): 8.00
ProCards **ProCards**
☐ 370 Rob Dopson (G) ☐ 371 John Callander
☐ 372 Chris Clifford (G) ☐ 373 Sandy Smith
☐ 374 Jim Kyte ☐ 375 Mike Needham
☐ 376 Mitch Wilson ☐ 377 Dave Goertz
☐ 378 Mark Kachowski ☐ 379 Perry Ganchar
☐ 380 Mark Major ☐ 381 Joel Gardner
☐ 382 Scott Gruhl ☐ 383 Todd Nelson
☐ 384 Darren Stolk ☐ 385 Scott Shaunessy
☐ 386 Mike Mersch ☐ 387 Glenn Mulvenna
☐ 388 Brad Aitken ☐ 389 Dave Michayluk
☐ 390 MacDonald, Coach ☐ 391 P. Russell, A Coach
☐ 392 Lumberjacks Checklist

INDIANAPOLIS ICE - IHL

Dominik Hasek is the most expensive player at $10-15.
Team Set (22 cards): 20.00
ProCards **ProCards**
☐ 393 Sean Williams ☐ 394 Ryan McGill
☐ 395 Mike Eagles ☐ 396 Jim Johannson
☐ 397 Marty Nanne ☐ 398 Jim Playfair
☐ 399 Warren Rychel ☐ 400 Cam Russell
☐ 401 Jim Waite (G) ☐ 402 Mike Stapleton
☐ 403 Trevor Dam ☐ 404 Tracey Egeland
☐ 405 Owen Lessard ☐ 406 Jeff Sirkka
☐ 407 Mike Dagenais ☐ 408 Alex Roberts
☐ 409 Dominik Hasek (G) ☐ 410 Martin Desjardins
☐ 411 Frantisek Kucera ☐ 412 Carl Mokosak
☐ 413 Dave McDowall, Coach ☐ 414 Ice Checklist

NEW HAVEN NIGHTHAWKS - AHL

Team Set (27 cards): 8.00
ProCards **ProCards**
☐ 415 Paul Saundercook ☐ 416 Darryl Williams
☐ 417 Micah Aivazoff ☐ 418 Robb Stauber (G)
☐ 419 Tom Martin ☐ 420 Billy O'Dwyer
☐ 421 Scott Harlow ☐ 422 Jim Thomson
☐ 423 Jim Pavese ☐ 424 Ron Scott (G)
☐ 425 Dave Pasin ☐ 426 Serge Roy
☐ 427 Darryl Gilmour (G) ☐ 428 Mike Donnelly
☐ 429 René Chapdelaine ☐ 430 Brandy Semchuk
☐ 431 Paul Holden ☐ 432 Bob Berg
☐ 433 Ladislav Tresl ☐ 434 Eric Ricard
☐ 435 Brumwell, Coach ☐ 436 Shawn McCosh
☐ 437 Ross Wilson ☐ 438 Scott Young
☐ 439 David Moylan ☐ 440 M. Comeau, Coach
☐ 441 Nighthawks Checklist

HALIFAX CITADELS - AHL

Stéphane Fiset is the most expensive player at $2-3.
Team Set (27 cards): 8.00
ProCards **ProCards**
☐ 442 David Espe ☐ 443 Mario Doyon
☐ 444 Gerald Bzdel ☐ 445 Claude Lapointe
☐ 446 Hopkins, A Coach ☐ 447 Jodoin, G.M./Coach
☐ 448 Kevin Kaminski ☐ 449 Jamie Baker
☐ 450 Mark Vermette ☐ 451 Iiro Jarvi
☐ 452 Kip Miller ☐ 453 Greg Smyth
☐ 454 Serge Roberge ☐ 455 Stéphane Morin
☐ 456 Brent Severyn ☐ 457 Jean-Marc Richard
☐ 458 Ken Quinney ☐ 459 Jeff Jackson
☐ 460 Jaroslav Sevcik ☐ 461 Dave Latta
☐ 462 Trevor Stienburg ☐ 463 Miroslav Ihnacak
☐ 464 Jim Sprott ☐ 465 Mike Bishop (G)
☐ 466 Stéphane Fiset (G) ☐ 467 Scott Gordon (G)
☐ 468 Citadels Checklist

ADIRONDACK RED WINGS - AHL

Team Set (25 cards): 8.00
ProCards **ProCards**
☐ 469 Gord Kruppke ☐ 470 Glenn Merkosky
☐ 471 Dennis Holland ☐ 472 Chris McRae
☐ 473 Al Conroy ☐ 474 Yves Racine
☐ 475 Nill, A. Coach ☐ 476 B. Melrose, Coach
☐ 477 Bob Wilkie ☐ 478 Guy Dupuis
☐ 479 Doug Houda ☐ 480 Tom Bissett
☐ 481 Bill McDougall ☐ 482 Glen Goodall
☐ 483 Kory Kocur ☐ 484 Chris Luongo

☐ 485 Serge Anglehart ☐ 486 Marc Potvin
☐ 487 Stewart Malgunas ☐ 488 John Chabot
☐ 489 Daniel Shank ☐ 490 Randy Hansch (G)
☐ 491 Dave Gagnon (G) ☐ 492 Scott King (G)
☐ 493 Red Wings Checklist

CAPITAL DISTRICT ISLANDERS - AHL

Team Set (21 cards): 8.00

ProCards ProCards
☐ 494 Derek Laxdal ☐ 495 Sean Lebrun
☐ 496 Shawn Byram ☐ 497 Wayne Doucet
☐ 498 Rich Kromm ☐ 499 Pryor, Plyr/A Coach
☐ 500 G. Maneluk (G) ☐ 501 Brad Lauer
☐ 502 Wayne McBean ☐ 503 Jeff Finley
☐ 504 Jim Culhane ☐ 505 Paul Cohen (G)
☐ 506 Brent Grieve ☐ 507 Kevin Cheveldayoff
☐ 508 Dennis Vaske ☐ 509 Dave Chyzowski
☐ 510 Travis Green ☐ 511 Dean Chynoweth
☐ 512 Rob DiMaio ☐ 513 Paul Guay
☐ 514 Islanders Checklist

ALBANY CHOPPERS - IHL

Team Set (21 cards): 8.00

ProCards ProCards
☐ 515 Rick Knickle (G) ☐ 516 Curtis Hunt
☐ 517 Bruce Racine (G) ☐ 518 Yves Heroux
☐ 519 Joe Stefan ☐ 520 Torrie Robertson
☐ 521 Nicholas Beaulieu ☐ 522 Dave Richter
☐ 523 Jeff Waver ☐ 524 Gordon Paddock
☐ 525 Darryl Noren ☐ 526 Byron Lomow
☐ 527 Ivan Matulik ☐ 528 Dan Woodley
☐ 529 Dale Henry ☐ 530 Soren True
☐ 531 Stuart Burnie ☐ 532 Rob MacInnis
☐ 533 Vern Smith ☐ 534 Paul Laus
☐ 535 Choppers Checklist

FORT WAYNE KOMETS - IHL

Team Set (21 cards): 8.00

ProCards ProCards
☐ 536 Robin Bawa ☐ 537 Steven Fletcher
☐ 538 Lonnie Loach ☐ 539 Al Sims, Coach
☐ 540 Colin Chin ☐ 541 Boudreau, A. Coach
☐ 542 Bob Lasko ☐ 543 John Anderson
☐ 544 Kevin Kaminski ☐ 545 Bruce Major
☐ 546 Stéphane Brochu ☐ 547 Peter Hankinson
☐ 548 Carey Lucyk ☐ 549 Tom Karalis
☐ 550 Bob Jay ☐ 551 Mike Butters
☐ 552 Brian McKee ☐ 553 Ray LeBlanc (G)
☐ 554 Tom Draper (G) ☐ 555 Steve Laurin (G)
☐ 556 Komets Checklist

UTICA DEVILS - AHL

Team Set (25 cards): 8.00

ProCards ProCards
☐ 557 Sergei Starikov ☐ 558 Claude Vilgrain
☐ 559 Jeff Sharples ☐ 560 Bob Woods
☐ 561 Perry Anderson ☐ 562 Brennan Maley
☐ 563 Mike Posma ☐ 564 McVie, G. M./Coach
☐ 565 Chris Palmer ☐ 566 Bill Huard
☐ 567 Marc Laniel ☐ 568 Neil Brady
☐ 569 Jason Simon ☐ 570 Kevin Todd
☐ 571 Jeff Madill ☐ 572 Jeff Christian
☐ 573 Todd Copeland ☐ 574 Mike Bodnarchuk
☐ 575 Chris Kiene ☐ 576 Myles O'Connor
☐ 577 Jamie Huscroft ☐ 578 Mark Romaine (G)
☐ 579 Rollie Melanson (G) ☐ 580 Team Photo
☐ 581 Devils Checklist

KANSAS CITY BLADES - IHL

Team Set (21 cards): 8.00

ProCards ProCards
☐ 582 Ron Handy ☐ 583 Cam Plante
☐ 584 Lee Giffin ☐ 585 Jim Latos
☐ 586 Stu Kulak ☐ 587 Claude Julien
☐ 588 Rick Barkovich ☐ 589 Randy Exelby (G)
☐ 590 Mark Vichorek ☐ 591 Darin Smith
☐ 592 Mike Kelfer ☐ 593 Andy Akervik
☐ 594 Mike Hiltner ☐ 595 Kevin Sullivan
☐ 596 Troy Frederick ☐ 597 Claudio Scremin
☐ 598 Kurt Semandel ☐ 599 Mike Colman
☐ 600 Jeff Odgers ☐ 601 Wade Flaherty (G)
☐ 602 Blades Checklist

SALT LAKE GOLDEN EAGLES - IHL

Team Set (26 cards): 8.00

ProCards ProCards
☐ 603 Marc Bureau ☐ 604 Darryl Olsen
☐ 605 Rick Lessard ☐ 606 Kevin Grant
☐ 607 Rich Chernomaz ☐ 608 Randy Bucyk
☐ 609 Wayne Cowley (G) ☐ 610 Ken Sabourin
☐ 611B. Francis, Coach ☐ 612 Jamie Hislop, Coach
☐ 613 Kevan Melrose ☐ 614 Scott McCrady
☐ 615 Corey Lyons ☐ 616 Martin Simard
☐ 617 C. J. Young ☐ 618 Mark Osiecki
☐ 619 Bryan Deasley ☐ 620 Kerry Clark
☐ 621 Paul Kruse ☐ 622 Darren Banks
☐ 623 Richard Zemlak ☐ 624 Todd Harkins
☐ 625 W. Sharples (G) ☐ 626 Andrew McKim
☐ 627 S. Guenette (G) ☐ 628 Golden Eagles CL

1990 - 91 SCORE

This series has two versions: the American version (English) and the Canadian version (Bilingual). The logo on the back of promo cards is eight mm high as opposed to six mm high on regular cards.

The most expensive single is Wayne Gretzky at $1.00-1.50. The most expensive rookie cards are Eric Lindros ($5-10), Martin Brodeur ($5-10), Jaromir Jagr ($4-5) and Olaf Kölzig ($2-3). The Lindros "B" cards sell for 50-75¢. All other singles and rookie cards sell between 20¢ and $1.00. Please see Canadian Sports Collector for up-to-date pricing.

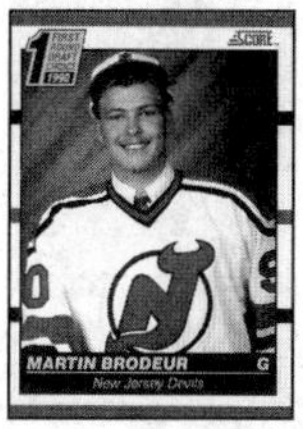

♦ A Martin Brodeur card graded BGS 9.5 closed at $340.30 U.S. (approx. $510 Cdn.) in an April 20-27 Internet auction at eBay.

Imprint: © 1990 SCORE

Complete Set (440 cards):	20.00	20.00
Factory Set (445 cards):	22.00	22.00
Common Player:	.20	.20
Promo	**U.S.**	**Cdn.**
☐ 1 W. Gretzky, LosA., Error (Catches)	20.00	
☐ 1 Wayne Gretzky, LosA., Corrected	15.00	
☐ 10 Patrick Roy (G), Mont.		15.00
☐ 40 Gary Leeman, Toro.		2.00
☐ 100 Mark Messier, Edmo.		5.00
☐ 100 Mark Messier, Edmo.		5.00
☐ 179 Jeremy Roenick, Chic.	3.00	
☐ 200 Ray Bourque, Bost.	5.00	

Score Score
☐☐ 1 Wayne Gretzky ☐☐ 2 Mario Lemieux
☐☐ 3 Steve Yzerman ☐☐ 4 Cam Neely
☐☐ 5 Al MacInnis ☐☐ 6 Paul Coffey
☐☐ 7 Brian Bellows ☐☐ 8 Joe Sakic
☐☐ 9 Bernie Nicholls ☐☐ 10 Patrick Roy (G)
☐☐ 11 Doug Houda RC ☐☐ 12 David Volek
☐☐ 13 Esa Tikkanen ☐☐ 14 Thomas Steen
☐☐ 15 Chris Chelios ☐☐ 16 Bobby Carpenter
☐☐ 17 Dirk Graham ☐☐ 18 Garth Butcher
☐☐ 19 Patrik Sundstrom ☐☐ 20 Rod Langway
☐☐ 21 Scott Young ☐☐ 22 Ulf Dahlén
☐☐ 23 Mike Ramsey ☐☐ 24 Peter Zezel
☐☐ 25 Ron Hextall (G) ☐☐ 26 Steve Duchesne
☐☐ 27 Allan Bester (G) ☐☐ 28 Everett Sanipass RC
☐☐ 29 Steve Konroyd ☐ 30 Nieuwendyk, Err. USA
☐☐ 30 Nieuwendyk ("feel") ☐☐ 31 Ashton (no position)
☐☐ 31 Brent Ashton ☐☐ 32 Trevor Linden
☐☐ 33 Mike Ridley ☐☐ 34 Sean Burke (G)
☐☐ 35 Pat Verbeek ☐☐ 36 Rob Ramage
☐☐ 37 Kelly Kisio ☐☐ 38 Muni (b: Simpson]
☐☐ 38 Craig Muni, Corr. ☐☐ 39 Brent Sutter
☐☐ 40 Gary Leeman ☐☐ 41 Jeff Brown
☐☐ 42 Greg Millen (G) ☐☐ 43 Alex. Mogilny RC
☐☐ 44 Dale Hunter ☐☐ 45 Randy Moller
☐☐ 46 Sidorkiewicz (G) ☐☐ 47 Terry Carkner
☐☐ 48 Tony Granato ☐☐ 49 Shawn Burr
☐☐ 50 Dale Hawerchuk ☐☐ 51 Don Sweeney RC
☐☐ 52 Vernon (G), Error ☐☐ 53 Kevin Stevens RC
☐☐ 54 Bryan Fogarty RC ☐☐ 55 Dan Quinn
☐☐ 56 Murray Craven ☐☐ 57 Shawn Chambers
☐☐ 58 Craig Simpson ☐☐ 59 Doug Crossman
☐☐ 60 Daren Puppa (G) ☐☐ 61 Bobby Smith
☐☐ 62 V. Fetisov RC ☐☐ 63 Gino Cavallini
☐☐ 64 Jimmy Carson ☐☐ 65 David Ellett
☐☐ 66 Steve Thomas ☐☐ 67 Mike Lalor RC
☐☐ 68 Mike Liut (G) ☐☐ 69 Tom Laidlaw
☐☐ 70 Ron Francis ☐☐ 71 Sergei Makarov RC
☐☐ 72 Randy Burridge ☐☐ 73 Doug Lidster
☐☐ 74 Mike Richter (G) RC ☐☐ 75 Stéphane Richer
☐☐ 76 Randy Hillier ☐☐ 77 Christian Ruuttu
☐☐ 78 Marc Fortier ☐☐ 79 Bill Ranford (G)
☐☐ 80 Rick Tocchet ☐☐ 81 Fredrik Olausson
☐☐ 82 Adam Creighton ☐☐ 83 Sylvain Côté
☐☐ 84 Brian Mullen ☐☐ 85 Adam Oates
☐☐ 86 Gary Nylund ☐☐ 87 Cheveldae (G) RC
☐☐ 88 Gary Suter ☐☐ 89 John Tonelli
☐☐ 90 Kevin Hatcher ☐☐ 91 Guy Carbonneau
☐☐ 92 Curtis Leschyshyn ☐☐ 93 Kirk McLean (G)
☐☐ 94 Curt Giles ☐☐ 95 Damphousse
☐☐ 96 Peter Stastny ☐☐ 97 Glen Wesley
☐☐ 98 David Shaw ☐☐ 99 Brad Shaw RC
☐☐ 100 Mark Messier ☐☐ 101 Rick Zombo RC
☐ 102 Mark Fitzpatrick (G) RC, Error (Catches R) (CDN)
☐☐ 102 Fitzpatrick (G) RC ☐☐ 103 Rick Vaive
☐☐ 104 Mark Osborne ☐☐ 105 Rob Brown
☐☐ 106 Gary Roberts ☐☐ 107 Riendeau (G) RC
☐☐ 108 Dave Gagner ☐☐ 109 Bruce Driver
☐☐ 110 Pierre Turgeon ☐☐ 111 Claude Lemieux
☐☐ 112 Essensa (G) RC ☐☐ 113 John Ogrodnick
☐☐ 114 Glenn Anderson ☐☐ 115 Kelly Hrudey (G)
☐☐ 116 Sylvain Turgeon ☐☐ 117 Gord Murphy RC
☐☐ 118 Craig Janney ☐☐ 119 Randy Wood
☐☐ 120 Mike Modano RC ☐☐ 121 Tom Barrasso (G)
☐☐ 122 Daniel Marois ☐☐ 123 Igor Larionov RC
☐☐ 124 Geoff Courtnall ☐☐ 125 Denis Savard
☐☐ 126 Ron Tugnutt (G) ☐☐ 127 M. Schneider RC
☐☐ 128 Joel Otto ☐☐ 129 Steve Smith
☐☐ 130 Mike Gartner ☐☐ 131 Brind'Amour RC
☐☐ 132 Jyrki Lumme RC ☐☐ 133 Mike Foligno
☐☐ 134 Ray Ferraro ☐☐ 135 Steve Larmer
☐☐ 136 Randy Carlyle ☐☐ 137 Tony Tanti
☐☐ 138 Jeff Chychrun RC ☐☐ 139 Gerald Diduck
☐☐ 140 Andy Moog (G) ☐☐ 141 Paul Gillis
☐☐ 142 Tom Kurvers ☐☐ 143 Bob Probert
☐☐ 144 Neal Broten ☐☐ 145 Phil Housley
☐☐ 146 Shanahan ☐☐ 147 Bob Rouse
☐☐ 148 Russ Courtnall ☐☐ 149 Normand Rochefort
☐☐ 150 Luc Robitaille ☐☐ 151 Cu. Joseph (G) RC
☐☐ 152 Ulf Samuelsson ☐☐ 153 Ron Sutter
☐☐ 154 Petri Skriko ☐☐ 155 Doug Gilmour
☐☐ 156 Paul Fenton ☐☐ 157 Jeff Norton
☐☐ 158 Jari Kurri ☐☐ 159 Réjean Lemelin (G)
☐☐ 160 Kirk Muller ☐☐ 161 Keith Brown
☐☐ 162 A. Broten (Photo is Dave Archibald)
☐☐ 163 Adam Graves RC ☐☐ 164 John Cullen
☐☐ 165 Craig Ludwig ☐☐ 166 Dave Taylor
☐☐ 167 Craig Wolanin RC ☐☐ 168 Kelly Miller
☐☐ 169 Uwe Krupp ☐☐ 170 Kevin Lowe
☐☐ 171 Wendel Clark ☐☐ 172 Dave Babych
☐☐ 173 Paul Reinhart ☐☐ 174 Patrick Flatley
☐☐ 175 Vanbiesbrouck (G) ☐☐ 176 T. Numminen RC
☐☐ 177 Tim Kerr ☐☐ 178 Ken Daneyko
☐☐ 179 J. Roenick RC ☐☐ 180 Gerard Gallant
☐☐ 181 Allen Pedersen ☐☐ 182 Jon Casey (G)
☐☐ 183 T. Sandström ☐☐ 184 Brad McCrimmon
☐☐ 185 Paul Cavallini ☐☐ 186 Mark Recchi RC
☐☐ 187 Michel Petit ☐☐ 188 Scott Stevens
☐☐ 189 Dave Andreychuk ☐☐ 190 John MacLean
☐☐ 191 Petr Svoboda ☐☐ 192 Dave Tippett
☐☐ 193 Dave Manson ☐☐ 194 James Patrick
☐☐ 195 Al Iafrate ☐☐ 196 Doug Smail
☐☐ 197 Kjell Samuelsson ☐☐ 198 Brian Bradley
☐☐ 199 Charlie Huddy ☐☐ 200 Ray Bourque
☐☐ 201 Joey Kocur RC ☐☐ 202 Jim Johnson
☐☐ 203 Paul MacLean ☐☐ 204 Tim Watters
☐☐ 205 Pat Elynuik ☐☐ 206 Larry Murphy
☐☐ 207 C. Loiselle RC ☐☐ 208 Joe Mullen
☐☐ 209 A. Kasatonov RC ☐☐ 210 Ed Olczyk
☐☐ 211 Doug Bodger ☐☐ 212 Kevin Dineen
☐☐ 213 Shayne Corson ☐☐ 214 Steve Chiasson
☐☐ 215 Don Beaupré (G) ☐☐ 216 Jamie Macoun
☐☐ 217 David Poulin ☐☐ 218 Zarley Zalapski
☐☐ 219 Brad Marsh ☐☐ 220 Mark Howe
☐☐ 221 Michel Goulet ☐☐ 222 H. McDonough RC
☐☐ 223 Frantisek Musil ☐☐ 224 S. Momesso RC
☐☐ 225 Brian Leetch ☐☐ 226 Theoren Fleury
☐☐ 227 Mike Krushelnyski ☐☐ 228 Glen Hanlon (G)
☐☐ 229 Mario Marois ☐☐ 230 Dino Ciccarelli
☐☐ 231 McLlwain (shot R) ☐☐ 231 McLlwain, Corr.
☐☐ 232 Petr Klima ☐☐ 233 Grant Ledyard RC
☐☐ 234 Phil Bourque ☐☐ 235 Bob Sweeney
☐☐ 236 Luke Richardson ☐☐ 237 Todd Krygier RC
☐☐ 238 Brian Skrudland ☐☐ 239 C. Terreri (G) RC
☐☐ 240 Greg Adams ☐☐ 241 D. Turcotte RC
☐☐ 242 Scott Mellanby ☐☐ 243 Troy Murray
☐☐ 244 Stewart Gavin ☐☐ 245 Gord Roberts
☐☐ 246 John Druce RC ☐☐ 247 Steve Kasper
☐☐ 248 Paul Ranheim RC ☐☐ 249 Greg Paslawski
☐☐ 250 Pat LaFontaine ☐☐ 251 Scott Arniel
☐☐ 252 Bernie Federko ☐☐ 253 Garry Galley RC
☐☐ 254 Carey Wilson ☐☐ 255 Bob Errey
☐☐ 256 Tony Hrkac ☐☐ 257 Andrew McBain
☐☐ 258 Craig MacTavish ☐☐ 259 D. Evason
☐ 259 Dean Evason (reversed negative, US version)
☐☐ 260 Larry Robinson ☐☐ 261 Basil McRae
☐☐ 262 S. Lebeau RC ☐☐ 263 Ken Wregget (G)
☐☐ 264 Greg Gilbert ☐☐ 265 K. Baumgartner RC
☐☐ 266 Franceschetti RC ☐☐ 267 Rick Meagher
☐☐ 268 Michal Pivonka RC ☐☐ 269 Brian Propp
☐☐ 270 Bryan Trottier ☐☐ 271 Marty McSorley
☐☐ 272 Jan Erixon ☐☐ 273 Vladimir Krutov RC
☐☐ 274 Dana Murzyn ☐☐ 275 Grant Fuhr (G)
☐☐ 276 R. Cunneyworth ☐☐ 277 John Chabot
☐☐ 278 Walt Poddubny ☐☐ 279 Stephen Leach
☐☐ 280 Doug Wilson ☐☐ 281 Rick Sutter
☐☐ 282 B'regard (G) RC Er. ☐☐ 283 John Carter RC
☐☐ 284 Don Barber RC ☐☐ 285 Tom Fergus
☐☐ 286 Ilkka Sinisalo ☐☐ 287 Kevin McClelland
☐☐ 288 Troy Mallette RC ☐☐ 289 Clint Malarchuk (G)
☐☐ 290 Guy Lafleur ☐☐ 291 Bob Joyce
☐☐ 292 Trent Yawney ☐☐ 293 Joe Murphy RC
☐☐ 294 G. Healy (G) RC ☐☐ 295 Dave Christian
☐☐ 296 Paul MacDermid ☐☐ 297 Todd Elik RC
☐☐ 298 W. Young (G) RC ☐☐ 299 Dean Kennedy RC
☐☐ 300 B. Hull, SLou. ☐ C 301 M. Gelinas RC
☐ US 301 Keith Acton ☐ C 302 Ric Nattress
☐ US 302 Yvon Corriveau ☐ C 303 Jim Sandlak
☐ US 303 Don Maloney ☐ C 304 B. Hayward (G)
☐ US 304 M. Tinordi RC ☐ C 305 Joe Cirella
☐ US 305 B. Kudelski RC ☐ C 306 Randall Gregg
☐ US 306 Brian Benning ☐ C 307 Lefebvre RC
☐ US 307 Alan Kerr ☐ C 308 M. Lamb RC
☐ US 308 Per-Erik Eklund ☐ C 309 R. Wamsley (G)
☐ US 309 C. Johansson ☐ C 310 Moe Mantha
☐ US 310 D. Maley RC ☐ C 311 Tony McKegney
☐ US 311 Chris Nilan ☐☐ 312 AS Patrick Roy (G)
☐☐ 313 AS Ray Bourque ☐☐ 314 AS Al MacInnis
☐☐ 315 AS Mark Messier ☐☐ 316 AS Luc Robitaille
☐☐ 317 AS Brett Hull ☐☐ 318 AS D. Puppa (G)
☐☐ 319 AS Paul Coffey ☐☐ 320 AS Doug Wilson
☐☐ 321 AS W. Gretzky ☐☐ 322 AS Brian Bellows
☐☐ 323 AS Cam Neely ☐☐ 324 Bob Essensa (G)
☐☐ 325 Brad Shaw ☐☐ 326 Geoff Smith
☐☐ 327 Mike Modano ☐☐ 328 Rod Brind'Amour
☐☐ 329 Sergei Makarov ☐ C 330 Generals
☐ U 330 K. Miller RC ☐☐ 331 Ranford with Cup
☐☐ 332 Paul Coffey ☐☐ 333 Mike Gartner
☐☐ 334 Al Iafrate ☐☐ 335 Al MacInnis
☐☐ 336 Wayne Gretzky ☐☐ 337 Mario Lemieux
☐☐ 338 Wayne Gretzky ☐☐ 339 Steve Yzerman
☐☐ 340 Cam Neely ☐☐ 341 Scott Stevens
☐☐ 342 Esa Tikkanen ☐☐ 343 Jan Erixon
☐☐ 344 Patrick Roy (G) ☐☐ 345 Bill Ranford (G)
☐☐ 346 Brett Hull ☐☐ 347 Wayne Gretzky
☐☐ 348 Jari Kurri ☐☐ 349 Paul Cavallini
☐☐ 350 Sergei Makarov ☐☐ 351 Brett Hull
☐☐ 352 Wayne Gretzky ☐☐ 353 Wayne Gretzky
☐☐ 354.Roy (G)/ Liut (G) ☐☐ 355 Gilbert Perreault
☐☐ 356 Bill Barber ☐☐ 357 Fern Flaman
☐☐ 358 Bill Ranford (G) ☐☐ 359 Rick Meagher
☐☐ 360 Mark Messier ☐☐ 361 Wayne Gretzky
☐☐ 362 Sergei Makarov ☐☐ 363 Ray Bourque
☐☐ 364 Patrick Roy (G) ☐☐ 365 Lemelin/ Moog (G)
☐☐ 366 Brett Hull ☐☐ 367 Gord Kluzak
☐☐ 368 BOST vs. WASH ☐☐ 369 EDMO vs. CHIC
☐☐ 370 Adam Burt RC ☐☐ 371 Troy Loney RC
☐☐ 372 D. Chyzowski RC ☐☐ 373 Geoff Smith RC
☐☐ 374 Stan Smyl ☐☐ 375 Gaetan Duchesne
☐☐ 376 Bob Murray ☐☐ 377 Daniel Shank RC
☐☐ 378 Tommy Albelin ☐☐ 379 Perry Berezan RC
☐☐ 380 Ken Linseman ☐☐ 381 S. Matteau RC
☐☐ 382 Mario Thyer RC ☐☐ 383 N. Emerson RC
☐☐ 384 Kory Kocur RC ☐☐ 385 Bob Beers RC
☐☐ 386 J. Hrivnak (G) RC ☐☐ 387 Mark Pederson RC
☐☐ 388 J. Hackett (G) RC ☐☐ 389 Eric Weinrich RC
☐☐ 390 Steven Rice RC ☐☐ 391 Stu Barnes RC
☐☐ 392 O. Kölzig (G) RC ☐☐ 393 F. Leroux RC
☐☐ 394 A. Plavsic RC ☐☐ 395 M. Mongeau RC
☐☐ 396 Rick Corriveau RC ☐☐ 397 Wayne Doucet RC
☐☐ 398 Mats Sundin RC ☐☐ 399 Murray Baron RC
☐☐ 400 Rick Bennett RC ☐☐ 401 Jon Morris RC
☐☐ 402 Whitmore (G) RC ☐☐ 403 Peter Lappin RC
☐☐ 404 Kris Draper RC ☐☐ 405 S. Stevenson RC
☐☐ 406 P. Ysebaert RC ☐☐ 407 Waite (G) RC (R)
☐☐ 407 Waite (G) RC Corr. ☐☐ 408 Cam Russell RC
☐☐ 409 Kim Issel RC ☐☐ 410 Darrin Shannon RC
☐☐ 411 Link Gaetz RC ☐☐ 412 Craig Fisher RC
☐☐ 413 B. Hoffort (G) RC ☐☐ 414 Peter Ing (G) RC
☐☐ 415 S. Fiset (G) RC ☐☐ 416 Dominic Lavoie RC
☐☐ 417 Steve Maltais RC ☐☐ 418 Wes Walz RC
☐☐ 419 Terry Yake RC ☐☐ 420 Jamie Leach RC
☐☐ 421 Rob Blake RC ☐☐ 422 A. Cassels RC
☐☐ 423 Marc Bureau RC ☐☐ 424 Scott Allison RC
☐☐ 425 Darryl Sydor RC ☐☐ 426 T. Stevenson RC
☐☐ 427 Brad May RC ☐☐ 428 Jaromir Jagr RC
☐☐ 429 Shawn Antoski RC ☐☐ 430 Derian Hatcher RC
☐☐ 431 Mark Greig RC ☐☐ 432 Scott Scissons RC
☐☐ 433 Mike Ricci RC ☐☐ 434 D. Berehowsky RC
☐☐ 435 Owen Nolan RC ☐☐ 436 Keith Primeau RC
☐☐ 437 Karl Dykhuis RC ☐☐ 438 Trevor Kidd (G) RC
☐☐ 439 M. Brodeur (G) RC ☐☐ 440 Eric Lindros RC
☐☐ B1 Eric Lindros ☐☐ B2 Eric Lindros
☐☐ B3 Eric Lindros ☐☐ B4 Eric Lindros
☐☐ B5 Eric Lindros

ROOKIE & TRADED

The most expensive singles are Eric Lindros ($3-5), Jaromir Jagr ($2-3), Mats Sundin ($1-2) and Wayne Gretzky ($1-2). The most expensive rookie cards are Sergei Fedorov ($1-2), Peter Bondra ($1-2) and Ed Belfour ($1-2). All other singles sell between 20¢ and $1.00.

Complete Set (110 cards): 10.00

Score Score
☐ 1T Denis Savard ☐ 2T Dale Hawerchuk
☐ 3T Phil Housley ☐ 4T Chris Chelios
☐ 5T Geoff Courtnall ☐ 6T Peter Zezel
☐ 7T Joe Mullen ☐ 8T Craig Ludwig
☐ 9T Claude Lemieux ☐ 10T Bobby Holik
☐ 11T Peter Ing (G) ☐ 12T Rod Buskas
☐ 13T Tim Sweeney ☐ 14T Don Barber
☐ 15T Ray Ferraro ☐ 16T Peter Taglianetti
☐ 17T Johan Garpenlov ☐ 18T Kevin Miller
☐ 19T Frantisek Musil ☐ 20T S. Fedorov (RC)
☐ 21T Aaron Broten ☐ 22T Chris Nilan
☐ 23T Gerald Diduck ☐ 24T Marc Habscheid
☐ 25T Glen Featherstone ☐ 26T Mikko Makela
☐ 27T Paul Stanton ☐ 28T Mark Osborne
☐ 29T Dave Tippett ☐ 30T Robert Reichel (RC)
☐ 31T Grant Jennings ☐ 32T Troy Gamble (G)
☐ 33T Mark Janssens ☐ 34T Brian Propp
☐ 35T Donald Dufresne ☐ 36T Martin Hostak
☐ 37T Brad McCrimmon ☐ 38T Dave Lowry
☐ 39T Anatoli Semenov ☐ 40T Scott Stevens
☐ 41T Paul Broten ☐ 42T Carey Wilson
☐ 43T Troy Crowder ☐ 44T Vladimir Ruzicka
☐ 45T Rich Pilon ☐ 46T John McIntyre
☐ 47T Mike Krushelnyski ☐ 48T Dave Snuggerud
☐ 49T Robert McGill ☐ 50T Petr Nedved
☐ 51T Ed Olczyk ☐ 52T Doug Crossman
☐ 53T Mikhail Tatarinov ☐ 54T Michel Petit
☐ 55T F. Pietrangelo (G) ☐ 56T Brian MacLellan
☐ 57T Paul Fenton ☐ 58T Eric Desjardins
☐ 59T Mike Craig ☐ 60T Mike Ricci
☐ 61T Harold Snepsts ☐ 62T John Byce
☐ 63T Laurie Boschman ☐ 64T Randy Velischek
☐ 65T Robert Kron ☐ 66T Jocelyn Lemieux
☐ 67T David Ellett ☐ 68T Scott Arniel
☐ 69T Doug Smail ☐ 70T Jaromir Jagr
☐ 71T Peter Bondra RC ☐ 72T Paul Cyr
☐ 73T D. Berthiaume (G) ☐ 74T Lee Norwood
☐ 75T Bobby Smith ☐ 76T Kris King
☐ 77T Mark Hunter ☐ 78T Brian Hayward (G)
☐ 79T Greg Hawgood ☐ 80T Owen Nolan
☐ 81T Cliff Ronning ☐ 82T Zdeno Ciger
☐ 83T Gord Roberts ☐ 84T Rick Green
☐ 85T Ken Hodge ☐ 86T Derek King
☐ 87T Brent Gilchrist ☐ 88T Eric Lindros
☐ 89T Steve Bozek ☐ 90T Keith Primeau
☐ 91T Roger Johansson ☐ 92T Wayne Presley
☐ 93T Ilkka Sinisalo ☐ 94T Mario Marois
☐ 95T Ken Linseman ☐ 96T Greg Brown
☐ 97T Ray Sheppard ☐ 98T Mike Lalor
☐ 99T Norman Lacombe ☐ 100T Mats Sundin
☐ 101T Jergus Baca ☐ 102T Mike Keane
☐ 103T Ed Belfour (G) ☐ 104T Mark Hardy
☐ 105T Dave Capuano ☐ 106T Bryan Trottier
☐ 107T Per Olav Djoos ☐ 108T Sylvain Turgeon
☐ 109T David Reid ☐ 110T Wayne Gretzky

1990 - 91 SCORE HOT CARDS

Score renumbered 100 cards from the regular issue set for Publications International, Ltd. They included these cards in Value Packs which also contained a Hottest and Rising Star book.

Complete Set (100 cards):	15.00
Album:	3.00
Common Card:	.30

Score	Hot
1 Wayne Gretzky, LosA.	5.00
2 Craig Simpson, Edmo.	.25
3 Brian Bellows, Minn.	.25
4 Steve Yzerman, Detr.	3.00
5 Bernie Nicholls, NYRa.	.25
6 Esa Tikkanen, Edmo.	.25
7 Joe Sakic, Québ.	2.00
8 Thomas Steen, Winn.	.25
9 Chris Chelios, Mont.	.25
10 Patrik Sundström, NJer.	.25
11 Rod Langway, Wash.	.25
12 Scott A. Young, Hart.	.25
13 Mike Ramsey, Buff.	.25
14 Ron Hextall (G), Phil.	.25
15 Steve Duchesne, LosA.	.25
16 Trevor Linden, Vanc.	.25
17 Sean Burke (G), NJer.	.25
18 Pat Verbeek, Hart.	.25
19 Brent Sutter, NYIs.	.25
20 Gary Leeman, Toro.	.25
21 Shawn Burr, Detr.	.25
22 Dale Hawerchuk, Winn.	.25
23 Mike Vernon (G), Calg.	.25
24 Dan Quinn, Vanc.	.25
25 Patrick Roy (G), Mont.	3.00
26 Daren Puppa (G), Buff.	.25
27 Gino Cavallini, SLou.	.25
28 Jimmy Carson, Detr.	.25
29 Dave Ellett, Winn.	.25
30 Steve Thomas, Chic.	.25
31 Jeremy Roenick, Chic.	1.00
32 Mike Liut (G), Wash.	.25
33 Mark Messier, Edmo.	1.00
34 Mario Lemieux, Pitt.	3.00
35 Raymond Bourque, Bost.	1.00
36 Al MacInnis, Calg.	.25
37 Ron Francis, Hart.	.25
38 Stéphane J.J. Richer, Mont.	.25
39 Bill Ranford (G), Edmo.	.25
40 Rick Tocchet, Phil.	.25
41 Adam Oates, SLou.	.25
42 Kevin Hatcher, Wash.	.25
43 Guy Carbonneau, Mont.	.25
44 Curtis Leschyshyn, Québ.	.25
45 Joe Nieuwendyk, Calg.	.25
46 Kirk McLean (G), Vanc.	.25
47 Vincent Damphousse, Toro.	.25
48 Peter Stastny, NJer.	.25
49 Rick Zombo, Detr.	.25
50 Mark Fitzpatrick (G), NYIs.	.25
51 Rob (Jr.) Brown, Pitt.	.25
52 Dave Gagner, Minn.	.25
53 Pierre Turgeon, Buff.	.25
54 Glenn Anderson, Edmo.	.25
55 Kelly Hrudey (G), LosA.	.25
56 Gord Murphy, Phil.	.25
57 Glen Wesley, Bost.	.25
58 Craig Janney, Bost.	.25
59 Denis Savard, Chic.	.25
60 Mike Gartner, NYRa.	1.00
61 Steve Larmer, Chic.	.25
62 Andy Moog (G), Bost.	.25
63 Phil Housley, Buff.	.25
64 Ulf Samuelsson, Hart.	.25
65 Paul Coffey, Pitt.	.25
66 Luc Robitaille, LosA.	1.00
67 Cam Neely, Bost.	1.00
68 Doug Wilson, Chic.	.25
69 Doug Gilmour, Calg.	.25
70 Jeff Norton, NYIs.	.25
71 Kirk Muller, NJer.	.25
72 Aaron Broten, Minn.	.25
73 John Cullen, Pitt.	.25
74 Craig Ludwig, Mont.	.25
75 Kevin Lowe, Edmo.	.25
76 John Vanbiesbrouck (G), NYRa.	.25
77 Tim Kerr, Phil.	.25
78 Gerard Gallant, Detr.	.25
79 Tomas Sandström, LosA.	.25
80 Jon Casey (G), Minn.	.25
81 Mark Recchi, Pitt.	.25
82 Scott Stevens, Wash.	.25
83 John MacLean, NJer.	.25
84 James Patrick, NYRa.	.25
85 Al Iafrate, Toro.	.25
86 Pat Elynuik, Winn.	.25
87 Dave Andreychuk, Buff.	.25
88 Joe Mullen, Calg.	.25
89 Ed Olczyk, Toro.	.25
90 Kevin Dineen, Hart.	.25
91 Shayne Corson, Mont.	.25
92 Mark Howe, Phil.	.25
93 Brian Leetch, NYRa.	.25
94 Dino Ciccarelli, Wash.	.25
95 Pat LaFontaine, NYIs.	.25
96 Guy Lafleur, Québ.	2.00
97 Mike Modano, Minn.	1.00
98 Rod Brind'Amour, SLou.	.25
99 Sergei Makarov, Calg.	.25
100 Brett Hull, SLou.	1.00

1990 - 91 SCORE YOUNG SUPERSTARS

The most expensive singles are Eric Lindros ($3-4), Mats Sundin (75¢-$1.00) and Curtis Joseph (75¢-$1.00). All other singles sell between 20¢ and $1.00.

Imprint: © 1990 SCORE

Complete Set (40 cards): 10.00

Score	Score
1 Pierre Turgeon	2 Brian Leetch
3 Daniel Marois	4 P. Sidorkiewicz (G)
5 Rob Brown	6 Theoren Fleury
7 Mats Sundin	8 Glen Wesley
9 Sergei Fedorov	10 Joe Sakic
11 Sean Burke (G)	12 Dave Chyzowski
13 Gord Murphy	14 Scott Young
15 Curtis Joseph (G)	16 Darren Turcotte
17 Kevin Stevens	18 Mathieu Schneider
19 Trevor Linden	20 Mike Modano
21 Martin Gelinas	22 Stéphane Fiset (G)
23 Brendan Shanahan	24 Jeremy Roenick
25 John Druce	26 Alexander Mogilny
27 Mike Richter (G)	28 Pat Elynuik
29 Robert Reichel	30 Craig Janney
31 Rod Brind'Amour	32 Mark Fitzpatrick (G)
33 Tony Granato	34 Bobby Holik
35 Mark Recchi	36 Owen Nolan
37 Petr Nedved	38 Keith Primeau
39 Mike Ricci	40 Eric Lindros

1990 - 91 SEMIC ELISTERIEN STICKERS

The most expensive singles are Nicklas Lidström at $4-8, Markus Näslund at $4-8, Mikael Renberg at $3-4, and Borje Salming at $3-4. Singles start at 25¢; stars and regional favourites sell at $1.00 or more.

Sticker Size: 3" x 2 1/8"

Complete Set (294 stickers): 40.00

Album: 6.00

Semic	Semic
1 MoDo Logo	2 MoDo Photo
3 Fredrik Andersson	4 Goran Ammark
5 Ari Salo	6 Anders Berglund
7 Lars Jansson	8 Hans Lodin
9 Ove Pettersson	10 Jorgen Eriksson
11 Tony Olofsson	12 Tomas Nanzen
13 Michael Hjälm	14 Erik Holmberg
15 Urban Nordin	16 Kent Lantz
17 Lars Bystrom	18 Jens Ohman
19 Ulf Odmark	20 Mikael Stahl
21 Ingemar Strom	22 Tommy Pettersson
23 Markus Näslund	24 Per Wallin
25 Frolunda Logo	26 Frolunda Photo
27 Ake Lilljebjorn	28 Hakan Algotsson
29 Leif Carlsson	30 Jonas Heed
31 Hakan Nordin	32 Joacim Esbjors
33 Stefan Axelsson	34 Stefan Larsson
35 Jorgen Palm	36 Oscar Ackerstrom
37 Patrik Carnback	38 Mats Lundstrom
39 Niklas Andersson	40 Serge Boisvert
41 Arto Sirvio	42 Terho Koskela
43 Kari Jaako	44 Peter Berndtsson
45 Mikael Andersson	46 Per Edlund
47 Jonas Andersson	48 Johan Witehall
49 Sodertalje Logo	50 Sodertalje Photo
51 Reino Sundberg	52 Jari Luoma
53 Mats Kilstrom	54 Stefan Jonsson
55 Peter Ekroth	56 Mats Waltin
57 Jan Bergman	58 Hans Pettersson
59 Stefan Nyman	60 Conny Jansson
61 Thomas Eklund	62 Otto Hascak
63 Morgan Samuelsson	64 Reine Landgren
65 Bjorn Carlsson	66 Ola Andersson
67 Tomaz Eriksson	68 Bert-Olav Karlsson
69 Ola Rosander	70 Stefan Olsson
71 Scott Moore	72 Anders Frykbo
73 AIK Logo	74 AIK Photo
75 Thomas Ostlund	76 Sami Lindstahl
77 Borje Salming	78 Mats Thelin
79 Petter Salsten	80 Petri Liimatainen
81 Rikard Franzen	82 Stefan Claesson
83 Torbjorn Mattsson	84 Daniel Jardemyre
85 Robert Burakovsky	86 Peter Gradin
87 Thomas Bjuhr	88 Heinz Ehlers
89 Tommy Lehmann	90 Peter Hammarstrom
91 Patric Kjellberg	92 Patric Englund
93 Mats Lindberg	94 Peter Johansson
95 Kristian Gahn	96 Niklas Sundblad
97 Erik Andersson	98 HV 71 Logo
99 HV 71 Photo	100 Peter Aslin
101 Kenneth Johansson	102 Arto Ruotanen
103 Fredrik Stillman	104 Lars Ivarsson
105 Klas Heed	106 Per Gustafsson
107 Mathias Svedberg	108 Tommy Fritz
109 Mats Nilsson	110 Peter Eriksson
111 Risto Kurkinen	112 Thomas Ljungbergh
113 Ove Thornberg	114 Mats Loov
115 Eddy Ericsson	116 Stefan Ornskog
117 Patrik Ross	118 Stefan Persson
119 Dennis Strom	120 Peter Ekelund
121 Jonas Jonsson	122 Torbjorn Persson
123 Malmo IF Logo	124 Malmo IF Photo
125 Peter Lindmark	126 R. Nordström (G)
127 Timo Blomqvist	128 Peter Andersson
129 Mats Lusth	130 Johan Salle
131 Roger Ohman	132 Anders Svensson
133 Peter Imhauser	134 Johan Norgren
135 Raimo Helminen	136 Peter Sundstrom
137 Mats Hallin	138 Matti Pauna
139 Patrik Gustavsson	140 Hakan Ahlund
141 Daniel Rydmark	142 L. Hermansson
143 Carl-Erik Larsson	144 Rick Erdall
145 Bo Svanberg	146 Frerik Johansson
147 Jens Hemstrom	149 Vasteras IK Logo
150 Vasteras IK Photo	150 Mats Ytter (G)
151 Par Hellenberg	152 Nicklas Lidström
153 Leif Rohlin	154 Peter Popovic
155 Jan Karlsson	156 Henrik Andersson
157 Tore Lindgren	158 Peter Jacobsson
159 Pierre Ivarsson	160 Jan Eriksson
161 Goran Sjoberg	162 Mishat Fahrutdinov
163 Anders Berglund	164 Claes Lindblom
165 Jorgen Holmberg	166 Stefan Hellkvist
167 Tomas Strandberg	168 Bjorn Akerblom
169 Ronny Hansen	170 Fredrik Nilsson
171 Patrik Juhlin	172 Henrik Nilsson
173 Brynas IF Logo	174 Brynas IF Photo
175 Michael Sundlov	176 Lars Eriksson
177 Tommy Sjodin	178 Brad Berry
179 Niklas Gallstedt	180 Mikael Lindman
181 Urban Molander	182 Jan-Erik Stormqvist
183 Stefan Klockare	184 Tommy Melkersson
185 Anders Carlsson	186 Patrik Erickson
187 Anders Huuss	188 Jan Larsson
189 Peter Larsson	190 Anders Gozzi
191 Joakim Persson	192 Peter Gustafsson
193 Peter Eriksson	194 Johan Brummer
195 Tomas Olund	196 Kenneth Andersson
197 Leksands IF Logo	198 Leksands IF Photo
199 O. Sundstrom	200 Lars-Erik Lord
201 Jonas Leven	202 Tomas Jonsson
203 Ricard Persson	204 Per Lundell
205 Tomas Nord	206 Mattias Andersson
207 Henric Bjorkman	208 Orjan Lindmark
209 Tomas forslund	210 Niklas Eriksson
211 Peter Lundmark	212 Per-Olof Carlsson
213 Marcus Thuresson	214 Jens Nielsen
215 Kenneth Soderlund	216 Markus Akerblom
217 Ronny Reichenberg	218 Fredrik Olsson
219 Niklas Hillblom	220 Magnus Gustafsson
221 Fredrik Jax	222 Lulea HF Logo
223 Lulea HF Photo	224 Robert skoog
225 Tomas Javeblad	226 Timo Jutila
227 Per Ljusterang	228 Lars Modig
229 Torbjorn Lindberg	230 Tomas Lilja
231 Osmo Soutukorva	232 Jan-Ove Mettavainio
233 Roger Åkerström	234 Johan Stromvall
235 Ulf Sandstrom	236 L-G Pettersson
237 Pauli Jarvinen	238 Lars Hurtig
239 Tomas Berglund	240 Stefan Nilsson
241 Mikael Renberg	242 Hans Hjalmar
243 Jens Hellgren	244 Lars Edstrom
245 Robert Nordberg	246 Farjestads BK Logo
247 Farjestads Photo	248 Anders Bergman
249 Jorgen Ryden	250 Patrik Haltia
251 T. Samuelsson	252 Jim Leavins
253 Peter Hasselblad	254 Jesper Duus
255 Mattis Olsson	256 Greger Artursson
257 Jacob Karlsson	258 Thomas Rhodin
259 Bengt Gustafsson	260 Hakan Loob
261 Thomas Rundqvist	262 Kjell Dahlin
263 Magnus Roupe	264 Jan Ingman
265 Lars Karlsson	266 Mikael Holmberg
267 Staffan Lundh	268 Peter Ottosson
269 Jonas Hoglund	270 Clas Eriksson
271 Djurgardens Logo	272 Djurgardens Photo
273 T. Söderström (G)	274 Joakim Persson
275 Thomas Eriksson	276 Arto Blomsten
277 Kenneth Kennholt	278 Christian Due-Boje
279 Orvar Stambert	280 Per Nygards
281 Marcus Ragnarsson	282 Thomas Johansson
283 Ronnie Pettersson	284 Charles Berglund
285 Jan Viktorsson	286 Jens Ohling
287 Ola Josefsson	288 Peter Nilsson
289 Anders Jonsson	290 Hakan Sodergren
291 Stefan Gustavson	292 Magnus Jansson
293 Mikael Johansson	294 Johan Lindstedt

1990 - 91 7TH INNING SKETCH LHJMQ

The most expensive singles are Martin Brodeur at $4-6 and Félix Potvin at $2-3. NHL stars sell between 35¢ and $1.50. All other singles sell between 20¢ and $1.00.

Imprint: © 1990 7th Inning Sketch

Complete Set (268 cards): 20.00

QMJHL	QMJHL
1 Patrick Poulin	2 Steve Lupien (G)
3 Pierre Gagnon (G)	4 Eric Plante
5 Stéphane Desjardins	6 Peter Valenta
7 Alexandre Legault	8 Patrice Brisebois
9 Martin Charrois	10 Eric Dandenault
11 Claude Jutras	12 David Pekarek
13 Denis Chassé	14 Ian Laperrière
15 Roger Larche	16 Dave Paquet
17 Pascal Lebrasseur	18 Eric Meloche
19 The Face Off, Action	20 Sylvain Rodrigue (G)
21 Dany Girard	22 Eric Rochette
23 Steve Gosselin	24 Martin Lavallée
27 Martin Lacombe	28 Patrice Martineau
29 Dave Tremblay	30 Steve Larouche
31 Danny Beauregard	32 François Bélanger
33 Michel St-Jacques	34 Patrick Bisaillon
35 Félix Potvin (G)	36 Sébastien Parent
37 Eric Duchesne	38 Gilles Bouchard
39 Martin Gagné	40 S. Charbonneau
41 Martin Beaupré	42 Daniel Paradis
43 Joe Canale, Coach	44 George Vezina Arena
45 François Leblanc (G)	46 Martin Chaput
47 Marc Beaucage	48 Carl Mantha
49 Jim Bermingham	50 Philippe Boucher
51 Denis Chalifoux	52 Sylvain Naud
53 Jean Roberge	54 Sandy McCarthy
55 Eric Dubois	56 Jean Blouin
57 Jason Brousseau	58 Pierre Sandke
59 Benoît Larose	60 Yannick Fréchette
61 Pierre Calder	62 Patrick Grisé
63 Martin Balleux	64 Boris Rousson (G)
65 Martin Trudel	66 Carl Leblanc
67 Martin Brochu (G)	68 Benoît Thérrien
69 Q.M.J.H.L. Action	70 Pascal Vincent
71 Christian Tardif	72 Christian Campeau
73 Eric Raymond (G)	74 John Kovacs
75 Steve Arès	76 Pascal Dufalt
77 Greg MacEachern	78 Rémi Belliveau
79 Jocelyn Langlois	80 Carl Ménard, Error
81 Sébastien Fortier	82 J-F Grégoire
83 Normand Demers	84 Nicolas Lefebvre
85 Dominic Maltais	86 Mario Thérrien
87 Daniel Thibault	88 J-F Labbé (G)
91 Patrick Nadeau	92 Claude Poirier
93 Stéphane Julien	94 Patrice René
95 F. Courturier, Error	96 Guy Lefebvre
97 Carl Boudreau	98 Jacques Parent
99 Stéphane Bourget	100 Yanic Perreault
101 Yvan Bergeron	102 J-F Rivard (G)
105 Yvan Charrois	106 Patrick Genest
107 Hervé Lapointe	108 J-F Jomphe
109 Marc Tardif	110 Eric Cardinal
111 Denis Cloutier	112 Q.M.J.H.L. Action
113 Sanscartier Coach	114 Marquis Mathieu
115 S. Tartari, Error	116 Q.M.J.H.L. Action
117 Q.M.J.H.L. Action	118 Martin Roy
119 David Boudreau	120 Mario Dumoulin
121 J-F Picard	122 Q.M.J.H.L. Action
123 Q.M.J.H.L. Action	124 Maxime Gagné
125 Stéphane Ouellet	126 Steven Paiement
127 François Paquette	128 Eric Cool
129 Simon Toupin	130 Shane Doiron
131 Todd Sparks	132 Bruno Lajeunesse
133 M. Cousineau (G)	134 C-C Sauriol, Err.
135 Eric Bellerose	136 Q.M.J.H.L. Action
137 Q.M.J.H.L. Action	138 Martin Lepage
139 Michal Longauer	140 Frédéric Boivin
141 Steven Dionl	142 Q.M.J.H.L. Action
143 Q.M.J.H.L. Action	144 Dan Paolucci
145 Bruno Villeneuve	146 Les Draveurs, Err.
147 Les Bisons, Error	148 Stefan Simoes
149 Joel Blain	150 Eric Lavigne
151 Le Titan de Laval	152 St-Hyacinthe Laser
153 Robert Melanson	154 Brian Rogger
155 Lynx de St-Jean	156 Olympiques, Error
157 F. Ouellette (G)	158 Q.M.J.H.L. Action
159 Saguenéens, Error	160 Les Voltigeurs, Error
161 Le College Français	162 Victoriaville Tigres
163 Q.M.J.H.L. Action	164 Q.M.J.H.L. Action
165 Les Harfangs, Error	166 Les Cataractes
167 Q.M.J.H.L. Action	168 Q.M.J.H.L. Action
169 Pierre Fillion	170 Yanick Degrâce (G)
171 Paul Daigneault,	172 Stacy Dallaire
173 Steve Searles	174 Todd Gillingham
175 Yves Sarault	176 Jason Downey
177 Paul Brousseau	178 Raymond Delarosbil
179 Yvan Corbin	180 G. Drapeau, Coach
181 The Celebration	182 Reginald Brézeault
183 Eric Lafrance	184 Martin Lavallée (G)
185 S. Lavallière, Error	186 Martin Lefebvre
187 Richard Hamelin	188 Eric Beauvais
189 Hughes Mongeon	190 Alain Côté
191 É. Desrochers (G)	192 Eric Joyal
193 Steve Dontigny	194 Frédérick Lefebvre
195 Patrick Hébert	196 Johnny Lorenzo (G)
197 Sylvain Cormier	198 Q.M.J.H.L. Action
199 Dave Morissette	200 Yanick Dupré
201 Eric Marcoux	202 Bruno Ducharme
203 Martin Caron	204 Yves Meunier
205 Eric Bissonette	206 Jason Underhill
207 Dave Béliveau	208 Steve Lapointe
209 Dean Melanson	210 Trevor Duhaime
211 Jacques Leblanc	212 Norm Paquet
213 Hughes Laliberté	214 Craig Prior
215 Patrick Labrecque	216 Patrick Cloutier
217 Michael Bazinet	218 Christian Proulx
219 Action Card	220 Charles Poulin
221 Christian Larivière	222 Martin Brodeur (G)
223 Yanick Lemay	224 Denis Leblanc
225 François Groleau	226 Pierre Sévigny
227 Pierre Allard	228 Craig Martin
229 Karl Dykhuis	230 Etienne Lavoie
231 Stan Melanson	232 Dominic Rhéaume
233 Mario Nobili	234 Martin Gendron
235 Stéphane Ménard	236 David St. Pierre
237 Yan Arsenault	238 Norman Flynn
239 Action Card	240 Dave Chouinard
241 Robert Guillet	242 Martin Lajeunesse
243 Nichol Cloutier	244 Joel Bouchard
245 Donald Brashear	246 Sébastien Tremblay
247 D. Grandmaison	248 Nicolas Lefebvre
249 Joseph Napolitano	250 Marc Savard
251 Alain Gauthier	252 Patrick Côté
253 Richard Aimonette	254 Martin Laitre
255 Carl Lamothe	256 Action Card
257 André Durocher	258 Jocelyn Martel
259 Jeannot Ferland	260 Claude Savoie
262 Denis Beauchamp	263 J-F Gagnon
264 André Bouliane	265 Paul-Emile Exantus
266 Danny Nolet	267 Jean Lebreau
268 Claude Barthe	

1990 - 91 7TH INNING SKETCH OHL

The most expensive singles are Eric Lindros at $4-6 and Michael Peca at $2-3. NHL stars sell between 35¢ and $1.50. All other singles sell between 20¢ and $1.00.

Imprint: © 1991 7th Inning Sketch

Complete Set (400 cards): 20.00

Promo	Promo
1 Eric Lindros Promo	6.00

OHL	OHL
1 Eric Lindros	2 G. Dreveny (G), Error
3 TC: Chris Varga	4 Richard Fatrola, Error

☐ 5 Craig Fraser	☐ 6 Robert Frayn
☐ 7 Brent Gretzky	☐ 8 Jake Grimes
☐ 9 Darren Hurley	☐ 10 Rick Marshall
☐ 11 TC: Keli Corpse	☐ 12 Darren McCarty
☐ 13 D. Morin, Belleville	☐ 14 Sean O'Reilly
☐ 15 Rob Pearson, Error	☐ 15 Pearson, Corrected
☐ 16 John Porco	☐ 17 Ken Rowbotham
☐ 18 Ken Ruddick	☐ 19 Jim Sonmez
☐ 20 Brad Teichmann (G)	☐ 21 Chris Varga
☐ 22 TC: J. Stevenson	☐ 23 Larry Mavety, Coach
☐ 24 R. Fullum, Variation	☐ 25 Lafayette, Variation
☐ 28 Shawn Caplice	☐ 29 Mike Cavanagh
☐ 30 Jason Cirone	☐ 31 Chris Clancy
☐ 32 Mark DeSantis	☐ 33 Rob Dykeman (G)
☐ 34 Shayne Gaffar	☐ 35 Ilpo Kauhanen (G)
☐ 36 Rob Kinghan	☐ 37 Dave Lemay
☐ 38 Guy Leveque	☐ 39 Matt McGuffin
☐ 40 Marcus Middleton	☐ 41 Thomas Nemeth
☐ 42 Rod Pasma	☐ 43 R. Raymond, Error
☐ 44 Jeff Reid	☐ 45 Jerry Ribble
☐ 46 J-A Schneider	☐ 47 John Slaney,
☐ 48 Jeremy Stevenson	☐ 49 R. VandenBussche
☐ 50 M. Crawford, Coach	☐ 51 Tony Bella
☐ 52 Berehowsky, Error	☐ 53 Jason Chipman (G)
☐ 54 Tony Cimellaro	☐ 55 Keli Corpse
☐ 56 Mike Dawson, Error	☐ 56 M. Dawson, Corr.
☐ 57 Sean Gauthier (G)	☐ 58 Fred Goltz, Error
☐ 59 Gord Harris	☐ 60 Tony Iob
☐ 61 John Bernie	☐ 62 Dale Junkin
☐ 63 Nathan Lafayette	☐ 64 Blake Martin
☐ 65 Mark McCague	☐ 66 Bob McKillop
☐ 67 Justin Morrison	☐ 68 Bill Robinson
☐ 69 Joel Sandie	☐ 70 Kevin King
☐ 71 Dave Stewart	☐ 72 Joel Washkurak
☐ 73 Brock Woods	☐ 74 Randy Hall, Coach
☐ 75 John Vary, Error	☐ 75 John Vary, Corrected
☐ 76 Peter Ambroziak	☐ 77 Troy Binnie
☐ 78 Curt Bowen	☐ 79 Andrew Brodie
☐ 80 TC: Grant Marshall	☐ 81 Greg Clancy
☐ 82 Jerrett DeFazio	☐ 83 Kris Draper
☐ 84 Wade Gibson	☐ 85 Ryan Kuwabara
☐ 86 Joni Lehto	☐ 87 Donald MacPherson
☐ 88 Grant Marshall	☐ 89 Pete McGlynn (G)
☐ 90 Maurice O'Brien	☐ 91 Jeff Ricciardi
☐ 92 Brett Seguin	☐ 93 L. DeVuono, Error
☐ 93 L. DeVuono, Corr.	☐ 94 Gerry Skrypec
☐ 95 Chris Snell	☐ 96 Jason Snow
☐ 97 Sean Spencer (G)	☐ 98 Brad Spry
☐ 99 Matt Stone	☐ 100 Brian Kilrea, Coach
☐ 101 K. Butt (G), Error	☐ 102 Glen Craig
☐ 103 Paul Doherty	☐ 104 Mark Donahue
☐ 105 Jeff Gardiner	☐ 106 Trent Gleason
☐ 107 Troy Gleason	☐ 108 Mark Lawrence
☐ 109 T. McIvor, Error	☐ 110 Paul Mitton
☐ 111 David Myles	☐ 112 Jeff Nolan, Error
☐ 113 Rob Papineau	☐ 114 Pat Peake, Error
☐ 114 Peake, Corrected	☐ 115 Chris Phelps
☐ 116 John Pinches	☐ 117 J. Shea (G), Error
☐ 117 J. Shea (G), Corr.	☐ 118 J. Sheehan, Error
☐ 118 J. Sheehan, Corr.	☐ 119 John Stios, Error
☐ 120 Tom Sullivan	☐ 121 John Wynne
☐ 122 R. Thorpe, Error	☐ 123 David Benn
☐ 124 Weidenbach, Coach	☐ 125 TC: Pat Peake
☐ 126 David Anderson	☐ 127 S. Basilio (G), Error
☐ 128 Brent Brownlee (G)	☐ 129 Rick Corriveau
☐ 130 Derrick Crane	☐ 131 Chris Crombie
☐ 132 Louie DeBrusk	☐ 133 Mark Guy
☐ 134 Brett Marietti	☐ 135 Steve Martell
☐ 136 Scott McKay	☐ 137 Aaron Nagy
☐ 138 Brett Nicol	☐ 139 Barry Potomski
☐ 140 Dennis Purdie	☐ 141 Kelly Reed
☐ 142 Gregory Ryan	☐ 143 Brad Smyth
☐ 144 Nick Stajduhar	☐ 145 J. Tanner (G), Error
☐ 146 Chris Taylor	☐ 147 Mark Visheau
☐ 148 Agnew, Coach, Err.	☐ 149 TC: Mark Visheau
☐ 150 TC: Jarrett Reid	☐ 151 David Babcock
☐ 152 Drew Bannister	☐ 153 Bob Boughner
☐ 154 Joe Busillo, Error	☐ 155 Mike DeCoff
☐ 156 Jason Denomme	☐ 157 Adam Foote
☐ 158 Kevin Hodson (G)	☐ 159 Shaun Imber, Error
☐ 160 Ralph Intranuovo	☐ 161 Kevin King
☐ 162 Rick Kowalsky	☐ 163 C. Kraemer, Error
☐ 164 Denny Lambert	☐ 165 Mike Lenarduzzi (G)
☐ 166 Tom MacDonald	☐ 167 Mark Matier
☐ 168 David Matsos	☐ 169 Colin Miller
☐ 170 Perry Pappas	☐ 171 Jarret Reid
☐ 172 Kevin Reid	☐ 173 Brad Tiley, Error
☐ 174 TC: Todd Warriner	☐ 175 Wade Whitten
☐ 176 Ted Nolan	☐ 177 Sean Burns
☐ 178 J. Cirone, Error	☐ 179 John Copley
☐ 180 Tyler Ertel	☐ 181 Brian Forestell
☐ 182 Rival Fullum, Error	☐ 183 Steve Gibson
☐ 184 L. MacDonald	☐ 185 Mike Speer, Error
☐ 186 Kevin MacKay	☐ 187 Ryan Merritt
☐ 188 Doug Minor	☐ 189 Rick Morton
☐ 190 Sean O'Hagan (G)	☐ 191 Mike Polano
☐ 192 Cory Stillman	☐ 193 Jason Stos
☐ 194 Trevor Walsh	☐ 195 Todd Warriner
☐ 196 Jeff Wilson (G)	☐ 197 Jason York
☐ 198 Jason Zohil, Error	☐ 199 Steve Smith, Error
☐ 200 Brad Smith, Coach	☐ 201 Jeff Bes
☐ 202 Ken Blum	☐ 203 Sean Brown
☐ 204 Darcy Cahill	☐ 205 Dale Chokan
☐ 206 Chris Code	☐ 207 George Dourian (G)
☐ 208 Todd Gleason	☐ 209 TC: Jeff Bes
☐ 210 Michael Hartwick	☐ 211 Scott Jenkins
☐ 212 Rob Leask	☐ 213 Gordon Pell
☐ 214 Michael Reier	☐ 215 Kayle Short
☐ 216 Jason Skellett	☐ 217 Gairin Smith
☐ 218 Jeff Smith	☐ 219 Jason Soules
☐ 220 Alek Stojanov	☐ 221 Dan Tanevski (G)
☐ 222 Gary Taylor	☐ 223 Brent Watson
☐ 224 Steve Woods	☐ 225 J. Johnston, Coach
☐ 226 Mike Allen	☐ 227 Brad Barton
☐ 228 Richard Borgo	☐ 229 Justin Cullen
☐ 230 L. DeVuono, Error	☐ 231 Norman Dezainde
☐ 232 Jason Firth	☐ 233 Derek Gauthier
☐ 234 Jamie Israel	☐ 235 Chris LiPuma
☐ 236 Tony McCabe	☐ 237 P. McCallion, Error
☐ 237 P. McCallion, Corr.	☐ 238 Shayne McCosh
☐ 239 Rod Saarinen	☐ 240 Steve Smith
☐ 241 J. St. Aubin, Error	☐ 242 Rob Stopar (G)
☐ 243 Jason Zohil, Error	☐ 244 Mike Torchia (G)
☐ 245 Gib Tucker	☐ 246 John Uniac
☐ 247 Jack Williams	☐ 248 McDonnell, Coach
☐ 249 Steve Rice, Error	☐ 250 Mike Polano, Error
☐ 251 Greg Allen	☐ 252 Roch Belley (G)
☐ 253 Andy Bezeau	☐ 254 Derek Booth, Error
☐ 255 Kevin Brown	☐ 256 Mark Cardiff
☐ 257 Jason Coles	☐ 258 Todd Coopman
☐ 259 Rick Girhiny	☐ 260 Brian Holk
☐ 261 John Johnson	☐ 262 Dan Krisko
☐ 263 M. Legace (G), Err.	☐ 264 Brad May
☐ 265 Don McConnell	☐ 266 TC: Steve Staios
☐ 267 Aaron Morrison	☐ 268 Cory Pageau
☐ 269 Geoff Rawson	☐ 270 Todd Simon
☐ 271 Steve Staios	☐ 272 Jeff Walker
☐ 273 Todd Wetzel	☐ 274 Jason Winch
☐ 275 Paul Wolanski	☐ 276 TC: G. Maynard
☐ 277 Andrew Brunette	☐ 278 Wyatt Buckland
☐ 279 Jason Buetow	☐ 280 Jason Castellan
☐ 281 Trent Cull	☐ 282 Robert Deschamps
☐ 283 Chris Driscoll	☐ 284 Bryan Drury
☐ 285 Todd Hunter (G)	☐ 286 Troy Hutchinson
☐ 287 Kirk Maltby	☐ 288 Geordie Maynard
☐ 289 K. McDougall (G)	☐ 290 Ted Miskolczi
☐ 291 Steven Parson	☐ 292 Jeff Perry
☐ 293 Grayden Reid	☐ 294 Mike Speer, Error
☐ 295 Mark Strohack	☐ 296 Mark Vilneff
☐ 297 Keith Whitmore	☐ 298 Jim Brown
☐ 299 McNamara Coach	☐ 300 D. Branch, Error
☐ 301 Shayne Antoski	☐ 302 Jason Beaton
☐ 303 Ron Bertrand (G)	☐ 304 Michael Burman
☐ 305 J. Caruso, Error	☐ 305 Jamie Caruso, Corr.
☐ 306 Allan Cox, Error	☐ 307 Tim Favot
☐ 308 Trevor Halverson	☐ 309 Derian Hatcher
☐ 310 Bill Lang	☐ 311 Jason MacDonald
☐ 312 Gary Miller	☐ 313 Chris Ottmann
☐ 314 Chad Penney	☐ 315 R. Pollard (G), Error
☐ 316 Bradley Shepard	☐ 317 John Spoltore
☐ 318 Derek Switzer	☐ 319 Karl Taylor
☐ 320 John Vary	☐ 321 Kevin White
☐ 322 B. Wright	☐ 323 Templeton, Coach
☐ 324 TC: J. MacDonald	☐ 325 TC: Mike Côté
☐ 326 Jan Benda	☐ 327 Fred Brathwaite (G)
☐ 328 M. Brunner	☐ 329 T. Burgess, Error
☐ 330 Clair Cornish	☐ 331 Mike Cote
☐ 332 David Craievich	☐ 333 Dale Craigwell
☐ 334 Jean-Paul Davis	☐ 335 Mark Deazeley
☐ 336 Mike Fountain (G)	☐ 337 Brian Grieve
☐ 338 M. Hoffman, Error	☐ 339 Scott Hollis
☐ 340 Scott Boston	☐ 341 Scott Luik
☐ 342 Craig Lutes, Error	☐ 342 Craig Lutes, Corr.
☐ 343 MacPherson, Error	☐ 344 Paul O'Hagan
☐ 345 Wade Simpson	☐ 346 J. Skalde, [Osha.]
☐ 346 J. Skalde, Corr.	☐ 347 Troy Sweet
☐ 348 J. Weaver, [Lutes]	☐ 349 Cornacchia, Coach
☐ 350 The Trophy, Error	☐ 351 Greg Bailey
☐ 352 Ryan Black	☐ 353 Bojcun (G) [Rev.]
☐ 354 Toby Burkitt, Error	☐ 355 Scott Campbell
☐ 356 Jassen Cullimore	☐ 357 Jason Dawe
☐ 358 Dan Ferguson	☐ 359 Bryan Gendron
☐ 360 Mike Harding	☐ 361 Joe Hawley
☐ 362 TC: Ryan Black	☐ 363 Geordie Kinnear
☐ 364 Chris Longo, Error	☐ 365 Dale McTavish
☐ 366 Mark Myles	☐ 367 Don O'Neill
☐ 368 Jamie Pegg	☐ 369 Brent Pope
☐ 370 TC: S. McCosh	☐ 371 Douglas Searle
☐ 372 Stephens [/bRev.]	☐ 373 Mike Tomlinson
☐ 374 Brent Tully	☐ 375 Andrew Verner (G)
☐ 376 Todd, Coa. [/b:Rev.]	☐ 377 J. Tanner (G), Error
☐ 377 J. Tanner (G), Corr.	☐ 378 Adam Bennett (G)
☐ 379 Kyle Blacklock (G)	☐ 380 Terry Chitaroni
☐ 381 Brandon Convery	☐ 382 J.D. Eaton (G)
☐ 383 Derek Etches	☐ 384 Rod Hinks
☐ 385 Bill Kovacs	☐ 386 Alain Laforge, Error
☐ 387 Jamie Matthews	☐ 388 Glen Murray
☐ 389 Dean Cull, Error	☐ 390 Sean O'Donnell
☐ 391 TC: Michael Peca	☐ 392 Michael Peca, Error
☐ 393 Shawn Rivers, Error	☐ 394 Dan Ryder (G)
☐ 395 Alastair Still	☐ 396 Michael Yeo
☐ 397 Barry Young	☐ 398 Jason Young
☐ 399 MacKenzie, Coach	☐ 400 Bob Berg, Error

Christmas	**OHL**
☐ White card stock	4.00
☐ Silver foil card stock	8.00

1990 - 91 7TH INNING SKETCH WHL

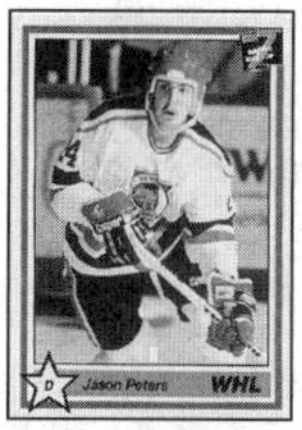

The most expensive single is Chris Osgood at $2-3. NHL stars sell between 35¢ and $1.50. All other singles sell between 20¢ and $1.00. Card 120 was not issued.

Imprint: © 1991 7th Inning Sketch

Complete Set (347 cards):	**20.00**

WHL	**WHL**
☐ 1 Brent Bilodeau	☐ 2 Craig Chapman
☐ 3 Jeff Jubenville	☐ 4 Al Kinisky
☐ 5 Kevin Malgunas	☐ 6 Andy MacIntyre
☐ 7 Darren McAusland	☐ 8 Mike Seaton
☐ 9 Turner Stevenson	☐ 10 Lindsay Vallis
☐ 11 Dave Wilkie	☐ 12 Jesse Wilson
☐ 13 Dody Wood	☐ 14 Bradley Zavisha
☐ 15 Vince Boe	☐ 16 Scott Davis
☐ 17 Troy Hyatt	☐ 18 Trevor Pennock
☐ 19 Corey Schwab (G)	☐ 20 S. Bellefontaine (G)
☐ 21 Travis Kelln	☐ 22 P. Anholt, Coach/GM
☐ 23 Sonny Mignacca (G)	☐ 24 Chris Osgood (G)
☐ 25 Murray Garbutt	☐ 26 Kalvin Knibbs
☐ 27 Jason Krywulak	☐ 28 Jason Miller
☐ 29 Rob Niedermayer	☐ 30 Clayton Norris
☐ 31 Jason Prosofsky	☐ 32 Dana Rieder
☐ 33 Kevin Riehl	☐ 34 Tyler Romanchuk
☐ 35 Dave Shute	☐ 36 Lorne Toews
☐ 37 Scott Townsend	☐ 38 David Cooper
☐ 39 Jon Duval	☐ 40 Dan Kordic
☐ 41 Mike Rathje	☐ 42 Tim Bothwell, Coach
☐ 43 Brent Thompson	☐ 44 Jeff Knight
☐ 45 Van Burgess	☐ 46 Kimbi Daniels
☐ 47 Curtis Friesen	☐ 48 Todd Holt
☐ 49 Blake Knox	☐ 50 Trent McCleary
☐ 51 Mark McFarlane	☐ 52 Eddie Patterson
☐ 53 Lloyd Pellitier	☐ 54 Geoff Sanderson
☐ 55 Andrew Schneider	☐ 56 Tyler Wright
☐ 57 Joel Dyck	☐ 58 Len MacAusland
☐ 59 Evan Marble	☐ 60 David Podlubny
☐ 61 Kurt Seher	☐ 62 Jason Smith
☐ 63 Justin Burke (G)	☐ 64 Kelly Thiessen (G)
☐ 65 Todd Esselmont	☐ 66 G. James, Coa./ GM
☐ 67 Chris Herperger	☐ 68 Mark McCoy
☐ 69 Dean Malkoc	☐ 70 Dennis Sproxton (G)
☐ 71 Centennial Civic	☐ 72 Kimbi Daniels
☐ 73 Shane Calder	☐ 74 Mark Franks
☐ 75 Greg Leahy	☐ 76 Dean Rambo
☐ 77 Scott Scissons	☐ 78 David Struch
☐ 79 Derek Tibbatts	☐ 80 Shawn Yakimishyn
☐ 81 Trent Coghill	☐ 82 Robert Lelacheur
☐ 83 Richard Matvichuk	☐ 84 Mark Raiter
☐ 85 Trevor Sherban	☐ 86 Mark Wotton
☐ 87 Cam Moon (G)	☐ 88 Trevor Robins (G)
☐ 89 Jeff Buchanan	☐ 90 Ryan Strain
☐ 91 Tim Cox	☐ 92 T. Ruskowski, Coach
☐ 93 Saskatchewan Place	☐ 94 Darin Bader
☐ 95 Gaetan Blouin	☐ 96 Kozuback, Coa./GM
☐ 97 Jason Bowen	☐ 98 Fran Deferenza
☐ 99 Terry Degner	☐ 100 Devin Derksen
☐ 101 Martin Svetlik	☐ 102 Jeremy Warring (G)
☐ 103 Corey Jones (G)	☐ 104 Dean Tiltgen
☐ 105 Ryan Fujita	☐ 106 Jeff Fancy
☐ 107 Terry Virtue	☐ 108 Dennis Pinfold
☐ 109 Kyle Reeves	☐ 110 Steve McNutt
☐ 111 Todd Klassen	☐ 112 Darren Hastman
☐ 113 Bill Lindsay	☐ 114 Brian Sakic
☐ 115 Dan Sherstenka	☐ 116 Don Blishen (G)
☐ 117 Jason Marshall	☐ 118 Dean Zayonce
☐ 119 Brad Loring	☐ 121 Darcy Austin (G)
☐ 122 Darcy Werenka	☐ 123 Shane Peacock
☐ 124 Bob Hartnell	☐ 125 Brad Zimmer
☐ 126 Allan Egeland	☐ 127 Brad Rubachuk
☐ 128 Jamie Pushor	☐ 129 J. McLennan (G)
☐ 130 Lance Burns	☐ 131 Ryan Smith
☐ 132 Jason McBain	☐ 133 Duane Maruschak
☐ 134 Kevin St. Jacques	☐ 135 Jason Sorochan
☐ 136 Jason Widmer	☐ 137 Bob Loucks, Coach
☐ 138 Jason Ruff	☐ 139 Pat Pylypuik
☐ 140 Scott Adair	☐ 141 Radek Sip
☐ 142 Russ West	☐ 143 Scott Thomas
☐ 144 Kent Staniforth	☐ 145 Travis Thiessen
☐ 146 Marc Hussey	☐ 147 Kevin Masters
☐ 148 Todd Johnson	☐ 149 Bob Loucks
☐ 150 Rob Reimer	☐ 151 Jeff Petruic
☐ 152 Chris Schmidt	☐ 153 Scott Barnstable
☐ 154 Ian Layton	☐ 155 Kevin Smyth
☐ 156 Kim Deck	☐ 157 Jason White
☐ 158 Peter Cox	☐ 159 Jeff Calvert (G)
☐ 160 Paul Dyck	☐ 161 Derek Kletzel
☐ 162 J. Fitzsimmons (G)	☐ 163 Darcy Jerome
☐ 164 Hal Christiansen	☐ 165 Terry Hollinger
☐ 166 Mike Risdale (G)	☐ 167 Jamie Heward
☐ 168 Louis Dumont	☐ 169 Cory Dosdall
☐ 170 Terry Bendera	☐ 171 Jamie Hayden
☐ 172 Kelly Chotowetz	☐ 173 Brad Scott
☐ 174 Jeff Shantz	☐ 175 Kelly Markwart
☐ 176 Garry Pearce	☐ 177 Kerry Biette
☐ 178 Jamie Splett	☐ 179 Frank Kovacs
☐ 180 Greg Pankewicz	☐ 181 Colin Ruck
☐ 182 B. Tippett, Coach	☐ 183 Dusty Imoo (G)
☐ 184 Derek Eberle	☐ 185 Heath Weenk
☐ 186 Mike Sillinger	☐ 187 Erin Thornton
☐ 188 Mike Chrun	☐ 189 Pat Falloon
☐ 190 Bobby House	☐ 191 Mike Jickling
☐ 192 Trevor Tovell	☐ 193 Steve Junker
☐ 194 Shane Maitland	☐ 195 Chris Lafrenière
☐ 196 Frank Evans	☐ 197 Jon Klemm
☐ 198 Shawn Dietrich (G)	☐ 199 Dennis Saharachuk
☐ 200 Mark Woolf	☐ 201 Ray Whitney
☐ 202 Scott Bailey (G)	☐ 203 Mike Ruark
☐ 204 Brent Thurston	☐ 205 Dan Faassen
☐ 206 Kerry Toporowski	☐ 207 Des Christopher (G)
☐ 208 Geoff Grandberg	☐ 209 B. Maxwell, Coach
☐ 210 Cam Danyluk	☐ 211 Bram Vanderkracht
☐ 212 Calvin Thudium	☐ 213 Mark Szoke
☐ 214 McCrimmon Coach	☐ 215 Kevin Robertson
☐ 216 Brian Purdy	☐ 217 Hardy Sauter
☐ 218 D. Gylywoychuk	☐ 219 Bart Cote
☐ 220 Merv Priest	☐ 221 Jeff Hoad
☐ 222 Glen Gulutzan	☐ 223 Johan Skillgard
☐ 224 B. Penstock (G)	☐ 225 Mike Vandenberghe
☐ 226 Trevor Kidd (G)	☐ 227 Dan Kopec
☐ 228 Greg Hutchings	☐ 229 Chris Constant
☐ 230 Glen Webster	☐ 231 Rob Puchniak
☐ 232 Calvin Flint	☐ 233 Stuart Scantlebury
☐ 234 Jason White	☐ 235 Gary Audette
☐ 236 Kevin Schmalz	☐ 237 Dwayne Newman
☐ 238 Chris Catellier	☐ 239 Todd Harris
☐ 240 Mike Shemko	☐ 241 John Badduke
☐ 242 Mark Cipriano	☐ 243 Brad Bagu
☐ 244 Ross Harris	☐ 245 Dino Caputo
☐ 246 Cam Bristow	☐ 247 Jarret Zukiwsky
☐ 248 Jason Knox	☐ 249 Gerry St. Cyr
☐ 250 Larry Woo	☐ 251 Jason Peters
☐ 252 Shane Stangby	☐ 253 Dave McMillen
☐ 254 Colin Gregor	☐ 255 Steve Passmore (G)
☐ 256 Shayne Green	☐ 257 Kevin Koopman (G)
☐ 258 Lanny Watkins	☐ 259 Scott Fukami
☐ 260 R. Hopper, Coach	☐ 261 Laurie Billeck
☐ 262 R. Daum, Coach	☐ 263 Mark Stowe
☐ 264 Curtis Regnier	☐ 265 David Neilson
☐ 266 Brian Pellerin	☐ 267 Dean McAmmond
☐ 268 Darren Van Impe	☐ 269 Troy Neumeier
☐ 270 Mike Langen (G)	☐ 271 Dan Kesa
☐ 272 Travis Laycock (G)	☐ 273 Scott Allison
☐ 274 Jeff Gorman	☐ 275 Lee J. Leslie
☐ 276 Jason Kwiatkowski	☐ 277 Donevan Hextall
☐ 278 Shane Zulyniak	☐ 279 Darren Perkins
☐ 280 Chad Seibel	☐ 281 Jeff Nelson
☐ 282 Troy Hjertaas	☐ 283 Jamie Linden
☐ 284 Zac Boyer	☐ 285 Jarret Bousquet
☐ 286 Steven Yule	☐ 287 Tom Renney, Coach
☐ 288 Lance Johnson	☐ 289 Scott Niedermayer
☐ 290 Ryan Harrison	☐ 291 Ed Patterson
☐ 292 Jeff Watchorn	☐ 293 Cal McGowan
☐ 294 Dale Masson (G)	☐ 295 Joey Mittelsteadt
☐ 296 Scott Loucks	☐ 297 Shea Esselmont
☐ 298 Craig Bonner	☐ 299 Mike Mathers
☐ 300 Fred Hettle	☐ 301 Craig Lyons
☐ 302 Murray Duval	☐ 303 Jamie Barnes
☐ 304 Bryan Gourlie	☐ 305 Chad Berezniuk
☐ 306 Corey Hirsch (G)	☐ 307 Darryl Sydor
☐ 308 Jarrett Deuling	☐ 309 Cory Stock
☐ 310 Chris Rowland	☐ 311 Mike Ruark
☐ 312 S. Konowalchuk	☐ 313 Jeff Sebastian
☐ 314 Brandon Smith	☐ 315 Greg Gatto
☐ 316 Brad Richardson	☐ 317 Brantt Myhres
☐ 318 Jamie Black	☐ 319 Colin Foley
☐ 320 Cam Danyluk	☐ 321 Dean Dorchak
☐ 322 Ryan Slemko	☐ 323 Kim Deck
☐ 324 Kelly Harris	☐ 325 Murray Bokenfohr
☐ 326 Dean Intwert (G)	☐ 327 Dennis Saharchuk
☐ 328 Shane Seiker	☐ 329 Terry Virtue
☐ 330 Josh Erdman	☐ 331 Layne Roland
☐ 332 Michel Michon	☐ 333 Scott Mydan
☐ 334 CL: Trevor Kidd	☐ 335 CL: Moose Jaw
☐ 336 CL: G. Sanderson	☐ 337 CL: Regina
☐ 338 CL: Saskatoon	☐ 339 CL: Medicine Hat
☐ 340 The Goalmouth	☐ 341 CL: Portland
☐ 342 CL: Kamloops	☐ 343 CL: Victoria
☐ 344 CL: Brian Sakic	☐ 345 CL: Pat Falloon
☐ 346 CL: Brent Bilodeau	☐ 347 CL: Jason Ruff
☐ 348 CL: Prince Albert	

Christmas	**WHL**
☐ White card stock - Christmas	4.00
☐ Silver foil card stock- Christmas	8.00

1990 - 91 SPORTS ILLUSTRATED FOR KIDS

These cards were distributed as part of nine-card perforated sheets included in *Sports Illustrated for Kids*. While these cards were intended for editorial purposes, they have made their way onto the secondary market. Cards issued in the twelve issues between July 1990 and June 1991 were numbered 163-270.

1990-91 Sports Illustrated for Kids	
☐ Oct. 1990 • 193 Brett Hull, SLou.	4.00
☐ Dec. 1990 • 214 Gordie Howe, Detr.	8.00
☐ Jan. 1991 • 224 Ron Hextall (G), Phil.	3.00
☐ Feb. 1991 • 228 Bernie Nicholls, NYRa.	1.00
☐ Mar. 1991 • 238 Chris Chelios, Chic.	1.00
☐ Apr. 1991 • 250 Mike Liut (G), Wash.	1.00
☐ Apr. 1991 • 252 Joe Mullen, Pitt.	1.00
☐ May 1991 • 254 Steve Larmer, Chic.	1.00

1990 - 91 TIM HORTON

These cards were issued to advertise the Sports Collectible Show in Oakville, Ontario, during May 1991.

Description	**Horton**
☐ 1 Tim Horton	3.00

1990 - 91 UPPER DECK

These cards have two versions: an English issue and a French issue.

Imprint: 1990 The Upper Deck Co.

Low Series Set (400 cards):	**70.00**	**45.00**
High Series Set (150 cards):	**50.00**	**30.00**
Common Player:	**.30**	**.20**

Promo	**Promo**
☐ 241 Wayne Gretzky, LosA.	30.00
☐ 241 Patrick Roy (G), Mont.	25.00

Upper Deck	Fre.	Eng.
1 David Volek, NYIs.	.30	.20
2 Brian Propp, Bost.	.30	.20
3 Wendel Clark, Toro.	.50	.20
4 Adam Creighton, Chic.	.30	.20
5 Mark Osborne, Toro.	.30	.20
6 Murray Craven, Phil.	.30	.20
7 Doug Crossman, NYIs.	.30	.20
8 Mario Marois, Québ.	.30	.20
9 Curt Giles, Minn.	.30	.20
10 Rick Wamsley (G), Calg.	.30	.20
11 Troy Mallette, NYRa. RC	**.50**	**.40**
12 John Cullen, Pitt.	.30	.20
13 Miloslav Horava, NYRa. RC	**.50**	**.40**
14 Kevin Stevens, Pitt. RC	**1.00**	**.50**
15 David Shaw, NYRa.	.30	.20
16 Randy Wood, NYIs.	.30	.20
17 Peter Zezel, SLou.	.30	.20
18 Glenn Healy (G), NYIs. RC	**1.00**	**.50**
19 Sergio Momesso, SLou. RC	**.50**	**.40**
20 Don Maloney, NYIs.	.30	.20
21 Craig Muni, Edmo.	.30	.20
22 Phil Housley, Buff.	.30	.20
23 Martin Gélinas, Edmo. RC	**1.00**	**.50**
24 Alexander Mogilny, Buff. RC	**2.50**	**1.50**
25 J. Byce, Bost. RC	**.50**	**.40**
26 Joe Nieuwendyk, Calg.	.30	.20
27 Ron Tugnutt (G), Québ.	.30	.20
28 Don Barber, Minn. RC	**.50**	**.40**
29 Gary Roberts, Calg.	.30	.20
30 Basil McRae, Minn.	.30	.20
31 Phil Bourque, Pitt.	.30	.20
32 Mike Richter (G), NYRa. RC	**2.50**	**1.50**
33 Zarley Zalapski, Pitt.	.30	.20
34 Bernie Nicholls, NYRa.	.30	.20
35 Corkum, Buff. RC	**.50**	**.40**
36 Rod Brind'Amour, SLou. RC	**2.00**	**1.00**
37 Mark Fitzpatrick (G), NYIs. RC	**.50**	**.50**
38 Gino Cavallini, SLou.	.30	.20
39 Mick Vukota, NYIs. RC	**.50**	**.40**
40 Mike Lalor, SLou. RC	**.50**	**.40**
41 Dave Andreychuk, Buff.	.30	.20
42 Bill Ranford (G), Edmo.	.30	.20
43 Pierre Turgeon, Buff.	.30	.20
44 Mark Messier w/ Stanley Cup	.50	.50
45 Rob Blake, LosA. RC	**3.00**	**2.00**
46 Mike Modano, Minn. RC	**7.00**	**3.50**
47 Theoren Fleury, Calg.	.30	.20
48 Neal Broten, Minn.	.30	.20
49 Paul Gillis, Québ.	.30	.20
50 Doug Bodger, Buff.	.30	.20
51 Stéphan Lebeau, Mont. RC	**.50**	**.40**
52 Larry Robinson, LosA.	.30	.20
53 Dale Hawerchuk, Winn.	.30	.20
54 Wayne Gretzky, LosA.	3.00	2.00
55 Ed Belfour (G), Chic. RC	**7.00**	**3.50**
56 Steve Yzerman, Detr.	1.50	1.00
57 Rod Langway, Wash.	.30	.20
58 Bernie Federko, Detr.	.30	.20
59 M. Lemieux, Pitt. [Scoring Streak]	2.00	1.50
60 Doug Lidster, Vanc.	.30	.20
61 Dave Christian, Bost.	.30	.20
62 Rob Ramage, Toro.	.30	.20
63 Jeremy Roenick, Chic. RC	**5.50**	**3.00**
64 Raymond Bourque, Bost.	.50	.50
65 Jon Morris, NJer. RC	**.50**	**.40**
66 Sean Burke (G), NJer.	.30	.20
67 Ron Francis, Hart.	.30	.20
68 Ron Sutter, Phil.	.30	.20
69 Peter Sidorkiewicz (G), Hart.	.30	.20
70 Sylvain Turgeon, NJer.	.30	.20
71 Dave Ellett, Winn.	.30	.20
72 Bobby Smith, Mont.	.30	.20
73 Luc Robitaille, LosA.	.50	.20
74 Pat Elynuik, Winn.	.30	.20
75 J. Soules, Edmo. Draft RC	**.50**	**.40**
76 Dino Ciccarelli, Wash.	.30	.20
77 Vladimir Krutov, Vanc. RC	**1.00**	**.50**
78 Lee Norwood, Detr.	.30	.20
79 Brian Bradley, Vanc.	.30	.20
80 Michal Pivonka, Wash. RC	**.50**	**.40**
81 Mark LaForest (G), Toro. RC	**.50**	**.40**
82 Trent Yawney, Chic.	.30	.20
83 Tom Fergus, Toro.	.30	.20
84 Andy Brickley, Bost.	.30	.20
85 Dave Manson, Chic.	.30	.20
86 Gord Murphy, Phil. RC	**.50**	**.40**
87 Scott Young, Hart.	.30	.20
88 Tommy Albelin, NJer.	.30	.20
89 Ken Wregget (G), Phil.	.30	.20
90 Brad Shaw, Hart. RC	**.50**	**.40**
91 Mario Gosselin (G), LosA.	.30	.20
92 Paul Fenton, Winn.	.30	.20
93 Brian Skrudland, Mont.	.30	.20
94 Thomas Steen, Winn.	.30	.20
95 John Tonelli, LosA.	.30	.20
96 Steve Chiasson, Detr.	.30	.20
97 Mike Ridley, Wash.	.30	.20
98 Garth Butcher, Vanc.	.30	.20
99 Daniel Shank, Detr. RC	**.50**	**.40**
100 Checklist	.30	.20
101 Jamie Macoun, Calg.	.30	.20
102 Wendell Young (G), Pitt. RC	**.50**	**.50**
103 Laurie Boschman, Winn.	.30	.20
104 Paul Ranheim, Calg. RC	**.50**	**.50**
105 Doug Smail, Winn.	.30	.20
106 Shawn Chambers, Minn.	.30	.20
107 Steve Weeks (G), Vanc.	.30	.20
108 Gaétan Duchesne, Minn.	.30	.20
109 Kevin Hatcher, Wash.	.30	.20
110 Paul Reinhart, Vanc.	.30	.20
111 Shawn Burr, Detr.	.30	.20
112 Troy Murray, Chic.	.30	.20
113 John Chabot, Detr.	.30	.20
114 Jacques Cloutier (G), Chic. RC	**.50**	**.50**
115 Rick Zombo, Detr. RC	**.50**	**.40**
116 Kjell Samuelsson, Phil.	.30	.20
117 Tim Watters, LosA.	.30	.20
118 Patrick Flatley, NYIs.	.30	.20
119 Tom Laidlaw, LosA.	.30	.20
120 Ilkka Sinisalo, Phil.	.30	.20
121 Tom Barrasso (G), Pitt.	.30	.20
122 Bob Essensa (G), Winn. RC	**1.00**	**.50**
123 Sergei Makarov, Calg. RC	**2.00**	**1.50**
124 Paul Coffey, Pitt.	.30	.20
125 Bob Beers, Bost. RC	**.50**	**.40**
126 Brian Bellows, Minn.	.30	.20
127 Mike Liut (G), Wash.	.30	.20
128 Igor Larionov, Vanc. RC	**3.00**	**2.00**
129 Craig Simpson, Edmo.	.30	.20
130 Kelly Miller, Wash.	.30	.20
131 Dirk Graham, Chic.	.30	.20
132 Jimmy Carson, Detr.	.30	.20
133 Michel Goulet, Chic.	.30	.20
134 Gerard Gallant, Detr.	.30	.20
135 Bruce Hoffort (G), Phil. RC	**.50**	**.40**
136 Steve Duchesne, LosA.	.30	.20
137 Bryan Trottier, NYIs.	.50	.50
138 Pelle Eklund, Phil.	.30	.20
139 Gary Nylund, NYIs.	.30	.20
140 Steve Kasper, LosA.	.30	.20
141 Joel Otto, Calg.	.30	.20
142 Rob (Jr.) Brown, Pitt.	.30	.20
143 Al MacInnis, Calg.	.30	.20
144 Mario Lemieux, Pitt.	2.00	1.50
145 Peter Eriksson, Edmo. RC	**.50**	**.40**
146 Jari Kurri, Edmo.	.50	.50
147 Petri Skriko, Vanc.	.30	.20
148 J. Steve Smith, Edmo.	.30	.20
149 Calle Johansson, Wash.	.30	.20
150 Stewart Gavin, Minn.	.30	.20
151 Randy Ladouceur, Hart.	.30	.20
152 Vincent Riendeau (G), SLou. RC	**.50**	**.50**
153 Patrick Roy (G), Mont.	2.00	1.50
154 Brett Hull, SLou.	.50	.50
155 Craig Fisher, Phil. RC	**.50**	**.40**
156 Cam Neely, Bost.	.50	.50
157 Al Iafrate, Toro.	.30	.20
158 Bob Carpenter, Bost.	.30	.20
159 Doug Brown, NJer.	.30	.20
160 Tom Kurvers, Toro.	.30	.20
161 John MacLean, NJer.	.30	.20
162 Guy Lafleur, Québ.	1.50	1.00
163 Peter Stastny, NJer.	.30	.20
164 Joe Sakic, Québ.	1.00	.50
165 Robb Stauber (G), LosA. RC	**.50**	**.50**
166 Daren Puppa (G), Buff.	.30	.20
167 Esa Tikkanen w/ Stanley Cup	.30	.20
168 Mike Ramsey, Buff.	.30	.20
169 Craig MacTavish, Edmo.	.30	.20
170 Christian Ruuttu, Buff.	.30	.20
171 Brian Hayward (G), Mont.	.30	.20
172 Pat Verbeek, Hart.	.30	.20
173 Adam Oates, SLou.	.30	.20
174 Chris Chelios, Mont.	.30	.20
175 Curtis Joseph (G), SLou. RC	**5.00**	**3.50**
176 Viacheslav Fetisov, NJer. RC	**3.00**	**2.00**
177 Dave Poulin, Bost.	.30	.20
178 Mark Recchi, Pitt. RC	**2.00**	**1.50**
179 Daniel Marois, Toro.	.30	.20
180 Mark Johnson, NJer.	.30	.20
181 Michel Petit, Québ.	.30	.20
182 Brian Mullen, NYRa.	.30	.20
183 Chris Terreri (G), NJer. RC	**.50**	**.50**
184 Tony Hrkac, Québ.	.30	.20
185 James Patrick, NYRa.	.30	.20
186 Craig Ludwig, Mont.	.30	.20
187 Uwe Krupp, Buff.	.30	.20
188 Guy Carbonneau, Mont.	.30	.20
189 Dave Snuggerud, Buff. RC	**.50**	**.40**
190 Joe Murphy, Edmo. RC	**.50**	**.50**
191 Jeff R. Brown, SLou.	.30	.20
192 Dean Evason, Hart.	.30	.20
193 Petr* Svoboda, Mont.	.30	.20
194 Dave Babych, Hart.	.30	.20
195 Steve Tuttle, SLou.	.30	.20
196 Randy Burridge, Bost.	.30	.20
197 Tony Tanti, Pitt.	.30	.20
198 Bob Sweeney, Bost.	.30	.20
199 Brad Marsh, Toro.	.30	.20
200 Checklist	.30	.20
201 Bill Ranford (G), Edmo.	.30	.20
202 Sergei Makarov, Awards (Calg.)	.30	.20
203 Brett Hull, Awards (SLou.)	.30	.20
204 Raymond Bourque, Awards (Bost.)	.30	.20
205 Wayne Gretzky, Awards (LosA.)	1.50	1.00
206 Mark Messier, Awards (Edmo.)	.30	.20
207 Patrick Roy (G), Awards (Mont.)	1.00	.50
208 Rick Meagher, Awards (SLou.)	.30	.20
209 Lemelin / Moog, Awards (Bost.)	.30	.20
210 Aaron Broten, Minn.	.30	.20
211 John Carter, Bost. RC	**.50**	**.40**
212 Marty McSorley, LosA.	.30	.20
213 Greg Millen (G), Chic.	.30	.20
214 Dave Taylor, LosA.	.30	.20
215 Réjean Lemelin (G), Bost.	.30	.20
216 Dave McLlwain, Winn.	.30	.20
217 Don Beaupré (G), Wash.	.30	.20
218 Paul MacDermid, Winn.	.30	.20
219 Dale Hunter, Wash.	.30	.20
220 Brent Ashton, Winn.	.30	.20
221 Steve Thomas, Chic.	.30	.20
222 Ed Olczyk, Toro.	.30	.20
223 Doug Wilson, Chic.	.30	.20
224 Vincent Damphousse, Toro.	.30	.20
225 Rob DiMaio, NYIs. RC	**.50**	**.50**
226 Hubie McDonough, NYIs. RC	**.50**	**.40**
227 Ron Hextall (G), Phil.	.30	.20
228 Dave Chyzowski, NYIs. RC	**.50**	**.40**
229 Larry Murphy, Minn.	.30	.20
230 Mike Bullard, Phil.	.30	.20
231 Kelly Hrudey (G), LosA.	.30	.20
232 Andy Moog (G), Bost.	.30	.20
233 Todd Elik, LosA. RC	**.50**	**.40**
234 Craig Janney, Bost.	.30	.20
235 Peter Lappin, Minn. RC	**.50**	**.40**
236 Scott Stevens, Wash.	.30	.20
237 Fredrik Olausson, Winn.	.30	.20
238 Geoff Courtnall, Wash.	.30	.20
239 Greg Paslawski, Winn.	.30	.20
240 Alan May, Wash. RC	**.50**	**.40**
241 Allan Bester (G), Toro.	.30	.20
242 Steve Larmer, Chic.	.30	.20
243 Gary Leeman, Toro.	.30	.20
244 Denis Savard, Chic.	.30	.20
245 Eric Weinrich, NJer. RC	**.50**	**.40**
246 Pat LaFontaine, NYIs.	.30	.20
247 Tim Kerr, Phil.	.30	.20
248 Dave Gagner, Minn.	.30	.20
249 Brent Sutter, NYIs.	.30	.20
250 Claude Vilgrain, NJer. RC	**.50**	**.40**
251 Tomas Sandström, LosA.	.30	.20
252 Joe Mullen, Calg.	.30	.20
253 Brian Leetch, NYRa.	.30	.20
254 Mike Vernon (G), Calg.	.30	.20
255 Daniel Doré, Québ. RC	**.50**	**.40**
256 Trevor Linden, Vanc.	.30	.20
257 Dave Barr, Detr.	.30	.20
258 John Ogrodnick, NYRa.	.30	.20
259 Russ Courtnall, Mont.	.30	.20
260 Dan Quinn, Vanc.	.30	.20
261 Mark Howe, Phil.	.30	.20
262 Kevin Lowe, Edmo.	.30	.20
263 Rick Tocchet, Phil.	.30	.20
264 Grant Fuhr (G), Edmo.	.30	.20
265 Andrew Cassels, Mont. RC	**1.00**	**.50**
266 Kevin Dineen, Hart.	.30	.20
267 Kirk Muller, NJer.	.30	.20
268 Randy Cunneyworth, Hart.	.30	.20
269 Brendan Shanahan, NJer.	.50	.50
270 Dave Tippett, Hart.	.30	.20
271 Doug Gilmour, Calg.	.30	.20
272 Tony Granato, LosA.	.30	.20
273 Gary Suter, Calg.	.30	.20
274 Darren Turcotte, NYRa. RC	**.50**	**.50**
275 Murray Baron, Phil. RC	**.50**	**.40**
276 Stéphane J.J. Richer, Mont.	.30	.20
277 Mike Gartner, NYRa.	.50	.20
278 Kirk McLean (G), Vanc.	.30	.20
279 John Vanbiesbrouck (G), NYRa.	.30	.20
280 Shayne Corson, Mont.	.30	.20
281 Paul Cavallini, SLou.	.30	.20
282 Petr Klima, Edmo.	.30	.20
283 Ulf Dahlén, Minn.	.30	.20
284 Glenn Anderson, Edmo.	.30	.20
285 Rick Meagher, SLou.	.30	.20
286 Alexei Kasatonov, NJer. RC	**1.00**	**.50**
287 Ulf Samuelsson, Hart.	.30	.20
288 Patrik Sundström, NJer.	.30	.20
289 Ray Ferraro, Hart.	.30	.20
290 Janne Ojanen, NJer. RC	**.50**	**.40**
291 Jeff Jackson, Québ.	.30	.20
292 Jiri Hrdina, Calg. RC	**.50**	**.50**
293 Joe Cirella, Québ.	.30	.20
294 Brad McCrimmon, Calg.	.30	.20
295 Curtis Leschyshyn, Québ. RC	**.50**	**.50**
296 Kelly Kisio, NYRa.	.30	.20
297 Jyrki Lumme, Vanc. RC	**1.00**	**.50**
298 Mark Janssens, NYRa. RC	**.50**	**.40**
299 Stan Smyl, Vanc.	.30	.20
300 Checklist	.30	.20
301 Joe Sakic, Québ. [TL]	.50	.20
302 Petri Skriko, Vanc. [TL]	.30	.20
303 Steve Yzerman, Detr. [TL]	.50	.50
304 Tim Kerr, Phil. [TL]	.30	.20
305 Mario Lemieux, Pitt. [TL]	1.00	.50
306 Pat LaFontaine, NYIs. [TL]	.30	.20
307 Wayne Gretzky, LosA. [TL]	1.50	1.00
308 Brian Bellows, Minn. [TL]	.30	.20
309 Rod Langway, Wash. [TL]	.30	.20
310 Gary Leeman, Toro. [TL]	.30	.20
311 Kirk Muller, NJer. [TL]	.30	.20
312 Brett Hull, SLou. [TL]	.30	.20
313 Thomas Steen, Winn. [TL]	.30	.20
314 Ron Francis, Hart. [TL]	.30	.20
315 Brian Leetch, NYRa. [TL]	.30	.20
316 Jeremy Roenick, Chic. [TL]	.30	.20
317 Patrick Roy (G), Mont. [TL]	1.00	.50
318 Pierre Turgeon, Buff. [TL]	.30	.20
319 Al MacInnis, Calg. [TL]	.30	.20
320 Raymond Bourque, Bost. [TL]	.30	.20
321 Mark Messier, Edmo. [TL]	.30	.20
322 Jody Hull, Hart. RC	**.50**	**.40**
323 Chris Joseph, Edmo. RC	**.50**	**.40**
324 Adam Burt, Hart. RC	**.50**	**.40**
325 Jason Herter, Vanc. RC	**.50**	**.40**
326 G. Smith, Edmo. [All-Rookie] RC	**.50**	**.40**
327 Brad Shaw, Hart. [All-Rookie]	.30	.20
328 Rich Sutter, SLou.	.30	.20
329 Barry Pederson, Pitt.	.30	.20
330 Paul MacLean, SLou.	.30	.20
331 Randy Carlyle, Winn.	.30	.20
332 Donald Dufresne, Mont. RC	**.50**	**.40**
333 Brent* Hughes, Winn. RC	**.50**	**.40**
334 Mathieu Schneider, Mont. RC	**1.00**	**.50**
335 Jason Miller, NJer. RC	**.50**	**.40**
336 Sergei Makarov, Calg. [All-Rookie]	.30	.20
337 B. Essensa (G), Winn. [All-Rookie]	.30	.20
338 Claude Loiselle, Québ. RC	**.50**	**.40**
339 Wayne Presley, Chic.	.30	.20
340 Tony McKegney, Québ.	.30	.20
341 Charlie Huddy, Edmo.	.30	.20
342 G. Adams, Vanc. [Photo Larionov]	.50	.20
343 Mike Tomlak, Hart. RC	**.50**	**.40**
344 Adam Graves, Edmo. RC	**2.00**	**1.50**
345 Michel Mongeau, SLou. RC	**.50**	**.40**
346 Mike Modano, Minn. [All-Rookie]	.50	.50
347 Brind'Amour, SLou. [All-Rookie]	.30	.20
348 Dana Murzyn, Calg.	.30	.20
349 Dave Lowry, SLou. RC	**1.00**	**.50**
350 Star Rookie Checklist	.30	.20
351 Draft Picks Checklist	.50	.20
352 Owen Nolan, Québ. RC	**3.00**	**2.00**
353 Petr Nedved, Vanc. RC	**1.50**	**1.00**
354 Keith Primeau, Detr. RC	**2.00**	**1.50**
355 Mike Ricci, Phil. RC	**1.50**	**1.00**
356 Jaromir Jagr, Pitt. RC	**7.00**	**5.00**
357 Scott Scissons, NYIs. RC	**.50**	**.40**
358 Darryl Sydor, LosA. RC	**1.00**	**1.00**
359 Derian Hatcher, Dall. RC	**1.50**	**1.00**
360 John Slaney, Wash. RC	**1.00**	**.50**
361 Drake Berehowsky, Toro. RC	**.50**	**.50**
362 Luke Richardson, Toro.	.30	.20
363 Lucien DeBlois, Québ.	.30	.20
364 David Reid, Toro. RC	**.50**	**.50**
365 Mats Sundin, Québ. RC	**5.00**	**3.50**
366 Jan Erixon, NYRa.	.30	.20
367 Troy Loney, Pitt. RC	**.50**	**.40**
368 Chris Nilan, NYRa.	.30	.20
369 Gord Dineen, Pitt.	.30	.20
370 Jeff Bloemberg, NYRa. RC	**.50**	**.40**
371 John Druce, Wash. RC	**.50**	**.40**
372 Brian MacLellan, Calg.	.30	.20
373 Bruce Driver, NJer.	.30	.20
374 Marc Habscheid, Detr.	.30	.20
375 Paul Ysebaert, NJer. RC	**.50**	**.40**
376 Rick Vaive, Buff.	.30	.20
377 Glen Wesley, Bost.	.30	.20
378 Mike Foligno, Buff.	.30	.20
379 Garry Galley, Bost. RC	**.50**	**.40**
380 Dean Kennedy, Buff. RC	**.50**	**.40**
381 Daniel Berthiaume (G), Minn.	.30	.20
382 Mike Keane, Mont. RC	**.50**	**.50**
383 Frantisek Musil, Minn.	.30	.20
384 Mike McPhee, Mont.	.30	.20
385 Jon Casey (G), Minn.	.30	.20
386 Jeff Norton, NYIs.	.30	.20
387 John Tucker, Wash.	.30	.20
388 Alan Kerr, NYIs.	.30	.20
389 Bob Rouse, Wash.	.30	.20
390 Gerald Diduck, NYIs.	.30	.20
391 Greg Hawgood, Bost.	.30	.20
392 Randy Velischek, NJer.	.30	.20
393 Tim Cheveldae (G), Detr. RC	**.50**	**.50**
394 Mike Krushelnyski, LosA.	.30	.20
395 Glen Hanlon (G), Detr.	.30	.20
396 Lou Franceschetti, Toro. RC	**.50**	**.40**
397 Scott Arniel, Buff.	.30	.20
398 Terry Carkner, Phil.	.30	.20
399 Clint Malarchuk, Buff.	.30	.20
400 Checklist	.30	.20
401 Mikhail Tatarinov, Wash. RC	**.50**	**.50**
402 Benoît Hogue, Buff.	.30	.20
403 Frank Pietrangelo (G), Pitt. RC	**1.00**	**.50**
404 Paul Stanton, Pitt. RC	**.50**	**.50**
405 Anatoli Semenov, Edmo. RC	**.50**	**.50**
406 Bobby Smith, Minn.	.30	.20
407 Derek King, NYIs.	.30	.20
408 J-C Bergeron (G), Mont. RC	**1.00**	**.50**
409 Brian Propp, Bost.	.30	.20
410 Jiri Latal, Phil. RC	**.50**	**.50**
411 Joey Kocur, Detr. RC	**1.00**	**.50**
412 Daniel Berthiaume (G), LosA.	.30	.20
413 Dave Ellett, Toro.	.30	.20
414 Jay Miller, LosA. RC	**.50**	**.50**
415 S. Beauregard (G), Winn. RC	**1.00**	**.50**
416 Mark Hardy, NYRa.	.30	.20
417 Todd Krygier, Hart. RC	**.50**	**.50**
418 Randy Moller, NYRa.	.30	.20
419 Doug Crossman, Hart.	.30	.20
420 Ray Sheppard, NYRa.	.30	.20
421 Sylvain Lefebvre, Mont. RC	**1.00**	**.50**
422 Chris Chelios, Chic.	.30	.20
423 Joe Mullen, Pitt.	.30	.20
424 Pete Peeters (G), Phil.	.30	.20
425 Bryan Trottier, Pitt.	.50	.50
426 Denis Savard, Mont.	.30	.20
427 Ken Daneyko, NJer.	.30	.20
428 Éric Desjardins, Mont. RC	**2.00**	**1.50**
429 Zdeno Ciger, NJer. RC	**1.00**	**.50**
430 Brad McCrimmon, Detr.	.30	.20
431 Ed Olczyk, Winn.	.30	.20
432 Peter Ing (G), Toro. RC	**1.00**	**.50**
433 Bob Kudelski, LosA. RC	**.50**	**.50**
434 Troy Gamble (G), Vanc. RC	**1.00**	**.50**
435 Phil Housley, Winn.	.30	.20
436 Scott Stevens, SLou.	.30	.20
437 Normand Rochefort, NYRa.	.30	.20
438 Geoff Courtnall, SLou.	.30	.20
439 Ken Baumgartner, NYIs. RC	**.50**	**.50**
440 Kris King, NYRa. RC	**1.00**	**.50**
441 Troy Crowder, NJer. RC	**1.00**	**.50**
442 Chris Nilan, Bost.	.30	.20
443 Dale Hawerchuk, Buff.	.30	.20
444 Kevin Miller, NYRa. RC	**.50**	**.50**
445 Keith Acton, Phil.	.30	.20
446 Jeff Chychrun, Phil. RC	**.50**	**.50**
447 Claude Lemieux, NJer.	.30	.20
448 Bob Probert, Detr.	.30	.20
449 Brian Hayward (G), Minn.	.30	.20
450 Craig Berube, Phil. RC	**1.00**	**.50**
451 Canada Juniors	.30	.20
452 Mike Sillinger, Canada RC	**1.00**	**.50**
453 Jason Marshall, Canada RC	**.50**	**.50**
454 Patrice Brisebois, Canada RC	**1.00**	**.50**
455 Brad May, Canada RC	**1.00**	**.50**
456 Pierre Sévigny, Canada RC	**.50**	**.50**
457 John Slaney, Canada	.50	.50
458 Félix Potvin (G), Canada RC	**12.50**	**4.00**
459 Scott Thornton, Canada RC	**.50**	**.50**
460 Greg Johnson, Canada RC	**1.00**	**.50**
461 S. Niedermayer, Canada RC	**2.00**	**1.50**
462 Steven Rice, Canada RC	**.50**	**.50**
463 Trevor Kidd (G), Canada RC	**2.00**	**1.50**

□□	**464 Dale Craigwell, Canada RC**	.50	.50
□□	**465 Kent Manderville, Canada RC**	.50	.50
□□	**466 Kris Draper, Canada RC**	1.50	1.00
□□	**467 Martin Lapointe, Canada RC**	3.50	2.00
□□	**468 Chris Snell, Canada RC**	.50	.50
□□	**469 Pat Falloon, Canada RC**	1.00	.50
□□	**470 David Harlock, Canada RC**	.50	.50
□□	**471 Karl Dykhuis, Canada RC**	.50	.50
□□	**472 Mike Craig, Canada RC**	.50	.50
□□	473 Canada Captains	2.00	1.00
□□	474 Brett Hull, All-Star (SLou.)	.50	.50
□□	475 Darren Turcotte, All-Star (NYRa.)	.30	.20
□□	476 Wayne Gretzky, All-Star (LosA.)	3.00	2.00
□□	477 Steve Yzerman, All-Star (Detr.)	1.50	1.00
□□	478 Theoren Fleury, All-Star (Calg.)	.30	.20
□□	479 Pat LaFontaine, All-Star (NYIs.)	.30	.20
□□	480 Trevor Linden, All-Star (Vanc.)	.30	.20
□□	481 Jeremy Roenick, All-Star (Chic.)	.50	.20
□□	482 Scott Stevens, All-Star (SLou.)	.30	.20
□□	483 Adam Oates, All-Star (SLou.)	.30	.20
□□	484 V. Damphousse, All-Star (Toro.)	.30	.20
□□	485 Brian Leetch, All-Star (NYRa.)	.30	.20
□□	486 Kevin Hatcher, All-Star (Wash.)	.30	.20
□□	487 Mark Recchi, All-Star (Pitt.)	.30	.20
□□	488 Rick Tocchet, All-Star (Phil.)	.30	.20
□□	489 Raymond Bourque, All-Star (Bost.)	.50	.50
□□	490 Joe Sakic, All-Star (Québ.)	1.00	.50
□□	491 Chris Chelios, All-Star (Chic.)	.30	.20
□□	492 John Cullen, All-Star (Pitt.)	.30	.20
□□	493 Cam Neely, All-Star (Bost.)	.50	.50
□□	494 Mark Messier Edmo.	.50	.50
□□	495 Mike Vernon (G), Calg.	.30	.20
□□	496 Patrick Roy (G), Mont.	2.00	1.50
□□	497 Al MacInnis, All-Star (Calg.)	.30	.20
□□	498 Paul Coffey, All-Star (Pitt.)	.30	.20
□□	499 Steve Larmer, Chic.	.30	.20
□□	500 Checklist	.30	.20
□□	501 Heroes Checklist	.30	.20
□□	502 Red Kelly, Heroes	.30	.20
□□	503 Eric Nesterenko, Chic.	.30	.20
□□	504 Darryl Sittler, Heroes	.50	.20
□□	505 Jim Schoenfeld, Heroes	.30	.20
□□	506 Serge Savard, Heroes	.30	.20
□□	507 Glenn (Chico) Resch, Heroes	.30	.20
□□	508 Lanny McDonald, Heroes	.50	.20
□□	509 Bobby Clarke, Heroes	.50	.20
□□	510 Phil Esposito, Heroes	.50	.50
□□	511 Harry Howell, Heroes	.30	.20
□□	512 Rod Gilbert, Heroes	.30	.20
□□	513 Pit Martin, Chic.	.30	.20
□□	514 Jimmy* Watson, Heroes	.30	.20
□□	515 Denis Potvin, Heroes	.50	.20
□□	**516 Rob Ray, Buff. RC**	1.50	1.00
□□	**517 Danton Cole, Winn. RC**	.50	.50
□□	**518 Gino Odjick, Vanc. RC**	1.00	.50
□□	**519 Donald Audette, Buff. RC**	6.00	2.00
□□	**520 Rick Tabaracci, Winn. RC**	1.00	.50
□□	521 Young Guns Checklist	1.00	.50
□□	**522 Kip Miller, Québ. RC**	1.00	.50
□□	**523 Johan Garpenlöv, Detr. RC**	.50	.50
□□	**524 Stéphane Morin, Québ. RC**	.50	.50
□□	**525 Sergei Fedorov, Detr. RC**	15.00	7.00
□□	**526 Pavel Bure, USSR (Vanc.) RC**	14.00	5.00
□□	**527 Wes Walz, Bost. RC**	1.50	1.00
□□	**528 Robert Kron, Vanc. RC**	1.00	.50
□□	**529 Ken (Jr.) Hodge, Bost. RC**	.50	.50
□□	**530 Garry Valk, Vanc. RC**	.50	.50
□□	**531 Tim Sweeney, Calg. RC**	.50	.50
□□	**532 Mark Pederson, Mont. RC**	.50	.50
□□	**533 Robert Reichel, Calg. RC**	2.00	1.50
□□	**534 Bobby Holik, Hart. RC**	3.00	1.50
□□	**535 Stéphane Matteau, Calg. RC**	1.00	.50
□□	**536 Peter Bondra, Wash. RC**	4.50	3.00
□□	**537 Dmitri Khristich, Wash. RC**	1.00	.50
□□	**538 Vladimir Ruzicka, Bost. RC**	1.50	1.00
□□	539 Al Iafrate, Wash.	.30	.20
□□	**540 Rick Bennett, NYRa. RC**	.50	.50
□□	**541 Daryl Reaugh (G), Hart. RC**	.50	.50
□□	**542 Martin Hostak, Phil. RC**	.50	.50
□□	**543 Kari Takko (G), Edmo. RC**	.50	.50
□□	**544 Jocelyn Lemieux, Chic. RC**	.50	.50
□□	545 W. Gretzky, LosA. [2000th Point]	3.00	2.00
□□	546 Brett Hull [50/50]	.50	.50
□□	**547 Neil Wilkinson, Minn. RC**	.50	.50
□□	**548 Bryan Fogarty, Québ. RC**	.50	.50
□□	549 Frank J. Zamboni	.30	.20
□□	550 Checklist	.30	.20

STEREOGRAM STICKERS

These hologram cards were inserted in both Low Series and High Series packs.

	Sticker	UD
□	Wayne Gretzky, LosA.	2.00
□	Wayne Gretzky, LosA.	2.00
□	Wayne Gretzky, LosA.	2.00
□	Brett Hull and Mark Messier	.50
□	Brett Hull and Steve Yzerman	1.00
□	Brett Hull, SLou.	.50
□	Mark Messier, Edmo.	.50
□	Steve Yzerman and Mark Messier	1.00
□	Steve Yzerman, Detr.	1.00
□	Steve Yzerman, Detr.	1.00

1990 - 91 UPPER DECK – BUYBACKS

These cards were purchased by The Upper Deck Company and reinserted as autographed cards in new 2000-01 and 2001-02 products.

	Buyback Autograph	UD
□	**32 Mike Richter, NYRa. RC ✍ {#/6}**	
□	**36 Rod Brind'Amour, SLou. RC ✍ {#/90}**	
□	44 Mark Messier, Edmo. ✍ {#/1}	
□	**45 Rob Blake, LosA. RC ✍ {#/4}**	
□	**46 Mike Modano, Minn. RC ✍ {#/75}**	
□	**46 Mike Modano, Minn. RC ✍ {#/56}**	
□	54 Wayne Gretzky, LosA. ✍ {#/1}	
□	56 Steve Yzerman, Detr. ✍ {#/1}	
□	64 Raymond Bourque, Bost. ✍ {#/1}	
□	73 Luc Robitaille, LosA. ✍ {#/10}	
□	**175 Curtis Joseph, SLou. RC ✍ {#/6}**	
□	204 Raymond Bourque, NHL Awards ✍ {#/2}	
□	303 Steve Yzerman, Detr. Team Leader ✍ {#/1}	
□	320 Raymond Bourque, Bost. Team Leader ✍ {#/1}	
□	321 Mark Messier, Edmo. Team Leader ✍ {#/1}	
□	346 Mike Modano, Minn. ✍ {#/13}	
□	**526 Pavel Bure, USSR Jrs. RC ✍ {#/6}**	
□	**536 Peter Bondra, Wash. RC ✍ {#/10}**	

1991 C55 REPRINTS

This series was published by Windhill Publishing and was limited to 50,000 copies.

Card Size: 1 1/2" x 2 1/2"

Complete Set (45 cards): 25.00

Album: 5.00

	Reprint	C55
□	1 Paddy Moran (G), Québec	1.00
□	2 Joe Hall, Québec	1.00
□	3 Barney Holden, Québec	.50
□	4 Joe Malone, Québec	2.00
□	5 Ed Oatman, Québec	.50
□	6 Tommy Dunderdale, Québec	1.00
□	7 Ken Mallen, Québec	.50
□	8 Jack McDonald, Québec	.50
□	9 Fred Lake, Ott.	.50
□	10 Albert Kerr, Ott.	.50
□	11 Marty Walsh, Ott.	1.00
□	12 Hamby Shore, Ott.	.50
□	13 Alex Currie, Ott.	.50
□	14 Bruce Ridpath, Ott.	.50
□	15 Bruce Stuart, Ott.	1.00
□	16 Percy Lesueur (G), Ott.	1.00
□	17 Jack Darragh, Ott.	1.00
□	18 Steve Vair, Renfrew	.50
□	19 Don Smith, Renfrew	.50
□	20 Fred Taylor, Renfrew	3.00
□	21 Bert Lindsay (G), Renfrew	.50
□	22 Larry Gilmour, Renfrew	.50
□	23 Bobby Rowe, Renfrew	.50
□	24 Sprague Cleghorn, Renfrew	1.00
□	25 Odie Cleghorn, Renfrew	.50
□	26 Skein Ronan, Renfrew	.50
□	27 Walter Smaill, Montréal W.	.50
□	28 Ernie Johnson, Montréal W.	1.00
□	29 Jack Marshall, Montréal W.	1.00
□	30 Harry Hyland, Montréal W.	1.00
□	31 Art Ross, Montréal W.	1.00
□	32 Riley Hern (G), Montréal W.	1.00
□	33 Gord Roberts, Montréal W.	1.00
□	34 Frank Glass, Montréal W.	.50
□	35 Ernest Russell, Montréal W.	1.00
□	36 James Gardiner, Montréal W.	.50
□	37 Art Bernier, Montréal C.	.50
□	38 Georges Vézina (G), Montréal C.	6.00
□	39 Henri Dellaire, Montréal C.	.50
□	40 R. Power, Montréal C.	.50
□	41 Didier Pitre, Montréal C.	1.00
□	42 Edouard Lalonde, Montréal C.	2.50
□	43 Eugene Payan, Montréal C.	.50
□	44 Georges Poulin, Montréal C.	.50
□	45 Jack Laviolette, Montréal C.	.50

1991 CANADA CUP - J.L. PRODUCTIONS

Card Size: 8" x 10"

Imprint: JL Productions

Complete Set (22 cards): 50.00

Album: 10.00

	Player	8x10
□	Paul Coffey	2.00
□	Shayne Corson	2.00
□	Russ Courtnall	2.00
□	Éric Desjardins	2.00
□	Theoren Fleury	2.00
□	Dirk Graham	2.00
□	Wayne Gretzky	15.00
□	Dale Hawerchuk	2.00
□	Steve Larmer	2.00
□	Eric Lindros	3.00
□	Al MacInnis	2.00
□	Mark Messier	3.00
□	Larry Murphy	2.00
□	Bill Ranford (G)	2.00
□	Luc Robitaille	3.00
□	Brendan Shanahan	3.00
□	J. Steve Smith	2.00
□	Scott Stevens	2.00
□	Brent Sutter	2.00
□	Mark Tinordi	2.00
□	Rick Tocchet	2.00
□	Canada	4.00

1991 IVAN FIODOROV SPORT UNITES HEARTS

There were 50,000 sets produced. Singes sell for 50¢-$2 each.

Complete Set (11 cards): 8.00

	Description		Description
□	1 Soviet Union	□	2 Sergei Fedorov
□	3 Viacheslav Fetisov	□	4 Alexei Gusarov
□	5 Alexei Kasatonov	□	6 Vladimir Konstantinov
□	7 Igor Larionov	□	8 Sergei Makarov
□	9 Alexander Mogilny	□	10 Mikhail Tatarinov
□	11 Vladislav Tretiak (G)		

1991 PRO SET NHL AWARDS

Cards 1-16 were given out June 5, 1991 at the NHL Awards Banquet in Toronto, while cards 17-23 were given out June 6, 1991 at the Hockey News Sponsor Awards also in Toronto. Cards have the same design as the 1991-92 Pro Set basic set.

Awards Special Set (17 cards): 350.00

Sponsor Awards Set (8 cards): 80.00

	Pro Set	
□	Title Card: 1990-91 NHL Awards Special	3.00
□	AC1 Ed Belfour (G), Chic.	30.00
□	AC2 Mike Richter (G), NYRa.	10.00
□	AC3 Patrick Roy (G), Mont.	90.00
□	AC4 Wayne Gretzky, LosA.	120.00
□	AC5 Joe Sakic, Québ.	45.00
□	AC6 Brett Hull, SLou.	30.00
□	AC7 Ray Bourque, Bost.	35.00
□	AC8 Al MacInnis, Calg.	10.00
□	AC9 Luc Robitaille, LosA.	20.00
□	AC10 Sergei Fedorov, Detr.	30.00
□	AC11 Ken Hodge, Bost.	3.00
□	AC12 Dirk Graham, Chic.	3.00
□	AC13 Steve Larmer, Chic.	10.00
□	AC14 Esa Tikkanen, Edmo.	3.00
□	AC15 Chris Chelios Chic.	15.00
□	AC16 Dave Taylor, LosA.	5.00
□	Title Card: 1990-91 NHL Sponsor Awards	3.00
□	AC17 Kevin Dineen, Hart.	3.00
□	AC18 Brett Hull, SLou.	30.00
□	AC19 Ed Belfour, Chic.	30.00
□	AC20 Theoren Fleury, Calg.	15.00
□	AC21 Marty McSorley, LosA.	5.00
□	AC22 Mike Ilitch, Owner, Detr.	10.00
□	AC23 Rod Gilbert, NYRa.	10.00

1991 SEMIC STICKERS

There are at least two versions of each of these stickers: "Marabou" backs and "Milky Way" backs. Each version has the same value. There are also some blank-back versions. The most expensive stickers are Wayne Gretzky ($6-10), Gordie Howe ($4-8) and Bobby Orr ($4-8). Other key stickers include Patrick Roy (G) ($3-6), Steve Yzerman ($3-5), Dominik Hasek ($2-5), Pavel Bure ($2-5), Jaromir Jagr ($3-5) and Bobby Hull ($2-5). Other NHL stars sell for 50¢-$4. Other singles sell for 20¢-$1.50.

Complete Set (250 stickers): 50.00

Common Player: .20

Semic	Semic
□□ 1 Finland	□□ 2 Markus Ketterer (G)
□□ 3 Sakari Lindfors (G)	□□ 4 Jukka Tammi (G)
□□ 5 Time Jutila	□□ 6 Hannu Virta
□□ 7 Simo Saarinen	□□ 8 Jukka Marttila
□□ 9 Ville Siren	□□ 10 Pasi Huura
□□ 11 Hannu Henriksson	□□ 12 Arte Ruotanen
□□ 13 Ari Haanpää	□□ 14 Pauli Järvinen
□□ 15 Teppo Kivelä	□□ 16 Risto Kurkinen
□□ 17 Mika Nieminen	□□ 18 Jari Kurri
□□ 19 Esa Keskinen	□□ 20 Raimo Summanen
□□ 21 Teemu Selänne	□□ 22 Jari Torkki
□□ 23 Hannu Järvenpää	□□ 24 Raimo Helminen
□□ 25 Time Peltomaa	□□ 26 Sweden
□□ 27 Peter Lindmark	□□ 28 Rolf Ridderwall
□□ 29 T. Söderström (G)	□□ 30 Thomas Eriksson
□□ 31 Nicklas Lidström	□□ 32 Tomas Jonsson
□□ 33 Tommy Samuelsson	□□ 34 Fredrik Stillman
□□ 35 Peter Andersson	□□ 36 Peter Andersson
□□ 37 Kenneth Kennholt	□□ 38 Håkan Loob
□□ 39 Thomas Rundqvist	□□ 40 Håkan Åhlund
□□ 41 Jan Viktorsson	□□ 42 Charles Berglund
□□ 43 Mikael Johansson	□□ 44 Robert Burakovsky
□□ 45 Bengt Gustafsson	□□ 46 Patrik Carnbäck
□□ 47 Patrik Erickson	□□ 48 Anders Carlsson
□□ 49 Mats Naslund	□□ 50 Kent Nilsson
□□ 51 Canada	□□ 52 Patrick Roy (G)
□□ 53 Ed Belfour (G)	□□ 54 D. Berthiaume (G)
□□ 55 Ray Bourque	□□ 56 Scott Stevens
□□ 57 Al MacInnis	□□ 58 Paul Coffey
□□ 59 Paul Cavallini	□□ 60 Zarley Zalapski
□□ 61 Steve Duchesne	□□ 62 Dave Ellett
□□ 63 Mark Messier	□□ 64 Wayne Gretzky
□□ 65 Steve Yzerman	□□ 66 Pierre Turgeon
□□ 67 Bernie Nicholls	□□ 68 Cam Neely
□□ 69 Joe Nieuwendyk	□□ 70 Luc Robitaille
□□ 71 Kevin Dineen	□□ 72 John Cullen
□□ 73 Steve Larmer	□□ 74 Mark Recchi
□□ 75 Joe Sakic	□□ 76 Soviet Union
□□ 77 Arturs Irbe (G)	□□ 78 Alexei Marjin
□□ 79 M. Shtalenkov (G)	□□ 80 Vladimir Malakhov
□□ 81 V. Konstantinov	□□ 82 Igor Kravchuk
□□ 83 Ilja Byakin	□□ 84 Dimitri Mironov
□□ 85 Vladimir Tiurikov	□□ 86 Vyacheslav Uvajev
□□ 87 Vladimir Fedosov	□□ 88 Valeri Kamensky
□□ 89 Pavel Bure	□□ 90 V. Butsayev
□□ 91 Igor Maslennikov	□□ 92 Evgeny Davydov
□□ 93 Andrei Kovalev	□□ 94 Alexander Semak
□□ 95 Alexei Zhamnov	□□ 96 Sergei Nemchinov
□□ 97 Viktor Gordiouk	□□ 98 Vyacheslav Kozlov
□□ 99 Andrei Khomutov	□□ 100 Vyacheslav Bykov
□□ 101 Czechoslovakia	□□ 102 Petr Briza (G)
□□ 103 Dominik Hasek (G)	□□ 104 E. Hartmann (G)
□□ 105 Bedrich Scerban	□□ 106 Jiri Slegr
□□ 107 Josef Reznicek	□□ 108 Petr Pavlas
□□ 109 Peter Slanina	□□ 110 Martin Maskarinec
□□ 111 Antonin Stavjana	□□ 112 Stanislav Medrik
□□ 113 Dusan Pasek	□□ 114 Jiri Lala
□□ 115 Darius Rusnak	□□ 116 Otto Hascak
□□ 117 Radek Toupal	□□ 118 Pavel Pycha
□□ 119 Lubomir Kolnik	□□ 120 Libor Dolana
□□ 121 Ladislav Lubina	□□ 122 Tomas Jelinek
□□ 123 Petr Vlk	□□ 124 Vladimir Petovka
□□ 125 Richard Zemlicka	□□ 126 USA
□□ 127 Vanbiesbrouck (G)	□□ 128 Mike Richter (G)
□□ 129 Chris Terreri (G)	□□ 130 Chris Chelios
□□ 131 Brian Leetch	□□ 132 Gary Suter
□□ 133 Phil Housley	□□ 134 Mark Howe
□□ 135 Al Iafrate	□□ 136 Kevin Hatcher
□□ 137 Mathieu Schneider	□□ 138 Pat LaFontaine
□□ 139 Darren Turcotte	□□ 140 Neal Broten
□□ 141 Mike Modano	□□ 142 Dave Christian
□□ 143 Craig Janney	□□ 144 Brett Hull
□□ 145 Kevin Stevens	□□ 146 Joe Mullen
□□ 147 Tony Granato	□□ 148 Ed Olczyk
□□ 149 Jeremy Roenick	□□ 150 Jimmy Carson
□□ 151 Germany	□□ 152 Helmut De Raaf
□□ 153 Josef Heiss (G)	□□ 154 Karl Friessen
□□ 155 Uli Hiemer	□□ 156 Harold Kreiss
□□ 157 Udo Kiessling	□□ 158 Michael Schmidt
□□ 159 Michael Heidt	□□ 160 Andreas Polorny
□□ 161 Bernd Wagner	□□ 162 Uwe Krupp
□□ 163 Gerd Truntschka	□□ 164 Bernd Truntschka
□□ 165 Thomas Brandl	□□ 166 Peter Draisaitl
□□ 167 A. Brockmann	□□ 168 Ulrich Liebsch
□□ 169 Ralf Hantschke	□□ 170 Thomas Schinko
□□ 171 Anton Krinner	□□ 172 Thomas Werner
□□ 173 Dieter Hegen	□□ 174 Selmut Steiger
□□ 175 Georg Franz	□□ 176 Switzerland
□□ 177 Renato Tosio (G)	□□ 178 Reto Pavoni (G)
□□ 179 Dino Stecher	□□ 180 Sven Leuenberger
□□ 181 Rick Tschumi	□□ 182 Patrice Brasey
□□ 183 Didier Massy	□□ 184 Sandro Bertaggia
□□ 185 Samuel Palmer	□□ 186 Martin Rauch
□□ 187 Marc Leuenberger	□□ 188 Jörg Eberle
□□ 189 Fredy Luhti	□□ 190 Andy Ton
□□ 191 Raymond Walder	□□ 192 Manuele Celio
□□ 193 Roman Wäger	□□ 194 Felix Hollenstein
□□ 195 Andre Rötheli	□□ 196 Christian Weber
□□ 197 Peter Jaks	□□ 198 Gil Montandon
□□ 199 Oliver Hoffman	□□ 200 Thomas Vrabec
□□ 201 Teppo Numminen	□□ 202 Jyrki Lumme
□□ 203 Esa Tikkanen	□□ 204 Petri Skriko
□□ 205 Christian Ruuttu	□□ 206 Ilkka Sinisalo
□□ 207 Calle Johansson	□□ 208 Tomas Sandström
□□ 209 Thomas Steen	□□ 210 Per-Erik Eklund
□□ 211 Mats Sundin	□□ 212 Johan Garpenlöv
□□ 213 Viacheslav Fetisov	□□ 214 Alexei Kasatonov
□□ 215 Michail Tatarinov	□□ 216 Sergei Makarov
□□ 217 Igor Larionov	□□ 218 Alexander Mogilny
□□ 219 Sergei Fedorov	□□ 220 Petr Klima
□□ 221 David Volek	□□ 222 Michal Pivonka
□□ 223 Robert Reichel	□□ 224 Bobby Holik
□□ 225 Jaromir Jagr	□□ 226 Urpo Ylönen
□□ 227 Ilpo Koskela	□□ 228 Pekka Rautakallio
□□ 229 Lasse Oksanen	□□ 230 Veli-Pekka Ketola
□□ 231 Leif Holmqvist (G)	□□ 232 Lennart Svedberg
□□ 233 Sven Tumba	□□ 234 Ulf Sterner
□□ 235 Anders Hedberg	□□ 236 Ken Dryden
□□ 237 Bobby Orr	□□ 238 Gordie Howe
□□ 239 Bobby Hull	□□ 240 Phil Esposito
□□ 241 V. Tretiak (G)	□□ 242 Aleksandr Ragulin
□□ 243 Anatoli Firsov	□□ 244 Valeri Kharlamov
□□ 245 Alexander Maltsev	□□ 246 Jiri Holecek
□□ 247 Jan Suchy	□□ 248 Josef Golonka
□□ 249 V. Nedomansky	□□ 250 Ivan Hlinka

1991 7TH INNING SKETCH MEMORIAL CUP

Issued in 1991 as a limited edition, this set was packaged in a display box and numbered of 20,000. The most expensive regular singles are Félix Potvin and Chris Osgood at $3-4 each. NHL stars sell between 50¢ and $1.25. Seventeen cards were withdrawn after an early print (approximately 1,300 sets). The most expensive single is Eric Lindros at $30-60. Withdrawn NHL stars sell between $2-4. All other withdrawn singles sell between $2-3.

Imprint: © 1990 7th Inning Sketch

Complete Set (130 cards): 180.00

	Description		Description
□	1 Mike Lenarduzzi (G)	□	2 Kevin Hodson (G)

3 OHL Action	4 Bob Boughner
5 Adam Foote	6 Brad Tilley
7 Brian Goudie	8 Wade Whitten
9 Jason Denomme	10 David Matsos
11 Rick Kowalsky	12 Jarret Reid
13 Perry Pappas	14 Tom MacDonald
15 Mike DeCoff	16 Joe Busillo
17 Denny Lambert	18 Mark Matier
19 Shaun Imber	20 Ralph Intranuovo
21 Chris Snell, (W/D)	22 Tony Iob
23 Colin Miller	24 Ted Nolan, Coach
25 Sylvain Rodigue (G)	26 Félix Potvin (G)
27 Martin Lavallée	28 Eric Brulé
29 Steve Larouche	30 Michel St-Jacques
31 Patrick Clement	32 Patrick Bisaillon
33 Checklist (W/D)	33 CL (62 to 131) Repla.
34 Gilles Bouchard	35 Eric Rochette
36 Dykeman (G) (W/D)	37 CL (1 to 61), (W/D)
37 CL (1 to 61), Corr.	38 Patrice Martineau
39 Danny Beauregard	40 François Bélanger
41 Sébastien Parent	42 Martin Gagné
43 S. Charbonneau	44 Martin Beaupré
45 Daniel Paradis	46 Joe Canale, Coach
47 OHL Action	48 Jubilation
49 Steve Lupien (G)	50 Pierre Gagnon (G)
51 Alexandre Legault	52 Martin Charrois
53 Eric Dandenault	54 Denis Chassé
55 Guy Lehoux	56 Ian Laperrière
57 Hugo Proulx	58 Dave Whittom
59 Yanick Dupré	60 Eric Plante
61 Stéphane Desjardins	62 Patrice Brisebois
63 René Corbet	64 Marc Kropf
65 Claude Jutras	66 David Pekarek
67 Roger Larche, Error	68 Dave Paquet
69 Eric Meloche	70 CHL Action
71 The Celebration	72 MVP: Félix Potvin (G)
73 Scott Bailey (G)	74 Trevor Kidd (G)
75 Chris Lafreniere	76 Frank Evans
77 Jon Klemm	78 Brent Thurston
79 Jamie McLennan	80 Steve Junker
81 Mark Szoke	82 Ray Whitney
83 Geoff Grandberg	84 Cam Danyluk
85 Kerry Toporowski	86 Trevor Tovell
87 Pat Falloon	88 Bram Vanderkracht
89 Mike Jickling	90 Murray Garbutt
91 Calvin Thudium	92 Mark Woolf
93 Shane Maitland	94 Bart Cote
95 B. Maxwell, Coach	96 Eric Lindros (W/D)
97 Scott Niedermayer	98 Patrick Poulin
99 Brent Bilodeau	100 Pat Falloon
101 Darcy Werenka	102 Martin Lapointe
103 Philippe Bouche	104 Jeff Nelson
105 René Corbet	106 Pat Peake (W/D)
107 Steve Staios (W/D)	108 Richard Matvichuk
109 Dean McAmmond	110 Alex Stojanov (W/D)
111 Glen Murray (W/D)	112 Tyler Wright
113 Jason Dawe (W/D)	114 N. Lafayette (W/D)
115 Yanic Perreault	116 Guy Léveque (W/D)
117 Darren Van Impe	118 S. Antoski (W/D)
119 Eric Lindros (W/D)	120 Dennis Perdie (W/D)
121 T. Chitaroni (W/D)	122 Jamie Pushor
123 Chris Osgood	124 J. Matthews (W/D)
125 Yves Sarault	126 Yanick Dupré
127 Brad Zimmer	128 Copps Coliseum
129 Jason Widmer	130 Marc Savard

1991 - 92 AIR CANADA SJHL

Rod Brind'Amour is the most expensive card at $4.00. Singles start at 20¢; regional stars start at 75¢.

Complete Set (250 cards): 25.00
Common Player: .20

SJHL	SJHL
1 Jeff Kungle	2 Jay Dunn
3 Kevin Dickie, Coach	4 Martin Smith
5 Jeff Cole	6 Trent Hamm
7 Kent Rogers	8 Dean Gerard
9 Jim McLarty	10 M. Kostuchenko
11 Mark Scollan	12 Brad Federenko
13 Rob Beck	14 Bryce Bohun
15 Kory Karlander	16 Scott Christion
17 Tyler Kuhn	18 Corri Moffatt
19 Layne Douglas	20 Shane Holunga
21 Mike Matteucci	22 Bart Vanstaalduinen
23 B. McEwen, G.M.	24 Kim Maier
25 Jamie Ling	26 Dean Seymour
27 Derek Crimin	28 Evan Anderson
29 Craig Matatall	30 Keith Murphy
31 Jason Feiffer	32 Michel Cook
33 Rod Krushel	34 Tyler Rice
35 Gerald Tallaire	36 Richard Nagy
37 Taras Lendzyk	38 Jeff Knight
39 Darren Opp	40 Dwayne Rhinehart
41 Minot Americans AS	42 S.Bellefontaine (G)
43 Darren Maloney	44 '92 SJHL N. Division
45 Yorkton Terriers AS	46 Melville AS
47 1992 Best AS Team	48 Evan All-Stars
49 Notre Dame AS	50 B. Robson, Coach
A1 Dean Normand	A2 Dan Meyers
A3 Tyson Balog	A4 Tyler McMillan
A5 Jason Selkirk	A6 Bryce Bohun
A7 Blaire Hornung	A8 Craig McKechnie
A9 Rejean Stringer	A10 Corri Moffat
A11 Dion Johnson	A12 Rod Krushel
A13 Mike Langen (G)	A14 Jeff Hassman
A15 Dean Moore	A16 Trevor Wathen
A17 Curtis Knight	A18 Chris Morgan
A19 Trevor Thurston	A20 Wayne Filipenko
A21 Jason Feiffer	A22 Layne Douglas
A23 Dave Gardner	A24 Ryan Sandholm
A25 Corey McKee	A26 Trevor Schmiess
A27 Todd Hollinger (G)	A28 Jay Dunn
A29 Jamie Ling	A30 Todd Small
A31 Barret Kropf	A32 Dean Gerard
A33 Christian Dutil (G)/ Aaron Campbell	
A34 Tyler Scheidt	A35 Dean Sideroff
A36 Dan Dufresne	A37 Cam Yager (G)
A38 Richard Nagy (G)	A39 Aaron Cain
A40 Rob Beck	A41 Blair Wagar
A42 Kim Maier	A43 Brent Hoiness
A44 Troy Edwards	A45 Evan Anderson
A46 Carlin Nordstrom	A47 Dean Seymour
A48 Scott Wotton	A49 Curtis Joseph
B1 Richard Boscher (G)	B2 James Schaeffler
B3 Wes Rommel	B4 Corey Thompson
B5 Rob Phillips	B6 Jim McLean
B7 Trevor Warrener	B8 Peter Boake
B9 Kevin Riffel (G)	B10 Tom Perry
B11 Mark Baird	B12 Stacy Prevost
B13 Taras Lendzyk (G)	B14 Shawn Reis (G)
B15 Shawn Thompson	B16 Curtis Kleisinger
B17 Kent Rogers	B18 Scott Christion (G)
B19 Gerald Tallaire	B20 Kelly Hollingshead
B21 Mike Savard (G)	B22 Darren Maloney
B23 Jason Hynd	B24 Scott Stewart
B25 Scott Beattie	B26 Dave McAmmond
B27 Myles Gibb	B28 Ryan Bach (G)
B29 Martin Smith	B30 Leigh Brookbank
B31 Todd Markus	B32 The Boys From PA
B33 Randy Muise	B34 George Gervais
B35 Keith Harris	B36 Jamie Stelmak (G)
B37 B. Vanstaalduinen	B38 Scott Murray, Minn.
B39 Danny Galarneau	B40 Keith Murphy
B41 Jeff Kungle	B42 Michel Cook
B43 Daryl Krauss	B44 Derek Wynne, Minn.
B45 Derek Crimin	B46 Jason Brown
B47 Bruce Matatall	B48 Chris Hatch
B49 Kurtise Souchotte	B50 Michael Brennan
B51 Orrin Hergott	C1 Craig Matatall
C2 Brad Prefontaine	C3 Mike Evans
C4 Jody Reiter	C5 Jeremy Mylymok
C6 Dave Doucet	C7 Randy Kerr
C8 Gordon McCann	C9 Quinn Fair
C10 Kyle Niemegeers	C11 Ryan Smith
C12 Mike Hillock, Minn.	C13 Vern Anderson
C14 Trent Hamm	C15 Curtis Folkett
C16 Warren Pickford	C17 Craig Volstad (G)
C18 Sean Tallaire	C19 Jason Yaganiski
C20 Jim McLarty	C21 Jamie Byfuglien
C22 Terry Metro	C23 Todd Kozak
C24 Jeff Huckle	C25 Darren McLean
C26 Bret Mohninger	C27 Tim Slukynsky
C28 Roman Mrhalek	C29 Joel Martinson
C30 Ron Patterson	C31 Mark Gorgi
C32 Tom Thomson	C33 Greg Wahl
C34 Craig Perrett	C35 Mike Harder
C36 Jeff Cole	C37 Justin Christoffer
C38 Nolan Weir	C39 Jeff Knight
C40 Lyle Vaughan	C41 S. Bellefontaine (G)
C42 Trevor Mathias	C43 Chris Schinkel (G)
C44 Scott Rogers	C45 Shane Holunga
C46 Dwayne Rhinehart	C47 Eddy Marchant
C48 Travis Smith	C49 Not issued
C50 Mike Hidlebaugh	D1 Darcy Herlick
D2 Joel Appleton	D3 Bobby Standish
D4 Kory Karlander	D5 Brett Kinaschuk
D6 Kevin Messer	D7 Jason Martin
D8 Devin Zimmer	D9 David Foster
D10 Bob Schwark	D11 Ted Grayling
D12 Travis Vantighem	D13 Darren Houghton
D14 Wade Welte	D15 1991 NB All Stars
D16 Kevin Powel	D17 Returning Hounds
D18 Dennis Budeau	D19 Darren Opp
D20 Jeff Greenwood	D21 Mark Daniels
D22 Todd Murphy	D23 Scott Weaver
D24 Robby Bear	D25 Nigel Werenka
D26 Sean Timmins	D27 Ken Melenfant
D28 Greg Taylor	D29 Sheldon Bylsma
D30 Clint Hooge (G)	D31 Bob McIntosh
D32 Dave Lovsin	D33 Jeremy Mathies
D34 Blaine Fomradas	D35 Cory Borys
D36 Brad Purdie	D37 J Sotropa
D38 Duane Vardale	D39 Jim Nellis
D40 Brent Sheppard	D41 Cam Bristow
D42 Steve Brent	D43 Mike Matteucci
D44 Bryan Cossette	D45 Tyler Kuhn
D46 Dave Debusschere	D47 Darryl Dickson
D48 Derek Meikle	D49 Parris Duffus (G)
D50 Lance Wakefield	D51 Rod Brind'Amour

1991 - 92 ARENA

These cards have four versions: an English issue, a French issue, a silver-ink autographed and a gold-ink autographed. There are 667 silver autographs (English) and 333 gold autographs (French). Unsigned cards sell for 20¢ to $1.50.

Complete Set (33 cards):	170.00	270.00
Hologram	**Hologram**	
Pat Falloon	2.00	
Player	**Silver**	**Gold**
1 Pat Falloon ✍	5.00	6.00
2 Scott Niedermayer ✍	10.00	20.00
3 Scott Lachance ✍	5.00	6.00
4 Peter Forsberg ✍	60.00	85.00
5 Alek Stojanov ✍	3.00	6.00
6 Richard Matvichuk ✍	5.00	10.00
7 Patrick Poulin ✍	5.00	6.00
8 Martin Lapointe ✍	10.00	20.00
9 Tyler Wright ✍	3.00	6.00
10 Philippe Boucher ✍	3.00	6.00
11 Pat Peake ✍	3.00	6.00
12 Markus Näslund ✍	35.00	50.00
13 Brent Bilodeau ✍	3.00	6.00
14 Glen Murray ✍	15.00	20.00
15 Niklas Sundblad ✍	3.00	6.00
16 Trevor Halverson ✍	3.00	6.00
17 Dean McAmmond ✍	5.00	6.00
18 René Corbet ✍	5.00	6.00
19 Eric Lavigne ✍	3.00	6.00
20 Steve Staios ✍	3.00	6.00
21 Jim Campbell ✍	3.00	6.00
22 Jassen Cullimore ✍	3.00	6.00
23 Jamie Pushor ✍	3.00	6.00
24 Donevan Hextall ✍	3.00	6.00
25 Andrew Verner (G) ✍	5.00	6.00
26 Jason Dawe ✍	3.00	6.00
27 Jeff Nelson ✍	3.00	6.00
28 Darcy Werenka ✍	3.00	6.00
29 François Groleau ✍	3.00	6.00
30 Guy Lévêque ✍	3.00	6.00
31 Yanic Perreault ✍	10.00	20.00
32 S. Lachance/P. Falloon		
33 Checklist		

1991 - 92 AVANT GARDE

This series features players from the BCJHL. Paul Kariya's cards (84, 86, 91, 93, 168) are the most expensive at $30-40 a piece. Bill Muckalt (#82) $10, Jason Podollan (#104) $4. Singles start at 20¢, regional stars start at 75¢.

Imprint: 91-92 Avant Garde

Complete Set (170 cards):	120.00
Common Player:	.20
Autograph	**BCJHL**
Paul Kariya ✍	250.00

BCJHL	BCJHL
1 Vernon Lakers	2 Scott Longstaff
3 Rick Crowe	4 Sheldon Wolitski
5 Kevan Rilcof	6 Greg Buchanan
7 Vernon Lakers	8 Murray Caton
9 Adrian Bubola	10 Troy Becker
11 Shawn Potyok	12 John Morabito
13 Peter Zurba	14 Chad Schraeder
15 Shawn Bourgeois	16 Michal Sup
17 Rick Eremenko	18 David Lemanowicz
19 Dan Blasko	20 Gary Audette
21 Graeme Harder	22 Ryan Nessman
23 Jason Switzer	24 Roland Ramoser
25 Dusty McLellan	26 Dustin Green
27 Steve Roberts	28 Jason Lowe
29 Brad Knight	30 Pavel Suchanek
31 Ken Crockett	32 Adam Smith
33 Glen Pullishy	34 Mike Zambon
35 Scott Chartier	36 Donny Hearn
37 Jeff Denham	38 Jamie Marriott
39 Silverio Mirao	40 Darren Tymchyshyn
41 Mark Basanta	42 Trevor Prest
43 Jim Lessard	44 Jade Kersey
45 Geordie Young	46 Darren Holmes
47 Wade Dayley	48 Dan Murphy
49 Paul Taylor	50 Sjon Wynia
51 Ryan Loxam	52 Andy Faulkner
53 Scott Kowalski	54 Mickey McGuire
55 Jason Disiewich	56 Jim Ingram
57 Ryan Keller	58 Brian Schiebel
59 Shawn York	60 Sean Krause
61 Casey Hungle	62 Chris Jones
63 Doug Stewart	64 Jason Sirota
65 Dave Dunnigan	66 Aaron Hoffman
67 Jason Timewell	68 Pat Meehan
69 Mike Leduc	70 Brad Koopmans
71 Guy Prince	72 Dorel Gecse
73 Scott Salmond	74 Brian Zakall
75 Mike Josephson	76 Derrek Harper
77 John Graham	78 Dan Morrissey
79 Glenn Calder	80 Jason Northard
81 Chris Kerr	82 Bill Muckalt
83 Greg Hunt	84 Paul Kariya
85 Dean Rowland	86 Paul Kariya
87 David Kilduff	88 Jeff Tory
89 Mike Newman	90 Tyler Boucher
91 Paul Kariya	92 Phil Valk
93 Paul Kariya	94 Bob Lewis
95 Steve Williams	96 James Pelzer
97 Shawn Carter	98 Ryan Erasmas
99 John Dehart	100 David Green
101 Derek Gecse	102 Brian Barnes
103 Jason Given	104 Jason Podollan
105 Brian Veale	106 Rob Tallas (G)
107 Bob McBurnie	108 Paul McMillan
109 Ryan Donovan	110 Kevin Robertson
111 Milt Mastad	112 Kees Roodbol
113 Carey Causey	114 Patrick O'Flaherty
115 Chad Vestergaard	116 Tyler Quiring
117 Loui Mellios	118 Bob Bell
119 Rob Tallas, (G)	120 Clint MacDonald
121 Bart Taylor	122 Mark Basanta
123 Don McCusker	124 Jason Howse
125 Mike McKinlay	126 Trevor Pennock
127 Dean Shmyr	128 Chris Kerr
129 Erin Thornton	130 Dennis Archibald
131 Brian McDonald	132 Bob Quinnell
133 Clint Black	134 Jason Peters
135 Doug Ast	136 Jason Bilous
137 Lee Schill	138 Jason Sanford
139 Jeff Hokanson	140 Marc Gagnon
141 Gunnar Henrikson	142 Jamie Lund
143 Jason White	144 Jag Bal
145 Brad Loring	146 Marc Gagnon
147 Brian Veale	148 Checklist
149 Checklist	150 The Centennial Cup
151 Brian Law	152 Al Radke
153 Faulkner/ Disiewich/ Holmes/ Hungle/ Jones	
154 Team Photo	
155 McLellan/ Ramoser/ Eremenko/ Wolitski/ Potok/ Longstaff	
156 Hendrikson/ Anchikoski/ Gagnon/ White	
157 Graham/ Dunnigan	
158 Chartier/ Zambon/ Taylor/ Low	
159 Tory/ Boucher/ Kilduff/ Davidson/ Dehart/ Burns	
160 Didmon/ Bentham/ Marsh/ Walsh	
161 Lipsett/ McNeil/ Klyn/ Edgington	
162 All-Stars	163 Eight players
164 John Dehart	165 John Craighead
166 Mike Josephson	167 Wayne Anchikoski
168 Paul Kariya	169 Jim Lessard
170 Tommy Virkgunen	

1991 - 92 BOWMAN

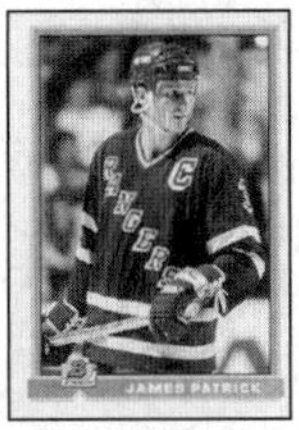

The most expensive singles are Wayne Gretzky at $1.50-2.00 and John LeClair at $1.00-1.50. All other singles sell between 20¢ and $1.00. Playoff and Hat Trick subset cards were inserted one card per pack. The promo cards were originally issued as a nine-card sheet with five Topps promo cards.

Imprint: © 1991 THE TOPPS COMPANY, INC.

Complete Set (429 cards):	12.00
Bowman	**Promo**
Raymond Bourque, Bost.	2.00
Wayne Gretzky, LosA.	5.00
Mark Messier, Edmo.	2.00
Steve Yzerman, Detr.	3.00

Description	No. Player
1 John Cullen	2 Todd Krygier
3 Kay Whitmore (G)	4 Terry Yake
5 Randy Ladouceur	6 Kevin Dineen
7 Jim McKenzie	8 Brad Shaw
9 Mark Hunter	10 Dean Evason
11 Mikael Andersson	12 Pat Verbeek
13 P. Sidorkiewicz (G)	14 Mike Tomlak
15 Zarley Zalapski	16 Rob Brown
17 Sylvain Côté	18 Bobby Holik
19 Daryl Reaugh (G)	20 Paul Cyr
21 Doug Bodger	22 Dave Andreychuk
23 Clint Malarchuk (G)	24 Darrin Shannon
25 Christian Ruuttu	26 Uwe Krupp
27 Pierre Turgeon	28 Kevin Haller RC
29 Dave Snuggerud	30 Alexander Mogilny
31 Dale Hawerchuk	32 Mike Ramsey
33 Darcy Wakaluk (G)	34 Tony Tanti
35 Jay Wells	36 Mikko Makelä
37 Daren Puppa (G)	38 Benoît Hogue
39 Rick Vaive	40 Grant Ledyard
41 Steve Yzerman	42 Steve Yzerman
43 Shawn Burr	44 Yves Racine
45 Johan Garpenlov	46 Keith Primeau
47 Tim Cheveldae (G)	48 Brad McCrimmon
49 David Barr	50 Sergei Fedorov
51 Brent Fedyk	52 Jimmy Carson
53 Paul Ysebaert	54 Rick Zombo
55 Bob Probert	56 Gerard Gallant
57 Kevin Miller	58 Randy Moller
59 Kris King	60 Corey Millen RC
61 Brian Mullen	62 Darren Turcotte
63 R. Sheppard	64 David Shaw
65 Troy Mallette	66 James Patrick
67 Mark Janssens	68 J.Vanbiesbrouck (G)
69 Joey Kocur	70 Mike Richter (G)
71 John Ogrodnick	72 Kelly Kisio
73 Normand Rochefort	74 Mike Gartner
75 Brian Leetch	76 Bernie Nicholls
77 Jan Erixon	78 Larry Murphy
79 Joe Mullen	80 Tom Barrasso (G)
81 Paul Coffey	82 Jiri Hrdina
83 Mark Recchi	84 Randy Gilhen
85 Bob Errey	86 Scott Young
87 Mario Lemieux	88 Ulf Samuelsson
89 F. Pietrangelo (G)	90 Ron Francis
91 Paul Stanton	92 Kevin Stevens
93 Bryan Trottier	94 Phil Bourque
95 Jaromir Jagr	96 Petr Klima
97 Adam Graves	98 Esa Tikkanen
99 Norm Maciver RC	100 Craig MacTavish
101 Bill Ranford (G)	102 Martin Gelinas
103 Charlie Huddy	104 Petr Klima
105 Ken Linseman	106 Steve Smith
107 Craig Simpson	108 Chris Joseph
109 Joe Murphy	110 Jeff Beukeboom
111 Grant Fuhr (G)	112 Geoff Smith
113 Anatoli Semenov	114 Mark Messier
115 Kevin Lowe	116 Glenn Anderson
117 Bobby Smith	118 Doug Small

☐ 119 Jon Casey (G) ☐ 120 Gaetan Duchesne
☐ 121 Neal Broten ☐ 122 B. Hayward (G)
☐ 123 Brian Propp ☐ 124 Mark Tinordi
☐ 125 Mike Modano ☐ 126 Marc Bureau
☐ 127 Ulf Dahlen ☐ 128 Chris Dahlquist
☐ 129 Brian Bellows ☐ 130 Mike Craig
☐ 131 Dave Gagner ☐ 132 Brian Glynn
☐ 133 Joe Sakic ☐ 134 Owen Nolan
☐ 135 Everett Sanipass ☐ 136 Jamie Baker RC
☐ 137 Mats Sundin ☐ 138 Craig Wolanin
☐ 139 Kip Miller ☐ 140 Steven Finn
☐ 141 Tony Hrkac ☐ 142 Curtis Leschyshyn
☐ 143 Mike McNeill ☐ 144 Mike Hough
☐ 145 A. Gusarov RC ☐ 146 J. Cloutier (G)
☐ 147 Shawn Anderson ☐ 148 Stéphane Morin
☐ 149 Bryan Fogarty ☐ 150 Scott Pearson
☐ 151 Ron Tugnutt (G) ☐ 152 Randy Velischek
☐ 153 Dave Reid ☐ 154 Rob Ramage
☐ 155 David Hannan ☐ 156 Wendel Clark
☐ 157 Peter Ing (G) ☐ 158 Michel Petit
☐ 159 Brian Bradley ☐ 160 Rob Cimetta
☐ 161 Gary Leeman ☐ 162 Aaron Broten
☐ 163 David Ellett ☐ 164 Peter Zezel
☐ 165 Daniel Marois ☐ 166 Mike Krushelnyski
☐ 167 Luke Richardson ☐ 168 Scott Thornton
☐ 169 Mike Foligno ☐ 170 V. Damphousse
☐ 171 Todd Gill ☐ 172 Kevin Maguire
☐ 173 Wayne Gretzky ☐ 174 Tomas Sandström
☐ 175 John Tonelli ☐ 176 Wayne Gretzky
☐ 177 Larry Robinson ☐ 178 Jay Miller
☐ 179 Tomas Sandström ☐ 180 John McIntyre
☐ 181 Brad Jones RC ☐ 182 Rob Blake
☐ 183 Kelly Hrudey (G) ☐ 184 Marty McSorley
☐ 185 Todd Elik ☐ 186 DaveTaylor
☐ 187 Steve Kasper ☐ 188 Luc Robitaille
☐ 189 Bob Kudelski ☐ 190 D. Berthiaume (G)
☐ 191 S. Duchesne ☐ 192 Tony Granato
☐ 193 Bob Essensa (G) ☐ 194 Phil Sykes
☐ 195 Paul MacDermid ☐ 196 Dave McLlwain
☐ 197 Phil Housley ☐ 198 Pat Elynuik
☐ 199 Randy Carlyle ☐ 200 Thomas Steen
☐ 201 Teppo Numminen ☐ 202 Danton Cole
☐ 203 Doug Evans ☐ 204 Ed Olczyk
☐ 205 Moe Mantha ☐ 206 Scott Arniel
☐ 207 Rick Tabaracci (G) ☐ 208 B. Marchment RC
☐ 209 Mark Osborne ☐ 210 Fredrik Olausson
☐ 211 Brent Ashton ☐ 212 Ray Ferraro
☐ 213 Mark Fitzpatrick (G) ☐ 214 Hubie McDonough
☐ 215 Joe Reekie ☐ 216 Bill Berg RC
☐ 217 Wayne McBean ☐ 218 Patrick Flatley
☐ 219 J. Hackett (G) ☐ 220 Derek King
☐ 221 Craig Ludwig ☐ 222 Pat LaFontaine
☐ 223 David Volek ☐ 224 Glenn Healy (G)
☐ 225 Jeff Norton ☐ 226 Brent Sutter
☐ 227 Randy Wood ☐ 228 Gary Nylund
☐ 229 David Chyzowski ☐ 230 Rick Tocchet
☐ 231 Ken Wregget (G) ☐ 232 Terry Carkner
☐ 233 Martin Hostak ☐ 234 Ron Hextall (G)
☐ 235 Gord Murphy ☐ 236 S. Mellanby
☐ 237 Pete Peeters (G) ☐ 238 Ron Sutter
☐ 239 Murray Craven ☐ 240 Kjell Samuelsson
☐ 241 Per-Erik Eklund ☐ 242 Mark Pederson
☐ 243 Murray Baron ☐ 244 Keith Acton
☐ 245 Derrick Smith ☐ 246 Mike Ricci
☐ 247 Dale Kushner ☐ 248 Normand Lacombe
☐ 249 Hat Trick: T. Fleury ☐ 250 HT: S. Makarov
☐ 251 Paul Ranheim ☐ 252 Joe Nieuwendyk
☐ 253 Mike Vernon (G) ☐ 254 Gary Suter
☐ 255 Doug Gilmour ☐ 256 Paul Fenton
☐ 257 Roger Johansson ☐ 258 Stéphane Matteau
☐ 259 Frantisek Musil ☐ 260 Joel Otto
☐ 261 Tim Sweeney ☐ 262 Al MacInnis
☐ 263 Gary Roberts ☐ 264 Sergei Makarov
☐ 265 Carey Wilson ☐ 266 Ric Nattress
☐ 267 Robert Reichel ☐ 268 Rick Wamsley (G)
☐ 269 B.MacLellan ☐ 270 Theoren Fleury
☐ 271 Claude Lemieux ☐ 272 John MacLean
☐ 273 Viacheslav Fetisov ☐ 274 Kirk Muller
☐ 275 Sean Burke (G) ☐ 276 Alexei Kasatonov
☐ 277 Claude Lemieux ☐ 278 Eric Weinrich
☐ 279 Patrik Sundstrom ☐ 280 Zdeno Ciger
☐ 281 Bruce Driver ☐ 282 Laurie Boschman
☐ 283 Chris Terreri (G) ☐ 284 Ken Daneyko
☐ 285 Doug Brown ☐ 286 Jon Morris
☐ 287 Peter Stastny ☐ 288 B. Shanahan
☐ 289 John MacLean ☐ 290 Mike Liut (G)
☐ 291 Michal Pivonka ☐ 292 Kelly Miller
☐ 293 John Druce ☐ 294 Calle Johansson
☐ 295 Alan May ☐ 296 Kevin Hatcher
☐ 297 Tim Bergland ☐ 298 M. Tatarinov
☐ 299 Peter Bondra ☐ 300 Al Iafrate
☐ 301 Nick Kypreos ☐ 302 Dino Ciccarelli
☐ 303 Dale Hunter ☐ 304 Don Beaupré (G)
☐ 305 Jim Hrivnak (G) ☐ 306 S. Leach
☐ 307 D. Khristich ☐ 308 Mike Ridley
☐ 309 Sergio Momesso ☐ 310 Kirk McLean (G)
☐ 311 Greg Adams ☐ 312 Adrien Plavsic
☐ 313 Cliff Ronning ☐ 314 Garry Valk
☐ 315 Troy Gamble (G) ☐ 316 Gino Odjick
☐ 317 Doug Lidster ☐ 318 Geoff Courtnall
☐ 319 Tom Kurvers ☐ 320 Robert Kron
☐ 321 Jyrki Lumme ☐ 322 Jay Mazur RC
☐ 323 Dave Capuano ☐ 324 Petr Nedved
☐ 325 Steven Bozek ☐ 326 Igor Larionov
☐ 327 Trevor Linden ☐ 328 Shayne Corson
☐ 329 Eric Desjardins ☐ 330 Stéphane Richer
☐ 331 Brian Skrudland ☐ 332 Sylvain Lefebvre
☐ 333 Stéphan Lebeau ☐ 334 Mike Keane
☐ 335 Patrick Roy (G)
☐ 336 Brent Gilchrist ☐ 337 A. Racicot (G) RC
☐ 338 Guy Carbonneau ☐ 339 Mike McPhee
☐ 340 Andrew Cassels ☐ 341 Petr Svoboda
☐ 342 Denis Savard ☐ 343 Mathieu Schneider
☐ 344 John LeClair RC ☐ 345 Tom Chorske
☐ 346 Russ Courtnall ☐ 347 Ken Hodge
☐ 348 Cam Neely ☐ 349 R. Burridge
☐ 350 Glen Wesley ☐ 351 Chris Nilan
☐ 352 Jeff Lazaro RC ☐ 353 Wes Walz
☐ 354 Réjean Lemelin (G) ☐ 355 Craig Janney
☐ 356 Raymond Bourque ☐ 357 Bob Sweeney
☐ 358 David Christian ☐ 359 Dave Poulin
☐ 360 Garry Galley ☐ 361 Andy Moog (G)
☐ 362 Ken Hodge ☐ 363 Jim Wiemer
☐ 364 Petri Skriko ☐ 365 Don Sweeney
☐ 366 Cam Neely ☐ 367 Brett Hull
☐ 368 Gino Cavallini ☐ 369 Scott Stevens
☐ 370 Rich Sutter ☐ 371 G. Featherstone
☐ 372 V. Riendeau (G) ☐ 373 Dave Lowry
☐ 374 Rod Brind'Amour ☐ 375 Brett Hull
☐ 376 Dan Quinn ☐ 377 Tom Tilley
☐ 378 Paul Cavallini ☐ 379 Bob Bassen
☐ 380 Mario Marois ☐ 381 Darin Kimble
☐ 382 Ron Wilson ☐ 383 Garth Butcher
☐ 384 Adam Oates ☐ 385 Jeff Brown
☐ 386 Jeremy Roenick ☐ 387 Tony McKegney
☐ 388 Troy Murray ☐ 389 Dave Manson
☐ 390 Ed Belfour (G) ☐ 391 Steve Thomas
☐ 392 Michel Goulet ☐ 393 Trent Yawney
☐ 394 Adam Creighton ☐ 395 Steve Larmer
☐ 396 Jimmy Waite (G) ☐ 397 Dirk Graham
☐ 398 Chris Chelios ☐ 399 Mike Hudson
☐ 400 Doug Wilson ☐ 401 Greg Gilbert
☐ 402 Wayne Presley ☐ 403 Jeremy Roenick
☐ 404 Frantisek Kucera ☐ 405 Action
☐ 406 Adam Oates ☐ 407 Grant Fuhr (G)
☐ 408 Action ☐ 409 Action
☐ 410 Action ☐ 411 Action
☐ 412 Action ☐ 413 Action
☐ 414 Russ Courtnall ☐ 415 Action
☐ 416 Action ☐ 417 Action
☐ 418 Action ☐ 419 Action
☐ 420 Action ☐ 421 Action
☐ 422 Action ☐ 423 Action
☐ 424 Action ☐ 425 MVP: M. Lemieux
☐ 426 Checklist ☐ 427 Checklist
☐ 428 Checklist ☐ 429 Checklist

1991 - 92 CANADIAN OLYMPIC TEAM

Trevor Kidd and Sean Burke are the most expensive singles at $2-3. Singles start at 50¢.

Complete Set (24 cards): 20.00

Canada	Canada
☐ Dave Archibald	☐ Todd Brost
☐ Sean Burke (G)	☐ Terry Crisp
☐ Kevin Dahl	☐ Karl Dykhuis
☐ Wayne Fleming	☐ Curt Giles
☐ Joé Juneau	☐ Trevor Kidd (G)
☐ Chris Lindberg	☐ Kent Manderville
☐ Dave King G.M./ Coach	☐ Chris Kontos
☐ Scott Scissons	☐ Randy Smith
☐ Stéphane Roy	☐ Brad Schlegel
☐ Adrien Plavsic	☐ Dan Ratushny
☐ Jason Woolley	☐ Title Card
☐ Gord Hynes	☐ Fabian Joseph

1991 - 92 CLASSIC DRAFT PICKS

The most expensive singles are Eric Lindros at $2-3 and Peter Forsberg at $1-2. All other singles sell between 20¢ and $1.00. Both English and bilingual cards sell at the same price.

Imprint: 1991 Classic Games, Inc.

Complete Set (50 cards): 6.00

Classic	Promo
☐ Eric Lindros	6.00
☐ Pat Falloon	2.00

Description	No. Player
☐ ☐ 1 Eric Lindros	☐ ☐ 2 Pat Falloon
☐ ☐ 3 Scott Niedermayer	☐ ☐ 4 Scott Lachance
☐ ☐ 5 Peter Forsberg	☐ ☐ 6 Alek Stojanov
☐ ☐ 7 Richard Matvichuk	☐ ☐ 8 Patrick Poulin
☐ ☐ 9 Martin Lapointe	☐ ☐ 10 Tyler Wright
☐ ☐ 11 Philippe Boucher	☐ ☐ 12 Pat Peake
☐ ☐ 13 Markus Näslund	☐ ☐ 14 Brent Bilodeau
☐ ☐ 15 Glen Murray	☐ ☐ 16 Niklas Sundblad
☐ ☐ 17 Martin Rucinsky	☐ ☐ 18 Trevor Halverson
☐ ☐ 19 Dean McAmmond	☐ ☐ 20 Ray Whitney
☐ ☐ 21 René Corbet	☐ ☐ 22 Eric Lavigne
☐ ☐ 23 Zigmund Palffy	☐ ☐ 24 Steve Staios
☐ ☐ 25 Jim Campbell	☐ ☐ 26 Jassen Cullimore
☐ ☐ 27 Martin Hamrlik	☐ ☐ 28 Jamie Pushor
☐ ☐ 29 Donevan Hextall	☐ ☐ 30 Andrew Verner (G)
☐ ☐ 31 Jason Dawe	☐ ☐ 32 Jeff Nelson
☐ ☐ 33 Darcy Werenka	☐ ☐ 34 Jozef Stumpel
☐ ☐ 35 François Groleau	☐ ☐ 36 Guy Léveque
☐ ☐ 37 Jamie Matthews	☐ ☐ 38 Dody Wood
☐ ☐ 39 Yanic Perreault	☐ ☐ 40 Jamie McLennan (G)
☐ ☐ 41 Yanick Dupré	☐ ☐ 42 Sandy McCarthy
☐ ☐ 43 Chris Osgood (G)	☐ ☐ 44 Fredrik Lindquist
☐ ☐ 45 Jason Young	☐ ☐ 46 Steve Konowalchuk
☐ ☐ 47 Michael Nylander	☐ ☐ 48 Shane Peacock
☐ ☐ 49 Yves Sarault	☐ ☐ 50 M. Cousineau (G)

Classic	Rocket
☐ ☐ Rocket Ismail	.75

1991 - 92 CLASSIC GAMES FOUR-SPORT

This 230-card four-sport set features only 50 hockey players. Both English and bilingual cards sell at the same price. A 230-card set sells at $15. Unsigned cards sell for 20¢ to $1.50

Classic	Promo
☐ Pat Falloon	2.00

Classic	Aut.
☐ ☐ 1 Future Stars (Eric Lindros)	–
☐ ☐ ☐ 2 Pat Falloon ✍	5.00
☐ ☐ ☐ 3 Scott Niedermayer, Kamloops ✍	10.00
☐ ☐ ☐ 4 Scott Lachance, Boston U. ✍	5.00
☐ ☐ 5 Peter Forsberg, Phil.	–
☐ ☐ ☐ 6 Alek Stojanov, Hamilton ✍	3.00
☐ ☐ 7 Richard Matvichuk, Saskatoon	–
☐ ☐ ☐ 8 Patrick Poulin, St-Hyacinthe ✍	5.00
☐ ☐ 9 Martin Lapointe, Laval	–
☐ ☐ ☐ 10 Tyler Wright , WHL All-Stars ✍	3.00
☐ ☐ ☐ 11 Philippe Boucher, QMJHL All-Stars ✍	3.00
☐ ☐ ☐ 12 Pat Peake, Detroit-OHL ✍	3.00
☐ ☐ 13 Markus Näslund, Pitt.	–
☐ ☐ ☐ 14 Brent Bilodeau, WHL All-Stars ✍	3.00
☐ ☐ ☐ 15 Glen Murray, Sudbury ✍	20.00
☐ ☐ ☐ 16 Niklas Sundblad, Calg. ✍	3.00
☐ ☐ ☐ 17 Martin Rucinsky, CSR. ✍	10.00
☐ ☐ ☐ 18 Trevor Halverson, North Bay ✍	3.00
☐ ☐ ☐ 19 Dean McAmmond, Prince Albert ✍	5.00
☐ ☐ ☐ 20 Ray Whitney, Spokane ✍	10.00
☐ ☐ ☐ 21 René Corbet, Drummondville ✍	5.00
☐ ☐ ☐ 22 Eric Lavigne, QMJHL All-Stars ✍	3.00
☐ ☐ 23 Zigmund Palffy, CSR.	–
☐ ☐ ☐ 24 Steve Staios, Niagara Falls ✍	3.00
☐ ☐ ☐ 25 Jim Campbell, Northwood ✍	3.00
☐ ☐ ☐ 26 Jassen Cullimore, Peterborough ✍	3.00
☐ ☐ 27 Martin Hamrlik, CSR.	–
☐ ☐ ☐ 28 Jamie Pushor, Lethbridge ✍	3.00
☐ ☐ ☐ 29 Donevan Hextall, Prince Albert ✍	3.00
☐ ☐ ☐ 30 Andrew Verner (G), Peterborough ✍	5.00
☐ ☐ ☐ 31 Jason Dawe, Peterborough ✍	3.00
☐ ☐ ☐ 32 Jeff Nelson, WHL All-Stars ✍	3.00
☐ ☐ ☐ 33 Darcy Werenka, Lethbridge ✍	3.00
☐ ☐ 34 Jozef Stumpel, CSR.	–
☐ ☐ ☐ 35 François Groleau, Shawinigan ✍	3.00
☐ ☐ ☐ 36 Guy Lévèque, Cornwall ✍	3.00
☐ ☐ ☐ 37 Jamie Matthews, Sudbury ✍	3.00
☐ ☐ ☐ 38 Dody Wood, Seattle ✍	3.00
☐ ☐ ☐ 39 Yanic Perreault, QMJHL All-Stars ✍	10.00
☐ ☐ ☐ 40 Jamie McLennan (G), Lethbridge ✍	5.00
☐ ☐ ☐ 41 Yanick Dupré, Drummondville ✍•	15.00
☐ ☐ ☐ 42 Sandy McCarthy, Laval ✍	5.00
☐ ☐ ☐ 43 Chris Osgood (G), Medicine Hat ✍	25.00
☐ ☐ ☐ 44 Fredrik Lindquist, Djugarden ✍	3.00
☐ ☐ ☐ 45 Jason Young, Sudbury ✍	3.00
☐ ☐ ☐ 46 Steve Konowalchuk, Portland-WHL ✍	10.00
☐ ☐ ☐ 47 Michael Nylander, Hart. ✍	10.00
☐ ☐ ☐ 48 Shane Peacock, Lethbridge ✍	3.00
☐ ☐ ☐ 49 Yves Sarault, St-Jean ✍	3.00
☐ ☐ ☐ 50 Marcel Cousineau (G), Beauport ✍	3.00

1991 - 92 FUTURE TRENDS '72 HOCKEY CANADA

These cards have two versions: an English issue and a French issue. 36 players have a third autographed version signed in gold ink. Cards were produced by 7th Inning Sketch and distributed through Hudson Bay stores in Canada.

The most expensive English version card is the Henderson vs. Tretiak card which sells for 50¢-$1.50. Hall of Famers sell for 25¢-$1.00; all other singles sell for 5¢-50¢. French version cards sell for 1.5-2 times English version cards.

Imprint: 1991 Future Trends Experience Ltd. Printed in Canada

Complete Set (101 cards): 10.00

Summit Series	Promo
☐ Phil Esposito Promo	3.00
☐ Paul Henderson Promo	3.00
☐ Vladislav Tretiak Promo	3.00

Summit Series	Summit Series
☐ ☐ 1 In the Beginning	☐ ☐ 2 Backyard rink/ ...
☐ ☐ 3 It Didn't Take Long	☐ ☐ 4 Anatoli Tarasov
☐ ☐ 5 More Hours a Day	☐ ☐ 6 Coming Out Party
☐ ☐ 7 Never in Doubt	☐ ☐ 8 Team Canada
☐ ☐ 9 Pat Stapleton	☐ ☐ 10 Vsevolod Bobrov
☐ ☐ 11 V. Tretiak (G)	☐ ☐ 12 Faceoff
☐ ☐ 13 30 Seconds	☐ ☐ 14 Yevgeny Zimin
☐ ☐ 15 Bill White	☐ ☐ 16 7-3/ Stats
☐ ☐ 17 Don Awrey	☐ ☐ 18 Mickey Redmond
☐ ☐ 19 Alexander Gusev	☐ ☐ 20 Alexander Maltsev
☐ ☐ 21 Rod Seiling	☐ ☐ 22 Dale Tallon
☐ ☐ 23 Coming Back	☐ ☐ 24 Unforgettable/ Stats
☐ ☐ 25 Wayne Cashman	☐ ☐ 26 Frank Mahovlich
☐ ☐ 27 Peter Mahovlich	☐ ☐ 28 Soviet players
☐ ☐ 29 Yuri Shatalov	☐ ☐ 30 The Brothers
☐ ☐ 31 The Goalies	☐ ☐ 32 Alexander Bodunov
☐ ☐ 33 All Even/ Stats	☐ ☐ 34 Yuri Blinov
☐ ☐ 35 Jocelyn Guevremont	☐ ☐ 36 Vic Hadfield
☐ ☐ 37 Yuri Lebedev	☐ ☐ 38 Starshinov/ Poladiev
☐ ☐ 39 Disaster/ Stats	☐ ☐ 40 Address...nation
☐ ☐ 41 Victor Kuzkin	☐ ☐ 42 Vladimir Lutchenko
☐ ☐ 43 Boris Mikhailov	☐ ☐ 44 Grace under...
☐ ☐ 45 Afraid to Lose...	☐ ☐ 46 Ready to Win/ Stats
☐ ☐ 47 Vladimir Vikulov	☐ ☐ 48 Red Berenson
☐ ☐ 49 Richard Martin	☐ ☐ 50 A. Martynyuk
☐ ☐ 51 Gilbert Perreault	☐ ☐ 52 Vladimir Petrov
☐ ☐ 53 Serge Savard	☐ ☐ 54 Vladimir Shadrin
☐ ☐ 55 Da Da Ka-na-da/ ...	☐ ☐ 56 One Step Back
☐ ☐ 57 Bobby Clarke	☐ ☐ 58 Valeri Kharlamov
☐ ☐ 59 Alexander Volchkov	☐ ☐ 60 Standing Guard
☐ ☐ 61 Stan Mikita	☐ ☐ 62 One More to Go
☐ ☐ 63 The Winner	☐ ☐ 64 The Fans Go Wild
☐ ☐ 65 Alexander Ragulin	☐ ☐ 66 Jean Ratelle
☐ ☐ 67 Gennady Tsygankov	☐ ☐ 68 Valeri Vasiliev
☐ ☐ 69 ..Dialogue	☐ ☐ 70 Series Stars
☐ ☐ 71 Series Stars	☐ ☐ 72 No Solitudes/ ...
☐ ☐ 73 2 - 2/ 3 - 3	☐ ☐ 74 Rod Gilbert
☐ ☐ 75 Yevgeny Mishakov	☐ ☐ 76 Ron Ellis
☐ ☐ 77 5 - 4/ 5 - 5	☐ ☐ 78 Different../Interlude
☐ ☐ 79 Bill Goldsworthy	☐ ☐ 80 .../'1:30 To Go
☐ ☐ 81 The Moment	☐ ☐ 82 Yvan Cournoyer
☐ ☐ 83 Yuri Liapkin	☐ ☐ 84 Phil Esposito
☐ ☐ 85 Ken Dryden (G)	☐ ☐ 86 Peace/ Stats
☐ ☐ 87 Gary Bergman	☐ ☐ 88 Brian Glennie
☐ ☐ 89 Dennis Hull	☐ ☐ 90 Vyacheslav Anisin
☐ ☐ 91 Marcel Dionne	☐ ☐ 92 Guy Lapointe
☐ ☐ 93 Ed Johnston (G)	☐ ☐ 94 Harry Sinden, Coach
☐ ☐ 95 Brad Park	☐ ☐ 96 Tony Esposito (G)
☐ ☐ 97 Alexander Yakushev	☐ ☐ 98 Paul Henderson
☐ ☐ 99 Jean-Paul Parise	☐ ☐ 100 V. Kharlamov
☐ ☐ 101 Checklist	

Autograph	Auto.
☐ 9 Pat Stapleton ✍	8.00
☐ 11 Vladislav Tretiak ✍	120.00
☐ 15 Bill White ✍	8.00
☐ 17 Don Awrey ✍	8.00
☐ 18 Mickey Redmond ✍	8.00
☐ 21 Rod Seiling ✍	8.00
☐ 22 Dale Tallon ✍	8.00
☐ 25 Wayne Cashman ✍	8.00
☐ 26 Frank Mahovlich ✍	35.00
☐ 27 Peter Mahovlich ✍	15.00
☐ 35 Jocelyn Guevremont ✍	8.00
☐ 36 Vic Hadfield ✍	8.00
☐ 48 Red Berenson ✍	8.00
☐ 49 Rick Martin ✍	8.00
☐ 51 Gilbert Perreault ✍	35.00
☐ 53 Serge Savard ✍	20.00
☐ 57 Bobby Clarke ✍	35.00
☐ 61 Stan Mikita ✍	35.00
☐ 66 Jean Ratelle ✍	15.00
☐ 74 Rod Gilbert ✍	15.00
☐ 76 Ron Ellis ✍	8.00
☐ 79 Bill Goldsworthy ✍•	50.00
☐ 82 Yvan Cournoyer ✍	25.00
☐ 84 Phil Esposito ✍	40.00
☐ 85 Ken Dryden ✍	100.00
☐ 87 Gary Bergman ✍•	25.00
☐ 88 Brian Glennie ✍	8.00
☐ 89 Dennis Hull ✍	8.00
☐ 91 Marcel Dionne ✍	40.00
☐ 92 Guy Lapointe ✍	15.00
☐ 93 Ed Johnston ✍	8.00
☐ 94 Harry Sinden ✍	8.00
☐ 95 Brad Park ✍	25.00
☐ 96 Tony Esposito ✍	40.00
☐ 98 Paul Henderson ✍	30.00
☐ 99 Jean-Paul Parise ✍	8.00

1991 - 92 GILLETTE

The most expensive cards are Mario Lemieux at $3-4, Jaromir Jagr at $2-3, Joe Sakic at $2-2.50 and Pavel Bure at $2-2.50. Regional stars sell at 50¢-$1.50; commons start at 10-25¢.

Complete Set (48 cards): 20.00

Gillette	Gillette
☐ Smythe Division	☐ 1 Luc Robitaille
☐ 2 Esa Tikkanen	☐ 3 Pat Falloon
☐ 4 Theoren Fleury	☐ 5 Trevor Linden
☐ 6 Rob Blake	☐ 7 Al MacInnis
☐ 8 Bob Essensa (G)	☐ 9 Bill Ranford (G)
☐ 10 Pavel Bure	☐ Norris Division
☐ 11 Wendel Clark	☐ 12 Sergei Fedorov
☐ 13 Jeremy Roenick	☐ 14 Brett Hull
☐ 15 Mike Modano	☐ 16 Chris Chelios
☐ 17 Dave Ellett	☐ 18 Ed Belfour (G)
☐ 19 Grant Fuhr (G)	☐ 20 Martin Lapointe
☐ Adams Division	☐ 21 Kirk Muller
☐ 22 Joe Sakic	☐ 23 Pat LaFontaine
☐ 24 Pat Verbeek	☐ 25 Owen Nolan
☐ 26 Raymond Bourque	☐ 27 Eric Desjardins
☐ 28 Patrick Roy (G)	☐ 29 Andy Moog (G)
☐ 30 Valeri Kamensky	☐ Patrick Division
☐ 31 Mark Messier	☐ 32 Mike Ricci
☐ 33 Mario Lemieux	☐ 34 Jaromir Jagr
☐ 35 Pierre Turgeon	☐ 36 Kevin Hatcher
☐ 37 Paul Coffey	☐ 38 Chris Terreri (G)
☐ 39 Mike Richter (G)	☐ 40 Kevin Todd
☐ Trivia Card	☐ Trivia Card
☐ Trivia Card	☐ Trivia Card

1991 - 92 JYVAS HYVA

A set of 12 unnumbered team logos and 72 numbered stickers from the Finnish National League. We have little pricing information on this set. Teemu Selänne is the most expensive single at $15.00. Singles start at 20¢.

Sticker Size: 1 5/8" x 4 1/4"

Jyvas Hyva	Jyvas Hyva
☐ HIFK Helsinki	☐ 1 Sakari Lindfors (G)
☐ 2 Jukka Seppo	☐ 3 Pekka Tuomisto
☐ 4 Harri Tuohimaa	☐ 5 Pertti Lehtonen
☐ 6 Simo Saarinen	☐ HPK Hameenlinna
☐ 7 Timo Lehkonen (G)	☐ 8 Teppo Kivela
☐ 9 Markku Piikkio	☐ 10 Pekka Peltola
☐ 11 Hannu Henriksson	☐ 12 Jari Haapamaki
☐ Ilves Tampere	☐ 13 Jukka Tammi (G)
☐ 14 Risto Jalo	☐ 15 Timo Peltomaa
☐ 16 Raimo Summanen	☐ 17 Ville Siren
☐ 18 Risto Siltanen	☐ Jokerit Helsinki
☐ 19 Markus Ketterer (G)	☐ 20 Pekka Jarvela
☐ 21 Teemu Selänne	☐ 22 Keijo Sailynoja
☐ 23 Mika Stromberg	☐ 24 Waltteri Immonen
☐ JyPHT Jyvaskyla	☐ 25 AP Siekkinen (G)
☐ 26 Jari Lindroos	☐ 27 Ari Haanpaa
☐ 28 Jiri Dolezal	☐ 29 Harri Laurila
☐ 30 Leo Gudas	☐ KalPa Kuopio
☐ 31 Mika Rautio (G)	☐ 32 Pekka Tirkkonen
☐ 33 Jarmo Kekalainen	☐ 34 Juha Jokiharju
☐ 35 Juha Tuohimaa	☐ 36 Erik Hamalainen
☐ Joensuun Kiekkopojat	☐ 37 J. Jaaskelainen (G)
☐ 38 Rostislav Vlach	☐ 39 Jouni Mustonen
☐ 40 Markku Kyllonen	☐ 41 Antonin Stavjana
☐ 42 Ossi Piitulainen	☐ Rauman Lukko
☐ 43 Petr Briza (G)	☐ 44 Mika Nieminen
☐ 45 Jari Torkki	☐ 46 Tommi Pullola
☐ 47 Jarmo Kuusisto	☐ 48 Pasi Huura
☐ Hockey Reipa Lahti	☐ 49 Jaromir Sindel (G)
☐ 50 Marko Jantunen	☐ 51 Erkki Laine
☐ 52 Erkki Makela	☐ 53 Niko Marttila
☐ 54 Erik Kakko	☐ Tappara Tampere
☐ 55 Jari Halme (G)	☐ 56 Kari Heikkinen
☐ 57 Jiri Kucera	☐ 58 Vesa Viitakoski
☐ 59 Jukka Marttila	☐ 60 Pekka Laksola
☐ Turun Palloseura	☐ 61 Jouni Rokama (G)
☐ 62 Esa Keskinen	☐ 63 Jukka Vilander
☐ 64 Jari Pulliainen	☐ 65 Jouko Narvanmaa
☐ 66 Hannu Virta	☐ Assat Pori
☐ 67 Kari Takko (G)	☐ 68 Janne Virtanen
☐ 69 Arto Javanainen	☐ 70 Oleg Znarok
☐ 71 Tapio Levo	☐ 72 Harry Nikander

1991 - 92 KELLOGG'S - SCORE

Complete Set (24 cards): 14.00
Album: 5.00

	Player	Score
☐	1 Patrick Roy (G), Mont.	3.50
☐	2 Rick Tocchet, Phil.	.25
☐	3 Wendel Clark, Toro.	1.00
☐	4 Mike Modano, Minn.	1.00
☐	5 Jeremy Roenick, Chic.	1.00
☐	6 Pierre Turgeon, Buff.	.50
☐	7 Kevin Hatcher, Wash.	.25
☐	8 Brian Leetch, NYRa.	.50
☐	9 Mark Recchi, Pitt.	.50
☐	10 Andy Moog (G), Bost.	.50
☐	11 Kevin Dineen, Hart.	.25
☐	12 Joe Sakic, Québ.	2.00
☐	13 John MacLean, Njer.	.25
☐	14 Steve Yzerman, Detr.	3.00
☐	15 Pat LaFontaine, NYIs.	.50
☐	16 Al MacInnis, Calg.	.50
☐	17 Petr Klima, Edmo.	.25
☐	18 Ed Olczyk, Winn.	.25
☐	19 Doug Wilson, Chic.	.25
☐	20 Trevor Linden, Vanc.	.50
☐	21 Brett Hull, Slou.	2.00
☐	22 Rob Blake, LosA.	.50
☐	23 Dave Ellett, Toro.	.25
☐	24 Cornelius Rooster	.25

1991 - 92 KRAFT

Cards 1-20/22-40/64 (red backs) were issued on the backs of KraftDinner; cards 41-56 (red backs) were issued on the backs of Kraft Spirals; cards 21/57-63 (red backs) were issued on the backs of Kraft Noodles; disks 67-88 were issued under caps of Kraft Peanut Butter.

Imprint: KRAFT
Disk Diameter: 2 3/4"
Complete Set (88 cards): 90.00
Album: 30.00

	Description	NRMT-MT
☐	1 Mario Lemieux, Pitt.	7.50
☐	2 Mark Recchi, Pitt.	1.00
☐	3 Jaromír Jágr, Pitt.	2.50
☐	4 Mats Sundin, Québ.	2.50
☐	5 Adam Oates, SLou.	1.00
☐	6 M. Richard / J. Plante	5.50
☐	7 Brendan Shanahan, SLou.	2.50
☐	8 Pat Falloon, SanJ.	.75
☐	9 Grant Fuhr (G), Toro.	1.50
☐	10 Gary Leeman, Toro.	.75
☐	11 Petr Nedved, Vanc.	.75
☐	12 Kirk Muller, Mont.	.75
☐	13 Theoren Fleury, Calg.	1.50
☐	14 Dino Ciccarelli, Wash.	.75
☐	15 Geoff Courtnall, Vanc.	.75
☐	16 Mark Messier, NYRa.	2.50
☐	17 Ken (Jr.) Hodge, Bost.	.75
☐	18 Chris Chelios, Chic.	1.50
☐	19 Mike Vernon (G), Calg.	1.00
☐	20 Kevin Hatcher, Wash.	.75
☐	21 Stéphane J.J. Richer, NJer.	.75
☐	22 Mark Tinordi, Minn.	.75
☐	23 Pat Verbeek, Hart.	.75
☐	24 John Cullen, Hart.	.75
☐	25 Pat LaFontaine, Buff.	1.50
☐	26 Stéphan Lebeau, Mont.	.75
☐	27 Mike Gartner, NYRa.	2.00
☐	28 Bob Baun, Toro.	1.50
☐	29 Shayne Corson, Mont.	.75
☐	30 Trevor Linden, Vanc.	1.00
☐	31 Craig Janney, Bost.	.75
☐	32 Al MacInnis, Calg.	1.00
☐	33 Phil Housley, Winn.	.75
☐	34 Doug Wilson, SanJ.	.75
☐	35 Tony Granato, LosA.	.75
☐	36 Dale Hawerchuk, Buff.	1.50
☐	37 Broda / Durnan	2.00
☐	38 Brian Bellows, Minn.	.75
☐	39 Bob Gainey, Mont.	1.50
☐	40 Darryl Sittler, Toro.	2.00
☐	41 Joe Sakic, Québ.	4.00
☐	42 Wendel Clark, Toro.	2.00
☐	43 Brent Sutter, Chic.	.75
☐	44 Bill Ranford (G), Edmo.	1.00
☐	45 Rick Tocchet, Phil.	.75
☐	46 Paul Ysebaert, Detr.	.75
☐	47 Adam Creighton, NYIs.	.75
☐	48 Mike Modano, Minn.	2.50
☐	49 Russ Courtnall, Mont.	.75
☐	50 Syl (Sr.) Apps, Toro.	2.00
☐	51 Sergei Fedorov, Detr.	2.50
☐	52 Mike Ricci, Phil.	.75
☐	53 Scott Stevens, NJer.	1.00
☐	54 Bobby Clarke, Phil.	2.00
☐	55 Owen Nolan, Québ.	1.50
☐	56 Jeremy Roenick, Chic.	2.00
☐	57 Raymond Bourque, Bost.	3.00
☐	58 Gerard Gallant, Detr.	.75
☐	59 Andy Moog (G), Bost.	1.00
☐	60 Alexander Mogilny, Buff.	1.00
☐	61 Denis Potvin, NYIs.	2.00
☐	62 Ed Olczyk, Winn.	.75
☐	63 Tomas Sandström, LosA.	.75
☐	64 Checklist	.75
☐	65 W. Gretzky / M. Richard	12.00
☐	66 Br. Hull / G. Lafleur	5.00
☐	67 B. Clarke / J. Kurri	3.00
☐	68 J. Béliveau / S. Yzerman	8.00
☐	69 S. Larmer / P. Stapleton	1.00
☐	70 T. Lindsay / L. Robitaille	3.00
☐	71 D. Harvey / L. Murphy	2.00
☐	72 D. Potvin / G. Suter	1.00

	Description	NRMT-MT
☐	73 H. Howell / B. Leetch	1.00
☐	74 P. Coffey / B. Gadsby	2.00
☐	75 J. Casey (G) / T. Sawchuk (G)	4.00
☐	76 J. Plante (G) / P. Roy (G)	8.00
☐	77 D. Savard / S. Savard	1.00
☐	78 B. Baun / D. Gilmour	1.00
☐	79 G. Carbonneau / Y. Cournoyer	1.00
☐	80 G. Perreault / L. Robinson	2.00
☐	81 R. Kelly / C. Simpson	1.00
☐	82 R. Gilbert / Bo. Smith	1.00
☐	83 S. Apps / P. Stastny	2.00
☐	84 V. Damphousse / B. Geoffrion	2.00
☐	85 M. Dionne / S. Smith	2.00
☐	86 K. Dineen / T. Horton	2.00
☐	87 M. Goulet / F. Mahovlich	2.00
☐	88 H. Richard / M. Richter	2.00
☐	Blackhawks	.75
☐	Bruins	.75
☐	Canadiens	.75
☐	Maple Leafs	.75
☐	Rangers	.75
☐	Red Wings	.75
☐	Stanley Cup	1.00

1991 - 92 MCDONALD'S - UPPER DECK

Imprint: 1991 The Upper Deck Co.
Complete Set (31 cards): 25.00

	McDonald's	All-Stars
☐	Mc-01 Cam Neely	1.00
☐	Mc-02 Rick Tocchet	.35
☐	Mc-03 Kevin Stevens	.35
☐	Mc-04 Mark Recchi	.35
☐	Mc-05 Joe Sakic	1.50
☐	Mc-06 Pat LaFontaine	.50
☐	Mc-07 Darren Turcotte	.35
☐	Mc-08 Patrick Roy	3.00
☐	Mc-09 Andy Moog	.35
☐	Mc-10 Raymond Bourque	1.00
☐	Mc-11 Paul Coffey	.50
☐	Mc-12 Brian Leetch	.50
☐	Mc-13 Brett Hull	1.00
☐	Mc-14 Luc Robitaille	.50
☐	Mc-15 Steve Larmer	.35
☐	Mc-16 Vincent Damphousse	.50
☐	Mc-17 Wayne Gretzky	4.00
☐	Mc-18 Theoren Fleury	.50
☐	Mc-19 Steve Yzerman	2.00
☐	Mc-20 Mike Vernon	.35
☐	Mc-21 Bill Ranford	.35
☐	Mc-22 Chris Chelios	.50
☐	Mc-23 Al MacInnis	.35
☐	Mc-24 Scott Stevens	.35
☐	Mc-25 Checklist	.35
	McDonald's	**Sticker**
☐	McH-1 Wayne Gretzky	5.00
☐	McH-2 Chris Chelios	1.00
☐	McH-3 Raymond Bourque	1.50
☐	McH-4 Brett Hull	1.00
☐	McH-5 Cam Neely	1.00
☐	McH-6 Patrick Roy	3.50

1991 - 92 O-PEE-CHEE / TOPPS

Promo cards were issued as a nine-card promo sheet along with your Bowman promo cards. The regular cards have two versions: the O-Pee-Chee (Canadian, Bilingual) issue and the Topps (American, English) issue.

Pricing for both issues is identical. The most expensive singles are Wayne Gretzky and John LeClair at $1.50-2.00. All other singles sell between 20¢ and $1.00

OPC Imprint: © 1991 O-Pee-Chee Co. Ltd.
Topps Imprint: © 1991 The Topps Company, Inc.
Complete Set (528 cards): 15.00

	Topps Promo	Promo
☐	Ed Belfour (G), Chic.	2.00
☐	Brett Hull, SLou.	2.00
☐	Pat LaFontaine, NYIs.	2.00
☐	Mario Lemieux, Pitt.	5.00
☐	Joe Sakic, Québ.	3.00

OPC / Topps	OPC / Topps
☐☐ 1 Guy Lafleur	☐☐ 2 Guy Lafleur
☐☐ 3 Guy Lafleur	☐☐ 4 Ed Belfour (G)
☐☐ 5 Ken Hodge	☐☐ 6 Rob Blake
☐☐ 7 Bobby Holik	☐☐ 8 S. Fedorov
☐☐ 9 Jaromir Jagr	☐☐ 10 Eric Weinrich
☐☐ 11 Mike Richter (G)	☐☐ 12 Mats Sundin
☐☐ 13 Mike Ricci	☐☐ 14 Eric Desjardins
☐☐ 15 Paul Ranheim	☐☐ 16 Joe Sakic
☐☐ 17 Curt Giles	☐☐ 18 Mike Foligno
☐☐ 19 Brad Marsh	☐☐ 20 Ed Belfour (G)
☐☐ 21 Steve Smith	☐☐ 22 Kirk Muller
☐☐ 23 Kelly Chase	☐☐ 24 J. McKenzie RC
☐☐ 25 Mick Vukota	☐☐ 26 T. Amonte RC
☐☐ 27 Danton Cole	☐☐ 28 Jay Mazur RC
☐☐ 29 Pete Peeters (G)	☐☐ 30 Petri Skriko
☐☐ 31 S. Duchesne	☐☐ 32 TC: Buffalo Sabres
☐☐ 33 Phil Bourque	☐☐ 34 Tim Bergland
☐☐ 35 Tim Cheveldae (G)	☐☐ 36 B. Armstrong RC
☐☐ 37 John McIntyre	☐☐ 38 D. Andreychuk
☐☐ 39 Curtis Leschyshyn	☐☐ 40 Jaromir Jagr
☐☐ 41 Craig Janney	☐☐ 42 Doug Brown
☐☐ 43 Ken Sabourin	☐☐ 44 TC: B. Bellows
☐☐ 45 F. Olausson	☐☐ 46 Mike Gartner
☐☐ 47 M. Fitzpatrick (G)	☐☐ 48 Joe Murphy
☐☐ 49 Doug Wilson	☐☐ 50 B. MacLellan
☐☐ 51 Bob Bassen	☐☐ 52 Robert Kron
☐☐ 53 Roger Johansson	☐☐ 54 Guy Carbonneau
☐☐ 55 R. Ramage	☐☐ 56 Bobby Holik
☐☐ 57 Alan May	☐☐ 58 Rick Meagher
☐☐ 59 Cliff Ronning	☐☐ 60 TC: Red Wings
☐☐ 61 Bob Kudelski	☐☐ 62 Wayne McBean
☐☐ 63 Craig MacTavish	☐☐ 64 Owen Nolan
☐☐ 65 Dale Hawerchuk	☐☐ 66 Raymond Bourque
☐☐ 67 Sean Burke (G)	☐☐ 68 Frantisek Musil
☐☐ 69 Joe Mullen	☐☐ 70 D. Berehowsky
☐☐ 71 Darren Turcotte	☐☐ 72 Randy Carlyle
☐☐ 73 Paul Cyr	☐☐ 74 Dave Gagner
☐☐ 75 Steve Larmer	☐☐ 76 Petr Svoboda
☐☐ 77 Keith Acton	☐☐ 78 Dmitri Khristich
☐☐ 79 Brad McCrimmon	☐☐ 80 Pat LaFontaine
☐☐ 81 Jeff Reese (G)	☐☐ 82 Mario Marois
☐☐ 83 Rob Brown	☐☐ 84 Grant Fuhr (G)
☐☐ 85 Carey Wilson	☐☐ 86 Garry Galley
☐☐ 87 T. Murray	☐☐ 88 Tony Granato
☐☐ 89 Gord Murphy	☐☐ 90 Brent Gilchrist
☐☐ 91 Mike Richter (G)	☐☐ 92 Eric Weinrich
☐☐ 93 Marc Bureau	☐☐ 94 Bob Errey
☐☐ 95 Dave McLlwain	☐☐ 96 TC: Nordiques
☐☐ 97 Clint Malarchuk (G)	☐☐ 98 Shawn Antoski
☐☐ 99 Bob Sweeney	☐☐ 100 S. Leach
☐☐ 101 Gary Nylund	☐☐ 102 Lucien DeBlois
☐☐ 103 TC: Norm Maciver	☐☐ 104 Jimmy Carson
☐☐ 105 Rod Langway	☐☐ 106 Jeremy Roenick
☐☐ 107 Mike Vernon (G)	☐☐ 108 Brian Leetch
☐☐ 109 Mark Hunter	☐☐ 110 Brian Bellows
☐☐ 111 Per-Erik Eklund	☐☐ 112 Rob Blake
☐☐ 113 Mike Hough	☐☐ 114 F. Pietrangelo (G)
☐☐ 115 Christian Ruuttu	☐☐ 116 B. Marchment RC
☐☐ 117 Garry Valk	☐☐ 118 Ken Daneyko
☐☐ 119 Russ Courtnall	☐☐ 120 Ron Wilson
☐☐ 121 Shayne Stevenson	☐☐ 122 Bill Berg RC
☐☐ 123 TC: L. Richardson	☐☐ 124 Glenn Anderson
☐☐ 125 Kevin Miller	☐☐ 126 C. Johansson
☐☐ 127 Jim Waite (G)	☐☐ 128 A. Pedersen
☐☐ 129 Brian Mullen	☐☐ 130 Ron Francis
☐☐ 131 Jergus Baca	☐☐ 132 Checklist 1
☐☐ 133 Tony Tanti	☐☐ 134 Wes Walz
☐☐ 135 Stéphan Lebeau	☐☐ 136 Ken Wregget (G)
☐☐ 137 Scott Arniel	☐☐ 138 Dave Taylor
☐☐ 139 Steven Finn	☐☐ 140 B. Shanahan
☐☐ 141 Petr Nedved	☐☐ 142 Chris Dahlquist
☐☐ 143 Rich Sutter	☐☐ 144 Joe Reekie
☐☐ 145 Peter Ing (G)	☐☐ 146 Ken Linseman
☐☐ 147 Dave Barr	☐☐ 148 Al Iafrate
☐☐ 149 Greg Gilbert	☐☐ 150 C. Ludwig
☐☐ 151 Gary Suter	☐☐ 152 Jan Erixon
☐☐ 153 Mario Lemieux	☐☐ 154 Mike Liut (G)
☐☐ 155 Uwe Krupp	☐☐ 156 Darin Kimble
☐☐ 157 Shayne Corson	☐☐ 158 TC: Winnipeg Jets
☐☐ 159 Stéphane Morin	☐☐ 160 Rick Tocchet
☐☐ 161 John Tonelli	☐☐ 162 Adrien Plavsic
☐☐ 163 Jason Miller	☐☐ 164 Tim Kerr
☐☐ 165 Brent Sutter	☐☐ 166 Michel Petit
☐☐ 167 Adam Graves	☐☐ 168 Jamie Macoun
☐☐ 169 Terry Yake	☐☐ 170 TC: Boston Bruins
☐☐ 171 A. Mogilny	☐☐ 172 Karl Dykhuis
☐☐ 173 T. Sandström	☐☐ 174 Bernie Nicholls
☐☐ 175 Viacheslav Fetisov	☐☐ 176 Andrew Cassels
☐☐ 177 Ulf Dahlen	☐☐ 178 Brian Hayward (G)
☐☐ 179 Doug Lidster	☐☐ 180 Dave Lowry
☐☐ 181 Ron Tugnutt (G)	☐☐ 182 Ed Olczyk
☐☐ 183 Paul Coffey	☐☐ 184 Shawn Burr
☐☐ 185 TC: Whalers	☐☐ 186 Mark Janssens
☐☐ 187 Mike Craig	☐☐ 188 Gary Leeman
☐☐ 189 Phil Sykes	☐☐ 190 Brett Hull
☐☐ 191 TC: Devils	☐☐ 192 Cam Neely
☐☐ 193 Petr Klima	☐☐ 194 Mike Ricci
☐☐ 195 Kelly Hrudey (G)	☐☐ 196 Mark Recchi
☐☐ 197 Mikael Andersson	☐☐ 198 Bob Probert
☐☐ 199 Craig Wolanin	☐☐ 200 S. Mellanby
☐☐ 201 HL:W. Gretzky	☐☐ 202 Laurie Boschman
☐☐ 203 Gino Odjick	☐☐ 204 Garth Butcher
☐☐ 205 Randy Wood	☐☐ 206 John Druce
☐☐ 207 Doug Bodger	☐☐ 208 Doug Gilmour
☐☐ 209 John LeClair RC	☐☐ 210 Steve Thomas
☐☐ 211 Kjell Samuelsson	☐☐ 212 Daniel Marois
☐☐ 213 Jiri Hrdina	☐☐ 214 Darrin Shannon
☐☐ 215 TC: Rangers	☐☐ 216 Robert McGill
☐☐ 217 Dirk Graham	☐☐ 218 Thomas Steen
☐☐ 219 Mats Sundin	☐☐ 220 Kevin Lowe
☐☐ 221 Kirk McLean (G)	☐☐ 222 Jeff Brown
☐☐ 223 Joe Nieuwendyk	☐☐ 224 LL: Wayne Gretzky
☐☐ 225 Marty McSorley	☐☐ 226 John Cullen
☐☐ 227 Brian Propp	☐☐ 228 Yves Racine
☐☐ 229 Dale Hunter	☐☐ 230 Dennis Vaske RC
☐☐ 231 Sylvain Turgeon	☐☐ 232 Ron Sutter
☐☐ 233 Chris Chelios	☐☐ 234 Brian Bradley
☐☐ 235 Scott Young	☐☐ 236 Mike Ramsey
☐☐ 237 Jon Casey (G)	☐☐ 238 Nevin Markwart
☐☐ 239 John MacLean	☐☐ 240 Brent Ashton
☐☐ 241 Tony Hrkac	☐☐ 242 TC: Steve Bozek
☐☐ 243 Jeff Norton	☐☐ 244 Martin Gelinas
☐☐ 245 Mike Ridley	☐☐ 246 Pat Jablonski (G)
☐☐ 247 TC: Mike Vernon	☐☐ 248 Paul Ysebaert
☐☐ 249 Sylvain Côté	☐☐ 250 M. Habscheid
☐☐ 251 Todd Elik	☐☐ 252 Mike McPhee
☐☐ 253 James Patrick	☐☐ 254 Murray Craven
☐☐ 255 Trent Yawney	☐☐ 256 Rob Cimetta
☐☐ 257 LL: W. Gretzky	☐☐ 258 AS: Wayne Gretzky
☐☐ 259 AS: Brett Hull	☐☐ 260 Luc Robitaille
☐☐ 261 AS: R. Bourque	☐☐ 262 AS: Al MacInnis
☐☐ 263 AS: E. Belfour (G)	☐☐ 264 AS: Checklist 2
☐☐ 265 AS: Adam Oates	☐☐ 266 AS: Cam Neely
☐☐ 267 AS: K. Stevens	☐☐ 268 AS: Chris Chelios
☐☐ 269 AS: Brian Leetch	☐☐ 270 AS: Patrick Roy (G)
☐☐ 271 LL: Ed Belfour (G)	☐☐ 272 Rob Zettler
☐☐ 273 Donald Audette	☐☐ 274 Teppo Numminen
☐☐ 275 Peter Stastny	☐☐ 276 David Christian
☐☐ 277 Larry Murphy	☐☐ 278 Johan Garpenlov
☐☐ 279 Tom Fitzgerald	☐☐ 280 Gerald Diduck
☐☐ 281 Gino Cavallini	☐☐ 282 Theoren Fleury
☐☐ 283 TC: Brian Benning	☐☐ 284 Jeff Beukeboom
☐☐ 285 Kevin Dineen	☐☐ 286 J. Cloutier (G)
☐☐ 287 Tom Chorske	☐☐ 288 LL: Ed Belfour
☐☐ 289 Ray Sheppard	☐☐ 290 Olaf Kolzig (G)
☐☐ 291 Terry Carkner	☐☐ 292 Benoît Hogue
☐☐ 293 Mike Peluso	☐☐ 294 Bruce Driver
☐☐ 295 Jari Kurri	☐☐ 296 P. Sidorkiewicz (G)
☐☐ 297 Scott Pearson	☐☐ 298 TC: Canadiens
☐☐ 299 V. Damphousse	☐☐ 300 John Carter
☐☐ 301 Geoff Smith	☐☐ 302 S. Kasper
☐☐ 303 Brett Hull	☐☐ 304 Ray Ferraro
☐☐ 305 Geoff Courtnall	☐☐ 306 David Shaw
☐☐ 307 Bob Essensa (G)	☐☐ 308 Mark Tinordi
☐☐ 309 Keith Primeau	☐☐ 310 Kevin Hatcher
☐☐ 311 Chris Nilan	☐☐ 312 Trevor Kidd (G)
☐☐ 313 D. Berthiaume (G)	☐☐ 314 Adam Creighton
☐☐ 315 E. Sanipass	☐☐ 316 Ken Baumgartner
☐☐ 317 Sheldon Kennedy	☐☐ 318 Dave Capuano
☐☐ 319 Don Sweeney	☐☐ 320 Gary Roberts
☐☐ 321 Wayne Gretzky	☐☐ 322 Fleury/ McSorley
☐☐ 323 Ulf Samuelsson	☐☐ 324 Mike Krushelnyski
☐☐ 325 Dean Evason	☐☐ 326 Pat Elynuik
☐☐ 327 Michal Pivonka	☐☐ 328 Paul Cavallini
☐☐ 329 TC: Flyers	☐☐ 330 Denis Savard
☐☐ 331 Paul Fenton	☐☐ 332 Jon Morris
☐☐ 333 Daren Puppa (G)	☐☐ 334 Doug Smail
☐☐ 335 Kelly Kisio	☐☐ 336 Michel Goulet
☐☐ 337 Mike Sillinger	☐☐ 338 Andy Moog (G)

□ □ 339 Paul Stanton □ □ 340 Greg Adams
□ □ 341 Doug Crossman □ □ 342 Kelly Miller
□ □ 343 Patrick Flatley □ □ 344 Zarley Zalapski
□ □ 345 Mark Osborne □ □ 346 Mark Messier
□ □ 347 TC: Adam Oates □ □ 348 Neil Wilkinson
□ □ 349 Brian Skrudland □ □ 350 Lyle Odelein
□ □ 351 Luke Richardson □ □ 352 Zdeno Ciger
□ □ 353 Vanbiesbrouck (G) □ □ 354 Franceschetti
□ □ 355 Alexei Gusarov □ □ 356 Bill Ranford (G)
□ □ 357 N. Lacombe □ □ 358 R. Burridge
□ □ 359 Brian Benning □ □ 360 Dave Hannan
□ □ 361 Todd Gill □ □ 362 Peter Bondra
□ □ 363 Mike Hartman □ □ 364 Trevor Linden
□ □ 365 John Ogrodnick □ □ 366 Steve Konroyd
□ □ 367 Mike Modano □ □ 368 Glenn Healy (G)
□ □ 369 Stéphane Richer □ □ 370 V. Riendeau (G)
□ □ 371 Randy Moller □ □ 372 TC: Tom Barrasso
□ □ 373 Murray Baron □ □ 374 Troy Crowder
□ □ 375 R. Tabaracci (G) □ □ 376 Brent Fedyk
□ □ 377 Randy Velischek □ □ 378 Esa Tikkanen
□ □ 379 Richard Pilon □ □ 380 Jeff Lazaro RC
□ □ 381 David Ellett □ □ 382 Jeff Hackett (G)
□ □ 383 S. Matteau □ □ 384 TC: Dave Tippett
□ □ 385 Wayne Presley □ □ 386 Grant Ledyard
□ □ 387 Kip Miller □ □ 388 Dean Kennedy
□ □ 389 H. McDonough □ □ 390 Anatoli Semenov
□ □ 391 Daryl Reaugh (G) □ □ 392 Mathieu Schneider
□ □ 393 Dan Quinn □ □ 394 Claude Lemieux
□ □ 395 Phil Housley □ □ 396 Checklist 3
□ □ 397 Steven Bozek □ □ 398 Bobby Smith
□ □ 399 Mark Pederson □ □ 400 Kevin Todd
□ □ 401 Sergei Fedorov □ □ 402 Tom Barrasso (G)
□ □ 403 HL: Brett Hull □ □ 404 Bob Carpenter
□ □ 405 Luc Robitaille □ □ 406 Mark Hardy
□ □ 407 Neil Sheehy □ □ 408 Mike McNeill
□ □ 409 Dave Manson □ □ 410 Mike Tomlak
□ □ 411 Robert Reichel □ □ 412 New York Islanders
□ □ 413 Patrick Roy (G) □ □ 414 S. Van Allen RC
□ □ 415 Dale Kushner □ □ 416 Pierre Turgeon
□ □ 417 Curtis Joseph (G) □ □ 418 Randy Gilhen
□ □ 419 Jyrki Lumme □ □ 420 Neal Broten
□ □ 421 Kevin Stevens □ □ 422 Chris Terreri (G)
□ □ 423 David Reid □ □ 424 Steve Yzerman
□ □ 425 LL: Ed Belfour □ □ 426 Jim Johnson
□ □ 427 Joey Kocur □ □ 428 Joel Otto
□ □ 429 Dino Ciccarelli □ □ 430 TC: Blackhawks
□ □ 431 Claude Lapointe □ □ 432 Chris Joseph
□ □ 433 Gaetan Duchesne □ □ 434 Mike Keane
□ □ 435 David Chyzowski □ □ 436 Glen Featherstone
□ □ 437 Jim Paek RC □ □ 438 Doug Evans
□ □ 439 A. Kasatonov □ □ 440 Ken Hodge
□ □ 441 Dave Snuggerud □ □ 442 Brad Shaw
□ □ 443 Gerard Gallant □ □ 444 Jiri Latal
□ □ 445 Peter Zezel □ □ 446 Troy Gamble (G)
□ □ 447 Craig Coxe □ □ 448 Adam Oates
□ □ 449 Todd Krygier □ □ 450 A. Racicot (G) RC
□ □ 451 Patrik Sundstrom □ □ 452 Glen Wesley
□ □ 453 Jocelyn Lemieux □ □ 454 Rick Zombo
□ □ 455 Derek King □ □ 456 J.J. Daigneault
□ □ 457 Rick Vaive □ □ 458 Larry Robinson
□ □ 459 Rick Wamsley (G) □ □ 460 Craig Simpson
□ □ 461 C. Millen RC □ □ 462 Sergio Momesso
□ □ 463 Paul MacDermid □ □ 464 Wendel Clark
□ □ 465 M. Tatarinov □ □ 466 Mark Howe
□ □ 467 Jay Miller □ □ 468 Grant Jennings
□ □ 469 Paul Gillis □ □ 470 Ron Hextall (G)
□ □ 471 A. Godynyuk RC □ □ 472 Bryan Trottier
□ □ 473 K. Haller RC □ □ 474 Troy Mallette
□ □ 475 James Wiemer □ □ 476 David Maley
□ □ 477 Moe Mantha □ □ 478 Brad Jones RC
□ □ 479 Craig Muni □ □ 480 Igor Larionov
□ □ 481 Scott Stevens □ □ 482 Sergei Makarov
□ □ 483 Mike Lalor □ □ 484 Tony McKegney
□ □ 485 Perry Berezan □ □ 486 Derrick Smith
□ □ 487 Jim Hrivnak (G) □ □ 488 David Volek
□ □ 489 Sylvain Lefebvre □ □ 490 Rod Brind'Amour
□ □ 491 Al MacInnis □ □ 492 Jamie Leach
□ □ 493 Robert Dirk □ □ 494 Gord Roberts
□ □ 495 Mike Hudson □ □ 496 François Breault
□ □ 497 R. Lemelin (G) □ □ 498 Kris King
□ □ 499 Pat Verbeek □ □ 500 Bryan Fogarty
□ □ 501 P. Anderson RC □ □ 502 Joe Cirella
□ □ 503 Mikko Makela □ □ 504 HL: Paul Coffey
□ □ 505 D. Beaupré (G) □ □ 506 Brian Glynn
□ □ 507 Dave Poulin □ □ 508 Steve Chiasson
□ □ 509 M. O'Connor RC □ □ 510 Ilkka Sinisalo
□ □ 511 Nick Kypreos □ □ 512 Doug Houda
□ □ 513 V. Kamensky □ □ 514 Sergei Nemchinov
□ □ 515 Dimitri Mironov □ □ 516 AW: Brett Hull
□ □ 517 AW: R. Bourque □ □ 518 AW: Ed Belfour
□ □ 519 AW: Ed Belfour □ □ 520 AW: W. Gretzky
□ □ 521 AW: Dirk Graham □ □ 522 AW: W. Gretzky
□ □ 523 AW: M. Lemieux □ □ 524 HL: Gretzky 700
□ □ 525 Sharks Roster □ □ 526 Lightning
□ □ 527 Ottawa Senators □ □ 528 Checklist 4

OPC - SAN JOSE / SOVIET UNION

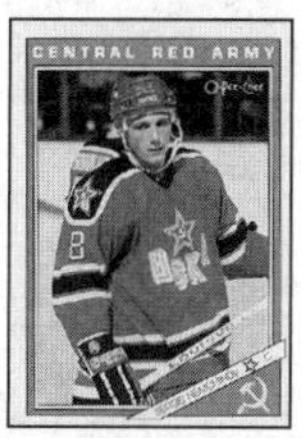

The most expensive singles are Alexei Zhamnov ($1.50) and Sergei Zubov at ($1). All other singles sell between 20¢ and $1.00.

Insert Set (66 cards): 8.00

O-Pee-Chee **O-Pee-Chee**
□ 1S Link Gaetz □ 2S Bengt Gustafsson
□ 3S Dan Keczmer RC □ 4S Dean Kolstad RC
□ 5S Peter Lappin □ 6S Jeff Madill RC
□ 7S Michael McHugh □ 8S Jarmo Myllys (G)
□ 9S Doug Zmolek RC □ 10S Sharks Checklist
□ 11R V. Brezgunov RC □ 12R V. Butsayev RC
□ 13R Ilya Byakin □ 14R Igor Chibirev RC
□ 15R Viktor Gordijuk RC □ 16R Yuri Khmylev RC
□ 17R Pavel Kostichkin □ 18R A. Kovalenko RC
□ 19R Igor Kravchuk RC □ 20R Igor Malykhin
□ 21R Igor Maslennikov □ 22R M. Mikhailovsky
□ 23R Dimitri Mironov □ 24R S. Nemchinov
□ 25R Alex Prokopjev RC □ 26R Igor Stelnov RC
□ 27R S. Vostrikov RC □ 28R Sergei Zubov RC
□ 29R Mikhailovsky (G) □ 30R Zubov/ Mikhailovsky
□ 31R A. Andreivsky RC □ 32R Igor Dorofeyev RC
□ 33R A. Galchenyuk RC □ 34R Roman Ilyin RC
□ 35R A. Karpovtsev RC □ 36R R. Khaidarov RC
□ 37R Igor Korolev RC □ 38R A. Kovalyov RC
□ 39R Yuri Leonov RC □ 40R A. Lomakin
□ 41R E. Popikhin RC □ 42R A. Semak RC
□ 43R Shtalenkov (G) RC □ 44R S. Sorokin RC
□ 45R A. Treflov (G) RC □ 46R Ravil Yakubov RC
□ 47R A. Yudin RC □ 48R A. Zhamnov RC
□ 49R A. Basalgin RC □ 50R L. Berdichevsky RC
□ 51R Kapkaikin (G) RC □ 52R K. Kurashov
□ 53R A. Kvartalnov RC □ 54R Albert Malgin RC
□ 55R Nikolai Maslov RC □ 56R Anatoli Naida RC
□ 57R Roman Oksiuta RC □ 58R Sergei Selyanin RC
□ 59R Valeri Shiryev □ 60R A. Smirnov
□ 61R Leonid Trukhno RC □ 62R Igor Ulanov RC
□ 63R A. Yakovenko RC □ 64R Oleg Yashin RC
□ 65R V. Zelepukin RC □ 66R Checklist

TOPPS - SCORING LEADERS

The most expensive singles are Wayne Gretzky at $2-3 and Steve Yzerman at $1.00-1.50. All other singles sell between 20¢ and $1.00.

Imprint: © 1991 THE TOPPS COMPANY, INC.

Insert Set (21 cards): 8.00

Topps **Topps**
□ 1 Pat Verbeek □ 2 Dale Hawerchuk
□ 3 Steve Yzerman □ 4 Brian Leetch
□ 5 Mark Recchi □ 6 Esa Tikkanen
□ 7 Dave Gagner □ 8 Joe Sakic
□ 9 V. Damphousse □ 10 Wayne Gretzky
□ 11 Phil Housley □ 12 Pat LaFontaine
□ 13 Rick Tocchet □ 14 Theoren Fleury
□ 15 John MacLean □ 16 Kevin Hatcher
□ 17 Trevor Linden □ 18 Russ Courtnall
□ 19 Raymond Bourque □ 20 Brett Hull
□ 21 Steve Larmer

1991 - 92 O-PEE-CHEE PREMIER

The most expensive singles are Wayne Gretzky and John LeClair at $1.50-2.00. All other singles sell between 20¢ and $1.00. The error Vladimir Konstantinov card (#118) sells at $15.00.

Imprint: © 1992 O-PEE-CHEE CO. LTD.

Complete Set (198 cards): 12.00

OPC Premier **OPC Premier**
□ 1 Dale Hawerchuk □ 2 Ray Sheppard
□ 3 Wayne Gretzky □ 4 John MacLean
□ 5 Pat Verbeek □ 6 Doug Wilson
□ 7 Adam Oates □ 8 Robert McGill
□ 9 Mike Vernon (G) □ 10 Glenn Anderson
□ 11 Tony Amonte RC □ 12 Stephen Leach
□ 13 Steve Duchesne □ 14 Patrick Roy (G)
□ 15 Jarmo Myllys (G) □ 16 Yanic Dupré RC
□ 17 Chris Chelios □ 18 Bill Ranford (G)
□ 19 Ed Belfour (G) □ 20 Michel Picard RC
□ 21 Rob Zettler □ 22 Kevin Todd RC
□ 23 Mike Ricci □ 24 Jaromir Jagr
□ 25 Sergei Nemchinov □ 26 Kevin Stevens
□ 27 Dan Quinn □ 28 Adam Graves
□ 29 P. Jablonski (G) RC □ 30 Scott Mellanby
□ 31 Tomas Forslund □ 32 D. Weight RC
□ 33 Peter Ing (G) □ 34 Luc Robitaille
□ 35 Scott Niedermayer □ 36 Dean Evason
□ 37 John Tonelli □ 38 Ron Hextall (G)
□ 39 Troy Mallette □ 40 Tony Hrkac
□ 41 Ken Hodge □ 42 Kip Miller
□ 43 Randy Burridge □ 44 Rob Blake
□ 45 Sergei Makarov □ 46 Luke Richardson
□ 47 Craig Berube □ 48 Joe Nieuwendyk
□ 49 Brett Hull □ 50 Phil Housley
□ 51 Mark Messier □ 52 Jeremy Roenick
□ 53 David Christian □ 54 Dave Barr
□ 55 Sergio Momesso □ 56 Pat Falloon
□ 57 Brian Leetch □ 58 Russ Courtnall
□ 59 Pierre Turgeon □ 60 Steve Larmer
□ 61 Petr Klima □ 62 Mikhail Tatarinov
□ 63 Rick Tocchet □ 64 Pat LaFontaine
□ 65 Rob Pearson RC □ 66 Glen Featherstone
□ 67 Pavel Bure □ 68 Sergei Fedorov
□ 69 Kelly Kisio □ 70 Joe Sakic
□ 71 Denis Savard □ 72 Andrew Cassels
□ 73 Steve Yzerman □ 74 Todd Elik
□ 75 Troy Murray □ 76 Rob Ramage
□ 77 Trevor Linden □ 78 Mike Richter (G)
□ 79 Paul Coffey □ 80 Craig Ludwig
□ 81 Al MacInnis □ 82 Tomas Sandström
□ 83 Tim Kerr □ 84 Scott Stevens
□ 85 Steve Kasper □ 86 Kirk Muller
□ 87 Pat MacLeod RC □ 88 Kevin Hatcher
□ 89 Wayne Presley □ 90 Darryl Sydor
□ 91 Tom Chorske □ 92 Theoren Fleury
□ 93 Craig Janney □ 94 Rod Brind'Amour
□ 95 Ron Sutter □ 96 M. DelGuidice (G) RC
□ 97 Rollie Melanson (G) □ 98 Tom Kurvers
□ 99 B. Marchment RC □ 100 Grant Fuhr (G)
□ 101 Geoff Courtnall □ 102 Joel Otto
□ 103 Tom Barrasso (G) □ 104 V. Damphousse
□ 105 John LeClair RC □ 106 Gary Leeman
□ 107 Cam Neely □ 108 Jeff Hackett (G)
□ 109 Stu Barnes □ 110 Neil Wilkinson
□ 111 Jari Kurri □ 112 Jon Casey (G)
□ 113 Stéphane Richer □ 114 Mario Lemieux
□ 115 Brad Jones RC □ 116 Wendel Clark
□ 117 N. Lidström RC □ 118 Vlad. Konstantinov
□ 118 Vladimir Konstantinov, Error (b/ Lidström)
□ 119 Raymond Bourque □ 120 Ron Francis
□ 121 Esa Tikkanen □ 122 Randy Hillier
□ 123 Randy Gilhen □ 124 Barry Pederson
□ 125 Charlie Huddy □ 126 Gary Roberts
□ 127 John Cullen □ 128 Dave Gagner
□ 129 Bob Kudelski □ 130 Brendan Shanahan
□ 131 Dirk Graham □ 132 Checklist 1 (1 to 99)
□ 133 Andy Moog (G) □ 134 06: Gary Leeman
□ 135 06: Steve Larmer □ 136 Steve Smith
□ 137 Dave Manson □ 138 Nelson Emerson
□ 139 06: Doug Weight □ 140 Uwe Krupp
□ 141 06: Peter Douris □ 142 06: Steve Yzerman
□ 143 Derian Hatcher □ 144 06: V. Ruzicka
□ 145 06: Kirk Muller □ 146 Darrin Shannon
□ 147 06: Mike Gartner □ 148 06: Bob Carpenter
□ 149 J. Beranek RC □ 150 06: Chris Chelios
□ 151 06: Bob Rouse □ 152 06: G. Carbonneau
□ 153 Joe Mullen □ 154 06: Ken Hodge
□ 155 06: V. Konstantinov □ 156 Brent Sutter
□ 157 06: Eric Desjardins □ 158 Kirk McLean (G)
□ 159 06: John Tonelli □ 160 06: Rob Cimetta
□ 161 Shayne Corson □ 162 R. Romaniuk RC
□ 163 06: Nicklas Lidström □ 164 Mike Gartner
□ 165 Curtis Joseph (G) □ 166 Brian Mullen
□ 167 Jimmy Carson □ 168 06: Petr Svoboda
□ 169 Troy Crowder □ 170 06: Patrick Roy (G)
□ 171 Adam Creighton □ 172 06: James Patrick
□ 173 06: Sergei Fedorov □ 174 06: Jeremy Roenick
□ 175 06: Cheveldae (G) □ 176 Dimitri Khristich
□ 177 06: Wendel Clark □ 178 Andrei Lomakin
□ 179 Benoît Hogue □ 180 06: David Ellett
□ 181 06: M. Schneider □ 182 Kay Whitmore (G)
□ 183 06: Brian Leetch □ 184 06: S. Turgeon
□ 185 06: Brian Bradley □ 186 06: John LeClair
□ 187 Paul Fenton □ 188 06: Alain Côté
□ 189 06: Krushelnyski □ 190 Brian Bradley
□ 191 06: Grant Fuhr (G) □ 192 06: R. Bourque
□ 193 Owen Nolan □ 194 06: Russ Courtnall
□ 195 Steve Thomas □ 196 Ed Olczyk
□ 197 Chris Terreri (G) □ 198 Checklist 2

1991 - 92 PANINI STICKERS

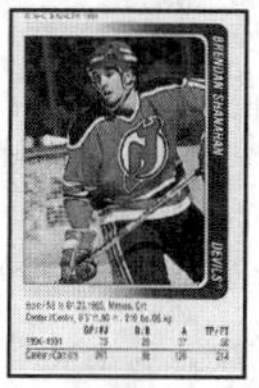

The most expensive singles are Wayne Gretzky at $2 and Mario Lemieux, Patrick Roy and Jaromir Jagr each between $1.00-1.50. All other singles sell between 20¢ and $1.00.

One of four different wrappers were available: Wayne Gretzky/ Al MacInnis, Mario Lemieux/ Steve Yzerman, Ray Bourque/ Mark Recchi and Brett Hull/ Patrick Roy.

Sticker Size: 1 13/16" x 2 7/8"

Complete Set (344 stickers): 35.00

Album: 5.00

Panini **Panini**
□ 1 NHL Logo □ 2 NHLPA Logo
□ 3 NHL 75th Ann. Logo □ 4 NHL 75th Ann. Logo
□ 5 Campbell Conference □ 6 Wales Conference
□ 7 Stanley Cup Logo □ 8 Steve Larmer
□ 9 Ed Belfour (G) □ 10 Chris Chelios
□ 11 Michel Goulet □ 12 Jeremy Roenick
□ 13 Adam Creighton □ 14 Steve Thomas
□ 15 Dave Manson □ 16 Dirk Graham
□ 17 Troy Murray □ 18 Doug Wilson
□ 19 Wayne Presley □ 20 Jocelyn Lemieux
□ 21 Keith Brown □ 22 Curtis Joseph (G)
□ 23 Jeff Brown □ 24 Gino Cavallini
□ 25 Brett Hull □ 26 Scott Stevens
□ 27 Dan Quinn □ 28 Garth Butcher
□ 29 Bob Bassen □ 30 Rod Brind'Amour
□ 31 Adam Oates □ 32 Dave Lowry
□ 33 Rich Sutter □ 34 Ron Wilson
□ 35 Paul Cavallini □ 36 Trevor Linden
□ 37 Troy Gamble (G) □ 38 Geoff Courtnall
□ 39 Greg Adams □ 40 Doug Lidster
□ 41 Dave Capuano □ 42 Igor Larionov
□ 43 Tom Kurvers □ 44 Sergio Momesso
□ 45 Kirk McLean (G) □ 46 Cliff Ronning
□ 47 Robert Kron □ 48 Steve Bozek
□ 49 Petr Nedved □ 50 Al MacInnis
□ 51 Theoren Fleury □ 52 Gary Roberts
□ 53 Joe Nieuwendyk □ 54 Paul Ranheim
□ 55 Mike Vernon (G) □ 56 Carey Wilson
□ 57 Gary Suter □ 58 Sergei Makarov
□ 59 Doug Gilmour □ 60 Joel Otto
□ 61 Jamie Macoun □ 62 Stéphane Matteau
□ 63 Robert Reichel □ 64 Ed Olczyk
□ 65 Phil Housley □ 66 Pat Elynuik
□ 67 Fredrik Olausson □ 68 Thomas Steen
□ 69 Paul MacDermid □ 70 Brent Ashton
□ 71 Teppo Numminen □ 72 Danton Cole
□ 73 Dave McLlwain □ 74 Scott Arniel
□ 75 Bob Essensa (G) □ 76 Randy Carlyle
□ 77 Mark Osborne □ 78 Wayne Gretzky
□ 79 Tomas Sandström □ 80 Steve Duchesne
□ 81 Kelly Hrudey (G) □ 82 Larry Robinson
□ 83 Tony Granato □ 84 Marty McSorley
□ 85 Todd Elik □ 86 Rob Blake
□ 87 Bob Kudelski □ 88 Steve Kasper
□ 89 Dave Taylor □ 90 John Tonelli
□ 91 Luc Robitaille □ 92 V. Damphousse
□ 93 Brian Bradley □ 94 Dave Ellett
□ 95 Daniel Marois □ 96 Rob Ramage
□ 97 Mike Krushelnyski □ 98 Michel Petit
□ 99 Peter Ing (G) □ 100 Lucien DeBlois
□ 101 Bob Rouse □ 102 Wendel Clark
□ 103 Peter Zezel □ 104 David Reid
□ 105 Aaron Broten □ 106 Brian Hayward (G)
□ 107 Neal Broten □ 108 Brian Bellows
□ 109 Mark Tinordi □ 110 Ulf Dahlen
□ 111 Doug Smail □ 112 Dave Gagner
□ 113 Bobby Smith □ 114 Brian Glynn
□ 115 Brian Propp □ 116 Mike Modano
□ 117 Gaetan Duchesne □ 118 Jon Casey (G)
□ 119 Basil McRae □ 120 Glenn Anderson
□ 121 Steve Smith □ 122 Adam Graves
□ 123 Esa Tikkanen □ 124 Mark Messier
□ 125 Bill Ranford (G) □ 126 Petr Klima
□ 127 Anatoli Semenov □ 128 Martin Gelinas
□ 129 Charlie Huddy □ 130 Craig Simpson
□ 131 Kevin Lowe □ 132 Craig MacTavish
□ 133 Craig Muni □ 134 Steve Yzerman
□ 135 Shawn Burr □ 136 Tim Cheveldae (G)
□ 137 Rick Zombo □ 138 Marc Habscheid
□ 139 Jimmy Carson □ 140 Brent Fedyk
□ 141 Yves Racine □ 142 Gerard Gallant
□ 143 Steve Chiasson □ 144 Johan Garpenlov
□ 145 Sergei Fedorov □ 146 Bob Probert
□ 147 Rick Green □ 148 Blackhawks
□ 149 Detroit Red Wings □ 150 North Stars
□ 151 St. Louis Blues □ 152 Toronto Maple Leafs
□ 153 Calgary Flames □ 154 Edmonton Oilers
□ 155 Los Angeles Kings □ 156 San Jose Sharks
□ 157 Vancouver Canucks □ 158 Winnipeg Jets
□ 159 Boston Bruins □ 160 Buffalo Sabres
□ 161 Hartford Whalers □ 162 Montréal Canadiens
□ 163 Québec Nordiques □ 164 New Jersey Devils
□ 165 New York Islanders □ 166 New York Rangers
□ 167 Philadelphia Flyers □ 168 Pittsburgh Penguins
□ 169 Capitals □ 170 Craig Janney
□ 171 Ray Bourque □ 172 R. Lemelin (G)
□ 173 Dave Christian □ 174 Randy Burridge
□ 175 Garry Galley □ 176 Cam Neely
□ 177 Bob Sweeney □ 178 Ken Hodge
□ 179 Andy Moog (G) □ 180 Don Sweeney
□ 181 Bob Carpenter □ 182 Glen Wesley
□ 183 Chris Nilan □ 184 Patrick Roy (G)
□ 185 Petr Svoboda □ 186 Russ Courtnall
□ 187 Denis Savard □ 188 Mike McPhee
□ 189 Eric Desjardins □ 190 Mike Keane
□ 191 Stéphan Lebeau □ 192 J.J. Daigneault
□ 193 Stéphane Richer □ 194 Brian Skrudland
□ 195 Mathieu Schneider □ 196 Shayne Corson
□ 197 Guy Carbonneau □ 198 Kevin Hatcher
□ 199 Mike Ridley □ 200 John Druce
□ 201 Don Beaupré (G) □ 202 Kelly Miller
□ 203 Dale Hunter □ 204 Nick Kypreos
□ 205 Calle Johansson □ 206 Michal Pivonka
□ 207 Dino Ciccarelli □ 208 Al Iafrate
□ 209 Rod Langway □ 210 Mikhail Tatarinov
□ 211 Stephen Leach □ 212 Sean Burke (G)
□ 213 John MacLean □ 214 Lee Norwood
□ 215 Laurie Boschman □ 216 Alexei Kasatonov
□ 217 Patrik Sundstrom □ 218 Ken Daneyko
□ 219 Kirk Muller □ 220 Peter Stastny
□ 221 Chris Terreri (G) □ 222 Brendan Shanahan
□ 223 Eric Weinrich □ 224 Claude Lemieux
□ 225 Bruce Driver □ 226 Tim Kerr
□ 227 Ron Hextall (G) □ 228 Per-Erik Eklund
□ 229 Rick Tocchet □ 230 Gord Murphy
□ 231 Mike Ricci □ 232 Derrick Smith
□ 233 Ron Sutter □ 234 Murray Craven
□ 235 Terry Carkner □ 236 Ken Wregget (G)
□ 237 Keith Acton □ 238 Scott Mellanby
□ 239 Kjell Samuelsson □ 240 Jeff Hackett (G)
□ 241 David Volek □ 242 Craig Ludwig
□ 243 Pat LaFontaine □ 244 Randy Wood
□ 245 Patrick Flatley □ 246 Brent Sutter
□ 247 Derek King □ 248 Jeff Norton
□ 249 Glenn Healy (G) □ 250 Ray Ferraro
□ 251 Gary Nylund □ 252 Joe Reekie
□ 253 David Chyzowski □ 254 Mike Hough
□ 255 Mats Sundin □ 256 Curtis Leschyshyn
□ 257 Joe Sakic □ 258 S. Fiset (G)
□ 259 Bryan Fogarty □ 260 Alexei Gusarov
□ 261 Steven Finn □ 262 Everett Sanipass
□ 263 Stéphane Morin □ 264 Craig Wolanin
□ 265 Randy Velischek □ 266 Owen Nolan
□ 267 Ron Tugnutt (G) □ 268 Mario Lemieux
□ 269 Kevin Stevens □ 270 Larry Murphy
□ 271 Tom Barrasso (G) □ 272 Phil Bourque
□ 273 Scott Young □ 274 Paul Stanton
□ 275 Jaromir Jagr □ 276 Paul Coffey
□ 277 Ulf Samuelsson □ 278 Joe Mullen
□ 279 Bob Errey □ 280 Mark Recchi
□ 281 Ron Francis □ 282 Vanbiesbrouck (G)
□ 283 Jan Erixon □ 284 Brian Leetch
□ 285 Darren Turcotte □ 286 Ray Sheppard
□ 287 James Patrick □ 288 Bernie Nicholls
□ 289 Brian Mullen □ 290 Mike Richter (G)
□ 291 Kelly Kisio □ 292 Mike Gartner
□ 293 John Ogrodnick □ 294 David Shaw

□ 295 Troy Mallette
□ 296 Dale Hawerchuk
□ 297 Rick Vaive
□ 298 Daren Puppa (G)
□ 299 Mike Ramsey
□ 300 Benoît Hogue
□ 301 C. Malarchuk (G)
□ 302 Mikko Makelä
□ 303 Pierre Turgeon
□ 304 Alexander Mogilny
□ 305 Uwe Krupp
□ 306 Christian Ruuttu
□ 307 Doug Bodger
□ 308 Dave Snuggerud
□ 309 Dave Andreychuk
□ 310 P. Sidorkiewicz (G)
□ 311 Brad Shaw
□ 312 Dean Evason
□ 313 Pat Verbeek
□ 314 John Cullen
□ 315 Rob Brown
□ 316 Bobby Holik
□ 317 Todd Krygier
□ 318 Adam Burt
□ 319 Mike Tomlak
□ 320 R. Cunneyworth
□ 321 Paul Cyr
□ 322 Zarley Zalapski
□ 323 Kevin Dineen
□ 324 AS: Luc Robitaille
□ 325 AS: Brett Hull
□ 326 All-Star Game Logo
□ 327 AS: W. Gretzky
□ 328 AS: M. Vernon (G)
□ 329 AS: Chris Chelios
□ 330 AS: Al MacInnis
□ 331 AS: Rick Tocchet
□ 332 AS: Cam Neely
□ 333 AS: Patrick Roy (G)
□ 334 AS: Joe Sakic
□ 335 AS: Ray Bourque
□ 336 AS: Paul Coffey
□ 337 Ed Belfour (G)
□ 338 Mike Ricci
□ 339 Rob Blake
□ 340 Sergei Fedorov
□ 341 Ken Hodge
□ 342 Bobby Holik
□ 343 Robert Reichel
□ 344 Jaromir Jagr

1991 - 92 PARKHURST

The most expensive singles are Wayne Gretzky at $2 and Patrick Roy, Mario Lemieux and Jaromir Jagr at $1.00-1.50. The most expensive rookie cards are John LeClair at $3, Dominik Hasek at $5-7 and Keith Tkachuk at $4. All other singles (1-450) sell between 20¢ and $1.00.

These cards have two versions: an English issue and a French issue. Only cards 451-475 do not come in a French version. Both English and French cards sell at the same price.

Imprint: Pro Set Inc.

Complete Set (450 cards):	**20.00**
Final Update (451-475):	**185.00**
Parkhurst	**Promo**
□ Doug Gilmour Promo	6.00
□ Robert Reichel Promo	3.00
Parkhurst	**PH**

□□ **1 Matt DelGuidice, Bost. RC [Rookie] .40**
□□ 2 Ken (Jr.) Hodge, Bost. .20
□□ 3 Vladimir Ruzicka, Bost. [Error: Ruzika] .20
□□ 4 Craig Janney, Bost. .20
□□ 5 Glen Wesley, Bost. .20
□□ 6 Stephen Leach, Bost. .20
□□ 7 Garry Galley, Bost. .20
□□ 8 Andy Moog, Bost. .20
□□ 9 Raymond Bourque, Bost. .50
□□ 10 Brad May, Buff. [Rookie] .20
□□ 11 Donald Audette, Buff. [Rookie] .20
□□ 12 Alexander Mogilny, Buff. .20
□□ 13 Randy Wood, Buff. .20
□□ 14 Daren Puppa, Buff. .20
□□ 15 Doug Bodger, Buff. .20
□□ 16 Pat LaFontaine, Buff. .20
□□ 17 Dave Andreychuk, Buff. .20
□□ 18 Dale Hawerchuk, Buff. .20
□□ 19 Mike Ramsey, Buff. .20
□□ **20 Tomas Forslund, Calg. RC [Rookie] .40**
□□ 21 Robert Reichel, Calg. .20
□□ 22 Theoren Fleury, Calg. .20
□□ 23 Joe Nieuwendyk, Calg. .20
□□ 24 Gary Roberts, Calg. .20
□□ 25 Gary Suter, Calg. .20
□□ 26 Doug Gilmour, Calg. .20
□□ 27 Mike Vernon, Calg. .20
□□ 28 Al MacInnis, Calg. .20
□□ 29 Jeremy Roenick, Chic. .20
□□ 30 Ed Belfour, Chic. .50
□□ 31 J. Steve Smith, Chic. .20
□□ 32 Chris Chelios, Chic. .20
□□ 33 Dirk Graham, Chic. .20
□□ 34 Steve Larmer, Chic. .20
□□ 35 Brent Sutter, Chic. .20
□□ 36 Michel Goulet, Chic. .20
□□ **37 Lidström, Detr. RC [Rookie] [Niklas] 1.50**
□□ 38 Sergei Fedorov, Detr. .50
□□ 39 Tim Cheveldae, Detr. .20
□□ 40 Kevin Miller, Detr. .20
□□ 41 Ray Sheppard, Detr. .20
□□ 42 Paul Ysebaert, Detr. .20
□□ 43 Jimmy Carson, Detr. .20
□□ 44 Steve Yzerman, Detr. 1.00
□□ 45 Shawn Burr, Detr. .20
□□ **46 Vladimir Konstantinov, Detr. RC .50**
□□ **47 Josef Beranek, Edmo. RC [Rookie] .40**
□□ 48 Vincent Damphousse, Edmo. .20
□□ 49 Dave Manson, Edmo. .20
□□ 50 Scott Mellanby, Edmo. .20
□□ 51 Kevin Lowe, Edmo. .20
□□ 52 Joe Murphy, Edmo. .20
□□ 53 Bill Ranford, Edmo. .20
□□ 54 Craig Simpson, Edmo. .20
□□ 55 Esa Tikkanen, Edmo. .20
□□ **56 Michel Picard, Hart. RC [Rookie] .40**
□□ **57 Geoff Sanderson, Hart. RC [Rookie] .50**
□□ 58 Kay Whitmore, Hart. .20
□□ 59 John Cullen, Hart. .20
□□ 60 Rob (Jr.) Brown, Hart. .20
□□ 61 Zarley Zalapski, Hart. .20
□□ 62 Brad Shaw, Hart. .20
□□ 63 Mikael Andersson, Hart. .20
□□ 64 Pat Verbeek, Hart. .20
□□ **65 Peter Ahola, LosA. RC [Rookie] .40**
□□ 66 Tony Granato, LosA. .20
□□ 67 Dave Taylor, LosA. .20
□□ 68 Luc Robitaille, LosA. .20
□□ 69 Marty McSorley, LosA. .20
□□ 70 Tomas Sandström, LosA. .20
□□ 71 Kelly Hrudey, LosA. .20
□□ 72 Jari Kurri, LosA. .50
□□ 73 Wayne Gretzky, LosA. 2.00
□□ 74 Larry Robinson, LosA. .20
□□ 75 Derian Hatcher, Minn. [Rookie] .20
□□ 76 Ulf Dahlén, Minn. .20
□□ 77 Jon Casey, Minn. .20
□□ 78 Dave Gagner, Minn. .20
□□ 79 Brian Bellows, Minn. .20
□□ 80 Neal Broten, Minn. .20
□□ 81 Mike Modano, Minn. .50
□□ 82 Brian Propp, Minn. .20
□□ 83 Bobby Smith, Minn. .20
□□ **84 John LeClair, Mont. RC [Rookie] 2.00**
□□ 85 Eric Desjardins, Mont. .20
□□ 86 Shayne Corson, Mont. .20
□□ 87 Stéphan Lebeau, Mont. .20
□□ 88 Mathieu Schneider, Mont. .20
□□ 89 Kirk Muller, Mont. .20
□□ 90 Patrick Roy, Mont. 1.50
□□ 91 Sylvain Turgeon, Mont. .20
□□ 92 Guy Carbonneau, Mont. .20
□□ 93 Denis Savard, Mont. .20
□□ 94 Scott Niedermayer, NJer. [Rookie] .20
□□ 95 Tom Chorske, NJer. .20
□□ 96 Viacheslav Fetisov, NJer. .20
□□ **97 Kevin Todd, NJer. RC [Rookie] .40**
□□ 98 Chris Terreri, NJer. .20
□□ 99 David Maley, NJer. .20
□□ 100 Stéphane J.J. Richer, NJer. .20
□□ 101 Claude Lemieux, NJer. .20
□□ 102 Scott Stevens, NJer. .20
□□ 103 Peter Stastny, NJer. .20
□□ 104 David Volek, NYIs. .20
□□ 105 Steve Thomas, NYIs. .20
□□ 106 Pierre Turgeon, NYIs. .20
□□ 107 Glenn Healy, NYIs. [Error: b/ Healey] .20
□□ 108 Derek King, NYIs. .20
□□ 109 Uwe Krupp, NYIs. .20
□□ 110 Ray Ferraro, NYIs. .20
□□ 111 Patrick Flatley, NYIs. .20
□□ 112 Tom Kurvers, NYIs. .20
□□ 113 Adam Creighton, NYIs. .20
□□ **114 Tony Amonte, NYRa. RC [Rookie] 1.50**
□□ 115 John Ogrodnick, NYRa. .20
□□ **116 Doug Weight, NYRa. RC [Rookie] 1.50**
□□ 117 Mike Richter, NYRa. .20
□□ 118 Darren Turcotte, NYRa. .20
□□ 119 Brian Leetch, NYRa. .20
□□ 120 James Patrick, NYRa. .20
□□ 121 Mark Messier, NYRa. .50
□□ 122 Mike Gartner, NYRa. .20
□□ 123 Mike Ricci, Phil. .20
□□ 124 Rod Brind'Amour, Phil. .20
□□ 125 Steve Duchesne, Phil. .20
□□ 126 Ron Hextall, Phil. .20
□□ **127 Brad Jones, Phil. RC .40**
□□ 128 Per-Erik (Pelle) Eklund, Phil. .20
□□ 129 Rick Tocchet, Phil. .20
□□ 130 Mark Howe, Phil. .20
□□ 131 Andrei Lomakin, Phil. .20
□□ 132 Jaromír Jágr, Pitt. .50
□□ **133 Jim Paek, Pitt. RC [Rookie] .40**
□□ 134 Mark Recchi, Pitt. .20
□□ 135 Kevin Stevens, Pitt. .20
□□ 136 Phil Bourque, Pitt. .20
□□ 137 Mario Lemieux, Pitt. 1.50
□□ 138 Bob Errey, Pitt. .20
□□ 139 Tom Barrasso, Pitt. .20
□□ 140 Paul Coffey, Pitt. .20
□□ 141 Joe Mullen, Pitt. .20
□□ 142 Kip Miller, Québ. [Rookie] .20
□□ 143 Owen Nolan, Québ. .20
□□ 144 Mats Sundin, Québ. .50
□□ 145 Mikhail Tatarinov, Québ. .20
□□ 146 Bryan Fogarty, Québ. .20
□□ 147 Stéphane Morin, Québ. .20
□□ 148 Joe Sakic, Québ. .50
□□ 149 Ron Tugnutt, Québ. .20
□□ 150 Mike Hough, Québ. .20
□□ **151 Nelson Emerson, SLou. RC [Rookie] .40**
□□ 152 Curtis Joseph, SLou. .50
□□ 153 Brendan Shanahan, SLou. .50
□□ 154 Paul Cavallini, SLou. .20
□□ 155 Adam Oates, SLou. .20
□□ 156 Jeff R. Brown, SLou. .20
□□ 157 Brett Hull, SLou. .50
□□ 158 Ron Sutter, SLou. .20
□□ 159 Dave Christian, SLou. .20
□□ 160 Pat Falloon, SanJ. [Rookie] .20
□□ **161 Pat MacLeod, SanJ. RC [Rookie] .40**
□□ 162 Jarmo Myllys, SanJ. .20
□□ 163 Wayne Presley, SanJ. .20
□□ **164 Perry Anderson, SanJ. RC .40**
□□ 165 Kelly Kisio, SanJ. .20
□□ 166 Brian Mullen, SanJ. .20
□□ 167 Brian Lawton, SanJ. .20
□□ 168 Doug Wilson, SanJ. .20
□□ **169 Rob Pearson, Toro. RC [Rookie] .40**
□□ 170 Wendel Clark, Toro. .20
□□ 171 Brian Bradley, Toro. .20
□□ 172 Dave Ellett, Toro. .20
□□ 173 Gary Leeman, Toro. .20
□□ 174 Peter Zezel, Toro. .20
□□ 175 Grant Fuhr, Toro. .20
□□ 176 Bob Rouse, Toro. .20
□□ 177 Glenn Anderson, Toro. .20
□□ 178 Petr Nedved, Vanc. .20
□□ 179 Trevor Linden, Vanc. .20
□□ 180 Jyrki Lumme, Vanc. .20
□□ 181 Kirk McLean, Vanc. .20
□□ 182 Cliff Ronning, Vanc. .20
□□ 183 Greg A. Adams, Vanc. .20
□□ 184 Doug Lidster, Vanc. .20
□□ 185 Sergio Momesso, Vanc. .20
□□ 186 Geoff Courtnall, Vanc. .20
□□ 187 Dave Babych, Vanc. .20
□□ 188 Peter Bondra, Wash. .20
□□ 189 Dmitri Khristich, Wash. .20
□□ 190 Randy Burridge, Wash. .20
□□ 191 Kevin Hatcher, Wash. .20
□□ 192 Mike Ridley, Wash. .20
□□ 193 Dino Ciccarelli, Wash. .20
□□ 194 Al Iafrate, Wash. .20
□□ 195 Dale Hunter, Wash. .20
□□ 196 Mike Liut, Wash. .20
□□ 197 Rod Langway, Wash. .20
□□ **198 Russ Romaniuk, Winn. RC [Rookie] .40**
□□ 199 Bob Essensa, Winn. .20
□□ 200 Teppo Numminen, Winn. .20
□□ 201 Darrin Shannon, Winn. .20
□□ 202 Pat Elynuik, Winn. .20
□□ 203 Fredrik Olausson, Winn. .20
□□ 204 Ed Olczyk, Winn. .20
□□ 205 Phil Housley, Winn. .20
□□ 206 Troy Murray, Winn. .20
□□ 207 Wayne Gretzky, LosA. [1000-Point Club] 2.00
□□ 208 Bryan Trottier, Pitt. [1000-Point Club] .50
□□ 209 Peter Stastny, NJer. [1000-Point Club] .20
□□ 210 Jari Kurri, LosA. [1000-Point Club] .50
□□ 211 Denis Savard, Mont. [1000-Point Club] .20
□□ 212 Paul Coffey, Pitt. [1000-Point Club] .20
□□ 213 Mark Messier, NYRa. [1000-Point Club] .50
□□ 214 Dave Taylor, LosA. [1000-Point Club] .20
□□ 215 Michel Goulet, Chic. [1000-Point Club] .20
□□ 216 Dale Hawerchuk, Buff. [1000-Point Club] .20
□□ 217 Bobby Smith, Minn. [1000-Point Club] .20
□□ 218 Ed Belfour, Chic. [Leader] .50
□□ 219 Brett Hull, SLou. [Leader] .50
□□ 220 Patrick Roy, NHL All-Star 1.50
□□ 221 Raymond Bourque, NHL All-Star '91 .50
□□ 222 Wayne Gretzky, NHL All-Star 2.00
□□ 223 Jari Kurri, NHL All-Star '90 .50
□□ 224 Luc Robitaille, NHL All-Star .20
□□ 225 Paul Coffey, NHL All-Star '91 .20
□□ 226 Bob Carpenter, Bost. .20
□□ 227 Gord Murphy, Bost. .20
□□ 228 Don Sweeney, Bost. .20
□□ **229 Glen Murray, Bost. RC 1.00**
□□ **230 Ted Donato, Bost. RC .40**
□□ **231 Jozef Stümpel, Bost. RC .50**
□□ **232 Stephen Heinze, Bost. RC .40**
□□ 233 Adam Oates, Bost. .20
□□ **234 Joé Juneau, Bost. RC .50**
□□ **235 Gord Hynes, Bost. RC .40**
□□ 236 Tony Tanti, Buff. .20
□□ 237 Petr* Svoboda, Buff. .20
□□ 238 Bob Corkum, Buff. .20
□□ **239 Ken Sutton, Buff. RC .40**
□□ **240 Tom Draper, Buff. RC .40**
□□ 241 Grant Ledyard, Buff. .20
□□ 242 Christian Ruuttu, Buff. .20
□□ 243 Brad Miller, Buff. .20
□□ 244 Clint Malarchuk, Buff. .20
□□ 245 Trent Yawney, Calg. .20
□□ 246 Craig Berube, Calg. .20
□□ 247 Sergei* Makarov, Calg. .20
□□ 248 Alexander Godynyuk, Calg. .20
□□ 249 Paul Ranheim, Calg. .20
□□ 250 Jeff Reese, Calg. .20
□□ **251 Chris Lindberg, Calg. RC .40**
□□ 252 Michel Petit, Calg. .20
□□ 253 Joel Otto, Calg. .20
□□ 254 Gary Leeman, Calg. .20
□□ **255 Ray LeBlanc, Chic. RC .40**
□□ 256 Jocelyn Lemieux, Chic. .20
□□ **257 Igor Kravchuk, Chic. RC .40**
□□ 258 Rob (Jr.) Brown, Chic. .20
□□ 259 Stéphane Matteau, Chic. .20
□□ 260 Mike Hudson, Chic. .20
□□ 261 Keith Brown, Chic. .20
□□ 262 Karl Dykhuis, Chic. .20
□□ **263 Dominik Hasek, Chic. RC 7.00**
□□ 264 Brian Noonan, Chic. .20
□□ 265 Yves Racine, Detr. .20
□□ **266 Vyacheslav (Slava) Kozlov, Detr. RC .40**
□□ 267 Martin Lapointe, Detr. .20
□□ 268 Steve Chiasson, Detr. .20
□□ 269 Gerard Gallant, Detr. .20
□□ 270 Brent Fedyk, Detr. .20
□□ 271 Brad McCrimmon, Detr. .20
□□ 272 Bob Probert, Detr. .20
□□ 273 Alan Kerr, Detr. .20
□□ 274 Luke Richardson, Edmo. .20
□□ 275 Kelly Buchberger, Edmo. .20
□□ 276 Craig MacTavish, Edmo. .20
□□ 277 Ron Tugnutt, Edmo. .20
□□ 278 Bernie Nicholls, Edmo. .20
□□ 279 Anatoli Semenov, Edmo. .20
□□ 280 Petr Klima, Edmo. .20
□□ **281 Louie DeBrusk, Edmo. RC .40**
□□ **282 Norm Maciver, Edmo. RC .40**
□□ 283 Martin Gélinas, Edmo. .20
□□ 284 Randy Cunneyworth, Hart. .20
□□ 285 Andrew Cassels, Hart. .20
□□ 286 Peter Sidorkiewicz, Hart. .20
□□ 287 Steve Konroyd, Hart. .20
□□ 288 Murray Craven, Hart. .20
□□ 289 Randy Ladouceur, Hart. .20
□□ 290 Bobby Holik, Hart. .20
□□ 291 Adam Burt, Hart. .20
□□ **292 Corey Millen, LosA. RC .40**
□□ 293 Rob Blake, LosA. .20
□□ **294 Mike Donnelly, LosA. RC .40**
□□ **295 Kyosti Karjalainen, LosA. RC .40**
□□ 296 John* McIntyre, LosA. .20
□□ 297 Paul Coffey, LosA. .20
□□ 298 Charlie Huddy, LosA. .20
□□ 299 Bob Kudelski, LosA. .20
□□ 300 Todd Elik, LosA. .20
□□ 301 Mike Craig, Minn. .20
□□ 302 Marc Bureau, Minn. .20
□□ 303 Jim* Johnson, Minn. .20
□□ 304 Mark Tinordi, Minn. .20
□□ 305 Gaétan Duchesne, Minn. .20
□□ **306 Darcy Wakaluk, Minn. RC .40**
□□ 307 Sylvain Lefebvre, Mont. .20
□□ 308 Russ Courtnall, Mont. .20
□□ 309 Patrice Brisebois, Mont. .20
□□ 310 Mike McPhee, Mont. .20
□□ 311 Mike Keane, Mont. .20
□□ 312 J-J Daigneault, Mont. .20
□□ **313 Gilbert Dionne, Mont. RC .40**
□□ 314 Brian Skrudland, Mont. .20
□□ 315 Brent Gilchrist, Mont. .20
□□ 316 Laurie Boschman, NJer. .20
□□ 317 Ken Daneyko, NJer. .20
□□ 318 Eric Weinrich, NJer. .20
□□ 319 Alexei Kasatonov, NJer. .20
□□ **320 Craig Billington, NJer. RC .40**
□□ 321 Claude Vilgrain, NJer. .20
□□ 322 Bruce Driver, NJer. .20
□□ **323 Alexander Semak, NJer. RC .40**
□□ **324 Valeri Zelepukin, NJer. RC .40**
□□ 325 Rob DiMaio, NYIs. .20
□□ **326 Scott Lachance, NYIs. RC .40**
□□ **327 Marty McInnis, NYIs. RC .40**
□□ 328 Joe Reekie, NYIs. .20
□□ 329 Daniel Marois, NYIs. .20
□□ 330 Wayne McBean, NYIs. .20
□□ 331 Jeff Norton, NYIs. .20
□□ 332 Benoît Hogue, NYIs. .20
□□ 333 Tie Domi, NYRa. .20
□□ 334 Sergei Nemchinov, NYRa. .20
□□ 335 Randy Gilhen, NYRa. .20
□□ 336 Paul Broten, NYRa. .20
□□ 337 Kris King, NYRa. .20
□□ 338 John Vanbiesbrouck, NYRa. .20
□□ 339 Adam Graves, NYRa. .20
□□ 340 Joe Cirella, NYRa. .20
□□ 341 Jeff Beukeboom, NYRa. .20
□□ 342 Terry Carkner, Phil. .20
□□ **343 Mark Freer, Phil. RC .40**
□□ **344 Corey Foster, Phil. RC .40**
□□ 345 Mark Pederson, Phil. .20
□□ **346 Kimbi Daniels, Phil. RC .40**
□□ 347 Mark Recchi, Phil. .20
□□ 348 Kevin Dineen, Phil. .20
□□ 349 Kerry Huffman, Phil. .20
□□ 350 Garry Galley, Phil. .20
□□ 351 Dan Quinn, Phil. .20
□□ 352 Troy Loney, Pitt. .20
□□ 353 Ron Francis, Pitt. .20
□□ 354 Rick Tocchet, Pitt. .20
□□ **355 Shawn McEachern, Pitt. RC .50**
□□ 356 Kjell Samuelsson, Pitt. .20
□□ 357 Ken Wregget, Pitt. .20
□□ 358 Larry Murphy, Pitt. .20
□□ 359 Ken Priestlay, Pitt. .20
□□ 360 Bryan Trottier, Pitt. .50
□□ 361 Ulf Samuelsson, Pitt. .20
□□ 362 Valeri Kamensky, Québ. .20
□□ 363 Stéphane Fiset, Québ. .20
□□ **364 Alexei Gusarov, Québ. RC .40**
□□ 365 Greg Paslawski, Québ. .20
□□ **366 Martin Rucinsky, Québ. RC .50**
□□ 367 Curtis Leschyshyn, Québ. .20
□□ 368 Jacques Cloutier, Québ. .20
□□ 369 Craig Wolanin, Québ. .20
□□ **370 Claude Lapointe, Québ. RC .40**
□□ **371 Adam Foote, Québ. RC .50**
□□ 372 Rich Sutter, SLou. .20
□□ 373 Lee Norwood, SLou. .20
□□ 374 Garth Butcher, SLou. .20
□□ **375 Philippe Bozon, SLou. RC .40**
□□ 376 Dave Lowry, SLou. .20
□□ 377 Darin Kimble, SLou. .20
□□ 378 Craig Janney, SLou. .20
□□ 379 Bob Bassen, SLou. .20
□□ 380 Rick Zombo, SLou. .20
□□ 381 Perry Berezan, SanJ. .20
□□ 382 Neil Wilkinson, SanJ. .20
□□ **383 Mike Sullivan, SanJ. RC .40**
□□ **384 David Bruce, SanJ. RC .40**
□□ 385 Johan Garpenlöv, SanJ. .20
□□ **386 Jeff Odgers, SanJ. RC .40**
□□ **387 Jayson More, SanJ. RC .40**
□□ 388 Dean Evason, SanJ. .20
□□ 389 Dale Craigwell, SanJ. .20
□□ **390 Darryl Shannon, Toro. RC .40**
□□ 391 Dmitri Mironov, Toro. .20
□□ 392 Kent Manderville, Toro. .20
□□ 393 Todd Gill, Toro. .20
□□ 394 Rick Wamsley, Toro. .20
□□ **395 Joe Sacco, Toro. RC .40**
□□ 396 Doug Gilmour, Toro. .20
□□ 397 Mike Bullard, Toro. .20
□□ 398 Félix Potvin, Toro. .20
□□ **399 Guy Larose, Toro. RC .40**
□□ 400 Tom Fergus, Vanc. .20
□□ 401 Ryan Walter, Vanc. .20
□□ 402 Troy Gamble, Vanc. .20
□□ 403 Robert Dirk, Vanc. .20
□□ 404 Pavel Bure, Vanc. .20
□□ 405 Jim Sandlak, Vanc. .20
□□ 406 Igor Larionov, Vanc. .20
□□ 407 Gerald Diduck, Vanc. .20
□□ 408 Todd Krygier, Wash. .20
□□ 409 Tim Bergland, Wash. .20
□□ 410 Calle Johansson, Wash. .20
□□ 411 Nick Kypreos, Wash. .20
□□ 412 Michal Pivonka, Wash. .20
□□ **413 Brad Schlegel, Wash. RC .40**
□□ 414 Kelly Miller, Wash. .20
□□ 415 John Druce, Wash. .20
□□ 416 Don Beaupré, Wash. .20
□□ 417 Alan May, Wash. .20
□□ 418 Randy Carlyle, Winn. .20
□□ 419 Stu Barnes, Winn. .20

□□ 420 Mike Eagles, Winn. .20
□□ **421 Igor Ulanov, Winn. RC .40**
□□ **422 Evgeny (Gene) Davydov, Winn. RC .40**
□□ 423 Shawn Cronin, Winn. .20
□□ **424 Keith Tkachuk, Winn. RC 1.50**
□□ **425 Luciano Borsato, Winn. RC .40**
□□ 426 Stéphane Beauregard, Winn. .20
□□ 427 Mike Lalor, Winn. .20
□□ 428 Michel Goulet, Chic. .20
□□ 429 Wayne Gretzky, LosA. 2.00
□□ 430 Mike Gartner, NYRa. .20
□□ 431 Bryan Trottier, NYIs. .50
□□ 432 Brett Hull, SLou. [League Leader] .50
□□ 433 Wayne Gretzky, LosA. [League Leader] 2.00
□□ 434 Steve Yzerman, Detr. [League Leader] 1.00
□□ 435 Paul Ysebaert, Detr. [League Leader] .20
□□ 436 Gary Roberts, Calg. [League Leader] .20
□□ 437 Dave Andreychuk, Buff. [League Leader] .20
□□ 438 Brian Leetch, NYRa. [League Leader] .20
□□ 439 Jeremy Roenick, Chic. [League Leader] .20
□□ 440 Kirk McLean, Vanc. [League Leader] .20
□□ 441 Tim Cheveldae, Detr. [League Leader] .20
□□ 442 Patrick Roy, Mont. [League Leader] 1.50
□□ 443 Tony Amonte, NYRa. [League Leader] .20
□□ 444 Kevin Todd, NJer. [League Leader] .20
□□ 445 Nicklas Lidström, Detr. [League Leader] .20
□□ 446 Pavel Bure, Vanc. [League Leader] .20
□□ 447 Gilbert Dionne, Mont. [League Leader] .20
□□ 448 Tom Draper, Buff. [League Leader] .20
□□ 449 Dominik Hasek, Chic. [League Leader] .50
□□ 450 Dominic Roussel, Phil. [League Leader] .20
□ 451 Checklist .50
□ **452 Trent Klatt, Minn. RC 2.00**
□ **453 Bill Guerin, NJer. RC 40.00**
□ **454 Ray Whitney, SanJ. RC 5.00**
□ 455 Action .50
□ 456 Action .50
□ 457 Action .50
□ 458 Action .50
□ 459 Action (Lemieux, et al) 2.00
□ 460 Action .50
□ 461 Action (Trottier, et al) 1.00
□ 462 Pavel Bure, Vanc. 2.00
□ 436 Patrick Roy (G), Mont. 9.00
□ 464 Brian Leetch, NYRa. 2.00
□ 465 Wayne Gretzky, LosA. 12.00
□ 466 Guy Carbonneau, Mont. 1.00
□ 467 Mario Lemieux, Pitt. 9.00
□ 468 Mark Messier, NYRa. 3.00
□ 469 Raymond Bourque, Bost. 4.00
□ 470 Patrick Roy (G), Mont. 9.00
□ 471 Brian Leetch, NYRa. 2.00
□ 472 Raymond Bourque, Bost. 4.00
□ 473 Kevin Stevens, Pitt. .50
□ 474 Brett Hull, SLou. 3.00
□ 475 Mark Messier, NYRa. 3.00

Insert NRMT-MT
□□ PHC1 Gordie Howe, Detr. 3.50
□□ PHC2 Alex Delvecchio, Detr. .50
□□ PHC3 Ken (Jr.) Hodge, Bost. .25
□□ PHC4 Robert Kron, Vanc. .25
□□ PHC5 Sergei Fedorov, Detr. 1.00
□□ PHC6 Brett Hull, SLou. 1.00
□□ PHC7 Mario Lemieux, Pitt. 3.50
□□ PHC8 Rangers 1.00
□□ PHC9 Terry Sawchuk (G), Detr. 2.50
□□ Santa Claus .50

1991 - 92 PINNACLE

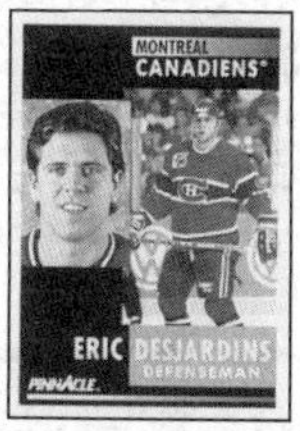

The most expensive English singles are Eric Lindros at $2-3 and Wayne Gretzky at $1.50-2.00. Regional stars sell for 25¢-$1.50; commons start at 5-20¢. The most expensive rookie cards are John LeClair at $2.50-3.50, Nicklas Lidström at $1.50-2.50 and Doug Weight at $1.50-2.50. All other rookie cards sell for 25¢-$2.00.
These cards have two versions: an English issue and a French issue. French cards sell for approximately 10-25% more than the English cards.
Imprint: © 1991 SCORE
English Set (420 cards): 30.00
French Set (420 cards): 40.00

Promo Panel (#s: 73, 78, 82, 87): 5.00
Promo Panel (#s: 12, 17, 23, 28): 5.00

Description / **No. Player**

□□□ 1 Mario Lemieux
□□ 2 Trevor Linden
□□□ 3 Kirk Muller
□□ 4 Phil Housley
□□□ 5 Mike Modano
□□ 6 Adam Oates
□□□ 7 Tom Kurvers
□□ 8 Doug Bodger
□□□ 9 Rod Brind'Amour
□□ 10 Mats Sundin
□□□ 11 Gary Suter
□□ 12 Glenn Anderson
□□□ 13 Doug Wilson
□□ 14 Stéphane J.J. Richer
□□□ 15 Raymond Bourque
□□ 16 Adam Graves
□□□ 17 Luc Robitaille
□□ 18 J. Steve Smith
□□□ 19 Uwe Krupp
□□ 20 Rick Tocchet
□□□ 21 Tim Cheveldae
□□ 22 Kay Whitmore
□□□ 23 Kelly Miller
□□ 24 Esa Tikkanen
□□□ 25 Pat LaFontaine
□□ 26 James Patrick
□□□ 27 Daniel Marois
□□ 28 Denis Savard
□□□ 29 Steve Larmer
□□ 30 Pierre Turgeon
□□□ 31 Gary Leeman
□□ 32 Mike Ricci
□□□ 33 Troy Murray
□□ 34 Sergio Momesso
□□□ 35 Marty McSorley
□□ 36 Paul Ysebaert
□□□ 37 Gary Roberts
□□ 38 Mike Hudson
□□□ 39 Kelly Hrudey
□□ 40 Dale Hunter
□□□ 41 Brendan Shanahan
□□ 42 Steve Duchesne
□□□ 43 Pat Verbeek
□□ 44 Tom Barrasso
□□□ 45 Scott Mellanby
□□ 46 Stephen Leach
□□□ 47 Darren Turcotte
□□ 48 Jari Kurri
□□□ 49 Michel Petit
□□ 50 Mark Messier
□□□ 51 Terry Carkner
□□ 52 Tim Kerr
□□□ 53 Jaromír Jágr
□□ 54 Joe Nieuwendyk
□□□ 55 Randy Burridge
□□ 56 Robert Reichel
□□□ 57 Craig Janney
□□ 58 Chris Chelios
□□□ 59 Bryan Fogarty
□□ 60 Christian Ruuttu
□□□ 61 Steve Bozek
□□ 62 Dave Manson
□□□ 63 Bruce Driver
□□ 64 Mike Ramsey
□□□ 65 Bobby Holik
□□ 66 Bob Essensa
□□□ 67 Patrick Flatley
□□ 68 Wayne Presley
□□□ 69 Mike Bullard
□□ 70 Claude Lemieux
□□□ 71 Dave Gagner
□□ 72 Jeff R. Brown
□□□ 73 Éric Desjardins
□□ 74 Fredrik Olausson
□□□ 75 Steve Yzerman
□□ 76 Tony Granato
□□□ 77 Adam Burt
□□ 78 Cam Neely
□□□ 79 Brent Sutter
□□ 80 Dale Hawerchuk
□□□ 81 Scott Stevens
□□ 82 Adam Creighton
□□□ 83 Brian Hayward
□□ 84 Dan Quinn
□□□ 85 Garth Butcher
□□ 86 Shawn Burr
□□□ 87 Peter Bondra
□□ 88 Brad Shaw
□□□ 89 Eric Weinrich
□□ 90 Brian Bradley
□□□ 91 V. Damphousse
□□ 92 Doug Gilmour
□□□ 93 Martin Gélinas
□□ 94 Mike Ridley
□□□ 95 Ron Sutter
□□ 96 Mark Osborne
□□□ 97 Mikhail Tatarinov
□□ 98 Bob McGill
□□□ 99 Bob Carpenter
□□ 100 Wayne Gretzky
□□□ 101 V. Fetisov
□□ 102 Shayne Corson
□□□ 103 Clint Malarchuk
□□ 104 Randy Wood
□□□ 105 Curtis Joseph
□□ 106 Cliff Ronning
□□□ 107 Derek King
□□ 108 Neil Wilkinson
□□□ 109 Michel Goulet
□□ 110 Zarley Zalapski
□□□ 111 Dave Ellett
□□ 112 Glen Wesley
□□□ 113 Bob Kudelski
□□ 114 Jamie Macoun
□□□ 115 John MacLean
□□ 116 Steve Thomas
□□□ 117 Pat Elynuik
□□ 118 Ron Hextall
□□□ 119 Jeff Hackett
□□ 120 Jeremy Roenick
□□□ 121 J. Vanbiesbrouck
□□ 122 Dave Andreychuk
□□□ 123 Ray Ferraro
□□ 124 Ron Tugnutt
□□□ 125 John Cullen
□□ 126 Andy Moog
□□□ 127 Ed Belfour
□□ 128 Dino Ciccarelli
□□□ 129 Brian Bellows
□□ 130 Guy Carbonneau
□□□ 131 Kevin Hatcher
□□ 132 Mike Vernon
□□□ 133 Kevin Miller
□□ 134 Pelle Eklund
□□□ 135 Brian Mullen
□□ 136 Brian Leetch
□□□ 137 Daren Puppa
□□ 138 Steven Finn
□□□ 139 Stéphan Lebeau
□□ 140 Gord Murphy
□□□ 141 Rob (Jr.) Brown
□□ 142 Ken Daneyko
□□□ 143 Larry Murphy
□□ 144 Jon Casey
□□□ 145 John Ogrodnick
□□ 146 Benoît Hogue
□□□ 147 Mike McPhee
□□ 148 Don Beaupré
□□□ 149 Kjell Samuelsson
□□ 150 Joe Sakic
□□□ 151 Mark Recchi
□□ 152 Ulf Dahlén
□□□ 153 Dean Evason
□□ 154 Keith Brown
□□□ 155 Ray Sheppard
□□ 156 Owen Nolan
□□□ 157 Sergei Fedorov
□□ 158 Kirk McLean
□□□ 159 Petr Klima
□□ 160 Brian Skrudland
□□□ 161 Neal Broten
□□ 162 Dmitri Khristich
□□□ 163 Alexander Mogilny
□□ 164 Mike Richter
□□□ 165 D. Berthiaume
□□ 166 Teppo Numminen
□□□ 167 Ron Francis
□□ 168 Grant Fuhr
□□□ 169 Mike Liut
□□ 170 Bill Ranford
□□□ 171 Garry Galley
□□ 172 Jeff Norton
□□□ 173 Jimmy Carson
□□ 174 Peter Zezel
□□□ 175 Patrick Roy
□□ 176 Joe Mullen
□□□ 177 Murray Craven
□□ 178 Tomas Sandström
□□□ 179 Joel Otto
□□ 180 Steve Konroyd
□□□ 181 Vladimír Ruzicka
□□ 182 Paul Cavallini
□□□ 183 Bob Probert
□□ 184 Brian Propp
□□□ 185 Glenn Healy
□□ 186 Paul Coffey
□□□ 187 Jan Erixon
□□ 188 Kevin Lowe
□□□ 189 Doug Lidster
□□ 190 Theoren Fleury
□□□ 191 Kevin Stevens
□□ 192 Petr Nedved
□□□ 193 Ed Olczyk
□□ 194 Mike Hough
□□□ 195 Rod Langway
□□ 196 Craig Simpson
□□□ 197 Petr* Svoboda
□□ 198 David Volek
□□□ 199 Mark Tinordi
□□ 200 Brett Hull
□□□ 201 Rob Blake
□□ 202 Mike Gartner
□□□ 203 Ken (Jr.) Hodge
□□ 204 Murray Baron
□□□ 205 Gerard Gallant
□□ 206 Joe Murphy
□□□ 207 Al Iafrate
□□ 208 Larry Robinson
□□□ 209 M. Schneider
□□ 210 Bobby Smith
□□□ 211 Gerald Diduck
□□ 212 Luke Richardson
□□□ 213 Rob Zettler
□□ 214 Brad McCrimmon
□□□ 215 Craig MacTavish
□□ 216 Gino Cavallini
□□□ 217 Craig Wolanin
□□ 218 Greg A. Adams
□□□ 219 Mike Craig
□□ 220 Al MacInnis
□□□ 221 Sylvain Côté
□□ 222 Bob Sweeney
□□□ 223 Dave Snuggerud
□□ 224 Randy Ladouceur
□□□ 225 Charlie Huddy
□□ 226 Sylvain Turgeon
□□□ 227 Phil Bourque
□□ 228 Rob Ramage
□□□ 229 Jeff Beukeboom
□□ 230 Alexei Gusarov RC
□□□ 231 Kelly Kisio
□□ 232 Calle Johansson
□□□ 233 Yves Racine
□□ 234 Peter Sidorkiewicz
□□□ 235 Jim* Johnson
□□ 236 Brent Gilchrist
□□□ 237 Jyrki Lumme
□□ 238 Randy Gilhen
□□□ 239 Ken Baumgartner
□□ 240 Joey Kocur
□□□ 241 Bryan Trottier
□□ 242 Todd Krygier
□□□ 243 Darrin Shannon
□□ 244 Dave Christian
□□□ 245 Stéphane Morin
□□ 246 Kevin Dineen
□□□ 247 Chris Terreri
□□ 248 Craig Ludwig
□□□ 249 DaveTaylor
□□ 250 Wendel Clark
□□□ 251 David Shaw
□□ 252 Paul Ranheim
□□□ 253 Mark Hunter
□□ 254 Russ Courtnall
□□□ 255 Alexei Kasatonov
□□ 256 Randy Moller
□□□ 257 Bob Errey
□□ 258 Curtis Leschyshyn
□□□ 259 Rick Zombo
□□ 260 Dana Murzyn
□□□ 261 Dirk Graham
□□ 262 Craig Muni
□□□ 263 Geoff Courtnall
□□ 264 Todd Elik
□□□ 265 Mike Keane
□□ 266 Peter Stastny
□□□ 267 Ulf Samuelsson
□□ 268 Rich Sutter
□□□ 269 Mike Krushelnyski
□□ 270 Dave Babych
□□□ 271 Sergei Makarov
□□ 272 David Maley
□□□ 273 N. Rochefort
□□ 274 Gord** Roberts
□□□ 275 Thomas Steen
□□ 276 Dave Lowry
□□□ 277 Michal Pivonka
□□ 278 Todd Gill
□□□ 279 Paul MacDermid
□□ 280 Brent Ashton
□□□ 281 Randy Hillier
□□ 282 Frantisek Musil
□□□ 283 Geoff Smith
□□ 284 John Tonelli
□□□ 285 Joe Reekie
□□ 286 Greg Paslawski
□□□ 287 Perry Berezan
□□ 288 Randy Carlyle
□□□ 289 Chris Nilan
□□ 290 Patrik Sundström
□□□ 291 Garry Valk
□□ 292 Mike Foligno
□□□ 293 Igor Larionov
□□ 294 Jim Sandlak
□□□ 295 Tom Chorske
□□ 296 Claude Loiselle
□□□ 297 Mark Howe
□□ 298 Steve Chiasson
□□□ 299 Mike Donnelly RC
□□ 300 Bernie Nicholls
□□□ 301 Tony Amonte RC
□□ 302 Brad May
□□□ 303 Josef Beránek RC
□□ 304 Rob Pearson RC
□□□ 305 Andrei Lomakin
□□ 306 Kip Miller
□□□ 307 Kevin Haller RC
□□ 308 Kevin Todd RC
□□□ 309 G. Sanderson RC
□□ 310 Doug Weight RC
□□□ 311 V. Konstantinov
□□ 312 Peter Ahola RC
□□□ 313 C. Lapointe RC
□□ 314 Nelson Emerson
□□□ 315 Pavel Bure
□□ 316 Jimmy Waite
□□□ 317 S. Nemchinov
□□ 318 Alex. Godynyuk RC
□□□ 319 Stu Barnes
□□ 320 N. Lidström RC
□□□ 321 Darryl Sydor
□□ 322 John LeClair RC
□□□ 323 Arturs Irbe
□□ 324 Russ Romaniuk RC
□□□ 325 Ken Sutton RC
□□ 326 Bob Beers
□□□ 327 Michel Picard RC
□□ 328 Derian Hatcher
□□□ 329 Pat Falloon
□□ 330 Donald Audette
□□□ 331 Pat Jablonski RC
□□ 332 Corey Foster RC
□□□ 333 T. Forslund RC
□□ 334 Steven Rice
□□□ 335 Marc Bureau
□□ 336 Kimbi Daniels RC
□□□ 337 Adam Foote RC
□□ 338 Dan Kordic RC
□□□ 339 Link Gaetz
□□ 340 Valeri Kamensky
□□□ 341 Tom Draper RC
□□ 342 Jayson More RC
□□□ 343 D. Roussel RC
□□ 344 Jim Paek RC
□□□ 345 Félix Potvin
□□ 346 Dan Lambert RC
□□□ 347 Louie DeBrusk RC
□□ 348 Jamie Baker RC
□□□ 349 Scott Niedermayer
□□ 350 Paul DiPietro RC
□□□ 351 Chris Winnes RC
□□ 352 Mark Greig
□□□ 353 L. Borsato RC
□□ 354 V. Zelepukin RC
□□□ 355 Martin Lapointe
□□ 356 Brett Hull
□□□ 357 Steve Larmer
□□ 358 Theoren Fleury
□□□ 359 Jeremy Roenick
□□ 360 Mark Recchi
□□□ 361 Brad Marsh
□□ 362 Kris King
□□□ 363 Doug Brown
□□ 364 Carey Wilson
□□□ 365 Eric Lindros
□□ 366 Kevin Dineen
□□□ 367 J. Vanbiesbrouck
□□ 368 Raymond Bourque
□□□ 369 Doug Wilson
□□ 370 Keith Brown
□□□ 371 Kevin Lowe
□□ 372 Kelly Miller
□□□ 373 Dave Taylor
□□ 374 Guy Carbonneau
□□□ 375 Tim Hunter
□□ 376 Brett Hull
□□□ 377 Paul Coffey
□□ 378 Adam Oates
□□□ 379 Andy Moog
□□ 380 Mario Lemieux
□□□ 381 Sakic/ Gretzky
□□ 382 Blake/ Robinson
□□□ 383 Weight/ Yzerman
□□ 384 Richter/ Parent
□□□ 385 Robitaille/ Dionne
□□ 386 Olczyk/ Clarke
□□□ 387 Roy / Vachon
□□ 388 Belfour / Esposito
□□□ 389 Sundin/ Näslund
□□ 390 Amonte/ Messier
□□□ 391 Cullen/ Cullen
□□ 392 Suter/ Orr
□□□ 393 Zombo/ Resch
□□ 394 Krygier/ Perreault
□□□ 395 Druce/ Gainey
□□ 396 Bob Carpenter
□□□ 397 Clint Malarchuk
□□ 398 Jim Kyte
□□□ 399 Al MacInnis
□□ 400 Ed Belfour
□□□ 401 Brad Marsh
□□ 402 Brian Benning
□□□ 403 Larry Robinson
□□ 404 Craig Ludwig
□□□ 405 Patrick Flatley
□□ 406 Gary Nylund
□□□ 407 Kjell Samuelsson
□□ 408 Dan Quinn
□□□ 409 Garth Butcher
□□ 410 Rick Zombo
□□□ 411 Paul Cavallini
□□ 412 Link Gaetz
□□□ 413 Dave Hannan
□□ 414 Peter Zezel
□□□ 415 Randy Gregg
□□ 416 Pat Elynuik
□□□ 417 Rod Buskas
□□ 418 Mark Howe
□□□ 419 Don Sweeney
□□ 420 Mark Hardy

TEAM PINNACLE

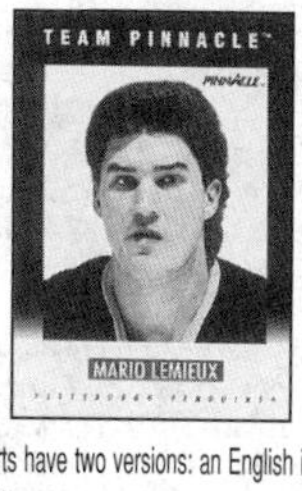

These inserts have two versions: an English issue and a French issue.

Insert Set (12 cards):	245.00	325.00
Description	English	French
□ B-1 Patrick Roy (G), Mont.	60.00	80.00
□ B-2 Raymond Bourque, Bost.	20.00	30.00
□ B-3 Brian Leetch, NYRa.	10.00	15.00
□ B-4 Kevin Stevens, Pitt.	10.00	15.00
□ B-5 Mario Lemieux, Pitt.	60.00	80.00
□ B-6 Cam Neely, Bost.	20.00	20.00
□ B-7 Bill Ranford, Edmo.	10.00	15.00
□ B-8 Al MacInnis, Calg.	10.00	15.00
□ B-9 Chris Chelios, Chic.	10.00	15.00
□ B-10 Luc Robitaille, LosA.	10.00	20.00
□ B-11 Wayne Gretzky, LosA.	90.00	110.00
□ B-12 Brett Hull, SLou.	20.00	20.00

1991 - 92 PRO SET

These cards have two versions: an English issue and a French issue. The French issue was released a little later than the English edition and shows the new Minnesota North Stars logos instead of the old ones.
The most expensive singles are Wayne Gretzky at $1.00-2.00, Dominik Hasek at $2.00-4.00 and John LeClair at $1.00-1.50. All other singles sell between 20¢ and $1.00.
Imprint: Pro Set
Complete Set (615 cards): 15.00

Promo
□ Title Card:
□ Bob Essensa (G)
□ Gord Murphy
□ Dave Reid, Tor.
□ Craig Wolanin
□ Randy Wood

Pro Set
□□□ 1 Glen Wesley
□□ 2 Craig Janney
□□□ 3 Ken Hodge
□□ 4 R. Burridge
□□□ 5 Cam Neely
□□ 6 Bob Sweeney
□□□ 7 Garry Galley
□□ 8 Petri Skriko
□□□ 9 Ray Bourque
□□ 10 Andy Moog (G)
□□□ 11 David Christian
□□ 12 Dave Poulin
□□□ 13 Jeff Lazaro RC
□□ 14 Darrin Shannon
□□□ 15 Turgeon, Err. (8-28)
□□ 16 A. Mogilny
□□□ 17 Hogue, Err (b: Win.)
□□ 18 Dave Snuggerud
□□□ 19 Doug Bodger
□□ 20 Uwe Krupp
□□□ 21 Daren Puppa (G)
□□ 22 Christian Ruuttu
□□□ 23 Dave Andreychuk
□□ 24 Dale Hawerchuk
□□□ 25 Mike Ramsey
□□ 26 Rick Vaive
□□□ 27 Stéphane Matteau
□□ 28 Theoren Fleury
□□□ 29 Joe Nieuwendyk
□□ 30 Gary Roberts
□□□ 31 Paul Ranheim
□□ 32 Gary Suter
□□□ 33 Al MacInnis
□□ 34 Doug Gilmour
□□□ 35 Mike Vernon (G)
□□ 36 Carey Wilson
□□□ 37 Joel Otto
□□ 38 Jamie Macoun
□□□ 39 Sergei Makarov
□□ 40 Jeremy Roenick
□□□ 41 Dave Manson
□□ 42 Adam Creighton
□□□ 43 Ed Belfour (G)
□□ 44 Wayne Presley
□□□ 45 Steve Thomas
□□ 46 Troy Murray
□□□ 47 Bob McGill
□□ 48 Chris Chelios
□□□ 49 Steve Larmer
□□ 50 Michel Goulet
□□□ 51 Dirk Graham
□□ 52 Doug Wilson
□□□ 53 Sergei Fedorov
□□ 54 Yves Racine
□□□ 55 Jimmy Carson
□□ 56 Johan Garpenlov
□□□ 57 Tim Cheveldae (G)
□□ 58 Shawn Burr
□□□ 59 Paul Ysebaert
□□ 60 Kevin Miller
□□□ 61 Bob Probert
□□ 62 Steve Yzerman
□□□ 63 Gerard Gallant
□□ 64 Rick Zombo
□□□ 65 David Barr
□□ 66 Martin Gelinas
□□□ 67 Adam Graves
□□ 68 Joe Murphy
□□□ 69 Craig Simpson
□□ 70 Bill Ranford (G)
□□□ 71 Esa Tikkanen
□□ 72 Petr Klima
□□□ 73 Steve Smith
□□ 74 Mark Messier
□□□ 75 Glenn Anderson
□□ 76 Kevin Lowe
□□□ 77 Craig MacTavish
□□ 78 Grant Fuhr (G)
□□□ 79 Bobby Holik
□□ 80 Rob Brown
□□□ 81 Doug Houda
□□ 82 Sylvain Côté
□□□ 83 Todd Krygier
□□ 84 Dean Evason
□□□ 85 John Cullen
□□ 86 Pat Verbeek
□□□ 87 Brad Shaw
□□ 88 Paul Cyr
□□□ 89 Kevin Dineen
□□ 90 P. Sidorkiewicz (G)
□□□ 91 Zarley Zalapski
□□ 92 Rob Blake
□□□ 93 Jari Kurri
□□ 94 Todd Elik
□□□ 95 Luc Robitaille
□□ 96 S. Duchesne
□□□ 97 Tomas Sandström
□□ 98 Tony Granato
□□□ 99 Bob Kudelski
□□ 100 Marty McSorley
□□□ 101 Wayne Gretzky
□□ 102 Kelly Hrudey (G)
□□□ 103 Dave Taylor
□□ 104 Larry Robinson
□□□ 105 Mike Modano
□□ 106 Ulf Dahlen
□□□ 107 Mark Tinordi
□□ 108 Dave Gagner
□□□ 109 Brian Bellows
□□ 110 Gaetan Duchesne
□□□ 111 Jon Casey (G)
□□ 112 Neal Broten
□□□ 113 Brian Propp
□□ 114 Curt Giles
□□□ 115 Bobby Smith
□□ 116 Jim Johnson
□□□ 117 Doug Smail
□□ 118 Eric Desjardins
□□□ 119 Mathieu Schneider
□□ 120 Stéphan Lebeau
□□□ 121 Mike Keane
□□ 122 Stéphane Richer
□□□ 123 Petr Svoboda
□□ 124 J.J. Daigneault
□□□ 125 Patrick Roy (G)
□□ 126 Russ Courtnall
□□□ 127 Brian Skrudland
□□ 128 Denis Savard
□□□ 129 Mike McPhee
□□ 130 Guy Carbonneau
□□□ 131 Brendan Shanahan
□□ 132 Sean Burke (G)
□□□ 133 Eric Weinrich
□□ 134 Kirk Muller
□□□ 135 Claude Lemieux
□□ 136 John MacLean
□□□ 137 Chris Terreri (G)
□□ 138 Doug Brown
□□□ 139 Ken Daneyko
□□ 140 Bruce Driver
□□□ 141 Patrik Sundstrom
□□ 142 Viacheslav Fetisov
□□□ 143 Peter Stastny
□□ 144 Wayne McBean
□□□ 145 Bill Berg RC
□□ 146 Derek King
□□□ 147 David Volk
□□ 148 Jeff Norton
□□□ 149 Pat LaFontaine
□□ 150 Gary Nylund
□□□ 151 Randy Wood
□□ 152 Patrick Flatley
□□□ 153 Glenn Healy (G)
□□ 154 Brent Sutter
□□□ 155 Craig Ludwig
□□ 156 Ray Ferraro
□□□ 157 Troy Mallette
□□ 158 Mark Janssens
□□□ 159 Brian Leetch
□□ 160 Darren Turcotte
□□□ 161 Mike Richter (G)
□□ 162 Ray Sheppard
□□□ 163 Randy Moller
□□ 164 James Patrick
□□□ 165 Brian Mullen
□□ 166 Bernie Nicholls
□□□ 167 Mike Gartner
□□ 168 Kelly Kisio
□□□ 169 John Ogrodnick
□□ 170 Mike Ricci
□□□ 171 Gord Murphy
□□ 172 Scott Mellanby
□□□ 173 Terry Carkner
□□ 174 Derrick Smith
□□□ 175 Murray Craven
□□ 176 Ron Hextall (G)
□□□ 177 Rick Tocchet
□□ 178 Ron Sutter
□□□ 179 Per-Erik Eklund
□□ 180 Tim Kerr
□□□ 181 Kjell Samuelsson
□□ 182 Mark Howe
□□□ 183 Jaromir Jagr
□□ 184 Mark Recchi
□□□ 185 Kevin Stevens
□□ 186 T. Barrasso (G)
□□□ 187 Bob Errey
□□ 188 Ron Francis
□□□ 189 Phil Bourque
□□ 190 Paul Coffey
□□□ 191 Joe Mullen
□□ 192 Bryan Trottier
□□□ 193 Larry Murphy
□□ 194 Mario Lemieux
□□□ 195 Scott Young
□□ 196 Owen Nolan
□□□ 197 Mats Sundin
□□ 198 C. Leschyshyn
□□□ 199 Joe Sakic
□□ 200 Bryan Fogarty
□□□ 201 Stéphane Morin
□□ 202 Ron Tugnutt (G)
□□□ 203 Craig Wolanin
□□ 204 Steven Finn
□□□ 205 Tony Hrkac
□□ 206 Randy Velischek
□□□ 207 A. Gusarov RC
□□ 208 Scott Pearson
□□□ 209 Dan Quinn
□□ 210 Garth Butcher
□□□ 211 Rod Brind'Amour
□□ 212 Jeff Brown
□□□ 213 V. Riendeau (G)
□□ 214 Paul Cavallini

□□ 215 Brett Hull □□ 216 Scott Stevens
□□ 217 Rich Sutter □□ 218 Gino Cavallini
□□ 219 Adam Oates □□ 220 Ron Wilson
□□ 221 Bob Bassen □□ 222 Peter Ing (G)
□□ 223 Daniel Marois □□ 224 V. Damphousse
□□ 225 Wendel Clark □□ 226 Todd Gill
□□ 227 Peter Zezel □□ 228 Bob Rouse
□□ 229 David Reid □□ 230 Dave Ellett
□□ 231 Gary Leeman □□ 232 R. Ramage
□□ 233 Mike Krushelnyski □□ 234 Tom Fergus
□□ 235 Petr Nedved □□ 236 Trevor Linden
□□ 237 Dave Capuano □□ 238 Troy Gamble (G)
□□ 239 Robert Kron □□ 240 Jyrki Lumme
□□ 241 Cliff Ronning □□ 242 Sergio Momesso
□□ 243 Greg Adams □□ 244 T. Kurvers
□□ 245 Geoff Courtnall □□ 246 Igor Larionov
□□ 247 Doug Lidster □□ 248 Calle Johansson
□□ 249 Kevin Hatcher □□ 250 Al Iafrate
□□ 251 John Druce □□ 252 Michal Pivonka
□□ 253 Stephen Leach □□ 254 Mike Ridley
□□ 255 Mike Lalor □□ 256 Kelly Miller
□□ 257 Don Beaupré (G) □□ 258 Dino Ciccarelli
□□ 259 Rod Langway □□ 260 Dimitri Khristich
□□ 261 Teppo Numminen □□ 262 Pat Elynuik
□□ 263 Danton Cole □□ 264 Fredrik Olausson
□□ 265 Ed Olczyk □□ 266 Bob Essensa (G)
□□ 267 Phil Housley □□ 268 Shawn Cronin
□□ 269 Paul MacDermid □□ 270 Mark Osborne
□□ 271 Thomas Steen □□ 272 Brent Ashton
□□ 273 Randy Carlyle □□ 274 AS: T. Fleury
□□ 275 AS: Al MacInnis □□ 276 AS: Gary Suter
□□ 277 AS: M. Vernon (G) □□ 278 AS: Chris Chelios
□□ 279 AS: Steve Larmer □□ 280 AS: J. Roenick
□□ 281 AS: Steve Yzerman □□ 282 AS: M. Messier
□□ 283 AS: B. Ranford (G) □□ 284 AS: Steve Smith
□□ 285 AS: W. Gretzky □□ 286 AS: L. Robitaille
□□ 287 AS: T.Sandström □□ 288 AS: Dave Gagner
□□ 289 AS: Bobby Smith □□ 290 AS: Brett Hull
□□ 291 AS: Adam Oates □□ 292 AS: Scott Stevens
□□ 293 AS: Damphousse □□ 294 AS: Trevor Linden
□□ 295 AS: Phil Housley □□ 296 AS: Ray Bourque
□□ 297 AS: D. Christian □□ 298 AS: Garry Galley
□□ 299 AS: A. Moog (G) □□ 300 AS: Cam Neely
□□ 301 AS: Uwe Krupp □□ 302 AS: John Cullen
□□ 303 AS: Pat Verbeek □□ 304 AS: P. Roy (G)
□□ 305 AS: Denis Savard □□ 306 AS: B. Skrudland
□□ 307 AS: John MacLean □□ 308 AS: P.LaFontaine
□□ 309 AS: Brian Leetch □□ 310 AS: D. Turcotte
□□ 311 AS: Rick Tocchet □□ 312 AS: Paul Coffey
□□ 313 AS: Mark Recchi □□ 314 AS: K. Stevens
□□ 315 AS: Joe Sakic □□ 316 AS: K. Hatcher
□□ 317 AS: Guy Lafleur □□ 318 Mario Lemieux
□□ 319 AW: Penguins □□ 320 AW: Brett Hull
□□ 321 AW: Belfour (G) □□ 322 AW: Ray Bourque
□□ 323 AW: Dirk Graham □□ 324 AW: W. Gretzky
□□ 325 AW: Dave Taylor □□ 326 AW: Brett Hull
□□ 327 Brian Hayward (G) □□ 328 Neil Wilkinson
□□ 329 Craig Coxe □□ 330 Rob Zettler
□□ 331 Jeff Hackett (G) □□ 332 Joe Malone
□□ 333 Georges Vézina □□ 334 The Modern Arena
□□ 335 Ace Bailey Game □□ 336 Howie Morenz
□□ 337 Punch Line □□ 338 Kid Line
□□ 339 Before.. Zamboni □□ 340 Bill Barilko
□□ 341 J. Plante (G) □□ 342 Arena Designs
□□ 343 Terry Sawchuk □□ 344 Gordie Howe
□□ 345 Guy Carbonneau □□ 346 Stephen Leach
□□ 347 Peter Douris □□ 348 David Reid
□□ 349 Bob Carpenter □□ 350 Stéphane Quintal
□□ 351 Barry Pederson □□ 352 Brent Ashton
□□ 353 Vladimir Ruzicka □□ 354 Brad Miller
□□ 355 Rob Ray □□ 356 Colin Patterson
□□ 357 Gord Donnelly □□ 358 Pat LaFontaine
□□ 359 Randy Wood □□ 360 Randy Hillier
□□ 361 Robert Reichel □□ 362 Ron Stern
□□ 363 Ric Nattress □□ 364 Tim Sweeney
□□ 365 Marc Habscheid □□ 366 Tim Hunter
□□ 367 R. Wamsley (G) □□ 368 Frantisek Musil
□□ 369 Mike Hudson □□ 370 Steve Smith
□□ 371 Keith Brown □□ 372 Greg Gilbert
□□ 373 John Tonelli □□ 374 Brent Sutter
□□ 375 Brad Lauer □□ 376 Alan Kerr
□□ 377 Brad McCrimmon □□ 378 Brad Marsh
□□ 379 Brent Fedyk □□ 380 Ray Sheppard
□□ 381 V. Damphousse □□ 382 Craig Muni
□□ 383 Scott Mellanby □□ 384 Geoff Smith
□□ 385 Kelly Buchberger □□ 286 Bernie Nicholls
□□ 387 Luke Richardson □□ 388 Peter Ing (G)
□□ 389 Dave Manson □□ 390 Mark Hunter
□□ 391 J.McKenzie RC □□ 392 R. Cunneyworth
□□ 393 Murray Craven □□ 394 Mikael Andersson
□□ 395 Andrew Cassels □□ 396 Randy Ladouceur
□□ 397 Marc Bergevin □□ 398 Brian Benning
□□ 399 M. Donnelly RC □□ 400 Charlie Huddy
□□ 401 John McIntyre □□ 402 Jay Miller
□□ 403 Randy Gilhen □□ 404 Stewart Gavin
□□ 405 Mike Craig □□ 406 Brian Glynn
□□ 407 Rob Ramage □□ 408 Chris Dahlquist
□□ 409 Basil McRae □□ 410 Todd Elik
□□ 411 Craig Ludwig □□ 412 Kirk Muller
□□ 413 Shayne Corson □□ 414 Brent Gilchrist
□□ 415 M. Roberge RC □□ 416 Sylvain Turgeon
□□ 417 Alain Côté □□ 418 Donald Dufresne
□□ 419 Todd Ewen □□ 420 Stéphane Richer
□□ 421 David Maley □□ 422 Randy McKay
□□ 423 Scott Stevens □□ 424 Jon Morris
□□ 425 Claude Vilgrain □□ 426 Laurie Boschman
□□ 427 Pat Conacher □□ 428 Tom Kurvers
□□ 429 Joe Reekie □□ 430 Rob DiMaio
□□ 431 Tom Fitzgerald □□ 432 K. Baumgartner
□□ 433 Pierre Turgeon □□ 434 Dave McLlwain
□□ 435 Benoît Hogue □□ 436 Uwe Krupp
□□ 437 Adam Creighton □□ 438 Steve Thomas
□□ 439 Mark Messier □□ 440 Tie Domi
□□ 441 Sergei Nemchinov □□ 442 Mark Hardy
□□ 443 Adam Graves □□ 444 Jeff Beukeboom
□□ 445 Kris King □□ 446 Tim Kerr
□□ 447 Vanbiesbrouck (G) □□ 448 Steve Duchesne
□□ 449 Steve Kasper □□ 450 Ken Wregget (G)
□□ 451 Kevin Dineen □□ 452 Dave Brown
□□ 453 Rod Brind'Amour □□ 454 Jiri Latal
□□ 455 Tony Horacek □□ 456 Brad Jones RC
□□ 457 Paul Stanton □□ 458 Gord Roberts
□□ 459 Ulf Samuelsson □□ 460 K. Priestlay RC
□□ 461 Jiri Hrdina □□ 462 Mikhail Tatarinov
□□ 463 Mike Hough □□ 464 Don Barber
□□ 465 Greg Smyth RC □□ 466 Doug Smail
□□ 467 Mike McNeill □□ 468 John Kordic
□□ 469 Greg Paslawski □□ 470 Herb Raglan
□□ 471 David Christian □□ 472 Murray Baron
□□ 473 Curtis Joseph (G) □□ 474 Rick Zombo
□□ 475 Brendan Shanahan □□ 476 Ron Sutter
□□ 477 Mario Marois □□ 478 Doug Wilson
□□ 479 Kelly Kisio □□ 480 Bob McGill
□□ 481 P. Anderson RC □□ 482 Brian Lawton
□□ 483 Neil Wilkinson □□ 484 Ken Hammond
□□ 485 David Bruce RC □□ 486 Steven Bozek
□□ 487 Perry Berezan □□ 488 Wayne Presley
□□ 489 Brian Bradley □□ 490 D. Shannon RC
□□ 491 Lucien DeBlois □□ 492 Michel Petit
□□ 493 Claude Loiselle □□ 494 Grant Fuhr (G)
□□ 495 Craig Berube □□ 496 Mike Bullard
□□ 497 Jim Sandlak □□ 498 Dana Murzyn
□□ 499 Garry Valk □□ 500 Andrew McBain
□□ 501 Kirk McLean (G) □□ 502 Gerald Diduck
□□ 503 Dave Babych □□ 504 Ryan Walter
□□ 505 Gino Odjick □□ 506 Dale Hunter
□□ 507 Tim Bergland □□ 508 Alan May
□□ 509 Jim Hrivnak (G) □□ 510 Randy Burridge
□□ 511 Peter Bondra □□ 512 Sylvain Côté
□□ 513 Nick Kypreos □□ 514 Troy Murray
□□ 515 Darrin Shannon □□ 516 Bryan Erickson
□□ 517 Petri Skriko □□ 518 Mike Eagles
□□ 519 Mike Hartman □□ 520 Bob Beers RC
□□ 521 DelGuidice (G) RC □□ 522 C. Winnes RC
□□ 523 Brad May □□ 524 Donald Audette
□□ 525 Kevin Haller RC □□ 526 M. Simard RC
□□ 527 T. Forslund RC □□ 528 M. Osiecki RC
□□ 529 D. Hasek (G) RC □□ 530 Jimmy Waite (G)
□□ 531 Nicklas Lidström RC, Err. (Niklas)
□□ 532 Martin Lapointe □□ 533 V. Konstantinov
□□ 534 J. Beranek RC □□ 535 L. DeBrusk RC
□□ 536 G. Sanderson RC □□ 537 Mark Greig RC
□□ 538 Michel Picard RC □□ 539 C. Tancill RC
□□ 540 Peter Ahola RC □□ 541 F. Breault RC
□□ 542 Darryl Sydor □□ 543 Derian Hatcher
□□ 544 Marc Bureau RC □□ 545 J. LeClair RC
□□ 546 Paul DiPietro RC
□□ 547 Scott Niedermayer, Err. (Neidermayer)
□□ 548 Kevin Todd RC □□ 549 D. Weight RC
□□ 550 T. Amonte RC □□ 551 C. Foster RC
□□ 552 D. Roussel (G) RC □□ 553 Dan Kordic RC
□□ 554 Jim Paek RC □□ 555 Kip Miller
□□ 556 C. Lapointe RC □□ 557 Nelson Emerson
□□ 558 Pat Falloon □□ 559 P. MacLeod RC
□□ 560 Rick Lessard RC □□ 561 Link Gaetz RC
□□ 562 Rob Pearson RC □□ 563 Alex. Godynyuk RC
□□ 564 Pavel Bure □□ 565 R. Romaniuk RC
□□ 566 Stu Barnes □□ 567 Ray Bourque
□□ 568 Mike Ramsey □□ 569 Joe Nieuwendyk
□□ 570 Dirk Graham □□ 571 Steve Yzerman
□□ 572 Kevin Lowe □□ 573 Randy Ladouceur
□□ 574 Wayne Gretzky □□ 575 Mark Tinordi
□□ 576 Guy Carbonneau □□ 577 Bruce Driver
□□ 578 Pat Flatley □□ 579 Mark Messier
□□ 580 Rick Tocchet □□ 581 Mario Lemieux
□□ 582 Mike Hough □□ 583 Garth Butcher
□□ 584 Doug Wilson □□ 585 Wendel Clark
□□ 586 Trevor Linden □□ 587 Rod Langway
□□ 588 Troy Murray □□ 589 Canadiens Practice
□□ 590 Shape Up... □□ 591 Bruins Cartoon
□□ 592 ML Gardens □□ 593 Rod Gilbert
□□ 594 Phil Esposito □□ 595 Dale Tallon
□□ 596 Gilbert Perreault □□ 597 Bernie Federko
□□ 598 All-Star Game □□ 599 Patrick Roy (G)
□□ 600 Ed Belfour (G) □□ 601 Don Beaupré (G)
□□ 602 Bob Essensa (G) □□ 603 K. McLean (G), Err.
□□ 604 Mike Gartner □□ 605 Jeremy Roenick
□□ 606 Rob Brown □□ 607 Ulf Dahlen
□□ 608 Paul Ysebaert □□ 609 Brad McCrimmon
□□ 610 Nicklas Lidström □□ 611 Kelly Miller
□□ 612 Jim Kyte □□ 613 Patrick Roy (G)
□□ 614 Alan May □□ 615 Kelly Miller

INSERTS

Cards CC1,CC2 and CC5-CC9 have both an English and a French issue; cards CC3 and CC4 are only available in English. French "CC" cards have the same value as English "CC" cards. Roy's card #125 autograph was inserted in French series one packs; Roy's card #599 autograph was inserted in French series two packs; McLean's card #501 autograph was inserted into English packs. The 75th Anniversary logo holograms were serial numbered to 10,000 copies.

	Description	NRMT-MT
□□	CC1 1991 Draft	.25
□□	CC2 Patrick Roy (G), Mont. [Mask]	3.00
□□	CC3 Pat Falloon, SanJ. Draft	4.00
□□	CC4 Scott Niedermayer, NJer.	8.00
□□	CC5 Wayne Gretzky, LosA.	4.00
□□	CC6 Brett Hull, SLou.	1.00
□□	CC7 Adam Oates, SLou.	.25
□□	CC8 Mark Recchi, Pitt.	.25
□□	CC9 John Cullen, Hart.	.25
□	125 Patrick Roy (G) Autograph	200.00
□	501 Kirk McLean (G) Autograph	20.00
□	599 Patrick Roy (G) Autograph	200.00
□	NHL 75th Anniversary logo	35.00

MISCELLANEOUS PRO SET CARDS

	Gazette	NRMT-MT
□	2 Patrick Roy (G), Mont.	4.00
	Hall of Fame	**NRMT-MT**
□	1 Mike Bossy, NYIs.	15.00
□	2 Denis Potvin, NYIs.	15.00
□	3 Bob Pulford	8.00
□	4 Scott Bowman	15.00
□	5 Neil P. Armstrong	8.00
□	6 Clint Smith	8.00
□	7 Silver Seven	6.00
□	8 Silver Seven	6.00
□	9 Senators	6.00
□	10 Senators	6.00
□	11 Senators	6.00
□	12 Senators	6.00
□	13 Senators	6.00
	No. Midwest Show	**NRMT-MT**
□	1of4 Adam Oates, SLou.	8.00
□	2of4 Paul Cavallini, SLou.	3.00
□	3of4 Rick Meagher, SLou.	3.00
□	4of4 Brett Hull, SLou.	12.00
	Description of the Month	**NRMT-MT**
□	P1 Kirk McLean (G), Vanc.	3.00
□	P2 Kevin Stevens, Pitt.	3.00
□	P3 Mario Lemieux, Pitt.	18.00
□	P4 Pat LaFontaine, NYIs.	3.00
□	P5 Andy Moog (G), Bost.	3.00
□	P6 Luc Robitaille, LosA.	5.00

1991 - 92 PRO SET PLATINUM

The most expensive singles are Wayne Gretzky, Dominik Hasek at $4.00 and John LeClair at $1.00-1.50. All other singles sell between 20¢ and $1.00.

Imprint: Series One: Pro Set NHL & NHLPA 1991
Series Two: PRO SET NHL AND NHLPA 1992
Complete Set (300 cards) 12.00

Description **No. Player**

□ 1 Cam Neely □ 2 Ray Bourque
□ 3 Craig Janney □ 4 Andy Moog (G)
□ 5 Dave Poulin □ 6 Ken Hodge
□ 7 Glen Wesley □ 8 Dave Andreychuk
□ 9 Daren Puppa (G) □ 10 Pierre Turgeon
□ 11 Dale Hawerchuk □ 12 Doug Bodger
□ 13 Mike Ramsey □ 14 Alexander Mogilny
□ 15 Sergei Makarov □ 16 Theoren Fleury
□ 17 Joel Otto □ 18 Joe Nieuwendyk
□ 19 Al MacInnis □ 20 Gary Suter
□ 21 Mike Vernon (G) □ 22 John Tonelli
□ 23 Dirk Graham □ 24 Jeremy Roenick
□ 25 Chris Chelios □ 26 Ed Belfour (G)
□ 27 Steve Smith □ 28 Steve Larmer
□ 29 Johan Garpenlov □ 30 Sergei Fedorov
□ 31 Tim Cheveldae (G) □ 32 Steve Yzerman
□ 33 Jimmy Carson □ 34 Bob Probert
□ 35 V. Damphousse □ 36 Bill Ranford (G)
□ 37 Petr Klima □ 38 Kevin Lowe
□ 39 Esa Tikkanen □ 40 Craig Simpson
□ 41 Peter Ing (G) □ 42 Rob Brown
□ 43 Bobby Holik □ 44 Pat Verbeek
□ 45 Brad Shaw □ 46 Kevin Dineen
□ 47 Zarley Zalapski □ 48 Jari Kurri
□ 49 Tony Granato □ 50 Luc Robitaille
□ 51 Rob Blake □ 52 Wayne Gretzky
□ 53 Tomas Sandström □ 54 Kelly Hrudey (G)
□ 55 Mike Modano □ 56 Jon Casey
□ 57 Todd Elik □ 58 Mark Tinordi
□ 59 Brian Bellows □ 60 Dave Gagner
□ 61 Patrick Roy (G) □ 62 Russ Courtnall
□ 63 Guy Carbonneau □ 64 Denis Savard
□ 65 Petr Svoboda □ 66 Kirk Muller
□ 67 Stéphane Richer □ 68 Chris Terreri (G)
□ 69 Bruce Driver □ 70 John MacLean
□ 71 Patrik Sundstrom □ 72 Scott Stevens
□ 73 Glenn Healy (G) □ 74 Brent Sutter
□ 75 David Volek □ 76 Ray Ferraro
□ 77 Patrick Flatley □ 78 Jeff Norton
□ 79 Brian Leetch □ 80 Tim Kerr
□ 81 Mark Messier □ 82 James Patrick
□ 83 Mike Richter (G) □ 84 Mike Gartner
□ 85 Mike Ricci □ 86 Steve Duchesne
□ 87 Ron Hextall (G) □ 88 Rick Tocchet
□ 89 Per-Erik Eklund □ 90 Rod Brind'Amour
□ 91 Mario Lemieux □ 92 Jaromir Jagr
□ 93 Kevin Stevens □ 94 Paul Coffey
□ 95 Ulf Samuelsson □ 96 Tom Barrasso (G)
□ 97 Mark Recchi □ 98 Ron Tugnutt (G)
□ 99 Mats Sundin □ 100 Stéphane Morin
□ 101 Owen Nolan □ 102 Joe Sakic
□ 103 Bryan Fogarty □ 104 Kelly Kisio
□ 105 Tony Hrkac □ 106 Brian Mullen
□ 107 Doug Wilson □ 108 Rich Sutter
□ 109 Brett Hull □ 110 Dave Christian
□ 111 Brendan Shanahan □ 112 V. Riendeau (G)
□ 113 Adam Oates □ 114 Jeff Brown
□ 115 Gary Leeman □ 116 Dave Ellett
□ 117 Grant Fuhr (G) □ 118 Daniel Marois
□ 119 Mike Krushelnyski □ 120 Wendel Clark
□ 121 Troy Gamble (G) □ 122 Robert Kron
□ 123 Geoff Courtnall □ 124 Trevor Linden
□ 125 Greg Adams □ 126 Igor Larionov
□ 127 Kevin Hatcher □ 128 Mike Ridley
□ 129 John Druce □ 130 Al Iafrate
□ 131 Dino Ciccarelli □ 132 Michal Pivonka
□ 133 Fredrik Olausson □ 134 Ed Olczyk
□ 135 Bob Essensa (G) □ 136 Pat Elynuik
□ 137 Phil Housley □ 138 Thomas Steen
□ 139 Don Beaupré (G) □ 140 Boston Bruins
□ 141 Blackhawks □ 142 Kings (/b: Gretzky)
□ 143 North Stars □ 144 Pittsburgh Penguins
□ 145 Boston Bruins □ 146 Blackhawks
□ 147 Detroit Red Wings □ 148 Montréal Canadiens
□ 149 New York Rangers □ 150 Toronto Maple Leafs
□ 151 Stephen Leach □ 152 Vladimir Ruzicka
□ 153 Don Sweeney □ 154 Bob Carpenter
□ 155 Brent Ashton □ 156 Gord Murphy
□ 157 Pat LaFontaine □ 158 Randy Hillier
□ 159 Clint Malarchuk □ 160 Randy Wood
□ 161 Gary Roberts □ 162 Gary Leeman
□ 163 Robert Reichel □ 164 Brent Sutter
□ 165 Brian Noonan □ 166 Michel Goulet
□ 167 Paul Ysebaert □ 168 Kevin Miller
□ 169 Ray Sheppard □ 170 Brad McCrimmon
□ 171 Joe Murphy □ 172 Dave Manson
□ 173 Scott Mellanby □ 174 Bernie Nicholls
□ 175 John Cullen □ 176 Marc Bergevin
□ 177 Steve Konroyd □ 178 Kay Whitmore (G)
□ 179 Murray Craven □ 180 Mikael Andersson
□ 181 Bob Kudelski □ 182 Brian Benning
□ 183 Mike Donnelly □ 184 Marty McSorley
□ 185 Corey Millen RC □ 186 Ulf Dahlen
□ 187 Brian Propp □ 188 Neal Broten
□ 189 Mike Craig □ 190 Stéphan Lebeau
□ 191 Mike Keane □ 192 Brent Gilchrist
□ 193 Eric Desjardins □ 194 Peter Stastny
□ 195 Claude Vilgrain □ 196 Claude Lemieux
□ 197 Craig Billington (G) RC (Error: photo is Terreri)
□ 198 Alexei Kasatonov □ 199 Viacheslav Fetisov
□ 200 Benoît Hogue □ 201 Derek King
□ 202 Uwe Krupp □ 203 Steve Thomas
□ 204 John Ogrodnick □ 205 S. Nemchinov
□ 206 Jeff Beukeboom □ 207 Adam Graves
□ 208 Andrei Lomakin □ 209 Dan Quinn
□ 210 Ken Wreggett (G) □ 211 Garry Galley
□ 212 Terry Carkner □ 213 Larry Murphy
□ 214 Ron Francis □ 215 Bob Errey
□ 216 Bryan Trottier □ 217 Mike Hough
□ 218 Mikhail Tatarinov □ 219 Jacques Cloutier
□ 220 Greg Paslawski □ 221 A. Gusarov RC
□ 222 Ron Sutter □ 223 Garth Butcher
□ 224 Paul Cavallini □ 225 Curtis Joseph (G)
□ 226 Jeff Hackett (G) □ 227 David Bruce RC
□ 228 Wayne Presley □ 229 Neil Wilkinson
□ 230 Dean Evason □ 231 Brian Bradley
□ 232 Peter Zezel □ 233 Mike Bullard
□ 234 Doug Gilmour □ 235 Jamie Macoun
□ 236 Cliff Ronning □ 237 Jyrki Lumme
□ 238 Tom Fergus □ 239 Kirk McLean (G)
□ 240 Sergio Momesso □ 241 Randy Burridge
□ 242 Dimitri Khristich □ 243 Calle Johansson
□ 244 Peter Bondra □ 245 Dale Hunter
□ 246 Darrin Shannon □ 247 Troy Murray
□ 248 Teppo Numminen □ 249 Donald Audette
□ 250 Kevin Haller RC □ 251 A. Godynyuk RC
□ 252 D. Hasek (G) RC □ 253 N. Lidström RC
□ 254 V. Konstantinov □ 255 J. Beranek RC
□ 256 G. Sanderson RC □ 257 Peter Ahola RC
□ 258 Derian Hatcher □ 259 John LeClair RC
□ 260 Kevin Todd RC □ 261 V. Zelepukin RC
□ 262 Tony Amonte RC □ 263 Doug Weight RC
□ 264 Claude Boivin RC □ 265 Corey Foster RC
□ 266 Jim Paek RC □ 267 C. Lapointe RC
□ 268 Adam Foote RC □ 269 Nelson Emerson
□ 270 Arturs Irbe (G) □ 271 Pat Falloon
□ 272 Pavel Bure □ 273 Stu Barnes
□ 274 R. Romaniuk RC □ 275 L. Borsato RC
□ 276 Al MacInnis □ 277 Sergei Fedorov
□ 278 Ray Bourque □ 279 Mike Richter (G)
□ 280 Campbell Conf. □ 281 Wales Conference
□ 282 Brett Hull □ 283 Alexander Mogilny
□ 284 Brian Leetch □ 285 Bob Essensa (G)
□ 286 Derek King □ 287 Steve Larmer
□ 288 Chris Terreri (G) □ 289 Terry O'Reilly
□ 290 Burton Cummins □ 291 Marv Albert
□ 292 Larry King □ 293 Jim Kelly
□ 294 David Wheaton □ 295 Ralph Macchio
□ 296 Rick Hansen □ 297 Fred Rogers
□ 298 Gaetan Boucher □ 299 S. Saint James
□ 300 James Belushi

INSERTS

The most expensive card is Gretzky at $4. All other singles sell between 25¢ and $1.

Insert Set (20 cards): 8.00

Pro Set **Pro Set**

□ PC1 John Vanbiesbrouck (G) □ PC2 Pete Peeters (G)
□ PC3 Tom Barrasso (G) □ PC4 Wayne Gretzky
□ PC5 Brett Hull □ PC6 Kelly Hrudey (G)
□ PC7 Sergei Fedorov □ PC8 Rob Blake
□ PC9 Ken (Jr.) Hodge □ PC10 Eric Weinrich
□ PC11 Mike Gartner □ PC12 Paul Coffey
□ PC13 Bobby Smith □ PC14 Wayne Gretzky
□ PC15 Michel Goulet □ PC16 Mike Liut (G)
□ PC17 Brian Propp □ PC18 Denis Savard
□ PC19 Bryan Trottier □ PC20 Mark Messier

1991 - 92 PROCARDS

Singles start at 25¢. Regional stars start at 1.00.
Imprint: 1991 ProCards, Inc. Made in USA
Complete Set (620 cards): 120.00

ROCHESTER AMERICANS - AHL

Team Set (24 cards): 8.00

ProCards	ProCards
1 Bill Houlder	2 Brian Curran
3 Dan Frawley	4 Darcy Loewen
5 Jiri Sejba	6 Lindy Ruff
7 Chris Snell	8 Bob Corkum
9 Dave Baseggio	10 Sean O'Donnell
11 Brad Rubachuk	12 Peter Ciavaglia
13 Joel Savage	14 Jason Winch
15 Steve Ludzik	16 Don McSween
17 David DiVita	18 Greg Brown
19 David Littman (G)	20 Tom Draper (G)
21 Jody Gage	22 T. Martin, A. Coach
23 Don Lever, Coach	24 Americans Checklist

PEORIA RIVERMEN - IHL

Guy Hebert is the most expensive player at $2-3.
Team Set (23 cards): 8.00

ProCards	ProCards
25 Jason Marshall	26 Michel Mongeau
27 Derek Frenette	28 Kevin Miehm
29 Guy Hebert (G)	30 Greg Poss
31 Dave Mackey	32 Dan Fowler
33 Mark Bassen	34 Yves Heroux
35 H. Snepsts, Coach	36 Bruce Shoebottom
37 Jaan Luik	38 Alain Raymond (G)
39 Kyle Reeves	40 Brian McKee
41 Steve Tuttle	42 Rob Tustian
43 Richard Pion	44 Joe Hawley
45 Brian Pellerin	46 Jason Ruff
47 Rivermen Checklist	

MAINE MARINERS - AHL

Team Set (22 cards): 8.00

ProCards	ProCards
48 Wes Walz	49 Steve Bancroft
50 John Blue (G)	51 Rick Allain
52 Mike Walsh	53 Dave Thomlinson
54 Dennis Smith	55 Jack Capuano
56 Mike Rossetti	57 Petr Prajsler
58 Matt Glennon	59 John Byce
60 Howie Rosenblatt	61 Brad Tiley
62 Lou Crawford	63 Matt Hervey
64 Peter Douris	65 Jeff Lazaro
66 Dave Reid	67 E. J. McGuire, Coach
68 F. Bathe, A. Coach	69 Mariners Checklist

FREDERICTON CANADIENS - AHL

Team Set (23 cards): 8.00

ProCards	ProCards
70 Paul DiPietro	71 Darcy Simon
72 Patrick Lebeau	73 Gilbert Dionne
74 John Ferguson	75 Norman Desjardins
76 Luc Gauthier	77 J.C. Bergeron (G)
78 André Racicot (G)	79 Steve Veilleux
80 Patrice Brisebois	81 Tom Sagissor
82 Lindsay Vallis	83 Steve Larouche
84 Sean Hill	85 Jesse Belanger
86 Stéphane Richer	87 Marc Labelle
88 Pierre Sévigny	89 Eric Charron
90 Ed Ronan	91 P. Bordeleau, Coach
92 Canadiens Checklist	

SPRINGFIELD INDIANS - AHL

Team Set (25 cards): 8.00

ProCards	ProCards
93 Daryl Reaugh (G)	94 Jergus Baca
95 Karl Johnston	96 Shawn Evans
97 Scott Humeniuk	98 Cam Brauer
99 Scott Eichstadt	100 Paul Cyr
101 James Black	102 Chris Govedaris
103 Joe Day	104 Chris Tancill
105 Kerry Russell	106 Denis Chalifoux
107 Blair Atcheynum	108 John Stevens
109 Brian Chapman	110 Chris Bright
111 Jim Burke	112 Scott Daniels
113 Kelly Ens	114 Mike Tomlak
115 Mario Gosselin (G)	116 Jay Leach, Coach
117 Indians Checklist	

ADIRONDACK RED WINGS - AHL

Keith Primeau is the most expensive player at $4-5.
Team Set (25 cards): 10.00

ProCards	ProCards
118 Allan Bester (G)	119 Daniel Shank
120 Lonnie Loach	121 Mark Reimer (G)
122 Kirk Tomlinson	123 Stewart Malgunas
124 Serge Anglehart	125 Chris Luongo
126 Keith Primeau	127 Ken Quinney
128 Dave Flanagan	129 Pete Stauber
130 Mike Sillinger	131 Micah Aivazoff
132 Gary Shuchuk	133 Bill McDougall
134 Sheldon Kennedy	135 Derek Mayer
136 Darin Bannister	137 Guy Dupuis
138 Gord Kruppke	139 Jason York
140 B. Melrose, Coach	141 Merkosky, A. Coach
142 Red Wings Checklist	

KALAMAZOO WINGS - IHL

Team Set (21 cards): 8.00

ProCards	ProCards
143 Larry Dyck (G)	144 Roy Mitchell
145 Greg Spenrath	146 Steve Herniman
147 Brad Berry	148 Jim Nesich
149 Tim Lenardon	150 Steve Guenette (G)
151 Paul Jerrard	152 Cal McGowan
153 Scott Robinson	154 Mitch Messier
155 Tony Joseph	156 Steve Maltais
157 Steve Gotaas	158 Doug Barrault
159 Dave Moylan	160 Mario Thyer
161 Hoffmeyer, Coach	162 Dawson, A. Coach
163 Wings Checklist	

MONCTON HAWKS - AHL

Team Set (26 cards): 8.00

ProCards	ProCards
164 Rob Murray	165 Chris Kiene
166 Lee Davidson	167 Rudy Poeschek
168 Kent Paynter	169 John LeBlanc
170 Dallas Eakins	171 Claude Julien
172 Bob Joyce	173 Derek Langille
174 Rob Cowie	175 Warren Rychel
176 Tom Karalis	177 Kris Draper
178 Ken Gernander	179 Tod Hartje
180 Sean Gauthier (G)	181 Tyler Larter
182 Scott Levins	183 Jason Cirone
184 Mark Kumpel	185 Rick Tabaracci (G)
186 Luciano Borsato	187 Farrish, H.C./G.M.
188 Prior, Goal Coach	189 Hawks Checklist

BINGHAMTON RANGERS - AHL

Team Set (25 cards): 8.00

ProCards	ProCards
190 Peter Fiorentino	191 Glen Goodall
192 John Mokosak	193 Sam St. Laurent (G)
194 Daniel Lacroix	195 Guy LaRose
196 Mike Hurlbut	197 Peter Laviolette
198 Rick Bennett	199 Steven King
200 Boris Rousson (G)	201 Jody Hull
202 Shaun Sabol	203 Joe Paterson
204 Rob Zamuner	205 Don Biggs
206 Chris Cichocki	207 Ross Fitzpatrick
208 Mark LaForest	209 Brian McReynolds
210 Jeff Bloemberg	211 Kord Cernich
212 Ron Smith, Coach	213 Al Hill, Asst. Coach
214 Rangers Checklist	

CAPE BRETON OILERS - AHL

Martin Rucinsky is the most expensive player at $1-2.
Team Set (24 cards): 8.00

ProCards	ProCards
215 François Leroux	216 Marc Laforge
217 Max Middendorf	218 Shjon Podein
219 Jason Soules	220 Collin Bauer
221 Shaun Van Allen	222 Eldon Reddick (G)
223 E. Belosheikin (G)	224 David Haas
225 Norm Foster (G)	226 Greg Hawgood
227 Steven Rice	228 Dan Currie
229 Peter Soberlak	230 Martin Rucinsky
231 Tomas Kapusta	232 Dean Antos
233 Craig Fisher	234 Tomas Srsen
235 MacAdam, Coach	236 Ferguson, A. Coach
237 Coaching Staff	238 Oilers Checklist

FORT WAYNE KOMETS - IHL

Team Set (24 cards): 8.00

ProCards	ProCards
239 Peter Hankinson	240 Chris McRae
241 Craig Martin	242 Carey Lucyk
243 Jean-Marc Richard	244 Grant Richison
245 Mark Turner	246 Todd Flichel
247 Scott Shaunessy	248 Darin Smith
249 Ian Boyce	250 Colin Chin
251 Bob Jones	252 Bob Jay
253 Kelly Hurd	254 Scott Gruhl
255 Kory Kocur	256 Steven Fletcher
257 Bob Lakso	258 Dusty Imoo (G)
259 Mike O'Neill (G)	260 Boudreau, A. Coach
261 Al Sims, Coach	262 Komets Checklist

HERSHEY BEARS - AHL

Team Set (25 cards): 8.00

ProCards	ProCards
263 R. Letourneau (G)	264 Marc D'Amour (G)
265 D. Roussel (G)	266 Bill Armstrong
267 Al Conroy	268 Dale Kushner
269 Toni Porkka	270 Mike Stothers
271 Darren Rumble	272 Reid Simpson
273 Claude Boivn	274 Len Barrie
275 Chris Jensen	276 Pat Murray
277 Eric Dandenault	278 Rod Dallman
279 Mark Freer	280 Bill Armstrong
281 Tim Tookey	282 Jamie Cooke
283 David Fenyves	284 Steve Morrow
285 Martin Hostak	286 Mike Eaves, Coach
287 Bears Checklist	

MUSKEGON LUMBERJACKS - IHL

Team Set (23 cards): 8.00

ProCards	ProCards
288 Dave Michayluk	289 Glenn Mulvenna
290 Jean Blouin	291 Jock Callander
292 Perry Ganchar	293 Paul Laus
294 Mark Major	295 Bruce Racine (G)
296 Daniel Gauthier	297 Mike Needham
298 Jeff Daniels	299 Sandy Smith
300 Gilbert Delorme	301 Rob Dopson (G)
302 Eric Brule	303 Alain Morissette (G)
304 Paul Dyck	305 Jason Smart
306 Gord Dineen	307 Todd Nelson
308 Jamie Heward	309 Phil Russell, Coach
310 Lumberjacks Checklist	

SAN DIEGO GULLS - IHL

Team Set (24 cards): 8.00

ProCards	ProCards
311 Soren True	312 Murray Duval
313 Dmitri Kvartalnov	314 Larry Floyd
315 Alan Leggett	316 Alan Hepple
317 Ron Duguay	318 Len Hachborn
319 Steve Martinson	320 Rick Knickle (G)
321 Darcy Norton	322 Keith Gretzky
323 Brian Straub	324 Denny Lambert
325 Jason Prosofsky	326 Bruce Hoffort (G)
327 Sergei Starikov	328 Dave Korol
329 Robbie Nichols	330 Kord Cernich
331 Brent Sapergia	332 Don Waddell, Coach
333 Simmer, A. Coach	334 Gulls Checklist

ST. JOHN'S MAPLE LEAFS - AHL

Félix Potvin is the most expensive player at $10.00. Damian Rhodes and Marc Crawford sell at $2.00 each.
Team Set (25 cards): 12.00

ProCards	ProCards
235 Rob Mendel	336 Curtis Hunt
337 Jeff Serowik	338 Bruce Bell
339 Yanic Perreault	340 Brad Aitken
341 Keith Osborne	342 Todd Hawkins
343 Andrew McKim	344 Kevin McClelland
345 Mike Stevens	346 Dave Tomlinson
347 Kevin Maguire	348 Mike MacWilliam
349 Greg Walters	350 Guy Lehoux
351 Todd Gillingham	352 Len Esau
353 Greg Johnston	354 Félix Potvin (G)
355 D. Rhodes (G)	356 Quenneville,ACoach
357 Crawford, Coach	358 Mike Eastwood
359 Maple Leafs Checklist	

NEW HAVEN NIGHTHAWKS - AHL

Team Set (24 cards): 8.00

ProCards	ProCards
360 Lou Franceschetti	361 John Anderson
362 Scott Schneider	363 Jérôme Béchard
364 Mario Doyon	365 Jeff Jackson
366 John Tanner (G)	367 Al Tuer
368 Paul Willett	369 Darryl Williams
370 G. Maneluk (G)	371 Eric Ricard
372 Trevor Stienburg	373 Jerry Tarrant
374 Michael McEwen	375 Brian Dobbin
376 David Latta	377 Jim Sprott
378 Trevor Pochipinski	379 Stan Drulia
380 Kent Hulst	381 Brad Turner
382 Carpenter, Coach	383 Nighthawks CL

PHOENIX ROADRUNNERS - IHL

Team Set (24 cards): 8.00

ProCards	ProCards
384 Bob Berg	385 Steve Jaques
386 Chris Norton	387 Vern Smith
388 Kevin MacDonald	389 Ross Wilson
390 Shawn McCosh	391 Mike Vukonich
392 Marc Saumier	393 Mike Ruark
394 Kris Miller	395 Tim Breslin
396 Paul Holden	397 Jeff Rohlicek
398 Kyosti Karjalainen	399 David Goverde (G)
400 John Van Kessel	401 Sean Whyte
402 Brent Thompson	403 Darryl Gilmour (G)
404 Scott Bjugstad	405 Backstrom, Coach
406 Kozuback, A.Coach	407 Roadrunners CL

UTICA DEVILS - AHL

Team Set (20 cards): 8.00

ProCards	ProCards
408 Brent Severyn	409 Dean Malkoc
410 Matt Ruchty	411 Jarrod Skalde
412 Brian Sullivan	413 B. Hankinson, Error
414 Bill Huard	415 Jeff Christian
416 Corey Schwab (G)	417 Kevin Dean
418 Todd Copeland	419 Mike Bodnarchuk
420 Jason Miller	421 Chad Erickson (G)
422 David Craievich	423 Jim Dowd
424 Jamie Huscroft	425 Myles O'Connor
426 Jon Morris	427 Valeri Zelepukin
428 Devils Checklist	

FLINT BULLDOGS - COLONIAL LEAGUE

Team Set (23 cards): 8.00

ProCards	ProCards
429 Brad Beck	430 Brett MacDonald
431 Jacques Mailhot	432 Francis Ouellette
433 Ron Kinghorn (G)	434 Dennis Miller
435 Darren Miciak	436 Tom Sasso
437 Peter Corbett	438 Brian Horan
439 John Messuri	440 E.J. Sauer
441 Tom Mutch	442 Jason Simon
443 Steve Sullivan	444 Scott Allen
445 Stéphane Brochu	446 Ken Spangler
447 Lee Odelein	448 Antti Autere
449 John Reid	450 Probst, Coach/G.M.
451 Bulldogs Checklist	

CAPITAL DISTRICT ISLANDERS - AHL

Team Set (25 cards): 8.00

ProCards	ProCards
452 Dean Ewen	453 Brett Grieve
454 Jim Culhane	455 Joni Lehto
456 G. Townshend	457 Danny Lorenz (G)
458 Phil Huber	459 Kevin Cheveldayoff
460 Dennis Vaske	461 Wayne Doucet
462 Greg Parks	463 Dean Chynoweth
464 Lee Giffin	465 Richard Kromm
466 Derek Laxdal	467 Travis Green
468 Iain Fraser	469 Rick Hayward
470 Jeff Finley	471 Dave Chyzowski
472 M. Fitzpatrick (G)	473 Hubie McDonough
474 Sean LeBrun	475 Chris Pryor
476 Islanders Checklist	

INDIANAPOLIS ICE - IHL

Dominik Hasek is the most expensive player at $10-12.
Team Set (28 cards): 18.00

ProCards	ProCards
477 Jeff Sirkka	478 Owen Lessard
479 Jim Playfair	480 Dan Vincelette
481 Tracey Egeland	482 Shawn Byram
483 Trevor Dam	484 Martin Desjardins
485 Milan Tichy	486 Cam Russell
487 Mike Speer	488 Sean Williams
489 Paul Gillis	490 Brad Lauer
491 Trent Yawney	492 Craig Woodcroft
493 Justin Lafayette	494 Robb Conn
495 Frantisek Kucera	496 Mike Peluso
497 Roch Belley (G)	498 Ryan McGill
499 Kerry Toporowski	500 Dominik Hasek (G)
501 Adam Bennett	502 Ray LeBlanc (G)
503 John Marks, Coach	504 Ice Checklist

KANSAS CITY BLADES - IHL

Team Set (23 cards): 8.00

ProCards	ProCards
505 Mikhail Kravets	506 Gary Emmons
507 Ed Courtenay	508 Claudio Scremin
509 Jarmo Myllys (G)	510 Mike Colman
511 Kevin Evans	512 Troy Frederick
513 Ron Handy	514 Murray Garbutt
515 Gord Frantti	516 Dale Craigwell
517 Wade Flaherty (G)	518 Dean Kolstad
519 Rick Lessard	520 Craig Coxe
521 Jeff Madill	522 Peter Lappin
523 Duane Joyce	524 Larry DePalma
525 Pat MacLeod	526 Andy Akervik
527 Blades Checklist	

HALIFAX CITADELS - AHL

Stéphane Fiset is the most expensive player at $2-3.
Team Set (19 cards): 8.00

ProCards	ProCards
528 Mike Dagenais	529 Gerald Bzdel
530 Stéphane Fiset (G)	531 David Espe
532 P. Labrecque (G)	533 Niclas Andersson
534 Jon Klemm	535 Denis Chassé
536 S. Charbonneau	537 Ivan Matulik
538 Serge Roberge	539 Daniel Doré
540 Sergei Kharin	541 Jamie Baker
542 Ken McRae	543 Dave Marcinyshyn
544 C. Jodoin, Coach	545 Hopkins, A. Coach
546 Citadels Checklist	

BALTIMORE SKIPJACKS - AHL

Olaf Kolzig is the most expensive player at $4-5.
Team Set (27 cards): 8.00

ProCards	ProCards
547 Jeff Greenlaw	548 Byron Dafoe (G)
549 Jim Hrivnak (G)	550 Olaf Kolzig (G)
551 John Purves	552 Bobby Reynolds
553 Simon Wheeldon	554 Jim Mathieson
555 Trevor Halverson	556 Steve Seftel
557 Ken Lovsin	558 Victor Gervais
559 Steve Martell	560 Chris Clarke
561 Brent Hughes	562 Jiri Vykoukal
563 Tim Taylor	564 Richie Walcott
565 Harry Mews	566 Craig Duncanson
567 Todd Hlushko	568 Mark Ferner
569 Bob Babcock	570 Reggie Savage
571 Rob Laird, Coach	572 B. Trotz, A. Coach
573 Skipjacks Checklist	

SALT LAKE GOLDEN EAGLES - IHL

Team Set (21 cards): 8.00

ProCards	ProCards
574 Kevan Melrose	575 Kevin Grant
576 Kevan Guy	577 Darryl Olsen
578 Kevin Wortman	579 Darren Stolk
580 Bryan Deasley	581 Paul Kruse
582 Darren Banks	583 Corey Lyons
584 Kerry Clark	585 Todd Strueby
586 Rich Chernomaz	587 Tim Harris
588 Shawn Heaphy	589 Todd Harkins
590 Richard Zemlak	591 W. Sharples (G)
592 J. Muzzatti (G)	593 Dennis Holland
594 Golden Eagles Checklist	

MILWAUKEE ADMIRALS - IHL

Team Set (26 cards): 8.00

ProCards	ProCards
595 Shawn Antoski	596 Peter Bakovic
597 Robin Bawa	598 Cam Brown
599 Neil Eisenhut	600 Jason Herter
601 Ian Kidd	602 Troy Neumeier
603 Carl Valimont	604 Phil Von Stefenelli
605 Andrew McBain	606 Eric Murano
607 Rob Murphy	608 Brian Blad
609 Randy Boyd	610 Don Gibson
611 Paul Guay	612 Jay Mazur
613 Jeff Larmer	614 Ladislav Tresl
615 Dennis Snedden	616 Corrie D'Alessio (G)
617 Bob Mason (G)	618 McIlhargey, Coach
619 Fraser, A. Coach	620 Admirals Checklist

1991 - 92 PUCK - PRO SET

Three of 30 different cards were packaged with a chocolate, peanut and caramel candy bar.
Imprint: Pro Set Inc.

Complete Set (30 cards): 10.00

Pro Set	Puck
1 Raymond Bourque, Bost.	1.00
2 Andy Moog (G), Bost.	.25
3 Doug Bodger, Buff.	.25
4 Theoren Fleury, Calg.	.50
5 Al MacInnis, Calg.	.25
6 Jeremy Roenick, Chic.	.50
7 Tim Cheveldae (G), Detr.	.25
8 Steve Yzerman, Detr.	2.00
9 Craig Simpson, Edmo.	.25
10 Pat Verbeek, Hart.	.25
11 Wayne Gretzky, LosA.	4.00
12 Luc Robitaille, LosA.	.50
13 Brian Bellows, Minn.	.25
14 Patrick Roy (G), Mont.	3.00
15 Guy Carbonneau, Mont.	.25
16 Peter Stastny, NJer.	.50
17 Adam Creighton, NYIs.	.25
18 Glenn Healy (G), NYIs.	.25
19 Mark Messier, NYRa.	1.00
20 Rod Brind'Amour, Phil.	.25
21 Paul Coffey, Pitt.	.50
22 Tom Barrasso (G), Pitt.	.25
23 Joe Sakic, Québ.	1.50
24 Brett Hull, SLou.	1.00
25 Adam Oates, SLou.	.25
26 Kelly Kisio, SanJ.	.25
27 Grant Fuhr (G), Toro.	.50
28 Kirk McLean (G), Vanc.	.25
29 Kevin Hatcher, Wash.	.25
30 Phil Housley, Winn.	.25

Pro Set		Promo
☐	Kirk McLean (G), Vanc.	1.00
☐	Andy Moog (G), Bost.	2.00
☐	Pat Verbeek, Hart.	1.00

1991 - 92 RED ACE

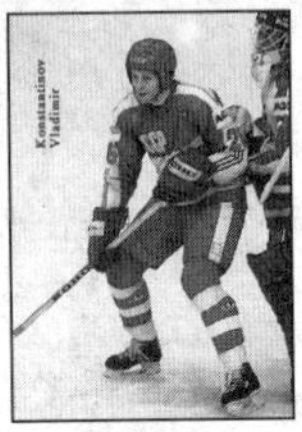

Complete Set (17 cards with folder): 10.00

	Description	NRMT-MT
☐	Pavel Bure	2.00
☐	Evgeny Davydov	.25
☐	Sergei Fedorov	2.50
☐	Viacheslav Fetisov	1.50
☐	Alexei Gusarov	.25
☐	Valeri Kamensky	.50
☐	Alexei Kasatonov	.50
☐	Ravil Khaidarov	.25
☐	Vladimir Konstantinov	.50
☐	Igor Kravchuk	.25
☐	Igor Larionov	1.50
☐	Andrei Lomakin	.25
☐	Sergei Makarov	1.00
☐	Alexander Mogilny	1.00
☐	Sergei Nemchinov	.50
☐	Anatoli Semenov	.25
☐	Mikhail Tatarinov	.25

1991 - 92 SCORE

The American issue of 1991-92 Score features a purple border as compared to the red or blue border in Score Canadian. The U.S. set was released as a single 440 card series. The most expensive singles are Dominik Hasek at $2.00-4.00 and Wayne Gretzky, John LeClair and Eric Lindros at $1.00-1.50. All other singles sell between 20¢ and $1.00.

Imprint: © 1991 SCORE

Complete Set (440 cards): 12.00

Description	No. Player
☐ 1 Brett Hull	☐ 2 Al MacInnis
☐ 3 Luc Robitaille	☐ 4 Pierre Turgeon
☐ 5 Brian Leetch	☐ 6 Cam Neely
☐ 7 John Cullen	☐ 8 Trevor Linden
☐ 9 Rick Tocchet	☐ 10 J. Vanbiesbrouck (G)
☐ 11 Steve Smith	☐ 12 Doug Smail
☐ 13 Craig Ludwig	☐ 14 Paul Fenton
☐ 15 Dirk Graham	☐ 16 Brad McCrimmon
☐ 17 Dean Evason	☐ 18 Fredrik Olausson
☐ 19 Guy Carbonneau	☐ 20 Kevin Hatcher
☐ 21 Paul Ranheim	☐ 22 Claude Lemieux
☐ 23 V. Riendeau (G)	☐ 24 Garth Butcher
☐ 25 Joe Sakic	☐ 26 Rick Vaive
☐ 27 Rob Blake	☐ 28 Mike Ricci
☐ 29 Patrick Flatley	☐ 30 Bill Ranford (G)
☐ 31 Larry Murphy	☐ 32 Bobby Smith
☐ 33 Mike Krushelnyski	☐ 34 Gerard Gallant
☐ 35 Doug Wilson	☐ 36 John Ogrodnick
☐ 37 Mikhail Tatarinov	☐ 38 Doug Crossman
☐ 39 Mark Osborne	☐ 40 Scott Stevens
☐ 41 Ron Tugnutt (G)	☐ 42 Russ Courtnall
☐ 43 Gord Murphy	☐ 44 Greg Adams
☐ 45 Christian Ruuttu	☐ 46 Ken Daneyko
☐ 47 Glenn Anderson	☐ 48 Ray Ferraro
☐ 49 Tony Tanti	☐ 50 Ray Bourque
☐ 51 Sergei Makarov	☐ 52 Jim Johnson
☐ 53 Troy Murray	☐ 54 Shawn Burr
☐ 55 Peter Ing (G)	☐ 56 Dale Hunter
☐ 57 Tony Granato	☐ 58 Curtis Leschyshyn
☐ 59 Brian Mullen	☐ 60 Ed Olczyk
☐ 61 Mike Ramsey	☐ 62 Dan Quinn
☐ 63 Rich Sutter	☐ 64 Terry Carkner
☐ 65 Shayne Corson	☐ 66 Peter Stastny
☐ 67 Craig Muni	☐ 68 Glenn Healy (G)
☐ 69 Phil Bourque	☐ 70 Pat Verbeek
☐ 71 Garry Galley	☐ 72 Dave Gagner
☐ 73 Bob Probert	☐ 74 Craig Wolanin
☐ 75 Patrick Roy (G)	☐ 76 Keith Brown
☐ 77 Gary Leeman	☐ 78 Brent Ashton
☐ 79 Randy Moller	☐ 80 Mike Vernon (G)
☐ 81 Kelly Miller	☐ 82 Ulf Samuelsson
☐ 83 Todd Elik	☐ 84 Uwe Krupp
☐ 85 Rod Brind'Amour	☐ 86 Dave Capuano
☐ 87 Geoff Smith	☐ 88 David Volek
☐ 89 Bruce Driver	☐ 90 Andy Moog (G)
☐ 91 Per-Erik Eklund	☐ 92 Joey Kocur
☐ 93 Mark Tinordi	☐ 94 Steve Thomas
☐ 95 Petr Svoboda	☐ 96 Joel Otto
☐ 97 Todd Krygier	☐ 98 Jaromir Jagr
☐ 99 Mike Liut (G)	☐ 100 Wayne Gretzky
☐ 101 Teppo Numminen	☐ 102 Randy Burridge
☐ 103 Michel Petit	☐ 104 Tony McKegney
☐ 105 Mathieu Schneider	☐ 106 Daron Puppa (G)
☐ 107 Paul Cavallini	☐ 108 Tim Kerr
☐ 109 Kevin Lowe	☐ 110 Kirk Muller
☐ 111 Zarley Zalapski	☐ 112 Mike Hough
☐ 113 Ken Hodge	☐ 114 Grant Fuhr (G)
☐ 115 Paul Coffey	☐ 116 Wendel Clark
☐ 117 Patrik Sundstrom	☐ 118 Kevin Dineen
☐ 119 Eric Desjardins	☐ 120 Mike Richter (G)
☐ 121 Sergio Momesso	☐ 122 Tony Hrkac
☐ 123 Joe Reekie	☐ 124 Petr Nedved
☐ 125 Randy Carlyle	☐ 126 Kevin Miller
☐ 127 Réjean Lemelin (G)	☐ 128 Dino Ciccarelli
☐ 129 Sylvain Côté	☐ 130 Mats Sundin
☐ 131 Eric Weinrich	☐ 132 D. Berthiaume (G)
☐ 133 Keith Acton	☐ 134 Benoît Hogue
☐ 135 Mike Gartner	☐ 136 Petr Klima
☐ 137 Curt Giles	☐ 138 Scott Pearson
☐ 139 Luke Richardson	☐ 140 Steve Larmer
☐ 141 Ken Wregget (G)	☐ 142 Frantisek Musil
☐ 143 Owen Nolan	☐ 144 Keith Primeau
☐ 145 Mark Recchi	☐ 146 Don Sweeney
☐ 147 Mike McPhee	☐ 148 Ken Baumgartner
☐ 149 Dave Lowry	☐ 150 Geoff Courtnall
☐ 151 Chris Terreri (G)	☐ 152 Dave Manson
☐ 153 Bobby Holik	☐ 154 Bob Kudelski
☐ 155 Calle Johansson	☐ 156 Mark Hunter
☐ 157 Randy Gilhen	☐ 158 Yves Racine
☐ 159 Martin Gelinas	☐ 160 Brian Bellows
☐ 161 David Shaw	☐ 162 Bob Carpenter
☐ 163 Doug Brown	☐ 164 Ulf Dahlén
☐ 165 Denis Savard	☐ 166 Paul Ysebaert
☐ 167 Derek King	☐ 168 Igor Larionov
☐ 169 Bob Errey	☐ 170 Joe Nieuwendyk
☐ 171 Normand Rochefort	☐ 172 John Tonelli
☐ 173 David Reid	☐ 174 Tom Kurvers
☐ 175 Dimitri Khristich	☐ 176 Bob Sweeney
☐ 177 Rick Zombo	☐ 178 Troy Mallette
☐ 179 Bob Bassen	☐ 180 John Druce
☐ 181 Mike Craig	☐ 182 John McIntyre
☐ 183 Murray Baron	☐ 184 Viacheslav Fetisov
☐ 185 Don Beaupré (G)	☐ 186 Brian Benning
☐ 187 David Barr	☐ 188 Petri Skriko
☐ 189 Steve Konroyd	☐ 190 Steve Yzerman
☐ 191 Jon Casey (G)	☐ 192 Gary Nylund
☐ 193 Michal Pivonka	☐ 194 Alexei Kasatonov
☐ 195 Garry Valk	☐ 196 Darren Turcotte
☐ 197 Chris Nilan	☐ 198 Thomas Steen
☐ 199 Gary Roberts	☐ 200 Mario Lemieux
☐ 201 Michel Goulet	☐ 202 Craig MacTavish
☐ 203 P. Sidorkiewicz (G)	☐ 204 Johan Garpenlov
☐ 205 Steve Duchesne	☐ 206 Dave Snuggerud
☐ 207 Kjell Samuelsson	☐ 208 Sylvain Turgeon
☐ 209 Al Iafrate	☐ 210 John MacLean
☐ 211 Brian Hayward (G)	☐ 212 Cliff Ronning
☐ 213 Ray Sheppard	☐ 214 Dave Taylor
☐ 215 Doug Lidster	☐ 216 Peter Bondra
☐ 217 Marty McSorley	☐ 218 Doug Gilmour
☐ 219 Paul MacDermid	☐ 220 Jeremy Roenick
☐ 221 Wayne Presley	☐ 222 Jeff Norton
☐ 223 Brian Propp	☐ 224 Jimmy Carson
☐ 225 Tom Barrasso (G)	☐ 226 Theoren Fleury
☐ 227 Carey Wilson	☐ 228 Rod Langway
☐ 229 Bryan Trottier	☐ 230 James Patrick
☐ 231 Kelly Hrudey (G)	☐ 232 Dave Poulin
☐ 233 Rob Ramage	☐ 234 Stéphane Richer
☐ 235 Chris Chelios	☐ 236 Alexander Mogilny
☐ 237 Bryan Fogarty	☐ 238 Adam Oates
☐ 239 Ron Hextall (G)	☐ 240 Bernie Nicholls
☐ 241 Esa Tikkanen	☐ 242 Jyrki Lumme
☐ 243 Brent Sutter	☐ 244 Gary Suter
☐ 245 Sean Burke (G)	☐ 246 Rob Brown
☐ 247 Mike Modano	☐ 248 Kevin Stevens
☐ 249 Mike Lalor	☐ 250 Sergei Fedorov
☐ 251 Bob Essensa (G)	☐ 252 Mark Howe
☐ 253 Craig Janney	☐ 254 Daniel Marois
☐ 255 Craig Simpson	☐ 256 Steve Kasper
☐ 257 Randy Velischek	☐ 258 Gino Cavallini
☐ 259 Dale Hawerchuk	☐ 260 Pat LaFontaine
☐ 261 Kirk McLean (G)	☐ 262 Murray Craven
☐ 263 Robert Reichel	☐ 264 Jan Erixon
☐ 265 Adam Creighton	☐ 266 M. Fitzpatrick (G)
☐ 267 Ron Francis	☐ 268 Joe Mullen
☐ 269 Peter Zezel	☐ 270 Tomas Sandström
☐ 271 Phil Housley	☐ 272 Tim Cheveldae (G)
☐ 273 Glen Wesley	☐ 274 Stéphan Lebeau
☐ 275 Dave Ellett	☐ 276 Jeff Brown
☐ 277 Dave Andreychuk	☐ 278 Steven Finn
☐ 279 Scott Mellanby	☐ 280 Neal Broten
☐ 281 Randy Wood	☐ 282 Troy Gamble (G)
☐ 283 Mike Ridley	☐ 284 Jamie Macoun
☐ 285 Mark Messier	☐ 286 Brendan Shanahan
☐ 287 Scott Young	☐ 288 Kelly Kisio
☐ 289 Brad Shaw	☐ 290 Ed Belfour (G)
☐ 291 Larry Robinson	☐ 292 Dave Christian
☐ 293 Steve Chiasson	☐ 294 Brian Skrudland
☐ 295 Pat Elynuik	☐ 296 Curtis Joseph (G)
☐ 297 Doug Bodger	☐ 298 Ron Sutter
☐ 299 Joe Murphy	☐ 300 V. Damphousse
☐ 301 Cam Neely	☐ 302 Rick Tocchet
☐ 303 Scott Stevens	☐ 304 Ulf Samuelsson
☐ 305 Jeremy Roenick	☐ 306 Hunter bros.
☐ 307 Broten bros.	☐ 308 Cavallini bros.
☐ 309 Miller bros.	☐ 310 Dennis Vaske RC
☐ 311 Rob Pearson RC	☐ 312 Jason Miller
☐ 313 John LeClair RC	☐ 314 B. Marchment RC
☐ 315 Gary Shuchuk RC	☐ 316 D.Hasek (G) RC
☐ 317 Michel Picard RC	☐ 318 Corey Millen RC
☐ 319 Joe Sacco RC	☐ 320 R. Savage RC
☐ 321 Pat Murray	☐ 322 M. O'Connor RC
☐ 323 Shawn Antoski	☐ 324 G. Sanderson RC
☐ 325 Chris Govedaris	☐ 326 A. Gusarov RC
☐ 327 Mike Sillinger	☐ 328 Bob Wilkie RC
☐ 329 P. Jablonski (G) RC	☐ 330 David Emma
☐ 331 TF: Kirk Muller	☐ 332 TF: P. LaFontaine
☐ 333 TF: Brian Leetch	☐ 334 TF: Rick Tocchet
☐ 335 TF: Mario Lemieux	☐ 336 TF: Joe Sakic
☐ 337 TF: Brett Hull	☐ 338 TF: V. Damphousse
☐ 339 TF: Trevor Linden	☐ 340 TF: Kevin Hatcher
☐ 341 TF: Pat Elynuik	☐ 342 Patrick Roy (G)
☐ 343 Brian Leetch	☐ 344 Ray Bourque
☐ 345 Luc Robitaille	☐ 346 Wayne Gretzky
☐ 347 Brett Hull	☐ 348 Ed Belfour (G)
☐ 349 Rob Blake	☐ 350 Eric Weinrich
☐ 351 Jaromir Jagr	☐ 352 Sergei Fedorov
☐ 353 Ken Hodge	☐ 354 Eric Lindros
☐ 355 Eric Lindros	☐ 356 Eric Lindros
☐ 357 Dana Murzyn	☐ 358 Adam Graves
☐ 359 Ken Linseman	☐ 360 Mike Keane
☐ 361 Stéphane Morin	☐ 362 Grant Ledyard
☐ 363 Kris King	☐ 364 Paul Gillis
☐ 365 Chris Dahlquist	☐ 366 Paul Stanton
☐ 367 Jeff Hackett (G)	☐ 368 Robert McGill
☐ 369 Neil Wilkinson	☐ 370 Rob Zettler
☐ 371 Brett Hull	☐ 372 Paul Coffey
☐ 373 Mark Messier	☐ 374 Dave Taylor
☐ 375 Michel Goulet	☐ 376 Dale Hawerchuk
☐ 377 Turgeon bros.	☐ 378 Sutter bros.
☐ 379 Mullen bros.	☐ 380 Courtnall bros.
☐ 381 Trevor Kidd (G)	☐ 382 Patrice Brisebois
☐ 383 Mark Greig	☐ 384 Kip Miller
☐ 385 Drake Berehowsky	☐ 386 Kevin Haller RC
☐ 387 David Gagnon (G)	☐ 388 Jason Marshall
☐ 389 Donald Audette	☐ 390 P. Lebeau RC
☐ 391 A. Godynyuk RC	☐ 392 J. Skalde RC
☐ 393 Ken Sutton RC	☐ 394 S. Kharin RC
☐ 395 A.Racicot (G) RC	☐ 396 Doug Weight RC
☐ 397 Kevin Todd RC	☐ 398 Tony Amonte RC
☐ 399 Kimbi Daniels RC	☐ 400 Jeff Daniels RC
☐ 401 G. Lafleur	☐ 402 G. Lafleur
☐ 403 HOF: Guy Lafleur	☐ 404 LL: Brett Hull
☐ 405 LL: Wayne Gretzky	☐ 406 LL: Wayne Gretzky
☐ 407 LL: Fleury/McSorley	☐ 408 LL: Sergei Fedorov
☐ 409 LL: Al MacInnis	☐ 410 LL: Ed Belfour (G)
☐ 411 LL: Ed Belfour (G)	☐ 412 HL: Brett Hull
☐ 413 HL: Wayne Gretzky	☐ 414 S.J Sharks Checklist
☐ 415 TF: Ray Bourque	☐ 416 TF: Pierre Turgeon
☐ 417 TF: Al MacInnis	☐ 418 TF: J. Roenick
☐ 419 TF: Steve Yzerman	☐ 420 TF: Mark Messier
☐ 421 TF: John Cullen	☐ 422 TF: Wayne Gretzky
☐ 423 TF: Mike Modano	☐ 424 TF: Patrick Roy (G)
☐ 425 Penguins	☐ 426 AW: M. Lemieux
☐ 427 AW: W. Gretzky	☐ 428 AW: Brett Hull
☐ 429 AW: Ray Bourque	☐ 430 AW: Ed Belfour (G)
☐ 431 AW: Ed Belfour (G)	☐ 432 AW: Dirk Graham
☐ 433 AW: Ed Belfour (G)	☐ 434 AW: W. Gretzky
☐ 435 AW: Dave Tippett	☐ 436 Randy Ladouceur
☐ 437 Dave Tippett	☐ 438 Clint Malarchuk (G)
☐ 439 Gord Roberts	☐ 440 F. Pietrangelo (G)

ROOKIE AND TRADED

Rookie and Traded cards have a green border and act as an update to the American series. The 110-card set was sold as a set on its own. Eric Lindros is the most expensive card at $3.00-4.00. All other singles sell between 20¢ and $1.00.

Complete Set (110 cards): 8

Description	No. Player
☐ 1T Doug Wilson	☐ 2T Brian Mullen
☐ 3T Kelly Kisio	☐ 4T Brian Hayward (G)
☐ 5T Tony Hrkac	☐ 6T Steven Bozek
☐ 7T John Carter	☐ 8T Neil Wilkinson
☐ 9T Wayne Presley	☐ 10T Bob McGill
☐ 11T Craig Ludwig	☐ 12T Mikhail Tatarinov
☐ 13T Todd Elik	☐ 14T Randy Burridge
☐ 15T Tim Kerr	☐ 16T Randy Gilhen
☐ 17T John Tonelli	☐ 18T Tom Kurvers
☐ 19T Steve Duchesne	☐ 20T Charlie Huddy
☐ 21T Adam Creighton	☐ 22T Brent Ashton
☐ 23T Rob Ramage	☐ 24T Steve Kasper
☐ 25T Scott Mellanby	☐ 26T Steve Leach
☐ 27T Scott Niedermayer	☐ 28T Craig Berube
☐ 29T Greg Paslawski	☐ 30T Randy Hillier
☐ 31T Stéphane Richer	☐ 32T Brian MacLellan
☐ 33T Marc Habscheid	☐ 34T Dave Babych
☐ 35T Troy Murray	☐ 36T Ray Sheppard
☐ 37T Glen Featherstone	☐ 38T Brendan Shanahan
☐ 39T Dave Christian	☐ 40T Mike Bullard
☐ 41T Ryan Walter	☐ 42T Randy Wood
☐ 43T V. Riendeau (G)	☐ 44T Adam Graves
☐ 45T Scott Stevens	☐ 46T Sylvain Côté
☐ 47T David Barr	☐ 48T Randy Gregg
☐ 49T Pavel Bure	☐ 50T Jari Kurri
☐ 51T Steve Thomas	☐ 52T Troy Crowder
☐ 53T Brad Jones	☐ 54T Randy McKay
☐ 55T Scott Thornton	☐ 56T Bryan Marchment
☐ 57T Andrew Cassels	☐ 58T Grant Fuhr (G)
☐ 59T V. Damphousse	☐ 60T Rick Zombo
☐ 61T Glenn Anderson	☐ 62T Peter Ing (G)
☐ 63T Tom Chorske	☐ 64T Kirk Muller
☐ 65T Dan Quinn	☐ 66T Murray Baron
☐ 67T Sergei Nemchinov	☐ 68T Rod Brind'Amour
☐ 69T Ron Sutter	☐ 70T Luke Richardson
☐ 71T N. Lidström RC	☐ 72T Petri Skriko
☐ 73T Steve Smith	☐ 74T Dave Manson
☐ 75T Kay Whitmore (G)	☐ 76T Valeri Kamensky
☐ 77T Russ Romaniuk	☐ 78T Brad May
☐ 79T Tomas Forslund	☐ 80T Stu Barnes
☐ 81T Darryl Sydor	☐ 82T Jimmy Waite (G)
☐ 83T Vladimir Ruzicka	☐ 84T Dave Brown
☐ 85T Mark Messier	☐ 86T Neil Sheehy
☐ 87T Todd Krygier	☐ 88T Eric Lindros
☐ 89T Nelson Emerson	☐ 90T Pat Falloon
☐ 91T Dean Evason	☐ 92T Jeff Hackett (G)
☐ 93T Rob Zettler	☐ 94T Perry Berezan
☐ 95T Pat MacLeod	☐ 96T Craig Coxe
☐ 97T Ken Hammond	☐ 98T Brian Lawton
☐ 99T Perry Anderson	☐ 100T Pat LaFontaine
☐ 101T Pierre Turgeon	☐ 102T Dave McLlwain
☐ 103T Brent Sutter	☐ 104T Uwe Krupp
☐ 105T Martin Lapointe	☐ 106T Derian Hatcher
☐ 107T Darrin Shannon	☐ 108T Benoît Hogue
☐ 109T V. Konstantinov	☐ 110T Andrei Lomakin

HOT CARD

Insert Set (10 cards): 17.00

	Bubble Pack Insert	Score
☐	1 Eric Lindros, Oshawa Generals	1.50
☐	2 Wayne Gretzky, LosA.	6.00
☐	3 Brett Hull, SLou.	1.50
☐	4 Sergei Fedorov, Detr.	1.50
☐	5 Mario Lemieux, Pitt.	4.50
☐	6 Adam Oates, SLou.	1.00
☐	7 Theoren Fleury, Calg.	1.00
☐	8 Jaromír Jágr, Pitt.	1.50
☐	9 Ed Belfour, Chic.	1.50
☐	10 Jeremy Roenick, Chic.	1.00

BOBBY ORR

Regular inserts sell for $10-12; autographed cards sell for $200-250.

Bobby Orr	Bobby Orr
☐ ☐ Junior Star	☐ ☐ Hall of Famer
☐ ☐ Rookie	☐ ☐ Cup Hero
☐ ☐ Scoring Leader	☐ ☐ Award Winner

PROMOS

The Gretzky promo sells for $10-20, the Roy promo sells for $5-10. All other Score promos sell for $1-6.

Score Promo	Score Promo
☐ 1 Brett Hull	☐ 50 Raymond Bourque
☐ 2 Al MacInnis	☐ 70 Patrick Roy (G)
☐ 3 Luc Robitaille	☐ 100 Wayne Gretzky

SCORE CANADIAN

The Canadian issue has two versions: a card with English only text and a card with both French and English test. Series One cards (1-330) have a red border, while Series Two cards (331-660) have a blue border. Pricing for both versions are the same. The most expensive singles are Dominik Hasek at $3.00-4.00 and Wayne Gretzky, John LeClair and Eric Lindros at $1.00-1.50. All other singles sell between 20¢ and $1.00.

Imprint: © 1991 SCORE

Complete Set (660 cards): 15.00

Description	No. Player
☐ ☐ 1 Brett Hull	☐ ☐ 2 Al MacInnis
☐ ☐ 3 Luc Robitaille	☐ ☐ 4 Pierre Turgeon
☐ ☐ 5 Brian Leetch	☐ ☐ 6 Cam Neely
☐ ☐ 7 John Cullen	☐ ☐ 8 Trevor Linden
☐ ☐ 9 Rick Tocchet	☐ ☐ 10 Vanbiesbrouck (G)
☐ ☐ 11 Steve Smith	☐ ☐ 12 Doug Smail
☐ ☐ 13 Craig Ludwig	☐ ☐ 14 Paul Fenton
☐ ☐ 15 Dirk Graham	☐ ☐ 16 Brad McCrimmon
☐ ☐ 17 Dean Evason	☐ ☐ 18 F. Olausson
☐ ☐ 19 Guy Carbonneau	☐ ☐ 20 Kevin Hatcher
☐ ☐ 21 Paul Ranheim	☐ ☐ 22 Claude Lemieux
☐ ☐ 23 V. Riendeau (G)	☐ ☐ 24 Garth Butcher
☐ ☐ 25 Joe Sakic	☐ ☐ 26 Rick Vaive
☐ ☐ 27 Rob Blake	☐ ☐ 28 Mike Ricci
☐ ☐ 29 Patrick Flatley	☐ ☐ 30 Bill Ranford (G)
☐ ☐ 31 Larry Murphy	☐ ☐ 32 Bobby Smith
☐ ☐ 33 Mike Krushelnyski	☐ ☐ 34 Gerard Gallant
☐ ☐ 35 Doug Wilson	☐ ☐ 36 John Ogrodnick
☐ ☐ 37 Mikhail Tatarinov	☐ ☐ 38 Doug Crossman
☐ ☐ 39 Mark Osborne	☐ ☐ 40 Scott Stevens
☐ ☐ 41 Ron Tugnutt (G)	☐ ☐ 42 Russ Courtnall
☐ ☐ 43 Gord Murphy	☐ ☐ 44 Greg Adams
☐ ☐ 45 Christian Ruuttu	☐ ☐ 46 Ken Daneyko
☐ ☐ 47 Glenn Anderson	☐ ☐ 48 Ray Ferraro
☐ ☐ 49 Tony Tanti	☐ ☐ 50 Ray Bourque
☐ ☐ 51 Sergei Makarov	☐ ☐ 52 Jim Johnson
☐ ☐ 53 Troy Murray	☐ ☐ 54 Shawn Burr
☐ ☐ 55 Peter Ing (G)	☐ ☐ 56 Dale Hunter
☐ ☐ 57 Tony Granato	☐ ☐ 58 C. Leschyshyn
☐ ☐ 59 Brian Mullen	☐ ☐ 60 Ed Olczyk
☐ ☐ 61 Mike Ramsey	☐ ☐ 62 Dan Quinn
☐ ☐ 63 Rich Sutter	☐ ☐ 64 Terry Carkner
☐ ☐ 65 Shayne Corson	☐ ☐ 66 Peter Stastny
☐ ☐ 67 Craig Muni	☐ ☐ 68 Glenn Healy (G)
☐ ☐ 69 Phil Bourque	☐ ☐ 70 Pat Verbeek
☐ ☐ 71 Garry Galley	☐ ☐ 72 Dave Gagner
☐ ☐ 73 Bob Probert	☐ ☐ 74 Craig Wolanin
☐ ☐ 75 Patrick Roy (G)	☐ ☐ 76 Keith Brown
☐ ☐ 77 Gary Leeman	☐ ☐ 78 Brent Ashton
☐ ☐ 79 Randy Moller	☐ ☐ 80 Mike Vernon (G)
☐ ☐ 81 Kelly Miller	☐ ☐ 82 Ulf Samuelsson
☐ ☐ 83 Todd Elik	☐ ☐ 84 Uwe Krupp
☐ ☐ 85 Rod Brind'Amour	☐ ☐ 86 Dave Capuano
☐ ☐ 87 Geoff Smith	☐ ☐ 88 David Volek
☐ ☐ 89 Bruce Driver	☐ ☐ 90 Andy Moog (G)
☐ ☐ 91 Per-Erik Eklund	☐ ☐ 92 Joey Kocur
☐ ☐ 93 Mark Tinordi	☐ ☐ 94 Steve Thomas

☐☐ 95 Petr Svoboda ☐☐ 96 Joel Otto
☐☐ 97 Todd Krygier ☐☐ 98 Jaromir Jagr
☐☐ 99 Mike Liut (G) ☐☐ 100 Wayne Gretzky
☐☐ 101 Teppo Numminen ☐☐ 102 Randy Burridge
☐☐ 103 Michel Petit ☐☐ 104 Tony McKegney
☐☐ 105 Mathieu Schneider ☐☐ 106 Daren Puppa (G)
☐☐ 107 Paul Cavallini ☐☐ 108 Tim Kerr
☐☐ 109 Kevin Lowe ☐☐ 110 Kirk Muller
☐☐ 111 Zarley Zalapski ☐☐ 112 Mike Hough
☐☐ 113 Ken Hodge ☐☐ 114 Grant Fuhr (G)
☐☐ 115 Paul Coffey ☐☐ 116 Wendel Clark
☐☐ 117 Patrik Sundstrom ☐☐ 118 Kevin Dineen
☐☐ 119 Eric Desjardins ☐☐ 120 M. Richter (G)
☐☐ 121 Sergio Momesso ☐☐ 122 Tony Hrkac
☐☐ 123 Joe Reekie ☐☐ 124 Petr Nedved
☐☐ 125 Randy Carlyle ☐☐ 126 Kevin Miller
☐☐ 127 R. Lemelin (G) ☐☐ 128 Dino Ciccarelli
☐☐ 129 Sylvain Côté ☐☐ 130 Mats Sundin
☐☐ 131 Eric Weinrich ☐☐ 132 D. Berthiaume (G)
☐☐ 133 Keith Acton ☐☐ 134 Benoît Hogue
☐☐ 135 Mike Gartner ☐☐ 136 Petr Klima
☐☐ 137 Curt Giles ☐☐ 138 Scott Pearson
☐☐ 139 Luke Richardson ☐☐ 140 Steve Larmer
☐☐ 141 Ken Wregget (G) ☐☐ 142 Frantisek Musil
☐☐ 143 Owen Nolan ☐☐ 144 Keith Primeau
☐☐ 145 Mark Recchi ☐☐ 146 Don Sweeney
☐☐ 147 Mike McPhee ☐☐ 148 K. Baumgartner
☐☐ 149 Dave Lowry ☐☐ 150 Geoff Courtnall
☐☐ 151 Chris Terreri (G) ☐☐ 152 Dave Manson
☐☐ 153 Bobby Holik ☐☐ 154 Bob Kudelski
☐☐ 155 Calle Johansson ☐☐ 156 Mark Hunter
☐☐ 157 Randy Gilhen ☐☐ 158 Yves Racine
☐☐ 159 Martin Gelinas ☐☐ 160 Brian Bellows
☐☐ 161 David Shaw ☐☐ 162 Bob Carpenter
☐☐ 163 Doug Brown ☐☐ 164 Ulf Dahlen
☐☐ 165 Denis Savard ☐☐ 166 Paul Ysebaert
☐☐ 167 Derek King ☐☐ 168 Igor Larionov
☐☐ 169 Bob Errey ☐☐ 170 Joe Nieuwendyk
☐☐ 171 N. Rochefort ☐☐ 172 John Tonelli
☐☐ 173 David Reid ☐☐ 174 Tom Kurvers
☐☐ 175 Dimitri Khristich ☐☐ 176 Bob Sweeney
☐☐ 177 Rick Zombo ☐☐ 178 Troy Mallette
☐☐ 179 Bob Bassen ☐☐ 180 John Druce
☐☐ 181 Mike Craig ☐☐ 182 John McIntyre
☐☐ 183 Murray Baron ☐☐ 184 Viacheslav Fetisov
☐☐ 185 Don Beaupré (G) ☐☐ 186 Brian Benning
☐☐ 187 Dave Barr ☐☐ 188 Petri Skriko
☐☐ 189 Steve Konroyd ☐☐ 190 Steve Yzerman
☐☐ 191 Jon Casey (G) ☐☐ 192 Gary Nylund
☐☐ 193 Michal Pivonka ☐☐ 194 Alexei Kasatonov
☐☐ 195 Garry Valk ☐☐ 196 Darren Turcotte
☐☐ 197 Chris Nilan ☐☐ 198 Thomas Steen
☐☐ 199 Gary Roberts ☐☐ 200 Mario Lemieux
☐☐ 201 Michel Goulet ☐☐ 202 Craig MacTavish
☐☐ 203 P. Sidorkiewicz (G) ☐☐ 204 Johan Garpenlov
☐☐ 205 Steve Duchesne ☐☐ 206 Dave Snuggerud
☐☐ 207 Kjell Samuelsson ☐☐ 208 Sylvain Turgeon
☐☐ 209 Al Iafrate ☐☐ 210 John MacLean
☐☐ 211 Brian Hayward (G) ☐☐ 212 Cliff Ronning
☐☐ 213 Ray Sheppard ☐☐ 214 Dave Taylor
☐☐ 215 Doug Lidster ☐☐ 216 Peter Bondra
☐☐ 217 Marty McSorley ☐☐ 218 Doug Gilmour
☐☐ 219 Paul MacDermid ☐☐ 220 Jeremy Roenick
☐☐ 221 Wayne Presley ☐☐ 222 Jeff Norton
☐☐ 223 Brian Propp ☐☐ 224 Jimmy Carson
☐☐ 225 Tom Barrasso (G) ☐☐ 226 Theoren Fleury
☐☐ 227 Carey Wilson ☐☐ 228 Rod Langway
☐☐ 229 Bryan Trottier ☐☐ 230 James Patrick
☐☐ 231 Dana Murzyn ☐☐ 232 Rick Wamsley (G)
☐☐ 233 Dave McLlwain ☐☐ 234 Tom Fergus
☐☐ 235 Adam Graves ☐☐ 236 J. Cloutier (G)
☐☐ 237 Gino Odjick ☐☐ 238 Andrew Cassels
☐☐ 239 Ken Linseman ☐☐ 240 Danton Cole
☐☐ 241 Dave Hannan ☐☐ 242 S. Matteau
☐☐ 243 Gerald Diduck ☐☐ 244 R. Tabaracci (G)
☐☐ 245 Sylvain Lefebvre ☐☐ 246 Bob Rouse
☐☐ 247 Charlie Huddy ☐☐ 248 Mike Foligno
☐☐ 249 Ric Nattress ☐☐ 250 Aaron Broten
☐☐ 251 Mike Keane ☐☐ 252 Steven Bozek
☐☐ 253 Jeff Beukeboom ☐☐ 254 Stéphane Morin
☐☐ 255 Brian Bradley ☐☐ 256 Scott Arniel
☐☐ 257 Robert Kron ☐☐ 258 Anatoli Semenov
☐☐ 259 Brent Gilchrist ☐☐ 260 Jim Sandlak
☐☐ 261 HL: Brett Hull ☐☐ 262 HL: Paul Coffey
☐☐ 263 HL: Mark Messier ☐☐ 264 HL: Dave Taylor
☐☐ 265 HL: Michel Goulet ☐☐ 266 HL: D. Hawerchuk
☐☐ 267 Turgeon bros. ☐☐ 268 Sutter bros.
☐☐ 269 Mullen bros. ☐☐ 270 Courtnall bros.
☐☐ 271 Trevor Kidd (G) ☐☐ 272 Patrice Brisebois
☐☐ 273 Mark Greig ☐☐ 274 Kip Miller
☐☐ 275 Drake Berehowsky ☐☐ 276 K. Haller RC
☐☐ 277 David Gagnon (G) ☐☐ 278 Jason Marshall
☐☐ 279 Don Audette ☐☐ 280 P. Lebeau RC
☐☐ 281 A. Godynyuk RC ☐☐ 282 J. Skalde RC
☐☐ 283 Ken Sutton RC ☐☐ 284 S. Kharin RC
☐☐ 285 A. Racicot (G) RC ☐☐ 286 D. Weight RC
☐☐ 287 Kevin Todd RC ☐☐ 288 T. Amonte RC
☐☐ 289 Kimbi Daniels RC ☐☐ 290 J. Daniels RC
☐☐ 291 Guy Lafleur ☐☐ 292 Guy Lafleur
☐☐ 293 Guy Lafleur ☐☐ 294 LL: Brett Hull
☐☐ 295 LL: Wayne Gretzky ☐☐ 296 LL: W. Gretzky
☐☐ 297 LL: Fleury ☐☐ 298 LL: S. Fedorov
☐☐ 299 LL: Al MacInnis ☐☐ 300 LL: E. Belfour (G)
☐☐ 301 LL: Ed Belfour (G) ☐☐ 302 HL: Brett Hull
☐☐ 303 HL: W. Gretzky ☐☐ 304 Sharks Checklist
☐☐ 305 Cam Neely ☐☐ 306 Rick Tocchet
☐☐ 307 Scott Stevens ☐☐ 308 Ulf Samuelsson
☐☐ 309 Jeremy Roenick ☐☐ 310 Mark Messier
☐☐ 311 John Cullen ☐☐ 312 Wayne Gretzky
☐☐ 313 Mike Modano ☐☐ 314 Patrick Roy (G)
☐☐ 315 Penguins ☐☐ 316 Mario Lemieux
☐☐ 317 Wayne Gretzky ☐☐ 318 Brett Hull
☐☐ 319 Ray Bourque ☐☐ 320 Ed Belfour (G)
☐☐ 321 Ed Belfour (G) ☐☐ 322 Dirk Graham
☐☐ 323 Ed Belfour (G) ☐☐ 324 Wayne Gretzky
☐☐ 325 Dave Taylor ☐☐ 326 Jeff Hackett (G)
☐☐ 327 Robert McGill ☐☐ 328 Neil Wilkinson
☐☐ 329 Eric Lindros ☐☐ 330 Eric Lindros
☐☐ 331 TF: Ray Bourque ☐☐ 332 TF: Pierre Turgeon
☐☐ 333 TF: Al MacInnis ☐☐ 334 TF: J. Roenick
☐☐ 335 TF: Steve Yzerman ☐☐ 336 Hunter bros.
☐☐ 337 Broten bros. ☐☐ 338 Cavallini bros.
☐☐ 339 Miller bros. ☐☐ 340 D. Vaske RC
☐☐ 341 Rob Pearson RC ☐☐ 342 Jason Miller
☐☐ 343 John LeClair RC ☐☐ 344 B. Marchment RC
☐☐ 345 Gary Shuchuk RC ☐☐ 346 D. Hasek (G) RC
☐☐ 347 Michel Picard RC ☐☐ 348 C. Millen RC
☐☐ 349 Joe Sacco RC ☐☐ 350 R. Savage RC
☐☐ 351 Pat Murray ☐☐ 352 M. O'Connor RC
☐☐ 353 Shawn Antoski ☐☐ 354 G. Sanderson RC
☐☐ 355 Chris Govedaris ☐☐ 356 A. Gusarov RC
☐☐ 357 Mike Sillinger ☐☐ 358 Bob Wilkie RC
☐☐ 359 Jablonski (G) RC ☐☐ 360 Spokane Chiefs
☐☐ 361 TF: Kirk Muller ☐☐ 362 TF: P. LaFontaine
☐☐ 363 TF: Brian Leetch ☐☐ 364 TF: Rick Tocchet
☐☐ 365 TF: Mario Lemieux ☐☐ 366 TF: Joe Sakic
☐☐ 367 TF: Brett Hull ☐☐ 368 TF: Damphousse
☐☐ 369 TF: Trevor Linden ☐☐ 370 TF: K. Hatcher
☐☐ 371 TF: Pat Elynuik ☐☐ 372 Patrick Roy (G)
☐☐ 373 Brian Leetch ☐☐ 374 Ray Bourque
☐☐ 375 Luc Robitaille ☐☐ 376 Wayne Gretzky
☐☐ 377 Brett Hull ☐☐ 378 Ed Belfour (G)
☐☐ 379 Rob Blake ☐☐ 380 Eric Weinrich
☐☐ 381 Jaromir Jagr ☐☐ 382 Sergei Fedorov
☐☐ 383 Ken Hodge ☐☐ 384 Eric Lindros
☐☐ 385 Lindros/ Pearson ☐☐ 386 Senators
☐☐ 387 Mick Vukota ☐☐ 388 L. Franceschetti
☐☐ 389 Mike Hudson ☐☐ 390 Frantisek Kucera
☐☐ 391 Basil McRae ☐☐ 392 Donald Dufresne
☐☐ 393 Tommy Albelin ☐☐ 394 N. Lacombe
☐☐ 395 Lucien DeBlois ☐☐ 396 Tony Twist RC
☐☐ 397 Rob Murphy ☐☐ 398 Ken Sabourin
☐☐ 399 Doug Evans ☐☐ 400 Walt Poddubny
☐☐ 401 Grant Ledyard ☐☐ 402 Kris King
☐☐ 403 Paul Gillis ☐☐ 404 Chris Dahlquist
☐☐ 405 Zdeno Ciger ☐☐ 406 Paul Stanton
☐☐ 407 Randy Ladouceur ☐☐ 408 Ron Stern
☐☐ 409 Dave Tippett ☐☐ 410 Jeff Reese (G)
☐☐ 411 Vladimir Ruzicka ☐☐ 412 Brent Fedyk
☐☐ 413 Paul Cyr ☐☐ 414 Mike Eagles
☐☐ 415 Chris Joseph ☐☐ 416 Brad Marsh
☐☐ 417 Rich Pilon ☐☐ 418 Jiri Hrdina
☐☐ 419 C. Malarchuk (G) ☐☐ 420 Steven Rice
☐☐ 421 Mark Janssens ☐☐ 422 Gord Roberts
☐☐ 423 Shawn Cronin ☐☐ 424 R. Cunneyworth
☐☐ 425 F. Pietrangelo (G) ☐☐ 426 David Maley
☐☐ 427 Rod Buskas ☐☐ 428 Dennis Vial
☐☐ 429 Kelly Buchberger ☐☐ 430 Wes Walz
☐☐ 431 Dean Kennedy ☐☐ 432 Nick Kypreos
☐☐ 433 Stewart Gavin ☐☐ 434 N. Maciver RC
☐☐ 435 Mark Pederson ☐☐ 436 Laurie Boschman
☐☐ 437 Stéphane Quintal ☐☐ 438 Darrin Shannon
☐☐ 439 Trent Yawney ☐☐ 440 Gaetan Duchesne
☐☐ 441 Joe Cirella ☐☐ 442 Doug Houda
☐☐ 443 Dave Chyzowski ☐☐ 444 Derrick Smith
☐☐ 445 Jeff Lazaro ☐☐ 446 Brian Glynn
☐☐ 447 Jocelyn Lemieux ☐☐ 448 Peter Taglianetti
☐☐ 449 Adam Burt ☐☐ 450 H. McDonough
☐☐ 451 Kelly Hrudey (G) ☐☐ 452 Dave Poulin
☐☐ 453 Mark Hardy ☐☐ 454 Mike Hartman
☐☐ 455 Chris Chelios ☐☐ 456 Alexander Mogilny
☐☐ 457 Bryan Fogarty ☐☐ 458 Adam Oates
☐☐ 459 Ron Hextall (G) ☐☐ 460 Bernie Nicholls
☐☐ 461 Esa Tikkanen ☐☐ 462 Jyrki Lumme
☐☐ 463 Brent Sutter ☐☐ 464 Gary Suter
☐☐ 465 Sean Burke (G) ☐☐ 466 Rob Brown
☐☐ 467 Mike Modano ☐☐ 468 Kevin Stevens
☐☐ 469 Mike Lalor ☐☐ 470 Sergei Fedorov
☐☐ 471 Bob Essensa (G) ☐☐ 472 Mark Howe
☐☐ 473 Craig Janney ☐☐ 474 Daniel Marois
☐☐ 475 Craig Simpson ☐☐ 476 Marc Bureau
☐☐ 477 Randy Velischek ☐☐ 478 Gino Cavallini
☐☐ 479 Dale Hawerchuk ☐☐ 480 Pat LaFontaine
☐☐ 481 Kirk McLean (G) ☐☐ 482 Murray Craven
☐☐ 483 Robert Reichel ☐☐ 484 Jan Erixon
☐☐ 485 Adam Creighton ☐☐ 486 M. Fitzpatrick (G)
☐☐ 487 Ron Francis ☐☐ 488 Joe Mullen
☐☐ 489 Peter Zezel ☐☐ 490 Tomas Sandström
☐☐ 491 Phil Housley ☐☐ 492 T. Cheveldae (G)
☐☐ 493 Glen Wesley ☐☐ 494 Stéphan Lebeau
☐☐ 495 David Ellett ☐☐ 496 Jeff Brown
☐☐ 497 Dave Andreychuk ☐☐ 498 Steven Finn
☐☐ 499 M. Donnelly RC ☐☐ 500 Neal Broten
☐☐ 501 Randy Wood ☐☐ 502 Troy Gamble (G)
☐☐ 503 Mike Ridley ☐☐ 504 Jamie Macoun
☐☐ 505 Mark Messier ☐☐ 506 Moe Mantha
☐☐ 507 Scott Young ☐☐ 508 Robert Dirk
☐☐ 509 Brad Shaw ☐☐ 510 Ed Belfour (G)
☐☐ 511 Larry Robinson ☐☐ 512 Dale Kushner
☐☐ 513 Steve Chiasson ☐☐ 514 Brian Skrudland
☐☐ 515 Pat Elynuik ☐☐ 516 Curtis Joseph (G)
☐☐ 517 Doug Bodger ☐☐ 518 Greg Brown
☐☐ 519 Joe Murphy ☐☐ 520 J.J. Daigneault
☐☐ 521 Todd Gill ☐☐ 522 Troy Loney
☐☐ 523 Tim Watters ☐☐ 524 Jody Hull
☐☐ 525 Colin Patterson ☐☐ 526 Darin Kimble
☐☐ 527 Perry Berezan ☐☐ 528 Lee Norwood
☐☐ 529 Mike Peluso ☐☐ 530 Wayne McBean
☐☐ 531 Grant Jennings ☐☐ 532 Claude Loiselle
☐☐ 533 Ron Wilson ☐☐ 534 Phil Sykes
☐☐ 535 Jim Wiemer ☐☐ 536 Herb Raglan
☐☐ 537 Tim Hunter ☐☐ 538 Mike Tomlak
☐☐ 539 Greg Gilbert ☐☐ 540 Jiri Latal
☐☐ 541 Bill Berg RC ☐☐ 542 Shane Churla
☐☐ 543 Jay Miller ☐☐ 544 Pete Peeters (G)
☐☐ 545 Alan May ☐☐ 546 Mario Marois
☐☐ 547 Jim Kyte ☐☐ 548 Jon Morris
☐☐ 549 Mikko Makelä ☐☐ 550 Nelson Emerson
☐☐ 551 Doug Wilson ☐☐ 552 Brian Mullen
☐☐ 553 Kelly Kisio ☐☐ 554 Brian Hayward (G)
☐☐ 555 Tony Hrkac ☐☐ 556 Steve Bozek
☐☐ 557 John Carter ☐☐ 558 Neil Wilkinson
☐☐ 559 Wayne Presley ☐☐ 560 Robert McGill
☐☐ 561 Craig Ludwig ☐☐ 562 Mikhail Tatarinov
☐☐ 563 Todd Elik ☐☐ 564 Randy Burridge
☐☐ 565 Tim Kerr ☐☐ 566 Randy Gilhen
☐☐ 567 John Tonelli ☐☐ 568 Tom Kurvers
☐☐ 569 Steve Duchesne ☐☐ 570 Charlie Huddy
☐☐ 571 Alan Kerr ☐☐ 572 Shawn Chambers
☐☐ 573 Rob Ramage ☐☐ 574 Steve Kasper
☐☐ 575 Scott Mellanby ☐☐ 576 Stephen Leach
☐☐ 577 Scott Niedermayer ☐☐ 578 Craig Berube
☐☐ 579 Greg Paslawski ☐☐ 580 Randy Hillier
☐☐ 581 Stéphane Richer ☐☐ 582 Brian MacLellan
☐☐ 583 Marc Habscheid ☐☐ 584 Dave Babych
☐☐ 585 Troy Murray ☐☐ 586 Ray Sheppard
☐☐ 587 Glen Featherstone ☐☐ 588 Brendan Shanahan
☐☐ 589 Dave Christian ☐☐ 590 Mike Bullard
☐☐ 591 Ryan Walter ☐☐ 592 Doug Smail
☐☐ 593 Paul Fenton ☐☐ 594 Adam Graves
☐☐ 595 Scott Stevens ☐☐ 596 Sylvain Côté
☐☐ 597 David Barr ☐☐ 598 Randy Gregg
☐☐ 599 Allen Pedersen ☐☐ 600 Jari Kurri
☐☐ 601 Troy Mallette ☐☐ 602 Troy Crowder
☐☐ 603 Brad Jones ☐☐ 604 Randy McKay
☐☐ 605 Scott Thornton ☐☐ 606 B. Marchment RC
☐☐ 607 Andrew Cassels ☐☐ 608 Grant Fuhr (G)
☐☐ 609 V. Damphousse ☐☐ 610 Rob Ray
☐☐ 611 Glenn Anderson ☐☐ 612 Peter Ing (G)
☐☐ 613 Tom Chorske ☐☐ 614 Kirk Muller
☐☐ 615 Dan Quinn ☐☐ 616 Murray Baron
☐☐ 617 S. Nemchinov ☐☐ 618 R. Brind'Amour
☐☐ 619 Ron Sutter ☐☐ 620 Luke Richardson
☐☐ 621 N. Lidström RC ☐☐ 622 Ken Linseman
☐☐ 623 Steve Smith ☐☐ 624 Dave Manson
☐☐ 625 Kay Whitmore (G) ☐☐ 626 Jeff Chychrun
☐☐ 627 R. Romaniuk RC ☐☐ 628 Brad May
☐☐ 629 T. Forslund RC ☐☐ 630 Stu Barnes
☐☐ 631 Darryl Sydor ☐☐ 632 Jimmy Waite (G)
☐☐ 633 Peter Douris ☐☐ 634 Dave Brown
☐☐ 635 Mark Messier ☐☐ 636 Neil Sheehy
☐☐ 637 Todd Krygier ☐☐ 638 S. Beauregard (G)
☐☐ 639 Barry Pederson ☐☐ 640 Pat Falloon
☐☐ 641 Dean Evason ☐☐ 642 Jeff Hackett (G)
☐☐ 643 Rob Zettler ☐☐ 644 David Bruce RC
☐☐ 645 Pat MacLeod RC ☐☐ 646 Craig Coxe
☐☐ 647 K. Hammond RC ☐☐ 648 Brian Lawton
☐☐ 649 P. Anderson RC ☐☐ 650 K. Evans RC
☐☐ 651 Mike McHugh RC ☐☐ 652 Mark Lamb
☐☐ 653 D. Wakaluk (G) RC ☐☐ 654 Pat Conacher
☐☐ 655 Martin Lapointe ☐☐ 656 Derian Hatcher
☐☐ 657 Bryan Erickson ☐☐ 658 K. Priestlay RC
☐☐ 659 V. Konstantinov ☐☐ 660 Andrei Lomakin

SCORE SHOW PROMOS

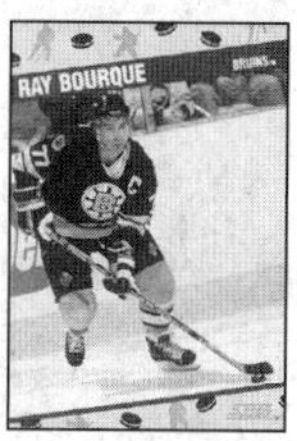

These cards were handed out at the 12th National Sports Collectors Convention in Anaheim, the National Candy Wholesalers Convention and the Toronto Baseball Fanfest (no mention of event on back). Each version sells for approximately the same amount although some dealers place a premium on the Toronto Baseball Fanfest versions

Complete Set (10 cards): 30.00

	Description	NRMT-MT
☐☐☐	1 Wayne Gretzky, LosA.	10.00
☐☐☐	2 Brett Hull, SLou.	2.50
☐☐☐	3 Raymond Bourque, Bost.	3.00
☐☐☐	4 Al MacInnis, SLou.	1.00
☐☐☐	5 Luc Robitaille, LosA.	2.00
☐☐☐	6 Ed Belfour, Chic.	2.50
☐☐☐	7 Steve Yzerman, Detr.	6.00
☐☐☐	8 Cam Neely, Bost.	2.50
☐☐☐	9 Paul Coffey, Detr.	1.50
☐☐☐	10 Patrick Roy (G), Mont.	7.50

ERIC LINDROS ON FIRE

	Description	NRMT-MT
☐	1 Eric Lindros A real corker!	2.00
☐	2 Eric Lindros A little bit of heaven	2.00
☐	3 Eric Lindros Graduation day	2.00

YOUNG SUPERSTARS

The most expensive singles are Eric Lindros at $1-2 and Jaromir Jagr at $1.00-1.50. All other singles sell between 20¢ and $1.00.

Complete Set (40 cards): 5.00

Score	Score
☐ 1 S. Fedorov, Detr.	☐ 2 M. Richter (G), NYRa.
☐ 3 Mats Sundin, Québ.	☐ 4 Theoren Fleury, Calg.
☐ 5 John Cullen, Hart.	☐ 6 D. Khristich, Wash.
☐ 7 S. Lebeau, Mont.	☐ 8 Rob Blake, LosA.
☐ 9 Ken Hodge, Bost.	☐ 10 Mike Ricci, Pitt.
☐ 11 Trevor Linden, Vanc.	☐ 12 Peter Ing (G), Edmo.
☐ 13 A. Mogilny, Buff.	☐ 14 M. Gelinas, Edmo.
☐ 15 C. Terreri (G), NJer.	☐ 16 Jeff Norton, NYIs.
☐ 17 Essensa (G), Winn.	☐ 18 Mark Tinordi, Minn.
☐ 19 Joseph (G), SLou.	☐ 20 Joe Sakic, Québ.
☐ 21 J. Roenick, Chic.	☐ 22 Mark Recchi, Pitt.
☐ 23 É. Desjardins, Mont.	☐ 24 Robert Reichel, Calg.
☐ 25 Cheveldae (G), Detr.	☐ 26 Eric Weinrich, NJer.
☐ 27 M. Barron, SLou.	☐ 28 D. Turcotte, NYRa.
☐ 29 T. Gamble (G), Vanc.	☐ 30 Eric Lindros, Osh.
☐ 31 Benoit Hogue, Buff.	☐ 32 Ed Belfour (G), Chic.
☐ 33 Tugnutt (G), Québ.	☐ 34 Pat Elynuik, Winn.
☐ 35 Mike Modano, Minn.	☐ 36 Bobby Holik, Hart.
☐ 37 Yves Racine, Detr.	☐ 38 Jaromir Jagr, Pitt.
☐ 39 S. Morin, Québ.	☐ 40 Kevin Miller, Detr.

1991 - 92 SEMIC ELITSERIEN STICKERS

The most expensive singles are Peter Forsberg at $10-15, Mats Sundin at $6-8, Nicklas Lidström at $2-3 and Borje Salming at $1-2. Singles start at 20¢.

Sticker Size: 3" x 2 1/8"

Complete Set (360 stickers) 40.00

Semic	Semic
☐ 1 AIK Logo	☐ 2 Thomas Ostlund
☐ 3 Sam Lindstahl	☐ 4 Borje Salming
☐ 5 Petri Liimatainen	☐ 6 Mats Thelin
☐ 7 Rikard Franzen	☐ 8 Petter Sahlsten
☐ 9 Daniel Jardemyr	☐ 10 Thomas Nilsson
☐ 11 Niclas Havelid	☐ 12 Mattias Norstrom
☐ 13 Peter Gradin	☐ 14 Peter Hammarstrom
☐ 15 Patrik Ericksson	☐ 16 Thomas Bjuhr
☐ 17 Thomas Strandberg	☐ 18 Tommy Lehmann
☐ 19 Mats Lindberg	☐ 20 Patric Kjellberg
☐ 21 Michael Nylander	☐ 22 Patric Englund
☐ 23 Niclas Sundblad	☐ 24 Kristian Gahn
☐ 25 Erik Andersson	☐ 26 Björn Ahlström
☐ 27 Brynas Logo	☐ 28 Michael Sundlov
☐ 29 Lars Eriksson	☐ 30 Lars Karlsson
☐ 31 Tommy Sjokin	☐ 32 Nikolaj Davydkin
☐ 33 Niklas Gallstedt	☐ 34 Mikael Lindman
☐ 35 Tommy Melkersson	☐ 36 Mikael Enander
☐ 37 Ruban Molander	☐ 38 Stefan Klockare
☐ 39 Anders Huss	☐ 40 Mikael Lindholm
☐ 41 Jan Larsson	☐ 42 Anders Gozzi
☐ 43 Peter Larsson	☐ 44 Thomas Tallberg
☐ 45 Peter Gustafsson	☐ 46 Joakim Persson
☐ 47 Peter Eriksson	☐ 48 Ove Molin
☐ 49 Jonas Johnson	☐ 50 Johan Schillgard
☐ 51 Andreas Dackell	☐ 52 Tom Bissett
☐ 53 Djurgarden Logo	☐ 54 T. Söderström (G)
☐ 55 Joakim Persson	☐ 56 Petter Ronnqvist
☐ 57 Thomas Eriksson	☐ 58 Kenneth Kennholt
☐ 59 Arto Blomsten	☐ 60 Orvar Stambert
☐ 61 Christian Due-Boje	☐ 62 Marcus Ragnarsson
☐ 63 Per Nygards	☐ 64 Thomas Johansson
☐ 65 Mikael Johansson	☐ 66 Charles Berglund
☐ 67 Jan Viktorsson	☐ 68 Ola Josefsson
☐ 69 Jens Ohlin	☐ 70 Magnus Jansson
☐ 71 Peter Nilsson	☐ 72 Fredrik Lingvist
☐ 73 Mariusz Czerkawski	☐ 74 Johan Lindstedt
☐ 75 Stefan Ketola	☐ 76 Erik Huusko
☐ 77 Anders Huusko	☐ 78 Farjestad Logo
☐ 79 Anders Bergman	☐ 80 Jorgen Ryden
☐ 81 Patrik Haltia	☐ 82 Tommy Samuelsson
☐ 83 Per Lundell	☐ 84 Leif Carlsson
☐ 85 Jesper Duus	☐ 86 Mattias Olsson
☐ 87 Thomas Rhodin	☐ 88 Jacob Karlsson
☐ 89 Greger Artursson	☐ 90 Thomas Rundqvist
☐ 91 Bengt Gustafsson	☐ 92 Hakan Loob
☐ 93 Lars Karlsson	☐ 94 Magnus Roupe
☐ 95 Kjell Dahlin	☐ 96 Staffan Lundh
☐ 97 Peter Ottosson	☐ 98 Niklas Brannstrom
☐ 99 Jonas Höglund	☐ 100 Clas Eriksson
☐ 101 Andreas Johansson	☐ 102 Mathias Johansson
☐ 103 HV 71 Logo	☐ 104 Peter Aslin
☐ 105 Boo Ahl (G)	☐ 106 Stefan Magnusson
☐ 107 Fredrik Stillman	☐ 108 Lars Ivarsson
☐ 109 Klas Heed	☐ 110 Arto Ruotanen
☐ 111 Per Gustafsson	☐ 112 Tommy Fritz
☐ 113 Mathias Svedberg	☐ 114 Kristian Pedersen
☐ 115 Peter Eriksson	☐ 116 Risto Kurkinen
☐ 117 Ove Thornberg	☐ 118 Stefan Ornskog
☐ 119 Thomas Ljungberg	☐ 120 Patrik Ross
☐ 121 Eddy Ericsson	☐ 122 Dennis Strom
☐ 123 Torbjorn Persson	☐ 124 Jonas Jonsson
☐ 125 Peter Ekelund	☐ 126 Stefan Falk
☐ 127 Ronny Nilsson	☐ 128 Leksand Logo
☐ 129 Olow Sundstrom	☐ 130 Jonas Leven
☐ 131 Tomas Jonsson	☐ 132 Ricard Persson
☐ 133 Magnus Svensson	☐ 134 Mattias Andersson
☐ 135 Henric Bjorkman	☐ 136 Orjan Lindmark
☐ 137 Orjan Nilsson	☐ 138 Tomas Ring
☐ 139 Roger Johansson	☐ 140 Marcus Thuresson
☐ 141 Per-Olof Carlsson	☐ 142 Jens Nielsen
☐ 143 Cenneth Soderlund	☐ 144 Markus Akerblom
☐ 145 Fredrik Jax	☐ 146 Reine Rauhala
☐ 147 Niklas Eriksson	☐ 148 Martin Wiita
☐ 149 Jonas Bergqvist	☐ 150 Hannu Jarvenpaa
☐ 151 Lulea Logo	☐ 152 Robert Skoog
☐ 153 Erik Granqvist	☐ 154 Timo Jutila
☐ 155 Tomas Lilja	☐ 156 Lars Modig
☐ 157 Per Ljusterang	☐ 158 Jari Gronstrand
☐ 159 Torbjorn Lindberg	☐ 160 Patrik Hoglund
☐ 161 Petter Nilsson	☐ 162 Daniel Behm
☐ 163 Johan Stromvall	☐ 164 Pauli Jarvinen
☐ 165 Lars Edstrom	☐ 166 L-G Pettersson
☐ 167 Stefan Nilsson	☐ 168 Lars Hurtig
☐ 169 Tomas Berglund	☐ 170 Robert Nordberg
☐ 171 Mikael Renberg	☐ 172 Ulf Sandstrom
☐ 173 Jens Hellgren	☐ 174 Mikael engstrom
☐ 175 Malmo Logo	☐ 176 Peter Lindmark
☐ 177 R. Nordström (G)	☐ 178 Johan Mansson
☐ 179 Timo Blomqvist	☐ 180 Peter Andersson
☐ 181 Mats Lusth	☐ 182 Roger Ohman

☐ 183 Johan Salle	☐ 184 Anders Svensson
☐ 185 Johan Norgren	☐ 186 Raimo Helminen
☐ 187 Mats Hallin	☐ 188 Mats Näslund
☐ 189 Robert Burakovsky	☐ 190 Hakan Ahlund
☐ 191 Peter Sundstrom	☐ 192 Daniel Rydmark
☐ 193 Matti Pauna	☐ 194 Roger Hansson
☐ 195 Patrik Gustavsson	☐ 196 Rick Erdall
☐ 197 Bo Svanberg	☐ 198 Jesper Mattsson
☐ 199 Jonas Hakansson	☐ 200 MoDo Logo
☐ 201 Fredrik Andersson	☐ 202 Goran Arnmark
☐ 203 Miroslav Horava	☐ 204 Hans Lodin
☐ 205 Iras Jansson	☐ 206 Jorgen Eriksson
☐ 208 Anders Berglund	☐ 208 Osmo Soutokorva
☐ 209 Tomas Nanzen	☐ 210 Hans Jonsson
☐ 211 Fredrik Bergqvist	☐ 212 Erik Holmberg
☐ 213 Peter Forsberg	☐ 214 Markus Näslund
☐ 215 Magnus Wernblom	☐ 216 Lars Bystrom
☐ 217 Kent Lantz	☐ 218 Per Wallin
☐ 219 Lennart Henriksson	☐ 220 Ingemar Strom
☐ 221 Ulf Odmark	☐ 222 Jens Ohman
☐ 223 Tommy Pettersson	☐ 224 A. Salomonsson
☐ 225 Sodertalje Logo	☐ 226 Roino Sundberg
☐ 227 Stefan Dernestal	☐ 228 Mats Kilstrom
☐ 229 Stefan Jonsson	☐ 230 Jan Bergman
☐ 231 Peter Ekroth	☐ 232 Stefan Nyman
☐ 233 Thomas Carlsson	☐ 234 Stefan Claesson
☐ 235 Oto Hascak	☐ 236 Morgan Samuelsson
☐ 237 Tomaz Eriksson	☐ 238 Thom Eklund
☐ 239 Conny Jansson	☐ 240 Bjorn Carlsson
☐ 241 Scott Moore	☐ 242 Reine Landgren
☐ 243 Ola Rosander	☐ 244 Stefan Olsson
☐ 245 Anders Frykbo	☐ 246 Ola Andersson
☐ 247 Joe Tracy	☐ 248 Christer Ljungberg
☐ 249 Patrik Nyberg	☐ 250 Joakim Skold
☐ 251 Västerås logo	☐ 252 Mats Ytter (G)
☐ 253 Par Hellenberg	☐ 254 Tommy Salo (G)
☐ 255 Nicklas Lidström	☐ 256 Robert Nordmark
☐ 257 Leif Rohlin	☐ 258 Roger Åkerström
☐ 259 Peter Popovic	☐ 260 Jan Karlsson
☐ 261 Tore Lindgren	☐ 262 Peter Jacobsson
☐ 263 Pierre Ivarsson	☐ 264 Mishat Fahrutdinov
☐ 265 Paul Andersson	☐ 266 Patrik Juhlin
☐ 267 Henrik Nilsson	☐ 268 Anders Berglund
☐ 269 Claes Lindblom	☐ 270 Jorgen Holmberg
☐ 271 Stefan Hellkvist	☐ 272 Fredrik Nilsson
☐ 273 Johan Brummer	☐ 274 Micael Karlberg
☐ 275 Niclas Lundberg	☐ 276 Frolunda Logo
☐ 277 Ake Liljebjorn	☐ 278 Hakan Algotsson
☐ 279 Hakan Nordin	☐ 280 Jonas Heed
☐ 281 Joacim Esbjors	☐ 282 Stefan Larsson
☐ 283 Stefan Axelsson	☐ 284 Oscar Ackestrom
☐ 285 Jerk Hogstrom	☐ 286 Patric Aberg
☐ 287 Patrik Carnback	☐ 288 Serge Boisvert
☐ 289 Mats Lundstrom	☐ 290 Mikael Andersson
☐ 291 Kari Jaako	☐ 292 Terho Koskela
☐ 293 Lars Dahlstrom	☐ 294 Jerry Persson
☐ 295 Peter Berndtsson	☐ 296 Thomas Sjogren
☐ 297 Par Edlund	☐ 298 Christian Lechtaler
☐ 299 Jonas Esbjors	☐ 300 Dennis Fredriksson
☐ 301 Mats Hjalmarsson	☐ 302 L. Holmgren, Coach
☐ 303 T. Sandlin, Coach	☐ 304 Lars Falk, Coach
☐ 305 H. Luckner, Coach	☐ 306 Lundstrom, Coach
☐ 307 S. Tholson, Coach	☐ 309 F. Lindfors, Coach
☐ 309 T. Lahtinen, Coach	☐ 310 Andersson, Coach
☐ 311 C-G Wallin, Coach	☐ 312 Lundstrom, Coach
☐ 313 Leif Boork, Coach	☐ 314 Thomas Rundqvist
☐ 315 Hakan Loob	☐ 316 T. Söderström (G)
☐ 317 Niklas Andersson	☐ 318 Hakan Loob
☐ 319 Tomas Sandström	☐ 320 Rolf Ridderwall
☐ 321 Thomas Eriksson	☐ 322 Niklas Lidström
☐ 323 Mats Sundin	☐ 324 Thomas Rundqvist
☐ 325 Hakan Loob	☐ 326 Marcus Karlsson
☐ 327 Anders Eriksson	☐ 328 Mats Lindgren
☐ 329 Mikael Hakansson	☐ 330 Mathias Johansson
☐ 331 Niklas Sundstrom	☐ 332 Jesper Mattsson
☐ 333 Anders Soderberg	☐ 334 Swedish Ice Hockey
☐ 335 World Champions	☐ 336 Rolf Ridderwall
☐ 337 Peter Lindmark	☐ 338 T. Söderström (G)
☐ 339 Kjell Samuelsson	☐ 340 Calle Johansson
☐ 341 Nicklas Lidström	☐ 342 Tomas Jonsson
☐ 343 Peter Andersson	☐ 344 Kenneth Kennholt
☐ 345 Fredrik Stillman	☐ 346 Thomas Rundqvist
☐ 347 Hakan Loob	☐ 348 Bengt Gustafsson
☐ 349 Mats Näslund	☐ 350 Mikael Johansson
☐ 351 Charles Berglund	☐ 352 Jan Viktorsson
☐ 353 Johan Garpenlov	☐ 354 Anders Carlsson
☐ 355 Patrik Ericksson	☐ 356 Jonas Bergqvist
☐ 357 Mats Sundin	☐ 358 Per-Erik Eklun
☐ 359 Conny Evensson	☐ 360 Curt Lundmark

1991 - 92 7TH INNING SKETCH QMJHL

Card numbers 66 and 256 do not exist. The most expensive singles are Martin Brodeur ($3-5), Jocelyn Thibault ($2-3), Manny Fernandez ($1-2) and Patrick Lalime ($1-2). NHL stars sell between 35¢ and $1.50. All other singles sell between 20¢ and $1.00.

Imprint: 1991 7th Inning Sketch Printed in Canada

Complete Set (298 cards): 20.00

QMJHL	QMJHL
☐ 1 Martin Brodeur (G)	☐ 2 Normand Paquet
☐ 3 David Desnoyers	☐ 4 Carlo Colombi
☐ 5 Stéphane Ménard (G)	☐ 6 Sébastien Bérubé
☐ 7 Marc Desgagne	☐ 8 Mil Sukovic
☐ 9 Patrick Belisle	☐ 10 Patrick Poulin
☐ 11 Martin Trudel	☐ 12 Charles Poulin
☐ 13 Etienne Thibault	☐ 14 Pierre Allard
☐ 15 François Gagnon	☐ 16 Stéphane Huard
☐ 17 Yanick Lemay	☐ 18 Dany Fortin
☐ 19 Carl Ménard	☐ 20 Serge Labelle
☐ 21 Dean Melanson	☐ 22 Yves Meunier
☐ 23 P. Petroni, Coach	☐ 24 M. Pouliot, A.Coach
☐ 25 Alain Côté, Error	☐ 26 Hugues Laliberté
☐ 27 Martin Gendron	☐ 28 Stan Melanson
☐ 29 Carl Leblanc	☐ 30 Patrick Grisé
☐ 31 Yves Charron	☐ 32 Hughes Mongeon
☐ 33 Christian Tardif	☐ 34 Patrick Tessier
☐ 35 Christian Campeau	☐ 36 Mario Thérrien
☐ 37 Martin Balleux	☐ 38 Joel Brassard
☐ 39 Sébastien Fortier	☐ 40 Jocelyn Langlois
☐ 41 Guiseppe Argentos	☐ 42 Sylvain Brisson
☐ 43 Philippe Boucher	☐ 44 Martin Brochu (G)
☐ 45 Marc Rodgers	☐ 46 Pascal Gagnon
☐ 47 Benoît Thérrien	☐ 48 Robin Bouchard
☐ 49 Michel Savoie	☐ 50 J-S Boiteau
☐ 51 Patrick Lamoureux	☐ 52 Stéphane Giard (G)
☐ 53 Maxime Jean	☐ 54 Alain Côté
☐ 55 François Groleau	☐ 56 Richard Hamelin
☐ 57 Eric Beauvis	☐ 58 Steve Laplante
☐ 59 Yves Meunier	☐ 60 Steve Dontigny
☐ 61 Simon Roy	☐ 62 J-F Laroche
☐ 63 Patrick Traverse	☐ 64 Eric Joyal
☐ 65 J-F Grégoire	☐ 67 Jean Imbeau
☐ 68 François Bourdeau	☐ 69 Alain Savage, Jr.
☐ 70 Johnny Lorenzo (G)	☐ 71 Patrick Lalime (G)
☐ 72 Patrick Melfi	☐ 73 Marc Tardif
☐ 74 Marc Savard	☐ 75 A. Sanscartier, Coach
☐ 76 Pascal Lebrasseur	☐ 77 Checklist 1
☐ 78 Dany Girard	☐ 79 Eddy Gervais
☐ 80 Dave Tremblay	☐ 81 Dany Larochelle
☐ 82 Michel St-Jacques	☐ 83 Rodney Petawabano
☐ 84 Eric Duchesne	☐ 85 Patrick Clement
☐ 86 Steve Gosselin	☐ 87 Patrick Lacombe
☐ 88 Patrice Martineau	☐ 89 Danny Beauregard
☐ 90 Martin Lamarche	☐ 91 Sébastien Parent
☐ 92 Christian Caron	☐ 93 Sylvain Careau (G)
☐ 94 Martin Beaupré	☐ 95 Daniel Paradis
☐ 96 Sylvain Rodrigue (G)	☐ 97 Joe Canale, Coach
☐ 98 Patrick Lampron	☐ 99 Carl Blondin
☐ 100 Carl Wiseman	☐ 101 Hugo Hamelin
☐ 102 Claude Poirier	☐ 103 Charles Paquette
☐ 104 Carl Fleury	☐ 105 Paolo Racicot
☐ 106 Sébastien Moreau	☐ 107 Pascal Trépanier
☐ 108 Dominic Maltais	☐ 109 Steve Arés
☐ 110 Daniel Thibault	☐ 111 Eric Messier
☐ 112 Stéphane Julien	☐ 113 Dave Paquet
☐ 114 Nicolas Turmel	☐ 115 Pascal Rhéaume
☐ 116 Carl Boudreau	☐ 117 Dave Boudreault
☐ 118 Éric Bellerose	☐ 119 Steve Searles
☐ 120 Patrick Nadeau	☐ 121 Stephan Viens
☐ 122 J-F Labbé (G)	☐ 123 Jocelyn Thibault (G)
☐ 124 G. Drapeau, Coach	☐ 125 Checklist 2
☐ 126 Martin Lajeaunes	☐ 127 Etienne Lavoie
☐ 128 Dominic Rhéaume	☐ 129 Robert Guillet
☐ 130 François Rivard	☐ 131 P. DeRouville (G)
☐ 132 Andrej Dobrota	☐ 133 Pierre Gendron
☐ 134 Dave Chouinard	☐ 135 Martin Tanguay
☐ 136 Jacques Blouin	☐ 137 Martin Larochelle
☐ 138 Jean-Martin Morin	☐ 139 Donald Brashear
☐ 140 Stéphane Paradis	☐ 141 Jan Simcik
☐ 142 Yan Arsenault	☐ 143 Joel Bouchard
☐ 144 J-S Lefebvre	☐ 145 David St. Pierre
☐ 146 Mario Nobili	☐ 147 Stacy Dallaire
☐ 148 Carl Lamothe	☐ 149 André Bouliane (G)
☐ 150 Simon Arial	☐ 151 Stéphane Madore
☐ 152 Hughes Bouchard	☐ 153 Steve Decaen
☐ 154 Jason Downey	☐ 155 Raymond Delarosbil
☐ 156 Lino Salvo	☐ 157 Réginald Brézeault
☐ 158 Nathan Morin	☐ 159 Samuel Groleau
☐ 160 Patrick Carignan	☐ 161 Stéphane St-Amour
☐ 162 Marquis Mathieu	☐ 163 Yves Sarault
☐ 164 Dave Belliveau	☐ 165 Trevor Duhaime
☐ 166 Eric O'Connor	☐ 167 Christian Proulx
☐ 168 Martin Lavallée (G)	☐ 169 J.F.Gagnon (G)
☐ 170 Eric Lafrance	☐ 171 Enrico Scardocchio
☐ 172 David Bergeron	☐ 173 Guillaume Morin (G)
☐ 174 Charlie Boucher	☐ 175 Marti Rozon
☐ 176 Brandon Piccarreto	☐ 177 Simon Toupin
☐ 178 Jamie Bird	☐ 179 Hervé Lapointe
☐ 180 Ian Mclantyre	☐ 181 J-F Rivard (G)
☐ 182 A. Chainey, Coach	☐ 183 Daniel Laflamme
☐ 184 Patrice Paquin	☐ 185 Patrick Déraspé
☐ 186 Martin Roy	☐ 187 Jeannot Ferland
☐ 188 Patrick Genest	☐ 189 Matthew Barnaby
☐ 190 Jean-Guy Trudel	☐ 191 Eric Moreau
☐ 192 Eric Cool	☐ 193 Alexandre Legault
☐ 194 Gregg Pineo	☐ 195 LHJMQ
☐ 196 Radoslav Balaz	☐ 197 Stefan Simoes
☐ 198 Action - Québec	☐ 199 François Paquette
☐ 200 Paul MacDonald	☐ 201 Shane Doiron
☐ 202 Michal Longauer	☐ 203 Joe Crowley
☐ 204 Joey Deliva	☐ 205 P-F Lalonde
☐ 206 Paul Brousseau	☐ 207 Martin Lepage
☐ 208 Y. DeGrâce (G)	☐ 209 Jim Campbell
☐ 210 S. Bordeleau	☐ 211 Marc Legault (G)
☐ 212 Joel Blain	☐ 213 Claude Jutras
☐ 214 Eric Lavigne	☐ 215 Todd Sparks
☐ 216 Sylvain Lapointe	☐ 217 Eric Lecompte
☐ 218 Thierry Mayer	☐ 219 Harold Hersh, Error
☐ 219 Harold Hersh, Corr.	☐ 220 Frédéric Boivin
☐ 221 Steven Dion	☐ 222 A. Vigneault, Coach
☐ 223 Checklist 3	☐ 224 Petr Valenta
☐ 225 Action - Québec	☐ 226 Jim Bermingham
☐ 227 Yanick Dubé	☐ 228 Sandy McCarthy
☐ 229 Dany Michaud	☐ 230 Jason Brousseau
☐ 231 Marc Beaucage	☐ 232 Eric Cardinal
☐ 233 Martin Chaput	☐ 234 Jean Roberge
☐ 235 Philip Gathercole	☐ 236 Michael Gaul
☐ 237 Yannick Fréchette	☐ 238 Sylvain Bloiun
☐ 239 David Pekorek	☐ 240 John Kovacs
☐ 241 Eric Raymond (G)	☐ 242 M. Fernandez (G)
☐ 243 Yan St. Pierre	☐ 244 Brant Blackned
☐ 245 Eric Veilleux	☐ 246 Pascal Vincent
☐ 247 Benoît Larose	☐ 248 Olivier Guillaume
☐ 249 A. Gauthier (G)	☐ 250 B. Ducharme (G)
☐ 251 P. Charbonneau (G)	☐ 252 Daniel Germain
☐ 253 Pascal Chiasson	☐ 254 Marc Thibeault
☐ 255 Martin Woods	☐ 257 D. Grandmaison
☐ 258 Carl Poirier	☐ 259 Stéphane Larocque
☐ 260 Mario Dumoulin	☐ 261 Yvan Laterreur
☐ 262 Claude Savoie	☐ 263 Denis Beauchamp
☐ 264 Patrick Bisaillon	☐ 265 Pascal Bernier
☐ 266 Nicolas Lefebvre	☐ 267 LHJMQ Action
☐ 268 Joseph Napolitano	☐ 269 Sébastien Tremblay
☐ 270 Alexandre Daigle	☐ 271 Pierre Pillion
☐ 272 Lambert, A. Coach	☐ 273 Pierre Aubry, Coach
☐ 274 Yves Loubier (G)	☐ 275 Peter Sandke
☐ 276 Louis Bernard	☐ 277 Alain Nasreddine
☐ 278 Sylvain Ducharme	☐ 279 Jeremy Caissie
☐ 280 Eric Meloche	☐ 281 Ian Laperrière
☐ 282 Hugo Proulx	☐ 283 Dave Whittom
☐ 284 Yannick Dupré	☐ 285 Eric Plante
☐ 286 S. Desjardins	☐ 287 René Corbet
☐ 288 David Lessard	☐ 289 Eric Marcoux
☐ 290 A. Duchesne	☐ 291 Maxime Petitclerc
☐ 292 P. Gagnon (G)	☐ 293 Roger Larche
☐ 294 J. Hamel, Coach	☐ 295 Alexandre Gaumond
☐ 296 Paul-Emile Exantus	☐ 297 LHJMQ Action
☐ 298 LHJMQ Action	

LHJMQ TEAMS

Insert Set (12 cards): 5.00

Common Team Insert: .50

QMJHL	QMJHL
☐ Q1 Harfangs	☐ Q2 Saguenéens
☐ Q3 Voltigeurs	☐ Q4 Hull Olympiques
☐ Q5 Laval Titan	☐ Q6 College de Verdun
☐ Q7 Laser	☐ Q8 St-Jean Lynx
☐ Q9 Cataractes	☐ Q10 Draveurs
☐ Q11 Victoriaville Tigres	☐ Q12 Granby Bisons

1991 - 92 7TH INNING SKETCH OHL

There are several card number errors in this set. Card 293 is unknown. The most expensive singles are Jason Allison ($3-4), Chris Pronger ($3-4), Jason Arnott ($2-3) and Michael Peca ($1-2). NHL stars sell between 35¢ and $1.50. All other singles sell between 20¢ and $1.00.

Imprint: 1991 7TH Inning Sketch

Complete Set (383 cards): 20.00

OHL	OHL
☐ The Dream	☐ 1 John Slaney
☐ 2 Jason Meloch	☐ 3 Mark DeSantis
☐ 4 Richard Raymond	☐ 5 Dave Lemay
☐ 6 Matt McGuffin	☐ 7 Sam Oliveira
☐ 8 Jeremy Stevenson	☐ 9 Todd Walker
☐ 10 Jean-Alain Schneider	☐ 11 Guy Lévêque
☐ 12 Shayne Gaffar	☐ 13 Mike Prokopec
☐ 14 Nathan Lafayette	☐ 15 Larry Courville
☐ 16 Chris Clancy	☐ 17 Thomas Nemeth
☐ 18 Jeff Reid	☐ 19 Ilpo Kauhanen (G)
☐ 20 Rob Dykeman (G)	☐ 21 Rival Fullum
☐ 22 R. VandenBussche	☐ 23 Gordon Pell
☐ 24 P. Andrea (Osh.)	☐ 25 Lovell,Coach (Osh.)
☐ 26 Alan Letang	☐ 27 Chris Phelps
☐ 28 John Wynne	☐ 29 Rob Kinghan
☐ 30 Glen Craig	☐ 31 Eric Cairns
☐ 32 John Pinches	☐ 33 Todd Harvey
☐ 34 Craig Fraser	☐ 35 Pat Peake
☐ 36 Chris Skoryna	☐ 37 Bob Wren
☐ 38 Chris Varga	☐ 39 David Benn
☐ 40 Mark Lawrence	☐ 41 Jeff Kostuch
☐ 42 J.D. Eaton	☐ 43 Derek Etches
☐ 44 Jeff Gardiner	☐ 45 James Shea (G)
☐ 46 Brad Teichmann (G)	☐ 47 J. Rutherford, Coach
☐ 48 Derek Wilkinson	☐ 49 OHL Action
☐ 50 OHL Action	☐ 51 Sandy Allan (G)
☐ 52 Ron Bertrand (G)	☐ 53 Brad Brown
☐ 54 Dennis Bonvie	☐ 55 Bradley Shepard
☐ 56 Allan Cox	☐ 57 Jack Williams
☐ 58 Chad Penney	☐ 59 Jason Firth
☐ 60 Bill Lang	☐ 61 Ryan Merritt
☐ 62 Michael Burman	☐ 63 Billy Wright
☐ 64 Dave Szabo	☐ 65 James Sheehan
☐ 66 John Spoltore	☐ 67 Paul Rushforth
☐ 68 Jeff Shevalier	☐ 69 Robert Thorpe
☐ 70 Berehowsky, Error	☐ 71 Patrick Barton
☐ 72 B. Templeton, Coach	☐ 73 Wade Gibson
☐ 74 C.J. Denomme (G)	☐ 75 Mike Torchia (G)
☐ 76 Mike Polano	☐ 77 Tony McCabe
☐ 78 Chris Kraemer	☐ 79 Tim Spitzig
☐ 80 Trevor Gallant	☐ 81 Yvan Corbin
☐ 82 Norman Dezainde	☐ 83 Marc Robillard
☐ 84 Derek Gauthier	☐ 85 Gib Tucker
☐ 86 Paul McCallion	☐ 87 Eric Manlow
☐ 88 James Caruso	☐ 89 Gary Miller
☐ 90 Jason Stevenson	☐ 91 Shayne McCosh
☐ 92 Jason Gladney	☐ 93 Brad Barton
☐ 94 Chris LiPuma	☐ 95 Justin Cullen
☐ 96 Bill Smith, Scout	☐ 97 J. McDonnell, Coach
☐ 98 Schucask (# 000)	☐ 99 Brent Gretzky
☐ 100 Gairin Smith	☐ 101 Blair Scott
☐ 102 Daniel Godbout	☐ 103 Dan Preston
☐ 104 Ian Keiller	☐ 105 Rick Marshall
☐ 106 Aaron Morrison	☐ 107 Dominic Belanger
☐ 108 Kevin Brown	☐ 109 Tony Cimellaro
☐ 110 L. Mavety, Coach	☐ 111 Jake Grimes
☐ 112 Greg Dreveny (G)	☐ 113 Darren McCarty
☐ 114 Doug Doull	☐ 115 Scott Boston
☐ 116 Dale Chokan	☐ 117 Darren Hurley
☐ 118 Mielko, Error (# 61)	☐ 119 Gallace, Err. (# 65)
☐ 120 Shayne Antoski	☐ 121 Greg Bailey
☐ 122 Keith Redmond	☐ 123 Dick Todd, Coach
☐ 124 Scott Turner	☐ 125 Colin Wilson
☐ 126 Mike Tomlinson	☐ 127 Dale McTavish
☐ 128 Chris Longo	☐ 129 Chad Lang (G)
☐ 130 Brent Tully	☐ 131 Shawn Heins
☐ 132 Geordie Kinnear	☐ 133 Jeff Walker
☐ 134 Chris Pronger	☐ 135 Chad Grills
☐ 136 Michael Harding	☐ 137 Matt St. Germain
☐ 138 Don O'Neill	☐ 139 Dave Roche
☐ 140 Doug Searle	☐ 141 Bryan Gendron
☐ 142 Kelly Vipond	☐ 143 Andrew Verner (G)
☐ 144 Ryan Black	☐ 145 Jason Dawe
☐ 146 Jassen Cullimore	☐ 148 Jason Arnott
☐ 149 Jan Benda	☐ 150 Todd Bradley
☐ 151 Markus Brunner	☐ 152 Jason Campeau
☐ 153 Mark Deazeley	☐ 154 Matt Hoffman
☐ 155 Scott Hollis	☐ 156 Neil Iserhoff
☐ 157 Darryl LaFrance	☐ 158 B.J. MacPherson
☐ 159 Troy Swee	☐ 160 Jason Weaver
☐ 161 Stéphane Yelle	☐ 162 Trevor Burgess
☐ 163 Joe Cook	☐ 164 Jean-Paul Davis
☐ 165 Brian Grieve	☐ 166 Rob Leask
☐ 167 Wade Simpson	☐ 168 Kevin Spero
☐ 169 Fred Brathwaite (G)	☐ 170 Mike Fountain (G)
☐ 171 Cornacchia, Coach	☐ 172 Checklist
☐ 173 Todd Warriner	☐ 174 Reuben Castella
☐ 175 Cory Stillman	☐ 176 Steve Gibson
☐ 177 Trent Cull	☐ 178 John Copley
☐ 179 Craig Binns	☐ 180 Ryan O'Neill
☐ 181 Matthew Mullin (G)	☐ 182 Todd Hunter
☐ 183 Jason Stos	☐ 184 Robert Frayn, Error
☐ 185 L. MacDonald	☐ 186 Tom Sullivan
☐ 187 Steve Smith	☐ 188 Bill Bowler
☐ 189 James Allison	☐ 190 Kevin MacKay
☐ 191 David Myles	☐ 192 Maxner, GM/ Coach
☐ 193 Prpich, A. Coach	☐ 194 Brady Blain
☐ 195 Eric Stamp	☐ 196 OHL Action
☐ 197 David Babcock	☐ 198 Brad Love
☐ 199 Dale Junkin	☐ 200 Rick Corriveau
☐ 201 Scott Campbell	☐ 202 Jason Clarke
☐ 203 Burnett, Coach	☐ 204 Ryan Tocher
☐ 205 Dennis Maxwell	☐ 206 Greg Scott (G)
☐ 207 Mark Cardiff	☐ 208 Neil Fewster
☐ 209 Jason Coles	☐ 210 R. Hall, A. Coach
☐ 211 Todd Simon	☐ 212 Ethan Moreau
☐ 213 Todd Wetzel	☐ 214 Tom Moores
☐ 215 Geoff Rawson	☐ 216 Dan Krisko
☐ 217 Manny Legace (G)	☐ 218 Kevin Brown
☐ 219 Steve Staios	☐ 220 Checklist
☐ 221 Checklist	☐ 222 Tony Bella
☐ 223 Shawn Caplice	☐ 224 Keli Corpse
☐ 225 Chris Gratton	☐ 226 Gord Harris
☐ 227 Cory Johnson	☐ 228 Kevin King
☐ 229 Justin Morrison	☐ 230 Alastair Still
☐ 231 Chris Scharf	☐ 232 Brian Stagg
☐ 233 Mike Dawson	☐ 234 Rod Pasma
☐ 235 Craig Rivet	☐ 236 Dave Stewart
☐ 237 John Vary	☐ 238 Jason Wadel
☐ 239 Joel Yates	☐ 240 Marc Lamothe (G)
☐ 241 Pete McGlynn (G)	☐ 242 OHL Action
☐ 243 Checklist 4	☐ 244 Joel Sandie
☐ 245 Glen Murray	☐ 246 Derek Armstrong
☐ 247 Michael Peca	☐ 248 Barry Young
☐ 249 Bernie Joh	☐ 250 Terry Chitaroni
☐ 251 Jason Young	☐ 252 Rod Hinks
☐ 253 Michael Yeo	☐ 254 Kyle Blacklock
☐ 255 Dan Ryder (G)	☐ 256 Mason, Asst. Coach
☐ 257 Jamie Rivers	☐ 258 Brandon Convery
☐ 259 Barrie Moore	☐ 260 Shawn Rivers
☐ 261 Jamie Matthews	☐ 262 Tim Favot
☐ 263 Bob MacIsaac	☐ 264 Sean Gagnon
☐ 265 MacKenzie, Coach	☐ 266 G. Dourian, Err.
☐ 267 MacKnz., A.Coach	☐ 268 Jason Zohil
☐ 269 Tarasuk, Coach	☐ 270 James Storr (G)
☐ 271 Sean Basilio (G)	☐ 272 Rick Morton
☐ 273 Jason Hughes	☐ 274 Scott Walker
☐ 275 Willie Skilliter	☐ 276 Shawn Krueger
☐ 277 Jason MacDonald	☐ 278 Kirk Maltby
☐ 279 Brock Woods	☐ 280 Troy Hutchinson
☐ 281 Geordie Maynard	☐ 282 Luigi Calce
☐ 283 Steven Parson	☐ 284 Andrew Brunette
☐ 285 Robert MacKenzie	☐ 286 Jason Buetow
☐ 287 Wyatt Buckland	☐ 288 Jim Brown
☐ 289 Gord Dickie	☐ 290 Jeff Smith
☐ 291 Peter Ambroziak	☐ 292 Mark O'Donnell
☐ 294 G. Reid, Error	☐ 295 Sean Spencer (G)
☐ 296 Gerry Skrypec	☐ 297 Billy Hall
☐ 298 Sean Gawley	☐ 299 Grant Marshall
☐ 300 Michael Johnson	☐ 301 Brett Seguin
☐ 302 Chris Coveny	☐ 303 Ryan Kuwabara
☐ 304 Jeff Ricciardi	☐ 305 Curt Bowen
☐ 306 Zbynek Kukacka	☐ 307 Chris Gignac
☐ 308 Steve Washburn	☐ 309 Brian Kilrea, Coach
☐ 310 M. Lenarduzzi (G)	☐ 311 Matt Stone
☐ 312 Ken Belanger	☐ 313 Chris Simon
☐ 314 Kiley Hill	☐ 315 Chris Grenville
☐ 316 Aaron Gavey	☐ 317 Briane Thompson
☐ 318 Ted Nolan, Coach	☐ 319 Perry Pappas
☐ 320 Kevin Hodson (G)	☐ 321 Colin Miller
☐ 322 Tom MacDonald	☐ 323 Shaun Imber
☐ 324 Jarret Reid	☐ 325 Tony Iob
☐ 326 Mark Matier	☐ 327 Drew Bannister
☐ 328 Jason Denomme	☐ 329 David Matsos
☐ 330 Rick Kowalsky	☐ 331 Tim Bacik (G)
☐ 332 Ralph Intranuovo	☐ 333 Jonas Rudberg
☐ 334 Jeff Toms	☐ 335 Jason Julian

☐ 336 Brian Goudie ☐ 337 Gary Roach
☐ 338 Brad Baber ☐ 339 Todd Gleason
☐ 340 Chris McMurty ☐ 341 Matt Turek
☐ 342 Shane Johnson ☐ 343 Grant Pritchett
☐ 344 Mike Cote ☐ 345 Duane Harmer
☐ 346 Jeff Bes ☐ 347 Wade Whitten
☐ 347 Dan Taveski ☐ 348 Bill Kovacs
☐ 349 Kayle Short ☐ 350 Sylvain Cloutier
☐ 351 Brent Watson ☐ 352 Brent Pope
☐ 353 Craig Lutes ☐ 354 Michael Hartwick
☐ 355 Kevin Reid ☐ 356 Toby Burkitt
☐ 357 Todd Bertuzzi ☐ 358 Angelo Amore (G)
☐ 359 Jeff Pawluk ☐ 361 Gordon Ross
☐ 362 Dennis Purdie ☐ 363 Dave Gilmore
☐ 364 Brent Brownlee (G) ☐ 365 Aaron Nagy
☐ 366 Barry Potomski ☐ 367 Steve Smillie
☐ 368 Kelly Reed ☐ 369 Gary Agnew, Coach
☐ 370 Chris Taylor ☐ 371 Brett Marietti
☐ 372 Cory Evans ☐ 373 Brian Stacey
☐ 374 Chris Crombie ☐ 375 Derrick Crane
☐ 376 Scott McKay ☐ 377 Gregory Ryan
☐ 378 Mark Visheau ☐ 379 Gerry Arcella
☐ 380 Nick Stajduhar ☐ 381 Jason Allison
☐ 382 Sean O'Reilly ☐ 383 Paul Wolanski

THE TEAMS

Insert Set (16 cards): 6.00
Common Team Insert: .50

OHL OHL
☐ O1 Cornwall Royals ☐ O2 Detroit Ambassadors
☐ O3 Guelph Storm ☐ O4 Kingston Frontenacs
☐ O5 London Knights ☐ O6 Thunder
☐ O7 Centennials ☐ O8 Oshawa Generals
☐ O9 Ottawa 67's ☐ O10 Kitchener Rangers
☐ O11 Platers ☐ O12 Peterborough Petes
☐ O13 Greyhounds ☐ O14 Sudbury Wolves
☐ O15 Windsor Spitfires ☐ O16 Belleville Bulls

1991 - 92 7TH INNING SKETCH WHL

Card numbers 233 and 234 do not exist. The most expensive single is Chris Osgood at $3-4. NHL stars sell between 35¢ and $1.50. All other singles sell between 20¢ and $1.00.

Imprint: 1991 7th Inning Sketch
Complete Set (360 cards): 20.00

WHL WHL
☐ 1 Valeri Bure ☐ 2 Hardy Sauter
☐ 3 Bryan Maxwell, Coach ☐ 4 Scott Bailey
☐ 5 Mike Gray ☐ 6 Mark Szoke
☐ 7 Mike Jickling ☐ 8 Frank Evans
☐ 9 Steve Junker ☐ 10 Greg Gatto
☐ 11 Jared Bednar ☐ 12 Justin Hocking
☐ 13 Paxton Schulte ☐ 14 Brad Toporowski
☐ 15 Shane Maitland ☐ 16 Aaron Boh
☐ 17 Ryan Duthie ☐ 18 Craig Reichert
☐ 19 Danny Faassen ☐ 20 Randy Toye
☐ 21 Geoff Grandberg ☐ 22 Jeremy Warring (G)
☐ 23 Tyler Romanchuck ☐ 24 Jamie Linden
☐ 25 90/91 Champs ☐ 26 Corey Jones (G)
☐ 27 Brandon Smith ☐ 28 Mike Williamson
☐ 29 Adam Murray ☐ 30 Steve Konowalchuk
☐ 31 Shawn Stone ☐ 32 Adam Deadmarsh0
☐ 33 Rick Mearns ☐ 34 Chris Rowland
☐ 35 Brandon Coates ☐ 36 Dave Cammock
☐ 37 Colin Foley ☐ 38 Dennis Saharchuk
☐ 39 Jiri Beranek ☐ 40 Chad Seibel
☐ 41 Kelly Harris ☐ 42 Layne Roland
☐ 43 Cale Hulse ☐ 44 Ken Hodge, Coach
☐ 45 Peter Cox ☐ 46 Joaquin Cage (G)
☐ 47 Peterson, Co-Coach ☐ 48 Jason McBain
☐ 49 John Badduke ☐ 50 Rick Hopper, GM
☐ 51 Dave Hamilton (G) ☐ 52 Dwayne Newman
☐ 53 Chris Catellier ☐ 54 Fran Defrenza
☐ 55 Randy Chadney ☐ 56 David Hebky
☐ 57 Craig Fletcher ☐ 58 Kane Chaloner
☐ 59 Ross Harris ☐ 60 Mike Barrie
☐ 61 Steve Lingren ☐ 62 Shea Esselmont
☐ 63 Matt Smith ☐ 64 Gerry St. Cyr
☐ 65 Andrew Laming ☐ 66 Jeff Fancy
☐ 67 Ryan Pellaers ☐ 68 Scott Fukami
☐ 69 Darcy Mattersdorfer ☐ 70 Chris Hawes
☐ 72 The Goalies 1 ☐ 73 Checklist
☐ 74 Riverside Coliseum ☐ 75 Tom Renney, Coach
☐ 76 Corey Hirsch (G) ☐ 77 Scott Ferguson
☐ 78 Steve Yule ☐ 79 Todd Johnson
☐ 80 Jarrett Bousquet ☐ 81 Mike Mathers
☐ 82 Rod Stevens ☐ 83 Lance Johnson
☐ 84 Zac Boyer ☐ 85 Craig Lyons
☐ 86 Dale Masson (G) ☐ 87 Scott Loucks
☐ 88 Darcy Tucker ☐ 89 Shayne Green
☐ 90 Micheal Sup ☐ 91 Craig Bonner
☐ 92 Jeff Watchorn ☐ 93 Jarrett Dueling
☐ 94 Ed Patterson ☐ 95 David Wilkie
☐ 96 The Goalies II ☐ 97 A Goal
☐ 98 Andy MacIntyre ☐ 99 Rhett Trombley
☐ 100 L. Molleken, Coach ☐ 101 Trevor Robins (G)
☐ 102 Jeff Buchanan ☐ 103 Mark Raiter
☐ 104 Bryce Goebel ☐ 105 Paul Buczkowski
☐ 106 James Startup ☐ 107 Chad Rusnak
☐ 108 Sean McFatridge ☐ 109 Shane Calder
☐ 110 Ryan Fujita ☐ 111 Derek Tibbatts
☐ 112 Glen Gulutzan ☐ 113 Richard Matvichuk
☐ 114 Chad Michalchuk ☐ 115 Mark Wotton
☐ 116 Mark Franks ☐ 117 Norm Maracle (G)
☐ 118 Jason Becker ☐ 119 Shawn Yakimishyn
☐ 120 Ed Chynoweth ☐ 121 Checklist 2
☐ 122 Craig Chapman ☐ 123 Jeff Jubenville
☐ 124 George Zajankala ☐ 125 Turner Stevenson
☐ 126 Rob Tallas (G) ☐ 127 Ryan Brown
☐ 128 Andrew Kemper ☐ 129 Brendan Witt
☐ 130 Troy Hyatt ☐ 131 Mike Kennedy
☐ 132 Jesse Wilson ☐ 133 Kurt Seher
☐ 134 Dody Wood ☐ 135 Darren McAusland
☐ 136 Jeff Sebastian ☐ 137 Eric Bouchard
☐ 138 Joel Dyck ☐ 139 Blake Knox
☐ 140 Peter Anholt, Coach ☐ 141 Chris Wells
☐ 142 Andrew Reimer (G) ☐ 143 Along The Boards
☐ 144 Which Way Is Up ☐ 145 Checklist
☐ 146 Tacoma Dome ☐ 147 Ceremonies
☐ 148 M. Comeau, Coach ☐ 149 D. Clark, A. Coach
☐ 150 John Varga ☐ 151 Joey Young
☐ 152 Laurie Billeck ☐ 153 Jeff Calvert (G)
☐ 154 Tuomas Gronman ☐ 155 Jason Knox
☐ 156 Kevin Malgunas ☐ 157 Dave McMillen
☐ 158 D. Onofrychuk (G) ☐ 159 Mike Piersol
☐ 160 Lasse Pirjeta ☐ 161 Drew Schoneck
☐ 162 Corey Stock ☐ 163 Ryan Strain
☐ 164 Michal Sykora ☐ 165 Scott Thomas
☐ 166 Toby Weishaar ☐ 167 Jeff Whittle
☐ 168 The Rockettes ☐ 169 Allan Egeland
☐ 170 Van Burgess ☐ 171 Trever Fraser
☐ 172 Jamie Black ☐ 173 WHL Action
☐ 174 Andy Schneider ☐ 175 John McMulkin
☐ 176 Rick Girard ☐ 177 Shane Hnidy
☐ 178 Jason Krywulak ☐ 179 Jeremy Riehl
☐ 180 Brent Bilodeau ☐ 181 Mark McCoy
☐ 182 Matt Young ☐ 183 Dan Sherstenka
☐ 184 Jarrod Daniel (G) ☐ 185 Lennie MacAusland
☐ 186 Keith McCambridge ☐ 187 Jason Horvath
☐ 188 Kevin Koopman (G) ☐ 189 Chris Herperger
☐ 190 Trent McCleary ☐ 191 Tyler Wright
☐ 192 Todd Holt ☐ 193 Ashley Buckberger
☐ 194 Bram Vanderkracht ☐ 195 Ken Zilka
☐ 196 Chris Osgood (G) ☐ 197 Rob Puchniak
☐ 198 Todd Dutiaume ☐ 199 Mike Maneluk
☐ 200 Shawn Dietrich (G) ☐ 201 Chris Johnston
☐ 202 Brian Purdy ☐ 203 Mike Chrun
☐ 204 Dan Kopec ☐ 205 Ryan Smith
☐ 206 Marty Murray ☐ 207 Merv Priest
☐ 208 Bobby House ☐ 209 Chris Constant
☐ 210 D. Gylywoychuk ☐ 211 Stu Scantlebury
☐ 212 Mark Kolesar ☐ 213 Craig Geekie
☐ 214 Terran Sandwith ☐ 215 Jeff Hoad
☐ 216 McCrimmon, Coach ☐ 217 Carlos Bye
☐ 218 Trevor Hanas ☐ 219 Jeff Shantz
☐ 220 Heath Weenk ☐ 221 Nathan Dempsey
☐ 222 Louis Dumont ☐ 223 Garry Pearce
☐ 224 Terry Bendera ☐ 225 Hal Christiansen
☐ 226 Jason Smith ☐ 227 K. Biette
☐ 228 Barry Becker (G) ☐ 229 Derek Eberle
☐ 230 Ken Richardson ☐ 231 Niklas Barklund
☐ 232 Frank Kovacs ☐ 235 Lloyd Pelletier
☐ 236 D.Vossen, A.Coach ☐ 237 A.J. Kelham
☐ 238 Mike Risdale (G) ☐ 239 Brad Bagu
☐ 240 Niko Ovaska ☐ 241 Brad Tippett, Coach
☐ 242 The Goalies II ☐ 243 Lee J. Leslie
☐ 244 Darren Perkins ☐ 245 Jason Kwiatkowski
☐ 246 J. Renard ☐ 247 Dan Kesa
☐ 248 Jason Klassen ☐ 249 N.Polychronopoulos
☐ 250 David Neilson ☐ 251 Merv Haney
☐ 252 Troy Hjertaas ☐ 253 Curt Regnier
☐ 254 Dean McAmmond ☐ 255 Travis Laycock (G)
☐ 256 Jeff Lank ☐ 257 Barkley Swenson
☐ 258 Darren Van Impe ☐ 259 Ryan Pisiak
☐ 260 Jeff Gorman ☐ 261 Stan Matwijiw (G)
☐ 262 M. Fedorko, Coach ☐ 263 Odnokon, A. Coach
☐ 264 Shane Zulyniak ☐ 265 Jeff Nelson
☐ 266 Donevan Hextall ☐ 267 Kevin Masters
☐ 268 C. Schmidt ☐ 269 Jeff Budai
☐ 270 Bill Hooson ☐ 271 Fred Hettle
☐ 272 Kent Staniforth ☐ 273 T. Stevenson
☐ 274 David Jesiolowski ☐ 275 Babcock, Coach
☐ 276 Scott Allison ☐ 277 Travis Thiessen
☐ 278 Marc Hussey ☐ 279 Kevin Smyth
☐ 280 J. Fitzsimmons (G) ☐ 281 Jeff Petruic
☐ 282 Russ West ☐ 283 Derek Kletzel0
☐ 284 Jarret Zukiwsky ☐ 285 J. Carey
☐ 286 Close Checking ☐ 287 Checklist
☐ 288 Jason Bowen ☐ 289 Dean Tiltgen
☐ 290 Terry Degner ☐ 291 J. Murphy
☐ 292 Brian Sakic ☐ 293 Jamie Barnes
☐ 294 Darren Hastman ☐ 295 Todd Klassen
☐ 296 Mirsad Mujcin ☐ 297 Trevor Sherban
☐ 298 Chadden Cabana ☐ 299 Adam Rettschlag
☐ 300 Mark Toljanich ☐ 301 Kory Mullin
☐ 302 Byron Penstock (G) ☐ 303 Vladimir Vujtek
☐ 304 Bill Lindsay ☐ 305 Jeff Cej
☐ 306 M. Busniak, Coach ☐ 307 Todd Harris
☐ 308 Cory Dosdall ☐ 309 Jason Smith
☐ 310 Mark Dawkins (G) ☐ 311 Dan O'Rourke
☐ 312 Darby Walker ☐ 313 Olaf Kjenstadt
☐ 314 S. Mignacca (G) ☐ 315 Jon Duval
☐ 316 Lorne Toews ☐ 317 Dana Rieder
☐ 318 Clayton Norris ☐ 319 David Cooper
☐ 320 Lanny Watkins ☐ 321 Evan Marble
☐ 322 Scott Lindsay ☐ 323 Ryan Petz
☐ 324 Jeramie Heistad ☐ 325 Scott Townsend
☐ 326 Stacy Roest ☐ 327 Rob Niedermayer
☐ 328 T. Bothwell, Coach ☐ 329 Kevin Riehl
☐ 330 Mike Rathje ☐ 331 Bryan McCabe
☐ 332 MHT Tiger ☐ 333 Dean Intwert (G)
☐ 334 M. Vandenberghe ☐ 335 Cam Danyluk
☐ 336 Darcy Austin (G) ☐ 337 Jason Knight
☐ 338 Lee Sorochan ☐ 339 Al Kinisky
☐ 340 Rob Hartnell ☐ 341 Radek Sip
☐ 342 Jamie Pushor ☐ 343 Shane Peacock
☐ 344 Cadrin Smart ☐ 345 Maurice Meagher
☐ 346 Lance Burns ☐ 347 Dominic Pittis
☐ 348 Todd MacIsaac ☐ 349 Brad Zimmer
☐ 350 Jason Sorochan ☐ 351 Darcy Werenka
☐ 352 Kevin St. Jacques ☐ 353 David Trofimenkoff
☐ 354 Terry Hollinger ☐ 355 Travis Munday
☐ 356 Slade Stephenson ☐ 357 Jason Widmer
☐ 358 Brad Zavisha ☐ 359 Bob Loucks, Coach
☐ 360 Brantt Myrhes ☐ no# Garfield Henderson

THE TEAMS

Insert Set (15 cards): 6.00
Common Team Insert: .50

WHL WHL
☐ W1 Spokane Chiefs ☐ W2 Winterhawks
☐ W3 Victoria Cougars ☐ W4 Kamloops Blazers
☐ W5 Saskatoon Blades ☐ W6 Seattle Thunderbirds
☐ W7 Tacoma Rockets ☐ W8 Broncos
☐ W9 Wheat Kings ☐ W10 Pats
☐ W11 Raiders ☐ W12 Warriors
☐ W13 Americans ☐ W14 Tigers
☐ W15 Lethbridge Hurricanes

1991 - 1992 SPORTS ILLUSTRATED FOR KIDS

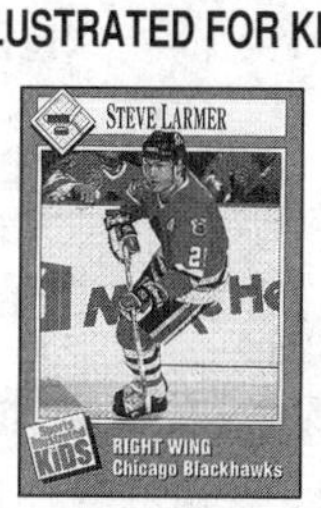

These cards were distributed as part of nine-card perforated sheets included in *Sports Illustrated for Kids*. While these cards were intended for editorial purposes, they have made their way onto the secondary market. Cards issued in the six issues between July 1991 and December 1991 were numbered 271-324. Cards issued in the six issues between January 1992 and June 1992 were numbered 1-54.

1991-92 Sports Illustrated for Kids
☐ Oct. 1991 • 300 Paul Coffey, Pitt. 1.00
☐ Dec. 1991 • 317 Bobby Orr, Bost. 10.00
1991-92 Sports Illustrated for Kids
☐ Jan. 1992 • 9 Tom Barrasso (G), Pitt. 1.00
☐ Feb. 1992 • 10 Mike Eruzione, United States 2.00
☐ Mar. 1992 • 20 Brian Bellows, Minn. 1.00
☐ Apr. 1992 • 33 Ed Belfour (G), Chic. 3.00
☐ May 1992 • 42 Mark Messier, NYRa. 3.00

1991 - 92 STAR PICS

The most expensive unsigned cards are Jean Béliveau, Peter Forsberg, Pavel Bure and Jaromir Jagr each at $1-2. Other singles sell between 5¢-$1.00. A number of players also signed cards in this series.

Imprint: © 1991 Star Pics, Inc.
Complete Set (72 cards): 7.00

Star Picks Star Picks
☐ 1 Draft Overview ☐ 2 Pat Falloon
☐ 3 Jamie Pushor ☐ 4 HOF: Jean Béliveau
☐ 5 Martin Lapointe ☐ 6 Jamie Matthews
☐ 7 HOF: Rod Gilbert ☐ 8 Niklas Sunblad
☐ 9 Steve Konowalchuk ☐ 10 Alex Delvecchio
☐ 11 Donevan Hextall ☐ 12 Dody Wood
☐ 13 Scott Niedermayer ☐ 14 Trevor Halverson
☐ 15 Terry Chitaroni ☐ 16 Tyler Wright
☐ 17 Andrey Lomakin ☐ 18 Martin Hamrlik
☐ 19 Dmitri Filimonov ☐ 20 E.Belfour (G)
☐ 21 Andrew Verner (G) ☐ 22 Yanic Perreault
☐ 23 Michael Nylander ☐ 24 Scott Lachance
☐ 25 Pavel Bure ☐ 26 Mike Torchia (G)
☐ 27 Frank Mahovlich ☐ 28 Philippe Boucher
☐ 29 Jiri Slegr ☐ 30 Sergei Fedorov
☐ 31 René Corbet ☐ 32 Jamie McLennan (G)
☐ 33 Shane Peacock ☐ 34 Mario Nobili
☐ 35 Peter Forsberg ☐ 36 Prospects
☐ 37 Arturs Irbe (G) ☐ 38 Alexei Zhitnik
☐ 39 Pat Peake ☐ 40 Adam Oates
☐ 41 Markus Näslund ☐ 42 Eric Lavigne
☐ 43 Jeff Nelson ☐ 44 Yanick Dupré
☐ 45 Justin Morrison ☐ 46 Alek Stojanov
☐ 47 M. Cousineau (G) ☐ 48 Alexei Kovalev
☐ 49 Andrey Trefilov (G) ☐ 50 Mats Sundin
☐ 51 Steve Staios ☐ 52 HOF: Glenn Hall (G)
☐ 53 Brent Bilodeau ☐ 54 Darcy Werenka
☐ 55 Chris Osgood (G) ☐ 56 Nathan LaFayette
☐ 57 Richard Matvichuk ☐ 58 Dmitri Mironov
☐ 59 Jason Dawe ☐ 60 Mike Ricci
☐ 61 Gerry Cheevers ☐ 62 Jim Campbell
☐ 65 Jason Young ☐ 66 Dean McAmmond
☐ 63 François Groleau ☐ 64 Glen Murray
☐ 67 Guy Lévêque ☐ 68 Patrick Poulin
☐ 69 Bobby House ☐ 70 Jaromir Jagr
☐ 71 Jassen Cullimore ☐ 72 Checklist

1991 - 92 TOPPS STADIUM CLUB

The most expensive cards are Wayne Gretzky ($2-3), Patrick Roy ($1.50-2.50) and Mario Lemieux ($1.50-2.50). Other singles sell between 20¢-$1.50.

Imprint: © 1991 THE TOPPS COMPANY, INC.
Complete Set (440 cards): 25.00
Common Player: .20

TSC TSC
☐ 1 Wayne Gretzky ☐ 2 Randy Moller
☐ 3 Ray Ferraro ☐ 4 Craig Wolanin
☐ 5 Shayne Corson ☐ 6 Chris Chelios
☐ 7 Joe Mullen ☐ 8 Ken Wregget
☐ 9 Robert Cimetta ☐ 10 Mike Liut
☐ 11 Martin Gélinas ☐ 12 Mario Marois
☐ 13 Rick Vaive ☐ 14 Brad McCrimmon
☐ 15 Mark Hunter ☐ 16 Jim Wiemer
☐ 17 Sergio Momesso ☐ 18 Claude Lemieux
☐ 19 Brian Hayward ☐ 20 Patrick Flatley
☐ 21 Mark Osborne ☐ 22 Mike Hudson
☐ 23 Réjean Lemelin ☐ 24 Viacheslav Fetisov
☐ 25 Bobby Smith ☐ 26 Kris King
☐ 27 Randy Velischek ☐ 28 Steve Bozek
☐ 29 Mike Foligno ☐ 30 Scott Arniel
☐ 31 Sergei Makarov ☐ 32 Rick Zombo
☐ 33 Christian Ruuttu ☐ 34 Gino Cavallini
☐ 35 Rick Tocchet ☐ 36 Jiri Hrdina
☐ 37 Peter Bondra ☐ 38 Craig Ludwig
☐ 39 Mikael Andersson ☐ 40 Bob Kudelski
☐ 41 Guy Carbonneau ☐ 42 Geoff Smith
☐ 43 Russ Courtnall ☐ 44 Michal Pivonka
☐ 45 Todd Krygier ☐ 46 Jeremy Roenick
☐ 47 Doug Brown ☐ 48 Paul Cavallini
☐ 49 Ron Sutter ☐ 50 Paul Ranheim
☐ 51 Mike Gartner ☐ 52 Greg A. Adams
☐ 53 Dave Capuano ☐ 54 Mike Krushelnyski
☐ 55 Ulf Dahlén ☐ 56 Steven Finn
☐ 57 Ed Olczyk ☐ 58 Steve Duchesne
☐ 59 Bob Probert ☐ 60 Joe Nieuwendyk
☐ 61 Petr Klima ☐ 62 Uwe Krupp
☐ 63 Jay Miller ☐ 64 Cam Neely
☐ 65 Phil Housley ☐ 66 Michel Goulet
☐ 67 Brett Hull ☐ 68 Mike Ridley
☐ 69 Esa Tikkanen ☐ 70 Kjell Samuelsson
☐ 71 Corey Millen RC ☐ 72 Doug Lidster
☐ 73 Ron Francis ☐ 74 Scott A. Young
☐ 75 Bob Sweeney ☐ 76 Sean Burke
☐ 77 Pierre Turgeon ☐ 78 David Reid
☐ 79 Al MacInnis ☐ 80 Mike Hough
☐ 81 Steve Yzerman ☐ 82 Derek King
☐ 83 Brad Shaw ☐ 84 Trevor Linden
☐ 85 Rick Meagher ☐ 86 Stéphane J.J. Richer
☐ 87 Brian Bellows ☐ 88 Pete Peeters
☐ 89 Adam Creighton ☐ 90 Brent Ashton
☐ 91 Bryan Trottier ☐ 92 Mike Richter
☐ 93 Dave Andreychuk ☐ 94 Randy Carlyle
☐ 95 Dave Christian ☐ 96 Doug Gilmour
☐ 97 Tony Granato ☐ 98 Jeff Norton
☐ 99 Neal Broten ☐ 100 Jody Hull
☐ 101 Shawn Burr ☐ 102 Pat Verbeek
☐ 103 Ken Daneyko ☐ 104 Peter Zezel
☐ 105 Kirk McLean ☐ 106 Kelly Miller
☐ 107 Patrick Roy (G) ☐ 108 Adam Oates
☐ 109 Steve Thomas ☐ 110 Scott Mellanby
☐ 111 Mark Messier ☐ 112 Larry Murphy
☐ 113 Mark Janssens ☐ 114 Doug Bodger
☐ 115 Ron Tugnutt ☐ 116 Glenn Anderson
☐ 117 Dave Gagner ☐ 118 Dino Ciccarelli
☐ 119 Randy Burridge ☐ 120 Kelly Hrudey
☐ 121 Jimmy Carson ☐ 122 Bruce Driver
☐ 123 Pat LaFontaine ☐ 124 Wendel Clark
☐ 125 Peter Sidorkiewicz ☐ 126 Gary Roberts
☐ 127 Petr' Svoboda ☐ 128 Vincent Riendeau
☐ 129 Brian Skrudland ☐ 130 Tim Kerr
☐ 131 Doug Wilson ☐ 132 Pat Elynuik
☐ 133 Craig MacTavish ☐ 134 Troy Mallette
☐ 135 Mike Ramsey ☐ 136 Tony Hrkac
☐ 137 Craig Simpson ☐ 138 Jon Casey
☐ 139 Steve Kasper ☐ 140 Kevin Hatcher
☐ 141 Dave Barr ☐ 142 Brad Lauer
☐ 143 Gary Suter ☐ 144 John MacLean
☐ 145 Dean Evason ☐ 146 V. Damphousse
☐ 147 Craig Janney ☐ 148 Jeff R. Brown
☐ 149 Geoff Courtnall ☐ 150 Igor Larionov
☐ 151 Jan Erixon ☐ 152 Bob Essensa
☐ 153 Gaëtan Duchesne ☐ 154 Jyrki Lumme
☐ 155 Tom Barrasso ☐ 156 Curtis Leschyshyn
☐ 157 Benoît Hogue ☐ 158 Gary Leeman
☐ 159 Luc Robitaille ☐ 160 Jamie Macoun
☐ 161 Bob Carpenter ☐ 162 Kevin Dineen
☐ 163 Gary Nylund ☐ 164 Dale Hunter
☐ 165 Gerard Gallant ☐ 166 Jacques Cloutier
☐ 167 Troy Murray ☐ 168 Phil Bourque
☐ 169 Grant Ledyard ☐ 170 Joel Otto
☐ 171 Paul Ysebaert ☐ 172 Luke Richardson
☐ 173 Ron Hextall ☐ 174 Mario Lemieux
☐ 175 Garry Galley ☐ 176 Murray Craven
☐ 177 Walt Poddubny ☐ 178 Scott Pearson
☐ 179 Kevin Lowe ☐ 180 Brent Sutter
☐ 181 Dirk Graham ☐ 182 Pelle Eklund
☐ 183 Sylvain Côté ☐ 184 Rod Brind'Amour
☐ 185 Fredrik Olausson ☐ 186 Kelly Kisio
☐ 187 Mike Modano ☐ 188 Calle Johansson
☐ 189 John Tonelli ☐ 190 Glen Wesley
☐ 191 Bob Errey ☐ 192 Rich Sutter
☐ 193 Kirk Muller ☐ 194 Rob Zettler
☐ 195 Alexander Mogilny ☐ 196 Adrien Plavsic
☐ 197 Daniel Marois ☐ 198 Yves Racine
☐ 199 Brendan Shanahan ☐ 200 Rob (Jr.) Brown
☐ 201 Brian Leetch ☐ 202 Dave McLlwain
☐ 203 Charlie Huddy ☐ 204 David Volek

☐ 205 Trent Yawney	☐ 206 Brian MacLellan
☐ 207 Thomas Steen	☐ 208 Sylvain Lefebvre
☐ 209 Tomas Sandström	☐ 210 Mike McPhee
☐ 211 Andy Moog	☐ 212 Paul Coffey
☐ 213 Denis Savard	☐ 214 Éric Desjardins
☐ 215 Wayne Presley	☐ 216 Stéphane Morin
☐ 217 Ric Nattress	☐ 218 Troy Gamble
☐ 219 Terry Carkner	☐ 220 Dave Hannan
☐ 221 Randy Wood	☐ 222 Brian Mullen
☐ 223 Garth Butcher	☐ 224 Tim Cheveldae
☐ 225 Rod Langway	☐ 226 Stephen Leach
☐ 227 Perry Berezan	☐ 228 Zarley Zalapski
☐ 229 Patrik Sundström	☐ 230 J. Steve Smith
☐ 231 Daren Puppa	☐ 232 Dave (Stitch) Taylor
☐ 233 Raymond Bourque	☐ 234 Kevin Stevens
☐ 235 Frantisek Musil	☐ 236 Mike Keane
☐ 237 Brian Propp	☐ 238 Brent Fedyk
☐ 239 Rob Ramage	☐ 240 Robert Kron
☐ 241 Mike McNeill	☐ 242 Greg Gilbert
☐ 243 Dan Quinn	☐ 244 Chris Nilan
☐ 245 Bernie Nicholls	☐ 246 Don Beaupré
☐ 247 Keith Acton	☐ 248 Gord Murphy
☐ 249 Bill Ranford	☐ 250 Dave Chyzowski
☐ 251 Clint Malarchuk	☐ 252 Larry Robinson
☐ 253 Dave Poulin	☐ 254 Paul MacDermid
☐ 255 Doug Smail	☐ 256 Mark Recchi
☐ 257 Brian Bradley	☐ 258 Grant Fuhr
☐ 259 Owen Nolan	☐ 260 Hubie McDonough
☐ 261 Mikko Mäkelä	☐ 262 Mathieu Schneider
☐ 263 Peter Stastny	☐ 264 Jim Hrivnak
☐ 265 Scott Stevens	☐ 266 Mike Tomlak
☐ 267 Marty McSorley	☐ 268 Johan Garpenlöv
☐ 269 Mike Vernon	☐ 270 Steve Larmer
☐ 271 Phil Sykes	☐ 272 Jay Mazur RC
☐ 273 John Ogrodnick	☐ 274 Dave Ellett
☐ 275 Randy Gilhen	☐ 276 Tom Chorske
☐ 277 James Patrick	☐ 278 Darin Kimble
☐ 279 Paul Cyr	☐ 280 Petr Nedved
☐ 281 Tony McKegney	☐ 282 Alexei Kasatonov
☐ 283 Stéphan Lebeau	☐ 284 Everett Sanipass
☐ 285 Tony Tanti	☐ 286 Kevin Miller
☐ 287 Moe Mantha	☐ 288 Alan May
☐ 289 John Cullen	☐ 290 Daniel Berthiaume
☐ 291 Mark Pederson	☐ 292 Laurie Boschman
☐ 293 Neil Wilkinson	☐ 294 Rick Wamsley
☐ 295 Ken Linseman	☐ 296 Jamie Leach
☐ 297 Chris Terreri	☐ 298 Cliff Ronning
☐ 299 Bobby Holik	☐ 300 Mats Sundin
☐ 301 Carey Wilson	☐ 302 Teppo Numminen
☐ 303 Dave Lowry	☐ 304 Joe Reekie
☐ 305 Keith Primeau	☐ 306 David Shaw
☐ 307 Nick Kypreos	☐ 308 Dave Manson
☐ 309 Mick Vukota	☐ 310 Todd Elik
☐ 311 Michel Petit	☐ 312 Dale Hawerchuk
☐ 313 Joe Murphy	☐ 314 Chris Dahlquist
☐ 315 Petri Skriko	☐ 316 Sergei Fedorov
☐ 317 Lee Norwood	☐ 318 Garry Valk
☐ 319 Glen Featherstone	☐ 320 Dave Snuggerud
☐ 321 Doug Evans	☐ 322 Marc Bureau
☐ 323 J. Vanbiesbrouck	☐ 324 John* McIntyre
☐ 325 Wes Walz	☐ 326 Daryl Reaugh
☐ 327 Paul Fenton	☐ 328 Ulf Samuelsson
☐ 329 Andrew Cassels	☐ 330 Alexei Gusarov RC
☐ 331 John Druce	☐ 332 Adam Graves
☐ 333 Ed Belfour	☐ 334 Murray Baron
☐ 335 John Tucker	☐ 336 Todd Gill
☐ 337 Martin Hostak	☐ 338 Gino Odjick
☐ 339 Eric Weinrich	☐ 340 Todd Ewen
☐ 341 Mike Hartman	☐ 342 Danton Cole
☐ 343 Jaromír Jágr	☐ 344 Mike Craig
☐ 345 Mark Fitzpatrick	☐ 346 Darren Turcotte
☐ 347 Ron L. Wilson	☐ 348 Rob Blake
☐ 349 Dale Kushner	☐ 350 Jeff Beukeboom
☐ 351 Tim Bergland	☐ 352 Peter Ing
☐ 353 Wayne McBean	☐ 354 Jim McKenzie RC
☐ 355 Theoren Fleury	☐ 356 Jocelyn Lemieux
☐ 357 Ken (Jr.) Hodge	☐ 358 Shawn Anderson
☐ 359 Dmitri Khristich	☐ 360 Jon Morris
☐ 361 Darrin Shannon	☐ 362 Chris Joseph
☐ 363 Normand Lacombe	☐ 364 Frank Pietrangelo
☐ 365 Joey Kocur	☐ 366 Anatoli Semenov
☐ 367 Bob Bassen	☐ 368 Brad Jones RC
☐ 369 Glenn Healy	☐ 370 Don Sweeney
☐ 371 Brad Dalgarno	☐ 372 Al Iafrate
☐ 373 Patrick Lebeau RC	☐ 374 Terry Yake
☐ 375 Roger Johansson	☐ 376 Paul Broten
☐ 377 André Racicot RC	☐ 378 Scott Thornton
☐ 379 Zdeno Ciger	☐ 380 Paul Stanton
☐ 381 Ray Sheppard	☐ 382 Kevin Haller RC
☐ 383 Vladimir Ruzicka	☐ 384 B. Marchment RC
☐ 385 Bill Berg RC	☐ 386 Mike Ricci
☐ 387 Pat Conacher	☐ 388 Brian Glynn RC
☐ 389 Joe Sakic	☐ 390 Mikhail Tatarinov
☐ 391 Stéphane Matteau	☐ 392 Mark Tinordi
☐ 393 Robert Reichel	☐ 394 Tim Sweeney
☐ 395 Rick Tabaracci	☐ 396 Ken Sabourin
☐ 397 Jeff Lazaro RC	☐ 398 Checklist
☐ 399 Checklist	☐ 400 Checklist

CHARTER MEMBERS SET

These cards say "Charter Member" on the card front. For "Members Only" cards, please see "1992 Topps Stadium Club Members Only".

Imprint: © 1991 the topps company, inc.

Complete Set (9 cards): 9.00

Player	TSC
☐ Ed Belfour [Vézina]	.50
☐ Ed Belfour [Top Goalie]	.50
☐ Raymond Bourque	.50
☐ Paul Coffey [1000]	.50
☐ Wayne Gretzky [2000]	3.00
☐ Wayne Gretzky [700]	3.00
☐ Brett Hull [Hart]	.50
☐ Brett Hull	.50
☐ Mario Lemieux [Club MVP]	2.00

1991 - 92 TRI-GLOBE FROM RUSSIA WITH PUCK

Pavel Bure is the most expensive single at $2-3. All other singles sell between 25¢ and $1.00.

Complete Set (24 cards): 10.00

Description	No. Player
☐ 1 Igor Larionov	☐ 2 Igor Larionov
☐ 3 Andrei Lomakin	☐ 4 Andrei Lomakin
☐ 5 Pavel Bure	☐ 6 Pavel Bure
☐ 7 Alexei Zhamnov	☐ 8 Alexei Zhamnov
☐ 9 Sergei Krivokrasov	☐ 10 Sergei Krivokrasov
☐ 11 Valeri Kamensky	☐ 12 Valeri Kamensky
☐ 13 Vyacheslav Kozlov	☐ 14 Vyacheslav Kozlov
☐ 15 Valeri Zelepukin	☐ 16 Valeri Zelepukin
☐ 17 Igor Kravchuk	☐ 18 Igor Kravchuk
☐ 19 Vladimir Malakhov	☐ 20 Vladimir Malakhov
☐ 21 Boris Mironov	☐ 22 Boris Mironov
☐ 23 Arturs Irbe (G)	☐ 24 Arturs Irbe (G)

1991 - 92 TRI-GLOBE MAGNIFICENT FIVE

Pavel Bure singles sell at $1-2; all other singles sell between 50¢ and $1.00.

Complete Set (26 cards): 18.00

Description	No. Player
☐ 1 Valeri Kamensky	☐ 2 Valeri Kamensky
☐ 3 Valeri Kamensky	☐ 4 Valeri Kamensky
☐ 5 Valeri Kamensky	☐ 6 Pavel Bure
☐ 7 Pavel Bure	☐ 8 Pavel Bure
☐ 9 Pavel Bure	☐ 10 Pavel Bure
☐ 11 Anatoli Semenov	☐ 12 Anatoli Semenov
☐ 13 Anatoli Semenov	☐ 14 Anatoli Semenov
☐ 15 Anatoli Semenov	☐ 16 Arturs Irbe (G)
☐ 17 Arturs Irbe (G)	☐ 18 Arturs Irbe (G)
☐ 19 Arturs Irbe (G)	☐ 20 Arturs Irbe (G)
☐ CL: Sergei Fedorov	☐ 1 Sergei Fedorov
☐ 2 Sergei Fedorov	☐ 3 Sergei Fedorov
☐ 4 Sergei Fedorov	☐ 5 Sergei Fedorov

1991 - 92 ULTIMATE DRAFT

These cards have two versions an English issue and a French issue. Fifty-one players have also signed both English and French cards. The most expensive unsigned card is Peter Forsberg (50¢-$1.50); unsigned singles sell for 20¢-$1.

Complete Set (90 cards): 6.00

Promo	NRMT-MT
☐ Pat Falloon	.50
☐ Alex Stojanov	.50
☐ Mike Torchia (G)	.50

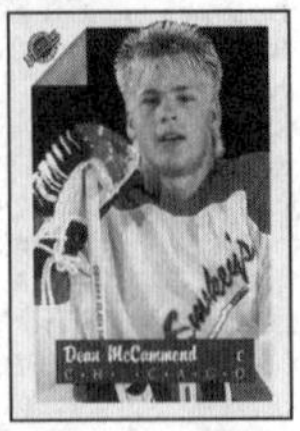

Description	Description
☐☐ 1 Ultimate / Preview	☐☐ 2 Pat Falloon
☐☐ 3 Scott Niedermayer	☐☐ 4 Scott Lachance
☐☐ 5 Peter Forsberg	☐☐ 6 Alek Stojanov
☐☐ 7 Richard Matvichuk	☐☐ 8 Patrick Poulin
☐☐ 9 Martin Lapointe	☐☐ 10 Tyler Wright
☐☐ 11 Philippe Boucher	☐☐ 12 Pat Peake
☐☐ 13 Markus Näslund	☐☐ 14 Brent Bilodeau
☐☐ 15 Glen Murray	☐☐ 16 Niklas Sundblad
☐☐ 17 Trevor Halverson	☐☐ 18 Dean McAmmond
☐☐ 19 Jim Campbell	☐☐ 20 René Corbet
☐☐ 21 Eric Lavigne	☐☐ 22 Steve Staios
☐☐ 23 Jassen Cullimore	☐☐ 24 Jamie Pushor
☐☐ 25 Donevan Hextall	☐☐ 26 Andrew Verner (G)
☐☐ 27 Jason Dawe	☐☐ 28 Jeff Nelson
☐☐ 29 Darcy Werenka	☐☐ 30 François Groleau
☐☐ 31 Guy Lévêque	☐☐ 32 Jamie Matthews
☐☐ 33 Dody Wood	☐☐ 34 Yanic Perreault
☐☐ 35 Jamie McLellan (G)	☐☐ 36 Yanick Dupré
☐☐ 37 Checklist	☐☐ 38 Chris Osgood (G)
☐☐ 39 Fredrik Lindqvist	☐☐ 40 Jason Young
☐☐ 41 Steve Konowalchuk	☐☐ 42 Michael Nylander
☐☐ 43 Shane Peacock	☐☐ 44 Yves Sarault
☐☐ 45 M. Cousineau (G)	☐☐ 46 Nathan Lafayette
☐☐ 47 Bobby House	☐☐ 48 Terry Toporowski
☐☐ 49 Terry Chitaroni	☐☐ 50 Mike Torchia (G)
☐☐ 51 Mario Nobili	☐☐ 52 Justin Morrison
☐☐ 53 Grayden Reid	☐☐ 54 Yanic Perreault
☐☐ 55 Checklist	☐☐ 56 Draft Picks
☐☐ 57 The Goalies	☐☐ 58 Pat Falloon
☐☐ 59 Scott Niedermayer	☐☐ 60 Scott Lachance
☐☐ 61 Peter Forsberg	☐☐ 62 Alek Stojanov
☐☐ 63 Richard Matvichuk	☐☐ 64 Patrick Poulin
☐☐ 65 Martin Lapointe	☐☐ 66 Tyler Wright
☐☐ 67 Philippe Boucher	☐☐ 68 Pat Peake
☐☐ 69 Markus Näslund	☐☐ 70 Brent Bilodeau
☐☐ 71 Glen Murray	☐☐ 72 Niklas Sundblad
☐☐ 73 Trevor Halverson	☐☐ 74 Dean McAmmond
☐☐ 75 Draft Picks	☐☐ 76 Draft Picks
☐☐ 77 Checklist	☐☐ 78 Pat Falloon
☐☐ 79 Scott Niedermayer	☐☐ 80 Draft Picks
☐☐ 81 Scott Lachance	☐☐ 82 Philippe Boucher
☐☐ 83 Markus Näslund	☐☐ 84 Glen Murray
☐☐ 85 Niklas Sundblad	☐☐ 86 Jason Dawe
☐☐ 87 Yanick Perreault	☐☐ 88 Draft Picks
☐☐ 89 Overview	☐☐ 90 Checklist

AUTOGRAPHS

No. Autograph	FRE	ENG
☐☐ 14 Brent Bilodeau ✍	4.00	3.00
☐☐ 67 Philippe Boucher ✍	4.00	3.00
☐☐ 19 Jim Campbell ✍	4.00	3.00
☐☐ 49 Terry Chitaroni ✍	4.00	3.00
☐☐ 20 René Corbet ✍	4.00	3.00
☐☐ 45 Marcel Cousineau (G) ✍	4.00	3.00
☐☐ 23 Jassen Cullimore ✍	4.00	3.00
☐☐ 27 Jason Dawe ✍	4.00	3.00
☐☐ 36 Yanick Dupré ✍•	8.00	10.00
☐☐ 58 Pat Falloon ✍	4.00	3.00
☐☐ 5 Peter Forsberg ✍	45.00	35.00
☐☐ 30 François Groleau ✍	4.00	3.00
☐☐ 73 Trevor Halverson ✍	4.00	3.00
☐☐ 25 Donevan Hextall ✍	4.00	3.00
☐☐ 47 Bobby House ✍	4.00	3.00
☐☐ 41 Steve Konowalchuk ✍	8.00	5.00
☐☐ 81 Scott Lachance ✍	4.00	3.00
☐☐ 46 Nathan Lafayette ✍	4.00	3.00
☐☐ 65 Martin Lapointe ✍	12.00	10.00
☐☐ 21 Éric Lavigne ✍	4.00	3.00
☐☐ 31 Guy Lévêque ✍	4.00	3.00
☐☐ 39 Fredrik Lindquist ✍	4.00	3.00
☐☐ 32 Jamie Matthews ✍	4.00	3.00
☐☐ 63 Richard Matvichuk ✍	8.00	5.00
☐☐ 74 Dean McAmmond ✍	4.00	3.00
☐☐ 35 Jamie McLennan (G) ✍	4.00	3.00
☐☐ 52 Justin Morrison ✍	4.00	3.00
☐☐ 15 Glen Murray ✍	16.00	10.00
☐☐ 83 Markus Näslund ✍	30.00	25.00
☐☐ 28 Jeff Nelson ✍	4.00	3.00
☐☐ 3 Scott Niedermayer ✍	10.00	5.00
☐☐ 51 Mario Nobili ✍	4.00	3.00
☐☐ 42 Michael Nylander ✍	8.00	5.00
☐☐ 38 Chris Osgood (G) ✍	20.00	15.00
☐☐ 43 Shane Peacock ✍	4.00	3.00
☐☐ 12 Pat Peake ✍	4.00	3.00
☐☐ 34 Yanic Perreault ✍	10.00	5.00
☐☐ 8 Patrick Poulin ✍	4.00	3.00
☐☐ 24 Jamie Pushor ✍	4.00	3.00
☐☐ 53 Grayden Reid ✍	4.00	3.00
☐☐ 44 Yves Sarault ✍	4.00	3.00
☐☐ 22 Steve Staios ✍	4.00	3.00
☐☐ 62 Alek Stojanov ✍	4.00	3.00
☐☐ 16 Niklas Sundblad ✍	4.00	3.00
☐☐ 48 Kerry Toporowski ✍	4.00	3.00
☐☐ 50 Mike Torchia (G) ✍	4.00	3.00
☐☐ 26 Andrew Verner (G) ✍	4.00	3.00
☐☐ 29 Darcy Werenka ✍	4.00	3.00
☐☐ 33 Dody Wood ✍	4.00	3.00
☐☐ 10 Tyler Wright ✍	4.00	3.00
☐☐ 40 Jason Young ✍	4.00	3.00

1991 - 92 ULTIMATE ORIGINAL SIX

These cards have two versions an English issue and a French issue. 59 players have a third autographed version. Unsigned singles sell for 20¢-$1.00.

Complete Set (90 cards): 6.00

Promo	NRMT-MT
☐ Bernie Geoffrion	.50
☐ Bobby Hull	2.00

Description	No. Player
☐☐ 1 Montréal Canadiens	☐☐ 2 New York Rangers
☐☐ 3 Toronto Maple Leafs	☐☐ 4 Boston Bruins
☐☐ 5 Chicago Blackhawks	☐☐ 6 Detroit Red Wings
☐☐ 7 Ralph Backstrom	☐☐ 8 Emile Bouchard
☐☐ 9 John Ferguson	☐☐ 10 Bernie Geoffrion
☐☐ 11 Phil Goyette	☐☐ 12 Doug Harvey
☐☐ 13 Don Marshall	☐☐ 14 Henri Richard
☐☐ 15 Dollard St. Laurent	☐☐ 16 Jean-Guy Talbot
☐☐ 17 Gump Worsley (G)	☐☐ 18 Andy Bathgate
☐☐ 19 Lou Fontinato	☐☐ 20 Ed Giacomin (G)
☐☐ 21 Vic Hadfield	☐☐ 22 Camille Henry
☐☐ 23 Harry Howell	☐☐ 24 Orland Kurtenbach
☐☐ 25 Jim Neilson	☐☐ 26 Bob Nevin
☐☐ 27 Dean Prentice	☐☐ 28 Leo Reise
☐☐ 29 Red Sullivan	☐☐ 30 Bobby Baun
☐☐ 31 Gus Bodnar	☐☐ 32 Johnny Bower (G)
☐☐ 33 Bob Davidson	☐☐ 34 Ron Ellis
☐☐ 35 Billy Harris	☐☐ 36 Larry Hillman
☐☐ 37 Tim Horton	☐☐ 38 Red Kelly
☐☐ 39 Dave Keon	☐☐ 40 Frank Mahovlich
☐☐ 41 Eddie Shack	☐☐ 42 Tod Sloan
☐☐ 43 Sid Smith	☐☐ 44 Allan Stanley
☐☐ 45 Gaye Stewart	☐☐ 46 Harry Watson
☐☐ 47 Wayne Carleton	☐☐ 48 Fern Flaman
☐☐ 49 Ken Hodge	☐☐ 50 Leo Labine
☐☐ 51 Harry Lumley (G)	☐☐ 52 John McKenzie
☐☐ 53 Doug Mohns	☐☐ 54 Fred Stanfield
☐☐ 55 Jerry Toppazzini	☐☐ 56 Ed Westfall
☐☐ 57 Bobby Hull	☐☐ 58 Ed Litzenberger
☐☐ 59 Gilles Marotte	☐☐ 60 Ab McDonald
☐☐ 61 Bill Mosienko	☐☐ 62 Jim Pappin
☐☐ 63 Pierre Pilote	☐☐ 64 Elmer Vasko
☐☐ 65 Johnny Wilson	☐☐ 66 Sid Abel
☐☐ 67 Gary Bergman	☐☐ 68 Alex Delvecchio
☐☐ 69 Bill Gadsby	☐☐ 70 Ted Lindsay
☐☐ 71 Marcel Pronovost	☐☐ 72 Norm Ullman
☐☐ 73 Bernie Geoffrion	☐☐ 74 Andy Bathgate
☐☐ 75 Allan Stanley	☐☐ 76 Fern Flaman
☐☐ 77 Bobby Hull	☐☐ 78 Norm Ullman
☐☐ 79 Red Kelly	☐☐ 80 Johnny Bower (G)
☐☐ 81 Henri Richard	☐☐ 82 Bobby Hull
☐☐ 83 Bernie Geoffrion	☐☐ 84 Tim Horton
☐☐ 85 Bill Friday	☐☐ 86 Bruce Hood
☐☐ 87 Ron Wicks	☐☐ 88 Bobby Hull
☐☐ 89 Bobby Hull	☐☐ 90 Bobby Hull
☐☐ 91 Bobby Hull	☐☐ 92 Bobby Hull
☐☐ 93 HL: Bobby Baun	☐☐ 94 HL: Ted Lindsay
☐☐ 95 HL: Henri Richard	☐☐ 96 HL: Bobby Hull
☐☐ 97 HL: Tim Horton	☐☐ 98 Keith McCreary
☐☐ 99 Checklist	☐☐ 100 Checklist

No. Holograms	NRMT
☐ Bobby Hull	20.00
☐ Bobby Hull Autograph ✍	100.00

AUTOGRAPHS

Autograph	ENG
☐ 7 Ralph Backstrom ✍	6.00
☐ 8 Emile Bouchard ✍	10.00
☐ 9 John Ferguson ✍	8.00
☐ 11 Phil Goyette ✍	3.00
☐ 13 Don Marshall ✍	3.00
☐ 14 Henri Richard ✍	25.00
☐ 15 Dollard St. Laurent ✍	3.00
☐ 17 Gump Worsley (G) ✍	20.00
☐ 18 Andy Bathgate ✍	12.00
☐ 19 Lou Fontinato ✍	4.00
☐ 20 Ed Giacomin (G) ✍	20.00
☐ 21 Vic Hadfield ✍	6.00
☐ 22 Camille Henry ✍	3.00
☐ 23 Harry Howell ✍	10.00
☐ 24 Orland Kurtenbach ✍	3.00
☐ 25 Jim Neilson ✍	3.00
☐ 26 Bob Nevin ✍	3.00
☐ 27 Dean Prentice ✍	3.00
☐ 28 Leo Reise ✍	3.00
☐ 29 Red Sullivan ✍	4.00
☐ 31 Gus Bodnar ✍	3.00
☐ 33 Bob Davidson ✍	4.00
☐ 34 Ron Ellis ✍	8.00
☐ 35 Billy Harris ✍•	15.00
☐ 36 Larry Hillman ✍	3.00
☐ 39 Dave Keon ✍	20.00
☐ 40 Frank Mahovlich ✍	20.00
☐ 41 Eddie Shack ✍	10.00
☐ 42 Tod Sloan ✍	6.00
☐ 43 Sid Smith ✍	3.00
☐ 44 Allan Stanley ✍	10.00
☐ 45 Gaye Stewart ✍	3.00
☐ 46 Harry Watson ✍	10.00
☐ 47 Wayne Carleton ✍	3.00
☐ 48 Fern Flaman ✍	10.00
☐ 49 Ken Hodge ✍	6.00
☐ 50 Leo Labine ✍	3.00
☐ 51 Harry Lumley (G) ✍	3.00
☐ 52 John McKenzie ✍	3.00
☐ 53 Doug Mohns ✍	3.00
☐ 54 Fred Stanfield ✍	3.00
☐ 56 Ed Westfall ✍	3.00
☐ 59 Gilles Marotte ✍	3.00
☐ 60 Ab McDonald ✍	3.00
☐ 61 Bill Mosienko ✍•	25.00
☐ 62 Jim Pappin ✍	3.00
☐ 63 Pierre Pilote ✍	12.00
☐ 64 Elmer Vasko ✍	3.00
☐ 65 Johnny Wilson ✍	3.00
☐ 66 Sid Abel ✍•	20.00
☐ 67 Gary Bergman ✍•	15.00
☐ 68 Alex Delvecchio ✍	12.00
☐ 69 Bill Gadsby ✍	12.00
☐ 70 Ted Lindsay ✍	25.00
☐ 71 Marcel Pronovost ✍	10.00
☐ 72 Norm Ullman ✍	12.00
☐ 79 Red Kelly ✍	15.00
☐ 80 Johnny Bower (G) ✍	15.00
☐ 83 Bernie Geoffrion ✍	20.00

1991 - 92 UPPER DECK

These cards have two versions: an English issue and a French issue. Both versions sell at the same price.

Imprint: © 1991 or 1992 Upper Deck Co.

Low Numbers Set (500 cards): 30.00

High Numbers Set (200 cards): 15.00

Common Player: .20

Description	UD
☐☐ 1 Vlad. Malakhov, C.I.S. Nationals	.20
☐☐ **2 Alexei Zhamnov, C.I.S. Nationals RC**	**1.00**
☐☐ **3 Dmitri Filimonov, C.I.S. Nationals RC**	**.20**
☐☐ **4 Alexander Semak, C.I.S. Nationals RC**	**.20**
☐☐ 5 Vyacheslav Kozlov, C.I.S. Nationals	.50
☐☐ 6 Sergei Fedorov, C.I.S. Nationals	.50
☐☐ 7 Canada Cup Checklist	.50
☐☐ 8 Al MacInnis, Canada	.20
☐☐ 9 Eric Lindros, Canada	2.00
☐☐ 10 Bill Ranford, Canada	.20
☐☐ 11 Paul Coffey, Canada	.20

	Card	Price
□□	12 Dale Hawerchuk, Canada	.20
□□	13 Wayne Gretzky, Canada	2.00
□□	14 Mark Messier, Canada	.50
□□	15 Steve Larmer, Canada	.20
□□	16 Zigmund Palffy, Czechoslovakia	1.50
□□	17 Josef Beránek, Czechoslovakia	.20
□□	**18 Jiri Slégr, Czechoslovakia RC**	**.50**
□□	19 Martin Rucinsky, Czechoslovakia	.50
□□	20 Jaromír Jágr, Czechoslovakia	.50
□□	**21 Teemu Selänne, Finland RC**	**3.50**
□□	**22 Janne Laukkanen, Finland RC**	**.20**
□□	**23 Markus Ketterer, Finland RC**	**.50**
□□	24 Jari Kurri, Finland	.50
□□	25 Janne Ojanen, Finland	.20
□□	**26 N. Lidström, Sweden [Error: Niklas] RC**	**2.50**
□□	**27 Tomas Forslund, Sweden RC**	**.20**
□□	28 Johan Garpenlöv, Sweden	.20
□□	**29 Niklas Andersson, Sweden RC**	**.20**
□□	30 Tomas Sandström, Sweden	.20
□□	31 Mats Sundin, Sweden	.50
□□	32 Mike Modano, U.S.A.	.50
□□	33 Brett Hull, U.S.A.	.50
□□	34 Mike Richter, U.S.A.	.20
□□	35 Brian Leetch, U.S.A.	.20
□□	36 Jeremy Roenick, U.S.A.	.20
□□	37 Chris Chelios, U.S.A.	.20
□□	38 W. Gretzky, LosA. / Edmo. [Gretzky 99]	2.00
□□	39 Ed Belfour, Upper Deck (Chic.)	.50
□□	40 Sergei Fedorov, Upper Deck (Detr.)	.50
□□	41 Ken (Jr.) Hodge, Upper Deck (Bost.)	.20
□□	42 Jaromír Jágr, Upper Deck (Pitt.)	.50
□□	43 Rob Blake, Upper Deck (LosA.)	.20
□□	44 Eric Weinrich, Upper Deck (NJer.)	.20
□□	45 W. Gretzky / B. Hull / M. Lemieux	1.00
□□	**46 Russ Romaniuk, Winn. RC**	**.20**
□□	47 Mario Lemieux and George Bush	1.50
□□	**48 Michel Picard, Hart. RC**	**.20**
□□	**49 Dennis Vaske, NYIs. RC**	**.20**
□□	**50 Eric Murano, Vanc. RC**	**.20**
□□	**51 Enrico Ciccone, Minn. RC**	**.50**
□□	**52 Shaun Van Allen, Edmo. RC**	**.50**
□□	53 Stu Barnes, Winn.	.20
□□	54 Pavel Bure, (Vanc.)	.50
□□	55 Neil Wilkinson, SanJ.	.20
□□	56 Tony Hrkac, SanJ.	.20
□□	57 Brian Mullen, SanJ.	.20
□□	58 Jeff Hackett, SanJ.	.20
□□	59 Brian Hayward, SanJ.	.20
□□	60 Craig Coxe, SanJ.	.20
□□	61 Rob Zettler, SanJ.	.20
□□	62 Bob McGill, SanJ.	.20
□□	63 Draft choice checklist	.20
□□	**64 Peter Forsberg, Phil. Draft RC**	**6.00**
□□	**65 Patrick Poulin, Hart. Draft RC**	**.50**
□□	66 Martin Lapointe, (Detr. Draft)	.50
□□	**67 Tyler Wright, Edmo. Draft RC**	**.20**
□□	**68 Philippe Boucher, Buff. Draft RC**	**.20**
□□	**69 Glen Murray, Bost. Draft RC**	**3.00**
□□	**70 Martin Rucinsky, Edmo. Draft RC**	**1.00**
□□	**71 Zigmund Palffy, Czechoslovakia RC**	**3.00**
□□	**72 Jassen Cullimore, Vanc. Draft RC**	**.20**
□□	**73 Jamie Pushor, Detr. Draft RC**	**.20**
□□	**74 Andrew Verner, Edmo. RC**	**.50**
□□	**75 Jason Dawe, Buff. Draft RC**	**.20**
□□	**76 Jamie Matthews, Chic. Draft RC**	**.20**
□□	**77 Sandy McCarthy, Calg. Draft RC**	**.50**
□□	78 Cam Neely, Bost. [Team Checklist]	.50
□□	79 Dale Hawerchuk, Buff. [Team Checklist]	.20
□□	80 Theoren Fleury, Calg. [Team Checklist]	.20
□□	81 Ed Belfour, Chic. [Team Checklist]	.50
□□	82 Sergei Fedorov, Detr. [Team Checklist]	.50
□□	83 Esa Tikkanen, Edmo. [Team Checklist]	.20
□□	84 John Cullen, Hart. [Team Checklist]	.20
□□	85 Tomas Sandström, LosA. [Team Checklist]	.20
□□	86 Dave Gagner, Minn. [Team Checklist]	.20
□□	87 Russ Courtnall, Mont. [Team Checklist]	.20
□□	88 John MacLean, NJer. [Team Checklist]	.20
□□	89 David Volek, NYIs. [Team Checklist]	.20
□□	90 Darren Turcotte, NYRa. [Team Checklist]	.20
□□	91 Rick Tocchet, Phil. [Team Checklist]	.20
□□	92 Mark Recchi, Pitt. [Team Checklist]	.20
□□	93 Mats Sundin, Québ. [Team Checklist]	.50
□□	94 Adam Oates, SLou. [Team Checklist]	.20
□□	95 Neil Wilkinson, SanJ. [Team Checklist]	.20
□□	96 Dave Ellett, Toro. [Team Checklist]	.20
□□	97 Trevor Linden, Vanc. [Team Checklist]	.20
□□	98 Kevin Hatcher, Wash. [Team Checklist]	.20
□□	99 Ed Olczyk, Winn. [Team Checklist]	.20
□□	100 Checklist	.20
□□	101 Bob Essensa, Winn.	.20
□□	102 Uwe Krupp, Buff.	.20
□□	103 Pelle Eklund, Phil.	.20
□□	104 Christian Ruuttu, Buff.	.20
□□	105 Kevin Dineen, Hart.	.20
□□	106 Phil Housley, Winn.	.20
□□	**107 Pat Jablonski, SLou. RC**	**.50**
□□	**108 Jarmo Kekäläinen, Bost. RC**	**.20**
□□	109 Pat Elynuik, Winn.	.20
□□	**110 Corey Millen, NYRa. RC**	**.20**
□□	111 Petr Klima, Edmo.	.20
□□	112 Mike Ridley, Wash.	.20
□□	113 Peter Stastny, NJer.	.20
□□	114 Jyrki Lumme, Vanc.	.20
□□	115 Chris Terreri, NJer.	.20
□□	116 Tom Barrasso, Pitt.	.20
□□	117 Bill Ranford, Edmo.	.20
□□	118 Peter Ing, Toro.	.20
□□	119 John Tanner, Québ.	.20
□□	120 Troy Gamble, Vanc.	.20
□□	121 Stéphane Matteau, Calg.	.20
□□	122 Rick Tocchet, Phil.	.20
□□	123 Wes Walz, Bost.	.20
□□	124 Dave Andreychuk, Buff.	.20
□□	125 Mike Craig, Minn.	.20
□□	126 Dale Hawerchuk, Buff.	.20
□□	127 Dean Evason, Hart.	.20
□□	128 Craig Janney, Bost.	.20
□□	129 Tim Cheveldae, Detr.	.20
□□	130 Rick Wamsley, Calg.	.20
□□	131 Peter Bondra, Wash.	.20
□□	132 Scott Stevens, SLou.	.20
□□	133 Kelly Miller, Wash.	.20
□□	134 Mats Sundin, Québ.	.50
□□	135 Mick Vukota, NYIs.	.20
□□	136 Vincent Damphousse, Toro.	.20
□□	137 Patrick Roy (G), Mont.	1.50
□□	138 Hubie McDonough, NYIs.	.20
□□	139 Curtis Joseph, SLou.	.50
□□	140 Brent Sutter, NYIs.	.20
□□	141 Tomas Sandström, LosA.	.20
□□	142 Kevin Miller, Detr.	.20
□□	143 Mike Ricci, Phil.	.20
□□	144 Sergei Fedorov, Detr.	.50
□□	145 Luc Robitaille, LosA.	.20
□□	146 Steve Yzerman, Detr.	1.00
□□	147 Andy Moog, Bost.	.20
□□	148 Rob Blake, LosA.	.20
□□	149 Kirk Muller, NJer.	.20
□□	150 Daniel Berthiaume, LosA.	.20
□□	151 John Druce, Wash.	.20
□□	152 Garry Valk, Vanc.	.20
□□	153 Brian Leetch, NYRa.	.20
□□	154 Kevin Stevens, Pitt.	.20
□□	155 Darren Turcotte, NYRa.	.20
□□	156 Mario Lemieux, Pitt. [w/ Stanley Cup]	1.50
□□	157 Dmitri Khristich, Wash.	.20
□□	**158 Brian Glynn, Minn. RC**	**.20**
□□	159 Benoît Hogue, Buff.	.20
□□	160 Mike Modano, Minn.	.50
□□	161 Jimmy Carson, Detr.	.20
□□	162 Steve Thomas, Chic.	.20
□□	163 Mike Vernon, Calg.	.20
□□	164 Ed Belfour, Chic.	.50
□□	165 Joel Otto, Calg.	.20
□□	166 Jeremy Roenick, Chic.	.20
□□	167 Johan Garpenlöv, Detr.	.20
□□	168 Russ Courtnall, Mont.	.20
□□	169 John MacLean, NJer.	.20
□□	170 J.J. Daigneault, Mont.	.20
□□	171 Sylvain Lefebvre, Mont.	.20
□□	172 Tony Granato, LosA.	.20
□□	173 David Volek, NYIs.	.20
□□	174 Trevor Linden, Vanc.	.20
□□	175 Mike Richter, NYRa.	.20
□□	176 Pierre Turgeon, Buff.	.20
□□	177 P. Coffey, Pitt. [b/ Stanley Cup, Lemieux]	.20
□□	178 Jan Erixon, NYRa.	.20
□□	179 Rick Vaive, Buff.	.20
□□	180 Dave Gagner, Minn.	.20
□□	181 Thomas Steen, Winn.	.20
□□	182 Esa Tikkanen, Edmo.	.20
□□	183 Sean Burke, NJer.	.20
□□	184 Paul Cavallini, SLou.	.20
□□	185 Alexei Kasatonov, NJer.	.20
□□	186 Kevin Lowe, Edmo.	.20
□□	187 Gino Cavallini, SLou.	.20
□□	188 Doug Gilmour, Calg.	.20
□□	189 Rod Brind'Amour, SLou.	.20
□□	190 Gary Roberts, Calg.	.20
□□	191 Kirk McLean, Vanc.	.20
□□	**192 Kevin Haller, Buff. RC**	**.20**
□□	193 Pat Verbeek, Hart.	.20
□□	194 Dave Snuggerud, Buff.	.20
□□	195 Gino Odjick, Vanc.	.20
□□	196 Dave Ellett, Toro.	.20
□□	197 Don Beaupré, Wash.	.20
□□	198 Rob (Jr.) Brown, Hart.	.20
□□	199 Marty McSorley, LosA.	.20
□□	200 Checklist	.20
□□	201 Joe Mullen, Pitt.	.20
□□	202 Dave Capuano, Vanc.	.20
□□	203 Paul Stanton, Pitt.	.20
□□	204 Terry Carkner, Phil.	.20
□□	205 Jon Casey, Minn.	.20
□□	206 Ken Wregget, Phil.	.20
□□	207 Gaétan Duchesne, Minn.	.20
□□	208 Cliff Ronning, Vanc.	.20
□□	209 Dale Hunter, Wash.	.20
□□	210 Danton Cole, Winn.	.20
□□	211 Jeff R. Brown, SLou.	.20
□□	212 Mike Foligno, Toro.	.20
□□	213 Michel Mongeau, SLou.	.20
□□	214 Doug Brown, NJer.	.20
□□	215 Todd Krygier, Hart.	.20
□□	216 Jon Morris, NJer.	.20
□□	217 David Reid, Toro.	.20
□□	218 John* McIntyre, LosA.	.20
□□	219 Guy Lafleur, Québ.	1.00
□□	220 V. Riendeau, SLou. [Signing autograph]	.20
□□	221 Tim Hunter, Calg.	.20
□□	222 Dave McLlwain, Winn.	.20
□□	223 Robert Reichel, Calg.	.20
□□	224 Glenn Healy, NYIs.	.20
□□	225 Robert Kron, Vanc.	.20
□□	226 Patrick Flatley, NYIs.	.20
□□	227 Petr Nedved, Vanc.	.20
□□	228 Mark Janssens, NYRa.	.20
□□	229 Michal Pivonka, Wash.	.20
□□	230 Ulf Samuelsson, Pitt.	.20
□□	231 Zarley Zalapski, Hart.	.20
□□	232 Neal Broten, Minn.	.20
□□	233 Bobby Holik, Hart.	.20
□□	234 Cam Neely, Bost.	.50
□□	235 John Cullen, Hart.	.20
□□	236 Brian Bellows, Minn.	.20
□□	237 Chris Nilan, Bost.	.20
□□	238 Mikael Andersson, Hart.	.20
□□	239 Bob Probert, Detr.	.20
□□	240 Teppo Numminen, Winn.	.20
□□	241 Peter Zezel, Toro.	.20
□□	242 Denis Savard, Mont.	.20
□□	243 Al MacInnis, Calg.	.20
□□	244 Stéphane J.J. Richer, Mont.	.20
□□	245 Theoren Fleury, Calg.	.20
□□	246 Mark Messier, Edmo.	.50
□□	247 Mike Gartner, NYRa.	.20
□□	248 Daren Puppa, Buff.	.20
□□	**249 Louie DeBrusk, NYRa. RC**	**.20**
□□	250 Glenn Anderson, Edmo.	.20
□□	251 Ken (Jr.) Hodge, Bost.	.20
□□	252 Adam Oates, SLou.	.20
□□	253 Pat LaFontaine, NYIs.	.20
□□	254 Adam Creighton, Chic.	.20
□□	255 Raymond Bourque, Bost.	.50
□□	256 Jaromír Jágr, Pitt.	.50
□□	257 Steve Larmer, Chic.	.20
□□	258 Keith Primeau, Detr.	.20
□□	259 Mike Liut, Wash.	.20
□□	260 Brian Propp, Minn.	.20
□□	261 Stéphan Lebeau, Mont.	.20
□□	262 Kelly Hrudey, LosA.	.20
□□	263 Joe Nieuwendyk, Calg.	.20
□□	264 Grant Fuhr, Edmo.	.20
□□	265 Guy Carbonneau, Mont.	.20
□□	266 Martin Gélinas, Edmo.	.20
□□	267 Alexander Mogilny, Buff.	.20
□□	268 Adam Graves, Edmo.	.20
□□	269 Anatoli Semenov, Edmo.	.20
□□	270 Dave (Stitch) Taylor, LosA.	.20
□□	271 Dirk Graham, Chic.	.20
□□	272 Gary Leeman, Toro.	.20
□□	273 Valeri Kamensky, Québ.	.50
□□	274 Marc Bureau, Minn.	.20
□□	275 James Patrick, NYRa.	.20
□□	276 Dino Ciccarelli, Wash.	.20
□□	277 Ron Tugnutt, Québ.	.20
□□	278 Paul Ysebaert, Detr.	.20
□□	279 Laurie Boschman, NJer.	.20
□□	280 Dave Manson, Chic.	.20
□□	281 Dave Chyzowski, NYIs.	.20
□□	282 Shayne Corson, Mont.	.20
□□	283 Steve Chiasson, Detr.	.20
□□	284 Craig MacTavish, Edmo.	.20
□□	285 Petr* Svoboda, Mont.	.20
□□	286 Craig Simpson, Edmo.	.20
□□	**287 Ron Hoover, Bost. RC**	**.20**
□□	288 Vladimír Ruzicka, Bost.	.20
□□	289 Randy Wood, NYIs.	.20
□□	290 Doug Lidster, Vanc.	.20
□□	291 Kay Whitmore, Hart.	.20
□□	292 Bruce Driver, NJer.	.20
□□	293 Bobby Smith, Minn.	.20
□□	294 Claude Lemieux, NJer.	.20
□□	295 Mark Tinordi, Minn.	.20
□□	296 Mark Osborne, Winn.	.20
□□	297 Brad Shaw, Hart.	.20
□□	298 Igor Larionov, Vanc.	.20
□□	299 Ron Francis, Pitt. [w/ Stanley Cup]	.20
□□	300 Checklist	.20
□□	301 Bob Kudelski, LosA.	.20
□□	302 Larry Murphy, Pitt.	.20
□□	303 Brent Ashton, Winn.	.20
□□	**304 Brad Jones, LosA. RC**	**.20**
□□	305 Gord Donnelly, Winn.	.20
□□	306 Murray Craven, Phil.	.20
□□	307 Chris Dahlquist, Minn.	.20
□□	**308 Jim Paek, Pitt. [b/ Stanley Cup] RC**	**.20**
□□	309 Ron Sutter, Phil.	.20
□□	310 Mike Tomlak, Hart.	.20
□□	311 Ray Ferraro, NYIs.	.20
□□	312 Dave Hannan, Toro.	.20
□□	313 Randy McKay, Detr.	.20
□□	314 Rod Langway, Wash.	.20
□□	315 Shawn Burr, Detr.	.20
□□	316 Calle Johansson, Wash.	.20
□□	317 Rich Sutter, SLou.	.20
□□	318 Al Iafrate, Wash.	.20
□□	319 Bob Bassen, SLou.	.20
□□	320 Mike Krushelnyski, Toro.	.20
□□	321 Sergei Makarov, Calg.	.20
□□	322 Darrin Shannon, Buff.	.20
□□	323 Terry Yake, Hart.	.20
□□	324 John Vanbiesbrouck, NYRa.	.20
□□	325 Peter Sidorkiewicz, Hart.	.20
□□	326 Troy Mallette, NYRa.	.20
□□	327 Ron Hextall, Phil.	.20
□□	328 Mathieu Schneider, Mont.	.20
□□	329 Bryan Trottier, Pitt.	.50
□□	330 Kris King, NYRa.	.20
□□	331 Daniel Marois, Toro.	.20
□□	332 Shayne Stevenson, Bost.	.20
□□	333 Joe Sakic, Québ.	.50
□□	334 Petri Skriko, Bost.	.20
□□	**335 Dominik Hasek, Chic. RC**	**4.00**
□□	336 Scott Pearson, Québ.	.20
□□	337 Bryan Fogarty, Québ.	.20
□□	338 Don Sweeney, Bost.	.20
□□	339 Rick Tabaracci, Winn.	.20
□□	340 Steven Finn, Québ.	.20
□□	341 Gary Suter, Calg.	.20
□□	342 Troy Crowder, NJer.	.20
□□	343 Jim Hrivnak, Wash.	.20
□□	344 Eric Weinrich, NJer.	.20
□□	**345 John LeClair, Mont. RC**	**3.50**
□□	346 Mark Recchi, Pitt.	.20
□□	**347 Dan Currie, Edmo. RC**	**.20**
□□	348 Ulf Dahlén, Minn.	.20
□□	349 Rob Ray, Buff.	.20
□□	350 J. Steve Smith, Edmo.	.20
□□	351 Shawn Antoski, Vanc.	.20
□□	352 Cam Russell, Chic.	.20
□□	353 Scott Thornton, Toro.	.20
□□	354 Chris Chelios, Chic.	.20
□□	355 Sergei Nemchinov, NYRa.	.20
□□	356 Bernie Nicholls, NYRa.	.20
□□	357 Jeff Norton, NYIs.	.20
□□	358 Dan Quinn, SLou.	.20
□□	359 Michel Petit, Toro.	.20
□□	360 Éric Desjardins, Mont.	.20
□□	361 Kevin Hatcher, Wash.	.20
□□	**362 Jiri Sejba, Buff. RC**	**.20**
□□	363 Mark Pederson, Phil.	.20
□□	**364 Jeff Lazaro, Bost. RC**	**.20**
□□	**365 Alexei Gusarov, Québ. RC**	**.50**
□□	366 Jari Kurri, LosA.	.50
□□	367 Owen Nolan, Québ.	.20
□□	368 Clint Malarchuk, Buff.	.20
□□	369 Patrik Sundström, NJer.	.20
□□	370 Glen Wesley, Bost.	.20
□□	371 Wayne Presley, Chic.	.20
□□	372 Craig Muni, Edmo.	.20
□□	373 Brent Fedyk, Detr.	.20
□□	374 Michel Goulet, Chic.	.20
□□	375 Tim Sweeney, Calg.	.20
□□	**376 Gary Shuchuk, Detr. RC**	**.20**
□□	**377 André Racicot, Mont. RC**	**.50**
□□	**378 Jay Mazur, Vanc. RC**	**.20**
□□	379 Andrew Cassels, Mont.	.20
□□	380 Brian Noonan, Chic.	.20
□□	**381 Sergei Kharin, Winn. RC**	**.20**
□□	382 Derek King, NYIs.	.20
□□	383 Fredrik Olausson, Winn.	.20
□□	384 Tom Fergus, Toro.	.20
□□	385 Zdeno Ciger, NJer.	.20
□□	386 Wendel Clark, Toro.	.20
□□	387 Ed Olczyk, Winn.	.20
□□	388 Basil McRae, Minn.	.20
□□	389 Tom Fitzgerald, NYIs.	.20
□□	390 Ray Sheppard, NYRa.	.20
□□	391 Bob Sweeney, Bost.	.20
□□	392 Gord Murphy, Phil.	.20
□□	393 John Chabot, Detr.	.20
□□	394 Jeff Beukeboom, Edmo.	.20
□□	395 Rick Zombo, Detr.	.20
□□	396 Kjell Samuelsson, Phil.	.20
□□	397 Garth Butcher, SLou.	.20
□□	398 Phil Bourque, Pitt.	.20
□□	399 Lou Franceschetti, Buff.	.20
□□	400 Checklist	.20
□□	**401 Kevin Todd, NJer. RC**	**.20**
□□	402 Ken Baumgartner, NYIs.	.20
□□	403 Peter Douris, Bost.	.20
□□	404 Jiri Latal, Phil.	.20
□□	**405 Marc Potvin, Detr. RC**	**.20**
□□	406 Gary Nylund, NYIs.	.20
□□	407 Yvon Corriveau, Hart.	.20
□□	408 Sheldon Kennedy, Detr.	.20
□□	409 David Shaw, NYRa.	.20
□□	410 Viacheslav Fetisov, NJer.	.20
□□	**411 Mario Doyon, Québ. RC**	**.20**
□□	412 Jamie Macoun, Calg.	.20
□□	413 Curtis Leschyshyn, Québ.	.20
□□	414 Mike Peluso, Chic.	.20
□□	415 Brian Benning, LosA.	.20
□□	**416 Stu Grimson, Chic. RC**	**1.00**
□□	417 Ken Sabourin, Wash.	.20
□□	418 Luke Richardson, Toro.	.20
□□	**419 Ken Quinney, Québ. RC**	**.20**
□□	**420 Mike Donnelly, LosA. RC**	**.20**
□□	**421 Darcy Loewen, Buff. RC**	**.20**
□□	422 Brian Skrudland, Mont.	.20
□□	**423 Joel Savage, Buff. RC**	**.20**
□□	424 Adrien Plavsic, Vanc.	.20
□□	425 Jergus Baca, Hart.	.20
□□	426 Greg A. Adams, Vanc.	.20
□□	427 Tom Chorske, Mont.	.20
□□	428 Scott Scissons, NYIs.	.20
□□	429 Dale Kushner, Phil.	.20
□□	**430 Todd Richards, Hart. RC**	**.20**
□□	431 Kip Miller, Québ.	.20
□□	**432 Jason Prosofsky, NYRa. RC**	**.20**
□□	433 Stéphane Morin, Québ.	.20
□□	**434 Brian McReynolds, NYRa. RC**	**.20**
□□	435 Ken Daneyko, NJer.	.20
□□	436 Chris Joseph, Edmo.	.20
□□	437 Wayne Gretzky, LosA.	2.00
□□	438 Jocelyn Lemieux, Chic.	.20
□□	439 Garry Galley, Bost.	.20
□□	440 Star Rookies	.20
□□	441 Steven Rice, NYRa.	.20
□□	442 Patrice Brisebois, Mont.	.20
□□	443 Jimmy Waite, Chic.	.20
□□	**444 Doug Weight, NYRa. RC**	**2.50**
□□	445 Nelson Emerson, SLou.	.20
□□	**446 Jarrod Skalde, NJer. RC**	**.20**
□□	447 Jamie Leach, Pitt.	.20
□□	**448 Gilbert Dionne, Mont. RC**	**.20**
□□	449 Trevor Kidd, Spokane Chiefs (Calg.)	.20
□□	**450 Tony Amonte, NYRa. RC**	**2.50**
□□	451 Pat Murray, Phil.	.20
□□	452 Stéphane Fiset, Québ.	.20
□□	**453 Patrick Lebeau, Mont. RC**	**.20**
□□	**454 Chris Taylor, NYIs. RC**	**.20**
□□	**455 Chris Tancill, Hart. RC**	**.20**
□□	456 Mark Greig, Hart.	.20
□□	457 Mike Sillinger, Detr.	.20
□□	**458 Ken Sutton, Buff. RC**	**.20**
□□	**459 Len Barrie, Phil. RC**	**.20**
□□	460 Félix Potvin, Chicoutimi (Toro.)	.50
□□	**461 Brian Sakic, Tri-City (Wash.) RC**	**.20**
□□	**462 Vyacheslav Kozlov, Detr. RC**	**1.00**
□□	**463 Matt DelGuidice, Bost. RC**	**.50**
□□	464 Brett Hull, SLou.	.50
□□	**465 Norm Foster, Bost. RC**	**.50**
□□	**466 Alexander Godynyuk, Toro. RC**	**.20**
□□	467 Geoff Courtnall, Vanc.	.20
□□	468 Frantisek Kucera, Chic.	.20
□□	**469 Benoît Brunet, Mont. RC**	**.20**
□□	**470 Mark Vermette, Québ. RC**	**.20**
□□	471 Tim Watters, LosA.	.20
□□	472 Paul Ranheim, Calg.	.20
□□	473 Martin Hostak, Phil.	.20
□□	474 Joe Murphy, Edmo.	.20
□□	**475 Claude Boivin, Phil. RC**	**.20**
□□	476 John Ogrodnick, NYRa.	.20
□□	477 Doug Bodger, Buff.	.20
□□	478 Shawn Cronin, Winn.	.20
□□	479 Mark Hunter, Hart.	.20
□□	480 Dave Tippett, Wash.	.20
□□	481 Rob DiMaio, NYIs.	.20
□□	482 Lyle Odelein, Mont.	.20
□□	483 Joe Reekie, NYIs.	.20
□□	484 Randy Velischek, Québ.	.20
□□	**485 Myles O'Connor, NJer. RC**	**.20**
□□	486 Craig Wolanin, Québ.	.20

□□	487 Mike McPhee, Mont.	.20
□□	**488 Claude Lapointe, Québ. RC**	**.50**
□□	489 Troy Loney, Pitt.	.20
□□	490 Bob Beers, Bost.	.20
□□	**491 Sylvain Couturier, LosA. RC**	**.20**
□□	**492 Kimbi Daniels, Phil. RC**	**.20**
□□	**493 Darryl Shannon, Toro. RC**	**.20**
□□	**494 Jim McKenzie, Hart. RC**	**.20**
□□	**495 Don Gibson, Vanc. RC**	**.20**
□□	**496 Ralph Barahona, Bost. RC**	**.20**
□□	497 Murray Baron, Phil.	.20
□□	498 Yves Racine, Detr.	.20
□□	499 Larry Robinson, LosA.	.20
□□	500 Checklist	.20
□□	501 Canada Cup checklist	.50
□□	502 Dirk Graham, Canada	.20
□□	503 Rick Tocchet, Canada	.20
□□	504 Eric Desjardins, Canada	.20
□□	505 Shayne Corson, Canada	.20
□□	506 Theoren Fleury, Canada	.20
□□	507 Luc Robitaille, Canada	.20
□□	508 Tony Granato, U.S.A.	.20
□□	509 Eric Weinrich, U.S.A.	.20
□□	510 Gary Suter, U.S.A.	.20
□□	511 Kevin Hatcher, U.S.A.	.20
□□	512 Craig Janney, U.S.A.	.20
□□	513 Darren Turcotte, U.S.A.	.20
□□	**514 Chris Winnes, Bost. RC**	**.20**
□□	515 Kelly Kisio, SanJ.	.20
□□	**516 Joe Day, Hart. RC**	**.20**
□□	**517 Ed Courtenay, SanJ. RC**	**.20**
□□	518 Andrei Lomakin, Phil.	.20
□□	519 Kirk Muller, Mont.	.20
□□	**520 Rick Lessard, SanJ. RC**	**.20**
□□	521 Scott Thornton, Edmo.	.20
□□	522 Luke Richardson, Edmo.	.20
□□	523 Mike Eagles, Winn.	.20
□□	524 Mike McNeill, Québ.	.20
□□	**525 Ken Priestlay, Pitt. RC**	**.20**
□□	526 Louie DeBrusk, Edmo.	.20
□□	527 Dave McLlwain, NYIs.	.20
□□	528 Gary Leeman, Calg.	.20
□□	**529 Adam Foote, Québ. RC**	**1.00**
□□	530 Kevin Dineen, Phil.	.20
□□	531 David Reid, Bost.	.20
□□	532 Arturs Irbe, SanJ.	.20
□□	**533 Mark Osiecki, Calg. RC**	**.20**
□□	534 Steve Thomas, NYIs.	.20
□□	535 Vincent Damphousse, Edmo.	.20
□□	536 Stéphane J.J. Richer, NJer.	.20
□□	537 Jarmo Myllys, SanJ.	.20
□□	538 Carey Wilson, Calg.	.20
□□	539 Scott Stevens, NJer.	.20
□□	540 Uwe Krupp, NYIs.	.20
□□	541 Dave Christian, SLou.	.20
□□	542 Scott Mellanby, Edmo.	.20
□□	**543 Peter Ahola, LosA. RC**	**.20**
□□	544 Todd Elik, Minn.	.20
□□	545 Mark Messier, NYRa.	.50
□□	546 Derian Hatcher, Minn.	.20
□□	547 Rod Brind'Amour, Phil.	.20
□□	548 Dave Manson, Edmo.	.20
□□	549 Darryl Sydor, LosA.	.20
□□	550 Paul Broten, NYRa.	.20
□□	551 Andrew Cassels, Hart.	.20
□□	**552 Tom Draper, Buff. RC**	**.50**
□□	553 Grant Fuhr, Toro.	.20
□□	554 Pierre Turgeon, NYIs.	.20
□□	555 Pavel Bure, Vanc.	.20
□□	556 Pat LaFontaine, Buff.	.20
□□	557 Dave Thomlinson, Bost.	.20
□□	558 Doug Gilmour, Toro.	.20
□□	**559 Craig Billington, NJer. RC**	**.50**
□□	560 Dean Evason, SanJ.	.20
□□	561 Brendan Shanahan, SLou.	.50
□□	562 Mike Hough, Québ.	.20
□□	563 Dan Quinn, Phil.	.20
□□	**564 Jeff Daniels, Pitt. RC**	**.20**
□□	565 Troy Murray, Winn.	.20
□□	566 Bernie Nicholls, Edmo.	.20
□□	567 Randy Burridge, Wash.	.20
□□	**568 Todd Hartje, Winn. RC**	**.20**
□□	569 Charlie Huddy, LosA.	.20
□□	570 Steve Duchesne, Phil.	.20
□□	571 Sergio Momesso, Vanc.	.20
□□	572 Brian Lawton, SanJ.	.20
□□	573 Ray Sheppard, Detr.	.20
□□	574 Adam Graves, NYRa.	.20
□□	575 Rollie Melanson, Mont.	.20
□□	576 Steve Kasper, Phil.	.20
□□	577 Jim Sandlak, Vanc.	.20
□□	**578 Pat MacLeod, SanJ. RC**	**.20**
□□	579 Sylvain Turgeon, Mont.	.20
□□	**580 James H. Black, Hart. RC**	**.20**
□□	581 Darrin Shannon, Winn.	.20
□□	582 Todd Krygier, Wash.	.20
□□	**583 Dominic Roussel, Phil. RC**	**.50**
□□	584 Nicklas Lidström, Detr. [Checklist]	.20
□□	585 Donald Audette, Buff. [Young Guns]	.20
□□	586 Tomas Forslund, Calg. [Young Guns]	.20
□□	587 Nicklas Lidström, Detr. [Young Guns]	.50
□□	**588 G. Sanderson, Hart. [Young Guns] RC**	**1.00**
□□	**589 V. Zelepukin, NJer. [Young Guns] RC**	**.20**
□□	**590 Igor Ulanov, Winn. [Young Guns] RC**	**.50**
□□	**591 Corey Foster, Phil. [Young Guns] RC**	**.20**
□□	**592 Dan Lambert, Québ. [Young Guns] RC**	**.20**
□□	593 Pat Falloon, SanJ. [Young Guns]	.20
□□	594 V. Konstantinov, Detr. [Young Guns]	.50
□□	**595 J. Beránek, Edmo. [Young Guns] RC**	**.50**
□□	596 Brad May, Buff. [Young Guns]	.20
□□	**597 Jeff Odgers, SanJ. [Young Guns] RC**	**.50**
□□	**598 Rob Pearson, Toro. [Young Guns] RC**	**.20**
□□	**599 L. Borsato, Winn. [Young Guns] RC**	**.20**
□□	600 Checklist	.20
□□	601 Peter Douris, Bost.	.20
□□	602 Mark Fitzpatrick, NYIs.	.20
□□	603 Randy Gilhen, NYRa.	.20
□□	604 Corey Millen, LosA.	.20
□□	**605 Jason Cirone, Winn. RC**	**.20**
□□	**606 Kyosti Karjalainen, LosA. RC**	**.20**
□□	607 Garry Galley, Phil.	.20
□□	**608 Brent Thompson, LosA. RC**	**.20**
□□	609 Alexander Godynyuk, Calg.	.20
□□	610 All-Star checklist	.20
□□	611 Mario Lemieux, All-Star	1.00
□□	612 Brian Leetch, All-Star	.20
□□	613 Kevin Stevens, All-Star	.20
□□	614 Patrick Roy (G), All-Star	1.00
□□	615 Paul Coffey, All-Star	.20
□□	616 Joe Sakic, All-Star	.50
□□	617 Jaromir Jagr, All-Star	.20
□□	618 Alexander Mogiln, All-Star	.20
□□	619 Owen Nolan, All-Star	.20
□□	620 Mark Messier, All-Star	.20
□□	621 Wayne Gretzky, All-Star	1.50
□□	622 Brett Hull, All-Star	.20
□□	623 Luc Robitaille, All-Star	.20
□□	624 Phil Housley, All-Star	.20
□□	625 Ed Belfour (G), All-Star	.20
□□	626 Steve Yzerman, All-Star	.50
□□	627 Adam Oates, All-Star	.20
□□	628 Trevor Linden, All-Star	.20
□□	629 Jeremy Roenick, All-Star	.20
□□	630 Theoren Fleury, All-Star	.20
□□	631 Sergei Fedorov, All-Star	.20
□□	632 Al MacInnis, All-Star	.20
□□	633 Raymond Bourqu, All-Stare	.20
□□	634 Mike Richter, All-Star	.20
□□	635 Al Secord, Chic. [Heroes of the NHL]	.20
□□	636 Marcel Dionne, LosA. [Heroes of the NHL]	.50
□□	637 Ken Morrow, NYIs. [Heroes of the NHL]	.20
□□	638 Guy Lafleur, Mont. [Heroes of the NHL]	1.00
□□	639 Ed Mio, NYRa. [Heroes of the NHL]	.20
□□	640 Clark Gillies, NYIs. [Heroes of the NHL]	.20
□□	641 Bob Nystrom, NYIs. [Heroes of the NHL]	.20
□□	642 Pete Peeters, Wash. [Heroes of the NHL]	.20
□□	643 Ulf Nilsson, NYRa. [Heroes of the NHL]	.20
□□	644 Lebeau brothers	.20
□□	645 Sutter brothers	.20
□□	646 Cavallini brothers	.20
□□	647 Bure brothers	.20
□□	648 Ferraro twins	.20

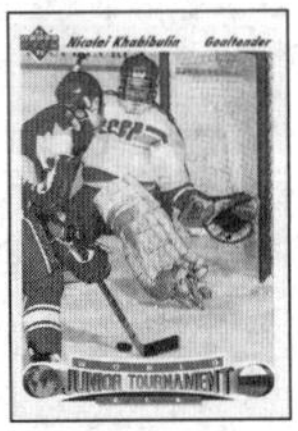

□□	649 C.I.S. Juniors	.20
□□	**650 Darius Kasparaitis, C.I.S. RC**	**1.00**
□□	**651 Alexei Yashin, C.I.S. RC**	**2.50**
□□	**652 Nikolai Khabibulin, C.I.S. RC**	**1.50**
□□	**653 Denis Metlyuk, C.I.S. RC**	**.20**
□□	**654 Konstantin Korotkov, C.I.S. RC**	**.20**
□□	**655 Alexei Kovalev, C.I.S. RC**	**2.50**
□□	**656 Alexander Kuzminsky, C.I.S. RC**	**.20**
□□	**657 Alexander Cherbayev, C.I.S. RC**	**.20**
□□	**658 Sergei Krivokrasov, C.I.S. RC**	**.50**
□□	**659 Sergei Zholtok, C.I.S. RC**	**.50**
□□	**660 Alexei Zhitnik, C.I.S. RC**	**.50**
□□	**661 Sandis Ozolinsh, C.I.S. RC**	**1.00**
□□	**662 Boris Mironov, C.I.S. RC**	**.50**
□□	**663 Pauli Jaks (G), Switzerland RC**	**.20**
□□	**664 Gaetan Voisard, Switzerland RC**	**.20**
□□	**665 Nicola Celio, Switzerland RC**	**.20**
□□	**666 Marc Weber, Switzerland RC**	**.20**
□□	**667 Bernhard Schumperli, Switzerland RC**	**.20**
□□	**668 Laurent Bucher, Switzerland RC**	**.20**
□□	**669 Michael Blaha, Switzerland RC**	**.20**
□□	**670 Tiziano Gianini, Switzerland RC**	**.20**
□□	**671 Marko Kiprusoff, Finland RC**	**.20**
□□	**672 Janne Grönvall, Finland RC**	**.20**
□□	**673 Juha Ylönen, Finland RC**	**.50**
□□	**674 Sami Kapanen, Finland RC**	**1.00**
□□	**675 Marko Tuomainen, Finland RC**	**.20**
□□	**676 Jarkko Varvio, Finland RC**	**1.00**
□□	**677 Tuomas Grönman, Finland RC**	**.20**
□□	**678 Andreas Naumann, Germany RC**	**.20**
□□	**679 Steffan Ziesche, Germany RC**	**.20**
□□	**680 Jens Schwabe, Germany RC**	**.20**
□□	**681 Thomas Schubert, Germany RC**	**.20**
□□	**682 Hans-Jörg Mayer, Germany RC**	**.20**
□□	**683 Marc Seliger, Germany RC**	**.20**
□□	684 Trevor Kidd, Canada	.20
□□	685 Martin Lapointe, Canada	.20
□□	686 Tyler Wright, Canada	.20
□□	687 Kimbi Daniels, Canada	.20
□□	688 Karl Dykhuis, Canada	.20
□□	**689 Jeff Nelson, Canada RC**	**.20**
□□	690 Jassen Cullimore, Canada	.20
□□	691 Turner Stevenson, Canada	.20
□□	**692 Scott Lachance, U.S.A. RC**	**.50**
□□	**693 Mike Dunham, U.S.A. RC**	**1.50**
□□	**694 Brent Bilodeau, U.S.A. RC**	**.20**
□□	**695 Ryan Sittler, U.S.A. RC**	**.20**
□□	**696 Peter Ferraro, U.S.A. RC**	**.50**
□□	**697 Pat Peake, U.S.A. RC**	**.20**
□□	**698 Keith Tkachuk, U.S.A. RC**	**2.50**
□□	**699 Brian Rolston, U.S.A. RC**	**1.00**
□□	700 Checklist	.20
□□	SP1 Glasnost on ice	4.00

HOCKEY HEROES

Insert Set (10 cards):		**4.00**
□	Brett Hull Auto. ✍	100.00
	Insert	**NRMT-MT**
□□	1 Brett Hull	.50
□□	2 Brett Hull	.50
□□	3 Brett Hull	.50
□□	4 Brett Hull	.50
□□	5 Brett Hull	.50
□□	6 Brett Hull	.50
□□	7 Brett Hull	.50
□□	8 Brett Hull	.50
□□	9 Brett Hull	.50
□□	Header Card	.75

AWARD WINNERS

Insert Set (9 cards):		**8.00**
	Insert	**NRMT-MT**
□	AW1 Wayne Gretzky, LosA.	3.00
□	AW2 Ed Belfour, Chic.	.50
□	AW3 Brett Hull, SLou.	.50
□	AW4 Ed Belfour, Chic.	.50
□	AW5 Raymond Bourque, Bost.	.50
□	AW6 Wayne Gretzky, LosA.	3.00
□	AW7 Ed Belfour, Chic.	.50
□	AW8 Dirk Graham, Chic.	.25
□	AW9 Mario Lemieux, Pitt.	2.00

EURO-STARS

Insert Set (18 cards):		**7.00**
	Insert	**NRMT-MT**
□□	E1 Jarmo Kekäläinen, Bost.	.25
□□	E2 Alexander Mogilny, Buff.	.50
□□	E3 Bobby Holik, Hart.	.25
□□	E4 Anatoli Semenov, Edmo.	.25
□□	E5 Petr Nedved, Vanc.	.25
□□	E6 Jaromír Jágr, Pitt.	1.00
□□	E7 Tomas Sandström, LosA.	.25
□□	E8 Robert Kron, Vanc.	.25
□□	E9 Sergei Fedorov, Detr.	1.00
□□	E10 Esa Tikkanen, Edmo.	.25
□□	E11 Christian Ruuttu, Buff.	.25
□□	E12 Peter Bondra, Wash.	.25
□□	E13 Mats Sundin, Toro.	1.00
□□	E14 Dominik Hasek, Chic.	3.00
□□	E15 Johan Garpenlöv, SanJ.	.25
□□	E16 Alexander Godynyuk, Toro.	.25
□□	E17 Ulf Samuelsson, Pitt.	.25
□□	E18 Igor Larionov, Vanc.	.50

1991 - 92 UPPER DECK – BUYBACKS

These cards were purchased by The Upper Deck Company and reinserted as autographed cards in new 2000-01 and 2001-02 products.

	Buyback Autograph	**UD**
□	32 Mike Modano, U.S.A. Nationals ✍ {#/5}	
□	34 Mike Richter, U.S.A. Nationals ✍ {#/1}	
□	145 Luc Robitaille, LosA. ✍ {#/12}	
□	146 Steve Yzerman, Detr. ✍ {#/1}	
□	160 Mike Modano, Dall. ✍ {#/12}	
□	175 Mike Richter, NYRa. ✍ {#/1}	
□	255 Raymond Bourque, Bost. ✍ {#/2}	
□	**345 John LeClair, Mont. RC ✍ {#/4}**	
□	**444 Doug Weight, NYRa. RC ✍ {#/20}**	
□	507 Luc Robitaille, Canada Nationals ✍ {#/5}	
□	Mark Messier ✍ {#/1}	
□	623 Luc Robitaille, All-Star ✍ {#/2}	

1991 - 92 UPPER DECK WORLD JUNIORS

This set was released for the 1992 World Junior Games in the Czech Republic.

Complete Set (102 cards):		**55.00**
Common Player:		**.25**
Album:		**6.00**
	Description	**WJC**
□	1 Description Card	.25
□	2 Vladislav Buljin	.25
□	3 Ravil Gusmanov	.25
□	4 Denis Vinokurov	.25
□	5 Mikhail Volkov	.25
□	6 Alexei Troschinsky	.25
□	7 Andrei Nikolishin	.50
□	8 Alexander Sverztov	.25
□	9 Artim Kopot	.25
□	10 Ildar Mukhometov	.25
□	11 Darius Kasparaitis	1.00
□	12 Alexei Yashin	4.00
□	13 Nikolai Khabibulin (G)	3.00
□	14 Denis Metlyuk	.25
□	15 Konstantin Korotkov	.25
□	16 Alexei Kovalev	4.00
□	17 Alexander Kuzminsky	.25
□	18 Slexander Cherbayev	.25
□	19 Sergei Krivokrasov	.50
□	20 Sergei Zholtok	.50
□	21 Alexei Zhitnik	.50
□	22 Sandis Ozolinsh	1.00
□	23 Boris Mironov	.50
□	24 Pauli Jaks (G)	.25
□	25 Gaetan Voisard	.25
□	26 Nicola Celio	.25
□	27 Marc Weber	.25
□	28 Bernhard Schumperli	.25
□	29 Laurent Bucher	.25
□	30 Michael Blaha	.25
□	31 Tiziano Gianini	.25
□	32 Tero Lehtera	.25
□	33 Mikko Luovi	.25
□	34 Marko Kiprusoff	.25
□	35 Janne Gronvall	.25
□	36 Juha Ylönen	.50
□	37 Sami Kapanen	2.00
□	38 Marko Tuomainen	.25
□	39 Jarkko Varvio	.50
□	40 Tuomas Gronman	.25
□	41 Andreas Naumann	.25
□	42 Steffen Ziesche	.25
□	43 Jens Schwabe	.25
□	44 Thomas Schubert	.25
□	45 Hans-Jorg Mayer	.25
□	46 Marc Seliger (G)	.25
□	47 Ryan Hughes	.25
□	48 Richard Matvichuk	.50
□	49 David St. Pierre	.25
□	50 Paul Kariya	18.00
□	51 Patrick Poulin	.50
□	52 Mike Fountain (G)	.25
□	53 Scott Niedermayer	.50
□	54 John Slaney	.25
□	55 Brad Bombardir	.25
□	56 Andy Schneider	.25
□	57 Steve Junker	.25
□	58 Trevor Kidd (G)	.50
□	59 Martin Lapointe	1.00
□	60 Tyler Wright	.25
□	61 Kimbi Daniels	.25
□	62 Karl Dykhuis	.25
□	63 Jeff Nelson	.25
□	64 Jassen Cullimore	.25
□	65 Turner Stevenson	.25
□	66 Brian Mueller	.50
□	67 Chris Tucker	.50
□	68 Marty Schriner	.50
□	69 Mike Pendergast	.50
□	70 John Lilley	.50
□	71 Jim Campbell	.50
□	72 Brian Holzinger	1.00
□	73 Steve Konowalchuk	1.50
□	74 Chris Ferraro	.50
□	75 Chris Imes	.50
□	76 Rich Brennan	.50
□	77 Todd Hall	.50
□	78 Brian Rafalski	2.00
□	79 Scott Lachance	.50
□	80 Mike Dunham (G)	2.00
□	81 Brent Bilodeau	.25
□	82 Ryan Sittler	.25
□	83 Peter Ferraro	.50
□	84 Pat Peake	.25
□	85 Keith Tkachuk	4.50
□	86 Brian Rolston	2.00
□	87 Milan Hnilicka	2.00
□	88 Roman Hamrlik	1.00
□	89 Milan Nedoma	.25
□	90 Patrik Luza	.25
□	91 Jan Caloun	.25
□	92 Viktor Ujcik	1.00
□	93 Robert Petrovicky	.50
□	94 Roman Meluzin	.25
□	95 Jan Vopat	.25
□	96 Martin Prochazka	.25
□	97 Zigmund Palffy	3.00
□	98 Ivan Droppa	.25
□	99 Martin Straka	1.50
□	100 Checklist	.25
□	Hologram: Wayne Gretzky, Art Ross	5.00
□	Hologram: Wayne Gretzky, Lady Byng	5.00

1992 CANADIAN WINTER OLYMPICS

This 200-card multi-sport set features 18 hockey players. A 200-card set sells at $20.00. Hockey singles sell for 20¢-$1.00.

Imprint: © B.N.A. CANADIAN OLYMPIC HOPEFULS 1992

	Description		**No. Player**
□	174 Kevin Dahl	□	175 Stéphane Roy
□	179 Curt Giles	□	180 Dave Archibald
□	184 Chris Kontos	□	185 Sean Burke (G)

☐ 189 Plasvic (Plausic) ☐ 190 Chris Lindberg
☐ 191 Todd Brost ☐ 192 Joé Juneau
☐ 193 Randy Smith ☐ 194 Woolley (Wooley)
☐ 195 Dan Ratushny ☐ 196 Fabian Joseph
☐ 197 Kent Manderville ☐ 198 Brad Schlegel
☐ 199 Karl Dykhuis ☐ 200 Trevor Kidd (G)

1992 NATIONAL GAME

Artwork by Paul Beare. We have no pricing information on this set.

Complete Set (29 cards)

National Pride **National Pride**
☐ Title Card ☐ 1 Brian Mulroney
☐ 2 Robert Bourassa ☐ 3 Joe Clark
☐ 4 Jacques Parizeau ☐ 5 Preston Manning
☐ 6 Jean Chrétien ☐ 7 Clyde Kirby Wells
☐ 8 Bob Rae ☐ 9 Donald Getty
☐ 10 Ovide Mecredi ☐ 11 Pierre Elliot Trudeau
☐ 12 William Vander Zalm ☐ 13 Mordecai Richler
☐ 14 Keith Spicer ☐ 15 Réné Levesque
☐ 16 Joseph Smallwood ☐ 17 S. Champelain
☐ 18 Marquis de Montcalm & Général James Wolfe
☐ 19 Sir John A. Macdonald ☐ 20 Louis Riel
☐ 21 Eric Lindros ☐ 22 Don Cherry
☐ 23 John Candy ☐ 24 Joe Canuck
☐ 25 J.P. Canuck ☐ 26 Camrose Canuck
☐ 27 Team Canuck ☐ Referendum (3 1/2" x 5")

1992 QUÉBEC INTERNATIONAL PEE WEE

A complete regular set sells for $175; Regular singles start at 20¢.

Regional stars in the regular series start at $1.00. Notable stars are priced below each team sub-heading.

Complete Set (1903 cards): 185.00

BURLINGTON
☐ 1 Sean Dwyer ☐ 2 Kelvin Mangaroo
☐ 3 Greg Judge ☐ 4 Graig Richter
☐ 5 Shane McKay ☐ 6 Richard Pitirri
☐ 7 Paul Robbins ☐ 8 James Austin
☐ 9 Shawn Cardy ☐ 10 Andrew Proskynicki
☐ 11 Mike Lankshear ☐ 12 Wayne Liu
☐ 13 Derek Boyer ☐ 14 Brent MacMillan
☐ 15 Brad Hunt ☐ 16 Brian Stremble
☐ 17 Mike Fox ☐ 18 Team Checklist

SAINTE-FOY
☐ 19 Dominick Samson ☐ 20 David Brisson
☐ 21 Patrick Gagné ☐ 22 Jabar Askerow
☐ 23 Alexandre Rioux ☐ 24 Pierre Renaud
☐ 25 J-F Métras ☐ 26 Derek Power
☐ 27 Martin Paqueur ☐ 28 William Girard
☐ 29 Rémi Boyer ☐ 30 Simon Dubuc
☐ 31 Frédéric Thibault ☐ 32 Benoit Chouinard
☐ 33 Martin Trudel ☐ 34 P.M. Vaillancourt
☐ 35 Bobby Larochelle ☐ 36 Team Checklist

DISRAËLI-COLÉRAINE
☐ 37 Sébastien Thibodeau ☐ 38 Éric Bouffard
☐ 39 Simon Croteau ☐ 40 Simon Lapointe
☐ 41 Pascal Goulet ☐ 42 Sylvain Binette
☐ 43 Patrick Dubois ☐ 44 Martin Durocher
☐ 45 Richard Audet ☐ 46 Jean Houle
☐ 47 Christian Houle ☐ 48 Alain Bellegarde
☐ 49 Martin Binette ☐ 50 Pierre Thibodeau
☐ 51 Kevin Marcoux ☐ 52 Team Checklist
☐ 1895 Yannick Therrien

ASBESTOS WARWICK
☐ 53 Dominic Vincent ☐ 54 Sylvain Martel
☐ 55 Justin Chabot ☐ 56 David Lamontagne
☐ 57 Mathieu Provencher ☐ 58 Bernard Thibodeau
☐ 59 Luc Pépin ☐ 60 Jean Régis
☐ 61 Simon Roy ☐ 62 Jean-Mathieu Dion
☐ 63 Yan Marcotte ☐ 64 Jean-Nicholas Milot
☐ 65 Simon Massé ☐ 66 Valérie Hamel
☐ 67 Paul Dion ☐ 68 Marc Simoneau
☐ 69 Team Checklist

MONTMAGNY
☐ 70 Philippe Lord ☐ 71 Steeve Martin
☐ 72 Eric Picard ☐ 73 Mathieu Ringuet
☐ 74 Sylvain Trépanier ☐ 75 Pierre-Luc Bélanger
☐ 76 Patrick Boivin ☐ 77 Réjean Cloutier
☐ 78 François Corriveau ☐ 79 H. Coulombe, Jr.
☐ 80 Jean-Philippe Fortin ☐ 81 Jérôme Gaudreau
☐ 82 Martin Guinard ☐ 83 Marc Lachance
☐ 84 Benoit Langlois ☐ 85 Maxime Lemieux
☐ 86 Michel Ringuet ☐ 87 Team Checklist

BOIS-FRANCS
☐ 88 Yanick Grimard ☐ 89 Dany St-Cyr
☐ 90 Yannick Béliveau ☐ 91 Gino Pinette
☐ 92 Martin Crochetière ☐ 93 Steve St-Laurent
☐ 94 Mathieu Guay ☐ 95 Sylvain Gagnon
☐ 96 M-A Perreault ☐ 97 Martin Tanguay
☐ 98 P. Boissonneault ☐ 99 Samuel St-Pierre
☐ 100 Patrice Girouard ☐ 101 Claude Gélinas
☐ 102 Jonathan Picard ☐ 103 Pascal Roux
☐ 104 Dominic Mailhot ☐ 105 Team Checklist

RIVIÈRE-DU-LOUP
☐ 106 Gilles Berger ☐ 107 Frédéric Bélanger
☐ 108 Dave Malenfant ☐ 109 J-P Soucy
☐ 110 Alexis Roy ☐ 111 Ludovic Berger
☐ 112 S. Lévesque ☐ 113 Éric Marquis
☐ 114 Simon Dubé ☐ 115 Hugo Pelletier
☐ 116 Mathieu Plourde ☐ 117 Patrick Mailloux
☐ 118 François Chenard ☐ 119 Jonathan Lantagne
☐ 120 Pascal Dubé ☐ 121 Bruce Ouellet
☐ 122 Jonathan Pelletier ☐ 123 François Landry
☐ 124 Team Checklist

POINTE-LEVY
☐ 125 Guillaume Ferland ☐ 126 Martin Leclerc
☐ 127 Martin Duquet ☐ 128 Rémi Roy
☐ 129 Sébastien Dumont ☐ 130 Daniel Auger
☐ 131 J-P Vachon ☐ 132 François Mesonero
☐ 133 Yves Deschesne ☐ 134 Éric Lavoie
☐ 135 Nicolas Moriset ☐ 136 Philippe Levasseur
☐ 137 L-B Forgues ☐ 138 Éric Barbeau
☐ 139 Jacques Moriset ☐ 140 Pierre-Luc Hins
☐ 141 David Labrecque ☐ 142 Team Checklist

SÉLECTS SAINTE-FOY
☐ 143 C. Noël de Tilly ☐ 144 François Mecteau
☐ 145 Sébastien Bédard ☐ 146 C. Abbott-Leblanc
☐ 147 Martin Fleury ☐ 148 Daniel Auclair
☐ 149 Nicolas Jolin ☐ 150 Éric Laflamme
☐ 151 Louis-Charles Roy ☐ 152 Stéphane Avard
☐ 153 Alexandre Pelletier ☐ 154 Kévin Demers
☐ 155 J.F. Boisbriand ☐ 156 Philippe Plante
☐ 157 Zachary Louder ☐ 158 Frédéric Nadeau
☐ 159 Jim Vaillantcourt ☐ 160 Team Checklist

LA CHAUDIÈRE
☐ 161 Claude Latulippe ☐ 162 Étienne Gilbert
☐ 163 Mathieu Grenier ☐ 164 S. Chapdelaine
☐ 165 Bruno Bergeron ☐ 166 David Lapointe
☐ 167 S. Rousseau ☐ 168 Mathieu Landry
☐ 169 Yannick Doyon ☐ 170 J.F. Boudreault
☐ 171 François Latulippe ☐ 172 Mathieu Létourneau
☐ 173 J-P Lacroix ☐ 174 Éric Lapierre
☐ 175 Marc Harvey ☐ 176 Jonathan Ruel
☐ 177 Philippe Grondin ☐ 178 Dany Chenel
☐ 179 Pierre Martin ☐ 180 Team Checklist

DRUMMONDVILLE
Gordie Dwyer is the most expensive single at $1-2.
☐ 181 Alexandre Poirier ☐ 182 Jasmin Gélinas
☐ 183 Danny Senay ☐ 184 Sylvain Laflamme
☐ 185 Gordie Dwyer ☐ 186 David Lizotte
☐ 187 Christophe Pagé ☐ 188 Francis Caron
☐ 189 Jonathan Cloutier ☐ 190 Yannick Rivard
☐ 191 Mark Philippe ☐ 192 Martin Gagné
☐ 193 Dominic Gervais ☐ 194 Julien Lessard
☐ 195 Denis Larivière ☐ 196 Mathieu Houle
☐ 197 Team Checklist

RICHELIEU-EXPRESS
☐ 198 David Lépine ☐ 199 Michel St-Georges
☐ 200 Éric Drouin ☐ 201 Martin Cornellier
☐ 202 Guillaume Boucher ☐ 203 Philippe Imbault
☐ 204 David Bernier ☐ 205 Patrick Marsan
☐ 206 Benoit Malboeuf ☐ 207 Sébastien Beaudoin
☐ 208 Alexandre Messier ☐ 209 Alexandre Bernard
☐ 210 Jarrod Gosselin ☐ 211 Mathieu Normandin
☐ 212 Jacques Aubertin ☐ 213 Richard Imbeault
☐ 214 Frédérique Morin ☐ 215 Stéphane Pouliot
☐ 216 Team Checklist

BELLECHASSE
☐ 217 J-F Samson ☐ 218 Pierre-Luc Nadeau
☐ 219 Nicolas Audet ☐ 220 Frédéric Côté
☐ 221 Pascal Patry ☐ 222 Patrick Baillargeon
☐ 223 Patrick Bolduc ☐ 224 Mitchel Roy
☐ 225 Sylvain Desnoyers ☐ 226 Nicolas Comeau
☐ 227 Patrick Fournier ☐ 228 Joanes Tanguay
☐ 229 Sylvain Lapierre ☐ 230 Bruno Goulet
☐ 231 Carl Gosselin ☐ 232 Mathieu Lapierre
☐ 233 Mario Beaudoin ☐ 234 Team Checklist

TORONTO YOUNG NATIONALS
☐ 235 Peter Zavodny ☐ 236 Robert Elele
☐ 237 Paul Howes ☐ 238 Michael Heather
☐ 239 Andrew Long ☐ 240 Mark Angeli
☐ 241 Mark Capizzano ☐ 242 Paul Reader
☐ 243 Rod Hynes ☐ 244 Scott Reiart
☐ 245 Rocky Kim ☐ 246 Suad Cejvanovic
☐ 247 Trevor Gryzbowski ☐ 248 Kevin Franch
☐ 249 Peter Seessle ☐ 250 Paul Griffin
☐ 251 David Cinelli ☐ 252 Nello Deluca
☐ 253 Team Checklist

ST-AUGUSTIN/ CAP-ROUGE
☐ 254 Jean-Philippe Gingras ☐ 255 Mathieu Julien
☐ 256 Jasmin De Blois ☐ 257 Mathieu Lemaire
☐ 258 Philippe Fortin ☐ 259 Guillaume Cantin
☐ 260 Frédéric Morin ☐ 261 Jérôme Smith
☐ 262 Maxime** Ouellet ☐ 263 Christian Dubois
☐ 264 Patrick Renaud ☐ 265 Louis Thellend
☐ 266 François Vincent ☐ 267 Philippe Laferrière
☐ 268 Marc-Andrée Fortin ☐ 269 Martin Pagé
☐ 270 Sylvain Guay ☐ 271 Team Checklist

MOOSE JAW
☐ 272 Warren Pilsner ☐ 273 Scott Shepherd
☐ 274 Aaron Tweet ☐ 275 Jason Gray
☐ 276 Bert Bechfold ☐ 277 Darren Pratte
☐ 278 Alvin Shea ☐ 279 Jason Miller
☐ 280 Kris Parker ☐ 281 Nolan Closs
☐ 282 Kent Silbernagel ☐ 283 Jason Smith
☐ 284 Jason Dutchak ☐ 285 Scott Arnold
☐ 286 Michael Beausoleil ☐ 287 Shaun Muchowski
☐ 288 Brant Arnold ☐ 289 Team Checklist

MISSISSAUGA REDS
Jeff Brown is the most expensive single at $1-2.
☐ 290 Mike Pinkney ☐ 291 Chris Grant
☐ 292 Shawn Dalrymple ☐ 293 Scott Bowman
☐ 294 Matt Luskey ☐ 295 Chris Pirie
☐ 296 Jeff Goldsmith ☐ 297 Jamie Hughes
☐ 298 Randy Fitzgerald ☐ 299 Matt Rimmer
☐ 300 Brian Moniz ☐ 301 Steve Palmer
☐ 302 Jeff Brown ☐ 303 John Rogers
☐ 304 J.J. Interbartolo ☐ 305 Mark Armstrong
☐ 306 Team Checklist

BRAMALEA
☐ 307 Lorne Hanson ☐ 308 Carlos Lopez
☐ 309 Geoff Harding ☐ 310 Paolo Puzzo
☐ 311 Adam Lee ☐ 312 Steve Mitrovic
☐ 313 Jason Allan ☐ 314 Raymond Draper
☐ 315 Ashton Whittle ☐ 316 Ryan Richard
☐ 317 Frank Tullio ☐ 318 Michael Weaver
☐ 319 Mike Mantione ☐ 320 Mark Falconer
☐ 321 Jeffery McCoy ☐ 322 Michael Bednarz
☐ 323 Joe Abraham ☐ 324 Team Checklist

MISSISSAUGA BLACKHAWKS
☐ 325 Michael Gesualdi ☐ 326 Samer Diab
☐ 327 Michael Hinde ☐ 328 Eddie Woo
☐ 329 Earl Kim ☐ 330 Domenic Sanelli
☐ 331 Sam Zakula ☐ 332 Jason Metcalfe
☐ 333 Matthew Reda ☐ 334 Kris Koutoula
☐ 335 Jason Maryuen ☐ 336 Peter Giardino
☐ 337 Tim Lindeau ☐ 338 Al Reisman
☐ 339 David Smiley ☐ 340 Eugène Kennedy
☐ 341 Team Checklist

RICHMOND HILL
Nick Boynton is the most expensive single at $2-3.
☐ 342 Sandro Mignosa ☐ 343 Nick Boynton
☐ 344 Jason Derose ☐ 345 Ricky Payne
☐ 346 Giorgio Scocco ☐ 347 David D'Ammizio
☐ 348 Jimmy Vitale ☐ 349 Eric Hobor
☐ 350 Stephen Johnson ☐ 351 Michael Laceby
☐ 352 Craig Kewitt ☐ 353 Robert Tusa
☐ 354 Tony Tersigni ☐ 355 Andy Kent
☐ 356 Michael Monaco ☐ 357 Robert Ciccolini
☐ 358 Lindsay Hofford ☐ 359 Marcello Martella
☐ 360 Joey Menonte ☐ 361 Team Checklist

TORONTO MAPLE LEAFS
☐ 362 Jeff Carter ☐ 363 Nick Kovachev
☐ 364 Kent Nobes ☐ 365 Jeremy Murphy
☐ 366 David Defrancesco ☐ 367 Stecen Kaxe
☐ 368 Wilson Westbrook ☐ 369 Billy-Joe Majchrzak
☐ 370 Jason McGowan ☐ 371 Daniel Puger
☐ 372 Jody Robinson ☐ 373 Joseph Muszynski
☐ 374 Ryan Ruznisky ☐ 375 Ryan Persi
☐ 376 Wayne Murphy ☐ 377 Mike Anderson
☐ 378 Paul Zarnett ☐ 379 Team Checklist

REPENTIGNY
☐ 380 Alexandre Mathieu ☐ 381 Shaun McGrath
☐ 382 Frédéric Dionne ☐ 383 Francis Dansereau
☐ 384 Marc Lavoie ☐ 385 Hugo Duzyk
☐ 386 Marc Ouimet ☐ 387 Alexandre Gagné
☐ 388 Francis Hervieux ☐ 389 J.F. Normand
☐ 390 Christian Ringuet ☐ 391 Germain Caron
☐ 392 Benoit Nadeau ☐ 393 J-F Dulude
☐ 394 Yves Ouimet ☐ 395 Pierre Mathieu
☐ 396 J-P Perreault ☐ 397 Cédric Thibault
☐ 398 Team Checklist

QUÉBEC CASTORS
☐ 399 Christian Roy ☐ 400 Justin Maryeski
☐ 401 Samuel Bonneau ☐ 402 Sébastien Cimon
☐ 403 Patrick Vallerand ☐ 404 Patrick Dion
☐ 405 François Blanchet ☐ 406 Ian Caron
☐ 407 Luc Live ☐ 408 Sylvain Daigle
☐ 409 René Morissette ☐ 410 Yannick Gagné
☐ 411 Rémi Landry ☐ 412 Olivier Giroux
☐ 413 Jacques Genois ☐ 414 A. Jutras-Ouimet
☐ 415 Team Checklist

QUINTE
Matt Cooke is the most expensive single at $3-4.
☐ 416 Dale Clarke ☐ 417 Grek Coulter
☐ 418 Matt Jarmin ☐ 419 Jordy McMurter
☐ 420 Rick Watters ☐ 421 Matt Cooke
☐ 422 Scott Weese ☐ 423 Andrew McFadzean
☐ 424 Michael Holmes ☐ 425 Brian Phillips
☐ 426 Mike Masterson ☐ 427 Bryan McAlpine
☐ 428 Noël Burkitt ☐ 429 Don Weese
☐ 430 David Green ☐ 431 Darryl McCaw
☐ 432 Team Checklist

BEAUPORT HARFANGS
☐ 433 Denis Perron ☐ 434 Martin Langlois
☐ 435 Kevin Bolduc ☐ 436 Philippe Tremblay
☐ 437 Benoit Bouchard ☐ 438 Jérôme Tremblay
☐ 439 Pascal Couture ☐ 440 Martin Morency
☐ 441 Sylvain Tremblay ☐ 442 Martin Renaud
☐ 443 Éric Martineau ☐ 444 Simon Tremblay
☐ 445 Carl Mainguy ☐ 446 Sébastien Robert
☐ 447 Stéphane Hains ☐ 448 Éric Hains
☐ 449 Mathieu Roy ☐ 450 Team Checklist

LANAUDIÈRE
☐ 451 Jonathan Salvas ☐ 452 Steve Boulet
☐ 453 Martin Côté ☐ 454 Luc Dansereau
☐ 455 Alexandre Beaudoin ☐ 456 Sébastien Gadoury
☐ 457 Yan Courchesne ☐ 458 Rémi Labelle
☐ 459 François Paquet ☐ 460 Yan Boivin
☐ 461 Rémy Lavoie ☐ 462 Frédéric Desjardins
☐ 463 Frédéric Daoust ☐ 464 Claude Aubut
☐ 465 Jonathan Labonté ☐ 466 J.F. Masson
☐ 467 Team Checklist

VAL BÉLAIR
☐ 468 Éric Jalbert ☐ 469 Benoit Cloutier
☐ 470 Érik St-Hilaire ☐ 471 Kevin Banville
☐ 472 Kevin Patenaude ☐ 473 Jimmy Bédard
☐ 474 Patrick Cloutier ☐ 475 Jimmy Grondin
☐ 476 Sylvain Lapérière ☐ 477 Nicolas Berryman
☐ 478 Martin Légaré ☐ 479 Dominic Côté
☐ 480 J.S. Crépeault ☐ 481 Pierre-Yves Grenier
☐ 482 Denis Cloutier ☐ 483 François Dion
☐ 484 Christian Lessard ☐ 485 Team Checklist

TORONTO RED WINGS
The most expensive singles are Daniel Tkaczuk at $2-3 and Brad Tapper at $2-3.
☐ 486 J. Davis Monkman ☐ 487 Quincy Warner
☐ 488 Brent Reilly ☐ 489 Éric Pacey
☐ 490 James Olufemi ☐ 491 Brad Tapper
☐ 492 Chris Gallucci ☐ 493 Kevin Taylor
☐ 494 Ryan Coles ☐ 495 Daniel Tkaczuk
☐ 496 Shane Nash ☐ 497 Adam Colagiacomo
☐ 498 Chris Heron ☐ 499 Brett Hurlock
☐ 500 Brandon Sugden ☐ 501 Bryan Hurlock
☐ 502 Al Neilly ☐ 503 Luca Santoro
☐ 504 Joey Walters ☐ 505 Team Checklist

VERDUN
☐ 506 Stéphane Mantha ☐ 507 Vincent Mallette
☐ 508 J-F Ritchie ☐ 509 Yannick Martinelli
☐ 510 Dominic Bédard ☐ 511 Steven
☐ 512 Riccardo Rossi ☐ 513 Patrick Laforce
☐ 514 Vincent Scalzo ☐ 515 Danny Dubreuil
☐ 516 D. Romanelli ☐ 517 Benjamin Guîté
☐ 518 Matthew Kuzniar ☐ 519 Jason Rodgers
☐ 520 Martin Gallant ☐ 521 Gilles Laroche
☐ 522 Mathieu Boily ☐ 523 F. Bonhomme
☐ 524 Team Checklist

CHICOUTIMI
☐ 525 M-É Hubert ☐ 526 Martin Tremblay
☐ 527 Sacha Fillion ☐ 528 Dave Côté
☐ 529 Luc Langlois ☐ 530 Carl Perron
☐ 531 Jean-Benoît Hudon ☐ 532 Pierre-Luc Poirier
☐ 533 Marc-André Côté ☐ 534 Manuel Jean
☐ 535 Éric DeChamplain ☐ 536 Patrice Côté
☐ 537 Jean-Fabrice ☐ 538 C. Maisonneuve
☐ 539 Richard Fecteau ☐ 540 Jean Étienne
☐ 541 Yanick Méthot ☐ 542 Team Checklist

ÉTOILES DE L'EST
☐ 543 Martin Bédard ☐ 544 Mauro Dipaolo
☐ 545 B. Destroismaisons ☐ 546 Martin Foisy
☐ 547 Martin Ledoux ☐ 548 Yannick Thériault
☐ 549 B. Mastroberardino ☐ 550 Yannick Girard
☐ 551 Luc Lambert ☐ 552 Robert Albert
☐ 553 M-A Bourque ☐ 554 J.F. Durocher
☐ 555 Frédérick Dufour ☐ 556 Jean Deraîche
☐ 557 S. Desjardins ☐ 558 Martin Fortier
☐ 725 Olivier Lefebvre ☐ 559 Team Checklist

CANADIENS-MONTRÉAL
The most expensive single is J-P Dumont as $3-5.
☐ 560 J-P Dumont ☐ 561 Brando Dituri
☐ 562 François Méthot ☐ 563 Dany Gauthier
☐ 564 Jean-Marc Caron ☐ 565 Antoine Brisebois
☐ 566 J-M Malouf ☐ 567 Joe Cardillo
☐ 568 R. Beauchamp ☐ 569 Jean-François Jobin
☐ 570 Domenico Scali ☐ 571 Mario Larocque
☐ 572 Marc-André Houle ☐ 573 François Latreille
☐ 574 Stéphane Sabourin ☐ 575 Mathieu Lachance
☐ 576 Francis Goudreau ☐ 577 Jean-François Pivin
☐ 578 Team Checklist

CHICOUTIMI-NORD
☐ 579 Yannick Bouchard ☐ 580 Yannick Munger
☐ 581 Michaël Tremblay ☐ 582 Michaël Potvin
☐ 583 Dave Méthot ☐ 584 Patrice Fortin
☐ 585 Jean-Pierre Côté ☐ 586 Jérôme Dufour
☐ 587 Étienne Guay ☐ 588 Jonathan Gagnon
☐ 589 Gérald Côté ☐ 590 Stéphane Piché
☐ 591 Martin Bélanger ☐ 592 Carol Brassard
☐ 593 Mario Fillion ☐ 594 Pierre-Luc Mallette
☐ 595 Rémi Bergeron ☐ 596 Team Checklist

CHAMPLAIN-RICHELIEU
The most expensive singles are Daniel Corso at $2-3 and Jean-Marc Pelletier at $2-3.
☐ 597 Jeoff Comeau ☐ 598 Maxime Legault
☐ 599 David Couture ☐ 600 Étienne Lacoursière
☐ 601 Joshua Mc Intyre ☐ 602 Sébastien Dupuis
☐ 603 Maxime Bugeaud ☐ 604 Daniel Corso
☐ 605 François Pelletier ☐ 606 Steve Villeneuve
☐ 607 Nicholas Benjamin ☐ 608 Bruno Lussier
☐ 609 Frédéric Martin ☐ 610 Frédéric Bélanger
☐ 611 Mauric Duguay ☐ 612 Jean-Marc Pelletier
☐ 613 Dominic Larose ☐ 614 Team Checklist
☐ 1898 Franco Bergamin

CHARLESBOURG
☐ 615 M-A Gagnon ☐ 616 J-T Beaulieu
☐ 617 J-F Gingras ☐ 618 Rémy St-Jean
☐ 619 Jérôme Simard ☐ 620 Frédérick Marcotte
☐ 621 Mathieu Chicoine ☐ 622 Éric Boucher
☐ 623 Tony McHugh ☐ 624 Éric Bédard
☐ 625 Christian Simard ☐ 626 Christian Papillon
☐ 627 Patrick Gingras ☐ 628 Patrick Carbonneau
☐ 629 Olivier Lépine ☐ 630 Pierre Lambert
☐ 631 Patrick Couture ☐ 632 Patrick Rhéaume
☐ 1896 David Bertrand ☐ 1897 Martin Ferland
☐ 633 Team Checklist, Err.

SHERBROOKE
☐ 634 François Lessard ☐ 635 J-F Houde
☐ 636 J.F. Letourneau ☐ 637 Francis Cournoyer
☐ 638 Francis Leblanc ☐ 639 Francis Trudeau
☐ 640 Jonathan Roy ☐ 641 David Labonté
☐ 642 Patrick Paquin ☐ 643 Vincent Roy
☐ 644 Yan Robert ☐ 645 Jérôme Langlois
☐ 646 Alain Lemay ☐ 647 Alain Paquin
☐ 648 Jacques Morin ☐ 649 Martin Perusse
☐ 650 Jean-François Gagné ☐ 651 Team Checklist

PAPINEAU
☐ 652 Marcel Séguin ☐ 653 Martin Gunville
☐ 654 Bertrand Trottier ☐ 655 Casey Leggett
☐ 656 Patrick Desjardins ☐ 657 Rodney Leggett
☐ 658 Sylvain Lanthier ☐ 659 Patrick Bigras
☐ 660 Serge Dumoulin ☐ 661 Mathieu Lacasse
☐ 662 Martin Leduc ☐ 663 Stéphane Laleur
☐ 664 Pierre Lafrance ☐ 665 André Secours
☐ 666 Denis Lafrance ☐ 667 Frédéric Jutras
☐ 668 Martin Blais ☐ 669 Team Checklist

QUÉBEC NORDIQUES
☐ 670 Nicolas Dufac ☐ 671 Dominic Laflamme
☐ 672 Éric Demers ☐ 673 Patrice Auger
☐ 674 S. Larouche ☐ 675 Charles Dubois
☐ 676 Simon Gravel ☐ 677 Étienne Morin
☐ 678 G. Fontaine ☐ 679 Marc-Antoine Barré
☐ 680 S. Tremblay ☐ 681 Martin Fillion
☐ 682 Luc Bastien ☐ 683 J.F. Duchesne

- ☐ 684 Michel Pelletier ☐ 685 Pierre-Alex Nadeau
- ☐ 686 Christine Simms ☐ 687 Team Checklist

VOILIER BEAUPORT

- ☐ 688 Frédirick Gravel ☐ 689 Simon Chenel
- ☐ 690 Christian Perreault ☐ 691 David Cloutier
- ☐ 692 Mathieu Genest ☐ 693 Rémi Leclerc
- ☐ 694 Jean-Daniel Lavoie ☐ 695 Jimmy Lapointe
- ☐ 696 Jonathan Maheux ☐ 697 Pascal Lachance
- ☐ 698 Jonathan Fortin ☐ 699 François Fortier
- ☐ 700 Joé Bussière ☐ 701 Simon Rodrigue
- ☐ 702 Matthieu Lépine ☐ 703 Luc Bédard
- ☐ 704 François Goulet ☐ 705 Team Checklist

CHAMPLAIN-RICHELIEU

- ☐ 706 Christopher Greene ☐ 707 Patrick Dixon
- ☐ 708 Terry Summerton ☐ 709 Olivier Gagné
- ☐ 710 M-A Lapointe ☐ 711 Dominic Landry
- ☐ 712 Neil Barrett ☐ 713 Frédéric Bourget
- ☐ 714 Yanic Carpentier ☐ 715 Étienne Pagé
- ☐ 716 Frédéric Langevin ☐ 717 P. Brousseau Jr.
- ☐ 718 Yannick Senez ☐ 719 Patrice Bernier
- ☐ 720 Olivier Lafontaine ☐ 721 John Greene
- ☐ 722 Stéphane Moquin ☐ 723 David Crowdis
- ☐ 724 Team Checklist

ST-GEORGES BEAUCE

- ☐ 726 David Lessard ☐ 727 David Jacques
- ☐ 728 Jean-Nicol Cliche ☐ 729 Sylvain Veilleux
- ☐ 730 Mathieu Giguère ☐ 731 Patrick Poirier
- ☐ 732 Louis-Jean Labbé ☐ 733 Dimmy Roy
- ☐ 734 Yannick Poulin ☐ 735 Vincent Gonthier
- ☐ 736 Philippe Cloutier ☐ 737 Mike Allan
- ☐ 738 Marco Grondin ☐ 739 L-P Gauthier
- ☐ 740 Michel Roy ☐ 741 Marc Poulin
- ☐ 742 Steve Gaudreau ☐ 743 Team Checklist

LAC-MÉGANTIC

- ☐ 744 Vincent Morin ☐ 745 Philippe Inkel
- ☐ 746 Stéphane Morin ☐ 747 Mathieu Therrien
- ☐ 748 Jocelyn Dugré ☐ 749 Martin Louis XVI
- ☐ 750 F. Charbonneau ☐ 751 Simon Poulin
- ☐ 752 Steve Fortier ☐ 753 Jonathan Clusiault
- ☐ 754 Maxime Paradis ☐ 755 Frédéric Michaud
- ☐ 756 Vincent Beaudoin ☐ 757 Mathieu Bégin
- ☐ 758 Gabriel Dugré ☐ 759 Jérôme Morin
- ☐ 760 Martin Robert ☐ 761 Team Checklist

CENTRE-MAURICIE

The most expensive single is Jean François Damphousse at $2-3.

- ☐ 762 David Morin ☐ 763 Guy Théberge
- ☐ 764 Benoit Dusablon ☐ 765 David Gélinas
- ☐ 766 Martin Ricard ☐ 767 David Bélanger
- ☐ 768 Patrick Salois ☐ 769 Yannick Dupuis
- ☐ 770 Tommi Houde ☐ 771 Jonathan Baril
- ☐ 772 B. Carpentier ☐ 773 Charles Grenier
- ☐ 774 J-S Lemay ☐ 775 J-N Bordeleau
- ☐ 776 René Perron ☐ 777 Damphousse (G)
- ☐ 778 Steve St.Arnaud ☐ 779 Team Checklist

SEIGNEURS MILLE-ÎLES

- ☐ 780 Frédéric Girard ☐ 781 Jonathan Cécile
- ☐ 782 Benoît Lacasse ☐ 783 Denis Bradley
- ☐ 784 Michel Jasmin ☐ 785 Cédric Bourgeois
- ☐ 786 A. Lachance ☐ 787 Michel Lachaine
- ☐ 788 S. Deschatelets ☐ 789 Mathieu Villeneuve
- ☐ 790 Mathieu Meloche ☐ 791 J-F Gamelin
- ☐ 792 Luc Laplante ☐ 793 André Viau
- ☐ 794 Alexandre Mathys ☐ 795 Sébastien Matte
- ☐ 796 Team Checklist

AMOS

- ☐ 797 Michel Bolduc ☐ 798 Bernard Guertin
- ☐ 799 Vincent Larochelle ☐ 800 Daniel Massé
- ☐ 801 Jonathan Lemerise ☐ 802 David Chouinard
- ☐ 803 Vincent Jolin ☐ 804 Frédérik Ouellet
- ☐ 805 Simon Lavoie ☐ 806 Richard Nadeau
- ☐ 807 Yan Patry ☐ 808 Dave Mc Cann
- ☐ 809 Dany Poitras ☐ 810 Francis Quevillon
- ☐ 811 Sébastien Audet ☐ 812 Bernard Boulianne
- ☐ 813 Hervé Gagnon ☐ 814 Cédric Fontaine
- ☐ 815 Team Checklist ☐ 1900 Simon Jolin
- ☐ 1901 J.F. Chouinard ☐ 1902 Dyno Doyon

PASPÉBIAC

- ☐ 816 J-F Moulin ☐ 817 Mathieu Corbet
- ☐ 818 Simon Grenier ☐ 819 Germain Babin
- ☐ 820 Gianni Horth ☐ 821 Philipe Leblanc
- ☐ 822 Frédéric Minville ☐ 823 Carol Poirier
- ☐ 824 Josian Delarosbil ☐ 825 Patrick Joseph
- ☐ 826 François Whittom ☐ 827 Jonathan Boudreau
- ☐ 828 Silvain Poirier ☐ 829 Alexandre Arsenault
- ☐ 830 Janel Huard ☐ 831 Team Checklist

FRANCHE VILLE

The most expensive single is Steve Bégin at $2-3.

- ☐ 832 François Abel ☐ 833 Dominic Parent
- ☐ 834 J-P Doyon ☐ 835 Benoit Côté
- ☐ 836 Steve Bégin ☐ 837 Daniel Cassivi
- ☐ 838 Maxime Hains ☐ 839 David Thibeault
- ☐ 840 B. Montembault ☐ 841 Marc-André Gaudet
- ☐ 842 Martin Janvier ☐ 843 Martin Bilodeau
- ☐ 844 Yannick Houle ☐ 845 Team Checklist
- ☐ 1899 Maxime Toupin

GATINEAU

- ☐ 846 Ghislain Daoust ☐ 847 Marc Desgagné
- ☐ 848 Simon Deschêsnes ☐ 849 Éric Durocher
- ☐ 850 Patrick Lafleur ☐ 851 Simon Dagenais
- ☐ 852 Sébastien Brisson ☐ 853 Marc Durand
- ☐ 854 Martin Dubois ☐ 855 Sébastien Guitard
- ☐ 856 P. Charbonneau ☐ 857 Michel Savard
- ☐ 858 Philippe Brennan ☐ 859 Michel Pariseau
- ☐ 860 Michel Desgagné ☐ 861 Ian Olsen
- ☐ 862 Martin Pleau ☐ 863 Team Checklist

CHARLEVOIX

- ☐ 864 Frédéric Dufour ☐ 865 Jérémy Harvey
- ☐ 866 A. Vigneault ☐ 867 Christian Harvey
- ☐ 868 Simon Bouchard ☐ 869 Pascal Lavoie
- ☐ 870 Sébastien Harvey ☐ 871 Pascal Tremblay
- ☐ 872 Luc Lavoie ☐ 873 Denis Lajoie
- ☐ 874 Pascal McNicoll ☐ 875 Pascal Fillion
- ☐ 876 Benoit Tremblay ☐ 877 Jérome Savard
- ☐ 878 Jérôme Tremblay ☐ 879 Guillaume Dufour
- ☐ 880 Gaston Tremblay ☐ 881 Frédéric Bergeron
- ☐ 882 Stéphane McNicoll ☐ 883 Team Checklist

ST-LOUIS BLUES

- ☐ 884 Todd Weinhams ☐ 885 Steve Shuert
- ☐ 886 Travis Rice-Wood ☐ 887 Chris Rakel
- ☐ 888 Chad Moroni ☐ 889 Kris Margherio
- ☐ 890 Kevin Landy ☐ 891 Keith Kleiner
- ☐ 892 Jason Kempt ☐ 893 Bob Huber
- ☐ 894 Eddie Hanneke ☐ 895 Nathan Fletcher
- ☐ 896 Brad Coombe ☐ 897 Mike Bergae
- ☐ 898 Tom Arenos ☐ 899 Joe Nahm
- ☐ 900 Justin Stiehr ☐ 901 Team Checklist

LAC ST-LOUIS

- ☐ 902 G. Archambault ☐ 903 Tyler Coleman
- ☐ 904 Marek Driver ☐ 905 Jonathan Lamy
- ☐ 906 Gian-Paolo Venuta ☐ 907 Simon Prieur
- ☐ 908 Oliver Gagnon ☐ 909 Jason Mikula
- ☐ 910 James Davidson ☐ 911 Enrik Brassard
- ☐ 912 RT Carr ☐ 913 Alexandre Tomaras
- ☐ 914 Casey Wolak ☐ 915 John Austen
- ☐ 916 Antoine Lejeune ☐ 917 Bernardo Bellini
- ☐ 918 Team Checklist ☐ 1894 Jason Lumsden

SMITHS FALLS

- ☐ 919 Larry Leadbeater ☐ 920 Lane Brennan
- ☐ 921 Kris Loughren ☐ 922 Derrick Rathwell
- ☐ 923 Ryan Richmond ☐ 924 Dave Korell
- ☐ 925 Josh Dixon ☐ 926 Kurt Dolinki
- ☐ 927 Jame Leadbeater ☐ 928 Aaron Graham
- ☐ 929 Jed Thompson ☐ 930 Dan Stanberg
- ☐ 931 Craig Ronan ☐ 932 Matt Johnston
- ☐ 933 Dave Mc Carthy ☐ 934 Robert Heffernan
- ☐ 935 Team Checklist

EDMONTON KINGS

- ☐ 936 Marc Forgues ☐ 937 Jim Tsirekas
- ☐ 938 Scott James ☐ 939 Erik Dmyruk
- ☐ 940 Cade Barry ☐ 941 Matt Mitchell
- ☐ 942 Adrian Bryksa ☐ 943 Matt Krahn
- ☐ 944 Luke Marco ☐ 945 Mark Mossey
- ☐ 946 Garreth Davies ☐ 947 Chris Chiu
- ☐ 948 Jeremy Pestun ☐ 949 Kiyoshi Morikawa
- ☐ 950 Dave Lynass ☐ 951 Lance Popke
- ☐ 952 Pat Tsirekas ☐ 953 Russ Dmytruk
- ☐ 954 Team Checklist

WASHINGTON CAPITALS

- ☐ 955 Ryan Goins ☐ 956 Carey Gutmann
- ☐ 957 Zac Jackson ☐ 958 Trevor Macknak
- ☐ 959 Josh Myerberg ☐ 960 Jason Noe
- ☐ 961 Justin Porter ☐ 962 Paul Tilch
- ☐ 963 Anthony Uccellini ☐ 964 Thomas Windsor
- ☐ 965 Dave Friedman ☐ 966 David Crenshaw
- ☐ 967 Doug Brotherton ☐ 968 Nick Carso
- ☐ 969 Bobby Dameron ☐ 970 Trevor Shattuck
- ☐ 971 Walker Coady ☐ 972 John Osidach
- ☐ 973 Team Checklist

NEW JERSEY DEVILS

- ☐ 974 Darian Redouane ☐ 975 Dennis Palaia
- ☐ 976 Chris Orlando ☐ 977 Brian Manley
- ☐ 978 Chris Baboulis ☐ 979 Josh Mandel
- ☐ 980 Peter Lauro ☐ 981 Derek Fisher
- ☐ 982 Craig Roser ☐ 983 Danny Casella
- ☐ 984 Bill Stepien ☐ 985 Mike Sweeney
- ☐ 986 Luke Williams ☐ 1327 Timothy Halewicz
- ☐ 1328 Nicholas Miro ☐ 1329 Craig Bland
- ☐ 987 Team Checklist

BEVERLY

- ☐ 988 Matthew Dennehy ☐ 989 Dwight Ware
- ☐ 990 Alex Tatum ☐ 991 Michael Souza
- ☐ 992 Nick Scola ☐ 993 Mickey Philbin
- ☐ 994 Stephen Perma ☐ 995 Graham Morrell
- ☐ 996 Jason Lamae ☐ 997 Scott Hayes
- ☐ 998 Jonathan Gregorio ☐ 999 Shawn Grasso
- ☐ 1000 Nicky Gillis ☐ 1001 John Duval
- ☐ 1002 Bobby Allen ☐ 1003 Matthew Carney
- ☐ 1004 Patrick Nigro ☐ 1005 Paul Vincent
- ☐ 1006 Team Checklist

VANCOUVER CANUCKS

The most expensive single is Scott Hannan at $1-2.

- ☐ 1007 Jeffrey Bubar ☐ 1008 Kevin Gavin
- ☐ 1009 Dean Shields ☐ 1010 Michael Little
- ☐ 1011 Ryan Berry ☐ 1012 Brad Blystone
- ☐ 1013 Bobby Russell ☐ 1014 Scott Donaldson
- ☐ 1015 Scott Hannan ☐ 1016 Derek Lensink
- ☐ 1017 Jamie Low ☐ 1018 Tyler Vanhorn
- ☐ 1019 Jeff Mc Bride ☐ 1020 Doug Griffin
- ☐ 1021 Chris Tibbles ☐ 1022 Randy Downes
- ☐ 1023 Team Checklist

ÉLITES RIVE-NORD

- ☐ 1024 Francis Lessard ☐ 1025 F. Deschamps
- ☐ 1026 Benoit Lampton ☐ 1027 Jimmy Verdule
- ☐ 1028 Sébastien Deschamps ☐ 1029 Danny Piata
- ☐ 1030 Marc-André Girard ☐ 1031 Benoît Duchesne
- ☐ 1032 Francis Morin ☐ 1033 Bernard Sylvain
- ☐ 1034 André Lamarche, Jr. ☐ 1035 Éric Riopel
- ☐ 1036 Carl Champagne ☐ 1037 Sébastien Fournier
- ☐ 1038 Alexandre Guy ☐ 1039 Luc Beaudoin
- ☐ 1040 Team Checklist

CHICAGO BLACKHAWKS

- ☐ 1041 Todd Vodnansky ☐ 1042 Michael Redden
- ☐ 1043 Michael Harper ☐ 1044 Jamie Ori
- ☐ 1045 Matt Pfaff ☐ 1046 Darren Beck
- ☐ 1047 Harly Fisher ☐ 1048 Adam Wald
- ☐ 1049 Steve Baran ☐ 1050 Adam Bryniczka
- ☐ 1051 Kevin Cline ☐ 1052 Phil Fisher
- ☐ 1053 Tom Koziol ☐ 1054 Team Checklist
- ☐ 1886 Marc Brown ☐ 1887 Kalajian Raffie
- ☐ 1888 Tom Cloherty ☐ 1889 Ryan O'Leary
- ☐ 1890 Chris Zuccaro ☐ 1891 Michael Redden

ANCIENNE-LORETTE

- ☐ 1055 Nicolas Roberge ☐ 1056 Jonathan Moore
- ☐ 1057 François Drolet ☐ 1058 Éric Coulombe
- ☐ 1059 Michel Auclair ☐ 1060 Charles Turcotte
- ☐ 1061 C-É Lamontagne ☐ 1062 Vincent Ruel
- ☐ 1063 Steve Gamache ☐ 1064 Carl Ménard
- ☐ 1065 Jonathan Dubé ☐ 1066 Éric Gagné
- ☐ 1067 C-É Drouin ☐ 1068 J-P Lizotte
- ☐ 1069 Gilles Gosselin ☐ 1070 Team Checklist

NORTH YORK

- ☐ 1071 Stephen Nowlan ☐ 1072 Alan Yousif
- ☐ 1073 Brenton Atkins ☐ 1074 Mark Cooper
- ☐ 1075 Jason Haines ☐ 1076 Joe Stangis
- ☐ 1077 Alex Palerno ☐ 1078 Duane Rushton
- ☐ 1079 Niles Cirone ☐ 1080 Shane Mitchell
- ☐ 1081 Mike Forshee ☐ 1082 Chris Beck
- ☐ 1083 Jason Madigan ☐ 1084 Tom Cowie
- ☐ 1085 Danny Coles ☐ 1086 Team Checklist

JONQUIÈRE ORIOLES

- ☐ 1087 Martin Labonté ☐ 1088 Martin Pedneault
- ☐ 1089 Jonathan Fortin ☐ 1090 Steve Girard
- ☐ 1091 Marc Gravel ☐ 1092 Marc Simard
- ☐ 1093 Tommy Dallaire ☐ 1094 Louis Paradis
- ☐ 1095 J-C Duplain ☐ 1096 Jonathan Brassard
- ☐ 1097 Steve Blackburn ☐ 1098 Joël Tremblay
- ☐ 1099 Jérôme Blackburn ☐ 1100 Martin Gervais
- ☐ 1101 François Paré ☐ 1102 S. Larocque
- ☐ 1103 Claude Bouchard ☐ 1104 Team Checklist

TORONTO WEXFORD

- ☐ 1105 Duncan Dalmao ☐ 1106 Mauricio Alvarez
- ☐ 1107 Johnny Dibattista ☐ 1108 Mike Duffy
- ☐ 1109 Joe Elek ☐ 1110 Wade Dawe
- ☐ 1111 Michael Tilson ☐ 1112 Jason Doyle
- ☐ 1113 Derek Minto ☐ 1114 Brad Simms
- ☐ 1115 Hugh Devlin ☐ 1116 Kevin Graham
- ☐ 1117 Allan Hitchen ☐ 1118 Kevin Burrett
- ☐ 1119 Team Checklist

PHILADELPHIA

- ☐ 1120 Chris Bala ☐ 1121 Mark Bove
- ☐ 1122 Vince Clevenger ☐ 1123 Luke Cunningham
- ☐ 1124 Todd Daily ☐ 1125 Brad Faleska
- ☐ 1126 Peter Hillsley ☐ 1127 Justin Holmes
- ☐ 1128 Mike Holmes ☐ 1129 Delaware Hood
- ☐ 1130 Todd Johnson ☐ 1131 John Lyons
- ☐ 1132 Tim Wood ☐ 1133 Trevor Martin
- ☐ 1134 J.B. Weaver ☐ 1135 Herb Holmes
- ☐ 1884 Hugh McGee ☐ 1885 Ryan Touchton
- ☐ 1892 Frank Bottino ☐ 1893 Jeremy Bean
- ☐ 1136 Team Checklist

NEW YORK RANGERS

- ☐ 1137 Matt Macleod ☐ 1138 Peter Campbell
- ☐ 1139 Bryan Gallacher ☐ 1140 John Heffers
- ☐ 1141 Eric Zink ☐ 1142 Josh Voorhees
- ☐ 1143 Jedd Morin ☐ 1144 Matthew Labet
- ☐ 1145 M. Heintzelman ☐ 1146 Niels Heilmann
- ☐ 1147 Matthew Fromkin ☐ 1148 Jason Faucher
- ☐ 1149 Kevin Connell ☐ 1150 Scott Bradbury
- ☐ 1151 Owen Weihman ☐ 1152 Team Checklist

DON MILLS

- ☐ 1153 Fabio Boccalon ☐ 1154 Eri Abayof
- ☐ 1155 John Lourie ☐ 1156 Brad Wood
- ☐ 1157 Willie Hunter ☐ 1158 Ken Shadlock
- ☐ 1159 James Cho ☐ 1160 Harkie Singh
- ☐ 1161 Jonathon Cartile ☐ 1162 Tim Dillon
- ☐ 1163 David Brady ☐ 1164 Mathew Davis
- ☐ 1165 Mark Mc Clymont ☐ 1166 Craig Wakeford
- ☐ 1167 Alex Morin ☐ 1168 Team Checklist

SAN JOSE SHARKS

- ☐ 1169 Christopher Miller ☐ 1170 Ronnie Solorio
- ☐ 1171 J. Reichenberg ☐ 1172 Jimmy Truitt
- ☐ 1173 Josh McGuire ☐ 1174 Billy Cox
- ☐ 1175 R. Glassman ☐ 1176 C.J. MacDonald
- ☐ 1177 Gary Levy ☐ 1178 Ryan Jones
- ☐ 1179 S. Tornabee ☐ 1180 Guy Manchuk
- ☐ 1181 Bryan Howard ☐ 1182 Mike Robert
- ☐ 1183 Team Checklist

GRENOBLE

- ☐ 1184 Team Checklist ☐ 1185 Aurelien Chaignet
- ☐ 1186 Philippe Combe ☐ 1187 Boris Costa
- ☐ 1188 Cyril Cothenet ☐ 1189 Gauthier Fontanel
- ☐ 1190 Thibault Fontanel ☐ 1191 Julien Girard
- ☐ 1192 Wily Grando ☐ 1193 J-A Guillemot
- ☐ 1194 Sandro Inebria ☐ 1195 Guillaume Megy
- ☐ 1196 Laurent Meunier ☐ 1197 Noël Roudet
- ☐ 1198 Fabien Roussel ☐ 1199 Mathieu Salamand
- ☐ 1200 Loïc Sassone ☐ 1201 Cyril Trabichet

THOMPSON

- ☐ 1202 Stefan Cherneski ☐ 1203 Daren Thompson
- ☐ 1204 Curtis Huculak ☐ 1205 Clifford Duchesne
- ☐ 1206 Karl Merasty ☐ 1207 Jared Morin
- ☐ 1208 David Waye ☐ 1209 Jason Weiss
- ☐ 1210 Corey Miller ☐ 1211 Bernie Miller
- ☐ 1212 Kane Doran ☐ 1213 Lyndon Thompson
- ☐ 1214 David Haywood ☐ 1215 Dustin Levesque
- ☐ 1216 Colin Daniels ☐ 1217 Ray Miller
- ☐ 1218 Team Checklist

CALIFORNIA KINGS

- ☐ 1219 Ian Wesson ☐ 1220 Justin Morrison
- ☐ 1221 Paul Killeen ☐ 1222 Matt Stanfield
- ☐ 1223 Donovan Tar ☐ 1224 Cory Mayes
- ☐ 1225 Nick Besherd ☐ 1226 Adam Nichols
- ☐ 1227 Darwin Nercestan ☐ 1228 Justin Cimo
- ☐ 1229 Patrick Johnson ☐ 1230 Chris Antzoulatos
- ☐ 1231 John Merandi ☐ 1232 Nylo Henderson
- ☐ 1233 David Griffiths ☐ 1234 Nick Berendt
- ☐ 1235 Scott Holsinger ☐ 1236 Glenn Herz
- ☐ 1237 Nick Vella ☐ 1238 Vic Venasky
- ☐ 1239 Team Checklist

BEAUCE AMIANTE

The most expensive single is Alex Tanguay at $6-10

- ☐ 1240 Éric Binet ☐ 1241 Frédéric Lessard
- ☐ 1242 Alexandre Poulin ☐ 1243 Pierre Gilbert
- ☐ 1244 Hugo Gingère ☐ 1245 Patrick Asselin
- ☐ 1246 Jérôme Pelchat ☐ 1247 M-A Pomerleau
- ☐ 1248 Marco Lachance ☐ 1249 Antoine Goulet
- ☐ 1250 Karl Fortier ☐ 1251 Dominic Côté
- ☐ 1252 Alex Tanguay ☐ 1253 Steve Camiré
- ☐ 1254 Jimmy Cloutier ☐ 1255 Marc Tanguay
- ☐ 1256 Francis Leblond ☐ 1257 Claude Binet
- ☐ 1258 Team Checklist

QUÉBEC CITADELLES

- ☐ 1259 Jean-François Bernier ☐ 1260 Patrick Savard
- ☐ 1261 Patrick Hébert ☐ 1262 Éric Moreau
- ☐ 1263 Pascal Mercier ☐ 1264 Éric Larrivée
- ☐ 1265 Glenn Donovan ☐ 1266 Martin Côté
- ☐ 1267 Philippe Couture ☐ 1268 Martin Berthelot
- ☐ 1269 Rémi Arial ☐ 1270 Martin Chabot
- ☐ 1271 Étienne Drapeau ☐ 1272 Mario Laflamme
- ☐ 1273 Dominic Lachance ☐ 1274 Maxime Gingras
- ☐ 1275 André Robitaille ☐ 1276 Team Checklist

ONTARIO JETS

- ☐ 1277 Jay Tyacke ☐ 1278 Nicholas Bugnacki
- ☐ 1279 Noah Clarke ☐ 1280 Mark Madell
- ☐ 1281 Trevor Martin ☐ 1282 Omar Mibis
- ☐ 1283 Chad Salsbury ☐ 1284 Casey Flanigan
- ☐ 1285 Tony Mascotto ☐ 1286 Johnny Mc Bryan
- ☐ 1287 Bryan Johnson ☐ 1288 Courtney Martin
- ☐ 1289 Brian Marsh ☐ 1290 John Mc Bryan
- ☐ 1291 Marc Goodwin ☐ 1292 Team Checklist

THETFORD

- ☐ 1293 Joey Bolduc ☐ 1294 Philippe Beaudoin
- ☐ 1295 Michel Lehoux ☐ 1296 Dave Picard
- ☐ 1297 P-É Bernard ☐ 1298 M-É Julien
- ☐ 1299 Vincent Lessard ☐ 1300 André Perron
- ☐ 1301 Michel Dodier ☐ 1302 Steve Grandmont
- ☐ 1303 Charles Paré ☐ 1304 Martin Rousseau
- ☐ 1305 François Landry ☐ 1306 Christian Lavoie
- ☐ 1307 Michel Boulet ☐ 1308 Claude Perron
- ☐ 1309 Team Checklist

TARDIVEL RAPID'EAU

- ☐ 1310 François Paquet ☐ 1311 Yves Soulard
- ☐ 1312 Tomy Bédard ☐ 1313 Jonathan Cyr
- ☐ 1314 Sébastien Rivard ☐ 1315 Luc Drolet
- ☐ 1316 Yannick Leclerc ☐ 1317 Steeve Langlois
- ☐ 1318 J-F Trudel ☐ 1319 Pierre-Félix Lemay
- ☐ 1320 Daniel Drolet ☐ 1321 Frédéric Matte
- ☐ 1322 F. Robitaille ☐ 1323 Benoît Côté
- ☐ 1324 Martin Delisle ☐ 1325 Jacques Paradis
- ☐ 1326 Team Checklist

CALGARY RANGERS

- ☐ 1330 Rangers Coach ☐ 1331 Ryan Thompson
- ☐ 1332 Aaron Lane ☐ 1333 Brett Thompson
- ☐ 1334 Dennis Lywood ☐ 1335 Jasper Lee
- ☐ 1336 Jason Day ☐ 1337 Paul Cabana
- ☐ 1338 Moe Halat ☐ 1339 Christopher Josue
- ☐ 1340 Shane Lodhar ☐ 1341 Chris MacDonald
- ☐ 1342 Adam Redmond ☐ 1343 Michael Krenzel
- ☐ 1344 Brandon Fleece ☐ 1345 Clark Palmer
- ☐ 1346 David Wandler ☐ 1347 Team Checklist

EDMONTON OILERS

The most expensive single is Darren Van Oene at $1-2.

- ☐ 1348 Darren Van Oene ☐ 1349 Thomas Fisher
- ☐ 1350 Mike Lazaruk ☐ 1351 Jeff Kuspira
- ☐ 1352 Tom Zavediuk ☐ 1353 Trevor Deeks
- ☐ 1354 Jeff Ryan ☐ 1355 Scott Roles
- ☐ 1356 Ben Bagnall ☐ 1357 Warren King
- ☐ 1358 Del Simpson ☐ 1359 Jason Rasher
- ☐ 1360 Ryan Schulha ☐ 1361 Marc Lachance
- ☐ 1362 Kenton Reilly ☐ 1363 Checklist, Err.

TARDIVEL ELANS

- ☐ 1364 David Mainguy ☐ 1365 Dominic Soulard
- ☐ 1366 Pierre-Luc Brière ☐ 1367 David Genois
- ☐ 1368 Christian Soulard ☐ 1369 Luka Lefebvre
- ☐ 1370 Olivier Pacquet ☐ 1371 J-P Piché
- ☐ 1372 David Verreault ☐ 1373 Mathieu Pagé
- ☐ 1374 P-L Carpentier ☐ 1375 Frédérick Duplain
- ☐ 1376 Dominic Gauvin ☐ 1377 Éric Moisan
- ☐ 1378 M-A Angers ☐ 1379 Jérôme Pagé
- ☐ 1380 Guy Patterson ☐ 1381 Team Checklist

SUISSE ROMANDE

The most expensive single is David Aebischer at $3-5.

- ☐ 1382 Jean-Pierre Kast ☐ 1383 Team Checklist
- ☐ 1384 Manfred Scnidrig ☐ 1385 Julien Vauclair
- ☐ 1386 Pascal Braillard ☐ 1387 Philippe Yerly
- ☐ 1388 Elvis Clavien ☐ 1389 Daniel Malara
- ☐ 1390 Jérôme Zahno ☐ 1391 Raphaël Berger
- ☐ 1392 Cédric Favre ☐ 1393 Toni Nelli
- ☐ 1394 Nicolas Gastaldo ☐ 1395 Michel Dolci
- ☐ 1396 Alain Demuth ☐ 1397 Laurent Faller
- ☐ 1398 Sacha Dudan ☐ 1399 Josselin Haller
- ☐ 1400 Jérôme Magnin ☐ 1401 Allan Thonney
- ☐ 1402 David Rochy ☐ 1403 D. Aebischer (G)

PITTSBURGH PENGUINS

- ☐ 1404 Keith Mitro ☐ 1405 Jason McBride
- ☐ 1406 Mike Lang ☐ 1407 Justin Kenepp
- ☐ 1408 Dan Frattaroli ☐ 1409 Brett Fisher
- ☐ 1410 J. Dohanich ☐ 1411 Tyler Dishong
- ☐ 1412 John Conti ☐ 1413 Michael Conley
- ☐ 1414 Chris Sam ☐ 1415 Tim Brooks
- ☐ 1416 Nick Lordi ☐ 1417 Keith Sachko
- ☐ 1418 Derek Powell ☐ 1419 Bernie Piesik
- ☐ 1420 Team Checklist

PHILADELPHIA FLYERS

- ☐ 1422 Dan McDonald ☐ 1423 T. McMonagle
- ☐ 1424 Anthony Switek ☐ 1425 Kevin Meehan
- ☐ 1426 Ron Mongeau ☐ 1427 Travis Howe
- ☐ 1428 Lee Jelenic ☐ 1429 Brendan Gallagher
- ☐ 1430 Dan Hovck ☐ 1431 Paul Dorn
- ☐ 1432 Michael Franco ☐ 1433 Jeremy Domish
- ☐ 1434 Paul Dabrowski ☐ 1435 John Larnera
- ☐ 1436 Jason Teck ☐ 1437 Team Checklist

HERSHEY

- ☐ 1438 Dave Roldan ☐ 1439 Bobby Stremmel
- ☐ 1440 Tom Ritz ☐ 1441 Chris Dietz
- ☐ 1442 J. Heitsenrether ☐ 1443 Erik Bechtold
- ☐ 1444 Brian Wrobble ☐ 1445 Bruce Bingaman
- ☐ 1446 Nick Castelli ☐ 1447 Eric Schork
- ☐ 1448 Doug Erain ☐ 1449 B.J. Stephens
- ☐ 1450 Zachary Stauffer ☐ 1451 Scott Wasilefski

☐ 1452 Drek Knaub ☐ 1453 Sean Knaub
☐ 1454 Jason Wood ☐ 1455 Team Checklist

KHARKOV

The most expensive singles are Dainius Zubrus at $2-3 and Andrei Zyuzin at $1-2.

☐ 1456 Andrei Lupandin ☐ 1457 Dmitry Yakushin
☐ 1458 Gennady Razin ☐ 1459 Sergei Drigulas
☐ 1460 R. Marakhovskiy ☐ 1461 Anatoly Buliga
☐ 1462 Andrei Zyuzin ☐ 1463 K. S. Kalmikov
☐ 1464 Dainius G. Zubrus ☐ 1465 Denis Shiryaev
☐ 1466 M. N. Starchenko ☐ 1467 Vladislav Serov
☐ 1468 Oleg Timchenko ☐ 1469 Dmitry Kluchko
☐ 1470 Dmitry Sirenko ☐ 1471 Oleg Panasenko
☐ 1472 A. Barankovskiy ☐ 1473 D. Romanukha
☐ 1474 Ivan Pravilov ☐ 1475 Team Checklist

BOSTON BRAVES

☐ 1476 Mark White ☐ 1477 Jerry Toomey
☐ 1478 Daniel Walsh ☐ 1479 James Swallow
☐ 1480 TJ Bannister ☐ 1481 Doug Bell
☐ 1482 Mike Bliss ☐ 1483 John Berriola
☐ 1484 Paul Carroll ☐ 1485 Michael Clabrese
☐ 1486 Joe Flammia ☐ 1487 Jim Conway
☐ 1488 Danny Doucette ☐ 1489 Jonathan Killeen
☐ 1490 Mike Lucenta ☐ 1491 Bobby Miele
☐ 1492 Sean Powers ☐ 1493 John McDonough
☐ 1494 Skip Rice ☐ 1495 Daniel Walsh
☐ 1421 Team Checklist

BUDAPEST

☐ 1496 Viktor Molnar ☐ 1497 Gergely Szongoth
☐ 1498 Csaba Gergely ☐ 1499 Tibor Marton
☐ 1500 Csaba Janosi ☐ 1501 Anras Kis
☐ 1502 Attila Hoffman ☐ 1503 Roland Nyari
☐ 1503 Roland Nyari ☐ 1504 Z. Kolbenheyer
☐ 1505 Mihaly Filip ☐ 1506 Botond Gergely
☐ 1507 Laszlo Miele ☐ 1508 Laszlo Almasi
☐ 1509 Adam Milus ☐ 1510 B. Czvikovski
☐ 1511 Kisztian Nagy ☐ 1512 Gergely Hausmann
☐ 1513 Csaba Bognar ☐ 1514 Akos Gergely
☐ 1515 Team Checklist

HARTFORD WHALERS

☐ 1516 Anders Johnson ☐ 1517 Russ Bartlett
☐ 1518 Robert Winslow ☐ 1519 Kyle Moore
☐ 1520 Jason Ferranti ☐ 1521 Kichael Herard
☐ 1522 Anthony Spinella ☐ 1523 Michael O'Keefe
☐ 1524 Mike Cacace ☐ 1525 Jason Therrien
☐ 1526 Michael Rizzotti ☐ 1527 John Castline
☐ 1528 Ryan Lynch ☐ 1529 Joey Exter
☐ 1530 Matt Powell ☐ 1531 Paul Therrien
☐ 1532 Team Checklist

NORTH VANCOUVER

☐ 1533 Gram Smith ☐ 1534 Mark Stewart
☐ 1535 Kelly Sickavish ☐ 1536 Jeff Oldenborger
☐ 1537 Rob Nikkel ☐ 1538 Keith Miller
☐ 1539 Jason Maxwell ☐ 1540 J.J. Martin
☐ 1541 Dusty Leonhardt ☐ 1542 Shane Klein
☐ 1543 Peter Horak ☐ 1544 Glen Burlingame
☐ 1545 Drew Barker ☐ 1546 Scott Hewson
☐ 1547 Graham Kennedy ☐ 1548 Josh Scuby
☐ 1549 James Brown ☐ 1550 Team Checklist

LOS ANGELES KINGS

☐ 1551 Micah Wouters ☐ 1552 Levon Bastegyan
☐ 1553 James Wagner ☐ 1554 Marc Gasway
☐ 1555 Michael Kratochvil ☐ 1556 Torrey Diroberto
☐ 1557 Shane Warschaw ☐ 1558 Luis Bodadilla
☐ 1559 Allen Shoham ☐ 1560 Eric DeJong
☐ 1561 Anders Eisnef ☐ 1562 Albert Diroberto
☐ 1563 Team Checklist

DETROIT RED WINGS

The most expensive single is Michael York at $3-5.

☐ 1564 Erik Anderon ☐ 1565 Josh Carter
☐ 1566 Scott Matzka ☐ 1567 Doug Schmidt
☐ 1568 Rob Hodge ☐ 1569 Tim Tracy
☐ 1570 Adam Patterson ☐ 1571 Joey Rakowicz
☐ 1572 Storm Kirschenbaum ☐ 1573 Ryan Fultz
☐ 1574 Jason Cannon ☐ 1575 Rick Smith
☐ 1576 Michael York ☐ 1577 Mike Gladchun
☐ 1578 Brian Rogers ☐ 1579 Neil Carnes
☐ 1580 Team Checklist

BUFFALO SABRES

☐ 1581 Henry Jurek ☐ 1582 Jamine Giambrone
☐ 1583 Patrick Blair ☐ 1584 Kevin Hansen
☐ 1585 John Frank ☐ 1586 Chad Corp
☐ 1587 Nick Wierzba ☐ 1588 Dave Cavanaugh
☐ 1589 Chris Fattey ☐ 1590 Ron Smith
☐ 1591 Nik Fattey ☐ 1592 Eric Kreutzer
☐ 1593 Mike Ginal ☐ 1594 Team Checklist

HALIFAX

☐ 1595 Clark Udle ☐ 1596 Weston Fader
☐ 1597 Tim Boyce ☐ 1598 Paul Dunphy
☐ 1599 Matt Stephens ☐ 1600 Shawn Philips
☐ 1601 Doug Clarke ☐ 1602 Tim Stephenson
☐ 1603 Scott McPhee ☐ 1604 Darrin Sutherland
☐ 1605 John Mullaly ☐ 1606 Jeff Pulsifer
☐ 1607 Jeff Sutherland ☐ 1608 Geoff Carter
☐ 1609 Mark Robbins ☐ 1610 Barry Martin
☐ 1611 Pat Berrigan ☐ 1612 Darryl Cameron
☐ 1613 Team Checklist

ZURICH

☐ 1614 Team Checklist ☐ 1615 Andreas Zücher
☐ 1616 Markus Kleiner ☐ 1617 Boris Ullmann
☐ 1618 Adriano Lombardo ☐ 1619 A. Baumgartner
☐ 1620 Alan Wittwer ☐ 1621 Lars Hottinger
☐ 1622 Martin Kröni ☐ 1623 Gino Gaduff
☐ 1624 Luca Lafranchi ☐ 1625 Frederick Marek
☐ 1626 Mario Schocher ☐ 1627 Pietro Stefanoni
☐ 1628 Daniel Bosshard ☐ 1629 Ronnie Lehmann
☐ 1630 René Stüssi ☐ 1631 Thomas Ziegler
☐ 1632 Roman Leonhard ☐ 1633 Daniel Hitz
☐ 1634 Werner Bayer ☐ 1635 Team Checklist

BOSTON BRUINS

☐ 1635 Dan Stone ☐ 1636 Phil Gambardella
☐ 1637 Tommy Sullivan ☐ 1638 James McCourt
☐ 1639 Heath Gordon ☐ 1640 Scott Perry
☐ 1641 Will Lyons ☐ 1642 David Gove
☐ 1643 Charlie Pero ☐ 1644 Tim Gallagher
☐ 1645 Michael Comer ☐ 1646 Patrick Rissmiller
☐ 1647 Joe Kealty ☐ 1648 Kevin Caulfield
☐ 1649 Michael Callahan ☐ 1650 Joey Robinson
☐ 1651 Douglas Garison ☐ 1652 Donald Duvall
☐ 1653 Kenneth Robinson ☐ 1654 Brian Murphy
☐ 1770 Team Checklist

MINNESOTA STARS

☐ 1655 Randy Johnson ☐ 1656 Josh DiMarzo
☐ 1657 Anoy Hyatt ☐ 1658 Jarod Soper
☐ 1659 Marc Sawyer ☐ 1660 Bobby Garrison
☐ 1661 Mike Saporito ☐ 1662 Scott Macre
☐ 1663 Rick Horch ☐ 1664 Kevin DeHond
☐ 1665 Tom Paolini ☐ 1666 Andy Green
☐ 1667 Joel Begert ☐ 1668 Sanjay Marwaha
☐ 1669 Alex Vigneri ☐ 1670 Richard DiMarzo
☐ 1671 Team Checklist, Error

BADEN WÜTTEMBERG

The most expensive single is Sascha Goc at $1-2.

☐ 1672 Team Checklist ☐ 1673 Björn Petersen
☐ 1674 Tobias Zappe ☐ 1675 Thomas Dolak
☐ 1676 Patrick Butscher ☐ 1677 M. Baumgarthaher
☐ 1678 Florian Weisheit ☐ 1679 Philip Schumacher
☐ 1680 I. Daniel Novak ☐ 1681 David Volek
☐ 1682 Marc Reimer ☐ 1683 Patrick Heitzmann
☐ 1684 J. Weibehrieder ☐ 1685 Mabte Kleerisch
☐ 1686 Marlon Blank ☐ 1687 Frank Martin
☐ 1688 Sascha Goc ☐ 1689 Christoph Jäger
☐ 1690 Steffen Karg ☐ 1691 Thorstev Scharf
☐ 1692 Clemens Frick

SHEDIAC

☐ 1693 Michel Savoie ☐ 1694 André** Roy
☐ 1695 René Goguen ☐ 1696 Jason Clements
☐ 1697 Brian Maillet ☐ 1698 Martin Allain
☐ 1699 Craig Roper ☐ 1700 M-A Goguen
☐ 1701 Benoît Allain ☐ 1702 Rémi Melanson
☐ 1703 Serge Després ☐ 1704 Joël Boudreau
☐ 1705 Mathieu Leblanc ☐ 1706 Martin Boudreau
☐ 1707 Brian Breau ☐ 1708 Dominic Blouin
☐ 1709 Léonard Allain ☐ 1710 Team Checklist

BRATISLAVA

The most expensive single is Marian Cisar at $1-2.

☐ 1711 Peter Fatul ☐ 1712 Roman Tomasek
☐ 1713 Daniel Mucka ☐ 1714 Martin Nemcek
☐ 1715 Erik Weissman ☐ 1716 Andrej Szöke
☐ 1717 Radoslav Pirohar ☐ 1718 Jan Veres
☐ 1719 Mariam Cisar ☐ 1720 Robert Liscak
☐ 1721 Roman Syrora ☐ 1722 Peter Udvardy
☐ 1723 Marek Rezkik ☐ 1724 Jaroslav Smatrala
☐ 1725 Milos Masarik ☐ 1726 Tomas Jozefcik
☐ 1727 Lubomir Krejci ☐ 1728 Matej Jurkovic
☐ 1729 Martin Rucera ☐ 1730 Martin Spilar
☐ 1883 Team Checklist

SLOVENSKO

The most expensive singles are Andrej Podkonicky at $2-3 and Robert Dome at $1-2.

☐ 1731 Andrej Podkonicky ☐ 1732 Pavol Sasik
☐ 1733 Karol Nesladek ☐ 1734 Robert Kostan
☐ 1735 Frantisek Kovac ☐ 1736 Henrich Beutel
☐ 1737 Jan Jas ☐ 1738 Marek Pramuka
☐ 1739 Pavol Reciciar ☐ 1740 Dusan Strelec
☐ 1741 Robert Dome ☐ 1742 Peter Ballo
☐ 1743 Milan Sejna ☐ 1744 Andrej Majesky
☐ 1745 Juraj Vondrak ☐ 1746 Peter Sopkovic
☐ 1747 Marek Topoli ☐ 1748 Chorvat Peter
☐ 1749 Martin Haviar ☐ 1750 Jan Simick
☐ 1881 Team Checklist

CALGARY FLAMES

☐ 1751 Kyle Stuckert ☐ 1752 Scott Williams
☐ 1753 Andy Préfontaine ☐ 1754 Ryan Epp
☐ 1755 Curtis Spitula ☐ 1756 Ryan Proulx
☐ 1757 Shane Sutherland ☐ 1758 Colin Kendall
☐ 1759 Brodie Chalmers ☐ 1760 Curis Mah
☐ 1761 Bobby Kendall ☐ 1762 Lawrence Nycholat
☐ 1763 Reed Woofter ☐ 1764 Travis Bell
☐ 1765 Riley Papero ☐ 1766 Jason Patterson
☐ 1767 René Préfontaine ☐ 1768 Team Checklist
☐ 1769 Richard Wright

MOSCOW

The most expensive singles are Sergei Samsonov at $8-10 and Oleg Kvasha at $2-3.

☐ 1771 Andrei Korpenko ☐ 1772 Andrei Chourupov
☐ 1773 Alexei Krovopuskov ☐ 1774 Andrei Petrunin
☐ 1775 Michel Korolev ☐ 1776 Sergei Samsonov
☐ 1777 Maxim Spiridenov ☐ 1778 Oleg Kvasha
☐ 1779 Michel Bouturlin ☐ 1780 Igor Iliin
☐ 1781 Levon Mickcelian ☐ 1782 Dmitri Zaes
☐ 1783 Nikolay Ignatov ☐ 1784 Dimtry Kakhankin
☐ 1785 Andrei Koteskov ☐ 1786 A. Korsakevitch
☐ 1787 Denis Khlopotnov ☐ 1788 Sergei Gimhev
☐ 1789 Team Checklist

MT. PEARL

☐ 1790 Michail Connors ☐ 1791 Ryan Walsh
☐ 1792 Keith Evans ☐ 1793 Scott Riggs
☐ 1794 Mark Rowe ☐ 1795 Robin Purcell
☐ 1796 Jeff Mahar ☐ 1797 C.J. Nolan
☐ 1798 Andrew Norris ☐ 1799 Curtis Singleton
☐ 1800 Mark Steeve ☐ 1801 Dave Woolridge
☐ 1802 D. Barrington ☐ 1803 Sean Jones
☐ 1804 Lee Kenny ☐ 1805 Tony Fitzgerald
☐ 1806 Glen Tucker ☐ 1807 Chris Mahar
☐ 1808 Team Checklist

LYNNFIELD

☐ 1809 Dominic Biscardi ☐ 1810 Scott Bertolami
☐ 1811 Michael Bethune ☐ 1812 Jamie Dalton
☐ 1813 Stephen Conley ☐ 1814 BG Gardner
☐ 1815 Michael Dalton ☐ 1816 Katlyn Hurton
☐ 1817 Philip Doucette ☐ 1818 David Ostuni
☐ 1819 Luke Milbury ☐ 1820 Mark Swansburg
☐ 1821 Kelly Park ☐ 1822 Keven Doherty
☐ 1823 Grant Rowland ☐ 1824 Joey Burns
☐ 1825 Ken Rowland ☐ 1826 Team Checklist

NEW YORK ISLANDERS

☐ 1827 Robbie Scuderi ☐ 1828 John Boynton
☐ 1829 Justin Shaberly ☐ 1830 Eddie Cassin
☐ 1831 Alan Richartz ☐ 1832 Andrew Merrick
☐ 1833 Brian Telesmanic ☐ 1834 Eric Lind
☐ 1835 Greg Bradley ☐ 1836 Bobby Bianco
☐ 1837 Graig Mischler ☐ 1838 Kirk Shimizuishi
☐ 1839 Jon Bokelman ☐ 1840 Joseph Zangari
☐ 1841 Kurt Gentile ☐ 1842 Martin Hughes
☐ 1843 Brett Chodorow ☐ 1844 Chris Schwartz
☐ 1845 John Stewart ☐ 1846 Wayne Merrick

DETROIT LITTLE CAESARS

The most expensive single is Matt Elich at $2-3.

☐ 1847 David D'Ailleboust ☐ 1848 Dominic Riggio
☐ 1849 J. Weinberger ☐ 1850 Todd Mason
☐ 1851 Jack Redwood ☐ 1852 Matthew Elich
☐ 1853 C. Kiehler ☐ 1854 Jason Durbin
☐ 1855 Andy Gering ☐ 1856 Jeff Lukasak
☐ 1857 Jason Basile ☐ 1858 Richard Kelly
☐ 1859 Jeff Logas ☐ 1860 Mike Nichols
☐ 1861 Andrew Arbanas ☐ 1862 Steve Nichols
☐ 1863 Team Checklist

FRASER

☐ 1864 Adam Trombley ☐ 1865 Rod Johnston
☐ 1866 Dave Francis ☐ 1867 Brett Doll
☐ 1868 Bill Faber ☐ 1869 Mike Herceg
☐ 1870 Chris Sturk ☐ 1871 Jay Vancik
☐ 1872 Ron Willette ☐ 1873 Josh Prues
☐ 1874 Doug Hartwig ☐ 1875 Mike McCauley
☐ 1876 Jeff Tessmer ☐ 1877 Brian Ringler
☐ 1878 Ron Tackett ☐ 1879 Bill McCauley
☐ 1880 Team Checklist ☐ 1882 Talor Agh

MISCELLANEOUS

☐ 1903 Additions Checklist ☐ P1 Guy Lafleur

1992 SEMIC STICKERS

The most expensive stickers are Wayne Gretzky ($5-10), Patrick Roy ($3-6), Steve Yzerman ($3-5), Dominik Hasek ($2-5), Pavel Bure ($2-5) and Jaromir Jagr ($3-5). Other NHL stars sell for 50¢-$4. Other singles sell for 20¢-$1.50.

Complete Set (288 stickers): 50.00
Common Player: .20

Semic / Semic

☐ 1 Finland ☐ 2 Pentti Matikainen
☐ 3 Markus Ketterer (G) ☐ 4 Sakari Lindfors (G)
☐ 5 Teppo Numminen ☐ 6 Jyrki Lumme
☐ 7 Janne Laukkanen ☐ 8 Ville Siren
☐ 9 Mikko Haapakoski ☐ 10 Simo Saarinen
☐ 11 Teemu Selänne ☐ 12 Petri Skriko
☐ 13 Iiro Järvi ☐ 14 Esa Tikkanen
☐ 15 Christian Ruuttu ☐ 16 Raimo Summanen
☐ 17 Jari Kurri ☐ 18 Time Peltomaa
☐ 19 Mika Nieminen ☐ 20 Mikko Mäkelä
☐ 21 Janne Ojanen ☐ 22 Jarmo Kekäläinen
☐ 23 Keijo Säilynoja ☐ 24 Esa Keskinen
☐ 25 Norway ☐ 26 Bengt Ohlsson
☐ 27 Jim Marthinsen ☐ 28 Steven Allman
☐ 29 Fetter Salsten ☐ 30 Åge Ellingsen
☐ 31 Kim Sogaard ☐ 32 Jan Roar Fagerli
☐ 33 Tommy Jakobsen ☐ 34 Cato Tom Andersen
☐ 35 Arne Billkvam ☐ 36 Øystein Olsen
☐ 37 Geir Hoff ☐ 38 Erik Kristiansen
☐ 39 Ørjan Lijvdal ☐ 40 Espen Knutsen
☐ 41 Ole Eskild Dahlstöm ☐ 42 Rune Gulliksen
☐ 43 Marius Rath ☐ 44 Petter Thoresen
☐ 45 Tom Johanssen ☐ 46 Stephen Foyn
☐ 47 Stig Johansen ☐ 48 Per Christian Knold
☐ 49 Sweden ☐ 50 Conny Evensson
☐ 51 T. Söderström (G) ☐ 52 Fredrik Andersson
☐ 53 Thomas Eriksson ☐ 54 Peter Andersson
☐ 55 Peter Andersson ☐ 56 Nicklas Lidström
☐ 57 Calle Johansson ☐ 58 Ulf Samuelsson
☐ 59 Fredrik Olausson ☐ 60 Börje Salming
☐ 61 Håkan Loob ☐ 62 Thomas Rundqvist
☐ 63 Mats Näslund ☐ 64 Mikael Johansson
☐ 65 B-A Gustavsson ☐ 66 Peter Ottoson
☐ 67 Markus Näslund ☐ 68 Daniel Rydmark
☐ 69 Tomas Sandström ☐ 70 Thomas Steen
☐ 71 Per-Erik Eklund ☐ 72 Mats Sundin
☐ 73 Canada ☐ 74 Dave King
☐ 75 Bill Ranford (G) ☐ 76 Ed Belfour (G)
☐ 77 Al MacInnis ☐ 78 Scott Stevens
☐ 79 Steve Smith ☐ 80 Ray Bourque
☐ 81 Paul Coffey ☐ 82 Larry Murphy
☐ 83 Mark Tinordi ☐ 84 Wayne Gretzky
☐ 85 Mark Messier ☐ 86 Mario Lemieux
☐ 87 Steve Yzerman ☐ 88 Eric Lindros
☐ 89 Luc Robitaille ☐ 90 Theoren Fleury
☐ 91 Steve Larmer ☐ 92 Brent Sutter
☐ 93 Shayne Corson ☐ 94 Dale Hawerschuk
☐ 95 Russ Courtnall ☐ 96 Rick Tocchet
☐ 97 Soviet Union ☐ 98 Victor Tikhonov
☐ 99 Andrei Trefilov (G) ☐ 100 M. Shtalenkov (G)
☐ 101 Alexei Kasatonov ☐ 102 Mikhail Tatarinov
☐ 103 Igor Kravchuk ☐ 104 Vladimir Malakhov
☐ 105 Alex Gusarov ☐ 106 Dimitri Filimonov
☐ 107 Dimitri Mironov ☐ 108 V. Konstantinov
☐ 109 Sergei Fedorov ☐ 110 Alexei Zhamnov
☐ 111 Vyacheslav Kozlov ☐ 112 Valeri Kamensky
☐ 113 Alexander Semak ☐ 114 V. Butsayev
☐ 115 Andrei Lomakin ☐ 116 Pavel Bure
☐ 117 Andrei Kovalenko ☐ 118 Ravil Khaidarov
☐ 119 Victor Gordiouk ☐ 120 Vitali Prokhorov
☐ 121 Czechoslovakia ☐ 122 Ivan Hlinka Coach
☐ 123 O. Svoboda (G) ☐ 124 Dominik Hasek (G)
☐ 125 Leo Gudas ☐ 126 Frantisek Musil
☐ 127 Kamil Prachar ☐ 128 Frantisek Kucera
☐ 129 Richard Smehlik ☐ 130 Jergus Baca
☐ 131 Jiri Slegr ☐ 132 Petr Hrbek
☐ 133 Kamil Kastak ☐ 134 Richard Zemlicka
☐ 135 Jaromir Jagr ☐ 136 Martin Rucinsky
☐ 137 Josef Beranek ☐ 138 Michael Pivonka
☐ 139 Robert Kron ☐ 140 Zigmund Palffy
☐ 141 Tomas Jelinek ☐ 142 Robert Reichel
☐ 143 Lubomir Kolnik ☐ 144 Zdeno Ciger
☐ 145 USA ☐ 146 Tim Taylor
☐ 147 Vanbiesbrouck (G) ☐ 148 Mike Richter (G)
☐ 149 Phil Housley ☐ 150 Brian Leetch
☐ 151 Kevin Hatcher ☐ 152 Gary Suter
☐ 153 Chris Chelios ☐ 154 Erich Weinrich
☐ 155 Jim Johnson ☐ 156 Brett Hull
☐ 157 Mike Modano ☐ 158 Jeremy Roenick
☐ 159 Pat LaFontaine ☐ 160 Craig Janney
☐ 161 Ed Olczyk ☐ 162 Tony Granato
☐ 163 Joe Mullen ☐ 164 Dave Christian
☐ 165 Doug Brown ☐ 166 Kevin Miller
☐ 167 Joel Otto ☐ 168 Randy Wood
☐ 169 Germany ☐ 170 Ludek Bukac
☐ 171 Klaus Merk (G) ☐ 172 Josef Heiss (G)
☐ 173 Harold Kreiss ☐ 174 Michael Heidt
☐ 175 Jörg Mayr ☐ 176 Marco Rentzsch
☐ 177 Heinrich Schiffel ☐ 178 Stefan Steinecker
☐ 179 Torsten Kienass ☐ 180 Raimund Hilger
☐ 181 Ernst Köpf ☐ 182 Peter Draisaitl
☐ 183 Axel Kammerer ☐ 184 Michael Rumrich
☐ 185 Jurgen Rumrich ☐ 186 Georg Holzmann
☐ 187 Lorenz Funk ☐ 188 Thomas Schinko
☐ 189 Andreas Lupzig ☐ 190 Tobias Abstreiter
☐ 191 Michael Pohl ☐ 192 Antony Vogel
☐ 193 Switzerland ☐ 194 Juhani Tamminen
☐ 195 Renato Tosio (G) ☐ 196 Reto Pavoni (G)
☐ 197 Rick Tschumi ☐ 198 Patrice Brasey
☐ 199 Didier Massy ☐ 200 Sandro Bertaggia
☐ 201 Sven Leuenberger ☐ 202 Samuel Palmer
☐ 203 Martin Rauch ☐ 204 Dino Kessler
☐ 205 Raymond Walder ☐ 206 Peter Jaks
☐ 207 Andy Ton ☐ 208 Jörg Eberle
☐ 209 Felix Hollenstein ☐ 210 Fredy Luthi
☐ 211 Manuele Celio ☐ 212 Christian Weber
☐ 213 Andre Rotheli ☐ 214 Gil Montandon
☐ 215 Thomas Vrabec ☐ 216 Patrick Howald
☐ 217 France ☐ 218 Kjell Larsson
☐ 219 J-M Dijan (G) ☐ 220 Petri Ylönen (G)
☐ 221 Stéphane Botteri ☐ 222 Michel Leblanc
☐ 223 J-P Lemoine ☐ 224 Denis Perez
☐ 225 Bruno Saunier ☐ 226 Steven Woodburn
☐ 227 Serge Poudrier ☐ 228 Michael Babin
☐ 229 Stéphane Barin ☐ 230 Philippe Bozon
☐ 231 Arnaud Briand ☐ 232 Yves Crettenand
☐ 233 Patrick Dunn ☐ 234 Yannick Goicoechea
☐ 235 Benoît Laporte ☐ 236 Christian Pouget
☐ 237 Antoine Richer ☐ 238 Christophe Ville
☐ 239 Peter Almasy ☐ 240 Pierre Pousse
☐ 241 Italy ☐ 242 Gene Ubriaco
☐ 243 David Delfino (G) ☐ 244 Mike Zanier (G)
☐ 245 Erwin Kostner ☐ 246 Roberto Oberrauch
☐ 247 Jim Camazzola ☐ 248 Anthony Circelli
☐ 249 Michael de Angelis ☐ 250 Giovanni Marchetti
☐ 251 Alessandro Batiani ☐ 252 Georg Comploi
☐ 253 Gaetano Orlando ☐ 254 Bruno Zarrillo
☐ 255 Emilio Iovio ☐ 256 Frank Nigro
☐ 257 Marco Scapinello ☐ 258 Giuseppe Foglietta
☐ 259 Rick Morocco ☐ 260 Santino Pellegrino
☐ 261 Lucio Topatigh ☐ 262 Mario Simioni
☐ 263 Ivano Cloch ☐ 264 Martino Soracreppa
☐ 265 Poland ☐ 266 Leszek Lejcyk
☐ 267 Andrzej Hanisz (G) ☐ 268 Mariusz Kieca (G)
☐ 269 Henryk Gruth ☐ 270 Janusz Syposz
☐ 271 Robert Szopinski ☐ 272 Marek Cholewa
☐ 273 Jacek Zamojski ☐ 274 Rafal Stroka
☐ 275 Dariusz Garbocz ☐ 276 Stanislaw Cyrwus
☐ 277 Janusz Adamiec ☐ 278 Miroslav Copija
☐ 279 Piotr Zdunek ☐ 280 Krzysztof Bujar
☐ 281 Ludwik Czapka ☐ 282 Andrzej Kotonski
☐ 283 Janusz Hajnos ☐ 284 Slawomir Wieloch
☐ 285 Wojciech Matczak ☐ 286 Jedrzej Kasperczyk
☐ 287 Wojciech Tkacs ☐ 288 Mariusz Czerkawski

1992 7TH INNING SKETCH AWARD WINNERS

Complete Set (30 cards): 10.00

Awards / Awards

☐ 1 Eric Lindros ☐ 2 Dale Craigwell
☐ 3 Nathan LaFayette ☐ 4 Chris Snell
☐ 5 Cory Stillman ☐ 6 Mike Torchia (G)
☐ 7 George Burnett ☐ 8 Eric Lindros
☐ 9 Sherwood Bassin ☐ 10 Eric Lindros
☐ 11 Scott Niedermayer ☐ 12 Pat Falloon
☐ 13 Scott Niedermayer ☐ 14 Darryl Sydor
☐ 15 Donevan Hextall ☐ 16 Jamie McLennan
☐ 17 Tom Renney ☐ 18 Frank Evans
☐ 19 Bob Brown ☐ 20 Ray Whitney
☐ 21 Phillippe Boucher ☐ 22 Yanic Perreault
☐ 23 Benoît Larose ☐ 24 Patrice Brisebois
☐ 25 Phillippe Boucher ☐ 26 Félix Potvin (G)
☐ 27 Joe Canale ☐ 28 Christian Larivière
☐ 29 Roland Janellem ☐ 30 Yanic Perreault

1992 TOPPS STADIUM CLUB MEMBERS ONLY

These cards say "Members Only" on the card front.

Complete Set (13 cards):	9.00
Player	TSC
☐ Pavel Bure	.50
☐ Guy Carbonneau	.50
☐ Paul Coffey	.50
☐ Mike Gartner	.50
☐ Mike Gartner	.50
☐ Michel Goulet	.50
☐ Wayne Gretzky	2.00
☐ Brett Hull	.50
☐ Brian Leetch	.50
☐ Mario Lemieux	1.50
☐ Mario Lemieux	1.50
☐ Mark Messier	.50
☐ Patrick Roy (G)	1.50

1992 - 93 ALL-WORLD

These cards start at $3-6.

- ☐ M. Lemieux green border / English
- ☐ M. Lemieux green border / French
- ☐ M. Lemieux green border / Spanish
- ☐ M. Lemieux foil border / English
- ☐ M. Lemieux foil border / French
- ☐ M. Lemieux foil border / Spanish

1992 - 93 AMERICAN LICORICE SOUR PUNCH CAPS

Imprint: 1993 American Licorice Co.

Complete Set (9 cards):	7.00
Player	NM-MT
☐ 1 Theoren Fleury, Calg.	.50
☐ 2 Guy Lafleur, Mont.	2.00
☐ 3 Chris Chelios, Chic.	.50
☐ 4 Stan Mikita, Chic.	.50
☐ 5 Maurice Richard, Mont.	2.50
☐ 6 Steve Thomas, Chic.	.25
☐ 7 Checklist	.25
☐ 8 Checklist	.25
☐ P Bobby Hull, Chic.	1.50

1992 - 93 BAYBANK

Imprint: ® Baybank

Complete Set (3 cards):	25.00
Player	NM-MT
☐ 1 Bobby Orr, Bost.	10.00
☐ 2 Bobby Orr, Bost.	10.00
☐ 3 Bobby Orr, Bost.	10.00

1992 - 93 BCJHL

Brendan Morrison is the most expensive card at $4-6. NHL Stars sell at $1-4. Singles start at 20¢; regional stars sell at 75¢-$2.

Complete Set (246 cards): 20.00

BCJHL	BCJHL
☐ 1 Tom Wittenberg	☐ 2 Kendel Kelly
☐ 3 Gus Rettschlag	☐ 4 Don Barr
☐ 5 Dave Kirkpatrick	☐ 6 Josh Flett
☐ 7 Paul McKenna	☐ 8 Brad Wingfield
☐ 9 Derek Gesce	☐ 10 Garry Gulash
☐ 11 Tim Bell	☐ 12 Dean Stork
☐ 13 Wes Reusse	☐ 14 Jason Peipmann
☐ 15 Tyler Johnston	☐ 16 Jason Delesoy
☐ 17 The Ice Man	☐ 18 Don Barr
☐ 19 Brad Swain	☐ 20 Wes Rudy
☐ 21 Michael Sigouin	☐ 22 Kevan Rilcof
☐ 23 Brian Preston	☐ 24 Doug Ast
☐ 25 Knut Engqvist	☐ 26 Zac George
☐ 27 Clint Black	☐ 28 Cameron Campbell
☐ 29 Dan Davies	☐ 30 Bryce Munro
☐ 31 Ryan Dayman	☐ 32 Kevin Kimura
☐ 33 Paul Nicolls	☐ 34 Thomas Kraft
☐ 35 Erin Thornton	☐ 36 Brad Loring
☐ 37 Jag Bal	☐ 38 Jeff Grabinsky
☐ 39 Johan Ahrgren	☐ 40 The Lethal Weapon
☐ 41 Chilliwach Chiefs	☐ 42 Judd Lambert
☐ 43 Brian Schiebel	☐ 44 Dennis Archibald
☐ 45 David Longbroek	☐ 46 Silverio Mirao
☐ 47 Jason Haakstad	☐ 48 Lee Grant
☐ 49 Ryan Esselmont	☐ 50 Steve Roberts
☐ 51 Curtis Fry	☐ 52 Daid Dollard
☐ 53 Diano Zol	☐ 54 Bob Needham
☐ 55 Dustin Green	☐ 56 Darren Tymchyshyn
☐ 57 Peter Arvanitis	☐ 58 Don Hearn
☐ 59 Title Card	☐ 60 Martin Masa
☐ 61 Steffon Walby	☐ 62 Joel Irwin
☐ 63 Brent Bradford	☐ 64 Dieter Kochan
☐ 65 Brendan Kenny	☐ 66 Marty Craigdallie
☐ 67 Graeme Harder	☐ 68 Pavel Suchanek
☐ 69 Shane Johnson	☐ 70 Burt Henderson
☐ 71 Tyler Willis	☐ 72 Mike Olaski
☐ 73 Daivd Green	☐ 74 Tom Mix
☐ 75 Walter (Guy) Prince	☐ 76 Joseph Rybar
☐ 77 Bill Muckalt	☐ 78 Jason Mansoff
☐ 79 Duane Puga	☐ 80 Aaron Hoffman
☐ 81 Dan Blasko	☐ 82 Rob Szatmary
☐ 83 Mike Minnis	☐ 84 Pat Meehan
☐ 85 Andre Robichaud	☐ 86 The Terminator
☐ 87 Derrek Harper	☐ 88 Dan Morrissey
☐ 89 Joey Kennedy	☐ 90 Derrek Harper
☐ 91 Lawrence Klyne	☐ 92 Ryan Beamin
☐ 93 Sjon Wynia	☐ 94 Jason Disiewich
☐ 95 Jason Sanford	☐ 96 Casey (G) Hungle
☐ 97 Brent Murcheson	☐ 98 Glenn Calder
☐ 99 Jade Kersey	☐ 100 Shawn York
☐ 101 Bob Quinnell	☐ 102 Geordie Dunstan
☐ 103 Cory Crowther	☐ 104 Jason Hodson
☐ 105 Chris Jones	☐ 106 Cory Green
☐ 107 Chris Buie	☐ 108 Shaun Peet
☐ 109 Jason Wood	☐ 110 Dan Murphy
☐ 111 Jason Disiewich	☐ 112 Cory Dayley
☐ 113 Brian Veale	☐ 114 Jason northard
☐ 115 Phil Valk	☐ 116 Wade Dayley
☐ 117 Brendan Morrison	☐ 118 Marcel Sakac
☐ 119 Tyler Boucher	☐ 120 Ray Guze
☐ 121 Brian Barnes	☐ 122 Jason Given
☐ 123 Michael Dairon	☐ 124 Mike Newman
☐ 125 Craig Fletcher	☐ 126 Ty Davidson
☐ 127 Miki Antonik	☐ 128 Rob Pennoyer
☐ 129 Dave Whitworth	☐ 130 Steve Williams
☐ 131 Robbie Trampuh	☐ 132 Mark Filipenko
☐ 133 Clint MacDonald	☐ 134 Colin Ryder
☐ 135 David Kilduff	☐ 136 Mickey McGuire
☐ 137 Randy Polacik	☐ 138 Jeff Tory
☐ 139 Chris Buckman	☐ 140 Bill Moddy
☐ 141 Rick McLarren	☐ 142 The Phantom
☐ 143 Jason Zaichkowski	☐ 144 Tony Hrycukk
☐ 145 Cameron Knox	☐ 146 Mike Warriner
☐ 147 Robb Gordon	☐ 148 Mike Pawluk
☐ 149 Tim Harris	☐ 150 Mike Bzdel
☐ 151 Chad Wilson	☐ 152 Andrew Plumb
☐ 153 Andy MacIntosh	☐ 154 Stefan Brannare
☐ 155 Matt Sharrers	☐ 156 Brent Berry
☐ 157 Ryan Douglas	☐ 158 Heath Dennison
☐ 159 Chad Vizzutti	☐ 160 Adam Lord
☐ 161 Brad Klyn	☐ 162 Andrew Young
☐ 163 Casey Lemanski	☐ 164 Mike McKinlay
☐ 165 Derek Robinson	☐ 166 Kees Roodbol
☐ 167 Scott Boucher	☐ 168 Shawn Gervais
☐ 169 Ryan Schaffer	☐ 170 Kevin Robertson
☐ 171 Ryan Donovan	☐ 172 Bart Taylor
☐ 173 Greg Hunt	☐ 174 Darcy George
☐ 175 Shane Tidsbury	☐ 176 Rob Smillie
☐ 177 Chad Vestergaard	☐ 178 Al Kinisky
☐ 179 Patrick O'Flaherty	☐ 180 Loui Mellios
☐ 181 Lorin Murdock	☐ 182 Jason Genik
☐ 183 Rob Herrington	☐ 184 Loui Mellios
☐ 185 Cal Benazic	☐ 186 Richard Kraus
☐ 187 Geoff White	☐ 188 Kirk Buchanan
☐ 189 Peter Zurba	☐ 190 John Morabito
☐ 191 Corey Kruchkowski	☐ 192 Spencer Ward
☐ 193 Danny Shermerhorn	☐ 194 Mark Davies
☐ 195 Jason Rushton	☐ 196 Chad Buckle
☐ 197 Serge Beauchesne	☐ 198 Todd Kelman
☐ 199 Jason Switzer	☐ 200 Eon MacFarlane
☐ 201 Terry Ryan	☐ 202 Shawn Bourgeois
☐ 203 Chad Schraeder	☐ 204 Dusty McLellan
☐ 205 The Predator	☐ 206 Danny Shermerhorn
☐ 207 Chris Godard	☐ 208 Jason Chipman
☐ 209 Christian Twomey	☐ 210 Ryan Loxam
☐ 211 Greg Buchanan	☐ 212 Kees Roodbol
☐ 213 Ryan Keller	☐ 214 Kevin Paschal
☐ 215 David Hebky	☐ 216 Vince Devlin
☐ 217 Mike Cole	☐ 218 Daljit Takhar
☐ 219 Scott Hall	☐ 220 Derek Lawrence
☐ 221 Mark Basanta	☐ 222 Jan Kloboucek
☐ 223 Randy Barker	☐ 224 Kris Gailloux
☐ 225 Tyson Scheuer	☐ 226 Brent Wormald
☐ 227 Vince Devlin	☐ 228 Gus Miller
☐ 229 Todd McKave	☐ 230 Lawrence Oliver
☐ 231 Scott Garvin	☐ 232 Rob Milliken
☐ 233 Roman Kobrc	☐ 234 Dan Skene
☐ 235 Blair Marsh	☐ 236 Maco Balkovec
☐ 237 Scott Kirton	☐ 238 Blaine Moore
☐ 239 Nigel Creightney	☐ 240 Bill Zapt
☐ 241 Jason Elders	☐ 242 BCJHL Officials
☐ 243 Black Panther	☐ 244 Puck Pirate
☐ 245 Mike Pawluk	☐ 246 Steffon Walby

1992 - 93 BOWMAN

Gold Foil All-Stars (199-220 / 222-243 /442) were inserted one per pack. Short-printed All-Stars are marked with an asterisk (*).

Imprint: 1992 THE TOPPS COMPANY, INC.

Complete Set (442 cards):	225.00
Common Player:	.25
Player	NM-MT
☐ 1 Wayne Gretzky, LosA.	5.00
☐ 2 Mike Krushelnyski, Toro.	.25
☐ 3 Raymond Bourque, Bost.	1.50
☐ 4 Keith Brown, Chic.	.25
☐ 5 Bob Sweeney, Bost.	.25
☐ 6 Dave Christian, SLou.	.25
☐ 7 Frantisek Kucera, Chic.	.25
☐ 8 John LeClair, Mont.	1.00
☐ 9 Jamie Macoun, Toro.	.25
☐ 10 Bob Carpenter, Bost.	.25
☐ 11 Garry Galley, Phil.	.25
☐ 12 Bob Kudelski, LosA.	.25
☐ 13 Doug Bodger, Buff.	.25
☐ 14 Craig Janney, SLou.	.25
☐ 15 Glen Wesley, Bost.	.25
☐ 16 Daren Puppa (G), Buff.	.25
☐ 17 Andy Brickley, Bost.	.25
☐ 18 Steve Konroyd, Hart.	.25
☐ 19 Dave Poulin, Bost.	.25
☐ 20 Phil Housley, Winn.	.25
☐ 21 Kevin Todd, NJer.	.25
☐ 22 Tomas Sandström, LosA.	.25
☐ 23 Pierre Turgeon, NYIs.	.50
☐ 24 J. Steve Smith, Chic.	.25
☐ 25 Ray Sheppard, Detr.	.25
☐ 26 Stu Barnes, Winn.	.25
☐ 27 Grant Ledyard, Buff.	.25
☐ 28 Benoît Hogue, NYIs.	.25
☐ 29 Randy Burridge, Wash.	.25
☐ 30 Clint Malarchuk (G), Buff.	.25
☐ 31 Steve Duchesne, Phil.	.25
☐ **32 Guy Hebert (G), SLou. RC**	**1.50**
☐ 33 Steve Kasper, Phil.	.25
☐ 34 Alexander Mogilny, Buff.	.50
☐ 35 Marty McSorley, LosA.	.25
☐ 36 Doug Weight, NYRa.	.50
☐ 37 Dave (Stitch) Taylor, LosA.	.25
☐ 38 Guy Carbonneau, Mont.	.25
☐ 39 Brian Benning, Phil.	.25
☐ 40 Nelson Emerson, SLou.	.25
☐ 41 Craig Wolanin, Québ.	.25
☐ 42 Kelly Hrudey (G), LosA.	.25
☐ 43 Chris Chelios, Chic.	.50
☐ 44 Dave Andreychuk, Buff.	.25
☐ 45 Russ Courtnall, Mont.	.25
☐ 46 Stéphane Richer, NJer.	.25
☐ 47 Petr* Svoboda, Buff.	.25
☐ 48 Barry Pederson, Bost.	.25
☐ 49 Claude Lemieux, NJer.	.25
☐ 50 Tony Granato, LosA.	.25
☐ 51 Al MacInnis, Calg.	.50
☐ 52 Luciano Borsato, Winn.	.25
☐ 53 Sergei Makarov, Calg.	.50
☐ 54 Bobby Smith, Minn.	.25
☐ 55 Gary Suter, Calg.	.25
☐ 56 Tom Draper (G), Buff.	.25
☐ 57 Corey Millen, LosA.	.25
☐ 58 Joe Mullen, Pitt.	.50
☐ 59 Joe Nieuwendyk, Calg.	.50
☐ 60 Brian Hayward (G), SanJ.	.25
☐ 61 Steve Larmer, Chic.	.50
☐ 62 Cam Neely, Bost.	1.00
☐ 63 Ric Nattress, Toro.	.25
☐ 64 Denis Savard, Mont.	.50
☐ 65 Gerald Diduck, Vanc.	.25
☐ 66 Pat Jablonski (G), SLou.	.25
☐ 67 Brad McCrimmon, Detr.	.25
☐ 68 Dirk Graham, Chic.	.25
☐ 69 Joel Otto, Calg.	.25
☐ 70 Luc Robitaille, LosA.	1.00
☐ 71 Dana Murzyn, Vanc.	.25
☐ 72 Jocelyn Lemieux, Chic.	.25
☐ 73 Mike Hudson, Chic.	.25
☐ 74 Patrick Roy (G), Mont.	3.50
☐ 75 Doug Wilson, SanJ.	.25
☐ 76 Wayne Presley, Buff.	.25
☐ 77 Félix Potvin (G), Toro.	.50
☐ 78 Jeremy Roenick, Chic.	1.00
☐ 79 Andy Moog (G), Bost.	.50
☐ 80 Joey Kocur, NYRa.	.25
☐ 81 Neal Broten, Minn.	.25
☐ 82 Shayne Corson, Mont.	.25
☐ 83 Doug Gilmour, Toro.	.50
☐ 84 Rob Zettler, SanJ.	.25
☐ 85 Bob Probert, Detr.	.25
☐ 86 Mike Vernon (G), Calg.	.50
☐ 87 Rick Zombo, SLou.	.25
☐ 88 Adam Creighton, NYIs.	.25
☐ 89 Mike McPhee, Mont.	.25
☐ 90 Ed Belfour (G), Chic.	1.00
☐ 91 Steve Chiasson, Detr.	.25
☐ 92 Dominic Roussel (G), Phil.	.25
☐ 93 Troy Murray, Winn.	.25
☐ 94 Jari Kurri, LosA.	1.00
☐ 95 Geoff Smith, Edmo.	.25
☐ 96 Paul Ranheim, Calg.	.25
☐ 97 Rick Wamsley (G), Toro.	.25
☐ 98 Brian Noonan, Chic.	.25
☐ 99 Kevin Lowe, Edmo.	.25
☐ 100 Josef Beránek, Edmo.	.25
☐ 101 Michel Petit, Calg.	.25
☐ 102 Craig Billington (G), NJer.	.25
☐ 103 Steve Yzerman, Detr.	3.00
☐ 104 Glenn Anderson, Toro.	.25
☐ 105 Perry Berezan, SanJ.	.25
☐ 106 Bill Ranford (G), Edmo.	.50
☐ 107 Randy Ladouceur, Hart.	.25
☐ 108 Jimmy Carson, Detr.	.25
☐ 109 Gary Roberts, Calg.	.50
☐ 110 Checklist	.25
☐ 111 Brad Shaw, Hart. (Otta.)	.25
☐ 112 Pat Verbeek, Hart.	.25
☐ 113 Mark Messier, NYRa.	1.00
☐ 114 Grant Fuhr (G), Toro.	.50
☐ 115 Sylvain Côté, Wash.	.25
☐ 116 Mike Sullivan, SanJ.	.25
☐ 117 Steve Thomas, NYIs.	.25
☐ 118 Craig MacTavish, Edmo.	.25
☐ 119 Dave Babych, Vanc.	.25
☐ 120 Jimmy Waite (G), Chic.	.25
☐ 121 Kevin Dineen, Phil.	.25
☐ 122 Shawn Burr, Detr.	.25
☐ 123 Ron Francis, Pitt.	.50
☐ 124 Garth Butcher, SLou.	.25
☐ 125 Jarmo Myllys (G), Toro.	.25
☐ 126 Doug Brown, NJer.	.25
☐ 127 James Patrick, NYRa.	.25
☐ 128 Ray Ferraro, NYIs.	.25
☐ 129 Terry Carkner, Phil.	.25
☐ 130 John MacLean, NJer.	.25
☐ 131 Randy Velischek, Québ.	.25
☐ 132 John Vanbiesbrouck (G), NYRa.	.50
☐ 133 Dean Evason, SanJ.	.25
☐ 134 Patrick Flatley, NYIs.	.25
☐ 135 Petr Klima, Edmo.	.25
☐ 136 Geoff Sanderson, Hart.	.25
☐ 137 Joe Reekie, NYIs. (Tamp.)	.25
☐ 138 Kirk Muller, Mont.	.25
☐ 139 Brian Mullen, SanJ.	.25
☐ 140 Daniel Berthiaume (G), Bost.	.25
☐ 141 David Shaw, Minn.	.25
☐ 142 Pat LaFontaine, Buff.	.50
☐ 143 Ulf Dahlén, Minn.	.25
☐ 144 Esa Tikkanen, Edmo.	.25
☐ 145 Viacheslav Fetisov, NJer.	.50
☐ 146 Mike Gartner, NYRa.	1.00
☐ 147 Brent Sutter, Chic.	.25
☐ 148 Darcy Wakaluk (G), Minn.	.25
☐ 149 Brian Leetch, NYRa.	.50
☐ 150 Craig Simpson, Edmo.	.25
☐ 151 Mike Modano, Minn.	1.00
☐ 152 Bryan Trottier, Pitt.	1.00
☐ 153 Larry Murphy, Pitt.	.25
☐ 154 Pavel Bure, Vanc.	1.00
☐ 155 Kay Whitmore (G), Hart.	.25
☐ 156 Darren Turcotte, NYRa.	.25
☐ 157 Frantisek Musil, Calg.	.25
☐ 158 Mikael Andersson, Hart. (Tamp.)	.25
☐ 159 Rick Tocchet, Pitt.	.25
☐ 160 Scott Stevens, NJer.	.50
☐ 161 Bernie Nicholls, Edmo.	.25
☐ 162 Peter Sidorkiewicz (G), Hart. (Otta.)	.25
☐ 163 Scott Mellanby, Edmo.	.25
☐ 164 Alexander Semak, NJer.	.25
☐ 165 Kjell Samuelsson, Pitt.	.25
☐ 166 Kelly Kisio, SanJ.	.25
☐ 167 Sylvain Turgeon, Mont. (Otta.)	.25
☐ 168 Rob (Jr.) Brown, Chic.	.25
☐ 169 Gerard Gallant, Detr.	.25
☐ 170 Jyrki Lumme, Vanc.	.25
☐ 171 Dave Gagner, Minn.	.25
☐ 172 Tony Tanti, Buff.	.25
☐ 173 Zarley Zalapski, Hart.	.25
☐ 174 Joe Murphy, Edmo.	.25
☐ 175 Ron Sutter, SLou.	.25
☐ 176 Dino Ciccarelli, Detr.	.25
☐ 177 Jim* Johnson, Minn.	.25
☐ 178 Mike Hough, Québ.	.25
☐ 179 Pelle Eklund, Phil.	.25
☐ 180 John Druce, Wash.	.25
☐ 181 Paul Coffey, LosA.	.50
☐ 182 Ken Wregget (G), Pitt.	.25
☐ 183 Brendan Shanahan, SLou.	1.00
☐ 184 Keith Acton, Phil.	.25
☐ 185 Steven Finn, Québ.	.25
☐ 186 Brett Hull, SLou.	1.00
☐ 187 Rollie Melanson (G), Mont.	.25
☐ 188 Derek King, NYIs.	.25
☐ 189 Mario Lemieux, Pitt.	3.50
☐ 190 Mathieu Schneider, Mont.	.25
☐ 191 Claude Vilgrain, NJer.	.25
☐ 192 Gary Leeman, Calg.	.25
☐ 193 Paul Cavallini, SLou.	.25
☐ 194 John Cullen, Hart.	.25
☐ 195 Ron Hextall (G), Québ. (G)	.50
☐ 196 David Volek, NYIs.	.25
☐ 197 Gord** Roberts, Bost.	.50
☐ 198 Dale Craigwell, SanJ.	.25
☐ 199 AS: Ed Belfour (G)	3.00
☐ 200 AS: Brian Bellows (*)	6.00
☐ 201 AS: Chris Chelios	2.00
☐ 202 AS: Tim Cheveldae (G) (*)	6.00
☐ 203 AS: Vincent Damphousse, Error	2.00
☐ 203 AS: Vincent Damphousse, Corrected	2.00
☐ 204 AS: Dave Ellett	1.00
☐ 205 AS: Sergei Fedorov (*)	20.00
☐ 206 AS: Theoren Fleury	2.00
☐ 207 AS: Wayne Gretzky	15.00
☐ 208 AS: Phil Housley	1.00
☐ 209 AS: Brett Hull	3.00
☐ 210 AS: Trevor Linden (*)	6.00
☐ 211 AS: Al MacInnis (*)	6.00
☐ 212 AS: Kirk McLean (G) (*)	6.00
☐ 213 AS: Adam Oates	1.00
☐ 214 AS: Gary Roberts (*)	6.00
☐ 215 AS: Larry Robinson	2.00
☐ 216 AS: Luc Robitaille	3.00
☐ 217 AS: Jeremy Roenick (*)	10.00
☐ 218 AS: Mark Tinordi	1.00
☐ 219 AS: Doug Wilson	1.00
☐ 220 AS: Steve Yzerman	9.00

☐	221 Checklist	.25
☐	222 AS: Don Beaupré (G) (*)	6.00
☐	223 AS: Raymond Bourque	4.00
☐	224 AS: Rod Brind'Amour (*)	6.00
☐	225 AS: Randy Burridge (*)	6.00
☐	226 AS: Paul Coffey (*)	10.00
☐	227 AS: John Cullen (*)	6.00
☐	228 AS: Eric Desjardins (*)	6.00
☐	229 AS: Ray Ferraro (*)	6.00
☐	230 AS: Kevin Hatcher	1.00
☐	231 AS: Jaromir Jagr	3.00
☐	232 AS: Brian Leetch (*)	10.00
☐	233 AS: Mario Lemieux	10.00
☐	234 AS: Mark Messier	3.00
☐	235 AS: Alexander Mogilny	1.00
☐	236 AS: Kirk Muller	1.00
☐	237 AS: Owen Nolan	2.00
☐	238 AS: Mike Richter (G)	1.00
☐	239 AS: Patrick Roy (G)	10.00
☐	240 AS: Joe Sakic (*)	25.00
☐	241 AS: Kevin Stevens	1.00
☐	242 AS: Scott Stevens	1.00
☐	243 AS: Bryan Trottier (*)	15.00
☐	244 Joe Sakic, Québ.	2.00
☐	245 Daniel Marois, NYIs.	.25
☐	246 Randy Wood, Buff.	.25
☐	247 Jeff R. Brown, SLou.	.25
☐	248 Peter Bondra, Wash.	.50
☐	249 Peter Stastny, NJer.	.50
☐	250 Tom Barrasso (G), Pitt.	.50
☐	251 Al Iafrate, Wash.	.25
☐	252 James H. Black, Hart.	.25
☐	253 Jan Erixon, NYRa.	.25
☐	254 Brian Lawton, SanJ.	.25
☐	255 Luke Richardson, Edmo.	.25
☐	256 Rich Sutter, SLou.	.25
☐	257 Jeff Chychrun, Pitt.	.25
☐	258 Adam Oates, Bost.	.50
☐	259 Tom Kurvers, NYIs.	.25
☐	260 Brian Bellows, Minn.	.25
☐	261 Trevor Linden, Vanc.	.50
☐	262 Vincent Riendeau (G), Detr.	.25
☐	263 Peter Zezel, Toro.	.25
☐	264 Richard Pilon, NYIs.	.25
☐	265 Paul Broten, NYRa.	.25
☐	266 Gaétan Duchesne, Minn.	.25
☐	267 Doug Lidster, Vanc.	.25
☐	268 Rod Brind'Amour, Phil.	.25
☐	269 Jon Casey (G), Minn.	.25
☐	270 Pat Elynuik, Winn.	.25
☐	271 Kevin Hatcher, Wash.	.25
☐	272 Brian Propp, Minn.	.25
☐	273 Tom Fergus, Vanc.	.25
☐	274 Steve Weeks, LosA. (Otta.)	.25
☐	275 Calle Johansson, Wash.	.25
☐	276 Russ Romaniuk, Winn.	.25
☐	277 Greg Paslawski, Québ.	.25
☐	278 Ed Olczyk, Winn.	.25
☐	279 Rod Langway, Wash.	.50
☐	280 Murray Craven, Hart.	.25
☐	281 Guy Larose, Toro.	.25
☐	282 Paul MacDermid, Wash.	.25
☐	283 Brian Bradley, Toro. (Tamp.)	.25
☐	284 Paul Stanton, Pitt.	.25
☐	285 Kirk McLean (G), Vanc.	.25
☐	286 Andrei Lomakin, Phil.	.25
☐	287 Randy Carlyle, Winn.	.25
☐	288 Donald Audette, Buff.	.50
☐	289 Dan Quinn, Phil.	.25
☐	290 Mike Keane, Mont.	.25
☐	291 Dave Ellett, Toro.	.25
☐	292 Joé Juneau, Bost.	.25
☐	293 Phil Bourque, Pitt.	.25
☐	294 Michal Pivonka, Wash.	.25
☐	295 Fredrik Olausson, Winn.	.25
☐	296 Randy McKay, NJer.	.25
☐	297 Don Beaupré (G), Wash.	.25
☐	298 Stephen Leach, Bost.	.25
☐	299 Teppo Numminen, Winn.	.25
☐	300 Vyacheslav Kozlov, Detr.	.25
☐	301 Kevin Haller, Mont.	.25
☐	302 Jaromir Jagr, Pitt.	1.00
☐	303 Dale Hunter, Wash.	.25
☐	304 Bob Errey, Pitt.	.25
☐	305 Nicklas Lidström, Detr.	.50
☐	306 Bob Essensa, Winn.	.25
☐	307 Sylvain Lefebvre, Mont.	.25
☐	308 Dale Hawerchuk, Buff.	.50
☐	309 Dave Snuggerud, SanJ.	.25
☐	310 Michel Goulet, Chic.	.50
☐	311 Éric Desjardins, Mont.	.25
☐	312 Thomas Steen, Winn.	.25
☐	313 Scott Niedermayer, NJer.	.25
☐	314 Mark Recchi, Phil.	.50
☐	315 Gord Murphy, Bost.	.25
☐	316 Sergio Momesso, Vanc.	.25
☐	317 Todd Elik, Minn.	.25
☐	318 Louie DeBrusk, Edmo.	.25
☐	319 Mike Lalor, Winn.	.25
☐	320 Jamie Leach, Pitt.	.25
☐	321 Darryl Sydor, LosA.	.25
☐	322 Brent Gilchrist, Mont.	.25
☐	323 Alexei Kasatonov, NJer.	.25
☐	324 Rick Tabaracci (G), Winn.	.25
☐	325 Wendel Clark, Toro.	1.00
☐	326 Vladimir Konstantinov, Detr.	.25
☐	327 Randy Gilhen, NYRa.	.25
☐	328 Owen Nolan, Québ.	.50
☐	329 Vincent Damphousse, Edmo.	.50
☐	330 Checklist	.25
☐	331 Yves Racine, Detr.	.25
☐	332 Jacques Cloutier (G), Québ.	.25
☐	333 Greg A. Adams, Vanc.	.25
☐	334 Mike Craig, Minn.	.25
☐	335 Curtis Leschyshyn, Québ.	.25
☐	336 John* McIntyre, LosA.	.25
☐	337 Stéphane Quintal, SLou.	.25
☐	338 Kelly Miller, Wash.	.25
☐	339 Dave Manson, Edmo.	.25
☐	340 Stéphane Matteau, Chic.	.25
☐	341 Christian Ruuttu, Winn.	.25
☐	342 Mike Donnelly, LosA.	.25
☐	343 Eric Weinrich, NJer.	.25
☐	344 Mats Sundin, Québ.	1.00
☐	345 Geoff Courtnall, Vanc.	.25
☐	346 Stéphan Lebeau, Mont.	.25
☐	347 Jeff Beukeboom, NYRa.	.25
☐	348 Jeff Hackett (G), SanJ.	.25
☐	349 Uwe Krupp, NYIs.	.25
☐	350 Igor Larionov, Vanc.	.50
☐	351 Ulf Samuelsson, Pitt.	.25
☐	352 Marty McInnis, NYIs.	.25
☐	353 Peter Ahola, LosA.	.25
☐	354 Mike Richter (G), NYRa.	.50
☐	355 Theoren Fleury, Calg.	.50
☐	356 Dan Lambert, Québ.	.25
☐	357 Brent Ashton, Bost.	.25
☐	358 David Bruce, SanJ.	.25
☐	359 Chris Dahlquist, Minn.	.25
☐	360 Mike Ridley, Wash.	.25
☐	361 Pat Falloon, SanJ.	.25
☐	362 Doug Smail, Québ.	.25
☐	363 Adrien Plavsic, Vanc.	.25
☐	364 Ron L. Wilson, SLou.	.25
☐	365 Derian Hatcher, Minn.	.25
☐	366 Kevin Stevens, Pitt.	.25
☐	367 Rob Blake, LosA.	.50
☐	368 Curtis Joseph (G), SLou.	1.00
☐	369 Tom Fitzgerald, NYIs.	.25
☐	370 Dave Lowry, SLou.	.25
☐	371 J.J. Daigneault, Mont.	.25
☐	372 Jim Hrivnak (G), Wash.	.25
☐	373 Adam Graves, NYRa.	.50
☐	374 Brad May, Buff.	.25
☐	375 Todd Gill, Toro.	.25
☐	376 Paul Ysebaert, Detr.	.25
☐	377 David* Williams, SanJ.	.25
☐	378 Bob Bassen, SLou.	.25
☐	379 Brian Glynn, Edmo.	.25
☐	380 Kris King, NYRa.	.25
☐	381 Rob Pearson, Toro.	.25
☐	382 Marc Bureau, Minn.	.25
☐	383 Jim Paek, Pitt.	.25
☐	384 Tomas Forslund, Calg.	.25
☐	385 Darrin Shannon, Winn.	.25
☐	386 Chris Terreri (G), NJer.	.25
☐	387 Andrew Cassels, Hart.	.25
☐	388 Jayson More, SanJ.	.25
☐	389 Tony Amonte, NYRa.	.50
☐	390 Mark Pederson, Phil.	.25
☐	391 Kevin Miller, Detr. (Wash.)	.25
☐	392 Igor Ulanov, Winn.	.25
☐	393 Kelly Buchberger, Edmo.	.25
☐	394 Mark Fitzpatrick (G), NYIs.	.25
☐	395 Mikhail Tatarinov, Québ.	.25
☐	396 Petr Nedved, Vanc.	.25
☐	397 Jeff Odgers, SanJ.	.25
☐	398 Stéphane Fiset (G), Québ.	.25
☐	399 Mark Tinordi, Minn.	.25
☐	400 Johan Garpenlöv, SanJ.	.25
☐	401 Robert Reichel, Calg.	.25
☐	402 Don Sweeney, Bost.	.25
☐	403 Rob DiMaio, NYIs. (Tamp.)	.25
☐	**404 Bill Lindsay, Québ. RC**	**.50**
☐	405 Stéphane Beauregard (G), Winn.	.25
☐	406 Mike Ricci, Québ.	.25
☐	407 Bobby Holik, Hart.	.25
☐	408 Igor Kravchuk, Chic.	.25
☐	409 Murray Baron, SLou.	.25
☐	410 Troy Gamble (G), Vanc.	.25
☐	411 Cliff Ronning, Vanc.	.25
☐	412 Jeff Reese (G), Calg.	.25
☐	413 Robert Kron, Vanc.	.25
☐	414 Benoît Brunet, Mont.	.25
☐	415 Shawn McEachern, Pitt.	.25
☐	416 Sergei Fedorov, Detr.	1.00
☐	417 Joe Sacco, Toro.	.25
☐	418 Bryan Marchment, Chic.	.25
☐	**419 John LeBlanc, Winn. RC**	**.25**
☐	420 Tim Cheveldae (G), Detr.	.25
☐	421 Claude Lapointe, Québ.	.25
☐	422 Ken Sutton, Buff.	.25
☐	423 Anatoli Semenov, Edmo. (Tamp.)	.25
☐	424 Mike McNeill, Québ.	.25
☐	425 Norm Maciver, Edmo.	.25
☐	426 Sergei Nemchinov, NYRa.	.25
☐	427 Dmitri Khristich, Wash.	.25
☐	428 Dominik Hasek (G), Chic.	3.50
☐	429 Bob McGill, Tamp.	.25
☐	430 Valeri Zelepukin, NJer.	.25
☐	431 Vladimir Ruzicka, Bost.	.25
☐	432 Valeri Kamensky, Québ.	.25
☐	433 Pat MacLeod, SanJ.	.25
☐	434 Glenn Healy (G), NYIs.	.25
☐	435 Patrice Brisebois, Mont.	.25
☐	436 Jamie Baker, Québ.	.25
☐	437 Michel Picard, Hart.	.25
☐	438 Scott Lachance, NYIs.	.25
☐	439 Gilbert Dionne, Mont.	.25
☐	440 AW: Mario Lemieux, Pitt.	10.00
☐	441 Checklist	.25
☐	442 Eric Lindros, Phil.	3.50

1992 - 93 CANADIAN OLYMPIC TEAM

Vladislav Tretiak is the most expensive single at $2-3. Singles start at 50¢.

Complete Set (22 cards): 18.00

	Canada		Canada
☐	Dominic Amodeo	☐	Mark Astley
☐	Adrian Aucoin	☐	Mark Bassen
☐	Eric Bellerose	☐	Mike Brewer
☐	Dany Dubé	☐	Mike Fountain (G)
☐	Keith Morris	☐	Jackson Penney
☐	Garth Premak	☐	Tom Renney
☐	Allain Roy	☐	Stéphane Roy
☐	Trevor Sim	☐	Vladislav Tretiak
☐	Title Card	☐	Mike Myers
☐	Todd Hlushko	☐	Hank Lammens
☐	Derek Laxdal	☐	Derek Mayer

1992 - 93 CANADIAN CARD NEWS

These cards were included as cardboard sheets in the magazine, *Canadian Card News*. Only hockey singles are listed below. Other hockey singles may exist. Cards 6-10 were included in the Fall '92 issue while cards 18-20 were included in the Spring '93 issue. Cards 7 & 9 are football players while card 8 is a baseball player.

	Player
☐	6 Mario Lemieux, Pitt.
☐	10 Brett Hull, SLou.
☐	18 Kirk McLean (G), Vanc.
☐	19 Mark Messier, NYRa.
☐	20 Kevin Stevens, Pitt.

1992 - 93 CANADIAN SPORTSCARD COLLECTOR

Each card on this sheet cut out to the 2 1/2" x 3 1/2" size. The sheet was an insert in CSC presents '92-93 Hockey Card Preview and sells for $4.

	Player	No.	Player
☐	5 R. Hamrlik, Tamp.	☐	6 D. Kasparaitis, NYIs.
☐	7 Cory Stillman, Calg.	☐	8 Mike Rathje, SanJ.
☐	9 D. Kvartalnov, Bost.	☐	10 B. Convery, Toro.

1992 - 93 CLASSIC DRAFT PICKS

Imprint: 1992 Classic Games, Inc.

		Gold	Reg.
	Complete Set (120 cards):	40.00	15.00
	Common Player:	.30	.20
☐	Roman Hamrlik Promo		1.00
☐	Mario Lemieux Promo		6.00
☐	Ray Whitney Promo		1.00
	Player	**Gold**	**Reg.**
☐☐	1 Roman Hamrlik, Cze.	.50	.20
☐☐	2 Alexei Yashin, CIS.	1.50	.50
☐☐	3 Mike Rathje, Medicine Hat	.30	.20
☐☐	4 Darius Kasparaitis, CIS.	.50	.20
☐☐	5 Cory Stillman, Windsor	.50	.20
☐☐	6 Robert Petrovicky, Cze.	.30	.20
☐☐	7 Andrei Nazarov, CIS.	.30	.20
☐☐	8 CL: Cory Stillman, Windsor	.30	.20
☐☐	9 Jason Bowen, Tri-City	.30	.20
☐☐	10 Jason Smith, Regina	.30	.20
☐☐	11 David Wilkie, Kamloops	.30	.20
☐☐	12 Curtis Bowen, Ottawa	.30	.20
☐☐	13 Grant Marshall, Ottawa	.30	.20
☐☐	14 Valeri Bure, Spokane	.50	.20
☐☐	15 Jeff Shantz, Regina	.30	.20
☐☐	16 Justin Hocking, Spokane	.30	.20
☐☐	17 Michael Peca, Sudbury	1.00	.20
☐☐	18 Marc Hussey, Moose Jaw	.30	.20
☐☐	19 Sandy Allan (G), North Bay	.30	.20
☐☐	20 Kirk Maltby, Owen Sound	.30	.20
☐☐	21 Cale Hulse, Portland	.30	.20
☐☐	22 Sylvain Cloutier, Guelph	.30	.20
☐☐	23 Martin Gendron, St. Hyacinthe	.30	.20
☐☐	24 Kevin Smyth, Moose Jaw	.30	.20
☐☐	25 Jason McBain, Portland	.30	.20
☐☐	26 Lee J. Leslie, Prince Albert	.30	.20
☐☐	27 Ralph Intranuovo, S.S. Marie	.30	.20
☐☐	28 Martin Reichel, Freiburg	.30	.20
☐☐	29 Stefan Ustorf, Ger.	.30	.20
☐☐	30 Jarkko Varvio, Fin.	.30	.20
☐☐	31 Jere Lehtinen, Fin.	.30	.20
☐☐	32 Janne Gronvall, Fin.	.30	.20
☐☐	33 Martin Straka, Cze.	.50	.20
☐☐	34 Libor Polasek, Cze.	.30	.20
☐☐	35 Jozef Cierny, Cze.	.30	.20
☐☐	36 Jan Vopat, Cze.	.30	.20
☐☐	37 Ondrej Steiner, Cze.	.30	.20
☐☐	38 Jan Caloun, Cze.	.30	.20
☐☐	39 Petr Hrbek, Cze.	.30	.20
☐☐	40 Richard Smehlik, Cze.	.30	.20
☐☐	41 CL: Sergei Gonchar, CIS	.30	.20
☐☐	42 Sergei Krivokrasov, CIS.	.30	.20
☐☐	43 Sergei Gonchar, CIS.	.30	.20
☐☐	44 Boris Mironov, CIS.	.30	.20
☐☐	45 Denis Metliuk, CIS.	.30	.20
☐☐	46 Sergei Klimovich, CIS.	.30	.20
☐☐	47 Sergei Brylin, CIS.	.30	.20
☐☐	48 Andrei Nikolishin,CIS.	.30	.20
☐☐	49 Alexander Cherbayev, CIS.	.30	.20
☐☐	50 Sergei Zholtok, CIS.	.30	.20
☐☐	51 Vitali Prokhorov, USSR	.30	.20
☐☐	52 Nikolai Borschevsky, CIS.	.30	.20
☐☐	53 Vitali Tomilin, CIS.	.30	.20
☐☐	54 Alexander Alexeyev, Tacoma	.30	.20
☐☐	55 Roman Zolotov, CIS.	.30	.20
☐☐	56 Konstantin Korotkov, CIS.	.30	.20
☐☐	57 Jacques and Daniel Laperrière,	.30	.20
☐☐	58 Martin and Eric Lacroix	.30	.20
☐☐	59 Manon Rhéaume (G)	9.00	3.00
☐☐	60 CL: Hamrlik/ Yashin/ Rathje	.50	.20
☐☐	61 CL: Viktor Kozlov, CIS.	.30	.20
☐☐	62 Victor Kozlov, CIS.	.50	.20
☐☐	63 CL: Denny Felsner, Michigan	.30	.20
☐☐	64 Denny Felsner, Michigan	.30	.20
☐☐	65 Darrin Madeley (G), Lake Superior	.30	.20
☐☐	66 Flashback: Mario Lemieux, Laval	4.50	1.50
☐☐	67 Sandy Moger, Lake Superior	.30	.20
☐☐	68 Dave Karpa, Ferris State	.30	.20
☐☐	69 Martin Jiranek, Bowling Green	.30	.20
☐☐	70 Dwayne Norris, Michigan State	.30	.20
☐☐	71 Michael Stewart, Michigan State	.30	.20
☐☐	72 Joby Messier, Michigan State	.30	.20
☐☐	73 Mike Bales (G), Pro-AM	.30	.20
☐☐	74 Scott Thomas, Clarkson	.30	.20
☐☐	75 Daniel Laperrière, St. Lawrence	.30	.20
☐☐	76 Mike Lappin, St. Lawrence	.30	.20
☐☐	77 Eric Lacroix, St. Lawrence	.30	.20
☐☐	78 Martin Lacroix, St. Lawrence	.30	.20
☐☐	79 Scott LaGrand (G), Boston College	.30	.20
☐☐	80 Jean-Yves Roy, Maine	.30	.20
☐☐	81 Scott Pellerin, Maine	.30	.20
☐☐	82 Rob Gaudreau, Providence	.30	.20
☐☐	83 Mike Boback, Providence	.30	.20
☐☐	84 Dixon Ward, North Dakota	.30	.20
☐☐	85 Jeff McLean, North Dakota	.30	.20
☐☐	86 Dallas Drake, North Michigan	.30	.20
☐☐	87 Bret Hedican, USA.	.30	.20
☐☐	88 Doug Zmolek, Minnesota	.30	.20
☐☐	89 Trent Klatt, Minnesota	.30	.20
☐☐	90 Larry Olimb, Minnesota	.30	.20
☐☐	91 Duane Derksen (G), Wisonsin	.30	.20
☐☐	92 Doug MacDonald, Wisonsin	.30	.20
☐☐	93 CL: Dmitri Kvartalnov, San Diego	.30	.20
☐☐	94 Jim Cummins, Adirondack	.30	.20
☐☐	95 Lonnie Loach, Adirondack	.30	.20
☐☐	96 Keith Jones, Baltimore	.30	.20
☐☐	97 Jason Woolley, Baltimore	.30	.20
☐☐	98 Rob Zamuner, Binghampton	.50	.20
☐☐	99 Brad Werenka, North Michigan	.30	.20
☐☐	100 Brent Grieve, Captial District	.30	.20
☐☐	101 Sean Hill, Fredericton	.30	.20
☐☐	102 Keith Carney, Rochester	.30	.20
☐☐	103 Peter Ciavaglia, Rochester	.30	.20
☐☐	104 David Littman (G), Rochester	.30	.20
☐☐	105 Bill Guerin, USA.	1.00	.20
☐☐	106 Mikhail Kravets, Kansas City	.30	.20
☐☐	107 J.F. Quintin, Kansas City	.30	.20
☐☐	108 Mike Needham, Muskegon	.30	.20
☐☐	109 Jason Ruff, Peoria	.30	.20
☐☐	110 Mike Vukonich, Phoenix	.30	.20
☐☐	111 Shawn McCosh, Phoenix	.30	.20
☐☐	112 Dave Tretowicz, Phoenix	.30	.20
☐☐	113 Todd Harkins, Salt Lake	.30	.20
☐☐	114 Jason Muzzatti (G), Salt Lake	.30	.20
☐☐	115 Paul Kruse, Salt Lake	.30	.20
☐☐	116 Kevin Wortman, Salt Lake	.30	.20
☐☐	117 Sean Burke (G), San Diego	.50	.20
☐☐	118 Keith Gretzky, San Diego	.30	.20
☐☐	119 Ray Whitney, San Diego	.50	.20
☐☐	120 Dmitri Kvartalnov, San Diego	.30	.20

	Insert	MINT
☐	SP1 Mario Lemieux	20.00
☐	Bure Brothers Autograph ✍✍ (#/6000)	40.00
☐	Mario Lemieux Autograph ✍ (#/2000)	150.00

LIMITED PRINT

	Insert Set (10 cards):	7.00
	Insert (#/1500)	**NM-MT**
☐	LP1 Roman Hamrlik, Cze.	.50
☐	LP2 Alexei Yashin, CIS.	5.00
☐	LP3 Mike Rathje, Medicine Hat	1.00
☐	LP4 Darius Kasparaitis, CIS.	2.00
☐	LP5 Cory Stillman, Windsor	2.00
☐	LP6 Dmitri Kvartalnov, San Diego	.50
☐	LP7 David Wilkie	.50
☐	LP8 Curtis Bowen	.50
☐	LP9 Valeri Bure, CIS.	2.00
☐	LP10 Joby Messier	.50

1992 - 93 CLASSIC FOUR SPORT

This 225-card four-sport set features only 75 hockey cards. A 225-card set sells for $20. The most expensive hockey single is Manon Rhéaume at $3-4. Hockey stars sell for 25-75¢. Commons start at 20¢.

	No. Promo	NM-MT
☐	PR3 Roman Hamrlik, Cze. (Promo)	2.00

No.	Player	No.	Player
151	Roman Hamrlik	152	Alexei Yashin
153	Mike Rathje	154	Darius Kasparaitis
155	Cory Stillman	156	Robert Petrovicky
157	Andrei Nazarov	158	Jason Bowen
159	Jason Smith	160	David Wilkie
161	Curtis Bowen	162	Grant Marshall
163	Valeri Bure	164	Jeff Shantz
165	Justin Hocking	166	Michael Peca
167	Marc Hussey	168	Sandy Allen (G)
169	Kirk Maltby	170	Cale Hulse
171	Sylvain Cloutier	172	Martin Gendron
173	Kevin Smyth	174	Jason McBain
175	Lee J. Leslie	176	Ralph Intranuovo
177	Martin Reichel	178	Stefan Ustorf
179	Jarkko Varvio	180	Martin Straka
181	Libor Polasek	182	Jozef Cierny
183	Sergei Krivokrasov	184	Sergei Gonchar
185	Boris Mironov	186	Denis Metliuk
187	Sergei Klimovich	188	Sergei Brylin
189	Andrei Nikolishin	190	A. Cherbayev
191	Vitali Tomilin	192	Sandy Moger
193	Darrin Madeley (G)	194	Denny Felsner
195	Dwayne Norris	196	Joby Messier
197	Michael Stewart	198	Scott Thomas
199	Daniel LaPerriere	200	Martin Lacroix
201	Scott Lagrand (G)	202	Scott Pellerin
203	Jean-Yves Roy	204	Rob Gaudreau
205	Jeff McLean	206	Dallas Drake
207	Doug Zmolek	208	Duane Derksen (G)
209	Jim Cummins	210	Lonnie Loach
211	Rob Zamuner	212	Brad Werenka
213	Brent Grieve	214	Sean Hill
215	Peter Ciavaglia	216	Jason Ruff
217	Shawn McCosh	218	Dave Tretowicz
219	Mike Vukonich	220	Kevin Wortman
221	Jason Muzzatti (G)	222	Dmitri Kvartalnov
223	Ray Whitney	224	M. Rhéaume (G)
225	Viktor Kozlov		

INSERTS

Bonus Card	NM-MT
BC7 Roman Hamrlik	.50
BC8 Valeri Bure	.50
BC9 Dallas Drake	.50
BC10 Dmitri Kvartalnov	.50
BC11 Manon Rhéaume	9.00
BC12 Viktor Kozlov	.50
Limited Print	**NM-MT**
LP22 Roman Hamrlik	1.00
LP23 Mike Rathje	.50
LP24 Valeri Bure	1.00
LP25 Alexei Yashin	3.00
Autograph	**Auto.**
Jason Bowen ✍	3.00
Libor Polásek ✍	3.00
Roman Hamrlik ✍	10.00
Justin Hocking ✍	3.00
Cale Hulse ✍	3.00
Joby Messier ✍	3.00
Boris Mironov ✍	5.00
Sandy Moger ✍	3.00
Dwayne Norris ✍	3.00
Mike Rathje ✍	3.00
Jason Smith ✍	3.00
Cory Stillman ✍	5.00
Doug Zmolek ✍	3.00

1992 - 93 CLASSIC PRO PROSPECTS

The most expensive singles are Manon Rhéaume (each at $2-3) and Patrick Roy ($1-2). NHL stars sell between 25¢-$1.00; all other singles sell at 20-75¢.

Imprint: © 1993 Classic Games, Inc.

Complete Set (150 cards):	15.00
Common Player:	.20
PR1 Steve King Promo	1.00
PR2 Manon Rhéaume Promo	6.00

No.	Player	No.	Player
1	Manon Rhéaume	2	Manon Rhéaume
3	Manon Rhéaume	4	Manon Rhéaume
5	Manon Rhéaume	6	Manon Rhéaume
7	Manon Rhéaume	8	Oleg Petrov
9	Shjon Podein	10	AS: Alexei Kovalev
11	Roman Oksiuta	12	Dave Tomlinson
13	Jason Miller	14	Andrew McKim
15	Dallas Drake	16	Rob Gaudreau
17	Darrin Madeley (G)	18	Scott Pellerin
19	Scott Thomas	20	AS: Chris Tancil
21	Patric Kjellberg	22	Jim Dowd
23	Daniel Gauthier	24	Mark Beaufait
25	AS: Milan Tichy	26	Chris Osgood (G)
27	Charles Poulin	28	Patrick Lebeau
29	Chris Govedaris	30	AS: A. Trefilov (G)
31	Kevin Stevens	32	Dmitri Kvartalnov
33	Patrick Roy (G)	34	Mark Recchi
35	Adam Oates	36	Patrik Augusta
37	Gerry Fleming	38	Sergei Krivokrasov
39	Mike O'Neill (G)	40	AS: D. Madeley (G)
41	Lindsay Vallis	42	Todd Nelson
43	Keith Jones	44	Howie Rosenblatt
45	AS: Jason Ruff	46	Robert Lang
47	André Faust	48	Steve Bancroft
49	Iain Fraser	50	AS: Roman Hamrlik
51	Pierre Sévigny	52	Jeff Levy (G)
53	Len Barrie	54	David Goverde (G)
55	AS: V. Malakhov	56	Scott White
57	Dmitri Motkov	58	Jason Herter
59	Drake Berehowsky	60	AS: Steve King
61	Doug Barrault	62	Martin Hamrlik
63	Kevin Miehm	64	Shaun Van Allen
65	AS: C. Hirsch (G)	66	Dwayne Norris
67	Petr Hrbek	68	Philippe Boucher
69	Denis Chervyakov	70	AS: Sergei Zubov
71	Geoff Sarjeant (G)	72	Les Kuntar (G)
73	Byron Dafoe (G)	74	Checklist
75	AS: A. Andrievski	76	Checklist
77	Brian Sullivan	78	Steve Larouche
79	Denis Chassé	80	AS: Félix Potvin (G)
81	Josef Beranek	82	Ken Klee
83	Jozef Stümpel	84	Andrew Verner (G)
85	AS: Keith Osborne	86	Igor Malykhin
87	Gilbert Dionne	88	Viktor Gordiouk
89	Glen Murray	90	AS: Scott Pellerin
91	T. Söderström (G)	92	Terry Chitaroni
93	Viktor Kozlov	94	M. Shtalenkov (G)
95	Leonid Toropchenko	96	Alex Galchenyuk
97	Anatoli Fedotov	98	Igor Chibirev
99	Keith Gretzky	100	M. Rhéaume (G)
101	Sean Whyte	102	Steve Konowalchuk
103	Richard Borgo	104	Paul DiPietro
105	AS: P. Camback	106	Mike Fountain (G)
107	Jamie Heward	108	David St. Pierre
109	Sean O'Donnell	110	AS: Greg Andrusak
111	D. Rhodes (G)	112	Ted Crowley
113	Chris Taylor	114	Terran Sandwith
115	AS: J. Bélanger	116	Justin Duberman
117	Arturs Irbe (G)	118	Chris LiPuma
119	Mike Torchia (G)	120	AS: N. Andersson
121	Rick Knickle (G)	122	RB: Scott Gruh
123	HL: D. Michayluk	124	Guy Levêque
125	AS: Scott Thomas	126	Travis Green
127	Joby Messier	128	Victor Ignatjev
129	Brad Tiley	130	AS: G. Panteleyev
133	Marty McInnis	134	Ed Ronan
131	V. Butsayev	132	Danny Lorenz (G)
135	AS: Vy. Kozlov	136	Kevin St. Jacques
137	Pavel Kostichkin	138	Mike Hurlbut
139	Tomas Forslund	140	AS: Rob Gaudreau
141	Shawn Heaphy	142	Radek Hamr
143	Jaroslav Otevrel	144	Keith Redmond
145	AS: Tom Pederson	146	Jaroslav Modry
147	Darren McCarty	148	Terry Yake
149	Ivan Droppa	150	Oilers trio

Autograph	Auto.
Dmitri Kvartalnov Autograph ✍	3.00
Manon Rhéaume Autograph ✍	30.00

BONUS CARDS

Insert Set (20 cards):	35.00

Player	NM-MT
BC1 Alexei Kovalev, Binghampton	6.00
BC2 Andrei Trefilov (G), Salt Lake	.50
BC3 Roman Hamrlik, Atlanta	2.00
BC4 Vladimir Malakov, Capital District	1.50
BC5 Corey Hirsch (G), Binghampton	.50
BC6 Sergei Zubov, Binghampton	2.00
BC7 Félix Potvin (G)	6.00
BC8 Tommy Söderström (G), Hershey	.50
BC9 Victor Kozlov, Russia	3.00
BC10 Manon Rhéaume (G)	12.00
BC11 Jesse Bélanger	.50
BC12 Rick Knickle (G), San Diego	.50
BC13 Joby Messier, Binghampton	.50
BC14 Viachealav Butsayev	.50
BC15 Tomas Forslund, Salt Lake	.50
BC16 Jozef Stümpel, Providence	2.00
BC17 Dmitri Kvartlanov	.50
BC18 Adam Oates	4.00
BC19 Dallas Drake	.50
BC20 Mark Recchi, Muskegon	4.00

LIMITED PRINT

Insert Set (5 cards):	15.00
Player	**NM-MT**
LP1 Manon Rhéaume (G)	10.00
LP2 Alexei Kovalev	7.50
LP3 Rob Gaudreau, Kansas City	.50
LP4 Viktor Kozlov, Russia	2.50
LP5 Dallas Drake, Adirondack	1.00

1992 - 93 DURIVAGE / DIANA - PANINI STICKERS

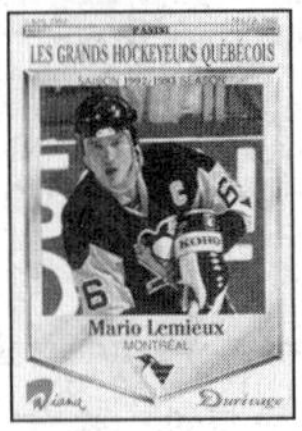

Complete Set (50 stickers):	20.00
Album:	3.00
Player	**NM-MT**
1 Guy Carbonneau, Mont.	.50
2 Lucien DeBlois, Winn.	.50
3 Benoît Hogue, NYIs.	.50
4 Steve Kasper, Phil.	.50
5 Mike Krushelnyski, Toro.	.50
6 Claude Lapointe, Québ.	.50
7 Stéphan Lebeau, Mont.	.50
8 Mario Lemieux, Pitt.	5.00
9 Stéphane Morin, Québ.	.50
10 Denis Savard, Mont.	.50
11 Pierre Turgeon, NYIs.	.50
12 Kevin Dineen, Phil.	.50
13 Gord Donnelly, Buff.	.50
14 Claude Lemieux, NJer.	.50
15 Jocelyn Lemieux, Chic.	.50
16 Daniel Marois, NYIs.	.50
17 Scott Mellanby, Edmo.	.50
18 Stéphane Richer, NJer.	.50
19 Benoît Brunet, Mont.	.50
20 Vincent Damphousse, Mont.	1.00
21 Gilbert Dionne, Mont.	.50
22 Gaétan Duchesne, Minn.	.50
23 Bob Errey, Pitt.	.50
24 Michel Goulet, Chic.	.50
25 Mike Hough, Québ.	.50
26 Sergio Momesso, Vanc.	.50
27 Mario Roberge, Mont.	.50
28 Luc Robitaille, LosA.	1.00
29 Sylvain Turgeon, Otta.	.50
30 Marc Bergevin, Tamp.	.50
31 Raymond Bourque, Bost.	2.00
32 Patrice Brisebois, Mont.	.50
33 Jeff Chychrun, Pitt.	.50
34 Sylvain Côté, Wash.	.50
35 J.J. Daigneault, Mont.	.50
36 Éric Desjardins, Mont.	.50
37 Gord Dineen, Otta.	.50
38 Steve Duchesne, Québ.	.50
39 Donald Dufresne, Mont.	.50
40 Steven Finn, Québ.	.50
41 Garry Galley, Phil.	.50
42 Kevin Lowe, Edmo.	.50
43 Michel Petit, Calg.	.50
44 Normand Rochefort, NYRa.	.50
45 Randy Velischek, Québ.	.50
46 Jacques Cloutier (G), Québ.	.50
47 Stéphane Fiset (G), Québ.	.50
48 Réjean Lemelin, Bost.	.50
49 André Racicot (G), Mont.	.50
50 Patrick Roy (G), Mont.	5.00
Autograph	**Auto.**
Patrick Roy (G), Mont. ✍	125.00

1992 - 93 FLEER ULTRA

Imprint: © 1992 FLEER CORP.

Series One Set (250 cards):	30.00
Series Two Set (200 cards):	25.00
Common Player:	.20
Player	**FU**
1 Brent Ashton, Bost.	.20
2 Raymond Bourque, Bost.	.50
3 Stephen Heinze, Bost. [Rookie]	.20
4 Joé Juneau, Bost. [Rookie]	.20
5 Stephen Leach, Bost.	.20
6 Andy Moog (G), Bost.	.20
7 Cam Neely, Bost.	.50
8 Adam Oates, Bost.	.20
9 Dave Poulin, Bost.	.20
10 Vladimir Ruzicka, Bost.	.20
11 Glen Wesley, Bost.	.20
12 Dave Andreychuk, Buff.	.20
13 Keith Carney, Buff. [Rookie] RC	**.50**
14 Tom Draper (G), Buff.	.20
15 Dale Hawerchuk, Buff.	.20
16 Pat LaFontaine, Buff.	.20
17 Brad May, Buff.	.20
18 Alexander Mogilny, Buff.	.20
19 Mike Ramsey, Buff.	.20
20 Ken Sutton, Buff.	.20
21 Theoren Fleury, Calg.	.20
22 Gary Leeman, Calg.	.20
23 Al MacInnis, Calg.	.20
24 Sergei Makarov, Calg.	.20
25 Joe Nieuwendyk, Calg.	.20
26 Joel Otto, Calg.	.20
27 Paul Ranheim, Calg.	.20
28 Robert Reichel, Calg.	.20
29 Gary Roberts, Calg.	.20
30 Gary Suter, Calg.	.20
31 Mike Vernon (G), Calg.	.20
32 Ed Belfour (G), Chic.	.50
33 Rob (Jr.) Brown, Chic.	.20
34 Chris Chelios, Chic.	.20
35 Michel Goulet, Chic.	.20
36 Dirk Graham, Chic.	.20
37 Mike Hudson, Chic.	.20
38 Igor Kravchuk, Chic.	.20
39 Steve Larmer, Chic.	.20
40 Dean McAmmond, Chic. [Rookie] RC	**.50**
41 Jeremy Roenick, Chic.	.20
42 J. Steve Smith, Chic.	.20
43 Brent Sutter, Chic.	.20
44 Shawn Burr, Detr.	.20
45 Jimmy Carson, Detr.	.20
46 Tim Cheveldae (G), Detr.	.20
47 Dino Ciccarelli, Detr.	.20
48 Sergei Fedorov, Detr.	.50
49 Vladimir Konstantinov, Detr.	.20
50 Vyacheslav Kozlov, Detr. [Rookie]	.20
51 Nicklas Lidström, Detr.	.20
52 Brad McCrimmon, Detr.	.20
53 Bob Probert, Detr.	.20
54 Paul Ysebaert, Detr.	.20
55 Steve Yzerman, Detr.	1.00
56 Josef Beránek, Edmo.	.20
57 Shayne Corson, Mont. (Edmo.)	.20
58 Brian Glynn, Edmo.	.20
59 Petr Klima, Edmo.	.20
60 Kevin Lowe, Edmo.	.20
61 Norm Maciver, Edmo.	.20
62 Dave Manson, Edmo.	.20
63 Joe Murphy, Edmo.	.20
64 Bernie Nicholls, Edmo.	.20
65 Bill Ranford (G), Edmo.	.20
66 Craig Simpson, Edmo.	.20
67 Esa Tikkanen, Edmo.	.20
68 Sean Burke (G), Hart.	.20
69 Adam Burt, Hart.	.20
70 Andrew Cassels, Hart.	.20
71 Murray Craven, Hart.	.20
72 John Cullen, Hart.	.20
73 Randy Cunneyworth, Hart.	.20
74 Tim Kerr, Hart.	.20
75 Geoff Sanderson, Hart.	.20
76 Eric Weinrich, NJer. (Hart.)	.20
77 Zarley Zalapski, Hart.	.20
78 Peter Ahola, LosA.	.20
79 Rob Blake, LosA.	.20
80 Paul Coffey, LosA.	.20
81 Mike Donnelly, LosA.	.20
82 Tony Granato, LosA.	.20
83 Wayne Gretzky, LosA.	2.00
84 Kelly Hrudey (G), LosA.	.20
85 Jari Kurri, LosA.	.50
86 Corey Millen, LosA.	.20
87 Luc Robitaille, LosA.	.20
88 Tomas Sandström, LosA.	.20
89 Neal Broten, Minn.	.20
90 Jon Casey (G), Minn.	.20
91 Russ Courtnall, Mont. (Minn.)	.20
92 Ulf Dahlén, Minn.	.20
93 Todd Elik, Minn.	.20
94 Dave Gagner, Minn.	.20
95 Jim* Johnson, Minn.	.20
96 Mike Modano, Minn.	.50
97 Bobby Smith, Minn.	.20
98 Mark Tinordi, Minn.	.20
99 Darcy Wakaluk (G), Minn.	.20
100 Brian Bellows, Minn. (Mont.)	.20
101 Benoît Brunet, Mont.	.20
102 Guy Carbonneau, Mont.	.20
103 Vincent Damphousse, Edmo. (Mont.)	.20
104 Éric Desjardins, Mont.	.20
105 Gilbert Dionne, Mont.	.20
106 Mike Keane, Mont.	.20
107 Kirk Muller, Mont.	.20
108 Patrick Roy (G), Mont.	1.50
109 Denis Savard, Mont.	.20
110 Mathieu Schneider, Mont.	.20
111 Brian Skrudland, Mont.	.20
112 Tom Chorske, NJer.	.20
113 Zdeno Ciger, NJer.	.20
114 Claude Lemieux, NJer.	.20
115 John MacLean, NJer.	.20
116 Scott Niedermayer, NJer. [Rookie]	.20
117 Stéphane Richer, NJer.	.20
118 Peter Stastny, NJer.	.20
119 Scott Stevens, NJer.	.20
120 Chris Terreri (G), NJer.	.20
121 Kevin Todd, NJer.	.20
122 Valeri Zelepukin, NJer.	.20
123 Ray Ferraro, NYIs.	.20
124 Mark Fitzpatrick (G), NYIs.	.20
125 Patrick Flatley, NYIs.	.20
126 Glenn Healy (G), NYIs.	.20
127 Benoît Hogue, NYIs.	.20
128 Derek King, NYIs.	.20
129 Uwe Krupp, NYIs.	.20
130 Scott Lachance, NYIs. [Rookie]	.20
131 Steve Thomas, NYIs.	.20
132 Pierre Turgeon, NYIs.	.20
133 Tony Amonte, NYRa.	.20
134 Paul Broten, NYRa.	.20
135 Mike Gartner, NYRa.	.20
136 Adam Graves, NYRa.	.20
137 Alexei Kovalev, NYRa. [Rookie]	.50
138 Brian Leetch, NYRa.	.20
139 Mark Messier, NYRa.	.50
140 Sergei Nemchinov, NYRa.	.20
141 James Patrick, NYRa.	.20
142 Mike Richter (G), NYRa.	.20
143 Darren Turcotte, NYRa.	.20
144 John Vanbiesbrouck (G), NYRa.	.20
145 Dominic Lavoie, Otta.	.20
146 Lonnie Loach, Otta. [Rookie] RC	**.50**
147 Andrew McBain, Otta.	.20
148 Darren Rumble, Otta. [Rookie] RC	**.50**
149 Sylvain Turgeon, Otta.	.20
150 Peter Sidorkiewicz (G), Hart. (Otta.)	.20
151 Brian Benning, Phil.	.20
152 Rod Brind'Amour, Phil.	.20
153 Viacheslav Butsayev, Phil. [Rookie] RC	**.20**
154 Kevin Dineen, Phil.	.20
155 Pelle Eklund, Phil.	.20
156 Garry Galley, Phil.	.20
157 Eric Lindros, Phil. [Rookie]	1.00
158 Mark Recchi, Phil.	.20
159 Dominic Roussel (G), Phil. [Rookie]	.20
160 Tommy Söderström, Phil. [Rookie] RC	**.50**
161 Dmitry Yushkevich, Phil. [Rookie] RC	**1.0**

☐ 162 Tom Barrasso (G), Pitt. .20
☐ 163 Ron Francis, Pitt. .20
☐ 164 Jaromir Jagr, Pitt. .50
☐ 165 Mario Lemieux, Pitt. 1.50
☐ 166 Joe Mullen, Pitt. .20
☐ 167 Larry Murphy, Pitt. .20
☐ 168 Jim Paek, Pitt. .20
☐ 169 Kjell Samuelsson, Pitt. .20
☐ 170 Ulf Samuelsson, Pitt. .20
☐ 171 Kevin Stevens, Pitt. .20
☐ 172 Rick Tocchet, Pitt. .20
☐ 173 Alexei Gusarov, Québ. .20
☐ 174 Ron Hextall (G), Phil. (Québ.) .20
☐ 175 Mike Hough, Québ. .20
☐ 176 Claude Lapointe, Québ. .20
☐ 177 Owen Nolan, Québ. .20
☐ 178 Mike Ricci, Phil. (Québ.) .20
☐ 179 Joe Sakic, Québ. .50
☐ 180 Mats Sundin, Québ. .50
☐ 181 Mikhail Tatarinov, Québ. .20
☐ 182 Bob Bassen, SLou. .20
☐ 183 Jeff R. Brown, SLou. .20
☐ 184 Garth Butcher, SLou. .20
☐ 185 Paul Cavallini, SLou. .20
☐ 186 Brett Hull, SLou. .50
☐ 187 Craig Janney, SLou. .20
☐ 188 Curtis Joseph (G), SLou. .50
☐ 189 Brendan Shanahan, SLou. .50
☐ 190 Ron Sutter, SLou. .20
☐ 191 David Bruce, SanJ. .20
☐ 192 Dale Craigwell, SanJ. .20
☐ 193 Dean Evason, SanJ. .20
☐ 194 Pat Falloon, SanJ. .20
☐ 195 Jeff Hackett (G), SanJ. .20
☐ 196 Kelly Kisio, SanJ. .20
☐ 197 Brian Lawton, SanJ. .20
☐ 198 Neil Wilkinson, SanJ. .20
☐ 199 Doug Wilson, SanJ. .20
☐ 200 Marc Bergevin, Tamp. .20
☐ **201 Roman Hamrlik, Tamp. [Rookie] RC 1.00**
☐ 202 Pat Jablonski (G), Tamp. .20
☐ 203 Michel Mongeau, Tamp. .20
☐ 204 Peter Taglianetti, Pitt. (Tamp.) .20
☐ 205 Steve Tuttle, Tamp. .20
☐ 206 Wendell Young (G), Pitt. (Tamp.) .20
☐ 207 Glenn Anderson, Toro. .20
☐ 208 Wendel Clark, Toro. .20
☐ 209 Dave Ellett, Toro. .20
☐ 210 Grant Fuhr (G), Toro. .20
☐ 211 Doug Gilmour, Toro. .20
☐ 212 Jamie Macoun, Toro. .20
☐ 213 Félix Potvin (G), Toro. [Rookie] .20
☐ 214 Bob Rouse, Toro. .20
☐ 215 Joe Sacco, Toro. .20
☐ 216 Peter Zezel, Toro. .20
☐ 217 Greg A. Adams, Vanc. .20
☐ 218 Dave Babych, Vanc. .20
☐ 219 Pavel Bure, Vanc. .20
☐ 220 Geoff Courtnall, Vanc. .20
☐ 221 Doug Lidster, Vanc. .20
☐ 222 Trevor Linden, Vanc. .20
☐ 223 Jyrki Lumme, Vanc. .20
☐ 224 Kirk McLean (G), Vanc. .20
☐ 225 Sergio Momesso, Vanc. .20
☐ 226 Petr Nedved, Vanc. .20
☐ 227 Cliff Ronning, Vanc. .20
☐ 228 Jim Sandlak, Vanc. .20
☐ 229 Don Beaupré (G), Wash. .20
☐ 230 Peter Bondra, Wash. .20
☐ 231 Kevin Hatcher, Wash. .20
☐ 232 Dale Hunter, Wash. .20
☐ 233 Al Iafrate, Wash. .20
☐ 234 Calle Johansson, Wash. .20
☐ 235 Dmitri Khristich, Wash. .20
☐ 236 Kelly Miller, Wash. .20
☐ 237 Michal Pivonka, Wash. .20
☐ 238 Mike Ridley, Wash. .20
☐ 239 Luciano Borsato, Winn. .20
☐ 240 Bob Essensa, Winn. .20
☐ 241 Phil Housley, Winn. .20
☐ 242 Troy Murray, Winn. .20
☐ 243 Teppo Numminen, Winn. .20
☐ 244 Fredrik Olausson, Winn. .20
☐ 245 Ed Olczyk, Winn. .20
☐ 246 Darrin Shannon, Winn. .20
☐ 247 Thomas Steen, Winn. .20
☐ 248 Checklist .20
☐ 249 Checklist .20
☐ 250 Checklist .20
☐ 251 Ted Donato, Bost. [Rookie] .20
☐ **252 Dmitri Kvartalnov, Bost. [Rookie] RC .50**
☐ 253 Gord Murphy, Bost. .20
☐ **254 Grigori Panteleev, Bost. [Rookie] RC .50**
☐ 255 Gord** Roberts, Bost. .20
☐ 256 David Shaw, Bost. .20
☐ 257 Don Sweeney, Bost. .20
☐ 258 Doug Bodger, Buff. .20
☐ 259 Gord Donnelly, Buff. .20
☐ **260 Yuri Khmylev, Buff. [Rookie] RC .20**
☐ 261 Daren Puppa (G), Buff. .20
☐ **262 Richard Smehlik, Buff. [Rookie] RC .50**
☐ 263 Petr* Svoboda, Buff. .20
☐ 264 Bob Sweeney, Buff. .20
☐ 265 Randy Wood, Buff. .20
☐ **266 Kevin Dahl, Calg. [Rookie] RC .50**
☐ 267 Chris Dahlquist, Calg. .20
☐ 268 Roger Johansson, Calg. .20
☐ 269 Chris Lindberg, Calg. [Rookie] .20
☐ 270 Frantisek Musil, Calg. .20
☐ 271 Ronnie Stern, Calg. .20
☐ 272 Carey Wilson, Calg. .20
☐ 273 Dave Christian, Chic. .20
☐ 274 Karl Dykhuis, Chic. [Rookie] .20
☐ 275 Greg Gilbert, Chic. .20
☐ 276 Sergei Krivokrasov, Chic. [Rookie] .20
☐ 277 Frantisek Kucera, Chic. .20
☐ 278 Bryan Marchment, Chic. .20
☐ 279 Stéphane Matteau, Chic. .20
☐ 280 Brian Noonan, Chic. .20
☐ 281 Christian Ruuttu, Chic. .20
☐ 282 Steve Chiasson, Detr. .20
☐ 283 Dino Ciccarelli, Detr. .20
☐ 284 Gerard Gallant, Detr. .20
☐ 285 Mark Howe, Detr. .20
☐ 286 Keith Primeau, Detr. .20
☐ 287 Yves Racine, Detr. .20
☐ 288 Vincent Riendeau (G), Detr. .20
☐ 289 Ray Sheppard, Detr. .20
☐ 290 Mike Sillinger, Detr. [Rookie] .20
☐ 291 Kelly Buchberger, Edmo. .20
☐ 292 Shayne Corson, Edmo. .20
☐ 293 Brent Gilchrist, Edmo. .20
☐ 294 Craig MacTavish, Edmo. .20
☐ 295 Scott Mellanby, Edmo. .20
☐ 296 Craig Muni, Edmo. .20
☐ 297 Luke Richardson, Edmo. .20
☐ 298 Ron Tugnutt, Edmo. .20
☐ 299 Shaun Van Allen, Edmo. [Rookie] .20
☐ 300 Steve Konroyd, Hart. .20
☐ 301 Nick Kypreos, Hart. .20
☐ **302 Robert Petrovicky, Hart. [Rookie] RC .50**
☐ 303 Frank Pietrangelo, Hart. .20
☐ 304 Patrick Poulin, Hart. [Rookie] .20
☐ 305 Pat Verbeek, Hart. .20
☐ 306 Eric Weinrich, Hart. .20
☐ **307 Jim Hiller, LosA. [Rookie] RC .50**
☐ 308 Charlie Huddy, LosA. .20
☐ 309 Lonnie Loach, LosA. [Rookie] .20
☐ 310 Marty McSorley, LosA. .20
☐ 311 Robb Stauber (G), LosA. [Rookie] .20
☐ 312 Darryl Sydor, LosA. [Rookie] .20
☐ 313 Dave (Stitch) Taylor, LosA. .20
☐ 314 Alexei Zhitnik, LosA. [Rookie] .20
☐ 315 Shane Churla, Minn. .20
☐ 316 Russ Courtnall, Minn. .20
☐ 317 Mike Craig, Minn. .20
☐ 318 Gaétan Duchesne, Minn. .20
☐ 319 Derian Hatcher, Minn. .20
☐ 320 Craig Ludwig, Minn. .20
☐ **321 Richard Matvichuk, Minn. [Rookie] RC 1.00**
☐ 322 Mike McPhee, Minn. .20
☐ **323 Tommy Sjödin, Minn. [Rookie] RC .50**
☐ 324 Brian Bellows, Mont. .20
☐ 325 Patrice Brisebois, Mont. .20
☐ 326 J.J. Daigneault, Mont. .20
☐ 327 Kevin Haller, Mont. .20
☐ **328 Sean Hill, Mont. [Rookie] RC .50**
☐ 329 Stéphan Lebeau, Mont. .20
☐ 330 John LeClair, Mont. .20
☐ 331 Lyle Odelein, Mont. .20
☐ 332 André Racicot (G), Mont. .20
☐ **333 Ed Ronan, Mont. [Rookie] RC .50**
☐ 334 Craig Billington (G), NJer. .20
☐ 335 Ken Daneyko, NJer. .20
☐ 336 Bruce Driver, NJer. .20
☐ 337 Viacheslav Fetisov, NJer. .20
☐ **338 Bill Guerin, NJer. [Rookie] RC 1.00**
☐ 339 Bobby Holik, NJer. .20
☐ 340 Alexei Kasatonov, NJer. .20
☐ 341 Alexander Semak, NJer. .20
☐ 342 Tom Fitzgerald, NYIs. .20
☐ **343 Travis Green, NYIs. [Rookie] RC 1.00**
☐ 344 Darius Kasparaitis, NYIs. [Rookie] .20
☐ **345 Danny Lorenz (G), NYIs. [Rookie] RC .50**
☐ 346 Vladimir Malakhov, NYIs. [Rookie] .20
☐ 347 Marty McInnis, NYIs. [Rookie] .20
☐ 348 Brian Mullen, NYIs. .20
☐ 349 Jeff Norton, NYIs. .20
☐ 350 David Volek, NYIs. .20
☐ 351 Jeff Beukeboom, NYRa. .20
☐ 352 Phil Bourque, NYRa. .20
☐ 353 Paul Broten, NYRa. .20
☐ 354 Mark Hardy, NYRa. .20
☐ **355 Steven King, NYRa. [Rookie] RC .20**
☐ 356 Kevin Lowe, NYRa. .20
☐ 357 Ed Olczyk, NYRa. .20
☐ 358 Doug Weight, NYRa. .20
☐ **359 Sergei Zubov, NYRa. [Rookie] RC .50**
☐ 360 Jamie Baker, Otta. .20
☐ 361 Daniel Berthiaume (G), Otta. .20
☐ **362 Chris Luongo, Otta. [Rookie] RC .50**
☐ 363 Norm Maciver, Otta. .20
☐ 364 Brad Marsh, Otta. .20
☐ 365 Mike Peluso, Otta. .20
☐ 366 Brad Shaw, Otta. .20
☐ 367 Peter Sidorkiewicz (G), Otta. .20
☐ 368 Keith Acton, Phil. .20
☐ 369 Stéphane Beauregard (G), Phil. .20
☐ 370 Terry Carkner, Phil. .20
☐ 371 Brent Fedyk, Phil. .20
☐ 372 Andrei Lomakin, Phil. .20
☐ **373 Ryan McGill, Phil. [Rookie] RC .50**
☐ 374 Ric Nattress, Phil. .20
☐ 375 Greg Paslawski, Phil. .20
☐ 376 Peter Ahola, Pitt. .20
☐ 377 Jeff Daniels, Pitt. [Rookie] .20
☐ 378 Troy Loney, Pitt. .20
☐ 379 Shawn McEachern, Pitt. [Rookie] .20
☐ **380 Mike Needham, Pitt. [Rookie] RC .50**
☐ 381 Paul Stanton, Pitt. .20
☐ **382 Martin Straka, Pitt. [Rookie] RC 1.50**
☐ 383 Ken Wregget (G), Pitt. .20
☐ 384 Steve Duchesne, Québ. .20
☐ 385 Ron Hextall (G), Québ. .20
☐ 386 Kerry Huffman, Québ. .20
☐ **387 Andrei Kovalenko, Québ. [Rookie] RC .20**
☐ **388 Bill Lindsay, Québ. [Rookie] RC .50**
☐ 389 Mike Ricci, Québ. .20
☐ 390 Martin Rucinsky, Québ. [Rookie] .20
☐ 391 Scott A. Young, Québ. .20
☐ 392 Philippe Bozon, SLou. [Rookie] .20
☐ 393 Nelson Emerson, SLou. .20
☐ **394 Guy Hebert (G), SLou. [Rookie] RC 1.00**
☐ 395 Igor Korolev, SLou. [Rookie] .20
☐ 396 Kevin Miller, SLou. .20
☐ **397 Vitali Prokhorov, SLou. [Rookie] RC .50**
☐ 398 Rich Sutter, SLou. .20
☐ 399 John Carter, SanJ. .20
☐ 400 Johan Garpenlöv, SanJ. .20
☐ 401 Arturs Irbe (G), SanJ. [Rookie] .20
☐ 402 Sandis Ozolinsh, SanJ. [Rookie] .20
☐ **403 Tom Pederson, SanJ. [Rookie] RC .50**
☐ 404 Michel Picard, SanJ. .20
☐ **405 Doug Zmolek, SanJ. [Rookie] RC .20**
☐ 406 Mikael Andersson, Tamp. .20
☐ 407 Bob Beers, Tamp. .20
☐ 408 Brian Bradley, Tamp. .20
☐ 409 Adam Creighton, Tamp. .20
☐ 410 Doug Crossman, Tamp. .20
☐ 411 Ken (Jr.) Hodge, Tamp. .20
☐ **412 Chris Kontos, Tamp. RC .50**
☐ 413 Rob Ramage, Tamp. .20
☐ 414 John Tucker, Tamp. .20
☐ **415 Rob Zamuner, Tamp. [Rookie] RC 1.00**
☐ 416 Ken Baumgartner, Toro. .20
☐ 417 Drake Berehowsky, Toro. [Rookie] .20
☐ **418 Nikolai Borschevsky, Toro. [Rookie] RC .50**
☐ 419 John Cullen, Toro. .20
☐ 420 Mike Foligno, Toro. .20
☐ 421 Mike Krushelnyski, Toro. .20
☐ 422 Dmitri Mironov, Toro. [Rookie] .20
☐ 423 Rob Pearson, Toro. .20
☐ 424 Gerald Diduck, Vanc. .20
☐ 425 Robert Dirk, Vanc. .20
☐ 426 Tom Fergus, Vanc. .20
☐ 427 Gino Odjick, Vanc. .20
☐ 428 Adrien Plavsic, Vanc. .20
☐ 429 Anatoli Semenov, Vanc. .20
☐ 430 Jiří Šlégr, Vanc. [Rookie] .20
☐ **431 Dixon Ward, Vanc. [Rookie] RC .50**
☐ 432 Paul Cavallini, Wash. .20
☐ 433 Sylvain Côté, Wash. .20
☐ 434 Pat Elynuik, Wash. .20
☐ 435 Jim Hrivnak (G), Wash. .20
☐ **436 Keith Jones, Wash. [Rookie] RC .50**
☐ **437 Steve Konowalchuk, Wash. [Rookie] RC 1.00**
☐ 438 Todd Krygier, Wash. .20
☐ 439 Paul MacDermid, Wash. .20
☐ **440 Sergei Bautin, Winn. [Rookie] RC .50**
☐ 441 Evgeny Davydov, Winn. [Rookie] .20
☐ 442 John Druce, Winn. .20
☐ 443 Troy Murray, Winn. .20
☐ 444 Teemu Selänne, Winn. [Rookie] .50
☐ 445 Rick Tabaracci (G), Winn. .20
☐ 446 Keith Tkachuk, Winn. [Rookie] .50
☐ 447 Alexei Zhamnov, Winn. [Rookie] .20
☐ 448 Checklist .20
☐ 449 Checklist .20
☐ 450 Checklist .20

ALL-STARS

Series One Insert Set (12 cards): 20.00

	Player	NM-MT
☐	1 Paul Coffey, Error	1.00
☐	2 Raymond Bourque	2.00
☐	3 Patrick Roy (G)	6.00
☐	4 Mario Lemieux	6.00
☐	5 Kevin Stevens, Error	.75
☐	6 Jaromir Jagr	2.00
☐	7 Chris Chelios	1.00
☐	8 Al MacInnis	.75
☐	9 Ed Belfour, (G)	2.00
☐	10 Wayne Gretzky	8.00
☐	11 Luc Robitaille	1.00
☐	12 Brett Hull	2.00

AWARD WINNERS

Series One Insert Set (10 cards): 25.00

	Player	NM-MT
☐	1 Mark Messier, NHL Awards (NYRa.)	2.00
☐	2 Brian Leetch, NHL Awards (NYRa.)	1.00
☐	3 Guy Carbonneau, NHL Awards (Mont.)	.75
☐	4 Patrick Roy (G), NHL Awards (Mont.)	7.00
☐	5 Mario Lemieux, NHL Awards (Pitt.)	7.00
☐	6 Wayne Gretzky, NHL Awards (LosA.)	10.00
☐	7 Mark Fitzpatrick (G), NHL Awards (NYIs.)	.75
☐	8 Raymond Bourque, NHL Awards (Bost.)	3.00
☐	9 Pavel Bure, NHL Awards (Vanc.)	2.00
☐	10 Mark Messier, NHL Awards (NYRa.)	2.00

ULTRA IMPORTS

Series Two Insert Set (25 cards): 20.00

	Player	NM-MT
☐	1 Nikolai Borschevsky, Toro.	.25
☐	2 Pavel Bure, Vanc.	3.00
☐	3 Sergei Fedorov, Detr.	3.00
☐	4 Roman Hamrlik, Tamp.	.25
☐	5 Arturs Irbe (G), SanJ.	1.00
☐	6 Jaromir Jagr, Pitt.	3.00
☐	7 Dmitri Khristich, Wash.	.25
☐	8 Petr Klima, Edmo.	.25
☐	9 Andrei Kovalenko, Québ.	.25
☐	10 Alexei Kovalev, NYRa.	4.00
☐	11 Jari Kurri, LosA.	3.00
☐	12 Dmitri Kvartalnov, Bost.	.25
☐	13 Nicklas Lidström, Detr.	2.00
☐	14 Vladimir Malakhov, NYIs.	.25
☐	15 Dmitri Mironov, Toro.	.25
☐	16 Alexander Mogilny, Buff.	1.00
☐	17 Petr Nedved, Vanc.	1.00
☐	18 Fredrik Olausson, Winn.	.25
☐	19 Sandis Ozolinsh, SanJ.	.25
☐	20 Ulf Samuelsson, Pitt.	.25
☐	21 Teemu Selänne, Winn.	3.00
☐	22 Richard Smehlik, Buff.	.25
☐	23 Tommy Söderström, Phil.	.25
☐	24 Peter Stastny, NJer.	2.00
☐	25 Mats Sundin, Québ.	3.00

PERFORMANCE HIGHLIGHTS

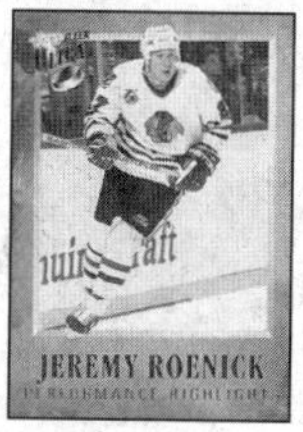

Series One Insert Set (12 cards): 15.00

	Player	NM-MT
☐	1 Jeremy Roenick	1.00
☐	2 Jeremy Roenick	1.00
☐	3 Jeremy Roenick	1.00
☐	4 Jeremy Roenick	1.00
☐	5 Jeremy Roenick	1.00
☐	6 Jeremy Roenick	1.00
☐	7 Jeremy Roenick	1.00
☐	8 Jeremy Roenick	1.00
☐	9 Jeremy Roenick	1.00
☐	10 Jeremy Roenick	1.00
☐	11 Jeremy Roenick Redeemed	5.00
☐	12 Jeremy Roenick Redeemed	5.00
	Autograph	**Auto.**
☐	Jeremy Roenick ✍	125.00

ULTRA ROOKIES

Series One Insert Set (8 cards): 8.00

	Player	NM-MT
☐	1 Tony Amonte, NYRa.	2.00
☐	2 Donald Audette, Buff.	1.00
☐	3 Pavel Bure, Vanc.	3.00
☐	4 Gilbert Dionne, Mont.	.50
☐	5 Nelson Emerson, SLou.	.50
☐	6 Pat Falloon, SanJ.	.50
☐	7 Nicklas Lidström, Detr.	2.00
☐	8 Kevin Todd, NJer.	.50

1992 - 93 FLEER ULTRA THE COLLECTION

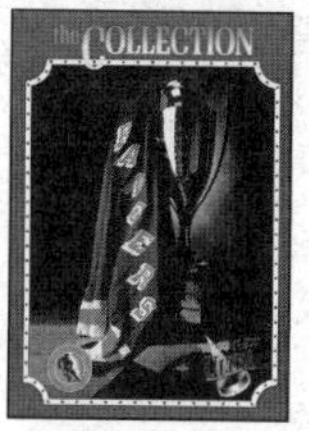

We do have have full information on this set.

Description

☐
☐
☐
☐
☐
☐
☐
☐
☐
☐ 9 Andy Bathgate Collection

1992 - 93 FUTURE TRENDS CANADA CUP '76

These cards were produced by 7th Inning Sketch. Cards 1-101 are part of the 1991-92 Future Trends Canada '72 series. The most expensive singles are Bobby Orr at $1.00-1.50, Vladislav Tretiak at 50¢-$1.00, and card 176 (Clarke and Pierre Trudeau) at 50¢-$1.00. Singles start at 20¢; regional stars sell at 40-75¢.

Imprint: 1992 Future Trends Experience Ltd.

Complete Set (100 cards): 10.00

Promo Sheet Canada Cup '76:	5.00
Promo Sheet Team Canada:	5.00
Promo Sheet Team U.S.A.:	5.00
Promo	**NM-MT**
☐ Vladislav Tretiak (G), Promo	5.00

Player	No. Player
☐ 102 Phil Esposito	☐ 103 Vladislav Tretiak (G)
☐ 104 Bobby Orr	☐ 105 The Goal
☐ 106 A. Yakushov	☐ 107 Bobby Hull
☐ 108 V. Tretiak (G)	☐ 109 Great Goalies
☐ 110 What If Series?	☐ 111 A Soviet Suprise
☐ 112 World Champs	☐ 113 Underdogs
☐ 114 Sweden's Best Ever	☐ 115 Team U.S.A. Trains
☐ 116 Canada Cup Camp	☐ 117 Serge Savard
☐ 118 Team Finland	☐ 119 Team Sweden
☐ 120 Czechoslovakia	☐ 121 Soviets
☐ 122 Team U.S.A.	☐ 123 Team Canada
☐ 124 Opening Barrage	☐ 125 Richard Martin
☐ 126 Bobby Orr	☐ 127 Power Play
☐ 128 Ivan Hlinka	☐ 129 CSSR 5 - CCCP 3
☐ 130 Helmut Balderis	☐ 131 Peter Stastny
☐ 132 Valeri Vasiliev	☐ 133 Out Of Contention
☐ 134 Standing Alone	☐ 135 Miracle..Almost
☐ 136 Josef Augusta	☐ 137 A Soviet Rout
☐ 138 Viktor Zhluktov	☐ 139 Hull's A Hit
☐ 140 Bob Gainey	☐ 141 Anders Hedberg
☐ 142 Bobby Hull	☐ 143 Ulf Nilsson
☐ 144 Sergei Kapustin	☐ 145 Börje Salming
☐ 146 Well Enough	☐ 147 Biggest Upset
☐ 148 Matti Hagman	☐ 149 Unbeatable
☐ 150 Boris Alexandrov	☐ 151 A Goaltending Duel
☐ 152 V. Dzurilla (G)	☐ 153 Phil Esposito
☐ 154 R. Vachon (G)	☐ 155 Milan Novy
☐ 156 Vladimir Martinec	☐ 157 Good For Hockey
☐ 158 Bill Nyrop	☐ 159 Pride
☐ 160 Another Summit	☐ 161 Alexander Maltsev
☐ 162 Gilbert Perreault	☐ 163 V. Tretiak (G)
☐ 164 Vladimir Vikulov	☐ 165 Final, Game 1
☐ 166 Not There Yet	☐ 167 Fast & Furious
☐ 167 Final, Game 2	☐ 168 4 - 3 / 4-4
☐ 169 Bill Barber	☐ 170 The Grapevine
☐ 171 Guy Lapointe	☐ 172 Reggie Leach
☐ 173 Sittler's Goal	☐ 174 Lanny McDonald
☐ 175 Darryl Sittler	☐ 176 Clarke / Trudeau
☐ 177 Bobby Clarke	☐ 178 Last Time For #9
☐ 179 Marcel Dionne	☐ 180 Peter Mahovlich
☐ 181 Denis Potvin	☐ 182 Larry Robinson
☐ 183 Steve Shutt	☐ 184 MVP: Bobby Orr
☐ 185 MVP: Vachon (G)	☐ 186 MVP: Milan Novy
☐ 187 MVP: Hagman	☐ 188 MVP: Börje Salming
☐ 189 MVP: Ftorek	☐ 190 MVP: Alex. Maltsev
☐ 191 Series Totals	☐ 192 Canada Totals
☐ 193 CSSR Totals	☐ 194 CSSR Totals
☐ 195 AS: Vachon (G)	☐ 196 AS: Orr
☐ 197 AS: Salming	☐ 198 AS: Novy
☐ 199 AS: Sittler	☐ 200 AS: Maltsev
☐ 201 Checklist	

AUTOGRAPHED CARDS

Insert Set (5 cards)	**270.00**
Player	**Auto.**
☐ Bobby Clarke ✍	25.00
☐ Bobby Hull ✍	40.00
☐ Bobby Orr ✍	210.00
☐ Darryl Sittler ✍	35.00
☐ Rogatien Vachon (G) ✍	15.00

1992 - 93 HIGH FIVE PREVIEW

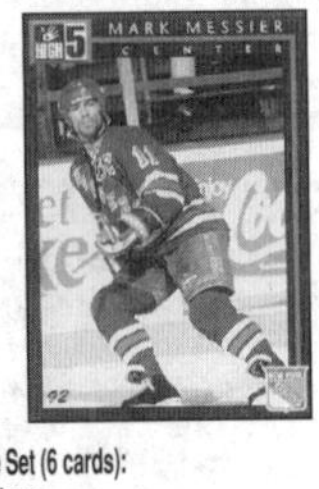

Complete Set (6 cards):	**50.00**
Player	**NM-MT**
☐ P1 Raymond Bourque, Bost. (**)	8.00
☐ P2 Brett Hull, SLou.	5.00
☐ P3 Wayne Gretzky, LosA.	25.00
☐ P4 Mark Messier, NYRa.	5.00
☐ P5 Mario Lemieux, Pitt.	20.00
☐ P6 Ed Belfour (G), Chic. (**)	5.00

1992 - 93 HIGH FIVE – BUYBACK

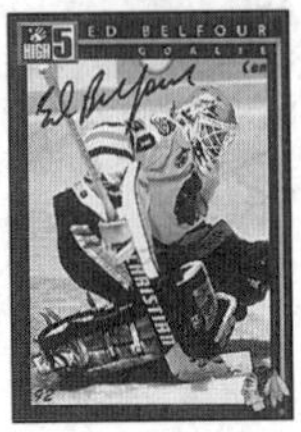

This card was inserted into packs of 1995-96 Future Legends.

Buyback autograph	**Auto.**
☐ P6 E. Belfour (G), Chic. ✍	50.00

1992 - 93 HIGH LINER CENTENNIAL SERIES

Two of 28 different cards were found in specially marked boxes of High Liner. Singles sell between $2-5.

Imprint: Made and printed in USA. Fait et imprimé aux États-Unis

Complete Set (28 cards): **50.00**

No. Team	No. Team
☐ 1 Montréal AAA	☐ 2 Winnipeg Victorias
☐ 3 Montréal Victorias	☐ 4 Montréal Shamrocks
☐ 5 Ottawa Silver Seven	☐ 6 Kenora Thistles
☐ 7 Montréal Wanderers	☐ 8 Québec Bulldogs
☐ 9 Toronto Blueshirts	☐ 10 Vanc. Millionaires
☐ 11 Seattle Metropolitans	☐ 12 Toronto Arenas
☐ 13 Toronto St. Patricks	☐ 14 Victoria Cougars
☐ 15 Ottawa Senators	☐ 16 Montréal Maroons0
☐ 17 New York Rangers	☐ 18 Detroit Red Wings
☐ 19 Montréal Canadiens	☐ 20 Chicago Blackhawks
☐ 21 Toronto Maple Leafs	☐ 22 Boston Bruins
☐ 23 Philadelphia Flyers	☐ 24 New York Islanders
☐ 25 Edmonton Oilers	☐ 26 Calgary Flames
☐ 27 Pittsburgh Penguins	☐ 28 Checklist

1992 - 93 HUMPTY DUMPTY

Card Size: 1 1/2"x2"	
Series One Set (26 cards):	**15.00**
Series Two Set (26 cards):	**10.00**
Album:	**5.00**
No. Series One	**NM-MT**
☐ Raymond Bourque, Bost.	1.00
☐ Rod Brind'Amour, Phil.	.35
☐ Chris Chelios, Chic.	.50
☐ Wendel Clark, Toro.	.50
☐ Gilbert Dionne, Mont.	.35
☐ Pat Falloon, SanJ.	.35
☐ Ray Ferraro, NYIs.	.35
☐ Theoren Fleury, Calg.	.50
☐ Grant Fuhr (G), Toro.	.50
☐ Wayne Gretzky, LosA.	4.00
☐ Kevin Hatcher, Wash.	.35
☐ Valeri Kamensky, Québ.	.35
☐ Mike Keane, Mont.	.35
☐ Brian Leetch, NYRa.	.50
☐ Kirk McLean (G), Vanc.	.35
☐ Alexander Mogilny, Buff.	.35
☐ Troy Murray, Winn.	.35
☐ Patrick Roy (G), Mont.	3.00
☐ Joe Sakic, Québ.	1.50
☐ Brendan Shanahan, SLou.	1.00
☐ Kevin Stevens, Pitt.	.35
☐ Scott Stevens, NJer.	.35
☐ Mark Tinordi, Minn.	.35
☐ Steve Yzerman, Detr.	2.00
☐ Zarley Zalapski, Hart.	.35
☐ Checklist	.35
No. Series Two	**NM-MT**
☐ Drake Berehowsky, Toro.	.35
☐ Shayne Corson, Mont.	.35
☐ Russ Courtnall, Mont.	.35
☐ Dave Ellett, Toro.	.35
☐ Sergei Fedorov, Detr.	1.00
☐ Dave Gagner, Minn.	.35
☐ Doug Gilmour, Toro.	.50
☐ Phil Housley, Winn.	.35
☐ Brett Hull, SLou.	1.00
☐ Jaromir Jagr, Pitt.	1.00
☐ Pat LaFontaine, Buff.	.50
☐ Mario Lemieux, Pitt.	3.00
☐ Trevor Linden, Vanc.	.35
☐ Al MacInnis, Calg.	.35
☐ Mark Messier, NYRa.	1.00
☐ Cam Neely, Bost.	1.00
☐ Owen Nolan, Québ.	.50
☐ Bill Ranford (G), Edmo.	.35
☐ Luc Robitaille, LosA.	.50
☐ Jeremy Roenick, Chic.	.50
☐ Mats Sundin, Québ.	1.00
☐ Chris Terreri (G), NJer.	.35
☐ Steve Thomas, NYIs.	.35
☐ Pat Verbeek, Hart.	.35
☐ Neil Wilkinson, SanJ.	.35
☐ Checklist	.35

1992 - 93 JYVAS HYVA

A set of 204 stickers plus a collecting album for the Finnish National League. We have little pricing information on this set. The most expensive single is Saku Koivu at $15.00. Singles start at 20¢.

Size: 2" x 3 1/4"

Complete Set (204 cards):

Jyvas Hyva	Jyvas Hyva
☐ 1 Harri Rindel	☐ 2 Sakari Lindfors (G)
☐ 3 Simo Saarinen	☐ 4 Pertti Lehtonen
☐ 5 Kari Laitinen	☐ 6 Teppo Kivela
☐ 7 Darren Boyko	☐ 8 Kai Rautio
☐ 9 Drahomir Kadlec	☐ 10 Mika Kortelainen
☐ 11 Jukka Seppo	☐ 12 Pekka Tuomisto
☐ 13 Pasi Sormunen	☐ 14 Kai Tervonen
☐ 15 Ville Peltonen	☐ 16 Valeri Krykov
☐ 17 Iiro Jarvi	☐ 18 Hannu Jortikka
☐ 19 Timo Lehkonen (G)	☐ 20 Timo Nykopp
☐ 21 Janne Laukkanen	☐ 22 Marko Palo
☐ 23 Juha Ylonen	☐ 24 Jarkko Varvio
☐ 25 Marko Allen	☐ 26 Marko Tuulola
☐ 27 Jarkko Nikander	☐ 28 Radek Toupal
☐ 29 Tommi Varjonen	☐ 30 Niko Marttila
☐ 31 Jari Haapamäki	☐ 32 Pasi Kivela
☐ 33 Tony Virta	☐ 34 Markku Piikkila
☐ 35 Anatoli Bogdanov	☐ 36 Jukka Tammi (G)
☐ 37 Jani Nikko	☐ 38 Jukka Ollila
☐ 39 Tommi Kiiski	☐ 40 Mikko Luovi
☐ 41 Juha Jarvenpaa	☐ 42 Juha Lampinen
☐ 43 Janne Seva	☐ 44 Timo Peltomaa
☐ 45 Mika Arvaja	☐ 46 Esa Tommila
☐ 47 Kristian Taubert	☐ 48 Jarkko Glad
☐ 49 Hannu Mattila	☐ 50 Pasi Maattanen
☐ 51 Petri Sullamaa	☐ 52 Boris Majorov
☐ 53 Markus Ketterer (G)	☐ 54 Waltteri Immonen
☐ 55 Mika Stromberg	☐ 56 Keijo Sailynoja
☐ 57 Otakar Janecky	☐ 58 Jiri Sejba
☐ 59 Kari Martikainen	☐ 60 Erik Hamalainen
☐ 61 Timo Norppa	☐ 62 Pekka Jarvela
☐ 63 Juha Salo	☐ 64 Heikki Riihijarvi
☐ 65 Ari Salo	☐ 66 Hannu Jarvenpaa
☐ 67 Jali Wahlsten	☐ 68 Juha Jokiharju
☐ 69 Hannu Aravirta	☐ 70 A-P Siekkinen (G)
☐ 71 Jarmo Jokilahti	☐ 72 Harri Laurila
☐ 73 Juha Riihijarvi	☐ 74 Jari Lindroos
☐ 75 Marko Virtanen	☐ 76 Jari Munck
☐ 77 Markku Heikkinen	☐ 78 Lasse Nieminen
☐ 79 Tero Lehikoinen	☐ 80 Ari Haanpaa
☐ 81 Jarmo Rantanen	☐ 82 VeliPekka Hard
☐ 83 Mika Paananen	☐ 84 Joni Lius
☐ 85 Risto Kurkinen	☐ 86 Juha Junno
☐ 87 Pasi Kuivalainen (G)	☐ 88 Jari Jarvinen
☐ 89 Vesa Salo	☐ 90 Vesa Karjalainen
☐ 91 Darius Rusnak	☐ 92 Arto Sirvio
☐ 93 Vesa Ruotsalainen	☐ 94 Juha Tuohimaa
☐ 95 Jari Hamalainen	☐ 96 Pekka Tirkkonen
☐ 97 Jari Laukkanen	☐ 98 Antti Tuomenoksa
☐ 99 Janne Leppanen	☐ 100 Marko Jantunen
☐ 101 Dusan Pasek	☐ 102 Sami Kapanen
☐ 103 Martti Merra	☐ 104 Sami Aikaa (G)
☐ 105 Teemu Sillanpaa	☐ 106 Sami Nuutinen
☐ 107 Jere Lehtinen	☐ 108 Jan Langbacka
☐ 109 Tero Lehtera	☐ 110 Robert Salo
☐ 111 Jimi Helin	☐ 112 Sami Kokko
☐ 113 Riku Kuusisto	☐ 114 Markku Tiinus
☐ 115 Pasi Heinisto	☐ 116 Petri Pulkkinen
☐ 117 Tom Laaksonen	☐ 118 Jarmo Muukkonen
☐ 119 Petro Koivunen	☐ 120 Matti Keinonen
☐ 121 Petr Briza (G)	☐ 122 Timo Kulonen
☐ 123 Allan Measures	☐ 124 Harri Suvanto
☐ 125 Timo Saarikoski	☐ 126 Mika Alatalo
☐ 127 Kari-Pekka Friman	☐ 128 Jarmo Kuusisto
☐ 129 Mika Valila	☐ 130 Jari Torkki
☐ 131 Pekka Peltola	☐ 132 Pasi Huura
☐ 133 Matti Forss	☐ 134 Kalle Sahlstedt
☐ 135 Tommi Pullola	☐ 136 Tero Arkiomaa
☐ 137 Esko Nokelainen	☐ 138 Petri Engman (G)
☐ 139 Timo Kahelin	☐ 140 Pasi Ruponen
☐ 141 Petteri Sihvonen	☐ 142 Toni Sihvonen
☐ 143 Sami Wikstrom	☐ 144 Erik Kakko
☐ 145 Jari Parviainen	☐ 146 Jonni Vauhkonen
☐ 147 Jari Kauppila	☐ 148 Erkki Makela
☐ 149 Jarkko Hamalainen	☐ 150 Petri Koski
☐ 151 Sami Lekkerimaki	☐ 152 Toni Koivunen
☐ 153 Jani Uski	☐ 154 Pertti Hasanen
☐ 155 Jaromir Sindel (G)	☐ 156 Tommi Haapsaari
☐ 157 Jukka Marttila	☐ 158 Jarmo Kekalainen
☐ 159 Tommi Pohja	☐ 160 Pauli Jarvinen
☐ 161 Timo Jutila	☐ 162 Janne Gronvall
☐ 163 J-P Jarvinen	☐ 164 Kari Heikkinen
☐ 165 Marko Ek	☐ 166 VeliPekka Kautonen
☐ 167 Pekka Laksola	☐ 168 Pasi Forsberg
☐ 169 Marko Lapinkoski	☐ 170 Mikko Peltola
☐ 171 Vladimir Yursinov	☐ 172 Jouni Rokama (G)
☐ 173 Mikko Haapakoski	☐ 174 Kari Harila
☐ 175 Kari Kanervo	☐ 176 Esa Keskinen
☐ 177 Saku Koivu	☐ 178 Jouko Narvanmaa
☐ 179 Alexander Smirnov	☐ 180 Reijo Mikkolainen
☐ 181 Mikko Makela	☐ 182 Raimo Summanen
☐ 183 Hannu Virta	☐ 184 Jukka Virtanen
☐ 185 German Titov	☐ 186 Jukka Vilander
☐ 187 Ari Vuori	☐ 188 Vasili Tihonov
☐ 189 Kari Takko (G)	☐ 190 Sami Saarinen
☐ 191 Marko Sten	☐ 192 Arto Javanainen
☐ 193 Janne Virtanen	☐ 194 Arto Heiskanen
☐ 195 Jouni Vento	☐ 196 Olli Kaski
☐ 197 Vjatseslav Fandul	☐ 198 Jokke Heinanen
☐ 199 Petri Varis	☐ 200 Harry Nikander
☐ 201 Jarno Miikkulainen	☐ 202 Jari Korpisalo
☐ 203 Rauli Raitanen	☐ 204 Jari Levonen

1992 - 93 KELLOGG'S ALL-STAR POSTERS

Poster Size: 14" x 9 1/4"

Imprint: KELLOGG'S CANADA INC. 1992

Complete Set (3 posters):	**4.00**
Player	**NM-MT**
☐ Campbell Conference All-Stars	2.00
☐ Wales Conference All-Stars	2.00
☐ Snap, Crackle, Pop	1.00

1992 - 93 KELLOGG'S MINI POSTERS

Poster Size: 9 1/4" x 14 1/8"

Complete Set (5 posters):	**10.00**
☐ Mario Lemieux, Man of Steel	5.00
☐ Mark Messier, Power Broker	3.00
☐ Luc Robitaille, Robo Shot	2.00
☐ Patrick Roy (G), Road Block	5.00
☐ Cornelius Rooster, Frequent Flyer	.75

1992 - 93 KELLOGG'S RICE KRISPIES TROPHIES

Card Size: 2 1/2" x 3 1/2"

Complete Set (11 cards): **5.00**

No. Trophy	No. Trophy
☐ 1 Stanley Cup	☐ 2 Presidents' Trophy
☐ 3 Hart Trophy	☐ 4 Conn Smythe Trophy
☐ 5 Vezina Trophy	☐ 6 James Trophy
☐ 7 Calder Trophy	☐ 8 Selke Trophy
☐ 9 Lady Byng Trophy	☐ 10 Art Ross Trophy
☐ 11 Jack Adams Award	

1992 - 93 KRAFT

Complete Set (48 cards):	**55.00**
Album:	**35.00**

KRAFT DINNER

One of 24 different team photos were found on the back of specially marked Kraft Dinner boxes.

Panel Size: 3 1/2" x 5 1/4"

Teams Set (24 cards):	**20.00**
Common Team:	**1.00**

Team	Team
☐ Boston Bruins	☐ Buffalo Sabres
☐ Calgary Flames	☐ Chicago Blackhawks
☐ Detroit Red Wings	☐ Edmonton Oilers
☐ Hartford Whalers	☐ Los Angeles Kings
☐ Minnesota North Stars	☐ Montréal Canadiens
☐ New Jersey Devils	☐ New York Islanders
☐ New York Rangers	☐ Ottawa Senators
☐ Philadelphia Flyers	☐ Pittsburgh Penguins
☐ Québec Nordiques	☐ St. Louis Blues
☐ San Jose Sharks	☐ Tampa Bay Lightning

☐ Toronto Maple Leafs	☐ Vancouver Canucks
☐ Washington Capitals	☐ Winnipeg Jets

KRAFT SINGLES

One of 3 different panels was found in specially marked packages of Kraft Singles. Each panel could be cut out into 4 cards each measuring 1 3/4" x 2 1/2". Gretzky is the most expensive cut-out single at $5.00.
Panel Size: 3 1/2" x 7 1/2"

All-Star Set (3 panels):	22.00
Player	NM-MT
☐ Chelios/ Gretzky/ Bourque/ Coffey	10.00
☐ Hull/ Linden/ Jagr/ Lemieux	8.00
☐ Roenick/ Yzerman/ Messier/ Roy (G)	8.00

PEANUT BUTTER

One of 12 different disks were found under the lids of specially marked jars of Kraft Peanut Butter.
Disk Diameter: 2 1/2"

Goalies Set (12 disks):	20.00
Player	NM-MT
☐ Tim Cheveldae (G)/ Sean Burke (G)	1.00
☐ Don Beaupré (G)/ Bob Essensa (G)	1.00
☐ Andy Moog (G)/ Mark Fitzpatrick (G)	1.00
☐ Peter Sidorkiewicz (G)/ Grant Fuhr (G)	1.00
☐ Jeff Hackett (G)/ Kirk McLean (G)	1.00
☐ Dominik Hasek (G)/ Chris Terreri (G)	2.00
☐ Ron Hextall (G)/ Curtis Joseph (G)	4.00
☐ Bill Ranford (G)/ Kelly Hrudey (G)	1.00
☐ Jon Casey (G)/ Dominic Roussel (G)	1.00
☐ Patrick Roy (G)/ John Vanbiesbrouck (G)	8.00
☐ Mike Vernon (G)/ Ed Belfour (G)	3.00
☐ Tom Barrasso (G)/ Wendal Young (G)	1.00

1992 - 93 LEGENDS OF HOCKEY

Artwork by Doug West. The most expensive singles are Bobby Orr at $15-20, Maurice Richard at $12-15 and Gordie Howe at $12-15. All other Hall of Famers sell between $8-12.
Card Size: 3 1/2" x 5 1/2"
Series One Set (18 cards): 120.00

Player	No. Player
☐ 1 Harry Lumley (G)	☐ 2 Conn Smythe
☐ 3 Maurice Richard	☐ 4 Bobby Orr
☐ 5 Bernie Geoffrion	☐ 6 Hobey Baker
☐ 7 Phil Esposito, Bost.	☐ 8 Francis (King) Clancy
☐ 9 Gordie Howe, Detr.	☐ 10 Emile Francis (G)
☐ 11 Jacques Plante (G)	☐ 12 Sid Abel
☐ 13 Foster Hewitt	☐ 14 Charlie Conacher
☐ 15 Stan Mikita	☐ 16 Bobby Clarke
☐ 17 Norm Ullman	☐ 18 Lord Stanley

1992 - 93 MARIO BUN

This premium three-card set was issued by Clark Candy.
Imprint: none

Complete Set (3 cards):	5.00
Player	NM-MT
☐ Mario Lemieux, Pitt.	2.00
☐ Mario Lemieux, Pitt.	2.00
☐ Mario Lemieux, Pitt.	2.00

1992 - 93 MCDONALD'S - UPPER DECK

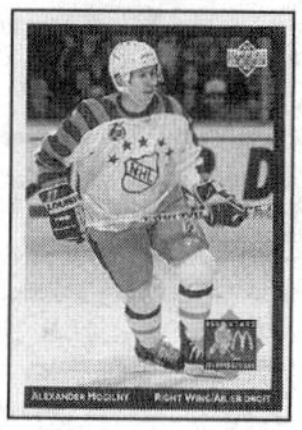

Imprint: 1992 The Upper Deck Co.

Complete Set (34 cards):	25.00
McDonald's	NM-MT
☐ McD01 Ed Belfour (G)	1.00
☐ McD02 Brian Bellows	.35
☐ McD03 Chris Chelios	.50
☐ McD04 Vincent Damphousse	.50
☐ McD05 David Ellet	.35
☐ McD06 Sergei Fedorov	1.00
☐ McD07 Theoren Fleury	.50
☐ McD08 Phil Housley	.35
☐ McD09 Trevor Linden	.35
☐ McD10 Al MacInnis	.35
☐ McD11 Adam Oates	.35
☐ McD12 Luc Robitaille	.50
☐ McD13 Jeremy Roenick	.50
☐ McD14 Steve Yzerman	2.00
☐ McD15 Don Beaupré (G)	.35
☐ McD16 Rod Brind'Amour	.35
☐ McD17 Paul Coffey	.50
☐ McD18 John Cullen	.35
☐ McD19 Kevin Hatcher	.35
☐ McD20 Jaromir Jagr	1.00
☐ McD21 Mario Lemieux	3.00
☐ McD22 Alexander Mogilny	.35
☐ McD23 Kirk Muller	.35
☐ McD24 Owen Nolan	.50
☐ McD25 Mike Richter (G)	.35
☐ McD26 Joe Sakic	1.50
☐ McD27 Scott Stevens	.35
☐ Checklist	1.00
☐ McH01 Mark Messier	2.00
☐ McH02 Brett Hull	2.00
☐ McH03 Kevin Stevens	2.00
☐ McH04 Raymond Bourque	2.00
☐ McH05 Brian Leetch	2.00
☐ McH06 Patrick Roy (G)	3.50

1992 - 93 MCDONALD'S TRANSFERS

Complete Set (26 transfers): 20.00
Common Team: 1.00

Team	Team
☐ Boston Bruins	☐ Buffalo Sabres
☐ Calgary Flames	☐ Chicago Blackhawks
☐ Dallas Stars	☐ Detroit Red Wings
☐ Edmonton Oilers	☐ Hartford Whalers
☐ Los Angeles Kings	☐ Montréal Canadiens
☐ New Jersey Devils	☐ New York Islanders
☐ New York Rangers	☐ Ottawa Senators
☐ Philadelphia Flyers	☐ Pittsburgh Penguins
☐ Québec Nordiques	☐ St. Louis Blues
☐ San Jose Sharks	☐ Tampa Bay Lightning
☐ Toronto Maple Leafs	☐ Vancouver Canucks
☐ Washington Capitals	☐ Winnipeg Jets
☐ McDonald's All-Star	

1992 - 93 MPS PHOTOGRAPHICS

This 168-card set represents the players of the 1992 - 93 Saskatchewan Junior Hockey League.
Complete Set (168 cards): 30.00
Common Player: .20

Player	No. Player
☐ 1 Troy Edwards	☐ 2 Simon Olivier
☐ 3 Gerald Tallaire	☐ 4 Blair Allison (G)
☐ 5 Mads True	☐ 6 Steve Brent
☐ 7 Jay Dobrescu	☐ 8 Dave Debusschere
☐ 9 Bryan Cossette	☐ 10 Brooke Battersby
☐ 11 Kyle Niemegeers	☐ 12 Darren McLean
☐ 13 Carson Cardinal	☐ 14 Bill McKay
☐ 15 Chris Hatch	☐ 16 Nolan Weir
☐ 17 Karl Johnson	☐ 18 Jason Brown
☐ 19 Tyler Kuhn	☐ 20 Daniel Dennis (G)
☐ 21 Wally Spence	☐ 22 Rob Beck
☐ 23 Aaron Cain	☐ 24 Darryl Dickson
☐ 25 Travis Cheyne	☐ 26 Mark Leoppky
☐ 27 Jason Ahenakew	☐ 28 Kyle Paul
☐ 29 Dean Normand	☐ 30 Brett Kinaschuk
☐ 31 Darren Schmidt	☐ 32 Chris Schinkel (G)
☐ 33 David Foster	☐ 34 Jason Zimmerman
☐ 35 Tom Perry	☐ 36 Kent Kinsachuk
☐ 37 Colin Froese	☐ 38 Shawn Zimmerman
☐ 39 Lary Empey	☐ 40 Curtis Knight
☐ 41 Blake Shipley	☐ 42 Cory Heon
☐ 43 Steve Pashulka	☐ 44 Rob Kinch
☐ 45 Dean Gerard	☐ 46 Matt Desmarais
☐ 47 Chad Rusnak	☐ 48 Brad Bagu
☐ 49 Cam Bristow	☐ 50 Derek Simonson
☐ 51 Ken Ruddock	☐ 52 Tyler Deis
☐ 53 Steve Tansowny (G)	☐ 54 Bill Stait
☐ 55 Garfield Henderson	☐ 56 Lonny Deobald
☐ 57 Lyle Ehrmantraut	☐ 58 Layne Humenny
☐ 59 Darren Balcombe	☐ 60 Jeff McCutheon
☐ 61 Trevor Wathen	☐ 62 Derek Wynne
☐ 63 Matt Russo	☐ 64 Bruce Matatall
☐ 65 Derek Crimin	☐ 66 Chad Crumley
☐ 67 Mike Hillock	☐ 68 Art Houghton (G)
☐ 69 Lee Materi	☐ 70 Nick Dyhr
☐ 71 Darren Maloney	☐ 72 Kurtise Souchotte
☐ 73 Noel Kamel	☐ 74 Trent Harper
☐ 75 Ted Grayling	☐ 76 Keith Harris
☐ 77 Corri Moffat	☐ 78 Travis Vantighem
☐ 79 Darren Houghton	☐ 80 Wade Welte
☐ 81 Dave Doucet	☐ 82 Jason Prokopetz
☐ 83 Gordon McCann	☐ 84 Clint Hooge (G)
☐ 85 Glen McGillvary	☐ 86 Regan Simpson
☐ 87 Mike Masse	☐ 88 Jeremy Procyshyn
☐ 89 Jim Nellis	☐ 90 Todd Kozak
☐ 91 Brent Hoiness	☐ 92 Josh Welter
☐ 93 Eldon Barker, Trainer	☐ 94 Duane Vandale
☐ 95 Brad McEwen	☐ 96 Trent Tibbatts
☐ 97 Jody Reiter	☐ 98 Greg Moore
☐ 99 Jon Rowe	☐ 100 Mike Evans
☐ 101 Jason Krug	☐ 102 Jon Bracco (G)
☐ 103 Ryan Sandholm	☐ 104 Darryl Sangster
☐ 105 Brett Colborne	☐ 106 Dean Moore
☐ 107 Chris Dechaine	☐ 108 Steve McKenna
☐ 109 Tony Bergin	☐ 110 Tim Murray
☐ 111 Casey Kesselring	☐ 112 Todd Barth
☐ 113 Ryan McConnell	☐ 114 Ian Adamson
☐ 115 Warren Pickford	☐ 116 Todd Murphy
☐ 117 Rob Phillips	☐ 118 Trevor Demmans
☐ 119 Jeff Greenwood	☐ 120 Kevin Messer
☐ 121 Dion Johnson	☐ 122 Rejean Stringer
☐ 123 Scott Mead	☐ 124 Jeff Lawson
☐ 125 Scot Newberry	☐ 126 Bill Reid
☐ 127 Chris Winkler	☐ 128 Kyle Girgan
☐ 129 Trevor Warrener	☐ 130 Richard Boscher (G)
☐ 131 Tom Thomson	☐ 132 Mike Wevers
☐ 133 Barton Holt	☐ 134 Kent Rogers
☐ 135 Richard Gibbs	☐ 136 Jared Witt
☐ 137 Jamie Stelmak	☐ 138 Greg Wahl
☐ 139 J. Sotropa	☐ 140 Mark Pivetz
☐ 141 Travis Kirby (G)	☐ 142 Jason Scanzano
☐ 143 Tyson Balog	☐ 144 Daryl Krauss
☐ 145 Mike Harder	☐ 146 Tyler McMillan
☐ 147 Darcy Herlick	☐ 148 Dave Zwyer
☐ 149 Craig McKechnie	☐ 150 Cam Cook
☐ 151 Derek Bruselinck	☐ 152 Travis Smith
☐ 153 Daryl Jones	☐ 154 Mike Savard (G)
☐ 155 Jeremy Matthies	☐ 156 Michel Cook
☐ 157 Leigh Brookbank	☐ 158 Christian Dutil (G)
☐ 159 Scott Heshka	☐ 160 Danny Galarneau
☐ 161 Jamie Dunn	☐ 162 Nigel Werenka
☐ 163 Steve Sabo	☐ 164 Tony Toth
☐ 165 Sebastien Moreau	☐ 166 Tim Slukynsky
☐ 167 Sheldon Bylsma	☐ 168 Stacy Prevost

1992 - 93 O-PEE-CHEE

The most expensive regular singles are Wayne Gretzky at $1-2, Mario Lemieux at $0.75-1.50, Patrick Roy at $0.75-1.25 and Bill Guerin at $1.00-1.50. Regional stars sell at 25¢-$1; commons start at 20¢. Retro-style cards sell at approximately the same price as the Anniversary Series reprints listed below.

O-Pee-Chee (396 cards):	20.00
25th Anniversary Factory Set:	75.00
Common Player:	.20
9-Card Promo Sheet:	10.00

OPC	OPC
☐ 1 Kevin Todd	☐ 2 Robert Kron
☐ 3 David Volek	☐ 4 Teppo Numminen
☐ 5 Paul Coffey	☐ 6 Luc Robitaille
☐ 7 Steven Finn	☐ 8 Gord Hynes
☐ 9 Dave Ellett	☐ 10 Alexander Godynyuk
☐ 11 Darryl Sydor	☐ 12 Randy Carlyle
☐ 13 Chris Chelios	☐ 14 Kent Manderville
☐ 15 Wayne Gretzky	☐ 16 Jon Casey (G)
☐ 17 Mark Tinordi	☐ 18 Dale Hunter
☐ 19 Martin Gélinas	☐ 20 Todd Elik
☐ 21 Bob Sweeney	☐ 22 Chris Dahlquist
☐ 23 Joe Mullen	☐ 24 Shawn Burr
☐ 25 Pavel Bure	☐ 26 Randy Gilhen
☐ 27 Brian Bradley	☐ 28 Don Beaupré (G)
☐ 29 Kevin Stevens	☐ 30 Michal Pivonka
☐ 31 Grant Fuhr (G)	☐ 32 Steve Larmer
☐ 33 Gary Leeman	☐ 34 Tony Tanti
☐ 35 Denis Savard	☐ 36 Paul Ranheim
☐ 37 Andrei Lomakin	☐ 38 Perry Anderson
☐ 39 Stu Barnes	☐ 40 Don Sweeney
☐ 41 Jamie Baker	☐ 42 Ray Ferraro
☐ 43 Bobby Clarke Retro	☐ 44 Kelly Hrudey (G)
☐ 45 Brian Skrudland	☐ 46 Paul Ysebaert
☐ 47 Pierre Turgeon	☐ 48 Keith Brown
☐ 49 Rod Brind'Amour	☐ 50 Wayne McBean
☐ 51 Doug Lidster	☐ 52 Bernie Nicholls
☐ 53 Daren Puppa (G)	☐ 54 Joe Sakic
☐ 55 Joe Sakic Retro	☐ 56 Dave Manson
☐ 57 Denis Potvin Retro	☐ 58 Daniel Marois
☐ 59 Martin Brodeur	☐ 60 Brent Sutter
☐ 61 Steve Yzerman	☐ 62 Neal Broten
☐ 63 Darcy Wakaluk (G)	☐ 64 Troy Murray
☐ 65 Tony Granato	☐ 66 Frantisek Musil
☐ 67 Claude Lemieux	☐ 68 Brian Benning
☐ 69 Stéphane Matteau	☐ 70 Tomas Forslund
☐ 71 Dmitri Mironov	☐ 72 Gary Roberts
☐ 73 Félix Potvin (G)	☐ 74 Glen Murray
☐ 75 Stéphane Fiset (G)	☐ 76 Stéphane Richer
☐ 77 Jeff Reese (G)	☐ 78 Marc Bureau
☐ 79 Derek King	☐ 80 Dave Gagner
☐ 81 Ed Belfour (G)	☐ 82 Joel Otto
☐ 83 Anatoli Semenov	☐ 84 Ron Hextall (G)
☐ 85 Adam Creighton	☐ 86 Kris King
☐ 87 Brett Hull	☐ 88 Zdeno Ciger
☐ 89 Petr Nedved	☐ 90 Sergei Makarov
☐ 91 Tomas Sandström	☐ 92 Stephen Heinze
☐ 93 Robert Reichel	☐ 94 Cliff Ronning
☐ 95 Eric Weinrich	☐ 96 Wendel Clark
☐ 97 Rick Zombo	☐ 98 Ric Nattress
☐ 99 Theoren Fleury	☐ 100 Joe Murphy
☐ 101 Gord Murphy	☐ 102 Jaromir Jagr
☐ 103 Mike Craig	☐ 104 John Cullen
☐ 105 John Druce	☐ 106 Peter Bondra
☐ 107 Bryan Trottier Retro	☐ 108 J. Steve Smith
☐ 109 Petr* Svoboda	☐ 110 Mats Sundin
☐ 111 Patrick Roy Retro	☐ 112 Stephen Leach
☐ 113 J. Cloutier (G)	☐ 114 Doug Weight
☐ 115 Frank Pietrangelo	☐ 116 Guy Hebert (G)
☐ 117 Donald Audette	☐ 118 Craig MacTavish
☐ 119 G. Fuhr Retro (G)	☐ 120 Trevor Linden
☐ 121 Fredrik Olausson	☐ 122 Geoff Sanderson
☐ 123 Derian Hatcher	☐ 124 Brett Hull Retro
☐ 125 Kelly Buchberger	☐ 126 Raymond Bourque
☐ 127 Murray Craven	☐ 128 Tim Cheveldae (G)
☐ 129 Ulf Dahlén	☐ 130 Bryan Trottier
☐ 131 Bob Carpenter	☐ 132 Benoît Hogue
☐ 133 Claude Vilgrain	☐ 134 Glenn Anderson
☐ 135 Marty McInnis	☐ 136 Rob Pearson
☐ 137 Bill Ranford (G)	☐ 138 Mario Lemieux
☐ 139 Bob Bassen	☐ 140 Scott Mellanby
☐ 141 Dave Andreychuk	☐ 142 Kelly Miller
☐ 143 Gaétan Duchesne	☐ 144 Mike Sullivan
☐ 145 Kevin Hatcher	☐ 146 Doug Bodger
☐ 147 Craig Berube	☐ 148 Rick Tocchet
☐ 149 Luciano Borsato	☐ 150 Glen Wesley
☐ 151 Mike Donnelly	☐ 152 Jimmy Carson
☐ 153 Jocelyn Lemieux	☐ 154 Ray Sheppard
☐ 155 Tony Amonte	☐ 156 Adrien Plavsic
☐ 157 Mark Pederson	☐ 158 Adam Graves
☐ 159 Igor Larionov	☐ 160 Steve Chiasson
☐ 161 Igor Kravchuk	☐ 162 Viacheslav Fetisov
☐ 163 Gerard Gallant	☐ 164 Patrick Roy (G)
☐ 165 Ken Sutton	☐ 166 Mathieu Schneider
☐ 167 L. Robinson Retro	☐ 168 Jim Sandlak
☐ 169 Joey Kocur	☐ 170 Rob (Jr.) Brown
☐ 171 Luke Richardson	☐ 172 Adam Oates Retro
☐ 173 Uwe Krupp	☐ 174 Cam Neely
☐ 175 P. Sidorkiewicz (G)	☐ 176 Geoff Courtnall
☐ 177 Doug Gilmour	☐ 178 Josef Beránek
☐ 179 Michel Picard	☐ 180 Terry Carkner
☐ 181 Nelson Emerson	☐ 182 Perry Berezan
☐ 183 Checklist	☐ 184 Andy Moog (G)
☐ 185 Michel Petit	☐ 186 Mark Greig
☐ 187 Paul Coffey Retro	☐ 188 Ron Francis
☐ 189 Joé Juneau	☐ 190 Jeff Odgers
☐ 191 Darryl Sittler Retro	☐ 192 Damphousse
☐ 193 Greg Paslawski	☐ 194 Esposito Retro (G)
☐ 195 Sergei Fedorov	☐ 196 Doug Smail
☐ 197 Pat Verbeek	☐ 198 Roussel (G)
☐ 199 Mike McPhee	☐ 200 Kevin Dineen
☐ 201 Pat Elynuik	☐ 202 Tom Kurvers
☐ 203 Chris Joseph	☐ 204 Mark Fitzpatrick (G)
☐ 205 Jari Kurri	☐ 206 Guy Carbonneau
☐ 207 Jan Erixon	☐ 208 Mark Messier
☐ 209 Larry Murphy	☐ 210 Dirk Graham
☐ 211 Ron Tugnutt	☐ 212 Dale Hawerchuk
☐ 213 Dave Babych	☐ 214 Mikael Andersson
☐ 215 James Patrick	☐ 216 Peter Stastny
☐ 217 Parent Retro (G)	☐ 218 Jeff Hackett (G)
☐ 219 Dave Lowry	☐ 220 Gretzky Retro
☐ 221 Brent Gilchrist	☐ 222 Andrew Cassels
☐ 223 Calle Johansson	☐ 224 Joe Reekie
☐ 225 Craig Simpson	☐ 226 Bob Essensa
☐ 227 Pat Falloon	☐ 228 Vladimir Ruzicka
☐ 229 Igor Ulanov	☐ 230 Kjell Samuelsson
☐ 231 Shayne Corson	☐ 232 Kelly Kisio
☐ 233 Gord** Roberts	☐ 234 Brian Noonan
☐ 235 Vyacheslav Kozlov	☐ 236 Checklist
☐ 237 Jeff Beukeboom	☐ 238 Steve Konroyd
☐ 239 Patrice Brisebois	☐ 240 Mario Lemieux
☐ 241 Dana Murzyn	☐ 242 Pelle Eklund
☐ 243 Rob Blake	☐ 244 Brendan Shanahan
☐ 245 HL: Mike Gartner	☐ 246 David Bruce
☐ 247 Mike Vernon (G)	☐ 248 Zarley Zalapski
☐ 249 Dino Ciccarelli	☐ 250 David* Williams
☐ 251 Scott Stevens Retro	☐ 252 Bob Probert
☐ 253 Mikhail Tatarinov	☐ 254 Bobby Holik
☐ 255 Tony Amonte Retro	☐ 256 Brad May
☐ 257 Philippe Bozon	☐ 258 Mark Messier Retro
☐ 259 Mike Richter (G)	☐ 260 Brian Mullen
☐ 261 Marty McSorley	☐ 262 Glenn Healy (G)
☐ 263 Russ Romaniuk	☐ 264 Dan Quinn
☐ 265 Jyrki Lumme	☐ 266 Valeri Kamensky
☐ 267 Konstantinov	☐ 268 Peter Ahola
☐ 269 Guy Larose	☐ 270 Ulf Samuelsson
☐ 271 Dale Craigwell	☐ 272 Adam Oates
☐ 273 Pat MacLeod	☐ 274 Mike Keane
☐ 275 Vanbiesbrouck (G)	☐ 276 Brian Lawton
☐ 277 Sylvain Côté	☐ 278 Gary Suter
☐ 279 Alexander Mogilny	☐ 280 Garth Butcher
☐ 281 Doug Wilson	☐ 282 Chris Terreri (G)
☐ 283 Phil Esposito Retro	☐ 284 Russ Courtnall
☐ 285 Pat LaFontaine	☐ 286 Dmitri Khristich
☐ 287 John LeBlanc	☐ 288 Randy Velischek
☐ 289 Dave Christian	☐ 290 Kevin Haller
☐ 291 Kevin Miller	☐ 292 Lemieux Retro
☐ 293 Stéphan Lebeau	☐ 294 Marcel Dionne Retro
☐ 295 Barry Pederson	☐ 296 Steve Duchesne
☐ 297 Yves Racine	☐ 298 Phil Housley
☐ 299 Randy Ladouceur	☐ 300 Mike Gartner
☐ 301 Dominik Hasek (G)	☐ 302 Kevin Lowe
☐ 303 Sylvain Lefebvre	☐ 304 J.J. Daigneault
☐ 305 Mike Ridley	☐ 306 Curtis Leschyshyn
☐ 307 Gilbert Dionne	☐ 308 Bill Guerin

☐ 309 Gerald Diduck	☐ 310 Rick Wamsley (G)
☐ 311 Pat Jablonski (G)	☐ 312 Jayson More
☐ 313 Mike Modano	☐ 314 Checklist
☐ 315 Sylvain Turgeon	☐ 316 Sergei Nemchinov
☐ 317 Garry Galley	☐ 318 HL: Paul Coffey
☐ 319 Esa Tikkanen	☐ 320 Claude Lapointe
☐ 321 Yzerman Retro	☐ 322 Mark Lamb
☐ 323 Bob Errey	☐ 324 Pavel Bure Retro
☐ 325 Craig Janney	☐ 326 Bob Kudelski
☐ 327 Kirk Muller	☐ 328 Jim Paek
☐ 329 Mike Ricci	☐ 330 Al MacInnis
☐ 331 Mike Hudson	☐ 332 Darrin Shannon
☐ 333 Doug Brown	☐ 334 Corey Millen
☐ 335 Mike Krushelnyski	☐ 336 Scott Stevens
☐ 337 Peter Zezel	☐ 338 Geoff Smith
☐ 339 Curtis Joseph (G)	☐ 340 Tom Barrasso (G)
☐ 341 Al Iafrate	☐ 342 Patrick Flatley
☐ 343 Cheevers Retro (G)	☐ 344 Norm Maciver
☐ 345 Jeremy Roenick	☐ 346 Keith Tkachuk
☐ 347 Rod Langway	☐ 348 HL: Bourque
☐ 349 Kirk McLean (G)	☐ 350 Brian Propp
☐ 351 John Ogrodnick	☐ 352 Benoît Brunet
☐ 353 Alexei Kasatonov	☐ 354 Joe Nieuwendyk
☐ 355 Joe Sacco	☐ 356 Tom Fergus
☐ 357 Dan Lambert	☐ 358 Michel Goulet
☐ 359 Shawn McEachern	☐ 360 Eric Desjardins
☐ 361 Paul Stanton	☐ 362 Ron Sutter
☐ 363 Derrick Smith	☐ 364 Paul Broten
☐ 365 Greg A. Adams	☐ 366 Rob Zettler
☐ 367 Dave Poulin	☐ 368 Keith Acton
☐ 369 Nicklas Lidström	☐ 370 Randy Burridge
☐ 371 Jamie Macoun	☐ 372 Craig Billington (G)
☐ 373 Mark Recchi	☐ 374 Kris Draper
☐ 375 Ed Olczyk	☐ 376 Tom Draper (G)
☐ 377 Sergio Momesso	☐ 378 Brian Leetch
☐ 379 Paul Cavallini	☐ 380 Paul Fenton
☐ 381 Dean Evason	☐ 382 Owen Nolan
☐ 383 Roenick Retro	☐ 384 Brian Bellows
☐ 385 Thomas Steen	☐ 386 John LeClair
☐ 387 Darren Turcotte	☐ 388 James H. Black
☐ 389 Alexei Gusarov	☐ 390 Scott Lachance
☐ 391 Mike Bossy Retro	☐ 392 Mike Hough
☐ 393 Grant Ledyard	☐ 394 Tom Fitzgerald
☐ 395 Steve Thomas	☐ 396 Bobby Smith

25TH ANNIVERSARY

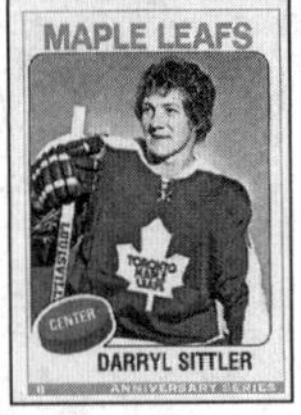

Insert Set (26 cards): 15.00

	Player	Reprint
☐	1 Bernie Parent (G), Phil.	.50
☐	2 Tony Esposito (G), Chic.	1.00
☐	3 Bobby Clarke, Phil.	.50
☐	4 Marcel Dionne, Detr.	1.00
☐	5 Gerry Cheevers (G), Cincinatti	.50
☐	6 Larry Robinson, Mont.	.50
☐	7 Denis Potvin, NYIs.	.50
☐	8 Darryl Sittler, Toro.	.50
☐	9 Bryan Trottier, NYIs.	1.00
☐	10 Phil Esposito, NYRa.	1.00
☐	11 Mike Bossy, NYIs.	1.50
☐	12 Wayne Gretzky, Edmo.	4.00
☐	13 Mark Messier, Edmo.	1.00
☐	14 Paul Coffey, Edmo.	.50
☐	15 Grant Fuhr (G), Edmo.	.50
☐	16 Scott Stevens, Wash.	.25
☐	17 Steve Yzerman, Detr.	2.00
☐	18 Mario Lemieux, Pitt.	3.00
☐	19 Patrick Roy (G), Mont.	3.00
☐	20 Adam Oates, Detr.	.25
☐	21 Brett Hull, SLou.	1.00
☐	22 Joe Sakic, Québ.	1.50
☐	23 Jeremy Roenick, Chic.	.50
☐	24 Tony Amonte, NYRa.	.50
☐	25 Pavel Bure, Vanc.	.50
☐	26 Checklist	.25

BOX BOTTOMS

One of four different large size cards were found on the bottom of O-Pee-Chee boxes.

Card Size: 5" x 6 3/4"

Complete Set (4 cards): 7.00

	Player	NM-MT
☐	AW: Pavel Bure	2.00
☐	AW: Brian Leetch	1.00
☐	AW: Mark Messier	1.00
☐	AW: Patrick Roy (G)	5.00

1992 - 93 O-PEE-CHEE PREMIER

The most expensive single is Eric Lindros at $1.00 -1.50. All other singles sell between 20¢ and $1.00.

Imprint: © 1993 O-PEE-CHEE CO. LTD

Complete Set (132 cards): 10.00

Player	No. Player
☐ 1 Dave Christian	☐ 2 Christian Ruuttu
☐ 3 Vincent Damphousse	☐ 4 Chris Lindberg
☐ 5 Bill Lindsay RC	☐ 6 D. Kvartalnov RC
☐ 7 Darcy Loewen RC	☐ 8 Ed Courtenay RC
☐ 9 Sergei Krivokrasov	☐ 10 Shawn Antoski
☐ 11 André Racicot (G)	☐ 12 Marty McInnis
☐ 13 Alexei Zhamnov	☐ 14 Keith Jones RC
☐ 15 S. Konowalchuk RC	☐ 16 Darryl Sydor
☐ 17 Janne Ojanen	☐ 18 Doug Zmolek
☐ 19 M. Nylander RC	☐ 20 Russ Courtnall
☐ 21 Martin Straka RC	☐ 22 Kevin Dahl RC
☐ 23 Kent Manderville	☐ 24 Steve Heinze
☐ 25 Philippe Bozon	☐ 26 Brent Fedyk
☐ 27 Kris Draper	☐ 28 Brad Schlegel
☐ 29 Patrik Kjellberg RC	☐ 30 Ted Donato
☐ 31 V. Butsayev	☐ 32 Tyler Wright
☐ 33 Tom Pederson RC	☐ 34 Jim Hiller RC
☐ 35 Chris Luongo RC	☐ 36 R. Petrovicky RC
☐ 37 J-F Quintin RC	☐ 38 Chris Dahlquist
☐ 39 D. Laperrière RC	☐ 40 Guy Hebert (G) RC
☐ 41 Ed Ronan RC	☐ 42 Shawn Cronin
☐ 43 Keith Tkachuk	☐ 44 Dino Ciccarelli
☐ 45 Doug Evans	☐ 46 R. Hamrlik RC
☐ 47 Robert Lang RC	☐ 48 Kerry Huffman
☐ 49 Pat Conacher	☐ 50 Dominik Hasek (G)
☐ 51 Dominic Roussel (G)	☐ 52 Glen Murray
☐ 53 Igor Korolev	☐ 54 Jiri Slegr
☐ 55 Mikael Andersson	☐ 56 B. Babcock RC
☐ 57 Ron Hextall (G)	☐ 58 Jeff Daniels
☐ 59 Doug Crossman	☐ 60 V. Gordijuk
☐ 61 Adam Creighton	☐ 62 Rob DiMaio
☐ 63 Eric Weinrich	☐ 64 V. Prokhorov RC
☐ 65 D. Yushkevich RC	☐ 66 Evgeny Davydov
☐ 67 Dixon Ward RC	☐ 68 Teemu Selänne
☐ 69 Rob Zamuner RC	☐ 70 Joe Reekie
☐ 71 Vyacheslav Kozlov	☐ 72 Philippe Boucher
☐ 73 Phil Bourque	☐ 74 Yvon Corriveau
☐ 75 Brian Bellows, Mont.	☐ 76 Wendell Young (G)
☐ 77 Bobby Holik	☐ 78 Bob Carpenter
☐ 79 Scott Lachance	☐ 80 John Druce
☐ 81 Keith Carney RC	☐ 82 Neil Brady
☐ 83 R. Matvichuk RC	☐ 84 Sergei Bautin RC
☐ 85 Patrick Poulin	☐ 86 Gord Roberts
☐ 87 Kay Whitmore (G)	☐ 88 S. Beauregard (G)
☐ 89 Vladimir Malakhov	☐ 90 R. Smehlik RC
☐ 91 Mike Ricci	☐ 92 Sean Burke (G)
☐ 93 A. Kovalenko	☐ 94 Shawn McEachern
☐ 95 Pat Jablonski (G)	☐ 96 Oleg Petrov RC
☐ 97 G. Mulvenna RC	☐ 98 J. Woolley RC
☐ 99 Mark Greig RC	☐ 100 N. Borschevsky RC
☐ 101 Joé Juneau	☐ 102 Eric Lindros
☐ 103 Darius Kasparaitis	☐ 104 Sandis Ozolinsh
☐ 105 Stan Drulia RC	☐ 106 M. Needham RC
☐ 107 Norm Maciver	☐ 108 Sylvain Lefebvre
☐ 109 Tommy Sjodin RC	☐ 110 Bob Sweeney
☐ 111 Brian Mullen	☐ 112 P. Sidorkiewicz (G)
☐ 113 Scott Niedermayer	☐ 114 Félix Potvin (G)
☐ 115 Robb Stauber (G)	☐ 116 Sylvain Turgeon
☐ 117 Mark Janssens	☐ 118 D. Banks RC
☐ 119 Pat Elynuik	☐ 120 Bill Guerin RC
☐ 121 Reggie Savage	☐ 122 Enrico Ciccone
☐ 123 Chris Kontos RC	☐ 124 Martin Rucinsky
☐ 125 Alexei Zhitnik	☐ 126 Alexei Kovalev
☐ 127 Tim Kerr	☐ 128 Guy Larose RC
☐ 129 Brent Gilchrist	☐ 130 Steve Duchesne
☐ 131 Drake Berehowsky	☐ 132 Checklist

STAR PERFORMERS

Insert Set (22 cards): 10.00

	Player	NM-MT
☐	1 Ray Ferraro, NYIs.	.25
☐	2 Dale Hunter, Wash.	.25
☐	3 Murray Craven, Hart.	.25
☐	4 Paul Coffey, LosA.	.50
☐	5 Jeremy Roenick, Chic.	1.00
☐	6 Denis Savard, Mont.	.50
☐	7 Jon Casey (G), Minn.	.25
☐	8 Doug Gilmour, Toro.	.50
☐	9 Rod Brind'Amour, Phil.	.25
☐	10 Pavel Bure, Vanc.	1.00
☐	11 Joe Sakic, Québ.	2.00
☐	12 Pat Falloon, SanJ.	.25
☐	13 Adam Oates, Bost.	.50
☐	14 Gary Roberts, Calg.	.50
☐	15 Mark Messier, NYRa.	1.00
☐	16 Phil Housley, Winn.	.25
☐	17 Pat LaFontaine, Buff.	.50
☐	18 Stéphane Richer, NJer.	.25
☐	19 Bill Ranford (G), Edmo.	.50
☐	20 Sergei Fedorov, Detr.	1.00
☐	21 Brett Hull, SLou.	1.00
☐	22 Mario Lemieux, Pitt.	3.50

TOP ROOKIES

Insert Set (4 cards): 3.50

	Player	NM-MT
☐	1 Eric Lindros, Phil.	3.00
☐	2 Roman Hamrlik, Tamp.	.25
☐	3 Dominic Roussel (G), Phil.	.25
☐	4 Félix Potvin (G), Toro.	.50

1992 - 93 PANINI STICKERS

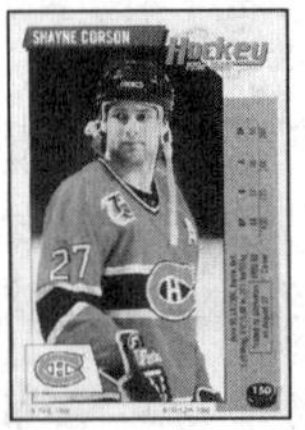

The most expensive regular singles are Wayne Gretzky $1.50-2.00, Mario Lemieux at 75¢-$1.50 and Patrick Roy at 75¢-$1.25. All other regular singles sell between 20¢ and $1.00. The most expensive Glitter singles are Jaromir Jagr and Eric Lindros at $1.50-2.50 each. All other Glitter singles sell between $0.25-1.00. French version singles sell at at 25-50% premium. Uncut six-sticker panels also exist.

Complete Set (330 stickers): 15.00

Player	No. Player
☐☐ 1 Stanley Cup	☐☐ 2 Blackhawks
☐☐ 3 Ed Belfour (G)	☐☐ 4 Jeremy Roenick
☐☐ 5 Steve Larmer	☐☐ 6 Michel Goulet
☐☐ 7 Dirk Graham	☐☐ 8 Jocelyn Lemieux
☐☐ 9 Brian Noonan	☐☐ 10 Rob (Jr.) Brown
☐☐ 11 Chris Chelios	☐☐ 12 J. Steve Smith
☐☐ 13 Keith Brown	☐☐ 14 Blues
☐☐ 15 Curtis Joseph (G)	☐☐ 16 Brett Hull
☐☐ 17 Brendan Shanahan	☐☐ 18 Ron L. Wilson
☐☐ 19 Rich Sutter	☐☐ 20 Ron Sutter
☐☐ 21 Dave Lowry	☐☐ 22 Craig Janney
☐☐ 23 Paul Cavallini	☐☐ 24 Garth Butcher
☐☐ 25 Jeff R. Brown	☐☐ 26 Canucks
☐☐ 27 Kirk McLean (G)	☐☐ 28 Trevor Linden
☐☐ 29 Geoff Courtnall	☐☐ 30 Cliff Ronning
☐☐ 31 Petr Nedved	☐☐ 32 Igor Larionov
☐☐ 33 Robert Kron	☐☐ 34 Jim Sandlak
☐☐ 35 Dave Babych	☐☐ 36 Jyrki Lumme
☐☐ 37 Doug Lidster	☐☐ 38 Flames
☐☐ 39 Mike Vernon (G)	☐☐ 40 Joe Nieuwendyk
☐☐ 41 Gary Leeman	☐☐ 42 Robert Reichel
☐☐ 43 Joel Otto	☐☐ 44 Paul Ranheim
☐☐ 45 Gary Roberts	☐☐ 46 Theoren Fleury
☐☐ 47 Sergei Makarov	☐☐ 48 Gary Suter
☐☐ 49 Al MacInnis	☐☐ 50 Jets
☐☐ 51 Bob Essensa	☐☐ 52 Teppo Numminen
☐☐ 53 Thomas Steen	☐☐ 54 Pat Elynuik
☐☐ 55 Ed Olczyk	☐☐ 56 Danton Cole
☐☐ 57 Troy Murray	☐☐ 58 Darrin Shannon
☐☐ 59 Russ Romaniuk	☐☐ 60 Fredrik Olausson
☐☐ 61 Phil Housley	☐☐ 62 Kings
☐☐ 63 Kelly Hrudey (G)	☐☐ 64 Wayne Gretzky
☐☐ 65 Luc Robitaille	☐☐ 66 Jari Kurri
☐☐ 67 Tomas Sandström	☐☐ 68 Tony Granato
☐☐ 69 Bob Kudelski	☐☐ 70 Corey Millen
☐☐ 71 Rob Blake	☐☐ 72 Paul Coffey
☐☐ 73 Marty McSorley	☐☐ 74 Maple Leafs
☐☐ 75 Grant Fuhr (G)	☐☐ 76 Glenn Anderson
☐☐ 77 Doug Gilmour	☐☐ 78 Mike Krushelnyski
☐☐ 79 Wendel Clark	☐☐ 80 Rob Pearson
☐☐ 81 Peter Zezel	☐☐ 82 Todd Gill
☐☐ 83 Dave Ellett	☐☐ 84 Mike Foligno
☐☐ 85 Ken Baumgartner	☐☐ 86 North Stars
☐☐ 87 Jon Casey (G)	☐☐ 88 Brian Bellows
☐☐ 89 Neal Broten	☐☐ 90 Dave Gagner
☐☐ 91 Mike Modano	☐☐ 92 Ulf Dahlén
☐☐ 93 Brian Propp	☐☐ 94 Jim* Johnson
☐☐ 95 Mike Craig	☐☐ 96 Bobby Smith
☐☐ 97 Mark Tinordi	☐☐ 98 Oilers
☐☐ 99 Bill Ranford (G)	☐☐ 100 Joe Murphy
☐☐ 101 Craig MacTavish	☐☐ 102 Craig Simpson
☐☐ 103 Esa Tikkanen	☐☐ 104 Damphousse
☐☐ 105 Petr Klima	☐☐ 106 Martin Gélinas
☐☐ 107 Kevin Lowe	☐☐ 108 Dave Manson
☐☐ 109 Bernie Nicholls	☐☐ 110 Red Wings
☐☐ 111 Tim Cheveldae (G)	☐☐ 112 Steve Yzerman
☐☐ 113 Sergei Fedorov	☐☐ 114 Jimmy Carson
☐☐ 115 Kevin Miller	☐☐ 116 Gerard Gallant
☐☐ 117 Keith Primeau	☐☐ 118 Paul Ysebaert
☐☐ 119 Yves Racine	☐☐ 120 Steve Chiasson
☐☐ 121 Ray Sheppard	☐☐ 122 Sharks
☐☐ 123 Jeff Hackett (G)	☐☐ 124 Kelly Kisio
☐☐ 125 Brian Mullen	☐☐ 126 David Bruce
☐☐ 127 Rob Zettler	☐☐ 128 Neil Wilkinson
☐☐ 129 Doug Wilson	☐☐ 130 Jeff Odgers
☐☐ 131 Dean Evason	☐☐ 132 Brian Lawton
☐☐ 133 Dale Craigwell	☐☐ 134 Bruins
☐☐ 135 Andy Moog (G)	☐☐ 136 Adam Oates
☐☐ 137 Dave Poulin	☐☐ 138 Vladimir Ruzicka
☐☐ 139 Jeff Lazaro	☐☐ 140 Bob Carpenter
☐☐ 141 Peter Douris	☐☐ 142 Glen Murray
☐☐ 143 Cam Neely	☐☐ 144 Raymond Bourque
☐☐ 145 Glen Wesley	☐☐ 146 Canadiens
☐☐ 147 Patrick Roy (G)	☐☐ 148 Kirk Muller
☐☐ 149 Guy Carbonneau	☐☐ 150 Shayne Corson
☐☐ 151 Stéphan Lebeau	☐☐ 152 Denis Savard
☐☐ 153 Brent Gilchrist	☐☐ 154 Russ Courtnall
☐☐ 155 Patrice Brisebois	☐☐ 156 Éric Desjardins
☐☐ 157 Mathieu Schneider	☐☐ 158 Capitals
☐☐ 159 Don Beaupré (G)	☐☐ 160 Dino Ciccarelli
☐☐ 161 Michal Pivonka	☐☐ 162 Mike Ridley
☐☐ 163 Randy Burridge	☐☐ 164 Peter Bondra
☐☐ 165 Dale Hunter	☐☐ 166 Kelly Miller
☐☐ 167 Kevin Hatcher	☐☐ 168 Al Iafrate
☐☐ 169 Rod Langway	☐☐ 170 Devils
☐☐ 171 Chris Terreri (G)	☐☐ 172 Claude Lemieux
☐☐ 173 Stéphane Richer	☐☐ 174 Peter Stastny
☐☐ 175 Zdeno Ciger	☐☐ 176 Alexander Semak
☐☐ 177 Valeri Zelepukin	☐☐ 178 Bruce Driver
☐☐ 179 Scott Niedermayer	☐☐ 180 Alexei Kasatonov
☐☐ 181 Scott Stevens	☐☐ 182 Flyers
☐☐ 183 D. Roussel (G)	☐☐ 184 Mike Ricci
☐☐ 185 Mark Recchi	☐☐ 186 Kevin Dineen
☐☐ 187 Rod Brind'Amour	☐☐ 188 Mark Pederson
☐☐ 189 Pelle Eklund	☐☐ 190 Terry Carkner
☐☐ 191 Mark Howe	☐☐ 192 Steve Duchesne
☐☐ 193 Andrei Lomakin	☐☐ 194 Islanders
☐☐ 195 Fitzpatrick (G)	☐☐ 196 Pierre Turgeon
☐☐ 197 Benoît Hogue	☐☐ 198 Ray Ferraro
☐☐ 199 Derek King	☐☐ 200 David Volek
☐☐ 201 Patrick Flatley	☐☐ 202 Uwe Krupp
☐☐ 203 Steve Thomas	☐☐ 204 Adam Creighton
☐☐ 205 Jeff Norton	☐☐ 206 Nordiques
☐☐ 207 S. Fiset (G)	☐☐ 208 Mikhail Tatarinov
☐☐ 209 Joe Sakic	☐☐ 210 Owen Nolan
☐☐ 211 Mike Hough	☐☐ 212 Mats Sundin
☐☐ 213 Claude Lapointe	☐☐ 214 Stéphane Morin
☐☐ 215 Alexei Gusarov	☐☐ 216 Steven Finn
☐☐ 217 Curtis Leschyshyn	☐☐ 218 Penguins
☐☐ 219 Tom Barrasso (G)	☐☐ 220 Mario Lemieux
☐☐ 221 Kevin Stevens	☐☐ 222 Shawn McEachern
☐☐ 223 Joe Mullen	☐☐ 224 Ron Francis
☐☐ 225 Phil Bourque	☐☐ 226 Rick Tocchet
☐☐ 227 Bryan Trottier	☐☐ 228 Larry Murphy
☐☐ 229 Ulf Samuelsson	☐☐ 230 Rangers
☐☐ 231 Mike Richter (G)	☐☐ 232 Vanbiesbrouck (G)
☐☐ 233 Mark Messier	☐☐ 234 Sergei Nemchinov
☐☐ 235 Darren Turcotte	☐☐ 236 Doug Weight
☐☐ 237 Mike Gartner	☐☐ 238 Adam Graves
☐☐ 239 Brian Leetch	☐☐ 240 James Patrick
☐☐ 241 Jan Erixon	☐☐ 242 Sabres
☐☐ 243 Tom Draper (G)	☐☐ 244 Grant Ledyard
☐☐ 245 Doug Bodger	☐☐ 246 Pat LaFontaine
☐☐ 247 Dale Hawerchuk	☐☐ 248 Alexander Mogilny
☐☐ 249 Dave Andreychuk	☐☐ 250 Christian Ruuttu
☐☐ 251 Randy Wood	☐☐ 252 Brad May
☐☐ 253 Mike Ramsey	☐☐ 254 Whalers
☐☐ 255 Kay Whitmore (G)	☐☐ 256 Pat Verbeek
☐☐ 257 John Cullen	☐☐ 258 Mikael Andersson
☐☐ 259 Yvon Corriveau	☐☐ 260 Cunneyworth
☐☐ 261 Bobby Holik	☐☐ 262 Murray Craven
☐☐ 263 Zarley Zalapski	☐☐ 264 Adam Burt
☐☐ 265 Brad Shaw	☐☐ 266 Lightning
☐☐ 267 Lightning	☐☐ 268 Senators
☐☐ 269 Senators	☐☐ 270 Tony Amonte
☐☐ 271 Pavel Bure	☐☐ 272 Gilbert Dionne
☐☐ 273 Pat Falloon	☐☐ 274 Nicklas Lidström
☐☐ 275 Kevin Todd	☐☐ 276 Wales Conference
☐☐ 277 Patrick Roy	☐☐ 278 Paul Coffey
☐☐ 279 Raymond Bourque	☐☐ 280 Mario Lemieux
☐☐ 281 Kevin Stevens	☐☐ 282 Jaromir Jagr
☐☐ 283 Campbell Conf..	☐☐ 284 Ed Belfour
☐☐ 285 Al MacInnis	☐☐ 286 Chris Chelios
☐☐ 287 Wayne Gretzky	☐☐ 288 Luc Robitaille
☐☐ 289 Brett Hull	☐☐ 290 Pavel Bure
☐☐ 291 Sergei Fedorov	☐☐ 292 Dominik Hasek (G)
☐☐ 293 Bobby Holik	☐☐ 294 Jaromir Jagr
☐☐ 295 Valeri Kamensky	☐☐ 296 Alexander Semak
☐☐ 297 Igor Kravchuk	☐☐ 298 Nicklas Lidström
☐☐ 299 Alexander Mogilny	☐☐ 300 Petr Nedved
☐☐ 301 Robert Reichel	☐☐ 302 Mats Sundin
☐☐ 303 Calder Trophy	☐☐ 304 Hart Trophy
☐☐ 305 Lady Byng Trophy	☐☐ 306 Norris Trophy
☐☐ 307 Selke Trophy	☐☐ 308 Vézina Trophy
☐☐ A Igor Kravchuk	☐☐ B Nelson Emerson
☐☐ C Pavel Bure	☐☐ D Tomas Forslund
☐☐ E Luciano Borsato	☐☐ F Darryl Sydor
☐☐ G Félix Potvin (G)	☐☐ H Derian Hatcher
☐☐ I Josef Beránek	☐☐ J Nicklas Lidström
☐☐ K Pat Falloon	☐☐ L Joé Juneau
☐☐ M Gilbert Dionne	☐☐ N Dmitri Khristich
☐☐ O Kevin Todd	☐☐ P Eric Lindros
☐☐ Q Scott Lachance	☐☐ R Valeri Kamensky
☐☐ S Jaromir Jagr	☐☐ T Tony Amonte
☐☐ U Donald Audette	☐☐ V Geoff Sanderson

1992 - 93 PANINI ACTION FREAKS

Imprint: None

Complete Set (110 stickers):	**10.00**
French Set (110 stickers):	**10.00**
Common Sticker:	**.20**

1992 - 93 PARKHURST

These cards have two versions: the regular card and an Emerald Ice parallel.

Imprint: © 1993 Pro Set Inc.

Series 1 Set (240 cards):	**95.00**	**20.00**
Series 2 Set (240 cards):	**80.00**	**15.00**
Final Update Set (30 cards):	**40.00**	**10.00**
Common Player (1-480):	**.35**	**.20**
Common Player (481-510):	**.35**	**.20**

	Player	Emerald	Parkie
☐☐	1 Raymond Bourque, Bost.	4.50	.50
☐☐	2 Joé Juneau, Bost. [CC]	.50	.20
☐☐	3 Andy Moog (G), Bost.	1.50	.20
☐☐	4 Adam Oates, Bost.	1.50	.20
☐☐	5 Vladimír Ruzicka, Bost.	.50	.20
☐☐	6 Glen Wesley, Bost.	.50	.20
☐☐	**7 Dmitri Kvartalnov, Bost. RC**	**.50**	**.50**
☐☐	8 Ted Donato, Bost. [CC]	.35	.20
☐☐	9 Glen Murray, Bost. [CC]	1.50	.20
☐☐	10 Dave Andreychuk, Buff.	1.00	.20

□□ 11 Dale Hawerchuk, Buff.	2.00	.20
□□ 12 Pat LaFontaine, Buff.	2.00	.20
□□ 13 Alexander Mogilny, Buff.	1.50	.20
□□ **14 Richard Smehlik, Buff. [CC] RC**	**.50**	**.50**
□□ **15 Keith Carney, Buff. [CC] RC**	**1.00**	**.50**
□□ 16 Philippe Boucher, Buff. [CC]	.35	.20
□□ 17 Viktor Gordiouk, Buff. [CC]	.35	.20
□□ 18 Donald Audette, Buff.	1.50	.20
□□ 19 Theoren Fleury, Calg.	2.00	.20
□□ 20 Al MacInnis, Calg.	1.50	.20
□□ 21 Joe Nieuwendyk, Calg.	1.50	.20
□□ 22 Gary Roberts, Calg.	1.50	.20
□□ 23 Gary Suter, Calg.	.50	.20
□□ 24 Mike Vernon (G), Calg.	1.50	.20
□□ 25 Sergei Makarov, Calg.	1.50	.20
□□ 26 Robert Reichel, Calg.	1.00	.20
□□ 27 Chris Lindberg, Calg. [CC]	.35	.20
□□ 28 Ed Belfour (G), Chic.	3.50	.50
□□ 29 Chris Chelios, Chic.	2.00	.20
□□ 30 Steve Larmer, Chic.	1.50	.20
□□ 31 Jeremy Roenick, Chic.	3.00	.20
□□ 32 J. Steve Smith, Chic.	.50	.20
□□ 33 Brent Sutter, Chic.	.50	.20
□□ 34 Christian Ruuttu, Chic.	.50	.20
□□ 35 Igor Kravchuk, Chic.	.50	.20
□□ 36 Sergei Krivokrasov, Chic. [CC]	.50	.20
□□ 37 Tim Cheveldae (G), Detr.	.50	.20
□□ 38 Mike Sillinger, Detr. [CC]	.50	.20
□□ 39 Sergei Fedorov, Detr.	3.50	.50
□□ 40 Vyacheslav Kozlov, Detr. [CC]	.50	.20
□□ 41 Bob Probert, Detr.	1.00	.20
□□ 42 Nicklas Lidström, Detr.	2.00	.20
□□ 43 Paul Ysebaert, Detr.	.35	.20
□□ 44 Steve Yzerman, Detr.	9.00	1.00
□□ 45 Dino Ciccarelli, Detr.	1.00	.20
□□ 46 Esa Tikkanen, Edmo.	.50	.20
□□ 47 Dave Manson, Edmo.	.50	.20
□□ 48 Craig MacTavish, Edmo.	.50	.20
□□ 49 Bernie Nicholls, Edmo.	.50	.20
□□ 50 Bill Ranford (G), Edmo.	1.50	.20
□□ 51 Craig Simpson, Edmo.	.50	.20
□□ 52 Scott Mellanby, Edmo.	.50	.20
□□ 53 Shayne Corson, Edmo.	1.00	.20
□□ 54 Petr Klima, Edmo.	.50	.20
□□ 55 Murray Craven, Hart.	.50	.20
□□ 56 Eric Weinrich, Hart.	.35	.20
□□ 57 Sean Burke (G), Hart.	2.00	.20
□□ 58 Pat Verbeek, Hart.	1.00	.20
□□ 59 Zarley Zalapski, Hart.	.35	.20
□□ 60 Patrick Poulin, Hart. [CC]	.50	.20
□□ **61 Robert Petrovicky, Hart. [CC] RC**	**1.00**	**.50**
□□ 62 Geoff Sanderson, Hart.	.50	.20
□□ 63 Paul Coffey, LosA.	2.00	.20
□□ **64 Robert Lang, LosA. [CC] RC**	**1.50**	**1.00**
□□ 65 Wayne Gretzky, LosA.	15.00	2.00
□□ 66 Kelly Hrudey (G), LosA.	1.00	.20
□□ 67 Jari Kurri, LosA.	3.50	.50
□□ 68 Luc Robitaille, LosA.	3.00	.20
□□ 69 Darryl Sydor, LosA. [CC]	.50	.20
□□ **70 Jim Hiller, LosA. [CC] RC**	**.50**	**.50**
□□ 71 Alexei Zhitnik, LosA. [CC]	.50	.20
□□ 72 Derian Hatcher, Minn.	1.00	.20
□□ 73 Jon Casey (G), Minn.	.50	.20
□□ **74 Richard Matvichuk, Minn. [CC] RC**	**1.50**	**1.00**
□□ 75 Mike Modano, Minn.	3.50	.50
□□ 76 Mark Tinordi, Minn.	.50	.20
□□ 77 Todd Elik, Minn.	.35	.20
□□ 78 Russ Courtnall, Minn.	.50	.20
□□ **79 Tommy Sjödin, Minn. RC**	**.50**	**.50**
□□ 80 Éric Desjardins, Mont.	1.00	.20
□□ 81 Gilbert Dionne, Mont.	.35	.20
□□ 82 Stéphan Lebeau, Mont.	.35	.20
□□ 83 Kirk Muller, Mont.	1.00	.20
□□ 84 Patrick Roy (G), Mont.	10.00	1.50
□□ 85 Denis Savard, Mont.	1.50	.20
□□ 86 Vincent Damphousse, Mont.	2.00	.20
□□ 87 Brian Bellows, Mont.	.50	.20
□□ **88 Ed Ronan, Mont. [CC] RC**	**.50**	**.50**
□□ 89 Claude Lemieux, NJer.	1.00	.20
□□ 90 John MacLean, NJer.	.50	.20
□□ 91 Stéphane Richer, NJer.	.50	.20
□□ 92 Scott Stevens, NJer.	1.50	.20
□□ 93 Chris Terreri (G), NJer.	.50	.20
□□ 94 Kevin Todd, NJer.	.35	.20
□□ 95 Scott Niedermayer, NJer. [CC]	1.00	.20
□□ 96 Bobby Holik, NJer.	1.00	.20
□□ 97 Bill Guerin, NJer. [CC]	4.50	.50
□□ 98 Ray Ferraro, NYIs.	.50	.20
□□ 99 Mark Fitzpatrick (G), NYIs.	.50	.20
□□ 100 Derek King, NYIs.	.50	.20
□□ 101 Uwe Krupp, NYIs.	.35	.20
□□ 102 Darius Kasparaitis, NYIs. [CC]	.50	.20
□□ 103 Pierre Turgeon, NYIs.	1.50	.20
□□ 104 Benoît Hogue, NYIs.	.50	.20
□□ 105 Scott Lachance, NYIs. [CC]	.50	.20
□□ 106 Marty McInnis, NYIs. [CC]	.50	.20
□□ 107 Tony Amonte, NYRa.	2.00	.20
□□ 108 Mike Gartner, NYRa.	3.00	.20
□□ 109 Alexei Kovalev, NYRa. [CC]	4.50	.50
□□ 110 Brian Leetch, NYRa.	2.00	.20
□□ 111 Mark Messier, NYRa.	3.50	.50
□□ 112 Mike Richter (G), NYRa.	1.50	.20
□□ 113 James Patrick, NYRa.	.35	.20
□□ 114 Sergei Nemchinov, NYRa.	.50	.20
□□ 115 Doug Weight, NYRa.	2.00	.20
□□ 116 Mark Lamb, Otta.	.35	.20
□□ 117 Norm Maciver, Otta.	.35	.20
□□ 118 Mike Peluso, Otta.	.35	.20
□□ 119 Jody Hull, Otta.	.35	.20
□□ 120 Peter Sidorkiewicz (G), Otta.	.50	.20
□□ 121 Sylvain Turgeon, Otta.	.50	.20
□□ 122 Laurie Boschman, Otta.	.35	.20
□□ 123 Brad Marsh, Otta.	.35	.20
□□ 124 Neil Brady, Otta.	.35	.20
□□ 125 Brian Benning, Phil.	.35	.20
□□ 126 Rod Brind'Amour, Phil.	1.00	.20
□□ 127 Kevin Dineen, Phil.	.50	.20
□□ 128 Eric Lindros, Phil. [CC]	7.50	1.00
□□ 129 Dominic Roussel (G), Phil. [CC]	.50	.20
□□ 130 Mark Recchi, Phil.	1.50	.20
□□ 131 Brent Fedyk, Phil.	.35	.20
□□ 132 Greg Paslawski, Phil.	.35	.20
□□ **133 D. Yushkevich, Phil. [CC] RC**	**1.50**	**1.00**
□□ 134 Tom Barrasso (G), Pitt.	1.50	.20
□□ 135 Jaromir Jagr, Pitt.	3.50	.50
□□ 136 Mario Lemieux, Pitt.	10.00	1.50
□□ 137 Larry Murphy, Pitt.	.50	.20
□□ 138 Kevin Stevens, Pitt.	.50	.20
□□ 139 Rick Tocchet, Pitt.	1.00	.20
□□ **140 Martin Straka, Pitt. [CC] RC**	**2.00**	**1.50**
□□ 141 Ron Francis, Pitt.	2.00	.20
□□ 142 Shawn McEachern, Pitt. [CC]	1.00	.20
□□ 143 Steve Duchesne, Québ.	.50	.20
□□ 144 Ron Hextall (G), Québ.	2.00	.20
□□ 145 Owen Nolan, Québ.	2.00	.20
□□ 146 Mike Ricci, Québ.	1.00	.20
□□ 147 Joe Sakic, Québ.	6.00	.50
□□ 148 Mats Sundin, Québ.	3.50	.50
□□ 149 Martin Rucinsky, Québ. [CC]	.50	.20
□□ 150 Andrei Kovalenko, Québ. [CC]	.50	.20
□□ **151 Dave Karpa, Québ. [CC] RC**	**.50**	**.50**
□□ 152 Nelson Emerson, SLou.	.50	.20
□□ 153 Brett Hull, SLou.	3.50	.50
□□ 154 Craig Janney, SLou.	.50	.20
□□ 155 Curtis Joseph (G), SLou.	3.50	.50
□□ 156 Brendan Shanahan, SLou.	3.50	.50
□□ **157 Vitali Prokhorov, SLou. [CC] RC**	**.50**	**.50**
□□ 158 Igor Korolev, SLou. [CC]	.50	.20
□□ 159 Philippe Bozon, SLou. [CC]	.35	.20
□□ 160 Ray Whitney, SanJ.	2.50	.20
□□ 161 Pat Falloon, SanJ.	.50	.20
□□ 162 Jeff Hackett (G), SanJ.	1.00	.20
□□ 163 Brian Lawton, SanJ.	.50	.20
□□ 164 Sandis Ozolinsh, SanJ. [CC]	.50	.20
□□ 165 Neil Wilkinson, SanJ.	.35	.20
□□ 166 Kelly Kisio, SanJ.	.35	.20
□□ 167 Doug Wilson, SanJ.	1.00	.20
□□ 168 Dale Craigwell, SanJ.	.35	.20
□□ 169 Mikael Andersson, Tamp.	.35	.20
□□ 170 Wendell Young (G), Tamp.	.50	.20
□□ **171 Rob Zamuner, Tamp. [CC] RC**	**1.50**	**1.00**
□□ 172 Adam Creighton, Tamp.	.35	.20
□□ **173 Roman Hamrlik, Tamp. [CC] RC**	**1.50**	**1.00**
□□ 174 Brian Bradley, Tamp.	.35	.20
□□ 175 Rob Ramage, Tamp.	.50	.20
□□ **176 Chris Kontos, Tamp. RC**	**.50**	**.50**
□□ **177 Stan Drulia, Tamp. [CC] RC**	**.50**	**.50**
□□ 178 Glenn Anderson, Toro.	1.00	.20
□□ 179 Wendel Clark, Toro.	3.00	.20
□□ 180 John Cullen, Toro.	.50	.20
□□ 181 Dave Ellett, Toro.	.50	.20
□□ 182 Grant Fuhr (G), Toro.	2.00	.20
□□ 183 Doug Gilmour, Toro.	2.00	.20
□□ 184 Kent Manderville, Toro. [CC]	.35	.20
□□ 185 Joe Sacco, Toro.	.35	.20
□□ **186 Nikolai Borschevsky, Toro. RC**	**.50**	**.50**
□□ 187 Félix Potvin (G), Toro. [CC]	2.00	.20
□□ 188 Pavel Bure, Vanc.	3.00	.20
□□ 189 Geoff Courtnall, Vanc.	.50	.20
□□ 190 Trevor Linden, Vanc.	1.50	.20
□□ 191 Jyrki Lumme, Vanc.	.50	.20
□□ 192 Kirk McLean (G), Vanc.	1.00	.20
□□ 193 Cliff Ronning, Vanc.	.50	.20
□□ **194 Dixon Ward, Vanc. [CC] RC**	**.50**	**.50**
□□ 195 Greg A. Adams, Vanc.	.35	.20
□□ 196 Jirí Slégr, Vanc. [CC]	.50	.20
□□ 197 Don Beaupré (G), Wash.	.50	.20
□□ 198 Kevin Hatcher, Wash.	.50	.20
□□ 199 Brad Schlegel, Wash. [CC]	.35	.20
□□ 200 Mike Ridley, Wash.	.50	.20
□□ 201 Calle Johansson, Wash.	.50	.20
□□ **202 Steve Konowalchuk, Wash. [CC] RC**	**1.50**	**1.00**
□□ 203 Al Iafrate, Wash.	.50	.20
□□ 204 Peter Bondra, Wash.	2.00	.20
□□ 205 Pat Elynuik, Wash.	.35	.20
□□ 206 Keith Tkachuk, Winn. [CC]	4.50	.50
□□ 207 Bob Essensa, Winn.	.50	.20
□□ 208 Phil Housley, Winn.	1.00	.20
□□ 209 Teemu Selänne, Winn. [CC]	6.00	.50
□□ 210 Alexei Zhamnov, Winn. [CC]	2.00	.20
□□ 211 Evgeny Davydov, Winn. [CC]	.35	.20
□□ 212 Fredrik Olausson, Winn.	.50	.20
□□ 213 Ed Olczyk, Winn.	.50	.20
□□ 214 Thomas Steen, Winn.	.50	.20
□□ 215 Darius Kasparaitis, NYIs. [IRS]	.50	.20
□□ 216 Nikolai Borschevsky, Toro. [IRS]	.35	.20
□□ 217 Teemu Selänne, Winn. [IRS]	6.00	.50
□□ 218 Alexander Mogilny, Buff. [IRS]	1.50	.20
□□ 219 Sergei Fedorov, Detr. [IRS]	3.50	.50
□□ 220 Jaromir Jagr, Pitt. [IRS]	3.50	.50
□□ 221 Mats Sundin, Québ. [IRS]	3.50	.50
□□ 222 Dmitri Kvartalnov, Bost. [IRS]	.35	.20
□□ 223 Andrei Kovalenko, Québ. [IRS]	1.00	.20
□□ 224 Tommy Sjödin, Minn. [IRS]	.35	.20
□□ 225 Alexei Kovalev, NYRa. [IRS]	4.50	.50
□□ 226 Evgeny Davydov, Winn. [IRS]	.35	.20
□□ 227 Robert Lang, LosA. [IRS]	.50	.20
□□ 228 Valeri Zelepukin, NJer. [SS]	.35	.20
□□ 229 Doug Weight, NYRa. [SS]	2.00	.20
□□ 230 Valeri Kamensky, Québ. [SS]	1.00	.20
□□ 231 Donald Audette, Buff. [SS]	1.50	.20
□□ 232 Nelson Emerson, SLou. [SS]	.50	.20
□□ 233 Pat Falloon, SanJ. [SS]	.50	.20
□□ 234 Pavel Bure, Vanc. [SS]	3.00	.20
□□ 235 Tony Amonte, NYRa. [SS]	2.00	.20
□□ 236 Sergei Nemchinov, NYRa. [SS]	.50	.20
□□ 237 Gilbert Dionne, Mont. [SS]	.35	.20
□□ 238 Kevin Todd, NJer. [SS]	.35	.20
□□ 239 Nicklas Lidström, Detr. [SS]	2.00	.20
□□ 240 Brad May, Buff. [SS]	.50	.20
□□ 241 Stephen Leach, Bost.	.35	.20
□□ 242 Dave Poulin, Bost.	.50	.20
□□ **243 Grigori Panteleev, Bost. [CC] RC**	**.50**	**.50**
□□ 244 Don Sweeney, Bost.	.50	.20
□□ **245 John Blue, Bost. RC**	**1.00**	**.50**
□□ **246 C.J. Young, Bost. [CC] RC**	**.50**	**.50**
□□ 247 Stephen Heinze, Bost. [CC]	.50	.20
□□ 248 Cam Neely, Bost.	3.50	.50
□□ 249 David Reid, Bost.	.50	.20
□□ 250 Grant Fuhr (G), Buff.	2.00	.20
□□ 251 Bob Sweeney, Buff.	.35	.20
□□ 252 Rob Ray, Buff.	.50	.20
□□ 253 Doug Bodger, Buff.	.35	.20
□□ 254 Ken Sutton, Buff.	.35	.20
□□ 255 Yuri Khmylev, Buff.	.50	.20
□□ 256 Mike Ramsey, Buff.	.50	.20
□□ 257 Brad May, Buff.	.50	.20
□□ 258 Brent Ashton, Calg.	.35	.20
□□ 259 Joel Otto, Calg.	.50	.20
□□ 260 Paul Ranheim, Calg.	.50	.20
□□ **261 Kevin Dahl, Calg. [CC] RC**	**.50**	**.50**
□□ 262 Trent Yawney, Calg.	.35	.20
□□ 263 Roger Johansson, Calg.	.35	.20
□□ 264 Jeff Reese (G), Calg.	.50	.20
□□ 265 Ronnie Stern, Calg.	.35	.20
□□ 266 Brian Skrudland, Calg.	.50	.20
□□ 267 Bryan Marchment, Chic.	.50	.20
□□ 268 Stéphane Matteau, Chic.	.50	.20
□□ 269 Frantisek Kucera, Chic.	.35	.20
□□ 270 Jimmy Waite (G), Chic.	.50	.20
□□ 271 Dirk Graham, Chic.	.50	.20
□□ 272 Michel Goulet, Chic.	1.50	.20
□□ 273 Joe Murphy, Chic.	.50	.20
□□ 274 Keith Brown, Chic.	.35	.20
□□ 275 Jocelyn Lemieux, Chic.	.35	.20
□□ 276 Paul Coffey, Detr.	2.00	.20
□□ 277 Keith Primeau, Detr.	1.50	.20
□□ 278 Vincent Riendeau (G), Detr.	.50	.20
□□ 279 Mark Howe, Detr.	1.00	.20
□□ 280 Ray Sheppard, Detr.	.50	.20
□□ 281 Jim Hiller, Detr. [CC]	.35	.20
□□ 282 Steve Chiasson, Detr.	.50	.20
□□ 283 Vladimir Konstantinov, Detr.	1.00	.20
□□ 284 Brian Benning, Edmo.	.35	.20
□□ 285 Kevin Todd, Edmo.	.35	.20
□□ 286 Zdeno Ciger, Edmo.	.35	.20
□□ 287 Brian Glynn, Edmo.	.35	.20
□□ 288 Shaun Van Allen, Edmo. [CC]	.50	.20
□□ **289 Brad Werenka, Edmo. [CC] RC**	**.50**	**.50**
□□ 290 Ron Tugnutt, Edmo.	1.50	.20
□□ 291 Igor Kravchuk, Edmo.	.50	.20
□□ 292 Todd Elik, Edmo.	.35	.20
□□ 293 Terry Yake, Hart.	.35	.20
□□ **294 M. Nylander, Hart. [CC] RC**	**1.50**	**1.00**
□□ 295 Yvon Corriveau, Hart.	.35	.20
□□ 296 Frank Pietrangelo, Hart.	.50	.20
□□ 297 Nick Kypreos, Hart.	.50	.20
□□ 298 Andrew Cassels, Hart.	.50	.20
□□ 299 Steve Konroyd, Hart.	.35	.20
□□ 300 Allen Pedersen, Hart.	.35	.20
□□ 301 Tony Granato, LosA.	.50	.20
□□ 302 Rob Blake, LosA.	2.00	.20
□□ 303 Robb Stauber (G), LosA. [CC]	.50	.20
□□ 304 Marty McSorley, LosA.	.50	.20
□□ **305 Lonnie Loach, LosA. [CC] RC**	**.50**	**.50**
□□ 306 Corey Millen, LosA.	.35	.20
□□ 307 Dave (Stitch) Taylor, LosA.	.50	.20
□□ 308 Jimmy Carson, LosA.	.50	.20
□□ **309 Warren Rychel, LosA. RC**	**.50**	**.50**
□□ 310 Ulf Dahlén, Minn.	.50	.20
□□ 311 Dave Gagner, Minn.	.50	.20
□□ **312 Brad Berry, Minn. RC**	**.50**	**.50**
□□ 313 Neal Broten, Minn.	.50	.20
□□ 314 Mike Craig, Minn.	.35	.20
□□ 315 Darcy Wakaluk (G), Minn.	.50	.20
□□ 316 Shane Churla, Minn.	.35	.20
□□ 317 Trent Klatt, Minn. [CC]	1.00	.20
□□ 318 Mike Keane, Mont.	.50	.20
□□ 319 Mathieu Schneider, Mont.	.50	.20
□□ 320 Patrice Brisebois, Mont.	.50	.20
□□ 321 André Racicot (G), Mont.	.50	.20
□□ 322 Mario Roberge, Mont.	.35	.20
□□ 323 Gary Leeman, Mont.	.50	.20
□□ 324 J.J. Daigneault, Mont.	.50	.20
□□ 325 Lyle Odelein, Mont.	.50	.20
□□ 326 John LeClair, Mont.	3.00	.20
□□ 327 Valeri Zelepukin, NJer.	.35	.20
□□ 328 Bernie Nicholls, NJer.	.50	.20
□□ 329 Alexander Semak, NJer.	.35	.20
□□ 330 Craig Billington (G), NJer.	.50	.20
□□ 331 Randy McKay, NJer.	.35	.20
□□ 332 Ken Daneyko, NJer.	.50	.20
□□ 333 Bruce Driver, NJer.	.35	.20
□□ 334 Viacheslav Fetisov, NJer.	2.00	.20
□□ 335 Dennis Vaske, NYIs.	.35	.20
□□ 336 Brad Dalgarno, NYIs.	.35	.20
□□ 337 Jeff Norton, NYIs.	.35	.20
□□ 338 Steve Thomas, NYIs.	.50	.20
□□ 339 Vladimir Malakhov, NYIs. [CC]	.50	.20
□□ 340 David Volek, NYIs.	.35	.20
□□ 341 Glenn Healy (G), NYIs.	.50	.20
□□ 342 Patrick Flatley, NYIs.	.35	.20
□□ **343 Travis Green, NYIs. [CC] RC**	**1.50**	**1.00**
□□ **344 Corey Hirsch, NYRa. [CC] RC**	**1.00**	**.50**
□□ 345 Darren Turcotte, NYRa.	.50	.20
□□ 346 Adam Graves, NYRa.	1.50	.20
□□ **347 Steven King, NYRa. [CC] RC**	**.50**	**.50**
□□ 348 Kevin Lowe, NYRa.	1.00	.20
□□ 349 John Vanbiesbrouck (G), NYRa.	1.50	.20
□□ 350 Ed Olczyk, NYRa.	.50	.20
□□ 351 Sergei Zubov, NYRa. [CC]	1.50	.50
□□ 352 Brad Shaw, Otta.	.35	.20
□□ 353 Jamie Baker, Otta.	.35	.20
□□ 354 Mark Freer, Otta.	.35	.20
□□ 355 Darcy Loewen, Otta. [CC]	.35	.20
□□ **356 Darren Rumble, Otta. RC**	**.50**	**.50**
□□ 357 Bob Kudelski, Otta.	.35	.20
□□ 358 Ken Hammond, Otta.	.35	.20
□□ 359 Daniel Berthiaume (G), Otta.	.50	.20
□□ 360 Josef Beránek, Phil.	.50	.20
□□ 361 Greg Hawgood, Phil.	.50	.20
□□ 362 Terry Carkner, Phil.	.35	.20
□□ 363 Viacheslav Butsayev, Phil. [CC]	.50	.20
□□ 364 Garry Galley, Phil.	.35	.20
□□ **365 André Faust, Phil. [CC] RC**	**.50**	**.50**
□□ **366 Ryan McGill, Phil. [CC] RC**	**.50**	**.50**
□□ **367 T. Söderström, Phil. [CC] RC**	**1.00**	**.50**
□□ 368 Joe Mullen, Pitt.	1.50	.20
□□ 369 Ulf Samuelsson, Pitt.	.50	.20
□□ **370 Mike Needham, Pitt. [CC] RC**	**.50**	**.50**
□□ 371 Ken Wregget (G), Pitt.	.50	.20
□□ 372 Dave Tippett, Pitt.	.35	.20
□□ 373 Kjell Samuelsson, Pitt.	.50	.20
□□ 374 Bob Errey, Pitt.	.50	.20
□□ 375 Jim Paek, Pitt.	.35	.20
□□ **376 Bill Lindsay, Québ. [CC] RC**	**.50**	**.50**
□□ 377 Valeri Kamensky, Québ.	1.00	.20
□□ 378 Stéphane Fiset (G), Québ.	1.00	.20
□□ 379 Steven Finn, Québ.	.35	.20
□□ 380 Mike Hough, Québ.	.35	.20
□□ 381 Scott Pearson, Québ.	.35	.20
□□ 382 Kerry Huffman, Québ.	.35	.20
□□ 383 Scott A. Young, Québ.	1.00	.20
□□ 384 Stéphane Quintal, SLou.	.50	.20
□□ **385 Bret Hedican, SLou. [CC] RC**	**.50**	**.50**
□□ **386 Guy Hebert (G), SLou. [CC] RC**	**1.50**	**1.00**
□□ **387 Vitali Karamnov, SLou. [CC] RC**	**.50**	**.50**
□□ 388 Doug Crossman, SLou.	.35	.20
□□ 389 Ron Sutter, SLou.	.50	.20
□□ 390 Garth Butcher, SLou.	.35	.20
□□ 391 Basil McRae, SLou.	.50	.20
□□ 392 Dean Evason, SanJ.	.35	.20
□□ 393 Doug Zmolek, SanJ. [CC]	.35	.20
□□ 394 Jayson More, SanJ.	.35	.20
□□ 395 Mike Sullivan, SanJ.	.35	.20
□□ 396 Arturs Irbe (G), SanJ. [CC]	3.00	.20
□□ 397 Johan Garpenlöv, SanJ.	.35	.20
□□ 398 Jeff Odgers, SanJ.	.50	.20
□□ **399 Jaroslav Otevrel, SanJ. [CC] RC**	**.50**	**.50**
□□ 400 Marc Bureau, Tamp.	.35	.20
□□ 401 Bob Beers, Tamp.	.35	.20
□□ 402 Rob DiMaio, Tamp.	.50	.20
□□ 403 Steve Kasper, Tamp.	.50	.20
□□ 404 Pat Jablonski (G), Tamp.	.50	.20
□□ 405 John Tucker, Tamp.	.35	.20
□□ 406 Shawn Chambers, Tamp.	.35	.20
□□ 407 Mike Hartman, Tamp.	.35	.20
□□ 408 Danton Cole, Tamp.	.35	.20
□□ 409 Dave Andreychuk, Toro.	1.00	.20
□□ 410 Peter Zezel, Toro.	.50	.20
□□ 411 Mike Krushelnyski, Toro.	.35	.20
□□ 412 Daren Puppa (G), Toro.	.50	.20
□□ 413 Ken Baumgartner, Toro.	.35	.20
□□ 414 Rob Pearson, Toro.	.35	.20
□□ 415 Mike Foligno, Toro.	.50	.20
□□ 416 Sylvain Lefebvre, Toro.	.50	.20
□□ 417 Dmitri Mironov, Toro.	.50	.20
□□ 418 Petr Nedved, Vanc.	1.00	.20
□□ 419 Gerald Diduck, Vanc.	.35	.20
□□ 420 Anatoli Semenov, Vanc.	.35	.20
□□ 421 Sergio Momesso, Vanc.	.35	.20
□□ 422 Gino Odjick, Vanc.	.50	.20
□□ 423 Kay Whitmore (G), Vanc.	.50	.20
□□ 424 Dave Babych, Vanc.	.50	.20
□□ 425 Robert Dirk, Vanc.	.35	.20
□□ 426 Reggie Savage, Wash. [CC]	.35	.20
□□ **427 Keith Jones, Wash. [CC] RC**	**1.00**	**.50**
□□ 428 Dmitri Khristich, Wash.	.50	.20
□□ **429 Jason Woolley, Wash. [CC] RC**	**.50**	**.50**
□□ 430 Jim Hrivnak (G), Wash.	.35	.20
□□ 431 Sylvain Côté, Wash.	.50	.20
□□ 432 Michal Pivonka, Wash.	.35	.20
□□ 433 Rod Langway, Wash.	1.50	.20
□□ 434 Tie Domi, Winn.	1.00	.20
□□ **435 Sergei Bautin, Winn. [CC] RC**	**.50**	**.50**
□□ 436 Darrin Shannon, Winn.	.35	.20
□□ 437 John Druce, Winn.	.35	.20
□□ 438 Teppo Numminen, Winn.	1.00	.20
□□ 439 Luciano Borsato, Winn.	.35	.20
□□ 440 Igor Ulanov, Winn.	.50	.20
□□ **441 Mike O'Neill, Winn. [CC] RC**	**.50**	**.50**
□□ 442 Kris King, Winn.	.50	.20
□□ 443 Roman Hamrlik, Tamp. [IRS]	.50	.20
□□ 444 J. Steve Smith, Chic. [IRS]	.50	.20
□□ 445 Jari Kurri, LosA. [IRS]	3.50	.50
□□ 446 Ulf Samuelsson, Pitt. [IRS]	.50	.20
□□ 447 Sergei Nemchinov, NYRa. [IRS]	.50	.20
□□ 448 Tommy Söderström, Phil. [IRS]	.50	.20
□□ 449 Petr Nedved, Vanc. [IRS]	1.00	.20
□□ 450 Peter Sidorkiewicz (G), Otta. [IRS]	.50	.20
□□ 451 Nicklas Lidström, Detr. [IRS]	2.00	.20
□□ 452 Philippe Bozon, SLou. [IRS]	.35	.20
□□ 453 Uwe Krupp, NYIs. [IRS]	.35	.20
□□ 454 Steve Thomas, NYIs. [IRS]	.50	.20
□□ 455 Owen Nolan, Québ. [IRS]	2.00	.20
□□ 456 Steve Yzerman, Detr. [All-Stars]	9.00	1.00
□□ 457 Chris Chelios, Chic. [All-Stars]	2.00	.20
□□ 458 Paul Coffey, Detr. [All-Stars]	2.00	.20
□□ 459 Brett Hull, SLou. [All-Stars]	3.50	.50
□□ 460 Pavel Bure, Vanc. [All-Stars]	3.00	.20
□□ 461 Ed Belfour (G), Chic. [All-Stars]	3.50	.50
□□ 462 Mario Lemieux, Pitt. [All-Stars]	10.00	1.50
□□ 463 Patrick Roy (G), Mont. [All-Stars]	10.00	1.50
□□ 464 Raymond Bourque, Bost. [All-Stars]	4.50	.50
□□ 465 Jaromir Jagr, Pitt. [All-Stars]	3.50	.50
□□ 466 Kevin Stevens, Pitt. [All-Stars]	.50	.20
□□ 467 Brian Leetch, NYRa. [All-Stars]	2.00	.20
□□ 468 Bobby Clarke, Phil. [Dynasty]	3.00	.20
□□ 469 Bill Barber, Phil. [Dynasty]	1.50	.20
□□ 470 Bernie Parent, Phil. [Dynasty]	3.00	.20
□□ 471 Reggie Leach, Phil. [Dynasty]	.50	.20
□□ 472 Rick MacLeish, Phil. [Dynasty]	.50	.20
□□ 473 Dave Schultz, Phil. [Dynasty]	1.00	.20
□□ 474 Joe Watson, Phil. [Dynasty]	.35	.20
□□ 475 Bobby Taylor, Phil. [Dynasty]	.35	.20
□□ 476 Orest Kindrachuk, Phil. [Dynasty]	.35	.20
□□ 477 Bob Kelly, Phil. [Dynasty]	.50	.20
□□ 478 Bill Clement, Phil. [Dynasty]	.50	.20
□□ 479 Ed Van Impe, Phil. [Dynasty]	.35	.20
□□ 480 Fred Shero, Phil. [Dynasty]	.50	.20
□□ **481 Bryan Smolinski, Bost. RC**	**1.00**	**.50**
□□ 482 Sergei Zholtok, Bost.	.50	.20
□□ **483 Matthew Barnaby, Buff. RC**	**.50**	**.50**
□□ 484 Gary Shuchuk, LosA.	.35	.20
□□ 485 Guy Carbonneau, Mont.	1.00	.20

□□	**486 Oleg Petrov, Mont. RC**	**2.00**	**1.50**
□□	**487 Sean Hill, Mont. RC**	**.50**	**.50**
□□	**488 Jesse Bélanger, Mont. RC**	**.50**	**.50**
□□	489 Paul DiPietro, Mont.	.35	.20
□□	490 Richard Pilon, NYIs.	.35	.20
□□	491 Greg Parks, NYIs.	.35	.20
□□	492 Jeff Daniels, Pitt.	.35	.20
□□	**493 Denny Felsner, SLou. RC**	**.50**	**.50**
□□	**494 Mike Eastwood, Toro. RC**	**.50**	**.50**
□□	495 Murray Craven, Vanc.	.50	.20
□□	496 V. Damphousse, Mont. [Playoffs]	2.00	.20
□□	497 Grant Fuhr (G), Buff. [Playoffs]	2.00	.20
□□	498 Mario Lemieux, Pitt. [Playoffs]	10.00	1.50
□□	499 Ray Ferraro, NYIs. [Playoffs]	.50	.20
□□	500 Teemu Selänne, Winn. [Playoffs]	3.00	.20
□□	501 Luc Robitaille, LosA. [Playoffs]	3.00	.20
□□	502 Doug Gilmour, Toro. [Playoffs]	2.00	.20
□□	503 Curtis Joseph (G), SLou. [Playoffs]	3.50	.50
□□	504 Kirk Muller, Mont. [Playoffs]	1.00	.20
□□	505 Glenn Healy (G), NYIs. [Playoffs]	.50	.20
□□	506 Pavel Bure, Vanc. [Playoffs]	3.00	.20
□□	507 Félix Potvin (G), Toro. [Playoffs]	2.00	.20
□□	508 Guy Carbonneau, Mont. [Playoffs]	1.00	.20
□□	509 Wayne Gretzky, LosA. [Playoffs]	15.00	2.00
□□	510 Patrick Roy (G), Mont. [Playoffs]	10.00	1.50

CHERRY PICKS

This 21-card set was randomly inserted in the Series Two regular and jumbo foil packs. The Don Cherry Thumbs Up autographed card was inserted only in jumbo Series Two foil packs.

Series Two Insert Set (CP1-CP20): **85.00**

	Player	**CP**
□	CP1 Doug Gilmour, Toro.	6.00
□	CP2 Jeremy Roenick, Chic.	8.00
□	CP3 Brent Sutter, Chic.	3.00
□	CP4 Mark Messier, NYRa.	10.00
□	CP5 Kirk Muller, Mont.	3.00
□	CP6 Eric Lindros, Phil.	10.00
□	CP7 Dale Hunter, Wash.	3.00
□	CP8 Gary Roberts, Calg.	4.00
□	CP9 Bob Probert, Detr.	3.00
□	CP10 Brendan Shanahan, SLou.	10.00
□	CP11 Wendel Clark, Toro.	8.00
□	CP12 Rick Tocchet, Pitt.	3.00
□	CP13 Owen Nolan, Québ.	6.00
□	CP14 Cam Neely, Bost.	10.00
□	CP15 Dave Manson, Edmo.	3.00
□	CP16 Chris Chelios, Chic.	6.00
□	CP17 Marty McSorley, LosA.	3.00
□	CP18 Scott Stevens, NJer.	4.00
□	CP19 John Blue, Bost.	3.00
□	CP20 Ron Hextall (G), Québ.	6.00
	Player	**NM-MT**
□	Don Cherry Checklist	25.00
□	Don Cherry Autograph ✍	175.00
□	CP1993 Doug Gilmour, Toro. [Update Insert]	12.00
□	Don Cherry Redemption	12.00

PARKIE REPRINTS

Series 1 Regular Pack (1-8/CL1): **60.00**
Series 1 Jumbo Pack (9-16/CL2): **45.00**
Series 2 Regular Pack (17-24/CL3): **35.00**
Series 2 Jumbo Pack (25-32/CL4): **60.00**

	Parkie	**Reprint**
□	PR-1 Jacques Plante, Mont. [1955-56 Parkie]	16.00
□	PR-2 Terry Sawchuk, Detr. [1951-52 Parkie]	20.00
□	PR-3 Johnny Bower, Toro. [1959-60 Parkie]	8.00
□	PR-4 Gump Worsley, NYRa. [1953-54 Parkie]	8.00
□	PR-5 Harry Lumley, Toro. [1953-54 Parkie]	5.00
□	PR-6 Turk Broda, Toro. [1951-52 Parkie]	8.00
□	PR-7 Jim Henry, Bost. [1952-53 Parkie]	5.00
□	PR-8 Al Rollins, Chic. [1954-55 Parkie]	5.00
□	Checklist 1 [1955-56 Parkie]	5.00
□	PR-9 Bill Gadsby, Chic. [1953-54Parkie]	5.00
□	PR-10 Red Kelly, Detr. [1954-55 Parkie]	6.00
□	PR-11 Allan Stanley, NYRa. [1952-53 Parkie]	5.00
□	PR-12 Bob Baun, Toro. [1959-60 Parkie]	5.00
□	PR-13 Carl Brewer, Toro. [1962-63 Parkie]	5.00
□	PR-14 Doug Harvey, Mont. [1954-55Parkie]	12.00
□	PR-15 Harry Howell, NYRa. [1953-54 Parkie]	5.00
□	PR-16 Tim Horton, Toro. [1955-56 Parkie]	12.00
□	Checklist 2 [1953-54 Parkie]	5.00
□	PR-17 G. Armstrong, Toro. [1953-54 Parkie]	5.00
□	PR-18 R. Backstrom, Mont. [1958-59 Parkie]	5.00
□	PR-19 Alex Delvecchio, Detr. [1963-64 Parkie]	5.00
□	PR-20 Bill Mosienko, Chic. [1953-54 Parkie]	5.00
□	PR-21 Dave Keon, Toro. [1961-62 Parkie]	8.00
□	PR-22 A. Bathgate, NYRa. [1953-54 Parkie]	5.00
□	PR-23 Milt Schmidt, Bost. [1952-53 Parkie]	6.00
□	PR-24 Dick Duff, Toro. [1958-59 Parkie]	5.00
□	Checklist 3 [1958-59 Parkie]	5.00
□	PR-25 Norm Ullman, Detr. [1962-63 Parkie]	5.00
□	PR-26 Dickie Moore, Mont. [1955-56 Parkie]	6.00
□	PR-27 Jerry Toppazzini, Bost.	5.00
□	PR-28 Henri Richard, Mont.	10.00
□	PR-29 Frank Mahovlich, Toro.	10.00
□	PR-30 Jean Béliveau, Mont.	22.00
□	PR-31 Ted Lindsay, Detr.	10.00
□	PR-32 Bernie Geoffrion, Mont.	8.00
□	Checklist 4 [1954-55 Parkie]	5.00
	Player	**NM-MT**
□	101 Don Cherry	40.00
□	101 Don Cherry Auto. ✍	175.00

1992 - 93 PINNACLE

These cards have two versions: an American (English only) and a Canadian (bilingual) issue. Player photos for both series are different.

Complete Set (420 cards): **30.00**
Common Player: **.20**
Promo Sheet (#s: 111, 165, 288, 387): **3.00**
Promo Sheet (#s: 66, 80, 110, 280): **4.00**
Promo Sheet (#s: 77, 175, 279, 406): **4.00**
Promo Sheet (#s: 6, 22, 36, 61, 88, 91): **7.00**

	Player	**NM-MT**
□□	1 Mark Messier, NYRa.	.50
□□	2 Raymond Bourque, Bost.	.50
□□	3 Gary Roberts, Calg.	.20
□□	4 Bill Ranford (G), Edmo.	.20
□□	5 Gilbert Dionne, Mont.	.20
□□	6 Owen Nolan, Québ.	.20
□□	7 Pat LaFontaine, Buff.	.20
□□	8 Nicklas Lidström, Detr.	.20
□□	9 Pat Falloon, SanJ.	.20
□□	10 Jeremy Roenick, Chic.	.20
□□	11 Kevin Hatcher, Wash.	.20
□□	12 Cliff Ronning, Vanc.	.20
□□	13 Jeff R. Brown, SLou.	.20
□□	14 Kevin Dineen, Phil.	.20
□□	15 Brian Leetch, NYRa.	.20
□□	16 Éric Desjardins, Mont.	.20
□□	17 Derek King, NYIs.	.20
□□	18 Mark Tinordi, Minn.	.20
□□	19 Kelly Hrudey (G), LosA.	.20
□□	20 Sergei Fedorov, Detr.	.50
□□	21 Mike Ramsey, Buff.	.20
□□	22 Michel Goulet, Chic.	.20
□□	23 Joe Murphy, Edmo.	.20
□□	24 Mark Fitzpatrick (G), NYIs.	.20
□□	25 Cam Neely, Bost.	.50
□□	26 Rod Brind'Amour, Phil.	.20
□□	27 Neil Wilkinson, SanJ.	.20
□□	28 Greg A. Adams, Vanc.	.20
□□	29 Thomas Steen, Winn.	.20
□□	30 Calle Johansson, Wash.	.20
□□	31 Joe Nieuwendyk, Calg.	.20
□□	32 Rob Blake, LosA.	.20
□□	33 Darren Turcotte, NYRa.	.20
□□	34 Derian Hatcher, Minn.	.20
□□	35 Mikhail Tatarinov, Québ.	.20
□□	36 Nelson Emerson, SLou.	.20
□□	37 Tim Cheveldae (G), Detr.	.20
□□	38 Donald Audette, Buff.	.20
□□	39 Brent Sutter, Chic.	.20
□□	40 Adam Oates, Bost.	.20
□□	41 Luke Richardson, Edmo.	.20
□□	42 Jon Casey (G), Minn.	.20
□□	43 Guy Carbonneau, Mont.	.20
□□	44 Patrick Flatley, NYIs.	.20
□□	45 Brian Benning, Phil.	.20
□□	46 Curtis Leschyshyn, Québ.	.20
□□	47 Trevor Linden, Vanc.	.20
□□	48 Don Beaupré (G), Wash.	.20
□□	49 Troy Murray, Winn.	.20
□□	50 Paul Coffey, LosA.	.20
□□	51 Frantisek Musil, Calg.	.20
□□	52 Doug Wilson, SanJ.	.20
□□	53 Pat Elynuik, Wash.	.20
□□	54 Curtis Joseph (G), SLou.	.50
□□	55 Tony Amonte, NYRa.	.20
□□	56 Bob Probert, Detr.	.20
□□	57 J. Steve Smith, Chic.	.20
□□	58 Dave Andreychuk, Buff.	.20
□□	59 Vladimír Ruzicka, Bost.	.20
□□	60 Jari Kurri, LosA.	.50
□□	61 Denis Savard, Mont.	.20
□□	62 Benoît Hogue, NYIs.	.20
□□	63 Terry Carkner, Phil.	.20
□□	64 Valeri Kamensky, Québ.	.20
□□	65 Jyrki Lumme, Vanc.	.20
□□	66 Al Iafrate, Wash.	.20
□□	67 Paul Ranheim, Calg.	.20
□□	68 Ulf Dahlén, Minn.	.20
□□	69 Tony Granato, LosA.	.20
□□	70 Phil Housley, Winn.	.20
□□	71 Brian Lawton, SanJ.	.20
□□	72 Garth Butcher, SLou.	.20
□□	73 Stephen Leach, Bost.	.20
□□	74 Steve Larmer, Chic.	.20
□□	75 Mike Richter (G), NYRa.	.20
□□	76 Vladimir Konstantinov, Detr.	.20
□□	77 Alexander Mogilny, Buff.	.20
□□	78 Craig MacTavish, Edmo.	.20
□□	79 Mathieu Schneider, Mont.	.20
□□	80 Mark Recchi, Phil.	.20
□□	81 Gerald Diduck, Vanc.	.20
□□	82 Peter Bondra, Wash.	.20
□□	83 Al MacInnis, Calg.	.20
□□	84 Bob Kudelski, LosA.	.20
□□	85 Dave Gagner, Minn.	.20
□□	86 Uwe Krupp, NYIs.	.20
□□	87 Randy Carlyle, Winn.	.20
□□	88 Eric Lindros, Phil.	1.00
□□	89 Rob Zettler, SanJ.	.20
□□	90 Mats Sundin, Québ.	.50
□□	91 Andy Moog (G), Bost.	.20
□□	92 Keith Brown, Chic.	.20
□□	93 Paul Ysebaert, Detr.	.20
□□	94 Mike Gartner, NYRa.	.20
□□	95 Kelly Buchberger, Edmo.	.20
□□	96 Dominic Roussel (G), Phil.	.20
□□	97 Doug Bodger, Buff.	.20
□□	98 Mike Donnelly, LosA.	.20
□□	99 Mike Craig, Minn.	.20
□□	100 Brett Hull, SLou.	.50
□□	101 Robert Reichel, Calg.	.20
□□	102 Jeff Norton, NYIs.	.20
□□	103 Garry Galley, Phil.	.20
□□	104 Dale Hunter, Wash.	.20
□□	105 Jeff Hackett (G), SanJ.	.20
□□	106 Darrin Shannon, Winn.	.20
□□	107 Craig Wolanin, Québ.	.20
□□	108 Adam Graves, NYRa.	.20
□□	109 Chris Chelios, Chic.	.20
□□	110 Pavel Bure, Vanc.	.20
□□	111 Kirk Muller, Mont.	.20
□□	112 Jeff Beukeboom, NYRa.	.20
□□	113 Mike Hough, Québ.	.20
□□	114 Brendan Shanahan, SLou.	.50
□□	115 Randy Burridge, Wash.	.20
□□	116 Dave Poulin, Bost.	.20
□□	117 Petr* Svoboda, Buff.	.20
□□	118 Ed Belfour (G), Chic.	.50
□□	119 Ray Sheppard, Detr.	.20
□□	120 Bernie Nicholls, Edmo.	.20
□□	121 Glenn Healy (G), NYIs.	.20
□□	122 Johan Garpenlöv, SanJ.	.20
□□	123 Mike Lalor, Winn.	.20
□□	124 Brad McCrimmon, Detr.	.20
□□	125 Theoren Fleury, Calg.	.20
□□	126 Randy Gilhen, NYRa.	.20
□□	127 Petr Nedved, Vanc.	.20
□□	128 Steve Thomas, NYIs.	.20
□□	129 Rick Zombo, SLou.	.20
□□	130 Patrick Roy (G), Mont.	1.50
□□	131 Rod Langway, Wash.	.20
□□	132 Gord Murphy, Bost.	.20
□□	133 Randy Wood, Buff.	.20
□□	134 Mike Hudson, Chic.	.20
□□	135 Gerard Gallant, Detr.	.20
□□	136 Brian Glynn, Edmo.	.20
□□	137 Jim* Johnson, Minn.	.20
□□	138 Corey Millen, LosA.	.20
□□	139 Daniel Marois, NYIs.	.20
□□	140 James Patrick, NYRa.	.20
□□	141 Claude Lapointe, Québ.	.20
□□	142 Bobby Smith, Minn.	.20
□□	143 Charlie Huddy, LosA.	.20
□□	144 Murray Baron, SLou.	.20
□□	145 Ed Olczyk, Winn.	.20
□□	146 Dmitri Khristich, Wash.	.20
□□	147 Doug Lidster, Vanc.	.20
□□	148 Perry Berezan, SanJ.	.20
□□	149 Pelle Eklund, Phil.	.20
□□	150 Joe Sakic, Québ.	.50
□□	151 Michal Pivonka, Wash.	.20
□□	152 Joey Kocur, NYRa.	.20
□□	153 Patrice Brisebois, Mont.	.20
□□	154 Ray Ferraro, NYIs.	.20
□□	155 Mike Modano, Minn.	.50
□□	156 Marty McSorley, LosA.	.20
□□	157 Norm Maciver, Otta.	.20
□□	158 Sergei Nemchinov, NYRa.	.20
□□	159 David Bruce, SanJ.	.20
□□	160 Kelly Miller, Wash.	.20
□□	161 Alexei Gusarov, Québ.	.20
□□	162 Andrei Lomakin, Phil.	.20
□□	163 Sergio Momesso, Vanc.	.20
□□	164 Mike Keane, Mont.	.20
□□	165 Pierre Turgeon, NYIs.	.20
□□	166 Martin Gélinas, Edmo.	.20
□□	167 Chris Dahlquist, Calg.	.20
□□	168 Kris King, NYRa.	.20
□□	169 Dean Evason, SanJ.	.20
□□	170 Mike Ridley, Wash.	.20
□□	171 Shawn Burr, Detr.	.20
□□	172 Dana Murzyn, Vanc.	.20
□□	173 Dirk Graham, Chic.	.20
□□	174 Trent Yawney, Calg.	.20
□□	175 Luc Robitaille, LosA.	.20
□□	176 Randy Moller, Buff.	.20
□□	177 Vincent Riendeau (G), Detr.	.20
□□	178 Brian Propp, Minn. [w/ 400th goal puck]	.20
□□	179 Don Sweeney, Bost.	.20
□□	180 Stéphane Matteau, Chic.	.20
□□	181 Garry Valk, Vanc.	.20
□□	182 Sylvain Côté, Wash.	.20
□□	183 Dave Snuggerud, SanJ.	.20
□□	184 Gary Leeman, Calg.	.20
□□	185 John Druce, Winn.	.20
□□	186 John Vanbiesbrouck (G), NYRa.	.20
□□	187 Geoff Courtnall, Vanc.	.20
□□	188 David Volek, NYIs.	.20
□□	189 Doug Weight, NYRa.	.20
□□	190 Bob Essensa, Winn.	.20
□□	191 Jan Erixon, NYRa.	.20
□□	192 Geoff Smith, Edmo.	.20
□□	193 Dave Christian, Chic.	.20
□□	194 Brian Noonan, Chic.	.20
□□	195 Gary Suter, Calg.	.20
□□	196 Craig Janney, SLou.	.20
□□	197 Brad May, Buff.	.20
□□	198 Gaétan Duchesne, Minn.	.20
□□	199 Adam Creighton, Tamp.	.20
□□	200 Wayne Gretzky, LosA.	2.00
□□	201 Dave Babych, Vanc.	.20
□□	202 Fredrik Olausson, Winn.	.20
□□	203 Bob Bassen, SLou.	.20
□□	204 Todd Krygier, Wash.	.20
□□	205 Grant Ledyard, Buff.	.20
□□	206 Michel Petit, Calg.	.20
□□	207 Todd Elik, Minn.	.20
□□	208 Josef Beránek, Edmo.	.20
□□	209 Neal Broten, Minn.	.20
□□	210 Jim Sandlak, Vanc.	.20
□□	211 Kevin Haller, Mont.	.20
□□	212 Paul Broten, NYRa.	.20
□□	213 Mark Pederson, Phil.	.20
□□	214 John* McIntyre, LosA.	.20
□□	215 Teppo Numminen, Winn.	.20
□□	216 Ken Sutton, Buff.	.20
□□	217 Ronnie Stern, Calg.	.20
□□	218 Luciano Borsato, Winn.	.20
□□	219 Claude Loiselle, NYIs.	.20
□□	220 Mark Hardy, NYRa.	.20
□□	221 Joé Juneau, Bost. [Rookie]	.20
□□	222 Keith Tkachuk, Winn. [Rookie]	.50
□□	223 Scott Lachance, NYIs. [Rookie]	.20
□□	224 Glen Murray, Bost. [Rookie]	.20
□□	225 Igor Kravchuk, Chic. [Rookie]	.20
□□	226 Evgeny Davydov, Winn. [Rookie]	.20
□□	227 Ray Whitney, SanJ. [Rookie]	.20
□□	**228 Bret Hedican, SLou. [Rookie] RC**	**.50**
□□	**229 Keith Carney, Buff. [Rookie] RC**	**.50**
□□	230 Vyacheslav Kozlov, Detr. [Rookie]	.20
□□	231 Drake Berehowsky, Toro. [Rookie]	.20
□□	232 Cam Neely, Bost. [Sidelines]	.50
□□	233 Doug Gilmour, Toro. [Sidelines]	.20
□□	234 Randy Wood, Buff. [Sidelines]	.20
□□	235 Luke Richardson, Edmo. [Sidelines]	.20
□□	236 Eric Lindros, Phil. [Sidelines]	1.00
□□	237 Dale Hunter, Wash. [Sidelines]	.20
□□	238 Pat Falloon, SanJ. [Sidelines]	.20
□□	239 Dean Kennedy, Winn. [Sidelines]	.20
□□	240 Uwe Krupp, NYIs. [Sidelines]	.20
□□	241 S. Niedermayer / S. Yzerman	.50
□□	242 G. Roberts / L. McDonald	.20
□□	243 P. Ahola / J. Kurri	.20
□□	244 S. Lachance / Mark Howe	.20
□□	245 R. Pearson / M. Bossy	.20
□□	246 K. McLean / B. Parent	.20
□□	247 D. Mironov / V. Fetisov	.20
□□	248 B. Shanahan / D. Sittler	.20
□□	249 P. Nedved / W. Gretzky	1.00
□□	250 T. Ewen / C. Gillies	.20
□□	251 Luc Robitaille, LosA. [Good Guy]	.20
□□	252 Mark Tinordi, Minn. [Good Guy]	.20
□□	253 Kris King, NYRa. [Good Guy]	.20
□□	254 Pat LaFontaine, Buff. [Good Guy]	.20
□□	255 Ryan Walter, Vanc. [Good Guy]	.20
□□	256 Jeremy Roenick, Chic. [Gamewinners]	.20
□□	257 Brett Hull, SLou. [Gamewinners]	.50
□□	258 Steve Yzerman, Detr. [Gamewinners]	1.00
□□	259 Claude Lemieux, NJer. [Gamewinners]	.20
□□	260 Mike Modano, Minn. [Gamewinners]	.50
□□	261 Vincent Damphousse, Mont. [Gamewinners]	.20
□□	262 Tony Granato, LosA. [Gamewinners]	.20
□□	263 Andy Moog (G), Bost. [Masks]	.20
□□	264 Curtis Joseph (G), SLou. [Masks]	.50
□□	265 Ed Belfour (G), Chic. [Masks]	.50
□□	266 Brian Hayward (G), SanJ. [Masks]	.20
□□	267 Grant Fuhr (G), Toro. [Masks]	.20
□□	268 Don Beaupré (G), Wash. [Masks]	.20
□□	269 Tim Cheveldae (G), Detr. [Masks]	.20
□□	270 Mike Richter (G), NYRa. [Masks]	.20
□□	271 Zarley Zalapski, Hart.	.20
□□	272 Kevin Todd, NJer.	.20
□□	273 Dave Ellett, Toro.	.20
□□	274 Chris Terreri (G), NJer.	.20
□□	275 Jaromir Jagr, Pitt.	.50
□□	276 Wendel Clark, Toro.	.20
□□	277 Bobby Holik, NJer.	.20
□□	278 Bruce Driver, NJer.	.20
□□	279 Doug Gilmour, Toro.	.20
□□	280 Scott Stevens, NJer.	.20
□□	281 Murray Craven, Hart.	.20
□□	282 Rick Tocchet, Pitt.	.20
□□	283 Peter Zezel, Toro.	.20
□□	284 Claude Lemieux, NJer.	.20
□□	285 John Cullen, Hart.	.20
□□	286 Valeri Zelepukin, NJer.	.20
□□	287 Rob Pearson, Toro.	.20
□□	288 Kevin Stevens, Pitt.	.20
□□	289 Alexei Kasatonov, NJer.	.20
□□	290 Todd Gill, Toro.	.20
□□	291 Randy Ladouceur, Hart.	.20
□□	292 Larry Murphy, Pitt.	.20
□□	293 Tom Chorske, NJer.	.20
□□	294 Jamie Macoun, Toro.	.20
□□	295 Sean Burke (G), Hart.	.20
□□	296 Ulf Samuelsson, Pitt.	.20
□□	297 Eric Weinrich, Hart.	.20
□□	298 Tom Barrasso (G), Pitt.	.20
□□	299 Viacheslav Fetisov, NJer.	.20
□□	300 Mario Lemieux, Pitt.	1.50
□□	301 Grant Fuhr (G), Toro.	.20
□□	302 Zdeno Ciger, NJer.	.20
□□	303 Ron Francis, Pitt.	.20
□□	304 Scott Niedermayer, NJer.	.20
□□	305 Mark Osborne, Toro.	.20
□□	306 Kjell Samuelsson, Pitt.	.20
□□	307 Geoff Sanderson, Hart.	.20
□□	308 Paul Stanton, Pitt.	.20
□□	309 Frank Pietrangelo, Hart.	.20
□□	310 Bob Errey, Pitt.	.20
□□	311 Dino Ciccarelli, Detr.	.20
□□	312 Gord** Roberts, Bost.	.20
□□	313 Kevin Miller, Wash.	.20
□□	314 Mike Ricci, Québ.	.20
□□	315 Bob Carpenter, Wash.	.20
□□	316 Dale Hawerchuk, Buff.	.20
□□	317 Christian Ruuttu, Chic.	.20
□□	318 Mike Vernon (G), Calg.	.20
□□	319 Paul Cavallini, SLou.	.20
□□	320 Steve Duchesne, Québ.	.20
□□	321 Craig Simpson, Edmo.	.20

□□	322 Mark Howe, Detr.	.20
□□	323 Shayne Corson, Edmo.	.20
□□	324 Tom Kurvers, NYIs.	.20
□□	325 Brian Bellows, Mont.	.20
□□	326 Glen Wesley, Bost.	.20
□□	327 Daren Puppa (G), Buff.	.20
□□	328 Joel Otto, Calg.	.20
□□	329 Jimmy Carson, Detr.	.20
□□	330 Kirk McLean (G), Vanc.	.20
□□	331 Rob (Jr.) Brown, Chic.	.20
□□	332 Yves Racine, Detr.	.20
□□	333 Brian Mullen, NYIs.	.20
□□	334 Dave Manson, Edmo.	.20
□□	335 Sergei Makarov, Calg.	.20
□□	336 Esa Tikkanen, Edmo.	.20
□□	337 Russ Courtnall, Minn.	.20
□□	338 Kevin Lowe, Edmo.	.20
□□	339 Steve Chiasson, Detr.	.20
□□	340 Ron Hextall (G), Québ.	.20
□□	341 Stéphan Lebeau, Mont.	.20
□□	342 Mike McPhee, Minn.	.20
□□	343 David Shaw, Bost.	.20
□□	344 Petr Klima, Edmo.	.20
□□	345 Tomas Sandström, LosA.	.20
□□	346 Scott Mellanby, Edmo.	.20
□□	347 Brian Skrudland, Mont.	.20
□□	348 Pat Verbeek, Hart.	.20
□□	349 Vincent Damphousse, Mont.	.20
□□	350 Steve Yzerman, Detr.	1.00
□□	351 John MacLean, NJer.	.20
□□	352 Steve Konroyd, Hart.	.20
□□	353 Phil Bourque, NYRa.	.20
□□	354 Ken Daneyko, NJer.	.20
□□	355 Glenn Anderson, Toro.	.20
□□	356 Ken Wregget (G), Pitt.	.20
□□	357 Brent Gilchrist, Edmo.	.20
□□	358 Bob Rouse, Toro.	.20
□□	359 Peter Stastny, NJer.	.20
□□	360 Joe Mullen, Pitt.	.20
□□	361 Stéphane Richer, NJer.	.20
□□	362 Kelly Kisio, SanJ.	.20
□□	363 Keith Acton, Phil.	.20
□□	364 Félix Potvin (G), Toro.	.20
□□	365 Martin Lapointe, Detr.	.20
□□	366 Ron Tugnutt, Edmo.	.20
□□	367 Dave Taylor, LosA.	.20
□□	368 Tim Kerr, Hart.	.20
□□	369 Carey Wilson, Calg.	.20
□□	370 Greg Paslawski, Phil.	.20
□□	371 Peter Sidorkiewicz (G), Otta.	.20
□□	372 Brad Shaw, Otta.	.20
□□	373 Sylvain Turgeon, Otta.	.20
□□	374 Mark Lamb, Otta.	.20
□□	375 Laurie Boschman, Otta.	.20
□□	376 Mark Osiecki, Otta.	.20
□□	377 Doug Smail, Otta.	.20
□□	378 Brad Marsh, Otta.	.20
□□	379 Mike Peluso, Otta.	.20
□□	380 Steve Weeks, Otta.	.20
□□	381 Wendell Young (G), Tamp.	.20
□□	382 Joe Reekie, Tamp.	.20
□□	383 Peter Taglianetti, Tamp.	.20
□□	384 Mikael Andersson, Tamp.	.20
□□	385 Marc Bergevin, Tamp.	.20
□□	386 Anatoli Semenov, Tamp.	.20
□□	387 Brian Bradley, Tamp.	.20
□□	388 Michel Mongeau, Tamp.	.20
□□	389 Rob Ramage, Tamp.	.20
□□	390 Ken (Jr.) Hodge, Tamp.	.20
□□	**391 Richard Matvichuk, Minn. [Rookie] RC**	**1.00**
□□	392 Alexei Zhitnik, LosA. [Rookie]	.20
□□	**393 Richard Smehlik, Buff. [Rookie] RC**	**.50**
□□	**394 Dmitry Yushkevich, Phil. [Rookie] RC**	**1.00**
□□	395 Andrei Kovalenko, Québ. [Rookie]	.20
□□	**396 Vladimir (Jr.) Vujtek, Edmo. [Rookie] RC**	**.50**
□□	**397 Nikolai Borschevsky, Toro. [Rookie] RC**	**.50**
□□	**398 Vitali Karamnov, SLou. [Rookie] RC**	**.50**
□□	**399 Jim Hiller, LosA. [Rookie] RC**	**.50**
□□	**400 Michael Nylander, Hart. [Rookie] RC**	**1.00**
□□	**401 Tommy Sjödin, Minn. [Rookie] RC**	**.50**
□□	**402 Robert Petrovicky, Hart. [Rookie] RC**	**.50**
□□	403 Alexei Kovalev, NYRa. [Rookie]	.50
□□	**404 Vitali Prokhorov, SLou. [Rookie] RC**	**.50**
□□	**405 Dmitri Kvartalnov, Bost. [Rookie] RC**	**.50**
□□	406 Teemu Selänne, Winn. [Rookie]	.50
□□	407 Darius Kasparaitis, NYIs. [Rookie]	.20
□□	**408 Roman Hamrlik, Tamp. [Rookie] RC**	**1.00**
□□	409 Vladimir Malakhov, NYIs. [Rookie]	.20
□□	410 Sergei Krivokrasov, Chic. [Rookie]	.20
□□	**411 Robert Lang, LosA. [Rookie] RC**	**1.00**
□□	412 Jozef Stümpel, Bost. [Rookie]	.20
□□	**413 Denny Felsner, SLou. [Rookie] RC**	**.50**
□□	**414 Rob Zamuner, Tamp. [Rookie] RC**	**1.00**
□□	**415 Jason Woolley, Wash. [Rookie] RC**	**.50**
□□	416 Alexei Zhamnov, Winn. [Rookie]	.20
□□	417 Igor Korolev, SLou. [Rookie]	.20
□□	418 Patrick Poulin, Hart. [Rookie]	.20
□□	419 Dmitri Mironov, Toro. [Rookie]	.20
□□	420 Shawn McEachern, Pitt. [Rookie]	.20

TEAM 2000

Insert Set (30 cards): 18.00

	Player	T2K
□□	1 Eric Lindros, Phil.	3.00
□□	2 Mike Modano, Minn.	2.00
□□	3 Nicklas Lidström, Detr.	1.00
□□	4 Tony Amonte, NYRa.	1.00
□□	5 Félix Potvin (G), Toro.	1.00
□□	6 Scott Lachance, NYIs.	.25
□□	7 Mats Sundin, Québ.	2.00
□□	8 Pavel Bure, Vanc.	1.00
□□	9 Éric Desjardins, Mont.	.25
□□	10 Owen Nolan, Québ.	1.00
□□	11 Dominic Roussel (G), Phil.	.25
□□	12 Scott Niedermayer, NJer.	.25
□□	13 Vyacheslav Kozlov, Detr.	.25
□□	14 Patrick Poulin, Hart.	.25
□□	15 Jaromir Jagr, Pitt.	2.00
□□	16 Rob Blake, LosA.	1.00
□□	17 Pierre Turgeon, NYIs.	.25
□□	18 Rod Brind'Amour, Phil.	.25
□□	19 Joé Juneau, Bost.	.25
□□	20 Tim Cheveldae (G), Detr.	.25
□□	21 Joe Sakic, Québ.	3.00
□□	22 Kevin Todd, NJer.	.25
□□	23 Rob Pearson, Toro.	.25
□□	24 Trevor Linden, Vanc.	.25
□□	25 Dmitri Khristich, Wash.	.25
□□	26 Pat Falloon, SanJ.	.25
□□	27 Jeremy Roenick, Chic.	1.00
□□	28 Alexander Mogilny, Buff.	.25
□□	29 Gilbert Dionne, Mont.	.25
□□	30 Sergei Fedorov, Detr.	2.00

TEAM PINNACLE

Insert Set (6 cards): 45.00

	Player	NM-MT
□□	1 E. Belfour (G) / M. Richter (G)	5.00
□□	2 C. Chelios / R. Bourque	5.00
□□	3 P. Coffey / B. Leetch	5.00
□□	4 P. Bure / K. Stevens	5.00
□□	5 W. Gretzky / E. Lindros	25.00
□□	6 Br. Hull / J. Jagr	10.00

1992 - 93 PINNACLE ROAD TO THE NHL

Complete Set (30 cards): 20.00
Common Eric Lindros: 1.00

□	1 St. Michael's Buzzers	□	2 Detroit Compuware
□	3 Oshawa Generals	□	4 Oshawa Generals
□	5 Oshawa Generals	□	6 Oshawa Generals
□	7 Memorial Cup	□	8 World Juniors
□	9 World Juniors	□	10 World Juniors
□	11 Canada Cup	□	12 Canada Cup
□	13 Canada Nationals	□	14 Canada Nationals
□	15 Canada Nationals	□	16 Canada Nationals
□	17 First-Round Pick	□	18 Trade to Philadelphia
□	19 Happy Flyer	□	20 Preseason Action
□	21 Preseason Action	□	22 Season Debut
□	23 First NHL Goal	□	24 Game-Winning Goal
□	25 First NHL Hat Trick	□	26 Playing Golf
□	27 Backyard Fun	□	28 Fan Favorite
□	29 Welcome to Philly	□	30 Philly Hero

1992 - 93 PRO SET

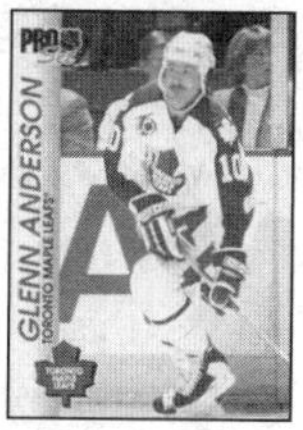

An intended second series was never issued. The most expensive single is Wayne Gretzky at $1.00-1.50. All other singles sell between 20¢ and $1.00.

Imprint: © 1992 PRO SET INC.

Complete Set (270 cards): 12.00

	Pro Set		Pro Set
□	1 Mario Lemieux	□	2 Patrick Roy (G)
□	3 Adam Oates	□	4 Raymond Bourque
□	5 Vladimir Ruzicka	□	6 Stephen Leach
□	7 Andy Moog (G)	□	8 Cam Neely
□	9 Dave Poulin	□	10 Glen Wesley
□	11 Gord Murphy	□	12 Dale Hawerchuk
□	13 Pat LaFontaine	□	14 Tom Draper (G)
□	15 Dave Andreychuk	□	16 Petr Svoboda
□	17 Doug Bodger	□	18 Donald Audette
□	19 Alexander Mogilny	□	20 Randy Wood
□	21 Gary Roberts	□	22 Al MacInnis
□	23 Theoren Fleury	□	24 Sergei Makarov
□	25 Mike Vernon (G)	□	26 Joe Nieuwendyk
□	27 Gary Suter	□	28 Joel Otto
□	29 Paul Ranheim	□	30 Jeremy Roenick
□	31 Steve Larmer	□	32 Michel Goulet
□	33 Ed Belfour (G)	□	34 Chris Chelios
□	35 Igor Kravchuk	□	36 Brent Sutter
□	37 Steve Smith	□	38 Dirk Graham
□	39 Steve Yzerman	□	40 Sergei Fedorov
□	41 Paul Ysebaert	□	42 Nicklas Lidström
□	43 Tim Cheveldae (G)	□	44 Vlad. Konstantinov
□	45 Shawn Burr	□	46 Bob Probert
□	47 Ray Sheppard	□	48 Kelly Buchberger
□	49 Joe Murphy	□	50 Norm Maciver
□	51 Bill Ranford (G)	□	52 Bernie Nicholls
□	53 Esa Tikkanen	□	54 Scott Mellanby
□	55 Dave Manson	□	56 Craig Simpson
□	57 John Cullen	□	58 Pat Verbeek
□	59 Zarley Zalapski	□	60 Murray Craven
□	61 Bobby Holik	□	62 Steve Konroyd
□	63 Geoff Sanderson	□	64 F. Pietrangelo (G)
□	65 M. Andersson	□	66 Wayne Gretzky
□	67 Rob Blake	□	68 Jari Kurri
□	69 Marty McSorley	□	70 Kelly Hrudey (G)
□	71 Paul Coffey	□	72 Luc Robitaille
□	73 Peter Ahola	□	74 Tony Granato
□	75 Derian Hatcher	□	76 Mike Modano
□	77 Dave Gagner	□	78 Mark Tinordi
□	79 Craig Ludwig	□	80 Ulf Dahlen
□	81 Bobby Smith	□	82 Jon Casey (G)
□	83 Jim Johnson	□	84 Denis Savard
□	85 Patrick Roy (G)	□	86 Eric Desjardins
□	87 Kirk Muller	□	88 Guy Carbonneau
□	89 Shayne Corson	□	90 B. Gilchrist
□	91 Mathieu Schneider	□	92 Gilbert Dionne
□	93 Stéphane Richer	□	94 Kevin Todd
□	95 Scott Stevens	□	96 Viacheslav Fetisov
□	97 Chris Terreri (G)	□	98 Claude Lemieux
□	99 Bruce Driver	□	100 Peter Stastny
□	101 Alexei Kasatonov	□	102 Patrick Flatley
□	103 A. Creighton	□	104 Pierre Turgeon
□	105 Ray Ferraro	□	106 Steve Thomas
□	107 Mark Fitzpatrick (G)	□	108 Benoît Hogue
□	109 Uwe Krupp	□	110 Derek King
□	111 Mark Messier	□	112 Brian Leetch
□	113 Mike Gartner	□	114 Darren Turcotte
□	115 Adam Graves	□	116 Mike Richter (G)
□	117 Sergei Nemchinov	□	118 Tony Amonte
□	119 James Patrick	□	120 Andrew McBain
□	121 Rob Murphy	□	122 Mike Peluso
□	123 Sylvain Turgeon	□	124 Brad Shaw
□	125 P. Sidorkiewicz (G)	□	126 Brad Marsh
□	127 Mark Freer	□	128 Marc Fortier
□	129 R. Hextall (G)	□	130 Claude Boivin
□	131 Mark Recchi	□	132 Rod Brind'Amour
□	133 Mike Ricci	□	134 Kevin Dineen
□	135 Brian Benning	□	136 K. Huffman
□	137 S. Duchesne	□	138 Rick Tocchet
□	139 Mario Lemieux	□	140 Kevin Stevens
□	141 Jaromir Jagr	□	142 Joe Mullen
□	143 Ulf Samuelsson	□	144 Ron Francis
□	145 Tom Barrasso (G)	□	146 Larry Murphy
□	147 Alexei Gusarov	□	148 Valeri Kamensky
□	149 Mats Sundin	□	150 Joe Sakic
□	151 Claude Lapointe	□	152 Stéphane Fiset (G)
□	153 Owen Nolan	□	154 Mike Hough
□	155 Greg Paslawski	□	156 Brett Hull
□	157 Craig Janney	□	158 Jeff Brown
□	159 Paul Cavallini	□	160 Garth Butcher
□	161 Nelson Emerson	□	162 Ron Sutter
□	163 Brendan Shanahan	□	164 Curtis Joseph (G)
□	165 Doug Wilson	□	166 Pat Falloon
□	167 Kelly Kisio	□	168 Neil Wilkinson
□	169 Jay More	□	170 David Bruce
□	171 Jeff Hackett (G)	□	172 David Williams RC
□	173 Brian Lawton	□	174 Brian Bradley
□	175 Jock Callander RC	□	176 Basil McRae
□	177 Rob Ramage	□	178 Pat Jablonski (G)
□	179 Joe Reekie	□	180 Doug Crossman
□	181 Jim Benning	□	182 Ken Hodge
□	183 Grant Fuhr (G)	□	184 Doug Gilmour
□	185 Glenn Anderson	□	186 David Ellett
□	187 Peter Zezel	□	188 Jamie Macoun
□	189 Wendel Clark	□	190 Bob Halkidis RC
□	191 Rob Pearson	□	192 Pavel Bure
□	193 Kirk McLean (G)	□	194 Sergio Momesso
□	195 Cliff Ronning	□	196 Jyrki Lumme
□	197 Trevor Linden	□	198 Geoff Cortnall
□	199 Doug Lidster	□	200 Dave Babych
□	201 Michal Pivonka	□	202 Dale Hunter
□	203 Calle Johansson	□	204 Kevin Hatcher
□	205 Al Iafrate	□	206 Don Beaupré (G)
□	207 Randy Burridge	□	208 Dimitri Khristich
□	209 Peter Bondra	□	210 Teppo Numminen
□	211 Bob Essensa (G)	□	212 Phil Housley
□	213 Ed Olczyk	□	214 Pat Elynuik
□	215 Troy Murray	□	216 Igor Ulanov
□	217 Thomas Steen	□	218 Darrin Shannon
□	219 Joé Juneau	□	220 Steve Heinze
□	221 Ted Donato	□	222 Glen Murray
□	223 Keith Carney RC	□	224 D. McAmmond RC
□	225 Vyacheslav Kozlov	□	226 Martin Lapointe
□	227 Patrick Poulin	□	228 Darryl Sydor
□	229 Trent Klatt RC	□	230 Bill Guerin RC
□	231 Jerrod Skalde	□	232 Scott Niedermayer
□	233 Marty McInnis	□	234 Scott Lachance
□	235 D. Roussel (G)	□	236 Eric Lindros
□	237 Shawn McEachern	□	238 Martin Rucinsky
□	239 Bill Lindsay RC	□	240 Bret Hedican RC
□	241 Ray Whitney RC	□	242 Félix Potvin (G)
□	243 Keith Tkachuk	□	244 Evgeny Davydov
□	245 Brett Hull	□	246 Wayne Gretzky
□	247 Steve Yzerman	□	248 Paul Ysebaert
□	249 Dave Andreychuk	□	250 Kirk McLean (G)
□	251 Tim Cheveldae (G)	□	252 Jeremy Roenick
□	253 Pro Set Youth Clinic	□	254 Pro Set Clinic
□	255 NHL All-Time Team	□	256 Mike Gartner
□	257 Brian Propp	□	258 Dave Taylor
□	259 Bobby Smith	□	260 Denis Savard
□	261 Raymond Bourque	□	262 Joe Mullen
□	263 John Tonelli	□	264 Brad Marsh
□	265 Randy Carlyle	□	266 Mike Hough
□	267 Bob Essensa (G)	□	268 Mike Lalor
□	269 Terry Carkner	□	270 Todd Krygier

AWARD WINNERS

Insert Set (5 cards): 13.00

	Player	NM-MT
□	CC1 Mark Messier, NYRa.	3.00
□	CC2 Patrick Roy (G), Mont.	9.00
□	CC3 Pavel Bure, Vanc.	2.00
□	CC4 Brian Leetch, NYRa.	1.00
□	CC5 Guy Carbonneau, Mont.	1.00

PARKHURST PREVIEWS

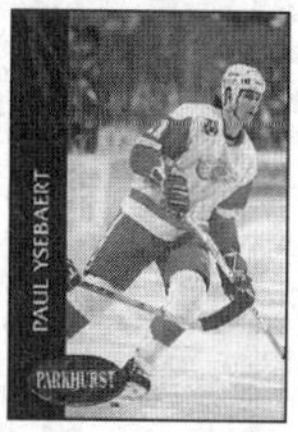

Insert Set (5 cards): 2.00

	Player	NM-MT
□	PV1 Paul Ysebaert, Detr.	.50
□	PV2 Sean Burke (G), Hart.	1.00
□	PV3 Gilbert Dionne, Mont.	.50
□	PV4 Ken Hammond, Otta.	.50
□	PV5 Grant Fuhr (G), Toro.	1.00

ROOKIE GOAL LEADERS

Insert Set (12 cards): 10.00

	Player	NM-MT
□	1 Tony Amonte, NYRa.	1.00
□	2 Pavel Bure, Vanc.	2.00
□	3 Donald Audette, Buff.	1.00
□	4 Pat Falloon, SanJ.	1.00
□	5 Nelson Emerson, SLou.	1.00
□	6 Gilbert Dionne, Mont.	1.00
□	7 Kevin Todd, NJer.	1.00
□	8 Luciano Borsato, Winn.	1.00
□	9 Rob Pearson, Toro.	1.00
□	10 Valeri Zelepukin, NJer.	1.00
□	11 Geoff Sanderson, Hart.	1.00
□	12 Claude Lapointe, Québ.	1.00

TEAM LEADERS

Insert Set (15 cards): 25.00

	Player	NM-MT
□	1 Gary Roberts, Calg.	1.00
□	2 Jeremy Roenick, Chic.	2.00
□	3 Steve Yzerman, Detr.	6.00
□	4 Nicklas Lidström, Detr.	1.00
□	5 Vincent Damphousse, Edmo.	1.00
□	6 Wayne Gretzky, LosA.	10.00
□	7 Mike Modano, Minn.	2.00
□	8 Brett Hull, SLou.	2.00
□	9 Nelson Emerson, SLou.	.50
□	10 Pat Falloon, SanJ.	.50
□	11 Doug Gilmour, Toro.	1.00
□	12 Trevor Linden, Vanc.	1.00
□	13 Pavel Bure, Vanc.	2.00
□	14 Phil Housley, Winn.	.50
□	15 Luciano Borsato, Winn.	.50

1992 - 93 RED ACE

Light Blue Set (36 cards): 5.00
Purple Set (37 cards): 5.00

	Light Blue		Light Blue
□	1 D. Kasparaitis	□	2 Alexei Zhamnov
□	3 Dimitri Khristich	□	4 Andrei Trefilov (G)
□	5 Vitali Prokhorov	□	6 Dmitri Filimonov
□	7 Valeri Zelepukin	□	8 Alexei Kovalev
□	9 Dmitri Kvartalnov	□	10 Igor Korolev
□	11 N. Borschevsky	□	12 Igor Boldin
□	13 A. Irbe (G)	□	14 V. Butsayev
□	15 Boris Mironov	□	16 Sergei Bautin
□	17 A. Kharlamov	□	18 Vyacheslav Kozlov
□	19 M. Shtalenkov (G)	□	20 Roman Oksyuta

☐ 21 S. Ozolnish ☐ 22 Dmitri Mironov
☐ 23 Sergei Brylin ☐ 24 Vladimir Grachev
☐ 25 Dmitri Starostenko ☐ 26 Andrei Nazarov
☐ 27 Alexei Yashin ☐ 28 Vladimir Malakhov
☐ 29 Ravil Yakubov ☐ 30 Sergei Klimovich
☐ 31 Artur Oktjabrev ☐ 32 Lev Berdichevsky
☐ 33 Yan Kaminski ☐ 34 Andrei Kovalenko
☐ 35 Dmitri Yushkevich ☐ Title card/Checklist (no#)

Purple / Purple

☐ 1 Alexander Barkov ☐ 2 Sergei Bautin
☐ 3 Igor Boldin ☐ 4 Nikolai Borshevsky
☐ 5 Sergei Brylin ☐ 6 Vyacheslav Butsayev
☐ 7 Alexander Cherbayev ☐ 8 Evgeny Garanin
☐ 9 Sergei Gonchar ☐ 10 A. Karpovtsev
☐ 11 Darius Kasparaitis ☐ 12 Alexander Kharlamov
☐ 13 Yuri Khmylev ☐ 14 Sergei Klimovich
☐ 15 Igor Korolev ☐ 16 Andrei Kovalenko
☐ 17 Alexei Kovalev ☐ 18 Dmitri Kvartalnov
☐ 19 Vladimir Malakhov ☐ 20 M. Mikhailovsky (G)
☐ 21 Boris Mironov ☐ 22 Dmitri Mironov
☐ 23 Andrei Nazarov ☐ 24 Roman Oksiuta
☐ 25 Arthur Oktjabrev ☐ 26 Sergei Petrenko
☐ 27 Oleg Petrov ☐ 28 Andrei Potaichuk
☐ 29 Vitali Prokhorov ☐ 30 Alexander Semak
☐ 31 Dmitri Starostenkov ☐ 32 Ravil Yakubov
☐ 33 Alexei Yashin ☐ 34 Dmitri Yushkevich
☐ 35 Alexei Zhamnov ☐ 36 Alexei Zhitnik
☐ 37 Checklist

1992 - 93 SCORE

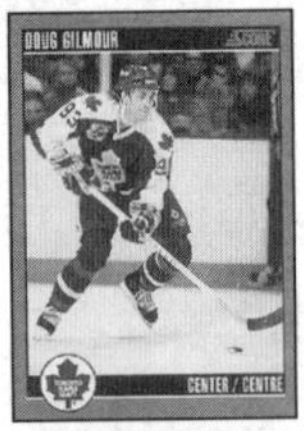

The Canadian set has a blue border, while the U.S. set has a white border. The most expensive singles are Wayne Gretzky, Eric Lindros and Maurice Richard at $1.00-1.50. All other singles sell between 20¢ and $1.00.

Imprint: © 1992 SCORE

Complete Cdn. Set (550 cards):	15.00
Promo Sheet (#s: 8, 16, 23, 25):	2.00
Promo Sheet (#s: 2, 6, 16, 25):	2.00

Player / No. Player

☐☐ 1 Wayne Gretzky ☐☐ 2 Chris Chelios
☐☐ 3 Joe Mullen ☐☐ 4 Russ Courtnall
☐☐ 5 Mike Richter (G) ☐☐ 6 Pat LaFontaine
☐☐ 7 Mark Tinordi ☐☐ 8 Claude Lemieux
☐☐ 9 Jimmy Carson ☐☐ 10 Cam Neely
☐☐ 11 Al Iafrate ☐☐ 12 Steve Thomas
☐☐ 13 Fredrik Olausson ☐☐ 14 Pavel Bure
☐☐ 15 Doug Wilson ☐☐ 16 Esa Tikkanen
☐☐ 17 Gary Suter ☐☐ 18 Murray Craven
☐☐ 19 Garry Galley ☐☐ 20 Grant Fuhr (G)
☐☐ 21 Craig Wolanin ☐☐ 22 Paul Cavallini
☐☐ 23 Eric Desjardins ☐☐ 24 Joey Kocur
☐☐ 25 Kevin Stevens ☐☐ 26 Marty McSorley
☐☐ 27 Dirk Graham ☐☐ 28 Mike Ramsey
☐☐ 29 Gord Murphy ☐☐ 30 John MacLean
☐☐ 31 Vlad. Konstantinov ☐☐ 32 Neal Broten
☐☐ 33 Dimitri Khristich ☐☐ 34 Gerald Diduck
☐☐ 35 Ken Baumgartner ☐☐ 36 Darrin Shannon
☐☐ 37 Steven Bozek ☐☐ 38 Michel Petit
☐☐ 39 Kevin Lowe ☐☐ 40 Doug Gilmour
☐☐ 41 P. Sidorkiewicz (G) ☐☐ 42 Gino Cavallini
☐☐ 43 Dan Quinn ☐☐ 44 Steven Finn
☐☐ 45 Larry Murphy ☐☐ 46 Brent Gilchrist
☐☐ 47 Darren Puppa (G) ☐☐ 48 Steve Smith
☐☐ 49 Dave Taylor ☐☐ 50 Mike Gartner
☐☐ 51 Derian Hatcher ☐☐ 52 Bob Probert
☐☐ 53 Ken Daneyko ☐☐ 54 Stephen Leach
☐☐ 55 Kelly Miller ☐☐ 56 Jeff Norton
☐☐ 57 Kelly Kisio ☐☐ 58 Igor Larionov
☐☐ 59 Paul MacDermid ☐☐ 60 Mike Vernon (G)
☐☐ 61 Randy Ladouceur ☐☐ 62 Luke Richardson
☐☐ 63 Daniel Marois ☐☐ 64 Mike Hough
☐☐ 65 Garth Butcher ☐☐ 66 Terry Carkner
☐☐ 67 Mike Donnelly ☐☐ 68 Keith Brown
☐☐ 69 Mathieu Schneider ☐☐ 70 Tom Barrasso (G)
☐☐ 71 Adam Graves ☐☐ 72 Brian Propp
☐☐ 73 Randy Wood ☐☐ 74 Yves Racine
☐☐ 75 Scott Stevens ☐☐ 76 Chris Nilan
☐☐ 77 Uwe Krupp ☐☐ 78 Sylvain Côté
☐☐ 79 Sergio Momesso ☐☐ 80 Thomas Steen
☐☐ 81 Craig Muni ☐☐ 82 Jeff Hackett. (G)
☐☐ 83 Frantisek Musil ☐☐ 84 Mike Ricci
☐☐ 85 Brad Shaw ☐☐ 86 Ron Sutter
☐☐ 87 Curtis Leschyshyn ☐☐ 88 Jamie Macoun
☐☐ 89 Brian Noonan ☐☐ 90 Ulf Samuelsson
☐☐ 91 Mike McPhee ☐☐ 92 Charlie Huddy
☐☐ 93 Tim Kerr ☐☐ 94 Craig Ludwig
☐☐ 95 Paul Ysebaert ☐☐ 96 Brad May
☐☐ 97 Viacheslav Fetisov ☐☐ 98 Todd Krygier
☐☐ 99 Patrick Flatley ☐☐ 100 Ray Bourque
☐☐ 101 Petr Nedved ☐☐ 102 T. Numminen
☐☐ 103 Dean Evason ☐☐ 104 Ron Hextall (G)
☐☐ 105 Josef Beranek ☐☐ 106 Robert Reichel
☐☐ 107 Mikhail Tatarinov ☐☐ 108 Geoff Sanderson
☐☐ 109 Dave Lowry ☐☐ 110 Wendel Clark
☐☐ 111 Corey Millen ☐☐ 112 Brent Sutter
☐☐ 113 Jaromir Jagr ☐☐ 114 Petr Svoboda
☐☐ 115 Sergei Nemchinov ☐☐ 116 Tony Tanti
☐☐ 117 Stewart Gavin ☐☐ 118 Doug Brown
☐☐ 119 Gerard Gallant ☐☐ 120 Andy Moog (G)
☐☐ 121 John Druce ☐☐ 122 Dave McLlwain
☐☐ 123 Bob Essensa (G) ☐☐ 124 Doug Lidster
☐☐ 125 Pat Falloon ☐☐ 126 Kelly Buchberger
☐☐ 127 Carey Wilson ☐☐ 128 Bobby Holik
☐☐ 129 Andrei Lomakin ☐☐ 130 Bob Rouse
☐☐ 131 Adam Foote ☐☐ 132 Bob Bassen
☐☐ 133 Brian Benning ☐☐ 134 Greg Gilbert
☐☐ 135 Paul Stanton ☐☐ 136 Brian Skrudland
☐☐ 137 Jeff Beukeboom ☐☐ 138 C. Malarchuk (G)
☐☐ 139 Mike Modano ☐☐ 140 Stéphane Richer
☐☐ 141 Brad McCrimmon ☐☐ 142 Bob Carpenter
☐☐ 143 Rod Langway ☐☐ 144 Adam Creighton
☐☐ 145 Ed Olczyk ☐☐ 146 Greg Adams
☐☐ 147 Jayson More ☐☐ 148 Scott Mellanby
☐☐ 149 Paul Ranheim ☐☐ 150 John Cullen
☐☐ 151 Steve Duchesne ☐☐ 152 Dave Ellett
☐☐ 153 Mats Sundin ☐☐ 154 Rick Zombo
☐☐ 155 Kelly Hrudey (G) ☐☐ 156 Mike Hudson
☐☐ 157 Bryan Trottier ☐☐ 158 Shayne Corson
☐☐ 159 Kevin Haller ☐☐ 160 J. Vanbiesbrock (G)
☐☐ 161 Jim Johnson ☐☐ 162 Kevin Todd
☐☐ 163 Ray Sheppard ☐☐ 164 Brent Ashton
☐☐ 165 Peter Bondra ☐☐ 166 Dave Volek
☐☐ 167 Randy Carlyle ☐☐ 168 Dana Murzyn
☐☐ 169 Perry Berezan ☐☐ 170 V. Damphousse
☐☐ 171 Gary Leeman ☐☐ 172 Steve Konroyd
☐☐ 173 Per-Erik Eklund ☐☐ 174 Peter Zezel
☐☐ 175 Greg Paslawski ☐☐ 176 Murray Baron
☐☐ 177 Rob Blake ☐☐ 178 Ed Belfour (G)
☐☐ 179 Mike Keane ☐☐ 180 Mark Recchi
☐☐ 181 Kris King ☐☐ 182 Dave Snuggerud
☐☐ 183 David Shaw ☐☐ 184 Tom Chorske
☐☐ 185 Steve Chiasson ☐☐ 186 Don Sweeney
☐☐ 187 Mike Ridley ☐☐ 188 Glenn Healy (G)
☐☐ 189 Troy Murray ☐☐ 190 Tom Fergus
☐☐ 191 Rob Zettler ☐☐ 192 Geoff Smith
☐☐ 193 Joe Nieuwendyk ☐☐ 194 Mark Hunter
☐☐ 195 Kjell Samuelsson ☐☐ 196 Todd Gill
☐☐ 197 Doug Smail ☐☐ 198 Dave Christian
☐☐ 199 Tomas Sandström ☐☐ 200 Jeremy Roenick
☐☐ 201 Gord Roberts ☐☐ 202 Denis Savard
☐☐ 203 James Patrick ☐☐ 204 D. Andreychuk
☐☐ 205 Bobby Smith ☐☐ 206 Valeri Zelepukin
☐☐ 207 Shawn Burr ☐☐ 208 Vladimir Ruzicka
☐☐ 209 Calle Johansson ☐☐ 210 M. Fitzpatrick (G)
☐☐ 211 Dean Kennedy ☐☐ 212 Dave Babych
☐☐ 213 Wayne Presley ☐☐ 214 Dave Manson
☐☐ 215 Mikael Andersson ☐☐ 216 Trent Yawney
☐☐ 217 Mark Howe ☐☐ 218 Mike Bullard
☐☐ 219 Claude Lapointe ☐☐ 220 Jeff Brown
☐☐ 221 Bob Kudelski ☐☐ 222 Michel Goulet
☐☐ 223 Phil Bourque ☐☐ 224 Darren Turcotte
☐☐ 225 Kirk Muller ☐☐ 226 Doug Bodger
☐☐ 227 Dave Gagner ☐☐ 228 Craig Billington (G)
☐☐ 229 Kevin Miller ☐☐ 230 Glen Wesley
☐☐ 231 Dale Hunter ☐☐ 232 Tom Kurvers
☐☐ 233 Pat Elynuik ☐☐ 234 Geoff Courtnall
☐☐ 235 Neil Wilkinson ☐☐ 236 Bill Ranford (G)
☐☐ 237 Ron Stern ☐☐ 238 Zarley Zalapski
☐☐ 239 Kerry Huffman ☐☐ 240 Joe Sakic
☐☐ 241 Glenn Anderson ☐☐ 242 Stéphane Quintal
☐☐ 243 Tony Granato ☐☐ 244 Rob Brown
☐☐ 245 Rick Tocchet ☐☐ 246 Stéphan Lebeau
☐☐ 247 Mark Hardy ☐☐ 248 Alexander Mogilny
☐☐ 249 Jon Casey (G) ☐☐ 250 Adam Oates
☐☐ 251 Bruce Driver ☐☐ 252 Sergei Fedorov
☐☐ 253 Michal Pivonka ☐☐ 254 Cliff Ronning
☐☐ 255 Derek King ☐☐ 256 Luciano Borsato
☐☐ 257 Paul Fenton ☐☐ 258 Craig Berube
☐☐ 259 Brian Bradley ☐☐ 260 Craig Simpson
☐☐ 261 Adam Burt ☐☐ 262 C. Joseph (G)
☐☐ 263 Mark Pederson ☐☐ 264 Alexei Gusarov
☐☐ 265 Paul Coffey ☐☐ 266 Steve Larmer
☐☐ 267 Ron Francis ☐☐ 268 Randy Gilhen
☐☐ 269 Guy Carbonneau ☐☐ 270 Chris Terreri (G)
☐☐ 271 Mike Craig ☐☐ 272 Dale Hawerchuk
☐☐ 273 Kevin Hatcher ☐☐ 274 Ken Hodge
☐☐ 275 Tim Cheveldae (G) ☐☐ 276 Benoît Hogue
☐☐ 277 Mark Osborne ☐☐ 278 Brian Mullen
☐☐ 279 Robert Dirk ☐☐ 280 Theoren Fleury
☐☐ 281 Martin Gelinas ☐☐ 282 Pat Verbeek
☐☐ 283 Mike Krushelnyski ☐☐ 284 Kevin Dineen
☐☐ 285 Craig Janney ☐☐ 286 Owen Nolan
☐☐ 287 Bob Errey ☐☐ 288 Bryan Marchment
☐☐ 289 Randy Moller ☐☐ 290 Luc Robitaille
☐☐ 291 Peter Stastny ☐☐ 292 Ken Sutton
☐☐ 293 Brad Marsh ☐☐ 294 Chris Dahlquist
☐☐ 295 Patrick Roy (G) ☐☐ 296 Andy Brickley
☐☐ 297 Randy Burridge ☐☐ 298 Ray Ferraro
☐☐ 299 Phil Housley ☐☐ 300 Mark Messier
☐☐ 301 David Bruce ☐☐ 302 Al MacInnis
☐☐ 303 Craig MacTavish ☐☐ 304 K. Whitmore (G)
☐☐ 305 Trevor Linden ☐☐ 306 Steve Kasper
☐☐ 307 Todd Elik ☐☐ 308 Eric Weinrich
☐☐ 309 Jocelyn Lemieux ☐☐ 310 Peter Ahola
☐☐ 311 J.J. Daigneault ☐☐ 312 Colin Patterson
☐☐ 313 Darcy Wakaluk (G) ☐☐ 314 Doug Weight
☐☐ 315 David Barr ☐☐ 316 Keith Primeau
☐☐ 317 Bob Sweeney ☐☐ 318 Jyrki Lumme
☐☐ 319 Stu Barnes ☐☐ 320 Don Beaupré (G)
☐☐ 321 Joe Murphy ☐☐ 322 Gary Roberts
☐☐ 323 Andrew Cassels ☐☐ 324 Rod Brind'Amour
☐☐ 325 Pierre Turgeon ☐☐ 326 Claude Vilgrain
☐☐ 327 Rich Sutter ☐☐ 328 Claude Loiselle
☐☐ 329 John Ogrodnick ☐☐ 330 Ulf Dahlen
☐☐ 331 Gilbert Dionne ☐☐ 332 Joel Otto
☐☐ 333 Rob Pearson ☐☐ 334 Christian Ruuttu
☐☐ 335 Brian Bellows ☐☐ 336 Anatoli Semenov
☐☐ 337 Brent Fedyk ☐☐ 338 Gaetan Duchesne
☐☐ 339 Randy McKay ☐☐ 340 Bernie Nicholls
☐☐ 341 Keith Acton ☐☐ 342 John Tonelli
☐☐ 343 Brian Lawton ☐☐ 344 Ric Nattress
☐☐ 345 Mike Eagles ☐☐ 346 Frantisek Kucera
☐☐ 347 John McIntyre ☐☐ 348 Troy Loney
☐☐ 349 Norm Maciver ☐☐ 350 Brett Hull
☐☐ 351 Rob Ramage ☐☐ 352 Claude Boivin
☐☐ 353 Paul Broten ☐☐ 354 S. Fiset (G)
☐☐ 355 Garry Valk ☐☐ 356 Basil McRae
☐☐ 357 Alan May ☐☐ 358 Grant Ledyard
☐☐ 359 Dave Poulin ☐☐ 360 Valeri Kamensky
☐☐ 361 Brian Glynn ☐☐ 362 Jan Erixon
☐☐ 363 Mike Lalor ☐☐ 364 Jeff Chychrun
☐☐ 365 Ron Wilson ☐☐ 366 Shawn Cronin
☐☐ 367 Sylvain Turgeon ☐☐ 368 Mike Liut (G)
☐☐ 369 Joe Cirella ☐☐ 370 David Maley
☐☐ 371 Lucien DeBlois ☐☐ 372 Per Djoos
☐☐ 373 Dominik Hasek (G) ☐☐ 374 Laurie Boschman
☐☐ 375 Brian Leetch ☐☐ 376 Nelson Emerson
☐☐ 377 Normand Rochefort ☐☐ 378 J. Cloutier (G)
☐☐ 379 Jim Sandlak ☐☐ 380 David Reid
☐☐ 381 Gary Nylund ☐☐ 382 Sergei Makarov
☐☐ 383 Petr Klima ☐☐ 384 Peter Douris
☐☐ 385 Kirk McLean (G) ☐☐ 386 Robert McGill
☐☐ 387 Ron Tugnutt (G) ☐☐ 388 Patrice Brisebois
☐☐ 389 Tony Amonte ☐☐ 390 Mario Lemieux
☐☐ 391 Nicklas Lidström ☐☐ 392 Brendan Shanahan
☐☐ 393 Donald Audette ☐☐ 394 Alexei Kasatonov
☐☐ 395 Dino Ciccarelli ☐☐ 396 V. Riendeau (G)
☐☐ 397 Joe Reekie ☐☐ 398 Jari Kurri
☐☐ 399 Ken Wregget (G) ☐☐ 400 Steve Yzerman
☐☐ 401 Scott Niedermayer ☐☐ 402 S. Beauregard (G)
☐☐ 403 Tim Hunter ☐☐ 404 Marc Bergevin
☐☐ 405 Sylvain Lefebvre ☐☐ 406 Johan Garpenlöv
☐☐ 407 Tony Hrkac ☐☐ 408 Tie Domi
☐☐ 409 Martin Lapointe ☐☐ 410 Darryl Sydor
☐☐ 411 LL: Brett Hull ☐☐ 412 LL: W. Gretzky
☐☐ 413 LL: Mario Lemieux ☐☐ 414 LL: P.Ysebaert
☐☐ 415 LL: Tony Amonte ☐☐ 416 LL: B. Leetch
☐☐ 417 LL: McLean (G)/ Cheveldae (G)
☐☐ 418 LL: Patrick Roy (G)
☐☐ 419 Ray Bourque ☐☐ 420 Pat LaFontaine
☐☐ 421 Al MacInnis ☐☐ 422 Jeremy Roenick
☐☐ 423 Steve Yzerman ☐☐ 424 Bill Ranford (G)
☐☐ 425 John Cullen ☐☐ 426 Wayne Gretzky
☐☐ 427 Mike Modano ☐☐ 428 Patrick Roy (G)
☐☐ 429 Scott Stevens ☐☐ 430 Pierre Turgeon
☐☐ 431 Mark Messier ☐☐ 432 Eric Lindros
☐☐ 433 Mario Lemieux ☐☐ 434 Joe Sakic
☐☐ 435 Brett Hull ☐☐ 436 Pat Falloon
☐☐ 437 Grant Fuhr (G) ☐☐ 438 Trevor Linden
☐☐ 439 Kevin Hatcher ☐☐ 440 Phil Housley
☐☐ 441 HL: Paul Coffey ☐☐ 442 HL: Brett Hull
☐☐ 443 HL: Mike Gartner ☐☐ 444 HL: M. Goulet
☐☐ 445 HL: Mike Gartner ☐☐ 446 HL: Bobby Smith
☐☐ 447 HL: Ray Bourque ☐☐ 448 HL: M. Lemieux
☐☐ 449 Scott Lachance ☐☐ 450 Keith Tkachuk
☐☐ 451 Alexander Semak ☐☐ 452 John Tanner (G)
☐☐ 453 Joé Juneau ☐☐ 454 Igor Kravchuk
☐☐ 455 Brent Thompson ☐☐ 456 Evgeny Davydov
☐☐ 457 Arturs Irbe (G) ☐☐ 458 Kent Manderville
☐☐ 459 Shawn McEachern ☐☐ 460 G. Hebert (G) RC
☐☐ 461 Keith Carney RC ☐☐ 462 Karl Dykhuis
☐☐ 463 Bill Lindsay RC ☐☐ 464 D. Roussel (G)
☐☐ 465 Marty McInnis ☐☐ 466 Dale Craigwell
☐☐ 467 Igor Ulanov ☐☐ 468 Dimitri Mironov
☐☐ 469 D. McAmmond RC ☐☐ 470 Bill Guerin RC
☐☐ 471 Bret Hedican ☐☐ 472 Félix Potvin (G)
☐☐ 473 Vyacheslav Kozlov ☐☐ 474 Martin Rucinsky
☐☐ 475 Ray Whitney RC ☐☐ 476 Stephen Heinze
☐☐ 477 Brad Schlegel ☐☐ 478 Patrick Poulin
☐☐ 479 Ted Donato ☐☐ 480 Martin Brodeur (G)
☐☐ 481 Denny Felsner RC ☐☐ 482 Trent Klatt RC
☐☐ 483 Gord Hynes ☐☐ 484 Glen Murray
☐☐ 485 Chris Lindberg ☐☐ 486 Ray LeBlanc (G)
☐☐ 487 Y. Perreault RC ☐☐ 488 J-F Quintin RC
☐☐ 489 Patrick Roy (G) ☐☐ 490 Ray Bourque
☐☐ 491 Brian Leetch ☐☐ 492 Kevin Stevens
☐☐ 493 Mark Messier ☐☐ 494 Jaromir Jagr
☐☐ 495 Bill Ranford (G) ☐☐ 496 Al MacInnis
☐☐ 497 Chris Chelios ☐☐ 498 Luc Robitaille
☐☐ 499 Jeremy Roenick ☐☐ 500 Brett Hull
☐☐ 501 Félix Potvin (G) ☐☐ 502 Nicklas Lidström
☐☐ 503 Vlad. Konstantinov ☐☐ 504 Pavel Bure
☐☐ 505 Nelson Emerson ☐☐ 506 Tony Amonte
☐☐ 507 Lightning CL ☐☐ 508 Shawn Chambers
☐☐ 509 Basil McRae ☐☐ 510 Joe Reekie
☐☐ 511 W. Young (G) ☐☐ 512 Senators CL
☐☐ 513 Laurie Boschman ☐☐ 514 Mark Lamb
☐☐ 515 P. Sidorkiewicz (G) ☐☐ 516 Sylvain Turgeon
☐☐ 517 Kevin & Bill Dineen ☐☐ 518 1992 Cup Champs
☐☐ 519 AW: M. Lemieux ☐☐ 520 AW: R. Bourque
☐☐ 521 AW: Mark Messier ☐☐ 522 AW: B. Leetch
☐☐ 523 AW: Pavel Bure ☐☐ 524 AW: Carbonneau
☐☐ 525 AW: W. Gretzky ☐☐ 526 AW: Fitzpatrick
☐☐ 527 AW: Roy (G) ☐☐ 528 Blazers
☐☐ 529 Rick Tabaracci (G) ☐☐ 530 Tom Draper (G)
☐☐ 531 Adrien Plavsic ☐☐ 532 Joe Sacco
☐☐ 533 Mike Sullivan ☐☐ 534 Zdeno Ciger
☐☐ 535 F. Pietrangelo (G) ☐☐ 536 Mike Peluso
☐☐ 537 Jim Paek ☐☐ 538 Dave Hannan
☐☐ 539 D. Williams RC ☐☐ 540 Gino Odjick
☐☐ 541 Yvon Corriveau ☐☐ 542 Grant Jennings
☐☐ 543 Stéphane Matteau ☐☐ 544 Patrick Conacher
☐☐ 545 Steven Rice ☐☐ 546 Marc Habscheid
☐☐ 547 Steve Weeks (G) ☐ 548 Maurice Richard
☐ 548 Jay Wells ☐ 549 Maurice Richard
☐ 549 Mick Vukota ☐☐ 550 Eric Lindros

	Player	NM-MT
☐	Eric Lindros, Phil. [Press Conference]	30.00

SHARP SHOOTERS

	Insert Set (30 cards):	8.00
	Player	NM-MT
☐☐	1 Gary Roberts, Calg.	.50
☐☐	2 Sergei Makarov, Calg.	.50
☐☐	3 Ray Ferraro, NYIs.	.25
☐☐	4 Dale Hunter, Wash.	.25
☐☐	5 Sergei Nemchinov, NYRa.	.25
☐☐	6 Mike Ridley, Wash.	.25
☐☐	7 Gilbert Dionne, Mont.	.25
☐☐	8 Pat LaFontaine, Buff.	.50
☐☐	9 Jimmy Carson, Detr.	.25
☐☐	10 Jeremy Roenick, Chic.	1.00
☐☐	11 Kelly Buchberger, Edmo.	.25
☐☐	12 Owen Nolan, Québ.	.50
☐☐	13 Igor Larionov, Vanc.	.50
☐☐	14 Claude Vilgrain, NJer.	.25
☐☐	15 Derek King, NYIs.	.25
☐☐	16 Greg Paslawski, Québ.	.25
☐☐	17 Bob Probert, Detr.	.25
☐☐	18 Mark Recchi, Phil.	.50
☐☐	19 Donald Audette, Buff.	.50
☐☐	20 Ray Sheppard, Detr.	.25
☐☐	21 Benoît Hogue, NYIs.	.25
☐☐	22 Rob (Jr.) Brown, Chic.	.25
☐☐	23 Pat Elynuik, Winn.	.25
☐☐	24 Petr Klima, Edmo.	.25
☐☐	25 Pierre Turgeon, NYIs.	.50
☐☐	26 Corey Millen, LosA.	.25
☐☐	27 Dmitri Khristich, Wash.	.25
☐☐	28 Anatoli Semenov, Edmo.	.25
☐☐	29 Kirk Muller, Mont.	.25
☐☐	30 Craig Simpson, Edmo.	.25

USA GREATS

	American Insert Set (15 cards):	50.00
	Player	NM-MT
☐	1 Pat LaFontaine, Buff.	6.00
☐	2 Chris Chelios, Chic.	6.00
☐	3 Jeremy Roenick, Chic.	8.00
☐	4 Tony Granato, LosA.	2.00
☐	5 Mike Modano, Minn.	10.00
☐	6 Mike Richter (G), NYRa.	4.00
☐	7 John Vanbiesbrouck (G), NYRa.	4.00
☐	8 Brian Leetch, NYRa.	6.00
☐	9 Joe Mullen, Pitt.	4.00
☐	10 Kevin Stevens, Pitt.	2.00
☐	11 Craig Janney, SLou.	2.00
☐	12 Brian Mullen, SanJ.	2.00
☐	13 Kevin Hatcher, Wash.	2.00
☐	14 Kelly Miller, Wash.	2.00
☐	15 Ed Olczyk, Winn.	2.00

CANADIAN OLYMPIC HEROES

	Canadian Insert Set (15 cards):	40.00
	Player	NM-MT
☐	1 Eric Lindros	14.00
☐	2 Joé Juneau	6.00
☐	3 Dave Archibald	2.00
☐	4 Randy Smith RC	3.00
☐	5 Gord Hynes	2.00
☐	6 Chris Lindberg	2.00
☐	7 Jason Woolley RC	3.00
☐	8 Fabian Joseph RC	3.00
☐	9 Brad Schlegel	2.00
☐	10 Kent Manderville	2.00
☐	11 Adrien Plavsic	2.00
☐	12 Trevor Kidd	4.00
☐	13 Sean Burke (G)	7.00

MAURICE RICHARD

	Player	Score
☐	Maurice Richard, Mont.	16.00
☐	Maurice Richard, Mont.	16.00
☐	Maurice Richard, Mont. ✍	200.00
☐	Maurice Richard, Mont. ✍	200.00

1992 - 93 SCORE YOUNG SUPERSTARS

Complete Set (40 cards): 8.00

	Player	NM-MT
☐	1 Eric Lindros, Phil.	.25
☐	2 Tony Amonte, NYRa.	.25
☐	3 Mats Sundin, Québ.	.25
☐	4 Jaromir Jagr, Pitt.	.25
☐	5 Sergei Fedorov, Detr.	.25
☐	6 Gilbert Dionne, Mont.	.25
☐	7 Mark Recchi, Phil.	.25
☐	8 Alexander Mogilny, Buff.	.25
☐	9 Mike Richter (G), NYRa.	.25
☐	10 Jeremy Roenick, Chic.	.25
☐	11 Nicklas Lidström, Detr.	.25
☐	12 Scott Lachance, NYIs.	.25
☐	13 Nelson Emerson, SLou.	.25
☐	14 Pat Falloon, SanJ.	.25
☐	15 Dmitri Khristich, Wash.	.25
☐	16 Trevor Linden, Vanc.	.25
☐	17 Curtis Joseph (G), SLou.	.25
☐	18 Rob Pearson, Toro.	.25
☐	19 Kevin Todd, NJer.	.25
☐	20 Joe Sakic, Québ.	.25
☐	21 Tim Cheveldae (G), Detr.	.25
☐	22 Joé Juneau, Wash.	.25
☐	23 Vladimir Konstantinov, Detr.	.25
☐	24 Valeri Kamensky, Québ.	.25
☐	25 Ed Belfour (G), Chic.	.25
☐	26 Rod Brind'Amour, Phil.	.25
☐	27 Pierre Turgeon, NYIs.	.25
☐	28 Éric Desjardins, Mont.	.25
☐	29 Keith Tkachuk, Winn.	.25
☐	30 Pavel Bure, Vanc.	.25
☐	31 Patrick Poulin, Hart.	.25
☐	32 Vyacheslav Kozlov, Detr.	.25
☐	33 Scott Niedermayer, NJer.	.25
☐	34 Jyrki Lumme, Vanc.	.25
☐	35 Paul Ysebaert, Detr.	.25
☐	36 Dominic Roussel (G), Phil.	.25
☐	37 Owen Nolan, Québ.	.25
☐	38 Rob Blake, LosA.	.25
☐	39 Félix Potvin (G), Toro.	.25
☐	40 Mike Modano, Dall.	.25

1992 - 93 SEASONS ACTION PLAYER PATCHES

The patches were made of soft cloth and intended to patch clothing. The set is considered complete without the prototype patch (#22, Grant Mulvey).

Patch Size: 3 1/8" x 4 3/8"

Imprint (on packaging): SEASONS TM/MC

Complete Set (71 patches): 150.00

	Player	NM-MT
☐	1 Jeremy Roenick, Chic.	2.00
☐	2 Steve Larmer, Chic.	2.00
☐	3 Ed Belfour (G), Chic.	2.00
☐	4 Chris Chelios, Chic.	2.00
☐	5 Sergei Fedorov, Detr.	2.00
☐	6 Steve Yzerman, Detr.	8.00
☐	7 Tim Cheveldae (G), Detr.	2.00
☐	8 Bob Probert, Detr.	2.00
☐	9 Wayne Gretzky, LosA.	14.00
☐	10 Luc Robitaille, LosA.	2.00
☐	11 Tony Granato, LosA.	2.00
☐	12 Kelly Hrudey (G), LosA.	2.00
☐	13 Brett Hull, SLou.	2.00
☐	14 Curtis Joseph (G), SLou.	2.00
☐	15 Brendan Shanahan, SLou.	2.00
☐	16 Nelson Emerson, SLou.	2.00
☐	17 Raymond Bourque, Bost.	4.00
☐	18 Joé Juneau, Bost.	2.00
☐	19 Andy Moog (G), Bost.	2.00
☐	20 Adam Oates, Bost.	2.00
☐	21 Patrick Roy (G), Mont.	10.00
☐	22 Grant Mulvey Prototype	20.00
☐	23 Denis Savard, Mont.	2.00
☐	24 Gilbert Dionne, Mont.	2.00
☐	25 Kirk Muller, Mont.	2.00
☐	26 Mark Messier, NYRa.	2.00
☐	27 Tony Amonte, NYRa.	2.00
☐	28 Brian Leetch, NYRa.	2.00
☐	29 Mike Richter (G), NYRa.	2.00
☐	30 Trevor Linden, Vanc.	2.00
☐	31 Pavel Bure, Vanc.	2.00
☐	32 Cliff Ronning, Vanc.	2.00
☐	33 Geoff Courtnall, Vanc.	2.00
☐	34 Mario Lemieux, Pitt.	10.00
☐	35 Jaromir Jagr, Pitt.	2.00
☐	36 Tom Barrasso (G), Pitt.	2.00
☐	37 Rick Tocchet, Phil.	2.00
☐	38 Eric Lindros, Phil.	2.00
☐	39 Rod Brind'Amour, Phil.	2.00
☐	40 Dominic Roussel (G), Phil.	2.00
☐	41 Mark Recchi, Phil.	2.00
☐	42 Pat LaFontaine, Buff.	2.00
☐	43 Donald Audette, Buff.	2.00
☐	44 Pat Verbeek, Hart.	2.00
☐	45 John Cullen, Hart.	2.00
☐	46 Owen Nolan, Québ.	2.00
☐	47 Joe Sakic, Québ.	6.00
☐	48 Kevin Hatcher, Wash.	2.00
☐	49 Don Beaupré (G), Wash.	2.00
☐	50 Scott Stevens, NJer.	2.00
☐	51 Chris Terreri (G), NJer.	2.00
☐	52 Scott Lachance, NJer.	2.00
☐	53 Pierre Turgeon, NYIs.	2.00
☐	54 Grant Fuhr (G), Toro.	2.00
☐	55 Doug Gilmour, Toro.	2.00
☐	56 Dave Manson, Edmo.	2.00
☐	57 Bill Ranford (G), Edmo.	2.00
☐	58 Troy Murray, Chic.	2.00
☐	59 Phil Housley, Winn.	2.00
☐	60 Al MacInnis, Calg.	2.00
☐	61 Mike Vernon (G), Calg.	2.00
☐	62 Pat Falloon, SanJ.	2.00
☐	63 Doug Wilson, SanJ.	2.00
☐	64 Jon Casey (G), Minn.	2.00
☐	65 Mike Modano, Minn.	2.00
☐	66 Kevin Stevens, Pitt.	2.00
☐	67 Al Iafrate, Wash.	2.00
☐	68 Dale Hawerchuk, Buff.	2.00
☐	69 Igor Kravchuk, Chic.	2.00
☐	70 Wendel Clark, Toro.	2.00
☐	71 Kirk McLean (G), Vanc.	2.00

1992 - 93 SEMIC ELITSERIEN STICKERS

The most expensive single is Johan Hedberg at $3-5. Singles start at 20¢.

Size: 3" x 2 1/8"

Complete Set (356 stickers): 40.00

Common Player: .20

Player	No. Player
☐ 1 AIK Photo LH	☐ 2 AIK Photo RH
☐ 3 Brynas Photo LH	☐ 4 Brynas Photo RH
☐ 5 Djurgardens Photo LH	☐ 6 Djurgardens Photo RH
☐ 7 Farjestad Photo LH	☐ 8 Farjestad Photo RH
☐ 9 HV 71 Photo LH	☐ 10 HV 71 Photo RH
☐ 11 Leksands Photo LH	☐ 12 Leksands Photo RH
☐ 13 Lulea Photo LH	☐ 14 Lulea Photo RH
☐ 15 Malmo Photo LH	☐ 16 Malmo Photo RH
☐ 17 MoDo Photo LH	☐ 18 MoDo Photo RH
☐ 19 Rogle Photo LH	☐ 20 Rogle Photo RH
☐ 21 Västerås Photo LH	☐ 22 Västerås Photo RH
☐ 23 Frolunda Photo LH	☐ 24 Frolunda Photo RH
☐ 25 AIK Logo	☐ 26 Rolf Ridderwall
☐ 27 Sam Lindstahl	☐ 28 Ronnie Karlsson
☐ 29 Mats Thelin	☐ 30 Mattias Norstrom
☐ 31 Dick Tarnstrom	☐ 32 Petri Liimatainen
☐ 33 Rikard Franzen	☐ 34 Daniel Jardemyr
☐ 35 Niclas Havelid	☐ 36 Börje Salming
☐ 37 Thomas Bjuhr	☐ 38 Peter Hammarstrom
☐ 39 Thomas Strandberg	☐ 40 Mats Lindberg
☐ 41 Anders Bjork	☐ 42 Anders Johnson
☐ 43 Patrik Erickson	☐ 44 Torbjorn Ohrlund
☐ 45 Björn Ahlström	☐ 46 Niclas Sundblad
☐ 47 Patric Englund	☐ 48 Kristian Gahn
☐ 49 Morgan Samuelsson	☐ 50 Brynas Logo
☐ 51 Michael Sundlov	☐ 52 Lars Karlsson
☐ 53 Bedrick Scerban	☐ 54 Mikael Lindman
☐ 55 Tommy Melkersson	☐ 56 Stefan Klockare
☐ 57 Mikael Enander	☐ 58 Roger Karlsson
☐ 59 Niklas Gallstedt	☐ 60 Christer Olsson
☐ 61 Anders Carlsson	☐ 62 Thomas Tallberg
☐ 63 Tom Bissett	☐ 64 Andreas Dackell
☐ 65 Mikael Wahlberg	☐ 66 Jan Larsson
☐ 67 Anders Gozzi	☐ 68 Ove Molin
☐ 69 Anders Huss	☐ 70 Peter Gustafsson
☐ 71 Jonas Johnson	☐ 72 Peter Larsson
☐ 73 Mikael Lindholm	☐ 74 Djurgarden Logo
☐ 75 Thomas Ostlund	☐ 76 Petter Ronnquist
☐ 77 Christian Due-Boje	☐ 78 Arto Blomsten
☐ 79 Kenneth Kennholt	☐ 80 Marcus Ragnarsson
☐ 81 Thomas Johansson	☐ 82 Joakim Lundberg
☐ 83 Thomas Eriksson	☐ 84 Bjorn Nord
☐ 85 Mikael Magnusson	☐ 86 Charles Berglund
☐ 87 Erik Huusko	☐ 88 Anders Huusko
☐ 89 Tony Skopac	☐ 90 Jens Ohling
☐ 91 Peter Nilsson	☐ 92 Magnus Jonsson
☐ 93 Kent Nilsson	☐ 94 Mikael Hakansson
☐ 95 Ola Josefsson	☐ 96 Jerry Friman
☐ 97 Fredrik Lindquist	☐ 98 Mathias Hallback
☐ 99 Jan Viktorsson	☐ 100 Farjestad Logo
☐ 101 Anders Bergman	☐ 102 Jonas Eriksson
☐ 103 Patrik Haltia	☐ 104 Tommy Samuelsson
☐ 105 Jesper Duus	☐ 106 Leif Carlsson
☐ 107 Per Lundell	☐ 108 Jacob Karlsson
☐ 109 Thomas Rhodin	☐ 110 Mattias Olsson
☐ 111 Hakan Loob	☐ 112 Thomas Rundqvist
☐ 113 Andreas Johansson	☐ 114 Staffan Lundh
☐ 115 Jonas Hoglund	☐ 116 B-A Gustafsson
☐ 117 Mattias Johansson	☐ 118 Clas Eriksson
☐ 119 Peter Ottosson	☐ 120 Niklas Brannstrom
☐ 121 Lars Karlsson	☐ 122 Peter Hagstrom
☐ 123 Kjell Dahlin	☐ 124 HV 71 Logo
☐ 125 Peter Aslin	☐ 126 Boo Ahl
☐ 127 Antonin Stavjana	☐ 128 Klas Heed
☐ 129 Tommy Fritz	☐ 130 Kristian Pedersen
☐ 131 Per Gustafsson	☐ 132 Mathias Svedberg
☐ 133 Niklas Rahm	☐ 134 Martin Canielsson
☐ 135 Fredrik Stillman	☐ 136 Lars Ivarsson
☐ 137 Ove Thornberg	☐ 138 Peter Ekelund
☐ 139 Eddy Eriksson	☐ 140 Stefan Ornskog
☐ 141 Patrik Ross	☐ 142 Torbjorn Persson
☐ 143 Kamil Kastak	☐ 144 Dennis Strom
☐ 145 Peter Eriksson	☐ 146 Magnus Axelsson
☐ 147 Stefan Falk	☐ 148 Thomas Ljungberg
☐ 149 Leksand Logo	☐ 150 Ake Lilljeborn
☐ 151 Jonas Leven	☐ 152 Johan Hedberg
☐ 153 Tomas Jonsson	☐ 154 Henric Bjorkman
☐ 155 Mattias Andersson	☐ 156 Rickard Persson
☐ 157 Orjan Nilsson	☐ 158 Magnus Svensson
☐ 159 Orjan Lindmark	☐ 160 Jan Huokko
☐ 161 Reine Rauhala	☐ 162 Emil Skoglund
☐ 163 Jens Nielsen	☐ 164 Marcus Thuresson
☐ 165 Niklas Eriksson	☐ 166 Tomas Srsen
☐ 167 Jonas Bergqvist	☐ 168 Per-Olof Carlsson
☐ 169 Markus Akerblom	☐ 170 Greg Parks
☐ 171 Mattias Loof	☐ 172 Cenneth Soderlund
☐ 173 Jarmo Makitalo	☐ 174 Lulea Logo
☐ 175 Robert Skoog	☐ 176 Erik Grankvist
☐ 177 Lars Modig	☐ 178 Patrik Hoglund
☐ 179 Niklas Bjornoft	☐ 180 Torbjorn Lindberg
☐ 181 Ville Siren	☐ 182 Petter Nilsson
☐ 183 Joakim Gunler	☐ 184 Tomas Lilja
☐ 185 Stefan Jonsson	☐ 186 Stefan Nilsson
☐ 187 Johan Stromvall	☐ 188 Robert Nordberg
☐ 189 Tomas Berglund	☐ 190 Mikael Renberg
☐ 191 L G Pettersson	☐ 192 Lars Edstrom
☐ 193 Kyosti Karjalainen	☐ 194 Lars Hurtig
☐ 195 Fredrik Oberg	☐ 196 Mikael Engstrom
☐ 197 Mika Nieminen	☐ 198 Malmo Logo
☐ 199 Peter Lindmark	☐ 200 R. Nordström (G)
☐ 201 Johan Mansson	☐ 202 Anders Svensson
☐ 203 Timo Blomqvist	☐ 204 Johan Norgren
☐ 205 Mats Lusth	☐ 206 Peter Hasselblad
☐ 207 Robert Svehla	☐ 208 Johan Salle
☐ 209 Roger Ohman	☐ 210 Raimo Helminen
☐ 211 Roger Hansson	☐ 212 Per Rosenqvist
☐ 213 Bo Svanberg	☐ 214 Daniel Rydmark
☐ 215 Patrik Sylvegard	☐ 216 Jonas Hakansson
☐ 217 Jesper Mattsson	☐ 218 Hakan Ahlund
☐ 219 Peter Sundström	☐ 220 Mats Näslund
☐ 221 Robert Burakovsky	☐ 222 MoDo Logo
☐ 223 Fredrik Andersson	☐ 224 Anders Nasstrom
☐ 225 Anders Berglund	☐ 226 Miroslav Horava
☐ 227 Hans Lodin	☐ 228 Lars Jansson
☐ 229 Jorgen Eriksson	☐ 230 Anders Eriksson
☐ 231 Hans Jonsson	☐ 232 Tomas Nazen
☐ 233 Mattias Timander	☐ 234 Fredrik Bergqvist
☐ 235 Magnus Wernblom	☐ 236 Martin Hostak
☐ 237 Mikael Pettersson	☐ 238 L. Hermansson
☐ 239 Tommy Lehmann	☐ 240 Markus Näslund
☐ 241 Ulf Odmark	☐ 242 Peter Forsberg
☐ 243 A. Salomonsson	☐ 244 Niklas Sundstrom
☐ 245 Lars Bystrom	☐ 246 Erik Holmberg
☐ 247 Henrik Gradin	☐ 248 Rogle Logo
☐ 249 Kenneth Johansson	☐ 250 Billy Nilsson
☐ 251 Orjan Jacobsson	☐ 252 Daniel Johansson
☐ 253 Kenny Jonsson	☐ 254 Kari Eloranta
☐ 255 Kari Suoraniemi	☐ 256 Hakan Persson
☐ 257 Rikar Gronborg	☐ 258 Stefa Nilsson
☐ 259 Per Ljusterang	☐ 260 Igor Stelnov
☐ 261 Peter Lundmark	☐ 262 Heinz ehlers
☐ 263 Michael Hjalm	☐ 264 Jan Ericson
☐ 265 Pelle Svensson	☐ 266 Mats Loov
☐ 267 Stefan Elvenes	☐ 268 Roger Elvenes
☐ 269 Peter Wennberg	☐ 270 Per Wallin
☐ 271 Torgny Lowgren	☐ 272 Jorgen Jonsson
☐ 273 Vasteras Logo	☐ 274 Mats Ytter(G)
☐ 275 Tommy Salo (G)	☐ 276 Erik Bergstrom
☐ 277 Pierre Ivarsson	☐ 278 Peter Popovic
☐ 279 Sergei Fokin	☐ 280 Edvin Frylen
☐ 281 Leif Rohlin	☐ 282 Peter Karlsson
☐ 283 Peter Jacobsson	☐ 294 Roger Åkerström
☐ 285 Robert Nordmark	☐ 286 Patrik Juhlin
☐ 287 Mishat Fahrutdinov	☐ 288 Henrik Nilsson
☐ 289 Mikael Pettersson	☐ 290 Fredrik Nilsson
☐ 291 Stefan Hellkvist	☐ 292 Henrik Pettersson
☐ 293 Mikael Karlberg	☐ 294 Anders Berglund
☐ 295 Claes Lindblom	☐ 296 Johan Brummer
☐ 297 Patrik Ulin	☐ 298 Paul Andersson
☐ 299 Frolunda Logo	☐ 300 Hakan Algotsson
☐ 301 Mikael Sandberg	☐ 302 Patric Aberg
☐ 303 Joacim Esbjors	☐ 304 Oscar Ackestrom
☐ 305 Jonas Heed	☐ 306 Stefan Axelsson
☐ 308 Ronnie Sundin	☐ 308 Stefan Larsson
☐ 309 J. Hagrenius	☐ 310 Serge Boisvert
☐ 311 Jerry Persson	☐ 312 Trond Magnussen
☐ 313 Terho Koskela	☐ 314 Peter Derndtsson
☐ 315 Mikael Persson	☐ 316 Mats Hjalmarsson
☐ 317 Henrik Lundin	☐ 318 Jonas Esbjors
☐ 319 Daniel Alfredsson	☐ 320 Stefan Ketola
☐ 321 Lars Dahlstrom	☐ 322 Par Edlund
☐ 323 Thomas Sjogren	☐ 324 L. Holmgren, Coach
☐ 325 Sandlin, Coach	☐ 326 Lars Falk, Coach
☐ 327 Luckner, Coach	☐ 328 Lundstrom, Coach
☐ 329 Fleming, Coach	☐ 330 Lindfors, Coach
☐ 331 Cahtinen, Coach	☐ 332 Forsberg, Coach
☐ 333 Abrahm., Coach	☐ 334 Lundstrom, Coach
☐ 335 Leif Boork, Coach	☐ 336 Tommy Sjodin
☐ 337 Hakan Loob	☐ 338 Michael Nylander
☐ 339 Michael Nylander	☐ 340 Hakan Loob
☐ 341 Calle Johansson	☐ 342 Tommy Sandlin
☐ 343 Söderström (G)	☐ 344 Tommy Sjodin
☐ 345 Peter Andersson	☐ 346 Hakan Loob
☐ 347 Peter Forsberg	☐ 348 Mats Sundin
☐ 349 Jonas Forsberg	☐ 350 Stefan Bjork
☐ 351 Edvin Frylen	☐ 352 Mikael Tjallden
☐ 353 Johan Davidsson	☐ 354 Markus Eriksson
☐ 355 Fredrik Lindh	☐ 356 Peter Nylander
☐ 353 Johan Davidsson	☐ 354 Markus Eriksson
☐ 355 Fredrik Lindh	☐ 356 Peter Nylander

1992 - 93 SEMIC NORDISK

A 242-card set sells for approximately $250-300.

- ☐ 1 Jim Marthinsen
- ☐ 2 Jarl Eriksen
- ☐ 3 Erik Tveten
- ☐ 4 Carl_G Gundersen
- ☐ 5 Nick Carone
- ☐ 6 Jaromir Latal
- ☐ 7 Tom Johansen
- ☐ 8 Asgault Moe
- ☐ 9 Øscar Olsen
- ☐ 10 Atle Olsen
- ☐ 11 Roy Johansen
- ☐ 12 Marius Rath
- ☐ 13 Svenn_Erik Bjørnstad
- ☐ 14 Jon_Magne Karlstad
- ☐ 15 Pål Kristiansen
- ☐ 16 Espen Knutsen
- ☐ 17 Stig Johansen
- ☐ 18 Geir Myhre
- ☐ 19 Remo Martinsen
- ☐ 20 Jan_Tore Rønningen
- ☐ 21 Jon_Hroard Nordstrøm
- ☐ 22 Tom_Erik Olsen
- ☐ 23 Peter Madach
- ☐ 24 Rune Gulliksen
- ☐ 25 Carl_Oscar Andersen
- ☐ 26 Martin Åhlberg
- ☐ 27 Erik Kristiansen
- ☐ 28 Tommy Larsen
- ☐ 29 Åge Ellingsen
- ☐ 30 Patrick Eide
- ☐ 31 Svein_H Arnesen
- ☐ 32 Petter Thoresen
- ☐ 33 Pål Martinsen
- ☐ 34 Ole_Eskild Dahlstrøm
- ☐ 35 Nikolai Davydkin
- ☐ 36 Lennart Åhlberg
- ☐ 37 Tommie Eriksen
- ☐ 38 Jan_Roar Fagerli
- ☐ 39 Erik Nerell
- ☐ 40 Knut Walbye
- ☐ 41 Pål Dahlstrøm
- ☐ 42 Martin Andersen
- ☐ 43 Geir Hoff
- ☐ 44 Cato Andersen
- ☐ 45 Per_O Walbye
- ☐ 46 Cato_Tom Andersen
- ☐ 47 Frode Hansen
- ☐ 48 Petter Salsten
- ☐ 49 Arne Billkvam
- ☐ 50 Jarle Friis
- ☐ 51 Steve Allmann
- ☐ 52 Torbjørn Orskaug
- ☐ 53 Christian Kjeldsberg
- ☐ 54 Bjørn Mathisrud
- ☐ 55 Pål Gjermundsen
- ☐ 56 Ketil Martinsen
- ☐ 57 Vidar Andersen
- ☐ 58 Rene Hansen
- ☐ 59 Martin Friis
- ☐ 60 Ørjan Løvdal
- ☐ 61 Lars_H Andersen
- ☐ 62 Robert Sundt
- ☐ 63 Henrik Buskoven
- ☐ 64 Morten Finstad
- ☐ 65 M Christoffersen
- ☐ 66 Roar Larsen
- ☐ 67 Oldrich Valdek
- ☐ 68 Zdenek Albrecht
- ☐ 69 Fredrik Jacobsen
- ☐ 70 Rune Hansen
- ☐ 71 Lars Jacobsen
- ☐ 72 Staffan Tholson
- ☐ 73 Lasse Syversen
- ☐ 74 Kim Søgaard
- ☐ 75 Jan_Erik Thoresen
- ☐ 76 Pål_Andre Eriksen
- ☐ 77 Bjørn_F Bekkerud
- ☐ 78 Kjell_Erik Myreng
- ☐ 79 Lars Eilertsen
- ☐ 80 Reino Johansen
- ☐ 81 Igor Mishukov
- ☐ 82 Ole_P Dahlene
- ☐ 83 Jon Gundersen
- ☐ 84 Pål_Raab Lien
- ☐ 85 Vadim Tunikov
- ☐ 86 Tommy Skaarberg
- ☐ 87 Per_Chr Knold
- ☐ 88 Stephen Foyn
- ☐ 89 Glenn Åsland
- ☐ 90 Bjørte Olsson
- ☐ 91 Gorm Gundersen
- ☐ 92 Morgan Andersen
- ☐ 93 Vegar Barlie
- ☐ 94 Øystein Tronrud
- ☐ 95 Kim Fagerhøi
- ☐ 96 Tor Nilsen
- ☐ 97 Arne Bergseng
- ☐ 98 Timo Laituri
- ☐ 99 Sjur_Robert Nilsen
- ☐ 100 Mattis Haakensen
- ☐ 101 Lars Bergseng
- ☐ 102 Svein_E Nørstebø
- ☐ 103 Tor_A Jacobsen
- ☐ 104 Jørgen Salsten
- ☐ 105 Tommy Jakobsen
- ☐ 106 Tim Budy
- ☐ 107 Martin Wiita
- ☐ 108 Lenny Eriksson
- ☐ 109 Ståle Berg

☐ 110 Bjørn_A Dahl
☐ 111 Geir_Tore Dahl
☐ 112 Dallas Gaume
☐ 113 Geir Haugen
☐ 114 Roar Husby
☐ 115 Robert Nielsen
☐ 116 Lars_Erik Lunde
☐ 117 Kåre Nordnes
☐ 118 Magne Nordnes
☐ 119 Geir Leknes
☐ 120 Rob Doroshuk
☐ 121 Roger Olsen
☐ 122 Øyvind Sørli
☐ 123 Gunnar Bye
☐ 124 Per_K Vellan
☐ 125 Marc Laniel
☐ 126 Dallas Gaume
☐ 127 Rob Schistad
☐ 128 Jan_P Løschbrandt
☐ 129 Tore Kristensen
☐ 130 Eskil Eide
☐ 131 Erik Brodahl
☐ 132 Morten Nordhus
☐ 133 Erik Pettersen
☐ 134 Hans Bekken
☐ 135 Jan Bekken
☐ 136 Jon_Erik Haaland
☐ 137 Richard Little
☐ 138 Eivind Olsen
☐ 139 Morten Gilje
☐ 140 Sverre Høgemark
☐ 141 Eirik Paulsen
☐ 142 Kyle McDonough
☐ 143 Steffen Trettenes
☐ 144 Richard David
☐ 145 Odd Nilsen
☐ 146 Per Martinsen
☐ 147 Johnny Nilsen
☐ 148 Per_Chr. Fjeldstad
☐ 149 Christian Hafsmoe
☐ 150 Ryamond Lunde
☐ 151 Rene Lemire
☐ 152 Thomas Kristiansen
☐ 153 Vidar Wold
☐ 154 Hans_Petter Halla
☐ 155 Michael Smithurst
☐ 156 Lars_Erik Solberg
☐ 157 Kenneth Fjell
☐ 158 Morten Hem
☐ 159 Dag Høyem
☐ 160 Vince Guidotti
☐ 161 Glen Engevik
☐ 162 Joe Clarke
☐ 163 Lars_Erik Kjaer
☐ 164 Gorm Laursen
☐ 165 Per_R Johansen
☐ 166 Anders Martinsen
☐ 167 Jørn_A Flatha
☐ 168 Rune Hansen
☐ 169 Stian Kraft
☐ 170 Geir Svendsberget
☐ 171 Andre Aass
☐ 172 Erik_S Nilsen
☐ 173 Frode Sletner
☐ 174 Petter Syversen
☐ 175 Jarle Gundersen
☐ 176 Terje Wikstrøm
☐ 177 Steve McDonald
☐ 178 Sjur Kinder
☐ 179 Morten Fjeldstad
☐ 180 George Tower
☐ 181 Espen Knutsen [Årets Spiller]
☐ 182 Karlstad [Gullpucken]
☐ 183 Jakobsen [Supporterprisen]
☐ 184 Valenga [Norgesmester]
☐ 185 Tik [Elitseriemester]
☐ 186 Dallas Gaume [Toppscorer]
☐ 187 Dahl [Årets Rookie]
☐ 188 Eriksen [Toppkeeper'n]
☐ 189 Fioretti [Backstoppen]
☐ 190 Tutt [Mest Utvist]
☐ 191 Marthinsen [Årets Lag]
☐ 192 Tutt [Årets Lag]
☐ 193 Jaromir Latal [Årets Lag]
☐ 194 Dallas Gaume [Årets Lag]
☐ 195 Espen Knutsen [Årets Lag]
☐ 196 Valek [Årets Lag]
☐ 197 Skaare [Draften Av NHL]
☐ 198 Walbye [Draften Av NHL]
☐ 199 Ellingsen [Draften Av NHL]
☐ 200 Espen Knutsen [Draften Av NHL]
☐ 201 Dahlstrøm [Draften Av NHL]
☐ 202 Eriksen [Draften Av NHL]
☐ 203 Barlie [Draften Av NHL]
☐ 204 Jessesen [Rookie]
☐ 205 Alseth [Rookie]
☐ 206 Vellan [Rookie]
☐ 207 Hatteland [Rookie]
☐ 208 Aaby [Rookie]
☐ 209 Nilsen [Rookie]
☐ 210 Svendsberget [Rookie]
☐ 211 Eggen [Rookie]
☐ 212 Brunvoll [Rookie]
☐ 213 Hansen [Rookie]
☐ 214 Christiansen [Rookie]
☐ 215 Dahl [Rookie]
☐ 216 Kraft [Rookie]
☐ 217 Lubo Sikela
☐ 218 Rune Fjeldstad
☐ 219 Sven_Arild Olsen
☐ 220 Kent_Inge Kristiansen
☐ 221 Sjur_Rakstad Larsen
☐ 222 Børre Østvang
☐ 223 Harald Bastiansen
☐ 224 Jon Warset
☐ 225 Jo_Espen Leibnitz
☐ 226 Arild Syversen
☐ 227 Terje Haukali
☐ 228 Geir Dalene
☐ 229 Jonas Larsen
☐ 230 Thomas Hanssen
☐ 231 Stig Olsen
☐ 232 Lars Hansen
☐ 233 Hans_M Anonsen
☐ 234 Ketil Kristiansen
☐ 235 Bjørnar Sørensen
☐ 236 Tom Jøstne
☐ 237 John Klears
☐ 238 Arve Jansen
☐ 239 Ørjan Gjertsen
☐ 240 Checklist
☐ 241 Checklist
☐ 242 Checklist

1992 - 93 SPORT FLASH

	Player	Card
☐	1 Jacques Laperrière	.75
☐	2 Larry Carrière	.75
☐	3 Chuck Rayner	.75
☐	4 Jean Béliveau	1.50
☐	5 Bernie Geoffrion	.75
☐	6 Gilles Gilbert	.75
☐	7 Marcel Bonin	.75
☐	8 Léon Rochefort	.75
☐	9 Maurice Richard	2.00
☐	10 Réjean Houle	.75
☐	11 Pierre Mondou	.75
☐	12 Yvan Cournoyer	.75
☐	13 Henri Richard	.75
☐	Checklist	

AUTOGRAPHS

	Player	Aut.
☐	1 Jacques Laperrière ✍	10.00
☐	2 Larry Carrière ✍	10.00
☐	3 Chuck Rayner ✍	10.00
☐	4 Jean Béliveau ✍	30.00
☐	5 Bernie Geoffrion ✍	10.00
☐	6 Gilles Gilbert ✍	10.00
☐	7 Marcel Bonin ✍	10.00
☐	8 Léon Rochefort ✍	10.00
☐	9 Maurice Richard ✍ •	50.00
☐	10 Réjean Houle ✍	10.00
☐	11 Pierre Mondou ✍	10.00
☐	12 Yvan Cournoyer ✍	10.00
☐	13 Henri Richard ✍	15.00

1992 - 93 SPORTS ILLUSTRATED FOR KIDS

These cards were distributed as part of nine-card perforated sheets included in *Sports Illustrated for Kids*. While these cards were intended for editorial purposes, they have made their way onto the secondary market. Cards issued in the 12 issues between July 1992 and June 1993 were numbered 55-162.

1992-93 Sports Illustrated for Kids

☐	Nov. 1992 • 93 Patrick Roy (G), Mont.	10.00
☐	Jan. 1993 • 117 Jaromir Jagr, Pitt.	4.00
☐	Feb. 1993 • 125 Mario Lemieux, Pitt.	10.00
☐	Mar. 1993 • 134 Eric Lindros, Phil.	3.00
☐	May 1993 • 153 Wayne Gretzky, LosA.	15.00
☐	Jun. 1993 • 154 Alexander Mogilny, Buff.	1.00

1992 - 93 TOPPS

These cards have two versions: the regular issue and a one per pack Topps Gold parallel. Short prints in the Topps Gold series are priced accordingly.

Imprint: © 1992 THE TOPPS COMPANY, INC.

Complete Set (529 cards): 350.00 20.00
Common Player: .35 .20

	Player	Gold	Topps
☐☐	1 Wayne Gretzky, LosA.	40.00	1.50
☐☐	2 Brett Hull, SLou.	10.00	.20
☐☐	3 Félix Potvin (G), Toro.	2.00	.20
☐☐	4 Mark Tinordi, Minn.	.35	.20
☐☐	5 Paul Coffey, Pitt. (LosA.) [Highlight]	2.00	.20
☐☐	6 Tony Amonte, NYRa.	2.00	.20
☐☐	7 Pat Falloon, SanJ.	.35	.20
☐☐	8 Pavel Bure, Vanc.	3.00	.20
☐☐	9 Nicklas Lidström, Detr.	2.00	.20
☐☐	10 Dominic Roussel (G), Phil.	.35	.20
☐☐	11 Nelson Emerson, SLou.	.35	.20
☐☐	12 Donald Audette, Buff.	1.00	.20
☐☐	13 Gilbert Dionne, Mont.	.35	.20
☐☐	14 Vladimir Konstantinov, Detr.	1.00	.20
☐☐	15 Kevin Todd, NJer.	.35	.20
☐☐	16 Stephen Leach, Bost.	.35	.20
☐☐	17 Ed Olczyk, Winn.	.35	.20
☐☐	18 Jim Hrivnak (G), Wash.	.35	.20
☐☐	19 Gilbert Dionne, Mont.	.35	.20
☐☐	20 Mike Vernon (G), Calg.	1.00	.20
☐☐	21 Dave Christian, SLou.	.35	.20
☐☐	22 Ed Belfour (G), Chic.	3.00	.20
☐☐	23 Andrew Cassels, Hart.	.35	.20
☐☐	24 Jaromir Jagr, Pitt.	3.00	.20
☐☐	25 Arturs Irbe (G), SanJ.	1.00	.20
☐☐	26 Petr Klima, Edmo.	.35	.20
☐☐	27 Randy Gilhen, NYRa.	.35	.20
☐☐	28 Ulf Dahlén, Minn.	.35	.20
☐☐	29 Kelly Hrudey (G), LosA.	1.00	.20
☐☐	30 Dave Ellett, Toro.	.35	.20
☐☐	31 Tom Fitzgerald, NYIs.	.35	.20
☐☐	32 Cam Neely, Bost.	3.00	.20
☐☐	33 Greg Paslawski, Québ.	.35	.20
☐☐	34 Brad May, Buff.	.35	.20
☐☐	35 Vyacheslav Kozlov, Detr.	.35	.20
☐☐	36 Mark Hunter, Hart. (Wash.)	.35	.20
☐☐	37 Steve Chiasson, Detr.	.35	.20
☐☐	38 Joe Murphy, Edmo.	.35	.20
☐☐	39 Darryl Sydor, LosA.	.35	.20
☐☐	40 Ron Hextall (G), Phil. (Québ.)	2.00	.20
☐☐	41 Jim Sandlak, Vanc.	.35	.20
☐☐	42 Dave Lowry, SLou.	.35	.20
☐☐	43 Claude Lemieux, NJer.	1.00	.20
☐☐	44 Gerald Diduck, Vanc.	.35	.20
☐☐	45 Mike McPhee, Mont.	.35	.20
☐☐	46 Rod Langway, Wash.	1.00	.20
☐☐	47 Guy Larose, Toro.	.35	.20
☐☐	48 Craig Billington (G), NJer.	.35	.20
☐☐	49 Daniel Marois, NYIs.	.35	.20
☐☐	**50 Todd Nelson, Pitt. RC**	**1.00**	**.20**
☐☐	51 Jari Kurri, LosA.	3.00	.20
☐☐	52 Keith Brown, Chic.	.35	.20
☐☐	53 Valeri Kamensky, Québ.	1.00	.20
☐☐	54 Jim* Johnson, Minn.	.35	.20
☐☐	55 Vincent Damphousse, Edmo.	2.00	.20
☐☐	56 Pat Elynuik, Winn.	.35	.20
☐☐	57 Jeff Beukeboom, NYRa.	.35	.20
☐☐	58 Paul Ysebaert, Detr.	.35	.20
☐☐	59 Ken Sutton, Buff.	.35	.20
☐☐	60 Dale Craigwell, SanJ.	.35	.20
☐☐	61 Marc Bergevin, Hart. (Tamp.)	.35	.20
☐☐	62 Stéphane Beauregard (G), Winn.	.35	.20
☐☐	63 Bob Probert, Detr.	1.00	.20
☐☐	64 Jergus Baca, Hart.	.35	.20
☐☐	65 Brian Propp, Minn.	.35	.20
☐☐	66 Jacques Cloutier (G), Québ.	.35	.20
☐☐	**67 Jim* Thomson, LosA. (Otta.) RC**	**1.00**	**.20**
☐☐	68 Anatoli Semenov, Edmo. (Tamp.)	.35	.20
☐☐	69 Stéphan Lebeau, Mont.	.35	.20
☐☐	70 Rick Tocchet, Pitt.	1.00	.20
☐☐	71 James Patrick, NYRa.	.35	.20
☐☐	72 Rob (Jr.) Brown, Chic.	.35	.20
☐☐	73 Peter Ahola, LosA.	.35	.20
☐☐	74 Bob Corkum, Buff.	.35	.20
☐☐	75 Brent Sutter, Chic.	.35	.20
☐☐	76 Neil Wilkinson, SanJ.	.35	.20
☐☐	77 Mark Osborne, Toro.	.35	.20
☐☐	78 Ron L. Wilson, SLou.	.35	.20
☐☐	79 Todd Richards, Hart.	.35	.20
☐☐	80 Robert Kron, Vanc.	.35	.20
☐☐	81 Cliff Ronning, Vanc.	.35	.20
☐☐	82 Zarley Zalapski, Hart.	.35	.20
☐☐	83 Randy Burridge, Wash.	.35	.20
☐☐	84 Jarrod Skalde, NJer.	.35	.20
☐☐	85 Gary Leeman, Calg.	.35	.20
☐☐	86 Mike Ricci, Phil. (Québ.)	1.00	.20
☐☐	87 Dennis Vaske, NYIs.	.35	.20
☐☐	**88 John LeBlanc, Winn. RC**	**1.00**	**.20**
☐☐	89 Brad Shaw, Hart. (Otta.)	.35	.20
☐☐	90 Rod Brind'Amour, Phil.	5.00	.20
☐☐	91 Colin Patterson, Buff.	.35	.20
☐☐	92 Gerard Gallant, Detr.	.35	.20
☐☐	93 Per Djoos, NYRa.	.35	.20
☐☐	94 Claude Lapointe, Québ.	.35	.20
☐☐	95 Bob Errey, Pitt.	.35	.20
☐☐	96 Norm Maciver, Edmo.	.35	.20
☐☐	97 Todd Elik, Minn.	.35	.20
☐☐	98 Chris Chelios, Chic.	2.00	.20
☐☐	99 Keith Primeau, Detr.	1.00	.20
☐☐	100 Jimmy Waite (G), Chic.	.35	.20
☐☐	101 Luc Robitaille, LosA.	3.00	.20
☐☐	102 Keith Tkachuk, Winn.	4.00	.20
☐☐	103 Benoît Hogue, NYIs.	.35	.20
☐☐	104 Brian Mullen, SanJ.	.35	.20
☐☐	105 Joe Nieuwendyk, Calg.	1.00	.20
☐☐	106 Randy McKay, NJer.	.35	.20
☐☐	107 Michal Pivonka, Wash.	.35	.20
☐☐	108 Darcy Wakaluk (G), Minn.	.35	.20
☐☐	109 Andy Brickley, Bost.	.35	.20
☐☐	110 Patrick Roy (G), Mont.	10.00	1.00
☐☐	111 Bob Sweeney, Bost.	.35	.20
☐☐	**112 Guy Hebert (G), SLou. RC**	**4.00**	**.20**
☐☐	113 Joe Mullen, Pitt.	1.00	.20
☐☐	114 Gord Murphy, Bost.	.35	.20
☐☐	115 Evgeny Davydov, Winn.	.35	.20
☐☐	116 Gary Roberts, Calg.	1.00	.20
☐☐	117 Pelle Eklund, Phil.	.35	.20
☐☐	118 Tom Kurvers, NYIs.	.35	.20
☐☐	119 John Tonelli, Québ.	.35	.20
☐☐	120 Fredrik Olausson, Winn.	.35	.20
☐☐	121 Mike Donnelly, LosA.	.35	.20
☐☐	122 Doug Gilmour, Toro.	2.00	.20
☐☐	123 Wayne Gretzky, LosA.	25.00	1.00
☐☐	124 Curtis Leschyshyn, Québ.	.35	.20
☐☐	125 Guy Carbonneau, Mont.	1.00	.20
☐☐	126 Bill Ranford (G), Edmo.	1.00	.20
☐☐	127 Ulf Samuelsson, Pitt.	.35	.20
☐☐	128 Joey Kocur, NYRa.	.35	.20
☐☐	129 Kevin Miller, Detr. (Wash.)	.35	.20
☐☐	130 Kirk McLean (G), Vanc.	1.00	.20
☐☐	131 Kevin Dineen, Phil.	.35	.20
☐☐	132 John Cullen, Hart.	.35	.20
☐☐	133 Al Iafrate, Wash.	.35	.20
☐☐	134 Craig Janney, SLou.	.35	.20
☐☐	135 Patrick Flatley, NYIs.	.35	.20
☐☐	136 Dominik Hasek (G), Chic.	3.00	.20
☐☐	137 Benoît Brunet, Mont.	.35	.20
☐☐	138 Dave Babych, Vanc.	.35	.20
☐☐	139 Doug Brown, NJer.	.35	.20
☐☐	140 Mike Lalor, Winn.	.35	.20
☐☐	141 Thomas Steen, Winn.	.35	.20
☐☐	142 Frantisek Musil, Calg.	.35	.20
☐☐	143 Dan Quinn, Phil.	.35	.20
☐☐	144 Dmitri Mironov, Toro.	.35	.20
☐☐	145 Bob Kudelski, LosA.	.35	.20
☐☐	146 Mike Bullard, Toro.	.35	.20
☐☐	147 Randy Carlyle, Winn.	.35	.20
☐☐	148 Kent Manderville, Toro.	.35	.20
☐☐	149 Kevin Hatcher, Wash.	.35	.20
☐☐	150 Steve Kasper, Phil.	.35	.20
☐☐	151 Mikael Andersson, Hart. (Tamp.)	.35	.20
☐☐	152 Alexei Kasatonov, NJer.	.35	.20
☐☐	153 Jan Erixon, NYRa.	.35	.20
☐☐	154 Craig Ludwig, Minn.	.35	.20
☐☐	155 Dave Poulin, Bost.	.35	.20
☐☐	156 Scott Stevens, NJer.	1.00	.20
☐☐	157 Robert Reichel, Calg.	1.00	.20
☐☐	158 Uwe Krupp, NYIs.	.35	.20
☐☐	159 Brian Noonan, Chic.	.35	.20
☐☐	160 Stéphane Richer, NJer.	.35	.20
☐☐	161 Brent Thompson, LosA.	.35	.20
☐☐	162 Glenn Anderson, Toro.	1.00	.20
☐☐	163 Joe Cirella, NYRa.	.35	.20
☐☐	164 Dave Andreychuk, Buff.	5.00	.20
☐☐	165 Vladimir Konstantinov, Detr.	1.00	.20
☐☐	166 Mike McNeill, Québ.	.35	.20
☐☐	167 Darrin Shannon, Winn.	.35	.20
☐☐	168 Rob Pearson, Toro.	.35	.20
☐☐	169 John Vanbiesbrouck (G), NYRa.	1.00	.20
☐☐	170 Randy Wood, Buff.	.35	.20
☐☐	171 Marty McSorley, LosA.	.35	.20
☐☐	172 Mike Hudson, Chic.	.35	.20
☐☐	173 Paul Fenton, SanJ.	.35	.20
☐☐	174 Jeff R. Brown, SLou.	.35	.20
☐☐	175 Mark Greig, Hart.	.35	.20
☐☐	176 Gord** Roberts, Pitt. (Bost.)	1.00	.20
☐☐	177 Josef Beránek, Edmo.	.35	.20
☐☐	178 Shawn Burr, Detr.	.35	.20
☐☐	179 Marc Bureau, Minn.	.35	.20
☐☐	180 Mikhail Tatarinov, Québ.	.35	.20
☐☐	181 Robert Cimetta, Toro.	.35	.20
☐☐	182 Paul Coffey, Pitt. (LosA.)	2.00	.20
☐☐	183 Bob Essensa, Winn.	.35	.20
☐☐	184 Joe Reekie, NYIs. (Tamp.)	.35	.20
☐☐	185 Jeff Hackett (G), SanJ.	1.00	.20
☐☐	186 Tomas Forslund, Calg.	.35	.20
☐☐	187 Claude Vilgrain, NJer.	.35	.20
☐☐	188 John Druce, Wash.	.35	.20
☐☐	189 Patrice Brisebois, Mont.	.35	.20
☐☐	190 Peter Douris, Bost.	.35	.20
☐☐	191 Brent Ashton, Bost.	.35	.20
☐☐	192 Éric Desjardins, Mont.	1.00	.20
☐☐	193 Nick Kypreos, Wash. (Hart.)	.35	.20
☐☐	194 Dana Murzyn, Vanc.	.35	.20
☐☐	195 Don Beaupré (G), Wash.	5.00	.20
☐☐	196 Jeff Chychrun, Pitt.	.35	.20
☐☐	197 Dave Barr, NJer.	.35	.20
☐☐	198 Brian Glynn, Edmo.	.35	.20
☐☐	199 Keith Acton, Phil.	.35	.20
☐☐	200 Igor Kravchuk, Chic.	.35	.20
☐☐	201 Shayne Corson, Mont.	1.00	.20
☐☐	202 Curt Giles, SLou.	.35	.20
☐☐	203 Darren Turcotte, NYRa.	.35	.20
☐☐	204 David Volek, NYIs.	.35	.20
☐☐	**205 Ray Whitney, SanJ. RC**	**4.00**	**.20**
☐☐	206 Donald Audette, Buff.	1.00	.20
☐☐	207 Steve Yzerman, Detr.	9.00	.50
☐☐	208 Craig Berube, Calg.	.35	.20
☐☐	209 Bob McGill, Detr. (Tamp.)	.35	.20
☐☐	210 Stu Barnes, Winn.	.35	.20
☐☐	211 Rob Blake, LosA.	2.00	.20
☐☐	212 Mario Lemieux, Pitt.	10.00	1.00
☐☐	213 Dominic Roussel (G), Phil.	.35	.20
☐☐	214 Sergio Momesso, Vanc.	.35	.20
☐☐	215 Brad Marsh, Detr. (Otta.)	.35	.20
☐☐	216 Mark Fitzpatrick (G), NYIs.	.35	.20
☐☐	217 Ken Baumgartner, Toro.	.35	.20
☐☐	218 Greg Gilbert, Chic.	.35	.20
☐☐	219 Ric Nattress, Toro.	.35	.20
☐☐	220 Theoren Fleury, Calg.	2.00	.20
☐☐	221 Raymond Bourque, Bost.	4.00	.20
☐☐	222 Steve Thomas, NYIs.	.35	.20
☐☐	223 Scott Niedermayer, NJer.	1.00	.20
☐☐	224 Jeff Lazaro, Bost. (Otta.)	.35	.20
☐☐	225 League leaders	5.00	.20
☐☐	226 Marc Fortier, Québ.	.35	.20
☐☐	227 Rob Zettler, SanJ.	.35	.20
☐☐	228 Kevin Todd, NJer.	.35	.20
☐☐	229 Tony Amonte, NYRa.	2.00	.20
☐☐	230 Mark Lamb, Otta.	.35	.20
☐☐	231 Chris Dahlquist, Minn.	.35	.20
☐☐	232 James H. Black, Hart.	.35	.20
☐☐	233 Paul Cavallini, SLou.	.35	.20
☐☐	234 Gino Cavallini, Québ.	.35	.20
☐☐	235 Tony Tanti, Buff.	.35	.20
☐☐	236 Mike Ridley, Wash.	.35	.20
☐☐	237 Curtis Joseph (G), SLou.	3.00	.20
☐☐	238 Mike Craig, Minn.	.35	.20
☐☐	239 Luciano Borsato, Winn.	.35	.20
☐☐	240 Brian Bellows, Minn.	.35	.20
☐☐	241 Barry Pederson, Bost.	.35	.20
☐☐	242 Tony Granato, LosA.	.35	.20
☐☐	243 Jim Paek, Pitt.	.35	.20
☐☐	244 Tim Bergland, Wash. (Tamp.)	.35	.20
☐☐	245 Jayson More, SanJ.	.35	.20
☐☐	246 Laurie Boschman, NJer. (Otta.)	.35	.20
☐☐	247 Doug Bodger, Buff.	.35	.20
☐☐	248 Murray Craven, Hart.	.35	.20
☐☐	249 Kris Draper, Winn.	.35	.20
☐☐	250 Brian Benning, Phil.	.35	.20
☐☐	251 Jarmo Myllys (G), SanJ. (Toro.)	.35	.20
☐☐	252 Sergei Fedorov, Detr.	3.00	.20
☐☐	253 Mathieu Schneider, Mont.	.35	.20
☐☐	254 Dave Gagner, Minn.	.35	.20
☐☐	255 Michel Goulet, Chic.	1.00	.20
☐☐	256 Alexander Godynyuk, Calg.	.35	.20
☐☐	257 Ray Sheppard, Detr.	.35	.20
☐☐	258 Mark Messier, NYRa. [All-Star]	3.00	.20
☐☐	259 Kevin Stevens, Pitt. [All-Star]	.35	.20
☐☐	260 Brett Hull, SLou. [All-Star]	3.00	.20
☐☐	261 Brian Leetch, NYRa. [All-Star]	2.00	.20
☐☐	262 R. Bourque, Bost. [All-Star]	4.00	.20
☐☐	263 Patrick Roy (G), Mont. [All-Star]	10.00	1.00
☐☐	264 Mike Gartner, NYRa. [Highlight]	3.00	.20

265 Mario Lemieux, Pitt. [All-Star]	10.00	1.00
266 Luc Robitaille, LosA. [All-Star]	3.00	.20
267 Mark Recchi, Phil. [All-Star]	1.00	.20
268 Phil Housley, Winn. [All-Star]	1.00	.20
269 Scott Stevens, NJer. [All-Star]	1.00	.20
270 Kirk McLean (G), Vanc. [All-Star]	1.00	.20
271 Steve Duchesne, Phil. (Québ.)	.35	.20
272 Jiri Hrdina, Pitt.	5.00	.20
273 John MacLean, NJer.	.35	.20
274 Mark Messier, NYRa.	3.00	.20
275 Geoff Smith, Edmo.	.35	.20
276 Russ Courtnall, Mont.	.35	.20
277 Yves Racine, Detr.	.35	.20
278 Tom Draper (G), Buff.	.35	.20
279 Charlie Huddy, LosA.	.35	.20
280 Trevor Kidd, Calg.	1.00	.20
281 Garth Butcher, SLou.	.35	.20
282 Mike Sullivan, SanJ.	.35	.20
283 Adam Burt, Hart.	.35	.20
284 Troy Murray, Winn.	.35	.20
285 Stéphane Fiset (G), Québ.	1.00	.20
286 Perry Anderson, SanJ.	.35	.20
287 Sergei Nemchinov, NYRa.	.35	.20
288 Rick Zombo, SLou.	.35	.20
289 Pierre Turgeon, NYIs.	1.00	.20
290 Kevin Lowe, Edmo.	1.00	.20
291 Brian Bradley, Toro. (Tamp.)	.35	.20
292 Martin Gélinas, Edmo.	.35	.20
293 Brian Leetch, NYRa.	2.00	.20
294 Peter Bondra, Wash.	2.00	.20
295 Brendan Shanahan, SLou.	3.00	.20
296 Dale Hawerchuk, Buff.	2.00	.20
297 Mike Hough, Québ.	.35	.20
298 Rollie Melanson (G), Mont.	.35	.20
299 Brad Jones, Phil.	.35	.20
300 Jocelyn Lemieux, Chic.	.35	.20
301 Brad McCrimmon, Detr.	.35	.20
302 Marty McInnis, NYIs.	.35	.20
303 Chris Terreri (G), NJer.	.35	.20
304 Dean Evason, SanJ.	.35	.20
305 Glenn Healy (G), NYIs.	.35	.20
306 Ken (Jr.) Hodge, Bost.	.35	.20
307 Mike Liut, Wash.	5.00	.20
308 Gary Suter, Calg.	.35	.20
309 Neal Broten, Minn.	.35	.20
310 Tim Cheveldae (G), Detr.	.35	.20
311 Tom Fergus, Vanc.	.35	.20
312 Petr* Svoboda, Buff.	.35	.20
313 Tom Chorske, NJer.	.35	.20
314 Paul Ysebaert, Detr.	.35	.20
315 J. Steve Smith, Chic.	.35	.20
316 Stéphane Morin, Québ.	.35	.20
317 Pat MacLeod, SanJ.	.35	.20
318 Dino Ciccarelli, Detr.	1.00	.20
319 Peter Zezel, Toro.	.35	.20
320 Chris Lindberg, Calg.	.35	.20
321 Grant Ledyard, Buff.	.35	.20
322 Ron Francis, Pitt.	2.00	.20
323 Adrien Plavsic, Vanc.	.35	.20
324 Ray Ferraro, NYIs.	5.00	.20
325 Wendel Clark, Toro.	3.00	.20
326 Corey Millen, LosA.	.35	.20
327 Mark Pederson, Phil.	.35	.20
328 Patrick Poulin, Hart.	.35	.20
329 Adam Graves, NYRa.	1.00	.20
330 Bobby Holik, Hart.	1.00	.20
331 Kelly Kisio, SanJ.	.35	.20
332 Peter Sidorkiewicz (G), Hart. (Otta.)	.35	.20
333 Vladimír Ruzicka, Bost.	.35	.20
334 J.J. Daigneault, Mont.	.35	.20
335 Troy Mallette, NJer.	.35	.20
336 Craig MacTavish, Edmo.	5.00	.20
337 Michel Petit, Calg.	.35	.20
338 Claude Loiselle, NYIs.	.35	.20
339 Teppo Numminen, Winn.	1.00	.20
340 Brett Hull, SLou.	3.00	.20
341 Sylvain Lefebvre, Mont.	.35	.20
342 Perry Berezan, SanJ.	.35	.20
343 Kevin Stevens, Pitt.	.35	.20
344 Randy Ladouceur, Hart.	.35	.20
345 Pat LaFontaine, Buff.	2.00	.20
346 Glen Wesley, Bost.	.35	.20
347 Michel Goulet, Chic. [Highlight]	1.00	.20
348 Jamie Macoun, Toro.	.35	.20
349 Owen Nolan, Québ.	2.00	.20
350 Grant Fuhr (G), Toro.	2.00	.20
351 Tim Kerr, NYRa. (Hart.)	.35	.20
352 Kjell Samuelsson, Pitt.	.35	.20
353 Pavel Bure, Vanc.	8.00	.20
354 Murray Baron, SLou.	.35	.20
355 Paul Broten, NYRa.	.35	.20
356 Craig Simpson, Edmo.	.35	.20
357 Ken Daneyko, NJer.	.35	.20
358 Greg Hawgood, Edmo.	.35	.20
359 Johan Garpenlöv, SanJ.	.35	.20
360 Garry Galley, Phil.	.35	.20
361 Paul DiPietro, Mont.	.35	.20
362 Jamie Leach, Pitt.	.35	.20
363 Clint Malarchuk (G), Buff.	.35	.20
364 Dan Lambert, Québ.	.35	.20
365 Joé Juneau, Bost.	.35	.20
366 Scott Lachance, NYIs.	5.00	.20
367 Mike Richter (G), NYRa.	1.00	.20
368 Sheldon Kennedy, Detr.	.35	.20
369 John* McIntyre, LosA.	.35	.20
370 Glen Murray, Bost.	1.00	.20
371 Ron Sutter, SLou.	.35	.20
372 David* Williams, SanJ. RC	**1.00**	**.20**
373 Bill Lindsay, Québ. RC	**1.00**	**.20**
374 Todd Gill, Toro.	.35	.20
375 Sylvain Turgeon, Mont. (Otta.)	.35	.20
376 Dirk Graham, Chic.	.35	.20
377 Brad Schlegel, Wash.	.35	.20
378 Bob Carpenter, Wash.	.35	.20
379 Jon Casey (G), Minn.	.35	.20
380 Andrei Lomakin, Phil.	.35	.20
381 Kay Whitmore (G), Hart.	.35	.20
382 Alexander Mogilny, Buff.	1.00	.20
383 Garry Valk, Vanc.	.35	.20
384 Bruce Driver, NJer.	.35	.20
385 Jeff Reese (G), Calg.	.35	.20
386 Brent Gilchrist, Mont.	.35	.20
387 Kerry Huffman, Phil. (Québ.)	.35	.20
388 Bobby Smith, Minn.	1.00	.20
389 Dave Manson, Edmo.	.35	.20
390 Russ Romaniuk, Winn.	.35	.20
391 Paul MacDermid, Wash.	.35	.20
392 Louie DeBrusk, Edmo.	.35	.20
393 Dave McLlwain, Toro.	.35	.20
394 Andy Moog (G), Bost.	1.00	.20
395 Tie Domi, NYRa.	1.00	.20
396 Pat Jablonski (G), SLou. (Tamp.)	.35	.20
397 Troy Loney, Pitt.	.35	.20
398 Jimmy Carson, Detr.	.35	.20
399 Eric Weinrich, NJer.	.35	.20
400 Jeremy Roenick, Chic.	3.00	.20
401 Brent Fedyk, Detr.	.35	.20
402 Geoff Sanderson, Hart.	.35	.20
403 Doug Lidster, Vanc.	.35	.20
404 Mike Gartner, NYRa.	3.00	.20
405 Derian Hatcher, Minn.	1.00	.20
406 Gaétan Duchesne, Minn.	.35	.20
407 Randy Moller, Buff.	.35	.20
408 Brian Skrudland, Mont.	.35	.20
409 Luke Richardson, Edmo.	.35	.20
410 Mark Recchi, Phil.	1.00	.20
411 Steve Konroyd, Hart.	.35	.20
412 Troy Gamble (G), Vanc.	.35	.20
413 Greg Johnston, Toro.	5.00	.20
414 Denis Savard, Mont.	1.00	.20
415 Mats Sundin, Québ.	3.00	.20
416 Bryan Trottier, Pitt.	3.00	.20
417 Don Sweeney, Bost.	.35	.20
418 Pat Falloon, SanJ.	.35	.20
419 Alexander Semak, NJer.	.35	.20
420 David Shaw, Minn.	5.00	.20
421 Tomas Sandström, LosA.	.35	.20
422 Petr Nedved, Vanc.	1.00	.20
423 Peter Ing, Edmo.	.35	.20
424 Wayne Presley, Buff.	.35	.20
425 Rick Wamsley (G), Toro.	.35	.20
426 R. Zamuner, NYRa. (Tamp.) RC	**4.00**	**.20**
427 Claude Boivin, Phil.	.35	.20
428 Sylvain Côté, Wash.	.35	.20
429 Kevin Stevens, Pitt. [Highlight]	.35	.20
430 Randy Velischek, Québ.	.35	.20
431 Derek King, NYIs.	.35	.20
432 Terry Yake, Hart.	.35	.20
433 Philippe Bozon, SLou.	.35	.20
434 Rich Sutter, SLou.	.35	.20
435 Brian Lawton, SanJ.	.35	.20
436 Brian Hayward (G), SanJ.	.35	.20
437 Robert Dirk, Vanc.	.35	.20
438 Bernie Nicholls, Edmo.	.35	.20
439 Michel Picard, Hart.	.35	.20
440 Nicklas Lidström, Detr.	2.00	.20
441 Mike Modano, Minn.	3.00	.20
442 Phil Bourque, Pitt.	.35	.20
443 Wayne McBean, NYIs.	.35	.20
444 Scott Mellanby, Edmo.	.35	.20
445 Kevin Haller, Mont.	.35	.20
446 Dave (Stitch) Taylor, LosA.	.35	.20
447 Larry Murphy, Pitt.	.35	.20
448 David Bruce, SanJ.	.35	.20
449 Steven Finn, Québ.	.35	.20
450 Mike Krushelnyski, Toro.	.35	.20
451 Adam Creighton, NYIs.	.35	.20
452 Al MacInnis, Calg.	1.00	.20
453 Rick Tabaracci (G), Winn.	.35	.20
454 Bob Bassen, SLou.	.35	.20
455 Kelly Buchberger, Edmo.	.35	.20
456 Phil Housley, Winn.	1.00	.20
457 Daren Puppa (G), Buff.	.35	.20
458 Viacheslav Fetisov, NJer.	2.00	.20
459 Doug Smail, Québ.	.35	.20
460 Paul Stanton, Pitt.	.35	.20
461 Steve Weeks, LosA. (Wash.)	.35	.20
462 Valeri Zelepukin, NJer.	.35	.20
463 Stéphane Matteau, Chic.	.35	.20
464 Dale Hunter, Wash.	1.00	.20
465 Terry Carkner, Phil.	.35	.20
466 Vincent Riendeau (G), Detr.	.35	.20
467 Sergei Makarov, Calg.	1.00	.20
468 Igor Ulanov, Winn.	.35	.20
469 Peter Stastny, NJer.	2.00	.20
470 Dmitri Khristich, Wash.	.35	.20
471 Joel Otto, Calg.	.35	.20
472 Geoff Courtnall, Vanc.	.35	.20
473 Mike Ramsey, Buff.	.35	.20
474 Yvon Corriveau, Hart.	.35	.20
475 Adam Oates, Bost.	1.00	.20
476 Esa Tikkanen, Edmo.	.35	.20
477 Doug Weight, NYRa.	2.00	.20
478 Mike Keane, Mont.	.35	.20
479 Kelly Miller, Wash.	.35	.20
480 Nelson Emerson, SLou.	.35	.20
481 Shawn McEachern, Pitt.	1.00	.20
482 Doug Wilson, SanJ.	1.00	.20
483 Jeff Odgers, SanJ.	.35	.20
484 Stéphane Quintal, SLou.	.35	.20
485 Christian Ruuttu, Winn.	.35	.20
486 Paul Ranheim, Calg.	.35	.20
487 Craig Wolanin, Québ.	.35	.20
488 Rob DiMaio, NYIs. (Tamp.)	.35	.20
489 Shawn Cronin., Winn.	.35	.20
490 Kirk Muller, Mont.	1.00	.20
491 Patrick Roy (G), Mont.	10.00	1.00
492 Richard Pilon, NYIs.	.35	.20
493 Pat Verbeek, Hart.	1.00	.20
494 Ken Wregget (G), Pitt.	.35	.20
495 Joe Sakic, Québ.	6.00	.50
496 Zdeno Ciger, NJer.	.35	.20
497 Steve Larmer, Chic.	5.00	.20
498 Calle Johansson, Wash.	.35	.20
499 Trevor Linden, Vanc.	1.00	.20
500 John LeClair, Mont.	3.00	.20
501 Bryan Marchment, Chic.	.35	.20
502 Todd Krygier, Wash.	.35	.20
503 Tom Barrasso (G), Pitt.	1.00	.20
504 Mario Lemieux, Pitt.	10.00	1.00
505 Daniel Berthiaume (G), Winn.	.35	.20
506 Jamie Baker, Québ.	.35	.20
507 Greg A. Adams, Vanc.	.35	.20
508 Patrick Roy (G), Mont.	33.00	1.00
509 Kris King, NYRa.	.35	.20
510 Jyrki Lumme, Vanc.	.35	.20
511 Darin Kimble, Tamp.	.35	.20
512 Igor Larionov, Vanc.	2.00	.20
513 Martin Brodeur, NJer.	16.00	1.00
514 Denny Felsner, SLou. RC	**1.00**	**.20**
515 Yanick Dupré, Phil.	.35	.20
516 Bill Guerin, NJer. RC	**7.00**	**.50**
517 Bret Hedican, SLou. RC	**1.00**	**.20**
518 Mike Hartman, Winn. (Tamp.)	.35	.20
519 Stephen Heinze, Bost.	.35	.20
520 Frantisek Kucera, Chic.	.35	.20
521 David Reid, Bost.	.35	.20
522 Frank Pietrangelo, Hart.	.35	.20
523 Martin Rucinsky, Québ.	.35	.20
524 Tony Hrkac, Chic.	.35	.20
525 Checklist	-	.20
526 Checklist	-	.20
527 Checklist	-	.20
528 Checklist	-	.20
529 Eric Lindros, Phil.	15.00	.50
525 Allan Conroy, Phil. RC	**2.00**	-
526 Jeff Norton, NYIs.	2.00	-
527 Rob Robinson, Tamp. RC	**2.00**	-
528 Adam Foote, Québ.	2.00	-

1992 - 93 TOPPS STADIUM CLUB

The most expensive singles are Wayne Gretzky ($1.50-2.00), Eric Lindros ($1.00-1.50), Mario Lemieux ($0.75-1.50), Patrick Roy ($0.65-1.25), Bill Guerin ($1.25-1.75) and Guy Hebert ($1.00-1.50). Regional stars sell at 25¢-$1; singles start at 20¢.

Imprint: © 1992 THE TOPPS COMPANY, INC.

Complete Set (501 cards):	**25.00**
Common Player:	**.20**
Player	**TSC**
1 Brett Hull, SLou.	**.50**
2 Theoren Fleury, Calg.	.20
3 Joe Sakic, Québ.	.50
4 Mike Modano, Minn.	.50
5 Dmitri Mironov, Toro.	.20
6 Yves Racine, Detr.	.20
7 Igor Kravchuk, Chic.	.20
8 Philippe Bozon, SLou.	.20
9 Stéphane J.J. Richer, NJer.	.20
10 Dave Lowry, SLou.	.20
11 Dean Evason, SanJ.	.20
12 Mark Fitzpatrick, NYIs.	.20
13 Dave Poulin, Bost.	.20
14 Phil Housley, Winn.	.20
15 Adrien Plavsic, Vanc.	.20
16 Claude Boivin, Phil.	.20
17 Bill Guerin, NJer.	.20
18 Wayne Gretzky, LosA.	2.00
19 Steve Yzerman, Detr.	1.00
20 Joe Mullen, Pitt.	.20
21 Brad McCrimmon, Detr.	.20
22 Dan Quinn, Phil.	.20
23 Rob Blake, LosA.	.20
24 Wayne Presley, (Buff.) [On Motorcycle]	.20
25 Zarley Zalapski, Hart.	.20
26 Bryan Trottier, Pitt.	.50
27 Peter Sidorkiewicz, Hart. (Otta.)	.20
28 John MacLean, NJer.	.20
29 Brad Schlegel, Wash.	.20
30 Marc Bureau, Minn.	.20
31 Troy Murray, Winn.	.20
32 Tony Amonte, NYRa.	.20
33 Rob DiMaio, NYIs. (Tamp.)	.20
34 Joe Murphy, Edmo.	.20
35 Jimmy Waite, Chic.	.20
36 Ron Sutter, SLou.	.20
37 Joe Nieuwendyk, Calg.	.20
38 Kevin Haller, Mont.	.20
39 Andrew Cassels, Hart.	.20
40 Dale Hunter, Wash.	.20
41 Craig Janney, SLou.	.20
42 Sergio Momesso, Vanc.	.20
43 Nicklas Lidström, Detr.	.20
44 Luc Robitaille, LosA.	.20
45 Adam Creighton, NYIs.	.20
46 Norm Maciver, Edmo.	.20
47 Mikhail Tatarinov, Québ.	.20
48 Gary Roberts, Calg.	.20
49 Gord Hynes, Bost.	.20
50 Claude Lemieux, NJer.	.20
51 Brad May, Buff.	.20
52 Paul Stanton, Pitt.	.20
53 Rick Wamsley, Toro.	.20
54 Steve Larmer, Chic.	.20
55 Darrin Shannon, Winn.	.20
56 Pat Falloon, SanJ.	.20
57 Chris Dahlquist, Minn.	.20
58 John Vanbiesbrouck, NYRa.	.20
59 Sylvain Turgeon, Mont. (Otta.)	.20
60 Jayson More, SanJ.	.20
61 Randy Burridge, Wash.	.20
62 Vyacheslav (Slava) Kozlov, Detr.	.20
63 Daniel Marois, NYIs.	.20
64 Curt Giles, SLou.	.20
65 Brad Shaw, Hart. (Otta.)	.20
66 Bill Ranford, Edmo.	.20
67 Frantisek (Frank) Musil, Calg.	.20
68 Stephen Leach, Bost.	.20
69 Michel Goulet, Chic.	.20
70 Mathieu Schneider, Mont.	.20
71 Steve Kasper, Phil.	.20
72 Darryl Sydor, LosA.	.20
73 Brian Leetch, NYRa.	.20
74 Chris Terreri, NJer.	.20
75 Jim* Johnson, Minn.	.20
76 Rick Tocchet, Pitt.	.20
77 Teppo Numminen, Winn.	.20
78 Owen Nolan, Québ.	.20
79 Grant Ledyard, Buff.	.20
80 Trevor Linden, Vanc.	.20
81 Luciano Borsato, Winn.	.20
82 Derek King, NYIs.	.20
83 Robert Cimetta, Toro.	.20
84 Geoff Smith, Edmo.	.20
85 Ray Sheppard, Detr.	.20
86 Dmitri Khristich, Wash.	.20
87 Chris Chelios, Chic.	.20
88 Alexander Godynyuk, Calg.	.20
89 Perry Anderson, SanJ.	.20
90 Neal Broten, Minn.	.20
91 Brian Benning, Phil.	.20
92 Brent Thompson, LosA.	.20
93 Claude Lapointe, Québ.	.20
94 Mario Lemieux, Pitt.	1.50
95 Pat LaFontaine, Buff.	.20
96 Frank Pietrangelo, Hart.	.20
97 Gerald Diduck, Vanc.	.20
98 Paul DiPietro, Mont.	.20
99 Valeri Zelepukin, NJer.	.20
100 Rick Zombo, SLou.	.20
101 Daniel Berthiaume, Bost. (Winn.)	.20
102 Tom Fitzgerald, NYIs.	.20
103 Ken Baumgartner, Toro.	.20
104 Esa Tikkanen, Edmo.	.20
105 Steve Chiasson, Detr.	.20
106 Bobby Holik, Hart.	.20
107 Dominik Hasek, Chic.	.50
108 Jeff Hackett, SanJ.	.20
109 Paul Broten, NYRa.	.20
110 Kevin Stevens, Pitt.	.20
111 Geoff Sanderson, Hart.	.20
112 Donald Audette, Buff.	.20
113 Jarmo Myllys, SanJ. (Toro.)	.20
114 Brian Skrudland, Mont.	.20
115 Andrei Lomakin, Phil.	.20
116 Keith Tkachuk, Winn.	.50
117 John* McIntyre, LosA.	.20
118 Jacques Cloutier, Québ.	.20
119 Michel Picard, Hart.	.20
120 Dave Babych, Vanc.	.20
121 Dave Gagner, Minn.	.20
122 Bob Carpenter, Bost. (Wash.)	.20
123 Ray Ferraro, NYIs.	.20
124 Glenn Anderson, Toro.	.20
125 Craig MacTavish, Edmo.	.20
126 Shawn Burr, Detr.	.20
127 Tim Bergland, Wash. (Tamp.)	.20
128 Al MacInnis, Calg.	.20
129 Jeff Beukeboom, NYRa.	.20
130 Ken Wregget, Pitt.	.20
131 Arturs Irbe, SanJ.	.20
132 Dave Andreychuk, Buff.	.20
133 Patrick Roy, Mont.	1.50
134 Benoît Brunet, Mont.	.20
135 Rick Tabaracci, (Winn.) [On Motorcycle]	.20
136 Jamie Baker, Québ.	.20
137 Yanick Dupré, Phil.	.20
138 Jari Kurri, LosA.	.50
139 Adam Burt, Hart.	.20
140 Peter Stastny, NJer.	.20
141 Brad Jones, Phil.	.20
142 Jeff Odgers, SanJ.	.20
143 Anatoli Semenov, Edmo. (Tamp.)	.20
144 Paul Ranheim, Calg.	.20
145 Sylvain Côté, Wash.	.20
146 Brent Ashton, Bost.	.20
147 Doug Bodger, Buff.	.20
148 Bryan Marchment, Chic.	.20
149 Bob Kudelski, LosA.	.20
150 Adam Graves, NYRa.	.20
151 Scott Stevens, NJer.	.20
152 Russ Courtnall, Mont.	.20
153 Darcy Wakaluk, Minn.	.20
154 Per-Erik (Pelle) Eklund, Phil.	.20
155 Robert Kron, Vanc.	.20
156 Randy Ladouceur, Hart.	.20
157 Ed Olczyk, Winn.	.20
158 Jiri Hrdina, Pitt.	.20
159 John Tonelli, Québ.	.20
160 John Cullen, Hart.	.20
161 Jan Erixon, NYRa.	.20
162 David Shaw, Minn.	.20
163 Brian Bradley, Toro. (Tamp.)	.20
164 Russ Romaniuk, Winn.	.20
165 Eric Weinrich, NJer.	.20
166 Stephen Heinze, Bost.	.20
167 Jeremy Roenick, Chic.	.20
168 Mark Pederson, Phil.	.20
169 Paul Coffey, LosA.	.20
170 Bob Errey, Pitt.	.20
171 Brian Lawton, SanJ.	.20
172 Vincent Riendeau, Detr.	.20
173 Marc Fortier, Québ.	.20
174 Marc Bergevin, Hart. (Tamp.) [vs. S.Larmer]	.20
175 Jim Sandlak, Vanc.	.20
176 Bob Bassen, SLou.	.20
177 Uwe Krupp, NYIs.	.20
178 Paul MacDermid, Wash.	.20
179 Bob Corkum, Buff.	.20
180 Robert Reichel, Calg.	.20
181 John LeClair, Mont.	.20

☐ 182 Mike Hudson, Chic. .20
☐ 183 Mark Recchi, Phil. .20
☐ 184 Rollie Melanson, Mont. .20
☐ 185 Gord** Roberts, Pitt. (Bost.) .20
☐ 186 Clint Malarchuk, Buff. .20
☐ 187 Kris King, NYRa. .20
☐ 188 Adam Oates, Bost. .20
☐ 189 Jarrod Skalde, NJer. .20
☐ 190 Mike Lalor, Winn. .20
☐ 191 Vincent Damphousse, Edmo. .20
☐ 192 Peter Ahola, LosA. .20
☐ 193 Kirk McLean, Vanc. .20
☐ 194 Murray Baron, SLou. .20
☐ 195 Michel Petit, Calg. .20
☐ 196 Stéphane Fiset, Québ. .20
☐ 197 Pat Verbeek, Hart. [vs. P.Brisebois] .20
☐ 198 Jon Casey, Minn. .20
☐ 199 Tim Cheveldae, Detr. .20
☐ 200 Mike Ridley, Wash. .20
☐ 201 Scott Lachance, NYIs. .20
☐ 202 Rod Brind'Amour, Phil. .20
☐ **203 Bret Hedican, SLou. RC [Error: Brett] .20**
☐ 204 Wendel Clark, Toro. .20
☐ 205 Shawn McEachern, Pitt. .20
☐ 206 Randy Wood, Buff. .20
☐ 207 Ulf Dahlén, Minn. .20
☐ 208 Andy Brickley, Bost. .20
☐ 209 Scott Niedermayer, NJer. .20
☐ 210 Bob Essensa, Winn. .20
☐ 211 Patrick Poulin, Hart. .20
☐ 212 Johan Garpenlöv, SanJ. .20
☐ 213 Marty McInnis, NYIs. .20
☐ 214 Josef Beránek, Edmo. .20
☐ 215 Rod Langway, Wash. .20
☐ 216 Dave Christian, SLou. .20
☐ 217 Sergei* Makarov, Calg. .20
☐ 218 Gerard Gallant, Detr. .20
☐ 219 Neil Wilkinson, SanJ. [On Motorcycle] .20
☐ 220 Tomas Sandström, LosA. .20
☐ 221 Shayne Corson, Mont. .20
☐ 222 John Ogrodnick, NYRa. .20
☐ 223 Keith Acton, Phil. .20
☐ 224 Paul Fenton, SanJ. .20
☐ 225 Rob Zettler, SanJ. [On Motorcycle] .20
☐ 226 Todd Elik, Minn. .20
☐ 227 Petr* Svoboda, Buff. .20
☐ 228 Zdeno Ciger, NJer. .20
☐ 229 Kevin Miller, Detr. (Wash.) .20
☐ 230 Richard Pilon, NYIs. .20
☐ 231 Pat Jablonski, SLou. (Tamp.) .20
☐ 232 Greg A. Adams, Vanc. .20
☐ 233 Martin Brodeur, NJer. 1.50
☐ 234 Dave (Stitch) Taylor, LosA. .20
☐ 235 Kelly Buchberger, Edmo. .20
☐ 236 Steve Konroyd, Hart. .20
☐ 237 Guy Larose, Toro. .20
☐ 238 Patrice Brisebois, Mont. .20
☐ 239 Checklist , .20
☐ 240 Checklist , .20
☐ 241 Mark Messier, NYRa. [Members Choice] .50
☐ 242 Mike Richter, NYRa. [Members Choice] .20
☐ 243 Ed Belfour, Chic. [Members Choice] .50
☐ 244 Sergei Fedorov, Detr. [Members Choice] .50
☐ 245 Adam Oates, Bost. [Members Choice] .20
☐ 246 Pavel Bure, Vanc. [Members Choice] .20
☐ 247 Luc Robitaille, LosA. [Members Choice] .20
☐ 248 Brian Leetch, NYRa. [Members Choice] .20
☐ 249 Bourque, NHL Awards (Bost.) [MC] .50
☐ 250 Tony Amonte, NYRa. [Members Choice] .20
☐ 251 Mario Lemieux, Pitt. [w/ Cup] [MC] 1.50
☐ 252 Patrick Roy, Mont. [Members Choice] 1.50
☐ 253 Nicklas Lidström, Detr. [Members Choice] .20
☐ 254 Steve Yzerman, Detr. [Members Choice] 1.00
☐ 255 Jeremy Roenick, Chic. [Members Choice] .20
☐ 256 Wayne Gretzky, LosA. [Members Choice] 2.00
☐ 257 Kevin Stevens, Pitt. [w/ Stanley Cup] [MC] .20
☐ 258 Brett Hull, SLou. [Members Choice] .50
☐ 259 Pat Falloon, SanJ. [Members Choice] .20
☐ 260 Guy Carbonneau, Awards (Mont.) [MC] .20
☐ 261 Todd Gill, Toro. .20
☐ 262 Mike Sullivan, SanJ. .20
☐ 263 Jeff R. Brown, SLou. .20
☐ 264 Joe Reekie, Tamp. .20
☐ 265 Geoff Courtnall, Vanc. .20
☐ 266 Mike Richter, NYRa. .20
☐ 267 Raymond Bourque, Bost. .50
☐ 268 Mike Craig, Minn. .20
☐ **269 Scott King, Detr. RC .20**
☐ 270 Don Beaupré, Wash. .20
☐ 271 Ted Donato, Bost. .20
☐ 272 Gary Leeman, Calg. .20
☐ 273 Steve Weeks, LosA. (Wash.) .20
☐ 274 Keith Brown, Chic. .20
☐ 275 Greg Paslawski, Québ. .20
☐ 276 Pierre Turgeon, NYIs. .20
☐ 277 Jimmy Carson, Detr. .20
☐ 278 Tom Fergus, Vanc. .20
☐ 279 Glen Wesley, Bost. .20
☐ 280 Tomas Forslund, Calg. .20
☐ 281 Tony Granato, LosA. .20
☐ 282 Phil Bourque, Pitt. .20
☐ 283 Dave Ellett, Toro. .20
☐ 284 David Bruce, SanJ. .20
☐ 285 Stu Barnes, Winn. .20
☐ 286 Peter Bondra, Wash. .20
☐ 287 Garth Butcher, SLou. .20
☐ 288 Ron Hextall, Phil. (Québ.) .20
☐ 289 Guy Carbonneau, Mont. .20
☐ 290 Louie DeBrusk, Edmo. .20
☐ 291 Dave Barr, NJer. .20
☐ 292 Ken Sutton, Buff. .20
☐ 293 Brian Bellows, Minn. .20
☐ 294 Mike McNeill, Québ. .20
☐ 295 Rob (Jr.) Brown, Chic. .20
☐ 296 Corey Millen, LosA. .20
☐ 297 Joé Juneau, Bost. .20
☐ 298 Jeff Chychrun, Pitt. [Error: Chychurn] .20
☐ 299 Igor Larionov, Vanc. .20
☐ 300 Sergei Fedorov, Detr. .50
☐ 301 Kevin Hatcher, Wash. .20
☐ 302 Al Iafrate, Wash. .20
☐ 303 James H. Black, Hart. .20
☐ 304 Stéphane Beauregard, Winn. .20
☐ 305 Joel Otto, Calg. .20
☐ 306 Nelson Emerson, SLou. .20
☐ 307 Gaétan Duchesne, Minn. .20
☐ 308 J-J Daigneault, Mont. .20
☐ 309 Jamie Macoun, Toro. .20
☐ 310 Laurie Boschman, NJer. (Otta.) .20
☐ 311 Mike Gartner, NYRa. [cameo: Paul Broten] .20
☐ 312 Tony Tanti, Buff. .20
☐ 313 Steve Duchesne, Phil. (Québ.) .20
☐ 314 Martin Gélinas, Edmo. .20
☐ 315 Dominic Roussel, Phil. .20
☐ 316 Cam Neely, Bost. .50
☐ 317 Craig Wolanin, Québ. .20
☐ 318 Randy Gilhen, NYRa. .20
☐ 319 David Volek, NYIs. .20
☐ 320 Alexander Mogilny, Buff. .20
☐ 321 Jyrki Lumme, Vanc. .20
☐ 322 Jeff Reese, Calg. .20
☐ 323 Greg Gilbert, Chic. .20
☐ 324 Jeff Norton, NYIs. .20
☐ 325 Jim Hrivnak, Wash. .20
☐ 326 Éric Desjardins, Mont. .20
☐ 327 Curtis Joseph, SLou. .50
☐ 328 Ric Nattress, Toro. .20
☐ 329 Jamie Leach, Pitt. .20
☐ 330 Christian Ruuttu, Buff. (Winn.) .20
☐ 331 Doug Brown, NJer. .20
☐ 332 Randy Carlyle, Winn. .20
☐ 333 Ed Belfour, Chic. .50
☐ 334 Doug Smail, Québ. .20
☐ 335 Hubie McDonough, NYIs. .20
☐ 336 Pat MacLeod, SanJ. .20
☐ 337 Don Sweeney, Bost. .20
☐ 338 Félix Potvin, Toro. .20
☐ 339 Kent Manderville, Toro. .20
☐ 340 Sergei Nemchinov, NYRa. .20
☐ 341 Calle Johansson, Wash. .20
☐ 342 Dirk Graham, Chic. .20
☐ 343 Craig Billington, NJer. .20
☐ 344 Valeri Kamensky, Québ. .20
☐ 345 Mike Vernon, Calg. .20
☐ 346 Fredrik Olausson, Winn. .20
☐ 347 Peter Ing, Edmo. .20
☐ 348 Mikael Andersson, Hart. (Tamp.) .20
☐ 349 Mike Keane, Mont. .20
☐ 350 Stéphane Quintal, SLou. .20
☐ 351 Tom Chorske, NJer. .20
☐ 352 Ron Francis, Pitt. .20
☐ 353 Dana Murzyn, Vanc. .20
☐ 354 Craig Ludwig, Minn. .20
☐ 355 Bob Probert, Detr. .20
☐ 356 Glenn Healy, NYIs. .20
☐ 357 Troy Loney, Pitt. .20
☐ 358 Vladimír Ruzicka, Bost. .20
☐ 359 Doug Gilmour, Toro. .20
☐ 360 Darren Turcotte, NYRa. .20
☐ 361 Kelly Miller, Wash. .20
☐ 362 Dennis Vaske, NYIs. .20
☐ 363 Stéphane Matteau, Chic. .20
☐ 364 Brian Hayward, SanJ. .20
☐ 365 Kevin Dineen, Phil. .20
☐ 366 Igor Ulanov, Winn. .20
☐ 367 Sylvain Lefebvre, Mont. .20
☐ 368 Petr Klima, Edmo. .20
☐ 369 Steve Thomas, NYIs. .20
☐ 370 Daren Puppa, Buff. .20
☐ 371 Brendan Shanahan, SLou. .50
☐ 372 Charlie Huddy, LosA. .20
☐ 373 Cliff Ronning, Vanc. .20
☐ 374 Brian Propp, Minn. .20
☐ 375 Larry Murphy, Pitt. .20
☐ 376 Bruce Driver, NJer. .20
☐ 377 Rob Pearson, Toro. .20
☐ 378 Paul Ysebaert, Detr. .20
☐ 379 Mark Osborne, Toro. .20
☐ 380 Doug Weight, NYRa. .20
☐ 381 Kerry Huffman, Phil. .20
☐ 382 Michal Pivonka, Wash. .20
☐ 383 J. Steve Smith, Chic. .20
☐ 384 Steven Finn, Québ. .20
☐ 385 Kevin Lowe, Edmo. .20
☐ 386 Mike Ramsey, Buff. .20
☐ 387 Kirk Muller, Mont. .20
☐ **388 John LeBlanc, Winn. RC .20**
☐ 389 Rich Sutter, SLou. .20
☐ 390 Brent Fedyk, Detr. .20
☐ 391 Kelly Hrudey, LosA. .20
☐ 392 Viacheslav Fetisov, NJer. .20
☐ 393 Glen Murray, Bost. [Error: Glenn] .20
☐ 394 James Patrick, NYRa. .20
☐ 395 Tom Draper, Buff. .20
☐ 396 Mark Hunter, Hart. (Wash.) .20
☐ 397 Wayne McBean, NYIs. .20
☐ 398 Joe Sacco, Toro. .20
☐ 399 Dino Ciccarelli, Wash. (Detr.) .20
☐ 400 Brian Noonan, Chic. .20
☐ **401 Guy Hebert, SLou. RC .50**
☐ 402 Peter Douris, Bost. .20
☐ 403 Gilbert Dionne, Mont. .20
☐ 404 Doug Lidster, Vanc. .20
☐ 405 John Druce, Wash. .20
☐ 406 Alexei Kasatonov, NJer. .20
☐ 407 Chris Lindberg, Calg. .20
☐ 408 Mike Ricci, Québ. [On golf caddie] .20
☐ 409 Tom Kurvers, NYIs. .20
☐ 410 Pat Elynuik, Winn. [At card store] .20
☐ 411 Mike Donnelly, LosA. .20
☐ 412 Grant Fuhr, Toro. .20
☐ 413 Curtis Leschyshyn, Québ. .20
☐ 414 Derian Hatcher, Minn. .20
☐ 415 Michel Mongeau, SLou. (Tamp.) .20
☐ 416 Tom Barrasso, Pitt. .20
☐ 417 Joey Kocur, NYRa. .20
☐ 418 Vladimir Konstantinov, Detr. .20
☐ 419 Dale Hawerchuk, Buff. .20
☐ 420 Brian Mullen, SanJ. .20
☐ 421 Mark Greig, Hart. .20
☐ 422 Claude Vilgrain, NJer. .20
☐ 423 Gary Suter, Calg. .20
☐ 424 Garry Galley, Phil. .20
☐ 425 Benoît Hogue, NYIs. .20
☐ **426 Jeff Finley, NYIs. RC .20**
☐ 427 Bobby Smith, Minn. .20
☐ 428 Brent Sutter, Chic. .20
☐ 429 Ron L. Wilson, SLou. .20
☐ 430 Andy Moog, Bost. .20
☐ 431 Stéphan Lebeau, Mont. .20
☐ 432 Troy Mallette, NJer. .20
☐ 433 Peter Zezel, Toro. .20
☐ 434 Mike Hough, Québ. .20
☐ 435 Mark Tinordi, Minn. .20
☐ 436 Dave Manson, Edmo. .20
☐ 437 Jim Paek, Pitt. .20
☐ 438 Frantisek Kucera, Chic. .20
☐ **439 Rob Zamuner, NYRa. (Tamp.) RC .50**
☐ 440 Ulf Samuelsson, Pitt. .20
☐ 441 Perry Berezan, SanJ. .20
☐ 442 Murray Craven, Hart. .20
☐ 443 Mark Messier, NYRa. .50
☐ 444 Alexander Semak, NJer. .20
☐ 445 Gord Murphy, Bost. .20
☐ 446 Jocelyn Lemieux, Chic. .20
☐ 447 Paul Cavallini, SLou. .20
☐ 448 Bernie Nicholls, Edmo. .20
☐ 449 Brent Gilchrist, Mont. .20
☐ 450 Randy McKay, NJer. .20
☐ 451 Alexei Gusarov, Québ. .20
☐ 452 Mike McPhee, Mont. .20
☐ 453 Kimbi Daniels, Phil. .20
☐ 454 Kelly Kisio, SanJ. .20
☐ 455 Bob Sweeney, Bost. .20
☐ 456 Luke Richardson, Edmo. .20
☐ 457 Petr Nedved, Vanc. .20
☐ 458 Craig Berube, Calg. .20
☐ 459 Kay Whitmore, Hart. .20
☐ 460 Randy Velischek, Québ. .20
☐ **461 David* Williams, SanJ. RC .20**
☐ 462 Scott Mellanby, Edmo. .20
☐ 463 Terry Carkner, Phil. .20
☐ 464 Dale Craigwell, SanJ. .20
☐ 465 Kevin Todd, NJer. .20
☐ 466 Kjell Samuelsson, Pitt. .20
☐ 467 Denis Savard, Mont. .20
☐ 468 Adam Foote, Québ. .20
☐ 469 Stéphane Morin, Québ. .20
☐ 470 Doug Wilson, SanJ. .20
☐ 471 Shawn Cronin, Winn. .20
☐ 472 Brian Glynn, Edmo. .20
☐ 473 Craig Simpson, Edmo. .20
☐ 474 Todd Krygier, Wash. .20
☐ 475 Brad Miller, Buff. (Otta.) .20
☐ 476 Yvon Corriveau, Hart. .20
☐ 477 Patrick Flatley, NYIs. .20
☐ 478 Mats Sundin, Québ. .50
☐ 479 Joe Cirella, NYRa. .20
☐ 480 Gino Cavallini, Québ. .20
☐ 481 Marty McSorley, LosA. .20
☐ 482 Brad Marsh, Detr. (Otta.) .20
☐ 483 Bob McGill, Detr. (Tamp.) .20
☐ 484 Randy Moller, Buff. .20
☐ 485 Keith Primeau, Detr. .20
☐ 486 Darin Kimble, SLou. (Tamp.) .20
☐ 487 Mike Krushelnyski, Toro. .20
☐ 488 Rich & Ron Sutter .20
☐ 489 Pavel Bure, Vanc. .20
☐ 490 Ray Whitney, SanJ. .20
☐ 491 Dave McLlwain, Toro. .20
☐ 492 Per Djoos, NYRa. .20
☐ 493 Garry Valk, Vanc. .20
☐ 494 Mike Bullard, Toro. .20
☐ 495 Greg Hawgood, Edmo. .20
☐ 496 Terry Yake, Hart. .20
☐ 497 Mike Hartman, Winn. (Tamp.) .20
☐ 498 Jaromir Jagr, Pitt. .50
☐ 499 Checklist , .20
☐ 500 Checklist , .20
☐ 501 Eric Lindros, Phil. 1.00

1992 - 93 TOPPS STADIUM CLUB MEMBERS ONLY

Imprint: **© 1992 the topps company, inc.

	Player	TSC
Complete Set (5 cards):		**.00**
☐	Neil Brady, Otta.	.25
☐	Chris Kontos, Tamp.	.25
☐	Jari Kurri, LosA.	1.00
☐	Eric Lindros, Phil.	1.00
☐	Reggie Savage, Wash.	.25

1992 - 93 UPPER DECK

Card 88 (Eric Lindros) was only inserted into Low Series packs.

Imprint: 1992 The Upper Deck Company
Low Numbers Set (440 cards): 20.00
High Numbers Set (200 cards): 40.00
Common Player: .20

Player **NM-MT**

☐ 1 Andy Moog (G), Bost. [Checklist] .25
☐ 2 Donald Audette, Buff. [Checklist] .25
☐ 3 Tomas Forslund, Calg. [Checklist] .25
☐ 4 Steve Larmer, Chic. [Checklist] .25
☐ 5 Tim Cheveldae (G), Detr. [Checklist] .25
☐ 6 Vincent Damphousse, Edmo. [Checklist] .25
☐ 7 Pat Verbeek, Hart. [Checklist] .25
☐ 8 Luc Robitaille, LosA. [Checklist] .25
☐ 9 Mike Modano, Minn. [Checklist] .50
☐ 10 Denis Savard, Mont. [Checklist] .25
☐ 11 Kevin Todd, NJer. [Checklist] .25
☐ 12 Ray Ferraro, NYIs. [Checklist] .25
☐ 13 Tony Amonte, NYRa. [Checklist] .25
☐ 14 Peter Sidorkiewicz (G), Otta. [Checklist] .25
☐ 15 Rod Brind'Amour, Phil. [Checklist] .25
☐ 16 Jaromir Jagr, Pitt. [Checklist] .50
☐ 17 Owen Nolan, Québ. [Checklist] .25
☐ 18 Nelson Emerson, SLou. [Checklist] .25
☐ 19 Pat Falloon, SanJ. [Checklist] .25
☐ 20 Anatoli Semenov, Tamp. [Checklist] .25
☐ 21 Doug Gilmour, Toro. [Checklist] .25
☐ 22 Kirk McLean (G), Vanc. [Checklist] .25
☐ 23 Don Beaupré (G), Wash. [Checklist] .25
☐ 24 Phil Housley, Winn. [Checklist] .25
☐ 25 Wayne Gretzky, LosA. 2.00
☐ 26 Mario Lemieux, Pitt. 1.50
☐ 27 Valeri Kamensky, Québ. .25
☐ 28 Jaromir Jagr, Pitt. .50
☐ 29 Brett Hull, SLou. .50
☐ 30 Neil Wilkinson, SanJ. .25
☐ 31 Dominic Roussel (G), Phil. .25
☐ 32 Kent Manderville, Toro. .25
☐ 33 HL: Wayne Gretzky, LosA. 2.00
☐ 34 New York Rangers .25
☐ 35 Miller brothers .25
☐ 36 Sakic brothers .25
☐ 37 Gretzky brothers .50
☐ 38 Linden brothers .25
☐ 39 Courtnall brothers .25
☐ 40 Dale Craigwell, SanJ. .25
☐ 41 Peter Ahola, LosA. .25
☐ 42 Robert Reichel, Calg. .25
☐ 43 Chris Terreri (G), NJer. .25
☐ 44 John Vanbiesbrouck (G), NYRa. .25
☐ 45 Alexander Semak, NJer. .25
☐ 46 Mike Sullivan, SanJ. .25
☐ 47 Bob Sweeney, Bost. .25
☐ 48 Corey Millen, LosA. .25
☐ 49 Murray Craven, Hart. .25
☐ 50 Dennis Vaske, NYIs. .25
☐ **51 David* Williams, SanJ. RC .50**
☐ 52 Tom Fitzgerald, NYIs. .25
☐ 53 Corey Foster, Phil. .25
☐ 54 Al Iafrate, Wash. .25
☐ 55 John LeClair, Mont. .25
☐ 56 Stéphane Richer, NJer. .25
☐ 57 Claude Boivin, Phil. .25
☐ 58 Rick Tabaracci (G), Winn. .25
☐ 59 Johan Garpenlöv, SanJ. .25
☐ 60 Checklist .25
☐ 61 Stephen Leach, Bost. .25
☐ 62 Trent Klatt, Minn. .25
☐ 63 Darryl Sydor, LosA. .25
☐ 64 Brian Glynn, Edmo. .25
☐ 65 Mike Craig, Minn. .25
☐ 66 Gary Leeman, Calg. .25
☐ 67 Jimmy Waite (G), Chic. .25
☐ 68 Jason Marshall, SLou. .25
☐ 69 Robert Kron, Vanc. .25
☐ **70 Yanic Perreault, Toro. RC 2.50**
☐ 71 Daniel Marois, NYIs. .25
☐ 72 Mark Osborne, Toro. .25
☐ 73 Mark Tinordi, Minn. .25
☐ 74 Brad May, Buff. .25
☐ 75 Kimbi Daniels, Phil. .25
☐ 76 Kay Whitmore (G), Hart. .25
☐ 77 Luciano Borsato, Winn. .25
☐ 78 Kris King, NYRa. .25
☐ 79 Félix Potvin (G), Toro. .25
☐ 80 Benoît Brunet, Mont. .25
☐ 81 Shawn Antoski, Vanc. .25
☐ 82 Randy Gilhen, NYRa. .25
☐ 83 Dmitri Mironov, Toro. .25
☐ 84 Dave Manson, Edmo. .25
☐ 85 Sergio Momesso, Vanc. .25
☐ 86 Cam Neely, Bost. .50
☐ 87 Mike Krushelnyski, Toro. .25
☐ 88 Eric Lindros, Phil. 2.00
☐ 89 Wendel Clark, Toro. .25
☐ 90 Enrico Ciccone, Minn. .25
☐ 91 Jarrod Skalde, NJer. .25
☐ 92 Dominik Hasek (G), Chic. .50
☐ 93 Dave McLlwain, Toro. .25
☐ 94 Russ Courtnall, Mont. .25
☐ 95 Tim Sweeney, Calg. .25
☐ 96 Alexei Kasatonov, NJer. .25
☐ 97 Chris Lindberg, Calg. .25
☐ 98 Steven Rice, Edmo. .25
☐ 99 Tie Domi, NYRa. .25
☐ 100 Paul Stanton, Pitt. .25
☐ 101 Brad Schlegel, Wash. .25
☐ 102 David Bruce, SanJ. .25
☐ 103 Mikael Andersson, Tamp. .25
☐ 104 Shawn Chambers, Tamp. .25
☐ 105 Rob Ramage, Tamp. .25
☐ 106 Joe Reekie, Tamp. .25
☐ 107 Sylvain Turgeon, Otta. .25

- 108 Rob Murphy, Otta. .25
- 109 Brad Shaw, Otta. .25
- **110 Darren Rumble, Otta. RC .50**
- 111 Kyosti Karjalainen, LosA. .25
- 112 Mike Vernon (G), Calg. .25
- 113 Michel Goulet, Chic. .25
- 114 Garry Valk, Vanc. .25
- 115 Peter Bondra, Wash. .25
- 116 Paul Coffey, LosA. .25
- 117 Brian Noonan, Chic. .25
- 118 John* McIntyre, LosA. .25
- 119 Scott Mellanby, Edmo. .25
- 120 Jim Sandlak, Vanc. .25
- 121 Mats Sundin, Québ. .50
- 122 Brendan Shanahan, SLou. .50
- 123 Kelly Buchberger, Edmo. .25
- 124 Doug Smail, Québ. .25
- 125 Craig Janney, SLou. .25
- 126 Mike Gartner, NYRa. .25
- 127 Alexei Gusarov, Québ. .25
- 128 Joe Nieuwendyk, Calg. .25
- 129 Troy Murray, Winn. .25
- 130 Jamie Baker, Québ. .25
- 131 Dale Hunter, Wash. .25
- 132 Darrin Shannon, Winn. .25
- 133 Adam Oates, Bost. .25
- 134 Trevor Kidd, Calg. .25
- 135 Steve Larmer, Chic. .25
- 136 Fredrik Olausson, Winn. .25
- 137 Jyrki Lumme, Vanc. .25
- 138 Tony Amonte, NYRa. .25
- 139 Calle Johansson, Wash. .25
- 140 Rob Blake, LosA. .25
- 141 Phil Bourque, Pitt. .25
- 142 Yves Racine, Detr. .25
- 143 Rich Sutter, SLou. .25
- 144 Joe Mullen, Pitt. .25
- 145 Mike Richter (G), NYRa. .25
- 146 Pat MacLeod, SanJ. .25
- 147 Claude Lapointe, Québ. .25
- 148 Paul Broten, NYRa. .25
- 149 Patrick Roy (G), Mont. 1.50
- 150 Doug Wilson, SanJ. .25
- 151 Jim Hrivnak (G), Wash. .25
- 152 Joe Murphy, Edmo. .25
- 153 Randy Burridge, Wash. .25
- 154 Thomas Steen, Winn. .25
- 155 Steve Yzerman, Detr. 1.00
- 156 Pavel Bure, Vanc. .25
- 157 Sergei Fedorov, Detr. .50
- 158 Trevor Linden, Vanc. .25
- 159 Chris Chelios, Chic. .25
- 160 Cliff Ronning, Vanc. .25
- 161 Jeff Beukeboom, NYRa. .25
- 162 Denis Savard, Mont. .25
- 163 Claude Lemieux, NJer. .25
- 164 Mike Keane, Mont. .25
- 165 Pat LaFontaine, Buff. .25
- 166 Nelson Emerson, SLou. .25
- 167 Alexander Mogilny, Buff. .25
- 168 Jamie Leach, Pitt. .25
- 169 Darren Turcotte, NYRa. .25
- 170 Checklist .25
- 171 Steve Thomas, NYIs. .25
- 172 Brian Bellows, Minn. .25
- 173 Mike Ridley, Wash. .25
- 174 Dave Gagner, Minn. .25
- 175 Pierre Turgeon, NYIs. .25
- 176 Paul Ysebaert, Detr. .25
- 177 Brian Propp, Minn. .25
- 178 Nicklas Lidström, Detr. .25
- 179 Kelly Miller, Wash. .25
- 180 Kirk Muller, Mont. .25
- 181 Bob Bassen, SLou. .25
- 182 Tony Tanti, Buff. .25
- 183 Mikhail Tatarinov, Québ. .25
- 184 Ron Sutter, SLou. .25
- 185 Tony Granato, LosA. .25
- 186 Curtis Joseph (G), SLou. .50
- 187 Uwe Krupp, NYIs. .25
- 188 Esa Tikkanen, Edmo. .25
- 189 Ulf Samuelsson, Pitt. .25
- 190 Jon Casey (G), Minn. .25
- 191 Derek King, NYIs. .25
- 192 Greg A. Adams, Vanc. .25
- 193 Ray Ferraro, NYIs. .25
- 194 Dave Christian, SLou. .25
- 195 Eric Weinrich, NJer. .25
- 196 Josef Beránek, Edmo. .25
- 197 Tim Cheveldae (G), Detr. .25
- 198 Kevin Hatcher, Wash. .25
- 199 Brent Sutter, Chic. .25
- 200 Bruce Driver, NJer. .25
- 201 Tom Draper (G), Buff. .25
- 202 Ted Donato, Bost. .25
- 203 Ed Belfour (G), Chic. .50
- 204 Pat Verbeek, Hart. .25
- 205 John Druce, Wash. .25
- 206 Neal Broten, Minn. .25
- 207 Doug Bodger, Buff. .25
- 208 Troy Loney, Pitt. .25
- 209 Mark Pederson, Phil. .25
- 210 Todd Elik, Minn. .25
- 211 Ed Olczyk, Winn. .25
- 212 Paul Cavallini, SLou. .25
- 213 Stéphan Lebeau, Mont. .25
- 214 Dave Ellett, Toro. .25
- 215 Doug Gilmour, Toro. .25
- 216 Luc Robitaille, LosA. .25
- 217 Bob Essensa, Winn. .25
- 218 Jari Kurri, LosA. .50
- 219 Dmitri Khristich, Wash. .25
- 220 Joel Otto, Calg. .25
- 221 Checklist, Sweden Juniors .25
- **222 Jonas Höglund, Sweden Juniors RC 1.00**
- **223 Rolf Wanhainen, Sweden Juniors RC .50**
- **224 Stefan Klockare, Sweden Juniors RC .50**
- **225 Johan Norgren, Sweden Juniors RC .50**
- **226 Roger Kyrö, Sweden Juniors RC .50**
- **227 Niklas Sundblad, Sweden Juniors RC .50**
- **228 Calle Carlsson, Sweden Juniors RC .50**
- **229 Jakob Karlsson, Sweden Juniors RC .50**
- **230 Fredrik Jax, Sweden Juniors RC .50**
- **231 Björn Nord, Sweden Juniors RC .50**
- **232 Kristian Gahn, Sweden Juniors RC .50**
- **233 Mikael Renberg, Sweden Juniors RC 2.00**
- **234 Markus Näslund, Sweden Juniors RC 6.00**
- 235 Peter Forsberg, Sweden Juniors 1.00
- **236 Michael Nylander, Sweden Juniors RC 1.50**
- 237 Stanley Cup Centennial .25
- 238 Rick Tocchet, Pitt. .25
- 239 Igor Kravchuk, Chic. .25
- 240 Geoff Courtnall, Vanc. .25
- 241 Larry Murphy, Pitt. .25
- 242 Mark Messier, NYRa. .50
- 243 Tom Barrasso (G), Pitt. .25
- 244 Glen Wesley, Bost. .25
- 245 Randy Wood, Buff. .25
- 246 Gerard Gallant, Detr. .25
- 247 Kip Miller, Minn. .25
- 248 Bob Probert, Detr. .25
- 249 Gary Suter, Calg. .25
- 250 Ulf Dahlén, Minn. .25
- 251 Dan Lambert, Québ. .25
- 252 Bobby Holik, Hart. .25
- 253 Jimmy Carson, Detr. .25
- 254 Ken (Jr.) Hodge, Bost. .25
- 255 Joe Sakic, Québ. .50
- 256 Kevin Dineen, Phil. .25
- 257 Al MacInnis, Calg. .25
- 258 Vladimír Ruzicka, Bost. .25
- 259 Ken Daneyko, NJer. .25
- 260 Guy Carbonneau, Mont. .25
- 261 Michal Pivonka, Wash. .25
- 262 Bill Ranford (G), Edmo. .25
- 263 Petr Nedved, Vanc. .25
- 264 Rod Brind'Amour, Phil. .25
- 265 Raymond Bourque, Bost. .50
- 266 Joe Sacco, Toro. .25
- 267 Vladimir Konstantinov, Detr. .25
- 268 Éric Desjardins, Mont. .25
- 269 Dave Andreychuk, Buff. .25
- 270 Kelly Hrudey (G), LosA. .25
- 271 Grant Fuhr (G), Toro. .25
- 272 Dirk Graham, Chic. .25
- 273 Frank Pietrangelo, Hart. .25
- 274 Jeremy Roenick, Chic. .25
- 275 Kevin Stevens, Pitt. .25
- 276 Phil Housley, Winn. .25
- 277 Patrice Brisebois, Mont. .25
- 278 Viacheslav Fetisov, NJer. .25
- 279 Doug Weight, NYRa. .25
- 280 Checklist .25
- 281 Dean Evason, SanJ. .25
- 282 Martin Gélinas, Edmo. .25
- 283 Philippe Bozon, SLou. .25
- 284 Brian Leetch, NYRa. .25
- 285 Theoren Fleury, Calg. .25
- 286 Pat Falloon, SanJ. .25
- 287 Derian Hatcher, Minn. .25
- 288 Andrew Cassels, Hart. .25
- 289 Gary Roberts, Calg. .25
- 290 Bernie Nicholls, Edmo. .25
- 291 Ron Francis, Pitt. .25
- 292 Tom Kurvers, NYIs. .25
- 293 Geoff Sanderson, Hart. .25
- 294 Vyacheslav Kozlov, Detr. .25
- 295 Valeri Zelepukin, NJer. .25
- 296 Ray Sheppard, Detr. .25
- 297 Scott Stevens, NJer. .25
- 298 Sergei Nemchinov, NYRa. .25
- 299 Kirk McLean (G), Vanc. .25
- 300 Igor Ulanov, Winn. .25
- 301 Brian Benning, Phil. .25
- 302 Dale Hawerchuk, Buff. .25
- 303 Kevin Todd, NJer. .25
- 304 John Cullen, Hart. .25
- 305 Mike Modano, Minn. .50
- 306 Donald Audette, Buff. .25
- 307 Vincent Damphousse, Edmo. .25
- 308 Jeff Hackett (G), SanJ. .25
- 309 Craig Simpson, Edmo. .25
- 310 Don Beaupré (G), Wash. .25
- 311 Adam Creighton, NYIs. .25
- 312 Pat Elynuik, Winn. .25
- 313 David Volek, NYIs. .25
- 314 Sergei Makarov, Calg. .25
- 315 Craig Billington (G), NJer. .25
- 316 Zarley Zalapski, Hart. .25
- 317 Brian Mullen, SanJ. .25
- 318 Rob Pearson, Toro. .25
- 319 Garry Galley, Phil. .25
- 320 James Patrick, NYRa. .25
- 321 Owen Nolan, Québ. .25
- 322 Marty McSorley, LosA. .25
- 323 James H. Black, Hart. .25
- 324 Jacques Cloutier (G), Québ. .25
- 325 Benoît Hogue, NYIs. .25
- 326 Teppo Numminen, Winn. .25
- 327 Mark Recchi, Phil. .25
- 328 Paul Ranheim, Calg. .25
- 329 Andy Moog (G), Bost. .25
- 330 Shayne Corson, Mont. .25
- 331 J.J. Daigneault, Mont. .25
- 332 Mark Fitzpatrick (G), NYIs. .25
- 333 Russian Stars , Dynamo Moscow [Checklist] .25
- 334 Alexei Yashin, Dynamo Moscow .25
- 335 Darius Kasparaitis, Dynamo Moscow .25
- 336 Alexander Yudin, Dynamo Moscow .25
- 337 Sergei Bautin, Dynamo Moscow .25
- 338 Igor Korolev, Dynamo Moscow .25
- **339 Sergei Klimovich, Dynamo Moscow RC .50**
- **340 Andrei Nikolishin, Dynamo Moscow RC 1.00**
- 341 Vitali Karamnov, Dynamo Moscow .25
- 342 Alexander Andrijevski, Dynamo Moscow .25
- 343 Sergei Sorokin, Dynamo Moscow .25
- **344 Yan Kaminsky, Dynamo Moscow RC .50**
- 345 Andrei Trefilov, Dynamo Moscow .25
- **346 Sergei Petrenko, Dynamo Moscow RC .50**
- 347 Ravil Khaidarov, Dynamo Moscow .25
- 348 Dmitri Frolov, Dynamo Moscow .25
- 349 Ravil Yakubov, Dynamo Moscow .25
- 350 Dmitry Yushkevich, Dynamo Moscow .25
- 351 Alexander Karpovtsev, Dynamo Moscow .25
- 352 Igor Dorofeyev, Dynamo Moscow .25
- 353 Alexander Galchenyuk, Dynamo Moscow .25
- 354 Joé Juneau, Bost. [Rookie Report] .25
- 355 Pat Falloon, SanJ. [Rookie Report] .25
- 356 Gilbert Dionne, Mont. [Rookie Report] .25
- 357 Vladimir Konstantinov, Detr. [Rookie Report] .25
- 358 Rick Tabaracci (G), Winn. [Rookie Report] .25
- 359 Tony Amonte, NYRa. [Rookie Report] .25
- 360 Scott Lachance, NYIs. [Rookie Report] .25
- 361 Tom Draper (G), Buff. [Rookie Report] .25
- 362 Pavel Bure, Vanc. [Rookie Report] .25
- 363 Nicklas Lidström, Detr. [Rookie Report] .25
- 364 Keith Tkachuk, Winn. [Rookie Report] .50
- 365 Kevin Todd, NJer. [Rookie Report] .25
- 366 Dominik Hasek (G), Chic. [Rookie Report] .50
- 367 Igor Kravchuk, Chic. [Rookie Report] .25
- 368 Shawn McEachern, Pitt. [Rookie Report] .25
- 369 World Championships checklist .50
- **370 Dieter Hegen, Germany Nationals RC .50**
- **371 Stefan Ustorf, Germany Nationals RC .50**
- **372 Ernst Köpf, Germany Nationals RC .50**
- **373 Raimond Hilger, Germany Nationals RC .50**
- 374 Mats Sundin, Sweden Nationals .50
- 375 Peter Forsberg, Sweden Nationals 1.00
- **376 Arto Blömsten, Sweden Nationals RC .20**
- 377 Tommy Söderström, Sweden Nationals .25
- 378 Michael Nylander, Sweden Nationals .25
- **379 David A. Jensen, U.S.A. Nationals RC .50**
- 380 Chris Winnes, U.S.A. Nationals .25
- 381 Ray LeBlanc, U.S.A. Nationals .25
- 382 Joe Sacco, U.S.A. Nationals .25
- 383 Dennis Vaske, U.S.A. Nationals .25
- **384 Jörg Eberle, Switzerland Nationals RC .50**
- 385 Trevor Kidd, Canada Nationals .25
- 386 Pat Falloon, Canada Nationals .25
- 387 Rob (Jr.) Brown, Chic. .25
- 388 Adam Graves, NYRa. .25
- 389 Peter Zezel, Toro. .25
- 390 Checklist .25
- 391 Don Sweeney, Bost. .25
- 392 Sean Hill, U.S.A. Nationals .25
- 393 Ted Donato, U.S.A. Nationals .25
- 394 Marty McInnis, U.S.A. Nationals .25
- **395 C.J. Young, U.S.A. Nationals RC .50**
- **396 Ted Drury, U.S.A. Nationals RC .50**
- 397 Scott A. Young, U.S.A. Nationals .25
- 398 Star Rookies checklist .25
- 399 Joé Juneau, Bost. .25
- 400 Stephen Heinze, Bost. .25
- 401 Glen Murray, Bost. .25
- **402 Keith Carney, Buff. RC 1.00**
- **403 Dean McAmmond, Chic. RC 1.00**
- 404 Karl Dykhuis, Chic. .25
- 405 Martin Lapointe, Detr. .25
- 406 Scott Niedermayer, NJer. .25
- 407 Ray Whitney, SanJ. .50
- 408 Martin Brodeur, NJer. 1.50
- 409 Scott Lachance, NYIs. .25
- 410 Marty McInnis, NYIs. .25
- 411 Bill Guerin, NJer. 1.00
- 412 Shawn McEachern, Pitt. .25
- **413 Denny Felsner, SLou. RC .50**
- **414 Bret Hedican, SLou. RC .50**
- 415 Drake Berehowsky, Toro. .25
- 416 Patrick Poulin, Hart. .25
- **417 Vladimir (Jr.) Vujtek, Mont. RC .50**
- **418 Steve Konowalchuk, Wash. RC 1.50**
- 419 Keith Tkachuk, Winn. .50
- 420 Evgeny Davydov, Winn. .25
- 421 Yanick Dupré, Phil. .25
- **422 Jason Woolley, Wash. RC .50**
- 423 W. Gretzky / Br. Hull 1.00
- 424 Tomas Sandström, LosA. .25
- 425 Craig MacTavish, Edmo. .25
- 426 Stu Barnes, Winn. .25
- 427 Gilbert Dionne, Mont. .25
- 428 Andrei Lomakin, Phil. .25
- 429 Tomas Forslund, Calg. .25
- 430 André Racicot (G), Mont. .25
- 431 Pavel Bure, Vanc. [Calder Trophy] .25
- 432 Mark Messier, NYRa. [Pearson Award] .50
- 433 Mario Lemieux, Pitt. [Art Ross Trophy] 1.50
- 434 Brian Leetch, NYRa. [Norris Trophy] .25
- 435 Wayne Gretzky, LosA. [Byng Trophy] 2.00
- 436 Lemieux, Pitt. [w/ Cup, Smythe Trophy] 1.50
- 437 Mark Messier, NYRa. [Hart Trophy] .50
- 438 Patrick Roy (G), Mont. [Vezina Trophy] 1.50
- 439 Guy Carbonneau, Mont. [Selke Trophy] .25
- 440 Patrick Roy (G), Mont. [Jennings Trophy] 1.50
- 441 Russ Courtnall, Minn. .25
- 442 Jeff Reese (G), Calg. .25
- 443 Brent Fedyk, Phil. .25
- 444 Kerry Huffman, Québ. .25
- 445 Mark Freer, Otta. .25
- 446 Christian Ruuttu, Chic. .25
- 447 Nick Kypreos, Hart. .25
- **448 Mike Hurlbut, NYRa. RC .50**
- 449 Bob Sweeney, Buff. .25
- 450 Checklist .25
- 451 Perry Berezan, SanJ. .25
- 452 Phil Bourque, NYRa. .25
- 453 A. Graves / M. Messier / T. Amonte .25
- 454 R. Tocchet / M. Lemieux / K. Stevens .50
- 455 J. Juneau / A. Oates / D. Kvartalnov .25
- 456 D. Andreychuk / P. LaFontaine / A. Mogilny .25
- 457 Zdeno Ciger, NJer. .25
- 458 Pat Jablonski (G), Tamp. .25
- 459 Brent Gilchrist, Edmo. .25
- 460 Yvon Corriveau, SanJ. .25
- 461 Dino Ciccarelli., Detr. .25
- 462 David Emma, NJer. .25
- **463 Corey Hirsch, NYRa. RC 1.00**
- 464 Jamie Baker, Otta. .25
- 465 John Cullen, Toro. .25
- **466 Lonnie Loach, LosA. RC .50**
- 467 Louie DeBrusk, Edmo. .25
- 468 Brian Mullen, NYIs. .25
- 469 Gaétan Duchesne, Minn. .25
- 470 Eric Lindros, Phil. 1.00
- 471 Brian Bellows, Mont. .25
- **472 Bill Lindsay, Québ. RC .50**
- 473 Dave Archibald, Otta. .25
- 474 Reggie Savage, Wash. .25
- **475 Tommy Söderström, Phil. RC 1.00**
- 476 Vincent Damphousse, Mont. .25
- 477 Mike Ricci, Québ. .25
- 478 Bob Carpenter, Wash. .25
- 479 Kevin Haller, Mont. .25
- 480 Peter Sidorkiewicz (G), Otta. .25
- **481 Peter** Andersson, NYRa. RC .50**
- 482 Kevin Miller, SLou. .25
- **483 Jean-François Quintin, SanJ. RC .50**
- 484 Philippe Boucher, Buff. .25
- 485 Jozef Stümpel, Bost. .25
- **486 Vitali Prokhorov, SLou. RC .50**
- **487 Stan Drulia, Tamp. RC .50**
- 488 Jayson More, SanJ. .25
- **489 Mike Needham, Pitt. RC .50**
- **490 Glenn Mulvenna, Phil. RC .50**
- **491 Ed Ronan, Mont. RC .50**
- **492 Grigori Panteleev, Bost. RC .50**
- **493 Kevin Dahl, Calg. RC .50**
- **494 Ryan McGill, Phil. RC .50**
- 495 Robb Stauber (G), LosA. .25
- 496 Vladimír (Jr.) Vujtek, Edmo. .25
- **497 Tomas Jelinek, Otta. RC .50**
- **498 Patric Kjellberg, Mont. RC 1.00**
- **499 Sergei Bautin, Winn. RC .50**
- 500 Bobby Holik, NJer. .25
- **501 Guy Hebert (G), SLou. RC 1.50**
- **502 Chris Kontos, Tamp. RC .50**
- 503 Viacheslav Butsayev, Phil. .25
- 504 Yuri Khmylev, Buff. .25
- **505 Richard Matvichuk, Minn. RC 1.50**
- 506 Dominik Hasek (G), Buff. .50
- 507 Ed Courtenay, SanJ. .25
- 508 Jeff Daniels, Pitt. .25
- 509 Doug Zmolek, SanJ. .25
- **510 Vitali Karamnov, SLou. RC .50**
- 511 Norm Maciver, Otta. .25
- 512 Terry Yake, Hart. .25
- 513 Steve Duchesne, Québ. .25
- 514 Andrei Trefilov, Calg. .25
- 515 Jiří Slégr, Vanc. .25
- 516 Sergei Zubov, NYRa. .50
- **517 Dave Karpa, Québ. RC .50**
- 518 Sean Burke (G), Hart. .25
- 519 Adrien Plavsic, Vanc. .25
- 520 Michael Nylander, Hart. .25
- 521 John MacLean, NJer. .25
- **522 Jason Ruff, SLou. RC .50**
- **523 Sean Hill, Mont. RC .50**
- 524 Mike Sillinger, Detr. .25
- **525 Daniel Laperrière, SLou. RC .50**
- 526 Peter Ahola, Pitt. .25
- 527 Guy Larose, Toro. .25
- **528 Tommy Sjödin, Minn. RC .50**
- 529 Rob DiMaio, Tamp. .25
- 530 Mark Howe, Detr. .25
- 531 Greg Paslawski, Phil. .25
- 532 Ron Hextall (G), Québ. .25
- **533 Keith Jones, Wash. RC 1.00**
- **534 Chris Luongo, Otta. RC .50**
- 535 Anatoli Semenov, Vanc. .25
- 536 Stéphane Beauregard (G), Phil. .25
- 537 Pat Elynuik, Wash. .25
- 538 Mike McPhee, Minn. .25
- 539 Jody Hull, Otta. .25
- 540 Stéphane Matteau, Chic. .25
- 541 Shayne Corson, Edmo. .25
- **542 Mikhail Kravets, SanJ. RC .50**
- **543 Kevin Miehm, SLou. RC .50**
- 544 Brian Bradley, Tamp. [vs K.Buchberger] .25
- 545 Mathieu Schneider, Mont. .25
- 546 Steve Chiasson, Detr. .25
- **547 Warren Rychel, LosA. RC .50**
- 548 John Tucker, Tamp. .25
- 549 Todd Ewen, Mont. .25
- 550 Checklist .25
- 551 Petr Klima, Edmo. .25
- **552 Robert Lang, LosA. RC 1.50**
- 553 Eric Weinrich, Hart. .25
- 554 Young Guns checklist .25
- **555 Roman Hamrlik, Tamp. RC 1.50**
- 556 Martin Rucinsky, Québ. .25
- 557 Patrick Poulin, Hart. .25
- 558 Tyler Wright, Edmo. .25
- **559 Martin Straka, Pitt. RC 2.00**
- **560 Jim Hiller, LosA. RC .50**
- **561 Dmitri Kvartalnov, Bost. RC .50**
- 562 Scott Niedermayer, NJer. .25
- 563 Darius Kasparaitis, NYIs. .25
- **564 Richard Smehlik, Buff. RC .50**
- 565 Shawn McEachern, Pitt. .25
- 566 Alexei Zhitnik, LosA. .25
- 567 Andrei Kovalenko, Québ. .25
- 568 Sandis Ozolinsh, SanJ. .25
- **569 Robert Petrovicky, Hart. RC 1.00**
- **570 Dmitry Yushkevich, Phil. RC 1.50**
- 571 Scott Lachance, NYIs. .25
- **572 Nikolai Borschevsky, Toro. RC .50**
- 573 Alexei Kovalev, NYRa. .50
- 574 Teemu Selänne, Winn. .50
- **575 Steven King, NYRa. RC .25**
- **576 Guy Lévêque, LosA. RC .50**
- 577 Vladimir Malakhov, NYIs. .25
- 578 Alexei Zhamnov, Winn. .25
- 579 Viktor Gordiouk, Buff. .25
- **580 Dixon Ward, Vanc. RC .50**
- 581 Igor Korolev, SLou. .25
- 582 Sergei Krivokrasov, Chic. .25
- **583 Rob Zamuner, Tamp. RC 1.50**

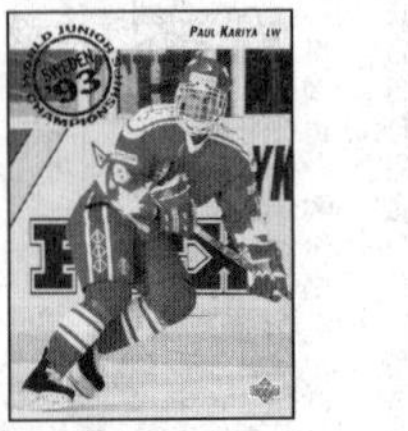

☐ 584 World Junior checklist .25
☐ **585 Manny Legace, Canada Juniors RC 2.50**
☐ **586 Paul Kariya, Canada Juniors RC 15.00**
☐ **587 Alexandre Daigle, Canada Juniors RC 1.00**
☐ **588 Nathan Lafayette, Canada Juniors RC .50**
☐ **589 Mike Rathje, Canada Juniors RC 1.00**
☐ **590 Chris Gratton, Canada Juniors RC 1.50**
☐ **591 Chris Pronger, Canada Juniors RC 5.00**
☐ **592 Brent Tully, Canada Juniors RC .50**
☐ **593 Rob Niedermayer, Canada Juniors RC 1.50**
☐ **594 Darcy Werenka, Canada Juniors RC .50**
☐ 595 Peter Forsberg, Sweden Juniors 1.00
☐ **596 Kenny Jönsson, Sweden Juniors RC 1.00**
☐ **597 Niklas Sundström, Sweden Juniors RC 1.50**
☐ **598 Reine Rauhala, Sweden Juniors RC .50**
☐ **599 Daniel Johansson, Sweden Juniors RC .50**
☐ **600 David Vyborny, Czech & Slovak Jrs. RC 1.00**
☐ **601 Jan Vopat, Czech & Slovak Jrs. RC .50**
☐ **602 Pavol Demitra, Czech & Slovak Jrs. RC 2.50**
☐ **603 Michal Cerny, Czech & Slovak Jrs. RC .50**
☐ **604 Ondrej Steiner, Czech & Slovak Jrs. RC .50**
☐ **605 Jim Campbell, U.S.A. Juniors RC .50**
☐ **606 Todd Marchant, U.S.A. Juniors RC 1.50**
☐ **607 Mike Pomichter, U.S.A. Juniors RC .50**
☐ **608 John Emmons, U.S.A. Juniors RC .50**
☐ **609 Adam Deadmarsh, U.S.A. Juniors RC 3.00**
☐ **610 Nikolai Semin, Russia Juniors RC .50**
☐ **611 Igor Alexandrov, Russia Juniors RC .50**
☐ **612 Vadim Sharifijanov, Russia Juniors RC .50**
☐ **613 Viktor Kozlov, Russia Juniors RC 2.00**
☐ **614 Nikolai Tsulygin, Russia Juniors RC .50**
☐ **615 Jere Lehtinen, Finland Juniors RC 2.00**
☐ **616 Ville Peltonen, Finland Juniors RC .50**
☐ **617 Saku Koivu, Finland Juniors RC 8.00**
☐ **618 Kimmo Rintanen, Finland Juniors RC .50**
☐ **619 Jonni Vauhkonen, Finland Juniors RC .50**
☐ 620 Brett Hull, SLou. [Profiles] .50
☐ 621 Wayne Gretzky, LosA. [Profiles] 2.00
☐ 622 Jaromir Jagr, Pitt. [Profiles] .50
☐ 623 Darius Kasparaitis, NYIs. [Profiles] .25
☐ 624 Bernie Nicholls, Edmo. [Profiles] .25
☐ 625 Gilbert Dionne, Mont. [Profiles] .25
☐ 626 Raymond Bourque, Bost. [Profiles] .50
☐ 627 Mike Ricci, Québ. [Profiles] .25
☐ 628 Phil Housley, Winn. [Profiles] .25
☐ 629 Chris Chelios, Chic. [Profiles] .25
☐ 630 Kevin Stevens, Pitt. [Profiles] .25
☐ 631 Roman Hamrlik, Tamp. [Profiles] .25
☐ 632 Sergei Fedorov, Detr. [Profiles] .50
☐ 633 Alexei Kovalev, NYRa. [Profiles] .50
☐ 634 Shawn McEachern, Pitt. [Profiles] .25
☐ 635 Tony Amonte, NYRa. [Profiles] .25
☐ 636 Brian Bellows, Mont. [Profiles] .25
☐ 637 Adam Oates, Bost. [Profiles] .25
☐ 638 Denis Savard, Mont. [Profiles] .25
☐ 639 Doug Gilmour, Toro. [Profiles] .25
☐ 640 Brian Leetch, NYRa. [Profiles] .25

Player NM-MT
☐ SP2 Pavel Bure, Vanc. 4.00
☐ SP3 Canada Juniors 4.00
☐ SP3 Canada Juniors [Oversize] 5.00

ALL-ROOKIE TEAM

Series 1 Insert Set (7 cards): 30.00
Insert [1:25] AR
☐ AR1 Tony Amonte, Upper Deck (NYRa.) 6.00
☐ AR2 Gilbert Dionne, Upper Deck (Mont.) 1.00
☐ AR3 Kevin Todd, Upper Deck (NJer.) 1.00
☐ AR4 Nicklas Lidström, Upper Deck (Detr.) 6.00
☐ AR5 Vladimir Konstantinov, Upper Deck (Detr.) 3.00
☐ AR6 Dominik Hasek (G), Upper Deck (Chic.) 10.00
☐ AR7 All-Rookie Team checklist 10.00

ALL-WORLD TEAM

Series 1 Insert Set (7 cards): 15.00
Canadian-Pack Insert AW
☐ W1 Wayne Gretzky, LosA. 10.00
☐ W2 Brett Hull, SLou. 2.00
☐ W3 Jaromir Jagr, Pitt. 2.00
☐ W4 Nicklas Lidström, Detr. 1.00
☐ W5 Vladimir Konstantinov, Detr. 1.00
☐ W6 Patrick Roy (G), Mont. 7.00

AMERI/CAN ROOKIE TEAM

Series 2 Insert Set (6 cards): 10.00
Insert [1:25] AC
☐ AC1 Joé Juneau, Bost. 2.00
☐ AC2 Keith Tkachuk, Winn. 6.00
☐ AC3 Stephen Heinze, Bost. 1.00
☐ AC4 Scott Lachance, NYIs. 1.00
☐ AC5 Scott Niedermayer, NJer. 3.00
☐ AC6 Dominic Roussel (G), Phil. 1.00

CALDER CANDIDATES

Series 2 Insert Set (20 cards): 30.00
Insert [1:9 Retail] CC
☐ CC1 Dixon Ward, Vanc. .75
☐ CC2 Igor Korolev, SLou. 1.00
☐ CC3 Félix Potvin (G), Toro. 3.00
☐ CC4 Rob Zamuner, Tamp. 1.00
☐ CC5 Scott Niedermayer, NJer. 2.00
☐ CC6 Eric Lindros, Phil. 6.00
☐ CC7 Alexei Zhitnik, LosA. 1.00
☐ CC8 Roman Hamrlik, Tamp. 1.00
☐ CC9 Joé Juneau, Bost. 1.00
☐ CC10 Teemu Selänne, Winn. 5.00
☐ CC11 Alexei Kovalev, NYRa. 7.00
☐ CC12 Vladimir Malakhov, NYIs. 1.00
☐ CC13 Darius Kasparaitis, NYIs. 1.00
☐ CC14 Shawn McEachern, Pitt. 2.00
☐ CC15 Keith Tkachuk, Winn. 3.00
☐ CC16 Scott Lachance, NYIs. 1.00
☐ CC17 Andrei Kovalenko, Québ. 1.00
☐ CC18 Patrick Poulin, Hart. 1.00
☐ CC19 Evgeny Davydov, Winn. .75
☐ CC20 Dmitry Yushkevich, Phil. 1.00

EURO ROOKIES

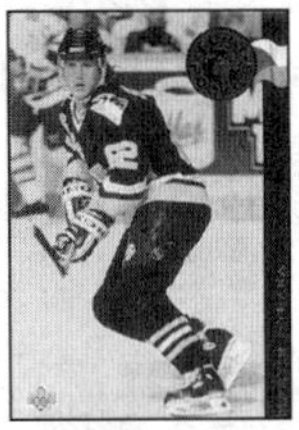

Series 2 Insert Set (20 cards): 8.00
Insert [1:1 Jumbo] ER
☐ ER1 Richard Smehlik, Buff. .25
☐ ER2 Michael Nylander, Hart. .25
☐ ER3 Igor Korolev, SLou. .25
☐ ER4 Robert Lang, LosA. .25
☐ ER5 Sergei Krivokrasov, Chic. .25
☐ ER6 Teemu Selänne, Winn. 2.00
☐ ER7 Darius Kasparaitis, NYIs. .25
☐ ER8 Alexei Zhamnov, Winn. .25
☐ ER9 Jirí Slégr, Vanc. .25
☐ ER10 Alexei Kovalev, NYRa. 3.00
☐ ER11 Roman Hamrlik, Tamp. .25
☐ ER12 Dmitry Yushkevich, Phil. .25
☐ ER13 Alexei Zhitnik, LosA. .25
☐ ER14 Andrei Kovalenko, Québ. .25
☐ ER15 Vladimir Malakhov, NYIs. .25
☐ ER16 Sandis Ozolinsh, SanJ. .25
☐ ER17 Evgeny Davydov, Winn. .25
☐ ER18 Viktor Gordiouk, Buff. .25
☐ ER19 Martin Straka, Pitt. .25
☐ ER20 Robert Petrovicky, Hart. .25

EURO STARS

Series 1 Insert Set (20 cards): 12.00
Insert [1:1 Jumbo] ES
☐ E1 Sergei Fedorov, Detr. 2.00
☐ E2 Pavel Bure, Vanc. 2.00
☐ E3 Dominik Hasek (G), Chic. 2.00
☐ E4 Vladimir Ruzicka, Bost. .25
☐ E5 Peter Ahola, LosA. .25
☐ E6 Kyosti Karjalainen, LosA. .25
☐ E7 Igor Kravchuk, Chic. .25
☐ E8 Evgeny Davydov, Winn. .25
☐ E9 Nicklas Lidström, Detr. 1.00
☐ E10 Vladimir Konstantinov, Detr. .25
☐ E11 Josef Beránek, Edmo. .25
☐ E12 Valeri Zelepukin, NJer. .25
☐ E13 Sergei Nemchinov, NYRa. .25
☐ E14 Jaromir Jagr, Pitt. 2.00
☐ E15 Igor Ulanov, Winn. .25
☐ E16 Sergei Makarov, Calg. 1.00
☐ E17 Andrei Lomakin, Phil. .25
☐ E18 Mats Sundin, Québ. 2.00
☐ E19 Jarmo Myllys (G), SanJ. .25
☐ E20 Valeri Kamensky, Québ. .25

EURO-ROOKIE TEAM

Series 1 Insert Set (7 cards): 8.00
Insert [1:25] ERT
☐ ERT1 Pavel Bure, Vanc. 3.00
☐ ERT2 Nicklas Lidström, Detr. 2.00
☐ ERT3 Dominik Hasek (G), Chic. 4.00
☐ ERT4 Peter Ahola, LosA. .75
☐ ERT5 Alexander Semak, NJer. .75
☐ ERT6 Tomas Forslund, Calg. .75

GORDON HOWE SELECTS

Series 2 Insert Set (20 cards): 40.00
Insert [1:12 Hobby] G
☐ G1 Brian Bellows, Mont. .75
☐ G2 Luc Robitaille, LosA. 2.00
☐ G3 Pat LaFontaine, Buff. 1.00
☐ G4 Kevin Stevens, Pitt. .75
☐ G5 Wayne Gretzky, LosA. 12.00
☐ G6 Steve Larmer, Chic. 1.00
☐ G7 Brett Hull, SLou. 3.00
☐ G8 Jeremy Roenick, Chic. 2.00
☐ G9 Mario Lemieux, Pitt. 9.00
☐ G10 Steve Yzerman, Detr. 7.00
☐ G11 Joé Juneau, Bost. .75
☐ G12 Vladimir Malakhov, NYIs. .75
☐ G13 Alexei Kovalev, NYRa. 3.00
☐ G14 Eric Lindros, Phil. 3.00
☐ G15 Teemu Selänne, Winn. 2.00
☐ G16 Dave Poulin, Bost. .75
☐ G17 Shawn McEachern, Pitt. .75
☐ G18 Keith Tkachuk, Winn. 1.00
☐ G19 Andrei Kovalenko, Québ. .75
☐ G20 Ted Donato, Bost. .75

HOCKEY HEROES

Series 1 Insert Set (10 cards): 35.00
Series 2 Insert Set (10 cards): 15.00
Player HH
☐ 10 Wayne Gretzky, Sault Ste. Marie 5.00
☐ 11 Wayne Gretzky, Edmo. 5.00
☐ 12 Wayne Gretzky, NHL Awards 5.00
☐ 13 Wayne Gretzky, Edmo. [w/ Stanley Cup] 5.00
☐ 14 Wayne Gretzky, Canada Nationals 5.00
☐ 15 Wayne Gretzky, LosA. 5.00
☐ 16 Wayne Gretzky, Edmo. (LosA.) 5.00
☐ 17 Wayne Gretzky, LosA. 5.00
☐ 18 Wayne Gretzky [Checklist] 5.00
☐ Header Card [Gretzky Set] 4.00
☐ 19 Gordie Howe, Detr. 2.00
☐ 20 Gordie Howe, Detr. 2.00
☐ 21 Production Line 2.00
☐ 22 Gordie Howe, Detr. 2.00
☐ 23 Gordie Howe, Detr. 2.00
☐ 24 Gordie Howe, HHOF 2.00
☐ 25 Howe family 2.00
☐ 26 Gordie Howe [w/ Gretzky] 3.00
☐ 27 Gordie Howe [Checklist] 2.00
☐ Header Card [Howe Set] 1.00

WORLD JUNIOR GRADS

Series 2 Insert Set (20 cards): 100.00
Canadian-Pack Insert WG
☐ WG1 Scott Niedermayer, NJer. 2.00
☐ WG2 Vyacheslav Kozlov, Detr. 2.00
☐ WG3 Chris Chelios, Chic. 3.00
☐ WG4 Jari Kurri, LosA. 6.00
☐ WG5 Pavel Bure, Vanc. 5.00
☐ WG6 Jaromir Jagr, Pitt. 6.00
☐ WG7 Steve Yzerman, Detr. 15.00
☐ WG8 Joe Sakic, Québ. 10.00
☐ WG9 Alexei Kovalev, NYRa. 7.00
☐ WG10 Wayne Gretzky, LosA. 25.00
☐ WG11 Mario Lemieux, Pitt. 18.00
☐ WG12 Eric Lindros, Phil. 6.00
☐ WG13 Pat Falloon, SanJ. 2.00
☐ WG14 Trevor Linden, Vanc. 2.00
☐ WG15 Brian Leetch, NYRa. 3.00
☐ WG16 Sergei Fedorov, Detr. 6.00
☐ WG17 Mats Sundin, Toro. 6.00
☐ WG18 Alexander Mogilny, Buff. 3.00
☐ WG19 Jeremy Roenick, Chic. 5.00
☐ WG20 Luc Robitaille, LosA. 5.00

1992 - 93 UPPER DECK – BUYBACKS

These cards were purchased by The Upper Deck Company and reinserted as autographed cards in new 2000-01 and 2001-02 products.

Buyback Autograph UD
☐ 8 Luc Robitaille, LosA. ✍ {#/6}
☐ 9 Mike Modano, Minn. ✍ {#/10}
☐ 25 Wayne Gretzky, LosA. ✍ {#/1}
☐ 33 Wayne Gretzky, LosA. ✍ {#/1}
☐ 34 Mark Messier, NYRa. ✍ {#/1}
☐ 55 John LeClair, Mont. ✍ {#/2}
☐ 145 Mike Richter (G), NYRa. ✍ {#/1}
☐ 155 Steve Yzerman, Detr. ✍ {#/1}
☐ 186 Curtis Joseph (G), SLou. ✍ {#/1}
☐ 216 Luc Robitaille, LosA. ✍ {#/13}
☐ 242 Mark Messier, NYRa. ✍ {#/1}
☐ 265 Raymond Bourque, Bost. ✍ {#/2}
☐ 305 Mike Modano, Minn. ✍ {#/69}
☐ 364 Keith Tkachuk, Winn. ✍ {#/2}
☐ 398 Keith Tkachuk, Winn. ✍ {#/2}
☐ 408 Martin Brodeur (G), NJer. ✍ {#/2}
☐ 419 Keith Tkachuk, Winn. ✍ {#/2}
☐ 621 Wayne Gretzky, LosA. ✍ {#/1}
☐ 626 Raymond Bourque, Bost. ✍ {#/1}

Buyback Autograph • Hockey Heroes
☐ 19 Gordie Howe, Detr. ✍ {#/1}
☐ 20 Gordie Howe, Detr. ✍ {#/1}
☐ 21 Gordie Howe, Detr. ✍ {#/1}
☐ 22 Gordie Howe, Detr. ✍ {#/1}
☐ 23 Gordie Howe, Detr. ✍ {#/1}
☐ 24 Gordie Howe, HHOF ✍ {#/1}
☐ 25 Gordie Howe [w/ family] ✍ {#/1}
☐ 26 Gordie Howe [w/ Gretzky] ✍ {#/1}
☐ 27 Gordie Howe [Checklist] ✍ {#/1}

1992 - 93 UPPER DECK LOCKER ALL-STAR

Complete Set (60 cards): 25.00
Player NM-MT
☐ 1 Peter Bondra .25
☐ 2 Steve Duchesne .25
☐ 3 Jaromir Jagr .50
☐ 4 Pat LaFontaine .25
☐ 5 Brian Leetch .25
☐ 6 Mario Lemieux 2.00
☐ 7 Mark Messier .50
☐ 8 Alexander Mogilny .25
☐ 9 Kirk Muller .25
☐ 10 Adam Oates .25
☐ 11 Mark Recchi .25
☐ 12 Patrick Roy (G) 2.00
☐ 13 Joe Sakic 1.00
☐ 14 Kevin Stevens .25
☐ 15 Scott Stevens .25
☐ 16 Rick Tocchet .25
☐ 17 Pierre Turgeon .25
☐ 18 Zarley Zalapski .25
☐ 19 Ed Belfour (G) .50
☐ 20 Brian Bradley .25
☐ 21 Pavel Bure .50
☐ 22 Chris Chelios .25
☐ 23 Paul Coffey .25
☐ 24 Doug Gilmour .25
☐ 25 Wayne Gretzky 3.00
☐ 26 Phil Housley .25
☐ 27 Brett Hull .50
☐ 28 Kelly Kisio .25
☐ 29 Jari Kurri .50
☐ 30 Dave Manson .25
☐ 31 Mike Modano .50
☐ 32 Gary Roberts .25
☐ 33 Luc Robitaille .50
☐ 34 Jeremy Roenick .50
☐ 35 Teemu Selänne .50
☐ 36 Steve Yzerman 1.50
☐ 37 Al Iafrate .25
☐ 38 Mike Gartner .50
☐ 39 Raymond Bourque .50

☐	40 Jon Casey (G)	.25
☐	41 Bob Gainey	.25
☐	42 Gordie Howe	2.00
☐	43 Bobby Hull	1.00
☐	44 Frank Mahovlich	.50
☐	45 Lanny McDonald	.50
☐	46 Stan Mikita	.50
☐	47 Henri Richard	.50
☐	48 Larry Robinson	.25
☐	49 Glen Sather	.25
☐	50 Bryan Trottier	.50
☐	51 Tony Amonte	.25
☐	52 Pat Falloon	.25
☐	53 Joé Juneau	.25
☐	54 Alexei Kovalev	.50
☐	55 Dmitri Kvartalnov	.25
☐	56 Eric Lindros	1.00
☐	57 Vladimir Malakhov	.25
☐	58 Félix Potvin (G)	.25
☐	59 Mats Sundin	.50
☐	60 Alexei Zhamnov	.25
	Autograph	**UD**
☐	Gordie Howe ✍	275.00

1992 - 93 ZELLERS MASTERS OF HOCKEY

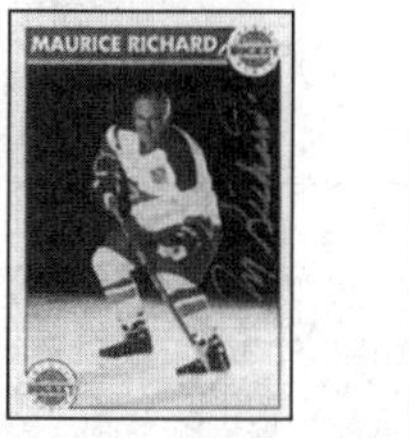

There are 10,000 copies of each card and 1,000 copies of each autographed card. Unsigned Richard cards sell for $5 while unsigned cards of other players sell for $1-3.

Imprint: ZELLERS

Complete Set (6 cards):		**130.00**
	Player	**Auto.**
☐ ☐	Johnny Bower (G) ✍	20.00
☐ ☐	Rod Gilbert ✍	20.00
☐ ☐	Ted Lindsay ✍	25.00
☐ ☐	Frank Mahovlich ✍	25.00
☐ ☐	Stan Mikita ✍	20.00
☐ ☐	Maurice Richard ✍•	70.00

1993 KOULULAINEN

A 9 card sheet issued by the magazine Koululainen.

Card Size: 2 5/8" x 3 4/16

Complete Set (6 cards): 20.00

Player	Player
☐ Jari Kurri	☐ Mario Lemieux
☐ Jyrki Lumme	☐ Teppo Numminen
☐ Janne Ojanen	☐ Christian Ruuttu
☐ Teemu Selänne	☐ Esa Tikkanen
☐ Title Card	

1993 QUÉBEC INTERNATIONAL PEE WEE

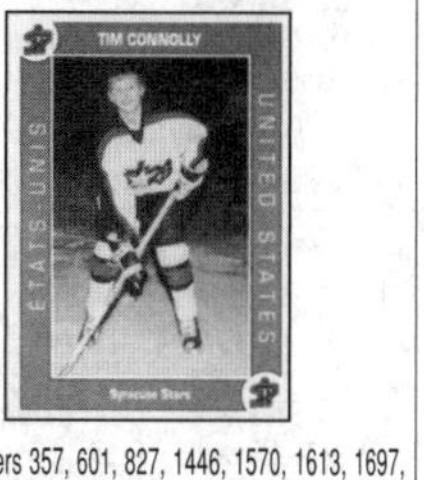

Card numbers 357, 601, 827, 1446, 1570, 1613, 1697, 1736, 1738, 1741, 1744, 1746, 1747, 1757, 1780, 1807 were never printed. Card numbers 1613, 1807 appear on the team checklists but were not printed.

There are two versions of each card: the regular card and a McDonald's parallel. Regular singles start at 25¢; McDonald's singles start at 35¢. Regional stars in the regular series start at $1.00 while regional stars in the McDonald's series start at $2.00. Notable stars are priced below each team sub-heading.

Imprint: Tournoi international de hockey Pee-Wee de Québec

Complete Set (1,794 cards): 190.00

Complete McDonald's Set (1,794 cards): 450.00

AMBASSADEURS DE LA VALLÉE

☐ ☐ 1 Vincent Dionne ☐ ☐ 2 Bryan Ouellet
☐ ☐ 3 Simon Gagnon ☐ ☐ 4 Jérome Landry
☐ ☐ 5 Sylvain Guenette ☐ ☐ 6 François Paquet
☐ ☐ 7 Martin-Benoît Leclerc ☐ ☐ 8 Michel Thériault
☐ ☐ 9 Frédérick Pilote ☐ ☐ 10 Dany Doucet
☐ ☐ 11 Carl Dancause ☐ ☐ 12 Simon Paquet
☐ ☐ 13 Kaven McNicoll ☐ ☐ 14 David Dupéré
☐ ☐ 15 Sébastien Caron ☐ ☐ 16 Team Checklist

LAKESHORE BRAVES

☐ ☐ 17 Marc Scheuer ☐ ☐ 18 Derek Legault
☐ ☐ 19 Valérie Desjardins ☐ ☐ 20 Éric Langill
☐ ☐ 21 Sean Landry ☐ ☐ 22 Jeremy Maher
☐ ☐ 23 Stéphane White ☐ ☐ 24 Martin Dubeau
☐ ☐ 25 François Duffy ☐ ☐ 26 Steven Côté
☐ ☐ 27 Mathieu Soulier ☐ ☐ 28 Louis Archambault
☐ ☐ 29 Robbie Boivin ☐ ☐ 30 Wesley Scanzano
☐ ☐ 31 Shawn Scanzano ☐ ☐ 32 Team Checklist

LEAFS DE VERDUN

☐ ☐ 33 Éric Fragapane ☐ ☐ 34 Francis Gagnier
☐ ☐ 35 Jan Marcigliese ☐ ☐ 36 Marc-André Guay
☐ ☐ 37 Maxime Venne ☐ ☐ 38 Arduino Patuli
☐ ☐ 39 Shean Briffey ☐ ☐ 40 Michael Scalzo
☐ ☐ 41 Dino Fabrizio ☐ ☐ 42 Sébastien Dorval
☐ ☐ 43 Marco Painchaud ☐ ☐ 44 Marc Simon
☐ ☐ 45 Patrick Sagala ☐ ☐ 46 Martin Prince
☐ ☐ 47 Sean Mclean ☐ ☐ 48 Team Checklist

SPHINX DE ST. MARC-DES-CARRIÈRES

☐ ☐ 49 Éric Petitclerc ☐ ☐ 50 Tommy Tessier
☐ ☐ 51 Mathieu Perrault ☐ ☐ 52 Éric Trottier
☐ ☐ 53 J-F Garneau ☐ ☐ 54 Martin Naud
☐ ☐ 55 Steve Durocher ☐ ☐ 56 Frédéric Boivin
☐ ☐ 57 David Matte ☐ ☐ 58 Jérémy Soler
☐ ☐ 59 Pierre-Olivier Cantin ☐ ☐ 60 Rémy Marcotte
☐ ☐ 61 Jasmin Naud ☐ ☐ 62 Jonathan Perron
☐ ☐ 253 Kavin Coulombe ☐ ☐ 63 Team Checklist

LES ÉPERVIERS DE MASCOUCHE M.L.L.

☐ ☐ 64 Monelle Quevilleon ☐ ☐ 65 Hugo Lusignan
☐ ☐ 66 Patrick Girard ☐ ☐ 67 Mathieu St-Marc
☐ ☐ 68 Sacha Paquette ☐ ☐ 69 Dany Cloutier
☐ ☐ 70 Mike Pistilli ☐ ☐ 71 Martin Bourgeois
☐ ☐ 72 Dominic Ranzi ☐ ☐ 75 Ugo Larouche, Err #
☐ ☐ 74 Jocelyn Dubord ☐ ☐ 75 Marc-André Ménard
☐ ☐ 76 Jonathan Dionne ☐ ☐ 77 Benoit Dumont
☐ ☐ 78 François Boucher ☐ ☐ 79 Benoit Poirier
☐ ☐ 80 Team Checklist

NATIONAL LA PRESQU'ÎLE

☐ ☐ 81 John Volk ☐ ☐ 82 Jason Roy
☐ ☐ 83 Manuel Fréchette ☐ ☐ 84 Vincent Parent
☐ ☐ 85 Steve Madison ☐ ☐ 86 Patrice Di Cola
☐ ☐ 87 Jeremy Welik ☐ ☐ 88 Benoit Chénier
☐ ☐ 89 Marc Belhumeur ☐ ☐ 90 Olivier Lebrun
☐ ☐ 91 Martin Fréchette ☐ ☐ 92 Cedrick Noël
☐ ☐ 93 Mathieu Lefrançois ☐ ☐ 94 Richard Sweezey
☐ ☐ 95 Éric Legault ☐ ☐ 96 J-F Tousignant
☐ ☐ 97 Team Checklist

CARAVELLES DE L'ÉRABLE

☐ ☐ 98 Dominic Rouleau ☐ ☐ 99 Steeve Allaire
☐ ☐ 100 J-P Beaudoin ☐ ☐ 101 Yannick Rousseau
☐ ☐ 102 Éric Fortier ☐ ☐ 103 Ghislain Robichaud
☐ ☐ 104 A. Beaudoin ☐ ☐ 105 F. Beauchesne
☐ ☐ 106 Serge Crochetière ☐ ☐ 107 Domonic Gouin
☐ ☐ 108 J-P Parent ☐ ☐ 109 Frédéric Paris
☐ ☐ 110 Éric Vigneault ☐ ☐ 111 Sébastien Faucher
☐ ☐ 112 Tommy Sévigny ☐ ☐ 113 Hugues Filion
☐ ☐ 114 Team Checklist

SHERBROOKE MÉTROPOLITAIN

The most expensive singles is Éric Chouinard (card $2-3, McD's $4-6)

☐ ☐ 115 J. Baillargeon ☐ ☐ 116 Éric Chouinard
☐ ☐ 117 David Boissinot ☐ ☐ 118 Francis Côté
☐ ☐ 119 David Sylvain ☐ ☐ 120 F. Desrosiers
☐ ☐ 121 Simon Francoeur ☐ ☐ 122 Jasmin Gaudet
☐ ☐ 123 J-F Gagné ☐ ☐ 124 Yannick Gilbert
☐ ☐ 125 Alexandre Landry ☐ ☐ 126 Dave Laurendeau
☐ ☐ 127 P-Y Lemelin ☐ ☐ 128 Alexandre Lessard
☐ ☐ 129 J-F Pichette ☐ ☐ 130 Francis Trudeau
☐ ☐ 200 Pascal Langevin ☐ ☐ 131 Team Checklist

TIGRES LAC ST-LOUIS OUEST

☐ ☐ 132 Alexandre Tomaras ☐ ☐ 133 Martin Lavergne
☐ ☐ 134 Allen Morris ☐ ☐ 135 Nicholas Bilotto
☐ ☐ 136 Patrick Soucy ☐ ☐ 137 James Desmarais
☐ ☐ 138 Christian Pichette ☐ ☐ 139 Ryan Lubell-Smith
☐ ☐ 140 Marc Lauzon ☐ ☐ 141 Antoine Lejeune
☐ ☐ 142 Simon Prieur ☐ ☐ 143 John Lachance
☐ ☐ 144 James Davidson ☐ ☐ 145 Justin Humes
☐ ☐ 146 Shaun McCarty ☐ ☐ 147 Jonathan Lemy
☐ ☐ 148 Team Checklist

BANFF PEE WEE BEARS

☐ ☐ 149 Charlie Powderface ☐ ☐ 150 Paul Grygorasz
☐ ☐ 151 Mineki Yamada ☐ ☐ 152 Matt Stambaugh
☐ ☐ 153 Cody Seguin ☐ ☐ 154 Jared Smyth
☐ ☐ 155 Bobby Mason ☐ ☐ 156 Ken Okabe
☐ ☐ 157 Takeshi Miiyazoe ☐ ☐ 158 Shane Mooney
☐ ☐ 159 Marty Goulet ☐ ☐ 160 Taisuka Hasumi
☐ ☐ 161 Mike DeMichels ☐ ☐ 162 Patrick Goon
☐ ☐ 163 Michael Campbell ☐ ☐ 164 Warren Beddow
☐ ☐ 165 Team Checklist

CALGARY FLAMES

☐ ☐ 166 Oliver Powderface ☐ ☐ 167 Craig Dow
☐ ☐ 168 Mark Darrah ☐ ☐ 169 Ryan Epp
☐ ☐ 170 David Duncan ☐ ☐ 171 Matthew Johnson
☐ ☐ 172 Bobby Kendall ☐ ☐ 173 Derek Kogut
☐ ☐ 174 Colin Mah ☐ ☐ 175 Lawrence Nycholat
☐ ☐ 176 Darren Malin ☐ ☐ 177 Riley Papero
☐ ☐ 178 John Stady ☐ ☐ 179 Michael J. Zimmer
☐ ☐ 180 Joshua Woitas ☐ ☐ 181 Team Checklist

MOUNT PEARL BLADES

☐ ☐ 182 Cory Benson ☐ ☐ 183 Stephen Murphy
☐ ☐ 184 Ian Daley ☐ ☐ 185 Keith Rickert
☐ ☐ 186 Francis Mooney ☐ ☐ 187 Brad Kerrivan
☐ ☐ 188 Adam Nolan ☐ ☐ 189 Wesley McGuire
☐ ☐ 190 Matthew McGuire ☐ ☐ 191 Blair Evans
☐ ☐ 192 Chris Furlong ☐ ☐ 193 Chad Jarvis
☐ ☐ 194 Ryan Lauzon ☐ ☐ 195 Scott Clarke
☐ ☐ 196 Douglas Spurrell ☐ ☐ 197 Keith Evans
☐ ☐ 198 Mark Steele ☐ ☐ 199 Team Checklist

L'EXCEL CENTRE MAURICE

☐ ☐ 201 S. Van Den Elzen ☐ ☐ 202 Daniel St-Amant
☐ ☐ 203 Maxime Samson ☐ ☐ 204 Martin Quessy
☐ ☐ 205 Benoît St-Hilaire ☐ ☐ 206 Steve Mongrain
☐ ☐ 207 François Pichette ☐ ☐ 208 Francis Mongrain
☐ ☐ 209 Sébastien Huard ☐ ☐ 210 J-F Hamel
☐ ☐ 211 Tommi Houde ☐ ☐ 212 M-A Garceau
☐ ☐ 213 Hugo Gélinas ☐ ☐ 214 Simon Dessureault
☐ ☐ 215 Yannick Dupuis ☐ ☐ 216 Team Checklist

VICTORIAVILLE

☐ ☐ 217 Francis Rhéault ☐ ☐ 218 Yannick Allaire
☐ ☐ 219 Jonathan Picard ☐ ☐ 220 Samuel St-Pierre
☐ ☐ 221 Éric Côté ☐ ☐ 222 Michael Côté
☐ ☐ 223 David Roberge ☐ ☐ 224 Martin Tanguay
☐ ☐ 225 David Bilodeau ☐ ☐ 226 Yannick Bouchard
☐ ☐ 227 Éric Lecompte ☐ ☐ 228 Simon Roy
☐ ☐ 229 F. Olivier Lafond ☐ ☐ 230 Jean Régis
☐ ☐ 231 Dominic Vincent ☐ ☐ 232 Vincent Daigle
☐ ☐ 233 François Cloutier ☐ ☐ 234 Simon Mailhot
☐ ☐ 235 Team Checklist

LES CANOTIERS DE MONTMAGNY

☐ ☐ 236 J-P Morency ☐ ☐ 237 Jérôme Morin
☐ ☐ 238 Dominic Jacques ☐ ☐ 239 Martin Guinard
☐ ☐ 240 Guillaume Boulet ☐ ☐ 241 François Corriveau
☐ ☐ 242 Daniel Gaudreau ☐ ☐ 243 Réaume Caron
☐ ☐ 244 J-F Dubé ☐ ☐ 245 J-P Caron
☐ ☐ 246 Mathieu Lapierre ☐ ☐ 247 Steve Bernier
☐ ☐ 248 Alexandre Thibault ☐ ☐ 249 Yves Caron
☐ ☐ 250 Vincent Boulet ☐ ☐ 251 Mathieu Ringuet
☐ ☐ 252 Team Checklist

HARFANGS DE BEAUPORT

☐ ☐ 254 J-F Collia ☐ ☐ 255 David Lachance
☐ ☐ 256 Simon Villeneuve ☐ ☐ 257 C. Zounimbiat
☐ ☐ 258 Dominic Paradis ☐ ☐ 259 Joë Bussières
☐ ☐ 260 Nicholas Lemelin ☐ ☐ 261 Carl Labbé
☐ ☐ 262 Francis Dumont ☐ ☐ 263 Cédric Pouliot
☐ ☐ 264 Jean-Daniel Lavoie ☐ ☐ 265 Dominic Latouche
☐ ☐ 266 Frédéric Parent ☐ ☐ 267 Daniel Jobin
☐ ☐ 268 J-F Gauthier ☐ ☐ 269 Jonathan Fournier
☐ ☐ 270 Team Checklist

LADUFO CÔTE DE BEAUPRÉ

☐ ☐ 271 S. Malenfant ☐ ☐ 272 Simon Lajeunesse
☐ ☐ 273 Jasmyn Laroche ☐ ☐ 274 Danny Labbé
☐ ☐ 275 Dany Racine ☐ ☐ 276 Karl Giguère
☐ ☐ 277 Carl Ferland ☐ ☐ 278 Frédérick Verret
☐ ☐ 279 C. Lachance, Jr. ☐ ☐ 280 Éric Paquet
☐ ☐ 281 A. Tremblay ☐ ☐ 282 Jean Langevin
☐ ☐ 283 Carl Bussière ☐ ☐ 284 Bruno Julien
☐ ☐ 285 Claude Boucher ☐ ☐ 286 Frédéric Couture
☐ ☐ 287 Team Checklist

LES SEIGNEURS DE BEAUBOURG

☐ ☐ 288 Sylvain Turgeon ☐ ☐ 289 Jérôme Tremblay
☐ ☐ 290 Michael Thomassin ☐ ☐ 291 Frédérick Marcotte
☐ ☐ 292 J-F Lavoie ☐ ☐ 293 Philippe Lord
☐ ☐ 294 Simon Gauthier ☐ ☐ 295 Jimmy Lapointe
☐ ☐ 296 François Fortier ☐ ☐ 297 Patrick Fournel
☐ ☐ 298 Mathieu Chicoine ☐ ☐ 299 Daniel Chapados
☐ ☐ 300 P. De Carvalhos ☐ ☐ 301 F. Brindamour
☐ ☐ 302 Karl Bédard ☐ ☐ 303 Éric Boucher
☐ ☐ 304 Team Checklist

CHARNY-BERNIÈRES

☐ ☐ 305 Jean-François Ruel ☐ ☐ 306 Nicolas Pelletier
☐ ☐ 307 Jean-René Ouellet ☐ ☐ 308 David Paradis
☐ ☐ 309 Éric Martineau ☐ ☐ 310 Éric Lapierre
☐ ☐ 311 Alexandre Langlois ☐ ☐ 312 Éric Laflamme
☐ ☐ 313 Éric Genest ☐ ☐ 314 Jérôme Hinse
☐ ☐ 315 Marc Dubreuil ☐ ☐ 316 Sébastien Dubois
☐ ☐ 317 J-F Cantin ☐ ☐ 318 Laurent Bilodeau
☐ ☐ 319 Jérôme Allard ☐ ☐ 320 Mathieu Bergeron
☐ ☐ 321 Team Checklist

LAC-MÉGANTIC BESTAR

☐ ☐ 322 Mathieu Thérien ☐ ☐ 323 Simon Bilodeau
☐ ☐ 324 J-F Drouin ☐ ☐ 325 Éric Turmel
☐ ☐ 326 J-F Hallée ☐ ☐ 327 Berthier Poulin
☐ ☐ 328 Jérome Morin ☐ ☐ 329 Vincent Morin
☐ ☐ 330 Luc Tanguay ☐ ☐ 331 Julien Dostie
☐ ☐ 332 Rémy Gosselin ☐ ☐ 333 Michel Demers
☐ ☐ 334 Frédéric Michaud ☐ ☐ 335 M-A Lacroix
☐ ☐ 336 J. Clusiault ☐ ☐ 337 Steve Fortier
☐ ☐ 338 M. Charbonneau ☐ ☐ 339 François Paré
☐ ☐ 340 Team Checklist

LES GOUVERNEURS DE SAINTE-FOY

The most expensive single is Simon Gagné (card $10-15, McD's $22-30).

☐ ☐ 341 Patrick Alain ☐ ☐ 342 Simon Gagné
☐ ☐ 343 Dominick Samson ☐ ☐ 344 Dominic Soulard
☐ ☐ 345 Jonathan Beaulieu ☐ ☐ 346 Carl Ménard
☐ ☐ 347 Steve Boutet ☐ ☐ 348 J-F Damphousse
☐ ☐ 349 Benoit Dusablon ☐ ☐ 350 Sébastien Bédard
☐ ☐ 351 Marc-André Cantin ☐ ☐ 352 Mathieu Julien
☐ ☐ 353 Alexandre Rioux ☐ ☐ 354 Frédéric Thibault
☐ ☐ 355 P.M. Vaillancourt ☐ ☐ 356 Team Checklist

ÉLITE BEAUCE-AMIANTE

The most expensive singles is Alex Tanguay (card $5-10, McD's $8-15).

☐ ☐ 358 Philippe Cloutier ☐ ☐ 359 Mike Allen
☐ ☐ 360 Éric Binet ☐ ☐ 361 Karl Fortier
☐ ☐ 362 J-P Cliche ☐ ☐ 363 Marco Lachance
☐ ☐ 364 Philippe Cliche ☐ ☐ 365 Jason Lehoux
☐ ☐ 366 Jérôme Nadeau ☐ ☐ 367 Charles Paré
☐ ☐ 368 Martin Roy ☐ ☐ 369 Kevin Marcoux
☐ ☐ 370 J-F Tanguay ☐ ☐ 371 Francis Binet
☐ ☐ 372 Vincent Boulianne ☐ ☐ 523 Alex Tanguay
☐ ☐ 373 Team Checklist

NATIONAL DE LA BAIE

☐ ☐ 374 David Boudreault ☐ ☐ 375 Patrice Morin
☐ ☐ 376 J-F Minier ☐ ☐ 377 Michaël Harvey
☐ ☐ 378 Cédric Boivin ☐ ☐ 379 Daniel Maltais
☐ ☐ 380 J-P Gagné ☐ ☐ 381 Dave McNicoll
☐ ☐ 382 Steve Gagné ☐ ☐ 383 Steeve Laberge
☐ ☐ 384 Marc-André Boivin ☐ ☐ 385 Patrice Boudreault
☐ ☐ 386 Pierre-Luc Gobeil ☐ ☐ 387 Éric Bélanger
☐ ☐ 388 S. Tremblay ☐ ☐ 389 Donald Lavoie
☐ ☐ 390 Team Checklist

BEAUCE-CENTRE

☐ ☐ 391 Frédéric Paré ☐ ☐ 392 Jonathan Poulin
☐ ☐ 393 Julien Veilleux ☐ ☐ 394 Jérôme Roy
☐ ☐ 395 Charles Fortin ☐ ☐ 396 Junior Lessard
☐ ☐ 397 Pierre-Jean Roy ☐ ☐ 398 Keven Cloutier
☐ ☐ 399 J-P Lessard ☐ ☐ 400 Mathieu Lachance
☐ ☐ 401 Simon Veilleux ☐ ☐ 402 Philippe Boily
☐ ☐ 403 Dominic Bourret ☐ ☐ 404 Maxime Paris
☐ ☐ 405 Julien Boudreault ☐ ☐ 406 Vincent Maheux
☐ ☐ 407 Team Checklist

CHAMPLAIN DE RICHELIEU

☐ ☐ 408 Steve Farnham ☐ ☐ 409 David St-Germain
☐ ☐ 410 Olivier Fontaine ☐ ☐ 411 Yann Joseph
☐ ☐ 412 L.A. Lehoux ☐ ☐ 413 Patrice Boijoli
☐ ☐ 414 Étienne Pagé ☐ ☐ 415 Alexandre Lessnick
☐ ☐ 416 Olivier Duguay ☐ ☐ 417 J-F Boulay
☐ ☐ 418 Jason Mihalik ☐ ☐ 419 Steve Simoes
☐ ☐ 420 Nicolas Rousseau ☐ ☐ 421 Guy Lamontagne
☐ ☐ 422 Jonathan Pilotte ☐ ☐ 423 Team Checklist

FAUCONS POINTE-LÉVY

☐ ☐ 424 Dominic Vincent ☐ ☐ 425 J.S. Grudelle
☐ ☐ 426 Jérôme Fournier ☐ ☐ 427 Éric Carrier
☐ ☐ 428 Pierre-Luc Hins ☐ ☐ 429 M-A Fournier
☐ ☐ 430 Martin Brisson ☐ ☐ 431 Jérôme Dumont
☐ ☐ 432 Sébastien Caron ☐ ☐ 433 Jean-Philippe Guay
☐ ☐ 434 Jean-Philippe Dion ☐ ☐ 435 G. Chamberland
☐ ☐ 436 Maxime Demers ☐ ☐ 437 Pascal Aubut
☐ ☐ 438 Grégoire LeBlanc ☐ ☐ 439 David Guérette
☐ ☐ 440 Team Checklist

LES RÉGENTS RIVE-SUD

☐ ☐ 441 Nicolas Bougie ☐ ☐ 442 Martin Poirier
☐ ☐ 443 Brian Laflamme ☐ ☐ 444 Sébastien Allard
☐ ☐ 445 Pierre Julien ☐ ☐ 446 Jérôme Marcotte
☐ ☐ 447 S-P Blouin ☐ ☐ 448 Nicolas Demers
☐ ☐ 449 L-C Warren ☐ ☐ 450 Simon Fontaine
☐ ☐ 451 Jonathan Roy ☐ ☐ 452 Martin Gionet
☐ ☐ 453 Tommy Larochelle ☐ ☐ 454 Patrick Boivin
☐ ☐ 455 Patrick Boulay ☐ ☐ 456 Maxime Boucher
☐ ☐ 457 Team Checklist

ÉLANS DE CHARLESBOURG

☐ ☐ 458 Hugo Welsh ☐ ☐ 459 Jonathan Verreault
☐ ☐ 460 S-P Gingras ☐ ☐ 461 Séb. Létourneau
☐ ☐ 462 Olivier Morin ☐ ☐ 463 Dominick Giguère
☐ ☐ 464 Yanick Bérubé ☐ ☐ 465 Frédérick Pépin
☐ ☐ 466 Nicolas Doré ☐ ☐ 467 Patrick Mathieu
☐ ☐ 468 Jocelyn Dugré ☐ ☐ 469 Marc Lafrance
☐ ☐ 470 Éric Grenier ☐ ☐ 471 Vincent Roy
☐ ☐ 472 Bryan Cooper ☐ ☐ 473 Olivier Simard
☐ ☐ 474 Team Checklist

TORONTO YOUNG NATIONALS

☐ ☐ 475 Andrew Robillard ☐ ☐ 476 Stuart Gowans
☐ ☐ 477 Mike DePetrillo ☐ ☐ 478 Cody Leibel
☐ ☐ 479 Jamie Drover ☐ ☐ 480 Gian. Innocentin
☐ ☐ 481 Greg Willers ☐ ☐ 482 Michael Laceby
☐ ☐ 483 Brett Cerqua ☐ ☐ 484 Craig Mumby
☐ ☐ 485 Eddie Fines ☐ ☐ 486 Andrew Kirwin
☐ ☐ 487 Marc Ancheloni ☐ ☐ 488 Bryan Pandovski
☐ ☐ 1699 Kevin McKeown ☐ ☐ 1700 Chris. McKeown
☐ ☐ 489 Team Checklist

NORTH YORK CANADIENS

☐ ☐ 490 Michael Ignatz ☐ ☐ 491 Jason Hurlbut
☐ ☐ 492 Adrano Fiacconi ☐ ☐ 493 Jeremy Wenzel
☐ ☐ 494 Andrew Ritchie ☐ ☐ 495 Robert Meanchoff
☐ ☐ 496 Craig Telfer ☐ ☐ 497 Willis Shawana
☐ ☐ 498 Anton Strgacic ☐ ☐ 499 David Delmonte
☐ ☐ 500 Andrew Taylor ☐ ☐ 501 Ken Fox
☐ ☐ 502 Colin Nash ☐ ☐ 503 Simon Bieber
☐ ☐ 504 Morris Fabrizi ☐ ☐ 505 Team Checklist

HALIFAX HAWKS

☐ ☐ 506 Tom Baxter ☐ ☐ 507 Pat Berrigan
☐ ☐ 508 Paul Dunphy ☐ ☐ 509 Matt Fry
☐ ☐ 510 Matt Jardine ☐ ☐ 511 Alex Johnstone
☐ ☐ 512 Peter Lawrence ☐ ☐ 513 Andrew Lowery
☐ ☐ 514 Scott McPhee ☐ ☐ 515 Pat Miller
☐ ☐ 516 Tim Moran ☐ ☐ 517 Anthony Purchase
☐ ☐ 518 Mike Quackenbush ☐ ☐ 519 Matt Stephens
☐ ☐ 520 Jeff Sutherland ☐ ☐ 521 John Walker
☐ ☐ 522 Team Checklist

CHARLEVOIX

☐ ☐ 524 Frédéric Bergeron ☐ ☐ 525 Pascal McNicoll
☐ ☐ 526 Pascal Lavoie ☐ ☐ 527 A. Vigneault
☐ ☐ 528 Sébastien Harvey ☐ ☐ 529 Mathieu Boulianne
☐ ☐ 530 Ian Belisle ☐ ☐ 531 Daniel Boulianne
☐ ☐ 532 Pascal Turcotte ☐ ☐ 533 Frédéric Harvey
☐ ☐ 534 Jérôme Tremblay ☐ ☐ 535 Patrick Sullivan
☐ ☐ 536 Yan Chouinard ☐ ☐ 537 Pascal Fillion
☐ ☐ 538 Sylvain Plamondon ☐ ☐ 539 Jean-Luc Néron
☐ ☐ 540 Martin Dufour ☐ ☐ 541 Team Checklist

PETERBOROUGH

The most expensive singles is Jay Legault (card $1-2, McD's $2-4).

☐ ☐ 542 Robert Kitchen ☐ ☐ 543 Shaun Hartwick
☐ ☐ 544 Adam Collins ☐ ☐ 545 Scott Johnson
☐ ☐ 546 Chris Kerr ☐ ☐ 547 Scott Self
☐ ☐ 548 Aaron Shill ☐ ☐ 549 Kelly Sullivan
☐ ☐ 550 Josh Burdick ☐ ☐ 551 Darren Mahoney
☐ ☐ 552 Stephen Evans ☐ ☐ 553 Nick Robinson
☐ ☐ 554 Jay Legault ☐ ☐ 555 Joel Johnston
☐ ☐ 556 Brad McCamus ☐ ☐ 557 Craig O'Brien
☐ ☐ 558 Joey Lester ☐ ☐ 559 Team Checklist

MAPLE LEAFS DE TORONTO

The most expensive singles are Daniel Tkaczuk (card $2-3, McD's $3-5), Peter Sarno (card $1-2, McD's $2-4).

☐ ☐ 560 Joey Arko ☐ ☐ 561 Luke MacBride
☐ ☐ 562 Daniel Tkaczuk ☐ ☐ 563 Steve Montabor
☐ ☐ 564 Matt Sirman ☐ ☐ 565 Peter Sarno
☐ ☐ 566 Sam Katsuras ☐ ☐ 567 Darryl Slaney
☐ ☐ 568 Damien Medina ☐ ☐ 569 Brad Gladwish
☐ ☐ 570 Justin Norwood ☐ ☐ 571 Darryl Somerville
☐ ☐ 572 Brant Somerville ☐ ☐ 573 Danny Nicoletti
☐ ☐ 574 Erik Epner ☐ ☐ 575 Team Checklist

SMITH FALLS BEARS

☐ ☐ 576 Matte Thake ☐ ☐ 577 Mason Black
☐ ☐ 578 Jed Thompson ☐ ☐ 579 Larry Leadbeater
☐ ☐ 580 Kris Loughren ☐ ☐ 581 Robert Garvin
☐ ☐ 582 Dan Stranberg ☐ ☐ 583 Greg Pilon
☐ ☐ 584 Keith Abbass ☐ ☐ 585 Ryan Poll
☐ ☐ 586 Derrick Rathwell ☐ ☐ 587 Jon Hull
☐ ☐ 588 David Ambler ☐ ☐ 589 Shaun Johnson
☐ ☐ 590 Jason Fielding ☐ ☐ 591 Team Checklist

SOUTH SHORE KINGS

The most expensive singles is Paul Mara (card $2-3, McD's $4-6).

☐ ☐ 592 Paul Nihigian ☐ ☐ 593 Ryan Murray
☐ ☐ 594 Mike Murray ☐ ☐ 595 Mike Morrison

□ □ 596 Nick Mosca □ □ 597 Paul Mara
□ □ 598 Mike Maturo □ □ 599 R.J. Longchamps
□ □ 600 Pat Libitz □ □ 602 Chris Knight
□ □ 603 Bob Gordon □ □ 604 Mike Higgins
□ □ 605 Lauren Goldstein □ □ 606 Chris Dyment
□ □ 607 Adam Bouchard □ □ 608 John Petricig
□ □ 609 Team Checklist

SAN JOSE SHARKS

□ □ 610 Nic Guida □ □ 611 Ryan Jones
□ □ 612 Andy Quandt □ □ 613 Jim Truitt
□ □ 614 Gary Levy □ □ 615 Tye Nielsen
□ □ 616 Margan McShan □ □ 617 George Kiessling
□ □ 618 Josh McGuire □ □ 619 Jason Luker
□ □ 620 C.J. MacDonald □ □ 621 Scott Feeney
□ □ 622 Tommy Reed □ □ 623 Billy Cox
□ □ 624 Aaron Kocian □ □ 625 Team Checklist

LYNNFIELD PIONEERS

□ □ 626 Todd Boling □ □ 627 Tom Manning
□ □ 628 Sean McKeever □ □ 629 Bernie Caniff
□ □ 630 Taylor Morrison □ □ 631 Michael Brainerd
□ □ 632 Joe Burns □ □ 633 James Aborn
□ □ 634 Ben Santonelli □ □ 635 Scott Conley
□ □ 636 Danny Skinner □ □ 637 Eric Silva
□ □ 638 Justin Stone □ □ 639 Jamie Dalton
□ □ 640 Michael Wendt □ □ 641 Brendon Hughes
□ □ 642 Team Checklist

BOSTON JR. BRAVES

□ □ 643 John Vereker □ □ 644 Mike Di Mella
□ □ 645 Nick De Monico □ □ 646 Joey Roy
□ □ 647 Jeff Perry □ □ 648 Carl Corazzini
□ □ 649 T.J. Scaparotti □ □ 650 Tim Vafides
□ □ 651 Eddie Owens □ □ 652 Jim Quigley
□ □ 653 Nick Kreus □ □ 654 Jackie Wallace
□ □ 655 Ryan Bailey □ □ 656 Chris Gannon
□ □ 657 Dan Genovese □ □ 658 Tom Gottwald
□ □ 659 Eric Langley □ □ 660 Bob Donovan
□ □ 661 Darrell Doucette □ □ 662 Ben Oberto
□ □ 663 Team Checklist

SYRACUSE STARS

The most expensive singles is Tim Connolly (card $5-7, McD's $10-12).

□ □ 664 Tim Connolly ($5-8) □ □ 665 Justin Brown
□ □ 667 Jon Downs □ □ 668 Brian Ford
□ □ 669 Nicole Kirnan □ □ 670 Brad Wolcott
□ □ 671 Rob Krenrich □ □ 672 Bratt Merritt
□ □ 673 Chris Madden □ □ 674 Bill Palmer
□ □ 675 Matt Murley □ □ 676 Dominick Sereno
□ □ 677 Don Patrick □ □ 678 Matt Weber
□ □ 679 Tim Stay □ □ 680 Dana Hopps
□ □ 681 Tom Williams □ □ 682 Team Checklist

BOSTON JR. BRUINS

□ □ 683 Ben Weiss □ □ 684 J.P. Berkery
□ □ 685 Scott Cooper □ □ 686 Jay Gleason
□ □ 687 Tim Wood □ □ 688 Bobby Young
□ □ 689 Joseph Russo □ □ 690 Ryan Maher
□ □ 691 Greg Mitchell □ □ 692 John Lynch
□ □ 693 Eric Wood □ □ 694 Chris Goulart
□ □ 695 Adam Aguilar □ □ 696 Matt Langille
□ □ 697 Jonathan Morse □ □ 698 Jason LeBlanc
□ □ 699 Greg Berks □ □ 700 Brian Beaton
□ □ 701 Brendon Cashman □ □ 702 Team Checklist

CHICAGO BLACKHAWKS

The most expensive singles is Nikos Tselios (card $2-3, McD's $3-6).

□ □ 703 Chris Cichon □ □ 704 Nikos Tselios
□ □ 705 Mike Chesney □ □ 706 Dan Cotuno
□ □ 707 Darren Malia □ □ 708 Chris Henning
□ □ 709 Paul Caponigri □ □ 710 Kevin Spiewak
□ □ 711 Marc Harris □ □ 712 Eric T. Richardson
□ □ 713 W. P. Rutherford □ □ 714 Chris Knupp
□ □ 715 Matt Snyder □ □ 716 Alex Katz
□ □ 717 Matt Donan □ □ 718 Kris Koski
□ □ 719 Chris Campbell □ □ 720 Team Checklist

NEW JERSEY DEVILS

□ □ 721 Craig Casella □ □ 722 Derek Fisher
□ □ 723 Philip Lagola □ □ 724 Kyle Frigon
□ □ 725 Jesse Elhai □ □ 726 Bryan Eberenz
□ □ 727 Tommy Nastasi □ □ 728 Joshua Mandel
□ □ 729 Gary Tashjian □ □ 730 Scott Dutcher
□ □ 731 Nick Vlasidis □ □ 732 Danny Perry
□ □ 733 Michael Sweeney □ □ 734 Joshua Goldfarb
□ □ 735 Andor Kish □ □ 736 Michael Sarro
□ □ 737 Team Checklist

TAMPA BAY LIGHTNING

□ □ 738 Jesse Goldstein □ □ 739 Scott Driscoll
□ □ 740 Jason Fogelson □ □ 741 Derek Nowak
□ □ 742 David Dymnicki □ □ 743 David Saunders
□ □ 744 Sean O'Neill □ □ 745 Curt Colarullo
□ □ 746 Kayser Dixon □ □ 747 Scott Lensky
□ □ 748 David Cohen □ □ 749 Tim Neary
□ □ 750 Jaime Moorhead □ □ 751 Christian Sturz
□ □ 752 John Boynton □ □ 753 Ryan Fitzgerald
□ □ 754 Jeff Guiliano □ □ 755 Chris Lombardo
□ □ 756 Team Checklist

PITTSBURGH PENGUINS

□ □ 757 Jordan Spallone □ □ 758 Gene Spadaro
□ □ 759 Michael Roth □ □ 760 Derek Powell
□ □ 761 Sean Murphy □ □ 762 Michael Conley
□ □ 763 Nathan Kush □ □ 764 Marty Martorelli
□ □ 765 Justin Kenepp □ □ 766 Ryan Bollard
□ □ 767 Jeff Bevacqua □ □ 768 Kevin Barefoot
□ □ 769 Brandon Marian □ □ 770 Ryan Patrick
□ □ 771 Josh Allison □ □ 772 Team Checklist

HERSHEY CUBS

□ □ 773 Seth Schell □ □ 774 Eric Schork
□ □ 775 Ryan Nade □ □ 776 Ryan Haley
□ □ 777 Bruce Bingman □ □ 778 Zach Stauffer
□ □ 779 Roald Llado □ □ 780 Nate Tulli
□ □ 781 Sean Knaub □ □ 782 Tony Morrell
□ □ 783 Ethan Holmes □ □ 784 B.J. Heckendorn
□ □ 785 David Thomas □ □ 786 T. Willits-Kelley
□ □ 787 John Heitsenrether □ □ 788 Dan Zorger
□ □ 789 Nick Castelli □ □ 790 Jon Kuhn
□ □ 791 Kevin Hollenbush □ □ 792 Team Checklist

BUFFALO SABRES

□ □ 793 David Cavanaugh □ □ 794 Keith Kashuba
□ □ 795 Rick Poveromo □ □ 796 Blue Hill
□ □ 797 Ron Smith □ □ 798 Justin Spicer
□ □ 799 Jeremy Osborne □ □ 800 Scott Wojcinski
□ □ 801 Nik Fattey □ □ 802 Nick Wierzba
□ □ 803 Mark D'Agostino □ □ 804 Mike Kauzala
□ □ 805 Sean Lafferty □ □ 806 J. Obstarczyk
□ □ 807 Jason Snusz □ □ 808 Jeff Alotta
□ □ 809 Team Checklist

HARTFORD WHALERS

□ □ 810 Eric Albano □ □ 811 Alain Solesky
□ □ 812 Joe Carpenter □ □ 813 Ryan Beauvais
□ □ 814 Scott Cunningham □ □ 815 Luke Earl
□ □ 816 R.J. Gates □ □ 817 Eric Gustason
□ □ 818 Craig Laramee □ □ 819 Chuck Kaiton
□ □ 820 Gregg Reynolds □ □ 821 Kris Vrolyk
□ □ 822 B.L. Reid □ □ 823 Justin Picone
□ □ 824 Mike Mello □ □ 825 Jon Veisor
□ □ 826 Rob Martin

BEVERLY

□ □ 828 Chris Maniatis □ □ 829 Myles Dudley
□ □ 830 Chris Torri □ □ 831 Nick Stead
□ □ 832 Mick Philbin □ □ 833 Peter Catalano
□ □ 834 T.C. Harris □ □ 835 N. Dimitrakos
□ □ 836 Shaun Sutter □ □ 837 Al Salvia
□ □ 838 Brian Marcaurelle □ □ 839 Peter Metcalf
□ □ 840 Adam Kozlowski □ □ 841 Mark Nunan
□ □ 842 Sean Donahue □ □ 843 Gary Ford
□ □ 844 Chris Connolly □ □ 845 D.J. Gravell

MICHIGAN NATIONALS

□ □ 847 Mike Vigilante □ □ 848 Jeff Reynaert
□ □ 849 Jeff Pustulka □ □ 850 J.P. Piontek
□ □ 851 Jesse Paul □ □ 852 Larry Mylek
□ □ 853 Ryan Melnechuk □ □ 854 Jerod Lutz
□ □ 855 Josh Johnson □ □ 856 Brandon Love
□ □ 857 Jake Heisler □ □ 858 Patrick Jesue
□ □ 859 Brad Fraser □ □ 860 David Hague
□ □ 861 Jesse Cortez □ □ 862 Chris Desjardins
□ □ 863 Scott Abraham □ □ 864 Jeremy Bachusz
□ □ 865 Team Checklist, Err.

MINNESOTA NORTH STAR

The most expensive singles is Brian Gionta (card $4-6, McD's $10-12).

□ □ 866 Lou Ferrari □ □ 867 Chris Dietz
□ □ 868 Sean Corcoran □ □ 869 Gerry Snyder
□ □ 870 Anthony Scorsone □ □ 871 Don Phillips
□ □ 872 S. McSweeney □ □ 873 B.J. Busch
□ □ 874 Kyle Langdon □ □ 875 Chuckie Healey
□ □ 876 Cameron Boyd □ □ 877 Brian Gionta
□ □ 878 Justin Booth □ □ 879 Shawn Fowler
□ □ 880 Scott Behrens □ □ 881 Mack Hodges
□ □ 882 Justin Knight □ □ 883 Team Checklist

ST-LOUIS BLUES

□ □ 884 Bobby Kern □ □ 885 Brian Elder
□ □ 886 Andrew Geiger □ □ 887 Christopher Kellogg
□ □ 888 Matt Knop □ □ 889 Trevor Rice-Wood
□ □ 890 Brad Bokal □ □ 891 Mark Turnipseed
□ □ 892 Tom Kaiman □ □ 893 Gary Opitz
□ □ 894 Geoff Hartwig □ □ 895 Justin Baisch
□ □ 896 Joseph Cabo □ □ 897 Mike Summers
□ □ 898 Timothy Carbery □ □ 899 Mike Jost
□ □ 900 Travis Rice-Wood □ □ 901 Team Checklist

SÉLECTS DU NORD

□ □ 902 Benoit Vézina □ □ 903 Jonathan Girard
□ □ 904 Patrick Léveillé □ □ 905 Guillaume Barbe
□ □ 906 Francis Lalande □ □ 907 Benoit Laroche
□ □ 908 David Ouellette □ □ 909 D. St-Germain
□ □ 910 Daniel Brouillard □ □ 911 Éric Bertrand
□ □ 912 Luc Vachon □ □ 913 Éric Pinoul
□ □ 914 Guillaume Marcoux □ □ 915 Julien Louis-Seize
□ □ 916 Éric Desjardins □ □ 917 Team Checklist

ST-GEORGES

□ □ 918 A. Mottand □ □ 919 J-F Lavoie
□ □ 920 Éric Talbot □ □ 921 Pascal Paradis
□ □ 922 Frédéric Deblois □ □ 923 Marco Grondin
□ □ 924 David Lessard □ □ 925 Mathieu Pouliot
□ □ 926 Vincent Gonthier □ □ 927 Sébastien Vachon
□ □ 928 Rémy Doyon □ □ 929 Jean-Pierre Talbot
□ □ 930 Steve Leclair □ □ 931 Louis-Jean Labbé
□ □ 932 Marc Poulin □ □ 933 Éric Grenier
□ □ 934 Team Checklist

LAC-ETCHEMIN

□ □ 935 Rémi Gilbert □ □ 936 Patrice Giguère
□ □ 937 Pierre Bouchard □ □ 938 Alexandre Audet
□ □ 939 Dominic Drouin □ □ 940 Philippe Deblois
□ □ 941 Jean-François Côté □ □ 942 Marco Bouffard
□ □ 943 Johny Carrier □ □ 944 Philippe Deblois
□ □ 945 Pierre-Luc Gégin □ □ 946 J-P Chabot
□ □ 947 S. Carbonneau □ □ 948 Stéphane Turcott
□ □ 949 Jérôme Drouin □ □ 950 Bernard Lachance
□ □ 951 Team Checklist

CASCADES – AMOS

□ □ 952 Terry Rankin □ □ 953 Christian Viens
□ □ 954 Luis Arseneault □ □ 955 Hervé Gagnon
□ □ 956 J-F Caron □ □ 957 Daniel Massé
□ □ 958 Dave McCann □ □ 959 Jérôme Petit
□ □ 960 Jonathan Audet □ □ 961 Simon Lavoie
□ □ 962 Martin Rondeau □ □ 963 Jonathan Lemerise
□ □ 964 B. Constantineau □ □ 965 Sébastien Audet
□ □ 966 Michel Bolduc □ □ 967 Team Checklist

SÉLECTS DE SAINTE-FOY

□ □ 968 Alexis Beaudouin □ □ 969 François Houde
□ □ 970 M-M Lavoie □ □ 971 Mathieu Louder
□ □ 972 Marc Forrier □ □ 973 François Béland
□ □ 974 Dominic Jolin □ □ 975 Jean-René Plante
□ □ 976 J-P Émard □ □ 977 Martin Bouffard
□ □ 978 J-P Côté □ □ 979 Mathieu Ouellet
□ □ 980 Luc Brisson □ □ 981 Paul Blanchard
□ □ 982 J-F Plante □ □ 983 Steve Jobidon
□ □ 984 Team Checklist

ROYAUX DE SAINTE-FOY

□ □ 985 Marc-André Poirier □ □ 986 J-S Poulin
□ □ 987 Charles Gélinas □ □ 988 Vincent Lecompte
□ □ 989 Guillaume Brochu □ □ 990 Dennis Burns
□ □ 991 Kevin Bélanger □ □ 992 Alexandre Born
□ □ 993 Dave Gagnon □ □ 994 J-F Doyon
□ □ 995 Patrick Lachance □ □ 996 L-V Lemelin
□ □ 997 Santino De Toni □ □ 998 G-C Gosselin
□ □ 999 Yanick Fiset □ □ 1000 Team Checklist

LES ÉPAULARDS

□ □ 1001 J-P Côté □ □ 1002 Simon Bussières
□ □ 1003 Kim Cloutier □ □ 1004 Jean-Luc Martin
□ □ 1005 Mathieu Lelièvre □ □ 1006 Jasmin Thibault
□ □ 1007 Steve Fortin □ □ 1008 Éric Martin
□ □ 1009 J. Harbour □ □ 1010 Martin Fournier
□ □ 1011 Sami Jalbert □ □ 1012 François Monier
□ □ 1013 Kevin Lapointe □ □ 1014 J-F Dionne
□ □ 1015 Frédéric Dreyer □ □ 1016 Gyslain Thibault
□ □ 1017 David Whittom □ □ 1018 David Cantin
□ □ 1019 J-F Sylvain □ □ 1020 Team Checklist

POINTE-LÉVY

□ □ 1021 Charles Latulippe □ □ 1022 Frédéric Nadeau
□ □ 1023 J-F Nolet □ □ 1024 M. L'Hébreux
□ □ 1025 L-C Garant □ □ 1026 V. L. Ramsay
□ □ 1027 J-P Morin □ □ 1028 Mario Vallières
□ □ 1029 J. Levasseur □ □ 1030 Nicolas Carrier
□ □ 1031 Maxime Perreault □ □ 1032 Jérôme Guay
□ □ 1033 Dave Labrecque □ □ 1034 N. Vaillancourt
□ □ 1035 Éric Carrier □ □ 1036 L-O Gervais
□ □ 1037 Team Checklist

SEIGNEURS DES MILLE ÎLES

The most expensive singles is Philippe Sauvé (card $2-4, McD's $4-8).

□ □ 1038 J-F Gamelin □ □ 1039 J-F Fortier
□ □ 1040 Cédric Bourgeois □ □ 1041 Pascal Brazeau
□ □ 1042 A. Lachance □ □ 1043 Benoit Lacasse
□ □ 1044 Michel Lachaine □ □ 1045 Pascal Dupuis
□ □ 1046 Frédéric Girard □ □ 1047 David Comeau
□ □ 1048 S. Deschatelets □ □ 1049 Jonathan Cécile
□ □ 1050 J-P Cloutier □ □ 1051 M. Villeneuve
□ □ 1052 Sébastien Matte □ □ 1053 P. Sauvé (G)
□ □ 1054 Team Checklist

BELLECHASSE

□ □ 1055 Joel Couture □ □ 1056 Vincent Caron
□ □ 1057 Stéphane Blouin □ □ 1058 Steve Bédard
□ □ 1059 Olivier Moreau □ □ 1060 S. Thivierge
□ □ 1061 R. Lamontagne □ □ 1062 Patrice Labrecque
□ □ 1063 J-F Roy □ □ 1064 Jonathan Argouin
□ □ 1065 R. Gagné, Jr. □ □ 1066 Olivier Dumais
□ □ 1067 Patrice Lachance □ □ 1068 Mathieu Patry
□ □ 1069 Vincent Gravel □ □ 1070 Raby Philippe
□ □ 1071 Team Checklist

FRONTENAC DE QUÉBEC

□ □ 1072 Yannick Turcotte □ □ 1073 Denis Vaillancourt
□ □ 1074 Carl Rousseau □ □ 1075 Mathieu Tanguay
□ □ 1076 Jonathan Petit □ □ 1077 Olivier Marier
□ □ 1078 Martin Légaré □ □ 1079 Justin Lemay
□ □ 1080 J-F Fortin □ □ 1081 Éric Dumont
□ □ 1082 Luc Dantine □ □ 1083 Stéphane Demers
□ □ 1084 Sébastien Cimon □ □ 1085 François Cantin
□ □ 1086 M-C Allard □ □ 1087 Nicolas Brown
□ □ 1088 Team Checklist

CAVALIERS DE SAINTE-FOY

□ □ 1089 Dave Tessier □ □ 1090 Vincent Ruel
□ □ 1091 Martin Roy □ □ 1092 Jérôme Fréchette
□ □ 1093 J-S Angers □ □ 1094 Jacmin Fiset
□ □ 1095 David Barabé □ □ 1096 Nelson Lévesque
□ □ 1097 Nicolas Jolin □ □ 1098 Korran Rivers
□ □ 1099 Fracis Mainguy □ □ 1100 François Mecteau
□ □ 1101 Daniel Auclair □ □ 1102 Jérôme Lessard
□ □ 1103 Dominic Carignan □ □ 1104 Chantale Maheux
□ □ 1105 David Grenier □ □ 1106 Team Checklist

NORDIQUES DE QUÉBEC

□ □ 1107 Isabelle Simon □ □ 1108 François Latulippe
□ □ 1109 Carl Gosselin □ □ 1110 Benoit Langlois
□ □ 1111 Patrice Auger □ □ 1112 Philippe Grondin
□ □ 1113 François Fortin □ □ 1114 Tommy Thibault
□ □ 1115 David Côté □ □ 1116 Danny Bernier
□ □ 1117 D. Laflamme □ □ 1118 L. De Beaumont
□ □ 1119 J-F Filion □ □ 1120 M. Deslauriers
□ □ 1121 S. Desnoyers □ □ 1122 Guy Roy
□ □ 1123 Team Checklist

SAGUENÉENS DE CHICOUTIMI

□ □ 1124 S. Melançon □ □ 1125 Charles Turgeon
□ □ 1126 Philippe Matteau □ □ 1127 Jean Étienne
□ □ 1128 Jean Hamel □ □ 1129 Luc Langlois
□ □ 1130 Étienne Guay □ □ 1131 Pascal Gauthier
□ □ 1132 J-M Drolet □ □ 1133 Érik Gagnon
□ □ 1134 Patrice Côté □ □ 1135 É. De Champlain
□ □ 1136 Simon Boivin □ □ 1137 Alexandre Boutin
□ □ 1138 Dominic Boily □ □ 1139 Charles Boily
□ □ 1140 Team Checklist

EDMONTON OILERS

The most expensive singles is Mike Comrie (card $10-15, McD's $22-30).

□ □ 1141 Mark Woytiuk □ □ 1142 Pat Stachniak
□ □ 1143 Mike Starrett □ □ 1144 Tim Salter
□ □ 1145 Andy Penny □ □ 1146 Oliver McGee
□ □ 1147 Charles Mietcalfe □ □ 1148 Shane McDodeye
□ □ 1149 Jeremy Glasgow □ □ 1150 Joey Bastien
□ □ 1151 Mike Graves □ □ 1152 Mike Comrie
□ □ 1153 Greg Dowell □ □ 1154 Rick Dowell
□ □ 1155 Paul Esdale □ □ 1156 Lloyd Fobes
□ □ 1157 Richard Forest □ □ 1158 Team Checklist

RICHMOND HILL

□ □ 1159 Richard Charter □ □ 1160 Sean Hodges
□ □ 1161 Philip Barski □ □ 1162 Robert Diblasio
□ □ 1163 John Gallo □ □ 1164 Kevin Baker
□ □ 1165 Jeffrey Morrison □ □ 1166 Adrian Firmani
□ □ 1167 Dominic Walters □ □ 1168 Thomas Jason Hill
□ □ 1169 Steven Pocock □ □ 1170 Anthony Doria
□ □ 1171 Gregory Dunlap □ □ 1172 Kenneth Dunlap
□ □ 1173 Trevor Padgett □ □ 1174 Peter Genua
□ □ 1175 Team Checklist

OAKVILLE

□ □ 1176 Adam Rosso □ □ 1177 Todd McNaught
□ □ 1178 Adam Richards □ □ 1179 Scott Nelson
□ □ 1180 André Kalata □ □ 1181 Jeff Kubacki
□ □ 1182 Kirk Joudrey □ □ 1183 Sasha Frankovic
□ □ 1184 Jeff Wilson □ □ 1185 Chad Blundy
□ □ 1186 Jason Gauthier □ □ 1187 Chris Kline
□ □ 1188 Michael Muldoon □ □ 1189 Ross Fiore
□ □ 1190 Curtis Hamilton □ □ 1191 Brad McDonald
□ □ 1192 Team Checklist

BERESFORD

□ □ 1193 Jeanot Savoie □ □ 1194 Christian Roy
□ □ 1195 Éric Roy □ □ 1196 Paul Ross
□ □ 1197 Martin Paré □ □ 1198 Sébastien Paradis
□ □ 1199 Andrew Milton □ □ 1200 Érik Gionet
□ □ 1201 Kyle Jamieson □ □ 1202 Jim Gallant
□ □ 1203 Stéphane Fortin □ □ 1204 Philippe Cormier
□ □ 1205 Ricky Doucet □ □ 1206 Craig Branch
□ □ 1207 Ghislain Bryar □ □ 1208 André Leblanc
□ □ 1209 Hugues Michaud □ □ 1210 Team Checklist

NORTH RIVER

□ □ 1211 Ryan Gallant □ □ 1212 Billy Frizzell
□ □ 1213 Mike McLaine □ □ 1214 Kent Macissac
□ □ 1215 Nathan Carragher □ □ 1216 Alex Mac Pherson
□ □ 1217 Kevin Crozier □ □ 1218 Billy Murphy
□ □ 1219 Jonathan Stavert □ □ 1220 Robbie Robert
□ □ 1221 Joshua Proud □ □ 1222 D. MacKinnon
□ □ 1223 Mark McKenzie □ □ 1224 Jasmin Barrett
□ □ 1225 Kris MacPhee □ □ 1698 Anthony Maclean
□ □ 1226 Team Checklist

LANGLEY EAGLES

□ □ 1227 Jason Labarbera □ □ 1228 Wes Jorundson
□ □ 1229 Steve Harrington □ □ 1230 Tyler Jackson
□ □ 1231 Jeff Webster □ □ 1232 Jordan Landry
□ □ 1233 Jesse Swett □ □ 1234 Jeremy Johnson
□ □ 1235 Jeff Franklin □ □ 1236 Brad Fehr
□ □ 1237 Peron Desnoyers □ □ 1238C.s Cunningham
□ □ 1239 Mark Ewing □ □ 1240 Brodie Norman
□ □ 1241 Peter Mihalewch □ □ 1242 Team Checklist

CALIFORNIA KINGS

□ □ 1243 Alex Kim □ □ 1244 Stephen Faulk
□ □ 1245 Shane Warschaw □ □ 1246 Scott Holsinger
□ □ 1247 Noah Clarke □ □ 1248 Patrick Johnson
□ □ 1249 Jon Wilkins □ □ 1250 Jay Tyacke
□ □ 1251 Manu Mau'u □ □ 1252 Justin Morrison
□ □ 1253 Micah Wouters □ □ 1254 Garrett Stafford
□ □ 1255 Eric DeJong □ □ 1256 Stephen Novodor
□ □ 1257 G. Yokoyama □ □ 1258 Justin Dixon
□ □ 1259 Martin Trevor □ □ 1260 Team Checklist

WASHINGTON CAPITALS

□ □ 1261 Justin Roe □ □ 1262 Matthew Kim
□ □ 1263 Paul R. Tilch □ □ 1264 Corey Segal
□ □ 1265 B. M. Dameron □ □ 1266 Jeff Sepanski
□ □ 1267 Zakary T. LeBlanc □ □ 1268 Michael Abner
□ □ 1269 Cam Donahue □ □ 1270 Michael Goldkind
□ □ 1271 Tom Daniel □ □ 1272 A. D. McKenzie
□ □ 1273 Brian Rice □ □ 1274 Tyler Scott
□ □ 1275 David Crenshaw □ □ 1276 Z. C. Jackson
□ □ 1277 M. Weyermann □ □ 1278 Kevin B. Knupp
□ □ 1279 John Lee □ □ 1280 Team Checklist

NEW YORK RANGERS

□ □ 1281 Lenny Raimondi □ □ 1282 Brendan Tuohy
□ □ 1283 Chris Wolff □ □ 1284 Craig Sliva
□ □ 1285 A. Townsend □ □ 1286 David Gibson
□ □ 1287 Keith Anthony □ □ 1288 Chris Migliore
□ □ 1289 Matt Celentano □ □ 1290 Geoff Barlow
□ □ 1291 Chris Dunn □ □ 1292 Jack Kennedy
□ □ 1293 John Longo □ □ 1294 Erik Mikan
□ □ 1295 Scott Savenelli □ □ 1296 Joe Snecinski
□ □ 1297 Derek Saunders □ □ 1298 Karl Bradford
□ □ 1298 Team Checklist

DETROIT GDP

□ □ 1299 Mike Swistak □ □ 1300 Erik Wright
□ □ 1301 Dustin Kuk □ □ 1302 Terry Brennan
□ □ 1303 Tim Hearon □ □ 1304 Matt Preter
□ □ 1305 Jason Bruneel □ □ 1306 David Tigay
□ □ 1307 Scot Curtin □ □ 1308 Phil Osaer
□ □ 1309 D. McGowan □ □ 1310 Nicholas Jardine
□ □ 1311 Jeff Bassett □ □ 1312 Shawn Fisher
□ □ 1313 Mike Porter □ □ 1314 Chris Tom
□ □ 1315 Team Checklist

CHICAGO YOUNG AMERICANS

□ □ 1316 Jejuan Collins □ □ 1317 Michael Gingrie
□ □ 1318 Toby Grahouec □ □ 1319 John Johnson
□ □ 1320 Jeremiah Kimento □ □ 1321 Nick Kalwinski
□ □ 1322 Adam Rogowin □ □ 1323 Kraig Roberts
□ □ 1324 Anthony Battaglia □ □ 1325 David Schneider
□ □ 1326 Peter Chelios □ □ 1327 Nick Chin
□ □ 1328 Kenny Marsch □ □ 1329 Gabe Poisky
□ □ 1330 Troy Linna □ □ 1331 Brent Kozel
□ □ 1332 Team Checklist

ÉLITES RIVE-NORD

□ □ 1333 Didier Tremblay □ □ 1334 A. Mathieu
□ □ 1335 Frédérick Jean □ □ 1336 Francis Morin
□ □ 1337 J-M Raymond □ □ 1338 Francis Lessard
□ □ 1339 Marc Ouimet □ □ 1340 Tom Dessureault
□ □ 1341 Christian Ringuet □ □ 1342 Sébastien Cyr
□ □ 1343 J.F. Normand □ □ 1344 Stéphane Girard
□ □ 1345 Steve Vendette □ □ 1346 Jonathan Dionne
□ □ 1347 S. Fournier □ □ 1348 Alexandre Guy
□ □ 1349 Team Checklist

ALMA

□ □ 1350 Mathieu Bouchard □ □ 1351 Sébastien Renaud
□ □ 1352 Sylvain Lacroix □ □ 1353 Frédéric Boily
□ □ 1354 Pierre-Marc Côté □ □ 1355 Dany Privé
□ □ 1356 Frédérick Côté □ □ 1357 Marc Fortin
□ □ 1358 Steve Vandal □ □ 1359 Alexandre Plourde
□ □ 1360 S. Gaudreault □ □ 1361 Éric Malaison
□ □ 1362 Patrice Gagnon □ □ 1363 A. Tremblay Jr.
□ □ 1364 Pierre-Luc Gagné □ □ 1365 M. Villeneuve
□ □ 1366 Alexandre Côté □ □ 1367 Team Checklist

CITADELLE DE QUÉBEC

☐☐ 1368 Érik St-Hilaire ☐☐ 1369 Éric Simon
☐☐ 1370 Simon Roy ☐☐ 1371 M-A Proulx
☐☐ 1372 Simon Ouellet ☐☐ 1373 Éric Moreau
☐☐ 1374 Tony McHugh ☐☐ 1375 Pascal Mercier
☐☐ 1376 Luc Live ☐☐ 1377 Pascal Lévesque
☐☐ 1378 D. Lachance ☐☐ 1379 Christian Lessard
☐☐ 1380 Frédéric Cloutier ☐☐ 1381 Alexandre Garant
☐☐ 1382 N. Berryman ☐☐ 1383 Donald Blouin
☐☐ 1384 Team Checklist

CANADIENS DE MONTRÉAL

The most expensive singles are Mike Ribeiro (card $3-5, McD's $5-10) and baseball player Netema Ndunigidi (card $2-4, McD's $4-8).

☐☐ 1385 K. G. Parenti ☐☐ 1386 Benoît Héroux
☐☐ 1387 M-P Lavoie ☐☐ 1388 Steve Souca
☐☐ 1389 B. Denis-Cartier ☐☐ 1390 Patrick Héroux
☐☐ 1391 Mike Ribeiro ☐☐ 1392 Éric Cyr
☐☐ 1393 N. Ndunigidi ☐☐ 1394 Yves Engler
☐☐ 1395 Jean Themens ☐☐ 1396 Jonatan Turcot
☐☐ 1397 Francis Leclerc ☐☐ 1398 Patrick Desrosiers
☐☐ 1399 J-F Fecteau ☐☐ 1400 S. Villandré
☐☐ 1401 Team Checklist

TORONTO RED WINGS

The most expensive singles is Adam Colagiacomo (card $1-2, McD's $2-4).

☐☐ 1402 Jay Greer ☐☐ 1403 Matt Laxton
☐☐ 1404 Randy Fitzgerald ☐☐ 1405 Chris Heron
☐☐ 1406 T. Kotsopoulos ☐☐ 1407 Shane Nash
☐☐ 1408 A. Colagiacomo ☐☐ 1409 Greg Jossa
☐☐ 1410 Marc Valcic ☐☐ 1411 Scott Crawford
☐☐ 1412 Clarke Walford ☐☐ 1413 Greg Dunn
☐☐ 1414 Robert Mulick ☐☐ 1415 Terry Lenyk
☐☐ 1416 Team Checklist

DON MILLS FLYERS

☐☐ 1417 Michael Ryder ☐☐ 1418 Aaron Fox
☐☐ 1419 Anthony A. Dynak ☐☐ 1420 Adam Neave
☐☐ 1421 Cerron P. Natale ☐☐ 1422 Micheal Idannou
☐☐ 1423 George Lopes ☐☐ 1424 C. Hunter
☐☐ 1425 Adam Murray ☐☐ 1426 T. Kotsopoulos
☐☐ 1427 Trevor Tuckey ☐☐ 1428 Robert Burns
☐☐ 1429 Jerry Rusin ☐☐ 1430 Mario Belano
☐☐ 1431 Team Checklist

MISSISSAUGA REPS

The most expensive single is Matt Zultek (card $1-2, McD's $2-4).

☐☐ 1432 Mark Meredith ☐☐ 1433 Trevor Mador
☐☐ 1434 Ryan Duke ☐☐ 1435 Vince Corinci
☐☐ 1436 Jamie McLerador ☐☐ 1437 Joey Bizzarro
☐☐ 1438 Matthew Strunach ☐☐ 1439 Chris Gram
☐☐ 1440 Alexander Boyle ☐☐ 1441 Matt Zultek
☐☐ 1442 Mike Leap ☐☐ 1443 Jason Spalding
☐☐ 1444 Ron Greco ☐☐ 1445 J.R. Mayers
☐☐ 1745 Blair Piggott

VANCOUVER THUNDERBIRDS

☐☐ 1447 Gary Toor ☐☐ 1448 Dustin Paul
☐☐ 1449 Ben Ngui ☐☐ 1450 Judd Medak
☐☐ 1451 Chris McKane ☐☐ 1452 Les Kasiotis
☐☐ 1453 Abraham Jang ☐☐ 1454 Chad Hahn
☐☐ 1455 Chris Daum ☐☐ 1456 Paul Condon
☐☐ 1457 John Buchanan ☐☐ 1458 Scott Arnold
☐☐ 1459 Brian Alexander ☐☐ 1460 Tyrone Lingley
☐☐ 1461 Jason Lang ☐☐ 1462 Team Checklist

WEXFORD

☐☐ 1463 Kyle Adams ☐☐ 1464 Geoff Anderson
☐☐ 1465 Brett Barrer ☐☐ 1466 Scott Cuthbertson
☐☐ 1467 Wes Harkin ☐☐ 1468 Colin McKenna
☐☐ 1469 B. McDonough ☐☐ 1470 Mike McLoughlin
☐☐ 1471 David Oh ☐☐ 1472 David Runge
☐☐ 1473 Matt Selby ☐☐ 1474 Chris Sinopoli
☐☐ 1475 Corey Somerville ☐☐ 1476 M. Thompson
☐☐ 1477 Alex Tzounzouris ☐☐ 1478 Jamie Ward
☐☐ 1479 Mike Weisz ☐☐ 1480 Team Checklist

FRANCE (BRULEURS DE LOUPS)

☐☐ 1481 Mattieu Billot ☐☐ 1482 M. Salamand
☐☐ 1483 Yorick Treille ☐☐ 1484 Arnaud Guetz
☐☐ 1485 Cyril Trabichet ☐☐ 1486 Laurent Meunier
☐☐ 1487 Julien Stager ☐☐ 1488 Gauthier Fontanel
☐☐ 1489 Maxime Augris ☐☐ 1490 Thibault Fontanel
☐☐ 1491 Philippe Combe ☐☐ 1492 Philippe Guers
☐☐ 1493 Marc Billieras ☐☐ 1494 T. Bergamelli
☐☐ 1495 Roland Fougère ☐☐ 1496 Benoit Sarzier
☐☐ 1497 Clement Berruex ☐☐ 1498 Nicolas Golleret
☐☐ Team Checklist

POLAND

☐☐ 1500 Arkadiusz Bizub ☐☐ 1501 Marek Raczka
☐☐ 1502 Lukasz Bizub ☐☐ 1503 Jacek Siedzik
☐☐ 1504 R. Smreczynski ☐☐ 1505 Piotr Fryzlewicz
☐☐ 1506 M. Grzegorczyk ☐☐ 1507 Jaroslaw Molenda
☐☐ 1508 Tomasz Kajzer ☐☐ 1509 Damian Siabon
☐☐ 1510 M. Kolodziejczyk ☐☐ 1511 Miroslaw Kolacz
☐☐ 1512 Zareba Zdzislaw ☐☐ 1513 Golak Tomasz
☐☐ 1514 P. Slowakiewicz ☐☐ 1515 Bartiomij Iskrzycki
☐☐ 1516 Grzegorz Brejta ☐☐ 1517 Rafal Kowalski
☐☐ 1518 K. Lipkowski ☐☐ 1519 Marek Dabrowski
☐☐ 1520 Team Checklist

AUSTRIA

The most expensive singles is Gregor Baumgartner (card $1-2, McD's $2-4).

☐☐ 1521 Winfried Rac ☐☐ 1522 Markus Painter
☐☐ 1523 K. Tschemernjak ☐☐ 1524 Elger Oberwelz
☐☐ 1525 T. Eichberger ☐☐ 1526 Gerhard Göttfried
☐☐ 1527 Jens Kraiger ☐☐ 1528 A. Lichtblau
☐☐ 1529 G. Baumgartner ☐☐ 1530 Hans Peter Mitter
☐☐ 1531 Christian Höller ☐☐ 1532 A. Lechner
☐☐ 1533 R. Wolfgang ☐☐ 1534 Gerhard Struger
☐☐ 1535 André Drechsel ☐☐ 1536 Andreas Kofler
☐☐ 1537 Thomas Strauss ☐☐ 1538 Patrik Schneider
☐☐ 1539 Rene Vallant ☐☐ 1540 T. Scheucher
☐☐ 1541 Styblo Ludek ☐☐ 1542 Team Checklist

BRATISLAVA

The most expensive singles are Marián Hossa (card $10-15, McD's $22-305) and Robert Dome (card $1-2, McD's $2-4).

☐☐ 1543 Pavol Spila ☐☐ 1544 Thomas Ziegler
☐☐ 1545 Tomas Kurina ☐☐ 1546 Martin Ochaba
☐☐ 1547 S. Pavlovic ☐☐ 1548 Lubomir Pistek
☐☐ 1549 Jaroslav Malik ☐☐ 1550 Michal Krupa
☐☐ 1551 Branislav Kosc ☐☐ 1552 Marek Kristek
☐☐ 1553 Alexander Jezo ☐☐ 1554 Marian Hossa
☐☐ 1555 V. Hiadlovsky ☐☐ 1556 Jan Holly
☐☐ 1557 Miroslav Hala ☐☐ 1558 Marek Havel
☐☐ 1559 Adrian Daniel ☐☐ 1560 Robert Dome
☐☐ 1561 Martin Galik ☐☐ 1562 Michal Cesnek
☐☐ 1563 Jozef Capka ☐☐ 1564 Robert Frajkor
☐☐ 1565 Daniel Borik ☐☐ 1566 Pavol Bolebruch
☐☐ 1567 Jan Bezdek ☐☐ 1568 Petr Bohunicky
☐☐ 1569 Team Checklist

PHILADELPHIA LITTLE FLYERS

☐☐ 1571 Kevin Meehan ☐☐ 1572 Josh Spiegel
☐☐ 1573 Anthony Switek ☐☐ 1574 Paul Dorn
☐☐ 1575 Rob Silvia ☐☐ 1576 Tom McMonagie
☐☐ 1577 Jimmy Henkel ☐☐ 1578 James Laux
☐☐ 1579 Russel Mocgut ☐☐ 1580 Daniel Houck
☐☐ 1581 John F. Larnerd ☐☐ 1582 Jerramie Domish
☐☐ 1583 Brian Wrobble ☐☐ 1584 Paul Dabrowski
☐☐ 1585 Danny McDonald ☐☐ 1586 B. Gallagher
☐☐ 1587 Jeremy Bean ☐☐ 1588 Team Checklist

DRAVEURS DE LA MAURICIE

☐☐ 1589 Hugues Gosselin ☐☐ 1590 Jonathan Violy
☐☐ 1591 M. Beauchesne ☐☐ 1592 Jonathan Blais
☐☐ 1593 J. Marchand ☐☐ 1594 J.F. Daneau
☐☐ 1595 F. Tanguay ☐☐ 1596 Maxime Toupin
☐☐ 1597 Benoît Côté ☐☐ 1598 Mathieu Dubois
☐☐ 1599 P-J Gaudet ☐☐ 1600 J-F Lemay
☐☐ 1601 François Doucet ☐☐ 1602 Maxime Hains
☐☐ 1603 Martin Bilodeau ☐☐ 1604 Team Checklist

VANCOUVER CANUCKS

☐☐ 1605 Jerry Merta ☐☐ 1606 Ken Richmond
☐☐ 1607 David Stewart ☐☐ 1608 Justin Gough
☐☐ 1609 Mike Greschner ☐☐ 1610 Brent Giesbrech
☐☐ 1611 Ryan Killam ☐☐ 1612 Jason Rich
☐☐ 1614 Mike Morin ☐☐ 1615 Chad Euverman
☐☐ 1616 Cam Laker ☐☐ 1617 Jon Cisecki
☐☐ 1618 Ryan Allford ☐☐ 1619 Team Checklist

TEAM ZURICK SUISSE

☐☐ 1620 Olivier Stattler ☐☐ 1621 Adrian Wichser
☐☐ 1622 Seiler Daniel ☐☐ 1623 Patrick Schraner
☐☐ 1624 R. Schnüriger ☐☐ 1625 Cornel Prinz
☐☐ 1626 Beat Meier ☐☐ 1627 Benjamin Plüss
☐☐ 1628 Martin Höhener ☐☐ 1629 Ronny Keller
☐☐ 1630 Philipp Folghera ☐☐ 1631 Marcel Franzi
☐☐ 1632 Stefan Eberhard ☐☐ 1633 Ronny Derrer
☐☐ 1634 Marco Bührer ☐☐ 1635 Marco Bonderer
☐☐ 1636 Morenso Biglel ☐☐ 1637 Peter Birrer
☐☐ 1638 O. Aeschlimann ☐☐ 1639 Fabio Beccareli
☐☐ 1640 Team Checklist

AQUITAIN DE BORDEAUX

☐☐ 1641 Yannis Boudeau ☐☐ 1642 Julien Valton
☐☐ 1643 Yann Vonachen ☐☐ 1644 Ludovic Hardouin
☐☐ 1645 Mathieu Palau ☐☐ 1646 Guillaume Arnoult
☐☐ 1647 Dominique Carré ☐☐ 1648 Jill Cauly
☐☐ 1649 Stéphane Labayle ☐☐ 1650 Julien Hortholary
☐☐ 1651 C. Pieddrafita ☐☐ 1652 A. Crampes
☐☐ 1653 P-É Bordas ☐☐ 1654 Olivier Benoît
☐☐ 1655 Étienne Lamande ☐☐ 1656 Julien Barthelemy
☐☐ 1657 Thomas Yulzari ☐☐ 1658 Benoît Lubeigt
☐☐ 1659 Team Checklist

PHILADELPHIA JR. FLYERS

☐☐ 1660 Timothy Ralston ☐☐ 1661 Jonathan Grabie
☐☐ 1662 J.J Taylor ☐☐ 1663 Philip Cohen
☐☐ 1664 James Whitacre ☐☐ 1665 James R. Zitzer
☐☐ 1666 Philip Amoroso ☐☐ 1667 Kevin J. Audit
☐☐ 1668 Blake Greene ☐☐ 1669 Kyle Neary
☐☐ 1670 Z. S. Bender ☐☐ 1671 Rich Giorman
☐☐ 1672 Bill Emerick ☐☐ 1673 Matt Silverio
☐☐ 1674 P. A. Hagopian ☐☐ 1675 Andrew R. Testa
☐☐ 1676 Jimmy Gilbert ☐☐ 1677 M. Herneisen
☐☐ 1678 Gregory Marinari ☐☐ 1679 Jonathan Drake
☐☐ 1680 Team Checklist

MISSISSAUGA SENATORS

☐☐ 1681 Eric Toressan ☐☐ 1682 Steven Williams
☐☐ 1683 Jared Gardner ☐☐ 1684 Richard Williams
☐☐ 1685 Colin Young ☐☐ 1686 Chris Daigle
☐☐ 1687 M. Bournazakis ☐☐ 1688 L. Clarfield
☐☐ 1689 Jeff Boyes ☐☐ 1690 Mark Trafford
☐☐ 1691 P.J Spadafora ☐☐ 1692 Matthew Thomas
☐☐ 1693 Randy Stolec ☐☐ 1694 Ryan Steele
☐☐ 1695 Matthew Currah ☐☐ 1696 Team Checklist

SLOVAKIA

The most expensive single is Ladislav Nagy (card $2-3, McD's $3-5).

☐☐ 1701 Tomás Baluch ☐☐ 1702 Jozef Contofalsky
☐☐ 1703 Tomás Schlosser ☐☐ 1704 Ladislav Nagy
☐☐ 1705 Gönczi Severin ☐☐ 1706 Peter Smrek
☐☐ 1707 Zoltán Bátovsky ☐☐ 1708 Martin Liba
☐☐ 1709 Michal Jandel ☐☐ 1710 Martin Kvietok
☐☐ 1711 Simo Stanislav ☐☐ 1712 Peter Grecko
☐☐ 1713 Kristian Peter ☐☐ 1714 Marián Bodnár
☐☐ 1715 Peter Dejna ☐☐ 1716 Marian Koleda
☐☐ 1717 Ján Lasák ☐☐ 1718 Peter Kassa
☐☐ 1719 Ján Supuka ☐☐ 1720 Stanislav Gejdos
☐☐ 1721 Rastilav Jacico ☐☐ 1722 Branislav Prásek
☐☐ 1723 Team Checklist

NEW YORK ISLANDERS

☐☐ 1724 Brian Rocheford ☐☐ 1725 J.P. Griandi
☐☐ 1726 Sean Mcquade ☐☐ 1727 Kevon Young
☐☐ 1728 John Cappelio ☐☐ 1729 Jon Olson
☐☐ 1730 Ronnie D'Angello ☐☐ 1731 David Rush
☐☐ 1732 Brett Henning ☐☐ 1733 Don Richardson
☐☐ 1734 Ales Colinar ☐☐ 1735 John Bombard
☐☐ 1737 Alan Steiger ☐☐ 1739 Matt Miracolo
☐☐ 1740 Chris Wolff ☐☐ 1742 Ryan Belling
☐☐ 1743 Ted Schiff

DETROIT RED WINGS

The most expensive singles is David Legwand (card $4-8, McD's $9-15).

☐☐ 1748 Brian Eovaldi ☐☐ 1749 Ernie Hartlieb
☐☐ 1750 Gregory Job ☐☐ 1751 Jason B. Deskins
☐☐ 1752 Joseph Gerbe ☐☐ 1753 Mike Bozoian
☐☐ 1754 Justin Brewer ☐☐ 1755 Mark Brian Felker
☐☐ 1756 J. R. Blackburn ☐☐ 1757 Donald Pierce
☐☐ 1759 Ronald Kolito ☐☐ 1760 David Legwand
☐☐ 1761 Rael Blair ☐☐ 1762 Esward Close
☐☐ 1763 Garrett M. Henkel ☐☐ 1764 Team Checklist

GERMANY

The most expensive single is Sascha Goc (card $1-2, McD's $2-4).

☐☐ 1765 Jiri Kratschmar ☐☐ 1766 Christoph Jager
☐☐ 1767 Sebastian Krause ☐☐ 1768 Felix Jentzmik
☐☐ 1769 Marc Wuhrer ☐☐ 1770 Oliver Reimer
☐☐ 1771 Matthias Vater ☐☐ 1772 Steffen Karl
☐☐ 1773 Marc Dell'Anna ☐☐ 1774 Alex. Dexheimer
☐☐ 1775 Sascha Goc ☐☐ 1776 Tobias Zappe
☐☐ 1777 Thomas Dolak ☐☐ 1778 Norman Thimm
☐☐ 1779 Thomas Jetter

SLOVANIA

☐☐ 1781 Anze Ulcar ☐☐ 1782 Dusan Brulc
☐☐ 1783 Jure Penko ☐☐ 1784 Mitja Sivic
☐☐ 1785 Ajosa Javor ☐☐ 1786 Luka Rebolj
☐☐ 1787 Gorazd Knezevic ☐☐ 1788 Erik Blatnik
☐☐ 1789 Martin Pirnat ☐☐ 1790 Uros Peruzzi
☐☐ 1791 Daniel Glumac ☐☐ 1792 Ales Baton
☐☐ 1793 Denis Samec ☐☐ 1794 Edo Terglav
☐☐ 1795 Matjav Vodnjov ☐☐ 1796 Tomaz Razinger
☐☐ 1797 Tine Troha ☐☐ 1798 Jure Rozman
☐☐ 1799 Jurij Golicic ☐☐ 1800 Marjan Bizjak
☐☐ 1801 Miha Zhontar ☐☐ 1802 Grega Matjasic
☐☐ 1803 Luka Kamsek ☐☐ 1804 Rudi Hiti
☐☐ 1805 Gregor Pesjak ☐☐ 1806 Bostian Kolaric

INSERTS

	Player	NM-MT
☐	1 Guy Chouinard	4.00
☐	2 Brad Park	4.00
☐	3 Manon Rhéaume	10.00

1993 SEMIC STICKERS

The most expensive stickers are Wayne Gretzky ($5-10), Patrick Roy ($3-6), Steve Yzerman ($3-5), Dominik Hasek ($2-5), Pavel Bure ($2-5) and Jaromir Jagr ($3-5). Other NHL stars sell for 50¢-$4. Other singles sell for 20¢-$1.50.

Complete Set (288 stickers): 50.00
Common Player: .20
Album: 6.00

	Player		No. Player
☐	1 Peter Åslin	☐	2 Håkan Algotsson
☐	3 Kenneth Kennholt	☐	4 Arto Blomsten
☐	5 Tomas Jonsson	☐	6 Fredrik Stillman
☐	7 Stefan Larsson	☐	8 Peter Popovic
☐	9 Håkan Loob	☐	10 Thomas Rundqvist
☐	11 Patrick Juhlin	☐	12 Mikael Renberg
☐	13 Peter Forsberg	☐	14 Markus Näslund
☐	15 B-A Gustafsson	☐	16 Jan Larsson
☐	17 Fredrik Nilsson	☐	18 Roger Hansson
☐	19 T. Söderström (G)	☐	20 Anders Eldebrink
☐	21 Ulf Samuelsson	☐	22 Kjell Samuelsson
☐	23 Nicklas Lidström	☐	24 Tommy Sjödin
☐	25 Calle Johansson	☐	26 Fredrik Olaussen
☐	27 Peter Andersson	☐	28 Tommy Albelin
☐	29 Roger Johansson	☐	30 Per Djoos
☐	31 Mikael Johansson	☐	32 Tomas Sandström
☐	33 Mats Sundin	☐	34 Ulf Dahlen
☐	35 Jan Erixon	☐	36 Thomas Steen
☐	37 Mikael Andersson	☐	38 Johan Garpenlöv
☐	39 Per-Erik Eklund	☐	40 Michael Nylander
☐	41 Thomas Forslund	☐	42 Patric Kjellberg
☐	43 Patrick Carnbäck	☐	44 Niclas Andersson
☐	45 Markus Ketterer (G)	☐	46 Sakari Lindfors (G)
☐	47 Jarmo Myllys (G)	☐	48 Peter Ahola
☐	49 Mikko Haapakoski	☐	50 Kari Harila
☐	51 Pasi Huura	☐	52 Walteri Immonen
☐	53 Timo Jutila	☐	54 Janne Laukkanen
☐	55 Harri Laurila	☐	56 Jyrki Lumme
☐	57 Teppo Numminen	☐	58 Sami Nuutinen
☐	59 Ville Siren	☐	60 Pasi Sormunen
☐	61 Mika Strömberg	☐	62 Mika Alatalo
☐	63 Raimo Helminen	☐	64 Pauli Järvinen
☐	65 Jarmo Kekäläinen	☐	66 Jari Korpisalo
☐	67 Jari Kurri	☐	68 Mikko Mäkelä
☐	69 Mika Nieminen	☐	70 Timo Norppa
☐	71 Janne Ojanen	☐	72 Timo Norppa
☐	73 Rauli Raitanen	☐	74 Juha Riihijärvi
☐	75 Christian Ruuttu	☐	76 Timo Saarikoski
☐	77 Teemu Selänne	☐	78 Jukka Seppo
☐	79 Petri Skriko	☐	80 Esa Tikkanen
☐	81 Pekka Tuomisto	☐	82 Petri Varis
☐	83 Jarkko Varvio	☐	84 Vesa Viitakoski
☐	85 Marko Virtanen	☐	86 Jali Wahlsten
☐	87 Sami Wahlsten	☐	88 Pentti Matikainen
☐	89 Petr Briza (G)	☐	90 Roman Turek (G)
☐	91 Milos Holan	☐	92 Drahomir Kadlec
☐	93 Bedrich Scerban	☐	94 Frantisek Prochazka
☐	95 Richard Zemlicka	☐	96 Roman Horak
☐	97 Lubos Rob	☐	98 Jiri Kucera
☐	99 Tomas Kapusta	☐	100 Roman Rysanek
☐	101 Roman Hamrlik	☐	102 Robert Svehla
☐	103 Tomas Jelinek	☐	104 Petr Klima
☐	105 Josef Beranek	☐	106 Robert Petrovecky
☐	107 Kamil Kastak	☐	108 David Volek
☐	109 Renato Tosio (G)	☐	110 Patrick Schöpf
☐	111 Samuel Palmer	☐	112 Andreas Beautler
☐	113 Patrice Brasey	☐	114 Rick Tschumi
☐	115 Sven Leuenberger	☐	116 Sandro Bertaggia
☐	117 Patrick Howard	☐	118 Andy Ton
☐	119 Keith Fair	☐	120 Mario Brodman
☐	121 Fredy Luthi	☐	122 Jörg Eberle
☐	123 Roman Wäger	☐	124 Manuel Celio
☐	125 Christian Weber	☐	126 Roger Thöny
☐	127 Felix Hollenstein	☐	128 Gil Montandon
☐	129 N. Khalibulin (G)	☐	130 Alexei Chervyakov
☐	131 Ilja Byakin	☐	132 Dmitri Filimonov
☐	133 A. Karpovstev	☐	134 Sergei Sorokin
☐	135 A. Sapozhnikov	☐	136 Alexei Yashin
☐	137 A. Cherbayev	☐	138 K. Astrakhantsev
☐	139 Sergei Petrenko	☐	140 Viktor Kozlov
☐	141 Roman Oksiuta	☐	142 Vladimir Malakhov
☐	143 Andrei Lomakin	☐	144 Dmitri Yushkevich
☐	145 Igor Korolev	☐	146 Darius Kasparaitis
☐	147 Vyacheslav Bykov	☐	148 Andrei Khomutov
☐	149 Helmut de Raaf (G)	☐	150 Klaus Merk (G)
☐	151 Michael Heidt	☐	152 Michael Schmidt
☐	153 Uli Hiemer	☐	154 Andreas Niederberg
☐	155 Rick Amann	☐	156 Andreas Brockmann
☐	157 Gerd Truntschka	☐	158 Dieter Hegen
☐	159 Stefan Usdorf	☐	160 Georg Holzmann
☐	161 Ernst Köpf	☐	162 Bernd Truntschka
☐	163 Raimund Hilger	☐	164 Wolfgang Kummer
☐	165 Georg Franz	☐	166 Thomas Brandl
☐	167 Michael Rumrich	☐	168 Uwe Krupp
☐	169 Tom Barraso (G)	☐	170 Mike Richter (G)
☐	171 Brian Leetch	☐	172 Chris Chelios
☐	173 Al Iafrate	☐	174 Phil Housley
☐	175 Kevin Hatcher	☐	176 Gary Suter
☐	177 Mathieu Schneider	☐	178 Joe Mullen
☐	179 Kevin Stevens	☐	180 Jeremy Roenick
☐	181 Tony Granato	☐	182 Mike Modano
☐	183 Pat LaFontaine	☐	184 Ed Olczyk
☐	185 Brett Hull	☐	186 Craig Janney
☐	187 Jimmy Carson	☐	188 Tony Amonte
☐	189 Patrick Roy (G)	☐	190 Kirk McLean (G)
☐	191 Larry Murphy	☐	192 Ray Bourque
☐	193 Al MacInnis	☐	194 Steve Duchesne
☐	195 Eric Desjardins	☐	196 Scott Stevens
☐	197 Paul Coffey	☐	198 Mario Lemieux
☐	199 Wayne Gretzky	☐	200 Rick Tocchet
☐	201 Eric Lindros	☐	202 Mark Messier
☐	203 Steve Yzerman	☐	204 Luc Robitaille
☐	205 Mark Recchi	☐	206 Joe Sakic
☐	207 Owen Nolan	☐	208 Gary Roberts
☐	209 David Delfino	☐	210 Michael Rosati (G)
☐	211 Robert Oberrauch	☐	212 Jim Camazzola
☐	213 Bill Stewart	☐	214 Mike de Angelis
☐	215 Anthony Circelli	☐	216 Georg Comploy
☐	217 Frank di Muzio	☐	218 Gates Orlando
☐	219 John Vecchiarelli	☐	220 Joe Foglietta
☐	221 Lucio Topatigh	☐	222 Carmine Vani
☐	223 Lino de Toni	☐	224 Mario Chitarroni
☐	225 Bruno Zarillo	☐	226 Maurizio Mansi
☐	227 Stefan Figliuzzi	☐	228 Santino Pellegrino
☐	229 Jim Marthinsen	☐	230 Rob Schistad
☐	231 Petter Salsten	☐	232 Cato Tom Andersen
☐	233 Tommy Jakobsen	☐	234 Svein E. Nöstebö
☐	235 Jon Magne Karlstad	☐	236 Klm Sögaard
☐	237 Geir Hoff	☐	238 Erik Kristiansen
☐	239 Petter Thoresen	☐	240 Ole Eskil Dahlström
☐	241 Espen Knutsen	☐	242 Öystein Olsen
☐	243 Roy Johansen	☐	244 Trond Magnussen
☐	245 Arne Billkvam	☐	246 Marius Rath
☐	247 Tom Erik Olsen	☐	248 Morten Finstad
☐	249 Petri Ylönen (G)	☐	250 Michel Vallière
☐	251 Stéphane Botteri	☐	252 Serge Poudrier
☐	253 Eric Durand	☐	254 J-P Lemoine
☐	255 Denis Perez	☐	256 Sébastian Marquet
☐	257 Michael Babin	☐	258 Stéphane Barin
☐	259 Arnaud Briand	☐	260 Yves Crettenand
☐	261 Laurent Deschaume	☐	262 Roger Dubé
☐	263 Patrick Dunn	☐	264 Franck Pajonkowski
☐	265 Pierre Pousse	☐	266 Antoine Richer
☐	267 Christophe Ville	☐	268 Mario Schaden
☐	269 Brian Stankiewicz	☐	270 Claus Dalpiaz (G)
☐	271 Michael Shea	☐	272 Robin Doyle
☐	273 Martin Ulrich	☐	274 Martin Krainz
☐	275 Erich Solderer	☐	276 Michael Günter
☐	277 Friedrich Ganster	☐	278 Wayne Groulx
☐	279 Dieter Kalt	☐	280 Werner Kerth
☐	281 Arno Maier	☐	282 Richard Nasheim
☐	283 Christian Perthaler	☐	284 Andreas Puschning
☐	285 Gerhard Punschnik	☐	286 Walter Putnik
☐	287 Reinhart Lampert	☐	288 Mario Schaden

1993 UPPER DECK WORLD CUP OF SOCCER

This soccer series included a four-card Honorary Captains insert set. Each Honorary Captains insert had a Gold parallel.

Imprint: © 1993 The Upper Deck Company

	Honorary Captains	Gold	Reg.
☐☐	H4 Wayne Gretzky	30.00	15.00

1993 - 94 ACTION PACKED

Imprint: Action Packed, Inc. Copyright 1993

Hall of Fame Set (10 cards):	**40.00**
Bobby Hull Set (2 cards):	**5.00**
Player	**HOF**
□ 1 Edgar Laprade	5.00
□ 2 Guy Lapointe, Mont.	5.00
□ 3 Billy Smith (G), NYIs.	10.00
□ 4 Steve Shutt, Mont.	5.00
□ 5 John D'Amico	4.00
□ 6 Al Shaver	4.00
□ 7 Seymour Knox	4.00
□ 8 Frank Griffiths	4.00
□ 9 Fred Page	4.00
□ 10 Al Strachan	4.00
Player	**Hull**
□ BH1 Bobby Hull, Chic.	4.00
□ BH2 Bobby Hull (Gold), Chic.	4.00

1993 - 94 CANADIAN OLYMPIC TEAM

Complete Set (23 cards): **20.00**

Canada	Canada
□ Dwayne Norris	□ Tom Renney, Coach
□ Russ Romaniuk	□ Brian Savage
□ Trevor Sim	□ Chris Therien
□ Todd Warriner	□ Craig Woodcroft
□ Sponsor Card	
□ Fabian Joseph	□ Paul Kariya
□ Chris Kontos	□ Manny Legacé (G)
□ Brett Lindros	□ Ken Lovsin
□ Jason Marshall	□ Derek Mayer
□ Adrian Aucion	□ Todd Brost
□ Dany Dubé	□ David Harlock
□ Corey Hirsch (G)	□ Todd Hlushko

1993 - 94 CLASSIC

The most expensive cards are Manon Rhéaume at $2-3 and Paul Kariya at $1-2. Regional stars sell at 15¢-$1; all other singles start at 20¢.

Imprint: © 1993 Classic Games, Inc.

Complete Set (150 cards):	**15.00**
Common Player:	**.10**
Postcard (Kariya, Rhéame, Mogilny; 5 1/4" x 7 3/4"):	**5.00**
Promo	**Classic**
□ PR3 Pavel Bure Promo	5.00

Classic

Classic	
□ 1 Alexandre Daigle	□ 2 Chris Pronger
□ 3 Chris Gratton	□ 4 Paul Kariya
□ 5 Rob Niedermayer	□ 6 Viktor Kozlov
□ 7 Jason Arnott	□ 8 Niklas Sundstrom
□ 9 Todd Harvey	□ 10 Jocelyn Thibault (G)
□ 11 Checklist	□ 12 Pat Peake
□ 13 Jason Allison	□ 14 Todd Bertuzzi
□ 15 Maxim Bets	□ 16 Curtis Bowen
□ 17 Kevin Brown	□ 18 Valeri Bure
□ 19 Jason Dawe	□ 20 Adam Deadmarsh
□ 21 Aaron Gavey	□ 22 Nathan Lafayette
□ 23 Eric Lecompte	□ 24 Manny Legacé (G)
□ 25 Michael Peca	□ 26 Denis Pederson
□ 27 Jeff Shantz	□ 28 Nick Stadjuhar
□ 29 Cory Stillman	□ 30 Michal Sykora
□ 31 Brent Tully	□ 32 Mike Wilson
□ 33 Wings	□ 34 Checklist
□ 35 Antti Aalto	□ 36 Radim Bicanek
□ 37 Vladimir Chebaturkin	□ 38 Alexander Cherbayev
□ 39 Markus Ketterer (G)	□ 40 Saku Koivu
□ 41 Vladimir Krechin	□ 42 Alexei Kudashov
□ 43 Janne Laukkanen	□ 44 Janne Niinimaa
□ 45 Juha Riihijarvi	□ 46 Nikolai Tsulygin
□ 47 Vesa Viitakoski	□ 48 David Vyborny
□ 49 Nikolai Zavarukhin	□ 50 Alexandre Daigle
□ 51 Alexandre Daigle	□ 52 Alexandre Daigle
□ 53 Alexandre Daigle	□ 54 Alexandre Daigle
□ 55 Jim Montgomery	□ 56 Mike Dunham (G)
□ 57 Matt Martin	□ 58 Garth Snow (G)
□ 59 Shawn Walch	□ 60 Bavis bros.
□ 61 Scott Chartier	□ 62 Craig Darby
□ 63 Ted Drury	□ 64 Steve Dubinsky
□ 65 Joe Frederick	□ 66 Cammi Granato
□ 67 Brett Hauer	□ 68 Jon Hillebrandt (G)
□ 69 Ryan Hughes	□ 70 Dean Hullet
□ 71 Kevin O'Sullivan	□ 72 Dan Plante
□ 73 Derek Plante	□ 74 Travis Richards
□ 75 Barry Richter	□ 76 David Roberts
□ 77 Chris Rogles (G)	□ 78 Jon Rohloff
□ 79 Brian Rolston	□ 80 David Sacco
□ 81 Brian Savage	□ 82 Mike Smith
□ 83 Chris Tamer	□ 84 Chris Therien
□ 85 Aaron Ward	□ 86 Russian Celebration
□ 87 V. Butsayev	□ 88 Yan Kaminsky
□ 89 A. Karpovtsev	□ 90 Valeri Karpov
□ 91 Sergei Petrenko	□ 92 Andrei Sapozhniko
□ 93 Sergei Sorokin	□ 94 German Titov
□ 95 Andrei Trefilov (G)	□ 96 Alexei Yashin
□ 97 Dimitri Yushkevich	□ 98 Radek Bonk
□ 99 Jason Bonsignore	□ 100 Brad Brown
□ 101 Chris Drury	□ 102 Jeff Freisen
□ 103 Sean Haggerty	□ 104 Jeff Kealty
□ 105 A. Kharlamov	□ 106 Stanislav Neckar
□ 107 Tom O'Connor	□ 108 Jeff O'Neill
□ 109 Deron Quint	□ 110 Vadim Sharifianov
□ 111 Oleg Tverdovsky	□ 112 M. Rhéaume (G)
□ 113 Paul Kariya	□ 114 Alexandre Daigle
□ 115 Jeff O'Neill	□ 116 Mike Bossy
□ 117 Pavel Bure	□ 118 Chris Chelios
□ 119 Doug Gilmour	□ 120 Roman Hamrlik
□ 121 Jari Kurri	□ 122 Alexander Mogilny
□ 123 Félix Potvin (G)	□ 124 Teemu Selänne
□ 125 T. Soderström (G)	□ 126 Mike Bales (G)
□ 127 Jozef Cierny	□ 128 Ivan Droppa
□ 129 Anders Eriksson	□ 130 Anatoli Fedotov
□ 131 Martin Gendron	□ 132 Daniel Guérard
□ 133 Corey Hirsch (G)	□ 134 Milos Holan
□ 135 Kenny Jonsson	□ 136 Steven King
□ 137 Alexei Kovalev	□ 138 Sergei Krivokrasov
□ 139 Mats Lindgren	□ 140 Grant Marshall
□ 141 Jesper Mattsson	□ 142 Sandy McCarthy
□ 143 Dean Melanson	□ 144 Robert Petrovicky
□ 145 Mike Rathje	□ 146 M. Rhéaume (G)
□ 147 Claude Savoie	□ 148 M. Shtalenkov (G)
□ 149 M. Rhéaume (G)	□ 150 M. Rhéaume (G)

Acetate Insert	**NRMT-MT**
□ MR1 Manon Rhéaume (G)	15.00

CLASS OF 1994

Insert Set (7 cards):	**10.00**
Player	**CL**
□ CL1 Jeff O'Neill, Guelph	4.00
□ CL2 Jason Bonsignore	1.50
□ CL3 Jeff Friesen, Regina	3.00
□ CL4 Radek Bonk, Las Vegas	3.00
□ CL5 Deron Quint	1.50
□ CL6 Vadim Sharifjanov	1.50
□ CL7 Tom O'Connor, PRO-AM	1.50

AUTOGRAPHS

Autograph	Aut
□ Mike Bossy ✍ {#/975}	40.00
□ Pavel Bure ✍ {#/900}	30.00
□ Chris Chelios ✍ {#/1,800}	15.00
□ Doug Gilmour ✍ {#/1,850}	15.00
□ Alexander Mogilny ✍ {#/950}	15.00
□ Jim Montgomery ✍ {#/1,800}	4.00
□ Rob Niedermayer ✍ {#/2,500}	5.00
□ Jeff O'Neill ✍ {#/2,225}	10.00
□ Pat Peake ✍ {#/790}	4.00
□ Mark Recchi ✍ {#/1,725}	10.00
□ Manon Rhéaume ✍ {G} ✍ {#/1,500}	30.00
□ Geoff Sanderson ✍ {#/875}	5.00

CRASH NUMBERED

Insert Set (10 cards):	**30.00**
Insert (#/15,000)	**NRMT-MT**
□ N1 Alexandre Daigle, Victoriaville	2.00
□ N2 Paul Kariya, Cdn.	5.00
□ N3 Jeff O'Neill, Guelph	2.00
□ N4 Jason Bonsignore, Newmarket	2.00
□ N5 Teemu Selänne, Fin.	5.00
□ N6 Pavel Bure, USSR	5.00
□ N7 Alexandre Mogilny, USSR	2.00
□ N8 Manon Rhéaume (G), Atlanta	10.00
□ N9 Félix Potvin (G), St. John's	2.00
□ N10 Radek Bonk, Las Vegas	2.00

TEAM CANADA

Insert Set (7 cards):	**10.00**
Player	**TC**
□ TC1 Greg Johnson, Cdn.	2.00
□ TC2 Paul Kariya, Cdn.	5.00
□ TC3 Brian Savage, Cdn.	2.00
□ TC4 Bill Ranford (G), Cdn.	2.00
□ TC5 Mark Recchi, Cdn.	2.00
□ TC6 Geoff Sanderson, Cdn.	2.00
□ TC7 Adam Graves, Cdn.	2.00

TOP TEN

Insert Set (10 cards):	**15.00**
Player	**DP**
□ DP1 Alexandre Daigle, Victoriaville	1.50
□ DP2 Chris Pronger, Peterborough	2.00
□ DP3 Chris Gratton, Kingston	1.50
□ DP4 Paul Kariya, Cdn.	5.00
□ DP5 Rob Niedermayer, CHL All-Stars	1.50
□ DP6 Viktor Kozlov, Russia	1.50
□ DP7 Jason Arnott, Oshawa	3.00
□ DP8 Niklas Sundstrom, Binghampton	1.50
□ DP9 Todd Harvey, Detroit	1.50
□ DP10 Jocelyn Thibault (G), CHL All-Stars	1.50

1993 - 94 CLASSIC FOUR-SPORT

This 325-card four-sport set features 75 hockey players. Each card has two versions: the regular card and a gold parallel. A 325-card set sells at $15. The most expensive hockey cards are Manon Rhéaume at $2-3, Cammi Granato at $2-3, Paul Kariya at $1-2, and Todd Bertuzzi at $1-2. Regional stars sell at 30¢-$1; all other singles start at 20¢.

Imprint: © 1993 Classic Games, Inc.

Classic	Classic
□ 185 Alexandre Daigle	□ 186 Chris Pronger
□ 187 Chris Gratton	□ 188 Paul Kariya
□ 189 Rob Niedermayer	□ 190 Viktor Kozlov
□ 191 Jason Arnott	□ 192 Niklas Sundstrom
□ 193 Todd Havery	□ 194 Jocelyn Thibault (G)
□ 195 Kenny Jonsson	□ 196 Denis Pederson
□ 197 Adam Deadmarsh	□ 198 Mats Lindgren
□ 199 Nick Stajduhar	□ 200 Jason Allison
□ 201 Jesper Mattsson	□ 202 Saku Koivu
□ 203 Anders Eriksson	□ 204 Todd Bertuzzi
□ 205 Eric Lecompte	□ 206 Nikolai Tsulygin
□ 207 Janne Niinimaa	□ 208 Maxim Bets
□ 209 Rory Fitzpatrick	□ 210 Eric Manlow
□ 211 David Roche	□ 212 V. Chebaturkin
□ 213 Bill McCauley	□ 214 Chad Lang
□ 215 Cosmo Dupaul	□ 216 Bob Wren
□ 217 Chris Simon	□ 218 Ryan Brown
□ 219 M. Shtalenkov (G)	□ 220 Vladimir Krechin
□ 221 Jason Saal (G)	□ 222 Dion Darling
□ 223 Chris Kelleher	□ 224 Antti Aalto
□ 225 Alain Nasreddine	□ 226 Paul Vincent
□ 227 Manny Legacé (G)	□ 228 Igor Chibirev
□ 229 Tom Noble (G)	□ 230 Mike Bales (G)
□ 231 Jozef Cierny	□ 232 Ivan Droppa
□ 233 Anatoli Fedotov	□ 234 Martin Gendron
□ 235 Daniel Guerard	□ 236 Corey Hirsch (G)
□ 237 Steven King	□ 238 Sergei Krivokrasov
□ 239 Darrin Madeley (G)	□ 240 Grant Marshall
□ 241 Sandy McCarthy	□ 242 Bill McDougall
□ 243 Dean Melanson	□ 244 Roman Oksiuta
□ 245 Robert Petrovicky	□ 246 Mike Rathje
□ 247 Eldon Reddick (G)	□ 248 Andrei Trefilov (G)
□ 249 Jiri Slegr	□ 250 Leonid Toropchenko
□ 251 Dody Wood	□ 252 Kevin Paden
□ 253 M. Rhéaume (G)	□ 254 Cammi Granato
□ 255 P. Charboneaum	□ 256 Curtis Bowen
□ 257 Kevin Brown	□ 258 Valeri Bure
□ 259 Janne Laukkanen	

INSERTS

This four-sport series featured the following hockey inserts: five hockey players amongst the 30 Autograph cards; two hockey players in the Acetate insert (12-card set sells at $45); three hockey players in the Draft Stars insert (20-card set sells at $20); four hockey players in the Limited Print insert (25-card set sells for $30); three hockey players in the Power Picks insert (20-card set sells for $20); one hockey trio in the five-card Tri-Card insert.

Acetate	**NRMT-MT**
□ 11 Alexandre Daigle	1.50
□ 12 Chris Pronger	3.00
Autograph	**NRMT-MT**
□ Adam Deadmarsh ✍ {#/4250}	4.00
□ Chris Gratton ✍ {#/3900}	4.00
□ Rob Niedermayer ✍ {#/4500}	4.00
□ Denis Pederson ✍ {#/2050}	4.00
□ Manon Rhéaume (G) ✍ {#/1250}	90.00
Draft Series	**DS**
□ DS58 Alexandre Daigle	.50
□ DS59 Chris Pronger	1.00
□ DS60 Chris Gratton	.50
Limited Print	**LP**
□ LP22 Alexandre Daigle	.50
□ LP23 Chris Pronger	1.00
□ LP24 Chris Gratton	.50
□ LP25 Paul Kariya	3.00
Power Picks	**PP**
□ PP18 Alexandre Daigle	.50
□ PP19 Chris Pronger	1.00
□ PP20 Chris Gratton	.50
Tri-Card	**TC**
□ TC4 A. Daigle/ C. Pronger/ C. Gratton	2.00

1993 - 94 CLASSIC IMAGES FOUR SPORT

This 150-card four-sport set features only 29 hockey players. A 150-card set sells at $15. The most expensive hockey cards are Manon Rhéaume at $2-3 and Paul Kariya at $1-2. Regional stars sell at 30¢-$1; all other singles start at 20¢.

Classic	Classic
□ 4 Alexandre Daigle	□ 8 Chris Pronger
□ 16 Jim Montgomery	□ 17 Todd Marchant
□ 20 Mike Dunham (G)	□ 21 Garth Snow (G)
□ 24 Barry Richter	□ 28 Matt Martin
□ 30 Rob Niedermayer	□ 32 Jesse Belanger
□ 35 Peter Ferraro	□ 38 Ted Drury
□ 43 Derek Plante	□ 46 Jim Campbell
□ 56 Chris Osgood (G)	□ 62 Jason Arnott
□ 74 Jocelyn Thibault (G)	□ 86 Chris Gratton
□ 92 Mike Rathje	□ 101 Martin Brodeur (G)
□ 106 Paul Kariya	□ 111 M. Rhéaume (G)
□ 121 Félix Potvin (G)	□ 125 Alexei Yashin
□ 130 Alexei Yashin	□ 135 Chris Pronger
□ 138 Chris Gratton	□ 142 Jason Arnott
□ 147 Manon Rhéaume (G)	

INSERTS

This four-sport series featured the following hockey inserts: five hockey players amongst the 30 Autograph cards; two hockey players in the Acetate insert (12-card set sells at $45); three hockey players in the Draft Stars insert (20-card set sells at $20); four hockey players in the Limited Print insert (25-card set sells for $30); three hockey players in the Power Picks insert (20-card set sells for $20); one hockey trio in the five-card Tri-Card insert.

Chrome	**NRMT-MT**
□ CC13 Alexei Yashin	4.00
□ CC14 Alexandre Daigle	1.50
□ CC15 Manon Rhéaume (G)	15.00
□ CC16 Radek Bonk	2.00
Sudden Impact	**NRMT-MT**

□ SI6 Rob Niedermayer	.50
□ SI7 Jocelyn Thibault (G)	1.00
□ SI8 Derek Plante	.50

1993 - 94 CLASSIC PRO PROSPECTS

The most expensive cards are Manon Rhéaume at $2-3, Cammi Granato at $2-3, and Paul Kariya at $1-2. Regional stars sell at 30¢-$1; all other singles start at 20¢.

Imprint: © 1994 Classic Games, Inc.

Complete Set (250 cards):	**15.00**
Common Player:	**.20**

Player	Player
1 Radek Bonk	2 Radek Bonk
3 Radek Bonk	4 Vlastimil Kroupa
5 Mattias Norstrom	6 Jaroslav Nedved
7 Steve Dubinsky	8 Christian Proulx
9 Michal Grosek	10 Pat Neaton
11 Jason Arnott	12 Martin Brodeur (G)
13 Alexandre Daigle	14 Ted Drury
15 Iain Fraser	16 Chris Gratton
17 Greg Johnson	18 Paul Kariya
19 A. Karpovtsev	20 Chris LiPuma
21 Kirk Maltby	22 Sandy McCarthy
23 Darren McCarty	24 Jaroslav Modry
25 Jim Montgomery	26 Markus Näslund
27 Rob Niedermayer	28 Chris Osgood (G)
29 Pat Peake	30 Derek Plante
31 Chris Pronger	32 Mike Rathje
33 Mikael Renberg	34 Damian Rhodes (G)
35 Garth Snow (G)	36 Cam Stewart
37 Jim Storm	38 Michal Sykora
39 Jocelyn Thibault (G)	40 Alexei Yashin
41 Checklist 1 (1 - 84)	42 Vesa Viitakoski
43 Jake Grimes	44 Jim Dowd
45 Craig Ferguson	46 Mike Boback
47 François Groleau	48 Juha Riihijarvi
49 M. Shtalenkov (G)	50 Zigmund Palffy
51 Félix Potvin (G)	52 Alexei Kovalev
53 Larry Robinson	54 John LeClair
55 D. Roussel (G)	56 Geoff Sanderson
57 Greg Pankewicz	58 Brent Bilodeau
59 Brandon Convery	60 Fred Knipscheer
61 Igor Chibirev	62 Anatoli Fedotov
63 Bob Kellogg	64 Mike Maurice
65 Chad Penney	66 Mike Bavis
67 Eric Veilleux	68 Parris Duffus (G)
69 Daniel Lacroix	70 Milos Holan
71 Mike Muller	72 Michah Aivazoff
73 Krzysztop Oliwa	74 Ryan Hughes
75 Christian Soucy (G)	76 Keith Redmond
77 Mark DeSantis	78 Craig Martin
79 Mike Kennedy	80 Pauli Jaks (G)
81 Colin Chin	82 Jody Gage
83 Don Biggs	84 Tim Tookey
85 Clint Malarchuk (G)	86 Jozef Cierny
87 Radek Hamr	88 Jason Dawe
89 Chris Longo	90 Brian Rolston
91 Mike McKee	92 Vitali Prokhorov
93 Chris Snell	94 Martin Brochu (G)
95 Dan Plante	96 Darcy Werenka
97 Steffon Walby	98 David Emma
99 Dan Stiver	100 Radek Bonk
101 Mark Visheau	102 Dean Melanson
103 Vladimir Tsyplakov	104 Mikhail Volkov
105 Aaron Miller	106 Alexei Kudashov
107 Shawn Rivers	108 Ladislav Karabin
109 Matt Mallgrave	110 Craig Darby
111 M. Cousineau (G)	112 J. McLennan (G)
113 Yanic Perreault	114 Zac Boyer
115 Sergei Zubov	116 Dan Kesa
117 Jim Hiller	118 Dmitri Starostenko
119 Chris Tamer	120 Aaron Ward
121 Claude Savoie	122 Jamie Black
123 J-F Jomphe	124 Paxton Schulte
125 Jarkko Varvio	126 Jaroslav Otevrel
127 Dane Jackson	128 Brent Grieve
129 CL: Rhéaume	130 René Corbet
131 Joe Frederick	132 Martin Tanguay
133 Fredrik Jax	134 Jamie Linden
135 Jason Smith	136 Rick Kowalsky
137 Dino Grossi	138 Aris Brimanis
130 Jeff McLean	140 Tyler Wright
141 Roman Gorev	142 Dean Hulett
143 Niklas Sundblad	144 Jeff Bes
145 Pascal Rhéaume	146 Donald Brashear
147 Hugo Belanger	148 Blair Scott
149 Steve Staios	150 Matt Martin
151 Richard Matvichuk	152 Paul Brousseau
153 E. Namestnikov	154 Michael Peca
155 Jeff Nelson	156 Greg Andrusak
157 Norm Batherson	158 Martin Bakula
159 Ed Patterson	160 Steve Larouche
161 Libor Polasek	162 Jon Hillebrandt (G)
163 Guy Lévesque	164 Eric Lacroix
165 Scott Walker	166 Robert Burakovsky
167 M. Ketterer (G)	168 Mike Speer
169 Martin Jiranek	170 Andy Schneider
171 Terry Hollinger	172 Mark Lawrence
173 Martin Lapointe	174 Vaclav Prospal
175 Mike Fountain (G)	176 Alexander Kerch
177 Oleg Petrov	178 Derek Armstrong
179 Matthew Barnaby	180 Andrei Nazarov
181 Andrei Trefilov (G)	182 Jean-Yves Roy
183 Boris Rousson (G)	184 Daniel Laperrière
185 Yan Kaminsky	186 Ralph Intranuovo
187 Sandy Moger	188 Grant Marshall
189 Denny Felsner	190 Cory Stillman
191 Eric Lavigne	192 Jarrod Skalde
193 Steve Junker	194 A. Cherbayev
195 Nathan Lafayette	196 Ed Ward
197 Harijs Vitolinsh	198 Jarmo Kekäläinen
199 Neil Eisenhut	200 Radek Bonk
201 Jason Bonsignore	202 Jeff Friesen
203 Ed Jovanovski	204 Brett Lindros
205 Jeff O'Neill	206 Deron Quint
207 Vadim Sharifjanov	208 Oleg Tverdovsky
209 CL: Friesen/ O'Neill	210 David Cooper
211 Doug MacDonald	212 Leonid Toropchenko
213 Chris Rogles (G)	214 Vyacheslav Kozlov
215 Denis Metlyuk	216 Scott McKay
217 Brian Loney	218 Kevin Hodson (G)
219 Bobby House	220 Sergei Krivokrasov
221 Brett Harkins	222 Cale Hulse
223 Marc Tardif	224 Jon Rohloff
225 Kevin Smyth	226 Jason Young
227 Sergei Zholtok	228 Todd Simon
229 Jerome Bechard	230 Matt Robbins
231 Joe Cook	232 John Brill
233 Dan Goldie	234 Dan Gravelle
235 Shawn Wheeler	236 Brad Harrison
237 Joe Dragon	238 Jason Jennings
239 M. Rhéaume (G)	240 Jamie Steer
241 Scott Rogers	242 Lyle Wildgoose
243 Darren Colbourne	244 Mike Smith
245 Chris Bright	246 Chris Belanger
247 Darren Schwartz	248 Cammi Granato
249 Erin Whitten (G)	250 M. Rhéaume (G)

Autographs	Aut
Radek Bonk ✍ {#/2,400}	5.00
Jason Bonsignore ✍ {#/2,450}	3.00
Jeff Friesen ✍ {#/2,450}	5.00
Joé Juneau ✍ {#/1,370}	5.00
Alexei Kovalev ✍ {#/1,900}	15.00
Chris Pronger ✍ {#/1,400}	20.00
Manon Rhéaume (G) ✍ {#/1,900}	50.00
Erin Whitten (G) ✍ {#/1,800}	10.00
Alexei Yashin ✍ {#/1,400}	20.00

ICE AMBASSADORS

Insert Set (20 cards): **9.00**

Player	IA
IA1 Adrian Aucoin, Cdn.	.25
IA2 Corey Hirsch (G), Cdn.	.25
IA3 Paul Kariya, Cdn.	3.00
IA4 David Harlock, Cdn.	.25
IA5 Manny Legacé (G), Cdn.	1.00
IA6 Chris Therien, Cdn.	.25
IA7 Todd Warriner, Cdn.	.25
IA8 Todd Marchant, USA.	.25
IA9 Matt Martin, USA.	.25
IA10 Peter Ferraro, USA.	.25
IA11 Brian Rolston, USA.	.25
IA12 Jim Campbell, USA.	.25
IA13 Mike Dunham (G), USA.	1.00
IA14 Craig Johnson, USA.	.25
IA15 Saku Koivu, Fin.	2.00
IA16 Jere Lehtinen, Fin.	.25
IA17 Viktor Kozlov, CIS.	.25
IA18 Andrei Nikolishin, CIS.	.25
IA19 Sergei Gonchar, CIS.	.25
IA20 Valeri Karpov, CIS.	.25

INTERNATIONAL HEROES

Insert Set (25 cards): **30.00**

Player	NRMT-MT
LP1 Jim Campbell, USA.	1.00
LP2 Ted Drury, USA.	1.00
LP3 Mike Dunham (G), USA.	3.00
LP4 Chris Ferraro, USA.	1.00
LP5 Peter Ferraro, USA.	1.00
LP6 Darby Hendrickson, USA.	1.00
LP7 Craig Johnson, USA.	1.00
LP8 Todd Marchant, USA.	1.00
LP9 Matt Martin, USA.	1.00
LP10 Brian Rolston, USA.	1.00
LP11 Adrian Aucoin, Cdn.	1.00
LP12 Martin Gendron, Cdn.	1.00
LP13 David Harlock, Cdn.	1.00
LP14 Corey Hirsch (G), Cdn.	1.00
LP15 Paul Kariya, Cdn.	5.00
LP16 Manny Legacé (G), Cdn.	2.00
LP17 Brett Lindros, Cdn.	1.00
LP18 Brian Savage, Cdn.	1.00
LP19 Chris Terrien, Cdn.	1.00
LP20 Todd Warriner, Cdn.	1.00
LP21 Radek Bonk	1.00
LP22 Pavel Bure	4.00
LP23 Teemu Selänne	4.00
LP24 Mark Recchi	2.00
LP25 Alexei Yashin	3.00

1993 - 94 COCA-COLA THE GREAT ONE POGS

These caps were available at Mac's Milk in Canada. Singles sell at $1.50.

Cap Diameter: 1 3/4 "

Imprint: © 1994 WPF

Complete Set (18 caps): **20.00**

Gretzky	Gretzky
1 Wayne Gretzky	2 Wayne Gretzky
3 Wayne Gretzky	4 Wayne Gretzky
5 Wayne Gretzky	6 Wayne Gretzky
7 Wayne Gretzky	8 Wayne Gretzky
9 Wayne Gretzky	10 Wayne Gretzky
11 Wayne Gretzky	12 Wayne Gretzky
13 Wayne Gretzky	14 Wayne Gretzky
15 Wayne Gretzky	16 Wayne Gretzky
17 Wayne Gretzky	18 Wayne Gretzky

1993 - 94 DONRUSS

Imprint: 1993 LEAF INC.

Series One Set (400 cards): **20.00**

Update Set (110 cards): **10.00**

Common Player: **.20**

Player	NRMT-MT
1 Steven King, Anah.	.20
2 Joe Sacco, Anah.	.20
3 Anatoli Semenov, Anah.	.20
4 Terry Yake, Anah.	.20
5 Alexei Kasatonov, Anah.	.20
6 Patrik Carnbäck, Anah. RC	**.50**
7 Sean Hill, Anah.	.20
8 Bill Houlder, Anah.	.20
9 Todd Ewen, Anah.	.20
10 Bob Corkum, Anah.	.20
11 Tim Sweeney, Anah.	.20
12 Ron Tugnutt (G), Anah.	.20
13 Guy Hebert (G), Anah.	.20
14 Shaun Van Allen, Anah.	.20
15 Stu Grimson, Anah.	.20
16 Jon Casey (G), Bost.	.20
17 Daniel Marois, Bost.	.20
18 Adam Oates, Bost.	.20
19 Glen Wesley, Bost.	.20
20 Cam Stewart, Bost. RC	**.50**
21 Don Sweeney, Bost.	.20
22 Glen Murray, Bost.	.20
23 Jozef Stumpel, Bost.	.20
24 Raymond Bourque, Bost.	.50
25 Ted Donato, Bost.	.20
26 Joé Juneau, Bost.	.20
27 Dmitri Kvartalnov, Bost.	.20
28 Stephen Leach, Bost.	.20
29 Cam Neely, Bost.	.50
30 Bryan Smolinski, Bost.	.20
31 Craig Simpson, Buff.	.20
32 Donald Audette, Buff.	.20
33 Doug Bodger, Buff.	.20
34 Grant Fuhr (G), Buff.	.20
35 Dale Hawerchuk, Buff.	.20
36 Yuri Khmylev, Buff.	.20
37 Pat LaFontaine, Buff.	.20
38 Brad May, Buff.	.20
39 Alexander Mogilny, Buff.	.20
40 Richard Smehlik, Buff.	.20
41 Petr' Svoboda, Buff.	.20
42 Matthew Barnaby, Buff.	.20
43 Sergei Petrenko, Buff.	.20
44 Mark Astley, Buff. RC	**.50**
45 Derek Plante, Buff. RC	**.50**
46 Theoren Fleury, Calg.	.20
47 Al MacInnis, Calg.	.20
48 Joe Nieuwendyk, Calg.	.20
49 Joel Otto, Calg.	.20
50 Paul Ranheim, Calg.	.20
51 Robert Reichel, Calg.	.20
52 Gary Roberts, Calg.	.20
53 Gary Suter, Calg.	.20
54 Mike Vernon (G), Calg.	.20
55 Kelly Kisio, Calg.	.20
56 German Titov, Calg. RC	**.50**
57 Wes Walz, Calg.	.20
58 Ted Drury, Calg.	.20
59 Sandy McCarthy, Calg.	.20
60 Vesa Viitakoski, Calg. RC	**.50**
61 Jeff Hackett (G), Chic.	.20
62 Neil Wilkinson, Chic.	.20
63 Dirk Graham, Chic.	.20
64 Ed Belfour (G), Chic.	.50
65 Chris Chelios, Chic.	.20
66 Joe Murphy, Chic.	.20
67 Jeremy Roenick, Chic.	.50
68 J. Steve Smith, Chic.	.20
69 Brent Sutter, Chic.	.20
70 Steve Dubinsky, Chic. RC	**.50**
71 Michel Goulet, Chic.	.20
72 Christian Ruuttu, Chic.	.20
73 Bryan Marchment, Chic.	.20
74 Sergei Krivokrasov, Chic.	.20
75 Jeff Shantz, Chic. RC	**.50**
76 Mike Modano, Dall.	.50
77 Derian Hatcher, Dall.	.20
78 Ulf Dahlén, Dall.	.20
79 Mark Tinordi, Dall.	.20
80 Russ Courtnall, Dall.	.20
81 Mike Craig, Dall.	.20
82 Trent Klatt, Dall.	.20
83 Dave Gagner, Dall.	.20
84 Chris Tancill, Dall.	.20
85 James H. Black, Dall.	.20
86 Dean Evason, Dall.	.20
87 Andy Moog (G), Dall.	.20
88 Paul Cavallini, Dall.	.20
89 Grant Ledyard, Dall.	.20
90 Jarkko Varvio, Dall.	.20
91 Vyacheslav Kozlov, Detr.	.20
92 Mike Sillinger, Detr.	.20
93 Aaron Ward, Detr. RC	**.50**
94 Greg Johnson, Detr.	.20
95 Steve Yzerman, Detr.	1.50
96 Tim Cheveldae (G), Detr.	.20
97 Steve Chiasson, Detr.	.20
98 Dino Ciccarelli, Detr.	.20
99 Paul Coffey, Detr.	.20
100 Dallas Drake, Detr. RC	**.50**
101 Sergei Fedorov, Detr.	.50
102 Nicklas Lidström, Detr.	.20
103 Darren McCarty, Detr. RC	**1.50**
104 Bob Probert, Detr.	.20
105 Ray Sheppard, Detr.	.20
106 Scott Pearson, Edmo.	.20
107 Steven Rice, Edmo.	.20
108 Louie DeBrusk, Edmo.	.20
109 Dave Manson, Edmo.	.20
110 Dean McAmmond, Edmo.	.20
111 Roman Oksiuta, Edmo.	.20
112 Geoff Smith, Edmo.	.20
113 Zdeno Ciger, Edmo.	.20
114 Shayne Corson, Edmo.	.20
115 Luke Richardson, Edmo.	.20
116 Igor Kravchuk, Edmo.	.20
117 Bill Ranford (G), Edmo.	.20
118 Doug Weight, Edmo.	.20
119 Fred Brathwaite (G), Edmo. RC	**1.50**
120 Jason Arnott, Edmo. RC	**2.00**
121 Tom Fitzgerald, Flor.	.20
122 Mike Hough, Flor.	.20
123 Jesse Bélanger, Flor.	.20
124 Brian Skrudland, Flor.	.20
125 Dave Lowry, Flor.	.20
126 Scott Mellanby, Flor.	.20
127 Evgeny Davydov, Flor.	.20
128 Andrei Lomakin, Flor.	.20
129 Brian Benning, Flor.	.20
130 Scott Levins, Flor. RC	**.50**
131 Gord Murphy, Flor.	.20
132 John Vanbiesbrouck (G), Flor.	.20
133 Mark Fitzpatrick (G), Flor.	.20
134 Rob Niedermayer, Flor.	.20
135 Alexander Godynyuk, Flor.	.20
136 Eric Weinrich, Hart.	.20
137 Mark Greig, Hart.	.20
138 Jim Sandlak, Hart.	.20
139 Adam Burt, Hart.	.20
140 Nick Kypreos, Hart.	.20
141 Sean Burke (G), Hart.	.20
142 Andrew Cassels, Hart.	.20
143 Robert Kron, Hart.	.20
144 Michael Nylander, Hart.	.20
145 Robert Petrovicky, Hart.	.20
146 Patrick Poulin, Hart.	.20
147 Geoff Sanderson, Hart.	.20
148 Pat Verbeek, Hart.	.20
149 Zarley Zalapski, Hart.	.20
150 Chris Pronger, Hart.	.20
151 Jari Kurri, LosA.	.50
152 Wayne Gretzky, LosA.	2.50
153 Pat Conacher, LosA.	.20
154 Shawn McEachern, LosA.	.20
155 Mike Donnelly, LosA.	.20
156 Warren Rychel, LosA.	.20
157 Gary Shuchuk, LosA.	.20
158 Rob Blake, LosA.	.20
159 Jimmy Carson, LosA.	.20
160 Tony Granato, LosA.	.20
161 Kelly Hrudey (G), LosA.	.20
162 Luc Robitaille, LosA.	.50
163 Tomas Sandström, LosA.	.20
164 Darryl Sydor, LosA.	.20
165 Alexei Zhitnik, LosA.	.20
166 Benoît Brunet, Mont.	.20
167 Lyle Odelein, Mont.	.20
168 Kevin Haller, Mont.	.20
169 Pierre Sévigny, Mont.	.20
170 Brian Bellows, Mont.	.20
171 Patrice Brisebois, Mont.	.20
172 Vincent Damphousse, Mont.	.20
173 Éric Desjardins, Mont.	.20
174 Gilbert Dionne, Mont.	.20
175 Stéphan Lebeau, Mont.	.20
176 John LeClair, Mont.	.50
177 Kirk Muller, Mont.	.20
178 Patrick Roy (G), Mont.	1.50
179 Mathieu Schneider, Mont.	.20
180 Peter Popovic, Mont. RC	**.50**
181 Corey Millen, NJer.	.20
182 Jason Smith, NJer. RC	**.50**
183 Bobby Holik, NJer.	.20
184 John MacLean, NJer.	.20
185 Bruce Driver, NJer.	.20
186 Bill Guerin, NJer.	.20
187 Claude Lemieux, NJer.	.20
188 Bernie Nicholls, NJer.	.20
189 Scott Niedermayer, NJer.	.20
190 Stéphane J.J. Richer, NJer.	.20
191 Alexander Semak, NJer.	.20
192 Scott Stevens, NJer.	.20
193 Valeri Zelepukin, NJer.	.20
194 Chris Terreri (G), NJer.	.20
195 Martin Brodeur (G), NJer.	1.00
196 Ron Hextall (G), NYIs.	.50
197 Brad Dalgarno, NYIs.	.20
198 Ray Ferraro, NYIs.	.20
199 Patrick Flatley, NYIs.	.20
200 Travis Green, NYIs.	.20
201 Benoît Hogue, NYIs.	.20
202 Steve Junker, NYIs. RC	**.50**
203 Darius Kasparaitis, NYIs.	.20
204 Derek King, NYIs.	.20
205 Uwe Krupp, NYIs.	.20
206 Scott Lachance, NYIs.	.20
207 Vladimir Malakhov, NYIs.	.20
208 Steve Thomas, NYIs.	.20
209 Pierre Turgeon, NYIs.	.20
210 Scott Scissons, NYIs.	.20
211 Glenn Healy (G), NYRa.	.20
212 Alexander Karpovtsev, NYRa.	.20
213 James Patrick, NYRa.	.20
214 Sergei Nemchinov, NYRa.	.20
215 Esa Tikkanen, NYRa.	.20
216 Corey Hirsch (G), NYRa.	.20
217 Tony Amonte, NYRa.	.20
218 Mike Gartner, NYRa.	.50
219 Adam Graves, NYRa.	.20
220 Alexei Kovalev, NYRa.	.20
221 Brian Leetch, NYRa.	.20
222 Mark Messier, NYRa.	.50
223 Mike Richter (G), NYRa.	.20
224 Darren Turcotte, NYRa.	.20
225 Sergei Zubov, NYRa.	.20
226 Craig Billington (G), Otta.	.20

☐	227 Troy Mallette, Otta.	.20
☐	228 Vladimír Ruzicka, Otta.	.20
☐	**229 Darrin Madeley (G), Otta. RC**	**.50**
☐	230 Mark Lamb, Otta.	.20
☐	231 Dave Archibald, Otta.	.20
☐	232 Bob Kudelski, Otta.	.20
☐	233 Norm Maciver, Otta.	.20
☐	234 Brad Shaw, Otta.	.20
☐	235 Sylvain Turgeon, Otta.	.20
☐	236 Brian Glynn, Otta.	.20
☐	237 Alexandre Daigle, Otta.	.20
☐	238 Alexei Yashin, Otta.	.50
☐	239 Dmitri Filimonov, Otta.	.20
☐	240 Pavol Demitra, Otta.	.20
☐	**241 Jason Bowen, Phil. RC**	**.50**
☐	242 Eric Lindros, Phil.	.50
☐	243 Dominic Roussel (G), Phil.	.20
☐	**244 Milos Holan, Phil. RC**	**.50**
☐	245 Greg Hawgood, Phil.	.20
☐	246 Yves Racine, Phil.	.20
☐	247 Josef Beránek, Phil.	.20
☐	248 Rod Brind'Amour, Phil.	.20
☐	249 Kevin Dineen, Phil.	.20
☐	250 Pelle Eklund, Phil.	.20
☐	251 Garry Galley, Phil.	.20
☐	252 Mark Recchi, Phil.	.20
☐	253 Tommy Söderström (G), Phil.	.20
☐	254 Dmitry Yushkevich, Phil.	.20
☐	255 Mikael Renberg, Phil.	.20
☐	256 Marty McSorley, Pitt.	.20
☐	257 Joe Mullen, Pitt.	.20
☐	258 Doug Brown, Pitt.	.20
☐	259 Kjell Samuelsson, Pitt.	.20
☐	260 Tom Barrasso (G), Pitt.	.20
☐	261 Ron Francis, Pitt.	.20
☐	262 Mario Lemieux, Pitt.	1.50
☐	263 Larry Murphy, Pitt.	.20
☐	264 Ulf Samuelsson, Pitt.	.20
☐	265 Kevin Stevens, Pitt.	.20
☐	266 Martin Straka, Pitt.	.20
☐	267 Rick Tocchet, Pitt.	.20
☐	268 Bryan Trottier, Pitt.	.50
☐	269 Markus Näslund, Pitt.	.50
☐	270 Jaromir Jagr, Pitt.	.50
☐	271 Martin Gélinas, Québ.	.20
☐	272 Adam Foote, Québ.	.20
☐	273 Curtis Leschyshyn, Québ.	.20
☐	274 Stéphane Fiset (G), Québ.	.20
☐	**275 Jocelyn Thibault (G), Québ. RC**	**2.00**
☐	276 Steve Duchesne, Québ.	.20
☐	277 Valeri Kamensky, Québ.	.20
☐	278 Andrei Kovalenko, Québ.	.20
☐	279 Owen Nolan, Québ.	.20
☐	280 Mike Ricci, Québ.	.20
☐	281 Martin Rucinsky, Québ.	.20
☐	282 Joe Sakic, Québ.	1.00
☐	283 Mats Sundin, Québ.	.50
☐	284 Scott Young, Québ.	.20
☐	285 Claude Lapointe, Québ.	.20
☐	286 Brett Hull, SLou.	.50
☐	287 Vitali Karamnov, SLou.	.20
☐	288 Ron Sutter, SLou.	.20
☐	289 Garth Butcher, SLou.	.20
☐	290 Vitali Prokhorov, SLou.	.20
☐	291 Bret Hedican, SLou.	.20
☐	292 Tony Hrkac, SLou.	.20
☐	293 Jeff R. Brown, SLou.	.20
☐	294 Phil Housley, SLou.	.20
☐	295 Craig Janney, SLou.	.20
☐	296 Curtis Joseph (G), SLou.	.50
☐	297 Igor Korolev, SLou.	.20
☐	298 Kevin Miller, SLou.	.20
☐	299 Brendan Shanahan, SLou.	.50
☐	**300 Jim Montgomery, SLou. RC**	**.50**
☐	301 Gaétan Duchesne, SanJ.	.20
☐	302 Jimmy Waite (G), SanJ.	.20
☐	303 Jeff Norton, SanJ.	.20
☐	304 Sergei Makarov, SanJ.	.20
☐	305 Igor Larionov, SanJ.	.20
☐	306 Mike Lalor, SanJ.	.20
☐	**307 Michal Sykora, SanJ. RC**	**.50**
☐	308 Pat Falloon, SanJ.	.20
☐	309 Johan Garpenlöv, SanJ.	.20
☐	**310 Rob Gaudreau, SanJ. RC**	**.50**
☐	311 Arturs Irbe (G), SanJ.	.20
☐	312 Sandis Ozolinsh, SanJ.	.20
☐	313 Doug Zmolek, SanJ.	.20
☐	314 Mike Rathje, SanJ.	.20
☐	**315 Vlastimil Kroupa, SanJ. RC**	**.50**
☐	316 Daren Puppa (G), Tamp.	.20
☐	317 Petr Klima, Tamp.	.20
☐	**318 Brent Gretzky, Tamp. RC**	**.50**
☐	319 Denis Savard, Tamp.	.20
☐	320 Gerard Gallant, Tamp.	.20
☐	321 Joe Reekie, Tamp.	.20
☐	322 Mikael Andersson, Tamp.	.20
☐	**323 Bill McDougall, Tamp. RC**	**.50**
☐	324 Brian Bradley, Tamp.	.20
☐	325 Shawn Chambers, Tamp.	.20
☐	326 Adam Creighton, Tamp.	.20
☐	327 Roman Hamrlik, Tamp.	.20
☐	328 John Tucker, Tamp.	.20
☐	329 Rob Zamuner, Tamp.	.20
☐	330 Chris Gratton, Tamp.	.20
☐	331 Sylvain Lefebvre, Toro.	.20
☐	332 Nikolai Borschevsky, Toro.	.20
☐	333 Bob Rouse, Toro.	.20
☐	334 John Cullen, Toro.	.20
☐	335 Todd Gill, Toro.	.20
☐	336 Drake Berehowsky, Toro.	.20
☐	337 Wendel Clark, Toro.	.50
☐	338 Peter Zezel, Toro.	.20
☐	339 Rob Pearson, Toro.	.20
☐	340 Glenn Anderson, Toro.	.20
☐	341 Doug Gilmour, Toro.	.20
☐	342 Dave Andreychuk, Toro.	.20
☐	343 Félix Potvin (G), Toro.	.20
☐	344 Dave Ellett, Toro.	.20
☐	**345 Alexei Kudashov, Toro. RC**	**.50**
☐	346 Gino Odjick, Vanc.	.20
☐	347 Jyrki Lumme, Vanc.	.20
☐	348 Dana Murzyn, Vanc.	.20
☐	349 Sergio Momesso, Vanc.	.20
☐	350 Greg A. Adams, Vanc.	.20
☐	351 Pavel Bure, Vanc.	.50
☐	352 Geoff Courtnall, Vanc.	.20
☐	353 Murray Craven, Vanc.	.20
☐	354 Trevor Linden, Vanc.	.20
☐	355 Kirk McLean (G), Vanc.	.20
☐	356 Petr Nedved, Vanc.	.20
☐	357 Cliff Ronning, Vanc.	.20
☐	358 Jiri Slégr, Vanc.	.20
☐	359 Kay Whitmore (G), Vanc.	.20
☐	360 Gerald Diduck, Vanc.	.20
☐	361 Pat Peake, Wash.	.20
☐	362 Dave Poulin, Wash.	.20
☐	363 Rick Tabaracci (G), Wash.	.20
☐	364 Jason Woolley, Wash.	.20
☐	365 Kelly Miller, Wash.	.20
☐	366 Peter Bondra, Wash.	.20
☐	367 Sylvain Côté, Wash.	.20
☐	368 Pat Elynuik, Wash.	.20
☐	369 Kevin Hatcher, Wash.	.20
☐	370 Dale Hunter, Wash.	.20
☐	371 Al Iafrate, Wash.	.20
☐	372 Calle Johansson, Wash.	.20
☐	373 Dmitri Khristich, Wash.	.20
☐	374 Michal Pivonka, Wash.	.20
☐	375 Mike Ridley, Wash.	.20
☐	376 Paul Ysebaert, Winn.	.20
☐	377 Stu Barnes, Winn.	.20
☐	378 Sergei Bautin, Winn.	.20
☐	379 Kris King, Winn.	.20
☐	380 Alexei Zhamnov, Winn.	.20
☐	381 Tie Domi, Winn.	.20
☐	382 Bob Essensa (G), Winn.	.20
☐	383 Nelson Emerson, Winn.	.20
☐	384 Boris Mironov, Winn.	.20
☐	385 Teppo Numminen, Winn.	.20
☐	386 Fredrik Olausson, Winn.	.20
☐	387 Teemu Selänne, Winn.	.50
☐	388 Darrin Shannon, Winn.	.20
☐	389 Thomas Steen, Winn.	.20
☐	390 Keith Tkachuk, Winn.	.20
☐	391 Panthers	.20
☐	392 Mighty Ducks	.20
☐	393 Draft Picks	.20
☐	394 Record breakers	.50
☐	395 Record breakers	1.50
☐	396 Checklist	.20
☐	397 Checklist	.20
☐	398 Checklist	.20
☐	399 Checklist	.20
☐	400 Checklist	.20
☐	401 Garry Valk, Anah.	.20
☐	402 Al Iafrate, Bost.	.20
☐	403 David Reid, Bost.	.20
☐	404 Jason Dawe, Buff.	.20
☐	405 Craig Muni, Buff.	.20
☐	406 Dan Keczmer, Calg. RC	.20
☐	407 Michael Nylander, Calg.	.20
☐	408 James Patrick, Calg.	.20
☐	409 Andrei Trefilov (G), Calg.	.20
☐	410 Zarley Zalapski, Calg.	.20
☐	411 Tony Amonte, Chic.	.20
☐	412 Keith Carney, Chic.	.20
☐	413 Randy Cunneyworth, Chic.	.20
☐	**414 Ivan Droppa, Chic. RC**	**.50**
☐	415 Gary Suter, Chic.	.20
☐	416 Eric Weinrich, Chic.	.20
☐	417 Paul Ysebaert, Chic.	.20
☐	418 Richard Matvichuk, Dall.	.20
☐	419 Alan May, Dall.	.20
☐	420 Darcy Wakaluk (G), Dall.	.20
☐	**421 Micah Aivazoff, Detr. RC**	**.50**
☐	422 Terry Carkner, Detr.	.20
☐	423 Kris Draper, Detr.	.20
☐	**424 Chris Osgood (G), Detr. RC**	**3.00**
☐	425 Keith Primeau, Detr.	.20
☐	426 Bob Beers, Edmo.	.20
☐	427 Ilya Byakin, Edmo.	.20
☐	**428 Kirk Maltby, Edmo. RC**	**1.00**
☐	429 Boris Mironov, Edmo.	.20
☐	430 Fredrik Olausson, Edmo.	.20
☐	**431 Peter White, Edmo. RC**	**.50**
☐	432 Stu Barnes, Flor.	.20
☐	433 Mike Foligno, Flor.	.20
☐	434 Bob Kudelski, Flor.	.20
☐	435 Geoff Smith, Flor.	.20
☐	436 Igor Chibirev, Hart. RC	.20
☐	437 Ted Drury, Hart.	.20
☐	438 Alexander Godynyuk, Hart.	.20
☐	439 Frantisek Kucera, Hart.	.20
☐	440 Jocelyn Lemieux, Hart.	.20
☐	441 Brian Propp, Hart.	.20
☐	442 Paul Ranheim, Hart.	.20
☐	443 Jeff Reese (G), Hart.	.20
☐	**444 Kevin Smyth, Hart. RC**	**.50**
☐	**445 Jim Storm, Hart. RC**	**.50**
☐	**446 Phil Crowe, LosA. RC**	**.50**
☐	447 Marty McSorley, LosA.	.20
☐	**448 Keith Redmond, LosA. RC**	**.50**
☐	449 Dixon Ward, LosA.	.20
☐	450 Guy Carbonneau, Mont.	.20
☐	451 Mike Keane, Mont.	.20
☐	452 Oleg Petrov, Mont.	.20
☐	453 Ron Tugnutt (G), Mont.	.20
☐	454 Randy McKay, NJer.	.20
☐	**455 Jaroslav Modry, NJer. RC**	**.50**
☐	456 Yan Kaminsky, NYIs.	.20
☐	457 Marty McInnis, NYIs.	.20
☐	**458 Jamie McLennan (G), NYIs. RC**	**.50**
☐	459 Zigmund Palffy, NYIs.	.20
☐	460 Glenn Anderson, NYRa.	.20
☐	461 Steve Larmer, NYRa.	.20
☐	462 Craig MacTavish, NYRa.	.20
☐	463 Stéphane Matteau, NYRa.	.20
☐	464 Brian Noonan, NYRa.	.20
☐	**465 Mattias Norström, NYRa. RC**	**1.00**
☐	466 Scott Levins, Otta.	.20
☐	**467 Derek Mayer, Otta. RC**	**.50**
☐	**468 Andy Schneider, Otta. RC**	**.50**
☐	**469 Todd Hlushko, Phil. RC**	**.50**
☐	**470 Stewart Malgunas, Phil. RC**	**.50**
☐	**471 Justin Duberman, Pitt. RC**	**.50**
☐	**472 Ladislav Karabin, Pitt. RC**	**.50**
☐	473 Shawn McEachern, Pitt.	.20
☐	**474 Ed Patterson, Pitt. RC**	**.50**
☐	475 Tomas Sandström, Pitt.	.20
☐	476 Bob Bassen, Québ.	.20
☐	477 Garth Butcher, Québ.	.20
☐	**478 Iain Fraser, Québ. RC**	**.50**
☐	**479 Mike McKee, Québ. RC**	**.50**
☐	**480 Dwayne Norris, Québ. RC**	**.50**
☐	**481 Garth Snow (G), Québ. RC**	**1.50**
☐	482 Ron Sutter, Québ.	.20
☐	483 Kelly Chase, SLou.	.20
☐	484 Steve Duchesne, SLou.	.20
☐	485 Daniel Laperrière, SLou.	.20
☐	486 Petr Nedved, SLou.	.20
☐	487 Peter Stastny, SLou.	.20
☐	488 Ulf Dahlén, SanJ.	.20
☐	489 Todd Elik, SanJ.	.20
☐	**490 Andrei Nazarov, SanJ. RC**	**.50**
☐	491 Danton Cole, Tamp.	.20
☐	492 Chris Joseph, Tamp.	.20
☐	**493 Chris LiPuma, Tamp. RC**	**.50**
☐	494 Mike Gartner, Toro.	.50
☐	495 Mark Greig, Toro.	.20
☐	496 David Harlock, Toro.	.20
☐	**497 Matt Martin, Toro. RC**	**.50**
☐	498 Shawn Antoski, Vanc.	.20
☐	499 Jeff R. Brown, Vanc.	.20
☐	500 Jimmy Carson, Vanc.	.20
☐	501 Martin Gélinas, Vanc.	.20
☐	**502 Yevgeny (John) Namestnikov, Vanc. RC**	**.50**
☐	503 Randy Burridge, Wash.	.20
☐	504 Joé Juneau, Wash.	.20
☐	**505 Kevin Kaminski, Wash. RC**	**.50**
☐	506 Arto Blomsten, Winn.	.20
☐	507 Tim Cheveldae (G), Winn.	.20
☐	508 Dallas Drake, Winn.	.20
☐	509 Dave Manson, Winn.	.20
☐	510 Checklist	.20

	Premier Edition	**PE**
☐	**EC Mario Lemieux, Pitt.**	**30.00**
☐	**WC Luc Robitaille, LosA.**	**9.00**

SPECIAL PRINT

	Insert Set (26 cards):	**95.00**
	Player (#/20,000)	**SP**
☐	A Ron Tugnutt (G), Anah.	2.00
☐	B Adam Oates, Bost.	2.00
☐	C Alexander Mogilny, Buff.	2.00
☐	D Theoren Fleury, Calg.	2.00
☐	E Jeremy Roenick, Chic.	5.00
☐	F Mike Modano, Dall.	5.00
☐	G Steve Yzerman, Detr.	15.00
☐	H Jason Arnott, Edmo.	5.00
☐	I Rob Niedermayer, Flor.	2.00
☐	J Chris Pronger, Hart.	2.00
☐	K Wayne Gretzky, LosA.	25.00
☐	L Patrick Roy (G), Mont.	15.00
☐	M Scott Niedermayer, NJer.	2.00
☐	N Pierre Turgeon, NYIs.	2.00
☐	O Mark Messier, NYRa.	5.00
☐	P Alexandre Daigle, Otta.	2.00
☐	Q Eric Lindros, Phil.	5.00
☐	R Mario Lemieux, Pitt.	15.00
☐	S Mats Sundin, Québ.	5.00
☐	T Pat Falloon, SanJ.	2.00
☐	U Brett Hull, SLou.	5.00
☐	V Chris Gratton, Tamp.	2.00
☐	W Félix Potvin (G), Toro.	2.00
☐	X Pavel Bure, Vanc.	5.00
☐	Y Al Iafrate, Wash.	2.00
☐	Z Teemu Selänne, Winn.	5.00

ELITE SERIES

	Insert Set (15 cards):	**170.00**
	Player (#/10,000)	**ES**
☐	1 Mario Lemieux, Pitt.	35.00
☐	2 Alexandre Daigle, Otta.	6.00
☐	3 Teemu Selänne, Winn.	10.00
☐	4 Eric Lindros, Phil.	10.00
☐	5 Brett Hull, SLou.	10.00
☐	6 Jeremy Roenick, Chic.	10.00
☐	7 Doug Gilmour, Toro.	6.00
☐	8 Alexander Mogilny, Buff.	6.00
☐	9 Patrick Roy (G), Mont.	35.00
☐	10 Wayne Gretzky, LosA.	50.00
☐	U1 Mikael Renberg, Phil.	6.00
☐	U2 Sergei Fedorov, Detr.	10.00
☐	U3 Félix Potvin (G), Toro.	6.00
☐	U4 Cam Neely, Bost.	10.00
☐	U5 Alexei Yashin, Otta.	6.00

ICE KINGS

	Insert Set (10 cards):	**20.00**
	Player (art by Dick Perez)	**IK**
☐	1 Patrick Roy (G), Mont.	6.00
☐	2 Pat LaFontaine, Buff.	1.00
☐	3 Jaromir Jagr, Pitt.	2.00
☐	4 Wayne Gretzky, LosA.	8.00
☐	5 Chris Chelios, Chic.	1.00
☐	6 Félix Potvin (G), Toro.	1.00
☐	7 Mario Lemieux, Pitt.	6.00
☐	8 Pavel Bure, Vanc.	1.00
☐	9 Eric Lindros, Phil.	2.00
☐	10 Teemu Selänne, Winn.	1.00

RATED ROOKIE

	Insert Set (15 cards):	**20.00**
	Player	**RR**
☐	1 Alexandre Daigle, Otta.	.50
☐	2 Chris Gratton, Tamp.	1.00
☐	3 Chris Pronger, Hart.	3.00
☐	4 Rob Niedermayer, Flor.	1.00
☐	5 Mikael Renberg, Phil.	1.00
☐	6 Jarkko Varvio, Dall.	1.00
☐	7 Alexei Yashin, Otta.	3.00
☐	8 Markus Näslund, Pitt.	5.00
☐	9 Boris Mironov, Winn.	.50
☐	10 Martin Brodeur (G), NJer.	8.00
☐	11 Jocelyn Thibault (G), Québ.	2.00
☐	12 Jason Arnott, Edmo.	4.00
☐	13 Jim Montgomery, SLou.	.50
☐	14 Ted Drury, Calg.	.50
☐	15 Roman Oksiuta, Edmo.	.50

WORLD JUNIOR CHAMPIONSHIP

	Insert Set (15 cards):	**20.00**
	Player	**WJC**
☐	**CAN1 Jason Allison, Canada Juniors RC**	**3.50**
☐	**CAN2 Chris Armstrong, Canada Juniors RC**	**.50**
☐	**CAN3 Drew Bannister, Canada Juniors RC**	**.50**
☐	**CAN4 Jason Botterill, Canada Juniors RC**	**.50**
☐	**CAN5 Joël Bouchard, Canada Juniors RC**	**.50**
☐	**CAN6 Curtis Bowen, Canada Juniors RC**	**.50**
☐	**CAN7 Anson Carter, Canada Juniors RC**	**1.50**
☐	**CAN8 B. Convery, Canada Juniors RC**	**.50**
☐	**CAN9 Yannick Dubé, Canada Juniors RC**	**.50**
☐	**CAN10 M. Fernandez, Canada Juniors RC**	**2.00**
☐	**CAN11 Jeff Friesen, Canada Juniors RC**	**1.50**
☐	**CAN12 Aaron Gavey, Canada Juniors RC**	**.50**
☐	**CAN13 Martin Gendron, Canada Juniors RC**	**.50**
☐	**CAN14 Rick Girard, Canada Juniors RC**	**.50**
☐	**CAN15 Todd Harvey, Canada Juniors RC**	**.50**
☐	**CAN16 Bryan McCabe, Canada Juniors RC**	**1.00**
☐	**CAN17 Marty Murray, Canada Juniors RC**	**.50**
☐	**CAN18 Michael Peca, Canada Juniors RC**	**2.00**
☐	**CAN19 Nick Stajduhar, Canada Juniors RC**	**.50**
☐	**CAN20 Jamie Storr (G), Canada Juniors RC**	**.50**
☐	CAN21 Brent Tully, Canada Juniors	.50
☐	**CAN22 Brendan Witt, Canada Juniors RC**	**.50**
☐	**USA1 Kevyn Adams, U.S.A. Juniors RC**	**.50**
☐	**USA2 Jason Bonsignore, U.S.A. Juniors RC**	**.50**
☐	**USA3 Andy Brink, U.S.A. Juniors RC**	**.50**
☐	**USA4 Jon Coleman, U.S.A. Juniors RC**	**.50**
☐	USA5 Adam Deadmarsh, U.S.A. Juniors	1.00
☐	**USA6 Aaron Ellis, U.S.A. Juniors RC**	**.50**
☐	USA7 John Emmons, U.S.A. Juniors	.50
☐	**USA8 Ashlin Halfnight, U.S.A. Juniors RC**	**.50**
☐	**USA9 Kevin Hilton, U.S.A. Juniors RC**	**.50**
☐	**USA10 Jason Karmanos, U.S.A. Juniors RC**	**.50**
☐	**USA11 Toby Kvalevog, U.S.A. Juniors RC**	**.50**
☐	**USA12 Bob Lachance, U.S.A. Juniors RC**	**.50**
☐	**USA13 Langenbrunner, U.S.A. Juniors RC**	**1.00**
☐	**USA14 Jason McBain, U.S.A. Juniors RC**	**.50**
☐	**USA15 Chris O'Sullivan, U.S.A. Juniors RC**	**.50**
☐	**USA16 Jay Pandolfo, U.S.A. Juniors RC**	**.50**
☐	**USA17 Richard Park, U.S.A. Juniors RC**	**.50**
☐	**USA18 Deron Quint, U.S.A. Juniors RC**	**.50**
☐	USA19 Ryan Sittler, U.S.A. Juniors	.50
☐	**USA20 Blake Sloan, U.S.A. Juniors RC**	**.50**

□	**USA21 John Varga, U.S.A. Juniors RC**	**.50**
□	**USA22 David Wilkie, U.S.A. Juniors RC**	**.50**
□	Checklist	.50

1993 - 94 DURIVAGE / DIANA - SCORE

Imprint: Score

Complete Set (51 cards): 25.00

	Player	Score
□	1 Alexandre Daigle, Otta.	.35
□	2 Pierre Sévigny, Mont.	.35
□	3 Jocelyn Thibault (G), Québ.	.50
□	4 Philippe Boucher, Buff.	.35
□	5 Martin Brodeur (G), NJer.	3.00
□	6 Martin Lapointe, Detr.	.50
□	7 Patrice Brisebois, Mont.	.35
□	8 Benoît Brunet, Mont.	.35
□	9 Guy Carbonneau, Mont.	.50
□	10 J.J. Daigneault, Mont.	.35
□	11 Vincent Damphousse, Mont.	1.00
□	12 Eric Desjardins, Mont.	.50
□	13 Gilbert Dionne, Mont.	.35
□	14 Stéphan Lebeau, Mont.	.35
□	15 André Racicot (G), Mont.	.35
□	16 Mario Roberge, Mont.	.35
□	17 Patrick Roy (G), Mont.	5.00
□	18 Jacques Cloutier (G), Québ.	.35
□	19 Alain Côté, Québ.	.35
□	20 Steve Finn, Québ.	.35
□	21 Stéphane Fiset (G), Québ.	.50
□	22 Martin Gélinas, Québ.	.35
□	23 Reginald Savage, Québ.	.35
□	24 Claude Lapointe, Québ.	.35
□	25 Denis Savard, Tamp.	.50
□	26 Ray Bourque, Bost.	2.00
□	27 Joé Juneau, Bost.	.35
□	28 Ron Stern, Calg.	.35
□	29 Benoît Hogue, NYIs.	.35
□	30 Pierre Turgeon, NYIs.	.50
□	31 Mike Krushelnyski, Toro.	.35
□	32 Félix Potvin (G), Toro.	1.00
□	33 Sergio Momesso, Vanc.	.35
□	34 Yves Racine, Phil.	.35
□	35 Sylvain Côté, Wash.	.35
□	36 Sylvain Turgeon, Otta.	.35
□	37 Kevin Dineen, Phil.	.35
□	38 Garry Galley, Phil.	.35
□	39 Dominic Roussel (G), Phil.	.35
□	40 Gaetan Duchesne, Dall.	.35
□	41 Luc Robitaille, LosA.	1.00
□	42 Michel Goulet, Chic.	.50
□	43 Jocelyn Lemieux, Chic.	.35
□	44 Stéphane Matteau, Chic.	.35
□	45 Mike Hough, Flor.	.35
□	46 Scott Mellanby, Flor.	.35
□	47 Claude Lemieux, NJer.	.50
□	48 Stéphane Richer, NJer.	.35
□	49 Jimmy Waite (G), SanJ.	.35
□	50 Patrick Poulin, Hart.	.35
□	Checklist 1 (1 - 50)	.35

	Player	Auto.
□	Patrick Roy (G), Mont. ✍	120.00
□	Jocelyn Thibault (G), Québ. ✍	30.00

1993 - 94 EA SPORTS

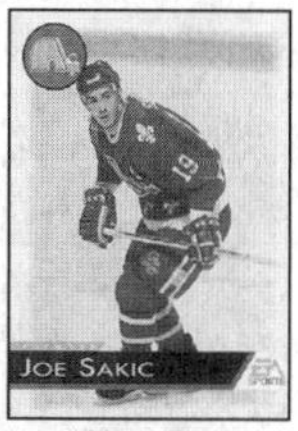

Complete Set (225 cards): 65.00

Common Player: .25

	Player	NRMT-MT
□	1 Alexei Kasatonov, NJer. (Anah.)	.50
□	2 Randy Ladouceur, Hart. (Anah.)	.25
□	3 Terry Yake, Hart. (Anah.)	.25
□	4 Troy Loney, Pitt. (Anah.)	.25
□	5 Anatoli Semenov, Edmo. (Anah.)	.25
□	6 Guy Hebert (G), SLou. (Anah.)	.50
□	7 Raymond Bourque, Bost.	3.00
□	8 Adam Oates, Bost.	1.00
□	8 Don Sweeney, Bost.	.25
□	11 Cam Neely, Bost.	2.50
□	12 Andy Moog (G), Bost.	1.00
□	13 Doug Bodger, Buff.	.25
□	14 Petr* Svoboda, Buff.	.50
□	15 Pat LaFontaine, Buff.	1.50
□	16 Dale Hawerchuk, Buff.	1.50
□	17 Alexander Mogilny, Buff.	1.00
□	18 Grant Fuhr (G), Buff.	1.50
□	19 Joé Juneau, Bost.	.50
□	19 Gary Suter, Calg.	.50
□	20 Al MacInnis, Calg.	1.00
□	21 Joe Nieuwendyk, Calg.	1.00
□	22 Gary Roberts, Calg.	1.00
□	23 Theoren Fleury, Calg.	1.50
□	24 Mike Vernon (G), Calg.	1.00
□	25 Chris Chelios, Chic.	1.50
□	26 J. Steve Smith, Chic.	.50
□	27 Jeremy Roenick, Chic.	2.00
□	28 Michel Goulet, Chic.	1.00
□	29 Steve Larmer, Chic.	1.00
□	30 Ed Belfour (G), Chic.	2.50
□	31 Mark Tinordi, Dall.	.25
□	32 Tommy Sjödin, Dall.	.25
□	33 Mike Modano, Dall.	2.50
□	34 Dave Gagner, Dall.	.25
□	35 Russ Courtnall, Dall.	.50
□	36 Jon Casey (G), Dall.	.25
□	37 Paul Coffey, Detr.	1.50
□	38 Steve Chiasson, Detr.	.25
□	39 Steve Yzerman, Detr.	6.00
□	40 Sergei Fedorov, Detr.	2.50
□	41 Dino Ciccarelli, Detr.	.50
□	42 Tim Cheveldae (G), Detr.	.25
□	43 Dave Manson, Edmo.	.25
□	44 Igor Kravchuk, Edmo.	.25
□	45 Doug Weight, Edmo.	1.50
□	46 Shayne Corson, Edmo.	.50
□	47 Petr Klima, Edmo.	.25
□	48 Bill Ranford (G), Edmo.	1.00
□	49 Joe Cirella, NYRa. (Flor.)	.25
□	50 Gord Murphy, Phil. (Flor.)	.25
□	51 Brian Skrudland, Calg. (Flor.)	.25
□	52 Andrei Lomakin, Phil. (Flor.)	.25
□	53 Scott Mellanby, Edmo. (Flor.)	.50
□	54 John Vanbiesbrouck (G), NYRa. (Flor.)	1.00
□	55 Zarley Zalapski, Hart.	.25
□	56 Eric Weinrich, Hart.	.25
□	57 Andrew Cassels, Hart.	.50
□	58 Geoff Sanderson, Hart.	.50
□	59 Pat Verbeek, Hart.	.50
□	60 Sean Burke (G), Hart.	1.50
□	61 Rob Blake, LosA.	1.50
□	62 Marty McSorley, LosA.	.50
□	63 Wayne Gretzky, LosA.	10.00
□	64 Luc Robitaille, LosA.	2.00
□	65 Tomas Sandström, LosA.	.50
□	66 Kelly Hrudey (G), LosA.	1.00
□	67 Éric Desjardins, Mont.	.50
□	68 Mathieu Schneider, Mont.	.50
□	69 Kirk Muller, Mont.	.50
□	70 Vincent Damphousse, Mont.	1.50
□	71 Brian Bellows, Mont.	.50
□	72 Patrick Roy (G), Mont.	7.50
□	73 Scott Stevens, NJer.	1.00
□	74 Viacheslav Fetisov, NJer.	1.50
□	75 Alexander Semak, NJer.	.25
□	76 Stéphane J.J. Richer, NJer.	.50
□	77 Claude Lemieux, NJer.	.50
□	78 Chris Terreri (G), NJer.	.50
□	79 Vladimir Malakhov, NYIs.	.25
□	80 Darius Kasparaitis, NYIs.	.50
□	81 Pierre Turgeon, NYIs.	1.00
□	82 Steve Thomas, NYIs.	.25
□	83 Benoît Hogue, NYIs.	.25
□	84 Glenn Healy (G), NYIs.	.50
□	85 Brian Leetch, NYRa.	1.50
□	86 James Patrick, NYRa.	.25
□	87 Mark Messier, NYRa.	2.50
□	88 The Wong ,	.25
□	89 Mike Gartner, NYRa.	2.00
□	90 Mike Richter (G), NYRa.	1.00
□	91 Norm Maciver, Otta.	.25
□	92 Brad Shaw, Otta.	.25
□	93 Jamie Baker, Otta.	.25
□	94 Sylvain Turgeon, Otta.	.25
□	95 Bob Kudelski, Otta.	.25
□	96 Peter Sidorkiewicz (G), Otta.	.50
□	97 Garry Galley, Phil.	.25
□	98 Dmitry Yushkevich, Phil.	.50
□	99 Eric Lindros, Phil.	2.50
□	100 Rod Brind'Amour, Phil.	.50
□	101 Mark Recchi, Phil.	1.00
□	102 Tommy Söderström (G), Phil.	.50
□	103 Larry Murphy, Pitt.	.50
□	104 Ulf Samuelsson, Pitt.	.25
□	105 Mario Lemieux, Pitt.	5.00
□	106 Kevin Stevens, Pitt.	.50
□	107 Jaromir Jagr, Pitt.	2.50
□	108 Tom Barrasso (G), Pitt.	1.00
□	109 Steve Duchesne, Québ.	.50
□	110 Curtis Leschyshyn, Québ.	.25
□	111 Mats Sundin, Québ.	2.50
□	112 Joe Sakic, Québ.	4.00
□	113 Owen Nolan, Québ.	1.50
□	114 Ron Hextall (G), Québ.	2.00
□	115 Doug Wilson, SanJ.	.50
□	116 Neil Wilkinson, SanJ.	.25
□	117 Kelly Kisio, SanJ.	.25
□	118 Johan Garpenlöv, SanJ.	.25
□	119 Pat Falloon, SanJ.	.25
□	120 Arturs Irbe (G), SanJ.	1.00
□	121 Jeff R. Brown, SLou.	.25
□	122 Garth Butcher, SLou. [Error: b/ Bourque]	.25
□	123 Craig Janney, SLou.	.50
□	124 Brendan Shanahan, SLou.	2.50
□	125 Brett Hull, SLou.	2.50
□	126 Curtis Joseph (G), SLou.	2.50
□	127 Bob Beers, Tamp.	.25
□	128 Roman Hamrlik, Tamp.	.50
□	129 Brian Bradley, Tamp.	.25
□	130 Mikael Andersson, Tamp.	.25
□	131 Chris Kontos, Tamp.	.25
□	132 Wendell Young (G), Tamp.	.50
□	133 Todd Gill, Toro.	.25
□	134 Dave Ellett, Toro.	.25
□	135 Doug Gilmour, Toro. [Error: b/ Bure]	1.50
□	136 Dave Andreychuk, Toro.	.50
□	137 Nikolai Borschevsky, Toro.	.25
□	138 Félix Potvin (G), Toro.	1.50
□	139 Jyrki Lumme, Vanc.	.50
□	140 Doug Lidster, Vanc.	.25
□	141 Cliff Ronning, Vanc.	.50
□	142 Geoff Courtnall, Vanc.	.25
□	143 Pavel Bure, Vanc.	2.00
□	144 Kirk McLean (G), Vanc.	.50
□	145 Phil Housley, Winn.	.50
□	146 Teppo Numminen, Winn.	.25
□	147 Alexei Zhamnov, Winn.	.50
□	148 Thomas Steen, Winn.	.25
□	149 Teemu Selänne, Winn.	2.00
□	150 Bob Essensa (G), Winn.	.50
□	151 Kevin Hatcher, Wash.	.25
□	152 Al Iafrate, Wash.	.50
□	153 Mike Ridley, Wash.	.25
□	154 Dmitri Khristich, Wash.	.25
□	155 Peter Bondra, Wash.	1.50
□	156 Don Beaupré (G), Wash.	.50
□	157 Eastern Conference	.25
□	158 West Conference	.25
□	159 Mighty Ducks	.25
□	160 Bruins	.25
□	161 Sabres	.25
□	162 Flames	.25
□	163 Blackhawks	.25
□	164 Red Wings	.25
□	165 Oilers	.25
□	166 Panthers	.25
□	167 Whalers	.25
□	168 Kings	.25
□	169 Stars	.25
□	170 Canadiens	.25
□	171 Devils	.25
□	172 Islanders	.25
□	173 Rangers	.25
□	174 Senators	.25
□	175 Flyers	.25
□	176 Penguins	.25
□	177 Nordiques	.25
□	178 Sharks	.25
□	179 Blues	.25
□	180 Lightning	.25
□	181 Maple Leafs	.25
□	182 Canucks	.25
□	183 Capitals	.25
□	184 Jets	.25
□	185 Raymond Bourque, Bost. [Checking]	3.00
□	186 Chris Chelios, Chic. [Defence]	1.50
□	187 Ed Belfour (G), Chic. [Goaltending]	2.50
□	188 Adam Oates, Bost. [Passing]	1.00
□	189 Mario Lemieux, Pitt. [Shot Accuracy]	5.00
□	190 Al Iafrate, Wash. [Shot Power]	.50
□	191 Alexander Mogilny, Buff. [Skating]	1.00
□	192 Wayne Gretzky, LosA. [Stickhandling]	10.00
□	193 Four-Way Play	.25
□	194 Auto-Line Changes [Derian Hatcher]	.25
□	195 Bench Checks [Dmitri Kvartlanov]	.25
□	196 Board Checks [Randy Wood]	.25
□	197 Clear Zone [Gord Murphy]	.25
□	198 Crowd Records	.25
□	199 Expansion Teams	.25
□	200 Jimmy Waite (G), SanJ. [Goalie Control]	.50
□	201 Hot/ Cold Streaks [Terry Yake]	.25
□	202 Local Organ [Mark Fitzpatrick]	.25
□	203 More Stats [Brad Shaw]	.25
□	204 NHL Logos	.50
□	205 One Timers [Jyrki Lumme]	.25
□	206 Penalty Shots [Peter Sidorkiewicz]	.25
□	207 Player Cards [Gord Murphy]	.25
□	208 Player Profiles [Viacheslav Fetisov]	.25
□	209 Player Records [Stéphan Lebeau]	.25
□	210 Reverse Angle	.25
□	211 Shootout Game [Dominik Hasek]	.25
□	212 User Records [Cam Neely]	.25
□	213 The Brook	.25
□	214 The Costa	.25
□	215 The Hogan	.25
□	216 The Lange	.25
□	217 The Lesser	.25
□	218 The Matulac	.25
□	219 The Scott	.25
□	220 The Probin	.25
□	221 The Rogers	.25
□	222 The Rubinelli	.25
□	223 The Shin	.25
□	224 The White	.25
□	225 The Wike	.25

1993 - 94 FAX PAX WORLD OF SPORT

This 40-card multi-sport set was printed in the U.K. and features three hockey players. A 40-card set sells for $15.

Imprint: Fax Pax

	Player	NRMT-MT
□	25 Wayne Gretzky, LosA.	4.00
□	26 Brett Hull, SLou.	1.00
□	27 Eric Lindros, Phil.	1.00

1993 - 94 FLEER ULTRA

Imprint: © 1993 FLEER CORP.

Series One Set (250 cards): 35.00

Series Two Set (250 cards): 45.00

Common Player: .20

8-Card Promo Sheet: 5.00

	Player	NRMT-MT
□	1 Raymond Bourque, Bost.	.50
□	2 Andy Moog (G), Bost. (Dall.)	.20
□	3 Brian Benning, Edmo.	.20
□	4 Brian Bellows, Mont.	.20
□	5 Claude Lemieux, NJer.	.20
□	6 Jamie Baker, Otta.	.20
□	7 Steve Duchesne, Québ.	.20
□	8 Ed Courtenay, SanJ.	.20
□	9 Glenn Anderson, Toro.	.20
□	10 Sergei Bautin, Winn.	.20
□	11 Al Iafrate, Wash.	.20
□	12 Gary Shuchuk, LosA.	.20
□	13 Matthew Barnaby, Buff.	.20
□	14 Tim Cheveldae (G), Detr.	.20
□	15 Sean Burke (G), Hart.	.20
□	16 Ray Ferraro, NYIs.	.20
□	17 Josef Beránek, Phil.	.20
□	18 Bob Beers, Tamp.	.20
□	19 Greg A. Adams, Vanc.	.20
□	20 John Cullen, Toro.	.20
□	21 Kirk Muller, Mont.	.20
□	22 Ed Belfour (G), Chic.	.50
□	23 Kevin Dahl, Calg.	.20
□	24 Rob Blake, LosA.	.20
□	25 Mike Gartner, NYRa.	.50
□	26 Tom Barrasso (G), Pitt.	.20
□	27 Garth Butcher, SLou.	.20
□	28 Don Beaupré (G), Wash.	.20
□	29 Kirk McLean (G), Vanc.	.20
□	30 Félix Potvin (G), Toro.	.20
□	31 Doug Bodger, Buff.	.20
□	32 Dino Ciccarelli, Detr.	.20
□	33 Andrew Cassels, Hart.	.20
□	34 Patrick Flatley, NYIs.	.20
□	**35 Jason Bowen, Phil. RC**	**.50**
□	36 Brian Bradley, Tamp.	.20
□	37 Pavel Bure, Vanc.	.50
□	38 Dave Ellett, Toro.	.20
□	39 Patrick Roy (G), Mont.	1.50
□	40 Chris Chelios, Chic.	.20
□	41 Theoren Fleury, Calg.	.20
□	42 Jimmy Carson, LosA.	.20
□	43 Adam Graves, NYRa.	.20
□	44 Ron Francis, Pitt.	.20
□	45 Nelson Emerson, SLou.	.20
□	46 Peter Bondra, Wash.	.20
□	47 Sergio Momesso, Vanc.	.20
□	48 Teemu Selänne, Winn.	.50
□	49 Joé Juneau, Bost.	.20
□	50 Russ Courtnall, Minn. (Dall.)	.20
□	51 Shayne Corson, Edmo.	.20
□	52 Patrice Brisebois, Mont.	.20
□	53 John MacLean, NJer.	.20
□	54 Daniel Berthiaume (G), Otta.	.20
□	55 Stéphane Fiset (G), Québ.	.20
□	56 Pat Falloon, SanJ.	.20
□	57 Dave Andreychuk, Toro.	.20
□	58 Evgeny Davydov, Winn.	.20
□	59 Dmitri Khristich, Wash.	.20
□	60 Darryl Sydor, LosA.	.20
□	61 Dirk Graham, Chic.	.20
□	62 Chris Lindberg, Calg.	.20
□	63 Tony Granato, LosA.	.20
□	64 Corey Hirsch (G), NYRa.	.20
□	65 Jaromir Jagr, Pitt.	.50
□	66 Bret Hedican, SLou.	.20
□	67 Pat Elynuik, Wash.	.20
□	68 Petr Nedved, Vanc.	.20
□	69 Thomas Steen, Winn.	.20
□	70 Philippe Boucher, Buff.	.20
□	71 Paul Coffey, Detr.	.20
□	**72 Mike Lenarduzzi (G), Hart. RC**	**.50**
□	**73 Iain Fraser, NYIs. RC**	**.50**
□	74 Rod Brind'Amour, Phil.	.20
□	75 Shawn Chambers, Tamp.	.20
□	76 Geoff Courtnall, Vanc.	.20
□	77 Todd Gill, Toro.	.20
□	78 Mathieu Schneider, Mont.	.20
□	79 Vincent Damphousse, Mont.	.20
□	80 Igor Kravchuk, Edmo.	.20
□	81 Ulf Dahlén, Minn. (Dall.)	.20
□	82 Dmitri Kvartalnov, Bost.	.20
□	83 Johan Garpenlöv, SanJ.	.20
□	84 Valeri Kamensky, Québ.	.20
□	85 Bob Kudelski, Otta.	.20
□	86 Bernie Nicholls, NJer.	.20
□	87 Alexei Zhitnik, LosA.	.20
□	88 Kelly Miller, Wash.	.20
□	89 Bob Essensa (G), Winn.	.20
□	90 Drake Berehowsky, Toro.	.20
□	91 Jon Casey (G), Minn. (Bost.)	.20
□	92 Dave Gagner, Minn. (Dall.)	.20
□	93 Dave Manson, Edmo. Edmo.	.20
□	94 Éric Desjardins, Mont. Mont.	.20
□	95 Scott Niedermayer, NJer. NJer.	.20
□	96 Chris Luongo, Otta. (NYIs.)	.20
□	97 Dave Karpa, Québ.	.20
□	**98 Rob Gaudreau, SanJ. RC**	**.50**
□	99 Nikolai Borschevsky, Toro.	.20
□	100 Phil Housley, Winn.	.20
□	101 Michal Pivonka, Wash.	.20
□	102 Dixon Ward, Vanc.	.20
□	103 Grant Fuhr (G), Buff.	.20
□	**104 Dallas Drake, Detr. RC**	**.50**
□	105 Michael Nylander, Hart.	.20
□	106 Glenn Healy (G), NYIs. (NYRa.)	.20
□	107 Kevin Dineen, Phil.	.20
□	108 Roman Hamrlik, Tamp.	.20

□ 109 Trevor Linden, Vanc. .20
□ 110 Doug Gilmour, Toro. .20
□ 111 Keith Tkachuk, Winn. .20
□ 112 Sergei Krivokrasov, Chic. .20
□ 113 Al MacInnis, Calg. .20
□ 114 Wayne Gretzky, LosA. 2.50
□ 115 Alexei Kovalev, NYRa. .20
□ 116 Mario Lemieux, Pitt. 1.50
□ 117 Brett Hull, SLou. .50
□ 118 Kevin Hatcher, Wash. .20
□ 119 Cliff Ronning, Vanc. .20
□ 120 Viktor Gordiouk, Buff. .20
□ 121 Sergei Fedorov, Detr. .50
□ 122 Patrick Poulin, Hart. .20
□ 123 Benoît Hogue, NYIs. .20
□ 124 Garry Galley, Phil. .20
□ 125 Pat Jablonski (G), Tamp. .20
□ 126 Jyrki Lumme, Vanc. .20
□ 127 Dmitri Mironov, Toro. .20
□ 128 Alexei Zhamnov, Winn. .20
□ 129 Steve Larmer, Chic. .20
□ 130 Joe Nieuwendyk, Calg. .20
□ 131 Kelly Hrudey (G), LosA. .20
□ 132 Brian Leetch, NYRa. .20
□ 133 Shawn McEachern, Pitt. .20
□ 134 Craig Janney, SLou. .20
□ 135 Dale Hunter, Wash. .20
□ 136 Jirí Slégr, Vanc. .20
□ 137 Mats Sundin, Québ. .50
□ 138 Cam Neely, Bost. .50
□ 139 Derian Hatcher, Minn. (Dall.) .20
□ **140 Shjon Podein, Edmo. RC 1.00**
□ 141 Gilbert Dionne, Mont. .20
□ **142 Scott Pellerin, NJer. RC .50**
□ 143 Norm Maciver, Otta. .20
□ 144 Andrei Kovalenko, Québ. .20
□ 145 Arturs Irbe (G), SanJ. .20
□ 146 Wendel Clark, Toro. .50
□ 147 Fredrik Olausson, Winn. .20
□ 148 Mike Ridley, Wash. .20
□ 149 Dale Hawerchuk, Buff. .20
□ 150 Vladimir Konstantinov, Detr. .20
□ 151 Geoff Sanderson, Hart. .20
□ 152 Stéphane J.J. Richer, NJer. .20
□ 153 Darren Rumble, Otta. .20
□ 154 Owen Nolan, Québ. .20
□ 155 Kelly Kisio, SanJ. .20
□ 156 Adam Oates, Bost. .20
□ 157 Trent Klatt, Minn. (Dall.) .20
□ 158 Bill Ranford (G), Edmo. .20
□ 159 Paul DiPietro, Mont. .20
□ 160 Darius Kasparaitis, NYIs. .20
□ 161 Eric Lindros, Phil. .50
□ 162 Chris Kontos, Tamp. .20
□ 163 Joe Murphy, Chic. .20
□ 164 Robert Reichel, Calg. .20
□ 165 Jari Kurri, LosA. .50
□ 166 Alexander Semak, NJer. .20
□ 167 Brad Shaw, Otta. .20
□ 168 Mike Ricci, Québ. .20
□ 169 Sandis Ozolinsh, SanJ. .20
□ **170 Joby Messier, NYRa. RC .50**
□ 171 Joe Mullen, Pitt. .20
□ 172 Curtis Joseph (G), SLou. .50
□ 173 Yuri Khmylev, Buff. .20
□ 174 Vyacheslav Kozlov, Detr. .20
□ 175 Pat Verbeek, Hart. .20
□ 176 Derek King, NYIs. .20
□ 177 Ryan McGill, Phil. .20
□ **178 Chris LiPuma, Tamp. RC .50**
□ 179 Grigori Panteleev, Bost. .20
□ 180 Richard Matvichuk, Minn. (Dall.) .20
□ 181 Steven Rice, Edmo. .20
□ 182 Sean Hill, Mont. (Anah.) .20
□ 183 Mark Messier, NYRa. .50
□ 184 Larry Murphy, Pitt. .20
□ 185 Igor Korolev, SLou. .20
□ 186 Jeremy Roenick, Chic. .50
□ 187 Gary Roberts, Calg. .20
□ 188 Robert Lang, LosA. .20
□ 189 Scott Stevens, NJer. .20
□ 190 Sylvain Turgeon, Otta. .20
□ 191 Martin Rucinsky, Québ. .20
□ 192 Jean-François Quintin, SanJ. .20
□ 193 Dave Poulin, Bost. .20
□ 194 Mike Modano, Minn. (Dall.) .50
□ 195 Doug Weight, Edmo. .20
□ 196 Mike Keane, Mont. .20
□ 197 Pierre Turgeon, NYIs. .20
□ 198 Dmitry Yushkevich, Phil. .20
□ 199 Rob Zamuner, Tamp. .20
□ 200 Richard Smehlik, Buff. .20
□ 201 Steve Yzerman, Detr. 1.50
□ 202 Tony Amonte, NYRa. .20
□ 203 Sergei Nemchinov, NYRa. .20
□ 204 Ulf Samuelsson, Pitt. .20
□ 205 Kevin Miehm, SLou. .20
□ 206 Brent Sutter, Chic. .20
□ 207 Mike Vernon (G), Calg. .20
□ 208 Luc Robitaille, LosA. .50
□ 209 Chris Terreri (G), NJer. .20
□ 210 Philippe Bozon, SLou. .20
□ 211 John Tucker, Tamp. .20
□ 212 Jozef Stumpel, Bost. .20
□ 213 Mark Tinordi, Minn. (Dall.) .20
□ 214 Bruce Driver, NJer. .20
□ 215 John LeClair, Mont. .50
□ 216 Steve Thomas, NYIs. .20
□ 217 Tommy Söderström (G), Phil. .20
□ 218 Kevin Miller, SLou. .20
□ 219 Pat LaFontaine, Buff. .20
□ 220 Nicklas Lidström, Detr. .20
□ 221 Terry Yake, Hart. (Anah.) .20
□ 222 Valeri Zelepukin, NJer. .20
□ 223 Jeff R. Brown, SLou. .20
□ **224 Chris Simon, Québ. RC 1.00**
□ 225 Rick Tocchet, Pitt. .20
□ 226 Gary Suter, Calg. .20
□ 227 Marty McSorley, LosA. .20
□ 228 Mike Richter (G), NYRa. .20
□ 229 Kevin Stevens, Pitt. .20
□ 230 Doug Wilson, SanJ. .20
□ 231 J. Steve Smith, Chic. .20
□ 232 Bryan Smolinski, Bost. .20
□ 233 Tommy Sjödin, Minn. (Dall.) .20
□ 234 Zarley Zalapski, Hart. .20
□ 235 Vladimir Malakhov, NYIs. .20
□ 236 Mark Recchi, Phil. .20
□ **237 David Littman (G), Tamp. RC .50**
□ 238 Alexander Mogilny, Buff. .20
□ 239 Keith Primeau, Detr. .20
□ 240 Tyler Wright, Edmo. .20
□ 241 Stéphan Lebeau, Mont. .20
□ 242 Joe Sakic, Québ. 1.00
□ 243 Sergei Zubov, NYRa. .20
□ 244 Martin Straka, Pitt. .20
□ 245 Brendan Shanahan, SLou. .50
□ 246 Tomas Sandström, LosA. .20
□ **247 Milan Tichy, Chic. (Flor.) RC .50**
□ 248 C.J. Young, Bost. .20
□ 249 Checklist .20
□ 250 Checklist .20
□ **251 Patrik Carnbäck, Anah. RC .50**
□ 252 Todd Ewen, Anah. .20
□ 253 Stu Grimson, Anah. .20
□ 254 Guy Hebert (G), Anah. .20
□ 255 Sean Hill, Anah. .20
□ 256 Bill Houlder, Anah. .20
□ 257 Alexei Kasatonov, Anah. .20
□ 258 Steven King, Anah. .20
□ 259 Troy Loney, Anah. .20
□ 260 Joe Sacco, Anah. .20
□ 261 Anatoli Semenov, Anah. .20
□ 262 Tim Sweeney, Anah. .20
□ 263 Ron Tugnutt (G), Anah. .20
□ 264 Shaun Van Allen, Anah. .20
□ 265 Terry Yake, Anah. .20
□ 266 Jon Casey (G), Bost. .20
□ 267 Ted Donato, Bost. .20
□ 268 Stephen Leach, Bost. .20
□ 269 David Reid, Bost. .20
□ **270 Cam Stewart, Bost. RC .50**
□ 271 Don Sweeney, Bost. .20
□ 272 Glen Wesley, Bost. .20
□ 273 Donald Audette, Buff. .20
□ 274 Dominik Hasek (G), Buff. .50
□ 275 Sergei Petrenko, Buff. .20
□ **276 Derek Plante, Buff. RC .50**
□ 277 Craig Simpson, Buff. .20
□ 278 Bob Sweeney, Buff. .20
□ 279 Randy Wood, Buff. .20
□ 280 Ted Drury, Calg. .20
□ 281 Trevor Kidd (G), Calg. .20
□ 282 Kelly Kisio, Calg. .20
□ 283 Frantisek Musil, Calg. .20
□ **284 Jason Muzzatti (G), Calg. RC .50**
□ 285 Joel Otto, Calg. .20
□ 286 Paul Ranheim, Calg. .20
□ 287 Wes Walz, Calg. .20
□ **288 Ivan Droppa, Chic. RC .50**
□ 289 Michel Goulet, Chic. .20
□ 290 Stéphane Matteau, Chic. .20
□ 291 Brian Noonan, Chic. .20
□ 292 Patrick Poulin, Chic. .20
□ 293 Rich Sutter, Chic. .20
□ 294 Kevin Todd, Chic. .20
□ 295 Eric Weinrich, Chic. .20
□ 296 Neal Broten, Dall. .20
□ 297 Mike Craig, Dall. .20
□ 298 Dean Evason, Dall. .20
□ 299 Grant Ledyard, Dall. .20
□ 300 Mike McPhee, Dall. .20
□ 301 Andy Moog (G), Dall. .20
□ 302 Jarkko Varvio, Dall. .20
□ **303 Micah Aivazoff, Detr. RC .50**
□ 304 Terry Carkner, Detr. .20
□ 305 Steve Chiasson, Detr. .20
□ 306 Greg Johnson, Detr. .20
□ **307 Darren McCarty, Detr. RC 1.50**
□ **308 Chris Osgood (G), Detr. RC 3.00**
□ 309 Bob Probert, Detr. .20
□ 310 Ray Sheppard, Detr. .20
□ 311 Mike Sillinger, Detr. .20
□ **312 Jason Arnott, Edmo. RC 2.00**
□ **313 Fred Brathwaite (G), Edmo. RC 1.50**
□ 314 Kelly Buchberger, Edmo. .20
□ 315 Zdeno Ciger, Edmo. .20
□ 316 Craig MacTavish, Edmo. .20
□ 317 Dean McAmmond, Edmo. .20
□ 318 Luke Richardson, Edmo. .20
□ 319 Vladimír (Jr.) Vujtek, Edmo. .20
□ 320 Jesse Bélanger, Flor. .20
□ 321 Brian Benning, Flor. .20
□ 322 Keith Brown, Flor. .20
□ 323 Evgeny Davydov, Flor. .20
□ 324 Tom Fitzgerald, Flor. .20
□ 325 Alexander Godynyuk, Flor. .20
□ **326 Scott Levins, Flor. RC .50**
□ 327 Andrei Lomakin, Flor. .20
□ 328 Scott Mellanby, Flor. .20
□ 329 Gord Murphy, Flor. .20
□ 330 Rob Niedermayer, Flor. .20
□ **331 Brent Severyn, Flor. RC .50**
□ 332 Brian Skrudland, Flor. .20
□ 333 John Vanbiesbrouck (G), Flor. .20
□ 334 Mark Greig, Hart. .20
□ 335 Bryan Marchment, Hart. .20
□ 336 James Patrick, Hart. .20
□ 337 Robert Petrovicky, Hart. .20
□ 338 Frank Pietrangelo (G), Hart. .20
□ 339 Chris Pronger, Hart. .50
□ 340 Brian Propp, Hart. .20
□ 341 Darren Turcotte, Hart. .20
□ 342 Pat Conacher, LosA. .20
□ 343 Mark Hardy, LosA. .20
□ 344 Charlie Huddy, LosA. .20
□ 345 Shawn McEachern, LosA. .20
□ 346 Warren Rychel, LosA. .20
□ 347 Robb Stauber (G), LosA. .20
□ 348 Dave Taylor, LosA. .20
□ 349 Benoît Brunet, Mont. .20
□ 350 Guy Carbonneau, Mont. .20
□ 351 J.J. Daigneault, Mont. .20
□ 352 Kevin Haller, Mont. .20
□ 353 Gary Leeman, Mont. .20
□ 354 Lyle Odelein, Mont. .20
□ 355 André Racicot (G), Mont. .20
□ 356 Ron L. Wilson, Mont. .20
□ 357 Martin Brodeur (G), NJer. 1.00
□ 358 Ken Daneyko, NJer. .20
□ 359 Bill Guerin, NJer. .20
□ 360 Bobby Holik, NJer. .20
□ 361 Corey Millen, NJer. .20
□ **362 Jaroslav Modry, NJer. RC .50**
□ **363 Jason Smith, NJer. RC .50**
□ 364 Brad Dalgarno, NYIs. .20
□ 365 Travis Green, NYIs. .20
□ 366 Ron Hextall (G), NYIs. .50
□ **367 Steve Junker, NYIs. RC .50**
□ 368 Tom Kurvers, NYIs. .20
□ 369 Scott Lachance, NYIs. .20
□ 370 Marty McInnis, NYIs. .20
□ 371 Glenn Healy (G), NYRa. .20
□ 372 Alexander Karpovtsev, NYRa. .20
□ 373 Steve Larmer, NYRa. .20
□ 374 Doug Lidster, NYRa. .20
□ 375 Kevin Lowe, NYRa. .20
□ **376 Mattias Norström, NYRa. RC 1.00**
□ 377 Esa Tikkanen, NYRa. .20
□ 378 Craig Billington (G), Otta. .20
□ **379 Robert Burakovsky, Otta. RC .50**
□ 380 Alexandre Daigle, Otta. .20
□ 381 Dmitri Filimonov, Otta. .20
□ **382 Darrin Madeley (G), Otta. RC .50**
□ 383 Vladimír Ruzicka, Otta. .20
□ 384 Alexei Yashin, Otta. .50
□ 385 Viacheslav Butsayev, Phil. .20
□ 386 Pelle Eklund, Phil. .20
□ 387 Brent Fedyk, Phil. .20
□ 388 Greg Hawgood, Phil. .20
□ **389 Milos Holan, Phil. RC .50**
□ **390 Stewart Malgunas, Phil. RC .50**
□ 391 Mikael Renberg, Phil. .20
□ 392 Dominic Roussel (G), Phil. .20
□ 393 Doug Brown, Pitt. .20
□ 394 Marty McSorley, Pitt. .20
□ 395 Markus Näslund, Pitt. 1.00
□ 396 Mike Ramsey, Pitt. .20
□ 397 Peter Taglianetti, Pitt. .20
□ 398 Bryan Trottier, Pitt. .50
□ 399 Ken Wregget (G), Pitt. .20
□ 400 Iain Fraser, Québ. .20
□ 401 Martin Gélinas, Québ. .20
□ 402 Kerry Huffman, Québ. .20
□ 403 Claude Lapointe, Québ. .20
□ 404 Curtis Leschyshyn, Québ. .20
□ 405 Chris Lindberg, Québ. .20
□ **406 Jocelyn Thibault (G), Québ. RC 2.00**
□ 407 Murray Baron, SLou. .20
□ 408 Bob Bassen, SLou. .20
□ 409 Phil Housley, SLou. .20
□ 410 Jim Hrivnak (G), SLou. .20
□ 411 Tony Hrkac, SLou. .20
□ 412 Vitali Karamnov, SLou. .20
□ **413 Jim Montgomery, SLou. RC .50**
□ **414 Vlastimil Kroupa, SanJ. RC .50**
□ 415 Igor Larionov, SanJ. .20
□ 416 Sergei Makarov, SanJ. .20
□ 417 Jeff Norton, SanJ. .20
□ 418 Mike Rathje, SanJ. .20
□ 419 Jimmy Waite (G), SanJ. .20
□ 420 Ray Whitney, SanJ. .20
□ 421 Mikael Andersson, Tamp. .20
□ 422 Donald Dufresne, Tamp. .20
□ 423 Chris Gratton, Tamp. .20
□ **424 Brent Gretzky, Tamp. RC .50**
□ 425 Petr Klima, Tamp. .20
□ **426 Bill McDougall, Tamp. RC .50**
□ 427 Daren Puppa (G), Tamp. .20
□ 428 Denis Savard, Tamp. .20
□ 429 Ken Baumgartner, Toro. .20
□ 430 Sylvain Lefebvre, Toro. .20
□ 431 Jamie Macoun, Toro. .20
□ **432 Matt Martin, Toro. RC .50**
□ 433 Mark Osborne, Toro. .20
□ 434 Rob Pearson, Toro. .20
□ **435 Damian Rhodes (G), Toro. RC 1.00**
□ 436 Peter Zezel, Toro. .20
□ 437 Shawn Antoski, Vanc. .20
□ **438 José Charbonneau, Vanc. RC .50**
□ 439 Murray Craven, Vanc. .20
□ 440 Gerald Diduck, Vanc. .20
□ 441 Dana Murzyn, Vanc. .20
□ 442 Gino Odjick, Vanc. .20
□ 443 Kay Whitmore (G), Vanc. .20
□ 444 Randy Burridge, Wash. .20
□ 445 Sylvain Côté, Wash. .20
□ 446 Keith Jones, Wash. .20
□ 447 Olaf Kölzig (G), Wash. .50
□ 448 Todd Krygier, Wash. .20
□ 449 Pat Peake, Wash. .20
□ 450 Dave Poulin, Wash. .20
□ 451 Stéphane Beauregard, Winn. .20
□ 452 Luciano Borsato, Winn. .20
□ 453 Nelson Emerson, Winn. .20
□ 454 Boris Mironov, Winn. .20
□ 455 Teppo Numminen, Winn. .20
□ 456 Stéphane Quintal, Winn. .20
□ 457 Paul Ysebaert, Winn. .20
□ **458 Adrian Aucoin, Canada Nationals RC .50**
□ **459 Todd Brost, Canada Nationals RC .50**
□ **460 Martin Gendron, Canada Nationals RC .50**
□ 461 David Harlock, Canada Nationals .20
□ 462 Corey Hirsch (G), Canada Nationals .20
□ **463 Todd Hlushko, Canada Nationals RC .50**
□ 464 Fabian Joseph, Canada Nationals RC .20
□ 465 Paul Kariya, Canada Nationals 1.50
□ **466 Brett Lindros, Canada Nationals RC 1.50**
□ **467 Ken Lovsin, Canada Nationals RC .50**
□ 468 Jason Marshall, Canada Nationals .20
□ **469 Derek Mayer, Canada Nationals RC .50**
□ **470 Dwayne Norris, Canada Nationals RC .50**
□ 471 Russ Romaniuk, Canada Nationals .20
□ **472 Brian Savage, Canada Nationals RC 1.50**
□ **473 Trevor Sim, Canada Nationals RC .50**
□ **474 Chris Therien, Canada Nationals RC .50**
□ **475 Brad Turner, Canada Nationals RC .50**
□ **476 Todd Warriner, Canada Nationals RC .50**
□ **477 Craig Woodcroft, Canada Nationals RC .50**
□ **478 Mark Beaufait, U.S.A. Nationals RC .50**
□ 479 Jim Campbell, U.S.A. Nationals .20
□ **480 Ted Crowley, U.S.A. Nationals RC .50**
□ 481 Mike Dunham (G), U.S.A. Nationals .20
□ **482 Chris Ferraro, U.S.A. Nationals RC .50**
□ 483 Peter Ferraro, U.S.A. Nationals .20
□ **484 Brett Hauer, U.S.A. Nationals RC .50**
□ **485 Darby Hendrickson, U.S.A. Nationals RC .50**
□ **486 Chris Imes, U.S.A. Nationals RC .50**
□ **487 Craig Johnson, U.S.A. Nationals RC .50**
□ **488 Peter Laviolette, U.S.A. Nationals RC 2.00**
□ 489 Jeff Lazaro, U.S.A. Nationals .20
□ **490 John Lilley, U.S.A. Nationals RC .50**
□ 491 Todd Marchant, U.S.A. Nationals .20
□ **492 Ian Moran, U.S.A. Nationals RC .50**
□ **493 Travis Richards, U.S.A. Nationals RC .50**
□ **494 Barry Richter, U.S.A. Nationals RC .50**
□ **495 David Roberts, U.S.A. Nationals RC .50**
□ 496 Brian Rolston, U.S.A. Nationals .20
□ **497 David Sacco, U.S.A. Nationals RC .50**
□ 498 Checklist .20
□ 499 Checklist .20
□ 500 Checklist .20

ALL-ROOKIE SERIES

Series One Insert Set (10 cards): 25.00
Insert (1:20 Jumbo) ARS

□ 1 Philippe Boucher, Buff. 2.00
□ 2 Viktor Gordiouk, Buff. 2.00
□ 3 Corey Hirsch (G), NYRa. 6.00
□ 4 Chris LiPuma, Tamp. 2.00
□ 5 David Littman (G), Tamp. 3.00
□ 6 Joby Messier, NYRa. 2.00
□ 7 Chris Simon, Québ. 6.00
□ 8 Bryan Smolinski, Bost. 4.00
□ 9 Jozef Stumpel, Bost. 6.00
□ 10 Milan Tichy, Chic. 2.00

ALL-STAR

Series One Insert Set (18 cards): 35.00
Insert (1:12) AS

□ 1 Patrick Roy (G), NHL All-Star 7.00
□ 2 Raymond Bourque, NHL All-Star 3.00
□ 3 Pierre Turgeon, NHL All-Star 1.00
□ 4 Pat LaFontaine, NHL All-Star 1.00
□ 5 Alexander Mogilny, NHL All-Star 1.00
□ 6 Kevin Stevens, NHL All-Star .75
□ 7 Adam Oates, NHL All-Star 1.00
□ 8 Al Iafrate, NHL All-Star .75
□ 9 Kirk Muller, NHL All-Star .75
□ 10 Ed Belfour (G), NHL All-Star 2.00
□ 11 Teemu Selänne, NHL All-Star 2.00
□ 12 Steve Yzerman, NHL All-Star 6.00
□ 13 Luc Robitaille, NHL All-Star 2.00
□ 14 Chris Chelios, NHL All-Star 1.00
□ 15 Wayne Gretzky, NHL All-Star 10.00
□ 16 Doug Gilmour, NHL All-Star 1.00
□ 17 Pavel Bure, NHL All-Star 2.00
□ 18 Phil Housley, NHL All-Star .75

AWARD WINNER

Series One Insert Set (6 cards): 10.00
Insert (1:35) AW

□ 1 Ed Belfour (G), NHL Awards 2.00
□ 2 Chris Chelios, NHL Awards 1.00
□ 3 Doug Gilmour, NHL Awards 1.00
□ 4 Mario Lemieux, NHL Awards 7.00
□ 5 Dave Poulin, NHL Awards .75
□ 6 Teemu Selänne, NHL Awards 2.00

CAREER HIGHLIGHTS

	Complete Set (12 cards):	5.00
	Insert	CH
☐	1 Adam Oates, Bost.	.50
☐	2 Adam Oates, Bost.	.50
☐	3 Adam Oates, Detr.	.50
☐	4 Adam Oates, Detr.	.50
☐	5 Adam Oates, Detr.	.50
☐	6 Adam Oates, SLou.	.50
☐	7 Adam Oates, SLou.	.50
☐	8 Adam Oates, NHL All-Star	.50
☐	9 Adam Oates, Bost.	.50
☐	10 Adam Oates, NHL All-Star (Bost.)	.50
☐	11 Adam Oates Redemption	1.00
☐	12 Adam Oates Redemption	1.00
☐	Adam Oates Autograph ✍	100.00

PREMIER PIVOTS

	Series Two Insert Set (10 cards):	22.00
	Insert (1:5)	PP
☐	1 Doug Gilmour, Toro.	1.00
☐	2 Wayne Gretzky, LosA.	8.00
☐	3 Pat LaFontaine, Buff.	1.00
☐	4 Mario Lemieux, Pitt.	6.00
☐	5 Eric Lindros, Phil.	2.00
☐	6 Mark Messier, NYRa.	2.00
☐	7 Adam Oates, Bost.	.50
☐	8 Jeremy Roenick, Chic.	1.00
☐	9 Pierre Turgeon, NYIs.	.50
☐	10 Steve Yzerman, Detr.	4.00

RED LIGHT SPECIALS

	Series Two Insert Set (10 cards):	15.00
	Insert (1:10)	RLS
☐	1 Dave Andreychuk, Toro.	.75
☐	2 Pavel Bure, Vanc.	2.00
☐	3 Mike Gartner, NYRa.	2.00
☐	4 Brett Hull, SLou.	2.00
☐	5 Jaromir Jagr, Pitt.	2.00
☐	6 Mario Lemieux, Pitt.	7.00
☐	7 Alexander Mogilny, Buff.	1.00
☐	8 Mark Recchi, Phil.	1.00
☐	9 Luc Robitaille, LosA.	2.00
☐	10 Teemu Selänne, Winn.	2.00

SCORING KING

	Series One Insert Set (6 cards):	20.00
	Insert (1:10)	SK
☐	1 Pat LaFontaine, Buff.	1.00
☐	2 Wayne Gretzky, LosA.	10.00
☐	3 Brett Hull, SLou.	2.00
☐	4 Mario Lemieux, Pitt.	5.00
☐	5 Pierre Turgeon, NYIs.	1.00
☐	6 Steve Yzerman, Detr.	6.00

SPEED MERCHANT

	Series Two Insert Set (10 cards):	60.00
	Insert (Jumbo packs)	SM
☐	1 Pavel Bure, Vanc.	10.00
☐	2 Russ Courtnall, Dall.	4.00
☐	3 Sergei Fedorov, Detr.	15.00
☐	4 Mike Gartner, NYRa.	10.00
☐	5 Al Iafrate, Wash.	4.00
☐	6 Pat LaFontaine, Buff.	5.00
☐	7 Alexander Mogilny, Buff.	7.00
☐	8 Rob Niedermayer, Flor.	4.00
☐	9 Geoff Sanderson, Hart.	4.00
☐	10 Teemu Selänne, Winn.	10.00

ULTRA PROSPECT

	Series One Insert Set (10 cards):	5.00
	Insert	UP
☐	1 Iain Fraser, NYIs.	.50
☐	2 Rob Gaudreau, SanJ.	.50
☐	3 Dave Karpa, Québ.	.50
☐	4 Trent Klatt, Minn.	1.00
☐	5 Mike Lenarduzzi (G), Hart.	.50
☐	6 Kevin Miehm, SLou.	.50
☐	7 Michael Nylander, Hart.	1.50
☐	8 Jean-François Quintin, SanJ.	.50
☐	9 Gary Shuchuk, LosA.	.50
☐	10 Tyler Wright, Edmo.	.50

WAVE OF THE FUTURE

	Series Two Insert Set (10 cards):	15.00
	Insert	WotF
☐	1 Jason Arnott, Edmo.	2.00
☐	2 Martin Brodeur (G), NJer.	4.00
☐	3 Alexandre Daigle, Otta.	.50
☐	4 Ted Drury, Calg.	.50
☐	5 Chris Gratton, Tamp.	.50
☐	6 Milos Holan, Phil.	.50
☐	7 Greg Johnson, Detr.	.50
☐	8 Boris Mironov, Winn.	.50
☐	9 Jaroslav Modry, NJer.	.50
☐	10 Markus Näslund, Pitt.	2.00
☐	11 Rob Niedermayer, Flor.	.50
☐	12 Chris Osgood (G), Detr.	2.00
☐	13 Derek Plante, Buff.	.50
☐	14 Chris Pronger, Hart.	1.00
☐	15 Mike Rathje, SanJ.	.50
☐	16 Mikael Renberg, Phil.	.50
☐	17 Jason Smith, NJer.	.50
☐	18 Jocelyn Thibault (G), Québ.	1.00
☐	19 Jarkko Varvio, Dall.	.50
☐	20 Alexei Yashin, Otta.	1.00

1993 - 94 GLOBAL TELECOMMUNICATIONS

Card Size: 2" x 3 1/4"

Complete Set (26 phonecards):

	Team		Team
☐	Anah. Mighty Ducks	☐	Bost. Bruins
☐	Buff. Sabres	☐	Calg. Flames
☐	Chic. Blackhawks	☐	Dall. Stars
☐	Detr. Red Wings	☐	Edmo. Oilers
☐	Flor. Panthers	☐	Hart. Whalers
☐	LosA. Kings	☐	Mont. Canadiens
☐	NJer. Devils	☐	New York Islanders
☐	New York Rangers	☐	Otta. Senators
☐	Phil. Flyers	☐	Pitt. Penguins
☐	Québ. Nordiques	☐	SanJ. Sharks
☐	SLou. Blues	☐	Tamp. Lightning
☐	Toro. Maple Leafs	☐	Vanc. Canucks
☐	Wash. Capitals	☐	Winn. Jets

1993 - 94 HIGH LINER GREATEST GOALIES

One of 15 cards was found in specially marked boxes of High Liner. A factory-cut set and album was also available through the mail.

	Complete Set (15 cards):	12.00
	Album:	5.00
	Player	NRMT-MT
☐	1 Patrick Roy (G), Mont.	3.00
☐	2 Ed Belfour (G), Chic.	1.00
☐	3 Grant Fuhr (G), Buff.	.50
☐	4 Ron Hextall (G), Québ.	1.00
☐	5 John Vanbiesbrouck (G), NYRa.	.50
☐	6 Tom Barrasso (G), Pitt.	.50
☐	7 Bernie Parent (G), Phil.	1.00
☐	8 Tony Esposito (G), Chic.	1.00
☐	9 Johnny Bower (G), Toro.	1.00
☐	10 Jacques Plante (G), Mont.	2.00
☐	11 Terry Sawchuk (G), Detr.	2.00
☐	12 Bill Durnan (G), Mont.	1.00
☐	13 Félix Potvin (G), Toro.	.50
☐	14 The Evolution of the Mask	.50
☐	15 Vézina Trophy	.50

1993 - 94 HOCKEY WIT

Card Size: 2 1/2" x 3 7/16"

	Complete Set (108 cards):	20.00
	Common Player:	.20
	Player	NRMT-MT
☐	1 Mike Richter (G), NYRa.	.20
☐	2 Tony Amonte, NYRa.	.50
☐	3 Patrick Roy (G), Mont.	3.00
☐	4 Craig Janney, SLou.	.20
☐	5 Adam Oates, Bost.	.20
☐	6 Geoff Sanderson, Hart.	.20
☐	7 Pavel Bure, Vanc.	.50
☐	8 Steve Duchesne, Québ.	.20
☐	9 Gordie Howe, Detr.	2.50
☐	10 Brad Park, NYRa.	.50
☐	11 Brian Bellows, Minn.	.20
☐	12 Chris Chelios, Chic.	.50
☐	13 Bill Barber, Phil.	.20
☐	14 Lorne (Gump) Worsley (G), NYRa.	.50
☐	15 Stanley Cup	.20
☐	16 Maurice Richard, Mont.	2.50
☐	17 Kevin Hatcher, Wash.	.20
☐	18 Ed Belfour (G), Chic.	1.00
☐	19 Kirk Muller, Mont.	.20
☐	20 Kevin Stevens, Pitt.	.20
☐	21 Dave Taylor, LosA.	.20
☐	22 Dale Hawerchuk, Buff.	.50
☐	23 Jean Béliveau, Mont.	2.00
☐	24 Rogatien Vachon (G), LosA.	.20
☐	25 Tom Barrasso (G), Pitt.	.20
☐	26 Rod Langway, Wash.	.20
☐	27 Pierre Turgeon, NYIs.	.20
☐	28 Derek King, NYIs.	.20
☐	29 Brendan Shanahan, SLou.	1.00
☐	30 Darren Turcotte, NYRa.	.20
☐	31 Chris Terreri (G), NJer.	.20
☐	32 Tony Granato, LosA.	.20
☐	33 Michel Goulet, Chic.	.20
☐	34 Félix Potvin (G), Toro.	.50
☐	35 Curtis Joseph (G), SLou.	1.00
☐	36 Cam Neely, Bost.	1.00
☐	37 Börje Salming, Toro.	.50
☐	38 Denis Savard, Mont.	.20
☐	39 Stan Mikita, Chic.	.50
☐	40 Grant Fuhr (G), Buff.	.50
☐	41 Gary Suter, Calg.	.20
☐	42 Serge Savard, Mont.	.20
☐	43 Steve Larmer, Chic.	.20
☐	44 Bryan Trottier, Pitt.	1.00
☐	45 Mike Vernon (G), Calg.	.20
☐	46 Paul Coffey, Detr.	.50
☐	47 Bernie Federko, SLou.	.20
☐	48 Larry Murphy, Pitt.	.20
☐	49 Scotty Bowman, Detr. [Coach]	.50
☐	50 Glenn Anderson, Toro.	.20
☐	51 Mats Sundin, Québ.	1.00
☐	52 Henri Richard, Mont.	1.00
☐	53 Ron Francis, Pitt.	.50
☐	54 Scott Niedermayer, NJer.	.20
☐	55 Teemu Selänne, Winn.	.50
☐	56 Frank Mahovlich, Toro.	1.00
☐	57 Owen Nolan, Québ.	.50
☐	58 Rick Tocchet, Pitt.	.20
☐	59 Rod Brind'Amour, Phil.	.20
☐	60 Mike Modano, Minn. (Dall.)	1.00
☐	61 Doug Gilmour, Toro.	.50
☐	62 Jimmy Carson, LosA.	.20
☐	63 Mike Keane, Mont.	.20
☐	64 Bernie Nicholls, NJer.	.20
☐	65 Scott Stevens, NJer.	.20
☐	66 Mario Lemieux, Pitt.	3.00
☐	67 Keith Primeau, Detr.	.20
☐	68 Bob Carpenter, Bost.	.20
☐	69 Sergei Fedorov, Detr.	1.00
☐	70 Peter Stastny, NJer.	.50
☐	71 Brian Leetch, NYRa.	.50
☐	72 Vincent Damphousse, Mont.	.50
☐	73 Darryl Sittler, Toro.	.50
☐	74 Al Iafrate, Wash.	.20
☐	75 Alexander Mogilny, Buff.	.20
☐	76 Bill Ranford (G), Edmo.	.20
☐	77 Raymond Bourque, Bost.	1.00
☐	78 Joe Mullen, Pitt.	.20
☐	79 Mike Ricci, Québ.	.20
☐	80 Bobby Clarke, Phil.	.50
☐	81 Gerry Cheevers (G), Bost.	.50
☐	82 Joe Nieuwendyk, Calg.	.20
☐	83 Terry Sawchuk (G), Toro.	2.00
☐	84 Ray Ferraro, NYIs.	.20
☐	85 Lanny McDonald, Calg.	.50
☐	86 Adam Graves, NYRa.	.20
☐	87 Tomas Sandström, LosA.	.20
☐	88 Eric Lindros, Phil.	1.00
☐	89 Jari Kurri, LosA.	.50
☐	90 Al MacInnis, Canada Nationals (Calg.)	.20
☐	91 Alexandre Daigle, Otta.	.20
☐	92 Larry Robinson, LosA.	.50
☐	93 Kelly Hrudey (G), LosA.	.20
☐	94 Theoren Fleury, Calg.	.50
☐	95 Billy Smith (G), NYIs.	.50
☐	96 Luc Robitaille, LosA.	.50
☐	97 Brett Hull, SLou.	1.00
☐	98 Pat Falloon, SanJ.	.20
☐	99 Wayne Gretzky, LosA.	4.00
☐	100 Joe Sakic, Québ.	1.50
☐	101 Phil Housley, Winn.	.20
☐	102 Mark Messier, NYRa.	1.00
☐	103 Jeremy Roenick, Chic.	.50
☐	104 Mark Recchi, Phil.	.20
☐	105 Pat LaFontaine, Buff.	.50
☐	106 Trevor Linden, Vanc.	.20
☐	107 Jaromir Jagr, Pitt.	1.00
☐	108 Steve Yzerman, Detr.	2.00

1993 - 94 JYVAS HYVA HOCKEY LIIGA

A set of 348 stickers plus a collecting album for the Finnish National League. There are three player stickers to each panel. Team panels are made up of 12 stickers. Stickers numbered 30, 60, 90, 120, 150, 180, 210, 240, 270, 300 and 330 were never issued. We have little pricing information on this set. The Saku Koivu panel is the most expensive single at $10.00. Singles start at 20¢.

Size: 2" x 3 3/8"

	Jyvas Hyva		Jyvas Hyva
☐	1 HIFK Helsinki	☐	2 HIFK Helsinki
☐	3 HIFK Helsinki	☐	4 HIFK Helsinki
☐	5 HIFK Helsinki	☐	6 HIFK Helsinki
☐	7 HIFK Helsinki	☐	8 HIFK Helsinki
☐	9 HIFK Helsinki	☐	10 HIFK Helsinki
☐	11 HIFK Helsinki	☐	12 HIFK Helsinki
☐	13 Harri Rindell	☐	14 Sakari Lindfors (G)
☐	15 Simo Saarinen	☐	16 Pertti Lehtonen
☐	17 Jari Laukkanen	☐	18 Valeri Krykov
☐	19 Iiro Jarvi	☐	20 Jari Munck
☐	21 Pasi Sormunen	☐	22 Pekka Peltola
☐	23 Teppo Kivela	☐	24 Pekka Tuomisto
☐	25 Kai Tervonen	☐	26 Dan Lambert
☐	27 Marco Poulsen	☐	28 Ville Peltonen
☐	29 Kim Ahlroos	☐	31 HPK Hameenlinna
☐	32 HPK Hameenlinna	☐	33 HPK Hameenlinna
☐	34 HPK Hameenlinna	☐	35 HPK Hameenlinna
☐	36 HPK Hameenlinna	☐	37 HPK Hameenlinna
☐	38 HPK Hameenlinna	☐	39 HPK Hameenlinna
☐	40 HPK Hameenlinna	☐	41 HPK Hameenlinna
☐	42 HPK Hameenlinna	☐	43 Pentti Matikainen
☐	44 Kari Rosenberg (G)	☐	45 Mikko Myllykoski
☐	46 Janne Laukkanen	☐	47 Jarkko Nikander
☐	48 Tomas Kapusta	☐	49 Mika Lartama
☐	50 Niko Marttila	☐	51 Jari Haapamaki
☐	52 Tommi Varjonen	☐	53 Toni Virta
☐	54 Marko Palo	☐	55 Marko Allen
☐	56 Miikka Ruohonen	☐	57 Jani Hassinen
☐	58 Pasi Kivila	☐	59 Markku Piikkila
☐	61 Ilves Tampere	☐	62 Ilves Tampere
☐	63 Ilves Tampere	☐	64 Ilves Tampere
☐	65 Ilves Tampere	☐	66 Ilves Tampere
☐	67 Ilves Tampere	☐	68 Ilves Tampere
☐	69 Ilves Tampere	☐	70 Ilves Tampere
☐	71 Ilves Tampere	☐	72 Ilves Tampere
☐	73 Jukka Jalonen	☐	74 Jukka Tammi (G)
☐	75 Jani Nikko	☐	76 Hannu Henriksson
☐	77 Juha Jarvenpaa	☐	78 Hannu Mattila
☐	79 Timo Peltomaa	☐	80 Jukka Ollila
☐	81 JuhaMatti Marijarvi	☐	82 Mikko Luovi
☐	83 Jarno Peltonen	☐	84 Pasi Maattanen
☐	85 Juha Lampinen	☐	86 Allan Measures
☐	87 Janne Seva	☐	88 Risto Jalo
☐	89 Esa Tommila	☐	91 Jokerit Helsinki
☐	92 Jokerit Helsinki	☐	93 Jokerit Helsinki
☐	94 Jokerit Helsinki	☐	95 Jokerit Helsinki
☐	96 Jokerit Helsinki	☐	97 Jokerit Helsinki
☐	98 Jokerit Helsinki	☐	99 Jokerit Helsinki
☐	100 Jokerit Helsinki	☐	101 Jokerit Helsinki
☐	102 Jokerit Helsinki	☐	103 Alpo Suhonen
☐	104 Ari Sulander (G)	☐	105 Kari Martikainen
☐	106 Erik Hämäläinen	☐	107 Juha Jokiharju
☐	108 Otakar Janecky	☐	109 Petri Varis
☐	110 Waltteri Immonen	☐	111 Mika Stromberg
☐	112 Keijo Sailynoja	☐	113 Timo Saarikoski
☐	114 Juha Ylonen	☐	115 Ari Salo
☐	116 Heikki Riihijarvi	☐	117 Timo Norppa
☐	118 Jali Wahlsten	☐	119 Rami Koivisto
☐	121 JyP HT Jyvaskyla	☐	122 JyP HT Jyvaskyla
☐	123 JyP HT Jyvaskyla	☐	124 JyP HT Jyvaskyla
☐	125 JyP HT Jyvaskyla	☐	126 JyP HT Jyvaskyla
☐	127 JyP HT Jyvaskyla	☐	128 JyP HT Jyvaskyla
☐	129 JyP HT Jyvaskyla	☐	130 JyP HT Jyvaskyla
☐	131 JyP HT Jyvaskyla	☐	132 JyP HT Jyvaskyla
☐	133 Kari Savolainen	☐	134 A-P Siekkinen (G)
☐	135 Harri Laurila	☐	136 Markku Heikkinen
☐	137 Jari Lindroos	☐	138 Lasse Nieminen
☐	139 Risto Kurkinen	☐	140 Jarmo Jokilahti
☐	141 VeliPekka Hard	☐	142 Joni Lius
☐	143 Jyrki Jokinen	☐	144 Mika Arvaja
☐	145 Vesa Ponto	☐	146 Jarmo Rantanen
☐	147 Mika Paananen	☐	148 Marko Virtanen
☐	149 Marko Ek	☐	151 Kalpa Kuopio
☐	152 Kalpa Kuopio	☐	153 Kalpa Kuopio
☐	154 Kalpa Kuopio	☐	155 Kalpa Kuopio
☐	156 Kalpa Kuopio	☐	157 Kalpa Kuopio
☐	158 Kalpa Kuopio	☐	159 Kalpa Kuopio
☐	160 Kalpa Kuopio	☐	161 Kalpa Kuopio
☐	162 Kalpa Kuopio	☐	163 Hannu Kapanen
☐	164 P. Kuivalainen (G)	☐	165 Kimmo Timonen
☐	166 Vesa Salo	☐	167 Jani Rautio
☐	168 Pekka Tirkkonen	☐	169 Dimitri Zinine
☐	170 Antti Tuomenoksa	☐	171 Jari Jarvinen
☐	172 Tuomas Kalliomaki	☐	173 Tommi Miettinen
☐	174 Sami Kapanen	☐	175 Vesa Ruotsalainen
☐	176 Mikko Tavi	☐	177 Sami Mettovaara
☐	178 V-P Pekkarinen	☐	179 Arto Sirvio
☐	181 Kiekko-Espoo	☐	182 Kiekko-Espoo

☐ 183 Kiekko-Espoo	☐ 184 Kiekko-Espoo
☐ 185 Kiekko-Espoo	☐ 186 Kiekko-Espoo
☐ 187 Kiekko-Espoo	☐ 188 Kiekko-Espoo
☐ 189 Kiekko-Espoo	☐ 190 Kiekko-Espoo
☐ 191 Kiekko-Espoo	☐ 192 Kiekko-Espoo
☐ 193 Martti Merra	☐ 194 Timo Maki (G)
☐ 195 Sami Nuutinen	☐ 196 Teemu Sillanpaa
☐ 197 Tero Lehtera	☐ 198 Jan Langbacka
☐ 199 Jukka Tiilikainen	☐ 200 Petri Pulkkinen
☐ 201 Robert Salo	☐ 202 Petro Koivunen
☐ 203 Juha Ikonen	☐ 204 Mikko Lempiainen
☐ 205 Marko Halonen	☐ 206 Jimi Helin
☐ 207 Timo Hirvonen	☐ 208 Mikko Halonen
☐ 209 Kimmo MakiKokkila	☐ 211 Rauman Lukko
☐ 212 Rauman Lukko	☐ 213 Rauman Lukko
☐ 214 Rauman Lukko	☐ 215 Rauman Lukko
☐ 216 Rauman Lukko	☐ 217 Rauman Lukko
☐ 218 Rauman Lukko	☐ 219 Rauman Lukko
☐ 220 Rauman Lukko	☐ 221 Rauman Lukko
☐ 222 Rauman Lukko	☐ 223 Vaclav Sykora
☐ 224 Jarmo Myllys (G)	☐ 225 KariPekka Friman
☐ 226 Timo Kulonen	☐ 227 Pasi Saarela
☐ 228 Kalle Sahlstedt	☐ 229 Kimmo Rintanen
☐ 230 Jarmo Kuusisto	☐ 231 Tuomas Gronman
☐ 232 Tero Arkiomaa	☐ 233 Petr Korinek
☐ 234 Mika Alatalo	☐ 235 Marko Tuulola
☐ 236 Pasi Huura	☐ 237 Tommi Pullola
☐ 238 Mika Valila	☐ 239 Jari Torkki
☐ 241 Reipas Lahti	☐ 242 Reipas Lahti
☐ 243 Reipas Lahti	☐ 244 Reipas Lahti
☐ 245 Reipas Lahti	☐ 246 Reipas Lahti
☐ 247 Reipas Lahti	☐ 248 Reipas Lahti
☐ 249 Reipas Lahti	☐ 250 Reipas Lahti
☐ 251 Reipas Lahti	☐ 252 Reipas Lahti
☐ 253 Kari Makinen	☐ 254 Oldrich Svoboda (G)
☐ 255 Timo Kahelin	☐ 256 Pasi Ruponen
☐ 257 Tommy Kiviaho	☐ 258 Jari Multanen
☐ 259 Erkki Makela	☐ 260 Jari Parviainen
☐ 261 Petri Koski	☐ 262 Jonni Vauhkonen
☐ 263 Toni Koivunen	☐ 264 Sami Wikstrom
☐ 265 Jarkko Hämäläinen	☐ 266 Sami Helenius
☐ 267 Sami Lekkerimaki	☐ 268 Jari Kauppila
☐ 269 Jani Uski	☐ 271 Tappara Tampere
☐ 272 Tappara Tampere	☐ 273 Tappara Tampere
☐ 274 Tappara Tampere	☐ 275 Tappara Tampere
☐ 276 Tappara Tampere	☐ 277 Tappara Tampere
☐ 278 Tappara Tampere	☐ 279 Tappara Tampere
☐ 280 Tappara Tampere	☐ 281 Tappara Tampere
☐ 282 Tappara Tampere	☐ 283 Boris Majorov
☐ 284 Timo Hankela (G)	☐ 285 Timo Jutila
☐ 286 Samuli Rautio	☐ 287 Ari Haanpaa
☐ 288 Mikko Peltola	☐ 289 Pauli Jarvinen
☐ 290 Pekka Laksola	☐ 291 Janne Gronvall
☐ 292 Kari Heikkinen	☐ 293 Tommi Pohja
☐ 294 Petri Aaltonen	☐ 295 Petri Kalteva
☐ 296 Tommi Haapsaari	☐ 297 Teemu Numminen
☐ 298 Pasi Forsberg	☐ 299 VeliPekka Kautonen
☐ 301 TPS Turku	☐ 302 TPS Turku
☐ 303 TPS Turku	☐ 304 TPS Turku
☐ 305 TPS Turku	☐ 306 TPS Turku
☐ 307 TPS Turku	☐ 308 TPS Turku
☐ 309 TPS Turku	☐ 310 TPS Turku
☐ 311 TPS Turku	☐ 312 TPS Turku
☐ 313 Vladimir Yursinov	☐ 314 Jouni Rokama (G)
☐ 315 Hannu Virta	☐ 316 Erik Kakko
☐ 317 Jukka Vilander	☐ 318 Esa Keskinen
☐ 319 Ari Vuori	☐ 320 Jouko Narvanmaa
☐ 321 Marko Kiprusoff	☐ 322 Jere Lehtinen
☐ 323 Saku Koivu	☐ 324 Marko Jantunen
☐ 325 Kari Harila	☐ 326 Aleksander Smirnov
☐ 327 Toni Sihvonen	☐ 328 Harri Sillgren
☐ 329 Kai Nurminen	☐ 331 Assat Pori
☐ 332 Assat Pori	☐ 333 Assat Pori
☐ 334 Assat Pori	☐ 335 Assat Pori
☐ 336 Assat Pori	☐ 337 Assat Pori
☐ 338 Assat Pori	☐ 339 Assat Pori
☐ 340 Assat Pori	☐ 341 Assat Pori
☐ 342 Assat Pori	☐ 343 Veli-Pekka Ketola
☐ 344 Kari Takko (G)	☐ 345 Olli Kaski
☐ 346 Karri Kivi	☐ 347 Arto Heiskanen
☐ 348 Janne Virtanen	☐ 349 Mikael Kotkaniemi
☐ 350 Stanislav Meciar	☐ 351 Jarno Miikkulainen
☐ 352 Jokke Heinanen	☐ 353 Vjatseslav Fandul
☐ 354 Ari Saarinen	☐ 355 Jouni Vento
☐ 356 Arto Javanainen	☐ 357 Jari Korpisalo
☐ 358 Rauli Raitanen	☐ 359 Jari Levonen

1993 - 94 KRAFT

Complete Set (61 cards): 90.00
Album: 30.00

JELL-O PUDDING SNACKS

One of 8 different panels were found under tops of specially marked boxes of JELL-O pudding (4x142g).

Panel Size: 3 11/16" x 5 3/16"
Complete Set (8 panels): 20.00

	Player	JELL-O
☐	Tom Barrasso/ Mario Lemieux	5.00
☐	Kirk McLean/ Pavel Bure	2.00
☐	Stéphane Fiset/ Joe Sakic	2.00
☐	Félix Potvin/ Doug Gilmour	2.00
☐	Wayne Gretzky/ Kelly Hrudey	5.00
☐	Eric Lindros/ Dominic Roussel	2.00
☐	Kirk Muller/ Patrick Roy	5.00
☐	Joe Nieuwendyk/ Mike Vernon (G)	2.00

KRAFT DINNER

One of 26 different cards was issued on the backs of specially marked boxes of Kraft Dinner.

Card Size: 3 1/2" x 5 1/4"
Complete Set (24 cards): 25.00

	Player	KD
☐	Ed Belfour (G), Chic.	2.00
☐	Brian Bradley, Tamp.	1.00
☐	Pavel Bure, Vanc.	2.00
☐	Paul Coffey, Detr.	1.00
☐	Russ Courtnall, Dall.	1.00
☐	Alexandre Daigle, Otta.	1.00
☐	Pat Falloon, SanJ.	1.00
☐	Theoren Fleury, Calg.	1.00
☐	Doug Gilmour, Toro.	1.00
☐	Adam Graves, NYRa.	1.00
☐	Stu Grimson, Anah.	1.00
☐	Al Iafrate, Wash.	1.00
☐	Jaromir Jagr, Pitt.	2.00
☐	Joé Juneau, Bost.	1.00
☐	Eric Lindros, Phil.	2.00
☐	Alexander Mogilny, Buff.	1.00
☐	Kirk Muller, Mont.	1.00
☐	Bill Ranford (G), Edmo.	1.00
☐	Mike Ricci, Québ.	1.00
☐	Luc Robitaille, LosA.	2.00
☐	Geoff Sanderson, Hfd.	1.00
☐	Teemu Selänne, Winn.	2.00
☐	Brendan Shanahan, SLou.	2.00
☐	Pierre Turgeon, NYIs.	1.00
☐	John Vanbiesbrouck (G), Flor.	1.00
☐	Valeri Zelepukin, N.J.	1.00

KRAFT DINNER / GOLD EDITION

This set was originally issued as a six-card panel. Panels were inserted in specially marked 12-box cases of Kraft Dinner

Card Size: 3 1/2" x 5 1/4"
Complete Set (6 cards): 15.00

	Player	KD Gold
☐	Jason Arnott, Edmo.	1.00
☐	Chris Chelios, Chic.	1.00
☐	Mario Lemieux, Pitt.	7.00
☐	Rob Niedermayer, Flor.	1.00
☐	Chris Pronger, Hart.	1.00
☐	Patrick Roy (G), Mont. [w/ Cup]	9.00

KRAFT PEANUT BUTTER

Two of 23 different captains and coaches disks were found under the lids of specially marked jars of Kraft Peanut Butter.

Disk Diameter: 2 1/2"
Complete Set (24 cards): 40.00

	Player	PB
☐	Ray Bourque, Bost./ Patrick Flatley, NYIs.	2.00
☐	Guy Carbonneau, Mont./ Jeremy Roenick, Chic.	2.00
☐	Wayne Gretzky, LosA./ Wendel Clark, Toro.	10.00
☐	Kevin Dineen, Phil./ Kevin Hatcher, Wash.	1.00
☐	Mario Lemieux, Pitt./ Mark Messier, NYRa.	7.00
☐	Trevor Linden, Vanc./ Troy Loney, Anah.	1.00
☐	Joe Nieuwendyk, Calg./ Joe Sakic, Mont.	3.00
☐	Dean Kennedy, Winn./ Denis Savard, Tamp.	1.00
☐	Brett Hull, SLou./ Brad Shaw, Otta.	2.00
☐	Craig MacTavish, Edmo./ Brian Skrudland, Flor.	1.00
☐	Mike Lalor, SanJ./ Mark Tinordi, Dall.	1.00
☐	Pat LaFontaine, Buff./ Pat Verbeek, Hfd.	1.00
☐	Scott Stevens, N.J./ Steve Yzerman, Detr.	5.00
☐	Al Arbour, Coach, NYIs.	1.00
☐	Bob Berry, Coach, SLou.	1.00
☐	Scott Bowman, Coach, Detr.	2.00
☐	Pat Burns, Coach, Toro.	1.00
☐	Jacques Demers, Coach, Mont.	1.00
☐	Eddie Johnston, Coach, Pitt.	1.00
☐	Dave King, Coach, Calg.	1.00
☐	Barry Melrose, Coach, LosA.	1.00
☐	John Muckler, Coach, Buff.	1.00
☐	Pierre Pagé, Coach, Québ.	1.00

1993 - 94 LEAF

Imprint: 1993 Leaf, Inc.
Series One Set (220 cards): 25.00
Series Two Set (220 cards): 25.00
Common Player: .20

	Player	NRMT-MT
☐	1 Mario Lemieux, Pitt.	1.50
☐	2 Curtis Joseph (G), SLou.	.50
☐	3 Stephen Leach, Bost.	.20
☐	4 Vincent Damphousse, Mont.	.20
☐	5 Murray Craven, Vanc.	.20
☐	6 Pat Elynuik, Wash.	.20
☐	7 Bill Guerin, NJer.	.20
☐	8 Zarley Zalapski, Hart.	.20
☐	**9 Rob Gaudreau, SanJ. RC**	**.50**
☐	10 Pavel Bure, Vanc.	.50
☐	11 Brad Shaw, Otta.	.20
☐	12 Pat LaFontaine, Buff.	.20
☐	13 Teemu Selänne, Winn.	.50
☐	14 Trent Klatt, Minn. (Dall.)	.20
☐	15 Kevin Todd, Edmo.	.20
☐	16 Larry Murphy, Pitt.	.20
☐	17 Tony Amonte, NYRa.	.20
☐	18 Dino Ciccarelli, Detr.	.20
☐	19 Doug Bodger, Buff.	.20
☐	20 Luc Robitaille, LosA.	.50
☐	21 John Tucker, Tamp.	.20
☐	22 Todd Gill, Toro.	.20
☐	23 Mike Ricci, Québ.	.20
☐	24 Evgeny Davydov, Winn.	.20
☐	25 Pierre Turgeon, NYIs.	.20
☐	26 Rod Brind'Amour, Phil.	.20
☐	27 Jeremy Roenick, Chic.	.50
☐	28 Joel Otto, Calg.	.20
☐	29 Jeff R. Brown, SLou.	.20
☐	30 Brendan Shanahan, SLou.	.50
☐	31 Jiri Slégr, Vanc.	.20
☐	32 Vladimir Malakhov, NYIs.	.20
☐	33 Patrick Roy (G), Mont.	1.50
☐	34 Kevin Hatcher, Wash.	.20
☐	35 Alexander Semak, NJer.	.20
☐	36 Gary Roberts, Calg.	.20
☐	37 Tommy Söderström (G), Phil.	.20
☐	38 Bob Essensa (G), Winn.	.20
☐	39 Kelly Hrudey (G), LosA.	.20
☐	40 Shawn Chambers, Tamp.	.20
☐	41 Glenn Anderson, Toro.	.20
☐	42 Owen Nolan, Québ.	.20
☐	43 Patrick Flatley, NYIs.	.20
☐	44 Ray Sheppard, Detr.	.20
☐	45 Darren Turcotte, NYRa.	.20
☐	46 Shayne Corson, Edmo.	.20
☐	47 Brad May, Buff.	.20
☐	48 Bob Kudelski, Otta.	.20
☐	49 Pat Falloon, SanJ.	.20
☐	50 Andrew Cassels, Hart.	.20
☐	51 Chris Chelios, Chic.	.20
☐	52 Sylvain Côté, Wash.	.20
☐	53 Mathieu Schneider, Mont.	.20
☐	54 Ted Donato, Bost.	.20
☐	55 Kirk McLean (G), Vanc.	.20
☐	56 Bruce Driver, NJer.	.20
☐	57 Uwe Krupp, NYIs.	.20
☐	58 Brent Fedyk, Phil.	.20
☐	59 Robert Reichel, Calg.	.20
☐	60 Scott Stevens, NJer.	.20
☐	61 Phil Housley, Winn.	.20
☐	62 Ed Belfour (G), Chic.	.50
☐	63 Dave Andreychuk, Toro.	.20
☐	64 Claude Lapointe, Québ.	.20
☐	65 Russ Courtnall, Minn. (Dall.)	.20
☐	66 Grant Fuhr (G), Buff.	.20
☐	67 Paul Coffey, Detr.	.20
☐	68 Bill Ranford (G), Edmo.	.20
☐	69 Kevin Stevens, Pitt.	.20
☐	70 Brian Leetch, NYRa.	.20
☐	71 Dale Hawerchuk, Buff.	.20
☐	72 Geoff Courtnall, Vanc.	.20
☐	73 Sandis Ozolinsh, SanJ.	.20
☐	74 Sylvain Turgeon, Otta.	.20
☐	75 Nelson Emerson, SLou.	.20
☐	76 Brian Bellows, Mont.	.20
☐	77 Geoff Sanderson, Hart.	.20
☐	78 Petr Nedved, Vanc.	.20
☐	79 Peter Bondra, Wash.	.20
☐	80 Scott Niedermayer, NJer.	.20
☐	81 Steve Thomas, NYIs.	.20
☐	82 Dmitry Yushkevich, Phil.	.20
☐	83 Mike Vernon (G), Calg.	.20
☐	84 Alexei Zhamnov, Winn.	.20
☐	85 Adam Creighton, Tamp.	.20
☐	86 Dave Ellett, Toro.	.20
☐	87 Joe Sakic, Québ.	1.00
☐	88 Mike Craig, Minn. (Dall.)	.20
☐	89 Nicklas Lidström, Detr.	.20
☐	90 Ed Olczyk, NYRa.	.20
☐	91 Alexander Mogilny, Buff.	.20
☐	92 Ulf Samuelsson, Pitt.	.20
☐	93 Doug Gilmour, Toro.	.20
☐	94 Michael Nylander, Hart.	.20
☐	95 J. Steve Smith, Chic.	.20
☐	96 Igor Korolev, SLou.	.20
☐	97 Dixon Ward, Vanc.	.20
☐	98 John LeClair, Mont.	.50
☐	99 Cam Neely, Bost.	.50
☐	100 Canadiens	.50
☐	101 Darius Kasparaitis, NYIs.	.20
☐	102 Mike Ridley, Wash.	.20
☐	103 Josef Beránek, Phil.	.20
☐	104 Valeri Zelepukin, NJer.	.20
☐	105 Keith Tkachuk, Winn.	.20
☐	106 Tomas Sandström, LosA.	.20
☐	107 Peter Zezel, Toro.	.20
☐	108 Scott Young, Québ.	.20
☐	109 Rick Tocchet, Pitt.	.20
☐	110 Teemu Selänne, Awards (Winn.) [Checklist]	.50
☐	111 Steve Chiasson, Detr.	.20
☐	112 Doug Zmolek, SanJ.	.20
☐	113 Patrick Poulin, Hart.	.20
☐	114 Stéphane Matteau, Chic.	.20
☐	115 Yves Racine, Detr.	.20
☐	116 Stephen Heinze, Bost.	.20
☐	117 Gilbert Dionne, Mont.	.20
☐	118 Dale Hunter, Wash.	.20
☐	119 Derek King, NYIs.	.20
☐	120 Garry Galley, Phil.	.20
☐	121 Ray Ferraro, NYIs.	.20
☐	122 Andrei Kovalenko, Québ.	.20
☐	123 Alexei Zhitnik, LosA.	.20
☐	124 Fredrik Olausson, Winn.	.20
☐	125 Claude Lemieux, NJer.	.20
☐	126 Joe Nieuwendyk, Calg.	.20
☐	127 Travis Green, NYIs.	.20
☐	128 Dave Gagner, Minn. (Dall.)	.20
☐	129 Sergei Fedorov, Detr.	.50
☐	130 Adam Graves, NYRa.	.20
☐	131 Petr* Svoboda, Buff.	.20
☐	132 Sean Burke (G), Hart.	.20
☐	133 Johan Garpenlöv, SanJ.	.20
☐	134 Jamie Baker, Otta.	.20
☐	135 Teppo Numminen, Winn.	.20
☐	136 Mats Sundin, Québ.	.50
☐	137 Nikolai Borschevsky, Toro.	.20
☐	138 Stéphane J.J. Richer, NJer.	.20
☐	139 Scott Lachance, NYIs.	.20
☐	140 Gary Suter, Calg.	.20
☐	141 Al Iafrate, Wash.	.20
☐	142 Brent Sutter, Chic.	.20
☐	143 Dmitri Kvartalnov, Bost.	.20
☐	144 Pat Verbeek, Hart.	.20
☐	145 Ed Courtenay, SanJ.	.20
☐	146 Mark Tinordi, Minn. (Dall.)	.20
☐	147 Alexei Kovalev, NYRa.	.20
☐	**148 Dallas Drake, Detr. RC**	**.50**
☐	149 Jimmy Carson, LosA.	.20
☐	150 Panthers , Flor.	.20
☐	151 Roman Hamrlik, Tamp.	.20
☐	152 Martin Rucinsky, Québ.	.20
☐	153 Calle Johansson, Wash.	.20
☐	154 Theoren Fleury, Calg.	.20
☐	155 Benoît Hogue, NYIs.	.20
☐	156 Kevin Dineen, Phil.	.20
☐	157 Jody Hull, Otta.	.20
☐	158 Mark Messier, NYRa.	.50
☐	159 Dave Manson, Edmo.	.20
☐	160 Chris Kontos, Tamp.	.20
☐	161 Ron Francis, Pitt.	.20
☐	162 Steve Yzerman, Detr.	1.50
☐	163 Igor Kravchuk, Edmo.	.20
☐	164 Sergei Zubov, NYRa.	.20
☐	165 Thomas Steen, Winn.	.20
☐	166 Wendel Clark, Toro.	.50
☐	**167 Scott Pellerin, NJer. RC**	**.50**
☐	168 Dmitri Khristich, Wash.	.20
☐	169 Bernie Nicholls, NJer.	.20
☐	170 Paul Ranheim, Calg.	.20
☐	171 Robert Kron, Hart.	.20
☐	172 Rob Blake, LosA.	.20
☐	173 Rob Zamuner, Tamp.	.20
☐	174 Rob Pearson, Toro.	.20
☐	175 Ed Belfour (G), Awards (Chic.) [Checklist]	.50
☐	176 Steve Duchesne, Québ.	.20
☐	177 Pelle Eklund, Phil.	.20
☐	178 Michal Pivonka, Wash.	.20
☐	179 Joe Murphy, Chic.	.20
☐	180 Al MacInnis, Calg.	.20
☐	181 Craig Janney, SLou.	.20
☐	182 Kirk Muller, Mont.	.20
☐	183 Cliff Ronning, Vanc.	.20
☐	184 Doug Weight, Edmo.	.20
☐	185 Mike Richter (G), NYRa.	.20
☐	186 Bob Probert, Detr.	.20
☐	187 Robert Petrovicky, Hart.	.20
☐	188 Richard Smehlik, Buff.	.20
☐	189 Norm Maciver, Otta.	.20
☐	190 Stéphan Lebeau, Mont.	.20
☐	191 Patrice Brisebois, Mont.	.20
☐	192 Kevin Miller, SLou.	.20
☐	193 Trevor Linden, Vanc.	.20
☐	194 Darrin Shannon, Winn.	.20
☐	195 Tim Cheveldae (G), Detr.	.20
☐	196 Tom Barrasso (G), Pitt.	.20
☐	197 Zdeno Ciger, Edmo.	.20
☐	198 Ulf Dahlén, Minn. (Dall.)	.20
☐	199 Arturs Irbe (G), SanJ.	.20
☐	200 Mighty Ducks , Anah.	.20
☐	201 Tony Granato, LosA.	.20
☐	202 Mike Modano, Minn. (Dall.)	.50
☐	203 Éric Desjardins, Mont.	.20
☐	204 Bryan Smolinski, Bost.	.20
☐	205 Mark Recchi, Phil.	.20
☐	206 Darryl Sydor, LosA.	.20
☐	207 Valeri Kamensky, Québ.	.20
☐	208 Kelly Kisio, SanJ.	.20
☐	209 Brian Bradley, Tamp.	.20
☐	210 Mario Lemieux, Awards (Pitt.) [Checklist]	1.50
☐	211 Yuri Khmylev, Buff.	.20
☐	212 Derian Hatcher, Minn. (Dall.)	.20
☐	213 Mike Gartner, NYRa.	.50
☐	214 Mike Needham, Pitt.	.20
☐	215 Raymond Bourque, Bost.	.50
☐	216 Tie Domi, Winn.	.20
☐	217 Shawn McEachern, Pitt.	.20
☐	218 Joé Juneau, Bost.	.20
☐	219 Greg A. Adams, Vanc.	.20
☐	220 Martin Straka, Pitt.	.20
☐	221 Tom Fitzgerald, Flor.	.20
☐	222 Gary Shuchuk, LosA.	.20
☐	223 Kevin Haller, Mont.	.20
☐	224 Bryan Marchment, Chic.	.20
☐	225 Louie DeBrusk, Edmo.	.20

☐ 226 Randy Wood, Buff. .20
☐ 227 Bobby Holik, NJer. .20
☐ 228 Troy Mallette, Otta. .20
☐ 229 Adam Foote, Québ. .20
☐ 230 Bob Rouse, Toro. .20
☐ 231 Jyrki Lumme, Vanc. .20
☐ 232 James Patrick, NYRa. .20
☐ 233 Eric Lindros, Phil. .50
☐ 234 Joe Reekie, Tamp. .20
☐ 235 Adam Oates, Bost. .20
☐ 236 Frantisek Musil, Calg. .20
☐ 237 Vladimir Konstantinov, Detr. .20
☐ 238 Dave Lowry, Flor. .20
☐ 239 Garth Butcher, SLou. .20
☐ 240 Jari Kurri, LosA. .50
☐ 241 Rick Tabaracci (G), Wash. .20
☐ 242 Sergei Bautin, Winn. .20
☐ 243 Scott Scissons, NYIs. .20
☐ 244 Dominic Roussel (G), Phil. .20
☐ 245 John Cullen, Toro. .20
☐ 246 Sheldon Kennedy, Detr. .20
☐ 247 Mike Hough, Flor. .20
☐ 248 Paul DiPietro, Mont. .20
☐ 249 David Shaw, Bost. .20
☐ 250 Sergio Momesso, Vanc. .20
☐ 251 Jeff Daniels, Pitt. .20
☐ 252 Sergei Nemchinov, NYRa. .20
☐ 253 Kris King, Winn. .20
☐ 254 Kelly Miller, Wash. .20
☐ 255 Brett Hull, SLou. .50
☐ 256 Dominik Hasek (G), Buff. .50
☐ 257 Chris Pronger, Hart. .50
☐ **258 Derek Plante, Buff. RC .50**
☐ 259 Mark Howe, Detr. .20
☐ 260 Oleg Petrov, Mont. .20
☐ 261 Ronnie Stern, Calg. .20
☐ 262 Scott Mellanby, Flor. .20
☐ 263 Warren Rychel, LosA. .20
☐ 264 John MacLean, NJer. .20
☐ **265 Radek Hamr, Otta. RC .50**
☐ 266 Greg Hawgood, Phil. .20
☐ 267 Sylvain Lefebvre, Toro. .20
☐ 268 Glen Wesley, Bost. .20
☐ 269 Joe Cirella, Flor. .20
☐ 270 Dirk Graham, Chic. .20
☐ 271 Eric Weinrich, Hart. .20
☐ 272 Donald Audette, Buff. .20
☐ 273 Jason Woolley, Wash. .20
☐ 274 Kjell Samuelsson, Pitt. .20
☐ 275 Ron Sutter, SLou. .20
☐ 276 Keith Primeau, Detr. .20
☐ 277 Ron Tugnutt (G), Anah. .20
☐ 278 Jesse Bélanger, Flor. .20
☐ 279 Mike Keane, Mont. .20
☐ 280 Adam Burt, Hart. .20
☐ 281 Don Sweeney, Bost. .20
☐ 282 Mike Donnelly, LosA. .20
☐ 283 Lyle Odelein, Mont. .20
☐ 284 Gord Murphy, Flor. .20
☐ 285 Mikael Andersson, Tamp. .20
☐ 286 Bret Hedican, SLou. .20
☐ 287 Bill Berg, Toro. .20
☐ 288 Esa Tikkanen, NYRa. .20
☐ 289 Markus Näslund, Pitt. 1.00
☐ 290 Chris Chelios, Awards (Chic.) [Checklist] .20
☐ 291 Kerry Huffman, Québ. .20
☐ 292 Dana Murzyn, Vanc. .20
☐ 293 Rob Niedermayer, Flor. .20
☐ 294 André Racicot (G), Mont. .20
☐ 295 Ken Sutton, Buff. .20
☐ 296 Shawn Burr, Detr. .20
☐ 297 Scott Pearson, Edmo. .20
☐ **298 Joby Messier, NYRa. RC .50**
☐ **299 Darrin Madeley (G), Otta. RC .50**
☐ 300 Joe Mullen, Pitt. .20
☐ 301 Stéphane Fiset (G), Québ. .20
☐ 302 Geoff Smith, Edmo. .20
☐ 303 Vyacheslav Kozlov, Detr. .20
☐ 304 Wayne Gretzky, LosA. 2.50
☐ 305 Curtis Leschyshyn, Québ. .20
☐ 306 Mike Sillinger, Detr. .20
☐ 307 Viacheslav Butsayev, Phil. .20
☐ 308 Mark Lamb, Otta. .20
☐ **309 German Titov, Calg. RC .50**
☐ 310 Gerard Gallant, Tamp. .20
☐ 311 Alexandre Daigle, Otta. .20
☐ 312 Jim Hrivnak (G), SLou. .20
☐ 313 Corey Hirsch (G), NYRa. .20
☐ 314 Craig Berube, Wash. .20
☐ 315 Bill Houlder, Anah. .20
☐ 316 Ron L. Wilson, Mont. .20
☐ 317 Glen Murray, Bost. .20
☐ 318 Bryan Trottier, Pitt. .50
☐ 319 Jeff Hackett (G), Chic. .20
☐ 320 Brad Dalgarno, NYIs. .20
☐ 321 Petr Klima, Tamp. .20
☐ 322 Jon Casey (G), Bost. .20
☐ 323 Mikael Renberg, Phil. .20
☐ 324 Jimmy Waite (G), SanJ. .20
☐ 325 Brian Skrudland, Flor. .20
☐ 326 Vitali Prokhorov, SLou. .20
☐ 327 Glenn Healy (G), NYRa. .20
☐ 328 Brian Benning, Flor. .20
☐ 329 Tony Hrkac, SLou. .20
☐ 330 Stu Grimson, Anah. .20
☐ 331 Chris Gratton, Tamp. .20
☐ 332 Dave Poulin, Wash. .20
☐ 333 Jarrod Skalde, Anah. .20
☐ 334 Christian Ruuttu, Chic. .20
☐ 335 Mark Fitzpatrick (G), Flor. .20
☐ 336 Martin Lapointe, Detr. .20
☐ **337 Cam Stewart, Bost. RC .50**
☐ 338 Anatoli Semenov, Anah. .20
☐ 339 Gaétan Duchesne, SanJ. .20
☐ 340 Pierre Turgeon, Awards (NYIs.) [Checklist] .20
☐ 341 Ron Hextall (G), NYIs. .20
☐ 342 Mikhail Tatarinov, Bost. .20
☐ 343 Danny Lorenz (G), NYIs. .20
☐ 344 Craig Simpson, Buff. .20
☐ 345 Martin Brodeur (G), NJer. 1.00
☐ 346 Jaromir Jagr, Pitt. .50
☐ 347 Tyler Wright, Edmo. .20
☐ 348 Greg Gilbert, NYRa. .20
☐ 349 Dave Tippett, Phil. .20
☐ 350 Stu Barnes, Winn. .20
☐ **351 Daniel Lacroix, NYRa. RC .50**
☐ 352 Marty McSorley, Pitt. .20
☐ 353 Sean Hill, Anah. .20
☐ 354 Craig Billington (G), Otta. .20
☐ 355 Donald Dufresne, Tamp. .20
☐ 356 Guy Hebert (G), Anah. .20
☐ 357 Neil Wilkinson, Chic. .20
☐ 358 Sandy McCarthy, Calg. .20
☐ **359 Aaron Ward, Detr. RC .50**
☐ **360 Scott Thomas, Buff. RC .50**
☐ 361 Corey Millen, NJer. .20
☐ 362 Matthew Barnaby, Buff. .20
☐ 363 Benoît Brunet, Mont. .20
☐ 364 Boris Mironov, Winn. .20
☐ 365 Doug Lidster, NYRa. .20
☐ 366 Pavol Demitra, Otta. .50
☐ **367 Damian Rhodes (G), Toro. RC 1.00**
☐ 368 Shawn Antoski, Vanc. .20
☐ 369 Andy Moog (G), Dall. .20
☐ 370 Greg Johnson, Detr. .20
☐ 371 John Vanbiesbrouck (G), Flor. .20
☐ 372 Denis Savard, Tamp. .20
☐ 373 Michel Goulet, Chic. .20
☐ 374 Dave Taylor, LosA. .20
☐ 375 Enrico Ciccone, Wash. .20
☐ 376 Sergei Zholtok, Bost. .20
☐ 377 Bob Errey, SanJ. .20
☐ 378 Doug Brown, Pitt. .20
☐ **379 Bill McDougall, Tamp. RC .50**
☐ 380 Pat Conacher, LosA. .20
☐ 381 Alexei Kasatonov, Anah. .20
☐ **382 Jason Arnott, Edmo. RC 2.00**
☐ 383 Jarkko Varvio, Dall. .20
☐ 384 Sergei Makarov, SanJ. .20
☐ 385 Trevor Kidd (G), Calg. .20
☐ 386 Alexei Yashin, Otta. .50
☐ 387 Gerald Diduck, Vanc. .20
☐ 388 Paul Ysebaert, Winn. .20
☐ **389 Jason Smith, NJer. RC .50**
☐ 390 Jeff Norton, SanJ. .20
☐ 391 Igor Larionov, SanJ. .20
☐ 392 Pierre Sévigny, Mont. .20
☐ 393 Wes Walz, Calg. .20
☐ 394 Grant Ledyard, Dall. .20
☐ 395 Brad McCrimmon, Hart. .20
☐ 396 Martin Gélinas, Québ. .20
☐ 397 Paul Cavallini, Dall. .20
☐ 398 Brian Noonan, Chic. .20
☐ 399 Mike Lalor, SanJ. .20
☐ 400 Dmitri Filimonov, Otta. .20
☐ 401 Andrei Lomakin, Flor. .20
☐ **402 Steve Junker, NYIs. RC .50**
☐ 403 Daren Puppa (G), Tamp. .20
☐ 404 Jozef Stumpel, Bost. .20
☐ **405 Jeff Shantz, Chic. RC .50**
☐ 406 Terry Yake, Anah. .20
☐ 407 Mike Peluso, NJer. .20
☐ 408 Vitali Karamnov, SLou. .20
☐ 409 Félix Potvin (G), Toro. .20
☐ 410 Steven King, Anah. .20
☐ 411 Roman Oksiuta, Edmo. RC .20
☐ 412 Mark Greig, Hart. .20
☐ 413 Wayne McBean, NYIs. .20
☐ 414 Nick Kypreos, Hart. .20
☐ 415 Dominic Lavoie, LosA. .20
☐ **416 Chris Simon, Québ. RC 1.00**
☐ **417 Peter Popovic, Mont. RC .50**
☐ 418 Gino Odjick, Vanc. .20
☐ 419 Mike Rathje, SanJ. .20
☐ 420 Keith Acton, Wash. .20
☐ 421 Bob Carpenter, NJer. .20
☐ 422 Steven Finn, Québ. .20
☐ **423 Ian Herbers, Edmo. RC .50**
☐ 424 Ted Drury, Calg. .20
☐ 425 Sergei Petrenko, Buff. .20
☐ **426 Mattias Norström, NYRa. RC 1.00**
☐ 427 Todd Ewen, Anah. .20
☐ **428 Jocelyn Thibault (G), Québ. RC 2.00**
☐ **429 Robert Burakovsky, Otta. RC .50**
☐ 430 Chris Terreri (G), NJer. .20
☐ **431 Michal Sykora, SanJ. RC .50**
☐ 432 Craig Ludwig, Dall. .20
☐ **433 Vesa Viitakoski, Calg. RC .50**
☐ 434 Sergei Krivokrasov, Chic. .20
☐ **435 Darren McCarty, Detr. RC 1.50**
☐ 436 Dean McAmmond, Edmo. .20
☐ 437 J.J. Daigneault, Mont. .20
☐ 438 Vladimír Ruzicka, Otta. .20
☐ **439 Vlastimil Kroupa, SanJ. RC .50**
☐ 440 Doug Gilmour, Awards (Toro.) [Checklist] .20

FRESHMAN PHENOMS

Series Two Insert Set (10 cards): 15.00

	Insert	FP
☐	1 Alexandre Daigle, Otta.	.75
☐	2 Chris Pronger, Hart.	3.00
☐	3 Chris Gratton, Tamp.	1.00
☐	4 Markus Näslund, Pitt.	5.00
☐	5 Mikael Renberg, Phil.	1.00
☐	6 Rob Niedermayer, Flor.	1.00
☐	7 Jason Arnott, Edmo.	4.00
☐	8 Jarkko Varvio, Dall.	1.00
☐	9 Alexei Yashin, Otta.	3.00
☐	10 Jocelyn Thibault (G), Québ.	2.00

GOLD LEAF ALL-STARS

Insert Set (10 cards): 50.00

	Insert	GLAS
☐	1 P. LaFontaine / M. Lemieux	10.00
☐	2 C. Chelios / L. Murphy	2.00
☐	3 Br. Hull / T. Selänne	5.00
☐	4 D. Andreychuk / K. Stevens	2.00
☐	5 T. Barrasso / P. Roy	10.00
☐	6 D. Gilmour / W. Gretzky	15.00
☐	7 R. Bourque / P. Coffey	5.00
☐	8 P. Bure / A. Mogilny	2.00
☐	9 L. Robitaille / B. Shanahan	5.00
☐	10 E. Belfour / F. Potvin	5.00

GOLD LEAF ROOKIE

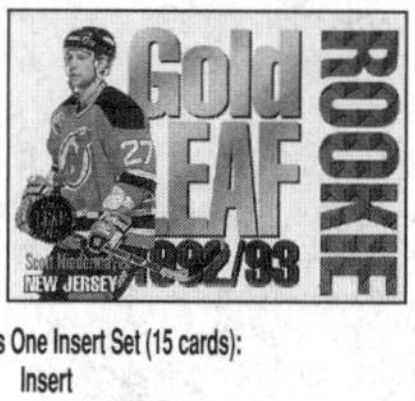

Series One Insert Set (15 cards): 9.00

	Insert	GLR
☐	1 Teemu Selänne, Winn.	2.00
☐	2 Joé Juneau, Bost.	.50
☐	3 Eric Lindros, Phil.	2.00
☐	4 Félix Potvin (G), Toro.	1.00
☐	5 Alexei Zhamnov, Winn.	.50
☐	6 Andrei Kovalenko, Québ.	.50
☐	7 Shawn McEachern, Pitt.	.50
☐	8 Alexei Zhitnik, LosA.	.50
☐	9 Vladimir Malakhov, NYIs.	.50
☐	10 Patrick Poulin, Hart.	.50
☐	11 Keith Tkachuk, Winn.	1.00
☐	12 Tommy Söderström (G), Phil.	.50
☐	13 Darius Kasparaitis, NYIs.	.50
☐	14 Scott Niedermayer, NJer.	.50
☐	15 Darryl Sydor, LosA.	.50

HAT TRICK ARTISTS

Insert Set (10 cards): 15.00

	Insert	HTA
☐	1 Mario Lemieux, Pitt. [Title Card]	3.00
☐	2 Alexander Mogilny, Buff.	.50
☐	3 Teemu Selänne, Winn.	1.00
☐	4 Mario Lemieux, Pitt.	6.00
☐	5 Pierre Turgeon, NYIs.	.50
☐	6 Kevin Dineen, Phil.	.50
☐	7 Eric Lindros, Phil.	2.00
☐	8 Adam Oates, Bost.	.50
☐	9 Kevin Stevens, Pitt.	.50
☐	10 Steve Yzerman, Detr.	4.00

LEMIEUX COLLECTION

Insert Set (10 cards): 22.00

	Insert	LC
☐	1 Mario Lemieux	3.00
☐	2 Mario Lemieux	3.00
☐	3 Mario Lemieux	3.00
☐	4 Mario Lemieux	3.00
☐	5 Mario Lemieux	3.00
☐	6 Mario Lemieux	3.00
☐	7 Mario Lemieux	3.00
☐	8 Mario Lemieux	3.00
☐	9 Mario Lemieux	3.00
☐	10 Mario Lemieux	3.00
☐	Mario Lemieux Autograph ✍	300.00

PAINTED WARRIORS

Insert Set (10 cards): 15.00

	Insert	PW
☐	1 Félix Potvin (G), Toro.	1.50
☐	2 Curtis Joseph (G), SLou.	3.00
☐	3 Kirk McLean (G), Vanc.	.75
☐	4 Patrick Roy (G), Mont.	9.00
☐	5 Grant Fuhr (G), Buff.	1.50
☐	6 Ed Belfour (G), Chic.	3.00
☐	7 Mike Vernon (G), Calg.	1.00
☐	8 John Vanbiesbrouck (G), Flor.	1.00
☐	9 Tom Barrasso (G), Pitt.	1.00
☐	10 Bill Ranford (G), Edmo.	1.00

STUDIO SIGNATURE SERIES

Insert Set (10 cards): 25.00

	Insert	SSS
☐	1 Doug Gilmour, Toro.	1.00
☐	2 Pat Falloon, SanJ.	.50
☐	3 Pat LaFontaine, Buff.	1.00

☐	4 Wayne Gretzky, LosA.	10.00
☐	5 Steve Yzerman, Detr.	6.00
☐	6 Patrick Roy (G), Mont.	7.00
☐	7 Jeremy Roenick, Chic.	2.00
☐	8 Brett Hull, SLou.	2.00
☐	9 Alexandre Daigle, Otta.	.50
☐	10 Eric Lindros, Phil.	2.00

1993 - 94 LEGENDS OF HOCKEY

Artwork by Doug West. Singles sell between $8 and $12.
Card Size: 3 1/2" x 5 1/2"
Series Two Set (18 cards): 125.00

Player	Player
☐ 19 Ted Lindsay	☐ 20 Duke Keats
☐ 21 Jack Adams	☐ 22 Bill Mosienko
☐ 23 Johnny Bower (G)	☐ 24 Tim Horton
☐ 25 Punch Imlach	☐ 26 Georges Vézina (G)
☐ 27 Earl Seibert	☐ 28 Bryan Hextall
☐ 29 Babe Pratt	☐ 30 Gump Worsley (G)
☐ 31 Ed Giacomin (G)	☐ 32 Ace Bailey
☐ 33 Harry Sinden	☐ 34 Lanny McDonald
☐ 35 Tommy Ivan	☐ 36 Frank Calder

1993 - 94 MCDONALD'S - UPPER DECK

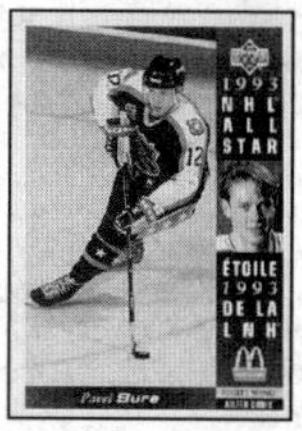

Imprint: © 1993 The Upper Deck Company
Complete Set (34 cards): 20.00

	Player	McD
☐	McD-01 Brian Bradley, NHL All-Star	.35
☐	McD-02 Pavel Bure, NHL All-Star	.50
☐	McD-03 Jon Casey (G), NHL All-Star	.35
☐	McD-04 Paul Coffey, NHL All-Star	.50
☐	McD-05 Doug Gilmour, NHL All-Star	.50
☐	McD-06 Phil Housley, NHL All-Star	.35
☐	McD-07 Brett Hull, NHL All-Star	1.00
☐	McD-08 Jari Kurri, NHL All-Star	1.00
☐	McD-09 Dave Manson, NHL All-Star	.35
☐	McD-10 Mike Modano, NHL All-Star	1.00
☐	McD-11 Gary Roberts, NHL All-Star	.35
☐	McD-12 Jeremy Roenick, NHL All-Star	.50
☐	McD-13 Steve Yzerman, NHL All-Star	2.00
☐	McD-14 Steve Duchesne, NHL All-Star	.35
☐	McD-15 Mike Gartner, NHL All-Star	.50
☐	McD-16 Al Iafrate, NHL All-Star	.35
☐	McD-17 Jaromir Jagr, NHL All-Star	1.00
☐	McD-18 Pat LaFontaine, NHL All-Star	.50
☐	McD-19 Alexander Mogilny, NHL All-Star	.35
☐	McD-20 Kirk Muller, NHL All-Star	.35
☐	McD-21 Adam Oates, NHL All-Star	.35
☐	McD-22 Mark Recchi, NHL All-Star	.35
☐	McD-23 Patrick Roy (G), NHL All-Star	3.00
☐	McD-24 Joe Sakic, NHL All-Star	1.50
☐	McD-25 Kevin Stevens, NHL All-Star	.35
☐	McD-26 Scott Stevens, NHL All-Star	.35
☐	McD-27 Pierre Turgeon, NHL All-Star	.35
☐	McH-01 Mario Lemieux, NHL All-Star	3.50
☐	McH-02 Teemu Selänne, NHL All-Star	1.00
☐	McH-03 Luc Robitaille, NHL All-Star	1.00
☐	McH-04 Raymond Bourque, NHL All-Star	1.50
☐	McH-05 Chris Chelios, NHL All-Star	.50
☐	McH-06 Ed Belfour (G), NHL All-Star	1.00
☐	Checklist	1.00
	5x7 Insert	**NRMT-MT**
☐	McD-23 Patrick Roy (G), NHL All-Star	8.00

AUTOGRAPHS

Collector Jim Sinclair reported that six players signed autographs for this series. Each player was reported to sign 100 cards. Any more information on this series would be appreciated.

□ Doug Gilmour ✍

1993 - 94 PANINI STICKER

The most expensive Glitter singles are Wayne Gretzky $1.50-2.00, Mario Lemieux at 75¢-$1.50 and Patrick Roy at 75¢-$1.25. All other regular singles sell between 20¢ and $1.00.

Sticker Size: 2 1/2" x 3 1/2"
Imprint: Panini

Complete Set (300 stickers):	**15.00**
Common Player:	**.20**
English Album:	**3.00**
French Album:	**3.00**

Players	Player
□ 1 Bruins	□ 2 Adam Oates
□ 3 Cam Neely	□ 4 Dave Poulin
□ 5 Stephen Leach	□ 6 Glen Wesley
□ 7 Dmitri Kvartalnov	□ 8 Ted Donato
□ 9 Andy Moog (G)	□ 10 Raymond Bourque
□ 11 Don Sweeney	□ 12 Canadiens
□ 13 V. Damphousse	□ 14 Kirk Muller
□ 15 Brian Bellows	□ 16 Stéphan Lebeau
□ 17 Denis Savard	□ 18 Gilbert Dionne
□ 19 Guy Carbonneau	□ 20 Benoît Brunet
□ 21 Éric Desjardins	□ 22 Mathieu Schneider
□ 23 Capitals	□ 24 Peter Bondra
□ 25 Mike Ridley	□ 26 Dale Hunter
□ 27 Michal Pivonka	□ 28 Dmitri Khristich
□ 29 Pat Elynuik	□ 30 Kelly Miller
□ 31 Calle Johansson	□ 32 Al Iafrate
□ 33 Don Beaupré (G)	□ 34 Devils
□ 35 Claude Lemieux	□ 36 Alexander Semak
□ 37 Stéphane J.J. Richer	□ 38 Valeri Zelepukin
□ 39 Bernie Nicholls	□ 40 John MacLean
□ 41 Peter Stastny	□ 42 Scott Niedermayer
□ 43 Scott Stevens	□ 44 Bruce Driver
□ 45 Flyers	□ 46 Mark Recchi
□ 47 Rod Brind'Amour	□ 48 Brent Fedyk
□ 49 Kevin Dineen	□ 50 Keith Acton
□ 51 Pelle Eklund	□ 52 Andrei Lomakin
□ 53 Garry Galley	□ 54 Terry Carkner
□ 55 T. Söderström (G)	□ 56 Islanders
□ 57 Steve Thomas	□ 58 Derek King
□ 59 Benoît Hogue	□ 60 Patrick Flatley
□ 61 Brian Mullen	□ 62 Marty McInnis
□ 63 Scott Lachance	□ 64 Jeff Norton
□ 65 Glenn Healy (G)	□ 66 Mark Fitzpatrick (G)
□ 67 Nordiques	□ 68 Mats Sundin
□ 69 Mike Ricci	□ 70 Owen Nolan
□ 71 Andrei Kovalenko	□ 72 Valeri Kamensky
□ 73 Scott Young	□ 74 Martin Rucinsky
□ 75 Steven Finn	□ 76 Steve Duchesne
□ 77 Ron Hextall (G)	□ 78 Penguins
□ 79 Kevin Stevens	□ 80 Rick Tocchet
□ 81 Ron Francis	□ 82 Jaromir Jagr
□ 83 Joe Mullen	□ 84 Shawn McEachern
□ 85 Dave Tippett	□ 86 Larry Murphy
□ 87 Ulf Samuelsson	□ 88 Tom Barrasso (G)
□ 89 Rangers	□ 90 Tony Amonte
□ 91 Mike Gartner	□ 92 Adam Graves
□ 93 Sergei Nemchinov	□ 94 Darren Turcotte
□ 95 Esa Tikkanen	□ 96 Brian Leetch
□ 97 Kevin Lowe	□ 98 J. Vanbiesbrouck (G)
□ 99 Mike Richter (G)	□ 100 Sabres
□ 101 Pat LaFontaine	□ 102 Dale Hawerchuk
□ 103 Donald Audette	□ 104 Bob Sweeney
□ 105 Randy Wood	□ 106 Yuri Khmylev
□ 107 Wayne Presley	□ 108 Grant Fuhr (G)
□ 109 Doug Bodger	□ 110 Richard Smehlik
□ 111 Senators	□ 112 Norm Maciver
□ 113 Jamie Baker	□ 114 Bob Kudelski
□ 115 Jody Hull	□ 116 Mike Peluso
□ 117 Mark Lamb	□ 118 Mark Freer
□ 119 Neil Brady	□ 120 Brad Shaw
□ 121 Sidorkiewicz (G)	□ 122 Whalers
□ 123 Andrew Cassels	□ 124 Pat Verbeek
□ 125 Terry Yake	□ 126 Patrick Poulin
□ 127 Mark Janssens	□ 128 Michael Nylander
□ 129 Zarley Zalapski	□ 130 Eric Weinrich
□ 131 Sean Burke (G)	□ 132 F. Pietrangelo (G)
□ 133 LL: Phil Housley	□ 134 LL: Paul Coffey
□ 135 LL: Larry Murphy	□ 136 LL: Mario Lemieux
□ 137 LL: Pat LaFontaine	□ 138 LL: Adam Oates
□ 139 LL: Félix Potvin (G)	□ 140 LL: Ed Belfour (G)
□ 141 LL: Barrasso (G)	□ 142 LL: Teemu Selänne
□ 143 LL: Joé Juneau	□ 144 LL: Eric Lindros
□ 145 Blackhawks	□ 146 Steve Larmer
□ 147 Dirk Graham	□ 148 Michel Goulet
□ 149 Brian Noonan	□ 150 Stéphane Matteau
□ 151 Brent Sutter	□ 152 Jocelyn Lemieux
□ 153 Chris Chelios	□ 154 J. Steve Smith
□ 155 Ed Belfour (G)	□ 156 Blues
□ 157 Craig Janney	□ 158 Brendan Shanahan
□ 159 Nelson Emerson	□ 160 Rich Sutter
□ 161 Ron Sutter	□ 162 Ron L. Wilson
□ 163 Bob Bassen	□ 164 Garth Butcher
□ 165 Jeff R. Brown	□ 166 Curtis Joseph (G)
□ 167 Canucks	□ 168 Cliff Ronning
□ 169 Murray Craven	□ 170 Geoff Courtnall
□ 171 Petr Nedved	□ 172 Trevor Linden
□ 173 Greg A. Adams	□ 174 Anatoli Semenov
□ 175 Jyrki Lumme	□ 176 Doug Lidster
□ 177 Kirk McLean (G)	□ 178 Flames
□ 179 Theoren Fleury	□ 180 Robert Reichel
□ 181 Gary Roberts	□ 182 Joe Nieuwendyk
□ 183 Sergei Makarov	□ 184 Paul Ranheim
□ 185 Joel Otto	□ 186 Gary Suter
□ 187 Jeff Reese (G)	□ 188 Mike Vernon (G)
□ 189 Jets	□ 190 Alexei Zhamnov
□ 191 Thomas Steen	□ 192 Darrin Shannon
□ 193 Keith Tkachuk	□ 194 Evgeny Davydov
□ 195 Luciano Borsato	□ 196 Phil Housley
□ 197 Teppo Numminen	□ 198 Fredrik Olausson
□ 199 Bob Essensa (G)	□ 200 Kings
□ 201 Luc Robitaille	□ 202 Jari Kurri
□ 203 Tony Granato	□ 204 Jimmy Carson
□ 205 Tomas Sandström	□ 206 Dave Taylor
□ 207 Corey Millen	□ 208 Marty McSorley
□ 209 Rob Blake	□ 210 Kelly Hrudey (G)
□ 211 Lightning	□ 212 John Tucker
□ 213 Chris Kontos	□ 214 Rob Zamuner
□ 215 Adam Creighton	□ 216 Mikael Andersson
□ 217 Bob Beers	□ 218 Rob DiMaio
□ 219 Shawn Chambers	□ 220 J-C Bergeron (G)
□ 221 Wendell Young (G)	□ 222 Maple Leafs
□ 223 Dave Andreychuk	□ 224 Nikolai Borschevsky
□ 225 Glenn Anderson	□ 226 John Cullen
□ 227 Wendel Clark	□ 228 Mike Foligno
□ 229 Mike Krushelnyski	□ 230 Jamie Macoun
□ 231 Dave Ellett	□ 232 Félix Potvin (G)
□ 233 Oilers	□ 234 Petr Klima
□ 235 Doug Weight	□ 236 Shayne Corson
□ 237 Craig Simpson	□ 238 Todd Elik
□ 239 Zdeno Ciger	□ 240 Craig MacTavish
□ 241 Kelly Buchberger	□ 242 Dave Manson
□ 243 Scott Mellanby	□ 244 Red Wings
□ 245 Dino Ciccarelli	□ 246 Sergei Fedorov
□ 247 Ray Sheppard	□ 248 Paul Ysebaert
□ 249 Bob Probert	□ 250 Keith Primeau
□ 251 Steve Chiasson	□ 252 Paul Coffey
□ 253 Nicklas Lidström	□ 254 Tim Cheveldae (G)
□ 255 Sharks	□ 256 Kelly Kisio
□ 257 Johan Garpenlöv	□ 258 Rob Gaudreau
□ 259 Dean Evason	□ 260 Jeff Odgers
□ 261 Ed Courtenay	□ 262 Mike Sullivan
□ 263 Doug Zmolek	□ 264 Doug Wilson
□ 265 Brian Hayward (G)	□ 266 Stars
□ 267 Brian Propp	□ 268 Russ Courtnall
□ 269 Dave Gagner	□ 270 Ulf Dahlén
□ 271 Mike Craig	□ 272 Neal Broten
□ 273 Gaëtan Duchesne	□ 274 Derian Hatcher
□ 275 Mark Tinordi	□ 276 Jon Casey (G)
□ A Joé Juneau	□ B Patrick Roy (G)
□ C Kevin Hatcher	□ D Chris Terreri (G)
□ E Eric Lindros	□ F Pierre Turgeon
□ G Joe Sakic	□ H Mario Lemieux
□ I Mark Messier	□ J Alexander Mogilny
□ K Sylvain Turgeon	□ L Geoff Sanderson
□ M Jeremy Roenick	□ N Brett Hull
□ O Pavel Bure	□ P Al MacInnis
□ Q Teemu Selänne	□ R Wayne Gretzky
□ S Doug Gilmour	□ T Brian Bradley
□ U Bill Ranford (G)	□ V Steve Yzerman
□ W Pat Falloon	□ X Mike Modano

1993 - 94 PARKHURST

These cards have two versions: the regular card and an Emerald Ice parallel. Cards 404 and 478 are repeated while cards 398 and 498 were never issued.

Imprint: © 1993 The Upper Deck Company

Series One Set (270 cards):	**120.00**	**20.00**
Series Two Set (270 cards):	**90.00**	**20.00**
Common Player:	**.35**	**.20**

Player	E.I.	Regular
□□ 1 Steven King, Anah.	.35	.20
□□ 2 Sean Hill, Anah.	.35	.20
□□ 3 Anatoli Semenov, Anah.	.35	.20
□□ 4 Garry Valk, Anah.	.35	.20
□□ 5 Todd Ewen, Anah.	.35	.20
□□ 6 Bob Corkum, Anah.	.35	.20
□□ 7 Tim Sweeney, Anah.	.35	.20
□□ **8 Patrik Carnbäck, Anah. RC**	**.50**	**.50**
□□ 9 Troy Loney, Anah.	.35	.20
□□ 10 Cam Neely, Bost.	2.50	.50
□□ 11 Adam Oates, Bost.	1.00	.20
□□ 12 Jon Casey (G), Bost.	.35	.20
□□ 13 Don Sweeney, Bost.	.35	.20
□□ 14 Raymond Bourque, Bost.	3.00	.50
□□ 15 Jozef Stumpel, Bost.	.50	.20
□□ 16 Glen Murray, Bost.	1.00	.20
□□ 17 Glen Wesley, Bost.	.35	.20
□□ **18 Fred Knipscheer, Bost. RC**	**.50**	**.50**
□□ 19 Craig Simpson, Buff.	.35	.20
□□ 20 Richard Smehlik, Buff.	.35	.20
□□ 21 Alexander Mogilny, Buff.	1.00	.20
□□ 22 Grant Fuhr (G), Buff.	1.50	.20
□□ 23 Dale Hawerchuk, Buff.	1.50	.20
□□ 24 Philippe Boucher, Buff.	.35	.20
□□ **25 Scott Thomas, Buff. RC**	**.50**	**.50**
□□ 26 Donald Audette, Buff.	1.00	.20
□□ 27 Brad May, Buff.	.35	.20
□□ 28 Theoren Fleury, Calg.	1.50	.20
□□ 29 Andrei Trefilov (G), Calg.	.35	.20
□□ 30 Sandy McCarthy, Calg.	.35	.20
□□ 31 Joe Nieuwendyk, Calg.	1.00	.20
□□ 32 Paul Ranheim, Calg.	.35	.20
□□ 33 Kelly Kisio, Calg.	.35	.20
□□ 34 Joel Otto, Calg.	.35	.20
□□ 35 Ted Drury, Calg.	.35	.20
□□ 36 Al MacInnis, Calg.	1.00	.20
□□ 37 Kevin Todd, Chic.	.35	.20
□□ 38 Joe Murphy, Chic.	.35	.20
□□ 39 Christian Ruuttu, Chic.	.35	.20
□□ **40 Steve Dubinsky, Chic. RC**	**.50**	**.50**
□□ 41 Stéphane Matteau, Chic.	.35	.20
□□ **42 Ivan Droppa, Chic. RC**	**.50**	**.50**
□□ 43 Jocelyn Lemieux, Chic.	.35	.20
□□ 44 Ed Belfour (G), Chic.	2.50	.50
□□ 45 Chris Chelios, Chic.	1.50	.20
□□ 46 Derian Hatcher, Minn. (Dall.)	.50	.20
□□ 47 Andy Moog (G), Dall.	1.00	.20
□□ 48 Trent Klatt, Dall.	.35	.20
□□ 49 Mike Modano, Minn. (Dall.)	2.50	.50
□□ 50 Paul Cavallini, Dall.	.35	.20
□□ 51 Mike McPhee, Minn. (Dall.)	.35	.20
□□ 52 Brent Gilchrist, Minn. (Dall.)	.35	.20
□□ 53 Russ Courtnall, Minn. (Dall.)	.50	.20
□□ 54 Neal Broten, Minn. (Dall.)	.50	.20
□□ 55 Steve Chiasson, Detr.	.35	.20
□□ 56 Paul Coffey, Detr.	1.50	.20
□□ 57 Vyacheslav Kozlov, Detr.	.50	.20
□□ 58 Sergei Fedorov, Detr.	2.50	.50
□□ 59 Tim Cheveldae (G), Detr.	.35	.20
□□ 60 Dino Ciccarelli, Detr.	.50	.20
□□ **61 Dallas Drake, Detr. RC**	**1.00**	**.50**
□□ 62 Nicklas Lidström, Detr.	1.50	.20
□□ 63 Martin Lapointe, Detr.	1.00	.20
□□ 64 Dean McAmmond, Edmo.	.35	.20
□□ 65 Igor Kravchuk, Edmo.	.35	.20
□□ **66 Shjon Podein, Edmo. RC**	**1.50**	**1.00**
□□ 67 Bill Ranford (G), Edmo.	1.00	.20
□□ 68 Brad Werenka, Edmo.	.35	.20
□□ 69 Doug Weight, Edmo.	1.50	.20
□□ **70 Ian Herbers, Edmo. RC**	**.50**	**.50**
□□ 71 Todd Elik, Edmo.	.35	.20
□□ 72 Steven Rice, Edmo.	.35	.20
□□ 73 John Vanbiesbrouck (G), Flor.	1.00	.20
□□ 74 Alexander Godynyuk, Flor.	.35	.20
□□ 75 Brian Skrudland, Flor.	.35	.20
□□ 76 Jody Hull, Flor.	.35	.20
□□ **77 Brent Severyn, Flor. RC**	**.50**	**.50**
□□ 78 Evgeny Davydov, Flor.	.35	.20
□□ 79 Dave Lowry, Flor.	.50	.20
□□ **80 Scott Levins, Flor. RC**	**.50**	**.50**
□□ 81 Scott Mellanby, Flor.	.50	.20
□□ 82 Dan Keczmer, Hart.	.50	.20
□□ 83 Michael Nylander, Hart.	.50	.20
□□ 84 Jim Sandlak, Hart.	.35	.20
□□ 85 Brian Propp, Hart.	.50	.20
□□ 86 Geoff Sanderson, Hart.	.50	.20
□□ **87 Mike Lenarduzzi (G), Hart. RC**	**.50**	**.50**
□□ 88 Zarley Zalapski, Hart.	.35	.20
□□ 89 Robert Petrovicky, Hart.	.35	.20
□□ 90 Robert Kron, Hart.	.35	.20
□□ 91 Luc Robitaille, LosA.	2.00	.20
□□ 92 Alexei Zhitnik, LosA.	.35	.20
□□ 93 Tony Granato, LosA.	.50	.20
□□ 94 Rob Blake, LosA.	1.50	.20
□□ 95 Gary Shuchuk, LosA.	.35	.20
□□ 96 Darryl Sydor, LosA.	.50	.20
□□ 97 Kelly Hrudey (G), LosA.	.50	.20
□□ 98 Warren Rychel, LosA.	.35	.20
□□ 99 Wayne Gretzky, LosA.	10.00	2.00
□□ 100 Patrick Roy (G), Mont.	7.50	1.50
□□ 101 Gilbert Dionne, Mont.	.35	.20
□□ 102 Éric Desjardins, Mont.	.50	.20
□□ **103 Peter Popovic, Mont. RC**	**.50**	**.50**
□□ 104 Vincent Damphousse, Mont.	1.50	.20
□□ 105 Patrice Brisebois, Mont.	.35	.20
□□ 106 Pierre Sévigny, Mont.	.35	.20
□□ 107 John LeClair, Mont.	2.00	.20
□□ 108 Paul DiPietro, Mont.	.35	.20
□□ 109 Alexander Semak, NJer.	.35	.20
□□ 110 Claude Lemieux, NJer.	.50	.20
□□ 111 Scott Niedermayer, NJer.	.50	.20
□□ 112 Chris Terreri (G), NJer.	.35	.20
□□ 113 Stéphane J.J. Richer, NJer.	.50	.20
□□ 114 Scott Stevens, NJer.	1.00	.20
□□ 115 John MacLean, NJer.	.35	.20
□□ **116 Scott Pellerin, NJer. RC**	**1.00**	**.50**
□□ 117 Bernie Nicholls, NJer.	.50	.20
□□ 118 Ron Hextall (G), NYIs.	1.50	.20
□□ 119 Derek King, NYIs.	.35	.20
□□ 120 Scott Lachance, NYIs.	.35	.20
□□ 121 Scott Scissons, NYIs.	.35	.20
□□ 122 Darius Kasparaitis, NYIs.	.50	.20
□□ 123 Ray Ferraro, NYIs.	.35	.20
□□ 124 Steve Thomas, NYIs.	.50	.20
□□ 125 Vladimir Malakhov, NYIs.	.35	.20
□□ 126 Travis Green, NYIs.	.50	.20
□□ 127 Mark Messier, NYRa.	2.50	.50
□□ 128 Sergei Nemchinov, NYRa.	.50	.20
□□ 129 Mike Richter (G), NYRa.	1.00	.20
□□ 130 Alexei Kovalev, NYRa.	1.50	.20
□□ 131 Brian Leetch, NYRa.	1.50	.20
□□ 132 Tony Amonte, NYRa.	1.50	.20
□□ 133 Sergei Zubov, NYRa.	.50	.20
□□ 134 Adam Graves, NYRa.	1.00	.20
□□ 135 Esa Tikkanen, NYRa.	.35	.20
□□ 136 Sylvain Turgeon, Otta.	.35	.20
□□ 137 Norm Maciver, Otta.	.35	.20
□□ 138 Craig Billington (G), Otta.	.35	.20
□□ 139 Dmitri Filimonov, Otta.	.35	.20
□□ 140 Pavol Demitra, Otta.	1.00	.20
□□ 141 Brian Glynn, Otta.	.35	.20
□□ **142 Darrin Madeley (G), Otta. RC**	**1.00**	**.50**
□□ **143 Radek Hamr, Otta. RC**	**.50**	**.50**
□□ **144 Robert Burakovsky, Otta. RC**	**.50**	**.50**
□□ 145 Dmitry Yushkevich, Phil.	.50	.20
□□ 146 Claude Boivin, Phil.	.35	.20
□□ 147 Pelle Eklund, Phil.	.35	.20
□□ 148 Brent Fedyk, Phil.	.35	.20
□□ 149 Mark Recchi, Phil.	1.00	.20
□□ 150 Tommy Söderström (G), Phil.	.35	.20
□□ 151 Viacheslav Butsayev, Phil.	.35	.20
□□ 152 Rod Brind'Amour, Phil.	.50	.20
□□ 153 Josef Beránek, Phil.	.35	.20
□□ 154 Jaromir Jagr, Pitt.	2.50	.50
□□ 155 Ulf Samuelsson, Pitt.	.35	.20
□□ 156 Martin Straka, Pitt.	.50	.20
□□ 157 Tom Barrasso (G), Pitt.	1.00	.20
□□ 158 Kevin Stevens, Pitt.	.50	.20
□□ 159 Joe Mullen, Pitt.	1.00	.20
□□ 160 Ron Francis, Pitt.	1.50	.20
□□ 161 Marty McSorley, Pitt.	.50	.20
□□ 162 Larry Murphy, Pitt.	.50	.20
□□ 163 Owen Nolan, Québ.	1.50	.20
□□ 164 Stéphane Fiset (G), Québ.	.50	.20
□□ 165 Dave Karpa, Québ.	.35	.20
□□ 166 Martin Gélinas, Québ.	.50	.20
□□ 167 Andrei Kovalenko, Québ.	.35	.20
□□ 168 Steve Duchesne, Québ.	.50	.20
□□ 169 Joe Sakic, Québ.	4.00	.50
□□ 170 Martin Rucinsky, Québ.	.50	.20
□□ **171 Chris Simon, Québ. RC**	**1.50**	**1.00**
□□ 172 Brendan Shanahan, SLou.	2.50	.50
□□ 173 Jeff R. Brown, SLou.	.35	.20
□□ 174 Phil Housley, SLou.	.50	.20
□□ 175 Curtis Joseph (G), SLou.	2.50	.50
□□ **176 Jim Montgomery, SLou. RC**	**.50**	**.50**
□□ 177 Bret Hedican, SLou.	.35	.20
□□ 178 Kevin Miller, SLou.	.35	.20
□□ 179 Philippe Bozon, SLou.	.35	.20
□□ 180 Brett Hull, SLou.	2.50	.50
□□ 181 Jimmy Waite (G), SanJ.	.35	.20
□□ 182 Ray Whitney, SanJ.	.50	.20
□□ 183 Pat Falloon, SanJ.	.35	.20
□□ 184 Tom Pederson, SanJ.	.35	.20
□□ 185 Igor Larionov, SanJ.	1.50	.20
□□ **186 Dody Wood, SanJ. RC**	**.50**	**.50**
□□ 187 Sandis Ozolinsh, SanJ.	.50	.20
□□ 188 Sergei Makarov, SanJ.	1.00	.20
□□ **189 Rob Gaudreau, SanJ. RC**	**.50**	**.50**
□□ 190 Roman Hamrlik, Tamp.	.50	.20
□□ 191 Stan Drulia, Tamp.	.35	.20
□□ 192 Pat Jablonski (G), Tamp.	.35	.20
□□ 193 Denis Savard, Tamp.	1.00	.20
□□ 194 Rob Zamuner, Tamp.	.50	.20
□□ 195 Petr Klima, Tamp.	.35	.20
□□ 196 Rob DiMaio, Tamp.	.35	.20
□□ 197 Chris Kontos, Tamp.	.35	.20
□□ 198 Mikael Andersson, Tamp.	.35	.20
□□ 199 Drake Berehowsky, Toro.	.35	.20
□□ 200 Dave Andreychuk, Toro.	.50	.20
□□ 201 Glenn Anderson, Toro.	.50	.20
□□ 202 Félix Potvin (G), Toro.	1.50	.20
□□ 203 Nikolai Borschevsky, Toro.	.35	.20
□□ 204 Kent Manderville, Toro.	.35	.20
□□ 205 Dave Ellett, Toro.	.35	.20
□□ 206 Peter Zezel, Toro.	.35	.20
□□ 207 Ken Baumgartner, Toro.	.35	.20
□□ 208 Murray Craven, Vanc.	.35	.20
□□ 209 Dixon Ward, Vanc.	.35	.20
□□ 210 Cliff Ronning, Vanc.	.50	.20
□□ 211 Pavel Bure, Vanc.	2.00	.20
□□ 212 Sergio Momesso, Vanc.	.35	.20
□□ 213 Kirk McLean (G), Vanc.	.50	.20
□□ 214 Jirí Slégr, Vanc.	.35	.20
□□ 215 Trevor Linden, Vanc.	1.00	.20
□□ 216 Geoff Courtnall, Vanc.	.35	.20
□□ 217 Al Iafrate, Wash.	.50	.20
□□ 218 Mike Ridley, Wash.	.35	.20
□□ 219 Enrico Ciccone, Wash.	.35	.20
□□ 220 Dmitri Khristich, Wash.	.35	.20
□□ 221 Kevin Hatcher, Wash.	.35	.20
□□ 222 Peter Bondra, Wash.	1.50	.20
□□ 223 Steve Konowalchuk, Wash.	.50	.20
□□ 224 Pat Elynuik, Wash.	.35	.20
□□ 225 Don Beaupré (G), Wash.	.35	.20
□□ 226 Stu Barnes, Winn.	.35	.20
□□ 227 Fredrik Olausson, Winn.	.50	.20
□□ 228 Keith Tkachuk, Winn.	1.50	.20
□□ 229 Mike Eagles, Winn.	.35	.20
□□ 230 Tie Domi, Winn.	.50	.20
□□ 231 Teppo Numminen, Winn.	.50	.20
□□ 232 Arto Blömsten, Winn.	.50	.20
□□ 233 Teemu Selänne, Winn.	2.00	.20
□□ 234 Bob Essensa (G), Winn.	.50	.20
□□ 235 Teemu Selänne, Winn.	2.00	.20
□□ 236 Eric Lindros, Phil. [Soph.]	2.50	.50
□□ 237 Félix Potvin (G), Toro. [Soph.]	1.50	.20
□□ 238 Alexei Kovalev, NYRa. [Soph.]	1.50	.20
□□ 239 Vladimir Malakhov, NYIs. [Soph.]	.35	.20
□□ 240 Scott Niedermayer, NJer. [Soph.]	.50	.20
□□ 241 Joé Juneau, Bost. [Soph.]	.50	.20
□□ 242 Shawn McEachern, LosA. [Soph.]	.50	.20
□□ 243 Alexei Zhamnov, Winn. [Soph.]	.50	.20
□□ 244 Alexandre Daigle, Otta.	.35	.20
□□ 245 Markus Näslund, Pitt.	2.50	1.00
□□ 246 Rob Niedermayer, Flor.	.50	.20
□□ **247 Thibault (G), Québ. RC**	**3.00**	**2.00**
□□ **248 B. Gretzky, Tamp. RC**	**1.00**	**.50**
□□ 249 Chris Pronger, Hart.	1.50	.50
□□ 250 Chris Gratton, Tamp.	.50	.20
□□ 251 Mikael Renberg, Phil.	.50	.20
□□ 252 Jarkko Varvio, Dall.	.50	.20
□□ **253 Micah Aivazoff, Detr. RC**	**.50**	**.50**
□□ 254 Alexei Yashin, Otta.	1.50	.50
□□ **255 German Titov, Calg. RC**	**.50**	**.50**
□□ **256 Mattias Norström, NYRa. RC**	**1.50**	**1.00**
□□ **257 Michal Sykora, SanJ. RC**	**1.00**	**.50**
□□ 258 Roman Oksiuta, Edmo.	.50	.20
□□ 259 Bryan Smolinski, Bost.	.35	.20
□□ **260 Alexei Kudashov, Toro. RC**	**.50**	**.50**
□□ **261 Jason Arnott, Edmo. RC**	**3.50**	**2.00**
□□ **262 Aaron Ward, Detr. RC**	**1.00**	**.50**
□□ **263 Vesa Viitakoski, Calg. RC**	**.50**	**.50**
□□ 264 Boris Mironov, Winn.	.35	.20
□□ **265 Darren McCarty, Detr. RC**	**2.00**	**1.50**
□□ **266 Vlastimil Kroupa, SanJ. RC**	**.50**	**.50**
□□ 267 Denny Felsner, SLou.	.35	.20
□□ **268 Milos Holan, Phil. RC**	**.50**	**.50**
□□ 269 Alexander Karpovtsev, NYRa.	.35	.20

□□	270 Greg Johnson, Detr.	.35	.20
□□	271 Terry Yake, Anah.	.35	.20
□□	272 Bill Houlder, Anah.	.35	.20
□□	273 Joe Sacco, Anah.	.35	.20
□□	274 Myles O'Connor, Anah.	.35	.20
□□	**275 Mark Ferner, Anah. RC**	**.50**	**.50**
□□	276 Alexei Kasatonov, Anah.	.50	.20
□□	277 Stu Grimson, Anah.	.50	.20
□□	278 Shaun Van Allen, Anah.	.35	.20
□□	279 Guy Hebert (G), Anah.	.50	.20
□□	280 Joé Juneau, Bost.	.50	.20
□□	281 Sergei Zholtok, Bost.	.35	.20
□□	282 Daniel Marois, Bost.	.35	.20
□□	283 Ted Donato, Bost.	.35	.20
□□	**284 Cam Stewart, Bost. RC**	**.50**	**.50**
□□	285 Stephen Leach, Bost.	.35	.20
□□	286 Darren Banks, Bost.	.35	.20
□□	287 Dmitri Kvartalnov, Bost.	.35	.20
□□	288 Paul Stanton, Bost.	.35	.20
□□	289 Pat LaFontaine, Buff.	1.50	.20
□□	290 Bob Sweeney, Buff.	.35	.20
□□	291 Craig Muni, Buff.	.35	.20
□□	292 Sergei Petrenko, Buff.	.35	.20
□□	**293 Derek Plante, Buff. RC**	**1.00**	**.50**
□□	294 Wayne Presley, Buff.	.35	.20
□□	**295 Mark Astley, Buff. RC**	**.50**	**.50**
□□	296 Matthew Barnaby, Buff.	.35	.20
□□	297 Randy Wood, Buff.	.35	.20
□□	298 Kevin Dahl, Calg.	.35	.20
□□	299 Gary Suter, Calg.	.50	.20
□□	300 Robert Reichel, Calg.	.50	.20
□□	301 Mike Vernon (G), Calg.	1.00	.20
□□	302 Gary Roberts, Calg.	1.00	.20
□□	303 Ronnie Stern, Calg.	.35	.20
□□	304 Michel Petit, Calg.	.35	.20
□□	305 Wes Walz, Calg.	.50	.20
□□	306 Brad Miller, Calg.	.35	.20
□□	307 Patrick Poulin, Chic.	.35	.20
□□	308 Brent Sutter, Chic.	.50	.20
□□	309 Jeremy Roenick, Chic.	2.00	.20
□□	310 J. Steve Smith, Chic.	.50	.20
□□	311 Eric Weinrich, Chic.	.35	.20
□□	312 Jeff Hackett (G), Chic.	.50	.20
□□	313 Michel Goulet, Chic.	1.00	.20
□□	**314 Jeff Shantz, Chic. RC**	**.50**	**.50**
□□	315 Neil Wilkinson, Chic.	.35	.20
□□	316 Shane Churla, Dall.	.35	.20
□□	317 Dave Gagner, Dall.	.35	.20
□□	318 Chris Tancill, Dall.	.35	.20
□□	319 Dean Evason, Dall.	.35	.20
□□	320 Mark Tinordi, Dall.	.35	.20
□□	321 Grant Ledyard, Dall.	.35	.20
□□	322 Ulf Dahlén, Dall.	.35	.20
□□	323 Mike Craig, Dall.	.35	.20
□□	324 Paul Broten, Dall.	.35	.20
□□	325 Vladimir Konstantinov, Detr.	.35	.20
□□	326 Steve Yzerman, Detr.	6.00	1.00
□□	327 Keith Primeau, Detr.	1.00	.20
□□	328 Shawn Burr, Detr.	.35	.20
□□	**329 Chris Osgood (G), Detr. RC**	**4.50**	**3.00**
□□	330 Ray Sheppard, Detr.	.35	.20
□□	331 Mike Sillinger, Detr.	.35	.20
□□	332 Terry Carkner, Detr.	.35	.20
□□	333 Bob Probert, Detr.	.50	.20
□□	**334 Adam Bennett, Edmo. RC**	**.50**	**.50**
□□	335 Dave Manson, Edmo.	.35	.20
□□	336 Zdeno Ciger, Edmo.	.35	.20
□□	337 Louie DeBrusk, Edmo.	.35	.20
□□	338 Shayne Corson, Edmo.	.50	.20
□□	339 Vladimír (Jr.) Vujtek, Edmo.	.35	.20
□□	340 Tyler Wright, Edmo.	.35	.20
□□	341 Ilya Byakin, Edmo.	.50	.20
□□	342 Craig MacTavish, Edmo.	.35	.20
□□	343 Brian Benning, Flor.	.35	.20
□□	344 Mark Fitzpatrick (G), Flor.	.35	.20
□□	345 Gord Murphy, Flor.	.35	.20
□□	346 Jesse Bélanger, Flor.	.35	.20
□□	347 Joe Cirella, Flor.	.35	.20
□□	348 Tom Fitzgerald, Flor.	.35	.20
□□	349 Andrei Lomakin, Flor.	.35	.20
□□	350 Bill Lindsay, Flor.	.35	.20
□□	351 Len Barrie, Flor.	.35	.20
□□	352 Frank Pietrangelo (G), Hart.	.35	.20
□□	353 Pat Verbeek, Hart.	.50	.20
□□	**354 Jim Storm, Hart. RC**	**.50**	**.50**
□□	355 Mark Janssens, Hart.	.35	.20
□□	356 Darren Turcotte, Hart.	.35	.20
□□	357 Jim McKenzie, Hart. [vs. G.Dineen]	.35	.20
□□	358 Brad McCrimmon, Hart.	.35	.20
□□	359 Andrew Cassels, Hart.	.50	.20
□□	360 James Patrick, Hart.	.35	.20
□□	**361 Bob Jay, LosA. RC**	**.50**	**.50**
□□	362 Tomas Sandström, LosA.	.50	.20
□□	363 Pat Conacher, LosA.	.35	.20
□□	364 Shawn McEachern, LosA.	.50	.20
□□	365 Jari Kurri, LosA.	2.50	.50
□□	366 Dominic Lavoie, LosA.	.35	.20
□□	367 Dave Taylor, LosA.	.50	.20
□□	368 Jimmy Carson, LosA.	.35	.20
□□	369 Mike Donnelly, LosA.	.35	.20
□□	370 Lyle Odelein, Mont.	.35	.20
□□	371 Brian Bellows, Mont.	.50	.20
□□	372 Guy Carbonneau, Mont.	.50	.20
□□	373 Mathieu Schneider, Mont.	.50	.20
□□	374 Stéphan Lebeau, Mont.	.35	.20
□□	375 Benoît Brunet, Mont.	.35	.20
□□	376 Kevin Haller, Mont.	.35	.20
□□	377 J.J. Daigneault, Mont.	.35	.20
□□	378 Kirk Muller, Mont.	.35	.20
□□	**379 Jason Smith, NJer. RC**	**1.00**	**.50**
□□	380 Martin Brodeur (G), NJer.	4.00	.50
□□	381 Corey Millen, NJer.	.35	.20
□□	382 Bill Guerin, NJer.	1.00	.20
□□	383 Valeri Zelepukin, NJer.	.35	.20
□□	384 Tom Chorske, NJer.	.35	.20
□□	385 Bobby Holik, NJer.	.50	.20
□□	**386 Jaroslav Modry, NJer. RC**	**.50**	**.50**
□□	387 Ken Daneyko, NJer.	.50	.20
□□	388 Uwe Krupp, NYIs.	.35	.20
□□	389 Pierre Turgeon, NYIs.	1.00	.20
□□	390 Marty McInnis, NYIs.	.35	.20
□□	391 Patrick Flatley, NYIs.	.35	.20
□□	392 Tom Kurvers, NYIs.	.35	.20
□□	393 Brad Dalgarno, NYIs.	.35	.20
□□	**394 Steve Junker, NYIs. RC**	**.50**	**.50**
□□	395 David Volek, NYIs.	.35	.20
□□	396 Benoît Hogue, NYIs.	.35	.20
□□	397 Zigmund Palffy, NYIs.	1.50	.20
□□	**399 Joby Messier, NYRa. RC**	**.50**	**.50**
□□	400 Mike Gartner, NYRa.	2.00	.20
□□	401 Joey Kocur, NYRa.	.35	.20
□□	402 Ed Olczyk, NYRa.	.50	.20
□□	403 Doug Lidster, NYRa.	.35	.20
□□	404 Greg Gilbert, NYRa.	.35	.20
□□	404 Steve Larmer, NYRa.	1.00	.20
□□	405 Glenn Healy (G), NYRa.	.50	.20
□□	406 Dennis Vial, Otta.	.35	.20
□□	407 Darcy Loewen, Otta.	.35	.20
□□	408 Bob Kudelski, Otta.	.35	.20
□□	**409 Hank Lammens, Otta. RC**	**.50**	**.50**
□□	410 Jarmo Kekäläinen, Otta.	.35	.20
□□	411 Darren Rumble, Otta.	.35	.20
□□	412 François Leroux, Otta.	.35	.20
□□	413 Troy Mallette, Otta.	.35	.20
□□	**414 Bill Huard, Otta. RC**	**.50**	**.50**
□□	415 Ryan McGill, Phil.	.35	.20
□□	416 Eric Lindros, Phil.	2.50	.50
□□	417 Dominic Roussel (G), Phil.	.35	.20
□□	**418 Jason Bowen, Phil. RC**	**.50**	**.50**
□□	419 André Faust, Phil.	.35	.20
□□	**420 Stewart Malgunas, Phil. RC**	**.50**	**.50**
□□	421 Kevin Dineen, Phil.	.35	.20
□□	422 Yves Racine, Phil.	.35	.20
□□	423 Garry Galley, Phil.	.35	.20
□□	424 Doug Brown, Pitt.	.35	.20
□□	425 Mario Lemieux, Pitt.	7.50	1.50
□□	**426 Ladislav Karabin, Pitt. RC**	**.50**	**.50**
□□	427 Grant Jennings, Pitt.	.35	.20
□□	428 Rick Tocchet, Pitt.	.50	.20
□□	429 Jeff Daniels, Pitt.	.35	.20
□□	430 Peter Taglianetti, Pitt.	.35	.20
□□	431 Bryan Trottier, Pitt.	2.50	.50
□□	432 Kjell Samuelsson, Pitt.	.35	.20
□□	**433 René Corbet, Québ. RC**	**1.00**	**.50**
□□	**434 Iain Fraser, Québ. RC**	**.50**	**.50**
□□	435 Mats Sundin, Québ.	2.50	.50
□□	436 Curtis Leschyshyn, Québ.	.35	.20
□□	437 Claude Lapointe, Québ.	.35	.20
□□	438 Valeri Kamensky, Québ.	.50	.20
□□	439 Mike Ricci, Québ.	.50	.20
□□	440 Chris Lindberg, Québ.	.35	.20
□□	441 Alexei Gusarov, Québ.	.35	.20
□□	442 Tom Tilley, SLou.	.35	.20
□□	443 Craig Janney, SLou.	.50	.20
□□	444 Vitali Karamnov, SLou.	.35	.20
□□	445 Bob Bassen, SLou.	.35	.20
□□	446 Igor Korolev, SLou.	.35	.20
□□	447 Kevin Miehm, SLou.	.35	.20
□□	448 Tony Hrkac, SLou.	.35	.20
□□	449 Garth Butcher, SLou.	.35	.20
□□	450 Vitali Prokhorov, SLou.	.35	.20
□□	451 Arturs Irbe (G), SanJ.	1.00	.20
□□	452 Jayson More, SanJ.	.35	.20
□□	453 Bob Errey, SanJ.	.35	.20
□□	454 Mike Sullivan, SanJ.	.35	.20
□□	455 Jeff Norton, SanJ.	.35	.20
□□	456 Gaétan Duchesne, SanJ.	.35	.20
□□	457 Doug Zmolek, SanJ.	.35	.20
□□	458 Mike Rathje, SanJ.	.35	.20
□□	459 Jamie Baker, SanJ.	.35	.20
□□	460 Joe Reekie, Tamp.	.35	.20
□□	461 Marc Bureau, Tamp.	.35	.20
□□	462 John Tucker, Tamp.	.35	.20
□□	**463 Bill McDougall, Tamp. RC**	**.50**	**.50**
□□	464 Danton Cole, Tamp.	.35	.20
□□	465 Brian Bradley, Tzamp.	.35	.20
□□	466 Jason Lafrenière, Tamp.	.35	.20
□□	467 Donald Dufresne, Tamp.	.35	.20
□□	468 Daren Puppa (G), Tamp.	.50	.20
□□	469 Doug Gilmour, Toro.	1.50	.20
□□	**470 Damian Rhodes (G), Toro. RC**	**1.50**	**1.00**
□□	**471 Matt Martin, Toro. RC**	**.50**	**.50**
□□	472 Bill Berg, Toro.	.35	.20
□□	473 John Cullen, Toro.	.50	.20
□□	474 Rob Pearson, Toro.	.35	.20
□□	475 Wendel Clark, Toro.	2.00	.20
□□	476 Mark Osborne, Toro.	.35	.20
□□	477 Dmitri Mironov, Toro.	.35	.20
□□	478 Kris King, Winn.	.35	.20
□□	478 Kay Whitmore (G), Vanc.	.35	.20
□□	479 Shawn Antoski, Vanc.	.35	.20
□□	480 Greg A. Adams, Vanc.	.35	.20
□□	481 Dave Babych, Vanc.	.35	.20
□□	482 John* McIntyre, Vanc.	.35	.20
□□	483 Jyrki Lumme, Vanc.	.50	.20
□□	**484 José Charbonneau, Vanc. RC**	**.50**	**.50**
□□	485 Gino Odjick, Vanc.	.35	.20
□□	486 Dana Murzyn, Vanc.	.35	.20
□□	487 Michal Pivonka, Wash.	.35	.20
□□	488 Dave Poulin, Wash.	.35	.20
□□	489 Sylvain Côté, Wash.	.35	.20
□□	490 Pat Peake, Wash.	.35	.20
□□	491 Kelly Miller, Wash.	.35	.20
□□	492 Randy Burridge, Wash.	.35	.20
□□	**493 Kevin Kaminski, Wash. RC**	**.50**	**.50**
□□	494 John Slaney, Wash.	.35	.20
□□	495 Keith Jones, Wash.	.35	.20
□□	496 Harijs Vitolinsh, Winn.	.35	.20
□□	497 Nelson Emerson, Winn.	.35	.20
□□	499 Darrin Shannon, Winn.	.35	.20
□□	500 Stéphane Quintal, Winn.	.35	.20
□□	501 Luciano Borsato, Winn.	.35	.20
□□	502 Thomas Steen, Winn.	.35	.20
□□	503 Alexei Zhamnov, Winn.	.50	.20
□□	504 Paul Ysebaert, Winn.	.35	.20
□□	**505 Jeff Friesen, Canada RC**	**2.00**	**1.50**
□□	506 Niklas Sundström, Sweden	.50	.20
□□	**507 Nick Stajduhar, Canada RC**	**.50**	**.50**
□□	**508 Jamie Storr (G), Canada RC**	**1.50**	**1.00**
□□	509 Valeri Bure, Russia	.50	.20
□□	**510 J. Bonsignore, U.S.A. RC**	**.50**	**.50**
□□	511 Mats Lindgren, Sweden	.35	.20
□□	**512 Yannick Dubé, Canada RC**	**.50**	**.50**
□□	**513 Todd Harvey, Canada RC**	**1.50**	**1.00**
□□	**514 Lad. Prokupek, Czech Jrs. RC**	**.50**	**.50**
□□	**515 Tomás Vlasák, Czech Jrs. RC**	**.50**	**.50**
□□	**516 Josef Marha, Czech Jrs. RC**	**.50**	**.50**
□□	**517 Tomás Blazek, Czech Jrs. RC**	**.50**	**.50**
□□	**518 Zdenek Nedved, Czech Jrs. RC**	**.50**	**.50**
□□	**519 Jar. Miklenda, Czech Jrs. RC**	**.50**	**.50**
□□	**520 Janne Niinimaa, Finland RC**	**1.50**	**1.00**
□□	521 Saku Koivu, Finland	6.00	1.00
□□	**522 Tommi Miettinen, Finland RC**	**.50**	**.50**
□□	523 Tuomas Grönman, Finland	.35	.20
□□	**524 Jani Nikko, Finland RC**	**.50**	**.50**
□□	525 Jonni Vauhkonen, Finland	.35	.20
□□	526 Nikolai Tsulygin, Russia	.35	.20
□□	527 Vadim Sharifijanov, Russia	.35	.20
□□	**528 Valeri Bure, Russia RC**	**2.00**	**1.50**
□□	**529 A. Kharlamov, Russia RC**	**.50**	**.50**
□□	**530 Nikolai Zavarukhin, Russia RC**	**.50**	**.50**
□□	**531 Oleg Tverdovsky, Russia RC**	**1.00**	**.50**
□□	**532 Sergei Kondrashkin, Russia RC**	**.50**	**.50**
□□	**533 E. Ryabchikov (G), Russia. RC**	**1.00**	**.50**
□□	**534 Mats Lindgren, Sweden RC**	**1.00**	**.50**
□□	535 Kenny Jönsson, Sweden	.50	.20
□□	**536 Edvin Frylén, Sweden RC**	**.50**	**.50**
□□	**537 Mattias Johansson, Sweden RC**	**.50**	**.50**
□□	**538 Johan Davidsson, Sweden RC**	**.50**	**.50**
□□	**539 Mikael Håkansson, Sweden RC**	**.50**	**.50**
□□	**540 Anders Eriksson, Sweden RC**	**.50**	**.50**

EAST & WEST STARS

Series One Insert Set (10 cards):		**120.00**
	Insert	**E/W**
□	E1 Eric Lindros, Phil.	5.00
□	E2 Mario Lemieux, Pitt.	20.00
□	E3 Alexandre Daigle, Otta.	4.00
□	E4 Patrick Roy (G), Mont.	20.00
□	E5 Rob Niedermayer, Flor.	4.00
□	E6 Chris Gratton, Tamp.	4.00
□	E7 Alexei Yashin, Otta.	4.00
□	E8 Pat LaFontaine, Buff.	4.00
□	E9 Joe Sakic, Québ.	10.00
□	E10 Pierre Turgeon, NYIs.	4.00
□	W1 Wayne Gretzky, LosA.	30.00
□	W2 Pavel Bure, Vanc.	5.00
□	W3 Teemu Selänne, Winn.	5.00
□	W4 Doug Gilmour, Toro.	4.00
□	W5 Steve Yzerman, Detr.	15.00
□	W6 Jeremy Roenick, Chic.	5.00
□	W7 Brett Hull, SLou.	5.00
□	W8 Jason Arnott, Edmo.	5.00
□	W9 Félix Potvin (G), Toro.	4.00
□	W10 Sergei Fedorov, Detr.	5.00

CANADA / USA GOLD

Series One Insert Set (10 cards):		**70.00**
	Insert	**G**
□	G1 Wayne Gretzky, LosA. [USA]	25.00
□	G2 Mario Lemieux, Pitt. [USA]	15.00
□	G3 Eric Lindros, Phil. [USA]	5.00
□	G4 Brett Hull, SLou. [USA]	5.00
□	G5 Rob Niedermayer, Flor. [USA]	3.00
□	G6 Alexandre Daigle, Otta. [Canada]	3.00
□	G7 Pavel Bure, Vanc. [Canada]	5.00
□	G8 Teemu Selänne, Winn. [Canada]	5.00
□	G9 Patrick Roy (G), Mont. [Canada]	15.00
□	G10 Doug Gilmour, Toro. [Canada]	3.00

CALDER CANDIDATES

Series Two Insert Set (20 cards):		**50.00**	**35.00**
	Insert	**Gold**	**Silver**
□□	C1 Alexandre Daigle, Otta.	1.50	1.00
□□	C2 Chris Pronger, Hart.	6.00	4.00
□□	C3 Chris Gratton, Tamp.	2.00	1.00
□□	C4 Rob Niedermayer, Flor.	2.00	1.00
□□	C5 Markus Näslund, Pitt.	10.00	7.00
□□	C6 Jason Arnott, Edmo.	6.00	4.00
□□	C7 Pierre Sévigny, Mont.	2.00	1.00
□□	C8 Jarkko Varvio, Dall.	2.00	1.00
□□	C9 Dean McAmmond, Edmo.	2.00	1.00
□□	C10 Alexei Yashin, Otta.	6.00	4.00
□□	C11 Philippe Boucher, Buff.	2.00	1.00
□□	C12 Mikael Renberg, Phil.	3.00	2.00
□□	C13 Chris Simon, Québ.	2.00	1.00
□□	C14 Brent Gretzky, Tamp.	2.00	1.00
□□	C15 Jesse Bélanger, Flor.	2.00	1.00
□□	C16 Jocelyn Thibault (G), Québ.	4.00	3.00
□□	C17 Chris Osgood (G), Detr.	10.00	5.00
□□	C18 Derek Plante, Buff.	2.00	1.00
□□	C19 Iain Fraser, Québ.	2.00	1.00
□□	C20 Vesa Viitakoski, Calg.	2.00	1.00
	Insert	**Gold**	**Silver**
□	Trade Card (Expired)	1.00	.50

CHERRY'S PLAYOFF HEROES

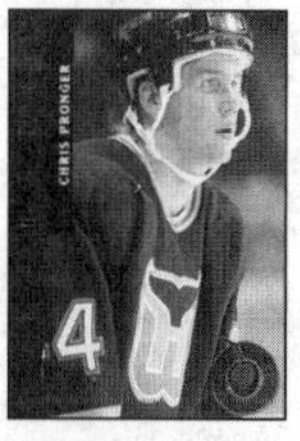

Series Two Insert Set (20 cards):		**240.00**
	Canadian Insert	**D**
□	D1 Wayne Gretzky, LosA.	50.00
□	D2 Mario Lemieux, Pitt.	35.00
□	D3 Al MacInnis, Calg.	5.00
□	D4 Mark Messier, NYRa.	10.00
□	D5 Dino Ciccarelli, Detr.	5.00
□	D6 Dale Hunter, Wash.	5.00
□	D7 Grant Fuhr (G), Buff.	5.00
□	D8 Paul Coffey, Detr.	5.00
□	D9 Doug Gilmour, Toro.	5.00
□	D10 Patrick Roy (G), Mont.	35.00
□	D11 Alexandre Daigle, Otta.	5.00
□	D12 Chris Gratton, Tamp.	5.00
□	D13 Chris Pronger, Hart.	5.00
□	D14 Félix Potvin (G), Toro.	5.00
□	D15 Eric Lindros, Phil.	10.00
□	D16 Maurice Richard, Mont.	35.00
□	D17 Gordie Howe, Detr.	35.00
□	D18 Henri Richard, Mont.	10.00
□	D19 Reggie Leach, Phil.	5.00
□	D20 Don Cherry [Checklist]	10.00

FIRST OVERALL

Series One Insert Set (10 cards):		**40.00**
	Insert	**F**
□	F1 Alexandre Daigle, Otta.	2.00
□	F2 Roman Hamrlik, Tamp.	2.00
□	F3 Eric Lindros, Phil.	5.00
□	F4 Owen Nolan, Québ.	2.00
□	F5 Mats Sundin, Québ.	5.00
□	F6 Mike Modano, Dall.	5.00
□	F7 Pierre Turgeon, NYIs.	2.00
□	F8 Joe Murphy, Chic.	2.00
□	F9 Wendel Clark, Toro.	5.00
□	F10 Mario Lemieux, Pitt.	20.00

PARKIE REPRINTS

Photo Photo-
hk934_Parkhurst_Reprint

Series 1 Regular Pack Set (33-41/CL5):	**80.00**
Series 1 Jumbo Pack Set (42-50/CL6):	**70.00**
Series 2 Regular Pack Set (51-59/CL7):	**60.00**
Series 2 Jumbo Pack Set (60-68/CL8):	**60.00**
Series 1 Case Inserts (DPR1-DPR6):	**50.00**
Series 2 Case Insers (DPR7-DPR12)	**35.00**

Player	**Reprint**	
□	PR33 Gordie Howe, Detr.	25.00
□	PR34 Tim Horton, Toro. [1952-53 Parkie]	10.00
□	PR35 Bill Barilko, Toro. [1951-52 Parkie]	6.00
□	PR36 Lach & Richard [1953-54 Parkie]	15.00
□	PR37 T. Sawchuk (G), Detr. [1961-62 Parkie]	20.00
□	PR38 FG. Armstrong, Toro. [1959-60 Parkie]	6.00
□	PR39 Billy E.Harris, Toro. [1963-64 Parkie]	6.00
□	PR40 Doug Harvey, Mont. [1957-58 Parkie]	10.00
□	PR41 G. Worsley (G), Mont. [1963-64 Parkie]	6.00
□	Checklist [1961-62 Parkie]	6.00
□	PR42 Gordie Howe, Detr. [1951-52 Parkie]	25.00
□	PR43 J. Plante (G), Mont. [1960-61 Parkie]	15.00
□	PR44 F. Mahovlich, Toro. [1962-63 Parkie]	10.00
□	PR45 Fern Flaman,	6.00
□	PR46 Bernie Geoffrion, Mont.	6.00
□	PR47 Toe Blake, Mont. [1963-64 Parkie]	6.00
□	PR48 Maurice Richard, Mont.	25.00
□	PR49 Ted Lindsay, Detr.	10.00
□	PR50 Camille Henry, NYRa. [1954-55 Parkie]	6.00
□	Checklist [1957-58 Parkie]	6.00
□	PR51 Gordie Howe, Detr. [1961-62 Parkie]	25.00
□	PR52 J-G Talbot, Mont. [1959-60 Parkie]	6.00
□	PR53 T. Sawchuk (G), Detr. [1954-55 Parkie]	20.00
□	PR54 Warren Godfrey, Bost. [1953-54 Parkie]	6.00
□	PR55 Tom Johnson, Mont. [1955-56 Parkie]	6.00
□	PR56 Bert Olmstead, Mont. [1960-61 Parkie]	6.00
□	PR57 Cal Gardner, Bost. [1953-54 Parkie]	6.00
□	PR58 Red Kelly, Toro. [1963-64 Parkie]	6.00
□	PR59 Phil Goyette, Mont. [1959-60 Parkie]	6.00
□	Checklist [1963-64 Parkie]	6.00
□	PR60 Gordie Howe, Detr.	25.00
□	PR61 Lou Fontinato, NYRa.	6.00
□	PR62 Bill Dineen, Detr.	6.00
□	PR63 Maurice Richard, Mont.	25.00
□	PR64 Vic Stasiuk, Bost.	6.00
□	PR65 Marcel Pronovost, Detr.	6.00
□	PR66 Ed Litzenberger, Chic.	6.00
□	PR67 Dave Keon, Toro.	6.00
□	PR68 D. St-Laurent, Mont. [1955-56 Parkie]	6.00
□	Checklist [1963-64 Parkie]	6.00
□	DPR-1 Gordie Howe, Detr. [1963-64 Parkie]	25.00
□	DPR-2 Milt Schmidt, Bost. [1954-55 Parkie]	6.00
□	DPR-3 Tim Horton, Toro. [1962-63 Parkie]	10.00
□	DPR-4 Al Rollins (G), Toro. [1951-52 Parkie]	6.00

☐	DPR-5 M. Richard, Mont. [1955-56 Parkie]	25.00
☐	DPR-6 Harry Howell, NYRa. [1954-55 Parkie]	6.00
☐	DPR-7 Gordie Howe, Detr.	25.00
☐	DPR-8 Johnny Bower (G), Toro.	6.00
☐	DPR-9 Dean Prentice, NYRa. [1954-55 Parkie]	6.00
☐	DPR-10 Leo Labine, Bost. [1953-54 Parkie]	6.00
☐	DPR-11 Harry P. Watson, Chic.	6.00
☐	DPR-12 Dickie Moore, Mont.	6.00

1993 - 94 PARKHURST MISSING LINK '56-57

Complete Set (180 cards): 35.00
Common Player: .25

	Player	Promo
Album: 18.00		
☐	Doug Harvey Promo	1.00

	Player	Parkie
☐	1 Jerry Toppazzini, Bost.	.25
☐	2 Fern Flaman, Bost.	.50
☐	3 Fleming MacKell, Bost.	.25
☐	4 Léo Labine, Bost.	.25
☐	5 John Peirson, Bost.	.25
☐	6 Don McKenney, Bost.	.25
☐	7 Bob Armstrong, Bost.	.25
☐	8 Réal Cheverfils, Bost.	.25
☐	9 Vic Stasiuk, Bost.	.25
☐	10 Cal Gardner, Bost.	.25
☐	11 Leo Boivin, Bost.	.50
☐	12 Jack Caffery, Bost.	.25
☐	13 Bob Beckett, Bost.	.25
☐	14 Jack Bionda, Bost.	.25
☐	15 Claude Pronovost (G), Bost.	.25
☐	16 Lerry Regan, Bost.	.25
☐	17 Terry Sawchuk (G), Bost.	3.00
☐	18 Doug Mohns, Bost.	.25
☐	19 Marcel Bonin, Bost.	.25
☐	20 Allan Stanley, Bost.	.50
☐	21 Milt Schmidt, Coach, Bost.	.50
☐	22 Al Dewsbury, Chic.	.25
☐	23 Glen Skov, Chic.	.25
☐	24 Ed Litzenberger, Chic.	.25
☐	25 Nick Mickoski, Chic.	.25
☐	26 Wally Hergesheimer, Chic.	.25
☐	27 Jack McIntyre, Chic.	.25
☐	28 Al Rollins (G), Chic.	.25
☐	29 Hank Ciesla, Chic.	.25
☐	30 Gus Mortson, Chic.	.25
☐	31 Elmer Vasko, Chic.	.25
☐	32 Pierre Pilote, Chic.	.50
☐	33 Ron Ingram, Chic.	.25
☐	34 Frank Martin, Chic.	.25
☐	35 Forbes Kennedy, Chic.	.25
☐	36 Harry Watson, Chic.	.50
☐	37 Eddie Kachur, Chic.	.25
☐	38 Hec Lalonde, Chic.	.25
☐	39 Eric Nesterenko, Chic.	.25
☐	40 Ben Woit, Chic.	.25
☐	41 Ken Mosdell, Chic.	.25
☐	42 Tommy Ivan, Coach, Chic.	.25
☐	43 Gordie Howe, Detr.	4.00
☐	44 Ted Lindsay, Detr.	1.50
☐	45 Norm Ullman, Detr.	.50
☐	46 Glenn Hall (G), Detr.	1.50
☐	47 Bill Dea, Detr.	.25
☐	48 Bill McNeill, Detr.	.25
☐	49 Earl Reibel, Detr.	.25
☐	50 Bill Dineen, Detr.	.25
☐	51 Warren Godfrey, Detr.	.25
☐	52 Red Kelly, Detr.	.50
☐	53 Marty Pavelich, Detr.	.25
☐	54 Lorne Ferguson, Detr.	.25
☐	55 Larry Hillman, Detr.	.25
☐	56 John Bucyk, Detr.	.50
☐	57 Motro Prystai, Detr.	.25
☐	58 Marcel Pronovost, Detr.	.50
☐	59 Alex Delvecchio, Detr.	.50
☐	60 Murray Costello, Detr.	.25
☐	61 Al Arbour, Detr.	.25
☐	62 Bucky Hollingworth, Detr.	.25
☐	63 Jim Skinner, Coach, Detr.	.25
☐	64 Jean Béliveau, Mont.	3.00
☐	65 Maurice Richard, Mont.	4.00
☐	66 Henri Richard, Mont.	1.50
☐	67 Doug Harvey, Mont.	1.50
☐	68 Bernie Geoffrion, Mont.	1.00
☐	69 Dollard St. Laurent, Mont.	.25
☐	70 Dickie Moore, Mont.	.50
☐	71 Bert Olmstead, Mont.	.50
☐	72 Jacques Plante (G), Mont.	2.00
☐	73 Claude Provost, Mont.	.25
☐	74 Phil Goyette, Mont.	.25
☐	75 André Pronovost, Mont.	.25
☐	76 Don Marshall, Mont.	.25
☐	77 Ralph Backstrom, Mont.	.25
☐	78 Floyd Curry, Mont.	.25
☐	79 Tom Johnson, Mont.	.50
☐	80 Jean-Guy Talbot, Mont.	.25
☐	81 Bob Turner, Mont.	.25
☐	82 Connie Broden, Mont.	.25
☐	83 Jackie Leclair, Mont.	.25
☐	84 Toe Blake, Mont.	1.00
☐	85 Frank Selke, Coach, Mont.	.50
☐	86 George Sullivan, NYRa.	.25
☐	87 Larry Cahan, NYRa.	.25
☐	88 Jean-Guy Gendron, NYRa.	.25
☐	89 Bill Gadsby, NYRa.	.50
☐	90 Andy Bathgate, NYRa.	.50
☐	91 Dean Prentice, NYRa.	.25
☐	92 Gump Worsley (G), NYRa.	1.00
☐	93 Lou Fontinato, NYRa.	.25
☐	94 Gerry Foley, NYRa.	.25
☐	95 Larry Popein, NYRa.	.25
☐	96 Harry Howell, NYRa.	.50
☐	97 Andy Hebenton, NYRa.	.25
☐	98 Danny Lewicki, NYRa.	.25
☐	99 Dave Creighton, NYRa.	.25
☐	100 Camille Henry, NYRa.	.25
☐	101 Jack Evans, NYRa.	.25
☐	102 Ron Murphy, NYRa.	.25
☐	103 Johnny Bower (G), NYRa.	1.00
☐	104 Parker MacDonald, NYRa.	.25
☐	105 Bronco Horvath, NYRa.	.25
☐	106 Bruce Cline, NYRa.	.25
☐	107 Ivan Irwin, NYRa.	.25
☐	108 Phil Watson, Coach, NYRa.	.25
☐	109 Sid Smith, Toro.	.25
☐	110 Ron Stewart, Toro.	.25
☐	111 Rudy Migay, Toro.	.25
☐	112 Tod Sloan, Toro.	.25
☐	113 Bob Pulford, Toro.	.50
☐	114 Marc Réaume, Toro.	.25
☐	115 Jim Morrison, Toro.	.25
☐	116 Ted Kennedy, Toro.	.50
☐	117 Gerry James, Toro.	.25
☐	118 Brian Cullen, Toro.	.25
☐	119 Jim Thompson, Toro.	.25
☐	120 Barry Cullen, Toro.	.25
☐	121 Al MacNeil, Toro.	.25
☐	122 Gary Aldcorn, Toro.	.25
☐	123 Bob Baun, Toro.	.25
☐	124 Hugh Bolton, Toro.	.25
☐	125 George Armstrong, Toro.	.50
☐	126 Dick Duff, Toro.	.25
☐	127 Tim Horton, Toro.	1.50
☐	128 Ed Chadwick (G), Toro.	.25
☐	129 Billy Harris, Toro.	.25
☐	130 Mike Nykoluk, Toro.	.25
☐	131 Noel Price, Toro.	.25
☐	132 Ken Girard, Toro.	.25
☐	133 Howie Meeker, Toro.	.50
☐	134 Hap Day, Coach, Toro.	.50
☐	135 AS: Jacques Plante (G), Mont.	1.00
☐	136 AS: Doug Harvey, Mont.	1.00
☐	137 AS: Bill Gadsby, NYRa.	.50
☐	138 AS: Jean Béliveau, Mont.	1.50
☐	139 AS: Maurice Richard, Mont.	2.50
☐	140 AS: Ted Lindsay, Detr.	.50
☐	141 AS: Glenn Hall (G), Detr.	.50
☐	142 AS: Red Kelly, Detr.	.50
☐	143 AS: Tom Johnson, Mont.	.50
☐	144 AS: Tod Sloan, Toro.	.25
☐	145 AS: Gordie Howe, Detr.	2.50
☐	146 AS: Bert Olmstead, Mont.	.50
☐	147 AW: Earl Reibel, Detr.	.25
☐	148 AW: Doug Harvey, Mont.	.50
☐	149 AW: Jean Béliveau, Mont.	1.00
☐	150 AW: Jean Béliveau, Mont.	1.00
☐	151 AW: Jacques Plante (G), Mont.	.50
☐	152 AW: Glenn Hall (G), Detr.	.50
☐	153 Terry Sawchuk (G) (Action)	1.00
☐	154 Action Shot	.50
☐	155 Action Shot	.50
☐	156 Jean Béliveau (Action)	1.00
☐	157 Jean Béliveau (Action)	1.00
☐	158 Action Shot	.50
☐	159 Action Shot	.50
☐	160 Gordie Howe (Action)	1.00
☐	161 Jacques Plante (G) (Action)	.50
☐	162 Gordie Howe (Action)	1.50
☐	163 Jacques Plante (G) (Action)	.50
☐	164 Action Shot	.50
☐	165 Action Shot	.50
☐	166 Action Shot	.50
☐	167 Terry Sawchuk (G) (Action)	1.00
☐	168 Terry Sawchuk (G) (Action)	1.00
☐	169 LL: Vic Stasiuk, Bost.	.25
☐	170 LL: Red Sullivan, Chic.	.25
☐	171 LL: Gordie Howe, Detr.	1.00
☐	172 LL: Jean Béliveau, Mont.	1.00
☐	173 LL: Andy Bathgate, NYRa.	.25
☐	174 LL: Tod Sloan, Toro.	.25
☐	175 Stanley Cup Playoffs	.50
☐	176 Stanley Cup Playoffs	.50
☐	177 Stanley Cup Playoffs	1.00
☐	178 Stanley Cup Playoffs	.25
☐	179 Checklist 1	.25
☐	180 Checklist 2	.25

AUTOGRAPHS

Insert Set (6 cards): 600.00

	Insert (#/956)	A956
☐	A-1 Gordie Howe, Detr. ✍	180.00
☐	A-2 Maurice Richard, Mont. ✍	200.00
☐	A-3 Bernie Geoffrion, Mont. ✍	80.00
☐	A-4 Gump Worsley (G), NYRa. ✍	80.00
☐	A-5 Jean Béliveau, Mont. ✍	100.00
☐	A-6 Frank Mahovlich, Toro. ✍	80.00

FUTURE STARS

Insert Set (6 cards): 80.00

	Insert	FS
☐	FS-1 Carl Brewer	8.00
☐	FS-2 Dave Keon	20.00
☐	FS-3 Stan Mikita	20.00
☐	FS-4 Eddie Shack	10.00
☐	FS-5 Frank Mahovlich	30.00
☐	FS-6 Charlie Hodge (G)	8.00

POP UPS

Cards 1-6 were inserted into Canadian packs while cards 7-12 were inserted into American packs.

Insert Set (12 cards): 325.00

	Insert	P
☐	P-1 Howie Morenz, Mont.	60.00
☐	P-2 George Hainsworth (G), Mont.	20.00
☐	P-3 Georges Vézina (G), Mont.	80.00
☐	P-4 King Clancy, Toro.	30.00
☐	P-5 Syl Apps, Toro.	30.00
☐	P-6 Turk Broda (G), Toro.	30.00
☐	P-7 Eddie Shore, Bost.	50.00
☐	P-8 Bill Cook, NYRa.	20.00
☐	P-9 Woody Dumart, Bost.	20.00
☐	P-10 Lester Patrick, NYRa.	30.00
☐	P-11 Doug Bentley, Chic.	20.00
☐	P-12 Earl Seibert, NYRa.	20.00

1993 - 94 PINNACLE

These cards have two versions: an American (English text) issue and a Canadian (Bilingual) issue. Both versions are priced similarly below. Card 512 (Wayne Gretzky) was a late addition in Series Two.

Imprint: Series One: © 1993 SCORE
Series Two: 1994 PINNACLE BRANDS, INC. PRINTED IN U.S.A.

Series One Set (236 cards): 15.00
Series Two Set (276 cards): 30.00
Common Player: .20
Promo Panel (Cards 1-6): 5.00

	Player	NRMT-MT
☐ ☐	1 Eric Lindros, Phil.	.50
☐ ☐	2 Mats Sundin, Québ.	.50
☐ ☐	3 Tom Barrasso (G), Pitt.	.20
☐ ☐	4 Teemu Selänne, Winn.	.50
☐ ☐	5 Joé Juneau, Bost.	.20
☐ ☐	6 Tony Amonte, NYRa.	.20
☐ ☐	7 Bob Probert, Detr.	.20
☐ ☐	8 Chris Kontos, Tamp.	.20
☐ ☐	9 Geoff Sanderson, Hart.	.20
☐ ☐	10 Alexander Mogilny, Buff.	.20
☐ ☐	11 Kevin Lowe, NYRa.	.20
☐ ☐	12 Nikolai Borschevsky, Toro.	.20
☐ ☐	13 Dale Hunter, Wash.	.20
☐ ☐	14 Gary Suter, Calg.	.20
☐ ☐	15 Curtis Joseph (G), SLou.	.50
☐ ☐	16 Mark Tinordi, Dall.	.20
☐ ☐	17 Doug Weight, Edmo.	.20
☐ ☐	18 Benoît Hogue, NYIs.	.20
☐ ☐	19 Tommy Söderström (G), Phil.	.20
☐ ☐	20 Pat Falloon, SanJ.	.20
☐ ☐	21 Jyrki Lumme, Vanc.	.20
☐ ☐	22 Brian Bellows, Mont.	.20
☐ ☐	23 Alexei Zhitnik, LosA.	.20
☐ ☐	24 Dirk Graham, Chic.	.20
☐ ☐	25 Scott Stevens, NJer.	.20
☐ ☐	26 Adam Foote, Québ.	.20
☐ ☐	27 Mike Gartner, NYRa.	.50
☐ ☐	**28 Dallas Drake, Detr. RC**	**.50**
☐ ☐	29 Ulf Samuelsson, Pitt.	.20
☐ ☐	30 Cam Neely, Bost.	.50
☐ ☐	31 Sean Burke (G), Hart.	.20
☐ ☐	32 Petr' Svoboda, Buff.	.20
☐ ☐	33 Keith Tkachuk, Winn.	.20
☐ ☐	34 Roman Hamrlik, Tamp.	.20
☐ ☐	35 Robert Reichel, Calg.	.20
☐ ☐	36 Igor Kravchuk, Edmo.	.20
☐ ☐	37 Mathieu Schneider, Mont.	.20
☐ ☐	38 Bob Kudelski, Otta.	.20
☐ ☐	39 Jeff R. Brown, SLou.	.20
☐ ☐	40 Mike Modano, Dall.	.50
☐ ☐	**41 Rob Gaudreau, SanJ. RC**	**.50**
☐ ☐	42 Dave Andreychuk, Toro.	.20
☐ ☐	43 Trevor Linden, Vanc.	.20
☐ ☐	44 Dmitri Khristich, Wash.	.20
☐ ☐	45 Joe Murphy, Chic.	.20
☐ ☐	46 Rob Blake, LosA.	.20
☐ ☐	47 Alexander Semak, NJer.	.20
☐ ☐	48 Ray Ferraro, NYIs.	.20
☐ ☐	49 Curtis Leschyshyn, Québ.	.20
☐ ☐	50 Mark Recchi, Phil.	.20
☐ ☐	51 Sergei Nemchinov, NYRa.	.20
☐ ☐	52 Larry Murphy, Pitt.	.20
☐ ☐	53 Stephen Heinze, Bost.	.20
☐ ☐	54 Sergei Fedorov, Detr.	.50
☐ ☐	55 Gary Roberts, Calg.	.20
☐ ☐	56 Alexei Zhamnov, Winn.	.20
☐ ☐	57 Derian Hatcher, Dall.	.20
☐ ☐	58 Kelly Buchberger, Edmo.	.20
☐ ☐	59 Éric Desjardins, Mont.	.20
☐ ☐	60 Brian Bradley, Tamp.	.20
☐ ☐	61 Patrick Poulin, Hart.	.20
☐ ☐	62 Scott Lachance, NYIs.	.20
☐ ☐	63 Johan Garpenlöv, SanJ.	.20
☐ ☐	64 Sylvain Turgeon, Otta.	.20
☐ ☐	65 Grant Fuhr (G), Buff.	.20
☐ ☐	66 Garth Butcher, SLou.	.20
☐ ☐	67 Michal Pivonka, Wash.	.20
☐ ☐	68 Todd Gill, Toro.	.20
☐ ☐	69 Cliff Ronning, Vanc.	.20
☐ ☐	70 J. Steve Smith, Chic.	.20
☐ ☐	71 Bobby Holik, NJer.	.20
☐ ☐	72 Garry Galley, Phil.	.20
☐ ☐	73 Stephen Leach, Bost.	.20
☐ ☐	74 Ron Francis, Pitt.	.20
☐ ☐	75 Jari Kurri, LosA.	.50
☐ ☐	76 Alexei Kovalev, NYRa.	.20
☐ ☐	77 Dave Gagner, Dall.	.20
☐ ☐	78 Steve Duchesne, Québ.	.20
☐ ☐	79 Theoren Fleury, Calg.	.20
☐ ☐	80 Paul Coffey, Detr.	.20
☐ ☐	81 Bill Ranford (G), Edmo.	.20
☐ ☐	82 Doug Bodger, Buff.	.20
☐ ☐	83 Nick Kypreos, Hart.	.20
☐ ☐	84 Darius Kasparaitis, NYIs.	.20
☐ ☐	85 Vincent Damphousse, Mont.	.20
☐ ☐	86 Arturs Irbe (G), SanJ.	.20
☐ ☐	87 Shawn Chambers, Tamp.	.20
☐ ☐	88 Murray Craven, Vanc.	.20
☐ ☐	89 Rob Pearson, Toro.	.20
☐ ☐	90 Kevin Hatcher, Wash.	.20
☐ ☐	91 Brent Sutter, Chic.	.20
☐ ☐	92 Teppo Numminen, Winn.	.20
☐ ☐	93 Shawn Burr, Detr.	.20
☐ ☐	94 Valeri Zelepukin, NJer.	.20
☐ ☐	95 Ron Sutter, SLou.	.20
☐ ☐	96 Craig MacTavish, Edmo.	.20
☐ ☐	97 Dominic Roussel (G), Phil.	.20
☐ ☐	98 Nicklas Lidström, Detr.	.20
☐ ☐	99 Adam Graves, NYRa.	.20
☐ ☐	100 Doug Gilmour, Toro.	.20
☐ ☐	101 Frantisek Musil, Calg.	.20
☐ ☐	102 Ted Donato, Bost.	.20
☐ ☐	103 Andrew Cassels, Hart.	.20
☐ ☐	104 Vladimir Malakhov, NYIs.	.20
☐ ☐	105 Shawn McEachern, Pitt.	.20
☐ ☐	106 Petr Nedved, Vanc.	.20
☐ ☐	107 Calle Johansson, Wash.	.20
☐ ☐	108 Rich Sutter, SLou.	.20
☐ ☐	109 Evgeny Davydov, Winn.	.20
☐ ☐	110 Mike Ricci, Québ.	.20
☐ ☐	111 Scott Niedermayer, NJer.	.20
☐ ☐	112 John LeClair, Mont.	.50
☐ ☐	113 Darryl Sydor, LosA.	.20
☐ ☐	114 Paul DiPietro, Mont.	.20
☐ ☐	115 Stéphane Fiset (G), Québ.	.20
☐ ☐	116 Christian Ruuttu, Chic.	.20
☐ ☐	117 Doug Zmolek, SanJ.	.20
☐ ☐	118 Bob Sweeney, Buff.	.20
☐ ☐	119 Brent Fedyk, Phil.	.20
☐ ☐	120 Norm Maciver, Otta.	.20
☐ ☐	121 Rob Zamuner, Tamp.	.20
☐ ☐	122 Joe Mullen, Pitt.	.20
☐ ☐	123 Trent Yawney, Calg.	.20
☐ ☐	124 David Shaw, Bost.	.20
☐ ☐	125 Mark Messier, NYRa.	.50
☐ ☐	126 Kevin Miller, SLou.	.20
☐ ☐	127 Dino Ciccarelli, Detr.	.20
☐ ☐	128 Derek King, NYIs.	.20
☐ ☐	129 Scott Young, Québ.	.20
☐ ☐	130 Craig Janney, SLou.	.20
☐ ☐	131 Jamie Macoun, Toro.	.20
☐ ☐	132 Geoff Courtnall, Vanc.	.20
☐ ☐	133 Bob Essensa (G), Winn.	.20
☐ ☐	134 Ken Daneyko, NJer.	.20
☐ ☐	135 Mike Ridley, Wash.	.20
☐ ☐	136 Stéphan Lebeau, Mont.	.20
☐ ☐	137 Tony Granato, LosA.	.20
☐ ☐	138 Kay Whitmore (G), Vanc.	.20
☐ ☐	139 Luke Richardson, Edmo.	.20
☐ ☐	140 Jeremy Roenick, Chic.	.50
☐ ☐	141 Brad May, Buff.	.20
☐ ☐	142 Sandis Ozolinsh, SanJ.	.20
☐ ☐	143 Stéphane J.J. Richer, NJer.	.20
☐ ☐	144 John Tucker, Tamp.	.20
☐ ☐	145 Luc Robitaille, LosA.	.50
☐ ☐	146 Dmitry Yushkevich, Phil.	.20
☐ ☐	147 Sean Hill, Anah.	.20
☐ ☐	148 John Vanbiesbrouck (G), Flor.	.20
☐ ☐	149 Kevin Stevens, Pitt.	.20
☐ ☐	150 Patrick Roy (G), Mont.	1.50
☐ ☐	151 Owen Nolan, Québ.	.20
☐ ☐	152 Richard Smehlik, Buff.	.20
☐ ☐	153 Ray Sheppard, Detr.	.20
☐ ☐	154 Ed Olczyk, NYRa.	.20
☐ ☐	155 Al MacInnis, Calg.	.20
☐ ☐	156 Sergei Zubov, NYRa.	.20
☐ ☐	157 Wendel Clark, Toro.	.50
☐ ☐	158 Kirk McLean (G), Vanc.	.20
☐ ☐	159 Thomas Steen, Winn.	.20
☐ ☐	160 Pierre Turgeon, NYIs.	.20
☐ ☐	161 Dmitri Kvartalnov, Bost.	.20
☐ ☐	162 Brian Noonan, Chic.	.20
☐ ☐	163 Mike McPhee, Dall.	.20
☐ ☐	164 Peter Bondra, Wash.	.20
☐ ☐	165 Bernie Nicholls, NJer.	.20
☐ ☐	166 Michael Nylander, Hart.	.20
☐ ☐	167 Guy Hebert (G), Anah.	.20
☐ ☐	168 Scott Mellanby, Flor.	.20
☐ ☐	169 Bob Bassen, SLou.	.20
☐ ☐	170 Rod Brind'Amour, Phil.	.20
☐ ☐	171 Andrei Kovalenko, Québ.	.20
☐ ☐	172 Mike Donnelly, LosA.	.20
☐ ☐	173 Steve Thomas, NYIs.	.20
☐ ☐	174 Rick Tocchet, Pitt.	.20
☐ ☐	175 Steve Yzerman, Detr.	1.50
☐ ☐	176 Dixon Ward, Vanc.	.20
☐ ☐	177 Randy Wood, Buff.	.20
☐ ☐	178 Dean Kennedy, Winn.	.20
☐ ☐	179 Joel Otto, Calg.	.20
☐ ☐	180 Kirk Muller, Mont.	.20
☐ ☐	181 Chris Chelios, Chic.	.20
☐ ☐	182 Richard Matvichuk, Dall.	.20
☐ ☐	183 John MacLean, NJer.	.20
☐ ☐	184 Joey Kocur, NYRa.	.20
☐ ☐	185 Adam Oates, Bost.	.20
☐ ☐	186 Bob Beers, Tamp.	.20
☐ ☐	187 Ron Tugnutt (G), Anah.	.20
☐ ☐	188 Brian Skrudland, Flor.	.20
☐ ☐	189 Al Iafrate, Wash.	.20
☐ ☐	190 Félix Potvin (G), Toro.	.20
☐ ☐	191 David Reid, Bost.	.20
☐ ☐	192 Jim' Johnson, Dall.	.20
☐ ☐	193 Kevin Haller, Mont.	.20
☐ ☐	194 Steve Chiasson, Detr.	.20
☐ ☐	195 Jaromir Jagr, Pitt.	.50
☐ ☐	196 Martin Rucinsky, Québ.	.20
☐ ☐	197 Sergei Bautin, Winn.	.20

□□	198 Joe Nieuwendyk, Calg.	.20
□□	199 Gilbert Dionne, Mont.	.20
□□	200 Brett Hull, SLou.	.50
□□	201 Yuri Khmylev, Buff.	.20
□□	202 Todd Elik, Edmo.	.20
□□	203 Patrick Flatley, NYIs.	.20
□□	204 Martin Straka, Pitt.	.20
□□	205 Brendan Shanahan, SLou.	.50
□□	**206 Mark Beaufait, SanJ. RC**	**.50**
□□	**207 Mike Lenarduzzi (G), Hart. RC**	**.50**
□□	**208 Chris LiPuma, Tamp. RC**	**.50**
□□	209 André Faust, Phil.	.20
□□	**210 Ben Hankinson, NJer. RC**	**.50**
□□	**211 Darrin Madeley (G), Otta. RC**	**.50**
□□	212 Oleg Petrov, Mont.	.20
□□	213 Philippe Boucher, Buff.	.20
□□	214 Tyler Wright, Edmo.	.20
□□	**215 Jason Bowen, Phil. RC**	**.50**
□□	216 Matthew Barnaby, Buff.	.20
□□	217 Bryan Smolinski, Bost.	.20
□□	218 Dan Keczmer, Hart.	.20
□□	**219 Chris Simon, Québ. RC**	**1.00**
□□	220 Corey Hirsch (G), NYRa.	.20
□□	221 Mario Lemieux, Pitt. [Award Winner]	1.50
□□	222 Teemu Selänne, Winn. [Award Winner]	.50
□□	223 Chris Chelios, Chic. [Award Winner]	.20
□□	224 Ed Belfour (G), Chic. [Award Winner]	.50
□□	225 Pierre Turgeon, NYIs. [Award Winner]	.20
□□	226 Doug Gilmour, Toro. [Award Winner]	.20
□□	227 Ed Belfour (G), Chic. [Award Winner]	.50
□□	228 Patrick Roy (G), Mont. [Award Winner]	1.50
□□	229 Dave Poulin, Bost. [Award Winner]	.20
□□	230 Mario Lemieux, Pitt. [Award Winner]	1.50
□□	231 Mike Vernon (G), Calg. [Hometown]	.20
□□	232 Vincent Damphousse, Mont. [Hometown]	.20
□□	233 Chris Chelios, Chic. [Hometown]	.20
□□	234 Cliff Ronning, Vanc. [Hometown]	.20
□□	235 Mark Howe, Detr. [Hometown]	.20
□□	236 Alexandre Daigle, Otta.	.20
□□	237 W. Gretzky, LosA. Edmo. [Then & Now]	2.50
□□	238 Mark Messier, NYRa. Edmo. [Then & Now]	.50
□□	239 Dino Ciccarelli, Detr. Minn. [Then & Now]	.20
□□	240 Joe Mullen, Pitt. SLou. [Then & Now]	.20
□□	241 Mike Gartner, NYRa. Wash. [Then & Now]	.50
□□	242 Mike Richter (G), NYRa.	.20
□□	243 Pat Verbeek, Hart.	.20
□□	244 Valeri Kamensky, Québ.	.20
□□	245 Nelson Emerson, Winn.	.20
□□	246 James Patrick, Hart.	.20
□□	247 Greg A. Adams, Vanc.	.20
□□	248 Ulf Dahlén, Dall.	.20
□□	249 Shayne Corson, Edmo.	.20
□□	250 Raymond Bourque, Bost.	.50
□□	251 Claude Lemieux, NJer.	.20
□□	252 Kelly Hrudey (G), LosA.	.20
□□	253 Patrice Brisebois, Mont.	.20
□□	254 Mark Howe, Detr.	.20
□□	255 Ed Belfour (G), Chic.	.50
□□	256 Pelle Eklund, Phil.	.20
□□	257 Zarley Zalapski, Hart.	.20
□□	258 Sylvain Côté, Wash.	.20
□□	259 Uwe Krupp, NYIs.	.20
□□	260 Dale Hawerchuk, Buff.	.20
□□	261 Alexei Gusarov, Québ.	.20
□□	262 Dave Ellett, Toro.	.20
□□	263 Tomas Sandström, LosA.	.20
□□	264 Vladimir Konstantinov, Detr.	.20
□□	265 Paul Ranheim, Calg.	.20
□□	266 Darrin Shannon, Winn.	.20
□□	267 Chris Terreri (G), NJer.	.20
□□	268 Russ Courtnall, Dall.	.20
□□	269 Don Sweeney, Bost.	.20
□□	270 Kevin Todd, Chic.	.20
□□	271 Brad Shaw, Otta.	.20
□□	272 Adam Creighton, Tamp.	.20
□□	273 Dana Murzyn, Vanc.	.20
□□	274 Donald Audette, Buff.	.20
□□	275 Brian Leetch, NYRa.	.20

1993 PINNACLE – BASEBALL

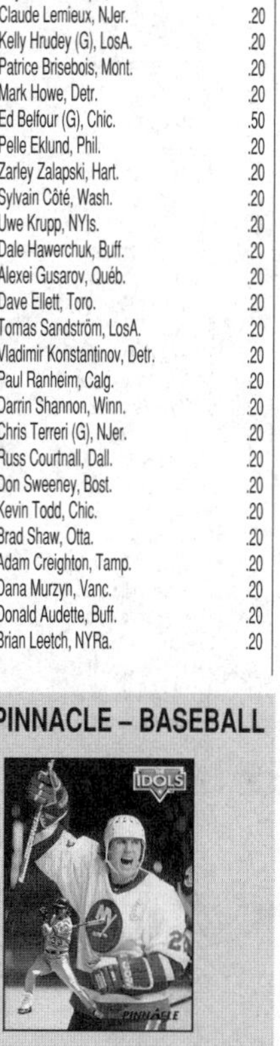

	Pinnacle	Pinnacle
□	299 Larry Walker / Mike Bossy	.50

□□	276 Kevin Dineen, Phil.	.20
□□	277 Bruce Driver, NJer.	.20
□□	278 Jim Paek, Pitt.	.20
□□	279 Esa Tikkanen, NYRa.	.20
□□	280 Guy Carbonneau, Mont.	.20
□□	281 Eric Weinrich, Chic.	.20
□□	282 Tim Cheveldae (G), Detr.	.20
□□	283 Bryan Marchment, Hart.	.20
□□	284 Kelly Miller, Wash.	.20
□□	285 Jimmy Carson, LosA.	.20
□□	286 Terry Carkner, Detr.	.20
□□	287 Mike Sullivan, SanJ.	.20
□□	288 Joe Reekie, Tamp.	.20
□□	289 Bob Rouse, Toro.	.20
□□	290 Joe Sakic, Québ.	1.00
□□	291 Gerald Diduck, Vanc.	.20
□□	292 Don Beaupré (G), Wash.	.20
□□	293 Kjell Samuelsson, Pitt.	.20
□□	294 Claude Lapointe, Québ.	.20
□□	295 Tie Domi, Winn.	.20
□□	296 Charlie Huddy, LosA.	.20
□□	297 Peter Zezel, Toro.	.20
□□	298 Craig Muni, Buff.	.20
□□	299 Rick Tabaracci (G), Wash.	.20
□□	300 Pat LaFontaine, Buff.	.20
□□	301 Lyle Odelein, Mont.	.20
□□	302 Jocelyn Lemieux, Chic.	.20
□□	303 Craig Ludwig, Dall.	.20
□□	304 Marc Bergevin, Tamp.	.20
□□	305 Bill Guerin, NJer.	.20
□□	306 Rick Zombo, SLou.	.20
□□	307 Steven Finn, Québ.	.20
□□	308 Gino Odjick, Vanc.	.20
□□	309 Jeff Beukeboom, NYRa.	.20
□□	310 Mario Lemieux, Pitt.	1.50
□□	311 J.J. Daigneault, Mont.	.20
□□	312 Vincent Riendeau (G), Detr.	.20
□□	313 Adam Burt, Hart.	.20
□□	314 Mike Craig, Dall.	.20
□□	315 Bret Hedican, SLou.	.20
□□	316 Kris King, Winn.	.20
□□	317 Sylvain Lefebvre, Toro.	.20
□□	318 Troy Murray, Chic.	.20
□□	319 Gord** Roberts, Bost.	.20
□□	320 Pavel Bure, Vanc.	.50
□□	321 Marc Bureau, Tamp.	.20
□□	322 Randy McKay, NJer.	.20
□□	323 Mark Lamb, Otta.	.20
□□	324 Brian Mullen, NYIs.	.20
□□	325 Ken Wregget (G), Pitt.	.20
□□	326 Stéphane Quintal, Winn.	.20
□□	327 Robert Dirk, Vanc.	.20
□□	328 Mike Krushelnyski, Toro.	.20
□□	329 Mikael Andersson, Tamp.	.20
□□	330 Paul Stanton, Bost.	.20
□□	331 Phil Bourque, NYRa.	.20
□□	332 André Racicot (G), Mont.	.20
□□	333 Brad Dalgarno, NYIs.	.20
□□	334 Neal Broten, Dall.	.20
□□	335 John Blue (G), Bost.	.20
□□	336 Ken Sutton, Buff.	.20
□□	337 Greg Paslawski, Calg.	.20
□□	338 Robb Stauber (G), LosA.	.20
□□	339 Mike Keane, Mont.	.20
□□	340 Terry Yake, Anah.	.20
□□	341 Brian Benning, Flor.	.20
□□	342 Brian Propp, Hart.	.20
□□	343 Frank Pietrangelo (G), Hart.	.20
□□	344 Stéphane Matteau, Chic.	.20
□□	345 Steven King, Anah.	.20
□□	346 Joe Cirella, Flor.	.20
□□	347 Andy Moog (G), Dall.	.20
□□	348 Paul Ysebaert, Winn.	.20
□□	349 Petr Klima, Tamp.	.20
□□	350 Corey Millen, NJer.	.20
□□	351 Phil Housley, SLou.	.20
□□	352 Craig Billington (G), Otta.	.20
□□	353 Jeff Norton, SanJ.	.20
□□	354 Neil Wilkinson, Chic.	.20
□□	355 Doug Lidster, NYRa.	.20
□□	356 Steve Larmer, NYRa.	.20
□□	357 Jon Casey (G), Bost.	.20
□□	358 Brad McCrimmon, Hart.	.20
□□	359 Alexei Kasatonov, Anah.	.20
□□	360 Andrei Lomakin, Flor.	.20
□□	361 Daren Puppa (G), Tamp.	.20
□□	362 Sergei Makarov, SanJ.	.20
□□	363 Dave Manson, Edmo.	.20
□□	364 Jim Sandlak, Hart.	.20
□□	365 Glenn Healy (G), NYRa.	.20
□□	366 Martin Gélinas, Québ.	.20
□□	367 Igor Larionov, SanJ.	.20
□□	368 Anatoli Semenov, Anah.	.20
□□	369 Mark Fitzpatrick (G), Flor.	.20
□□	370 Paul Cavallini, Dall.	.20
□□	371 Jimmy Waite (G), SanJ.	.20
□□	372 Yves Racine, Phil.	.20
□□	373 Jeff Hackett (G), Chic.	.20
□□	374 Marty McSorley, Pitt.	.20
□□	375 Scott Pearson, Edmo.	.20
□□	376 Ron Hextall (G), NYIs.	.20
□□	377 Gaétan Duchesne, SanJ.	.20
□□	378 Jamie Baker, SanJ.	.20
□□	379 Troy Loney, Anah.	.20
□□	380 Gord Murphy, Flor.	.20
□□	381 Peter Sidorkiewicz (G), NJer.	.20
□□	382 Pat Elynuik, Tamp.	.20
□□	383 Glen Wesley, Bost.	.20
□□	384 Dean Evason, Dall.	.20
□□	385 Mike Peluso, NJer.	.20
□□	386 Darren Turcotte, Hart.	.20
□□	387 Dave Poulin, Wash.	.20
□□	388 John Cullen, Toro.	.20
□□	389 Randy Ladouceur, Anah.	.20
□□	390 Tom Fitzgerald, Flor.	.20
□□	391 Denis Savard, Tamp.	.20
□□	392 Fredrik Olausson, Edmo.	.20
□□	393 Sergio Momesso, Vanc.	.20
□□	394 Mike Ramsey, Pitt.	.20
□□	395 Kelly Kisio, Calg.	.20
□□	396 Craig Simpson, Buff.	.20
□□	397 Viacheslav Fetisov, NJer.	.20
□□	398 Glenn Anderson, Toro.	.20
□□	399 Michel Goulet, Chic.	.20
□□	400 Wayne Gretzky, LosA.	2.50
□□	401 Stu Grimson, Anah.	.20
□□	402 Mike Hough, Flor.	.20
□□	403 Dominik Hasek (G), Buff.	.50
□□	404 Gerard Gallant, Tamp.	.20
□□	405 Greg Gilbert, NYRa.	.20
□□	406 Vladimir Ruzicka, Otta.	.20
□□	407 Jim Hrivnak (G), SLou.	.20
□□	408 Dave Lowry, Flor.	.20
□□	409 Todd Ewen, Anah.	.20
□□	410 Bob Errey, SanJ.	.20
□□	411 Bryan Trottier, Pitt.	.50
□□	412 Dave Taylor, LosA.	.20
□□	413 Grant Ledyard, Dall.	.20
□□	414 Chris Dahlquist, Calg.	.20
□□	415 Brent Gilchrist, Dall.	.20
□□	416 Geoff Smith, Edmo.	.20
□□	417 Jiri Slégr, Vanc.	.20
□□	418 Randy Burridge, Wash.	.20
□□	419 Sergei Krivokrasov, Chic.	.20
□□	420 Keith Primeau, Detr.	.20
□□	421 Robert Kron, Hart.	.20
□□	422 Keith Brown, Flor.	.20
□□	423 David Volek, NYIs.	.20
□□	424 Josef Beránek, Phil.	.20
□□	425 Wayne Presley, Buff.	.20
□□	426 Stu Barnes, Winn.	.20
□□	**427 Milos Holan, Phil. RC**	**.50**
□□	**428 Jeff Shantz, Chic. RC**	**.50**
□□	**429 Brent Gretzky, Tamp. RC**	**.50**
□□	430 Jarkko Varvio, Dall.	.20
□□	**431 Chris Osgood (G), Detr. RC**	**3.00**
□□	**432 Aaron Ward, Detr. RC**	**.50**
□□	**433 Jason Smith, NJer. RC**	**.50**
□□	**434 Cam Stewart, Bost. RC**	**.50**
□□	**435 Derek Plante, Buff. RC**	**.50**
□□	436 Pat Peake, Wash.	.20
□□	437 Alexander Karpovtsev, NYRa.	.20
□□	**438 Jim Montgomery, SLou. RC**	**.50**
□□	439 Rob Niedermayer, Flor.	.20
□□	**440 Jocelyn Thibault (G), Québ. RC**	**2.00**
□□	**441 Jason Arnott, Edmo. RC**	**2.00**
□□	442 Mike Rathje, SanJ.	.20
□□	443 Chris Gratton, Tamp.	.20
□□	**444 Vesa Viitakoski, Calg. RC**	**.50**
□□	**445 Alexei Kudashov, Toro. RC**	**.50**
□□	446 Pavol Demitra, Otta.	.50
□□	447 Ted Drury, Calg.	.20
□□	**448 René Corbet, Québ. RC**	**.50**
□□	449 Markus Näslund, Pitt.	1.00
□□	450 Dmitri Filimonov, Otta.	.20
□□	451 Roman Oksiuta, Edmo.	.20
□□	**452 Michal Sykora, SanJ. RC**	**.50**
□□	453 Greg Johnson, Detr.	.20
□□	454 Mikael Renberg, Phil.	.20
□□	455 Alexei Yashin, Otta.	.50
□□	456 Chris Pronger, Hart.	.50
□□	**457 Manny Fernandez, Canada RC**	**2.00**
□□	**458 Jamie Storr (G), Canada Juniors RC**	**1.00**
□□	**459 Chris Armstrong, Canada Juniors RC**	**.50**
□□	**460 Drew Bannister, Canada Juniors RC**	**.50**
□□	**461 Joël Bouchard, Canada Juniors RC**	**.50**
□□	**462 Bryan McCabe, Canada Juniors RC**	**1.00**
□□	**463 Nick Stajduhar, Canada Juniors RC**	**.50**
□□	464 Brent Tully, Canada Juniors	.20
□□	**465 Brendan Witt, Canada Juniors RC**	**.50**
□□	**466 Jason Allison, Canada Juniors RC**	**3.00**
□□	**467 Jason Botterill, Canada Juniors RC**	**.50**
□□	**468 Curtis Bowen, Canada Juniors RC**	**.50**
□□	**469 Anson Carter, Canada Juniors RC**	**2.00**
□□	**470 Brandon Convery, Canada Juniors RC**	**.50**
□□	**471 Yannick Dubé, Canada Juniors RC**	**.50**
□□	**472 Jeff Friesen, Canada Juniors RC**	**1.50**
□□	**473 Aaron Gavey, Canada Juniors RC**	**.50**
□□	**474 Martin Gendron, Canada Juniors RC**	**.50**
□□	**475 Rick Girard, Canada Juniors RC**	**.50**
□□	**476 Todd Harvey, Canada Juniors RC**	**1.00**
□□	**477 Marty Murray, Canada Juniors RC**	**.50**
□□	**478 Michael Peca, Canada Juniors RC**	**2.00**
□□	**479 Aaron Ellis, U.S.A. Juniors RC**	**.50**
□□	**480 Toby Kvalevog, U.S.A. Juniors RC**	**.50**
□□	**481 Jon Coleman, U.S.A. Juniors RC**	**.50**
□□	**482 Ashlin Halfnight, U.S.A. Juniors RC**	**.50**
□□	**483 Jason McBain, U.S.A. Juniors RC**	**.50**
□□	**484 Chris O'Sullivan, U.S.A. Juniors RC**	**.50**
□□	**485 Deron Quint, U.S.A. Juniors RC**	**.50**
□□	**486 Blake Sloan, U.S.A. Juniors RC**	**.50**
□□	**487 David Wilkie, U.S.A. Juniors RC**	**.50**
□□	**488 Kevyn Adams, U.S.A. Juniors RC**	**.50**
□□	**489 Jason Bonsignore, U.S.A. Juniors RC**	**.50**
□□	**490 Andy Brink, U.S.A. Juniors RC**	**.50**
□□	491 Adam Deadmarsh, U.S.A. Juniors	.20
□□	492 John Emmons, U.S.A. Juniors	.20
□□	**493 Kevin Hilton, U.S.A. Juniors RC**	**.50**
□□	**494 Jason Karmanos, U.S.A. Juniors RC**	**.50**
□□	**495 Bob Lachance, U.S.A. Juniors RC**	**.50**
□□	**496 J. Langenbrunner, U.S.A. Juniors RC**	**1.00**
□□	**497 Jay Pandolfo, U.S.A. Juniors RC**	**.50**
□□	**498 Richard Park, U.S.A. Juniors RC**	**.50**
□□	499 Ryan Sittler, U.S.A. Juniors	.20
□□	**500 John Varga, U.S.A. Juniors RC**	**.50**
□□	**501 Valeri Bure, Russia Juniors RC**	**1.50**
□□	**502 Maxim Bets, Russia Juniors RC**	**.50**
□□	503 Vadim Sharifijanov, Russia Juniors	.20
□□	**504 A. Kharlamov, Russia Juniors RC**	**.50**
□□	**505 Pavel Desyatkov, Russia Juniors RC**	**.50**
□□	**506 Oleg Tverdovsky, Russia Juniors RC**	**.50**
□□	507 Nikolai Tsulygin, Russia Juniors	.20
□□	**508 E. Ryabchikov (G), Russia Juniors RC**	**.50**
□□	**509 Sergei Brylin, Russia Juniors RC**	**.50**
□□	**510 Maxim Sushinsky, Russia Juniors RC**	**.50**
□□	**511 Sergei Kondrashkin, Russia Juniors RC**	**.50**
□□	512 Wayne Gretzky, LosA. [802]	10.00

	Insert	Auto.
□	236 Alexandre Daigle Autograph ✍	25.00
□	Eric Lindros Autograph ✍	100.00
□□	Brett & Eric Lindros	10.00

CAPTAINS

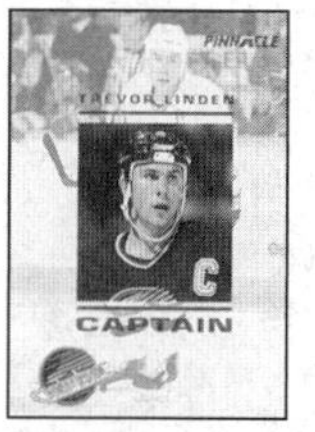

These cards have two versions: an American issue and a Canadian issue. Photos in each set are different.

	Series Two Insert Set (27 cards):	150.00
	Insert (1:4 Jumbo)	CA
□□	CA1 Troy Loney, Anah.	3.00
□□	CA2 Raymond Bourque, Bost.	10.00
□□	CA3 Pat LaFontaine, Buff.	5.00
□□	CA4 Joe Nieuwendyk, Calg.	3.00
□□	CA5 Dirk Graham, Chic.	3.00
□□	CA6 Mark Tinordi, Dall.	3.00
□□	CA7 Steve Yzerman, Detr.	20.00
□□	CA8 Craig MacTavish, Edmo.	3.00
□□	CA9 Brian Skrudland, Flor.	3.00
□□	CA10 Pat Verbeek, Hart.	3.00
□□	CA11 Wayne Gretzky, LosA.	40.00
□□	CA12 Guy Carbonneau, Mont.	3.00
□□	CA13 Scott Stevens, NJer.	3.00
□□	CA14 Patrick Flatley, NYIs.	3.00
□□	CA15 Mark Messier, NYRa.	10.00
□□	CA16 Mark Lamb, Otta.	3.00
□□	CA17 Kevin Dineen, Phil.	3.00
□□	CA18 Mario Lemieux, Pitt.	30.00
□□	CA19 Joe Sakic, Québ.	15.00
□□	CA20 Brett Hull, SLou.	10.00
□□	CA21 Bob Errey, SanJ.	3.00
□□	CA22 Lightning captains	3.00
□□	CA23 Wendel Clark, Toro.	5.00
□□	CA24 Trevor Linden, Vanc.	3.00
□□	CA25 Kevin Hatcher, Wash.	3.00
□□	CA26 Keith Tkachuk, Winn.	5.00
□□	CA27 Checklist	10.00

EXPANSION

	Series One Insert Set (6 cards):	10.00
	Insert (Hobby Packs)	Expan.
□	1 G. Hebert (G) / J. Vanbiesbrouck (G)	5.00
□	2 R. Ladouceur / G. Murphy	1.00
□	3 S. Hill / J. Cirella	1.00
□	4 T. Loney / D. Lowry	2.00
□	5 T. Yake / B. Skrudland	1.00
□	6 S. King / S. Mellanby	2.00

MASKS

	Series One Insert Set (10 cards):	90.00
	Insert (1:24)	Mask
□	1 Grant Fuhr (G), Buff.	20.00
□	2 Mike Vernon (G), Calg.	15.00
□	3 Robb Stauber (G), LosA.	10.00
□	4 Dominic Roussel (G), Phil.	10.00
□	5 Pat Jablonski (G), Tamp.	10.00
□	6 Stéphane Fiset (G), Québ.	10.00
□	7 Wendell Young (G), Tamp.	10.00
□	8 Ron Hextall (G), NYIs.	20.00
□	9 John Vanbiesbrouck (G), Flor.	15.00
□	10 Peter Sidorkiewicz (G), Otta.	10.00

NIFTY FIFTY

	Series Two Insert Set (15 cards):	130.00
	Insert (1:36)	NF
□	1 Checklist	10.00
□	2 Alexander Mogilny, Buff.	5.00
□	3 Teemu Selänne, Winn.	10.00
□	4 Mario Lemieux, Pitt.	35.00
□	5 Luc Robitaille, LosA.	10.00
□	6 Pavel Bure, Vanc.	10.00
□	7 Pierre Turgeon, NYIs.	5.00
□	8 Steve Yzerman, Detr.	30.00
□	9 Kevin Stevens, Pitt.	4.00
□	10 Brett Hull, SLou.	10.00
□	11 Dave Andreychuk, Toro.	4.00
□	12 Pat LaFontaine, Buff.	5.00
□	13 Mark Recchi, Phil.	5.00
□	14 Brendan Shanahan, SLou.	10.00
□	15 Jeremy Roenick, Chic.	10.00

SUPER ROOKIES

These cards have two versions: an American issue and a Canadain issue. Photos in each series are different.

	Series Two Insert Set (9 cards):	10.00
	Insert (1:36)	SR
□□	SR1 Alexandre Daigle, Otta.	1.00
□□	SR2 Chris Pronger, Hart.	2.00
□□	SR3 Chris Gratton, Tamp.	1.00
□□	SR4 Rob Niedermayer, Flor.	1.00
□□	SR5 Alexei Yashin, Otta.	2.00
□□	SR6 Mikael Renberg, Phil.	1.00
□□	SR7 Jason Arnott, Edmo.	3.00
□□	SR8 Markus Näslund, Pitt.	3.00
□□	SR9 Pat Peake, Wash.	1.00

TEAM 2001

Series One Insert Set (30 cards):	**35.00**
Insert (1:1 Jumbo)	**T2K1**
1 Eric Lindros, Phil.	3.50
2 Alexander Mogilny, Buff.	1.50
3 Pavel Bure, Vanc.	3.00
4 Joé Juneau, Bost.	.50
5 Félix Potvin (G), Toro.	2.00
6 Nicklas Lidström, Detr.	2.00
7 Alexei Kovalev, NYRa.	2.00
8 Patrick Poulin, Hart.	.50
9 Shawn McEachern, Pitt.	1.00
10 Teemu Selänne, Winn.	3.00
11 Rod Brind'Amour, Phil.	1.00
12 Jaromir Jagr, Pitt.	3.00
13 Pierre Turgeon, NYIs.	1.50
14 Scott Niedermayer, NJer.	1.00
15 Mats Sundin, Québ.	3.50
16 Trevor Linden, Vanc.	1.50
17 Mike Modano, Dall.	3.50
18 Roman Hamrlik, Tamp.	.50
19 Tony Amonte, NYRa.	2.00
20 Jeremy Roenick, Chic.	3.00
21 Scott Lachance, NYIs.	.50
22 Mike Ricci, Québ.	1.00
23 Dmitri Khristich, Wash.	.50
24 Sergei Fedorov, Detr.	3.50
25 Joe Sakic, Québ.	6.00
26 Pat Falloon, SanJ.	.50
27 Mathieu Schneider, Mont.	.50
28 Owen Nolan, Québ.	2.00
29 Brendan Shanahan, SLou.	3.50
30 Mark Recchi, Phil.	1.50

TEAM PINNACLE

Insert Set (12 cards):	**325.00**
Insert (1:90)	**TP**
1 E. Belfour / P. Roy	70.00
2 C. Chelios / B. Leetch	20.00
3 A. MacInnis / S. Stevens	10.00
4 L. Robitaille / K. Stevens	10.00
5 W. Gretzky / M. Lemieux	130.00
6 Br. Hull / J. Jagr	30.00
7 T. Barrasso / K. McLean	10.00
8 R. Bourque / P. Coffey	30.00
9 P. Housley / A. Iafrate	10.00
10 P. Bure / V. Damphousse	20.00
11 E. Lindros / J. Roenick	30.00
12 A. Mogilny / T. Selänne	20.00

1993 - 94 POWER PLAY

Card Size: 2 1/2" x 4 3/4"
Imprint: © 1993 Fleer Corp.

Series One Set (280 cards):	**40.00**
Series Two Set (240 cards):	**50.00**
Common Player	**.20**
Player	**NRMT-MT**
1 Stu Grimson, Anah.	.20
2 Guy Hebert (G), Anah.	.20
3 Sean Hill, Anah.	.20
4 Bill Houlder, Anah.	.20
5 Alexei Kasatonov, Anah.	.20
6 Steven King, Anah.	.20
7 Lonnie Loach, Anah.	.20
8 Troy Loney, Anah.	.20
9 Joe Sacco, Anah.	.20
10 Anatoli Semenov, Anah.	.20
11 Jarrod Skalde, Anah.	.20
12 Tim Sweeney, Anah.	.20
13 Ron Tugnutt (G), Anah.	.20
14 Terry Yake, Anah.	.20
15 Shaun Van Allen, Anah.	.20
16 Raymond Bourque, Bost.	.50
17 Jon Casey (G), Bost.	.20
18 Ted Donato, Bost.	.20
19 Joé Juneau, Bost.	.20
20 Dmitri Kvartalnov, Bost.	.20
21 Stephen Leach, Bost.	.20
22 Cam Neely, Bost.	.50
23 Adam Oates, Bost.	.20
24 Don Sweeney, Bost.	.20
25 Glen Wesley, Bost.	.20
26 Doug Bodger, Buff.	.20
27 Grant Fuhr (G), Buff.	.20
28 Viktor Gordiouk, Buff.	.20
29 Dale Hawerchuk, Buff.	.20
30 Yuri Khmylev, Buff.	.20
31 Pat LaFontaine, Buff.	.20
32 Alexander Mogilny, Buff.	.20
33 Richard Smehlik, Buff.	.20
34 Bob Sweeney, Buff.	.20
35 Randy Wood, Buff.	.20
36 Theoren Fleury, Calg.	.20
37 Kelly Kisio, Calg.	.20
38 Al MacInnis, Calg.	.20
39 Joe Nieuwendyk, Calg.	.20
40 Joel Otto, Calg.	.20
41 Robert Reichel, Calg.	.20
42 Gary Roberts, Calg.	.20
43 Ronnie Stern, Calg.	.20
44 Gary Suter, Calg.	.20
45 Mike Vernon (G), Calg.	.20
46 Ed Belfour (G), Chic.	.50
47 Chris Chelios, Chic.	.20
48 Karl Dykhuis, Chic.	.20
49 Michel Goulet, Chic.	.20
50 Dirk Graham, Chic.	.20
51 Sergei Krivokrasov, Chic.	.20
52 Steve Larmer, Chic.	.20
53 Joe Murphy, Chic.	.20
54 Jeremy Roenick, Chic.	.50
55 J. Steve Smith, Chic.	.20
56 Brent Sutter, Chic.	.20
57 Neal Broten, Dall.	.20
58 Russ Courtnall, Dall.	.20
59 Ulf Dahlén, Dall.	.20
60 Dave Gagner, Dall.	.20
61 Derian Hatcher, Dall.	.20
62 Trent Klatt, Dall.	.20
63 Mike Modano, Dall.	.50
64 Andy Moog (G), Dall.	.20
65 Tommy Sjödin, Dall.	.20
66 Mark Tinordi, Dall.	.20
67 Tim Cheveldae (G), Detr.	.20
68 Steve Chiasson, Detr.	.20
69 Dino Ciccarelli, Detr.	.20
70 Paul Coffey, Detr.	.20
71 Dallas Drake, Detr. RC	**1.00**
72 Sergei Fedorov, Detr.	.50
73 Vladimir Konstantinov, Detr.	.20
74 Nicklas Lidström, Detr.	.20
75 Keith Primeau, Detr.	.20
76 Ray Sheppard, Detr.	.20
77 Steve Yzerman, Detr.	1.50
78 Zdeno Ciger, Edmo.	.20
79 Shayne Corson, Edmo.	.20
80 Todd Elik, Edmo.	.20
81 Igor Kravchuk, Edmo.	.20
82 Craig MacTavish, Edmo.	.20
83 Dave Manson, Edmo.	.20
84 Shjon Podein, Edmo. RC	**1.50**
85 Bill Ranford (G), Edmo.	.20
86 Steven Rice, Edmo.	.20
87 Doug Weight, Edmo.	.20
88 Doug Barrault, Flor. RC	**.50**
89 Jesse Bélanger, Flor.	.20
90 Brian Benning, Flor.	.20
91 Joe Cirella, Flor.	.20
92 Mark Fitzpatrick (G), Flor.	.20
93 Randy Gilhen, Flor.	.20
94 Mike Hough, Flor.	.20
95 Bill Lindsay, Flor.	.20
96 Andrei Lomakin, Flor.	.20
97 Dave Lowry, Flor.	.20
98 Scott Mellanby, Flor.	.20
99 Gord Murphy, Flor.	.20
100 Brian Skrudland, Flor.	.20
101 Milan Tichy, Flor. RC	**.50**
102 John Vanbiesbrouck (G), Flor.	.20
103 Sean Burke (G), Hart.	.20
104 Andrew Cassels, Hart.	.20
105 Nick Kypreos, Hart.	.20
106 Michael Nylander, Hart.	.20
107 Robert Petrovicky, Hart.	.20
108 Patrick Poulin, Hart.	.20
109 Geoff Sanderson, Hart.	.20
110 Pat Verbeek, Hart.	.20
111 Eric Weinrich, Hart.	.20
112 Zarley Zalapski, Hart.	.20
113 Rob Blake, LosA.	.20
114 Jimmy Carson, LosA.	.20
115 Tony Granato, LosA.	.20
116 Wayne Gretzky, LosA.	3.00
117 Kelly Hrudey (G), LosA.	.20
118 Jari Kurri, LosA.	.50
119 Shawn McEachern, LosA.	.20
120 Luc Robitaille, LosA.	.50
121 Tomas Sandström, LosA.	.20
122 Darryl Sydor, LosA.	.20
123 Alexei Zhitnik, LosA.	.20
124 Brian Bellows, Mont.	.20
125 Patrice Brisebois, Mont.	.20
126 Guy Carbonneau, Mont.	.20
127 Vincent Damphousse, Mont.	.20
128 Éric Desjardins, Mont.	.20
129 Mike Keane, Mont.	.20
130 Stéphan Lebeau, Mont.	.20
131 Kirk Muller, Mont.	.20
132 Lyle Odelein, Mont.	.20
133 Patrick Roy (G), Mont.	2.00
134 Mathieu Schneider, Mont.	.20
135 Bruce Driver, NJer.	.20
136 Viacheslav Fetisov, NJer.	.20
137 Claude Lemieux, NJer.	.20
138 John MacLean, NJer.	.20
139 Bernie Nicholls, NJer.	.20
140 Scott Niedermayer, NJer.	.20
141 Stéphane J.J. Richer, NJer.	.20
142 Alexander Semak, NJer.	.20
143 Scott Stevens, NJer.	.20
144 Chris Terreri (G), NJer.	.20
145 Valeri Zelepukin, NJer.	.20
146 Patrick Flatley, NYIs.	.20
147 Ron Hextall (G), NYIs.	.50
148 Benoît Hogue, NYIs.	.20
149 Darius Kasparaitis, NYIs.	.20
150 Derek King, NYIs.	.20
151 Uwe Krupp, NYIs.	.20
152 Scott Lachance, NYIs.	.20
153 Vladimir Malakhov, NYIs.	.20
154 Steve Thomas, NYIs.	.20
155 Pierre Turgeon, NYIs.	.20
156 Tony Amonte, NYRa.	.20
157 Mike Gartner, NYRa.	.50
158 Adam Graves, NYRa.	.20
159 Alexei Kovalev, NYRa.	.20
160 Brian Leetch, NYRa.	.20
161 Joby Messier, NYRa. RC	**.50**
163 Sergei Nemchinov, NYRa.	.20
164 James Patrick, NYRa.	.20
165 Mike Richter (G), NYRa.	.20
162 Mark Messier, NYRa.	.50
166 Darren Turcotte, NYRa.	.20
167 Sergei Zubov, NYRa.	.20
168 Dave Archibald, Otta.	.20
169 Craig Billington (G), Otta.	.20
170 Bob Kudelski, Otta.	.20
171 Mark Lamb, Otta.	.20
172 Norm Maciver, Otta.	.20
173 Darren Rumble, Otta.	.20
174 Vladimír Ruzicka, Otta.	.20
175 Brad Shaw, Otta.	.20
176 Sylvain Turgeon, Otta.	.20
177 Josef Beránek, Phil.	.20
178 Rod Brind'Amour, Phil.	.20
179 Kevin Dineen, Phil.	.20
180 Pelle Eklund, Phil.	.20
181 Brent Fedyk, Phil.	.20
182 Garry Galley, Phil.	.20
183 Eric Lindros, Phil.	.50
184 Mark Recchi, Phil.	.20
185 Tommy Söderström (G), Phil.	.20
186 Dmitry Yushkevich, Phil.	.20
187 Tom Barrasso (G), Pitt.	.20
188 Ron Francis, Pitt.	.20
189 Jaromir Jagr, Pitt.	.50
190 Mario Lemieux, Pitt.	2.00
191 Marty McSorley, Pitt.	.20
192 Joe Mullen, Pitt.	.20
193 Larry Murphy, Pitt.	.20
194 Ulf Samuelsson, Pitt.	.20
195 Kevin Stevens, Pitt.	.20
196 Rick Tocchet, Pitt.	.20
197 Steve Duchesne, Québ.	.20
198 Stéphane Fiset (G), Québ.	.20
199 Valeri Kamensky, Québ.	.20
200 Andrei Kovalenko, Québ.	.20
201 Owen Nolan, Québ.	.20
202 Mike Ricci, Québ.	.20
203 Martin Rucinsky, Québ.	.20
204 Joe Sakic, Québ.	1.00
205 Mats Sundin, Québ.	.50
206 Scott Young, Québ.	.20
207 Jeff R. Brown, SLou.	.20
208 Garth Butcher, SLou.	.20
209 Nelson Emerson, SLou.	.20
210 Bret Hedican, SLou.	.20
211 Brett Hull, SLou.	.50
212 Craig Janney, SLou.	.20
213 Curtis Joseph (G), SLou.	.50
214 Igor Korolev, SLou.	.20
215 Kevin Miller, SLou.	.20
216 Brendan Shanahan, SLou.	.50
217 Ed Courtenay, SanJ.	.20
218 Pat Falloon, SanJ.	.20
219 Johan Garpenlöv, SanJ.	.20
220 Rob Gaudreau, SanJ. RC	**.50**
221 Arturs Irbe (G), SanJ.	.20
222 Sergei Makarov, SanJ.	.20
223 Jeff Norton, SanJ.	.20
224 Jeff Odgers, SanJ.	.20
225 Sandis Ozolinsh, SanJ.	.20
226 Tom Pederson, SanJ.	.20
227 Bob Beers, Tamp.	.20
228 Brian Bradley, Tamp.	.20
229 Shawn Chambers, Tamp.	.20
230 Gerard Gallant, Tamp.	.20
231 Roman Hamrlik, Tamp.	.20
232 Petr Klima, Tamp.	.20
233 Chris Kontos, Tamp.	.20
234 Daren Puppa (G), Tamp.	.20
235 John Tucker, Tamp.	.20
236 Rob Zamuner, Tamp.	.20
237 Glenn Anderson, Toro.	.20
238 Dave Andreychuk, Toro.	.20
239 Drake Berehowsky, Toro.	.20
240 Nikolai Borschevsky, Toro.	.20
241 Wendel Clark, Toro.	.50
242 John Cullen, Toro.	.20
243 Dave Ellett, Toro.	.20
244 Doug Gilmour, Toro.	.20
245 Dmitri Mironov, Toro.	.20
246 Félix Potvin (G), Toro.	.20
247 Greg A. Adams, Vanc.	.20
248 Pavel Bure, Vanc.	.50
249 Geoff Courtnall, Vanc.	.20
250 Gerald Diduck, Vanc.	.20
251 Trevor Linden, Vanc.	.20
252 Jyrki Lumme, Vanc.	.20
253 Kirk McLean (G), Vanc.	.20
254 Petr Nedved, Vanc.	.20
255 Cliff Ronning, Vanc.	.20
256 Jiri Slégr, Vanc.	.20
257 Dixon Ward, Vanc.	.20
258 Peter Bondra, Wash.	.20
259 Sylvain Côté, Wash.	.20
260 Pat Elynuik, Wash.	.20
261 Kevin Hatcher, Wash.	.20
262 Dale Hunter, Wash.	.20
263 Al Iafrate, Wash.	.20
264 Dmitri Khristich, Wash.	.20
265 Michal Pivonka, Wash.	.20
266 Mike Ridley, Wash.	.20
267 Rick Tabaracci (G), Wash.	.20
268 Sergei Bautin, Winn.	.20
269 Evgeny Davydov, Winn.	.20
270 Bob Essensa (G), Winn.	.20
271 Phil Housley, Winn.	.20
272 Teppo Numminen, Winn.	.20
273 Fredrik Olausson, Winn.	.20
274 Teemu Selänne, Winn.	.50
275 Thomas Steen, Winn.	.20
276 Keith Tkachuk, Winn.	.20
277 Paul Ysebaert, Winn.	.20
278 Alexei Zhamnov, Winn.	.20
279 Checklist	.20
280 Checklist	.20
281 Patrik Carnbäck, Anah. RC	**.50**
282 Bob Corkum, Anah.	.20
283 Bobby Dollas, Anah. RC	**.50**
284 Peter Douris, Anah.	.20
285 Todd Ewen, Anah.	.20
286 Garry Valk, Anah.	.20
287 John Blue (G), Bost.	.20
288 Glen Featherstone, Bost.	.20
289 Stephen Heinze, Bost.	.20
290 David Reid, Bost.	.20
291 Bryan Smolinski, Bost.	.20
292 Cam Stewart, Bost. RC	**.50**
293 Jozef Stumpel, Bost.	.20
294 Sergei Zholtok, Bost.	.20
295 Donald Audette, Buff.	.20
296 Philippe Boucher, Buff.	.20
297 Dominik Hasek (G), Buff.	.50
298 Brad May, Buff.	.20
299 Craig Muni, Buff.	.20
300 Derek Plante, Buff. RC	**1.00**
301 Craig Simpson, Buff.	.20
302 Scott Thomas, Buff. RC	**.50**
303 Ted Drury, Calg.	.20
304 Dan Keczmer, Calg.	.20
305 Trevor Kidd (G), Calg.	.20
306 Sandy McCarthy, Calg.	.20
307 Frantisek Musil, Calg.	.20
308 Michel Petit, Calg.	.20
309 Paul Ranheim, Calg.	.20
310 German Titov, Calg. RC	**.50**
311 Andrei Trefilov (G), Calg.	.20
312 Jeff Hackett (G), Chic.	.20
313 Stéphane Matteau, Chic.	.20
314 Brian Noonan, Chic.	.20
315 Patrick Poulin, Chic.	.20
316 Jeff Shantz, Chic. RC	**.50**
317 Rich Sutter, Chic.	.20
318 Kevin Todd, Chic.	.20
319 Eric Weinrich, Chic.	.20
320 Dave Barr, Dall.	.20
321 Paul Cavallini, Dall.	.20
322 Mike Craig, Dall.	.20
323 Dean Evason, Dall.	.20
324 Brent Gilchrist, Dall.	.20
325 Grant Ledyard, Dall.	.20
326 Mike McPhee, Dall.	.20
327 Darcy Wakaluk (G), Dall.	.20
328 Terry Carkner, Detr.	.20
329 Mark Howe, Detr.	.20
330 Greg Johnson, Detr.	.20
331 Vyacheslav Kozlov, Detr.	.20
332 Martin Lapointe, Detr.	.20
333 Darren McCarty, Detr. RC	**2.00**
334 Chris Osgood (G), Detr. RC	**3.50**
335 Bob Probert, Detr.	.20
336 Mike Sillinger, Detr.	.20
337 Jason Arnott, Edmo. RC	**3.00**
338 Bob Beers, Edmo.	.20
339 Fred Brathwaite (G), Edmo. RC	**2.00**
340 Kelly Buchberger, Edmo.	.20
341 Ilya Byakin, Edmo.	.20
342 Fredrik Olausson, Edmo.	.20
343 Vladimír (Jr.) Vujtek, Edmo.	.20
344 Peter White, Edmo. RC	**.50**
345 Stu Barnes, Flor.	.20
346 Mike Foligno, Flor.	.20
347 Greg Hawgood, Flor.	.20
348 Bob Kudelski, Flor.	.20
349 Rob Niedermayer, Flor.	.20
350 Igor Chibirev, Hart.	.20
351 Robert Kron, Hart.	.20
352 Bryan Marchment, Hart.	.20
352 Warren Rychel, LosA.	.20
353 James Patrick, Hart.	.20
354 Chris Pronger, Hart.	.50
355 Jeff Reese (G), Hart.	.20
356 Jim Storm, Hart. RC	**.50**
357 Darren Turcotte, Hart.	.20
358 Pat Conacher, LosA.	.20
359 Mike Donnelly, LosA.	.20
360 John Druce, LosA.	.20
361 Charlie Huddy, LosA.	.20
363 Robb Stauber (G), LosA.	.20
364 Dave Taylor, LosA.	.20
365 Dixon Ward, LosA.	.20
366 Benoît Brunet, Mont.	.20
367 J.J. Daigneault, Mont.	.20
368 Gilbert Dionne, Mont.	.20
369 Paul DiPietro, Mont.	.20
370 Kevin Haller, Mont.	.20
371 Oleg Petrov, Mont.	.20
372 Peter Popovic, Mont. RC	**.50**
373 Ron L. Wilson, Mont.	.20
374 Martin Brodeur (G), NJer.	1.00
375 Tom Chorske, NJer.	.20
376 Jim Dowd, NJer. RC	**.50**
377 David Emma, NJer.	.20
378 Bobby Holik, NJer.	.20
379 Corey Millen, NJer.	.20
380 Jaroslav Modry, NJer. RC	**.50**
381 Jason Smith, NJer. RC	**1.00**
382 Ray Ferraro, NYIs.	.20
383 Travis Green, NYIs.	.20
384 Tom Kurvers, NYIs.	.20
385 Marty McInnis, NYIs.	.20
386 Jamie McLennan (G), NYIs. RC	**1.00**
387 Dennis Vaske, NYIs.	.20
388 David Volek, NYIs.	.20
389 Jeff Beukeboom, NYRa.	.20
390 Glenn Healy (G), NYRa.	.20
391 Alexander Karpovtsev, NYRa.	.20
392 Steve Larmer, NYRa.	.20
393 Kevin Lowe, NYRa.	.20
394 Ed Olczyk, NYRa.	.20
395 Esa Tikkanen, NYRa.	.20
396 Alexandre Daigle, Otta.	.20
397 Evgeny Davydov, Otta.	.20
398 Dmitri Filimonov, Otta.	.20
399 Brian Glynn, Otta.	.20
400 Darrin Madeley (G), Otta. RC	**1.00**

□ 401 Troy Mallette, Otta. .20
□ 402 Dave McLlwain, Otta. .20
□ 403 Alexei Yashin, Otta. .50
□ **404 Jason Bowen, Phil. RC .50**
□ 405 Jeff Finley, Phil. .20
□ 406 Yves Racine, Phil. .20
□ 407 Rob Ramage, Phil. .20
□ 408 Mikael Renberg, Phil. .20
□ 409 Dominic Roussel (G), Phil. .20
□ 410 Dave Tippett, Phil. .20
□ 411 Doug Brown, Pitt. .20
□ 412 Markus Näslund, Pitt. 1.50
□ **413 Pat Neaton, Pitt. RC .50**
□ 414 Kjell Samuelsson, Pitt. .20
□ 415 Martin Straka, Pitt. .20
□ 416 Bryan Trottier, Pitt. .50
□ 417 Ken Wregget (G), Pitt. .20
□ 418 Adam Foote, Québ. .20
□ **419 Iain Fraser, Québ. RC .50**
□ 420 Alexei Gusarov, Québ. .20
□ 421 Dave Karpa, Québ. .20
□ 422 Claude Lapointe, Québ. .20
□ 423 Curtis Leschyshyn, Québ. .20
□ **424 Mike McKee, Québ. RC .50**
□ **425 Garth Snow (G), Québ. RC 2.00**
□ **426 Jocelyn Thibault (G), Québ. RC 2.50**
□ 427 Phil Housley, SLou. .20
□ 428 Jim Hrivnak (G), SLou. .20
□ 429 Vitali Karamnov, SLou. .20
□ 430 Basil McRae, SLou. .20
□ **431 Jim Montgomery, SLou. RC .50**
□ 432 Vitali Prokhorov, SLou. .20
□ 433 Gaétan Duchesne, SanJ. .20
□ 434 Todd Elik, SanJ. .20
□ 435 Bob Errey, SanJ. .20
□ 436 Igor Larionov, SanJ. .20
□ 437 Mike Rathje, SanJ. .20
□ 438 Jimmy Waite (G), SanJ. .20
□ 439 Ray Whitney, SanJ. .20
□ 440 Mikael Andersson, Tamp. .20
□ 441 Danton Cole, Tamp. .20
□ 442 Pat Elynuik, Tamp. .20
□ 443 Chris Gratton, Tamp. .20
□ 444 Pat Jablonski (G), Tamp. .20
□ 445 Chris Joseph, Tamp. .20
□ **446 Chris LiPuma, Tamp. RC .50**
□ 447 Denis Savard, Tamp. .20
□ 448 Ken Baumgartner, Toro. .20
□ 449 Todd Gill, Toro. .20
□ 450 Sylvain Lefebvre, Toro. .20
□ 451 Jamie Macoun, Toro. .20
□ 452 Mark Osborne, Toro. .20
□ 453 Rob Pearson, Toro. .20
□ **454 Damian Rhodes (G), Toro. RC 1.50**
□ 455 Peter Zezel, Toro. .20
□ 456 Dave Babych, Vanc. .20
□ **457 José Charbonneau, Vanc. RC .50**
□ 458 Murray Craven, Vanc. .20
□ **459 Neil Eisenhut, Vanc. RC .50**
□ **460 Dan Kesa, Vanc. RC .50**
□ 461 Gino Odjick, Vanc. .20
□ 462 Kay Whitmore (G), Vanc. .20
□ 463 Don Beaupré (G), Wash. .20
□ 464 Randy Burridge, Wash. .20
□ 465 Calle Johansson, Wash. .20
□ 466 Keith Jones, Wash. .20
□ 467 Todd Krygier, Wash. .20
□ 468 Kelly Miller, Wash. .20
□ 469 Pat Peake, Wash. .20
□ 470 Dave Poulin, Wash. .20
□ 471 Luciano Borsato, Winn. .20
□ 472 Nelson Emerson, Winn. .20
□ 473 Randy Gilhen, Winn. .20
□ 474 Boris Mironov, Winn. .20
□ 475 Stéphane Quintal, Winn. .20
□ 476 Thomas Steen, Winn. .20
□ 477 Igor Ulanov, Winn. .20
□ **478 Adrian Aucoin, Canada Nationals RC 1.00**
□ **479 Todd Brost, Canada Nationals RC .50**
□ **480 Martin Gendron, Canada Nationals RC .50**
□ 481 David Harlock, Canada Nationals .20
□ 482 Corey Hirsch (G), Canada Nationals .20
□ **483 Todd Hlushko, Canada Nationals RC .50**
□ 484 Fabian Joseph, Canada Nationals .20
□ 485 Paul Kariya, Canada Nationals 2.50
□ **486 Brett Lindros, Canada Nationals RC 2.00**
□ **487 Ken Lovsin, Canada Nationals RC .50**
□ 488 Jason Marshall, Canada Nationals .20
□ **489 Derek Mayer, Canada Nationals RC .50**
□ 490 Petr Nedved, Canada Nationals .20
□ **491 Dwayne Norris, Canada Nationals RC .50**
□ 492 Russ Romaniuk, Canada Nationals .20
□ **493 Brian Savage, Canada Nationals RC 2.00**
□ **494 Trevor Sim, Canada Nationals RC .50**
□ **495 Chris Therien, Canada Nationals RC .50**
□ **496 Todd Warriner, Canada Nationals RC 1.00**
□ **497 Craig Woodcroft, Canada Nationals RC .50**
□ **498 Mark Beaufait, U.S.A. Nationals RC .50**
□ 499 Jim Campbell, U.S.A. Nationals .20
□ **500 Ted Crowley, U.S.A. Nationals RC .50**
□ 501 Mike Dunham (G), U.S.A. Nationals .50
□ **502 Chris Ferraro, U.S.A. Nationals RC 1.00**
□ 503 Peter Ferraro, U.S.A. Nationals .20
□ **504 Brett Hauer, U.S.A. Nationals RC .50**
□ **505 D. Hendrickson, U.S.A. Nationals RC 1.00**
□ **506 Chris Imes, U.S.A. Nationals RC .50**
□ **507 Craig Johnson, U.S.A. Nationals RC .50**
□ **508 Peter Laviolette, U.S.A. Nationals RC 2.50**
□ 509 Jeff Lazaro, U.S.A. Nationals .20
□ **510 John Lilley, U.S.A. Nationals RC .50**
□ 511 Todd Marchant, U.S.A. Nationals .20
□ **512 Ian Moran, U.S.A. Nationals RC .50**
□ **513 Travis Richards, U.S.A. Nationals RC .50**
□ **514 Barry Richter, U.S.A. Nationals RC .50**
□ **515 David Roberts, U.S.A. Nationals RC .50**
□ 516 Brian Rolston, U.S.A. Nationals .20
□ **517 David Sacco, U.S.A. Nationals RC .50**
□ 518 Checklist .20
□ 519 Checklist .20
□ 520 Checklist .20

2ND YEAR STARS

Series One Insert Set (12 cards): 6.00
Insert (1:3) SYS

□ 1 Rob Gaudreau, SanJ. .35
□ 2 Joé Juneau, Bost. .35
□ 3 Darius Kasparaitis, NYIs. .35
□ 4 Dmitri Kvartalnov, Bost. .35
□ 5 Eric Lindros, Phil. 2.00
□ 6 Vladimir Malakhov, NYIs. .35
□ 7 Shawn McEachern, Pitt. (LosA.) .35
□ 8 Félix Potvin (G), Toro. 1.00
□ 9 Patrick Poulin, Hart. .35
□ 10 Teemu Selänne, Winn. 1.00
□ 11 Tommy Söderström (G), Phil. .35
□ 12 Alexei Zhamnov, Winn. .35

GAMEBREAKERS

Series Two Insert Set (10 cards): 15.00
Insert (1:4) GB

□ 1 Sergei Fedorov, Detr. 1.00
□ 2 Doug Gilmour, Toro. .75
□ 3 Wayne Gretzky, LosA. 6.00
□ 4 Curtis Joseph (G), SLou. 1.00
□ 5 Mario Lemieux, Pitt. 4.00
□ 6 Eric Lindros, Phil. 1.00
□ 7 Félix Potvin (G), Toro. .75
□ 8 Jeremy Roenick, Chic. 1.00
□ 9 Patrick Roy (G), Mont. 4.00
□ 10 Steve Yzerman, Detr. 3.00

GLOBAL GREATS

Series Two Insert Set (10 cards): 6.00
Insert (1:4) GG

□ 1 Pavel Bure, Vanc. 1.00
□ 2 Sergei Fedorov, Detr. 1.00
□ 3 Jaromir Jagr, Pitt. 1.00
□ 4 Jari Kurri, LosA. 1.00
□ 5 Alexander Mogilny, Buff. .50
□ 6 Mikael Renberg, Phil. .50
□ 7 Teemu Selänne, Winn. 1.00
□ 8 Mats Sundin, Québ. 1.00
□ 9 Esa Tikkanen, NYRa. .50
□ 10 Alexei Yashin, Otta. .50

NETMINDERS

Series One Insert Set (8 cards): 45.00
Insert (1:8) NM

□ 1 Tom Barrasso (G), Pitt. 3.00
□ 2 Ed Belfour (G), Chic. 5.00
□ 3 Grant Fuhr (G), Buff. 5.00
□ 4 Curtis Joseph (G), SLou. 5.00
□ 5 Félix Potvin (G), Toro. 5.00
□ 6 Bill Ranford (G), Edmo. 3.00
□ 7 Patrick Roy (G), Mont. 25.00
□ 8 Tommy Söderström (G), Phil. 3.00

POINT LEADERS

Series One Insert Set (20 cards): 20.00
Insert (1:2) PL

□ 1 Pavel Bure, Vanc. 1.00
□ 2 Doug Gilmour, Toro. .50
□ 3 Wayne Gretzky, LosA. 6.00
□ 4 Brett Hull, SLou. 1.00
□ 5 Jaromir Jagr, Pitt. 1.00
□ 6 Joé Juneau, Bost. .50
□ 7 Pat LaFontaine, Buff. .50
□ 8 Mario Lemieux, Pitt. 4.00
□ 9 Mark Messier, NYRa. 1.00
□ 10 Alexander Mogilny, Buff. .50
□ 11 Adam Oates, Bost. .50
□ 12 Mark Recchi, Phil. .50
□ 13 Luc Robitaille, LosA. 1.00
□ 14 Jeremy Roenick, Chic. 1.00
□ 15 Joe Sakic, Québ. 2.00
□ 16 Teemu Selänne, Winn. 1.00
□ 17 Kevin Stevens, Pitt. .50
□ 18 Mats Sundin, Québ. 1.00
□ 19 Pierre Turgeon, NYIs. .50
□ 20 Steve Yzerman, Detr. 3.00

RISING STARS

Series Two Insert Set (10 cards): 5.00
Insert (1:10) RisS

□ 1 Arturs Irbe (G), SanJ. 1.00
□ 2 Vyacheslav Kozlov, Detr. .75
□ 3 Félix Potvin (G), Toro. 2.00
□ 4 Keith Primeau, Detr. 1.00
□ 5 Robert Reichel, Calg. 1.00
□ 6 Geoff Sanderson, Hart. .75
□ 7 Martin Straka, Pitt. 1.00
□ 8 Keith Tkachuk, Winn. 2.00
□ 9 Alexei Zhamnov, Winn. 1.00
□ 10 Sergei Zubov, NYRa. .75

ROOKIE STANDOUTS

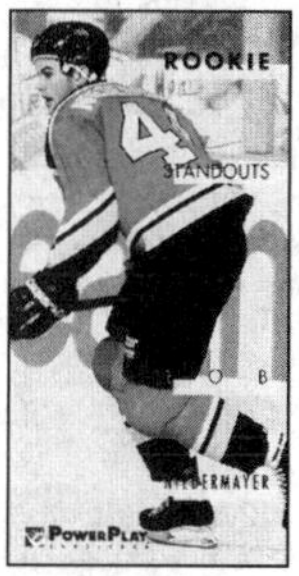

Series Two Insert Set (16 cards): 9.00
Insert (1:5) RooS

□ 1 Jason Arnott, Edmo. 2.00
□ 2 Jesse Bélanger, Flor. .35
□ 3 Alexandre Daigle, Otta. .35
□ 4 Iain Fraser, Québ. .35
□ 5 Chris Gratton, Tamp. .35
□ 6 Boris Mironov, Winn. .35
□ 7 Jaroslav Modry, NJer. .35
□ 8 Rob Niedermayer, Flor. .35
□ 9 Chris Osgood (G), Detr. 2.00
□ 10 Pat Peake, Wash. .35
□ 11 Derek Plante, Buff. .35
□ 12 Chris Pronger, Hart. 1.00
□ 13 Mikael Renberg, Phil. .35
□ 14 Bryan Smolinski, Bost. .35
□ 15 Jocelyn Thibault (G), Québ. 1.00
□ 16 Alexei Yashin, Otta. 1.00

SLAPSHOT ARTIST

Series Two Insert Set (10 cards): 20.00
Insert (1:10) SA

□ 1 Dave Andreychuk, Toro. 1.00
□ 2 Raymond Bourque, Bost. 4.00
□ 3 Sergei Fedorov, Detr. 3.00
□ 4 Brett Hull, SLou. 3.00
□ 5 Al Iafrate, Wash. 1.00
□ 6 Brian Leetch, NYRa. 2.00
□ 7 Al MacInnis, Calg. 1.00
□ 8 Mike Modano, Dall. 3.00
□ 9 Teemu Selänne, Winn. 3.00
□ 10 Brendan Shanahan, SLou. 3.00

1993 - 94 PREMIER

There are four versions to this series: an O-Pee-Chee card, a Topps card, an O-Pee-Chee Gold parallel and a Topps Gold parallel. O-Pee-Chee and Topps base cards have the same value. TheO-Pee-Chee vartiations were sold in Canada while the Topps variations were sold in the United States.

	OG	TG	Prmr
Complete Set (528 cards):	**200.00**	**150.00**	**30.00**
9-card Promo Sheet:	**-**	**-**	**6.00**
Common Player:	**.40**	**.30**	**.20**
Player	**OG**	**TG**	**Prmr**
□□□□1 Patrick Roy (G), Mont.	10.00	7.00	1.50
□□□□2 Alexei Zhitnik, LosA.	.40	.30	.20
□□□□3 Uwe Krupp, NYIs.	.40	.30	.20
□□□□4 Todd Gill, Toro.	.40	.30	.20
□□□□5 Paul Stanton, Pitt.	.40	.30	.20
□□□□6 Petr Nedved, Vanc.	1.00	.30	.20
□□□□7 Dale Hawerchuk, Buff.	2.00	1.00	.20
□□□□8 Kevin Miller, SLou.	.40	.30	.20
□□□□9 Nicklas Lidström, Detr.	2.00	1.00	.20
□□□□10 Joe Sakic, Québ.	6.00	4.00	.50
□□□□11 Thomas Steen, Winn.	.40	.30	.20
□□□□12 Peter Bondra, Wash.	2.00	1.00	.20
□□□□13 Brian Noonan, Chic.	.40	.30	.20
□□□□14 Glen Featherstone, Bost.	.40	.30	.20
□□□□15 Mike Vernon (G), Calg.	1.00	1.00	.20
□□□□16 Janne Ojanen, NJer.	.40	.30	.20
□□□□17 Neil Brady, Otta.	.40	.30	.20
□□□□18 Dmitry Yushkevich, Phil.	.40	.30	.20
□□□□19 Rob Zamuner, Tamp.	.40	.30	.20
□□□□20 Zarley Zalapski, Hart.	.40	.30	.20
□□□□21 Mike Sullivan, SanJ.	.40	.30	.20
□□□□22 Jamie Baker, Otta.	.40	.30	.20
□□□□23 Craig MacTavish, Edmo.	.40	.30	.20
□□□□24 Mark Tinordi, Minn. (Dall.)	.40	.30	.20
□□□□25 Brian Leetch, NYRa.	2.00	1.00	.20
□□□□26 Brian Skrudland, Flor.	.40	.30	.20
□□□□27 Keith Tkachuk, Winn.	2.00	1.00	.20
□□□□28 Patrick Flatley, NYIs.	.40	.30	.20
□□□□29 Doug Bodger, Buff.	.40	.30	.20
□□□□30 Félix Potvin (G), Toro.	2.00	1.00	.20
□□□□31 Shawn Antoski, Vanc.	.40	.30	.20
□□□□32 Éric Desjardins, Mont.	1.00	.30	.20
□□□□33 Mike Donnelly, LosA.	.40	.30	.20
□□□□34 Kjell Samuelsson, Pitt.	.40	.30	.20
□□□□35 Nelson Emerson, SLou.	.40	.30	.20
□□□□36 Phil Housley, Winn.	1.00	.30	.20
□□□□37 LL: Mario Lemieux, Pitt.	10.00	7.00	1.50
□□□□38 Shayne Corson, Edmo.	1.00	.30	.20
□□□□39 J. Steve Smith, Chic.	.40	.30	.20
□□□□40 Bob Kudelski, Otta.	.40	.30	.20
□□□□41 Joe Cirella, Flor.	.40	.30	.20
□□□□42 Sergei Nemchinov, NYRa.	.40	.30	.20
□□□□43 Kerry Huffman, Québ.	.40	.30	.20
□□□□44 Bob Beers, Tamp.	.40	.30	.20
□□□□45 Al Iafrate, Wash.	.40	.30	.20
□□□□46 M. Modano, Minn. (Dall.)	3.00	2.00	.50
□□□□47 Pat Verbeek, Hart.	1.00	.30	.20
□□□□48 Joel Otto, Calg.	.40	.30	.20
□□□□49 Dino Ciccarelli, Detr.	1.00	.30	.20
□□□□50 Adam Oates, Bost.	1.00	1.00	.20
□□□□51 Pat Elynuik, Wash.	.40	.30	.20
□□□□52 Bobby Holik, NJer.	1.00	.30	.20
□□□□53 Johan Garpenlöv, SanJ.	.40	.30	.20
□□□□54 Jeff Beukeboom, NYRa.	.40	.30	.20
□□□□55 T. Söderström (G), Phil.	.40	.30	.20
□□□□56 Rob Blake, LosA.	2.00	1.00	.20
□□□□57 Marty McInnis, NYIs.	.40	.30	.20
□□□□58 Dixon Ward, Vanc.	.40	.30	.20
□□□□59 Patrice Brisebois, Mont.	.40	.30	.20
□□□□60 Ed Belfour (G), Chic.	3.00	2.00	.50
□□□□61 Donald Audette, Buff.	1.00	1.00	.20
□□□□62 Mike Ricci, Québ.	1.00	.30	.20
□□□□63 Fredrik Olausson, Winn.	.40	.30	.20
□□□□64 Norm Maciver, Otta.	.40	.30	.20
□□□□65 Andrew Cassels, Hart.	.40	.30	.20
□□□□66 Tim Cheveldae (G), Detr.	.40	.30	.20
□□□□67 David Reid, Bost.	.40	.30	.20
□□□□68 Philippe Bozon, SLou.	.40	.30	.20
□□□□69 Drake Berehowsky, Toro.	.40	.30	.20
□□□□70 Tony Amonte, NYRa.	2.00	1.00	.20
□□□□71 Dave Manson, Edmo.	.40	.30	.20
□□□□72 Rick Tocchet, Pitt.	1.00	.30	.20
□□□□73 Steve Kasper, Tamp.	.40	.30	.20
□□□□74 LL: Adam Oates, Bost.	1.00	1.00	.20
□□□□75 Ulf Dahlén, Minn. (Dall.)	.40	.30	.20
□□□□76 Chris Lindberg, Calg.	.40	.30	.20
□□□□77 Doug Wilson, SanJ.	1.00	.30	.20
□□□□78 Mike Ridley, Wash.	.40	.30	.20
□□□□79 Viacheslav Butsayev, Phil.	.40	.30	.20
□□□□80 Scott Stevens, NJer.	1.00	1.00	.20
□□□□81 Cliff Ronning, Vanc.	.40	.30	.20
□□□□82 Andrei Lomakin, Flor.	.40	.30	.20
□□□□83 Shawn Burr, Detr.	.40	.30	.20
□□□□84 Benoît Brunet, Mont.	.40	.30	.20
□□□□85 Valeri Kamensky, Québ.	1.00	.30	.20
□□□□86 Randy Carlyle, Winn.	.40	.30	.20
□□□□87 Chris Joseph, Edmo.	.40	.30	.20
□□□□88 Dirk Graham, Chic.	.40	.30	.20
□□□□89 Ken Sutton, Buff.	.40	.30	.20
□□□□90 AS: Luc Robitaille, LosA.	3.00	2.00	.20
□□□□91 AS: Mario Lemieux, Pitt.	10.00	7.00	1.50
□□□□92 AS: Teemu Selänne, Winn.	3.00	2.00	.20
□□□□93 AS: R. Bourque, Bost.	4.00	3.00	.50
□□□□94 AS: Chris Chelios, Chic.	2.00	1.00	.20

□□□□95 AS: Ed Belfour (G), Chic. 3.00 2.00 .50
□□□□96 Keith Jones, Wash. .40 .30 .20
□□□□97 Sylvain Turgeon, Otta. .40 .30 .20
□□□□98 Jim* Johnson, Minn. (Dall.) .40 .30 .20
□□□□99 Michael Nylander, Hart. .40 .30 .20
□□□□100 Theoren Fleury, Calg. 2.00 1.00 .20
□□□□101 S. Chambers, Tamp. .40 .30 .20
□□□□102 Alexander Semak, NJer. .40 .30 .20
□□□□103 Ron Sutter, SLou. .40 .30 .20
□□□□104 Glenn Anderson, Toro. 1.00 .30 .20
□□□□105 Jaromir Jagr, Pitt. 3.00 2.00 .50
□□□□106 Adam Graves, NYRa. 1.00 1.00 .20
□□□□107 N. Borschevsky, Toro. .40 .30 .20
□□□□108 V. Konstantinov, Detr. 1.00 .30 .20
□□□□109 Robb Stauber (G), LosA. .40 .30 .20
□□□□110 Arturs Irbe (G), SanJ. 2.00 1.00 .20
□□□□111 LL: F. Potvin (G), Toro. 2.00 1.00 .20
□□□□112 Darius Kasparaitis, NYIs. .40 .30 .20
□□□□113 Kirk McLean (G), Vanc. 1.00 1.00 .20
□□□□114 Glen Wesley, Bost. .40 .30 .20
□□□□115 Rod Brind'Amour, Phil. 1.00 .30 .20
□□□□116 Mike Eagles, Winn. .40 .30 .20
□□□□117 Brian Bradley, Tamp. .40 .30 .20
□□□□118 Dave Christian, Chic. .40 .30 .20
□□□□119 Randy Wood, Buff. .40 .30 .20
□□□□120 Craig Janney, SLou. .40 .30 .20
□□□□121 SR: Eric Lindros, Phil. 3.00 2.00 .50
□□□□122 SR: Söderström (G), Phil. .40 .30 .20
□□□□123 SR: S. McEachern, Pitt. 1.00 .30 .20
□□□□124 SR: Kovalenko, Québ. .40 .30 .20
□□□□125 SR: Joé Juneau, Bost. .40 .30 .20
□□□□126 SR: F. Potvin (G), Toro. 2.00 1.00 .20
□□□□127 SR: Dixon Ward, Vanc. .40 .30 .20
□□□□128 SR: A. Zhamnov, Winn. 1.00 .30 .20
□□□□129 SR: V. Malakhov, NYIs. .40 .30 .20
□□□□130 SR: Selänne, Winn. 3.00 2.00 .20
□□□□131 Neal Broten, Minn. (Dall.) .40 .30 .20
□□□□132 Ulf Samuelsson, Pitt. .40 .30 .20
□□□□133 Mark Janssens, Hart. .40 .30 .20
□□□□134 Claude Lemieux, NJer. 1.00 .30 .20
□□□□135 Mike Richter (G), NYRa. 1.00 1.00 .20
□□□□136 Doug Weight, Edmo. 2.00 1.00 .20
□□□□137 Rob Pearson, Toro. .40 .30 .20
□□□□138 Côté, Wash. [vs. J.Jagr] .40 .30 .20
□□□□139 Mike Keane, Mont. .40 .30 .20
□□□□140 Benoît Hogue, NYIs. .40 .30 .20
□□□□141 Michel Petit, Calg. .40 .30 .20
□□□□142 Mark Freer, Otta. .40 .30 .20
□□□□143 Doug Zmolek, SanJ. .40 .30 .20
□□□□144 Tony Granato, LosA. .40 .30 .20
□□□□145 Paul Coffey, Detr. 2.00 1.00 .20
□□□□146 Ted Donato, Bost. .40 .30 .20
□□□□147 Brent Sutter, Chic. .40 .30 .20
□□□□148 League leaders 2.00 1.00 .20
□□□□149 James Patrick, NYRa. .40 .30 .20
□□□□150 Mikael Andersson, Tamp. .40 .30 .20
□□□□151 Steve Duchesne, Québ. .40 .30 .20
□□□□152 Terry Carkner, Phil. .40 .30 .20
□□□□153 R. Courtnall, Minn. (Dall.) .40 .30 .20
□□□□154 Brian Mullen, NYIs. .40 .30 .20
□□□□155 Martin Straka, Pitt. 1.00 .30 .20
□□□□156 Geoff Sanderson, Hart. .40 .30 .20
□□□□157 Mark Howe, Detr. 1.00 .30 .20
□□□□158 Stéphane Richer, NJer. .40 .30 .20
□□□□159 Doug Crossman, SLou. .40 .30 .20
□□□□160 Vanbiesbrouck (G), Flor. 1.00 1.00 .20
□□□□161 Bob Essensa (G), Winn. .40 .30 .20
□□□□162 Wayne Presley, Buff. .40 .30 .20
□□□□163 Mathieu Schneider, Mont. .40 .30 .20
□□□□164 Jirí Slégr, Vanc. .40 .30 .20
□□□□165 S. Fiset (G), Québ. 1.00 .30 .20
□□□□166 W. Young (G), Tamp. .40 .30 .20
□□□□167 Kevin Dineen, Phil. .40 .30 .20
□□□□168 Sandis Ozolinsh, SanJ. .40 .30 .20
□□□□169 Mike Krushelnyski, Toro. .40 .30 .20
□□□□170 AS: Kevin Stevens, Pitt. .40 .30 .20
□□□□171 AS: LaFontaine, Buff. 2.00 1.00 .20
□□□□172 AS: A. Mogilny, Buff. 1.00 1.00 .20
□□□□173 AS: Larry Murphy, Pitt. .40 .30 .20
□□□□174 AS: Al Iafrate, Wash. .40 .30 .20
□□□□175 AS: Barrasso (G), Pitt. 1.00 1.00 .20
□□□□176 Derek King, NYIs. .40 .30 .20
□□□□177 Bob Probert, Detr. 1.00 .30 .20
□□□□178 Gary Suter, Calg. .40 .30 .20
□□□□179 David Shaw, Bost. .40 .30 .20
□□□□180 Luc Robitaille, LosA. 3.00 2.00 .20
□□□□181 John LeClair, Mont. 3.00 2.00 .20
□□□□182 Troy Murray, Chic. .40 .30 .20
□□□□183 D. Gagner, Minn. (Dall.) .40 .30 .20
□□□□184 Darcy Loewen, Otta. .40 .30 .20
□□□□185 LL: M. Lemieux, Pitt. 10.00 7.00 1.50
□□□□186 Pat Jablonski (G), Tamp. .40 .30 .20
□□□□187 Alex Kovalev, NYRa. 2.00 1.00 .20
□□□□188 Todd Krygier, Wash. .40 .30 .20
□□□□189 Larry Murphy, Pitt. .40 .30 .20

□□□□190 Pierre Turgeon, NYIs. 1.00 1.00 .20
□□□□191 C. Ludwig, Minn. (Dall.) .40 .30 .20
□□□□192 Brad May, Buff. .40 .30 .20
□□□□193 John MacLean, NJer. .40 .30 .20
□□□□194 Ron L. Wilson, SLou. .40 .30 .20
□□□□195 Eric Weinrich, Hart. .40 .30 .20
□□□□196 Steve Chiasson, Detr. .40 .30 .20
□□□□197 Dmitri Kvartalnov, Bost. .40 .30 .20
□□□□198 Andrei Kovalenko, Québ. .40 .30 .20
□□□□**199 Gaudreau, SanJ. RC 1.00 1.00 .50**
□□□□200 Evgeny Davydov, Winn. .40 .30 .20
□□□□201 Adrien Plavsic, Vanc. .40 .30 .20
□□□□202 Brian Bellows, Mont. .40 .30 .20
□□□□203 Doug Evans, Phil. .40 .30 .20
□□□□204 LL: Barrasso (G), Pitt. 1.00 1.00 .20
□□□□205 Joe Nieuwendyk, Calg. 1.00 1.00 .20
□□□□206 Jari Kurri, LosA. 3.00 2.00 .50
□□□□207 Bob Rouse, Toro. .40 .30 .20
□□□□208 Yvon Corriveau, Hart. .40 .30 .20
□□□□209 John Blue (G), Bost. .40 .30 .20
□□□□210 Dmitri Khristich, Wash. .40 .30 .20
□□□□211 Brent Fedyk, Phil. .40 .30 .20
□□□□212 Jody Hull, Otta. .40 .30 .20
□□□□213 Chris Terreri (G), NJer. .40 .30 .20
□□□□214 M. McPhee, Minn. (Dall.) .40 .30 .20
□□□□215 Chris Kontos, Tamp. .40 .30 .20
□□□□216 Greg Gilbert, Chic. .40 .30 .20
□□□□217 Sergei Zubov, NYRa. .40 .30 .20
□□□□218 Grant Fuhr (G), Buff. 2.00 1.00 .20
□□□□219 Charlie Huddy, LosA. .40 .30 .20
□□□□220 Mario Lemieux, Pitt. 10.00 7.00 1.50
□□□□221 Sheldon Kennedy, Detr. .40 .30 .20
□□□□222 LL: Joseph (G), SLou. 3.00 2.00 .50
□□□□223 Brad Dalgarno, NYIs. .40 .30 .20
□□□□224 Bret Hedican, SLou. .40 .30 .20
□□□□225 Trevor Linden, Vanc. 1.00 1.00 .20
□□□□226 Darryl Sydor, LosA. .40 .30 .20
□□□□227 Jayson More, SanJ. .40 .30 .20
□□□□228 Dave Poulin, Bost. .40 .30 .20
□□□□229 Frantisek Musil, Calg. .40 .30 .20
□□□□230 Mark Recchi, Phil. 1.00 1.00 .20
□□□□231 Craig Simpson, Edmo. .40 .30 .20
□□□□232 Gino Cavallini, Québ. .40 .30 .20
□□□□233 Damphousse, Mont. 2.00 1.00 .20
□□□□234 Luciano Borsato, Winn. .40 .30 .20
□□□□235 Dave Andreychuk, Toro. 1.00 .30 .20
□□□□236 Ken Daneyko, NJer. .40 .30 .20
□□□□237 Chris Chelios, Chic. 2.00 1.00 .20
□□□□238 Andrew McBain, Otta. .40 .30 .20
□□□□239 Rick Tabaracci (G), Wash. .40 .30 .20
□□□□240 Steve Larmer, Chic. 1.00 1.00 .20
□□□□241 Sean Burke (G), Hart. 2.00 1.00 .20
□□□□242 Rob DiMaio, Tamp. .40 .30 .20
□□□□243 Jim Paek, Pitt. .40 .30 .20
□□□□244 Dave Lowry, Flor. .40 .30 .20
□□□□245 Alexander Mogilny, Buff. 1.00 1.00 .20
□□□□246 Darren Turcotte, NYRa. .40 .30 .20
□□□□247 B. Shanahan, SLou. 3.00 2.00 .50
□□□□248 Peter Taglianetti, Pitt. .40 .30 .20
□□□□249 Scott Mellanby, Flor. .40 .30 .20
□□□□250 Guy Carbonneau, Mont. 1.00 .30 .20
□□□□251 Claude Lapointe, Québ. .40 .30 .20
□□□□252 Pat Conacher, LosA. .40 .30 .20
□□□□253 Roger Johansson, Calg. .40 .30 .20
□□□□254 Cam Neely, Bost. 3.00 2.00 .50
□□□□255 Garry Galley, Phil. .40 .30 .20
□□□□256 Keith Primeau, Detr. 1.00 1.00 .20
□□□□257 Scott Lachance, NYIs. .40 .30 .20
□□□□258 Bill Ranford (G), Edmo. 1.00 1.00 .20
□□□□259 Pat Falloon, SanJ. .40 .30 .20
□□□□260 Pavel Bure, Vanc. 3.00 2.00 .20
□□□□261 Darrin Shannon, Winn. .40 .30 .20
□□□□262 Mike Foligno, Toro. .40 .30 .20
□□ 263 Checklist .40 .30 .20
□□ 264 Checklist .40 .30 .20
□□□□265 Peter Douris, Anah. .40 .30 .20
□□□□266 Warren Rychel, LosA. .40 .30 .20
□□□□267 Owen Nolan, Québ. 2.00 1.00 .20
□□□□268 Mark Osborne, Toro. .40 .30 .20
□□□□269 Teppo Numminen, Winn. 1.00 .30 .20
□□□□270 Rob Niedermayer, Flor. 1.00 1.00 .20
□□□□271 Mark Lamb, Otta. .40 .30 .20
□□□□272 Curtis Joseph (G), SLou. 3.00 2.00 .50
□□□□273 Joe Murphy, Chic. .40 .30 .20
□□□□274 Bernie Nicholls, NJer. .40 .30 .20
□□□□275 Gord** Roberts, Bost. 1.00 1.00 .20
□□□□276 Al MacInnis, Calg. 1.00 1.00 .20
□□□□277 Ken Wregget (G), Pitt. 1.00 .30 .20
□□□□278 Calle Johansson, Wash. .40 .30 .20
□□□□279 Tom Kurvers, NYIs. .40 .30 .20
□□□□280 Steve Yzerman, Detr. 9.00 6.00 1.00
□□□□281 Roman Hamrlik, Tamp. .40 .30 .20
□□□□282 Esa Tikkanen, NYRa. .40 .30 .20
□□□□**283 Madeley (G), Otta. RC 3.00 2.00 .50**
□□□□284 Robert Dirk, Vanc. .40 .30 .20

□□□□**285 Derek Plante, Buff. RC 3.00 2.00 .50**
□□□□286 Ron Tugnutt (G), Anah. 1.00 1.00 .20
□□□□287 Pietrangelo (G), Hart. .40 .30 .20
□□□□288 Paul DiPietro, Mont. .40 .30 .20
□□□□289 A. Godynyuk, Flor. .40 .30 .20
□□□□**290 K. Maltby, Edmo. RC 4.00 3.00 1.00**
□□□□291 Olaf Kölzig (G), Wash. 3.00 2.00 .20
□□□□292 Vitali Karamnov, SLou. .40 .30 .20
□□□□293 Alexei Gusarov, Québ. .40 .30 .20
□□□□294 Bryan Erickson, Winn. .40 .30 .20
□□□□295 Jocelyn Lemieux, Chic. .40 .30 .20
□□□□296 Bryan Trottier, Pitt. 3.00 2.00 .50
□□□□297 Dave Ellett, Toro. .40 .30 .20
□□□□298 Tim Watters, LosA. .40 .30 .20
□□□□299 Joé Juneau, Bost. .40 .30 .20
□□□□300 Steve Thomas, NYIs. .40 .30 .20
□□□□301 Mark Greig, Hart. .40 .30 .20
□□□□302 Jeff Reese (G), Calg. .40 .30 .20
□□□□303 Steven King, Anah. .40 .30 .20
□□□□304 Don Beaupré (G), Wash. .40 .30 .20
□□□□305 Denis Savard, Tamp. 1.00 1.00 .20
□□□□306 Greg Smyth, Flor. .40 .30 .20
□□□□**307 J. Modry, NJer. RC 1.00 1.00 .50**
□□□□308 Petr* Svoboda, Buff. .40 .30 .20
□□□□309 Mike Craig, Dall. .40 .30 .20
□□□□310 Eric Lindros, Phil. 3.00 2.00 .50
□□□□311 Dana Murzyn, Vanc. .40 .30 .20
□□□□312 Sean Hill, Anah. .40 .30 .20
□□□□313 A. Racicot (G), Mont. .40 .30 .20
□□□□314 Vanbiesbrouck (G), Flor. 1.00 1.00 .20
□□□□315 Doug Lidster, NYRa. .40 .30 .20
□□□□316 Garth Butcher, SLou. .40 .30 .20
□□□□317 Alexei Yashin, Otta. 4.00 3.00 .50
□□□□318 Sergei Fedorov, Detr. 3.00 2.00 .50
□□□□319 Louie DeBrusk, Edmo. .40 .30 .20
□□□□320 Hasek (G), Buff. [CSR.] 3.00 2.00 .50
□□□□321 Pivonka, Wash. [CSR.] .40 .30 .20
□□□□322 Holik, NJer. [CSR.] 1.00 .30 .20
□□□□323 Hamrlik, Tamp. [CSR.] .40 .30 .20
□□□□324 Svoboda, Buff. [CSR.] .40 .30 .20
□□□□325 Jagr, Pitt. [CSR.] 3.00 2.00 .50
□□□□326 Steven Finn, Québ. .40 .30 .20
□□□□**327 S.J.G. Richer, Flor. RC 1.00 1.00 .50**
□□□□328 Claude Loiselle, NYIs. .40 .30 .20
□□□□329 Joe Sacco, Anah. .40 .30 .20
□□□□330 Wayne Gretzky, LosA. 15.00 10.00 2.00
□□□□331 Sylvain Lefebvre, Toro. .40 .30 .20
□□□□332 Sergei Bautin, Winn. .40 .30 .20
□□□□333 Craig Simpson, Buff. .40 .30 .20
□□□□334 Don Sweeney, Bost. .40 .30 .20
□□□□335 D. Roussel (G), Phil. .40 .30 .20
□□□□**336 S. Thomas, Buff. RC 1.00 1.00 .50**
□□□□337 Geoff Courtnall, Vanc. .40 .30 .20
□□□□338 Tom Fitzgerald, Flor. .40 .30 .20
□□□□339 Kevin Haller, Mont. .40 .30 .20
□□□□340 Troy Loney, Anah. .40 .30 .20
□□□□341 Ronnie Stern, Calg. .40 .30 .20
□□□□**342 Mark Astley, Buff. RC 1.00 1.00 .50**
□□□□343 Jeff Daniels, Pitt. .40 .30 .20
□□□□344 Marc Bureau, Tamp. .40 .30 .20
□□□□**345 M. Aivazoff, Detr. RC 1.00 1.00 .50**
□□□□346 Matthew Barnaby, Buff. .40 .30 .20
□□□□347 C.J. Young, Flor. .40 .30 .20
□□□□348 Dale Craigwell, SanJ. .40 .30 .20
□□□□349 Ray Ferraro, NYIs. .40 .30 .20
□□□□350 R. Bourque, Bost. 4.00 3.00 .50
□□□□351 Stu Barnes, Winn. .40 .30 .20
□□□□352 Allan Conroy, Phil. RC 1.00 1.00 .20
□□□□353 S. McEachern, LosA. 1.00 .30 .20
□□□□354 Garry Valk, Anah. .40 .30 .20
□□□□355 Christian Ruuttu, Chic. .40 .30 .20
□□□□356 Darren Rumble, Otta. .40 .30 .20
□□□□357 Stu Grimson, Anah. .40 .30 .20
□□□□358 A. Karpovtsev, NYRa. .40 .30 .20
□□□□359 Wendel Clark, Toro. 3.00 2.00 .20
□□□□360 Michal Pivonka, Wash. .40 .30 .20
□□□□**361 P. Popovic, Mont. RC 1.00 1.00 .50**
□□□□362 Kevin Dahl, Calg. .40 .30 .20
□□□□363 Jeff R. Brown, SLou. .40 .30 .20
□□□□364 D. Puppa (G), Tamp. 1.00 .30 .20
□□□□**365 D. Drake, Detr. RC 3.00 2.00 .50**
□□□□366 Dean McAmmond, Edmo. .40 .30 .20
□□□□367 Martin Rucinsky, Québ. .40 .30 .20
□□□□368 S. Churla, Minn. (Dall.) .40 .30 .20
□□□□369 Todd Ewen, Anah. .40 .30 .20
□□□□370 Kevin Stevens, Pitt. .40 .30 .20
□□□□371 David Volek, NYIs. .40 .30 .20
□□□□372 J.J. Daigneault, Mont. .40 .30 .20
□□□□373 Marc Bergevin, Tamp. .40 .30 .20
□□□□374 Craig Billington (G), Otta. .40 .30 .20
□□□□375 Mike Gartner, NYRa. 3.00 2.00 .20
□□□□376 Jimmy Carson, LosA. .40 .30 .20
□□□□377 Bruce Driver, NJer. .40 .30 .20
□□□□378 Stephen Heinze, Bost. .40 .30 .20
□□□□**379 Carnbäck, Anah. RC 1.00 1.00 .50**

□□□□380 Gretzky, LosA. [Can.] 15.00 10.00 2.00
□□□□381 Brown, SLou. [Can.] .40 .30 .20
□□□□382 Roberts, Calg. [Can.] 1.00 1.00 .20
□□□□383 Bourque, Bost. [Can.] 4.00 3.00 .50
□□□□384 Gartner, NYRa. [Can.] 3.00 2.00 .20
□□□□385 Potvin (G), Toro. [Can.] 2.00 1.00 .20
□□□□386 Michel Goulet, Chic. 1.00 1.00 .20
□□□□387 Dave Tippett, Phil. .40 .30 .20
□□□□388 Jimmy Waite (G), SanJ. .40 .30 .20
□□□□389 Yuri Khmylev, Buff. .40 .30 .20
□□□□390 Doug Gilmour, Toro. 2.00 1.00 .20
□□□□391 Brad McCrimmon, Hart. .40 .30 .20
□□□□**392 B. Severyn, Flor. RC 1.00 1.00 .50**
□□□□**393 Thibault (G), Québ. RC 7.00 5.00 2.00**
□□□□394 Boris Mironov, Winn. .40 .30 .20
□□□□395 Marty McSorley, Pitt. .40 .30 .20
□□□□396 Shaun Van Allen, Anah. .40 .30 .20
□□□□397 Gary Leeman, Mont. .40 .30 .20
□□□□398 Ed Olczyk, NYRa. .40 .30 .20
□□□□399 Wakaluk (G), Minn. (Dall.) .40 .30 .20
□□□□400 Murray Craven, Vanc. .40 .30 .20
□□□□401 M. Brodeur (G), NJer. 6.00 4.00 .50
□□□□**402 Paul Laus, Flor. RC 1.00 1.00 .50**
□□□□403 Bill Houlder, Anah. .40 .30 .20
□□□□404 Robert Reichel, Calg. 1.00 .30 .20
□□□□405 Alexandre Daigle, Otta. 1.00 .30 .20
□□□□406 Brent Thompson, LosA. .40 .30 .20
□□□□407 Keith Acton, NYIs. .40 .30 .20
□□□□408 Dave Karpa, Québ. .40 .30 .20
□□□□409 Igor Korolev, SLou. .40 .30 .20
□□□□410 Chris Gratton, Tamp. 1.00 1.00 .20
□□□□411 V. Riendeau (G), Detr. .40 .30 .20
□□□□**412 D. McCarty, Detr. RC 6.00 4.00 1.50**
□□□□413 Bob Carpenter, NJer. .40 .30 .20
□□□□414 Joe Cirella, Flor. .40 .30 .20
□□□□415 Stéphane Matteau, Chic. .40 .30 .20
□□□□416 Jozef Stumpel, Bost. .40 .30 .20
□□□□417 Richard Pilon, NYIs. .40 .30 .20
□□□□**418 Norström, NYRa. RC 4.00 3.00 1.00**
□□□□419 Dmitri Mironov, Toro. .40 .30 .20
□□□□420 Alexei Zhamnov, Winn. 1.00 .30 .20
□□□□421 Bill Guerin, NJer. 1.00 1.00 .20
□□□□422 Greg Hawgood, Phil. .40 .30 .20
□□□□423 Cunneyworth, Hart. .40 .30 .20
□□□□424 Ron Francis, Pitt. 2.00 1.00 .20
□□□□425 Brett Hull, SLou. 3.00 2.00 .50
□□□□426 Tim Sweeney, Anah. .40 .30 .20
□□□□427 Mike Rathje, SanJ. 1.00 .30 .20
□□□□428 Dave Babych, Vanc. .40 .30 .20
□□□□429 Chris Tancill, Dall. .40 .30 .20
□□□□430 Mark Messier, NYRa. 3.00 2.00 .50
□□□□431 Bob Sweeney, Buff. .40 .30 .20
□□□□432 Terry Yake, Anah. .40 .30 .20
□□□□433 Joe Reekie, Tamp. .40 .30 .20
□□□□434 Tomas Sandström, LosA. .40 .30 .20
□□□□435 Kevin Hatcher, Wash. .40 .30 .20
□□□□436 Bill Lindsay, Flor. .40 .30 .20
□□□□437 Jon Casey (G), Bost. .40 .30 .20
□□□□438 Dennis Vaske, NYIs. .40 .30 .20
□□□□439 Allen Pedersen, Hart. .40 .30 .20
□□□□440 Bure, Vanc. [Rus.] 3.00 2.00 .20
□□□□441 Fedorov, Detr. [Rus.] 3.00 2.00 .50
□□□□442 Irbe (G), SanJ. [Latv.] 2.00 1.00 .20
□□□□443 Kasparaitis, NYIs. [Lith.] .40 .30 .20
□□□□444 E. Davydov, Flor. [Rus.] .40 .30 .20
□□□□445 Malakhov, NYIs. [Rus.] .40 .30 .20
□□□□446 Tom Barrasso (G), Pitt. 1.00 1.00 .20
□□□□447 Jeff Norton, SanJ. .40 .30 .20
□□□□448 David Emma, NJer. .40 .30 .20
□□□□449 Pelle Eklund, Phil. .40 .30 .20
□□□□450 Jeremy Roenick, Chic. 3.00 2.00 .20
□□□□451 Jesse Bélanger, Flor. .40 .30 .20
□□□□452 Vitali Prokhorov, SLou. .40 .30 .20
□□□□453 Arto Blomsten, Winn. .40 .30 .20
□□□□454 Peter Zezel, Toro. .40 .30 .20
□□□□455 Kelly Kisio, Calg. .40 .30 .20
□□□□456 Zdeno Ciger, Edmo. .40 .30 .20
□□□□457 Greg Johnson, Detr. 1.00 .30 .20
□□□□458 Dave Archibald, Otta. .40 .30 .20
□□□□459 V. Vujtek, Edmo. .40 .30 .20
□□□□460 Mats Sundin, Québ. 3.00 2.00 .50
□□□□461 Dan Keczmer, Hart. 1.00 1.00 .20
□□□□462 Stéphan Lebeau, Mont. .40 .30 .20
□□□□463 D. Hasek (G), Buff. 3.00 2.00 .50
□□□□464 Kevin Lowe, NYRa. 1.00 .30 .20
□□□□465 Gord Murphy, Flor. .40 .30 .20
□□□□466 Bryan Smolinski, Bost. .40 .30 .20
□□□□467 Josef Beránek, Phil. .40 .30 .20
□□□□468 Ron Hextall (G), NYIs. 3.00 2.00 .20
□□□□469 R. Ladouceur, Anah. .40 .30 .20
□□□□470 S. Niedermayer, NJer. 1.00 .30 .20
□□□□471 K. Hrudey (G), LosA. 1.00 1.00 .20
□□□□472 Mike Needham, Pitt. .40 .30 .20
□□□□473 John Tucker, Tamp. .40 .30 .20
□□□□474 Kelly Miller, Wash. .40 .30 .20

□□□□475 Jyrki Lumme, Vanc. .40 .30 .20
□□□□476 Andy Moog (G), Dall. 1.00 1.00 .20
□□□□477 Glen Murray, Bost. 1.00 1.00 .20
□□□□**478 M. Ferner, Anah. RC 1.00 1.00 .50**
□□□□479 John Cullen, Toro. .40 .30 .20
□□□□480 Gilbert Dionne, Mont. .40 .30 .20
□□□□481 Paul Ranheim, Calg. .40 .30 .20
□□□□482 Mike Hough, Flor. .40 .30 .20
□□□□483 Teemu Selänne, Winn. 3.00 2.00 .20
□□□□**484 Aaron Ward, Detr. RC 3.00 2.00 .50**
□□□□485 Chris Pronger, Hart. 4.00 3.00 .50
□□□□486 Glenn Healy (G), NYRa. .40 .30 .20
□□□□487 C. Leschyshyn, Québ. .40 .30 .20
□□□□**488 Montgomery, SLou. RC 1.00 1.00 .50**
□□□□489 Travis Green, NYIs. .40 .30 .20
□□□□490 Pat LaFontaine, Buff. 2.00 1.00 .20
□□□□**491 B. Dollas, Anah. RC 1.00 1.00 .50**
□□□□492 Alexei Kasatonov, Anah. .40 .30 .20
□□□□493 Corey Millen, NJer. .40 .30 .20
□□□□494 Vyacheslav Kozlov, Detr. .40 .30 .20
□□□□495 Igor Kravchuk, Edmo. .40 .30 .20
□□□□496 Dmitri Filimonov, Otta. .40 .30 .20
□□□□497 Jeff Odgers, SanJ. .40 .30 .20
□□□□498 Joe Mullen, Pitt. 1.00 1.00 .20
□□□□499 Gary Shuchuk, LosA. .40 .30 .20
□□□□500 Roenick, Chic. [U.S.A.] 3.00 2.00 .20
□□□□501 Barrasso (G), Pitt. [U.S.A.] 1.00 1.00 .20
□□□□502 Tkachuk, Winn. [U.S.A.] 2.00 1.00 .20
□□□□503 Housley, SLou. [U.S.A.] 1.00 .30 .20
□□□□504 Granato, LosA. [U.S.A.] .40 .30 .20
□□□□505 Leetch, NYRa. [U.S.A.] 2.00 1.00 .20
□□□□506 Anatoli Semenov, Anah. .40 .30 .20
□□□□507 Stephen Leach, Bost. .40 .30 .20
□□□□508 Brian Skrudland, Flor. .40 .30 .20
□□□□509 Kirk Muller, Mont. 1.00 .30 .20
□□□□510 Gary Roberts, Calg. 1.00 1.00 .20
□□□□511 Gerard Gallant, Tamp. .40 .30 .20
□□□□512 Joey Kocur, NYRa. .40 .30 .20
□□□□513 Tie Domi, Winn. .40 .30 .20
□□□□514 Kay Whitmore (G), Vanc. .40 .30 .20
□□□□515 Vladimir Malakhov, NYIs. .40 .30 .20
□□□□**516 S. Malgunas, Phil. RC 1.00 1.00 .50**
□□□□517 Jamie Macoun, Toro. .40 .30 .20
□□□□518 Alan May, Wash. .40 .30 .20
□□□□519 Guy Hebert (G), Anah. 1.00 .30 .20
□□□□520 D. Hatcher, Minn. (Dall.) 1.00 .30 .20
□□□□521 Richard Smehlik, Buff. .40 .30 .20
□□□□**522 J. Messier, NYRa. RC 1.00 1.00 .50**
□□□□523 Trent Klatt, Dall. .40 .30 .20
□□□□524 Tom Chorske, NJer. .40 .30 .20
□□□□**525 Iain Fraser, Québ. RC 1.00 1.00 .50**
□□□□526 Daniel Laperrière, SLou. .40 .30 .20
□□ 527 Checklist - - .20
□□ 528 Checklist - - .20

	Gold	OG	TG	Prmr
□□	263 Martin Lapointe, Detr.	1.50	1.00	-
□□	264 Kevin Miehm, SLou.	1.00	.75	-
□□	527 Myles O'Connor, Anah.	1.00	.75	-
□□	528 Jamie Leach, Flor.	1.00	.75	-

O-PEE-CHEE / BLACK GOLD

O-Pee-Chee Insert Set (24 cards): 100.00

	Insert	OPC
□	1 Wayne Gretzky, LosA.	20.00
□	2 Vincent Damphousse, Mont.	3.00
□	3 Adam Oates, Bost.	2.00
□	4 Phil Housley, Winn.	2.00
□	5 Mike Vernon (G), Calg.	2.00
□	6 Mats Sundin, Québ.	5.00
□	7 Pavel Bure, Vanc.	4.00
□	8 Patrick Roy (G), Mont.	15.00
□	9 Tom Barrasso (G), Pitt.	2.00
□	10 Alexander Mogilny, Buff.	2.00
□	11 Doug Gilmour, Toro.	3.00
□	12 Eric Lindros, Phil.	5.00
□	13 Theoren Fleury, Calg.	3.00
□	14 Pat LaFontaine, Buff.	3.00
□	15 Joe Sakic, Québ.	5.00
□	16 Ed Belfour (G), Chic.	5.00
□	17 Félix Potvin (G), Toro.	3.00
□	18 Mario Lemieux, Pitt.	15.00
□	19 Jaromir Jagr, Pitt.	5.00
□	20 Teemu Selänne, Winn.	4.00

□	21 Raymond Bourque, Bost.	6.00
□	22 Brett Hull, SLou.	5.00
□	23 Steve Yzerman, Detr.	10.00
□	24 Kirk Muller, Mont.	2.00

TOPPS / BLACK GOLD

Topps Insert Set (24 cards):		**60.00**
	Insert (1:72)	**Topps**
□	1 Teemu Selänne, Winn.	3.00
□	2 Steve Duchesne, Québ.	.75
□	3 Félix Potvin (G), Toro.	.75
□	4 Shawn McEachern, Pitt.	.75
□	5 Adam Oates, Bost.	1.00
□	6 Paul Coffey, Detr.	2.00
□	7 Wayne Gretzky, LosA.	15.00
□	8 Alexei Zhamnov, Winn.	1.00
□	9 Mario Lemieux, Pitt.	10.00
□	10 Gary Suter, Calg.	.75
□	11 Tom Barrasso (G), Pitt.	1.00
□	12 Joé Juneau, Bost.	.75
□	13 Eric Lindros, Phil.	3.00
□	14 Ed Belfour (G), Chic.	3.00
□	15 Raymond Bourque, Bost.	4.00
□	16 Steve Yzerman, Detr.	5.00
□	17 Andrei Kovalenko, Québ.	.75
□	18 Curtis Joseph (G), SLou.	3.00
□	19 Phil Housley, SLou.	1.00
□	20 Pierre Turgeon, NYIs.	.75
□	21 Brett Hull, SLou.	3.00
□	22 Patrick Roy (G), Mont.	10.00
□	23 Larry Murphy, Pitt.	.75
□	24 Pat LaFontaine, Buff.	.75
	Expired Redemption	**NRMT-MT**
□	Winner A (1-12)	.50
□	Winner B (13-24)	.50
□	Winner A and B (1-24)	1.00

FINEST

Series Two Insert Set (12 cards):		**25.00**
	Insert (1:18)	**Finest**
□	1 Alexandre Daigle, Otta.	.50
□	2 Roman Hamrlik, Tamp.	.50
□	3 Eric Lindros, Phil.	3.00
□	4 Owen Nolan, Québ.	2.00
□	5 Mats Sundin, Québ.	3.00
□	6 Mike Modano, Dall.	3.00
□	7 Pierre Turgeon, NYIs.	1.00
□	8 Joe Murphy, Detr.	.50
□	9 Wendel Clark, Toro.	3.00
□	10 Mario Lemieux, Pitt.	10.00
□	11 Dale Hawerchuk, Buff.	2.00
□	12 Rob Ramage, Phil.	.50
	Expired Redemption	**NRMT-MT**
□	Winner (One Card)	.50
□	Winner (12-card Set)	.50

TOPPS / USA HOCKEY

Topps Series Two Insert Set (23 cards):		**20.00**
	Insert (1:12)	**USA**
□	1 Mike Dunham (G), U.S.A.	4.00
□	**2 Peter Laviolette, U.S.A. RC**	**4.00**
□	**3 Ian Moran, U.S.A. RC**	**1.00**
□	**4 Darby Hendrickson, U.S.A. RC**	**1.00**
□	5 Brian Rolston, U.S.A.	1.00
□	**6 Mark Beaufait, U.S.A. RC**	**1.00**
□	**7 Travis Richards, U.S.A. RC**	**1.00**
□	**8 John Lilley, U.S.A. RC**	**1.00**
□	**9 Chris Ferraro, U.S.A. RC**	**1.00**
□	**10 Jon Hillebrandt, U.S.A. RC**	**1.00**
□	**11 Chris Imes, U.S.A. RC**	**1.00**
□	**12 Ted Crowley, U.S.A. RC**	**1.00**
□	**13 David Sacco, U.S.A. RC**	**1.00**
□	14 Todd Marchant, U.S.A.	1.00
□	15 Peter Ferraro, U.S.A.	.50
□	**16 David Roberts, U.S.A. RC**	**1.00**
□	17 Jim Campbell, U.S.A.	.50
□	**18 Barry Richter, U.S.A. RC**	**1.00**
□	**19 Craig Johnson, U.S.A. RC**	**1.00**
□	**20 Brett Hauer, U.S.A. RC**	**1.00**
□	21 Jeff Lazaro, U.S.A. [Photo is John Lilley]	.50
□	**22 Jim Storm, U.S.A. RC**	**1.00**
□	**23 Matt Martin, U.S.A. RC**	**1.00**

O-PEE-CHEE / HOCKEY CANADA

O-Pee-Chee Series Two Insert Set (19 cards):		**20.00**
	Insert	**Canada**
□	**1 Brett Lindros, Canada RC**	**3.00**
□	2 Manny Legace, Canada	2.00
□	**3 Adrian Aucoin, Canada RC**	**1.00**
□	**4 Ken Lovsin, Canada RC**	**1.00**
□	**5 Craig Woodcroft, Canada RC**	**1.00**
□	**6 Derek Mayer, Canada RC**	**1.00**
□	7 Fabian Joseph, Canada	.50
□	**8 Todd Brost, Canada RC**	**1.00**
□	**9 Chris Therien, Canada RC**	**1.00**
□	**10 Brad Turner, Canada RC**	**1.00**
□	**11 Trevor Sim, Canada RC**	**1.00**
□	**12 Todd Hlushko, Canada RC**	**1.00**
□	**13 Dwayne Norris, Canada RC**	**1.00**
□	14 Chris Kontos, Canada	.50
□	15 Petr Nedved, Canada	1.00
□	**16 Brian Savage, Canada RC**	**3.00**
□	17 Paul Kariya, Canada	8.00
□	18 Corey Hirsch (G), Canada	1.00
□	**19 Todd Warriner, Canada RC**	**1.00**

1993 - 94 SCORE

These cards have two versions: an American (English) card and a Canadian (bilingual) card. Series Two cards (497-662) have a third American Gold Rush parallel and fourth Canadian Gold Rush parallel version. Cards 1-6 also have a Sample variation.

The most expensive Series One cards are Wayne Gretzky at $1-2, Mario Lemieux at $0.75-1.50 and Patrick Roy at $0.65-1.25. Regional stars sell at 20¢-$1.00; all other singles start at 20¢. The Alexandre Daigle redeemed card (#496) sells at $0.25-$1.00. Pricing for Canadian and American versions is the same.

Series One Set (496 cards):	**15.00**
Series Two Set (166 cards):	**10.00**
Score Gold Rush Set (166 cards):	**55.00**
Common Player:	**.20**

Player	Player
□□□ 1 Eric Lindros	□□□ 2 Mike Gartner
□□□ 3 Steve Larmer	□□□ 4 Brian Bellows
□□□ 5 Félix Potvin (G)	□□□ 6 Pierre Turgeon
□□ 7 Joe Mullen	□□ 8 Craig MacTavish
□□ 9 Mats Sundin	□□ 10 Pat Verbeek
□□ 11 Andy Moog (G)	□□ 12 Dirk Graham
□□ 13 Gary Suter	□□ 14 Brent Fedyk
□□ 15 Brad Shaw	□□ 16 Benoît Hogue
□□ 17 Cliff Ronning	□□ 18 Mathieu Schneider
□□ 19 Bernie Nicholls	□□ 20 V. Konstantinov
□□ 21 Doug Bodger	□□ 22 Peter Stastny
□□ 23 Larry Murphy	□□ 24 Darren Turcotte
□□ 25 Doug Crossman	□□ 26 Bob Essensa (G)
□□ 27 Kelly Kisio	□□ 28 Nelson Emerson
□□ 29 Raymond Bourque	□□ 30 Kelly Miller
□□ 31 Peter Zezel	□□ 32 Owen Nolan
□□ 33 Sergei Makarov	□□ 34 Stéphane J.J. Richer
□□ 35 Adam Graves	□□ 36 Rob Ramage
□□ 37 Ed Olczyk	□□ 38 Jeff Hackett (G)
□□ 39 Ron Sutter	□□ 40 Dale Hunter
□□ 41 Nikolai Borschevsky	□□ 42 Curtis Leschyshyn
□□ 43 Mike Vernon (G)	□□ 44 Brent Sutter
□□ 45 Rod Brind'Amour	□□ 46 Sylvain Turgeon
□□ 47 Kirk McLean (G)	□□ 48 Derek King
□□ 49 Murray Craven	□□ 50 Jaromir Jagr
□□ 51 Guy Carbonneau	□□ 52 Tony Granato
□□ 53 Mark Tinordi	□□ 54 Brad McCrimmon
□□ 55 Randy Wood	□□ 56 Scott Young
□□ 57 Jamie Baker	□□ 58 Don Beaupré (G)
□□ 59 Bob Probert	□□ 60 Ray Ferraro
□□ 61 Alexei Kasatonov	□□ 62 Corey Millen
□□ 63 Scott Mellanby	□□ 64 Brian Benning
□□ 65 Doug Lidster	□□ 66 Doug Gilmour
□□ 67 Shawn McEachern	□□ 68 Tim Cheveldae (G)
□□ 69 Jeff Norton	□□ 70 Ed Belfour (G)
□□ 71 Thomas Steen	□□ 72 Stéphan Lebeau
□□ 73 James Patrick	□□ 74 Joel Otto
□□ 75 Grant Fuhr (G)	□□ 76 Calle Johansson
□□ 77 Donald Audette	□□ 78 Geoff Courtnall
□□ 79 Fredrik Olausson	□□ 80 Dmitri Khristich
□□ 81 John MacLean	□□ 82 Dominic Roussel (G)
□□ 83 Ray Sheppard	□□ 84 Christian Ruuttu
□□ 85 Mike McPhee	□□ 86 Adam Creighton
□□ 87 Uwe Krupp	□□ 88 Stephen Leach
□□ 89 Kevin Miller	□□ 90 Charlie Huddy
□□ 91 Mark Howe	□□ 92 Sylvain Côté
□□ 93 Anatoli Semenov	□□ 94 Jeff Beukeboom
□□ 95 Gord Murphy	□□ 96 Rob Pearson
□□ 97 Esa Tikkanen	□□ 98 Dave Gagner
□□ 99 Mike Richter (G)	□□ 100 Jari Kurri
□□ 101 Chris Chelios	□□ 102 P. Sidorkiewicz (G)
□□ 103 Scott Lachance	□□ 104 Zarley Zalapski
□□ 105 Denis Savard	□□ 106 Paul Coffey
□□ 107 Ulf Dahlén	□□ 108 Shayne Corson
□□ 109 Jimmy Carson	□□ 110 Petr* Svoboda
□□ 111 Scott Stevens	□□ 112 Kevin Lowe
□□ 113 Chris Kontos	□□ 114 Evgeny Davydov
□□ 115 Doug Wilson	□□ 116 Curtis Joseph (G)
□□ 117 Trevor Linden	□□ 118 Michal Pivonka
□□ 119 Dave Ellett	□□ 120 Mike Ricci
□□ 121 Al MacInnis	□□ 122 Kevin Dineen
□□ 123 Norm Maciver	□□ 124 Darius Kasparaitis
□□ 125 Adam Oates	□□ 126 Sean Burke (G)
□□ 127 Dave Manson	□□ 128 Éric Desjardins
□□ 129 Tomas Sandström	□□ 130 Russ Courtnall
□□ 131 Roman Hamrlik	□□ 132 Teppo Numminen
□□ 133 Pat Falloon	□□ 134 Jyrki Lumme
□□ 135 Joe Sakic	□□ 136 Kevin Hatcher
□□ 137 Wendel Clark	□□ 138 Neil Wilkinson
□□ 139 Craig Simpson	□□ 140 Kelly Hrudey (G)
□□ 141 Steve Thomas	□□ 142 Mike Modano
□□ 143 Garry Galley	□□ 144 Jim* Johnson
□□ 145 Rod Langway	□□ 146 Bobby Sweeney
□□ 147 Gary Leeman	□□ 148 Alexei Zhitnik
□□ 149 Adam Foote	□□ 150 Mark Recchi
□□ 151 Ron Francis	□□ 152 Ron Hextall (G)
□□ 153 Michel Goulet	□□ 154 Vladimír Ruzicka
□□ 155 Bill Ranford (G)	□□ 156 Mike Craig
□□ 157 Vladimir Malakhov	□□ 158 Nicklas Lidström
□□ 159 Dale Hawerchuk	□□ 160 Claude Lemieux
□□ 161 Ulf Samuelsson	□□ 162 Vanbiesbrouck (G)
□□ 163 Patrice Brisebois	□□ 164 Andrew Cassels
□□ 165 Paul Ranheim	□□ 166 Neal Broten
□□ 167 Joe Reekie	□□ 168 Derian Hatcher
□□ 169 Don Sweeney	□□ 170 Mike Keane
□□ 171 M. Fitzpatrick (G)	□□ 172 Paul Cavallini
□□ 173 Garth Butcher	□□ 174 Andrei Kovalenko
□□ 175 Shawn Burr	□□ 176 Mike Donnelly
□□ 177 Glenn Healy (G)	□□ 178 Gilbert Dionne
□□ 179 Mike Ramsey	□□ 180 Glenn Anderson
□□ 181 Pelle Eklund	□□ 182 Kerry Huffman
□□ 183 Johan Garpenlöv	□□ 184 Kjell Samuelsson
□□ 185 Todd Elik	□□ 186 Craig Janney
□□ 187 Dmitri Kvartalnov	□□ 188 Al Iafrate
□□ 189 John Cullen	□□ 190 Steve Duchesne
□□ 191 Theoren Fleury	□□ 192 J. Steve Smith
□□ 193 Jon Casey (G)	□□ 194 Jeff R. Brown
□□ 195 Keith Tkachuk	□□ 196 Greg A. Adams
□□ 197 Mike Ridley	□□ 198 Bobby Holik
□□ 199 Joe Nieuwendyk	□□ 200 Mark Messier
□□ 201 Jim Hrivnak (G)	□□ 202 Patrick Poulin
□□ 203 Alexei Kovalev	□□ 204 Robert Reichel
□□ 205 David Shaw	□□ 206 Brent Gilchrist
□□ 207 Craig Billington (G)	□□ 208 Bob Errey
□□ 209 Dmitri Mironov	□□ 210 Dixon Ward
□□ 211 Rick Zombo	□□ 212 Marty McSorley
□□ 213 Geoff Sanderson	□□ 214 Dino Ciccarelli
□□ 215 Tony Amonte	□□ 216 Dmitry Yushkevich
□□ 217 Scott Niedermayer	□□ 218 Sergei Nemchinov
□□ 219 Steve Konroyd	□□ 220 Patrick Flatley
□□ 221 Steve Chiasson	□□ 222 Alexander Mogilny
□□ 223 Pat Elynuik	□□ 224 Jamie Macoun
□□ 225 Tom Barrasso (G)	□□ 226 Gaétan Duchesne
□□ 227 Eric Weinrich	□□ 228 Dave Poulin
□□ 229 Viacheslav Fetisov	□□ 230 Brian Bradley
□□ 231 Petr Nedved	□□ 232 Phil Housley
□□ 233 Terry Carkner	□□ 234 Kirk Muller
□□ 235 Brian Leetch	□□ 236 Rob Blake
□□ 237 Chris Terreri (G)	□□ 238 Brendan Shanahan
□□ 239 Paul Ysebaert	□□ 240 Jeremy Roenick
□□ 241 Gary Roberts	□□ 242 Petr Klima
□□ 243 Glen Wesley	□□ 244 V. Damphousse
□□ 245 Luc Robitaille	□□ 246 Dallas Drake RC
□□ 247 Rob Gaudreau RC	□□ 248 Tommy Sjödin
□□ 249 Richard Smehlik	□□ 250 Sergei Fedorov
□□ 251 Stephen Heinze	□□ 252 Luke Richardson
□□ 253 Doug Weight	□□ 254 Martin Rucinsky
□□ 255 Sergio Momesso	□□ 256 Alexei Zhamnov
□□ 257 Bob Kudelski	□□ 258 Brian Skrudland
□□ 259 Terry Yake	□□ 260 Alexei Gusarov
□□ 261 Sandis Ozolinsh	□□ 262 Ted Donato
□□ 263 Bruce Driver	□□ 264 Yves Racine
□□ 265 Mike Peluso	□□ 266 Craig Muni
□□ 267 Bob Carpenter	□□ 268 Kevin Haller
□□ 269 Brad May	□□ 270 Joey Kocur
□□ 271 Igor Korolev	□□ 272 Troy Murray
□□ 273 Daren Puppa (G)	□□ 274 Gord** Roberts
□□ 275 Michel Petit	□□ 276 V. Riendeau (G)
□□ 277 Robert Petrovicky	□□ 278 Valeri Zelepukin
□□ 279 Bob Bassen	□□ 280 Darrin Shannon
□□ 281 Dominik Hasek (G)	□□ 282 Craig Ludwig
□□ 283 Lyle Odelein	□□ 284 Alexander Semak
□□ 285 Richard Matvichuk	□□ 286 Ken Daneyko
□□ 287 Jan Erixon	□□ 288 Robert Dirk
□□ 289 Laurie Boschman	□□ 290 Greg Paslawski
□□ 291 Rob Zamuner	□□ 292 Todd Gill
□□ 293 Neil Brady	□□ 294 Murray Baron
□□ 295 Peter Taglianetti	□□ 296 Wayne Presley
□□ 297 Paul Broten	□□ 298 Dana Murzyn
□□ 299 J.J. Daigneault	□□ 300 Wayne Gretzky
□□ 301 Keith Acton	□□ 302 Yuri Khmylev
□□ 303 Frantisek Musil	□□ 304 Bob Rouse
□□ 305 Greg Gilbert	□□ 306 Geoff Smith
□□ 307 Adam Burt	□□ 308 Phil Bourque
□□ 309 Igor Kravchuk	□□ 310 Steve Yzerman
□□ 311 Darryl Sydor	□□ 312 Tie Domi
□□ 313 Sergei Zubov	□□ 314 Chris Dahlquist
□□ 315 Patrick Roy (G)	□□ 316 Mark Osborne
□□ 317 Kelly Buchberger	□□ 318 John LeClair
□□ 319 Randy McKay	□□ 320 Jody Hull
□□ 321 Paul Stanton	□□ 322 Steven Finn
□□ 323 Rich Sutter	□□ 324 Ray Whitney
□□ 325 Kevin Stevens	□□ 326 Valeri Kamensky
□□ 327 Doug Zmolek	□□ 328 Mikhail Tatarinov
□□ 329 Ken Wregget (G)	□□ 330 Joé Juneau
□□ 331 Teemu Selänne	□□ 332 Trent Yawney
□□ 333 Pavel Bure	□□ 334 Jim Paek
□□ 335 Brett Hull	□□ 336 T. Söderström (G)
□□ 337 Grigori Panteleev	□□ 338 Kevin Todd
□□ 339 Mark Janssens	□□ 340 Rick Tocchet
□□ 341 Wendell Young (G)	□□ 342 Cam Neely
□□ 343 D. Andreychuk	□□ 344 Peter Bondra
□□ 345 Pat LaFontaine	□□ 346 Robb Stauber (G)
□□ 347 Brian Mullen	□□ 348 Joe Murphy
□□ 349 Pat Jablonski (G)	□□ 350 Mario Lemieux
□□ 351 Sergei Bautin	□□ 352 Claude Lapointe
□□ 353 Dean Evason	□□ 354 John Tucker
□□ 355 D. Berehowsky	□□ 356 Gerald Diduck
□□ 357 Todd Krygier	□□ 358 Adrien Plavsic
□□ 359 Sylvain Lefebvre	□□ 360 Kay Whitmore (G)
□□ 361 Sheldon Kennedy	□□ 362 Kris King
□□ 363 Marc Bergevin	□□ 364 Keith Primeau
□□ 365 Jimmy Waite (G)	□□ 366 Dean Kennedy
□□ 367 Mike Krushelnyski	□□ 368 Ron Tugnutt (G)
□□ 369 Bob Beers	□□ 370 Randy Burridge
□□ 371 David Reid	□□ 372 Frantisek Kucera
□□ 373 Scott Pellerin RC	□□ 374 Brad Dalgarno
□□ 375 Martin Straka	□□ 376 Scott Pearson
□□ 377 Arturs Irbe (G)	□□ 378 Jiri Slégr
□□ 379 Stéphane Fiset (G)	□□ 380 Stu Barnes
□□ 381 Ric Nattress	□□ 382 Steven King
□□ 383 Michael Nylander	□□ 384 Keith Brown
□□ 385 Gino Odjick	□□ 386 Bryan Marchment
□□ 387 Mike Foligno	□□ 388 Zdeno Ciger
□□ 389 Dave Taylor	□□ 390 Mike Sullivan
□□ 391 Shawn Chambers	□□ 392 Brad Marsh
□□ 393 Mike Hough	□□ 394 Jeff Reese (G)
□□ 395 Bill Guerin	□□ 396 Greg Hawgood
□□ 397 Jim Sandlak	□□ 398 Stéphane Matteau
□□ 399 John Blue (G)	□□ 400 Tony Twist
□□ 401 Luciano Borsato	□□ 402 Gerard Gallant
□□ 403 Rick Tabaracci (G)	□□ 404 Nick Kypreos
□□ 405 Marty McInnis	□□ 406 Craig Wolanin
□□ 407 Mark Lamb	□□ 408 Martin Gélinas
□□ 409 Ronnie Stern	□□ 410 Ken Sutton
□□ 411 Brian Noonan	□□ 412 Stéphane Quintal
□□ 413 Rob Zettler	□□ 414 Gino Cavallini
□□ 415 Mark Hardy	□□ 416 Jay Wells
□□ 417 Keith Jones	□□ 418 Dave McLlwain
□□ 419 F. Pietrangelo (G)	□□ 420 Jocelyn Lemieux
□□ 421 Vyacheslav Kozlov	□□ 422 Randy Moller
□□ 423 Kevin Dahl	□□ 424 Shjon Podein RC
□□ 425 Shane Churla	□□ 426 Guy Hebert (G)
□□ 427 Mikael Andersson	□□ 428 Robert Kron
□□ 429 Mike Eagles	□□ 430 Alan May
□□ 431 Ron L. Wilson	□□ 432 Darcy Wakaluk
□□ 433 Rob Ray	□□ 434 Brent Ashton
□□ 435 Jason Woolley	□□ 436 Basil McRae
□□ 437 André Racicot (G)	□□ 438 Brad Werenka
□□ 439 Josef Beránek	□□ 440 Dave Christian
□□ 441 Theoren Fleury	□□ 442 Mark Recchi
□□ 443 Cliff Ronning	□□ 444 Tony Granato
□□ 445 Vanbiesbrouck (G)	□□ 446 Jari Kurri
□□ 447 Mike Gartner	□□ 448 Steve Yzerman
□□ 449 Glenn Anderson	□□ 450 Capitals defence
□□ 451 Luc Robitaille	□□ 452 Penguins
□□ 453 Corey Hirsch (G)	□□ 454 Jesse Bélanger
□□ 455 Philippe Boucher	□□ 456 Robert Lang
□□ 457 Doug Barrault RC	□□ 458 Steve Konowalchuk
□□ 459 Oleg Petrov	□□ 460 Niklas Andersson
□□ 461 Milan Tichy RC	□□ 462 D. Madeley (G) RC
□□ 463 Tyler Wright	□□ 464 Sergei Krivokrasov
□□ 465 Vladimír Vujtek	□□ 466 Rick Knickle RC
□□ 467 Gord Kruppke RC	□□ 468 David Emma
□□ 469 Scott Thomas RC	□□ 470 Shawn Rivers RC
□□ 471 Jason Bowen RC	□□ 472 Bryan Smolinski
□□ 473 Chris Simon RC	□□ 474 Peter Ciavaglia RC
□□ 475 Sergei Zholtok	□□ 476 Radek Hamr RC
□□ 477 Mogilny / Selänne	□□ 478 Adam Oates
□□ 479 Mario Lemieux	□□ 480 Mario Lemieux
□□ 481 Dave Andreychuk	□□ 482 Phil Housley
□□ 483 Tom Barrasso (G)	□□ 484 Félix Potvin (G)
□□ 485 Ed Belfour (G)	□□ 486 Greyhounds
□□ 487 Canadiens	□□ 488 Mighty Ducks
□□ 489 Guy Hebert (G)	□□ 490 Sean Hill
□□ 491 Panthers	□□ 492 Vanbiesbrouck (G)
□□ 493 Tom Fitzgerald	□□ 494 Paul DiPietro
□□ 495 David Volek	□□ 496 Alexandre Daigle
□ Expired Trade Card	

Player	GR	Reg.
□□□□497 Shawn McEachern, LosA.	.50	.20
□□□□498 Rich Sutter, Chic.	.50	.20
□□□□499 Evgeny Davydov, Otta.	.30	.20
□□□□500 Sean Hill, Anah.	.30	.20
□□□□501 John Vanbiesbrouck (G), Flor.	1.00	.20
□□□□502 Guy Hebert (G), Anah.	.50	.20
□□□□503 Scott Mellanby, Flor.	.50	.20
□□□□504 Ron Tugnutt (G), Anah.	1.00	.20
□□□□505 Brian Skrudland, Flor.	.30	.20
□□□□506 Nelson Emerson, Winn.	.30	.20
□□□□507 Kevin Todd, Chic.	.30	.20
□□□□508 Terry Carkner, Detr.	.30	.20
□□□□509 Stéphane Quintal, Winn.	.30	.20
□□□□510 Paul Stanton, Bost.	.30	.20
□□□□511 Terry Yake, Anah.	.30	.20
□□□□512 Brian Benning, Flor.	.30	.20
□□□□513 Brian Propp, Hart.	.50	.20
□□□□514 Steven King, Anah.	.30	.20
□□□□515 Joe Cirella, Flor.	.30	.20
□□□□516 Andy Moog (G), Dall.	1.00	.20
□□□□517 Paul Ysebaert, Winn.	.30	.20
□□□□518 Petr Klima, Tamp.	.30	.20
□□□□519 Corey Millen, NJer.	.30	.20
□□□□520 Phil Housley, SLou.	.50	.20
□□□□521 Craig Billington (G), Otta.	.50	.20
□□□□522 Jeff Norton, SanJ.	.30	.20
□□□□523 Neil Wilkinson, Chic.	.30	.20
□□□□524 Doug Lidster, NYRa.	.30	.20
□□□□525 Steve Larmer, NYRa.	1.00	.20
□□□□526 Jon Casey (G), Bost.	.30	.20
□□□□527 Brad McCrimmon, Hart.	.30	.20
□□□□528 Alexei Kasatonov, Anah.	.50	.20
□□□□529 Andrei Lomakin, Flor.	.30	.20
□□□□530 Daren Puppa (G), Tamp.	.50	.20
□□□□531 Sergei Makarov, SanJ.	1.00	.20
□□□□532 Jim Sandlak, Hart.	.30	.20
□□□□533 Glenn Healy (G), NYRa.	.50	.20
□□□□534 Martin Gélinas, Vanc.	.50	.20
□□□□535 Igor Larionov, SanJ.	1.50	.20
□□□□536 Anatoli Semenov, Anah.	.30	.20
□□□□537 Mark Fitzpatrick (G), Flor.	.30	.20

□□□□538 Paul Cavallini, Dall. .30 .20
□□□□539 Jimmy Waite (G), SanJ. .50 .20
□□□□540 Yves Racine, Phil. .30 .20
□□□□541 Jeff Hackett (G), Chic. .50 .20
□□□□542 Marty McSorley, Pitt. .50 .20
□□□□543 Scott Pearson, Edmo. .30 .20
□□□□544 Ron Hextall (G), NYIs. 2.00 .20
□□□□545 Gaétan Duchesne, SanJ. .30 .20
□□□□546 Jamie Baker, SanJ. .30 .20
□□□□547 Troy Loney, Anah. .30 .20
□□□□548 Gord Murphy, Flor. .30 .20
□□□□549 Bob Kudelski, Flor. .30 .20
□□□□550 Dean Evason, Dall. .30 .20
□□□□551 Mike Peluso, NJer. .30 .20
□□□□552 Dave Poulin, Wash. .30 .20
□□□□553 Randy Ladouceur, Anah. .30 .20
□□□□554 Tom Fitzgerald, Flor. .30 .20
□□□□555 Denis Savard, Tamp. 1.00 .20
□□□□556 Kelly Kisio, Calg. .30 .20
□□□□557 Craig Simpson, Buff. .30 .20
□□□□558 Stu Grimson, Anah. .50 .20
□□□□559 Mike Hough, Flor. .30 .20
□□□□560 Gerard Gallant, Tamp. .30 .20
□□□□561 Greg Gilbert, NYRa. .30 .20
□□□□562 Vladimír Ruzicka, Otta. .50 .20
□□□□563 Jim Hrivnak (G), SLou. .30 .20
□□□□564 Dave Lowry, Flor. .50 .20
□□□□565 Todd Ewen, Anah. .30 .20
□□□□566 Bob Errey, SanJ. .30 .20
□□□□567 Bryan Trottier, Pitt. 2.50 .50
□□□□568 Grant Ledyard, Dall. .30 .20
□□□□569 Keith Brown, Flor. .30 .20
□□□□570 Darren Turcotte, Hart. .30 .20
□□□□571 Patrick Poulin, Chic. .30 .20
□□□□572 Jimmy Carson, Vanc. .30 .20
□□□□573 Eric Weinrich, Chic. .30 .20
□□□□574 James Patrick, Hart. .30 .20
□□□□575 Bob Beers, Edmo. .30 .20
□□□□576 Chris Joseph, Tamp. .30 .20
□□□□577 Bryan Marchment, Hart. .30 .20
□□□□578 Bob Carpenter, NJer. .50 .20
□□□□579 Craig Muni, Buff. .30 .20
□□□□580 Pat Elynuik, Tamp. .30 .20
□□□□581 Todd Elik, SanJ. .30 .20
□□□□582 Doug Brown, Pitt. .30 .20
□□□□583 Dave McLlwain, Otta. .30 .20
□□□□584 Dave Tippett, Phil. .30 .20
□□□□585 Jesse Bélanger, Flor. .30 .20
□□□□586 Chris Pronger, Hart. 3.00 .50
□□□□587 Alexandre Daigle, Otta. .50 .20
□□□□**588 Cam Stewart, Bost. RC** **1.00** **.50**
□□□□**589 Derek Plante, Buff. RC** **1.50** **.50**
□□□□590 Pat Peake, Wash. .50 .20
□□□□591 Alexander Karpovtsev, NYRa. .50 .20
□□□□592 Rob Niedermayer, Flor. 1.00 .20
□□□□**593 J. Thibault (G), Québ. RC** **4.00** **2.00**
□□□□**594 Jason Arnott, Edmo. RC** **4.50** **2.00**
□□□□595 Mike Rathje, SanJ. .50 .20
□□□□596 Chris Gratton, Tamp. 1.00 .20
□□□□597 Markus Näslund, Pitt. 5.00 1.00
□□□□598 Dmitri Filimonov, Otta. .50 .20
□□□□599 Andrei Trefilov (G), Calg. .50 .20
□□□□**600 Michal Sykora, SanJ. RC** **1.50** **.50**
□□□□601 Greg Johnson, Detr. .50 .20
□□□□602 Mikael Renberg, Phil. 1.50 .20
□□□□603 Alexei Yashin, Otta. 3.00 .50
□□□□**604 D. Rhodes (G), Toro. RC** **2.00** **1.00**
□□□□**605 Jeff Shantz, Chic. RC** **1.00** **.50**
□□□□**606 Brent Gretzky, Tamp. RC** **1.50** **.50**
□□□□607 Boris Mironov, Winn. .30 .20
□□□□608 Ted Drury, Calg. .50 .20
□□□□**609 Chris Osgood (G), Detr. RC** **6.00** **3.00**
□□□□**610 Jim Storm, Hart. RC** **1.00** **.50**
□□□□611 Dave Karpa, Québ. .30 .20
□□□□**612 Stewart Malgunas, Phil. RC** **1.00** **.50**
□□□□**613 Jason Smith, NJer. RC** **1.50** **.50**
□□□□**614 German Titov, Calg. RC** **1.00** **.50**
□□□□**615 Patrik Carnbäck, Anah. RC** **1.00** **.50**
□□□□**616 Jaroslav Modry, NJer. RC** **1.00** **.50**
□□□□**617 Scott Levins, Otta. RC** **1.00** **.50**
□□□□**618 F. Brathwaite (G), Edmo. RC** **3.00** **1.50**
□□□□619 Ilya Byakin, Edmo. 1.00 .20
□□□□620 Jarkko Varvio, Dall. 1.00 .20
□□□□**621 Jim Montgomery, SLou. RC** **1.00** **.50**
□□□□**622 Vesa Viitakoski, Calg. RC** **1.00** **.50**
□□□□**623 Alexei Kudashov, Toro. RC** **1.00** **.50**
□□□□624 Pavol Demitra, Otta. 2.00 .20
□□□□**625 Iain Fraser, Québ. RC** **1.00** **.50**
□□□□**626 Peter Popovic, Mont. RC** **1.00** **.50**
□□□□**627 Kirk Maltby, Edmo. RC** **2.00** **1.00**
□□□□**628 Garth Snow (G), Québ. RC** **3.00** **1.50**
□□□□**629 Peter White, Edmo. RC** **1.00** **.50**
□□□□**630 Mike McKee, Québ. RC** **1.00** **.50**
□□□□**631 Darren McCarty, Detr. RC** **3.00** **1.50**
□□□□**632 Pat Neaton, Pitt. RC** **1.00** **.50**
□□□□633 Sandy McCarthy, Calg. .30 .20
□□□□634 Pierre Sévigny, Mont. .30 .20
□□□□**635 Matt Martin, Toro. RC** **1.00** **.50**
□□□□636 John Slaney, Wash. .30 .20
□□□□637 Bob Corkum, Anah. .30 .20
□□□□**638 Mike Stapleton, RC** **1.00** **.50**
□□□□639 Bill Houlder, Anah. .30 .20
□□□□640 Ron Sutter, .50 .20
□□□□641 Garry Valk, Anah. .30 .20
□□□□642 Greg Hawgood, Flor. .30 .20
□□□□643 Bob Bassen, Québ. .30 .20
□□□□644 Stu Barnes, Flor. .30 .20
□□□□645 Fredrik Olausson, Edmo. .50 .20
□□□□646 Geoff Smith, Flor. .30 .20
□□□□647 Mike Foligno, Flor. .50 .20
□□□□648 Martin Brodeur (G), NJer. 4.00 .50
□□□□649 Ryan McGill, Phil. .30 .20
□□□□650 Jeff Reese (G), Hart. .50 .20
□□□□651 Mike Sillinger, Detr. .30 .20
□□□□**652 Brent Severyn, Flor. RC** **1.00** **.50**
□□□□653 Rob Ramage, Phil. .50 .20
□□□□654 Dixon Ward, LosA. .30 .20
□□□□655 Danton Cole, Tamp. .30 .20
□□□□656 Viacheslav Butsayev, SanJ. .30 .20
□□□□657 Garth Butcher, .30 .20
□□□□658 Paul Broten, Dall. .30 .20
□□□□659 Steve Duchesne, SLou. .50 .20
□□□□660 Trevor Kidd (G), Calg. 1.00 .20
□□□□661 Travis Green, NYIs. .50 .20
□□□□662 Wayne Gretzky, LosA. 12.00 2.50

Player **NRMT-MT**
□ Eric Lindros, NHL All-Star '94 35.00

DREAM TEAM

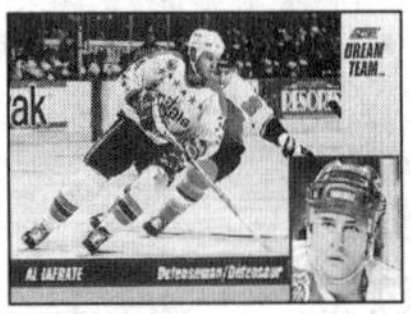

Series One Insert Set (24 cards): **145.00**
Canadian Insert (1:24) **DT**
□ 1 Tom Barrasso (G), Pitt. 3.00
□ 2 Patrick Roy (G), Mont. 20.00
□ 3 Chris Chelios, Chic. [vs. A.Cassels] 4.00
□ 4 Al MacInnis, Calg. 3.00
□ 5 Scott Stevens, NJer. 3.00
□ 6 Brian Leetch, NYRa. 4.00
□ 7 Raymond Bourque, Bost. 5.00
□ 8 Paul Coffey, Detr. 4.00
□ 9 Al Iafrate, Wash. 3.00
□ 10 Mario Lemieux, Pitt. 20.00
□ 11 Wayne Gretzky, LosA. 30.00
□ 12 Eric Lindros, Phil. 5.00
□ 13 Pat LaFontaine, Buff. 4.00
□ 14 Joe Sakic, Québ. 10.00
□ 15 Pierre Turgeon, NYIs. 3.00
□ 16 Steve Yzerman, Detr. 15.00
□ 17 Adam Oates, Bost. 3.00
□ 18 Brett Hull, SLou. 7.00
□ 19 Pavel Bure, Vanc. 5.00
□ 20 Alexander Mogilny, Buff. 3.00
□ 21 Teemu Selänne, Winn. 5.00
□ 22 Steve Larmer, Chic. 3.00
□ 23 Kevin Stevens, Pitt. 3.00
□ 24 Luc Robitaille, LosA. 6.00

DYNAMIC DUO

Series Two Canadian Insert Set (9 cards): **75.00**
Series Two American Insert Set (9 cards): **100.00**
Canadian Insert (1:48) **DD**
□ DD1 D. Andreychuk / D. Gilmour 6.00
□ DD2 A. Zhamnov / T. Selänne 6.00
□ DD3 A. Yashin / A. Daigle 6.00
□ DD4 Gar. Roberts / J. Nieuwendyk 6.00
□ DD5 M. Sundin / J. Sakic 20.00
□ DD6 K. Muller / B. Bellows 6.00
□ DD7 S. Corson / B. Bellows 13.00
□ DD8 K. Stevens / M. Lemieux 25.00
□ DD9 P. Turgeon / Der. King 6.00

American Insert (1:36) **DD**
□ DD1 E. Lindros / M. Recchi 10.00
□ DD2 P. LaFontaine / A. Mogilny 6.00
□ DD3 J. Juneau / A. Oates 6.00
□ DD4 Br. Hull / C. Janney 10.00
□ DD5 A. Graves / M. Messier 10.00
□ DD6 J. Murphy / J. Roenick 6.00
□ DD7 J. Kurri / W. Gretzky 40.00
□ DD8 I. Larionov / S. Makarov 6.00
□ DD9 S. Fedorov / S. Yzerman 25.00

INTERNATIONAL STARS

Series One Insert Set (22 cards): **20.00**
Insert (1:1 Jumbo) **IS**
□□ 1 Pavel Bure, Vanc. 3.00
□□ 2 Teemu Selänne, Winn. 3.00
□□ 3 Sergei Fedorov, Detr. 3.00
□□ 4 Peter Bondra, Wash. 2.00
□□ 5 Tommy Söderström (G), Phil. .30
□□ 6 Robert Reichel, Calg. 1.00
□□ 7 Jari Kurri, LosA. 3.00
□□ 8 Alexander Mogilny, Buff. 1.00
□□ 9 Jaromir Jagr, Pitt. 3.00
□□ 10 Mats Sundin, Québ. 3.00
□□ 11 Uwe Krupp, NYIs. .30
□□ 12 Nikolai Borschevsky, Toro. .30
□□ 13 Ulf Dahlén, Minn. .30
□□ 14 Alexander Semak, NJer. .30
□□ 15 Michal Pivonka, Wash. .30
□□ 16 Sergei Nemchinov, NYRa. .30
□□ 17 Darius Kasparaitis, NYIs. .30
□□ 18 Sandis Ozolinsh, SanJ. .30
□□ 19 Alexei Kovalev, NYRa. 2.00
□□ 20 Dmitri Khristich, Wash. .30
□□ 21 Tomas Sandström, LosA. .30
□□ 22 Petr Nedved, Vanc. 1.00

PINNACLE ALL-STAR

These cards have two versions: an American issue and a Canadian issue. Photo variations for the Canadian [CDN] and American [U.S.] series are explained in brackets.

Insert Set (45 cards): **10.00**
Redemption Set (46-50): **8.00**
Common Player: **.20**
Insert (1:1) **PAS**
□ 1 Craig Billington (G) [CDN-Net to his right] .30
□ 1 Craig Billington (G) [U.S.] .30
□ 2 Zarley Zalapski [CDN-McDonald's ad] .30
□ 2 Zarley Zalapski [U.S.-Molson Canadian ad] .30
□ 3 Kevin Lowe [CDN-Coca-Cola ad] .30
□ 3 Kevin Lowe [U.S.-XZX: K. Kisio] .30
□ 4 Scott Stevens [CDN-Blue line visible] .30
□ 4 Scott Stevens [U.S.-UPS ad] .30
□ 5 Pierre Turgeon [CDN-XZX: Z. Zalapski] .30
□ 5 Pierre Turgeon [U.S.-XZX: Wales bench] .30
□ 6 Mark Recchi [CDN-Goal crease visible] .30
□ 6 Mark Recchi [U.S.-Coca-Cola ad] .30
□ 7 Kirk Muller [CDN-McDonald's ad] .30
□ 7 Muller [U.S.-XZX: Oates, Recchi & Duchesne] .30
□ 8 Mike Gartner [CDN-XZX: Wayne Gretzky] .30
□ 8 Mike Gartner [U.S.-XZX: Bourque, Lowe] .30
□ 9 Adam Oates [CDN-Kellogg's ad] .30
□ 9 Adam Oates [U.S.-Referee visible] .30
□ 10 Brad Marsh [CDN-Coca-Cola ad] .30
□ 10 Brad Marsh [U.S.-Molson Export ad] .30
□ 11 Pat LaFontaine [CDN-XZX: Wayne Gretzky] .30
□ 11 Pat LaFontaine [U.S.-Gillette Sensor ad] .30
□ 12 Peter Bondra [CDN-Molson Export ad] .30
□ 12 Peter Bondra [U.S.-Molson Canadian ad] .30
□ 13 Joe Sakic [CDN-XZX: Campbell bench] .30
□ 13 Joe Sakic [U.S.] .30
□ 14 Rick Tocchet [CDN-XZX: P. Housley] .30
□ 14 Rick Tocchet [U.S.] .30
□ 15 Kevin Stevens [CDN-XZX: Campbell bench] .30
□ 15 Kevin Stevens [U.S.-XZX: K. Kisio] .30
□ 16 Steve Duchesne [CDN-XZX: Wales bench] .30
□ 16 Steve Duchesne [U.S.-Molson Canadian ad] .30
□ 17 Peter Sidorkiewicz (G) [CDN-Net mid-left] .30
□ 17 Peter Sidorkiewicz (G) [U.S.] .30
□ 18 Patrick Roy (G) [CDN-Hugging post] 1.00
□ 18 Patrick Roy (G) [U.S.] 1.00
□ 19 Al Iafrate [CDN-XZX: L. Robitaille] .30
□ 19 Al Iafrate [U.S.-Molson Canadian ad] .30
□ 20 Jaromir Jagr [CDN-Sony a.] .30
□ 20 Jaromir Jagr [U.S.-68 mirror image] .30
□ 21 Ray Bourque [CDN-McDonald's ad] .30
□ 21 Ray Bourque [U.S.-XZX: D. Gilmour] .30
□ 22 Alexander Mogilny [CDN-XZX: M. Vernon] .30
□ 22 Alexander Mogilny [U.S.-XZX: S. Chiasson] .30
□ 23 Steve Chiasson [CDN-XZX: Wales bench] .30
□ 23 Steve Chiasson [U.S.-McDonald's ad] .30
□ 24 Garth Butcher [CDN-Front view] .30
□ 24 Garth Butcher [U.S.-Esso ad] .30
□ 25 Phil Housley [CDN-XZX: M. Gartner] .30
□ 25 Phil Housley [U.S.-XZX: A. Mogilny] .30
□ 26 Chris Chelios [CDN-XZX: J. Jagr] .30
□ 26 Chris Chelios [U.S.-Coca-Cola ad] .30
□ 27 Randy Carlyle [CDN-Photo from ankles up] .30
□ 27 Randy Carlyle [U.S.-Photo from skates up] .30
□ 28 Mike Modano [CDN-McDonald's ad] .30
□ 28 Mike Modano [U.S.] .30
□ 29 Gary Roberts [CDN-Molson Export ad] .30
□ 29 Gary Roberts [U.S.-McDonald's ad] .30
□ 30 Kelly Kisio [CDN-Coca-Cola ad] .30
□ 30 Kelly Kisio [U.S.-XZX: Wayne Gretzky] .30
□ 31 Pavel Bure [CDN-Glidden ad] .30
□ 31 Pavel Bure [U.S.-XZX: A. Iafrate] .30
□ 32 Selänne [CDN-Someone's stick blade] .30
□ 32 Teemu Selänne [U.S.] .30
□ 33 Brian Bradley [CDN-McDonald's ad] .30
□ 33 Bradley [U.S.-XZX: Robit., Selänne, Roen.] .30
□ 34 Brett Hull [CDN-UPS ad] .30
□ 34 Brett Hull [U.S] .30
□ 35 Jari Kurri [CDN-UPS ad] .30
□ 35 Jari Kurri [U.S.] .30
□ 36 Steve Yzerman [CDN-Esso ad] 1.00
□ 36 Steve Yzerman [U.S.-XZX: M.Gartner] 1.00
□ 37 Luc Robitaille [CDN-XZX: P. Sidorkiewicz] .30
□ 37 Luc Robitaille [U.S.-Esso ad] .30
□ 38 Dave Manson [CDN-Kellogg's ad] .30
□ 38 Dave Manson [U.S.] .30
□ 39 Jeremy Roenick [CDN-Gillette ad] .30
□ 39 Jeremy Roenick [U.S.-Open ice] .30
□ 40 Mike Vernon (G) [CDN-Molson Export ad] .30
□ 40 Mike Vernon (G) [U.S.] .30
□ 41 Jon Casey (G) [CDN-Coca-Cola ad] .30
□ 41 Jon Casey (G) [U.S.-Esso ad] .30
□ 42 Ed Belfour (G) [CDN-Photo from pads up] .30
□ 42 Ed Belfour (G) [U.S.-Canadian stick] .30
□ 43 Paul Coffey [CDN-Photo from skates up] .30
□ 43 Paul Coffey [U.S.-Photo from ankles up] .30
□ 44 Doug Gilmour [CDN-Opponent's skates] .30
□ 44 Doug Gilmour [U.S.-Esso ad] .30
□ 45 Wayne Gretzky [CDN-XZX: J. Sakic] 2.00
□ 45 Wayne Gretzky [U.S.] 2.00

Redemption **NRMT-MT**
□□ 46 Mike Gartner, NYRa. [Esso ad.] 4.00
□□ 47 Al Iafrate, Wash. [Coca-Cola ad.] 1.00
□□ 48 Raymond Bourque, Bost. 6.00
□□ 49 Jon Casey (G), Minn. 1.00
□□ 50 All-Stars 1.00

THE FRANCHISE

Series One Insert Set (24 cards): **145.00**
American Insert (1:24) **TF**
□ 1 Raymond Bourque, Bost. 5.00
□ 2 Pat LaFontaine, Buff. 4.00
□ 3 Al MacInnis, Calg. 3.00
□ 4 Jeremy Roenick, Chic. 6.00
□ 5 Mike Modano, Dall. 7.00
□ 6 Steve Yzerman, Detr. 15.00
□ 7 Bill Ranford (G), Edmo. 3.00
□ 8 Sean Burke (G), Hart. 4.00
□ 9 Wayne Gretzky, LosA. 30.00
□ 10 Patrick Roy (G), Mont. 20.00
□ 11 Scott Stevens, NJer. 3.00
□ 12 Pierre Turgeon, NYIs. 3.00
□ 13 Brian Leetch, NYRa. 4.00
□ 14 Peter Sidorkiewicz (G), Otta. 3.00
□ 15 Eric Lindros, Phil. 5.00
□ 16 Mario Lemieux, Pitt. 20.00
□ 17 Joe Sakic, Québ. 10.00
□ 18 Brett Hull, SLou. 7.00
□ 19 Pat Falloon, SanJ. 3.00
□ 20 Brian Bradley, Tamp. 3.00
□ 21 Doug Gilmour, Toro. 4.00
□ 22 Pavel Bure, Vanc. 5.00
□ 23 Kevin Hatcher, Wash. 3.00
□ 24 Teemu Selänne, Winn. 5.00

1993 - 94 SEASONS ACTION PATCHES

Patch Size: 3 1/8" x 4 3/8"
Imprint: (on packaging) SEASONS TM/MC
Complete Set (20 patches): **65.00**
Player **NRMT-MT**
□ 1 Ed Belfour (G), Chic. 3.00
□ 2 Pavel Bure, Vanc. 3.00
□ 3 Paul Coffey, Detr. 2.00
□ 4 Doug Gilmour, Toro. 2.00
□ 5 Wayne Gretzky, LosA. 15.00
□ 6 Brett Hull, SLou. 3.00
□ 7 Jaromir Jagr, Pitt. 2.00
□ 8 Joé Juneau, Bost. 2.00
□ 9 Mario Lemieux, Pitt. 10.00
□ 10 Eric Lindros, Phil. 3.00
□ 11 Shawn McEachern, Pitt. 2.00
□ 12 Alexander Mogilny, Buff. 2.00
□ 13 Adam Oates, Bost. 2.00
□ 14 Félix Potvin (G), Toro. 2.00
□ 15 Jeremy Roenick, Chic. 3.00
□ 16 Patrick Roy (G), Mont. 10.00
□ 17 Joe Sakic, Québ. 6.00
□ 18 Teemu Selänne, Winn. 3.00
□ 19 Kevin Stevens, Pitt. 2.00
□ 20 Steve Yzerman, Detr. 5.00

1993 - 94 SISU

The most expensive singles are Saku Koivu (#41 at $8-10, subsets $3-5) and Jere Lehtinen ($3-5). NHL stars sell at $1-2. All other singles sell between 20¢ and $1.00.
Imprint: © 1993 Leaf
Complete Set (396 cards): **40.00**

Sisu	Sisu
□ 1 Jokerit Helsinki Logo	□ 2 Alpo Suhonen, Coach
□ 3 Ari Sulander (G)	□ 4 Marko Rantanen
□ 5 Ari Salo	□ 6 Kalle Koskinen
□ 7 Sebastian Sulku	□ 8 Waltteri Immonen
□ 9 Mika Strömberg	□ 10 Heikki Riihijärvi
□ 11 Kari Martikainen	□ 12 Erik Hämäläinen
□ 13 Juha Jokiharju	□ 14 Timo Norppa
□ 15 Rami Koivisto	□ 16 Antti Törmänen
□ 17 Keijo Säilynoja	□ 18 Jere Keskinen
□ 19 Jali Wahlsten	□ 20 Mikko Konttila
□ 21 Juha Ylönen	□ 22 Jussi Veinonen
□ 23 Petri Varis	□ 24 Juha Lind
□ 25 Timo Saarikoski	□ 26 Otakar Janecky
□ 27 TPS Turku Logo	□ 28 Yursinov, Coach
□ 29 Juoni Rokama (G)	□ 30 Kimmo Lecklin
□ 31 Jouko Narvanmaa	□ 32 Petteri Nummelin
□ 33 Erik Kakko	□ 34 Tom Koivisto
□ 35 Marko Kiprusoff	□ 36 Kari Harila
□ 37 Hannu Virta	□ 38 Aki Berg
□ 39 Alexander Smirnov	□ 40 Esa Keskinen
□ 41 Saku Koivu $12	□ 42 Jukka Vilander
□ 43 Antti Aalto	□ 44 Mika Karapuu
□ 45 Toni Sihvonen	□ 46 Pavel Torgajev
□ 47 Jere Lehtinen	□ 48 Kai Nurminen
□ 49 Harri Sillgren	□ 50 Niko Mikkola
□ 51 Ari Vuori	□ 52 Lasse Pirjetä
□ 53 Reijo Mikkolainen	□ 54 Marko Jantunen
□ 55 Mikko Virolainen	□ 56 Tappara Logo

- ☐ 57 Boris Majorov, Coach ☐ 58 Jaromir Sindel (G)
- ☐ 59 Timo Hankela (G) ☐ 60 Teemu Kivinen
- ☐ 61 Petri Kalteva ☐ 62 Jari Harjumäki
- ☐ 63 Timo Jutila ☐ 64 Janne Grönvall
- ☐ 65 Jari Grönstand ☐ 66 Pekka Laksola
- ☐ 67 Tommi Haapsaari ☐ 68 Veli-Pekka Kautonen
- ☐ 69 Mikko Peltola ☐ 70 Kari Heikkinen
- ☐ 71 Teemu Numminen ☐ 72 Jiri Kucera
- ☐ 73 Pauli Järvinen ☐ 74 Pasi Forsberg
- ☐ 75 Tero Toivola ☐ 76 Ari Haanpää
- ☐ 77 Tommi Pohja ☐ 78 Samuli Rautio
- ☐ 79 Markus Oijennus ☐ 80 Petri Aaltonen
- ☐ 81 HIFK, Helsinki Logo ☐ 82 Harri Rindell, Coach
- ☐ 83 Sakari Lindfors (G) ☐ 84 Mikael Granlund (G)
- ☐ 85 Kimmo Hyttinen ☐ 86 Jere Karalahti
- ☐ 87 Dan Lambert ☐ 88 Simo Saarinen
- ☐ 89 Pasi Sormunen ☐ 90 Tommi Hämäläinen
- ☐ 91 Pertti Lehtonen ☐ 92 Jari Munck
- ☐ 93 Kai Tervonen ☐ 94 Kim Ahlroos
- ☐ 95 Teppo Kivelä ☐ 96 Darren Boyko
- ☐ 97 Pekka Peltola ☐ 98 Marco Poulsen
- ☐ 99 Valeri Krykov ☐ 100 Jari Laukkanen
- ☐ 101 Ville Peltonen ☐ 102 Pekka Tuomisto
- ☐ 103 Miro Haapaniemi ☐ 104 Mika Kortelainen
- ☐ 105 Marko Ojanen ☐ 106 Iiro Järvi
- ☐ 107 Ilves Tampere Logo ☐ 108 Jalonen, Coach
- ☐ 109 Jukka Tammi (G) ☐ 110 Mika Manninen (G)
- ☐ 111 Jani Nikko ☐ 112 Jukka Ollila
- ☐ 113 Juha Lampinen ☐ 114 Hannu Henriksson
- ☐ 115 Sami Lehtonen ☐ 116 Mikko Niemi
- ☐ 117 Juha-Matti Märijärvi ☐ 118 Jarkko Glad
- ☐ 119 Allan Measures ☐ 120 Mikko Luovi
- ☐ 121 Risto Jalo ☐ 122 Juha Järvenpää
- ☐ 123 Jarno Peltonen ☐ 124 Matti Kaipainen
- ☐ 125 Timo Peltomaa ☐ 126 Esa Tommila
- ☐ 127 Hannu Mattila ☐ 128 Jari Neuvonen
- ☐ 129 Pasi Määttänen ☐ 130 Juha Hautamaa
- ☐ 131 Janne Seva ☐ 132 Sami Ahlberg
- ☐ 133 Jari Virtanen ☐ 134 JyP HT Logo
- ☐ 135 Savolainen, Coach ☐ 136 AP Siekkinen (G)
- ☐ 137 Marko Leinonen (G) ☐ 138 Jan Latvala
- ☐ 139 Markku Heikkinen ☐ 140 Jarmo Jokilahti
- ☐ 141 Veli-Pekka Hård ☐ 142 Kalle Koskinen
- ☐ 143 Vesa Ponto ☐ 144 Petri Kujala
- ☐ 145 Jarmo Rantanen ☐ 146 Harri Laurila
- ☐ 147 Lasse Nieminen ☐ 148 Mika Paananen
- ☐ 149 Mika Arvaja ☐ 150 Marko Virtanen
- ☐ 151 Marko Ek ☐ 152 Joni Lius
- ☐ 153 Teemu Kohvakka ☐ 154 Jari Lindroos
- ☐ 155 Marko Kupari ☐ 156 Markku Ikonen
- ☐ 157 Jyrki Jokinen ☐ 158 Risto Kurkinen
- ☐ 159 KalPa Logo ☐ 160 H. Kapanen, Coach
- ☐ 161 P. Kuivalainen (G) ☐ 162 Kimmo Kapanen
- ☐ 163 Kimmo Timonen ☐ 164 Jari Järvinen
- ☐ 165 Mikko Tavi ☐ 166 Jermu Pisto
- ☐ 167 Antti Tuomenoksa ☐ 168 Vesa Ruotsalainen
- ☐ 169 Vesa Salo ☐ 170 V-P Pekkarinen
- ☐ 171 Tuomas Kalliomäki ☐ 172 Dimitri Zinine
- ☐ 173 Jani Rautio ☐ 174 Janne Kekäläinen
- ☐ 175 Arto Sirviö ☐ 176 Sami Mettovaara
- ☐ 177 Sami Simonen ☐ 178 Pekka Tirkkonen
- ☐ 179 Sami Kapanen ☐ 180 Jussi Tarvainen
- ☐ 181 Lukko Logo ☐ 182 V. Sykora, Coach
- ☐ 183 Jarmo Myllys (G) ☐ 184 Kimmo Vesa (G)
- ☐ 185 Mika Yli-Mäenpää ☐ 186 Jarmo Kuusisto
- ☐ 187 Marko Tuulola ☐ 188 Tuomas Grönman
- ☐ 189 Timo Kulonen ☐ 190 Kari-Pekka Friman
- ☐ 191 Pasi Huura ☐ 192 Harri Suvanto
- ☐ 193 Kamil Kastak ☐ 194 Jari Torkki
- ☐ 195 Kalle Sahlstedt ☐ 196 Tommi Pullola
- ☐ 197 Mika Välilä ☐ 198 Tero Arkiomaa
- ☐ 199 Pasi Saarela ☐ 200 Matti Forss
- ☐ 201 Jussi Kiuru ☐ 202 Mika Alatalo
- ☐ 203 Kimmo Rintanen ☐ 204 Petri Lätti
- ☐ 205 Petr Korinek ☐ 206 Assat Pori Logo
- ☐ 207 V-P Ketola, Coach ☐ 208 Kari Takko (G)
- ☐ 209 Timo Järvinen (G) ☐ 210 Marko Sten
- ☐ 211 Pasi Peltonen ☐ 212 Olli Kaski
- ☐ 213 Jarno Miikkulainen ☐ 214 Juoni Vento
- ☐ 215 Karri Kivi ☐ 216 Stanislav Meciar
- ☐ 217 Nemo Nokkosmäki ☐ 218 Arto Javanainen
- ☐ 219 Janne Virtanen ☐ 220 Vjatseslav Fandul
- ☐ 221 Jari Levonen ☐ 222 Jarno Levonen
- ☐ 223 Jari Korpisalo ☐ 224 Jokke Heinänen
- ☐ 225 Harri Lönnberg ☐ 226 Ari Saarinen
- ☐ 227 Kari Syväsalmi ☐ 228 Jarno Mäkelä
- ☐ 229 Rauli Raitanen ☐ 230 Arto Heiskanen
- ☐ 231 Mikael Kotkaniemi ☐ 232 HPK Logo
- ☐ 233 Matikainen, Coach ☐ 234 Kari Rosenberg (G)
- ☐ 235 Petri Vilen (G) ☐ 236 Marko Allen
- ☐ 237 Mikko Myllykoski ☐ 238 Kim Vähänen
- ☐ 239 Janne Laukkanen ☐ 240 Jari Haapamäki
- ☐ 241 Niko Marttila ☐ 242 Esa Sateri
- ☐ 243 Toni Virta ☐ 244 Marko Palo
- ☐ 245 Markku Piikkilä ☐ 246 Jani Hassinen
- ☐ 247 Jarkko Nikander ☐ 248 Pasi Kivilä
- ☐ 249 Mika Lartama ☐ 250 Tomas Kapusta
- ☐ 251 Tommi Varjonen ☐ 252 Teemu Tamminen
- ☐ 253 Jukka Seppo ☐ 254 Kiekko-Espoo Logo
- ☐ 255 Martti Merra, Coach ☐ 256 Scott Brower (G)
- ☐ 257 Timo Mäki (G) ☐ 258 Petri Pulkkinen
- ☐ 259 Robert Salo ☐ 260 Sami Nuutinen
- ☐ 261 Teemu Sillanpää ☐ 262 Marko Halonen
- ☐ 263 Jimi Helin ☐ 264 Kari Haakana
- ☐ 265 Jukka Tiilikainen ☐ 266 Jan Långbacka
- ☐ 267 Jarmo Muukkonen ☐ 268 Timo Hirvonen
- ☐ 269 Pasi Heinistö ☐ 270 Kimmo Maki-Kokkila
- ☐ 271 Mikko Lempiäinen ☐ 272 Tero Lehterä
- ☐ 273 Hannu Järvenpää ☐ 274 Riku Kuusisto
- ☐ 275 Mikko Halonen ☐ 276 Markku Takala
- ☐ 277 Petro Koivunen ☐ 278 Reipas Lahti Logo
- ☐ 279 K. Mäkinen, Coach ☐ 280 Oldrich Svoboda (G)
- ☐ 281 Pekka Ilmivalta (G) ☐ 282 Matti Vuorio
- ☐ 283 Jari Parviainen ☐ 284 Timo Kahelin
- ☐ 285 Ville Skinnari ☐ 286 Petri Koski
- ☐ 287 Jarkko Hämäläinen ☐ 288 Pasi Ruponen
- ☐ 289 Oldrich Valek ☐ 290 Juha Nurminen
- ☐ 291 Erkki Laine ☐ 292 Sami Lekkerimaki
- ☐ 293 Tommy Kiviaho ☐ 294 Jyrki Poikolainen
- ☐ 295 Sami Wikström ☐ 296 Jonni Vauhkonen
- ☐ 297 Erkki Mäkelä ☐ 298 Jani Uski
- ☐ 299 Jari Multanen ☐ 300 Toni Koivunen
- ☐ 301 Action 1 ☐ 302 Action 2
- ☐ 303 Action 3 ☐ 304 Action 4
- ☐ 305 Action 5 ☐ 306 Action 6
- ☐ 307 Action 7 ☐ 308 Action 8
- ☐ 309 Action 9 ☐ 310 Action 10 (S. Koivu)
- ☐ 311 Action 11 ☐ 312 Action 12
- ☐ 313 Action 13 ☐ 314 Action 14
- ☐ 315 Action 15 ☐ 316 Action 16
- ☐ 317 Action 17 ☐ 318 Action 18
- ☐ 319 Action 19 ☐ 320 Action 20
- ☐ 321 Action 21 ☐ 322 Action 22
- ☐ 323 Action 23 ☐ 324 Action 24
- ☐ 325 Action 25 ☐ 326 Action 26
- ☐ 327 Action 27 ☐ 328 Action 28
- ☐ 329 Action 29 ☐ 330 Action 30
- ☐ 331 Action 31 ☐ 332 Action 32
- ☐ 333 Action 33 ☐ 334 Action 34
- ☐ 335 Action 35 ☐ 336 Action 36
- ☐ 337 Action 37 ☐ 338 Action 38
- ☐ 339 Action 39 ☐ 340 Action 40
- ☐ 341 Action 41 ☐ 342 Action 42
- ☐ 343 Action 43 ☐ 344 Action 44
- ☐ 345 Playoffs 1 ☐ 346 Playoffs 2
- ☐ 347 Playoffs 3 ☐ 348 Playoffs 4
- ☐ 349 HPK - Lukko ☐ 350 Jokerit
- ☐ 351 Jokerit - ässät ☐ 352 TPS - Ilves
- ☐ 353 HPK - JyP HT ☐ 354 Väleriä TPS - ässät
- ☐ 355 Pronssiottelu ☐ 356 Finaali
- ☐ 357 Finaali ☐ 358 Finaali
- ☐ 359 Finaali ☐ 360 LL: Esa Keskinen
- ☐ 361 LL: Tomas Kapusta ☐ 362 LL: Erik Hämäläinen
- ☐ 363 LL: Brian Tutt ☐ 364 LL: Otakar Janecky
- ☐ 365 LL: Ville Peltonen ☐ 366 AS: Petr Briza (G)
- ☐ 367 AS: Jan. Laukkanen ☐ 368 AS: Timo Jutila
- ☐ 369 AS: J. Riihijarvi ☐ 370 AS: Esa Keskinen
- ☐ 371 AS: Jarkko Varvio ☐ 372 Esa Keskinen
- ☐ 373 Vladimir Yursinov ☐ 374 Erik Hämäläinen
- ☐ 375 Timo Lehkonen (G) ☐ 376 German Titov
- ☐ 377 Raimo Summanen ☐ 378 Mikko Haapakoski
- ☐ 379 Marko Palo ☐ 380 S. Mäkelä, Referee
- ☐ 381 TPS Team Card ☐ 382 HPK Hämeenlinna
- ☐ 383 JyP HT Jyväskylä ☐ 384 Juha Riihijärvi
- ☐ 385 Jukka Virtanen ☐ 386 Kari Jalonen
- ☐ 387 Matti Forss ☐ 388 Arto Javanainen
- ☐ 389 Saku Koivu ☐ 390 Janne Niinimaa
- ☐ 391 Ville Peltonen ☐ 392 Jonni Vauhkonen
- ☐ 393 Petri Varis ☐ 394 Antti Aalto
- ☐ 395 Jere Karalaht ☐ 396 Kimmo Timonen

1993 - 94 SLAPSHOT TEAM SETS

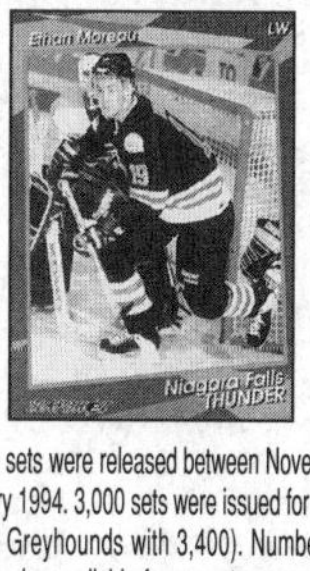

These team sets were released between November 1993 and February 1994. 3,000 sets were issued for each team (except the Greyhounds with 3,400). Numbered uncut sheets were also available for every team except for the Wolves.

PROMOTIONAL CARD

Player	NRMT-MT
☐ Trevor Gallant	.75

DETROIT JR. RED WINGS

Complete Set (25 cards): 15.00

Player / Player
- ☐ 1 Todd Harvey ☐ 2 Jason Saal (G)
- ☐ 3 Aaron Ellis (G) ☐ 4 Chris Mailloux (G)
- ☐ 5 Robin Lacour ☐ 6 Mike Rucinski
- ☐ 7 Eric Cairns ☐ 8 Matt Ball
- ☐ 9 Dale Junkin ☐ 10 Bill McCauley
- ☐ 11 Jeremy Meehan ☐ 12 Mike Harding
- ☐ 13 Brad Cook ☐ 14 Jeff Mitchell
- ☐ 15 Jamie Allison ☐ 16 Dan Pawlaczyk
- ☐ 17 Kevin Brown ☐ 18 Duane Harmer
- ☐ 19 Gerry Skrypec ☐ 20 Shayne McCosh
- ☐ 21 Sean Haggerty ☐ 22 Nic Beaudoin
- ☐ 23 Paul Maurice, Coach ☐ 24 DeBoer, A. Coach
- ☐ 25 Bob Wren

DRUMMONDVILLE VOLTIGEURS

Complete Set (28 cards): 10.00

Player / Player
- ☐ 1 Checklist ☐ 2 Stéphane Routhier (G)
- ☐ 3 Yannick Gagnon (G) ☐ 4 Sébastien Bety
- ☐ 5 Martin Latulippe ☐ 6 Nicolas Savage
- ☐ 7 Sylvain Ducharme ☐ 8 Yan St. Pierre
- ☐ 9 Emmanuel Labranche ☐ 10 Ian Laperrière
- ☐ 11 Louis Bernard ☐ 12 Stéphane St Amour
- ☐ 13 Vincent Tremblay ☐ 14 Denis Gauthier
- ☐ 15 Eric Plante ☐ 16 Christian Marcoux
- ☐ 17 Patrice Charbonneau ☐ 18 Raymond Delarosbil
- ☐ 19 Patrick Livernoche ☐ 20 Luc Decelles
- ☐ 21 François Sasseville ☐ 22 Steve Tardif
- ☐ 23 Mathieu Sunderland ☐ 24 Alexandre Duchesne
- ☐ 25 J. Hamel, Trainer ☐ 26 M. Carrier, A.Trainer
- ☐ 27 A. Lepage, Trainer ☐ 28 Slapshot Calender

GUELPH STORM

Complete Set (30 cards): 12.00

Player / Player
- ☐ 1 Title Card ☐ 2 Jeff O'Neill
- ☐ 3 Mark McArthur (G) ☐ 4 Kayle Short
- ☐ 5 Ryan Risidore ☐ 6 Mike Rusk
- ☐ 7 Regan Stocco ☐ 8 Duane Harmer
- ☐ 9 Sylvain Cloutier ☐ 10 Eric Landry
- ☐ 11 Jamie Wright ☐ 12 Todd Norman
- ☐ 13 Mike Pittman ☐ 14 Ken Belanger
- ☐ 15 Viktor Reuta ☐ 16 Mike Prokopec
- ☐ 17 Jeff Williams ☐ 18 Chris Skoryna
- ☐ 19 Stéphane Lefebvre ☐ 20 Jeff Cowan
- ☐ 21 Murray Hogg ☐ 22 Andy Adams (G)
- ☐ 23 Todd Bertuzzi ☐ 24 Grant Pritchett
- ☐ 25 Rumun Ndur ☐ 26 Jeff O'Neill
- ☐ 27 P. Brydges, A. Coach ☐ 28 John Lovell, Coach
- ☐ 29 Team Picture ☐ 30 Domino's Pizza

KINGSTON FRONTENACS

Complete Set (24 cards): 10.00

Player / Player
- ☐ 1 Greg Lovell (G) ☐ 2 Marc Lamothe (G)
- ☐ 3 T.J. Moss (G) ☐ 4 Marc Moro
- ☐ 5 Trevor Doyle ☐ 6 Jeff Dacosta
- ☐ 7 Gord Walsh ☐ 8 Brian Scott
- ☐ 9 Jason Disher ☐ 10 Alexander Zhurik
- ☐ 11 Ken Boone ☐ 12 Cail Maclean
- ☐ 13 Bill Marandiuk ☐ 14 Martin Sychra
- ☐ 15 Duncan Fader ☐ 16 David Ling
- ☐ 17 Chad Kilger ☐ 18 Greg Kraemer
- ☐ 19 Trent Cull ☐ 20 Steve Parson
- ☐ 21 Craig Rivet ☐ 22 Keli Corpse
- ☐ 23 Brett Lindros ☐ 24 D. Allison/ M. Allison

KITCHENER RANGERS

Complete Set (30 cards): 10.00

Player / Player
- ☐ 1 Checklist ☐ 2 David Belitski (G)
- ☐ 3 Darryl Whyte (G) ☐ 4 Greg McLean
- ☐ 5 Jason Hughes ☐ 6 Gord Dickie
- ☐ 7 Travis Riggin ☐ 8 Norm Dezainde
- ☐ 9 Tim Spitzig ☐ 10 Trevor Gallant
- ☐ 11 Chris Pittman ☐ 12 Ryan Pawluk
- ☐ 13 Jason Morgan ☐ 14 James Boyd
- ☐ 15 Todd Warriner ☐ 16 Mark Donahue
- ☐ 17 Peter Brearley ☐ 18 Andrew Taylor
- ☐ 19 Jason Gladney ☐ 20 Wes Swinson
- ☐ 21 Matt O'Dette ☐ 22 Darren Schmidt
- ☐ 23 Jason Johnson ☐ 24 Eric Manlow
- ☐ 25 Jeff Lillie (G) ☐ 26 Sergei Olympiev
- ☐ 27 J. McDonnell, Coach ☐ 28 R. Chambers, Trainer
- ☐ 29 Rangers trio ☐ 30 Domino's Pizza

NIAGARA FALLS THUNDER

Complete Set (28 cards): 10.00

Player / Player
- ☐ 1 Checklist ☐ 2 Jimmy Hibbert (G)
- ☐ 3 Darryl Foster (G) ☐ 4 Gerry Skrypec
- ☐ 5 Greg de Vries ☐ 6 Tim Thompson
- ☐ 7 Joel Yates ☐ 8 Yianni Loannou
- ☐ 9 Steve Nimigon ☐ 10 Jeff Johnstone
- ☐ 11 Brandon Convery ☐ 12 Dale Junkin
- ☐ 13 Ethan Moreau ☐ 14 Derek Grant
- ☐ 15 Neil Fewster ☐ 16 Jason Reesor
- ☐ 17 Tom Moores ☐ 18 Matthew Mayo
- ☐ 19 Bogdon Savenko ☐ 20 Corey Bricknell
- ☐ 21 Derek Sylvester ☐ 22 Anatoli Filatov
- ☐ 23 Jason Bonsignore ☐ 24 Mike Perna
- ☐ 25 M. Legacé (G) ☐ 26 R. Hall, Coach/ GM
- ☐ 27 C. Johnstone, A.G.M. ☐ 28 Wolves

NORTH BAY CENTENNIALS

Complete Set (25 cards): 10.00

Player / Player
- ☐ 1 Brad Brown ☐ 2 Sandy Allan (G)
- ☐ 3 Rob Lave ☐ 4 Steve McLaren
- ☐ 5 Andy Delmore ☐ 6 Corey Neilson
- ☐ 7 Jason Campeau ☐ 8 Jim Ensom
- ☐ 9 Bill Lang ☐ 10 Ryan Gillis
- ☐ 11 Michael Burman ☐ 12 Stefan Rivard
- ☐ 13 B.J. MacPherson ☐ 14 Lee Jinman
- ☐ 15 Scott Cherrey ☐ 16 Damian Bloye
- ☐ 17 Denis Gaudet ☐ 18 Bob Thornton
- ☐ 19 John Guirestante ☐ 20 Jeff Shevalier
- ☐ 21 Scott Roche (G) ☐ 22 Vitali Yachmenev
- ☐ 23 B. Templeton, Coach ☐ 24 R. Kirsch, A Coach
- ☐ 25 B. Brown/ V.Yachmenev

OSHAWA GENERALS

Complete Set (26 cards): 10.00

Player / Player
- ☐ 1 Checklist ☐ 2 Joel Gagnon (G)
- ☐ 3 Ken Shepard (G) ☐ 4 Jan Snopek
- ☐ 5 David Froh ☐ 6 Brandon Gray
- ☐ 7 Damon Hardy ☐ 8 Sean Brown
- ☐ 9 Jeff Andrews ☐ 10 Stéphane Yelle
- ☐ 11 Stéphane Soullière ☐ 12 Andrew Power
- ☐ 13 Todd Bradley ☐ 14 Darryl Lafrance
- ☐ 15 Darryl Moxam ☐ 16 Robert Dubois
- ☐ 17 Kevin Vaughan ☐ 18 Rob McQuat
- ☐ 19 B.J. Johnston ☐ 20 Paul Doherty
- ☐ 21 Eric Boulton ☐ 22 Marc Savard
- ☐ 23 Chris Hall ☐ 24 Jason McQuat
- ☐ 25 Ryan Lindsay ☐ 26 Generals

PETERBOROUGH PETES

Complete Set (30 cards): 12.00

Player / Player
- ☐ 1 1992-93 OHL Champions ☐ 2 Jonathan Murphy
- ☐ 3 Dave Roche ☐ 4 Rob Giffin
- ☐ 5 Mike Harding ☐ 6 Tim Hill
- ☐ 7 Darryl Moxam ☐ 8 Pat Paone
- ☐ 9 Brent Tully ☐ 10 Zac Bierk (G)
- ☐ 11 Chad Grills ☐ 12 Matt St. Germain
- ☐ 13 Henrik Eppers ☐ 14 Rick Emmett
- ☐ 15 Chad Lang (G) ☐ 16 Cameron Mann
- ☐ 17 Steve Hogg ☐ 18 Mike Williams
- ☐ 19 Ryan Nauss ☐ 20 Jamie Langenbrunner
- ☐ 21 Ryan Douglas (G) ☐ 22 Matt Johnson
- ☐ 23 Kelvin Solari ☐ 24 Dan Delmonte
- ☐ 25 Quade Loghtbody ☐ 26 Adrian Murray
- ☐ 27 Jason Dawe ☐ 28 Mike Harding
- ☐ 29 Chris Pronger ☐ 30 Cardball Heroes

SAULT STE. MARIE GREYHOUNDS

Complete Set (30 cards): 10.00

Player / Player
- ☐ 1 Andrea Carpano (G) ☐ 2 Ryan Douglas (G)
- ☐ 3 Dan Cloutier (G) ☐ 4 Oliver Pastinsky
- ☐ 5 Scott King ☐ 6 Drew Bannister
- ☐ 7 Sean Gagnon ☐ 8 Andre Payette
- ☐ 9 Peter Mackeller ☐ 10 Richard Uniacke
- ☐ 11 Steve Zoryk ☐ 12 Brad Baber
- ☐ 13 Gary Roach ☐ 14 Jeff Gies
- ☐ 15 Tom MacDonald ☐ 16 Rhett Trombley
- ☐ 17 Joe Van Volsen ☐ 18 Andrew Clark
- ☐ 19 Briane Thompson ☐ 20 Aaron Gavey
- ☐ 21 Wade Gibson ☐ 22 Chad Grills
- ☐ 23 Jeff Toms ☐ 24 Steve Sullivan
- ☐ 25 Jeremy Stevenson ☐ 26 Corey Moylan
- ☐ 27 Steve Spina ☐ 28 Dave Mayville, GM
- ☐ 29 Ted Nolan, Coach ☐ 30 D. Flynn/ M. Zuke

SUDBURY WOLVES

Complete Set (24 cards): 12.00

Player / Player
- ☐ 1 Shawn Silver (G) ☐ 2 Jeff Melnechuk (G)
- ☐ 3 Jay McKee ☐ 4 Chris McMurtry
- ☐ 5 Rory Fitzpatrick ☐ 6 Mike Wilson
- ☐ 7 Shawn Frappier ☐ 8 Jamie Rivers
- ☐ 9 Zdenek Nedved ☐ 10 Ryan Shanahan
- ☐ 11 Sean Venedam ☐ 12 Andrew Dale
- ☐ 13 Mark Giannetti ☐ 14 Rick Bodkin
- ☐ 15 Barrie Moore ☐ 16 Jamie Matthews
- ☐ 17 Gary Coupal ☐ 18 Ilya Lysenko
- ☐ 19 Simon Sherry ☐ 20 Steve Potvin
- ☐ 21 Joel Poirier ☐ 22 Mike Yeo
- ☐ 23 Bob MacIssac ☐ 24 Legend: Paul DiPietro

WINDSOR SPITFIRES

Complete Set (26 cards): 10.00

Player / Player
- ☐ 1 Ed Jovanovski ☐ 2 Shawn Silver (G)
- ☐ 3 Travis Scott (G) ☐ 4 Mike Martin
- ☐ 5 Daryl Lavoie ☐ 6 Craig Lutes
- ☐ 7 David Pluck ☐ 8 Bill Bowler
- ☐ 9 David Green ☐ 10 Adam Young
- ☐ 11 Mike Loach ☐ 12 Brady Blain
- ☐ 13 Shayne McCosh ☐ 14 Rob Shearer
- ☐ 15 Joel Poirier ☐ 16 Cory Evans
- ☐ 17 Vladimir Kretchine ☐ 18 Dave Roche
- ☐ 19 Ryan Stewart ☐ 20 Dave Geris
- ☐ 21 Dan West ☐ 22 Luke Clowes
- ☐ 23 John Cooper ☐ 24 Akil Adams
- ☐ 25 Pizza Hut ☐ 26 Steve Bell, AM800

1993 - 94 SPORTS ILLUSTRATED FOR KIDS

These cards were distributed as part of nine-card perforated sheets included in *Sports Illustrated for Kids*. While these cards were intended for editorial purposes, they have made their way onto the secondary market. Cards issued in the 12 issues between July 1993 and June 1994 were numbered 163-270.

1993-94 Sports Illustrated for Kids	
☐ Oct. 1993 • 191 Manon Rhéaume (G)	8.00
☐ Nov. 1993 • 200 Teemu Selänne, Winn.	3.00
☐ Dec. 1993 • 211 Bobby Hull	3.00
☐ Mar. 1994 • 241 Luc Robitaille	2.00
☐ Apr 1994 • 246 Mike Gartner	2.00
☐ May 1993 • 259 Sergei Fedorov, Detr.	2.00
☐ Jun. 1993 • 265 Cam Neely, Bost.	2.00

1993 - 94 STARTING LINEUP

Two cards were packaged with each figure.

Complete Set (24 cards): 45.00

Player	Card
☐ Ed Belfour (G), Chic.	2.00
☐ Ed Belfour (G), Chic.	2.00
☐ 504087 Raymond Bourque, Bost.	2.00
☐ 504109 Raymond Bourque, Bost. [Hit Man]	2.00
☐ Grant Fuhr (G), Buff. [U.S. only]	1.00
☐ Grant Fuhr (G), Buff.	1.00
☐ Brett Hull, SLou.	2.00
☐ Brett Hull, SLou.	2.00
☐ 504112 Jaromir Jagr, Pitt. [Superstar Scorer]	2.00
☐ Jaromir Jagr, Pitt.	2.00
☐ Pat LaFontaine, Buff.	1.00
☐ Pat LaFontaine, Buff.	1.00
☐ 504082 Mario Lemieux, Pitt.	6.00
☐ 504104 M. Lemieux, Pitt. [Superstar Scorer]	6.00
☐ 504091 Eric Lindros, Phil.	2.00
☐ 504113 Eric Lindros, Phil.	2.00
☐ 504085 Mark Messier, NYRa.	2.00
☐ 504107 Mark Messier, NYRa.	2.00
☐ Jeremy Roenick, Chic.	1.00
☐ Jeremy Roenick, Chic.	1.00
☐ Patrick Roy (G), Mont.	6.00
☐ Patrick Roy (G), Mont.	6.00
☐ Steve Yzerman, Detr.	4.00
☐ Steve Yzerman, Detr.	4.00

FIGURES

Most figures were available in both American (English text) and Canadian (bilingual text) packaging. The figures and cards in each type of package are the same. Priced below are retail selling prices for packaged figures (each package includes two cards) and loose figures.

Canadian Set (11 packages): 275.00
American Set (12 packages): 550.00
Figure Set (12 loose figures): 75.00

Player	US	CAN	Loose

Ed Belfour (G), Chic.	125.00	75.00	15.00
Raymond Bourque, Bost.	30.00	25.00	4.00
Grant Fuhr, Buff.	200.00	-	35.00
Brett Hull, SLou.	15.00	15.00	3.00
Jaromir Jagr, Pitt.	35.00	25.00	4.00
Pat LaFontaine, Buff.	90.00	50.00	5.00
Mario Lemieux, Pitt.	30.00	25.00	4.00
Eric Lindros, Phil.	40.00	25.00	4.00
Mark Messier, NYRa.	30.00	20.00	3.00
Jeremy Roenick, Chic.	25.00	20.00	3.00
Patrick Roy (G), Mont.	100.00	80.00	15.00
Steve Yzerman, Detr.	35.00	25.00	4.00

1993 - 94 TITREX / POWER PLAY

We do not have pricing information on this set.

Titrex	Titrex
1 Guy Lafleur	2 Guy Lafleur
3 Guy Lafleur	4 Guy Lafleur
5 Guy Lafleur	6 Guy Lafleur
7 Guy Lafleur	8 Guy Lafleur
9 Guy Lafleur	10 Guy Lafleur
11 Guy Lafleur	12 Guy Lafleur
13 Guy Lafleur	14 Guy Lafleur
15 Guy Lafleur	16 Guy Lafleur
17 Guy Lafleur	18 Guy Lafleur
19 Guy Lafleur	20 Guy Lafleur
21 Guy Lafleur	22 Guy Lafleur
23 Guy Lafleur	24 Guy Lafleur

Promotional Postcards	Titrex
Guy Lafleur 5" x 7"	
Guy Lafleur Flower Power 4" x 6"	

1993 - 94 TOPPS STADIUM CLUB

This series features up to five versions: a Topps card (1-500), an O-Pee-Chee (1-250, "PTD in U.S.A."), a Topps First Day Issue (1-500), an O-Pee-Chee First Day Issue (1-250, "PTD. in U.S.A.") and a Members Only parallel (1-500). O-Pee-Chee regular cards may carry a 10-50% premium over Topps regular cards and O-Pee-Chee First Day Issues carry a 10-25% premium over Topps First Day Issues.

Imprint: © 1993 the topps company, inc.

Series One (250 cards):	**-1100.00**	**20.00**	
Series Two (250 cards):	**- 800.00**	**20.00**	
Members Only Set (558 cards):	**2900.00**	**-**	**-**
Common Player:	**5.00**	**3.50**	**.20**

Player	MO	FDI	TSC
1 Guy Carbonneau, Mont.	10.00	5.00	.20
2 Joe Cirella, Flor.	5.00	3.00	.20
3 Laurie Boschman, Otta.	5.00	3.00	.20
4 Arturs Irbe (G), SanJ.	10.00	10.00	.20
5 Adam Creighton, Tamp.	5.00	3.00	.20
6 M. McPhee, Minn. (Dall.)	5.00	3.00	.20
7 Jeff Beukeboom, NYRa.	5.00	3.00	.20
8 Kevin Todd, Edmo.	5.00	3.00	.20
9 Yvon Corriveau, Hart.	5.00	3.00	.20
10 Eric Lindros, Phil.	30.00	25.00	.50
11 Martin Rucinsky, Québ.	5.00	5.00	.20
12 Michel Goulet, Chic.	15.00	10.00	.20
13 S. Pellerin, NJer. RC	**10.00**	**5.00**	**.50**
14 Mike Eagles, Winn.	5.00	3.00	.20
15 Stephen Heinze, Bost.	5.00	3.00	.20
16 Gerard Gallant, Detr.	5.00	3.00	.20
17 Kelly Miller, Wash.	5.00	3.00	.20
18 Petr Nedved, Vanc.	10.00	5.00	.20
19 Joe Mullen, Pitt.	10.00	10.00	.20
20 Pat LaFontaine, Buff.	15.00	15.00	.20
21 Garth Butcher, SLou.	5.00	3.00	.20
22 Jeff Reese (G), Calg.	5.00	3.00	.20
23 Dave Andreychuk, Toro.	10.00	5.00	.20
24 Patrick Flatley, NYIs.	5.00	3.00	.20
25 T. Sandström, LosA.	5.00	5.00	.20
26 André Racicot (G), Mont.	5.00	3.00	.20
27 Patrice Brisebois, Mont.	5.00	3.00	.20
28 N. Broten, Minn. (Dall.)	5.00	5.00	.20
29 Mark Freer, Otta.	5.00	3.00	.20
30 Kelly Kisio, SanJ.	5.00	3.00	.20
31 Scott Mellanby, Flor.	5.00	5.00	.20
32 Joe Sakic, Québ.	50.00	40.00	.50
33 Kerry Huffman, Québ.	5.00	3.00	.20
34 Evgeny Davydov, Winn.	5.00	3.00	.20
35 Mark Messier, NYRa.	30.00	25.00	.50
36 Pat Verbeek, Hart.	10.00	5.00	.20
37 G. Gilbert, Chic. (NYRa.)	5.00	3.00	.20
38 John Tucker, Tamp.	5.00	3.00	.20
39 Claude Lemieux, NJer.	10.00	5.00	.20
40 Shayne Corson, Edmo.	10.00	5.00	.20
41 Gord** Roberts, Bost.	10.00	10.00	.20
42 Jirí Slégr, Vanc.	5.00	3.00	.20
43 Kevin Dineen, Phil.	5.00	3.00	.20
44 Johan Garpenlöv, SanJ.	5.00	3.00	.20
45 Sergei Fedorov, Detr.	30.00	25.00	.50
46 Rich Sutter, SLou.	5.00	5.00	.20
47 Dave Hannan, Buff.	5.00	3.00	.20
48 Sylvain Lefebvre, Toro.	5.00	3.00	.20
49 Pat Elynuik, Wash.	5.00	3.00	.20
50 Ray Ferraro, NYIs.	5.00	3.00	.20
51 Brent Ashton, Calg.	5.00	3.00	.20
52 Paul Stanton, Pitt.	5.00	3.00	.20
53 Kevin Haller, Mont.	5.00	3.00	.20
54 Kelly Hrudey (G), LosA.	10.00	5.00	.20
55 R. Courtnall, Minn. (Dall.)	5.00	5.00	.20
56 Alexei Zhamnov, Winn.	10.00	5.00	.20
57 Andrei Lomakin, Flor.	5.00	3.00	.20
58 Keith Brown, Chic.	5.00	3.00	.20
59 Glen Murray, Bost.	15.00	10.00	.20
60 Kay Whitmore (G), Vanc.	5.00	3.00	.20
61 Stéphane Richer, NJer.	5.00	5.00	.20
62 Todd Gill, Toro.	5.00	3.00	.20
63 Bob Sweeney, Buff.	5.00	3.00	.20
64 M. Richter (G), NYRa.	15.00	10.00	.20
65 Brett Hull, SLou.	30.00	25.00	.50
66 Sylvain Côté, Wash.	5.00	3.00	.20
67 Kirk Muller, Mont.	10.00	5.00	.20
68 Ronnie Stern, Calg.	5.00	3.00	.20
69 Josef Beránek, Phil.	5.00	3.00	.20
70 Steve Yzerman, Detr.	75.00	60.00	1.00
71 Don Beaupré (G), Wash.	5.00	3.00	.20
72 Ed Courtenay, SanJ.	5.00	3.00	.20
73 Zdeno Ciger, Edmo.	5.00	3.00	.20
74 Andrew Cassels, Hart.	5.00	5.00	.20
75 Roman Hamrlik, Tamp.	5.00	5.00	.20
76 Benoît Hogue, NYIs.	5.00	3.00	.20
77 Andrei Kovalenko, Québ.	5.00	3.00	.20
78 R. Brind'Amour, Phil.	10.00	5.00	.20
79 Tom Barrasso (G), Pitt.	10.00	10.00	.20
80 Al Iafrate, Wash.	5.00	5.00	.20
81 Bret Hedican, SLou.	5.00	3.00	.20
82 Peter Bondra, Wash.	15.00	15.00	.20
83 Ted Donato, Bost.	5.00	3.00	.20
84 Chris Lindberg, Calg.	5.00	3.00	.20
85 Vanbiesbrouck (G), Flor.	15.00	10.00	.20
86 Ron Sutter, SLou.	5.00	5.00	.20
87 Luc Robitaille, LosA.	25.00	20.00	.20
88 Brian Leetch, NYRa.	15.00	15.00	.20
89 Randy Wood, Buff.	5.00	3.00	.20
90 Dirk Graham, Chic.	5.00	3.00	.20
91 A. Mogilny, Buff.	15.00	10.00	.20
92 Mike Keane, Mont.	5.00	3.00	.20
93 Adam Oates, Bost.	10.00	10.00	.20
94 V. Butsayev, Phil.	5.00	3.00	.20
95 John LeClair, Mont.	25.00	20.00	.20
96 Joe Nieuwendyk, Calg.	10.00	10.00	.20
97 M. Andersson, Tamp.	5.00	3.00	.20
98 Jaromir Jagr, Pitt.	30.00	25.00	.50
99 Ed Belfour (G), Chic.	30.00	25.00	.50
100 David Reid, Bost.	5.00	3.00	.20
101 D. Kasparaitis, NYIs.	5.00	5.00	.20
102 Zarley Zalapski, Hart.	5.00	3.00	.20
103 Christian Ruuttu, Chic.	5.00	3.00	.20
104 Phil Housley, Winn.	10.00	5.00	.20
105 Al MacInnis, Calg.	10.00	10.00	.20
106 T. Sjödin, Minn. (Dall.)	5.00	3.00	.20
107 Richard Smehlik, Buff.	5.00	3.00	.20
108 Jyrki Lumme, Vanc.	5.00	5.00	.20
109 D. Roussel (G), Phil.	5.00	3.00	.20
110 Mike Gartner, NYRa.	25.00	20.00	.20
111 Bernie Nicholls, NJer.	5.00	5.00	.20
112 Mark Howe, Detr.	10.00	5.00	.20
113 Richard Pilon, NYIs.	5.00	3.00	.20
114 Jeff Odgers, SanJ.	5.00	3.00	.20
115 Gilbert Dionne, Mont.	5.00	3.00	.20
116 Peter Zezel, Toro.	5.00	3.00	.20
117 Don Sweeney, Bost.	5.00	3.00	.20
118 Jimmy Carson, LosA.	5.00	3.00	.20
119 Igor Korolev, SLou.	5.00	3.00	.20
120 Bob Kudelski, Otta.	5.00	3.00	.20
121 Dave Lowry, Flor.	5.00	3.00	.20
122 Kasper v.Lindros	10.00	5.00	.20
123 Ridley v.Lindros	10.00	5.00	.20
124 Dave Tippett, Pitt.	5.00	3.00	.20
125 Cliff Ronning, Vanc.	5.00	5.00	.20
126 Bruce Driver, NJer.	5.00	3.00	.20
127 S. Matteau, Chic.	5.00	3.00	.20
128 Joel Otto, Calg.	5.00	3.00	.20
129 Alexei Kovalev, NYRa.	15.00	15.00	.20
130 Modano, Minn. (Dall.)	30.00	25.00	.50
131 B. Ranford (G), Edmo.	10.00	10.00	.20
132 Petr* Svoboda, Buff.	5.00	5.00	.20
133 Roger Johansson, Calg.	5.00	3.00	.20
134 Marc Bureau, Tamp.	5.00	3.00	.20
135 Keith Tkachuk, Winn.	15.00	15.00	.20
136 Mark Recchi, Phil.	10.00	10.00	.20
137 Bob Probert, Detr.	10.00	5.00	.20
138 Uwe Krupp, NYIs.	5.00	3.00	.20
139 Mike Sullivan, SanJ.	5.00	3.00	.20
140 Doug Gilmour, Toro.	15.00	15.00	.20
141 Selänne, Awards	25.00	20.00	.20
142 Dave Poulin, Awards	5.00	3.00	.20
143 M. Lemieux, Awards	90.00	75.00	1.50
144 Belfour (G), Awards	5.00	5.00	.20
145 P. Turgeon, Awards	10.00	10.00	.20
146 M. Lemieux, Awards	90.00	75.00	1.50
147 Chris Chelios, Awards	15.00	15.00	.20
148 M. Lemieux, Awards	90.00	75.00	1.50
149 Doug Gilmour, Awards	15.00	15.00	.20
150 Belfour (G), Awards	5.00	5.00	.20
151 Paul Ranheim, Calg.	5.00	3.00	.20
152 Gino Cavallini, Québ.	5.00	3.00	.20
153 Kevin Hatcher, Wash.	5.00	3.00	.20
154 Marc Bergevin, Tamp.	5.00	3.00	.20
155 Marty McSorley, LosA.	5.00	5.00	.20
156 Bellows with Cup	5.00	5.00	.20
157 Patrick Poulin, Hart.	5.00	3.00	.20
158 Kevin Stevens, Pitt.	5.00	5.00	.20
159 Bobby Holik, NJer.	10.00	5.00	.20
160 R. Bourque, Bost.	35.00	30.00	.50
161 Bryan Marchment, Chic.	5.00	3.00	.20
162 Cu. Joseph (G), SLou.	30.00	25.00	.50
163 K. McLean (G), Vanc.	10.00	5.00	.20
164 T. Numminen, Winn.	10.00	5.00	.20
165 Kevin Lowe, NYRa.	10.00	5.00	.20
166 Cheveldae (G), Detr.	5.00	3.00	.20
167 Brad Dalgarno, NYIs.	5.00	3.00	.20
168 Glenn Anderson, Toro.	10.00	5.00	.20
169 Frantisek Musil, Calg.	5.00	5.00	.20
170 Éric Desjardins, Mont.	10.00	5.00	.20
171 Doug Zmolek, SanJ.	5.00	3.00	.20
172 Mark Lamb, Otta.	5.00	3.00	.20
173 Ludwig, Minn. (Dall.)	5.00	3.00	.20
174 Gaudreau, SanJ. RC	**5.00**	**5.00**	**.50**
175 Bob Carpenter, Wash.	5.00	5.00	.20
176 Mike Ricci, Québ.	10.00	5.00	.20
177 Brian Skrudland, Flor.	5.00	3.00	.20
178 D. Hasek (G), Buff.	30.00	25.00	.50
179 Pat Conacher, LosA.	5.00	3.00	.20
180 Mark Janssens, Hart.	5.00	3.00	.20
181 Brent Fedyk, Phil.	5.00	3.00	.20
182 Rob DiMaio, Tamp.	5.00	3.00	.20
183 Dave Manson, Edmo.	5.00	3.00	.20
184 Janne Ojanen, NJer.	5.00	3.00	.20
185 Ryan Walter, Vanc.	5.00	3.00	.20
186 Michael Nylander, Hart.	5.00	5.00	.20
187 Stephen Leach, Bost.	5.00	3.00	.20
188 Jeff R. Brown, SLou.	5.00	3.00	.20
189 S. McEachern, Pitt.	10.00	5.00	.20
190 J. Roenick, Chic.	25.00	20.00	.20
191 Darrin Shannon, Winn.	5.00	3.00	.20
192 Wendel Clark, Toro.	25.00	20.00	.20
193 Kevin Miller, SLou.	5.00	3.00	.20
194 Paul DiPietro, Mont.	5.00	3.00	.20
195 Steve Thomas, NYIs.	5.00	5.00	.20
196 Nicklas Lidström, Detr.	15.00	15.00	.20
197 Ed Olczyk, NYRa.	5.00	5.00	.20
198 Robert Reichel, Calg.	10.00	5.00	.20
199 Neil Brady, Otta.	5.00	3.00	.20
200 W. Gretzky, LosA.	125.00	100.00	2.00
201 Adrien Plavsic, Vanc.	5.00	3.00	.20
202 Joé Juneau, Bost.	5.00	5.00	.20
203 Brad May, Buff.	5.00	3.00	.20
204 Igor Kravchuk, Edmo.	5.00	3.00	.20
205 Keith Acton, Phil.	5.00	3.00	.20
206 Ken Daneyko, NJer.	5.00	3.00	.20
207 Sean Burke (G), Hart.	15.00	15.00	.20
208 Jayson More, SanJ.	5.00	3.00	.20
209 John Cullen, Toro.	5.00	5.00	.20
210 T. Selänne, Winn.	25.00	20.00	.20
211 Brent Sutter, Chic.	5.00	5.00	.20
212 Brian Bradley, Tamp.	5.00	3.00	.20
213 Donald Audette, Buff.	10.00	10.00	.20
214 Philippe Bozon, SLou.	5.00	3.00	.20
215 Derek King, NYIs.	5.00	3.00	.20
216 Cam Neely, Bost.	30.00	25.00	.50
217 Keith Primeau, Detr.	10.00	10.00	.20
218 J. Steve Smith, Chic.	5.00	5.00	.20
219 Ken Sutton, Buff.	5.00	3.00	.20
220 Dale Hawerchuk, Buff.	15.00	15.00	.20
221 Alexei Zhitnik, LosA.	5.00	3.00	.20
222 Glen Wesley, Bost.	5.00	3.00	.20
223 Nelson Emerson, SLou.	5.00	3.00	.20
224 Pat Falloon, SanJ.	5.00	3.00	.20
225 Darryl Sydor, LosA.	5.00	5.00	.20
226 Tony Amonte, NYRa.	15.00	15.00	.20
227 Brian Mullen, NYIs.	5.00	3.00	.20
228 Gary Suter, Calg.	5.00	5.00	.20
229 David Shaw, Bost.	5.00	3.00	.20
230 Troy Murray, Chic.	5.00	3.00	.20
231 P. Roy (G), Mont.	90.00	75.00	1.50
232 Michel Petit, Calg.	5.00	3.00	.20
233 Wayne Presley, Buff.	5.00	3.00	.20
234 Keith Jones, Wash.	5.00	3.00	.20
235 Gary Roberts, Calg.	10.00	10.00	.20
236 Steve Larmer, Chic.	10.00	10.00	.20
237 V. Kamensky, Québ.	10.00	5.00	.20
238 Ulf Dahlén, Minn. (Dall.)	5.00	3.00	.20
239 Danton Cole, Tamp.	5.00	3.00	.20
240 Damphousse, Mont.	15.00	15.00	.20
241 Yuri Khmylev, Buff.	5.00	3.00	.20
242 Stéphane Quintal, SLou.	5.00	3.00	.20
243 Peter Taglianetti, Pitt.	5.00	3.00	.20
244 Gary Leeman, Mont.	5.00	3.00	.20
245 S. Nemchinov, NYRa.	5.00	5.00	.20
246 Rob Blake, LosA.	15.00	15.00	.20
247 Steve Chiasson, Detr.	5.00	3.00	.20
248 V. Malakhov, NYIs.	5.00	3.00	.20
249 Checklist	5.00	3.00	.20
250 Checklist	5.00	3.00	.20
251 Kjell Samuelsson, Pitt.	5.00	3.00	.20
252 Terry Carkner, Detr.	5.00	3.00	.20
253 Bill Lindsay, Flor.	5.00	3.00	.20
254 Bob Essensa (G), Winn.	5.00	3.00	.20
255 Jocelyn Lemieux, Chic.	5.00	3.00	.20
256 Joe Sacco, Anah.	5.00	3.00	.20
257 Marty McInnis, NYIs.	5.00	3.00	.20
258 Warren Rychel, LosA.	5.00	3.00	.20
259 David Maley, SanJ.	5.00	3.00	.20
260 Grant Fuhr (G), Buff.	15.00	15.00	.20
261 Scott Young, Québ.	10.00	5.00	.20
262 Ed Ronan, Mont.	5.00	3.00	.20
263 M. Aivazoff, Detr. RC	**5.00**	**5.00**	**.50**
264 Murray Craven, Vanc.	5.00	3.00	.20
265 V. Fetisov, NJer.	15.00	15.00	.20
266 Chris Dahlquist, Calg.	5.00	3.00	.20
267 Norm Maciver, Otta.	5.00	3.00	.20
268 A. Godynyuk, Flor.	5.00	3.00	.20
269 Mikael Renberg, Phil.	20.00	15.00	.20
270 Adam Graves, NYRa.	10.00	10.00	.20
271 R. Ladouceur, Anah.	5.00	3.00	.20
272 F. Pietrangelo (G), Hart.	5.00	3.00	.20
273 Basil McRae, SLou.	5.00	3.00	.20
274 Bryan Smolinski, Bost.	5.00	3.00	.20
275 D. Puppa (G), Tamp.	5.00	3.00	.20
276 Wakaluk (G), Minn. (Dall.)	5.00	3.00	.20
277 Dmitri Khristich, Wash.	5.00	3.00	.20
278 Vladimír Vujtek, Edmo.	5.00	3.00	.20
279 Tom Kurvers, NYIs.	5.00	3.00	.20
280 Félix Potvin (G), Toro.	15.00	15.00	.20
281 Keith Brown, Flor.	5.00	3.00	.20
282 Thomas Steen, Winn.	5.00	3.00	.20
283 Larry Murphy, Pitt.	5.00	5.00	.20
284 Bob Corkum, Anah.	5.00	3.00	.20
285 Tony Granato, LosA.	5.00	5.00	.20
286 Cam Russell, Chic.	5.00	3.00	.20
287 John MacLean, NJer.	5.00	3.00	.20
288 Shawn Antoski, Vanc.	5.00	3.00	.20
289 Pelle Eklund, Phil.	5.00	3.00	.20
290 Chris Pronger, Hart.	35.00	30.00	.50
291 A. Karpovtsev, NYRa.	5.00	5.00	.20
292 Paul Laus, Flor. RC	**5.00**	**5.00**	**.50**
293 Jaroslav Otevrel, SanJ.	5.00	3.00	.20
294 Dino Ciccarelli, Detr.	10.00	5.00	.20
295 Guy Hebert (G), Anah.	5.00	5.00	.20
296 Dave Karpa, Québ.	5.00	3.00	.20
297 Denis Savard, Tamp.	10.00	10.00	.20
298 Jim* Johnson, Dall.	5.00	3.00	.20
299 K. Maltby, Edmo. RC	**15.00**	**10.00**	**1.00**
300 A. Daigle, Otta.	10.00	5.00	.20
301 Dave Poulin, Wash.	5.00	3.00	.20
302 James Patrick, Hart.	5.00	3.00	.20
303 Jon Casey (G), Bost.	5.00	3.00	.20
304 Yves Racine, Phil.	5.00	3.00	.20
305 Craig Simpson, Buff.	5.00	3.00	.20
306 M. Krushelnyski, Toro.	5.00	3.00	.20
307 M. Fitzpatrick (G), Flor.	5.00	3.00	.20
308 Charlie Huddy, LosA.	5.00	3.00	.20
309 Todd Ewen, Anah.	5.00	3.00	.20
310 Mario Lemieux, Pitt.	90.00	75.00	1.50
311 Mark Astley, Buff. RC	**5.00**	**5.00**	**.50**
312 Sergei Zubov, NYRa.	5.00	5.00	.20
313 Shawn Burr, Detr.	5.00	3.00	.20
314 Valeri Zelepukin, NJer.	5.00	3.00	.20
315 S. Fiset (G), Québ.	10.00	5.00	.20
316 C.J. Young, Flor.	5.00	3.00	.20
317 Luciano Borsato, Winn.	5.00	3.00	.20
318 Darcy Loewen, Otta.	5.00	3.00	.20
319 M. Vernon (G), Calg.	10.00	10.00	.20
320 Chris Gratton, Tamp.	15.00	10.00	.20
321 M. Barnaby, Buff.	5.00	3.00	.20
322 Mike Rathje, SanJ.	10.00	5.00	.20
323 Sergio Momesso, Vanc.	5.00	3.00	.20
324 David Volek, NYIs.	5.00	3.00	.20
325 R. Tugnutt (G), Anah.	10.00	10.00	.20
326 Jeff Hackett (G), Chic.	10.00	5.00	.20
327 R. Stauber (G), LosA.	5.00	3.00	.20
328 Chris Terreri (G), NJer.	5.00	3.00	.20
329 Rick Tocchet, Pitt.	10.00	5.00	.20
330 V'b'sbrouck (G), Flor.	15.00	10.00	.20
331 D. Berehowsky, Toro.	5.00	3.00	.20
332 Alexei Kasatonov, Anah.	5.00	5.00	.20
333 V. Konstantinov, Detr.	10.00	5.00	.20
334 John Blue (G), Bost.	5.00	3.00	.20
335 Craig Janney, SLou.	5.00	5.00	.20
336 C. Leschyshyn, Québ.	5.00	3.00	.20
337 Todd Krygier, Wash.	5.00	3.00	.20
338 Boris Mironov, Winn.	10.00	5.00	.20
339 J. Messier, NYRa. RC	**5.00**	**5.00**	**.50**
340 T. Söderström (G), Phil.	5.00	3.00	.20
341 R. Cunneyworth, Hart.	5.00	3.00	.20
342 M. Ferner, Anah. RC	**5.00**	**5.00**	**.50**
343 Stéphan Lebeau, Mont.	5.00	3.00	.20
344 Jody Hull, Flor.	5.00	3.00	.20
345 J. Arnott, Edmo. RC	**30.00**	**20.00**	**2.00**
346 Gerard Gallant, Tamp.	5.00	3.00	.20
347 S. JG. Richer, Flor. RC	**5.00**	**5.00**	**.50**
348 Jeff Shantz, Chic. RC	**5.00**	**5.00**	**.50**
349 Brian Skrudland, Flor.	5.00	3.00	.20
350 Osgood (G), Detr. RC	**35.00**	**30.00**	**3.00**
351 Gary Shuchuk, LosA.	5.00	3.00	.20
352 M. Brodeur (G), NJer.	50.00	40.00	.50
353 Bob Rouse, Toro.	5.00	3.00	.20
354 Doug Bodger, Buff.	5.00	3.00	.20
355 Mike Craig, Minn. (Dall.)	5.00	3.00	.20
356 Ulf Samuelsson, Pitt.	5.00	3.00	.20
357 Trevor Linden, Vanc.	10.00	10.00	.20
358 Dennis Vaske, NYIs.	5.00	3.00	.20
359 Alexei Yashin, Otta.	35.00	30.00	.50
360 Paul Ysebaert, Winn.	5.00	3.00	.20
361 Shaun Van Allen, Anah.	5.00	3.00	.20
362 Sandis Ozolinsh, SanJ.	5.00	5.00	.20
363 Todd Elik, SanJ.	5.00	3.00	.20
364 G. Titov, Calg. RC	**5.00**	**5.00**	**.50**
365 Alexander Semak, NJer.	5.00	3.00	.20
366 Allen Pedersen, Hart.	5.00	3.00	.20
367 Greg Johnson, Detr.	10.00	5.00	.20
368 Anatoli Semenov, Anah.	5.00	3.00	.20
369 Scott Mellanby, Flor.	5.00	5.00	.20
370 Mats Sundin, Québ.	30.00	25.00	.50
371 Norström, NYRa. RC	**15.00**	**10.00**	**1.00**
372 G. Featherstone, Bost.	5.00	3.00	.20
373 Sergei Petrenko, Buff.	5.00	5.00	.20
374 Mike Donnelly, LosA.	5.00	3.00	.20
375 N. Borschevsky, Toro.	5.00	3.00	.20
376 Rob Zamuner, Tamp.	5.00	5.00	.20
377 Steven King, Anah.	5.00	3.00	.20
378 R. Tabaracci (G), Wash.	5.00	3.00	.20
379 Dave Lowry, Flor.	5.00	5.00	.20
380 Pierre Turgeon, NYIs.	10.00	10.00	.20
381 Garry Galley, Phil.	5.00	3.00	.20
382 Doug Weight, Edmo.	15.00	15.00	.20
383 Scott Stevens, NJer.	10.00	10.00	.20
384 M. Tinordi, Minn. (Dall.)	5.00	3.00	.20
385 Ron Francis, Pitt.	15.00	15.00	.20
386 Mark Greig, Hart.	5.00	3.00	.20
387 Sean Hill, Anah.	5.00	3.00	.20
388 Vy. Kozlov, Detr.	5.00	5.00	.20
389 B. Shanahan, SLou.	30.00	25.00	.50
390 Theoren Fleury, Calg.	15.00	15.00	.20
391 M. Schneider, Mont.	5.00	5.00	.20
392 Tom Fitzgerald, Flor.	5.00	3.00	.20
393 Markus Näslund, Pitt.	60.00	50.00	1.00
394 Travis Green, NYIs.	5.00	5.00	.20
395 Troy Loney, Anah.	5.00	3.00	.20
396 Gord Donnelly, Buff.	5.00	3.00	.20
397 Owen Nolan, Québ.	15.00	15.00	.20
398 Steve Larmer, NYRa.	10.00	10.00	.20
399 Dave Archibald, Otta.	5.00	3.00	.20
400 Jari Kurri, LosA.	30.00	25.00	.50

401 Jim Paek, Pitt.	5.00	3.00	.20
402 Andrei Lomakin, Flor.	5.00	3.00	.20
403 S. Niedermayer, NJer.	10.00	5.00	.20
404 Bob Errey, SanJ.	5.00	3.00	.20
405 Michal Pivonka, Wash.	5.00	3.00	.20
406 Doug Lidster, NYRa.	5.00	3.00	.20
407 Garry Valk, Anah.	5.00	3.00	.20
408 Geoff Sanderson, Hart.	5.00	5.00	.20
409 S. Malgunas, Phil. RC	**5.00**	**5.00**	**.50**
410 C. MacTavish, Edmo.	5.00	3.00	.20
411 J. Modry, NJer. RC	**5.00**	**5.00**	**.50**
412 S. Chambers, Tamp.	5.00	3.00	.20
413 Geoff Courtnall, Vanc.	5.00	3.00	.20
414 Mark Hardy, LosA.	5.00	3.00	.20
415 Martin Straka, Pitt.	10.00	5.00	.20
416 Randy Burridge, Wash.	5.00	3.00	.20
417 Kent Manderville, Toro.	5.00	3.00	.20
418 Darren Rumble, Otta.	5.00	3.00	.20
419 Bill Houlder, Anah.	5.00	3.00	.20
420 Chris Chelios, Chic.	15.00	15.00	.20
421 Jim Hrivnak (G), SLou.	5.00	3.00	.20
422 Benoît Brunet, Mont.	5.00	3.00	.20
423 Aaron Ward, Detr. RC	**10.00**	**5.00**	**.50**
424 Alexei Gusarov, Québ.	5.00	3.00	.20
425 Sundin, Québ. [Swe.]	30.00	25.00	.50
426 K.Samuelsson, Pitt. [Swe.]	5.00	3.00	.20
427 M. Andersson, Tamp. [Swe.]	5.00	3.00	.20
428 Ulf Dahlén, Dall. [Swe.]	5.00	3.00	.20
429 Lidström, Detr. [Swe.]	15.00	15.00	.20
430 Söderström (G), Phil. [Swe.]	5.00	3.00	.20
431 Madeley (G), Otta. RC	**10.00**	**5.00**	**.50**
432 Kevin Dahl, Calg.	5.00	3.00	.20
433 Ron Hextall (G), NYIs.	15.00	15.00	.20
434 P. Carnbäck, Anah. RC	**5.00**	**5.00**	**.50**
435 Randy Moller, Buff.	5.00	3.00	.20
436 Dave Gagner, Dall.	5.00	3.00	.20
437 Corey Millen, NJer.	5.00	3.00	.20
438 Olaf Kölzig (G), Wash.	15.00	15.00	.20
439 Gord Murphy, Flor.	5.00	3.00	.20
440 C. Stewart, Bost. RC	**5.00**	**5.00**	**.50**
441 D. McCarty, Detr. RC	**20.00**	**15.00**	**1.50**
442 Frantisek Kucera, Chic.	5.00	3.00	.20
443 Ted Drury, Calg.	5.00	5.00	.20
444 Troy Mallette, Otta.	5.00	3.00	.20
445 R. Bawa, Anah. RC	**5.00**	**5.00**	**.50**
446 Steven Rice, Edmo.	5.00	3.00	.20
447 Pat Elynuik, Tamp.	5.00	3.00	.20
448 J. Cummins, Phil. RC	**5.00**	**5.00**	**.50**
449 R. Niedermayer, Flor.	15.00	10.00	.20
450 Paul Coffey, Detr.	15.00	15.00	.20
451 Calle Johansson, Wash.	5.00	5.00	.20
452 Mike Needham, Pitt.	5.00	3.00	.20
453 Glenn Healy (G), NYRa.	5.00	3.00	.20
454 Dixon Ward, Vanc.	5.00	3.00	.20
455 Iafrate, Wash. [USA.]	5.00	5.00	.20
456 Casey (G), Bost. [USA.]	5.00	3.00	.20
457 K. Stevens, Pitt. [USA.]	5.00	3.00	.20
458 Amonte, NYRa. [USA.]	15.00	15.00	.20
459 Chelios, Chic. [USA.]	15.00	15.00	.20
460 LaFontaine, Buff. [USA.]	15.00	15.00	.20
461 Jamie Baker, SanJ.	5.00	3.00	.20
462 André Faust, Phil.	5.00	3.00	.20
463 B. Dollas, Anah. RC	**5.00**	**5.00**	**.50**
464 Steven Finn, Québ.	5.00	3.00	.20
465 Scott Lachance, NYIs.	5.00	3.00	.20
466 Mike Hough, Flor.	5.00	3.00	.20
467 Bill Guerin, NJer.	10.00	10.00	.20
468 Dmitri Filimonov, Otta.	5.00	5.00	.20
469 Dave Ellett, Toro.	5.00	3.00	.20
470 Andy Moog (G), Dall.	10.00	10.00	.20
471 Sc. Thomas, Buff. RC	**5.00**	**5.00**	**.50**
472 Trent Yawney, Calg.	5.00	3.00	.20
473 Tim Sweeney, Anah.	5.00	3.00	.20
474 S. Podein, Edmo. RC	**15.00**	**10.00**	**1.00**
475 J.J. Daigneault, Mont.	5.00	3.00	.20
476 Darren Turcotte, Hart.	5.00	3.00	.20
477 Esa Tikkanen, NYRa.	5.00	3.00	.20
478 Vitali Karamnov, SLou.	5.00	3.00	.20
479 Thibault (G), Québ. RC	**25.00**	**20.00**	**2.00**
480 Pavel Bure, Vanc.	25.00	20.00	.20
481 Konowalchuk, Wash.	5.00	5.00	.20
482 Sylvain Turgeon, Otta.	5.00	3.00	.20
483 Jeff Daniels, Pitt.	5.00	3.00	.20
484 D. Drake, Detr. RC	**10.00**	**5.00**	**.50**
485 Iain Fraser, Québ. RC	**5.00**	**5.00**	**.50**
486 Joe Reekie, Tamp.	5.00	3.00	.20
487 Evgeny Davydov, Flor.	5.00	3.00	.20
488 Jozef Stumpel, Bost.	5.00	5.00	.20
489 Brent Thompson, LosA.	5.00	3.00	.20
490 Terry Yake, Anah.	5.00	3.00	.20
491 De. Plante, Buff. RC	**10.00**	**5.00**	**.50**
492 Dmitry Yushkevich, Phil.	5.00	5.00	.20
493 Wayne McBean, NYIs.	5.00	3.00	.20
494 Derian Hatcher, Dall.	10.00	5.00	.20
495 Jeff Norton, SanJ.	5.00	3.00	.20
496 Adam Foote, Québ.	10.00	5.00	.20
497 Mike Peluso, NJer.	5.00	3.00	.20
498 Rob Pearson, Toro.	5.00	3.00	.20
499 Checklist	5.00	3.00	.20
500 Checklist	5.00	3.00	.20

O-PEE-CHEE

Player	FDI	OPC
1 Guy Carbonneau, Mont.	5.00	.20
2 Joe Cirella, Flor.	3.00	.20
3 Laurie Boschman, Otta.	3.00	.20
4 Arturs Irbe (G), SanJ.	10.00	.20
5 Adam Creighton, Tamp.	3.00	.20
6 Mike McPhee, Minn. (Dall.)	3.00	.20
7 Jeff Beukeboom, NYRa.	3.00	.20
8 Kevin Todd, Edmo.	3.00	.20
9 Yvon Corriveau, Hart.	3.00	.20
10 Eric Lindros, Phil.	25.00	.50
11 Martin Rucinsky, Québ.	5.00	.20
12 Michel Goulet, Chic.	10.00	.20
13 Scott Pellerin, NJer. RC	**5.00**	**.50**
14 Mike Eagles, Winn.	3.00	.20
15 Stephen Heinze, Bost.	3.00	.20
16 Gerard Gallant, Detr.	3.00	.20
17 Kelly Miller, Wash.	3.00	.20
18 Petr Nedved, Vanc.	5.00	.20
19 Joe Mullen, Pitt.	10.00	.20
20 Pat LaFontaine, Buff.	15.00	.20
21 Garth Butcher, SLou.	3.00	.20
22 Jeff Reese (G), Calg.	3.00	.20
23 Dave Andreychuk, Toro.	5.00	.20
24 Patrick Flatley, NYIs.	3.00	.20
25 Tomas Sandström, LosA.	5.00	.20
26 André Racicot (G), Mont.	3.00	.20
27 Patrice Brisebois, Mont.	3.00	.20
28 Neal Broten, Minn. (Dall.)	5.00	.20
29 Mark Freer, Otta.	3.00	.20
30 Kelly Kisio, SanJ.	3.00	.20
31 Scott Mellanby, Flor.	5.00	.20
32 Joe Sakic, Québ.	40.00	.50
33 Kerry Huffman, Québ.	3.00	.20
34 Evgeny Davydov, Winn.	3.00	.20
35 Mark Messier, NYRa.	25.00	.50
36 Pat Verbeek, Hart.	5.00	.20
37 Greg Gilbert, Chic. (NYRa.)	3.00	.20
38 John Tucker, Tamp.	3.00	.20
39 Claude Lemieux, NJer.	5.00	.20
40 Shayne Corson, Edmo.	5.00	.20
41 Gord** Roberts, Bost.	10.00	.20
42 Jiri Slégr, Vanc.	3.00	.20
43 Kevin Dineen, Phil.	3.00	.20
44 Johan Garpenlöv, SanJ.	3.00	.20
45 Sergei Fedorov, Detr.	25.00	.50
46 Rich Sutter, SLou.	5.00	.20
47 Dave Hannan, Buff.	3.00	.20
48 Sylvain Lefebvre, Toro.	3.00	.20
49 Pat Elynuik, Wash.	3.00	.20
50 Ray Ferraro, NYIs.	3.00	.20
51 Brent Ashton, Calg.	3.00	.20
52 Paul Stanton, Pitt.	3.00	.20
53 Kevin Haller, Mont.	3.00	.20
54 Kelly Hrudey (G), LosA.	5.00	.20
55 Russ Courtnall, Minn. (Dall.)	5.00	.20
56 Alexei Zhamnov, Winn.	5.00	.20
57 Andrei Lomakin, Flor.	3.00	.20
58 Keith Brown, Chic.	3.00	.20
59 Glen Murray, Bost.	10.00	.20
60 Kay Whitmore (G), Vanc.	3.00	.20
61 Stéphane J.J. Richer, NJer.	5.00	.20
62 Todd Gill, Toro.	3.00	.20
63 Bob Sweeney, Buff.	3.00	.20
64 Mike Richter (G), NYRa.	10.00	.20
65 Brett Hull, SLou.	25.00	.50
66 Sylvain Côté, Wash.	3.00	.20
67 Kirk Muller, Mont.	5.00	.20
68 Ronnie Stern, Calg.	3.00	.20
69 Josef Beránek, Phil.	3.00	.20
70 Steve Yzerman, Detr.	60.00	1.00
71 Don Beaupré (G), Wash.	3.00	.20
72 Ed Courtenay, SanJ.	3.00	.20
73 Zdeno Ciger, Edmo.	3.00	.20
74 Andrew Cassels, Hart.	5.00	.20
75 Roman Hamrlik, Tamp.	5.00	.20
76 Benoît Hogue, NYIs.	3.00	.20
77 Andrei Kovalenko, Québ.	3.00	.20
78 Rod Brind'Amour, Phil.	5.00	.20
79 Tom Barrasso (G), Pitt.	10.00	.20
80 Al Iafrate, Wash.	3.00	.20
81 Bret Hedican, SLou.	3.00	.20
82 Peter Bondra, Wash.	15.00	.20
83 Ted Donato, Bost.	3.00	.20
84 Chris Lindberg, Calg.	3.00	.20
85 J. Vanbiesbrouck (G), Flor.	10.00	.20
86 Ron Sutter, SLou.	5.00	.20
87 Luc Robitaille, LosA.	20.00	.20
88 Brian Leetch, NYRa.	15.00	.20
89 Randy Wood, Buff.	3.00	.20
90 Dirk Graham, Chic.	3.00	.20
91 Alexander Mogilny, Buff.	10.00	.20
92 Mike Keane, Mont.	3.00	.20
93 Adam Oates, Bost.	10.00	.20
94 Viacheslav Butsayev, Phil.	3.00	.20
95 John LeClair, Mont.	20.00	.20
96 Joe Nieuwendyk, Calg.	10.00	.20
97 Mikael Andersson, Tamp.	3.00	.20
98 Jaromir Jagr, Pitt.	25.00	.50
99 Ed Belfour (G), Chic.	25.00	.50
100 David Reid, Bost.	3.00	.20
101 Darius Kasparaitis, NYIs.	5.00	.20
102 Zarley Zalapski, Hart.	3.00	.20
103 Christian Ruuttu, Chic.	3.00	.20
104 Phil Housley, Winn.	5.00	.20
105 Al MacInnis, Calg.	10.00	.20
106 Tommy Sjödin, Minn. (Dall.)	3.00	.20
107 Richard Smehlik, Buff.	3.00	.20
108 Jyrki Lumme, Vanc.	5.00	.20
109 Dominic Roussel (G), Phil.	3.00	.20
110 Mike Gartner, NYRa.	20.00	.20
111 Bernie Nicholls, NJer.	5.00	.20
112 Mark Howe, Detr.	5.00	.20
113 Richard Pilon, NYIs.	3.00	.20
114 Jeff Odgers, SanJ.	3.00	.20
115 Gilbert Dionne, Mont.	3.00	.20
116 Peter Zezel, Toro.	3.00	.20
117 Don Sweeney, Bost.	3.00	.20
118 Jimmy Carson, LosA.	3.00	.20
119 Igor Korolev, SLou.	3.00	.20
120 Bob Kudelski, Otta.	3.00	.20
121 Dave Lowry, Flor.	5.00	.20
122 S. Kasper, Wash. [v.Lindros]	5.00	.20
123 M. Ridley, Wash. [v.Lindros]	5.00	.20
124 Dave Tippett, Pitt.	3.00	.20
125 Cliff Ronning, Vanc.	5.00	.20
126 Bruce Driver, NJer.	3.00	.20
127 Stéphane Matteau, Chic.	3.00	.20
128 Joel Otto, Calg.	3.00	.20
129 Alexei Kovalev, NYRa.	15.00	.20
130 Mike Modano, Minn. (Dall.)	25.00	.50
131 Bill Ranford (G), Edmo.	10.00	.20
132 Petr* Svoboda, Buff.	5.00	.20
133 Roger Johansson, Calg.	3.00	.20
134 Marc Bureau, Tamp.	3.00	.20
135 Keith Tkachuk, Winn.	15.00	.20
136 Mark Recchi, Phil.	10.00	.20
137 Bob Probert, Detr.	5.00	.20
138 Uwe Krupp, NYIs.	3.00	.20
139 Mike Sullivan, SanJ.	3.00	.20
140 Doug Gilmour, Toro.	15.00	.20
141 Teemu Selänne, Awards	20.00	.20
142 Dave Poulin, Awards	3.00	.20
143 Mario Lemieux, Awards	75.00	1.50
144 Ed Belfour (G), Awards	5.00	.20
145 Pierre Turgeon, Awards	10.00	.20
146 Mario Lemieux, Awards	75.00	1.50
147 Chris Chelios, Awards	15.00	.20
148 Mario Lemieux, Awards	75.00	1.50
149 Doug Gilmour, Awards	15.00	.20
150 Ed Belfour (G), Awards	5.00	.20
151 Paul Ranheim, Calg.	3.00	.20
152 Gino Cavallini, Québ.	3.00	.20
153 Kevin Hatcher, Wash.	3.00	.20
154 Marc Bergevin, Tamp.	3.00	.20
155 Marty McSorley, LosA.	5.00	.20
156 Brian Bellows, Mont. [w/ Cup]	5.00	.20
157 Patrick Poulin, Hart.	3.00	.20
158 Kevin Stevens, Pitt.	5.00	.20
159 Bobby Holik, NJer.	5.00	.20
160 Raymond Bourque, Bost.	30.00	.50
161 Bryan Marchment, Chic.	3.00	.20
162 Curtis Joseph (G), SLou.	25.00	.50
163 Kirk McLean (G), Vanc.	5.00	.20
164 Teppo Numminen, Winn.	5.00	.20
165 Kevin Lowe, NYRa.	5.00	.20
166 Tim Cheveldae (G), Detr.	3.00	.20
167 Brad Dalgarno, NYIs.	3.00	.20
168 Glenn Anderson, Toro.	5.00	.20
169 Frantisek Musil, Calg.	5.00	.20
170 Éric Desjardins, Mont.	5.00	.20
171 Doug Zmolek, SanJ.	3.00	.20
172 Mark Lamb, Otta.	3.00	.20
173 Craig Ludwig, Minn. (Dall.)	3.00	.20
174 Rob Gaudreau, SanJ. RC	**5.00**	**.50**
175 Bob Carpenter, Wash.	5.00	.20
176 Mike Ricci, Québ.	5.00	.20
177 Brian Skrudland, Flor.	3.00	.20
178 Dominik Hasek (G), Buff.	25.00	.50
179 Pat Conacher, LosA.	3.00	.20
180 Mark Janssens, Hart.	3.00	.20
181 Brent Fedyk, Phil.	3.00	.20
182 Rob DiMaio, Tamp.	3.00	.20
183 Dave Manson, Edmo.	3.00	.20
184 Janne Ojanen, NJer.	3.00	.20
185 Ryan Walter, Vanc.	3.00	.20
186 Michael Nylander, Hart.	5.00	.20
187 Stephen Leach, Bost.	3.00	.20
188 Jeff R. Brown, SLou.	3.00	.20
189 Shawn McEachern, Pitt.	5.00	.20
190 Jeremy Roenick, Chic.	20.00	.20
191 Darrin Shannon, Winn.	3.00	.20
192 Wendel Clark, Toro.	20.00	.20
193 Kevin Miller, SLou.	3.00	.20
194 Paul DiPietro, Mont.	3.00	.20
195 Steve Thomas, NYIs.	5.00	.20
196 Nicklas Lidström, Detr.	15.00	.20
197 Ed Olczyk, NYRa.	5.00	.20
198 Robert Reichel, Calg.	5.00	.20
199 Neil Brady, Otta.	3.00	.20
200 Wayne Gretzky, LosA.	100.00	2.00
201 Adrien Plavsic, Vanc.	3.00	.20
202 Joé Juneau, Bost.	5.00	.20
203 Brad May, Buff.	3.00	.20
204 Igor Kravchuk, Edmo.	3.00	.20
205 Keith Acton, Phil.	3.00	.20
206 Ken Daneyko, NJer.	5.00	.20
207 Sean Burke (G), Hart.	15.00	.20
208 Jayson More, SanJ.	3.00	.20
209 John Cullen, Toro.	5.00	.20
210 Teemu Selänne, Winn.	20.00	.20
211 Brent Sutter, Chic.	5.00	.20
212 Brian Bradley, Tamp.	3.00	.20
213 Donald Audette, Buff.	10.00	.20
214 Philippe Bozon, SLou.	3.00	.20
215 Derek King, NYIs.	3.00	.20
216 Cam Neely, Bost.	25.00	.50
217 Keith Primeau, Detr.	10.00	.20
218 J. Steve Smith, Chic.	5.00	.20
219 Ken Sutton, Buff.	3.00	.20
220 Dale Hawerchuk, Buff.	15.00	.20
221 Alexei Zhitnik, LosA.	3.00	.20
222 Glen Wesley, Bost.	3.00	.20
223 Nelson Emerson, SLou.	3.00	.20
224 Pat Falloon, SanJ.	3.00	.20
225 Darryl Sydor, LosA.	5.00	.20
226 Tony Amonte, NYRa.	15.00	.20
227 Brian Mullen, NYIs.	3.00	.20
228 Gary Suter, Calg.	5.00	.20
229 David Shaw, Bost.	3.00	.20
230 Troy Murray, Chic.	3.00	.20
231 Patrick Roy (G), Mont.	75.00	1.50
232 Michel Petit, Calg.	3.00	.20
233 Wayne Presley, Buff.	3.00	.20
234 Keith Jones, Wash.	3.00	.20
235 Gary Roberts, Calg.	10.00	.20
236 Steve Larmer, Chic.	10.00	.20
237 Valeri Kamensky, Québ.	5.00	.20
238 Ulf Dahlén, Minn. (Dall.)	3.00	.20
239 Danton Cole, Tamp.	3.00	.20
240 Vincent Damphousse, Mont.	15.00	.20
241 Yuri Khmylev, Buff.	3.00	.20
242 Stéphane Quintal, SLou.	3.00	.20
243 Peter Taglianetti, Pitt.	3.00	.20
244 Gary Leeman, Mont.	3.00	.20
245 Sergei Nemchinov, NYRa.	5.00	.20
246 Rob Blake, LosA.	15.00	.20
247 Steve Chiasson, Detr.	3.00	.20
248 Vladimir Malakhov, NYIs.	3.00	.20
249 Checklist	3.00	.20
250 Checklist	3.00	.20

MASTER PHOTO

Insert Set (24 cards):	15.00	15.00
Series One Insert	5x7	Insert
1 Pat LaFontaine, Buff.	1.00	1.00
2 Doug Gilmour, Toro.	1.00	1.00
3 Raymond Bourque, Bost.	1.00	2.00
4 Teemu Selänne, Winn.	1.00	1.50
5 Eric Lindros, Phil.	1.00	2.00
6 Ray Ferraro, NYIs.	1.00	.50
7 Patrick Roy (G), Mont.	4.00	6.00
8 Wayne Gretzky, LosA.	6.00	8.00
9 Brett Hull, SLou.	1.00	2.00
10 John Vanbiesbrouck (G), Flor.	1.00	.50
11 Adam Oates, Bost.	1.00	.50
12 Tom Barrasso (G), Pitt.	1.00	.50

Series Two Insert	5x7	Insert
1 Esa Tikkanen, Edmo.	1.00	.50
2 Jari Kurri, LosA.	1.00	2.00
3 Grant Fuhr (G), Buff.	1.00	1.00
4 Scott Lachance, NYIs.	1.00	.50
5 Theoren Fleury, Calg.	1.00	1.00
6 Adam Graves, NYRa.	1.00	.50
7 Rick Tabaracci (G), Wash.	1.00	.50
8 Pierre Turgeon, NYIs.	1.00	.50
9 Steven Finn, Québ.	1.00	.50
10 Craig Janney, SLou.	1.00	.50
11 Mathieu Schneider, Mont.	1.00	.50
12 Félix Potvin (G), Toro.	1.00	1.00

ALL-STARS

These cards have three versions: a Topps insert, an O-Pee-Chee insert and a Members Only subset.

Insert Set (23 cards):		60.00
Insert	MO	TSC
E. Belfour / P. Roy	35.00	15.00
J. Casey / C. Billington	5.00	2.00
K. Kisio / P. Bondra	5.00	2.00
P. Coffey / R. Bourque	15.00	5.00
A. Oates / B. Bradley	5.00	2.00
P. Bure / K. Stevens	5.00	2.00
G. Butcher / K. Lowe	5.00	2.00
R. Carlyle / B. Marsh	5.00	2.00
C. Chelios / A. Iafrate	5.00	2.00
S. Chiasson / S. Duchesne	5.00	2.00
T. Selänne / M. Gartner	15.00	5.00
D. Gilmour / J. Sakic	20.00	5.00
W. Gretzky / M. Lemieux	65.00	30.00
P. Housley / S. Stevens	5.00	2.00
Br. Hull / J. Jagr	15.00	5.00
J. Kurri / A. Mogilny	10.00	5.00
S. Yzerman / P. LaFontaine	25.00	10.00
D. Manson / Z. Zalapski	5.00	2.00
M. Modano / P. Turgeon	10.00	5.00
G. Roberts / K. Muller	5.00	2.00
L. Robitaille / M. Recchi	10.00	5.00
J. Roenick / R. Tocchet	10.00	2.00
M. Vernon / P. Sidorkiewicz	5.00	2.00

FINEST

These cards have two versions: a Topps insert and a Members Only subset.

Insert Set (12 cards):		25.00
Insert	M.O.	Insert
1 Wayne Gretzky, LosA.	75.00	15.00
2 Jeff R. Brown, SLou.	5.00	.75
3 Brett Hull, SLou.	15.00	3.00
4 Paul Coffey, Detr.	10.00	2.00
5 Félix Potvin (G), Toro.	10.00	2.00
6 Mike Gartner, NYRa.	15.00	3.00
7 Luc Robitaille, LosA.	15.00	3.00
8 Marty McSorley, Pitt.	5.00	.75
9 Gary Roberts, Calg.	5.00	1.00
10 Mario Lemieux, Pitt.	55.00	10.00
11 Patrick Roy (G), Mont.	55.00	10.00
12 Raymond Bourque, Bost.	20.00	4.00

TEAM U.S.A.

These cards have two versions: a Topps insert and a Members Only subset.

Insert Set (23 cards):		10.00
Insert	M.O.	Insert
1 Mark Beaufait, U.S.A. RC	5.00	1.00
2 Jim Campbell, U.S.A.	5.00	.50
3 Ted Crowley, U.S.A. RC	5.00	1.00
4 Mike Dunham (G), U.S.A.	10.00	2.00
5 Chris Ferraro, U.S.A. RC	5.00	1.00

6 Peter Ferraro, U.S.A.	5.00	.50
7 Brett Hauer, U.S.A. RC	5.00	1.00
8 Darby Hendrickson, U.S.A. RC	5.00	1.00
9 Jon Hillebrandt, U.S.A. RC	5.00	1.00
10 Chris Imes, U.S.A. RC	5.00	1.00
11 Craig Johnson, U.S.A. RC	5.00	1.00
12 Peter Laviolette, U.S.A. RC	10.00	4.00
13 Jeff Lazaro, U.S.A.	5.00	.50
14 John Lilley, U.S.A. RC	5.00	1.00
15 Todd Marchant, U.S.A.	5.00	1.00
16 Matt Martin, U.S.A. RC	5.00	1.00
17 Ian Moran, U.S.A. RC	5.00	1.00
18 Travis Richards, U.S.A. RC	5.00	1.00
19 Barry Richter, U.S.A. RC	5.00	1.00
20 David Roberts, U.S.A. RC	5.00	1.00
21 Brian Rolston, U.S.A.	10.00	1.00
22 David Sacco, U.S.A. RC	5.00	1.00
23 Jim Storm, U.S.A. RC	5.00	1.00

1993 - 94 TOPPS STADIUM CLUB MEMBERS ONLY

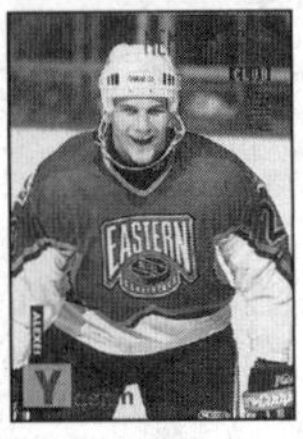

Complete Set (50 cards): 20.00

Player	TSC
1 Félix Potvin (G), NHL All-Star	.50
2 Chris Chelios, NHL All-Star	.50
3 Paul Coffey, NHL All-Star	.50
4 Pavel Bure, NHL All-Star	.50
5 Wayne Gretzky, NHL All-Star	4.00
6 Brett Hull, NHL All-Star	1.00
7 Al MacInnis, NHL All-Star	.25
8 Rob Blake, NHL All-Star	.50
9 Alexei Kasatonov, NHL All-Star	.25
10 Teemu Selänne, NHL All-Star	.50
11 Sandis Ozolinsh, NHL All-Star	.25
12 Shayne Corson, NHL All-Star	.25
13 Dave Andreychuk, NHL All-Star	.25
14 Dave Taylor, NHL All-Star	.25
15 Sergei Fedorov, NHL All-Star	1.00
16 Brendan Shanahan, NHL All-Star	1.00
17 Arturs Irbe (G), NHL All-Star	.25
18 Joe Nieuwendyk, NHL All-Star	.25
19 Russ Courtnall, NHL All-Star	.25
20 Jeremy Roenick, NHL All-Star	.50
21 Doug Gilmour, NHL All-Star	.50
22 Curtis Joseph (G), NHL All-Star	1.00
23 Patrick Roy (G), NHL All-Star	3.00
24 Brian Leetch, NHL All-Star	.50
25 Raymond Bourque, NHL All-Star	1.00
26 Alexander Mogilny, NHL All-Star	.25
27 Mark Messier, NHL All-Star	1.00
28 Eric Lindros, NHL All-Star	1.00
29 Garry Galley, NHL All-Star	.25
30 Scott Stevens, NHL All-Star	.25
31 Al Iafrate, NHL All-Star	.25
32 Larry Murphy, NHL All-Star	.25
33 Joe Mullen, NHL All-Star	.25
34 Mark Recchi, NHL All-Star	.25
35 Adam Graves, NHL All-Star	.25
36 Geoff Sanderson, NHL All-Star	.25
37 Adam Oates, NHL All-Star	.25
38 Pierre Turgeon, NHL All-Star	.25
39 Joe Sakic, NHL All-Star	1.50
40 John Vanbiesbrouck (G), NHL All-Star	.25
41 Brian Bradley, NHL All-Star	.25
42 Alexei Yashin, NHL All-Star	.50
43 Bob Kudelski, NHL All-Star	.25
44 Jaromir Jagr, NHL All-Star	1.00
45 Mike Richter (G), NHL All-Star	.25
46 Martin Brodeur (G), NJer.	1.50
47 Mikael Renberg, Phil.	.25
48 Derek Plante, Buff.	.25
49 Jason Arnott, Edmo.	.50
50 Alexandre Daigle, Otta.	.25

1993 - 94 UPPER DECK

Imprint: © 1993 The Upper Deck Company

Series One Set (310 cards):	20.00
Series Two Set (265 cards):	25.00
Common Player:	.20

Player	NRMT-MT
1 Guy Hebert (G), Anah.	.20
2 Bob Bassen, SLou.	.20
3 Theoren Fleury, Calg.	.20
4 Ray Whitney, SanJ.	.20
5 Donald Audette, Buff.	.20
6 Martin Rucinsky, Québ.	.20
7 Lyle Odelein, Mont.	.20
8 John Vanbiesbrouck (G), Flor.	.20
9 Tim Cheveldae (G), Detr.	.20
10 Jock Callander, Tamp.	.20
11 Nick Kypreos, Hart.	.20
12 Jarrod Skalde, Anah.	.20
13 Gary Shuchuk, LosA.	.20
14 Kris King, Winn.	.20
15 Josef Beránek, Phil.	.20
16 Sean Hill, Anah.	.20
17 Bob Kudelski, Otta.	.20
18 Jirí Slégr, Vanc.	.20
19 Dmitri Kvartalnov, Bost.	.20
20 Drake Berehowsky, Toro.	.20
21 Jean-François Quintin, SanJ.	.20
22 Randy Wood, Buff.	.20
23 Jim McKenzie, Hart.	.20
24 Steven King, Anah.	.20
25 Scott Niedermayer, NJer.	.20
26 Alexander Andrijevski, Chic.	.20
27 Alexei Kovalev, NYRa.	.20
28 Steve Konowalchuk, Wash.	.20
29 Vladimir Malakhov, NYIs.	.20
30 Eric Lindros, Phil.	.50
31 Mathieu Schneider, Mont.	.20
32 Russ Courtnall, Minn. (Dall.)	.20
33 Ron Sutter, SLou.	.20
34 Radek Hamr, Otta. RC	**.50**
35 Pavel Bure, Vanc.	.20
36 Joe Sacco, Anah.	.20
37 Robert Petrovicky, Hart.	.20
38 Anatoli Fedotov, Anah. RC	**.50**
39 Pat Falloon, SanJ.	.20
40 Martin Straka, Pitt.	.20
41 Brad Werenka, Edmo.	.20
42 Mike Richter (G), NYRa.	.20
43 Mike McPhee, Minn. (Dall.)	.20
44 Sylvain Turgeon, Otta.	.20
45 Tom Barrasso (G), Pitt.	.20
46 Anatoli Semenov, Anah.	.20
47 Joe Murphy, Chic.	.20
48 Rob Pearson, Toro.	.20
49 Patrick Roy (G), Mont.	1.50
50 Dallas Drake, Detr. RC	**.50**
51 Mark Messier, NYRa.	.50
52 Scott Pellerin, NJer. RC	**.50**
53 Teppo Numminen, Winn.	.20
54 Chris Kontos, Tamp.	.20
55 Richard Matvichuk, Minn. (Dall.)	.20
56 Dale Craigwell, SanJ.	.20
57 Mike Eastwood, Toro.	.20
58 Bernie Nicholls, NJer.	.20
59 Travis Green, NYIs.	.20
60 Shjon Podein, Edmo. RC	**1.00**
61 Darrin Madeley (G), Otta. RC	**.50**
62 Dixon Ward, Vanc.	.20
63 André Faust, Phil.	.20
64 Tony Amonte, NYRa.	.20
65 Joe Cirella, Flor.	.20
66 Michel Petit, Calg.	.20
67 Dave Lowry, Flor.	.20
68 Shawn Chambers, Tamp.	.20
69 Joe Sakic, Québ.	.50
70 Michael Nylander, Hart.	.20
71 Peter** Andersson, NYRa.	.20
72 Sandis Ozolinsh, SanJ.	.20
73 Joby Messier, NYRa. RC	**.50**
74 John Blue (G), Bost.	.20
75 Pat Elynuik, Wash.	.20
76 Keith Osborne, Tamp. RC	**.50**
77 Greg A. Adams, Vanc.	.20
78 Chris Gratton, Tamp.	.20
79 Louie DeBrusk, Edmo.	.20
80 Todd Harkins, Calg. RC	**.50**
81 Neil Brady, Otta.	.20
82 Philippe Boucher, Buff.	.20
83 Darryl Sydor, LosA.	.20
84 Oleg Petrov, Mont.	.20
85 Andrei Kovalenko, Québ.	.20
86 Dave Andreychuk, Toro.	.20
87 Jeff Daniels, Pitt.	.20
88 Kevin Todd, Edmo.	.20
89 Mark Tinordi, Minn. (Dall.)	.20
90 Garry Galley, Phil.	.20
91 Shawn Burr, Detr.	.20
92 Tom Pederson, SanJ.	.20
93 Warren Rychel, LosA.	.20
94 Stu Barnes, Winn.	.20
95 Peter Bondra, Wash.	.20
96 Brian Skrudland, Flor.	.20
97 Doug MacDonald, Buff. RC	**.50**
98 Rob Niedermayer, Flor.	.20
99 Wayne Gretzky, LosA.	2.00
100 Peter Taglianetti, Pitt.	.20
101 Don Sweeney, Bost.	.20
102 Andrei Lomakin, Flor.	.20
103 Checklist	.20
104 Sergio Momesso, Vanc.	.20
105 Dave Archibald, Otta.	.20
106 Karl Dykhuis, Chic.	.20
107 Scott Mellanby, Flor.	.20
108 Paul DiPietro, Mont.	.20
109 Neal Broten, Minn. (Dall.)	.20
110 Chris Terreri (G), NJer.	.20
111 Craig MacTavish, Edmo.	.20
112 Jody Hull, Otta.	.20
113 Philippe Bozon, SLou.	.20
114 Geoff Courtnall, Vanc.	.20
115 Ed Olczyk, NYRa.	.20
116 Raymond Bourque, Bost.	.50
117 Gilbert Dionne, Mont.	.20
118 Valeri Kamensky, Québ.	.20
119 Scott Stevens, NJer.	.20
120 Pelle Eklund, Phil.	.20
121 Brian Bradley, Tamp.	.20
122 Steve Thomas, NYIs.	.20
123 Don Beaupré (G), Wash.	.20
124 Joel Otto, Calg.	.20
125 Arturs Irbe (G), SanJ.	.20
126 Kevin Stevens, Pitt.	.20
127 Dmitry Yushkevich, Phil.	.20
128 Adam Graves, NYRa.	.20
129 Chris Chelios, Chic.	.20
130 Jeff R. Brown, SLou.	.20
131 Paul Ranheim, Calg.	.20
132 Shayne Corson, Edmo.	.20
133 Curtis Leschyshyn, Québ.	.20
134 John MacLean, NJer.	.20
135 Dmitri Khristich, Wash.	.20
136 Dino Ciccarelli, Detr.	.20
137 Pat LaFontaine, Buff.	.20
138 Patrick Poulin, Hart.	.20
139 Jaromir Jagr, Pitt.	.50
140 Kevin Hatcher, Wash.	.20
141 Christian Ruuttu, Chic.	.20
142 Ulf Samuelsson, Pitt.	.20
143 Ted Donato, Bost.	.20
144 Bob Essensa (G), Winn.	.20
145 Dave Gagner, Minn. (Dall.)	.20
146 Tony Granato, LosA.	.20
147 Ed Belfour (G), Chic.	.50
148 Kirk Muller, Mont. [w/ Stanley Cup]	.20
149 Rob Gaudreau, SanJ. RC	**.50**
150 Nicklas Lidström, Detr.	.20
151 Gary Roberts, Calg.	.20
152 Trent Klatt, Minn. (Dall.)	.20
153 Ray Ferraro, NYIs.	.20
154 Michal Pivonka, Wash.	.20
155 Mike Foligno, Toro.	.20
156 Kirk McLean (G), Vanc.	.20
157 Curtis Joseph (G), SLou.	.50
158 Roman Hamrlik, Tamp.	.20
159 Félix Potvin (G), Toro.	.20
160 Brett Hull, SLou.	.50
161 Alexei Zhitnik, LosA.	.20
162 Alexei Zhamnov, Winn.	.20
163 Grant Fuhr (G), Buff.	.20
164 Nikolai Borschevsky, Toro.	.20
165 Tomas Jelinek, Otta.	.20
166 Thomas Steen, Winn.	.20
167 John LeClair, Mont.	.20
168 Vladimir (Jr.) Vujtek, Edmo.	.20
169 Richard Smehlik, Buff.	.20
170 Alexandre Daigle, Otta.	.20
171 Sergei Fedorov, Detr.	.50
172 Steve Larmer, Chic.	.20
173 Darius Kasparaitis, NYIs.	.20
174 Igor Kravchuk, Edmo.	.20
175 Owen Nolan, Québ.	.20
176 Rob DiMaio, Tamp.	.20
177 Mike Vernon (G), Calg.	.20
178 Alexander Semak, NJer.	.20
179 Rick Tocchet, Pitt.	.20
180 Bill Ranford (G), Edmo.	.20
181 Sergei Zubov, NYRa.	.20
182 Tommy Söderström (G), Phil.	.20
183 Al Iafrate, Wash.	.20
184 Éric Desjardins, Mont.	.20
185 Bret Hedican, SLou.	.20
186 Joe Mullen, Pitt.	.20
187 Doug Bodger, Buff.	.20
188 Tomas Sandström, LosA.	.20
189 Glen Murray, Bost.	.20
190 Chris Pronger, Hart.	.50
191 Mike Craig, Minn. (Dall.)	.20
192 Jim Paek, Pitt.	.20
193 Doug Zmolek, SanJ.	.20
194 Yves Racine, Detr.	.20
195 Keith Tkachuk, Winn.	.20
196 Chris Lindberg, Calg.	.20
197 Kelly Buchberger, Edmo.	.20
198 Mark Janssens, Hart.	.20
199 Peter Zezel, Toro.	.20
200 Bob Probert, Detr.	.20
201 Brad May, Buff.	.20
202 Rob Zamuner, Tamp.	.20
203 Stéphane Fiset (G), Québ.	.20
204 Derian Hatcher, Minn. (Dall.)	.20
205 Mike Gartner, NYRa.	.20
206 Checklist	.20
207 Todd Krygier, Wash.	.20
208 Glen Wesley, Bost.	.20
209 Fredrik Olausson, Winn.	.20
210 Patrick Flatley, NYIs.	.20
211 Cliff Ronning, Vanc.	.20
212 Kevin Dineen, Phil.	.20
213 Zarley Zalapski, Hart.	.20
214 Stéphane Matteau, Chic.	.20
215 Dave Ellett, Toro.	.20
216 Kelly Hrudey (G), LosA.	.20
217 Steve Duchesne, Québ.	.20
218 Bobby Holik, NJer.	.20
219 Brad Dalgarno, NYIs.	.20
220 Mats Sundin, Québ. [Checklist]	.50
221 Pat LaFontaine, Buff.	.20
222 Mark Recchi, Phil.	.20
223 Joe Sakic, Québ.	.50
224 Pierre Turgeon, NYIs.	.20
225 Craig Janney, SLou.	.20
226 Adam Oates, Bost.	.20
227 Steve Yzerman, Detr.	1.00
228 Mats Sundin, Québ.	.50
229 Theoren Fleury, Calg.	.20
230 Kevin Stevens, Pitt.	.20
231 Luc Robitaille, LosA.	.20
232 Brett Hull, SLou.	.50
233 Rick Tocchet, Pitt.	.20
234 Alexander Mogilny, Buff.	.20
235 Jeremy Roenick, Chic.	.20
236 Guy Lévêque, LosA. [CL, w/ Stevenson]	.20
236 Turner Stevenson, Mont. [CL, w/ Leveque]	.20
237 Adam Bennett, Chic. [Star Rookie] RC	**.50**
238 Dody Wood, SanJ. [Star Rookie] RC	**.50**
239 Niklas Andersson, Québ. [Star Rookie]	.20
240 Jason Bowen, Phil. [Star Rookie] RC	**.50**
241 Steve Junker, NYIs. [Star Rookie] RC	**.50**
242 Bryan Smolinski, Bost. [Star Rookie]	.20
243 Chris Simon, Québ. [Star Rookie] RC	**1.00**
244 Sergei Zholtok, Bost. [Star Rookie]	.20
245 Dan Ratushny, Vanc. [Star Rookie] RC	**.50**
246 Guy Lévêque, LosA. [Star Rookie]	.20
247 Scott Thomas, Buff. [Star Rookie] RC	**.50**
248 Turner Stevenson, Mont. [Star Rookie]	.20
249 Dan Keczmer, Hart. [Star Rookie]	.20
250 Alexandre Daigle, Canada Juniors [CL]	.20
251 Adrian Aucoin, Canada Juniors RC	**.50**
252 Jason Smith, Canada Juniors RC	**.50**
253 Ralph Intranuovo, Canada Juniors RC	**.50**
254 Jason Dawe, Canada Juniors	.20
255 Jeff Bes, Canada Juniors RC	**.50**
256 Tyler Wright, Canada Juniors	.20
257 Martin Lapointe, Canada Juniors	.20
258 Jeff Shantz, Canada Juniors	.20
259 Martin Gendron, Canada Juniors RC	**.50**
260 P. DeRouville, Canada Juniors RC	**.50**
261 Frantisek* Kaberle, Czech & Slovak RC	**.50**
262 Radim Bicanek, Czech & Slovak RC	**.50**
263 Tomas Klimt, Czech & Slovak RC	**.50**
264 Tomas Nemcicky, Czech & Slovak RC	**.50**
265 Richard Kapus, Czech & Slovak RC	**.50**
266 Patrik Krisak, Czech & Slovak RC	**.50**
267 Roman Kadera, Czech & Slovak RC	**.50**
268 Kimmo Timonen, Finland Juniors RC	**.50**
269 Jukka Ollila, Finland Juniors RC	**.50**
270 Tuomas Grönman, Finland Juniors	.20
271 Mikko Luovi, Finland Juniors RC	**.50**
272 Sergei Gonchar, Russia Juniors RC	**2.00**
273 Maxim Galanov, Russia Juniors RC	**.50**
274 Oleg Belov, Russia Juniors RC	**.50**
275 Sergei Klimovich, Russia Juniors	.20
276 Sergei Brylin, Russia Jrs. RC [Error: Unknown player]	**.50**
277 Alexei Yashin, Russia Juniors	.50
278 Vitali Tomilin, Russia Juniors RC	**.50**
279 Alexander Cherbayev, Russia Juniors	.20
280 Eric Lindros, Phil. [All-Rookie Team]	.50
281 Teemu Selänne, Winn. [All-Rookie Team]	.20
282 Joé Juneau, Bost. [All-Rookie Team]	.20
283 Vladimir Malakhov, NYIs. [All-Rookie Team]	.20
284 Scott Niedermayer, NJer. [All-Rookie Team]	.20
285 Félix Potvin (G), Toro. [All-Rookie Team]	.20
286 Adam Oates, Bost. [Team Leader]	.20
287 Pat LaFontaine, Buff. [Team Leader]	.20
288 Theoren Fleury, Calg. [Team Leader]	.20
289 Jeremy Roenick, Chic. [Team Leader]	.20
290 Steve Yzerman, Detr. [Team Leader]	1.00
291 Klima / Weight [Edmo. Team Leaders]	.20
292 Geoff Sanderson, Hart. [Team Leader]	.20
293 Luc Robitaille, LosA. [Team Leader]	.20
294 Mike Modano, Minn. (Dall.) [Team Leader]	.50
295 Vincent Damphousse, Mont. [Team Leader]	.20
296 Claude Lemieux, NJer. [Team Leader]	.20
297 Pierre Turgeon, NYIs. [Team Leader]	.20
298 Mark Messier, NYRa. [Team Leader]	.50
299 Norm Maciver, Otta. [Team Leader]	.20
300 Mark Recchi, Phil. [Team Leader]	.20
301 Mario Lemieux, Pitt. [Team Leader]	1.50
302 Mats Sundin, Québ. [Team Leader]	.50
303 Craig Janney, SLou. [Team Leader]	.20
304 Kelly Kisio, SanJ. [Team Leader]	.20
305 Brian Bradley, Tamp. [Team Leader]	.20
306 Doug Gilmour, Toro. [Team Leader]	.20
307 Pavel Bure, Vanc. [Team Leader]	.20
308 Peter Bondra, Wash. [Team Leader]	.20
309 Teemu Selänne, Winn. [Team Leader]	.20
310 Checklist	.20
311 Terry Yake, Anah.	.20
312 Bob Sweeney, Buff.	.20
313 Robert Reichel, Calg.	.20
314 Jeremy Roenick, Chic.	.20
315 Paul Coffey, Detr.	.20
316 Geoff Sanderson, Hart.	.20
317 Rob Blake, LosA.	.20
318 Patrice Brisebois, Mont.	.20
319 Jaroslav Modry, NJer. RC	**.50**
320 Scott Lachance, NYIs.	.20
321 Glenn Healy (G), NYRa.	.20
322 Martin Gélinas, Québ.	.20
323 Craig Janney, SLou.	.20
324 Bill McDougall, Tamp. RC	**.50**
325 Shawn Antoski, Vanc.	.20
326 Olaf Kölzig (G), Wash.	.20
327 Adam Oates, Bost.	.20
328 Dirk Graham, Chic.	.20
329 Brent Gilchrist, Dall.	.20
330 Zdeno Ciger, Edmo.	.20
331 Pat Verbeek, Hart.	.20
332 Jari Kurri, LosA.	.50
333 Kevin Haller, Mont.	.20
334 Martin Brodeur (G), NJer.	.50
335 Norm Maciver, Otta.	.20
336 Dominic Roussel (G), Phil.	.20
337 Iain Fraser, Québ. RC	**.50**
338 Vitali Karamnov, SLou.	.20
339 René Corbet, Québ. RC	**.50**
340 Wendel Clark, Toro.	.20
341 Mike Ridley, Wash.	.20
342 Nelson Emerson, Winn.	.20
343 Joé Juneau, Bost.	.20
344 Vesa Viitakoski, Calg. RC	**.50**
345 Steve Chiasson, Detr.	.20
346 Andrew Cassels, Hart.	.20
347 Pierre Turgeon, NYIs.	.20
348 Brian Leetch, NYRa.	.20
349 Alexei Yashin, Otta.	.20
350 Mark Recchi, Phil.	.50
351 Ron Francis, Pitt.	.20
352 Mike Ricci, Québ.	.20
353 Igor Korolev, SLou.	.20

☐	**354 Brent Gretzky, Tamp. RC**	**.50**
☐	355 Dave Poulin, Wash.	.20
☐	356 Cam Neely, Bost.	.50
☐	357 Gary Suter, Calg.	.20
☐	358 Dave Manson, Edmo.	.20
☐	359 Robert Kron, Hart.	.20
☐	360 Ulf Dahlén, Minn. (Dall.)	.20
☐	361 Rod Brind'Amour, Phil.	.20
☐	362 Alexei Gusarov, Québ.	.20
☐	363 Vitali Prokhorov, SLou.	.20
☐	**364 Damian Rhodes (G), Toro. RC**	**1.00**
☐	365 Paul Ysebaert, Winn.	.20
☐	366 Vladimir Konstantinov, Detr.	.20
☐	367 Steven Rice, Edmo.	.20
☐	368 Brian Propp, Hart.	.20
☐	369 Valeri Zelepukin, NJer.	.20
☐	370 David Volek, NYIs.	.20
☐	371 Sergei Nemchinov, NYRa.	.20
☐	372 Pavol Demitra, Otta.	.20
☐	373 Brent Fedyk, Phil.	.20
☐	374 Larry Murphy, Pitt.	.20
☐	375 Dave Karpa, Québ.	.20
☐	376 Dave Babych, Vanc.	.20
☐	377 Keith Jones, Wash.	.20
☐	378 Neil Wilkinson, Chic.	.20
☐	379 Jozef Stumpel, Bost.	.20
☐	380 Vincent Damphousse, Mont.	.20
☐	381 Tom Kurvers, NYIs.	.20
☐	382 Doug Gilmour, Toro.	.20
☐	383 Trevor Linden, Vanc.	.20
☐	384 Kelly Miller, Wash.	.20
☐	385 Tim Sweeney, Anah.	.20
☐	386 Mikhail Tatarinov, Bost.	.20
☐	387 Dominik Hasek (G), Buff.	.50
☐	388 Steve Yzerman, Detr.	1.00
☐	389 Scott Pearson, Edmo.	.20
☐	390 Brian Bellows, Mont.	.20
☐	391 Claude Lemieux, NJer.	.20
☐	392 Marty McInnis, NYIs.	.20
☐	393 Jim Sandlak, Hart.	.20
☐	**394 Jocelyn Thibault (G), Québ. RC**	**2.00**
☐	395 John Cullen, Toro.	.20
☐	396 Joe Nieuwendyk, Calg.	.20
☐	397 Mike Modano, Minn. (Dall.)	.50
☐	398 Ray Sheppard, Detr.	.20
☐	399 Trevor Kidd (G), Calg.	.20
☐	400 Checklist	.20
☐	401 Frank Pietrangelo (G), Hart.	.20
☐	402 Stéphan Lebeau, Mont.	.20
☐	403 Stéphane J.J. Richer, NJer.	.20
☐	404 Greg Gilbert, NYRa.	.20
☐	405 Dmitri Filimonov, Otta.	.20
☐	406 Viacheslav Butsayev, Phil.	.20
☐	407 Mario Lemieux, Pitt.	1.50
☐	408 Kevin Miller, SLou.	.20
☐	409 John Tucker, Tamp.	.20
☐	410 Murray Craven, Vanc.	.20
☐	411 Dale Hawerchuk, Buff.	.20
☐	412 Al MacInnis, Calg.	.20
☐	413 Keith Primeau, Detr.	.20
☐	414 Luc Robitaille, LosA.	.20
☐	415 Benoît Brunet, Mont.	.20
☐	416 Tom Chorske, NJer.	.20
☐	417 Derek King, NYIs.	.20
☐	418 Troy Mallette, Otta.	.20
☐	419 Mats Sundin, Québ.	.50
☐	420 Kent Manderville, Toro.	.20
☐	421 Kip Miller, SanJ.	.20
☐	422 Jarkko Varvio, Dall.	.20
☐	**423 Jason Arnott, Edmo. RC**	**2.00**
☐	424 Craig Billington (G), Otta.	.20
☐	**425 Stewart Malgunas, Phil. RC**	**.50**
☐	426 Ron Tugnutt (G), Anah.	.20
☐	**427 Alexei Kudashov, Toro. RC**	**.50**
☐	428 Harijs Vitolinsh, Winn.	.20
☐	429 Bill Houlder, Anah.	.20
☐	430 Craig Simpson, Buff.	.20
☐	431 Wes Walz, Calg.	.20
☐	**432 Micah Aivazoff, Detr. RC**	**.50**
☐	**433 Scott Levins, Flor. RC**	**.50**
☐	434 Ron Hextall (G), NYIs.	.20
☐	**435 Fred Brathwaite (G), Edmo. RC**	**1.50**
☐	**436 Chad Penney, Otta. RC**	**.50**
☐	**437 Vlastimil Kroupa, SanJ. RC**	**.50**
☐	438 Troy Loney, Anah.	.20
☐	439 Matthew Barnaby, Buff.	.20
☐	440 Kevin Todd, Chic.	.20
☐	441 Paul Cavallini, Dall.	.20
☐	442 Doug Weight, Edmo.	.20
☐	443 Evgeny Davydov, Flor.	.20
☐	444 Dominic Lavoie, LosA.	.20
☐	**445 Peter Popovic, Mont. RC**	**.50**
☐	446 Sergei Makarov, SanJ.	.20
☐	**447 Matt Martin, Toro. RC**	**.50**
☐	448 Teemu Selänne, Winn.	.20
☐	449 Todd Ewen, Anah.	.20
☐	450 Sergei Petrenko, Buff.	.20
☐	**451 Jeff Shantz, Chic. RC**	**.50**
☐	452 Greg Johnson, Detr.	.20
☐	**453 Brent Severyn, Flor. RC**	**.50**
☐	454 Shawn McEachern, LosA.	.20
☐	455 Pierre Sévigny, Mont.	.20
☐	456 Benoît Hogue, NYIs.	.20
☐	457 Esa Tikkanen, NYRa.	.20
☐	458 Brian Glynn, Otta.	.20
☐	459 Doug Brown, Pitt.	.20
☐	460 Mike Rathje, SanJ.	.20
☐	**461 Rudy Poeschek, Tamp. RC**	**.50**
☐	462 Jason Woolley, Wash.	.20
☐	**463 Patrik Carnbäck, Anah. RC**	**.50**
☐	**464 Cam Stewart, Bost. RC**	**.50**
☐	465 Petr* Svoboda, Buff.	.20
☐	466 Ted Drury, Calg.	.20
☐	**467 Ladislav Karabin, Pitt. RC**	**.50**
☐	468 Paul Broten, Dall.	.20
☐	469 Alexander Godynyuk, Flor.	.20
☐	**470 Bob Jay, LosA. RC**	**.50**
☐	471 Steve Larmer, NYRa.	.20
☐	**472 Jim Montgomery, SLou. RC**	**.50**
☐	473 Daren Puppa (G), Tamp.	.20
☐	474 Alexei Kasatonov, Anah.	.20
☐	**475 Derek Plante, Buff. RC**	**.50**
☐	**476 German Titov, Calg. RC**	**.50**
☐	**477 Steve Dubinsky, Chic. RC**	**.50**
☐	478 Andy Moog (G), Dall.	.20
☐	**479 Aaron Ward, Detr. RC**	**.50**
☐	480 Dean McAmmond, Edmo.	.20
☐	481 Randy Gilhen, Flor.	.20
☐	**482 Jason Muzzatti (G), Calg. RC**	**.50**
☐	483 Corey Millen, NJer.	.20
☐	484 Alexander Karpovtsev, NYRa.	.20
☐	**485 Bill Huard, Otta. RC**	**.50**
☐	486 Mikael Renberg, Phil.	.20
☐	487 Marty McSorley, Pitt.	.20
☐	488 Alexander Mogilny, Buff.	.20
☐	**489 Michal Sykora, SanJ. RC**	**.50**
☐	490 Checklist	.20
☐	491 Tom Tilley, SLou.	.20
☐	492 Boris Mironov, Winn.	.20
☐	493 Sandy McCarthy, Calg.	.20
☐	**494 Mark Astley, Buff. RC**	**.50**
☐	495 Vyacheslav Kozlov, Detr.	.20
☐	496 Brian Benning, Flor.	.20
☐	497 Eric Weinrich, Chic.	.20
☐	**498 Robert Burakovsky, Otta. RC**	**.50**
☐	499 Patrick Lebeau, Flor.	.20
☐	500 Markus Näslund, Pitt.	1.00
☐	501 Jimmy Waite (G), SanJ.	.20
☐	502 Denis Savard, Tamp.	.20
☐	**503 José Charbonneau, Vanc. RC**	**.50**
☐	504 Randy Burridge, Wash.	.20
☐	505 Arto Blömsten, Winn.	#NAME?
☐	506 Shaun Van Allen, Anah.	.20
☐	507 Jon Casey (G), Bost.	.20
☐	**508 Darren McCarty, Detr. RC**	**1.50**
☐	509 Roman Oksiuta, Edmo. RC	.20
☐	510 Jody Hull, Flor.	.20
☐	511 Scott Scissons, NYIs.	.20
☐	512 Jeff Norton, SanJ.	.20
☐	513 Dmitri Mironov, Toro.	.20
☐	514 Sergei Bautin, Winn.	.20
☐	515 Garry Valk, Anah.	.20
☐	516 Keith Carney, Chic.	.20
☐	517 James H. Black, Minn. (Dall.)	.20
☐	518 Pat Peake, Wash.	.20
☐	**519 Chris Osgood (G), Detr. RC**	**3.00**
☐	**520 Kirk Maltby, Edmo. RC**	**1.00**
☐	521 Gord Murphy, Flor.	.20
☐	**522 Mattias Norström, NYRa. RC**	**1.00**
☐	**523 Milos Holan, Phil. RC**	**.50**
☐	524 Dave McLlwain, Otta.	.20
☐	525 Phil Housley, SLou.	.20
☐	526 Petr Klima, Tamp.	.20
☐	527 John McIntyre, Vanc.	.20
☐	528 Enrico Ciccone, Wash.	.20
☐	529 Stéphane Quintal, Winn.	.20

☐	530 Brent Tully, Canada Juniors [Checklist]	.20
☐	**531 Anson Carter, Canada Juniors RC**	**2.00**
☐	**532 Jeff Friesen, Canada Juniors RC**	**1.50**
☐	**533 Yannick Dubé, Canada Juniors RC**	**.50**
☐	**534 Jason Botterill, Canada Juniors RC**	**.50**
☐	**535 Todd Harvey, Canada Juniors RC**	**1.00**
☐	**536 Manny Fernandez, Canada Juniors RC**	**2.00**
☐	**537 Jason Allison, Canada Juniors RC**	**3.00**
☐	**538 Jamie Storr (G), Canada Juniors RC**	**1.00**
☐	**539 Rick Girard, Canada Juniors RC**	**.50**
☐	540 Martin Gendron, Canada Juniors	.20
☐	**541 Joël Bouchard, Canada Juniors RC**	**.50**
☐	**542 Michael Peca, Canada Juniors RC**	**2.00**
☐	**543 Nick Stajduhar, Canada Juniors RC**	**.50**
☐	**544 Brendan Witt, Canada Juniors RC**	**.50**
☐	**545 Aaron Gavey, Canada Juniors RC**	**.50**
☐	**546 Chris Armstrong, Canada Juniors RC**	**.50**
☐	**547 Curtis Bowen, Canada Juniors RC**	**.50**
☐	**548 Brandon Convery, Canada Juniors RC**	**.50**
☐	**549 Bryan McCabe, Canada Juniors RC**	**1.00**
☐	**550 Marty Murray, Canada Juniors RC**	**.50**
☐	551 Ryan Sittler, U.S.A. Juniors	.20
☐	**552 Jason McBain, U.S.A. Juniors RC**	**.50**
☐	**553 Richard Park, U.S.A. Juniors RC**	**.50**
☐	**554 Aaron Ellis, U.S.A. Juniors RC**	**.50**
☐	**555 Toby Kvalevog, U.S.A. Juniors RC**	**.50**
☐	**556 Jay Pandolfo, U.S.A. Juniors RC**	**.50**
☐	557 John Emmons, U.S.A. Juniors	.20
☐	**558 David Wilkie, U.S.A. Juniors RC**	**.50**
☐	**559 John Varga, U.S.A. Juniors RC**	**.50**
☐	**560 Jason Bonsignore, U.S.A. Juniors RC**	**.50**
☐	**561 Deron Quint, U.S.A. Juniors RC**	**.50**
☐	562 Adam Deadmarsh, U.S.A. Juniors	.20
☐	**563 Jon Coleman, U.S.A. Juniors RC**	**.50**
☐	**564 Bob Lachance, U.S.A. Juniors RC**	**.50**
☐	**565 Chris O'Sullivan, U.S.A. Juniors RC**	**.50**
☐	**566 J. Langenbrunner, U.S.A. Juniors RC**	**1.00**
☐	**567 Kevin Hilton, U.S.A. Juniors RC**	**.50**
☐	**568 Kevyn Adams, U.S.A. Juniors RC**	**.50**
☐	569 Saku Koivu, Finland Juniors	1.00
☐	**570 Mats Lindgren, Sweden Juniors RC**	**.50**
☐	**571 Valeri Bure, Russia Juniors RC**	**1.50**
☐	**572 Edvin Frylén, Sweden Juniors RC**	**.50**
☐	**573 Jaro. Miklenda (G), Czech Jrs. RC**	**.50**
☐	574 Vadim Sharifijanov, Russia Juniors	.20
☐	**575 Checklist**	**.20**
	Insert	**NRMT-MT**
☐	SP4 Teemu Selänne, Winn.	2.00
☐	99 Wayne Gretzky, LosA. [Gold]	12.00
☐	99 Wayne Gretzky, LosA. [Silver]	25.00

AWARD WINNERS

	Canadian Insert Set (8 cards):	**25.00**
	Insert (1:30)	**AW**
☐	AW1 Mario Lemieux, Pitt.	10.00
☐	AW2 Teemu Selänne, Winn.	3.00
☐	AW3 Ed Belfour (G), Chic.	3.00
☐	AW4 Patrick Roy (G), Mont.	10.00
☐	AW5 Chris Chelios, Chic.	2.00
☐	AW6 Doug Gilmour, Toro.	2.00
☐	AW7 Pierre Turgeon, NYIs.	1.00
☐	AW8 Dave Poulin, Bost.	.75

GRETZKY'S GREAT ONES

	Insert Set (10 cards):	**5.00**
	Insert (1:1 Jumbo)	**GG**
☐	GG1 Denis Savard, Mont.	.35
☐	GG2 Chris Chelios, Mont.	.35
☐	GG3 Brett Hull, SLou.	1.00
☐	GG4 Mario Lemieux, Pitt.	4.00
☐	GG5 Mark Messier, Edmo.	1.00
☐	GG6 Paul Coffey, Pitt.	.35
☐	GG7 Theoren Fleury, Calg.	.35
☐	GG8 Luc Robitaille, NHL All-Star	1.00
☐	GG9 Marty McSorley, LosA.	.35
☐	GG10 Grant Fuhr (G), Edmo.	.35

FUTURE HEROES

	American Insert Set (10 cards):	**70.00**
	Insert (1:30)	**FH**
☐	28 Félix Potvin (G), Toro.	7.00
☐	29 Pat Falloon, SanJ.	4.00
☐	30 Pavel Bure, Vanc.	10.00
☐	31 Eric Lindros, Phil.	10.00
☐	32 Teemu Selänne, Winn.	10.00
☐	33 Jaromir Jagr, Pitt.	10.00
☐	34 Alexander Mogilny, Buff.	6.00
☐	35 Joé Juneau, Bost.	4.00
☐	36 Checklist	10.00
☐	Title Card	15.00

HAT TRICKS

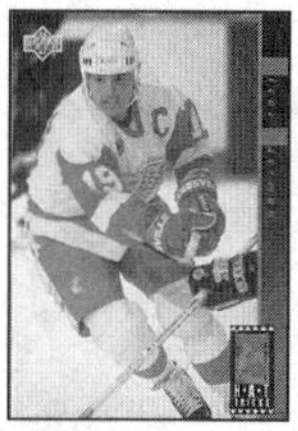

	Insert Set (20 cards):	**5.00**
	Insert (1:1 Jumbo)	**HT**
☐	HT1 Adam Graves, NYRa.	.35
☐	HT2 Geoff Sanderson, Hart.	.35
☐	HT3 Gary Roberts, Calg.	.35
☐	HT4 Robert Reichel, Calg.	.35
☐	HT5 Adam Oates, Bost.	.35
☐	HT6 Steve Yzerman, Detr.	3.00
☐	HT7 Alexei Kovalev, NYRa.	.35
☐	HT8 Vincent Damphousse, Mont.	.35
☐	HT9 Rob Gaudreau, SanJ.	.35
☐	HT10 Pat LaFontaine, Buff.	.35
☐	HT11 Pierre Turgeon, NYIs.	.35
☐	HT12 Rick Tocchet, Pitt.	.35
☐	HT13 Michael Nylander, Hart.	.35
☐	HT14 Steve Larmer, Chic.	.35
☐	HT15 Alexander Mogilny, Buff.	.35
☐	HT16 Owen Nolan, Québ.	.35
☐	HT17 Luc Robitaille, LosA.	1.00
☐	HT18 Jeremy Roenick, Chic.	1.00
☐	HT19 Kevin Stevens, Pitt.	.35
☐	HT20 Mats Sundin, Québ.	1.00

NEXT IN LINE

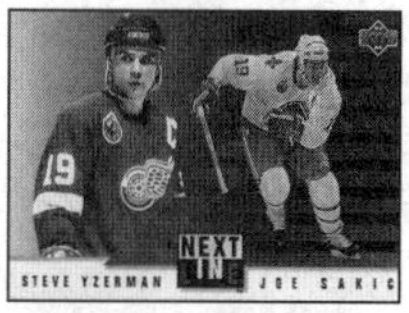

	Insert Set (6 cards):	**15.00**
	Insert (1:36)	**NL**
☐	NL1 W. Gretzky / M. Nylander	5.00
☐	NL2 Br. Hull / P. Poulin	1.00
☐	NL3 S. Yzerman / J. Sakic	5.00
☐	NL4 R. Bourque / B. Leetch	1.00
☐	NL5 D. Gilmour / K. Tkachuk	1.00
☐	NL6 P. Roy / F. Potvin	5.00

NHL'S BEST

	American Insert Set (10 cards):	**120.00**
	Insert (1:30 Retail)	**HB**
☐	HB1 Alexander Mogilny, Buff.	6.00
☐	HB2 Rob Gaudreau, SanJ.	6.00
☐	HB3 Brett Hull, SLou.	10.00
☐	HB4 Dallas Drake, Detr.	6.00
☐	HB5 Pavel Bure, Vanc.	10.00
☐	HB6 Alexei Kovalev, NYRa.	7.00
☐	HB7 Mario Lemieux, Pitt.	35.00
☐	HB8 Eric Lindros, Phil.	10.00
☐	HB9 Wayne Gretzky, LosA.	50.00
☐	HB10 Joé Juneau, Bost.	6.00

PROGRAM OF EXCELLENCE

	Canadian Insert Set (15 cards):	**250.00**
	Insert (1:30)	**E**
☐	**E1 Adam Smith, Canada Juniors RC**	**8.00**
☐	**E2 Jason Podollan, Canada Juniors RC**	**8.00**
☐	**E3 Jason Wiemer, Canada Juniors RC**	**8.00**
☐	**E4 Jeff O'Neill, Canada Juniors RC**	**30.00**
☐	**E5 Daniel Goneau, Canada Juniors RC**	**8.00**
☐	**E6 Christian Laflamme, Canada Juniors RC**	**8.00**
☐	**E7 D. Langkow, Canada Juniors RC**	**15.00**
☐	E8 Jeff Friesen, Canada Juniors	25.00
☐	**E9 Wayne Primeau, Canada Juniors RC**	**12.00**
☐	E10 Paul Kariya, Canada Juniors	40.00
☐	E11 Rob Niedermayer, Flor.	8.00
☐	E12 Eric Lindros, Phil.	20.00
☐	E13 Mario Lemieux, Pitt.	60.00
☐	E14 Steve Yzerman, Detr.	45.00
☐	E15 Alexandre Daigle, Otta.	8.00

SILVER SKATES

	Hobby Insert Set (10 cards):	**-**	**35.00**
	Retail Insert Set (10 cards):	**65.00**	**45.00**
	Insert (1:30)	**Gold**	**Silver**
☐	H1 Mario Lemieux, Pitt.	-	15.00
☐	H2 Pavel Bure, Vanc.	-	4.00
☐	H3 Eric Lindros, Phil.	-	5.00
☐	H4 Rob Niedermayer, Flor.	-	2.00
☐	H5 Chris Pronger, Hart.	-	3.00
☐	H6 Adam Oates, Bost.	-	2.00
☐	H7 Pierre Turgeon, NYIs.	-	2.00
☐	H8 Alexei Yashin, Otta.	-	3.00
☐	H9 Joe Sakic, Québ.	-	5.00
☐	H10 Alexander Mogilny, Buff.	-	2.00
☐ ☐	R1 Wayne Gretzky, LosA.	30.00	20.00
☐ ☐	R2 Teemu Selänne, Winn.	6.00	4.00
☐ ☐	R3 Alexandre Daigle, Otta.	2.00	2.00
☐ ☐	R4 Chris Gratton, Tamp.	2.00	2.00
☐ ☐	R5 Brett Hull, SLou.	7.00	5.00
☐ ☐	R6 Steve Yzerman, Detr.	15.00	10.00
☐ ☐	R7 Doug Gilmour, Toro.	4.00	3.00
☐ ☐	R8 Jaromir Jagr, Pitt.	5.00	5.00
☐ ☐	R9 Jason Arnott, Edmo.	5.00	3.00
☐ ☐	R10 Jeremy Roenick, Chic.	6.00	4.00
	Expired Trade Card	**Gold**	**Silver**
☐ ☐	Wayne Gretzky, LosA.	90.00	50.00

SP

	Complete Set (180 cards):	**80.00**
	Player	**SP**
☐	1 Sean Hill, Anah.	.35
☐	2 Troy Loney, Anah.	.35
☐	3 Joe Sacco, Anah.	.35
☐	4 Anatoli Semenov, Anah.	.35
☐	5 Ron Tugnutt (G), Anah.	1.00
☐	6 Terry Yake, Anah.	.35
☐	7 Raymond Bourque, Bost.	3.00
☐	8 Jon Casey (G), Bost.	.35

☐ 9 Joé Juneau, Bost. .50
☐ 10 Cam Neely, Bost. 2.50
☐ 11 Adam Oates, Bost. 1.00
☐ 12 Bryan Smolinski, Bost. .35
☐ 13 Matthew Barnaby, Buff. .35
☐ 14 Philippe Boucher, Buff. .35
☐ 15 Grant Fuhr (G), Buff. 1.50
☐ 16 Dale Hawerchuk, Buff. 1.50
☐ 17 Pat LaFontaine, Buff. 1.50
☐ 18 Alexander Mogilny, Buff. 1.00
☐ 19 Craig Simpson, Buff. .35
☐ 20 Ted Drury, Calg. .35
☐ 21 Theoren Fleury, Calg. 1.50
☐ 22 Al MacInnis, Calg. 1.00
☐ 23 Joe Nieuwendyk, Calg. 1.00
☐ 24 Joel Otto, Calg. .35
☐ 25 Gary Roberts, Calg. 1.00
☐ 26 Vesa Viitakoski, Calg. .35
☐ 27 Ed Belfour (G), Chic. 2.50
☐ 28 Chris Chelios, Chic. 1.50
☐ 29 Joe Murphy, Chic. .35
☐ 30 Patrick Poulin, Chic. .35
☐ 31 Jeremy Roenick, Chic. 2.00
☐ 32 Jeff Shantz, Chic. .35
☐ 33 Kevin Todd, Chic. .35
☐ 34 Neal Broten, Minn. (Dall.) .50
☐ 35 Paul Cavallini, Dall. .35
☐ 36 Russ Courtnall, Minn. (Dall.) .50
☐ 37 Derian Hatcher, Minn. (Dall.) .50
☐ 38 Mike Modano, Minn. (Dall.) 2.50
☐ 39 Andy Moog (G), Dall. 1.00
☐ 40 Jarkko Varvio, Dall. .50
☐ 41 Dino Ciccarelli, Detr. .50
☐ 42 Paul Coffey, Detr. 1.50
☐ 43 Dallas Drake, Detr. .50
☐ 44 Sergei Fedorov, Detr. 2.50
☐ 45 Keith Primeau, Detr. 1.00
☐ 46 Bob Probert, Detr. .50
☐ 47 Steve Yzerman, Detr. 6.00
☐ 48 Jason Arnott, Edmo. 1.50
☐ 49 Shayne Corson, Edmo. .50
☐ 50 Dave Manson, Edmo. .35
☐ 51 Dean McAmmond, Edmo. .35
☐ 52 Bill Ranford (G), Edmo. 1.00
☐ 53 Doug Weight, Edmo. 1.50
☐ 54 Brad Werenka, Edmo. .35
☐ 55 Evgeny Davydov, Flor. .35
☐ 56 Scott Levins, Flor. .35
☐ 57 Scott Mellanby, Flor. .50
☐ 58 Rob Niedermayer, Flor. .50
☐ 59 Brian Skrudland, Flor. .35
☐ 60 John Vanbiesbrouck (G), Flor. 1.00
☐ 61 Robert Kron, Hart. .35
☐ 62 Michael Nylander, Hart. .50
☐ 63 Robert Petrovicky, Hart. .35
☐ 64 Chris Pronger, Hart. 1.50
☐ 65 Geoff Sanderson, Hart. .50
☐ 66 Darren Turcotte, Hart. .35
☐ 67 Pat Verbeek, Hart. .50
☐ 68 Rob Blake, LosA. 1.50
☐ 69 Tony Granato, LosA. .50
☐ 70 Wayne Gretzky, LosA. 10.00
☐ 71 Kelly Hrudey (G), LosA. .50
☐ 72 Shawn McEachern, LosA. .50
☐ 73 Luc Robitaille, LosA. 2.00
☐ 74 Darryl Sydor, LosA. .50
☐ 75 Alexei Zhitnik, LosA. .35
☐ 76 Brian Bellows, Mont. .50
☐ 77 Vincent Damphousse, Mont. 1.50
☐ 78 Stéphan Lebeau, Mont. .35
☐ 79 John LeClair, Mont. 2.00
☐ 80 Kirk Muller, Mont. .50
☐ 81 Patrick Roy (G), Mont. 7.50
☐ 82 Pierre Sévigny, Mont. .35
☐ 83 Claude Lemieux, NJer. .50
☐ 84 Corey Millen, NJer. .35
☐ 85 Bernie Nicholls, NJer. .50
☐ 86 Scott Niedermayer, NJer. .50
☐ 87 Stéphane J.J. Richer, NJer. .50
☐ 88 Alexander Semak, NJer. .35
☐ 89 Scott Stevens, NJer. 1.00
☐ 90 Ray Ferraro, NYIs. .35
☐ 91 Darius Kasparaitis, NYIs. .50
☐ 92 Scott Lachance, NYIs. .35
☐ 93 Vladimir Malakhov, NYIs. .35
☐ 94 Marty McInnis, NYIs. .35
☐ 95 Steve Thomas, NYIs. .50
☐ 96 Pierre Turgeon, NYIs. 1.00
☐ 97 Tony Amonte, NYRa. 1.50
☐ 98 Mike Gartner, NYRa. 2.00
☐ 99 Adam Graves, NYRa. 1.00
☐ 100 Alexander Karpovtsev, NYRa. .35
☐ 101 Alexei Kovalev, NYRa. 1.50
☐ 102 Brian Leetch, NYRa. 1.50
☐ 103 Mark Messier, NYRa. 2.50
☐ 104 Esa Tikkanen, NYRa. .35
☐ 105 Craig Billington (G), Otta. .35
☐ 106 Robert Burakovsky, Otta. .35
☐ 107 Alexandre Daigle, Otta. .35
☐ 108 Pavol Demitra, Otta. 1.00
☐ 109 Dmitri Filimonov, Otta. .35
☐ 110 Bob Kudelski, Otta. .35
☐ 111 Norm Maciver, Otta. .35
☐ 112 Alexei Yashin, Otta. 1.50
☐ 113 Josef Beránek, Phil. .35
☐ 114 Rod Brind'Amour, Phil. .50
☐ 115 Milos Holan, Phil. .35
☐ 116 Eric Lindros, Phil. 2.50
☐ 117 Mark Recchi, Phil. 1.00
☐ 118 Mikael Renberg, Phil. .50
☐ 119 Dmitry Yushkevich, Phil. .50
☐ 120 Tom Barrasso (G), Pitt. 1.00
☐ 121 Jaromir Jagr, Pitt. 2.50
☐ 122 Mario Lemieux, Pitt. 7.50
☐ 123 Markus Näslund, Pitt. 2.50
☐ 124 Kevin Stevens, Pitt. .50
☐ 125 Martin Straka, Pitt. .50
☐ 126 Rick Tocchet, Pitt. .50
☐ 127 Martin Gélinas, Québ. .50
☐ 128 Owen Nolan, Québ. 1.50
☐ 129 Mike Ricci, Québ. .50
☐ 130 Joe Sakic, Québ. 4.00
☐ 131 Chris Simon, Québ. .50
☐ 132 Mats Sundin, Québ. 2.50
☐ 133 Jocelyn Thibault (G), Québ. 1.50
☐ 134 Philippe Bozon, SLou. .35
☐ 135 Jeff R. Brown, SLou. .35
☐ 136 Phil Housley, SLou. .50
☐ 137 Brett Hull, SLou. 2.50
☐ 138 Craig Janney, SLou. .50
☐ 139 Curtis Joseph (G), SLou. 2.50
☐ 140 Brendan Shanahan, SLou. 2.50
☐ 141 Pat Falloon, SanJ. .35
☐ 142 Johan Garpenlöv, SanJ. .35
☐ 143 Rob Gaudreau, SanJ. .35
☐ 144 Vlastimil Kroupa, SanJ. .35
☐ 145 Sergei Makarov, SanJ. 1.00
☐ 146 Sandis Ozolinsh, SanJ. .50
☐ 147 Mike Rathje, SanJ. .35
☐ 148 Brian Bradley, Tamp. .35
☐ 149 Chris Gratton, Tamp. .50
☐ 150 Brent Gretzky, Tamp. .50
☐ 151 Roman Hamrlik, Tamp. .50
☐ 152 Petr Klima, Tamp. .35
☐ 153 Denis Savard, Tamp. 1.00
☐ 154 Rob Zamuner, Tamp. .50
☐ 155 Dave Andreychuk, Toro. .50
☐ 156 Nikolai Borschevsky, Toro. .35
☐ 157 Dave Ellett, Toro. .35
☐ 158 Doug Gilmour, Toro. 1.50
☐ 159 Alexei Kudashov, Toro. .35
☐ 160 Félix Potvin (G), Toro. 1.50
☐ 161 Greg A. Adams, Vanc. .35
☐ 162 Pavel Bure, Vanc. 2.00
☐ 163 Geoff Courtnall, Vanc. .35
☐ 164 Trevor Linden, Vanc. 1.00
☐ 165 Kirk McLean (G), Vanc. .50
☐ 166 Jiri Slégr, Vanc. .35
☐ 167 Dixon Ward, Vanc. .35
☐ 168 Peter Bondra, Wash. 1.50
☐ 169 Kevin Hatcher, Wash. .35
☐ 170 Al Iafrate, Wash. .50
☐ 171 Dmitri Khristich, Wash. .35
☐ 172 Pat Peake, Wash. .35
☐ 173 Mike Ridley, Wash. .35
☐ 174 Arto Blömsten, Winn. .35
☐ 175 Nelson Emerson, Winn. .35
☐ 176 Boris Mironov, Winn. .35
☐ 177 Teemu Selänne, Winn. 2.00
☐ 178 Keith Tkachuk, Winn. 1.50
☐ 179 Paul Ysebaert, Winn. .35
☐ 180 Alexei Zhamnov, Winn. .50

1993 - 94 UPPER DECK – BUYBACKS

Buyback Autograph

UD
☐ 231 Luc Robitaille, LosA. ✍ {#/12}
☐ 293 Luc Robitaille, LosA. ✍ {#/5}
☐ 294 Mike Modano, Minn. (Dall.) ✍ {#/2}
☐ 397 Mike Modano, Minn. (Dall.) ✍ {#/5}
☐ 414 Luc Robitaille, LosA. ✍ {#/13}
☐ Steve Yzerman, Detr. ✍ {#/1}

Buyback Autograph • SP

SP
☐ 31 Jeremy Roenick, Chic. ✍ {#/11}
☐ 47 Steve Yzerman, Detr. ✍ {#/3}
☐ 47 Steve Yzerman, Detr. ✍ {#/3}
☐ 73 Luc Robitaille, LosA. ✍ {#/16}

1993 - 94 UPPER DECK BE A PLAYER

Cards 1-18 feature the photography of Walter Iooss.

Complete Set (45 cards): 30.00

	Player	BAP
☐	1 Tony Amonte, NHLPA	.50
☐	2 Chris Chelios, NHLPA	.50
☐	3 Alexandre Daigle, NHLPA	.25
☐	4 Dave Ellett, NHLPA	.25
☐	5 Sergei Fedorov, NHLPA	1.50
☐	6 Chris Gratton, NHLPA	.25
☐	7 Wayne Gretzky, NHLPA	6.00
☐	8 Brett Hull, NHLPA	1.50
☐	9 Brian Leetch, NHLPA	.50
☐	10 Rob Niedermayer, NHLPA	.25
☐	11 Félix Potvin (G), NHLPA	.50
☐	12 Luc Robitaille, NHLPA	1.00
☐	13 Jeremy Roenick, NHLPA	1.00
☐	14 Joe Sakic, NHLPA	2.00
☐	15 Teemu Selänne, NHLPA	1.00
☐	16 Brendan Shanahan, NHLPA	1.50
☐	17 Alexei Yashin, NHLPA	.50
☐	18 Steve Yzerman, NHLPA	3.50
☐	19 Jason Arnott, NHLPA	1.00
☐	20 Pavel Bure, NHLPA	1.00
☐	21 Theoren Fleury, NHLPA	.50
☐	22 Mike Gartner, NHLPA	1.00
☐	23 Kevin Haller, NHLPA	.25
☐	24 Derian Hatcher, NHLPA	.25
☐	25 Howe Family	2.00
☐	26 Al Iafrate, NHLPA	.25
☐	27 Joé Juneau, NHLPA	.25
☐	28 Pat LaFontaine, NHLPA	.50
☐	29 Eric Lindros, NHLPA	1.50
☐	30 Dave Manson, NHLPA	.25
☐	31 Mike Modano, NHLPA	1.50
☐	32 Scott Niedermayer, NHLPA	.25
☐	33 Owen Nolan, NHLPA	.50
☐	34 Joel Otto, NHLPA	.25
☐	35 Chris Pronger, NHLPA	.50
☐	36 Scott Stevens, NHLPA	.50
☐	37 Pierre Turgeon, NHLPA	.50
☐	38 Pat Verbeek, NHLPA	.25
☐	39 Doug Weight, NHLPA	.50
☐	40 Terry Yake, NHLPA	.25
☐	41 Doug Gilmour, NHLPA	.50
☐	42 Doug Gilmour, NHLPA	.50
☐	43 Doug Gilmour, NHLPA	.50
☐	44 Doug Gilmour, NHLPA	.50
☐	45 Doug Gilmour, NHLPA	.50

1993 - 94 UPPER DECK BE A PLAYER / ROOTS

Complete Set (30 cards): 20.00

	Player	NRMT-MT
☐	1 Trevor Linden, NHLPA	.50
☐	2 Guy Carbonneau, NHLPA	.25
☐	3 Félix Potvin (G), NHLPA	.50
☐	4 Steve Yzerman, NHLPA	3.50
☐	5 Doug Gilmour, NHLPA	.50
☐	6 Wendel Clark, NHLPA	1.00
☐	7 Kirk McLean (G), NHLPA	.25
☐	8 Larry Murphy, NHLPA	.25
☐	9 Patrick Roy (G), NHLPA	4.50
☐	10 Mike Ricci, NHLPA	.25
☐	11 Doug Gilmour, NHLPA	.50
☐	12 Sergei Fedorov, NHLPA	1.50
☐	13 Shayne Corson, NHLPA	.25
☐	14 Alexei Yashin, NHLPA	.50
☐	15 Pavel Bure, NHLPA	1.00
☐	16 Joe Sakic, NHLPA	2.00
☐	17 Teemu Selänne, NHLPA	1.00
☐	18 Dave Andreychuk, NHLPA	.25
☐	19 Al MacInnis, NHLPA	.50
☐	20 Rob Blake, NHLPA	.50
☐	21 Doug Gilmour, NHLPA	.50
☐	22 Steve Larmer, NHLPA	.50
☐	23 Eric Lindros, NHLPA	1.50
☐	24 Mike Modano, NHLPA	1.50
☐	25 Vincent Damphousse, NHLPA	.50
☐	26 Mike Gartner, NHLPA	1.00
☐	27 John Vanbiesbrouck (G), NHLPA	.50
☐	28 Theoren Fleury, NHLPA	.50
☐	29 Ken Baumgartner, NHLPA	.25
☐	30 Jeremy Roenick, NHLPA	1.00

1993 - 94 ZELLERS MASTERS OF HOCKEY

This 8-card set is unnumbered and listed here alphabetically. There are 10,000 copies of each card and 2,100 copies of each autographed card. Unsigned cards sell for 25¢-$1.00.

Imprint: ZELLERS

Complete Set (8 cards): 150.00

	Player	Auto.
☐☐	Andy Bathgate ✍	15.00
☐☐	John Bucyk ✍	20.00
☐☐	Yvan Cournoyer ✍	20.00
☐☐	Marcel Dionne ✍	30.00
☐☐	Bobby Hull ✍	35.00
☐☐	Brad Park ✍	20.00
☐☐	Jean Ratelle ✍	15.00
☐☐	Gump Worsley (G) ✍	30.00

1994 KOULULAINEN

A 9-card sheet issued by the magazine Koululainen.

Card Size: 2 5/8" x 3 3/8"

Complete Set (9 cards): 30.00

Koululainen	Koululainen
☐ Ray Bourque, Bost.	☐ Sergei Fedorov, Detr.
☐ Doug Gilmour, Toro.	☐ Wayne Gretzky, LosA.
☐ Mario Lemieux, Pitt.	☐ Eric Lindros, Phil.
☐ Mark Messier, NYRa.	☐ Alexander Mogilny, Buff.
☐ Patrick Roy (G), Mont.	

1994 PANINI OLYMPIC STICKERS

We have no pricing information on these stickers.

Player	Player
☐ 273 Hockey logo	☐ 274 Russia
☐ 275 Russia	☐ 276 Russia
☐ 277 Russia	☐ 278 Russia
☐ 279 Russia	☐ 280 Konst. Astrahantsev
☐ 281 Vyacheslav Bykov	☐ 282 Sergei
☐ 283 Alexander Smirnov	☐ 284 Sweden
☐ 285 Sweden	☐ 286 Sweden
☐ 287 Sweden	☐ 288 Sweden
☐ 289 Sweden	☐ 290 Markus Näslund
☐ 291 Peter Forsberg	☐ 292 Mats Sundin
☐ 293 Mikael Renberg	☐ 294 Tommy Söderström
☐ 295 Finland	☐ 296 Finland
☐ 297 Finland	☐ 298 Finland
☐ 299 Finland	☐ 300 Finland
☐ 301 Markus Ketterer	☐ 302 Vesa Viitakoski
☐ 303 Esa Tikkanen	☐ 304 Erik Hämäläinen
☐ 305 Norway	☐ 306 Norway
☐ 307 Norway	☐ 308 Norway
☐ 309 Norway	☐ 310 Norway
☐ 311 Jim Martinsen	☐ 312 Erik Kristiansen
☐ 313 Petter Sahlsten	☐ 314 Eric Lindros
☐ 315 Greg Johnson	☐ 316 Allain Roy
☐ 317 Hank Lammens	☐ 318 Leo Gudas
☐ 319 Petr Briza	☐ 320 Petr Rosol
☐ 321 Otakar Janecky	☐ 322 Mike Richter
☐ 323 Brett Hull	☐ 324 Chris Chelios
☐ 325 Pat LaFontaine	☐ 326 Klaus Dalpiaz
☐ 327 Stéphane Barin	☐ 328 Gerd Truntschka

1994 QUÉBEC INTERNATIONAL PEE WEE

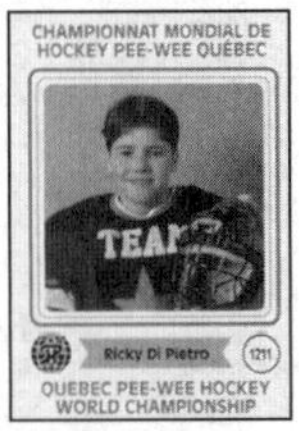

Complete Set (1,853 cards): 325.00

NORTH SHORE PEE WEE

The most expensive single is Vincent Lecavalier at $35-45.

☐ 1 Shawn Scanzano	☐ 2 Éric Groulx
☐ 3 David Gauvin	☐ 4 Brian Kerr
☐ 5 Mathieu Lendick	☐ 6 Daniel Vena
☐ 7 Jean-François Pilon	☐ 8 Alan Stevenson
☐ 9 Dominic Lalli	☐ 10 Wesley Scanzano
☐ 11 Vincent Lecavalier	☐ 12 Philippe Parent
☐ 13 Éric Lavigne	☐ 14 Chris Lyness
☐ 15 Philippe Lagrange	☐ 16 J. Angers-Frappier
☐ 17 Alexandre Beaudet	☐ 18 Instructeurs

MAURICIE PEE WEE

☐ 19 F. Benoît-Dupuis	☐ 20 P-L Courchesne
☐ 21 Mathieu Dubois	☐ 22 Marc-André Dubois
☐ 23 A. Normandin	☐ 24 Dave Moreau
☐ 25 Philippe Roussel	☐ 26 Yan St-Louis
☐ 27 Mathieu Prud'homme	☐ 28 Jonathan Blais
☐ 29 Luc Carrier	☐ 30 Martin Beauchesne
☐ 31 F-J Lavergne	☐ 32 Jean-François Lemay
☐ 33 Jérôme Fréchette	☐ 34 Philippe Turcotte

PHILADELPHIA PEE WEE LITTLE FLYERS

☐ 36 John Zimmerman	☐ 38 Scott Selig
☐ 39 Robert Christini	☐ 40 Kevin Emore
☐ 41 Tyler Kolarik	☐ 42 Christopher Yorty
☐ 43 Robert Weller	☐ 44 Mark Vizzacco
☐ 46 Anthony Voce	☐ 47 Joseph Testa
☐ 49 Thomas Arthur	☐ 50 Matthew Fishbone
☐ 51 Daniel Fox	☐ 51 Justin Pastglione
☐ 51 Ryan Shaw	☐ 52 Instructeurs

GRENOBLE PEE WEE

☐ 53 Nicolas Favarin	☐ 54 Mathieu Bellet
☐ 55 Luc Peretti	☐ 56 Nicolas Golleret
☐ 57 Yonick Treille	☐ 58 Philippe Guers
☐ 59 Arnaud Goetz	☐ 60 Julien Staeger
☐ 61 Marc-André Billeras	☐ 62 Nicolas Antonoff
☐ 63 Roman Laurens	☐ 64 Cyprien Coutens
☐ 65 Jonathan Lussier	☐ 66 Rémy Martinet
☐ 67 Sylvain Giet	☐ 68 Antoine Goudot
☐ 69 Lilian Martinez	☐ 70 Jonathan Martin
☐ 71 Instructeurs	

CALGARY PEE WEE FLAMES

☐ 72 Scott Wenz	☐ 73 Richard Sinclair
☐ 74 Adam Skulsky	☐ 75 Cody Brown
☐ 76 Ross Wichenheiser	☐ 77 Blake Pawsey
☐ 78 Aaron Monti	☐ 79 Kurtis Lamb
☐ 80 Robin Marquardt	☐ 81 Michael Fowlie
☐ 82 Travis Churchman	☐ 83 Michael Greeves
☐ 84 Kevin Ainsworth	☐ 85 Kyle Schonknecht
☐ 86 Derek Rupprecht	☐ 87 Rick Fraud
☐ 88 Instructeurs	

MONCTON PEE WEE

☐ 89 Robbie Fraser	☐ 90 Matthew Wilkins
☐ 91 P-L Bastarache	☐ 92 Jon Sheen
☐ 93 Denis Richard	☐ 94 Scott Prime
☐ 95 Kevin Lutzac	☐ 96 Troy MacMillan
☐ 97 Geoff Baird	☐ 98 J-F Auffrey
☐ 99 François Bourque	☐ 100 Adam Mills
☐ 101 Dominique Lacasse	☐ 102 André Leblanc
☐ 103 Justin Gautreau	☐ 104 Marc Léger

LOTBINIÈRE PEE WEE

☐ 106 Éric Lamontagne	☐ 107 Danny Dallaire
☐ 108 Sébastien Fournier	☐ 109 Frédérick Lemieux
☐ 110 Daniel Bergeron (G)	☐ 111 Vincent Noël

☐ 112 Marc Desrochers ☐ 113 Rick Martin
☐ 114 Karl Paquet ☐ 115 Frédérick Guérard
☐ 116 Éric Boivert ☐ 117 Rémi Champagne
☐ 118 Jacques Garon ☐ 119 Jimmy Boivin
☐ 120 Félix Garneau ☐ 121 Jérôme Cayer
☐ 122 Charles Gingras ☐ 123 Instructeurs

DRUMMONDVILLE PEE WEE

☐ 124 Nicolas Bahl ☐ 125 Marc Dumoulin
☐ 126 Simon Delisle ☐ 127 Sébastien Comeau
☐ 128 Joel Dugas ☐ 129 Jonathan Lussier
☐ 130 Dave Laflamme ☐ 131 Mathieu Simard
☐ 132 Yan Verhoef ☐ 133 J. Dauphinais
☐ 134 Bryan Fontaine ☐ 135 Francis-José Lapierre
☐ 136 Martin Pagé ☐ 137 Dominic Desmarais
☐ 138 Philippe Paris ☐ 139 Martin Paré
☐ 140 Instructeurs

RIMOUSKI PEE WEE

☐ 141 Dave Lévesque ☐ 142 Éric Morissette
☐ 143 Julien Desrosiers ☐ 144 Mathieu Dufour
☐ 145 J-O Gauvin ☐ 146 Mathieu Pigeon
☐ 147 Jérôme Pelletier ☐ 148 Martin Leblond
☐ 149 Justin Dionne ☐ 150 Martin Tremblay
☐ 151 Steven Couturier ☐ 152 Christian Lavoie
☐ 153 Sébastien Rouleau ☐ 154 Alexandre Desbiens
☐ 155 David Dorsonnens ☐ 156 Maxim Brunet
☐ 156 Serge Hébert ☐ 157 Instructeurs

BOSTON PEE WEE BRAVES

☐ 158 Brian McHugh ☐ 159 Kyle Hintlian
☐ 160 Brian Manning ☐ 161 Sean Ober
☐ 162 Tim Horgan ☐ 163 Ryan Carr
☐ 164 Tony Johnson ☐ 165 Nicky Dimella
☐ 166 John Ronan ☐ 167 Daniel Roselando
☐ 169 Ryan Foley ☐ 170 Jeremy Wilson
☐ 171 Mark Mullen ☐ 172 Todd Bryson
☐ 173 Joel Verrecchia ☐ 174 Robbie Laquaglia
☐ 175 Instructeurs

ST-ROMUALD PEE WEE

☐ 176 Dominik Tanguay ☐ 177 Guillaume Dubé
☐ 178 Sylvain Renaud ☐ 179 Simon Talbot
☐ 180 Alexandre Jacques ☐ 181 Alain Bilodeau
☐ 182 Frédéric Tellier ☐ 183 Patrice Dubois
☐ 184 Frédéric Blais ☐ 185 Patrick Bastien
☐ 186 Stéphane Cliché ☐ 187 Sébastien Bouchard
☐ 188 Érick Auger ☐ 189 Daniel Fortin
☐ 190 Patrick* Gosselin ☐ 191 Vincent Roy
☐ 192 Luc Boivin ☐ 193 Frédéric Allard
☐ 194 Jonathan Lemay ☐ 195 Instructeurs

PITTSBURGH PEE WEE

☐ 196 Joel Bartlett ☐ 197 J. D'Allessandro
☐ 198 Robbie Fried ☐ 199 Rob Garber
☐ 200 David Glatz ☐ 201 Rob Hammel
☐ 202 Shawn Jonnet ☐ 203 Rob Mastylak
☐ 204 Todd Myers ☐ 205 Brett Naugle
☐ 206 Paul Ondo ☐ 207 Steve Padgelak
☐ 208 Geoff Rulong ☐ 209 George Strasbaugh
☐ 210 Ryan Vesely ☐ 211 D.J. Vogt
☐ 212 Mike Woods ☐ 213 Instructeurs

CHICAGO PEE WEE BLACKHAWKS

☐ 214 Nicky Aulich ☐ 215 Stephen Baby
☐ 216 Gregg Cooper ☐ 217 Paul Glynn
☐ 218 R. Scott Jackson ☐ 219 Aaron Kim
☐ 220 Rich Kohler ☐ 221 Joe Locallo
☐ 222 Mike Lubesnick ☐ 223 Daniel Lynch
☐ 224 Jason Mals ☐ 225 Denis Nam
☐ 226 Michael Pihos ☐ 227 Justin Pitrack
☐ 228 Tim Woods ☐ 229 Adam Wallace
☐ 230 Jon Lother

FLORIDA PEE WEE PANTHERS

☐ 232 Manu Man'u ☐ 233 Adam York
☐ 234 Todd Grant ☐ 235 Matt Cline
☐ 236 Quinn Connelly ☐ 237 Stephen Novador
☐ 238 A. Riazantsev ☐ 239 Michael Pinkowski
☐ 240 Charlie Pulley ☐ 241 Jeremy Laster
☐ 242 Marc Deitsch ☐ 243 Jason Deitsch
☐ 244 John Zaka ☐ 245 A.J. Rivers
☐ 246 John Michael Liles ☐ 247 Michael Morton
☐ 248 Jason Huntley ☐ 249 Instructeurs

POINTE-LÉVY PEE WEE

☐ 250 Mathieu Roy ☐ 251 JF Turgeon
☐ 252 Dominic Laurin ☐ 253 Bryan Patry
☐ 254 Frédéric Parent ☐ 255 Dany Dumont
☐ 256 Jean-Philippe Morin ☐ 257 Mario Vallières
☐ 258 Nicolas Carrier ☐ 259 Nicolas Vaillancourt
☐ 260 J-F Lemieux ☐ 261 Jérôme Levasseur
☐ 262 Charles-André Maheux ☐ 263 Michel Léveillé
☐ 264 Olivier Grenier ☐ 265 Justin Grenier
☐ 266 Instructeurs

ROCK FOREST PEE WEE

☐ 267 J-F Bélisle ☐ 268 Pierre-Luc Noël
☐ 269 Éric Laurendeau ☐ 270 Jonathan Parr

☐ 271 Ghyslain Proulx ☐ 272 M-É Lemay
☐ 273 Benjamin Tremblay ☐ 274 Simon Rodrigue
☐ 275 Martin Cloutier ☐ 276 Paul-André Côté
☐ 277 Nicolas Fournier ☐ 278 Sébastien Couture
☐ 279 Christian Salvail ☐ 280 J_F Perron
☐ 281 Simon Robidas ☐ 282 Patrick Guay
☐ 283 J-F Quirion ☐ 284 Instructeurs

CHICOUTIMI PEE WEE

☐ 285 Jacques Tremblay ☐ 286 J.P. DeLaunière
☐ 287 M-A Savard ☐ 288 Éric Harvey
☐ 289 Frédéric Boily ☐ 290 C-D Dufour
☐ 291 Philippe Lavoie ☐ 292 Alain Provencher
☐ 293 David Corneau ☐ 294 Dave Verville
☐ 295 Martin Lavoie ☐ 296 Martin Brisson
☐ 297 Francis Gagnon ☐ 298 Marc-André Allard
☐ 298 Bruno Villeneuve ☐ 299 Instructeurs

BEAUCE-NORD PEE WEE

☐ 300 Marc Labrecque ☐ 301 Pascal Doyon
☐ 302 Hugo Lehoux ☐ 303 François Giroux
☐ 304 J-F Labrecque ☐ 305 François Larose
☐ 306 Frédéric Allen ☐ 307 Jérôme Joubert
☐ 308 Guillaume Ferland ☐ 309 Patrick* Vachon
☐ 310 Steve Allen ☐ 311 J-F Talbot
☐ 312 Martin Odesse ☐ 313 Jean-François Dion
☐ 314 Patrick Ferland ☐ 315 Jérôme Nadeau
☐ 316 Instructeurs

MONTMAGNY PEE WEE

☐ 317 J-F Poitras ☐ 318 Ghislain Poitras
☐ 319 Jérôme* Morin ☐ 320 Simon Heppell
☐ 321 Dominic Jacques ☐ 322 J-P Bélanger
☐ 323 Maxim Cloutier ☐ 324 Antoine Lemay
☐ 325 Dominic Bernier ☐ 326 Hubert Gagné
☐ 327 G. Charbonneau ☐ 328 J-P Gaudreau
☐ 329 J-F Couillard ☐ 330 Jérôme Gagnon
☐ 331 Steve Bernier ☐ 332 Frédéric Caron
☐ 332 Éric Langlois ☐ 332 Éric Masson
☐ 333 Instructeurs

SHERBROOKE PEE WEE

The most expensive single is Éric Chouinard at $2-4.

☐ 334 G. Théberge ☐ 335 M. Riendeau
☐ 336 Ben Price ☐ 337 Maxime Pothier
☐ 338 Charles Moreault ☐ 339 Christian Lavoie
☐ 340 Dave Laurendeau ☐ 341 Frédéric Gosselin
☐ 342 Alexandre Gosselin ☐ 343 Simon Francoeur
☐ 344 Stéphane Dubreuil ☐ 345 Éric Chouinard
☐ 346 David Chapdelaine ☐ 347 A. Champagne
☐ 348 Miguel Boisvert ☐ 349 Simon Bélanger
☐ 350 Instructeurs

HERSHEY PEE WEE

☐ 351 Aaron Davis ☐ 352 Kevin Hollenbush
☐ 353 Matt Pauli ☐ 354 Jon Kuhn
☐ 355 Craig Stern ☐ 356 T. Willits-Kelley
☐ 357 Lee Taylor ☐ 358 David Thomas
☐ 359 B.J. Heckendorn ☐ 360 Ethan Holmes
☐ 361 Joel Buchenauer ☐ 362 Erich Schork
☐ 363 Ryan Ford ☐ 364 Mike Patton
☐ 365 Brendan McCartin ☐ 366 Tony Morrell
☐ 367 Ronald Llado ☐ 368 Nate Tulli
☐ 369 Instructeurs

ROUYN-NORANDA PEE WEE

☐ 370 Frédéric Laperle ☐ 371 Jocelyn Potvin
☐ 372 Pierre-Marc Lajoie ☐ 373 Stéphane Plante
☐ 374 Philippe Moreau ☐ 375 Jonathan Morin
☐ 376 P-M Coulombe ☐ 377 Mathieu Gagnon
☐ 378 C-Philippe Lajoie ☐ 379 Simon Rodrigue
☐ 380 Éric Cloutier ☐ 381 M. Charbonneau
☐ 382 Christian Côté ☐ 383 Christian Pilotte
☐ 384 Jonathan Boucher ☐ 384 Mathieu Mercier-B
☐ 384 D. Lavoie-Mercier ☐ 385 Instructeurs

AUSTRIA PEE WEE

☐ 382 David Schuller ☐ 386 Günter D'Ameros
☐ 387 Josef Wimmer ☐ 388 Richard Wildmann
☐ 389 Gerhard Göttfried ☐ 390 Christian Höller
☐ 391 Christian Müller ☐ 393 Helmut Fischer
☐ 394 Andres Seelhofer ☐ 395 Gerald Seifried
☐ 396 Alexander Mellitzer ☐ 397 Thomas Pock
☐ 398 Manuel Hagen ☐ 399 Markus Peintner
☐ 400 Robert Strauss ☐ 401 Michael Mayer
☐ 402 Hannes Ezenhofer ☐ 403 C. Anderhuber
☐ 404 Alexander Lichtblan ☐ 405 Sébastien Koncilia
☐ 406 Walter Fusse ☐ 407 Michael Pfleger
☐ 408 Bernhard Bock ☐ 408 Philippe Lakos
☐ 409 Instructeurs

LONGEUIL PEE WEE

The most expensive single is Ramzi Abid at $3-5.

☐ 410 J. Sanscartier ☐ 411 Jonathan Gagnon
☐ 412 Patrick Dupré ☐ 413 Martin Delaunière
☐ 414 Dominic David ☐ 415 François Bramucci
☐ 416 Mathieu Bourdeau ☐ 417 J-M Blanchette
☐ 418 Ramzi Abid ☐ 419 Mathieu Shank

☐ 420 Guillaume Larivière ☐ 421 Yan Laliberté
☐ 422 André Cadorette ☐ 423 Danny Vézina
☐ 424 Steve Vallée ☐ 425 Instructeurs

BELLECHASSE PEE WEE

☐ 426 Olivier Couture ☐ 427 R. Lamontagne
☐ 428 J-F Tanguay ☐ 429 Jean-Michel Leclerc
☐ 430 Olivier Audet ☐ 431 Jérôme Mercier
☐ 432 Olivier Dumais ☐ 433 Guillaume Couture
☐ 434 Guillaume Huot ☐ 435 Sébastien Pelletier
☐ 436 Sébastien Roy ☐ 437 Gabriel Turgeon
☐ 438 Philippe Raby ☐ 439 Patrice* Lachance
☐ 440 S. Lamontagne ☐ 441 Dave Bernard

VICTORIAVILLE PEE WEE

☐ 443 Frédérick Ling ☐ 444 Sébastien Larivée
☐ 445 Éric Fortier ☐ 446 Jean-Luc Parizeau
☐ 447 Christian Boucher ☐ 448 Frédéric Paris
☐ 449 Sébastien Faucher ☐ 450 Jimmy Bilodeau
☐ 451 Simon Mailhot ☐ 452 Dominic Robichaud
☐ 453 Serge Crochetière ☐ 454 P. André Pircard
☐ 455 Guillaume Morin ☐ 456 Steve Castonguay
☐ 457 Martin Hamel ☐ 458 Dominic Rouleau
☐ 459 Instructeurs

SAN JOSE PEE WEE SHARKS

☐ 460 Nyjer Moran ☐ 461 John Kennard
☐ 462 Scott Feeney ☐ 463 Jason (Nic) Guida
☐ 464 Bodey Dressler ☐ 465 Tye Neilson
☐ 466 Todd Lathrop ☐ 467 Owen Richey
☐ 468 Joshua Angevine ☐ 469 Michael Tornabene
☐ 470 David Fuhrer ☐ 471 Jason Flatt
☐ 472 Christian Beerman ☐ 473 Ryan Wiggins
☐ 474 Matthew Yourkin ☐ 475 Tommy (Jr.) Reed

BOSTON PEE WEE BRUINS

☐ 477 Matthew Quagliozzi ☐ 478 Jonathan McCourt
☐ 479 Scott Kushner ☐ 481 Michael Powers
☐ 482 Robert Irving ☐ 483 Michael* Sullivan
☐ 484 Gavin Grant ☐ 485 William McNamara
☐ 486 Matthew Beck ☐ 487 Sean Guilfoy
☐ 488 Gregory Kim ☐ 489 Matthew Blake
☐ 490 Corey Clark ☐ 491 Mark Haley
☐ 492 David Hines ☐ 493 Michael Freeman
☐ 494 Scott Rissimiller ☐ 495 Jeffrey Czarnowski
☐ 496 Instructeurs

SEIGNEURS MILLES-ILES PEE WEE

The most expensive single is Mathieu Chouinard at $2-4.

☐ 497 Mathieu Chouinard ☐ 498 Martin Meilleur
☐ 499 David Thibodeau ☐ 500 Alain Brassard
☐ 501 Marc Lajoie ☐ 502 Martin Gauthier
☐ 503 Sylvain Castilloux ☐ 504 Marc Bonneville
☐ 507 J-F Gauvin ☐ 507 Dominic Périard
☐ 508 Daniel Boileau ☐ 509 J-P Glaude
☐ 510 Jonathan Plouffe ☐ 510 Mathieu Plouffe
☐ 511 M-A Lalande ☐ 512 Philippe Sauvé
☐ 513 Instructeurs

MONTREAL PEE WEE NOROIS

☐ 514 Sébastien Drouin ☐ 515 Patrick Fournier
☐ 516 Marc-André Brunet ☐ 517 Mario Arcand
☐ 518 Seneque Hyacinthe ☐ 519 Philippe Alarie
☐ 520 Jason Jalbert ☐ 521 Mathieu Bertrand
☐ 522 Hong Ly ☐ 523 Patrick Aumont
☐ 524 M-A Pinheiro ☐ 525 Michel Brisebois
☐ 526 Quintal-Rodrigues ☐ 527 José Luis Urrutuia
☐ 528 M.A. Dixon ☐ 529 Éric Charest
☐ 530 Instructeurs

HARTFORD PEE WEE WHALERS

☐ 532 Shaun* Burke ☐ 533 Christo Baldwin
☐ 534 Jeffrey Griffin ☐ 535 Danny Cavanaugh
☐ 536 D.J. Janik ☐ 537 Dennis Guyer
☐ 538 Keith Kirley ☐ 539 Sean Keane
☐ 540 Billy Manwaring ☐ 541 Mike Liebro
☐ 542 William Rothfuss ☐ 543 Jeff McMinn
☐ 544 Raymond Veilleux ☐ 545 Dominic Torretti
☐ 546 J.R. Zavusha ☐ 547 Matthew Wooten
☐ 548 Instructeurs

EXPRESS RIVE-SUD PEE WEE

☐ 549 Michael Pion ☐ 550 François Tremblay
☐ 551 Patrick Bergeron ☐ 552 Francis Godbout
☐ 553 Vincent Blanchette ☐ 554 Steve Bienvenue
☐ 555 Jean-Luc Lévesque ☐ 556 Benoît Richard
☐ 557 Guillaume Gauthier ☐ 558 A. Lamoureux
☐ 559 Dave** Williams ☐ 560 Yannick Langlois
☐ 561 J-F Cartier ☐ 562 Simon Laliberté
☐ 563 P-L Beauchemin ☐ 564 Instructeurs

SAULT STE. MARIE PEE WEE

The most expensive singles are Rico Fata at $2-4 and Seamus Kotyk at $2-3.

☐ 565 Seamus Kotyk ☐ 566 Ben Brown
☐ 567 Chad Finn ☐ 568 Mike Lattimer
☐ 569 Darren McMillan ☐ 570 Robbie Palahnuk
☐ 571 Jeff Cochrane ☐ 572 Mark Chambers
☐ 573 Rico Fata ☐ 574 Paul Best

☐ 575 Travis Jourdin ☐ 576 Preston Mizzi
☐ 577 Christo Ladubec ☐ 578 Joey Mancuso
☐ 579 Ryan Leonard ☐ 580 Instructeurs

LANAUDIÈRE PEE WEE

☐ 581 David Thibodeau ☐ 582 A. Caumartin-S.
☐ 583 Claude Majeu ☐ 584 Simon Laverdière
☐ 585 Martin Larose ☐ 586 L-P Laporte
☐ 587 Billy-Joe Houle-B. ☐ 588 Joël Guertin
☐ 589 David Grégoire ☐ 590 Daniel Gervais
☐ 591 Sébastien Favreau ☐ 592 Benoît Crépeault
☐ 593 T. Brind'Amour ☐ 594 M. Champagne
☐ 595 Jean-Samuël Bacon ☐ 596 Louis-Pier Asselin
☐ 597 Instructeurs

JONQUIÈRE PEE WEE ORIOLES

☐ 598 Marc-Olivier Tellier ☐ 599 J-F Rousseau
☐ 600 Yannick Couillard ☐ 601 Hugo Dessureault
☐ 602 Patrick Barriault ☐ 603 Éric Vigneault
☐ 604 Éric Bélanger ☐ 606 Pascal Rousseau
☐ 607 Jonathan Tremblay ☐ 607 Simon Tremblay
☐ 608 Vincent Harvey ☐ 609 Mathieu Lavoie
☐ 610 J-F Potvin ☐ 611 David** Tremblay
☐ 612 Patrick Chouinard ☐ 613 Nicolas Paradis

MONTREAL PEE WEE CANADIENS

The most expensive singles are Jonathan Girard at $2-3 and Martin Grenier at $2-3.

☐ 615 P-H Piché ☐ 616 Andrew McKay
☐ 617 Jonathan Girard ☐ 618 Sylvain Léroux
☐ 619 Luc Vachon ☐ 620 Jean-Michel Soulard
☐ 621 Éric Joly ☐ 622 David* Thibault
☐ 623 J-F Labelle ☐ 624 Cameron Lowe
☐ 625 Francis Lalande ☐ 626 Éric Piché
☐ 627 Marc-André Leclerc ☐ 628 Martin Grenier
☐ 629 Marc Desjardins ☐ 630 Simon Desjardins
☐ 630 Équipe ☐ 631 Instructeurs

SYRACUSE PEE WEE

The most expensive single is Tim Connolly at $10-15.

☐ 632 A.J. McCutcheon ☐ 633 John Corr
☐ 634 Josh Downs ☐ 635 Dan Addy
☐ 636 Dan Bunnell ☐ 637 Gary Baronick
☐ 638 Daniel Baquer ☐ 639 Drew Bucktooth
☐ 640 Justin Brown ☐ 641 Stephen Pakan
☐ 642 Anthony Pace ☐ 643 Bill Houze
☐ 644 Jeremy Downs ☐ 645 Justin Forrest
☐ 646 Doug MacCormack ☐ 647 Michael Saracent
☐ 648 Patrick Lannon ☐ 649 Tim Connolly
☐ 650 Todd Jackson ☐ 651 Instructeurs

TORONTO PEE WEE MAPLE LEAFS

The most expensive single is Michael Henrich at $2-3.

☐ 652 Brandon Cook ☐ 653 Nikolas Balkos
☐ 654 Chris Dennis ☐ 655 Joey Bartley
☐ 656 Michael Henrich ☐ 657 Joseph Dolby
☐ 658 Chris Kelly ☐ 659 David Inman
☐ 660 Jeff Milroy ☐ 661 Kenneth Mair
☐ 662 Kevin Robinson ☐ 663 Jamie Novak
☐ 664 Ryan Ward ☐ 665 Michael Shanab
☐ 666 Ryan Wilson ☐ 667 Michael Tedesco
☐ 668 Instructeurs

NEW YORK PEE WEE RANGERS

☐ 669 Keith Seltzer ☐ 670 James Sedoruk
☐ 671 Erik Nates ☐ 672 Geoffrey Moss
☐ 673 Daniel Morrell ☐ 674 Kevin Mitchell
☐ 675 Garrett Martinez ☐ 676 Tazio Lombardo
☐ 677 Jordy Karp ☐ 678 Chad Holzer
☐ 679 Joe Fontanetta ☐ 680 Tom Egan
☐ 681 Joey Dudek ☐ 682 Garrett Dionne
☐ 683 Charles Carson ☐ 684 Robert Brescia
☐ 685 Jason Breen ☐ 686 Instructeurs

PHILADELPHIA PEE WEE FLYERS

☐ 687 Jason Swavely ☐ 688 Michael Billingsley
☐ 689 Gregory Marinari ☐ 690 Ryan Lochhead
☐ 691 David* Taylor ☐ 692 John Longo
☐ 693 Nathaniel Smith ☐ 694 Ryan Cohen
☐ 695 Brett Bergman ☐ 696 Chris Fulton
☐ 697 Matthew Ciancio ☐ 698 Sean Dillon
☐ 699 Matthew Herneisen ☐ 700 Matt Silverio
☐ 701 Philip Ditoro ☐ 702 Marc Abels
☐ 703 Philip A. Hagopian ☐ 704 Bryan Aronchik
☐ 705 Jared Roberts ☐ 706 Matt Gallagher
☐ 707 Instructeurs

ÉTOILES PEE WEE DU ST-LAURENT

☐ 708 François St-André ☐ 709 Sébastien Lussier
☐ 710 Luc Lavoie ☐ 711 P-O Éloquin
☐ 712 Guy La Roche ☐ 713 Karl Chassé
☐ 714 Martin Lazure ☐ 715 Louis Mongrain
☐ 716 Sébastien Richard ☐ 717 Martin Deragon
☐ 718 M-A Gaudreau ☐ 719 Jean-Michel Fortin
☐ 720 Jonathan Laramée ☐ 721 Jean-Luc Turcot
☐ 722 Francis Montpetit ☐ 723 Instructeurs

JONQUIÈRE PEE WEE MARQUIS

☐ 724 Maxime Dallaire ☐ 725 Marc Dallaire
☐ 727 François Dubé ☐ 728 Danick Jomphe
☐ 729 Frédéric Gagnon ☐ 730 J-F Murray
☐ 731 Claude La Haye ☐ 732 Bernie** Parent

☐ 733 Yan Pageau ☐ 734 Sébastien Potvin
☐ 735 Michael Pomerleau ☐ 736 Dominic Dufour
☐ 736 Nicolas St-Pierre ☐ 737 Frédéric St-Pierre
☐ 738 R. Vaillancourt ☐ 739 Maxime Tremblay
☐ 740 Instructeurs

BUFFALO PEE WEE SABRES

☐ 741 Mark Branden ☐ 742 Marc Fattey
☐ 743 Paul Dombrowski ☐ 744 James Lorentz
☐ 745 John Lenz ☐ 746 Joseph Matis
☐ 747 Paul Marranca ☐ 748 Michael** Newman
☐ 749 Matthew McGirr ☐ 750 Joseph Saitino
☐ 751 Justin Niefer ☐ 752 Sean Stickler
☐ 753 Willie Sundown ☐ 754 Andrew Tinti
☐ 755 Thomas Pawlak ☐ 756 Michael Nellany
☐ 757 Jeffrey Wilczewski

REPENTIGNY PEE WEE

☐ 759 Yan* Martel ☐ 760 Jonathan Cournoyer
☐ 761 Mario Courbin ☐ 762 Sébastien Rouillard
☐ 763 Patrick Forget ☐ 764 P-O Loiselle
☐ 765 Jonathan Lauzon ☐ 766 Sébastien Hamel
☐ 767 Frédéric Arbour ☐ 768 Hugo Mudie
☐ 769 François Mayer ☐ 770 Mathieu Loiselle
☐ 771 Stéphan Doiron ☐ 772 Jean-Philippe Ashby
☐ 773 Mathieu Dionne ☐ 774 Philippe Marsolais
☐ 774 Simon Piette ☐ 775 Instructeurs

STE-FOY PEE WEE ROYAUX

☐ 776 Dave Beaupré ☐ 777 J-A Borne
☐ 778 R. Bissonnette ☐ 779 Mathieu Boure
☐ 780 François Bouliane ☐ 781 Yanick Fiset
☐ 782 Danny Delisle ☐ 783 Michel Larouche
☐ 784 Cédrick Larochelle ☐ 785 Gino Ricci
☐ 786 Jocelyn Lépine ☐ 787 Hugo Trépanier
☐ 788 André Thomassin ☐ 789 Nicolas Vimard
☐ 790 David Vachon ☐ 791 Instructeurs

OTTAWA PEE WEE SENATORS

The most expensive single is Justin Papineau at $2-4.

☐ 792 Blake Cushing ☐ 793 Alistair Donaghy
☐ 794 D. Edward Labelle ☐ 795 Ryan Hartman
☐ 796 Bill Hughes ☐ 797 Jeff Jones
☐ 798 Erik** Lind ☐ 799 Michael McKenna
☐ 800 Nicholas Michaud ☐ 801 John Mitchell
☐ 802 Allan Muldoon ☐ 803 Fernando Multari
☐ 804 Stefan Nichols ☐ 805 Steve Orchard
☐ 806 Justin Papineau ☐ 807 Ryan Parent
☐ 808 Donald Rowat ☐ 809 Instructeurs

RIVIÈRE-DU-LOUP PEE WEE

☐ 810 Pierre Dufour ☐ 811 François Chénard
☐ 812 Jérôme Paquet ☐ 813 Simon Malenfant
☐ 814 Frédéric Busseau ☐ 815 Martin St-Pierre
☐ 816 Simon Desjardins ☐ 817 P.-Étienne Cadrin
☐ 818 David Ouellet ☐ 819 Pierre Lévesque
☐ 820 Grégoire Pelletier ☐ 821 Alexandre Belzile
☐ 822 Hugo Lévesque ☐ 823 Pierre-Marc Roy
☐ 824 Sébastien Lavoie ☐ 825 Instructeurs

VANCOUVER PEE WEE CANUCKS

The most expensive single is David Morisset at $2-3.

☐ 826 Daryl Sampson ☐ 827 Tim Preston
☐ 828 Craig Reid ☐ 829 David* Morisset
☐ 830 Randy Ponte ☐ 831 C. Lorenzetto
☐ 832 Peter Mihalech ☐ 833 Wesley Jorundson
☐ 834 Cameron Jow ☐ 835 Steven Harrington
☐ 836 Brent Jackson ☐ 837 Jesse Ferguson
☐ 838 Derek Franco ☐ 839 Perry Billings
☐ 840 Bradley Blatz ☐ 841 Bryce Ayers
☐ 842 Richard Batten ☐ 843 Instructeurs

LAC-MÉGANTIC PEE WEE

☐ 844 J-F Hallée ☐ 845 David Lachance
☐ 846 Simon Laprade ☐ 847 Marc-André Roy
☐ 848 Vincent Gobeil ☐ 849 Rémy Gosselin
☐ 850 Marc-André Lacroix ☐ 851 Francis* Paré
☐ 852 Simon Bolduc ☐ 853 J-P Nadeau
☐ 854 Martin Fortier ☐ 855 Philippe Proteau
☐ 856 Francis Bédard ☐ 857 René Paré
☐ 858 Michel Demers ☐ 859 Tim McLean
☐ 860 Instructeurs

CHARNY PEE WEE

☐ 862 Jonathan Samson ☐ 861 J-F Cantin
☐ 864 Francis Lemay ☐ 863 Pierre-Luc* Turgeon
☐ 866 Olivier Hamel ☐ 865 Vincent Hinse
☐ 868 Mathieu Gosselin ☐ 867 Vincent Desrochers
☐ 870 David Boilard ☐ 869 David Cloutier
☐ 872 Jonathan Fortin ☐ 871 François Paradis
☐ 874 Sébastien Gingras ☐ 873 Jérôme Allard
☐ 876 Jonathan Côté ☐ 875 Vincent Auclair
☐ 876 Tommy Roy ☐ 876 Martin Lambert
☐ 877 Instructeurs

DETROIT PEE WEE RED WINGS

The most expensive single is David Legwand at $5-8.

☐ 878 Matt York ☐ 879 Frank Werner
☐ 880 Ryan Vanbuskirk ☐ 881 Joe Tome

☐ 882 Scott Titus ☐ 883 Johnny Shouneyia
☐ 884 Todd Reibling ☐ 885 Jason Porter
☐ 886 Mark Mink ☐ 887 Michael Mantua
☐ 888 David Legwand ☐ 889 Eric Kelemen
☐ 890 Jonathan Insana ☐ 891 Kevin Holdridge
☐ 892 David Bowen ☐ 893 Patrick Brush
☐ 894 Instructeurs

BEAUCE-AMIANTE PEE WEE

☐ 895 Francis Lachance ☐ 897 Éric Turmel
☐ 898 Pascal Paradis ☐ 899 Philippe Deblois
☐ 900 J. Blanchette ☐ 901 Simon Bilodeau
☐ 902 Lucien Lessard ☐ 903 Martin Roy
☐ 904 Christian Labbé ☐ 905 Nicolas Caouette
☐ 906 J_F Lehoux ☐ 907 Carol Lecours
☐ 908 S. Veilleux ☐ 909 Philippe Cliché
☐ 910 Julien Dostie ☐ 911 Instructeurs

PHOENIX PEE WEE

☐ 912 Daniel Hemken ☐ 913 Casey Gast
☐ 914 Jeffrey** Daniels ☐ 915 Roman Gelfand
☐ 916 Mathew Morgan ☐ 917 Jeremy Smith
☐ 918 Nick Fouts ☐ 919 Jay Campbell
☐ 920 Jeffrey Domingos ☐ 921 Jacob Schnaible
☐ 922 Ian Itsell ☐ 923 Justin Hogge
☐ 924 Patrick Racine ☐ 925 Matthew Greven
☐ 926 J.W. MacArthur ☐ 927 Michael Larter
☐ 928 Devin Fairchild ☐ 929 Michael Salafia
☐ 930 Julien Trudeau ☐ 931 Walker McBain

SLOVÉNIE PEE WEE

☐ 933 Ales Kranjc ☐ 934 Marcel Rodman
☐ 935 Grega Solar ☐ 936 Ziga Pavlic
☐ 937 Miha Zbontar ☐ 938 Uros Gantar
☐ 939 Rudi Hiti ☐ 940 Jure Penko
☐ 941 Grega Polonicic ☐ 942 Edo Terglav
☐ 943 Ziga Petac ☐ 944 Gregor Matjasic
☐ 945 Saso Zura ☐ 946 Blaz Emersic
☐ 947 Uros Vidmar ☐ 948 Bostjan Kolaric
☐ 949 Ales Petrovcic ☐ 950 Anze Terlikar
☐ 951 Borut Biteznik ☐ 952 Tomo Hafner
☐ 953 Yuri Golicic ☐ 954 Ales Burnik
☐ 955 Dennis Kropec ☐ 956 Instructeurs

BEAUCE-CENTRE PEE WEE

☐ 957 Keven Cloutier ☐ 958 Jean-Marc Poulin
☐ 959 Patrice* Voyer ☐ 960 Philippe Boulet
☐ 961 Pierre-Luc Paré ☐ 962 Jean Vallières
☐ 963 J-P Lessard ☐ 964 André Giguère
☐ 965 Mathieu Lachance ☐ 966 J. Champagne
☐ 967 Jérôme Roy ☐ 968 Philippe Grenier
☐ 969 Jean-Martin Roy ☐ 970 Cédric Maheux
☐ 971 M. Longchamps ☐ 972 Benoît Lessard
☐ 973 Sébastien Paquet ☐ 973 Cédric Perron
☐ 973 Jean-François Roy ☐ 974 Instructeurs

ST-GEORGES BEAUCE PEE WEE

☐ 975 Samuel Beaulé ☐ 976 Yannick Parent
☐ 977 Alex Gilbert ☐ 978 François Beaudoin
☐ 979 Nicolas Poirier ☐ 980 Dave Lagrange
☐ 981 J-F Lavoie ☐ 982 Frédéric Deblois
☐ 983 M-A Dion ☐ 984 Israël Laplante
☐ 985 Pierre Boulanger ☐ 986 Pascal Maheux
☐ 987 M-A Genest ☐ 988 Mathieu Pouliot
☐ 989 Alexandre Mottand ☐ 990 Bernard Lalomalec
☐ 991 Guillaume Deblois ☐ 992 Maxime Maheux
☐ 993 Instructeurs

BEAUPORT PEE WEE HARFANGS

☐ 994 Simon Laberge ☐ 995 P-L Gamache
☐ 996 Simon Beaulieu ☐ 997 Louis Grenier
☐ 998 Pascal Morin ☐ 999 Jocelyn Larouche
☐ 1000 L-M Langevin ☐ 1001 Maxime Guimond
☐ 1002 Martin Leclerc ☐ 1003 Brian Pichette
☐ 1004 Sylvain* Sénéchal ☐ 1005 Frédérick Tremblay
☐ 1006 J-P Picard ☐ 1008 Philippe Gauthier
☐ 1008 Luc Tremblay ☐ 1009 Simon Pichette
☐ 1010 Jonathan Michel ☐ 1011 Instructeurs

TORONTO PEE WEE RED WINGS

The most expensive single is Norm Milley at $2-3.

☐ 1012 George Trifon ☐ 1013 Darryl Baker
☐ 1014 Jason Trinetti ☐ 1015 Nickolas Harper
☐ 1016 A. Wamsteeker ☐ 1017 Randy Davidson
☐ 1018 Stacey Britstone ☐ 1019 Joe Goodenow
☐ 1020 Ryan Crane ☐ 1021 N. Marjanovic
☐ 1022 David Cornacchia ☐ 1023 Brian Passmore
☐ 1024 Adam Lay ☐ 1025 Norm Milley
☐ 1026 T.J. Coletti ☐ 1027 Dean Jackson
☐ 1028 Corey Batten ☐ 1028 Instructeurs

ZURICH PEE WEE

☐ 1029 Björn Christen ☐ 1030 Marco Nef
☐ 1031 Adrian Wischer ☐ 1032 Detlev Müller
☐ 1033 Marc Eichmann ☐ 1034 Patrick Meichtry
☐ 1035 Rico Beltrame ☐ 1036 Sven Gasser
☐ 1037 Martin Höhener ☐ 1038 André Bielmann
☐ 1039 Reto Taborgna ☐ 1040 Simon Wanner

☐ 1041 P. Tiegermann ☐ 1042 Thomas Widmer
☐ 1043 Andreas Nauser ☐ 1044 Remo Brunner
☐ 1045 Serge Maurer

SUISSE ROMANDE PEE WEE

☐ 1047 Christophe Busset ☐ 1048 Guillaume Zanoli
☐ 1049 Goran Bezina ☐ 1050 Lionel D'Urso
☐ 1051 J. Forgeoux ☐ 1052 Vincent Kunzi
☐ 1053 Gregory Pedat ☐ 1054 Alain Rey
☐ 1055 J-C Wysling ☐ 1056 Julien Boddi
☐ 1057 Loic Burkhalter ☐ 1058 Jan Cadieux
☐ 1059 Adrien Chauvy ☐ 1060 Flavien Conne
☐ 1061 Patrick Giove ☐ 1062 Yannick Imesch
☐ 1063 Thierry Métrailler ☐ 1064 Norman Perrin
☐ 1065 Réal Raemy ☐ 1066 Sébastien Reuille
☐ 1067 Loic Rogenmoser ☐ 1068 V. Schuepbach
☐ 1069 Instructeurs

STE-FOY PEE WEE

The most expensive single is Simon Gagné at $15-20.

☐ 1070 Luc Brisson ☐ 1071 Martin Roy
☐ 1072 Jean-René Plante ☐ 1073 P-A Paquet
☐ 1074 Mathieu Jouder ☐ 1075 Jérôme Lessard
☐ 1076 Patrick Gaudreau ☐ 1077 Simon Gagné
☐ 1078 Maxime Éthier ☐ 1079 Dominic Carignan
☐ 1080 Paul Blanchard ☐ 1081 Jonathan Beaulieu
☐ 1082 Vincent Lemelin ☐ 1083 Chantale Maheux
☐ 1084 Guillaume Drewitt ☐ 1085 Instructeurs

RICHMOND HILL PEE WEE

☐ 1086 Joey Sbergio ☐ 1087 Ryan Nolan
☐ 1088 Michael Rende ☐ 1089 Domenic Manzone
☐ 1090 Brian Merkley ☐ 1091 Bradley Hewit
☐ 1092 Christophe Idrovo ☐ 1093 Marco Di Cocco
☐ 1094 Russell Drewitt ☐ 1095 Bryan Carrigan
☐ 1096 Nickolis De Luca ☐ 1097 Doug Boyd
☐ 1098 Brock Burford ☐ 1099 Michael Andreoli
☐ 1100 Daniel Avery ☐ 1101 Instructeurs

HALIFAX PEE WEE

☐ 1102 Patrick Taiani ☐ 1103 Brian Sutherland
☐ 1104 Robbie Sutherland ☐ 1105 Mike Quackenbush
☐ 1106 Ryan Savary ☐ 1107 Steve Pamenter
☐ 1108 Anthony Purchase ☐ 1109 Scott Macintosh
☐ 1110 Tommy Maclean ☐ 1111 Andrew Lowery
☐ 1112 P.J. Lynch ☐ 1113 Scott Howard
☐ 1114 Ryan Lauzon ☐ 1115 Mike Fougère
☐ 1116 Adam Fredericks ☐ 1117 Greg Crawford
☐ 1118 Andrew Carnell ☐ 1119 Instructeurs

CHARLESBOURG CITADINS PEE WEE

☐ 1120 Maxime Blouin ☐ 1121 Guillaume Morin
☐ 1122 Yves Pelletier ☐ 1123 Patrick Dubé
☐ 1124 Christian Plante ☐ 1125 Éric Morin
☐ 1126 Yves Lecompte ☐ 1127 Pierre-Luc Lafond
☐ 1128 Michel Côté ☐ 1129 Frédéric Bélanger
☐ 1130 David Thoral ☐ 1131 J-F Gravel
☐ 1132 Steve Morency ☐ 1133 Yannick Gosselin
☐ 1134 Simon Bussières ☐ 1136 Martin Plante
☐ 1137 Vincent Métivier ☐ 1138 Karl Juneau
☐ 1139 Mathieu Lelièvre ☐ 1140 Instructeurs

BEAUBOURG PEE WEE

The most expensive single is Maxime Ouellet at $4-6.

☐ 1141 A. Vigneault ☐ 1142 Jonathan Verreault
☐ 1143 M. Thomassin ☐ 1144 Vincent Roy
☐ 1145 Cédric Pouliot ☐ 1146 Yannick Poirier
☐ 1147 Dominic Paradis ☐ 1148 Maxime* Ouellet
☐ 1149 Christian Laforest ☐ 1150 David Lachance
☐ 1151 Simon Gauthier ☐ 1152 J. Francoeur
☐ 1153 P-O Dufour ☐ 1154 Yan Chouinard
☐ 1155 Tommy Bolduc ☐ 1156 Jérôme Bergeron
☐ 1157 Instructeurs

SURREY PEE WEE THUNDER

The most expensive single is Jordan Krestanovich at $2-3.

☐ 1158 Greg Scurr ☐ 1159 Paul Fraser
☐ 1160 Kevin Caruso ☐ 1161 Geoff Oleschuk
☐ 1162 Jimmy Druska ☐ 1163 Paul Elliott
☐ 1164 Daniel Meneghin ☐ 1165 Chad Sharp
☐ 1166 Robert Arcino ☐ 1167 Scott Chartier
☐ 1168 Richard Kellington ☐ 1169 J. Krestanovich
☐ 1170 Scott** Bailey ☐ 1171 Colin Hemingway
☐ 1172 Éric Allard ☐ 1173 Kevin Hogg
☐ 1174 Ryan Foreman ☐ 1175 Instructeurs

LOS ANGELES PEE WEE KINGS

☐ 1176 Wayne Russell ☐ 1177 Brian Tudrick
☐ 1178 Mike O'Donnell ☐ 1179 Stephen Novobar
☐ 1180 Willie Lévesque ☐ 1181 Mike Mounsey
☐ 1182 Brian Eklund ☐ 1183 Ray Kirby
☐ 1184 Alex Cochrane ☐ 1185 Ryan Cordeiro
☐ 1186 Bill Cass ☐ 1187 Ray Cattaneo
☐ 1188 Eddie Boudreau ☐ 1189 Ricky Casavant
☐ 1190 Scott Bradley ☐ 1190 Scott Brien
☐ 1190 Craig Wadman ☐ 1191 Instructeurs

BEVERLY PEE WEE

The most expensive single is Rick DiPietro at $10-15.

☐ 1192 Brian Sjostrom ☐ 1193 Craig Robinson
☐ 1194 Shaun Sutter ☐ 1195 Ryan Tipping
☐ 1196 Bobby Pate ☐ 1197 Joe Seeley
☐ 1198 Matt Needel ☐ 1199 John Nigro
☐ 1200 Scott McGrane ☐ 1201 Ben Murphy
☐ 1202 Fred Meyer ☐ 1203 Tom Milward
☐ 1204 Tye Korbl ☐ 1205 Greg Lecolst
☐ 1206 Peter Hams ☐ 1207 Eddie Hill
☐ 1208 Mark Camarata ☐ 1209 Craig Falite
☐ 1210 Greg Harrison ☐ 1211 Rick DiPietro (G)
☐ 1212 Kyle Kilimonis

ST-EPHREM BEAUCE PEE WEE

☐ 1214 Frédéric** Cloutier ☐ 1215 Vincent Plante
☐ 1216 Jason Bernard ☐ 1217 Kevin Bilodeau
☐ 1218 Marco Veilleux ☐ 1219 Étienne Roy
☐ 1220 Carl Beaudoin ☐ 1221 Jean-Pierre Marois
☐ 1222 Guillaume Paré ☐ 1223 Stéphane Rodrigue
☐ 1224 Sylvain Roy ☐ 1225 Vincent Turcotte
☐ 1226 Yannick Labonté ☐ 1227 Sylvain Labbé
☐ 1228 Rémi Roy ☐ 1229 David Hamel
☐ 1230 Alexandre Roy ☐ 1231 J-F Poulin

CAP ROUGE CAMPUS PEE WEE

☐ 1233 Alexis Léger ☐ 1234 Jeff Aubry
☐ 1235 Dany Blais ☐ 1236 David Lord
☐ 1237 François Tremblay ☐ 1238 Charles Tassidu
☐ 1239 Hugo Blouin ☐ 1240 J-P Létourneau
☐ 1241 P-L Laliberté ☐ 1242 Philippe Veilleux
☐ 1243 V. Roof-Racine ☐ 1244 Simon Veillette
☐ 1245 Julien St-Pierre ☐ 1246 Étienne Audet
☐ 1247 Patrice Bégin ☐ 1248 Yannick Lévesque
☐ 1249 Antoine Dufour ☐ 1250 Étienne Grondin
☐ 1251 Yannick** Martel ☐ 1252 Instructeurs

SOUTH SHORE KINGS PEE WEE

☐ 1253 Michael Sayre ☐ 1254 Walter Siggins
☐ 1255 Michael Roberson ☐ 1256 Michael Ryan
☐ 1257 Michael Matik ☐ 1258 Chris McCloud
☐ 1259 Stephen Greeley ☐ 1260 Brad Kent
☐ 1261 Christopher Haidul ☐ 1262 M. Hunter Greeley
☐ 1263 Justin Dziame ☐ 1264 Nicolas Fish
☐ 1265 Saul Chase ☐ 1266 Anthony D'Arpino
☐ 1267 Jack Baker ☐ 1268 Michael Bovaro
☐ 1269 Michael Ayers ☐ 1269 Trevor Byrne
☐ 1269 Brian Collins ☐ 1269 Luke Smith
☐ 1269 Jimmy Walsh ☐ 1270 Instructeurs

STE-FOY GOUVERNEURS PEE WEE

☐ 1271 Alexandre Lebel ☐ 1272 Bruno Gagné
☐ 1273 Marc Fortier ☐ 1274 David Fournier
☐ 1275 J-P Marcotte ☐ 1276 François Béland
☐ 1277 Dominic Jolin ☐ 1278 David Grenier
☐ 1279 Daniel Clermont ☐ 1280 J-F Plante
☐ 1281 Dave* Gagnon ☐ 1282 Marc Brisson
☐ 1283 Steve Jobidon ☐ 1284 Jocelyn Nadeau
☐ 1285 Patrick Marois ☐ 1293 François Bouchard

LORETTEVILLE PEE WEE

☐ 1287 Mathieu Sioui ☐ 1288 Bernard Martel
☐ 1289 Stéphane Vallée ☐ 1290 David Vachon
☐ 1291 Nicolas Roy ☐ 1292 Yvon* Racine
☐ 1294 Kevin Bouchard ☐ 1295 Jean-François Roy
☐ 1296 Thiery Girard ☐ 1297 Hugo Patry
☐ 1298 Martin Fournier ☐ 1299 Marc Piché
☐ 1300 Nicolas Therrien ☐ 1301 J-P Therrien
☐ 1302 Simon Drolet

CHARLESBOURG ÉPAULARDS PEE WEE

☐ 1304 Martin Raîche ☐ 1305 Antoine Joubert
☐ 1306 Frédéric Dreyer ☐ 1307 Steve Racicot
☐ 1308 Mathieu Laplante ☐ 1309 Kim Cloutier
☐ 1310 Mathieu Charest ☐ 1311 David Caron
☐ 1312 René Beauchesne ☐ 1313 David Alain
☐ 1314 Étienne Ouellet ☐ 1315 Richard Talbot
☐ 1316 Sébastien Rouleau ☐ 1317 Patrick Fortin
☐ 1318 Simon Bertrand ☐ 1319 Tony Paquet
☐ 1320 Jonathan Harbour ☐ 1321 Martin Dionne
☐ 1322 Vincent Boucher ☐ 1323 Instructeurs

TARDIVEL EST PEE WEE

☐ 1324 G. Chevalier ☐ 1325 Hugo Delisle
☐ 1326 Jean Vaillancourt ☐ 1327 Jonathan Côté
☐ 1328 Jimmy Gilbert ☐ 1329 G. Lefebvre
☐ 1330 David Savard ☐ 1331 François Leclerc
☐ 1332 Jérôme Leclerc ☐ 1333 Bobby Paquet
☐ 1334 D. Dionne-Laroche ☐ 1335 Simon Marcotte
☐ 1336 S. Ouarhani ☐ 1337 Mathieu Bussières
☐ 1338 Élie Dufour ☐ 1339 Philippe Allard
☐ 1340 Instructeurs

CAMPUS ST-AUGUSTIN PEE WEE

☐ 1341 Tommy Bussières ☐ 1342 Mathieu Blouin
☐ 1343 Dominic Bourque ☐ 1344 Christian Drolet
☐ 1345 Hugo Girard ☐ 1346 Simon Gallichand

☐ 1347 Dominic Précourt ☐ 1348 Pierre-Luc Boivin
☐ 1349 J-F Labbé ☐ 1350 F. Blanchette
☐ 1351 Patrice Boudreault ☐ 1352 Alexandre Nicolle
☐ 1353 Dominic Lévesque ☐ 1354 Steve Munro
☐ 1355 David Jacques ☐ 1356 Cédric Fortin
☐ 1356 Instructeurs

SUISSE CENTRALE PEE WEE

☐ 1358 Stefan Jenni ☐ 1359 C. Decurtins
☐ 1360 Philippe Félix ☐ 1361 Reto Kobach
☐ 1362 C. Rezdeusek ☐ 1363 Silvano Worni
☐ 1364 Matthias Wust ☐ 1365 Marc Bachmann
☐ 1366 Claudio Bitzi ☐ 1367 Gregory Bosshard
☐ 1368 Stefan Burch ☐ 1369 Joel Camenzind
☐ 1370 Stefan Niggli ☐ 1371 Stefan Probst
☐ 1372 Luc Vizek ☐ 1373 Mario Zumbühl
☐ 1374 Reto Müller ☐ 1375 Instructeurs

BOSTON PEE WEE TERRIERS

☐ 1376 Mike Ziolkowski ☐ 1378 Chris Vail
☐ 1379 Steven Tobio ☐ 1380 Andrew Segal
☐ 1381 Mike Notartomaso ☐ 1382 Matt McCarthy
☐ 1383 Chris Macleod ☐ 1384 Chris Kern
☐ 1385 Tim Kollcher ☐ 1386 Mel Fiore
☐ 1387 John Cronin ☐ 1388 Nick Cammarata
☐ 1389 Kyle Bunstein ☐ 1390 Jamie Atkinson
☐ 1391 Mark Angeloni ☐ 1392 Instructeurs

CENTRE-MAURICE PEE WEE

☐ 1393 Y. Boissonneault ☐ 1394 J-H Flageolle
☐ 1395 Benoît Bélanger ☐ 1396 Maxime Turcotte
☐ 1397 S. Robitaille ☐ 1398 David Bournival
☐ 1399 Francis Mongrain ☐ 1400 Simon Dessureault
☐ 1401 Bruno Bélanger ☐ 1402 David Paquin
☐ 1403 J-F Gélinas ☐ 1404 Tommy Tessier
☐ 1405 Benoît Boutet ☐ 1406 Daniel St-Amant
☐ 1407 François Pichette ☐ 1408 Frédéric Gignac
☐ 1408 Yannick Lachance ☐ 1409 Instructeurs

LONDON PEE WEE REBELS

The most expensive single is Jason Williams at $4-6.

☐ 1410 Michael Gryp ☐ 1411 Brian Kilcan
☐ 1412 Josh Robinson ☐ 1413 David Bureigh
☐ 1414 Ryan Wilcox ☐ 1415 Brent L'Heureux
☐ 1416 Matt Meyer ☐ 1417 Jason** Allison
☐ 1418 Jason Williams ☐ 1419 Jason Hnatyk
☐ 1420 Mike Jennings ☐ 1421 Matt Dodgson
☐ 1422 Chris Legg ☐ 1423 Todd Hunt
☐ 1424 Sean Ogrady ☐ 1425 Jeff Kaufman
☐ 1426 Bryce Holliday

DETROIT PEE WEE LITTLE CAESARS

☐ 1428 Trevor Wolfe ☐ 1429 J.J. Swistak
☐ 1430 Ian Smith ☐ 1431 Neck Shrader
☐ 1432 Richard Scheele ☐ 1433 Craig Piscopink
☐ 1434 Charly Pak ☐ 1435 Brad Matthews
☐ 1436 Tony Maci ☐ 1437 Nick Luxon
☐ 1438 Chris Lieckfield ☐ 1439 Scott Hamilton
☐ 1440 Beau Fritz ☐ 1441 Chad Ellis
☐ 1442 Sean Connolly ☐ 1443 Chad Bennetts
☐ 1444 Dan Bachmann ☐ 1445 Instructeurs

NEW YORK PEE WEE ISLANDERS

☐ 1446 Chris Purslow ☐ 1447 Brian Karbot
☐ 1448 Ryan Tonelli ☐ 1449 Travers Breen
☐ 1450 Peter Dirkes ☐ 1451 John-Paul Barnych
☐ 1452 Evan Munno ☐ 1453 Steven D'Auria
☐ 1454 Ryan Radonis ☐ 1455 Chris Ferazzali
☐ 1456 Richard Hansen ☐ 1457 Mike Zeibaq
☐ 1458 Justin Cynar ☐ 1459 Chris D'Auria
☐ 1460 David Sell ☐ 1461 Brett Henning
☐ 1462 Chris Pedota ☐ 1463 Evan Mankoff
☐ 1464 Chris Hartsburgh

NEW JERSEY PEE WEE DEVILS

☐ 1466 Matthew Blaszka ☐ 1467 Michael Cacace
☐ 1468 John Dibble ☐ 1469 Jason Daunno
☐ 1470 Benoît Halewicz ☐ 1471 J. Ryan Grabowski
☐ 1472 Anthony Inverno ☐ 1473 Gordon Inverno
☐ 1474 Andor Kish ☐ 1475 Stephen Jeffers
☐ 1476 Jourdan Ozga ☐ 1477 Leonard Luciano
☐ 1478 Victor Sceneche ☐ 1479 Daniel Percella
☐ 1480 J. Skowronski ☐ 1481 Scott Seedorf
☐ 1482 Instructeurs

ANAHEIM PEE WEE

☐ 1483 Mark Adamek ☐ 1484 Chris Davis
☐ 1485 Mike Adamek ☐ 1486 Jacques Goulet
☐ 1487 Nathan Espiritu ☐ 1488 Aaron Holliday
☐ 1489 Tony Gutilla ☐ 1490 Tony Mutalipassi
☐ 1491 Scott Irby ☐ 1492 Brett Peterson
☐ 1493 Blake Pickett ☐ 1494 Eric Rosenberg
☐ 1495 Quentin Pickett ☐ 1496 Chris White
☐ 1497 Dustin MacIsaac ☐ 1497 Pat Sweeney
☐ 1497 Cassie Talbot ☐ 1498 Instructeurs

ST. LOUIS PEE WEE BLUES

☐ 1499 Dan Schuerman ☐ 1500 Thomas Poe
☐ 1501 Adam Parker ☐ 1502 Jeff Highill

☐ 1503 Tony Marbury ☐ 1504 Travis Revelle
☐ 1505 Mike Dlugos ☐ 1506 Trevor Wood
☐ 1507 Michael Cox ☐ 1508 Matt Crosby
☐ 1509 Ryan Wachter ☐ 1510 Ben Lamperti
☐ 1511 Nathan Mayfield ☐ 1512 Chris Peterson
☐ 1513 Éric Ortlip ☐ 1514 Dan Hauck
☐ 1515 Connor Dunlop ☐ 1516 Instructeurs

FRASER PEE WEE

☐ 1517 Ronald Terry ☐ 1518 Daniel Sluka
☐ 1519 Ryan Sanders ☐ 1520 Ryan Reed
☐ 1521 Troy Milam ☐ 1522 A. Hutchinson
☐ 1523 Matthew Gossett ☐ 1524 Joseph Giambra
☐ 1525 Brandon Burd ☐ 1526 Charles Braun
☐ 1527 Francis Beaudoin ☐ 1528 James Aato
☐ 1529 Steven Rondeau ☐ 1530 Colin Morawski
☐ 1530 Barry Pochmara ☐ 1531 Instructeurs

WINNIPEG PEE WEE

☐ 1532 Kevin Barkman ☐ 1533 Luc Bergeron
☐ 1534 Kevin Brewer ☐ 1535 Jason Brothers
☐ 1536 Daniel Charette ☐ 1537 Danny Filion
☐ 1538 Dominic Fournier ☐ 1539 Sean Griffin
☐ 1540 Dominic Lacroix ☐ 1541 Francis Lallier
☐ 1542 Ryan Martin ☐ 1543 Ryan McAllister
☐ 1544 Jamie Mitchell ☐ 1545 Ryan Simpson
☐ 1546 Adam Switzer ☐ 1547 Ryan Warsh

ILLINOIS PEE WEE

☐ 1548 Neil Watanabe ☐ 1550 A. Mantagano
☐ 1551 Mike Thivel ☐ 1552 Jimmy Caruso
☐ 1553 Joe Kautz ☐ 1554 Joe Pagone
☐ 1555 Matt Doman ☐ 1556 Paul Kroll
☐ 1557 Ryan Reid ☐ 1558 Craig Anderson
☐ 1559 Pat Patel ☐ 1560 Brad Rebic
☐ 1561 Matt Spanton ☐ 1562 Ryan Feil
☐ 1563 Philip Slovitt ☐ 1564 Tony Demola
☐ 1565 Matt Rzepecki ☐ 1566 Instructeurs

DALLAS PEE WEE

☐ 1567 Scott Dibella ☐ 1568 Brian Dimarzo
☐ 1569 Steve Bottini ☐ 1570 Michael Bateman
☐ 1571 Kevin Dudley ☐ 1572 Jim Devine
☐ 1573 David Grenier ☐ 1574 Bill Gilchrist
☐ 1575 Kim Insalaco ☐ 1576 Jason Heberger
☐ 1577 Joe McArdle ☐ 1578 Jim Mazzullo
☐ 1579 Kevin Mooney ☐ 1580 Jason McMullen
☐ 1581 Sam Paolini ☐ 1582 Danny Murray
☐ 1583 Adam Prescott ☐ 1584 Jeremy Paris
☐ 1585 Ryan Soper ☐ 1586 Chris Satiora
☐ 1587 Instructeurs

MISSISSAUGA REPS PEE WEE

The most expensive single is Manny Malhotra at $4-7.

☐ 1588 Alfredo Moniz ☐ 1589 Wole James
☐ 1590 Mike Hipditch ☐ 1591 Joey D'Urzo
☐ 1592 Jason Southwell ☐ 1593 Mike Miculinic
☐ 1594 Fraser Vernon ☐ 1595 Vince Zumpano
☐ 1596 Lawrence Longo ☐ 1597 R.J. Sones
☐ 1598 Mike Pincoe ☐ 1599 Jeff Hladysh
☐ 1600 Manny Malhotra ☐ 1601 Simon Mangos
☐ 1602 Allan Rourke ☐ 1603 Brandon Verner

DON MILLS PEE WEE

☐ 1605 Jesse Watt ☐ 1606 Jim Stamatopoulos
☐ 1607 Dominic Moore ☐ 1608 M. Dzieduszycki
☐ 1609 Bryan Friechman ☐ 1610 Jeff Scruton
☐ 1611 Louis Foulidis ☐ 1612 Jamie Ritskos
☐ 1613 Jason Pinizzotto ☐ 1614 Danny Yungblut
☐ 1615 Elliott Morris ☐ 1616 John McKenna
☐ 1617 Christian Joakim

EDMONTON PEE WEE OILERS

☐ 1619 Cameron Agnew ☐ 1620 Bobby Almeida
☐ 1621 Michael Alexander ☐ 1622 David Boychuk
☐ 1623 Mark Behiels ☐ 1624 Chad Forsberg
☐ 1625 Shawn Charney ☐ 1626 Brad Hutchinson
☐ 1627 D. Holowaychwk ☐ 1628 Keith Ketza
☐ 1629 Stephen Johnson ☐ 1630 Shaun Myskiw
☐ 1631 Kris Liber ☐ 1632 Chris Standing
☐ 1633 Jason Sand ☐ 1634 Ryan Van De Ligt
☐ 1635 James Turner ☐ 1636 Instructeurs

WASHINGTON PEE WEE

☐ 1637 Tim Judy ☐ 1638 Brad Watts
☐ 1639 Paul Cohen ☐ 1640 Iem Vithaya
☐ 1641 Dave Stockdale ☐ 1642 Danny Collins
☐ 1643 Dave Hubbard ☐ 1644 Matt Mondorff
☐ 1645 Tony Sweeney ☐ 1646 Jon Hurst
☐ 1647 Connor Hills ☐ 1648 Tyler Scott
☐ 1649 Craig Eiring ☐ 1650 Jeff Earley
☐ 1651 Kevin Early ☐ 1652 Kevin* Lyons
☐ 1653 Jason Costa ☐ 1654 Instructeurs

VICTORIA PEE WEE

The most expensive single is Matt Pettinger at $2-3.

☐ 1655 Matt Pettinger ☐ 1656 Sean O'Connor
☐ 1657 Curtis Smith ☐ 1658 Nathan Forster
☐ 1659 Sean Wilson ☐ 1660 David Neale

☐ 1661 K.C. Timmons ☐ 1662 Mark Campbell
☐ 1663 Blake Munro ☐ 1664 Joey Matheson
☐ 1665 Graham Cool ☐ 1666 Trevor McCall
☐ 1667 Jesse Phillips ☐ 1668 Bryce McFadden
☐ 1669 Aaron Sproule ☐ 1670 Instructeurs

QUÉBEC PEE WEE NORDIQUES

☐ 1671 Jonathan Pelletier ☐ 1672 Vincent Picard
☐ 1673 Frédéric' Cloutier ☐ 1674 Sylvain Watt
☐ 1675 Donald Blouin ☐ 1676 Éric Dumont
☐ 1677 Alex Paul ☐ 1678 Bruno Cliché
☐ 1679 Simon Roy ☐ 1680 Jonathan Petit
☐ 1681 Justin Lemay ☐ 1682 Denis Vaillancourt
☐ 1683 Jérôme Marois ☐ 1684 Olivier Marier
☐ 1685 Sylvain Nadeau ☐ 1687 Instructeurs

HOCHELAGA PEE WEE

The most expensive single is Mike Ribeiro at $3-5.

☐ 1688 Jean Themens ☐ 1689 Joey Rullier
☐ 1690 Carl Durand ☐ 1691 Éric Servant
☐ 1692 Christian Gagnon ☐ 1693 Martin Lefebvre
☐ 1694 Frédéric Chiasson ☐ 1695 Michael Lanthier
☐ 1696 Sébastien Crête ☐ 1697 Maxime Campeau
☐ 1698 Steve Dupont ☐ 1699 Daniel Dumont
☐ 1700 Éric Naud ☐ 1701 Mike Ribeiro
☐ 1702 Jason Harvey ☐ 1703 M. (Jr.) Giantorno
☐ 1704 Instructeurs

TORONTO PEE WEE YOUNG NATS

The most expensive singles are Sheldon Keefe at $3-4 and Mike (Jefferson) Danton at $2-3.

☐ 1705 Daniel McLarty ☐ 1706 Lance Galbraith
☐ 1707 Richard Williams ☐ 1708 Trevor Large
☐ 1709 Matthew House ☐ 1710 Mike Danton
☐ 1711 Shawn Cation ☐ 1712 Adam Lowe
☐ 1713 Stephen Samson ☐ 1714 Christopher Harry
☐ 1715 Stace Page ☐ 1716 Brad Keeling
☐ 1717 Sheldon Keefe ☐ 1718 Ryan Bell
☐ 1719 D Dufour ☐ 1719 Ian Forbes
☐ 1720 Instructeurs

RIVE-SUDE PEE WEE

☐ 1721 Patrice' Labrecque ☐ 1722 Jérôme Dumont
☐ 1723 Steven St-Onge ☐ 1724 Jonathan Roy
☐ 1725 Yannick Picard ☐ 1726 J-P Guay
☐ 1727 J-F Turgeon ☐ 1728 Grégoire Leblanc
☐ 1729 Guillaume Caron ☐ 1730 Mathieu Bergeron
☐ 1731 G. Chamberland ☐ 1732 L. De Beaumont
☐ 1733 Martin Gionet ☐ 1734 François Fortin
☐ 1735 Mathieu Saindon ☐ 1736 Martin Poirier

CHARLESBOURG ÉLANS PEE WEE

The most expensive single is Mathieu Biron at $2-4.

☐ 1738 Hugo Welsh ☐ 1739 J-F Sylvain
☐ 1740 Éric Rhéaume ☐ 1741 J-P Paradis
☐ 1742 Kévin Lapointe ☐ 1743 Mathieu Langevin
☐ 1744 François Gravel ☐ 1745 Maxime Gagnon
☐ 1746 J-P Côté ☐ 1748 David Cantin
☐ 1749 J-S Boutet ☐ 1750 Martin Boucher
☐ 1751 Martin Bouchard ☐ 1752 Mathieu Biron
☐ 1753 Simon Bertrand

OLOMOUC PEE WEE

The most expensive single is Jaroslav Svoboda at $3-5.

☐ 1755 Lukas Fiala ☐ 1756 Michal Cech
☐ 1757 Miloslav Kolacek ☐ 1758 Jan Kasparu
☐ 1759 Jaroslav Svoboda ☐ 1760 Ivan Svitak
☐ 1761 Jakub Wurzel ☐ 1762 Jaromir Vesely
☐ 1763 Zbynek Hubler ☐ 1764 Daniel Visalek
☐ 1765 Radim Houdulik ☐ 1766 David Hamernik
☐ 1767 David Dostalik ☐ 1768 Marek Kubin
☐ 1769 Karel Rarousky ☐ 1770 Pavel Jasensky
☐ 1771 Petr Serafin ☐ 1772 Ondrej Syrinek
☐ 1773 Libor Wavrzacz ☐ 1774 David Vychodil
☐ 1774 David Vychodil ☐ 1775 Libor Wawarzacz
☐ 1776 Instructeurs

KIEV PEE WEE

☐ 1777 Andrei Krakhmal ☐ 1778 Alexandre Khmil
☐ 1779 Viktor Konkov ☐ 1780 Andrei Dolnik
☐ 1781 E. Pissarenko ☐ 1782 Vitalii Lioutkevitche
☐ 1783 Timour Ekpaev ☐ 1784 Vitalei Zhidkikh
☐ 1785 Maxime Oleinik ☐ 1786 Denis Motchouin
☐ 1787 Eugenei Lahanov ☐ 1788 A. Boutotchnov
☐ 1789 Andrei Kitcha ☐ 1790 Kirill Rechetnikov
☐ 1791 Evgueni Sidorov ☐ 1792 Vitalli Gritsan
☐ 1793 A. Ponikorovskii ☐ 1794 Instructeurs

MEXICO PEE WEE

☐ 1796 Lior Miller ☐ 1797 Pedro Pardo
☐ 1798 J.P. Calvert ☐ 1799 Darian Aguilera
☐ 1800 J.P. Arramburu ☐ 1801 Manolo Sierra
☐ 1802 Axel Molet ☐ 1803 Carlos Orvananos
☐ 1804 M. Couchonnal ☐ 1805 Gabriel Kleiman
☐ 1806 J. Diez-Canedo ☐ 1807 A Belausteguigoitia
☐ 1808 David Goldsweig ☐ 1809 Victor Ibarra
☐ 1810 Antonio Scheffler ☐ 1811 Javier Velasquez
☐ 1812 Jim Stugles ☐ 1813 Raul Orozco
☐ 1814 Sergio Peralta ☐ 1815 Patricio Jordain

SUISSE ITALIENNE PEE WEE

☐ 1817 Mark Tschudy ☐ 1818 Jessica Naretto
☐ 1819 Andrea Pellandini ☐ 1820 Mirko Grimani
☐ 1821 Lorenzo Barenco ☐ 1822 Ludovic Stefanick
☐ 1823 Gabriele Cozzi ☐ 1824 Alvaro Peverelli
☐ 1825 Leopoldo Rossini ☐ 1826 A. Barbaro
☐ 1827 Massimo Jamusci ☐ 1828 Roberto Dazio
☐ 1829 Mirko Lunini ☐ 1830 Paolo Duca
☐ 1831 Luca Gilardini ☐ 1832 Luca Bonfanti
☐ 1833 Gabrio Baldi ☐ 1834 Luca Cereda
☐ 1835 Andres Vassena ☐ 1836 A. Untersee
☐ 1837 Instructeurs

TAMPA BAY PEE WEE

☐ 1220 Instructeurs ☐ 1838 Jacob Sifers
☐ 1839 Rich Wunder ☐ 1840 Todd Marr
☐ 1841 D.J. Pelletier ☐ 1842 Hunter MacDonnel
☐ 1843 Adam Major ☐ 1844 Jamie Falk
☐ 1845 Tiffany Hayes ☐ 1846 Jeffrey Dwyer
☐ 1847 Grayson Ferhg ☐ 1848 Brad D'Arce
☐ 1848 Brad D'Arce ☐ 1849 John Dawson
☐ 1850 Jamie Bruno ☐ 1851 Peter Broccoli
☐ 1852 Bill Clifford ☐ 1853 Sotheby Chung

1994 PINNACLE – TORONTO EXPO AT THE PINNACLE

Player
☐ Dave Andreychuk, Toro.

1994 SEMIC

Complete Set (360 cards):	**50.00**
Common Player:	**.20**
Album:	**6.00**

Player	NRMT-MT
☐ 1 Jarmo Myllys (G), Fin.	.20
☐ 2 Pasi Kuivalainen (G), Fin.	.20
☐ 3 Jukka Tammi (G), Fin.	.20
☐ 4 Markus Ketterer (G), Fin.	.20
☐ 5 Timo Jutila, Fin.	.20
☐ 6 Mikko Jaapakoski, Fin.	.20
☐ 7 Marko Tuulola, Fin.	.20
☐ 8 Jyrki Lumme, Fin.	.20
☐ 9 Kari Harila, Fin.	.20
☐ 10 Teppo Numminen, Fin.	.20
☐ 11 Pasi Sormunen, Fin.	.20
☐ 12 Petteri Nummelin, Fin.	.20
☐ 13 Harri Laurila, Fin.	.20
☐ 14 Mika Strömberg, Fin.	.20
☐ 15 Ville Siren, Fin.	.20
☐ 16 Pekka Laksola, Fin.	.20
☐ 17 Janne Laukkanen, Fin.	.20
☐ 18 Marko Kiprusoff, Fin.	.20
☐ 19 Waltteri Immonen, Fin.	.20
☐ 20 Teemu Selänne, Fin.	.50
☐ 21 Mika Alatalo, Fin.	.20
☐ 22 Vesa Viitakoski, Fin.	.20
☐ 23 Tero Arkiomaa, Fin.	.20
☐ 24 Jari Kurri, Fin.	1.00
☐ 25 Pekka Tirkkonen, Fin.	.20
☐ 26 Jarmo Kekäläinen, Fin.	.20
☐ 27 Saku Koivu, Fin.	.50
☐ 28 Antti Törmänen, Fin.	.20
☐ 29 Mikko Mäkelä, Fin.	.20
☐ 30 Jere Lehtinen, Fin.	.20
☐ 31 Raimo Helminen, Fin.	.20
☐ 32 Marko Jantunen, Fin.	.20
☐ 33 Ville Peltonen, Fin.	.20
☐ 34 Esa Tikkanen, Fin.	.20
☐ 35 Janne Ojanen, Fin.	.20
☐ 36 Mika Nieminen, Fin.	.20
☐ 37 Marko Palo, Fin.	.20
☐ 38 Rauli Raitanen, Fin.	.20
☐ 39 Sami Kapanen, Fin.	.20
☐ 40 Juha Riihijärvi, Fin.	.20
☐ 41 Esa Keskinen, Fin.	.20
☐ 42 Jari Korpisalo, Fin.	.20
☐ 43 Christian Ruutu, Fin.	.20
☐ 44 Jarkko Varvio, Fin.	.20
☐ 45 Sami Wahlsten, Fin.	.20
☐ 46 Petri Varis, Fin.	.20
☐ 47 Timo Saarikoski, Fin.	.20
☐ 48 Timo Norppa, Fin.	.20
☐ 49 Marko Virtanen, Fin.	.20
☐ 50 Pauli Järvinen, Fin.	.20
☐ 51 Håkan Algotsson (G), Swe.	.20
☐ 52 Tommy Söderström (G), Swe.	.20
☐ 53 Rolf Ridderwall, Swe.	.20
☐ 54 Tomas Jonsson, Swe.	.20
☐ 55 Christer Due-Boje, Swe.	.20
☐ 56 Peter Popovic, Swe.	.20
☐ 57 Fredrik Stillman, Swe.	.20
☐ 58 Magnus Svensson, Swe.	.20
☐ 59 Fredrik Nilsson, Swe.	.20
☐ 60 Tommy Albelin, Swe.	.20
☐ 61 Joacim Esbjörs, Swe.	.20
☐ 62 Roger Johansson, Swe.	.20
☐ 63 Stefan Nilsson, Swe.	.20
☐ 64 Håkan Loob, Swe.	.20
☐ 65 Peter Ottosson, Swe.	.20
☐ 66 Daniel Rydmark, Swe.	.20
☐ 67 Mikael Renberg, Swe.	.20
☐ 68 Patrik Juhlin, Swe.	.20
☐ 69 Thomas Rundqvist, Swe.	.20
☐ 70 Andreas Johansson, Swe.	.20
☐ 71 Stefan Örnskog, Swe.	.20
☐ 72 Niklas Eriksson, Swe.	.20
☐ 73 Jonas Bergqvist, Swe.	.20
☐ 74 Mats Sundin, Swe.	1.00
☐ 75 Peter Forsberg, Swe.	1.00
☐ 76 Stefan Elvenes, Swe.	.20
☐ 77 Tomas Forslund, Swe.	.20
☐ 78 Patric Kjellberg, Swe.	.20
☐ 79 Bill Ranford (G), Cdn.	.20
☐ 80 Corey Hirsh (G), Cdn.	.20
☐ 81 Larry Murphy, Cdn.	.20
☐ 82 Mark Tinordi, Cdn.	.20
☐ 83 Scott Stevens, Cdn.	.20
☐ 84 Al MacInnis, Cdn.	.20
☐ 85 Steve Smith, Cdn.	.20
☐ 86 Paul Coffey, Cdn.	.50
☐ 87 Eric Desjardins, Cdn.	.20
☐ 88 Eric Lindros, Cdn.	1.00
☐ 89 Dale Hawerchuk, Cdn.	.50
☐ 90 Steve Larmer, Cdn.	.20
☐ 91 Brent Sutter, Cdn.	.20
☐ 92 Luc Robitaille, Cdn.	.50
☐ 93 Shayne Corson, Cdn.	.20
☐ 94 Mark Messier, Cdn.	1.00
☐ 95 Rick Tocchet, Cdn.	.20
☐ 96 Theoren Fleury, Cdn.	.50
☐ 97 Dirk Graham, Cdn.	.20
☐ 98 Russ Courtnall, Cdn.	.20
☐ 99 Wayne Gretzky, Cdn.	4.00
☐ 100 Brendan Shanahan, Cdn.	1.00
☐ 101 Mark Recchi, Cdn.	.20
☐ 102 David Harlock, Cdn.	.20
☐ 103 Craig Woodcroft, Cdn.	.20
☐ 104 Paul Kariya, Cdn.	1.00
☐ 105 Jason Marshall, Cdn.	.20
☐ 106 Brett Lindros, Cdn.	.20
☐ 107 Mike Richter (G), USA.	.20
☐ 108 Mike Dunham (G), USA.	.20
☐ 109 Craig Wolanin, USA.	.20
☐ 110 Jim Johnson, USA.	.20
☐ 111 Chris Chelios, USA.	.50
☐ 112 Eric Weinrich, USA.	.20
☐ 113 Brian Leetch, USA.	.50
☐ 114 Kevin Hatcher, USA.	.20
☐ 115 Ed Olczyk, USA.	.20
☐ 116 Kevin Miller, USA.	.20
☐ 117 Doug Brown, USA.	.20
☐ 118 Joe Mullen, USA.	.20
☐ 119 Craig Janney, USA.	.20
☐ 120 Pat LaFontaine, USA.	.50
☐ 121 Gary Suter, USA.	.20
☐ 122 Jeremy Roenick, USA.	.50
☐ 123 Brett Hull, USA.	1.00
☐ 124 Joel Otto, USA.	.20
☐ 125 Mike Modano, USA.	1.00
☐ 126 Tony Granato, USA.	.20
☐ 127 Dave Christian, USA.	.20
☐ 128 Brian Mullen, USA.	.20
☐ 129 Chris Ferraro, USA.	.20
☐ 130 John Lilley, USA.	.20
☐ 131 Jeff Lazaro, USA.	.20
☐ 132 Peter Ferraro, USA.	.20
☐ 133 Brian Rolston, USA.	.20
☐ 134 Dave Roberts, USA.	.20
☐ 135 Nikolai Khabibulin (G), Rus.	.50
☐ 136 Andrei Trefilov (G), Rus.	.20
☐ 137 Vladimir Malakhov, Rus.	.20
☐ 138 Alexander Karpovstev, Rus.	.20
☐ 139 Alexander Smirnov, Rus.	.20
☐ 140 Sergei Zubov, Rus.	.20
☐ 141 Sergei Seljanin, Rus.	.20
☐ 142 Sergei Shendelev, Rus.	.20
☐ 143 Alexei Kasatonov, Rus.	.20
☐ 144 Sergei Sorokin, Rus.	.20
☐ 145 Vyacheslav Bykov, Rus.	.20
☐ 146 Sergei Fedorov, Rus.	1.00
☐ 147 Alexei Yashin, Rus.	.50
☐ 148 Vjatseslav Butsajev, Rus.	.20
☐ 149 Konstantin Astrahantsev, Rus.	.20
☐ 150 Alexei Zhamnov, Rus.	.20
☐ 151 Dimitri Frolov, Rus.	.20
☐ 152 Vyacheslav Kozlov, Rus.	.20
☐ 153 Sergei Pushkov, Rus.	.20
☐ 154 Andrei Khomutov, Rus.	.20
☐ 155 Sergei Makarov, Rus.	.20
☐ 156 Igor Larionov, Rus.	.50
☐ 157 Valeri Kamensky, Rus.	.20
☐ 158 Alexander Semak, Rus.	.20
☐ 159 Alexei Gusarov, Rus.	.20
☐ 160 Andrei Lomakin, Rus.	.20
☐ 161 Igor Korolev, Rus.	.20
☐ 162 Ravil Khaidarov, Rus.	.20
☐ 163 Dominik Hasek (G), Cze.	1.00
☐ 164 Oldrich Svoboda (G), Cze.	.20
☐ 165 Peter Briza (G), Cze.	.50
☐ 166 Leov Gudas, Cze.	.20
☐ 167 Kamil Prachar, Cze.	.20
☐ 168 Richard Smehlik, Cze.	.20
☐ 169 Frantisek Kucera, Cze.	.20
☐ 170 Drahomir Kadlec, Cze.	.20
☐ 171 Jan Vopat, Cze.	.20
☐ 172 Frantisek Prohazka, Cze.	.20
☐ 173 Antonin Stavjana, Cze.	.20
☐ 174 Bedrich Scerban, Cze.	.20
☐ 175 Kamil Kastak, Cze.	.20
☐ 176 Josef Beranek, Cze.	.20
☐ 177 Martin Rucinsky, Cze.	.20
☐ 178 Michal Pivonka, Cze.	.20
☐ 179 Tomas Jelinek, Cze.	.20
☐ 180 Richard Zemlicka, Cze.	.20
☐ 181 Robert Kron, Cze.	.20
☐ 182 Jiri Slegr, Cze.	.20
☐ 183 Jaromir Jagr, Cze.	1.00
☐ 184 Robert Reichel, Cze.	.20
☐ 185 David Vyborny, Cze.	.20
☐ 186 Robert Lang, Cze.	.20
☐ 187 Petr Rosol, Cze.	.20
☐ 188 Otakar Janeckv, Cze.	.20
☐ 189 Martin Hostak, Cze.	.20
☐ 190 Jiri Kucera, Cze.	.20
☐ 191 Eduard Hartmannn (G), Slo.	.20
☐ 192 Lubomir Sekeras, Slo.	.20
☐ 193 Marian Smerciak, Slo.	.20
☐ 194 Jan Varholik, Slo.	.20
☐ 195 Lubomir Rybovic, Slo.	.20
☐ 196 Miroslav Marcinko, Slo.	.20
☐ 197 Stanislav Medrik, Slo.	.20
☐ 198 Zdeno Ciger, Slo.	.20
☐ 199 Jergus Baca, Slo.	.20
☐ 200 Peter Stastny, Slo.	.50
☐ 201 Peter Veselovsky, Slo.	.20
☐ 202 Anton Stastny, Slo.	.20
☐ 203 Lubomir Kolnik, Slo.	.20
☐ 204 Roman Kontsek, Slo.	.20
☐ 205 Rene Pucher, Slo.	.20
☐ 206 Slavomir Ilavsky, Slo.	.20
☐ 207 Zigmund Palffy, Slo.	.50
☐ 208 Vlastimil Plavucha, Slo.	.20
☐ 209 Dusan Pohorelec, Slo.	.20
☐ 210 Robert Petrovicky, Slo.	.20
☐ 211 Michel Valliere (G), Fra.	.20
☐ 212 Petri Ylönen (G), Fra.	.20
☐ 213 Jean-Philippe Lemoin, Fra.	.20
☐ 214 Christophe Moyon, Fra.	.20
☐ 215 Denis Perez, Fra.	.20
☐ 216 Bruno Saunier, Fra.	.20
☐ 217 Stéphane Botteri, Fra.	.20
☐ 218 Michel Breistroff, Fra.	.20
☐ 219 Gerald Guennelon, Fra.	.20
☐ 220 Serge Poudrier, Fra.	.20
☐ 221 Benjamin Agnel, Fra.	.20
☐ 222 Stéphane Arcangeloni, Fra.	.20
☐ 223 Pierrick Maia, Fra.	.20
☐ 224 Antoine Richer, Fra.	.20
☐ 225 Christophe Ville, Fra.	.20
☐ 226 Michael Babin, Fra.	.20
☐ 227 Lionel Orsolini, Fra.	.20
☐ 228 Stéphane Barin, Fra.	.20
☐ 229 Arnauld Briand, Fra.	.20
☐ 230 Franck Pajonkowski, Fra.	.20
☐ 231 Klaus Dalpiaz (G), Aut.	.20
☐ 232 Brian Stankiewicz, Aut.	.20
☐ 233 Robin Doyle, Aut.	.20
☐ 234 Michael Günter, Aut.	.20
☐ 235 Martin Krainz, Aut.	.20
☐ 236 Michael Shea, Aut.	.20
☐ 237 Martin Ulrich, Aut.	.20
☐ 238 Erich Solderer, Aut.	.20
☐ 239 Wayne Groulx, Aut.	.20
☐ 240 Andreas Puschnig, Aut.	.20
☐ 241 Dieter Kalt, Aut.	.20
☐ 242 Gerhard Puschnik, Aut.	.20
☐ 243 Werner Kerth, Aut.	.20
☐ 244 Richard Nasheim, Aut.	.20
☐ 245 Arno Maier, Aut.	.20
☐ 246 Mario Schaden, Aut.	.20
☐ 247 Reinhart Lampert, Aut.	.20
☐ 248 Karl Heinzle, Aut.	.20
☐ 249 Wolfgang Kromp, Aut.	.20
☐ 250 Marty Dallman , Aut.	.20
☐ 251 Jim Marthinsen (G), Nor.	.20
☐ 252 Robert Schistad, Nor.	.20
☐ 253 Cato Tom Andersen, Nor.	.20
☐ 254 Anders Myrvold, Nor.	.20
☐ 255 Svein Enok Norstebb, Nor.	.20
☐ 256 Tommy Jakobsen, Nor.	.20
☐ 257 Pål Kristiansen, Nor.	.20
☐ 258 Petter Salsten, Nor.	.20
☐ 259 Ole Eskild Dahlström, Nor.	.20
☐ 260 Morten Finstad, Nor.	.20
☐ 261 Espen Knutsen, Nor.	.20
☐ 262 Erik Kristiansen, Nor.	.20
☐ 263 Geir Hoff, Nor.	.20
☐ 264 Roy Johansen, Nor.	.20
☐ 265 Trend Magnussen, Nor.	.20
☐ 266 Marius Rath, Nor.	.20
☐ 267 Vegar Barlie, Nor.	.20
☐ 268 Arne Billkvam, Nor.	.20
☐ 269 Tom Johanssen, Nor.	.20
☐ 270 Petter Thoresen, Nor.	.20
☐ 271 Klaus Merk (G), Ger.	.20
☐ 272 Josef Heiss (G), Ger.	.20
☐ 273 Rick Amann, Ger.	.20
☐ 274 Torsten Kienass, Ger.	.20
☐ 275 Mirco Ludemann, Ger.	.20
☐ 276 Jason Meyer, Ger.	.20
☐ 277 Uli Hiemer, Ger.	.20
☐ 278 Karsten Mende, Ger.	.20
☐ 279 Andreas Niederberger, Ger.	.20
☐ 280 Thomas Brandl, Ger.	.20
☐ 281 Benoît Doucet, Ger.	.20
☐ 282 Robert Hock, Ger.	.20
☐ 283 Georg Franz, Ger.	.20
☐ 284 Ernst Kopf, Ger.	.20
☐ 285 Reemt Pyka, Ger.	.20
☐ 286 Jurgen Rumrich, Ger.	.20
☐ 287 Dieter Hegen, Ger.	.20
☐ 288 Raimund Hilger, Ger.	.20
☐ 289 Thomas Schinko, Ger.	.20
☐ 290 Leo Stefan, Ger.	.20
☐ 291 David Delfino (G), Ita.	.20
☐ 292 Elmar Parth, Ita.	.20
☐ 293 Luigi Da Corte, Ita.	.20
☐ 294 Phil Gaetano, Ita.	.20
☐ 295 Ralph Di Fiore, Ita.	.20
☐ 296 Giorgio Comploi, Ita.	.20
☐ 297 Alexander Thaler, Ita.	.20
☐ 298 Giovanni Marchetti, Ita.	.20
☐ 299 Gates Orlando, Ita.	.20
☐ 300 Frank Di Muzio, Ita.	.20
☐ 301 Joe Foglietta, Ita.	.20
☐ 302 Stefan Figliuzzi, Ita.	.20
☐ 303 John Vecchiarelli, Ita.	.20
☐ 304 Maurizio Mansi, Ita.	.20
☐ 305 Santino Pellegrino, Ita.	.20
☐ 306 Line De Toni, Ita.	.20
☐ 307 Mario Chitarroni, Ita.	.20
☐ 308 Bruno Zarillo, Ita.	.20
☐ 309 Armando Chelodi, Ita.	.20
☐ 310 Carmine Vani, Ita.	.20
☐ 311 Martin McKay (G), G.B.	.20
☐ 312 Scott O'Connor, G.B.	.20
☐ 313 John McCrone, G.B.	.20
☐ 314 Stephen Cooper, G.B.	.20
☐ 315 Mike O'Connor, G.B.	.20
☐ 316 Chris Kelland, G.B.	.20
☐ 317 Graham Waghorn, G.B.	.20
☐ 318 Nickey Chinn, G.B.	.20

□	319 Damien Smith, G.B.	.20
□	320 Tim Cranston, G.B.	.20
□	321 Scott Morrison, G.B.	.20
□	322 Anthony Johnson, G.B.	.20
□	323 Tony Hand, G.B.	.20
□	324 Kevin Conway, G.B.	.20
□	325 Rick Fera, G.B.	.20
□	326 Doug McEwen, G.B.	.20
□	327 Scott Neil, G.B.	.20
□	328 John Iredale, G.B.	.20
□	329 Iain Robertson, G.B.	.20
□	330 Ian Cooper, G.B.	.20
□	331 Bill Ranford (G), Cdn.	.20
□	332 Jarmo Myllys (G), Fin.	.20
□	333 Dominik Hasek (G), Cze.	1.00
□	334 Tommy Söderström (G), Swe.	.20
□	335 Teppo Numminen, Fin.	.20
□	336 Mikhail Tatarinov, Rus.	.20
□	337 Paul Coffey, Cdn.	.50
□	338 Chris Chelios, USA.	.50
□	339 Brian Leetch, USA.	.50
□	340 Al MacInnis, Cdn.	.20
□	341 Vladimir Malakhov, Rus.	.20
□	342 Kevin Hatcher, USA.	.20
□	343 Jiri Slegr, Cze.	.20
□	344 Wayne Gretzky, Cdn.	4.00
□	345 Teemu Selänne, Fin.	.50
□	346 Jari Kurri, Fin.	1.00
□	347 Brett Hull, USA.	1.00
□	348 Sergei Fedorov, Rus.	1.00
□	349 Esa Tikkanen, Fin.	.20
□	350 Mark Messier, Cdn.	1.00
□	351 Jaromir Jagr, Cze.	1.00
□	352 Jeremy Roenick, USA.	.50
□	353 Luc Robitaille, Cdn.	.50
□	354 Tomas Sandström, Swe.	.20
□	355 Peter Forsberg, Fin.	1.00
□	356 Alexei Zhamnov, Rus.	.20
□	357 Theoren Fleury, Cdn.	.50
□	358 Rick Tocchet, Cdn.	.20
□	359 Pat LaFontaine, USA.	.50
□	360 Eric Lindros, Cdn.	1.00

1994 SPORTFLICS

This four-card multi-sport set featured two hockey players. These cards were given out at the 1994 National Sports Collectors Convention in Houston.

	Player	NRMT-MT
□	N4 Derian Hatcher, Dall	2.00
□	Mike Modano, Dall.	5.00

1994 TOPPS FINEST BRONZE

Each card is bonded to a bed of solid bronze.

Complete Set (6 cards): 100.00

	Player	NRMT-MT
□	1 Jaromir Jagr, Pitt.	15.00
□	2 Eric Lindros, Phil.	15.00
□	3 Patrick Roy (G), Mont.	50.00
□	4 Pavel Bure, Vanc.	15.00
□	5 Teemu Selänne, Winn.	15.00
□	6 Doug Gilmour, Toro.	15.00

1994 UPPER DECK WORLD CUP OF SOCCER

This soccer series included a ten-card Honorary Captains insert set. Multi-language variations exist.

Imprint: © 1994 The Upper Deck Company

	Honorary Captains	NRMT-MT
□	C5 Gordie Howe	12.00
□	C6 Wayne Gretzky	20.00

1994 - 95 ACTION PACKED

Action Packed had plans of releasing a series of player pins (Badges of Honour), player coasters, oversized photos and an 84-card Big Picture set. Promos and test issues were released for most if not all of these sets. Big Picture cards are standard-sized issues with a 5 3/4" x 6 1/2" paper photo folded inside. The cards open up at bottom to unfold the oversize action shot. Two different styles of Jeremy Roenick's Big Picture card are known to exist: one card that opens up at the bottom (like a notepad) and one card that opens up from the side (like a booklet). A 4" x 5" checklist card was also available that listed the 84 intended players for this never released product. We have no pricing information on these promos and little information on excatly which cards were released in each series.

BADGE OF HONOR

	Player	BH
□	Sergei Fedorov, Detr.	10.00
□	Doug Gilmour, Toro.	4.00
□	Mike Modano, Dall.	4.00
□	Patick Roy, Mont.	15.00

BIG PICTURE

	Player	BP
□	BP1 Jeremy Roenick, Chic.	4.00
□	BP1 Jeremy Roenick, Chic.	
□	BP2 John Vanbiesbrouck, Flor. (G)	4.00
□	BP3 Jaromir Jagr, Pitt.	10.00
□	BP4 Steve Yzerman, Detr.	15.00

COASTER

	Player		Player
□	Mario Lemieux	□	Trevor Linden
□	Mark Messier	□	Félix Potvin
□	Luc Robitaille	□	Teemu Selänne
□	Brendan Shanahan		

MAMMOTH

	Player	
□	MM1 Chris Chelios, Chic.	5.00
□	Pavel Bure, Vanc.	5.00
□	Brett Hull, SLou.	5.00
□	Adam Oates, Bost.	5.00

1994 - 95 APS

The most expensive single is Jaromir Jagr at $35-50. Other expensive singles include Patrik Elias ($12-15), Milan Hejduk ($12-15), Roman Cechmanek ($8-12), Martin Straka ($6-10), Roman Turek ($3-5), Martin Rucinsky ($3-5) and Jan Hlavac ($3-5). NHL. Other NHL stars sell at $1-4. Other singles sell between 20¢ and $1.00.

Complete Set (300 cards): 90.00
Common Player: .25

	Player		Player
□	1 Pavel Cagas (G)	□	2 Ladislav Blazek (G)
□	3 Ales Flasar	□	4 Petr Tejkl
□	5 Jaromir Latal	□	6 Ales Tomasek
□	7 Jiri Kuntos	□	8 Jan Vavrecka
□	9 Martin Smetak	□	10 Patrik Rimmel
□	11 Michal Slavik	□	12 Milan Navratil
□	13 Petr Fabian	□	14 Zdenek Eichenmann
□	15 Miroslav Chalanek	□	16 Pavel Nohel
□	17 Radim Radevic	□	18 Tomas Martinec
□	19 Alex Zima	□	20 Ivo Hrstka
□	21 Richard Brancik	□	22 Martin Janecek
□	23 Robert Holy	□	24 Radovan Biegl (G)
□	25 Dusan Salficky (G)	□	26 Jiri Malinsky
□	27 Jan Filip	□	28 Jaroslav Spelda
□	29 Petr Jancarik	□	30 Robert Kostka
□	31 Kamil Ioupal	□	32 Tomas Pacal
□	33 Ales Pisa	□	34 Milan Hejduk
□	35 Josef Zajic	□	36 Stanislav Prochazka
□	37 Jiri Sejba	□	38 Marek Zadina
□	39 Milan Filipi	□	40 David Pospisil
□	41 Tomas Blazek	□	42 Patrik Weber
□	43 Richard Kral	□	44 Martin Sekera
□	45 Ladislav Lubina	□	46 Jiri Provznik
□	47 Martin Chlad (G)	□	48 Tomas Vokoun (G)
□	49 Pavel Trnka	□	50 Petr Kuda
□	51 Frantisek Kaberle	□	52 Libor Prochazka
□	53 Jan Dlouhy	□	54 Otakar Cerny
□	55 Martin Ancicka	□	56 Marke Zidlicky
□	57 Martin Prochazka	□	58 Pavel Patera
□	59 Otakar Vejvoda	□	60 Jan Blaha
□	61 David Cernak	□	62 Petr Ton
□	63 Miroslav Mach	□	64 Patrik Elias
□	65 Martin Stepanek	□	66 Tomas Mikolasek
□	67 Milan Rucha	□	68 Jaromir Jagr
□	69 Milos Kajer	□	70 Jaromir Sindel (G)
□	71 Ivo Capek (G)	□	72 Jan Bohacek
□	73 Zdenek Touzimsky	□	74 Jan Krulis
□	75 Frantisek Musil	□	76 Jaroslav Nedved
□	77 Frantisek Ptacek	□	78 Pavel Taborsky
□	79 Frantisek Kucera	□	80 Pavel Srek
□	81 Martin Simek	□	82 Zbynek Kukacka
□	83 Jiri Zelenka	□	84 Jan Hlavac
□	85 Patrik Martinec	□	86 David Bruk
□	87 Pavel Geffert	□	88 Michal Sup
□	89 Jaromir Kverka	□	90 Miroslav Hlinka
□	91 Milan Kastner	□	92 Andrej Potajcuk
□	93 Roman Turek (G)	□	94 Ladislav Gula (G)
□	95 Robert Slavik (G)	□	96 Jiri Hala
□	97 Jaroslav Modry	□	98 Petr Sedy
□	99 Petr Hodek	□	100 Petr Mainer
□	101 Michael Kubicek	□	102 Milan Nedoma
□	103 Rudolf Suchanek	□	104 Libor Zabransky
□	105 Jaroslav Brabec	□	106 Lubos Rob
□	107 Zdenek Sperger	□	108 Ondrej Vosta
□	109 Filip Turek	□	110 Radek Belohlav
□	111 Frantisek Sevcik	□	112 Roman Bozek
□	113 Roman Horak	□	114 Pavel Pycha
□	115 Arpad Gyori	□	116 Tomas Vasicek (G)
□	117 Michal Hlinka (G)	□	118 Daniel Kysela
□	119 Rudolf Wolf	□	120 Antonin Planovsky
□	121 Tomas Kramny	□	122 Vitezslav Skuta
□	123 Pavel Marecek	□	124 Miroslav Javin
□	125 Kamil Pribyla	□	126 Michal Cerny
□	127 Juris Opulskis	□	128 Richard Smehlik
□	129 Ales Badal	□	130 Robert Simicek
□	131 Vladimir Vujtek	□	132 Tomas Chlubna
□	133 Michal Piskor	□	134 Petr Folta
□	135 Roman Kadera	□	136 Lumir Kotala
□	137 Jan Peterek	□	138 Roman Rysanek
□	139 Rudolf Pejchar (G)	□	140 Jiri Kucera (G)
□	141 Stanislav Benes	□	142 Karel Smid
□	143 Martin Kovarik	□	144 Kiri Jonak
□	145 Alexander Savickij	□	146 Vaclav Ruprecht
□	147 Ivan Vlcek	□	149 Jaroslav Spacek
□	150 Peter Veselovsky	□	150 Milan Cerny
□	151 Milan Volak	□	152 Dusan Huml
□	153 Tomas Kucharcik	□	154 Martin Zivny
□	155 Martin Straka	□	156 Michal Straka
□	157 Jiri Beranek	□	158 Ondrej Steiner
□	159 Josef Rybar	□	160 Jaroslav Kreuzmann
□	161 David Trachta	□	162 Marek Novotny (G)
□	163 Pavel Falta (G)	□	164 Antonin Necas
□	165 Roman Cech	□	166 Pavel Zmrhal
□	167 Petr Buzek	□	168 Jaroslav Benak
□	169 Michael Vyhlidal	□	170 Petr Kuchyna
□	171 Josef Marha	□	172 Leos Pipa
□	173 Jiri Poukar	□	174 Libor Dolana
□	175 Viktor Ujcik	□	176 Ladislav Prokupek
□	177 Jiri Cihlar	□	178 Patrik Fink
□	179 Oldrich Valek	□	180 Zdenek Cely
□	181 Jaroslav Kames (G)	□	182 Pavel Malac (G)
□	183 Martin Maskarinec	□	184 Pavel Rajnoha
□	185 Pavel Kowalczyk	□	186 Miloslav Guren
□	187 Radim Tesarik	□	188 Jan Krajicek
□	189 Patrik Hucko	□	190 Roman Kankovsky
□	191 Jaroslav Hub	□	192 Petr Kankovsky
□	193 Pavel Janku	□	194 Miroslav Okal
□	195 Zdenek Okal	□	196 Roman Mejzlik
□	197 Juraj Jurik	□	198 Roman Meluzin
□	199 Josef Straub	□	200 Martin Kotasek
□	201 Zdenek Sedlak	□	202 Petr Cajanek
□	203 Zdenek Orct (G)	□	204 Petr Franek (G)
□	205 Petr Svoboda	□	206 Angel Nikolov
□	207 Petr Molnar	□	208 Kamil Prachar
□	209 Jiri Slegr	□	210 Radek Mrazek
□	211 Jan Vopat	□	212 Ondrej Zetek
□	213 Martin Stelcich	□	214 Zdenek Skorepa
□	215 Stanislav Rosa	□	216 Radek Sip
□	217 Martin Rousek	□	218 Tomas Vlasak
□	219 Radim Piroutek	□	220 Robert Kysela
□	221 Martin Rucinsky	□	222 Robert Lang
□	223 Ivo Prorok	□	224 Jan Alinc
□	225 Vladimir Machulda	□	226 Kamil Kolacek
□	227 David Balazs	□	228 R. Cechmanek (G)
□	229 Ivo Pesat (G)	□	230 Antonin Stavjana
□	231 Pavel Augusta	□	232 Daniel Vrla
□	233 Alexej Jaskin	□	234 Radek Mesicek
□	235 Marek Tichy	□	236 Stanislav Pavelec
□	237 Jan Srdinko	□	238 Zbynek Marak
□	239 Andrej Galkin	□	240 Miroslav Stavjana
□	241 Libor Forch	□	242 Roman Stantien
□	243 Josef Beranek	□	244 Lubos Jenacek
□	245 Michal Tomek	□	246 Rostislav Vlach
□	247 Miroslav Barus	□	248 Josef Podlaha
□	249 Pavel Rohlik	□	250 Martin Altrichter (G)
□	251 Radek Toth (G)	□	252 V. Hudacek (G)
□	253 Miloslav Horava	□	254 Meptr Macek
□	255 Pavel Blaha	□	256 Radomir Brazda
□	257 Jiri Hes	□	258 Romas Arnost
□	259 Miroslav Hosek	□	260 Jan Penk
□	261 Tomas Jelinek	□	262 Jiri Hlinka
□	263 Lubos Pazler	□	264 Roman Blazek
□	265 Vladimir Ruzicka	□	266 Tomas Kupka
□	267 Lubos Dopita	□	268 Ladislav Slizek
□	269 Milan Antos	□	270 Vadim Kulabuchov
□	271 Anatoli Naida	□	272 Tomas Hyka
□	273 Vaclav Eiselt	□	274 Tomas Placatka
□	275 Jan Nemecek	□	276 J. Augusta, Coach
□	277 L. Fischer, Coach	□	278 J. Piecechtel, Coach
□	279 Ma. Sykora, Coach	□	280 P. Hernsky, Coach
□	281 Jan Neliba, Coach	□	282 Z. Muller, Coach
□	283 F. Vyborny, Coach	□	284 S. Berger, Coach
□	285 K. Prazak, Coach	□	286 V. Caldr, Coach
□	287 Hadamczik, Coach	□	288 Bochensky, Coach
□	289 K. Trachta, Coach	□	290 Setikovsky, Coach
□	291 Ja. Holik, Coach	□	292 Jan Hrbaty, Coach
□	293 V. Vujtek, Coach	□	294 Z. Cech, Coach
□	295 F. Vorlicek, Coach	□	296 Weissmann, Coach
□	297 H. Valasek, Coach	□	298 Z. Tabara, Coach
□	299 P. Richter, Coach	□	300 B. Kopriva, Coach

1994 - 95 ASSETS

This 100-card four-sport set features only 14 hockey players. Half the cards (excluding the checklists) have a Silver Signatures parallel, a one minute Sprint phonecard and a $2 Sprint phonecard. A 100-card regular set sells at $25 while a 48-card Silver Signatures set sells for $135. A 48-card on -minute set sells at $150 while a 48-card $2 set sells at $275.

Bonk, Jovanovski and Rhéaume (Canadian National Team uniform) were available in series one while Fichaud, O'Neill, Sykora and Rhéaume (Las Vegas Thunder uniform) were available in series two. There are reportedly 20,605 first series one minute phonecards, 2,587 first series $2 phonecards and 3,117 second series $2 phonecards.

Rhéaume's series one card has a $25 phonecard version (808 copies) and a $1,000 phonecard version (4 copies) while her series two card has a $5 phonecard version (2,562 copies) and a $2,000 phonecard version (4 copies). All phonecards are unnumbered. Prices below are for unused phonecards.

	Player	Silver	Base
□□	8 Ed Jovanovski, Windsor	1.00	0.25
□□	20 Radek Bonk, Las Vegas	0.50	0.25
□□	21 Manon Rhéaume (G), Cdn.	4.50	1.50
□	33 Ed Jovanovski, Windsor	-	0.25
□	45 Radek Bonk, Las Vegas	-	0.25
□	46 Manon Rhéaume (G), Cdn.	-	1.50
□□	57 Jeff O'Neill, Guelph	1.00	0.25
□□	60 Petr Sykora, Detroit	1.00	0.25
□□	62 Éric Fichaud (G), Chicoutimi	0.50	0.25
□□	72 Rhéaume (G), Las Vegas	4.50	1.50
□	82 Jeff O'Neill, Guelph	-	0.25
□	85 Petr Sykora, Detroit	-	0.25
□	87 Éric Fichaud (G), Chicoutimi	-	0.25
□	97 Manon Rhéaume (G), Las Vegas	-	1.50

	Phonecard	$2	1-min
□□	8 Ed Jovanovski, Windsor	3.00	2.00
□□	20 Radek Bonk, Las Vegas	2.00	1.50
□□	21 Manon Rhéaume (G), Cdn.	9.00	6.00
□□	57 Jeff O'Neill, Guelph	3.00	2.00
□□	60 Petr Sykora, Detroit	3.00	2.00
□□	62 Éric Fichaud (G), Chicoutimi	2.00	1.00
□□	72 Rhéaume (G), Las Vegas	9.00	6.00

	Player	Unused
□	$5 Manon Rhéaume (G), Las Vegas	10.00
□	$25 Manon Rhéaume (G), Canada Nationals	60.00
□	$1000 Manon Rhéaume (G), Canada Nationals	-
□	$2000 Manon Rhéaume (G), Las Vegas	-

DIE-CUT

This 25-card multi-sport set features three hockey players. A 25-card set sells at $175.

	Player	NRMT-MT
□	DC9 Ed Jovanovski, Windsor	4.00
□	DC10 Manon Rhéaume (G), Canada	18.00
□	DC24 Éric Fichaud (G), Chicoutimi	1.00

1994 - 95 BE A PLAYER MAGAZINE CARDS

These cards were inserted in the NHLPA's Be A Player magazine.

	Player	BAP
□	Félix Potvin (G) (no #)	2.00
□	Teemu Selänne (no #)	2.00
□	3 Paul Kariya	4.00
□	4 Joe Sakic	4.00

1994 - 95 CLASSIC

There are two versions: the regular card and a gold parallel. The most expensive regular card is Manon Rhéaume (G) at $2-3. Regional stars sell at $0.25-1.00; commons start at 20¢. The most expensive gold card is Manon Rhéaume (G) at $8-10. Gold cards for regional stars sell at $0.50-3.00 (approx. 2-3 times regular card); commons start at 25¢.

Imprint: 1994 Classic Games, Inc.

Complete Set (120 cards):	**12.00**
Gold Set (120 cards):	**60.00**

Promo

☐ Jason Arnott

Player	Player
☐ ☐ 1 Ed Jovanovski	☐ ☐ 2 Oleg Tverdovsky
☐ ☐ 3 Radek Bonk	☐ ☐ 4 Jason Bonsignore
☐ ☐ 5 Jeff O'Neill	☐ ☐ 6 Ryan Smyth
☐ ☐ 7 Jamie Storr (G)	☐ ☐ 8 Jason Wiemer
☐ ☐ 9 Nolan Baumgartner	☐ ☐ 10 Jeff Friesen
☐ ☐ 11 Wade Belak	☐ ☐ 12 Ethan Moreau
☐ ☐ 13 A. Kharlamov	☐ ☐ 14 Éric Fichaud (G)
☐ ☐ 15 Wayne Primeau	☐ ☐ 16 Brad Brown
☐ ☐ 17 Chris Dingman	☐ ☐ 18 E. Ryabchikov (G)
☐ ☐ 19 Yan Golubovsky	☐ ☐ 20 Chris Wells
☐ ☐ 21 Vadim Sharifijanov	☐ ☐ 22 Dan Cloutier (G)
☐ ☐ 23 CL: Pirates	☐ ☐ 24 J. Langenbrunner
☐ ☐ 25 Kenny Jönsson	☐ ☐ 26 Curtis Bowen
☐ ☐ 27 Sergei Gonchar	☐ ☐ 28 Stefan Bergqvist
☐ ☐ 29 Vaclav Prospal	☐ ☐ 30 Valeri Bure
☐ ☐ 31 R. Shulmistra (G)	☐ ☐ 32 Chris Armstrong
☐ ☐ 33 Brian Farrell	☐ ☐ 34 Brian Savage
☐ ☐ 35 Blaine Lacher (G)	☐ ☐ 36 Kevin Brown
☐ ☐ 37 Joe Dziedzic	☐ ☐ 38 Peter Ferraro
☐ ☐ 39 Chris Ferraro	☐ ☐ 40 Todd Harvey
☐ ☐ 41 Eric Lecompte	☐ ☐ 42 Dean Grillo
☐ ☐ 43 Valeri Karpov	☐ ☐ 44 Andrew Shier
☐ ☐ 45 Vesa Viitakoski	☐ ☐ 46 Xavier Majic
☐ ☐ 47 Kevin Smyth	☐ ☐ 48 Jeff Nelson
☐ ☐ 49 Cory Stillman	☐ ☐ 50 Clayton Beddoes
☐ ☐ 51 Craig Conroy	☐ ☐ 52 Dean Fedorchuk
☐ ☐ 53 John Gruden	☐ ☐ 54 Chris McAlpine
☐ ☐ 55 Sean McCann	☐ ☐ 56 Derek Maguire
☐ ☐ 57 David Oliver	☐ ☐ 58 Mike Pomichter
☐ ☐ 59 Jamie Ram (G)	☐ ☐ 60 Shawn Reid
☐ ☐ 61 D. Roloson (G)	☐ ☐ 62 Steve Shields (G)
☐ ☐ 63 Brian Wiseman	☐ ☐ 64 Drew Bannister
☐ ☐ 65 Matt Johnson	☐ ☐ 66 Scott Malone
☐ ☐ 67 Sergei Berezin	☐ ☐ 68 Chad Penney
☐ ☐ 69 Ian Laperrière	☐ ☐ 70 Andrei Nikolishin
☐ ☐ 71 Kelly Fairchild	☐ ☐ 72 Jere Lehtinen
☐ ☐ 73 Ravil Gusmanov	☐ ☐ 74 CL: Atlanta Knights
☐ ☐ 75 Neil Little (G)	☐ ☐ 76 Brian Rolston
☐ ☐ 77 David Vyborny	☐ ☐ 78 Nikolai Tsulygin
☐ ☐ 79 Niklas Sundström	☐ ☐ 80 Patrik Juhlin
☐ ☐ 81 Dan Plante	☐ ☐ 82 Brandon Convery
☐ ☐ 83 Nick Stajduhar	☐ ☐ 84 Garth Snow (G)
☐ ☐ 85 Corey Hirsch (G)	☐ ☐ 86 Craig Darby
☐ ☐ 87 Andrei Nazarov	☐ ☐ 88 Todd Marchant
☐ ☐ 89 Jeff Nielson	☐ ☐ 90 Brendan Witt
☐ ☐ 91 Denis Metlyuk	☐ ☐ 92 Maxim Bets
☐ ☐ 93 Sean Pronger	☐ ☐ 94 Chris Tamer
☐ ☐ 95 Saku Koivu	☐ ☐ 96 Mattias Norstrom
☐ ☐ 97 Ville Peltonen	☐ ☐ 98 René Corbet
☐ ☐ 99 Brent Gretzky	☐ ☐ 100 Chris Marinucci
☐ ☐ 101 Ian Moran	☐ ☐ 102 Janne Laukkanen
☐ ☐ 103 Todd Bertuzzi	☐ ☐ 104 Darby Hendrickson
☐ ☐ 105 Janne Niinimaa	☐ ☐ 106 David Roberts
☐ ☐ 107 Pat Neaton	☐ ☐ 108 Todd Warriner
☐ ☐ 109 Mats Lindgren	☐ ☐ 110 Jason Allison
☐ ☐ 111 Radim Bicanek	☐ ☐ 112 Denis Pederson
☐ ☐ 113 Viktor Kozlov	☐ ☐ 114 Mike Murray
☐ ☐ 115 Aaron Gavey	☐ ☐ 116 Michael Peca
☐ ☐ 117 Jason Zent	☐ ☐ 118 Jason MacDonald
☐ ☐ 119 Aaron Israel (G)	☐ ☐ 120 M. Rhéaume (G)

CHL ALL-STARS

Insert Set (10 cards):	**25.00**
Insert (#/2000)	**CHL**
☐ C1 Jason Allison	7.00
☐ C2 Yannick Dubé	1.00
☐ C3 Éric Fichaud (G)	2.00
☐ C4 Jeff Friesen	4.00
☐ C5 Aaron Gavey	1.00
☐ C6 Ed Jovanovski	5.00
☐ C7 Jeff O'Neill	5.00
☐ C8 Ryan Smyth	6.00
☐ C9 Jamie Storr (G)	3.00
☐ C10 Brendan Witt	1.00

ALL-ROOKIE TEAM

Insert Set (6 cards):	**10.00**
Player	**ART**
☐ AR1 Martin Brodeur (G), Utica	8.00
☐ AR2 Jason Arnott	2.00
☐ AR3 Alexei Yashin	3.00
☐ AR4 Oleg Petrov	1.00
☐ AR5 Chris Pronger	3.00
☐ AR6 Alexander Karpovtsev	.50

AUTOGRAPHS

Autograph	**Auto.**
☐ Mike Bavis ✍ {#/1,955}	4.00
☐ Radek Bonk ✍ {#/4,940}	4.00
☐ Jason Bonsignore ✍ {#/4,300}	4.00
☐ Scott Chartier ✍ {#/1,930}	4.00
☐ Craig Darby ✍ {#/1,915}	4.00
☐ Dallas Drake ✍ {#/960}	4.00
☐ Ted Drury ✍ {#/1,920}	4.00
☐ Mike Dunham (G) ✍ {#/1,955}	10.00
☐ Eric Fenton ✍ {#/1,845}	4.00
☐ Chris Ferraro ✍ {#/4,770}	4.00
☐ Peter Ferraro ✍ {#/4,875}	4.00
☐ Jeff Friesen ✍ {#/6,145}	4.00
☐ Doug Gilmour ✍ {#/1,950}	15.00
☐ Chris Gratton ✍ {#/2,000}	6.00
☐ Brett Harkins ✍ {#/1,885}	4.00
☐ Brett Hauer ✍ {#/1,930}	4.00
☐ Jon Hillebrandt ✍ {#/1,570}	4.00
☐ Ryan Hughes ✍ {#/1,940}	4.00
☐ Dean Hullet ✍ {#/1,955}	4.00
☐ Fred Knipsheer ✍ {#/1,945}	4.00
☐ John Lilley ✍ {#/2,460}	4.00
☐ Stanislav Neckar ✍ {#/4,645}	4.00
☐ Cam Neely ✍ {#/1,850}	25.00
☐ Rob Niedermayer ✍ {#/950}	7.00
☐ Jeff O'Neill ✍ {#/5,380}	5.00
☐ Derek Plante ✍ {#/1,970}	4.00
☐ Manon Rhéaume (G) ✍ {#/2,400}	40.00
☐ Travis Richards ✍ {#/1,950}	4.00
☐ Barry Richter ✍ {#/1,935}	4.00
☐ David Roberts ✍ {#/1,970}	4.00
☐ Chris Rögles ✍ {#/1,920}	4.00
☐ Jon Rohloff ✍ {#/2,010}	4.00
☐ Brian Rolston ✍ {#/2,400}	7.00
☐ David Sacco ✍ {#/1,975}	4.00
☐ Brian Savage ✍ {#/4,930}	4.00
☐ Cam Stewart ✍ {#/970}	4.00
☐ Jim Storm ✍ {#/1,950}	4.00
☐ Chris Tamer ✍ {#/1,900}	4.00
☐ Aaron Ward ✍ {#/1,965}	4.00

CHL PREVIEW

Insert Set (6 cards):	**2.50**
Player	**CHL**
☐ CP1 Wayne Primeau, Owen Sound	.50
☐ CP2 Éric Fichaud (G), Chicoutimi	.50
☐ CP3 Wade Redden, Brandon	1.00
☐ CP4 Jason Doig, St-Jean	.50
☐ CP5 Vitali Yachmenev, North Bay	.50
☐ CP6 Nolan Baumgartner, Kamloops	.50

DRAFT PICKS

Insert Set (5 cards):	**10.00**
Player	**DP**
☐ CP11 Ed Jovanovski	2.00
☐ CP12 Oleg Tverdovsky	1.00
☐ CP13 Radek Bonk	1.00
☐ CP14 Jason Allison	3.00
☐ CP15 Manon Rhéaume (G)	6.00

COLLEGE ALL-AMERICAN

Insert Set (10 cards):	**15.00**
Player	**AA**
☐ AA1 Craig Conroy	4.00
☐ AA2 John Gruden	1.50
☐ AA3 Chris Marinucci	1.50
☐ AA4 Chris McAlpine	1.50
☐ AA5 Sean McCann	1.50
☐ AA6 David Oliver	1.50
☐ AA7 Mike Pomichter	1.50
☐ AA8 Jamie Ram (G)	2.00
☐ AA9 Shawn Reid	1.50
☐ AA10 Dwayne Roloson (G)	2.00

DRAFT PROSPECTS

Insert Set (10 cards):	**20.00**
Player	**DP**
☐ DP1 Bubba Berenzweig	1.50
☐ DP2 Aki Berg	2.00
☐ DP3 Chad Kilger	3.00
☐ DP4 Daymond Langkow	3.00
☐ DP5 Alyn McCauley	4.00
☐ DP6 Igor Melyakov	1.50
☐ DP7 Erik Rasmussen	3.00
☐ DP8 Marty Reasoner	3.00
☐ DP9 Scott Roche	1.50
☐ DP10 Petr Sykora	5.00

ENFORCERS

Insert Set (10 cards):	**15.00**
☐ PR1 Richard Zemlick	2.00
Player	**E**
☐ E1 Donald Brashear, Fredericton	3.00
☐ E2 Daniel Lacroix, Binghampton	2.00
☐ E3 Dale Henry, Milwaukee	2.00
☐ E4 John Badduke, Hamilton	2.00
☐ E5 Corey Schwab (G), Albany	2.00
☐ E6 Craig Martin, Adirondack	2.00
☐ E7 Kerry Clark, Portland-AHL	2.00
☐ E8 Kevin Kaminski, Portland-AHL	2.00
☐ E9 Jim Kyte, Las Vegas	2.00
☐ E10 Mark DeSantis, San Diego	2.00

R.O.Y. SWEEPSTAKES

Insert Set (20 cards):	**40.00**
Player	**ROYS**
☐ R1 Jason Allison, Portland-AHL	6.00
☐ R2 Radek Bonk	3.00
☐ R3 Jason Bonsignore	1.50
☐ R4 Valeri Bure	3.00
☐ R5 Jeff Friesen	3.00
☐ R6 Aaron Gavey	1.50
☐ R7 Todd Harvey	2.00
☐ R8 Kenny Jönsson, Swe.	2.00
☐ R9 Ed Jovanovski	4.00
☐ R10 Patrik Juhlin	1.50
☐ R11 Valeri Karpov	1.50
☐ R12 Viktor Kozlov	3.00
☐ R13 Blaine Lacher (G)	1.50
☐ R14 Andrei Nikolishin	1.50
☐ R15 Jeff O'Neill	4.00
☐ R16 David Oliver	1.50
☐ R17 Garth Snow (G)	3.00
☐ R18 Jamie Storr (G), Owen Sound	2.00
☐ R19 Oleg Tverdovsky	1.50
☐ R20 Field Card	1.50

TRI-CARDS

Insert Set (26 cards):	**40.00**
Player	**Tri**
☐ T1-3 V. Karpov/ N. Tsulygin/ O.Tverdovsky	1.50
☐ T4-6 Knipscheeer/ Lacher (G)/ Ryabchikov (G)	1.50
☐ T7-10 D. Cooper/ W. Primeau/ S. Shields (G)	1.50
☐ T10-12 C. Dingman/ C. Stillman/ V. Vitakoski	1.50
☐ T13-15 E. Lecompte/ E. Moreau/ M. Pomichter	1.50
☐ T16-18 Harvey/ Langenbrunner/ Lehtinen	2.00
☐ T19-21 Bowen/ Golubovsky/ Hodson (G)	1.50
☐ T22-24 J. Bonsignore/ M. Lindgren/ D. Oliver	1.50
☐ T25-27 C. Armstrong/ Jovanovski/ Podollan	2.00
☐ T28-30 A. Nikolishin/ J. O'Neill/ K. Smyth	2.00
☐ T31-33 K. Brown/ M. Johnson/ J. Storr (G)	1.50
☐ T34-36 V. Bure/ S. Koivu/ B. Savage	5.00
☐ T37-39 Pederson/ Rolston/ Sharifijanov	1.50
☐ T40-42 T. Bertuzzi/ C. Marinucci/ D. Plante	4.00
☐ T43-45 Hirsch (G)/ Sundström/ S. Malone	1.50
☐ T46-48 R. Bicanek/ R. Bonk/ C. Penney	1.50
☐ T49-51 P. Juhlin/ D. Metlyuk/ J. Niinimaa	1.50
☐ T52-54 G. Andrusak/ P. Neaton/ C. Wells	1.50
☐ T55-57 Corbet/ A. Deadmarsh/ G. Snow (G)	2.00
☐ T58-60 D. Roberts/ I. Laperrière/ P. Tardif	1.50
☐ T61-63 J. Friesen/ V. Kozlov/ V. Peltonen	2.00
☐ T64-66 A. Gavey/ B. Gretzky/ J. Weimer	1.50
☐ T67-69 B. Convery/ Fichaud (G)/ K. Jönsson	1.50
☐ T70-72 M. Fountain/ R. Girard/ M. Peca	2.00
☐ T73-75 J. Allison/ A. Kharlamov/ B. Witt	2.00
☐ T76-78 M. Alatalo/ R. Gusmanov/ D. Quint	1.50

WOMEN OF HOCKEY

Insert Set (40 cards):	**25.00**
Player	**W**
☐ **W1 Manon Rhéaume (G) RC**	**6.00**
☐ **W2 France St-Louis RC**	**1.50**
☐ **W3 Cheryl Pounder RC**	**1.50**
☐ **W4 Thérèse Brisson RC**	**1.00**
☐ **W5 Cassie Campbell RC**	**3.00**
☐ **W6 Angela James RC**	**3.00**
☐ **W7 Danielle Goyette RC**	**1.50**
☐ **W8 Jane Robinson RC**	**.50**
☐ **W9 Stacy Wilson RC**	**1.00**
☐ **W10 Margot Page RC**	**.50**
☐ **W11 Laura Leslie RC**	**.50**
☐ **W12 Judy Diduck RC**	**1.00**
☐ **W13 Hayley Wickenheiser RC**	**6.00**
☐ **W14 Nathalie Picard RC**	**.50**
☐ **W15 Leslie Reddon (G) RC**	**.50**
☐ **W16 Marianne Grnak RC**	**.50**
☐ **W17 Andria Hunter RC**	**.50**
☐ **W18 Nancy Drolet RC**	**1.50**
☐ **W19 Geraldine Heaney RC**	**1.50**
☐ **W20 Karen Nystrom RC**	**1.00**
☐ W21 CL: Rhéaume/ Grnak/ Heaney	1.50
☐ **W22 Kelly Dyer (G) RC**	**.50**
☐ **W23 Vicki Movsessian RC**	**.50**
☐ **W24 Lisa Brown RC**	**.50**
☐ **W25 Shawna Davidson RC**	**.50**
☐ **W26 Colleen Coyne RC**	**.50**
☐ **W27 Karyne Bye RC**	**.50**
☐ **W28 Suzanne Merz RC**	**.50**
☐ **W29 Gretzhen Ulion RC**	**.50**
☐ **W30 Sandra Whyte RC**	**.50**
☐ **W31 Cindy Curley RC**	**.50**
☐ **W32 Michele DiFronze RC**	**.50**
☐ **W33 Stephanie Boyd RC**	**.50**
☐ **W34 Shelley Looney RC**	**1.50**
☐ **W35 Jeanine Sobek RC**	**.50**
☐ **W36 Beth Beagan RC**	**.50**
☐ **W37 Cammi Granato RC**	**6.00**
☐ **W38 Christina Bailey RC**	**.50**
☐ **W39 Kelly O'Leary RC**	**.50**
☐ **W40 Erin Whitten (G) RC**	**2.00**

1994 - 95 CLASSIC DRAFT DAY

Complete Set (10 cards):	**30.00**
Player	**NRMT-MT**
☐ Anah.: Radek Bonk, Las Vegas	3.00
☐ Flor.: Radek Bonk, Las Vegas	3.00
☐ Otta.: Radek Bonk, Las Vegas	3.00
☐ Edmo.: Jason Bonsignore, Niagara Falls	2.00
☐ Anah.: Jeff O'Neill, Guelph	4.00
☐ Flor.: Jeff O'Neill, Guelph	4.00
☐ Otta.: Jeff O'Neill, Guelph	4.00
☐ Anah.: Ed Jovanovski, Windsor	5.00
☐ Flor.: Ed Jovanovski, Windsor	5.00
☐ Otta.: Ed Jovanovski, Windsor	5.00

1994 - 95 CLASSIC FOUR SPORT

This 200-card four-sport set features 46 hockey players. Each card has two verions: the regular card and a gold parallel. A 200-card regular set sells at $15 and a 200-card gold set sells at $40.

Regional stars sell at $0.25-1.00; commons start at 20¢. Gold cards for regional stars sell at $0.50-3.00 (approx. 2-3 times regular card); commons start at 25¢.

Player	Player
☐ ☐ 115 Ed Jovanovski	☐ ☐ 116 Oleg Tverdovsky
☐ ☐ 117 Radek Bonk	☐ ☐ 118 Jason Bonsignore
☐ ☐ 119 Jeff O'Neill	☐ ☐ 120 Ryan Smyth
☐ ☐ 121 Jamie Storr (G)	☐ ☐ 122 Jason Wiemer
☐ ☐ 123 E. Ryabchikov (G)	☐ ☐ 124 Nolan Baumgartner
☐ ☐ 125 Jeff Friesen	☐ ☐ 126 Wade Belak
☐ ☐ 127 Maxim Bets	☐ ☐ 128 Ethan Moreau
☐ ☐ 129 A. Kharlamov	☐ ☐ 130 Éric Fichaud (G)
☐ ☐ 131 Wayne Primeau	☐ ☐ 132 Brad Brown
☐ ☐ 133 Chris Dingman	☐ ☐ 134 Craig Darby
☐ ☐ 135 Darby Hendrickson	☐ ☐ 136 Yan Golubovsky
☐ ☐ 137 Chris Wells	☐ ☐ 138 Vadim Sharifijanov
☐ ☐ 139 Dan Cloutier (G)	☐ ☐ 140 Todd Marchant
☐ ☐ 141 David Roberts	☐ ☐ 142 Brian Rolston
☐ ☐ 143 Garth Snow (G)	☐ ☐ 144 Cory Stillman
☐ ☐ 145 Chad Penney	☐ ☐ 146 Jeff Nelson
☐ ☐ 147 Michael Stewart	☐ ☐ 148 Mike Dunham (G)
☐ ☐ 149 Joe Frederick	☐ ☐ 150 Mark DeSantis
☐ ☐ 151 David Cooper	☐ ☐ 152 Andrei Buschan
☐ ☐ 153 Mike Greenlay	☐ ☐ 154 Geoff Sarjeant (G)
☐ ☐ 155 Pauli Jaks (G)	☐ ☐ 156 Greg Andrusak
☐ ☐ 157 Denis Metlyuk	☐ ☐ 158 Mike Fountain (G)
☐ ☐ 159 Brent Gretzky	☐ ☐ 160 Jason Allison

INSERTS

A 20-card Bonus Card set sells at $25. A five-card Tri-Card set sells at $30.

Insert	**NRMT-MT**
☐ BC17 Ed Jovanovski	1.00
☐ BC18 Radek Bonk	.50
☐ BC19 Jeff O'Neill	1.00
☐ BC20 Ethan Moreau	.50

Insert	**NRMT-MT**
☐ TC4 Radek Bonk/ Chris Wells/ Jeff O'Neill	4.00

Insert	NRMT-MT
□ CP25 Ethan Moreau	3.00

Insert	NRMT-MT
□ Four in One: Ed Jovanovski, et al.	15.00

Insert	NRMT-MT
□ HV4 Ed Jovanovski	5.00
□ HV8 Oleg Tverdovsky	2.00
□ HV12 Radek Bonk	4.00
□ HV16 Jason Bonsignore	1.00
□ HV19 Jeff O'Neill	5.00

SPRINT PHONECARDS

This eight-card four-sport insert set features two hockey players. Each card has five denominations: A one dollar, a two dollar, a three dollar, a four dollar and a five dollar card. Prices below are for unused phonecards. Two-dollar phonecards are valued twice as much as one-dollar phonecards; three-dollar phonecards are valued three times as much as one-dollar phonecards.

Player	$1	$4	$5
□□□□□ Jeff O'Neill	3.00	10.00	12.00
□□□□□ Ed Jovanovski	3.00	10.00	12.00

1994 - 95 CLASSIC IMAGES

These cards have a gold parallel. NHL logos are covered in this set.

The most expensive regular card is Manon Rhéaume (G) at $3-4. Regional stars sell at $0.35-1.25; commons start at 20¢. The most expensive gold card is Manon Rhéaume (G) at $8-10. Gold cards for regional stars sell at $0.75-4.00 (approx. 2-3 times regular card); commons start at 35¢.

Complete Set (100 cards): 15.00
Gold Set (100 cards): 40.00

Player	Player
□□ 1 Bryan Berard	□□ 2 Jeff Friesen
□□ 3 Tommy Salo (G)	□□ 4 Jim Carey (G)
□□ 5 Wade Redden	□□ 6 Jocelyn Thibault (G)
□□ 7 Ian Laperriere	□□ 8 Todd Marchant
□□ 9 Blaine Lacher (G)	□□ 10 Pavel Bure
□□ 11 Alexei Vasilevski	□□ 12 Jason Doig
□□ 13 Éric Fichaud (G)	□□ 14 Eric Dazé
□□ 15 Ed Jovanovski	□□ 16 A. Selivanov
□□ 17 Brent Gretzky	□□ 18 Terry Ryan
□□ 19 Chris Wells	□□ 20 Wade Belak
□□ 21 Kevin Dineen	□□ 22 Craig Fisher
□□ 23 Jan Caloun	□□ 24 M. Fernandez (G)
□□ 25 Radek Bonk	□□ 26 Dave Christian
□□ 27 Patrice Tardif	□□ 28 Kevin Brown
□□ 29 Hubie McDonough	□□ 30 Yan Golubovsky
□□ 31 Steve Larouche	□□ 32 Chris Therien
□□ 33 Craig Darby	□□ 34 Dwayne Norris
□□ 35 Roman Oksiuta	□□ 36 Steve Washburn
□□ 37 Todd Bertuzzi	□□ 38 Cory Stillman
□□ 39 Steve Kelly	□□ 40 Nathan Lafayette
□□ 41 D. Roloson (G)	□□ 42 N. Khabibulin (G)
□□ 43 Radim Bicanek	□□ 44 Jeff O'Neill
□□ 45 Jason Bonsignore	□□ 46 Shean Donovan
□□ 47 Wayne Primeau	□□ 48 J. Langenbrunner
□□ 49 Dan Cloutier (G)	□□ 50 Ethan Moreau
□□ 51 Brad Bombardir	□□ 52 Jason Muzzatti (G)
□□ 53 Jassen Cullimore	□□ 54 Jason Zent
□□ 55 Sergei Gonchar	□□ 56 Steve Rucchin
□□ 57 Rob Cowie	□□ 58 Miroslav Satan
□□ 59 Kenny Jönsson	□□ 60 Adam Deadmarsh
□□ 61 Mike Dunham (G)	□□ 62 Corey Hirsch (G)
□□ 63 Janne Laukkanen	□□ 64 Craig Conroy
□□ 65 Ryan Sittler	□□ 66 Jeff Nelson
□□ 67 Michel Picard	□□ 68 Mark Astley
□□ 69 Lonny Bohonos	□□ 70 E. Ryabchikov (G)
□□ 71 Chris Osgood (G)	□□ 72 M. Rhéaume (G)
□□ 73 Mike Kennedy	□□ 74 Deron Quint
□□ 75 Jamie Storr (G)	□□ 76 Aris Brimanis
□□ 77 Valeri Bure	□□ 78 René Corbet
□□ 79 David Oliver	□□ 80 Chris McAlpine
□□ 81 Petr Sykora	□□ 82 Brad Church
□□ 83 Daymond Langkow	□□ 84 Chad Kilger
□□ 85 Shane Doan	□□ 86 Jeff Ware
□□ 87 Christian Laflamme	□□ 88 Cory Cross
□□ 89 Al Secord	□□ 90 Jason Woolley
□□ 91 Bryan McCabe	□□ 92 Travis Richards
□□ 93 Andrei Nazarov	□□ 94 Mike Pomichter
□□ 95 Chris Marinucci	□□ 96 Jean-Yves Roy
□□ 97 Brian Rolston	□□ 98 Aaron Ward
□□ 99 CL: Jim Carey (G)	□□ 100 CL: Pavel Bure

AUTOGRAPHS

Twenty-two players also have a third autographed version (no card number, serial numbered). Each player signed between 970 (Radek Bonk) and 1,500 autographs.

Player	NRMT-MT
□ Radek Bonk ✍	8.00
□ Jason Bonsignore ✍	4.00
□ Aris Brimanis ✍	4.00
□ Craig Conroy ✍	8.00
□ Adam Deadmarsh ✍	7.00
□ Shean Donovan ✍	4.00
□ Jeff Friesen ✍	7.00
□ Yan Golubovsky ✍	4.00
□ Kenny Jönsson ✍	5.00
□ Blaine Lacher (G) ✍	4.00
□ Jamie Langenbrunner ✍	5.00
□ Chris Marinucci ✍	4.00
□ Chris McAlpine ✍	4.00
□ David Oliver ✍	4.00
□ Mike Pomichter ✍	4.00
□ Deron Quint ✍	4.00
□ Dwayne Roloson (G) ✍	4.00
□ Petr Sykora ✍	9.00
□ Jocelyn Thibault (G) ✍	10.00
□ Aaron Ward ✍	4.00
□ Steve Washburn ✍	4.00
□ Jason Zent ✍	4.00

CLEAR EXCITEMENT

Insert Set (20 cards):	220.00
□ CE4 Promo Jim Carey (G)	5.00
Insert (#/350)	**CE**
□ CE1 Bryan Berard, Detroit-OHL	10.00
□ CE2 Jeff Friesen, Regina	10.00
□ CE3 Tommy Salo (G), Denver	15.00
□ CE4 Jim Carey (G), Portland-AHL	5.00
□ CE5 Wade Redden, Brandon	10.00
□ CE6 Jocelyn Thibault (G), Sherbrooke	15.00
□ CE7 Ian Laperrière, Peoria	5.00
□ CE8 Todd Marchant, Cape Breton	5.00
□ CE9 Blaine Lacher (G), Providence	5.00
□ CE10 Pavel Bure, Vanc.	30.00
□ CE11 Petr Sykora, Detroit-IHL	15.00
□ CE12 Manny Fernandez (G), Kalamazoo	15.00
□ CE13 Radek Bonk, Las Vegas	10.00
□ CE14 Patrice Tardif, Peoria	4.00
□ CE15 Jeff Nelson, Portland-AHL	4.00
□ CE16 Jeff O'Neill, Guelph	15.00
□ CE17 Ed Jovanovski, Windsor	15.00
□ CE18 Jason Doig, Laval	4.00
□ CE19 Chris Marinucci, Denver	4.00
□ CE20 Manon Rhéaume (G), Las Vegas	65.00

PLATINUM PLAYERS

Insert Set (10 cards):	20.00
□ PL5 Promo Claude Lemieux	1.00
Insert	**PL**
□ PL1 Pavel Bure, Vanc.	6.00
□ PL2 Tony Granato, LosA.	2.00
□ PL3 Kevin Dineen, Phil.	2.00
□ PL4 Ron Hextall (G), Phil.	4.00
□ PL5 Claude Lemieux, NJer.	2.00
□ PL6 Mark Recchi	3.00
□ PL7 Benoît Hogue	2.00
□ PL8 Tim Cheveldae (G), Winn.	2.00
□ PL9 Darcy Wakaluk (G)	2.00
□ PL10 Todd Gill, Toro.	2.00

PLATINUM PROSPECTS

Insert Set (10 cards):	20.00
Player	**PR**
□ PR1 Jeff Nelson, Portland-AHL	2.00
□ PR2 Jim Carey (G), Portland-AHL	2.00
□ PR3 Ian Laperrière, Peoria	2.00
□ PR4 Chris Osgood (G), Adirondack	4.00
□ PR5 Todd Marchant, Cape Breton	2.00
□ PR6 Radek Bonk, Las Vegas	2.00
□ PR7 Chris Marinucci, Denver	2.00
□ PR8 Tommy Salo (G), Denver	3.00
□ PR9 Manny Fernandez (G), Kalamazoo	3.00
□ PR10 Jan Caloun, Kansas City	2.00

PREMIER DRAFT CHOICES

The Bryan Berard winner card could be redeemed for a Manon Rhéaume (G) autographed phonecard.

Insert Set (10 cards):	20.00
Player	**PD**
□ PD1 Bryan Berard, Detroit-OHL (WIN)	7.00
□ PD2 Wade Redden, Brandon	2.00
□ PD3 Steve Kelly, London	2.00
□ PD4 Petr Sykora, Detroit-IHL	3.00
□ PD5 Brad Church, Prince Albert	2.00
□ PD6 Daymond Langkow, Tri-City	2.00
□ PD7 Chad Kilger, Kingston	2.00
□ PD8 Terry Ryan, Tri-City	2.00
□ PD9 Jason Doig, Laval	2.00
□ PD10 Field Card (Brandon players)	2.00
Autograph	**Auto.**
□ Manon Rhéaume (G) ✍	60.00

1994 - 95 CLASSIC IMAGES FOUR SPORT

This 120-card set features only 25 hockey players. A 120-card regular set sells at $35.

The most expensive regular card is Manon Rhéaume (G) at $3-4. Regional stars sell at $0.35-1.25; commons start at 20¢. The most expensive gold card is Manon Rhéaume (G) at $8-10. Gold cards for regional stars sell at $0.75-4.00 (approx. 2-3 times regular card); commons start at 35¢.

Classic Images	Classic Images
□ 94 Ed Jovanovski	□ 95 Oleg Tverdovsky
□ 96 Radek Bonk	□ 97 Jason Bonsignore
□ 98 Jeff O'Neill	□ 99 Ryan Smyth
□ 100 Jamie Storr (G)	□ 101 Jason Wiemer
□ 102 N. Baumgartner	□ 103 Jeff Friesen
□ 104 Wade Belak	□ 105 Ethan Moreau
□ 106 A. Kharlamov	□ 107 Éric Fichaud (G)
□ 108 Wayne Primeau	□ 109 Brad Brown
□ 110 Chris Dingman	□ 111 Chris Wells
□ 112 Vadim Sharifjanov	□ 113 Dan Cloutier (G)
□ 114 Jason Allison	□ 115 Todd Marchant
□ 116 Brent Gretzky	□ 117 Petr Sykora
□ 118 M. Rhéaume (G)	

INSERTS

Cards with the prefix "CP" are part of the 20-card Classic Performers insert set. Cards with the prefix "E" are part of the five-card Clear Excitement insert set.

Classic Performers	CP
□ CP19 Ed Jovanovski	8.00
□ CP20 Éric Fichaud (G)	3.00
Clear Excitement	**E**
□ E5 Manon Rhéaume (G)	50.00

1994 - 95 DEL

The most expensive singles are Sergei Berezin at $3-5 and Jiri Dopita at $2-3. NHL stars sell at $1-2. Other singles sell between 30¢ and $1.00.

Complete Set (440 cards): 65.00

Player	Player
□ 1 International Hockey	□ 2 DEL 1994-95
□ 3 Season 1994-95	□ 4 TC: Augsburger
□ 5 Gunnar Leiborg	□ 6 Gary Prior
□ 7 Campbell	□ 8 Dieter Medicus
□ 9 Duanne Moeser	□ 10 Daniel Naud
□ 11 Andy Romer	□ 12 Thomas Groger
□ 13 Sven Zywitza	□ 14 Fritz Meyer
□ 15 Christian Curth	□ 16 Toni Krinner
□ 17 Patrik Pysz	□ 18 Heinrich Romer
□ 19 Ales Polcar	□ 20 Philip Kukuk
□ 21 Dietrich Adam	□ 22 Tim Schnobrich
□ 23 Tim Ferguson	□ 24 Robert Heidt
□ 25 Alfred Burkhard	□ 26 Charly Fliegauf
□ 27 Robert Paclik	□ 28 Stefan Mayer
□ 29 Reinhard Haider	□ 30 Dennis Schrapp
□ 31 TC: Eisbaren Berlin	□ 32 Walter Jaroslav
□ 33 Klaus Schroder	□ 34 Andre Dietsch
□ 35 Juri Stumpf	□ 36 Torsten Deutscher
□ 37 Frank Kannewurf	□ 38 Thomas Graul
□ 39 Sven Felski	□ 40 Moritz Schmidt
□ 41 Marco Swibenko	□ 42 Holger Mix
□ 43 Jiri Dopita	□ 44 Dirk Perschau
□ 45 Guido Hiller	□ 46 Daniel Held
□ 47 Richard Zemlicka	□ 48 Jan Schertz
□ 49 Mike losch	□ 50 Patrick Solf
□ 51 Rupert Meister	□ 52 TC: BSC Preussen
□ 53 Billy Flynn	□ 54 Tony Tanti
□ 55 Jochen Molling	□ 56 Andreas Schubert
□ 57 Stefan Steinecker	□ 58 Josef Lebner
□ 59 Tom O'Regan	□ 60 Gaetan Malo
□ 61 Michael Komma	□ 62 Marco Schinko
□ 63 Marco Rentzsch	□ 64 Georg Holzmann
□ 65 Mark Kosturik	□ 66 Jurgen Rumrich
□ 67 John Chabot	□ 68 Harald Windler
□ 69 Mark Teevens	□ 70 Klaus Merk (G)
□ 71 Stephen Sinner	□ 72 Mark Gronau
□ 73 Bruce Hardy	□ 74 Fabian Brannstrom
□ 75 Daniel Poudrier	□ 76 TC: Dusseldorfer EG
□ 77 Hans Zach	□ 78 Helmut DeRaaf
□ 79 Markus Kehle	□ 80 Christian Schmitz
□ 81 Lorenz Funk	□ 82 Chris Valentine
□ 83 Rafael Jedamzik	□ 84 Torsten Keinass
□ 85 Christopher Kreutzer	□ 86 Benoît Doucet
□ 87 Bernd Kuhnhauser	□ 88 A. Niederberger
□ 89 Rick Amann	□ 90 Thorsten Van Leyen
□ 91 Bruce Eakin	□ 92 Pierre Rioux
□ 93 Andreas Brockmann	□ 94 Uli Heimer
□ 95 Bernd Truntschka	□ 96 Wolfgang Kummer
□ 97 Carston Gossman	□ 98 Ernst Kopf
□ 99 Robert Sterflinger	□ 100 Kevin LaVallée
□ 101 Rainer Zerwesz	□ 102 TC: Frankfurt Lions
□ 103 Pjotr Vorobiev	□ 104 Peter Obresa
□ 105 Vladimir Quapp	□ 106 Florian Storf
□ 107 Alexander Wedl	□ 108 Olaf Scholz
□ 109 Ilya Vorobjev	□ 110 Ladislav Stompf
□ 111 Udo Dohler	□ 112 Alexander Wunsch
□ 113 Jiri Lala	□ 114 Andrej Jaufmann
□ 115 Thomas Muhlbauer	□ 116 Markus Kempf
□ 117 Igor Schultz	□ 118 Martin Schultz
□ 119 Michael Raubal	□ 120 Rudi Gorgenlander
□ 121 Jurgen Schaal	□ 122 Patrick Vozar
□ 123 Rochus Schneider	□ 124 Toni Raubal
□ 125 Stefan Koniger	□ 126 TC: EC Hannover
□ 127 Hartmut Nickel	□ 128 Joachim Lempio
□ 129 Torsten Hanusch	□ 130 Thomas Jungwirth
□ 131 David Reierson	□ 132 F. Bogelsack
□ 133 Thomas Werner	□ 134 Dirk Rohrbach
□ 135 Harald Kuhnke	□ 136 Florian Funk
□ 137 Mark Maroste	□ 138 Anton Maidl
□ 139 Rene Reuter	□ 140 Rene Ledock
□ 141 Marco Hebst	□ 142 Milos Vanik
□ 143 Gunther Preuss	□ 144 Troy Tumbach
□ 145 Marc Wittbrock	□ 146 Roger Mede
□ 147 Craig Topolinsky	□ 148 J. Schlickenriede
□ 149 Marcus Bleicher	□ 150 TC: EC Kassel
□ 151 Ross Yates	□ 152 Josef Kontny
□ 153 Milan Mokros	□ 154 Alexander Engel
□ 155 Greg Johnston	□ 156 Jedrzej Kasperczyk
□ 157 Dave Morrison	□ 158 Jaro Mucha
□ 159 Mike Millar	□ 160 Ireneusz Pacula
□ 161 Vitalij Grossmann	□ 162 Murray McIntosh
□ 163 Manfred Ahne	□ 164 Peter Kwasigroch
□ 165 Georg Guttler	□ 166 Falk Ozellis
□ 167 Mario Naster	□ 168 Sergej Wikulow
□ 169 Gerhard Hegen	□ 170 Brian Hannon
□ 171 Tino Boos	□ 172 TC: Kaufbeurer
□ 173 Peter Kathan	□ 174 Kenneth Karpuk
□ 175 Michael Olbrich	□ 176 Drahomir Kadlec
□ 177 C. Seeberger	□ 178 Elmar Boiger
□ 179 Otto Hascak	□ 180 Thorsten Rau
□ 181 Tomas Martinec	□ 182 Norbert Zabel
□ 183 Daniel Kunce	□ 184 Hans-Jorg Mayer
□ 185 Manfred Jorde	□ 186 Roland Timoschuk
□ 187 Jim Hoffmann	□ 188 Andreas Volland
□ 189 Rolf Hammer	□ 190 Manuel Hess
□ 191 Timo Gschwill	□ 192 Marc Pethke
□ 193 Axel Kammerer	□ 194 Jurgen Simon
□ 195 Patrick Lange	□ 196 Ronny Martin
□ 197 TC: Kolner EC	□ 198 Vladimir Vassiliev
□ 199 Bernd Haake	□ 200 Joseph Heiss (G)
□ 201 Jorg Mayr	□ 202 Thomas Brandl
□ 203 Stephan Mann	□ 204 Tony Reddo
□ 205 Mirco Ludemann	□ 206 Leo Stefan
□ 207 Andreas Pokorny	□ 208 Peter Draisaitl
□ 209 Ralf Dobrzynski	□ 210 Andreas Lupzig
□ 211 Karsten Mende	□ 212 Frank Hohenadl
□ 213 Marco Heinrichs	□ 214 Michael Rumrich
□ 215 Martin Ondrejka	□ 216 H. Hohenberger
□ 217 Thorsten Sendt	□ 218 Thorsten Koslowski
□ 219 Olaf Grundmann	□ 220 Franz Demmel
□ 221 Sergei Berezin	□ 222 TC: Krefelder EV
□ 223 Michael Zettel	□ 224 Frank Brunsing
□ 225 Karel Lang	□ 226 Markus Krawinkel
□ 227 Earl Spry	□ 228 Andre Grein
□ 229 Greg Evtushevski	□ 230 Herberts Vasiljevs
□ 231 Ken Petrash	□ 232 Greg Thomson
□ 233 Reemt Pyka	□ 234 Brad Bergen
□ 235 Chris Lindberg	□ 236 Markus Kranwinkel
□ 237 Martin Gebel	□ 238 François Sills
□ 239 Klaus Micheller	□ 240 Peter Ihnacak
□ 241 Marek Strebnicki	□ 242 Johnny Walker
□ 243 Gunter Oswald	□ 244 James Hanlon
□ 245 Rene Bielke	□ 246 TC: EV Landshut
□ 247 Bernhard Johnston	□ 248 Mark Stuckey
□ 249 Michael Bresagk	□ 250 Bernd Wagner
□ 251 Eduard Uvria	□ 252 Mike Smazal
□ 253 Jacek Plachta	□ 254 Georg Franz
□ 255 Stephan Retzer	□ 256 Henri Macoux
□ 257 Andreas Loth	□ 258 Mike Bullard
□ 259 Markus Berwanger	□ 260 Petr Briza (G)
□ 261 Wally Schreiber	□ 262 Peter Gulda
□ 263 Ralf Hantschke	□ 264 Steve McNeill
□ 265 Christian Kunast	□ 266 Jorg Hendrick
□ 267 Helmut Steiger	□ 268 Udo Kiessling
□ 269 Mike Lay	□ 270 TC: Adler Mannheim
□ 271 Lance Nethery	□ 272 Marcus Kuhl
□ 273 Joachim Appel	□ 274 Harold Kries
□ 275 Mike Heidt	□ 276 Mario Gehrig
□ 277 Pavel Gross	□ 278 Steffen Michel
□ 279 Daniel Korber	□ 280 Robert Cimetta
□ 281 Dale Krentz	□ 282 Jochen Hecht
□ 283 Till Feser	□ 284 Lars Brüggemann
□ 285 Toni Plattner	□ 286 Alexander Schuster
□ 287 Dieter Willmann	□ 288 Markus Flemming
□ 289 Rick Goldmann	□ 290 Damian Adamus
□ 291 Frederik Ledlin	□ 292 David Musial
□ 293 Michael Gabler	□ 294 Sven Valenti
□ 295 TC: Munchen	□ 296 Robert Murdoch
□ 297 Alexander Genze	□ 298 Greg Muller
□ 299 Mike Schmidt	□ 300 Zdenek Travnicek
□ 301 Christian Lukes	□ 302 Gordon Sherven
□ 303 Anthony Vogel	□ 304 Michael Hreus
□ 305 Dale Derkatch	□ 306 Sergei Schendelew
□ 307 Christian Brittig	□ 308 Harald Waibel
□ 309 Rainer Lutz	□ 310 Ewald Steiger
□ 311 Didi Hegen	□ 312 Ralf Reisinger
□ 313 Henrik Holscher	□ 314 Karl Friesen
□ 315 Christian Frutel	□ 316 Tobias Abstreiter
□ 317 C. Sandner	□ 318 Harald Birk
□ 319 Chris Strausse	□ 320 TC: Nurnberg
□ 321 Josef Golonka	□ 322 Christian Gerum
□ 323 Paul Geddes	□ 324 Ian Young
□ 325 Stefan Steinbock	□ 326 Doug Irwin
□ 327 Christian Flugge	□ 328 Klaus Birk
□ 329 Jurgen Lechl	□ 330 Thomas Popiesch
□ 331 Miroslav Maly	□ 332 Stephan Eder
□ 333 Arno Brux	□ 334 Jiri Dolezal
□ 335 R. Vorderbruggen	□ 336 Thomas Sterflinger
□ 337 B. Engelbrecht	□ 338 Michael Weinfürter
□ 339 Sepp Wassermann	□ 340 Stephan Bauer
□ 341 Otto Sykora	□ 342 TC: Lowen
□ 343 Bill Lochead	□ 344 Pavel Mann
□ 345 Christian Kohmann	□ 346 Sven Prusa
□ 347 Otto Keresztes	□ 348 Frank Kovacs
□ 349 Jiri Smicek	□ 350 Richard Brodnicke
□ 351 Andrej Fuchs	□ 352 Oliver Kasper
□ 353 Michael Kratz	□ 354 Klaus Striemitzer
□ 355 Oliver Schwartz	□ 356 Boris Fuchs
□ 357 Christian Althoff	□ 358 W. Novosjolov
□ 359 Thomas Imdahl	□ 360 Helmut Elters
□ 361 Andrej Hanisz	□ 362 Peter Lutter
□ 363 Martem Janov	□ 364 Mark Bassen
□ 365 Udo Schmid	□ 366 Mark Bassen
□ 367 TC: Rosenheim	□ 368 Ernst Hofner
□ 369 Ludek Bukac	□ 370 Markus Wieland
□ 371 Andreas Schneider	□ 372 Raphael Kruger
□ 373 Michael Tattner	□ 374 Richard Boehm
□ 375 Robert Hock	□ 376 Joachim Reil
□ 377 Radek Toupal	□ 378 Martin Reichel
□ 379 Ron Fischer	□ 380 Raimund Hilger
□ 381 Petr Hrbek	□ 382 Oliver Hausler
□ 383 C. Gegenfurth	□ 384 Marc Seliger (G)
□ 385 Venci Sebek	□ 386 Florian Keller
□ 387 Heinrich Schiffl	□ 388 Michael Pohl
□ 389 TC: Fuchse	□ 390 Jiri Kochta
□ 391 Boris Capla	□ 392 Matthias Kliemann
□ 393 Josef Rednicek	□ 394 Branjo Heisig
□ 395 Jens Schwabe	□ 396 Frank Peschke
□ 397 Thomas Schubert	□ 398 Torsten Eisebitt
□ 399 Marcel Lichnovsky	□ 400 Jari Gronstrand
□ 401 Thomas Knobloch	□ 402 Falk Herzig
□ 403 Thomas Wagner	□ 404 Jan Tabor
□ 405 Sebastian Klenner	□ 406 Peter Hofmann
□ 407 Terry Cambell	□ 408 Antonio Fonso
□ 409 Thomas Bresagk	□ 410 Peter Franke
□ 411 Andreas Ott	□ 412 Michael Flemming
□ 413 Janusz Janikowski	□ 414 TC: Schwenningen
□ 415 Miroslav Berek	□ 416 Bob Burns
□ 417 Thomas Gaus	□ 418 Richard Trojan
□ 419 Ilmar Toman	□ 420 Alan Young
□ 421 Michael Pastika	□ 422 Thomas Schadler
□ 423 Andrei Kovalev	□ 424 Alexander Horn
□ 425 Petr Kopta	□ 426 Robert Brezina
□ 427 Wayne Hynes	□ 428 Frantisek Frosch
□ 429 Carsten Solbach	□ 430 George Fritz
□ 431 Mike Bader	□ 432 Thomas Deiter

☐ 433 Daniel Nowak	☐ 434 Peter Heinold
☐ 435 Matthias Hoppe	☐ 436 Grant Martin
☐ 437 Roger Bruns	☐ 438 Andreas Renz
☐ 439 Karsten Schulz	☐ 440 Alfie Turcotte

1994 - 95 DONRUSS

Imprint: © 1994 DONRUSS, INC.
Complete Set (330 cards): 40.00
Common Player: .20

Player	Donruss
☐ 1 Steve Yzerman, Detr.	1.00
☐ 2 Paul Ysebaert, Chic.	.20
☐ 3 Doug Weight, Edmo.	.20
☐ 4 Trevor Kidd (G), Calg.	.20
☐ 5 Mario Lemieux, Pitt.	1.50
☐ 6 Andrei Kovalenko, Québ.	.20
☐ 7 Arturs Irbe (G), SanJ.	.20
☐ 8 Doug Gilmour, Toro.	.20
☐ 9 Mark Messier, NYRa.	.50
☐ 10 Milos Holan, Phil.	.20
☐ 11 Kevin Miller, SLou.	.20
☐ 12 Félix Potvin (G), Toro.	.20
☐ 13 Josef Beránek, Phil.	.20
☐ 14 Mikael Andersson, Tamp.	.20
☐ 15 Stéphane Matteau, NYRa.	.20
☐ **16 Todd Simon, Buff. RC**	**.50**
☐ 17 Darcy Wakaluk (G), Dall.	.20
☐ 18 Kelly Buchberger, Edmo.	.20
☐ 19 Pavel Bure, Vanc.	.20
☐ 20 Dave Lowry, Flor.	.20
☐ 21 Bryan Smolinski, Bost.	.20
☐ 22 Kirk McLean (G), Vanc.	.20
☐ 23 Pierre Turgeon, NYIs.	.20
☐ 24 Martin Brodeur (G), NJer.	.50
☐ 25 Jason Arnott, Edmo.	.20
☐ 26 Steve Dubinsky, Chic.	.20
☐ 27 Larry Murphy, Pitt.	.20
☐ 28 Craig Janney, SLou.	.20
☐ 29 Patrik Carnbäck, Anah.	.20
☐ 30 Derek King, NYIs.	.20
☐ 31 Peter Bondra, Wash.	.20
☐ 32 Jason Bowen, Phil.	.20
☐ 33 Maxim Bets, Anah.	.20
☐ 34 Matt Martin, Toro.	.20
☐ 35 Jeff Hackett (G), Chic.	.20
☐ 36 Kevin Dineen, Phil.	.20
☐ 37 Trent Klatt, Dall.	.20
☐ 38 Joe Murphy, Chic.	.20
☐ 39 Sandy McCarthy, Calg.	.20
☐ 40 Brian Bradley, Tamp.	.20
☐ 41 Scott Lachance, NYIs.	.20
☐ 42 Scott Mellanby, Flor.	.20
☐ 43 Adam Graves, NYRa.	.20
☐ 44 Dale Hawerchuk, Buff.	.20
☐ 45 Owen Nolan, Québ.	.20
☐ 46 Keith Primeau, Detr.	.20
☐ 47 Jim Dowd, NJer.	.20
☐ **48 Dan Plante, NYIs. RC**	**.50**
☐ 49 Rick Tabaracci (G), Wash.	.20
☐ 50 Geoff Courtnall, Vanc.	.20
☐ 51 Markus Näslund, Pitt.	.50
☐ 52 Kelly Miller, Wash.	.20
☐ 53 Kirk Maltby, Edmo.	.20
☐ 54 Paul Coffey, Detr.	.20
☐ 55 Gord Murphy, Flor.	.20
☐ 56 Joe Nieuwendyk, Calg.	.20
☐ 57 Ulf Dahlén, SanJ.	.20
☐ 58 Dmitri Mironov, Toro.	.20
☐ 59 Kevin Smyth, Hart.	.20
☐ 60 Tie Domi, Winn.	.20
☐ 61 Oleg Petrov, Mont.	.20
☐ 62 Bill Guerin, NJer.	.20
☐ 63 Alexei Yashin, Otta.	.20
☐ 64 Joe Sacco, Anah.	.20
☐ **65 Aris Brimanis, Phil. RC**	**.50**
☐ 66 Randy Burridge, Wash.	.20
☐ 67 Neal Broten, Dall.	.20
☐ 68 Raymond Bourque, Bost.	.50
☐ 69 Ron Tugnutt (G), Mont.	.20
☐ 70 Darryl Sydor, LosA.	.20
☐ 71 Jocelyn Thibault (G), Québ.	.20
☐ 72 Shawn Chambers, Tamp.	.20
☐ 73 Alexei Zhamnov, Winn.	.20
☐ 74 Michael Nylander, Calg.	.20
☐ 75 Travis Green, NYIs.	.20
☐ 76 Brad May, Buff.	.20
☐ 77 Geoff Sanderson, Hart.	.20
☐ 78 Derek Plante, Buff.	.20
☐ 79 Stéphane J.J. Richer, NJer.	.20
☐ 80 Rod Brind'Amour, Phil.	.20
☐ 81 Guy Hebert (G), Anah.	.20
☐ 82 Claude Lemieux, NJer.	.20
☐ 83 Pat Falloon, SanJ.	.20
☐ 84 Alexei Kudashov, Toro.	.20
☐ 85 Andrei Lomakin, Flor.	.20
☐ 86 Dino Ciccarelli, Detr.	.20
☐ 87 John Tucker, Tamp.	.20
☐ 88 Jamie McLennan (G), NYIs.	.20
☐ 89 Peter Taglianetti, Pitt.	.20
☐ 90 Bobby Holik, NJer.	.20
☐ 91 Sergei Krivokrasov, Chic.	.20
☐ 92 Alexander Mogilny, Buff.	.20
☐ 93 Jari Kurri, LosA.	.50
☐ 94 Dominik Hasek (G), Buff.	.50
☐ 95 Shawn McEachern, Pitt.	.20
☐ 96 Bob Corkum, Anah.	.20
☐ 97 Dmitri Filimonov, Otta.	.20
☐ 98 John LeClair, Mont.	.20
☐ 99 Theoren Fleury, Calg.	.20
☐ 100 Daren Puppa (G), Tamp.	.20
☐ 101 Greg A. Adams, Vanc.	.20
☐ 102 Joel Otto, Calg.	.20
☐ 103 Sergei* Makarov, SanJ.	.20
☐ 104 Mike Ricci, Québ.	.20
☐ 105 Sylvain Turgeon, Otta.	.20
☐ 106 Igor Larionov, SanJ.	.20
☐ 107 Tony Amonte, Chic.	.20
☐ 108 Andy Moog (G), Dall.	.20
☐ 109 Jeff R. Brown, Vanc.	.20
☐ 110 Checklist	.20
☐ 111 Mike Gartner, Toro.	.20
☐ 112 Craig Simpson, Buff.	.20
☐ 113 Rob Niedermayer, Flor.	.20
☐ 114 Robert Kron, Hart.	.20
☐ **115 Jason York, Detr. RC**	**.50**
☐ 116 Valeri Kamensky, Québ.	.20
☐ 117 Ray Whitney, SanJ.	.20
☐ 118 Chris Chelios, Chic.	.20
☐ 119 Scott Levins, Otta.	.20
☐ 120 Sandis Ozolinsh, SanJ.	.20
☐ 121 Mark Recchi, Phil.	.20
☐ 122 Ron Francis, Pitt.	.20
☐ 123 Dean McAmmond, Edmo.	.20
☐ 124 Terry Yake, Anah.	.20
☐ 125 Sergei Nemchinov, NYRa.	.20
☐ 126 Vitali Prokhorov, SLou.	.20
☐ 127 Wayne Gretzky, LosA.	2.00
☐ 128 Roman Hamrlik, Tamp.	.20
☐ 129 Jarkko Varvio, Dall.	.20
☐ 130 Brian Skrudland, Flor.	.20
☐ 131 Murray Craven, Vanc.	.20
☐ 132 Jeff Norton, SanJ.	.20
☐ 133 Pavol Demitra, Otta.	.20
☐ 134 Mike Keane, Mont.	.20
☐ 135 Paul Cavallini, Dall.	.20
☐ 136 Richard Smehlik, Buff.	.20
☐ 137 Eric Lindros, Phil.	.50
☐ **138 Mariusz Czerkawski, Bost. RC**	**1.00**
☐ 139 Darrin Shannon, Winn.	.20
☐ 140 Brian Noonan, NYRa.	.20
☐ 141 Joe Sakic, Québ.	.50
☐ 142 Steve Thomas, NYIs.	.20
☐ 143 Gary Roberts, Calg.	.20
☐ 144 Patrick Poulin, Chic.	.20
☐ 145 Tony Granato, LosA.	.20
☐ **146 Donald Brashear, Mont. RC**	**1.00**
☐ 147 Ron Hextall (G), NYIs.	.20
☐ 148 Corey Millen, NJer.	.20
☐ 149 Dale Hunter, Wash.	.20
☐ 150 Greg Johnson, Detr.	.20
☐ 151 John MacLean, NJer.	.20
☐ 152 Brian Leetch, NYRa.	.20
☐ 153 Sylvain Côté, Wash.	.20
☐ 154 Thomas Steen, Winn.	.20
☐ 155 Ted Donato, Bost.	.20
☐ 156 Nathan Lafayette, Vanc.	.20
☐ 157 Kelly Chase, SLou.	.20
☐ 158 Sean Burke (G), Hart.	.20
☐ 159 Jaromir Jagr, Pitt.	.50
☐ 160 Checklist	.20
☐ 161 Scott Niedermayer, NJer.	.20
☐ 162 Ray Ferraro, NYIs.	.20
☐ 163 Todd Elik, SanJ.	.20
☐ 164 Dave Gagner, Dall.	.20
☐ 165 Mike Richter (G), NYRa.	.20
☐ 166 Garry Galley, Phil.	.20
☐ 167 Russ Courtnall, Dall.	.20
☐ 168 Marty McSorley, LosA.	.20
☐ 169 Robert Reichel, Calg.	.20
☐ 170 Mike Rathje, SanJ.	.20
☐ 171 Bill Ranford (G), Edmo.	.20
☐ 172 Danton Cole, Tamp.	.20
☐ 173 Sergei Fedorov, Detr.	.50
☐ 174 Brendan Shanahan, SLou.	.50
☐ **175 Byron Dafoe (G), Wash. RC**	**2.00**
☐ 176 John Vanbiesbrouck (G), Flor.	.20
☐ 177 Éric Desjardins, Mont.	.20
☐ 178 Andrew Cassels, Hart.	.20
☐ **179 John Gruden, Bost. RC**	**.50**
☐ 180 Vyacheslav Kozlov, Detr.	.20
☐ 181 Trevor Linden, Vanc.	.20
☐ 182 Kris Draper, Detr.	.20
☐ 183 J. Steve Smith, Chic.	.20
☐ 184 André Faust, Phil.	.20
☐ 185 James Patrick, Calg.	.20
☐ 186 Ted Drury, Hart.	.20
☐ 187 Daniel Laperrière, SLou.	.20
☐ 188 Benoît Hogue, NYIs.	.20
☐ 189 Chris Gratton, Tamp.	.20
☐ 190 Jyrki Lumme, Vanc.	.20
☐ 191 Peter Stastny, SLou.	.20
☐ 192 Keith Tkachuk, Winn.	.20
☐ 193 Mike Modano, Dall.	.50
☐ 194 Nicklas Lidström, Detr.	.20
☐ 195 Pierre Sévigny, Mont.	.20
☐ 196 Scott Pearson, Edmo.	.20
☐ 197 Jaroslav Modry, NJer.	.20
☐ 198 Garry Valk, Anah.	.20
☐ 199 Kevin Hatcher, Wash.	.20
☐ **200 Denis Tsygurov, Buff. RC**	**.50**
☐ 201 Paul Laus, Flor.	.20
☐ 202 Alexander Godynyuk, Hart.	.20
☐ 203 Brian Bellows, Mont.	.20
☐ 204 Michal Sykora, SanJ.	.20
☐ 205 Al Iafrate, Bost.	.20
☐ 206 Mark Tinordi, Dall.	.20
☐ 207 Kelly Hrudey (G), LosA.	.20
☐ 208 Tom Barrasso (G), Pitt.	.20
☐ 209 Craig Billington (G), Otta.	.20
☐ 210 Teemu Selänne, Winn.	.20
☐ 211 Alexandre Daigle, Otta.	.20
☐ 212 Grant Fuhr (G), Buff.	.20
☐ 213 Doug Brown, Pitt.	.20
☐ 214 Tim Sweeney, Anah.	.20
☐ 215 Chris Pronger, Hart.	.20
☐ 216 Alexei Gusarov, Québ.	.20
☐ 217 Gary Suter, Chic.	.20
☐ 218 Boris Mironov, Edmo.	.20
☐ 219 Sergei Zubov, NYRa.	.20
☐ 220 Checklist	.20
☐ 221 Shayne Corson, Edmo.	.20
☐ 222 Jeremy Roenick, Chic.	.20
☐ 223 John Druce, LosA.	.20
☐ 224 Martin Straka, Pitt.	.20
☐ 225 Stéphane Fiset (G), Québ.	.20
☐ 226 Vincent Damphousse, Mont.	.20
☐ 227 Bob Kudelski, Flor.	.20
☐ 228 German Titov, Calg.	.20
☐ 229 Kevin Stevens, Pitt.	.20
☐ 230 Dave Ellett, Toro.	.20
☐ 231 Steve Larmer, NYRa.	.20
☐ 232 Glen Wesley, Bost.	.20
☐ 233 Mathieu Schneider, Mont.	.20
☐ 234 Stéphan Lebeau, Anah.	.20
☐ 235 Mark Fitzpatrick (G), Flor.	.20
☐ 236 Mikael Renberg, Phil.	.20
☐ 237 Darren McCarty, Detr.	.20
☐ 238 Todd Nelson, Wash.	.20
☐ 239 Igor Korolev, SLou.	.20
☐ 240 Warren Rychel, LosA.	.20
☐ 241 Gino Odjick, Vanc.	.20
☐ 242 Dave Manson, Winn.	.20
☐ 243 Calle Johansson, Wash.	.20
☐ 244 Andrei Trefilov (G), Calg.	.20
☐ 245 Jason Dawe, Buff.	.20
☐ 246 Glen Murray, Bost.	.20
☐ 247 Jeff Shantz, Chic.	.20
☐ 248 Zarley Zalapski, Calg.	.20
☐ 249 Petr Klima, Tamp.	.20
☐ 250 Patrice Brisebois, Mont.	.20
☐ 251 Chris Osgood (G), Detr.	.20
☐ 252 Darius Kasparaitis, NYIs.	.20
☐ 253 Chris Joseph (G), Tamp.	.20
☐ 254 Glenn Anderson, NYRa.	.20
☐ 255 Kirk Muller, Mont.	.20
☐ 256 Jason Smith, NJer.	.20
☐ 257 Bob Bassen, Québ.	.20
☐ 258 Joé Juneau, Wash.	.20
☐ 259 Igor Kravchuk, Edmo.	.20
☐ 260 John Lilley, Anah.	.20
☐ 261 Philippe Bozon, SLou.	.20
☐ 262 Scott Stevens, NJer.	.20
☐ 263 Dominic Roussel (G), Phil.	.20
☐ 264 Dmitri Khristich, Wash.	.20
☐ 265 Ed Patterson, Pitt.	.20
☐ 266 Michael Peca, Vanc.	.20
☐ 267 Teppo Numminen, Winn.	.20
☐ 268 Alex Kovalev, NYRa.	.20
☐ 269 Cam Neely, Bost.	.50
☐ 270 Iain Fraser, Québ.	.20
☐ 271 Tomas Sandström, Pitt.	.20
☐ 272 Lyle Odelein, Mont.	.20
☐ 273 Norm Maciver, Otta.	.20
☐ 274 Zdeno Cíger, Edmo.	.20
☐ 275 Ed Belfour (G), Chic.	.50
☐ 276 Brian Savage, Mont.	.20
☐ 277 Vlastimil Kroupa, SanJ.	.20
☐ 278 Cliff Ronning, Vanc.	.20
☐ 279 Alexei Zhitnik, LosA.	.20
☐ 280 Jim Storm, Hart.	.20
☐ 281 Don Sweeney, Bost.	.20
☐ 282 Mike Donnelly, LosA.	.20
☐ 283 Glenn Healy (G), NYRa.	.20
☐ 284 Denis Savard, Tamp.	.20
☐ 285 Chris Terreri (G), NJer.	.20
☐ 286 Darren Turcotte, Hart.	.20
☐ 287 Curtis Joseph (G), SLou.	.50
☐ 288 Ken Baumgartner, Toro.	.20
☐ 289 Matthew Barnaby, Buff.	.20
☐ 290 Brent Sutter, Chic.	.20
☐ 291 Valeri Zelepukin, NJer.	.20
☐ 292 Michal Pivonka, Wash.	.20
☐ 293 Ray Sheppard, Detr.	.20
☐ 294 Jiri Slegr, Vanc.	.20
☐ 295 Vesa Viitakoski, Calg.	.20
☐ 296 Ulf Samuelsson, Pitt.	.20
☐ 297 Nelson Emerson, Winn.	.20
☐ 298 John Slaney, Wash.	.20
☐ 299 Pat Verbeek, Hart.	.20
☐ 300 Pat LaFontaine, Buff.	.20
☐ 301 Johan Garpenlöv, SanJ.	.20
☐ 302 Eric Weinrich, Chic.	.20
☐ 303 Richard Matvichuk, Dall.	.20
☐ 304 Steve Duchesne, SLou.	.20
☐ 305 Donald Audette, Buff.	.20
☐ 306 Stu Barnes, Flor.	.20
☐ 307 Vladimir Malakhov, NYIs.	.20
☐ 308 Dmitry Yushkevich, Phil.	.20
☐ 309 David Sacco, Toro.	.20
☐ 310 Scott A. Young, Québ.	.20
☐ 311 Marty McInnis, NYIs.	.20
☐ 312 Grant Ledyard, Dall.	.20
☐ 313 Peter Popovic, Mont.	.20
☐ 314 Mikhail Shtalenkov (G), Anah.	.20
☐ 315 Dave McLlwain, Otta.	.20
☐ 316 Cam Stewart, Bost.	.20
☐ 317 Derian Hatcher, Dall.	.20
☐ 318 Pat Peake, Wash.	.20
☐ 319 Wes Walz, Calg.	.20
☐ 320 Fred Brathwaite, Edmo.	.20
☐ 321 Jesse Bélanger, Flor.	.20
☐ 322 Jozef Stumpel, Bost.	.20
☐ 323 Dave Andreychuk, Toro.	.20
☐ 324 Yuri Khmylev, Buff.	.20
☐ 325 Tim Cheveldae (G), Winn.	.20
☐ 326 Anatoli Semenov, Anah.	.20
☐ 327 Alexander Karpovtsev, NYRa.	.20
☐ 328 Patrick Roy (G), Mont.	1.50
☐ 329 Troy Mallette, Otta.	.20
☐ 330 Checklist	.20

DOMINATORS

Insert Set (8 cards): 40.00

Insert (1:36)	Dom.
☐ 1 M. Lemieux / E. Lindros / M. Messier	10.00
☐ 2 R. Bourque / B. Leetch / S. Stevens	4.00
☐ 3 D. Hasek (G) / P. Roy / J. Vanbiesbrouck (G)	8.00
☐ 4 J. Jagr / C. Neely / M. Renberg	4.00
☐ 5 S. Fedorov / W. Gretzky / J. Roenick	12.00
☐ 6 C. Chelios / P. Coffey / A. MacInnis	3.00
☐ 7 E. Belfour (G) / A. Irbe (G) / F. Potvin	4.00
☐ 8 P. Bure / Br. Hull / T. Selänne	4.00

ELITE SERIES

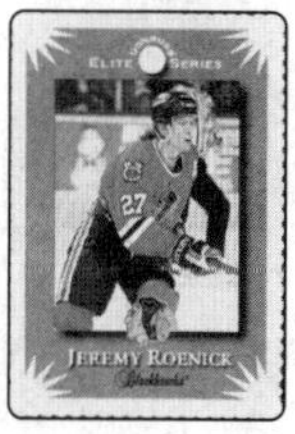

Insert Set (10 cards): 155.00

Insert (#/10,000)	ES
☐ 1 Jason Arnott, Edmo.	8.00
☐ 2 Martin Brodeur (G), NJer.	20.00
☐ 3 Pavel Bure, Vanc.	10.00
☐ 4 Sergei Fedorov, Detr.	10.00
☐ 5 Wayne Gretzky, LosA.	50.00
☐ 6 Mario Lemieux, Pitt.	30.00
☐ 7 Eric Lindros, Phil.	10.00
☐ 8 Félix Potvin (G), Toro.	8.00
☐ 9 Jeremy Roenick, Chic.	10.00
☐ 10 Patrick Roy (G), Mont.	30.00

ICE MASTERS

Insert Set (10 cards): 25.00

Insert (1:18)	IM
☐ 1 Ed Belfour (G), Chic.	2.00
☐ 2 Sergei Fedorov, Detr.	2.00
☐ 3 Doug Gilmour, Toro.	2.00
☐ 4 Wayne Gretzky, LosA.	10.00
☐ 5 Mario Lemieux, Pitt.	6.00
☐ 6 Eric Lindros, Phil.	2.00
☐ 7 Mark Messier, NYRa.	2.00
☐ 8 Mike Modano, Dall.	2.00
☐ 9 Luc Robitaille, Pitt.	2.00
☐ 10 John Vanbiesbrouck (G), Flor.	2.00

MASKED MARVELS

Insert Set (10 cards): 30.00

Insert (1:18)	MM
☐ 1 Ed Belfour (G), Chic.	4.00
☐ 2 Martin Brodeur (G), NJer.	6.00
☐ 3 Dominik Hasek (G), Buff.	4.00
☐ 4 Arturs Irbe (G), SanJ.	1.00
☐ 5 Curtis Joseph (G), SLou.	4.00
☐ 6 Kirk McLean (G), Vanc.	1.00
☐ 7 Félix Potvin (G), Toro.	2.00
☐ 8 Mike Richter (G), NYRa.	2.00
☐ 9 Patrick Roy (G), Mont.	12.00
☐ 10 John Vanbiesbrouck (G), Flor.	2.00

1994 - 95 FLAIR

Imprint: © 1994 FLEER CORP.
Complete Set (225 cards): 40.00
Common Player: .25

Player	Flair
☐ 1 Bob Corkum, Anah.	.25
☐ 2 Bobby Dollas, Anah.	.25
☐ 3 Guy Hebert (G), Anah.	.25
☐ 4 Paul Kariya, Anah.	2.50
☐ 5 Anatoli Semenov, Anah.	.25
☐ 6 Tim Sweeney, Anah.	.25
☐ 7 Garry Valk, Anah.	.25
☐ 8 Raymond Bourque, Bost.	1.50
☐ **9 Mariusz Czerkawski, Bost. RC**	**2.00**
☐ 10 Al Iafrate, Bost.	.25
☐ 11 Cam Neely, Bost.	1.00
☐ 12 Adam Oates, Bost.	.50
☐ 13 Vincent Riendeau (G), Bost.	.25
☐ 14 Don Sweeney, Bost.	.25
☐ 15 Donald Audette, Buff.	.50
☐ 16 Doug Bodger, Buff.	.25
☐ 17 Dominik Hasek (G), Buff.	1.00
☐ 18 Dale Hawerchuk, Buff.	.50
☐ 19 Pat LaFontaine, Buff.	.50
☐ 20 Alexander Mogilny, Buff.	.50
☐ 21 Craig Muni, Buff.	.25
☐ 22 Richard Smehlik, Buff.	.25
☐ **23 Denis Tsygurov, Buff. RC**	**1.00**
☐ 24 Theoren Fleury, Calg.	.50
☐ 25 Trevor Kidd (G), Calg.	.25
☐ 26 James Patrick, Calg.	.25
☐ 27 Robert Reichel, Calg.	.25

Player	NRMT-MT
28 Gary Roberts, Calg.	.50
29 German Titov, Calg.	.25
30 Zarley Zalapski, Calg.	.25
31 Ed Belfour (G), Chic.	1.00
32 Chris Chelios, Chic.	.50
33 Dirk Graham, Chic.	.25
34 Joe Murphy, Chic.	.25
35 Bernie Nicholls, Chic.	.25
36 Jeremy Roenick, Chic.	1.00
37 J. Steve Smith, Chic.	.25
38 Gary Suter, Chic.	.25
39 Neal Broten, Dall.	.25
40 Russ Courtnall, Dall.	.25
41 Todd Harvey, Dall.	.25
42 Grant Ledyard, Dall.	.25
43 Mike Modano, Dall.	1.00
44 Andy Moog (G), Dall.	.50
45 Mark Tinordi, Dall.	.25
46 Dino Ciccarelli, Detr.	.25
47 Paul Coffey, Detr.	.50
48 Sergei Fedorov, Detr.	1.00
49 Vladimir Konstantinov, Detr.	.25
50 Vyacheslav Kozlov, Detr.	.25
51 Keith Primeau, Detr.	.50
52 Ray Sheppard, Detr.	.25
53 Mike Vernon (G), Detr.	.50
54 Jason York, Detr. RC	**1.50**
55 Steve Yzerman, Detr.	3.00
56 Jason Arnott, Edmo.	.50
57 Shayne Corson, Edmo.	.25
58 Igor Kravchuk, Edmo.	.25
59 Dean McAmmond, Edmo.	.25
60 David Oliver, Edmo. RC	**1.00**
61 Bill Ranford (G), Edmo.	.50
62 Doug Weight, Edmo.	.50
63 Jesse Bélanger, Flor.	.25
64 Bob Kudelski, Flor.	.25
65 Scott Mellanby, Flor.	.25
66 Gord Murphy, Flor.	.25
67 Rob Niedermayer, Flor.	.25
68 Brian Skrudland, Flor.	.25
69 John Vanbiesbrouck (G), Flor.	.50
70 Sean Burke (G), Hart.	.50
71 Andrew Cassels, Hart.	.25
72 Alexander Godynyuk, Hart.	.25
73 Chris Pronger, Hart.	.50
74 Geoff Sanderson, Hart.	.25
75 Darren Turcotte, Hart.	.25
76 Pat Verbeek, Hart.	.25
77 Rob Blake, LosA.	.50
78 Mike Donnelly, LosA.	.25
79 Wayne Gretzky, LosA.	5.00
80 Kelly Hrudey (G), LosA.	.50
81 Jari Kurri, LosA.	1.00
82 Marty McSorley, LosA.	.25
83 Rick Tocchet, LosA.	.25
84 Brian Bellows, Mont.	.25
85 Patrice Brisebois, Mont.	.25
86 Valeri Bure, Mont.	.50
87 Vincent Damphousse, Mont.	.50
88 Éric Desjardins, Mont.	.25
89 Kirk Muller, Mont.	.25
90 Oleg Petrov, Mont.	.25
91 Patrick Roy (G), Mont.	3.50
92 Martin Brodeur (G), NJer.	2.00
93 David Emma, NJer.	.25
94 Bill Guerin, NJer.	.50
95 John MacLean, NJer.	.25
96 Scott Niedermayer, NJer.	.25
97 Stéphane J.J. Richer, NJer.	.25
98 Brian Rolston, NJer.	.50
99 Alexander Semak, NJer.	.25
100 Scott Stevens, NJer.	.50
101 Valeri Zelepukin, NJer.	.25
102 Patrick Flatley, NYIs.	.25
103 Derek King, NYIs.	.25
104 Brett Lindros, NYIs.	.50
105 Vladimir Malakhov, NYIs.	.25
106 Marty McInnis, NYIs.	.25
107 Jamie McLennan (G), NYIs.	.25
108 Steve Thomas, NYIs.	.25
109 Pierre Turgeon, NYIs.	.50
110 Jeff Beukeboom, NYRa.	.25
111 Adam Graves, NYRa.	.50
112 Alex Kovalev, NYRa.	.50
113 Steve Larmer, NYRa.	.50
114 Brian Leetch, NYRa.	.50
115 Mark Messier, NYRa.	1.00
116 Sergei Nemchinov, NYRa.	.25
117 Mike Richter (G), NYRa.	.50
118 Sergei Zubov, NYRa.	.25
119 Craig Billington (G), Otta.	.25
120 Alexandre Daigle, Otta.	.25
121 Sean Hill, Otta.	.25
122 Norm Maciver, Otta.	.25
123 Dave McLlwain, Otta.	.25
124 Alexei Yashin, Otta.	.50
125 Vladislav Boulin, Phil. RC	**1.00**
126 Rod Brind'Amour, Phil.	.25
127 Ron Hextall (G), Phil.	.50
128 Patrik Juhlin, Phil. RC	**1.00**
129 Eric Lindros, Phil.	1.00
130 Mark Recchi, Phil.	.50
131 Mikael Renberg, Phil.	.25
132 Chris Therien, Phil.	.25
133 Tom Barrasso (G), Pitt.	.50
134 Ron Francis, Pitt.	.50
135 Mario Lemieux, Pitt.	3.50
136 Shawn McEachern, Pitt.	.25
137 Larry Murphy, Pitt.	.25
138 Luc Robitaille, Pitt.	1.00
139 Ulf Samuelsson, Pitt.	.25
140 Kevin Stevens, Pitt.	.25
141 Martin Straka, Pitt.	.25
142 Wendel Clark, Québ.	1.00
143 René Corbet, Québ.	.25
144 Adam Deadmarsh, Québ.	.50
145 Stéphane Fiset (G), Québ.	.25
146 Peter Forsberg, Québ.	1.50
147 Valeri Kamensky, Québ.	.25
148 Janne Laukkanen, Québ.	.25
149 Sylvain Lefebvre, Québ.	.25
150 Mike Ricci, Québ.	.25
151 Joe Sakic, Québ.	2.00
152 Steve Duchesne, SLou.	.25
153 Brett Hull, SLou.	1.00
154 Craig Janney, SLou.	.25
155 Craig Johnson, SLou.	.25
156 Curtis Joseph (G), SLou.	1.00
157 Al MacInnis, SLou.	.50
158 Brendan Shanahan, SLou.	1.00
159 Peter Stastny, SLou.	.50
160 Esa Tikkanen, SLou.	.25
161 Ulf Dahlén, SanJ.	.25
162 Todd Elik, SanJ.	.25
163 Pat Falloon, SanJ.	.25
164 Jeff Friesen, SanJ.	.50
165 Johan Garpenlöv, SanJ.	.25
166 Arturs Irbe (G), SanJ.	.50
167 Sergei' Makarov, SanJ.	.50
168 Jeff Norton, SanJ.	.25
169 Sandis Ozolinsh, SanJ.	.25
170 Brian Bradley, Tamp.	.25
171 Shawn Chambers, Tamp.	.25
172 Aaron Gavey, Tamp.	.25
173 Chris Gratton, Tamp.	.25
174 Petr Klima, Tamp.	.25
175 Daren Puppa (G), Tamp.	.25
176 Jason Wiemer, Tamp.	.50
177 Dave Andreychuk, Toro.	.25
178 Dave Ellett, Toro.	.25
179 Éric Fichaud (G), Toro. RC	**1.50**
180 Mike Gartner, Toro.	1.00
181 Doug Gilmour, Toro.	.50
182 Kenny Jönsson, Toro.	.25
183 Dmitri Mironov, Toro.	.25
184 Félix Potvin (G), Toro.	.50
185 Mike Ridley, Toro.	.25
186 Mats Sundin, Toro.	1.00
187 Greg A. Adams, Vanc.	.25
188 Jeff R. Brown, Vanc.	.25
189 Pavel Bure, Vanc.	1.00
190 Nathan Lafayette, Vanc.	.25
191 Trevor Linden, Vanc.	.50
192 Jyrki Lumme, Vanc.	.25
193 Kirk McLean (G), Vanc.	.25
194 Cliff Ronning, Vanc.	.25
195 Jason Allison, Wash.	1.00
196 Peter Bondra, Wash.	.50
197 Randy Burridge, Wash.	.25
198 Sylvain Côté, Wash.	.25
199 Dale Hunter, Wash.	.25
200 Joé Juneau, Wash.	.25
201 Dmitri Khristich, Wash.	.25
202 Todd Nelson, Wash.	.25
203 Pat Peake, Wash.	.25
204 Rick Tabaracci (G), Wash.	.25
205 Tim Cheveldae (G), Winn.	.25
206 Dallas Drake, Winn.	.25
207 Dave Manson, Winn.	.25
208 Teppo Numminen, Winn.	.25
209 Teemu Selänne, Winn.	1.00
210 Darrin Shannon, Winn.	.25
211 Keith Tkachuk, Winn.	.50
212 Alexei Zhamnov, Winn.	.25
213 Sergei Fedorov, Detr. [MVP Series]	.50
214 Sergei Fedorov, Detr. [MVP Series]	.50
215 Sergei Fedorov, Detr. [MVP Series]	.50
216 Sergei Fedorov, Detr. [MVP Series]	.50
217 Sergei Fedorov, Detr. [MVP Series]	.50
218 Sergei Fedorov, Detr. [MVP Series]	.50
219 Sergei Fedorov, Detr. [MVP Series]	.50
220 Sergei Fedorov, Detr. [MVP Series]	.50
221 Sergei Fedorov, Detr. [MVP Series]	.50
222 Sergei Fedorov, All-Star [MVP Series]	.50
223 Checklist	.25
224 Checklist	.25
225 Checklist	.25

CENTER ICE SPOTLIGHT

Insert Set (10 cards):	25.00
Insert (1:4)	CIS
1 Jason Arnott, Edmo.	1.00
2 Sergei Fedorov, Detr.	2.00
3 Doug Gilmour, Toro.	1.00
4 Wayne Gretzky, LosA.	10.00
5 Pat LaFontaine, Buff.	1.00
6 Mario Lemieux, Pitt.	7.00
7 Eric Lindros, Phil.	2.00
8 Mark Messier, NYRa.	2.00
9 Mike Modano, Dall.	2.00
10 Jeremy Roenick, Chic.	2.00

HOT NUMBERS

Insert Set (10 cards):	85.00
Insert (1:16)	HN
1 Pavel Bure, Vanc.	4.00
2 Wayne Gretzky, LosA.	25.00
3 Dominik Hasek (G), Buff.	6.00
4 Brett Hull, SLou.	6.00
5 Mario Lemieux, Pitt.	18.00
6 Adam Oates, Bost.	4.00
7 Luc Robitaille, Pitt.	4.00
8 Patrick Roy (G), Mont.	18.00
9 Brendan Shanahan, SLou.	6.00
10 Steve Yzerman, Detr.	14.00

SCORING POWER

Insert Set (10 cards):	15.00
Insert (1:8)	SP
1 Pavel Bure, Vanc.	2.00
2 Alexandre Daigle, Otta.	2.00
3 Sergei Fedorov, Detr.	2.00
4 Alex Kovalev, NYRa.	2.00
5 Brian Leetch, NYRa.	2.00
6 Eric Lindros, Phil.	2.00
7 Mike Modano, Dall.	2.00
8 Alexander Mogilny, Buff.	2.00
9 Jeremy Roenick, Chic.	2.00
10 Alexei Yashin, Otta.	2.00

1994 - 95 FLEER

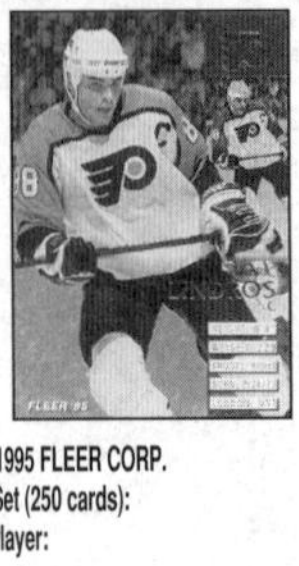

Imprint: © 1995 FLEER CORP.

Complete Set (250 cards):	25.00
Common Player:	.20

Player	NRMT-MT
1 Patrik Carnbäck, Anah.	.20
2 Bob Corkum, Anah.	.20
3 Paul Kariya, Anah.	1.00
4 Valeri Karpov, Anah. RC	**.50**
5 Tom Kurvers, Anah.	.20
6 John Lilley, Anah.	.20
7 Mikhail Shtalenkov (G), Anah.	.20
8 Oleg Tverdovsky, Anah.	.20
9 Raymond Bourque, Bost.	.50
10 Mariusz Czerkawski, Bost. RC	**1.50**
11 John Gruden, Bost. RC	**.50**
12 Al Iafrate, Bost.	.20
13 Blaine Lacher (G), Bost. RC	**1.00**
14 Mats Näslund, Bost.	.20
15 Cam Neely, Bost.	.50
16 Adam Oates, Bost.	.20
17 Bryan Smolinski, Bost.	.20
18 Don Sweeney, Bost.	.20
19 Donald Audette, Buff.	.20
20 Dominik Hasek (G), Buff.	.50
21 Dale Hawerchuk, Buff.	.20
22 Yuri Khmylev, Buff.	.20
23 Pat LaFontaine, Buff.	.20
24 Brad May, Buff.	.20
25 Alexander Mogilny, Buff.	.20
26 Derek Plante, Buff.	.20
27 Richard Smehlik, Buff.	.20
28 Steve Chiasson, Calg.	.20
29 Theoren Fleury, Calg.	.20
30 Phil Housley, Calg.	.20
31 Trevor Kidd (G), Calg.	.20
32 Joe Nieuwendyk, Calg.	.20
33 James Patrick, Calg.	.20
34 Robert Reichel, Calg.	.20
35 Gary Roberts, Calg.	.20
36 German Titov, Calg.	.20
37 Tony Amonte, Chic.	.20
38 Ed Belfour (G), Chic.	.50
39 Chris Chelios, Chic.	.20
40 Dirk Graham, Chic.	.20
41 Sergei Krivokrasov, Chic.	.20
42 Joe Murphy, Chic.	.20
43 Bernie Nicholls, Chic.	.20
44 Patrick Poulin, Chic.	.20
45 Jeremy Roenick, Chic.	.50
46 J. Steve Smith, Chic.	.20
47 Gary Suter, Chic.	.20
48 Russ Courtnall, Dall.	.20
49 Dave Gagner, Dall.	.20
50 Brent Gilchrist, Dall.	.20
51 Todd Harvey, Dall.	.20
52 Derian Hatcher, Dall.	.20
53 Kevin Hatcher, Dall.	.20
54 Mike Kennedy, Dall. RC	**.50**
55 Mike Modano, Dall.	.50
56 Andy Moog (G), Dall.	.20
57 Dino Ciccarelli, Detr.	.20
58 Paul Coffey, Detr.	.20
59 Sergei Fedorov, Detr.	.50
60 Vladimir Konstantinov, Detr.	.20
61 Vyacheslav Kozlov, Detr.	.20
62 Nicklas Lidström, Detr.	.20
63 Chris Osgood (G), Detr.	.20
64 Keith Primeau, Detr.	.20
65 Ray Sheppard, Detr.	.20
66 Mike Vernon (G), Detr.	.20
67 Steve Yzerman, Detr.	1.50
68 Jason Arnott, Edmo.	.20
69 Shayne Corson, Edmo.	.20
70 Igor Kravchuk, Edmo.	.20
71 Todd Marchant, Edmo.	.20
72 Roman Oksiuta, Edmo.	.20
73 Fredrik Olausson, Edmo.	.20
74 David Oliver, Edmo. RC	**.50**
75 Bill Ranford (G), Edmo.	.20
76 Stu Barnes, Flor.	.20
77 Jesse Bélanger, Flor.	.20
78 Keith Brown, Flor.	.20
79 Bob Kudelski, Flor.	.20
80 Scott Mellanby, Flor.	.20
81 Gord Murphy, Flor.	.20
82 Rob Niedermayer, Flor.	.20
83 John Vanbiesbrouck (G), Flor.	.20
84 Sean Burke (G), Hart.	.20
85 Jimmy Carson, Hart.	.20
86 Andrew Cassels, Hart.	.20
87 Andrei Nikolishin, Hart	.20
88 Chris Pronger, Hart.	.20
89 Geoff Sanderson, Hart.	.20
90 Darren Turcotte, Hart.	.20
91 Pat Verbeek, Hart. (NYRa.)	.20
92 Glen Wesley, Hart.	.20
93 Rob Blake, LosA.	.20
94 Wayne Gretzky, LosA.	2.50
95 Kelly Hrudey (G), LosA.	.20
96 Jari Kurri, LosA.	.50
97 Éric Lacroix, LosA. RC	**.50**
98 Marty McSorley, LosA.	.20
99 Jamie Storr (G), LosA.	.20
100 Rick Tocchet, LosA.	.20
101 Brian Bellows, Mont.	.20
102 Patrice Brisebois, Mont.	.20
103 Vincent Damphousse, Mont.	.20
104 Kirk Muller, Mont.	.20
105 Lyle Odelein, Mont.	.20
106 Mark Recchi, Mont.	.20
107 Patrick Roy (G), Mont.	1.50
108 Brian Savage, Mont.	.20
109 Mathieu Schneider, Mont.	.20
110 Turner Stevenson, Mont.	.20
111 Martin Brodeur (G), NJer.	1.00
112 Bill Guerin, NJer.	.20
113 Claude Lemieux, NJer.	.20
114 John MacLean, NJer.	.20
115 Scott Niedermayer, NJer.	.20
116 Stéphane J.J. Richer, NJer.	.20
117 Brian Rolston, NJer.	.20
118 Alexander Semak, NJer.	.20
119 Scott Stevens, NJer.	.20
120 Ray Ferraro, NYIs.	.20
121 Patrick Flatley, NYIs.	.20
122 Darius Kasparaitis, NYIs.	.20
123 Derek King, NYIs.	.20
124 Scott Lachance, NYIs.	.20
125 Brett Lindros, NYIs.	.20
126 Vladimir Malakhov, NYIs.	.20
127 Jamie McLennan (G), NYIs.	.20
128 Zigmund Palffy, NYIs.	.20
129 Steve Thomas, NYIs.	.20
130 Pierre Turgeon, NYIs.	.20
131 Jeff Beukeboom, NYRa.	.20
132 Adam Graves, NYRa.	.20
133 Alex Kovalev, NYRa.	.20
134 Steve Larmer, NYRa.	.20
135 Brian Leetch, NYRa.	.20
136 Mark Messier, NYRa.	.50
137 Petr Nedved, NYRa.	.20
138 Sergei Nemchinov, NYRa.	.20
139 Mike Richter (G), NYRa.	.20
140 Sergei Zubov, NYRa.	.20
141 Don Beaupré (G), Otta.	.20
142 Radek Bonk, Otta. RC	**2.00**
143 Alexandre Daigle, Otta.	.20
144 Pavol Demitra, Otta.	.20
145 Pat Elynuik, Otta.	.20
146 Rob Gaudreau, Otta.	.20
147 Sean Hill, Otta.	.20
148 Sylvain Turgeon, Otta.	.20
149 Alexei Yashin, Otta.	.20
150 Rod Brind'Amour, Phil.	.20
151 Éric Desjardins, Phil.	.20
152 Gilbert Dionne, Phil.	.20
153 Garry Galley, Phil.	.20
154 Ron Hextall (G), Phil.	.20
155 Patrik Juhlin, Phil. RC	**.50**
156 John LeClair, Phil.	.50
157 Eric Lindros, Phil.	.50
158 Mikael Renberg, Phil.	.20
159 Chris Therien, Phil.	.20
160 Dmitry Yushkevich, Phil.	.20
161 Len Barrie, Pitt.	.20
162 Ron Francis, Pitt.	.20
163 Jaromir Jagr, Pitt.	.50
164 Shawn McEachern, Pitt.	.20
165 Joe Mullen, Pitt.	.20
166 Larry Murphy, Pitt.	.20
167 Luc Robitaille, Pitt.	.50
168 Ulf Samuelsson, Pitt.	.20
169 Tomas Sandström, Pitt.	.20
170 Kevin Stevens, Pitt.	.20
171 Martin Straka, Pitt.	.20
172 Ken Wregget (G), Pitt.	.20
173 Wendel Clark, Québ.	.50
174 Adam Deadmarsh, Québ.	.20
175 Stéphane Fiset (G), Québ.	.20
176 Peter Forsberg, Québ.	.50
177 Valeri Kamensky, Québ.	.20
178 Andrei Kovalenko, Québ.	.20
179 Uwe Krupp, Québ.	.20
180 Sylvain Lefebvre, Québ.	.20
181 Owen Nolan, Québ.	.20
182 Mike Ricci, Québ.	.20
183 Joe Sakic, Québ.	1.00
184 Denis Chassé, SLou. RC	**.50**
185 Adam Creighton, SLou.	.20
186 Steve Duchesne, SLou.	.20
187 Brett Hull, SLou.	.50
188 Curtis Joseph (G), SLou.	.50
189 Ian Laperrière, SLou. RC	**1.00**

□ 190 Al MacInnis, SLou. .20
□ 191 Brendan Shanahan, SLou. .50
□ **192 Patrice Tardif, SLou. RC .50**
□ 193 Esa Tikkanen, SLou. .20
□ 194 Ulf Dahlén, SanJ. .20
□ 195 Pat Falloon, SanJ. .20
□ 196 Jeff Friesen, SanJ. .20
□ 197 Arturs Irbe (G), SanJ. .20
□ 198 Sergei* Makarov, SanJ. .20
□ 199 Andrei Nazarov, SanJ. .20
□ 200 Sandis Ozolinsh, SanJ. .20
□ 201 Michal Sykora, SanJ. .20
□ 202 Ray Whitney, SanJ. .20
□ 203 Brian Bradley, Tamp. .20
□ 204 Shawn Chambers, Tamp. .20
□ **205 Éric Charron, Tamp. RC .50**
□ 206 Chris Gratton, Tamp. .20
□ 207 Roman Hamrlik, Tamp. .20
□ 208 Petr Klima, Tamp. .20
□ 209 Daren Puppa (G), Tamp. .20
□ **210 Alexander Selivanov, Tamp. RC .50**
□ 211 Jason Wiemer, Tamp. .20
□ 212 Dave Andreychuk, Toro. .20
□ 213 Dave Ellett, Toro. .20
□ 214 Mike Gartner, Toro. .50
□ 215 Doug Gilmour, Toro. .20
□ 216 Kenny Jönsson, Toro. .20
□ 217 Dmitri Mironov, Toro. .20
□ 218 Félix Potvin (G), Toro. .20
□ 219 Mike Ridley, Toro. .20
□ 220 Mats Sundin, Toro. .50
□ 221 Josef Beránek, Vanc. .20
□ 222 Jeff R. Brown, Vanc. .20
□ 223 Pavel Bure, Vanc. .50
□ 224 Geoff Courtnall, Vanc. .20
□ 225 Trevor Linden, Vanc. .20
□ 226 Jyrki Lumme, Vanc. .20
□ 227 Kirk McLean (G), Vanc. .20
□ 228 Gino Odjick, Vanc. .20
□ 229 Michael Peca, Vanc. .20
□ 230 Cliff Ronning, Vanc. .20
□ 231 Jason Allison, Wash. .50
□ 232 Peter Bondra, Wash. .20
□ **233 Jim Carey, Wash. RC 1.00**
□ 234 Sylvain Côté, Wash. .20
□ 235 Dale Hunter, Wash. .20
□ 236 Joé Juneau, Wash. .20
□ 237 Dmitri Khristich, Wash. .20
□ 238 Pat Peake, Wash. .20
□ 239 Mark Tinordi, Wash. .20
□ 240 Nelson Emerson, Winn. .20
□ **241 Michal Grosek, Winn. RC .50**
□ 242 Nikolai Khabibulin (G), Winn. .20
□ 243 Dave Manson, Winn. .20
□ 244 Stéphane Quintal, Winn. .20
□ 245 Teemu Selänne, Winn. .50
□ 246 Keith Tkachuk, Winn. .20
□ 247 Alexei Zhamnov, Winn. .20
□ 248 Checklist .20
□ 249 Checklist .20
□ 250 Checklist .20

FRANCHISE FUTURES

Insert Set (10 cards): 5.00
Insert (1:7 Hobby) FF
□ 1 Jason Arnott, Edmo. .50
□ 2 Rob Blake, LosA. 1.00
□ 3 Adam Graves, NYRa. .50
□ 4 Arturs Irbe (G), SanJ. .50
□ 5 Joé Juneau, Wash. .50
□ 6 Sandis Ozolinsh, SanJ. .50
□ 7 Mikael Renberg, Phil. .50
□ 8 Keith Tkachuk, Winn. 1.00
□ 9 Alexei Yashin, Otta. 1.00
□ 10 Sergei Zubov, NYRa. .50

HEADLINERS

Insert Set (10 cards): 10.00
Insert (1:4) HL
□ 1 Pavel Bure, Vanc. 1.00
□ 2 Sergei Fedorov, Detr. 1.00
□ 3 Doug Gilmour, Toro. .50
□ 4 Wayne Gretzky, LosA. 5.00

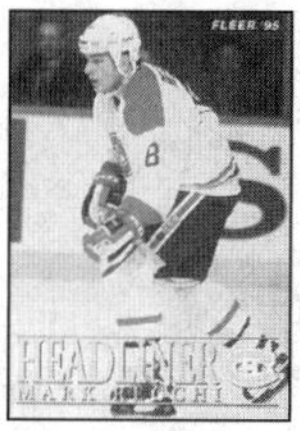

□ 5 Brian Leetch, NYRa. .50
□ 6 Eric Lindros, Phil. 1.00
□ 7 Mark Messier, NYRa. 1.00
□ 8 Cam Neely, Bost. 1.00
□ 9 Mark Recchi, Mont. .50
□ 10 Brendan Shanahan, SLou. 1.00

NETMINDERS

Insert Set (10 cards): 5.00
Insert (1:2) NM
□ 1 Ed Belfour (G), Chic. 1.00
□ 2 Martin Brodeur (G), NJer. 2.00
□ 3 Dominik Hasek (G), Buff. 1.00
□ 4 Arturs Irbe (G), SanJ. .50
□ 5 Curtis Joseph (G), SLou. 1.00
□ 6 Kirk McLean (G), Vanc. .50
□ 7 Félix Potvin (G), Toro. .50
□ 8 Mike Richter (G), NYRa. .50
□ 9 Patrick Roy (G), Mont. 3.50
□ 10 John Vanbiesbrouck (G), Flor. .50

ROOKIE SENSATION

Insert Set (10 cards): 30.00
Insert (1:7 Jumbo) RS
□ 1 Radek Bonk, Otta. 3.00
□ 2 Peter Forsberg, Québ. 10.00
□ 3 Jeff Friesen, SanJ. 3.00
□ 4 Todd Harvey, Dall. 2.00
□ 5 Paul Kariya, Anah. 10.00
□ 6 Blaine Lacher (G), Bost. 2.00
□ 7 Brett Lindros, NYIs. 3.00
□ 8 Michael Peca, Vanc. 4.00
□ 9 Jamie Storr (G), LosA. 2.00
□ 10 Oleg Tverdovsky, Anah. 2.00

SLAPSHOT ARTIST

Insert Set (10 cards): 20.00
Insert (1:12) SA
□ 1 Wendel Clark, Québ. 4.00
□ 2 Brett Hull, SLou. 5.00
□ 3 Al Iafrate, Bost. 1.00
□ 4 Jaromir Jagr, Pitt. 5.00
□ 5 Al MacInnis, SLou. 2.00
□ 6 Mike Modano, Dall. 5.00
□ 7 Stéphane J.J. Richer, NJer. 1.00
□ 8 Jeremy Roenick, Chic. 4.00
□ 9 Geoff Sanderson, Hart. 1.00
□ 10 Steve Thomas, NYIs. 1.00

1994 - 95 FLEER ULTRA

Imprint: © 1994 Fleer Corp. or © 1995 Fleer Corp.
Series One Set (250 cards): 30.00
Series Two Set (150 cards): 20.00
Common Player: .20
Player NRMT-MT
□ 1 Bob Corkum, Anah. .20
□ 2 Todd Ewen, Anah. .20
□ 3 Guy Hebert (G), Anah. .20
□ 4 Bill Houlder, Anah. .20
□ 5 Stéphan Lebeau, Anah. .20
□ 6 Joe Sacco, Anah. .20
□ 7 Anatoli Semenov, Anah. .20
□ 8 Tim Sweeney, Anah. .20
□ 9 Terry Yake, Anah. .20
□ 10 Raymond Bourque, Bost. .50
□ **11 Mariusz Czerkawski, Bost. RC 1.50**
□ 12 Ted Donato, Bost. .20
□ 13 Cam Neely, Bost. .50
□ 14 Adam Oates, Bost. .20
□ 15 Vincent Riendeau (G), Bost. .20
□ 16 Bryan Smolinski, Bost. .20
□ 17 Don Sweeney, Bost. .20
□ 18 Glen Wesley, Bost. .20
□ 19 Donald Audette, Buff. .20
□ 20 Doug Bodger, Buff. .20
□ 21 Jason Dawe, Buff. .20
□ 22 Dominik Hasek (G), Buff. .50
□ 23 Dale Hawerchuk, Buff. .20
□ 24 Pat LaFontaine, Buff. .20
□ 25 Brad May, Buff. .20
□ 26 Alexander Mogilny, Buff. .20
□ 27 Derek Plante, Buff. .20
□ 28 Richard Smehlik, Buff. .20
□ 29 Theoren Fleury, Calg. .20
□ 30 Trevor Kidd (G), Calg. .20
□ 31 Frantisek Musil, Calg. .20
□ 32 Michael Nylander, Calg. .20
□ 33 James Patrick, Calg. .20
□ 34 Robert Reichel, Calg. .20
□ 35 Gary Roberts, Calg. .20
□ 36 German Titov, Calg. .20
□ 37 Wes Walz, Calg. .20
□ 38 Zarley Zalapski, Calg. .20
□ 39 Ed Belfour (G), Chic. .50
□ 40 Chris Chelios, Chic. .20
□ 41 Dirk Graham, Chic. .20
□ 42 Bernie Nicholls, NJer. (Chic.) .20
□ 43 Patrick Poulin, Chic. .20
□ 44 Jeremy Roenick, Chic. .50
□ 45 J. Steve Smith, Chic. .20
□ 46 Gary Suter, Chic. .20
□ 47 Brent Sutter, Chic. .20
□ 48 Neal Broten, Dall. .20
□ 49 Paul Cavallini, Dall. .20
□ 50 Dean Evason, Dall. .20
□ 51 Dave Gagner, Dall. .20
□ 52 Derian Hatcher, Dall. .20
□ 53 Trent Klatt, Dall. .20
□ 54 Grant Ledyard, Dall. .20
□ 55 Mike Modano, Dall. .50
□ 56 Andy Moog (G), Dall. .20
□ 57 Mark Tinordi, Dall. .20
□ 58 Dino Ciccarelli, Detr. .20
□ 59 Paul Coffey, Detr. .20
□ 60 Sergei Fedorov, Detr. .50
□ 61 Vladimir Konstantinov, Detr. .20
□ 62 Nicklas Lidström, Detr. .20
□ 63 Darren McCarty, Detr. .20
□ 64 Chris Osgood (G), Detr. .20
□ 65 Keith Primeau, Detr. .20
□ 66 Ray Sheppard, Detr. .20
□ 67 Steve Yzerman, Detr. 1.50
□ 68 Jason Arnott, Edmo. .20
□ 69 Bob Beers, Edmo. .20
□ 70 Ilya Byakin, Edmo. .20
□ 71 Zdeno Ciger, Edmo. .20
□ 72 Igor Kravchuk, Edmo. .20
□ 73 Boris Mironov, Edmo. .20
□ 74 Fredrik Olausson, Edmo. .20
□ 75 Scott Pearson, Edmo. .20
□ 76 Bill Ranford (G), Edmo. .20
□ 77 Doug Weight, Edmo. .20
□ 78 Stu Barnes, Flor. .20
□ 79 Jesse Bélanger, Flor. .20
□ 80 Bob Kudelski, Flor. .20
□ 81 Andrei Lomakin, Flor. .20
□ 82 Dave Lowry, Flor. .20
□ 83 Gord Murphy, Flor. .20
□ 84 Rob Niedermayer, Flor. .20
□ 85 Brian Skrudland, Flor. .20
□ 86 John Vanbiesbrouck (G), Flor. .20
□ 87 Sean Burke (G), Hart. .20
□ 88 Ted Drury, Hart. .20
□ 89 Alexander Godynyuk, Hart. .20
□ 90 Robert Kron, Hart. .20
□ 91 Chris Pronger, Hart. .20
□ 92 Brian Propp, Hart. .20
□ 93 Geoff Sanderson, Hart. .20
□ 94 Darren Turcotte, Hart. .20
□ 95 Pat Verbeek, Hart. .20
□ 96 Rob Blake, LosA. .20
□ 97 Mike Donnelly, LosA. .20
□ 98 John Druce, LosA. .20
□ 99 Kelly Hrudey (G), LosA. .20
□ 100 Jari Kurri, LosA. .50
□ 101 Robert Lang, LosA. .20
□ 102 Marty McSorley, LosA. .20
□ 103 Luc Robitaille, LosA. .50
□ 104 Alexei Zhitnik, LosA. .20
□ 105 Brian Bellows, Mont. .20
□ 106 Patrice Brisebois, Mont. .20
□ 107 Vincent Damphousse, Mont. .20
□ 108 Éric Desjardins, Mont. .20
□ 109 Gilbert Dionne, Mont. .20
□ 110 Mike Keane, Mont. .20
□ 111 John LeClair, Mont. .50
□ 112 Lyle Odelein, Mont. .20
□ 113 Patrick Roy (G), Mont. 1.50
□ 114 Mathieu Schneider, Mont. .20
□ 115 Martin Brodeur (G), NJer. 1.00
□ 116 Jim Dowd, NJer. .20
□ 117 Bill Guerin, NJer. .20
□ 118 Claude Lemieux, NJer. .20
□ 119 John MacLean, NJer. .20
□ 120 Corey Millen, NJer. .20
□ 121 Scott Niedermayer, NJer. .20
□ 122 Stéphane J.J. Richer, NJer. .20
□ 123 Scott Stevens, NJer. .20
□ 124 Valeri Zelepukin, NJer. .20
□ 125 Patrick Flatley, NYIs. .20
□ 126 Travis Green, NYIs. .20
□ 127 Ron Hextall (G), NYIs. .20
□ 128 Benoît Hogue, NYIs. .20
□ 129 Darius Kasparaitis, NYIs. .20
□ 130 Vladimir Malakhov, NYIs. .20
□ 131 Marty McInnis, NYIs. .20
□ 132 Steve Thomas, NYIs. .20
□ 133 Pierre Turgeon, NYIs. .20
□ 134 Dennis Vaske, NYIs. .20
□ 135 Glenn Anderson, NYRa. .20
□ 136 Jeff Beukeboom, NYRa. .20
□ 137 Adam Graves, NYRa. .20
□ 138 Steve Larmer, NYRa. .20
□ 139 Brian Leetch, NYRa. .20
□ 140 Mark Messier, NYRa. .50
□ 141 Petr Nedved, SLou. (NYRa.) .20
□ 142 Sergei Nemchinov, NYRa. .20
□ 143 Mike Richter (G), NYRa. .20
□ 144 Sergei Zubov, NYRa. .20
□ 145 Craig Billington (G), Otta. .20
□ 146 Alexandre Daigle, Otta. .20
□ 147 Evgeny Davydov, Otta. .20
□ 148 Scott Levins, Otta. .20
□ 149 Norm Maciver, Otta. .20
□ 150 Troy Mallette, Otta. .20
□ 151 Brad Shaw, Otta. .20
□ 152 Alexei Yashin, Otta. .20
□ 153 Josef Beránek, Phil. .20
□ 154 Jason Bowen, Phil. .20
□ 155 Rod Brind'Amour, Phil. .20
□ 156 Kevin Dineen, Phil. .20
□ 157 Garry Galley, Phil. .20
□ 158 Mark Recchi, Phil. .20
□ 159 Mikael Renberg, Phil. .20
□ 160 Tommy Söderström (G), Phil. .20
□ 161 Dmitry Yushkevich, Phil. .20
□ 162 Tom Barrasso (G), Pitt. .20
□ 163 Ron Francis, Pitt. .20
□ 164 Jaromir Jagr, Pitt. .50
□ 165 Mario Lemieux, Pitt. 1.50
□ 166 Shawn McEachern, Pitt. .20
□ 167 Joe Mullen, Pitt. .20
□ 168 Larry Murphy, Pitt. .20
□ 169 Ulf Samuelsson, Pitt. .20
□ 170 Kevin Stevens, Pitt. .20
□ 171 Martin Straka, Pitt. .20
□ 172 Wendel Clark, Toro. (Québ.) .50
□ 173 Stéphane Fiset (G), Québ. .20
□ 174 Iain Fraser, Québ. .20
□ 175 Andrei Kovalenko, Québ. .20
□ 176 Sylvain Lefebvre, Toro. (Québ.) .20
□ 177 Owen Nolan, Québ. .20
□ 178 Mike Ricci, Québ. .20
□ 179 Martin Rucinsky, Québ. .20
□ 180 Joe Sakic, Québ. 1.00
□ 181 Scott A. Young, Québ. .20
□ 182 Steve Duchesne, SLou. .20
□ 183 Brett Hull, SLou. .50
□ 184 Curtis Joseph (G), SLou. .50
□ 185 Al MacInnis, Calg. (SLou.) .20
□ 186 Kevin Miller, SLou. .20
□ 187 Jim Montgomery, SLou. .20
□ 188 Vitali Prokhorov, SLou. .20
□ 189 Brendan Shanahan, SLou. .50
□ 190 Peter Stastny, SLou. .20
□ 191 Esa Tikkanen, NYRa. (SLou.) .20
□ 192 Ulf Dahlén, SanJ. .20
□ 193 Todd Elik, SanJ. .20
□ 194 Johan Garpenlöv, SanJ. .20
□ 195 Arturs Irbe (G), SanJ. .20
□ 196 Vlastimil Kroupa, SanJ. .20
□ 197 Igor Larionov, SanJ. .20
□ 198 Sergei* Makarov, SanJ. .20
□ 199 Jeff Norton, SanJ. .20
□ 200 Sandis Ozolinsh, SanJ. .20
□ 201 Mike Rathje, SanJ. .20
□ 202 Brian Bradley, Tamp. .20
□ 203 Shawn Chambers, Tamp. .20
□ 204 Danton Cole, Tamp. .20
□ 205 Chris Gratton, Tamp. .20
□ 206 Roman Hamrlik, Tamp. .20
□ 207 Chris Joseph (G), Tamp. .20
□ 208 Petr Klima, Tamp. .20
□ 209 Daren Puppa (G), Tamp. .20
□ 210 John Tucker, Tamp. .20
□ 211 Dave Andreychuk, Toro. .20
□ 212 Ken Baumgartner, Toro. .20
□ 213 Dave Ellett, Toro. .20
□ 214 Mike Gartner, Toro. .50
□ 215 Todd Gill, Toro. .20
□ 216 Doug Gilmour, Toro. .20
□ 217 Jamie Macoun, Toro. .20
□ 218 Dmitri Mironov, Toro. .20
□ 219 Félix Potvin (G), Toro. .20
□ 220 Mats Sundin, Québ. (Toro.) .50
□ 221 Jeff R. Brown, Vanc. .20
□ 222 Pavel Bure, Vanc. .50
□ 223 Murray Craven, Vanc. .20
□ 224 Bret Hedican, Vanc. .20
□ 225 Nathan Lafayette, Vanc. .20
□ 226 Trevor Linden, Vanc. .20
□ 227 Jyrki Lumme, Vanc. .20
□ 228 Kirk McLean (G), Vanc. .20
□ 229 Gino Odjick, Vanc. .20
□ 230 Cliff Ronning, Vanc. .20
□ 231 Peter Bondra, Wash. .20
□ 232 Sylvain Côté, Wash. .20
□ 233 Kevin Hatcher, Wash. .20
□ 234 Dale Hunter, Wash. .20
□ 235 Calle Johansson, Wash. .20
□ 236 Dmitri Khristich, Wash. .20
□ 237 Pat Peake, Wash. .20
□ 238 Michal Pivonka, Wash. .20
□ 239 Rick Tabaracci (G), Wash. .20
□ 240 Tim Cheveldae (G), Winn. .20
□ 241 Dallas Drake, Winn. .20
□ 242 Nelson Emerson, Winn. .20
□ 243 Dave Manson, Winn. .20
□ 244 Teppo Numminen, Winn. .20
□ 245 Stéphane Quintal, Winn. .20
□ 246 Teemu Selänne, Winn. .50
□ 247 Keith Tkachuk, Winn. .20
□ 248 Checklist .20
□ 249 Checklist .20
□ 250 Checklist .20
□ 251 John Lilley, Anah. .20
□ 252 Mikhail Shtalenkov (G), Anah. .20
□ 253 Garry Valk, Anah. .20
□ **254 John Gruden, Bost. RC .50**
□ 255 Brent* Hughes, Bost. .20
□ 256 Al Iafrate, Bost. .20
□ 257 Alexei Kasatonov, Bost. .20
□ 258 Mikko Mäkelä, Bost. .20
□ 259 Marc Potvin, Bost. .20
□ **260 Jon Rohloff, Bost. RC .50**
□ 261 Jozef Stumpel, Bost. .20
□ 262 Grant Fuhr (G), Buff. .20
□ 263 Viktor Gordiouk, Buff. .20
□ 264 Yuri Khmylev, Buff. .20
□ 265 Craig Muni, Buff. .20
□ 266 Craig Simpson, Buff. .20
□ **267 Denis Tsygurov, Buff. RC .50**

☐	268 Steve Chiasson, Calg.	.20
☐	269 Phil Housley, Calg.	.20
☐	270 Joel Otto, Calg.	.20
☐	271 Andrei Trefilov (G), Calg.	.20
☐	272 Vesa Viitakoski, Calg.	.20
☐	273 Tony Amonte, Chic.	.20
☐	**274 Brent Grieve, Chic. RC**	**.50**
☐	275 Bernie Nicholls, Chic.	.20
☐	**276 Christian Soucy (G), Chic. RC**	**1.00**
☐	277 Paul Ysebaert, Chic.	.20
☐	278 Shane Churla, Dall.	.20
☐	279 Russ Courtnall, Dall.	.20
☐	280 Craig Ludwig, Dall.	.20
☐	281 Jarkko Varvio, Dall.	.20
☐	282 Darcy Wakaluk (G), Dall.	.20
☐	283 Greg Johnson, Detr.	.20
☐	284 Vyacheslav Kozlov, Detr.	.20
☐	285 Martin Lapointe, Detr.	.20
☐	**286 Tim Taylor, Detr. RC**	**.50**
☐	287 Mike Vernon (G), Detr.	.20
☐	**288 Jason York, Detr. RC**	**1.00**
☐	289 Fred Brathwaite, Edmo.	.20
☐	290 Kelly Buchberger, Edmo.	.20
☐	291 Shayne Corson, Edmo.	.20
☐	292 Dean McAmmond, Edmo.	.20
☐	293 Vladimír (Jr.) Vujtek, Edmo.	.20
☐	294 Doug Barrault, Flor.	.20
☐	295 Keith Brown, Flor.	.20
☐	296 Mark Fitzpatrick (G), Flor.	.20
☐	297 Mike Hough, Flor.	.20
☐	298 Scott Mellanby, Flor.	.20
☐	299 Jimmy Carson, Hart.	.20
☐	300 Andrew Cassels, Hart.	.20
☐	301 Andrei Nikolishin, Hart.	.20
☐	302 Steven Rice, Hart.	.20
☐	303 Glen Wesley, Hart.	.20
☐	304 Rob (Jr.) Brown, LosA.	.20
☐	305 Tony Granato, LosA.	.20
☐	306 Wayne Gretzky, LosA.	2.50
☐	307 Dan Quinn, LosA.	.20
☐	308 Darryl Sydor, LosA.	.20
☐	309 Rick Tocchet, LosA.	.20
☐	**310 Donald Brashear, Mont. RC**	**1.50**
☐	311 Valeri Bure, Mont.	.20
☐	312 Jim Montgomery, Mont.	.20
☐	313 Kirk Muller, Mont.	.20
☐	314 Oleg Petrov, Mont.	.20
☐	315 Peter Popovic, Mont.	.20
☐	316 Yves Racine, Mont.	.20
☐	317 Turner Stevenson, Mont.	.20
☐	318 Ken Daneyko, NJer.	.20
☐	319 David Emma, NJer.	.20
☐	320 Zigmund Palffy, NYIs.	.20
☐	320 Brian Rolston, NJer.	.20
☐	321 Alexander Semak, NJer.	.20
☐	322 Jason Smith, NJer.	.20
☐	323 Chris Terreri (G), NJer.	.20
☐	324 Ray Ferraro, NYIs.	.20
☐	325 Derek King, NYIs.	.20
☐	326 Scott Lachance, NYIs.	.20
☐	327 Brett Lindros, NYIs.	.20
☐	328 Jamie McLennan (G), NYIs.	.20
☐	330 Corey Hirsch (G), NYRa.	.20
☐	331 Alex Kovalev, NYRa.	.20
☐	332 Stéphane Matteau, NYRa.	.20
☐	333 Petr Nedved, NYRa.	.20
☐	334 Mattias Norström, NYRa.	.20
☐	335 Mark Osborne, NYRa.	.20
☐	336 Randy Cunneyworth, Otta.	.20
☐	337 Pavol Demitra, Otta.	.20
☐	338 Pat Elynuik, Otta.	.20
☐	339 Sean Hill, Otta.	.20
☐	340 Darrin Madeley (G), Otta.	.20
☐	341 Sylvain Turgeon, Otta.	.20
☐	**342 Vladislav Boulin, Phil. RC**	**.50**
☐	343 Ron Hextall (G), Phil.	.20
☐	**344 Patrik Juhlin, Phil. RC**	**.50**
☐	345 Eric Lindros, Phil.	.50
☐	346 Shjon Podein, Phil.	.20
☐	347 Chris Therien, Phil.	.20
☐	348 John Cullen, Pitt.	.20
☐	349 Markus Näslund, Pitt.	.50
☐	350 Luc Robitaille, Pitt.	.50
☐	351 Kjell Samuelsson, Pitt.	.20
☐	352 Tomas Sandström, Pitt.	.20
☐	353 Ken Wregget (G), Pitt.	.20
☐	354 Wendel Clark, Québ.	.50
☐	355 Adam Deadmarsh, Québ.	.20
☐	356 Peter Forsberg, Québ.	.50
☐	357 Valeri Kamensky, Québ.	.20
☐	358 Uwe Krupp, Québ.	.20
☐	359 Janne Laukkanen, Québ.	.20
☐	360 Sylvain Lefebvre, Québ.	.20
☐	361 Jocelyn Thibault (G), Québ.	.20
☐	362 Bill Houlder, SLou.	.20
☐	363 Craig Janney, SLou.	.20
☐	364 Pat Falloon, SanJ.	.20
☐	365 Jeff Friesen, SanJ.	.20
☐	366 Viktor Kozlov, SanJ.	.20
☐	367 Andrei Nazarov, SanJ.	.20
☐	368 Jeff Odgers, SanJ.	.20
☐	369 Michal Sykora, SanJ.	.20
☐	370 Mikael Andersson, Tamp.	.20
☐	**371 Éric Charron, Tamp. RC**	**.50**
☐	372 Chris LiPuma, Tamp.	.20
☐	373 Denis Savard, Tamp.	.20
☐	374 Jason Wiemer, Tamp.	.20
☐	375 Nikolai Borschevsky, Toro.	.20
☐	**376 Éric Fichaud (G), Toro. RC**	**1.00**
☐	377 Kenny Jönsson, Toro.	.20
☐	378 Mike Ridley, Toro.	.20
☐	379 Mats Sundin, Toro.	.50
☐	380 Greg A. Adams, Vanc.	.20
☐	381 Shawn Antoski, Vanc.	.20
☐	382 Geoff Courtnall, Vanc.	.20
☐	383 Martin Gélinas, Vanc.	.20
☐	384 Sergio Momesso, Vanc.	.20
☐	385 Jiri Slegr, Vanc.	.20
☐	386 Jason Allison, Wash.	.50
☐	387 Don Beaupré (G), Wash.	.20
☐	388 Joé Juneau, Wash.	.20
☐	389 Steve Konowalchuk, Wash.	.20
☐	390 Kelly Miller, Wash.	.20
☐	391 Dave Poulin, Wash.	.20
☐	392 Tie Domi, Winn.	.20
☐	**393 Michal Grosek, Winn. RC**	**.50**
☐	394 Russ Romaniuk, Winn.	.20
☐	395 Darrin Shannon, Winn.	.20
☐	396 Thomas Steen, Winn.	.20
☐	397 Igor Ulanov, Winn.	.20
☐	398 Alexei Zhamnov, Winn.	.20
☐	399 Checklist	.20
☐	400 Checklist	.20

ALL-ROOKIE SERIES

Series One Insert Set (10 cards):		**90.00**
	Insert (1:37 Jumbo)	**ARS**
☐	1 Jason Arnott, Edmo.	10.00
☐	2 Martin Brodeur (G), NJer.	40.00
☐	3 Alexandre Daigle, Otta.	4.00
☐	4 Chris Gratton, Tamp.	5.00
☐	5 Boris Mironov, Edmo.	4.00
☐	6 Derek Plante, Buff.	4.00
☐	7 Chris Pronger, Hart.	15.00
☐	8 Mikael Renberg, Phil.	5.00
☐	9 Bryan Smolinski, Bost.	4.00
☐	10 Alexei Yashin, Otta.	15.00

ALL-STAR GAME

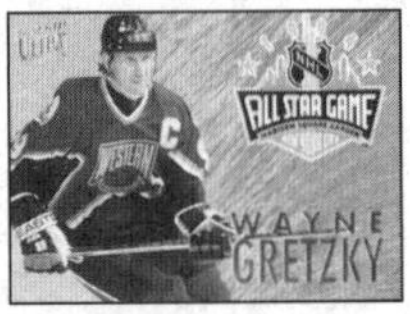

Series One Insert Set (12 cards):		**8.00**
	Insert (1:2)	**ASG**
☐	1 Raymond Bourque, All-Star	.50
☐	2 Brian Leetch, All-Star	.50
☐	3 Eric Lindros, All-Star	.50
☐	4 Mark Messier, All-Star	.50
☐	5 Alexander Mogilny, All-Star	.50
☐	6 Patrick Roy (G), All-Star	2.00
☐	7 Pavel Bure, All-Star	.50
☐	8 Chris Chelios, All-Star	.50
☐	9 Paul Coffey, All-Star	.50
☐	10 Wayne Gretzky, All-Star	3.00
☐	11 Brett Hull, All-Star	.50
☐	12 Félix Potvin, All-Star	.50

AWARD WINNER

Series One Insert Set (8 cards):		**10.00**
	Insert (1:7)	**AW**
☐	1 Raymond Bourque, Bost.	1.00
☐	2 Martin Brodeur (G), NJer.	2.00
☐	3 Sergei Fedorov, Detr.	1.00
☐	4 Adam Graves, NYRa.	.50
☐	5 Wayne Gretzky, LosA.	5.00

☐	6 Dominik Hasek (G), Buff.	1.00
☐	7 Brian Leetch, NYRa.	.50
☐	8 Cam Neely, Bost.	1.00

GLOBAL GREATS

Series Two Insert Set (10 cards):		**45.00**
	Insert (1:12 Jumbo)	**GG**
☐	1 Sergei Fedorov, Detr.	8.00
☐	2 Dominik Hasek (G), Buff.	8.00
☐	3 Arturs Irbe (G), SanJ.	3.00
☐	4 Jaromir Jagr, Pitt.	8.00
☐	5 Jari Kurri, LosA.	8.00
☐	6 Alexander Mogilny, Buff.	4.00
☐	7 Petr Nedved, NYRa.	3.00
☐	8 Mikael Renberg, Phil.	3.00
☐	9 Teemu Selänne, Winn.	6.00
☐	10 Alexei Yashin, Otta.	5.00

PERFORMANCE HIGHLIGHTS

Series One Insert Set (12 cards):		**10.00**
	Player	**PH**
☐	1 Sergei Fedorov	1.00
☐	2 Sergei Fedorov	1.00
☐	3 Sergei Fedorov	1.00
☐	4 Sergei Fedorov	1.00
☐	5 Sergei Fedorov	1.00
☐	6 Sergei Fedorov	1.00
☐	7 Sergei Fedorov	1.00
☐	8 Sergei Fedorov	1.00
☐	9 Sergei Fedorov	1.00
☐	10 Sergei Fedorov	1.00
☐	11 Sergei Fedorov Mail-In	2.00
☐	12 Sergei Fedorov Mail-In	2.00
	Autograph	**Auto.**
☐	**Sergei Fedorov, Detr. ✍**	**110.00**

PREMIER PAD MEN

Series One Insert Set (6 cards):		**35.00**
	Insert (1:37)	**PPM**
☐	1 Dominik Hasek (G), Buff.	5.00
☐	2 Arturs Irbe (G), SanJ.	4.00
☐	3 Curtis Joseph (G), SLou.	5.00
☐	4 Félix Potvin (G), Toro.	4.00
☐	5 Mike Richter (G), NYRa.	4.00
☐	6 Patrick Roy (G), Mont.	20.00

PREMIER PIVOTS

Series Two Insert Set (10 cards):		**65.00**
	Insert (1:4)	**PPM**
☐	1 Jason Arnott, Edmo.	4.00
☐	2 Sergei Fedorov, Detr.	5.00
☐	3 Doug Gilmour, Toro.	4.00
☐	4 Wayne Gretzky, LosA.	30.00
☐	5 Pat LaFontaine, Buff.	4.00
☐	6 Eric Lindros, Phil.	5.00
☐	7 Mark Messier, NYRa.	5.00
☐	8 Mike Modano, Dall.	5.00
☐	9 Adam Oates, Bost.	4.00
☐	10 Steve Yzerman, Detr.	15.00

RED LIGHT SPECIALS

Series Two Insert Set (10 cards):		**13.00**
	Insert	**RLS**
☐	1 Dave Andreychuk, Toro.	.75
☐	2 Pavel Bure, Vanc.	2.00
☐	3 Mike Gartner, Toro.	2.00
☐	4 Adam Graves, NYRa.	1.00
☐	5 Brett Hull, SLou.	2.00
☐	6 Cam Neely, Bost.	2.00
☐	7 Gary Roberts, Calg.	1.00
☐	8 Teemu Selänne, Winn.	2.00
☐	9 Brendan Shanahan, SLou.	2.00
☐	10 Kevin Stevens, Pitt.	.75

SCORING KING

Series One Insert Set (7 cards):		**20.00**
	Insert (1:8)	**SK**
☐	1 Pavel Bure, Vanc.	1.00
☐	2 Sergei Fedorov, Detr.	2.00
☐	3 Doug Gilmour, Toro.	1.00
☐	4 Wayne Gretzky, LosA.	8.00
☐	5 Mario Lemieux, Pitt.	6.00
☐	6 Eric Lindros, Phil.	2.00
☐	7 Steve Yzerman, Detr.	4.00

SPEED MERCHANT

Series Two Insert Set (10 cards):		**8.00**
	Insert	**NRMT-MT**
☐	1 Pavel Bure, Vanc.	1.00
☐	2 Russ Courtnall, Dall.	.50
☐	3 Sergei Fedorov, Detr.	2.00
☐	4 Al Iafrate, Bost.	.50
☐	5 Pat LaFontaine, Buff.	1.00
☐	6 Brian Leetch, NYRa.	1.00
☐	7 Mike Modano, Dall.	2.00
☐	8 Alexander Mogilny, Buff.	.50
☐	9 Jeremy Roenick, Chic.	1.00
☐	10 Geoff Sanderson, Hart.	.50

ULTRA POWER

Series One Insert Set (10 cards):		**20.00**
	Insert	**Power**
☐	1 Dave Andreychuk, Toro.	1.00
☐	2 Jason Arnott, Edmo.	2.00
☐	3 Chris Gratton, Tamp.	1.00
☐	4 Adam Graves, NYRa.	2.00
☐	5 Eric Lindros, Phil.	4.00
☐	6 Cam Neely, Bost.	4.00
☐	7 Mikael Renberg, Phil.	1.00
☐	8 Jeremy Roenick, Chic.	4.00

☐	9 Brendan Shanahan, SLou.	4.00
☐	10 Keith Tkachuk, Winn.	2.00

ULTRA PROSPECT

Series Two Insert Set (10 cards):		**20.00**
	Insert (1:12 Hobby)	**Prosp.**
☐	1 Peter Forsberg, Québ.	8.00
☐	2 Todd Harvey, Dall.	1.00
☐	3 Paul Kariya, Anah.	8.00
☐	4 Viktor Kozlov, SanJ.	2.00
☐	5 Brett Lindros, NYIs.	2.00
☐	6 Michael Peca, Vanc.	2.00
☐	7 Brian Rolston, NJer.	2.00
☐	8 Jamie Storr (G), LosA.	1.00
☐	9 Oleg Tverdovsky, Anah.	1.00
☐	10 Jason Wiemer, Tamp.	.50

1994 - 95 INCOMNET PHONECARDS

These $20 (U.S.) phonecards were issued by Incomnet. The NHLPA - licensed cards feature photos from the 1994 Four on Four Challenge.

Complete Set (8 cards):		**185.00**	**90.00**
	Player	**Unused**	**Used**
☐	Doug Gilmour, Team Ontario	20.00	10.00
☐	Brett Hull, Team U.S.A.	20.00	10.00
☐	Paul Kariya, Team West	30.00	15.00
☐	Eric Lindros,Team Ontario	30.00	15.00
☐	Luc Robitaille, Team Québec	20.00	10.00
☐	Jeremy Roenick,Team U.S.A.	20.00	10.00
☐	Patrick Roy (G), Team Québec	40.00	20.00
☐	J. Vanbiesbrouck (G), Team U.S.A.	20.00	10.00
☐	Team Ontario	20.00	10.00

1994 - 95 KRAFT

Complete Set (72 cards):	**85.00**
Album:	**30.00**

JELL-O INSTANT PUDDING / HOCKEY HEROES

One of 14 different cards was found on the back of specially marked boxes of JELL-O instant pudding.

Card Size: 3" x 4 1/4"

Complete Set (14 cards):		20.00
	Player	HH
☐	Dave Andreychuk, Toro.	1.00
☐	Chris Chelios, Chic.	1.00
☐	Wendel Clark, Toro.	1.00
☐	Theoren Fleury, Calg.	1.00
☐	Wayne Gretzky, LosA.	8.00
☐	Brett Hull, SLou.	2.00
☐	Al Iafrate, Bost.	1.00
☐	Jaromir Jagr, Pitt.	2.00
☐	Pat LaFontaine, Buff.	1.00
☐	Kirk Muller, Mont.	1.00
☐	Mark Recchi, Mont.	1.00
☐	Gary Roberts, Calg.	1.00
☐	Mats Sundin, Toro.	2.00
☐	Steve Yzerman, Detr.	4.00

JELL-O PUDDING / SHARP SHOOTERS

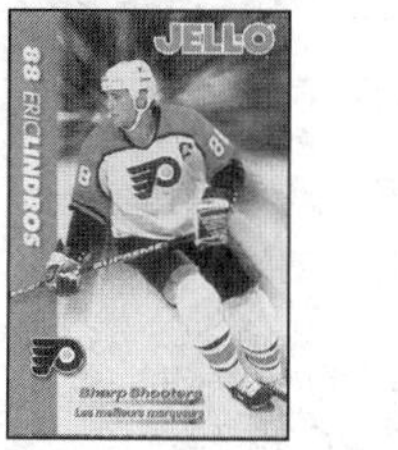

Two of 16 different cards were found under the tops of specially marked JELL-O pudding.

Card Size: 2 1/2" x 3 1/2"

Complete Set (16 cards):		15.00
	Player	SS
☐	Jason Arnott, Edmo.	1.00
☐	Vincent Damphousse, Mont.	1.00
☐	Doug Gilmour, Toro.	1.00
☐	Craig Janney, SLou.	1.00
☐	Joé Juneau, Wash.	1.00
☐	Trevor Linden, Vanc.	1.00
☐	Eric Lindros, Phil.	2.00
☐	Mark Messier, NYRa.	2.00
☐	Mike Modano, Dall.	2.00
☐	Alexander Mogilny, Buff.	1.00
☐	Adam Oates, Bost.	1.00
☐	Robert Reichel, Calg.	1.00
☐	Jeremy Roenick, Chic.	1.00
☐	Joe Sakic, Que.	3.00
☐	Keith Tkachuk, Winn.	1.00
☐	Alexei Yashin, Otta.	1.00

KRAFT DINNER / MASKED DEFENDERS

One of 26 different cards was found on the back of specially marked Kraft Dinner.

Card Size: 3" x 5"

Complete Set (26 cards):		30.00
	Player	MD
☐	Tom Barrasso (G), Pitt.	1.00
☐	Don Beaupré, Wash.	1.00
☐	Ed Belfour (G), Chic.	2.00
☐	Craig Billington (G), Otta.	1.00
☐	Martin Brodeur (G), NJer.	3.00
☐	Sean Burke (G), Hart.	1.00
☐	Tim Cheveldae (G), Winn.	1.00
☐	Stéphane Fiset (G), Québ.	1.00
☐	Dominik Hasek (G), Buff.	2.00
☐	Guy Hebert (G), Anah.	1.00
☐	Ron Hextall (G), Phil.	1.00
☐	Kelly Hrudey (G), LosA.	1.00
☐	Arturs Irbe (G), SanJ.	1.00
☐	Curtis Joseph (G), SLou.	2.00
☐	Trevor Kidd (G), Calg.	1.00
☐	Kirk McLean (G), Vanc.	1.00
☐	Jamie McLennan (G), NYIs.	1.00
☐	Andy Moog (G), Dall.	1.00
☐	Félix Potvin (G), Toro.	1.00
☐	Daren Puppa (G), Tamp.	1.00
☐	Bill Ranford (G), Edmo.	1.00
☐	Mike Richter (G), NYRa.	1.00
☐	Vincent Riendeau (G), Bost.	1.00
☐	Patrick Roy (G), Mont.	6.00
☐	John Vanbiesbrouck (G), Flor.	1.00
☐	Mike Vernon (G), Detr.	1.00

KRAFT PEANUT BUTTER / ALL-STARS AND AWARD WINNERS

Two of 16 different disks were found under caps of specially marked Kraft Peanut Butter.

Disk Diameter: 2 3/4"

Complete Set (16 cards):		30.00
	Player	AS/AW
☐	Raymond Bourque, Bost.	3.00
☐	AS: Raymond Bourque, Bost.	3.00
☐	Martin Brodeur (G), NJer.	4.00
☐	AS: Pavel Bure, Vanc.	2.00
☐	Sergei Fedorov, Detr.	2.00
☐	AS: Sergei Fedorov, Detr.	2.00
☐	Adam Graves, NYRa.	1.00
☐	Wayne Gretzky, LosA.	10.00
☐	AS: Dominik Hasek (G), Buff.	2.00
☐	Dominik Hasek (G), Buff.	2.00
☐	AS: Brian Leetch, NYRa.	1.00
☐	Jacques Lemaire, NJer.	1.00
☐	Cam Neely, Bost.	2.00
☐	AS: Brendan Shanahan, SLou.	2.00
☐	Scott Stevens, NJer.	1.00
☐	Devils	1.00

1994 - 95 KRAFT JUMBO MASKS

Complete Set (8 masks)		15.00
	Cardboard Mask	Mask
☐	Ed Belfour (G), Chic.	2.00
☐	Guy Hebert (G), Anah.	2.00
☐	Curtis Joseph (G), SLou.	2.00
☐	Andy Moog (G), Dall.	2.00
☐	Félix Potvin (G), Toro.	2.00
☐	Vincent Riendeau (G), Bost.	2.00
☐	Patrick Roy (G), Mont.	6.00
☐	John Vanbiesbrouck (G), Flor.	2.00

1994 - 95 LEAF

Imprint: © 1994 DONRUSS, INC.

Series One Set (330 cards):		25.00
Series Two Set (220 cards):		15.00
Common Player:		.20
☐	Doug Gilmour Swiss card 8" x 10" (#/2,500):	30.00
	Player	NRMT-MT
☐	1 Mario Lemieux, Pitt.	1.50
☐	2 Tony Amonte, Chic.	.20
☐	3 Steve Duchesne, SLou.	.20
☐	4 Glen Murray, Bost.	.20
☐	5 John LeClair, Mont.	.50
☐	6 Glen Wesley, Bost.	.20
☐	7 Chris Chelios, Chic.	.20
☐	8 Alexei Zhitnik, LosA.	.20
☐	9 Mike Modano, Dall.	.50
☐	10 Pavel Bure, Vanc.	.50
☐	11 Mark Messier, NYRa.	.50
☐	12 Rob Blake, LosA.	.20
☐	13 Tony Twist, Québ.	.20
☐	14 Glenn Anderson, NYRa.	.20
☐	15 Keith Redmond, LosA.	.20
☐	16 Brett Hull, SLou.	.50
☐	17 Valeri Zelepukin, NJer.	.20
☐	18 Mike Richter (G), NYRa.	.20
☐	19 Alexei Yashin, Otta.	.20
☐	20 Luc Robitaille, LosA.	.50
☐	21 Tim Sweeney, Anah.	.20
☐	22 Ted Drury, Hart.	.20
☐	23 Guy Carbonneau, Mont.	.20
☐	24 Stéphane J.J. Richer, NJer.	.20
☐	25 Ulf Dahlén, SanJ.	.20
☐	26 Fred Brathwaite, Edmo.	.20
☐	27 Darius Kasparaitis, NYIs.	.20
☐	28 Kris Draper, Detr.	.20
☐	29 Alexander Godynyuk, Hart.	.20
☐	30 Brent Sutter, Chic.	.20
☐	31 Josef Beránek, Phil.	.20
☐	32 Stéphane Matteau, NYRa.	.20
☐	33 Derek Plante, Buff.	.20
☐	34 Vesa Viitakoski, Calg.	.20
☐	35 Dave Ellett, Toro.	.20
☐	36 Martin Straka, Pitt.	.20
☐	37 Dmitry Yushkevich, Phil.	.20
☐	38 John Tucker, Tamp.	.20
☐	39 Rob Gaudreau, SanJ.	.20
☐	40 Doug Weight, Edmo.	.20
☐	41 Patrick Roy (G), Mont.	1.50
☐	42 Brian Bradley, Tamp.	.20
☐	43 Bob Beers, Edmo.	.20
☐	44 Dino Ciccarelli, Detr.	.20
☐	45 Dean Evason, Dall.	.20
☐	46 Ron Tugnutt (G), Mont.	.20
☐	47 Andy Moog (G), Dall.	.20
☐	48 Jason Dawe, Buff.	.20
☐	49 Ted Donato, Bost.	.20
☐	50 Ron Hextall (G), NYIs.	.20
☐	**51 Derek Armstrong, NYIs. RC**	**1.00**
☐	52 Craig Janney, SLou.	.20
☐	53 Geoff Courtnall, Vanc.	.20
☐	54 Mikael Renberg, Phil.	.20
☐	55 Theoren Fleury, Calg.	.20
☐	56 Martin Brodeur (G), NJer.	1.00
☐	57 Mattias Norström, NYRa.	.20
☐	58 David Sacco, Toro.	.20
☐	59 Jeff Reese (G), Hart.	.20
☐	60 Bill Ranford (G), Edmo.	.20
☐	61 Dan Quinn, Otta.	.20
☐	62 Joé Juneau, Wash.	.20
☐	63 Jeremy Roenick, Chic.	.50
☐	64 Donald Audette, Buff.	.20
☐	65 Zdeno Ciger, Edmo.	.20
☐	66 Cliff Ronning, Vanc.	.20
☐	67 Steve Thomas, NYIs.	.20
☐	68 Norm Maciver, Otta.	.20
☐	69 Vincent Damphousse, Mont.	.20
☐	70 John Vanbiesbrouck (G), Flor.	.20
☐	71 Andrei Kovalenko, Québ.	.20
☐	72 Dave Andreychuk, Toro.	.20
☐	73 Stu Barnes, Flor.	.20
☐	74 Jamie McLennan (G), NYIs.	.20
☐	75 Rudy Poeschek, Tamp.	.20
☐	76 Ken Wregget (G), Pitt.	.20
☐	77 Raymond Bourque, Bost.	.50
☐	78 Grant Fuhr (G), Buff.	.20
☐	79 Paul Cavallini, Dall.	.20
☐	80 Nelson Emerson, Winn.	.20
☐	81 Tim Cheveldae (G), Winn.	.20
☐	**82 Mariusz Czerkawski, Bost. RC**	**1.50**
☐	83 Pat Peake, Wash.	.20
☐	84 Craig Billington (G), Otta.	.20
☐	85 Sean Burke (G), Hart.	.20
☐	86 Chris Gratton, Tamp.	.20
☐	87 Andrei Trefilov (G), Calg.	.20
☐	88 Terry Yake, Anah.	.20
☐	89 Mark Recchi, Phil.	.20
☐	90 Igor Korolev, SLou.	.20
☐	91 Mark Tinordi, Dall.	.20
☐	92 Alex Kovalev, NYRa.	.20
☐	93 Bob Essensa, Detr.	.20
☐	94 Keith Tkachuk, Winn.	.20
☐	95 Pat Falloon, SanJ.	.20
☐	96 John Slaney, Wash.	.20
☐	97 Alexei Zhamnov, Winn.	.20
☐	98 Jeff Norton, SanJ.	.20
☐	99 Doug Gilmour, Toro.	.20
☐	100 Rick Tocchet, Pitt.	.20
☐	101 Robert Kron, Hart.	.20
☐	102 Patrik Carnbäck, Anah.	.20
☐	103 Tom Barrasso (G), Pitt.	.20
☐	104 Jari Kurri, LosA.	.50
☐	105 Iain Fraser, Québ.	.20
☐	106 Mike Donnelly, LosA.	.20
☐	107 Ray Sheppard, Detr.	.20
☐	108 Scott A. Young, Québ.	.20
☐	109 Kirk McLean (G), Vanc.	.20
☐	110 Checklist	.20
☐	111 Sergei Zubov, NYRa.	.20
☐	112 Ivan Droppa, Chic.	.20
☐	113 Brendan Shanahan, SLou.	.50
☐	114 Michal Pivonka, Wash.	.20
☐	115 Pavol Demitra, Otta.	.20
☐	116 Doug Brown, Pitt.	.20
☐	117 Valeri Kamensky, Québ.	.20
☐	118 Alexander Karpovtsev, NYRa.	.20
☐	119 Alexandre Daigle, Otta.	.20
☐	120 Dominik Hasek (G), Buff.	.50
☐	121 Murray Craven, Vanc.	.20
☐	122 Michal Sykora, SanJ.	.20
☐	**123 Aris Brimanis, Phil. RC**	**.50**
☐	124 Benoît Hogue, NYIs.	.20
☐	125 Arto Blomsten, Winn.	.20
☐	126 Russ Courtnall, Dall.	.20
☐	127 Bryan Marchment, Hart.	.20
☐	128 Jeff Hackett (G), Chic.	.20
☐	129 Kevin Miller, SLou.	.20
☐	130 Bryan Smolinski, Bost.	.20
☐	131 John Druce, LosA.	.20
☐	132 Roman Hamrlik, Tamp.	.20
☐	133 Jason Arnott, Edmo.	.20
☐	134 Chris Terreri (G), NJer.	.20
☐	135 Mike Gartner, Toro.	.50
☐	136 Darryl Sydor, LosA.	.20
☐	137 Lyle Odelein, Mont.	.20
☐	138 Martin Gélinas, Vanc.	.20
☐	139 Mike Rathje, SanJ.	.20
☐	140 Sylvain Côté, Wash.	.20
☐	141 Nicklas Lidström, Detr.	.20
☐	142 Guy Hebert (G), Anah.	.20
☐	143 Jozef Stumpel, Bost.	.20
☐	144 Owen Nolan, Québ.	.20
☐	145 Jesse Bélanger, Flor.	.20
☐	146 Bill Guerin, NJer.	.20
☐	147 Mike Stapleton, Edmo.	.20
☐	148 Steve Yzerman, Detr.	1.50
☐	149 Michael Nylander, Calg.	.20
☐	150 Rod Brind'Amour, Phil.	.20
☐	151 Jaromir Jagr, Pitt.	.50
☐	152 Darcy Wakaluk (G), Dall.	.20
☐	153 Sergei Nemchinov, NYRa.	.20
☐	154 Wes Walz, Calg.	.20
☐	155 Sergei Fedorov, Detr.	.50
☐	156 Daniel Laperrière, SLou.	.20
☐	157 Marty McInnis, NYIs.	.20
☐	158 Chris Joseph (G), Tamp.	.20
☐	159 Matt Martin, Toro.	.20
☐	160 Checklist	.20
☐	**161 Denis Tsygurov, Buff. RC**	**.50**
☐	162 Stéphan Lebeau, Anah.	.20
☐	163 Kirk Muller, Mont.	.20
☐	164 Shayne Corson, Edmo.	.20
☐	165 Joe Sakic, Québ.	1.00
☐	166 Denis Savard, Tamp.	.20
☐	167 Kevin Dineen, Phil.	.20
☐	168 Paul Coffey, Detr.	.20
☐	169 Sandis Ozolinsh, SanJ.	.20
☐	170 Stewart Malgunas, Phil.	.20
☐	171 Petr Klima, Tamp.	.20
☐	172 Pat Verbeek, Hart.	.20
☐	173 Yan Kaminsky, NYIs.	.20
☐	174 Marty McSorley, LosA.	.20
☐	175 Arturs Irbe (G), SanJ.	.20
☐	176 Peter Popovic, Mont.	.20
☐	177 Brian Skrudland, Flor.	.20
☐	178 John Lilley, Anah.	.20
☐	179 Boris Mironov, Edmo.	.20
☐	180 Garth Snow (G), Québ.	.20
☐	181 Alexei Kudashov, Toro.	.20
☐	182 Scott Mellanby, Flor.	.20
☐	183 Dale Hunter, Wash.	.20
☐	184 Tommy Söderström (G), Phil.	.20
☐	185 Claude Lemieux, NJer.	.20
☐	186 Félix Potvin (G), Toro.	.20
☐	187 Corey Millen, NJer.	.20
☐	188 Derek King, NYIs.	.20
☐	189 Kelly Hrudey (G), LosA.	.20
☐	190 Dmitri Khristich, Wash.	.20
☐	191 Sylvain Turgeon, Otta.	.20
☐	**192 John Gruden, Bost. RC**	**.50**
☐	193 Michael Peca, Vanc.	.20
☐	194 Vladimir Malakhov, NYIs.	.20
☐	195 Mathieu Schneider, Mont.	.20
☐	196 Jeff Shantz, Chic.	.20
☐	197 Darren McCarty, Detr.	.20
☐	198 Craig Simpson, Buff.	.20
☐	199 Jarkko Varvio, Dall.	.20
☐	200 Gino Odjick, Vanc.	.20
☐	201 Martin Lapointe, Detr.	.20
☐	202 Paul Ysebaert, Chic.	.20
☐	203 Mike McPhee, Dall.	.20
☐	204 John MacLean, NJer.	.20
☐	205 Ulf Samuelsson, Pitt.	.20
☐	206 Garry Valk, Anah.	.20
☐	207 Tomas Sandström, Pitt.	.20
☐	208 Curtis Joseph (G), SLou.	.50
☐	209 Mikhail Shtalenkov (G), Anah.	.20
☐	210 Darren Turcotte, Hart.	.20
☐	211 Markus Näslund, Pitt.	.50
☐	212 Al Iafrate, Bost.	.20
☐	213 Jim Storm, Hart.	.20
☐	**214 Dan Plante, NYIs. RC**	**.50**
☐	215 Brad May, Buff.	.20
☐	216 Nathan Lafayette, Vanc.	.20
☐	217 Brian Noonan, NYRa.	.20
☐	218 Brent* Hughes, Bost.	.20
☐	219 Geoff Sanderson, Hart.	.20
☐	220 Checklist	.20
☐	221 Eric Weinrich, Chic.	.20
☐	222 Greg A. Adams, Vanc.	.20
☐	223 Dominic Roussel (G), Phil.	.20
☐	224 Daren Puppa (G), Tamp.	.20
☐	225 Rob Niedermayer, Flor.	.20
☐	226 Todd Elik, SanJ.	.20
☐	**227 Donald Brashear, Mont. RC**	**1.50**
☐	228 Joe Nieuwendyk, Calg.	.20
☐	229 Tony Granato, LosA.	.20
☐	230 Kirk Maltby, Edmo.	.20
☐	231 Jocelyn Thibault (G), Québ.	.20
☐	232 Shawn McEachern, Pitt.	.20
☐	233 Teppo Numminen, Winn.	.20
☐	234 Johan Garpenlöv, SanJ.	.20
☐	235 Ron Francis, Pitt.	.20
☐	236 Vyacheslav Kozlov, Detr.	.20
☐	237 Scott Niedermayer, NJer.	.20
☐	238 Sergei Krivokrasov, Chic.	.20
☐	239 Dave Manson, Winn.	.20
☐	240 Mike Ricci, Québ.	.20
☐	241 Chad Penney, Otta.	.20
☐	242 Calle Johansson, Wash.	.20
☐	243 Robert Reichel, Calg.	.20
☐	244 Igor Kravchuk, Edmo.	.20
☐	245 Jason Smith, NJer.	.20
☐	246 Neal Broten, Dall.	.20
☐	247 Jeff R. Brown, Vanc.	.20
☐	248 Jason Bowen, Phil.	.20
☐	249 Larry Murphy, Pitt.	.20
☐	250 Gord Murphy, Flor.	.20
☐	251 Darrin Shannon, Winn.	.20
☐	252 Bobby Holik, NJer.	.20
☐	253 Zigmund Palffy, NYIs.	.20
☐	254 Dmitri Mironov, Toro.	.20
☐	255 Adam Graves, NYRa.	.20
☐	256 Alexander Mogilny, Buff.	.20
☐	257 J. Steve Smith, Chic.	.20
☐	258 Jim Montgomery, SLou.	.20
☐	259 Danton Cole, Tamp.	.20
☐	260 Dave McLlwain, Otta.	.20
☐	261 German Titov, Calg.	.20
☐	262 Tom Chorske, NJer.	.20
☐	263 Grant Ledyard, Dall.	.20
☐	264 Garry Galley, Phil.	.20
☐	265 Vlastimil Kroupa, SanJ.	.20
☐	266 Keith Primeau, Detr.	.20
☐	267 Cam Neely, Bost.	.50
☐	268 Chris Pronger, Hart.	.20
☐	269 Richard Matvichuk, Dall.	.20
☐	270 Steve Larmer, NYRa.	.20
☐	271 James Patrick, Calg.	.20
☐	272 Joel Otto, Calg.	.20
☐	273 Todd Nelson, Wash.	.20
☐	274 Joe Sacco, Anah.	.20
☐	**275 Jason York, Detr. RC**	**1.00**
☐	276 Andrew Cassels, Hart.	.20
☐	277 Peter Bondra, Wash.	.20
☐	278 Pat LaFontaine, Buff.	.20
☐	279 Nikolai Borschevsky, Toro.	.20
☐	**280 David Mackey, SLou. RC**	**.50**
☐	281 Cam Stewart, Bost.	.20
☐	282 Sergei* Makarov, SanJ.	.20
☐	**283 Byron Dafoe (G), Wash. RC**	**2.50**
☐	284 Joe Murphy, Chic.	.20
☐	285 Matthew Barnaby, Buff.	.20
☐	286 Derian Hatcher, Dall.	.20
☐	287 Jyrki Lumme, Vanc.	.20
☐	288 Travis Green, NYIs.	.20
☐	289 Milos Holan, Phil.	.20
☐	290 Ed Patterson, Pitt.	.20
☐	291 Randy Burridge, Wash.	.20
☐	292 Brian Savage, Mont.	.20
☐	293 Stéphane Quintal, Winn.	.20
☐	294 Zarley Zalapski, Calg.	.20
☐	295 Vitali Prokhorov, SLou.	.20
☐	296 Ed Belfour (G), Chic.	.50
☐	297 Yuri Khmylev, Buff.	.20
☐	298 Dean McAmmond, Edmo.	.20
☐	299 Bob Corkum, Anah.	.20
☐	300 Darrin Madeley (G), Otta.	.20
☐	301 Brian Bellows, Mont.	.20
☐	302 Andrei Lomakin, Flor.	.20
☐	303 Anatoli Semenov, Anah.	.20
☐	304 Claude Lapointe, Québ.	.20

☐	305 Adam Oates, Bost.	.20
☐	306 Richard Smehlik, Buff.	.20
☐	307 Jim Dowd, NJer.	.20
☐	308 Mark Fitzpatrick (G), Flor.	.20
☐	309 Pierre Sévigny, Mont.	.20
☐	310 Glenn Healy (G), NYRa.	.20
☐	311 Igor Larionov, SanJ.	.20
☐	312 Aaron Ward, Detr.	.20
☐	313 Dale Hawerchuk, Buff.	.20
☐	314 Bob Kudelski, Flor.	.20
☐	315 Chris Osgood (G), Detr.	.20
☐	316 Trent Klatt, Dall.	.20
☐	317 Gary Suter, Chic.	.20
☐	318 Tie Domi, Winn.	.20
☐	319 Dave Gagner, Dall.	.20
☐	320 Kevin Smyth, Hart.	.20
☐	321 Philippe Bozon, SLou.	.20
☐	322 Trevor Kidd (G), Calg.	.20
☐	323 Warren Rychel, LosA.	.20
☐	324 Steven Rice, Edmo.	.20
☐	325 Patrice Brisebois, Mont.	.20
☐	326 Gary Roberts, Calg.	.20
☐	327 Fredrik Olausson, Edmo.	.20
☐	328 Andrei Nazarov, SanJ.	.20
☐	329 Stéphane Fiset (G), Québ.	.20
☐	330 Checklist	.20
☐	331 Fred Knipscheer, Bost.	.20
☐	332 Shawn Chambers, Tamp.	.20
☐	333 Kelly Buchberger, Edmo.	.20
☐	334 Ray Ferraro, NYIs.	.20
☐	335 Dirk Graham, Chic.	.20
☐	336 Ken Daneyko, NJer.	.20
☐	337 Mark Lamb, Phil.	.20
☐	338 Shaun Van Allen, Anah.	.20
☐	339 Chris Simon, Québ.	.20
☐	340 Brent Gilchrist, Dall.	.20
☐	341 Greg Gilbert, NYRa.	.20
☐	342 Brent Severyn, Flor.	.20
☐	343 Craig Berube, Wash.	.20
☐	344 Randy Moller, Flor.	.20
☐	345 Wayne Gretzky, LosA.	2.50
☐	346 Shawn Anderson, Phil.	.20
☐	347 Mikael Andersson, Tamp.	.20
☐	348 Jim Montgomery, Mont.	.20
☐	349 Scott Pearson, Edmo.	.20
☐	350 Kevin Todd, LosA.	.20
☐	351 Ron Sutter, NYIs.	.20
☐	**352 Paul Kruse, Calg. RC**	**.50**
☐	353 Doug Lidster, SLou.	.20
☐	354 Oleg Petrov, Mont.	.20
☐	355 Greg Johnson, Detr.	.20
☐	356 Kevin Stevens, Pitt.	.20
☐	357 Doug Bodger, Buff.	.20
☐	358 Troy Mallette, Otta.	.20
☐	359 Keith Carney, Chic.	.20
☐	360 Petr Nedved, NYRa.	.20
☐	361 Mark Janssens, Hart.	.20
☐	362 Teemu Selänne, Winn.	.50
☐	363 Scott Stevens, NJer.	.20
☐	364 Shane Churla, Dall.	.20
☐	365 John* McIntyre, Vanc.	.20
☐	366 Geoff Smith, Flor.	.20
☐	367 Pierre Turgeon, NYIs.	.20
☐	368 Shawn Burr, Detr.	.20
☐	369 Kevin Hatcher, Wash.	.20
☐	370 Paul Ranheim, Hart.	.20
☐	371 Kevin Haller, Phil.	.20
☐	372 Scott Lachance, NYIs.	.20
☐	373 Craig Muni, Buff.	.20
☐	374 Mike Ridley, Toro.	.20
☐	375 Joby Messier, NYRa.	.20
☐	376 Thomas Steen, Winn.	.20
☐	377 Bruce Driver, NJer.	.20
☐	378 Mike Eastwood, Toro.	.20
☐	379 Brian Benning, Flor.	.20
☐	380 Dallas Drake, Winn.	.20
☐	381 Patrick Flatley, NYIs.	.20
☐	382 Cam Russell, Chic.	.20
☐	383 Bobby Dollas, Anah.	.20
☐	384 Marc Bergevin, Tamp.	.20
☐	385 Joe Mullen, Pitt.	.20
☐	386 Chris Dahlquist, Otta.	.20
☐	387 Robert Petrovicky, Hart.	.20
☐	388 Yves Racine, Mont.	.20
☐	389 Adam Bennett, Edmo.	.20
☐	390 Patrick Poulin, Chic.	.20
☐	391 Vladimir Konstantinov, Detr.	.20
☐	392 Frantisek Kucera, Hart.	.20
☐	393 Petr* Svoboda, Buff.	.20
☐	394 Mike Sillinger, Detr.	.20
☐	395 Kris King, Winn.	.20
☐	396 Kelly Chase, SLou.	.20
☐	397 Peter Douris, Anah.	.20
☐	398 Bob Errey, SanJ.	.20
☐	399 Ronnie Stern, Calg.	.20

☐	400 Randy McKay, NJer.	.20
☐	401 Benoît Brunet, Mont.	.20
☐	402 Gerald Diduck, Vanc.	.20
☐	403 Brian Leetch, NYRa.	.20
☐	404 Stephen Heinze, Bost.	.20
☐	405 Jimmy Waite (G), SanJ.	.20
☐	406 Nick Kypreos, NYRa.	.20
☐	407 J.J. Daigneault, Mont.	.20
☐	408 Alexei Gusarov, Québ.	.20
☐	409 Paul Broten, Dall.	.20
☐	410 Drake Berehowsky, Toro.	.20
☐	411 Sandy McCarthy, Calg.	.20
☐	412 John Cullen, Pitt.	.20
☐	413 Dan Quinn, LosA.	.20
☐	414 Dave Lowry, Flor.	.20
☐	415 Eric Lindros, Phil.	.50
☐	416 Igor Ulanov, Winn.	.20
☐	417 Bob Sweeney, Buff.	.20
☐	418 Jamie Macoun, Toro.	.20
☐	419 Brian Mullen, NYIs.	.20
☐	420 Stephen Leach, Bost.	.20
☐	421 Jamie Baker, SanJ.	.20
☐	422 Uwe Krupp, Québ.	.20
☐	423 Steve Konowalchuk, Wash.	.20
☐	424 Craig Ludwig, Dall.	.20
☐	425 Bret Hedican, Vanc.	.20
☐	426 Steve Dubinsky, Chic.	.20
☐	427 Rob Zamuner, Tamp.	.20
☐	428 Dave Brown, Phil.	.20
☐	429 Robert Lang, LosA.	.20
☐	430 Dave Babych, Vanc.	.20
☐	431 Scott Thornton, Edmo.	.20
☐	432 Dave Archibald, Otta.	.20
☐	433 Éric Desjardins, Mont.	.20
☐	434 Jim Cummins, Tamp.	.20
☐	435 Troy Loney, NYIs.	.20
☐	436 Bob Carpenter, NJer.	.20
☐	437 Joe Reekie, Wash.	.20
☐	438 Mike Krushelnyski, Detr.	.20
☐	439 Jeff Odgers, SanJ.	.20
☐	440 Checklist	.20
☐	441 Brian Rolston, NJer.	.20
☐	442 Adam Deadmarsh, Québ.	.20
☐	**443 Éric Fichaud (G), Toro. RC**	**1.00**
☐	444 Michel Petit, LosA.	.20
☐	445 Brett Lindros, NYIs.	.20
☐	446 Pat Jablonski (G), Toro.	.20
☐	447 Janne Laukkanen, Québ.	.20
☐	448 Ray Whitney, SanJ.	.20
☐	449 Tom Kurvers, Anah.	.20
☐	450 Phil Housley, Calg.	.20
☐	451 Viktor Kozlov, SanJ.	.20
☐	452 Aaron Gavey, Tamp.	.20
☐	453 Doug Zmolek, Dall.	.20
☐	454 Tony Twist, SLou.	.20
☐	455 Paul Kariya, Anah.	1.00
☐	**456 Vladislav Boulin, Phil. RC**	**.50**
☐	**457 Kevin Brown, LosA. RC**	**.50**
☐	458 David Wilkie, Mont.	.20
☐	459 Jamie Pushor, Detr.	.20
☐	460 Glen Wesley, Hart.	.20
☐	461 Al MacInnis, SLou.	.20
☐	462 Bernie Nicholls, Chic.	.20
☐	463 Luc Robitaille, Pitt.	.50
☐	464 Mike Vernon (G), Detr.	.20
☐	465 Alexander Cherbayev, SanJ.	.20
☐	466 Garth Butcher, Toro.	.20
☐	467 Todd Harvey, Dall.	.20
☐	468 Viktor Gordiouk, Buff.	.20
☐	469 Pat Neaton, Pitt.	.20
☐	470 Jason Muzzatti (G), Calg.	.20
☐	471 Valeri Bure, Mont.	.20
☐	472 Kenny Jönsson, Toro.	.20
☐	473 Alexei Kasatonov, Bost.	.20
☐	474 Rick Tocchet, LosA.	.20
☐	475 Peter Forsberg, Québ.	.50
☐	476 Sean Hill, Otta.	.20
☐	477 Steven Rice, Hart.	.20
☐	478 David Roberts, SLou.	.20
☐	**479 Justin Hocking, LosA. RC**	**.50**
☐	480 Chris Therien, Phil.	.20
☐	**481 Cale Hulse, NJer. RC**	**.50**
☐	482 Jeff Friesen, SanJ.	.20
☐	483 Brandon Convery, Toro.	.20
☐	**484 Ian Laperrière, SLou. RC**	**1.00**
☐	**485 Brent Grieve, Chic. RC**	**.50**
☐	**486 Valeri Karpov, Anah. RC**	**.50**
☐	487 Steve Chiasson, Calg.	.20
☐	488 Jassen Cullimore, Vanc.	.20
☐	489 Jason Wiemer, Tamp.	.20
☐	490 Checklist	.20
☐	491 Len Barrie, Pitt.	.20
☐	492 Turner Stevenson, Mont.	.20
☐	493 Kelly Kisio, Calg.	.20
☐	494 Dwayne Norris, Québ.	.20

☐	495 Ron Hextall (G), Phil.	.20
☐	496 Jaroslav Modry, NJer.	.20
☐	497 Todd Gill, Toro.	.20
☐	498 Ken Sutton, Buff.	.20
☐	499 Sergio Momesso, Vanc.	.20
☐	500 Dean Kennedy, Winn.	.20
☐	501 David Reid, Bost.	.20
☐	502 Jocelyn Lemieux, Hart.	.20
☐	503 Mark Osborne, NYRa.	.20
☐	504 Mike Hough, Flor.	.20
☐	505 Todd Marchant, Edmo.	.20
☐	506 Keith Jones, Wash.	.20
☐	507 Sylvain Lefebvre, Québ.	.20
☐	508 Sergei Zholtok, Bost.	.20
☐	509 Jayson More, SanJ.	.20
☐	510 Mike Craig, Toro.	.20
☐	511 Jason Allison, Wash.	.50
☐	512 Jim Paek, Otta.	.20
☐	**513 Chris Tamer, Pitt. RC**	**.50**
☐	514 Craig MacTavish, Phil.	.20
☐	515 Mikko Mäkelä, Bost.	.20
☐	516 Tom Fitzgerald, Flor.	.20
☐	517 Brent Fedyk, Phil.	.20
☐	518 Don Sweeney, Bost.	.20
☐	519 Kelly Miller, Wash.	.20
☐	520 Jiri Slegr, Vanc.	.20
☐	521 Wayne Presley, Buff.	.20
☐	522 Mark Greig, Calg.	.20
☐	523 Doug Houda, Buff.	.20
☐	524 Kay Whitmore (G), Vanc.	.20
☐	**525 Craig Ferguson, Mont. RC**	**.50**
☐	526 Kent Manderville, Toro.	.20
☐	527 Trevor Linden, Vanc.	.20
☐	528 Jeff Beukeboom, NYRa.	.20
☐	529 Adam Foote, Québ.	.20
☐	530 Mats Sundin, Toro.	.50
☐	531 Shjon Podein, Phil.	.20
☐	532 Louie DeBrusk, Edmo.	.20
☐	533 Peter Zezel, Dall.	.20
☐	534 Greg Hawgood, Pitt.	.20
☐	535 Pat Elynuik, Otta.	.20
☐	536 Mike Ramsey, Detr.	.20
☐	537 Bob Beers, NYIs.	.20
☐	538 David* Williams, Anah.	.20
☐	539 Philippe Boucher, Buff.	.20
☐	540 Rob (Jr.) Brown, LosA.	.20
☐	541 Marc Potvin, Bost.	.20
☐	542 Wendel Clark, Québ.	.50
☐	543 Alexander Semak, NJer.	.20
☐	544 Randy Wood, Buff.	.20
☐	545 Frantisek Musil, Calg.	.20
☐	546 Mike Peluso, NJer.	.20
☐	547 Gaétan Duchesne, SanJ.	.20
☐	548 Curtis Leschyshyn, Québ.	.20
☐	549 Rob DiMaio, Phil.	.20
☐	550 Checklist	.20

CREASE PATROL

Series Two Insert Set (10 cards):		**8.00**
	Insert (1:18)	**CP**
☐	1 Patrick Roy (G), Mont.	3.00
☐	2 Ed Belfour (G), Chic.	1.00
☐	3 Curtis Joseph (G), SLou.	1.00
☐	4 Félix Potvin (G), Toro.	.50
☐	5 John Vanbiesbrouck (G), Flor.	.50
☐	6 Dominik Hasek (G), Buff.	1.00
☐	7 Kirk McLean (G), Vanc.	.50
☐	8 Mike Richter (G), NYRa.	.50
☐	9 Martin Brodeur (G), NJer.	2.00
☐	10 Bill Ranford (G), Edmo.	.50

FIRE ON ICE

Series One Insert Set (12 cards):		**25.00**
	Insert (1:18)	**FOI**
☐	1 Sergei Fedorov, Detr.	2.00
☐	2 Jeremy Roenick, Chic.	2.00
☐	3 Pavel Bure, Vanc.	2.00

☐	4 Wayne Gretzky, LosA.	10.00
☐	5 Doug Gilmour, Toro.	1.00
☐	6 Eric Lindros, Phil.	2.00
☐	7 Joé Juneau, Wash.	1.00
☐	8 Paul Coffey, Detr.	1.00
☐	9 Mario Lemieux, Pitt.	7.00
☐	10 Alexander Mogilny, Buff.	1.00
☐	11 Mike Gartner, Toro.	2.00
☐	12 Teemu Selänne, Winn.	2.00

GOLD LEAF ROOKIE

Series One Insert Set (15 cards):		**30.00**
	Insert (1:18)	**GLR**
☐	1 Martin Brodeur (G), NJer.	10.00
☐	2 Jason Arnott, Edmo.	3.00
☐	3 Alexei Yashin, Otta.	4.00
☐	4 Chris Gratton, Tamp.	1.00
☐	5 Alexandre Daigle, Otta.	1.00
☐	6 Mikael Renberg, Phil.	2.00
☐	7 Rob Niedermayer, Flor.	1.00
☐	8 Boris Mironov, Edmo.	1.00
☐	9 Chris Pronger, Hart.	4.00
☐	10 Chris Osgood (G), Detr.	4.00
☐	11 Derek Plante, Buff.	1.00
☐	12 Pat Peake, Wash.	1.00
☐	13 Jason Allison, Wash.	4.00
☐	14 Bryan Smolinski, Bost.	1.00
☐	15 Jocelyn Thibault (G), Québ.	3.00

GOLD LEAF STARS

Insert Set (15 cards):		**325.00**
	Insert	**GLS**
☐	1 S. Fedorov / W. Gretzky	75.00
☐	2 D. Gilmour / J. Roenick	20.00
☐	3 M. Richter / P. Roy	50.00
☐	4 P. Bure / Br. Hull	25.00
☐	5 M. Messier / A. Yashin	25.00
☐	6 R. Bourque / B. Leetch	25.00
☐	7 E. Belfour (G) / Cu. Joseph	30.00
☐	8 M. Brodeur (G) / D. Hasek (G)	40.00
☐	9 C. Neely / M. Renberg	20.00
☐	10 J. Arnott / M. Modano	20.00
☐	11 M. Lemieux / E. Lindros	60.00
☐	12 R. Blake / S. Stevens	15.00
☐	13 F. Potvin / J. Vanbiesbrouck (G)	15.00
☐	14 P. LaFontaine / A. Oates	15.00
☐	15 J. Jagr / M. Recchi	20.00

LEAF LIMITED

Insert Set (28 cards):		**70.00**
	Insert	**LL**
☐	1 Guy Hebert (G), Anah.	2.00
☐	2 Adam Oates, Bost.	2.00
☐	3 Dominik Hasek (G), Buff.	2.00
☐	4 Robert Reichel, Calg.	2.00
☐	5 Jeremy Roenick, Chic.	2.00
☐	6 Mike Modano, Dall.	2.00
☐	7 Sergei Fedorov, Detr.	2.00
☐	8 Jason Arnott, Edmo.	2.00
☐	9 John Vanbiesbrouck (G), Flor.	2.00
☐	10 Chris Pronger, Hart.	2.00
☐	11 Wayne Gretzky, LosA.	15.00
☐	12 Patrick Roy (G), Mont.	10.00
☐	13 Martin Brodeur (G), NJer.	5.00
☐	14 Pierre Turgeon, NYIs.	2.00
☐	15 Mark Messier, NYRa.	2.00
☐	16 Alexei Yashin, Otta.	2.00
☐	17 Eric Lindros, Phil.	2.00
☐	18 Mario Lemieux, Pitt.	10.00
☐	19 Joe Sakic, Québ.	5.00
☐	20 Brendan Shanahan, SLou.	2.00

☐	21 Arturs Irbe (G), SanJ.	2.00
☐	22 Chris Gratton, Tamp.	2.00
☐	23 Doug Gilmour, Toro.	2.00
☐	24 Pavel Bure, Vanc.	2.00
☐	25 Joé Juneau, Wash.	2.00
☐	26 Teemu Selänne, Winn.	2.00
☐	27 Paul Kariya, Anah.	5.00
☐	28 Peter Forsberg, Québ.	5.00

PHENOMS

Series Two Insert Set (10 cards):		**16.00**
	Insert (1:36)	**Phen**
☐	1 Jamie Storr (G), LosA.	1.00
☐	2 Brett Lindros, NYIs.	1.00
☐	3 Peter Forsberg, Québ.	7.00
☐	4 Jason Wiemer, Tamp.	1.00
☐	5 Paul Kariya, Anah.	5.00
☐	6 Oleg Tverdovsky, Anah.	1.00
☐	7 Éric Fichaud (G), Toro.	1.00
☐	8 Viktor Kozlov, SanJ.	1.00
☐	9 Jeff Friesen, SanJ.	1.00
☐	10 Valeri Karpov, Anah.	1.00

1994 - 95 LEAF ELIT SET

The most expensive singles are Peter Forsberg ($10-12), Mats Sundin ($8-10), Johan Hedberg ($4-8) and Nicklas Lidström ($4-6). NHL stars sell between $1-3. All other singles sell between 20¢ and $1.00.

Series One Set (160 cards): **30.00**
Series Two Set (160 cards): **45.00**

	Player		Player
☐	1 Thomas Tallberg	☐	2 Hakan Algotsson (G)
☐	3 Mikael Magnusson	☐	4 Per Lundell
☐	5 Kenneth Kennholt	☐	6 Jan Huokko
☐	7 Petter Nilsson	☐	8 Johan Norgren
☐	9 Anders Berglund	☐	10 Kari Eloranta
☐	11 Sam Lindstahl	☐	12 Johan Rosen
☐	13 Jonas Johnsson	☐	14 Erik Huusko
☐	15 Thomas Rhodin	☐	16 Patric Kjellberg
☐	17 Fredrik Andersson	☐	18 Stefan Nilsson
☐	19 Petri Liimatainen	☐	20 Lars Jansson
☐	21 Per Wallin	☐	22 Mika Nieminen
☐	23 Lars Ivarsson	☐	24 Ronnie Sundin
☐	25 Bedrich Scerban	☐	26 Anders Huusko
☐	27 Erik Grenkvist	☐	28 Stefan Ornskog
☐	29 Marcus Thuresson	☐	30 John Stromvall
☐	31 Peter Hasselblad	☐	32 Anders Eriksson
☐	33 Roger Elvenes	☐	34 Stefan Larsson
☐	35 Alexei Salomatin	☐	36 Niclas Havelid
☐	37 Mikael Lindman	☐	38 Jens Ohling
☐	39 Håkan Loob	☐	40 Johan Hedberg (G)
☐	41 Niklas Eriksson	☐	42 Robert Norberg
☐	43 Robert Svehla	☐	44 Hans Honsson
☐	45 Tomas Srsen	☐	46 Thomas Sjogren
☐	47 Mishat Fahrutdinov	☐	48 Thomas Standberg
☐	49 Andreas Dackell	☐	50 Peter Nilsson
☐	51 Andreas Johnsson	☐	52 Stefan Falk
☐	53 Marcus Akerblom	☐	54 Peter Aslin (G)
☐	55 Ricard Persson	☐	56 Tomas Nänzén
☐	57 Per-Johan Svensson	☐	58 Terhom Koskela
☐	59 Henrik Nelsson	☐	60 Mats Lindberg
☐	61 Anders Huss	☐	62 Magnus Hansson
☐	63 Mats Lindgren	☐	64 Thomas Ljungberg
☐	65 Tomas Forslund	☐	66 Thomas Ostlund
☐	67 Raimo Helminen	☐	68 Magnus Wenblom
☐	69 Jörgen Jönsson	☐	70 Peter Berndtsson
☐	71 Stefan Hellkvist	☐	72 Tommy Lehmann
☐	73 Stefan Klockare	☐	74 Ola Josefsson
☐	75 Peter Lindmark (G)	☐	76 Ove Thornberg

☐ 77 Jarno Kakitalo	☐ 78 Tomas Berglund
☐ 79 Bo Svanberg	☐ 80 Lennart Hermansson
☐ 81 Stefan Elvenes	☐ 82 Daniel Alfredsson
☐ 83 Claes Lindblom	☐ 84 Björn Ahlström
☐ 85 Ove Molin	☐ 86 Fredrik Lindquist
☐ 87 Clas Ericksson	☐ 88 Pter Hammarstrom
☐ 89 Magnus Swardh	☐ 90 Lars Hurtig
☐ 91 Daniel Rydmark	☐ 92 Lars Bystrom
☐ 93 Mats Loov	☐ 94 Lars Dahlstrom
☐ 95 Johan Brummer	☐ 96 Patric Englund
☐ 97 Christer Olsson	☐ 98 Patrik Erickson
☐ 99 Peter Ottsosson	☐ 100 Tomas Jonsson
☐ 101 Lars Modig	☐ 102 Ake Liljebjorn (G)
☐ 103 Patrik Sylvegard	☐ 104 Danel Johansson
☐ 105 Edvin Frylen	☐ 106 Par Edlund
☐ 107 Paul Andersson	☐ 108 Rikard Franzen
☐ 109 Christian Due-Boje	☐ 110 Tommy Samuelsson
☐ 111 Mathias Svedberg	☐ 112 Hans Lodin
☐ 113 Jonas Eriksson	☐ 114 Mikael Engstrom
☐ 115 Hakan Ahlund	☐ 116 Kari Suoraniemi
☐ 117 Peter Jacobsson	☐ 118 Kristian Gahn
☐ 119 Tommy Melkersson	☐ 120 Oscar Ackestrom
☐ 121 Thomas Johansson	☐ 122 Jesper Duus
☐ 123 Hans Abrahamsson	☐ 124 Orjan Lindmark
☐ 125 Torbjorn Lindberg	☐ 126 Michael Sundlov
☐ 127 Peter Sundstrom	☐ 128 Pierre Johnsson
☐ 129 Thomas Carlsson	☐ 130 Stefan Axelsson
☐ 131 Robert Norkmark	☐ 132 Torbjorn Persson
☐ 133 Bjorn Nord	☐ 134 Mats Ytter
☐ 135 A.I.K.	☐ 136 Brynäs
☐ 137 Djurgårdens	☐ 138 Vastra Frolunda
☐ 139 Färjestads	☐ 140 HV 71
☐ 141 Leksands	☐ 142 Luleåa
☐ 143 Malmö	☐ 144 MoDo
☐ 145 Rögle	☐ 146 Västerås
☐ 147 A.I.K.	☐ 148 Brynäs
☐ 149 Djurgårdens	☐ 150 Vastra Frolunda
☐ 151 Färjestads	☐ 152 HV 71 Logo
☐ 153 Leksands	☐ 154 Luleå
☐ 155 Malmö	☐ 156 MoDo
☐ 157 Rögle	☐ 158 Västerås
☐ 159 Checklist	☐ 160 Checklist
☐ 161 Kenneth Johansson	☐ 162 Stefan Jonsson
☐ 163 Mikael Wahlberg	☐ 164 Per Djoos
☐ 165 Andreas Schultz	☐ 166 Sacha Molin
☐ 167 Marcus Ramén	☐ 168 Jergus Baca
☐ 169 Erik Bergström	☐ 170 Jonas Forsberg
☐ 171 Olli Kaski	☐ 172 Morgan Samuelsson
☐ 173 Anders Burström	☐ 174 Staninslav Meciar
☐ 175 Leif Rohlin	☐ 176 Lars Edström
☐ 177 Esa Keskinen	☐ 178 Daniel Casselstahl
☐ 179 Mattias Timander	☐ 180 Peter Nordström
☐ 181 Patric Aberg	☐ 182 Mikael Enander
☐ 183 Charles Berglund	☐ 184 Andersson-Junkka
☐ 185 Sergei Fokin	☐ 186 Boo Ahl (G)
☐ 187 Jiri Kucera	☐ 188 R. Nordström (G)
☐ 189 Peter Forsberg	☐ 190 Arto Ruotanen
☐ 191 Mikael Wiklander	☐ 192 Joakim Persson
☐ 193 Peter Larsson	☐ 194 Per Eklund
☐ 195 Joacim Esbjörs	☐ 196 Magnus Arvedsson
☐ 197 Marko Palo	☐ 198 Mikael Homberg
☐ 199 Mikael Renberg	☐ 200 Tero Lehterä
☐ 201 Fredrik Lindh	☐ 202 Johan Finnström
☐ 203 Peter Popovic	☐ 204 Tony Barthelson
☐ 205 Stefan Pöllä	☐ 206 Jonas Esbjörs
☐ 207 Roger Hansson	☐ 208 Mikael Håkanson
☐ 209 Daniel Tjarnqvist	☐ 210 Anders Carlsson
☐ 211 Dick Tarnstrom	☐ 212 Johan Tornberg
☐ 213 Joakim Lundberg	☐ 214 Marko Jantunen
☐ 215 Patrik Haltia	☐ 216 Fredrik Stillman
☐ 217 Andy Schneider	☐ 218 Tomas Holmström
☐ 219 Jens Hemström	☐ 220 Anders Soderberg
☐ 221 Peter Lundmark	☐ 222 Patrik Juhlin
☐ 223 Anders Gozzi	☐ 224 Marcus Ragnarsson
☐ 225 Mattias Olsson	☐ 226 Andreas Karlsson
☐ 227 Tomas Lilja	☐ 228 Stefan Ohman
☐ 229 Jarmo Kekalainen	☐ 230 Tony Skopac
☐ 231 Lars Karlsson	☐ 232 Mats Sundin
☐ 233 Peter Ström	☐ 234 Mattias Johansson
☐ 235 Johan Lindbom	☐ 236 Mats Lusth
☐ 237 Marcus Magnertoft	☐ 238 Martin Hostak
☐ 239 Mikael Pettersson	☐ 240 Johan Akerman
☐ 241 Mathias Hällback	☐ 242 Johan Davidsson
☐ 234 Pelle Eklund	☐ 244 Johan Sälle
☐ 245 Per Svartvadet	☐ 246 Ville Siren
☐ 247 Mattias Lööf	☐ 248 Per-Johan Axelsson
☐ 249 Peter Gerhardsson	☐ 250 Jonas Bergqvist
☐ 251 P-J Johansson	☐ 252 Mattias Bosson
☐ 253 Andreas Olsson	☐ 254 Patrik Zetterberg
☐ 255 Michael Johansson	☐ 256 Stefan Gustavson
☐ 257 Jerry Persson	☐ 258 Stefan Nilsson
☐ 259 Roger Johansson	☐ 260 Jarmo Myllys (G)
☐ 261 Kyosti Karjalainen	☐ 262 Thomas Eriksson
☐ 263 Michael Hjälm	☐ 264 Espen Knutsen
☐ 265 A. Salomonsson	☐ 266 Patrik Höglund
☐ 267 Peter Andersson	☐ 268 Brett Hauer
☐ 269 Stefan Ketola	☐ 270 Patrik Carnbäck
☐ 271 Petter Rönnqvist	☐ 272 Roger Ohman
☐ 273 F. Modin, Brynäs	☐ 274 Alexander Beliavski
☐ 275 Niklas Brännström	☐ 276 Per Gustafsson
☐ 277 Nicklas Nordquist	☐ 278 Roger Åkerström
☐ 279 Jiri Vykoukal	☐ 280 Jesper Mattsson
☐ 281 Henrik Nordfeldt	☐ 282 Joakim Musakka
☐ 283 Anders Johnson	☐ 284 Niklas Sundström
☐ 285 Nicklas Lidström	☐ 286 Tomas Sandström
☐ 287 Jens Nielsen	☐ 288 Mattias Öhlund
☐ 289 Markus Eriksson	☐ 290 Mikael Sandberg
☐ 291 Sergei Pushkov	☐ 292 Jonas Höglund
☐ 293 Peter Ekelund	☐ 294 Fredrik Bergqvist
☐ 295 T. Bendelin, Coach	☐ 296 T. Sandlin, Coach
☐ 297 T. Boustedt, Coach	☐ 298 C. Evensson, Coach
☐ 299 S. Bergman, Coach	☐ 300 W. Fleming, Coach
☐ 301 Bergstrom, Coach	☐ 302 H. Jortikka, Coach
☐ 303 Leif Boork, Coach	☐ 304 Abrahamss., Coach
☐ 305 R. Edmonds, Coach	☐ 306 U.Labraaten, Coach
☐ 307 AIK Team Photo	☐ 308 Brynäs Team Photo
☐ 309 Djurgårdens Photo	☐ 310 Färjestads Photo
☐ 311 HV71 Team Photo	☐ 312 Leksands Photo
☐ 313 Luleå Team Photo	☐ 314 Malmö Team Photo
☐ 315 MoDo Team Photo	☐ 316 Rögle Team Photo
☐ 317 Vasterås Photo	☐ 318 Frolunda Photo
☐ 319 Checklist	☐ 320 Checklist

CLEAN SWEEPERS

Inserts start at $4-5.

Series One Insert Set (10 cards): 45.00

Leaf Elit	Leaf Elit
☐ 1 Peter Lindmark (G)	☐ 2 Michael Sundlov (G)
☐ 3 Thomas Ostlund (G)	☐ 4 Jonas Eriksson (G)
☐ 5 Peter Aslin (G)	☐ 6 Ake Liljebjorn (G)
☐ 7 Johan Hedberg (G)	☐ 8 Henrik Arvsell (G)
☐ 9 F. Andersson (G)	☐ 10 Hakan Algotsson (G)

FOREIGN AFFAIRS

Inserts start at $2-3.

Series One Insert Set (10 cards): 30.00

Player	Player
☐ 1 Espen Knutsen	☐ 2 Esa Keskinen
☐ 3 Marko Jantunen	☐ 4 Jarmo Myllys (G)
☐ 5 Jiri Kucera	☐ 6 Jiri Vykoukal
☐ 7 Jarmo Kekalainen	☐ 8 Olli Kaski
☐ 9 Jergus Baca	☐ 10 Tero Lehtera

GOLD CARDS

Peter Forsberg is the most expensive insert at $15-25.
Inserts start at $2-3.

Series One Insert Set (24 cards): 80.00

Player	Player
☐ 1 Title Card	☐ 2 Andreas Dackell
☐ 3 Charles Berglund	☐ 4 Christian Due-Boje
☐ 5 Daniel Rydmark	☐ 6 Fredrik Stillman
☐ 7 Hakan Algotsson	☐ 8 Häkan Loob
☐ 9 Jonas Bergqvist	☐ 10 Jörgen Jönsson
☐ 11 Kenny Jönsson	☐ 12 Leif Rohlin
☐ 13 Magnus Svensson	☐ 14 Mats Näslund
☐ 15 Michael Sundlov	☐ 16 Niklas Eriksson
☐ 17 Patric Kjellberg	☐ 18 Patrick Juhlin
☐ 19 Peter Forsberg	☐ 20 Roger Hansson
☐ 21 Roger Johansson	☐ 22 Stefan Örnskog
☐ 23 Tomas Jönsson	☐ 24 Tommy Salo (G)

GUEST SPECIAL

Peter Forsberg is the most expensive insert at $25-35.
Inserts start at $3-4.

Series Two Insert Set (8 cards): 70.00

Player	Player
☐ 1 Mats Sundin	☐ 2 Tomas Sandström
☐ 3 Peter Forsberg	☐ 4 Nicklas Lidström
☐ 5 Mikael Renberg	☐ 6 Roger Johansson
☐ 7 Peter Popovic	☐ 8 Patrick Juhlin

NHL DRAFT

Daniel Alfredsson is the most expensive insert at $8-12.
Inserts start at $2-3.

Series Two Insert Set (10 cards): 30.00

Player	Player
☐ 1 Mattias Öhlund	☐ 2 Johan Davidsson
☐ 3 Fredrik Modin	☐ 4 Johan Finnstrom
☐ 5 Edvin Frylen	☐ 6 Daniel Alfredsson
☐ 7 Patrik Haltia	☐ 8 Peter Strom
☐ 9 Thomas Holmström	☐ 10 Dick Tarnstrom

PLAYMAKERS

Inserts start at $2-3.

Series One Insert Set (6 cards): 15.00

Player	Player
☐ 1 Title Card	☐ 2 Stefan Nilsson
☐ 3 Mika Nieminen	☐ 4 Raimo Helminen
☐ 5 Peter Larsson	☐ 6 Häkan Loob

ROOKIE ROCKETS

Inserts start at $2-3.

Series Two Insert Set (10 cards): 30.00

Player	Player
☐ 1 Fredrik Modin	☐ 2 J. Andersson-Junkka
☐ 3 Thomas Holmström	☐ 4 Mattias Öhlund
☐ 5 Per Eklund	☐ 6 Daniel Tjarnqvist
☐ 7 Joakim Persson	☐ 8 Patrik Haltia
☐ 9 Andreas Karlsson	☐ 10 Stefan Nilsson

STUDIO SIGNATURES

Inserts start at $2-3.

Series Two Insert Set (12 cards): 30.00

Player	Player
☐ 1 Rikard Franzen	☐ 2 Anders Huuss
☐ 3 Jens Ohling	☐ 4 Tommy Samuelsson
☐ 5 Fredrik Stillman	☐ 6 Jonas Bergqvist
☐ 7 Johan Stromvall	☐ 8 Roger Nordström
☐ 9 Lars Bystrom	☐ 10 Roger Elvenes
☐ 11 Leif Rohlin	☐ 12 Tero Koskela

TOP GUNS

Inserts start at $2-3.

Series Two Insert Set (12 cards): 35.00

Player	Player
☐ 1 Tomas Srsen	☐ 2 Häkan Loob
☐ 3 Lars Hurtig	☐ 4 Stefan Elvenes
☐ 5 Jörgen Jönsson	☐ 6 Robert Svehla
☐ 7 Daniel Rydmark	☐ 8 Ove Thornberg
☐ 9 Patric Kjellberg	☐ 10 Mats Loov

1994 - 95 LEAF LIMITED

Imprint: © 1995 DONRUSS, INC.

Complete Set (120 cards): 110.00

Common Player: .35

Player	NRMT-MT
☐ 1 Mario Lemieux, Pitt.	7.50
☐ 2 Brett Hull, SLou.	2.50
☐ 3 Ed Belfour (G), Chic.	2.50
☐ 4 Brian Rolston, NJer.	1.00
☐ 5 Garry Galley, Phil.	.35
☐ 6 Steve Thomas, NYIs.	.50
☐ **7 Kevin Brown, LosA. RC**	**1.00**
☐ 8 Doug Gilmour, Toro.	1.50
☐ 9 Bill Ranford (G), Edmo.	1.00
☐ 10 Wayne Gretzky, LosA.	10.00
☐ 11 Rob Niedermayer, Flor.	.50
☐ 12 Larry Murphy, Pitt.	.50
☐ 13 Glen Wesley, Hart.	.35
☐ 14 Pat Falloon, SanJ.	.35
☐ 15 Jocelyn Thibault (G), Québ.	1.00
☐ 16 Félix Potvin (G), Toro.	1.50
☐ 17 Mike Richter (G), NYRa.	1.00
☐ 18 Jeff R. Brown, Vanc.	.35
☐ 19 Jesse Bélanger, Flor.	.35
☐ 20 Benoit Hogue, NYIs.	.35
☐ 21 Viktor Kozlov, SanJ.	1.00
☐ 22 Chris Pronger, Hart.	1.50
☐ 23 Kirk McLean (G), Vanc.	.50
☐ 24 Oleg Tverdovsky, Anah.	.50
☐ 25 Derian Hatcher, Dall.	.50
☐ 26 Ray Sheppard, Detr.	.35
☐ 27 Pat Verbeek, Hart.	.50
☐ 28 Patrick Roy (G), Mont.	7.50
☐ **29 Mariusz Czerkawski, Bost. RC**	**3.50**
☐ 30 Ron Francis, Pitt.	1.50
☐ 31 Wendel Clark, Québ.	2.00
☐ 32 Rob Blake, LosA.	1.50
☐ 33 Brian Leetch, NYRa.	1.50
☐ 34 Dave Andreychuk, Toro.	.50
☐ 35 Russ Courtnall, Dall.	.50
☐ 36 Alexander Mogilny, Buff.	1.00
☐ 37 Kirk Muller, Mont.	.50
☐ 38 Joé Juneau, Wash.	.50
☐ 39 Robert Reichel, Calg.	.50
☐ 40 Scott Niedermayer, NJer.	.50
☐ 41 Owen Nolan, Québ.	1.50
☐ 42 Mats Sundin, Toro.	2.50
☐ 43 Sandis Ozolinsh, SanJ.	.50
☐ 44 Derek Plante, Buff.	.35
☐ **45 Éric Fichaud (G), Toro. RC**	**2.00**
☐ 46 Kevin Stevens, Pitt.	.50
☐ 47 Igor Larionov, SanJ.	1.50
☐ 48 Mikael Renberg, Phil.	.50
☐ 49 Cam Neely, Bost.	2.50
☐ 50 Brett Lindros, NYIs.	1.00
☐ **51 Valeri Karpov, Anah. RC**	**1.00**
☐ 52 Pierre Turgeon, NYIs.	1.00
☐ 53 Doug Weight, Edmo.	1.50
☐ 54 Geoff Sanderson, Hart.	.50
☐ 55 Vyacheslav Kozlov, Detr.	.50
☐ 56 Chris Gratton, Tamp.	.50
☐ 57 Bryan Smolinski, Bost.	.35
☐ 58 Eric Lindros, Phil.	2.50
☐ 59 Alex Kovalev, NYRa.	1.50
☐ 60 Mike Modano, Dall.	2.50
☐ 61 Jeremy Roenick, Chic.	2.00
☐ 62 Martin Straka, Pitt.	.50
☐ 63 Pat LaFontaine, Buff.	1.50
☐ 64 Vlastimil Kroupa, SanJ.	.35
☐ 65 Sergei Zubov, NYRa.	.50
☐ 66 Jason Arnott, Edmo.	1.00
☐ 67 Petr Nedved, NYRa.	.50
☐ 68 Teemu Selänne, Winn.	2.00
☐ 69 Geoff Courtnall, Vanc.	.35
☐ 70 Martin Brodeur (G), NJer.	4.00
☐ 71 Mark Recchi, Phil.	1.00
☐ 72 John Vanbiesbrouck (G), Flor.	1.00
☐ 73 Adam Graves, NYRa.	1.00
☐ 74 Arturs Irbe (G), SanJ.	1.00
☐ 75 Paul Coffey, Detr.	1.50
☐ 76 Ulf Dahlén, SanJ.	.35
☐ 77 Phil Housley, Calg.	.50
☐ 78 Rod Brind'Amour, Phil.	.50
☐ 79 Al MacInnis, SLou.	1.00
☐ 80 Alexei Yashin, Otta.	1.50
☐ 81 Sergei Fedorov, Detr.	2.50
☐ 82 Joe Nieuwendyk, Calg.	1.00
☐ 83 Chris Chelios, Chic.	1.50
☐ 84 Raymond Bourque, Bost.	3.00
☐ 85 Scott Stevens, NJer.	1.00
☐ 86 Jaromir Jagr, Pitt.	2.50
☐ 87 Alexandre Daigle, Otta.	.35
☐ 88 Luc Robitaille, Pitt.	2.00
☐ 89 Mark Messier, NYRa.	2.50
☐ 90 Vincent Damphousse, Mont.	1.50
☐ 91 Craig Janney, SLou.	.50
☐ 92 John MacLean, NJer.	.35
☐ 93 Steve Duchesne, SLou.	.50
☐ 94 Dale Hawerchuk, Buff.	1.50
☐ 95 Curtis Joseph (G), SLou.	2.50
☐ 96 Chris Osgood (G), Detr.	1.50
☐ 97 Brendan Shanahan, SLou.	2.50
☐ 98 Jason Allison, Wash.	2.00
☐ 99 Theoren Fleury, Calg.	1.50
☐ 100 Pavel Bure, Vanc.	2.00
☐ 101 Mathieu Schneider, Mont.	.50
☐ 102 Dominik Hasek (G), Buff.	2.50
☐ 103 Scott Mellanby, Flor.	.50
☐ 104 Adam Oates, Bost.	1.00
☐ 105 Jari Kurri, LosA.	2.50
☐ 106 Joe Sakic, Québ.	4.00
☐ 107 Paul Kariya, Anah.	5.00
☐ 108 Keith Tkachuk, Winn.	1.50
☐ 109 Daren Puppa (G), Tamp.	.50
☐ 110 Keith Primeau, Detr.	1.00
☐ 111 Alexei Zhitnik, LosA.	.35
☐ 112 Trevor Linden, Vanc.	1.00
☐ 113 Alexei Zhamnov, Winn.	.50
☐ 114 Gary Roberts, Calg.	1.00
☐ 115 Kenny Jönsson, Toro.	.50
☐ 116 Peter Forsberg, Québ.	3.50
☐ 117 Rick Tocchet, LosA.	.50
☐ 118 Aaron Gavey, Tamp.	.35
☐ 119 Jason Wiemer, Tamp.	1.00
☐ 120 Steve Yzerman, Detr.	6.00

GOLD

Insert Set (10 cards): 185.00

Insert (#/2500)	Gold
☐ 1 Mario Lemieux, Pitt.	45.00
☐ 2 Brett Hull, SLou.	15.00
☐ 3 Doug Gilmour, Toro.	12.00
☐ 4 Eric Lindros, Phil.	15.00
☐ 5 Paul Kariya, Anah.	20.00
☐ 6 Jaromir Jagr, Pitt.	15.00
☐ 7 Wayne Gretzky, LosA.	60.00
☐ 8 Jeremy Roenick, Chic.	12.00
☐ 9 Sergei Fedorov, Detr.	15.00
☐ 10 Pavel Bure, Vanc.	12.00

HOCKEY CANADA WORLD JUNIORS

Insert Set (10 cards): 70.00

Insert (#/5000)	CAN
☐ **1 Nolan Baumgartner, Canada Juniors RC**	**6.00**
☐ **2 Éric Dazé, Canada Juniors RC**	**12.00**
☐ 3 Jeff Friesen, Canada Juniors	6.00
☐ 4 Todd Harvey, Canada Juniors	6.00
☐ **5 Ed Jovanovski, Canada Juniors RC**	**12.00**
☐ 6 Jeff O'Neill, Canada Juniors	8.00
☐ **7 Wade Redden, Canada Juniors RC**	**8.00**
☐ **8 Jamie Rivers, Canada Juniors RC**	**6.00**
☐ **9 Ryan Smyth, Canada Juniors RC**	**14.00**
☐ 10 Jamie Storr (G), Canada Juniors	6.00

USA HOCKEY WORLD JUNIORS

Insert Set (10 cards): 50.00

Insert (#/5000)	USA
☐ **1 Bryan Berard, U.S.A. Juniors RC**	**8.00**
☐ **2 Doug Bonner, U.S.A. Juniors RC**	**6.00**
☐ 3 Jason Bonsignore, U.S.A. Juniors	6.00
☐ 4 Adam Deadmarsh, U.S.A. Juniors	6.00
☐ **5 Rory Fitzpatrick, U.S.A. Juniors RC**	**6.00**
☐ **6 Sean Haggerty, U.S.A. Juniors RC**	**6.00**
☐ 7 Jamie Langenbrunner, U.S.A. Juniors	6.00
☐ **8 Jeff Mitchell, U.S.A. Juniors RC**	**6.00**
☐ 9 Richard Park, U.S.A. Juniors	6.00
☐ 10 Deron Quint, U.S.A. Juniors	6.00

1994 - 95 LEGENDS OF HOCKEY

Artwork by Doug West. Singles sell between $8-12.

Card Size: 3 1/2" x 5 1/2"

Series Three Set (18 cards): 120.00

Player	Player
☐ 37 Red Storey	☐ 38 Harry Oliver
☐ 39 Tony Esposito (G)	☐ 40 Milt Schmidt
☐ 41 Ivan Johnson	☐ 42 Brad Park
☐ 43 Frank Mahovlich	☐ 44 Syd Howe
☐ 45 Woody Dumart	☐ 46 Jean Béliveau
☐ 47 Jack Walker	☐ 48 Frank Patrick
☐ 49 Hap Holmes	☐ 50 Elmer Lach
☐ 51 Cecil Dye	☐ 52 Sir Montagu Allan
☐ 53 Red Kelly	☐ 54 Marcel Dionne

1994 - 95 MCDONALD'S / UPPER DECK

Imprint: © 1995 The Upper Deck Compnay

Complete Set (40 cards): 20.00

Player	McD
☐ McD-01 Joe Sakic, Que.	1.50
☐ McD-02 Adam Graves, NYRa.	.35
☐ McD-03 Alexei Yashin, Otta.	.50
☐ McD-04 Patrick Roy (G), Mont.	3.00
☐ McD-05 Ray Bourque, Bos	1.00
☐ McD-06 Brian Leetch, NYRa.	.50

McD-07	Scott Stevens, NJer.	.35
McD-08	Alexander Mogilny, Buff.	.35
McD-09	Eric Lindros, Phil.	1.00
McD-10	Jaromir Jagr, Pitt.	1.00
McD-11	Sandis Ozolinsh, SanJ.	.35
McD-12	Sergei Fedorov, Detr.	1.00
McD-13	Brett Hull, SLou.	1.00
McD-14	Félix Potvin (G), Toro.	.50
McD-15	Al MacInnis, SLou.	.35
McD-16	Chris Chelios, Chic.	.50
McD-17	Rob Blake, LosA.	.50
McD-18	Dave Andreychuk, Toro.	.35
McD-19	Paul Coffey, Detr.	.50
McD-20	Jeremy Roenick, Chic.	.50
McD-21	Joe Nieuwendyk, Calg.	.35
McD-22	Cam Neely, Bost.	1.00
McD-23	Pavel Bure, Vanc.	.50
McD-24	Wendel Clark, Que.	.50
McD-25	Teemu Selänne, Winn.	.50
McD-26	Pierre Turgeon, NYIs.	.35
McD-27	Alexei Zhamnov, Winn.	.35
McD-28	Doug Gilmour, Toro.	.50
McD 29	Vincent Damphousse, Mont.	.50
McD-30	Brendan Shanahan, SLou.	1.00
McD-31	Peter Forsberg, Que.	1.00
McD-32	Paul Kariya, Anah.	1.00
McD-33	Viktor Kozlov, SanJ.	.35
McD-34	Brett Lindros, NYIs.	.35
McD-35	Martin Brodeur (G), NJer.	1.50
McD-36	Alexandre Daigle, Otta.	.35
McD-37	Jason Arnott, Edmo.	.35
McD-38	Alex Kovalev, NYRa.	.50
McD-39	Mikael Renberg, Phil.	.35
CL:	Mike Richter (G), NYRa.	.35

1994 - 95 PANINI STICKERS

The most expensive singles are Wayne Gretzky at $2-3 and Mario Lemieux at $1-2. Players are organized by team.

Imprint: Panini S. r. l. - Modena

Complete Set (276 stickers):	**20.00**
Common Player:	**.20**
Album:	**2.00**

Player	Player
1 Adam Oates	2 Ted Donato
3 Cam Neely	4 Brent* Hughes
5 Bruins	6 Glen Wesley
7 Al Iafrate	8 Raymond Bourque
9 Jon Casey	10 Guy Carbonneau
11 Pierre Sévigny	12 Kirk Muller
13 Canadiens	14 Vincent Damphousse
15 Gilbert Dionne	16 Mathieu Schneider
17 Éric Desjardins	18 Patrick Roy (G)
19 Joé Juneau	20 Dmitri Khristich
21 Dale Hunter	22 Capitals
23 Mike Ridley	24 Peter Bondra
25 Sylvain Côté	26 Kevin Hatcher
27 Don Beaupré (G)	28 Bernie Nicholls
29 Alexander Semak	30 John MacLean
31 Devils	32 Stéphane J.J. Richer
33 Valeri Zelepukin	34 Scott Stevens
35 Martin Brodeur (G)	36 Chris Terreri (G)
37 Rod Brind'Amour	38 Eric Lindros
39 Mark Recchi	40 Flyers
41 Kevin Dineen	42 Brent Fedyk
43 Garry Galley	44 Ryan McGill
45 Dominic Roussel (G)	46 Ray Ferraro
47 Benoît Hogue	48 Pierre Turgeon
49 Islanders	50 Patrick Flatley
51 Steve Thomas	52 Darius Kasparaitis
53 Vladimir Malakhov	54 Ron Hextall (G)
55 Mats Sundin	56 Joe Sakic
57 Nordiques	58 Claude Lapointe
59 Scott A. Young	60 Valeri Kamensky
61 Steven Finn	62 Jocelyn Thibault (G)
63 Stéphane Fiset (G)	64 Brian Skrudland
65 Bob Kudelski	66 Jody Hull
67 Scott Mellanby	68 Panthers
69 Dave Lowry	70 Mike Hough
71 Gord Murphy	72 J. Vanbiesbrouck (G)
73 Ron Francis	74 Mario Lemieux
75 Penguins	76 Jaromir Jagr
77 Rick Tocchet	78 Kevin Stevens
79 Ulf Samuelsson	80 Larry Murphy
81 Tom Barrasso (G)	82 Mark Messier
83 Alex Kovalev	84 Rangers
85 Sergei Nemchinov	86 Steve Larmer
87 Adam Graves	88 Brian Leetch
89 Sergei Zubov	90 Mike Richter (G)
91 Dale Hawerchuk	92 Pat LaFontaine
93 Donald Audette	94 Alexander Mogilny
95 Sabres	96 Yuri Khmylev
97 Brad May	98 Richard Smehlik
99 Dominik Hasek (G)	100 Dave McLlwain
101 Alexandre Daigle	102 Dave Archibald
103 Senators	104 Troy Murray
105 Sylvain Turgeon	106 Gord Dineen
107 Darren Rumble	108 Craig Billington (G)
109 Geoff Sanderson	110 Andrew Cassels
111 Whalers	112 Pat Verbeek
113 Jim Sandlak	114 Jocelyn Lemieux
115 Brian Propp	116 Frantisek Kucera
117 Sean Burke (G)	118 Anatoli Semenov
119 Stéphan Lebeau	120 Mighty Ducks
121 Terry Yake	122 Joe Sacco
123 Todd Ewen	124 Troy Loney
125 Sean Hill	126 Guy Hebert (G)
127 Jeremy Roenick	128 Tony Amonte
129 Joe Murphy	130 Blackhawks
131 Michel Goulet	132 Paul Ysebaert
133 Gary Suter	134 Chris Chelios
135 Ed Belfour (G)	136 Craig Janney
137 Petr Nedved	138 Blues
139 Kevin Miller	140 Brett Hull
141 Brendan Shanahan	142 Phil Housley
143 Steve Duchesne	144 Curtis Joseph (G)
145 Cliff Ronning	146 Pavel Bure
147 Trevor Linden	148 Canucks
149 Geoff Courtnall	150 Gino Odjick
151 Jyrki Lumme	152 Jeff R. Brown
153 Kirk McLean (G)	154 Robert Reichel
155 Joel Otto	156 Joe Nieuwendyk
157 Flames	158 German Titov
159 Theoren Fleury	160 Gary Roberts
161 Al MacInnis	162 Mike Vernon (G)
163 Alexei Zhamnov	164 Nelson Emerson
165 Jets	166 Teemu Selänne
167 Tie Domi	168 Keith Tkachuk
169 Teppo Numminen	170 Stéphane Quintal
171 Tim Cheveldae (G)	172 Wayne Gretzky
173 Jari Kurri	174 Luc Robitaille
175 Kings	176 Tony Granato
177 Rob Blake	178 Marty McSorley
179 Alexei Zhitnik	180 Kelly Hrudey (G)
181 Denis Savard	182 Brian Bradley
183 Lightning	184 Danton Cole
185 Petr Klima	186 Mikael Andersson
187 Shawn Chambers	188 Roman Hamrlik
189 Daren Puppa (G)	190 Doug Gilmour
191 Mike Gartner	192 Nikolai Borschevsky
193 Maple Leafs	194 Dave Andreychuk
195 Wendel Clark	196 Sylvain Lefebvre
197 Dave Ellett	198 Félix Potvin (G)
199 Doug Weight	200 Zdeno Ciger
201 Kelly Buchberger	202 Shayne Corson
203 Oilers	204 Scott Pearson
205 Igor Kravchuk	206 Luke Richardson
207 Bill Ranford (G)	208 Vyacheslav Kozlov
209 Steve Yzerman	210 Sergei Fedorov
211 Ray Sheppard	212 Red Wings
213 Bob Probert	214 Keith Primeau
215 Paul Coffey	216 Nicklas Lidström
217 Igor Larionov	218 Todd Elik
219 Pat Falloon	220 Sharks
221 Ulf Dahlén	222 Sergei* Makarov
223 Sandis Ozolinsh	224 Jeff Norton
225 Arturs Irbe (G)	226 Mike Modano
227 Dave Gagner	228 Mike Craig
229 Stars	230 Russ Courtnall
231 Derian Hatcher	232 Mark Tinordi
233 Craig Ludwig	234 Darcy Wakaluk (G)
235 a Bure / b Hull	
236 a Fedorov / b Andreychuk	
237 a Shanahan / b Sheppard	
238 a Graves / b Neely	
239 a Goal Club / b Modano	
A Bryan Smolinski	B Oleg Petrov
C Pat Peake	D Jaroslav Modry
E Mikael Renberg	F Yan Kaminsky
G Iain Fraser	H Rob Niedermayer
I Markus Näslund	J Alexander Karpovtsev
K Derek Plante	L Alexei Yashin
M Chris Pronger	N Patrik Carnbäck
O Jeff Shantz	P Vitali Karamnov
Q Nathan Lafayette	R Trevor Kidd (G)
S Dave Tomlinson	T Robert Lang
U Chris Gratton	V Alexei Kudashov
W Jason Arnott	X Chris Osgood (G)
Y Mike Rathje	Z Jarkko Varvio
AA Wayne Gretzky	BB Sergei Fedorov
CC Adam Oates	DD Mark Recchi
EE Brendan Shanahan	FF Doug Gilmour
GG Pavel Bure	HH Jeremy Roenick
II Jaromir Jagr	JJ Dave Andreychuk

1994 - 95 PARKHURST

These cards have two versions: the regular cards and a Parkie Gold parallel. An intended second series was never released.

Imprint: © 1994 The Upper Deck Company

	Gold	Regular
Complete Set (315 cards):	**800.00**	**20.00**
Common Player:	**2.00**	**.20**

Promo	Gold	Regular
458 Mikael Renberg, Phil.	-	.25

Player	Gold	Regular
1 Anatoli Semenov, Anah.	2.00	.20
2 Stéphan Lebeau, Anah.	2.00	.20
3 Stu Grimson, Anah.	3.00	.20
4 Mikhail Shtalenkov (G), Anah.	4.00	.20
5 Troy Loney, Anah.	2.00	.20
6 Sean Hill, Anah.	2.00	.20
7 Patrik Carnbäck, Anah.	2.00	.20
8 John Lilley, Anah.	3.00	.20
9 Tim Sweeney, Anah.	2.00	.20
10 Maxim Bets, Anah.	3.00	.20
11 Cam Neely, Bost.	14.00	.50
12 Bryan Smolinski, Bost.	2.00	.20
13 Raymond Bourque, Bost.	18.00	.50
14 Vincent Riendeau (G), Bost.	2.00	.20
15 Al Iafrate, Bost.	3.00	.20
16 Andrew McKim, Bost. RC	**7.00**	**.50**
17 Glen Wesley, Bost.	2.00	.20
18 Daniel Marois, Bost.	2.00	.20
19 Jozef Stumpel, Bost.	3.00	.20
20 Mariusz Czerkawski, Bost. RC	**18.00**	**1.00**
21 Alexander Mogilny, Buff.	7.00	.20
22 Yuri Khmylev, Buff.	2.00	.20
23 Donald Audette, Buff.	6.00	.20
24 Dominik Hasek (G), Buff.	15.00	.50
25 Randy Wood, Buff.	2.00	.20
26 Brad May, Buff.	2.00	.20
27 Wayne Presley, Buff.	2.00	.20
28 Richard Smehlik, Buff.	2.00	.20
29 Dale Hawerchuk, Buff.	9.00	.20
30 Rob Ray, Buff.	3.00	.20
31 Zarley Zalapski, Calg.	2.00	.20
32 Michael Nylander, Calg.	3.00	.20
33 Joe Nieuwendyk, Calg.	6.00	.20
34 Robert Reichel, Calg.	4.00	.20
35 Al MacInnis, Calg.	6.00	.20
36 Andrei Trefilov (G), Calg.	2.00	.20
37 Guy Larose, Calg.	2.00	.20
38 Wes Walz, Calg.	3.00	.20
39 Michel Petit, Calg.	2.00	.20
40 James Patrick, Calg.	2.00	.20
41 Ed Belfour (G), Chic.	14.00	.50
42 Christian Ruuttu, Chic.	2.00	.20
43 Eric Weinrich, Chic.	2.00	.20
44 Joe Murphy, Chic.	2.00	.20
45 Chris Chelios, Chic.	9.00	.20
46 Jeff Shantz, Chic.	2.00	.20
47 Gary Suter, Chic.	3.00	.20
48 Paul Ysebaert, Chic.	2.00	.20
49 Ivan Droppa, Chic.	2.00	.20
50 Keith Carney, Chic.	2.00	.20
51 Andy Moog (G), Dall.	6.00	.20
52 Russ Courtnall, Dall.	3.00	.20
53 Neal Broten, Dall.	3.00	.20
54 Mike Craig, Dall.	2.00	.20
55 Brent Gilchrist, Dall.	2.00	.20
56 Pelle (Pelle) Eklund, Dall.	2.00	.20
57 Richard Matvichuk, Dall.	3.00	.20
58 Dave Gagner, Dall.	2.00	.20
59 Mark Tinordi, Dall.	2.00	.20
60 Paul Broten, Dall.	2.00	.20
61 Nicklas Lidström, Detr.	9.00	.20
62 Shawn Burr, Detr.	2.00	.20
63 Paul Coffey, Detr.	9.00	.20
64 Bob Essensa, Detr.	3.00	.20
65 Dino Ciccarelli, Detr.	4.00	.20
66 Vyacheslav Kozlov, Detr.	3.00	.20
67 Keith Primeau, Detr.	6.00	.20
68 Steve Chiasson, Detr.	2.00	.20
69 Terry Carkner, Detr.	2.00	.20
70 Martin Lapointe, Detr.	6.00	.20
71 Bob Probert, Detr.	4.00	.20
72 Bill Ranford (G), Edmo.	6.00	.20
73 Scott Thornton, Edmo.	2.00	.20
74 Doug Weight, Edmo.	9.00	.20
75 Shayne Corson, Edmo.	4.00	.20
76 Zdeno Ciger, Edmo.	2.00	.20
77 Adam Bennett, Edmo.	2.00	.20
78 Scott Pearson, Edmo.	2.00	.20
79 Brent Grieve, Edmo. RC	**7.00**	**.50**
80 Gord Mark, Edmo. RC	**7.00**	**.50**
81 Shjon Podein, Edmo.	3.00	.20
82 Geoff Smith, Flor.	2.00	.20
83 Bob Kudelski, Flor.	2.00	.20
84 Andrei Lomakin, Flor.	2.00	.20
85 Scott Mellanby, Flor.	3.00	.20
86 Jesse Bélanger, Flor.	2.00	.20
87 Mark Fitzpatrick (G), Flor.	2.00	.20
88 Peter** Andersson, Flor.	2.00	.20
89 Jody Hull, Flor.	2.00	.20
90 Brent Severyn, Flor.	2.00	.20
91 Jim Sandlak, Hart.	2.00	.20
92 Pat Verbeek, Hart.	4.00	.20
93 Ted Crowley, Hart.	3.00	.20
94 Robert Petrovicky, Hart.	2.00	.20
95 Geoff Sanderson, Hart.	3.00	.20
96 Ted Drury, Hart.	2.00	.20
97 Andrew Cassels, Hart.	3.00	.20
98 Igor Chibirev, Hart.	2.00	.20
99 Kevin Smyth, Hart.	2.00	.20
100 Alexander Godynyuk, Hart.	2.00	.20
101 Alexei Zhitnik, LosA.	2.00	.20
102 Dixon Ward, LosA.	2.00	.20
103 Wayne Gretzky, LosA.	60.00	2.00
104 Jari Kurri, LosA.	14.00	.50
105 Rob Blake, LosA.	9.00	.20
106 Marty McSorley, LosA.	3.00	.20
107 Pat Conacher, LosA.	2.00	.20
108 Kevin Todd, LosA.	2.00	.20
109 Robb Stauber (G), LosA.	2.00	.20
110 Keith Redmond, LosA.	2.00	.20
111 John LeClair, Mont.	12.00	.20
112 Brian Bellows, Mont.	3.00	.20
113 Patrick Roy (G), Mont.	45.00	1.50
114 Les Kuntar (G), Mont. RC	**12.00**	**.50**
115 Vincent Damphousse, Mont.	9.00	.20
116 Patrice Brisebois, Mont.	2.00	.20
117 Pierre Sévigny, Mont.	2.00	.20
118 Éric Desjardins, Mont.	4.00	.20
119 Oleg Petrov, Mont.	4.00	.20
120 Kevin Haller, Mont.	2.00	.20
121 Christian Proulx, Mont. RC	**7.00**	**.50**
122 Corey Millen, NJer.	2.00	.20
123 Jaroslav Modry, NJer.	2.00	.20
124 Valeri Zelepukin, NJer.	2.00	.20
125 John MacLean, NJer.	2.00	.20
126 Martin Brodeur (G), NJer.	20.00	.50
127 Bill Guerin, NJer.	6.00	.20
128 Bobby Holik, NJer.	4.00	.20
129 Claude Lemieux, NJer.	4.00	.20
130 Jason Smith, NJer.	2.00	.20
131 Ken Daneyko, NJer.	3.00	.20
132 Derek King, NYIs.	2.00	.20
133 Darius Kasparaitis, NYIs.	3.00	.20
134 Ray Ferraro, NYIs.	2.00	.20
135 Pierre Turgeon, NYIs.	6.00	.20
136 Ron Hextall (G), NYIs.	9.00	.20
137 Travis Green, NYIs.	3.00	.20
138 Joe Day, NYIs.	2.00	.20
139 David Volek, NYIs.	2.00	.20
140 Scott Lachance, NYIs.	2.00	.20
141 Dennis Vaske, NYIs.	2.00	.20
142 Alex Kovalev, NYRa.	9.00	.20
143 Brian Noonan, NYRa.	2.00	.20
144 Sergei Zubov, NYRa.	3.00	.20
145 Craig MacTavish, NYRa.	2.00	.20
146 Steve Larmer, NYRa.	6.00	.20
147 Adam Graves, NYRa.	6.00	.20
148 Jeff Beukeboom, NYRa.	2.00	.20
149 Corey Hirsch (G), NYRa.	2.00	.20
150 Stéphane Matteau, NYRa.	2.00	.20
151 Brian Leetch, NYRa.	9.00	.20
152 Mattias Norström, NYRa.	3.00	.20
153 Sylvain Turgeon, Otta.	2.00	.20
154 Norm Maciver, Otta.	2.00	.20
155 Scott Levins, Otta.	2.00	.20
156 Derek Mayer, Otta.	2.00	.20
157 Dave McLlwain, Otta.	2.00	.20
158 Craig Billington (G), Otta.	2.00	.20
159 Claude Boivin, Otta.	2.00	.20
160 Troy Mallette, Otta.	2.00	.20
161 Evgeny Davydov, Otta.	2.00	.20
162 Dmitri Filimonov, Otta.	2.00	.20
163 Dmitry Yushkevich, Phil.	3.00	.20
164 Rob Zettler, Phil.	2.00	.20
165 Mark Recchi, Phil.	6.00	.20
166 Josef Beránek, Phil.	2.00	.20
167 Rod Brind'Amour, Phil.	4.00	.20
168 Yves Racine, Phil.	2.00	.20
169 Dominic Roussel (G), Phil.	2.00	.20
170 Brent Fedyk, Phil.	2.00	.20
171 Bob Wilkie, Phil.	2.00	.20
172 Kevin Dineen, Phil.	2.00	.20
173 Shawn McEachern, Pitt.	4.00	.20
174 Jaromir Jagr, Pitt.	15.00	.50
175 Tomas Sandström, Pitt.	3.00	.20
176 Ron Francis, Pitt.	9.00	.20
177 Kevin Stevens, Pitt.	3.00	.20
178 Jim McKenzie, Pitt.	2.00	.20
179 Larry Murphy, Pitt.	3.00	.20
180 Joe Mullen, Pitt.	6.00	.20
181 Greg Hawgood, Pitt.	2.00	.20
182 Tom Barrasso (G), Pitt.	6.00	.20
183 Ulf Samuelsson, Pitt.	2.00	.20
184 Bob Bassen, Québ.	2.00	.20
185 Mats Sundin, Québ.	14.00	.50
186 Mike Ricci, Québ.	4.00	.20
187 Iain Fraser, Québ.	2.00	.20
188 Garth Butcher, Québ.	2.00	.20
189 Jocelyn Thibault (G), Québ.	6.00	.20
190 Valeri Kamensky, Québ.	4.00	.20
191 Martin Rucinsky, Québ.	3.00	.20
192 Ron Sutter, Québ.	3.00	.20
193 René Corbet, Québ.	2.00	.20
194 Reggie Savage, Québ.	2.00	.20
195 Alexei Kasatonov, SLou.	3.00	.20
196 Brendan Shanahan, SLou.	14.00	.50
197 Phil Housley, SLou.	3.00	.20
198 Jim Montgomery, SLou.	2.00	.20
199 Curtis Joseph (G), SLou.	14.00	.50
200 Craig Janney, SLou.	3.00	.20
201 David Roberts, SLou.	3.00	.20
202 David Mackey, SLou. RC	**7.00**	**.50**
203 Peter Stastny, SLou.	9.00	.20
204 Terry Hollinger, SLou. RC	**7.00**	**.50**
205 Steve Duchesne, SLou.	3.00	.20
206 Vitali Prokhorov, SLou.	2.00	.20
207 Rob Gaudreau, SanJ.	2.00	.20
208 Sandis Ozolinsh, SanJ.	3.00	.20
209 Johan Garpenlöv, SanJ.	2.00	.20
210 Todd Elik, SanJ.	2.00	.20
211 Sergei* Makarov, SanJ.	6.00	.20
212 Jean-François Quintin, SanJ.	2.00	.20
213 Viacheslav Butsayev, SanJ.	2.00	.20
214 Jimmy Waite (G), SanJ.	2.00	.20
215 Ulf Dahlén, SanJ.	2.00	.20
216 Andrei Nazarov, SanJ.	2.00	.20
217 Denis Savard, Tamp.	6.00	.20
218 Brent Gretzky, Tamp.	2.00	.20
219 Petr Klima, Tamp.	2.00	.20
220 Chris Gratton, Tamp.	3.00	.20
221 Brian Bradley, Tamp.	2.00	.20
222 Adam Creighton, Tamp.	2.00	.20
223 Shawn Chambers, Tamp.	2.00	.20
224 Rob Zamuner, Tamp.	3.00	.20
225 Daren Puppa (G), Tamp.	3.00	.20
226 Mikael Andersson, Tamp.	2.00	.20
227 Dave Ellett, Toro.	2.00	.20
228 Mike Gartner, Toro.	12.00	.20
229 Félix Potvin (G), Toro.	9.00	.20
230 Yanic Perreault, Toro.	4.00	.20
231 Nikolai Borschevsky, Toro.	2.00	.20
232 Dmitri Mironov, Toro.	2.00	.20
233 Todd Gill, Toro.	2.00	.20
234 Éric Lacroix, Toro. RC	**7.00**	**.50**
235 Kent Manderville, Toro.	2.00	.20
236 Chris Govedaris, Toro.	2.00	.20
237 Frank Bialowas, Toro. RC	**7.00**	**.50**
238 Kirk McLean (G), Vanc.	4.00	.20
239 Jimmy Carson, Vanc.	2.00	.20
240 Geoff Courtnall, Vanc.	2.00	.20
241 Trevor Linden, Vanc.	6.00	.20
242 Murray Craven, Vanc.	2.00	.20
243 Bret Hedican, Vanc.	2.00	.20
244 Jeff R. Brown, Vanc.	2.00	.20
245 Michael Peca, Vanc.	12.00	.20
246 John Namestnikov, Vanc.	2.00	.20
247 Nathan Lafayette, Vanc.	3.00	.20
248 Shawn Antoski, Vanc.	2.00	.20
249 Sergio Momesso, Vanc.	2.00	.20
250 Mike Ridley, Wash.	2.00	.20
251 Peter Bondra, Wash.	9.00	.20
252 Dmitri Khristich, Wash.	2.00	.20

☐☐ 253 Dave Poulin, Wash.	2.00	.20
☐☐ 254 Dale Hunter, Wash.	4.00	.20
☐☐ 255 Rick Tabaracci (G), Wash.	2.00	.20
☐☐ 256 Kelly Miller, Wash.	2.00	.20
☐☐ 257 John Slaney, Wash.	2.00	.20
☐☐ 258 Todd Krygier, Wash.	2.00	.20
☐☐ 259 Kevin Hatcher, Wash.	2.00	.20
☐☐ 260 Alexei Zhamnov, Winn.	4.00	.20
☐☐ 261 Dallas Drake, Winn.	2.00	.20
☐☐ 262 Dave Manson, Winn.	2.00	.20
☐☐ 263 Thomas Steen, Winn.	2.00	.20
☐☐ 264 Keith Tkachuk, Winn.	8.00	.20
☐☐ 265 Russ Romaniuk, Winn.	2.00	.20
☐☐ **266 Michal Grosek, Winn. RC**	**7.00**	**.50**
☐☐ 267 Nelson Emerson, Winn.	2.00	.20
☐☐ 268 Mike O'Neill, Winn.	2.00	.20
☐☐ 269 Kris King, Winn.	2.00	.20
☐☐ 270 Teppo Numminen, Winn.	4.00	.20
☐☐ 271 Jason Arnott, Edmo.	7.00	.20
☐☐ 272 Mikael Renberg, Phil.	4.00	.20
☐☐ 273 Alexei Yashin, Otta.	9.00	.20
☐☐ 274 Chris Pronger, Hart.	9.00	.20
☐☐ 275 Jocelyn Thibault (G), Québ.	6.00	.20
☐☐ 276 Bryan Smolinski, Bost.	2.00	.20
☐☐ 277 Derek Plante, Buff.	2.00	.20
☐☐ 278 Martin Brodeur (G), NJer.	20.00	.50
☐☐ 279 Jim Dowd, NJer.	2.00	.20
☐☐ 280 Iain Fraser, Québ.	2.00	.20
☐☐ 281 Pat Peake, Wash.	2.00	.20
☐☐ 282 Chris Gratton, Tamp.	3.00	.20
☐☐ 283 Chris Osgood (G), Detr.	9.00	.20
☐☐ 284 Jesse Bélanger, Flor.	2.00	.20
☐☐ 285 Alexandre Daigle, Otta.	2.00	.20
☐☐ 286 Robert Lang, LosA.	3.00	.20
☐☐ 287 Markus Näslund, Pitt.	14.00	.50
☐☐ 288 Trevor Kidd (G), Calg.	4.00	.20
☐☐ 289 Jeff Shantz, Chic.	2.00	.20
☐☐ 290 Jaroslav Modry, NJer.	2.00	.20
☐☐ 291 Oleg Petrov, Mont.	4.00	.20
☐☐ 292 Scott Levins, Otta.	2.00	.20
☐☐ 293 Jozef Stumpel, Bost.	3.00	.20
☐☐ 294 Rob Niedermayer, Flor.	3.00	.20
☐☐ 295 Brent Gretzky, Tamp.	2.00	.20
☐☐ 296 Mario Lemieux, Pitt. [Best]	45.00	1.50
☐☐ 297 Pavel Bure, Vanc. [Best]	10.00	.20
☐☐ 298 Brendan Shanahan, SLou. [Best]	14.00	.50
☐☐ 299 Steve Yzerman, Detr. [Best]	35.00	1.00
☐☐ 300 Teemu Selänne, Winn. [Best]	12.00	.20
☐☐ 301 Eric Lindros, Phil. [Best]	15.00	.50
☐☐ 302 Jeremy Roenick, Chic. [Best]	12.00	.20
☐☐ 303 Dave Andreychuk, Toro. [Best]	4.00	.20
☐☐ 304 Raymond Bourque, Bost. [Best]	18.00	.50
☐☐ 305 Sergei Fedorov, Detr. [Best]	14.00	.50
☐☐ 306 Wayne Gretzky, LosA. [Best]	60.00	2.00
☐☐ 307 Adam Graves, NYRa. [Best]	6.00	.20
☐☐ 308 Mike Modano, Dall. [Best]	14.00	.50
☐☐ 309 Brett Hull, SLou. [Best]	14.00	.50
☐☐ 310 Pat LaFontaine, Buff. [Best]	9.00	.20
☐☐ 311 Adam Oates, Bost. [Best]	6.00	.20
☐☐ 312 Patrick Roy (G), Mont. [Best]	45.00	1.50
☐☐ 313 Doug Gilmour, Toro. [Best]	9.00	.20
☐☐ 314 Jaromir Jagr, Pitt. [Best]	15.00	.50
☐☐ 315 Mark Recchi, Phil. [Best]	6.00	.20

VINTAGE

Insert Set (90 cards): 30.00
Common Player: .25

Insert (1:1)	NRMT-MT
☐ V1 Dominik Hasek (G), Buff.	1.50
☐ V2 Mike Modano, Dall.	1.50
☐ V3 Shayne Corson, Edmo.	.25
☐ V4 Kirk Muller, Mont.	.25
☐ V5 Mike Richter (G), NYRa.	.50
☐ V6 Mario Lemieux, Pitt.	4.50
☐ V7 Sandis Ozolinsh, SanJ.	.25
☐ V8 Dave Ellett, Toro.	.25
☐ V9 Dave Manson, Winn.	.25
☐ V10 Terry Yake, Anah.	.25
☐ V11 Craig Simpson, Buff.	.25
☐ V12 Paul Cavallini, Dall.	.25
☐ V13 John Vanbiesbrouck (G), Flor.	.50
☐ V14 Gilbert Dionne, Mont.	.25
☐ V15 Brian Leetch, NYRa.	.50
☐ V16 Martin Straka, Pitt.	.25
☐ V17 Curtis Joseph (G), SLou.	1.50
☐ V18 Pavel Bure, Vanc.	1.00
☐ V19 Garry Valk, Anah.	.25
☐ V20 Theoren Fleury, Calg.	.50
☐ V21 Brent Gilchrist, Dall.	.25
☐ V22 Rob Niedermayer, Flor.	.25
☐ V23 Vincent Damphousse, Mont.	.50
☐ V24 Alex Kovalev, NYRa.	.50
☐ V25 Rick Tocchet, Pitt.	.25
☐ V26 Steve Duchesne, SLou.	.25
☐ V27 Jiri Slegr, Vanc.	.25
☐ V28 Patrik Carnbäck, Anah.	.25
☐ V29 Gary Roberts, Calg.	.50
☐ V30 Derian Hatcher, Dall.	.25
☐ V31 Jesse Bélanger, Flor.	.25
☐ V32 Mathieu Schneider, Mont.	.25
☐ V33 Mark Messier, NYRa.	1.50
☐ V34 Joe Sakic, Québ.	2.00
☐ V35 Brett Hull, SLou.	1.50
☐ V36 Martin Gélinas, Vanc.	.25
☐ V37 Maxim Bets, Anah.	.25
☐ V38 Joel Otto, Calg.	.25
☐ V39 Sergei Fedorov, Detr.	1.50
☐ V40 Chris Pronger, Hart.	.50
☐ V41 Scott Stevens, NJer.	.50
☐ V42 Alexandre Daigle, Otta.	.25
☐ V43 Owen Nolan, Québ.	.50
☐ V44 Petr Nedved, SLou.	.25
☐ V45 Jeff R. Brown, Vanc.	.25
☐ V46 Adam Oates, Bost.	.50
☐ V47 Robert Reichel, Calg.	.25
☐ V48 Vyacheslav Kozlov, Detr.	.25
☐ V49 Geoff Sanderson, Hart.	.25
☐ V50 Stéphane J.J. Richer, NJer.	.25
☐ V51 Sylvain Turgeon, Otta.	.25
☐ V52 Mike Ricci, Québ.	.25
☐ V53 Roman Hamrlik, Tamp.	.25
☐ V54 Kevin Hatcher, Wash.	.25
☐ V55 Mariusz Czerkawski, Bost.	.25
☐ V56 Tony Amonte, Chic.	.50
☐ V57 Steve Yzerman, Detr.	3.50
☐ V58 Andrew Cassels, Hart.	.25
☐ V59 Claude Lemieux, NJer.	.25
☐ V60 Derek Mayer, Otta.	.25
☐ V61 Jocelyn Thibault (G), Québ.	.50
☐ V62 Brent Gretzky, Tamp.	.25
☐ V63 Pat Peake, Wash.	.25
☐ V64 Cam Neely, Bost.	1.50
☐ V65 Jeremy Roenick, Chic.	1.00
☐ V66 Keith Primeau, Detr.	.50
☐ V67 Luc Robitaille, LosA.	1.00
☐ V68 Steve Thomas, NYIs.	.25
☐ V69 Eric Lindros, Phil.	1.50
☐ V70 Pat Falloon, SanJ.	.25
☐ V71 Brian Bradley, Tamp.	.25
☐ V72 Kelly Miller, Wash.	.25
☐ V73 Pat LaFontaine, Buff.	.50
☐ V74 Gary Suter, Chic.	.25
☐ V75 Bill Ranford (G), Edmo.	.50
☐ V76 Tony Granato, LosA.	.25
☐ V77 Vladimir Malakhov, NYIs.	.25
☐ V78 Mikael Renberg, Phil.	.25
☐ V79 Arturs Irbe (G), SanJ.	.50
☐ V80 Doug Gilmour, Toro.	.50
☐ V81 Teemu Selänne, Winn.	1.00
☐ V82 Dale Hawerchuk, Buff.	.50
☐ V83 Eric Weinrich, Chic.	.25
☐ V84 Jason Arnott, Edmo.	.50
☐ V85 Rob Blake, LosA.	.50
☐ V86 Ray Ferraro, NYIs.	.25
☐ V87 Garry Galley, Phil.	.25
☐ V88 Igor Larionov, SanJ.	.50
☐ V89 Dave Andreychuk, Toro.	.25
☐ V90 Dallas Drake, Winn.	.25

YOU CRASH THE GAME

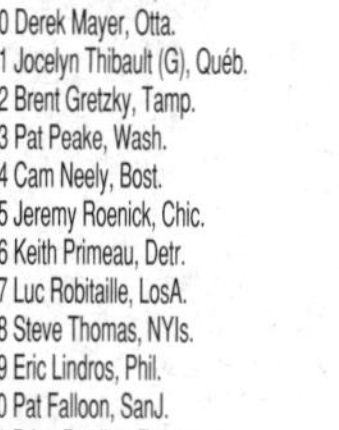

These cards have four versions: a Canadian insert (prefix C, red), a Hobby insert (prefix H, green), a Retail insert (prefix R, blue) and a redeemed card (prefix G, gold). Canadian, Hobby and Retail inserts all have identical pricing. Since the 1994-95 hockey season was shortened by an NHL-lockout, any insert could be redeemed for a complete gold set.

Insert Set (28 cards): 45.00 10.00

Player	Insert	Gold
☐☐☐☐ 1 Stéphan Lebeau, Anah.	1.00	.25
☐☐☐☐ 2 Raymond Bourque, Bost.	3.00	1.00
☐☐☐☐ 3 Pat LaFontaine, Buff.	1.00	.50
☐☐☐☐ 4 Joe Nieuwendyk, Calg.	1.00	.25
☐☐☐☐ 5 Jeremy Roenick, Chic.	2.00	.50
☐☐☐☐ 6 Mike Modano, Dall.	3.00	1.00
☐☐☐☐ 7 Sergei Fedorov, Detr.	3.00	1.00
☐☐☐☐ 8 Jason Arnott, Edmo.	1.00	.25
☐☐☐☐ 9 John Vanbiesbrouck (G), Flor.	1.00	.25
☐☐☐☐ 10 Geoff Sanderson, Hart.	1.00	.25
☐☐☐☐ 11 Wayne Gretzky, LosA.	12.00	4.00
☐☐☐☐ 12 Patrick Roy (G), Mont.	9.00	3.00
☐☐☐☐ 13 Scott Stevens, NJer.	1.00	.25
☐☐☐☐ 14 Pierre Turgeon, NYIs.	1.00	.25
☐☐☐☐ 15 Adam Graves, NYRa.	1.00	.25
☐☐☐☐ 16 Alexei Yashin, Otta.	1.00	.50
☐☐☐☐ 17 Eric Lindros, Phil.	3.00	1.00
☐☐☐☐ 18 Mario Lemieux, Pitt.	9.00	3.00
☐☐☐☐ 19 Joe Sakic, Québ.	4.00	1.50
☐☐☐☐ 20 Brett Hull, SLou.	3.00	1.00
☐☐☐☐ 21 Sandis Ozolinsh, SanJ.	1.00	.25
☐☐☐☐ 22 Chris Gratton, Tamp.	1.00	.25
☐☐☐☐ 23 Doug Gilmour, Toro.	1.00	.50
☐☐☐☐ 24 Pavel Bure, Vanc.	2.00	.50
☐☐☐☐ 25 Joé Juneau, Wash.	1.00	.25
☐☐☐☐ 26 Teemu Selänne, Winn.	2.00	.50
☐☐☐☐ 27 Mark Messier, All-Star	3.00	1.00
☐☐☐☐ 28 Wayne Gretzky, All-Star	12.00	4.00

1994 - 95 PARKHURST SE

These cards have two versions: the regular card and a "Parkie" gold parallel.

Imprint: © 1994 The Upper Deck Company
Complete Set (270 cards): 110.00 30.00
Common Player: .30 .20

Player	Gold	Reg.
☐☐ SE1 Guy Hebert (G), Anah.	.30	.20
☐☐ SE2 Bob Corkum, Anah.	.30	.20
☐☐ SE3 Randy Ladouceur, Anah.	.30	.20
☐☐ SE4 Tom Kurvers, Anah.	.30	.20
☐☐ SE5 Joe Sacco, Anah.	.30	.20
☐☐ **SE6 Valeri Karpov, Anah. RC**	**.50**	**.50**
☐☐ SE7 Garry Valk, Anah.	.30	.20
☐☐ SE8 Paul Kariya, Anah.	5.50	1.00
☐☐ SE9 Alexei Kasatonov, SLou.	.30	.20
☐☐ SE10 Sergei Zholtok, Bost.	.30	.20
☐☐ SE11 Glen Murray, Bost.	.50	.20
☐☐ SE12 David Reid, Bost.	.30	.20
☐☐ SE13 Adam Oates, Bost.	.50	.20
☐☐ SE14 Ted Donato, Bost.	.30	.20
☐☐ SE15 Don Sweeney, Bost.	.30	.20
☐☐ SE16 Philippe Boucher, Buff.	.30	.20
☐☐ SE17 Bob Sweeney, Buff.	.30	.20
☐☐ SE18 Pat LaFontaine, Buff.	1.00	.20
☐☐ SE19 Derek Plante, Buff.	.30	.20
☐☐ SE20 Jason Dawe, Buff.	.30	.20
☐☐ SE21 Petr* Svoboda, Buff.	.30	.20
☐☐ SE22 Craig Simpson, Buff.	.30	.20
☐☐ SE23 Viktor Gordiouk, Buff.	.30	.20
☐☐ SE24 Trevor Kidd (G), Calg.	.50	.20
☐☐ SE25 Todd Hlushko, Calg.	.30	.20
☐☐ SE26 German Titov, Calg.	.30	.20
☐☐ SE27 Gary Roberts, Calg.	.50	.20
☐☐ SE28 Theoren Fleury, Calg.	1.00	.20
☐☐ **SE29 Cory Stillman, Calg. RC**	**1.50**	**1.00**
☐☐ SE30 Phil Housley, Calg.	.50	.20
☐☐ SE31 Joel Otto, Calg.	.30	.20
☐☐ SE32 Patrick Poulin, Chic.	.30	.20
☐☐ **SE33 C. Soucy (G), Chic. RC**	**1.00**	**.50**
☐☐ SE34 Karl Dykhuis, Chic.	.30	.20
☐☐ SE35 Jeremy Roenick, Chic.	1.50	.20
☐☐ SE36 Tony Amonte, Chic.	1.00	.20
☐☐ SE37 Sergei Krivokrasov, Chic.	.30	.20
☐☐ SE38 Bernie Nicholls, Chic.	.30	.20
☐☐ SE39 Todd Harvey, Dall.	.50	.20
☐☐ SE40 Jarkko Varvio, Dall.	.30	.20
☐☐ SE41 Shane Churla, Dall.	.30	.20
☐☐ SE42 Paul Cavallini, Dall.	.30	.20
☐☐ SE43 Trent Klatt, Dall.	.30	.20
☐☐ SE44 Darcy Wakaluk (G), Dall.	.30	.20
☐☐ SE45 Derian Hatcher, Dall.	.50	.20
☐☐ SE46 Dean Evason, Dall.	.30	.20
☐☐ SE47 Mike Modano, Dall.	2.00	.50
☐☐ SE48 Greg Johnson, Detr.	.50	.20
☐☐ SE49 Ray Sheppard, Detr.	.30	.20
☐☐ SE50 Sergei Fedorov, Detr.	2.00	.50
☐☐ SE51 Bob Rouse, Detr.	.30	.20
☐☐ SE52 Mike Vernon (G), Detr.	.50	.20
☐☐ SE53 Vladimir Konstantinov, Detr.	.50	.20
☐☐ SE54 Chris Osgood (G), Detr.	1.00	.20
☐☐ SE55 Steve Yzerman, Detr.	4.50	1.00
☐☐ **SE56 Jason York, Detr. RC**	**1.00**	**.50**
☐☐ SE57 Boris Mironov, Edmo.	.30	.20
☐☐ SE58 Igor Kravchuk, Edmo.	.30	.20
☐☐ SE59 Jason Arnott, Edmo.	.50	.20
☐☐ **SE60 David Oliver, Edmo. RC**	**.50**	**.50**
☐☐ SE61 Todd Marchant, Edmo.	.50	.20
☐☐ SE62 Dean McAmmond, Edmo.	.30	.20
☐☐ SE63 Brian Skrudland, Flor.	.30	.20
☐☐ SE64 Tom Fitzgerald, Flor.	.30	.20
☐☐ SE65 Brian Benning, Flor.	.30	.20
☐☐ SE66 Stu Barnes, Flor.	.30	.20
☐☐ SE67 John Vanbiesbrouck (G), Flor.	.50	.20
☐☐ SE68 Rob Niedermayer, Flor.	.30	.20
☐☐ SE69 Jimmy Carson, Hart.	.30	.20
☐☐ SE70 Mark Janssens, Hart.	.30	.20
☐☐ SE71 Sean Burke (G), Hart.	1.00	.20
☐☐ SE72 Andrei Nikolishin, Hart.	.50	.20
☐☐ SE73 Chris Pronger, Hart.	1.00	.20
☐☐ SE74 Jeff Reese (G), Hart.	.30	.20
☐☐ SE75 Darren Turcotte, Hart.	.30	.20
☐☐ SE76 Robert Kron, Hart.	.30	.20
☐☐ **SE77 Kevin Brown, LosA. RC**	**.50**	**.50**
☐☐ SE78 Robert Lang, LosA.	.30	.20
☐☐ SE79 Rick Tocchet, LosA.	.50	.20
☐☐ SE80 Jamie Storr (G), LosA.	.50	.20
☐☐ SE81 Kelly Hrudey (G), LosA.	.50	.20
☐☐ SE82 Darryl Sydor, LosA.	.30	.20
☐☐ SE83 Tony Granato, LosA.	.30	.20
☐☐ SE84 Warren Rychel, LosA.	.30	.20
☐☐ SE85 Gary Shuchuk, LosA.	.30	.20
☐☐ SE86 Peter Popovic, Mont.	.30	.20
☐☐ SE87 Valeri Bure, Mont.	1.00	.20
☐☐ SE88 Kirk Muller, Mont.	.50	.20
☐☐ SE89 Lyle Odelein, Mont.	.30	.20
☐☐ SE90 Brian Savage, Mont.	1.00	.20
☐☐ SE91 Gilbert Dionne, Mont.	.30	.20
☐☐ SE92 Mathieu Schneider, Mont.	.30	.20
☐☐ SE93 Jim Montgomery, Mont.	.30	.20
☐☐ SE94 Chris Terreri (G), NJer.	.30	.20
☐☐ SE95 Scott Niedermayer, NJer.	.50	.20
☐☐ SE96 Bob Carpenter, NJer.	.30	.20
☐☐ SE97 Scott Stevens, NJer.	.50	.20
☐☐ SE98 Jim Dowd, NJer.	.30	.20
☐☐ SE99 Brian Rolston, NJer.	1.00	.20
☐☐ SE100 Stéphane J.J. Richer, NJer.	.30	.20
☐☐ SE101 Mick Vukota, NYIs.	.30	.20
☐☐ SE102 Steve Thomas, NYIs.	.30	.20
☐☐ SE103 Patrick Flatley, NYIs.	.30	.20
☐☐ SE104 Marty McInnis, NYIs.	.30	.20
☐☐ SE105 Richard Pilon, NYIs.	.30	.20
☐☐ SE106 Benoît Hogue, NYIs.	.30	.20
☐☐ SE107 Zigmund Palffy, NYIs.	1.00	.20
☐☐ SE108 Vladimir Malakhov, NYIs.	.30	.20
☐☐ SE109 Brett Lindros, NYIs.	1.00	.20
☐☐ SE110 Mike Richter (G), NYRa.	.50	.20
☐☐ SE111 Greg Gilbert, NYRa.	.30	.20
☐☐ SE112 Kevin Lowe, NYRa.	.50	.20
☐☐ SE113 Mark Messier, NYRa.	2.00	.50
☐☐ SE114 Alexander Karpovtsev, NYRa.	.30	.20
☐☐ SE115 Sergei Nemchinov, NYRa.	.30	.20
☐☐ SE116 Petr Nedved, NYRa.	.50	.20
☐☐ SE117 Glenn Healy (G), NYRa.	.30	.20
☐☐ SE118 Dave Archibald, Otta.	.30	.20
☐☐ SE119 Alexandre Daigle, Otta.	.30	.20
☐☐ SE120 Darrin Madeley (G), Otta.	.30	.20
☐☐ SE121 Pavol Demitra, Otta.	.50	.20
☐☐ SE122 Brad Shaw, Otta.	.30	.20
☐☐ SE123 Alexei Yashin, Otta.	1.00	.20
☐☐ SE124 Sean Hill, Otta.	.30	.20
☐☐ **SE125 Vladislav Boulin, Phil. RC**	**.50**	**.50**
☐☐ SE126 Kevin Haller, Phil.	.30	.20
☐☐ SE127 Chris Therien, Phil.	.30	.20
☐☐ SE128 Garry Galley, Phil.	.30	.20
☐☐ SE129 Mikael Renberg, Phil.	.50	.20
☐☐ SE130 Ron Hextall (G), Phil.	1.00	.20
☐☐ SE131 Eric Lindros, Phil.	2.00	.50
☐☐ SE132 Craig MacTavish, Phil.	.30	.20
☐☐ **SE133 Patrik Juhlin, Phil. RC**	**.50**	**.50**
☐☐ SE134 Martin Straka, Pitt.	.50	.20
☐☐ SE135 Doug Brown, Pitt. (Detr.)	.30	.20
☐☐ SE136 Markus Näslund, Pitt.	2.00	.50
☐☐ SE137 Luc Robitaille, Pitt.	1.50	.20
☐☐ SE138 Kjell Samuelsson, Pitt.	.30	.20
☐☐ SE139 Ken Wregget (G), Pitt.	.30	.20
☐☐ SE140 John Cullen, Pitt.	.30	.20
☐☐ SE141 Peter Taglianetti, Pitt.	.30	.20
☐☐ SE142 Janne Laukkanen, Québ.	.30	.20
☐☐ SE143 Owen Nolan, Québ.	1.00	.20
☐☐ SE144 Adam Deadmarsh, Québ.	1.00	.20
☐☐ SE145 Dave Karpa, Québ.	.30	.20
☐☐ SE146 Wendel Clark, Québ.	1.50	.20
☐☐ SE147 Joe Sakic, Québ.	3.00	.50
☐☐ SE148 Alexei Gusarov, Québ.	.30	.20
☐☐ SE149 Peter Forsberg, Québ.	2.50	.50
☐☐ SE150 Kevin Miller, SLou.	.30	.20
☐☐ SE151 Denny Felsner, SLou.	.30	.20
☐☐ SE152 Al MacInnis, SLou.	.50	.20
☐☐ SE153 Philippe Bozon, SLou.	.30	.20
☐☐ SE154 Brett Hull, SLou.	2.00	.50
☐☐ SE155 Guy Carbonneau, SLou.	.50	.20
☐☐ SE156 Igor Korolev, SLou.	.30	.20
☐☐ SE157 Esa Tikkanen, SLou.	.30	.20
☐☐ SE158 Jon Casey, SLou.	.30	.20
☐☐ SE159 Viktor Kozlov, SanJ.	1.00	.20
☐☐ SE160 Mike Rathje, SanJ.	.30	.20
☐☐ SE161 Bob Errey, SanJ.	.30	.20
☐☐ SE162 Arturs Irbe (G), SanJ.	.50	.20
☐☐ SE163 Ray Whitney, SanJ.	.30	.20
☐☐ SE164 Igor Larionov, SanJ.	1.00	.20
☐☐ SE165 Pat Falloon, SanJ.	.30	.20
☐☐ SE166 Jeff Friesen, SanJ.	1.00	.20
☐☐ SE167 Vlastimil Kroupa, SanJ.	.30	.20
☐☐ SE168 Chris Joseph (G), Tamp. (Pitt.)	.30	.20
☐☐ SE169 Danton Cole, Tamp.	.30	.20
☐☐ SE170 John Tucker, Tamp.	.30	.20
☐☐ SE171 Roman Hamrlik, Tamp.	.30	.20
☐☐ SE172 Jason Wiemer, Tamp.	.50	.20
☐☐ SE173 Kenny Jönsson, Toro.	.50	.20
☐☐ **SE174 Éric Fichaud (G), Toro. RC**	**1.00**	**.50**
☐☐ SE175 Mats Sundin, Toro.	2.00	.50
☐☐ SE176 Doug Gilmour, Toro.	1.00	.20
☐☐ SE177 Drake Berehowsky, Toro.	.30	.20
☐☐ SE178 Mike Ridley, Toro.	.30	.20
☐☐ SE179 Jamie Macoun, Toro.	.30	.20
☐☐ SE180 Alexei Kudashov, Toro.	.30	.20
☐☐ SE181 Bill Berg, Toro.	.30	.20
☐☐ SE182 Dave Andreychuk, Toro.	.50	.20
☐☐ SE183 Mike Eastwood, Toro.	.30	.20
☐☐ SE184 Martin Gélinas, Vanc.	.30	.20
☐☐ SE185 Greg A. Adams, Vanc.	.30	.20
☐☐ SE186 Gino Odjick, Vanc.	.30	.20
☐☐ SE187 Pavel Bure, Vanc.	1.50	.20
☐☐ SE188 Cliff Ronning, Vanc.	.30	.20
☐☐ SE189 Jiri Slegr, Vanc.	.30	.20
☐☐ SE190 Jyrki Lumme, Vanc.	.30	.20
☐☐ SE191 Jassen Cullimore, Vanc.	.30	.20
☐☐ SE192 Steve Konowalchuk, Wash.	.30	.20
☐☐ SE193 Sylvain Côté, Wash.	.30	.20
☐☐ SE194 Jason Allison, Wash.	2.00	.50
☐☐ SE195 Sergei Gonchar, Wash.	1.00	.20
☐☐ SE196 Pat Peake, Wash.	.30	.20
☐☐ SE197 Calle Johansson, Wash.	.30	.20
☐☐ SE198 Joé Juneau, Wash.	.30	.20
☐☐ SE199 Jeff Nelson, Wash.	.30	.20
☐☐ SE200 Luciano Borsato, Winn.	.30	.20
☐☐ SE201 Teemu Selänne, Winn.	1.50	.20
☐☐ SE202 Tie Domi, Winn.	.50	.20
☐☐ SE203 Tim Cheveldae (G), Winn.	.30	.20
☐☐ SE204 Darrin Shannon, Winn.	.30	.20
☐☐ **SE205 Ravil Gusmanov, Winn. RC**	**.50**	**.50**
☐☐ SE206 Todd Harvey, Canada	.50	.20
☐☐ **SE207 Ed Jovanovski, Canada RC**	**3.00**	**2.00**
☐☐ SE208 Jason Allison, Canada	2.00	.50
☐☐ SE209 Bryan McCabe, Canada	.50	.20
☐☐ **SE210 Dan Cloutier (G), Canada RC**	**3.00**	**2.00**
☐☐ **SE211 Ladislav Kohn, Czech RC**	**1.00**	**.50**
☐☐ **SE212 Marek Malik, Czech RC**	**.50**	**.50**
☐☐ **SE213 Jan Hlavac, Czech RC**	**1.50**	**1.00**
☐☐ **SE214 Petr Cajanek, Czech RC**	**.50**	**.50**
☐☐ **SE215 J. Markkanen, Finland RC**	**1.00**	**.50**
☐☐ **SE216 Jere Karalahti, Finland RC**	**.50**	**.50**
☐☐ SE217 Janne Niinimaa, Finland	.50	.20
☐☐ SE218 Kimmo Timonen, Finland	.30	.20
☐☐ **SE219 Mikko Helisten, Finland RC**	**.50**	**.50**
☐☐ **SE220 Niko Halttunen, Finland RC**	**.50**	**.50**
☐☐ SE221 Tommi Miettinen, Finland	.30	.20
☐☐ **SE222 V-P Nutikka, Finland RC**	**.50**	**.50**
☐☐ **SE223 Timo Salonen, Finland RC**	**.50**	**.50**
☐☐ **SE224 Tommi Sova, Finland RC**	**.50**	**.50**
☐☐ **SE225 J. Tarvainen, Finland RC**	**.50**	**.50**
☐☐ **SE226 T. Rajamäki, Finland RC**	**.50**	**.50**
☐☐ **SE227 Antti Aalto, Finland RC**	**.50**	**.50**
☐☐ **SE228 Alex. Korolyuk, Russia RC**	**.50**	**.50**
☐☐ **SE229 V. Yachmenev, Russia RC**	**1.00**	**.50**
☐☐ SE230 Nikolai Zavarukhin, Russia	.30	.20
☐☐ **SE231 V. Epantchinsev, Russia RC**	**.50**	**.50**
☐☐ **SE232 Dmitri Klevakin, Sweden RC**	**.50**	**.50**
☐☐ SE233 Anders Eriksson, Sweden	.30	.20

□□	**SE234 A. Söderberg, Sweden RC**	**.50**	**.50**
□□	**SE235 Per Svartvadet, Sweden RC**	**.50**	**.50**
□□	SE236 Johan Davidsson, Sweden	.30	.20
□□	SE237 Niklas Sundström, Sweden	.50	.20
□□	**SE238 Andersson-Junkka, Swe. RC**	**.50**	**.50**
□□	**SE239 D. Tarnstrom, Sweden RC**	**1.50**	**1.00**
□□	**SE240 Per Axelsson, Sweden RC**	**1.00**	**.50**
□□	**SE241 F. Johansson, Sweden RC**	**.50**	**.50**
□□	**SE242 Peter Ström, Sweden RC**	**.50**	**.50**
□□	**SE243 Mattias Öhlund, Sweden RC**	**2.50**	**1.50**
□□	**SE244 Jesper Mattsson, Sweden RC**	**.50**	**.50**
□□	**SE245 Jonas Forsberg, Sweden RC**	**.50**	**.50**
□□	SE246 Adam Deadmarsh, U.S.A.	1.00	.20
□□	SE247 Deron Quint, U.S.A.	.30	.20
□□	SE248 J. Langenbrunner, U.S.A.	.50	.20
□□	SE249 Richard Park, U.S.A.	.30	.20
□□	**SE250 Bryan Berard, U.S.A. RC**	**2.50**	**1.50**

□□	**SE251 D. Belitski (G), Canada RC**	**1.00**	**.50**
□□	**SE252 Mike McBain, Canada RC**	**.50**	**.50**
□□	**SE253 Hugh Hamilton, Canada RC**	**.50**	**.50**
□□	**SE254 Jason Doig, Canada RC**	**.50**	**.50**
□□	**SE255 Xavier Delisle, Canada RC**	**.50**	**.50**
□□	**SE256 Wade Redden, Canada RC**	**2.50**	**1.50**
□□	**SE257 Jeff Ware, Canada RC**	**.50**	**.50**
□□	**SE258 Christian Dubé, Canada RC**	**1.00**	**.50**
□□	**SE259 L-P Sévigny, Canada RC**	**.50**	**.50**
□□	**SE260 Jarome Iginla, Canada RC**	**6.00**	**4.00**
□□	**SE261 Daniel Brière, Canada RC**	**6.00**	**4.00**
□□	**SE262 Justin Kurtz, Canada RC**	**.50**	**.50**
□□	**SE263 Marc Savard, Canada RC**	**1.50**	**1.00**
□□	**SE264 Alyn McCauley, Canada RC**	**5.00**	**2.00**
□□	**SE265 Brad Mehalko, Canada RC**	**.50**	**.50**
□□	**SE266 Jeff Ambrosio, Canada RC**	**.50**	**.50**
□□	**SE267 Todd Norman, Canada RC**	**.50**	**.50**
□□	**SE268 Brian Scott, Canada RC**	**.50**	**.50**
□□	**SE269 Brad Larsen, Canada RC**	**.50**	**.50**
□□	**SE270 Giguère (G), Canada RC**	**15.00**	**12.00**

EURO-STARS

Insert Set (20 cards): **20.00**

	Insert (1:8)	NRMT-MT
□	ES-1 Peter Forsberg, Québ.	3.00
□	ES-2 Mats Sundin, Toro.	2.00
□	ES-3 Mikael Renberg, Phil.	.50
□	ES-4 Nicklas Lidström, Detr.	1.00
□	ES-5 Mariusz Czerkawski, Bost.	.50
□	ES-6 Ulf Dahlén, SanJ.	.50
□	ES-7 Kjell Samuelsson, Pitt.	.50
□	ES-8 Jyrki Lumme, Vanc.	.50
□	ES-9 Jari Kurri, LosA.	2.00
□	ES-10 Teppo Numminen, Winn.	.50
□	ES-11 Esa Tikkanen, SLou.	.50
□	ES-12 Christian Ruuttu, Chic.	.50
□	ES-13 Teemu Selänne, Winn.	2.00
□	ES-14 Alexander Mogilny, Buff.	1.00
□	ES-15 Pavel Bure, Vanc.	2.00
□	ES-16 Sergei Fedorov, Detr.	2.00
□	ES-17 Arturs Irbe (G), SanJ.	1.00
□	ES-18 Alex Kovalev, NYRa.	1.00
□	ES-19 Dominik Hasek (G), Buff.	2.00
□	ES-20 Jaromir Jagr, Pitt.	2.00

VINTAGE

Insert Set (45 cards): **55.00**

	Insert (1:6)	V
□	seV1 Paul Kariya, Anah.	3.50
□	seV2 Dino Ciccarelli, Detr.	.50
□	seV3 Patrick Roy (G), Mont.	7.50
□	seV4 Markus Näslund, Pitt.	2.50
□	seV5 Trevor Linden, Vanc.	1.00
□	seV6 Valeri Karpov, Anah.	.35
□	seV7 Pat Verbeek, Hart.	.50
□	seV8 Martin Brodeur (G), NJer.	4.00
□	seV9 Kevin Stevens, Pitt.	.50
□	seV10 Kirk McLean (G), Vanc.	.50
□	seV11 Stéphan Lebeau, Anah.	.35
□	seV12 Scott Niedermayer, NJer.	.50
□	seV13 Peter Bondra, Wash.	1.50
□	seV14 Ed Belfour (G), Chic.	2.50
□	seV15 Paul Coffey, Detr.	1.50
□	seV16 Chris Gratton, Tamp.	.50
□	seV17 Joé Juneau, Wash.	.50
□	seV18 Raymond Bourque, Bost.	3.00
□	seV19 Sergei Krivokrasov, Chic.	.35
□	seV20 Wayne Gretzky, LosA.	10.00
□	seV21 Alexei Yashin, Otta.	1.50
□	seV22 Al Iafrate, Bost.	.50
□	seV23 Doug Weight, Edmo.	1.50
□	seV24 Jari Kurri, LosA.	2.50
□	seV25 Rod Brind'Amour, Phil.	.50
□	seV26 Bryan Smolinski, Bost.	.35
□	seV27 Darius Kasparaitis, NYIs.	.50
□	seV28 Mark Recchi, Phil.	1.00
□	seV29 Mike Gartner, Toro.	2.00
□	seV30 Russ Courtnall, Dall.	.50
□	seV31 Pierre Turgeon, NYIs.	1.00
□	seV32 Félix Potvin (G), Toro.	1.50
□	seV33 Nelson Emerson, Winn.	.35
□	seV34 Alexander Mogilny, Buff.	1.00
□	seV35 Bob Kudelski, Flor.	.35
□	seV36 Brett Lindros, NYIs.	.50
□	seV37 Mats Sundin, Toro.	2.50
□	seV38 Keith Tkachuk, Winn.	1.50
□	seV39 Derek Plante, Buff.	.35
□	seV40 Oleg Petrov, Mont.	.50
□	seV41 Adam Graves, NYRa.	1.00
□	seV42 Jaromir Jagr, Pitt.	2.50
□	seV43 Viktor Kozlov, SanJ.	.50
□	seV44 Nathan Lafayette, Vanc.	.35
□	seV45 Alexei Zhamnov, Winn.	.50

1994 - 95 PARKHURST TALL BOYS '64-65

Imprint: © PARKHURST PRODUCTS
Card Size: 2 1/2" x 4 11/16"
Complete Set (180 cards): **25.00**
Common Player: **.25**
Album: **10.00**

	Player	NRMT-MT
□	1 John Bucyk, Bost.	.50
□	2 Murray Oliver, Bost.	.25
□	3 Ted Green, Bost.	.25
□	4 Tom Williams, Bost.	.25
□	5 Dean Prentice, Bost.	.25
□	6 Ed Westfall, Bost.	.25
□	7 Orland Kurtenbach, Bost.	.25
□	8 Reg Fleming, Bost.	.25
□	9 Leo Boivin, Bost.	.50
□	10 Bob McCord, Bost.	.25
□	11 Bob Leiter, Bost.	.25
□	12 Tom Johnson, Bost.	.50
□	13 Bob Woytowich, Bost.	.25
□	14 Ab MacDonald, Bost.	.25
□	15 Ed Johnston (G), Bost.	.25
□	16 Forbes Kennedy, Bost.	.25
□	17 Murray Balfour, Bost.	.25
□	18 Wayne Cashman, Bost.	.25
□	19 Don Awrey, Bost.	.25
□	20 Gary Dornhoefer, Bost.	.25
□	21 Ron Schock, Bost.	.25
□	22 Milt Schmidt, Coach, Bost.	.50
□	23 Ken Wharram, Chic.	.25
□	24 Chico Maki, Chic.	.25
□	25 Bobby Hull, Chic.	2.00
□	26 Stan Mikita, Chic.	1.00
□	27 Doug Mohns, Chic.	.25
□	28 Denis DeJordy (G), Chic.	.25
□	29 Phil Esposito, Chic.	1.50
□	30 Elmer Vasko, Chic.	.25
□	31 Pierre Pilote, Chic.	.50
□	32 Glenn Hall (G), Chic.	1.00
□	33 Eric Nesterenko, Chic.	.25
□	34 Doug Robinson, Chic.	.25
□	35 Matt Ravlich, Chic.	.25
□	36 John McKenzie, Chic.	.25
□	37 Fred Stanfield, Chic.	.25
□	38 Doug Jarrett, Chic.	.25
□	39 Dennis Hull, Chic.	.25
□	40 Al MacNeil, Chic.	.25
□	41 Wayne Hillman, Chic.	.25
□	42 Bill Hay, Chic.	.25
□	43 Billy Reay, Coach, Chic.	.25
□	44 Parker MacDonald, Detr.	.25
□	45 Floyd Smith, Detr.	.25
□	46 Gordie Howe, Detr.	3.50
□	47 Bruce MacGregor, Detr.	.25
□	48 Ron Murphy, Detr.	.25
□	49 Doug Barkley, Detr.	.25
□	50 Paul Henderson, Detr.	.50
□	51 Pit Martin, Detr.	.25
□	52 Al Langlois, Detr.	.25
□	53 Roger Crozier (G), Detr.	.25
□	54 Bill Gadsby, Detr.	.50
□	55 Marcel Pronovost, Detr.	.50
□	56 Alex Delvecchio, Detr.	.50
□	57 Gary Bergman, Detr.	.25
□	58 Norm Ullman, Detr.	.50
□	59 Larry Jeffrey, Detr.	.25
□	60 Lowell MacDonald, Detr.	.25
□	61 Pete Goegan, Detr.	.25
□	62 Andre Pronovost, Detr.	.25
□	63 Warren Godfrey, Detr.	.25
□	64 Ted Lindsay, Detr.	1.00
□	65 Sid Abel, Coach, Detr.	.50
□	66 John Ferguson, Mont.	.25
□	67 Henri Richard, Mont.	1.00
□	68 Dave Balon, Mont.	.25
□	69 Noel Picard, Mont.	.25
□	70 Claude Provost, Mont.	.25
□	71 Claude Larose, Mont.	.25
□	72 Jacques Laperrière, Mont.	.50
□	73 Ralph Backstrom, Mont.	.25
□	74 J-C Tremblay, Mont.	.25
□	75 Yvan Cournoyer, Mont.	.50
□	76 Jean-Guy Talbot, Mont.	.25
□	77 Gilles Tremblay, Mont.	.25
□	78 Ted Harris, Mont.	.25
□	79 Jim Roberts, Mont.	.25
□	80 Red Berenson, Mont.	.25
□	81 Gump Worsley (G), Mont.	1.00
□	82 Charlie Hodge (G), Mont.	.25
□	83 Terry Harper, Mont.	.25
□	84 Bobby Rousseau, Mont.	.25
□	85 Jean Béliveau, Mont.	2.50
□	86 Bill Hicke, Mont.	.25
□	87 Toe Blake, Coach, Mont.	1.00
□	88 Don Marshall, NYRa.	.25
□	89 Jean Ratelle, NYRa.	.50
□	90 Vic Hadfield, NYRa.	.25
□	91 Earl Ingarfield, NYRa.	.25
□	92 Harry Howell, NYRa.	.50
□	93 Rod Seiling, NYRa.	.25
□	94 Dave Richardson, NYRa.	.25
□	95 Val Fonteyne, NYRa.	.25
□	96 Lou Angotti, NYRa.	.25
□	97 Arnie Brown, NYRa.	.25
□	98 Don Johns, NYRa.	.25
□	99 Jim Mikol, NYRa.	.25
□	100 Jacques Plante (G), NYRa.	2.00
□	101 Marcel Paille (G), NYRa.	.25
□	102 Jim Neilson, NYRa.	.25
□	103 Bob Nevin, NYRa.	.25
□	104 Rod Gilbert, NYRa.	.50
□	105 Phil Goyette, NYRa.	.25
□	106 Dick Duff, NYRa.	.25
□	107 Camille Henry, NYRa.	.25
□	108 Red Sullivan, Coach, NYRa.	.25
□	109 Kent Douglas, Toro.	.25
□	110 Bob Pulford, Toro.	.50
□	111 Dave Keon, Toro.	1.00
□	112 Don McKenney, Toro.	.25
□	113 Pete Stemkowski, Toro.	.25
□	114 Carl Brewer, Toro.	.25
□	115 Allan Stanley, Toro.	.50
□	116 Dickie Moore, Toro.	.50
□	117 Eddie Shack, Toro.	.50
□	118 Larry Hillman, Toro.	.25
□	119 Terry Sawchuk (G), Toro.	2.50
□	120 Bobby Baun, Toro.	.25
□	121 Brit Selby, Toro.	.25
□	122 George Armstrong, Toro.	.50
□	123 Jim Pappin, Toro.	.25
□	124 Andy Bathgate, Toro.	.50
□	125 Ron Ellis, Toro.	.25
□	126 Billy Harris, Toro.	.25
□	127 Red Kelly, Toro.	.50
□	128 Ron Stewart, Toro.	.25
□	129 Johnny Bower (G), Toro.	1.00
□	130 Frank Mahovlich, Toro.	1.00
□	131 Tim Horton, Toro.	1.50
□	132 King Clancy, Ass. G.M., Toro.	1.00
□	133 AS: Glenn Hall (G), Chic.	1.00
□	134 AS: Pierre Pilote, Chic.	.50
□	135 AS: Tim Horton, Toro.	1.50
□	136 AS: Bobby Hull, Chic.	2.00
□	137 AS: Ken Wharram, Chic.	.25
□	138 AS: Stan Mikita, Chic.	1.00
□	139 AS: Charlie Hodge (G), Mont.	.25
□	140 AS: Jacques Laperrière, Mont.	.50
□	141 AS: Elmer Vasko, Chic.	.25
□	142 AS: Jean Béliveau, Mont.	2.50
□	143 AS: Frank Mahovlich, Toro.	1.00
□	144 AS: Gordie Howe, Detr.	3.50
□	145 AW: Pierre Pilote, Chic.	.50
□	146 AW: Jean Béliveau, Mont.	2.50
□	147 AW: Stan Mikita, Chic.	1.00
□	148 AW: Charlie Hodge (G), Mont.	.25
□	149 AW: Jacques Laperrière, Mont.	.50
□	150 AW: Ken Wharram, Chic.	.25
□	151 1964 All-Star Game	2.00
□	152 Jean Ratelle Invades Crease	.50
□	153 Center Ice Action	.25
□	154 Old Teammates Duel	2.00
□	155 All Eyes On The Puck	.50
□	156 Detroit Defense Stands Tall	.50
□	157 Roger Crozier Makes The Stretch	.25
□	158 Roger Crozier Plays Center Field	1.00
□	159 Hawks Eye Jean Béliveau	.50
□	160 Montreal's Speedy Rookie	.50
□	161 Jacques Laperrière Wins Race	1.00
□	162 Ron Ellis Robbed By Habs	.25
□	163 Terry Sawchuk Eyes Bouncing Disc	2.50
□	164 Eddie Shack Entertains	.50
□	165 "Mr. Goalie" In Action	1.00
□	166 Glenn Hall Holds His Ground	.50
□	167 Ed Johnston Freezes Action	.25
□	168 Ron Ellis Robbed By Ed Johnston	.25
□	169 LL: Murray Oliver, Bost.	.25
□	170 LL: Stan Mikita, Chic.	1.00
□	171 LL: Gordie Howe, Detr.	3.50
□	172 LL: Jean Béliveau, Mont.	2.50
□	173 LL: Phil Goyette, NYRa.	.25
□	174 LL: Andy Bathgate, Toro.	.50
□	175 Stanley Cup Semi-Finals	1.00
□	176 Stanley Cup Semi-Finals	.25
□	177 Stanley Cup Finals	1.50
□	178 Stanley Cup	.50
□	179 Checklist 1	.25
□	180 Checklist 2	.25

AUTOGRAPHS

Card Size: 2 1/2" x 4 11/16"
Insert Set (6 cards): **350.00**

	Autograph (#/964)	Auto.
□	A-1 Rod Gilbert, NYRa. ✍	50.00
□	A-2 Yvan Cournoyer, Mont. ✍	50.00
□	A-3 Bobby Hull, Chic. ✍	60.00
□	A-4 Phil Esposito, Chic. ✍	60.00
□	A-5 Gordie Howe, Detr. ✍	150.00
□	A-6 Dave Keon, Toro. ✍	60.00

CANADIAN/AMERICAN GREATS

Cards 1-6 were issued in Canadian packs while cards 7-12 were issued in American packs. These cards are limited to 1,000 copies.

Card Size: 2 1/2" x 4 11/16"
Insert Set (12 cards): **275.00**

	Player	NRMT-MT
□	1 Ace Bailey	20.00
□	2 Alex Levinsky	15.00
□	3 Babe Pratt	20.00
□	4 Elmer Lach	20.00
□	5 Maurice Richard	70.00
□	6 Bill Durnan (G)	40.00
□	7 Frank Brimsek	20.00
□	8 Dit Clapper	30.00
□	9 Tiny Thompson (G)	20.00
□	10 Bun Cook	20.00
□	11 Ching Johnson	20.00
□	12 Lionel Conacher	30.00

FUTURE STAR

Card Size: 2 1/2" x 4 11/16"
Insert Set (6 cards): **60.00**

	Player	FS
□	FS-1 Jacques Lemaire	10.00
□	FS-2 Gerry Cheevers (G)	20.00
□	FS-3 Ken Hodge	8.00
□	FS-4 Bernie Parent (G)	20.00
□	FS-5 Rogatien Vachon (G)	10.00
□	FS-6 Derek Sanderson	8.00

REDEMPTION

Card Size: 2 1/2" x 4 11/16"
Redemption Set (18 cards): **50.00**

	Player	NRMT-MT
□	AS1 Roger Crozier (G)	2.00
□	AS2 Pierre Pilote	2.00
□	AS3 Jacques Laperrière	2.00
□	AS4 Norm Ullman	2.00
□	AS5 Bobby Hull	9.00
□	AS6 Claude Provost	2.00
□	SL1 John Bucyk	3.00
□	SL2 Stan Mikita	4.00
□	SL3 Norm Ullman	2.00
□	SL4 Claude Provost	2.00
□	SL5 Rod Gilbert	2.00
□	SL6 Frank Mahovlich	5.00
□	TW1 Pierre Pilote	2.00
□	TW2 Bobby Hull	9.00
□	TW3 Stan Mikita	4.00
□	TW4 Terry Sawchuk/ Johnny Bower	7.00
□	TW5 Roger Crozier	2.00
□	TW6 Bobby Hull	9.00

1994 - 95 PINNACLE

These cards have three versions: the regular card, a Rink Collection parallel and an Artist's Proof parallel. Rink Collection parallels for cards 246-266 and 521-540 were available via redemption. Trade cards for each of these cards were inserted into packs. Expired trade cards sell at $1.00.

Imprint: © 1994 PINNACLE BRANDS, INC.

		A/P	Rink	Reg.
	Series One Set (270 cards):	**1,700.00**	**250.00**	**15.00**
	Series Two Set (270 cards):	**1,300.00**	**175.00**	**15.00**
	Common Player:	**5.00**	**1.00**	**.20**
	Player	A/P	Rink	Reg.
□□□	1 Eric Lindros, Phil.	40.00	7.00	.50
□□□	2 Alexandre Daigle, Otta.	5.00	1.00	.20
□□□	3 Mike Modano, Dall.	40.00	7.00	.50
□□□	4 V. Damphousse, Mont.	20.00	4.00	.20

□□□ 5 Dave Andreychuk, Toro. 10.00 2.00 .20
□□□ 6 Curtis Joseph (G), SLou. 40.00 7.00 .50
□□□ 7 Joé Juneau, Wash. 5.00 1.00 .20
□□□ 8 Trevor Linden, Vanc. 15.00 3.00 .20
□□□ 9 Rob Blake, LosA. 20.00 4.00 .20
□□□ 10 Mike Richter (G), NYRa. 15.00 3.00 .20
□□□ 11 Chris Pronger, Hart. 20.00 4.00 .20
□□□ 12 Robert Reichel, Calg. 10.00 2.00 .20
□□□ 13 Bryan Smolinski, Bost. 5.00 1.00 .20
□□□ 14 Ray Sheppard, Detr. 5.00 1.00 .20
□□□ 15 Guy Hebert (G), Anah. 5.00 1.00 .20
□□□ 16 Tony Amonte, Chic. 20.00 4.00 .20
□□□ 17 Richard Smehlik, Buff. 5.00 1.00 .20
□□□ 18 Doug Weight, Edmo. 20.00 4.00 .20
□□□ 19 Chris Gratton, Tamp. 5.00 1.00 .20
□□□ 20 Tom Barrasso (G), Pitt. 15.00 3.00 .20
□□□ 21 Brian Skrudland, Flor. 5.00 1.00 .20
□□□ 22 Sandis Ozolinsh, SanJ. 5.00 1.00 .20
□□□ 23 Bill Guerin, NJer. 15.00 3.00 .20
□□□ 24 C. Leschyshyn, Québ. 5.00 1.00 .20
□□□ 25 Teemu Selänne, Winn. 30.00 6.00 .50
□□□ 26 Darius Kasparaitis, NYIs. 5.00 1.00 .20
□□□ 27 Garry Galley, Phil. 5.00 1.00 .20
□□□ 28 Alexei Yashin, Otta. 20.00 4.00 .20
□□□ 29 Mark Tinordi, Dall. 5.00 1.00 .20
□□□ 30 Patrick Roy (G), Mont. 120.00 22.00 1.50
□□□ 31 Mike Gartner, Toro. 30.00 6.00 .50
□□□ 32 B. Shanahan, SLou. 40.00 7.00 .50
□□□ 33 Sylvain Côté, Wash. 5.00 1.00 .20
□□□ 34 Jeff R. Brown, Vanc. 5.00 1.00 .20
□□□ 35 Jari Kurri, LosA. 40.00 7.00 .50
□□□ 36 Sergei Zubov, NYRa. 5.00 1.00 .20
□□□ 37 Pat Verbeek, Hart. 10.00 2.00 .20
□□□ 38 Theoren Fleury, Calg. 20.00 4.00 .20
□□□ 39 Al Iafrate, Bost. 5.00 1.00 .20
□□□ 40 Keith Primeau, Detr. 15.00 3.00 .20
□□□ 41 Bobby Dollas, Anah. 5.00 1.00 .20
□□□ 42 Ed Belfour (G), Chic. 40.00 7.00 .50
□□□ 43 Dale Hawerchuk, Buff. 20.00 4.00 .20
□□□ 44 Shayne Corson, Edmo. 10.00 2.00 .20
□□□ 45 Danton Cole, Tamp. 5.00 1.00 .20
□□□ 46 Ulf Samuelsson, Pitt. 5.00 1.00 .20
□□□ 47 Stu Barnes, Flor. 5.00 1.00 .20
□□□ 48 Ulf Dahlén, SanJ. 5.00 1.00 .20
□□□ 49 Valeri Zelepukin, NJer. 5.00 1.00 .20
□□□ 50 Joe Sakic, Québ. 60.00 12.00 1.00
□□□ 51 Dave Manson, Winn. 5.00 1.00 .20
□□□ 52 Steve Thomas, NYIs. 5.00 1.00 .20
□□□ 53 Mark Recchi, Phil. 15.00 3.00 .20
□□□ 54 Dave McLlwain, Otta. 5.00 1.00 .20
□□□ 55 Derian Hatcher, Dall. 10.00 2.00 .20
□□□ 56 M. Schneider, Mont. 5.00 1.00 .20
□□□ 57 Bill Berg, Toro. 5.00 1.00 .20
□□□ 58 Nedved, SLou. (NYRa.) 10.00 2.00 .20
□□□ 59 Dmitri Khristich, Wash. 5.00 1.00 .20
□□□ 60 Kirk McLean (G), Vanc. 10.00 2.00 .20
□□□ 61 Marty McSorley, LosA. 5.00 1.00 .20
□□□ 62 Adam Graves, NYRa. 15.00 3.00 .20
□□□ 63 Geoff Sanderson, Hart. 5.00 1.00 .20
□□□ 64 Frantisek Musil, Calg. 5.00 1.00 .20
□□□ 65 Cam Neely, Bost. 40.00 7.00 .50
□□□ 66 Nicklas Lidström, Detr. 20.00 4.00 .20
□□□ 67 Stéphan Lebeau, Anah. 5.00 1.00 .20
□□□ 68 Joe Murphy, Chic. 5.00 1.00 .20
□□□ 69 Yuri Khmylev, Buff. 5.00 1.00 .20
□□□ 70 Zdeno Ciger, Edmo. 5.00 1.00 .20
□□□ 71 Daren Puppa (G), Tamp. 5.00 1.00 .20
□□□ 72 Ron Francis, Pitt. 20.00 4.00 .20
□□□ 73 Scott Mellanby, Flor. 5.00 1.00 .20
□□□ 74 Igor Larionov, SanJ. 20.00 4.00 .20
□□□ 75 S. Niedermayer, NJer. 10.00 2.00 .20
□□□ 76 Owen Nolan, Québ. 20.00 4.00 .20
□□□ 77 T. Numminen, Winn. 10.00 2.00 .20
□□□ 78 Pierre Turgeon, NYIs. 15.00 3.00 .20
□□□ 79 Mikael Renberg, Phil. 10.00 2.00 .20
□□□ 80 Norm Maciver, Otta. 5.00 1.00 .20
□□□ 81 Paul Cavallini, Dall. 5.00 1.00 .20
□□□ 82 Kirk Muller, Mont. 10.00 2.00 .20
□□□ 83 Félix Potvin (G), Toro. 20.00 4.00 .20
□□□ 84 Craig Janney, SLou. 5.00 1.00 .20
□□□ 85 Dale Hunter, Wash. 10.00 2.00 .20
□□□ 86 Jyrki Lumme, Vanc. 5.00 1.00 .20
□□□ 87 Alexei Zhitnik, LosA. 5.00 1.00 .20
□□□ 88 Steve Larmer, NYRa. 15.00 3.00 .20
□□□ 89 Jocelyn Lemieux, Hart. 5.00 1.00 .20
□□□ 90 Joe Nieuwendyk, Calg. 15.00 3.00 .20
□□□ 91 Don Sweeney, Bost. 5.00 1.00 .20
□□□ 92 Vyacheslav Kozlov, Detr. 5.00 1.00 .20
□□□ 93 Tim Sweeney, Anah. 5.00 1.00 .20
□□□ 94 Chris Chelios, Chic. 20.00 4.00 .20
□□□ 95 Derek Plante, Buff. 5.00 1.00 .20
□□□ 96 Igor Kravchuk, Edmo. 5.00 1.00 .20
□□□ 97 S. Chambers, Tamp. 5.00 1.00 .20
□□□ 98 Jaromir Jagr, Pitt. 40.00 7.00 .50
□□□ 99 Jeff Norton, SanJ. 5.00 1.00 .20
□□□ 100 V'b'sbrouck (G), Flor. 15.00 3.00 .20
□□□ 101 John MacLean, NJer. 5.00 1.00 .20
□□□ 102 S. Fiset (G), Québ. 10.00 2.00 .20
□□□ 103 Keith Tkachuk, Winn. 20.00 4.00 .20
□□□ 104 V. Malakhov, NYIs. 5.00 1.00 .20
□□□ 105 Mike McPhee, Dall. 5.00 1.00 .20
□□□ 106 Éric Desjardins, Mont. 10.00 2.00 .20
□□□ 107 Alex Kovalev, NYRa. 20.00 4.00 .20
□□□ 108 Steve Duchesne, SLou. 5.00 1.00 .20
□□□ 109 Peter Zezel, Toro. 5.00 1.00 .20
□□□ 110 Randy Burridge, Wash. 5.00 1.00 .20
□□□ 111 Jason Bowen, Phil. 5.00 1.00 .20
□□□ 112 Phil Bourque, Otta. 5.00 1.00 .20
□□□ 113 Cliff Ronning, Vanc. 5.00 1.00 .20
□□□ 114 Sean Burke (G), Hart. 20.00 4.00 .20
□□□ 115 Gary Roberts, Calg. 15.00 3.00 .20
□□□ 116 V. Konstantinov, Detr. 10.00 2.00 .20
□□□ 117 Brent Sutter, Chic. 5.00 1.00 .20
□□□ 118 Tony Granato, LosA. 5.00 1.00 .20
□□□ 119 Garry Valk, Anah. 5.00 1.00 .20
□□□ 120 Adam Oates, Bost. 15.00 3.00 .20
□□□ 121 Arturs Irbe (G), SanJ. 15.00 3.00 .20
□□□ 122 Jesse Bélanger, Flor. 5.00 1.00 .20
□□□ 123 Roman Hamrlik, Tamp. 5.00 1.00 .20
□□□ 124 Jason Arnott, Edmo. 15.00 3.00 .20
□□□ 125 A. Mogilny, Buff. 15.00 3.00 .20
□□□ 126 Bruce Driver, NJer. 5.00 1.00 .20
□□□ 127 S. McEachern, Pitt. 10.00 2.00 .20
□□□ 128 A. Kovalenko, Québ. 5.00 1.00 .20
□□□ 129 Benoît Hogue, NYIs. 5.00 1.00 .20
□□□ 130 T. Cheveldae (G), Winn. 5.00 1.00 .20
□□□ 131 Brian Noonan, NYRa. 5.00 1.00 .20
□□□ 132 Lyle Odelein, Mont. 5.00 1.00 .20
□□□ 133 Russ Courtnall, Dall. 5.00 1.00 .20
□□□ 134 Peter Stastny, SLou. 20.00 4.00 .20
□□□ 135 Doug Gilmour, Toro. 20.00 4.00 .20
□□□ 136 Pat Peake, Wash. 5.00 1.00 .20
□□□ 137 Gary Suter, Chic. 5.00 1.00 .20
□□□ 138 Paul Ranheim, Hart. 5.00 1.00 .20
□□□ 139 Troy Murray, Otta. 5.00 1.00 .20
□□□ 140 Pavel Bure, Vanc. 30.00 6.00 .50
□□□ 141 Gord Murphy, Flor. 5.00 1.00 .20
□□□ 142 Michael Nylander, Calg. 5.00 1.00 .20
□□□ 143 Craig Muni, Buff. 5.00 1.00 .20
□□□ 144 Bob Corkum, Anah. 5.00 1.00 .20
□□□ 145 M. Brodeur (G), NJer. 60.00 12.00 1.00
□□□ 146 Ted Donato, Bost. 5.00 1.00 .20
□□□ 147 Alexei Zhamnov, Winn. 10.00 2.00 .20
□□□ 148 Josef Beránek, Phil. 5.00 1.00 .20
□□□ 149 Joe Mullen, Pitt. 15.00 3.00 .20
□□□ 150 Sergei Fedorov, Detr. 40.00 7.00 .50
□□□ 151 Mike Keane, Mont. 5.00 1.00 .20
□□□ 152 S. Makarov, SanJ. 15.00 3.00 .20
□□□ 153 Marty McInnis, NYIs. 5.00 1.00 .20
□□□ 154 Steven Rice, Edmo. 5.00 1.00 .20
□□□ 155 Brian Leetch, NYRa. 20.00 4.00 .20
□□□ 156 Ch. Joseph (G), Tamp. 5.00 1.00 .20
□□□ 157 D. Wakaluk (G), Dall. 5.00 1.00 .20
□□□ 158 Kelly Miller, Wash. 5.00 1.00 .20
□□□ 159 Jim Montgomery, SLou. 5.00 1.00 .20
□□□ 160 N. Borschevsky, Toro. 5.00 1.00 .20
□□□ 161 Darren Turcotte, Hart. 5.00 1.00 .20
□□□ 162 Brad Shaw, Otta. 5.00 1.00 .20
□□□ 163 Mark Lamb, Phil. 5.00 1.00 .20
□□□ 164 Alexei Gusarov, Québ. 5.00 1.00 .20
□□□ 165 J. Roenick, Chic. 30.00 6.00 .50
□□□ 166 Stéphane Richer, NJer. 5.00 1.00 .20
□□□ 167 German Titov, Calg. 5.00 1.00 .20
□□□ 168 Rob Niedermayer, Flor. 5.00 1.00 .20
□□□ 169 Glen Murray, Bost. 15.00 3.00 .20
□□□ 170 Mario Lemieux, Pitt. 120.00 22.00 1.50
□□□ 171 Thomas Steen, Winn. 5.00 1.00 .20
□□□ 172 R. Tugnutt (G), Mont. 15.00 3.00 .20
□□□ 173 Pat Falloon, SanJ. 5.00 1.00 .20
□□□ 174 Tikkanen, NYRa. (SLou.) 5.00 1.00 .20
□□□ 175 D. Hasek (G), Buff. 40.00 7.00 .50
□□□ 176 Patrick Flatley, NYIs. 5.00 1.00 .20
□□□ 177 Gino Odjick, Vanc. 5.00 1.00 .20
□□□ 178 Charlie Huddy, LosA. 5.00 1.00 .20
□□□ 179 Dave Poulin, Wash. 5.00 1.00 .20
□□□ 180 Darren McCarty, Detr. 10.00 2.00 .20
□□□ 181 Todd Gill, Toro. 5.00 1.00 .20
□□□ 182 Tom Chorske, NJer. 5.00 1.00 .20
□□□ 183 Marc Bergevin, Tamp. 5.00 1.00 .20
□□□ 184 Dave Lowry, Flor. 5.00 1.00 .20
□□□ 185 Brent Gilchrist, Dall. 5.00 1.00 .20
□□□ 186 Eric Weinrich, Chic. 5.00 1.00 .20
□□□ 187 Ted Drury, Hart. 5.00 1.00 .20
□□□ 188 Boris Mironov, Edmo. 5.00 1.00 .20
□□□ 189 Patrik Carnbäck, Anah. 5.00 1.00 .20
□□□ 190 R. Bourque, Bost. 45.00 9.00 .50
□□□ 191 P. Brisebois, Mont. 5.00 1.00 .20
□□□ 192 Bob Errey, SanJ. 5.00 1.00 .20
□□□ 193 Scott Lachance, NYIs. 5.00 1.00 .20
□□□ 194 Brad May, Buff. 5.00 1.00 .20
□□□ 195 Jeff Beukeboom, NYRa. 5.00 1.00 .20
□□□ 196 James Patrick, Calg. 5.00 1.00 .20
□□□ 197 Doug Brown, Pitt. 5.00 1.00 .20
□□□ 198 Dana Murzyn, Vanc. 5.00 1.00 .20
□□□ 199 C. Osgood (G), Detr. 20.00 4.00 .20
□□□ 200 W. Gretzky, LosA. 160.00 30.00 2.50
□□□ 201 Bob Carpenter, NJer. 5.00 1.00 .20
□□□ 202 Evgeny Davydov, Otta. 5.00 1.00 .20
□□□ 203 Oleg Petrov, Mont. 10.00 2.00 .20
□□□ 204 Grant Ledyard, Dall. 5.00 1.00 .20
□□□ 205 J. Thibault (G), Québ. 15.00 3.00 .20
□□□ 206 Bill Houlder, Anah. 5.00 1.00 .20
□□□ 207 Tom Fitzgerald, Flor. 5.00 1.00 .20
□□□ 208 D. Roussel (G), Phil. 5.00 1.00 .20
□□□ 209 Dave Ellett, Toro. 5.00 1.00 .20
□□□ 210 Frantisek Kucera, Hart. 5.00 1.00 .20
□□□ 211 J. Steve Smith, Chic. 5.00 1.00 .20
□□□ 212 V. Riendeau (G), Bost. 5.00 1.00 .20
□□□ 213 Scott Pearson, Edmo. 5.00 1.00 .20
□□□ 214 John Slaney, Wash. 5.00 1.00 .20
□□□ 215 Larry Murphy, Pitt. 5.00 1.00 .20
□□□ 216 Travis Green, NYIs. 5.00 1.00 .20
□□□ 217 Joel Otto, Calg. 5.00 1.00 .20
□□□ 218 Randy Wood, Buff. 5.00 1.00 .20
□□□ 219 G. Duchesne, SanJ. 5.00 1.00 .20
□□□ 220 S. Nemchinov, NYRa. 5.00 1.00 .20
□□□ 221 Terry Carkner, Detr. 5.00 1.00 .20
□□□ 222 Randy McKay, NJer. 5.00 1.00 .20
□□□ 223 Mike Donnelly, LosA. 5.00 1.00 .20
□□□ 224 J.J. Daigneault, Mont. 5.00 1.00 .20
□□□ 225 Dallas Drake, Winn. 5.00 1.00 .20
□□□ 226 John Tucker, Tamp. 5.00 1.00 .20
□□□ 227 Dmitry Yushkevich, Phil. 5.00 1.00 .20
□□□ 228 Mike Stapleton, Edmo. 5.00 1.00 .20
□□□ 229 Dmitri Mironov, Toro. 5.00 1.00 .20
□□□ 230 Ken Wregget (G), Pitt. 5.00 1.00 .20
□□□ 231 Claude Lapointe, Québ. 5.00 1.00 .20
□□□ 232 Joe Sacco, Anah. 5.00 1.00 .20
□□□ 233 Craig Ludwig, Dall. 5.00 1.00 .20
□□□ 234 David Reid, Bost. 5.00 1.00 .20
□□□ 235 Rich Sutter, Chic. 5.00 1.00 .20
□□□ 236 M. Fitzpatrick (G), Flor. 5.00 1.00 .20
□□□ 237 Jim Storm, Hart. 5.00 1.00 .20
□□□ 238 Brad Dalgarno, NYIs. 5.00 1.00 .20
□□□ 239 Dixon Ward, LosA. 5.00 1.00 .20
□□□ 240 Greg A. Adams, Vanc. 5.00 1.00 .20
□□□ 241 Dino Ciccarelli, Detr. 10.00 2.00 .20
□□□ 242 Vlastimil Kroupa, SanJ. 5.00 1.00 .20
□□□ 243 Joey Kocur, NYRa. 5.00 1.00 .20
□□□ 244 Donald Audette, Buff. 15.00 3.00 .20
□□□ 245 Trent Yawney, Calg. 5.00 1.00 .20
□□□ **246 Czerkawski, Bost. RC 15.00 3.00 1.00**
□□□ 247 Jason Allison, Wash. 35.00 6.00 .50
□□□ 248 Brian Savage, Mont. 15.00 3.00 .20
□□□ 249 Fred Knipscheer, Bost. 5.00 1.00 .20
□□□ 250 J. McLennan (G), NYIs. 5.00 1.00 .20
□□□ 251 Aaron Gavey, Tamp. 5.00 1.00 .20
□□□ 252 Jeff Friesen, SanJ. 15.00 3.00 .20
□□□ 253 A. Deadmarsh, Québ. 15.00 3.00 .20
□□□ 254 Jamie Storr (G), LosA. 10.00 2.00 .20
□□□ 255 Brian Rolston, NJer. 15.00 3.00 .20
□□□ 256 Zigmund Palffy, NYIs. 20.00 4.00 .20
□□□ 257 Brett Lindros, NYIs. 15.00 3.00 .20
□□□ **258 D. Tsygurov, Buff. RC 5.00 1.00 .50**
□□□ **259 C. Tamer, Pitt. RC 5.00 1.00 .50**
□□□ 260 Michael Peca, Vanc. 20.00 4.00 .20
□□□ 261 Oleg Tverdovsky, Anah. 5.00 1.00 .20
□□□ 262 Todd Harvey, Dall. 10.00 2.00 .20
□□□ 263 Yan Kaminsky, NYIs. 5.00 1.00 .20
□□□ 264 Kenny Jönsson, Toro. 10.00 2.00 .20
□□□ 265 Paul Kariya, Anah. 80.00 15.00 1.00
□□□ 266 P. Forsberg, Québ. 55.00 10.00 .50
□□□ 267 Checklist 5.00 1.00 .20
□□□ 268 Checklist 5.00 1.00 .20
□□□ 269 Checklist 5.00 1.00 .20
□□□ 270 Checklist 5.00 1.00 .20
□□□ 271 Steve Yzerman, Detr. 95.00 18.00 1.50
□□□ 272 John LeClair, Mont. 30.00 6.00 .50
□□□ 273 R. Brind'Amour, Phil. 10.00 2.00 .20
□□□ 274 Ron Hextall (G), Phil. 20.00 4.00 .20
□□□ 275 Todd Elik, SanJ. 5.00 1.00 .20
□□□ 276 Geoff Courtnall, Vanc. 5.00 1.00 .20
□□□ 277 Ulf Samuelsson, Pitt. 5.00 1.00 .20
□□□ 278 Brian Bradley, Tamp. 5.00 1.00 .20
□□□ 279 Darrin Shannon, Winn. 5.00 1.00 .20
□□□ 280 Mike Ricci, Québ. 10.00 2.00 .20
□□□ 281 Peter Bondra, Wash. 20.00 4.00 .20
□□□ 282 T. Yake, Anah. (Toro.) 5.00 1.00 .20
□□□ 283 Patrick Poulin, Chic. 5.00 1.00 .20
□□□ 284 Bob Kudelski, Flor. 5.00 1.00 .20
□□□ 285 Bill Ranford (G), Edmo. 15.00 3.00 .20
□□□ 286 A. Godynyuk, Hart. 5.00 1.00 .20
□□□ 287 Claude Lemieux, NJer. 10.00 2.00 .20
□□□ 288 Sylvain Turgeon, Otta. 5.00 1.00 .20
□□□ 289 Kevin Miller, SLou. 5.00 1.00 .20
□□□ 290 Brian Bellows, Mont. 5.00 1.00 .20
□□□ 291 Murray Craven, Vanc. 5.00 1.00 .20
□□□ 292 K. Hrudey (G), LosA. 15.00 3.00 .20
□□□ 293 Neal Broten, Dall. 5.00 1.00 .20
□□□ 294 Craig Simpson, Buff. 5.00 1.00 .20
□□□ 295 Mark Howe, Detr. 10.00 2.00 .20
□□□ 296 Johan Garpenlöv, SanJ. 5.00 1.00 .20
□□□ 297 Jamie Macoun, Toro. 5.00 1.00 .20
□□□ 298 Stephen Leach, Bost. 5.00 1.00 .20
□□□ 299 Kevin Stevens, Pitt. 5.00 1.00 .20
□□□ 300 Mark Messier, NYRa. 40.00 7.00 .50
□□□ 301 Paul Ysebaert, Chic. 5.00 1.00 .20
□□□ 302 Derek King, NYIs. 5.00 1.00 .20
□□□ 303 F. Olausson, Edmo. 5.00 1.00 .20
□□□ 304 John Druce, LosA. 5.00 1.00 .20
□□□ 305 Calle Johansson, Wash. 5.00 1.00 .20
□□□ 306 Kelly Kisio, Calg. 5.00 1.00 .20
□□□ 307 Sergio Momesso, Vanc. 5.00 1.00 .20
□□□ 308 Joe Cirella, Flor. 5.00 1.00 .20
□□□ 309 T. Söderström (G), NYIs. 5.00 1.00 .20
□□□ 310 Scott Stevens, NJer. 15.00 3.00 .20
□□□ 311 Petr Klima, Tamp. 5.00 1.00 .20
□□□ 312 Steven Finn, Québ. 5.00 1.00 .20
□□□ 313 Tomas Sandström, Pitt. 5.00 1.00 .20
□□□ 314 Ray Ferraro, NYIs. 5.00 1.00 .20
□□□ 315 Andy Moog (G), Dall. 15.00 3.00 .20
□□□ 316 Ray Whitney, SanJ. 5.00 1.00 .20
□□□ 317 Dirk Graham, Chic. 5.00 1.00 .20
□□□ 318 Shawn Burr, Detr. 5.00 1.00 .20
□□□ 319 Andrew Cassels, Hart. 5.00 1.00 .20
□□□ 320 C. Billington (G), Otta. 5.00 1.00 .20
□□□ 321 Wayne Presley, Buff. 5.00 1.00 .20
□□□ 322 Anatoli Semenov, Anah. 5.00 1.00 .20
□□□ 323 Michal Pivonka, Wash. 5.00 1.00 .20
□□□ 324 Martin Gélinas, Vanc. 5.00 1.00 .20
□□□ 325 Nelson Emerson, Winn. 5.00 1.00 .20
□□□ 326 Brent Fedyk, Phil. 5.00 1.00 .20
□□□ 327 Bob Bassen, Québ. 5.00 1.00 .20
□□□ 328 Darryl Sydor, LosA. 5.00 1.00 .20
□□□ 329 S. Matteau, NYRa. 5.00 1.00 .20
□□□ 330 Ken Daneyko, NJer. 5.00 1.00 .20
□□□ 331 Shtalenkov (G), Anah. 5.00 1.00 .20
□□□ 332 K. Buchberger, Edmo. 5.00 1.00 .20
□□□ 333 Mike Hough, Flor. 5.00 1.00 .20
□□□ 334 Dave Gagner, Dall. 5.00 1.00 .20
□□□ 335 Chris Terreri (G), NJer. 5.00 1.00 .20
□□□ 336 Robert Kron, Hart. 5.00 1.00 .20
□□□ 337 Andrei Lomakin, Flor. 5.00 1.00 .20
□□□ 338 Kevin Lowe, NYRa. 10.00 2.00 .20
□□□ 339 Steve Konroyd, Otta. 5.00 1.00 .20
□□□ 340 Denis Savard, Tamp. 15.00 3.00 .20
□□□ 341 Stephen Heinze, Bost. 5.00 1.00 .20
□□□ 342 Zarley Zalapski, Calg. 5.00 1.00 .20
□□□ 343 V. Kamensky, Québ. 10.00 2.00 .20
□□□ 344 Tie Domi, Winn. 10.00 2.00 .20
□□□ 345 Kevin Hatcher, Wash. 5.00 1.00 .20
□□□ 346 Dean Evason, Dall. 5.00 1.00 .20
□□□ 347 Bobby Holik, NJer. 10.00 2.00 .20
□□□ 348 S. Konowalchuk, Wash. 5.00 1.00 .20
□□□ 349 Rob Gaudreau, SanJ. 5.00 1.00 .20
□□□ 350 Pat LaFontaine, Buff. 20.00 4.00 .20
□□□ 351 Joe Reekie, Wash. 5.00 1.00 .20
□□□ 352 Martin Straka, Pitt. 10.00 2.00 .20
□□□ 353 Dave Babych, Vanc. 5.00 1.00 .20
□□□ 354 Geoff Smith, Flor. 5.00 1.00 .20
□□□ 355 D. Beaupré (G), Wash. 5.00 1.00 .20
□□□ 356 Adam Burt, Hart. 5.00 1.00 .20
□□□ 357 Doug Bodger, Buff. 5.00 1.00 .20
□□□ 358 D. McAmmond, Edmo. 5.00 1.00 .20
□□□ 359 Gerald Diduck, Vanc. 5.00 1.00 .20
□□□ 360 Rob DiMaio, Phil. 5.00 1.00 .20
□□□ 361 Scott A. Young, Québ. 10.00 2.00 .20
□□□ 362 Alexander Semak, NJer. 5.00 1.00 .20
□□□ 363 Mike Rathje, SanJ. 5.00 1.00 .20
□□□ 364 A. Karpovtsev, NYRa. 5.00 1.00 .20
□□□ 365 Trevor Kidd (G), Calg. 10.00 2.00 .20
□□□ 366 Jason Dawe, Buff. 5.00 1.00 .20
□□□ 367 Vitali Prokhorov, SLou. 5.00 1.00 .20
□□□ 368 Keith Brown, Flor. 5.00 1.00 .20
□□□ 369 Bret Hedican, Vanc. 5.00 1.00 .20
□□□ 370 Markus Näslund, Pitt. 40.00 7.00 .50
□□□ 371 Rick Tocchet, LosA. 10.00 2.00 .20
□□□ 372 G. Carbonneau, SLou. 10.00 2.00 .20
□□□ 373 Kevin Haller, Phil. 5.00 1.00 .20
□□□ 374 Bob Rouse, Detr. 5.00 1.00 .20
□□□ 375 Rob Pearson, Wash. 5.00 1.00 .20
□□□ 376 Steve Chiasson, Calg. 5.00 1.00 .20
□□□ 377 M. Vernon (G), Detr. 15.00 3.00 .20
□□□ 378 Keith Jones, Wash. 5.00 1.00 .20
□□□ 379 Sylvain Lefebvre, Québ. 5.00 1.00 .20
□□□ 380 Tom Kurvers, Anah. 5.00 1.00 .20
□□□ 381 Pat Elynuik, Otta. 5.00 1.00 .20
□□□ 382 Uwe Krupp, Québ. 5.00 1.00 .20
□□□ 383 Ron Sutter, NYIs. 5.00 1.00 .20
□□□ 384 Mike Ridley, Toro. 5.00 1.00 .20
□□□ 385 Wendel Clark, Québ. 30.00 6.00 .50
□□□ 386 Mats Sundin, Toro. 40.00 7.00 .50
□□□ 387 Al MacInnis, SLou. 15.00 3.00 .20
□□□ 388 Glen Wesley, Hart. 5.00 1.00 .20
□□□ 389 Jim Paek, Otta. 5.00 1.00 .20
□□□ 390 Rudy Poeschek, Tamp. 5.00 1.00 .20
□□□ 391 Yves Racine, Mont. 5.00 1.00 .20
□□□ 392 Craig MacTavish, Phil. 5.00 1.00 .20
□□□ 393 Jon Casey, SLou. 5.00 1.00 .20
□□□ 394 Garth Butcher, Toro. 5.00 1.00 .20
□□□ 395 Sean Hill, Otta. 5.00 1.00 .20
□□□ 396 Troy Loney, NYIs. 5.00 1.00 .20
□□□ 397 John Cullen, Pitt. 5.00 1.00 .20
□□□ 398 A. Kasatonov, Bost. 5.00 1.00 .20
□□□ 399 Mike Craig, Toro. 5.00 1.00 .20
□□□ 400 Luc Robitaille, Pitt. 30.00 6.00 .50
□□□ 401 Randy Moller, Flor. 5.00 1.00 .20
□□□ 402 Chris Dahlquist, Otta. 5.00 1.00 .20
□□□ 403 Pat Conacher, LosA. 5.00 1.00 .20
□□□ 404 Bob Probert, Chic. 10.00 2.00 .20
□□□ 405 Robert Dirk, Anah. 5.00 1.00 .20
□□□ 406 R. Cunneyworth, Otta. 5.00 1.00 .20
□□□ 407 B. Marchment, Edmo. 5.00 1.00 .20
□□□ 408 Nick Kypreos, NYRa. 5.00 1.00 .20
□□□ 409 Doug Lidster, SLou. 5.00 1.00 .20
□□□ 410 Phil Housley, Calg. 10.00 2.00 .20
□□□ 411 Bob Sweeney, Buff. 5.00 1.00 .20
□□□ 412 Mike Ramsey, Detr. 5.00 1.00 .20
□□□ 413 Robert Lang, LosA. 5.00 1.00 .20
□□□ 414 Brian Benning, Flor. 5.00 1.00 .20
□□□ 415 Greg Gilbert, NYRa. 5.00 1.00 .20
□□□ 416 Martin Rucinsky, Québ. 5.00 1.00 .20
□□□ 417 Jason Smith, NJer. 5.00 1.00 .20
□□□ 418 Jozef Stumpel, Bost. 5.00 1.00 .20
□□□ 419 Bob Beers, NYIs. 5.00 1.00 .20
□□□ 420 Ed Olczyk, NYRa. 5.00 1.00 .20
□□□ 421 Grant Fuhr (G), Buff. 20.00 4.00 .20
□□□ 422 Gilbert Dionne, Mont. 5.00 1.00 .20
□□□ 423 Mike Peluso, NJer. 5.00 1.00 .20
□□□ 424 Petr* Svoboda, Buff. 5.00 1.00 .20
□□□ 425 Corey Millen, NJer. 5.00 1.00 .20
□□□ 426 Kevin Dineen, Phil. 5.00 1.00 .20
□□□ 427 Brad McCrimmon, Hart. 5.00 1.00 .20
□□□ 428 Bob Essensa, Detr. 5.00 1.00 .20
□□□ 429 Paul Coffey, Detr. 20.00 4.00 .20
□□□ 430 G. Healy (G), NYRa. 5.00 1.00 .20
□□□ 431 L. Richardson, Edmo. 5.00 1.00 .20
□□□ 432 Adam Foote, Québ. 10.00 2.00 .20
□□□ 433 Paul Broten, Dall. 5.00 1.00 .20
□□□ 434 Christian Ruuttu, Chic. 5.00 1.00 .20
□□□ 435 David Shaw, Bost. 5.00 1.00 .20
□□□ 436 Jimmy Carson, Hart. 5.00 1.00 .20
□□□ 437 Ken Sutton, Buff. 5.00 1.00 .20
□□□ 438 K. Whitmore (G), Vanc. 5.00 1.00 .20
□□□ 439 Jim Dowd, NJer. 5.00 1.00 .20
□□□ 440 Jim* Johnson, Wash. 5.00 1.00 .20
□□□ 441 Kirk Maltby, Edmo. 5.00 1.00 .20
□□□ 442 Trent Klatt, Dall. 5.00 1.00 .20
□□□ 443 Paul DiPietro, Mont. 5.00 1.00 .20
□□□ 444 R. Tabaracci (G), Wash. 5.00 1.00 .20
□□□ 445 Craig Wolanin, Québ. 5.00 1.00 .20
□□□ 446 Dave Hannan, Buff. 5.00 1.00 .20
□□□ 447 Rick Zombo, SLou. 5.00 1.00 .20
□□□ 448 Tom Pederson, SanJ. 5.00 1.00 .20
□□□ 449 Martin Lapointe, Detr. 15.00 3.00 .20
□□□ 450 Brett Hull, SLou. 40.00 7.00 .50
□□□ 451 M. Andersson, Tamp. 5.00 1.00 .20
□□□ 452 Benoît Brunet, Mont. 5.00 1.00 .20
□□□ 453 Nathan Lafayette, Vanc. 5.00 1.00 .20
□□□ 454 Kent Manderville, Toro. 5.00 1.00 .20
□□□ 455 Todd Krygier, Wash. 5.00 1.00 .20
□□□ 456 Dennis Vaske, NYIs. 5.00 1.00 .20
□□□ 457 Peter Popovic, Mont. 5.00 1.00 .20
□□□ 458 Jeff Shantz, Chic. 5.00 1.00 .20
□□□ 459 Darrin Madeley (G), Otta. 5.00 1.00 .20
□□□ 460 René Corbet, Québ. 5.00 1.00 .20
□□□ 461 Alex. Daigle, Otta. 5.00 1.00 .20
□□□ 462 M. Brodeur (G), NJer. 60.00 12.00 1.00
□□□ 463 Jason Arnott, Edmo. 15.00 3.00 .20
□□□ 464 Mikael Renberg, Phil. 10.00 2.00 .20
□□□ 465 Alexei Yashin, Otta. 20.00 4.00 .20
□□□ 466 Chris Pronger, Hart. 20.00 4.00 .20
□□□ 467 M. Czerkawski, Bost. 10.00 2.00 .20
□□□ 468 Chris Gratton, Tamp. 5.00 1.00 .20
□□□ 469 Rob Niedermayer, Flor. 5.00 1.00 .20
□□□ 470 Bryan Smolinski, Bost. 5.00 1.00 .20
□□□ 471 C. Osgood (G), Detr. 20.00 4.00 .20
□□□ 472 Derek Plante, Buff. 5.00 1.00 .20
□□□ 473 Brian Rolston, NJer. 10.00 2.00 .20
□□□ 474 Jason Allison, Wash. 20.00 4.00 .20
□□□ 475 Jamie Storr (G), LosA. 5.00 1.00 .20
□□□ 476 Kenny Jönsson, Toro. 5.00 1.00 .20
□□□ 477 Viktor Kozlov, SanJ. 15.00 3.00 .20
□□□ 478 Brett Lindros, NYIs. 10.00 2.00 .20
□□□ 479 Peter Forsberg, Québ. 55.00 10.00 .50

□□□ 480 Paul Kariya, Anah. 55.00 10.00 .50
□□□ 481 Viktor Kozlov, SanJ. 10.00 2.00 .20
□□□ **482 M. Grosek, Winn. RC 5.00 1.00 .50**
□□□ 483 Maxim Bets, Anah. 5.00 1.00 .20
□□□ 484 J. Wiemer, Tamp. 20.00 3.00 .20
□□□ 485 J. Laukkanen, Québ. 5.00 1.00 .20
□□□ **486 V. Karpov, Anah. RC 5.00 1.00 .50**
□□□ 487 Andrei Nikolishin, Hart. 5.00 1.00 .20
□□□ **488 Dan Plante, NYIs. RC 5.00 1.00 .50**
□□□ 489 M. Norström, NYRa. 5.00 1.00 .20
□□□ **490 D. Oliver, Edmo. RC 5.00 1.00 .50**
□□□ **491 Todd Simon, Buff. RC 5.00 1.00 .50**
□□□ 492 Valeri Bure, Mont. 15.00 3.00 .20
□□□ **493 Fichaud (G), Toro. RC 10.00 2.00 .50**
□□□ **494 C. Stillman, Calg. RC 15.00 3.00 1.00**
□□□ 495 Chris Therien, Phil. 5.00 1.00 .20
□□□ **496 M. Johnson, LosA. RC 5.00 1.00 .50**
□□□ 497 Joby Messier, NYRa. 5.00 1.00 .20
□□□ 498 V. Butsayev, SanJ. 5.00 1.00 .20
□□□ 499 Bernie Nicholls, Chic. 5.00 1.00 .20
□□□ 500 Mark Osborne, NYRa. 5.00 1.00 .20
□□□ 501 Stéphane Quintal, Winn. 5.00 1.00 .20
□□□ 502 Jamie Baker, SanJ. 5.00 1.00 .20
□□□ 503 Todd Ewen, Anah. 5.00 1.00 .20
□□□ 504 Dan Quinn, LosA. 5.00 1.00 .20
□□□ 505 Peter Taglianetti, Pitt. 5.00 1.00 .20
□□□ 506 Chris Simon, Québ. 5.00 1.00 .20
□□□ 507 Jay Wells, NYRa. 5.00 1.00 .20
□□□ 508 Tommy Albelin, NJer. 5.00 1.00 .20
□□□ 509 Warren Rychel, LosA. 5.00 1.00 .20
□□□ 510 Brent" Hughes, Bost. 5.00 1.00 .20
□□□ 511 Greg Johnson, Detr. 5.00 1.00 .20
□□□ 512 Stu Grimson, Anah. 5.00 1.00 .20
□□□ 513 Iain Fraser, Québ. 5.00 1.00 .20
□□□ 514 Rob Ray, Buff. 5.00 1.00 .20
□□□ 515 Craig Berube, Wash. 5.00 1.00 .20
□□□ 516 Shane Churla, Dall. 5.00 1.00 .20
□□□ 517 Checklist 5.00 1.00 .20
□□□ 518 Checklist 5.00 1.00 .20
□□□ 519 Checklist 5.00 1.00 .20
□□□ 520 Checklist 5.00 1.00 .20

□□□ 521 Jamie Storr (G) 10.00 2.00 .20
□□□ **522 Dan Cloutier (G) RC 30.00 6.00 2.00**
□□□ 523 Bryan McCabe 10.00 2.00 .20
□□□ **524 Ed Jovanovski RC 30.00 6.00 2.00**
□□□ **525 N. Baumgartner RC 5.00 1.00 .50**
□□□ **526 Jamie Rivers RC 5.00 1.00 .50**
□□□ **527 Wade Redden RC 25.00 4.00 1.50**
□□□ **528 Lee Sorochan RC 5.00 1.00 .50**
□□□ **529 Éric Dazé RC 30.00 6.00 2.00**
□□□ 530 Jason Allison 35.00 6.00 .50
□□□ 531 Alexandre Daigle 5.00 1.00 .20
□□□ 532 Jeff Friesen 15.00 3.00 .20
□□□ 533 Todd Harvey 10.00 2.00 .20
□□□ 534 Jeff O'Neill RC 30.00 6.00 2.00
□□□ **535 Ryan Smyth RC 35.00 7.00 2.00**
□□□ 536 Marty Murray 5.00 1.00 .20
□□□ **537 Darcy Tucker RC 15.00 3.00 1.00**
□□□ **538 D. Pederson RC 5.00 1.00 .50**
□□□ **539 S. Donovan RC 10.00 2.00 .50**
□□□ **540 Larry Courville RC 5.00 1.00 .50**

BOOMERS

Series One Insert Set (18 cards): 45.00
Insert (1:24 Hobby) BR
□ BR1 Al Iafrate, Bost. 1.00
□ BR2 Vladimir Malakhov, NYIs. 1.00
□ BR3 Al MacInnis, Calg. (SLou.) 2.00
□ BR4 Chris Chelios, Chic. 1.00
□ BR5 Mike Modano, Dall. 5.00
□ BR6 Brendan Shanahan, SLou. 5.00
□ BR7 Raymond Bourque, Bost. 5.00
□ BR8 Geoff Sanderson, Hart. 1.00
□ BR9 Brett Hull, SLou. 5.00
□ BR10 Rob Blake, LosA. 3.00
□ BR11 Steve Thomas, NYIs. 1.00
□ BR12 Cam Neely, Bost. 5.00
□ BR13 Pavel Bure, Vanc. 5.00
□ BR14 Stéphane J.J. Richer, NJer. 1.00
□ BR15 Teemu Selänne, Winn. 5.00
□ BR16 Eric Lindros, Phil. 5.00
□ BR17 Alexander Mogilny, Buff. 3.00
□ BR18 Rick Tocchet, Pitt. 2.00

GAMERS

Series One Insert Set (18 cards): 55.00
Insert (1:18) GR
□ GR1 Teemu Selänne, Winn. 4.00
□ GR2 Pat LaFontaine, Buff. 3.00
□ GR3 Sergei Fedorov, Detr. 5.00
□ GR4 Pavel Bure, Vanc. 4.00
□ GR5 Jaromir Jagr, Pitt. 5.00
□ GR6 Alexandre Daigle, Otta. 1.00
□ GR7 Kirk Muller, Mont. 1.00
□ GR8 Mike Modano, Dall. 5.00
□ GR9 Mark Messier, NYRa. 5.00
□ GR10 Brendan Shanahan, SLou. 5.00
□ GR11 Doug Gilmour, Toro. 3.00
□ GR12 Rick Tocchet, LosA. 1.00
□ GR13 Wendel Clark, Québ. 4.00
□ GR14 Jeremy Roenick, Chic. 4.00
□ GR15 Adam Graves, NYRa. 2.00
□ GR16 Eric Lindros, Phil. 5.00
□ GR17 Cam Neely, Bost. 5.00
□ GR18 Keith Tkachuk, Winn. 3.00

GOALTENDING GREATS

Series One Insert Set (18 cards): 85.00
Insert (1:9 Jumbo) GT
□ GT1 D. Hasek (G), Buff. [vs. G.Carbonneau] 10.00
□ GT2 Mike Richter (G), NYRa. 1.00
□ GT3 John Vanbiesbrouck (G), Flor. 1.00
□ GT4 Ed Belfour (G), Chic. 10.00
□ GT5 Patrick Roy (G), Mont. 30.00
□ GT6 Bill Ranford (G), Edmo. 1.00
□ GT7 Martin Brodeur (G), NJer. 15.00
□ GT8 Félix Potvin (G), Toro. 5.00
□ GT9 Arturs Irbe (G), SanJ. 1.00
□ GT10 Mike Vernon (G), Calg. (Detr.) 1.00
□ GT11 Kirk McLean (G), Vanc. 1.00
□ GT12 Sean Burke (G), Hart. 5.00
□ GT13 Curtis Joseph (G), SLou. 10.00
□ GT14 Andy Moog (G), Dall. 1.00
□ GT15 Daren Puppa (G), Tamp. 1.00
□ GT16 Chris Osgood (G), Detr. 5.00
□ GT17 Tom Barrasso (G), Pitt. 1.00
□ GT18 Jocelyn Thibault (G), Québ. 1.00

MASKS

Series One Insert Set (10 cards): 325.00
Insert (1:90 Canadian) Mask
□ MA1 Patrick Roy (G), Mont. 120.00
□ MA2 John Vanbiesbrouck (G), Flor. 35.00
□ MA3 Kelly Hrudey (G), LosA. 25.00
□ MA4 Guy Hebert (G), Anah. 20.00
□ MA5 Rick Tabaracci (G), Wash. 20.00
□ MA6 Ron Hextall (G), NYIs. 45.00
□ MA7 Trevor Kidd (G), Calg. 25.00
□ MA8 Andy Moog (G), Dall. 30.00
□ MA9 Jimmy Waite (G), SanJ. 20.00
□ MA10 Curtis Joseph (G), SLou. 60.00

MVP

Insert MVP
□ MVPC Pavel Bure, Vanc. 20.00
□ MVPU Dominik Hasek (G), Buff. 20.00

NORTHERN LIGHTS

Series One Insert Set (18 cards): 100.00
Insert (1:24 Canadian) NL
□ NL1 Patrick Roy (G), Mont. 25.00
□ NL2 Kirk Muller, Mont. 5.00

□ NL3 Vincent Damphousse, Mont. 5.00
□ NL4 Joe Sakic, Québ. 10.00
□ NL5 Wendel Clark, Toro. (Québ.) 7.00
□ NL6 Alexandre Daigle, Otta. 5.00
□ NL7 Alexei Yashin, Otta. 5.00
□ NL8 Doug Gilmour, Toro. 5.00
□ NL9 Félix Potvin (G), Toro. 5.00
□ NL10 Mats Sundin, Québ. 5.00
□ NL11 Teemu Selänne, Winn. 5.00
□ NL12 Keith Tkachuk, Winn. 5.00
□ NL13 Bill Ranford (G), Edmo. 5.00
□ NL14 Jason Arnott, Edmo. 5.00
□ NL15 Theoren Fleury, Calg. 5.00
□ NL16 Gary Roberts, Calg. 5.00
□ NL17 Pavel Bure, Vanc. 7.00
□ NL18 Trevor Linden, Vanc. 5.00

ROOKIE TEAM PINNACLE

These cards were produced with the dufex on either the front or the back of the card.

Series Two Insert Set (12 cards): 110.00
Insert (1:90) RTP
□□ RTP1 J. Storr (G) / C. Hirsch (G) 5.00
□□ RTP2 O. Tverdovsky / M. Norström 5.00
□□ RTP3 D. Tsygurov / J. Laukkanen 3.00
□□ RTP4 K. Jönsson / C. Tamer 5.00
□□ RTP5 Vik. Kozlov / Z. Palffy 15.00
□□ RTP6 M. Bets / R. Corbet 3.00
□□ RTP7 J. Friesen / Jas. Allison 15.00
□□ RTP8 M. Peca / B. Rolston 10.00
□□ RTP9 P. Kariya / P. Forsberg 50.00
□□ RTP10 T. Harvey / B. Savage 10.00
□□ RTP11 V. Karpov / B. Lindros 5.00
□□ RTP12 S. Krivokrasov / M. Czerkawski 5.00

TEAM PINNACLE

These cards were produced with the dufex on either the front or the back of the card.

Series One Insert Set (12 cards): 255.00
Insert (1:90) TP
□□ TP1 F. Potvin / P. Roy 45.00
□□ TP2 Cu. Joseph / M. Richter 15.00
□□ TP3 C. Chelios / R. Bourque 20.00
□□ TP4 R. Blake / B. Leetch 15.00
□□ TP5 P. Coffey / S. Stevens 10.00
□□ TP6 B. Shanahan / A. Graves 15.00
□□ TP7 L. Robitaille / K. Stevens 10.00
□□ TP8 S. Fedorov / E. Lindros 25.00
□□ TP9 W. Gretzky / M. Messier 75.00
□□ TP10 D. Gilmour / M. Lemieux 45.00
□□ TP11 Br. Hull / J. Jagr 25.00
□□ TP12 P. Bure / C. Neely 20.00

WORLD EDITION

Series Two Insert Set (18 cards): 55.00
Insert (1:18) WE
□ WE1 Teemu Selänne, Winn. 4.00
□ WE2 Doug Gilmour, Toro. 3.00
□ WE3 Jeremy Roenick, Chic. 4.00
□ WE4 Ulf Dahlén, SanJ. 1.00
□ WE5 Sergei Fedorov, Detr. 5.00
□ WE6 Dominik Hasek (G), Buff. 5.00
□ WE7 Jari Kurri, LosA. 5.00
□ WE8 Mario Lemieux, Pitt. 15.00
□ WE9 Mike Modano, Dall. 5.00
□ WE10 Mikael Renberg, Phil. 1.00
□ WE11 Sandis Ozolinsh, SanJ. 1.00
□ WE12 Alex Kovalev, NYRa. 3.00
□ WE13 Robert Reichel, Calg. 1.00
□ WE14 Eric Lindros, Phil. 5.00
□ WE15 Brian Leetch, NYRa. 3.00
□ WE16 Nicklas Lidström, Detr. 3.00
□ WE17 Alexei Yashin, Otta. 3.00
□ WE18 Petr Nedved, SLou. 1.00

1994 - 95 POG

This series was produced by Canada Games. Gretzky is the most expensive POG at $2-3. Singles start at 20¢.

Cap Diametre: 1 5/8"
Card Size: 2 1/8" 3 1/2"
Imprint: 1994 CGCL TM/MC & 1994 WPF
Complete Set (376 caps): 80.00
Common Player: .20

Player
□ 1 Kings
□ 2 Rangers
□ 3 Penguins
□ 4 Stars
□ 5 Senators
□ 6 Jets
□ 7 Canucks
□ 8 Capitals
□ 9 Mighty Ducks
□ 10 Bruins
□ 11 Sabres
□ 12 Flames
□ 13 Blackhawks
□ 14 Red Wings
□ 15 Oilers
□ 16 Panthers
□ 17 Whalers
□ 18 Canadiens
□ 19 Devils
□ 20 Islanders
□ 21 Flyers
□ 22 Nordiques
□ 23 Sharks
□ 24 Blues
□ 25 Lightning
□ 26 Maple Leafs
□ 27 Cliff Ronning
□ 28 Bob Corkum
□ 29 Joe Sacco
□ 30 Peter Douris
□ 31 Shaun Van Allen
□ 32 Stéphan Lebeau
□ 33 Stu Grimson
□ 34 Tim Sweeney
□ 35 Adam Oates
□ 36 Al Iafrate
□ 37 Alexei Kasatonov
□ 38 Bryan Smolinski
□ 39 Cam Neely
□ 40 Don Sweeney
□ 41 Glen Murray
□ 42 Raymond Bourque
□ 43 Ted Donato
□ 44 Alexander Mogilny
□ 45 Doug Gilmour
□ 46 Dale Hawerchuk
□ 47 Derek Plante
□ 48 Donald Audette
□ 49 Doug Bodger
□ 50 Pat LaFontaine
□ 51 Randy Wood
□ 52 Richard Smehlik
□ 53 Yuri Khmylev
□ 54 Theoren Fleury
□ 55 Kelly Kisio
□ 56 Joe Nieuwendyk
□ 57 Michael Nylander
□ 58 Joel Otto
□ 59 James Patrick
□ 60 Robert Reichel
□ 61 Gary Roberts
□ 62 Wes Walz
□ 63 Ulf Dahlén
□ 64 Zarley Zalapski
□ 65 Tony Amonte
□ 66 Dirk Graham
□ 67 Joe Murphy
□ 68 Bernie Nicholls
□ 69 Patrick Poulin
□ 70 Jeremy Roenick
□ 71 Christian Ruuttu
□ 72 Brent Sutter
□ 73 Chris Chelios
□ 74 J. Steve Smith
□ 75 Gary Suter
□ 76 Neal Broten
□ 77 Russ Courtnall
□ 78 Dean Evason
□ 79 Dave Gagner
□ 80 Mike McPhee
□ 81 Mike Modano
□ 82 Paul Cavallini
□ 83 Derian Hatcher
□ 84 Grant Ledyard
□ 85 Mark Tinordi
□ 86 Dino Ciccarelli
□ 87 Sergei Fedorov
□ 88 Vyacheslav Kozlov
□ 89 Darren McCarty
□ 90 Keith Primeau
□ 91 Ray Sheppard
□ 92 Steve Yzerman
□ 93 Paul Coffey
□ 94 Vladimir Konstantinov
□ 95 Nicklas Lidström
□ 96 Greg A. Adams
□ 97 Jason Arnott
□ 98 Kelly Buchberger
□ 99 Shayne Corson
□ 100 Scott Pearson
□ 101 Doug Weight
□ 102 Boris Mironov
□ 103 Fredrik Olausson
□ 104 Stu Barnes
□ 105 Bob Kudelski
□ 106 Andrei Lomakin
□ 107 Dave Lowry
□ 108 Scott Mellanby
□ 109 Rob Niedermayer
□ 110 Brian Skrudland
□ 111 Brian Benning
□ 112 Gord Murphy
□ 113 Andrew Cassels
□ 114 Hobert Kron
□ 115 Jocelyn Lemieux
□ 116 Paul Ranheim
□ 117 Geoff Sanderson
□ 118 Jim Sandlak
□ 119 Darren Turcotte
□ 120 Pat Verbeek
□ 121 Chris Pronger
□ 122 Pat Conacher
□ 123 Mike Donnelly
□ 124 John Druce
□ 125 Tony Granato
□ 126 Wayne Gretzky
□ 127 Jari Kurri
□ 128 Warren Rychel
□ 129 Rob Blake
□ 130 Marty McSorley
□ 131 Alexei Zhitnik
□ 132 Brian Bellows
□ 133 V. Damphousse
□ 134 Gilbert Dionne
□ 135 Mike Keane
□ 136 John LeClair
□ 137 Kirk Muller
□ 138 Oleg Petrov
□ 139 Éric Desjardins
□ 140 Lyle Odelein
□ 141 Peter Popovic
□ 142 Mathieu Schneider
□ 143 Trent Klatt
□ 144 Bobby Holik
□ 145 Claude Lemieux
□ 146 John MacLean
□ 147 Corey Millen
□ 148 Stéphane Richer
□ 149 Valeri Zelepukin
□ 150 Bruce Driver
□ 151 Gino Odjick
□ 152 Scott Stevens
□ 153 Brad Dalgarno
□ 154 Ray Ferraro
□ 155 Patrick Flatley
□ 156 Travis Green
□ 157 Derek King
□ 158 Marty McInnis
□ 159 Steve Thomas
□ 160 Pierre Turgeon
□ 161 Darius Kasparaitis
□ 162 Vladimir Malakhov
□ 163 Alex Kovalev
□ 164 Steve Larmer
□ 165 Stéphane Matteau
□ 166 Mark Messier
□ 167 Sergei Nemchinov
□ 168 Brian Noonan
□ 169 Petr Nedved
□ 170 Brian Leetch
□ 171 Kevin Lowe
□ 172 Sergei Zubov
□ 173 Sylvain Turgeon
□ 174 Alexei Yashin
□ 175 Norm Maciver
□ 176 Brad Shaw
□ 177 Brent Fedyk
□ 178 Mark Lamb
□ 179 Don McSween
□ 180 Mark Recchi
□ 181 Mikael Renberg
□ 182 Garry Galley
□ 183 Ron Francis
□ 184 Jaromir Jagr
□ 185 Mario Lemieux
□ 186 Shawn McEachern
□ 187 Joe Mullen
□ 188 Tomas Sandström
□ 189 Kevin Stevens
□ 190 Martin Straka
□ 191 Larry Murphy
□ 192 Kjell Samuelsson
□ 193 Ulf Samuelsson
□ 194 Wendel Clark
□ 195 Valeri Kamensky
□ 196 Andrei Kovalenko
□ 197 Owen Nolan
□ 198 Mike Ricci
□ 199 Joe Sakic
□ 200 Scott A. Young
□ 201 Uwe Krupp
□ 202 Curtis Leschyshyn
□ 203 Brett Hull
□ 204 Craig Janney
□ 205 Kevin Miller
□ 206 Vitali Prokhorov
□ 207 Brendan Shanahan
□ 208 Peter Stastny
□ 209 Esa Tikkanen
□ 210 Steve Duchesne
□ 211 Gaétan Duchesne
□ 212 Todd Elik
□ 213 POG Man
□ 214 Pat Falloon
□ 215 Johan Garpenlöv
□ 216 Igor Larionov
□ 217 Sergei" Makarov
□ 218 Jeff Norton
□ 219 Sandis Ozolinsh
□ 220 Mikael Andersson
□ 221 Brian Bradley
□ 222 Danton Cole
□ 223 Chris Gratton
□ 224 Petr Klima
□ 225 Denis Savard
□ 226 John Tucker
□ 227 Shawn Chambers
□ 228 Chris Joseph (G)
□ 229 Dave Andreychuk
□ 230 Nikolai Borschevsky
□ 231 Mike Craig
□ 232 Mike Eastwood
□ 233 Mike Gartner
□ 234 Doug Gilmour
□ 235 Kent Manderville
□ 236 Mike Ridley
□ 237 Mats Sundin
□ 238 Dave Ellett
□ 239 Todd Gill
□ 240 Jamie Macoun
□ 241 Dmitri Mironov
□ 242 Peter Bondra
□ 243 Randy Burridge
□ 244 Dale Hunter
□ 245 Joé Juneau
□ 246 Dmitri Khristich
□ 247 Kelly Miller
□ 248 Michal Pivonka
□ 249 Sylvain Côté
□ 250 Tie Domi
□ 251 Dallas Drake
□ 252 Nelson Emerson
□ 253 Teemu Selänne
□ 254 Darrin Shannon
□ 255 Thomas Steen
□ 256 Keith Tkachuk
□ 257 Dave Manson
□ 258 Stéphane Quintal
□ 259 Adam Graves
□ 260 Brian Leetch
□ 261 Vanbiesbrouck (G)
□ 262 Scott Stevens
□ 263 Raymond Bourque
□ 264 Al MacInnis
□ 265 Brendan Shanahan
□ 266 Pavel Bure
□ 267 Sergei Fedorov
□ 268 Wayne Gretzky
□ 269 Guy Hebert (G)
□ 270 Kirk McLean (G)
□ 271 John Blue (G)
□ 272 V. Riendeau (G)
□ 273 Grant Fuhr (G)
□ 274 Dominik Hasek (G)
□ 275 Trevor Kidd (G)
□ 276 Ed Belfour (G)
□ 277 Andy Moog (G)
□ 278 Mike Vernon (G)
□ 279 Bill Ranford (G)
□ 280 Vanbiesbrouck (G)
□ 281 Sean Burke (G)
□ 282 Kelly Hrudey (G)
□ 283 Patrick Roy (G)
□ 284 Martin Brodeur (G)
□ 285 Chris Terreri (G)
□ 286 J. McLennan (G)
□ 287 Glenn Healy (G)
□ 288 Mike Richter (G)
□ 289 Craig Billington (G)
□ 290 D. Roussel (G)
□ 291 Tom Barrasso (G)
□ 292 Stéphane Fiset (G)
□ 293 Curtis Joseph (G)
□ 294 Arturs Irbe (G)
□ 295 Daren Puppa (G)
□ 296 Félix Potvin (G)
□ 297 Tim Cheveldae (G)
□ 298 Don Beaupré (G)
□ 299 Rick Tabaracci (G)
□ 300 Mighty Ducks
□ 301 Bruins
□ 302 Sabres
□ 303 Flames
□ 304 Blackhawks
□ 305 Stars
□ 306 Red Wings
□ 307 Oilers
□ 308 Panthers
□ 309 Whalers
□ 310 Kings
□ 311 Canadiens
□ 312 Devils
□ 313 Jeff R. Brown
□ 314 Rangers
□ 315 Senators
□ 316 Flyers

317 Penguins	318 Nordiques
319 Blues	320 Sharks
321 Lightning	322 Maple Leafs
323 Canucks	324 Capitals
325 Jets	326 Martin Brodeur (G)
327 Raymond Bourque	328 Cam Neely
329 Geoff Courtnall	330 POG Federation
331 Wayne Gretzky	332 Dominik Hasek (G)
333 Dominik Hasek (G)	334 Brian Leetch
335 Martin Gélinas	336 Cam Neely
337 Mike Richter (G)	338 Luke Richardson
339 Jyrki Lumme	340 Nathan Lafayette
341 Pavel Bure	342 Sergio Momesso
343 Randy Burridge	344 Tie Domi
345 Scott Stevens	346 Teppo Numminen
347 Anatoli Semenov	348 Stephen Heinze
349 Tom Chorske	350 Bill Guerin
351 Scott Niedermayer	352 Adam Graves
353 Alexandre Daigle	354 Troy Mallette
355 Dave McLlwain	356 Josef Beránek
357 Kevin Dineen	358 Eric Lindros
359 Bob Rouse	360 Sergei Fedorov
361 Bob Errey	362 Brad May
363 Kevin Hatcher	364 Islanders
365 Randy Ladouceur	366 Bobby Dollas
367 Igor Kravchuk	368 Jesse Bélanger
369 POG Logo	370 Garry Valk
371 POG Logo	372 Ron Hextall (G)
373 Rod Brind'Amour	374 Benoît Hogue
375 Alexei Zhamnov	376 Pavel Bure
1 Checklist	2 Checklist
3 Checklist	4 Checklist
5 Checklist	6 Checklist
7 Checklist	8 Checklist

1994 - 95 POG WESTERN POWER TEAM

Complete Set (25 cards): 15.00
Unperforated set on board: 20.00

Player	NRMT-MT
1 Jason Arnott, Edmo.	1.50
2 Trevor Kidd (G), Calg.	1.00
Geoff Courtnall, Vanc.	.50
4 Joe Nieuwendyk, Calg.	1.50
5 Sandy McCarthy, Calg.	.50
6 Ronnie Stern, Calg.	.50
7 Pavel Bure, Vanc.	3.00
8 Bill Ranford (G), Edmo.	1.50
9 Shayne Corson, Edmo.	1.00
10 Luke Richardson, Edmo.	.50
Russ Courtnall, Vanc.	.50
12 David Oliver, Edmo.	.50
13 Kelly Buchberger, Edmo.	.50
14 Theoren Fleury, Calg.	2.00
15 Gino Odjick, Vanc.	.50
16 Kirk Maltby, Edmo.	.50
17 Jeff Brown, Vanc.	.50
18 Gary Roberts, Calg.	1.50
19 Kirk McLean (G), Vanc.	1.00
20 Zarley Zalapski, Calg.	.50
21 Trevor Linden, Vanc.	1.50
22 Doug Weight, Edmo.	2.00
23 Cliff Ronning, Vanc.	.50
24 Steve Chiasson, Calg.	.50

1994 - 95 POST

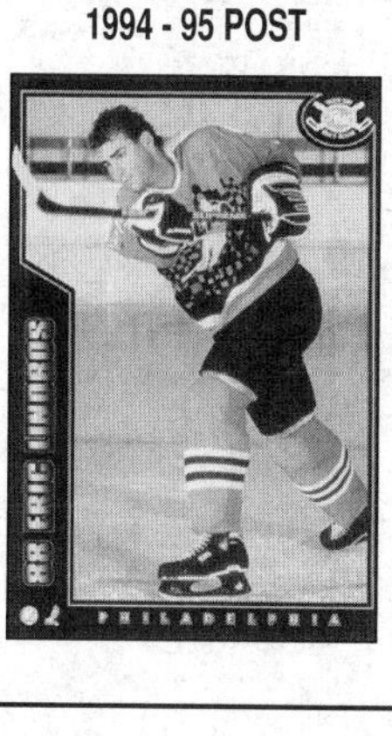

This series was licensed by the NHLPA and issued on the backs of specially marked boxes of Post Honey Comb and Post Sugar Crisp cereal. A complete 25-card factory set was available by mail. The title card was only available in the redeemed sets.

Card Size: 8 3/4" x 12 1/4"

Complete Set (25 cards): 55.00

Player	NRMT-MT
Tony Amonte, NHLPA	3.00
Jason Arnott, NHLPA	3.00
Raymond Bourque, NHLPA	3.00
Martin Brodeur (G), NHLPA	5.00
Pavel Bure, NHLPA	3.00
Chris Chelios, NHLPA	3.00
Geoff Courtnall, NHLPA	3.00
Russ Courtnall, NHLPA	3.00
Steve Duchesne, NHLPA	3.00
Sergei Fedorov, NHLPA	3.00
Theoren Fleury, NHLPA	3.00
Doug Gilmour, NHLPA	3.00
Wayne Gretzky, NHLPA	15.00
Jari Kurri, NHLPA	3.00
Eric Lindros, NHLPA	3.00
Marty McSorley, NHLPA	3.00
Alexander Mogilny, NHLPA	3.00
Kirk Muller, NHLPA	3.00
Rob Niedermayer, NHLPA	3.00
Félix Potvin (G), NHLPA	3.00
Luc Robitaille, NHLPA	3.00
Joe Sakic, NHLPA	5.00
Teemu Selänne, NHLPA	3.00
Alexei Yashin, NHLPA	3.00
Title Card	3.00

1994 - 95 PREMIER

These cards have four versions: an O-Pee-Chee regular card, an O-Pee-Chee Special FX parallel, a Topps regular card and a Topps Special FX parallel. The OPC and Topps regular cards have the same value.

Series One Imprint: © 1994 The Topps Company, Inc.
Series Two Imprint: © 1995 The Topps Company, Inc.

Complete Set (550 cards): 700.00 425.00 35.00
Common Player: .50 .35 .20

Player	O/FX	T/FX	Prmr
1 Mark Messie w/ Cup	7.00	4.50	.50
2 Darren Turcotte, Hart.	1.00	.50	.20
3 M. Shtalenkov (G), Anah.	6.00	3.50	.20
4 Rob Gaudreau, SanJ.	.50	.35	.20
5 Tony Amonte, Chic.	4.00	2.50	.20
6 Stéphane Quintal, Winn.	1.00	.50	.20
7 Iain Fraser, Québ.	.50	.35	.20
8 Doug Weight, Edmo.	4.00	2.50	.20
9 German Titov, Calg.	.50	.35	.20
10 Larry Murphy, Pitt.	1.00	1.00	.20
11 Danton Cole, Tamp.	.50	.35	.20
12 Pat Peake, Wash.	.50	.35	.20
13 Chris Terreri (G), NJer.	1.00	.50	.20
14 Yuri Khmylev, Buff.	.50	.35	.20
15 Paul Coffey, Detr.	4.00	2.50	.20
16 Brian Savage, Mont.	4.00	2.50	.20
17 Rod Brind'Amour, Phil.	2.00	1.00	.20
18 Nathan Lafayette, Vanc.	1.00	.50	.20
19 Gord Murphy, Flor.	.50	.35	.20
20 Al Iafrate, Bost.	1.00	1.00	.20
21 Kevin Miller, SLou.	.50	.35	.20
22 Peter Zezel, Toro.	1.00	.50	.20
23 Sylvain Turgeon, Otta.	1.00	.50	.20
24 Mark Tinordi, Dall.	1.00	.50	.20
25 Jari Kurri, LosA.	7.00	4.50	.50
26 Benoît Hogue, NYIs.	1.00	.50	.20
27 Jeff Reese (G), Hart.	1.00	.50	.20
28 Brian Noonan, NYRa.	.50	.35	.20
29 D. Tsygurov, Buff. RC	**3.00**	**2.00**	**.50**
30 James Patrick, Calg.	.50	.35	.20
31 Bob Corkum, Anah.	.50	.35	.20
32 Valeri Kamensky, Québ.	2.00	1.00	.20
33 Ray Whitney, SanJ.	1.00	1.00	.20
34 Joe Murphy, Chic.	1.00	.50	.20
35 AS: D. Hasek (G), Buff.	7.00	4.50	.50
36 AS: R. Bourque, Bost.	9.00	5.00	.50
37 AS: Brian Leetch, NYRa.	4.00	2.50	.20
38 AS: D. Andreychuk, Toro.	2.00	1.00	.20
39 AS: Pavel Bure, Vanc.	6.00	3.50	.20
40 AS: Sergei Fedorov, Detr.	7.00	4.50	.50
41 Bob Beers, Edmo.	.50	.35	.20
42 Dafoe (G), Wash. RC	**15.00**	**9.00**	**2.00**
43 Lyle Odelein, Mont.	1.00	.50	.20
44 Markus Näslund, Pitt.	7.00	4.50	.50
45 D. Chynoweth, NYIs. RC	**3.00**	**2.00**	**.50**
46 Trent Klatt, Dall.	1.00	.50	.20
47 Murray Craven, Vanc.	1.00	.50	.20
48 D. Mackey, SLou. RC	**3.00**	**2.00**	**.50**
49 Norm Maciver, Otta.	.50	.35	.20
50 Alexander Mogilny, Buff.	3.00	2.00	.20
51 David Reid, Bost.	1.00	.50	.20
52 Nicklas Lidström, Detr.	4.00	2.50	.20
53 Tom Fitzgerald, Flor.	.50	.35	.20
54 Roman Hamrlik, Tamp.	1.00	1.00	.20
55 Wendel Clark, Toro.	6.00	3.50	.20
56 D. Roussel (G), Phil.	1.00	.50	.20
57 Alexei Zhitnik, LosA.	1.00	.50	.20
58 Valeri Zelepukin, NJer.	.50	.35	.20
59 Calle Johansson, Wash.	1.00	1.00	.20
60 Craig Janney, SLou.	1.00	1.00	.20
61 Randy Wood, Buff.	.50	.35	.20
62 Curtis Leschyshyn, Québ.	1.00	.50	.20
63 Stéphan Lebeau, Anah.	.50	.35	.20
64 Dallas Drake, Winn.	1.00	.50	.20
65 V. Damphousse, Mont.	4.00	2.50	.20
66 Scott Lachance, NYIs.	1.00	.50	.20
67 Dirk Graham, Chic.	1.00	.50	.20
68 Kevin Smyth, Hart.	.50	.35	.20
69 Denis Savard, Tamp.	3.00	1.50	.20
70 Mike Richter (G), NYRa.	3.00	2.00	.20
71 Ronnie Stern, Calg.	.50	.35	.20
72 Kirk Maltby, Edmo.	1.00	1.00	.20
73 Kjell Samuelsson, Pitt.	1.00	.50	.20
74 Neal Broten, Dall.	1.00	1.00	.20
75 Trevor Linden, Vanc.	3.00	1.50	.20
76 Todd Elik, SanJ.	.50	.35	.20
77 Andrew McBain, Otta.	.50	.35	.20
78 Alexei Kudashov, Toro.	.50	.35	.20
79 Ken Daneyko, NJer.	1.00	1.00	.20
80 Fuhr (G) / Hasek (G)	6.00	3.50	.20
81 Moog (G) / Wakaluk	2.00	1.00	.20
82 F'patrick / V'bsbrouck (G)	3.00	2.00	.20
83 Brodeur (G) / Terreri (G)	6.00	3.50	.20
84 Barrasso (G) / Wregget (G)	2.00	1.00	.20
85 McLean / Whitmore (G)	1.00	1.00	.20
86 Darryl Sydor, LosA.	1.00	1.00	.20
87 Chris Osgood (G), Detr.	4.00	2.50	.20
88 Ted Donato, Bost.	.50	.35	.20
89 Dave Lowry, Flor.	1.00	1.00	.20
90 Mark Recchi, Phil.	3.00	1.50	.20
91 Jim Montgomery, SLou.	.50	.35	.20
92 Bill Houlder, Anah.	.50	.35	.20
93 Richard Smehlik, Buff.	.50	.35	.20
94 Benoît Brunet, Mont.	.50	.35	.20
95 Teemu Selänne, Winn.	6.00	3.50	.20
96 Paul Ranheim, Hart.	1.00	.50	.20
97 Andrei Kovalenko, Québ.	1.00	.50	.20
98 Grant Ledyard, Dall.	.50	.35	.20
99 B. Grieve, Edmo. RC	**3.00**	**2.00**	**.50**
100 Joé Juneau, Wash.	1.00	1.00	.20
101 Martin Gélinas, Vanc.	1.00	1.00	.20
102 Jamie Macoun, Toro.	.50	.35	.20
103 MacTavish w/ Cup	1.00	.50	.20
104 Micah Aivazoff, Detr.	.50	.35	.20
105 Stéphane Richer, NJer.	1.00	1.00	.20
106 Eric Weinrich, Chic.	.50	.35	.20
107 Pat Elynuik, Tamp.	.50	.35	.20
108 Tomas Sandström, Pitt.	1.00	1.00	.20
109 D. Madeley (G), Otta.	1.00	.50	.20
110 Al MacInnis, Calg.	3.00	1.50	.20
111 Cam Stewart, Bost.	.50	.35	.20
112 Dixon Ward, LosA.	.50	.35	.20
113 Vlastimil Kroupa, SanJ.	.50	.35	.20
114 Rob DiMaio, Phil.	1.00	.50	.20
115 Pierre Turgeon, NYIs.	3.00	1.50	.20
116 Mike Hough, Flor.	.50	.35	.20
117 John LeClair, Mont.	6.00	3.50	.20
118 Dave Hannan, Buff.	.50	.35	.20
119 Todd Ewen, Anah.	.50	.35	.20
120 Cup Champions	.50	.35	.20
121 Dave Manson, Winn.	1.00	.50	.20
122 Jocelyn Lemieux, Hart.	.50	.35	.20
123 J. Thibault (G), Québ.	3.00	1.50	.20
124 Scott Pearson, Edmo.	.50	.35	.20
125 AS: P. Roy (G), Mont.	22.00	12.00	1.50
126 AS: S. Stevens, NJer.	3.00	1.50	.20
127 AS: Al MacInnis, Calg.	3.00	1.50	.20
128 AS: A. Graves, NYRa.	3.00	1.50	.20
129 AS: Cam Neely, Bost.	7.00	4.50	.50
130 AS: W. Gretzky, LosA.	30.00	18.00	2.00
131 Tom Chorske, NJer.	.50	.35	.20
132 John Tucker, Tamp.	.50	.35	.20
133 J. Steve Smith, Chic.	1.00	1.00	.20
134 K. Whitmore (G), Vanc.	1.00	.50	.20
135 Adam Oates, Bost.	3.00	1.50	.20
136 Bill Berg, Toro.	.50	.35	.20
137 Wes Walz, Calg.	1.00	1.00	.20
138 Jeff Beukeboom, NYRa.	1.00	.50	.20
139 Ron Francis, Pitt.	4.00	2.50	.20
140 Alexandre Daigle, Otta.	1.00	.50	.20
141 Josef Beránek, Phil.	1.00	.50	.20
142 Tom Pederson, SanJ.	.50	.35	.20
143 J. McLennan (G), NYIs.	1.00	.50	.20
144 Scott Mellanby, Flor.	1.00	1.00	.20
145 Vy. Kozlov, Detr.	1.00	1.00	.20
146 Marty McSorley, LosA.	1.00	1.00	.20
147 Tim Sweeney, Anah.	.50	.35	.20
148 Luciano Borsato, Winn.	.50	.35	.20
149 Jason Dawe, Buff.	.50	.35	.20
150 LL: W. Gretzky, LosA.	30.00	18.00	2.00
151 LL: Pavel Bure, Vanc.	6.00	3.50	.20
152 LL: D. Hasek (G), Buff.	7.00	4.50	.50
153 LL: S. Stevens, NJer.	3.00	1.50	.20
154 LL: W. Gretzky, LosA.	30.00	18.00	2.00
155 LL: Richter (G), NYRa.	3.00	2.00	.20
156 LL: D. Hasek (G), Buff.	7.00	4.50	.50
157 Ted Drury, Hart.	.50	.35	.20
158 Peter Popovic, Mont.	.50	.35	.20
159 Alexei Kasatonov, SLou.	1.00	1.00	.20
160 Mats Sundin, Québ.	7.00	4.50	.50
161 Brad Shaw, Otta.	.50	.35	.20
162 Bret Hedican, Vanc.	.50	.35	.20
163 Mike McPhee, Dall.	1.00	.50	.20
164 Martin Straka, Pitt.	2.00	1.00	.20
165 Dmitri Mironov, Toro.	1.00	.50	.20
166 A. Trefilov (G), Calg.	1.00	.50	.20
167 Joe Reekie, Wash.	.50	.35	.20
168 Gary Suter, Chic.	1.00	1.00	.20
169 Gilbert, NYRa. [Parade]	.50	.35	.20
170 Igor Larionov, SanJ.	4.00	2.50	.20
171 Mike Sillinger, Detr.	1.00	.50	.20
172 Igor Kravchuk, Edmo.	1.00	.50	.20
173 Glen Murray, Bost.	3.00	2.00	.20
174 S. Chambers, Tamp.	.50	.35	.20
175 John MacLean, NJer.	1.00	.50	.20
176 Yves Racine, Phil.	.50	.35	.20
177 Andrei Lomakin, Flor.	.50	.35	.20
178 Patrick Flatley, NYIs.	.50	.35	.20
179 Igor Ulanov, Winn.	1.00	.50	.20
180 Pat LaFontaine, Buff.	4.00	2.50	.20
181 M. Schneider, Mont.	1.00	1.00	.20
182 Peter Stastny, SLou.	4.00	2.50	.20
183 Tony Granato, LosA.	1.00	1.00	.20
184 Peter Douris, Anah.	.50	.35	.20
185 Alex Kovalev w/ Cup	4.00	2.50	.20
186 Geoff Courtnall, Vanc.	1.00	.50	.20
187 Richard Matvichuk, Dall.	1.00	1.00	.20
188 Troy Murray, Otta.	.50	.35	.20
189 Todd Gill, Toro.	1.00	.50	.20
190 RS: Brodeur (G), NJer.	12.00	7.00	.50
191 RS: Renberg, Phil.	2.00	1.00	.20
192 RS: Yashin, Otta.	4.00	2.50	.20
193 RS: Arnott, Edmo.	3.00	2.00	.20
194 RS: Derek Plante, Buff.	1.00	.50	.20
195 RS: Daigle, Otta.	1.00	.50	.20
196 RS: Smolinski, Bost.	1.00	.50	.20
197 RS: J. Bélanger, Flor.	.50	.35	.20
198 RS: Pronger, Hart.	4.00	2.50	.20
199 RS: Osgood (G), Detr.	4.00	2.50	.20
200 Jeremy Roenick, Chic.	6.00	3.50	.20
201 Johan Garpenlöv, SanJ.	.50	.35	.20
202 Dave Karpa, Québ.	.50	.35	.20
203 Darren McCarty, Detr.	2.00	1.00	.20
204 Claude Lemieux, NJer.	2.00	1.00	.20
205 Geoff Sanderson, Hart.	1.00	1.00	.20
206 Tom Barrasso (G), Pitt.	3.00	1.50	.20
207 Kevin Dineen, Phil.	1.00	.50	.20
208 Sylvain Côté, Wash.	1.00	.50	.20
209 Brent Gretzky, Tamp.	1.00	.50	.20
210 Shayne Corson, Edmo.	2.00	1.00	.20
211 D. Kasparaitis, NYIs.	1.00	.50	.20
212 Peter** Andersson, Flor.	.50	.35	.20
213 Robert Reichel, Calg.	2.00	1.00	.20
214 Jozef Stumpel, Bost.	1.00	1.00	.20
215 B. Shanahan, SLou.	7.00	4.50	.50
216 Craig Muni, Buff.	.50	.35	.20
217 Alexei Zhamnov, Winn.	2.00	1.00	.20
218 Robert Lang, LosA.	1.00	1.00	.20
219 Brian Bellows, Mont.	1.00	1.00	.20
220 Steven* King, Anah.	.50	.35	.20
221 Sergei Zubov w/ Cup	1.00	1.00	.20
222 Kelly Miller, Wash.	1.00	.50	.20
223 Ilya Byakin, Edmo.	1.00	.50	.20
224 Chris Tamer, Pitt. RC	**3.00**	**2.00**	**.50**
225 Doug Gilmour, Toro.	4.00	2.50	.20
226 Shawn Antoski, Vanc.	.50	.35	.20
227 Andrew Cassels, Hart.	1.00	1.00	.20
228 Craig Wolanin, Québ.	.50	.35	.20
229 Jon Casey, Bost.	1.00	.50	.20
230 Mike Modano, Dall.	7.00	4.50	.50
231 Bill Guerin, NJer.	3.00	1.50	.20
232 G. Duchesne, SanJ.	.50	.35	.20
233 Steve Dubinsky, Chic.	.50	.35	.20
234 Jason Bowen, Phil.	.50	.35	.20
235 S. Yzerman, Detr.	18.00	10.00	1.00
236 Dave Poulin, Wash.	1.00	.50	.20
237 Michael Nylander, Calg.	1.00	1.00	.20
238 Félix Potvin (G), Toro.	4.00	2.50	.20
239 Sandis Ozolinsh, SanJ.	1.00	1.00	.20
240 S. Niedermayer, NJer.	2.00	1.00	.20
241 Eric Lindros, Phil.	7.00	4.50	.50
242 Keith Tkachuk, Winn.	4.00	2.50	.20
243 Teemu Selänne, Winn.	6.00	3.50	.20
244 Marty McInnis, NYIs.	1.00	.50	.20
245 Bob Kudelski, Flor.	.50	.35	.20
246 Paul Cavallini, Dall.	.50	.35	.20
247 Brian Bradley, Tamp.	.50	.35	.20
248 R. Stauber (G), LosA.	1.00	.50	.20
249 Jay Wells w/ Cup	.50	.35	.20
250 Mario Lemieux, Pitt.	22.00	12.00	1.50
251 Tommy Albelin, NJer.	1.00	.50	.20
252 Paul DiPietro, Mont.	.50	.35	.20
253 Mike Gartner, Toro.	6.00	3.50	.20
254 Darrin Shannon, Winn.	.50	.35	.20
255 A. Karpovtsev, NYRa.	.50	.35	.20
256 Dave Babych, Vanc.	1.00	.50	.20
257 Greg Johnson, Detr.	2.00	1.00	.20
258 Frantisek Musil, Calg.	1.00	1.00	.20
259 Michal Pivonka, Wash.	.50	.35	.20
260 Arturs Irbe (G), SanJ.	3.00	1.50	.20
261 Paul Broten, Dall.	1.00	.50	.20
262 Don Sweeney, Bost.	1.00	.50	.20
263 Doug Brown, Pitt.	.50	.35	.20
264 Bobby Dollas, Anah.	.50	.35	.20
265 Brian Skrudland, Flor.	1.00	.50	.20
266 Dan Plante, NYIs. RC	**3.00**	**2.00**	**.50**
267 Chad Penney, Otta.	.50	.35	.20
268 Stephen Leach, Bost.	.50	.35	.20
269 D. Rhodes (G), Toro.	1.00	1.00	.20
270 G. Anderson w/ Cup	2.00	1.00	.20
271 Randy McKay, NJer.	.50	.35	.20
272 Jeff R. Brown, Vanc.	.50	.35	.20
273 S. Konowalchuk, Wash.	1.00	1.00	.20
274 Checklist	-	-	.20
275 Checklist	-	-	.20
276 Sergei Fedorov, Detr.	7.00	4.50	.50
277 Adam Oates, Bost.	3.00	1.50	.20
278 Mark Messier, NYRa.	7.00	4.50	.50
279 Doug Gilmour, Toro.	4.00	2.50	.20
280 Wayne Gretzky, LosA.	30.00	18.00	2.00
281 Rick Tocchet, LosA.	2.00	1.00	.20
282 Guy Carbonneau, SLou.	2.00	1.00	.20
283 Peter Bondra, Wash.	4.00	2.50	.20
284 V. Karpov, Anah. RC	**3.00**	**2.00**	**.50**
285 Ed Belfour (G), Chic.	7.00	4.50	.50
286 Petr Nedved, NYRa.	2.00	1.00	.20
287 M. Andersson, Tamp.	.50	.35	.20
288 Boris Mironov, Edmo.	1.00	.50	.20
289 Donald Audette, Buff.	3.00	1.50	.20
290 Kevin Stevens, Pitt.	1.00	1.00	.20
291 Cliff Ronning, Vanc.	1.00	1.00	.20
292 Bruce Driver, NJer.	.50	.35	.20
293 Czerkawski, Bost. RC	**9.00**	**5.00**	**1.00**
294 Mikael Renberg, Phil.	2.00	1.00	.20
295 Theoren Fleury, Calg.	4.00	2.50	.20
296 Robert Kron, Hart.	1.00	.50	.20
297 Wendel Clark, Québ.	6.00	3.50	.20
298 Dave Gagner, Dall.	1.00	.50	.20
299 Ulf Dahlén, SanJ.	1.00	.50	.20
300 Keith Tkachuk, Winn.	4.00	2.50	.20
301 Mike Ridley, Toro.	1.00	.50	.20
302 Mike Vernon (G), Detr.	3.00	1.50	.20
303 Troy Mallette, Otta.	.50	.35	.20
304 Derek King, NYIs.	1.00	.50	.20
305 Kirk Muller, Mont.	2.00	1.00	.20
306 Rob Niedermayer, Flor.	1.00	1.00	.20
307 I. Laperrière, SLou. RC	**6.00**	**3.50**	**.50**
308 Mike Donnelly, LosA.	.50	.35	.20
309 Joe Sacco, Anah.	.50	.35	.20
310 P. Roy (G), Mont.	22.00	12.00	1.50
311 T. Barrasso (G), Pitt.	3.00	1.50	.20
312 D. Hasek (G), Buff.	7.00	4.50	.50
313 Félix Potvin (G), Toro.	4.00	2.50	.20
314 Mike Richter (G), NYRa.	3.00	2.00	.20
315 Bobby Holik, NJer.	2.00	1.00	.20
316 Patrick Poulin, Chic.	1.00	.50	.20
317 S. Matteau, NYRa.	1.00	.50	.20
318 Petr Klima, Tamp.	1.00	.50	.20
319 Fredrik Olausson, Edmo.	1.00	1.00	.20
320 Dale Hawerchuk, Buff.	4.00	2.50	.20
321 Jim Dowd, NJer.	.50	.35	.20
322 Chris Therien, Phil.	1.00	.50	.20

□□□□ **323 Gusmanov, Winn. RC**	**3.00**	**2.00**	**.50**
□□□□ 324 V. Riendeau (G), Bost.	1.00	.50	.20
□□□□ 325 Pavel Bure, Vanc.	6.00	3.50	.20
□□□□ 326 Jimmy Carson, Hart.	1.00	.50	.20
□□□□ 327 Steve Chiasson, Calg.	1.00	.50	.20
□□□□ 328 Ken Wregget (G), Pitt.	1.00	1.00	.20
□□□□ 329 Kenny Jönsson, Toro.	3.00	1.50	.20
□□□□ 330 Keith Primeau, Detr.	3.00	1.50	.20
□□□□ 331 Bob Errey, SanJ.	1.00	.50	.20
□□□□ 332 Derian Hatcher, Dall.	2.00	1.00	.20
□□□□ 333 S. Fiset (G), Québ.	2.00	1.00	.20
□□□□ 334 Brent Severyn, Flor.	.50	.35	.20
□□□□ 335 Ray Ferraro, NYIs.	1.00	.50	.20
□□□□ 336 Pavol Demitra, Otta.	3.00	1.50	.20
□□□□ 337 Valeri Bure, Mont.	4.00	2.50	.20
□□□□ 338 Guy Hebert (G), Anah.	1.00	1.00	.20
□□□□ **339 M. Johnson, LosA. RC**	**3.00**	**2.00**	**.50**
□□□□ 340 Cu. Joseph (G), SLou.	7.00	4.50	.50
□□□□ 341 Rob Pearson, Wash.	.50	.35	.20
□□□□ 342 Jeff Shantz, Chic.	.50	.35	.20
□□□□ **343 É. Charron, Tamp. RC**	**3.00**	**2.00**	**.50**
□□□□ 344 Jason Smith, NJer.	1.00	.50	.20
□□□□ 345 W. Clark / M. Sundin	6.00	4.00	.20
□□□□ 346 Robitaille / Tocchet	4.00	2.50	.20
□□□□ 347 Housley / MacInnis	2.00	1.50	.20
□□□□ 348 Chiasson / Vernon (G)	2.00	1.00	.20
□□□□ 349 Craig Simpson, Buff.	1.00	.50	.20
□□□□ 350 Adam Graves, NYRa.	3.00	1.50	.20
□□□□ 351 Kevin Haller, Phil.	.50	.35	.20
□□□□ 352 Nelson Emerson, Winn.	1.00	.50	.20
□□□□ 353 Phil Housley, Calg.	2.00	1.00	.20
□□□□ 354 S. McEachern, Pitt.	2.00	1.00	.20
□□□□ 355 Félix Potvin (G), Toro.	4.00	2.50	.20
□□□□ 356 Sergio Momesso, Vanc.	.50	.35	.20
□□□□ 357 Glen Wesley, Hart.	1.00	.50	.20
□□□□ 358 David Shaw, Bost.	.50	.35	.20
□□□□ 359 Terry Carkner, Detr.	.50	.35	.20
□□□□ 360 Vanbiesbrouck (G), Flor.	3.00	2.00	.20
□□□□ 361 Dean Evason, Dall.	.50	.35	.20
□□□□ 362 Michal Sykora, SanJ.	1.00	.50	.20
□□□□ 363 Troy Loney, NYIs.	.50	.35	.20
□□□□ 364 Sylvain Lefebvre, Québ.	1.00	.50	.20
□□□□ 365 Alexei Yashin, Otta.	4.00	2.50	.20
□□□□ 366 Gilbert Dionne, Mont.	.50	.35	.20
□□□□ 367 R. Tabaracci (G), Wash.	1.00	.50	.20
□□□□ 368 Paul Ysebaert, Chic.	.50	.35	.20
□□□□ 369 Craig Johnson, SLou.	1.00	.50	.20
□□□□ 370 Scott Stevens, NJer.	3.00	1.50	.20
□□□□ 371 Philippe Boucher, Buff.	.50	.35	.20
□□□□ 372 Garry Valk, Anah.	.50	.35	.20
□□□□ 373 Jason Muzzatti (G), Calg.	1.00	.50	.20
□□□□ 374 Chris Joseph (G), Tamp.	.50	.35	.20
□□□□ 375 W. Gretzky, LosA.	30.00	18.00	2.00
□□□□ 376 T. Numminen, Winn.	2.00	1.00	.20
□□□□ 377 Oleg Petrov, Mont.	2.00	1.00	.20
□□□□ **378 Patrik Juhlin, Phil. RC**	**3.00**	**2.00**	**.50**
□□□□ 379 Zarley Zalapski, Calg.	.50	.35	.20
□□□□ 380 Brodeur (G), NJer.	12.00	7.00	.50
□□□□ 381 Chris Pronger, Hart.	4.00	2.50	.20
□□□□ 382 Sergei Zubov, NYRa.	1.00	1.00	.20
□□□□ 383 Mikael Renberg, Phil.	2.00	1.00	.20
□□□□ 384 Brett Lindros, NYIs.	4.00	2.50	.20
□□□□ 385 Peter Forsberg, Québ.	10.00	6.00	.50
□□□□ 386 Brandon Convery, Toro.	1.00	.50	.20
□□□□ 387 Stephen Heinze, Bost.	1.00	.50	.20
□□□□ 388 Glenn Healy (G), NYRa.	1.00	1.00	.20
□□□□ 389 Brian Benning, Flor.	.50	.35	.20
□□□□ 390 Pat Verbeek, Hart.	2.00	1.00	.20
□□□□ 391 Ulf Samuelsson, Pitt.	1.00	.50	.20
□□□□ 392 T. Stevenson, Mont.	1.00	.50	.20
□□□□ 393 Bob Rouse, Detr.	.50	.35	.20
□□□□ 394 Steve Konroyd, Otta.	.50	.35	.20
□□□□ 395 Russ Courtnall, Dall.	1.00	1.00	.20
□□□□ 396 Sergei* Makarov, SanJ.	3.00	1.50	.20
□□□□ 397 Kirk McLean (G), Vanc.	2.00	1.00	.20
□□□□ 398 Steven Finn, Québ.	.50	.35	.20
□□□□ 399 Yan Kaminsky, NYIs.	.50	.35	.20
□□□□ 400 Eric Lindros, Phil.	7.00	4.50	.50
□□□□ 401 Steve Duchesne, SLou.	1.00	1.00	.20
□□□□ 402 John Slaney, Wash.	.50	.35	.20
□□□□ 403 Bernie Nicholls, Chic.	1.00	1.00	.20
□□□□ 404 K. Buchberger, Edmo.	1.00	.50	.20
□□□□ 405 Paul Kariya, Anah.	20.00	12.00	1.00
□□□□ 406 Michel Petit, LosA.	.50	.35	.20
□□□□ **407 Cale Hulse, NJer. RC**	**3.00**	**2.00**	**.50**
□□□□ 408 Sheldon Kennedy, Winn.	.50	.35	.20
□□□□ 409 Brad May, Buff.	1.00	.50	.20
□□□□ 410 D. Puppa (G), Tamp.	1.00	1.00	.20
□□□□ 411 J. Laukkanen, Québ.	1.00	.50	.20
□□□□ 412 Mats Sundin, Toro.	7.00	4.50	.50
□□□□ 413 Trevor Kidd (G), Calg.	2.00	1.00	.20
□□□□ 414 Greg A. Adams, Vanc.	1.00	.50	.20
□□□□ 415 Pavel Bure, Vanc.	6.00	3.50	.20
□□□□ 416 Teemu Selänne, Winn.	6.00	3.50	.20
□□□□ 417 Brett Hull, SLou.	7.00	4.50	.50
□□□□ 418 Steve Larmer, NYRa.	3.00	1.50	.20
□□□□ 419 Cam Neely, Bost.	7.00	4.50	.50
□□□□ 420 R. Bourque, Bost.	9.00	5.00	.50
□□□□ 421 Andrei Nikolishin, Hart.	2.00	1.00	.20
□□□□ 422 Jim Paek, Otta.	.50	.35	.20
□□□□ 423 John Cullen, Pitt.	1.00	1.00	.20
□□□□ 424 D. Wakaluk (G), Dall.	1.00	.50	.20
□□□□ 425 Peter Forsberg, Québ.	10.00	6.00	.50
□□□□ 426 Yves Racine, Mont.	.50	.35	.20
□□□□ 427 Jody Hull, Flor.	.50	.35	.20
□□□□ 428 Ron Sutter, NYIs.	1.00	1.00	.20
□□□□ 429 Ray Sheppard, Detr.	1.00	.50	.20
□□□□ 430 Sandis Ozolinsh, SanJ.	1.00	1.00	.20
□□□□ 431 Brent Grieve, Chic.	1.00	.50	.20
□□□□ 432 Shaun Van Allen, Anah.	1.00	.50	.20
□□□□ 433 Craig Berube, Wash.	1.00	.50	.20
□□□□ **434 V. Boulin, Phil. RC**	**3.00**	**2.00**	**.50**
□□□□ 435 Bill Ranford (G), Edmo.	3.00	1.50	.20
□□□□ 436 Denny Felsner, SLou.	.50	.35	.20
□□□□ 437 Jamie Storr (G), LosA.	3.00	2.00	.20
□□□□ 438 Brian Rolston, NJer.	4.00	2.50	.20
□□□□ 439 Chris Gratton, Tamp.	1.00	1.00	.20
□□□□ 440 D. Hasek (G), Buff.	7.00	4.50	.50
□□□□ 441 Garth Butcher, Toro.	.50	.35	.20
□□□□ 442 Jyrki Lumme, Vanc.	1.00	1.00	.20
□□□□ 443 S. Nemchinov, NYRa.	1.00	1.00	.20
□□□□ 444 Tie Domi, Winn.	2.00	1.00	.20
□□□□ 445 Gary Roberts, Calg.	3.00	1.50	.20
□□□□ 446 Dave McLlwain, Otta.	.50	.35	.20
□□□□ **447 Gruden, Bost. RC**	**3.00**	**2.00**	**.50**
□□□□ 448 V. Konstantinov, Detr.	2.00	1.00	.20
□□□□ 449 A. Deadmarsh, Québ.	4.00	2.50	.20
□□□□ 450 Brian Leetch, NYRa.	4.00	2.50	.20
□□□□ 451 Scott Stevens, NJer.	3.00	1.50	.20
□□□□ 452 Mark Tinordi, Dall.	1.00	.50	.20
□□□□ 453 Al Iafrate, Bost.	1.00	1.00	.20
□□□□ 454 R. Bourque, Bost.	9.00	5.00	.50
□□□□ 455 P. Roy (G), Mont.	22.00	12.00	1.50
□□□□ 456 Viktor Gordiouk, Buff.	.50	.35	.20
□□□□ 457 Owen Nolan, Québ.	4.00	2.50	.20
□□□□ 458 Stu Barnes, Flor.	.50	.35	.20
□□□□ 459 Zigmund Palffy, NYIs.	4.00	2.50	.20
□□□□ 460 Jaromir Jagr, Pitt.	7.00	4.50	.50
□□□□ 461 Andrei Nazarov, SanJ.	1.00	.50	.20
□□□□ 462 Kelly Hrudey (G), LosA.	3.00	2.00	.20
□□□□ 463 J. Wiemer, Tamp.	3.00	2.00	.20
□□□□ 464 Oleg Tverdovsky, Anah.	2.00	1.00	.20
□□□□ 465 Brett Hull, SLou.	7.00	4.50	.50
□□□□ 466 L. Richardson, Edmo.	1.00	.50	.20
□□□□ 467 Jason Allison, Wash.	9.00	5.00	.50
□□□□ 468 Dmitry Yushkevich, Phil.	1.00	1.00	.20
□□□□ **469 Todd Simon, Buff. RC**	**3.00**	**2.00**	**.50**
□□□□ 470 M. Brodeur (G), NJer.	12.00	7.00	.50
□□□□ 471 Thomas Steen, Winn.	1.00	.50	.20
□□□□ 472 Vesa Viitakoski, Calg.	.50	.35	.20
□□□□ 473 Todd Harvey, Dall.	3.00	2.00	.20
□□□□ 474 Kent Manderville, Toro.	.50	.35	.20
□□□□ 475 Chris Chelios, Chic.	4.00	2.50	.20
□□□□ 476 Joby Messier, NYRa.	.50	.35	.20
□□□□ 477 Jassen Cullimore, Vanc.	.50	.35	.20
□□□□ 478 Jamie Pushor, Detr.	.50	.35	.20
□□□□ 479 Bryan Smolinski, Bost.	1.00	.50	.20
□□□□ 480 Joe Sakic, Québ.	12.00	7.00	.50
□□□□ 481 David Wilkie, Mont.	1.00	.50	.20
□□□□ 482 C. Billington (G), Otta.	1.00	.50	.20
□□□□ 483 Pat Neaton, Pitt.	.50	.35	.20
□□□□ 484 Chris Pronger, Hart.	4.00	2.50	.20
□□□□ 485 Brian Leetch, NYRa.	4.00	2.50	.20
□□□□ 486 Chris Chelios, Chic.	4.00	2.50	.20
□□□□ 487 Jeff R. Brown, Vanc.	.50	.35	.20
□□□□ 488 Al MacInnis, SLou.	3.00	1.50	.20
□□□□ 489 Paul Coffey, Detr.	4.00	2.50	.20
□□□□ 490 R. Bourque, Bost.	9.00	5.00	.50
□□□□ 491 Phil Housley, Calg.	2.00	1.00	.20
□□□□ 492 Larry Murphy, Pitt.	1.00	1.00	.20
□□□□ 493 Sergei Zubov, NYRa.	1.00	1.00	.20
□□□□ 494 Scott Stevens, NJer.	3.00	1.50	.20
□□□□ 495 Steve Thomas, NYIs.	1.00	1.00	.20
□□□□ 496 Jimmy Waite (G), SanJ.	1.00	.50	.20
□□□□ 497 Mike Keane, Mont.	1.00	.50	.20
□□□□ 498 Rob Blake, LosA.	4.00	2.50	.20
□□□□ 499 John Lilley, Anah.	1.00	.50	.20
□□□□ 500 Brian Leetch, NYRa.	4.00	2.50	.20
□□□□ 501 Derek Plante, Buff.	1.00	.50	.20
□□□□ 502 T. Cheveldae (G), Winn.	1.00	.50	.20
□□□□ 503 Vladimir Vujtek, Edmo.	.50	.35	.20
□□□□ 504 Esa Tikkanen, SLou.	1.00	.50	.20
□□□□ 505 Cam Neely, Bost.	7.00	4.50	.50
□□□□ 506 Dale Hunter, Wash.	2.00	1.00	.20
□□□□ 507 Marc Bergevin, Tamp.	.50	.35	.20
□□□□ 508 Joel Otto, Calg.	1.00	.50	.20
□□□□ 509 Brent Fedyk, Phil.	.50	.35	.20
□□□□ 510 D. Andreychuk, Toro.	2.00	1.00	.20
□□□□ 511 Andy Moog (G), Dall.	3.00	1.50	.20
□□□□ 512 Jaroslav Modry, NJer.	.50	.35	.20
□□□□ 513 S. Krivokrasov, Chic.	1.00	.50	.20
□□□□ 514 Brett Lindros, NYIs.	2.00	1.00	.20
□□□□ **515 C. Stillman, Calg. RC**	**9.00**	**5.00**	**1.00**
□□□□ **516 Jon Rohloff, Bost. RC**	**3.00**	**2.00**	**.50**
□□□□ 517 Joe Mullen, Pitt.	3.00	1.50	.20
□□□□ 518 Evgeny Davydov, Otta.	.50	.35	.20
□□□□ 519 Scott A. Young, Québ.	2.00	1.00	.20
□□□□ 520 Sergei Fedorov, Detr.	7.00	4.50	.50
□□□□ 521 Pat Falloon, SanJ.	1.00	.50	.20
□□□□ 522 Bill Lindsay, Flor.	.50	.35	.20
□□□□ 523 R. Tugnutt (G), Mont.	3.00	1.50	.20
□□□□ 524 Anatoli Semenov, Anah.	.50	.35	.20
□□□□ 525 Geoff Courtnall, Vanc.	1.00	.50	.20
□□□□ 526 Luc Robitaille, Pitt.	6.00	3.50	.20
□□□□ 527 Geoff Sanderson, Hart.	1.00	1.00	.20
□□□□ 528 Esa Tikkanen, SLou.	1.00	.50	.20
□□□□ 529 B. Shanahan, SLou.	7.00	4.50	.50
□□□□ 530 Jason Arnott, Edmo.	3.00	2.00	.20
□□□□ **531 M. Grosek, Winn. RC**	**3.00**	**2.00**	**.50**
□□□□ 532 Steve Larmer, NYRa.	3.00	1.50	.20
□□□□ **533 Fichaud (G), Toro. RC**	**6.00**	**3.50**	**.50**
□□□□ 534 Dmitri Khristich, Wash.	1.00	.50	.20
□□□□ 535 Garry Galley, Phil.	.50	.35	.20
□□□□ 536 Aaron Gavey, Tamp.	1.00	.50	.20
□□□□ 537 Joe Nieuwendyk, Calg.	3.00	1.50	.20
□□□□ 538 Mike Craig, Toro.	.50	.35	.20
□□□□ 539 S. Niedermayer, NJer.	2.00	1.00	.20
□□□□ 540 Luc Robitaille, Pitt.	6.00	3.50	.20
□□□□ 541 Dino Ciccarelli, Detr.	2.00	1.00	.20
□□□□ 542 Sean Burke (G), Hart.	4.00	2.50	.20
□□□□ 543 Jiri Slegr, Vanc.	1.00	.50	.20
□□□□ 544 Jesse Bélanger, Flor.	.50	.35	.20
□□□□ 545 Sean Hill, Otta.	.50	.35	.20
□□□□ 546 V. Malakhov, NYIs.	1.00	.50	.20
□□□□ 547 Jeff Friesen, SanJ.	4.00	2.50	.20
□□□□ 548 Mike Ricci, Québ.	2.00	1.00	.20
□□ 549 Checklist	-	-	.20
□□ 550 Checklist	-	-	.20

Player	O/FX	T/FX	Prmr
□□ 274 Rudy Poeschek, Tamp.	1.00	1.00	-
□□ 275 Michael Peca, Vanc.	3.00	1.50	-
□ 549 John Druce, LosA.		1.00	-
□ 550 Matt Martin, Toro.		1.00	-

TOPPS / FINEST

Series One Insert Set (23 cards): 80.00

Insert (1:36)	Topps
□ 1 Pavel Bure, Vanc.	6.00
□ 2 Brett Hull, SLou.	7.00
□ 3 Sergei Fedorov, Detr.	7.00
□ 4 Dave Andreychuk, Toro.	2.00
□ 5 Brendan Shanahan, SLou.	7.00
□ 6 Ray Sheppard, Detr.	1.00
□ 7 Adam Graves, NYRa.	3.00
□ 8 Cam Neely, Bost.	7.00
□ 9 Mike Modano, Dall.	7.00
□ 10 Wendel Clark, Toro.	6.00
□ 11 Jeremy Roenick, Chic.	6.00
□ 12 Eric Lindros, Phil.	7.00
□ 13 Luc Robitaille, LosA.	6.00
□ 14 Steve Thomas, NYIs.	1.00
□ 15 Geoff Sanderson, Hart.	1.00
□ 16 Gary Roberts, Calg.	3.00
□ 17 Kevin Stevens, Pitt.	1.00
□ 18 Keith Tkachuk, Winn.	4.00
□ 19 Theoren Fleury, Calg.	4.00
□ 20 Robert Reichel, Calg.	2.00
□ 21 Mark Recchi, Phil.	3.00
□ 22 Vincent Damphousse, Mont.	4.00
□ 23 Bob Kudelski, Flor.	1.00

O-PEE-CHEE / FINEST

Series One Insert Set (23 cards): 40.00

Insert (1:36)	NRMT-MT
□ 1 Patrik Carnback, Anah.	1.00
□ 2 Bryan Smolinski, Bost.	1.00
□ 3 Derek Plante, Buff.	1.00
□ 4 Alexander Karpovtsev, Que.	1.00
□ 5 Trevor Kidd (G), Calg.	2.00
□ 6 Iain Fraser, Que.	1.00
□ 7 Alexandre Daigle, Otta.	1.00
□ 8 Chris Osgood (G), Detr.	4.00
□ 9 Rob Niedermayer, Flor.	1.00
□ 10 Jason Arnott, Edmo.	3.00
□ 11 Chris Pronger, Hfd.	4.00
□ 12 Jesse Belanger, Flor.	1.00
□ 13 Oleg Petrov, Mont.	2.00
□ 14 Martin Brodeur (G), NJer.	12.00
□ 15 Alexei Yashin, Otta.	4.00
□ 16 Mikael Renberg, Phil.	2.00
□ 17 Boris Mironov, Winn.	1.00
□ 18 Damian Rhodes (G), Toro.	1.00
□ 19 Darren McCarty, Detr.	2.00
□ 20 Chris Gratton, Tamp.	1.00
□ 21 Jamie McLennan (G), NYIs.	1.00
□ 22 Nathan Lafayette, Vanc.	1.00
□ 23 Jeff Shantz, Chic.	1.00

GO TO GUY

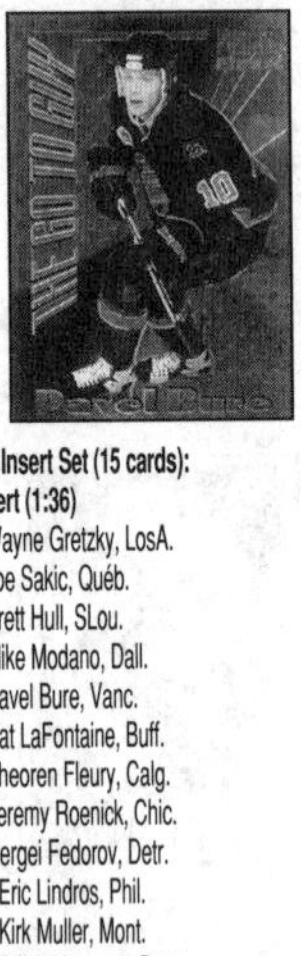

Series Two Insert Set (15 cards): 45.00

Insert (1:36)	NRMT-MT
□ 1 Wayne Gretzky, LosA.	15.00
□ 2 Joe Sakic, Québ.	6.00
□ 3 Brett Hull, SLou.	3.00
□ 4 Mike Modano, Dall.	3.00
□ 5 Pavel Bure, Vanc.	3.00
□ 6 Pat LaFontaine, Buff.	2.00
□ 7 Theoren Fleury, Calg.	2.00
□ 8 Jeremy Roenick, Chic.	3.00
□ 9 Sergei Fedorov, Detr.	3.00
□ 10 Eric Lindros, Phil.	3.00
□ 11 Kirk Muller, Mont.	2.00
□ 12 Steve Yzerman, Detr.	9.00
□ 13 Alexander Mogilny, Buff.	2.00
□ 14 Doug Gilmour, Toro.	2.00
□ 15 Mark Messier, NYRa.	3.00

1994 - 95 SCORE

These cards have two or three versions: a regular card (1-275), a Gold Line card and a Platinum (1-200, 216-262). Promo versions (clipped corner) exist for cards 1-7. There are two versions of the Gold Line parallel: the gold band crosses either to the right or to the left. This variation appears only in cards 216-262.

Gold Line team sets could be redeemed for Platinum Team sets. Only NHL team cards were redeemed in Platinum. Common Platinum Team sets sell for $15.00-20.00. The Kings' Platinum set sells for $90.00 and the Flyers' Platinum set sells for $70.00. Gold Line cards were returned with a perforation of the Pinnacle logo. While World Junior Platinum cards (201-215) were not redeemable, they do exist. We have no pricing information on these World Junior Platinum cards.

Imprint: © 1994 PINNACLE BRANDS, INC.

Complete Set (275 cards):	-	80.00	15.00
Platinum Set (260 cards):	600.00	-	-
Common Player:	2.00	.35	.20
Player	**Plat.**	**Gold**	**Reg.**
□□□□ 1 Eric Lindros, Phil.	25.00	2.50	.50
□□□□ 2 Pat LaFontaine, Buff.	15.00	1.50	.20
□□□□ 3 Wendel Clark, Toro.	20.00	2.00	.20
□□□□ 4 Cam Neely, Bost.	25.00	2.50	.50
□□□□ 5 Larry Murphy, Pitt.	6.00	.50	.20
□□□□ 6 Patrick Poulin, Chic.	4.00	.35	.20
□□□□ 7 Bob Beers, Edmo.	2.00	.35	.20
□□□ 8 James Patrick, Calg.	2.00	.35	.20
□□□ 9 Gino Odjick, Vanc.	4.00	.35	.20
□□□ 10 Arturs Irbe (G), SanJ.	10.00	1.00	.20
□□□ 11 Darius Kasparaitis, NYIs.	6.00	.50	.20
□□□ 12 Peter Bondra, Wash.	15.00	1.50	.20
□□□ 13 Garth Butcher, Québ.	2.00	.35	.20
□□□ 14 Sergei Nemchinov, NYRa.	6.00	.50	.20
□□□ 15 Doug Brown, Pitt.	2.00	.35	.20
□□□ 16 Anatoli Semenov, Anah.	2.00	.35	.20
□□□ 17 Mike McPhee, Dall.	4.00	.35	.20
□□□ 18 Joel Otto, Calg.	4.00	.35	.20
□□□ 19 Dino Ciccarelli, Detr.	8.00	.50	.20
□□□ 20 Marty McSorley, LosA.	6.00	.50	.20
□□□ 21 Ron Tugnutt (G), Mont.	10.00	1.00	.20
□□□ 22 Scott Niedermayer, NJer.	8.00	.50	.20
□□□ 23 John Tucker, Tamp.	2.00	.35	.20
□□□ 24 Norm Maciver, Otta.	2.00	.35	.20
□□□ 25 Kevin Miller, SLou.	2.00	.35	.20
□□□ 26 Garry Galley, Phil.	2.00	.35	.20
□□□ 27 Ted Donato, Bost.	2.00	.35	.20
□□□ 28 Bob Kudelski, Flor.	2.00	.35	.20
□□□ 29 Craig Muni, Buff.	2.00	.35	.20
□□□ 30 N. Borschevsky, Toro.	2.00	.35	.20
□□□ 31 Tom Barrasso (G), Pitt.	10.00	1.00	.20
□□□ 32 Brent Sutter, Chic.	6.00	.50	.20
□□□ 33 Igor Kravchuk, Edmo.	4.00	.35	.20
□□□ 34 Andrew Cassels, Hart.	6.00	.50	.20
□□□ 35 Jyrki Lumme, Vanc.	6.00	.50	.20
□□□ 36 Sandis Ozolinsh, SanJ.	6.00	.50	.20
□□□ 37 Steve Thomas, NYIs.	6.00	.50	.20
□□□ 38 Dave Poulin, Wash.	4.00	.35	.20
□□□ 39 Andrei Kovalenko, Québ.	4.00	.35	.20
□□□ 40 Steve Larmer, NYRa.	10.00	1.00	.20
□□□ 41 Nelson Emerson, Winn.	4.00	.35	.20
□□□ 42 Guy Hebert (G), Anah.	6.00	.50	.20
□□□ 43 Russ Courtnall, Dall.	6.00	.50	.20
□□□ 44 Gary Suter, Chic.	6.00	.50	.20
□□□ 45 Steve Chiasson, Detr.	4.00	.35	.20
□□□ 46 Guy Carbonneau, Mont.	8.00	.50	.20
□□□ 47 Rob Blake, LosA.	15.00	1.50	.20
□□□ 48 Roman Hamrlik, Tamp.	6.00	.50	.20
□□□ 49 Valeri Zelepukin, NJer.	2.00	.35	.20
□□□ 50 Mark Recchi, Phil.	10.00	1.00	.20
□□□ 51 Darrin Madeley (G), Otta.	4.00	.35	.20
□□□ 52 Steve Duchesne, SLou.	6.00	.50	.20
□□□ 53 Brian Skrudland, Flor.	4.00	.35	.20
□□□ 54 Craig Simpson, Buff.	4.00	.35	.20
□□□ 55 Todd Gill, Toro.	4.00	.35	.20
□□□ 56 Dirk Graham, Chic.	4.00	.35	.20
□□□ 57 Joe Mullen, Pitt.	10.00	1.00	.20
□□□ 58 Doug Weight, Edmo.	15.00	1.50	.20
□□□ 59 Michael Nylander, Calg.	6.00	.50	.20
□□□ 60 Kirk McLean (G), Vanc.	8.00	.50	.20
□□□ 61 Igor Larionov, SanJ.	15.00	1.50	.20
□□□ 62 Vladimir Malakhov, NYIs.	4.00	.35	.20
□□□ 63 Kelly Miller, Wash.	4.00	.35	.20
□□□ 64 Curtis Leschyshyn, Québ.	4.00	.35	.20
□□□ 65 Thomas Steen, Winn.	4.00	.35	.20
□□□ 66 Jeff Beukeboom, NYRa.	4.00	.35	.20
□□□ 67 Troy Loney, Anah.	2.00	.35	.20
□□□ 68 Mark Tinordi, Dall.	4.00	.35	.20
□□□ 69 Theoren Fleury, Calg.	15.00	1.50	.20
□□□ 70 Vyacheslav Kozlov, Detr.	6.00	.50	.20
□□□ 71 Tony Granato, LosA.	6.00	.50	.20
□□□ 72 Daren Puppa (G), Tamp.	6.00	.50	.20
□□□ 73 Brian Bellows, Mont.	6.00	.50	.20
□□□ 74 Bernie Nicholls, NJer.	6.00	.50	.20
□□□ 75 Rick Zombo, SLou.	2.00	.35	.20
□□□ 76 Brad Shaw, Otta.	2.00	.35	.20
□□□ 77 Josef Beránek, Phil.	4.00	.35	.20
□□□ 78 Hasek vs. Bure	25.00	2.50	.50
□□□ 79 Stephen Leach, Bost.	2.00	.35	.20
□□□ 80 David Reid, Bost.	4.00	.35	.20
□□□ 81 Dave Lowry, Flor.	6.00	.50	.20
□□□ 82 Martin Straka, Pitt.	8.00	.50	.20
□□□ 83 Dave Ellett, Toro.	4.00	.35	.20
□□□ 84 Sean Burke (G), Hart.	15.00	1.50	.20
□□□ 85 Craig MacTavish, NYRa.	4.00	.35	.20
□□□ 86 Cliff Ronning, Vanc.	6.00	.50	.20
□□□ 87 Bob Errey, SanJ.	4.00	.35	.20
□□□ 88 Marty McInnis, NYIs.	4.00	.35	.20
□□□ 89 Mats Sundin, Québ.	25.00	2.50	.50
□□□ 90 Randy Burridge, Wash.	4.00	.35	.20
□□□ 91 Teppo Numminen, Winn.	8.00	.50	.20
□□□ 92 Tony Amonte, Chic.	15.00	1.50	.20
□□□ 93 Terry Yake, Anah.	2.00	.35	.20
□□□ 94 Paul Cavallini, Dall.	2.00	.35	.20
□□□ 95 German Titov, Calg.	2.00	.35	.20
□□□ 96 V. Konstantinov, Detr.	8.00	.50	.20
□□□ 97 Darryl Sydor, LosA.	6.00	.50	.20
□□□ 98 Chris Joseph (G), Tamp.	2.00	.35	.20
□□□ 99 Corey Millen, LosA.	2.00	.35	.20

☐☐☐	100 Brett Hull, SLou.	25.00	2.50	.50
☐☐☐	101 Don Sweeney, Bost.	4.00	.35	.20
☐☐☐	102 Scott Mellanby, Flor.	6.00	.50	.20
☐☐☐	103 M. Schneider, Mont.	6.00	.50	.20
☐☐☐	104 Brad May, Buff.	4.00	.35	.20
☐☐☐	105 D. Roussel (G), Phil.	4.00	.35	.20
☐☐☐	106 Jamie Macoun, Toro.	2.00	.35	.20
☐☐☐	107 Bryan Marchment, Hart.	4.00	.35	.20
☐☐☐	108 S. McEachern, Pitt.	8.00	.50	.20
☐☐☐	109 Murray Craven, Vanc.	4.00	.35	.20
☐☐☐	110 Éric Desjardins, Mont.	8.00	.50	.20
☐☐☐	111 Jon Casey, Bost.	4.00	.35	.20
☐☐☐	112 Mike Gartner, Toro.	20.00	2.00	.20
☐☐☐	113 Neal Broten, Dall.	6.00	.50	.20
☐☐☐	114 Jari Kurri, LosA.	25.00	2.50	.50
☐☐☐	115 Bruce Driver, NJer.	2.00	.35	.20
☐☐☐	116 Patrick Flatley, NYIs.	2.00	.35	.20
☐☐☐	117 Gord Murphy, Flor.	2.00	.35	.20
☐☐☐	118 Dmitri Khristich, Wash.	4.00	.35	.20
☐☐☐	119 Nicklas Lidström, Detr.	15.00	1.50	.20
☐☐☐	120 Al MacInnis, Calg.	10.00	1.00	.20
☐☐☐	121 J. Steve Smith, Chic.	6.00	.50	.20
☐☐☐	122 Zdeno Ciger, Edmo.	4.00	.35	.20
☐☐☐	123 Tie Domi, Winn.	8.00	.50	.20
☐☐☐	124 Joé Juneau, Wash.	6.00	.50	.20
☐☐☐	125 Todd Elik, SanJ.	2.00	.35	.20
☐☐☐	126 S. Fiset (G), Québ.	8.00	.50	.20
☐☐☐	127 Craig Janney, SLou.	6.00	.50	.20
☐☐☐	128 Stéphan Lebeau, Anah.	2.00	.35	.20
☐☐☐	129 Richard Smehlik, Buff.	2.00	.35	.20
☐☐☐	130 Mike Richter (G), NYRa.	12.00	1.00	.20
☐☐☐	131 Danton Cole, Tamp.	2.00	.35	.20
☐☐☐	132 Rod Brind'Amour, Phil.	8.00	.50	.20
☐☐☐	133 Dave Archibald, Otta.	2.00	.35	.20
☐☐☐	134 Dana Murzyn, Vanc.	2.00	.35	.20
☐☐☐	135 Jaromir Jagr, Pitt.	25.00	2.50	.50
☐☐☐	136 Esa Tikkanen, NYRa.	4.00	.35	.20
☐☐☐	137 Rob Pearson, Toro.	2.00	.35	.20
☐☐☐	138 Stu Barnes, Flor.	2.00	.35	.20
☐☐☐	139 Frantisek Musil, Calg.	6.00	.50	.20
☐☐☐	140 Ron Hextall (G), NYIs.	15.00	1.50	.20
☐☐☐	141 Adam Oates, Bost.	10.00	1.00	.20
☐☐☐	142 Ken Daneyko, NJer.	6.00	.50	.20
☐☐☐	143 Dale Hunter, Wash.	8.00	.50	.20
☐☐☐	144 Geoff Sanderson, Hart.	6.00	.50	.20
☐☐☐	145 K. Hrudey (G), LosA.	12.00	1.00	.20
☐☐☐	146 Kirk Muller, Mont.	8.00	.50	.20
☐☐☐	147 F. Olausson, Edmo.	6.00	.50	.20
☐☐☐	148 Derian Hatcher, Dall.	8.00	.50	.20
☐☐☐	149 Ed Belfour (G), Chic.	25.00	2.50	.50
☐☐☐	150 Steve Yzerman, Detr.	60.00	6.00	1.00
☐☐☐	151 Adam Foote, Québ.	8.00	.50	.20
☐☐☐	152 Pat Falloon, SanJ.	4.00	.35	.20
☐☐☐	153 S. Chambers, Tamp.	2.00	.35	.20
☐☐☐	154 Alexei Zhamnov, Winn.	8.00	.50	.20
☐☐☐	155 B. Shanahan, SLou.	25.00	2.50	.50
☐☐☐	156 Ulf Samuelsson, Pitt.	4.00	.35	.20
☐☐☐	157 Donald Audette, Buff.	10.00	1.00	.20
☐☐☐	158 Bob Corkum, Anah.	2.00	.35	.20
☐☐☐	159 Joe Nieuwendyk, Calg.	10.00	1.00	.20
☐☐☐	160 Félix Potvin (G), Toro.	15.00	1.50	.20
☐☐☐	161 Geoff Courtnall, Vanc.	4.00	.35	.20
☐☐☐	162 Yves Racine, Phil.	2.00	.35	.20
☐☐☐	163 Tom Fitzgerald, Flor.	2.00	.35	.20
☐☐☐	164 Adam Graves, NYRa.	10.00	1.00	.20
☐☐☐	165 V. Damphousse, Mont.	15.00	1.50	.20
☐☐☐	166 Pierre Turgeon, NYIs.	10.00	1.00	.20
☐☐☐	167 C. Billington (G), Otta.	4.00	.35	.20
☐☐☐	168 Al Iafrate, Bost.	6.00	.50	.20
☐☐☐	169 Darren Turcotte, Hart.	4.00	.35	.20
☐☐☐	170 Joe Murphy, Chic.	4.00	.35	.20
☐☐☐	171 Alexei Zhitnik, LosA.	4.00	.35	.20
☐☐☐	172 John MacLean, NJer.	4.00	.35	.20
☐☐☐	173 Andy Moog (G), Dall.	10.00	1.00	.20
☐☐☐	174 Shayne Corson, Edmo.	8.00	.50	.20
☐☐☐	175 Ray Sheppard, Detr.	4.00	.35	.20
☐☐☐	176 Johan Garpenlöv, SanJ.	2.00	.35	.20
☐☐☐	177 Ron Sutter, Québ.	6.00	.50	.20
☐☐☐	178 T. Selänne, Winn.	20.00	2.00	.20
☐☐☐	179 Brian Bradley, Tamp.	2.00	.35	.20
☐☐☐	180 R. Bourque, Bost.	30.00	3.00	.50
☐☐☐	181 Cu. Joseph (G), SLou.	25.00	2.50	.50
☐☐☐	182 Kevin Stevens, Pitt.	6.00	.50	.20
☐☐☐	183 Alexei Kasatonov, SLou.	6.00	.50	.20
☐☐☐	184 Brian Leetch, NYRa.	15.00	1.50	.20
☐☐☐	185 Doug Gilmour, Toro.	15.00	1.50	.20
☐☐☐	186 Gary Roberts, Calg.	10.00	1.00	.20
☐☐☐	187 Mike Keane, Mont.	4.00	.35	.20
☐☐☐	188 Mike Modano, Dall.	25.00	2.50	.50
☐☐☐	189 Chris Chelios, Chic.	15.00	1.50	.20
☐☐☐	190 Pavel Bure, Vanc.	20.00	2.00	.20
☐☐☐	191 Bob Essensa, Detr.	6.00	.50	.20
☐☐☐	192 Dale Hawerchuk, Buff.	15.00	1.50	.20
☐☐☐	193 Scott Stevens, NJer.	10.00	1.00	.20
☐☐☐	194 Claude Lapointe, Québ.	4.00	.35	.20
☐☐☐	195 Scott Lachance, NYIs.	4.00	.35	.20
☐☐☐	196 G. Duchesne, SanJ.	2.00	.35	.20
☐☐☐	197 Kevin Dineen, Phil.	4.00	.35	.20
☐☐☐	198 Doug Bodger, Buff.	2.00	.35	.20
☐☐☐	199 Mike Ridley, Wash.	4.00	.35	.20
☐☐☐	200 A. Mogilny, Buff.	12.00	1.00	.20
☐☐☐	201 Jamie Storr (G), Canada	-	.50	.20
☐☐☐	202 Jason Botterill, Canada	-	.35	.20
☐☐☐	203 Jeff Friesen, Canada	-	1.00	.20
☐☐☐	204 Todd Harvey, Canada	-	.50	.20
☐☐☐	205 Brendan Witt, Canada	-	.35	.20
☐☐☐	206 Jason Allison, Canada	-	2.00	.20
☐☐☐	207 Aaron Gavey, Canada	-	.35	.20
☐☐☐	208 Deron Quint, U.S.A.	-	.50	.20
☐☐☐	209 J. Bonsignore, U.S.A.	-	.35	.20
☐☐☐	210 Richard Park, U.S.A.	-	.35	.20
☐☐☐	211 Kevyn Adams, U.S.A.	-	.50	.20
☐☐☐	212 V. Sharifijanov, Russia	-	.35	.20
☐☐☐	213 A. Kharlamov, Russia	-	.35	.20
☐☐☐	214 Oleg Tverdovsky, Russia	-	.50	.20
☐☐☐	215 Valeri Bure, Russia	-	1.50	.20
☐☐☐☐	**216 D. Jackson, Vanc. RC**	**5.00**	**1.00**	**.50**
☐☐☐☐	**217 J. Cierny, Edmo. RC**	**5.00**	**1.00**	**.50**
☐☐☐☐	218 J. Namestnikov, Vanc.	2.00	.35	.20
☐☐☐☐	219 Daniel Laperrière, SLou.	2.00	.35	.20
☐☐☐☐	220 Fred Knipscheer, Bost.	2.00	.35	.20
☐☐☐☐	221 Yan Kaminsky, NYIs.	2.00	.35	.20
☐☐☐☐	222 David Roberts, SLou.	5.00	.50	.20
☐☐☐☐	223 Derek Mayer, Otta.	2.00	.35	.20
☐☐☐☐	224 J. McLennan (G), NYIs.	4.00	.35	.20
☐☐☐☐	225 Kevin Smyth, Hart.	2.00	.35	.20
☐☐☐☐	226 Todd Marchant, Edmo.	12.00	1.00	.20
☐☐☐☐	**227 Czerkawski, Bost. RC**	**12.00**	**3.00**	**1.00**
☐☐☐☐	228 John Lilley, Anah.	5.00	.50	.20
☐☐☐☐	229 Aaron Ward, Detr.	4.00	.35	.20
☐☐☐☐	230 Brian Savage, Mont.	16.00	1.50	.20
☐☐☐☐	231 Jason Allison, Wash.	30.00	3.00	.50
☐☐☐☐	232 Maxim Bets, Anah.	5.00	.50	.20
☐☐☐☐	233 Ted Crowley, Hart.	5.00	.50	.20
☐☐☐☐	**234 Todd Simon, Buff. RC**	**5.00**	**1.00**	**.50**
☐☐☐☐	235 Zigmund Palffy, NYIs.	15.00	1.50	.20
☐☐☐☐	236 René Corbet, Québ.	4.00	.35	.20
☐☐☐☐	237 Michael Peca, Vanc.	20.00	2.00	.20
☐☐☐☐	238 Dwayne Norris, Québ.	2.00	.35	.20
☐☐☐☐	239 Andrei Nazarov, SanJ.	4.00	.35	.20
☐☐☐☐	240 David Sacco, Toro.	5.00	.50	.20
☐☐☐☐	241 HL: W. Gretzky, LosA.	100.00	10.00	2.00
☐☐☐☐	242 HL: M. Gartner, NYRa.	20.00	2.00	.20
☐☐☐☐	243 HL: D. Ciccarelli, Detr.	8.00	.50	.20
☐☐☐☐	244 HL: Ron Francis, Pitt.	15.00	1.50	.20
☐☐☐☐	245 HL: B. Nicholls, NJer.	6.00	.50	.20
☐☐☐☐	246 HL: D. Ciccarelli, Detr.	8.00	.50	.20
☐☐☐☐	247 HL: Brian Propp, Hart.	6.00	.50	.20
☐☐☐☐	248 YS: A. Daigle, Otta.	4.00	.35	.20
☐☐☐☐	249 YS: M. Renberg, Phil.	8.00	.50	.20
☐☐☐☐	250 YS: Thibault (G), Québ.	10.00	1.00	.20
☐☐☐☐	251 YS: Derek Plante, Buff.	4.00	.35	.20
☐☐☐☐	252 YS: C. Pronger, Hart.	15.00	1.50	.20
☐☐☐☐	253 YS: Alexei Yashin, Otta.	15.00	1.50	.20
☐☐☐☐	254 YS: J. Arnott, Edmo.	12.00	1.00	.20
☐☐☐☐	255 YS: B. Mironov, Edmo.	4.00	.35	.20
☐☐☐☐	256 YS: Osgood (G), Detr.	15.00	1.50	.20
☐☐☐☐	257 YS: J. Bélanger, Flor.	2.00	.35	.20
☐☐☐☐	258 YS: D. McCarty, Detr.	8.00	.50	.20
☐☐☐☐	259 YS: T. Kidd (G), Calg.	8.00	.50	.20
☐☐☐☐	260 YS: Oleg Petrov, Mont.	8.00	.50	.20
☐☐☐☐	261 YS: Mike Rathje, SanJ.	4.00	.35	.20
☐☐☐☐	262 YS: John Slaney, Wash.	2.00	.35	.20
☐☐☐	263 Mighty Ducks / Bruins	2.00	.35	.20
☐☐☐	264 Sabres / Flames	2.00	.35	.20
☐☐☐	265 Blackhawks / Stars	2.00	.35	.20
☐☐☐	266 Red Wings / Oilers	2.00	.35	.20
☐☐☐	267 Panthers / Whalers	2.00	.35	.20
☐☐☐	268 Kings / Canadiens	2.00	.35	.20
☐☐☐	269 Devils / Islanders	2.00	.35	.20
☐☐☐	270 Rangers / Senators	2.00	.35	.20
☐☐☐	271 Flyers / Penguins	2.00	.35	.20
☐☐☐	272 Nordiques / Blues	2.00	.35	.20
☐☐☐	273 Sharks / Lightning	2.00	.35	.20
☐☐☐	274 Maple Leafs / Canucks	2.00	.35	.20
☐☐☐	275 Capitals / Jets	2.00	.35	.20

CANADIAN TEAM

	Insert Set (24 cards):	70.00
	Insert (1:36 Canadian)	CT
☐	CT1 Paul Kariya, Canada Nationals	10.00
☐	CT2 Petr Nedved, Canada Nationals	4.00
☐	CT3 Todd Warriner, Canada Nationals	3.00
☐	CT4 Corey Hirsch (G), Canada Nationals	3.00
☐	CT5 Greg Johnson, Canada Nationals	3.00
☐	CT6 Chris Kontos, Canada Nationals	3.00
☐	CT7 Dwayne Norris, Canada Nationals	3.00
☐	CT8 Brian Savage, Canada Nationals	4.00
☐	CT9 Todd Hlushko, Canada Nationals	3.00
☐	CT10 Fabian Joseph, Canada Nationals	3.00
☐	CT11 Greg Parks, Canada Nationals	3.00
☐	CT12 Jean-Yves Roy, Canada Nationals RC	3.00
☐	CT13 Mark Astley, Canada Nationals	3.00
☐	CT14 Adrian Aucoin, Canada Nationals	3.00
☐	CT15 David Harlock, Canada Nationals	3.00
☐	CT16 Ken Lovsin, Canada Nationals	3.00
☐	CT17 Derek Mayer, Canada Nationals	3.00
☐	CT18 Brad Schlegel, Canada Nationals	3.00
☐	CT19 Chris Therien, Canada Nationals	3.00
☐	CT20 Manny Legacé (G), Canada Nationals	4.00
☐	CT21 Brad Werenka, Canada Nationals	3.00
☐	CT22 Wally Schrieber, Canada Nationals RC	3.00
☐	CT23 Allain Roy, Canada Nationals RC	3.00
☐	CT24 Brett Lindros, Canada Nationals	4.00

CHECK-IT

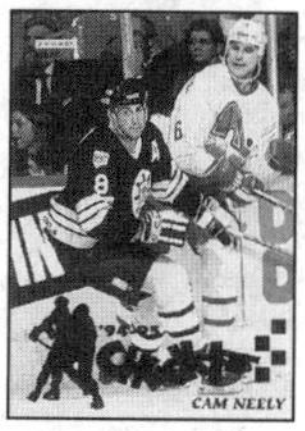

	Insert Set (18 cards):	325.00
	Insert (1:72 Canadian)	CI
☐	CI1 Eric Lindros, Phil. [vs. D.Hatcher]	70.00
☐	CI2 Scott Stevens, NJer.	15.00
☐	CI3 Darius Kasparaitis, NYIs.	10.00
☐	CI4 Kevin Stevens, Pitt. [vs. D.Kasparaitis]	10.00
☐	CI5 Brendan Shanahan, SLou. [vs. B.Benning]	40.00
☐	CI6 Jeremy Roenick, Chic. [vs. Y.Khymlev]	35.00
☐	CI7 Ulf Samuelsson, Pitt. [vs. C.Neely]	10.00
☐	CI8 Cam Neely, Bost. [vs. C.Wolanin]	40.00
☐	CI9 Adam Graves, NYRa. [vs. D.Cole]	15.00
☐	CI10 Kirk Muller, Mont. [vs. J.Reekie]	10.00
☐	CI11 Rick Tocchet, Pitt.	10.00
☐	CI12 Gary Roberts, Calg. [vs. V.Malakhov]	15.00
☐	CI13 Wendel Clark, Toro. [vs. K.Hammond]	35.00
☐	CI14 Keith Tkachuk, Winn. [vs. Islanders]	25.00
☐	CI15 Theoren Fleury, Calg. [vs. D.Craigwell]	20.00
☐	CI16 Claude Lemieux, NJer.	10.00
☐	CI17 Chris Chelios, Chic.	25.00
☐	CI18 Pat Verbeek, Hart.	10.00

DREAM TEAM

	Insert Set (24 cards):	145.00
	Insert (1:36)	NRMT-MT
☐	DT1 Patrick Roy (G), Mont.	20.00
☐	DT2 Félix Potvin (G), Toro.	4.00
☐	DT3 Raymond Bourque, Bost.	5.00
☐	DT4 Brian Leetch, NYRa.	4.00
☐	DT5 Scott Stevens, NJer.	4.00
☐	DT6 Paul Coffey, Detr.	4.00
☐	DT7 Al MacInnis, Calg.	4.00
☐	DT8 Chris Chelios, Chic.	4.00
☐	DT9 Adam Graves, NYRa.	4.00
☐	DT10 Luc Robitaille, LosA.	5.00
☐	DT11 Dave Andreychuk, Toro.	4.00
☐	DT12 Sergei Fedorov, Detr.	5.00
☐	DT13 Doug Gilmour, Toro.	4.00
☐	DT14 Wayne Gretzky, LosA.	30.00
☐	DT15 Mario Lemieux, Pitt.	20.00
☐	DT16 Mark Messier, NYRa.	5.00
☐	DT17 Mike Modano, Dall.	5.00
☐	DT18 Jeremy Roenick, Chic.	5.00
☐	DT19 Eric Lindros, Phil.	5.00
☐	DT20 Steve Yzerman, Detr.	15.00
☐	DT21 Alexandre Daigle, Otta.	4.00
☐	DT22 Brett Hull, SLou.	5.00
☐	DT23 Cam Neely, Bost.	5.00
☐	DT24 Pavel Bure, Vanc.	5.00

90-PLUS CLUB

	Insert Set (21 cards):	90.00
	Insert (1:4 Jumbo)	NRMT-MT
☐	NP1 Wayne Gretzky, LosA.	30.00
☐	NP2 Sergei Fedorov, Detr.	5.00
☐	NP3 Adam Oates, Bost.	3.00
☐	NP4 Doug Gilmour, Toro.	3.00
☐	NP5 Pavel Bure, Vanc.	5.00
☐	NP6 Jeremy Roenick, Chic.	5.00
☐	NP7 Mark Recchi, Phil.	3.00
☐	NP8 Brendan Shanahan, SLou.	5.00
☐	NP9 Jaromir Jagr, Pitt.	5.00
☐	NP10 Dave Andreychuk, Toro.	3.00
☐	NP11 Brett Hull, SLou.	5.00
☐	NP12 Eric Lindros, Phil.	5.00
☐	NP13 Rod Brind'Amour, Phil.	3.00
☐	NP14 Pierre Turgeon, NYIs.	3.00
☐	NP15 Ray Sheppard, Detr.	3.00
☐	NP16 Mike Modano, Dall.	5.00
☐	NP17 Robert Reichel, Calg.	3.00
☐	NP18 Ron Francis, Pitt.	3.00
☐	NP19 Joe Sakic, Québ.	10.00
☐	NP20 Vincent Damphousse, Mont.	3.00
☐	NP21 Raymond Bourque, Bost.	5.00

THE FRANCHISE

	Insert Set (26 cards):	375.00
	Insert (1:72)	NRMT-MT
☐	TF1 Guy Hebert (G), Anah.	6.00
☐	TF2 Cam Neely, Bost.	20.00
☐	TF3 Pat LaFontaine, Buff.	10.00
☐	TF4 Theoren Fleury, Calg.	10.00
☐	TF5 Jeremy Roenick, Chic.	15.00
☐	TF6 Mike Modano, Dall.	20.00
☐	TF7 Sergei Fedorov, Detr.	20.00
☐	TF8 Jason Arnott, Edmo.	6.00
☐	TF9 John Vanbiesbrouck (G), Flor.	6.00
☐	TF10 Geoff Sanderson, Hart.	6.00
☐	TF11 Wayne Gretzky, LosA.	80.00
☐	TF12 Patrick Roy (G), Mont.	60.00
☐	TF13 Scott Stevens, NJer.	6.00
☐	TF14 Pierre Turgeon, NYIs.	6.00
☐	TF15 Mark Messier, NYRa.	20.00
☐	TF16 Alexandre Daigle, Otta.	6.00
☐	TF17 Eric Lindros, Phil.	20.00
☐	TF18 Mario Lemieux, Pitt.	60.00
☐	TF19 Joe Sakic, Québ.	30.00
☐	TF20 Brett Hull, SLou.	20.00
☐	TF21 Arturs Irbe (G), SanJ.	6.00
☐	TF22 Daren Puppa (G), Tamp.	6.00
☐	TF23 Doug Gilmour, Toro.	10.00
☐	TF24 Pavel Bure, Vanc.	15.00
☐	TF25 Joé Juneau, Wash.	6.00
☐	TF26 Teemu Selänne, Winn.	15.00

TOP ROOKIE

	Redemption Set (10 cards):	35.00
	Expired Pro Debut cards:	.50
	Insert (1:72)	NRMT-MT
☐	TR1 Paul Kariya, Anah.	15.00
☐	TR2 Peter Forsberg, Québ.	15.00
☐	TR3 Brett Lindros, NYIs.	2.00
☐	TR4 Oleg Tverdovsky, Anah.	2.00
☐	TR5 Jamie Storr (G), LosA.	2.00
☐	TR6 Kenny Jönsson, Toro.	2.00
☐	TR7 Brian Rolston, NJer.	2.00
☐	TR8 Jeff Friesen, SanJ.	2.00
☐	TR9 Todd Harvey, Dall.	2.00
☐	TR10 Viktor Kozlov, SanJ.	2.00

1994 - 95 SELECT

These cards have a Certified Gold parallel.

Imprint: © 1995 PINNACLE BRANDS, Inc.

Complete Set (200 cards):	225.00	25.00
Common Player:	.50	.20

	Player	CG	Reg.
☐☐	1 Mark Messier, NYRa.	5.00	.50
☐☐	2 Rick Tocchet, LosA.	1.50	.20
☐☐	3 Alexandre Daigle, Otta.	.50	.20
☐☐	4 Owen Nolan, Québ.	3.00	.20
☐☐	5 Bill Ranford (G), Edmo.	2.00	.20
☐☐	6 Dave Gagner, Dall.	.50	.20
☐☐	7 John Vanbiesbrouck (G), Flor.	2.00	.20
☐☐	8 Sergei* Makarov, SanJ.	2.00	.20
☐☐	9 Derek King, NYIs.	.50	.20
☐☐	10 Sergei Fedorov, Detr.	5.00	.50
☐☐	11 Trevor Linden, Vanc.	2.00	.20
☐☐	12 Don Beaupré (G), Otta.	.50	.20
☐☐	13 Dave Manson, Winn.	.50	.20
☐☐	14 Sergei Zubov, NYRa.	1.00	.20
☐☐	15 Keith Primeau, Detr.	2.00	.20
☐☐	16 Joe Mullen, Pitt.	2.00	.20
☐☐	17 Bernie Nicholls, Chic.	1.00	.20
☐☐	18 Raymond Bourque, Bost.	6.00	.50
☐☐	19 Mike Ridley, Toro.	.50	.20
☐☐	20 Wendel Clark, Québ.	4.00	.50
☐☐	21 Mats Sundin, Toro.	5.00	.50
☐☐	22 Alexander Mogilny, Buff.	2.00	.20
☐☐	23 Mathieu Schneider, Mont.	1.00	.20
☐☐	24 Brian Leetch, NYRa.	3.00	.20
☐☐	25 Rob Niedermayer, Flor.	1.00	.20
☐☐	26 Donald Audette, Buff.	2.00	.20
☐☐	27 Doug Weight, Edmo.	3.00	.20
☐☐	28 Al MacInnis, SLou.	2.00	.20
☐☐	29 Jeremy Roenick, Chic.	4.00	.50
☐☐	30 Mark Recchi, Phil.	2.00	.20
☐☐	31 Chris Chelios, Chic.	3.00	.20
☐☐	32 Luc Robitaille, Pitt.	4.00	.50
☐☐	33 Dale Hunter, Wash.	1.50	.20
☐☐	34 Kelly Hrudey (G), LosA.	2.00	.20
☐☐	35 Steve Yzerman, Detr.	12.00	1.50
☐☐	36 Martin Straka, Pitt.	1.50	.20
☐☐	37 Arturs Irbe (G), SanJ.	2.00	.20
☐☐	38 Mike Modano, Dall.	5.00	.50
☐☐	39 Cam Neely, Bost.	5.00	.50
☐☐	40 Igor Larionov, SanJ.	3.00	.20
☐☐	41 Ray Ferraro, NYIs.	.50	.20
☐☐	42 Dale Hawerchuk, Buff.	3.00	.20
☐☐	43 Brian Bradley, Tamp.	.50	.20
☐☐	44 Joe Murphy, Chic.	.50	.20
☐☐	45 Daren Puppa (G), Tamp.	1.00	.20
☐☐	46 Pierre Turgeon, NYIs.	2.00	.20
☐☐	47 Shayne Corson, Edmo.	1.50	.20
☐☐	48 Adam Graves, NYRa.	2.00	.20
☐☐	49 Craig Billington (G), Otta.	.50	.20
☐☐	50 Derian Hatcher, Dall.	1.50	.20
☐☐	51 Alexei Zhamnov, Winn.	1.50	.20
☐☐	52 Dominik Hasek (G), Buff.	5.00	.50
☐☐	53 Ed Belfour (G), Chic.	5.00	.50
☐☐	54 Mike Vernon (G), Detr.	2.00	.20
☐☐	55 Bob Kudelski, Flor.	.50	.20
☐☐	56 Ray Sheppard, Detr.	.50	.20
☐☐	57 Pat LaFontaine, Buff.	3.00	.20
☐☐	58 Adam Oates, Bost.	2.00	.20
☐☐	59 Vincent Damphousse, Mont.	3.00	.20
☐☐	60 Jaromir Jagr, Pitt.	5.00	.50
☐☐	61 Mikael Renberg, Phil.	1.50	.20
☐☐	62 Joe Sakic, Québ.	8.00	1.00
☐☐	63 Sandis Ozolinsh, SanJ.	1.00	.20
☐☐	64 Kirk McLean (G), Vanc.	1.50	.20
☐☐	65 Stéphan Lebeau, Anah.	.50	.20
☐☐	66 Alex Kovalev, NYRa.	3.00	.20
☐☐	67 Ron Hextall (G), Phil.	3.00	.20
☐☐	68 Geoff Sanderson, Hart.	1.00	.20
☐☐	69 Doug Gilmour, Toro.	3.00	.20
☐☐	70 Russ Courtnall, Dall.	1.00	.20
☐☐	71 Jari Kurri, LosA.	5.00	.50
☐☐	72 Paul Coffey, Detr.	3.00	.20
☐☐	73 Claude Lemieux, NJer.	1.50	.20
☐☐	74 Teemu Selänne, Winn.	4.00	.50
☐☐	75 Keith Tkachuk, Winn.	3.00	.20
☐☐	76 Pat Verbeek, Hart.	1.50	.20
☐☐	77 Chris Gratton, Tamp.	1.00	.20
☐☐	78 Martin Brodeur (G), NJer.	8.00	1.00
☐☐	79 Guy Hebert (G), Anah.	1.00	.20
☐☐	80 Al Iafrate, Bost.	1.00	.20
☐☐	81 Glen Wesley, Hart.	.50	.20
☐☐	82 Scott Stevens, NJer.	2.00	.20
☐☐	83 Wayne Gretzky, LosA.	20.00	2.50

□□	84 Ron Francis, Pitt.	3.00	.20
□□	85 Scott Mellanby, Flor.	1.00	.20
□□	86 Joé Juneau, Wash.	1.00	.20
□□	87 Jason Arnott, Edmo.	2.00	.20
□□	88 Tom Barrasso (G), Pitt.	2.00	.20
□□	89 Peter Bondra, Wash.	3.00	.20
□□	90 Félix Potvin (G), Toro.	3.00	.20
□□	91 Brian Bellows, Mont.	1.00	.20
□□	92 Pavel Bure, Vanc.	4.00	.50
□□	93 Grant Fuhr (G), Buff.	3.00	.20
□□	94 Andy Moog (G), Dall.	2.00	.20
□□	95 Mike Gartner, Toro.	4.00	.50
□□	96 Patrick Roy (G), Mont.	15.00	1.50
□□	97 Brett Hull, SLou.	5.00	.50
□□	98 Rob Blake, LosA.	3.00	.20
□□	99 Dave Andreychuk, Toro.	1.50	.20
□□	100 Eric Lindros, Phil.	5.00	.50
□□	101 Scott Niedermayer, NJer.	1.50	.20
□□	102 Tim Cheveldae (G), Winn.	.50	.20
□□	103 Vyacheslav Kozlov, Detr.	1.00	.20
□□	104 Dmitri Khristich, Wash.	.50	.20
□□	105 Steve Thomas, NYIs.	1.00	.20
□□	106 Kevin Stevens, Pitt.	1.00	.20
□□	107 Kirk Muller, Mont.	1.50	.20
□□	108 Stéphane J.J. Richer, NJer.	1.00	.20
□□	109 Theoren Fleury, Calg.	3.00	.20
□□	110 Jeff R. Brown, Vanc.	.50	.20
□□	111 Chris Pronger, Hart.	3.00	.20
□□	112 Steve Larmer, NYRa.	2.00	.20
□□	113 Éric Desjardins, Mont.	1.50	.20
□□	114 Mike Ricci, Québ.	1.50	.20
□□	115 Tony Amonte, Chic.	3.00	.20
□□	116 Pat Falloon, SanJ.	.50	.20
□□	117 Garry Galley, Phil.	.50	.20
□□	118 Dino Ciccarelli, Detr.	1.50	.20
□□	119 Rod Brind'Amour, Phil.	1.50	.20
□□	120 Petr Nedved, NYRa.	1.50	.20
□□	121 Curtis Joseph (G), SLou.	5.00	.50
□□	122 Cliff Ronning, Vanc.	1.00	.20
□□	123 Ulf Dahlén, SanJ.	.50	.20
□□	124 Marty McSorley, LosA.	1.00	.20
□□	125 Nelson Emerson, Winn.	.50	.20
□□	126 Brian Skrudland, Flor.	.50	.20
□□	127 Sean Burke (G), Hart.	3.00	.20
□□	128 Sylvain Côté, Wash.	.50	.20
□□	129 Brendan Shanahan, SLou.	5.00	.50
□□	130 Benoît Hogue, NYIs.	.50	.20
□□	131 Joe Nieuwendyk, Calg.	2.00	.20
□□	132 Bryan Smolinski, Bost.	.50	.20
□□	133 Mike Richter (G), NYRa.	2.00	.20
□□	134 Nicklas Lidström, Detr.	3.00	.20
□□	135 Alexei Yashin, Otta.	3.00	.20
□□	136 John MacLean, NJer.	.50	.20
□□	137 Geoff Courtnall, Vanc.	.50	.20
□□	138 Robert Reichel, Calg.	1.50	.20
□□	139 Craig Janney, SLou.	1.00	.20
□□	140 Zarley Zalapski, Calg.	.50	.20
□□	141 Andrew Cassels, Hart.	1.00	.20
□□	142 Kevin Dineen, Phil.	.50	.20
□□	143 Larry Murphy, Pitt.	1.00	.20
□□	144 Valeri Kamensky, Québ.	1.50	.20
□□	145 Steve Duchesne, SLou.	1.00	.20
□□	146 Phil Housley, Calg.	1.50	.20
□□	147 Gary Roberts, Calg.	2.00	.20
□□	148 Kevin Hatcher, Dall.	.50	.20

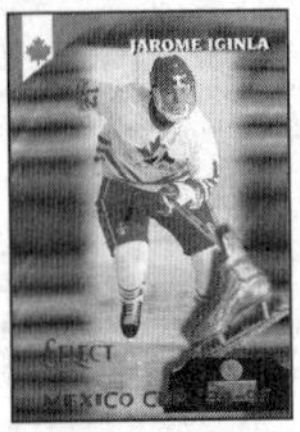

□□	**149 Bryan Berard, U.S.A. RC**	**6.00**	**2.00**
□□	**150 Marty Reasoner, U.S.A. RC**	**4.50**	**2.50**
□□	**151 A. Berenzweig, U.S.A. RC**	**2.00**	**.50**
□□	**152 R. Rasmussen, U.S.A. RC**	**4.50**	**1.50**
□□	**153 Luke Curtin, U.S.A. RC**	**2.00**	**.50**
□□	**154 Dan LaCouture, U.S.A. RC**	**2.00**	**.50**
□□	**155 Brian Boucher, U.S.A. RC**	**14.00**	**6.00**
□□	**156 Wyatt Smith, U.S.A. RC**	**2.00**	**.50**
□□	**157 M. Kuznetsov, Russia RC**	**2.00**	**.50**
□□	**158 A. Morozov, Russia RC**	**4.50**	**3.00**
□□	**159 D. Nabokov, Russia RC**	**3.00**	**1.00**
□□	**160 Wade Redden, Canada RC**	**6.00**	**2.00**
□□	**161 Jason Doig, Canada RC**	**2.00**	**.50**
□□	**162 A. McCauley, Canada RC**	**6.00**	**2.00**
□□	**163 Jeff Ware, Canada RC**	**2.00**	**.50**
□□	**164 Brad Larsen, Canada RC**	**2.00**	**.50**
□□	**165 J. Iginla, Canada RC**	**16.00**	**7.00**
□□	**166 Christian Dubé, Canada RC**	**3.00**	**1.00**
□□	**167 Mike McBain, Canada RC**	**2.00**	**.50**
□□	**168 Todd Norman, Canada RC**	**2.00**	**.50**
□□	169 Oleg Tverdovsky, Anah. [Rookie]	1.00	.20
□□	170 Jamie Storr (G), LosA. [Rookie]	1.50	.20
□□	171 J. Wiemer, Tamp. [Rookie]	2.50	.20
□□	172 Kenny Jönsson, Toro. [Rookie]	1.50	.20
□□	173 Paul Kariya, Anah. [Rookie]	10.00	1.00
□□	174 Viktor Kozlov, SanJ. [Rookie]	2.00	.20
□□	175 Peter Forsberg, Québ. [Rookie]	10.00	1.00
□□	176 Jeff Friesen, SanJ. [Rookie]	2.00	.20
□□	177 Brian Rolston, NJer. [Rookie]	2.00	.20
□□	178 Brett Lindros, NYIs. [Rookie]	2.00	.20
□□	179 A. Deadmarsh, Québ. [Rookie]	2.00	.20
□□	180 Aaron Gavey, Tamp. [Rookie]	.50	.20
□□	181 Janne Laukkanen, Québ. [Rookie]	.50	.20
□□	182 Todd Harvey, Dall. [Rookie]	1.50	.20
□□	**183 V. Karpov, Anah. [Rookie] RC**	**2.00**	**.50**
□□	184 Andrei Nikolishin, Hart. [Rookie]	1.00	.20
□□	185 Pavol Demitra, Otta. [Rookie]	3.00	.20
□□	**186 Radek Bonk, Otta. [Rookie] RC**	**6.00**	**2.00**
□□	187 Valeri Bure, Mont. [Rookie]	2.00	.20
□□	**188 É. Fichaud (G), Toro. [Rookie] RC**	**3.00**	**1.00**
□□	189 J. McLennan (G), NYIs. [Rookie]	1.00	.20
□□	**190 Czerkawski, Bost. [Rookie] RC**	**4.50**	**1.50**
□□	191 John Lilley, Anah. [Rookie]	.50	.20
□□	192 Brian Savage, Mont. [Rookie]	2.00	.20
□□	193 Jason Allison, Wash. [Rookie]	4.50	.50
□□	194 Mattias Norström, NYRa. [Rookie]	1.50	.20
□□	**195 T. Simon, Buff. [Rookie] RC**	**2.00**	**.50**
□□	196 Zigmund Palffy, NYIs. [Rookie]	4.50	.50
□□	197 René Corbet, Québ. [Rookie]	1.00	.20
□□	198 Michael Peca, Vanc. [Rookie]	3.00	.20
□□	199 Checklist	.50	.20
□□	200 Checklist	.50	.20

FIRST LINE

Insert Set (12 cards): 90.00

	Insert (1:48)	FL
□	FL1 Patrick Roy (G), Mont.	25.00
□	FL2 Raymond Bourque, Bost.	10.00
□	FL3 Brian Leetch, NYRa.	5.00
□	FL4 Brendan Shanahan, SLou.	5.00
□	FL5 Eric Lindros, Phil.	5.00
□	FL6 Pavel Bure, Vanc.	5.00
□	FL7 Mike Richter (G), NYRa.	3.00
□	FL8 Scott Stevens, NJer.	3.00
□	FL9 Chris Chelios, Chic.	5.00
□	FL10 Luc Robitaille, Pitt.	5.00
□	FL11 Wayne Gretzky, LosA.	35.00
□	FL12 Brett Hull, SLou.	5.00

YOUTH EXPLOSION

Insert Set (12 cards): 35.00

	Insert (1:48)	NRMT-MT
□	YE1 Jamie Storr (G), LosA.	2.00
□	YE2 Oleg Tverdovsky, Anah.	2.00
□	YE3 Janne Laukkanen, Québ.	2.00
□	YE4 Kenny Jönsson, Toro.	2.00
□	YE5 Paul Kariya, Anah.	10.00
□	YE6 Viktor Kozlov, SanJ.	2.00
□	YE7 Peter Forsberg, Québ.	10.00
□	YE8 Jason Allison, Wash.	4.00
□	YE9 Jeff Friesen, SanJ.	2.00
□	YE10 Brian Rolston, NJer.	2.00
□	YE11 Mariusz Czerkawski, Bost.	2.00
□	YE12 Brett Lindros, NYIs.	2.00

1994 - 95 SIGNATURE ROOKIES

Each player card has two versions: the regular card and a one per pack autograph parallel. Regular cards are limited to 45,000 copies while autographed cards are limited to 7,750 copies.

Imprint: © 1994 Signature Rookies

Complete Set (70 cards): 25.00

Common Player: .25

	Player	Reg.
□	1 Vaclav Varada, Cze.	.25
□	2 Roman Vopat, Cze.	.25
□	3 Yannick Dubé, Cdn.	.25
□	4 Colin Cloutier (G), Brandon	.20
□	5 Scott Cherrey, North Bay	.20
□	6 Johan Finnstrom, Swe.	.20
□	7 Fredrik Modin, Swe.	.25
□	8 Stéphane Roy, Val'd'or	.20
□	9 Evgeni Ryabchikov (G), Rus.	.25
□	10 José Théodore (G), St-Hyacinthe	10.00
□	11 Jason Holland, Kamloops	.25
□	12 Richard Park, Belleville	.25
□	13 Jason Podollan, Flor.	.25
□	14 Mattias Öhlund, Swe.	.50
□	15 Chris Wells, Pitt.	.25
□	16 Hugh Hamilton, Spokane	.20
□	17 Edvin Frylen, Swe.	.25
□	18 Wade Belak, Que.	.25
□	19 Sébastien Bety, Drummondville	.20
□	20 Chris Dingman, Brandon	.25
□	21 Peter Nylander, Swe.	.25
□	22 Daymond Langkow, Tri-City	.25
□	23 Kelly Fairchild, St. John's	.25
□	24 Norm Dezainde, Kitchener	.20
□	25 Nolan Baumgartner, Kamloops	.25
□	26 Deron Quint, USA.	.25
□	27 Sheldon Souray, NJer.	.25
□	28 Stefan Ustorf, Ger.	.25
□	29 Juha Vuovirta, Fin.	.25
□	30 Mark Seliger (G), Rosenheim	.25
□	31 Ryan Smyth, Edmo.	1.50
□	32 Dimitri Tabarin, CIS.	.20
□	33 Nikolai Tsulygin, Rus.	.25
□	34 Paul Vincent, Toro.	.20
□	35 Rhett Warrener, Flor.	.25
□	36 Jamie Rivers, SLou.	.25
□	37 Rumun Ndur, Buff.	.20
□	38 Phil Huber	.20
□	39 Radek Dvorak, Cze.	.25
□	40 Mike Barrie, Seattle	.20
□	41 Chris Hynnes	.20
□	42 Mike Dubinsky, Vanc.	.20
□	43 Steve Cheredaryk, Winn.	.20
□	44 Jim Carey (G), Wash.	.25
□	45 Dorian Anneck, Edmo.	.20
□	46 Jörgen Jönsson, Swe.	.25
□	47 Alyn McCauley, Ottawa-OHL	1.00
□	48 Corey Nielson, Edmo.	.20
□	49 Daniel Tjarnqvist, Swe.	.25
□	50 Vadim Epantchisev, Rus.	.25
□	51 Sean Haggerty, Detroit-OHL	.25
□	52 Milan Hejduk	8.00
□	53 Adam Magarrell, Phil.	.20
□	54 Dave Scatchard, Vanc.	.25
□	55 Sébastien Vallée, Phil.	.20
□	56 Milos Guren, Cze.	.25
□	57 Johan Davidsson, Anah.	.25
□	58 Byron Briske, Anah.	.20
□	59 Sylvain Blouin, NYRa.	.20
□	60 Bryan Berard, Detroit-OHL, Error (Brian)	.50
□	61 Tim Findlay, Windsor	.20
□	62 Doug Bonner, Seattle	.25
□	63 Curtis Brown, Buff.	.25
□	64 Brad Symes, Winn.	.20
□	65 Andrew Taylor, Kitchener	.20
□	66 Brad Bombardir, Albany	.25
□	67 Joe Dziedzic, Pitt.	.25
□	68 Valentin Morozov, CSKA	.20
□	69 Mark McArthur, Que.	.20
□	70 Checklist, Error (wrong numbering)	.25

REDEMPTION

Redemption Set (5 cards): 4.00

	Player	NRMT-MT
□	1 Sergei Luchinkin	1.00
□	2 Stefan Ustorf, Ger.	1.00
□	3 Brad Brown	1.00
□	4 Yannick Dubé	1.00
□	5 Vitali Yachmenev	1.00

AUTOGRAPHS

Autograph Set (69 cards): 250.00

	Autograph (#/7750)	NRMT-MT
□	1 Vaclav Varada, Cze. ✍	3.00
□	2 Roman Vopat, Cze. ✍	3.00
□	3 Yannick Dubé, Cdn. ✍	3.00
□	4 Colin Cloutier (G), Brandon ✍	3.00
□	5 Scott Cherrey, North Bay ✍	3.00
□	6 Johan Finnstrom, Swe. ✍	3.00
□	7 Fredrik Modin, Swe. ✍	5.00
□	8 Stéphane Roy, Val'd'or ✍	3.00
□	9 Evgeni Ryabchikov (G), Rus. ✍	3.00
□	10 José Théodore (G), St-Hyacinthe ✍	50.00
□	11 Jason Holland, Kamloops ✍	3.00
□	12 Richard Park, Belleville ✍	3.00
□	13 Jason Podollan, Flor. ✍	3.00
□	14 Mattias Öhlund, Swe. ✍	5.00
□	15 Chris Wells, Pitt. ✍	3.00
□	16 Hugh Hamilton, Spokane ✍	3.00
□	17 Edvin Frylen, Swe. ✍	3.00
□	18 Wade Belak, Que. ✍	3.00
□	19 Sébastien Bety, Drummondville ✍	3.00
□	20 Chris Dingman, Brandon ✍	3.00
□	21 Peter Nylander, Swe. ✍	3.00
□	22 Daymond Langkow, Tri-City ✍	5.00
□	23 Kelly Fairchild, St. John's ✍	3.00
□	24 Norm Dezainde, Kitchener ✍	3.00
□	25 Nolan Baumgartner, Kamloops ✍	3.00
□	26 Deron Quint, USA. ✍	3.00
□	27 Sheldon Souray, NJer. ✍	3.00
□	28 Stefan Ustorf, Ger. ✍	3.00
□	29 Juha Vuovirta, Fin. ✍	3.00
□	30 Mark Seliger (G), Rosenheim ✍	3.00
□	31 Ryan Smyth, Edmo. ✍	10.00
□	32 Dimitri Tabarin, CIS. ✍	3.00
□	33 Nikolai Tsulygin, Rus. ✍	3.00
□	34 Paul Vincent, Toro. ✍	3.00
□	35 Rhett Warrener, Flor. ✍	3.00
□	36 Jamie Rivers, SLou. ✍	3.00
□	37 Rumun Ndur, Buff. ✍	3.00
□	38 Phil Huber ✍	3.00
□	39 Radek Dvorak, Cze. ✍	5.00
□	40 Mike Barrie, Seattle ✍	3.00
□	41 Chris Hynnes ✍	3.00
□	42 Mike Dubinsky, Vanc. ✍	3.00
□	43 Steve Cheredaryk, Winn. ✍	3.00
□	44 Jim Carey (G), Wash. ✍	3.00
□	45 Dorian Anneck, Edmo. ✍	3.00
□	46 Jörgen Jönsson, Swe. ✍	5.00
□	47 Alyn McCauley, Ottawa-OHL ✍	5.00
□	48 Corey Nielson, Edmo. ✍	3.00
□	49 Daniel Tjarnqvist, Swe. ✍	3.00
□	50 Vadim Epantchisev, Rus. ✍	3.00
□	51 Sean Haggerty, Detroit-OHL ✍	3.00
□	52 Milan Hejduk ✍	35.00
□	53 Adam Magarrell, Phil. ✍	3.00
□	54 Dave Scatchard, Vanc. ✍	3.00
□	55 Sébastien Vallée, Phil. ✍	3.00
□	56 Milos Guren, Cze. ✍	3.00
□	57 Johan Davidsson, Anah. ✍	3.00
□	58 Byron Briske, Anah. ✍	3.00
□	59 Sylvain Blouin, NYRa. ✍	3.00
□	60 Bryan Berard, Detroit-OHL ✍	5.00
□	61 Tim Findlay, Windsor ✍	3.00
□	62 Doug Bonner, Seattle ✍	3.00
□	63 Curtis Brown, Buff. ✍	3.00
□	64 Brad Symes, Winn. ✍	3.00
□	65 Andrew Taylor, Kitchener ✍	3.00
□	66 Brad Bombardir, Albany ✍	3.00
□	67 Joe Dziedzic, Pitt. ✍	3.00
□	68 Valentin Morozov, CSKA ✍	3.00
□	69 Mark McArthur, Que. ✍	3.00

COOL FIVE

Insert Set (5 cards): 15.00

	Player	Insert
□	CF1 Radek Bonk, Las Vegas	1.00
□	CF2 Brad Park, Bost.	2.00
□	CF3 Brian Leetch, NYRa.	2.00
□	CF4 Maurice Richard, Mont.	12.00
□	CF5 Henri Richard, Mont.	4.00

COOL FIVE AUTOGRAPHS

Insert Set (5 cards): 85.00

	Player	Auto.
□	CF1 Radek Bonk, Las Vegas ✍	15.00
□	CF2 Brad Park, Bost. ✍	10.00
□	CF3 Brian Leetch, NYRa. ✍	10.00
□	CF4 Maurice Richard, Mont. ✍•	50.00
□	CF5 Henri Richard, Mont. ✍	20.00

FUTURE FLASH

Insert Set (10 cards): 20.00

	Player	Insert
□	FF1 Jeff Ambrosio	.50
□	FF2 Brad Brown, North Bay	.50
□	FF3 Patrik Juhlin	.50
□	FF4 Sergei Gorbachev, Dynamo	.50
□	FF5 Vasili Kamenev	.50
□	FF6 Oleg Orekhovski	.50
□	FF7 Maxim Kuznetsov	.50
□	FF8 Sergei Luchinkin, Rus.	.50
□	FF9 Scotte Roche	.50
□	FF10 Aleksey Morozov	2.00

FUTURE FLASH AUTOGRAPHS

Insert Set (10 cards): 45.00

	Player	Auto.
□	FF1 Jeff Ambrosio ✍	6.00
□	FF2 Brad Brown, North Bay ✍	6.00
□	FF3 Patrik Juhlin ✍	6.00
□	FF4 Sergei Gorbachev, Dynamo ✍	4.00
□	FF5 Vasili Kamenev ✍	4.00
□	FF6 Oleg Orekhovski ✍	4.00
□	FF7 Maxim Kuznetsov ✍	6.00
□	FF8 Sergei Luchinkin, Rus. ✍	4.00
□	FF9 Scotte Roche ✍	4.00
□	FF10 Aleksey Morozov ✍	14.00

1994 - 95 SIGNATURE ROOKIES AUTO-PHONEX

Complete Set (40 cards): 15.00

	Player	SRAP
□	1 Mika Alatalo	.50
□	2 Chad Allan	.50
□	3 Jonas Andersson-Junkka	.50
□	4 Serge Aubin	.50
□	5 David Belitski (G)	.50
□	6 Aki Berg	.50
□	7 Zac Bierk (G)	1.00
□	8 Lou Boddy	.25
□	9 Kevin Bolibruck	.25
□	10 Brian Boucher (G)	1.50
□	11 Jack Callahan	.25
□	12 Jake Deadmarsh	.25
□	13 Andy Delmore	1.00
□	14 Shane Doan	1.00
□	15 Dan Cleary	1.50
□	16 Ian Gordon	.25
□	17 Jochen Hecht, Ger.	1.00
□	18 Martin Hohenberger	.25
□	19 Tomas Holmström	1.00
□	20 Cory Keenan	.25
□	21 Shane Kenny, Owen Sound	.25
□	22 Pavel Kriz	.25
□	23 Justin Kurtz	.50
□	24 Jan Labraaten	.50
□	25 Brad Larsen	.50
□	26 Donald MacLean	.50
□	27 Tavis MacMillan	.25
□	28 Mike Martin	.25
□	29 Bryan Berard	1.50
□	30 Dmitri Nabokov	.50
□	31 Todd Norman	.50
□	32 Cory Peterson	.25
□	33 Johan Ramstedt	.50
□	34 Wade Redden	1.50
□	35 Kevin Riehl	.25
□	36 David Roberts	.50
□	37 Terry Ryan	.50
□	38 Brian Scott	.50
□	39 Alexander Selivanov	.50
□	40 Peter Wallin	.50

AUTOGRAPHED PHONECARDS

These autographed $3 Sprint phonecards came one per pack. Shane Doan (#14) did not sign. Autographs are serial numbered out of 3,000.

Autographed Set (39 cards):	150.00	100.00
Player	Unused	Used
☐ 1 Mika Alatalo	5.00	3.00
☐ 2 Chad Allan	5.00	3.00
☐ 3 Jonas Andersson-Junkka	4.00	3.00
☐ 4 Serge Aubin	5.00	3.00
☐ 5 David Belitski (G)	5.00	3.00
☐ 6 Aki Berg	5.00	3.00
☐ 7 Zac Bierk (G)	5.00	3.00
☐ 8 Lou Boddy	4.00	3.00
☐ 9 Kevin Bolibruck	4.00	3.00
☐ 10 Brian Boucher (G)	10.00	6.00
☐ 11 Jack Callahan	4.00	3.00
☐ 12 Jake Deadmarsh	4.00	3.00
☐ 13 Andy Delmore	5.00	3.00
☐ 15 Dan Cleary	10.00	6.00
☐ 16 Ian Gordon	4.00	3.00
☐ 17 Jochen Hecht, Ger.	5.00	3.00
☐ 18 Martin Hohenberger	4.00	3.00
☐ 19 Tomas Holmström	5.00	3.00
☐ 20 Cory Keenan	4.00	3.00
☐ 21 Shane Kenny, Owen Sound	4.00	3.00
☐ 22 Pavel Kriz	4.00	3.00
☐ 23 Justin Kurtz	4.00	3.00
☐ 24 Jan Labraaten	4.00	3.00
☐ 25 Brad Larsen	4.00	3.00
☐ 26 Donald MacLean	4.00	3.00
☐ 27 Tavis MacMillan	4.00	3.00
☐ 28 Mike Martin	4.00	3.00
☐ 29 Bryan Berard	10.00	6.00
☐ 30 Dmitri Nabokov	5.00	3.00
☐ 31 Todd Norman	4.00	3.00
☐ 32 Cory Peterson	4.00	3.00
☐ 33 Johan Ramstedt	4.00	3.00
☐ 34 Wade Redden	10.00	6.00
☐ 35 Kevin Riehl	4.00	3.00
☐ 36 David Roberts	4.00	3.00
☐ 37 Terry Ryan	4.00	3.00
☐ 38 Brian Scott	4.00	3.00
☐ 39 Alexander Selivanov	4.00	3.00
☐ 40 Peter Wallin	4.00	3.00

BEYOND 2000

Insert Set (5 cards):	20.00
Player	Insert
☐ B1 Jamie Rivers	4.00
☐ B2 Terry Ryan	4.00
☐ B3 Ryan Smyth	4.00
☐ B4 Nolan Baumgartner	4.00
☐ B5 José Théodore (G)	12.00

BEYOND 2000

These cards have two versions: the regular card and an autographed card.

Insert Set (5 cards):	90.00
Player	Auto.
☐ B1 Jamie Rivers ✍	10.00
☐ B2 Terry Ryan ✍	10.00
☐ B3 Ryan Smyth ✍	20.00
☐ B4 Nolan Baumgartner ✍	10.00
☐ B5 José Théodore (G) ✍	60.00

JAROMIR JAGR

Insert Set (5 cards):	15.00
☐ Jaromir Jagr Promo	5.00
Player	Insert
☐ JJ1 Jaromir Jagr	4.00
☐ JJ2 Jaromir Jagr	4.00
☐ JJ3 Jaromir Jagr	4.00
☐ JJ4 Jaromir Jagr	4.00
☐ JJ5 Jaromir Jagr	4.00

JAROMIR JAGR

These cards have two versions: the regular card and an autographed card.

Insert Set (5 cards):	125.00
Player	Auto.
☐ JJ1 Jaromir Jagr ✍	30.00
☐ JJ2 Jaromir Jagr ✍	30.00
☐ JJ3 Jaromir Jagr ✍	30.00
☐ JJ4 Jaromir Jagr ✍	30.00
☐ JJ5 Jaromir Jagr ✍	30.00

PRODIGIES

Insert Set (5 cards):	15.00
☐ Wade Redden Promo	1.00
Player	Insert
☐ P1 Bryan Berard	4.00
☐ P2 Daymond Langkow	3.00
☐ P3 Daniel Cleary	4.00
☐ P4 Aki Berg	3.00
☐ P5 Wade Redden	4.00

PRODIGIES

Insert Set (5 cards):	85.00
Player	Auto.
☐ P1 Bryan Berard ✍	25.00
☐ P2 Daymond Langkow ✍	20.00
☐ P3 Daniel Cleary ✍	25.00
☐ P4 Aki Berg ✍	10.00
☐ P5 Wade Redden ✍	25.00

PHONECARDS

We have little information on these Sprint phonecard inserts. Other singles may exist.

Insert	Unused	Used
☐ Wade Redden Promo $1,000	2.00	-
☐ Ryan Smyth Promo $6	4.00	-
☐ 6 Wade Redden	8.00	4.00
☐ 6 Terry Ryan	8.00	4.00

1994 - 95 SIGNATURE ROOKIES GOLD STANDARD

Player	NRMT-MT
☐ 76 Nolan Baumgartner	.25
☐ 77 Wade Belak	.25
☐ 78 Radek Bonk	1.00
☐ 79 Brad Brown	.25
☐ 80 Dan Cloutier (G)	1.50
☐ 81 Johan Davidsson	.25
☐ 82 Yannick Dubé	.25
☐ 83 Éric Fichaud (G)	.25
☐ 84 Johan Finnstrom	.25
☐ 85 Edvin Frylin	.25
☐ 86 Patrik Juhlin	.25
☐ 87 Valeri Karpov	.25
☐ 88 Nikolai Khabibulin (G)	1.50
☐ 89 Mattias Öhlund	1.00
☐ 90 Jason Podollan	.25
☐ 91 Vadim Sharifjanov	.25
☐ 92 Ryan Smyth	1.50
☐ 93 Dimitri Tabarin	.25
☐ 94 Nikolai Tsulygin	.25
☐ 95 Stefan Ustorf	.25
☐ 96 Paul Vincent	.25
☐ 97 Roman Vopat	.25
☐ 98 Rhett Warrener	.25
☐ 99 Vitali Yachmenev	.25
☐ 100 Vadim Epenchintrev	.25
☐ GS2 Nolan Baumgartner	.50
☐ GS3 Radek Bonk, Las Vegas	.75
☐ GS9 Valeri Karpov	.50
☐ GS18 Ryan Smyth	1.00
☐ HOF7 Tony Esposito (G)	3.00
☐ L1 Brian Leetch	3.00

1994 - 95 SIGNATURE ROOKIES MIRACLE ON ICE

We have little information on this set. Cards have two versions: the regular card and an autographed parallel. It is unsure whether players signed one or both of their cards. Action cards (45-50) were not signed. The most expensive autographs are Mike Eruzione at $30 and Neal Broten at $20. Common autographs start at $5.

Complete Set (50 cards):	.00
Player	NRMT-MT
☐ 1 Bill Baker	.50
☐ 2 Bill Baker	.50
☐ 3 Neal Broten	1.00
☐ 4 Neal Broten	1.00
☐ 5 Dave Christian	.50
☐ 6 Dave Christian	.50
☐ 7 Steve Christoff	.50
☐ 8 Steve Christoff	.50
☐ 9 Jim Craig (G)	1.00
☐ 10 Jim Craig (G)	1.00
☐ 11 Mike Eruzione	2.00
☐ 12 Mike Eruzione	2.00
☐ 13 John Harrington	.50
☐ 14 John Harrington	.50
☐ 15 Steve Janasak	.50
☐ 16 Steve Janasak	.50
☐ 17 Mark Johnson	.50
☐ 18 Mark Johnson	.50
☐ 19 Rob McClanahan	.50
☐ 20 Rob McClanahan	.50
☐ 21 Ken Morrow	1.50
☐ 22 Ken Morrow	1.50
☐ 23 Jack O'Callahan	.50
☐ 24 Jack O'Callahan	.50
☐ 25 Mark Pavelich	.50
☐ 26 Mark Pavelich	.50
☐ 27 Mike Ramsey	.50
☐ 28 Mike Ramsey	.50
☐ 29 Buzz Schneider	.50
☐ 30 Buzz Schneider	.50
☐ 31 Dave Silk	.50
☐ 32 Dave Silk	.50
☐ 33 Bob Suter	.50
☐ 34 Bob Suter	.50
☐ 35 Eric Strobel	.50
☐ 36 Eric Strobel	.50
☐ 37 Phil Verchota	.50
☐ 38 Phil Verchota	.50
☐ 39 Marc Wells	.50
☐ 40 Marc Wells	.50
☐ 41 Herb Brooks	.50
☐ 42 Herb Brooks	.50
☐ 43 Craig Patrick	1.50
☐ 44 Craig Patrick	1.50
☐ 45 U.S.A. Action	.50
☐ 46 U.S.A. Action	.50
☐ 47 Mike Eruzione (Action)	1.00
☐ 48 U.S.A. Celebration	.50
☐ 49 U.S.A. Action (Neal Broten)	1.00
☐ 50 Checklist	.25

PRODIGIES

Autograph (#/2000)	Auto.
☐ 1 Bill Baker ✍	5.00
☐ 2 Bill Baker ✍	5.00
☐ 3 Neal Broten ✍	10.00
☐ 4 Neal Broten ✍	10.00
☐ 5 Dave Christian ✍	5.00
☐ 6 Dave Christian ✍	5.00
☐ 7 Steve Christoff ✍	5.00
☐ 8 Steve Christoff ✍	5.00
☐ 9 Jim Craig (G) ✍	10.00
☐ 10 Jim Craig (G) ✍	10.00
☐ 11 Mike Eruzione ✍	20.00
☐ 12 Mike Eruzione ✍	20.00
☐ 13 John Harrington ✍	5.00
☐ 14 John Harrington ✍	5.00
☐ 15 Steve Janasak ✍	5.00
☐ 16 Steve Janasak ✍	5.00
☐ 17 Mark Johnson ✍	5.00
☐ 18 Mark Johnson ✍	5.00
☐ 19 Rob McClanahan ✍	5.00
☐ 20 Rob McClanahan ✍	5.00
☐ 21 Ken Morrow ✍	10.00
☐ 22 Ken Morrow ✍	10.00
☐ 23 Jack O'Callahan ✍	5.00
☐ 24 Jack O'Callahan ✍	5.00
☐ 25 Mark Pavelich ✍	5.00
☐ 26 Mark Pavelich ✍	5.00
☐ 27 Mike Ramsey ✍	5.00
☐ 28 Mike Ramsey ✍	5.00
☐ 29 Buzz Schneider ✍	5.00
☐ 30 Buzz Schneider ✍	5.00
☐ 31 Dave Silk ✍	5.00
☐ 32 Dave Silk ✍	5.00
☐ 33 Bob Suter ✍	5.00
☐ 34 Bob Suter ✍	5.00
☐ 35 Eric Strobel ✍	5.00
☐ 36 Eric Strobel ✍	5.00
☐ 37 Phil Verchota ✍	5.00
☐ 38 Phil Verchota ✍	5.00
☐ 39 Marc Wells ✍	5.00
☐ 40 Marc Wells ✍	5.00
☐ 42 Herb Brooks ✍	5.00
☐ 43 Craig Patrick ✍	10.00
☐ 44 Craig Patrick ✍	10.00

1994 - 95 SIGNATURE ROOKIES TETRAD

This 120-card multi-sport set has only 16 hockey cards. Each card has a regular version and autographed version.

Imprint: © 1994 Signature Rookies

Player	Card
☐ CIV Sven Butenschon	.25
☐ CIX Sergei Klimentiev, Buff. (Medicine Hat)	.25
☐ CV Dan Cloutier (G)	3.00
☐ CVI Pat Jablonski (G)	.25
☐ CVII Valeri Karpov, Rus.	.25
☐ CVIII Nikolai Khabibulin (G), CSKA	3.00
☐ CX Krzysztof Oliwa, NJer. (Raleigh)	1.50
☐ CXI Dimitri Rjabykin, Calg. (CSKA)	.25
☐ CXII Ryan Risidore, Hfd. (Guelph)	.25
☐ CXIII Shawn Rivers, Atlanta	.25
☐ CXIV Vadim Shariljanov, Rus.	.50
☐ CXV Mika Stromberg, Fin.	.25
☐ CXVI Tim Taylor, Adirondack	.25
☐ CXVII Vitali Yachmenev, North Bay	.25
☐ CXVIII Wendell Young (G), Tamp.	.25
☐ CXXII Bobby Hull	2.50

AUTOGRAPHS

Autograph	Auto.
☐ CIV Sven Butenschon ✍	5.00
☐ CIX Sergei Klimentiev, Buff. (Medicine Hat) ✍	3.00
☐ CV Dan Cloutier (G) ✍	20.00
☐ CVI Pat Jablonski (G) ✍	5.00
☐ CVII Valeri Karpov, Rus. ✍	5.00
☐ CVIII Nikolai Khabibulin (G), CSKA ✍	20.00
☐ CX Krzysztof Oliwa, NJer. (Raleigh) ✍	10.00
☐ CXI Dimitri Rjabykin, Calg. (CSKA) ✍	5.00
☐ CXII Ryan Risidore, Hfd. (Guelph) ✍	3.00
☐ CXIII Shawn Rivers, Atlanta ✍	5.00
☐ CXIV Vadim Shariljanov, Rus. ✍	5.00
☐ CXV Mika Stromberg, Fin. ✍	3.00
☐ CXVI Tim Taylor, Adirondack ✍	5.00
☐ CXVII Vitali Yachmenev, North Bay ✍	5.00
☐ CXVIII Wendell Young (G), Tamp. ✍	5.00
☐ CXXII Bobby Hull ✍	50.00

1994 - 95 SISU

The most expensive singles are Teemu Selänne ($6-8), Saku Koivu ($4-6), Jari Kurri ($2-3) and Jere Lehtinen ($2-3). NHL stars sell at $1-2. Other singles sell between 20¢ and $1.00.

Series One Set (200 cards): 40.00
Series Two Set (200 cards): 50.00

Player	Player
☐ 1 Pasi Kuivalainen	☐ 2 Jere Karalahti
☐ 3 Markku Heikkinen	☐ 4 Marko Allen
☐ 5 Jarmo Kuusisto	☐ 6 Marko Tuulola
☐ 7 Marko Kiprusoff	☐ 8 Vesa Ponto
☐ 9 Tero Lehtera	☐ 10 Darren Boyko
☐ 11 Kari Heikkinen	☐ 12 Niko Marttila
☐ 13 Jari Torkki	☐ 14 Jiri Kucera
☐ 15 Jari Levonen	☐ 16 Juha Ikonen
☐ 17 Joni Lius	☐ 18 Pekka Tuomisto
☐ 19 Petri Kokko	☐ 20 Jere Lehtinen
☐ 21 Janne Kekalainen	☐ 22 Ari Haanpaa
☐ 23 Hannu Jarvenpaa	☐ 24 Waltteri Immonen
☐ 25 Jari Lindroos	☐ 26 Jan Langbacka
☐ 27 Kari Takko (G)	☐ 28 Pasi Maattanen
☐ 29 Jan Latvala	☐ 30 Arto Heiskanen
☐ 31 Iiro Jarvi	☐ 32 Igor Boldin
☐ 33 Sami Simonen	☐ 34 Kari Rosenberg (G)
☐ 35 Sakari Lindfors (G)	☐ 36 Veli-Pekka Hard
☐ 37 Jari Halme	☐ 38 Jukka Tammi (G)
☐ 39 Kalle Koskinen	☐ 40 Pekka Tirkkonen
☐ 41 Ari Sulander (G)	☐ 42 Jani Hassinen
☐ 43 Timo Peltomaa	☐ 44 Sami Mettovaara
☐ 45 Mika Yli-Maenpaa	☐ 46 Toni Virta
☐ 47 Kimmo Lecklin	☐ 48 Rauli Raitanen
☐ 49 Juha Lind	☐ 50 A-P Siekkinen (G)
☐ 51 Kim Ahlroos	☐ 52 Jarkko Nikander
☐ 53 Jouni Vento	☐ 54 Juha Lampinen
☐ 55 Kalle Sahlstedt	☐ 56 Teemu Sillanpaa
☐ 57 Lasse Nieminen	☐ 58 Janne Niinimaa
☐ 59 Timo Jutila	☐ 60 Tommi Haapsaari
☐ 61 Allan Measures	☐ 62 Petteri Nummelin
☐ 63 Antti Törmänen	☐ 64 Pekka Laksola
☐ 65 Esa Sateri	☐ 66 Petro Koivunen
☐ 67 Jarmo Virtanen	☐ 68 Pekka Peltola
☐ 69 Matti Kaipainen	☐ 70 Sami Pekki
☐ 71 Jussi Tarvainen	☐ 72 Jari Virtanen
☐ 73 Kimmo Salminen	☐ 74 Tommi Varjonen
☐ 75 Pauli Jarvinen	☐ 76 Hannu Mattila
☐ 77 Aleksander Smirnov	☐ 78 Arto Kulmala
☐ 79 Roland Karlsson	☐ 80 Jarno Miikkulainen
☐ 81 Jarmo Muukkonen	☐ 82 Mika Paananen
☐ 83 Pasi Kivila	☐ 84 Jari Laukkanen
☐ 85 Tero Arkiomaa	☐ 86 Tommi Miettinen
☐ 87 Juha Järvenpää	☐ 88 Niko Mikkola
☐ 89 Antti Tuomenoksa	☐ 90 Ilkka Sinisalo
☐ 91 Otakar Janecky	☐ 92 Arto Sirviö
☐ 93 Robert Salo	☐ 94 Ari Saarinen
☐ 95 Kari Martikainen	☐ 96 Miro Haapaniemi
☐ 97 Fredrik Norrena (G)	☐ 98 Erik Hämäläinen
☐ 99 Simo Saarinen	☐ 100 Harri Suvanto
☐ 101 Kai Nurminen	☐ 102 Rami Koivisto
☐ 103 Pasi Peltonen	☐ 104 Kari-Pekka Friman
☐ 105 Mika Kortelainen	☐ 106 Timo Hirvonen
☐ 107 Jari Haapamaki	☐ 108 Mika Manninen
☐ 109 Ari Vuori	☐ 110 Markku Ikonen
☐ 111 Mikko Konttila	☐ 112 Harri Sillgren
☐ 113 Mikko Tavi	☐ 114 Markus Oijennus
☐ 115 Kimmo Hyttinen	☐ 116 Jokke Heinanen
☐ 117 Sami Ahlberg	☐ 118 Mika Rautio
☐ 119 Ari Salo	☐ 120 Juha Hautamaa
☐ 121 Kari Haakana	☐ 122 Sami Nuutinen
☐ 123 Lasse Pirjeta	☐ 124 Keijo Sailynoja
☐ 125 Mikael Kotkaniemi	☐ 126 Samuli Rautio
☐ 127 V-P Pekkarinen	☐ 128 Hannu Henriksson
☐ 129 Antti Aalto	☐ 130 Jyrki Jokinen
☐ 131 Marko Ek	☐ 132 Marko Ojanen
☐ 133 Mika Arvaja	☐ 134 Karri Kivi
☐ 135 Timo Saarikoski	☐ 136 Toni Sihvonen
☐ 137 Mika Laaksonen	☐ 138 HIFK Helsinki
☐ 139 HPK Hameenlinna	☐ 140 Ilves Tampere
☐ 141 Jokerit Helsinki	☐ 142 JyP HT Jyvaskyla
☐ 143 KalPa Kuopio	☐ 144 Kiekko-Espoo
☐ 145 Lukko Rauma	☐ 146 Tappara Tampere
☐ 147 TPS Turku	☐ 148 TuTo Turku

☐ 149 Assat Pori	☐ 150 CL 1: Juha Lind (G)
☐ 151 CL 2: K. Takko (G)	☐ 152 CL 3: V. Yursinov
☐ 153 CL 4: P. Nummelin	☐ 154 Marko Jantunen
☐ 155 Jere Lehtinen	☐ 156 Esa Keskinen
☐ 157 Jere Lehtinen	☐ 158 Timo Peltomaa
☐ 159 Janne Grönvall	☐ 160 AS: J. Myllys (G)
☐ 161 AS: Ma. Kiprusoff	☐ 162 AS: Timo Jutila
☐ 163 AS: Sami Kapaner	☐ 164 AS: Esa Keskinen
☐ 165 AS: Mika Alatalo	☐ 166 Ville Peltonen
☐ 167 Igor Boldin	☐ 168 Sami Lehtonen
☐ 169 Juha Jokiharju	☐ 170 Harri Laurila
☐ 171 Pekka Tirkkonen	☐ 172 Mikko Halonen
☐ 173 Tero Arkiomaa	☐ 174 Jonni Vauhkonen
☐ 175 Janne Grönvall	☐ 176 Marko Jantunen
☐ 177 Jouni Vento	☐ 178 HIFK/ ottelut
☐ 179 HPK/ ottelut	☐ 180 Ilves/ ottelut
☐ 181 Jokerit/ ottelut	☐ 182 JyP HT/ ottelut
☐ 183 KalPa/ ottelut	☐ 184 Kiekko-Espoo
☐ 185 Lukko/ ottelut	☐ 186 Reipas/ ottelut
☐ 187 Tappara/ ottelut	☐ 188 TPS/ ottelut
☐ 189 Assat/ ottelut	☐ 190 SM-kulta/ Jokerit
☐ 191 SM-hopea/ TPS	☐ 192 SM-pronssi/ Lukko
☐ 193 EM-kulta/ TPS	☐ 194 Puolivaliérat
☐ 195 Valierat	☐ 196 Pronssiottelu
☐ 197 1. finaali	☐ 198 2. finaali
☐ 199 3. finaali	☐ 200 4. finaali
☐ 201 Jouni Rokama	☐ 202 Sami Leinonen
☐ 203 Jani Nikko	☐ 204 Arto Vuoti
☐ 205 Petr Pavlas	☐ 206 Reijo Mikkolainen
☐ 207 Jari Kurri	☐ 208 Janne Ojanen
☐ 209 Sami Kapanen	☐ 210 Teppo Kivelä
☐ 211 Saku Koivu	☐ 212 Pekka Virta
☐ 213 Risto Jalo	☐ 214 Serjei Prjakhin
☐ 215 Aleksander Barkov	☐ 216 Ville Peltonen
☐ 217 Jari Korpisalo	☐ 218 Jari Liikkanen
☐ 219 Timo Lehkonen	☐ 220 Juha Ylönen
☐ 221 Harri Lönnberg	☐ 222 Teemu Vuorinen
☐ 223 Pertti Lehtonen	☐ 224 Tommi Pullola
☐ 225 Tomas Kapusta	☐ 226 J. Jääskeläinen
☐ 227 Jukka Tiilikainen	☐ 228 Jarno Kultanen
☐ 229 Kimmo Kapanen	☐ 230 Jari Kauppila
☐ 231 Jarkko Glad	☐ 232 Nemo Nokkosmäki
☐ 233 Petri Matikainen	☐ 234 Christian Ruuttu
☐ 235 Matti Järventie	☐ 236 Sami Salo
☐ 237 Timo Kulonen	☐ 238 Pasi Sormunen
☐ 239 Timo Nurmberg	☐ 240 Jari Hirsimäki
☐ 241 Tommi Hämäläinen	☐ 242 Vesa Salo
☐ 243 Juha Nurminen	☐ 244 Petr Korinek
☐ 245 Kimmo Vesa	☐ 246 Jukka Seppo
☐ 247 Jarno Mäkelä	☐ 248 Petri Varis
☐ 249 Marko Virtanen	☐ 250 Risto Siltanen
☐ 251 Juha Järvenpää	☐ 252 Raimo Summanen
☐ 253 Markus Hätinen	☐ 254 Kimmo Nurro
☐ 255 Timo Salonen	☐ 256 Jari Munck
☐ 257 Kimmo Rintanen	☐ 258 Jarno Levonen
☐ 259 Jarno Peltonen	☐ 260 Valeri Krykov
☐ 261 Kai Rautio	☐ 262 Timo Blomqvist
☐ 263 Teemu Selänne	☐ 264 Juha Virtanen
☐ 265 V-P Kautonen	☐ 266 Mikko Koivunoro
☐ 267 Mikko Luovi	☐ 268 Jaroslav Otevrel
☐ 269 Erik Kakko	☐ 270 Peter Ahola
☐ 271 Miikka Kemppi	☐ 272 Toni Mäkiaho
☐ 273 Pekka Poikolainen	☐ 274 Timo Norppa
☐ 275 Sebastian Sulku	☐ 276 Esa Tikkanen
☐ 277 Pasi Saarela	☐ 278 Ilpo Kauhanen
☐ 279 Mika Alatalo	☐ 280 Jukka Suomalainen
☐ 281 Tony Arima	☐ 282 Mika Puhakka
☐ 283 Jussi Kiuru	☐ 284 Jarkko Isotalo
☐ 285 Esa Tommila	☐ 286 Jouni Loponen
☐ 287 Jermu Pisto	☐ 288 Pasi Heinistö
☐ 289 Toni Porkka	☐ 290 Juha Vuorivirta
☐ 291 Vesa Karjalainen	☐ 292 Tom Koivisto
☐ 293 Markku Hurme	☐ 294 Mika Kannisto
☐ 295 Marko Rantanen	☐ 296 Petri Kalteva
☐ 297 Pasi Huura	☐ 298 Miikka Ruokonen
☐ 299 Tuomo Räty	☐ 300 Vadim Shaidullin
☐ 301 Juha Riihijärvi	☐ 302 Brad Turner
☐ 303 Marko Toivola	☐ 304 Kimmo Timonen
☐ 305 Kai Nurminen	☐ 306 Vesa Lehtonen
☐ 307 Mika Niittymäki	☐ 308 Sami Wahlsten
☐ 309 Pavel Torgajev	☐ 310 Pasi Kemppainen
☐ 311 Markku Kallio	☐ 312 Timo Mäki
☐ 313 Mika Strömberg	☐ 314 Tuomas Grönman
☐ 315 Tommi Rajamäki	☐ 316 Juri Kuznetsov
☐ 317 Mikko Myllykoski	☐ 318 Brian Tutt
☐ 319 Teemu Numminen	☐ 320 Juha Jokiharju
☐ 321 Mika Lehtinen	☐ 322 Jari Pulliainen
☐ 323 K. Mäki-Kokkila	☐ 324 Mikko Peltola
☐ 325 Risto Kurkinen	☐ 326 Harri Laurila
☐ 327 Vjatcheslav Fandul	☐ 328 Niklas Hede
☐ 329 Boris Rousson	☐ 330 Jukka Ollila
☐ 331 Jouni Tuominen	☐ 332 Marko Härkönen
☐ 333 Petri Engman	☐ 334 Mikko Halonen
☐ 335 Aki Berg	☐ 336 Kristian Fagerström
☐ 337 Jiri Veber	☐ 338 Tommy Kiviaho
☐ 339 K. Astrahantsev	☐ 340 Jukka Mäkitalo
☐ 341 Timo Nykopp	☐ 342 Sami Lehtonen
☐ 343 Joni Lehto	☐ 344 Jouko Myrrä
☐ 345 Mikko Mäkelä	☐ 346 Marco Poulsen
☐ 347 Janne Seva	☐ 348 Shawn McEachern
☐ 349 Jarkko Varvio	☐ 350 Mikko Konttila
☐ 351 Veli-Pekka Ahonen	☐ 352 Michael Nylander
☐ 353 Kristian Taubert	☐ 354 Ismo Kuoppala
☐ 355 Kimmo Hyttinen	☐ 356 Petri Lätti
☐ 357 Ted Donato	☐ 358 Jari Harjumäki
☐ 359 Teppo Numminen	☐ 360 Jyrki Lumme
☐ 361 German Titov	☐ 362 Kari Eloranta
☐ 363 Raimo Helminen	☐ 364 Marko Jantunen
☐ 365 Olli Kaski	☐ 366 Jarmo Kekäläinen
☐ 367 Esa Keskinen	☐ 368 Jarmo Mäkitalo
☐ 369 Mika Nieminen	☐ 370 Marko Palo
☐ 371 Ville Siren	☐ 372 Kari Suoraniemi
☐ 373 Otakar Janecky	☐ 374 Jari Lindroos
☐ 375 Teppo Kivelä	☐ 376 Petri Varis
☐ 377 Pekka Laksola	☐ 378 Jari Korpisalo
☐ 379 Iiro Järvi	☐ 380 Timo Saarikoski
☐ 381 Rauli Raitanen	☐ 382 Juha Riihijärvi
☐ 383 Juha Jokiharju	☐ 384 Vesa Salo
☐ 385 Kari Nieminen	☐ 386 Marko Jantunen
☐ 387 Jere Lehtinen	☐ 388 Ari Sulander (G)
☐ 389 Hannu Kapanen	☐ 390 Hannu Savolainen
☐ 391 Heikki Vesala	☐ 392 Hannu Aravirta
☐ 393 Kari Savolainen	☐ 394 Anatoli Bogdanov
☐ 395 Harri Rindell	☐ 396 Vaclav Sykora
☐ 397 Boris Majorov	☐ 398 Vladimir Yursinov
☐ 399 Seppo Suoraniemi	☐ 400 Veli-Pekka Ketola

NHL DRAFT

Singles start at $2-3.

Insert Set (8 cards): 20.00

Player	Player
☐ 1 Title Card	☐ 2 Marko Kiprusoff
☐ 3 Jussi Tarvainen	☐ 4 Arto Kuki
☐ 5 Tommi Rajamäki	☐ 6 Tero Lehterä
☐ 7 Tommi Miettinen	☐ 8 Antti Törmänen

FIRE ON ICE

Saku Koivu is the most expensive single at $8-10. Singles start at $2.

Insert Set (20 cards): 35.00

Player	Player
☐ 1 Saku Koivu	☐ 2 Esa Keskinen
☐ 3 Igor Boldin	☐ 4 Juha Nurminen
☐ 5 Marko Jantunen	☐ 6 Janne Ojanen
☐ 7 Sami Kapanen	☐ 8 Kai Nurminen
☐ 9 Jari Korpisalo	☐ 10 Tero Lehtera
☐ 11 Timo Jutila	☐ 12 Vjatseslav Fandul
☐ 13 Otakar Janecky	☐ 14 Tero Arkiomaa
☐ 15 Jari Torkki	☐ 16 Risto Kurkinen
☐ 17 Petr Korinek	☐ 18 Petro Koivunen
☐ 19 Tomas Kapusta	☐ 20 Pauli Jarvinen

GUEST SPECIAL

Teemu Selänne is the most expensive single at $8-10. Singles start at $2-3.

Insert Set (12 cards): 40.00

Player	Player
☐ 1 Ted Donato	☐ 2 Jari Kurri
☐ 3 Jyrki Lumme	☐ 4 Shawn McEachern
☐ 5 Mikko Mäkelä	☐ 6 Teppo Numminen
☐ 7 Michael Nylander	☐ 8 Christian Ruuttu
☐ 9 Teemu Selänne	☐ 10 Esa Tikkanen
☐ 11 German Titov	☐ 12 Jarkko Varvio

HOROSCOPES

Singles start at 75¢.

Insert Set (20 cards): 15.00

Player	Player
☐ 1 Juha Lind	☐ 2 Jukka Seppo
☐ 3 Antti Tuomenoksa	☐ 4 Tuomas Grönman
☐ 5 Peter Ahola	☐ 6 Ville Peltonen
☐ 7 Timo Saarikoski	☐ 8 Timo Peltomaa
☐ 9 Jari Levonen	☐ 10 Teppo Kivelä
☐ 11 Valeri Krykov	☐ 12 Juha Riihijärvi
☐ 13 Kai Nurminen	☐ 14 Mikko Luovi
☐ 15 Raimo Summanen	☐ 16 Tommy Kiviaho
☐ 17 Hannu Järvenpää	☐ 18 Marko Virtanen
☐ 19 Sami Lehtonen	☐ 20 Mika Alatalo

JUNIOR

Saku Koivu is the most expensive single at $6-8. Singles start at $1.50

Insert Set (10 cards): 20.00

Player	Player
☐ 1 Saku Koivu	☐ 2 Jokke Heinanen
☐ 3 Tommi Miettinen	☐ 4 Jere Karalahti
☐ 5 Kalle Koskinen	☐ 6 Kari Rosenberg (G)
☐ 7 Mika Manninen (G)	☐ 8 Jussi Tarvainen
☐ 9 Mika Stromberg	☐ 10 Kalle Sahlstedt

MA6IC NUM3ER5

Singles start at 75¢.

Insert Set (10 cards): 10.00

Player	Player
☐ 1 Pasi Kuivalainen	☐ 2 Petteri Nummelin
☐ 3 Jarmo Kuusisto	☐ 4 Janne Ojanen
☐ 5 Sami Kapanen	☐ 6 Pekka Virta
☐ 7 Antti Törmänen	☐ 8 Jari Korpisalo
☐ 9 Kimmo Salminen	☐ 10 Jukka Tammi (G)

NOLLA

Singles start at $3-4.

Insert Set (10 cards): 30.00

Player	Player
☐ 1 Mika Manninen (G)	☐ 2 Kari Takko (G)
☐ 3 Ari Sulander (G)	☐ 4 Jouni Rokama (G)
☐ 5 Kari Rosenberg (G)	☐ 6 A-P Siekkinen (G)
☐ 7 Allain Roy (G)	☐ 8 Pasi Kuivalainen (G)
☐ 9 Sakari Lindfors (G)	☐ 10 Mika Rautio (G)

SISU SPECIALS

Saku Koivu is the most expensive single at $8-10. Singles start at $1.50

Insert Set (10 cards): 25.00

Player	Player
☐ 1 Mika Alatalo	☐ 2 Jari Korpisalo
☐ 3 Petteri Nummelin	☐ 4 Janne Ojanen
☐ 5 Sami Kapanen	☐ 6 Kari Takko (G)
☐ 7 Esa Keskinen	☐ 8 Ari Sulander (G)
☐ 9 Jarmo Myllys (G)	☐ 10 Saku Koivu

SUPER CHASE

Player	NRMT-MT
☐ Canada Bowl	15.00
☐ Saku Koivu Autograph ✍	75.00

1994 - 95 SLAPSHOT

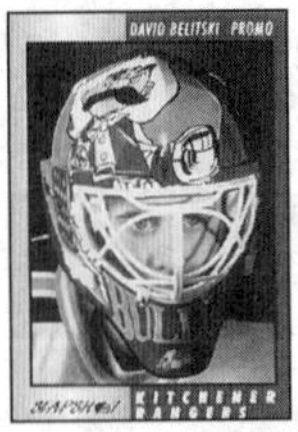

PROMO CARDS

Player	NRMT-MT
☐ David Belitski (G)	1.50
☐ Todd Norman	1.50
☐ Steve Rice	1.50
☐ Four Wolves	1.50

BRANTFORD SMOKE

Complete Set (25 cards): 10.00

Player	Player
☐ 1 Checklist	☐ 2 Bob Decomimière
☐ 3 Todd Francis	☐ 4 Petr Liptrott
☐ 5 Lorne Knauft	☐ 6 Paul Polillo
☐ 7 Rob Arabski	☐ 8 Derek Gauthier
☐ 9 Joe Simon	☐ 10 Brad Barton
☐ 11 Terry Chitaroni	☐ 12 Paul Mitton
☐ 13 Wayne MacPhee	☐ 14 Brian Blad
☐ 15 John Laan	☐ 16 Shane MacEachern
☐ 17 Wayne Muir	☐ 18 Ted Miskolczi
☐ 19 Marc Delorme	☐ 20 Mike Speer
☐ 21 Bob Baird/Ken Crabb	☐ 22 Ken Gratton, Coach
☐ 23 Team/Sponsor Card	☐ 24 Craig Newton
☐ 25 Joe Lowes	

DETROIT JR. RED WINGS

Complete Set (25 cards): 15.00

Player	Player
☐ 1 Checklist	☐ 2 Darryl Foster
☐ 3 Quade Lightbody	☐ 4 Ryan MacDonald
☐ 5 Mike Rucinski	☐ 6 Murray Sheehan
☐ 7 Matt Ball	☐ 8 Gerry Lanigan
☐ 9 Mike Morrone	☐ 10 Tom Buckley
☐ 11 Eric Manlow	☐ 12 Bill McCauley
☐ 13 Andrew Taylor	☐ 14 Scott Blair
☐ 15 Jeff Mitchell	☐ 16 Jason Saal (G)
☐ 17 Jamie Allison	☐ 18 Bryan Berard
☐ 19 Dan Pawlaczyk	☐ 20 Milan Kostolny
☐ 21 Duane Harmer	☐ 22 Shayne McCosh
☐ 23 Sean Haggerty	☐ 24 Nic Beaudoin
☐ 25 Paul Maurice, Coach	

GUELPH STORM

Complete Set (30 cards): 12.00

Player	Player
☐ 1 Checklist	☐ 2 Mark McArthur
☐ 3 Andy Adams	☐ 4 Bryan McKinney
☐ 5 Ryan Risidore	☐ 6 Joel Cort
☐ 7 Chris Hajt	☐ 8 Regan Stocco
☐ 9 Dwayne Hay	☐ 10 Andrew Clark
☐ 11 Neil Fewster	☐ 12 Jamie Wright
☐ 13 Jason Jackman	☐ 14 Pat Barton
☐ 15 Tom Johnson	☐ 16 Brian Wesenberg
☐ 17 Mike Pittman	☐ 18 Jeff Williams
☐ 19 Todd Norman	☐ 20 Mike Rusk
☐ 21 David Lylyk	☐ 22 Todd Bertuzzi
☐ 23 Jeff Cowan	☐ 24 Rumun Ndur
☐ 25 Jeff O'Neill	☐ 26 Andrew Long
☐ 27 C. Hartsburg, Coach	☐ 28 P. Brydges, A. Coach
☐ 29 Burger King Sponsor	☐ 30 Domino's Pizza

KITCHENER RANGERS

Complete Set (35 cards): 12.00

Player	Player
☐ 1 Checklist	☐ 2 David Belitski (G)
☐ 3 Darryl Whyte	☐ 4 Daniel Godbout
☐ 5 Greg McLean	☐ 6 Jason Hughes
☐ 7 Jason Byrnes	☐ 8 Paul Traynor
☐ 9 Travis Riggin	☐ 10 Tim Spitzig
☐ 11 Trevor Gallant	☐ 12 Chris Pittman
☐ 13 Rick Emmett	☐ 14 Jason Morgan
☐ 15 Luch Nasato	☐ 16 Ryan Pepperall
☐ 17 Keith Welsh	☐ 18 Bill McGuigen
☐ 19 Chris Brassard	☐ 20 Andrew Taylor
☐ 21 Rob Deciantis	☐ 22 Wes Swinson
☐ 23 Lucas Miller	☐ 24 Sergei Olympiev
☐ 25 Rob Maric	☐ 26 Eric Manlow
☐ 27 Geoff Ward, Coach	☐ 28 Bob Ertel, G.M.
☐ 29 Chambers/ Nicholls	☐ 30 Domino's Pizza
☐ 31 Brian Scott	☐ 32 Robin LaCour
☐ 33 Jim Ensom	☐ 34 Dylan Seca
☐ 35 Garrett Burnett	

NORTH BAY CENTENNIALS

Complete Set (25 cards): 10.00

Player	Player
☐ 1 Joel Gagnon	☐ 2 Scott Roche
☐ 3 Derek Lahnalampi	☐ 4 Brad Brown
☐ 5 Steve McLaren	☐ 6 Cam White
☐ 7 Corey Neilson	☐ 8 Jason Campeau
☐ 9 Steve Carpenter	☐ 10 Trevor Gallant
☐ 11 Alex Matvichuk	☐ 12 Ryan Gillis
☐ 13 Kris Cantu	☐ 14 Stefan Rivard
☐ 15 Brian Whitley	☐ 16 Dustin Virag
☐ 17 Lee Jinman	☐ 18 Scott Cherrey
☐ 19 Damian Bloye	☐ 20 Justin Robinson
☐ 21 Kody Grigg	☐ 22 John Guirestante
☐ 23 Gary Roach	☐ 24 Vitali Yachmenev
☐ 25 Shane Parker/ Tom Hedica	

SARNIA STING

Complete Set (30 cards): 10.00

Player	Player
☐ 1 Checklist	☐ 2 Ken Carroll
☐ 3 Scott Hay	☐ 4 Kam White
☐ 5 Joe Doyle	☐ 6 Tom Brown
☐ 7 Jeremy Miculinic	☐ 8 Darren Mortier
☐ 9 Aaron Brand	☐ 10 Chris George
☐ 11 Stephane Soulliere	☐ 12 Paul McInnes
☐ 13 Trevor Letowski	☐ 14 Dustin McArthur
☐ 15 Rob Massa	☐ 16 Brendan Yarema
☐ 17 Dan DelMonte	☐ 18 B.J. Johnston
☐ 19 Wes Mason	☐ 20 Rob Guinn
☐ 21 Jeff Brown	☐ 22 Dennis Maxwell
☐ 23 Damon Hardy	☐ 24 Alan Letang
☐ 25 Matt Hogan	☐ 26 Sasha Cucuz
☐ 27 Rich Brown, Coach	☐ 28 G. Hamilton, Trainer
☐ 29 D. Ciccarelli/ S. Burr	☐ 30 Mascot Buzz

SUDBURY WOLVES

Complete Set (25 cards): 10.00

Player	Player
☐ 1 Checklist	☐ 2 Dave MacDonald
☐ 3 Rory Fitzpatrick	☐ 4 Mike Wilson
☐ 5 Neal Martin	☐ 6 Shwan Frappier
☐ 7 Jamie Rivers	☐ 8 Zdenek Nedved
☐ 9 Ryan Shanahan	☐ 10 Sean Venedam
☐ 11 Andrew Dale	☐ 12 Rick Bodkin
☐ 13 Luc Gagne	☐ 14 Barrie Moore
☐ 15 Richard Rochefort	☐ 16 Krystof Secemski
☐ 17 Jason Bonsignore	☐ 18 Liam MacEachern
☐ 19 Simon Sherry	☐ 20 Ethan Moreau
☐ 21 Matt Mulin (G)	☐ 22 Aaron Starnyski
☐ 23 Ron Newhook	☐ 24 Merkosky/ T. Lalonde
☐ 25 Dan Lebold/ Jason Allen	

WINDSOR SPITFIRES

Complete Set (28 cards): 12.00

Player	Player
☐ 1 Checklist	☐ 2 Jamie Storr (G)
☐ 3 Travis Scott	☐ 4 Paul Beazley
☐ 5 Mike Martin	☐ 6 Chris Van Dyk
☐ 7 Denis Smith	☐ 8 Glenn Crawford
☐ 9 David Pluck	☐ 10 Bill Bowler
☐ 11 David Green	☐ 12 Adam Young
☐ 13 Wes Ward	☐ 14 Ed Jovanovski
☐ 15 Kevin Paden	☐ 16 Rob Shearer
☐ 17 Joel Poirier	☐ 18 Cory Evans
☐ 19 Vladimir Kretchine	☐ 20 David Roche
☐ 21 Rick Emmett	☐ 22 David Geris
☐ 23 Caleb Ward	☐ 24 Luke Clowes
☐ 25 John Cooper	☐ 26 Tim Findlay
☐ 27 Pizza Hut Sponsor	☐ 28 AM 800 Sponsor

1994 - 95 SLAPSHOT MEMORIAL CUP

Complete Set (110 cards): 40.00

Common Player: .25

Player	NM-MT
☐ 1 Rod Branch (G), Kamloops	.25
☐ 2 Jeff Oldenborger, Kamloops	.25
☐ 3 Jason Holland, Kamloops	.25
☐ 4 Nolan Baumgartner, Kamloops	.25
☐ 5 Keith McCambridge, Kamloops	.25
☐ 6 Ivan Vologjaninov, Kamloops	.25
☐ 7 Aaron Keller, Kamloops	.25
☐ 8 Greg Hart, Kamloops	.25
☐ 9 Jarome Iginla, Kamloops	8.00
☐ 10 Ryan Huska, Kamloops	.25
☐ 11 Jeff Ainsworth, Kamloops	.25
☐ 12 Darcy Tucker, Kamloops	1.50
☐ 13 Hnat Domenichelli, Kamloops	1.00
☐ 14 Tyson Nash, Kamloops	1.00
☐ 15 Shane Doan, Kamloops	1.50
☐ 16 Jeff Antonovich, Kamloops	.25
☐ 17 Donnie Kinney, Kamloops	.25
☐ 18 Ashley Buckberger, Kamloops	.25
☐ 19 Brad Lukowich, Kamloops	1.00
☐ 20 Bob Westerby, Kamloops	.25
☐ 21 Jason Strudwick, Kamloops	.50
☐ 22 Bob Maudie, Kamloops	.25
☐ 23 Randy Petruk (G), Kamloops	.25
☐ 24 Shawn McNeil, Kamloops	.25
☐ 25 Don Hay, Head Coach, Kamloops	.25
☐ 26 Byron Penstock (G), Brandon	.25
☐ 27 Brian Elder (G), Brandon	.25
☐ 28 Jeff Staples, Brandon	.25
☐ 29 Scott Laluk, Brandon	.25
☐ 30 Kevin Pozzo, Brandon	.25
☐ 31 Wade Redden, Brandon	2.00
☐ 32 Jusin Kurtz, Brandon	.25
☐ 33 Sven Butenschon, Brandon	.25
☐ 34 Bryan McCabe, Brandon	1.50
☐ 35 Kelly Smart, Brandon	.25
☐ 36 Bobby Brown, Brandon	.25
☐ 37 Mike Dubinsky, Brandon	.25
☐ 38 Mike Leclerc, Brandon	1.00
☐ 39 Dean Kletzel, Brandon	.25
☐ 40 Darren Ritchie, Brandon	.25
☐ 41 Mark Dutiaume, Brandon	.25

☐	42 Ryan Robson, Brandon	.25
☐	43 Chris Dingman, Brandon	1.00
☐	44 Darren Van Oene, Brandon	.25
☐	45 Colin Cloutier (G), Brandon	.25
☐	46 Darryl Stoclham, Brandon	.25
☐	47 Peter Schaefer, Brandon	1.00
☐	48 Marty Murray, Brandon	.50
☐	49 Alex Vasilevski, Brandon	.25
☐	50 Bob Lowes, Head Coach, Brandon	.25
☐	51 Michael Coveny, Hull	.25
☐	52 Jan Nemecek, Hull	.25
☐	53 Chris Hall, Hull	.25
☐	54 Jason Groleau, Hull	.25
☐	55 Alex Rodrigue, Hull	.25
☐	56 Jamie Bird, Hull	.25
☐	57 Jarold Hersh, Hull	.25
☐	58 Carl Prud'homme, Hull	.25
☐	59 Sean Farmer, Hull	.25
☐	60 Carl Beaudoin, Hull	.25
☐	61 Gordie Dwyer, Hull	.50
☐	62 Richard Safarik, Hull	.25
☐	63 Carl Charland, Hull	.25
☐	64 Jean-Guy Trudel, Hull	1.00
☐	65 François Cloutier, Hull	.25
☐	66 Roddie MacKenzie, Hull	.25
☐	67 Colin White, Hull	1.00
☐	68 Marin Menard, Hull	.25
☐	69 Sébastien Bordeleau, Hull	.50
☐	70 Jonathan Delisle, Hull	.25
☐	71 Peter Worrell, Hull	1.50
☐	72 Louis-Philippe Charbonneau, Hull	.25
☐	73 José Théodore (G), Hull	25.00
☐	74 Neil Savary (G), Hull	.25
☐	75 Michael McKay, Hull	.25
☐	76 Darryl Foster (G), Detroit-OHL	.25
☐	77 Quade Lightbody, Detroit-OHL	.25
☐	78 Ryan MacDonald, Detroit-OHL	.25
☐	79 Mike Rucinski, Detroit-OHL	.50
☐	80 Murray Sheehan, Detroit-OHL	.25
☐	81 Matt Ball, Detroit-OHL	.25
☐	82 Gerry Lanigan, Detroit-OHL	.25
☐	83 Mike Morrone, Detroit-OHL	.25
☐	84 Tom Buckley, Detroit-OHL	.25
☐	85 Eric Manlow, Detroit-OHL	.25
☐	86 Bill McCauley, Detroit-OHL	.25
☐	87 Andrew Taylor, Detroit-OHL	.25
☐	88 Scott Blair, Detroit-OHL	.25
☐	89 Jeff Mitchell, Detroit-OHL	.25
☐	90 Jason Saal (G), Detroit-OHL	.25
☐	91 Jamie Allison, Detroit-OHL	.25
☐	92 Bryan Berard, Detroit-OHL	2.00
☐	93 Dan Pawlaczyk, Detroit-OHL	.25
☐	94 Milan Kostolny, Detroit-OHL	.25
☐	95 Duane Harmer, Detroit-OHL	.25
☐	96 Shayne McCosh, Detroit-OHL	.25
☐	97 Sean Haggerty, Detroit-OHL	.25
☐	98 Nic Beaudoin, Detroit-OHL	.25
☐	99 Paul Maurice, Coach/ GM, Detroit-OHL	.25
☐	100 Pete DeBoe, Asst. Coach, Detroit-OHL	.25
☐	101 CL: Kamloops	.25
☐	102 CL: Brandon	.25
☐	103 CL: Hull	.25
☐	104 CL: Detroit	.25
☐	105 Kamloops Blazers	.25
☐	106 Detroit Jr. Red Wings	.25
☐	107 Hull Olympiques	.25
☐	OHL Card	.25
☐	QMJHL Card	.25
☐	WHL Card	.25

1994 - 95 SP

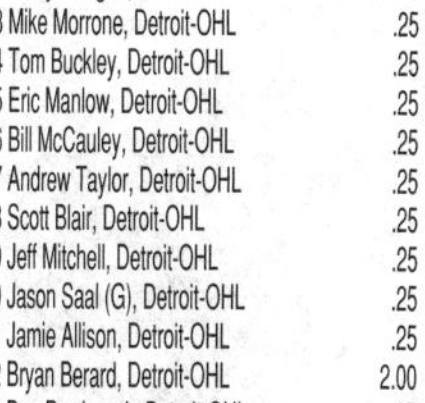

These cards have a Die-Cut parallel.

Imprint: © 1995 The Upper Deck Company

Complete Set (195 cards): 120.00 55.00

Common Player: .30 .20

	Player	D.C.	Reg.
☐ ☐	1 Paul Kariya, Anah.	4.00	2.00
☐ ☐	2 Oleg Tverdovsky, Anah.	.50	.20
☐ ☐	3 Stéphan Lebeau, Anah.	.35	.20
☐ ☐	4 Bob Corkum, Anah.	.35	.20
☐ ☐	5 Guy Hebert (G), Anah.	.35	.20
☐ ☐	6 Raymond Bourque, Bost.	2.00	1.00
☐ ☐	**7 Blaine Lacher (G), Bost. RC**	**1.50**	**1.50**
☐ ☐	8 Adam Oates, Bost.	.50	.20
☐ ☐	9 Cam Neely, Bost.	2.00	1.00
☐ ☐	**10 Mariusz Czerkawski, Bost. RC**	**2.00**	**2.00**
☐ ☐	11 Bryan Smolinski, Bost.	.35	.20
☐ ☐	12 Pat LaFontaine, Buff.	1.00	.50
☐ ☐	13 Alexander Mogilny, Buff.	.50	.20
☐ ☐	14 Dominik Hasek (G), Buff.	2.00	1.00
☐ ☐	15 Dale Hawerchuk, Buff.	1.00	.50
☐ ☐	16 Alexei Zhitnik, Buff.	.35	.20
☐ ☐	17 Theoren Fleury, Calg.	1.00	.50
☐ ☐	18 German Titov, Calg.	.35	.20
☐ ☐	19 Phil Housley, Calg.	.50	.20
☐ ☐	20 Joe Nieuwendyk, Calg.	.50	.20
☐ ☐	21 Trevor Kidd (G), Calg.	.50	.20
☐ ☐	22 Jeremy Roenick, Chic.	1.50	.50
☐ ☐	23 Chris Chelios, Chic.	1.00	.50
☐ ☐	24 Ed Belfour (G), Chic.	2.00	1.00
☐ ☐	25 Bernie Nicholls, Chic.	.35	.20
☐ ☐	26 Tony Amonte, Chic.	1.00	.50
☐ ☐	27 Joe Murphy, Chic.	.35	.20
☐ ☐	28 Mike Modano, Dall.	2.00	1.00
☐ ☐	29 Trent Klatt, Dall.	.35	.20
☐ ☐	30 Dave Gagner, Dall.	.35	.20
☐ ☐	31 Kevin Hatcher, Dall.	.35	.20
☐ ☐	32 Andy Moog (G), Dall.	.50	.20
☐ ☐	33 Sergei Fedorov, Detr.	2.00	1.00
☐ ☐	34 Steve Yzerman, Detr.	4.50	2.00
☐ ☐	35 Vyacheslav Kozlov, Detr.	.35	.20
☐ ☐	36 Paul Coffey, Detr.	1.00	.50
☐ ☐	37 Keith Primeau, Detr.	.50	.20
☐ ☐	38 Ray Sheppard, Detr.	.35	.20
☐ ☐	39 Doug Weight, Edmo.	1.00	.50
☐ ☐	40 Jason Arnott, Edmo.	.50	.20
☐ ☐	41 Bill Ranford (G), Edmo.	.50	.20
☐ ☐	42 Shayne Corson, Edmo.	.50	.20
☐ ☐	43 Stu Barnes, Flor.	.35	.20
☐ ☐	44 John Vanbiesbrouck (G), Flor.	.50	.20
☐ ☐	45 Johan Garpenlöv, Flor.	.35	.20
☐ ☐	46 Bob Kudelski, Flor.	.35	.20
☐ ☐	47 Scott Mellanby, Flor.	.35	.20
☐ ☐	48 Chris Pronger, Hart.	1.00	.50
☐ ☐	49 Darren Turcotte, Hart.	.35	.20
☐ ☐	50 Andrew Cassels, Hart.	.35	.20
☐ ☐	51 Sean Burke (G), Hart.	1.00	.50
☐ ☐	52 Geoff Sanderson, Hart.	.35	.20
☐ ☐	53 Rob Blake, LosA.	1.00	.50
☐ ☐	54 Wayne Gretzky, LosA.	8.00	4.00
☐ ☐	55 Rick Tocchet, LosA.	.50	.20
☐ ☐	56 Tony Granato, LosA.	.35	.20
☐ ☐	57 Jari Kurri, LosA.	2.00	1.00
☐ ☐	58 Vincent Damphousse, Mont.	1.00	.50
☐ ☐	59 Patrick Roy (G), Mont.	6.00	3.00
☐ ☐	60 Vladimir Malakhov, Mont.	.35	.20
☐ ☐	61 Pierre Turgeon, Mont.	.50	.20
☐ ☐	62 Mark Recchi, Mont.	.50	.20
☐ ☐	63 Martin Brodeur (G), NJer.	3.00	1.50
☐ ☐	64 Stéphane J.J. Richer, NJer.	.35	.20
☐ ☐	65 John MacLean, NJer.	.35	.20
☐ ☐	66 Scott Stevens, NJer.	.50	.20
☐ ☐	67 Scott Niedermayer, NJer.	.50	.20
☐ ☐	68 Kirk Muller, NYIs.	.50	.20
☐ ☐	69 Ray Ferraro, NYIs.	.35	.20
☐ ☐	70 Brett Lindros, NYIs.	3.50	.50
☐ ☐	71 Steve Thomas, NYIs.	.35	.20
☐ ☐	72 Pat Verbeek, NYRa.	.50	.20
☐ ☐	73 Mark Messier, NYRa.	2.00	1.00
☐ ☐	74 Brian Leetch, NYRa.	1.00	.50
☐ ☐	75 Mike Richter (G), NYRa.	1.00	.50
☐ ☐	76 Alex Kovalev, NYRa.	1.00	.50
☐ ☐	77 Adam Graves, NYRa.	.50	.20
☐ ☐	78 Sergei Zubov, NYRa.	.35	.20
☐ ☐	79 Alexei Yashin, Otta.	1.00	.50
☐ ☐	**80 Radek Bonk, Otta. RC**	**3.00**	**3.00**
☐ ☐	81 Alexandre Daigle, Otta.	.35	.20
☐ ☐	82 Don Beaupré (G), Otta.	.35	.20
☐ ☐	83 Mikael Renberg, Phil.	.50	.20
☐ ☐	84 Eric Lindros, Phil.	2.00	1.00
☐ ☐	85 John LeClair, Phil.	1.50	.50
☐ ☐	86 Rod Brind'Amour, Phil.	.50	.20
☐ ☐	87 Ron Hextall (G), Phil.	1.00	.50
☐ ☐	88 Ken Wregget (G), Pitt.	.35	.20
☐ ☐	89 Jaromir Jagr, Pitt.	2.00	1.00
☐ ☐	90 Tomas Sandström, Pitt.	.35	.20
☐ ☐	91 John Cullen, Pitt.	.35	.20
☐ ☐	92 Ron Francis, Pitt.	1.00	.50
☐ ☐	93 Luc Robitaille, Pitt.	1.50	.50
☐ ☐	94 Joe Sakic, Québ.	3.00	1.50
☐ ☐	95 Owen Nolan, Québ.	1.00	.50
☐ ☐	96 Peter Forsberg, Québ.	2.50	1.00
☐ ☐	97 Wendel Clark, Québ.	1.50	.50
☐ ☐	98 Mike Ricci, Québ.	.50	.20
☐ ☐	99 Stéphane Fiset (G), Québ.	.50	.20
☐ ☐	100 Brett Hull, SLou.	2.00	1.00
☐ ☐	101 Brendan Shanahan, SLou.	2.00	1.00
☐ ☐	102 Curtis Joseph (G), SLou.	2.00	1.00
☐ ☐	103 Esa Tikkanen, SLou.	.35	.20
☐ ☐	104 Al MacInnis, SLou.	.50	.20
☐ ☐	105 Arturs Irbe (G), SanJ.	.50	.20
☐ ☐	106 Ray Whitney, SanJ.	.35	.20
☐ ☐	107 Sergei" Makarov, SanJ.	.50	.20
☐ ☐	108 Sandis Ozolinsh, SanJ.	.35	.20
☐ ☐	109 Craig Janney, SanJ.	.35	.20
☐ ☐	110 Petr Klima, Tamp.	.35	.20
☐ ☐	111 Chris Gratton, Tamp.	.35	.20
☐ ☐	112 Roman Hamrlik, Tamp.	.35	.20
☐ ☐	**113 A. Selivanov, Tamp. RC**	**1.00**	**1.00**
☐ ☐	114 Brian Bradley, Tamp.	.35	.20
☐ ☐	115 Doug Gilmour, Toro.	1.00	.50
☐ ☐	116 Mats Sundin, Toro.	2.00	1.00
☐ ☐	117 Félix Potvin (G), Toro.	1.00	.50
☐ ☐	118 Mike Ridley, Toro.	.35	.20
☐ ☐	119 Dave Andreychuk, Toro.	.50	.20
☐ ☐	120 Dmitri Mironov, Toro.	.35	.20
☐ ☐	121 Pavel Bure, Vanc.	1.50	.50
☐ ☐	122 Trevor Linden, Vanc.	.50	.20
☐ ☐	123 Jeff R. Brown, Vanc.	.35	.20
☐ ☐	124 Kirk McLean (G), Vanc.	.50	.20
☐ ☐	125 Geoff Courtnall, Vanc.	.35	.20
☐ ☐	126 Joé Juneau, Wash.	.35	.20
☐ ☐	127 Dale Hunter, Wash.	.50	.20
☐ ☐	**128 Jim Carey, Wash. RC**	**1.50**	**1.50**
☐ ☐	129 Peter Bondra, Wash.	1.00	.50
☐ ☐	130 Dmitri Khristich, Wash.	.35	.20
☐ ☐	131 Teemu Selänne, Winn.	1.50	.50
☐ ☐	132 Keith Tkachuk, Winn.	1.00	.50
☐ ☐	133 Alexei Zhamnov, Winn.	.50	.20
☐ ☐	134 Dave Manson, Winn.	.35	.20
☐ ☐	135 Nelson Emerson, Winn.	.35	.20
☐ ☐	136 Alexandre Daigle, Canada	.50	.20
☐ ☐	137 Jamie Storr (G), Canada	.50	.20
☐ ☐	138 Todd Harvey, Canada	.50	.20
☐ ☐	**139 Wade Redden, Canada RC**	**3.00**	**3.00**
☐ ☐	**140 Ed Jovanovski, Canada RC**	**4.00**	**4.00**
☐ ☐	**141 Jamie Rivers, Canada RC**	**1.00**	**1.00**
☐ ☐	**142 Ryan Smyth, Canada RC**	**4.50**	**4.50**
☐ ☐	143 Jason Botterill, Canada	.35	.20
☐ ☐	**144 Denis Pederson, Canada RC**	**1.00**	**1.00**
☐ ☐	145 Jeff Friesen, Canada	1.00	.50
☐ ☐	**146 Dan Cloutier (G), Canada RC**	**4.00**	**4.00**
☐ ☐	**147 Lee Sorochan, Canada RC**	**1.00**	**1.00**
☐ ☐	148 Marty Murray, Canada	.35	.20
☐ ☐	**149 Shean Donovan, Canada RC**	**1.50**	**1.50**
☐ ☐	**150 Larry Courville, Canada RC**	**1.00**	**1.00**
☐ ☐	151 Jason Allison, Canada	2.00	1.00
☐ ☐	152 Jeff O'Neill, Canada	6.00	4.00
☐ ☐	153 Bryan McCabe, Canada	.50	.20
☐ ☐	**154 Miloslav Guren, Czech RC**	**1.00**	**1.00**
☐ ☐	**155 Petr Buzek, Czech RC**	**1.00**	**1.00**
☐ ☐	156 Tomás Blazek, Czech	.35	.20
☐ ☐	157 Josef Marha, Czech	.35	.20
☐ ☐	**158 Jan Hlavac, Czech RC**	**2.00**	**2.00**
☐ ☐	**159 Veli-Pekka Nutikka, Finland RC**	**1.00**	**1.00**
☐ ☐	160 Kimmo Timonen, Finland	.50	.20
☐ ☐	**161 Antti Aalto, Finland RC**	**1.00**	**1.00**
☐ ☐	162 Janne Niinimaa, Finland	.50	.20
☐ ☐	163 Nikolai Zavarukhin, Russia	.35	.20
☐ ☐	**164 V. Epantchinsev, Russia RC**	**1.00**	**1.00**
☐ ☐	**165 A. Korolyuk, Russia RC**	**1.00**	**1.00**
☐ ☐	**166 Dmitri Klevakin, Russia RC**	**1.00**	**1.00**
☐ ☐	**167 Vitali Yachmenev, Russia RC**	**1.50**	**1.50**
☐ ☐	168 Niklas Sundström, Sweden	.50	.20
☐ ☐	**169 A. Söderberg, Sweden RC**	**1.00**	**1.00**
☐ ☐	170 Anders Eriksson, Sweden	.35	.20
☐ ☐	**171 Jesper Mattsson, Sweden RC**	**1.00**	**1.00**
☐ ☐	**172 Mattias Öhlund, Sweden RC**	**3.00**	**3.00**
☐ ☐	173 Jason Bonsignore, U.S.A.	.35	.20
☐ ☐	**174 Bryan Berard, U.S.A. RC**	**3.00**	**3.00**
☐ ☐	175 Richard Park, U.S.A.	.35	.20

☐ ☐	**176 Mike McBain, Canada RC**	**1.00**	**1.00**
☐ ☐	**177 Jason Doig, Canada RC**	**1.00**	**1.00**
☐ ☐	**178 Xavier Delisle, Canada RC**	**1.00**	**1.00**
☐ ☐	**179 Christian Dubé, Canada RC**	**1.50**	**1.50**
☐ ☐	**180 L-P Sévigny, Canada RC**	**1.00**	**1.00**
☐ ☐	**181 Jarome Iginla, Canada RC**	**16.00**	**12.50**
☐ ☐	**182 Marc Savard, Canada RC**	**2.00**	**2.00**
☐ ☐	**183 A. McCauley, Canada RC**	**3.00**	**3.00**
☐ ☐	**184 Brad Mehalko, Canada RC**	**1.00**	**1.00**
☐ ☐	**185 Todd Norman, Canada RC**	**1.00**	**1.00**
☐ ☐	**186 Brian Scott, Canada RC**	**1.00**	**1.00**
☐ ☐	**187 Brad Larsen, Canada RC**	**1.00**	**1.00**
☐ ☐	**188 Jeff Ware, Canada RC**	**1.00**	**1.00**
☐ ☐	**189 S. Samsonov, Russia RC**	**15.00**	**10.00**
☐ ☐	**190 Andrei Petrunin, Russia RC**	**1.00**	**1.00**
☐ ☐	**191 Sean Haggerty, U.S.A. RC**	**1.00**	**1.00**
☐ ☐	**192 Rory Fitzpatrick, U.S.A. RC**	**1.00**	**1.00**
☐ ☐	193 Deron Quint, U.S.A.	.50	.20
☐ ☐	194 J. Langenbrunner, U.S.A.	.50	.20
☐ ☐	**195 Jeff Mitchell, U.S.A. RC**	**1.00**	**1.00**
	Player	**D.C.**	**-**
☐	SP1 Wayne Gretzky, LosA.	75.00	

PREMIER

These cards have have a Die-Cut parallel.

	Insert Set (30 cards):	300.00	60.00
	Player	**D.C.**	**Insert**
☐ ☐	1 Paul Kariya, Anah.	25.00	5.00
☐ ☐	2 Peter Forsberg, Québ.	25.00	5.00
☐ ☐	3 Viktor Kozlov, SanJ.	5.00	1.00
☐ ☐	4 Todd Marchant, Edmo.	.35	.20
☐ ☐	5 Oleg Tverdovsky, Anah.	.35	.20
☐ ☐	6 Todd Harvey, Dall.	.35	.20
☐ ☐	7 Kenny Jönsson, Toro.	.35	.20
☐ ☐	8 Blaine Lacher (G), Bost.	.35	.20
☐ ☐	9 Radek Bonk, Otta.	5.00	1.00
☐ ☐	10 Brett Lindros, NYIs.	5.00	1.00
☐ ☐	11 Valeri Bure, Mont.	5.00	1.00
☐ ☐	12 Brian Rolston, NJer.	5.00	1.00
☐ ☐	13 David Oliver, Edmo.	.35	.20
☐ ☐	14 Ian Laperrière, SLou.	.35	.20
☐ ☐	15 Adam Deadmarsh, Québ.	5.00	1.00
☐ ☐	16 Pavel Bure, Vanc.	15.00	3.00
☐ ☐	17 Wayne Gretzky, LosA.	75.00	15.00
☐ ☐	18 Jeremy Roenick, Chic.	15.00	3.00
☐ ☐	19 Dominik Hasek (G), Buff.	15.00	3.00
☐ ☐	20 Raymond Bourque, Bost.	20.00	4.00
☐ ☐	21 Doug Gilmour, Toro.	10.00	2.00
☐ ☐	22 Teemu Selänne, Winn.	15.00	3.00
☐ ☐	23 Cam Neely, Bost.	15.00	3.00
☐ ☐	24 Sergei Fedorov, Detr.	15.00	3.00
☐ ☐	25 Bernie Nicholls, Chic.	.35	.20
☐ ☐	26 Jaromir Jagr, Pitt.	15.00	3.00
☐ ☐	27 Joe Sakic, Québ.	30.00	6.00
☐ ☐	28 Mark Messier, NYRa.	15.00	3.00
☐ ☐	29 Brett Hull, SLou.	15.00	3.00
☐ ☐	30 Eric Lindros, Phil.	15.00	3.00

1994 - 95 SP – BUYBACKS

	Buyback Autograph	SP
☐	22 Jeremy Roenick, Chic. ✍ {#/71}	
☐	28 Mike Modano, Dall. ✍ {#/61}	
☐	34 Steve Yzerman, Detr. ✍ {#/22}	
☐	34 Steve Yzerman, Detr. ✍ {#/67}	
☐	54 Wayne Gretzky, LosA. ✍ {#/56}	
☐	54 Wayne Gretzky, LosA. ✍ {#/4}	
☐	73 Mark Messier, NYRa. ✍ {#/50}	
☐	75 Mike Richter (G), NYRa. ✍ {#/9}	
☐	85 John LeClair, Phil. ✍ {#/2}	
☐	85 John LeClair, Phil. ✍ {#/150}	
☐	93 Luc Robitaille, Pitt. ✍ {#/36}	
☐	93 Luc Robitaille, Pitt. ✍ {#/24}	
☐	100 Brett Hull, SLou. ✍ {#/92}	
☐	102 Curtis Joseph (G), SLou. ✍ {#/65}	
☐	121 Pavel Bure, Vanc. ✍ {#/69}	
☐	**189 Sergei Samsonov, Russia RC ✍ {#/3}**	
☐	**189 Sergei Samsonov, Russia RC ✍ {#/65}**	
	Buyback Autograph • Die-Cut parallel	**SP**
☐	22 Jeremy Roenick, Chic. ✍ {#/14}	
☐	34 Steve Yzerman, Detr. ✍ {#/2}	
☐	54 Wayne Gretzky, LosA. ✍ {#/1}	
☐	54 Wayne Gretzky, LosA. ✍ {#/1}	
☐	63 Martin Brodeur (G), NJer. ✍ {#/3}	
☐	85 John LeClair, Phil. ✍ {#/10}	
☐	93 Luc Robitaille, Pitt. ✍ {#/19}	
☐	100 Brett Hull, SLou. ✍ {#/1}	
☐	102 Curtis Joseph (G), SLou. ✍ {#/9}	
☐	121 Pavel Bure, Vanc. ✍ {#/4}	
☐	**189 Sergei Samsonov, Russia RC ✍ {#/15}**	
	Buyback Autograph • Premier insert	**SP**
☐	1 Pavel Bure, Vanc. ✍ {#/1}	

1994 - 95 SPORTS ILLUSTRATED FOR KIDS

These cards were distributed as part of nine-card perforated sheets included in *Sports Illustrated for Kids*. While these cards were intended for editorial purposes, they have made their way onto the secondary market. Cards issued in the 12 issues between July 1994 and June 1995 were numbered 271-378.

	1994-95 Sports Illustrated for Kids	
☐	Aug. 1994 • 284 Mike Richter (G), NYRa.	2.00
☐	Oct. 1994 • 303 Pavel Bure, Vanc.	3.00
☐	Nov. 1994 •309 Doug Gilmour, Toro.	2.00
☐	Dec. 1994 • 317 Phil Esposito	2.00
☐	Jan. 1994 • 333 Jeremy Roenick, Chic.	2.00
☐	Feb. 1994 • 338 J. Vanbiesbrouck (G), Flor.	2.00
☐	Mar. 1994 • 347 Mark Messier, NYRa.	2.00
☐	Apr. 1994 • 356 Félix Potvin (G), Toro.	3.00
☐	May 1994 • 366 Scott Stevens, NJer.	1.00
☐	Jun. 1994 • 377 Paul Kariya	6.00

1994 - 95 STARTING LINEUP

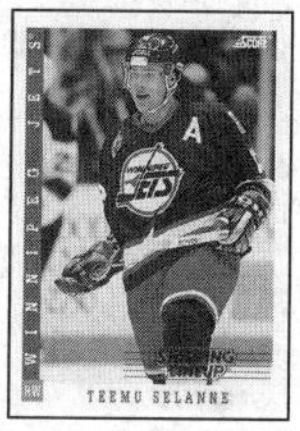

One Score card (1993-94 design) was packaged with each figure.

Complete Set (21 cards): 35.00

	Player	Card
☐	66 Doug Gilmour, Toro.	1.00
☐	125 Adam Oates, Bost.	1.00
☐	222 Alexander Mogilny, Buff.	1.00
☐	225 Tom Barrasso (G), Pitt.	1.00
☐	235 Brian Leetch, NYRa.	1.00
☐	310 Steve Yzerman, Detr.	4.50
☐	333 Pavel Bure, Vanc.	1.50
☐	335 Brett Hull, SLou.	3.00
☐	345 Pat LaFontaine, Buff.	1.50
☐	350 Mario Lemieux, Pitt.	6.00
☐	Raymond Bourque, Bost.	3.50
☐	Sergei Fedorov, Detr.	2.00
☐	Grant Fuhr (G), Buff.	2.00
☐	Arturs Irbe (G), SanJ.	1.00
☐	Jaromir Jagr, Pitt.	3.00
☐	Eric Lindros, Phil.	2.00
☐	Mark Messier, NYRa.	3.00
☐	Mike Richter (G), NYRa.	1.00
☐	Luc Robitaille, LosA.	1.50
☐	Jeremy Roenick, Chic.	2.00
☐	Teemu Selänne, Winn.	1.50

FIGURES

Figures were available in American (English text) and Canadian (bilingual text) packaging. The figures and cards in each type of package are the same. Priced below are retail selling prices for packaged figures (each package includes one card) and loose figures.

Canadian Set (13 packages): 250.00

American Set (20 packages): 400.00

Figure Set (21 loose figures): 75.00

	Figure	US	CAN	Loose
☐	Tom Barrasso (G), Pitt.	40.00	-	8.00
☐	Raymond Bourque, Bost.	30.00	-	4.00
☐	Pavel Bure, Vanc.	18.00	15.00	3.00
☐	Sergei Fedorov, Detr.	18.00	15.00	3.00
☐	Grant Fuhr (G), Buff.	-	85.00	10.00
☐	Doug Gilmour, Toro.	18.00	15.00	3.00
☐	Brett Hull, SLou.	15.00	-	3.00
☐	Arturs Irbe (G), SanJ.	40.00	-	8.00
☐	Jaromir Jagr, Pitt.	20.00	-	3.00
☐	Pat LaFontaine, Buff.	15.00	-	3.00
☐	Brian Leetch, NYRa.	15.00	15.00	3.00
☐	Mario Lemieux, Pitt.	30.00	20.00	4.00
☐	Eric Lindros, Phil.	30.00	20.00	4.00
☐	Mark Messier, NYRa.	60.00	-	5.00
☐	Alexander Mogilny, Buff.	20.00	15.00	3.00
☐	Adam Oates, Bost.	15.00	15.00	3.00
☐	Mike Richter (G), NYRa.	40.00	35.00	8.00
☐	Luc Robitaille, LosA.	20.00	15.00	3.00

Jeremy Roenick, Chic.	15.00	-	3.00
Teemu Selänne, Winn.	20.00	20.00	3.00
Steve Yzerman, Detr.	15.00	20.00	3.00
Collector's Club			**NRMT-MT**
John Vanbiesbrouck (G), Flor.			35.00

1994 - 95 TOPPS FINEST

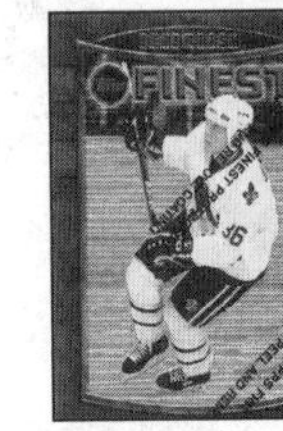

These cards have up to five versions: the regular card (1-165), a Refractor parallel (1-165), a Stanley Cup Champions card (1-165), a Conference Winners card (Red Wings and Devils only) and a Division Winners card (Red Wings, Flames, Flyers and Nordiques only). Stanley Cup Champions, Conference Winners and Division Winners all have identical pricing. Box-top versions for each card also exist.

Imprint: © 1995 THE TOPPS COMPANY, INC.

Complete Set (165 cards):	**200.00**	**80.00**
Common Player:	**6.00**	**.35**

Player	Refr.	Reg.
1 Peter Forsberg, Québ.	6.00	3.50
2 Oleg Tverdovsky, Anah.	6.00	.35
3 Radek Bonk, Otta. RC	**6.00**	**4.00**
4 Brian Rolston, NJer.	6.00	.50
5 K. Jönsson, Toro. [b/ Yashin]	6.00	.50
6 Patrik Juhlin, Phil. RC	**6.00**	**.75**
7 Paul Kariya, Anah.	6.00	3.50
8 Janne Laukkanen, Québ.	6.00	.35
9 Brett Lindros, NYIs.	6.00	.50
10 Andrei Nikolishin, Hart.	6.00	.35
11 Jeff Friesen, SanJ.	6.00	.50
12 Jamie Storr (G), LosA.	6.00	.50
13 Chris Therien, Phil.	6.00	.35
14 Alexander Cherbayev, SanJ.	6.00	.35
15 Kevin Brown, LosA. RC	**6.00**	**.75**
16 Mark Messier, NYRa.	6.00	2.50
17 Kevin Hatcher, Dall.	6.00	.35
18 Scott Stevens, NJer.	6.00	1.00
19 Keith Tkachuk, Winn.	6.00	1.50
20 Guy Hebert (G), Anah.	6.00	.50
21 Jason Arnott, Edmo.	6.00	1.00
22 Cam Neely, Bost.	6.00	2.50
23 Adam Graves, NYRa.	6.00	1.00
24 Pavel Bure, Vanc.	6.00	2.00
25 Mark Tinordi, Wash.	6.00	.35
26 Félix Potvin (G), Toro.	6.00	1.50
27 Nikolai Khabibulin (G), Winn.	6.00	1.00
28 Theoren Fleury, Calg.	6.00	1.50
29 Curtis Joseph (G), SLou.	6.00	2.50
30 Patrick Roy (G), Mont.	6.00	7.50
31 Adam Deadmarsh, Québ.	6.00	.50
32 Pat Falloon, SanJ.	6.00	.35
33 Jaromir Jagr, Pitt.	6.00	2.50
34 Chris Chelios, Chic.	6.00	1.50
35 Raymond Bourque, Bost.	6.00	3.00
36 Mike Vernon (G), Detr.	6.00	1.00
37 Steve Thomas, NYIs.	6.00	.50
38 Eric Lindros, Phil.	6.00	2.50
39 Dave Andreychuk, Toro.	6.00	.50
40 John Vanbiesbrouck (G), Flor.	6.00	1.00
41 Wayne Gretzky, LosA.	6.00	10.00
42 Brett Hull, SLou.	6.00	2.50
43 Dominik Hasek (G), Buff.	6.00	2.50
44 Kirk Muller, Mont.	6.00	.50
45 Rob Blake, LosA.	6.00	1.50
46 Viktor Kozlov, SanJ.	6.00	.50
47 Todd Harvey, Dall.	6.00	.50
48 Valeri Bure, Mont.	6.00	.50
49 Brian Leetch, NYRa.	6.00	1.50
50 Ray Sheppard, Detr.	6.00	.35
51 Ed Belfour (G), Chic.	6.00	2.50
52 Rick Tocchet, LosA.	6.00	.50
53 Daren Puppa (G), Tamp.	6.00	.50
54 Russ Courtnall, Dall.	6.00	.50
55 Jason Allison, Wash.	6.00	1.50
56 A. Yashin, Otta. [b/ Coffey]	6.00	1.50
57 Sandis Ozolinsh, SanJ.	6.00	.50
58 Chris Gratton, Tamp.	6.00	.50
59 Michael Peca, Vanc.	6.00	1.00
60 Glen Wesley, Hart.	6.00	.35
61 Kirk McLean (G), Vanc.	6.00	.50
62 Chris Pronger, Hart.	6.00	1.50
63 Steve Larmer, NYRa.	6.00	1.00
64 Michal Grosek, Winn. RC	**6.00**	**.75**
65 Sergei Fedorov, Detr.	6.00	2.50
66 Stu Barnes, Flor.	6.00	.35
67 Adam Oates, Bost.	6.00	1.00
68 P. Coffey, Detr. [b/ Mogilny]	6.00	1.50
69 Joe Sakic, Québ.	6.00	4.00
70 Pat LaFontaine, Buff.	6.00	1.50
71 Martin Brodeur (G), NJer.	6.00	4.00
72 Bob Corkum, Anah.	6.00	.35
73 Jeremy Roenick, Chic.	6.00	2.00
74 Shayne Corson, Edmo.	6.00	.50
75 German Titov, Calg.	6.00	.35
76 Teemu Selänne, Winn.	6.00	2.00
77 Éric Fichaud (G), Toro. RC	**6.00**	**2.00**
78 Pierre Turgeon, NYIs.	6.00	1.00
79 Alexander Selivanov, Tamp. RC	**6.00**	**.75**
80 Kevin Stevens, Pitt.	6.00	.50
81 Jari Kurri, LosA.	6.00	2.50
82 Gary Roberts, Calg.	6.00	1.00
83 Geoff Courtnall, Vanc.	6.00	.35
84 Steve Yzerman, Detr.	6.00	6.00
85 Rod Brind'Amour, Phil.	6.00	.50
86 Mike Richter (G), NYRa.	6.00	1.00
87 Bernie Nicholls, Chic.	6.00	.50
88 Alexandre Daigle, Otta.	6.00	.35
89 Luc Robitaille, Pitt.	6.00	2.00
90 John MacLean, NJer.	6.00	.35
91 Phil Housley, Calg.	6.00	.50
92 Brendan Shanahan, SLou.	6.00	2.50
93 Joé Juneau, Wash.	6.00	.50
94 Stéphane J.J. Richer, NJer.	6.00	.50
95 Blaine Lacher (G), Bost. RC	**6.00**	**2.00**
96 Mike Gartner, Toro.	6.00	2.00
97 René Corbet, Québ.	6.00	.35
98 Vincent Damphousse, Mont.	6.00	1.50
99 A. Mogilny, Buff. [b/ Jönsson]	6.00	1.00
100 Doug Gilmour, Toro.	6.00	1.50
101 Petr Nedved, NYRa.	6.00	.50
102 Alexei Zhamnov, Winn.	6.00	.50
103 Wendel Clark, Québ.	6.00	2.00
104 Arturs Irbe (G), SanJ.	6.00	1.00
105 Brian Bellows, Mont.	6.00	.50
106 Mike Modano, Dall.	6.00	2.50
107 Ravil Gusmanov, Winn. RC	**6.00**	**.75**
108 Geoff Sanderson, Hart.	6.00	.50
109 Mark Recchi, Mont.	6.00	1.00
110 Mats Sundin, Toro.	6.00	2.50
111 Pavol Demitra, Otta.	6.00	1.00
112 Richard Park	6.00	.35
113 Doug Bonner RC	**6.00**	**.75**
114 Bryan Berard RC	**6.00**	**4.00**
115 Rory Fitzpatrick RC	**6.00**	**.75**
116 Deron Quint	6.00	.50
117 Jason Bonsignore	6.00	.35
118 Adam Deadmarsh	6.00	1.00
119 Sean Haggerty RC	**6.00**	**.75**
120 Jamie Langenbrunner	6.00	.50
121 Jeff Mitchell RC	**6.00**	**.75**
122 Antti Aalto RC	**6.00**	**.75**
123 Tommi Rajamäki RC	**6.00**	**.75**
124 J. Markkanen RC	**6.00**	**2.00**
125 Miikka. Kiprusoff (G) RC	**6.00**	**10.00**
126 Jere Karalahti RC	**6.00**	**.75**
127 Petri Kokko RC	**6.00**	**.75**
128 Janne Niinimaa	6.00	.50
129 Kimmo Timonen	6.00	.50
130 M. Järventie RC	**6.00**	**2.00**
131 Mikko Helisten RC	**6.00**	**.75**
132 Niko Halttunen RC	**6.00**	**.75**
133 Tommi Miettinen	6.00	.35
134 Miska Kangasniemi RC	**6.00**	**.75**
135 V-P Nutikka RC	**6.00**	**.75**
136 Jani Hassinen RC	**6.00**	**.75**
137 Timo Salonen RC	**6.00**	**.75**
138 Tommi Sova RC	**6.00**	**.75**
139 Toni Mäkiaho RC	**6.00**	**.75**
140 T. Hämäläinen RC	**6.00**	**.75**
141 Juha Vuorivirta RC	**6.00**	**.75**
142 Jussi Tarvainen RC	**6.00**	**.75**
143 Miika Elomo RC	**6.00**	**.75**
144 Jason Botterill	6.00	.35
145 Dan Cloutier (G) RC	**6.00**	**6.00**
146 Jamie Storr (G)	6.00	.50
147 Chad Allan RC	**6.00**	**.75**
148 Nolan Baumgartner RC	**6.00**	**.75**
149 Ed Jovanovski RC	**6.00**	**6.00**
150 Bryan McCabe	6.00	.50
151 Wade Redden RC	**6.00**	**4.00**
152 Jamie Rivers RC	**6.00**	**.75**
153 Lee Sorochan RC	**6.00**	**.75**
154 Jason Allison	6.00	2.00
155 Alexandre Daigle	6.00	.50
156 Larry Courville RC	**6.00**	**.75**
157 Éric Dazé RC	**6.00**	**6.00**
158 Shean Donovan RC	**6.00**	**2.00**
159 Jeff Friesen	6.00	1.00
160 Todd Harvey	6.00	.50
161 Marty Murray	6.00	.35
162 Jeff O'Neill	6.00	6.00
163 Denis Pederson RC	**6.00**	**.75**
164 Darcy Tucker RC	**6.00**	**4.00**
165 Ryan Smyth RC	**6.00**	**8.00**

REDEMPTIONS

Player	SCC
1 Peter Forsberg, Québ.	10.00
2 Oleg Tverdovsky, Anah.	1.00
3 Radek Bonk, Otta. RC	**6.00**
4 Brian Rolston, NJer.	2.00
5 K. Jönsson, Toro. [b/ Yashin]	1.00
6 Patrik Juhlin, Phil. RC	**2.00**
7 Paul Kariya, Anah.	10.00
8 Janne Laukkanen, Québ.	1.00
9 Brett Lindros, NYIs.	2.00
10 Andrei Nikolishin, Hart.	1.00
11 Jeff Friesen, SanJ.	2.00
12 Jamie Storr (G), LosA.	1.00
13 Chris Therien, Phil.	1.00
14 Alexander Cherbayev, SanJ.	1.00
15 Kevin Brown, LosA. RC	**2.00**
16 Mark Messier, NYRa.	7.00
17 Kevin Hatcher, Dall.	1.00
18 Scott Stevens, NJer.	3.00
19 Keith Tkachuk, Winn.	4.00
20 Guy Hebert (G), Anah.	1.00
21 Jason Arnott, Edmo.	3.00
22 Cam Neely, Bost.	7.00
23 Adam Graves, NYRa.	3.00
24 Pavel Bure, Vanc.	6.00
25 Mark Tinordi, Wash.	1.00
26 Félix Potvin (G), Toro.	4.00
27 Nikolai Khabibulin (G), Winn.	3.00
28 Theoren Fleury, Calg.	4.00
29 Curtis Joseph (G), SLou.	7.00
30 Patrick Roy (G), Mont.	22.00
31 Adam Deadmarsh, Québ.	2.00
32 Pat Falloon, SanJ.	1.00
33 Jaromir Jagr, Pitt.	7.00
34 Chris Chelios, Chic.	4.00
35 Raymond Bourque, Bost.	9.00
36 Mike Vernon (G), Detr.	3.00
37 Steve Thomas, NYIs.	1.00
38 Eric Lindros, Phil.	7.00
39 Dave Andreychuk, Toro.	2.00
40 John Vanbiesbrouck (G), Flor.	3.00
41 Wayne Gretzky, LosA.	30.00
42 Brett Hull, SLou.	7.00
43 Dominik Hasek (G), Buff.	7.00
44 Kirk Muller, Mont.	2.00
45 Rob Blake, LosA.	4.00
46 Viktor Kozlov, SanJ.	2.00
47 Todd Harvey, Dall.	1.00
48 Valeri Bure, Mont.	2.00
49 Brian Leetch, NYRa.	4.00
50 Ray Sheppard, Detr.	1.00
51 Ed Belfour (G), Chic.	7.00
52 Rick Tocchet, LosA.	2.00
53 Daren Puppa (G), Tamp.	1.00
54 Russ Courtnall, Dall.	1.00
55 Jason Allison, Wash.	4.00
56 A. Yashin, Otta. [b/ Coffey]	4.00
57 Sandis Ozolinsh, SanJ.	1.00
58 Chris Gratton, Tamp.	1.00
59 Michael Peca, Vanc.	3.00
60 Glen Wesley, Hart.	1.00
61 Kirk McLean (G), Vanc.	2.00
62 Chris Pronger, Hart.	4.00
63 Steve Larmer, NYRa.	3.00
64 Michal Grosek, Winn. RC	**2.00**
65 Sergei Fedorov, Detr.	7.00
66 Stu Barnes, Flor.	1.00
67 Adam Oates, Bost.	3.00
68 P. Coffey, Detr. [b/ Mogilny]	4.00
69 Joe Sakic, Québ.	12.00
70 Pat LaFontaine, Buff.	4.00
71 Martin Brodeur (G), NJer.	12.00
72 Bob Corkum, Anah.	1.00
73 Jeremy Roenick, Chic.	6.00
74 Shayne Corson, Edmo.	2.00
75 German Titov, Calg.	1.00
76 Teemu Selänne, Winn.	6.00
77 Éric Fichaud (G), Toro. RC	**2.00**
78 Pierre Turgeon, NYIs.	3.00
79 Alexander Selivanov, Tamp. RC	**2.00**
80 Kevin Stevens, Pitt.	1.00
81 Jari Kurri, LosA.	7.00
82 Gary Roberts, Calg.	3.00
83 Geoff Courtnall, Vanc.	1.00
84 Steve Yzerman, Detr.	18.00
85 Rod Brind'Amour, Phil.	2.00
86 Mike Richter (G), NYRa.	3.00
87 Bernie Nicholls, Chic.	1.00
88 Alexandre Daigle, Otta.	1.00
89 Luc Robitaille, Pitt.	6.00
90 John MacLean, NJer.	1.00
91 Phil Housley, Calg.	2.00
92 Brendan Shanahan, SLou.	7.00
93 Joé Juneau, Wash.	1.00
94 Stéphane J.J. Richer, NJer.	1.00
95 Blaine Lacher (G), Bost. RC	**2.00**
96 Mike Gartner, Toro.	6.00
97 René Corbet, Québ.	1.00
98 Vincent Damphousse, Mont.	4.00
99 A. Mogilny, Buff. [b/ Jönsson]	3.00
100 Doug Gilmour, Toro.	4.00
101 Petr Nedved, NYRa.	2.00
102 Alexei Zhamnov, Winn.	2.00
103 Wendel Clark, Québ.	6.00
104 Arturs Irbe (G), SanJ.	3.00
105 Brian Bellows, Mont.	1.00
106 Mike Modano, Dall.	7.00
107 Ravil Gusmanov, Winn. RC	**2.00**
108 Geoff Sanderson, Hart.	1.00
109 Mark Recchi, Mont.	3.00
110 Mats Sundin, Toro.	7.00
111 Pavol Demitra, Otta.	3.00
112 Richard Park	1.00
113 Doug Bonner RC	**2.00**
114 Bryan Berard RC	**6.00**
115 Rory Fitzpatrick RC	**2.00**
116 Deron Quint	1.00
117 Jason Bonsignore	1.00
118 Adam Deadmarsh	3.00
119 Sean Haggerty RC	**2.00**
120 Jamie Langenbrunner	2.00
121 Jeff Mitchell RC	**2.00**
122 Antti Aalto RC	**2.00**
123 Tommi Rajamäki RC	**2.00**
124 J. Markkanen RC	**2.00**
125 Miikka. Kiprusoff (G) RC	**15.00**
126 Jere Karalahti RC	**2.00**
127 Petri Kokko RC	**2.00**
128 Janne Niinimaa	2.00
129 Kimmo Timonen	1.00
130 M. Järventie RC	**2.00**
131 Mikko Helisten RC	**2.00**
132 Niko Halttunen RC	**2.00**
133 Tommi Miettinen	1.00
134 Miska Kangasniemi RC	**2.00**
135 V-P Nutikka RC	**2.00**
136 Jani Hassinen RC	**2.00**
137 Timo Salonen RC	**2.00**
138 Tommi Sova RC	**2.00**
139 Toni Mäkiaho RC	**2.00**
140 T. Hämäläinen RC	**2.00**
141 Juha Vuorivirta RC	**2.00**
142 Jussi Tarvainen RC	**2.00**
143 Miika Elomo RC	**2.00**
144 Jason Botterill	1.00
145 Dan Cloutier (G) RC	**8.00**
146 Jamie Storr (G)	2.00
147 Chad Allan RC	**2.00**
148 Nolan Baumgartner RC	**2.00**
149 Ed Jovanovski RC	**8.00**
150 Bryan McCabe	2.00
151 Wade Redden RC	**6.00**
152 Jamie Rivers RC	**2.00**
153 Lee Sorochan RC	**2.00**
154 Jason Allison	6.00
155 Alexandre Daigle	1.00
156 Larry Courville RC	**2.00**
157 Éric Dazé RC	**8.00**
158 Shean Donovan RC	**2.00**
159 Jeff Friesen	3.00
160 Todd Harvey	2.00
161 Marty Murray	1.00
162 Jeff O'Neill	8.00
163 Denis Pederson RC	**2.00**
164 Darcy Tucker RC	**4.00**
165 Ryan Smyth RC	**10.00**

BOWMAN'S BEST BLUE

These cards have a Refractor parallel.

Insert Set (45 cards):	**650.00**	**100.00**
Blue Insert	**Ref.**	**Insert**
1 Raymond Bourque, Bost.	45.00	5.00
2 Mark Messier, NYRa.	35.00	5.00
3 Cam Neely, Bost.	35.00	5.00
4 Theoren Fleury, Calg.	20.00	3.00
5 Jeremy Roenick, Chic.	30.00	5.00
6 Mike Modano, Dall.	35.00	5.00
7 Sergei Fedorov, Detr.	35.00	5.00
8 John Vanbiesbrouck (G), Flor.	15.00	3.00
9 Pierre Turgeon, NYIs.	15.00	3.00
10 Kirk Muller, Mont.	12.00	3.00
11 Pavel Bure, Vanc.	30.00	5.00
12 Brian Leetch, NYRa.	20.00	3.00
13 Mike Richter (G), NYRa.	15.00	3.00
14 Teemu Selänne, Winn.	30.00	5.00
15 Brett Hull, SLou.	35.00	5.00
16 Eric Lindros, Phil.	35.00	5.00
17 Keith Tkachuk, Winn.	20.00	3.00
18 Joe Sakic, Québ.	60.00	10.00
19 Doug Gilmour, Toro.	20.00	3.00
20 Jaromir Jagr, Pitt.	35.00	5.00
Mirror Image Insert	**Ref.**	**Insert**
1 T. Fleury / P. Kariya	35.00	5.00
2 D. Gilmour / P. Forsberg	35.00	5.00
3 J. Sakic / R. Bonk	35.00	5.00
4 B. Leetch / O. Tverdovsky	12.00	3.00
5 C. Neely / J. Wiemer	20.00	3.00
Red Insert	**Ref.**	**Insert**
1 Paul Kariya, Anah.	50.00	10.00
2 Oleg Tverdovsky, Anah.	12.00	3.00
3 Blaine Lacher (G), Bost.	12.00	3.00
4 Todd Harvey, Dall.	12.00	3.00
5 Roman Oksiuta, Edmo.	12.00	3.00
6 David Oliver, Edmo.	12.00	3.00
7 Jamie Storr (G), LosA.	12.00	3.00
8 Brian Savage, Mont.	12.00	3.00
9 Brian Rolston, NJer.	12.00	3.00
10 Brett Lindros, NYIs.	12.00	3.00
11 Radek Bonk, Otta.	12.00	3.00
12 Peter Forsberg, Québ.	50.00	10.00
13 Adam Deadmarsh, Québ.	12.00	3.00
14 Jeff Friesen, SanJ.	12.00	3.00
15 Denis Chassé, SLou.	12.00	3.00
16 Jason Wiemer, Tamp.	12.00	3.00
17 Alexander Selivanov, Tamp.	12.00	3.00
18 Kenny Jönsson, Toro.	12.00	3.00
19 Todd Marchant, Edmo.	12.00	3.00
20 Mariusz Czerkawski, Bost.	12.00	3.00

DIVISION'S FINEST

Insert Set (20 cards):	**90.00**
ClearChrome Insert (1:12)	**DF**
1 Patrick Roy (G), Mont.	20.00
2 Raymond Bourque, Bost.	5.00
3 Adam Oates, Bost.	2.00
4 Luc Robitaille, Pitt.	5.00
5 Mark Recchi, Mont.	2.00
6 Mike Richter (G), NYRa.	2.00
7 Scott Stevens, NJer.	2.00
8 Eric Lindros, Phil.	5.00
9 Adam Graves, NYRa.	2.00
10 Stéphane J.J. Richer, NJer.	2.00
11 Ed Belfour (G), Chic.	5.00
12 Al MacInnis, SLou.	2.00
13 Sergei Fedorov, Detr.	5.00
14 Brendan Shanahan, SLou.	5.00
15 Brett Hull, SLou.	5.00
16 Arturs Irbe (G), SanJ.	2.00
17 Sandis Ozolinsh, SanJ.	2.00
18 Wayne Gretzky, LosA.	30.00
19 Gary Roberts, Calg.	2.00
20 Pavel Bure, Vanc.	5.00

RING LEADERS

Insert Set (20 cards):	**200.00**
Insert (1:24)	**NRMT-MT**
1 Mark Messier, NYRa.	15.00
2 Kevin Lowe, NYRa.	5.00
3 Jari Kurri, LosA.	15.00
4 Grant Fuhr (G), Buff.	10.00

□ 5 Wayne Gretzky, LosA. 75.00
□ 6 Paul Coffey, Detr. 10.00
□ 7 Craig Simpson, Buff. 3.00
□ 8 Craig MacTavish, Phil. 3.00
□ 9 Jeff Beukeboom, NYRa. 3.00
□ 10 Joe Mullen, Pitt. 5.00
□ 11 Marty McSorley, LosA. 3.00
□ 12 J. Steve Smith, Chic. 3.00
□ 13 Kevin Stevens, Pitt. 3.00
□ 14 Patrick Roy (G), Mont. 55.00
□ 15 Jaromir Jagr, Pitt. 15.00
□ 16 Ron Francis, Pitt. 10.00
□ 17 Bill Ranford (G), Edmo. 5.00
□ 18 Larry Murphy, Pitt. 3.00
□ 19 Tom Barrasso (G), Pitt. 5.00
□ 20 Adam Graves, NYRa. 5.00

1994 - 95 TOPPS STADIUM CLUB

These card have up to six versions: the regular card (1-270), a First Day Issue (1-270), a Stanley Cup Champions card (1-270), a Conference Winners card (Red Wings and Devils only); a Division Winners card (Red Wings, Flames, Flyers and Nordiques only) and a Members Only card (1-270). Stanley Cup, Conference and Division Winners all have the same value. An intended second series for 1994-95 Topps Stadium Club was never released. Instead, Topps released Topps Finest.

Imprint: © 1994 THE TOPPS COMPANY, INC.

Complete Set (270 cards): 1875.00 700.00 25.00
Common Player: 4.00 1.50 .20

□□□ 1 Mark Messier w/ Cup 40.00 14.00 .50
□□□ 2 Brad May, Buff. 5.00 2.00 .20
□□□ 3 Mike Ricci, Québ. 10.00 4.00 .20
□□□ 4 Scott Stevens, NJer. 15.00 6.00 .20
□□□ 5 Keith Tkachuk, Winn. 20.00 8.00 .20
□□□ 6 Guy Hebert (G), Anah. 5.00 2.00 .20
□□□ 7 Jason Arnott, Edmo. 15.00 6.00 .20
□□□ 8 Cam Neely, Bost. 40.00 14.00 .50
□□□ 9 Adam Graves, NYRa. 15.00 6.00 .20
□□□ 10 Pavel Bure, Vanc. 30.00 10.00 .50
□□□ 11 Jeff Odgers, SanJ. 5.00 2.00 .20
□□□ 12 Dmitri Khristich, Wash. 5.00 2.00 .20
□□□ 13 Patrick Poulin, Chic. 5.00 2.00 .20
□□□ 14 Mike Donnelly, LosA. 4.00 1.50 .20
□□□ 15 Félix Potvin (G), Toro. 20.00 8.00 .20
□□□ 16 Keith Primeau, Detr. 15.00 6.00 .20
□□□ 17 Fred Knipscheer, Bost. 4.00 1.50 .20
□□□ 18 Mike Keane, Mont. 5.00 2.00 .20
□□□ 19 Vitali Prokhorov, SLou. 4.00 1.50 .20
□□□ 20 Ray Ferraro & sons 5.00 2.00 .20
□□□ 21 Shane Churla, Dall. 4.00 1.50 .20
□□□ 22 Rob Niedermayer, Flor. 5.00 2.00 .20
□□□ 23 Adam Creighton, Tamp. 4.00 1.50 .20
□□□ 24 T. Söderström (G), Phil. 5.00 2.00 .20
□□□ 25 Theoren Fleury, Calg. 20.00 8.00 .20
□□□ 26 Jim Storm, Hart. 4.00 1.50 .20
□□□ 27 Bret Hedican, Vanc. 4.00 1.50 .20
□□□ 28 Sean Hill, Anah. 4.00 1.50 .20
□□□ 29 Bill Ranford (G), Edmo. 15.00 6.00 .20
□□□ 30 Derek Plante, Buff. 5.00 2.00 .20
□□□ 31 Dave McLlwain, Otta. 4.00 1.50 .20
□□□ 32 Iain Fraser, Québ. 4.00 1.50 .20
□□□ 33 Patrick Roy (G), Mont. 120.00 45.00 1.50
□□□ 34 Martin Straka, Pitt. 10.00 4.00 .20
□□□ 35 Bruce Driver, NJer. 4.00 1.50 .20
□□□ 36 Brian Skrudland, Flor. 5.00 2.00 .20
□□□ 37 Bob Errey, SanJ. 5.00 2.00 .20
□□□ 38 R. Cunneyworth, Chic. 5.00 2.00 .20
□□□ 39 John Slaney, Wash. 4.00 1.50 .20
□□□ 40 Ray Sheppard, Detr. 5.00 2.00 .20
□□□ 41 S. Nemchinov, NYRa. 5.00 2.00 .20
□□□ 42 Dave Ellett, Toro. 5.00 2.00 .20
□□□ 43 V. Riendeau (G), Bost. 5.00 2.00 .20
□□□ 44 Trent Yawney, Calg. 4.00 1.50 .20
□□□ 45 Dave Gagner, Dall. 5.00 2.00 .20
□□□ 46 Igor Korolev, SLou. 5.00 2.00 .20
□□□ 47 Gary Shuchuk, LosA. 4.00 1.50 .20
□□□ 48 Rob Zamuner, Tamp. 5.00 2.00 .20
□□□ 49 Frantisek Kucera, Hart. 4.00 1.50 .20
□□□ 50 Joe Mullen & sons 15.00 6.00 .20
□□□ 51 Ron Hextall (G), NYIs. 20.00 8.00 .20
□□□ 52 J.J. Daigneault, Mont. 5.00 2.00 .20
□□□ 53 Patrik Carnbäck, Anah. 4.00 1.50 .20
□□□ 54 Steven Rice, Edmo. 4.00 1.50 .20
□□□ 55 PP: B. Leetch, NYRa. 20.00 8.00 .20
□□□ 56 PP: Al MacInnis, Calg. 15.00 6.00 .20
□□□ 57 PP: L. Robitaille, LosA. 30.00 12.00 .50
□□□ 58 PP: Andreychuk, Toro. 10.00 4.00 .20
□□□ 59 PP: J. Roenick, Chic. 30.00 12.00 .50
□□□ 60 PP: M. Lemieux, Pitt. 120.00 45.00 1.50
□□□ 61 Dave Manson, Winn. 5.00 2.00 .20
□□□ 62 Pat Falloon, SanJ. 5.00 2.00 .20
□□□ 63 Jesse Bélanger, Flor. 4.00 1.50 .20
□□□ 64 Philippe Boucher, Buff. 4.00 1.50 .20
□□□ 65 Sergio Momesso, Vanc. 4.00 1.50 .20
□□□ 66 Evgeny Davydov, Otta. 4.00 1.50 .20
□□□ 67 Alexei Gusarov, Québ. 5.00 2.00 .20
□□□ 68 Jaromir Jagr, Pitt. 40.00 15.00 .50
□□□ 69 R. Ladouceur, Anah. 5.00 2.00 .20
□□□ 70 Chris Chelios, Chic. 20.00 8.00 .20
□□□ 71 John Druce, LosA. 4.00 1.50 .20
□□□ 72 Kris Draper, Detr. 5.00 2.00 .20
□□□ 73 Joey Kocur, NYRa. 5.00 2.00 .20
□□□ 74 Rick Tabaracci (G), Wash.5.00 2.00 .20
□□□ 75 Mikael Andersson, Tamp. 4.00 1.50 .20
□□□ 76 Mark Osborne, Toro. 4.00 1.50 .20
□□□ 77 R. Bourque, Bost. 45.00 18.00 .50
□□□ 78 Dmitry Yushkevich, Phil. 5.00 2.00 .20
□□□ 79 Mike Vernon (G), Calg. 15.00 6.00 .20
□□□ 80 Steve Thomas & son 5.00 2.00 .20
□□□ 81 Steve Duchesne, SLou. 5.00 2.00 .20
□□□ 82 Dean Evason, Dall. 4.00 1.50 .20
□□□ 83 Jason Smith, NJer. 5.00 2.00 .20
□□□ 84 Bryan Marchment, Hart. 5.00 2.00 .20
□□□ 85 Boris Mironov, Edmo. 5.00 2.00 .20
□□□ 86 Jeff Norton, SanJ. 4.00 1.50 .20
□□□ 87 Donald Audette, Buff. 15.00 6.00 .20
□□□ 88 Eric Lindros, Phil. 40.00 15.00 .50
□□□ 89 Garry Valk, Anah. 4.00 1.50 .20
□□□ 90 Mats Sundin, Québ. 40.00 14.00 .50
□□□ 91 Gerald Diduck, Vanc. 4.00 1.50 .20
□□□ 92 Jeff Shantz, Chic. 4.00 1.50 .20
□□□ 93 S. Niedermayer, NJer. 10.00 4.00 .20
□□□ 94 Troy Mallette, Otta. 4.00 1.50 .20
□□□ 95 Vanbiesbrouck & sons 15.00 6.00 .20
□□□ 96 Ron Francis, Pitt. 20.00 8.00 .20
□□□ 97 Vyacheslav Kozlov, Detr. 5.00 2.00 .20
□□□ 98 Ken Baumgartner, Toro. 4.00 1.50 .20
□□□ 99 Wayne Gretzky, LosA. 160.00 60.00 2.50
□□□ 100 Brett Hull, SLou. 40.00 14.00 .50
□□□ 101 Marc Bergevin, Tamp. 4.00 1.50 .20
□□□ 102 Owen Nolan, Québ. 20.00 8.00 .20
□□□ 103 Bryan Smolinski, Bost. 5.00 2.00 .20
□□□ 104 Lyle Odelein, Mont. 5.00 2.00 .20
□□□ 105 Mike Ridley, Wash. 5.00 2.00 .20
□□□ 106 Trevor Kidd (G), Calg. 10.00 4.00 .20
□□□ 107 Derian Hatcher, Dall. 10.00 4.00 .20
□□□ 108 Derek King, NYIs. 5.00 2.00 .20
□□□ 109 Rob Zettler, Phil. 4.00 1.50 .20
□□□ 110 GE: A. Daigle, Otta. 5.00 2.00 .20
□□□ 111 GE: C. Pronger, Hart. 20.00 8.00 .20
□□□ 112 GE: C. Gratton, Tamp. 5.00 2.00 .20
□□□ 113 GE: John Slaney, Wash.4.00 1.50 .20
□□□ 114 GE: Thibault (G), Québ.15.00 6.00 .20
□□□ 115 GE: Arnott, Edmo. 15.00 6.00 .20
□□□ 116 GE: Alexei Yashin, Otta.20.00 8.00 .20
□□□ 117 GE: R. Niedermayer, Flor.5.00 2.00 .20
□□□ 118 GE: Allison, Wash. 35.00 12.00 .50
□□□ 119 GE: Brodeur (G), NJer. 60.00 20.00 1.00
□□□ 120 Pat Verbeek, Hart. 10.00 4.00 .20
□□□ 121 K. Buchberger, Edmo. 5.00 2.00 .20
□□□ 122 Doug Lidster, NYRa. 4.00 1.50 .20
□□□ 123 Sergei* Makarov, SanJ.15.00 6.00 .20
□□□ 124 Kris King, Winn. 5.00 2.00 .20
□□□ 125 D. Hasek (G), Buff. 40.00 15.00 .50
□□□ 126 Martin Rucinsky, Québ. 5.00 2.00 .20
□□□ 127 Kerry Huffman, Otta. 4.00 1.50 .20
□□□ 128 Gord Murphy, Flor. 4.00 1.50 .20
□□□ 129 Bobby Holik, NJer. 10.00 4.00 .20
□□□ 130 Kirk Muller, Mont. 10.00 4.00 .20
□□□ 131 Christian Ruuttu, Chic. 5.00 2.00 .20
□□□ 132 Jyrki Lumme, Vanc. 5.00 2.00 .20
□□□ 133 Ken Wregget (G), Pitt. 5.00 2.00 .20
□□□ 134 Dale Hunter, Wash. 10.00 4.00 .20
□□□ 135 Rob Blake, LosA. 20.00 8.00 .20
□□□ 136 Petr Klima, Tamp. 5.00 2.00 .20
□□□ 137 Stephen Heinze, Bost. 5.00 2.00 .20
□□□ 138 C. Osgood (G), Detr. 20.00 8.00 .20
□□□ 139 John Lilley, Anah. 5.00 2.00 .20
□□□ 140 D. Andreychuk, Toro. 10.00 4.00 .20
□□□ 141 Zarley Zalapski, Calg. 4.00 1.50 .20
□□□ 142 Cu. Joseph (G), SLou. 40.00 14.00 .50
□□□ 143 Brent Gilchrist, Dall. 4.00 1.50 .20
□□□ 144 V. Malakhov, NYIs. 5.00 2.00 .20
□□□ 145 Mikael Renberg, Phil. 10.00 4.00 .20
□□□ 146 Robert Kron, Hart. 5.00 2.00 .20
□□□ 147 D. McAmmond, Edmo. 5.00 2.00 .20
□□□ 148 Doug Bodger, Buff. 4.00 1.50 .20
□□□ 149 Ray Whitney, SanJ. 5.00 2.00 .20
□□□ 150 Brian Leetch, NYRa. 20.00 8.00 .20
□□□ 151 Martin Lapointe, Detr. 15.00 6.00 .20
□□□ 152 T. Numminen, Winn. 10.00 4.00 .20
□□□ 153 Scott A. Young, Québ. 10.00 4.00 .20
□□□ 154 Nick Kypreos, NYRa. 5.00 2.00 .20
□□□ 155 Ed Belfour (G), Chic. 40.00 14.00 .50
□□□ 156 Greg A. Adams, Vanc. 5.00 2.00 .20
□□□ 157 Brian Benning, Flor. 4.00 1.50 .20
□□□ 158 Bob Carpenter, NJer. 5.00 2.00 .20
□□□ 159 V. Konstantinov, Detr. 10.00 4.00 .20
□□□ 160 Rick Tocchet, Pitt. 10.00 4.00 .20
□□□ 161 Joe Sacco, Anah. 4.00 1.50 .20
□□□ 162 D. Puppa (G), Tamp. 5.00 2.00 .20
□□□ 163 Randy Burridge, Wash. 5.00 2.00 .20
□□□ 164 Darryl Sydor, LosA. 5.00 2.00 .20
□□□ 165 Jayson More, SanJ. 4.00 1.50 .20
□□□ 166 Joe Nieuwendyk, Calg. 15.00 6.00 .20
□□□ 167 Mike Eastwood, Toro. 4.00 1.50 .20
□□□ 168 Murray Baron, SLou. 4.00 1.50 .20
□□□ 169 Brent Fedyk, Phil. 4.00 1.50 .20
□□□ 170 Russ Courtnall, Dall. 5.00 2.00 .20
□□□ 171 Sean Burke (G), Hart. 20.00 8.00 .20
□□□ 172 Uwe Krupp & son 4.00 1.50 .20
□□□ 173 Kevin Lowe, NYRa. 10.00 4.00 .20
□□□ 174 G. Carbonneau, Mont. 10.00 4.00 .20
□□□ 175 Alexei Yashin, Otta. 20.00 8.00 .20
□□□ 176 Thomas Steen, Winn. 5.00 2.00 .20
□□□ 177 Sandis Ozolinsh, SanJ. 5.00 2.00 .20
□□□ 178 ShO: Roy (G), Mont. 120.00 45.00 1.50
□□□ 179 ShO: Hasek (G), Buff. 40.00 15.00 .50
□□□ 180 ShO: Belfour (G), Chic. 40.00 14.00 .50
□□□ 181 ShO: Richter (G), NYRa.15.00 6.00 .20
□□□ 182 ShO: Hextall (G), NYIs.20.00 8.00 .20
□□□ 183 ShO: Puppa (G), Tamp. 5.00 2.00 .20
□□□ 184 ShO: Casey, Bost. 5.00 2.00 .20
□□□ 185 ShO: Potvin (G), Toro. 20.00 8.00 .20
□□□ 186 ShO: Brodeur (G), NJer.60.00 20.00 1.00
□□□ 187 ShO: Wakaluk (G), Dall. 5.00 2.00 .20
□□□ 188 ShO: McLean (G), Vanc.10.00 4.00 .20
□□□ 189 ShO: Vernon (G), Calg.15.00 6.00 .20
□□□ 190 ShO: Irbe (G), SanJ. 15.00 6.00 .20
□□□ 191 Dino Ciccarelli, Detr. 10.00 4.00 .20
□□□ 192 Steven Finn, Québ. 4.00 1.50 .20
□□□ 193 Pierre Sévigny, Mont. 4.00 1.50 .20
□□□ 194 Jim Dowd, NJer. 4.00 1.50 .20
□□□ 195 Chris Gratton, Tamp. 5.00 2.00 .20
□□□ 196 Wayne Presley, Buff. 4.00 1.50 .20
□□□ 197 Joel Otto, Calg. 5.00 2.00 .20
□□□ 198 F. Olausson, Edmo. 5.00 2.00 .20
□□□ 199 Jody Hull, Flor. 4.00 1.50 .20
□□□ 200 Cliff Ronning, Vanc. 5.00 2.00 .20
□□□ 201 Rink: D. Turcotte, Hart. 5.00 2.00 .20
□□□ 202 Rink: Al Iafrate, Bost. 5.00 2.00 .20
□□□ 203 Rink: E. Lindros, Phil. 40.00 15.00 .50
□□□ 204 Rink: Ozolinsh, SanJ. 5.00 2.00 .20
□□□ 205 Petr Nedved, SLou. 10.00 4.00 .20
□□□ 206 Mark Lamb, Phil. 4.00 1.50 .20
□□□ 207 Shaun Van Allen, Anah. 5.00 2.00 .20
□□□ 208 K. Hrudey (G), LosA. 15.00 6.00 .20
□□□ 209 N. Borschevsky, Toro. 4.00 1.50 .20
□□□ 210 Glen Wesley, Bost. 5.00 2.00 .20
□□□ 211 S. McEachern, Pitt. 10.00 4.00 .20
□□□ 212 Mark Janssens, Hart. 4.00 1.50 .20
□□□ 213 Brian Mullen & son 5.00 2.00 .20
□□□ 214 Craig Ludwig, Dall. 5.00 2.00 .20
□□□ 215 Mike Rathje, SanJ. 5.00 2.00 .20
□□□ 216 S. Matteau, NYRa. 5.00 2.00 .20
□□□ 217 T. Cheveldae (G), Winn. 5.00 2.00 .20
□□□ 218 Brent Sutter, Chic. 5.00 2.00 .20
□□□ 219 Gord Dineen, Otta. 4.00 1.50 .20
□□□ 220 Kevin Hatcher, Wash. 5.00 2.00 .20
□□□ **221 Todd Simon, Buff. RC 5.00 2.00 .50**
□□□ 222 Bill Lindsay, Flor. 4.00 1.50 .20
□□□ 223 K. McLean (G), Vanc. 10.00 4.00 .20
□□□ 224 Ch. Joseph (G), Tamp. 4.00 1.50 .20
□□□ 225 Valeri Zelepukin, NJer. 4.00 1.50 .20
□□□ 226 Terry Yake, Anah. 4.00 1.50 .20
□□□ 227 Benoît Brunet, Mont. 4.00 1.50 .20
□□□ 228 N. Lidström, Detr. 20.00 8.00 .20
□□□ 229 Zdeno Ciger, Edmo. 5.00 2.00 .20
□□□ 230 Gary Roberts, Calg. 15.00 6.00 .20
□□□ 231 Andy Moog (G), Dall. 15.00 6.00 .20
□□□ 232 Ed Patterson, Pitt. 4.00 1.50 .20
□□□ 233 Philippe Bozon, SLou. 4.00 1.50 .20
□□□ 234 Brent* Hughes, Bost. 4.00 1.50 .20
□□□ 235 Chris Pronger, Hart. 20.00 8.00 .20
□□□ 236 Travis Green, NYIs. 5.00 2.00 .20
□□□ 237 Pat Conacher, LosA. 4.00 1.50 .20
□□□ 238 Bob Rouse, Toro. 4.00 1.50 .20
□□□ 239 Yves Racine, Phil. 4.00 1.50 .20
□□□ 240 Nelson Emerson, Winn. 5.00 2.00 .20
□□□ 241 Oleg Petrov, Mont. 10.00 4.00 .20
□□□ 242 Steve Larmer, NYRa. 15.00 6.00 .20
□□□ 243 Daniel Laperrière, SLou. 4.00 1.50 .20
□□□ 244 John* McIntyre, Vanc. 4.00 1.50 .20
□□□ 245 A. Semak, NJer. 4.00 1.50 .20
□□□ 246 S. Fiset (G), Québ. 10.00 4.00 .20
□□□ 247 Peter Bondra, Wash. 20.00 8.00 .20
□□□ 248 D. Hawerchuk, Buff. 20.00 8.00 .20
□□□ 249 Jamie Baker, SanJ. 4.00 1.50 .20
□□□ 250 Sergei Fedorov, Detr. 40.00 14.00 .50
□□□ 251 Derek Mayer, Otta. 4.00 1.50 .20
□□□ 252 Ivan Droppa, Chic. 4.00 1.50 .20
□□□ 253 Kent Manderville, Toro. 4.00 1.50 .20
□□□ 254 Sergei Zholtok, Bost. 5.00 2.00 .20
□□□ 255 Murray Craven, Vanc. 5.00 2.00 .20
□□□ 256 Todd Krygier, Wash. 4.00 1.50 .20
□□□ **257 B. Grieve, Edmo. RC 5.00 2.00 .50**
□□□ 258 Esa Tikkanen, NYRa. 5.00 2.00 .20
□□□ 259 Brad Dalgarno, NYIs. 4.00 1.50 .20
□□□ 260 Russ Romaniuk, Winn. 4.00 1.50 .20
□□□ 261 Stu Barnes, Flor. 4.00 1.50 .20
□□□ 262 Dan Keczmer, Calg. 4.00 1.50 .20
□□□ 263 Éric Desjardins, Mont. 10.00 4.00 .20
□□□ 264 TW: Brodeur (G), NJer.50.00 18.00 1.00
□□□ 265 TW: Graves, NYRa. 10.00 4.00 .20
□□□ 266 TW: Neely, Bost. 30.00 12.00 .50
□□□ 267 TW: Bourque, Bost. 35.00 14.00 .50
□□□ 268 TW: Fedorov, Detr. 30.00 12.00 .50
□□□ 269 TW: Hasek (G), Buff. 30.00 12.00 .50
□□□ 270 TW: Gretzky, LosA. 125.00 45.00 2.50

REDEMPTIONS

Player SCC

□ 1 Mark Messier, NYRa. 5.00
□ 2 Brad May, Buff. .20
□□ 3 Mike Ricci, Québ. 1.00
□□ 4 Scott Stevens, NJer. 2.00
□ 5 Keith Tkachuk, Winn. 3.00
□ 6 Guy Hebert (G), Anah. 1.00
□ 7 Jason Arnott, Edmo. 2.00
□ 8 Cam Neely, Bost. 5.00
□ 9 Adam Graves, NYRa. 2.00
□ 10 Pavel Bure, Vanc. 4.00
□ 11 Jeff Odgers, SanJ. .20
□ 12 Dmitri Khristich, Wash. .20
□ 13 Patrick Poulin, Chic. .20
□ 14 Mike Donnelly, LosA. .20
□ 15 Félix Potvin (G), Toro. 3.00
□□□ 16 Keith Primeau, Detr. 2.00
□ 17 Fred Knipscheer, Bost. .20
□ 18 Mike Keane, Mont. .20
□ 19 Vitali Prokhorov, SLou. .20
□ 20 Ray Ferraro, NYIs. [w/ sons] .20
□ 21 Shane Churla, Dall. .20
□ 22 Rob Niedermayer, Flor. 1.00
□ 23 Adam Creighton, Tamp. .20
□□ 24 Tommy Söderström (G), Phil. .20
□□ 25 Theoren Fleury, Calg. 3.00
□ 26 Jim Storm, Hart. .20
□ 27 Bret Hedican, Vanc. .20
□ 28 Sean Hill, Anah. .20
□ 29 Bill Ranford (G), Edmo. 2.00
□ 30 Derek Plante, Buff. .20
□ 31 Dave McLlwain, Otta. .20
□□ 32 Iain Fraser, Québ. .20
□ 33 Patrick Roy (G), Mont. 15.00
□ 34 Martin Straka, Pitt. 1.00
□□ 35 Bruce Driver, NJer. .20
□ 36 Brian Skrudland, Flor. .20
□ 37 Bob Errey, SanJ. .20
□ 38 Randy Cunneyworth, Chic. .20
□ 39 John Slaney, Wash. .20
□□□ 40 Ray Sheppard, Detr. .20
□ 41 Sergei Nemchinov, NYRa. 1.00
□ 42 Dave Ellett, Toro. .20
□ 43 Vincent Riendeau (G), Bost. .20
□□ 44 Trent Yawney, Calg. .20
□ 45 Dave Gagner, Dall. .20
□ 46 Igor Korolev, SLou. .20
□ 47 Gary Shuchuk, LosA. .20
□ 48 Rob Zamuner, Tamp. 1.00
□ 49 Frantisek Kucera, Hart. .20
□ 50 Joe Mullen, All-Star [w/ sons] 2.00
□ 51 Ron Hextall (G), NYIs. 3.00
□ 52 J.J. Daigneault, Mont. .20
□ 53 Patrik Carnbäck, Anah. .20
□ 54 Steven Rice, Edmo. .20
□ 55 PP: Brian Leetch, NYRa. 3.00
□□ 56 PP: Al MacInnis, Calg. 2.00
□ 57 PP: Luc Robitaille, LosA. 4.00
□ 58 PP: Dave Andreychuk, Toro. 1.00
□ 59 PP: Jeremy Roenick, Chic. 4.00
□ 60 PP: Mario Lemieux, Pitt. 15.00
□ 61 Dave Manson, Winn. .20
□ 62 Pat Falloon, SanJ. .20
□ 63 Jesse Bélanger, Flor. .20
□ 64 Philippe Boucher, Buff. .20
□ 65 Sergio Momesso, Vanc. .20
□ 66 Evgeny Davydov, Otta. .20
□□ 67 Alexei Gusarov, Québ. .20
□ 68 Jaromir Jagr, Pitt. 5.00
□ 69 Randy Ladouceur, Anah. .20
□ 70 Chris Chelios, Chic. 3.00
□ 71 John Druce, LosA. .20
□□□ 72 Kris Draper, Detr. 1.00
□ 73 Joey Kocur, NYRa. .20
□ 74 Rick Tabaracci (G), Wash. .20
□ 75 Mikael Andersson, Tamp. .20
□ 76 Mark Osborne, Toro. .20
□ 77 Raymond Bourque, Bost. 6.00
□□ 78 Dmitry Yushkevich, Phil. 1.00
□□ 79 Mike Vernon (G), Calg. 2.00
□ 80 Steve Thomas, NYIs. [w/ son] 1.00
□ 81 Steve Duchesne, SLou. 1.00
□ 82 Dean Evason, Dall. .20
□□ 83 Jason Smith, NJer. .20
□ 84 Bryan Marchment, Hart. .20
□ 85 Boris Mironov, Edmo. .20
□ 86 Jeff Norton, SanJ. .20
□ 87 Donald Audette, Buff. 2.00
□□ 88 Eric Lindros, Phil. 5.00
□ 89 Garry Valk, Anah. .20
□□ 90 Mats Sundin, Québ. 5.00
□ 91 Gerald Diduck, Vanc. .20
□ 92 Jeff Shantz, Chic. .20
□□ 93 Scott Niedermayer, NJer. 1.00
□ 94 Troy Mallette, Otta. .20
□□ 95 V'b'sbrouck (G), AS [w/ sons] 2.00
□ 96 Ron Francis, Pitt. 3.00
□□□ 97 Vyacheslav Kozlov, Detr. 1.00
□ 98 Ken Baumgartner, Toro. .20
□ 99 Wayne Gretzky, LosA. 20.00
□ 100 Brett Hull, SLou. 5.00
□ 101 Marc Bergevin, Tamp. .20
□□ 102 Owen Nolan, Québ. 3.00
□ 103 Bryan Smolinski, Bost. .20
□ 104 Lyle Odelein, Mont. .20
□ 105 Mike Ridley, Wash. .20
□□ 106 Trevor Kidd (G), Calg. 1.00
□ 107 Derian Hatcher, Dall. 1.00
□ 108 Derek King, NYIs. .20
□□ 109 Rob Zettler, Phil. .20
□ 110 GE: Alexandre Daigle, Otta. .20
□ 111 GE: Chris Pronger, Hart. 3.00
□ 112 GE: Chris Gratton, Tamp. 1.00
□ 113 GE: John Slaney, Wash. .20
□□ 114 GE: Jocelyn Thibault (G), Québ. 2.00
□ 115 GE: Jason Arnott, Edmo. 2.00
□ 116 GE: Alexei Yashin, Otta. 3.00
□ 117 GE: Rob Niedermayer, Flor. 1.00
□ 118 GE: Jason Allison, Wash. 4.00
□□ 119 GE: Martin Brodeur (G), NJer. 8.00
□ 120 Pat Verbeek, Hart. 1.00
□ 121 Kelly Buchberger, Edmo. .20
□ 122 Doug Lidster, NYRa. .20
□ 123 Sergei* Makarov, SanJ. 2.00
□ 124 Kris King, Winn. .20
□ 125 Dominik Hasek (G), Buff. 5.00
□□ 126 Martin Rucinsky, Québ. 1.00
□ 127 Kerry Huffman, Otta. .20
□ 128 Gord Murphy, Flor. .20
□□ 129 Bobby Holik, NJer. 1.00
□ 130 Kirk Muller, Mont. 1.00
□ 131 Christian Ruuttu, Chic. .20
□ 132 Jyrki Lumme, Vanc. 1.00
□ 133 Ken Wregget (G), Pitt. 1.00
□ 134 Dale Hunter, Wash. 1.00
□ 135 Rob Blake, LosA. 3.00
□ 136 Petr Klima, Tamp. .20
□ 137 Stephen Heinze, Bost. .20
□□□ 138 Chris Osgood (G), Detr. 3.00
□ 139 John Lilley, Anah. 1.00
□ 140 Dave Andreychuk, Toro. 1.00
□□ 141 Zarley Zalapski, Calg. .20
□ 142 Curtis Joseph (G), SLou. 5.00
□ 143 Brent Gilchrist, Dall. .20
□ 144 Vladimir Malakhov, NYIs. .20
□□ 145 Mikael Renberg, Phil. 1.00
□ 146 Robert Kron, Hart. .20
□ 147 Dean McAmmond, Edmo. .20
□ 148 Doug Bodger, Buff. .20
□ 149 Ray Whitney, SanJ. 1.00
□ 150 Brian Leetch, NYRa. 3.00
□□□ 151 Martin Lapointe, Detr. 2.00
□ 152 Teppo Numminen, Winn. 1.00
□□ 153 Scott A. Young, Québ. 1.00
□ 154 Nick Kypreos, NYRa. 1.00
□ 155 Ed Belfour (G), Chic. 5.00
□ 156 Greg A. Adams, Vanc. .20

☐	157 Brian Benning, Flor.	.20
☐☐	158 Bob Carpenter, NJer.	1.00
☐☐☐	159 Vladimir Konstantinov, Detr.	1.00
☐	160 Rick Tocchet, Pitt.	1.00
☐	161 Joe Sacco, Anah.	.20
☐	162 Daren Puppa (G), Tamp.	1.00
☐	163 Randy Burridge, Wash.	.20
☐	164 Darryl Sydor, LosA.	1.00
☐	165 Jayson More, SanJ.	.20
☐☐	166 Joe Nieuwendyk, Calg.	2.00
☐	167 Mike Eastwood, Toro.	.20
☐	168 Murray Baron, SLou.	.20
☐☐	169 Brent Fedyk, Phil.	.20
☐	170 Russ Courtnall, Dall.	1.00
☐	171 Sean Burke (G), Hart.	3.00
☐	172 Uwe Krupp, NYIs. [w/ son]	.20
☐	173 Kevin Lowe, NYRa.	1.00
☐	174 Guy Carbonneau, Mont.	1.00
☐	175 Alexei Yashin, Otta.	3.00
☐	176 Thomas Steen, Winn.	.20
☐	177 Sandis Ozolinsh, SanJ.	1.00
☐	178 ShO: Patrick Roy (G), Mont.	15.00
☐	179 ShO: Dominik Hasek (G), Buff.	5.00
☐	180 ShO: Ed Belfour (G), Chic.	5.00
☐	181 ShO: Mike Richter (G), NYRa.	2.00
☐	182 ShO: Ron Hextall (G), NYIs.	3.00
☐	183 ShO: Daren Puppa (G), Tamp.	1.00
☐	184 ShO: Jon Casey, Bost.	.20
☐	185 ShO: Félix Potvin (G), Toro.	3.00
☐☐	186 ShO: Martin Brodeur (G), NJer.	8.00
☐	187 ShO: Darcy Wakaluk (G), Dall.	.20
☐	188 ShO: Kirk McLean (G), Vanc.	1.00
☐☐	189 ShO: Mike Vernon (G), Calg.	2.00
☐	190 ShO: Arturs Irbe (G), SanJ.	2.00
☐☐☐	191 Dino Ciccarelli, Detr.	1.00
☐☐	192 Steven Finn, Québ.	.20
☐	193 Pierre Sévigny, Mont.	.20
☐☐	194 Jim Dowd, NJer.	.20
☐	195 Chris Gratton, Tamp.	1.00
☐	196 Wayne Presley, Buff.	.20
☐☐	197 Joel Otto, Calg.	.20
☐	198 Fredrik Olausson, Edmo.	1.00
☐	199 Jody Hull, Flor.	.20
☐	200 Cliff Ronning, Vanc.	1.00
☐	201 Rink: Darren Turcotte, Hart.	.20
☐	202 Rink: Al Iafrate, Bost.	1.00
☐☐	203 Rink: Eric Lindros, Phil.	5.00
☐	204 Rink: Sandis Ozolinsh, SanJ.	1.00
☐	205 Petr Nedved, SLou.	1.00
☐☐	206 Mark Lamb, Phil.	.20
☐	207 Shaun Van Allen, Anah.	.20
☐	208 Kelly Hrudey (G), LosA.	2.00
☐	209 Nikolai Borschevsky, Toro.	.20
☐	210 Glen Wesley, Bost.	.20
☐	211 Shawn McEachern, Pitt.	1.00
☐	212 Mark Janssens, Hart.	.20
☐	213 Brian Mullen, NYIs. [w/ son]	.20
☐	214 Craig Ludwig, Dall.	.20
☐	215 Mike Rathje, SanJ.	.20
☐	216 Stéphane Matteau, NYRa.	.20
☐	217 Tim Cheveldae (G), Winn.	.20
☐	218 Brent Sutter, Chic.	1.00
☐	219 Gord Dineen, Otta.	.20
☐	220 Kevin Hatcher, Wash.	.20
☐	**221 Todd Simon, Buff. RC**	**1.00**
☐	222 Bill Lindsay, Flor.	.20
☐	223 Kirk McLean (G), Vanc.	1.00
☐	224 Chris Joseph (G), Tamp.	.20
☐☐	225 Valeri Zelepukin, NJer.	.20
☐	226 Terry Yake, Anah.	.20
☐	227 Benoît Brunet, Mont.	.20
☐☐☐	228 Nicklas Lidström, Detr.	3.00
☐	229 Zdeno Ciger, Edmo.	.20
☐☐	230 Gary Roberts, Calg.	2.00
☐	231 Andy Moog (G), Dall.	2.00
☐	232 Ed Patterson, Pitt.	.20
☐	233 Philippe Bozon, SLou.	.20
☐	234 Brent* Hughes, Bost.	.20
☐	235 Chris Pronger, Hart.	3.00
☐	236 Travis Green, NYIs.	1.00
☐	237 Pat Conacher, LosA.	.20
☐	238 Bob Rouse, Toro.	.20
☐☐	239 Yves Racine, Phil.	.20
☐	240 Nelson Emerson, Winn.	.20
☐	241 Oleg Petrov, Mont.	1.00
☐	242 Steve Larmer, NYRa.	2.00
☐	243 Daniel Laperrière, SLou.	.20
☐	244 John* McIntyre, Vanc.	.20
☐☐	245 Alexander Semak, NJer.	.20
☐☐	246 Stéphane Fiset (G), Québ.	1.00
☐	247 Peter Bondra, Wash.	3.00
☐	248 Dale Hawerchuk, Buff.	3.00
☐	249 Jamie Baker, SanJ.	.20
☐☐☐	250 Sergei Fedorov, Detr.	5.00
☐	251 Derek Mayer, Otta.	.20
☐	252 Ivan Droppa, Chic.	.20
☐	253 Kent Manderville, Toro.	.20
☐	254 Sergei Zholtok, Bost.	.20
☐	255 Murray Craven, Vanc.	.20
☐	256 Todd Krygier, Wash.	.20
☐	**257 Brent Grieve, Edmo. RC**	**1.00**
☐	258 Esa Tikkanen, NYRa.	.20
☐	259 Brad Dalgarno, NYIs.	.20
☐	260 Russ Romaniuk, Winn.	.20
☐	261 Stu Barnes, Flor.	.20
☐☐	262 Dan Keczmer, Calg.	.20
☐	263 Éric Desjardins, Mont.	1.00
☐☐	264 TW: Martin Brodeur (G), NJer.	6.00
☐	265 TW: Adam Graves, NYRa.	1.00
☐	266 TW: Cam Neely, Bost.	4.00
☐	267 TW: Raymond Bourque, Bost.	4.00
☐☐☐	268 TW: Sergei Fedorov, Detr.	4.00
☐	269 TW: Dominik Hasek (G), Buff.	4.00
☐	270 TW: Wayne Gretzky, LosA.	16.00

CHECKLISTS

☐	1 Checklist	.25
☐	2 Checklist	.25
☐	3 Checklist	.25
☐	Checklist (Blue)	.25
☐	Checklist (Green)	.25

DYNASTY AND DESTINY

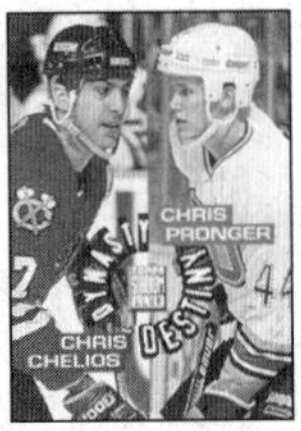

These cards have two versions: an insert (1:24) and an Members Only subset.

Insert Set (5 cards): **10.00**

	Players	M.O.	Insert
☐☐	1 A. Irbe (G) / T. Barrasso (G)	1.50	2.00
☐☐	2 E. Lindros / M. Messier	10.00	5.00
☐☐	3 P. Bure / Br. Hull	10.00	2.00
☐☐	4 M. Renberg / L. Robitaille	5.00	2.00
☐☐	5 C. Chelios / C. Pronger	5.00	2.00

FINEST

These cards have two versions: an insert (1:12) and an Members Only subset.

Insert Set (9 cards): **45.00**

	Players	M.O.	Insert
☐☐	1 Mario Lemieux, Pitt.	35.00	10.00
☐☐	2 Brett Hull, SLou.	10.00	3.00
☐☐	3 Mark Messier, NYRa.	10.00	3.00
☐☐	4 Wayne Gretzky, LosA.	45.00	15.00
☐☐	5 Pavel Bure, Vanc.	5.00	3.00
☐☐	6 Sergei Fedorov, Detr.	10.00	3.00
☐☐	7 Brian Leetch, NYRa.	5.00	3.00
☐☐	8 Raymond Bourque, Bost.	10.00	5.00
☐☐	9 Patrick Roy (G), Mont.	35.00	10.00

SUPER TEAM CARD

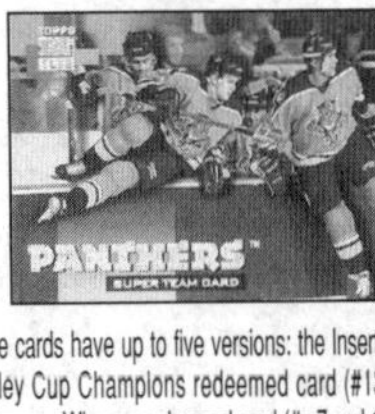

These cards have up to five versions: the Insert (1-26), a Stanley Cup Champions redeemed card (#13 only), a Conference Winners redeemed card (#s 7 and 13 only), a Division Winners redeemed card (#s 4, 7, 17 and 19 only), a Members Only card (1-26) and a Test Proof (1-26). A winner card was redeemed for a gold-stamped Topps Stadium Club/Topps Finest team set or in the case of the Devils, a complete 435-card gold-stamped Stanley Cup Champions set. Redeemed Super Team cards sell at 33% of the insert's value. A redeemed Devils Conference Winners set sells at $18; a redeemed Red Wings Conference Winners or Division Winners set sells at $20; a redeemed Flyers Division Winners set sells at $25; a redeemed Nordiques Division Winners set sells at $25; and a redeemed Flames set sells at $15.

Insert Set (26 cards): **105.00**

	Players	M.O.	Insert
☐☐☐	1 G. Valk / B. Corkum / etc.	1.50	3.00
☐☐☐	2 A. Oates / C. Neely	8.00	4.00
☐☐☐	3 Sabres aerial (inc. Hasek)	6.00	4.00
☐☐☐	4 A. Trefilov (G) / T. Fleury	4.00	4.00
☐☐☐	5 E. Belfour (G) / J. Roenick	10.00	6.00
☐☐☐	6 P. Broten (inc. Modano, Klatt)	6.00	4.00
☐☐☐	7 Red Wings bench (inc. Osgood, Fedorov)	8.00	14.00
☐☐☐	8 B. Ranford (G) / B. Beers	2.00	3.00
☐☐☐	9 Panthers bench (inc. Niederm.)	2.00	3.00
☐☐☐	10 S. Burke (G) / Storm / Crowley	4.00	3.00
☐☐☐	11 Kings bluelin (inc. Granato, Blake)	4.00	3.00
☐☐☐	12 P. Roy (G) / L. Odelein	18.00	10.00
☐☐☐	13 M. Brodeur (G) / Daneyko / Stevens	8.00	12.00
☐☐☐	14 D. Kasparaitis / Y. Kaminsky	2.00	3.00
☐☐☐	15 Rangers parade (inc. Messier, Leetch)	8.00	6.00
☐☐☐	16 Senators aerial	1.50	3.00
☐☐☐	17 M. Recchi (inc. Lindros back)	6.00	6.00
☐☐☐	18 R. Francis / J. Mullen	6.00	3.00
☐☐☐	19 O. Nolan (inc. J. Sakic)	10.00	10.00
☐☐☐	20 Cu. Joseph (G) / B. Shanahan	12.00	6.00
☐☐☐	21 T. Pederson / S. Makarov	2.00	3.00
☐☐☐	22 D. Savard (inc. Klima)	2.00	3.00
☐☐☐	23 D. Gilmour / D. Andreychuk	4.00	3.00
☐☐☐	24 Canucks bench (inc. Bure)	4.00	3.00
☐☐☐	25 Capitals aerial (inc. Dafoe)	2.00	3.00
☐☐☐	26 A. Zhamnov / T. Selänne	6.00	4.00

1994 - 95 TOPPS STADIUM CLUB MEMBERS ONLY

Imprint: © 1995 THE TOPPS COMPANY, INC.

Complete Set (50 cards): **25.00**

	Player	NRMT-MT
☐	1 Patrick Roy (G), Mont.	3.00
☐	2 Raymond Bourque, Bost.	1.00
☐	3 Brian Leetch, NYRa.	.50
☐	4 Cam Neely, Bost.	1.00
☐	5 Jaromir Jagr, Pitt.	1.00
☐	6 Alexander Mogilny, Buff.	.25
☐	7 John Vanbiesbrouck (G), Flor.	.25
☐	8 Geoff Sanderson, Hart.	.25
☐	9 Mark Recchi, Mont.	.25
☐	10 Scott Stevens, NJer.	.25
☐	11 Roman Hamrlik, Tamp.	.25
☐	12 Dominik Hasek (G), Buff.	1.00
☐	13 Joe Sakic, Québ.	1.50
☐	14 Alexei Yashin, Otta.	.50
☐	15 Eric Lindros, Phil.	1.00
☐	16 Adam Oates, Bost.	.25
☐	17 Ulf Samuelsson, Pitt.	.25
☐	18 Wendel Clark, Québ.	.50
☐	19 Mark Messier, NYRa.	1.00
☐	20 Pierre Turgeon, NYIs.	.25
☐	21 Mark Tinordi, Dall.	.25
☐	22 Ron Francis, Pitt.	.50
☐	23 Jeff R. Brown, Vanc.	.25
☐	24 Tom Kurvers, NYIs.	.25
☐	25 Mike Modano, Dall.	1.00
☐	26 Mats Sundin, Toro.	1.00
☐	27 Jeremy Roenick, Chic.	.50
☐	28 Kevin Hatcher, Dall.	.25
☐	29 Curtis Joseph (G), SLou.	1.00
☐	30 Paul Coffey, Detr.	.50
☐	31 Jason Arnott, Edmo.	.25
☐	32 Wayne Gretzky, LosA.	4.00
☐	33 Theoren Fleury, Calg.	.50
☐	34 Al MacInnis, SLou.	.25
☐	35 Ed Belfour (G), Chic.	1.00
☐	36 Sergei Fedorov, Detr.	1.00
☐	37 Brett Hull, SLou.	1.00
☐	38 Chris Chelios, Chic.	.50
☐	39 Keith Tkachuk, Winn.	.50
☐	40 Félix Potvin (G), Toro.	.50
☐	41 Pavel Bure, Vanc.	.50
☐	42 Ulf Dahlén, SanJ.	.25
☐	43 Teemu Selänne, Winn.	.50
☐	44 Doug Gilmour, Toro.	.50
☐	45 Phil Housley, Calg.	.25
☐	46 Paul Kariya, Anah.	1.00
☐	47 Peter Forsberg, Québ.	1.00
☐	48 Jim Carey (G), Wash.	.25
☐	49 Todd Marchant, Edmo.	.25
☐	50 Blaine Lacher (G), Bost.	.25

1994 - 95 UPPER DECK

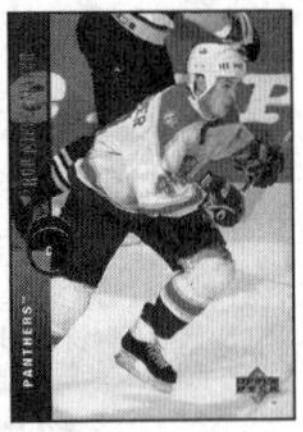

These cards have two versions: the regular card and an Electric Ice parallel.

Series One Imprint: © 1994 The Upper Deck Company
Series Two Imprint: © 1995 The Upper Deck Company

Series One Set (270 cards):	**575.00**	**25.00**
Series Two Set (300 cards):	**550.00**	**35.00**
Common Player:	**2.00**	**.20**
Series One Box Bottom (Gretzky):		**3.00**
Series Two Box Bottom (Renberg):		**1.00**
☐ 5" x 7" Wayne Gretzky Promo (#1):	-	10.00

	Player	Electric	Regular
☐☐	1 Wayne Gretzky, LosA.	60.00	2.50
☐☐	2 German Titov, Calg.	2.00	.20
☐☐	3 Guy Hebert (G), Anah.	2.00	.20
☐☐	4 Tony Amonte, Chic.	5.00	.20
☐☐	5 Dino Ciccarelli, Detr.	2.00	.20
☐☐	6 Geoff Sanderson, Hart.	2.00	.20
☐☐	7 Alexei Zhamnov, Winn.	2.00	.20
☐☐	8 John MacLean, NJer.	2.00	.20
☐☐	9 Brent Fedyk, Phil.	2.00	.20
☐☐	10 Adam Graves, NYRa.	5.00	.20
☐☐	11 Adam Oates, Bost.	5.00	.20
☐☐	12 Ron Francis, Pitt.	5.00	.20
☐☐	13 Bobby Dollas, Anah.	2.00	.20
☐☐	14 Ray Ferraro, NYIs.	2.00	.20
☐☐	15 Paul Broten, Dall.	2.00	.20
☐☐	16 Ulf Dahlén, SanJ.	2.00	.20
☐☐	17 Pat LaFontaine, Buff.	5.00	.20
☐☐	18 Craig Janney, SLou.	2.00	.20
☐☐	19 Garry Galley, Phil.	2.00	.20
☐☐	20 Gary Roberts, Calg.	5.00	.20
☐☐	21 Bill Ranford (G), Edmo.	5.00	.20
☐☐	22 Mario Lemieux, Pitt.	45.00	1.50
☐☐	22 Mike Sillinger, Detr.	2.00	.20
☐☐	23 Glen Murray, Bost.	5.00	.20
☐☐	24 Paul Coffey, Detr.	5.00	.20
☐☐	25 Corey Millen, NJer.	2.00	.20
☐☐	26 Chris Chelios, Chic.	5.00	.20
☐☐	27 Ronnie Stern, Calg.	2.00	.20
☐☐	28 Zdeno Ciger, Edmo.	2.00	.20
☐☐	29 Tony Granato, LosA.	2.00	.20
☐☐	30 Donald Audette, Buff.	5.00	.20
☐☐	31 Russ Courtnall, Dall.	2.00	.20
☐☐	32 Mike Gartner, Toro.	10.00	.50
☐☐	33 Marty McSorley, LosA.	2.00	.20
☐☐	34 Jeff R. Brown, Vanc.	2.00	.20
☐☐	35 Mark Janssens, Hart.	2.00	.20
☐☐	36 Patrick Poulin, Chic.	2.00	.20
☐☐	37 Sergei Fedorov, Detr.	15.00	.50
☐☐	38 Tim Sweeney, Anah.	2.00	.20
☐☐	39 John Slaney, Wash.	2.00	.20
☐☐	40 Steve Larmer, NYRa.	5.00	.20
☐☐	41 Dave Karpa, Québ.	2.00	.20
☐☐	42 Esa Tikkanen, SLou.	2.00	.20
☐☐	43 Joel Otto, Calg.	2.00	.20
☐☐	44 Doug Weight, Edmo.	5.00	.20
☐☐	45 Murray Craven, Vanc.	2.00	.20
☐☐	46 John Vanbiesbrouck (G), Flor.	5.00	.20
☐☐	47 Nelson Emerson, Winn.	2.00	.20
☐☐	48 Dean Evason, Dall.	2.00	.20
☐☐	49 Evgeny Davydov, Otta.	2.00	.20
☐☐	50 Craig Simpson, Buff.	2.00	.20
☐☐	51 Mats Sundin, Toro.	15.00	.50
☐☐	52 Chris Pronger, Hart.	5.00	.20
☐☐	53 Stéphan Lebeau, Anah.	2.00	.20
☐☐	54 Martin Gélinas, Vanc.	2.00	.20
☐☐	55 Bob Rouse, Detr.	2.00	.20
☐☐	56 Christian Ruuttu, Chic.	2.00	.20
☐☐	57 Gilbert Dionne, Mont.	2.00	.20
☐☐	58 Mike Modano, Dall.	15.00	.50
☐☐	59 Derek King, NYIs.	2.00	.20
☐☐	60 Peter Stastny, SLou.	5.00	.20
☐☐	61 Ted Donato, Bost.	2.00	.20
☐☐	62 Mark Messier w/ Stanley Cup	15.00	.50
☐☐	63 Dave Manson, Winn.	2.00	.20
☐☐	64 Johan Garpenlöv, SanJ.	2.00	.20
☐☐	65 Igor Larionov, SanJ.	5.00	.20
☐☐	65 Sergio Momesso, Vanc.	2.00	.20
☐☐	66 Kirk Muller, Mont.	2.00	.20
☐☐	67 Dave Ellett, Toro.	2.00	.20
☐☐	68 Dale Hunter, Wash.	2.00	.20
☐☐	69 Brent Gretzky, Tamp.	2.00	.20
☐☐	70 Tom Barrasso (G), Pitt.	5.00	.20
☐☐	71 Philippe Boucher, Buff.	2.00	.20
☐☐	72 Jesse Bélanger, Flor.	2.00	.20
☐☐	73 Scott Stevens, NJer.	5.00	.20
☐☐	74 Gary Suter, Chic.	2.00	.20
☐☐	75 Tim Cheveldae (G), Winn.	2.00	.20
☐☐	76 Dmitri Khristich, Wash.	2.00	.20
☐☐	77 Pierre Turgeon, NYIs.	5.00	.20
☐☐	78 Mike Richter (G), NYRa.	5.00	.20
☐☐	79 Michael Nylander, Calg.	2.00	.20
☐☐	80 Sergei Krivokrasov, Chic.	2.00	.20
☐☐	81 Andy Moog (G), Dall.	5.00	.20
☐☐	82 Al Iafrate, Bost.	2.00	.20
☐☐	83 Bernie Nicholls, Chic.	2.00	.20
☐☐	84 Darren Turcotte, Hart.	2.00	.20
☐☐	85 Igor Larionov, SanJ.	5.00	.20
☐☐	85 Sergio Momesso, Vanc.	2.00	.20
☐☐	86 Petr Klima, Tamp.	2.00	.20
☐☐	87 Alexandre Daigle, Otta.	2.00	.20
☐☐	88 Joé Juneau, Wash.	2.00	.20
☐☐	89 Glen Wesley, Hart.	2.00	.20
☐☐	90 Teemu Selänne, Winn.	10.00	.50
☐☐	91 Curtis Joseph (G), SLou.	15.00	.50
☐☐	92 Scott Mellanby, Flor.	2.00	.20
☐☐	93 Jaromir Jagr, Pitt.	15.00	.50
☐☐	94 Mark Recchi, Phil.	5.00	.20
☐☐	95 Jiri Slegr, Vanc.	2.00	.20
☐☐	96 Martin Brodeur (G), NJer.	20.00	1.00
☐☐	97 Scott Pearson, Edmo.	2.00	.20
☐☐	98 Eric Lindros, Phil.	15.00	.50
☐☐	99 Larry Murphy, Pitt.	2.00	.20
☐☐	100 Sergei Zubov, NYRa.	2.00	.20
☐☐	101 Mathieu Schneider, Mont.	2.00	.20
☐☐	102 Dale Hawerchuk, Buff.	5.00	.20
☐☐	103 Owen Nolan, Québ.	5.00	.20
☐☐	104 Darryl Sydor, LosA.	2.00	.20
☐☐	105 Anatoli Semenov, Anah.	2.00	.20
☐☐	106 Marty McInnis, NYIs.	2.00	.20
☐☐	107 Derek Mayer, Otta.	2.00	.20
☐☐	108 Steve Duchesne, SLou.	2.00	.20
☐☐	109 Geoff Smith, Flor.	2.00	.20
☐☐	110 Zarley Zalapski, Calg.	2.00	.20
☐☐	111 Rod Brind'Amour, Phil.	2.00	.20
☐☐	112 Nicklas Lidström, Detr.	5.00	.20
☐☐	113 Teppo Numminen, Winn.	2.00	.20
☐☐	114 Denny Felsner, SLou.	2.00	.20
☐☐	115 Wendel Clark, Québ.	10.00	.50
☐☐	116 Arturs Irbe (G), SanJ.	5.00	.20
☐☐	117 Josef Beránek, Phil.	2.00	.20
☐☐	118 Brian Bradley, Tamp.	2.00	.20
☐☐	119 Eric Weinrich, Chic.	2.00	.20
☐☐	120 Kevin Todd, LosA.	2.00	.20
☐☐	121 Patrick Roy (G), Mont.	45.00	1.50
☐☐	122 Guy Carbonneau, SLou.	2.00	.20
☐☐	123 Tom Kurvers, Anah.	2.00	.20
☐☐	124 Sergei* Makarov, SanJ.	5.00	.20
☐☐	125 Pat Peake, Wash.	2.00	.20
☐☐	126 Danton Cole, Tamp.	2.00	.20
☐☐	127 Derian Hatcher, Dall.	2.00	.20
☐☐	128 Kjell Samuelsson, Pitt.	2.00	.20
☐☐	129 Alexei Yashin, Otta.	5.00	.20
☐☐	130 Chris Osgood (G), Detr.	5.00	.20
☐☐	131 Kent Manderville, Toro.	2.00	.20
☐☐	132 Jim Montgomery, Mont.	2.00	.20
☐☐	133 Kirk McLean (G), Vanc.	2.00	.20
☐☐	134 Kelly Buchberger, Edmo.	2.00	.20
☐☐	135 Peter Bondra, Wash.	5.00	.20
☐☐	136 Stéphane Matteau, NYRa.	2.00	.20
☐☐	137 Oleg Petrov, Mont.	2.00	.20
☐☐	138 Doug Gilmour, Toro.	5.00	.20
☐☐	139 Vladimir Malakhov, NYIs.	2.00	.20
☐☐	140 Peter Zezel, Dall.	2.00	.20
☐☐	141 Mike Vernon (G), Detr.	5.00	.20
☐☐	142 Derek Plante, Buff.	2.00	.20
☐☐	143 Valeri Zelepukin, NJer.	2.00	.20
☐☐	144 Kevin Haller, Phil.	2.00	.20
☐☐	145 Keith Tkachuk, Winn.	5.00	.20

☐☐ 146 Claude Boivin, Otta. 2.00 .20
☐☐ 147 Jocelyn Thibault (G), Québ. 5.00 .20
☐☐ 148 Jyrki Lumme, Vanc. 2.00 .20
☐☐ 149 Ray Whitney, SanJ. 2.00 .20
☐☐ 150 Al MacInnis, SLou. 5.00 .20
☐☐ 151 Kelly Miller, Wash. 2.00 .20
☐☐ 152 Ray Sheppard, Detr. 2.00 .20
☐☐ 153 Aaron Ward, Detr. 2.00 .20
☐☐ 154 Damian Rhodes (G), Toro. 2.00 .20
☐☐ 155 Jozef Stumpel, Bost. 2.00 .20
☐☐ 156 Sergei Nemchinov, NYRa. 2.00 .20
☐☐ 157 Richard Matvichuk, Dall. 2.00 .20
☐☐ 158 Sean Burke (G), Hart. 5.00 .20
☐☐ 159 Todd Marchant, Edmo. 5.00 .20
☐☐ 160 Ryan McGill, Phil. 2.00 .20
☐☐ 161 Sean Hill, Otta. 2.00 .20
☐☐ 162 Iain Fraser, Québ. 2.00 .20
☐☐ 163 Shawn McEachern, Pitt. 2.00 .20
☐☐ 164 Petr Nedved, NYRa. 2.00 .20
☐☐ 165 John Lilley, Anah. 2.00 .20
☐☐ 166 Joe Sacco, Anah. 2.00 .20
☐☐ 167 Jason Dawe, Buff. 2.00 .20
☐☐ 168 Mike Rathje, SanJ. 2.00 .20
☐☐ 169 Phil Housley, Calg. 2.00 .20
☐☐ 170 Ron Hextall (G), Phil. 5.00 .20
☐☐ 171 Yves Racine, Mont. 2.00 .20
☐☐ 172 Boris Mironov, Edmo. 2.00 .20
☐☐ 173 Vitali Prokhorov, SLou. 2.00 .20
☐☐ 174 Roman Hamrlik, Tamp. 2.00 .20
☐☐ 175 Robert Lang, LosA. 2.00 .20
☐☐ 176 Jody Hull, Flor. 2.00 .20
☐☐ 177 Mike Ridley, Toro. 2.00 .20
☐☐ 178 Dmitri Filimonov, Otta. 2.00 .20
☐☐ 179 René Corbet, Québ. 2.00 .20
☐☐ 180 Rob Pearson, Wash. 2.00 .20
☐☐ 181 Richard Smehlik, Buff. 2.00 .20
☐☐ 182 Rob Gaudreau, SanJ. 2.00 .20
☐☐ 183 Bill Houlder, SLou. 2.00 .20
☐☐ 184 Igor Korolev, SLou. 2.00 .20
☐☐ 185 Chris Joseph (G), Tamp. 2.00 .20
☐☐ 186 Shane Churla, Dall. 2.00 .20
☐☐ 187 Rick Tabaracci (G), Wash. 2.00 .20
☐☐ 188 Alexander Godynyuk, Hart. 2.00 .20
☐☐ 189 Vladimir Konstantinov, Detr. 2.00 .20
☐☐ 190 Markus Näslund, Pitt. 15.00 .50
☐☐ 191 Tom Chorske, NJer. 2.00 .20
☐☐ 192 Thomas Steen, Winn. 2.00 .20
☐☐ 193 Patrice Brisebois, Mont. 2.00 .20
☐☐ 194 Luc Robitaille, Pitt. 10.00 .50
☐☐ 195 Michal Sykora, SanJ. 2.00 .20
☐☐ 196 Troy Mallette, Otta. 2.00 .20
☐☐ 197 Steve Chiasson, Calg. 2.00 .20
☐☐ 198 Jimmy Carson, Hart. 2.00 .20
☐☐ 199 Mike Donnelly, LosA. 2.00 .20
☐☐ 200 Mario Lemieux, Pitt. 45.00 1.50
☐☐ 200 Mike Sillinger, Detr. 2.00 .20
☐☐ 201 Martin Rucinsky, Québ. 2.00 .20
☐☐ 202 Adam Bennett, Edmo. 2.00 .20
☐☐ **203 Matt Johnson, LosA. RC 2.00 .50**
☐☐ 204 Daren Puppa (G), Tamp. 2.00 .20
☐☐ 205 Ted Drury, Hart. 2.00 .20
☐☐ 206 Jon Casey, SLou. 2.00 .20
☐☐ 207 Alex Kovalev, NYRa. 5.00 .20
☐☐ 208 Alexei Kasatonov, Bost. 2.00 .20
☐☐ 209 Ulf Samuelsson, Pitt. 2.00 .20
☐☐ **210 Justin Hocking, LosA. RC 2.00 .50**
☐☐ 211 Greg A. Adams, Vanc. 2.00 .20
☐☐ 212 Greg Johnson, Detr. 2.00 .20
☐☐ 213 Mike Craig, Toro. 2.00 .20
☐☐ 214 Steve Konowalchuk, Wash. 2.00 .20
☐☐ 215 Luke Richardson, Edmo. 2.00 .20
☐☐ 216 Pavol Demitra, Otta. 5.00 .20
☐☐ 217 Brian Benning, Flor. 2.00 .20
☐☐ 218 Corey Hirsch (G), NYRa. 2.00 .20
☐☐ 219 Alexander Semak, NJer. 2.00 .20
☐☐ 220 Travis Green, NYIs. 2.00 .20
☐☐ 221 Turner Stevenson, Mont. 2.00 .20
☐☐ 222 Dmitri Mironov, Toro. 2.00 .20
☐☐ **223 Christian Soucy (G), Chic. RC 5.00 1.00**
☐☐ 224 Rick Tocchet, LosA. 2.00 .20
☐☐ 225 Craig MacTavish, Phil. 2.00 .20
☐☐ 226 HL: Wayne Gretzky, LosA. 60.00 2.50
☐☐ 227 Pavel Bure, Vanc. [Shooter's] 10.00 .50
☐☐ 228 W. Gretzky, LosA. [Shooter's] 60.00 2.50
☐☐ 229 Brett Hull, SLou. [Shooter's] 15.00 .50
☐☐ 230 Mike Gartner, Toro. [Shooter's] 10.00 .50
☐☐ 231 Brian Leetch, NYRa. [Shooter's] 5.00 .20
☐☐ 232 Al MacInnis, SLou. [Shooter's] 5.00 .20
☐☐ 233 D. Hasek (G), Buff. [Shooter's] 15.00 .50
☐☐ 234 M. Messier, NYRa. [Shooter's] 15.00 .50
☐☐ 235 P. Kariya, Anah. 30.00 1.00
☐☐ 236 J. Storr (G), LosA. 5.00 .20
☐☐ 237 Jeff Friesen, SanJ. 5.00 .20
☐☐ 238 K. Jönsson, Toro. 5.00 .20
☐☐ **239 Mariusz Czerkawski, Bost. RC 10.00 1.50**
☐☐ 240 Brett Lindros, NYIs. 5.00 .20
☐☐ 241 Andrei Nikolishin, Hart. 2.00 .20
☐☐ 242 Jason Allison, Wash. 15.00 .50
☐☐ 243 Oleg Tverdovsky, Anah. 2.00 .20
☐☐ 244 Brian Savage, Mont. 5.00 .20
☐☐ 245 Peter Forsberg, Québ. 20.00 .50
☐☐ **246 Patrik Juhlin, Phil. RC 2.00 .50**
☐☐ 247 Jassen Cullimore, Vanc. 2.00 .20
☐☐ 248 Chris Therien, Phil. 2.00 .20
☐☐ **249 Kevin Brown, LosA. RC 2.00 .50**
☐☐ 250 Jeff Nelson, Wash. 2.00 .20
☐☐ 251 Janne Laukkanen, Québ. 2.00 .20
☐☐ 252 Jamie McLennan (G), NYIs. 2.00 .20
☐☐ 253 Craig Johnson, SLou. 2.00 .20
☐☐ **254 Ravil Gusmanov, Winn. RC 2.00 .50**
☐☐ 255 Valeri Bure, Mont. 5.00 .20
☐☐ **256 Valeri Karpov, Anah. RC 2.00 .50**
☐☐ 257 Michael Peca, Vanc. 10.00 .50
☐☐ 258 Brian Rolston, NJer. 5.00 .20
☐☐ 259 Brandon Convery, Toro. 2.00 .20
☐☐ **260 Mark Lawrence, Dall. RC 2.00 .50**
☐☐ 261 Adam Deadmarsh, Québ. 5.00 .20
☐☐ 262 Jason Wiemer, Tamp. 5.00 .20
☐☐ 263 Alexander Cherbayev, SanJ. 2.00 .20
☐☐ 264 Sergei Gonchar, Wash. 5.00 .20
☐☐ 265 Viktor Kozlov, SanJ. 5.00 .20
☐☐ **266 Vladislav Boulin, Phil. RC 2.00 .50**
☐☐ 267 Todd Harvey, Dall. 5.00 .20
☐☐ **268 Cory Stillman, Calg. RC 10.00 1.50**
☐☐ **269 David Oliver, Edmo. RC 2.00 .50**
☐☐ 270 Andrei Nazarov, SanJ. 2.00 .20
☐☐ 271 Mikael Renberg, Phil. 2.00 .20
☐☐ 272 Andrei Kovalenko, Québ. 2.00 .20
☐☐ 273 Neal Broten, Dall. 2.00 .20
☐☐ 274 Ed Olczyk, NYRa. 2.00 .20
☐☐ 275 Steve Thomas, NYIs. 2.00 .20
☐☐ 276 Joe Nieuwendyk, Calg. 5.00 .20
☐☐ 277 Rob Gaudreau, Otta. 2.00 .20
☐☐ 278 Pat Verbeek, Hart. 2.00 .20
☐☐ 279 Éric Desjardins, Phil. 2.00 .20
☐☐ 280 Vincent Damphousse, Mont. 5.00 .20
☐☐ 281 John Cullen, Pitt. 2.00 .20
☐☐ 282 Garry Valk, Anah. 2.00 .20
☐☐ 283 Daniel Lacroix, Bost. 2.00 .20
☐☐ 284 Mike Ricci, Québ. 2.00 .20
☐☐ 285 Dominik Hasek (G), Buff. 15.00 .50
☐☐ 286 Geoff Courtnall, Vanc. 2.00 .20
☐☐ 287 Rob Niedermayer, Flor. 2.00 .20
☐☐ 288 Alexander Karpovtsev, NYRa. 2.00 .20
☐☐ 289 Martin Straka, Pitt. 2.00 .20
☐☐ 290 Ed Belfour (G), Chic. 15.00 .50
☐☐ 291 Dave Lowry, Flor. 2.00 .20
☐☐ 292 Brendan Shanahan, SLou. 15.00 .50
☐☐ 293 Jari Kurri, LosA. 15.00 .50
☐☐ 294 Steven Rice, Hart. 2.00 .20
☐☐ 295 Scott Levins, Otta. 2.00 .20
☐☐ 296 Raymond Bourque, Bost. 15.00 .50
☐☐ 297 Mikael Andersson, Tamp. 2.00 .20
☐☐ 298 Darius Kasparaitis, NYIs. 2.00 .20
☐☐ 299 Chris Simon, Québ. 2.00 .20
☐☐ 300 Steve Yzerman, Detr. 35.00 1.50
☐☐ **301 Don McSween, Anah. RC 2.00 .50**
☐☐ 302 Brian Noonan, NYRa. 2.00 .20
☐☐ 303 Claude Lemieux, NJer. 2.00 .20
☐☐ **304 Radek Bonk, Otta. RC 10.00 2.00**
☐☐ 305 Jason Arnott, Edmo. 5.00 .20
☐☐ **306 Ian Laperrière, SLou. RC 5.00 1.00**
☐☐ 307 Pat Falloon, SanJ. 2.00 .20
☐☐ 308 Kris King, Winn. 2.00 .20
☐☐ 309 Brian Bellows, Mont. 2.00 .20
☐☐ 310 Uwe Krupp, Québ. 2.00 .20
☐☐ 311 Paul Cavallini, Dall. 2.00 .20
☐☐ 312 Shaun Van Allen, Anah. 2.00 .20
☐☐ 313 Dave Andreychuk, Toro. 2.00 .20
☐☐ 314 Bobby Holik, NJer. 2.00 .20
☐☐ 315 Theoren Fleury, Calg. 5.00 .20
☐☐ 316 Mark Osborne, NYRa. 2.00 .20
☐☐ 317 Andrew Cassels, Hart. 2.00 .20
☐☐ **318 Chris Tamer, Pitt. RC 2.00 .50**
☐☐ 319 Trevor Linden, Vanc. 5.00 .20
☐☐ 320 Tom Fitzgerald, Flor. 2.00 .20
☐☐ 321 Ron Tugnutt (G), Mont. 5.00 .20
☐☐ 322 Jeremy Roenick, Chic. 10.00 .50
☐☐ 323 Todd Marchant, Edmo. 2.00 .20
☐☐ 324 Scott Niedermayer, NJer. 2.00 .20
☐☐ **325 Tim Taylor, Detr. RC 2.00 .50**
☐☐ **326 Mike Kennedy, Dall. RC 2.00 .50**
☐☐ 327 Stephen Heinze, Bost. 2.00 .20
☐☐ 328 David Sacco, Anah. 2.00 .20
☐☐ 329 Sergei Brylin, NJer. 2.00 .20
☐☐ 330 John LeClair, Phil. 10.00 .50
☐☐ 331 Brian Skrudland, Flor. 2.00 .20
☐☐ 332 Kevin Hatcher, Dall. 2.00 .20
☐☐ 333 Brett Hull, SLou. 15.00 .50
☐☐ 334 Alexander Mogilny, Buff. 5.00 .20
☐☐ 335 Sylvain Lefebvre, Québ. 2.00 .20
☐☐ 336 Sylvain Turgeon, Otta. 2.00 .20
☐☐ 337 Keith Primeau, Detr. 5.00 .20
☐☐ **338 Éric Fichaud (G), Toro. RC 5.00 1.00**
☐☐ 339 Jeff Beukeboom, NYRa. 2.00 .20
☐☐ **340 Cory Cross, Tamp. RC 2.00 .50**
☐☐ 341 J.J. Daigneault, Mont. 2.00 .20
☐☐ 342 Stephen Leach, Bost. 2.00 .20
☐☐ 343 Zigmund Palffy, NYIs. 5.00 .20
☐☐ 344 Igor Korolev, Winn. 2.00 .20
☐☐ 345 Chris Gratton, Tamp. 2.00 .20
☐☐ 346 Joe Mullen, Pitt. 5.00 .20
☐☐ 347 Brent Gilchrist, Dall. 2.00 .20
☐☐ 348 Adam Creighton, SLou. 2.00 .20
☐☐ 349 Dmitry Yushkevich, Phil. 2.00 .20
☐☐ 350 Wes Walz, Calg. 2.00 .20
☐☐ 351 Shayne Corson, Edmo. 2.00 .20
☐☐ **352 Éric Lacroix, LosA. RC 2.00 .50**
☐☐ 353 Maxim Bets, Anah. 2.00 .20
☐☐ 354 Sylvain Côté, Wash. 2.00 .20
☐☐ 355 Valeri Kamensky, Québ. 2.00 .20
☐☐ 356 Shjon Podein, Phil. 2.00 .20
☐☐ 357 Robert Reichel, Calg. 2.00 .20
☐☐ 358 Cliff Ronning, Vanc. 2.00 .20
☐☐ 359 Bill Guerin, NJer. 5.00 .20
☐☐ 360 Dallas Drake, Winn. 2.00 .20
☐☐ 361 Robert Petrovicky, Hart. 2.00 .20
☐☐ 362 Ken Wregget (G), Pitt. 2.00 .20
☐☐ 363 Todd Elik, SanJ. 2.00 .20
☐☐ 364 Cam Neely, Bost. 15.00 .50
☐☐ 365 Darren McCarty, Detr. 2.00 .20
☐☐ **366 Shean Donovan, SanJ. RC 5.00 1.00**
☐☐ 367 Félix Potvin (G), Toro. 5.00 .20
☐☐ 368 Yuri Khmylev, Buff. 2.00 .20
☐☐ 369 Mark Tinordi, Wash. 2.00 .20
☐☐ 370 Craig Billington (G), Otta. 2.00 .20
☐☐ 371 Patrick Flatley, NYIs. 2.00 .20
☐☐ 372 Jocelyn Lemieux, Hart. 2.00 .20
☐☐ 373 Vyacheslav Kozlov, Detr. 2.00 .20
☐☐ 374 Trent Klatt, Dall. 2.00 .20
☐☐ **375 Geoff Sarjeant (G), SLou. RC 2.00 .50**
☐☐ 376 Bob Kudelski, Flor. 2.00 .20
☐☐ **377 Stanislav Neckar, Otta. RC 5.00 1.00**
☐☐ **378 Jon Rohloff, Bost. RC 2.00 .50**
☐☐ 379 Jeff Shantz, Chic. 2.00 .20
☐☐ 380 Dale Craigwell, SanJ. 2.00 .20
☐☐ 381 Adrien Plavsic, Vanc. 2.00 .20
☐☐ 382 Dave Gagner, Dall. 2.00 .20
☐☐ 383 Dave Archibald, Otta. 2.00 .20
☐☐ 384 Gilbert Dionne, Phil. 2.00 .20
☐☐ 385 Troy Loney, NYIs. 2.00 .20
☐☐ 386 Dean McAmmond, Edmo. 2.00 .20
☐☐ 387 Pauli Jaks (G), LosA. 2.00 .20
☐☐ 388 Stéphane J.J. Richer, NJer. 2.00 .20
☐☐ 389 Don Beaupré (G), Otta. 2.00 .20
☐☐ 390 Kevin Stevens, Pitt. 2.00 .20
☐☐ 391 Brad May, Buff. 2.00 .20
☐☐ 392 Neil Wilkinson, Winn. 2.00 .20
☐☐ 393 Kevin Lowe, NYRa. 2.00 .20
☐☐ 394 Fredrik Olausson, Edmo. 2.00 .20
☐☐ 395 Trevor Kidd (G), Calg. 2.00 .20
☐☐ **396 Brent Grieve, Chic. RC 2.00 .50**
☐☐ 397 Dominic Roussel (G), Phil. 2.00 .20
☐☐ 398 Bret Hedican, Vanc. 2.00 .20
☐☐ 399 Bryan Smolinski, Bost. 2.00 .20
☐☐ 400 Doug Lidster, SLou. 2.00 .20
☐☐ 401 Bob Errey, SanJ. 2.00 .20
☐☐ 402 Pierre Sévigny, Mont. 2.00 .20
☐☐ 403 Rob (Jr.) Brown, LosA. 2.00 .20
☐☐ 404 Joe Sakic, Québ. 20.00 1.00
☐☐ 405 Nikolai Borschevsky, Toro. 2.00 .20
☐☐ 406 Martin Lapointe, Detr. 5.00 .20
☐☐ **407 Jean-Yves Roy, NYRa. RC 2.00 .50**
☐☐ 408 Robert Kron, Hart. 2.00 .20
☐☐ 409 Tie Domi, Winn. 2.00 .20
☐☐ 410 Jim Dowd, NJer. 2.00 .20
☐☐ 411 Keith Jones, Wash. 2.00 .20
☐☐ 412 Scott Lachance, NYIs. 2.00 .20
☐☐ 413 Bob Corkum, Anah. 2.00 .20
☐☐ **414 Denis Chassé, SLou. RC 2.00 .50**
☐☐ 415 Denis Savard, Tamp. 5.00 .20
☐☐ 416 Joe Murphy, Chic. 2.00 .20
☐☐ 417 Viacheslav Butsayev, SanJ. 2.00 .20
☐☐ 418 Mattias Norström, NYRa. 2.00 .20
☐☐ 419 Sergei Zholtok, Bost. 2.00 .20
☐☐ 420 Nikolai Khabibulin (G), Winn. 10.00 .50
☐☐ 421 Pat Elynuik, Otta. 2.00 .20
☐☐ 422 Doug Brown, Detr. 2.00 .20
☐☐ 423 Dave McLlwain, Otta. 2.00 .20
☐☐ 424 James Patrick, Calg. 2.00 .20
☐☐ **425 Alexander Selivanov, Tamp. RC 2.00 .50**
☐☐ 426 Scott Thornton, Edmo. 2.00 .20
☐☐ 427 Todd Ewen, Anah. 2.00 .20
☐☐ 428 Peter Popovic, Mont. 2.00 .20
☐☐ 429 Jarkko Varvio, Dall. 2.00 .20
☐☐ 430 Paul Ranheim, Hart. 2.00 .20
☐☐ 431 Kevin Dineen, Phil. 2.00 .20
☐☐ 432 Kelly Hrudey (G), LosA. 5.00 .20
☐☐ **433 Michal Grosek, Winn. RC 2.00 .50**
☐☐ 434 Viacheslav Fetisov, NJer. 5.00 .20
☐☐ 435 Ivan Droppa, Chic. 2.00 .20
☐☐ 436 Benoît Hogue, NYIs. 2.00 .20
☐☐ 437 Sheldon Kennedy, Calg. 2.00 .20
☐☐ 438 Gord Murphy, Flor. 2.00 .20
☐☐ 439 Jamie Baker, SanJ. 2.00 .20
☐☐ 440 Todd Gill, Toro. 2.00 .20
☐☐ 441 Mark Recchi, Mont. 5.00 .20
☐☐ 442 Ted Crowley, Hart. 2.00 .20
☐☐ **443 Ryan Smyth, Edmo. RC 20.00 3.00**
☐☐ 444 Brian Leetch, NYRa. 5.00 .20
☐☐ 445 Bob Sweeney, Buff. 2.00 .20
☐☐ 446 Don Sweeney, Bost. 2.00 .20
☐☐ **447 Byron Dafoe (G), Wash. RC 15.00 2.50**
☐☐ 448 Nathan Lafayette, Vanc. 2.00 .20
☐☐ 449 Keith Carney, Chic. 2.00 .20
☐☐ 450 Stéphane Fiset (G), Québ. 2.00 .20
☐☐ 451 Kevin Miller, SLou. 2.00 .20
☐☐ **452 Craig Darby, Mont. RC 5.00 1.00**
☐☐ 453 Vlastimil Kroupa, SanJ. 2.00 .20
☐☐ 454 Rob Zettler, Phil. 2.00 .20
☐☐ 455 Glenn Healy (G), NYRa. 2.00 .20
☐☐ **456 Todd Simon, Buff. RC 2.00 .50**
☐☐ 457 Mark Fitzpatrick (G), Flor. 2.00 .20
☐☐ 458 Drake Berehowsky, Toro. 2.00 .20
☐☐ 459 Darcy Wakaluk (G), Dall. 2.00 .20
☐☐ 460 Enrico Ciccone, Tamp. 2.00 .20
☐☐ 461 Tomas Sandström, Pitt. 2.00 .20
☐☐ 462 Mikhail Shtalenkov (G), Anah. 2.00 .20
☐☐ 463 Igor Kravchuk, Edmo. 2.00 .20
☐☐ **464 Jamie* Allison, Calg. RC 2.00 .50**
☐☐ 465 Gino Odjick, Vanc. 2.00 .20
☐☐ 466 Norm Maciver, Otta. 2.00 .20
☐☐ 467 Terry Carkner, Detr. 2.00 .20
☐☐ 468 Rob Zamuner, Tamp. 2.00 .20
☐☐ 469 Pavel Bure, Vanc. 10.00 .50
☐☐ **470 Patrice Tardif, SLou. RC 2.00 .50**
☐☐ 471 Andrei Lomakin, Flor. 2.00 .20
☐☐ 472 Kirk Maltby, Edmo. 2.00 .20
☐☐ 473 Jaroslav Modry, NJer. 2.00 .20
☐☐ 474 Tommy Söderström (G), NYIs. 2.00 .20
☐☐ 475 Patrik Carnbäck, Anah. 2.00 .20
☐☐ 476 Jeff Reese (G), Hart. 2.00 .20
☐☐ 477 Todd Krygier, Anah. 2.00 .20
☐☐ 478 John* McIntyre, Vanc. 2.00 .20
☐☐ 479 Joey Kocur, NYRa. 2.00 .20
☐☐ **480 Steve Rucchin, Anah. RC 10.00 1.50**
☐☐ 481 Bob Bassen, Québ. 2.00 .20
☐☐ **482 Marek Malik, Hart. RC 2.00 .50**
☐☐ 483 Darryl Shannon, Winn. 2.00 .20
☐☐ 484 Shawn Burr, Detr. 2.00 .20
☐☐ 485 Louie DeBrusk, Edmo. 2.00 .20
☐☐ 486 Olaf Kölzig (G), Wash. 5.00 .20
☐☐ 487 Cam Stewart, Bost. 2.00 .20
☐☐ 488 Rob Blake, LosA. 5.00 .20
☐☐ **489 Éric Charron, Tamp. RC 2.00 .50**
☐☐ 490 Sandis Ozolinsh, SanJ. 2.00 .20
☐☐ 491 Paul Ysebaert, Chic. 2.00 .20
☐☐ 492 Kris Draper, Detr. 2.00 .20
☐☐ 493 Stu Barnes, Flor. 2.00 .20
☐☐ 494 Doug Bodger, Buff. 2.00 .20
☐☐ **495 Blaine Lacher (G), Bost. RC 5.00 1.00**
☐☐ **496 Ed Jovanovski, Canada RC 15.00 2.50**
☐☐ **497 Éric Dazé, Canada RC 15.00 2.50**
☐☐ **498 Dan Cloutier (G), Canada RC 15.00 2.50**
☐☐ **499 Chad Allan, Canada RC 2.00 .50**
☐☐ 500 Todd Harvey, Canada 5.00 .20
☐☐ **501 Jamie Rivers, Canada RC 2.00 .50**
☐☐ 502 Bryan McCabe, Canada 5.00 .20
☐☐ **503 Darcy Tucker, Canada RC 10.00 1.50**
☐☐ **504 Wade Redden, Canada RC 10.00 2.00**
☐☐ **505 N. Baumgartner, Canada RC 2.00 .50**
☐☐ 506 Marek Malik, Czech 2.00 .20
☐☐ **507 Petr Cajanek, Czech RC 2.00 .50**
☐☐ **508 Jan Hlavac, Czech RC 10.00 1.50**
☐☐ **509 Ladislav Kohn, Czech RC 5.00 1.00**
☐☐ 510 Kimmo Timonen, Finland 2.00 .20
☐☐ **511 Antti Aalto, Finland RC 2.00 .50**
☐☐ **512 Tommi Rajamäki, Finland RC 2.00 .50**
☐☐ **513 Vitali Yachmenev, Russia RC 5.00 1.00**
☐☐ **514 V. Epantchinsev, Russia RC 2.00 .50**
☐☐ **515 Dmitri Klevakin, Russia RC 2.00 .50**
☐☐ 516 Nikolai Zavarukhin, Russia 2.00 .20
☐☐ **517 A. Korolyuk, Russia RC 2.00 .50**
☐☐ 518 Anders Eriksson, Sweden 2.00 .20
☐☐ **519 Jesper Mattsson, Sweden RC 2.00 .50**
☐☐ **520 Mattias Öhlund, Sweden RC 10.00 2.00**
☐☐ **521 A. Söderberg, Sweden RC 2.00 .50**
☐☐ **522 Bryan Berard, U.S.A. RC 10.00 2.00**
☐☐ 523 Jason Bonsignore, U.S.A. 2.00 .20
☐☐ 524 Deron Quint, U.S.A. 2.00 .20
☐☐ 525 Richard Park, U.S.A. 2.00 .20
☐☐ 526 Jeff Friesen, SanJ. 2.00 .20
☐☐ 527 Paul Kariya, Anah. 20.00 .50
☐☐ 528 Peter Forsberg, Québ. 20.00 .50
☐☐ 529 Zigmund Palffy, NYIs. 5.00 .20
☐☐ 530 Kenny Jönsson, Toro. 2.00 .20
☐☐ 531 Jamie Storr (G), LosA. 2.00 .20
☐☐ 532 Alex. Selivanov, Tamp. 2.00 .20
☐☐ 533 Michael Peca, Vanc. 5.00 .20
☐☐ 534 M. Czerkawski, Bost. 5.00 .20
☐☐ 535 Jason Allison, Wash. 5.00 .20
☐☐ 536 Todd Harvey, Dall. 2.00 .20
☐☐ 537 Brett Lindros, NYIs. 2.00 .20
☐☐ 538 Radek Bonk, Otta. 5.00 .20
☐☐ 539 Blaine Lacher (G), Bost. 2.00 .20
☐☐ 540 Oleg Tverdovsky, Anah. 2.00 .20
☐☐ 541 Wayne Gretzky, LosA. [Tour] 60.00 2.50
☐☐ 542 Radek Bonk, Otta. [Tour] 5.00 .20
☐☐ 543 Mariusz Czerkawski, Bost. [Tour] 5.00 .20
☐☐ 544 Jaromir Jagr, Pitt. [Tour] 15.00 .50
☐☐ 545 Dominik Hasek (G), Buff. [Tour] 15.00 .50
☐☐ 546 Todd Harvey, Dall. [Tour] 2.00 .20
☐☐ 547 Michael Peca, Vanc. [Tour] 5.00 .20
☐☐ 548 Mats Sundin, Toro. [Tour] 15.00 .50
☐☐ 549 Doug Weight, Edmo. [Tour] 5.00 .20
☐☐ 550 Steve Yzerman, Detr. [Tour] 35.00 1.50
☐☐ 551 Brett Lindros, NYIs. [Tour] 2.00 .20
☐☐ 552 Alexander Mogilny, Buff. [Tour] 5.00 .20
☐☐ 553 Patrik Juhlin, Phil. [Tour] 2.00 .20
☐☐ 554 Alexei Yashin, Otta. [Tour] 5.00 .20
☐☐ 555 Peter Forsberg, Québ. [Tour] 20.00 .50
☐☐ 556 Michael Nylander, Calg. [Tour] 2.00 .20
☐☐ 557 Teemu Selänne, Winn. [Tour] 10.00 .50
☐☐ 558 Marek Malik, Hart. [Tour] 2.00 .20
☐☐ 559 Jari Kurri, LosA. [Tour] 15.00 .50
☐☐ 560 Kenny Jönsson, Toro. [Tour] 2.00 .20
☐☐ 561 Mikael Renberg, Phil. [Tour] 2.00 .20
☐☐ 562 Adam Deadmarsh, Québ. [Tour] 2.00 .20
☐☐ 563 Mark Messier, NYRa. [Tour] 15.00 .50
☐☐ 564 Rob Blake, LosA. [Tour] 5.00 .20
☐☐ 565 Janne Laukkanen, Québ. [Tour] 2.00 .20
☐☐ 566 Theoren Fleury, Calg. [Tour] 5.00 .20
☐☐ 567 Alex Kovalev, NYRa. [Tour] 5.00 .20
☐☐ 568 Jamie Storr (G), LosA. [Tour] 2.00 .20
☐☐ 569 Brett Hull, SLou. [Tour] 15.00 .50
☐☐ 570 Valeri Karpov, Anah. [Tour] 2.00 .20

AWARD PREDICTOR

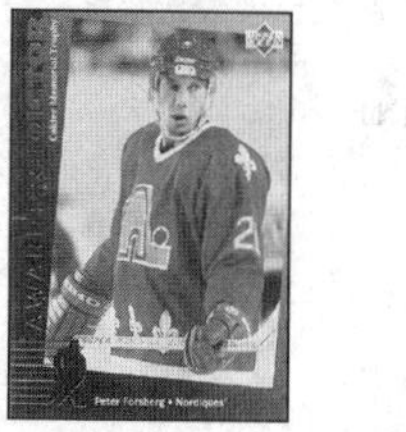

Only C1-C15 and H1-H15 have Silver and Gold redeemed versions. All other Predictor cards have only Gold redeemed versions.

Calder Set (C1-C15): 10.00 10.00 20.00
Pearson Set (C16-C25): - 15.00 35.00
Norris Set (C26-C35): - 5.00 15.00
Hart Set (H1-H15): 30.00 30.00 65.00
Art Ross Set (H16-H25): - 20.00 45.00
Vézina Set (H26-H35): - 15.00 30.00
Goals Set (R1-R10): - 10.00 20.00
Assists Set (R11-R20): - 15.00 30.00
Points Set (R21-R30): - 20.00 40.00

	Player	Silver	Gold	Insert
☐☐☐	C1 Forsberg, Québ. [Win]	3.00	3.00	6.00
☐☐☐	C2 Paul Kariya, Anah.	3.00	3.00	6.00
☐☐☐	C3 Viktor Kozlov, SanJ.	.50	.50	1.00
☐☐☐	C4 Jason Allison, Wash.	1.00	1.00	2.00
☐☐☐	C5 M. Czerkawski, Bost.	.50	.50	1.00
☐☐☐	C6 Valeri Karpov, Anah.	.50	.50	1.00
☐☐☐	C7 Brett Lindros, NYIs.	.50	.50	1.00
☐☐☐	C8 Valeri Bure, Mont.	.50	.50	1.00
☐☐☐	C9 Andrei Nikolishin, Hart.	.50	.50	1.00
☐☐☐	C10 Michael Peca, Vanc.	.50	.50	1.00
☐☐☐	C11 Kenny Jönsson, Toro.	.50	.50	1.00
☐☐☐	C12 A. Cherbayev, SanJ.	.50	.50	1.00
☐☐☐	C13 Brian Rolston, NJer.	.50	.50	1.00
☐☐☐	C14 Oleg Tverdovsky, Anah.	.50	.50	1.00
☐☐☐	C15 Long Shot	.50	.50	1.00
☐☐	C16 Wayne Gretzky, LosA.	-	9.00	18.00
☐☐	C17 Brett Hull, SLou.	-	2.00	4.00
☐☐	C18 Doug Gilmour, Toro.	-	1.00	2.00
☐☐	C19 Jeremy Roenick, Chic.	-	1.50	3.00
☐☐	C20 J. Vanbiesbrouck (G), Flor.	-	1.00	2.00
☐☐	C21 Sergei Fedorov, Detr.	-	2.00	4.00
☐☐	C22 Mark Messier, NYRa.	-	2.00	4.00

□□	C23 Eric Lindros, Phil. [Win]	-	2.00	4.00
□□	C24 Jaromir Jagr, Pitt. [Win]	-	2.00	4.00
□□	C25 Long Shot	-	.50	1.00
□□	C26 Raymond Bourque, Bost.	-	2.50	5.00
□□	C27 Sandis Ozolinsh, SanJ.	-	.50	1.00
□□	C28 Brian Leetch, NYRa.	-	1.00	2.00
□□	C29 Chris Chelios, Chic. [Win]	-	1.00	2.00
□□	C30 Scott Stevens, NJer.	-	.50	1.00
□□	C31 Paul Coffey, Detr. [Win]	-	1.00	2.00
□□	C32 Rob Blake, LosA.	-	1.00	2.00
□□	C33 Al MacInnis, SLou.	-	.50	1.00
□□	C34 Scott Niedermayer, NJer.	-	.50	1.00
□□	C35 Long Shot	-	.50	1.00
□□□	H1 Wayne Gretzky, LosA.	9.00	9.00	18.00
□□□	H2 Pavel Bure, Vanc.	1.50	1.50	3.00
□□□	H3 Doug Gilmour, Toro.	1.00	1.00	2.00
□□□	H4 Mark Messier, NYRa.	2.00	2.00	4.00
□□□	H5 Patrick Roy (G), Mont.	6.50	6.50	13.00
□□□	H6 Sergei Fedorov, Detr.	2.00	2.00	4.00
□□□	H7 Chris Chelios, Chic.	1.00	1.00	2.00
□□□	H8 Lindros, Phil. [Win Gold]	2.00	2.00	4.00
□□□	H9 Alexander Mogilny, Buff.	1.00	1.00	2.00
□□□	H10 Peter Forsberg, Québ.	3.00	3.00	6.00
□□□	H11 Brian Leetch, NYRa.	1.00	1.00	2.00
□□□	H12 M. Brodeur (G), NJer.	3.50	3.50	7.00
□□□	H13 Jeremy Roenick, Chic.	1.50	1.50	3.00
□□□	H14 Paul Kariya, Anah.	3.00	3.00	6.00
□□□	H15 Long Shot	.50	.50	1.00
□□	H16 Wayne Gretzky, LosA.	-	9.00	18.00
□□	H17 Joe Sakic, Québ.	-	3.50	7.00
□□	H18 Sergei Fedorov, Detr.	-	2.00	4.00
□□	H19 Pavel Bure, Vanc.	-	1.50	3.00
□□	H20 Adam Oates, Bost.	-	.50	1.00
□□	H21 Doug Gilmour, Toro.	-	1.00	2.00
□□	H22 Steve Yzerman, Detr.	-	5.00	10.00
□□	H23 Eric Lindros, Phil. [Win]	-	2.00	4.00
□□	H24 Jaromir Jagr, Pitt. [Win]	-	2.00	4.00
□□	H25 Long Shot,	-	.50	1.00
□□	H26 Patrick Roy (G), Mont.	-	6.50	13.00
□□	H27 Ed Belfour (G), Chic. [Win]	-	2.00	4.00
□□	H28 Félix Potvin (G), Toro.	-	1.00	2.00
□□	H29 Martin Brodeur (G), NJer.	-	3.50	7.00
□□	H30 Mike Richter (G), NYRa.	-	1.00	2.00
□□	H31 Dom. Hasek (G), Buff. [Win]	-	2.00	4.00
□□	H32 Vanbiesbrouck (G), Flor.	-	1.00	2.00
□□	H33 Curtis Joseph (G), SLou.	-	2.00	4.00
□□	H34 Kirk McLean (G), Vanc.	-	.50	1.00
□□	H35 Long Shot	-	.50	1.00
□□	R1 Pavel Bure, Vanc.	-	1.50	3.00
□□	R2 Brett Hull, SLou.	-	2.00	4.00
□□	R3 Teemu Selänne, Winn.	-	1.50	3.00
□□	R4 Sergei Fedorov, Detr.	-	2.00	4.00
□□	R5 Adam Graves, NYRa.	-	.50	1.00
□□	R6 Dave Andreychuk, Toro.	-	.50	1.00
□□	R7 Brendan Shanahan, SLou.	-	2.00	4.00
□□	R8 Jeremy Roenick, Chic.	-	1.50	3.00
□□	R9 Eric Lindros, Phil.	-	2.00	4.00
□□	R10 Long Shot	-	.50	1.00
□□	R11 Doug Gilmour, Toro.	-	1.00	2.00
□□	R12 Adam Oates, Bost.	-	.50	1.00
□□	R13 Brian Leetch, NYRa.	-	1.00	2.00
□□	R14 Raymond Bourque, Bost.	-	2.50	5.00
□□	R15 Joé Juneau, Wash.	-	.50	1.00
□□	R16 Craig Janney, SanJ.	-	.50	1.00
□□	R17 Pat LaFontaine, Buff.	-	1.00	2.00
□□	R18 Jaromir Jagr, Pitt.	-	2.00	4.00
□□	R19 Wayne Gretzky, LosA.	-	9.00	18.00
□□	R20 Long Shot	-	.50	1.00
□□	R21 Wayne Gretzky, LosA.	-	9.00	18.00
□□	R22 Pat LaFontaine, Buff.	-	1.00	2.00
□□	R23 Sergei Fedorov, Detr.	-	2.00	4.00
□□	R24 Steve Yzerman, Detr.	-	5.00	10.00
□□	R25 Pavel Bure, Vanc.	-	1.50	3.00
□□	R26 Adam Oates, Bost.	-	.50	1.00
□□	R27 Doug Gilmour, Toro.	-	1.00	2.00
□□	R28 Eric Lindros, Phil. [Win]	-	2.00	4.00
□□	R29 Jaromir Jagr, Pitt. [Win]	-	2.00	4.00
□□	R30 Long Shot	-	.50	1.00

ICE GALLERY

	Series One Insert Set (15 cards):	**40.00**
	Insert (1:25)	IG
□	IG1 Steve Yzerman, Detr.	9.00
□	IG2 Jason Arnott, Edmo.	1.00
□	IG3 Jeremy Roenick, Chic.	3.00
□	IG4 Brendan Shanahan, SLou.	3.00
□	IG5 Scott Stevens, NJer.	1.00
□	IG6 Scott Niedermayer, NJer.	1.00
□	IG7 Adam Graves, NYRa.	1.00
□	IG8 Mike Modano, Dall.	3.00
□	IG9 Kirk Muller, Mont.	1.00
□	IG10 Alexandre Daigle, Otta.	1.00
□	IG11 Martin Brodeur (G), NJer.	6.00
□	IG12 Garry Valk, Anah.	1.00
□	IG13 Teemu Selänne, Winn.	3.00
□	IG14 Pat LaFontaine, Buff.	2.00
□	IG15 Wayne Gretzky, LosA.	15.00

PLAYOFF PREDICTOR

	Playoff Goals Set (R31-R40):	**10.00**	**25.00**
	Playoff Assists Set (R41-R50):	**15.00**	**30.00**
	Playoff Points Set (R51-R60):	**15.00**	**35.00**
	Player	Gold	Insert
□□	R31 Pavel Bure, Vanc.	1.50	3.00
□□	R32 Brett Hull, SLou.	2.00	4.00
□□	R33 Cam Neely, Bost.	2.00	4.00
□□	R34 Mark Messier, NYRa.	2.00	4.00
□□	R35 Dave Andreychuk, Toro.	.50	1.00
□□	R36 Sergei Fedorov, Detr.	2.00	4.00
□□	R37 Mike Modano, Dall.	2.00	4.00
□□	R38 Adam Graves, NYRa.	.50	1.00
□□	R39 Jaromir Jagr, Pitt. [Win]	2.00	4.00
□□	R40 Long Shot	.50	1.00
□□	R41 Theoren Fleury, Calg.	1.00	2.00
□□	R42 Wayne Gretzky, LosA.	9.00	18.00
□□	R43 Steve Yzerman, Detr.	5.00	10.00
□□	R44 Adam Oates, Bost.	.50	1.00
□□	R45 Brian Leetch, NYRa.	1.00	2.00
□□	R46 Al MacInnis, SLou.	.50	1.00
□□	R47 Pat LaFontaine, Buff.	1.00	2.00
□□	R48 Scott Stevens, NJer.	.50	1.00
□□	R49 Doug Gilmour, Toro.	1.00	2.00
□□	R50 Long Shot	.50	1.00
□□	R51 Brian Leetch, NYRa.	1.00	2.00
□□	R52 Sergei Fedorov, Detr. [Win]	2.00	4.00
□□	R53 Pavel Bure, Vanc.	1.50	3.00
□□	R54 Mark Messier, NYRa.	2.00	4.00
□□	R55 Pat LaFontaine, Buff.	1.00	2.00
□□	R56 Doug Gilmour, Toro.	1.00	2.00
□□	R57 Brett Hull, SLou.	2.00	4.00
□□	R58 Theoren Fleury, Calg.	1.00	2.00
□□	R59 Wayne Gretzky, LosA.	9.00	18.00
□□	R60 Long Shot	.50	1.00

SP

These cards have a Die-Cut parallel.

	Series 1 Insert Set (90 cards):	**200.00**	**50.00**
	Series 2 Insert Set (90 cards):	**125.00**	**25.00**
	Common Player:	**.75**	**.30**
	Player	Die-Cut	SP
□□	SP-1 Maxim Bets, Anah.	.75	.30
□□	SP-2 Stéphan Lebeau, Anah.	.75	.30
□□	SP-3 Garry Valk, Anah.	.75	.30
□□	SP-4 Raymond Bourque, Bost.	9.50	2.00
□□	SP-5 Mariusz Czerkawski, Bost.	1.50	.30
□□	SP-6 Cam Neely, Bost.	8.00	2.00
□□	SP-7 Adam Oates, Bost.	3.00	.50
□□	SP-8 Dominik Hasek (G), Buff.	8.00	2.00
□□	SP-9 Dale Hawerchuk, Buff.	4.50	1.00
□□	SP-10 Alexander Mogilny, Buff.	3.50	.50
□□	SP-11 Theoren Fleury, Calg.	4.50	1.00
□□	SP-12 Trevor Kidd (G), Calg.	2.50	.50
□□	SP-13 Joe Nieuwendyk, Calg.	3.00	.50
□□	SP-14 Gary Roberts, Calg.	3.00	.50
□□	SP-15 Ed Belfour (G), Chic.	8.00	2.00
□□	SP-16 Chris Chelios, Chic.	4.50	1.00
□□	SP-17 Jeremy Roenick, Chic.	6.00	1.50
□□	SP-18 Neal Broten, Dall.	1.50	.30
□□	SP-19 Russ Courtnall, Dall.	1.50	.30
□□	SP-20 Derian Hatcher, Dall.	2.50	.50
□□	SP-21 Mike Modano, Dall.	8.00	2.00
□□	SP-22 Paul Coffey, Detr.	4.50	1.00
□□	SP-23 Vyacheslav Kozlov, Detr.	1.50	.30
□□	SP-24 Keith Primeau, Detr.	3.00	.50
□□	SP-25 Steve Yzerman, Detr.	19.00	4.50
□□	SP-26 Jason Arnott, Edmo.	3.50	.50
□□	SP-27 Bill Ranford (G), Edmo.	3.00	.50
□□	SP-28 Doug Weight, Edmo.	4.50	1.00
□□	SP-29 Bob Kudelski, Flor.	.75	.30
□□	SP-30 Rob Niedermayer, Flor.	1.50	.30
□□	SP-31 John Vanbiesbrouck (G), Flor.	3.50	.50
□□	SP-32 Andrew Cassels, Hart.	1.50	.30
□□	SP-33 Chris Pronger, Hart.	4.50	1.00
□□	SP-34 Geoff Sanderson, Hart.	1.50	.30
□□	SP-35 Rob Blake, LosA.	4.50	1.00
□□	SP-36 Wayne Gretzky, LosA.	32.00	8.00
□□	SP-37 Jari Kurri, LosA.	8.00	2.00
□□	SP-38 Alexei Zhitnik, LosA.	1.00	.30
□□	SP-39 Vincent Damphousse, Mont.	4.50	1.00
□□	SP-40 Kirk Muller, Mont.	2.50	.50
□□	SP-41 Oleg Petrov, Mont.	2.50	.50
□□	SP-42 Patrick Roy (G), Mont.	24.00	6.00
□□	SP-43 Martin Brodeur (G), NJer.	12.50	3.00
□□	SP-44 Stéphane J.J. Richer, NJer.	1.50	.30
□□	SP-45 Scott Stevens, NJer.	3.00	.50
□□	SP-46 Darius Kasparaitis, NYIs.	1.50	.30
□□	SP-47 Vladimir Malakhov, NYIs.	1.00	.30
□□	SP-48 Pierre Turgeon, NYIs.	3.00	.50
□□	SP-49 Alex Kovalev, NYRa.	4.50	1.00
□□	SP-50 Brian Leetch, NYRa.	4.50	1.00
□□	SP-51 Mark Messier, NYRa.	8.00	2.00
□□	SP-52 Mike Richter (G), NYRa.	3.50	.50
□□	SP-53 Craig Billington (G), Otta.	1.00	.30
□□	SP-54 Alexandre Daigle, Otta.	1.00	.30
□□	SP-55 Alexei Yashin, Otta.	4.50	1.00
□□	SP-56 Josef Beránek, Phil.	1.00	.30
□□	SP-57 Rod Brind'Amour, Phil.	2.50	.50
□□	SP-58 Mark Recchi, Phil.	3.00	.50
□□	SP-59 Mikael Renberg, Phil.	2.50	.50
□□	SP-60 Jaromir Jagr, Pitt.	8.00	2.00
□□	SP-61 Mario Lemieux, Pitt.	24.00	6.00
□□	SP-62 Kevin Stevens, Pitt.	1.50	.30
□□	SP-63 Owen Nolan, Québ.	4.50	1.00
□□	SP-64 Mike Ricci, Québ.	2.50	.50
□□	SP-65 Joe Sakic, Québ.	12.50	3.00
□□	SP-66 Brett Hull, SLou.	8.00	2.00
□□	SP-67 Craig Janney, SLou.	1.50	.30
□□	SP-68 Curtis Joseph (G), SLou.	8.00	2.00
□□	SP-69 Brendan Shanahan, SLou.	8.00	2.00
□□	SP-70 Ulf Dahlén, SanJ.	1.00	.30
□□	SP-71 Arturs Irbe (G), SanJ.	3.00	.50
□□	SP-72 Sergei" Makarov, SanJ.	3.00	.50
□□	SP-73 Sandis Ozolinsh, SanJ.	1.50	.30
□□	SP-74 Brian Bradley, Tamp.	.75	.30
□□	SP-75 Chris Gratton, Tamp.	1.50	.30
□□	SP-76 Denis Savard, Tamp.	3.00	.50
□□	SP-77 Dave Andreychuk, Toro.	2.50	.50
□□	SP-78 Mike Gartner, Toro.	6.00	1.50
□□	SP-79 Dmitri Mironov, Toro.	1.00	.30
□□	SP-80 Félix Potvin (G), Toro.	4.50	1.00
□□	SP-81 Jeff R. Brown, Vanc.	.75	.30
□□	SP-82 Geoff Courtnall, Vanc.	1.00	.30
□□	SP-83 Trevor Linden, Vanc.	3.00	.50
□□	SP-84 Kirk McLean (G), Vanc.	2.50	.50
□□	SP-85 Peter Bondra, Wash.	4.50	1.00
□□	SP-86 Kevin Hatcher, Wash.	1.00	.30
□□	SP-87 Dmitri Khristich, Wash.	1.00	.30
□□	SP-88 Teemu Selänne, Winn.	6.00	1.50
□□	SP-89 Keith Tkachuk, Winn.	4.50	1.00
□□	SP-90 Alexei Zhamnov, Winn.	2.50	.50
□□	SP-91 Paul Kariya, Anah.	10.00	2.50
□□	SP-92 Valeri Karpov, Anah.	.75	.30
□□	SP-93 Oleg Tverdovsky, Anah.	1.00	.30
□□	SP-94 Al Iafrate, Bost.	1.50	.30
□□	SP-95 Blaine Lacher (G), Bost.	1.00	.30
□□	SP-96 Bryan Smolinski, Bost.	1.00	.30
□□	SP-97 Donald Audette, Buff.	3.00	.50
□□	SP-98 Yuri Khmylev, Buff.	.75	.30
□□	SP-99 Pat LaFontaine, Buff.	4.50	1.00
□□	SP-100 Derek Plante, Buff.	1.00	.30
□□	SP-101 Steve Chiasson, Calg.	1.00	.30
□□	SP-102 Phil Housley, Calg.	2.50	.50
□□	SP-103 Michael Nylander, Calg.	1.50	.30
□□	SP-104 Robert Reichel, Calg.	2.50	.50
□□	SP-105 Tony Amonte, Chic.	4.50	1.00
□□	SP-106 Bernie Nicholls, Chic.	1.50	.30
□□	SP-107 Gary Suter, Chic.	1.50	.30
□□	SP-108 Paul Cavallini, Dall.	.75	.30
□□	SP-109 Todd Harvey, Dall.	1.50	.30
□□	SP-110 Kevin Hatcher, Dall.	1.00	.30
□□	SP-111 Andy Moog (G), Dall.	3.00	.50
□□	SP-112 Dino Ciccarelli, Detr.	2.50	.50
□□	SP-113 Sergei Fedorov, Detr.	8.00	2.00
□□	SP-114 Nicklas Lidström, Detr.	4.50	1.00
□□	SP-115 Mike Vernon (G), Detr.	3.00	.50
□□	SP-116 Shayne Corson, Edmo.	2.50	.50
□□	SP-117 David Oliver, Edmo.	.75	.30
□□	SP-118 Ryan Smyth, Edmo.	7.50	1.50
□□	SP-119 Jesse Bélanger, Flor.	.75	.30
□□	SP-120 Mark Fitzpatrick (G), Flor.	1.00	.30
□□	SP-121 Scott Mellanby, Flor.	1.50	.30
□□	SP-122 Andrei Nikolishin, Hart.	1.00	.30
□□	SP-123 Darren Turcotte, Hart.	1.00	.30
□□	SP-124 Pat Verbeek, Hart.	2.50	.50
□□	SP-125 Glen Wesley, Hart.	1.00	.30
□□	SP-126 Tony Granato, LosA.	1.50	.30
□□	SP-127 Marty McSorley, LosA.	1.50	.30
□□	SP-128 Jamie Storr (G), LosA.	1.50	.30
□□	SP-129 Rick Tocchet, LosA.	2.50	.50
□□	SP-130 Brian Bellows, Mont.	1.50	.30
□□	SP-131 Valeri Bure, Mont.	2.50	.50
□□	SP-132 Turner Stevenson, Mont.	1.00	.30
□□	SP-133 John MacLean, NJer.	1.00	.30
□□	SP-134 Scott Niedermayer, NJer.	2.50	.50
□□	SP-135 Brian Rolston, NJer.	2.50	.50
□□	SP-136 Brett Lindros, NYIs.	2.50	.50
□□	SP-137 Jamie McLennan (G), NYIs.	1.00	.30
□□	SP-138 Zigmund Palffy, NYIs.	4.50	1.00
□□	SP-139 Steve Thomas, NYIs.	1.50	.30
□□	SP-140 Adam Graves, NYRa.	3.00	.50
□□	SP-141 Petr Nedved, NYRa.	2.50	.50
□□	SP-142 Sergei Zubov, NYRa.	1.50	.30
□□	SP-143 Don Beaupré (G), Otta.	1.00	.30
□□	SP-144 Radek Bonk, Otta.	2.50	.50
□□	SP-145 Pavol Demitra, Otta.	3.00	.50
□□	SP-146 Sylvain Turgeon, Otta.	1.00	.30
□□	SP-147 Ron Hextall (G), Phil.	4.50	1.00
□□	SP-148 Patrik Juhlin, Phil.	.75	.30
□□	SP-149 Eric Lindros, Phil.	8.00	2.00
□□	SP-150 Ron Francis, Pitt.	4.50	1.00
□□	SP-151 Markus Näslund, Pitt.	8.00	2.00
□□	SP-152 Luc Robitaille, Pitt.	6.00	1.50
□□	SP-153 Martin Straka, Pitt.	2.50	.50
□□	SP-154 Wendel Clark, Québ.	6.00	1.50
□□	SP-155 Adam Deadmarsh, Québ.	2.50	.50
□□	SP-156 Peter Forsberg, Québ.	10.00	2.50
□□	SP-157 Janne Laukkanen, Québ.	.75	.30
□□	SP-158 Steve Duchesne, SLou.	1.50	.30
□□	SP-159 Al MacInnis, SLou.	3.00	.50
□□	SP-160 Esa Tikkanen, SLou.	1.00	.30
□□	SP-161 Jeff Friesen, SanJ.	2.50	.50
□□	SP-162 Viktor Kozlov, SanJ.	2.50	.50
□□	SP-163 Ray Whitney, SanJ.	1.50	.30
□□	SP-164 Roman Hamrlik, Tamp.	1.50	.30
□□	SP-165 Alexander Selivanov, Tamp.	.75	.30
□□	SP-166 Jason Wiemer, Tamp.	.75	.30
□□	SP-167 Doug Gilmour, Toro.	4.50	1.00
□□	SP-168 Kenny Jönsson, Toro.	1.50	.30
□□	SP-169 Mike Ridley, Toro.	1.00	.30
□□	SP-170 Mats Sundin, Toro.	8.00	2.00
□□	SP-171 Pavel Bure, Vanc.	6.00	1.50
□□	SP-172 Martin Gélinas, Vanc.	1.50	.30
□□	SP-173 Michael Peca, Vanc.	3.00	.50
□□	SP-174 Jason Allison, Wash.	4.50	1.00
□□	SP-175 Joé Juneau, Wash.	1.50	.30
□□	SP-176 Pat Peake, Wash.	.75	.30
□□	SP-177 Mark Tinordi, Wash.	1.00	.30
□□	SP-178 Tim Cheveldae (G), Winn.	1.00	.30
□□	SP-179 Nelson Emerson, Winn.	1.00	.30
□□	SP-180 Dave Manson, Winn.	1.00	.30

1994 - 95 UPPER DECK – BUYBACKS

	Buyback Autograph • Upper Deck	**UD**
□	58 Mike Modano, Dall. ✍ {#/8}	
□	62 Mark Messier, NYRa. ✍ {#/1}	
□	78 Mike Richter (G), NYRa. ✍ {#/1}	
□	91 Curtis Joseph (G), SLou. ✍ {#/1}	
□	96 Martin Brodeur (G), NJer. ✍ {#/1}	
□	145 Keith Tkachuk, Winn. ✍ {#/1}	
□	300 Steve Yzerman, Detr. ✍ {#/1}	
	Buyback Autograph • SP Insert	**UD-SP**
□	SP-17 Jeremy Roenick, Chic. ✍ {#/40}	
□	SP-25 Steve Yzerman, Detr. ✍ {#/34}	
□	SP-36 Wayne Gretzky, LosA. ✍ {#/16}	
□	SP-52 Mike Richter, NYRa. ✍ {#/8}	
□	SP-66 Brett Hull, SLou. ✍ {#/17}	
□	SP-66 Brett Hull, SLou. ✍ {#/7}	
□	SP-68 Curtis Joseph (G), SLou. ✍ {#/34}	
□	SP-114 Nicklas Lidström, Detr. ✍ {#/6}	
□	SP-138 Zigmund Palffy, NYIs. ✍ {#/79}	
□	SP-152 Luc Robitaille, Pitt. ✍ {#/60}	
□	SP-152 Luc Robitaille, Pitt. ✍ {#/8}	
□	SP-171 Pavel Bure, Vanc. ✍ {#/2}	
□	SP-171 Pavel Bure, Vanc. ✍ {#/64}	
	Buyback Autograph • SP Die-Cut parallel	**SP**
□	SP-17 Jeremy Roenick, Chic. ✍ {#/13}	
□	SP-25 Steve Yzerman, Detr. ✍ {#/4}	
□	SP-36 Wayne Gretzky, LosA. ✍ {#/5}	
□	SP-66 Brett Hull, SLou. ✍ {#/3}	
□	SP-68 Curtis Joseph (G), SLou. ✍ {#/4}	
□	SP-138 Zigmund Palffy, NYIs. ✍ {#/10}	
□	SP-152 Luc Robitaille, Pitt. ✍ {#/9}	
□	SP-171 Pavel Bure, Vanc. ✍ {#/2}	

1994 - 95 UPPER DECK BE A PLAYER

Imprint: © 1995 The Upper Deck Company

	Complete Set (180 cards):	**35.00**
	Common Player:	**.35**
	Player	NRMT-MT
□	R1 Doug Gilmour	.50
□	R2 Joel Otto	.35
□	R3 Kirk Muller	.35
□	R4 Marty McInnis	.35
□	R5 Dave Gagner	.35
□	R6 Geoff Courtnall	.35
□	R7 Dale Hawerchuk	.50
□	R8 Mike Modano	1.00
□	R9 Roman Hamrlik	.35
□	R10 Marty McSorley	.35
□	R11 Teemu Selänne	.50
□	R12 Jeremy Roenick	.50
□	R13 Glenn Healy (G)	.35
□	R14 Darren Turcotte	.35
□	R15 Derian Hatcher	.35
□	R16 Enrico Ciccone	.35
□	R17 Tony Amonte	.50
□	R18 Mark Recchi	.35
□	R19 Eric Weinrich	.35
□	R20 John Vanbiesbrouck (G)	.35
□	R21 Nick Kypreos	.35
□	R22 Gilbert Dionne	.35
□	R23 Theoren Fleury	.50
□	R24 Todd Gill	.35
□	R25 Jari Kurri	1.00
□	R26 Brad May	.35
□	R27 Russ Courtnall	.35
□	R28 Bill Ranford (G)	.35
□	R29 Steve Yzerman	2.00
□	R30 Alexandre Daigle	.35
□	R31 Mike Hudson	.35
□	R32 Raymond Bourque	1.00
□	R33 Dave Andreychuk	.35
□	R34 Jason Arnott	.35
□	R35 Pavel Bure	.50
□	R36 Keith Tkachuk	.50
□	R37 Scott Niedermayer	.35
□	R38 Johan Garpenlöv	.35
□	R39 Dino Ciccarelli	.35
□	R40 Rob Blake	.50
□	R41 Dave Manson	.35
□	R42 Adam Foote	.35
□	R43 Chris Pronger	.50
□	R44 Scott Lachance	.35
□	R45 Adam Oates	.35
□	R46 Brian Leetch	.50
□	R47 Guy Hebert (G)	.35
□	R48 Brett Hull	1.00
□	R49 Mike Ricci	.35
□	R50 Dave Ellett	.35
□	R51 Owen Nolan	.50
□	R52 Craig Janney	.35
□	R53 Trevor Linden	.35
□	R54 Ray Sheppard	.35
□	R55 Rob Niedermayer	.35
□	R56 Kevin Haller	.35
□	R57 Jeff Norton	.35
□	R58 Martin Brodeur (G)	1.50
□	R59 Robb Stauber (G)	.35
□	R60 Sylvain Turgeon	.35
□	R61 Pat Verbeek	.35
□	R62 J. Steve Smith	.35
□	R63 Jaromir Jagr	1.00
□	R64 Steve Duchesne	.35
□	R65 Tie Domi	.35
□	R66 Sylvain Lefebvre	.35
□	R67 Guy Carbonneau	.35
□	R68 Alexander Mogilny	.35
□	R69 Mario Lemieux	3.00
□	R70 Neil Wilkinson	.35
□	R71 Curtis Joseph (G)	1.00
□	R72 Wendel Clark	.50
□	R73 Kirk McLean (G)	.35
□	R74 Mikael Renberg	.35
□	R75 Shawn McEachern	.35
□	R76 Mats Sundin	1.00

□ R77 Craig Simpson .35
□ R78 Phil Housley .35
□ R79 Pat LaFontaine .50
□ R80 Pierre Turgeon .35
□ R81 Félix Potvin (G) .50
□ R82 Kevin Stevens .35
□ R83 Steve Chiasson .35
□ R84 Robert Petrovicky .35
□ R85 Joé Juneau .35
□ R86 Brendan Shanahan 1.00
□ R87 Joe Sacco .35
□ R88 David Reid .35
□ R89 Louie DeBrusk .35
□ R90 Darryl Sydor .35
□ R91 Paul Coffey [Training Tips] .50
□ R92 Alexei Yashin [Training Tips] .50
□ R93 Jason Arnott [Training Tips] .35
□ R94 Gary Suter [Training Tips] .35
□ R95 Luc Robitaille [Training Tips] .50
□ R96 Joe Sakic [Training Tips] 1.50
□ R97 Chris Chelios [Training Tips] .50
□ R98 Tony Granato [Training Tips] .35
□ R99 Wayne Gretzky [Training Tips] 4.00
□ R100 Joé Juneau [Training Tips] .35
□ R101 Curtis Joseph (G) [Training Tips] 1.00
□ R102 Vincent Damphousse [Training Tips] .50
□ R103 Paul Kariya [Training Tips] 1.00
□ R104 Brendan Shanahan [Training Tips] 1.00
□ R105 Éric Desjardins [Training Tips] .35
□ R106 Eric Lindros [Training Tips] 1.00
□ R107 Kirk McLean (G) [Snapshots] .35
□ R108 Mike Ricci [Snapshots] .35
□ R109 Chris Chelios [Snapshots] .50
□ R110 Chris Gratton [Snapshots] .35
□ R111 Doug Gilmour [Snapshots] .50
□ R112 Vincent Damphousse [Snapshots] .50
□ R113 Mark Osborne [Snapshots] .35
□ R114 Mike Modano [Snapshots] 1.00
□ R115 Steve Yzerman [Snapshots] 2.00
□ R116 Garry Valk [Snapshots] .35
□ R117 Adam Graves [Snapshots] .35
□ R118 Doug Weight [Snapshots] .50
□ R119 Rob Niedermayer [Snapshots] .35
□ R120 Craig Simpson [Snapshots] .35
□ R121 Patrick Roy (G) [Snapshots] 3.00
□ R122 Ronnie Stern [Snapshots] .35
□ R123 Jiri Slegr [Snapshots] .35
□ R124 Darren Turcotte [Snapshots] .35
□ R125 Vladimir Malakhov [Snapshots] .35
□ R126 Paul Kariya [Then and Now] 1.00
□ R127 Mike Gartner [Then and Now] .50
□ R128 Scott Niedermayer [Then and Now] .35
□ R129 Dino Ciccarelli [Then and Now] .35
□ R130 Martin Brodeur (G) [Then and Now] 1.50
□ R131 Kevin Hatcher [Then and Now] .35
□ R132 Pat LaFontaine [Then and Now] .50
□ R133 Joel Otto [Then and Now] .35
□ R134 Jason Arnott [Then and Now] .35
□ R135 John Vanbiesbrouck (G) [Then and Now] .35
□ R136 Derian Hatcher [Then and Now] .35
□ R137 Brendan Shanahan [Then and Now] 1.00
□ R138 Félix Potvin (G) [Then and Now] .50
□ R139 Trevor Linden [Then and Now] .35
□ R140 Ken Baumgartner [Then and Now] .35
□ R141 Dennis Leary [Dennis Leary On] .35
□ R142 Wendel Clark [Dennis Leary On] .50
□ R143 Cam Neely [Dennis Leary On] 1.00
□ R144 Jeremy Roenick [Dennis Leary On] .50
□ R145 Sergei Fedorov [Dennis Leary On] 1.00
□ R146 Scott Stevens [Dennis Leary On] .35
□ R147 Wayne Gretzky [Dennis Leary On] 4.00
□ R148 Darius Kasparaitis [Dennis Leary On] .35
□ R149 Brian Leetch [Dennis Leary On] .50
□ R150 Marty McSorley [Dennis Leary On] .35
□ R151 Paul Kariya [Rookie Headliners] 1.00
□ R152 Peter Forsberg [Rookie Headliners] 1.00
□ R153 Brett Lindros [Rookie Headliners] .35
□ R154 Kenny Jönsson [Rookie Headliners] .35
□ R155 Jason Allison [Rookie Headliners] .50
□ R156 Aaron Gavey [Rookie Headliners] .35
□ R157 Jamie Storr (G) [Rookie Headliners] .35
□ R158 Viktor Kozlov [Rookie Headliners] .35
□ R159 Valeri Bure [Rookie Headliners] .35
□ R160 Oleg Tverdovsky [Rookie Headliners] .35
□ R161 Brent Gretzky [Rookie Headliners] .35
□ R162 Todd Harvey [Rookie Headliners] .35
□ R163 Todd Warriner [Rookie Headliners] .35
□ R164 Jeff Friesen [Rookie Headliners] .35
□ R165 Adam Deadmarsh [Rookie Headliners] .35
□ R166 Ken Baumgartner [NHLPA Shootout] .35
□ R167 Terry Carkner [NHLPA Shootout] .35
□ R168 Tie Domi [NHLPA Shootout] .35
□ R169 Steve Larmer [NHLPA Shootout] .35
□ R170 Larry Murphy [NHLPA Shootout] .35
□ R171 Steve Thomas [NHLPA Shootout] .35
□ R172 Alexei Yashin [NHLPA Shootout] .50
□ R173 Félix Potvin (G) [NHLPA Shootout] .50
□ R174 Curtis Joseph (G) [NHLPA Shootout] 1.00
□ R175 Rob Zamuner [NHLPA Shootout] .35
□ R176 Wayne Gretzky [Fanimation] 4.00
□ R177 Pavel Bure [Fanimation] .50
□ R178 Eric Lindros [Fanimation] 1.00
□ R179 Patrick Roy (G) [Fanimation] 3.00
□ R180 Doug Gilmour [Fanimation] .50

AUTOGRAPHS

These autographs were inserted one per pack. Most signed approximately 2,400 cards. The Jiri Slegr autograph (#119) was only available via redemption.

Insert Set (178 cards): 3100.00
Common Autograph: 4.00

Player **NRMT-MT**

□ 1 Doug Gilmour ✍ {#/1250} 40.00
□ 2 Adam Foote ✍ 8.00
□ 3 M. Brodeur (G) ✍ [Gold Ink] 50.00
□ 4 Alexander Semak ✍ 4.00
□ 5 Dale Hawerchuk ✍ 15.00
□ 6 Derek King ✍ 4.00
□ 7 Mark Recchi ✍ [Gold Ink] 10.00
□ 8 Fredrik Olausson ✍ 6.00
□ 9 Dave McLlwain ✍ 4.00
□ 10 Marc Bergevin ✍ 4.00
□ 11 Teemu Selänne ✍ {#/600} 200.00
□ 12 Jeremy Roenick ✍ {#/600} 90.00
□ 13 Éric Lacroix ✍ 4.00
□ 14 Marty McInnis ✍ 4.00
□ 15 Kris King ✍ 4.00
□ 16 Bill Ranford (G) ✍ 10.00
□ 17 Gary Roberts ✍ 10.00
□ 18 Mark Osborne ✍ 4.00
□ 19 Dmitri Mironov ✍ 4.00
□ 20 John Vanbiesbrouck (G) ✍ {#/600} 70.00
□ 21 Alexei Zhamnov ✍ 8.00
□ 22 Brad May ✍ 4.00
□ 23 Doug Lidster ✍ 4.00
□ 24 Mikael Renberg ✍ 8.00
□ 25 Kris Draper ✍ 6.00
□ 26 Darryl Sydor ✍ 6.00
□ 27 Claude Lemieux ✍ 8.00
□ 28 Doug Brown ✍ 4.00
□ 29 Louie DeBrusk ✍ 4.00
□ 30 Andy Moog (G) ✍ 10.00
□ 31 Donald Audette ✍ 10.00
□ 32 Raymond Bourque ✍ {#/600} 175.00
□ 33 Brian Rolston ✍ 8.00
□ 34 Ted Drury ✍ 4.00
□ 35 Darren Turcotte ✍ [Gold Ink] 4.00
□ 36 Gary Shuchuk ✍ [Gold Ink] 4.00
□ 37 Mike Ricci ✍ 8.00
□ 38 Kirk Maltby ✍ 6.00
□ 39 Doug Bodger ✍ 4.00
□ 40 Kirk Muller ✍ 8.00
□ 41 Sylvain Lefebvre ✍ 4.00
□ 42 Brent Grieve ✍ 4.00
□ 43 Bill Houlder ✍ [Gold Ink] 4.00
□ 44 Neil Wilkinson ✍ 4.00
□ 45 Donald Dufresne ✍ 4.00
□ 46 Brian Leetch ✍ [Red Ink] ✍ {#/600} 100.00
□ 47 Bryan Smolinski ✍ [Gold Ink] 4.00
□ 48 Kevin Hatcher ✍ [Gold Ink] 4.00
□ 49 Steven Rice ✍ 4.00
□ 50 Bill Guerin ✍ 20.00
□ 51 Grant Jennings ✍ 4.00
□ 52 Dave Andreychuk ✍ 8.00
□ 53 Sean Burke (G) ✍ 15.00
□ 54 Nick Kypreos ✍ 6.00
□ 55 Drake Berehowsky ✍ 4.00
□ 56 Kevin Haller ✍ [Gold Ink] 4.00
□ 57 Bill Berg ✍ 4.00
□ 58 Chris Simon ✍ 6.00
□ 59 Owen Nolan ✍ 20.00
□ 60 Don Sweeney ✍ 4.00
□ 61 Johan Garpenlöv ✍ 4.00
□ 62 Garry Galley ✍ 4.00
□ 63 Pat LaFontaine ✍ 15.00
□ 64 Craig Berube ✍ 4.00
□ 65 Dave Ellett ✍ 4.00
□ 66 Robert Kron ✍ 4.00
□ 67 Alexander Godynyuk ✍ 4.00
□ 68 Markus Näslund ✍ [Gold Ink] 25.00
□ 69 Joel Otto ✍ [Gold Ink] 4.00
□ 70 Igor Ulanov ✍ 4.00
□ 71 Pat Verbeek ✍ 8.00
□ 72 Craig MacTavish ✍ 4.00
□ 73 Gary Leeman ✍ 4.00
□ 74 Kevin Todd ✍ 4.00
□ 75 Mike Sullivan ✍ 4.00
□ 76 Rob Pearson ✍ 4.00
□ 77 Dave Gagner ✍ 4.00
□ 78 Dirk Graham ✍ 4.00
□ 79 Joe Sacco ✍ 4.00
□ 80 Jassen Cullimore ✍ 4.00
□ 81 Glen Featherstone ✍ 4.00
□ 82 Scott Lachance ✍ 4.00
□ 83 Kerry Huffman ✍ 4.00
□ 84 Troy Loney ✍ 4.00
□ 85 Rob Gaudreau ✍ [Gold Ink] 4.00
□ 86 Brendan Shanahan ✍ {#/600} 175.00
□ 87 Joe Murphy ✍ 4.00
□ 88 Scott Niedermayer ✍ 8.00
□ 89 Dan Quinn ✍ 4.00
□ 90 Jeff Norton ✍ 4.00
□ 91 Jim Dowd ✍ 4.00
□ 92 Ray Ferraro ✍ [Gold Ink] 4.00
□ 93 Shawn Burr ✍ 4.00
□ 94 Denis Savard ✍ [Gold Ink] 10.00
□ 95 Dave Manson ✍ [Gold Ink] 4.00
□ 96 Joe Nieuwendyk ✍ 10.00
□ 97 Tony Amonte ✍ 15.00
□ 98 James Patrick ✍ 4.00
□ 99 Guy Hebert (G) ✍ 6.00
□ 100 Peter Zezel ✍ 4.00
□ 101 Shawn McEachern ✍ 8.00
□ 102 Dave Lowry ✍ 6.00
□ 103 David Reid ✍ 4.00
□ 104 Todd Gill ✍ 4.00
□ 105 John Cullen ✍ 6.00
□ 106 Guy Carbonneau ✍ 8.00
□ 107 Jeff Beukeboom ✍ 4.00
□ 108 Wayne Gretzky ✍ {#/300} 1300.00
□ 109 Curtis Joseph (G) ✍ 25.00
□ 110 Jason Arnott ✍ 12.00
□ 111 Éric Desjardins ✍ 8.00
□ 112 Gary Suter ✍ 6.00
□ 113 Luc Robitaille ✍ 20.00
□ 114 Tony Granato ✍ 6.00
□ 115 Steve Yzerman ✍ [Gold Ink] ✍ {#/600} 400.00
□ 116 Chris Gratton ✍ [Gold Ink] 6.00
□ 117 Doug Weight ✍ [Gold Ink] 15.00
□ 118 Garry Valk ✍ [Gold Ink] 4.00
□ 119 Jiri Slegr ✍ [Gold Ink] 40.00
□ 120 Vincent Damphousse ✍ [Gold Ink] 15.00
□ 121 Vladimir Malakhov ✍ [Gold Ink] 4.00
□ 122 Craig Simpson ✍ [Gold Ink] 4.00
□ 123 Theoren Fleury ✍ [Gold Ink] 15.00
□ 124 Dave Poulin ✍ 4.00
□ 125 Derian Hatcher ✍ 8.00
□ 126 Jimmy Waite (G) ✍ 4.00
□ 127 Norm Maciver ✍ [Gold Ink] 4.00
□ 128 Glenn Healy (G) ✍ 6.00
□ 129 Jocelyn Lemieux ✍ 4.00
□ 130 Steve Chiasson ✍ 20.00
□ 131 Keith Jones ✍ 4.00
□ 132 Enrico Ciccone ✍ [Gold Ink] 4.00
□ 133 Martin Lapointe ✍ 10.00
□ 134 John MacLean ✍ 4.00
□ 135 Geoff Courtnall ✍ 4.00
□ 136 David Shaw ✍ [Gold Ink] 4.00
□ 137 Steve Duchesne ✍ 6.00
□ 138 Dean Evason ✍ [Gold Ink] 4.00
□ 139 Eric Weinrich ✍ 4.00
□ 140 Kelly Hrudey (G) ✍ 12.00
□ 141 Ted Donato ✍ [Gold Ink] 4.00
□ 142 Darius Kasparaitis ✍ [Gold Ink] 6.00
□ 143 Tie Domi ✍ [Gold Ink] 8.00
□ 144 Terry Carkner ✍ [Gold Ink] 4.00
□ 145 Steve Thomas ✍ [Gold Ink] 6.00
□ 146 Steve Larmer ✍ 10.00
□ 147 Rob Zamuner ✍ 6.00
□ 148 Larry Murphy ✍ 6.00
□ 149 Ken Baumgartner ✍ [Gold Ink] 4.00
□ 150 Alexei Yashin ✍ {#/600} 75.00
□ 151 Paul Kariya ✍ {#/600} 250.00
□ 152 Todd Harvey ✍ 6.00
□ 153 Viktor Kozlov ✍ [Initials] 12.00
□ 153 Viktor Kozlov ✍ [Full name] 200.00
□ 154 Brent Gretzky ✍ 4.00
□ 155 Petr Klima ✍ [Gold Ink] 4.00
□ 156 Kent Manderville ✍ [Gold Ink] 4.00
□ 157 Mike Eagles ✍ [Gold Ink] 4.00
□ 158 Valeri Kamensky ✍ 8.00
□ 159 Thomas Steen ✍ 4.00
□ 160 Michal Pivonka ✍ 4.00
□ 161 Stephen Heinze ✍ [Gold Ink] 4.00
□ 162 Nicklas Lidström ✍ 15.00
□ 163 Uwe Krupp ✍ 4.00
□ 164 Pat Elynuik ✍ 4.00
□ 165 Michael Peca ✍ 10.00
□ 166 Sylvain Côté ✍ 4.00
□ 167 Trevor Kidd (G) ✍ 8.00
□ 168 Patrick Poulin ✍ 4.00
□ 169 Shane Churla ✍ 4.00
□ 170 Scott Mellanby ✍ 6.00
□ 171 Mike Sillinger ✍ 4.00
□ 172 Shayne Corson ✍ 8.00
□ 173 Micah Aivazoff ✍ 4.00
□ 174 Robert Lang ✍ 6.00
□ 175 Rod Brind'Amour ✍ [Gold Ink] 8.00
□ 176 Troy Murray ✍ [Gold Ink] 4.00
□ 177 Mike Krushelnyski ✍ 4.00
□ 178 Sergio Momesso ✍ [Gold Ink] 4.00

UP CLOSE AND PERSONAL

Insert Set (10 cards): 60.00
Insert (1:14) UC

□ UC-1 Wayne Gretzky, NHLPA 20.00
□ UC-2 Eric Lindros, NHLPA 5.00
□ UC-3 Pavel Bure, NHLPA 3.00
□ UC-4 Teemu Selänne, NHLPA 3.00
□ UC-5 Steve Yzerman, NHLPA 10.00
□ UC-6 Jeremy Roenick, NHLPA 3.00
□ UC-7 Sergei Fedorov, NHLPA 5.00
□ UC-8 Patrick Roy (G), NHLPA 15.00
□ UC-9 Paul Kariya, NHLPA 5.00
□ UC-10 Doug Gilmour, NHLPA 3.00

WAYNE GRETZKY'S 99 ALL-STARS

Insert Set (19 cards): 130.00
Insert (1:14) G

□ G1 Wayne Gretzky, Ninety-Nine All-Stars 50.00
□ G2 Paul Coffey, Ninety-Nine All-Stars 5.00
□ G3 Rob Blake, Ninety-Nine All-Stars 5.00
□ G4 Pat Conacher, Ninety-Nine All-Stars 2.00
□ G5 Russ Courtnall, Ninety-Nine All-Stars 2.00
□ G6 Sergei Fedorov, Ninety-Nine All-Stars 10.00
□ G7 Grant Fuhr (G), Ninety-Nine All-Stars 5.00
□ G8 Todd Gill, Ninety-Nine All-Stars 2.00
□ G9 Tony Granato, Ninety-Nine All-Stars 2.00
□ G10 Brett Hull, Ninety-Nine All-Stars 10.00
□ G11 Charlie Huddy, Ninety-Nine All-Stars 2.00
□ G12 Steve Larmer, Ninety-Nine All-Stars 5.00
□ G13 Kelly Hrudey (G), Ninety-Nine All-Stars 5.00
□ G14 Al MacInnis, Ninety-Nine All-Stars 5.00
□ G15 Marty McSorley, Ninety-Nine All-Stars 2.00
□ G16 Jari Kurri, Ninety-Nine All-Stars 10.00
□ G17 Kirk Muller, Ninety-Nine All-Stars 2.00
□ G18 Rick Tocchet, Ninety-Nine All-Stars 2.00
□ G19 Steve Yzerman, Ninety-Nine All-Stars 30.00

1994 - 95 UPPER DECK WORLD JUNIOR ALUMNI

Complete Set (15 cards): 6.00

Player **NRMT-MT**

□ 1 Title Card .25
□ 2 Manny Legacé (G), Canada Juniors .50
□ 3 Jeff Nelson, Canada Juniors .25
□ 4 Alexandre Daigle, Canada Juniors .25
□ 5 Paul Kariya, Canada Juniors 2.50
□ 6 Turner Stevenson, Canada Juniors .25
□ 7 Michael Peca, Canada Juniors .50
□ 8 Tyler Wright, Canada Juniors .25
□ 9 Brent Tully, Canada Juniors .25

□ 10 Trevor Kidd (G), Canada Juniors .50
□ 11 Martin Lapointe, Canada Juniors .50
□ 12 Scott Niedermayer, Canada Juniors .50
□ 13 Jeff Friesen, Canada Juniors .50
□ 14 Todd Harvey, Canada Juniors .25
□ 15 Jamie Storr (G), Canada Juniors .25

1994 - 95 ZELLERS MASTERS OF HOCKEY

There are 10,850 copies of each card and 1,100 copies of each autographed card. The unsigned cards sell for $1-3.

Imprint: ZELLERS

Complete Set (8 cards): 275.00

Player **Auto.**

□□ Jean Béliveau ✍ 70.00
□□ Gerry Cheevers (G) ✍ 40.00
□□ Red Kelly ✍ 30.00
□□ Dave Keon ✍ 50.00
□□ Lanny McDonald ✍ 40.00
□□ Pierre Pilote ✍ 25.00
□□ Henri Richard ✍ 50.00
□□ Norm Ullman ✍ 25.00

1995 GLOBE

Numerous cards in this series (specifically, cards of NHLPA members) were not licensed. As such, cards in this series are not recognized as rookie cards.

Imprint: Semic Sports Cards

Complete Set (270 cards): 60.00
Common Player: .20
Album: 6.00

Player **NRMT-MT**

□ 1 Tommy Söderström (G), Swe. .20
□ 2 Roger Nordström (G), Swe. .20
□ 3 Tommy Salo (G), Swe. .50
□ 4 Hakan Algotsson, Swe. .20
□ 5 Thomas Ostlund, Swe. .20
□ 6 Johan Hedberg (G), Swe. 5.00
□ 7 Ulf Samuelsson, Swe. .20
□ 8 Calle Johansson, Swe. .20
□ 9 Nicklas Lidström, Swe. .50
□ 10 Tommy Albein, Swe. .20
□ 11 Peter Andersson, Swe. .20
□ 12 Magnus Svensson, Swe. .20
□ 13 Mats Sundin, Swe. 1.00
□ 14 Tomas Jönsson, Swe. .20
□ 15 Kenny Jönsson, Swe. .20
□ 16 Tommy Sjödin, Swe. .20
□ 17 Fredrik Stillman, Swe. .20
□ 18 Marcus Ragnarsson, Swe. .20
□ 19 Peter Popovic, Swe. .20
□ 20 Arto Blomsten, Swe. .20
□ 21 Peter Forsberg, Swe. 1.50
□ 22 Roger Johansson, Swe. .20
□ 23 Leif Rohlin, Swe. .20

	Player	Price
□	24 Björn Nord, Swe.	.20
□	25 Stefan Larsson, Swe.	.20
□	26 Fredrik Olausson, Swe.	.20
□	27 Kjell Samuelsson, Swe.	.20
□	28 Tomas Sandström, Swe.	.20
□	29 Mikael Renberg, Swe.	.20
□	30 Mikael Johansson, Swe.	.20
□	31 Patrik Juhlin, Swe.	.20
□	32 Roger Hansson, Swe.	.20
□	33 Daniel Rydmark, Swe.	.20
□	34 Jonas Bergqvist, Swe.	.20
□	35 Michael Nylander, Swe.	.20
□	36 Johan Garpenlöv, Swe.	.20
□	37 Charles Berglund, Swe.	.20
□	38 Jörgen Jönsson, Swe.	.20
□	39 Stefan Örnskog, Swe.	.20
□	40 Thomas Steen, Swe.	.20
□	41 Patrik Carnbäck, Swe.	.20
□	42 Mikael Andersson, Swe.	.20
□	43 Markus Näslund, Swe.	1.00
□	44 Andreas Dackell, Swe.	.20
□	45 Erik Huusko, Swe.	.20
□	46 Tomas Forslund, Swe.	.20
□	47 Daniel Alfredsson, Swe.	.50
□	48 Ulf Dahlén, Swe.	.20
□	49 Anders Huusko, Swe.	.20
□	50 Tomas Holmström, Swe.	.20
□	51 Niklas Andersson, Swe.	.20
□	52 Hakan Loob, Swe.	.20
□	53 Pelle Eklund, Swe.	.20
□	54 Patrik Erickson, Swe.	.20
□	55 Jonas Forsberg (G), Swe.	.20
□	56 Daniel Johansson, Swe.	.20
□	57 Mattias Öhlund, Swe.	.20
□	58 Anders Eriksson, Swe.	.20
□	59 Fredrik Modin, Swe.	.20
□	60 Niklas Sundström, Swe.	.20
□	61 Jesper Mattsson, Swe.	.20
□	62 Johan Davidsson, Swe.	.20
□	63 Mats Lindgren, Swe.	.20
□	64 Leif Holmqvist (G), Swe.	.50
□	65 Pelle Lindberg (G), Swe.	.50
□	66 Lennart (Lill-Strimma) Svedberg, Swe.	.50
□	67 Börje Salming, Swe.	1.00
□	68 Sven (Tumba) Johansson, Swe.	.50
□	69 Ulf Sterner, Swe.	.50
□	70 Anders Hedberg, Swe.	.20
□	71 Kent Nilsson, Swe.	.20
□	72 Mats Näslund, Swe.	.20
□	73 Patrick Roy (G), Cdn.	3.50
□	74 Ed Belfour (G), Cdn.	1.00
□	75 Bill Ranford (G), Cdn.	.50
□	76 Paul Coffey, Cdn.	.50
□	77 Ray Bourque, Cdn.	1.50
□	78 Steve Smith, Cdn.	.20
□	79 Al MacInnis, Cdn.	.50
□	80 Mark Tinordi, Cdn.	.20
□	81 Scott Stevens, Cdn.	.50
□	82 Rob Blake, Cdn.	.50
□	83 Theoren Fleury, Cdn.	.50
□	84 Mark Messier, Cdn.	1.00
□	85 Mike Gartner, Cdn.	1.00
□	86 Brendan Shanahan, Cdn.	1.00
□	87 Mario Lemieux, Cdn.	3.50
□	88 Eric Lindros, Cdn.	1.00
□	89 Steve Yzerman, Cdn.	3.00
□	90 Adam Oates, Cdn.	.50
□	91 Paul Kariya, Cdn.	1.50
□	92 Rick Tocchet, Cdn.	.20
□	93 Doug Gilmour, Cdn.	.50
□	94 Luc Robitaille, Cdn.	1.00
□	95 Jason Arnott, Cdn.	.50
□	96 Adam Graves, Cdn.	.50
□	97 Petr Nedved, Cdn.	.20
□	98 mark Recchi, Cdn.	.50
□	99 Wayne Gretzky, Cdn.	5.00
□	100 Mike Richter (G), USA.	.50
□	101 John Vanbiesbrouck (G), USA.	.50
□	102 Tom Barrasso (G), USA.	.50
□	103 Brian Leetch, USA.	.50
□	104 Gary Suter, USA.	.20
□	105 Kevin Hatcher, USA.	.20
□	106 Phil Housley, USA.	.20
□	107 Chris Chelios, USA.	.50
□	108 Eric Weinrich, USA.	.20
□	109 Derian Hatcher, USA.	.20
□	110 Craig Wolanin, USA.	.20
□	111 Mike Modano, USA.	1.00
□	112 Joe Mullen, USA.	.50
□	113 Joel Otto, USA.	.20
□	114 Doug Brown, USA.	.20
□	115 Brett Hull, USA.	1.00
□	116 Pat LaFontaine, USA.	.50
□	117 Jeremy Roenick, USA.	1.00
□	118 Craig Janney, USA.	.20
□	119 Kevin Miller, USA.	.20
□	120 Tony Granato, USA.	.20
□	121 Tony Amonte, USA.	.50
□	122 Kevin Stevens, USA.	.20
□	123 Darren Turcotte, USA.	.20
□	124 Scott Young, USA.	.20
□	125 Doug Weight, USA.	.50
□	126 Phil Bourque, USA.	.20
□	127 Markus Ketterer (G), Fin.	.20
□	128 Jarmo Myllys (G), Fin.	.20
□	129 Jyrki Lumme, Fin.	.20
□	130 Timo Jutila, Fin.	.20
□	131 Marko Kiprusoff, Fin.	.20
□	132 Hannu Virta, Fin.	.50
□	133 Teppo Numminen, Fin.	.20
□	134 Janne Laukkanen, Fin.	.20
□	135 Mika Nieminen, Fin.	.20
□	136 Janne Ojanen, Fin.	.20
□	137 Jari Kurri, Fin.	1.00
□	138 Esa Tikkanen, Fin.	.20
□	139 Saku Koivu, Fin.	1.00
□	140 Teemu Selänne, Fin.	1.00
□	141 Raimo Helminen, Fin.	.20
□	142 Mikko Mäkelä, Fin.	.20
□	143 Christian Ruuttu, Fin.	.20
□	144 Esa Keskinen, Fin.	.20
□	145 Dominik Hasek (G), Cze.	1.00
□	146 Petr Briza (G), Cze.	.50
□	147 Richard Smehlik, Cze.	.20
□	148 Leo Gudas, Cze.	.20
□	149 Roman Hamrlik, Cze.	.20
□	150 Antonin Stavjana, Cze.	.20
□	151 Jiri Slegr, Cze.	.20
□	152 Jiri Vykoukal, Cze.	.20
□	153 Tomas Jelinek, Cze.	.20
□	154 Richard Zemlicka, Cze.	.20
□	155 Robert Lang, Cze.	.20
□	156 Michal Pivonka, Cze.	.20
□	157 Jaromir Jagr, Cze.	1.00
□	158 Josef Beranek, Cze.	.20
□	159 Robert Reichel, Cze.	.20
□	160 Petr Hrbek, Cze.	.20
□	161 Jiri Kucera, Cze.	.20
□	162 Kamil Kastak, Cze.	.20
□	163 Andrei Trefilov (G), Rus.	.20
□	164 Mikhail Shtalenkov (G), Rus.	.20
□	165 Sergei Zubov, Rus.	.20
□	166 Vladimir Malakhov, Rus.	.20
□	167 Igor Kravchuk, Rus.	.20
□	168 Alexei Gusarov, Rus.	.20
□	169 Alexei Zhitnik, Rus.	.20
□	170 Alexander Smirnov, Rus.	.20
□	171 Dimitri Yushkevich, Rus.	.20
□	172 Alexei Yashin, Rus.	.50
□	173 Alexei Zhamonov, Rus.	.20
□	174 Pavel Bure, Rus.	1.00
□	175 Sergei Fedorov, Rus.	1.00
□	176 Andrei Kovalenko, Rus.	.20
□	177 Alex Kovalev, Rus.	.50
□	178 Andrei Khomutov, Rus.	.20
□	179 Valeri Kamensky, Rus.	.20
□	180 Vyacheslav Bykov, Rus.	.20
□	181 Claus Dalpiaz (G), Aut.	.20
□	182 Michael Puschacher, Aut.	.20
□	183 Ken Strong, Aut.	.20
□	184 Martin Ulrich, Aut.	.20
□	185 Andreas Puschnig, Aut.	.20
□	186 Herbert Hohenberger, Aut.	.20
□	187 Marty Dallmann, Aut.	.20
□	188 James Burton, Aut.	.20
□	189 Michael Shea, Aut.	.20
□	190 Jim Marthinsen (G), Nor.	.20
□	191 Örjan Lövdal, Nor.	.20
□	192 Cato Tom Andersen, Nor.	.20
□	193 Geir Hoff, Nor.	.20
□	194 Tommy Jakobsen, Nor.	.20
□	195 Marius Rath, Nor.	.20
□	196 Trond Magnussen, Nor.	.20
□	197 Svein Enok Nörstebö, Nor.	.20
□	198 Espen Knutsen, Nor.	.20
□	199 Petri Ylönen (G), Fra.	.20
□	200 Michel Valliere, Fra.	.20
□	201 Franck Pajonkowski, Fra.	.20
□	202 Pierrick Maia, Fra.	.20
□	203 Christophe Ville, Fra.	.20
□	204 Serge Poudrier, Fra.	.20
□	205 Philippe Bozon, Fra.	.20
□	206 Gerald Guonnelon, Fra.	.20
□	207 Antoine Richer, Fra.	.20
□	208 Reto Pavoni (G), Sui.	.20
□	209 Renato Tosio (G), Sui.	.20
□	210 Jörg Eberle, Sui.	.20
□	211 Fredy Luthi, Sui.	.20
□	212 Christian Weber, Sui.	.20
□	213 Sandro Bertaggia, Sui.	.20
□	214 Patrick Howald, Sui.	.20
□	215 Gil Montandon, Sui.	.20
□	216 Rick Tschumi, Sui.	.20
□	217 Klaus Merk (G), Ger.	.20
□	218 Josef Heiss (G), Ger.	.20
□	219 Rich Amann, Ger.	.20
□	220 Michael Rumrich, Ger.	.20
□	221 Thomas Brandl, Ger.	.20
□	222 Andreas Niederberger, Ger.	.20
□	223 Leo Stefan, Ger.	.20
□	224 Stefan Ustorf, Ger.	.20
□	225 Dieter Hegen, Ger.	.20
□	226 Michael Rosati (G), Ita.	.50
□	227 Bruno Campese (G), Ita.	.20
□	228 Roberto Oberrauch, Ita.	.20
□	229 Anthony Circelli, Ita.	.20
□	230 Bill Stewart, Ita.	.20
□	231 Bruno Zarrillo, Ita.	.20
□	232 Gaetano Orlando, Ita.	.20
□	233 Stefan Figliuzzi, Ita.	.20
□	234 Jim Camazzola, Ita.	.20
□	235 Vladislav Tretiak (G), USSR	1.50
□	236 Viacheslav Fetisov, USSR	.50
□	237 Alexei Kasatonov, USSR	.20
□	238 Sergei Makarov, USSR	.50
□	239 Igor Larionov, USSR	.50
□	240 Vladimir Krutov, USSR	.20
□	241 Valeri Kharlamov, USSR	.50
□	242 Vladimir Petrov, USSR	.50
□	243 Boris Mikhailov, USSR	.50
□	244 OS-GULD 94	.20
□	245 OS-GULD 94	.20
□	246 OS-GULD 94	.20
□	247 VM-GULD 94	.20
□	248 VM-GULD 94	.20
□	249 VM-GULD 94	.20
□	250 Manon Rhéaume (G)	3.50
□	251 Tomas Brolin/ Espen Knutsen	.20
□	252 Mats Sundin/ Roger Andersson	1.00
□	253 Peter Forsberg	1.00
□	254 Peter Forsberg	1.00
□	255 Peter Forsberg	1.00
□	256 Mats Sundin	.50
□	257 Mats Sundin	.50
□	258 Mats Sundin	.50
□	259 Mikael Renberg	.20
□	260 Mikael Renberg	.20
□	261 Mikael Renberg	.20
□	262 Eric Lindros	.50
□	263 Eric Lindros	.50
□	264 Eric Lindros	.50
□	265 Wayne Gretzky	3.50
□	266 Wayne Gretzky	3.50
□	267 Wayne Gretzky	3.50
□	268 CL: Mikael Renberg	.20
□	269 CL: Mats Sundin	.50
□	270 CL: Peter Forsberg	.50

1995 HARTWALL KARJALA

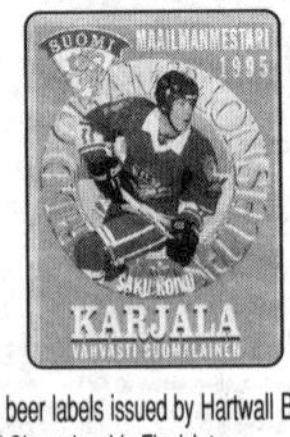

A set of 24 beer labels issued by Hartwall Brewery of the 1995 World Championship Finnish team.

Label Size: 2 1/4" x 3"

Complete Set (24 labels): 50.00

	Player	Hartwall
□	Raimo Helminen	2.00
□	Erik Hämäläinen	2.00
□	Timo Jutila	3.00
□	Sami Kapanen	3.00
□	Esa Keskinen	2.00
□	Marko Kiprusoff	2.00
□	Saku Koivu	12.00
□	Tero Lehtera	2.00
□	Jere Lehtinen	5.00
□	Curt Lindstrom	2.00
□	Jarmo Myllys (G)	3.00
□	Mika Nieminen	2.00
□	Janne Niinimaa	5.00
□	Petteri Nummelin	2.00
□	Janne Ojanen	2.00
□	Marko Palo	2.00
□	Ville Peltonen	2.00
□	Mika Stromberg	2.00
□	Ari Sulander	2.00
□	Raimo Summanen	2.00
□	Jukka Tammi	2.00
□	Antti Tormanen	2.00
□	Hannu Virta	2.00
□	Juha Ylönen	3.00

1995 KOULULAINEN

Two 2-card panels issued by the magazine Koululainen. We have no pricing information on this set.

Card Size: 1 7/8" x 4 1/8"

Koululainen

□ Wayne Gretzky □ Saku Koivu
□ Jari Kurri □ Esa Tikkanen

1995 LEAF LATKALIIGA

A set of 12 candy boxes issued by Leaf for the the Finnish National League.

Card Size: 1 7/8" x 2 3/16"

Complete Set (12 cards): 18.00

	Player		Player
□	1 Jere Lehtinen	□	2 Antti Törmänen
□	3 Jari Korpisalo	□	4 Ari-Pekka Siekkinen
□	5 Ville Peltonen	□	6 Mika Rautio
□	7 Juha Riihijarvi	□	8 Jukka Seppo
□	9 Pasi Kuivalainen	□	10 Kari Rosenberg
□	11 Mika Manninen	□	12 Janne Ojanen

1995 PANINI WORLD CHAMPIONSHIP STICKERS

These stickers were a European release.

Complete Set (300 stickers): 45.00

Common Player: .20

Album (Saku Koivu, et al):

	Player		Player
□	1 Bill Ranford (G)	□	2 Stéphane Fiset (G)
□	3 Steve Duchesne	□	4 Brad Schlegel
□	5 Luke Richardson	□	6 Darryl Sydor
□	7 Yves Racine	□	8 Rob Blake
□	9 Marc Bergevin	□	10 Paul Coffey
□	11 Jason Arnott	□	12 Geoff Sanderson
□	13 Shayne Corson	□	14 Mike Ricci
□	15 Kelly Buchberger	□	16 Brendan Shanahan
□	17 Pat Verbeek	□	18 Nelson Emerson
□	19 Rod Brind'Amour	□	20 Joe Sakic
□	21 Luc Robitaille	□	22 Steve Thomas
□	23 Paul Kariya	□	24 Theoren Fleury
□	25 Dave Gagner	□	26 Valeri Ivannikov (G)
□	27 M. Shtalenkov (G)	□	28 Nikolai Tsulygin
□	29 Dmitri Krasotkin	□	30 Morat Davydov
□	31 Andrei Sklopintsev	□	32 Oleg Davydov
□	33 Evgeny Gribko	□	34 Andrei Yakhanov
□	35 Igor Nikulin	□	36 Valeri Kamensky
□	37 Boris Timorfeyev	□	38 Dmitri Denisov
□	39 Rail Muftiev	□	40 Andrei Tarasyenko
□	41 Oleg Belov	□	42 Andrei Kovalenko
□	43 Igor Varitski	□	44 Ravil Yakubov
□	45 Vyacheslav Kozlov	□	46 A. Vinogradov
□	47 Yuri Tsyplakov	□	48 Stanislav Romanov
□	49 Vyacheslav Bykov	□	50 Andrei Khomutov
□	51 Joseph Heiss (G)	□	52 Klaus Merk (G)
□	53 Mirko Lüdemann	□	54 Ulrich Hiemer
□	55 Torsten Kienass	□	56 Jayson Meyer
□	57 Josef Lehner	□	58 Ron Fischer
□	59 Michael Bresagk	□	60 A. Niederberger
□	61 Peter Guida	□	62 Jan Benda
□	63 Thomas Brandl	□	64 Andreas Lupzig
□	65 Michael Rumrich	□	66 Benoit Doucet
□	67 Raimond Hilger	□	68 Georg Franz
□	69 Jörg Handrick	□	70 Dieter Hegen
□	71 Ernst Köpf	□	72 Günter Oswald
□	73 Georg Holzmann	□	74 Jürgen Rumrich
□	75 Leo Stefan	□	76 Bruno Campese (G)
□	77 Michael Rosati (G)	□	78 Giovanni Marchetti
□	79 Georg Comloi	□	80 Luigi de Corte
□	81 Robert Oberrauch	□	82 Anthony Circelli
□	83 Alex Thaler	□	84 Carlo Lorenzi
□	85 Michael de Angelis	□	86 Emilio Iovio
□	87 Gaetano Orlando	□	88 Lucio Topatigh
□	89 Stefano Figliuzzi	□	90 Bruno Zarrillo
□	91 Mark Montanari	□	92 Armando Chelodi
□	93 Mirko Moroder	□	94 Alex Gschliesser
□	95 Maurizio Mansi	□	96 Petri Ylönen (G)
□	97 Michel Valliere (G)	□	98 Serge Djelloul
□	99 Christophe Moyon	□	100 Gerald Guennelon
□	101 Philippe Lemoine	□	102 Denis Perez
□	103 Serge Poudrier	□	104 Steven Woodburn
□	105 Michael Babin	□	106 Benjamin Angnel
□	107 S. Arcangeloni	□	108 Laurent Deschaume
□	109 Pierre Pousse	□	110 Patrick Dunn
□	111 Pierrick Maia	□	112 Philippe Bozon
□	113 Christian Pouget	□	114 Antoine Richer
□	115 Richard Aimonetto	□	116 Reto Pavoni (G)
□	117 Renato Tosio (G)	□	118 Marco Bayer
□	119 Sandro Bertaggia	□	120 Frédy Bobillier
□	121 Dino Kessler	□	122 Sven Leuenberger
□	123 Martin Steinegger	□	124 Andreas Zehnder
□	125 Misko Antisin	□	126 Gian-Marco Crameri
□	127 Jörg Eberle	□	128 Patrick Fischer
□	129 Patrick Howald	□	130 Marcel Jenni
□	131 Gil Montandon	□	132 Pascal Schaller
□	133 Andy Ton	□	134 Roberto Triulzi
□	135 Theo Wittman	□	136 R. Nordström (G)
□	137 T. Östlund (G)	□	138 Magnus Svensson
□	139 Tommy Sjödin	□	140 Fredrik Stillman
□	141 Tomas Jönsson	□	142 Stefan Larsson
□	143 Leif Rohlin	□	144 Marcus Ragnarsson
□	145 Christer Olsson	□	146 Morgan Samuelsson
□	147 Andreas Dackell	□	148 Jonas Johnsson
□	149 Charles Berglund	□	150 Erik Huusko
□	151 Daniel Rydmark	□	152 Patrik Carnbäck
□	153 Mats Lindgren	□	154 Jonas Bergkvist
□	155 Stefan Örnskog	□	156 Pelle Eklund
□	157 Tomas Forslund	□	158 Roger Hansson
□	159 Håkan Åhlund	□	160 Daniel Alfredsson
□	161 Jarmo Myllys (G)	□	162 Jukka Tammi (G)
□	163 Mika Strömberg	□	164 Erik Hämäläinen
□	165 Karri Kivi	□	166 Timo Jutila
□	167 Petteri Nummelin	□	168 Hannu VIrta
□	169 Marko Kiprusov	□	170 Waltteri Immonen
□	171 Janne Ojanen	□	172 Esa Keskinen
□	173 Marko Jantunen	□	174 Saku Koivu
□	175 Marko Palo	□	176 Tero Lehterä
□	177 Mika Alatalo	□	178 Ville Peltonen
□	179 Raimo Helminen	□	180 Petri Varis
□	181 Jokke Heinänen	□	182 Timo Saarikoski
□	183 Sami Kapanen	□	184 Tero Arkiomaa
□	185 Mika Nieminen	□	186 Petr Briza (G)
□	187 Roman Turek (G)	□	188 Milos Holan
□	189 Drahomir Kadlec	□	190 Frantisek Kaberle
□	191 Bedrich Scerban	□	192 Roman Hamrlik
□	193 Jan Vopat	□	194 Antonin Stavjana
□	195 Jiri Vykoukal	□	196 Jiri Veber
□	197 Frantisek Musil	□	198 Richard Zemlicka
□	199 Kamil Kastak	□	200 Jiri Kucera
□	201 Roman Horak	□	202 Martin Rucinsky
□	203 Josef Beranek	□	204 Bobby Holik
□	205 Otakar Janecky	□	206 Jiri Dolezal
□	207 Martin Straka	□	208 Martin Hostak
□	209 Radek Toupal	□	210 Tomas Kapusta
□	211 Guy Hebert (G)	□	212 Mike Richter (G)
□	213 Shawn Chambers	□	214 Sean Hill
□	215 Don McSween	□	216 Pat Neaton
□	217 Barry Richter	□	218 Craig Wolanin
□	219 Gary Suter	□	220 Bob Beers
□	221 Brett Hauer	□	222 Peter Ciavaglia
□	223 Phil Bourque	□	224 Shjon Podein
□	225 John Lilley	□	226 Tim Sweeney
□	227 Scott Young	□	228 Craig Janney
□	229 Joe Sacco	□	230 Jeff Lazaro
□	231 Doug Weight	□	232 Thomas Bisset
□	233 Jim Campbell	□	234 Mark Beaufait
□	235 Peter Ferraro	□	236 Jim Marthinsen (G)
□	237 R. Schinstad (G)	□	238 Jan Roar Fagerli
□	239 Petter Salsten	□	240 C.O. Andersen
□	241 S.E. Nørstebø	□	242 Thommie Eriksen
□	243 Tom Erik Olsen	□	244 Geir Hoff
□	245 Bjørn Anders Dahl	□	246 Trond Magnussen
□	247 Ørjan Løvdal	□	248 Espen Knutsen
□	249 Rune Gulliksen	□	250 Erik Paulsen
□	251 Sjur Robert Nilsen	□	252 Petter Thoresen
□	253 Rune Fjeldstad	□	254 Erik Tveten
□	255 Henrik Aaby	□	256 M. Puschacher (G)

- ☐ 257 Claus Dalpiaz (G) ☐ 258 Michael Günter
- ☐ 259 Martin Ulrich ☐ 260 Peter Kasper
- ☐ 261 E. Linder ☐ 262 H. Hohenberger
- ☐ 263 G. Unterluggauer ☐ 264 Martin Krainz
- ☐ 265 Helmut Karel ☐ 266 Werner Kerth
- ☐ 267 Dieter Kalt ☐ 268 Patrick Pilloni
- ☐ 269 Mario Schaden ☐ 270 Wolfgang Kromp
- ☐ 271 Günter Lanzinger ☐ 272 Manfred Mühr
- ☐ 273 Gerald Ressmann ☐ 274 Siegfried Habert
- ☐ 275 Christoph Brandner ☐ 276 Wayne Gretzky
- ☐ 277 Mario Lemieux ☐ 278 Eric Lindros
- ☐ 279 Mark Messier ☐ 280 Steve Yzerman
- ☐ 281 Pavel Bure ☐ 282 Sergei Fedorov
- ☐ 283 Igor Larionov ☐ 284 Sergei Makarov
- ☐ 285 Alexander Mogilny ☐ 286 Ulf Dahlén
- ☐ 287 Peter Forsberg ☐ 288 Mikael Renberg
- ☐ 289 Ulf Samuelsson ☐ 290 Tomas Sandström
- ☐ 291 Thomas Steen ☐ 292 Mats Sundin
- ☐ 293 Jari Kurri ☐ 294 Teemu Selänne
- ☐ 295 Esa Tikkanen ☐ 296 Dominik Hasek (G)
- ☐ 297 Jaromir Jagr ☐ 298 Robert Reichel
- ☐ 299 Brett Hull ☐ 300 Brian Leetch

1995 PARKHURST PHONECARDS

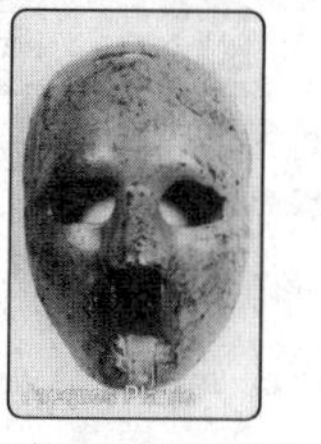

These phonecards premiered at the National sportscard Collectors Convention in St. Louis. These Incomnet phonecards are licensed by the NHLPA. We have no pricing information on these cards.

Player

- ☐ Ed Belfour (G), Chic.
- ☐ Br. Hull / Cu. Joseph / B. Shanahan
- ☐ Curtis Joseph (G), SLou.
- ☐ Kirk McLean (G), Vanc.
- ☐ Andy Moog (G), Dall.
- ☐ Jacques Plante, Mont.
- ☐ Félix Potvin (G), Toro.
- ☐ John Vanbiesbrouck (G), Flor.

1995 PARKHURST PHONECARDS

We have no pricing information on these cards.

Imprint: Canada Telecom Network Inc.

Player

- ☐ Doug Gilmour
- ☐ Brett Hull
- ☐ Jaromir Jagr
- ☐ Trevor Linden
- ☐ Eric Lindros
- ☐ Mark Messier
- ☐ Félix Potvin (G)
- ☐ Patrick Roy (G)

1995 QUÉBEC INTERNATIONAL PEE WEE

Complete Set (1436):

LA PRESQU'ÎLE PEE WEE

- ☐ 1 Jonathan Chevrier ☐ 2 Yen-I Chen
- ☐ 3 Luc Charlebois ☐ 4 Simon Granger
- ☐ 5 Alexandre Burrows ☐ 6 Clint Preston
- ☐ 7 Sébastien Corbeil ☐ 8 Jean-Nicolas Wilkins
- ☐ 9 Daniel Charlebois ☐ 10 Dario D'Andrea
- ☐ 11 Francis Chevrier ☐ 12 Charles Séguin
- ☐ 13 Sylvain Létourneau ☐ 14 Maxime Paré
- ☐ 15 Carl Michaelson ☐ 16 Philippe Lauzon

ST-HUBERT PEE WEE

- ☐ 17 Jonathan Émond ☐ 18 Bryan Messier
- ☐ 19 Pierre-Luc St-Louis ☐ 20 Mathieu Lessard
- ☐ 21 Karl Harbec ☐ 22 Steve Lessieur
- ☐ 23 Mathieu Gladu ☐ 24 Frédéric Hardy
- ☐ 25 Éric Tremblay ☐ 26 Daniel Boileau
- ☐ 27 Pierre-Luc Geneau ☐ 28 Sébastien Larivière
- ☐ 29 Mathieu Deleau ☐ 30 Mathieu Péladeau
- ☐ 31 Jean-Marc Bastien ☐ 32 Vincent Sirois

STE-FOY PEE WEE AA

- ☐ 33 Roberto Bissonnette ☐ 34 Mathieu Blouin
- ☐ 35 François Boulianne ☐ 36 Marc Brisson
- ☐ 37 Daniel Clemont ☐ 38 Antoine Dufour
- ☐ 39 David Fournier ☐ 40 Nicolas Geoffroy
- ☐ 41 David Jacques ☐ 42 Alexis Léger
- ☐ 43 Patrick Mébarga ☐ 44 Jocelyn Nadeau
- ☐ 45 Simon Paquet ☐ 46 David Savard
- ☐ 47 Nicolas Vimard

CAMPUS PEE WEE CAMP-ROUGE/ ST-AUGUSTINE/PORTNEUF

- ☐ 48 Patrice Bégin ☐ 49 Alexandre Blackburn
- ☐ 50 Jean-Philippe Brière ☐ 51 Alexandre Côté
- ☐ 52 J-P Côté ☐ 53 Jonathan Côté
- ☐ 54 Mathieu Döré ☐ 55 Élie Dufour
- ☐ 56 Frédéric Faucher ☐ 57 Maxime Ferland
- ☐ 58 Simon Gauthier ☐ 59 Marc-André Gosselin
- ☐ 60 Étienne Grondin ☐ 61 Sébastien Ouarhani
- ☐ 62 Nicolas Pelletier ☐ 63 Guillaume Roy

FINLAND PEE WEE

- ☐ 64 Jussi Ahopelto ☐ 65 Patri Haikonen
- ☐ 66 Aleksi Helander ☐ 67 Pasi Lehtinen
- ☐ 68 Matti Lievonen ☐ 69 Olli Malmivaara
- ☐ 70 Juha Metsälä ☐ 71 Toni Mustonen
- ☐ 72 Olli-Pekka Mäki ☐ 73 Antti Pihlgren
- ☐ 74 Tero Pylkänen ☐ 75 Aki Rissanen
- ☐ 76 Marko Sakko ☐ 77 Mikko Tylli
- ☐ 78 Jaakko Valkama ☐ 79 Niko Vuori
- ☐ 80 Tomi Vuori ☐ 81 Jarno Välimäki
- ☐ 82 Marko Salminen

POINTE-AUX-TREMBLES PEE WEE

- ☐ 83 Marc-André Leclerc ☐ 84 J-C Roberge
- ☐ 85 François Cardin ☐ 86 Jean-François Verret
- ☐ 87 Ian Liboiron ☐ 88 Danny Sansregret
- ☐ 89 Christian Beaulieu ☐ 90 Luc Beauchemin
- ☐ 91 Richard Roy ☐ 92 Frédérick Samson
- ☐ 93 Simon Trépanier ☐ 94 S. Létourneau
- ☐ 95 Yan* Tremblay ☐ 96 Marc-André Collins
- ☐ 97 Benoît Boisvert ☐ 98 Steve Gauthier

LAC ST-LOUIS PEE WEE

The most expensive singles are Mirko Murovic and Matthew Lombardi at $2-3 each.

- ☐ 99 Reid Allen ☐ 100 C. Davidson
- ☐ 101 Jared Nixon ☐ 102 David Kajaks
- ☐ 103 Matthew Lombardi ☐ 104 S. Lagacé-Daigle
- ☐ 105 M-A Maglieri ☐ 106 Brandon McCarthy
- ☐ 107 Mirko Murovic ☐ 108 Justin Quenneville
- ☐ 109 Brandon Reid ☐ 110 Tyler Reid
- ☐ 111 Brent Robinson ☐ 112 Patrice Thériault
- ☐ 113 Dustin Traylen

MOUNT-PEARL PEE WEE

- ☐ 115 Marko Kenny ☐ 116 Kevin Sullivan
- ☐ 117 Mark Reddy ☐ 118 David Norris
- ☐ 119 Darryl Butt ☐ 121 Brad Sturge
- ☐ 122 Stephen North ☐ 123 Paul Kielly
- ☐ 124 B.J. Robart ☐ 125 Brad Coles
- ☐ 126 Jason Garland ☐ 127 Victor Dray
- ☐ 128 Mark Tilley ☐ 129 Adam French
- ☐ 130 Garrett Gallivan ☐ 130 Robbie Harris

CAMPUS PEE WEE CAP-ROUGE/ ST-AUGUSTIN

- ☐ 131 Yannick Lévesque ☐ 132 J.-Philippe Bonneau
- ☐ 133 L-P Létourneau ☐ 134 Christian Barbeau
- ☐ 135 S-P Julien ☐ 136 Alexandre Bannon
- ☐ 137 Philippe Lavigne ☐ 138 Dominic Brisson
- ☐ 139 Jérôme Villeneuve ☐ 140 M-A St-Pierre
- ☐ 141 M-O Lefrançois ☐ 142 David Lord
- ☐ 143 Simon Plante ☐ 144 Pierre Laliberté
- ☐ 145 Bryan Denis ☐ 146 Philippe Veilleux

PITTSBURGH PEE WEE PENGUINS

- ☐ 147 Joey Bartlett ☐ 148 Adam Böhm
- ☐ 149 Chip Crispino ☐ 150 Rob Garber
- ☐ 151 David Glatz ☐ 152 Craig Hoolihan
- ☐ 153 Bo Jack ☐ 154 Bill Kristan
- ☐ 155 Sean Luketic ☐ 156 Doug Marsteller
- ☐ 157 P.J. Mastylak ☐ 158 Todd Meehan
- ☐ 159 Ben Myers ☐ 160 Steven Padgelek
- ☐ 161 Chris Perry ☐ 162 Ethan Riffe
- ☐ 163 George Strasbaugh

ST-LAMBERT PEE WEE

- ☐ 164 Joey Bazso ☐ 165 F. Berthiaume
- ☐ 166 James Botsford ☐ 168 C-É Brodeur
- ☐ 169 J-P Côté ☐ 170 J. L-Nadeau
- ☐ 171 M-A Lechasseur ☐ 172 Xavier Mignot
- ☐ 173 Patrick Ouellet ☐ 174 M. Pinsonneault
- ☐ 175 Jonathan Roux ☐ 176 Philippe Roux
- ☐ 177 M-A Sanscartier ☐ 178 Jean-François Shink
- ☐ 179 Jean-Luc Rajotte ☐ 1234 Patrick Bouchard

CALGARY PEE WEE FLAMES

- ☐ 180 Chris Bentson ☐ 181 Chad Bucar
- ☐ 182 Shane Buckley ☐ 183 Shawn Calafatis
- ☐ 184 Matthew Field ☐ 185 Matthew Forsyth
- ☐ 186 Kevin Gerlitz ☐ 187 Kurt Goodjohn
- ☐ 188 Scott Hammond ☐ 189 R. Homer-Dixon
- ☐ 190 Lucas Klapper ☐ 191 Troy Muspratt
- ☐ 192 Trevor Nychkalo ☐ 193 Craig Weller
- ☐ 194 Jeremy Young

THETFORD-MINES PEE WEE

- ☐ 195 J-F Tardif ☐ 196 Mathieu Bouchard
- ☐ 197 J-F Gosselin ☐ 198 Guillaume Brossard
- ☐ 199 Samuel Leblond ☐ 200 Jonathan Durocher
- ☐ 201 Keven Poulin ☐ 202 Nicolas Bouchard
- ☐ 203 Dave Lessard ☐ 204 Éric Laflamme
- ☐ 205 Patrick Bolduc ☐ 206 Martin Vachon
- ☐ 207 J-F Duguay ☐ 208 Sébastien Boutet
- ☐ 209 Marc Simoneau ☐ 210 Jonathan Fortin

TORONTO PEE WEE YOUNG NATS

- ☐ 211 Shawn Sullivan ☐ 212 Johnny Eminger
- ☐ 213 Brent Noon ☐ 214 Matt Bannan
- ☐ 215 Brad Pierce ☐ 216 Travis Davidson
- ☐ 217 P.J. Yedon ☐ 218 Pat Nailer
- ☐ 219 Ryan Penet ☐ 220 Jeff Fiorino
- ☐ 221 Tony Lawrence ☐ 222 Billy Kam Brothers
- ☐ 223 Tait Williamson ☐ 224 Jason Morris
- ☐ 225 Jason Cassels ☐ 226 Jason Bloor

BEAUCE-AMIANTE PEE WEE

The most expensive single is Simon Gamache at $2-3.

- ☐ 227 Rudy Boucher ☐ 228 Guillaume Deblois
- ☐ 229 Michael Parent ☐ 230 Alexandre Drouin
- ☐ 231 Dave Lagrange ☐ 232 Vincent Plante
- ☐ 233 Daniel Laflamme ☐ 234 Simon Gamache
- ☐ 235 Stéphane Veilleux ☐ 236 J-F Poulin
- ☐ 237 J. Blanchette ☐ 238 Sébastien Nadeau
- ☐ 239 Hugo Lehoux ☐ 240 David Turcotte
- ☐ 241 Étienne Roy

HALIFAX PEE WEE

- ☐ 242 Chad Leclair ☐ 243 Jordan Udle
- ☐ 244 Ryan Veinot ☐ 245 Jeff Flinn
- ☐ 246 Robb Dunphy ☐ 247 P.J. Lynch
- ☐ 248 Tommy Maclean ☐ 249 Nathan States
- ☐ 250 Bill Mosher ☐ 251 Robbie Sutherland
- ☐ 252 Mark Cody ☐ 253 Scott Smith
- ☐ 254 Melchior Schori ☐ 255 Mike Fougère
- ☐ 256 Brian Sutherland ☐ 257 Carlos Sayde

HERSHEY PEE WEE

- ☐ 258 Lowell Franko ☐ 259 Matt Junkins
- ☐ 260 Adam Bonenberger ☐ 261 Joel Buchenauer
- ☐ 262 Chris Connor ☐ 263 Ryan Ford
- ☐ 264 Brandon Love ☐ 265 Brendan McCartin
- ☐ 266 Nolan Meanor ☐ 267 Mike Patton
- ☐ 268 Robbie Roth ☐ 269 A.J. Skinner
- ☐ 270 Lee Taylor ☐ 271 David Thomas
- ☐ 272 Jason Weiland ☐ 273 Brent Weist
- ☐ 274 Bret Wilhite ☐ 275 T. Willits-Kelley
- ☐ 276 Alex Delaney

DAUPHINS CHAUDIÈRE PEE WEE

The most expensive single is Antoine Vermette at $2-3.

- ☐ 277 Kim Cauchy ☐ 278 Antoine Vermette
- ☐ 279 J-F Gosselin ☐ 280 Steve Vachon
- ☐ 281 Frédéric Bourget ☐ 282 Alexandre Roberge
- ☐ 283 Simon Baribeau ☐ 284 David Cloutier
- ☐ 285 Francis Martineau ☐ 286 Nicolas Roy
- ☐ 287 François Isabelle ☐ 288 Tommy Roy
- ☐ 289 Nicolas Boudrault ☐ 290 Marc-André Nolet
- ☐ 291 J-P Landry ☐ 292 Vincent Fréchette
- ☐ 293 Guillaume Allard

VICTORIAVILLE PEE WEE

- ☐ 294 J-F Martel ☐ 295 Olivier Dumas
- ☐ 296 Éric Fortier ☐ 297 André Martineau
- ☐ 298 Martin Thibault (G) ☐ 299 Jonathan Labonté
- ☐ 300 Julien Marcoux ☐ 301 Sébastien Lavigne
- ☐ 302 David Bouchard ☐ 303 Dave Pruneau
- ☐ 304 Denis Desmarais ☐ 305 François Cormier
- ☐ 306 Simon Bérubé ☐ 307 Jimmy Bilodeau
- ☐ 308 Dave Pinard ☐ 309 Jean (Jr.) Morin
- ☐ 310 Dominic Robichaud

ANCIENNE-LORETTE PEE WEE

- ☐ 311 Mathieu Beachesne ☐ 312 Éric Bédard
- ☐ 313 M-A Bélanger ☐ 314 Pierre-Luc Côté
- ☐ 315 Jérôme Drolet ☐ 316 Martin Gaboury
- ☐ 317 Sébastien Gagnon ☐ 318 Michel Gagnon
- ☐ 319 M-A Guérin ☐ 320 Luc Laberge
- ☐ 321 Jonathan Labrie ☐ 322 David Lavoie
- ☐ 323 Vincent Martel ☐ 324 Judyann Patry
- ☐ 325 Philippe Rochefort ☐ 326 Pascal St-Louis
- ☐ 327 J-M Tremblay

CHARLEVOIX PEE WEE

- ☐ 328 Philippe Bouchard ☐ 329 Philippe Larouche
- ☐ 330 D. Savard-Gagnon ☐ 331 Keven Tremblay
- ☐ 332 J-F Ménard ☐ 333 Stéphane Guay
- ☐ 334 Mathieu Lapointe ☐ 335 Éric* Gagnon
- ☐ 336 Guillaume Bourque ☐ 337 Patrice Gagné
- ☐ 338 Michael Côté ☐ 339 Francis Dufour
- ☐ 340 Martin Bradet ☐ 341 Jean-Nicolas Pilote
- ☐ 342 Rémy Tremblay ☐ 343 Jérôme Gagné

BEAUCE-NORD PEE WEE

- ☐ 344 Dominique Dion ☐ 345 Pierre Audet
- ☐ 346 Nicolas Bélanger ☐ 347 Nicolas Lehoux
- ☐ 348 Jimmy Poulin ☐ 349 David Hanzen
- ☐ 350 Jovane Drouin ☐ 351 Vincent Fortin
- ☐ 352 Tony Lafontaine ☐ 353 Guillaume Ferland
- ☐ 354 Jérôme Nadeau ☐ 355 Frédéric Allen
- ☐ 356 Dave Thibodeau ☐ 357 Cindy Côté
- ☐ 358 Sébastien Lemay ☐ 359 Alexandre Gilbert
- ☐ 360 J. Létourneau ☐ 361 Sylvain Grenier
- ☐ 362 Pascal Maheu

STE-FOY PEE WEE GOUVERNEURS B

- ☐ 363 Mathieu Vézina ☐ 364 Pierre-Marc Girard
- ☐ 365 Mathieu Latour ☐ 366 Simon Dancause
- ☐ 367 Étienne Garon ☐ 368 Bruno Gagné
- ☐ 369 Daniel McBryde ☐ 370 Jocelyn Lépine
- ☐ 371 René Auclair ☐ 372 Sylvain Ruel
- ☐ 373 Dany Martineau ☐ 374 Dave Beaupré
- ☐ 375 Dany Delisle ☐ 376 David Vachon
- ☐ 377 Mathieu Bouré

QUÉBEC PEE WEE NORDIQUES

The most expensive single is Maxime Ouellet at $4-8.

- ☐ 378 M. Ouellet (G) ☐ 379 Éric Savard
- ☐ 380 Éric Rhéaume ☐ 381 Michel Côté
- ☐ 382 Frédérick Tremblay ☐ 383 Jérôme Bergeron
- ☐ 384 Hugo Lévesque ☐ 385 J-P Paradis
- ☐ 386 Pascal Morin ☐ 387 Maxime Guimond
- ☐ 388 Martin Boucher ☐ 389 Jonathan Francoeur
- ☐ 390 P-O Dufour ☐ 391 Martin Leclerc
- ☐ 392 Maxime Gagnon ☐ 393 Tommy Bolduc

PAPINEAU PEE WEE

- ☐ 394 Philippe Demers ☐ 395 Simon Charbonneau
- ☐ 396 Jonathan Demers ☐ 397 Dominic Bastien
- ☐ 398 Daniel Blais ☐ 399 Bruno Boileau
- ☐ 400 Vincent D'Aoust ☐ 401 Steve Davis
- ☐ 402 Philippe Goulet ☐ 403 Patrice Lafleur
- ☐ 404 Carl Laframboise ☐ 405 Jérôme Laflamme
- ☐ 406 Francis Mongeon ☐ 407 Bertrand Plouffe
- ☐ 408 Éric Lanthier ☐ 409 Hugues Lagacé

QUÉBEC PEE WEE CARTIER

- ☐ 410 David Bergeron ☐ 411 J-F Bouchard
- ☐ 412 Steve* Boucher ☐ 413 Olivier Bourque
- ☐ 414 J-F Bureau ☐ 415 Nicolas Clusiault
- ☐ 416 Jackson Comeau ☐ 417 Guillaume Durand
- ☐ 418 Simon Gagnon ☐ 419 J-P Grenon
- ☐ 420 Jocelyn Lacroix ☐ 421 Sylvain Leclerc
- ☐ 422 Keven Lemay ☐ 423 J-F Madore
- ☐ 424 Vincent Paquet ☐ 425 Olivier St-Antoine
- ☐ 426 François Tailleur

LAC-ETCHEMIN PEE WEE

- ☐ 427 Joey Nolet ☐ 428 Keven Carrier
- ☐ 429 Cédric Dupont ☐ 430 Bobby Deblois
- ☐ 431 Cédric Labonté ☐ 432 Vincent Tanguay
- ☐ 433 François Quirion ☐ 434 Étienne Couture
- ☐ 435 David Vallières ☐ 436 M-A Gagnon-Pouliot
- ☐ 437 Julie Maheux ☐ 438 Richard Pelletier
- ☐ 439 Sébastien Jacques ☐ 440 François Rouillard
- ☐ 441 Jérémie Drouin ☐ 442 Dave Lehoux
- ☐ 443 Simon Nadeau

MONTRÉAL PEE WEE CANADIENS

The most expensive single is Marc-André Thinel at $3-5.

- ☐ 444 David Jarry ☐ 445 Dominic Léveillé
- ☐ 446 Sébastien Thinel ☐ 447 Alex Lapiere
- ☐ 448 Marc-André Thinel ☐ 449 Olivier Proulx
- ☐ 450 Victor Gervais ☐ 451 Patrick Lavoie
- ☐ 452 Eddie Bergeron ☐ 453 Alexandre Arel
- ☐ 454 Yann Danis ☐ 455 Christian Martel
- ☐ 456 Jean-Luc Legault ☐ 457 Robby Fournier
- ☐ 458 Nicolas Raymond ☐ 459 Frédéric Lachapelle

MATAPÉDIA PEE WEE

- ☐ 460 Jérôme Dupéré ☐ 461 Hugues Lévesque
- ☐ 462 Mike Ouellet ☐ 463 Billy Poirier
- ☐ 464 Francis Pelletier ☐ 465 Martin Dufour
- ☐ 466 Bruno Thériault ☐ 467 Sébastien Gagnon
- ☐ 468 Nicolas Pilote ☐ 469 G. Thibault (G)
- ☐ 470 Dave Ouellet ☐ 471 Carl McNicoll
- ☐ 472 David Chouinard ☐ 473 Dave Canuel
- ☐ 474 Yves Lamarre

BOSTON PEE WEE BRUINS

- ☐ 475 Robert Goulart ☐ 476 Didier Alther
- ☐ 477 Andrew Wyman ☐ 478 Christopher Breem
- ☐ 479 Michael MacNeil ☐ 480 Alan Pettinelli
- ☐ 481 Maxime Doctoroff ☐ 482 Matthew Hannon
- ☐ 483 Michael Pearce ☐ 484 Daniel Gyllstrom
- ☐ 485 Christopher Gauvin ☐ 486 Andrew McShea
- ☐ 487 Michael Warner ☐ 488 Stephen Crusco
- ☐ 489 Jason McDonald ☐ 490 Kevin Mitchell
- ☐ 491 Jason Sullivan ☐ 492 Joseph Barberio
- ☐ 493 Gerard Hickey ☐ 494 Ryan Krueger

MONTMAGNY PEE WEE

- ☐ 495 D. Ouellet-Beaudry ☐ 496 J-C Caron
- ☐ 497 Keven Chouinard ☐ 498 Michael Couillard
- ☐ 499 Marc-Antoine Dubé ☐ 500 Yannick Dubé
- ☐ 501 Patrice Dufresne ☐ 502 Pierre-Luc Émond
- ☐ 503 Hubert Gagné ☐ 504 Jérôme Gagnon
- ☐ 505 J-P Gaudreau ☐ 506 Yves Gonthier
- ☐ 507 Mathieu Mercier ☐ 508 Jean-Philippe Morin
- ☐ 509 Alexandre Ouellet ☐ 510 Mathieu Piette
- ☐ 511 Ghislain Poitras

SYRACUSE PEE WEE

The most expensive single is Tim Connolly at $4-6.

- ☐ 512 Daniel Bequer ☐ 513 Brian Balash
- ☐ 514 Gary Baronick ☐ 515 Drew Buctooth
- ☐ 516 Tim Connolly ☐ 517 Jeremy Downs
- ☐ 518 Joshua Downs ☐ 519 J.D. Forrest
- ☐ 520 Todd Jackson ☐ 521 Josh Jordan
- ☐ 522 Tom Leroux ☐ 523 Doug MacCormack
- ☐ 524 Matthew Maglione ☐ 525 Freddy Meyer
- ☐ 526 Anthony Pace ☐ 527 Steve Pakan
- ☐ 528 Mike Saraceni ☐ 529 Ricky Williams

CHARLESBOURG ÉLANS PEE WEE

- ☐ 530 P. Beauchesne ☐ 531 René Beauchesne
- ☐ 532 Bruno Bédard ☐ 533 Frédéric Bélanger
- ☐ 534 Patrick Bernier ☐ 535 Martin Bouchard
- ☐ 536 Dominic Dallaire ☐ 537 Maxime Genest-Cyr
- ☐ 538 T. Guérin-Comeau ☐ 539 Nicolas Lapointe
- ☐ 540 Frédéric Légaré ☐ 541 Steve Morency
- ☐ 542 J. Pelletier-Ouellet ☐ 543 Frédéric St-Martin
- ☐ 544 Carl Simard ☐ 545 David Thoral

NIAGARA FALLS PEE WEE

- ☐ 546 Justin Berbier ☐ 547 M. Catherwood
- ☐ 548 Jeff Corey ☐ 549 Kevin Dallman
- ☐ 550 Joshua Dunn ☐ 551 Michael Kelley
- ☐ 552 Zenon Konopka ☐ 553 Nathan Milani
- ☐ 554 Lorne Misita ☐ 555 David Morton
- ☐ 556 Michael Orr ☐ 557 John Pugliese
- ☐ 558 John Quaranta ☐ 559 Aaron Romanyk
- ☐ 560 Jason Shawana ☐ 561 Keith Thorne

AUSTRIA PEE WEE

- ☐ 562 Robert Steinwender ☐ 564 Gregor Hager
- ☐ 565 Thomas Pöck ☐ 566 Rene Wild
- ☐ 567 Olivier Oberrauner ☐ 568 Andreas Moschik
- ☐ 569 Martin Hager ☐ 570 Stephen Schweitzer
- ☐ 571 Chris Harand ☐ 572 B. Tschemernjak
- ☐ 573 M-P Kotnauer ☐ 574 Michael Pfleger
- ☐ 575 Clemens Pichler ☐ 576 Marc Hammerle
- ☐ 577 Mario Gesson ☐ 578 Bernd Brückler
- ☐ 579 Gerd Gruber ☐ 580 Hannes Luccini
- ☐ 581 Michael Mayer ☐ 582 Marco Hirz
- ☐ 583 Herbert Retz ☐ 584 Gerhard Salzer
- ☐ 585 Roland Kaspitz

MAURICIE PEE WEE

- ☐ 586 Jérôme Fréchette ☐ 587 S. Lesieur-Sirois
- ☐ 588 Marc-André Dubois ☐ 589 Keven Mongrain
- ☐ 590 Francis Dupuis ☐ 591 René Demontigny
- ☐ 592 Daniel Mongrain ☐ 593 Jonathan Massicotte
- ☐ 594 Pierre-Luc Doyon ☐ 595 Dominic Fraser
- ☐ 596 Maxime Thibodeau ☐ 597 Brian Bourassa
- ☐ 598 N. Mercure-Joliette ☐ 599 Mathieu Massicotte
- ☐ 600 P-L Courchesne ☐ 601 Tommy Lefebvre

LAMBTON PEE WEE

The most expensive singles are Michael Leighton, Dusty Jamieson and Jamie Chamberlain each at $2-3.

- ☐ 602 Ryan Chapman ☐ 603 Justin Thompson
- ☐ 604 Kyle Doyle ☐ 605 Jamie Schouten
- ☐ 606 Shawn Grondin ☐ 607 Dusty Jamieson
- ☐ 608 Michael Leighton ☐ 609 Marc Guilbeault
- ☐ 610 Kevin Fines ☐ 611 Dara Emslie
- ☐ 612 Nick Policelli ☐ 613 Michael Fleming
- ☐ 614 Craig Marshall ☐ 615 Michael Anning
- ☐ 616 Joël Willock ☐ 617 Jamie Chamberlain
- ☐ 618 Daniel Dimuzio

NEW YORK PEE WEE RANGERS

- ☐ 619 Justin Boening ☐ 620 Brian Boyle
- ☐ 621 Danny Di Lauro ☐ 622 Chris Gartman
- ☐ 623 C.J. Huber ☐ 624 Chauncey Hughes
- ☐ 625 David Hughes ☐ 626 Fankie Mingone
- ☐ 627 Peter Raimondi ☐ 628 Darren Seid
- ☐ 629 Bryan Smith ☐ 630 Guy Smith
- ☐ 631 Ken Turano ☐ 632 Ryan Vesce
- ☐ 633 Steve Viola ☐ 634 Evan Wax

ST-ÉPHREM BEAUCE PEE WEE

- ☐ 635 Alexandre Roy ☐ 636 Sylvain Plante
- ☐ 637 Sylvain Labbé ☐ 638 Julien Roy

☐ 639 Rémi Roy
☐ 640 Stéphane Roy
☐ 641 Jérôme Baillargeon
☐ 642 Étienne Champagne
☐ 643 Jason Bernard
☐ 644 Nicolas Léger
☐ 645 Nicolas Paré
☐ 646 Vincent Veilleux
☐ 647 Carl Baudoin
☐ 648 Paskal Métivier
☐ 649 Éric Fortin
☐ 650 Keven Bilodeau
☐ 651 Jean-Pierre Marois
☐ 652 Denis Rodrigue
☐ 653 René Grondin

BROSSARD PEE WEE

☐ 654 Bryan Lacireno
☐ 655 Gabriel Beauchamp
☐ 656 Pedro Rodrigues
☐ 657 Benoît Montmagny
☐ 658 Frédéric Camerlain
☐ 659 Kévin Sauvé
☐ 660 Patrick Freignoz
☐ 661 Charles Gill
☐ 662 Éric Tremblay
☐ 663 Stéphane Poirier
☐ 664 Danny Bouchard
☐ 665 Charles Taylor
☐ 666 Benoît Dépatie
☐ 667 Yves Lessard
☐ 668 Étienne Drouin

BUFFALO PEE WEE SABRES

☐ 669 Sean Apier
☐ 670 Thomas Amodeo
☐ 671 Mark Branden
☐ 672 Joseph Carosa
☐ 673 Nick DeMarco
☐ 674 Paul Dombrowski
☐ 675 Michael Drezek
☐ 676 Mark Horsch
☐ 677 John Lenz
☐ 678 Matt McGirr
☐ 679 Brian Mika
☐ 680 Justin Nieffer
☐ 681 Michael Nellany
☐ 682 Thomas Pawlak
☐ 683 Andy Tinti

QUINTE PEE WEE

The most expensive singles are Justin Williams at $3-5 and Jeff Bateman at $2-3.

☐ 684 Jeff Bateman
☐ 685 Andrew Cone
☐ 686 Justin Dorland
☐ 687 Lee Vanhuizen
☐ 688 Jeff Whitney
☐ 689 Andrew Gunning
☐ 690 James Lord
☐ 691 Justin Spencer
☐ 692 Justin Williams
☐ 693 Josh Thomas
☐ 694 Ben Lupenette
☐ 695 Lara Perks
☐ 696 Ian Turner
☐ 697 Ryan Korderas
☐ 698 Aaron Lee
☐ 699 Justin Miller
☐ 700 Ryan Spencer

GRAND-PRAIRIE PEE WEE

☐ 701 Brandon Jones
☐ 702 Garrett Larson
☐ 703 Peter MacLellan
☐ 704 Reilly Olson
☐ 705 Cory Kinnon
☐ 706 Justin Bain
☐ 707 Curtis Ames
☐ 708 Chris* Taylor
☐ 709 Sean Rogan
☐ 710 Morgan Lange
☐ 711 William Hampton
☐ 712 Jordan Menzies
☐ 713 Scott Charlesworth
☐ 714 Jordan Adams
☐ 715 Dean Farquhar
☐ 716 Tyler Bavol
☐ 717 Landon Thompson

PHILADELPHIA PEE WEE FLYERS

☐ 718 Ryan Cohen
☐ 719 David* Taylor
☐ 720 Billy Scaggs
☐ 721 Joseph Ciocco
☐ 722 John Zimmerman
☐ 723 Bryan Aronchik
☐ 724 Robi Bannon
☐ 725 Nate Smith
☐ 726 Matt Herneisen
☐ 727 Bryan Bonawitz
☐ 728 Danny Hindley
☐ 729 Joseph Testa
☐ 731 Patrick Wall
☐ 732 Danny Angeline
☐ 733 Jeffrey Corey
☐ 734 Matt Gallagher
☐ 735 Chase Watson
☐ 736 Tom Arthur
☐ 737 Ryan Lochhead

ST-PROSPER PEE WEE

☐ 738 J-P Gagné
☐ 739 Christian Buteau
☐ 740 Yannick** Poulin
☐ 741 Michel Bourque
☐ 742 David* Gosselin
☐ 743 Karl Morin
☐ 744 Marco Veilleux
☐ 745 M. Lamontagne
☐ 746 Jérôme Samson
☐ 747 Stéphane Hébert
☐ 748 Mathieu Bédard
☐ 749 Simon Labbé
☐ 750 Dave Quirion
☐ 751 Mathieu Boulet
☐ 752 David* Poulin
☐ 753 Richard Veilleux
☐ 754 Dave Thompson

DETROIT PEE WEE LITTLE CAESARS

The most expensive singles are Andy Hilbert at $4-6 and Damian Surma at $2-3.

☐ 755 Robbie Bonk
☐ 756 A.J. Walczak
☐ 757 Eric Mannix
☐ 758 Robert St-Laurent
☐ 759 Rocky Mulinaro
☐ 760 Karl Borguist
☐ 761 Mike Schultz
☐ 762 Andy Hilbert
☐ 763 Mike Falk
☐ 764 Damian Surma
☐ 765 Joe Tigay
☐ 766 Ryan Sinks
☐ 767 Chris Christensen
☐ 768 Vinnie Lacommare
☐ 769 Justin Kahle
☐ 770 Bret Postal
☐ 771 Jonathan Krall

STE-FOY PEE WEE GOUVERNEURS

☐ 772 Dominic Morin
☐ 773 Érik Larose
☐ 774 Antoine Filion
☐ 775 Frédéric Couet
☐ 776 D. Robitaille-Jacob
☐ 777 Olivier Doyon
☐ 778 Laurent Dionne
☐ 779 C. Laro.-Simard
☐ 780 Carl Fournel
☐ 781 G. Boisbriand
☐ 782 Dominic Bruneau
☐ 783 Hugo Trépanier
☐ 784 Dominic Bruneau
☐ 785 Frédéric Dumais
☐ 786 M. F.-Desrochers

ROBERVAL

☐ 787 Jean-François Boily
☐ 788 Yannick Boily
☐ 789 G. Bouchard
☐ 790 David Côté
☐ 791 Jessy Dominique
☐ 792 Daniel Dumont
☐ 793 Sébastien Genest
☐ 794 Daniel Hudon
☐ 795 Hugo Larouche
☐ 796 Mario Lemay
☐ 797 Yves Paul
☐ 798 Mathieu Privé
☐ 799 J-F Racine
☐ 800 Jean Stubbert
☐ 801 Julien Tremblay

HARTFORD PEE WEE WHALERS

☐ 802 Frank Carrano
☐ 803 Adam Lavorgna
☐ 804 John Cicarella
☐ 805 Wes Lippman
☐ 806 David Sandals
☐ 807 Mike Eresen
☐ 808 Steven Prebola
☐ 809 Justin Delavri
☐ 810 Adam Bell
☐ 811 Peter Giatrelis
☐ 812 Mike Coughlin
☐ 813 Mike Wolfe
☐ 814 David Fleet
☐ 815 Alex Rosso
☐ 816 Adam Mantin
☐ 817 Jesse Larusso
☐ 818 Peter Zingoni
☐ 819 Matthew Vagvolgyi
☐ 920 Jessie Sorrentino

WEXFORD PEE WEE

The most expensive single is Luke Sellars at $2-3.

☐ 821 David Kapur
☐ 822 Jeremy Weiss
☐ 823 Chad Wiseman
☐ 824 Cameron Deyoung
☐ 825 Ryan Micallef
☐ 826 Mark Norman
☐ 827 Mark McRae
☐ 828 Carmelo Scali
☐ 829 Robert Ackerman
☐ 830 Omar Medina
☐ 831 John Ross Holmes
☐ 832 Fraser Clair
☐ 833 Dustin Wood
☐ 834 Luke Sellars
☐ 835 Matthew McRae
☐ 836 Matthew Collaton

TORONTO PEE WEE MAPLE LEAFS

☐ 837 Michael Abbott
☐ 838 Adam Brunswick
☐ 839 B. Vanderklok
☐ 840 Sal Lettieri
☐ 841 Vincent Cheng
☐ 842 Edwin Chung
☐ 843 Andrew Marshall
☐ 844 Johnathan Harper
☐ 845 Rhys Herriott
☐ 846 Adrian Kremblewski
☐ 847 Joe Dibiase
☐ 848 Adam Crane
☐ 849 Daniel Sullivan
☐ 850 Darcy McConvey
☐ 851 Christopher Large
☐ 852 Matthew Pantalone
☐ 853 Michael Lecce

LOWELL PEE WEE

☐ 854 Bill Moss
☐ 855 Justin Platten
☐ 856 Michael Turner
☐ 857 Paul Crooker
☐ 858 Phil Martin
☐ 859 Michael* Murphy
☐ 860 Travis Lyle
☐ 861 Dan Cesere
☐ 862 John Sullivan
☐ 863 Stephen Pink
☐ 864 Jeff Abelli
☐ 865 T. O'Shaughnessy
☐ 866 Tom Riley
☐ 867 Adam Reel
☐ 868 Rob Barker
☐ 869 Brendon Clark
☐ 870 Christopher Dusault
☐ 871 Sean Sparks

POINTE-LÉVY PEE WEE

☐ 872 Audrey Samson
☐ 873 Marie-Claude Morin
☐ 874 Jonathan Leblond
☐ 875 Jean-Michel Asselin
☐ 876 Stéphane Caron
☐ 877 Danny Tondreau
☐ 878 Vincent Mercier
☐ 879 François Tremblay
☐ 880 C-A Maheux
☐ 881 Hakim Gheriet
☐ 882 Martin Vézina
☐ 883 Frédéric St-Pierre
☐ 884 Jonathan Ouellet
☐ 885 Jérôme Godbout
☐ 886 Jérôme Marceau
☐ 887 David Perron

CÔTÉ-DE-BEAUPRÉ PEE WEE

☐ 888 Samuel Bourget
☐ 889 Jonathan Vézina
☐ 890 Donald Grenier
☐ 891 Nelson Cloutier (G)
☐ 892 Simon Racine
☐ 893 Yoann Labranche
☐ 894 Samuel Dion
☐ 895 Pierre-Luc Ménard
☐ 896 Simon Noël
☐ 897 Thierry Kaszap
☐ 898 Vincent DeBlois
☐ 899 Jonathan Grenier
☐ 900 Michel Beaulieu
☐ 901 Nicolas Ferland
☐ 902 Sylvain Boivin
☐ 903 Frédéric Gauthier
☐ 904 Sean O'Neill
☐ 905 Sébastien Racine
☐ 906 Richard Lavoie
☐ 907 Eric Gauthier

CHANDLER PEE WEE

☐ 908 Maxime Albert
☐ 909 Alex Blais
☐ 910 Marc Bouchard
☐ 911 Joël Duguay
☐ 912 Julien Duguay
☐ 913 Tommy Dunn
☐ 914 Martin Fullum
☐ 915 Nelson Gionest
☐ 916 François Godin
☐ 917 Jonathan Grenier
☐ 918 Gabriel Huard
☐ 919 Julien Huard
☐ 920 Samuel Johnson
☐ 921 Serge Leblanc
☐ 922 Dominic Loiselle
☐ 923 Patrick Méthot
☐ 924 Jonathan Poirier
☐ 925 Marc Shannon
☐ 926 Tim Sutton

NEW YORK PEE WEE ISLANDERS

☐ 927 Robert Rochefort
☐ 928 Marc Forte
☐ 929 Adam Ramos
☐ 930 Matthew Stack
☐ 931 Richard Hansen
☐ 932 Joe Weber
☐ 933 Kevin Gardelli
☐ 934 Michael Brodsky
☐ 935 Brian Mandlakes
☐ 936 Andrew Hickcox
☐ 937 Steven Recher
☐ 938 Michael Camarinos
☐ 939 Philip Yovino
☐ 940 Sean Meade
☐ 941 Jonathan Sinex
☐ 942 Terry Gaslow
☐ 943 Joey Grasso
☐ 944 Jason Guerriero

TROY PEE WEE

The most expensive single is Dan Snyder at $2-3.

☐ 945 Josh Gela
☐ 946 James Corrigan
☐ 947 Philip Gauthier
☐ 948 Luke Parillo
☐ 949 Dan Snyder
☐ 950 Robert Fretto
☐ 951 David Ambuhl
☐ 952 Michael Tyburski
☐ 953 Ryan Bennett
☐ 954 Joe Bulmer
☐ 955 Joe Bulmer
☐ 956 Nicholas Colucci
☐ 957 Mike Paine
☐ 958 B.J. Sheehan
☐ 1183 Peter McCarthy

JONQUIÈRE PEE WEE

☐ 959 Maxime Tremblay
☐ 960 Patrick* Murray
☐ 961 Éric** Bouchard
☐ 962 J-F Blackburn
☐ 963 Mathieu Simard
☐ 964 Kenny Tremblay
☐ 965 Patrick Chouinard
☐ 966 Guillaume Lavoie
☐ 967 Nelson Kirouac
☐ 968 Dany Cossette
☐ 969 Yanic Savard
☐ 970 Pierre-Luc Martin
☐ 971 Stéphane Gareau
☐ 972 Jean-Michel Otis
☐ 973 Bruno Leblanc
☐ 974 J-F Rousseau

MONTRÉAL NOROIS PEE WEE

☐ 975 Simon Whilhelmy
☐ 976 A. Martin-Laval
☐ 977 Marx Gauthier
☐ 978 François Tremblay
☐ 979 Mario Daigle
☐ 980 Lino Quintieri
☐ 981 Maxime Yanire
☐ 982 Rubens Morne
☐ 983 Seneque Hyacinthe
☐ 984 Jason Jalbert
☐ 985 William Gibbs
☐ 986 Lee William
☐ 987 Duilio Grande
☐ 988 Marc-André David
☐ 989 Maxime Blais
☐ 990 G. Adamopoulos

QUÉBEC CHAMPLAINS PEE WEE

☐ 991 Steve Côté
☐ 992 Yan-Philippe Côté
☐ 993 Éric Courcy
☐ 994 Jonathan Croteau
☐ 995 A. Derepentigny
☐ 996 Jessy Laprade
☐ 997 Jérôme Matte
☐ 998 Steven McKinnon
☐ 999 Martin Nadeau
☐ 1000 Steve Plante
☐ 1001 Dannik Poulin
☐ 1002 Guillaume Pouliot
☐ 1003 J-F Richard
☐ 1004 G. Rodrigue
☐ 1005 Nicolas Tanguay

BELLECHASSE PEE WEE

☐ 1006 Patrick Audet
☐ 1007 J-P Boivin
☐ 1008 Dave Boucher
☐ 1009 J_F Drouin
☐ 1010 Olivier Fortier
☐ 1011 Nicolas Gagné
☐ 1012 Janik Guay
☐ 1013 J-S Labrie
☐ 1015 Étienne Lefebvre
☐ 1016 Kévin Moore
☐ 1017 Guillaume Ouellet
☐ 1018 Gabriel Prévost
☐ 1019 Mathieu Roberge
☐ 1020 Pierre-Olivier Roy
☐ 1021 Sébastien Roy
☐ 1022 Jonathan Royer

WASHINGTON PEE WEE CAPITALS

☐ 1023 Lenny Barnard
☐ 1024 Duncan Brooks
☐ 1025 David-John Brady
☐ 1026 Brooks Brumsted
☐ 1027 Eric Bull
☐ 1028 John Costa
☐ 1029 Kevin Earley
☐ 1030 Patrick Ellis
☐ 1031 Shane Farragher
☐ 1032 Phil Giampietro
☐ 1033 Eric Lederer
☐ 1034 Matt Mondorff
☐ 1035 Ryan Pastorek
☐ 1036 Patrick Schaeffer
☐ 1037 Kliff Snowden
☐ 1038 Bobby Steen

ST-HILAIRE PEE WEE

☐ 1039 Philip Brazeau
☐ 1040 Marc-Olivier Roy
☐ 1041 Patrick Teoli
☐ 1042 Nicolas Séguin
☐ 1043 G. Lemay-Tougas
☐ 1044 Charles Tremblay
☐ 1045 Philip* Sauvé
☐ 1046 Philippe Cholette
☐ 1047 Jonathan Coupal
☐ 1048 Jonathan Jalbert
☐ 1049 M-A Perron
☐ 1050 Virgile Cormier
☐ 1051 Charles Daigle
☐ 1052 Jonathan Potvin
☐ 1053 Yannick Noël

CHICAGO PEE WEE BLACKHAWKS

The most expensive single is Craig Andersson at $2-3.

☐ 1054 C. Andersson (G)
☐ 1055 Andy Bradford
☐ 1056 Tony Cacciatore
☐ 1057 Danny Calzada
☐ 1058 Peter Cecil
☐ 1059 James Claney
☐ 1060 John Eichelberger
☐ 1061 Adam Elzinga
☐ 1062 Tim Leahy
☐ 1063 Parker Millard
☐ 1064 Evan Nielsen
☐ 1065 Matt O'Connor
☐ 1066 Alex Pearl
☐ 1067 Justin Schabes
☐ 1068 Bobby Skalla
☐ 1069 Frank Zupancic

LACHUTE PEE WEE

☐ 1070 Patrick Joly
☐ 1071 Jonathan Diotte
☐ 1072 Martin Aubry
☐ 1073 Maxime Villeneuve
☐ 1074 G. Boucher
☐ 1075 Carl Modérie
☐ 1076 Dominik Gauthier
☐ 1077 Julien Gagné
☐ 1078 Étienne Therrien
☐ 1079 Derek Belvedère
☐ 1080 M-A Campeau
☐ 1081 Éric Vézeau
☐ 1082 Stéphane Parent
☐ 1083 Marc-André Landry
☐ 1084 René Laflamme

DETROIT PEE WEE RED WINGS

☐ 1085 Craig Kowalski
☐ 1086 Eric Williams
☐ 1087 Ken McKay
☐ 1088 Chris Sad
☐ 1089 Carl Voelker
☐ 1090 B. Shouneyia
☐ 1091 Brent Sroda
☐ 1092 Mike Roemensky
☐ 1093 Jeff Cluff
☐ 1094 Fred Lukanchoff
☐ 1095 Steve Jackson
☐ 1096 Dave Lawrence
☐ 1097 Brent Sullivan
☐ 1098 Marc Norrington
☐ 1099 Timothy Adams
☐ 1100 Jonathan Billy
☐ 1101 Mark (II) Juliano

KUUJJUAQ PEE WEE

☐ 1102 Maxime Tremblay
☐ 1103 Richard Adams
☐ 1104 Barnie Davies
☐ 1105 Guillaume Paré
☐ 1106 Andrew Labranche
☐ 1107 Ned Tooma
☐ 1108 Henry Saunders
☐ 1109 Alec Clunas
☐ 1110 Tommy Tooma
☐ 1111 Ahoyak Dupuis
☐ 1112 Ned Gordon
☐ 1113 J-J Saunders
☐ 1114 Daniel Suppa
☐ 1115 Peter Papak
☐ 1116 Larry White
☐ 1391 Johnny Lingard
☐ 1393 Etva Watkins

LOTBINIÈRE PEE WEE

☐ 1117 Rick Martin
☐ 1118 Jonathan Aubé
☐ 1119 Samuel Lemieux
☐ 1120 Jérôme Cayer
☐ 1121 Nelson Fillion
☐ 1122 Alain Rousseau
☐ 1123 Jacques Garon
☐ 1124 J. Desruisseaux
☐ 1125 P-L D'Anjou
☐ 1126 Frédéric Moreau
☐ 1127 Alain Goulet
☐ 1128 Julien Montminy
☐ 1129 P-L Labrecque
☐ 1130 René Belley
☐ 1131 Jocelytn Guimond
☐ 1132 Dany Dallaire

CHICOUTIMI-NORD PEE WEE

☐ 1133 Marc-André Allard
☐ 1134 Christian Chantal
☐ 1135 David Corneau
☐ 1136 A. Desbiens
☐ 1137 Guillaume Fillion
☐ 1138 Francis Gagnon
☐ 1139 Mathieu Gauthier
☐ 1140 S-P Harvey
☐ 1141 Patrick Lavoie
☐ 1142 Sébastien Lavoie
☐ 1143 François Lessard
☐ 1144 Sylvain Pedneault
☐ 1145 Stéphane Pelland
☐ 1146 Frédéric Simard
☐ 1147 Serge Tremblay

QUÉBEC PEE WEE CITADELLES

The most expensive single is Alexandre Giroux at $2-3.

☐ 1148 Guillaume Duval
☐ 1149 Jérôme Marois
☐ 1150 Frédéric Blouin
☐ 1151 Simon Tardif
☐ 1152 Mathieu Pigeon
☐ 1153 Alexandre Giroux
☐ 1154 Dominic Jalbert
☐ 1155 Félix Gagné
☐ 1156 Charles Cauchon
☐ 1157 David Wong
☐ 1158 C-J Massé
☐ 1159 Benoît Gendron
☐ 1160 Sébastien Gagnon
☐ 1161 Sylvain Watt
☐ 1162 Dale Paré
☐ 1163 Éric Roberge

ST-JOSEPH BEAUCE PEE WEE

☐ 1164 Sébastien Vachon
☐ 1165 Patrick Giguère
☐ 1166 Jean-Martin Roy
☐ 1167 David Drouin
☐ 1168 David Mathieu
☐ 1169 Éric Gosselin
☐ 1170 David Fortin
☐ 1170 Alexandre Vachon
☐ 1172 J-F Lambert
☐ 1173 Jean Vallières
☐ 1174 Cédric Maheux
☐ 1175 J-F Cliché
☐ 1176 Olivier Spénard
☐ 1177 Jérôme Lachance
☐ 1178 Olivier Latulippe
☐ 1179 Sylvain Turmel
☐ 1180 Philippe Grenier
☐ 1181 Guillaume Audet
☐ 1182 Mathieu Labbé

WEST MICHIGAN PEE WEE

☐ 1184 Aaron Copeland
☐ 1185 Mike Zalewski
☐ 1186 T. Eenigenberg
☐ 1187 Andy Burnes
☐ 1188 Eric Jensen
☐ 1189 Victor Zurek
☐ 1190 Mike Hall
☐ 1191 Daniel Schuemann
☐ 1192 Aaron Vidmar
☐ 1193 James Simmons
☐ 1194 Andy Reynolds
☐ 1195 Bryan Beck
☐ 1196 Bobby Gifford
☐ 1197 Nicholas Malina
☐ 1198 Nick Piechouwski
☐ 1199 Adam Slater

SUISSE ITALIAN PEE WEE

☐ 1200 Luigi Alberti
☐ 1201 Lorenzo Barenco
☐ 1202 Devis Bertolini
☐ 1203 Fabio Carrara
☐ 1204 Carlo Cattaneo
☐ 1205 Luca Careda
☐ 1206 Athos Comolli
☐ 1207 Diego Crivelli
☐ 1208 Ruban Doma
☐ 1209 Paolo Ducas
☐ 1210 Marco Fahndrich
☐ 1211 Mattias Fritz
☐ 1212 John Gobbi
☐ 1213 Nicola Martingnoni
☐ 1214 Thomas Renner
☐ 1215 Marco Rigoni
☐ 1216 Alfio Pronini
☐ 1217 Mark Tschudy

ZURICH PEE WEE

☐ 1218 Michel Frey
☐ 1219 Pasqual Sievert
☐ 1220 Patrick Ammann
☐ 1221 Marcel Debrunner
☐ 1222 Mauro Beccarelli
☐ 1223 Sven Breitenmoser
☐ 1224 Andy Cellar
☐ 1225 Martin Etter
☐ 1226 Patrick Haag
☐ 1227 Timo Helbling
☐ 1228 Sven Helfenstein
☐ 1229 Giancarlo Hendry
☐ 1230 C. Hiltebrand
☐ 1231 Michael Jackle
☐ 1232 Patrick Meier
☐ 1233 Francis Reichmuth
☐ 1234 G. Ronchetti
☐ 1235 Fabian Stephan
☐ 1236 Mike Stiffler

SPRINGFIELD PEE WEE

The most expensive single is Ron Hainsey at $3-4.

☐ 1237 Ryan Cournoyer
☐ 1238 Kevin Davry
☐ 1239 Jon DiSalvatore
☐ 1240 Jason Fortin
☐ 1241 Robert Fried
☐ 1242 Tyson Gajda
☐ 1243 Ron Hainsey
☐ 1244 Jerry Hayden
☐ 1245 Mike Healy
☐ 1246 Stephen Labrie
☐ 1247 Troy Mansell
☐ 1248 Brian Neary
☐ 1249 James Nowak
☐ 1250 James Pagnam
☐ 1251 Mattias Perella
☐ 1252 Ken Plourd
☐ 1253 Christof Snizek
☐ 1254 Michael Velez

ST. LOUIS PEE WEE

☐ 1255 Ed Alberding
☐ 1256 George Cantrall
☐ 1257 Adam Coombe
☐ 1258 Robert Dillender
☐ 1259 Connor Dunlop
☐ 1260 Chance Ernst
☐ 1261 Jordy Federko
☐ 1262 Kevin Helldoerfer
☐ 1263 Garret Hitchcock
☐ 1264 Neill Komadoski
☐ 1265 Pierre Labarge
☐ 1266 Michael Mesko
☐ 1267 Timo Niedbalski
☐ 1268 Ryan Rogers
☐ 1269 Ryan Schilli
☐ 1270 Ben Tobin
☐ 1271 Corey Weinhaus

RIVE-SUD PEE WEE

☐ 1272 G. St-Laurent
☐ 1273 Luc Boivin
☐ 1274 David Boilard
☐ 1275 Dominic Laurin
☐ 1276 Dominic Tanguay
☐ 1277 Simon Delmarre
☐ 1278 Olivier Couture
☐ 1279 L-P Lessard
☐ 1280 Guillaume Caron
☐ 1281 V. Desrochers
☐ 1282 Jérôme Couture
☐ 1283 Yannick Picard
☐ 1284 Olivier Grenier
☐ 1285 Daniel Bergeron
☐ 1286 Michel Léveillé
☐ 1287 J-P Bélanger
☐ 1288 Justin Grenier

COLLÈGE FRANÇAIS PEE WEE

☐ 1289 M-A Bélanger
☐ 1290 Sébastien Laprise
☐ 1291 J-C Charette
☐ 1293 M-A Demers
☐ 1294 Patric Provençal
☐ 1295 Étienne Germain
☐ 1296 Kevin Bergin
☐ 1297 Sébastien Tardif
☐ 1298 Alexandre Gravel
☐ 1299 Sébastien Lucier
☐ 1300 François Miville
☐ 1301 Samuel Séguin
☐ 1302 A. Turcotte
☐ 1303 V-O Pelletier
☐ 1305 Guillaume Kerrer

REPENTIGNY PEE WEE

☐ 1306 Hugo Mudie
☐ 1307 Jonathan Lauzon
☐ 1308 Guy Bibeau
☐ 1309 Francis Miron
☐ 1310 Mathieu Magny
☐ 1311 Sébastien Bond
☐ 1312 Martin Labonté
☐ 1313 Pascal Guay
☐ 1314 L-P Ratelle
☐ 1315 Jonathan Lebuis
☐ 1316 Patrick Deschênes
☐ 1317 M-A Nantais
☐ 1318 Jason Pomminville
☐ 1319 Marc Ledoux
☐ 1320 Mighel Croteau
☐ 1321 François Gauthier

TORONTO PEE WEE RED WINGS

☐ 1322 Brian Tatum
☐ 1323 Mike Walker
☐ 1324 Michael Renzi
☐ 1325 Joshua Legge
☐ 1326 Julius Halfkenny
☐ 1327 George Nistas
☐ 1328 Steve Nobili
☐ 1329 John Osborne
☐ 1330 Kevin Waldock
☐ 1331 David Guenette
☐ 1332 Alex Ward
☐ 1333 Thomas Sockett
☐ 1334 Trevor Freeman
☐ 1336 Darcey Morris

LAVAL PEE WEE

☐ 1337 M-A Therrien
☐ 1338 S. Cossette
☐ 1339 Martin Blanchet
☐ 1340 Jonathan Gauthier
☐ 1341 M-A Binette
☐ 1342 Éric Cloutier
☐ 1343 Henri-Pierre Ano
☐ 1344 Alain Melançon
☐ 1345 Sébastien Labelle
☐ 1346 Patrice Tassy
☐ 1347 Jonathan Therrien
☐ 1348 Philippe Angers
☐ 1349 Jonathan Farresse
☐ 1350 Simon Lachapelle
☐ 1351 Maxime Gagné
☐ 1352 Sébastien Thériault

VANCOUVER PEE WEE CANUCKS

☐ 1353 Chris Shaw
☐ 1354 Justin Kelly
☐ 1355 David Ullman
☐ 1356 Ian Cheyne
☐ 1357 Craig Pickell
☐ 1358 Greg Perih
☐ 1359 Jesse Gregory
☐ 1360 Aaron Deakin
☐ 1361 Bryce Parker
☐ 1362 Wayne Berg
☐ 1363 Adrian Deakin
☐ 1364 Ryan Thorpe
☐ 1365 Trevor Paul
☐ 1366 Scott May
☐ 1367 Adam Roberts
☐ 1368 Kevin Young
☐ 1369 Ryan Trsek

SUISSE CENTRALE PEE WEE

☐ 1370 Peter Mettler
☐ 1371 Simon Looser
☐ 1372 Levand Aytek
☐ 1373 T. Achermann
☐ 1374 Dominik Glaus
☐ 1375 Stephan Maag
☐ 1376 Michael Risi
☐ 1377 Samuel Schuler
☐ 1378 André Annen
☐ 1379 Nico Battaglia
☐ 1380 A. Camenzind
☐ 1381 Csaba Dekany
☐ 1382 Tobias Erni
☐ 1383 Michael Gnos
☐ 1384 Philipp Hodel
☐ 1386 Adrian Lechmann
☐ 1387 Oliver Scharer

SUISSE ROMANDE PEE WEE

☐ 1394 Ludwig Bochy
☐ 1395 Martin Zerzuben
☐ 1396 Gilles Catella
☐ 1397 David Jobin
☐ 1398 Jimmy Coia
☐ 1399 Nicolas Brasey
☐ 1400 J-C Wysling
☐ 1401 Olivier Jeanneret
☐ 1402 Xavier Durini
☐ 1403 Sébastien Reuille
☐ 1404 Valentin Wirz
☐ 1405 Pascal Faivet
☐ 1406 Ludovic Aubry
☐ 1407 Xavier Gattuso
☐ 1408 Thierry Bornard
☐ 1409 Nicolas Sciboz
☐ 1410 Lars Blatter
☐ 1411 Nicolas Burdet
☐ 1412 Cédric Melly
☐ 1413 Thibault Monnet
☐ 1415 David Favre

FREDERICTON PEE WEE

☐ 1416 Tim Dickinson ☐ 1417 Greg McGinnis
☐ 1418 Ryan Wilson ☐ 1419 Kent Staples
☐ 1420 Ian Appleton ☐ 1421 Chris Boulter
☐ 1422 Matt Sweehey ☐ 1423 Andy Harriman
☐ 1424 Marc Leblanc ☐ 1425 Nathan Doucetter
☐ 1426 Dusty McSorley ☐ 1427 Jan Pineo
☐ 1428 Shawn Mersereau ☐ 1429 Michael Grand
☐ 1430 Trevor Dean ☐ 1431 Steve Kelly
☐ 1432 Ryan" Murphy

EDMONTON PEE WEE

The most expensive single is Jamie Lundmark at $4-6.

☐ 1434 Kevin Flugleberg ☐ 1435 Blair Stevens
☐ 1436 Kevin Gardner ☐ 1437 Bryan Kosak
☐ 1438 Jamie Lundmark ☐ 1439 Mike Mulhooland
☐ 1440 James" Wright ☐ 1441 Eric Jonanssnon
☐ 1442 Doug Edmondson ☐ 1443 Alan Ciciarelli
☐ 1444 Galloway Carroll ☐ 1445 Curtis Dorfman
☐ 1446 Jezzy Letros ☐ 1447 Wendel Ward
☐ 1448 Paul Crosty ☐ 1449 Samuel Halaby
☐ 1450 Curtis Savage

1995 SEMIC

Numerous cards in this series (specifically, cards of NHLPA members) were not licensed. As such, cards in this series are not recognized as rookie cards.

Imprint: Semic Sport Cards
Complete Set (240 cards): 45.00
Common Player: .20

	Player	NRMT-MT
☐	1 Pasi Kuivalainen, Fin.	.20
☐	2 Marko Kiprusoff, Fin.	.20
☐	3 Tuomas Grönman, Fin.	.20
☐	4 Erik Hämäläinen, Fin.	.20
☐	5 Timo Jutila, Fin.	.20
☐	6 Pasi Sormunen, Fin.	.20
☐	7 Waltteri Immonen, Fin.	.20
☐	8 Janne Ojanen, Fin.	.20
☐	9 Esa Keskinen, Fin.	.20
☐	10 Kimmo Timonen, Fin.	.20
☐	11 Saku Koivu, Fin.	1.00
☐	12 Janne Laukkanen, Fin.	.20
☐	13 Marko Pale, Fin.	.20
☐	14 Raimo Helminen, Fin.	.20
☐	15 Mika Alatalo, Fin.	.20
☐	16 Ville Peltonen, Fin.	.20
☐	17 Jari Kurri, Fin.	1.00
☐	18 Jari Korpisalo, Fin.	.20
☐	19 Kimmo Rintanen, Fin.	.20
☐	20 Jere Lehtinen, Fin.	.20
☐	21 Kalle Sahlstedt, Fin.	.20
☐	22 Christian Ruuttu, Fin.	.20
☐	23 Hannu Virta, Fin.	.20
☐	24 Sami Kapanen, Fin.	.20
☐	25 Marko Tuulola, Fin.	.20
☐	26 Mika Strömberg, Fin.	.20
☐	27 Tero Lehterä, Fin.	.20
☐	28 Petri Varis, Fin.	.20
☐	29 Mikko Peltola, Fin.	.20
☐	30 Jukka Tammi (G), Fin.	.20
☐	31 Tero Arkiomaa, Fin.	.20
☐	32 Olli Kaski, Fin.	.20
☐	33 Pekka Laksola, Fin.	.20
☐	34 Mika Välilä, Fin.	.20
☐	35 Jarmo Myllys (G), Fin.	.20
☐	36 Harri Laurila, Fin.	.20
☐	37 Teppo Numminen, Fin.	.20
☐	38 Jyrki Lumme, Fin.	.20
☐	39 Petteti Nummelin, Fin.	.20
☐	40 Mika Nieminen, Fin.	.20
☐	41 Teemu Selänne, Fin.	1.00
☐	42 Mikko Mäkelä, Fin.	.20
☐	43 Esa Tikkanen, Fin.	.20
☐	44 Jarkko Varvio, Fin.	.20
☐	45 Vesa Viitakoski, Fin.	.20
☐	46 Juha Riihijärvi, Fin.	.20
☐	47 Markus Ketterer (G), Fin.	.20
☐	48 Mikko Haapakoski, Fin.	.20
☐	49 Antti Törmänen, Fin.	.20
☐	50 Time Peltomaa, Fin.	.20
☐	51 Rauli Raitanen, Fin.	.20
☐	52 Roger Nordström (G), Swe.	.20
☐	53 Tommy Salo (G), Swe.	.50
☐	54 Tommy Söderström (G), Swe.	.20
☐	55 Magnus Svensson, Swe.	.20
☐	56 Fredrik Stillman, Swe.	.20
☐	57 Nicklas Lidström, Swe.	.50
☐	58 Roger Johansson, Swe.	.20
☐	59 Kenny Jönsson, Swe.	.20
☐	60 Peter Andersson, Swe.	.20
☐	61 Tommy Sjödin, Swe.	.20
☐	62 Mats Sundin, Swe.	1.00
☐	63 Jonas Bergqvisd, Swe.	.20
☐	64 Peter Forsberg, Swe.	1.50
☐	65 Roger Hansson, Swe.	.20
☐	66 Jargen Jansson, Swe.	.20
☐	67 Charles Berglund, Swe.	.20
☐	68 Mikael Johansson, Swe.	.20
☐	69 Tomas Forslund, Swe.	.20
☐	70 Anders Dackell, Swe.	.20
☐	71 Stefan Öjrnskog, Swe.	.20
☐	72 Mikael Andersson, Swe.	.20
☐	73 Jan Larsson, Swe.	.20
☐	74 Patrik Carnbäck, Swe.	.20
☐	75 Håkan Loob, Swe.	.20
☐	76 Patrik Juhlin, Swe.	.20
☐	77 Bill Ranford (G), Cdn.	.50
☐	78 Ed Belfour (G), Cdn.	1.00
☐	79 Rob Blake, Cdn.	.50
☐	80 Yves Racine, Cdn.	.20
☐	81 Steve Smith, Cdn.	.20
☐	82 Paul Coffey, Cdn.	.50
☐	83 Larry Murphy, Cdn.	.20
☐	84 Mark Tinordi, Cdn.	.20
☐	85 Al MacInnis, Cdn.	.50
☐	86 Paul Kariya, Cdn.	1.50
☐	87 Joe Sakic, Cdn.	2.00
☐	88 Brendan Shanahan, Cdn.	1.00
☐	89 Luc Robitaille, Cdn.	1.00
☐	90 Rod Brind'Amour, Cdn.	.20
☐	91 Shayne Corson, Cdn.	.20
☐	92 Mike Ricci, Cdn.	.20
☐	93 Mario Lemieux, Cdn.	3.50
☐	94 Eric Lindros, Cdn.	1.00
☐	95 Russ Courtnall, Cdn.	.20
☐	96 Theoren Fleury, Cdn.	.50
☐	97 Mark Messier, Cdn.	1.00
☐	98 Rick Tocchet, Cdn.	.20
☐	99 Wayne Gretzky, Cdn.	5.00
☐	100 Steve Larmer, Cdn.	.50
☐	101 Brett Lindros, Cdn.	.20
☐	102 John Vanbiesbrouck (G), USA.	.50
☐	103 Craig Wolanin, USA.	.20
☐	104 Chris Chelios, USA.	.50
☐	105 Brian Leetch, USA.	.50
☐	106 Kevin Hatcher, USA.	.20
☐	107 Craig Janney, USA.	.20
☐	108 Tim Sweeney, USA.	.20
☐	109 Shawn Chambers, USA.	.20
☐	110 Scott Young, USA.	.20
☐	111 John Lilley, USA.	.20
☐	112 Joe Sacco, USA.	.20
☐	113 Brett Hull, USA.	1.00
☐	114 Pat LaFontaine, USA.	.50
☐	115 Joel Otto, USA.	.20
☐	116 Mike Modano, USA.	1.00
☐	117 Tony Granato, USA.	.20
☐	118 Jeremy Roenick, USA.	1.00
☐	119 Jeff Lazaro, USA.	.20
☐	120 Brian Mullen, USA.	.20
☐	121 Mikhail Shtalenkov (G), Rus.	.20
☐	122 Valeri Ivannikov, Rus.	.20
☐	123 Andrei Nikolishin, Rus.	.20
☐	124 Ilja Byakin, Rus.	.20
☐	125 Alexander Smirnov, Rus.	.20
☐	126 Dimitri Yushkevich, Rus.	.20
☐	127 Sergei Shendelev, Rus.	.20
☐	128 Alexei Zhitnik, Rus.	.20
☐	129 Igor Ulanov, Rus.	.20
☐	130 Dmitri Frolov, Rus.	.20
☐	131 Valeri Kamensky, Rus.	.20
☐	132 Igor Feduiov, Rus.	.20
☐	133 Andrei Kovalenko, Rus.	.20
☐	134 Valeri Bure, Rus.	.20
☐	135 Sergei Berezin, Rus.	.20
☐	136 Alexei Yashin, Rus.	.50
☐	137 Vyacheslav Kozlov, Rus.	.20
☐	138 Vyacheslav Bykov, Rus.	.20
☐	139 Andrei Khomutov, Rus.	.20
☐	140 Petr Briza (G), Cze.	.20
☐	141 Dominik Hasek (G), Cze.	1.00
☐	142 Roman Turek (G), Cze.	.50
☐	143 Jan Vopat, Cze.	.20
☐	144 Drahomir Kadlec, Cze.	.20
☐	145 Petr Pavlas, Cze.	.20
☐	146 Frantisek Kucera, Cze.	.20
☐	147 Jiri Veber, Cze.	.20
☐	148 David Vyborny, Cze.	.20
☐	149 Radek Toupalv, Cze.	.20
☐	150 Jiri Kucera, Cze.	.20
☐	151 Richard Zemlicka, Cze.	.20
☐	152 Martin Rucinsky, Cze.	.20
☐	153 Jiri Dolezal, Cze.	.20
☐	154 Josef Beranek, Cze.	.20
☐	155 Martin Prochazka, Cze.	.20
☐	156 Tomas Srsen, Cze.	.20
☐	157 Vavid Bruk, Cze.	.20
☐	158 Jaromir Jagr, Cze.	1.00
☐	159 Jan Caloun, Cze.	.20
☐	160 Martin Straka, Cze.	.20
☐	161 Roman Horak, Cze.	.20
☐	162 Frantisek Musil, Cze.	.20
☐	163 Peter Hrbek, Cze.	.20
☐	164 Jan Alino, Cze.	.20
☐	165 Joseph Heiss (G), Ger.	.20
☐	166 Peter Gulda, Ger.	.20
☐	167 Jason Meyer, Ger.	.20
☐	168 Ernst Köpf, Ger.	.20
☐	169 Raimund Hilger, Ger.	.20
☐	170 Richard Böhm, Ger.	.20
☐	171 Michael Rosati (G), Ita.	.50
☐	172 Michael de Angelis, Ita.	.20
☐	173 Anthony Circelli, Ita.	.20
☐	174 Gaetano Orlando, Ita.	.20
☐	175 Lucio Topatigh, Ita.	.20
☐	176 Martin Pavlu, Ita.	.20
☐	177 Jim Marthinsen (G), Nor.	.20
☐	178 Petter Salsten, Nor.	.20
☐	179 Tommy Jacobsen, Nor.	.20
☐	180 Morten Finstad, Nor.	.20
☐	181 Tom Andersen, Nor.	.20
☐	182 Magnus Rath, Nor.	.20
☐	183 Michael Puschacher (G), Aut.	.20
☐	184 James Burton, Aut.	.20
☐	185 Michael Shea, Aut.	.20
☐	186 Dieter Kalt, Aut.	.20
☐	187 Manfred Muhr, Aut.	.20
☐	188 Andreas Pusnik, Aut.	.20
☐	189 Renato Tosio (G), Sui.	.20
☐	190 Doug Honneger, Sui.	.20
☐	191 Felix Hollenstein, Sui.	.20
☐	192 Jörg Eberle, Sui.	.20
☐	193 Gil Montandon, Sui.	.20
☐	194 Roberto Triulzi, Sui.	.20
☐	195 Petri Yönen (G), Fra.	.20
☐	196 Bruno Maynort, Fra.	.20
☐	197 Michel Leblanc, Fra.	.20
☐	198 Benoit Laporte, Fra.	.20
☐	199 Christophe Ville, Fra.	.20
☐	200 Antoine Richer, Fra.	.20
☐	201 AS: Bill Ranford (G), Cdn.	.50
☐	202 AS: Timo Jutila, Fin.	.20
☐	203 AS: Magnus Svensson, Swe.	.20
☐	204 AS: Jari Kurri, Fin.	1.00
☐	205 AS: Saku Koivu, Fin.	1.00
☐	206 AS: Paul Kariya, Cdn.	1.50
☐	207 Jarmo Myllys (G), Fin.	.20
☐	208 Bill Ranford (G), Cdn.	.50
☐	209 Roger Nordström (G), Swe.	.20
☐	210 Guy Hebert (G), USA.	.20
☐	211 Mikail Shtalenkov (G), Rus.	.20
☐	212 Tommy Söderström (G), Swe.	.20
☐	213 Petr Briza (G), Cze.	.20
☐	214 Dominik Hasek (G), Cze.	1.00
☐	215 Tom Barrasso (G),	.50
☐	216 Jukka Tammi (G), Fin.	.20
☐	217 John Vanbiesbrouck (G), USA.	.50
☐	218 Mike Richter (G), USA.	.50
☐	219 Saku Koivu, Fin.	1.00
☐	220 Saku Koivu, Fin.	1.00
☐	221 Saku Koivu, Fin.	1.00
☐	222 Saku Koivu, Fin.	1.00
☐	223 Saku Koivu, Fin.	1.00
☐	224 Saku Koivu, Fin.	1.00
☐	225 Tuomas Grönman, Fin.	.20
☐	226 Jani Nikko, Fin.	.20
☐	227 Janne Niinimaa, Fin.	.20
☐	228 Jukka Tiilikainen, Fin.	.20
☐	229 Kimmo Rintanen, Fin.	.20
☐	230 Ville Peltonen, Fin.	.20
☐	231 Sami Kapanen, Fin.	.20
☐	232 Jere Lehtinen, Fin.	.20
☐	233 Kimmo Timonen, Fin.	.20
☐	234 Jonni Vauhkonen, Fin.	.20
☐	235 Juha Lind, Fin.	.20
☐	236 Tommi Miettinen, Fin.	.20
☐	237 Jere Karalahti, Fin.	.20
☐	238 Antti Aalto, Fin.	.20
☐	239 Teemu Kohvakka, Fin.	.20
☐	240 Niko Mikkola, Fin.	.20

1995 SUOMEN ALL-STAR

A set of 8 card covers.
Card Size: 3" x 4 1/2"
Complete Set (8 cards): 25.00

	Player	NRMT-MT
☐	1 Jarmo Myllys (G)	2.00
☐	2 Jari Kurri	6.00
☐	3 Saku Koivu	10.00
☐	4 Teemu Selänne	10.00
☐	5 Esa Tikkanen	2.00
☐	6 Christian Ruuttu	1.00
☐	7 Mika Nieminen	1.00
☐	8 Timo Jutila	2.00

1995 SUOMEN BECKETT ALL-STARS

A set of 8 ad cards.
Card Size: 2 7/8" x 4 1/2"
Complete Set (8 cards): 25.00

	Player	NRMT-MT
☐	1 Saku Koivu	10.00
☐	2 Jere Lehtinen	6.00
☐	3 Ville Peltonen	3.00
☐	4 Erik Hämäläinen	2.00
☐	5 Sami Kapanen	3.00
☐	6 Marko Kiprusoff	2.00
☐	7 Mika Stromberg	2.00
☐	8 Marko Palo	2.00

1995 TOPPS FINEST BRONZE

These oversized cards were sold by Topps as a complete set.
Series Two Set (7 cards): 150.00

	Player	NRMT-MT
☐	8 Brett Hull, SLou.	20.00
☐	9 Paul Kariya, Anah.	60.00
☐	10 Cam Neely, Bost.	15.00
☐	11 Mats Sundin, Toro.	20.00
☐	12 Martin Brodeur (G), NJer.	35.00
☐	13 Jeremy Roenick, Chic.	15.00
☐	14 Brian Leetch, NYRa.	15.00

1995 - 96 APS

We have little pricing information on this set. Our checklist is supposedly incomplete. Jaromir Jagr is the most expensive single at $15-20. Other sought-after singles include Milan Hejduk ($8-12), Roman Cechmanek ($4-6), Jiri Dopita ($4-6) and Roman Turek ($4-6), Dominik Hasek ($8-12). NHL stars sell at $1-4. Singles start at 25¢.

Player	Player
☐ 1 Horst Valasek, Coach	☐ 2 Zdislav Tabara, Coach
☐ 3 R. Cechmanek (G)	☐ 4 Ivo Pesat (G)
☐ 5 Alexei Jaskin	☐ 6 Stanislav Pavelec
☐ 7 Jan Srdinko	☐ 8 Antonin Stavjana
☐ 9 Pavel Taborsky	☐ 10 Jiri Veber
☐ 11 Daniel Vrla	☐ 12 Miroslav Barus
☐ 13 Ivan Padelek	☐ 14 Libor Forch
☐ 15 Andrei Galkin	☐ 16 Lubos Jenacek
☐ 17 Tomas Srsen	☐ 18 Rostislav Vlach
☐ 19 Zbynek Marak	☐ 20 Jiri Dopita
☐ 21 Ales Polcar	☐ 22 Roman Stantien
☐ 23 Michal Tomek	☐ 24 Jiri Zadrazil
☐ 25 Pavel Augusta	☐ 26 Tomas Jakes
☐ 27 V. Vujtek, Coach	☐ 28 Z. Cech (Coach)
☐ 29 Jaroslav Kames (G)	☐ 30 Pavel Malac (G)
☐ 31 Jan Vavrecka	☐ 32 Miroslav Javin
☐ 33 Stanislav Medrik	☐ 34 Pavel Kowalczyk
☐ 35 Miroslav Guren	☐ 36 Radim Tesarik
☐ 37 Jan Krajicek	☐ 38 Jiri Marusak
☐ 39 Josef Straub	☐ 40 Pavel Janku
☐ 41 Roman Meluzin	☐ 42 Miroslav Okal
☐ 43 Zdenek Okal	☐ 44 David Bruk
☐ 45 Jaroslav Hub	☐ 46 Petr Cajanek
☐ 47 Tomas Nemcicky	☐ 48 Martin Kotasek
☐ 49 Zdenek Sedlak	☐ 50 Petr Leska
☐ 51 V. Caldr, Coach	☐ 52 J. Liska, Coach
☐ 53 Oldrich Svoboda (G)	☐ 54 Robert Slavik (G)
☐ 55 Rudolf Suchanek	☐ 56 Milan Nedoma
☐ 57 Lukas Zib	☐ 58 Karel Soudek
☐ 59 Petr Sedy	☐ 60 Libor Zabransky
☐ 61 Kamil Toupal	☐ 62 Michal Kubicek
☐ 63 Martin Masak	☐ 64 Radek Belohlav
☐ 65 Radek Toupal	☐ 66 Pavel Pycha
☐ 67 Lubos Rob	☐ 68 Filip Turek
☐ 69 Ondrej Vosta	☐ 70 Roman Bozek
☐ 71 Jaroslav Brabec	☐ 72 Petr Sailer
☐ 73 M. Strba, Coach	☐ 74 Z. Sperger, Coach
☐ 75 Jan Neliba (G)	☐ 76 Zdenek Miller (G)
☐ 77 Martin Chlad	☐ 78 Jiri Kucera
☐ 79 Jan Dlouhy	☐ 80 Tomas Kaberle
☐ 81 Petr Kasik	☐ 82 Jan Krulis
☐ 83 Petr Kuda	☐ 84 Libor Prochazka
☐ 85 Martin Stepanek	☐ 86 Marek Zidlicky
☐ 87 Jiri Beranek	☐ 88 Jiri Burger
☐ 89 David Cermak	☐ 90 Milos Kajer
☐ 91 Miroslav Mach	☐ 92 Tomas Mikolasek
☐ 93 Pavel Patera	☐ 94 Martin Prochazka
☐ 95 Petr Ton	☐ 96 Otakar Vejvoda
☐ 97 Josef Zajic	☐ 98 J. Augusta, Coach
☐ 99 L. Fischer, Coach	☐ 100 Precechtel, Coach
☐ 101 Pavel Cagas (G)	☐ 102 Ladislav Blazek (G)
☐ 103 Jaromir Latal	☐ 104 Jiri Latal
☐ 105 Petr Tejkl	☐ 106 Jiri Kuntos
☐ 107 Patrik Rimmel	☐ 108 Robert Machalek
☐ 109 Jiri Polak	☐ 110 Martin Bakula
☐ 111 Michal Slavik	☐ 112 Pavel Nohel
☐ 113 Igor Cikl	☐ 114 Zdenek Eichenmann
☐ 115 Milan Navratil	☐ 116 Ales Zima
☐ 117 Tomas Matinec	☐ 118 Richard Brancik
☐ 119 Ondrej Kratena	☐ 120 Michal Bros
☐ 121 Juraj Jurik	☐ 122 Jan Tomajko
☐ 123 R. Farda, Coach	☐ 124 B. Kopriva, Coach
☐ 125 Martin Altrichter (G)	☐ 126 Radek Toth (G)
☐ 127 Miroslav Horava	☐ 128 Martin Maskarinec
☐ 129 Jakub Ficenec	☐ 130 Jiri Hes
☐ 131 Andrej Jakovenko	☐ 132 Petr Macek
☐ 133 Jan Penk	☐ 134 Robert Kostka
☐ 135 Vladimir Ruzicka	☐ 136 Viktor Ujcik
☐ 137 Ivo Prorok	☐ 138 Tomas Jelinek
☐ 139 Michal Sup	☐ 140 Milan Antos
☐ 141 Roman Blazek	☐ 142 Jiri Hlinka
☐ 143 Tomas Kupka	☐ 144 Vaclav Eiselt
☐ 145 Jaroslav Bednar	☐ 146 Ladislav Svoboda
☐ 147 Ladislav Kudrna	☐ 148 J. Beranek, Coach
☐ 149 V. Kyhos, Coach	☐ 150 Zdenek Orct (G)
☐ 151 Petr Franek (G)	☐ 152 Kamil Prachar
☐ 153 Angel Nikolov	☐ 154 Onderj Zetek
☐ 155 Tomas Arnost	☐ 156 Normunds Sejejs
☐ 157 Petr Kratky	☐ 158 Sergej Butko
☐ 159 Petr Molnar	☐ 160 Radek Mrazek
☐ 161 Radim Piroutek	☐ 162 David Balasz
☐ 163 Jindrich Kotrla	☐ 164 Jaroslav Buchal
☐ 165 Josef Straka	☐ 166 Michail Fadejev
☐ 167 Radek Sip	☐ 168 Martin Rousek
☐ 169 Tomas Vlasak	☐ 170 Robert Kysela
☐ 171 Jan Alinc	☐ 172 Vladimir Machulda
☐ 173 Vladimir Jerabek	☐ 174 F. Vorlicek, Coach
☐ 175 Jan Hrbaty, Coach	☐ 176 Marek Novotny (G)
☐ 177 Lukas Sablik (G)	☐ 178 Roman Kankovsky
☐ 179 Michael Vyhlidal	☐ 180 Jan Bohacek
☐ 181 Roman Cech	☐ 182 Zdenek Touzimsky
☐ 183 Marek Posmyk	☐ 184 Pavel Rajnoha
☐ 185 Martin Tupa	☐ 186 Libor Dolana
☐ 187 Petr Vlk	☐ 188 Petr Kankovsky
☐ 189 Jiri Cihlar	☐ 190 Jiri Poukar
☐ 191 Jaromir Kverka	☐ 192 Leos Pipa
☐ 193 Ladislav Prokupek	☐ 194 Patrik Fink
☐ 195 Marek Melenovsky	☐ 196 Jiri Holik
☐ 197 Miroslav Bruna	☐ 198 J. Walter, Coach
☐ 199 O. Zelezny, Coach	☐ 200 Libor Barta (G)
☐ 201 Pavel Nestak (G)	☐ 202 Leo Gudas
☐ 203 Karel Beran	☐ 204 Richard Adam
☐ 205 Pavel Zubicek	☐ 206 Alexander Elsner
☐ 207 Robert Kantor	☐ 208 Ladislav Tresl
☐ 209 Frantisek Sevcik	☐ 210 Michal Konecny

☐ 211 Richard Sebestu	☐ 212 Roman Mejzlik
☐ 213 Zdenek Cely	☐ 214 Jiri Vitek
☐ 215 Radek Haman	☐ 216 Tomas Krasny
☐ 217 Jiri Suhrada	☐ 218 Jaroslav Smolik
☐ 219 Hadamczik, Coach	☐ 220 K. Suchanek, Coach
☐ 221 Michal Hlinka (G)	☐ 222 Josef Lucak (G)
☐ 223 Karel Pavlik	☐ 224 Stanislav Meciar
☐ 225 Petr Mainer	☐ 226 Petr Pavlas
☐ 227 Lubomir Sekeras	☐ 228 Roman Sindel
☐ 229 Vaclav Slaby	☐ 230 Miroslav Cihal
☐ 231 Martin Palinek	☐ 232 Petr Zajonc
☐ 233 Michal Piskor	☐ 234 Roman Kadera
☐ 235 Marek Zadina	☐ 236 Richard Kral
☐ 237 Miroslav Skovira	☐ 238 Vladimir Machalek
☐ 239 Libor Zatopek	☐ 240 Dusan Adamcik
☐ 241 Jiri Novotny	☐ 242 K. Trachta, Coach
☐ 243 Setikovsky, Coach	☐ 244 Rudolf Pejchar (G)
☐ 245 Michal Marik (G)	☐ 246 Karel Smid
☐ 247 Martin Kovarik	☐ 248 Jiri Hanzlik
☐ 249 Jaroslav Spacek	☐ 250 Stanislav Benes
☐ 251 Robert Jindrich	☐ 252 Vaclav Ruprecht
☐ 253 Tomas Kucharcik	☐ 254 Michal Straka
☐ 255 Ondrej Steiner	☐ 256 Tomas Klimt
☐ 257 Martin Zivny	☐ 258 Milan Volak
☐ 259 Pavel Metlicka	☐ 260 Josef Rybar
☐ 261 Jaroslav Kreuzman	☐ 262 David Trachta
☐ 263 Anatolij Najda	☐ 264 Tomas Ruprecht
☐ 265 Dalibor Sanda	☐ 266 Jaroslav Brabec
☐ 267 F. Vyborny, Coach	☐ 268 S. Berger, Coach
☐ 269 Ivo Capek (G)	☐ 270 David Volek
☐ 271 Jiri Vykoukal	☐ 272 Vaclav Burda
☐ 273 Petr Kuchyna	☐ 274 Pavel Srek
☐ 275 Frantisek Ptacek	☐ 276 Radek Hamr
☐ 277 Jiri Krocak	☐ 278 Jaroslav Nedved
☐ 279 Jiri Zelenka	☐ 280 David Vyborny
☐ 281 Petr Hrbek	☐ 282 Roman Horak
☐ 283 Kamil Kastak	☐ 284 Patrik Martinec
☐ 285 Zbynek Kukacka	☐ 286 Miroslav Hlinka
☐ 287 Jaroslav Hlinka	☐ 288 Jan Hlavac
☐ 289 Andrej Potajcuk	☐ 290 Richard Zemlicka
☐ 291 V. Stransky, Coach	☐ 292 L. Svozil, Coach
☐ 293 Martin Prusek (G)	☐ 294 V. Hudacek (G)
☐ 295 Pavel Marecek	☐ 296 Rudolf Wolf
☐ 297 Tomas Kramny	☐ 298 Pavel Kubina
☐ 299 Rene Sevecek	☐ 300 Filip Kuba
☐ 301 Ales Tomasek	☐ 302 Roman Rysanek
☐ 303 Vladimir Vujtek	☐ 304 Petr Folta
☐ 305 Jan Peterek	☐ 306 Roman Simicek
☐ 307 Pavel Zdrahal	☐ 308 Pavel Sebesta
☐ 309 David Moravec	☐ 310 Tomas Chlubna
☐ 311 Ludek Krayzel	☐ 312 Waldemar Klisiak
☐ 313 Petr Fabian	☐ 314 J. Palacek, Coach
☐ 315 F. Strida, Coach	☐ 316 Radovan Biegl (G)
☐ 317 Dusan Salficky (G)	☐ 318 Petr Jancarik
☐ 319 Tomas Pacal	☐ 320 Radomir Brazda
☐ 321 Radek Mesicek	☐ 322 Jiri Antonin
☐ 323 Alexander Terekhov	☐ 324 Milan Beranek
☐ 325 Ladislav Lubina	☐ 326 David Pospisil
☐ 327 Milan Kastner	☐ 328 Stanislav Prochazka
☐ 329 Patrik Weber	☐ 330 Milan Hejduk
☐ 331 Tomas Blazek	☐ 332 Jiri Jantovsky
☐ 333 Jaroslav Kudrna	☐ 334 Tomas Pisa
☐ 335 Ales Pisa	☐ 336 Ivan Vasilev (G)
☐ 337 Milan Hnilicka (G)	☐ 338 Ales Flasar
☐ 339 Martin Smetak	☐ 340 Libor Polasek
☐ 341 Vitezslav Skuta	☐ 342 Ladislav Benysek
☐ 343 Jaroslav Smolik	☐ 344 Igor Cikl
☐ 345 Jan Czerlinski	☐ 346 Marek Vorel
☐ 347 Martin Ancicka	☐ 348 Pavel Skrbek
☐ 349 Petr Kadlec	☐ 350 Tomas Kucharcik
☐ 351 L. Bukac, Coach	☐ 352 Z. Uher, Coach
☐ 353 R. Cechmanek (G)	☐ 354 Roman Turek (G)
☐ 355 Petr Briza (G)	☐ 356 Jaroslav Kames (G)
☐ 357 Antonin Stavjana	☐ 358 Berdrich Scerban
☐ 359 Petr Kuchyna	☐ 360 Jiri Vykoukal
☐ 361 Frantisek Kaberle	☐ 362 Jan Vopat
☐ 363 Libor Prochazka	☐ 364 Jiri Kucera
☐ 365 Tomas Jelinek	☐ 366 Richard Zemlicka
☐ 367 Martin Hostak	☐ 368 Tomas Srsen
☐ 369 Jiri Dopita	☐ 370 Martin Prochazka
☐ 371 Pavel Patera	☐ 372 Otakar Vejvoda
☐ 373 Roman Horak	☐ 374 Radek Belohlav
☐ 375 Pavel Geffert	☐ 376 Jan Alinc
☐ 377 Roman Kadera	☐ 378 Viktor Ujcik
☐ 379 Roman Meluzin	☐ 380 Pavel Janku
☐ 381 Tomas Kucharcik	☐ 382 Zbynek Marak
☐ 383 Ales Zima	☐ 384 AW: Jaromir Jagr
☐ 385 AW: Pavel Patera	☐ 386 AW: M. Prochazka
☐ 387 AW: Pavel Janku	☐ 388 AW:Cechmanek (G)
☐ 389 AW: A. Stavjana	☐ 390 AW: Rostislav Vlach
☐ 391 AW: L. Jenacek	☐ 392 AW: D. Hasek (G)
☐ 393 Jiri Holik	☐ 394 Frantisek Pospisil
☐ 395 Ivan Hlinka	☐ 396 Vladimir Martinec
☐ 397 Jaroslav Pouzar	☐ 398 Karel Gut
☐ 399 Jan Benda	☐ 400 AS: Cechmanek (G)
☐ 401 AS: A. Stavjana	☐ 402 AS: Radim Tesarik
☐ 403 AS: Tomas Srsen	☐ 404 AS: Roman Meluzin
☐ 405 AS: Jiri Dopita	☐ 406 AS: J. Kames (G)
☐ 407 AS: Jiri Latal	☐ 408 AS: Leo Gudas
☐ 409 AS: Vladimir Vujtek	☐ 410 AS: Roman Kadera
☐ 411 AS: Rostislav Vlach	☐ 412 AS: R. Kankovsky
☐ 413 AS: Ales Tomasek	☐ 414 AS: Petr Kankovsky
☐ 415 AS: Jiri Poukar	☐ 416 AS: R. Rysanek
☐ 417 AS: Jiri Veber	☐ 418 AS: Jaromir Latal
☐ 419 AS: David Bruk	☐ 420 AS: Richard Kral
☐ 421 AS: Zbynek Marak	☐ 422 AS: Coaches
☐ 423 AS: O. Svoboda (G)	☐ 424 AS: J. Vykoukal
☐ 425 AS: L. Prochazka	☐ 426 AS: Otakar Vejvoda
☐ 427 AS: M. Prochazka	☐ 428 AS: Pavel Patera
☐ 429 AS: Ivo Capek (G)	☐ 430 AS: Miloslav Horava
☐ 431 AS: Vaclav Burda	☐ 432 AS: Andrei Potajcuk
☐ 433 AS: Radek Belohlav	☐ 434 AS: V. Ruzicka
☐ 435 AS: J. Spacek	☐ 436 AS: Libor Zabransky
☐ 437 AS: N. Sejejs	☐ 438 AS: Angel Nikolov
☐ 439 AS: David Prospisil	☐ 440 AS: Jan Alinc
☐ 441 AS: Tomas Jelinek	☐ 442 AS: Ladislav Lubina
☐ 443 AS: Radek Toupal	☐ 444 AS: Viktor Ujcik
☐ 445 AS: Coaches	☐ 446 AS: Team East
☐ 447 AS: Team West	Petr Nedved Top Card

1995 - 96 BICYCLE SPORTS ACES

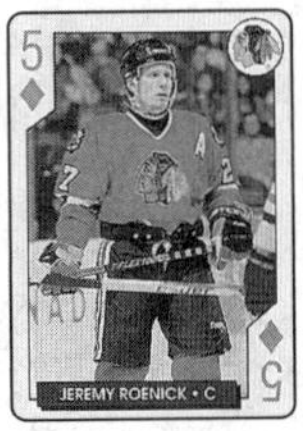

The most expensive single is Wayne Gretzky at $1.50-2.00. Commons start at 20¢.

Imprint: 1995•1996 Bicycle Sports Collection

Complete Deck (55 cards): 8.00

Player	Player
☐ 2♣ S. Stevens, NJer.	☐ 3♣ Ranford (G), Edmo.
☐ 4♣ B. Bradley, Tamp.	☐ 5♣ Ed Belfour (G), Chi.
☐ 6♣ B. Leetch, NYRa.	☐ 7♣ Ron Francis, Pitt.
☐ 8♣ T. Selänne, Winn.	☐ 9♣ Brodeur (G), NJer.
☐ 10♣ Nieuwendyk, Dall.	☐ J♣ M. Messier, NYRa.
☐ Q♣ M. Renberg, Phil.	☐ K♣ Joe Sakic, Québ.
☐ A♣ Paul Coffey, Detr.	☐ 2♦ Al MacInnis, SLou.
☐ 3♦ Mike Modano, Dall.	☐ 4♦ A. Daigle, Otta.
☐ 5♦ J. Roenick, Chi.	☐ 6♦ Jason Arnott, Edmo.
☐ 7♦ P. Bondra, Wash.	☐ 8♦ Ray Bourque, Bost.
☐ 9♦ Pavel Bure, Vanc.	☐ 10♦ Mats Sundin, Toro.
☐ J♦ Brett Hull, SLou.	☐ Q♦ Jaromir Jagr, Pitt.
☐ K♦ D. Hasek (G), Buff.	☐ A♦ W. Gretzky, LosA.
☐ 2♥ Craig Janney, SanJ.	☐ 3♥ Doug Gilmour, Toro.
☐ 4♥ C. Lemieux, NJer.	☐ 5♥ Trevor Linden, Vanc.
☐ 6♥ G. Sanderson, Hart.	☐ 7♥ Paul Kariya, Anah.
☐ 8♥ P. Turgeon, Mont.	☐ 9♥ P. Forsberg, Québ.
☐ 10♥ A. Oates, Bost.	☐ J♥ S. Fedorov, Detr.
☐ Q♥ M. Lemieux, Pitt.	☐ K♥ A. Zhamnov, Winn.
☐ A♥ Eric Lindros, Phil.	☐ 2′ Kirk Muller, NYIs.
☐ 3♠ S. Yzerman, Detr.	☐ 4♠ F. Potvin (G), Toro.
☐ 5♠ P. LaFontaine, Buff.	☐ 6♠ J. Carey (G), Wash.
☐ 7♠ V'sbrouck (G), Flor.	☐ 8♠ Alexei Yashin, Otta.
☐ 9♠ Chris Chelios, Chi.	☐ 10♠ Cam Neely, Bost.
☐ J♠ K. Tkachuk, Winn.	☐ Q♠ John LeClair, Phil.
☐ K♠ T. Fleury, Calg.	☐ A♠ P. Roy (G), Mont.
☐ Checklist	☐ Eastern Conference
☐ Western Conference	

1995 - 96 BOWMAN

These cards have two versions: the regular card and a foil parallel.

	Foil	Reg.
Complete Set (165 cards):	**115.00**	**30.00**
Common Player:	**.35**	**.20**
Player	**Foil**	**Reg.**
☐☐ 1 Wayne Gretzky, SLou.	10.00	2.50
☐☐ 2 Raymond Bourque, Bost.	3.00	.50
☐☐ 3 Craig Janney, SanJ.	.50	.20
☐☐ 4 Andrew Cassels, Hart.	.50	.20
☐☐ 5 Alexander Mogilny, Vanc.	1.00	.20
☐☐ 6 Pierre Turgeon, Mont.	1.00	.20
☐☐ 7 Dave Andreychuk, Toro.	.50	.20
☐☐ 8 Mark Messier, NYRa.	2.50	.50
☐☐ 9 Igor Korolev, Winn.	.35	.20
☐☐ 10 Tomas Sandström, Pitt.	.50	.20
☐☐ 11 Shayne Corson, SLou.	.50	.20
☐☐ 12 Chris Chelios, Chic.	1.50	.20
☐☐ 13 Claude Lemieux vs. McSorley	.50	.20
☐☐ 14 Stéphane Richer, NJer.	.50	.20
☐☐ 15 Patrick Roy (G), Colo.	7.50	1.50
☐☐ 16 Al MacInnis, SLou.	1.00	.20
☐☐ 17 Cam Neely, Bost.	2.50	.50
☐☐ 18 Doug Gilmour, Toro.	1.50	.20
☐☐ 19 Steve Thomas, NJer.	.50	.20
☐☐ 20 Jeremy Roenick, Chic.	2.00	.50
☐☐ 21 Steve Yzerman, Detr.	6.00	1.50
☐☐ 22 Petr Klima, Tamp.	.35	.20
☐☐ 23 Luc Robitaille, NYRa.	2.00	.50
☐☐ 24 Bill Ranford (G), Edmo.	1.00	.20
☐☐ 25 Grant Fuhr (G), SLou.	1.50	.20
☐☐ 26 Sean Burke (G), Hart.	1.50	.20
☐☐ 27 John MacLean, NJer.	.35	.20
☐☐ 28 Brendan Shanahan, Hart.	2.50	.50
☐☐ 29 Pat LaFontaine, Buff.	1.50	.20
☐☐ 30 John Vanbiesbrouck (G), Flor.	1.00	.20
☐☐ 31 Ron Francis, Pitt.	1.50	.20
☐☐ 32 Brian Leetch, NYRa.	1.50	.20
☐☐ 33 Dave Gagner, Dall.	.35	.20
☐☐ 34 Larry Murphy, Toro.	.50	.20
☐☐ 35 Mike Modano, Dall.	2.50	.50
☐☐ 36 Rick Tocchet, LosA.	.50	.20
☐☐ 37 Scott Mellanby, Flor.	.50	.20
☐☐ 38 Ron Hextall (G), Phil.	1.50	.20
☐☐ 39 Joé Juneau, Wash.	.50	.20
☐☐ 40 Mario Lemieux, Pitt.	7.50	1.50
☐☐ 41 Paul Coffey, Detr.	1.50	.20
☐☐ 42 Joe Sakic, Colo.	4.00	1.00
☐☐ 43 Brett Hull, SLou.	2.50	.50
☐☐ 44 Adam Oates, Bost.	1.00	.20
☐☐ 45 Wendel Clark, NYIs.	2.00	.50
☐☐ 46 Trevor Linden, Vanc.	1.00	.20
☐☐ 47 Tom Barrasso (G), Pitt.	1.00	.20
☐☐ 48 Kevin Hatcher, Dall.	.35	.20
☐☐ 49 Mats Sundin, Toro.	2.50	.50
☐☐ 50 Scott Stevens, NJer.	1.00	.20
☐☐ 51 Mark Recchi, Mont.	1.00	.20
☐☐ 52 Theoren Fleury, Calg.	1.50	.20
☐☐ 53 Ed Belfour (G), Chic.	2.50	.50
☐☐ 54 Adam Graves, NYRa.	1.00	.20
☐☐ 55 Peter Bondra, Wash.	1.50	.20
☐☐ 56 Dominik Hasek (G), Buff.	2.50	.50
☐☐ 57 Jaromir Jagr, Pitt.	2.50	.50
☐☐ 58 Owen Nolan, SanJ.	1.50	.20
☐☐ 59 Kevin Stevens, Bost.	.50	.20
☐☐ 60 Alexei Zhamnov, Winn.	.50	.20
☐☐ 61 Dmitri Khristich, LosA.	.35	.20
☐☐ 62 Chris Pronger, SLou.	1.50	.20
☐☐ 63 John LeClair, Phil.	2.00	.50
☐☐ 64 Scott Niedermayer, NJer.	.50	.20
☐☐ 65 Pavel Bure, Vanc.	2.00	.50
☐☐ 66 Chris Osgood (G), Detr.	1.50	.20
☐☐ 67 Geoff Sanderson, Hart.	.50	.20
☐☐ 68 Doug Weight, Edmo.	1.50	.20
☐☐ 69 Keith Tkachuk, Winn.	1.50	.20
☐☐ 70 Martin Brodeur (G), NJer.	4.00	1.00
☐☐ 71 Eric Lindros, Phil.	2.50	.50
☐☐ 72 Martin Straka, Otta.	.50	.20
☐☐ 73 Alexander Selivanov, Tamp.	.35	.20
☐☐ 74 Jim Carey (G), Wash.	.35	.20
☐☐ 75 Teemu Selänne, Winn.	2.00	.50
☐☐ 76 Rob Niedermayer, Flor.	.50	.20
☐☐ 77 Vyacheslav Kozlov, Detr.	.50	.20
☐☐ 78 Todd Harvey, Dall.	.50	.20
☐☐ 79 Félix Potvin (G), Toro.	1.50	.20
☐☐ 80 Sergei Fedorov, Detr.	2.50	.50
☐☐ 81 Mathieu Schneider, NYIs.	.50	.20
☐☐ 82 Roman Hamrlik, Tamp.	.50	.20
☐☐ 83 Mikael Renberg, Phil.	.50	.20
☐☐ 84 Jeff Friesen, SanJ.	.50	.20
☐☐ 85 Peter Forsberg, Colo.	3.50	.50
☐☐ 86 Kenny Jönsson, Toro.	.50	.20
☐☐ 87 Brian Savage, Mont.	.50	.20
☐☐ 88 Oleg Tverdovsky, Anah.	.35	.20
☐☐ 89 Nikolai Khabibulin (G), Winn.	1.00	.20
☐☐ 90 Paul Kariya, Anah.	3.50	.50
☐☐ 91 Zdenek Nedved, Toro.	.50	.20
☐☐ **92 Darren Langdon, NYRa. RC**	**1.50**	**1.00**
☐☐ **93 Lonny Bohonos, Vanc. RC**	**.50**	**.50**
☐☐ **94 Mike Wilson, Buff. RC**	**.50**	**.50**
☐☐ **95 Landon Wilson, Colo. RC**	**1.00**	**.50**
☐☐ 96 Bryan McCabe, NYIs.	1.00	.20
☐☐ 97 Byron Dafoe (G), LosA.	1.00	.20
☐☐ **98 Denny Lambert, Anah. RC**	**.50**	**.50**
☐☐ **99 Craig Mills, Winn. RC**	**.50**	**.50**
☐☐ 100 Ed Jovanovski, Flor.	2.00	.50
☐☐ 101 Jason Bonsignore, Edmo.	.50	.20
☐☐ **102 Clayton Beddoes, Bost. RC**	**.50**	**.50**
☐☐ 103 Jamie Pushor, Detr.	.35	.20
☐☐ 104 Drew Bannister, Tamp.	.50	.20
☐☐ **105 Ed Ward, Calg. RC**	**.50**	**.50**
☐☐ 106 Todd Warriner, Toro.	.50	.20
☐☐ 107 Deron Quint, Winn.	.50	.20
☐☐ **108 Rhett Warrener, Flor. RC**	**.50**	**.50**
☐☐ 109 Marko Kiprusoff, Mont.	.50	.20
☐☐ **110 Daniel Alfredsson, Otta. RC**	**4.50**	**3.00**
☐☐ **111 M. Ragnarsson, SanJ. RC**	**1.50**	**1.00**
☐☐ **112 Miroslav Satan, Edmo. RC**	**2.00**	**1.50**
☐☐ 113 Niklas Sundström, NYRa.	1.00	.20
☐☐ **114 Mathieu Dandenault, Detr. RC**	**1.00**	**.50**
☐☐ 115 Vitali Yachmenev, LosA.	.50	.20
☐☐ **116 Petr Sykora, NJer. RC**	**3.00**	**2.00**
☐☐ **117 Antti Törmänen, Otta. RC**	**.50**	**.50**
☐☐ 118 Jeff O'Neill, Hart.	2.00	.50
☐☐ **119 David Nemirovsky, Flor. RC**	**.50**	**.50**
☐☐ 120 Jason Doig, Winn.	.50	.20
☐☐ 121 Aaron Gavey, Tamp.	.35	.20
☐☐ 122 Ladislav Kohn, Calg.	.50	.20
☐☐ 123 Richard Park, Pitt.	.50	.20
☐☐ **124 Stéphane Yelle, Colo. RC**	**1.00**	**.50**
☐☐ 125 Éric Dazé, Chic.	2.00	.50
☐☐ 126 Niklas Andersson, NYIs.	.35	.20
☐☐ 127 Brendan Witt, Wash.	.50	.20
☐☐ 128 Jamie Storr (G), LosA.	.50	.20
☐☐ 129 Darby Hendrickson, Toro.	.50	.20
☐☐ **130 Radek Dvorak, Flor. RC**	**1.50**	**1.00**
☐☐ 131 Cory Stillman, Calg.	.50	.20
☐☐ 132 Jamie Rivers, SLou.	.50	.20
☐☐ 133 Ville Peltonen, SanJ.	.50	.20
☐☐ 134 Peter Ferraro, NYRa.	.50	.20
☐☐ **135 Trent McCleary, Otta. RC**	**1.00**	**.50**
☐☐ **136 Chris Wells, Pitt. RC**	**.50**	**.50**
☐☐ **137 Chad Kilger, Anah. RC**	**1.50**	**1.00**
☐☐ 138 Denis Pederson, NJer.	.50	.20
☐☐ **139 Roman Vopat, SLou. RC**	**.50**	**.50**
☐☐ 140 Shean Donovan, SanJ.	.35	.20
☐☐ **141 Alek Stojanov, Vanc. RC**	**.50**	**.50**
☐☐ **142 Mark Kolesar, Toro. RC**	**.50**	**.50**
☐☐ **143 Scott Walker, Vanc. RC**	**1.50**	**1.00**
☐☐ **144 Dave Roche, Pitt. RC**	**.50**	**.50**
☐☐ 145 Corey Hirsch, Vanc.	.35	.20
☐☐ **146 Aki Berg, LosA. RC**	**1.00**	**.50**
☐☐ 147 Stefan Ustorf, Wash.	.50	.20
☐☐ 148 Saku Koivu, Mont.	4.00	1.00
☐☐ **149 Shane Doan, Winn. RC**	**1.50**	**1.00**
☐☐ 150 Jere Lehtinen, Dall.	1.50	.20
☐☐ **151 Kyle McLaren, Bost. RC**	**1.50**	**1.00**
☐☐ 152 Marty Murray, Calg.	.50	.20
☐☐ **153 Sean Pronger, Anah. RC**	**.50**	**.50**
☐☐ **154 Joaquin Gage (G), Edmo. RC**	**1.00**	**.50**
☐☐ 155 Éric Fichaud (G), NYIs.	.35	.20
☐☐ **156 Todd Bertuzzi, NYIs. RC**	**9.00**	**6.00**
☐☐ **157 Wayne Primeau, Buff. RC**	**1.00**	**.50**
☐☐ **158 Scott Bailey, Bost. RC**	**1.00**	**.50**
☐☐ 159 Viktor Kozlov, SanJ.	.50	.20
☐☐ 160 Valeri Bure, Mont.	.50	.20
☐☐ 161 Dody Wood, SanJ.	.35	.20
☐☐ **162 Grant Marshall, Dall. RC**	**1.00**	**.50**
☐☐ **163 Ken Klee, Wash. RC**	**.50**	**.50**
☐☐ **164 Corey Schwab, NJer. RC**	**1.00**	**.50**
☐☐ **165 Brian Holzinger, Buff. RC**	**1.00**	**.50**

BOWMAN'S BEST

This series has two versions: a regular insert and a refractor version.

	Ref.	Reg.
Insert Set (30 cards):	**275.00**	**70.00**
Player	**Ref.**	**Reg.**
☐☐ BB1 Peter Forsberg, Colo.	20.00	4.00
☐☐ BB2 Teemu Selänne, Winn.	10.00	2.00
☐☐ BB3 Eric Lindros, Phil.	15.00	2.00
☐☐ BB4 Scott Stevens, NJer.	5.00	1.00
☐☐ BB5 Wayne Gretzky, SLou.	60.00	14.00
☐☐ BB6 Mark Messier, NYRa.	15.00	2.00
☐☐ BB7 Jaromir Jagr, Pitt.	15.00	2.00
☐☐ BB8 Martin Brodeur (G), NJer.	20.00	6.00
☐☐ BB9 Alexander Mogilny, Vanc.	5.00	1.00
☐☐ BB10 Mario Lemieux, Pitt.	45.00	10.00
☐☐ BB11 Joe Sakic, Colo.	20.00	6.00
☐☐ BB12 Sergei Fedorov, Detr.	15.00	2.00
☐☐ BB13 Pavel Bure, Vanc.	10.00	2.00
☐☐ BB14 Brian Leetch, NYRa.	5.00	2.00
☐☐ BB15 Paul Kariya, Anah.	20.00	4.00
☐☐ BB16 Daniel Alfredsson, Otta.	10.00	4.00
☐☐ BB17 Saku Koivu, Mont.	15.00	6.00
☐☐ BB18 Éric Dazé, Chic.	5.00	2.00
☐☐ BB19 Ed Jovanovski, Flor.	5.00	2.00
☐☐ BB20 Vitali Yachmenev, LosA.	5.00	1.00
☐☐ BB21 Niklas Sundström, NYRa.	5.00	1.00
☐☐ BB22 Radek Dvorak, Flor.	5.00	1.00
☐☐ BB23 Byron Dafoe (G), LosA.	5.00	2.00
☐☐ BB24 Shane Doan, Winn.	5.00	1.00
☐☐ BB25 Chad Kilger, Anah.	5.00	1.00
☐☐ BB26 Jeff O'Neill, Hart.	5.00	2.00
☐☐ BB27 Cory Stillman, Calg.	5.00	1.00
☐☐ BB28 Valeri Bure, Mont.	5.00	2.00
☐☐ BB29 Marcus Ragnarsson, SanJ.	5.00	1.00
☐☐ BB30 Todd Bertuzzi, NYIs.	25.00	12.00

DRAFT PROSPECT

Insert Set (30 cards):	**25.00**
Insert (1:1)	**BP**
☐ **P1 Johnathan Aitken, CHL Prospect RC**	**.50**
☐ **P2 Chris Allen, CHL Prospect RC**	**.50**
☐ **P3 Matt Bradley, CHL Prospect RC**	**1.00**
☐ P4 Daniel Brière, CHL Prospect	4.00
☐ **P5 Jeff Brown, CHL Prospect RC**	**.50**
☐ **P6 Jan Bulis, CHL Prospect RC**	**.50**
☐ **P7 Daniel Corso, CHL Prospect RC**	**1.00**
☐ P8 Luke Curtin, CHL Prospect	.50
☐ **P9 Matthieu Descôteaux, CHL Prospect RC**	**.50**
☐ **P10 Boyd Devereaux, CHL Prospect RC**	**1.50**
☐ **P11 Jason Doyle, CHL Prospect RC**	**.50**
☐ **P12 Étienne Drapeau, CHL Prospect RC**	**.50**
☐ **P13 Jean-Pierre Dumont, CHL Prospect RC**	**3.50**
☐ **P14 Mathieu Garon (G), CHL Prospect RC**	**3.00**
☐ **P15 Josh Green, CHL Prospect RC**	**1.00**
☐ **P16 Chris Hajt, CHL Prospect RC**	**.50**
☐ **P17 Matt Higgins, CHL Prospect RC**	**.50**
☐ **P18 Craig Hillier (G), CHL Prospect RC**	**.50**
☐ **P19 Josh Holden, CHL Prospect RC**	**1.00**
☐ **P20 Dan Focht, CHL Prospect RC**	**.50**
☐ **P21 Henry Kuster, CHL Prospect RC**	**.50**
☐ **P22 Francis Larivée, CHL Prospect RC**	**.50**
☐ **P23 Mario Larocque, CHL Prospect RC**	**.50**
☐ **P24 Wes Mason, CHL Prospect RC**	**.50**
☐ **P25 François Méthot, CHL Prospect RC**	**.50**
☐ **P26 Geoff Peters, CHL Prospect RC**	**.50**
☐ **P27 Randy Petruk, CHL Prospect RC**	**.50**
☐ **P28 Chris Phillips, CHL Prospect RC**	**2.00**
☐ **P29 Boris Protsenko, CHL Prospect RC**	**.50**
☐ **P30 Rémi Royer, CHL Prospect RC**	**.50**
☐ **P31 Cory Sarich, CHL Prospect RC**	**1.00**
☐ **P32 Jaroslav Svejkovsky, CHL Prospect RC**	**1.00**
☐ **P33 Curtis Tipler, CHL Prospect RC**	**.50**
☐ **P34 Darren Van Oene, CHL Prospect RC**	**.50**
☐ **P35 Jesse Wallin, CHL Prospect RC**	**.50**
☐ **P36 Kurt Walsh, CHL Prospect RC**	**.50**
☐ **P37 Lance Ward, CHL Prospect RC**	**.50**
☐ **P38 Steve Wasylko, CHL Prospect RC**	**.50**
☐ **P39 Trevor Wasyluk, CHL Prospect RC**	**.50**
☐ **P40 Jonathan Zukiwsky, CHL Prospect RC**	**.50**

1995 - 96 CLASSIC

There are five versions to Classic: the regular card, a silver foil-board parallel (Canadian packs), a gold foil-board parallel (American packs), a Printer's Proof parallel (Canadian Packs, "1 of 749") and a Printer's Proof Gold foil-board parallel (American packs, "1 of 249"). Prices for silver and gold parallels are the same.

Complete Set (100 cards):	**20.00**	**10.00**
Wade Redden Box Bottom:		**1.00**
Common Player:	**0.30**	**0.20**
Player	**Para.**	**Reg.**
1 Bryan Berard	1.00	.50
2 Wade Redden	.50	.20
3 Aki Berg	.30	.20
4 Chad Kilger	.50	.20
5 Daymond Langkow	.50	.20
6 Steve Kelly	.30	.20
7 Shane Doan	.50	.20
8 Terry Ryan	.30	.20
9 Mike Martin	.30	.20
10 Radek Dvorak	.50	.20
11 Jarome Iginla	3.00	1.50
12 Teemu Riihijarvi	.30	.20
13 J-S Giguère (G)	3.00	1.50
14 Peter Schaefer	.30	.20
15 Jeff Ware	.30	.20
16 Martin Biron (G)	1.50	.50
17 Brad Church	.30	.20
18 Petr Sykora	1.50	.50
19 Denis Gauthier	.30	.20
20 Sean Brown	.30	.20
21 Brad Isbister	.50	.20
22 Miikka Elomo	.30	.20
23 Mathieu Sunderland	.30	.20
24 Marc Moro	.30	.20
25 Jan Hlavac	.50	.20
26 Brian Wesenberg	.30	.20
27 Mike McBain	.30	.20
28 Georges Laraque	.30	.20
29 Marc Chouinard	.30	.20
30 Donald MacLean	.30	.20
31 Jason Doig	.30	.20
32 Aaron MacDonald	.30	.20
33 Patrick Côté	.30	.20
34 Christian Dubé	.30	.20
35 Chris McAllister	.30	.20
36 Denis Smith	.30	.20
37 Mark Dutiaume	.30	.20
38 Dwayne Hay	.30	.20
39 Nathan Perrott	.30	.20
40 Christian Laflamme	.30	.20
41 Paxton Schafer (G)	.30	.20
42 Shane Kenny	.30	.20
43 Nic Beaudoin	.30	.20
44 Philippe Audet	.30	.20
45 Brad Larsen	.30	.20
46 Ryan Pepperall	.30	.20
47 Mike Leclerc	.30	.20
48 Shane Willis	.50	.20
49 Darryl Laplante	.30	.20
50 Larry Courville	.30	.20
51 Mike O'Grady	.30	.20
52 Petr Buzek	.30	.20
53 Alyn McCauley	1.00	.50
54 Scott Roche (G)	.30	.20
55 John Tripp	.30	.20
56 Johnathan Aitken	.30	.20
57 Blake Bellefeuille	.30	.20
58 Daniel Brière	1.00	.50
59 Josh DeWolf	.30	.20
60 Josh Green	.30	.20
61 Chris Hajt	.30	.20
62 Josh Holden	.30	.20
63 Henry Kuster	.30	.20
64 Dan LaCouture	.30	.20
65 Oleg Orekhovsky	.30	.20
66 Andrei Petrunin	.30	.20
67 Tom Poti	.30	.20
68 Peter Ratchuk	.30	.20
69 Andrei Zyuzin	.30	.20
70 George Breen	.30	.20
71 Greg Bullock	.30	.20
72 Kent Fearns	.30	.20
73 Eric Flinton	.30	.20
74 Brian Holzinger	.30	.20
75 Chris Kenady	.30	.20
76 Kaj Linna	.30	.20
77 Brian Mueller	.30	.20
78 Brent Peterson	.30	.20
79 Chad Quenneville	.30	.20
80 Randy Stevens	.30	.20
81 Adam Wiesel	.30	.20
82 Barrie Colts	.30	.20
83 Belleville Bulls	.30	.20
84 Detroit Jr. Red Wings	.30	.20
85 Guelph Storm	.50	.20
86 Kingston Frontenacs	.30	.20
87 Kitchener Rangers	.30	.20
88 London Knights	.30	.20
89 Niagara Falls Thunder	.30	.20
90 North Bay Centennials	.30	.20
91 Oshawa Generals	.30	.20
92 Ottawa 67's	.30	.20
93 Owen Sound Platers	.30	.20
94 Peterborough Petes	.30	.20
95 Soo Greyhounds	.50	.20
96 Sarnia Sting	.30	.20
97 Sudbury Wolves	.30	.20
98 Windsor Spitfires	.30	.20
99 CL: Bryan Berard	.30	.20
100 CL: Wade Redden	.30	.20

PRINTER'S PROOF

Player	Prf.G	Proof
1 Bryan Berard	15.00	8.00
2 Wade Redden	10.00	6.00
3 Aki Berg	5.00	2.00
4 Chad Kilger	5.00	4.00
5 Daymond Langkow	5.00	4.00
6 Steve Kelly	5.00	2.00
7 Shane Doan	5.00	4.00
8 Terry Ryan	5.00	2.00
9 Mike Martin	5.00	2.00
10 Radek Dvorak	5.00	4.00
11 Jarome Iginla	40.00	20.00
12 Teemu Riihijarvi	5.00	2.00
13 J-S Giguère (G)	40.00	20.00
14 Peter Schaefer	5.00	2.00
15 Jeff Ware	5.00	2.00
16 Martin Biron (G)	20.00	12.00
17 Brad Church	5.00	2.00
18 Petr Sykora	20.00	10.00
19 Denis Gauthier	5.00	2.00
20 Sean Brown	5.00	2.00
21 Brad Isbister	10.00	6.00
22 Miikka Elomo	5.00	2.00
23 Mathieu Sunderland	5.00	2.00
24 Marc Moro	5.00	2.00
25 Jan Hlavac	10.00	6.00
26 Brian Wesenberg	5.00	2.00
27 Mike McBain	5.00	2.00
28 Georges Laraque	5.00	2.00
29 Marc Chouinard	5.00	2.00
30 Donald MacLean	5.00	2.00
31 Jason Doig	5.00	2.00
32 Aaron MacDonald	5.00	2.00
33 Patrick Côté	5.00	2.00
34 Christian Dubé	5.00	2.00
35 Chris McAllister	5.00	2.00
36 Denis Smith	5.00	2.00
37 Mark Dutiaume	5.00	2.00
38 Dwayne Hay	5.00	2.00
39 Nathan Perrott	5.00	2.00
40 Christian Laflamme	5.00	2.00
41 Paxton Schafer (G)	5.00	2.00
42 Shane Kenny	5.00	2.00
43 Nic Beaudoin	5.00	2.00
44 Philippe Audet	5.00	2.00
45 Brad Larsen	5.00	2.00
46 Ryan Pepperall	5.00	2.00
47 Mike Leclerc	5.00	2.00
48 Shane Willis	10.00	6.00
49 Darryl Laplante	5.00	2.00
50 Larry Courville	5.00	2.00
51 Mike O'Grady	5.00	2.00
52 Petr Buzek	5.00	2.00
53 Alyn McCauley	15.00	8.00
54 Scott Roche (G)	5.00	2.00
55 John Tripp	5.00	2.00
56 Johnathan Aitken	5.00	2.00
57 Blake Bellefeuille	5.00	2.00
58 Daniel Brière	15.00	8.00
59 Josh DeWolf	5.00	2.00
60 Josh Green	5.00	2.00
61 Chris Hajt	5.00	2.00
62 Josh Holden	5.00	2.00
63 Henry Kuster	5.00	2.00
64 Dan LaCouture	5.00	2.00
65 Oleg Orekhovsky	5.00	2.00
66 Andrei Petrunin	5.00	2.00
67 Tom Poti	5.00	2.00
68 Peter Ratchuk	5.00	2.00
69 Andrei Zyuzin	5.00	2.00
70 George Breen	5.00	2.00
71 Greg Bullock	5.00	2.00
72 Kent Fearns	5.00	2.00
73 Eric Flinton	5.00	2.00
74 Brian Holzinger	5.00	2.00
75 Chris Kenady	5.00	2.00
76 Kaj Linna	5.00	2.00
77 Brian Mueller	5.00	2.00
78 Brent Peterson	5.00	2.00
79 Chad Quenneville	5.00	2.00
80 Randy Stevens	5.00	2.00
81 Adam Wiesel	5.00	2.00
82 Barrie Colts	5.00	2.00
83 Belleville Bulls	5.00	2.00
84 Detroit Jr. Red Wings	5.00	2.00
85 Guelph Storm	10.00	6.00
86 Kingston Frontenacs	5.00	2.00
87 Kitchener Rangers	5.00	2.00
88 London Knights	5.00	2.00
89 Niagara Falls Thunder	5.00	2.00
90 North Bay Centennials	5.00	2.00
91 Oshawa Generals	5.00	2.00
92 Ottawa 67's	5.00	2.00
93 Owen Sound Platers	5.00	2.00
94 Peterborough Petes	5.00	2.00
95 Soo Greyhounds	10.00	6.00
96 Sarnia Sting	5.00	2.00
97 Sudbury Wolves	5.00	2.00
98 Windsor Spitfires	5.00	2.00
99 CL: Bryan Berard	5.00	2.00
100 CL: Wade Redden	5.00	2.00

AUTOGRAPHS

Each player signed a different amount of cards. Petr Sykora signed the least number of autographs (fewer than 1,000).

Player	NRMT-MT
George Breen ✍	3.00
Greg Bullock ✍	3.00
Petr Buzek ✍	3.00
Henry Custer ✍	3.00
Radek Dvorak ✍	5.00
Kent Fearns ✍	3.00
Eric Flinton ✍	3.00
Josh Green ✍	5.00
Josh Holden ✍	3.00
Brian Holzinger ✍	5.00
Ed Jovanovski ✍	15.00
Chris Kenady ✍	3.00
Josef Marha ✍	3.00
Brian Mueller ✍	3.00
Angel Nikolov ✍	3.00
Oleg Orekhovsky ✍	3.00
Brent Peterson ✍	3.00
Andrei Petrunin ✍	3.00
Chad Quenneville ✍	3.00
Manon Rhéaume (G) ✍	40.00
Miroslav Satan ✍	10.00
Randy Stevens ✍	3.00
Petr Sykora ✍	20.00
Adam Wiesel ✍	3.00
Andrei Zyuzin ✍	5.00

CHL ALL-STARS

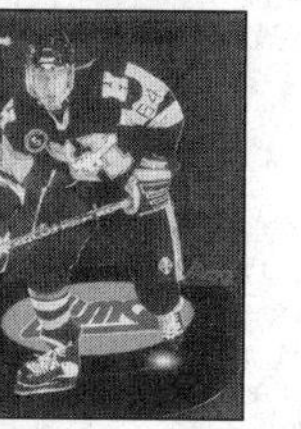

Insert Set (18 cards):	**80.00**
Insert (#/849)	**NRMT-MT**
AS1 Nolan Baumgartner	2.00
AS2 Wade Redden	8.00
AS3 Henry Kuster	2.00
AS4 Daymond Langkow	5.00
AS5 Shane Doan	6.00
AS6 Steve Kelly	2.00
AS7 Tyler Moss (G)	4.00
AS8 Bryan Berard	5.00
AS9 Ed Jovanovski	10.00
AS10 Chad Kilger	6.00
AS11 Daniel Cleary	5.00
AS12 Ethan Moreau	4.00
AS13 J.S. Giguère (G)	20.00
AS14 Daniel Gauthier	2.00
AS15 Jason Doig	2.00
AS16 Etienne Drapeau	2.00
AS17 Daniel Brière	12.00
AS18 Marc Chouinard	2.00

ICE BREAKERS

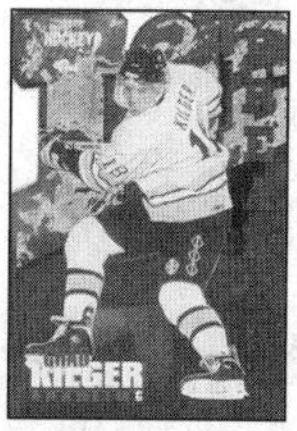

There are two versions to this set: the regular insert card (American packs only) and a die-cut insert (Canadian and American packs, "1 of 1,649").

Insert Set (20 cards):	**150.00**	**80.00**
Inserts	**DC1649**	**Reg.**
BK1 Bryan Berard	10.00	6.00
BK2 Wade Redden	10.00	6.00
BK3 Aki Berg	5.00	2.00
BK4 Chad Kilger	5.00	4.00
BK5 Daymond Langkow	5.00	4.00
BK6 Steve Kelly	4.00	2.00
BK7 Shane Doan	5.00	4.00
BK8 Terry Ryan	4.00	2.00
BK9 Radek Dvorak	5.00	4.00
BK10 Jarome Iginla	30.00	14.00
BK11 Teemu Riihijarvi	4.00	2.00
BK12 J.S. Giguère (G)	30.00	14.00
BK13 Martin Biron (G)	15.00	8.00
BK14 Jeff Ware	4.00	2.00
BK15 Brad Church	4.00	2.00
BK16 Petr Sykora	15.00	6.00
BK17 Jason Bonsignore	4.00	2.00
BK18 Brian Holzinger	5.00	2.00
BK19 Ed Jovanovski	15.00	6.00
BK20 Nolan Baumgartner	4.00	2.00

1995 - 96 CLASSIC ASSETS

This is a 50-card multi-sport set. Other hockey singles may exist.

Player	NRMT-MT
8 Radek Dvorak	.25
17 Ed Jovanovski	.50
45 Petr Sykora	1.00

1995 - 96 CLASSIC CLEAR ASSETS

This is a 50-card multi-sport set. Other hockey singles may exist.

Player	NRMT-MT	
56 Bryan Berard	.50	
57 Petr Sykora	1.00	
58 Ed Jovanovksi	.50	
59 Radek Dvorak	.25	
Insert	**Unused**	**Used**
5 Wade Redden ($2)	2.00	1.00
11 Manon Rhéaume (G) ($2)	6.00	4.00
22 Petr Sykora ($2)	4.00	2.00
16 Petr Sykora ($5)	6.00	3.00

1995 - 96 CLASSIC FIVE SPORT

This 200-card five-sport set features only 39 hockey cards. There are four versions to this set: the regular card, a die-cut parallel, a Printer's Proof parallel ("1 of 795") and an "Autograph Collection" parallel. A 200-card regular set sells at $15.

Player	PP	DC	Reg
123 Bryan Berard	6.00	3.00	.20
124 Wade Redden	6.00	3.00	.20
125 Aki Berg	3.00	1.50	.20
126 N. Baumgartner	2.00	1.00	.20
127 J. Bonsignore	2.00	1.00	.20
128 Steve Kelly	2.00	1.00	.20
129 George Breen	2.00	.75	.20
130 Terry Ryan	2.00	1.00	.20
131 Greg Bullock	2.00	.75	.20
132 Jarome Iginla	16.00	8.00	1.00
133 Petr Buzek	2.00	1.00	.20
134 Brad Church	2.00	1.00	.20
135 Jay McKee	2.00	1.00	.20
136 Jan Hlavak	4.00	2.00	.20
137 Petr Sykora	8.00	4.00	.50
138 Ed Jovanovski	8.00	4.00	.50
139 Chris Kenady	2.00	1.00	.20
140 Marc Moro	2.00	.75	.20
141 Kaj Linna	2.00	.75	.20
142 A. MacDonald	2.00	.75	.20
143 Chad Kilger	4.00	2.00	.20
144 Tyler Moss (G)	2.00	.75	.20
145 C. Laflamme	2.00	1.00	.20
146 Brian Mueller	2.00	.75	.20
147 D. Langkow	4.00	2.00	.20
148 Brent Peterson	2.00	1.00	.20
149 C. Quenneville	2.00	.75	.20
150 Chris Van Dyk	2.00	.75	.20
151 Kent Fearns	2.00	.75	.20
152 Adam Wiesel	2.00	.75	.20
153 Marc Chouinard	2.00	1.00	.20
154 Jason Doig	2.00	1.00	.20
155 Denis Smith	2.00	1.00	.20
156 Radek Dvorak	4.00	2.00	.20
157 D. MacLaren	2.00	1.00	.20
158 S. Kenny	2.00	.75	.20
159 B. Holzinger	3.00	1.50	.20
160 Eric Flinton	2.00	.75	.20
189 George Breen	2.00	.75	.20

AUTOGRAPHS

Other hockey autographs exist.

Player	NRMT-MT
Nolan Baumgartner ✍	3.00
Greg Bullock ✍	3.00
Jason Doig ✍	3.00
Kent Fearns ✍	3.00
Steve Kelly ✍	3.00
Aaron MacDonald ✍	3.00
Marc Moro ✍	3.00
Chad Quenneville ✍	3.00

BLUE AND RED SIGNINGS

This 100-card five-sport set features only nine hockey cards. There are two versions to this set: a blue card and a red card. We have no pricing information on this set.

Player
- 70 Bryan Berard
- 71 Wade Redden
- 72 Aki Berg
- 73 Nolan Baumgartner
- 74 Jason Bonsignore
- 75 Ed Jovanovski
- 76 Radek Dvorak
- 77 Brian Holzinger
- 78 Brad Church

INSERTS

Classic Standouts is a 10-card insert set with only one hockey card. Fast Track is a 20-card insert set with two hockey cards. Prices on phonecards are for unused copies.

Classic Standouts		**CS**
CS5 Bryan Berard, Detroit-OHL		5.00
Fast Track		**FT**
FT5 Bryan Berard		4.00
FT14 Petr Sykora		5.00
Phonecards	**Unused**	**Used**
($3) Brian Holzinger	8.00	4
($4) Wade Redden	12.00	6

STRIVE FOR 5

This 65-card set includes 13 hockey players.

Insert	NRMT-MT
2 Jan Hlavac	2.00
3 Brad Church	1.00
4 Steve Kelly, Prince Albert	1.00
5 Radek Dvorak	2.00
6 Jason Bonsignore	1.00
7 Petr Sykora	4.00
8 Daymond Langkow, Tri-City	2.00
9 Chad Kilger	2.00
10 Nolan Baumgartner	1.00
A Wade Redden	3.00
J Brian Holzinger	1.50
K Ed Jovanovski	4.00
Q Aki Berg	1.50

AUTOGRAPHED COLLECTION

These cards are not autographed.

Player	A.C.
☐ 123 Bryan Berard, Detroit-OHL	1.50
☐ 124 Wade Redden, Brendon	1.50
☐ 125 Aki Berg, Fin.	.50
☐ 126 N. Baumgartner, Kamloops	.50
☐ 127 J. Bonsignore, Sudbury	.50
☐ 128 Steve Kelly, Edmo.	.50
☐ 129 George Breen, Providence	.25
☐ 130 Terry Ryan, Mont.	.50
☐ 131 Greg Bullock, Lowell	.25
☐ 132 Jarome Iginla, Kamloops	4.00
☐ 133 Petr Buzek, Cze.	.50
☐ 134 Brad Church, Prince Albert	.50
☐ 135 Jay McKee, Buff.	.50
☐ 136 Jan Hlavak, Cze.	1.00
☐ 137 Petr Sykora, Detroit-IHL	2.00
☐ 138 Ed Jovanovski, Windsor	2.00
☐ 139 Chris Kenady, Denver U.	.50
☐ 140 Marc Moro, Kingston	.25
☐ 141 Kaj Linna, Boston U.	.25
☐ 142 A. MacDonald, Sw. Current	.25
☐ 143 Chad Kilger, Kingston	1.00
☐ 144 Tyler Moss (G), Kingston	.25
☐ 145 C. Laflamme, Beauport	.50
☐ 146 Brian Mueller, Clarkson	.25
☐ 147 D. Langkow, Tri-City	1.00
☐ 148 Brent Peterson, Michigan	.50
☐ 149 C. Quenneville, Providence	.25
☐ 150 Chris Van Dyk, Windsor	.25
☐ 151 Kent Fearns, Colorado	.25
☐ 152 Adam Wiesel, Clarkson	.25
☐ 153 Marc Chouinard, Beauport	.50
☐ 154 Jason Doig, Laval	.50
☐ 155 Denis Smith, Windsor	.50
☐ 156 Radek Dvorak, Cze.	1.00
☐ 157 D. MacLaren, Beauport	.50
☐ 158 S. Kenny, Owen Sound	.25
☐ 159 B. Holzinger, Bowl. Green	.50
☐ 160 Eric Flinton, U.N.H.	.25
☐ 189 George Breen, Providence	.25

1995 - 96 CLASSIC VISIONS

Other hockey singles may exist in this 150-card multi-sport set.

Player	NRMT-MT
☐ 82 Bryan Berard	.35
☐ 91 Petr Sykora	.50
☐ 92 Ed Jovanovski	.50
☐ 94 Manon Rhéaume (G)	2.50

1995 - 96 CLASSIC VISIONS SIGNINGS

This 100-card multi-sport set features only 19 hockey cards.

Player	NRMT-MT
☐ 61 Boyd Devereaux	.25
☐ 62 Alexandre Volchkov	.25
☐ 63 Trevor Wasyluk	.25
☐ 64 Luke Curtin	.25
☐ 65 Richard Jackman	.25
☐ 66 Jonathan Zukiwsky	.25
☐ 67 Geoff Peters	.25
☐ 68 Daniel Brière	1.00
☐ 69 Chris Allen	.25
☐ 70 Jason Sweitzer	.25
☐ 71 Steve Nimigon	.25
☐ 72 Jay McKee	.25
☐ 73 Henry Kuster	.25
☐ 74 Johnathan Aitken	.25
☐ 75 Ed Jovanovski	.50
☐ 76 Petr Sykora	.50
☐ 77 Bryan Berard	.50
☐ 78 Manon Rhéaume (G)	2.00
☐ 79 Radek Dvorak	.25
Artistry	**NRMT-MT**
☐ 6 Petr Sykora	10.00

AUTOGRAPHS

Each player signed a different number of autographs. We have no pricing information on this set. Gold parallel autographs possibly exist for the following list.

Player
- ☐ Johnathan Aitken
- ☐ Chris Allen
- ☐ Bryan Berard
- ☐ Daniel Brière
- ☐ Luke Curtin
- ☐ Boyd Devereaux
- ☐ Radek Dvorak
- ☐ Richard Jackman
- ☐ Ed Jovanovski
- ☐ Henry Kuster
- ☐ Jay McKee
- ☐ Steve Nimigon
- ☐ Geoff Peters
- ☐ Manon Rhéaume (G)
- ☐ Jason Sweitzer
- ☐ Petr Sykora
- ☐ Alexandre Volchkov
- ☐ Trevor Wasyluk
- ☐ Jonathan Zukiwsky

1995 - 96 DEL

The most expensive singles are Marco Sturm and Roman Turek at $3-5 each. Singles start at 30¢.

Complete Set (451 cards): 65.00

Player	Player
☐ 1 Gary Prior	☐ 2 Rupert Meister
☐ 3 Dennis Schrapp	☐ 4 Scott Campbell
☐ 5 Fritz Meyer	☐ 6 Rob Mendel
☐ 7 Kim Collins	☐ 8 Stefan Mayer
☐ 9 Torsten Fendt	☐ 10 Andrei Skopintsev
☐ 11 Bob Wilkie	☐ 12 Duanne Moeser
☐ 13 M. Nagler	☐ 14 Sven Zywitza
☐ 15 Marc Habscheid	☐ 16 Daniel Held
☐ 17 Heinrich Romer	☐ 18 R. Laycock
☐ 19 R. Francz	☐ 20 Tim Ferguson
☐ 21 Robert Heidt	☐ 22 E. Dylla
☐ 23 Harald Birk	☐ 24 Rochus Schneider
☐ 25 Billy Flynn	☐ 26 Andre Dietsch
☐ 27 Udo Dohler	☐ 28 Juri Stumpf
☐ 29 Torsten Deutscher	☐ 30 Frank Kannewurf
☐ 31 Thomas Graul	☐ 32 Dirk Perschau
☐ 33 Patrick Solf	☐ 34 Daniel Poudrier
☐ 35 B. Kaminski	☐ 36 C. Hadraschek
☐ 37 Sven Felski	☐ 38 Marco Swibenko
☐ 39 Holger Mix	☐ 40 Mark Maroste
☐ 41 Troy Tumbach	☐ 42 Jan Schertz
☐ 43 Mike Losch	☐ 44 A. Naumann
☐ 45 M. Garthe	☐ 46 I. Dorochin
☐ 47 T. Mitew	☐ 48 C. Lundmark
☐ 49 Chris Panek	☐ 50 Klaus Merk (G)
☐ 51 Mark Gronau	☐ 52 Stefan Steinecker
☐ 53 Josef Lehner	☐ 54 Tom O'Regan
☐ 55 Fredrik Stillmann	☐ 56 Marco Rentzsch
☐ 57 Stephan Sinner	☐ 58 Andreas Schubert
☐ 59 Tony Tanti	☐ 60 Gaetan Malo
☐ 61 Michael Komma	☐ 62 Thomas Schinko
☐ 63 Georg Holzmann	☐ 64 Mark Kosturik
☐ 65 Christian Brittig	☐ 66 Jurgen Rumrich
☐ 67 John Chabot	☐ 68 Andreas Dimbat
☐ 69 Ulrich Liebsch	☐ 70 Mark Teevens
☐ 71 Fabian Brannstom	☐ 72 D. Meyer
☐ 73 L Hoffman	☐ 74 Hardy Nilsson, Coach
☐ 75 Marcus Karlsson	☐ 76 Helmut DeRaaf
☐ 77 Kai Fischer	☐ 78 Carsten Gossmann
☐ 79 Torsten Keinass	☐ 80 Christopher Kreutzer
☐ 81 Brad Bergen	☐ 82 A. Niederberger
☐ 83 Rick Amann	☐ 84 Uli Hiemer
☐ 85 Sergei Sorokin	☐ 86 Robert Sterflinger
☐ 87 Lorenz Funk	☐ 88 Chris Valentine
☐ 89 Gord Sherven	☐ 90 Boris Lingemann
☐ 91 Benoit Doucet	☐ 92 Bernd Kuhnhauser
☐ 93 Bruce Eakin	☐ 94 Dieter Hegen
☐ 95 Andreas Brockmann	☐ 96 Bernd Truntschka
☐ 97 Wolfgang Kummer	☐ 98 Mikko Makela
☐ 99 Nikolaus Mondt	☐ 100 Piotr Vorobjew
☐ 101 Peter Obresa	☐ 102 Thierry Mayer
☐ 103 Marc Seliger (G)	☐ 104 Florian Storf
☐ 105 Ladislav Stompf	☐ 106 Greg Thompson
☐ 107 Sergei Schendelev	☐ 108 M. Duris
☐ 109 R. Gorgenlander	☐ 110 A. Raubal
☐ 111 Stephan Ziesche	☐ 112 Petr Kopta
☐ 113 Thomas Popiesch	☐ 114 Francois Sills
☐ 115 Jiri Lala	☐ 116 Robert Reichel
☐ 117 Markus Kempf	☐ 118 Igor Schultz
☐ 119 Martin Schultz	☐ 120 Brian Hannon
☐ 121 Jurgen Schaal	☐ 122 Patrick Vozar
☐ 123 Ron Kennedy	☐ 124 F. Bogelsack
☐ 125 Marco Herbst	☐ 126 Josef Schlickenriede
☐ 127 Torsten Hanusch	☐ 128 Thomas Jungwirth
☐ 129 David Reierson	☐ 130 Christian Curth
☐ 131 Anton Maidl	☐ 132 Marc Wittbrock
☐ 133 Brad Schlegel	☐ 134 Thomas Werner
☐ 135 Dirk Rohrbach	☐ 136 Bruce Hardy
☐ 137 Harald Kuhnke	☐ 138 Florian Funk
☐ 139 Rene Reuter	☐ 140 Milos Vanik
☐ 141 Gunther Preuss	☐ 142 Kevin LaVallée
☐ 143 Marcus Bleicher	☐ 144 Anton Krinner
☐ 145 Harald Waibel	☐ 146 Hans Zach
☐ 147 Josef Kontny	☐ 148 Gerhard Hegen
☐ 149 Milan Mokros	☐ 150 Venci Sebek
☐ 151 Alexander Engel	☐ 152 Alexander Wedl
☐ 153 Jaro Mucha	☐ 154 Murray McIntosh
☐ 155 Georg Guttler	☐ 156 Greg Johnston
☐ 157 Jederzej Kaspercyk	☐ 158 Dave Morrison
☐ 159 Mike Millar	☐ 160 Ireneusz Pacula
☐ 161 Vitalij Grossmann	☐ 162 I. Varitsky
☐ 163 Peter Kwasigroch	☐ 164 Branjo Heisig
☐ 165 Greg Evtushevski	☐ 166 Falk Ozellis
☐ 167 Tino Boos	☐ 168 J Tolvanen
☐ 169 Dieter Medicus	☐ 170 Michael Olbrich
☐ 171 Marc Pethke	☐ 172 Drahomir Kadlec
☐ 173 C. Seeberger	☐ 174 G. Kunce
☐ 175 Daniel Kunce	☐ 176 Timo Gschwill
☐ 177 M. Ettner	☐ 178 Jurgen Simon
☐ 179 A. Herbst	☐ 180 Elmar Boiger
☐ 181 Otto Hascak	☐ 182 Tim Schnobrich
☐ 183 Anthony Vogel	☐ 184 Tomas Martinec
☐ 185 Hans-Jörg Mayer	☐ 186 Roland Timoschuk
☐ 187 Jim Hoffmann	☐ 188 Andreas Volland
☐ 189 Rolf Hammer	☐ 190 Manuel Hess
☐ 191 Dale Derkatch	☐ 192 S. Schwele
☐ 193 Bob Murdoch	☐ 194 Bernd Haake
☐ 195 Joseph Heiss (G)	☐ 196 Olaf Grundmann
☐ 197 Alexander Genze	☐ 198 A. von Trzcinski
☐ 199 Jörg Mayr	☐ 200 Mirco Ludemann
☐ 201 Andreas Pokorny	☐ 202 Jason Meyer
☐ 203 Karsten Mende	☐ 204 H. Hohenberger
☐ 205 Thomas Brandt	☐ 206 Stefan Mann
☐ 207 Luciano Borsato	☐ 208 Leo Stefan
☐ 209 Peter Draisaitl	☐ 210 Andreas Lupzig
☐ 211 Ralf Reisinger	☐ 212 Rainer Zerwesz
☐ 213 Michael Rumrich	☐ 214 Martin Ondrejka
☐ 215 Tobias Abstreiter	☐ 216 Franz Demmel
☐ 217 Sergei Berezin	☐ 218 M. Berek, Coach
☐ 219 Karel Lang	☐ 220 Rene Bielke
☐ 221 Markus Krawinkel	☐ 222 Kenneth Karpuk
☐ 223 Klaus Micheller	☐ 224 Earl Spry
☐ 225 Andreas Ott	☐ 226 Petri Limatainen
☐ 227 Andre Grein	☐ 228 Ken Petrash
☐ 229 James Hanlon	☐ 230 Reemt Pyka
☐ 231 Thomas Imdahl	☐ 232 Chris Lindberg
☐ 233 J. Luknovsky	☐ 234 Peter Ihnacak
☐ 235 Marek Strebnicki	☐ 236 Johnny Walker
☐ 237 Arno Brux	☐ 238 R. Busch
☐ 239 Mark Bassen	☐ 240 Martin Gebel
☐ 241 Bernhard Johnston	☐ 242 Petr Briza (G)
☐ 243 Christian Kunast	☐ 244 Michael Bresagk
☐ 245 Eduard Uvria	☐ 246 Michael Heidt
☐ 247 Peter Gulda	☐ 248 Udo Kiessling
☐ 249 Dieter Bloem	☐ 250 Tony Vogel
☐ 251 Jacek Plachta	☐ 252 Georg Franz
☐ 253 Stephan Retzer	☐ 254 Henri Macoux
☐ 255 Andreas Loth	☐ 256 Mike Bullard
☐ 257 José Charbonneau	☐ 258 Wally Schreiber
☐ 259 Jorg Handrick	☐ 260 Holger Steiger
☐ 261 Marco Sturm	☐ 262 Lance Nethery
☐ 263 Markus Kuhl	☐ 264 Joachim Appel
☐ 265 Markus Flemming	☐ 266 Harold Kreis
☐ 267 Paul Stanton	☐ 268 Christian Lukes
☐ 269 Steffen Michel	☐ 270 S. J.G. Richer
☐ 271 Jorg Hanft	☐ 272 Erich Goldmann
☐ 273 Mario Gehrig	☐ 274 Pavel Gross
☐ 275 Daniel Korber	☐ 276 Rob Cimetta
☐ 277 Jochen Hecht	☐ 278 Till Feser
☐ 279 Alexander Serikow	☐ 280 Patrik Pysz
☐ 281 Darian Adamus	☐ 282 David Musial
☐ 283 Michael Hreus	☐ 284 Chris Strausse
☐ 285 Sven Valenti	☐ 286 Sebastien Thivierge
☐ 287 Jan Eysselt, Coach	☐ 288 R. Neubauer
☐ 289 Roman Turek (G)	☐ 290 Stefan Lahn
☐ 291 Christian Gerum	☐ 292 Heiko Smazal
☐ 293 Miroslav Maly	☐ 294 Thomas Sterflinger
☐ 295 M. Weinfürter	☐ 296 Stephan Bauer
☐ 297 Lars Brüggemenn	☐ 298 Markus Kehle
☐ 299 Paul Geddes	☐ 300 Ian Young
☐ 301 Stefan Steinbock	☐ 302 Jurgen Lechl
☐ 303 M. Goerlitz	☐ 304 Jiri Dolazal
☐ 305 Henrik Holscher	☐ 306 Sepp Wassermann
☐ 307 Otto Sykora	☐ 308 Bill Lochead
☐ 309 Patrick Lange	☐ 310 Ian Wood
☐ 311 H. Thorn	☐ 312 Doug Irwin
☐ 313 Christian Schmitz	☐ 314 Alexander Wunsch
☐ 315 Cory Holden	☐ 316 J. Bartman
☐ 317 Peter Lutter	☐ 318 Pavel Mann
☐ 319 Greg Muller	☐ 320 Christian Kohmann
☐ 321 Paul Beraldo	☐ 322 Thomas Groger
☐ 323 Andrej Fuchs	☐ 324 Klaus Birk
☐ 325 D. Rich	☐ 326 Boris Fuchs
☐ 327 T. Muhlbauer	☐ 328 Axel Kammerer
☐ 329 Jeff Lazaro	☐ 330 Olaf Scholz
☐ 331 Bobby Reynolds	☐ 332 Jaroslav Sevcik
☐ 333 P.M. Arnholt	☐ 334 G. Stranka
☐ 335 Vincent Riendeau	☐ 336 Michael Schmidt
☐ 337 T. Gobel	☐ 338 Vladimir Fedosov
☐ 339 R. Jadamzik	☐ 340 Frank Hohendahl
☐ 341 A. Raubal	☐ 342 C. Schonmoser
☐ 343 A. Ludwig	☐ 344 K. Ostler
☐ 345 Markus Berwanger	☐ 346 M Holzer
☐ 347 J. Feller	☐ 348 H. Domke
☐ 349 A. Maurer	☐ 350 A. Gebauer
☐ 351 Guntar Oswald	☐ 352 H. Buchwieser
☐ 353 B. Stewart	☐ 354 C. Sandner
☐ 355 J. Haglsperger	☐ 356 Robert Hock
☐ 357 Marl Jooris	☐ 358 Ernst Hofner
☐ 359 Gary Clark, Coach	☐ 360 Karl Friesen
☐ 361 Klaus Dalpiaz	☐ 362 Markus Wieland
☐ 363 Chris Clarke	☐ 364 Markus Pottinger
☐ 365 Raphael Kruger	☐ 366 Ron Fischer
☐ 367 C. Gegenfurte	☐ 368 Heinrich Schiffl
☐ 369 Andreas Schneider	☐ 370 V Mittelfellner
☐ 371 Richard Bohm	☐ 372 Dale Krentz
☐ 373 T. Schraven	☐ 374 Florian Keller
☐ 375 Doug Gerraugh	☐ 376 Martin Reichel
☐ 377 M. Draxler	☐ 378 Raimund Hilger
☐ 379 Michael Pohl	☐ 380 M. Kropf
☐ 381 Joel Savage	☐ 382 J. Eckmaier
☐ 383 R.R. Burns	☐ 384 Gunnar Leidborg
☐ 385 Carsten Solbach	☐ 386 Matthias Hoppe
☐ 387 Gord Hynes	☐ 388 Thomas Gaus
☐ 389 Zdenek Travnicek	☐ 390 Richard Trojan
☐ 391 Frantisek Frosch	☐ 392 Daniel Nowak
☐ 393 Andreas Renz	☐ 394 Alan Young
☐ 395 Robert Brezina	☐ 396 Wayne Hynes
☐ 397 George Fritz	☐ 398 Mike Bader
☐ 399 Grant Martin	☐ 400 Karsten Schulz
☐ 401 Mike Lay	☐ 402 Jackson Penney
☐ 403 Rich Chernomaz	☐ 404 Mark MacKay
☐ 405 Sana Hassan	☐ 406 Jiri Kochta
☐ 407 Thomas Bresagk	☐ 408 Peter Franke
☐ 409 Jochen Molling	☐ 410 Frantisek Prochazka
☐ 411 Josef Reznicek	☐ 412 Thomas Schubert
☐ 413 Ronny Martin	☐ 414 Marcel Lichnovsky
☐ 415 Matthias Kliemann	☐ 416 Ronny Reddo
☐ 417 Frank Peschke	☐ 418 Torsten Eisebitt
☐ 419 Janusz Janikowski	☐ 420 Thomas Knobloch
☐ 421 Falk Herzig	☐ 422 Thomas Wagner
☐ 423 Jan Tabor	☐ 424 J. Pohling
☐ 425 Pavel Vit	☐ 426 Vad. Kulabuchov
☐ 427 D. Cup Meister	☐ 428 Three players
☐ 429 Heiss (G)/ Lupzig	☐ 430 Brandl/ Mann
☐ 431 Doucet/ Nowak	☐ 432 Meyer/ Pyka
☐ 433 Hegen/ Kunce	☐ 434 Rumrich/ Ludemann
☐ 435 Benda/ Kosturik	☐ 436 Three players
☐ 437 Three players	☐ 438 A. Niederberger
☐ 439 Martin Reichel	☐ 440 Klaus Merk (G)

Player	NRMT-MT
☐ 441 Glenn Anderson	2.00
☐ 442 Pavel Bure	12.00
☐ 443 Vincent Damphousse	8.00
☐ 444 Uwe Krupp	1.00
☐ 445 Robert Reichel	2.00
☐ 446 Jeremy Roenick	12.00
☐ 447 Brendan Shanahan	14.00
☐ 448 Jozef Stumpel	2.00
☐ 449 Doug Weight	8.00
☐ 450 Scott Young	4.00
☐ Hologram Card	15.00

1995 - 96 DONRUSS

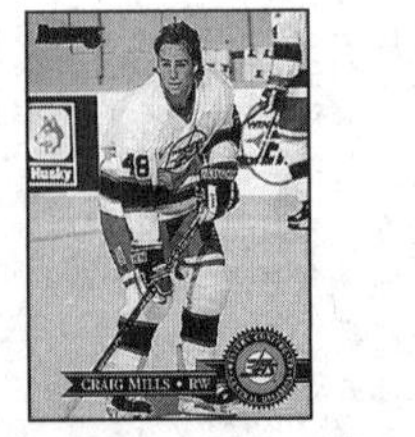

Series One Set (205 cards):	**15.00**
Series Two Set (185 cards):	**20.00**
Common Player:	**.20**
Player	**NRMT-MT**
☐ 1 Eric Lindros, Phil.	.50
☐ 2 Steve Larmer, NYRa.	.20
☐ 3 Oleg Tverdovsky, Anah.	.20
☐ 4 Vladimir Malakhov, Mont.	.20
☐ 5 Ian Laperrière, SLou.	.20
☐ **6 Chris Marinucci, NYIs. RC**	**.50**
☐ 7 Nelson Emerson, Winn.	.20
☐ 8 David Oliver, Edmo.	.20
☐ 9 Félix Potvin (G), Toro.	.20
☐ 10 Manny Fernandez (G), Dall.	.20
☐ 11 Jason Wiemer, Tamp.	.20
☐ 12 Dale Hunter, Wash.	.20
☐ 13 Wayne Gretzky, LosA.	2.00
☐ 14 Todd Gill, Toro.	.20
☐ 15 Radim Bicanek, Otta.	.20
☐ 16 Kirk McLean (G), Vanc.	.20
☐ 17 Esa Tikkanen, SLou.	.20
☐ 18 Yuri Khmylev, Buff.	.20
☐ 19 Peter Bondra, Wash.	.20
☐ 20 Brian Savage, Mont.	.20
☐ 21 Mariusz Czerkawski, Bost.	.20
☐ 22 Rob Blake, LosA.	.20
☐ 23 Chris Osgood (G), Detr.	.20
☐ 24 Bernie Nicholls, Chic.	.20
☐ 25 Doug Weight, Edmo.	.20
☐ 26 Shaun Van Allen, Anah.	.20
☐ 27 Jeremy Roenick, Chic.	.20
☐ 28 Sean Burke (G), Hart.	.20
☐ 29 Pat Verbeek, NYRa.	.20
☐ 30 Dino Ciccarelli, Detr.	.20
☐ 31 Trevor Kidd (G), Calg.	.20
☐ 32 Steve Thomas, NYIs.	.20
☐ 33 Dominik Hasek (G), Buff.	.50
☐ 34 Sandis Ozolinsh, SanJ.	.20
☐ 35 Bill Guerin, NJer.	.20
☐ 36 Scott A. Young, Québ.	.20
☐ 37 Scott Mellanby, Flor.	.20
☐ 38 Joe Mullen, Pitt.	.20
☐ **39 Steve Larouche, Otta. RC**	**.50**
☐ 40 Joe Nieuwendyk, Calg.	.20
☐ 41 Rick Tocchet, LosA.	.20
☐ 42 Keith Primeau, Detr.	.20
☐ 43 Darren Turcotte, Hart.	.20
☐ 44 Jason Arnott, Edmo.	.20
☐ **45 Brantt Myhres, Tamp. RC**	**.50**
☐ 46 Murray Craven, Chic.	.20
☐ 47 Martin Gendron, Wash.	.20
☐ 48 Mark Recchi, Mont.	.20
☐ 49 Uwe Krupp, Québ.	.20
☐ 50 Alexei Zhitnik, Buff.	.20
☐ 51 Rob Niedermayer, Flor.	.20
☐ 52 Sergei Brylin, NJer.	.20
☐ 53 Mats Näslund, Bost.	.20
☐ 54 Glenn Healy (G), NYRa.	.20
☐ 55 Mathieu Schneider, NYIs.	.20
☐ 56 Marko Tuomainen, Edmo.	.20
☐ 57 Paul Kariya, Anah.	.50
☐ 58 Dave Gagner, Dall.	.20
☐ 59 Mike Richter (G), NYRa.	.20
☐ 60 Patrik Juhlin, Phil.	.20
☐ 61 Pierre Turgeon, Mont.	.20
☐ 62 Mike Modano, Dall.	.50
☐ 63 Chris Pronger, Hart.	.20
☐ 64 Chris Joseph (G), Pitt.	.20
☐ 65 Peter Forsberg, Québ.	.50
☐ 66 Roman Oksiuta, Vanc.	.20
☐ 67 Jamie Storr (G), LosA.	.20
☐ 68 Brett Hull, SLou.	.50
☐ 69 Steve Chiasson, Calg.	.20
☐ 70 Benoît Hogue, Toro.	.20
☐ 71 Guy Hebert (G), Anah.	.20
☐ 72 Chris Therien, Phil.	.20
☐ 73 Darryl Sydor, LosA.	.20
☐ 74 Phil Housley, Calg.	.20
☐ 75 Jason Allison, Wash.	.20
☐ 76 Richard Smehlik, Buff.	.20
☐ 77 Shean Donovan, SanJ.	.20
☐ 78 Keith Tkachuk, Winn.	.20
☐ 79 Cliff Ronning, Vanc.	.20
☐ 80 Mikael Renberg, Phil.	.20
☐ 81 Steven Rice, Hart.	.20
☐ 82 Adam Graves, NYRa.	.20
☐ 83 Nicklas Lidström, Detr.	.20
☐ 84 Daren Puppa (G), Tamp.	.20
☐ 85 Todd Warriner, Toro.	.20
☐ 86 Jon Rohloff, Bost.	.20
☐ 87 Patrice Tardif, SLou.	.20
☐ 88 John MacLean, NJer.	.20
☐ 89 Ulf Samuelsson, Pitt.	.20
☐ 90 Alexander Selivanov, Tamp.	.20
☐ 91 Chris Chelios, Chic.	.20
☐ 92 Ulf Dahlén, SanJ.	.20
☐ 93 Brad May, Buff.	.20
☐ 94 Ron Francis, Pitt.	.20
☐ 95 Kevin Hatcher, Dall.	.20
☐ 96 Steve Yzerman, Detr.	1.00
☐ 97 Jocelyn Thibault (G), Québ.	.20
☐ 98 Dave Andreychuk, Toro.	.20
☐ 99 Gary Suter, Chic.	.20
☐ 100 Teemu Selänne, Winn.	.20
☐ 101 Don Sweeney, Bost.	.20
☐ 102 Valeri Bure, Mont.	.20
☐ 103 Todd Harvey, Dall.	.20
☐ 104 Luc Robitaille, Pitt.	.20
☐ 105 Scott Niedermayer, NJer.	.20
☐ 106 John Vanbiesbrouck (G), Flor.	.20
☐ 107 Alexei Yashin, Otta.	.20

	Card	Price
☐	108 Ed Belfour (G), Chic.	.50
☐	109 Jyrki Lumme, Vanc.	.20
☐	110 Petr Klima, Tamp.	.20
☐	111 Tony Granato, LosA.	.20
☐	112 Bob Corkum, Anah.	.20
☐	**113 Chris McAlpine, NJer. RC**	**.50**
☐	114 John LeClair, Phil.	.20
☐	115 Kenny Jönsson, Toro.	.20
☐	116 Garry Galley, Buff.	.20
☐	117 Jeff Norton, SLou.	.20
☐	118 Tomas Sandström, Pitt.	.20
☐	119 Paul Coffey, Detr.	.20
☐	120 Mike Ricci, Québ.	.20
☐	121 Tony Amonte, Chic.	.20
☐	122 Chris Gratton, Tamp.	.20
☐	123 Blaine Lacher (G), Bost.	.20
☐	124 Andrei Nikolishin, Hart.	.20
☐	125 Michal Grosek, Winn.	.20
☐	126 Shawn Chambers, NJer.	.20
☐	127 Raymond Bourque, Bost.	.50
☐	128 Jeff Nelson, Wash.	.20
☐	129 Kirk Muller, NYIs.	.20
☐	130 Sergei Zubov, NYRa.	.20
☐	131 Stanislav Neckar, Otta.	.20
☐	132 Stu Barnes, Flor.	.20
☐	133 Jari Kurri, LosA.	.50
☐	134 Vyacheslav Kozlov, Detr.	.20
☐	135 Curtis Joseph (G), SLou.	.50
☐	136 Joé Juneau, Wash.	.20
☐	137 Craig Janney, SanJ.	.20
☐	138 Bryan Smolinski, Bost.	.20
☐	139 Brian Bradley, Tamp.	.20
☐	140 Steve Rucchin, Anah.	.20
☐	141 Donald Audette, Buff.	.20
☐	142 Jaromir Jagr, Pitt.	.50
☐	**143 Mike Torchia, Dall. RC**	**.50**
☐	144 Ray Ferraro, NYIs.	.20
☐	145 Adam Deadmarsh, Québ.	.20
☐	146 Joe Murphy, Chic.	.20
☐	147 Ron Hextall (G), Phil.	.20
☐	148 Andrew Cassels, Hart.	.20
☐	149 Martin Brodeur (G), NJer.	.50
☐	150 Marek Malik, Hart.	.20
☐	151 Éric Desjardins, Phil.	.20
☐	152 Cory Stillman, Calg.	.20
☐	153 Owen Nolan, Québ.	.20
☐	154 Randy Wood, Toro.	.20
☐	155 Alexei Zhamnov, Winn.	.20
☐	156 John Cullen, Pitt.	.20
☐	157 Zdenek Nedved, Toro.	.20
☐	158 Greg A. Adams, Dall.	.20
☐	159 Kelly Miller, Wash.	.20
☐	160 Alexandre Daigle, Otta.	.20
☐	161 Gord Murphy, Flor.	.20
☐	162 Jeff Friesen, SanJ.	.20
☐	163 Scott Stevens, NJer.	.20
☐	164 Denis Chassé, SLou.	.20
☐	165 Cam Neely, Bost.	.50
☐	**166 Magnus Svensson, Flor. RC**	**.50**
☐	167 Joe Sakic, Québ.	.50
☐	168 Kevin Brown, LosA.	.20
☐	**169 Craig Conroy, Mont. RC**	**1.50**
☐	170 Pavel Bure, Vanc.	.20
☐	171 Viktor Kozlov, SanJ.	.20
☐	172 Pat LaFontaine, Buff.	.20
☐	173 Sergei Gonchar, Wash.	.20
☐	174 Brett Lindros, NYIs.	.20
☐	175 Jassen Cullimore, Vanc.	.20
☐	176 Mats Sundin, Toro.	.50
☐	177 Zarley Zalapski, Calg.	.20
☐	178 Stéphane Richer, NJer.	.20
☐	179 J. Steve Smith, Chic.	.20
☐	180 Brendan Shanahan, SLou.	.50
☐	181 Brian Leetch, NYRa.	.20
☐	182 Ken Wregget (G), Pitt.	.20
☐	183 Jeff R. Brown, Vanc.	.20
☐	184 Darby Hendrickson, Toro.	.20
☐	185 Nikolai Khabibulin (G), Winn.	.20
☐	186 Glen Wesley, Hart.	.20
☐	187 Andrei Nazarov, SanJ.	.20
☐	188 Rod Brind'Amour, Phil.	.20
☐	189 Jim Carey (G), Wash.	.20
☐	190 Derek Plante, Buff.	.20
☐	191 Valeri Karpov, Anah.	.20
☐	192 Mike Kennedy, Dall.	.20
☐	193 Wendel Clark, Québ.	.20
☐	194 Radek Bonk, Otta.	.20
☐	195 Jozef Stumpel, Bost.	.20
☐	**196 Tommy Salo (G), NYIs. RC**	**2.00**
☐	197 Michal Pivonka, Wash.	.20
☐	198 Ray Sheppard, Detr.	.20
☐	199 Russ Courtnall, Vanc.	.20
☐	200 Todd Marchant, Edmo.	.20
☐	201 Geoff Sanderson, Hart.	.20
☐	202 Vincent Damphousse, Mont.	.20
☐	203 Sergei Krivokrasov, Chic.	.20
☐	204 Jesse Bélanger, Flor.	.20
☐	205 Al MacInnis, SLou.	.20
☐	206 Philippe DeRouville, Pitt.	.20
☐	207 Mike Eastwood, Winn.	.20
☐	208 Travis Green, NYIs.	.20
☐	209 Jeff Shantz, Chic.	.20
☐	**210 Shane Doan, Winn. RC**	**1.00**
☐	211 Mike Sullivan, Calg.	.20
☐	212 Kevin Dineen, Phil.	.20
☐	213 Pat Falloon, SanJ.	.20
☐	214 Rick Tabaracci (G), Calg.	.20
☐	215 Kelly Hrudey (G), LosA.	.20
☐	216 Alexei Kovalev, NYRa.	.20
☐	217 Matt Johnson, LosA.	.20
☐	218 Turner Stevenson, Mont.	.20
☐	219 Mike Sillinger, Anah.	.20
☐	220 Bobby Holik, NJer.	.20
☐	221 Kevin Stevens, Bost.	.20
☐	222 Dave Lowry, Flor.	.20
☐	223 Martin Gélinas, Vanc.	.20
☐	**224 Darren Langdon, NYRa. RC**	**1.00**
☐	225 Tie Domi, Toro.	.20
☐	226 Doug Bodger, Buff.	.20
☐	227 Patrick Flatley, NYIs.	.20
☐	**228 Anders Myrvold, Colo. RC**	**.50**
☐	229 German Titov, Calg.	.20
☐	230 Pat Peake, Wash.	.20
☐	231 Robert Kron, Hart.	.20
☐	232 Mike Donnelly, Dall.	.20
☐	233 Denis Savard, Chic.	.20
☐	**234 Mathieu Dandenault, Detr. RC**	**.50**
☐	**235 Joe Dziedzic, Pitt. RC**	**.50**
☐	236 Valeri Kamensky, Colo.	.20
☐	**237 Joaquin Gage (G), Edmo. RC**	**.50**
☐	238 Geoff Courtnall, SLou.	.20
☐	239 Arturs Irbe (G), SanJ.	.20
☐	240 Dan Quinn, Otta.	.20
☐	241 Jean-Claude Bergeron, Tamp.	.20
☐	242 Brian Noonan, SLou.	.20
☐	243 Ulf Samuelsson, NYRa.	.20
☐	244 Jeff O'Neill, Hart.	.20
☐	**245 Sandy Moger, Bost. RC**	**.50**
☐	246 Don Beaupré (G), Otta.	.20
☐	247 Bob Probert, Chic.	.20
☐	248 Mattias Norström, NYRa.	.20
☐	249 Jason Bonsignore, Edmo.	.20
☐	250 Mike Ridley, Vanc.	.20
☐	251 Joe Mullen, Bost.	.20
☐	252 Petr Nedved, Pitt.	.20
☐	253 Jason Doig, Winn.	.20
☐	254 Olaf Kölzig (G), Wash.	.20
☐	255 Mark Tinordi, Wash.	.20
☐	256 Roman Hamrlik, Tamp.	.20
☐	257 Denis Pederson, NJer.	.20
☐	258 Paul Ysebaert, Tamp.	.20
☐	259 Neal Broten, NJer.	.20
☐	260 Jason Woolley, Flor.	.20
☐	261 Teppo Numminen, Winn.	.20
☐	262 Scott Thornton, Edmo.	.20
☐	263 Ted Donato, Bost.	.20
☐	**264 Marcus Ragnarsson, SanJ. RC**	**1.00**
☐	265 Dmitri Khristich, LosA.	.20
☐	266 Michael Peca, Vanc.	.20
☐	267 Dominic Roussel, Phil.	.20
☐	268 Owen Nolan, SanJ.	.20
☐	269 Patrick Poulin, Chic.	.20
☐	270 Mario Lemieux, Pitt.	1.50
☐	271 Mark Messier, NYRa.	.50
☐	272 Viacheslav Fetisov, Detr.	.20
☐	273 Andrei Trefilov, Buff.	.20
☐	274 Damian Rhodes (G), Toro.	.20
☐	275 Alexander Mogilny, Vanc.	.20
☐	276 Ray Sheppard, SanJ.	.20
☐	**277 Radek Dvorak, Flor. RC**	**1.00**
☐	278 Steve Duchesne, Otta.	.20
☐	279 Jason Smith, NJer.	.20
☐	**280 Wade Flaherty, SanJ. RC**	**.50**
☐	281 Lyle Odelein, Mont.	.20
☐	282 Keith Jones, Wash.	.20
☐	283 Saku Koivu, Mont.	.50
☐	284 Marty Murray, Calg.	.20
☐	285 Sergei Fedorov, Detr.	.50
☐	286 Brian Rolston, NJer.	.20
☐	**287 Dave Roche, Pitt. RC**	**.50**
☐	288 Sylvain Lefebvre, Colo.	.20
☐	289 Theoren Fleury, Calg.	.20
☐	290 Andy Moog (G), Dall.	.20
☐	291 Tom Barrasso (G), Pitt.	.20
☐	**292 Craig Mills, Winn. RC**	**.50**
☐	293 Mike Gartner, Toro.	.20
☐	294 Stefan Ustorf, Wash.	.20
☐	295 Darren Turcotte, Winn.	.20
☐	296 Steve Konowalchuk, Wash.	.20
☐	297 Ray Ferraro, NYRa.	.20
☐	**298 Brian Holzinger, Buff. RC**	**.50**
☐	**299 Daniel Alfredsson, Otta. RC**	**3.00**
☐	300 Derek King, NYIs.	.20
☐	301 Mark Fitzpatrick (G), Flor.	.20
☐	302 Joe Sacco, Anah.	.20
☐	**303 Scott Walker, Vanc. RC**	**1.00**
☐	**304 Ricard Persson, NJer. RC**	**.50**
☐	305 Mike Rathje, SanJ.	.20
☐	306 Petr* Svoboda, Phil.	.20
☐	**307 Roman Vopat, SLou. RC**	**.50**
☐	308 Ray Whitney, SanJ.	.20
☐	309 Calle Johansson, Wash.	.20
☐	310 Grant Fuhr (G), SLou.	.20
☐	311 John Tucker, Tamp.	.20
☐	312 Anatoli Semenov, Phil.	.20
☐	313 Darren McCarty, Detr.	.20
☐	314 Stéphane Quintal, Mont.	.20
☐	315 Jason Dawe, Buff.	.20
☐	316 Zigmund Palffy, NYIs.	.20
☐	317 Dave Manson, Winn.	.20
☐	318 Vitali Yachmenev, LosA.	.20
☐	319 Chris Pronger, SLou.	.20
☐	320 Valeri Zelepukin, NJer.	.20
☐	321 Ryan Smyth, Edmo.	.20
☐	322 Johan Garpenlöv, Flor.	.20
☐	323 Bill Ranford (G), Edmo.	.20
☐	324 Daymond Langkow, Tamp.	.50
☐	**325 Aki Berg, LosA. RC**	**.50**
☐	326 Derian Hatcher, Dall.	.20
☐	327 Bryan Smolinski, Pitt.	.20
☐	328 Michel Picard, Otta.	.20
☐	**329 Alek Stojanov, Vanc. RC**	**.50**
☐	330 Trent Klatt, Dall.	.20
☐	331 Richard Park, Pitt.	.20
☐	332 Jere Lehtinen, Dall.	.20
☐	333 Bryan McCabe, NYIs.	.20
☐	**334 Kyle McLaren, Bost. RC**	**1.00**
☐	335 Todd Krygier, Anah.	.20
☐	336 Adam Creighton, SLou.	.20
☐	337 Jamie Pushor, Detr.	.20
☐	338 Patrick Roy (G), Mont.	1.50
☐	339 Milos Holan, Anah.	.20
☐	340 Dave Ellett, Toro.	.20
☐	341 Brian Bellows, Tamp.	.20
☐	342 Jamie Rivers, SLou.	.20
☐	343 Claude Lemieux, Colo.	.20
☐	**344 Leif Rohlin, Vanc. RC**	**.50**
☐	345 Éric Dazé, Chic.	.20
☐	**346 Todd Bertuzzi, NYIs. RC**	**6.00**
☐	**347 Antti Törmänen, Otta. RC**	**.50**
☐	348 Luc Robitaille, NYRa.	.20
☐	349 Tim Taylor, Detr.	.20
☐	**350 Stéphane Yelle, Colo. [Photo is D.Friedman] RC**	**1.50**
☐	351 Marko Kiprusoff, Mont.	.20
☐	352 Igor Korolev, Winn.	.20
☐	353 Scott Lachance, NYIs.	.20
☐	354 Marty McSorley, LosA.	.20
☐	355 Joel Otto, Phil.	.20
☐	356 Josef Beranek, Vanc.	.20
☐	357 Sergei Zubov, Pitt.	.20
☐	**358 Rhett Warrener, Flor. RC**	**.50**
☐	359 Jimmy Carson, Hart.	.20
☐	360 Zdeno Ciger, Edmo.	.20
☐	361 Brendan Witt, Wash.	.20
☐	362 Byron Dafoe (G), LosA.	.20
☐	363 Steve Thomas, NJer.	.20
☐	364 Deron Quint, Winn.	.20
☐	365 Nelson Emerson, Hart.	.20
☐	366 Larry Murphy, Toro.	.20
☐	367 Benoît Brunet, Mont.	.20
☐	368 Kjell Samuelsson, Phil.	.20
☐	369 Aaron Gavey, Tamp.	.20
☐	**370 Robert Svehla, Flor. RC**	**1.00**
☐	371 René Corbet, Colo.	.20
☐	372 Gary Roberts, Calg.	.20
☐	373 Shawn McEachern, Bost.	.20
☐	374 Andrei Kovalenko, Colo.	.20
☐	375 Yanic Perreault, LosA.	.20
☐	376 Shayne Corson, SLou.	.20
☐	377 Brendan Shanahan, Hart.	.50
☐	378 Sergei Nemchinov, NYRa.	.20
☐	**379 Chad Kilger, Anah. RC**	**1.00**
☐	380 Sergio Momesso, Toro.	.20
☐	381 Craig Billington (G), Bost.	.20
☐	382 Niklas Sundström, NYRa.	.20
☐	383 Matthew Barnaby, Buff.	.20
☐	384 Dale Hawerchuk, SLou.	.20
☐	385 Trevor Linden, Vanc.	.20
☐	386 Adam Oates, Bost.	.20
☐	387 Dmitry Yushkevich, Toro.	.20
☐	388 Todd Elik, Bost.	.20
☐	389 Wendel Clark, NYIs.	.20
☐	390 Stéphane Fiset (G), Colo.	.20

	Insert	**NRMT-MT**
☐	1 Checklist	.20
☐	2 Checklist	.20
☐	3 Checklist	.20
☐	4 Checklist	.20
☐	5 Checklist	.20
☐	6 Checklist	.20
☐	7 Checklist	.20
☐	8 Checklist	.20

BETWEEN THE PIPES

These die-cut inserts were found in Series One and Series Two packs.

	Insert Set (10 cards):	**45.00**
	Insert (1:36)	**BTP**
☐	1 Blaine Lacher (G), Bost.	3.00
☐	2 Dominik Hasek (G), Buff.	6.00
☐	3 Mike Vernon (G), Detr.	3.00
☐	4 Trevor Kidd (G), Calg.	3.00
☐	5 Martin Brodeur (G), NJer.	12.00
☐	6 Jim Carey (G), Wash.	3.00
☐	7 Patrick Roy (G), Colo.	22.00
☐	8 Sean Burke (G), Hart.	4.00
☐	9 Félix Potvin (G), Toro.	4.00
☐	10 Ed Belfour (G), Chic.	6.00

CANADA: THREE TIME WORLD CHAMPIONS

These inserts were found in Series One and Series Two packs.

	Insert Set (22 cards):	**10.00**
	Insert (1:2)	**CTTWC**
☐	1 Jamie Storr (G), Canada Juniors	.50
☐	2 Dan Cloutier (G), Canada Juniors	1.00
☐	3 Nolan Baumgartner, Canada Juniors	.35
☐	4 Chad Allan, Canada Juniors	.35
☐	5 Wade Redden, Canada Juniors	.50
☐	6 Ed Jovanovski, Cdn.	1.00
☐	7 Jamie Rivers, Canada Juniors	.35
☐	8 Bryan McCabe, Canada Juniors	.50
☐	9 Lee Sorochan, Canada Juniors	.35
☐	10 Marty Murray, Canada Juniors	.35
☐	11 Larry Courville, Canada Juniors	.35
☐	12 Jason Allison, Canada Juniors	1.50
☐	13 Darcy Tucker, Canada Juniors	.50
☐	14 Jeff O'Neill, Canada Juniors	1.00
☐	15 Éric Dazé, Canada Juniors	1.00
☐	16 Alexandre Daigle, Canada Juniors	.35
☐	17 Todd Harvey, Canada Juniors	.50
☐	18 Jason Botterill, Canada Juniors	.35
☐	19 Shean Donovan, Canada Juniors	.35
☐	20 Denis Pederson, Canada Juniors	.35
☐	21 Jeff Friesen, Canada Juniors	.50
☐	22 Ryan Smyth, Canada Juniors	1.00

DOMINATORS

	Series Two Insert Set (8 cards):	**110.00**
	Insert (#/5000)	**Dom.**
☐	1 P. Forsberg / M. Lemieux / E. Lindros	30.00
☐	2 J. Jagr / J. LeClair / M. Renberg	10.00
☐	3 R. Bourque / B. Leetch / S. Zubov	10.00
☐	4 M. Brodeur / J. Carey / D. Hasek	10.00
☐	5 S. Fedorov / D. Gilmour / W. Gretzky	40.00
☐	6 P. Bure / Br. Hull / P. Kariya	15.00
☐	7 C. Chelios / P. Coffey / A. MacInnis	6.00
☐	8 E. Belfour / T. Kidd / F. Potvin	10.00

ELITE

	Insert Set (10 cards):	**115.00**
	Insert (#/10,000)	**ES**
☐	1 Alexei Zhamnov, Winn.	5.00
☐	2 Joe Sakic, Québ.	15.00
☐	3 Mikael Renberg, Phil.	5.00
☐	4 Sergei Fedorov, Detr.	10.00
☐	5 Paul Coffey, Detr.	5.00
☐	6 Paul Kariya, Anah.	10.00
☐	7 Wayne Gretzky, LosA.	40.00
☐	8 Eric Lindros, Phil.	10.00
☐	9 Mario Lemieux, Pitt.	30.00
☐	10 Jaromir Jagr, Pitt.	10.00

IGNITERS

	Series One Insert Set (10 cards):	**85.00**
	Insert (#/5000)	**I5000**
☐	1 Adam Oates, Bost.	6.00
☐	2 Paul Coffey, Detr.	6.00
☐	3 Doug Gilmour, Toro.	6.00
☐	4 Pierre Turgeon, Mont.	6.00
☐	5 Mark Messier, NYRa.	15.00
☐	6 Alexei Zhamnov, Winn.	6.00
☐	7 Jeremy Roenick, Chic.	10.00
☐	8 Steve Yzerman, Detr.	35.00
☐	9 Joe Nieuwendyk, Calg.	6.00
☐	10 Ron Francis, Pitt.	6.00

MARKSMEN

	Series One Insert Set (8 cards):	**65.00**
	Insert (1:24 Retail)	**M**
☐	1 Peter Bondra, Wash.	8.00
☐	2 Owen Nolan, Québ.	8.00
☐	3 Eric Lindros, Phil.	12.00
☐	4 Ray Sheppard, Detr.	5.00
☐	5 Jaromir Jagr, Pitt.	12.00
☐	6 Theoren Fleury, Calg.	8.00
☐	7 Brett Hull, SLou.	12.00
☐	8 Brendan Shanahan, SLou.	12.00

PRO POINTERS

	Series Two Insert Set (10 cards):	**7.00**
	Insert (1:1)	**PP**
☐	1 Jeremy Roenick, Chic. / U.S.A. Nationals	.50
☐	2 Pat LaFontaine, Buff. / U.S.A. Nationals	.35
☐	3 Jason Bonsignore, Edmo. / U.S.A. Juniors	.35
☐	4 Chris Chelios, Chic. / U.S.A. Nationals	.35
☐	5 Brian Leetch, NYRa. / U.S.A. Nationals	.35
☐	6 Brett Hull, SLou. / U.S.A. Nationals	.50
☐	7 Keith Tkachuk, Winn. / U.S.A. Nationals	.35
☐	8 Mike Modano, Dall. / U.S.A. Nationals	.50
☐	9 Brian Rolston, NJer. / U.S.A. Nationals	.35
☐	10 Darren Turcotte, Winn. / U.S.A. Nationals	.35
☐	11 Jeff Friesen, SanJ. / Canada Juniors	.35
☐	12 Theoren Fleury, Calg. / Canada Nationals	.35
☐	13 Eric Lindros, Phil. / Canada Juniors	.50
☐	14 Mario Lemieux, Pitt. / Canada Nationals	1.50
☐	15 Jamie Storr (G), LosA. / Canada Juniors	.35
☐	16 Trevor Kidd (G), Calg. / Canada Juniors	.35
☐	17 Chris Pronger, SLou. / Canada Juniors	.35
☐	18 Brendan Witt, Wash. / Canada Juniors	.35
☐	19 Paul Kariya, Anah. / Canada Juniors	.50
☐	20 Todd Harvey, Dall. / Canada Juniors	.35

RATED ROOKIE

	Player	
	Series Two Insert Set (16 cards):	**60.00**
	Insert (1:24 Retail)	**RR**
☐	1 Saku Koivu, Mont.	10.00
☐	2 Todd Bertuzzi, NYIs.	20.00
☐	3 Niklas Sundström, NYRa.	2.00
☐	4 Jeff O'Neill, Hart.	2.00
☐	5 Zdenek Nedved, Toro.	2.00
☐	6 Éric Dazé, Chic.	4.00
☐	7 Chad Kilger, Anah.	2.00
☐	8 Shane Doan, Winn.	2.00
☐	9 Vitali Yachmenev, LosA.	2.00
☐	10 Radek Dvorak, Flor.	2.00
☐	11 Marty Murray, Calg.	2.00
☐	12 Cory Stillman, Calg.	2.00
☐	13 Marcus Ragnarsson, SanJ.	2.00
☐	14 Daniel Alfredsson, Otta.	10.00
☐	15 Antti Törmänen, Otta.	2.00
☐	16 Petr Sykora, NJer.	5.00

ROOKIE TEAM

	Player	
	Series One Insert Set (9 cards):	**20.00**
	Insert (1:12)	**RT**
☐	1 Jim Carey (G), Wash.	2.00
☐	2 Peter Forsberg, Québ.	6.00
☐	3 Paul Kariya, Anah.	6.00
☐	4 David Oliver, Edmo.	2.00
☐	5 Blaine Lacher (G), Bost.	2.00
☐	6 Oleg Tverdovsky, Anah.	2.00
☐	7 Jeff Friesen, SanJ.	2.00
☐	8 Todd Marchant, Edmo.	2.00
☐	9 Todd Harvey, Dall.	2.00

1995 - 96 DONRUSS ELITE

There are three versions to Donruss Elite: a regular card, a die-cut stars parallel and an uncut die-cut stars parallel. There are reportedly 500 copies of each die-cut parallel while there is an undetermined number of uncut die-cut parallels that were "mistakenly" inserted into the packs.

	Player	UDC	DC	Reg.
	Complete Set (110 cards):	**475.00**	**925.00**	**30.00**
	Common Player:	**3.00**	**5.00**	**.25**
☐☐☐	1 J. Thibault (G), Mont.	5.00	10.00	.50
☐☐☐	2 Nicklas Lidström, Detr.	5.00	15.00	.50
☐☐☐	3 B. Shanahan, Hart.	15.00	25.00	1.00
☐☐☐	4 Kenny Jönsson, NYIs.	3.00	5.00	.25
☐☐☐	5 Doug Weight, Edmo.	5.00	15.00	.50
☐☐☐	6 Oleg Tverdovsky, Winn.	3.00	5.00	.25
☐☐☐	7 Brett Hull, SLou.	15.00	25.00	1.00
☐☐☐	8 Larry Murphy, Toro.	3.00	5.00	.25
☐☐☐	9 R. Bourque, Bost.	15.00	30.00	1.50
☐☐☐	10 Adam Graves, NYRa.	5.00	10.00	.50
☐☐☐	11 Gary Suter, Chic.	3.00	5.00	.25
☐☐☐	12 Bill Ranford (G), Bost.	5.00	10.00	.50
☐☐☐	13 Zigmund Palffy, NYIs.	5.00	15.00	.50
☐☐☐	14 Cam Neely, Bost.	15.00	25.00	1.00
☐☐☐	15 Al MacInnis, SLou.	5.00	10.00	.50
☐☐☐	16 Joe Sakic, Colo.	20.00	40.00	2.00
☐☐☐	17 Kevin Hatcher, Dall.	3.00	5.00	.25
☐☐☐	18 A. Mogilny, Vanc.	5.00	10.00	.50
☐☐☐	**19 R. Dvorak, Flor. RC**	**10.00**	**15.00**	**1.50**
☐☐☐	20 Ed Belfour (G), Chic.	15.00	25.00	1.00
☐☐☐	21 Jeff O'Neill, Hart.	5.00	15.00	1.00
☐☐☐	22 Valeri Kamensky, Colo.	3.00	5.00	.25
☐☐☐	23 John MacLean, NJer.	3.00	5.00	.25
☐☐☐	24 Zdeno Ciger, Edmo.	3.00	5.00	.25
☐☐☐	**25 Alfredsson, Otta. RC**	**25.00**	**45.00**	**4.50**
☐☐☐	26 Owen Nolan, SanJ.	5.00	15.00	.50
☐☐☐	27 Wendel Clark, Toro.	10.00	20.00	1.00
☐☐☐	28 Brian Savage, Mont.	3.00	5.00	.25
☐☐☐	29 Alexei Zhamnov, Winn.	3.00	5.00	.25
☐☐☐	30 D. Hasek (G), Buff.	15.00	25.00	1.00
☐☐☐	31 Paul Kariya, Anah.	20.00	35.00	1.50
☐☐☐	32 Mike Modano, Dall.	15.00	25.00	1.00
☐☐☐	33 Craig Janney, Winn.	3.00	5.00	.25
☐☐☐	34 Todd Harvey, Dall.	3.00	5.00	.25
☐☐☐	35 Jaromir Jagr, Pitt.	15.00	25.00	1.00
☐☐☐	36 Roman Hamrlik, Tamp.	3.00	5.00	.25
☐☐☐	37 Sergei Zubov, Pitt.	3.00	5.00	.25
☐☐☐	**38 Ragnarsson, SanJ. RC**	**10.00**	**15.00**	**1.50**
☐☐☐	39 Peter Forsberg, Colo.	20.00	35.00	1.50
☐☐☐	40 Ron Francis, Pitt.	5.00	15.00	.50
☐☐☐	41 German Titov, Calg.	3.00	5.00	.25
☐☐☐	42 Grant Fuhr (G), SLou.	5.00	15.00	.50
☐☐☐	43 M. Brodeur (G), NJer.	20.00	40.00	2.00
☐☐☐	44 Claude Lemieux, Colo.	3.00	5.00	.25
☐☐☐	45 Trevor Linden, Vanc.	5.00	10.00	.50
☐☐☐	46 Mark Messier, NYRa.	15.00	25.00	1.00
☐☐☐	47 Jeremy Roenick, Chic.	10.00	20.00	1.00
☐☐☐	48 Peter Bondra, Wash.	5.00	15.00	.50
☐☐☐	49 Donald Audette, Buff.	5.00	10.00	.50
☐☐☐	50 Joe Nieuwendyk, Dall.	5.00	10.00	.50
☐☐☐	51 M. Lemieux, Pitt. [CL]	20.00	35.00	1.50
☐☐☐	52 Vitali Yachmenev, LosA.	3.00	5.00	.25
☐☐☐	53 Sergei Fedorov, Detr.	15.00	25.00	1.00
☐☐☐	54 Kirk Muller, Toro.	3.00	5.00	.25
☐☐☐	**55 Chad Kilger, Winn. RC**	**10.00**	**15.00**	**1.50**
☐☐☐	56 John LeClair, Phil.	10.00	20.00	1.00
☐☐☐	**57 T. Bertuzzi, NYIs. RC**	**50.00**	**90.00**	**9.00**
☐☐☐	58 W. Gretzky, SLou.	60.00	100.00	5.00
☐☐☐	59 Cu. Joseph (G), Edmo.	15.00	25.00	1.00
☐☐☐	60 N. Sundström, NYRa.	3.00	5.00	.50
☐☐☐	61 Chris Chelios, Chic.	5.00	15.00	.50
☐☐☐	62 Radek Bonk, Otta.	3.00	5.00	.25
☐☐☐	63 Éric Dazé, Chic.	5.00	15.00	1.00
☐☐☐	64 Patrick Roy (G), Colo.	45.00	75.00	3.50
☐☐☐	65 Rob Niedermayer, Flor.	3.00	5.00	.25
☐☐☐	66 Mario Lemieux, Pitt.	45.00	75.00	3.50
☐☐☐	67 Saku Koivu, Mont.	15.00	30.00	2.00
☐☐☐	68 Ed Jovanovski, Flor.	5.00	15.00	1.00
☐☐☐	69 Jim Carey (G), Wash.	3.00	5.00	.25
☐☐☐	70 Scott Stevens, NJer.	5.00	10.00	.50
☐☐☐	71 Steve Thomas, NJer.	3.00	5.00	.25
☐☐☐	72 Mats Sundin, Toro.	15.00	25.00	1.00
☐☐☐	73 Teemu Selänne, Anah.	10.00	20.00	1.00
☐☐☐	74 Tomas Sandström, Pitt.	3.00	5.00	.25
☐☐☐	75 Pat LaFontaine, Buff.	5.00	15.00	.50
☐☐☐	76 Pat Verbeek, NYRa.	3.00	5.00	.25
☐☐☐	77 Pavel Bure, Vanc.	10.00	20.00	1.00
☐☐☐	78 Jeff R. Brown, Hart.	3.00	5.00	.25
☐☐☐	79 Alexei Yashin, Otta.	5.00	15.00	.50
☐☐☐	80 Adam Oates, Bost.	5.00	10.00	.50
☐☐☐	81 Keith Tkachuk, Winn.	5.00	15.00	.50
☐☐☐	82 Brian Bradley, Tamp.	3.00	5.00	.25
☐☐☐	83 Vanbiesbrouck (G), Flor.	5.00	10.00	.50
☐☐☐	84 A. Selivanov, Tamp.	3.00	5.00	.25
☐☐☐	85 Paul Coffey, Detr.	5.00	15.00	.50
☐☐☐	86 Scott Mellanby, Flor.	3.00	5.00	.25
☐☐☐	87 Vyacheslav Kozlov, Detr.	3.00	5.00	.25
☐☐☐	88 Eric Lindros, Phil.	15.00	25.00	1.00
☐☐☐	89 Deron Quint, Winn.	3.00	5.00	.25
☐☐☐	90 Pierre Turgeon, Mont.	5.00	10.00	.50
☐☐☐	91 Rod Brind'Amour, Phil.	3.00	5.00	.25
☐☐☐	92 Doug Gilmour, Toro.	5.00	15.00	.50
☐☐☐	93 Sandis Ozolinsh, Colo.	3.00	5.00	.25
☐☐☐	94 Mikael Renberg, Phil.	3.00	5.00	.25
☐☐☐	95 Kevin Stevens, LosA.	3.00	5.00	.25
☐☐☐	96 V. Damphousse, Mont.	5.00	15.00	.50
☐☐☐	97 Félix Potvin (G), Toro.	5.00	15.00	.50
☐☐☐	98 Brian Leetch, NYRa.	5.00	15.00	.50
☐☐☐	99 Steve Yzerman, Detr.	35.00	60.00	3.00
☐☐☐	100 Dale Hawerchuk, Phil.	5.00	15.00	.50
☐☐☐	101 Jason Arnott, Edmo.	5.00	10.00	.50
☐☐☐	102 Ray Sheppard, Flor.	3.00	5.00	.25
☐☐☐	103 Mark Recchi, Mont.	5.00	10.00	.50
☐☐☐	104 Joé Juneau, Wash.	3.00	5.00	.25
☐☐☐	105 Luc Robitaille, NYRa.	10.00	20.00	1.00
☐☐☐	106 Theoren Fleury, Calg.	5.00	15.00	.50
☐☐☐	107 Sean Burke (G), Hart.	5.00	15.00	.50
☐☐☐	108 Ron Hextall (G), Phil.	5.00	15.00	.50
☐☐☐	**109 S. Doan, Winn. RC**	**10.00**	**15.00**	**1.50**
☐☐☐	110 E. Lindros, Phil. [CL]	5.00	10.00	.50

	Expired Trade Card	Insert
☐	Lemieux/Lindros Cool Trade	3.00

CUTTING EDGE

	Player	
	Insert Set (15 cards):	**110.00**
	Insert (#/5000)	**CE**
☐	1 Eric Lindros, Phil.	6.00
☐	2 Mario Lemieux, Pitt.	22.00
☐	3 Wayne Gretzky, SLou.	30.00
☐	4 Peter Forsberg, Colo.	10.00
☐	5 Paul Kariya, Anah.	10.00
☐	6 Jaromir Jagr, Pitt.	6.00

	Player	
☐	7 Alexander Mogilny, Vanc.	4.00
☐	8 Mark Messier, NYRa.	6.00
☐	9 Sergei Fedorov, Detr.	6.00
☐	10 Pierre Turgeon, Mont.	4.00
☐	11 Mats Sundin, Toro.	6.00
☐	12 Brett Hull, SLou.	6.00
☐	13 Paul Coffey, Detr.	4.00
☐	14 Jeremy Roenick, Chic.	6.00
☐	15 Teemu Selänne, Anah.	6.00

HART TO HART (LINDROS/LEMIEUX)

	Player	NRMT-MT
☐	Lindros ✍ / Lemieux ✍ Autographs	300.00

LEMIEUX SERIES

	Player	
	Lemieux Set (7 cards):	**300.00**
	Insert (#/1066)	**LS**
☐	1 Mario Lemieux, Pitt.	30.00
☐	2 Mario Lemieux, Pitt.	30.00
☐	3 Mario Lemieux, Pitt.	30.00
☐	4 Mario Lemieux, Pitt.	30.00
☐	5 Mario Lemieux, Pitt.	30.00
☐	6 Mario Lemieux, Pitt.	30.00
☐	7 Mario Lemieux, Pitt. ✍	175.00

LINDROS SERIES

	Player	
	Lindros Set (7 cards):	**125.00**
	Insert (#/1088)	**LS**
☐	1 Eric Lindros, Phil.	10.00
☐	2 Eric Lindros, Phil.	10.00
☐	3 Eric Lindros, Phil.	10.00
☐	4 Eric Lindros, Phil.	10.00
☐	5 Eric Lindros, Phil.	10.00
☐	6 Eric Lindros, Phil.	10.00
☐	7 Eric Lindros, Phil. ✍	90.00

PAINTED WARRIORS

These inserts are serial numbered out of 2,500. Promo cards are numbered "XXXX of 2,500".

	Player	Promo	PW
	Insert Set (10 cards):	**17.00**	**135.00**
☐☐	1 Patrick Roy (G), Colo.	7.00	55.00
☐☐	2 Félix Potvin (G), Toro.	1.00	10.00
☐☐	3 Martin Brodeur (G), NJer.	4.00	30.00
☐☐	4 Ed Belfour (G), Chic.	2.00	15.00
☐☐	5 Guy Hebert (G), Anah.	1.00	8.00
☐☐	6 John Vanbiesbrouck (G), Flor.	1.00	8.00
☐☐	7 Jocelyn Thibault (G), Mont.	1.00	8.00
☐☐	8 Ron Hextall (G), Phil.	1.00	10.00
☐☐	9 Grant Fuhr (G), SLou.	1.00	10.00
☐☐	10 Jim Carey (G), Wash.	1.00	8.00

ROOKIE

	Player	
	Insert Set (15 cards):	**85.00**
	Insert (#/5000)	**Rookie**
☐	1 Éric Dazé, Chic.	6.00
☐	2 Vitali Yachmenev, LosA.	4.00
☐	3 Daniel Alfredsson, Otta.	8.00
☐	4 Todd Bertuzzi, NYIs.	26.00
☐	5 Byron Dafoe (G), LosA.	6.00
☐	6 Éric Fichaud (G), NYIs.	4.00
☐	7 Marcus Ragnarsson, SanJ.	4.00
☐	8 Saku Koivu, Mont.	12.00
☐	9 Chad Kilger, Anah.	4.00
☐	10 Radek Dvorak, Flor.	4.00
☐	11 Ed Jovanovski, Flor.	6.00
☐	12 Jeff O'Neill, Hart.	6.00
☐	13 Shane Doan, Winn.	4.00
☐	14 Niklas Sundström, NYRa.	4.00
☐	15 Kyle McLaren, Bost.	4.00

WORLD JUNIOR

	Player	
	Insert Set (44 cards):	**450.00**
	Insert (#/1000)	**WJC**
☐	**1 Marc Denis (G), Canada Juniors RC**	**24.00**
☐	**2 José Théodore (G), Canada Juniors RC**	**60.00**
☐	3 Chad Allan, Canada Juniors	6.00
☐	4 Nolan Baumgartner, Canada Juniors	6.00
☐	**5 Denis Gauthier, Canada Juniors RC**	**6.00**
☐	**6 Jason Holland, Canada Juniors RC**	**6.00**
☐	**7 Chris Phillips, Canada Juniors RC**	**12.00**
☐	8 Wade Redden, Canada Juniors	12.00
☐	**9 Rhett Warrener, Canada Juniors RC**	**6.00**
☐	10 Jason Botterill, Canada Juniors	6.00
☐	**11 Curtis Brown, Canada Juniors RC**	**8.00**
☐	**12 Hnat Domenichelli, Canada Juniors RC**	**8.00**
☐	13 Christian Dubé, Canada Juniors	6.00
☐	**14 Robb Gordon, Canada Juniors RC**	**6.00**
☐	15 Jarome Iginla, Canada Juniors	40.00
☐	16 Daymond Langkow, Canada Juniors	8.00
☐	17 Brad Larsen, Canada Juniors	6.00
☐	18 Alyn McCauley, Canada Juniors	12.00
☐	**19 Craig Mills, Canada Juniors RC**	**6.00**
☐	20 Jason Podollan, Canada Juniors	6.00
☐	**21 Mike Watt, Canada Juniors RC**	**6.00**
☐	**22 Jamie Wright, Canada Juniors RC**	**6.00**
☐	23 Brian Boucher (G), U.S.A. Juniors	16.00
☐	**24 Marc Magliarditi, U.S.A. Juniors RC**	**6.00**
☐	25 Bryan Berard, U.S.A. Juniors	16.00
☐	**26 Chris Bogas, U.S.A. Juniors RC**	**6.00**
☐	**27 Ben Clymer, U.S.A. Juniors RC**	**6.00**
☐	**28 Jeff Kealty, U.S.A. Juniors RC**	**6.00**
☐	29 Mike McBain, U.S.A. Juniors	6.00
☐	**30 Jeremiah McCarthy, U.S.A. Juniors RC**	**6.00**
☐	**31 Tom Poti, U.S.A. Juniors RC**	**8.00**
☐	**32 Reg Berg, U.S.A. Juniors RC**	**6.00**
☐	**33 Matt Cullen, U.S.A. Juniors RC**	**12.00**
☐	**34 Chris Drury, U.S.A. Juniors RC**	**40.00**
☐	**35 Jeff Farkas, U.S.A. Juniors RC**	**20.00**
☐	**36 Casey Hankinson, U.S.A. Juniors RC**	**6.00**
☐	**37 Matt Herr, U.S.A. Juniors RC**	**6.00**
☐	**38 Mark Parrish, U.S.A. Juniors RC**	**40.00**
☐	39 Erik Rasmussen, U.S.A. Juniors	8.00
☐	40 Marty Reasoner, U.S.A. Juniors	12.00
☐	41 Wyatt Smith, U.S.A. Juniors	6.00
☐	**42 Brian Swanson, U.S.A. Juniors RC**	**8.00**
☐	**43 Mike Sylvia, U.S.A. Juniors RC**	**6.00**
☐	**44 Mike York, U.S.A. Juniors RC**	**30.00**

1995 - 96 EDGE ICE

These cards have two versions: a regular card and a holoprism parallel. Holoprism parallel cards were seeded in specially marked team boxes. There are no holofoil parallels for the checklists.

	Player	Par.	Reg.
	Complete Set (200 cards):	**—**	**30.00**
	Holoprism Set (196 cards):	**250.00**	**—**
	Common Player:	**2.00**	**.20**
☐☐	1 Curtis Bowen, Adirondack	2.00	.20
☐☐	2 Anders Eriksson, Adirondack	2.00	.20
☐☐	3 Kevin Hodson (G), Adirondack	2.00	.50
☐☐	4 Martin Lapointe, Adirondack	4.00	1.00
☐☐	5 Aaron Ward, Adirondack	2.00	.20
☐☐	6 Mike Dunham (G), Albany	4.00	1.00
☐☐	7 Chris McAlpine, Albany	2.00	.20
☐☐	8 Brian Rolston, Albany	3.00	.50
☐☐	9 Corey Schwab (G), Albany	2.00	.20
☐☐	10 Steve Sullivan, Albany	3.00	.50
☐☐	11 Petr Sykora, Albany	4.00	1.00
☐☐	12 Darren Van Impe, Albany	2.00	.20
☐☐	13 Mike Maneluk, Baltimore	2.00	.20
☐☐	14 David Sacco, Baltimore	2.00	.20
☐☐	15 Jarrod Skalde, Baltimore	2.00	.20
☐☐	16 Nikolai Tsulygin, Baltimore	2.00	.20
☐☐	17 Peter Ferraro, Binghamton	2.00	.20
☐☐	18 Chris Ferraro, Binghamton	2.00	.20
☐☐	19 Corey Hirsch (G), Binghampton	2.00	.20
☐☐	20 Mattias Norstrom, Binghampton	2.00	.20
☐☐	21 Jamie Ram (G), Binghampton	2.00	.20
☐☐	22 Chris Armstrong, Carolina	2.00	.20
☐☐	23 Alexei Kudashov, Carolina	2.00	.20
☐☐	24 Todd MacDonald, Carolina	2.00	.20
☐☐	25 Steve Washburn, Carolina	2.00	.20
☐☐	26 Kevin Weekes (G), Carolina	2.00	.20
☐☐	27 René Corbet, Cornwall	2.00	.20
☐☐	28 Janne Laukkanen, Cornwall	2.00	.20
☐☐	29 Aaron Miller, Cornwall	2.00	.20
☐☐	30 Landon Wilson, Cornwall	2.00	.20
☐☐	31 Fred Brathwaite (G), Cape Breton	3.00	.50
☐☐	32 Ryan Haggerty, Cape Breton	2.00	.20
☐☐	33 Ralph Intranuovo, Cape Breton	2.00	.20
☐☐	34 Todd Marchant, Cape Breton	2.00	.20
☐☐	35 David Oliver, Cape Breton	2.00	.20
☐☐	36 Marko Tuomainen, Cape Breton	2.00	.20
☐☐	37 Peter White, Cape Breton	2.00	.20
☐☐	38 Sébastien Bordeleau, Fredericton	2.00	.20
☐☐	39 Martin Brochu (G), Fredericton	2.00	.20
☐☐	40 Valeri Bure, Fredericton	3.00	.50
☐☐	41 Craig Conroy, Fredericton	3.00	.50
☐☐	42 Darcy Tucker, Fredericton	2.00	.20
☐☐	43 David Wilkie, Fredericton	2.00	.20
☐☐	44 Paul Healey, Hershey	2.00	.20
☐☐	45 Chris Herperger, Hershey	2.00	.20
☐☐	46 Jim Montgomery, Hershey	2.00	.20
☐☐	47 Chris Therien, Hershey	2.00	.20
☐☐	48 Pavol Demitra, P.E.I.	4.00	1.00
☐☐	49 Michel Picard, P.E.I.	2.00	.20
☐☐	50 Jason Zent, P.E.I.	2.00	.20
☐☐	51 Patrick Boileau, Portland	2.00	.20
☐☐	52 Jim Carey (G), Portland	2.00	.20
☐☐	53 Sergei Gonchar, Portland	3.00	.50
☐☐	54 Jeff Nelson, Portland	2.00	.20
☐☐	55 Stefan Ustorf, Portland	2.00	.20
☐☐	56 Alexander Kharlamov, Portland	2.00	.20
☐☐	57 Ron Tugnutt (G), Portland	4.00	1.00
☐☐	58 Scott Bailey (G), Providence	2.00	.20
☐☐	59 Clayton Beddoes, Providence	2.00	.20
☐☐	60 André Roy, Providence	2.00	.20
☐☐	61 Evgeny Ryabchikov (G), Providence	2.00	.20
☐☐	62 Mark Astley, Rochester	2.00	.20
☐☐	63 Jody Gage, Rochester	2.00	.20
☐☐	64 Sergei Klimentiev, Rochester	2.00	.20
☐☐	65 Barrie Moore, Rochester	2.00	.20
☐☐	66 Mike Wilson, Rochester	2.00	.20
☐☐	67 Shayne Wright, Rochester	2.00	.20
☐☐	68 Michal Grosek, Springfield	2.00	.20
☐☐	69 Tavis Hansen, Springfield	2.00	.20
☐☐	70 Nikolai Khabibulin (G), Springfield	4.00	1.00
☐☐	71 Scott Langkow (G), Springfield	2.00	.20
☐☐	72 Jason McBain, Springfield	2.00	.20
☐☐	73 Dwayne Roloson (G), Saint John	2.00	.20

74 Cory Stillman, Saint John	2.00	.20
75 Jamie Allison, Saint John	2.00	.20
76 Jesper Mattson, Saint John	2.00	.20
77 David Ling, Saint John	2.00	.20
78 Brandon Convery, St. John's	2.00	.20
79 Darby Hendrickson, St. John's	2.00	.20
80 Janne Gronvall, St. John's	2.00	.20
81 Jason Saal (G), St. John's	2.00	.20
82 Brent Gretzky, St. John's	2.00	.20
83 Kent Manderville, St. John's	2.00	.20
84 Shayne Toporowski, St. John's	2.00	.20
85 Paul Vincent, St. John's	2.00	.20
86 Mark Kolesar, St. John's	2.00	.20
87 Lonny Bohonos, Syracuse	2.00	.20
88 Larry Courville, Syracuse	2.00	.20
89 Jassen Cullimore, Syracuse	2.00	.20
90 Scott Walker, Syracuse	2.00	.20
91 Mike Buzak, Worcester	2.00	.20
92 Craig Darby, Worcester	2.00	.20
93 Éric Fichaud (G), Worcester	2.00	.20
94 Andreas Johansson, Worcester	2.00	.20
95 Jamie Rivers, Worcester	2.00	.20
96 Jason Strudwick, Worcester	2.00	.20
97 Patrice Tardif, Worcester	2.00	.20
98 Alex Vasilevski, Worcester	2.00	.20
99 Drew Bannister, Atlanta	2.00	.20
100 Stan Drulia, Atlanta	2.00	.20
101 Aaron Gavey, Atlanta	2.00	.20
102 Reggie Sanders, Atlanta	2.00	.20
103 Derek Wilkinson, Atlanta	2.00	.20
104 Rob Brown, Chicago	2.00	.20
105 Dan Currie, Chicago	2.00	.20
106 Kevin MacDonald, Chicago	2.00	.20
107 Steve Maltais, Chicago	2.00	.20
108 Shawn Rivers, Chicago	2.00	.20
109 Wendell Young (G), Chicago	2.00	.20
110 Don Biggs, Cincinnati	2.00	.20
111 Dale DeGray, Cincinnati	2.00	.20
112 Paul Lawless, Cincinnati	2.00	.20
113 Danny Lorenz, Cincinnati	2.00	.20
114 Dave Tomlinson, Cincinnati	2.00	.20
115 Jock Callander, Cleveland	2.00	.20
116 Phillipe DeRouville (G), Cleveland	2.00	.20
117 Ryan Savoia, Cleveland	2.00	.20
118 Mike Stevens, Cleveland	2.00	.20
119 Chris Tamer, Cleveland	2.00	.20
120 Peter Bondra, Detroit	6.00	1.50
121 Peter Ciavaglia, Detroit	2.00	.20
122 Rick Knickle (G), Detroit	2.00	.20
123 Jamie Loach, Detroit	2.00	.20
124 Michal Pivonka, Detroit	2.00	.20
125 Andy Bezeau, Fort Wayne	2.00	.20
126 Bob Essensa (G), Fort Wayne	2.00	.20
127 Andrew McBain, Fort Wayne	2.00	.20
128 Kevin Miehm, Fort Wayne	2.00	.20
129 Scott Arniel, Houston	2.00	.20
130 Kevin Dineen, Houston	2.00	.20
131 Rob Dopson, Houston	2.00	.20
132 Mark Freer, Houston	2.00	.20
133 Troy Gamble (G), Houston	2.00	.20
134 Ethan Moreau, Indianapolis	2.00	.20
135 Sergei Klimovich, Indianapolis	2.00	.20
136 Eric Lecompte, Indianapolis	2.00	.20
137 Eric Manlow, Indianaplois	2.00	.20
138 Kip Miller, Indianapolis	2.00	.20
139 Manny Fernandez (G), Michigan	4.00	1.00
140 Mike Kennedy, Michigan	2.00	.20
141 Jamie Langenbrunner, Michigan	2.00	.20
142 Derrick Smith, Michigan	2.00	.20
143 Jordan Willis, Michigan	2.00	.20
144 Jan Caloun, Kansas City	2.00	.20
145 Viktor Kozlov, Kansas City	3.00	.50
146 Andrei Nazarov, Kansas City	2.00	.20
147 Geoff Sarjeant (G), Kansas City	2.00	.20
148 Patrik Augusta, Los Angeles	2.00	.20
149 Viktor Gordiouk, Los Angeles	2.00	.20
150 Dave Littman (G), Los Angeles	2.00	.20
151 Todd Gillingham, Los Angeles	2.00	.20
152 Greg Hawgood, Las Vegas	2.00	.20
153 Patrice Lefebvre, Las Vegas	2.00	.20
154 Eldon Reddick (G), Las Vegas	2.00	.20
155 Manon Rhéaume (G), Las Vegas	18.00	3.50
156 Jeff Sharples, Las Vegas	2.00	.20
157 Todd Simon, Las Vegas	2.00	.20
158 Radek Bonk, Las Vegas	3.00	.50
159 Gino Cavallini, Milwaukee	2.00	.20
160 Tom Draper (G), Milwaukee	2.00	.20
161 Tony Hrkac, Milwaukee	2.00	.20
162 Fabian Joseph, Milwaukee	2.00	.20
163 Mark LaForest (G), Milwaukee	2.00	.20
164 Dave Christian, Minnesota	2.00	.20
165 Bryan Fogarty, Minnesota	2.00	.20
166 Chris Goverdaris, Minnesota	2.00	.20
167 Mike Hurlbut, Minnesota	2.00	.20
168 Chris Imes, Minnesota	2.00	.20
169 Stéphane Morin, Minnesota	2.00	.20
170 Allan Bester (G), Orlando	2.00	.20
171 Kerry Clark, Orlando	2.00	.20
172 Neil Eisenhut, Orlando	2.00	.20
173 Craig Fisher, Orlando	2.00	.20
174 Patrick Neaton, Orlando	2.00	.20
175 Todd Richards, Orlando	2.00	.20
176 Jon Casey (G), Peoria	2.00	.20
177 Doug Evans, Peoria	2.00	.20
178 Michel Mongeau, Peoria	2.00	.20
179 Greg Paslawski, Peoria	2.00	.20
180 Darren Veitch, Peoria	2.00	.20
181 Frederick Beauben, Phoenix	2.00	.20
182 Kevin Brown, Phoenix	2.00	.20
183 Rob Cowie, Phoenix	2.00	.20
184 Yanic Perreault, Phoenix	3.00	.50
185 Chris Snell, Phoenix	2.00	.20
186 Jan Vopat, Phoenix	2.00	.20
187 Robin Bawa, San Francisco	2.00	.20
188 S. Beauregard (G), San Francisco	2.00	.20
189 Dale Craigwell, San Francisco	2.00	.20
190 John Purves, San Francisco	2.00	.20
191 Jeff Madill, San Francisco	2.00	.20
192 Gord Dineen, Utah	2.00	.20
193 Chris Marinucci, Utah	2.00	.20
194 Mark McArthur, Utah	2.00	.20
195 Zigmund Palffy, Utah	6.00	1.50
196 Tommy Salo (G), Utah	4.00	1.00
197 Checklist	–	.20
198 Checklist	–	.20
199 Checklist	–	.20
200 Checklist	–	.20

CRUCIBLES

Insert Set (24 cards):	60.00
Player	C
C1 David Roberts, Peoria	2.00
C2 Ian Laperrière, Peoria	2.00
C3 Kevin Dineen, Houston	2.00
C4 Kenny Jönsson, St. John's	2.00
C5 Jim Carey (G), Portland	2.00
C6 Todd Marchant, Cape Breton	3.00
C7 David Oliver, Cape Breton	2.00
C8 Yanic Perreault, Phoenix	4.00
C9 Chris Therien, Hershey	2.00
C10 Viktor Kozlov, Kansas City	4.00
C11 Valeri Bure, Fredericton	2.00
C12 Nikolai Khabibulin (G), Springfield	5.00
C13 Steven Rice, Cape Breton	2.00
C14 Mike Kennedy, Kalamazoo	2.00
C15 Peter Bondra, Detroit	5.00
C16 Sergei Zubov, Binghampton	3.00
C17 Vyacheslav Kozlov, Adirondack	3.00
C18 Chris Osgood (G), Adirondack	5.00
C19 Darren McCarty, Adirondack	4.00
C20 Jason Dawe, Rochester	2.00
C21 Trevor Kidd (G), Saint John	2.00
C22 Tommy Salo (G), Utah	5.00
C23 Michal Pivonka, Detroit	2.00
C24 Zigmund Palffy, Utah	5.00

LIVIN' LARGE

Insert Set (11 cards):	45.00
Player	LL
L1 Adam Graves	3.00
L2 Marty McSorley	3.00
L3 Adam Oates	3.00
L4 Keith Primeau	3.00
L5 Bill Ranford (G)	3.00
L6 Curtis Joseph (G)	10.00
L7 Félix Potvin (G)	5.00
L8 Mike Vernon (G)	3.00
L9 Theoren Fleury	5.00
L10 Kevin Stevens	3.00
L11 Martin Brodeur (G)	15.00

QUANTUM MOTION

Insert Set (12 cards):	
Insert (#/2000)	QM
1 Manny Fernandez (G), Kalamazoo	
2 Eldon Reddick (G), Las Vegas	
3 Yanic Perreault, Phoenix	
4 Rob Brown, Phoenix	
5 Hubie McDonough	
6 Stan Drulia, Atlanta	
7 Michel Picard, P.E.I.	
8 Jim Carey (G), Portland	
9 Martin Lapointe, Adirondack	
10 Valeri Bure, Fredericton	
11 Martin Brochu (G), Fredericton	
12 Corey Schwab (G), Albany	

THE WALL

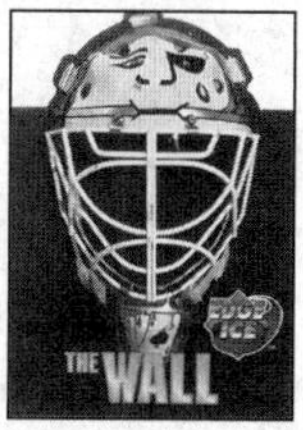

Insert Set (13 cards):	10.00
Player	TW
TW1 Ray Leblanc (G), Chicago	1.00
TW2 Manny Fernandez (G), Kalamazoo	2.00
TW3 Rick Knickle (G), Detroit	1.00
TW4 Troy Gamble (G), Houston	1.00
TW5 Eldon Reddick (G), Las Vegas	1.00
TW6 Wendell Young (G), Chicago	1.00
TW7 Jim Carey (G), Portland	1.00
TW8 Dwayne Roloson (G), Saint John	1.00
TW9 Les Kuntar (G), Fredericton	1.00
TW10 Mike Dunham (G), Albany	2.00
TW11 Éric Fichaud (G), St. John's	1.00
TW12 Kevin Hodson (G), Adirondack	1.00
Checklist (No #)	1.00

PROMOS

The seven-card promo pack acted as a sample to Edge Ice Hockey. The three Manon Rhéaume (G) cards had a design of their own and were handed out at the Toronto Fall Expo in November 1995.

Player	NRMT-MT
1 Manon Rhéaume (G), Las Vegas	4.00
2 Manon Rhéaume (G), Las Vegas	4.00
3 Manon Rhéaume (G), Las Vegas	4.00
PR-1 Todd Marchant, Cape Breton	1.00
PR-2 Tommy Salo (G), Utah	1.50
PR-3 Mike Dunham (G), Albany	1.50
PR-4 Viktor Kozlov, Kansas City	1.00
PR-5 Dwayne Roloson (G), Saint John	1.50
PR-6 Tony Hrkac, Milwaukee	1.00
Title Card	.75

1995 - 96 FLEER METAL

Imprint: © 1996 Fleer/Skybox International

Complete Set (200 cards):	30.00
Common Player:	.20
4-Card Promo Panel (Potvin/ Roenick/ Fleury/ Park):	3.00
Player	NRMT-MT
1 Guy Hebert (G), Anah.	.25
2 Paul Kariya, Anah.	1.00
3 Todd Krygier, Anah.	.25
4 Steve Rucchin, Anah.	.25
5 Oleg Tverdovsky, Anah.	.25
6 Raymond Bourque, Bost.	.50
7 Blaine Lacher (G), Bost.	.25
8 Shawn McEachern, Bost.	.25
9 Cam Neely, Bost.	.50
10 Adam Oates, Bost.	.25
11 Kevin Stevens, Bost.	.25
12 Donald Audette, Buff.	.25
13 Randy Burridge, Buff.	.25
14 Jason Dawe, Buff.	.25
15 Dominik Hasek (G), Buff.	.50
16 Pat LaFontaine, Buff.	.25
17 Alexei Zhitnik, Buff.	.25
18 Theoren Fleury, Calg.	.25
19 Phil Housley, Calg.	.25
20 Trevor Kidd (G), Calg.	.25
21 Joe Nieuwendyk, Calg.	.25
22 Michael Nylander, Calg.	.25
23 Ed Belfour (G), Chic.	.50
24 Chris Chelios, Chic.	.25
25 Joe Murphy, Chic.	.25
26 Bernie Nicholls, Chic.	.25
27 Patrick Poulin, Chic.	.25
28 Jeremy Roenick, Chic.	.50
29 Gary Suter, Chic.	.25
30 Adam Deadmarsh, Colo.	.25
31 Stéphane Fiset (G), Colo.	.25
32 Peter Forsberg, Colo.	1.00
33 Valeri Kamensky, Colo.	.25
34 Claude Lemieux, Colo.	.25
35 Sandis Ozolinsh, Colo.	.25
36 Joe Sakic, Colo.	1.00
37 Greg A. Adams, Dall.	.25
38 Dave Gagner, Dall.	.25
39 Todd Harvey, Dall.	.25
40 Derian Hatcher, Dall.	.25
41 Kevin Hatcher, Dall.	.25
42 Mike Modano, Dall.	.50
43 Andy Moog (G), Dall.	.25
44 Paul Coffey, Detr.	.25
45 Sergei Fedorov, Detr.	.50
46 Vladimir Konstantinov, Detr.	.25
47 Vyacheslav Kozlov, Detr.	.25
48 Nicklas Lidström, Detr.	.25
49 Chris Osgood (G), Detr.	.25
50 Keith Primeau, Detr.	.25
51 Steve Yzerman, Detr.	1.50
52 Jason Arnott, Edmo.	.25
53 Zdeno Ciger, Edmo.	.25
54 Todd Marchant, Edmo.	.25
55 David Oliver, Edmo.	.25
56 Bill Ranford (G), Edmo.	.25
57 Doug Weight, Edmo.	.25
58 Stu Barnes, Flor.	.25
59 Jody Hull, Flor.	.25
60 Scott Mellanby, Flor.	.25
61 Rob Niedermayer, Flor.	.25
62 John Vanbiesbrouck (G), Flor.	.25
63 Sean Burke (G), Hart.	.25
64 Andrew Cassels, Hart.	.25
65 Nelson Emerson, Hart.	.25
66 Geoff Sanderson, Hart.	.25
67 Brendan Shanahan, Hart.	.50
68 Glen Wesley, Hart.	.25
69 Rob Blake, LosA.	.25
70 Tony Granato, LosA.	.25
71 Wayne Gretzky, LosA.	3.00
72 Dmitri Khristich, LosA.	.25
73 Yanic Perreault, LosA.	.25
74 Rick Tocchet, LosA.	.25
75 Benoît Brunet, Mont.	.25
76 Vincent Damphousse, Mont.	.25
77 Mark Recchi, Mont.	.25
78 Patrick Roy (G), Mont.	2.00
79 Brian Savage, Mont.	.25
80 Pierre Turgeon, Mont.	.25
81 Martin Brodeur (G), NJer.	1.00
82 Neal Broten, NJer.	.25
83 John MacLean, NJer.	.25
84 Scott Niedermayer, NJer.	.25
85 Scott Stevens, NJer.	.25
86 Stéphane Richer, NJer.	.25
87 Esa Tikkanen, NJer.	.25
88 Steve Thomas, NJer.	.25
89 Wendel Clark, NYIs.	.50
90 Travis Green, NYIs.	.25
91 Kirk Muller, NYIs.	.25
92 Zigmund Palffy, NYIs.	.25
93 Mathieu Schneider, NYIs.	.25
94 Ray Ferraro, NYRa.	.25
95 Alexei Kovalev, NYRa.	.25
96 Brian Leetch, NYRa.	.25
97 Mark Messier, NYRa.	.50
98 Mike Richter (G), NYRa.	.25
99 Luc Robitaille, NYRa.	.50
100 Ulf Samuelsson, NYRa.	.25
101 Pat Verbeek, NYRa.	.25
102 Radek Bonk, Otta.	.25
103 Don Beaupré (G), Otta.	.25
104 Alexandre Daigle, Otta.	.25
105 Steve Duchesne, Otta.	.25
106 Dan Quinn, Otta.	.25
107 Martin Straka, Otta.	.25
108 Rod Brind'Amour, Phil.	.25
109 Éric Desjardins, Phil.	.25
110 Ron Hextall (G), Phil.	.25
111 John LeClair, Phil.	.50
112 Eric Lindros, Phil.	.50
113 Mikael Renberg, Phil.	.25
114 Chris Therien, Phil.	.25
115 Tom Barrasso (G), Pitt.	.25
116 Ron Francis, Pitt.	.25
117 Jaromir Jagr, Pitt.	.50
118 Mario Lemieux, Pitt.	2.00
119 Tomas Sandström, Pitt.	.25
120 Bryan Smolinski, Pitt.	.25
121 Sergei Zubov, Pitt.	.25
122 Shayne Corson, SLou.	.25
123 Grant Fuhr (G), SLou.	.25
124 Dale Hawerchuk, SLou.	.25
125 Brett Hull, SLou.	.50
126 Al MacInnis, SLou.	.25
127 Chris Pronger, SLou.	.25
128 Ulf Dahlén, SanJ.	.25
129 Jeff Friesen, SanJ.	.25
130 Arturs Irbe (G), SanJ.	.25
131 Craig Janney, SanJ.	.25
132 Andrei Nazarov, SanJ.	.25
133 Owen Nolan, SanJ.	.25
134 Ray Sheppard, SanJ.	.25
135 Brian Bradley, Tamp.	.25
136 Chris Gratton, Tamp.	.25
137 Roman Hamrlik, Tamp.	.25
138 Petr Klima, Tamp.	.25
139 Daren Puppa (G), Tamp.	.25
140 Alexander Selivanov, Tamp.	.25
141 Dave Andreychuk, Toro.	.25
142 Mike Gartner, Toro.	.50
143 Doug Gilmour, Toro.	.25
144 Kenny Jönsson, Toro.	.25
145 Larry Murphy, Toro.	.25
146 Félix Potvin (G), Toro.	.25
147 Mats Sundin, Toro.	.50
148 Jeff R. Brown, Vanc.	.25
149 Pavel Bure, Vanc.	.50
150 Russ Courtnall, Vanc.	.25
151 Trevor Linden, Vanc.	.25
152 Kirk McLean (G), Vanc.	.25
153 Alexander Mogilny, Vanc.	.25
154 Roman Oksiuta, Vanc.	.25
155 Mike Ridley, Vanc.	.25
156 Peter Bondra, Wash.	.25
157 Jim Carey (G), Wash.	.25
158 Sylvain Côté, Wash.	.25
159 Sergei Gonchar, Wash.	.25
160 Keith Jones, Wash.	.25
161 Joé Juneau, Wash.	.25
162 Nikolai Khabibulin (G), Winn.	.25
163 Igor Korolev, Winn.	.25
164 Teppo Numminen, Winn.	.25
165 Teemu Selänne, Winn.	.50
166 Keith Tkachuk, Winn.	.25
167 Darren Turcotte, Winn.	.25
168 Alexei Zhamnov, Winn.	.25
169 Daniel Alfredsson, Otta. [Rookie] RC	**3.50**
170 Aki Berg, LosA. [Rookie] RC	**1.00**
171 Todd Bertuzzi, NYIs. [Rookie] RC	**7.50**
172 Jason Bonsignore, Edmo. [Rookie]	.25
173 Byron Dafoe (G), LosA. [Rookie]	.50
174 Éric Dazé, Chic. [Rookie]	.50
175 Shane Doan, Winn. [Rookie] RC	**1.50**
176 Radek Dvorak, Flor. [Rookie] RC	**1.50**
177 Brian Holzinger, Buff. [Rookie] RC	**1.00**
178 Ed Jovanovski, Flor. [Rookie]	.50
179 Chad Kilger, Anah. [Rookie] RC	**1.50**
180 Saku Koivu, Mont. [Rookie]	1.00
181 Darren Langdon, NYRa. [Rookie] RC	**1.50**
182 Daymond Langkow, Tamp.	1.00
183 Jere Lehtinen, Dall. [Rookie]	.25
184 Kyle McLaren, Bost. [Rookie] RC	**1.50**
185 Marty Murray, Calg. [Rookie]	.25
186 Jeff O'Neill, Hart. [Rookie]	.50

187 Richard Park, Pitt. [Rookie]	.25
188 Deron Quint, Winn. [Rookie]	.25
189 M. Ragnarsson, SanJ. [Rookie] RC	**1.50**
190 Miroslav Satan, Edmo. [Rookie] RC	**2.00**
191 Tommy Salo (G), NYIs. [Rookie] RC	**2.50**
192 Jamie Storr (G), LosA. [Rookie]	.25
193 Niklas Sundström, NYRa. [Rookie]	.25
194 Robert Svehla, Flor. [Rookie] RC	**1.50**
195 Denis Pederson, NJer. [Rookie]	.25
196 Antti Törmänen, Otta. [Rookie] RC	**.50**
197 Brendan Witt, Wash. [Rookie]	.25
198 Vitali Yachmenev, LosA. [Rookie]	.25
199 Checklist	.25
200 Checklist	.25

HEAVY METAL

Insert Set (12 cards):	135.00
Insert (1:30)	HM
1 Pavel Bure, Vanc.	6.00
2 Sergei Fedorov, Detr.	10.00
3 Theoren Fleury, Calg.	6.00
4 Wayne Gretzky, LosA.	40.00
5 Brett Hull, SLou.	10.00
6 Jaromir Jagr, Pitt.	10.00
7 Paul Kariya, Anah.	10.00
8 Brian Leetch, NYRa.	6.00
9 Mario Lemieux, Pitt.	30.00
10 Mike Modano, Dall.	10.00
11 Adam Oates, Bost.	6.00
12 Joe Sakic, Colo.	15.00

INTERNATIONAL STEEL

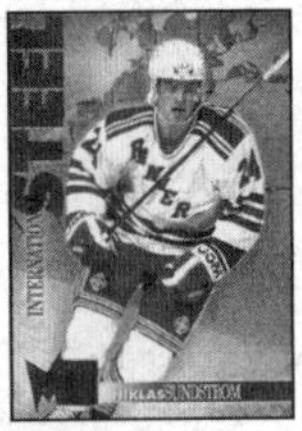

Insert Set (24 cards):	45.00
Insert (1:3)	IS
1 Pavel Bure, Vanc.	2.00
2 Chris Chelios, Chic.	1.00
3 Sergei Fedorov, Detr.	2.00
4 Peter Forsberg, Colo.	3.00
5 Wayne Gretzky, LosA.	10.00
6 Roman Hamrlik, Tamp.	.75
7 Dominik Hasek (G), Buff.	2.00
8 Brett Hull, SLou.	2.00
9 Jaromir Jagr, Pitt.	2.00
10 Saku Koivu, Mont.	4.00
11 Pat LaFontaine, Buff.	1.00
12 Brian Leetch, NYRa.	1.00
13 Jere Lehtinen, Dall.	.75
14 Mario Lemieux, Pitt.	7.00
15 Alexander Mogilny, Vanc.	1.00
16 Mikael Renberg, Phil.	.75
17 Jeremy Roenick, Chic.	2.00
18 Joe Sakic, Colo.	4.00
19 Teemu Selänne, Winn.	2.00
20 Mats Sundin, Toro.	2.00
21 Niklas Sundström, NYRa.	.75
22 Vitali Yachmenev, LosA.	.75
23 Alexei Zhamnov, Winn.	.75
24 Sergei Zubov, Pitt.	.75

IRON WARRIORS

Insert Set (15 cards):	50.00
Insert (1:12)	IW
1 Jason Arnott, Edmo.	2.50
2 Ed Belfour (G), Chic.	5.00
3 Theoren Fleury, Calg.	5.00
4 Ron Francis, Pitt.	5.00
5 John LeClair, Phil.	5.00
6 Claude Lemieux, NJer.	2.50
7 Eric Lindros, Phil.	5.00
8 Mark Messier, NYRa.	5.00
9 Cam Neely, Bost.	5.00
10 Keith Primeau, Detr.	3.00
11 Kevin Stevens, Bost.	2.50
12 Scott Stevens, NJer.	2.50
13 Brendan Shanahan, Hart.	5.00
14 Keith Tkachuk, Winn.	5.00
15 Rick Tocchet, LosA.	2.50

METAL WINNERS

Insert Set (9 cards):	65.00
Insert (1:60)	MW
1 Peter Forsberg, Colo.	20.00
2 Saku Koivu, Mont.	10.00
3 Alexei Kovalev, NYRa.	10.00
4 Eric Lindros, Phil.	15.00
5 Alexander Mogilny, Vanc.	5.00
6 Tommy Salo (G), NYIs.	7.00
7 Brian Savage, Mont.	5.00
8 Sergei Zubov, Pitt.	5.00
9 Alexei Zhamnov, Winn.	5.00

1995 - 96 FLEER ULTRA

Series One cards (1-200) have two versions: the regular issue and a Gold Medallion parallel. The series two set was called "Ultra Extra".

	G.M.	Reg.
Series One Set (200 cards):	**110.00**	**25.00**
Series Two Set (200 cards):	**—**	**30.00**
Common Player:	**.40**	**.20**
Player	**G.M.**	**Reg.**
1 Guy Hebert (G), Anah.	.40	.20
2 Milos Holan, Anah.	.40	.20
3 Paul Kariya, Anah.	4.00	.50
4 Denny Lambert, Anah. RC	**1.00**	**.50**
5 Stéphan Lebeau, Anah.	.40	.20
6 Oleg Tverdovsky, Anah.	.40	.20
7 Shaun Van Allen, Anah.	.40	.20
8 Raymond Bourque, Bost.	3.00	.50
9 Mariusz Czerkawski, Bost.	.40	.20
10 Blaine Lacher (G), Bost.	.40	.20
11 Sandy Moger, Bost. RC	**1.00**	**.50**
12 Cam Neely, Bost.	3.00	.50
13 Adam Oates, Bost.	1.00	.20
14 Bryan Smolinski, Bost.	.40	.20
15 Donald Audette, Buff.	1.00	.20
16 Jason Dawe, Buff.	.40	.20
17 Garry Galley, Buff.	.40	.20
18 Dominik Hasek (G), Buff.	3.00	.50
19 Brian Holzinger, Buff. RC	**1.00**	**.50**
20 Pat LaFontaine, Buff.	1.00	.20
21 Alexander Mogilny, Buff.	1.00	.20
22 Alexei Zhitnik, Buff.	.40	.20
23 Steve Chiasson, Calg.	.40	.20
24 Theoren Fleury, Calg.	1.00	.20
25 Phil Housley, Calg.	.40	.20
26 Trevor Kidd (G), Calg.	.40	.20
27 Joel Otto, Calg.	.40	.20
28 Gary Roberts, Calg.	1.00	.20
29 Zarley Zalapski, Calg.	.40	.20
30 Ed Belfour (G), Chic.	3.00	.50
31 Chris Chelios, Chic.	1.00	.20
32 Éric Dazé, Chic.	2.00	.50
33 Sergei Krivokrasov, Chic.	.40	.20
34 Bernie Nicholls, Chic.	.40	.20
35 Jeremy Roenick, Chic.	2.00	.50
36 Gary Suter, Chic.	.40	.20
37 Todd Harvey, Dall.	.40	.20
38 Derian Hatcher, Dall.	.40	.20
39 Mike Kennedy, Dall.	.40	.20
40 Grant Ledyard, Dall.	.40	.20
41 Mike Modano, Dall.	3.00	.50
42 Andy Moog (G), Dall.	1.00	.20
43 Mike Torchia, Dall. RC	**1.00**	**.50**
44 Paul Coffey, Detr.	1.00	.20
45 Sergei Fedorov, Detr.	3.00	.50
46 Vladimir Konstantinov, Detr.	.40	.20
47 Vyacheslav Kozlov, Detr.	.40	.20
48 Keith Primeau, Detr.	1.00	.20
49 Ray Sheppard, Detr.	.40	.20
50 Mike Vernon (G), Detr.	1.00	.20
51 Steve Yzerman, Detr.	7.00	1.50
52 Jason Arnott, Edmo.	1.00	.20
53 Shayne Corson, Edmo.	.40	.20
54 Igor Kravchuk, Edmo.	.40	.20
55 Todd Marchant, Edmo.	.40	.20
56 David Oliver, Edmo.	.40	.20
57 Bill Ranford (G), Edmo.	1.00	.20
58 Doug Weight, Edmo.	1.00	.20
59 Stu Barnes, Flor.	.40	.20
60 Jesse Bélanger, Flor.	.40	.20
61 Gord Murphy, Flor.	.40	.20
62 Rob Niedermayer, Flor.	.40	.20
63 Brian Skrudland, Flor.	.40	.20
64 John Vanbiesbrouck (G), Flor.	1.00	.20
65 Sean Burke (G), Hart.	1.00	.20
66 Andrew Cassels, Hart.	.40	.20
67 Frantisek Kucera, Hart.	.40	.20
68 Andrei Nikolishin, Hart.	.40	.20
69 Chris Pronger, Hart.	1.00	.20
70 Geoff Sanderson, Hart.	.40	.20
71 Kevin Smyth, Hart.	.40	.20
72 Darren Turcotte, Hart.	.40	.20
73 Rob Blake, LosA.	1.00	.20
74 Wayne Gretzky, LosA.	12.00	2.50
75 Kelly Hrudey (G), LosA.	.40	.20
76 Marty McSorley, LosA.	.40	.20
77 Jamie Storr (G), LosA.	.40	.20
78 Darryl Sydor, LosA.	.40	.20
79 Rick Tocchet, LosA.	.40	.20
80 Vincent Damphousse, Mont.	1.00	.20
81 Vladimir Malakhov, Mont.	.40	.20
82 Mark Recchi, Mont.	1.00	.20
83 Patrick Roy (G), Mont.	9.00	1.50
84 Brian Savage, Mont.	.40	.20
85 Pierre Turgeon, Mont.	1.00	.20
86 Martin Brodeur (G), NJer.	4.00	1.00
87 Neal Broten, NJer.	.40	.20
88 Sergei Brylin, NJer.	.40	.20
89 John MacLean, NJer.	.40	.20
90 Scott Niedermayer, NJer.	.40	.20
91 Scott Stevens, NJer.	1.00	.20
92 Stéphane Richer, NJer.	.40	.20
93 Ray Ferraro, NYIs.	.40	.20
94 Scott Lachance, NYIs.	.40	.20
95 Brett Lindros, NYIs.	.40	.20
96 Kirk Muller, NYIs.	.40	.20
97 Zigmund Palffy, NYIs.	1.00	.20
98 Tommy Salo (G), NYIs. RC	**4.00**	**2.00**
99 Mathieu Schneider, NYIs.	.40	.20
100 Tommy Söderström (G), NYIs.	.40	.20
101 Glenn Healy (G), NYRa.	.40	.20
102 Darren Langdon, NYRa. RC	**2.00**	**1.00**
103 Steve Larmer, NYRa.	1.00	.20
104 Brian Leetch, NYRa.	1.00	.20
105 Mark Messier, NYRa.	3.00	.50
106 Mattias Norström, NYRa.	.40	.20
107 Pat Verbeek, NYRa.	.40	.20
108 Sergei Zubov, NYRa.	.40	.20
109 Don Beaupré (G), Otta.	.40	.20
110 Radek Bonk, Otta.	.40	.20
111 Alexandre Daigle, Otta.	.40	.20
112 Steve Larouche, Otta. RC	**1.00**	**.50**
113 Stanislav Neckar, Otta.	.40	.20
114 Alexei Yashin, Otta.	1.00	.20
115 Rod Brind'Amour, Phil.	.40	.20
116 Éric Desjardins, Phil.	.40	.20
117 Ron Hextall (G), Phil.	1.00	.20
118 John LeClair, Phil.	2.00	.50
119 Eric Lindros, Phil.	3.00	.50
120 Mikael Renberg, Phil.	.40	.20
121 Chris Therien, Phil.	.40	.20
122 Ron Francis, Pitt.	1.00	.20
123 Jaromir Jagr, Pitt.	3.00	.50
124 Joe Mullen, Pitt.	1.00	.20
125 Larry Murphy, Pitt.	.40	.20
126 Ulf Samuelsson, Pitt.	.40	.20
127 Kevin Stevens, Pitt.	.40	.20
128 Ken Wregget (G), Pitt.	.40	.20
129 Wendel Clark, Québ.	2.00	.50
130 Adam Deadmarsh, Québ.	.40	.20
131 Stéphane Fiset (G), Québ.	.40	.20
132 Peter Forsberg, Québ.	4.00	.50
133 Curtis Leschyshyn, Québ.	.40	.20
134 Owen Nolan, Québ.	1.00	.20
135 Mike Ricci, Québ.	.40	.20
136 Joe Sakic, Québ.	4.00	1.00
137 Denis Chassé, SLou.	.40	.20
138 Steve Duchesne, SLou.	.40	.20
139 Brett Hull, SLou.	3.00	.50
140 Curtis Joseph (G), SLou.	3.00	.50
141 Ian Laperrière, SLou.	.40	.20
142 Brendan Shanahan, SLou.	3.00	.50
143 Esa Tikkanen, SLou.	.40	.20
144 Ulf Dahlén, SanJ.	.40	.20
145 Jeff Friesen, SanJ.	.40	.20
146 Arturs Irbe (G), SanJ.	1.00	.20
147 Craig Janney, SanJ.	.40	.20
148 Sergei Makarov, SanJ.	1.00	.20
149 Sandis Ozolinsh, SanJ.	.40	.20
150 Ray Whitney, SanJ.	.40	.20
151 Chris Gratton, Tamp.	.40	.20
152 Roman Hamrlik, Tamp.	.40	.20
153 Petr Klima, Tamp.	.40	.20
154 Brantt Myhres, Tamp. RC	**1.00**	**.50**
155 Daren Puppa (G), Tamp.	.40	.20
156 Jason Wiemer, Tamp.	.40	.20
157 Paul Ysebaert, Tamp.	.40	.20
158 Dave Andreychuk, Toro.	.40	.20
159 Tie Domi, Toro.	.40	.20
160 Doug Gilmour, Toro.	1.00	.20
161 Kenny Jönsson, Toro.	.40	.20
162 Félix Potvin (G), Toro.	1.00	.20
163 Mike Ridley, Toro.	.40	.20
164 Mats Sundin, Toro.	3.00	.50
165 Jeff R. Brown, Vanc.	.40	.20
166 Pavel Bure, Vanc.	2.00	.50
167 Geoff Courtnall, Vanc.	.40	.20
168 Russ Courtnall, Vanc.	.40	.20
169 Trevor Linden, Vanc.	1.00	.20
170 Kirk McLean (G), Vanc.	.40	.20
171 Roman Oksiuta, Vanc.	.40	.20
172 Peter Bondra, Wash.	1.00	.20
173 Jim Carey (G), Wash.	.40	.20
174 Martin Gendron, Wash.	.40	.20
175 Dale Hunter, Wash.	.40	.20
176 Calle Johansson, Wash.	.40	.20
177 Michal Pivonka, Wash.	.40	.20
178 Mark Tinordi, Wash.	.40	.20
179 Nelson Emerson, Winn.	.40	.20
180 Nikolai Khabibulin (G), Winn.	1.00	.20
181 Dave Manson, Winn.	.40	.20
182 Teppo Numminen, Winn.	.40	.20
183 Teemu Selänne, Winn.	2.00	.50
184 Keith Tkachuk, Winn.	1.00	.20
185 Alexei Zhamnov, Winn.	.40	.20
186 Martin Brodeur (G) [Champions]	4.00	1.00
187 Neal Broten [Champions]	.40	.20
188 Bob Carpenter [Champions]	.40	.20
189 Ken Daneyko [Champions]	.40	.20
190 Bruce Driver [Champions]	.40	.20
191 Bill Guerin [Champions]	1.00	.20
192 Claude Lemieux [Champions]	.40	.20
193 John MacLean [Champions]	.40	.20
194 Scott Niedermayer [Champions]	.40	.20
195 Stéphane Richer [Champions]	.40	.20
196 Scott Stevens [Champions]	1.00	.20
197 Scott Stevens, w/ Stanley Cup	1.00	.20
198 Checklist	.40	.20
199 Checklist	.40	.20
200 Checklist	.40	.20
201 Todd Krygier, Anah.		.20
202 Steve Rucchin, Anah.		.20
203 Mike Sillinger, Anah.		.20
204 Ted Donato, Bost.		.20
205 Shawn McEachern, Bost.		.20
206 Joe Mullen, Bost.		.20
207 Kevin Stevens, Bost.		.20
208 Don Sweeney, Bost.		.20
209 Mark Astley, Buff.		.20
210 Randy Burridge, Buff.		.20
211 Jason Dawe, Buff.		.20
212 Michael Peca, Buff.		.20
213 Michael Nylander, Calg.		.20
214 Cory Stillman, Calg.		.20
215 Pavel Torgajev, Calg. RC		**.50**
216 Tony Amonte, Chic.		.20
217 Joe Murphy, Chic.		.20
218 Bob Probert, Chic.		.20
219 Denis Savard, Chic.		.20
220 Stéphane Fiset (G), Colo.		.20
221 Valeri Kamensky, Colo.		.20
222 Sylvain Lefebvre, Colo.		.20
223 Claude Lemieux, Colo.		.20
224 Sandis Ozolinsh, Colo.		.20
225 Patrick Roy (G), Colo.		1.50
226 Scott A. Young, Colo.		.20
227 Greg A. Adams, Dall.		.20
228 Guy Carbonneau, Dall.		.20
229 Dave Gagner, Dall.		.20
230 Kevin Hatcher, Dall.		.20
231 Darcy Wakaluk, Dall.		.20
232 Dino Ciccarelli, Detr.		.20
233 Greg Johnson, Detr.		.20
234 Igor Larionov, Detr.		.20
235 Darren McCarty, Detr.		.20
236 Chris Osgood (G), Detr.		.20
237 Zdeno Ciger, Edmo.		.20
238 Bryan Marchment, Edmo.		.20
239 Boris Mironov, Edmo.		.20
240 Peter White, Edmo.		.20
241 Jody Hull, Flor.		.20
242 Scott Mellanby, Flor.		.20
243 Gord Murphy, Flor.		.20
244 Jason Woolley, Flor.		.20
245 Gerald Diduck, Hart.		.20
246 Nelson Emerson, Hart.		.20
247 Brendan Shanahan, Hart.		.50
248 Glen Wesley, Hart.		.20
249 Tony Granato, LosA.		.20
250 Dmitri Khristich, LosA.		.20
251 Jari Kurri, LosA.		.50
252 Éric Lacroix, LosA.		.20
253 Yanic Perreault, LosA.		.20
254 Patrice Brisebois, Mont.		.20
255 Benoît Brunet, Mont.		.20
256 Valeri Bure, Mont.		.20
257 Stéphane Quintal, Mont.		.20
258 Jocelyn Thibault (G), Mont.		.20
259 Shawn Chambers, NJer.		.20
260 Jim Dowd, NJer.		.20
261 Bill Guerin, NJer.		.20
262 Bobby Holik, NJer.		.20
263 Steve Thomas, NJer.		.20
264 Esa Tikkanen, NJer.		.20
265 Wendel Clark, NYIs.		.50
266 Travis Green, NYIs.		.20
267 Brett Lindros, NYIs.		.20
268 Kirk Muller, NYIs.		.20
269 Zigmund Palffy, NYIs.		.20
270 Mathieu Schneider, NYIs.		.20
271 Alexander Semak, NYIs.		.20
272 Dennis Vaske, NYIs.		.20
273 Ray Ferraro, NYRa.		.20
274 Adam Graves, NYRa.		.20
275 Alexei Kovalev, NYRa.		.20
276 Mike Richter (G), NYRa.		.20
277 Luc Robitaille, NYRa.		.50
278 Ulf Samuelsson, NYRa.		.20
279 Steve Duchesne, Otta.		.20
280 Trent McCleary, Otta. RC		**.50**
281 Dan Quinn, Otta.		.20
282 Martin Straka, Otta.		.20
283 Karl Dykhuis, Phil.		.20
284 Pat Falloon, Phil.		.20
285 Joel Otto, Phil.		.20
286 Kjell Samuelsson, Phil.		.20
287 Garth Snow (G), Phil.		.20
288 Mario Lemieux, Pitt.		1.50
289 Norm Maciver, Pitt.		.20
290 Dmitri Mironov, Pitt.		.20
291 Markus Näslund, Pitt.		.50
292 Petr Nedved, Pitt.		.20
293 Tomas Sandström, Pitt.		.20
294 Bryan Smolinski, Pitt.		.20
295 Sergei Zubov, Pitt.		.20
296 Shayne Corson, SLou.		.20
297 Geoff Courtnall, SLou.		.20
298 Grant Fuhr (G), SLou.		.20
299 Dale Hawerchuk, SLou.		.20
300 Al MacInnis, SLou.		.20
301 Brian Noonan, SLou.		.20
302 Chris Pronger, SLou.		.20
303 Andrei Nazarov, SanJ.		.20
304 Owen Nolan, SanJ.		.20
305 Ray Sheppard, SanJ.		.20
306 Chris Terreri (G), SanJ.		.20
307 Brian Bellows, Tamp.		.20
308 Brian Bradley, Tamp.		.20
309 John Cullen, Tamp.		.20
310 Alexander Selivanov, Tamp.		.20
311 Mike Gartner, Toro.		.50
312 Benoît Hogue, Toro.		.20
313 Sergio Momesso, Toro.		.20
314 Larry Murphy, Toro.		.20
315 Dave Babych, Vanc.		.20
316 Bret Hedican, Vanc.		.20

☐	317 Alexander Mogilny, Vanc.	.20
☐	318 Mike Ridley, Vanc.	.20
☐	319 Peter Bondra, Wash.	.20
☐	320 Jim Carey (G), Wash.	.20
☐	321 Sylvain Côté, Wash.	.20
☐	322 Sergei Gonchar, Wash.	.20
☐	323 Joé Juneau, Wash.	.20
☐	324 Steve Konowalchuk, Wash.	.20
☐	325 Pat Peake, Wash.	.20
☐	326 Dallas Drake, Winn.	.20
☐	327 Igor Korolev, Winn.	.20
☐	328 Darren Turcotte, Winn.	.20
☐	**329 Daniel Alfredsson, Otta. RC**	**3.00**
☐	**330 Aki Berg, LosA. RC**	**.50**
☐	**331 Todd Bertuzzi, NYIs. RC**	**6.00**
☐	332 Jason Bonsignore, Edmo.	.20
☐	**333 Curtis Brown, Buff. RC**	**.50**
☐	334 Byron Dafoe (G), LosA.	.50
☐	335 Éric Dazé, Chic.	.50
☐	**336 Shane Doan, Winn. RC**	**1.00**
☐	337 Jason Doig, Winn.	.20
☐	**338 Radek Dvorak, Flor. RC**	**1.00**
☐	**339 Joe Dziedzic, Pitt. RC**	**.50**
☐	340 Darby Hendrickson, Toro.	.20
☐	341 Brian Holzinger, Buff.	.20
☐	342 Ed Jovanovski, Flor.	.50
☐	**343 Chad Kilger, Anah. RC**	**1.00**
☐	344 Saku Koivu, Mont.	1.00
☐	345 Darren Langdon, NYRa.	.20
☐	346 Jamie Langenbrunner, Dall.	.20
☐	347 Jere Lehtinen, Dall.	.20
☐	348 Bryan McCabe, NYIs.	.20
☐	**349 Kyle McLaren, Bost. RC**	**1.00**
☐	350 Marty Murray, Calg.	.20
☐	351 Jeff O'Neill, Hart.	.50
☐	352 Deron Quint, Winn.	.20
☐	**353 Marcus Ragnarsson, SanJ. RC**	**1.00**
☐	354 Tommy Salo (G), NYIs.	.50
☐	**355 Miroslav Satan, Edmo. RC**	**1.50**
☐	356 Jamie Storr (G), LosA.	.20
☐	357 Niklas Sundström, NYRa.	.20
☐	**358 Robert Svehla, Flor. RC**	**1.00**
☐	359 Denis Pederson, NJer.	.20
☐	**360 Antti Törmänen, Otta. RC**	**.50**
☐	361 Brendan Witt, Wash.	.20
☐	362 Vitali Yachmenev, LosA.	.20
☐	**363 Stéphane Yelle, Colo. RC**	**.50**
☐	364 Tom Barrasso (G), Pitt. [No Entry]	.20
☐	365 Ed Belfour (G), Chic. [No Entry]	.50
☐	366 Martin Brodeur (G), NJer. [No Entry]	1.00
☐	367 Sean Burke (G), Hart. [No Entry]	.20
☐	368 Jim Carey (G), Wash. [No Entry]	.20
☐	369 Stéphane Fiset (G), Colo. [No Entry]	.20
☐	370 Dominik Hasek (G), Buff. [No Entry]	.50
☐	371 Ron Hextall (G), Phil. [No Entry]	.20
☐	372 N. Khabibulin (G), Winn. [No Entry]	.20
☐	373 Kirk McLean (G), Vanc. [No Entry]	.20
☐	374 Chris Osgood (G), Detr. [No Entry]	.20
☐	375 Félix Potvin (G), Toro. [No Entry]	.20
☐	376 Daren Puppa (G), Tamp. [No Entry]	.20
☐	377 Patrick Roy (G), Colo. [No Entry]	1.50
☐	378 J. Vanbiesbrouck (G), Flor. [No Entry]	.20
☐	379 Pavel Bure, Vanc. [Ultra Cool]	.50
☐	380 Chris Chelios, Chic. [Ultra Cool]	.20
☐	381 Sergei Fedorov, Detr. [Ultra Cool]	.50
☐	382 Theoren Fleury, Calg. [Ultra Cool]	.20
☐	383 Peter Forsberg, Colo. [Ultra Cool]	.50
☐	384 Ron Francis, Pitt. [Ultra Cool]	.20
☐	385 Wayne Gretzky, SLou. [Ultra Cool]	4.00
☐	386 Brett Hull, SLou. [Ultra Cool]	.50
☐	387 Jaromir Jagr, Pitt. [Ultra Cool]	.50
☐	388 Paul Kariya, Anah. [Ultra Cool]	.50
☐	389 Pat LaFontaine, Buff. [Ultra Cool]	.20
☐	390 Brian Leetch, NYRa. [Ultra Cool]	.20
☐	391 Mario Lemieux, Pitt. [Ultra Cool]	1.50
☐	392 Eric Lindros, Phil. [Ultra Cool]	.50
☐	393 Mark Messier, NYRa. [Ultra Cool]	.50
☐	394 Mike Modano, Dall. [Ultra Cool]	.50
☐	395 Adam Oates, Bost. [Ultra Cool]	.20
☐	396 Jeremy Roenick, Chic. [Ultra Cool]	.50
☐	397 Joe Sakic, Colo. [Ultra Cool]	1.00
☐	398 Alexei Zhamnov, Winn. [Ultra Cool]	.20
☐	399 Checklist	.20
☐	400 Checklist	.20

ALL-ROOKIE

There are two versions to this set: regular inserts and Gold Medallion.

Insert Set (10 cards):		50.00	20.00
	Insert	G.M.	AR
☐☐	1 Jim Carey (G), Wash.	4.00	2.00
☐☐	2 Mariusz Czerkawski, Bost.	4.00	2.00
☐☐	3 Peter Forsberg, Québ.	15.00	6.00
☐☐	4 Jeff Friesen, SanJ.	4.00	2.00
☐☐	5 Paul Kariya, Anah.	15.00	6.00
☐☐	6 Blaine Lacher (G), Bost.	4.00	2.00
☐☐	7 Ian Laperrière, SLou.	4.00	2.00
☐☐	8 Todd Marchant, Edmo.	4.00	2.00
☐☐	9 Roman Oksiuta, Vanc.	4.00	2.00
☐☐	10 David Oliver, Edmo.	4.00	2.00

CREASE CRASHERS

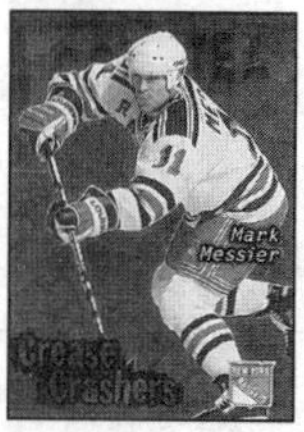

Series Two Insert Set (20 cards):		170.00
	Insert (1:18 Retail)	CC
☐	1 Jason Arnott, Edmo.	10.00
☐	2 Rod Brind'Amour, Phil.	5.00
☐	3 Theoren Fleury, Calg.	10.00
☐	4 Todd Harvey, Dall.	5.00
☐	5 John LeClair, Phil.	15.00
☐	6 Claude Lemieux, Colo.	5.00
☐	7 Trevor Linden, Vanc.	5.00
☐	8 Eric Lindros, Phil.	20.00
☐	9 Darren McCarty, Detr.	5.00
☐	10 Scott Mellanby, Flor.	5.00
☐	11 Mark Messier, NYRa.	20.00
☐	12 Cam Neely, Bost.	20.00
☐	13 Owen Nolan, Québ.	10.00
☐	14 Keith Primeau, Detr.	5.00
☐	15 Jeremy Roenick, Chic.	15.00
☐	16 Tomas Sandström, Pitt.	5.00
☐	17 Brendan Shanahan, Hart.	20.00
☐	18 Kevin Stevens, Bost.	5.00
☐	19 Rick Tocchet, LosA.	5.00
☐	20 Keith Tkachuk, Winn.	10.00

EXTRA ATTACKER

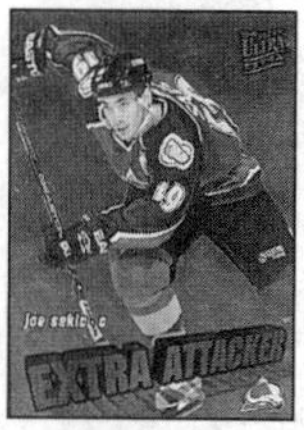

Series Two Insert Set (20 cards):		115.00
	Insert (1:18 Hobby)	EA
☐	1 Peter Bondra, Wash.	3.00
☐	2 Éric Dazé, Chic.	3.00
☐	3 Radek Dvorak, Flor.	3.00
☐	4 Sergei Fedorov, Detr.	5.00
☐	5 Peter Forsberg, Colo.	5.00
☐	6 Ron Francis, Pitt.	3.00
☐	7 Wayne Gretzky, LosA.	25.00
☐	8 Brett Hull, SLou.	5.00
☐	9 Jaromir Jagr, Pitt.	5.00
☐	10 Ed Jovanovski, Flor.	3.00
☐	11 Paul Kariya, Anah.	5.00
☐	12 Saku Koivu, Mont.	10.00
☐	13 Mario Lemieux, Pitt.	18.00
☐	14 Mike Modano, Dall.	5.00
☐	15 Alexander Mogilny, Vanc.	3.00
☐	16 Adam Oates, Bost.	3.00
☐	17 Joe Sakic, Colo.	10.00
☐	18 Niklas Sundström, NYRa.	3.00
☐	19 Mats Sundin, Toro.	5.00
☐	20 Steve Yzerman, Detr.	15.00

HIGH SPEED

Series Two Insert Set (20 cards):		30.00
	Insert (1:5)	HS
☐	1 Daniel Alfredsson, Otta.	4.00
☐	2 Jason Arnott, Edmo.	1.00
☐	3 Todd Bertuzzi, NYIs.	9.00
☐	4 Radek Bonk, Otta.	1.00
☐	5 Martin Brodeur (G), NJer.	5.00
☐	6 Alexandre Daigle, Otta.	.50
☐	7 Shane Doan, Winn.	.50
☐	8 Peter Forsberg, Colo.	5.00
☐	9 Roman Hamrlik, Tamp.	.50
☐	10 Todd Harvey, Dall.	.50
☐	11 Paul Kariya, Anah.	5.00
☐	12 Travis Green, NYIs.	.50
☐	13 Chris Osgood (G), Detr.	2.00
☐	14 Zigmund Palffy, NYIs.	2.00
☐	15 Marcus Ragnarsson, SanJ.	.50
☐	16 Mikael Renberg, Phil.	1.00
☐	17 Brian Savage, Mont.	1.00
☐	18 Robert Svehla, Flor.	.50
☐	19 Jocelyn Thibault (G), Mont.	1.00
☐	20 Brendan Witt, Wash.	.50

PREMIER PAD MEN

There are two versions to this set: regular inserts and Gold Medallion.

Insert Set (12 cards):		300.00	150.00
	Insert	G.M.	PPM
☐☐	1 Ed Belfour (G), Chic.	35.00	15.00
☐☐	2 Sean Burke (G), Hart.	20.00	10.00
☐☐	3 Martin Brodeur (G), NJer.	55.00	25.00
☐☐	4 Jim Carey (G), Wash.	15.00	8.00
☐☐	5 Dominik Hasek (G), Buff.	35.00	15.00
☐☐	6 Curtis Joseph (G), SLou.	35.00	15.00
☐☐	7 Blaine Lacher (G), Bost.	15.00	8.00
☐☐	8 Andy Moog (G), Dall.	15.00	8.00
☐☐	9 Félix Potvin (G), Toro.	20.00	10.00
☐☐	10 Patrick Roy (G), Mont.	100.00	50.00
☐☐	11 John Vanbiesbrouck (G), Flor.	15.00	8.00
☐☐	12 Mike Vernon (G), Detr.	15.00	8.00

PREMIER PIVOTS

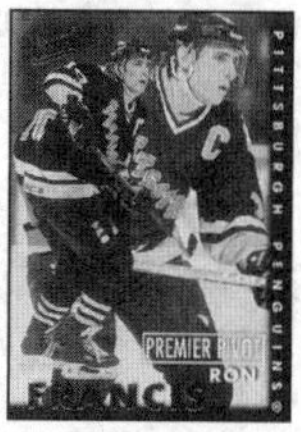

There are two versions to this set: regular inserts and Gold Medallion.

Insert Set (10 cards):		50.00	22.00
	Insert	G.M.	PP
☐☐	1 Sergei Fedorov, Detr.	5.00	2.00
☐☐	2 Ron Francis, Pitt.	3.00	1.00
☐☐	3 Wayne Gretzky, LosA.	20.00	10.00
☐☐	4 Eric Lindros, Phil.	5.00	2.00
☐☐	5 Mark Messier, NYRa.	5.00	2.00
☐☐	6 Adam Oates, Bost.	2.00	1.00
☐☐	7 Jeremy Roenick, Chic.	4.00	2.00
☐☐	8 Joe Sakic, Québ.	8.00	4.00
☐☐	9 Mats Sundin, Toro.	5.00	2.00
☐☐	10 Alexei Zhamnov, Winn.	2.00	1.00

RED LIGHT SPECIALS

There are two versions to this set: regular inserts and Gold Medallion.

Insert Set (10 cards):		15.00	6.00
	Insert	G.M.	RLS
☐☐	1 Peter Bondra, Wash.	2.00	1.00
☐☐	2 Theoren Fleury, Calg.	2.00	1.00
☐☐	3 Brett Hull, SLou.	3.00	1.00
☐☐	4 Jaromir Jagr, Pitt.	3.00	1.00
☐☐	5 John LeClair, Phil.	2.00	1.00
☐☐	6 Eric Lindros, Phil.	3.00	1.00
☐☐	7 Cam Neely, Bost.	3.00	1.00
☐☐	8 Owen Nolan, Québ.	2.00	1.00
☐☐	9 Ray Sheppard, Detr.	1.00	.50
☐☐	10 Alexei Zhamnov, Winn.	1.00	.50

RISING STARS

There are two versions to this set: regular inserts and Gold Medallion.

Insert Set (10 cards):		35.00	15.00
	Insert	G.M.	RS
☐☐	1 Jason Arnott, Edmo.	4.00	2.00
☐☐	2 Alexandre Daigle, Otta.	4.00	2.00
☐☐	3 Roman Hamrlik, Tamp.	4.00	2.00
☐☐	4 Trevor Kidd (G), Calg.	4.00	2.00
☐☐	5 Scott Niedermayer, NJer.	4.00	2.00
☐☐	6 Keith Primeau, Detr.	4.00	2.00
☐☐	7 Mikael Renberg, Phil.	4.00	2.00
☐☐	8 Jocelyn Thibault (G), Québ.	4.00	2.00
☐☐	9 Alexei Yashin, Otta.	6.00	3.00
☐☐	10 Alexei Zhitnik, Buff.	4.00	2.00

ULTRAVIEW

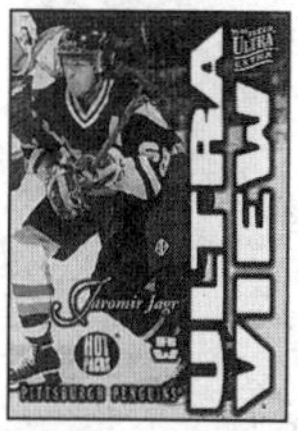

This set has two versions: the regular insert and Hot Packs inserts. "Hot Packs" versions came all in one pack.

Series Two Insert Set (10 cards):		40.00	100.00
	Insert	Hot Packs	UV
☐☐	1 Sergei Fedorov, Detr.	3.00	8.00
☐☐	2 Wayne Gretzky, LosA.	14.00	35.00
☐☐	3 Dominik Hasek (G), Buff.	3.00	8.00
☐☐	4 Jaromir Jagr, Pitt.	3.00	8.00
☐☐	5 Brian Leetch, NYRa.	3.00	6.00
☐☐	6 Mario Lemieux, Pitt.	10.00	25.00
☐☐	7 Eric Lindros, Phil.	3.00	8.00
☐☐	8 Jeremy Roenick, Chic.	3.00	6.00
☐☐	9 Joe Sakic, Colo.	6.00	14.00
☐☐	10 Alexei Zhamnov, Winn.	3.00	6.00

1995 - 96 FUTURE LEGENDS

Complete Set (50 cards):		35.00
Common Player:		.65
	Player	NRMT-MT
☐	1 Brad Bombardir, Albany	.65
☐	2 Niklas Andersson, Phoenix	.65
☐	3 Mike Dunham (G), Albany	1.50
☐	4 Anders Eriksson, Adirondack	.65
☐	5 Kelly Fairchild, St. John's	.65
☐	6 Chris Ferraro, Binghampton	.65
☐	7 Peter Ferraro, Binghampton	.65
☐	8 Éric Fichaud (G), Worcester	.65
☐	9 Manny Legacé (G), Springfield	1.00
☐	10 David Ling, Saint John	.65
☐	11 Jim Montgomery, Hershey	.65
☐	12 Chris Murray, Fredericton	.65
☐	13 Rob Brown, Chicago-IHL	.65
☐	14 Rem Murray, Cape Breton	.65
☐	15 Rob Murray, Springfield	.65
☐	16 Jan Caloun, Kansas City	.65
☐	17 Frédéric Chabot (G), Cincinatti	.65
☐	18 Craig Fischer, Orlando	.65
☐	19 Dwayne Roloson (G), Saint John	.65
☐	20 Brad Smyth, Carolina	.65
☐	21 Steve Sullivan, Albany	1.00
☐	22 Petr Sykora, Albany	1.50
☐	23 Darcy Tucker, Fredericton	.65
☐	24 Landon Wilson, Cornwall	.65
☐	25 Greg Hawgood, Las Vegas	.65
☐	26 Stéphane Beauregard (G), San Francisco	.65
☐	27 Aki Berg, Phoenix	.65
☐	28 Matt Johnson, Phoenix	.65
☐	29 Curtis Joseph (G), Las Vegas	4.00
☐	30 Dan Lambert, Los Angeles	.65
☐	31 Eric Lecompte, Indianapolis	.65
☐	32 Brett Lievers, Utah	.65
☐	33 Mark McArthur, Utah	.65
☐	34 Ethan Moreau, Indianapolis	.65
☐	35 Marty Murray, Saint John	.65
☐	36 Wayne Primeau, Rochester	.65
☐	37 John Purves, San Francisco	.65
☐	38 Manon Rhéaume (G)	4.50
☐	39 Barry Richter, Binghampton	.65
☐	40 Jamie Rivers, Worcester	.65
☐	41 Tommy Salo (G), Utah	1.50
☐	42 Jamie Storr (G), Phoenix	.65
☐	43 Tom Tilley, Milwaukee	.65
☐	44 Derek Wilkinson, Atlanta	.65
☐	45 Mike Wilson, Rochester	.65
☐	46 Sandis Ozolinsh, San Francisco	.65
☐	47 Andrew Brunette, Portland-AHL	.65
☐	48 James Black, Indianapolis	.65
☐	49 Terry Yake, Milwaukee	.65
☐	50 Mike Prokopec, Indianapolis	.65

HOT PICKS

Two autographed cards came cellophane wrapped in each foil box.

	Player	Auto.
☐	1 Chris Philips ✍	10.00
☐	2 Boyd Devereaux ✍	10.00
☐	3 Richard Jackman ✍	8.00
☐	4 Marcus Nilson ✍	8.00

PLATINUM CLUB

Insert Set (8 cards):		40.00
	Player	PC
☐	1 Mike Dunham (G), AHL All-Stars	10.00
☐	2 Eric Fichaud (G)	4.00
☐	3 Manny Legacé (G)	8.00
☐	4 Steve Sullivan	8.00
☐	5 Darcy Tucker	5.00
☐	6 Jamie Langenbrunner	5.00
☐	7 Ethan Moreau	4.00
☐	8 Jamie Storr (G)	5.00

SIGNED SEALED & DELIVERED

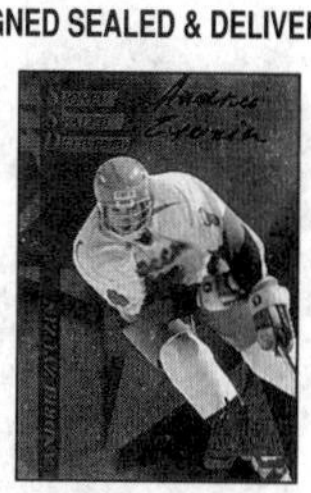

Card number 7 has not been confirmed to exist.

	Insert	Auto.
☐	1 Alexandre Volchkov ✍	5.00
☐	2 Chris Allen ✍	5.00
☐	3 Brian Bonin ✍	5.00
☐	4 Josh Green ✍	5.00
☐	5 Chris Hajt ✍	5.00

☐	6 Josh Holden ✍	5.00
☐	8 Andrei Zyuzin, Rus. ✍	5.00

1995 - 96 HOYLE EASTERN CONFERENCE

Patrick Roy is the most expensive single at $1.00-1.50. Singles start at 10¢.

Complete Deck (54 cards): 8.00

	Player		Player
☐	JOKER Alexei Yashin	☐	JOKER Sergei Zubov
☐	A♣ Joe Sakic	☐	2♣ Mikael Renberg
☐	3♣ Stéphane Richer	☐	4♣ Mike Richter (G)
☐	5♣ Luc Robitaille	☐	6♣ Geoff Sanderson
☐	7♣ Brian Smolinski	☐	8♣ Kevin Stevens
☐	9♣ Scott Stevens	☐	10♣ Steve Thomas
☐	J♣ Darren Turcotte	☐	Q♣ Vanbiesbrouck (G)
☐	K♣ New Jersey Devils	☐	A♦ Mark Messier
☐	2♦ Brian Leetch	☐	3♦ Alexander Mogilny
☐	4♦ Kirk Muller	☐	5♦ Cam Neely
☐	6♦ Rob Niedermayer	☐	7♦ Scott Niedermayer
☐	8♦ Owen Nolan	☐	9♦ Adam Oates
☐	10♦ Michal Pivonka	☐	J♦ Derek Plante
☐	Q♦ Chris Pronger	☐	K♦ Mark Recchi
☐	A♥ Eric Lindros	☐	2♥ Peter Bondra
☐	3♥ Radek Bonk	☐	4♥ Ray Bourque
☐	5♥ Brian Bradley	☐	6♥ Rod Brind'Amour
☐	7♥ Martin Brodeur (G)	☐	8♥ Wendel Clark
☐	9♥ Alexandre Daigle	☐	10♥ V. Damphousse
☐	J♥ Ray Ferraro	☐	Q♥ Stéphane Fiset (G)
☐	K♥ Peter Forsberg	☐	A♠ Patrick Roy (G)
☐	2♠ Chris Gratton	☐	3♠ Adam Graves
☐	4♠ Dominik Hasek (G)	☐	5♠ Ron Hextall (G)
☐	6♠ Jaromir Jagr	☐	7♠ Joé Juneau
☐	8♠ Dimitri Khristich	☐	9♠ Petr Klima
☐	10♠ Bob Kudelski	☐	J♠ Scott Lachance
☐	Q♠ Pat LaFontaine	☐	K♠ John LeClair

1995 - 96 HOYLE WESTERN CONFERENCE

Wayne Gretzky is the most expensive single at $1-2. Singles start at 10¢.

Complete Deck (54 cards): 8.00

	Player		Player
☐	JOKER Alexei Zhamnov	☐	JOKER Steve Yzerman
☐	A♣ Wayne Gretzky	☐	2♣ Joe Sacco
☐	3♣ Denis Savard	☐	4♣ Teemu Selänne
☐	5♣ B. Shanahan	☐	6♣ Ray Sheppard
☐	7♣ Mats Sundin	☐	8♣ Esa Tikkanen
☐	9♣ German Titov	☐	10♣ Keith Tkachuk
☐	J♣ Rick Tocchet	☐	Q♣ Doug Weight
☐	K♣ Detroit Red Wings	☐	A♦ Pavel Bure
☐	2♦ Jari Kurri	☐	3♦ Igor Larionov
☐	4♦ Nicklas Lidström	☐	5♦ Trevor Linden
☐	6♦ Marty McSorley	☐	7♦ Mike Modano
☐	8♦ Bernie Nicholls	☐	9♦ Joe Nieuwendyk
☐	10♦ David Oliver	☐	J♦ Félix Potvin (G)
☐	Q♦ Bill Ranford (G)	☐	K♦ Gary Roberts
☐	A♥ Jeremy Roenick	☐	2♥ Dave Andreychuk
☐	3♥ Jason Arnott	☐	4♥ Ed Belfour (G)
☐	5♥ Rob Blake	☐	6♥ Jeff Brown
☐	7♥ Patrik Carnback	☐	8♥ Chris Chelios
☐	9♥ T. Chevelade (G)	☐	10♥ Paul Coffey
☐	J♥ Shayne Corson	☐	Q♥ Geoff Courtnall
☐	K♥ Russ Courtnall	☐	A♠ Sergei Fedorov
☐	2♠ Ulf Dahlen	☐	3♠ Pat Falloon
☐	4♠ Theoren Fleury	☐	5♠ Doug Gilmour
☐	6♠ Todd Harvey	☐	7♠ Kevin Hatcher
☐	8♠ Guy Hebert (G)	☐	9♠ Phil Housley
☐	10♠ Brett Hull	☐	J♠ Arturs Irbe (G)
☐	Q♠ Curtis Joseph (G)	☐	K♠ Paul Kariya

1995 - 96 KELLOGG'S - DONRUSS

One of six different cards were found in specially marked boxes of Kellogg's cereal.

Complete Set (6 cards): 15.00

	Player	NRMT-MT
☐	Brett Hull - 50 in 50	2.00
☐	Brett Hull - Hart Trophy	2.00
☐	Mario Lemieux - 500 Goals	4.00
☐	Mario Lemieux - Return	4.00
☐	Mario Lemieux - The Fiver	4.00
☐	Mario Lemieux - Stanley Cup	4.00

1995 - 96 KELLOGG'S POP-UPS

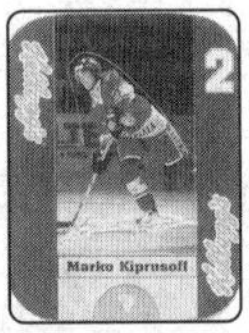

We have no pricing information on this set.

	Player
☐	1 Jarmo Myllys (G)
☐	2 Marko Kiprusoff
☐	3 Hannu Virta
☐	4 Ville Peltonen
☐	5 Saku Koivu
☐	6 Sami Kapanen

1995 - 96 KRAFT

Master Set (79 cards): 75.00
Album: 30.00

JELL-O INSTANT PUDDING / HOTTEST TICKET

Cards are on the back of specially marked boxes.
Card Size: 2 3/4" x 4 1/4"

Complete Set (14 cards): 15.00

	Player	NRMT-MT
☐	Jason Arnott, Edmo.	1.00
☐	Wendel Clark, NYIs.	1.50
☐	Alexandre Daigle, Otta.	1.00
☐	Sergei Fedorov, Detr.	2.00
☐	Peter Forsberg, Colo.	2.50
☐	Doug Gilmour, Toro.	1.00
☐	Phil Housley, Calg.	1.00
☐	Joé Juneau, Wash.	1.00
☐	Mario Lemieux, Pitt.	5.00
☐	Trevor Linden, Vanc.	1.00
☐	Cam Neely, Bost.	2.00
☐	Teemu Selänne, Winn.	1.50
☐	Scott Stevens, NJer.	1.00
☐	Pierre Turgeon, Mont.	1.00

JELL-O PUDDING SNACKS / CREASE KEEPERS

Two of 18 different cards were found on boxes of specially marked packages of JELL-O Pudding. JELL-O flavours and pairings were: Butterscotch (Burke & Hextall (G) or Vanbiesbrouck (G) & Richter); Chocolate (Belfour (G) & Puppa or Kidd (G) & Fuhr (G)); Chocolate Fudge (Belfour (G) & Puppa or Hasek (G) & Fiset); Chocolate Marshmellow (Kidd & Fuhr (G)); Banana (Vernon (G) & McLean); Vanilla (Vernon (G) & McLean); Raspberry (Potvin & Carey); and Strawberry (Moog (G) & Roy). Two of 8 different mini cards were found on boxes of specially marked packages of JELL-O Pudding.

Complete Set (26 cards): 25.00

	Player	NRMT-MT
☐	Tom Barrasso (G), Pitt.	1.00
☐	Don Beaupré (G), Otta.	1.00
☐	Ed Belfour (G), Chic.	2.00
☐	Martin Brodeur (G), NJer.	3.00
☐	Sean Burke (G), Hart.	1.00
☐	Jim Carey (G), Wash.	1.00
☐	Tim Chevelade (G), Winn.	1.00
☐	Stéphane Fiset (G), Colo.	1.00
☐	Grant Fuhr (G), SLou.	1.00
☐	Dominik Hasek (G), Buff.	2.00
☐	Guy Hebert (G), Anah.	1.00
☐	Ron Hextall (G), Phil.	1.00
☐	Kelly Hrudey (G), LosA.	1.00
☐	Arturs Irbe (G), SanJ.	1.00
☐	Trevor Kidd (G), Calg.	1.00
☐	Blaine Lacher (G), Bost.	1.00
☐	Kirk McLean (G), Vanc.	1.00
☐	Andy Moog (G), Bost.	1.00
☐	Félix Potvin (G), Toro.	1.00
☐	Daren Puppa (G), Tamp.	1.00
☐	Bill Ranford (G), Edmo.	1.00
☐	Mike Richter (G), NYRa.	1.00
☐	Patrick Roy (G), Mont.	6.00
☐	Tommy Söderström (G), NYIs.	1.00
☐	John Vanbiesbrouck (G), Flor.	1.00
☐	Mike Vernon (G), Detr.	1.00

KRAFT DINNER / SHOOTING STARS

One of 20 different cards could be found on the backs of specially marked 225g boxes of Kraft Dinner and one of six different cards were found on the back of specially marked 225g boxes of Kraft Dinner specialty flavours.

Complete Set (26 cards): 30.00

	Player	NRMT-MT
☐	Jesse Bélanger, Flor.	1.00
☐	Peter Bondra, Wash.	1.00
☐	Brian Bradley, Tamp.	1.00
☐	Pavel Bure, Vanc.	1.50
☐	Andrew Cassels, Hart.	1.00
☐	Paul Coffey, Detr.	1.00
☐	Ulf Dahlén, SanJ.	1.00
☐	Alexandre Daigle, Otta.	1.00
☐	Ray Ferraro, NYRa.	1.00
☐	Theoren Fleury, Calg.	1.00
☐	Dave Gagner, Dall.	1.00
☐	Wayne Gretzky, LosA.	5.00
☐	Brett Hull, SLou.	2.00
☐	Jaromir Jagr, Pitt.	1.00
☐	Paul Kariya, Anah.	1.00
☐	Eric Lindros, Phil.	2.00
☐	Mark Messier, NYRa.	2.00
☐	Alexander Mogilny, Vanc.	1.00
☐	Bernie Nicholls, Chic.	1.00
☐	Adam Oates, Bost.	1.00
☐	Mark Recchi, Mont.	1.00
☐	Stéphane Richer, NJer.	1.00
☐	Joe Sakic, Colo.	3.00
☐	Mats Sundin, Toro.	2.00
☐	Doug Weight, Edmo.	1.00
☐	Alexei Zhamnov, Winn.	1.00

KRAFT PEANUT BUTTER / ALL-STARS

One of 13 different disks were found under the lids of specially marked jars of Kraft Peanut Butter.

Complete Set (13 disks): 15.00

	Player	NRMT-MT
☐	Ed Belfour (G), Chic.	2.50
☐	Raymond Bourque, Bost.	3.00
☐	Chris Chelios, Chic.	1.50
☐	Paul Coffey, Detr.	1.50
☐	Theoren Fleury, Calg.	1.50
☐	Dominik Hasek (G), Buff.	2.50
☐	Jaromir Jagr, Pitt.	1.00
☐	John LeClair, Phil.	2.00
☐	Eric Lindros, Phil.	1.00
☐	Larry Murphy, Toro.	1.00
☐	Keith Tkachuk, Winn.	1.50
☐	Alexei Zhamnov, Winn.	1.00
☐	Devils	2.50

1995 - 96 LEAF

Complete Set (330 cards): 30.00
Common Player: .20

	Player	NRMT-MT
☐	1 Mario Lemieux, Pitt.	1.50
☐	2 Todd Harvey, Dall.	.20
☐	3 Blaine Lacher (G), Bost.	.20
☐	4 Alexei Zhitnik, Buff.	.20
☐	5 Cory Stillman, Calg.	.20
☐	6 Murray Craven, Chic.	.20
☐	7 Mike Kennedy, Dall.	.20
☐	8 Mike Vernon (G), Detr.	.20
☐	9 David Oliver, Edmo.	.20
☐	**10 Magnus Svensson, Flor. RC**	**.50**
☐	11 Andrei Nikolishin, Hart.	.20
☐	12 Jamie Storr (G), LosA.	.20
☐	13 David Roberts, SLou.	.20
☐	**14 Chris McAlpine, NJer. RC**	**.50**
☐	15 Brett Lindros, NYIs.	.20
☐	16 Pat Verbeek, NYRa.	.20
☐	17 Tony Amonte, Chic.	.20
☐	18 Chris Therien, Phil.	.20
☐	19 Ken Wregget (G), Pitt.	.20
☐	20 Peter Forsberg, Québ. (Colo.)	.50
☐	21 Jeff Friesen, SanJ.	.20
☐	22 Patrice Tardif, SLou.	.20
☐	23 Jason Wiemer, Tamp.	.20
☐	24 Kenny Jönsson, Toro.	.20
☐	25 Jassen Cullimore, Vanc.	.20
☐	26 Sergei Gonchar, Wash.	.20
☐	27 Nikolai Khabibulin (G), Winn.	.20
☐	28 Oleg Tverdovsky, Anah.	.20
☐	29 Rick Tocchet, LosA.	.20
☐	30 Garry Galley, Buff.	.20
☐	31 German Titov, Calg.	.20
☐	32 Sergei Krivokrasov, Chic.	.20
☐	33 Sylvain Turgeon, Otta.	.20
☐	34 Sergei Fedorov, Detr.	.50
☐	35 Ralph Intranuovo, Edmo.	.20
☐	36 Stu Barnes, Flor.	.20
☐	37 Mike Gartner, Toro.	.50
☐	38 Kevin Brown, LosA.	.20
☐	39 Valeri Bure, Mont.	.20
☐	40 Sergei Brylin, NJer.	.20
☐	41 Kirk Muller, NYIs.	.20
☐	42 Mike Richter (G), NYRa.	.20
☐	43 Stanislav Neckar, Otta.	.20
☐	44 Patrik Juhlin, Phil.	.20
☐	45 Ron Francis, Pitt.	.20
☐	46 Janne Laukkanen, Québ. (Colo.)	.20
☐	47 Shean Donovan, SanJ.	.20
☐	48 Igor Korolev, Winn.	.20
☐	49 Alexander Selivanov, Tamp.	.20
☐	50 Frantisek Kucera, Hart.	.20
☐	51 Russ Courtnall, Vanc.	.20
☐	52 Don Beaupré (G), Otta.	.20
☐	53 Michal Grosek, Winn.	.20
☐	54 Steve Rucchin, Anah.	.20
☐	55 Mariusz Czerkawski, Bost.	.20
☐	56 Dominik Hasek (G), Buff.	.50
☐	57 Trent Klatt, Dall.	.20
☐	58 Sergio Momesso, Vanc. (Toro.)	.20
☐	59 Mark Lawrence, Dall.	.20
☐	60 Steve Yzerman, Detr.	1.50
☐	61 Todd Marchant, Edmo.	.20
☐	62 Jesse Bélanger, Flor.	.20
☐	63 Sean Burke (G), Hart.	.20
☐	64 Matt Johnson, LosA.	.20
☐	65 Mark Recchi, Mont.	.20
☐	66 Martin Brodeur (G), NJer.	1.00
☐	67 Mathieu Schneider, NYIs.	.20
☐	68 Mark Messier, NYRa.	.50
☐	69 Radim Bicanek, Otta.	.20
☐	70 Éric Desjardins, Phil.	.20
☐	71 Jaromir Jagr, Pitt.	.50
☐	72 Adam Deadmarsh, Québ. (Colo.)	.20
☐	73 Viktor Kozlov, SanJ.	.20
☐	74 Jeff Norton, SLou.	.20
☐	**75 Brantt Myhres, Tamp. RC**	**.50**
☐	76 Darby Hendrickson, Toro.	.20
☐	77 Roman Oksiuta, Vanc.	.20
☐	78 Jim Carey (G), Wash. [Error]	.20
☐	79 Keith Tkachuk, Winn.	.20
☐	80 Valeri Karpov, Anah.	.20
☐	81 Adam Oates, Bost.	.20
☐	82 Eric Lindros, Phil.	.50
☐	83 Trevor Kidd (G), Calg.	.20
☐	84 Bernie Nicholls, Chic.	.20
☐	**85 Craig Conroy, Mont. RC**	**1.50**
☐	86 Bill Ranford (G), Edmo.	.20
☐	87 Scott Mellanby, Flor.	.20
☐	88 Geoff Sanderson, Hart.	.20
☐	89 Wayne Gretzky, LosA.	2.50
☐	90 Pierre Turgeon, Mont.	.20
☐	91 Stéphane Richer, NJer.	.20
☐	**92 Chris Marinucci, NYIs. RC**	**.50**
☐	93 Brian Leetch, NYRa.	.20
☐	**94 Steve Larouche, Otta. RC**	**.50**
☐	95 John LeClair, Phil.	.50
☐	96 Dmitri Mironov, Toro. (Pitt.)	.20
☐	97 Jocelyn Thibault (G), Québ. (Colo.)	.20
☐	98 Craig Janney, SanJ.	.20
☐	99 Ian Laperrière, SLou.	.20
☐	100 Dino Ciccarelli, Detr.	.20
☐	101 Todd Warriner, Toro.	.20
☐	102 Kirk McLean (G), Vanc.	.20
☐	103 Jason Allison, Wash.	.20
☐	104 Alexei Zhamnov, Winn.	.20
☐	105 Keith Jones, Wash.	.20
☐	106 Raymond Bourque, Bost.	.50
☐	107 John Druce, LosA.	.20
☐	**108 Scott Walker, Vanc. RC**	**1.00**
☐	109 Joe Murphy, Chic.	.20
☐	110 Checklist	.20
☐	111 Philippe DeRouville, Pitt.	.20
☐	112 Greg A. Adams, Dall.	.20
☐	113 Cam Neely, Bost.	.50
☐	114 Michael Peca, Vanc. (Buff.)	.20
☐	115 Theoren Fleury, Calg.	.20
☐	116 Jeremy Roenick, Chic.	.50
☐	117 Kevin Hatcher, Dall.	.20
☐	118 Ray Sheppard, Detr.	.20
☐	119 Jason Arnott, Edmo.	.20
☐	120 Mark Fitzpatrick (G), Flor.	.20
☐	121 Brendan Shanahan, SLou. (Hart.)	.50
☐	122 Jari Kurri, LosA.	.50
☐	123 Shayne Corson, Edmo. (SLou.)	.20
☐	124 Scott Stevens, NJer.	.20
☐	125 Steve Thomas, NYIs.	.20
☐	126 Sergei Zubov, NYRa. (Pitt.)	.20
☐	127 Denis Savard, Chic.	.20
☐	128 Mikael Renberg, Phil.	.20
☐	129 Luc Robitaille, Pitt. (NYRa.)	.50
☐	130 Andrei Kovalenko, Québ. (Colo.)	.20
☐	131 Andrei Nazarov, SanJ.	.20
☐	132 Denis Chassé, SLou.	.20
☐	133 Chris Gratton, Tamp.	.20
☐	134 Benoît Hogue, Dall.	.20
☐	135 Pavel Bure, Vanc.	.50

☐ 136 Peter Bondra, Wash. .20
☐ 137 Teemu Selänne, Winn. .50
☐ **138 Darren Van Impe, Anah. RC .50**
☐ 139 Dmitri Khristich, Wash. (LosA.) .20
☐ 140 Pat LaFontaine, Buff. .20
☐ 141 Phil Housley, Calg. .20
☐ 142 Chris Chelios, Chic. .20
☐ 143 Steve Duchesne, SLou. (Otta.) .20
☐ 144 Paul Coffey, Detr. .20
☐ 145 Doug Weight, Edmo. .20
☐ 146 Gord Murphy, Flor. .20
☐ 147 Andrew Cassels, Hart. .20
☐ 148 Rob Blake, LosA. .20
☐ 149 Vladimir Malakhov, Mont. .20
☐ 150 Scott Niedermayer, NJer. .20
☐ 151 Patrick Flatley, NYIs. .20
☐ 152 Adam Graves, NYRa. .20
☐ 153 Alexei Yashin, Otta. .20
☐ 154 Rod Brind'Amour, Phil. .20
☐ 155 Joe Mullen, Pitt. .20
☐ 156 Mike Ricci, Québ. (Colo.) .20
☐ 157 Ulf Dahlén, SanJ. .20
☐ 158 Dave Manson, Winn. .20
☐ 159 Brian Bradley, Tamp. .20
☐ 160 Félix Potvin (G), Toro. .20
☐ 161 Trevor Linden, Vanc. .20
☐ 162 Michal Pivonka, Wash. .20
☐ 163 Nelson Emerson, Winn. .20
☐ 164 Joe Sacco, Anah. .20
☐ 165 Todd Elik, SLou. (Bost.) .20
☐ 166 Derek Plante, Buff. .20
☐ 167 Mike Sullivan, Calg. .20
☐ 168 Randy Wood, Toro. .20
☐ 169 Manny Fernandez (G), Dall. .50
☐ 170 Keith Primeau, Detr. .20
☐ 171 Marko Tuomainen, Edmo. .20
☐ 172 John Vanbiesbrouck (G), Flor. .20
☐ 173 Darren Turcotte, Winn. .20
☐ 174 Tony Granato, LosA. .20
☐ 175 Brian Savage, Mont. .20
☐ 176 John MacLean, NJer. .20
☐ **177 Tommy Salo (G), NYIs. RC 2.00**
☐ 178 Steve Larmer, NYRa. .20
☐ 179 Alexandre Daigle, Otta. .20
☐ 180 Petr Svoboda, Phil. .20
☐ 181 John Cullen, Tamp. .20
☐ 182 Joe Sakic, Québ. (Colo.) 1.00
☐ 183 Sandis Ozolinsh, SanJ. .20
☐ 184 Dale Hawerchuk, Buff. (SLou.) .20
☐ 185 Paul Ysebaert, Tamp. .20
☐ 186 Larry Murphy, Toro. .20
☐ 187 Alexander Mogilny, Buff. (Vanc.) .20
☐ 188 Joé Juneau, Wash. .20
☐ **189 Craig Martin, Winn. RC .50**
☐ 190 Jason Marshall, Anah. .20
☐ 191 Don Sweeney, Bost. .20
☐ 192 Ron Hextall (G), Phil. .20
☐ 193 Steve Chiasson, Calg. .20
☐ 194 J. Steve Smith, Chic. .20
☐ 195 Lyle Odelein, Mont. .20
☐ 196 Ryan Smyth, Edmo. .20
☐ 197 Rob Niedermayer, Flor. .20
☐ 198 Steven Rice, Hart. .20
☐ 199 Darryl Sydor, LosA. .20
☐ 200 Patrick Roy (G), Mont. 1.50
☐ 201 Bill Guerin, NJer. .20
☐ 202 Scott Lachance, NYIs. .20
☐ 203 Alexei Kovalev, NYRa. .20
☐ 204 Ronnie Stern, Calg. .20
☐ 205 Kevin Dineen, Hart. .20
☐ 206 Ulf Samuelsson, Pitt. (NYRa.) .20
☐ 207 Wendel Clark, Toro. .50
☐ 208 Ray Whitney, SanJ. .20
☐ 209 Brett Hull, SLou. .50
☐ 210 Vyacheslav Kozlov, Detr. .20
☐ 211 Doug Gilmour, Toro. .20
☐ 212 Mike Ridley, Toro. (Vanc.) .20
☐ **213 Mike Torchia, Dall. (Wash.) RC .50**
☐ **214 Tavis Hansen, Winn. RC .50**
☐ 215 Dale Hunter, Wash. .20
☐ 216 Kevin Stevens, Pitt. (Bost.) .20
☐ 217 Mike Donnelly, Dall. .20
☐ 218 Sylvain Côté, Wash. .20
☐ 219 Gary Suter, Chic. .20
☐ 220 Checklist .20
☐ 221 Richard Park, Pitt. .20
☐ 222 Dave Gagner, Dall. .20
☐ 223 Jozef Stumpel, Bost. .20
☐ 224 Brad May, Buff. .20
☐ 225 Zarley Zalapski, Calg. .20
☐ 226 Éric Dazé, Chic. .50
☐ 227 Mike Modano, Dall. .50
☐ 228 Nicklas Lidström, Detr. .20
☐ 229 Jason Bonsignore, Edmo. .20
☐ **230 Robert Svehla, Flor. RC 1.00**
☐ 231 Glen Wesley, Hart. .20
☐ 232 Josef Beranek, Vanc. .20
☐ 233 Geoff Courtnall, Vanc. (SLou.) .20
☐ 234 Shawn Chambers, NJer. .20
☐ 235 Darius Kasparaitis, NYIs. .20
☐ 236 Sergei Nemchinov, NYRa. .20
☐ 237 Patrick Poulin, Chic. .20
☐ 238 Anatoli Semenov, Phil. .20
☐ 239 Bryan Smolinski, Bost. (Pitt.) .20
☐ 240 Owen Nolan, Québ. (Colo.) .20
☐ 241 Pat Falloon, SanJ. .20
☐ 242 Chris Pronger, Hart. (SLou.) .20
☐ 243 Daren Puppa (G), Tamp. .20
☐ 244 Mats Sundin, Toro. .50
☐ 245 Jeff R. Brown, Vanc. .20
☐ 246 Jeff Nelson, Wash. .20
☐ 247 Teppo Numminen, Winn. .20
☐ 248 Shaun Van Allen, Anah. .20
☐ 249 Yanic Perreault, LosA. .20
☐ **250 Brian Holzinger, Buff. RC .50**
☐ 251 Paul Kruse, Calg. .20
☐ 252 Jeff Shantz, Chic. .20
☐ 253 Martin Straka, Otta. .20
☐ 254 Chris Osgood (G), Detr. .20
☐ **255 Joaquin Gage (G), Edmo. RC .50**
☐ 256 Dave Lowry, Flor. .20
☐ 257 Robert Kron, Hart. .20
☐ 258 Dan Quinn, LosA. (Otta.) .20
☐ 259 David Wilkie, Mont. .20
☐ 260 Valeri Zelepukin, NJer. .20
☐ 261 Derek King, NYIs. .20
☐ **262 Darren Langdon, NYRa. RC 1.00**
☐ 263 Radek Bonk, Otta. .20
☐ 264 Karl Dykhuis, Phil. .20
☐ 265 Tomas Sandström, Pitt. .20
☐ 266 Uwe Krupp, Québ. (Colo.) .20
☐ 267 Arturs Irbe (G), SanJ. .20
☐ 268 Dallas Drake, Winn. .20
☐ 269 John Tucker, Tamp. .20
☐ 270 Dave Andreychuk, Toro. .20
☐ 271 Guy Hebert (G), Anah. .20
☐ **272 Sandy Moger, Bost. RC .50**
☐ 273 Craig Johnson, SLou. .20
☐ 274 Donald Audette, Buff. .20
☐ 275 Cory Cross, Tamp. .20
☐ 276 Richard Smehlik, Buff. .20
☐ 277 Gary Roberts, Calg. .20
☐ 278 Todd Gill, Toro. .20
☐ 279 Derian Hatcher, Dall. .20
☐ 280 Viacheslav Fetisov, Detr. .20
☐ 281 Curtis Joseph (G), SLou. (Edmo.) .50
☐ 282 Johan Garpenlöv, Flor. .20
☐ 283 Vladimir Konstantinov, Detr. .20
☐ 284 Ray Ferraro, NYIs. (NYRa.) .20
☐ 285 Turner Stevenson, Mont. .20
☐ 286 Neal Broten, NJer. .20
☐ **287 Jason Widmer, NYIs. RC .50**
☐ 288 Mattias Norström, NYRa. .20
☐ 289 Michel Picard, Otta. .20
☐ 290 Brent Fedyk, Phil. .20
☐ 291 Dmitry Yushkevich, Phil. (Toro.) .20
☐ 292 Sylvain Lefebvre, Québ. (Colo.) .20
☐ 293 Sergei Makarov, SanJ. .20
☐ 294 Brian Rolston, NJer. .20
☐ 295 Roman Hamrlik, Tamp. .20
☐ **296 Mark Wotton, Vanc. RC .50**
☐ **297 Alek Stojanov, Vanc. RC .50**
☐ 298 Calle Johansson, Wash. .20
☐ 299 Mike Eastwood, Winn. .20
☐ 300 Bob Corkum, Anah. .20
☐ 301 Petr Nedved, NYRa. (Pitt.) .20
☐ 302 Vincent Damphousse, Mont. .20
☐ **303 Brett Harkins, Bost. (Flor.) RC .50**
☐ 304 Paul Kariya, Anah. .50
☐ 305 Joe Nieuwendyk, Dall. .20
☐ **306 Dennis Bonvie, Edmo. RC .50**
☐ 307 Jason Woolley, Flor. .20
☐ 308 Jimmy Carson, Hart. .20
☐ 309 Marty McSorley, LosA. .20
☐ **310 Craig Rivet, Mont. RC .50**
☐ 311 Claude Lemieux, NJer. .20
☐ 312 Al MacInnis, SLou. .20
☐ 313 Gerald Diduck, Chic. (Hart.) .20
☐ 314 Randy McKay, NJer. .20
☐ 315 Bob Errey, Detr. .20
☐ **316 Rusty Fitzgerald, Pitt. RC .50**
☐ 317 Scott A. Young, Québ. (Colo.) .20
☐ 318 Igor Larionov, Detr. .20
☐ 319 Esa Tikkanen, SLou. .20
☐ 320 Darren McCarty, Detr. .20
☐ 321 Petr Klima, Tamp. .20
☐ 322 Jon Rohloff, Bost. .20
☐ 323 Steve Konowalchuk, Wash. .20
☐ 324 Milos Holan, Anah. .20
☐ 325 Checklist .20
☐ 326 Ted Donato, Bost. .20
☐ **327 Grant Marshall, Dall. RC .50**
☐ 328 Jyrki Lumme, Vanc. .20
☐ 329 Ed Belfour (G), Chic. .50
☐ 330 Checklist .20

FIRE ON ICE

Insert Set (12 cards): 105.00
Insert (#/10,000) FOI
☐ 1 Pavel Bure, Vanc. 5.00
☐ 2 Eric Lindros, Phil. 10.00
☐ 3 Alexei Zhamnov, Winn. 5.00
☐ 4 Paul Coffey, Detr. 5.00
☐ 5 Theoren Fleury, Calg. 5.00
☐ 6 Peter Forsberg, Québ. (Colo.) 10.00
☐ 7 Sergei Fedorov, Detr. 10.00
☐ 8 Mats Sundin, Toro. 10.00
☐ 9 Brett Hull, SLou. 10.00
☐ 10 Wayne Gretzky, LosA. 40.00
☐ 11 Paul Kariya, Anah. 10.00
☐ 12 Mikael Renberg, Phil. 5.00

FREEZE FRAME

Insert Set (8 cards): 60.00
Insert (#/10,000) FF
☐ 1 Jim Carey (G), Wash. 5.00
☐ 2 Pierre Turgeon, Mont. [XCX: Malakhov] 5.00
☐ 3 Mikael Renberg, Phil. 5.00
☐ 4 Jaromir Jagr, Pitt. 10.00
☐ 5 Alexei Zhamnov, Winn. 5.00
☐ 6 Devils with Stanley Cup 5.00
☐ 7 Mario Lemieux, Pitt. 30.00
☐ 8 Alexander Mogilny, Vanc. [cameo: P.Bure] 8.00

GOLD LEAF STAR

Retail Insert Set (6 cards): 35.00
Insert (#/5000) NRMT-MT
☐ 1 J. Carey / D. Hasek (G) 6.00
☐ 2 C. Chelios / P. Coffey 6.00
☐ 3 R. Bourque / B. Leetch 10.00
☐ 4 E. Lindros / A. Zhamnov 6.00
☐ 5 T. Fleury / J. Jagr 10.00
☐ 6 Br. Hull / M. Renberg 6.00

LEMIEUX'S BEST

Insert Set (10 cards): 50.00
Insert LB
☐ 1 Mario Lemieux, Pitt. [10/11/1984] 6.00
☐ 2 Lemieux, Canada (Pitt.) [09/15/1987] 6.00
☐ 3 Mario Lemieux, All-Star [02/09/1988] 6.00
☐ 4 Mario Lemieux, Pitt. [12/31/1988] 6.00
☐ 5 Mario Lemieux, Pitt. [1988] 6.00
☐ 6 Mario Lemieux, Pitt. [04/25/1989] 6.00
☐ 7 Mario Lemieux, All-Star [01/21/1990] 6.00
☐ 8 Mario Lemieux, Pitt. [05/25/1991] 6.00
☐ 9 Mario Lemieux, Pitt. [06/01/1992] 6.00
☐ 10 Mario Lemieux, Pitt. [03/02/1993] 6.00

ROAD TO THE CUP

Hobby Insert Set (10 cards): 75.00
Insert (#/5000) RTTC
☐ 1 Ray Whitney, SanJ. 6.00
☐ 2 Martin Brodeur (G), NJer. 20.00
☐ 3 Jaromir Jagr, Pitt. 15.00
☐ 4 Eric Lindros, Phil. 15.00
☐ 5 Paul Coffey, Detr. 6.00
☐ 6 Chris Chelios, Chic. 6.00
☐ 7 Neal Broten, NJer. 6.00
☐ 8 Vyacheslav Kozlov, Detr. 6.00
☐ 9 Scott Niedermayer, NJer. 6.00
☐ 10 Claude Lemieux, NJer. 6.00

STUDIO ROOKIE

Insert Set (20 cards): 30.00
Insert SR
☐ 1 Jim Carey (G), Wash. 1.00
☐ 2 Peter Forsberg, Québ. 9.00
☐ 3 Paul Kariya, Anah. 9.00
☐ 4 David Oliver, Edmo. 1.00
☐ 5 Blaine Lacher (G), Bost. 1.00
☐ 6 Oleg Tverdovsky, Anah. 1.00
☐ 7 Jeff Friesen, SanJ. 2.00
☐ 8 Todd Marchant, Edmo. 1.00
☐ 9 Todd Harvey, Dall. 1.00
☐ 10 Ian Laperrière, SLou. 1.00
☐ 11 Éric Dazé, Chic. 2.00
☐ 12 Jason Bonsignore, Edmo. 1.00
☐ 13 Jamie Storr (G), LosA. 1.00
☐ 14 Brian Holzinger, Buff. 1.00
☐ 15 Brian Savage, Mont. 2.00
☐ 16 Roman Oksiuta, Vanc. 1.00
☐ 17 Mariusz Czerkawski, Bost. 1.00
☐ 18 Sergei Krivokrasov, Chic. 1.00
☐ 19 Jason Wiemer, Tamp. 1.00
☐ 20 Radek Bonk, Otta. 2.00

1995 - 96 LEAF ELIT SET

The most expensive single is Johan Hedberg (G) at $4-5. NHL stars sell at $1-3. Other singles sell between 30¢ and $1.00.

Series One Set (150 cards): 40.00
Series Two Set (160 cards): 40.00

Player	Player
☐ 1 Håkan Loob	☐ 2 CL: AIK
☐ 3 AIK stats	☐ 4 Joakim Persson (G)
☐ 5 Niclas Hävelid	☐ 6 Tony Barthelsson
☐ 7 Patric Aberg	☐ 8 Johan Akerman
☐ 9 Dick Tarnström	☐ 10 Stefan Gustavson
☐ 11 Anders Gozzi	☐ 12 Morgan Samuelsson
☐ 13 CL: Brynäs	☐ 14 Brynas stats
☐ 15 Michael Sundlov (G)	☐ 16 Stefan Klockare
☐ 17 Bedrich Scerban	☐ 18 Andreas Dackell
☐ 19 Fredrik Modin	☐ 20 Ove Molin
☐ 21 Mikael Wahlberg	☐ 22 Thomas Tallberg
☐ 23 Peter Larsson	☐ 24 Stefan Ketola
☐ 25 CL: Djugardens	☐ 26 Djugardens stats
☐ 27 Jonas Forsberg (G)	☐ 28 Christian Due-Boje
☐ 29 Mikael Magnusson	☐ 30 Thomas Johansson
☐ 31 Joakim Musakka	☐ 32 Erik Huusko
☐ 33 Jens Ohling	☐ 34 Per Eklund
☐ 35 Espen Knutsen	☐ 36 Patrik Erickson
☐ 37 CL: Farjestads	☐ 38 Farjestads stats
☐ 39 Patrik Haltia (G)	☐ 40 Sergei Fokin
☐ 41 Thomas Rhodin	☐ 42 Stefan Nilsson
☐ 43 Magnus Arvedsson	☐ 44 Mattias Johansson
☐ 45 Clas Eriksson	☐ 46 Peter Ottosson
☐ 47 CL: HV71	☐ 48 HV71 stats
☐ 49 Boo Ahl (G)	☐ 50 Kenneth Kennholt
☐ 51 Hans Abrahamsson	☐ 52 Peter Hammarstrom
☐ 53 Johan Davidsson	☐ 54 Stefan Falk
☐ 55 Johan Lindbom	☐ 56 Esa Keskinen
☐ 57 Stefan Ornskog	☐ 58 Peter Ekelund
☐ 59 CL: Leksand	☐ 60 Leksand stats
☐ 61 Johan Hedberg (G)	☐ 62 Tomas Jonsson
☐ 63 Hans Lodin	☐ 64 Orjan Lindmark
☐ 65 Jan Huokko	☐ 66 Markus Eriksson
☐ 67 Andreas Karlsson	☐ 68 Mikael Holmberg
☐ 69 Jonas Bergqvist	☐ 70 Nicklas Eriksson
☐ 71 Per-Erik Eklund	☐ 72 CL: Lulea
☐ 73 Lulea stats	☐ 74 Jarmo Myllys (G)
☐ 75 Mattias Öhlund	☐ 76 Lars Modig
☐ 77 Torbjorn Lindberg	☐ 78 Roger Åkerström
☐ 79 Stefan Jonsson	☐ 80 Johan Rosen
☐ 81 Tomas Berglund	☐ 82 Robert Nordberg
☐ 83 Jiri Kucera	☐ 84 Thomas Holmstrom
☐ 85 CL: Malmo	☐ 86 Malmo stats
☐ 87 Peter Andersson	☐ 88 Roger Ohman
☐ 89 Marcus Magnertoft	☐ 90 Patrik Sylvegard
☐ 91 Hakan Ahlund	☐ 92 Jesper Matsson
☐ 93 Roger Hansson	☐ 94 Mattias Bosson
☐ 95 Bo Svanberg	☐ 96 Raimo Helminen
☐ 97 CL: MoDo	☐ 98 MoDo stats
☐ 99 Petter Ronnqvist (G)	☐ 100 Lars Jansson
☐ 101 Mattias Timmander	☐ 102 Hans Jonsson
☐ 103 Anders Soderberg	☐ 104 Martin Hostak
☐ 105 Kyosti Karjalainen	☐ 106 Mikael Hakansson
☐ 107 Per Svartvadet	☐ 108 A. Salomonsson
☐ 109 Lars Bystrom	☐ 110 Magnus Wernblom
☐ 111 CL: Rogle	☐ 112 Rogle stats
☐ 113 Magnus Sward (G)	☐ 114 Arto Ruotanen
☐ 115 Johan Finnstrom	☐ 116 Daniel Tjarnqvist
☐ 117 Pierre Johnsson	☐ 118 Per Wallin
☐ 119 Michael Johansson	☐ 120 P-J Svensson
☐ 121 Roger Elvenes	☐ 122 Mats Loov
☐ 123 Michael Hjalm	☐ 124 CL: Vasteras
☐ 125 Vasteras stats	☐ 126 Mats Ytter (G)
☐ 127 Erik Bergstrom	☐ 128 Lars Ivarsson
☐ 129 Mishat Fahrutdinov	☐ 130 Claes Lindblom
☐ 131 Paul Andersson	☐ 132 Henrik Nordfeldt
☐ 133 Alexei Salomatin	☐ 134 Mikael Pettersson
☐ 135 CL: Frolunda	☐ 136 Frolunda stats
☐ 137 H. Algotsson (G)	☐ 138 J. A-Junkka
☐ 139 Stefan Larsson	☐ 140 Par Djoos
☐ 141 Ronnie Sundin	☐ 142 Par Edlund
☐ 143 Peter Berndtsson	☐ 144 Joacim Esbjors
☐ 145 Alexander Beljavski	☐ 146 Jonas Esbjors
☐ 147 Marku Jantunen	☐ 148 Peter Strom
☐ 149 Checklist 1 - 75	☐ 150 Checklist 76 - 150
☐ 151 AIK	☐ 152 Tommy Lehmann
☐ 153 Mikael Nilsson	☐ 154 Juha Jokiharju
☐ 155 Stefan Andersson	☐ 156 Thomas Strandberg
☐ 157 Mats Lindberg	☐ 158 Peter Gerhardsson
☐ 159 Tommy Lehmann	☐ 160 Tommy Hedlund
☐ 161 Peter Wallin	☐ 162 Björn Ahlström
☐ 163 Erik Hamalainen	☐ 164 Patric Englund
☐ 165 Rikard Franzen	☐ 166 Brynas IF
☐ 167 Brynas	☐ 168 Lars Karlsson
☐ 169 Jonas Lofstrom	☐ 170 Stefan Polla
☐ 171 Mikael Lind	☐ 172 Brian Rafalski
☐ 173 Roger Kyro	☐ 174 P-J Johansson
☐ 175 Greg Parks	☐ 176 Per Lofstrom
☐ 177 Jonas Johnson	☐ 178 Mikael Lindman
☐ 179 Mikael Wiklander	☐ 180 Tommy Melkersson
☐ 181 Djugardens IF	☐ 182 Djugardens
☐ 183 Thomas Ostlund	☐ 184 Patrik Hofbauer
☐ 185 Magnus Jansson	☐ 186 Nichlas Falk
☐ 187 Ola Josefsson	☐ 188 Joakim Lundberg
☐ 189 Fredrik Lindquist	☐ 190 Patrik Kjellberg
☐ 191 Jan Viktorsson	☐ 192 Bjorn Nord
☐ 193 Tommy Jacobsen	☐ 194 Anders Huusko
☐ 195 Kristofer Ottosson	☐ 196 Vastra Frolunda HC
☐ 197 Frolunda	☐ 198 Mikael Sanberg
☐ 199 Jerry Persson	☐ 200 Peter Hogardh
☐ 201 Stefan Axelsson	☐ 202 Lars Edstrom
☐ 203 L-G Wiklander	☐ 204 Per-Johan Axelsson
☐ 205 Henrik Nilsson	☐ 206 Petteri Nummelin
☐ 207 Christian Ruuttu	☐ 208 Oscar Ackerstrom
☐ 209 Farjestad BK	☐ 210 Farjestad
☐ 211 M. Ketterer (G)	☐ 212 Bjorn Eriksson
☐ 213 Jonas Höglund	☐ 214 Peter Nordstrom
☐ 215 Jorgen Jonsson	☐ 216 Greger Artursson
☐ 217 Jesper Duus	☐ 218 Roger Johansson
☐ 219 Leif Carlsson	☐ 220 Per Lundell
☐ 221 Vitali Prokhorov	☐ 222 HV71
☐ 223 HV 71	☐ 224 Kennth Johansson
☐ 225 T. Gustavsson	☐ 226 Marcus Thuresson
☐ 227 Vesa Salo	☐ 228 Kai Nurminen
☐ 229 Johan Brummer	☐ 230 Daniel Johansson
☐ 231 Per Gustafsson	☐ 232 Niklas Rahm
☐ 233 Leksands IF	☐ 234 Leksands
☐ 235 P-R Bergkvist	☐ 236 Anders Carlsson
☐ 237 Micael Karlberg	☐ 238 Torgny Lowgren

☐ 239 Stefan Hellkvist	☐ 240 Markus Akerblom
☐ 241 Joakim Lindgren	☐ 242 Tomas Forslund
☐ 243 Torbjorn Johansson	☐ 244 Nicklas Nordquist
☐ 245 Lulea HF	☐ 246 Lulea
☐ 247 Erik Grankvist	☐ 248 Mikael Lindholm
☐ 249 Johan Stromvall	☐ 250 Anders Burstrom
☐ 251 Lars Hurtig	☐ 252 Stefan Nilsson
☐ 253 Jan Mertzig	☐ 254 Petter Nilsson
☐ 255 Malmo IF	☐ 256 Malmo IF
☐ 257 Peter Lindmark	☐ 258 Roger Nordstrom
☐ 259 Andres Lilja	☐ 260 Brian McReynolds
☐ 261 Ilja Byakin	☐ 262 Robert Burakovsky
☐ 263 Mikael Burakovsky	☐ 264 Stafn Elvenes
☐ 265 Johan Salle	☐ 266 Kim Johnsson
☐ 267 Peter Hasselblad	☐ 268 Marko Palo
☐ 269 MoDo Hockey	☐ 270 MoDo
☐ 271 Fredrik Andersson	☐ 272 Frantisek Kaberle
☐ 273 Samuel Pahlsson	☐ 274 Jan Larsson
☐ 275 PA Lundstrom	☐ 276 Tomas Nansen
☐ 277 Marcus Karlsson	☐ 278 Jan-Axel Alavaara
☐ 279 Kristian Gahn	☐ 280 Rogle BK
☐ 281 Rogle	☐ 282 Patrick Backlund
☐ 283 Peter Lundmark	☐ 284 Anders Berglund
☐ 285 Harijs Vitolins	☐ 286 Jens Nielsen
☐ 287 Greg Brown	☐ 288 Bjorn Linden
☐ 289 Vasteras IK	☐ 290 Vasteras
☐ 291 Jacob Karlsson	☐ 292 Patrik Zetterberg
☐ 293 Mattias Loof	☐ 294 Johan Tornberg
☐ 295 Andrei Korolev	☐ 296 Mattias Olsson
☐ 297 Roger Rosen	☐ 298 Andrei Lulin
☐ 299 Edvin Frylen	☐ 300 Mats Lusth
☐ 301 Fredrik Oberg	☐ 302 AS: J. Myllys (G)
☐ 303 AS: T. Jonsson	☐ 304 AS: P. Andersson
☐ 305 AS: Håkan Loob	☐ 306 AS: Esa Keskinen
☐ 307 AS: C. Ruuttu	☐ 308 Checklist
☐ 309 Checklist	☐ 310 Checklist: (Inserts)

Super Chase	NRMT-MT
☐ Per-Erik Eklund	25.00
☐ HV71 Jonkoping (#/2000)	20.00

CHAMPS

Series Two Insert Set (15 cards):	65.00
Insert (#/3000)	Champ
☐ 1 Tomas Jonsson	5.00
☐ 2 Patrik Kjellberg	5.00
☐ 3 Håkan Loob	8.00
☐ 4 Peter Lindmark	5.00
☐ 5 Anders Carlsson	5.00
☐ 6 Raimo Helminen	6.00
☐ 7 Esa Keskinen	5.00
☐ 8 Jan Larsson	5.00
☐ 9 Roger Johansson	5.00
☐ 10 Andreas Dackell	5.00
☐ 11 Stefan Ornskog	5.00
☐ 12 Michael Sundlov	5.00
☐ 13 Per-Erik Eklund	5.00
☐ 14 Kenneth Kennholt	5.00
☐ 15 Jan Viktorsson	5.00

FACE TO FACE

Series Two Insert Set (15 cards):	50.00
Insert	FTF
☐ 1 Morgan Samuelsson/ Thomas Strandberg	4.00
☐ 2 Bedrich Scerban/ Greg Parks	4.00
☐ 3 Erik Huusko/ Anders Huusko	4.00
☐ 4 Stefan Larsson/ Marko Jantunen	4.00
☐ 5 Hakan Loob/ Roger Johansson	6.00
☐ 6 Kenneth Kennholt/ Per Gustafsson	4.00
☐ 7 Stefan Hellkvist/ Tomas Forslund	4.00
☐ 8 Thomas Holmstrom/ Roger Åkerström	4.00
☐ 9 Stefan Elvenes/ Robert Burakovsky	4.00
☐ 10 Martin Hostak/ Mattias Timander	4.00
☐ 11 Mats Loov/ Michael Hjalm	4.00
☐ 12 Alexei Salomatin/ Fredrik Oberg	4.00
☐ 13 Patrik Erickson/ Espen Knutsen	5.00
☐ 14 Peter Andersson/ Peter Hasselblad	4.00
☐ 15 Tomas Jonsson/ Markus Akerblom	5.00

GOLDIES

Series One Insert Set (10 cards):	35.00
Insert	Goldies
☐ 1 Morgan Samuelsson	4.50
☐ 2 Ove Molin	4.50
☐ 3 Fredrik Lindqvist	4.50
☐ 4 Peter Strom	4.50
☐ 5 Mattias Johansson	4.50
☐ 6 Stefan Ornskog	4.50
☐ 7 Niklas Eriksson	4.50
☐ 8 Johan Rosen	4.50
☐ 9 Roger Ohman	4.50
☐ 10 Anders Soderberg	4.50

LEAF MEGA

Series One Insert Set (15 cards):	80.00
Insert	NRMT-MT
☐ 1 Michael Sundlov (G)	5.00
☐ 2 Jonas Bergqvist	5.00
☐ 3 Marko Jantunen	5.00
☐ 4 Thomas Ostlund	5.00
☐ 5 Tomas Jonsson	6.00
☐ 6 Esa Keskinen	5.00
☐ 7 Roger Nordstrom	5.00
☐ 8 Mattias Öhlund	12.00
☐ 9 Håkan Loob	12.00
☐ 10 Raimo Helminen	9.00
☐ 11 Per-Erik Eklund	6.00
☐ 12 Jarmo Myllys (G)	6.00
☐ 13 Rikard Franzen	5.00
☐ 14 Christer Olsson	5.00
☐ 15 Per Gustafsson	5.00

ROOKIE

Series Two Insert Set (9 cards):	30.00
Player	NRMT-MT
☐ 1 Peter Wallin	4.00
☐ 2 Jan-Axel Alavaara	4.00
☐ 3 Nichlas Falk	4.00
☐ 4 Lars-Goran Wiklander	4.00
☐ 5 Torbjorn Johansson	4.00
☐ 6 Jan Mertzig	4.00
☐ 7 Mikael Burakovsky	4.00
☐ 8 Marcus Karlsson	4.00
☐ 9 Roger Rosen	4.00

SPIDERMEN

Series Insert Set (14 cards):	70.00
Insert	NRMT-MT
☐ 1 Joakim Persson (G)	5.00
☐ 2 Michael Sundlov (G)	5.00
☐ 3 Thomas Ostlund (G)	5.00
☐ 4 Hakan Algotsson (G)	5.00
☐ 5 Patrik Haltia (G)	5.00
☐ 6 Boo Ahl (G)	5.00
☐ 7 Johan Hedberg (G)	18.00
☐ 8 Jarmo Myllys (G)	5.00
☐ 9 Jonas Forsberg (G)	5.00
☐ 10 Petter Ronnqvist (G)	5.00
☐ 11 Magnus Swardh (G)	5.00
☐ 12 Mats Ytter (G)	5.00
☐ 13 Mikael Sandberg (G)	5.00
☐ 14 Roger Nordstrom (G)	5.00

1995 - 96 LEAF LIMITED

Complete Set (121 cards):	95.00
Common Player:	.35
Player	LL
☐ 1 Mario Lemieux, Pitt.	7.00
☐ 2 Peter Forsberg, Colo.	3.50
☐ 3 Geoff Courtnall, SLou.	.35
☐ 4 Vincent Damphousse, Mont.	1.50
☐ 5 Jason Allison, Wash.	1.50
☐ 6 Theoren Fleury, Calg.	1.50
☐ **7 Shane Doan, Winn. RC**	**3.50**
☐ 8 Chris Gratton, Tamp.	.50
☐ 9 Paul Kariya, Anah.	3.50
☐ **10 Radek Dvorak, Flor. RC**	**3.50**
☐ 11 Adam Graves, NYRa.	1.00
☐ 12 Donald Audette, Buff.	1.00
☐ 13 Craig Janney, SanJ.	.50
☐ 14 Sean Burke (G), Hart.	1.50
☐ 15 Ed Belfour (G), Chic.	2.50
☐ 16 Raymond Bourque, Bost.	3.00
☐ 17 Pavel Bure, Vanc.	2.00
☐ 18 Martin Brodeur (G), NJer.	4.00
☐ **19 Todd Bertuzzi, NYIs. RC**	**18.00**
☐ **20 Aki Berg, LosA. RC**	**2.00**
☐ 21 Dave Andreychuk, Toro.	.50
☐ 22 Jason Arnott, Edmo.	1.00
☐ 23 Ron Francis, Pitt.	1.50
☐ 24 Paul Coffey, Detr.	1.50
☐ **25 Daniel Alfredsson, Otta. RC**	**9.00**
☐ 26 Todd Harvey, Dall.	.50
☐ 27 Claude Lemieux, Colo.	.50
☐ 28 Brett Hull, SLou.	2.50
☐ 29 Félix Potvin (G), Toro.	1.50
☐ 30 Peter Bondra, Wash.	1.50
☐ 31 Trevor Kidd (G), Calg.	.50
☐ 32 Igor Korolev, Winn.	.35
☐ 33 Roman Hamrlik, Tamp.	.50
☐ **34 Chad Kilger, Anah. RC**	**3.50**
☐ 35 Rob Niedermayer, Flor.	.50
☐ 36 Richard Park, Pitt.	.50
☐ **37 Mathieu Dandenault, Detr. RC**	**2.00**
☐ 38 Alexandre Daigle, Otta.	.35
☐ 39 Jere Lehtinen, Dall.	1.50
☐ 40 Chris Chelios, Chic.	1.50
☐ 41 Blaine Lacher (G), Bost.	.35
☐ 42 Trevor Linden, Vanc.	1.00
☐ 43 Scott Niedermayer, NJer.	.50
☐ 44 Teemu Selänne, Winn.	2.00
☐ 45 Daymond Langkow, Tamp.	2.50
☐ 46 Oleg Tverdovsky, Anah.	.35
☐ 47 John Vanbiesbrouck (G), Flor.	1.00
☐ 48 Alexei Kovalev, NYRa.	1.50
☐ 49 Sergei Fedorov, Detr.	2.50
☐ 50 Alexei Yashin, Otta.	1.50
☐ 51 Mike Modano, Dall.	2.50
☐ 52 Sandis Ozolinsh, Colo.	.50
☐ 53 Ian Laperrière, SLou.	.35
☐ 54 Mark Recchi, Mont.	1.00
☐ 55 Jim Carey (G), Wash.	.35
☐ 56 Joe Nieuwendyk, Calg.	1.00
☐ 57 Keith Tkachuk, Winn.	1.50
☐ 58 Daren Puppa (G), Tamp.	.50
☐ 59 Jason Bonsignore, Edmo.	.50
☐ 60 Tomas Sandström, Pitt.	.50
☐ 61 Chris Osgood (G), Detr.	1.50
☐ 62 Jeff Friesen, SanJ.	.50
☐ 63 Jeff O'Neill, Hart.	2.00
☐ 64 Joe Sakic, Colo.	4.00
☐ 65 Éric Dazé, Chic.	2.00
☐ 66 Patrick Roy (G), Colo.	7.00
☐ 67 Kirk McLean (G), Vanc.	.50
☐ 68 Stéphane Richer, NJer.	.50
☐ 69 Rod Brind'Amour, Phil.	.50
☐ 70 Wendel Clark, NYIs.	2.00
☐ 71 Rob Blake, LosA.	1.50
☐ 72 Doug Gilmour, Toro.	1.50
☐ 73 Jaromir Jagr, Pitt.	2.50
☐ 74 Sergei Zubov, Pitt.	.50
☐ 75 Mark Messier, NYRa.	2.50
☐ 76 Dominik Hasek (G), Buff.	2.50
☐ 77 Viktor Kozlov, SanJ.	.50
☐ **78 Marcus Ragnarsson, SanJ. RC**	**3.50**
☐ 79 Jocelyn Thibault (G), Mont.	1.00
☐ 80 Jeremy Roenick, Chic.	2.00
☐ 81 Cam Neely, Bost.	2.50
☐ 82 Brian Savage, Mont.	.50
☐ 83 Alexander Mogilny, Vanc.	1.00
☐ 84 Steve Thomas, NJer.	.50
☐ 85 John LeClair, Phil.	2.00
☐ 86 Brett Lindros, NYIs.	.50
☐ 87 Wayne Gretzky, LosA.	10.00
☐ 88 Kenny Jönsson, Toro.	.50
☐ 89 David Oliver, Edmo.	.35
☐ 90 Brian Leetch, NYRa.	1.50
☐ 91 Luc Robitaille, NYRa.	2.00
☐ 92 Keith Primeau, Detr.	1.00
☐ 93 Owen Nolan, SanJ.	1.50
☐ 94 Brendan Shanahan, Hart.	2.50
☐ 95 Al MacInnis, SLou.	1.00
☐ 96 Kevin Stevens, Bost.	.50
☐ 97 Larry Murphy, Toro.	.50
☐ 98 Joé Juneau, Wash.	.50
☐ 99 Eric Lindros, Phil.	2.50
☐ 100 Travis Green, NYIs.	.50
☐ 101 Jamie Storr (G), LosA.	.50
☐ 102 Pierre Turgeon, Mont.	1.00
☐ 103 Bill Ranford (G), Edmo.	1.00
☐ 104 Niklas Sundström, NYRa.	1.00
☐ 105 Steve Yzerman, Detr.	6.00
☐ 106 Ray Sheppard, SanJ.	.35
☐ 107 Chris Pronger, SLou.	1.50
☐ 108 Adam Oates, Bost.	1.00
☐ 109 Mike Gartner, Toro.	2.00
☐ 110 Doug Weight, Edmo.	1.50
☐ 111 Jason Dawe, Buff.	.35
☐ 112 Rick Tocchet, LosA.	.50
☐ 113 Pat LaFontaine, Buff.	1.50
☐ 114 Scott Mellanby, Flor.	.50
☐ 115 Vitali Yachmenev, LosA.	.50
☐ 116 Alexei Zhamnov, Winn.	.50
☐ 117 Brendan Witt, Wash.	.50
☐ 118 Saku Koivu, Mont.	4.00
☐ 119 Mikael Renberg, Phil.	.50
☐ 120 Mats Sundin, Toro.	2.50
☐ CL: M. Lemieux / E. Lindros	1.00

ROOKIE PHENOMS

Insert Set (10 cards):	55.00
Insert (#/5000)	RP
☐ 1 Marcus Ragnarsson, SanJ.	4.00
☐ 2 Daniel Alfredsson, Otta.	8.00
☐ 3 Chad Kilger, Anah.	4.00
☐ 4 Niklas Sundström, NYRa.	4.00
☐ 5 Vitali Yachmenev, LosA.	4.00
☐ 6 Éric Dazé, Chic.	6.00
☐ 7 Radek Dvorak, Flor.	4.00
☐ 8 Jeff O'Neill, Hart.	6.00
☐ 9 Saku Koivu, Mont.	12.00
☐ 10 Todd Bertuzzi, NYIs.	18.00

STARS OF THE GAME

Insert Set (12 cards):	100.00
Insert (#/5000)	SotG
☐ 1 Mario Lemieux, Pitt.	22.00
☐ 2 Eric Lindros, Phil.	6.00
☐ 3 Wayne Gretzky, LosA.	30.00
☐ 4 Peter Forsberg, Colo.	10.00
☐ 5 Paul Kariya, Anah.	10.00
☐ 6 Alexander Mogilny, Vanc.	5.00
☐ 7 Teemu Selänne, Winn.	6.00
☐ 8 Jaromir Jagr, Pitt.	6.00
☐ 9 Mats Sundin, Toro.	6.00
☐ 10 Brett Hull, SLou.	6.00
☐ 11 Sergei Fedorov, Detr.	6.00
☐ 12 Jeremy Roenick, Chic.	6.00

STICK SIDE

Insert Set (8 cards):	175.00
Insert (#/2500)	SS
☐ 1 Jim Carey (G), Wash.	10.00
☐ 2 Martin Brodeur (G), NJer.	40.00
☐ 3 Félix Potvin (G), Toro.	15.00
☐ 4 Patrick Roy (G), Colo.	70.00
☐ 5 Dominik Hasek (G), Buff.	25.00
☐ 6 John Vanbiesbrouck (G), Flor.	10.00
☐ 7 Ron Hextall (G), Phil.	15.00
☐ 8 Ed Belfour (G), Chic.	25.00

1995 - 96 LEGENDS OF HOCKEY

Singles sell between $8.00 and 12.00.

Complete Set (18 cards): 120.00

Player	Player
☐ 55 Bill Barber	☐ 56 Harry Howell
☐ 57 Dick Irvin	☐ 58 Dave Keon
☐ 59 Clint Smith	☐ 60 Lester Patrick
☐ 61 Rod Gilbert	☐ 62 Hooley Smith
☐ 63 Eddie Shore	☐ 64 Fred Maxwell
☐ 65 Ted Kennedy	☐ 66 Allan Stanley
☐ 67 Darryl Sittler	☐ 68 Red Horner
☐ 69 Howie Morenz	☐ 70 Bill Gadsby
☐ 71 Aurèle Joliat	☐ 72 Joe Malone

1995 - 96 MCDONALD'S - PINNACLE UC3

Complete Set (41 cards):	20.00
Player	NRMT-MT
☐ McD-1 Jaromir Jagr, Pitt.	1.00
☐ McD-2 Eric Lindros, Phil.	1.00
☐ McD-3 Alexei Zhamnov, Winn.	.35
☐ McD-4 Paul Coffey, Detr.	.50
☐ McD-5 Mark Messier, NYRa.	1.00
☐ McD-6 Brett Hull, SLou.	1.00
☐ McD-7 Peter Forsberg, Colo.	1.50
☐ McD-8 Pavel Bure, Vanc.	1.00
☐ McD-9 Doug Gilmour, Toro.	.50
☐ McD-10 Owen Nolan, SanJ.	.50
☐ McD-11 Paul Kariya, Anah.	1.50
☐ McD-12 Joe Nieuwendyk, Calg.	.50
☐ McD-13 Pierre Turgeon, Mont.	.50
☐ McD-14 Jason Arnott, Edmo.	.50
☐ McD-15 Mario Lemieux, Pitt.	3.50
☐ McD-16 Jeremy Roenick, Chic.	1.00
☐ McD-17 Sergei Fedorov, Detr.	1.00
☐ McD-18 Mats Sundin, Toro.	1.00
☐ McD-19 Teemu Selänne, Winn.	1.00
☐ McD-20 John LeClair, Phil.	1.00
☐ McD-21 Alexander Mogilny, Vanc.	.50
☐ McD-22 Mikael Renberg, Phil.	.35
☐ McD-23 Chris Chelios, Chic.	.50
☐ McD-24 Mark Recchi, Mont.	.50
☐ McD-25 Patrick Roy (G), Mont.	3.50
☐ McD-26 Félix Potvin (G), Toro.	.50
☐ McD-27 Martin Brodeur (G), NJer.	2.00
☐ McD-28 Dominik Hasek (G), Buff.	1.00
☐ McD-29 Ed Belfour (G), Chic.	1.00
☐ McD-30 Kirk McLean (G), Vanc.	.35
☐ McD-31 Jeff Friesen, SanJ.	.35
☐ McD-32 Todd Harvey, Dall.	.35
☐ McD-33 Brett Lindros, NYIs.	.35
☐ McD-34 Valeri Bure, Mont.	.35
☐ McD-35 Oleg Tverdovsky, Anah.	.35
☐ McD-36 Kenny Jönsson, Toro.	.35
☐ McD-37 Mariusz Czerkawski, Bost.	.35
☐ McD-38 Alexandre Daigle, Otta.	.35

□	McD-39 Saku Koivu, Mont.	1.00
□	McD-40 Jim Carey (G), Wash.	.35
□	Joe Sakic, Colo. [Checklist]	1.00

1995 - 96 MCDONALD'S MUPPET MANIA

The following "Free" teams came on the game card: Chicago, Calgary, Los Angeles, Colorado, Florida, Islanders, Washington, Hartford and Ottawa. We have no pricing information on this set.

	Team		Team
□	501 Dallas Stars	□	502 Detroit Red Wings
□	503 St. Louis Blues	□	504 Toro. Maple Leafs
□	505 Winnipeg Jets	□	506 Edmonton Oilers
□	507 Vancouver Canucks	□	508 San Jose Sharks
□	509 Anah. Mighty Ducks	□	510 Tamp. Lightning
□	511 New York Rangers	□	512 New Jersey Devils
□	513 Phil. Flyers	□	514 Pitt. Penguins
□	515 Montréal Canadiens	□	516 Boston Bruins
□	517 Buffalo Sabres		

1995 - 96 NHL-NHLPA / COOL TRADE

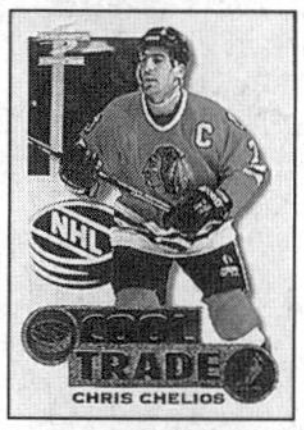

This 20-card set was available as a wrapper redemption offer. Four cards were produced by each company. Cool Trade parallel cards were available via a redemption card. Pinnacle's trade card was inserted into Pinnacle Summit packs; Upper Deck's trade card was inserted into Upper Deck Series Two packs; Fleer/SkyBox's trade card was inserted into Fleer Ultra Extra packs; Donruss' trade card was inserted into Donruss Elite packs; and Topps' trade card was inserted into Bowman packs.

	Redemption Set (20 cards):	175.00	20.00
	Player	Par.	Reg.
□ □	1 Cam Neely, Bost. [Pi. Summit]	4.00	1.00
□ □	2 W. Gretzky, LosA. [Upper Deck]	20.00	5.00
□ □	3 J. Roenick, Chic. [SBx Emotion]	15.00	1.00
□ □	4 M. Lemieux, Pitt. [Donruss Elite]	30.00	.35
□ □	5 Mark Messier, NYRa. [T. Finest]	6.00	1.00
□ □	6 R. Bourque, Bost. [Pi. Summit]	4.00	1.50
□ □	7 Sergei Fedorov, Detr. [Upper Deck]	4.00	1.00
□ □	8 Paul Kariya, Anah. [SBx Emotion]	25.00	1.50
□ □	9 Eric Lindros, Phil. [Donruss Elite]	10.00	1.00
□ □	10 Pavel Bure, Vanc. [T. Finest]	6.00	1.00
□ □	11 Chris Chelios, Chic. [Pi. Summit]	2.00	.50
□ □	12 P. Forsberg, Colo. [Upper Deck]	6.00	1.50
□ □	13 S. Koivu, Mont. [SBx Emotion]	15.00	1.00
□ □	14 E. Belfour (G), Chic. [D. Elite]	10.00	1.00
□ □	15 Brett Hull, SLou. [T. Finest]	6.00	1.00
□ □	16 P. Roy (G), Colo. [Pi. Summit]	10.00	.35
□ □	17 Doug Gilmour, Toro. [Upper Deck]	2.00	.50
□ □	18 Brodeur (G), NJer. [SBx Emotion]	30.00	2.00
□ □	19 A. Mogilny, Vanc. [Donruss Elite]	6.00	.50
□ □	20 Jaromir Jagr, Pitt. [T. Finest]	6.00	1.00

1995 - 96 NHL / FANFEST

These cards were handed out at the 1996 All-Star Fanfest in Boston.

	Complete Set (5 cards):	50.00
	Player	NRMT-MT
□	3 Phil Esposito, Bost.	5.00
□	Phil Esposito, Bost.	5.00
□	Phil Esposito, Bost.	5.00
□	Phil Esposito, Bost.	5.00
□	Phil Esposito, Bost.	5.00

1995 - 96 PANINI STICKER

Sticker Size: 2 1/8" x 3"

	Complete Set (306 stickers):	30.00
	Album:	3.00
	Player	NRMT-MT
□	1 Claude Lemieux, NJer. [Left Half]	.20
□	2 Claude Lemieux, NJer. [Right Half]	.20
□	3 Adam Oates, Bost.	.20
□	4 Ted Donato, Bost.	.20
□	5 Mariusz Czerkawski, Bost.	.20
□	6 Sandy Moger, Bost.	.20
□	7 Kevin Stevens, Bost.	.20
□	8 Cam Neely, Bost.	1.00
□	9 Raymond Bourque, Bost.	1.00
□	10 Bruins, Bost. [Logo]	.20
□	11 Don Sweeney, Bost.	.20
□	12 Al Iafrate, Bost.	.20
□	13 Blaine Lacher (G), Bost.	.20
□	14 Brian Holzinger, Buff.	.20
□	15 Pat LaFontaine, Buff.	.50
□	16 Derek Plante, Buff.	.20
□	17 Yuri Khmylev, Buff.	.20
□	18 Jason Dawe, Buff.	.20
□	19 Donald Audette, Buff.	.20
□	20 Alexei Zhitnik, Buff.	.20
□	21 Sabres, Buff. [Logo]	.20
□	22 Richard Smehlik, Buff.	.20
□	23 Garry Galley, Buff.	.20
□	24 Dominik Hasek (G), Buff.	1.00
□	25 Andrew Cassels, Hart.	.20
□	26 Jimmy Carson, Hart.	.20
□	27 Darren Turcotte, Hart.	.20
□	28 Geoff Sanderson, Hart.	.20
□	29 Andrei Nikolishin, Hart.	.20
□	30 Kevin Smyth, Hart.	.20
□	31 Brendan Shanahan, Hart.	1.00
□	32 Whalers, Hart. [Logo]	.20
□	33 Steven Rice, Hart.	.20
□	34 Frantisek Kucera, Hart.	.20
□	35 Sean Burke (G), Hart.	.50
□	36 Brian Savage, Mont.	.20
□	37 Pierre Turgeon, Mont.	.20
□	38 Vincent Damphousse, Mont.	.50
□	39 Benoît Brunet, Mont.	.20
□	40 Mike Keane, Mont.	.20
□	41 Mark Recchi, Mont.	.20
□	42 Vladimir Malakhov, Mont.	.20
□	43 Canadiens, Mont. [Logo]	.20
□	44 Patrice Brisebois, Mont.	.20
□	45 Stéphane Quintal, Mont.	.20
□	46 Patrick Roy (G), Mont.	3.00
□	47 Alexandre Daigle, Otta.	.20
□	48 Alexei Yashin, Otta.	.50
□	49 Dan Quinn, Otta.	.20
□	50 Radek Bonk, Otta.	.20
□	51 Scott Levins, Otta.	.20
□	52 Sylvain Turgeon, Otta.	.20
□	53 Pavol Demitra, Otta.	.20
□	54 Senators, Otta. [Logo]	.20
□	55 Steve Larouche, Otta.	.20
□	56 Sean Hill, Otta.	.20
□	57 Don Beaupré (G), Otta.	.20
□	58 Ron Francis, Pitt.	.50
□	59 Mario Lemieux, Pitt.	3.00
□	60 Bryan Smolinski, Pitt.	.20
□	61 Luc Robitaille, Pitt.	.50
□	62 Tomas Sandström, Pitt.	.20
□	63 Jaromir Jagr, Pitt.	1.00
□	64 Joe Mullen, Pitt.	.20
□	65 Penguins, Pitt. [Logo]	.20
□	66 Ulf Samuelsson, Pitt.	.20
□	67 Dmitri Mironov, Pitt.	.20
□	68 Ken Wregget (G), Pitt.	.20
□	69 Stu Barnes, Flor.	.20
□	70 Jesse Bélanger, Flor.	.20
□	71 Rob Niedermayer, Flor.	.20
□	72 Brian Skrudland, Flor.	.20
□	73 Dave Lowry, Flor.	.20
□	74 Jody Hull, Flor.	.20
□	75 Scott Mellanby, Flor.	.20
□	76 Panthers, Flor. [Logo]	.20
□	77 Gord Murphy, Flor.	.20
□	78 Magnus Svensson, Flor.	.20
□	79 John Vanbiesbrouck (G), Flor.	.20
□	80 Neal Broten, NJer.	.20
□	81 Bill Guerin, NJer.	.20
□	82 Claude Lemieux, NJer.	.20
□	83 John MacLean, NJer.	.20
□	84 Randy McKay, NJer.	.20
□	85 Stéphane Richer, NJer.	.20
□	86 Shawn Chambers, NJer.	.20
□	87 Devils, NJer. [Logo]	.20
□	88 Scott Niedermayer, NJer.	.20
□	89 Scott Stevens, NJer.	.20
□	90 Martin Brodeur (G), NJer.	1.50
□	91 Kirk Muller, NYIs.	.20
□	92 Derek King, NYIs.	.20
□	93 Patrick Flatley, NYIs.	.20
□	94 Brett Lindros, NYIs.	.20
□	95 Steve Thomas, NYIs.	.20
□	96 Darius Kasparaitis, NYIs.	.20
□	97 Scott Lachance, NYIs.	.20
□	98 Islanders, NYIs. [Logo]	.20
□	99 Mathieu Schneider, NYIs.	.20
□	100 Dennis Vaske, NYIs.	.20
□	101 Tommy Salo (G), NYIs.	.20
□	102 Mark Messier, NYRa.	1.00
□	103 Ray Ferraro, NYRa.	.20
□	104 Petr Nedved, NYRa.	.20
□	105 Adam Graves, NYRa.	.20
□	106 Alexei Kovalev, NYRa.	.50
□	107 Steve Larmer, NYRa.	.20
□	108 Pat Verbeek, NYRa.	.20
□	109 Rangers, NYRa. [Logo]	.20
□	110 Brian Leetch, NYRa.	.50
□	111 Sergei Zubov, NYRa.	.20
□	112 Mike Richter (G), NYRa.	.20
□	113 Eric Lindros, Phil.	1.00
□	114 Rod Brind'Amour, Phil.	.20
□	115 Joel Otto, Phil.	.20
□	116 John LeClair, Phil.	.50
□	117 Mikael Renberg, Phil.	.20
□	118 Chris Therien, Phil.	.20
□	119 Éric Desjardins, Phil.	.20
□	120 Flyers, Phil. [Logo]	.20
□	121 Dmitry Yushkevich, Phil.	.20
□	122 Karl Dykhuis, Phil.	.20
□	123 Ron Hextall (G), Phil.	.50
□	124 Brian Bradley, Tamp.	.20
□	125 John Tucker, Tamp.	.20
□	126 Chris Gratton, Tamp.	.20
□	127 Alexander Semak, Tamp.	.20
□	128 Brian Bellows, Tamp.	.20
□	129 Paul Ysebaert, Tamp.	.20
□	130 Petr Klima, Tamp.	.20
□	131 Lightning, Tamp. [Logo]	.20
□	132 Alexander Selivanov, Tamp.	.20
□	133 Roman Hamrlik, Tamp.	.20
□	134 Daren Puppa (G), Tamp.	.20
□	135 Dale Hunter, Wash.	.20
□	136 Michal Pivonka, Wash.	.20
□	137 Steve Konowalchuk, Wash.	.20
□	138 Joé Juneau, Wash.	.20
□	139 Peter Bondra, Wash.	.50
□	140 Keith Jones, Wash.	.20
□	141 Sergei Gonchar, Wash.	.20
□	142 Capitals, Wash. [Logo]	.20
□	143 Calle Johansson, Wash.	.20
□	144 Mark Tinordi, Wash.	.20
□	145 Jim Carey (G), Wash.	.20
□	146 Eric Lindros, Phil. [Award Winner]	1.00
□	147 Paul Coffey, Detr. [Award Winner]	.50
□	148 Peter Forsberg, Colo. [Award Winner]	1.00
□	149 Dominik Hasek (G), Buff. [Award Winner]	1.00
□	150 Jaromir Jagr, Pitt. [Award Winner]	1.00
□	151 Peter Bondra, Wash. [League Leader]	.50
□	152 Ron Francis, Pitt. [League Leader]	.50
□	153 Cam Neely, Bost. [League Leader]	1.00
□	154 Dominik Hasek (G), Buff. [League Leader]	1.00
□	155 Ian Laperrière, SLou. [League Leader]	.20
□	156 Bernie Nicholls, Chic.	.20
□	157 Jeremy Roenick, Chic.	.50
□	158 Patrick Poulin, Chic.	.20
□	159 Éric Dazé, Chic.	.20
□	160 Tony Amonte, Chic.	.50
□	161 Sergei Krivokrasov, Chic.	.20
□	162 Joe Murphy, Chic.	.20
□	163 Blackhawks, Chic. [Logo]	.20
□	164 Chris Chelios, Chic.	.50
□	165 Gary Suter, Chic.	.20
□	166 Ed Belfour (G), Chic.	1.00
□	167 Dave Gagner, Dall.	.20
□	168 Mike Modano, Dall.	1.00
□	169 Todd Harvey, Dall.	.20
□	170 Mike Donnelly, Dall.	.20
□	171 Mike Kennedy, Dall.	.20
□	172 Trent Klatt, Dall.	.20
□	173 Derian Hatcher, Dall.	.20
□	174 Stars, Dall. [Logo]	.20
□	175 Kevin Hatcher, Dall.	.20
□	176 Grant Ledyard, Dall.	.20
□	177 Andy Moog (G), Dall.	.20
□	178 Sergei Fedorov, Detr.	1.00
□	179 Steve Yzerman, Detr.	2.00
□	180 Vyacheslav Kozlov, Detr.	.20
□	181 Keith Primeau, Detr.	.20
□	182 Dino Ciccarelli, Detr.	.20
□	183 Ray Sheppard, Detr.	.20
□	184 Paul Coffey, Detr.	.50
□	185 Red Wings, Detr. [Logo]	.20
□	186 Nicklas Lidström, Detr.	.50
□	187 Chris Osgood (G), Detr.	.50
□	188 Mike Vernon (G), Detr.	.20
□	189 Dale Hawerchuk, SLou.	.50
□	190 Ian Laperrière, SLou.	.20
□	191 David Roberts, SLou.	.20
□	192 Esa Tikkanen, SLou.	.20
□	193 Geoff Courtnall, SLou.	.20
□	194 Brett Hull, SLou.	1.00
□	195 Steve Duchesne, SLou.	.20
□	196 Blues, SLou. [Logo]	.20
□	197 Al MacInnis, SLou.	.20
□	198 Chris Pronger, SLou.	.50
□	199 Jon Casey (G), SLou.	.20
□	200 Doug Gilmour, Toro.	.50
□	201 Mats Sundin, Toro.	1.00
□	202 Benoît Hogue, Toro.	.20
□	203 Dave Andreychuk, Toro.	.20
□	204 Mike Gartner, Toro.	.50
□	205 Dave Ellett, Toro.	.20
□	206 Todd Gill, Toro.	.20
□	207 Maple Leafs, Toro. [Logo]	.20
□	208 Kenny Jönsson, Toro.	.20
□	209 Larry Murphy, Toro.	.20
□	210 Félix Potvin (G), Toro.	.50
□	211 Dallas Drake, Winn.	.20
□	212 Alexei Zhamnov, Winn.	.20
□	213 Mike Eastwood, Winn.	.20
□	214 Keith Tkachuk, Winn.	.50
□	215 Igor Korolev, Winn.	.20
□	216 Nelson Emerson, Winn.	.20
□	217 Teemu Selänne, Winn.	.50
□	218 Jets, Winn. [Logo]	.20
□	219 Dave McLlwain, Winn.	.20
□	220 Teppo Numminen, Winn.	.20
□	221 Nikolai Khabibulin (G), Winn.	.20
□	222 Steve Rucchin, Anah.	.20
□	223 Shaun Van Allen, Anah.	.20
□	224 Patrik Carnbäck, Anah.	.20
□	225 Peter Douris, Anah.	.20
□	226 Todd Krygier, Anah.	.20
□	227 Paul Kariya, Anah.	1.00
□	228 Bobby Dollas, Anah.	.20
□	229 Mighty Ducks, Anah. [Logo]	.20
□	230 Milos Holan, Anah.	.20
□	231 Oleg Tverdovsky, Anah.	.20
□	232 Guy Hebert (G), Anah.	.20
□	233 Joe Nieuwendyk, Calg.	.20
□	234 German Titov, Calg.	.20
□	235 Paul Kruse, Calg.	.20
□	236 Gary Roberts, Calg.	.20
□	237 Theoren Fleury, Calg.	.50
□	238 Ronnie Stern, Calg.	.20
□	239 Steve Chiasson, Calg.	.20
□	240 Flames, Calg. [Logo]	.20
□	241 Phil Housley, Calg.	.20
□	242 Zarley Zalapski, Calg.	.20
□	243 Trevor Kidd (G), Calg.	.20
□	244 Peter Forsberg, Colo.	1.00
□	245 Mike Ricci, Colo.	.20
□	246 Joe Sakic, Colo.	1.50
□	247 Wendel Clark, Colo.	.50
□	248 Valeri Kamensky, Colo.	.20
□	249 Owen Nolan, Colo.	.50
□	250 Scott A. Young, Colo.	.20
□	251 Avalanche, Colo. [Logo]	.20
□	252 Uwe Krupp, Colo.	.20
□	253 Curtis Leschyshyn, Colo.	.20
□	254 Jocelyn Thibault (G), Colo.	.20
□	255 Jason Arnott, Edmo.	.20
□	256 Jason Bonsignore, Edmo.	.20
□	257 Todd Marchant, Edmo.	.20
□	258 Scott Thornton, Edmo.	.20
□	259 Doug Weight, Edmo.	.50
□	260 Shayne Corson, Edmo.	.20
□	261 Kelly Buchberger, Edmo.	.20
□	262 Oilers, Edmo. [Logo]	.20
□	263 David Oliver, Edmo.	.20
□	264 Igor Kravchuk, Edmo.	.20
□	265 Curtis Joseph (G), Edmo.	1.00
□	266 Wayne Gretzky, LosA.	4.00
□	267 Tony Granato, LosA.	.20
□	268 Dmitri Khristich, LosA.	.20
□	269 John Druce, LosA.	.20
□	270 Jari Kurri, LosA.	1.00
□	271 Rick Tocchet, LosA.	.20
□	272 Rob Blake, LosA.	.50
□	273 Kings, LosA. [Logo]	.20
□	274 Marty McSorley, LosA.	.20
□	275 Darryl Sydor, LosA.	.20
□	276 Kelly Hrudey (G), LosA.	.20
□	277 Craig Janney, SanJ.	.20
□	278 Jeff Friesen, SanJ.	.20
□	279 Viktor Kozlov, SanJ.	.20
□	280 Ray Whitney, SanJ.	.20
□	281 Ulf Dahlén, SanJ.	.20
□	282 Sergei Makarov, SanJ.	.20
□	283 Sandis Ozolinsh, SanJ.	.20
□	284 Sharks, SanJ. [Logo]	.20
□	285 Mike Rathje, SanJ.	.20
□	286 Michal Sykora, SanJ.	.20
□	287 Arturs Irbe (G), SanJ.	.20
□	288 Trevor Linden, Vanc.	.20
□	289 Mike Ridley, Vanc.	.20
□	290 Cliff Ronning, Vanc.	.20
□	291 Josef Beranek, Vanc.	.20
□	292 Roman Oksiuta, Vanc.	.20
□	293 Pavel Bure, Vanc.	.50
□	294 Alexander Mogilny, Vanc.	.20
□	295 Canucks, Vanc. [Logo]	.20
□	296 Russ Courtnall, Vanc.	.20
□	297 Jeff R. Brown, Vanc.	.20
□	298 Kirk McLean (G), Vanc.	.20
□	299 Peter Forsberg, Colo. [Foil]	1.00
□	300 Paul Kariya, Anah. [Foil]	1.00
□	301 Chris Therien, Phil. [Foil]	.20
□	302 Blaine Lacher (G), Bost. [Foil]	.20
□	303 Jim Carey (G), Wash. [Foil]	.20
□	304 Jeff Friesen, SanJ. [Foil]	.20
□	305 Ian Laperrière, SLou. [Foil]	.20
□	306 Kenny Jönsson, Toro. [Foil]	.20

1995 - 96 PARKHURST

These cards have two versions: the regular card and an Emerald Ice parallel. Seven cards also have a promo version. The promo card and Emerald Ice card have the same value.

Imprint: Parkhurst Products Inc.

Series One Set (270 cards):		**325.00**	**45.00**
Series Two Set (270 cards):		**225.00**	**45.00**
Common Player:		**.75**	**.20**
	Player	**Eme.**	**Reg**
□□	1 Patrik Carnbäck, Anah.	.75	.20
□□	2 Milos Holan, Anah.	.75	.20
□□	3 Paul Kariya, Anah.	7.00	.50
□□	4 Guy Hebert (G), Anah.	1.00	.20
□□	5 Garry Valk, Anah.	.75	.20
□□	6 Mikhail Shtalenkov, Anah.	.75	.20
□□	7 Randy Ladouceur, Anah.	.75	.20
□□	8 Shaun Van Allen, Anah.	.75	.20
□□	9 Oleg Tverdovsky, Anah.	.75	.20
□□	10 Kevin Stevens, Bost.	1.00	.20
□□	11 Raymond Bourque, Bost.	6.00	.50
□□	12 Cam Neely, Bost.	5.00	.50
□□	13 Jozef Stumpel, Bost.	1.00	.20
□□	14 Blaine Lacher (G), Bost.	.75	.20
□□	15 Alexei Kasatonov, Bost.	1.00	.20
□□	16 Adam Oates, Bost.	2.00	.20
□□	17 Ted Donato, Bost.	.75	.20
□□	18 Mariusz Czerkawski, Bost.	1.00	.20
□□	19 Alexei Zhitnik, Buff.	.75	.20
□□	20 Pat LaFontaine, Buff.	3.00	.20
□□	21 Garry Galley, Buff.	.75	.20
□□	22 Scott Pearson, Buff.	.75	.20
□□	23 Yuri Khmylev, Buff.	.75	.20
□□	24 Jason Dawe, Buff.	.75	.20
□□	25 Robb Stauber, Buff.	.75	.20
□□	26 Wayne Primeau, Buff.	3.00	.50
□□	**27 Brian Holzinger, Buff. RC**	**3.00**	**.50**
□□	28 German Titov, Calg.	.75	.20
□□	29 Theoren Fleury, Calg.	3.00	.20
□□	30 Phil Housley, Calg.	1.50	.20
□□	31 Zarley Zalapski, Calg.	.75	.20
□□	32 Rick Tabaracci (G), Calg.	.75	.20
□□	33 Joe Nieuwendyk, Calg.	2.00	.20
□□	34 Michael Nylander, Calg.	1.00	.20
□□	35 Trevor Kidd (G), Calg.	1.50	.20
□□	36 Dean Evason, Calg.	.75	.20
□□	37 Bernie Nicholls, Chic.	1.00	.20
□□	38 Chris Chelios, Chic.	3.00	.20
□□	39 Gary Suter, Chic.	1.00	.20
□□	40 Denis Savard, Chic.	2.00	.20
□□	41 Ed Belfour (G), Chic.	5.00	.50
□□	42 Patrick Poulin, Chic.	.75	.20
□□	43 J. Steve Smith, Chic.	1.00	.20
□□	44 Jeff Hackett (G), Chic.	1.50	.20
□□	45 Éric Dazé, Chic.	4.00	.50
□□	46 Joe Sakic, Colo.	8.00	1.00
□□	47 John Slaney, Colo.	.75	.20
□□	48 Valeri Kamensky, Colo.	1.50	.20
□□	49 Owen Nolan, Colo.	3.00	.20
□□	50 Uwe Krupp, Colo.	.75	.20
□□	51 Andrei Kovalenko, Colo.	.75	.20
□□	52 Janne Laukkanen, Colo.	.75	.20
□□	53 Jocelyn Thibault (G), Colo.	2.00	.20
□□	54 Adam Deadmarsh, Colo.	1.50	.20
□□	55 Mike Modano, Dall.	5.00	.50
□□	56 Kevin Hatcher, Dall.	.75	.20
□□	57 Mike Donnelly, Dall.	.75	.20
□□	58 Derian Hatcher, Dall.	1.50	.20
□□	59 Andy Moog (G), Dall.	2.00	.20
□□	60 Jamie Langenbrunner, Dall.	2.00	.20
□□	61 Shane Churla, Dall.	.75	.20
□□	62 Todd Harvey, Dall.	1.00	.20
□□	63 Manny Fernandez (G), Dall.	4.00	.50
□□	64 Nicklas Lidström, Detr.	3.00	.20
□□	65 Vyacheslav Kozlov, Detr.	1.00	.20
□□	66 Paul Coffey, Detr.	3.00	.20
□□	67 Chris Osgood (G), Detr.	3.00	.20
□□	68 Viacheslav Fetisov, Detr.	3.00	.20
□□	69 Vladimir Konstantinov, Detr.	1.50	.20
□□	70 Steve Yzerman, Detr.	12.00	1.50
□□	71 Aaron Ward, Detr.	.75	.20
□□	72 Keith Primeau, Detr.	2.00	.20
□□	73 Jason Arnott, Edmo.	2.00	.20
□□	74 Igor Kravchuk, Edmo.	.75	.20
□□	75 Boris Mironov, Edmo.	.75	.20
□□	76 David Oliver, Edmo.	.75	.20
□□	77 Kelly Buchberger, Edmo.	.75	.20
□□	78 Bill Ranford (G), Edmo.	2.00	.20
□□	79 Zdeno Ciger, Edmo.	.75	.20
□□	80 Jason Bonsignore, Edmo.	1.00	.20
□□	81 Louie DeBrusk, Edmo.	.75	.20
□□	82 Rob Niedermayer, Flor.	1.00	.20
□□	**83 Magnus Svensson, Flor. RC**	**2.00**	**.50**
□□	**84 Robert Svehla, Flor. RC**	**4.50**	**1.00**
□□□	85 John Vanbiesbrouck (G), Flor.	2.00	.20
□□	86 Stu Barnes, Flor.	.75	.20
□□	87 Jesse Bélanger, Flor.	.75	.20
□□	88 Mark Fitzpatrick (G), Flor.	.75	.20
□□	89 Jason Woolley, Flor.	.75	.20
□□	90 Johan Garpenlöv, Flor.	.75	.20
□□	91 Geoff Sanderson, Hart.	1.00	.20
□□	92 Robert Kron, Hart.	.75	.20
□□	93 Darren Turcotte, Hart.	.75	.20
□□	94 Andrei Nikolishin, Hart.	.75	.20
□□	95 Steven Rice, Hart.	.75	.20
□□	96 Sean Burke (G), Hart.	3.00	.20
□□	97 Brendan Shanahan, Hart.	5.00	.50
□□	98 Glen Wesley, Hart.	.75	.20
□□	99 Marek Malík, Hart.	.75	.20
□□	100 Wayne Gretzky, LosA.	20.00	2.50
□□	101 Robert Lang, LosA.	1.00	.20
□□□	102 Jari Kurri, LosA.	5.00	.50
□□	103 Kelly Hrudey (G), LosA.	1.50	.20
□□	104 Jamie Storr (G), LosA.	1.00	.20
□□	105 Marty McSorley, LosA.	1.00	.20
□□	106 Rob Blake, LosA.	3.00	.20
□□	107 Éric Lacroix, LosA.	.75	.20
□□	108 Dmitri Khristich, LosA.	.75	.20
□□	109 Pierre Turgeon, Mont.	2.00	.20
□□	110 Vincent Damphousse, Mont.	3.00	.20
□□	111 Peter Popovic, Mont.	.75	.20
□□	112 Brian Savage, Mont.	1.50	.20
□□□	113 Patrick Roy (G), Mont.	15.00	1.50
□□	114 Valeri Bure, Mont.	1.50	.20
□□	115 Vladimir Malakhov, Mont.	.75	.20
□□	116 Benoît Brunet, Mont.	.75	.20
□□	117 Stéphane Quintal, Mont.	.75	.20
□□	118 Stéphane Richer, NJer.	1.00	.20
□□	119 Sergei Brylin, NJer.	.75	.20
□□	120 Neal Broten, NJer.	1.00	.20
□□	121 Scott Stevens, NJer.	2.00	.20
□□	122 Martin Brodeur (G), NJer.	8.00	1.00
□□	123 John MacLean, NJer.	.75	.20
□□	124 Bill Guerin, NJer.	2.00	.20
□□	125 Bobby Holik, NJer.	1.50	.20
□□	126 Tommy Albelin, NJer. [b/ Cup]	.75	.20
□□	127 Tommy Söderström (G), NYIs.	.75	.20
□□	**128 Tommy Salo (G), NYIs. RC**	**8.00**	**2.00**
□□	129 Kirk Muller, NYIs.	1.50	.20
□□	130 Mathieu Schneider, NYIs.	1.00	.20
□□	131 Zigmund Palffy, NYIs.	3.00	.20
□□	132 Derek King, NYIs.	.75	.20
□□	133 Brett Lindros, NYIs.	1.50	.20
□□	134 Marty McInnis, NYIs.	.75	.20
□□	135 Alexander Semak, NYIs.	.75	.20
□□	136 Mark Messier, NYRa.	5.00	.50
□□	137 Adam Graves, NYRa.	2.00	.20
□□	138 Mike Richter (G), NYRa.	2.00	.20
□□	139 Alexei Kovalev, NYRa.	3.00	.20
□□	140 Luc Robitaille, NYRa.	4.00	.50
□□	141 Sergei Nemchinov, NYRa.	1.00	.20
□□	142 Alexander Karpovtsev, NYRa.	.75	.20
□□	143 Mattias Norström, NYRa.	1.00	.20
□□	144 Brian Leetch, NYRa.	3.00	.20
□□	145 Martin Straka, Otta.	1.50	.20
□□	146 Sylvain Turgeon, Otta.	.75	.20
□□	147 Radek Bonk, Otta.	1.50	.20
□□	148 Stanislav Neckar, Otta.	.75	.20
□□	149 Pavol Demitra, Otta.	2.00	.20
□□	150 Alexandre Daigle, Otta.	.75	.20
□□	151 Alexei Yashin, Otta.	3.00	.20
□□	152 Don Beaupré (G), Otta.	.75	.20
□□	153 Steve Duchesne, Otta.	1.00	.20
□□	154 Eric Lindros, Phil.	5.00	.50
□□	155 Kjell Samuelsson, Phil.	.75	.20
□□	156 Chris Therien, Phil.	.75	.20
□□	157 John LeClair, Phil.	4.00	.50
□□	158 Rod Brind'Amour, Phil.	1.50	.20
□□	159 Ron Hextall (G), Phil.	3.00	.20
□□	160 Patrik Juhlin, Phil.	.75	.20
□□□	161 Mikael Renberg, Phil.	1.50	.20
□□	162 Joel Otto, Phil.	.75	.20
□□	163 Markus Näslund, Pitt.	5.00	.50
□□	164 Ron Francis, Pitt.	3.00	.20
□□	165 Jaromir Jagr, Pitt.	5.00	.50
□□	166 Tomas Sandström, Pitt.	1.00	.20
□□	167 Ken Wregget (G), Pitt.	1.00	.20
□□	168 Bryan Smolinski, Pitt.	.75	.20
□□	169 Richard Park, Pitt.	1.00	.20
□□	170 Mario Lemieux, Pitt.	15.00	1.50
□□	171 Norm Maciver, Pitt.	.75	.20
□□	172 Brett Hull, SLou.	5.00	.50
□□	173 Esa Tikkanen, SLou.	.75	.20
□□	174 Shayne Corson, SLou.	1.50	.20
□□	175 Chris Pronger, SLou.	3.00	.20
□□	176 Ian Laperrière, SLou.	.75	.20
□□	177 Jon Casey (G), SLou.	.75	.20
□□	178 Al MacInnis, SLou.	2.00	.20
□□	179 David Roberts, SLou.	.75	.20
□□	180 Dale Hawerchuk, SLou.	3.00	.20
□□	181 Michal Sykora, SanJ.	.75	.20
□□	182 Jeff Friesen, SanJ.	1.50	.20
□□	183 Ray Whitney, SanJ.	1.00	.20
□□	184 Igor Larionov, SanJ.	3.00	.20
□□	185 Sandis Ozolinsh, SanJ.	1.00	.20
□□	186 Andrei Nazarov, SanJ.	.75	.20
□□	187 Viktor Kozlov, SanJ.	1.50	.20
□□	188 Arturs Irbe (G), SanJ.	2.00	.20
□□	**189 Wade Flaherty, SanJ. RC**	**3.00**	**.50**
□□	190 Brian Bradley, Tamp.	.75	.20
□□	191 Paul Ysebaert, Tamp.	.75	.20
□□	192 John Tucker, Tamp.	.75	.20
□□	193 Jason Wiemer, Tamp.	.75	.20
□□	194 Alexander Selivanov, Tamp.	.75	.20
□□	195 Daren Puppa (G), Tamp.	1.00	.20
□□	196 Mikael Andersson, Tamp.	.75	.20
□□	197 Petr Klima, Tamp.	.75	.20
□□	198 Roman Hamrlik, Tamp.	1.00	.20
□□	199 Doug Gilmour, Toro.	3.00	.20
□□	200 Damian Rhodes (G), Toro.	1.00	.20
□□	201 Mats Sundin, Toro.	5.00	.50
□□	202 Todd Gill, Toro.	.75	.20
□□	203 Kenny Jönsson, Toro.	1.00	.20
□□	204 Félix Potvin (G), Toro.	3.00	.20
□□	205 Tie Domi, Toro.	1.50	.20
□□	206 Mike Gartner, Toro.	4.00	.50
□□	207 Larry Murphy, Toro.	1.00	.20
□□	208 Josef Beranek, Vanc.	.75	.20
□□	209 Trevor Linden, Vanc.	2.00	.20
□□	210 Russ Courtnall, Vanc.	1.00	.20
□□	211 Roman Oksiuta, Vanc.	.75	.20
□□	212 Alexander Mogilny, Vanc.	2.00	.20
□□	213 Kirk McLean (G), Vanc.	1.50	.20
□□	214 Mike Ridley, Vanc.	.75	.20
□□	215 Jyrki Lumme, Vanc.	1.00	.20
□□	216 Bret Hedican, Vanc.	.75	.20
□□	217 Keith Jones, Wash.	.75	.20
□□	218 Calle Johansson, Wash.	1.00	.20
□□	219 Kelly Miller, Wash.	.75	.20
□□	220 Olaf Kölzig (G), Wash.	3.00	.20
□□	221 Joé Juneau, Wash.	1.00	.20
□□	222 Sylvain Côté, Wash.	.75	.20
□□	223 Dale Hunter, Wash.	1.50	.20
□□	224 Mark Tinordi, Wash.	.75	.20
□□	225 Sergei Gonchar, Wash.	1.50	.20
□□	226 Alexei Zhamnov, Winn.	1.50	.20
□□	227 Igor Korolev, Winn.	.75	.20
□□	228 Teppo Numminen, Winn.	1.50	.20
□□	**229 Craig Martin, Winn. RC**	**2.00**	**.50**
□□	230 Nikolai Khabibulin (G), Winn.	2.00	.20
□□	231 Michal Grosek, Winn.	.75	.20
□□□	232 Teemu Selänne, Winn.	4.00	.50
□□	233 Dave Manson, Winn.	.75	.20
□□	234 Tim Chevelade (G), Winn.	.75	.20
□□	235 Esa Tikkanen, SLou.	.75	.20
□□	236 Dominik Hasek (G), Buff.	5.00	.50
□□	237 Peter Forsberg, Colo.	7.00	.50
□□	238 Sergei Fedorov, Detr.	5.00	.50
□□	239 Jari Kurri, LosA.	5.00	.50
□□	240 Tommy Söderström (G), NYIs.	.75	.20
□□	241 Alexei Zhamnov, Winn.	1.50	.20
□□	242 Alexei Yashin, Otta.	3.00	.20
□□	243 Mikael Renberg, Phil.	1.50	.20
□□□	244 Jaromir Jagr, Pitt.	5.00	.50
□□	245 Ulf Dahlén, SanJ.	.75	.20
□□	246 Alexander Mogilny, Vanc.	2.00	.20
□□	247 Mats Sundin, Toro.	5.00	.50
□□	248 Pavel Bure, Vanc.	4.00	.50
□□	249 Viacheslav Fetisov, Detr.	3.00	.20
□□	250 Teemu Selänne, Winn.	4.00	.50
□□	251 Arturs Irbe (G), SanJ.	2.00	.20
□□	252 Nicklas Lidström, Detr.	3.00	.20
□□	**253 Aki Berg, LosA. RC**	**3.00**	**.50**
□□□	254 Zdenek Nedved, Toro.	1.00	.20
□□	**255 Chad Kilger, Anah. RC**	**4.50**	**1.00**
□□	256 Bryan McCabe, NYIs.	2.00	.20
□□	**257 Daniel Alfredsson, Otta. RC**	**12.00**	**3.00**
□□	258 Brendan Witt, Wash.	1.00	.20
□□	259 Jeff O'Neill, Hart.	4.00	.50
□□	**260 Radek Dvorak, Flor. RC**	**4.50**	**1.00**
□□	261 Niklas Sundström, NYRa.	2.00	.20
□□	**262 Kyle McLaren, Bost. RC**	**4.50**	**1.00**
□□	263 Saku Koivu, Mont.	8.00	1.00
□□	**264 Todd Bertuzzi, NYIs. RC**	**24.00**	**6.00**
□□	265 Jere Lehtinen, Dall.	3.00	.20
□□	266 Vitali Yachmenev, LosA.	1.50	.20
□□	**267 Shane Doan, Winn. RC**	**4.50**	**1.00**
□□	268 Marko Kiprusoff, Mont.	1.00	.20
□□	269 Deron Quint, Winn.	1.50	.20
□□	270 Daymond Langkow, Tamp.	4.50	.50
□□	**271 Alex Hicks, Anah. RC**	**2.00**	**.50**
□□	272 Steve Rucchin, Anah.	1.00	.20
□□	273 Dave Karpa, Anah.	.75	.20
□□	274 Mike Sillinger, Anah.	.75	.20
□□	275 Teemu Selänne, Anah.	4.00	.50
□□	276 Todd Krygier, Anah.	.75	.20
□□	277 Valeri Karpov, Anah.	.75	.20
□□	278 Peter Douris, Anah.	.75	.20
□□	279 Mighty Ducks, Anah. [Checklist]	.75	.20
□□	280 Shawn McEachern, Bost.	1.50	.20
□□	281 David Reid, Bost.	.75	.20
□□	282 Bill Ranford (G), Bost.	2.00	.20
□□	283 Don Sweeney, Bost.	.75	.20
□□	284 Stephen Leach, Bost.	.75	.20
□□	285 Craig Billington (G), Bost.	.75	.20
□□	**286 Clayton Beddoes, Bost. RC**	**2.00**	**.50**
□□	287 Rick Tocchet, Bost.	1.50	.20
□□	288 Bruins, Bost. [Checklist]	.75	.20
□□	289 Brad May, Buff.	.75	.20
□□	290 Michael Peca, Buff.	2.00	.20
□□	291 Dominik Hasek (G), Buff.	5.00	.50
□□	292 Donald Audette, Buff.	2.00	.20
□□	293 Randy Burridge, Buff.	.75	.20
□□	294 Derek Plante, Buff.	.75	.20
□□	**295 Martin Biron, Buff. RC**	**18.00**	**8.00**
□□	296 Andrei Trefilov, Buff.	.75	.20
□□	297 Sabres, Buff. [Checklist]	.75	.20
□□	298 Steve Chiasson, Calg.	.75	.20
□□	299 Cory Stillman, Calg.	1.00	.20
□□	300 Mike Sullivan, Calg.	.75	.20
□□	301 Gary Roberts, Calg.	2.00	.20
□□	**302 Pavel Torgajev, Calg. RC**	**2.00**	**.50**
□□	303 James Patrick, Calg.	.75	.20
□□	304 Corey Millen, Calg.	.75	.20
□□	**305 Ed Ward, Calg. RC**	**2.00**	**.50**
□□	306 Flames, Calg. [Checklist]	.75	.20
□□	307 Jeremy Roenick, Chic.	4.00	.50
□□	**308 Mike Prokopec, Chic. RC**	**2.00**	**.50**
□□	309 Joe Murphy, Chic.	.75	.20
□□	310 Eric Weinrich, Chic.	.75	.20
□□	311 Tony Amonte, Chic.	3.00	.20
□□	312 Bob Probert, Chic.	1.50	.20
□□	313 Murray Craven, Chic.	.75	.20
□□	314 Sergei Krivokrasov, Chic.	.75	.20
□□	315 Blackhawks, Chic. [Checklist]	.75	.20
□□	316 Peter Forsberg, Colo.	7.00	.50
□□	317 Stéphane Fiset (G), Colo.	1.50	.20
□□	318 Mike Ricci, Colo.	1.50	.20
□□	319 Claude Lemieux, Colo.	1.50	.20
□□	320 Sandis Ozolinsh, Colo.	1.00	.20
□□	321 Sylvain Lefebvre, Colo.	.75	.20
□□	322 Scott A. Young, Colo.	1.50	.20
□□	323 Patrick Roy (G), Colo.	15.00	1.50
□□	324 Avalanche, Colo. [Checklist]	.75	.20
□□	325 Brent Fedyk, Dall.	.75	.20
□□	326 Brent Gilchrist, Dall.	.75	.20
□□	327 Greg A. Adams, Dall.	.75	.20
□□	328 Richard Matvichuk, Dall.	1.00	.20
□□	329 Joe Nieuwendyk, Dall.	2.00	.20
□□	330 Benoît Hogue, Dall.	.75	.20
□□	331 Darcy Wakaluk, Dall.	.75	.20
□□	332 Guy Carbonneau, Dall.	1.50	.20
□□	333 Stars, Dall. [Checklist]	.75	.20
□□	334 Mike Vernon (G), Detr.	2.00	.20
□□	**335 Mathieu Dandenault, Detr. RC**	**3.00**	**.50**
□□	336 Igor Larionov, Detr.	3.00	.20
□□	337 Sergei Fedorov, Detr.	5.00	.50
□□	338 Greg Johnson, Detr.	.75	.20
□□	339 Dino Ciccarelli, Detr.	1.50	.20
□□	340 Martin Lapointe, Detr.	2.00	.20
□□	341 Darren McCarty, Detr.	1.50	.20
□□	342 Red Wings, Detr. [Checklist]	.75	.20
□□	**343 Joaquin Gage (G), Edmo. RC**	**3.00**	**.50**
□□	344 Jirí Slégr, Edmo.	.75	.20
□□	345 Mariusz Czerkawski, Edmo.	1.00	.20
□□	346 Doug Weight, Edmo.	3.00	.20
□□	347 Todd Marchant, Edmo.	1.00	.20
□□	**348 Miroslav Satan, Edmo. RC**	**6.00**	**1.50**
□□	349 Jeff Norton, Edmo.	.75	.20
□□	350 Curtis Joseph (G), Edmo.	5.00	.50
□□	351 Oilers, Edmo. [Checklist]	.75	.20
□□	352 Tom Fitzgerald, Flor.	.75	.20
□□	353 Jody Hull, Flor.	.75	.20
□□	354 Terry Carkner, Flor.	.75	.20
□□	355 Scott Mellanby, Flor.	1.00	.20
□□	356 Bill Lindsay, Flor.	.75	.20
□□	357 Gord Murphy, Flor.	.75	.20
□□	358 Brian Skrudland, Flor.	.75	.20
□□	**359 David Nemirovsky, Flor. RC**	**2.00**	**.50**
□□	360 Panthers, Flor. [Checklist]	.75	.20
□□	361 Paul Ranheim, Hart.	.75	.20
□□	362 Jason Muzzatti, Hart.	.75	.20
□□	363 Glen Featherstone, Hart.	.75	.20
□□	364 Andrew Cassels, Hart.	1.00	.20
□□	365 Jeff R. Brown, Hart.	.75	.20
□□	366 Kevin Dineen, Hart.	.75	.20
□□	367 Nelson Emerson, Hart.	.75	.20
□□	368 Gerald Diduck, Hart.	.75	.20
□□	369 Whalers, Hart. [Checklist]	.75	.20
□□	370 Kevin Stevens, LosA.	1.00	.20
□□	371 Darryl Sydor, LosA.	1.00	.20
□□	372 Yanic Perreault, LosA.	1.50	.20
□□	373 Arto Blomsten, LosA.	.75	.20
□□	374 Kevin Todd, LosA.	.75	.20
□□	375 Byron Dafoe (G), LosA.	2.00	.20
□□	376 Tony Granato, LosA.	1.00	.20
□□	**377 V. Tsyplakov, LosA. RC**	**2.00**	**.50**
□□	378 Kings, LosA. [Checklist]	.75	.20
□□	379 Martin Rucinsky, Mont.	1.00	.20
□□	380 Patrice Brisebois, Mont.	.75	.20
□□	381 Lyle Odelein, Mont.	.75	.20
□□	382 Andrei Kovalenko, Mont.	.75	.20
□□	383 Mark Recchi, Mont.	2.00	.20
□□	384 Jocelyn Thibault (G), Mont.	2.00	.20
□□	385 Turner Stevenson, Mont.	.75	.20
□□	386 Pat Jablonski, Mont.	.75	.20
□□	387 Canadiens, Mont. [Checklist]	.75	.20
□□	388 Scott Niedermayer, NJer.	1.50	.20
□□	**389 Corey Schwab, NJer. RC**	**3.00**	**.50**
□□	390 Steve Thomas, NJer.	1.00	.20
□□	391 Valeri Zelepukin, NJer.	.75	.20
□□	392 Shawn Chambers, NJer.	.75	.20
□□	393 Jocelyn Lemieux, NJer.	.75	.20
□□	394 Brian Rolston, NJer.	1.50	.20
□□	395 Denis Pederson, NJer.	1.00	.20
□□	396 Devils, NJer. [Checklist]	.75	.20
□□	397 Martin Straka, NYIs.	1.50	.20
□□	398 Niklas Andersson, NYIs.	.75	.20
□□	399 Wendel Clark, NYIs.	4.00	.50
□□	400 Travis Green, NYIs.	1.00	.20
□□	**401 Chris Marinucci, NYIs. RC**	**2.00**	**.50**
□□	402 Darius Kasparaitis, NYIs.	1.00	.20
□□	403 Patrick Flatley, NYIs.	.75	.20
□□	404 Jamie McLennan (G), NYIs.	.75	.20
□□	405 Islanders, NYIs. [Checklist]	.75	.20
□□	406 Glenn Healy (G), NYRa.	1.00	.20
□□	407 Pat Verbeek, NYRa.	1.50	.20
□□	408 Ian Laperrière, NYRa.	.75	.20
□□	409 Ray Ferraro, NYRa.	.75	.20
□□	410 Jeff Beukeboom, NYRa.	.75	.20
□□	411 Ulf Samuelsson, NYRa.	.75	.20
□□	412 Doug Lidster, NYRa.	.75	.20
□□	413 Bruce Driver, NYRa.	.75	.20
□□	414 Rangers, NYRa. [Checklist]	.75	.20
□□	**415 Antti Törmänen, Otta. RC**	**2.00**	**.50**
□□	416 Sean Hill, Otta.	.75	.20
□□	417 Damian Rhodes (G), Otta.	1.00	.20
□□	418 Jaroslav Modry, Otta.	.75	.20
□□	**419 Mike Bales, Otta. RC**	**3.00**	**.50**
□□	**420 Trent McCleary, Otta. RC**	**3.00**	**.50**
□□	421 Randy Cunneyworth, Otta.	.75	.20
□□	422 Ted Drury, Otta.	.75	.20
□□	423 Senators, Otta. [Checklist]	.75	.20
□□	424 Pat Falloon, Phil.	.75	.20
□□	425 Garth Snow (G), Phil.	1.50	.20
□□	426 Shjon Podein, Phil.	1.00	.20
□□	427 Petr* Svoboda, Phil.	1.00	.20
□□	428 Éric Desjardins, Phil.	1.50	.20
□□	429 Anatoli Semenov, Phil.	.75	.20
□□	430 Kevin Haller, Phil.	.75	.20
□□	431 Rob DiMaio, Phil.	.75	.20
□□	432 Flyers, Phil. [Checklist]	.75	.20
□□	433 Chris Joseph (G), Pitt.	.75	.20
□□	434 Sergei Zubov, Pitt.	1.00	.20
□□	435 Tom Barrasso (G), Pitt.	2.00	.20
□□	436 Chris Tamer, Pitt.	.75	.20
□□	437 Dmitri Mironov, Pitt.	.75	.20
□□	438 Petr Nedved, Pitt.	1.50	.20
□□	439 Neil Wilkinson, Pitt.	.75	.20
□□	440 Glen Murray, Pitt.	2.00	.20
□□	441 Penguins, Pitt. [Checklist]	.75	.20
□□	442 J.J. Daigneault, SLou.	.75	.20
□□	443 Grant Fuhr (G), SLou.	3.00	.20
□□	444 Adam Creighton, SLou.	.75	.20
□□	445 Brian Noonan, SLou.	.75	.20
□□	446 Stéphane Matteau, SLou.	.75	.20
□□	**447 Roman Vopat, SLou. RC**	**2.00**	**.50**
□□	448 Geoff Courtnall, SLou.	.75	.20
□□	449 Wayne Gretzky, SLou.	24.00	3.00
□□	450 Blues, SLou. [Checklist]	.75	.20
□□	451 Chris Terreri (G), SanJ.	.75	.20
□□	452 Ulf Dahlén, SanJ.	.75	.20
□□	453 Owen Nolan, SanJ.	3.00	.20
□□	454 Doug Bodger, SanJ.	.75	.20
□□	455 Craig Janney, SanJ.	1.00	.20
□□	456 Ville Peltonen, SanJ.	1.00	.20
□□	457 Ray Sheppard, SanJ.	.75	.20
□□	458 Shean Donovan, SanJ.	.75	.20
□□	459 Sharks, SanJ. [Checklist]	.75	.20
□□	460 Jeff Reese, Tamp.	.75	.20
□□	461 Shawn Burr, Tamp.	.75	.20
□□	462 Chris Gratton, Tamp.	1.00	.20
□□	463 John Cullen, Tamp.	1.00	.20
□□	464 Bill Houlder, Tamp.	.75	.20
□□	465 Jean-Claude Bergeron, Tamp.	.75	.20
□□	466 Brian Bellows, Tamp.	1.00	.20
□□	467 Drew Bannister, Tamp.	1.00	.20
□□	468 Lightning, Tamp. [Checklist]	.75	.20

469 Dmitry Yushkevich, Toro. 1.00 .20
470 Dave Andreychuk, Toro. 1.50 .20
471 Dave Gagner, Toro. .75 .20
472 Todd Warriner, Toro. 1.50 .20
473 Sergio Momesso, Toro. .75 .20
474 Kirk Muller, Toro. 1.50 .20
475 Dave Ellett, Toro. .75 .20
476 Ken Baumgartner, Toro. .75 .20
477 Maple Leafs, Toro. [Checklist] .75 .20
478 Esa Tikkanen, Vanc. .75 .20
479 Cliff Ronning, Vanc. 1.00 .20
480 Martin Gélinas, Vanc. 1.00 .20
481 Brian Loney, Vanc. RC 2.00 1.00
482 Pavel Bure, Vanc. 4.00 .50
483 Corey Hirsch, Vanc. .75 .20
484 Scott Walker, Vanc. RC 4.50 1.00
485 Jim Dowd, Vanc. .75 .20
486 Canucks, Vanc. [Checklist] .75 .20
487 Michal Pivonka, Wash. .75 .20
488 Pat Peake, Wash. .75 .20
489 Martin Gendron, Wash. 1.00 .20
490 Peter Bondra, Wash. 3.00 .20
491 Nolan Baumgartner, Wash. 1.00 .20
492 Jim Carey (G), Wash. .75 .20
493 Steve Konowalchuk, Wash. 1.00 .20
494 Jason Allison, Wash. 3.00 .20
495 Capitals, Wash. [Checklist] .75 .20
496 Oleg Tverdovsky, Winn. .75 .20
497 Craig Mills, Winn. RC 2.00 .50
498 Darren Turcotte, Winn. .75 .20
499 Norm Maciver, Winn. .75 .20
500 Chad Kilger, Winn. 2.00 .20
501 Keith Tkachuk, Winn. 3.00 .20
502 Kris King, Winn. .75 .20
503 Dallas Drake, Winn. .75 .20
504 Jets, Winn. [Checklist] .75 .20
505 Saku Koivu, Mont. 4.00 .50
506 Vitali Yachmenev, LosA. .75 .20
507 Daniel Alfredsson, Otta. 6.00 .50
508 Radek Dvorak, Flor. 2.00 .20
509 Miroslav Satan, Edmo. 3.00 .20
510 Aki Berg, LosA. 1.50 .20
511 Valeri Bure, Mont. 1.50 .20
512 Petr Sykora, NJer. 4.00 .50
513 Andrei Vasilyev, NYIs. RC 2.00 .50
514 Niklas Sundström, NYRa. 1.00 .20
515 Viktor Kozlov, SanJ. 1.50 .20
516 Sami Kapanen, Hart. 3.00 .20
517 Anders Myrvold, Colo. RC 3.00 .50
518 Jere Lehtinen, Dall. 1.50 .20
519 Marcus Ragnarsson, SanJ. 2.00 .20
520 Stefan Ustorf, Wash. 1.00 .20
521 Ville Peltonen, SanJ. .75 .20
522 Antti Törmänen, Otta. 1.00 .20
523 Petr Sykora, NJer. RC 8.00 2.00
524 Scott Bailey, Bost. RC 3.00 .50
525 Kevin Hodson, Detr. RC 4.50 3.00
526 Landon Wilson, Colo. RC 3.00 .50
527 Aaron Gavey, Tamp. .75 .20
528 D. Langdon, NYRa. RC 4.50 1.00
529 Jason Doig, Winn. 1.00 .20
530 Marty Murray, Calg. 1.00 .20
531 M. Ragnarsson, SanJ. RC 4.50 1.00
532 Peter Ferraro, NYRa. 1.50 .20
533 Grant Marshall, Dall. RC 3.00 .50
534 Mike Wilson, Buff. RC 2.00 .50
535 Rory Fitzpatrick, Mont. 1.00 .20
536 Ed Jovanovski, Flor. 4.00 .50
537 Éric Fichaud (G), NYIs. .75 .20
538 Stefan Ustorf, Wash. .75 .20
539 Stéphane Yelle, Colo. RC 3.00 .50
540 Ethan Moreau, Chic. RC 3.00 2.00

Oversize Cards - 5x7
Saku Koivu, Mont. - 5.00
Saku Koivu Autograph ✍ - 50.00

ALL-STAR

Series Two Insert Set (6 cards): 80.00
Insert (1:96) AS
1 W. Gretzky / M. Lemieux 55.00
2 B. Hull / J. Jagr 10.00
3 P. Bure / B. Shanahan 8.00
4 C. Chelios / S. Stevens 4.00
5 P. Coffey / R. Bourque 8.00
6 E. Belfour (G) / M. Brodeur 12.00

AUTOGRAPHS

These autographed cards were inserted in both Series One and Series Two packs.

Autograph Auto.
Martin Brodeur (G), NJer. ✍ 70.00
Saku Koivu, Mont. ✍ 35.00
Mikael Renberg, Phil. ✍ 12.00
Teemu Selänne, Winn. ✍ 30.00

CROWN COLLECTION

These cards have two versions: the regular insert and a gold parallel. Black border cards were inserted in series one packs and purple border cards were inserted in series two packs.

Black Insert Set (16 cards): 165.00 75.00
Purple Insert Set (16 cards): 170.00 75.00
Black GCC CC
1 Eric Lindros, Phil. 10.00 4.00
2 Félix Potvin (G), Toro. 6.00 2.00
3 Mario Lemieux, Pitt. 30.00 15.00
4 Paul Kariya, Anah. 14.00 6.00
5 Pavel Bure, Vanc. 8.00 4.00
6 Wayne Gretzky, LosA. 40.00 20.00
7 Mikael Renberg, Phil. 4.00 2.00
8 Paul Coffey, Detr. 6.00 2.00
9 Teemu Selänne, Winn. 8.00 4.00
10 Brett Hull, SLou. 10.00 4.00
11 Martin Brodeur (G), NJer. 16.00 8.00
12 Doug Gilmour, Toro. 6.00 2.00
13 Peter Forsberg, Colo. 14.00 6.00
14 Sergei Fedorov, Detr. 10.00 4.00
15 Saku Koivu, Mont. 12.00 6.00
16 Jim Carey (G), Wash. 4.00 2.00
Purple GCC CC
1 Jaromir Jagr, Pitt. 10.00 4.00
2 Patrick Roy (G), Colo. 30.00 15.00
3 Alexander Mogilny, Vanc. 4.00 2.00
4 Paul Kariya, Anah. 14.00 6.00
5 Dominik Hasek (G), Buff. 10.00 4.00
6 Peter Forsberg, Colo. 14.00 6.00
7 Mark Messier, NYRa. 10.00 4.00
8 Mats Sundin, Toro. 10.00 4.00
9 Raymond Bourque, Bost. 12.00 6.00
10 Wayne Gretzky, SLou. 40.00 20.00
11 Eric Lindros, Phil. 10.00 4.00
12 John Vanbiesbrouck (G), Flor. 4.00 2.00
13 Chris Chelios, Chic. 6.00 2.00
14 Brian Leetch, NYRa. 6.00 2.00
15 Daniel Alfredsson, Otta. 12.00 6.00
16 Éric Dazé, Chic. 8.00 4.00

GOAL PATROL

These series one goalie inserts are embossed.

Series One Insert Set (12 cards): 50.00
Insert (1:24) GP
1 Martin Brodeur (G), NJer. 12.00
2 Félix Potvin (G), Toro. 4.00
3 Patrick Roy (G), Mont. 22.00
4 Dominik Hasek (G), Buff. 6.00
5 Jim Carey (G), Wash. 2.00
6 Ed Belfour (G), Chic. 6.00
7 John Vanbiesbrouck (G), Flor. 2.00
8 Trevor Kidd (G), Calg. 2.00
9 Bill Ranford (G), Edmo. 2.00
10 Arturs Irbe (G), SanJ. 2.00
11 Kirk McLean (G), Vanc. 2.00
12 Mike Richter (G), NYRa. 2.00

INTERNATIONAL ALL-STAR

Series One Insert Set (6 cards): 50.00

Insert (1:96) IAS
1 D. Hasek (G) / A. Irbe (G) 10.00
2 N. Lidström / S. Ozolinsh 5.00
3 A. Zhitnik / S. Zubov 4.00
4 S. Fedorov / P. Forsberg 20.00
5 J. Jagr / T. Selänne 15.00
6 M. Renberg / M. Sundin 10.00

PARKIE PICKS

Series Two Insert Set (54 cards): 430.00
Insert (of 1000) PP
PP2 Eric Lindros, Phil. 10.00
PP2 Mario Lemieux, Pitt. 30.00
PP3 Sergei Fedorov, Detr. 10.00
PP4 Peter Forsberg, Colo. 14.00
PP5 John Vanbiesbrouck (G), Flor. 4.00
PP6 Mark Messier, NYRa. 10.00
PP7 Jaromir Jagr, Pitt. 10.00
PP8 Joe Sakic, Colo. 16.00
PP9 Grant Fuhr (G), SLou. 6.00
PP10 Eric Lindros, Phil. 10.00
PP11 Mario Lemieux, Pitt. 30.00
PP12 Mark Messier, NYRa. 10.00
PP13 Peter Forsberg, Colo. 14.00
PP14 Jaromir Jagr, Pitt. 10.00
PP15 Paul Kariya, Anah. 14.00
PP16 Joe Sakic, Colo. 16.00
PP17 Teemu Selänne, Anah. 8.00
PP18 Alexander Mogilny, Vanc. 4.00
PP19 Paul Coffey, Detr. 6.00
PP20 Chris Chelios, Chic. 6.00
PP21 Brian Leetch, NYRa. 6.00
PP22 Raymond Bourque, Bost. 12.00
PP23 Larry Murphy, Toro. 4.00
PP24 Nicklas Lidström, Detr. 6.00
PP25 Roman Hamrlik, Tamp. 4.00
PP26 Gary Suter, Chic. 4.00
PP27 Sergei Zubov, Pitt. 4.00
PP28 Dominik Hasek (G), Buff. 10.00
PP29 John Vanbiesbrouck (G), Flor. 4.00
PP30 Chris Osgood (G), Detr. 6.00
PP31 Mike Richter (G), NYRa. 6.00
PP32 Martin Brodeur (G), NJer. 16.00
PP33 Ron Hextall (G), Phil. 6.00
PP34 Grant Fuhr (G), SLou. 6.00
PP35 Patrick Roy (G), Colo. 30.00
PP36 Jim Carey (G), Wash. 4.00
PP37 Vitali Yachmenev, LosA. 4.00
PP38 Daniel Alfredsson, Otta. 12.00
PP39 Saku Koivu, Mont. 12.00
PP40 Éric Dazé, Chic. 4.00
PP41 Marcus Ragnarsson, SanJ. 4.00
PP42 Ed Jovanovski, Flor. 4.00
PP43 Petr Sykora, NJer. 8.00
PP44 Todd Bertuzzi, NYIs. 24.00
PP45 Radek Dvorak, Flor. 4.00
PP46 Paul Kariya, Anah. 14.00
PP47 Ron Francis, Pitt. 6.00
PP48 Alexander Mogilny, Vanc. 4.00
PP49 Pat LaFontaine, Buff. 6.00
PP50 Pierre Turgeon, Mont. 4.00
PP51 Teemu Selänne, Anah. 8.00
PP52 Sergei Fedorov, Detr. 10.00
PP53 Adam Oates, Bost. 4.00
PP54 Brett Hull, SLou. 10.00

TROPHY WINNERS

Series One Insert Set (6 cards): 20.00

Insert (1:24) TW
1 Eric Lindros, Phil. 5.00
2 Jaromir Jagr, Pitt. 5.00
3 Peter Forsberg, Colo. 5.00
4 Paul Coffey, Detr. 3.00
5 Dominik Hasek (G), Buff. 5.00
6 Ron Francis, Pitt. 3.00

1995 - 97 PARKHURST 24 KT. GOLD

The first nine cards were produced for 1995-96 while the Lemieux card was produced for 1996-97. Each card was serial numbered out of 1,000. The three prototypes for 1996-97 that are known to exist are Ray Bourque, Martin Brodeur (G) and Sergei Fedorov. It is estimated that only a handful of these prototypes exist.

Player NRMT-MT
Ed Belfour (G), Chic. 70.00
Peter Forsberg, Colo. 80.00
Jaromir Jagr, Pitt. 90.00
Paul Kariya, Anah. 90.00
Brian Leetch, NYRa. 70.00
Eric Lindros, Phil. 90.00
Jacques Plante, Mont. 80.00
Patrick Roy (G), Mont. 125.00
Teemu Selänne, Winn. 70.00

1995 - 96 PARKHURST REVOLUTION - '66-67

Numbers 1-120 have two versions: the regular card and a one per pack cap parallel. There are also five promo cards. These promo cards are valued at about 2 times the regular issue. The Paul Henderson cap, although said not to be short printed, is usually a tough find and thus the most expensive in the series.

Complete Set (150 cards): 25.00
Cap Set (120 wheels): 95.00
Album: 15.00
Bruins Shield: 10.00
Blackhawks Shield: 10.00
Red Wings Shield: 10.00
Canadiens Shield: 10.00
Rangers Shield: 10.00
Maple Leafs Shield: 10.00
Common Player: .60 .20
Player Cap Card
1 Pit Martin, Bost. .60 .20
2 Ron Stewart, Bost. .60 .20
3 Joe Watson, Bost. .60 .20
4 Ed Westfall, Bost. .60 .20
5 John Bucyk, Bost. 2.00 .50
6 Ted Green, Bost. .60 .20
7 Bobby Orr, Bost. 14.00 5.00
8 Bob Woytowich, Bost. .60 .20
9 Murray Oliver, Bost. .60 .20
10 John McKenzie, Bost. .60 .20
11 Tom Williams, Bost. .60 .20
12 Don Awrey, Bost. .60 .20
13 Ron Schock, Bost. .60 .20
14 Bernie Parent (G), Bost. 2.50 1.00
15 Ron Murphy, Bost. .60 .20
16 Gerry Cheevers (G), Bost. 2.50 1.00
17 Gilles Marotte, Bost. .60 .20
18 Ed Johnston, Bost. .60 .20
19 Derek Sanderson, Bost. 1.00 .20
20 Wayne Connelly, Bost. .60 .20
21 Bobby Hull, Chi. 6.00 2.00
22 Matt Pavelich, Chi. .60 .20
23 Ken Hodge, Chi. .60 .20
24 Stan Mikita, Chi. 2.50 1.00
25 Fred Stanfield, Chi. .60 .20
26 Eric Nesterenko, Chi. .60 .20
27 Doug Jarrett, Chi. .60 .20
28 Lou Angotti, Chi. .60 .20
29 Ken Wharram, Chi. .60 .20
30 Bill Hay, Chi. .60 .20
31 Glenn Hall (G), Chi. 3.50 1.00
32 Chico Maki, Chi. .60 .20
33 Phil Esposito, Chi. 4.00 1.50
34 Pierre Pilote, Chi. 1.50 .50
35 Doug Mohns, Chi. .60 .20
36 Ed Van Impe, Chi. .60 .20
37 Dennis Hull, Chi. 1.00 .20
38 Pat Stapleton, Chi. 1.00 .20
39 Dennis DeJordy (G), Chi. .60 .20
40 Paul Henderson, Detr. 15.00 .50
41 Gary Bergman, Detr. .60 .20
42 Gordie Howe, Detr. 8.00 3.50
43 Bob McCord, Detr. .60 .20
44 Andy Bathgate, Detr. 1.50 .50
45 Norm Ullman, Detr. 1.50 .50
46 Peter Mahovlich, Detr. 1.00 .50
47 Ted Hampson, Detr. .60 .20
48 Léo Boivin, Detr. 1.00 .50
49 Bruce MacGregor, Detr. .60 .20
50 Ab McDonald, Detr. .60 .20
51 Dean Prentice, Detr. .60 .20
52 Floyd Smith, Detr. .60 .20
53 Alex Delvecchio, Detr. 1.50 .50
54 Pete Goegan, Detr. .60 .20
55 Parker McDonald, Detr. .60 .20
56 Roger Crozier (G), Detr. .60 .20
57 Val Fonteyne, Detr. .60 .20
58 Henri Richard, Mont. 3.50 1.00
59 John Ferguson, Mont. 1.00 .20
60 Yvan Cournoyer, Mont. 2.00 .50
61 Claude Provost, Mont. .60 .20
62 Dave Balon, Mont. .60 .20
63 Ted Harris, Mont. .60 .20
64 Ralph Backstrom, Mont. .60 .20
65 Jacques Laperrière, Mont. 1.00 .50
66 Terry Harper, Mont. .60 .20
67 J.C. Tremblay, Mont. .60 .20
68 Jean Guy Talbot, Mont. .60 .20
69 Claude Larose, Mont. .60 .20
70 Charlie Hodge (G), Mont. 1.00 .20
71 Gilles Tremblay, Mont. .60 .20
72 Jim Roberts, Mont. .60 .20
73 Jean Béliveau, Mont. 6.00 2.50
74 Serge Savard, Mont. 1.50 .50
75 Rogatien Vachon (G), Mont. 1.00 .50
76 Gump Worsley (G), Mont. 2.50 1.00
77 Bobby Rousseau, Mont. .60 .20
78 Dick Duff, Mont. .60 .20
79 Rod Gilbert, NYRa. 1.00 .50
80 Harry Howell, NYRa. 1.00 .50
81 Jim Neilson, NYRa. .60 .20
82 Don Marshall, NYRa. .60 .20
83 Reg Fleming, NYRa. .60 .20
84 Wayne Hillman, NYRa. .60 .20
85 Bob Nevin, NYRa. .60 .20
86 Arnie Brown, NYRa. .60 .20
87 Earl Ingarfield, NYRa. .60 .20
88 Jean Ratelle, NYRa. 1.00 .50
89 Bernie Geoffrion, NYRa. 2.50 1.00
90 Orland Kurtenbach, NYRa. .60 .20
91 Bill Hicke, NYRa. .60 .20
92 Red Berenson, NYRa. .60 .20
93 Ed Giacomin (G), NYRa. 2.50 1.00
94 Al MacNeil, NYRa. .60 .20
95 Rod Seiling, NYRa. .60 .20
96 Doug Robinson, NYRa. .60 .20
97 Cesare Maniago (G), NYRa. .60 .20
98 Vic Hadfield, NYRa. .60 .20
99 Phil Goyette, NYRa. .60 .20
100 Dave Keon, Toro. 2.50 1.00
101 Mike Walton, Toro. .60 .20
102 Frank Mahovlich, Toro. 3.50 1.00
103 Tim Horton, Toro. 4.00 1.50
104 Larry Hillman, Toro. .60 .20
105 Kent Douglas, Toro. .60 .20
106 Ron Ellis, Toro. 1.00 .20
107 Jim Pappin, Toro. .60 .20
108 Marcel Pronovost, Toro. 1.00 .50
109 Red Kelly, Toro. 2.00 .50

110 Allan Stanley, Toro.	1.00	.50
111 Brit Selby, Toro.	.60	.20
112 Pete Stemkowski, Toro.	.60	.20
113 Eddie Shack, Toro.	1.00	.50
114 Bob Pulford, Toro.	1.00	.50
115 Larry Jeffrey, Toro.	.60	.20
116 George Armstrong, Toro.	1.00	.50
117 Bobby Baun, Toro.	1.00	.20
118 Bruce Gamble (G), Toro.	.60	.20
119 Johnny Bower (G), Toro.	2.50	1.00
120 Terry Sawchuk (G), Toro.	6.00	2.50
121 AS: Hall (G)/ Worsley (G)		1.00
122 AS: Laperrière/ Allan Stanley		.50
123 AS: Pierre Pilote/ Pat Stapleton		.50
124 AS: Bobby Hull/ Frank Mahovlich		1.50
125 AS: Stan Mikita/ Jean Béliveau		1.50
126 AS: Gordie Howe/ Bobby Rousseau		1.50
127 AW: Alex Delvecchio, Detr.		.50
128 AW: Jacques Laperrière, Mont.		.50
129 AW: Bobby Hull, Chi.		2.00
130 AW: Bobby Hull, Chi.		2.00
131 AW: Worsley (G)/ Hodge (G), Mont.		.50
132 AW: Brit Selby, Toro.		.20
133 All-Stars Eye Richard		.50
134 Boston Young Stars		1.50
135 Gump Stumps Golden Jet		.50
136 Ellis Beats Crozier		.20
137 Habs Protect Roggie		.20
138 Phil Fills The Crease		.50
139 All Hands on Deck		.20
140 TL: Murray Oliver, Bost.		.20
141 TL: Bobby Hull, Chi.		2.00
142 TL: Gordie Howe, Detr.		3.50
143 TL: Bobby Rousseau, Mont.		.20
144 TL: Bob Nevin, NYRa.		.20
145 TL: Frank Mahovlich/ Pulford, Toro.		.50
146 Semi-finals		.20
147 Semi-finals		1.00
148 Finals		1.00
149 Checklist		.20
150 Checklist		.20

MR. HOCKEY

There are four versions to this set: the regular insert ($15), an autographed card ($110), a cap parallel ($10) and a 5"x7" promo ($12).

Player	Player
MH1 Howe	MH2 Howe
MH3 Howe	MH4 Howe
MH5 Howe	

SUPER ROOKIE

There are four versions to this set: the regular insert ($20), an autographed card ($165), a cap parallel ($12) and a 5"x7" promo ($15).

Player	Player
SR1 Bobby Orr	SR2 Bobby Orr
SR3 Bobby Orr	SR4 Bobby Orr
SR5 Bobby Orr	

REDEMPTION

Each series of of six cards was available through a redemption offer.

Complete Set (18 cards):	45.00
Player	NRMT-MT
AS1 Ed Giacomin (G)	4.00
AS2 Pierre Pilote	2.00
AS3 Harry Howell	2.00
AS4 Bobby Hull	5.00
AS5 Stan Mikita	1.50
AS6 Ken Wharram	1.50
SL1 Johnny Bucyk	3.00
SL2 Stan Mikita	1.50
SL3 Norm Ullman	2.00
SL4 Bobby Rousseau	1.50
SL5 Phil Goyette	1.50
SL6 Dave Keon	4.00
TW1 Stan Mikita	1.50
TW2 Stan Mikita	1.50
TW3 Stan Mikita	1.50
TW4 Harry Howell	2.00
TW5 Bobby Orr	20.00
TW6 D. DeJordy (G)/ G. Hall (G)	1.50

1995 - 96 PINNACLE

These cards have three versions: a regular card, a Rink Collection parallel (dufex technology) and an Artist's Proof parallel (dufex with Artist's Proof stamp). Cards 100-125 have horizontal pictures. An intended second series was never released. Seven cards have a clipped promo version. Promo and regular cards have the same value.

Complete Set (225 cards):	1600.00	250.00	15.00
Common Player:	4.00	1.00	.20
Player	AP	Rink	Reg.
1 Pavel Bure, Vanc.	35.00	6.00	.50
2 Paul Kariya, Anah.	60.00	10.00	.50
3 Adam Oates, Bost.	15.00	2.00	.20
4 Garry Galley, Buff.	4.00	1.00	.20
5 Mark Messier, NYRa.	45.00	6.00	.50
6 Theoren Fleury, Calg.	25.00	4.00	.20
7 Alexandre Daigle, Otta.	6.00	1.00	.20
8 Joe Murphy, Chic.	6.00	1.00	.20
9 Eric Lindros, Phil.	45.00	6.00	.50
10 Kevin Hatcher, Dall.	6.00	1.00	.20
11 Jaromir Jagr, Pitt.	45.00	6.00	.50
12 O. Nolan, Québ. (Colo.)	25.00	4.00	.20
13 Ulf Dahlén, SanJ.	6.00	1.00	.20
14 Paul Coffey, Detr.	25.00	4.00	.20
15 Brett Hull, SLou.	45.00	6.00	.50
16 Jason Arnott, Edmo.	20.00	2.00	.20
17 Paul Ysebaert, Tamp.	4.00	1.00	.20
18 Jesse Bélanger, Flor.	4.00	1.00	.20
19 Mats Sundin, Toro.	45.00	6.00	.50
20 D. Turcotte & son	6.00	1.00	.20
21 Dale Hunter, Wash.	14.00	2.00	.20
22 Jari Kurri, LosA.	45.00	6.00	.50
23 Alexei Zhamnov, Winn.	14.00	2.00	.20
24 Mark Recchi, Mont.	15.00	2.00	.20
25 Dallas Drake, Winn.	6.00	1.00	.20
26 John MacLean, NJer.	6.00	1.00	.20
27 Keith Jones, Wash.	6.00	1.00	.20
28 M. Schneider, NYIs.	10.00	1.00	.20
29 Jeff R. Brown, Vanc.	4.00	1.00	.20
30 Patrick Flatley, NYIs.	4.00	1.00	.20
31 Dave Andreychuk, Toro.	14.00	2.00	.20
32 Bill Guerin w/ Cup	15.00	2.00	.20
33 Chris Gratton, Tamp.	10.00	1.00	.20
34 Pierre Turgeon, Mont.	15.00	2.00	.20
35 Stéphane Richer, NJer.	10.00	1.00	.20
36 Marty McSorley, LosA.	10.00	1.00	.20
37 Craig Janney, SanJ.	10.00	1.00	.20
38 Geoff Sanderson, Hart.	10.00	1.00	.20
39 Ron Francis, Pitt.	25.00	4.00	.20
40 Stu Barnes, Flor.	4.00	1.00	.20
41 Mikael Renberg, Phil.	14.00	2.00	.20
42 David Oliver, Edmo.	4.00	1.00	.20
43 Radek Bonk, Otta.	14.00	2.00	.20
44 Sergei Fedorov, Detr.	45.00	6.00	.50
45 Adam Graves, NYRa.	15.00	2.00	.20
46 U. Krupp, Québ. (Colo.)	4.00	1.00	.20
47 M. Richter (G), NYRa.	20.00	2.00	.20
48 Todd Harvey, Dall.	10.00	1.00	.20
49 Stanislav Neckar, Otta.	6.00	1.00	.20
50 Chris Chelios, Chic.	25.00	4.00	.20
51 John LeClair, Phil.	35.00	6.00	.50
52 German Titov, Calg.	4.00	1.00	.20
53 Garth Butcher, Toro.	4.00	1.00	.20
54 Pat LaFontaine, Buff.	25.00	4.00	.20
55 Jeff Friesen, SanJ.	14.00	2.00	.20
56 R. Bourque, Bost.	50.00	8.00	.50
57 Esa Tikkanen, SLou.	6.00	1.00	.20
58 Steve Rucchin, Anah.	10.00	1.00	.20
59 Roman Hamrlik, Tamp.	10.00	1.00	.20
60 Oleg Tverdovsky, Anah.	6.00	1.00	.20
61 Doug Gilmour, Toro.	25.00	4.00	.20
62 Jocelyn Lemieux, Hart.	4.00	1.00	.20
63 Roman Oksiuta, Vanc.	4.00	1.00	.20
64 Alexei Zhitnik, Buff.	6.00	1.00	.20
65 Sylvain Côté, Wash.	6.00	1.00	.20
66 Paul Kruse, Calg.	4.00	1.00	.20
67 Teppo Numminen, Winn.	14.00	2.00	.20
68 Gary Suter, Chic.	10.00	1.00	.20
69 Darrin Shannon, Winn.	4.00	1.00	.20
70 Derian Hatcher, Dall.	14.00	2.00	.20
71 Sergei Gonchar, Wash.	14.00	2.00	.20
72 Deadmarsh, Québ.(Colo.)	14.00	2.00	.20
73 Jyrki Lumme, Vanc.	10.00	1.00	.20
74 Dino Ciccarelli, Detr.	14.00	2.00	.20
75 Mike Gartner, Toro.	35.00	6.00	.50
76 Todd Marchant, Edmo.	10.00	1.00	.20
77 Jason Wiemer, Tamp.	4.00	1.00	.20
78 Scott Mellanby, Flor.	10.00	1.00	.20
79 Al MacInnis, SLou.	15.00	2.00	.20
80 Glen Wesley, Hart.	6.00	1.00	.20
81 Igor Larionov, SanJ.	25.00	4.00	.20
82 Éric Lacroix, LosA.	4.00	1.00	.20
83 Mike Keane, Mont.	6.00	1.00	.20
84 V. Damphousse, Mont.	25.00	4.00	.20
85 Robert Kron, Hart.	6.00	1.00	.20
86 Scott Stevens w/ Cup	15.00	2.00	.20
87 Don Beaupré (G), Otta.	6.00	1.00	.20
88 Zigmund Palffy, NYIs.	25.00	4.00	.20
89 Kevin Lowe, NYRa.	14.00	2.00	.20
90 T. Söderström (G), NYIs.	6.00	1.00	.20
91 Glenn Healy (G), NYRa.	10.00	1.00	.20
92 Randy McKay, NJer.	4.00	1.00	.20
93 Sean Hill, Otta.	4.00	1.00	.20
94 Brian Savage, Mont.	14.00	2.00	.20
95 Ron Hextall (G), Phil.	25.00	4.00	.20
96 Darryl Sydor, LosA.	10.00	1.00	.20
97 Tom Barrasso (G), Pitt.	15.00	2.00	.20
98 Andrei Nikolishin, Hart.	6.00	1.00	.20
99 Viktor Kozlov, SanJ.	14.00	2.00	.20
100 Rob Niedermayer, Flor.	10.00	1.00	.20
101 W. Gretzky, LosA.	180.00	30.00	2.50
102 Shaun Van Allen, Anah.	6.00	1.00	.20
103 Dave Manson, Winn.	6.00	1.00	.20
104 Donald Audette, Buff.	15.00	2.00	.20
105 D. Puppa (G), Tamp.	10.00	1.00	.20
106 Jeremy Roenick, Chic.	35.00	6.00	.50
107 Ken Wregget (G), Pitt.	10.00	1.00	.20
108 Mike Modano, Dall.	45.00	6.00	.50
109 Rod Brind'Amour, Phil.	14.00	2.00	.20
110 Éric Desjardins, Phil.	14.00	2.00	.20
111 Pat Verbeek, NYRa.	14.00	2.00	.20
112 Jeff Beukeboom, NYRa.	6.00	1.00	.20
113 John Druce, LosA.	4.00	1.00	.20
114 Andy Moog (G), Dall.	15.00	2.00	.20
115 Turner Stevenson, Mont.	6.00	1.00	.20
116 A. Selivanov, Tamp.	4.00	1.00	.20
117 Neal Broten, NJer.	10.00	1.00	.20
118 N. Khabibulin (G), Winn.	15.00	2.00	.20
119 Claude Lemieux, NJer.	14.00	2.00	.20
120 Sergei Brylin, NJer.	6.00	1.00	.20
121 Bob Corkum, Anah.	4.00	1.00	.20
122 K. Hrudey (G), LosA.	14.00	2.00	.20
123 Jason Dawe, Buff.	4.00	1.00	.20
124 Sean Burke (G), Hart.	25.00	4.00	.20
125 Dave Gagner, Dall.	6.00	1.00	.20
126 Kirk Maltby, Edmo.	10.00	1.00	.20
127 Ian Laperrière, SLou.	6.00	1.00	.20
128 Vy. Kozlov, Detr.	10.00	1.00	.20
129 V. Konstantinov, Detr.	14.00	2.00	.20
130 Kenny Jönsson, Toro.	8.00	1.00	.20
131 Lefebvre, Québ. (Colo.)	6.00	1.00	.20
132 Kirk McLean (G), Vanc.	14.00	2.00	.20
133 Brian Leetch, NYRa.	25.00	4.00	.20
134 Olaf Kölzig (G), Wash.	25.00	4.00	.20
135 Patrick Poulin, Chic.	6.00	1.00	.20
136 Chevelade (G), Winn.	6.00	1.00	.20
137 Gary Roberts, Calg.	15.00	2.00	.20
138 Jim Carey (G), Wash.	6.00	1.00	.20
139 D. Hasek (G), Buff.	45.00	6.00	.50
140 Josef Beranek, Vanc.	6.00	1.00	.20
141 Don Sweeney, Bost.	6.00	1.00	.20
142 Félix Potvin (G), Toro.	25.00	4.00	.20
143 Guy Hebert (G), Anah.	10.00	1.00	.20
144 G. Carbonneau, SLou.	14.00	2.00	.20
145 M. Shtalenkov, Anah.	6.00	1.00	.20
146 Kevin Miller, SanJ.	6.00	1.00	.20
147 Blaine Lacher (G), Bost.	6.00	1.00	.20
148 Craig MacTavish, Phil.	6.00	1.00	.20
149 Derek Plante, Buff.	6.00	1.00	.20
150 Kevin Dineen, Phil.	6.00	1.00	.20
151 Trevor Kidd (G), Calg.	14.00	2.00	.20
152 S. Nemchinov, NYRa.	10.00	1.00	.20
153 Ed Belfour (G), Chic.	45.00	6.00	.50
154 S. Krivokrasov, Chic.	6.00	1.00	.20
155 Mike Rathje, SanJ.	6.00	1.00	.20
156 Mike Donnelly, Dall.	4.00	1.00	.20
157 David Roberts, SLou.	4.00	1.00	.20
158 Thibault (G),Québ.(Colo.)	15.00	2.00	.20
159 Tie Domi, Toro.	14.00	2.00	.20
160 C. Osgood (G), Detr.	25.00	4.00	.20
161 Martin Gélinas, Vanc.	10.00	1.00	.20
162 Scott Thornton, Edmo.	4.00	1.00	.20
163 Bob Rouse, Detr.	4.00	1.00	.20
164 Randy Wood, Toro.	4.00	1.00	.20
165 Chris Therien, Phil.	4.00	1.00	.20
166 Steven Rice, Hart.	4.00	1.00	.20
167 Scott Lachance, NYIs.	6.00	1.00	.20
168 Petr' Svoboda, Phil.	10.00	1.00	.20
169 P. Roy (G), Mont.	135.00	22.00	1.50
170 Norm Maciver, Pitt.	4.00	1.00	.20
171 Todd Gill, Toro.	6.00	1.00	.20
172 Brian Rolston, NJer.	14.00	2.00	.20
173 W. Flaherty, SanJ. RC	**10.00**	**2.00**	**.50**
174 Valeri Bure, Mont.	14.00	2.00	.20
175 M. Fitzpatrick (G), Flor.	6.00	1.00	.20
176 Darren McCarty, Detr.	14.00	2.00	.20
177 Ken Daneyko, NJer.	10.00	1.00	.20
178 Yves Racine, Mont.	4.00	1.00	.20
179 Murray Craven, Chic.	6.00	1.00	.20
180 N. Lidström, Detr.	25.00	4.00	.20
181 Gord Murphy, Flor.	4.00	1.00	.20
182 Eric Weinrich, Chic.	4.00	1.00	.20
183 Todd Krygier, Anah.	4.00	1.00	.20
184 Cliff Ronning, Vanc.	10.00	1.00	.20
185 M. Czerkawski, Bost.	10.00	1.00	.20
186 Benoit Hogue, Toro.	6.00	1.00	.20
187 Richard Smehlik, Buff.	4.00	1.00	.20
188 Jeff Norton, SLou.	4.00	1.00	.20
189 Steve Chiasson, Calg.	6.00	1.00	.20
190 Andrei Nazarov, SanJ.	6.00	1.00	.20
191 J. Steve Smith, Chic.	10.00	1.00	.20
192 Mario Lemieux, Pitt.	135.00	22.00	1.50
193 Trent Klatt, Dall.	6.00	1.00	.20
194 Valeri Zelepukin, NJer.	4.00	1.00	.20
195 A. Foote, Québ. (Colo.)	14.00	2.00	.20
196 Lyle Odelein, Mont.	6.00	1.00	.20
197 Keith Primeau, Detr.	15.00	2.00	.20
198 Rob Blake, LosA.	25.00	4.00	.20
199 Dave Lowry, Flor.	10.00	1.00	.20
200 Adam Burt, Hart.	4.00	1.00	.20
201 Martin Gendron, Wash.	8.00	1.00	.20
202 T. Salo (G), NYIs. RC	**35.00**	**8.00**	**2.00**
203 Éric Dazé, Chic.	35.00	6.00	.50
204 Ryan Smyth, Edmo.	20.00	2.00	.20
205 B. Holzinger, Buff. RC	**10.00**	**2.00**	**.50**
206 C. Marinucci, NYIs. RC	**5.00**	**2.00**	**.50**
207 J. Bonsignore, Edmo.	8.00	1.00	.20
208 Craig Johnson, SLou.	4.00	1.00	.20
209 S. Larouche, Otta. RC	**5.00**	**2.00**	**.50**
210 C. McAlpine, NJer. RC	**5.00**	**2.00**	**.50**
211 Shean Donovan, SanJ.	6.00	1.00	.20
212 Cory Stillman, Calg.	10.00	1.00	.20
213 Craig Darby, NYIs.	6.00	1.00	.20
214 P. DeRouville, Pitt.	14.00	2.00	.20
215 Kevin Brown, LosA.	4.00	1.00	.20
216 Fernandez (G), Dall.	35.00	6.00	.50
217 Radim Bicanek, Otta.	8.00	1.00	.20
218 C. Conroy, Mont. RC	**25.00**	**6.00**	**1.50**
219 Todd Warriner, Toro.	14.00	2.00	.20
220 Richard Park, Pitt.	8.00	1.00	.20
221 Checklist	4.00	1.00	.20
222 Checklist	4.00	1.00	.20
223 Checklist	4.00	1.00	.20
224 Checklist	4.00	1.00	.20
225 Checklist	4.00	1.00	.20

GLOBAL GREATS

These cards are identical to the regular series except for a different numbering system and a Global Gold stamp on the front.

Insert Set (25 cards):	25.00
Insert (1:6 International)	GG
1 Pavel Bure, Vanc.	2.00
2 Jaromir Jagr, Pitt.	2.50
3 Mats Sundin, Toro.	2.50
4 Jari Kurri, LosA.	2.50
5 Mikael Renberg, Phil.	.75
6 Radek Bonk, Otta.	.75
7 Sergei Fedorov, Detr.	2.50
8 Uwe Krupp, Québ.	.75
9 German Titov, Calg.	.75
10 Esa Tikkanen, SLou.	.75
11 Oleg Tverdovsky, Anah.	.75
12 Teppo Numminen, Winn.	.75
13 Jyrki Lumme, Vanc.	.75
14 Zigmund Palffy, NYIs.	1.50
15 Tommy Söderström (G), NYIs.	.75
16 Viktor Kozlov, SanJ.	.75
17 Alexander Selivanov, Tamp.	.75
18 Sergei Brylin, NJer.	.75
19 Dominik Hasek (G), Buff.	2.50
20 Sergei Nemchinov, NYRa.	.75
21 Petr Svoboda, Phil.	.75
22 Valeri Bure, Mont.	.75
23 Nicklas Lidström, Detr.	1.50
24 Mariusz Czerkawski, Bost.	.75
25 Valeri Zelepukin, NJer.	.75

CLEAR SHOT

Insert Set (15 cards):	115.00
Insert (1:60)	CS
1 Martin Brodeur (G), NJer.	10.00
2 Brett Hull, SLou.	6.00

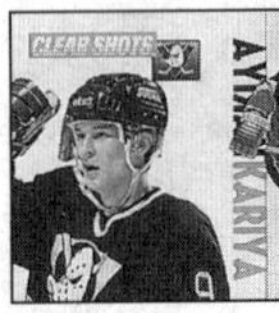

3 Paul Kariya, Anah.	8.00
4 Eric Lindros, Phil.	6.00
5 Cam Neely, Bost.	6.00
6 Doug Gilmour, Toro.	5.00
7 Sergei Fedorov, Detr.	6.00
8 Peter Forsberg, Québ. (Colo.)	8.00
9 Wayne Gretzky, LosA.	25.00
10 Patrick Roy (G), Mont.	18.00
11 Jaromir Jagr, Pitt.	6.00
12 Pavel Bure, Vanc.	5.00
13 Mario Lemieux, Pitt.	18.00
14 Pierre Turgeon, Mont.	5.00
15 Dominik Hasek (G), Buff.	6.00

FIRST STRIKE

Insert Set (15 cards):	50.00
Insert (1:24)	FS
1 Mark Messier, NYRa.	2.00
2 Wayne Gretzky, LosA.	14.00
3 Doug Gilmour, Toro.	2.00
4 Patrick Roy (G), Mont.	10.00
5 Cam Neely, Bost.	2.00
6 Brian Leetch, NYRa.	2.00
7 Ed Belfour (G), Chic.	2.00
8 Wendel Clark, Québ. (Colo.)	2.00
9 Chris Chelios, Chic.	2.00
10 Claude Lemieux, NJer.	2.00
11 Peter Forsberg, Québ. (Colo.)	4.00
12 Brett Hull, SLou.	2.00
13 Mario Lemieux, Pitt.	10.00
14 Dominik Hasek (G), Buff.	2.00
15 Theoren Fleury, Calg.	2.00

FULL CONTACT

Insert Set (12 cards):	45.00
Insert (1:9 Jumbo)	FC
1 Cam Neely, Bost. [vs. Yushkevich]	8.00
2 Scott Stevens, NJer. [vs. Knipscheer]	2.00
3 Owen Nolan, Québ. (Colo.)	4.00
4 Jeremy Roenick, Chic.	6.00
5 Brendan Shanahan, SLou. [vs. Granato]	10.00
6 Chris Chelios, Chic. [vs. Thomas]	4.00
7 Brett Lindros, NYIs. [vs. Laus]	2.00
8 Jason Arnott, Edmo. [vs. Smolinski]	4.00
9 Tie Domi, Toro.	2.00
10 Mark Tinordi, Wash. [vs. LeClair]	2.00
11 Keith Tkachuk, Winn. [vs. Chelios]	4.00
12 Mark Messier, NYRa. [vs. Savage]	8.00

MASKS

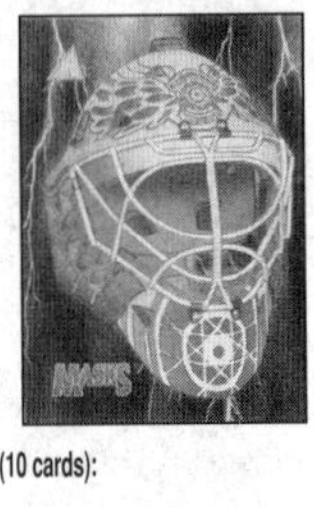

Insert Set (10 cards):	175.00

	Insert (1:90)	Mask
□	1 Blaine Lacher (G), Bost.	15.00
□	2 Martin Brodeur (G), NJer.	60.00
□	3 Jim Carey (G), Wash.	15.00
□	4 Félix Potvin (G), Toro.	20.00
□	5 Andy Moog (G), Dall.	15.00
□	6 Mike Vernon (G), Detr.	15.00
□	7 Mark Fitzpatrick (G), Flor.	15.00
□	8 Ron Hextall (G), Phil.	20.00
□	9 Sean Burke (G), Hart.	20.00
□	10 Jocelyn Thibault (G), Québ. (Colo.)	15.00

ROARING 20S

Insert Set (20 cards): 55.00

	Insert (1:19 Hobby)	R20s
□	1 Eric Lindros, Phil.	4.00
□	2 Paul Kariya, Anah.	6.00
□	3 Martin Brodeur (G), NJer.	6.00
□	4 Jeremy Roenick, Chic.	2.00
□	5 Mike Modano, Dall.	4.00
□	6 Sergei Fedorov, Detr.	4.00
□	7 Mats Sundin, Toro.	4.00
□	8 Pavel Bure, Vanc.	2.00
□	9 Jim Carey (G), Wash.	2.00
□	10 Félix Potvin (G), Toro.	2.00
□	11 Alexei Zhamnov, Winn.	2.00
□	12 Mikael Renberg, Phil.	2.00
□	13 Jaromir Jagr, Pitt.	4.00
□	14 Peter Bondra, Wash.	2.00
□	15 Peter Forsberg, Québ.	6.00
□	16 John LeClair, Phil.	2.00
□	17 Joe Sakic, Québ.	6.00
□	18 Brendan Shanahan, SLou.	4.00
□	19 Teemu Selänne, Winn.	2.00
□	20 Pierre Turgeon, Mont.	2.00

1995 - 96 PINNACLE FANTASY

Two-card packs were first handed out at the January 18-21 All-Star Game Fanfest weekend in Boston, Massachusetts.

Complete Set (31 cards): 45.00

	Player	NRMT-MT
□	1 Cam Neely, Bost.	2.00
□	2 Raymond Bourque, Bost.	2.00
□	3 Alexandre Daigle, Otta.	.50
□	4 Mariusz Czerkawski, Bost.	.50
□	5 Adam Oates, Bost.	.50
□	6 Brendan Shanahan, SLou.	2.00
□	7 Arturs Irbe (G), SanJ.	.50
□	8 Mario Lemieux, Pitt.	5.00
□	9 Theoren Fleury, Calg.	1.00
□	10 Patrick Roy (G), Mont.	5.00
□	11 Roman Hamrlik, Tamp.	.50
□	12 Pavel Bure, Vanc.	1.50
□	13 Wayne Gretzky, LosA.	5.00
□	14 Mike Modano, Dall.	2.00
□	15 Teemu Selänne, Winn.	1.50
□	16 John Vanbiesbrouck (G), Flor.	.50
□	17 Dominik Hasek (G), Buff.	2.00
□	18 Mark Messier, NYRa.	2.00
□	19 Martin Brodeur (G), NJer.	3.00
□	20 Jim Carey (G), Wash.	.50
□	21 Wendel Clark, Toro.	1.50
□	22 Jason Arnott, Edmo.	.50
□	23 Jeremy Roenick, Chic.	1.50
□	24 Brett Hull, SLou.	2.00
□	25 Peter Forsberg, Québ.	.50
□	26 Paul Kariya, Anah.	.50
□	27 Eric Lindros, Phil.	.50
□	28 Kevin Stevens, Pitt.	.50
□	29 Félix Potvin (G), Toro.	1.00
□	30 Sergei Fedorov, Detr.	2.00
□	31 Bobby Orr and Travis Roy	5.00

1995 - 96 PINNACLE SUMMIT

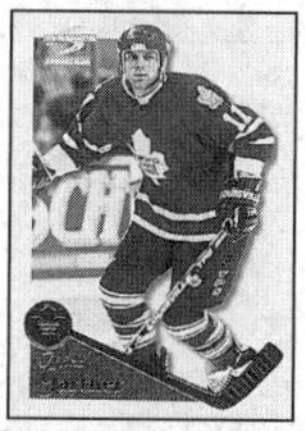

These cards have three versions: a regular card, the Summit Ice parallel and an Artist's Proof parallel. Seven regular cards also have a hole-punched promo version. Promo cards have the same value as the regular card.

Imprint: © 1996 Pinnacle Brands, Inc.

		AP	Ice	Reg.
	Complete Set (200 cards):	1800.00	275.00	20.00
	Common Player:	4.00	1.00	.20
	Player	AP	Ice	Reg.
□□□	1 Mark Messier, NYRa.	45.00	6.00	.50
□□□	2 Paul Kariya, Anah.	60.00	10.00	.50
□□□	3 Alexei Zhamnov, Winn.	14.00	2.00	.20
□□□	4 Adam Oates, Bost.	15.00	2.00	.20
□□□	5 Dale Hunter, Wash.	14.00	2.00	.20
□□□	6 Valeri Kamensky, Colo.	14.00	2.00	.20
□□□	7 Pavel Bure, Vanc.	35.00	6.00	.50
□□□	8 Theoren Fleury, Calg.	25.00	4.00	.20
□□□	9 Mats Sundin, Toro.	45.00	6.00	.50
□□□	10 Joe Murphy, Chic.	6.00	1.00	.20
□□□	11 Brian Bellows, Tamp.	10.00	1.00	.20
□□□	12 Owen Nolan, SanJ.	25.00	4.00	.20
□□□	13 Brett Hull, SLou.	45.00	6.00	.50
□□□	14 Mike Modano, Dall.	45.00	6.00	.50
□□□	15 Ulf Dahlén, SanJ.	6.00	1.00	.20
□□□□	16 Paul Coffey, Detr.	25.00	4.00	.20
□□□□	17 Jaromir Jagr, Pitt.	45.00	6.00	.50
□□□	18 Jason Arnott, Edmo.	20.00	2.00	.20
□□□	19 Eric Lindros, Phil.	45.00	6.00	.50
□□□	20 Jesse Bélanger, Flor.	4.00	1.00	.20
□□□	21 Alexandre Daigle, Otta.	6.00	1.00	.20
□□□	22 Darren Turcotte, Winn.	6.00	1.00	.20
□□□	23 Brian Leetch, NYRa.	25.00	4.00	.20
□□□	24 Wayne Gretzky, LosA.	180.00	30.00	2.50
□□□	25 M. Schneider, NYIs.	10.00	1.00	.20
□□□	26 Mark Recchi, Mont.	15.00	2.00	.20
□□□	27 M. Brodeur (G), NJer.	70.00	12.00	1.00
□□□	28 Igor Korolev, Winn.	6.00	1.00	.20
□□□	29 Thibault (G), Mont.	15.00	2.00	.20
□□□	30 Chris Pronger, SLou.	25.00	4.00	.20
□□□	31 Sergei Fedorov, Detr.	45.00	6.00	.50
□□□	32 Jari Kurri, LosA.	45.00	6.00	.50
□□□□	33 R. Bourque, Bost.	50.00	8.00	.50
□□□	34 Pat LaFontaine, Buff.	25.00	4.00	.20
□□□	35 Don Beaupré (G), Otta.	6.00	1.00	.20
□□□	36 Dave Andreychuk, Toro.	14.00	2.00	.20
□□□	37 Oleg Tverdovsky, Anah.	6.00	1.00	.20
□□□	38 Geoff Sanderson, Hart.	10.00	1.00	.20
□□□	39 Chris Chelios, Chic.	25.00	4.00	.20
□□□	40 Phil Housley, Calg.	14.00	2.00	.20
□□□	41 Kevin Hatcher, Dall.	6.00	1.00	.20
□□□	42 Ron Francis, Pitt.	25.00	4.00	.20
□□□□	43 Pierre Turgeon, Mont.	15.00	2.00	.20
□□□	44 Mikael Renberg, Phil.	14.00	2.00	.20
□□□	45 Chris Gratton, Tamp.	10.00	1.00	.20
□□□	46 T. Söderström (G), NYIs.	6.00	1.00	.20
□□□	47 Stu Barnes, Flor.	4.00	1.00	.20
□□□	48 A. Mogilny, Vanc.	20.00	2.00	.20
□□□	49 Craig Janney, SanJ.	10.00	1.00	.20
□□□	50 S. Niedermayer, NJer.	14.00	2.00	.20
□□□	51 Jim Carey (G), Wash.	6.00	1.00	.20
□□□	52 Stéphane Richer, NJer.	10.00	1.00	.20
□□□	53 Dave Gagner, Dall.	6.00	1.00	.20
□□□	54 Teemu Selänne, Winn.	35.00	6.00	.50
□□□	55 Kelly Hrudey (G), LosA.	14.00	2.00	.20
□□□	56 Roman Hamrlik, Tamp.	10.00	1.00	.20
□□□	57 Scott Mellanby, Flor.	10.00	1.00	.20
□□□	58 Guy Hebert (G), Anah.	10.00	1.00	.20
□□□	59 Gary Suter, Chic.	10.00	1.00	.20
□□□	60 Travis Green, NYIs.	10.00	1.00	.20
□□□□	61 Joe Sakic, Colo.	70.00	12.00	1.00
□□□	62 Doug Gilmour, Toro.	25.00	4.00	.20
□□□	63 Peter Bondra, Wash.	25.00	4.00	.20
□□□	64 V. Damphousse, Mont.	25.00	4.00	.20
□□□	65 Dino Ciccarelli, Detr.	14.00	2.00	.20
□□□	66 Adam Graves, NYRa.	15.00	2.00	.20
□□□	67 Kevin Stevens, Bost.	10.00	1.00	.20
□□□	68 Jeff Friesen, SanJ.	14.00	2.00	.20
□□□	69 Kirk McLean (G), Vanc.	14.00	2.00	.20
□□□	70 Brad May, Buff.	6.00	1.00	.20
□□□	71 Bill Ranford (G), Edmo.	15.00	2.00	.20
□□□	72 Derian Hatcher, Dall.	14.00	2.00	.20
□□□	73 Glen Wesley, Hart.	6.00	1.00	.20
□□□	74 Sergei Zubov, Pitt.	10.00	1.00	.20
□□□□	75 John LeClair, Phil.	35.00	6.00	.50
□□□	76 Igor Larionov, Detr.	25.00	4.00	.20
□□□	77 Ray Sheppard, SanJ.	6.00	1.00	.20
□□□	78 Ulf Samuelsson, NYRa.	6.00	1.00	.20
□□□	79 Rod Brind'Amour, Phil.	14.00	2.00	.20
□□□	80 Félix Potvin (G), Toro.	25.00	4.00	.20
□□□	81 Cam Neely, Bost.	45.00	6.00	.50
□□□	82 Jeremy Roenick, Chic.	35.00	6.00	.50
□□□	83 Vyacheslav Kozlov, Detr.	10.00	1.00	.20
□□□	84 Arturs Irbe (G), SanJ.	15.00	2.00	.20
□□□	85 D. Puppa (G), Tamp.	10.00	1.00	.20
□□□	86 Rob Blake, LosA.	25.00	4.00	.20
□□□	87 Stephen Heinze, Bost.	6.00	1.00	.20
□□□	88 Tom Barrasso (G), Pitt.	15.00	2.00	.20
□□□	89 Luc Robitaille, NYRa.	35.00	6.00	.50
□□□	90 Al MacInnis, SLou.	15.00	2.00	.20
□□□	91 Petr Nedved, Pitt.	14.00	2.00	.20
□□□	92 Joe Mullen, Bost.	15.00	2.00	.20
□□□	93 Mark Tinordi, Wash.	6.00	1.00	.20
□□□	94 Tomas Sandström, Pitt.	10.00	1.00	.20
□□□	95 Dale Hawerchuk, SLou.	25.00	4.00	.20
□□□	96 Andy Moog (G), Dall.	15.00	2.00	.20
□□□	97 Alexei Kovalev, NYRa.	25.00	4.00	.20
□□□	98 David Oliver, Edmo.	4.00	1.00	.20
□□□	99 Patrick Poulin, Chic.	6.00	1.00	.20
□□□	100 Tony Granato, LosA.	10.00	1.00	.20
□□□	101 Alexei Yashin, Otta.	25.00	4.00	.20
□□□	102 Trevor Linden, Vanc.	15.00	2.00	.20
□□□	103 Rick Tocchet, LosA.	14.00	2.00	.20
□□□	104 Brett Lindros, NYIs.	14.00	2.00	.20
□□□	105 Rob Niedermayer, Flor.	10.00	1.00	.20
□□□	106 John MacLean, NJer.	6.00	1.00	.20
□□□	107 Pat Verbeek, NYRa.	14.00	2.00	.20
□□□	108 Ray Ferraro, NYRa.	6.00	1.00	.20
□□□	109 Mike Ricci, Colo.	14.00	2.00	.20
□□□	110 Doug Weight, Edmo.	25.00	4.00	.20
□□□	111 Bill Guerin, NJer.	15.00	2.00	.20
□□□	112 Ken Wregget (G), Pitt.	10.00	1.00	.20
□□□	113 T. Numminen, Winn.	14.00	2.00	.20
□□□	114 Mike Vernon (G), Detr.	15.00	2.00	.20
□□□	115 Mike Richter (G), NYRa.	20.00	2.00	.20
□□□	116 Dan Quinn, Otta.	4.00	1.00	.20
□□□	117 Peter Forsberg, Colo.	60.00	10.00	.50
□□□	118 Mario Lemieux, Pitt.	135.00	22.00	1.50
□□□	119 Geoff Courtnall, SLou.	6.00	1.00	.20
□□□	120 Ed Belfour (G), Chic.	45.00	6.00	.50
□□□	121 Kirk Muller, NYIs.	14.00	2.00	.20
□□□	122 C. Osgood (G), Detr.	25.00	4.00	.20
□□□	123 Radek Bonk, Otta.	14.00	2.00	.20
□□□□	124 B. Shanahan, Hart.	45.00	6.00	.50
□□□	125 Sean Burke (G), Hart.	25.00	4.00	.20
□□□	126 Larry Murphy, Toro.	10.00	1.00	.20
□□□	127 Blaine Lacher (G), Bost.	6.00	1.00	.20
□□□	128 Russ Courtnall, Vanc.	10.00	1.00	.20
□□□	129 Claude Lemieux, Colo.	14.00	2.00	.20
□□□	130 V'b'sbrouck (G), Flor.	20.00	2.00	.20
□□□	131 Wendel Clark, NYIs.	35.00	6.00	.50
□□□	132 Nelson Emerson, Hart.	6.00	1.00	.20
□□□	133 Ron Hextall (G), Phil.	25.00	4.00	.20
□□□	134 Scott Stevens, NJer.	15.00	2.00	.20
□□□	135 Bernie Nicholls, Chic.	10.00	1.00	.20
□□□	136 Brian Skrudland, Flor.	6.00	1.00	.20
□□□	137 Sandis Ozolinsh, Colo.	10.00	1.00	.20
□□□	138 Trevor Kidd (G), Calg.	14.00	2.00	.20
□□□	139 Joé Juneau, Wash.	10.00	1.00	.20
□□□	140 Keith Primeau, Detr.	15.00	2.00	.20
□□□	141 Petr Klima, Tamp.	6.00	1.00	.20
□□□	142 Viktor Kozlov, SanJ.	14.00	2.00	.20
□□□	143 Mike Gartner, Toro.	35.00	6.00	.50
□□□	144 Zigmund Palffy, NYIs.	25.00	4.00	.20
□□□	145 Steve Duchesne, Otta.	10.00	1.00	.20
□□□	146 Brian Bradley, Tamp.	4.00	1.00	.20
□□□	147 Michal Pivonka, Wash.	4.00	1.00	.20
□□□	148 Todd Harvey, Dall.	10.00	1.00	.20
□□□	149 P. Roy (G), Colo.	135.00	22.00	1.50
□□□	150 Gary Roberts, Calg.	15.00	2.00	.20
□□□	151 Shayne Corson, SLou.	14.00	2.00	.20
□□□	152 Keith Tkachuk, Winn.	25.00	4.00	.20
□□□	153 Dmitri Khristich, LosA.	6.00	1.00	.20
□□□	154 Steve Yzerman, Detr.	105.00	18.00	1.50
□□□	155 S. McEachern, Bost.	14.00	2.00	.20
□□□	156 Bryan Smolinski, Pitt.	6.00	1.00	.20
□□□	157 V. Malakhov, Mont.	6.00	1.00	.20
□□□	158 Andrew Cassels, Hart.	10.00	1.00	.20
□□□	159 D. Hasek (G), Buff.	45.00	6.00	.50
□□□	160 S. Fiset (G), Colo.	14.00	2.00	.20
□□□	161 Steve Thomas, NJer.	10.00	1.00	.20
□□□	162 Joe Nieuwendyk, Dall.	15.00	2.00	.20
□□□	163 Sergio Momesso, Toro.	4.00	1.00	.20
□□□	164 Jyrki Lumme, Vanc.	10.00	1.00	.20
□□□	165 Tony Amonte, Chic.	25.00	4.00	.20
□□□	166 Yanic Perreault, LosA.	14.00	2.00	.20
□□□	167 Brian Savage, Mont.	14.00	2.00	.20
□□□	**168 B. Holzinger, Buff. RC**	**10.00**	**2.00**	**.50**
□□□	**169 R. Dvorak, Flor. RC**	**20.00**	**4.00**	**1.00**
□□□	170 Langenbrunner, Dall.	20.00	2.00	.20
□□□	171 Ed Jovanovski, Flor.	35.00	6.00	.50
□□□	172 Bryan McCabe, NYIs.	20.00	2.00	.20
□□□	173 Jere Lehtinen, Dall.	25.00	4.00	.20
□□□	**174 A. Törmänen, Otta. RC**	**5.00**	**2.00**	**.50**
□□□	**175 Aki Berg, LosA. RC**	**10.00**	**2.00**	**.50**
□□□	176 Ryan Smyth, Edmo.	20.00	2.00	.20
□□□	177 Shean Donovan, SanJ.	6.00	1.00	.20
□□□	178 D. Hendrickson, Toro.	14.00	2.00	.20
□□□	**179 C. Kilger, Anah. RC**	**20.00**	**4.00**	**1.00**
□□□	180 V. Yachmenev, LosA.	14.00	2.00	.20
□□□	181 Deron Quint, Winn.	14.00	2.00	.20
□□□	**182 Alfredsson, Otta. RC**	**50.00**	**12.00**	**3.00**
□□□	183 Jeff O'Neill, Hart.	35.00	6.00	.50
□□□	184 Corey Hirsch, Vanc.	6.00	1.00	.20
□□□	**185 S. Moger, Bost. RC**	**5.00**	**2.00**	**.50**
□□□	186 Saku Koivu, Mont.	70.00	12.00	1.00
□□□	187 N. Sundström, NYRa.	20.00	2.00	.20
□□□	**188 S. Doan, Winn. RC**	**20.00**	**4.00**	**1.00**
□□□	189 Brendan Witt, Wash.	8.00	1.00	.20
□□□	190 Éric Dazé, Chic.	35.00	6.00	.50
□□□	191 Marty Murray, Calg.	8.00	1.00	.20
□□□	192 Byron Dafoe (G), LosA.	15.00	2.00	.20
□□□	**193 Bertuzzi, NYIs. RC**	**100.00**	**26.00**	**6.00**
□□□	**194 McLaren, Bost. RC**	**20.00**	**4.00**	**1.00**
□□□	**195 Ragnarsson, SanJ. RC**	**20.00**	**4.00**	**1.00**
□□□	**196 R. Svehla, Flor. RC**	**20.00**	**4.00**	**1.00**
□□□	197 Valeri Bure, Mont.	14.00	2.00	.20
□□□	198 Paul Coffey, Detr. [HL]	25.00	4.00	.20
□□□	199 Checklist	4.00	1.00	.20
□□□	200 Checklist	4.00	1.00	.20

GM'S CHOICE

Insert Set (21 cards): 200.00

	Insert (1:37)	GMC
□	1 Patrick Roy (G), Colo.	30.00
□	2 Martin Brodeur (G), NJer.	15.00
□	3 Chris Chelios, Chic.	5.00
□	4 Brian Leetch, NYRa.	5.00
□	5 Eric Lindros, Phil.	10.00
□	6 Keith Tkachuk, Winn.	5.00
□	7 Pavel Bure, Vanc.	5.00
□	8 Scott Stevens, NJer.	3.00
□	9 Paul Coffey, Detr.	5.00
□	10 Mario Lemieux, Pitt.	30.00
□	11 Jaromir Jagr, Pitt.	10.00
□	12 Cam Neely, Bost.	10.00
□	13 Raymond Bourque, Bost.	10.00
□	14 Al MacInnis, SLou.	3.00
□	15 Sergei Fedorov, Detr.	10.00
□	16 Mark Messier, NYRa.	10.00
□	17 Brett Hull, SLou.	10.00
□	18 Wayne Gretzky, LosA.	40.00
□	19 Paul Kariya, Anah.	10.00
□	20 Brendan Shanahan, Hart.	10.00
□	21 Mike McPhee, Pinnacle (Dall.)	3.00

IN THE CREASE

Insert Set (15 cards): 225.00

	Insert (1:91)	ITC
□	1 Martin Brodeur (G), NJer.	40.00
□	2 Dominik Hasek (G), Buff.	25.00
□	3 Patrick Roy (G), Colo.	70.00
□	4 Ed Belfour (G), Chic.	25.00
□	5 Félix Potvin (G), Toro.	15.00
□	6 Jim Carey (G), Wash.	8.00
□	7 Jocelyn Thibault (G), Mont.	10.00
□	8 Stéphane Fiset (G), Colo.	8.00
□	9 Chris Osgood (G), Detr.	15.00
□	10 Ron Hextall (G), Phil.	14.00
□	11 Mike Richter (G), NYRa.	12.00
□	12 Andy Moog (G), Dall.	10.00
□	13 Sean Burke (G), Hart.	15.00
□	14 Kirk McLean (G), Vanc.	8.00
□	15 John Vanbiesbrouck (G), Flor.	12.00

MAD HATTER

Insert Set (15 cards): 40.00

		MH
□	Wendel Clark Promo	1.00
	Insert (1:23)	MH
□	1 E. Lindros / B. Nicholls / O. Nolan	4.00
□	2 Brett Hull, SLou.	4.00
□	3 John LeClair, Phil.	3.00
□	4 Cam Neely, Bost.	4.00
□	5 Alexei Zhamnov, Winn.	3.00
□	6 Jason Arnott, Edmo.	3.00
□	7 Pavel Bure, Vanc.	3.00
□	8 Wendel Clark, NYIs.	3.00
□	9 Sergei Fedorov, Detr.	4.00
□	10 Jaromir Jagr, Pitt.	4.00
□	11 Peter Bondra, Wash.	3.00
□	12 Alexei Yashin, Otta.	3.00
□	13 Joe Nieuwendyk, Dall.	3.00
□	14 Luc Robitaille, NYRa.	3.00
□	15 Todd Harvey, Dall.	3.00

1995 - 96 PINNACLE ZENITH

Seven regular cards also have a hole-punched promo version. Neely (#61) also has a second promo without the hole punch.

Complete Set (152 cards): 65.00

Common Player: .30

	Player	NRMT-MT
□	1 Brett Hull, SLou.	2.00
□	2 Paul Coffey, Detr.	1.00
□	3 Jaromir Jagr, Pitt.	2.00
□	4 Joe Murphy, Chic.	.30
□	5 Jim Carey (G), Wash.	.30
□	6 Eric Lindros, Phil.	2.00
□	7 Ulf Dahlén, SanJ.	.30
□	8 Mark Recchi, Mont.	.50
□	9 Pavel Bure, Vanc.	1.50
□	10 Adam Oates, Bost.	.50
□	11 Theoren Fleury, Calg.	1.00
□	12 Martin Brodeur (G), NJer.	3.00
□	13 Wayne Gretzky, LosA.	8.00
□	14 Geoff Sanderson, Hart.	.30
□	15 Chris Gratton, Tamp.	.30
□	16 Owen Nolan, SanJ.	1.00
□	17 Paul Kariya, Anah.	2.50
□	18 Mark Messier, NYRa.	2.00
□	19 Mats Sundin, Toro.	2.00
□□	20 Brian Savage, Mont.	.50
□	21 Mathieu Schneider, NYIs.	.30
□	22 Alexandre Daigle, Otta.	.30
□	23 Jason Arnott, Edmo.	.50
□	24 Mike Modano, Dall.	2.00
□□	25 Scott Mellanby, Flor.	.30
□	26 Alexei Zhamnov, Winn.	.50
□	27 Scott Niedermayer, NJer.	.50
□	28 Chris Pronger, SLou.	1.00
□	29 Raymond Bourque, Bost.	2.00
□	30 Sergei Fedorov, Detr.	2.00
□	31 Alexander Mogilny, Vanc.	.50
□□	32 Brian Leetch, NYRa.	1.00
□	33 Adam Graves, NYRa.	.50
□	34 Jocelyn Thibault (G), Mont.	.50
□□	35 Ron Francis, Pitt.	1.00
□	36 John Vanbiesbrouck (G), Flor.	.50
□	37 Chris Chelios, Chic.	1.00
□	38 Pierre Turgeon, Mont.	.50
□	39 Stéphane Richer, NJer.	.30
□	40 Al MacInnis, SLou.	.50
□	41 Dave Andreychuk, Toro.	.50
□	42 Mikael Renberg, Phil.	.50

□ 43 Nelson Emerson, Hart. .30
□ 44 Kevin Hatcher, Dall. .30
□ 45 Kirk Muller, NYIs. .50
□ 46 Bernie Nicholls, Chic. .30
□ 47 Bill Ranford (G), Edmo. .50
□ 48 Luc Robitaille, NYRa. 1.50
□ 49 Peter Bondra, Wash. 1.00
□ 50 Jari Kurri, LosA. 2.00
□ 51 Dino Ciccarelli, Detr. .50
□ 52 Kevin Stevens, Bost. .30
□ 53 Mike Richter (G), NYRa. .50
□ 54 Doug Gilmour, Toro. 1.00
□ 55 Kelly Hrudey (G), LosA. .50
□ 56 Dave Gagner, Dall. .30
□ 57 Kirk McLean (G), Vanc. .50
□ 58 Geoff Courtnall, SLou. .30
□ 59 John LeClair, Phil. 1.50
□ 60 Mike Vernon (G), Detr. .50
□□ 61 Cam Neely, Bost. 2.00
□ 62 Mike Gartner, Toro. 1.50
□□ 63 Igor Korolev, Winn. .30
□ 64 Joe Sakic, Colo. 3.00
□ 65 Jeff Friesen, SanJ. .50
□ 66 Sergei Zubov, Pitt. .30
□ 67 Trevor Kidd (G), Calg. .50
□ 68 Rod Brind'Amour, Phil. .50
□ 69 John MacLean, NJer. .30
□ 70 Peter Forsberg, Colo. 2.50
□ 71 Oleg Tverdovsky, Anah. .30
□ 72 Jeremy Roenick, Chic. 1.50
□ 73 Gary Suter, Chic. .30
□□ 74 Keith Tkachuk, Winn. 1.00
□ 75 Todd Harvey, Dall. .30
□ 76 Félix Potvin (G), Toro. 1.00
□ 77 Vincent Damphousse, Mont. 1.00
□ 78 Blaine Lacher (G), Bost. .30
□ 79 Tomas Sandström, Pitt. .30
□ 80 Chris Osgood (G), Detr. 1.00
□ 81 Arturs Irbe (G), SanJ. .50
□ 82 Pat Verbeek, NYRa. .50
□ 83 Keith Primeau, Detr. .50
□ 84 Brett Lindros, NYIs. .50
□ 85 Pat LaFontaine, Buff. 1.00
□ 86 Brendan Shanahan, Hart. 2.00
□ 87 Trevor Linden, Vanc. .50
□ 88 Rob Blake, LosA. 1.00
□ 89 Scott Stevens, NJer. .50
□ 90 Tom Barrasso (G), Pitt. .50
□ 91 Mike Ricci, Colo. .50
□ 92 Ray Sheppard, Flor. .30
□ 93 Steve Yzerman, Detr. 4.50
□ 94 Wendel Clark, NYIs. 1.50
□ 95 Ed Belfour (G), Chic. 2.00
□ 96 Joé Juneau, Wash. .30
□ 97 Ron Hextall (G), Phil. 1.00
□ 98 Shayne Corson, SLou. .50
□ 99 Guy Hebert (G), Anah. .30
□ 100 Sean Burke (G), Hart. 1.00
□ 101 Sandis Ozolinsh, Colo. .30
□ 102 Teemu Selänne, Winn. 1.50
□ 103 Petr Nedved, Pitt. .50
□ 104 Phil Housley, Calg. .50
□ 105 Andy Moog (G), Dall. .50
□ 106 Larry Murphy, Toro. .30
□ 107 Grant Fuhr (G), SLou. 1.00
□ 108 Mario Lemieux, Pitt. 6.00
□ 109 Dominik Hasek (G), Buff. 2.00
□ 110 Rob Niedermayer, Flor. .30
□ 111 Steve Duchesne, Otta. .30
□ 112 Joe Nieuwendyk, Dall. .50
□ 113 Yanic Perreault, LosA. .50
□ 114 Steve Thomas, NJer. .30
□ 115 Russ Courtnall, Vanc. .30
□ 116 Claude Lemieux, Colo. .50
□ 117 Patrick Roy (G), Colo. 6.00
□ 118 Rick Tocchet, LosA. .50
□ 119 Stéphane Fiset (G), Colo. .50
□ 120 Daren Puppa (G), Tamp. .30
□ 121 Ed Jovanovski, Flor. [Rookie] 1.50
□ 122 Éric Dazé, Chic. [Rookie] 1.50
□ 123 Cory Stillman, Calg. [Rookie] .50
□ 124 Brendan Witt, Wash. [Rookie] .30
□ 125 Valeri Bure, Mont. [Rookie] 1.00
□ **126 Brian Holzinger, Buff. [Rookie] RC 2.00**
□ **127 Kyle McLaren, Bost. [Rookie] RC 3.00**
□ 128 Niklas Sundström, NYRa. [Rookie] .50
□ 129 Jamie Langenbrunner, Dall. [Rookie] .50
□ 130 Jeff O'Neill, Hart. [Rookie] 1.50
□ 131 Vitali Yachmenev, LosA. [Rookie] .50
□ **132 Shane Doan, Winn. [Rookie] RC 3.00**
□ 133 Byron Dafoe (G), LosA. [Rookie] 1.50
□ 134 Corey Hirsch, Vanc. [Rookie] .50
□ **135 Antti Törmänen, Otta. [Rookie] RC 1.00**
□ 136 Jason Bonsignore, Edmo. [Rookie] .30
□ 137 Ryan Smyth, Edmo. [Rookie] 1.50
□ 138 Bryan McCabe, NYIs. [Rookie] .50
□ **139 Chad Kilger, Anah. [Rookie] RC 3.00**
□ **140 Todd Bertuzzi, NYIs. [Rookie] RC 15.00**
□ **141 Marcus Ragnarsson, SanJ. [Rookie] RC 3.00**
□ 142 Marty Murray, Calg. [Rookie] .30
□ 143 Daymond Langkow, Tamp. 2.00
□ 144 Saku Koivu, Mont. [Rookie] 3.00
□ 145 Jere Lehtinen, Dall. [Rookie] 1.00
□ **146 Aki Berg, LosA. [Rookie] RC 2.00**
□ **147 Radek Dvorak, Flor. [Rookie] RC 3.00**
□ **148 Robert Svehla, Flor. [Rookie] RC 3.00**
□ **149 Daniel Alfredsson, Otta. [Rookie] RC 7.00**
□ **150 Miroslav Satan, Edmo. [Rookie] RC 4.00**
□ Checklist 1 .30
□ Checklist 2 .30

GIFTED GRINDERS

Insert Set (18 cards): 25.00

	Insert	GG
□	1 Keith Tkachuk, Winn. [vs. Richardson]	2.00
□	2 Kevin Stevens, Bost. [vs. S.Duchesne]	1.00
□	3 Wendel Clark, NYIs.	4.00
□	4 Claude Lemieux, Colo.	1.00
□	5 Rick Tocchet, LosA.	1.00
□	6 Trevor Linden, Vanc. [vs. Sydor]	2.00
□	7 John LeClair, Phil. [vs. Pronger]	4.00
□	8 Mikael Renberg, Phil. [vs. Galley]	1.00
□	9 Owen Nolan, SanJ. [vs. Lidster]	2.00
□	10 Todd Harvey, Dall.	1.00
□	11 Dave Gagner, Dall.	1.00
□	12 Dale Hunter, Wash.	1.00
□	13 Dave Andreychuk, Toro. [vs. Bradley]	1.00
□	14 Mark Recchi, Mont. [vs. Lescyshyn]	2.00
□	15 Jason Arnott, Edmo.	2.00
□	16 Dino Ciccarelli, Detr.	1.00
□	17 Adam Graves, NYRa.	2.00
□	18 Steve Thomas, NJer.	1.00

ROOKIE ROLL CALL

Insert Set (18 cards): 140.00

	Insert (1:24)	RRC
□	1 Saku Koivu, Mont.	22.00
□	2 Radek Dvorak, Flor.	6.00
□	3 Brendan Witt, Wash.	5.00
□	4 Antti Törmänen, Otta.	5.00
□	5 Brian Holzinger, Buff.	5.00
□	6 Aki Berg, LosA.	5.00
□	7 Ed Jovanovski, Flor.	10.00
□	8 Marcus Ragnarsson, SanJ.	6.00
□	9 Todd Bertuzzi, NYIs.	34.00
□	10 Daniel Alfredsson, Otta.	16.00
□	11 Vitali Yachmenev, LosA.	5.00
□	12 Chad Kilger, Anah.	6.00
□	13 Éric Dazé, Chic.	10.00
□	14 Niklas Sundström, NYRa.	6.00
□	15 Shane Doan, Winn.	6.00
□	16 Cory Stillman, Calg.	6.00
□	17 Kyle McLaren, Bost.	6.00
□	18 Jeff O'Neill, Hart.	10.00

Z-TEAM

Insert Set (18 cards): 600.00

		ZT
	Martin Brodeur (G) Promo	5.00
	Insert (1:72)	ZT
□	1 Patrick Roy (G), Colo.	90.00
□	2 Martin Brodeur (G), NJer.	30.00
□	3 Mario Lemieux, Pitt.	90.00
□	4 Wayne Gretzky, LosA.	120.00
□	5 Mark Messier, NYRa.	30.00
□	6 Jeremy Roenick, Chic.	20.00
□	7 Eric Lindros, Phil.	30.00

□	8 Peter Forsberg, Colo.	40.00
□	9 Sergei Fedorov, Detr.	30.00
□	10 Mike Modano, Dall.	30.00
□	11 Jaromir Jagr, Pitt.	30.00
□	12 Pavel Bure, Vanc.	20.00
□	13 Joe Sakic, Colo.	40.00
□	14 Paul Kariya, Anah.	40.00
□	15 Brett Hull, SLou.	30.00
□	16 Brendan Shanahan, Hart.	30.00
□	17 Félix Potvin (G), Toro.	15.00
□	18 Jim Carey (G), Wash.	15.00

1995 - 96 PLAYOFF ONE-ON-ONE CHALLENGE

This series was later repackaged with the 1996 - 97 release.

Imprint: © 1995 Playoff Corporation

Master Set (330 cards + 26 dice): 575.00
Commons Set (110 cards): 15.00
Uncommons Set (110 cards): 20.00

Player NRMT-MT

□ 1 Guy Hebert (G), Anah. [Uncommon] .20
□ 2 Paul Kariya, Anah. [Uncommon] .50
□ 3 Mike Sillinger, Anah. [Uncommon] .20
□ 4 Oleg Tverdovsky, Anah. [Uncommon] .20
□ 5 Raymond Bourque, Bost. [Uncommon] .50
□ 6 Alexei Kasatonov, Bost. [Uncommon] .20
□ 7 Blaine Lacher (G), Bost. [Uncommon] .20
□ 8 Cam Neely, Bost. [Uncommon] .50
□ 9 Adam Oates, Bost. [Uncommon] .20
□ 10 Kevin Stevens, Bost. [Uncommon] .20
□ 11 Donald Audette, Buff. [Uncommon] .20
□ 12 Dominik Hasek (G), Buff. [Uncommon] .50
□ 13 Pat LaFontaine, Buff. [Uncommon] .20
□ 14 Alexei Zhitnik, Buff. [Uncommon] .20
□ 15 Steve Chiasson, Calg. [Uncommon] .20
□ 16 Theoren Fleury, Calg. [Uncommon] .20
□ 17 Phil Housley, Calg. [Uncommon] .20
□ 18 Joe Nieuwendyk, Calg. [Uncommon] .20
□ 19 Gary Roberts, Calg. [Uncommon] .20
□ 20 German Titov, Calg. [Uncommon] .20
□ 21 Ed Belfour (G), Chic. [Uncommon] .50
□ 22 Chris Chelios, Chic. [Uncommon] .20
□ 23 Bernie Nicholls, Chic. [Uncommon] .20
□ 24 Jeremy Roenick, Chic. [Uncommon] .20
□ 25 Peter Forsberg, Colo. [Uncommon] .50
□ 26 Sylvain Lefebvre, Colo. [Uncommon] .20
□ 27 Owen Nolan, Colo. [Uncommon] .20
□ 28 Joe Sakic, Colo. [Uncommon] .50
□ 29 Jocelyn Thibault (G), Colo. [Uncommon] .20
□ 30 Dave Gagner, Dall. [Uncommon] .20
□ 31 Mike Modano, Dall. [Uncommon] .50
□ 32 Andy Moog (G), Dall. [Uncommon] .20
□ 33 Paul Coffey, Detr. [Uncommon] .20
□ 34 Sergei Fedorov, Detr. [Uncommon] .50
□ 35 Keith Primeau, Detr. [Uncommon] .20
□ 36 Ray Sheppard, Detr. [Uncommon] .20
□ 37 Jason Arnott, Edmo. [Uncommon] .20
□ 38 David Oliver, Edmo. [Uncommon] .20
□ 39 Pat Stapleton, Edmo. [Uncommon] .20
□ 40 Jesse Bélanger, Edmo. [Uncommon] .20
□ 41 Paul Laus, Flor. [Uncommon] .20
□ 42 Rob Niedermayer, Flor. [Uncommon] .20
□ 43 Brian Skrudland, Flor. [Uncommon] .20
□ 44 John Vanbiesbrouck (G), Flor. [Uncommon] .20
□ 45 Sean Burke (G), Hart. [Uncommon] .20
□ 46 Andrew Cassels, Hart. [Uncommon] .20
□ 47 Brendan Shanahan, Hart. [Uncommon] .50
□ 48 Rob Blake, LosA. [Uncommon] .20
□ 49 Tony Granato, LosA. [Uncommon] .20
□ 50 Wayne Gretzky, LosA. [Uncommon] 2.00
□ 51 Marty McSorley, LosA. [Uncommon] .20
□ 52 Jamie Storr (G), LosA. [Uncommon] .20
□ 53 Vincent Damphousse, Mont. [Uncommon] .20
□ 54 Mark Recchi, Mont. [Uncommon] .20
□ 55 Patrick Roy (G), Mont. [Uncommon] 1.50
□ 56 Pierre Turgeon, Mont. [Uncommon] .20
□ 57 Martin Brodeur (G), NJer. [Uncommon] .50
□ 58 Bill Guerin, NJer. [Uncommon] .20
□ 59 Scott Niedermayer, NJer. [Uncommon] .20
□ 60 Stéphane Richer, NJer. [Uncommon] .20
□ 61 Scott Stevens, NJer. [Uncommon] .20
□ 62 Patrick Flatley, NYIs. [Uncommon] .20
□ 63 Brett Lindros, NYIs. [Uncommon] .20
□ 64 Mathieu Schneider, NYIs. [Uncommon] .20
□ 65 Kirk Muller, NYIs. [Uncommon] .20
□ 66 Adam Graves, NYRa. [Uncommon] .20
□ 67 Alexei Kovalev, NYRa. [Uncommon] .20
□ 68 Brian Leetch, NYRa. [Uncommon] .20
□ 69 Mike Richter (G), NYRa. [Uncommon] .20
□ 70 Pat Verbeek, NYRa. [Uncommon] .20
□ 71 Luc Robitaille, NYRa. [Uncommon] .20
□ 72 Radek Bonk, Otta. [Uncommon] .20
□ 73 Alexandre Daigle, Otta. [Uncommon] .20
□ 74 Alexei Yashin, Otta. [Uncommon] .20
□ 75 Éric Desjardins, Phil. [Uncommon] .20
□ 76 Eric Lindros, Phil. [Uncommon] .50
□ 77 Ron Francis, Pitt. [Uncommon] .20
□ 78 Jaromir Jagr, Pitt. [Uncommon] .50
□ 79 Mario Lemieux, Pitt. [Uncommon] 1.50
□ 80 Ken Wregget (G), Pitt. [Uncommon] .20
□ 81 François Leroux, Pitt. [Uncommon] .20
□ 82 Pat Falloon, SanJ. [Uncommon] .20
□ 83 Jeff Friesen, SanJ. [Uncommon] .20
□ 84 Arturs Irbe (G), SanJ. [Uncommon] .20
□ 85 Igor Larionov, SanJ. [Uncommon] .20
□ 86 Shayne Corson, SLou. [Uncommon] .20
□ 87 Geoff Courtnall, SLou. [Uncommon] .20
□ 88 Steve Duchesne, SLou. [Uncommon] .20
□ 89 Brett Hull, SLou. [Uncommon] .50
□ 90 Al MacInnis, SLou. [Uncommon] .20
□ 91 Brian Bellows, Tamp. [Uncommon] .20
□ 92 Chris Gratton, Tamp. [Uncommon] .20
□ 93 Dave Andreychuk, Toro. [Uncommon] .20
□ 94 Tie Domi, Toro. [Uncommon] .20
□ 95 Mike Gartner, Toro. [Uncommon] .20
□ 96 Doug Gilmour, Toro. [Uncommon] .20
□ 97 Larry Murphy, Toro. [Uncommon] .20
□ 98 Félix Potvin (G), Toro. [Uncommon] .20
□ 99 Mats Sundin, Toro. [Uncommon] .50
□ 100 Pavel Bure, Vanc. [Uncommon] .20
□ 101 Kirk McLean (G), Vanc. [Uncommon] .20
□ 102 Alexander Mogilny, Vanc. [Uncommon] .20
□ 103 Christian Ruuttu, Vanc. [Uncommon] .20
□ 104 Jim Carey (G), Wash. [Uncommon] .20
□ 105 Joé Juneau, Wash. [Uncommon] .20
□ 106 Jason Allison, Wash. [Uncommon] .20
□ 107 Teppo Numminen, Wash. [Uncommon] .20
□ 108 Teemu Selänne, Winn. [Uncommon] .20
□ 109 Keith Tkachuk, Winn. [Uncommon] .20
□ 110 Alexei Zhamnov, Winn. [Uncommon] .20
□ 111 Patrik Carnbäck, Anah. [Common] .30
□ 112 Bobby Dollas, Anah. [Common] .30
□ 113 Guy Hebert (G), Anah. [Common] .30
□ 114 Paul Kariya, Anah. [Common] 1.00
□ 115 Shaun Van Allen, Anah. [Common] .30
□ 116 Raymond Bourque, Bost. [Common] .50
□ 117 Mariusz Czerkawski, Bost. [Common] .30
□ 118 Todd Elik, Bost. [Common] .30
□ 119 Blaine Lacher (G), Bost. [Common] .30
□ 120 Cam Neely, Bost. [Common] .50
□ 121 Adam Oates, Bost. [Common] .30
□ 122 David Reid, Bost. [Common] .30
□ 123 Kevin Stevens, Bost. [Common] .30
□ 124 Garry Galley, Buff. [Common] .30
□ 125 Dominik Hasek (G), Buff. [Common] .50
□ 126 Brian Holzinger, Buff. [Common] .30
□ 127 Pat LaFontaine, Buff. [Common] .30
□ 128 Michael Peca, Buff. [Common] .30
□ 129 Phil Housley, Calg. [Common] .30
□ 130 Paul Kruse, Calg. [Common] .30
□ 131 Ronnie Stern, Calg. [Common] .30
□ 132 Zarley Zalapski, Calg. [Common] .30
□ 133 Patrick Poulin, Chic. [Common] .30
□ 134 Bob Probert, Chic. [Common] .30
□ 135 Jeremy Roenick, Chic. [Common] .50
□ 136 Adam Deadmarsh, Colo. [Common] .30
□ 137 Peter Forsberg, Colo. [Common] 1.00
□ 138 Andrei Kovalenko, Colo. [Common] .30
□ 139 Joe Sakic, Colo. [Common] 1.00
□ 140 Derian Hatcher, Dall. [Common] .30
□ 141 Grant Ledyard, Dall. [Common] .30
□ 142 Mike Modano, Dall. [Common] .50
□ 143 Paul Coffey, Detr. [Common] .30
□ 144 Sergei Fedorov, Detr. [Common] .50
□ 145 Vladimir Konstantinov, Detr. [Common] .30
□ 146 Nicklas Lidström, Detr. [Common] .30
□ 147 Steve Yzerman, Detr. [Common] 1.50
□ 148 Igor Kravchuk, Edmo. [Common] .30
□ 149 Kirk Maltby, Edmo. [Common] .30
□ 150 Boris Mironov, Edmo. [Common] .30
□ 151 Bill Ranford (G), Edmo. [Common] .30
□ 152 Stu Barnes, Flor. [Common] .30
□ 153 Jesse Bélanger, Flor. [Common] .30
□ 154 Scott Mellanby, Flor. [Common] .30
□ 155 Adam Burt, Hart. [Common] .30
□ 156 Steven Rice, Hart. [Common] .30
□ 157 Brendan Shanahan, Hart. [Common] .50
□ 158 Glen Wesley, Hart. [Common] .30
□ 159 Wayne Gretzky, LosA. [Common] 3.00
□ 160 Darryl Sydor, LosA. [Common] .30
□ 161 Rick Tocchet, LosA. [Common] .30
□ 162 Benoît Brunet, Mont. [Common] .30
□ 163 J.J. Daigneault, Mont. [Common] .30
□ 164 Saku Koivu, Mont. [Common] .50
□ 165 Lyle Odelein, Mont. [Common] .30
□ 166 Patrick Roy (G), Mont. [Common] 2.00
□ 167 Scott Stevens, NJer. [Common] .30
□ 168 Valeri Zelepukin, NJer. [Common] .30
□ 169 Steve Thomas, NJer. [Common] .30
□ 170 Dennis Vaske, NYIs. [Common] .30
□ 171 Brett Lindros, NYIs. [Common] .30
□ 172 Zigmund Palffy, NYIs. [Common] .30
□ 173 Ray Ferraro, NYIs. [Common] .30
□ 174 Brian Leetch, NYRa. [Common] .30
□ 175 Mark Messier, NYRa. [Common] .50
□ 176 Ulf Samuelsson, NYRa. [Common] .30
□ 177 Don Beaupré (G), Otta. [Common] .30
□ 178 Alexandre Daigle, Otta. [Common] .30
□ 179 Steve Larouche, Otta. [Common] .30
□ 180 Scott Levins, Otta. [Common] .30
□ 181 Ron Hextall (G), Phil. [Common] .30
□ 182 Eric Lindros, Phil. [Common] .50
□ 183 Mikael Renberg, Phil. [Common] .30
□ 184 Kjell Samuelsson, Phil. [Common] .30
□ 185 Jaromir Jagr, Pitt. [Common] .50
□ 186 Mario Lemieux, Pitt. [Common] 2.00
□ 187 Sergei Zubov, Pitt. [Common] .30
□ 188 Bryan Smolinski, Pitt. [Common] .30
□ 189 Dmitri Mironov, Pitt. [Common] .30
□ 190 Ulf Dahlén, SanJ. [Common] .30
□ 191 Arturs Irbe (G), SanJ. [Common] .30
□ 192 Craig Janney, SanJ. [Common] .30
□ 193 Sandis Ozolinsh, SanJ. [Common] .30
□ 194 Jon Casey (G), SLou. [Common] .30
□ 195 Brett Hull, SLou. [Common] .50
□ 196 Esa Tikkanen, SLou. [Common] .30
□ 197 Brian Bradley, Tamp. [Common] .30
□ 198 Daren Puppa (G), Tamp. [Common] .30
□ 199 Alexander Selivanov, Tamp. [Common] .30
□ 200 Rob Zamuner, Tamp. [Common] .30
□ 201 Ken Baumgartner, Toro. [Common] .30
□ 202 Doug Gilmour, Toro. [Common] .30
□ 203 Kenny Jönsson, Toro. [Common] .30
□ 204 Félix Potvin (G), Toro. [Common] .30
□ 205 Randy Wood, Toro. [Common] .30
□ 206 Jeff R. Brown, Vanc. [Common] .30
□ 207 Pavel Bure, Vanc. [Common] .50
□ 208 Trevor Linden, Vanc. [Common] .30
□ 209 Alexander Mogilny, Vanc. [Common] .30
□ 210 Roman Oksiuta, Vanc. [Common] .30
□ 211 Cliff Ronning, Vanc. [Common] .30
□ 212 Peter Bondra, Wash. [Common] .30
□ 213 Jim Carey (G), Wash. [Common] .30
□ 214 Pat Peake, Wash. [Common] .30
□ 215 Mark Tinordi, Wash. [Common] .30
□ 216 Mike Eastwood, Winn. [Common] .30
□ 217 Nelson Emerson, Winn. [Common] .30
□ 218 Dave Manson, Winn. [Common] .30
□ 219 Teemu Selänne, Winn. [Common] .50
□ 220 Keith Tkachuk, Winn. [Common] .30
□ 221 Bob Corkum, Anah. [Rare] .50
□ 222 Peter Douris, Anah. [Rare] .50
□ 223 Paul Kariya, Anah. [Ultra Rare] 25.00
□ 224 Todd Krygier, Anah. [Ultra Rare] 5.00
□ 225 Mike Sillinger, Anah. [Rare] .50
□ 226 Raymond Bourque, Bost. [Ultra Rare] 24.00
□ 227 Fred Knipscheer, Bost. [Rare] .50
□ 228 Cam Neely, Bost. [Ultra Rare] 20.00
□ 229 Adam Oates, Bost. [Ultra Rare] 8.00
□ 230 Jason Dawe, Buff. [Rare] .50
□ 231 Yuri Khmylev, Buff. [Rare] .50
□ 232 Bob Sweeney, Bost. [Ultra Rare] 5.00
□ 233 Trevor Kidd (G), Calg. [Rare] .50
□ 234 Éric Dazé, Chic. [Rare] 1.00
□ 235 Tony Amonte, Chic. [Rare] 1.50
□ 236 Jeremy Roenick, Chic. [Ultra Rare] 16.00
□ 237 Denis Savard, Chic. [Rare] 1.00
□ 238 Gary Suter, Chic. [Rare] .50

☐ 239 Peter Forsberg, Colo. [Ultra Rare] 28.00
☐ 240 Curtis Leschyshyn, Colo. [Rare] .50
☐ 241 Owen Nolan, Colo. [Ultra Rare] 12.00
☐ 242 Joe Sakic, Colo. [Ultra Rare] 30.00
☐ 243 Valeri Kamensky, Colo. [Rare] .50
☐ 244 Claude Lemieux, Colo. [Rare] .50
☐ 245 Bob Bassen, Dall. [Rare] .50
☐ 246 Shane Churla, Dall. [Rare] .50
☐ 247 Todd Harvey, Dall. [Rare] .50
☐ 248 Kevin Hatcher, Dall. [Ultra Rare] 5.00
☐ 249 Richard Matvichuk, Dall. [Rare] .50
☐ 250 Mike Modano, Dall. [Ultra Rare] 20.00
☐ 251 Dino Ciccarelli, Detr. [Rare] .50
☐ 252 Paul Coffey, Detr. [Ultra Rare] 12.00
☐ 253 Sergei Fedorov, Detr. [Ultra Rare] 20.00
☐ 254 Vyacheslav Kozlov, Detr. [Rare] .50
☐ 255 Mike Vernon (G), Detr. [Rare] 1.00
☐ 256 Jason Bonsignore, Edmo. [Rare] .50
☐ 257 Dean McAmmond, Edmo. [Rare] .50
☐ 258 Bill Ranford (G), Edmo. [Rare] 1.00
☐ 259 Doug Weight, Edmo. [Ultra Rare] 12.00
☐ 260 Bob Kudelski, Flor. [Rare] .50
☐ 261 Dave Lowry, Flor. [Rare] .50
☐ 262 Gord Murphy, Flor. [Rare] .50
☐ 263 Rob Niedermayer, Flor. [Ultra Rare] 5.00
☐ 264 Frantisek Kucera, Hart. [Rare] .50
☐ 265 Paul Ranheim, Hart. [Rare] .50
☐ 266 Geoff Sanderson, Hart. [Ultra Rare] 5.00
☐ 267 Darren Turcotte, Hart. [Rare] .50
☐ 268 Pat Conacher, LosA. [Rare] .50
☐ 269 Wayne Gretzky, LosA. [Ultra Rare] 80.00
☐ 270 Kelly Hrudey (G), LosA. [Rare] .50
☐ 271 Jari Kurri, LosA. [Rare] 2.50
☐ 272 Patrice Brisebois, Mont. [Rare] .50
☐ 273 Vladimir Malakhov, Mont. [Rare] .50
☐ 274 Patrick Roy (G), Mont. [Ultra Rare] 60.00
☐ 275 Martin Brodeur (G), NJer. [Ultra Rare] 30.00
☐ 276 Neal Broten, NJer. [Rare] .50
☐ 277 Sergei Brylin, NJer. [Rare] .50
☐ 278 John MacLean, NJer. [Rare] .50
☐ 279 Wendel Clark, NYIs. [Rare] 2.00
☐ 280 Travis Green, NYIs. [Rare] .50
☐ 281 Scott Lachance, NYIs. [Ultra Rare] 5.00
☐ 282 Tommy Salo (G), NYIs. [Rare] 1.00
☐ 283 Brian Leetch, NYRa. [Ultra Rare] 12.00
☐ 284 Mark Messier, NYRa. [Ultra Rare] 20.00
☐ 285 Sergei Nemchinov, NYRa. [Rare] .50
☐ 286 Luc Robitaille, NYRa. [Ultra Rare] 16.00
☐ 287 Sean Hill, Otta. [Rare] .50
☐ 288 Jim Paek, Otta. [Ultra Rare] 5.00
☐ 289 Martin Straka, Otta. [Rare] .50
☐ 290 Sylvain Turgeon, Otta. [Rare] .50
☐ 291 Rod Brind'Amour, Phil. [Ultra Rare] 6.00
☐ 292 Kevin Haller, Phil. [Rare] .50
☐ 293 John LeClair, Phil. [Rare] 2.00
☐ 294 Eric Lindros, Phil. [Ultra Rare] 20.00
☐ 295 Joel Otto, Phil. [Rare] .50
☐ 296 Chris Therien, Phil. [Rare] .50
☐ 297 Jaromir Jagr, Pitt. [Ultra Rare] 20.00
☐ 298 Mario Lemieux, Pitt. [Ultra Rare] 60.00
☐ 299 Glen Murray, Pitt. [Rare] 1.00
☐ 300 Petr Nedved, Pitt. [Rare] .50
☐ 301 Jamie Baker, SanJ. [Rare] .50
☐ 302 Arturs Irbe (G), SanJ. [Ultra Rare] 8.00
☐ 303 Jayson More, SanJ. [Rare] .50
☐ 304 Ray Whitney, SanJ. [Rare] .50
☐ 305 Geoff Courtnall, SLou. [Ultra Rare] 5.00
☐ 306 Dale Hawerchuk, SLou. [Rare] 1.50
☐ 307 Brett Hull, SLou. [Ultra Rare] 20.00
☐ 308 Ian Laperrière, SLou. [Rare] .50
☐ 309 Chris Pronger, SLou. [Rare] 1.50
☐ 310 Roman Hamrlik, Tamp. [Rare] .50
☐ 311 Petr Klima, Tamp. [Ultra Rare] 5.00
☐ 312 John Tucker, Tamp. [Rare] .50
☐ 313 Paul Ysebaert, Tamp. [Ultra Rare] 5.00
☐ 314 Ken Baumgartner, Toro. [Rare] .50
☐ 315 Doug Gilmour, Toro. [Ultra Rare] 12.00
☐ 316 Pavel Bure, Vanc. [Ultra Rare] 16.00
☐ 317 Bret Hedican, Vanc. [Rare] .50
☐ 318 Alexander Mogilny, Vanc. [Ultra Rare] 8.00
☐ 319 Mike Ridley, Vanc. [Rare] .50
☐ 320 Peter Bondra, Wash. [Rare] 1.50
☐ 321 Sylvain Côté, Wash. [Rare] .50
☐ 322 Dale Hunter, Wash. [Rare] .50
☐ 323 Keith Jones, Wash. [Ultra Rare] 5.00
☐ 324 Kelly Miller, Wash. [Rare] .50
☐ 325 Tim Chevelade (G), Winn. [Rare] .50
☐ 326 Dallas Drake, Winn. [Rare] .50
☐ 327 Igor Korolev, Winn. [Rare] .50
☐ 328 Teppo Numminen, Winn. [Rare] .50
☐ 329 Teemu Selänne, Winn. [Ultra Rare] 16.00
☐ 330 Alexei Zhamnov, Winn. [Ultra Rare] 6.00

ONE ON ONE DICE

Dice sell between $2-3 each.

Team	Team
☐ Anaheim Mighty Ducks	☐ Boston Bruins
☐ Buffalo Sabres	☐ Calgary Flames
☐ Chicago Blackhawks	☐ Colorado Avalanche
☐ Dallas Stars	☐ Detroit Red Wings
☐ Edmonton Oilers	☐ Florida Panthers
☐ Hartford Whalers	☐ Los Angeles Kings
☐ Montréal Canadiens	☐ New Jersey Devils
☐ New York Islanders	☐ New York Rangers
☐ Ottawa Senators	☐ Philadelphia Flyers
☐ Pittsburgh Penguins	☐ St. Louis Blues
☐ San Jose Sharks	☐ Tampa Bay Lightning
☐ Toronto Maple Leafs	☐ Vancouver Canucks
☐ Washington Capitals	☐ Winnipeg Jets

1995 - 96 POGS

Kinis come in blue, gold and purple but do not show a player photo.

Cap Diameter: 1 5/8"
Complete Set (296 POGs): 95.00
Common Player: .25

	Player	POG
☐	1 Pearson Award [xLindros]	4.00
☐	2 Art Ross Trohpy [xJagr]	4.00
☐	3 Masterton Trophy [xLaFontaine]	2.00
☐	4 Calder Trophy [xForsberg]	4.00
☐	5 Campbell Bowl [xRed Wings]	4.00
☐	6 Conn Smythe Trophy [xC.Lemieux]	1.00
☐	7 Selke Trophy [xFrancis]	2.00
☐	8 Hart Trophy [xLindros]	4.00
☐	9 Adams Trophy [xCrawford]	1.00
☐	10 Norris Trophy [xCoffey]	2.00
☐	11 King Clancy Trophy [xNieuwendyk]	1.00
☐	12 Lady Byng Trophy [xFrancis]	2.00
☐	13 Wales Trophy [xDevils]	4.00
☐	14 Stanley Cup [xDevils]	4.00
☐	15 Vézina Trophy [xHasek (G)]	4.00
☐	16 Jennings Trophy [xBelfour (G)]	4.00
☐	17 Paul Kariya, Anah.	1.00
☐	18 Peter Douris, Anah.	.25
☐	19 Valeri Karpov, Anah.	.25
☐	20 Todd Krygier, Anah.	.25
☐	21 Joe Sacco, Anah.	.25
☐	22 Mike Sillinger, Anah.	.25
☐	23 Shaun Van Allen, Anah.	.25
☐	24 Oleg Tverdovsky, Anah.	.25
☐	25 Bobby Dollas, Anah.	.25
☐	26 Steve Rucchin, Anah.	.25
☐	27 Guy Hebert (G), Anah.	.25
☐	28 Shawn McEachern, Bost.	.25
☐	29 Adam Oates, Bost.	.25
☐	30 Ted Donato, Bost.	.25
☐	31 Cam Neely, Bost.	1.00
☐	32 Joe Mullen, Bost.	.25
☐	33 Kevin Stevens, Bost.	.25
☐	34 Mariusz Czerkawski, Bost.	.25
☐	35 Don Sweeney, Bost.	.25
☐	36 Raymond Bourque, Bost.	1.00
☐	37 Alexei Kasatonov, Bost.	.25
☐	38 Blaine Lacher (G), Bost.	.25
☐	39 Brian Holzinger, Buff.	.25
☐	40 Derek Plante, Buff.	.25
☐	41 Michael Peca, Buff.	.25
☐	42 Pat LaFontaine, Buff.	.25
☐	43 Jason Dawe, Buff.	.25
☐	44 Brad May, Buff.	.25
☐	45 Yuri Khmylev, Buff.	.25
☐	46 Garry Galley, Buff.	.25
☐	47 Alexei Zhitnik, Buff.	.25
☐	48 Dominik Hasek (G), Buff.	1.00
☐	49 Joe Nieuwendyk, Calg.	.25
☐	50 German Titov, Calg.	.25
☐	51 Cory Stillman, Calg.	.25
☐	52 Theoren Fleury, Calg.	.25
☐	53 Paul Kruse, Calg.	.25
☐	54 Michael Nylander, Calg.	.25
☐	55 Gary Roberts, Calg.	.25
☐	56 Phil Housley, Calg.	.25
☐	57 Steve Chiasson, Calg.	.25
☐	58 Zarley Zalapski, Calg.	.25
☐	59 Ronnie Stern, Calg.	.25
☐	60 Trevor Kidd (G), Calg.	.25
☐	61 Jeremy Roenick, Chic.	1.00
☐	62 Denis Savard, Chic.	.25
☐	63 Tony Amonte, Chic.	.25
☐	64 Bernie Nicholls, Chic.	.25
☐	65 Sergei Krivokrasov, Chic.	.25
☐	66 Joe Murphy, Chic.	.25
☐	67 Patrick Poulin, Chic.	.25
☐	68 Bob Probert, Chic.	.25
☐	69 Gary Suter, Chic.	.25
☐	70 Chris Chelios, Chic.	.25
☐	71 Ed Belfour (G), Chic.	1.00
☐	72 Joe Sakic, Colo.	2.00
☐	73 Mike Ricci, Colo.	.25
☐	74 Valeri Kamensky, Colo.	.25
☐	75 Andrei Kovalenko, Colo.	.25
☐	76 Owen Nolan, Colo.	.25
☐	77 Peter Forsberg, Colo.	1.00
☐	78 Scott A. Young, Colo.	.25
☐	79 Uwe Krupp, Colo.	.25
☐	80 Curtis Leschyshyn, Colo.	.25
☐	81 Adam Deadmarsh, Colo.	.25
☐	82 Stéphane Fiset (G), Colo.	.25
☐	83 Bob Bassen, Dall.	.25
☐	84 Corey Millen, Dall.	.25
☐	85 Mike Modano, Dall.	1.00
☐	86 Dave Gagner, Dall.	.25
☐	87 Mike Donnelly, Dall.	.25
☐	88 Trent Klatt, Dall.	.25
☐	89 Kevin Hatcher, Dall.	.25
☐	90 Grant Ledyard, Dall.	.25
☐	91 Greg A. Adams, Dall.	.25
☐	92 Andy Moog (G), Dall.	.25
☐	93 Keith Primeau, Detr.	.25
☐	94 Kris Draper, Detr.	.25
☐	95 Sergei Fedorov, Detr.	1.00
☐	96 Steve Yzerman, Detr.	3.00
☐	97 Vyacheslav Kozlov, Detr.	.25
☐	98 Ray Sheppard, Detr.	.25
☐	99 Dino Ciccarelli, Detr.	.25
☐	100 Viacheslav Fetisov, Detr.	.25
☐	101 Nicklas Lidström, Detr.	.25
☐	102 Paul Coffey, Detr.	.25
☐	103 Darren McCarty, Detr.	.25
☐	104 Mike Vernon (G), Detr.	.25
☐	105 Doug Weight, Edmo.	.25
☐	106 Jason Arnott, Edmo.	.25
☐	107 Todd Marchant, Edmo.	.25
☐	108 David Oliver, Edmo.	.25
☐	109 Igor Kravchuk, Edmo.	.25
☐	110 Jirí Slégr, Edmo.	.25
☐	111 Kelly Buchberger, Edmo.	.25
☐	112 Scott Thornton, Edmo.	.25
☐	113 Bill Ranford (G), Edmo.	.25
☐	114 Jesse Bélanger, Flor.	.25
☐	115 Stu Barnes, Flor.	.25
☐	116 Scott Mellanby, Flor.	.25
☐	117 Bill Lindsay, Flor.	.25
☐	118 Dave Lowry, Flor.	.25
☐	119 Gaétan Duchesne, Flor.	.25
☐	120 Johan Garpenlöv, Flor.	.25
☐	121 Paul Laus, Flor.	.25
☐	122 Gord Murphy, Flor.	.25
☐	123 John Vanbiesbrouck (G), Flor.	.25
☐	124 Andrew Cassels, Hart.	.25
☐	125 Geoff Sanderson, Hart.	.25
☐	126 Brendan Shanahan, Hart.	1.00
☐	127 Paul Ranheim, Hart.	.25
☐	128 Steven Rice, Hart.	.25
☐	129 Frantisek Kucera, Hart.	.25
☐	130 Glen Wesley, Hart.	.25
☐	131 Sean Burke (G), Hart.	.25
☐	132 Wayne Gretzky, LosA.	5.00
☐	133 Dmitri Khristich, LosA.	.25
☐	134 Jari Kurri, LosA.	1.00
☐	135 John Druce, LosA.	.25
☐	136 Pat Conacher, LosA.	.25
☐	137 Rick Tocchet, LosA.	.25
☐	138 Rob Blake, LosA.	.25
☐	139 Tony Granato, LosA.	.25
☐	140 Marty McSorley, LosA.	.25
☐	141 Darryl Sydor, LosA.	.25
☐	142 Éric Lacroix, LosA.	.25
☐	143 Kelly Hrudey (G), LosA.	.25
☐	144 Brian Savage, Mont.	.25
☐	145 Pierre Turgeon, Mont.	.25
☐	146 Benoît Brunet, Mont.	.25
☐	147 Valeri Bure, Mont.	.25
☐	148 Vincent Damphousse, Mont.	.25
☐	149 Mike Keane, Mont.	.25
☐	150 Mark Recchi, Mont.	.25
☐	151 Vladimir Malakhov, Mont.	.25
☐	152 Patrice Brisebois, Mont.	.25
☐	153 J.J. Daigneault, Mont.	.25
☐	154 Yves Racine, Mont.	.25
☐	155 Patrick Roy (G), Mont.	.25
☐	156 Bob Carpenter, NJer.	.25
☐	157 Neal Broten, NJer.	.25
☐	158 Steve Thomas, NJer.	.25
☐	159 Bobby Holik, NJer.	.25
☐	160 John MacLean, NJer.	.25
☐	161 Mike Peluso, NJer.	.25
☐	162 Randy McKay, NJer.	.25
☐	163 Stéphane Richer, NJer.	.25
☐	164 Scott Niedermayer, NJer.	.25
☐	165 Scott Stevens, NJer.	.25
☐	166 Bill Guerin, NJer.	.25
☐	167 Martin Brodeur (G), NJer.	2.00
☐	168 Kirk Muller, NYIs.	.25
☐	169 Zigmund Palffy, NYIs.	.25
☐	170 Travis Green, NYIs.	.25
☐	171 Brett Lindros, NYIs.	.25
☐	172 Derek King, NYIs.	.25
☐	173 Patrick Flatley, NYIs.	.25
☐	174 Wendel Clark, NYIs.	1.00
☐	175 Bryan McCabe, NYIs.	.25
☐	176 Mathieu Schneider, NYIs.	.25
☐	177 Eric Fichaud (G), NYIs.	.25
☐	178 Ray Ferraro, NYRa.	.25
☐	179 Adam Graves, NYRa.	.25
☐	180 Mark Messier, NYRa.	1.00
☐	181 Sergei Nemchinov, NYRa.	.25
☐	182 Pat Verbeek, NYRa.	.25
☐	183 Luc Robitaille, NYRa.	1.00
☐	184 Alexei Kovalev, NYRa.	.25
☐	185 Jeff Beukeboom, NYRa.	.25
☐	186 Brian Leetch, NYRa.	.25
☐	187 Ulf Samuelsson, NYRa.	.25
☐	188 Alexander Karpovtsev, NYRa.	.25
☐	189 Mike Richter (G), NYRa.	.25
☐	190 Alexandre Daigle, Otta.	.25
☐	191 Alexei Yashin, Otta.	.25
☐	192 Dan Quinn, Otta.	.25
☐	193 Martin Straka, Otta.	.25
☐	194 Radek Bonk, Otta.	.25
☐	195 Pavol Demitra, Otta.	.25
☐	196 Steve Duchesne, Otta.	.25
☐	197 Chris Dahlquist, Otta.	.25
☐	198 Sean Hill, Otta.	.25
☐	199 Stanislav Neckar, Otta.	.25
☐	200 Don Beaupré (G), Otta.	.25
☐	201 Eric Lindros, Phil.	1.00
☐	202 Rod Brind'Amour, Phil.	.25
☐	203 Shjon Podein, Phil.	.25
☐	204 Brent Fedyk, Phil.	.25
☐	205 Joel Otto, Phil.	.25
☐	206 John LeClair, Phil.	1.00
☐	207 Kevin Dineen, Phil.	.25
☐	208 Petr* Svoboda, Phil.	.25
☐	209 Éric Desjardins, Phil.	.25
☐	210 Ron Hextall (G), Phil.	.25
☐	211 Mario Lemieux, Pitt.	.25
☐	212 Petr Nedved, Pitt.	.25
☐	213 Bryan Smolinski, Pitt.	.25
☐	214 Tomas Sandström, Pitt.	.25
☐	215 Ron Francis, Pitt.	.25
☐	216 Jaromir Jagr, Pitt.	1.00
☐	217 Sergei Zubov, Pitt.	.25
☐	218 Drake Berehowsky, Pitt.	.25
☐	219 Dmitri Mironov, Pitt.	.25
☐	220 Ken Wregget (G), Pitt.	.25
☐	221 Tom Barrasso (G), Pitt.	.25
☐	222 Igor Larionov, SanJ.	.25
☐	223 Jeff Friesen, SanJ.	.25
☐	224 Kevin Miller, SanJ.	.25
☐	225 Ray Whitney, SanJ.	.25
☐	226 Craig Janney, SanJ.	.25
☐	227 Pat Falloon, SanJ.	.25
☐	228 Ulf Dahlén, SanJ.	.25
☐	229 Viktor Kozlov, SanJ.	.25
☐	230 Michal Sykora, SanJ.	.25
☐	231 Sandis Ozolinsh, SanJ.	.25
☐	232 Jamie Baker, SanJ.	.25
☐	233 Arturs Irbe (G), SanJ.	.25
☐	234 Adam Creighton, SLou.	.25
☐	235 Ian Laperrière, SLou.	.25
☐	236 Brett Hull, SLou.	1.00
☐	237 Brian Noonan, SLou.	.25
☐	238 Dale Hawerchuk, SLou.	.25
☐	239 Esa Tikkanen, SLou.	.25
☐	240 Geoff Courtnall, SLou.	.25
☐	241 Shayne Corson, SLou.	.25
☐	242 Al MacInnis, SLou.	.25
☐	243 Chris Pronger, SLou.	.25
☐	244 Jeff Norton, SLou.	.25
☐	245 Grant Fuhr (G), SLou.	.25
☐	246 Brian Bradley, Tamp.	.25
☐	247 Chris Gratton, Tamp.	.25
☐	248 John Cullen, Tamp.	.25
☐	249 John Tucker, Tamp.	.25
☐	250 Paul Ysebaert, Tamp.	.25
☐	251 Petr Klima, Tamp.	.25
☐	252 Alexander Selivanov, Tamp.	.25
☐	253 Brian Bellows, Tamp.	.25
☐	254 Enrico Ciccone, Tamp.	.25
☐	255 Roman Hamrlik, Tamp.	.25
☐	256 Daren Puppa (G), Tamp.	.25
☐	257 Doug Gilmour, Toro.	.25
☐	258 Benoît Hogue, Toro.	.25
☐	259 Mats Sundin, Toro.	1.00
☐	260 Dave Andreychuk, Toro.	.25
☐	261 Mike Gartner, Toro.	1.00
☐	262 Randy Wood, Toro.	.25
☐	263 Tie Domi, Toro.	.25
☐	264 Dave Ellett, Toro.	.25
☐	265 Todd Gill, Toro.	.25
☐	266 Larry Murphy, Toro.	.25
☐	267 Kenny Jönsson, Toro.	.25
☐	268 Félix Potvin (G), Toro.	.25
☐	269 Cliff Ronning, Vanc.	.25
☐	270 Mike Ridley, Vanc.	.25
☐	271 Trevor Linden, Vanc.	.25
☐	272 Alexander Mogilny, Vanc.	.25
☐	273 Martin Gélinas, Vanc.	.25
☐	274 Pavel Bure, Vanc.	1.00
☐	275 Russ Courtnall, Vanc.	.25
☐	276 Jeff R. Brown, Vanc.	.25
☐	277 Jyrki Lumme, Vanc.	.25
☐	278 Kirk McLean (G), Vanc.	.25
☐	279 Steve Konowalchuk, Wash.	.25
☐	280 Kelly Miller, Wash.	.25
☐	281 Peter Bondra, Wash.	.25
☐	282 Keith Jones, Wash.	.25
☐	283 Joé Juneau, Wash.	.25
☐	284 Mark Tinordi, Wash.	.25
☐	285 Calle Johansson, Wash.	.25
☐	286 Sergei Gonchar, Wash.	.25
☐	287 Jim Carey (G), Wash.	.25
☐	288 Dallas Drake, Winn.	.25
☐	289 Alexei Zhamnov, Winn.	.25
☐	290 Mike Eastwood, Winn.	.25
☐	291 Igor Korolev, Winn.	.25
☐	292 Teemu Selänne, Winn.	1.00
☐	293 Keith Tkachuk, Winn.	.25
☐	294 Teppo Numminen, Winn.	.25
☐	295 Dave Manson, Winn.	.25
☐	296 Tim Chevelade (G), Winn.	.25
☐	Checklist	.25
☐	Checklist	.25
☐	Checklist	.25
☐	Checklist	.25
☐	Checklist	.25
☐	Checklist	.25
☐	Checklist	.25
☐	Checklist	.25

INSERT

Insert Set (35 caps): 50.00

	Player	NRMT-MT
☐	1 Wayne Gretzky, LosA.	10.00
☐	2 Mario Lemieux, Pitt.	5.00
☐	3 Cam Neely, Bost.	2.00
☐	4 Raymond Bourque, Bost.	3.00
☐	5 Patrick Roy (G), Colo.	5.00
☐	6 Mark Messier, NYRa.	2.00
☐	7 Brett Hull, SLou.	2.00
☐	8 Grant Fuhr (G), SLou.	1.00
☐	9 Eric Lindros, Phil.	.50
☐	10 John LeClair, Phil.	2.00
☐	11 Jaromir Jagr, Pitt.	.50
☐	12 Chris Chelios, Chic.	1.00
☐	13 Paul Coffey, Detr.	1.00
☐	14 Dominik Hasek (G), Buff.	.50
☐	15 Alexei Zhamnov, Winn.	.50
☐	16 Keith Tkachuk, Winn.	1.00
☐	17 Theoren Fleury, Calg.	1.00
☐	18 Raymond Bourque, Bost.	3.00
☐	19 Larry Murphy, Toro.	.50
☐	20 Ed Belfour (G), Chic.	2.00
☐	21 Pavel Bure, Vanc.	.50
☐	22 Doug Gilmour, Toro.	1.00
☐	23 Brett Hull, SLou.	2.00
☐	24 Mark Messier, NYRa.	2.00
☐	25 Cam Neely, Bost.	2.00
☐	26 Jeremy Roenick, Chic.	2.00
☐	27 Patrick Roy (G), Colo.	5.00
☐	28 Jim Carey (G), Wash.	.50
☐	29 Peter Forsberg, Colo.	.50
☐	30 Jeff Friesen, SanJ.	.50
☐	31 Kenny Jönsson, Toro.	.50
☐	32 Paul Kariya, Anah.	.50
☐	33 Ian Laperrière, SLou.	.50
☐	34 David Oliver, Edmo.	.50
☐	35 Kyle McLaren, Bost.	.50

1995 - 96 PRO MAGNET

There is believed to be 50-100 copies of each Test Proof. Only 100 of the 130 players in the magnet set have test proof cards. This series was issued by Chris Martin Enterprises.

Magnet Size: 2 7/16" x 3 11/16"

		Proof	Magnet
	Complete Set (130 magnets):	-	115.00
	Test Proofs Set (100 cards):	725.00	-
	Player	**Proof**	**Magnet**
☐☐	1 Ed Belfour (G), Chic.	20.00	3.50
☐☐	2 Chris Chelios, Chic.	12.00	2.00
☐☐	3 Joe Murphy, Chic.	2.00	.50
☐☐	4 Jeremy Roenick, Chic.	15.00	3.00
☐☐	5 Bernie Nicholls, Chic.	4.00	.50
☐☐	6 Brett Hull, SLou.	25.00	2.00
☐☐	7 Esa Tikkanen, SLou.	2.00	.50
☐☐	8 Chris Pronger, SLou.	12.00	2.00
☐☐	9 Al MacInnis, SLou.	8.00	1.50
☐☐	10 Geoff Courtnall, SLou.	2.00	.50
☐☐	11 Raymond Bourque, Bost.	30.00	4.00
☐☐	12 Blaine Lacher (G), Bost.	2.00	.50
☐☐	13 Cam Neely, Bost.	25.00	3.50
☐☐	14 Adam Oates, Bost.	8.00	1.50
☐☐	15 Kevin Stevens, Bost.	4.00	.50
☐☐	16 Vincent Damphousse, Mont.	12.00	2.00
☐☐	17 Mark Recchi, Mont.	8.00	1.50
☐☐	18 Pierre Turgeon, Mont.	8.00	1.50
☐☐	19 Patrick Roy (G), Mont.	120.00	10.00
☐☐	20 Valeri Bure, Mont.	6.00	1.00
☐☐	21 Pavel Bure, Vanc.	20.00	2.00
☐☐	22 Alexander Mogilny, Vanc.	8.00	1.50
☐☐	23 Trevor Linden, Vanc.	8.00	1.50
☐☐	24 Kirk McLean (G), Vanc.	6.00	1.00
☐☐	25 Cliff Ronning, Vanc.	4.00	.50
☐	26 Jim Carey (G), Wash.	-	.50
☐	27 Brendan Witt, Wash.	-	.50
☐	28 Joé Juneau, Wash.	-	.50
☐	29 Jason Allison, Wash.	-	2.00
☐	30 Dale Hunter, Wash.	-	1.00
☐☐	31 Martin Brodeur (G), NJer.	60.00	6.00
☐☐	32 John MacLean, NJer.	2.00	.50
☐☐	33 Scott Niedermayer, NJer.	6.00	1.00
☐☐	34 Stéphane Richer, NJer.	4.00	.50
☐☐	35 Scott Stevens, NJer.	8.00	1.50
☐☐	36 Patrik Carnbäck, Anah.	2.00	.50
☐☐	37 Oleg Tverdovsky, Anah.	2.00	.50
☐☐	38 Guy Hebert (G), Anah.	4.00	.50
☐☐	39 Paul Kariya, Anah.	55.00	4.00
☐☐	40 Garry Valk, Anah.	2.00	.50
☐☐	41 Theoren Fleury, Calg.	10.00	2.00
☐☐	42 German Titov, Calg.	2.00	.50
☐☐	43 Joe Nieuwendyk, Calg.	8.00	1.50
☐☐	44 Gary Roberts, Calg.	8.00	1.50
☐☐	45 Trevor Kidd (G), Calg.	6.00	1.00
☐☐	46 Rod Brind'Amour, Phil.	6.00	1.00
☐☐	47 Eric Lindros, Phil.	30.00	2.00
☐☐	48 John LeClair, Phil.	15.00	2.00
☐☐	49 Ron Hextall (G), Phil.	12.00	2.00
☐☐	50 Mikael Renberg, Phil.	6.00	1.00
☐	51 Patrick Flatley, NYIs.	-	.50
☐	52 Kirk Muller, NYIs.	-	1.00
☐	53 Mathieu Schneider, NYIs.	-	.50
☐	54 Wendel Clark, NYIs.	-	3.00
☐	55 Brett Lindros, NYIs.	-	1.00
☐	56 Tim Chevelade (G), Winn.	-	.50
☐	57 Dallas Drake, Winn.	-	.50
☐	58 Teemu Selänne, Winn.	-	2.00
☐	59 Keith Tkachuk, Winn.	-	2.00
☐	60 Alexei Zhamnov, Winn.	-	1.00
☐☐	61 Rob Blake, LosA.	12.00	2.00
☐☐	62 Wayne Gretzky, LosA.	160.00	14.00
☐☐	63 Jari Kurri, LosA.	25.00	2.00
☐☐	64 Jamie Storr (G), LosA.	4.00	.50
☐☐	65 Rick Tocchet, LosA.	6.00	1.00
☐☐	66 Brian Bradley, Tamp.	2.00	.50
☐☐	67 Roman Hamrlik, Tamp.	4.00	.50
☐☐	68 Rob Zamuner, Tamp.	4.00	.50
☐☐	69 Paul Ysebaert, Tamp.	2.00	.50
☐☐	70 Chris Gratton, Tamp.	4.00	.50
☐☐	71 Dave Andreychuk, Toro.	6.00	1.00
☐☐	72 Kenny Jönsson, Toro.	4.00	.50
☐☐	73 Doug Gilmour, Toro.	12.00	2.00
☐☐	74 Félix Potvin (G), Toro.	12.00	2.00
☐☐	75 Mats Sundin, Toro.	25.00	2.00
☐	76 Claude Lemieux, Colo.	-	1.00
☐	77 Peter Forsberg, Colo.	-	4.00
☐	78 Mike Ricci, Colo.	-	1.00
☐	79 Joe Sakic, Colo.	-	6.00
☐	80 Stéphane Fiset (G), Colo.	-	1.00
☐☐	81 Jason Arnott, Edmo.	8.00	1.50
☐☐	82 Jason Bonsignore, Edmo.	2.00	.50
☐☐	83 Doug Weight, Edmo.	12.00	2.00
☐☐	84 Bill Ranford (G), Edmo.	8.00	1.50
☐☐	85 Todd Marchant, Edmo.	4.00	.50
☐☐	86 Rob Niedermayer, Flor.	4.00	.50
☐☐	87 Jody Hull, Flor.	2.00	.50
☐☐	88 Bob Kudelski, Flor.	2.00	.50
☐☐	89 Scott Mellanby, Flor.	4.00	.50
☐☐	90 John Vanbiesbrouck (G), Flor.	8.00	1.50
☐☐	91 Bryan Smolinski, Pitt.	2.00	.50
☐☐	92 Mario Lemieux, Pitt.	120.00	10.00
☐☐	93 Jaromir Jagr, Pitt.	40.00	2.00
☐☐	94 Sergei Zubov, Pitt.	4.00	.50
☐☐	95 Ron Francis, Pitt.	12.00	2.00
☐☐	96 Adam Graves, NYRa.	8.00	1.50
☐☐	97 Brian Leetch, NYRa.	12.00	2.00
☐☐	98 Mark Messier, NYRa.	25.00	2.00
☐☐	99 Mike Richter (G), NYRa.	8.00	1.50
☐☐	100 Luc Robitaille, NYRa.	15.00	3.00
☐	101 Paul Coffey, Detr.	-	2.00
☐	102 Sergei Fedorov, Detr.	-	2.00
☐	103 Nicklas Lidström, Detr.	-	2.00
☐	104 Ray Sheppard, Detr.	-	.50
☐	105 Steve Yzerman, Detr.	-	8.00
☐☐	106 Dominik Hasek (G), Buff.	30.00	2.00
☐☐	107 Alexei Zhitnik, Buff.	2.00	.50
☐☐	108 Yuri Khmylev, Buff.	2.00	.50
☐☐	109 Pat LaFontaine, Buff.	12.00	2.00
☐☐	110 Donald Audette, Buff.	8.00	1.50
☐☐	111 Radek Bonk, Otta.	6.00	1.00
☐☐	112 Alexandre Daigle, Otta.	2.00	.50
☐☐	113 Steve Larouche, Otta.	2.00	.50
☐☐	114 Martin Straka, Otta.	6.00	1.00
☐☐	115 Randy Cunneyworth, Otta.	2.00	.50
☐☐	116 Pat Falloon, SanJ.	2.00	.50
☐☐	117 Arturs Irbe (G), SanJ.	8.00	1.50
☐☐	118 Ulf Dahlén, SanJ.	2.00	.50
☐☐	119 Craig Janney, SanJ.	4.00	.50
☐☐	120 Jeff Friesen, SanJ.	6.00	1.00
☐	121 Shane Churla, Dall.	-	.50
☐	122 Derian Hatcher, Dall.	-	1.00
☐	123 Todd Harvey, Dall.	-	.50
☐	124 Mike Modano, Dall.	-	2.00
☐	125 Andy Moog (G), Dall.	-	1.50
☐☐	126 Sean Burke (G), Hart.	12.00	2.00
☐☐	127 Andrew Cassels, Hart.	4.00	.50
☐☐	128 Darren Turcotte, Hart.	2.00	.50
☐☐	129 Geoff Sanderson, Hart.	4.00	.50
☐☐	130 Brendan Shanahan, Hart.	25.00	2.00

	Player	Magnet
☐	IC01 Ed Belfour (G), Chic.	5.00
☐	IC02 Martin Brodeur (G), NJer.	10.00
☐	IC03 Arturs Irbe (G), SanJ.	2.00
☐	IC04 Mike Richter (G), NYRa.	2.00
☐	IC05 Mike Vernon (G), Detr.	2.00
☐	IC06 Ron Hextall (G), Phil.	3.00
	Promo	**Magnet**
☐	01 Adam Oates, Bost.	2.00
☐	02 Pavel Bure, Vanc.	4.00
☐	03 Guy Hebert (G), Anah.	2.00
☐	04 Mark Messier, NYRa.	3.00
☐	05 Sergei Fedorov, Detr.	2.50
☐	06 Arturs Irbe (G), SanJ.	1.00
☐	MAG1 Wayne Gretzky, LosA.	10.00
☐	MAG2 Ed Belfour (G), Chi.	2.00
☐	MAG3 Mike Modano, Dall.	2.50
☐	NHL Logo	.50

1995 - 96 PRO STAMPS

These sticker/stamps feature the same photos as the Pro Magnets series.

Complete Set (12 panels): **30.00**

	Stickers		Stickers
☐	Panel 1	☐	Panel 2
☐	Panel 3	☐	Panel 4
☐	Panel 5	☐	Panel 6
☐	Panel 7	☐	Panel 8
☐	Panel 9	☐	Panel 10
☐	Panel 11	☐	Panel 12

1995 - 96 RADIO CITY POSTCARDS

We have no pricing information on this set.

Postcard Size: 4 1/4" x 6"

	Player		Player
☐	Timo Jutila	☐	Jarmo Myllys
☐	Petteri Nummelin	☐	Christian Ruuttu

1995 - 96 SCORE

These cards have three versions: a regular card, a Black Ice parallel and a Black Ice Artist's Proof parallel. Seven regular cards also have a promo version. Promo cards and regular cards have the same value.

		AP	BI	Reg.
	Complete Set (330 cards):	1500.00	165.00	20.00
	Common Player:	3.00	.35	.20
	Player	**AP**	**BI**	**Reg.**
☐☐☐	1 Jaromir Jagr, Pitt.	30.00	3.00	.20
☐☐☐	2 Adam Graves, NYRa.	10.00	1.00	.20
☐☐☐☐	3 Chris Chelios, Chic.	15.00	1.50	.20
☐☐☐	4 Félix Potvin (G), Toro.	15.00	1.50	.20
☐☐☐	5 Joe Sakic, Québ.	45.00	4.50	.50
☐☐☐	6 Chris Pronger, Hart.	15.00	1.50	.20
☐☐☐	7 Teemu Selänne, Winn.	20.00	2.00	.20
☐☐☐☐	8 Jason Arnott, Edmo.	10.00	1.00	.20
☐☐☐	9 John LeClair, Phil.	20.00	2.00	.20
☐☐☐☐	10 Mark Recchi, Mont.	10.00	1.00	.20
☐☐☐	11 Rob Blake, LosA.	15.00	1.50	.20
☐☐☐	12 Kevin Hatcher, Dall.	3.00	.35	.20
☐☐☐	13 Shawn Burr, Detr.	3.00	.35	.20
☐☐☐	14 Brett Lindros, NYIs.	5.00	.50	.20
☐☐☐	15 Craig Janney, SanJ.	5.00	.50	.20
☐☐☐	16 Oleg Tverdovsky, Anah.	3.00	.35	.20
☐☐☐	17 Blaine Lacher (G), Bost.	3.00	.35	.20
☐☐☐	18 Alexandre Daigle, Otta.	3.00	.35	.20
☐☐☐☐	19 Trevor Kidd (G), Calg.	5.00	.50	.20
☐☐☐	20 B. Shanahan, SLou.	30.00	3.00	.20
☐☐☐	21 A. Mogilny, Buff.	10.00	1.00	.20
☐☐☐	22 Stu Barnes, Flor.	3.00	.35	.20
☐☐☐	23 Jeff R. Brown, Vanc.	3.00	.35	.20
☐☐☐	24 Paul Coffey, Detr.	15.00	1.50	.20
☐☐☐☐	25 M. Brodeur (G), NJer.	45.00	4.50	.50
☐☐☐	26 Darryl Sydor, LosA.	5.00	.50	.20
☐☐☐	27 J. Steve Smith, Chic.	5.00	.50	.20
☐☐☐	28 Ted Donato, Bost.	3.00	.35	.20
☐☐☐	29 Bernie Nicholls, Chic.	5.00	.50	.20
☐☐☐	30 Kenny Jönsson, Toro.	5.00	.50	.20
☐☐☐	31 Peter Forsberg, Québ.	40.00	4.00	.50
☐☐☐	32 Sean Burke (G), Hart.	15.00	1.50	.20
☐☐☐☐	33 Keith Tkachuk, Winn.	15.00	1.50	.20
☐☐☐	34 Todd Marchant, Edmo.	5.00	.50	.20
☐☐☐	35 Mikael Renberg, Phil.	5.00	.50	.20
☐☐☐	36 V. Damphousse, Mont.	15.00	1.50	.20
☐☐☐	37 Rick Tocchet, LosA.	5.00	.50	.20
☐☐☐	38 Todd Harvey, Dall.	5.00	.50	.20
☐☐☐	39 Chris Gratton, Tamp.	5.00	.50	.20
☐☐☐	40 Darius Kasparaitis, NYIs.	5.00	.50	.20
☐☐☐	41 S. Nemchinov, NYRa.	5.00	.50	.20
☐☐☐	42 Bob Corkum, Anah.	3.00	.35	.20
☐☐☐	43 Bryan Smolinski, Bost.	3.00	.35	.20
☐☐☐	44 Kevin Stevens, Pitt.	5.00	.50	.20
☐☐☐	45 Phil Housley, Calg.	5.00	.50	.20
☐☐☐	46 Al MacInnis, SLou.	10.00	1.00	.20
☐☐☐	47 Alexei Zhitnik, Buff.	3.00	.35	.20
☐☐☐	48 Rob Niedermayer, Flor.	5.00	.50	.20
☐☐☐	49 Kirk McLean (G), Vanc.	5.00	.50	.20
☐☐☐	50 Mark Messier, NYRa.	30.00	3.00	.20
☐☐☐	51 Nicklas Lidström, Detr.	15.00	1.50	.20
☐☐☐	52 S. Niedermayer, NJer.	5.00	.50	.20
☐☐☐	53 Peter Bondra, Wash.	15.00	1.50	.20
☐☐☐	54 Luc Robitaille, Pitt.	20.00	2.00	.20
☐☐☐	55 Jeremy Roenick, Chic.	20.00	2.00	.20
☐☐☐	56 Mats Sundin, Toro.	30.00	3.00	.20
☐☐☐	57 Wendel Clark, Québ.	20.00	2.00	.20
☐☐☐	58 Todd Elik, SLou.	3.00	.35	.20
☐☐☐	59 Dave Manson, Winn.	3.00	.35	.20
☐☐☐	60 David Oliver, Edmo.	3.00	.35	.20
☐☐☐	61 Yuri Khmylev, Buff.	3.00	.35	.20
☐☐☐	62 Sergei Krivokrasov, Chic.	3.00	.35	.20
☐☐☐	63 Randy Wood, Toro.	3.00	.35	.20
☐☐☐	64 Andy Moog (G), Dall.	10.00	1.00	.20
☐☐☐	65 Petr Klima, Tamp.	3.00	.35	.20
☐☐☐	66 Ray Ferraro, NYIs.	3.00	.35	.20
☐☐☐	67 Sandis Ozolinsh, SanJ.	5.00	.50	.20
☐☐☐	68 Joe Sacco, Anah.	3.00	.35	.20
☐☐☐	69 Zarley Zalapski, Calg.	3.00	.35	.20
☐☐☐	70 Ron Tugnutt (G), Mont.	10.00	1.00	.20
☐☐☐	71 German Titov, Calg.	3.00	.35	.20
☐☐☐	72 Ian Laperrière, SLou.	3.00	.35	.20
☐☐☐	73 Doug Gilmour, Toro.	15.00	1.50	.20
☐☐☐	74 Brian Skrudland, Flor.	3.00	.35	.20
☐☐☐	75 Cliff Ronning, Vanc.	5.00	.50	.20
☐☐☐	76 Brian Savage, Mont.	5.00	.50	.20
☐☐☐	77 John MacLean, NJer.	3.00	.35	.20
☐☐☐	78 Jim Carey (G), Wash.	3.00	.35	.20
☐☐☐	79 Alexei Kovalev, NYRa.	15.00	1.50	.20
☐☐☐	80 Brian Rolston, NJer.	5.00	.50	.20
☐☐☐	81 Shawn McEachern, Pitt.	5.00	.50	.20
☐☐☐	82 Gary Suter, Chic.	5.00	.50	.20
☐☐☐	83 Owen Nolan, Québ.	15.00	1.50	.20
☐☐☐	84 Ray Whitney, SanJ.	5.00	.50	.20
☐☐☐	85 Alexei Zhamnov, Winn.	5.00	.50	.20
☐☐☐	86 Shawn Chambers, NJer.	3.00	.35	.20
☐☐☐	87 Ed Belfour (G), Chic.	30.00	3.00	.20
☐☐☐	88 Patrice Tardif, SLou.	3.00	.35	.20
☐☐☐	89 Greg A. Adams, Dall.	3.00	.35	.20
☐☐☐	90 Pierre Turgeon, Mont.	10.00	1.00	.20
☐☐☐	91 Jeff Friesen, SanJ.	5.00	.50	.20
☐☐☐	92 Marty McSorley, LosA.	5.00	.50	.20
☐☐☐	93 Dave Gagner, Dall.	3.00	.35	.20
☐☐☐	94 Guy Hebert (G), Anah.	5.00	.50	.20
☐☐☐	95 Keith Jones, Wash.	3.00	.35	.20
☐☐☐	96 Kirk Muller, NYIs.	5.00	.50	.20
☐☐☐	97 Gary Roberts, Calg.	10.00	1.00	.20
☐☐☐	98 Chris Therien, Phil.	3.00	.35	.20
☐☐☐	99 Steve Duchesne, SLou.	5.00	.50	.20
☐☐☐	100 Sergei Fedorov, Detr.	30.00	3.00	.20
☐☐☐	101 Donald Audette, Buff.	10.00	1.00	.20
☐☐☐	102 Jyrki Lumme, Vanc.	5.00	.50	.20
☐☐☐	103 Darrin Shannon, Winn.	3.00	.35	.20
☐☐☐	104 Gord Murphy, Flor.	3.00	.35	.20
☐☐☐	105 John Cullen, Pitt.	5.00	.50	.20
☐☐☐	106 Bill Guerin, NJer.	10.00	1.00	.20
☐☐☐	107 Dale Hunter, Wash.	5.00	.50	.20
☐☐☐	108 Uwe Krupp, Québ.	3.00	.35	.20
☐☐☐	109 Dave Andreychuk, Toro.	5.00	.50	.20
☐☐☐	110 Joe Murphy, Chic.	3.00	.35	.20
☐☐☐	111 Geoff Sanderson, Hart.	5.00	.50	.20
☐☐☐	112 Garry Galley, Buff.	3.00	.35	.20
☐☐☐	113 Ron Sutter, NYIs.	5.00	.50	.20
☐☐☐	114 Viktor Kozlov, SanJ.	5.00	.50	.20
☐☐☐	115 Jari Kurri, LosA.	30.00	3.00	.20
☐☐☐	116 Paul Ysebaert, Tamp.	3.00	.35	.20
☐☐☐	117 V. Malakhov, Mont.	3.00	.35	.20
☐☐☐	118 Josef Beranek, Vanc.	3.00	.35	.20
☐☐☐	119 Adam Oates, Bost.	10.00	1.00	.20
☐☐☐	120 Mike Modano, Dall.	30.00	3.00	.20
☐☐☐	121 Theoren Fleury, Calg.	15.00	1.50	.20
☐☐☐	122 Pat Verbeek, NYRa.	5.00	.50	.20
☐☐☐	123 Esa Tikkanen, SLou.	3.00	.35	.20
☐☐☐	124 Brian Leetch, NYRa.	15.00	1.50	.20
☐☐☐	125 Paul Kariya, Anah.	40.00	4.00	.50
☐☐☐	126 Ken Wregget (G), Pitt.	5.00	.50	.20
☐☐☐	127 Ray Sheppard, Detr.	3.00	.35	.20
☐☐☐	128 Jason Allison, Wash.	15.00	1.50	.20
☐☐☐	129 Dave Ellett, Toro.	3.00	.35	.20
☐☐☐	130 Stéphane Richer, NJer.	5.00	.50	.20
☐☐☐	131 J. Thibault (G), Québ.	10.00	1.00	.20
☐☐☐	132 Martin Straka, Otta.	5.00	.50	.20
☐☐☐	133 Tony Amonte, Chic.	15.00	1.50	.20
☐☐☐	134 Scott Mellanby, Flor.	5.00	.50	.20
☐☐☐	135 Pavel Bure, Vanc.	20.00	2.00	.20
☐☐☐	136 Andrew Cassels, Hart.	5.00	.50	.20
☐☐☐	137 Ulf Dahlén, SanJ.	3.00	.35	.20
☐☐☐	138 Valeri Bure, Mont.	5.00	.50	.20
☐☐☐	139 Teppo Numminen, Winn.	5.00	.50	.20
☐☐☐	140 Mike Richter (G), NYRa.	10.00	1.00	.20
☐☐☐	141 Rob Gaudreau, Otta.	3.00	.35	.20
☐☐☐	142 N. Khabibulin (G), Winn.	10.00	1.00	.20
☐☐☐	143 M. Czerkawski, Bost.	5.00	.50	.20
☐☐☐	144 Mark Tinordi, Wash.	3.00	.35	.20
☐☐☐	145 P. Roy (G), Mont.	90.00	9.00	1.00
☐☐☐	146 Steve Chiasson, Calg.	3.00	.35	.20
☐☐☐	147 Mike Donnelly, Dall.	3.00	.35	.20
☐☐☐	148 Patrice Brisebois, Mont.	3.00	.35	.20
☐☐☐	149 Jason Wiemer, Tamp.	3.00	.35	.20
☐☐☐	150 Eric Lindros, Phil.	30.00	3.00	.20
☐☐☐	151 Dmitri Khristich, Wash.	3.00	.35	.20
☐☐☐	152 T. Barrasso (G), Pitt.	10.00	1.00	.20
☐☐☐	153 C. Leschyshyn, Québ.	3.00	.35	.20
☐☐☐	154 Robert Kron, Hart.	3.00	.35	.20
☐☐☐	155 Jesse Bélanger, Flor.	3.00	.35	.20
☐☐☐	156 Brian Noonan, NYRa.	3.00	.35	.20
☐☐☐	157 Michael Peca, Vanc.	10.00	1.00	.20
☐☐☐	158 Patrick Poulin, Chic.	3.00	.35	.20
☐☐☐	159 Sergei Makarov, SanJ.	10.00	1.00	.20
☐☐☐	160 Scott Stevens, NJer.	10.00	1.00	.20
☐☐☐	161 Sergio Momesso, Vanc.	3.00	.35	.20
☐☐☐	162 Todd Gill, Toro.	3.00	.35	.20
☐☐☐	163 Don Sweeney, Bost.	3.00	.35	.20
☐☐☐	164 Randy Burridge, LosA.	3.00	.35	.20
☐☐☐	165 Vy. Kozlov, Detr.	5.00	.50	.20
☐☐☐	166 Shaun Van Allen, Anah.	3.00	.35	.20
☐☐☐	167 Steven Rice, Hart.	3.00	.35	.20
☐☐☐	168 A. Deadmarsh, Québ.	5.00	.50	.20
☐☐☐	169 Andrei Nikolishin, Hart.	3.00	.35	.20
☐☐☐	170 Valeri Karpov, Anah.	3.00	.35	.20
☐☐☐	171 Doug Bodger, Buff.	3.00	.35	.20
☐☐☐	172 Corey Millen, Dall.	3.00	.35	.20
☐☐☐	173 M. Fitzpatrick (G), Flor.	3.00	.35	.20
☐☐☐	174 Bob Errey, Detr.	3.00	.35	.20
☐☐☐	175 Dan Quinn, LosA.	3.00	.35	.20
☐☐☐	176 V. Konstantinov, Detr.	5.00	.50	.20
☐☐☐	177 Scott Lachance, NYIs.	3.00	.35	.20
☐☐☐	178 Jeff Norton, SLou.	3.00	.35	.20
☐☐☐	179 Valeri Zelepukin, NJer.	3.00	.35	.20
☐☐☐	180 Dmitri Mironov, Toro.	3.00	.35	.20
☐☐☐	181 Pat Peake, Wash.	3.00	.35	.20
☐☐☐	182 Dominic Roussel, Phil.	3.00	.35	.20
☐☐☐	183 Sylvain Côté, Wash.	3.00	.35	.20
☐☐☐	184 Pat Falloon, SanJ.	3.00	.35	.20
☐☐☐	185 Roman Hamrlik, Tamp.	5.00	.50	.20
☐☐☐	186 Joel Otto, Calg.	3.00	.35	.20
☐☐☐	187 Ron Francis, Pitt.	15.00	1.50	.20
☐☐☐	188 Sergei Zubov, NYRa.	5.00	.50	.20
☐☐☐	189 Arturs Irbe (G), SanJ.	10.00	1.00	.20
☐☐☐	190 Radek Bonk, Otta.	5.00	.50	.20
☐☐☐	191 John Tucker, Tamp.	3.00	.35	.20
☐☐☐	192 Sylvain Lefebvre, Québ.	3.00	.35	.20
☐☐☐	193 Doug Brown, Detr.	3.00	.35	.20
☐☐☐	194 Glen Wesley, Hart.	3.00	.35	.20
☐☐☐	195 Ron Hextall (G), Phil.	15.00	1.50	.20
☐☐☐	196 Patrick Flatley, NYIs.	3.00	.35	.20
☐☐☐	197 Darcy Wakaluk, Dall.	3.00	.35	.20
☐☐☐	198 Kelly Hrudey (G), LosA.	5.00	.50	.20
☐☐☐	199 R. Bourque, Bost.	35.00	3.50	.20
☐☐☐	200 D. Hasek (G), Buff.	30.00	3.00	.20
☐☐☐	201 Pat LaFontaine, Buff.	15.00	1.50	.20
☐☐☐	202 C. Osgood (G), Detr.	15.00	1.50	.20
☐☐☐	203 Ulf Samuelsson, Pitt.	3.00	.35	.20
☐☐☐	204 Mike Gartner, Toro.	20.00	2.00	.20
☐☐☐	205 S. Fiset (G), Québ.	5.00	.50	.20
☐☐☐	206 M. Schneider, NYIs.	5.00	.50	.20
☐☐☐	207 Éric Desjardins, Phil.	5.00	.50	.20
☐☐☐	208 Trevor Linden, Vanc.	10.00	1.00	.20
☐☐☐	209 Cam Neely, Bost.	30.00	3.00	.20
☐☐☐	210 D. Puppa (G), Tamp.	5.00	.50	.20
☐☐☐	211 Steve Larmer, NYRa.	10.00	1.00	.20
☐☐☐	212 T. Chevelade (G), Winn.	3.00	.35	.20
☐☐☐	213 Derek Plante, Buff.	3.00	.35	.20
☐☐☐	214 Murray Craven, Chic.	3.00	.35	.20
☐☐☐	215 T. Söderström (G), NYIs.	3.00	.35	.20
☐☐☐	216 Bob Bassen, Québ.	3.00	.35	.20
☐☐☐	217 Marty McInnis, NYIs.	3.00	.35	.20
☐☐☐	218 Dave Lowry, Flor.	5.00	.50	.20
☐☐☐	219 Mike Vernon (G), Detr.	10.00	1.00	.20
☐☐☐	220 Petr Nedved, NYRa.	5.00	.50	.20
☐☐☐	221 Yves Racine, Mont.	3.00	.35	.20
☐☐☐	222 Dale Hawerchuk, Buff.	15.00	1.50	.20
☐☐☐	223 Wayne Presley, Buff.	3.00	.35	.20
☐☐☐	224 Darren Turcotte, Hart.	3.00	.35	.20
☐☐☐	225 Derian Hatcher, Dall.	5.00	.50	.20
☐☐☐	226 Steve Thomas, NYIs.	5.00	.50	.20
☐☐☐	227 S. Matteau, NYRa.	3.00	.35	.20
☐☐☐	228 Grant Fuhr (G), LosA.	15.00	1.50	.20
☐☐☐	229 Joe Nieuwendyk, Calg.	10.00	1.00	.20
☐☐☐	230 Alexei Yashin, Otta.	15.00	1.50	.20
☐☐☐	231 Brian Bellows, Mont.	5.00	.50	.20
☐☐☐	232 Brian Bradley, Tamp.	3.00	.35	.20
☐☐☐	233 Tony Granato, LosA.	5.00	.50	.20
☐☐☐	234 Mike Ricci, Québ.	5.00	.50	.20
☐☐☐	235 Brett Hull, SLou.	30.00	3.00	.20
☐☐☐	236 Mike Ridley, Toro.	3.00	.35	.20
☐☐☐	237 Al Iafrate, Bost.	5.00	.50	.20
☐☐☐	238 Derek King, NYIs.	3.00	.35	.20
☐☐☐	239 Bill Ranford (G), Edmo.	10.00	1.00	.20
☐☐☐	240 Steve Yzerman, Detr.	70.00	7.00	1.00
☐☐☐	241 Vanbiesbrouck (G), Flor.	10.00	1.00	.20
☐☐☐	242 Russ Courtnall, Vanc.	5.00	.50	.20
☐☐☐	243 Chris Terreri (G), NJer.	3.00	.35	.20
☐☐☐	244 Rod Brind'Amour, Phil.	5.00	.50	.20
☐☐☐	245 Shayne Corson, Edmo.	5.00	.50	.20
☐☐☐	246 Don Beaupré (G), Otta.	3.00	.35	.20
☐☐☐	247 Dino Ciccarelli, Detr.	5.00	.50	.20
☐☐☐	248 Kevin Lowe, NYRa.	5.00	.50	.20
☐☐☐	249 Craig MacTavish, Phil.	3.00	.35	.20
☐☐☐	250 W. Gretzky, LosA.	120.00	12.00	1.50
☐☐☐	251 Cu. Joseph (G), SLou.	30.00	3.00	.20
☐☐☐	252 Joe Mullen, Pitt.	10.00	1.00	.20
☐☐☐	253 A. Kovalenko, Québ.	3.00	.35	.20
☐☐☐	254 Igor Larionov, SanJ.	15.00	1.50	.20
☐☐☐	255 Geoff Courtnall, Vanc.	3.00	.35	.20
☐☐☐	256 Joé Juneau, Wash.	5.00	.50	.20
☐☐☐	257 Bruce Driver, NJer.	3.00	.35	.20
☐☐☐	258 Michal Pivonka, Wash.	3.00	.35	.20
☐☐☐	259 Nelson Emerson, Winn.	3.00	.35	.20
☐☐☐	260 Larry Murphy, Pitt.	5.00	.50	.20
☐☐☐	261 Brent Gilchrist, Dall.	3.00	.35	.20
☐☐☐	262 Benoît Hogue, Toro.	3.00	.35	.20
☐☐☐	263 Doug Weight, Edmo.	15.00	1.50	.20
☐☐☐	264 Keith Primeau, Detr.	10.00	1.00	.20

265 Neal Broten, NJer.	5.00	.50	.20
266 Mike Keane, Mont.	3.00	.35	.20
267 Zigmund Palffy, NYIs.	15.00	1.50	.20
268 Valeri Kamensky, Québ.	5.00	.50	.20
269 Claude Lemieux, NJer.	5.00	.50	.20
270 B. Marchment, Edmo.	3.00	.35	.20
271 Kelly Miller, Wash.	3.00	.35	.20
272 Brent Sutter, Chic.	5.00	.50	.20
273 Glenn Healy (G), NYRa.	5.00	.50	.20
274 Sergei Brylin, NJer.	3.00	.35	.20
275 Tie Domi, Toro.	5.00	.50	.20
276 Norm Maciver, Pitt.	3.00	.35	.20
277 Kevin Dineen, Phil.	3.00	.35	.20
278 Scott A. Young, Québ.	5.00	.50	.20
279 Tomas Sandström, Pitt.	5.00	.50	.20
280 Guy Carbonneau, SLou.	5.00	.50	.20
281 D. Savard, Chic.	10.00	1.00	.20
282 Ed Olczyk, Winn.	5.00	.50	.20
283 Adam Creighton, SLou.	3.00	.35	.20
284 Tom Chorske, NJer.	3.00	.35	.20
285 Roman Oksiuta, Vanc.	3.00	.35	.20
286 David Roberts, SLou.	3.00	.35	.20
287 Petr* Svoboda, Phil.	5.00	.50	.20
288 Brad May, Buff.	3.00	.35	.20
289 Michael Nylander, Calg.	5.00	.50	.20
290 J.Casey (G), SLou. [b/ Joseph]	3.00	.35	.20
291 P. DeRouville, Pitt.	5.00	.50	.20
292 Craig Johnson, SLou.	3.00	.35	.20
293 C. McAlpine, NJer. RC	**3.00**	**.50**	**.20**
294 Ralph Intranuovo, Edmo.	3.00	.50	.20
295 Richard Park, Pitt.	3.00	.50	.20
296 Todd Warriner, Toro.	5.00	.50	.20
297 C. Conroy, Mont. RC	**10.00**	**2.50**	**1.00**
298 Marek Malík, Hart.	3.00	.35	.20
299 M. Fernandez (G), Dall.	15.00	2.00	.20
300 Cory Stillman, Calg.	5.00	.50	.20
301 Kevin Brown, LosA.	3.00	.35	.20
302 S. Larouche, Otta. RC	**3.00**	**.50**	**.20**
303 Chris Taylor, NYIs.	3.00	.35	.20
304 Ryan Smyth, Edmo.	10.00	1.00	.20
305 Craig Darby, NYIs.	3.00	.35	.20
306 Radim Bicanek, Otta.	3.00	.50	.20
307 Shean Donovan, SanJ.	3.00	.35	.20
308 Jason Bonsignore, Edmo.	3.00	.50	.20
309 C. Marinucci, NYIs. RC	**3.00**	**.50**	**.20**
310 B. Holzinger, Buff. RC	**5.00**	**1.00**	**.50**
311 Mike Torchia, Dall. RC	**5.00**	**1.00**	**.50**
312 Éric Dazé, Chic.	15.00	2.00	.20
313 J. Linden, Flor. RC	**3.00**	**.50**	**.20**
314 T. Salo (G), NYIs. RC	**15.00**	**3.50**	**1.50**
315 Martin Gendron, Wash.	3.00	.50	.20
316 F. Potvin (G)	15.00	1.50	.20
317 J. Carey (G)	3.00	.35	.20
318 E. Belfour (G)	30.00	3.00	.20
319 M. Vernon (G)	10.00	1.00	.20
320 S. Burke (G)	15.00	1.50	.20
321 M. Richter (G)	10.00	1.00	.20
322 J.Vanbiesbrouck (G)	10.00	1.00	.20
323 M. Brodeur (G)	45.00	4.50	.50
324 P. Roy (G)	90.00	9.00	1.00
325 D. Hasek (G)	30.00	3.00	.20
326 Checklist	3.00	.35	.20
327 Checklist	3.00	.35	.20
328 Checklist	3.00	.35	.20
329 Checklist	3.00	.35	.20
330 Checklist	3.00	.35	.20

BORDER BATTLE

Insert Set (15 cards):	**25.00**
Cam Neely Promo	1.00
Insert (1:12)	**BB**
1 Pierre Turgeon, Mont.	1.00
2 Wayne Gretzky, LosA.	10.00
3 Cam Neely, Bost.	2.00
4 Joe Sakic, Québ.	4.00
5 Doug Gilmour, Toro.	1.00
6 Brett Hull, SLou.	2.00
7 Pat LaFontaine, Buff.	1.00
8 Joe Mullen, Pitt.	1.00
9 Mike Modano, Dall.	2.00
10 Jeremy Roenick, Chic.	2.00
11 Pavel Bure, Vanc.	2.00
12 Alexei Zhamnov, Winn.	1.00
13 Sergei Fedorov, Detr.	2.00
14 Jaromir Jagr, Pitt.	2.00
15 Mats Sundin, Toro.	2.00

CHECK-IT

Insert Set (12 cards):	**85.00**
Insert (1:36)	**CI**
1 Eric Lindros, Phil. [vs. M.Pivonka]	16.00
2 Owen Nolan, Québ. [vs. S.Lachance]	10.00
3 Brett Lindros, NYIs. [vs. A.Graves]	4.00
4 Chris Gratton, Tamp. [vs. P.Popovic]	4.00
5 Chris Pronger, Hart. [vs. Do.Brown]	10.00
6 Adam Deadmarsh, Québ. [vs. D.Yushkevich]	4.00
7 Peter Forsberg, Québ. [vs/ A.Zhitnik]	24.00
8 Derian Hatcher, Dall. [vs. M.Sillinger]	4.00
9 Rob Blake, LosA. [vs. V.Butsayev]	10.00
10 Jeff Friesen, SanJ. [vs. I.Korolev]	4.00
11 Keith Tkachuk, Winn. [vs. C.Ludwig]	10.00
12 Mike Ricci, Québ.	4.00

DREAM TEAM

Insert Set (12 cards):	**60.00**
Insert (1:72)	**DT**
1 Wayne Gretzky, LosA.	20.00
2 Sergei Fedorov, Detr.	4.00
3 Eric Lindros, Phil.	4.00
4 Mark Messier, NYRa.	4.00
5 Peter Forsberg, Québ.	6.00
6 Doug Gilmour, Toro.	2.00
7 Paul Kariya, Anah.	6.00
8 Jaromir Jagr, Pitt.	4.00
9 Brett Hull, SLou.	4.00
10 Pavel Bure, Vanc.	4.00
11 Patrick Roy (G), Mont.	14.00
12 Jim Carey (G), Wash.	2.00

GOLDEN BLADES

Inset Set (20 cards):	**170.00**
Insert (1:18 Jumbo)	**GB**
1 Joe Sakic, Québ.	20.00
2 Teemu Selänne, Winn.	10.00
3 Alexander Mogilny, Buff.	6.00
4 Peter Bondra, Wash.	6.00
5 Paul Coffey, Detr.	6.00
6 Mike Modano, Dall.	10.00
7 Alexei Yashin, Otta.	6.00
8 Pat LaFontaine, Buff.	6.00
9 Paul Kariya, Anah.	15.00
10 Peter Forsberg, Québ.	15.00
11 Jeff Friesen, SanJ.	6.00
12 Steve Yzerman, Detr.	30.00
13 Theoren Fleury, Calg.	6.00
14 Stéphane Richer, NJer.	6.00
15 Mark Messier, NYRa.	10.00
16 Mats Sundin, Toro.	10.00
17 Brendan Shanahan, SLou.	10.00
18 Mark Recchi, Mont.	6.00
19 Jeremy Roenick, Chic.	10.00
20 Jason Arnott, Edmo.	6.00

LAMPLIGHTERS

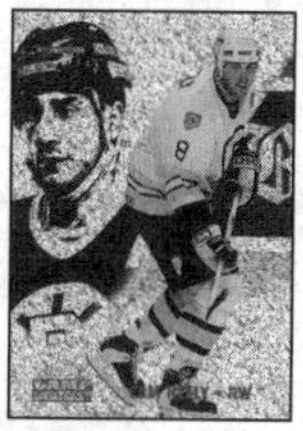

Insert Set (15 cards):	**80.00**
Insert (1:36 Hobby)	**LL**
1 Wayne Gretzky, LosA.	30.00
2 Pavel Bure, Vanc.	6.00
3 Cam Neely, Bost.	6.00
4 Owen Nolan, Québ.	4.00
5 Sergei Fedorov, Detr.	6.00
6 Pierre Turgeon, Mont.	2.00
7 Peter Bondra, Wash.	4.00
8 Mikael Renberg, Phil.	2.00
9 Luc Robitaille, Pitt.	6.00
10 Alexei Zhamnov, Winn.	2.00
11 Brett Hull, SLou.	6.00
12 Jaromir Jagr, Pitt.	6.00
13 Theoren Fleury, Calg.	4.00
14 Teemu Selänne, Winn.	6.00
15 Eric Lindros, Phil.	6.00

1995 - 96 SELECT CERTIFIED EDITION

These cards have two versions: a regular card and a Mirror Gold parallel. Seven cards also have a promo version. Regular cards and promos have the same value.

Complete Set (144 cards):	**.00**	**70.00**
Common Player:	**4.00**	**.35**
Player	**MG**	**Reg.**
1 Mario Lemieux, Pitt.	90.00	7.50
2 Chris Chelios, Chic.	15.00	1.50
3 Scott Mellanby, Flor.	5.00	.50
4 Brett Hull, SLou.	30.00	2.50
5 Theoren Fleury, Calg.	15.00	1.50
6 Alexei Zhamnov, Winn.	5.00	.50
7 Mats Sundin, Toro.	30.00	2.50
8 Mathieu Schneider, NYIs.	5.00	.50
9 Jason Arnott, Edmo.	10.00	1.00
10 Mark Recchi, Mont.	10.00	1.00
11 Adam Oates, Bost.	10.00	1.00
12 Jim Carey (G), Wash.	4.00	.35
13 Paul Kariya, Anah.	40.00	3.50
14 Mark Messier, NYRa.	30.00	2.50
15 Eric Lindros, Phil.	30.00	2.50
16 Pavel Bure, Vanc.	20.00	2.00
17 Mike Modano, Dall.	30.00	2.50
18 Pat LaFontaine, Buff.	15.00	1.50
19 Owen Nolan, SanJ.	15.00	1.50
20 Roman Hamrlik, Tamp.	5.00	.50
21 Paul Coffey, Detr.	15.00	1.50
22 Alexandre Daigle, Otta.	4.00	.35
23 Wayne Gretzky, LosA.	120.00	10.00
24 Martin Brodeur (G), NJer.	45.00	4.00
25 Ulf Dahlén, SanJ.	4.00	.35
26 Geoff Sanderson, Hart.	5.00	.50
27 Brian Leetch, NYRa.	15.00	1.50
28 Dave Andreychuk, Toro.	5.00	.50
29 Sergei Fedorov, Detr.	30.00	2.50
30 Jocelyn Thibault (G), Mont.	10.00	1.00
31 Mikael Renberg, Phil.	5.00	.50
32 Joe Nieuwendyk, Dall.	10.00	1.00
33 Craig Janney, SanJ.	5.00	.50
34 Raymond Bourque, Bost.	35.00	3.00
35 Jari Kurri, LosA.	30.00	2.50
36 Alexei Yashin, Otta.	15.00	1.50
37 Keith Tkachuk, Winn.	15.00	1.50
38 Jaromir Jagr, Pitt.	30.00	2.50
39 Stéphane Richer, NJer.	5.00	.50
40 Trevor Kidd (G), Calg.	5.00	.50
41 Kevin Hatcher, Dall.	4.00	.35
42 Mike Vernon (G), Detr.	10.00	1.00
43 Alexander Mogilny, Vanc.	10.00	1.00
44 John LeClair, Phil.	20.00	2.00
45 Joe Sakic, Colo.	45.00	4.00
46 Kevin Stevens, LosA.	5.00	.50
47 Adam Graves, NYRa.	10.00	1.00
48 Doug Gilmour, Toro.	15.00	1.50
49 Pierre Turgeon, Mont.	10.00	1.00
50 Joe Murphy, Chic.	4.00	.35
51 Peter Bondra, Wash.	15.00	1.50
52 Ron Francis, Pitt.	15.00	1.50
53 Luc Robitaille, NYRa.	20.00	2.00
54 Mike Gartner, Toro.	20.00	2.00
55 Bill Ranford (G), Bost.	10.00	1.00
56 Jeff Friesen, SanJ.	5.00	.50
57 Cam Neely, Bost.	30.00	2.50
58 Daren Puppa (G), Tamp.	5.00	.50
59 Rod Brind'Amour, Phil.	5.00	.50
60 Jeremy Roenick, Chic.	20.00	2.00
61 Brett Lindros, NYIs.	5.00	.50
62 Todd Harvey, Dall.	5.00	.50
63 Kirk McLean (G), Vanc.	5.00	.50
64 Brendan Shanahan, Hart.	30.00	2.50
65 Kelly Hrudey (G), LosA.	5.00	.50
66 Scott Stevens, NJer.	10.00	1.00
67 Sergei Zubov, Pitt.	5.00	.50
68 Peter Forsberg, Colo.	40.00	3.50
69 Félix Potvin (G), Toro.	15.00	1.50
70 Scott Niedermayer, NJer.	5.00	.50
71 Keith Primeau, Detr.	10.00	1.00
72 Al MacInnis, SLou.	10.00	1.00
73 Mike Richter (G), NYRa.	10.00	1.00
74 Rob Blake, LosA.	15.00	1.50
75 Vincent Damphousse, Mont.	15.00	1.50
76 Teemu Selänne, Winn. (Anah.)	20.00	2.00
77 Andy Moog (G), Dall.	10.00	1.00
78 Ron Hextall (G), Phil.	15.00	1.50
79 Oleg Tverdovsky, Anah. (Winn.)	4.00	.35
80 Joé Juneau, Wash.	5.00	.50
81 Patrick Roy (G), Colo.	90.00	7.50
82 Wendel Clark, NYIs.	20.00	2.00
83 Brian Bradley, Tamp.	4.00	.35
84 Curtis Joseph (G), Edmo.	30.00	2.50
85 John Vanbiesbrouck (G), Flor.	10.00	1.00
86 Phil Housley, Calg.	5.00	.50
87 Trevor Linden, Vanc.	10.00	1.00
88 Alexei Kovalev, NYRa.	15.00	1.50
89 Dominik Hasek (G), Buff.	30.00	2.50
90 Larry Murphy, Toro.	5.00	.50
91 Arturs Irbe (G), SanJ.	10.00	1.00
92 John MacLean, NJer.	4.00	.35
93 Ed Belfour (G), Chic.	30.00	2.50
94 Steve Yzerman, Detr.	70.00	6.00
95 Tom Barrasso (G), Pitt.	10.00	1.00
96 Rob Niedermayer, Flor.	5.00	.50
97 Dale Hawerchuk, SLou.	15.00	1.50
98 Rick Tocchet, Bost.	5.00	.50
99 Claude Lemieux, Colo.	5.00	.50
100 Sean Burke (G), Hart.	15.00	1.50
101 Shayne Corson, SLou.	5.00	.50
102 Dino Ciccarelli, Detr.	5.00	.50
103 Kirk Muller, Toro.	5.00	.50
104 Don Beaupré (G), Toro.	4.00	.35
105 Valeri Kamensky, Colo.	5.00	.50
106 Markus Näslund, Pitt.	30.00	2.50
107 Tomas Sandström, Pitt.	5.00	.50
108 Pat Verbeek, NYRa.	5.00	.50
109 Doug Weight, Edmo.	15.00	1.50
110 Brian Holzinger, Buff. RC	**10.00**	**2.00**
111 Antti Törmänen, Otta. RC	**5.00**	**1.00**
112 Tommy Salo (G), NYIs. RC	**35.00**	**6.00**
113 Jason Bonsignore, Edmo.	4.00	.50
114 Shane Doan, Winn. RC	**20.00**	**3.00**
115 Robert Svehla, Flor. RC	**20.00**	**3.00**
116 C. Kilger, Anah. (Winn.) RC	**20.00**	**3.00**
117 Saku Koivu, Mont.	35.00	4.00
118 Jeff O'Neill, Hart.	15.00	2.00
119 Brendan Witt, Wash.	4.00	.50
120 Byron Dafoe (G), LosA.	15.00	2.00
121 Ryan Smyth, Edmo.	20.00	2.00
122 D. Alfredsson, Otta. RC	**50.00**	**9.00**
123 Todd Bertuzzi, NYIs. RC	**100.00**	**18.00**
124 Daymond Langkow, Tamp.	20.00	3.00
125 Miroslav Satan, Edmo. RC	**25.00**	**4.00**
126 Bryan McCabe, NYIs.	10.00	1.00
127 Aki Berg, LosA. RC	**10.00**	**2.00**
128 Cory Stillman, Calg.	10.00	1.00
129 Deron Quint, Winn.	5.00	.50
130 Vitali Yachmenev, LosA.	5.00	.50
131 Valeri Bure, Mont.	10.00	1.50
132 Éric Dazé, Chic.	15.00	2.00
133 Radek Dvorak, Flor. RC	**20.00**	**3.00**
134 Landon Wilson, Colo. RC	**10.00**	**2.00**
135 Niklas Sundström, NYRa.	10.00	1.00
136 Jamie Storr (G), LosA.	10.00	1.00
137 Ed Jovanovski, Flor.	15.00	2.00
138 Marcus Ragnarsson, SanJ. RC	**20.00**	**3.00**
139 Kyle McLaren, Bost. RC	**20.00**	**3.00**
140 Sandy Moger, Bost. RC	**5.00**	**1.00**
141 Marty Murray, Calg.	4.00	.50
142 Darby Hendrickson, Toro.	5.00	.50
143 Corey Hirsch, Vanc.	5.00	.50
144 Petr Sykora, NJer. RC	**35.00**	**6.00**
1 Checklist	-	.20
2 Checklist	-	.20
3 Checklist	-	.20
4 Checklist	-	.20
5 Checklist	-	.20
6 Checklist	-	.20
7 Checklist	-	.20

CERTIFIED FUTURE

Insert Set (10 cards):	**80.00**
Insert (1:19)	**CF**
1 Peter Forsberg, Colo.	25.00
2 Jim Carey (G), Wash.	4.00
3 Paul Kariya, Anah.	25.00
4 Jocelyn Thibault (G), Mont.	6.00
5 Saku Koivu, Mont.	15.00
6 Brian Holzinger, Buff.	4.00
7 Todd Harvey, Dall.	4.00
8 Jeff O'Neill, Hart.	6.00
9 Oleg Tverdovsky, Anah.	4.00
10 Ed Jovanovski, Flor.	6.00

DOUBLE STRIKE

These cards have two versions: the regular insert (limited to 1,975 copies) and a Gold parallel (limited to 903 copies).

Insert Set (20 cards):	**325.00**	**150.00**
Inserts	**DSG**	**DS**
1 Doug Gilmour, Toro.	20.00	10.00
2 Ron Francis, Pitt.	20.00	10.00
3 Raymond Bourque, Bost.	45.00	22.00
4 Chris Chelios, Chic.	20.00	10.00
5 Adam Oates, Bost.	15.00	6.00
6 Mike Ricci, Colo.	10.00	6.00
7 Jeremy Roenick, Chic.	30.00	14.00
8 Jason Arnott, Edmo.	15.00	8.00
9 Brendan Shanahan, Hart.	35.00	18.00
10 Joe Nieuwendyk, Dall.	15.00	6.00
11 Trevor Linden, Vanc.	15.00	6.00
12 Mikael Renberg, Phil.	10.00	6.00
13 Theoren Fleury, Calg.	20.00	10.00
14 Sergei Fedorov, Detr.	35.00	18.00
15 Mark Messier, NYRa.	35.00	18.00
16 Keith Primeau, Detr.	15.00	6.00
17 Keith Tkachuk, Winn.	20.00	10.00
18 Scott Stevens, NJer.	15.00	6.00
19 Claude Lemieux, Colo.	10.00	6.00
20 Alexei Zhamnov, Winn.	10.00	6.00

GOLD TEAM

Insert Set (10 cards):	**300.00**
Pavel Bure Promo	5.00
Insert (1:41)	**GT**
1 Eric Lindros, Phil.	20.00
2 Wayne Gretzky, LosA.	90.00
3 Mario Lemieux, Pitt.	60.00

4 Jaromir Jagr, Pitt.	20.00
5 Pavel Bure, Vanc.	15.00
6 Brett Hull, SLou.	20.00
7 Cam Neely, Bost.	20.00
8 Joe Sakic, Colo.	30.00
9 Martin Brodeur (G), NJer.	35.00
10 Patrick Roy (G), Colo.	60.00

1995 - 96 SIGNATURE ROOKIES DRAFT DAY

Player	NRMT-MT
FF1 Bryan Berard	2.00
JC1 Jim Carey (G)	1.00
JC2 Jim Carey (G)	1.00
JC3 Jim Carey (G)	1.00
JC4 Jim Carey (G)	1.00
JC5 Jim Carey (G)	1.00
Aleksey Morozov	2.00

1995 - 96 SIGNATURE ROOKIES TETRAD

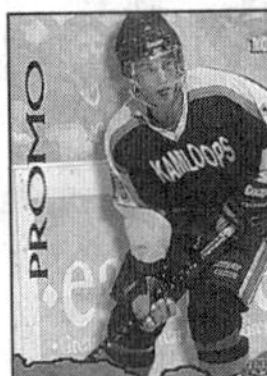

This 76-card multi-sport set includes seven hockey cards.

Player	NRMT-MT
Shane Doan Promo	.25
61 Aleksey Morozov	.25
62 Radek Dvorak	.25
66 Terry Ryan	.25
67 Shane Doan	.25
68 Brad Church	.25
69 Brian Boucher (G)	.50
70 Dmitri Nabokov	.25

SR FORCE

This 35-card insert set includes 10 hockey cards.

Player	NRMT-MT
F1 Nolan Baumgartner	.50
F2 Bryan Berard	1.00
F3 Aki Berg	.50
F4 Daymond Langkow	.50
F5 Wade Redden	1.00
F6 Martin Brodeur (G)	6.00
F7 Jim Carey (G)	.50
F8 Jaromir Jagr	4.00
F9 Maxim Kuznetsov	.50
F10 Terry Ryan	.50

1995 - 96 SIGNATURE ROOKIES TETRAD AUTOBILIA

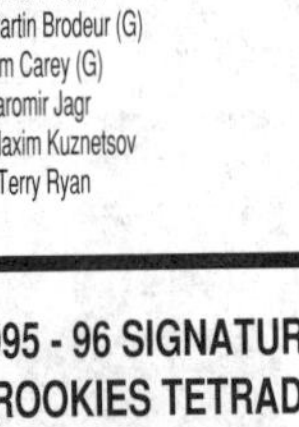

This 100-card multi-sport set includes 23 hockey cards.

Player	NRMT-MT
2 Jim Carey (G) Preview	.50
38 Nolan Baumgartner	.25
39 Bryan Berard	.50
40 Aki Berg	.25
41 Dan Cleary	.50
42 Radek Dvorak	.25
43 Patrick Juhlin	.25
44 Jan Labraaten	.25
45 Daymond Langkow	.25
46 Sergei Luchinkin	.25
47 Cameron Mann	.25
48 Aleksey Morozov	.25
49 Oleg Orekhovski	.25
50 Johan Ramstedt	.25
51 Wade Redden	.50
52 Sami-Ville Salomaa	.25
53 Alexei Vasiljev	.25
54 Peter Wallin, Swe.	.25
94 Brian Boucher (G)	.50
95 Martin Brodeur (G)	3.00
96 Brad Church	.25
97 Shane Doan	.25
98 Terry Ryan	.25
99 Ryan Smyth	.50

1995 - 96 SISU

The most expensive single is Saku Koivu at $3-4. NHL stars sell at $1-2. Other singles sell between 30¢ and $1.00.

Series One Set (200 cards):	**35.00**
Series Two Set (200 cards):	**35.00**

Player	Player
1 HIFK Helsinki	2 Kimmo Kapanen (G)
3 Yuri Kuznetsov	4 Simo Saarinen
5 Roland Carlsson	6 Veli-Pekka Kautonen
7 Kristian Fagerstrom	8 Mika Kortelainen
9 Jari Laukkanen	10 Juha Nurminen
11 Markku Jurme	12 Sami Kapanen
13 Darren Boyko	14 Marko Ojanen
15 HPK Hameenlinna	16 Kari Rosenberg (G)
17 Petri Engman	18 Niko Marttila
19 Jari Haapamaki	20 Marko Allen
21 Erik Kakko	22 Mikko Mylloykoski
23 Jani Hassinen	24 Risto Jalo
25 Juha Jarvenpaa	26 Jari Kauppila
27 Toni Makiaho	28 Ilves Tampere
29 Mika Manninen (G)	30 Hannu Henriksson
31 Petri Kokko	32 Martti Jarventie
33 Allan Measures	34 Pasi Huura
35 Janne Seva	36 Tommy Kiviaho
37 Reijo Mikkolainen	38 Hannu Mattila
39 Jari Virtanen	40 Sami Ahlberg
41 Juha Hautamaa	42 Jokerit Helsinki
43 Ari Sulander (G)	44 Santeri Immonen
45 Pasi Sormunen	46 Waltteri Immonen
47 Mika Stromberg	48 Kari Martikainen
49 Tommi Sova	50 Juha Lind
51 Niko Halttunen	52 Keijo Sailynoja
53 Otakar Janecky	54 Timo Saarikoski
55 JyP HT Jyvaskyla	56 A-P Siekkinen (G)
57 Vesa Ponto	58 Kalle Koskinen
59 Jouni Loponen	60 Miska Kangasniemi
61 Mika Paananen	62 Markku Ikonen
63 Kimmo Salminen	64 Joni Lius
65 Lasse Nieminen	66 Janne Kurjeniemi
67 Marko Virtanen	68 KalPa Kuopio
69 Jarkko Kortesoja (G)	70 Petri Matikainen
71 Mika Laaksonen	72 Kai Rautio
73 Jarno Kaultanen	74 Miika Ruokonen
75 Jussi Tarvainen	76 Mikko Honkonen
77 Sami Simonen	78 Petr Korinek
79 V-P Pekkarinen	80 Pekka Tirkkonen
81 Kiekko-Espoo	82 Iiro Itamies (G)
83 Tommi Nyyssönen	84 Robert Salo
85 Sami Nuutinen	86 Timo Blomqvist
87 Ismo Kuoppala	88 Mikko Koivunoro
89 Petro Koivunen	90 Jarmo Muukkonen
91 Sergei Prjahin	92 Teemu Riihijarvi
93 Juha Ikonen	94 Lukko Rauma
95 Boris Rousson (G)	96 Vesa Salo
97 Toni Porkka	98 Mika Yli-Maenpaa
99 Juha Riihijarvi	100 Petri Latti
101 Veli-Pekka Ahonen	102 Mikko Peltola
103 Kalle Sahlstedt	104 Jari Torkki
105 Jussi Kiuru	106 Sakari Palsola
107 Tappara Tampere	108 Ilpo Kauhanen (G)
109 Sami Lehtonen	110 Pasi Petrilainen
111 Pekka Laksola	112 Tommi Haapsaari
113 Ville Nieminen	114 Arto Kulmala
115 Valeri Krykov	116 Timo Nurmberg
117 Aleksander Barkov	118 Miikka Kemppi
119 Marko Toivola	120 Juha Vuorivirta
121 TPS Turku	122 Miikka Kiprusoff (G)
123 Kimmo Timonen	124 Sami Salo
125 Kari Harila	126 Tuomas Gronman
127 Vjatschelav Fandul	128 Mika Alatalo
129 Jukka Tiilikainen	130 Kimmo Rintanen
131 Hannes Hyvonen	132 Simo Rouvali
133 Harri Sillgren	134 Harri Suvanto
135 TuTo Turku	136 M. Korhonen (G)
137 Sebastien Sulku	138 Jukka Suomalainen
139 Timo Kulonen	140 Risto Siltanen
141 Sami Leinonen	142 Juha Virtanen
143 Jari Hirsimaki	144 Jouni Tuominen
145 Vesa Karjalainen	146 Pekka Virta
147 Jouko Myrra	148 Assat Pori
149 Kari Takko (G)	150 Timo Nykopp
151 Harri Laurila	152 Jarno Miikkulainen
153 Pasi Peltonen	154 Jari Korpisalo
155 Teppo Kivela	156 Jari Levonen
157 Janne Virtanen	158 Jarno Makela
159 Mikael Kotkaniemi	160 Ari Saarinen
161 AS: B. Rousson (G)	162 AS: Joni Lehto
163 AS: Marko Kiprusoff	164 AS: Jere Lehtinen
165 AS: Saku Koivu	166 AS: Kai Nurminen
167 AS: A. Sulander (G)	168 AS: Mika Stromberg
169 AS: Jarmo Kuusisto	170 AS: Tero Arkiomaa
171 AS: Otakar Janecky	172 AS: Ville Peltonen
173 HL: Tony Arima	174 HL: Darren Boyko
175 HL: K-P Friman	176 HL: Arto Heiskanen
177 HL: H. Henriksson	178 HL: Erik Hamalainen
179 HL: Risto Jalo	180 HL: Timo Jutila
181 HL: H. Jarvenpaa	182 HL: Jarmo Kuusisto
183 HL: Pekka Laksola	184 HL: Harri Laurila
185 HL: Pertti Lehtonen	186 HL: Jari Lindroos
187 HL: R. Mikkolainen	188 HL: Esa Tommila
189 HL: Jari Torkki	190 HL: A. Tuomenoksa
191 HL: Ari Vuori	192 TPS Turko
193 Jokerit Helsinki	194 Assat Pori
195 Jokerit Helsinki	196 TPS Turko
197 CL: Kai Nurminen	198 CL: V-P Kautonen
199 CL: Saku Koivu	200 CL: Marko Kiprusoff
201 HIFK Helsinki	202 Sakari Lindfors (G)
203 Lauri Puolanne	204 Pertti Lehtonen
205 Peter Ahola	206 Jere Karalahti
207 K. Maki-Kokkila	208 Tom Laaksonen
209 Tero Hamalainen	210 Miro Haapaniemi
211 Toni Sihvonen	212 Sami Laine
213 Iiro Jarvi	214 Pekka Tuomisto
215 HPK Hameenlinna	216 Mika Pietila
217 Tom Koivisto	218 Tommi Hamalainen
219 Kai Rautio	220 Jani Nikko
221 Mika Kannisto	222 Jason Miller
223 Niklas Hede	224 Tony Virta
225 A. Andrijevski	226 Mika Puhakka
227 Timo Peltomaa	228 Toni Saarinen
229 Ilves Tampere	230 Vesa Toskala (G)
231 P. Kangasalusta	232 Juha Lampinen
233 Pasi Saarinen	234 Teemu Vuorinen
235 Jarno Peltonen	236 Matti Kaipainen
237 Semi Pekki	238 Sami Karjalainen
239 Jouni Lahtinen	240 Pasi Maattanen
241 Petri Murtovaara	242 Tomi Hirvonen
243 Mikko Eloranta	244 Mika Arvaja
245 Juha Jarvenpaa	246 Jokerit Helsinki
247 Marko Rantanen	248 Marko Tuulola
249 Jani-Matti Loikala	250 Antti-Jussi Niemi
251 Janne Niinimaa	252 Jari Lindroos
253 Pasi Saarela	254 Yuha Ylonen
255 Mika Asikainen	256 Eero Somervuori
257 Tero Lehtera	258 Jukka Penttinen
259 Petri Varis	260 JyP HT Jyvaskyla
261 Marko Leinonen	262 Jan Latvala
263 Jukka Laamanen	264 Pekka Poikilainen
265 Thomas Sjogren	266 Pasi Kangas
267 Toni Koivunen	268 Lasse Jansen
269 Petri Kujala	270 Mikko Inkinen
271 KalPa Kuopio	272 Pasi Kuivalainen
273 Pasi Kolehmainen	274 Reijo Ruotsalainen
275 Jarkko Glad	276 Ivan Vlzek
277 Jarno Levonen	278 Janne Kekalainen
279 Veli-Pekka Nutikka	280 Mikko Konttila
281 Janne Virtanen	282 Pasi Kemppainen
283 Kiekko-Espoo	284 Mika Rautio
285 Teemu Sillanpaa	286
287 Timo Kykopp	288 Miikka Teimonen
289 Tero Tiainen	290 J. Jaaskelainen
291 Lubomir Kolnik	292 Arto Sirvio
293 Ilkka Sinisalo	294 Timo Hirvonen
295 Arto Kuki	296 Timo Norppa
297 Lukko Rauma	298 Timo Kaukanen
299 Joni Lehto	300 Jarmo Miikkulainen
301 Kimmo Lotvonen	302 Robert Nordmark
303 Riku Kallioniemi	304 Matti Raunio
305 Tommi Turunen	306 Jarkko Varvio
307 Tero Arkiomaa	308 Harri Lonnberg
309 Mikko Luovi	310 Tappara Tampere
311 Jussi Markkanen	312 Timo Jutila
313 Jukka Ollila	314 Antti Rahkonen
315 Derek Mayer	316 Petri Kalteva
317 Jarkko Nikander	318 Pauli Jarvinen
319 Mikko Helisten	320 Ari Haanpaa
321 Markus Oijennus	322 Janne Ojanen
323 TPS Turku	324 Fredrik Norrena (G)
325 Mika Lehtinen	326 Karlis Skrastins
327 Manu Laapas	328 Antti Aalto
329 Teemu Numminen	330 Tommi Miettienen
331 Lasse Pirjeta	332 Miuika Rousu
333 Marko Makinen	334 Mikko Markkanen
335 Tomi Kallio	336 Miika Elomo
337 Sami Mettovaara	338 TuTo Turku
339 Jukka Tammi	340 Kari-Pekka Friman
341 Veli-Pekka Hard	342 Antti Tirkkonen
343 Jukka Seppo	344 Kim Ahlroos
345 Marco Poulsen	346 Juha Kuusisaari
347 Mikko Laaksonen	348 Tuomas Jalava
349 Tommi Pullola	350 Tuomas Kalliomaki
351 Assat Pori	352 Karri Kivi
353 Olli Kaski	354 Jouni Vento
355 Tommi Rajamaki	356 Jokke Heinanen
357 Tomas Kapusta	358 Jaroslav Otevrel
359 Timo Salonen	360 Pekka Virta
361 Vesa Goman	362 Pekka Pelktola
363 Rauli Raitanen	364 Pasi Tuominen
365 Kari Syvasalmi	366 Timo Hakanen
367 A. Andrijevski	368 Aleksander Barkov
369 Darren Boyko	370 Vjatschelav Fandul
371 Otakar Janecky	372 Tomas Kapusta
373 Lubomir Kolnik	374 Petr Korinek
375 Derek Mayer	376 Allan Measures
377 Jason Miller	378 Robert Nordmark
379 Jaroslav Otevrel	380 Sergei Prjahin
381 Boris Rousson	382 Thomas Sjogren
383 Karlis Skrastins	384 Ivan Vlzek
385 Vladimir Jursinov	386 Hannu Aravirta
387 Veli-Pekka Ketola	388 Vaclav Sykora
389 Hannu Kapanen	390 Kari Savolainen
391 Harri Rindell	392 Anatoli Bogdanov
393 Sakari Pietila	394 Jukka Rautakorpi
395 Harri Jalava	396 Vladimir Yursinov
397 CL: Jere Lehtinen	398 Checklist
399 Checklist	400 CL: Saku Koivu

DOUBLE TROUBLE

Series Two Insert Set (8 cards):	**25.00**
Insert (1:17)	**DT**
1 Tuomas Gronman/ Kimmo Timonen	4.00
2 Waltteri Immonen/ Mika Stromberg	4.00
3 Olli Kaski/ Karri Kivi	4.00
4 Joni Lehto/ Robert Nordmark	4.00
5 Peter Ahola/ Pertti Lehtonen	4.00
6 Timo Blomqvist/ Sami Nuutinen	4.00
7 Reijo Ruotsalainen/ Ivan Vlzek	4.00
8 Timo Jutila/ Pekka Laksola	4.00

DRAFTED DOZEN

Series Two Insert Set (12 cards):	**55.00**
Insert (1:19)	**DD**
1 Aki Berg	6.00
2 Teemu Riihijarvi	4.00
3 Miikka Elomo	4.00
4 Marko Makinen	4.00
5 Tomi Kallio	6.00
6 Sami Kapanen	12.00
7 Vesa Toskala	4.00
8 Miikka Kiprusoff	12.00
9 Timo Hakanen	4.00
10 Juha Vuorivirta	4.00
11 Tomi Hirvonen	4.00
12 Mikko Markkanen	4.00

GHOST GOALIES

Series One Insert Set (10 cards):	**50.00**
Insert (1:24)	**GG**
1 Sakari Lindfors (G)	6.00
2 Boris Rousson (G)	6.00
3 Ari Sulander (G)	6.00
4 Kari Takko (G)	6.00
5 Fredrik Norrena (G)	6.00
6 Kari Rosenberg (G)	6.00
7 Ari-Pekka Siekkinen (G)	6.00
8 Jukka Tammi (G)	6.00
9 Pasi Kuivalainen (G)	6.00
10 Ilpo Kauhanen (G)	6.00

GOLD

Insert Set (24 cards):	**75.00**
Insert	**Gold**
1 Title Card	3.00
2 Jarmo Myllys (G)	3.00
3 Ari Sulander (G)	3.00
4 Jukka Tammi	3.00
5 Erik Hamalainen	3.00
6 Timo Jutila	4.00
7 Marko Kiprusoff	3.00
8 Janne Niinimaa	4.00
9 Petteri Nummelin	3.00
10 Mika Stromberg	3.00
11 Hannu Virta	3.00
12 Raimo Helminen	4.00
13 Sami Kapanen	6.00
14 Esa Keskinen	3.00
15 Saku Koivu	16.00
16 Tero Lehtera	3.00
17 Jere Lehtinen	6.00
18 Mika Nieminen	3.00
19 Janne Ojanen	3.00
20 Marko Palo	3.00
21 Ville Peltonen	3.00
22 Raimo Summanen	3.00
23 Antti Törmänen	3.00
24 Juha Ylonen	3.00

PAINKILLERS

Series One Insert Set (8 cards):	**20.00**
Insert (1:15)	**PK**
1 Jokke Hainanen	3.00
2 Mika Alatalo	3.00
3 Joni Lehto	3.00
4 Harri Lonnberg	3.00
5 Ville Peltonen	3.00
6 Harri Sillgren	3.00
7 Petri Varis	3.00
8 Marko Virtanen	3.00

SISU SPECIALS

Series One Insert Set (10 cards):	**75.00**
Insert (1:24)	**SS**
1 Petri Varis	6.00
2 Boris Rousson (G)	6.00
3 Saku Koivu	20.00
4 Jari Kurri	24.00
5 Jarmo Kuusisto	6.00
6 Janne Ojanen	6.00
7 Jere Lehtinen	8.00
8 Peter Ahola	6.00
9 Jukka Seppo	6.00
10 Michael Nylander	6.00

SPOTLIGHT

Series Two Insert Set (8 cards):	**12.00**
Insert (1:8)	**Spot.**
1 Otakar Janecky	2.00
2 Jari Korpisalo	2.00
3 Juha Riihijarvi	2.00
4 Iiro Jarvi	2.00
5 Thomas Sjogren	2.00
6 Risto Jalo	2.00
7 Jari Hirsimaka	2.00
8 Juha Hautamaa	2.00

SUPER CHASE

Insert	Super
Saku Koivu	60.00
Saku Koivu Golden Helmet	75.00
Janne Niinimaa	30.00

1995 - 96 SISU LIMITED

The wrappers featured one of three different players: Saku Koivu, Jari Kurri or Teemu Selänne.

Complete Set (108 cards):	**35.00**

Common Player: .30
☐ Saku Koivu Hologram 8.00
Player NRMT-MT
☐ 1 Frederik Norrena (G), TPS .50
☐ 2 Hannu Virta, TPS .50
☐ 3 Petteri Nummelin, TPS .50
☐ 4 Tuomas Gronman, TPS .30
☐ 5 Marko Kiprusoff, TPS .30
☐ 6 Saku Koivu, TPS 4.00
☐ 7 Raimo Summanen, TPS .30
☐ 8 Esa Keskinen, TPS .50
☐ 9 Jere Lehtinen, TPS 1.00
☐ 10 Ari Sulander (G), Jokerit .50
☐ 11 Waltteri Immonen, Jokerit .30
☐ 12 Mika Stromberg, Jokerit .30
☐ 13 Janne Niinimaa, Jokerit .50
☐ 14 Otakar Janecky, Jokerit .30
☐ 15 Teemu Selänne, Jokerit 4.00
☐ 16 Jari Kurri, Jokerit 5.00
☐ 17 Antti Tormanen, Jokerit .30
☐ 18 Petri Varis, Jokerit .30
☐ 19 Kari Takko (G), Ässät .30
☐ 20 Olli Kaski, Ässät .30
☐ 21 Rauli Raitanen, Ässät .30
☐ 22 Jari Korpisalo, Ässät .30
☐ 23 Teppo Kivela, Ässät .30
☐ 24 Jokka Heinanen, Ässät .30
☐ 25 Arto Javanainen, Ässät .30
☐ 26 Jari Levonen, Ässät .30
☐ 27 Arto Heiskanen, Ässät .30
☐ 28 Jarmo Myllys (G), Lukko .50
☐ 29 Boris Rousson (G), Lukko .50
☐ 30 Jarmo Kuusisto, Lukko .30
☐ 31 Joni Lehto, Lukko .30
☐ 32 Robert Nordmark, Lukko .30
☐ 33 Tero Arkiomaa, Lukko .30
☐ 34 Jari Torkki, Lukko .30
☐ 35 Juha Riihijarvi, Lukko .30
☐ 36 Matti Forss, Lukko .30
☐ 37 Sakari Lindfors (G), HIFK .50
☐ 38 Pertti Lehtonen, HIFK .30
☐ 39 Simo Saarinen, HIFK .30
☐ 40 Esa Tikkanen, HIFK .50
☐ 41 Ville Peltonen, HIFK .30
☐ 42 Christian Ruuttu, HIFK .50
☐ 43 Mika Kortelainen, HIFK .30
☐ 44 Darren Boyko, HIFK .30
☐ 45 Iiro Jarvi, HIFK .30
☐ 46 Ari-Pekka Siekkinen (G), JyPHT .50
☐ 47 Harri Laurila, JyPHT .30
☐ 48 Jouni Loponen, JyPHT .30
☐ 49 Joni Lius, JyPHT .30
☐ 50 Jari Lindroos, JyPHT .30
☐ 51 Risto Kurkinen, JyPHT .30
☐ 52 Thomas Sjogren, JyPHT .30
☐ 53 Marko Virtanen, JyPHT .30
☐ 54 Michael Nylander, JyPHT .50
☐ 55 Mika Rautio, Kiekko-Espoo .30
☐ 56 Sami Nuutinen, Kiekko-Espoo .30
☐ 57 Peter Ahola, Kiekko-Espoo .30
☐ 58 Timo Blomqvist, Kiekko-Espoo .30
☐ 59 Ilkka Sinisalo, Kiekko-Espoo .30
☐ 60 Petro Koivunen, Kiekko-Espoo .30
☐ 61 Sergei Pryakin, Kiekko-Espoo .30
☐ 62 Tero Lehtera, Kiekko-Espoo .30
☐ 63 Mariusz Czerkawski, Kiekko-Espoo .50
☐ 64 Pasi Kuivalainen, KalPa .50
☐ 65 Kimmo Timonen, KalPa .50
☐ 66 Reijo Ruotsalainen, KalPa 1.00
☐ 67 Vesa Salo, KalPa .30
☐ 68 Petr Korinek, KalPa .30
☐ 69 Marko Jantunen, KalPa .30
☐ 70 Pekka Tirkkonen, KalPa .30
☐ 71 Janne Kekalainen, KalPa .30
☐ 72 Sami Kapanen, KalPa 1.00
☐ 73 Timo Jutila, Tappara .50
☐ 74 Pekka Laksola, Tappara .30
☐ 75 Janne Gronvall, Tappara .30
☐ 76 Jiri Kucera, Tappara .30
☐ 77 Janne Ojanen, Tappara .30
☐ 78 Pauli Jarvinen, Tappara .30
☐ 79 Ari Haanpaa, Tappara .30
☐ 80 Aleksander Barkov, Tappara .30
☐ 81 Theoren Fleury, Tappara 2.00
☐ 82 Kari Rosenberg (G), HPK .50
☐ 83 Janne Laukkanen, HPK .30
☐ 84 Jani Nikko, HPK .30
☐ 85 Mika Lartama, HPK .30
☐ 86 Kai Nurminen, HPK .30
☐ 87 Tomas Kapusta, HPK .30
☐ 88 Marko Palo, HPK .30
☐ 89 Jarkko Varvio, HPK .30
☐ 90 Risto Jalo, HPK .30
☐ 91 Jukka Tammi (G), TuTo .50
☐ 92 Risto Siltanen, TuTo .30
☐ 93 Teppo Numminen, TuTo 1.00
☐ 94 Marco Poulsen, TuTo .30
☐ 95 Jukka Seppo, TuTo .30
☐ 96 Vesa Karjalainen, TuTo .30
☐ 97 Ted Donato, TuTo .30
☐ 98 Juha Virtanen, TuTo .30
☐ 99 Jari Hirsimaki, TuTo .30
☐ 100 Vesa Toskala (G), Ilves .30
☐ 101 Jyrki Lumme, Ilves .50
☐ 102 Hannu Henriksson, Ilves .30
☐ 103 Allan Measures, Ilves .30
☐ 104 Timo Peltomaa, Ilves .30
☐ 105 Juha Hautamaa, Ilves .30
☐ 106 Mikko Makela, Ilves .50
☐ 107 Juha Jarvenpaa, Ilves .30
☐ 108 Semi Pekki, Ilves .30

LEAF GALLERY

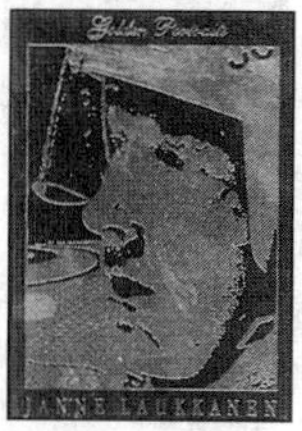

Insert Set (9 cards): 20.00
Insert (1:6) LG
☐ 1 Jyrki Lumme 4.00
☐ 2 Janne Laukkanen 3.00
☐ 3 Michael Nylander 3.00
☐ 4 Janne Ojanen 3.00
☐ 5 Peter Ahola 3.00
☐ 6 Kari Takko (G) 3.00
☐ 7 Hannu Virta 3.00
☐ 8 Juha Lind 3.00
☐ 9 Sakari Lindfors (G) 3.00

PLATINUM POWER

Insert (#/720) PP
☐ Peltonen/ Koivu/ Lehtinen 100.00

SIGNED AND SEALED

Insert Set (9 cards): 60.00
Insert (1:9) SAS
☐ 1 Sami Kapanen 6.00
☐ 2 Christian Ruuttu 4.00
☐ 3 Teemu Selänne 16.00
☐ 4 Aki Berg 4.00
☐ 5 Joni Lehto 4.00
☐ 6 Teppo Numminen 6.00
☐ 7 Jari Kurri 20.00
☐ 8 Esa Tikkanen 4.00
☐ 9 Theoren Fleury 12.00

1995 - 96 SKYBOX EMOTION

Complete Set (200 cards): 40.00
Common Player: .25
Promo Panel (Jeremy Roenick): 2.00
Player NRMT-MT
☐ 1 Bobby Dollas, Anah. [Blastin'] .25
☐ 2 Guy Hebert (G), Anah. [Floored] .25
☐ 3 Paul Kariya, Anah. [Exulted] 1.00
☐ 4 Oleg Tverdovsky, Anah. [Closin'] .25
☐ 5 Shaun Van Allen, Anah. [Crashin'] .25

☐ 6 Raymond Bourque, Bost. [Finesse] 1.00
☐ 7 Al Iafrate, Bost. [Relentless] .25
☐ 8 Blaine Lacher (G), Bost. [Magnifique; Err.-Manifique] .25
☐ 9 Joe Mullen, Bost. [Control] .25
☐ 10 Cam Neely, Bost. [Bruisin'] 1.00
☐ 11 Adam Oates, Bost. [Thrashin'] .25
☐ 12 Kevin Stevens, Bost. [Bold] .25
☐ 13 Don Sweeney, Bost. [Menacing] .25
☐ 14 Donald Audette, Buff. [Loose] .25
☐ 15 Garry Galley, Buff. [Galrin'] .25
☐ 16 Dominik Hasek (G), Buff. [Psyched] 1.00
☐ **17 Brian Holzinger, Buff. [Fluid] RC 1.00**
☐ 18 Pat LaFontaine, Buff. [Howlin'] .50
☐ 19 Alexei Zhitnik, Buff. [Pressure] .25
☐ 20 Steve Chiasson, Calg. [Chargin'] .25
☐ 21 Theoren Fleury, Calg. [Crush] .50
☐ 22 Phil Housley, Calg. [Pursuit] .25
☐ 23 Trevor Kidd (G), Calg. [Vision] .25
☐ 24 Joe Nieuwendyk, Calg. [Surge] .25
☐ 25 Gary Roberts, Calg. [Scorchin'] .25
☐ 26 Zarley Zalapski, Calg. [Brutal] .25
☐ 27 Ed Belfour (G), Chic. [Tough] 1.00
☐ 28 Chris Chelios, Chic. [Swift] .50
☐ 29 Sergei Krivokrasov, Chic. [Adrenalized] .25
☐ 30 Joe Murphy, Chic. [Loose] .25
☐ 31 Bernie Nicholls, Chic. [Drivin'] .25
☐ 32 Patrick Poulin, Chic. [Winded] .25
☐ 33 Jeremy Roenick, Chic. [Raw] .50
☐ 34 Gary Suter, Chic. [Explosive] .25
☐ 35 René Corbet, Colo. [Burnin'] .25
☐ 36 Peter Forsberg, Colo. [Explosive] 1.00
☐ 37 Valeri Kamensky, Colo. [Loose] .25
☐ 38 Uwe Krupp, Colo. [Tenacity] .25
☐ 39 Curtis Leschyshyn, Colo. [Fury] .25
☐ 40 Owen Nolan, Colo. [Guts] .50
☐ 41 Mike Ricci, Colo. [Adrenaline] .25
☐ 42 Joe Sakic, Colo. [Control] 1.50
☐ 43 Jocelyn Thibault (G), Colo. [Icy] .25
☐ 44 Bob Bassen, Dall. [Swift] .25
☐ 45 Dave Gagner, Dall. [Crazed] .25
☐ 46 Todd Harvey, Dall. [Bumpin'] .25
☐ 47 Derian Hatcher, Dall. [Solid] .25
☐ 48 Kevin Hatcher, Dall. [Searchin'] .25
☐ 49 Mike Modano, Dall. [Shinin'] 1.00
☐ 50 Andy Moog (G), Dall. [Roarin'] .25
☐ 51 Dino Ciccarelli, Detr. [Wheelin'] .25
☐ 52 Paul Coffey, Detr. [Squids!] .50
☐ 53 Sergei Fedorov, Detr. [Deadly] 1.00
☐ 54 Vladimir Konstantinov, Detr. [Fearless] .25
☐ 55 Vyacheslav Kozlov, Detr. [Sleek] .25
☐ 56 Nicklas Lidström, Detr. [Stormin'] .50
☐ 57 Keith Primeau, Detr. [Primo] .25
☐ 58 Ray Sheppard, Detr. [Hustlin'] .25
☐ 59 Mike Vernon (G), Detr. [Steady] .25
☐ 60 Steve Yzerman, Detr. [Contact] 2.00
☐ 61 Jason Arnott, Edmo. [Mayhem] .25
☐ 62 Curtis Joseph (G), SLou. (Edmo.) [Rabid] 1.00
☐ 63 Igor Kravchuk, Edmo. [Crucial] .25
☐ 64 Todd Marchant, Edmo. [Focused] .25
☐ 65 David Oliver, Edmo. [Instinct] .25
☐ 66 Bill Ranford (G), Edmo. [Denied] .25
☐ 67 Doug Weight, Edmo. [Slick] .50
☐ 68 Stu Barnes, Flor. [Glory] .25
☐ 69 Jesse Bélanger, Flor. [Clawin'] .25
☐ 70 Gord Murphy, Flor. [Slapshot] .25
☐ **71 Magnus Svensson, Flor. [Grit] RC .50**
☐ 72 John Vanbiesbrouck (G), Flor. [Snatched] .25
☐ 73 Sean Burke (G), Hart. [Snag] .50
☐ 74 Andrew Cassels, Hart. [Cool] .25
☐ 75 Frantisek Kucera, Hart. [Stern] .25
☐ 76 Andrei Nikolishin, Hart. [Hungry] .25
☐ 77 Geoff Sanderson, Hart. [Burnin'] .25
☐ 78 Brendan Shanahan, Hart. [Menace] 1.00
☐ 79 Darren Turcotte, Hart. [Strength] .25
☐ 80 Rob Blake, LosA. [Smooth] .50
☐ 81 Wayne Gretzky, LosA. [King] 4.00
☐ 82 Dmitri Khristich, LosA. [Intense] .25
☐ 83 Jari Kurri, LosA. [Tenacious] 1.00
☐ 84 Jamie Storr (G), LosA. [Vision] .25
☐ 85 Darryl Sydor, LosA. [Passion] .25
☐ 86 Rick Tocchet, LosA. [Bold] .25
☐ 87 Vincent Damphousse, Mont. [Havoc] .50
☐ 88 Vladimir Malakhov, Mont. [Berserk] .25
☐ 89 Stéphane Quintal, Mont. [Instinct] .25
☐ 90 Mark Recchi, Mont. [Power] .25
☐ 91 Patrick Roy (G), Mont. [Alert] 3.00
☐ 92 Brian Savage, Mont. [Destroyer] .25
☐ 93 Pierre Turgeon, Mont. [Instinct] .25
☐ 94 Martin Brodeur (G), NJer. [Awesome] 1.50
☐ 95 Neal Broten, NJer. [Fiery] .25
☐ 96 Shawn Chambers, NJer. [Burnin'] .25
☐ 97 Claude Lemieux, NJer. [Wicked] .25
☐ 98 John MacLean, NJer. [Control] .25
☐ 99 Randy McKay, NJer. [Possessed] .25
☐ 100 Scott Niedermayer, NJer. [Venom] .25
☐ 101 Stéphane Richer, NJer. [Stomp] .25
☐ 102 Scott Stevens, NJer. [Slam] .25
☐ **103 Todd Bertuzzi, NYIs. [Victory] RC 9.00**
☐ 104 Patrick Flatley, NYIs. [Wild] .25
☐ 105 Brett Lindros, NYIs. [Kickin'] .25
☐ 106 Kirk Muller, NYIs. [Tense] .25
☐ **107 Tommy Salo (G), NYIs. [Shield] RC 3.00**
☐ 108 Mathieu Schneider, NYIs. [Slap] .25
☐ 109 Alexander Semak, NYIs. [Glory] .25
☐ 110 Dennis Vaske, NYIs. [Pressure] .25
☐ 111 Ray Ferraro, NYRa. [Driven] .25
☐ 112 Adam Graves, NYRa. [Iced] .25
☐ 113 Alexei Kovalev, NYRa. [Steady] .50
☐ 114 Steve Larmer, NYRa. [Rough] .25
☐ 115 Brian Leetch, NYRa. [Poundin'] .50
☐ 116 Mark Messier, NYRa. [Victory] 1.00
☐ 117 Mike Richter (G), NYRa. [Clutch] .25
☐ 118 Luc Robitaille, NYRa. [Passion] .50
☐ 119 Ulf Samuelsson, NYRa. [Cagey] .25
☐ 120 Pat Verbeek, NYRa. [Pure] .25
☐ 121 Don Beaupré (G), Otta. [Force] .25
☐ 122 Radek Bonk, Otta. [Prime] .25
☐ 123 Alexandre Daigle, Otta. [Agile] .25
☐ 124 Steve Duchesne, Otta. [Hunger] .25
☐ **125 Steve Larouche, Otta. [Anguish] RC .50**
☐ 126 Dan Quinn, Otta. [Gliding] .25
☐ 127 Martin Straka, Otta. [Heart] .25
☐ 128 Alexei Yashin, Otta. [Style] .50
☐ 129 Rod Brind'Amour, Phil. [Soarin'] .25
☐ 130 Éric Desjardins, Phil. [Coup!] .25
☐ 131 Ron Hextall (G), Phil. [Hexed] .50
☐ 132 John LeClair, Phil. [Maitre] .50
☐ 133 Eric Lindros, Phil. [Pressure] 1.00
☐ 134 Mikael Renberg, Phil. [Courage] .25
☐ 135 Chris Therien, Phil. [Spirited] .25
☐ 136 Ron Francis, Pitt. [Psyched] .50
☐ 137 Jaromir Jagr, Pitt. [Lethal] 1.00
☐ 138 Mario Lemieux, Pitt. [Returnin'] 3.00
☐ 139 Dmitri Mironov, Pitt. [Absorbed] .25
☐ 140 Petr Nedved, Pitt. [Fierce] .25
☐ 141 Tomas Sandström, Pitt. [Tangled] .25
☐ 142 Bryan Smolinski, Pitt. [Clutch] .25
☐ 143 Ken Wregget (G), Pitt. [Primed] .25
☐ 144 Sergei Zubov, Pitt. [Agile] .25
☐ 145 Shayne Corson, SLou. [Relentless] .25
☐ 146 Geoff Courtnall, SLou. [Chillin'] .25
☐ 147 Dale Hawerchuk, SLou. [Rage] .50
☐ 148 Brett Hull, SLou. [Haulin'] 1.00
☐ 149 Ian Laperrière, SLou. [Jazzin'] .25
☐ 150 Al MacInnis, SLou. [Jammin'] .25
☐ 151 Chris Pronger, SLou. [Viscious] .50
☐ 152 David Roberts, SLou. [Savvy] .25
☐ 153 Esa Tikkanen, SLou. [Solo] .25
☐ 154 Ulf Dahlén, SanJ. [Poised] .25
☐ 155 Jeff Friesen, SanJ. [Lunge] .25
☐ 156 Arturs Irbe (G), SanJ. [Thrashin'] .25
☐ 157 Craig Janney, SanJ. [Absorbed] .25
☐ 158 Sergei Makarov, SanJ. [Lurking] .25
☐ 159 Sandis Ozolinsh, SanJ. [Hungry] .25
☐ 160 Mike Rathje, SanJ. [Frenzy] .25
☐ 161 Ray Whitney, SanJ. [Jaws] .25
☐ 162 Brian Bradley, Tamp. [Cruisin'] .25
☐ 163 Chris Gratton, Tamp. [Electric] .25
☐ 164 Roman Hamrlik, Tamp. [Steady] .25
☐ 165 Petr Klima, Tamp. [Fluid] .25
☐ 166 Daren Puppa (G), Tamp. [Wall] .25
☐ 167 Paul Ysebaert, Tamp. [Stormin'] .25
☐ 168 Dave Andreychuk, Toro. [Force] .25
☐ 169 Mike Gartner, Toro. [Pushin'] .50
☐ 170 Todd Gill, Toro. [Crack!] .25
☐ 171 Doug Gilmour, Toro. [Iced!] .50
☐ 172 Kenny Jönsson, Toro. [Iced!] .25
☐ 173 Larry Murphy, Toro. [Bruising] .25
☐ 174 Félix Potvin (G), Toro. [Nyet] .50
☐ 175 Mats Sundin, Toro. [Bruising] 1.00
☐ 176 Josef Beranek, Vanc. [Impact] .25
☐ 177 Jeff R. Brown, Vanc. [Primal, Err. (Photo on back Beranek)] .25
☐ 178 Pavel Bure, Vanc. [Travail] .50
☐ 179 Russ Courtnall, Vanc. [Aware] .25
☐ 180 Trevor Linden, Vanc. [Airborne] .25
☐ 181 Kirk McLean (G), Vanc. [Capture] .25
☐ 182 Alexander Mogilny, Vanc. [Primed] .25
☐ 183 Roman Oksiuta, Vanc. [Deadly] .25
☐ 184 Mike Ridley, Vanc. [Electric] .25
☐ 185 Jason Allison, Wash. [Breathin'] .50
☐ 186 Jim Carey (G), Wash. [Smokin'] .25
☐ 187 Sergei Gonchar, Wash. [Dynamo] .25
☐ 188 Dale Hunter, Wash. [Motorin'] .25
☐ 189 Calle Johansson, Wash. [Menace] .25
☐ 190 Joé Juneau, Wash. [Fury] .25
☐ 191 Joe Reekie, Wash. [Power] .25
☐ 192 Nelson Emerson, Winn. [Checked] .25
☐ 193 Nikolai Khabibulin (G), Winn. [Ready] .25
☐ 194 Dave Manson, Winn. [Soaring] .25
☐ 195 Teppo Numminen, Winn. [Lightning] .25
☐ 196 Teemu Selänne, Winn. [Marauder] .50
☐ 197 Keith Tkachuk, Winn. [Thrashin'] .50
☐ 198 Alexei Zhamnov, Winn. [Dangerous] .25
☐ 199 Checklist .25
☐ 200 Checklist .25

GENERATIONEXT

Insert Set (10 cards): 45.00
Insert (1:10) gN
☐ 1 Brian Holzinger, Buff. 2.00
☐ 2 Éric Dazé, Chic. 6.00
☐ 3 Jason Bonsignore, Edmo. 2.00
☐ 4 Jamie Storr (G), LosA. 2.00
☐ 5 Tommy Salo (G), NYIs. 6.00
☐ 6 Brendan Witt, Wash. 2.00
☐ 7 Saku Koivu, Mont. 12.00
☐ 8 Todd Bertuzzi, NYIs. 18.00
☐ 9 Ed Jovanovski, Flor. 6.00
☐ 10 Chad Kilger, Anah. 2.00

NTENSE POWER

Inset Set (10 cards): 60.00
Insert (1:30) NP
☐ 1 Cam Neely, Bost. 12.00
☐ 2 Keith Primeau, Detr. 4.00
☐ 3 Mark Messier, NYRa. 12.00
☐ 4 Eric Lindros, Phil. 12.00
☐ 5 Mikael Renberg, Phil. 4.00
☐ 6 Owen Nolan, Colo. 6.00
☐ 7 Brendan Shanahan, Hart. 12.00
☐ 8 Kevin Stevens, Bost. 3.00
☐ 9 Keith Tkachuk, Winn. 6.00
☐ 10 Rick Tocchet, LosA. 4.00

SKYMOTION

Insert SM
☐ Jeremy Roenick, Chic. 18.00

XCITED

Inset Set (20 cards): 35.00
Insert (1:3) XC
☐ 1 Theoren Fleury, Calg. 1.00
☐ 2 Jeremy Roenick, Chic. 2.00
☐ 3 Mike Modano, Dall. 2.00
☐ 4 Sergei Fedorov, Detr. 2.00
☐ 5 Wayne Gretzky, LosA. 10.00
☐ 6 Brian Leetch, NYRa. 1.00
☐ 7 Alexei Yashin, Otta. 1.00
☐ 8 Brett Hull, SLou. 2.00

☐	9 Jaromir Jagr, Pitt.	2.00
☐	10 Mario Lemieux, Pitt.	6.00
☐	11 Ron Francis, Pitt. [vs. R.Bourque]	1.00
☐	12 Keith Primeau, Detr.	1.00
☐	13 Joe Sakic, Colo.	4.00
☐	14 Peter Forsberg, Colo.	2.00
☐	15 Paul Kariya, Anah.	2.00
☐	16 Pavel Bure, Vanc.	2.00
☐	17 Alexei Zhamnov, Winn.	.50
☐	18 Martin Brodeur (G), NJer.	4.00
☐	19 Jim Carey (G), Wash.	.50
☐	20 Chris Chelios, Chic.	1.00

XCEL

Insert Set (10 cards):		160.00
	Insert (1:72)	XL
☐	1 Adam Oates, Bost.	6.00
☐	2 Jeremy Roenick, Chic.	12.00
☐	3 Sergei Fedorov, Detr.	14.00
☐	4 Wayne Gretzky, LosA.	60.00
☐	5 Alexei Yashin, Otta.	8.00
☐	6 Eric Lindros, Phil.	14.00
☐	7 Ron Francis, Pitt.	8.00
☐	8 Mario Lemieux, Pitt.	40.00
☐	9 Joe Sakic, Colo.	24.00
☐	10 Alexei Zhamnov, Winn.	6.00

1995 - 96 SKYBOX IMPACT

Complete Set (250 cards):		20.00
Common Player:		.20
Panel (Fleury/ Lacher (G)/ Lacher (G)/ Roenick):		3.00
	Player	NRMT-MT
☐	1 Bobby Dollas, Anah.	.20
☐	2 Guy Hebert (G), Anah.	.20
☐	3 Paul Kariya, Anah.	.50
☐	4 Todd Krygier, Anah.	.20
☐	5 Oleg Tverdovsky, Anah.	.20
☐	6 Shaun Van Allen, Anah. [vs. D.Quinn]	.20
☐	7 Raymond Bourque, Bost.	.50
☐	8 Al Iafrate, Bost.	.20
☐	9 Blaine Lacher (G), Bost.	.20
☐	10 Joe Mullen, Bost.	.20
☐	11 Cam Neely, Bost.	.50
☐	12 Adam Oates, Bost.	.20
☐	13 Kevin Stevens, Bost. [vs. P.Brisebois]	.20
☐	14 Donald Audette, Buff.	.20
☐	15 Garry Galley, Buff.	.20
☐	16 Dominik Hasek (G), Buff.	.50
☐	17 Pat LaFontaine, Buff.	.20
☐	18 Derek Plante, Buff.	.20
☐	19 Alexei Zhitnik, Buff.	.20
☐	20 Steve Chiasson, Calg.	.20
☐	21 Theoren Fleury, Calg.	.20
☐	22 Phil Housley, Calg.	.20
☐	23 Trevor Kidd (G), Calg.	.20
☐	24 Joe Nieuwendyk, Calg.	.20
☐	25 German Titov, Calg.	.20
☐	26 Zarley Zalapski, Calg.	.20
☐	27 Ed Belfour (G), Chic.	.50
☐	28 Chris Chelios, Chic.	.20
☐	29 Sergei Krivokrasov, Chic.	.20
☐	30 Joe Murphy, Chic.	.20
☐	31 Bernie Nicholls, Chic.	.20
☐	32 Patrick Poulin, Chic.	.20
☐	33 Jeremy Roenick, Chic.	.20
☐	34 Gary Suter, Chic. [vs. K.King]	.20
☐	35 Peter Forsberg, Colo.	.50
☐	36 Valeri Kamensky, Colo.	.20
☐	37 Claude Lemieux, Colo.	.20
☐	38 Curtis Leschyshyn, Colo. [vs. P.Kariya]	.20
☐	39 Sandis Ozolinsh, Colo.	.20
☐	40 Mike Ricci, Colo.	.20
☐	41 Joe Sakic, Colo.	.50
☐	42 Jocelyn Thibault (G), Colo.	.20
☐	43 Bob Bassen, Dall.	.20
☐	44 Dave Gagner, Dall. [vs. I.Kravchuk]	.20
☐	45 Todd Harvey, Dall.	.20
☐	46 Derian Hatcher, Dall.	.20
☐	47 Kevin Hatcher, Dall.	.20
☐	48 Mike Modano, Dall.	.50
☐	49 Andy Moog (G), Dall.	.20
☐	50 Dino Ciccarelli, Detr.	.20
☐	51 Paul Coffey, Detr.	.20
☐	52 Sergei Fedorov, Detr. [vs. J.Roenick]	.50
☐	53 Vladimir Konstantinov, Detr.	.20
☐	54 Vyacheslav Kozlov, Detr.	.20
☐	55 Nicklas Lidström, Detr.	.20
☐	56 Chris Osgood (G), Detr.	.20
☐	57 Keith Primeau, Detr.	.20
☐	58 Steve Yzerman, Detr.	1.00
☐	59 Jason Arnott, Edmo.	.20
☐	60 Curtis Joseph (G), SLou. (Edmo.)	.50
☐	61 Igor Kravchuk, Edmo.	.20
☐	62 Todd Marchant, Edmo.	.20
☐	63 David Oliver, Edmo.	.20
☐	64 Bill Ranford (G), Edmo.	.20
☐	65 Doug Weight, Edmo.	.20
☐	66 Stu Barnes, Flor.	.20
☐	67 Jesse Bélanger, Flor.	.20
☐	68 Gord Murphy, Flor.	.20
☐	**69 Magnus Svensson, Flor. RC**	**.50**
☐	70 John Vanbiesbrouck (G), Flor.	.20
☐	71 Sean Burke (G), Hart.	.20
☐	72 Andrew Cassels, Hart. [vs. S.Nemchinov]	.20
☐	73 Nelson Emerson, Hart.	.20
☐	74 Andrei Nikolishin, Hart.	.20
☐	75 Geoff Sanderson, Hart.	.20
☐	76 Brendan Shanahan, Hart. [vs. R.Bourque]	.50
☐	77 Glen Wesley, Hart.	.20
☐	78 Rob Blake, LosA.	.20
☐	79 Wayne Gretzky, LosA. [vs. P.Brisebois]	2.00
☐	80 Dmitri Khristich, LosA.	.20
☐	81 Jari Kurri, LosA. [vs. M.Keane]	.50
☐	82 Darryl Sydor, LosA.	.20
☐	83 Rick Tocchet, LosA.	.20
☐	84 Vincent Damphousse, Mont.	.20
☐	85 Vladimir Malakhov, Mont.	.20
☐	86 Mark Recchi, Mont.	.20
☐	87 Patrick Roy (G), Mont.	1.50
☐	88 Brian Savage, Mont.	.20
☐	89 Pierre Turgeon, Mont.	.20
☐	90 Martin Brodeur (G), NJer.	.50
☐	91 Neal Broten, NJer. [vs. S.Koivu]	.20
☐	92 Shawn Chambers, NJer.	.20
☐	93 John MacLean, NJer.	.20
☐	94 Randy McKay, NJer.	.20
☐	95 Scott Niedermayer, NJer.	.20
☐	96 Stéphane Richer, NJer.	.20
☐	97 Scott Stevens, NJer.	.20
☐	98 Steve Thomas, NJer.	.20
☐	99 Wendel Clark, NYIs.	.20
☐	100 Patrick Flatley, NYIs. [vs. G.Healy (G)]	.20
☐	101 Scott Lachance, NYIs.	.20
☐	102 Brett Lindros, NYIs.	.20
☐	103 Kirk Muller, NYIs. [vs. R.Ferraro]	.20
☐	**104 Tommy Salo (G), NYIs. RC**	**2.00**
☐	105 Mathieu Schneider, NYIs.	.20
☐	106 Dennis Vaske, NYIs.	.20
☐	107 Ray Ferraro, NYRa.	.20
☐	108 Adam Graves, NYRa.	.20
☐	109 Alexei Kovalev, NYRa.	.20
☐	110 Brian Leetch, NYRa.	.20
☐	111 Mark Messier, NYRa.	.50
☐	112 Mike Richter (G), NYRa.	.20
☐	113 Luc Robitaille, NYRa.	.20
☐	114 Ulf Samuelsson, NYRa.	.20
☐	115 Pat Verbeek, NYRa.	.20
☐	116 Don Beaupré (G), Otta.	.20
☐	117 Radek Bonk, Otta.	.20
☐	118 Alexandre Daigle, Otta.	.20
☐	119 Steve Duchesne, Otta.	.20
☐	120 Dan Quinn, Otta.	.20
☐	121 Martin Straka, Otta.	.20
☐	122 Alexei Yashin, Otta.	.20
☐	123 Rod Brind'Amour, Phil.	.20
☐	124 Éric Desjardins, Phil.	.20
☐	125 Ron Hextall (G), Phil.	.20
☐	126 John LeClair, Phil.	.20
☐	127 Eric Lindros, Phil.	.50
☐	128 Mikael Renberg, Phil.	.20
☐	129 Chris Therien, Phil.	.20
☐	130 Ron Francis, Pitt.	.20
☐	131 Jaromir Jagr, Pitt.	.50
☐	132 Mario Lemieux, Pitt.	1.50
☐	133 Petr Nedved, Pitt.	.20
☐	134 Tomas Sandström, Pitt. [xS.Stevens]	.20
☐	135 Bryan Smolinski, Pitt.	.20
☐	136 Ken Wregget (G), Pitt.	.20
☐	137 Sergei Zubov, Pitt.	.20
☐	138 Shayne Corson, SLou.	.20
☐	139 Geoff Courtnall, SLou.	.20
☐	140 Dale Hawerchuk, SLou.	.20
☐	141 Brett Hull, SLou.	.50
☐	142 Ian Laperrière, SLou.	.20
☐	143 Al MacInnis, SLou.	.20
☐	144 Chris Pronger, SLou.	.20
☐	145 Esa Tikkanen, SLou.	.20
☐	146 Ulf Dahlén, SanJ.	.20
☐	147 Jeff Friesen, SanJ.	.20
☐	148 Arturs Irbe (G), SanJ.	.20
☐	149 Craig Janney, SanJ.	.20
☐	150 Owen Nolan, SanJ.	.20
☐	151 Mike Rathje, SanJ.	.20
☐	152 Ray Sheppard, SanJ.	.20
☐	153 Brian Bradley, Tamp.	.20
☐	154 Chris Gratton, Tamp.	.20
☐	155 Roman Hamrlik, Tamp.	.20
☐	156 Petr Klima, Tamp.	.20
☐	157 Daren Puppa (G), Tamp.	.20
☐	158 Dave Andreychuk, Toro.	.20
☐	159 Mike Gartner, Toro.	.20
☐	160 Todd Gill, Toro.	.20
☐	161 Doug Gilmour, Toro.	.20
☐	162 Kenny Jönsson, Toro.	.20
☐	163 Larry Murphy, Toro. [cameo: F.Potvin]	.20
☐	164 Félix Potvin (G), Toro.	.20
☐	165 Mats Sundin, Toro.	.50
☐	166 Jeff R. Brown, Vanc. [vs. J.Kurri]	.20
☐	167 Pavel Bure, Vanc.	.20
☐	168 Russ Courtnall, Vanc.	.20
☐	169 Trevor Linden, Vanc.	.20
☐	170 Kirk McLean (G), Vanc.	.20
☐	171 Alexander Mogilny, Vanc.	.20
☐	172 Roman Oksiuta, Vanc.	.20
☐	173 Mike Ridley, Vanc.	.20
☐	174 Peter Bondra, Wash.	.20
☐	175 Jim Carey (G), Wash.	.20
☐	176 Sergei Gonchar, Wash.	.20
☐	177 Dale Hunter, Wash.	.20
☐	178 Calle Johansson, Wash.	.20
☐	179 Joé Juneau, Wash.	.20
☐	180 Michal Pivonka, Wash.	.20
☐	181 Nikolai Khabibulin (G), Winn.	.20
☐	182 Dave Manson, Winn.	.20
☐	183 Teppo Numminen, Winn.	.20
☐	184 Teemu Selänne, Winn.	.20
☐	185 Keith Tkachuk, Winn.	.20
☐	186 Darren Turcotte, Winn.	.20
☐	187 Alexei Zhamnov, Winn.	.20
☐	**188 Chad Kilger, Anah. RC**	**1.00**
☐	**189 Kyle McLaren, Bost. RC**	**1.00**
☐	**190 Brian Holzinger, Buff. RC**	**.50**
☐	191 Wayne Primeau, Buff.	.50
☐	192 Marty Murray, Calg.	.20
☐	193 Éric Dazé, Chic.	.20
☐	**194 Jon Klemm, Colo. RC**	**.50**
☐	195 Jere Lehtinen, Dall.	.20
☐	196 Jason Bonsignore, Edmo.	.20
☐	**197 Miroslav Satan, Edmo. RC**	**1.50**
☐	198 Ryan Smyth, Edmo.	.20
☐	199 Tyler Wright, Edmo.	.20
☐	200 Radek Dvorak, Flor.	.20
☐	201 Ed Jovanovski, Flor.	.20
☐	202 Jeff O'Neill, Hart.	.20
☐	**203 Aki Berg, LosA. RC**	**.50**
☐	204 Jamie Storr (G), LosA.	.20
☐	205 Vitali Yachmenev, LosA.	.20
☐	206 Saku Koivu, Mont.	.50
☐	207 Denis Pederson, NJer.	.20
☐	**208 Todd Bertuzzi, NYIs. RC**	**6.00**
☐	209 Bryan McCabe, NYIs.	.20
☐	210 Dan Plante, NYIs.	.20
☐	211 Peter Ferraro, NYRa.	.20
☐	**212 Darren Langdon, NYRa. RC**	**1.00**
☐	213 Niklas Sundström, NYRa.	.20
☐	**214 Daniel Alfredsson, Otta. RC**	**3.00**
☐	215 Garth Snow (G), Phil.	.20
☐	216 Ian Moran, Pitt.	.20
☐	217 Richard Park, Pitt.	.20
☐	218 Jamie Rivers, SLou.	.20
☐	**219 Roman Vopat, SLou. RC**	**.50**
☐	**220 Marcus Ragnarsson, SanJ. RC**	**1.00**
☐	221 Aaron Gavey, Tamp.	.20
☐	222 Daymond Langkow, Tamp.	.50
☐	223 Darby Hendrickson, Toro.	.20
☐	224 Martin Gendron, Wash.	.20
☐	225 Brendan Witt, Wash.	.20
☐	**226 Shane Doan, Winn. RC**	**1.00**
☐	227 Deron Quint, Winn.	.20
☐	228 Jim Carey (G), Wash. [Hockey's Hip]	.20
☐	229 Peter Forsberg, Colo. [Hockey's Hip]	.50
☐	230 Paul Kariya, Anah. [Hockey's Hip]	.50
☐	231 David Oliver, Edmo. [Hockey's Hip]	.20
☐	232 Blaine Lacher (G), Bost. [Hockey's Hip]	.20
☐	233 Todd Harvey, Dall. [Hockey's Hip]	.20
☐	234 Todd Marchant, Edmo. [Hockey's Hip]	.20
☐	235 Jeff Friesen, SanJ. [Hockey's Hip]	.20
☐	236 Oleg Tverdovsky, Anah. [Hockey's Hip]	.20
☐	237 Jason Arnott, Edmo. [Hockey's Hip]	.20
☐	238 Cam Neely, Bost. [Powerplay]	.50
☐	239 Keith Tkachuk, Winn. [Powerplay]	.20
☐	240 Owen Nolan, Colo. [Powerplay]	.20
☐	241 Keith Primeau, Detr. [Powerplay]	.20
☐	242 Peter Bondra, Wash. [Powerplay]	.20
☐	243 Jeremy Roenick, Chic. [Powerplay]	.20
☐	244 John LeClair, Phil. [Powerplay]	.20
☐	245 Mikael Renberg, Phil. [Powerplay]	.20
☐	246 Dave Andreychuk, Toro. [Powerplay]	.20
☐	247 Rick Tocchet, Bost. [Powerplay]	.20
☐	248 Checklist	.20
☐	249 Checklist	.20
☐	250 Checklist	.20

COUNTDOWN TO IMPACT

Insert Set (9 cards):		65.00
	Insert (1:60)	CTI
☐	1 Eric Lindros, Phil.	6.00
☐	2 Jaromir Jagr, Pitt.	6.00
☐	3 Mario Lemieux, Pitt.	18.00
☐	4 Wayne Gretzky, LosA.	24.00
☐	5 Mark Messier, NYRa.	6.00
☐	6 Sergei Fedorov, Detr.	6.00
☐	7 Paul Kariya, Anah.	8.00
☐	8 Doug Gilmour, Toro.	4.00
☐	9 Pavel Bure, Vanc.	4.00

DEFLECTORS

Insert Set (12 cards):		10.00
	Insert (1:10)	D
☐	1 Dominik Hasek (G), Buff.	2.00
☐	2 Jim Carey (G), Wash.	.50
☐	3 Félix Potvin (G), Toro.	1.00
☐	4 Sean Burke (G), Hart.	1.00
☐	5 Blaine Lacher (G), Bost.	.50
☐	6 John Vanbiesbrouck (G), Flor.	.50
☐	7 Jocelyn Thibault (G), Colo.	.50
☐	8 Patrick Roy (G), Mont.	5.00
☐	9 Ed Belfour (G), Chic.	2.00
☐	10 Trevor Kidd (G), Calg.	.50
☐	11 Martin Brodeur (G), NJer.	3.00
☐	12 Kirk McLean (G), Vanc.	.50

FOX, IT'S A BEAUTIFUL THING

Insert Set (18 cards):		5.00
	Insert (1:3)	Fox
☐	1 Mariusz Czerkawski, Bost.	.30
☐	2 Roman Oksiuta, Vanc.	.30
☐	3 David Oliver, Edmo.	.30
☐	4 Adam Deadmarsh, Colo.	.50
☐	5 Denis Chassé, SLou.	.30
☐	6 Sergei Krivokrasov, Chic.	.30
☐	7 Ian Laperrière, SLou.	.30
☐	8 Chris Therien, Phil.	.30
☐	9 Brian Savage, Mont.	.50
☐	10 Todd Marchant, Edmo.	.30
☐	11 Jeff O'Neill, Hart.	.50
☐	12 Brett Lindros, NYIs.	.50
☐	13 Kenny Jönsson, Toro.	.30
☐	14 Manny Fernandez (G), Dall.	.50
☐	15 Brian Holzinger, Buff.	.30
☐	16 Niklas Sundström, NYRa.	.30
☐	17 Éric Dazé, Chic.	.50
☐	18 Chad Kilger, Anah.	.30

ICEQUAKE

Insert Set (15 cards):		65.00
	Insert (1:20)	IQ
☐	1 Jaromir Jagr, Pitt.	4.00
☐	2 Brett Hull, SLou.	4.00
☐	3 Pavel Bure, Vanc.	4.00
☐	4 Eric Lindros, Phil.	4.00
☐	5 Mark Messier, NYRa.	4.00
☐	6 Wayne Gretzky, LosA.	20.00
☐	7 Mario Lemieux, Pitt.	14.00
☐	8 Peter Forsberg, Colo.	6.00
☐	9 Sergei Fedorov, Detr.	4.00
☐	10 Cam Neely, Bost.	4.00
☐	11 Owen Nolan, SanJ.	2.00
☐	12 Alexei Zhamnov, Winn.	2.00
☐	13 Theoren Fleury, Calg.	2.00
☐	14 Luc Robitaille, NYRa.	4.00
☐	15 Teemu Selänne, Winn.	4.00

SKYMOTION

	Blaine Lacher Inserts	NRMT-MT
☐	SkyMotion	3.00
☐	SkyMotion Offer Card	.10
☐	Slapshot Instant Win Game	.10

1995 - 96 SKYMINT

This card was available with the redemption of a trade card found in Fleer Metal packs.

	Player	NRMT-MT
☐	Joe Sakic, Colo.	25.00

1995 - 96 SLAPSHOT

Promotional samples were issued at the Toronto Sport Card & Memorabilia Fall Expo.

Complete Set (440 cards):		85.00
Common Player:		.20
	Player	NRMT-MT
☐	1 Title Card/ Checklist	.20
☐	2 Checklist Eastern	.20
☐	3 Checklist Central	.20
☐	4 Checklist Western	.20
☐	5 David Branch	.20
☐	6 Bert Templeton, Coach, Barrie	.20
☐	7 Chris George, Barrie	.20
☐	8 Chris Thompson (G), Barrie	.20
☐	9 Quade Lightbody, Barrie	.20

☐ 10 Shane Delaronde (G), Barrie .20
☐ 11 Justin Robinson, Barrie .20
☐ 12 Shawn Frappier, Barrie .20
☐ 13 Lucio Nasato, Barrie .20
☐ 14 Jason Payne, Barrie .20
☐ 15 Jason Cannon, Barrie .20
☐ 16 Alexandre Volchkov, Barrie .20
☐ 17 Daniel Tkaczuk, Barrie 1.50
☐ 18 Gerry Lanigan, Barrie .20
☐ 19 Darrell Woodley, Barrie .20
☐ 20 Brian Barker, Barrie .20
☐ 21 Mauricio Alvarez, Barrie .20
☐ 22 Brock Boucher, Barrie .20
☐ 23 Jeff Cowan, Barrie .50
☐ 24 Jan Bulis, Barrie .50
☐ 25 Jeff Tetzlaff, Barrie .20
☐ 26 Caleb Ward, Barrie .20
☐ 27 Mike White, Barrie .20
☐ 28 Jeremy Miculinic, Barrie .20
☐ 29 Andrew Morrison, Barrie .20
☐ 30 Robert Dubois, Barrie .20
☐ 31 Kory Cooper (G), Belleville .20
☐ 32 Jason Gaggi (G), Belleville .20
☐ 33 Mike Van Volsen, Belleville .20
☐ 34 Paul McInnes, Belleville .20
☐ 35 Harkie Singh, Belleville .20
☐ 36 Robin Lacour, Belleville .20
☐ 37 Jamie Sokolsky, Belleville .20
☐ 38 Marc Dupuis, Belleville .20
☐ 39 Daniel Cleary, Belleville 2.50
☐ 40 David Peca, Belleville .20
☐ 41 Adam Robbins, Belleville .20
☐ 42 Steve Tracze, Belleville .20
☐ 43 James Boyd, Belleville .20
☐ 44 Jake Irsag, Belleville .20
☐ 45 Ryan Ready, Belleville .20
☐ 46 Walker McDonald, Belleville .20
☐ 47 Rob Guinn, Belleville .20
☐ 48 Rob Fitzgerald, Belleville .20
☐ 49 Joe Coombs, Belleville .20
☐ 50 Daniel Reja, Belleville .20
☐ 51 Joe Van Volsen, Belleville .20
☐ 52 Craig Mills, Belleville .50
☐ 53 Murray Hogg, Belleville .20
☐ 54 Andrei Shurupov, Belleville .20
☐ 55 Andrew Williamson, Belleville .20
☐ 56 Mike Minard (G), Detroit .50
☐ 57 Robert Esche (G), Detroit 1.50
☐ 58 Lee Jinman, Detroit .20
☐ 59 Corey Neilson, Detroit .20
☐ 60 Troy Smith, Detroit .20
☐ 61 Mike Rucinski, Detroit .50
☐ 62 Colin Beardsmore, Detroit .20
☐ 63 Dan Pawlaczyk, Detroit .20
☐ 64 Scott Blair, Detroit .20
☐ 65 Mike Morrone, Detroit .20
☐ 66 Matt Ball, Detroit .20
☐ 67 Steve Dumonski, Detroit .20
☐ 68 Mike Sheehan, Detroit .20
☐ 69 Sean Haggerty, Detroit .50
☐ 70 Andrew Taylor, Detroit .20
☐ 71 Steve Wasylko, Detroit .50
☐ 72 Jan Vodrazka, Detroit .20
☐ 73 Dan Preston, Detroit .20
☐ 74 Jesse Boulerice, Detroit .50
☐ 75 Bryan Berard, Detroit 2.50
☐ 76 Nic Beaudoin, Detroit .20
☐ 77 Tom Buckley, Detroit .20
☐ 78 Mark Cadotte, Detroit .20
☐ 79 Greg Stephan, Coach, Detroit .20
☐ 80 Peter DeBoar, Coach, Detroit .20
☐ 81 Regan Stocco, Guelph .20
☐ 82 Andy Adams (G), Guelph .20
☐ 83 Brett Thompson (G), Guelph .20
☐ 84 Darryl McArthur, Guelph .20
☐ 85 Ryan Risidore, Guelph .20
☐ 86 Joel Cort, Guelph .20
☐ 87 Chris Hajt, Guelph .50
☐ 88 Bryan McKinney, Guelph .20
☐ 89 Dwayne Hay, Guelph .50
☐ 90 Andrew Clark, Guelph .20
☐ 91 Ryan Robichaud, Guelph .20
☐ 92 Mike Vellinga, Guelph .20
☐ 93 Jamie Wright, Guelph .50
☐ 94 Herbert Vasiljevs, Guelph .50
☐ 95 Dan Cloutier (G), Guelph 3.00
☐ 96 Brian Wesenberg, Guelph .50
☐ 97 Michael Pittman, Guelph .20
☐ 98 Jeff Williams, Guelph .20
☐ 99 Todd Norman, Guelph .50
☐ 100 Brian Willsie, Guelph .50
☐ 101 Jason Jackman, Guelph .20
☐ 102 Mike Lankshear, Guelph .20
☐ 103 Andrew Long, Guelph .20
☐ 104 Nick Bootland, Guelph .20
☐ 105 E.J. McGuire, Coach, Guelph .20
☐ 106 Bujar Amidovski (G), Kingston .50
☐ 107 John Hultberg (G), Kingston .20
☐ 108 Eric Olsen, Kingston .20
☐ 109 Chris Allen, Kingston .50
☐ 110 Michael Tilson, Kingston .20
☐ 111 Jeff DaCosta, Kingston .20
☐ 112 Gord Walsh, Kingston .20
☐ 113 Matt Bradley, Kingston .50
☐ 114 Robert Mailloux, Kingston .20
☐ 115 Justin Davis, Kingston .20
☐ 116 Marc Moro, Kingston .50
☐ 117 Cail MacLean, Kingston .20
☐ 118 Jason Sands, Kingston .20
☐ 119 Matt Price, Kingston .20
☐ 120 Zdenek Skorepa, Kingston .20
☐ 121 Jason Morgan, Kingston .50
☐ 122 Mike Oliveira, Kingston .20
☐ 123 Colin Chaulk, Kingston .20
☐ 124 Dylan Taylor, Kingston .20
☐ 125 Kurt Johnston, Kingston .20
☐ 126 Bill Minkhorst, Kingston .20
☐ 127 Wes Swinson, Kingston .20
☐ 128 Adam Fleming, Kingston .20
☐ 129 Chris MacDonald, Coach, Kingston .20
☐ 130 Gary Agnew, Coach, Kingston .20
☐ 131 David Belitski (G), Kitchener .50
☐ 132 Jarrett Rose (G), Kitchener .20
☐ 133 Ryan Mougenel, Kitchener .20
☐ 134 Rob Stanfield, Kitchener .20
☐ 135 Duncan Fader, Kitchener .20
☐ 136 Rob Maric, Kitchener .20
☐ 137 Mark McMahon, Kitchener .20
☐ 138 Serge Payer, Kitchener .50
☐ 139 Paul Traynor, Kitchener .20
☐ 140 Bogdan Rudenko, Kitchener .20
☐ 141 Rob DeCiantis, Kitchener .20
☐ 142 Andrew Dale, Kitchener .20
☐ 143 Jeff Ambrosio, Kitchener .50
☐ 144 Paul Doyle, Kitchener .20
☐ 145 Bryan Duce, Kitchener .20
☐ 146 Jason Byrnes, Kitchener .20
☐ 147 Ryan Pepperall, Kitchener .20
☐ 148 Wes Vander Wal, Kitchener .20
☐ 149 Boyd Devereaux, Kitchener 1.50
☐ 150 Keith Welsh, Kitchener .20
☐ 151 Joe Birch, Kitchener .20
☐ 152 Craig Nelson, Kitchener .20
☐ 153 Brian Hayden, Coach, Kitchener .20
☐ 154 Matt O'Dette, Kitchener .20
☐ 155 Geoff Ward, Coach, Kitchener .20
☐ 156 Frank Ivankovic (G), London .20
☐ 157 Eoin McInerney (G), London .20
☐ 158 Joel Dezainde, London .20
☐ 159 Duncan Dalmad, London .20
☐ 160 Brandon Sugden, London .20
☐ 161 Jamie Wentzell, London .20
☐ 162 Ryan Burgoyne, London .20
☐ 163 Todd Crane, London .20
☐ 164 Chad Cavanagh, London .20
☐ 165 Andrew Fagan, London .20
☐ 166 Ryan Gardner, London .20
☐ 167 Kevin Boyd, London .20
☐ 168 Kevin Barry, London .20
☐ 169 Richard Pitirri, London .20
☐ 170 Adam Colagiacomo, London .50
☐ 171 Jason Brooks, London .20
☐ 172 Justin McPolin, London .20
☐ 173 Travis Riggin, London .20
☐ 174 Steve Lowe, London .20
☐ 175 Todd St. Louis, London .20
☐ 176 Kevin Slota, London .20
☐ 177 Ryan McKie, London .20
☐ 178 Corey Isen, London .20
☐ 179 Sasha Cucuz, London .20
☐ 180 Tom Barrett, Coach, London .20
☐ 181 Ken Carroll (G), Niagara Falls .20
☐ 182 Ryan Penney (G), Niagara Falls .20
☐ 183 Jay McKee, Niagara Falls .50
☐ 184 Ryan Taylor, Niagara Falls .20
☐ 185 Jeff Paul, Niagara Falls .20
☐ 186 Jason Ward, Niagara Falls 1.00
☐ 187 Jesse Black, Niagara Falls .20
☐ 188 Steve Nimigon, Niagara Falls .20
☐ 189 Chris Haskett, Niagara Falls .20
☐ 190 Geoff Peters, Niagara Falls .50
☐ 191 Ryan Cirillo, Niagara Falls .20
☐ 192 David Froh, Niagara Falls .20
☐ 193 Jeff Johnstone, Niagara Falls .20
☐ 194 Shane Nash, Niagara Falls .20
☐ 195 Jason Robinson, Niagara Falls .20
☐ 196 Rich Vrataric, Niagara Falls .20
☐ 197 Colin Pepperall, Niagara Falls .20
☐ 198 Craig Jalbert, Niagara Falls .20
☐ 199 Andrew Williamson, Niagara Falls .20
☐ 200 Greg Tymchuk, Niagara Falls .20
☐ 201 Chester Gallant, Niagara Falls .20
☐ 202 Mike Perna, Niagara Falls .20
☐ 203 Adam Nittel, Niagara Falls .20
☐ 204 Dave Burkholder, Coach, Niagara Falls .20
☐ 205 Chris Johnstone, Coach, Niagara Falls .20
☐ 206 Elliott Faust (G), North Bay .20
☐ 207 Scott Roche (G), North Bay .20
☐ 208 Kam White, North Bay .20
☐ 209 Scott Atkins, North Bay .20
☐ 210 Luc Belliveau, North Bay .20
☐ 211 Jamie Vossen, North Bay .20
☐ 212 Ryan MacDonald, North Bay .20
☐ 213 Jim Midgley, North Bay .20
☐ 214 Steven Carpenter, North Bay .20
☐ 215 Jake Martel, North Bay .20
☐ 216 Alex Matvichuk, North Bay .20
☐ 217 Trevor Gallant, North Bay .20
☐ 218 Ryan Gillis, North Bay .20
☐ 219 Kris Cantu, North Bay .20
☐ 220 Mark Provenzano, North Bay .20
☐ 221 Brian Whitley, North Bay .20
☐ 222 Dustin Virag, North Bay .20
☐ 223 Lee Jinman, North Bay .20
☐ 224 Peter McCague, North Bay .20
☐ 225 Herb Bonvie, North Bay .20
☐ 226 Philippe Poirier, North Bay .20
☐ 227 Greg Labenski, North Bay .20
☐ 228 Milan Kostolny, North Bay .20
☐ 229 Ryan Power, North Bay .20
☐ 230 Shane Parker, Coach, North Bay .20
☐ 231 Travis Scott (G), Oshawa .50
☐ 232 Tyrone Garner (G), Oshawa .50
☐ 233 Marty Wilford, Oshawa .20
☐ 234 Ole Anderson, Oshawa .20
☐ 235 Ryan Tocher, Oshawa .20
☐ 236 Nathan Perrott, Oshawa .50
☐ 237 Brandon Coalter, Oshawa .20
☐ 238 John Tripp, Oshawa .20
☐ 239 Jay LeGault, Oshawa .20
☐ 240 Wayne Primeau, Oshawa 1.00
☐ 241 Trevor Edgar, Oshawa .20
☐ 242 Peter Hogan, Oshawa .20
☐ 243 Warren Holmes, Oshawa .20
☐ 244 Jason Metcalfe, Oshawa .20
☐ 245 Mike Zanutto, Oshawa .20
☐ 246 Jeff Ware, Oshawa .50
☐ 247 Ian MacNeil, Oshawa .20
☐ 248 Jan Snopek, Oshawa .20
☐ 249 Kurt Walsh, Oshawa .50
☐ 250 Marc Savard, Oshawa 1.50
☐ 251 Darcy O'Shea, Oshawa .20
☐ 252 Jason Sweitzer, Oshawa .20
☐ 253 Ryan Lindsay, Oshawa .20
☐ 254 Scott Seiling, Oshawa .20
☐ 255 Stan Butler, Coach, Oshawa .20
☐ 256 Tim Keyes (G), Ottawa .20
☐ 257 Craig Hillier (G), Ottawa .50
☐ 258 Craig Whynot, Ottawa .20
☐ 259 David Bell, Ottawa .20
☐ 260 Rich Bronilla, Ottawa .20
☐ 261 Roy Gray, Ottawa .20
☐ 262 Nick Boynton, Ottawa 1.00
☐ 263 Mike Sim, Ottawa .20
☐ 264 Billy-Jay Johnston, Ottawa .20
☐ 265 Niall Maynard, Ottawa .20
☐ 266 Dan Tudin, Ottawa .20
☐ 267 Jure Kovacevic, Ottawa .20
☐ 268 Ben Gustavson, Ottawa .20
☐ 269 Steve Zoryk, Ottawa .20
☐ 270 Darren Debrie, Ottawa .20
☐ 271 Troy Stonier, Ottawa .20
☐ 272 David Nemirovsky, Ottawa .50
☐ 273 Joel Trottier, Ottawa .20
☐ 274 Mike Lavell, Ottawa .20
☐ 275 Brian Campbell, Ottawa .50
☐ 276 Chris Despatis, Ottawa .20
☐ 277 Sean Blanchard, Ottawa .50
☐ 278 Alyn McCauley, Ottawa 2.50
☐ 279 Chris Pittman, Ottawa .20
☐ 280 Daryl Rivers, Ottawa .20
☐ 281 Brent Johnson (G), Owen Sound 3.00
☐ 282 Shaun Gallant (G), Owen Sound .20
☐ 283 Shane Kenny, Owen Sound .20
☐ 284 Chris Biagini, Owen Sound .20
☐ 285 Jim Ensom, Owen Sound .20
☐ 286 Marek Babic, Owen Sound .20
☐ 287 Oleg Tsirkounov, Owen Sound .20
☐ 288 Mike Loach, Owen Sound .20
☐ 289 Peter MacKellar, Owen Sound .20
☐ 290 Ryan Davis, Owen Sound .20
☐ 291 John Argiropoulos, Owen Sound .20
☐ 292 Jason Campbell, Owen Sound .20
☐ 293 Ryan Christie, Owen Sound .50
☐ 294 Dan Snyder, Owen Sound .50
☐ 295 Steve Gallace, Owen Sound .20
☐ 296 Scott Seiling, Owen Sound .20
☐ 297 Jeremy Rebek, Owen Sound .20
☐ 298 Adam Mair, Owen Sound .50
☐ 299 Matt Osborne, Owen Sound .50
☐ 300 Mike Galati, Owen Sound .20
☐ 301 Wayne Primeau, Owen Sound 1.00
☐ 302 Chris Wismer, Owen Sound .20
☐ 303 Larry Paleczny, Owen Sound .20
☐ 304 Kurt Walsh, Owen Sound .50
☐ 305 John Lovell, Coach, Owen Sound .20
☐ 306 Allan Hitchen (G), Peterborough .20
☐ 307 Zac Bierk (G), Peterborough 1.00
☐ 308 Mike Martone, Peterborough .20
☐ 309 Jonathan Murphy, Peterborough .20
☐ 310 Adrian Murray, Peterborough .20
☐ 311 Rob Giffin, Peterborough .20
☐ 312 Corey Crocker, Peterborough .20
☐ 313 Cameron Mann, Peterborough 1.00
☐ 314 Ryan Pawluk, Peterborough .20
☐ 315 Jason MacMillan, Peterborough .20
☐ 316 Shawn Thornton, Peterborough .20
☐ 317 Wade Dawe, Peterborough .20
☐ 318 Eric Landry, Peterborough .20
☐ 319 Steve Hogg, Peterborough .20
☐ 320 Kevin Bolibruck, Peterborough .20
☐ 321 Dave Duerden, Peterborough .50
☐ 322 Mike Williams, Peterborough .20
☐ 323 Andy Johnson, Peterborough .20
☐ 324 Jaret Nixon, Peterborough .20
☐ 325 Evgeny Korolev, Peterborough .50
☐ 326 Matthew Lahey, Peterborough .20
☐ 327 Ryan Schmidt, Peterborough .20
☐ 328 Scott Barney, Peterborough .50
☐ 329 Steve Jones, Peterborough .20
☐ 330 Dave McQueen, Coach, Peterborough .20
☐ 331 Jeff Salajko (G), Sarnia .20
☐ 332 Patrick DesRochers (G), Sarnia 1.00
☐ 333 Gerald Moriarity, Sarnia .20
☐ 334 Allan Carr, Sarnia .20
☐ 335 Tom Brown, Sarnia .20
☐ 336 Andy Delmore, Sarnia 1.00
☐ 337 Darren Mortier, Sarnia .20
☐ 338 Aaron Brand, Sarnia .20
☐ 339 Eric Boulton, Sarnia .50
☐ 340 Jonathan Sim, Sarnia .50
☐ 341 Trevor Letowski, Sarnia 1.00
☐ 342 Michael Hanson, Sarnia .20
☐ 343 Todd Miller, Sarnia .20
☐ 344 Brendan Yarema, Sarnia .20
☐ 345 Brad Simms, Sarnia .20
☐ 346 David Nemirovsky, Sarnia .50
☐ 347 Jeff Brown, Sarnia .20
☐ 348 Andrew Proskurnicki, Sarnia .20
☐ 349 Wes Mason, Sarnia .50
☐ 350 Scott Corbett, Sarnia .20
☐ 351 Dave Bourque, Sarnia .20
☐ 352 Sean Brown, Sarnia .50
☐ 353 Marcin Snita, Sarnia .20
☐ 354 Rich Brown, Coach, Sarnia .20
☐ 355 Mark Hunter, Coach, Sarnia .50
☐ 356 Michael Podolka (G), S.S. Marie .20
☐ 357 Dan Cloutier (G), S.S. Marie 3.00
☐ 358 Cory Murphy, S.S. Marie .20
☐ 359 Kevin Murnaghan, S.S. Marie .20
☐ 360 André Payette, S.S. Marie .20
☐ 361 Richard Uniacke, S.S. Marie .20
☐ 362 Joe Serosky, S.S. Marie .20
☐ 363 Joe Thornton, S.S. Marie 18.00
☐ 364 Ben Schust, S.S. Marie .20
☐ 365 Peter Cava, S.S. Marie .20
☐ 366 Darryl Green, S.S. Marie .20
☐ 367 Trevor Tokarczyk, S.S. Marie .20
☐ 368 Jeff Gies, S.S. Marie .20
☐ 369 Rico Fata, S.S. Marie 1.50
☐ 370 Brian Secord, S.S. Marie .20
☐ 371 Scott Cherrey, S.S. Marie .20
☐ 372 Brian Stacey, S.S. Marie .20
☐ 373 Lee Cole, S.S. Marie .20
☐ 374 Richard Jackman, S.S. Marie .50
☐ 375 Jason Doyle, S.S. Marie .50
☐ 376 Brian Stewart, S.S. Marie .20
☐ 377 Blaine Fitzpatrick, S.S. Marie .20
☐ 378 Robert Mulick, S.S. Marie .20
☐ 379 Andy Adams (G), S.S. Marie .20
☐ 380 Joe Paterson, Coach, S.S. Marie .20
☐ 381 Dave MacDonald (G), Sudbury .20
☐ 382 Stephen Valiquette (G), Sudbury .50
☐ 383 Tim Swartz, Sudbury .20
☐ 384 Gregg Lalonde, Sudbury .20
☐ 385 Tyson Flinn, Sudbury .20
☐ 386 Ryan Sly, Sudbury .20
☐ 387 Neal Martin, Sudbury .20
☐ 388 Kevin Hansen, Sudbury .20
☐ 389 Joe Lombardo, Sudbury .20
☐ 390 Darryl Moxam, Sudbury .20
☐ 391 Jeremy Adduono, Sudbury .20
☐ 392 Ryan Shanahan, Sudbury .20
☐ 393 Sean Venedam, Sudbury .20
☐ 394 Andrew Dale, Sudbury .20
☐ 395 Rob Butler, Sudbury .20
☐ 396 Brian Scott, Sudbury .50
☐ 397 Liam MacEachern, Sudbury .20
☐ 398 Luc Gagne, Sudbury .20
☐ 399 Richard Rochefort, Sudbury .20
☐ 400 Noel Burkitt, Sudbury .20
☐ 401 Simon Sherry, Sudbury .20
☐ 402 Brad Domonsky, Sudbury .20
☐ 403 Ron Newhook, Sudbury .20
☐ 404 Serge Dunphy, Sudbury .20
☐ 405 Todd Lalonde, Coach, Sudbury .20
☐ 406 Ryan Gelinas (G), Windsor .20
☐ 407 Terry Joss (G), Windsor .20
☐ 408 Mike Martin, Windsor .20
☐ 409 Chris Van Dyk, Windsor .20
☐ 410 Denis Smith, Windsor .50
☐ 411 Glenn Crawford, Windsor .50
☐ 412 Robert Blain, Windsor .20
☐ 413 Matt Masterson, Windsor .20
☐ 414 Adam Young, Windsor .20
☐ 415 Matt Cooke, Windsor 1.00
☐ 416 Jeff Zehr, Windsor .50
☐ 417 Wes Ward, Windsor .20
☐ 418 Matt Elich, Windsor .50
☐ 419 Rob Shearer, Windsor .50
☐ 420 Dean Mando, Windsor .20
☐ 421 Chris Kerr, Windsor .20
☐ 422 Vladimir Krechine, Windsor .20
☐ 423 Jeff Martin, Windsor .20
☐ 424 Valery Svoboda, Windsor .20
☐ 425 Dave Geris, Windsor .20
☐ 426 Ryan Pawluk, Windsor .20
☐ 427 Ryan Shaver, Windsor .20
☐ 428 Cameron Kincaid, Windsor .20
☐ 429 Tim Findlay, Windsor .20
☐ 430 Tim Bryan, Windsor .20
☐ 431 Alexandre Volchkov, Barrie .50
☐ 432 Boyd Devereaux, Kitcherer 1.50
☐ 433 Chris Allen, Kingston .50
☐ 434 Jason Doyle, S.S. Marie .50
☐ 435 Wes Mason, Sarnia .50
☐ 436 Chris Hajt, Guelph .50
☐ 437 Kurt Walsh, Owen Sound .50
☐ 438 Glen Crawford, Windsor .50
☐ 439 Jeff Brown, Sarnia .20
☐ 440 Geoff Peters, Niagara Falls .50

Player **NRMT-MT**
☐ Zac Bierk (G) Autographed ✍ 35.00
☐ Zac Bierk (G), Peterborough 6.00
☐ Nick Boynton, Ottawa 6.00
☐ Adam Colagiacomo, London 2.00
☐ Sean Haggerty, Detroit 2.00
☐ Cameron Mann, Peterborough 4.00
☐ Mike Martin, Windsor 2.00
☐ Jay McKee, Niagara Falls 2.50
☐ Ryan Pepperall, Kitchener 2.00
☐ Scott Roche (G), North Bay 2.00
☐ Zac Bierk (G) (Toronto Expo) 3.00
☐ Jay McKee (Tornton Expo) 3.00

1995 - 96 SP

Complete Set (188 cards): 55.00
Common Player: .20

Promo **NRMT-MT**
☐ 66 Wayne Gretzky, All-Star 10.00

Player **SP**
☐ 1 Paul Kariya, Anah. 1.50
☐ 2 Teemu Selänne, Anah. 1.00
☐ 3 Guy Hebert (G), Anah. .20
☐ 4 Steve Rucchin, Anah. .20
☐ 5 Raymond Bourque, All-Star 1.50
☐ 6 Cam Neely, Bost. 1.00
☐ 7 Adam Oates, Bost. .50
☐ **8 Kyle McLaren, Bost. RC 3.00**
☐ 9 Bill Ranford (G), Bost. .50
☐ 10 Shawn McEachern, Bost. .20

☐	11 Don Sweeney, Bost.	.20
☐	12 Pat LaFontaine, Buff.	.50
☐	13 Dominik Hasek (G), Buff.	1.00
☐	**14 Brian Holzinger, Buff. RC**	**2.00**
☐	15 Alexei Zhitnik, Buff.	.20
☐	16 Theoren Fleury, Calg.	.50
☐	17 Cory Stillman, Calg.	.20
☐	18 German Titov, Calg.	.20
☐	19 Phil Housley, Calg.	.20
☐	20 Michael Nylander, Calg.	.20
☐	21 Trevor Kidd (G), Calg.	.20
☐	22 Éric Dazé, Chic.	1.00
☐	23 Chris Chelios, Chic.	.50
☐	24 Jeremy Roenick, Chic.	1.00
☐	25 Gary Suter, Chic.	.20
☐	26 Bernie Nicholls, Chic.	.20
☐	27 Ed Belfour (G), Chic.	1.00
☐	28 Tony Amonte, Chic.	.50
☐	29 Peter Forsberg, Colo.	1.50
☐	30 Patrick Roy (G), Colo.	.20
☐	31 Joe Sakic, Colo.	2.00
☐	32 Sandis Ozolinsh, Colo. [vs. T.Marchant]	.20
☐	33 Adam Deadmarsh, Colo.	.20
☐	34 Stéphane Fiset (G), Colo.	.20
☐	35 Claude Lemieux, Colo.	.20
☐	36 Mike Modano, Dall.	1.00
☐	37 Kevin Hatcher, Dall.	.20
☐	38 Joe Nieuwendyk, Dall.	.50
☐	39 Todd Harvey, Dall.	.20
☐	40 Derian Hatcher, Dall.	.20
☐	41 Jere Lehtinen, Dall.	.20
☐	42 Nicklas Lidström, Detr.	.50
☐	**43 Mathieu Dandenault, Detr. RC**	**2.50**
☐	44 Sergei Fedorov, Detr.	1.00
☐	45 Paul Coffey, Detr.	.50
☐	46 Steve Yzerman, Detr.	3.00
☐	47 Keith Primeau, Detr. [cameo: S.Yzerman]	.50
☐	48 Chris Osgood (G), Detr.	.50
☐	49 Vyacheslav Kozlov, Detr.	.20
☐	50 Doug Weight, Edmo.	.50
☐	51 Jason Arnott, Edmo.	.50
☐	**52 Miroslav Satan, Edmo. RC**	**6.00**
☐	53 Zdeno Ciger, Edmo.	.20
☐	54 Curtis Joseph (G), Edmo.	1.00
☐	55 Scott Mellanby, Flor.	.20
☐	56 John Vanbiesbrouck (G), Flor.	.50
☐	57 Jody Hull, Flor.	.20
☐	58 Ed Jovanovski, Flor.	1.00
☐	**59 Radek Dvorak, Flor. RC**	**3.00**
☐	60 Rob Niedermayer, Flor.	.20
☐	61 Andrew Cassels, Hart.	.20
☐	62 Brendan Shanahan, Hart. [vs. G.Suter]	1.00
☐	63 Nelson Emerson, Hart.	.20
☐	64 Jeff O'Neill, Hart.	1.00
☐	65 Sean Burke (G), Hart.	.50
☐	66 Craig Johnson, LosA.	.20
☐	67 Dmitri Khristich, LosA.	.20
☐	68 Vitali Yachmenev, LosA.	.20
☐	**69 Aki Berg, LosA. RC**	**2.00**
☐	70 Byron Dafoe (G), LosA.	.50
☐	71 Pierre Turgeon, Mont.	.50
☐	72 Mark Recchi, Mont.	.50
☐	73 Saku Koivu, Mont.	2.00
☐	74 Valeri Bure, Mont.	.20
☐	75 Vincent Damphousse, Mont.	.50
☐	76 Jocelyn Thibault (G), Mont.	.50
☐	77 Patrice Brisebois, Mont.	.20
☐	78 John MacLean, NJer.	.20
☐	79 Martin Brodeur (G), NJer.	2.00
☐	80 Steve Thomas, NJer.	.20
☐	81 Scott Stevens, NJer.	.50
☐	82 Bill Guerin, NJer.	.50
☐	**83 Petr Sykora, NJer. RC**	**7.00**
☐	84 Scott Niedermayer, NJer.	.20
☐	85 Stéphane Richer, NJer.	.20
☐	86 Zigmund Palffy, NYIs.	.50
☐	87 Travis Green, NYIs.	.20
☐	**88 Todd Bertuzzi, NYIs. RC**	**25.00**
☐	89 Mathieu Schneider, NYIs.	.20
☐	90 Éric Fichaud (G), NYIs.	.20
☐	91 Bryan McCabe, NYIs.	.50
☐	92 Mark Messier, NYRa.	1.00
☐	93 Pat Verbeek, NYRa.	.20
☐	94 Brian Leetch, NYRa.	.50
☐	95 Mike Richter (G), NYRa.	.50
☐	96 Niklas Sundström, NYRa.	.50
☐	97 Luc Robitaille, NYRa.	1.00
☐	98 Adam Graves, NYRa.	.50
☐	99 Alexei Kovalev, NYRa.	.50
☐	**100 Daniel Alfredsson, Otta. RC**	**9.00**
☐	101 Alexei Yashin, Otta.	.50
☐	102 Radek Bonk, Otta.	.20
☐	103 Alexandre Daigle, Otta.	.20
☐	104 Damian Rhodes (G), Otta.	.20
☐	**105 Antti Törmänen, Otta. RC**	**1.00**
☐	106 Eric Lindros, Phil.	1.00
☐	107 Mikael Renberg, Phil.	.20
☐	108 John LeClair, Phil.	1.00
☐	109 Ron Hextall (G), Phil.	.50
☐	110 Rod Brind'Amour, Phil.	.20
☐	111 Joel Otto, Phil.	.20
☐	112 Éric Desjardins, Phil.	.20
☐	113 Mario Lemieux, Pitt.	.20
☐	114 Jaromir Jagr, Pitt.	1.00
☐	115 Ron Francis, All-Star	.50
☐	116 Markus Näslund, Pitt.	1.00
☐	117 Sergei Zubov, Pitt.	.20
☐	118 Tomas Sandström, Pitt.	.20
☐	119 Tom Barrasso (G), Pitt.	.50
☐	120 Richard Park, Pitt.	.20
☐	121 Brett Hull, SLou.	1.00
☐	122 Shayne Corson, SLou.	.20
☐	123 Dale Hawerchuk, SLou.	.50
☐	124 Chris Pronger, SLou.	.50
☐	125 Al MacInnis, SLou.	.50
☐	126 Grant Fuhr (G), SLou.	.50
☐	127 Wayne Gretzky, SLou.	5.00
☐	128 Geoff Courtnall, SLou.	.20
☐	129 Owen Nolan, SanJ.	.50
☐	130 Ray Sheppard, SanJ.	.20
☐	131 Chris Terreri (G), SanJ.	.20
☐	**132 Marcus Ragnarsson, SanJ. RC**	**3.00**
☐	133 Jeff Friesen, SanJ.	.20
☐	134 Doug Bodger, SanJ.	.20
☐	135 Roman Hamrlik, Tamp.	.20
☐	136 Petr Klima, Tamp.	.20
☐	137 Daren Puppa (G), Tamp.	.20
☐	138 Aaron Gavey, Tamp.	.20
☐	139 Daymond Langkow, Tamp.	2.00
☐	140 Alexander Selivanov, Tamp.	.20
☐	141 Mats Sundin, Toro.	1.00
☐	142 Kirk Muller, Toro.	.20
☐	143 Larry Murphy, Toro.	.20
☐	144 Doug Gilmour, Toro.	.50
☐	145 Darby Hendrickson, Toro.	.20
☐	146 Félix Potvin (G), Toro.	.50
☐	147 Kenny Jönsson, Toro.	.20
☐	148 Alexander Mogilny, Vanc.	.50
☐	149 Pavel Bure, Vanc.	1.00
☐	150 Trevor Linden, Vanc.	.50
☐	151 Corey Hirsch, Vanc.	.20
☐	152 Kirk McLean (G), Vanc.	.20
☐	153 Esa Tikkanen, Vanc.	.20
☐	154 Cliff Ronning, Vanc.	.20
☐	155 Peter Bondra, Wash.	.50
☐	156 Jim Carey (G), Wash.	.20
☐	157 Michal Pivonka, Wash.	.20
☐	158 Joé Juneau, Wash.	.20
☐	159 Dale Hunter, Wash.	.20
☐	160 S. Konowalchuk, Wash. [vs. M.Fitzpatrick]	.20
☐	161 Stefan Ustorf, Wash.	.20
☐	162 Brendan Witt, Wash.	.20
☐	**163 Chad Kilger, Winn. RC**	**3.00**
☐	164 Keith Tkachuk, Winn.	.50
☐	165 Deron Quint, Winn.	.20
☐	166 Oleg Tverdovsky, Winn.	.20
☐	167 Alexei Zhamnov, Winn.	.20
☐	168 Igor Korolev, Winn.	.20
☐	169 Wade Redden, Canada Juniors	.50
☐	170 Jarome Iginla, Canada Juniors	2.00
☐	171 Christian Dubé, Canada Juniors	.20
☐	172 Jason Podollan, Canada Juniors	1.00
☐	173 Alyn McCauley, Canada Juniors	.50
☐	174 Nolan Baumgartner, Canada Juniors	.50
☐	175 Jason Botterill, Canada Juniors	.20
☐	**176 Chris Phillips, Canada Juniors RC**	**3.00**
☐	177 Dimitri Nabokov, Russia Juniors	.20
☐	178 Andrei Petrunin, Russia Juniors	.20
☐	179 Alexander Korolyuk, Russia Juniors	.20
☐	180 Sergei Samsonov, Russia Juniors	1.50
☐	**181 Ilja Gorokhov, Russia Juniors RC**	**1.00**
☐	**182 Alexei Kolkunov, Russia Juniors RC**	**1.00**
☐	**183 Samuel Påhlsson, Sweden Juniors RC**	**2.00**
☐	184 Mattias Öhlund, Sweden Juniors	.50
☐	**185 Marcus Nilson, Sweden Juniors RC**	**2.00**
☐	**186 Daniel Tjärnqvist, Sweden Juniors RC**	**1.00**
☐	**187 Per Anton Lundström, Sweden Jrs. RC**	**1.00**
☐	**188 Fredrik Loven, Sweden Juniors RC**	**1.00**

GREAT CONNECTIONS

	Die-Cut Insert (1:381)	**NRMT-MT**
☐	GC1 Wayne Gretzky, SLou.	100.00
☐	GC2 Sergei Samsonov, Russia Juniors	35.00

ÉTOILES

These inserts have two versions: the regular silver insert and a gold parallel. Both versions are die-cut.

	Insert Set (30 cards):	**575.00**	**60.00**
	Inserts	**Gold**	**Reg.**
☐ ☐	É1 Paul Kariya, Anah.	25.00	2.00
☐ ☐	É2 Teemu Selänne, Anah.	15.00	2.00
☐ ☐	É3 Raymond Bourque, Bost.	20.00	2.00
☐ ☐	É4 Cam Neely, Bost.	20.00	2.00
☐ ☐	É5 Pat LaFontaine, Buff.	10.00	1.00
☐ ☐	É6 Theoren Fleury, Calg.	10.00	1.00
☐ ☐	É7 Jeremy Roenick, Chic.	15.00	2.00
☐ ☐	É8 Joe Sakic, Colo.	30.00	4.00
☐ ☐	É9 Patrick Roy (G), Colo.	60.00	6.00
☐ ☐	É10 Peter Forsberg, Colo.	25.00	2.00
☐ ☐	É11 Mike Modano, Dall.	20.00	2.00
☐ ☐	É12 Sergei Fedorov, Detr.	20.00	2.00
☐ ☐	É13 Paul Coffey, Detr.	10.00	1.00
☐ ☐	É14 Steve Yzerman, Detr.	45.00	6.00
☐ ☐	É15 Pierre Turgeon, Mont.	6.00	1.00
☐ ☐	É16 Brendan Shanahan, Hart.	20.00	2.00
☐ ☐	É17 Wayne Gretzky, SLou.	80.00	10.00
☐ ☐	É18 Martin Brodeur (G), NJer.	30.00	4.00
☐ ☐	É19 Mark Messier, NYRa.	20.00	2.00
☐ ☐	É20 Brian Leetch, NYRa.	10.00	1.00
☐ ☐	É21 Eric Lindros, Phil.	20.00	2.00
☐ ☐	É22 Mario Lemieux, Pitt.	60.00	6.00
☐ ☐	É23 Jaromir Jagr, Pitt.	20.00	2.00
☐ ☐	É24 Brett Hull, SLou.	20.00	2.00
☐ ☐	É25 Roman Hamrlik, Tamp.	6.00	1.00
☐ ☐	É26 Mats Sundin, Toro.	20.00	2.00
☐ ☐	É27 Félix Potvin (G), Toro.	10.00	1.00
☐ ☐	É28 Alexander Mogilny, Vanc.	6.00	1.00
☐ ☐	É29 Pavel Bure, Vanc.	15.00	2.00
☐ ☐	É30 Keith Tkachuk, Winn.	10.00	1.00

HOLOVIEW

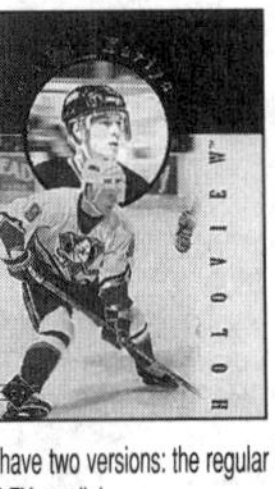

These inserts have two versions: the regular insert and a die-cut Special FX parallel.

	Insert Set (20 cards):	**475.00**	**85.00**
	Inserts	**Die-Cut**	**Reg.**
☐ ☐	FX2 Paul Kariya, Anah.	35.00	6.00
☐ ☐	FX3 Chris Chelios, Chic.	15.00	2.00
☐ ☐	FX4 Peter Forsberg, Colo.	35.00	6.00
☐ ☐	FX5 Sergei Fedorov, Detr.	25.00	4.00
☐ ☐	FX6 Paul Coffey, Detr.	15.00	2.00
☐ ☐	FX7 Steve Yzerman, Detr.	60.00	12.00
☐ ☐	FX8 Jason Arnott, Edmo.	10.00	2.00
☐ ☐	FX9 Doug Weight, Edmo.	15.00	2.00
☐ ☐	FX10 Wayne Gretzky, LosA.	100.00	20.00
☐ ☐	FX11 Vitali Yachmenev, LosA.	6.00	1.50
☐ ☐	FX12 Martin Brodeur (G), NJer.	40.00	8.00
☐ ☐	FX13 Scott Stevens, NJer.	10.00	2.00
☐ ☐	FX14 Mark Messier, NYRa.	25.00	4.00
☐ ☐	FX15 Daniel Alfredsson, Otta.	20.00	8.00
☐ ☐	FX16 Eric Lindros, Phil.	25.00	4.00
☐ ☐	FX17 Mario Lemieux, Pitt.	75.00	14.00
☐ ☐	FX18 Jaromir Jagr, Pitt.	25.00	4.00
☐ ☐	FX19 Shayne Corson, SLou.	6.00	1.50
☐ ☐	FX20 Pavel Bure, Vanc.	20.00	4.00

1995 - 96 SP – BUYBACKS

	Buyback Autograph	**SP**
☐	24 Jeremy Roenick, Chic. ✍ {#/3}	
☐	36 Mike Modano, Dall. ✍ {#/10}	
☐	42 Nicklas Lidström, Detr. ✍ {#/11}	
☐	46 Steve Yzerman, Detr. ✍ {#/2}	
☐	**52 Miroslav Satan, Buff. RC** ✍ **{#/6}**	
☐	66 Wayne Gretzky, All-Star ✍ {#/2}	
☐	70 Byron Dafoe (G) ✍ {#/7}	
☐	79 Martin Brodeur (G), NJer. ✍ {#/11}	
☐	92 Mark Messier, NYRa. ✍ {#/9}	
☐	95 Mike Richter (G), NYRa. ✍ {#/21}	
☐	97 Luc Robitaille, NYRa. ✍ {#/1}	
☐	108 John LeClair, Phil. ✍ {#/24}	
☐	113 Mario Lemieux, Pitt. ✍ {#/19}	
☐	121 Brett Hull, SLou. ✍ {#/2}	
☐	127 Wayne Gretzky, SLou. ✍ {#/}	
☐	164 Félix Potvin (G), Toro. ✍ {#/10}	
☐	149 Pavel Bure, Vanc. ✍ {#/3}	
☐	180 Sergei Samsonov, Russia ✍ {#/10}	
☐	180 Sergei Samsonov, Russia. ✍ {#/2}	
	Buyback Autograph • Étoiles insert	**SP**
☐	É24 Brett Hull, SLou. ✍ {#/4}	
	Buyback Autograph • Holoview insert	**SP**
☐	FX7 Steve Yzerman, Detr. ✍ {#/1}	
☐	FX20 Pavel Bure, Vanc. ✍ {#/1}	

1995 - 96 SPORTS ILLUSTRATED FOR KIDS

These cards were distributed as part of nine-card perforated sheets included in *Sports Illustrated for Kids*. While these cards were intended for editorial purposes, they have made their way onto the secondary market. Cards issued in the 12 issues between July 1995 and June 1996 were numbered 379-486.

	1995-96 Sports Illustrated for Kids	
☐	Jul. 1995 • 382 Jim Carey(G), Wash.	1.00
☐	Sep. 1995 • 399 Eric Lindros, Phil.	3.00
☐	Oct. 1995 • 413 Martin Brodeur (G), NJer.	3.00
☐	Nov. 1995 • 420 Paul Coffey, Detr.	1.00
☐	Dec. 1995 • 425 Peter Forsberg, Colo.	3.00
☐	Dec. 1995 • 432 Karen Bye, United States	3.00
☐	Jan. 1996 • 435 Peter Bondra, Wash.	1.00
☐	Feb. 1996 • 442 Dominik Hasek (G), Buff.	3.00
☐	Mar. 1996 • 453 Mario Lemieux, Pitt.	8.00
☐	Apr. 1996 • 465 Brendan Shanahan, Hart.	3.00
☐	May 1996 • 477 Steve Yzerman, Detr.	5.00

1995 - 96 STARTING LINEUP

One Fleer card (1994 - 95 design) was packaged with each figure.

	Complete Set (20 cards):	**25.00**
	Player	**NRMT-MT**
☐	39 Chris Chelios, Chic.	1.00
☐	Tom Barrasso (G), Pitt.	1.50
☐	Rob Blake, LosA.	1.00
☐	Martin Brodeur (G), NJer.	3.00
☐	Pavel Bure, Vanc.	1.50
☐	Bob Corkum, Anah.	1.00
☐	Sergei Fedorov, Detr.	4.00
☐	Theoren Fleury, Calg.	1.00
☐	Adam Graves, NYRa.	1.00
☐	Dominik Hasek (G), Buff.	2.00
☐	Brett Hull, SLou.	2.00
☐	Arturs Irbe (G), SanJ.	1.50
☐	Mike Modano, Dall.	2.00
☐	Kirk Muller, Mont.	1.00
☐	Cam Neely, Bost.	2.00
☐	Sandis Ozolinsh, SanJ.	1.00
☐	Félix Potvin (G), Toro.	1.00
☐	Luc Robitaille, NYRa.	3.00
☐	Brendan Shanahan, SLou.	2.00
☐	Scott Stevens, NJer.	1.00
☐	Pierre Turgeon, Mont.	1.50

FIGURES

Figures were available in American (English text) and Canadian (bilingual text) packaging. The figures and cards in each type of package are the same. Priced below are retail selling prices for packaged figures (each package includes one card) and loose figures.

Canadian Set (13 packages): - 200.00
American Set (19 packages): 250.00
Figure Set (21 loose figures): 65.00

	Player	**US**	**CAN**	**Loose**
☐	Arturs Irbe (G), SanJ.	-	20.00	5.00
☐	Tom Barrasso (G), Pitt.	-	25.00	5.00
☐	Rob Blake, LosA.	12.00	12.00	3.00
☐	Martin Brodeur (G), NJer.	30.00	30.00	8.00
☐	Pavel Bure, Vanc.	15.00	-	3.00
☐	Chris Chelios, Chic.	15.00	15.00	3.00
☐	Bob Corkum, Anah.	12.00	-	3.00
☐	Sergei Fedorov, Detr.	15.00	-	3.00
☐	Theoren Fleury, Calg.	15.00	15.00	3.00
☐	Adam Graves, NYRa.	12.00	12.00	3.00
☐	Dominik Hasek (G), Buff.	35.00	35.00	8.00
☐	Brett Hull, SLou.	15.00	-	3.00
☐	Mike Modano, Dall.	15.00	15.00	3.00
☐	Kirk Muller, Mont.	12.00	-	3.00
☐	Cam Neely, Bost.	12.00	12.00	3.00
☐	Sandis Ozolinsh, SanJ.	12.00	-	3.00
☐	Félix Potvin (G), Toro.	25.00	25.00	5.00
☐	Luc Robitaille, NYRa.	12.00	-	3.00
☐	Brendan Shanahan, SLou.	15.00	15.00	3.00
☐	Scott Stevens, NJer.	12.00	12.00	3.00
☐	Pierre Turgeon, Mont.	12.00	-	3.00

1995 - 96 STARTING LINEUP / CANADIAN LEGENDS

One card was packaged with each figure.

	Complete Set (6 cards):	**15.00**
	Player	**Card**
☐	Jean Béliveau, Mont.	4.00
☐	Phil Esposito, Bost.	2.00
☐	Tony Esposito, Chic.	2.00
☐	Gordie Howe, Detr.	5.50
☐	Bobby Hull, Chic.	3.50
☐	Maurice Richard, Mont.	5.50

FIGURES

Priced below are retail selling prices for packaged figures (each package includes one card) and loose figures.

	Complete Set (6 packages):	**100.00**	**20.00**
	Figure	**Pack.**	**Loose**
☐	Jean Béliveau, Mont.	20.00	4.00
☐	Phil Esposito, Bost.	15.00	4.00
☐	Tony Esposito, Chic.	15.00	4.00
☐	Gordie Howe, Detr.	25.00	5.00
☐	Bobby Hull, Chic.	20.00	4.00
☐	Maurice Richard, Mont.	25.00	5.00

1995 - 96 STARTING LINEUP / TIMELESS LEGENDS

This nine-figure set features only two hockey players.

	Player	**Pack.**	**Loose**
☐	Gordie Howe, Detr.	25.00	5.00
☐	Bobby Hull, Chic.	20.00	4.00

1995 - 96 SUPER STICKER

These stickers were issed by Imperial Toy. There is no set album. Team Decals feature a team logo and the facsimile of a player's signature. The most expensive single is Wayne Gretzky at $1-2. Stars sell at 25¢-$1.00; commons start at 10¢.

Imprint: 1996 Bashan - Shabtai LTD.

Complete Set (136 stickers): **20.00**
Common Player: **.20**

	Player		**NRMT-MT**
☐	1 Anah. Mighty Ducks	☐	2 Paul Kariya
☐	3 Chad Kilger	☐	4 Oleg Tverdovsky
☐	5 Boston Bruins	☐	6 Ray Bourque
☐	7 Cam Neely	☐	8 Adam Oates
☐	9 Kevin Stevens	☐	10 Buffalo Sabres
☐	11 Pat LaFontaine	☐	12 Dominik Hasek (G)
☐	13 Alexei Zhitnik	☐	14 Calgary Flames
☐	15 Theoren Fleury	☐	16 Phil Housley
☐	17 Trevor Kidd (G)	☐	18 Joe Nieuwendyk
☐	19 Zarley Zalapski	☐	20 Chicago Blackhawks
☐	21 Jeremy Roenick	☐	22 Chris Chelios
☐	23 Ed Belfour (G)	☐	24 Joe Murphy
☐	25 Patrick Poulin	☐	26 Colorado Avalanche
☐	27 Joe Sakic	☐	28 Peter Forsberg

☐ 29 Sandis Ozolinsh	☐ 30 Mike Ricci
☐ 31 Valeri Kamensky	☐ 32 Dallas Stars
☐ 35 Andy Moog (G)	☐ 36 Detroit Red Wings
☐ 33 Mike Modano	☐ 34 Kevin Hatcher
☐ 37 Steve Yzerman	☐ 38 Sergei Fedorov
☐ 39 Paul Coffey	☐ 40 Keith Primeau
☐ 41 Nicklas Lidström	☐ 42 Edmonton Oilers
☐ 43 Doug Weight	☐ 44 Jason Arnott
☐ 45 Bill Ranford (G)	☐ 46 Florida Panthers
☐ 49 Scott Mellanby	☐ 50 Rob Niedermayer
☐ 47 J. Vanbiesbrouck (G)	☐ 48 Stu Barnes
☐ 51 Hartford Whalers	☐ 52 Brendan Shanahan
☐ 53 Geoff Sanderson	☐ 54 Sean Burke (G)
☐ 55 Jeff O'Neill	☐ 56 Los Angeles Kings
☐ 57 Wayne Gretzky	☐ 58 Rob Blake
☐ 59 Rick Tocchet	☐ 60 Dimitri Khristich
☐ 63 Pierre Turgeon	☐ 64 Mark Recchi
☐ 61 Kelly Hrudey (G)	☐ 62 Montréal Canadiens
☐ 65 Saku Koivu	☐ 66 Patrick Roy (G)
☐ 67 Vincent Damphousse	☐ 68 New Jersey Devils
☐ 69 Stéphane Richer	☐ 70 Martin Brodeur (G)
☐ 71 Scott Niedermayer	☐ 72 Scott Stevens
☐ 73 New York Islanders	☐ 74 Kirk Muller
☐ 75 Mathieu Schneider	☐ 76 Derek King
☐ 77 Wendel Clark	☐ 78 New York Rangers
☐ 79 Brian Leetch	☐ 80 Mark Messier
☐ 81 Alexei Kovalev	☐ 82 Luc Robitaille
☐ 83 Mike Richter (G)	☐ 84 Ottawa Senators
☐ 87 Steve Duchesne	☐ 88 Radek Bonk
☐ 85 Dan Quinn	☐ 86 Alexandre Daigle
☐ 89 Philadelphia Flyers	☐ 90 Eric Lindros
☐ 91 Mikael Renberg	☐ 92 John LeClair
☐ 93 Eric Desjardins	☐ 94 Rod Brind'Amour
☐ 95 Pittsburgh Penguins	☐ 96 Jaromir Jagr
☐ 97 Mario Lemieux	☐ 98 Ron Francis
☐ 99 Sergei Zubov	☐ 100 St. Louis Blues
☐ 101 Brett Hull	☐ 102 Al MacInnis
☐ 103 Dale Hawerchuk	☐ 104 Chris Pronger
☐ 105 San Jose Sharks	☐ 106 Craig Janney
☐ 107 Pat Falloon	☐ 108 Arturs Irbe (G)
☐ 109 Ulf Dahlen	☐ 110 Owen Nolan
☐ 111 Tamp. Lightning	☐ 112 Roman Hamrlik
☐ 113 Brian Bradley	☐ 114 Chris Gratton
☐ 115 Brian Bellows	☐ 116 Toronto Maple Leafs
☐ 117 Doug Gilmour	☐ 118 Mats Sundin
☐ 119 Dave Andreychuk	☐ 120 Félix Potvin (G)
☐ 121 Larry Murphy	☐ 122 Vancouver Canucks
☐ 123 Pavel Bure	☐ 124 Alexander Mogilny
☐ 125 Trevor Linden	☐ 126 Jeff Brown
☐ 127 Kirk McLean (G)	☐ 128 Washington Capitals
☐ 129 Joé Juneau	☐ 130 Peter Bondra
☐ 131 Jim Carey (G)	☐ 132 Calle Johansson
☐ 135 Alexei Zhamnov	☐ 136 Keith Tkachuk
☐ 133 Winnipeg Jets	☐ 134 Teemu Selänne

DIE-CUT

Insert Set (25 stickers): 10.00

	Insert	DC
☐	1 Pierre Turgeon, Mont.	.35
☐	2 Patrick Roy (G), Mont.	2.00
☐	3 Pat LaFontaine, Buff.	.35
☐	4 Joe Sakic, Québ.	1.00
☐	5 Paul Coffey, Detr.	.35
☐	6 Raymond Bourque, Bost.	.50
☐	7 Brian Leetch, NYRa.	.35
☐	8 Joé Juneau, Wash.	.35
☐	9 Jeremy Roenick, Chic.	.50
☐	10 Chris Chelios, Chic.	.35
☐	11 Brett Hull, SLou.	.50
☐	12 Paul Kariya, Anah.	1.00
☐	13 Jason Arnott, Edmo.	.35
☐	14 Pavel Bure, Vanc.	.50
☐	15 Steve Duchesne, Otta.	.35
☐	16 Martin Brodeur (G), NJer.	1.00
☐	17 Eric Lindros, Phil.	.50
☐	18 Mikael Renberg, Phil.	.35
☐	19 Félix Potvin (G), Toro.	.35
☐	20 Roman Hamrlik, Tamp.	.35
☐	21 Wayne Gretzky, LosA.	3.00
☐	22 Brendan Shanahan, SLou.	.50
☐	23 Jaromir Jagr, Pitt.	.50
☐	24 Mario Lemieux, Pitt.	2.00
☐	25 Steve Yzerman, Detr.	1.50

1995 - 96 TOPPS

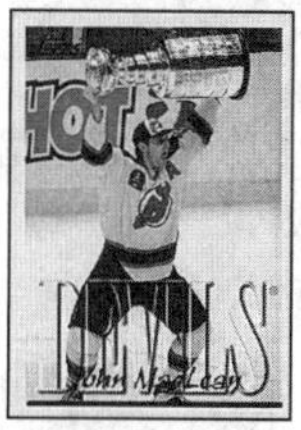

O-Pee-Chee parallel cards for numbers 1-385 were inserted into Series Two packs. O-Pee-Chee cards 257, 326, 333, 351, 359 and 373-385 are short printed.

Marquee Men cards have a third parallel called Power Boosters which were inserted in Series One (1-22) and Series Two (373-383) packs. Power Boosters are printed on a thicker card stock.

Complete Set (385 cards): — 585.00 40.00
Series One Power Booster Set (22 cards)565.00— —
Series Two Power Booster Set (11 cards)630.00— —
Common Player: 3.00 .50 .20

	Player	PB	OPC	Top.
☐☐☐	1 Lindros, Phil. [MM]	6.00	5.00	.50
☐☐☐	2 Hasek (G), Buff. [MM]	6.00	5.00	.50
☐☐☐	3 Roenick, Chic. [MM]	4.00	4.00	.20
☐☐☐	4 Paul Coffey, Detr. [MM]	3.00	3.00	.20
☐☐☐	5 Messier, NYRa. [MM]	6.00	5.00	.50
☐☐☐	6 Bondra, Wash. [MM]	3.00	3.00	.20
☐☐☐	7 Kariya, Anah. [MM]	8.00	7.00	.50
☐☐☐	8 Chelios, Chic. [MM]	3.00	3.00	.20
☐☐☐	9 Brodeur (G), NJer. [MM]	10.00	8.00	.50
☐☐☐	10 Brett Hull, SLou. [MM]	6.00	5.00	.50
☐☐☐	11 Vernon (G), Detr. [MM]	3.00	2.00	.20
☐☐☐	12 Linden, Vanc. [MM]	3.00	2.00	.20
☐☐☐	13 LaFontaine, Buff. [MM]	3.00	3.00	.20
☐☐☐	14 Sanderson, Hart. [MM]	3.00	1.00	.20
☐☐☐	15 Cam Neely, Bost. [MM]	6.00	5.00	.50
☐☐☐	16 Shanahan, SLou. [MM]	6.00	5.00	.50
☐☐☐	17 Arnott, Edmo. [MM]	3.00	2.00	.20
☐☐☐	18 Renberg, Phil. [MM]	3.00	1.50	.20
☐☐☐	19 Sundin, Toro. [MM]	6.00	5.00	.50
☐☐☐	20 Pavel Bure, Vanc. [MM]	4.00	4.00	.20
☐☐☐	21 Turgeon, Mont. [MM]	3.00	2.00	.20
☐☐☐	22 Zhamnov, Winn. [MM]	3.00	1.50	.20
☐☐	23 Blaine Lacher (G), Bost.		.50	.20
☐☐	**24 Brian Holzinger, Buff. RC**		**2.00**	**.50**
☐☐	25 Theoren Fleury, Calg.		3.00	.20
☐☐	26 Éric Dazé, Chic.		4.00	.20
☐☐	27 Mike Kennedy, Dall.		.50	.20
☐☐	28 Darren McCarty, Detr.		1.50	.20
☐☐	29 Todd Marchant, Edmo.		1.00	.20
☐☐	30 Andrew Cassels, Hart.		1.00	.20
☐☐	31 Rob Niedermayer, Flor.		1.00	.20
☐☐	32 Éric Lacroix, LosA.		.50	.20
☐☐	33 Steve Rucchin, Anah.		1.00	.20
☐☐	34 Turner Stevenson, Mont.		.50	.20
☐☐	35 Sergei Brylin, NJer.		.50	.20
☐☐	36 Mathieu Schneider, NYIs.		1.00	.20
☐☐	37 Pat Verbeek, NYRa.		1.50	.20
☐☐	**38 Steve Larouche, Otta. RC**		**1.50**	**.50**
☐☐	39 Rod Brind'Amour, Phil.		1.50	.20
☐☐	40 Luc Robitaille, Pitt.		4.00	.20
☐☐	41 Brett Lindros, NYIs.		1.50	.20
☐☐	42 Shean Donovan, SanJ.		.50	.20
☐☐	43 David Roberts, SLou.		.50	.20
☐☐	44 Cory Cross, Tamp.		.50	.20
☐☐	45 Todd Warriner, Toro.		1.50	.20
☐☐	46 Yevgeny Namestnikov, Vanc.		.50	.20
☐☐	47 Sergei Gonchar, Wash.		1.50	.20
☐☐	48 Nikolai Khabibulin (G), Winn.		2.00	.20
☐☐	49 Alexei Zhitnik, Buff.		.50	.20
☐☐	50 Raymond Bourque, Bost.		6.00	.50
☐☐	51 Paul Kruse, Calg.		.50	.20
☐☐	52 Murray Craven, Chic.		.50	.20
☐☐	53 Andy Moog (G), Dall.		2.00	.20
☐☐	54 Keith Primeau, Detr.		2.00	.20
☐☐	55 Shayne Corson, Edmo.		1.50	.20
☐☐	56 Johan Garpenlöv, Flor.		.50	.20
☐☐	57 Marek Malik, Hart.		.50	.20
☐☐	58 Tony Granato, LosA.		1.00	.20
☐☐	59 Bob Corkum, Anah.		.50	.20
☐☐	60 Patrick Roy (G), Mont.		15.00	1.50
☐☐	**61 Chris McAlpine, NJer. RC**		**1.50**	**.50**
☐☐	**62 Chris Marinucci, NYIs. RC**		**1.50**	**.50**
☐☐	63 Jeff Beukeboom, NYRa.		.50	.20
☐☐	64 Radek Bonk, Otta.		1.50	.20
☐☐	65 John LeClair, Phil.		4.00	.20
☐☐	66 Len Barrie, Pitt.		.50	.20
☐☐	67 Teppo Numminen, Winn.		1.50	.20
☐☐	68 Ray Whitney, SanJ.		1.00	.20
☐☐	69 Jeff Norton, SLou.		.50	.20
☐☐	70 Chris Gratton, Tamp.		1.00	.20
☐☐	71 Benoît Hogue, Toro.		.50	.20
☐☐	72 Bret Hedican, Vanc.		.50	.20
☐☐	73 Keith Jones, Wash.		.50	.20
☐☐	74 John Cullen, Tamp.		1.00	.20
☐☐	75 Brian Leetch, NYRa.		3.00	.20
☐☐	76 David Reid, Bost.		.50	.20
☐☐	77 Dino Ciccarelli, Detr.		1.50	.20
☐☐	78 Gary Roberts, Calg.		2.00	.20
☐☐	79 Tony Amonte, Chic.		3.00	.20
☐☐	80 Mike Modano, Dall.		5.00	.50
☐☐	81 Doug Brown, Detr.		.50	.20
☐☐	82 Scott Thornton, Edmo.		.50	.20
☐☐	83 Bill Lindsay, Flor.		.50	.20
☐☐	84 Frantisek Kucera, Hart.		.50	.20
☐☐	85 Wayne Gretzky, LosA.		20.00	2.00
☐☐	86 Joe Sacco, Anah.		.50	.20
☐☐	87 Benoît Brunet, Mont.		.50	.20
☐☐	88 Bill Guerin, NJer. [w/ Cup]		2.00	.20
☐☐	89 Travis Green, NYIs.		1.00	.20
☐☐	90 Alexei Kovalev, NYRa.		3.00	.20
☐☐	91 Stanislav Neckar, Otta.		.50	.20
☐☐	92 Rob DiMaio, Phil.		.50	.20
☐☐	93 Chris Joseph (G), Pitt.		.50	.20
☐☐	**94 Craig Martin, Winn. RC**		**1.50**	**.50**
☐☐	95 Craig Janney, SanJ.		1.00	.20
☐☐	96 Greg Gilbert, SLou.		.50	.20
☐☐	97 Alexander Semak, Tamp.		.50	.20
☐☐	98 Mike Gartner, Toro.		4.00	.20
☐☐	99 Cliff Ronning, Vanc.		1.00	.20
☐☐	100 Mario Lemieux, Pitt.		15.00	1.50
☐☐	101 Jassen Cullimore, Vanc.		.50	.20
☐☐	102 Steve Duchesne, SLou.		1.00	.20
☐☐	103 Derek Plante, Buff.		.50	.20
☐☐	104 John Gruden, Bost.		.50	.20
☐☐	105 Michal Sykora, SanJ.		.50	.20
☐☐	106 Trent Klatt, Dall.		.50	.20
☐☐	107 Nicklas Lidström, Detr.		3.00	.20
☐☐	108 Luke Richardson, Edmo.		.50	.20
☐☐	109 Steven Rice, Hart.		.50	.20
☐☐	110 Stu Barnes, Flor.		.50	.20
☐☐	111 John Druce, LosA.		.50	.20
☐☐	112 Guy Hebert (G), Anah.		1.00	.20
☐☐	113 Vladimir Malakhov, Mont.		.50	.20
☐☐	114 Claude Lemieux w/ Cup		1.50	.20
☐☐	115 Kirk Muller, NYIs.		1.50	.20
☐☐	**116 Darren Langdon, NYRa. RC**		**3.50**	**1.00**
☐☐	117 Rob Gaudreau, Otta.		.50	.20
☐☐	118 Karl Dykhuis, Phil.		.50	.20
☐☐	119 Richard Park, Pitt.		1.00	.20
☐☐	120 Dave Manson, Winn.		.50	.20
☐☐	121 Andrei Nazarov, SanJ.		.50	.20
☐☐	122 Bernie Nicholls, Chic.		1.00	.20
☐☐	123 Mikael Andersson, Tamp.		.50	.20
☐☐	124 Todd Gill, Toro.		.50	.20
☐☐	125 Trevor Linden, Vanc.		2.00	.20
☐☐	126 Kelly Miller, Wash.		.50	.20
☐☐	127 Don Sweeney, Bost.		.50	.20
☐☐	128 Jason Dawe, Buff.		.50	.20
☐☐	129 Steve Chiasson, Calg.		.50	.20
☐☐	130 Ed Belfour (G), Chic.		5.00	.50
☐☐	131 Kerry Huffman, Otta.		.50	.20
☐☐	132 Tim Taylor, Detr.		.50	.20
☐☐	133 Kirk Maltby, Edmo.		1.00	.20
☐☐	134 Jody Hull, Flor.		.50	.20
☐☐	135 Sean Burke (G), Hart.		3.00	.20
☐☐	136 Philippe Boucher, LosA.		.50	.20
☐☐	137 Valeri Karpov, Anah.		.50	.20
☐☐	138 Yves Racine, Mont.		.50	.20
☐☐	139 Patrick Flatley, NYIs.		.50	.20
☐☐	140 John MacLean w/ Cup		.50	.20
☐☐	141 Sergei Nemchinov, NYRa.		1.00	.20
☐☐	142 Don Beaupré (G), Otta.		.50	.20
☐☐	143 Kevin Dineen, Phil.		.50	.20
☐☐	144 Ulf Samuelsson, Pitt.		.50	.20
☐☐	145 Al MacInnis, SLou.		2.00	.20
☐☐	146 Igor Korolev, Winn.		.50	.20
☐☐	147 Pat Falloon, SanJ.		.50	.20
☐☐	148 Brian Bradley, Tamp.		.50	.20
☐☐	149 Josef Beranek, Vanc.		.50	.20
☐☐	150 Mats Sundin, Toro.		5.00	.50
☐☐	151 Sylvain Côté, Wash.		.50	.20
☐☐	152 Keith Tkachuk, Winn.		3.00	.20
☐☐	153 Mariusz Czerkawski, Bost.		1.00	.20
☐☐	154 Trevor Kidd (G), Calg.		1.50	.20
☐☐	155 Garry Galley, Buff.		.50	.20
☐☐	156 Gary Suter, Chic.		1.00	.20
☐☐	157 Grant Ledyard, Dall.		.50	.20
☐☐	158 Doug Weight, Edmo.		3.00	.20
☐☐	159 Jesse Bélanger, Flor.		.50	.20
☐☐	160 Mike Vernon (G), Detr.		2.00	.20
☐☐	161 Robert Kron, Hart.		.50	.20
☐☐	162 Marty McSorley, LosA.		1.00	.20
☐☐	163 Todd Krygier, Anah.		.50	.20
☐☐	164 Scott Niedermayer, NJer.		1.50	.20
☐☐	165 Mark Recchi, Mont.		2.00	.20
☐☐	166 Phil Housley, Calg.		1.50	.20
☐☐	167 Ron Hextall (G), Phil.		3.00	.20
☐☐	168 Richard Smehlik, Buff.		.50	.20
☐☐	169 Chris Tamer, Pitt.		.50	.20
☐☐	170 Alexei Yashin, Otta.		3.00	.20
☐☐	171 Sergei Makarov, SanJ.		2.00	.20
☐☐	172 Patrice Tardif, SLou.		.50	.20
☐☐	173 Milos Holan, Anah.		.50	.20
☐☐	174 J-C Bergeron, Tamp.		.50	.20
☐☐	175 Dave Andreychuk, Toro.		1.50	.20
☐☐	176 Martin Gélinas, Vanc.		1.00	.20
☐☐	177 Dale Hunter, Wash.		1.50	.20
☐☐	178 Kevin Haller, Phil.		.50	.20
☐☐	179 Jeff Shantz, Chic.		.50	.20
☐☐	180 Adam Oates, Bost.		2.00	.20
☐☐	181 Ronnie Stern, Calg.		.50	.20
☐☐	182 Jamie Langenbrunner, Dall.		2.00	.20
☐☐	183 Mark Fitzpatrick (G), Flor.		.50	.20
☐☐	184 Adam Burt, Hart.		.50	.20
☐☐	185 Sergei Fedorov, Detr.		5.00	.50
☐☐	186 Robert Lang, LosA.		1.00	.20
☐☐	**187 Craig Conroy, Mont. RC**		**4.00**	**1.50**
☐☐	188 Ken Daneyko w/ Cup		1.00	.20
☐☐	189 Marko Tuomainen, Edmo.		1.00	.20
☐☐	190 Ken Wregget (G), Pitt.		1.00	.20
☐☐	191 Mike Rathje, SanJ.		.50	.20
☐☐	192 Dmitry Yushkevich, Phil.		1.00	.20
☐☐	193 Roman Hamrlik, Tamp.		1.00	.20
☐☐	194 Russ Courtnall, Vanc.		1.00	.20
☐☐	195 Teemu Selänne, Winn.		4.00	.20
☐☐	196 Jon Rohloff, Bost.		.50	.20
☐☐	197 Derian Hatcher, Dall.		1.50	.20
☐☐	198 Mark Tinordi, Wash.		.50	.20
☐☐	199 Patrice Brisebois, Mont.		.50	.20
☐☐	200 Jaromir Jagr, Pitt.		5.00	.50
☐☐	201 Randy McKay, NJer.		.50	.20
☐☐	202 Derek King, NYIs.		.50	.20
☐☐	203 Tony Twist, SLou.		.50	.20
☐☐	204 Jyrki Lumme, Vanc.		1.00	.20
☐☐	205 J. Steve Smith, Chic.		1.00	.20
☐☐	206 Bob Rouse, Detr.		.50	.20
☐☐	207 Dave Ellett, Toro.		.50	.20
☐☐	**208 Kevin Dean, NJer. RC**		**1.50**	**.50**
☐☐	**209 Rusty Fitzgerald, Pitt. RC**		**1.50**	**.50**
☐☐	210 Jim Carey (G), Wash.		.50	.20
☐☐	211 Kenny Jönsson, Toro.		1.00	.20
☐☐	212 Mike Richter (G), NYRa.		2.00	.20
☐☐	213 Glen Wesley, Hart.		.50	.20
☐☐	214 Donald Audette, Buff.		2.00	.20
☐☐	215 Curtis Joseph (G), SLou.		5.00	.50
☐☐	216 Joé Juneau, Wash.		1.00	.20
☐☐	217 Paul Kariya, Anah.		7.00	.50
☐☐	218 Devils with Cup		.50	.20
☐☐	219 Checklist		.50	.20
☐☐	220 Checklist		.50	.20
☐☐	221 Cam Neely, Bost.		5.00	.50
☐☐	222 Wayne Primeau, Buff.		2.00	.50
☐☐	223 Yanic Perreault, LosA.		1.50	.20
☐☐	224 Pierre Turgeon, Mont.		2.00	.20
☐☐	225 Alexander Mogilny, Vanc.		2.00	.20
☐☐	226 Daren Puppa (G), Tamp.		1.00	.20
☐☐	227 Ulf Dahlén, SanJ.		.50	.20
☐☐	228 Tomas Sandström, Pitt.		1.00	.20
☐☐	229 Shayne Corson, SLou.		1.50	.20
☐☐	230 Chris Chelios, Chic.		3.00	.20
☐☐	231 Stéphane Richer, NJer.		1.00	.20
☐☐	232 Paul Ranheim, Hart.		.50	.20
☐☐	233 Joe Nieuwendyk, Calg.		2.00	.20
☐☐	234 Doug Gilmour, Toro.		3.00	.20
☐☐	235 Jeremy Roenick, Chic.		4.00	.20
☐☐	236 Joel Otto, Phil.		.50	.20
☐☐	237 Steve Yzerman, Detr.		12.00	1.00
☐☐	238 Petr Klima, Tamp.		.50	.20
☐☐	239 Jari Kurri, LosA.		5.00	.50
☐☐	240 Mark Messier, NYRa.		5.00	.50
☐☐	241 Bill Ranford (G), Edmo.		2.00	.20
☐☐	242 Grant Fuhr (G), SLou.		3.00	.20
☐☐	243 Brent Severyn, NYIs.		.50	.20
☐☐	244 Ron Francis, Pitt.		3.00	.20
☐☐	245 Ray Ferraro, NYRa.		.50	.20
☐☐	246 Martin Straka, Otta.		1.50	.20
☐☐	247 Gerald Diduck, Hart.		.50	.20
☐☐	248 Dmitri Khristich, LosA.		.50	.20
☐☐	**249 Wade Flaherty, SanJ. RC**		**2.00**	**.50**
☐☐	250 Pat LaFontaine, Buff.		3.00	.20
☐☐	251 Darren Turcotte, Winn.		.50	.20
☐☐	252 J. Vanbiesbrouck (G), Flor.		2.00	.20
☐☐	253 Brian Bellows, Tamp.		1.00	.20
☐☐	254 Dave Gagner, Dall.		.50	.20
☐☐	255 Larry Murphy, Toro.		1.00	.20
☐☐	256 Steve Thomas, NJer.		1.00	.20
☐☐	**257 Robert Svehla, Flor. RC**		**8.00**	**1.00**
☐☐	258 Deron Quint, Winn.		1.50	.20
☐☐	259 Kjell Samuelsson, Phil.		.50	.20
☐☐	260 Scott Mellanby, Flor.		1.00	.20
☐☐	261 Dan Quinn, Otta.		.50	.20
☐☐	262 Tom Barrasso (G), Pitt.		2.00	.20
☐☐	263 Zarley Zalapski, Calg.		.50	.20
☐☐	264 Rick Tocchet, LosA.		1.50	.20
☐☐	265 Paul Coffey, Detr.		3.00	.20
☐☐	266 Joe Sakic, Colo.		8.00	.50
☐☐	**267 Aki Berg, LosA. RC**		**2.00**	**.50**
☐☐	268 Jeff R. Brown, Vanc.		.50	.20
☐☐	269 Wendel Clark, NYIs.		4.00	.20
☐☐	270 Vincent Damphousse, Mont.		3.00	.20
☐☐	271 Dale Hawerchuk, SLou.		3.00	.20
☐☐	**272 Rhett Warrener, Flor. RC**		**1.50**	**.50**
☐☐	273 Kevin Hatcher, Dall.		.50	.20
☐☐	274 Calle Johansson, Wash.		1.00	.20
☐☐	275 Scott Stevens, NJer.		2.00	.20
☐☐	276 Geoff Courtnall, SLou.		.50	.20
☐☐	277 Kirk McLean (G), Vanc.		1.50	.20
☐☐	278 Stephen Heinze, Bost.		.50	.20
☐☐	279 Sylvain Lefebvre, Colo.		.50	.20
☐☐	280 Joe Murphy, Chic.		.50	.20
☐☐	281 Mike Keane, Mont.		.50	.20
☐☐	282 Kevin Stevens, Bost.		1.00	.20
☐☐	**283 Miroslav Satan, Edmo. RC**		**4.00**	**1.50**
☐☐	284 Stéphane Fiset (G), Colo.		1.50	.20
☐☐	285 Jeff O'Neill, Hart.		4.00	.20
☐☐	**286 Denny Lambert, Anah. RC**		**1.50**	**.50**
☐☐	**287 M. Ragnarsson, SanJ. RC**		**3.50**	**1.00**
☐☐	288 Adam Deadmarsh, Colo.		1.50	.20
☐☐	289 Eric Weinrich, Chic.		.50	.20
☐☐	290 Éric Desjardins, Phil.		1.50	.20
☐☐	291 Tim Chevelade (G), Winn.		.50	.20
☐☐	292 Glenn Healy (G), NYRa.		1.00	.20
☐☐	293 Byron Dafoe (G), LosA.		2.00	.20
☐☐	294 Tom Fitzgerald, Flor.		.50	.20
☐☐	295 Adam Graves, NYRa.		2.00	.20
☐☐	296 Arturs Irbe (G), SanJ.		2.00	.20
☐☐	297 Shaun Van Allen, Anah.		.50	.20
☐☐	298 Kelly Buchberger, Edmo.		.50	.20
☐☐	299 Bob Probert, Chic.		1.50	.20
☐☐	300 Pavel Bure, Vanc.		4.00	.20
☐☐	**301 Chad Kilger, Anah. RC**		**3.50**	**1.00**
☐☐	302 Dominik Hasek (G), Buff.		5.00	.50
☐☐	303 Bobby Holik, NJer.		1.50	.20
☐☐	304 Petr Nedved, Pitt.		1.50	.20
☐☐	305 Owen Nolan, SanJ.		3.00	.20
☐☐	306 Saku Koivu, Mont.		8.00	.50
☐☐	307 Rob Blake, LosA.		3.00	.20
☐☐	308 Chris Pronger, SLou.		3.00	.20
☐☐	**309 Kyle McLaren, Bost. RC**		**3.50**	**1.00**
☐☐	310 Peter Bondra, Wash.		3.00	.20
☐☐	311 Nelson Emerson, Hart.		.50	.20
☐☐	312 Bryan McCabe, NYIs.		2.00	.20
☐☐	313 Darcy Wakaluk, Dall.		.50	.20
☐☐	**314 Shane Doan, Winn. RC**		**3.50**	**1.00**
☐☐	315 Félix Potvin (G), Toro.		3.00	.20
☐☐	316 Jim Dowd, NJer.		.50	.20
☐☐	317 Roman Oksiuta, Vanc.		.50	.20
☐☐	318 Geoff Sanderson, Hart.		1.00	.20
☐☐	**319 Radek Dvorak, Flor. RC**		**3.50**	**1.00**
☐☐	320 Paul Ysebaert, Tamp.		.50	.20
☐☐	321 Shawn McEachern, Bost.		1.50	.20
☐☐	322 Vyacheslav Kozlov, Detr.		1.00	.20
☐☐	323 Marty McInnis, NYIs.		.50	.20
☐☐	324 Ted Donato, Bost.		.50	.20
☐☐	325 Martin Brodeur (G), NJer.		8.00	.50
☐☐	326 Patrick Poulin, Chic.		8.00	.20
☐☐	327 Eric Lindros, Phil.		5.00	.50
☐☐	328 Dallas Drake, Winn.		.50	.20
☐☐	329 Sean Hill, Otta.		.50	.20
☐☐	330 Michal Pivonka, Wash.		.50	.20
☐☐	331 Alexei Zhamnov, Winn.		1.50	.20
☐☐	332 Cory Stillman, Calg.		1.00	.20
☐☐	333 Sergei Zubov, Pitt.		8.00	.20
☐☐	334 T. Söderström (G), NYIs.		.50	.20
☐☐	335 Patrik Carnbäck, Anah.		.50	.20
☐☐	**336 Joe Dziedzic, Pitt. RC**		**1.50**	**.50**
☐☐	337 Steve Duchesne, Otta.		1.00	.20
☐☐	338 Marty Murray, Calg.		1.00	.20
☐☐	**339 Todd Bertuzzi, NYIs. RC**		**18.00**	**6.00**
☐☐	340 Jason Arnott, Edmo.		2.00	.20
☐☐	341 Niklas Sundström, NYRa.		2.00	.20
☐☐	342 Alexandre Daigle, Otta.		.50	.20
☐☐	343 Jocelyn Thibault (G), Mont.		2.00	.20
☐☐	344 Mikhail Shtalenkov, Anah.		.50	.20
☐☐	345 Chris Osgood (G), Detr.		3.00	.20
☐☐	346 Brendan Witt, Wash.		1.00	.20
☐☐	347 Ian Laperrière, SLou.		.50	.20
☐☐	348 Zigmund Palffy, NYIs.		3.00	.20
☐☐	349 Brian Savage, Mont.		1.50	.20
☐☐	350 Michael Peca, Buff.		2.00	.20
☐☐	351 Vitali Yachmenev, LosA.		8.00	.20
☐☐	352 Luc Robitaille, NYRa.		4.00	.20
☐☐	353 Mikael Renberg, Phil.		1.50	.20
☐☐	354 Ed Jovanovski, Flor.		4.00	.20

□ □	355 Jason Doig, Winn.		1.00	.20
□ □	356 Todd Harvey, Dall.		1.00	.20
□ □	357 Viktor Kozlov, SanJ.		1.50	.20
□ □	358 Valeri Bure, Mont.		1.50	.20
□ □	359 Peter Forsberg, Colo.		30.00	.50
□ □	360 Jeff Friesen, SanJ.		1.50	.20
□ □	361 Andrei Nikolishin, Hart.		.50	.20
□ □	362 Brian Rolston, NJer.		1.50	.20
□ □	363 Jamie Storr (G), LosA.		1.00	.20
□ □	364 Chris Therien, Phil.		.50	.20
□ □	365 Oleg Tverdovsky, Anah.		.50	.20
□ □	366 David Oliver, Edmo.		.50	.20
□ □	367 Alexander Selivanov, Tamp.		.50	.20
□ □	**368 Alek Stojanov, Vanc. RC**		**1.50**	**.50**
□ □	**369 D. Alfredsson, Otta. RC**		**9.00**	**3.00**
□ □	370 Brendan Shanahan, Hart.		5.00	.50
□ □	371 Yuri Khmylev, Buff.		.50	.20
□ □	372 Brett Hull, SLou.		5.00	.50
□ □ □	373 Fedorov, Detr. [MM]	6.00	20.00	.50
□ □ □	374 Jagr, Pitt. [MM]	6.00	20.00	.50
□ □ □	375 Gretzky, LosA. [MM]	24.00	100.00	2.00
□ □ □	376 Mogilny, Vanc. [MM]	3.00	10.50	.20
□ □ □	377 Roy (G), Mont. [MM]	18.00	65.00	1.50
□ □ □	378 Belfour (G), Chic. [MM]	6.00	20.00	.50
□ □ □	379 Robitaille, NYRa. [MM]	4.00	15.00	.20
□ □ □	380 Forsberg, Colo. [MM]	8.00	30.00	.50
□ □ □	381 Oates, Bost. [MM]	3.00	9.00	.20
□ □ □	382 Fleury, Calg. [MM]	3.00	10.00	.20
□ □ □	383 Carey (G), Wash. [MM]	3.00	8.00	.20
□ □	384 Checklist		8.00	.20
□ □	385 Checklist		8.00	.20

CANADIAN GOLD

Series One Insert Set (10 cards):		**80.00**
	Insert (1:36)	**CG**
□	1CG Patrick Roy (G), Mont.	35.00
□	2CG Alexei Yashin, Otta.	6.00
□	3CG Jason Arnott, Edmo.	6.00
□	4CG Trevor Kidd (G), Calg.	4.00
□	5CG Pavel Bure, Vanc.	10.00
□	6CG Theoren Fleury, Calg.	6.00
□	7CG Pierre Turgeon, Mont.	4.00
□	8CG Félix Potvin (G), Toro.	6.00
□	9CG Teemu Selänne, Winn.	10.00
□	10CG Mats Sundin, Toro.	12.00

CANADIAN WORLD JUNIORS

Series One Insert Set (22 cards):		**15.00**
	Insert (1:18)	**CJ**
□	1CJ Wade Redden, Canada Juniors	1.00
□	2CJ Jamie Storr (G), Canada Juniors	.50
□	3CJ Larry Courville, Canada Juniors	.50
□	4CJ Jason Allison, Canada Juniors	2.00
□	5CJ Alexandre Daigle, Canada Juniors	.50
□	6CJ Marty Murray, Canada Juniors	.50
□	7CJ Bryan McCabe, Canada Juniors	.50
□	8CJ Ryan Smyth, Canada Juniors	1.50
□	9CJ Lee Sorochan, Canada Juniors	.50
□	10CJ Todd Harvey, Canada Juniors	.50
□	11CJ Nolan Baumgartner, Canada Juniors	.50
□	12CJ Denis Pederson, Canada Juniors	.50
□	13CJ Shean Donovan, Canada Juniors	.50
□	14CJ Jason Botterill, Canada Juniors	.50
□	15CJ Jeff Friesen, Canada Juniors	1.00
□	16CJ Darcy Tucker, Canada Juniors	.50
□	17CJ Chad Allan, Canada Juniors	.50
□	18CJ Dan Cloutier (G), Canada Juniors	1.50
□	19CJ Éric Dazé, Canada Juniors	1.50
□	20CJ Jeff O'Neill, Canada Juniors	1.50
□	21CJ Jamie Rivers, Canada Juniors	.50
□	22CJ Ed Jovanovski, Canada Juniors	1.50

HIDDEN GEMS

Series One Insert Set (15 cards):		**35.00**
	Insert (1:24)	**HG**
□	1HG Theoren Fleury, Calg.	3.00
□	2HG Luc Robitaille, Pitt.	5.00
□	3HG Doug Gilmour, Toro.	3.00
□	4HG Dominik Hasek (G), Buff.	6.00
□	5HG Pavel Bure, Vanc.	5.00
□	6HG Peter Bondra, Wash.	3.00
□	7HG Steve Larmer, NYRa.	2.00
□	8HG David Oliver, Edmo.	1.00
□	9HG Gary Suter, Chic.	1.00
□	10HG Brett Hull, SLou.	6.00
□	11HG Kevin Stevens, Pitt.	1.00
□	12HG Ron Hextall (G), Phil.	3.00
□	13HG Kirk McLean (G), Vanc.	2.00
□	14HG Andy Moog (G), Dall.	2.00
□	15HG Rick Tocchet, LosA.	2.00

HOME GROWN CANADA

Cards 1-15 were inserted in retail packs while cards 16-30 were inserted in hobby packs.

Series One Cdn. Retail Set (15 cards):		**115.00**
Series Two Cdn. Hobby Set (15 cards):		**405.00**
	Insert	**HGC**
□	HGC1 Patrick Roy (G), Mont.	40.00
□	HGC2 Wendel Clark, NYIs.	10.00
□	HGC3 Pierre Turgeon, Mont.	5.00
□	HGC4 Doug Gilmour, Toro.	5.00
□	HGC5 Theoren Fleury, Calg.	5.00
□	HGC6 Eric Lindros, Phil.	10.00
□	HGC7 Paul Kariya, Anah.	15.00
□	HGC8 Bill Ranford (G), Edmo.	5.00
□	HGC9 Raymond Bourque, Bost.	15.00
□	HGC10 Brendan Shanahan, Hart.	10.00
□	HGC11 Paul Coffey, Detr.	5.00
□	HGC12 Trevor Linden, Vanc.	5.00
□	HGC13 Trevor Kidd (G), Calg.	3.00
□	HGC14 Alexandre Daigle, Otta.	3.00
□	HGC15 Chris Pronger, SLou.	5.00
□	HGC16 Steve Yzerman, Detr.	75.00
□	HGC17 Todd Harvey, Dall.	6.00
□	HGC18 Félix Potvin (G), Toro.	15.00
□	HGC19 Luc Robitaille, Pitt.	25.00
□	HGC20 Wayne Gretzky, LosA.	125.00
□	HGC21 Keith Primeau, Detr.	10.00
□	HGC22 Al MacInnis, SLou.	10.00
□	HGC23 Cam Neely, Bost.	30.00
□	HGC24 Ed Belfour (G), Chic.	30.00
□	HGC25 Joé Juneau, Wash.	6.00
□	HGC26 Adam Graves, NYRa.	10.00
□	HGC27 Mark Recchi, Mont.	10.00
□	HGC28 Stéphane Richer, NJer.	6.00
□	HGC29 Mark Messier, NYRa.	30.00
□	HGC30 Mario Lemieux, Pitt.	90.00

HOME GROWN U.S.A.

U.S. Set (10 cards):		**50.00**
	Insert (1:36)	**HGA**
□	HGA1 Brian Leetch, NYRa.	6.00
□	HGA2 Jeremy Roenick, Chic.	8.00
□	HGA3 Mike Modano, Dall.	10.00
□	HGA4 Pat LaFontaine, Buff.	6.00
□	HGA5 Keith Tkachuk, Winn.	6.00
□	HGA6 Chris Chelios, Chic.	6.00
□	HGA7 Darren Turcotte, Hart.	2.00
□	HGA8 John Vanbiesbrouck (G), Flor.	4.00
□	HGA9 John LeClair, Phil.	8.00
□	HGA10 Mike Richter (G), NYRa.	4.00

MYSTERY FINEST

Each card came with a black removable cover on the front. Three players (or four in the case of cards M19-M22) are depicted on the card back. Collectors would remove the black cover to find out which player was depicted on the front and whether the card was a regular insert or a refractor parallel.

Series Two Insert Set (22 cards):		**725.00**	**135.00**
	Insert (1:36)	**MFR**	**MF**
□ □	M1 Wayne Gretzky, LosA.	100.00	20.00
□ □	M2 Mario Lemieux, Pitt.	85.00	16.00
□ □	M3 Mark Messier, NYRa.	60.00	12.00
□ □	M4 Eric Lindros, Phil.	35.00	6.00
□ □	M5 Sergei Fedorov, Detr.	35.00	6.00
□ □	M6 Joe Sakic, Colo.	45.00	8.00
□ □	M7 Brett Hull, SLou.	30.00	6.00
□ □	M8 Jaromir Jagr, Pitt.	30.00	6.00
□ □	M9 Teemu Selänne, Winn.	25.00	4.00
□ □	M10 Brendan Shanahan, Hart.	25.00	4.00
□ □	M11 Cam Neely, Bost.	25.00	4.00
□ □	M12 Mikael Renberg, Phil.	15.00	3.00
□ □	M13 Paul Kariya, Anah.	35.00	6.00
□ □	M14 Keith Tkachuk, Winn.	25.00	4.00
□ □	M15 Pavel Bure, Vanc.	25.00	4.00
□ □	M16 Brian Leetch, NYRa.	15.00	3.00
□ □	M17 Scott Stevens, NJer.	15.00	3.00
□ □	M18 Chris Chelios, Chic.	15.00	3.00
□ □	M19 Dominik Hasek (G), Buff.	50.00	10.00
□ □	M20 Patrick Roy (G), Mont.	75.00	14.00
□ □	M21 Martin Brodeur (G), NJer.	55.00	10.00
□ □	M22 Félix Potvin (G), Toro.	45.00	8.00

NEW TO THE GAME

Series One Insert Set (22 cards):		**10.00**
	Insert (1:1 Retail)	**NG**
□	1NG Jim Carey (G), Wash.	.30
□	2NG Sergei Brylin, NJer.	.30
□	3NG Todd Marchant, Edmo.	.50
□	4NG Oleg Tverdovsky, Anah.	.30
□	5NG Paul Kariya, Anah.	3.50
□	6NG Adam Deadmarsh, Québ. (Colo.)	.50
□	7NG Mike Kennedy, Dall.	.30
□	8NG Roman Oksiuta, Vanc.	.30
□	9NG Kenny Jönsson, Toro.	.50
□	10NG Peter Forsberg, Québ. (Colo.)	3.50
□	11NG Alexander Selivanov, Tamp.	.30
□	12NG Chris Therien, Phil.	.30
□	13NG Brian Rolston, NJer.	.50
□	14NG David Oliver, Edmo.	.30
□	15NG Blaine Lacher (G), Bost.	.30
□	16NG Sergei Krivokrasov, Chic.	.30
□	17NG Todd Harvey, Dall.	.50
□	18NG Jeff Friesen, SanJ.	.50
□	19NG Mariusz Czerkawski, Bost.	.50
□	20NG Ian Laperrière, SLou.	.30
□	21NG Brian Savage, Mont.	.50
□	22NG Andrei Nikolishin, Hart.	.30

POWER LINES

Series One Insert Set (10 cards):		**10.00**
	Insert (1:12)	**PL**
□	1PL J. LeClair / E. Lindros / M. Renberg	4.00
□	2PL K. Tkachuk / A. Zhamnov / T. Selänne	1.50
□	3PL A. Graves / M. Messier / P. Verbeek	1.50
□	4PL P. Poulin / J. Roenick / T. Amonte	1.50
□	5PL K. Stevens / R. Francis / J. Jagr	1.50
□	6PL J. Dawe / P. LaFontaine / A. Mogilny	1.00
□	7PL M. Czerkawski / A. Oates / C. Neely	1.50
□	8PL D. Brown / S. Fedorov / Vy. Kozlov	1.00
□	9PL V. Damphousse / P. Turgeon / M. Recchi	1.00
□	10PL R. McKay / B. Holik / M. Peluso	.50

PROFILES BY MARK MESSIER

Insert Set (20 cards):		**45.00**
	Insert (1:12)	**PF**
□	PF1 Wayne Gretzky, LosA.	10.00
□	PF2 Brian Leetch, NYRa.	1.00
□	PF3 Patrick Roy (G), Mont.	6.00
□	PF4 Jaromir Jagr, Pitt.	2.00
□	PF5 Sergei Fedorov, Detr.	2.00
□	PF6 Martin Brodeur (G), NJer.	4.00
□	PF7 Eric Lindros, Phil.	2.00
□	PF8 Jeremy Roenick, Chic.	2.00
□	PF9 John Vanbiesbrouck (G), Flor.	1.00
□	PF10 Cam Neely, Bost.	2.00
□	PF11 Pavel Bure, Vanc.	2.00
□	PF12 Paul Coffey, Detr.	1.00
□	PF13 Scott Stevens, NJer.	1.00
□	PF14 Dominik Hasek (G), Buff.	2.00
□	PF15 Mario Lemieux, Pitt.	6.00
□	PF16 Ed Belfour (G), Chic.	2.00
□	PF17 Doug Gilmour, Toro.	1.00
□	PF18 Teemu Selänne, Winn.	2.00
□	PF19 Brett Hull, SLou.	2.00
□	PF20 Joe Sakic, Colo.	4.00

RINK LEADERS

Series One Insert Set (10 cards):		**75.00**
	Insert (1:36 Hobby)	**RL**
□	1RL Mark Messier, NYRa.	6.00
□	2RL Mario Lemieux, Pitt.	22.00
□	3RL Raymond Bourque, Bost.	8.00
□	4RL Brett Hull, SLou.	6.00
□	5RL Pat LaFontaine, Buff.	4.00
□	6RL Scott Stevens, NJer.	2.00
□	7RL Keith Tkachuk, Winn.	4.00
□	8RL Doug Gilmour, Toro.	4.00
□	9RL Chris Chelios, Chic.	4.00
□	10RL Wayne Gretzky, LosA.	30.00

YOUNG STARS

Series Two Insert Set (15 cards):		**25.00**
	Insert (1:24)	**YS**
□	YS1 Paul Kariya, Anah.	4.00
□	YS2 Martin Brodeur (G), NJer.	6.00
□	YS3 Mikael Renberg, Phil.	1.50
□	YS4 Peter Forsberg, Colo.	4.00
□	YS5 Alexei Yashin, Otta.	2.00
□	YS6 Jeff Friesen, SanJ.	1.50
□	YS7 Oleg Tverdovsky, Anah.	1.50
□	YS8 Jim Carey (G), Wash.	1.50
□	YS9 Alexei Kovalev, NYRa.	2.00
□	YS10 Jason Arnott, Edmo.	1.50
□	YS11 Teemu Selänne, Winn.	2.00
□	YS12 Chris Osgood (G), Detr.	2.00
□	YS13 Roman Hamrlik, Tamp.	1.50
□	YS14 Scott Niedermayer, NJer.	1.50
□	YS15 Jaromir Jagr, Pitt.	2.00

1995 - 96 TOPPS FINEST

One blank back bronze card was found on the top of every box. There is a blank back card for all 110 bronze cards. All 191 cards have a regular card and refractor parallel. Four basic designs were used: one for "Sterling", one for "Rookies", one for "Performers" and one for "Defenders".

Complete Set (191 cards):		**2400.00**	**600.00**
Commons Set (110 cards):		**550.00**	**40.00**
Uncommons Set (55 cards):		**500.00**	**100.00**
Rare Set (26 cards):		**1600.00**	**625.00**
Commons:		**4.00**	**.35**
	Player	**Refr.**	**Reg.**
□ □	1 Eric Lindros, Phil. [Bronze]	20.00	2.00
□ □	2 Raymond Bourque, Bost. [Gold]	90.00	35.00
□ □	3 Éric Dazé, Chic. [Bronze]	5.00	.50
□ □	4 Craig Janney, SanJ. [Silver]	10.00	2.50
□ □	5 Wayne Gretzky, SLou. [Bronze]	80.00	8.00
□ □	6 Dave Andreychuk, Toro. [Bronze]	5.00	.50
□ □	7 Phil Housley, Calg. [Bronze]	5.00	.50
□ □	8 Mike Gartner, Toro. [Bronze]	15.00	1.50
□ □	9 Cam Neely, Bost. [Bronze]	20.00	2.00
□ □	10 Brett Hull, SLou. [Bronze]	20.00	2.00
□ □	11 Daren Puppa (G), Tamp. [Silver]	10.00	2.50
□ □	12 Tomas Sandström, Pitt. [Silver]	10.00	2.50
□ □	13 Patrick Roy (G), Colo. [Gold]	225.00	90.00
□ □	14 Steve Thomas, NJer. [Bronze]	4.00	.35
□ □	15 Joe Sakic, Colo. [Bronze]	30.00	3.00
□ □	16 Ray Sheppard, SanJ. [Silver]	10.00	2.50
□ □	17 Steve Duchesne, Otta. [Bronze]	4.00	.35
□ □	18 Shayne Corson, SLou. [Silver]	10.00	2.50
□ □	19 Chris Chelios, Chic. [Gold]	40.00	15.00
□ □	20 J. Vanbiesbrouck (G), Flor. [Bronze]	5.00	.50
□ □	21 Randy Burridge, Buff. [Bronze]	4.00	.35
□ □	**22 Shane Doan, Winn. [Bronze] RC**	**10.00**	**3.00**
□ □	23 Brian Savage, Mont. [Bronze]	5.00	.50
□ □	24 Luc Robitaille, NYRa. [Bronze]	15.00	1.50
□ □	25 Jeremy Roenick, Chic. [Gold]	60.00	20.00
□ □	26 Peter Forsberg, Colo. [Bronze]	25.00	2.50
□ □	27 Jeff Friesen, SanJ. [Silver]	10.00	2.50
□ □	28 Aaron Gavey, Tamp. [Silver]	10.00	2.50
□ □	29 Kenny Jönsson, Toro. [Silver]	10.00	2.50
□ □	30 Theoren Fleury, Calg. [Gold]	40.00	15.00
□ □	31 Dave Gagner, Dall. [Silver]	10.00	2.50
□ □	32 A. Selivanov, Tamp. [Silver]	10.00	2.50
□ □	33 Scott Stevens, NJer. [Bronze]	5.00	.50
□ □	34 Valeri Bure, Mont. [Bronze]	5.00	.50
□ □	35 Teemu Selänne, Winn. [Gold]	60.00	20.00
□ □	36 Ray Ferraro, NYRa. [Silver]	10.00	2.50
□ □	37 Sylvain Côté, Wash. [Silver]	10.00	2.50
□ □	38 John MacLean, NJer. [Bronze]	4.00	.35
□ □	39 B. Shanahan, Hart. [Bronze]	20.00	2.00
□ □	40 Pat LaFontaine, Buff. [Bronze]	10.00	1.00
□ □	41 Brian Leetch, NYRa. [Gold]	40.00	15.00
□ □	42 Larry Murphy, Toro. [Bronze]	4.00	.35
□ □	43 Adam Oates, Bost. [Bronze]	5.00	.50
□ □	44 Rod Brind'Amour, Phil. [Bronze]	5.00	.50
□ □	45 Martin Brodeur (G), NJer. [Gold]	100.00	45.00
□ □	46 Pierre Turgeon, Mont. [Bronze]	5.00	.50
□ □	47 Claude Lemieux, Colo. [Bronze]	5.00	.50
□ □	48 Al MacInnis, SLou. [Silver]	15.00	2.50
□ □	49 Geoff Courtnall, SLou. [Silver]	10.00	2.50
□ □	50 Mark Messier, NYRa. [Bronze]	20.00	2.00
□ □	51 Bill Ranford (G), Bost. [Bronze]	5.00	.50
□ □	52 V. Damphousse, Mont. [Silver]	25.00	4.00
□ □	53 Jere Lehtinen, Dall. [Bronze]	5.00	.50
□ □	54 Bryan McCabe, NYIs. [Silver]	10.00	2.50
□ □	55 Doug Gilmour, Toro. [Gold]	40.00	15.00
□ □	56 Mathieu Schneider, NYIs. [Silver]	10.00	2.50
□ □	57 Igor Larionov, Detr. [Silver]	25.00	4.00
□ □	58 Joe Murphy, Chic. [Silver]	10.00	2.50
□ □	59 Niklas Sundström, NYRa. [Bronze]	4.00	.35
□ □	60 John LeClair, Phil. [Bronze]	15.00	1.50
□ □	61 Cory Stillman, Calg. [Bronze]	4.00	.35
□ □	62 David Oliver, Edmo. [Bronze]	4.00	.35
□ □	63 N. Khabibulin (G), Winn. [Bronze]	5.00	.50

64 Steve Rucchin, Anah. [Bronze] 4.00 .35
65 Brendan Shanahan, Hart. [Silver] 40.00 8.00
66 Jim Carey (G), Wash. [Bronze] 4.00 .35
67 B. Holzinger, Buff. [Silver] RC 20.00 8.00
68 Stu Barnes, Flor. [Silver] 10.00 2.50
69 Nicklas Lidström, Detr. [Bronze] 10.00 1.00
70 Jaromir Jagr, Pitt. [Bronze] 20.00 2.00
71 Donald Audette, Buff. [Silver] 15.00 2.50
72 D. Hasek (G), Buff. [Bronze] 20.00 2.00
73 Peter Bondra, Wash. [Silver] 25.00 4.00
74 Andrew Cassels, Hart. [Bronze] 4.00 .35
75 Pavel Bure, Vanc. [Bronze] 15.00 1.50
76 Ragnarsson, SanJ. [Bronze] RC 10.00 3.00
77 Raymond Bourque, Bost. [Silver] 50.00 10.00
78 Alexei Zhamnov, Winn. [Bronze] 5.00 .50
79 Travis Green, NYIs. [Silver] 10.00 2.50
80 Joe Sakic, Colo. [Bronze] 30.00 3.00
81 Chad Kilger, Anah. [Bronze] RC 10.00 3.00
82 Bill Guerin, NJer. [Silver] 15.00 2.50
83 Vyacheslav Kozlov, Detr. [Bronze] 4.00 .35
84 Igor Korolev, Winn. [Silver] 10.00 2.50
85 Saku Koivu, Mont. [Gold] 60.00 20.00
86 Ron Hextall (G), Phil. [Bronze] 10.00 1.00
87 Wendel Clark, NYIs. [Silver] 35.00 6.00
88 Eric Lindros, Phil. [Gold] 75.00 30.00
89 Richard Park, Pitt. [Bronze] 4.00 .35
90 Dominik Hasek (G), Buff. [Silver] 40.00 8.00
91 Shawn McEachern, Bost. [Bronze] 5.00 .50
92 Martin Straka, Otta. [Silver] 10.00 2.50
93 Roman Hamrlik, Tamp. [Bronze] 4.00 .35
94 Roman Oksiuta, Vanc. [Silver] 10.00 2.50
95 Sergei Fedorov, Detr. [Bronze] 20.00 2.00
96 Jeff O'Neill, Hart. [Silver] 15.00 2.50
97 Todd Harvey, Dall. [Silver] 10.00 2.50
98 Rob Niedermayer, Flor. [Bronze] 4.00 .35
99 Mark Messier, NYRa. [Gold] 70.00 30.00
100 Peter Forsberg, Colo. [Gold] 100.00 40.00
101 Deron Quint, Winn. [Bronze] 4.00 .35
102 Nelson Emerson, Hart. [Silver] 10.00 2.50
103 S. Niedermayer, NJer. [Bronze] 5.00 .50
104 Doug Weight, Edmo. [Silver] 25.00 4.00
105 Félix Potvin (G), Toro. [Bronze] 10.00 1.00
106 Brendan Witt, Wash. [Bronze] 4.00 .35
107 Zdeno Ciger, Edmo. [Bronze] 4.00 .35
108 Ed Belfour (G), Chic. [Silver] 40.00 8.00
109 Jody Hull, Flor. [Bronze] 4.00 .35
110 Cam Neely, Bost. [Silver] 40.00 8.00
111 K. McLaren, Bost. [Bronze] RC 10.00 3.00
112 Petr Klima, Tamp. [Silver] 10.00 2.50
113 Grant Fuhr (G), SLou. [Bronze] 10.00 1.00
114 Todd Krygier, Anah. [Bronze] 4.00 .35
115 Brian Leetch, NYRa. [Bronze] 10.00 1.00
116 Alfredsson, Otta. [Silver] RC 75.00 30.00
117 Zigmund Palffy, NYIs. [Bronze] 10.00 1.00
118 A. Törmänen, Otta. [Bronze] RC 5.00 1.00
119 Mark Recchi, Mont. [Bronze] 5.00 .50
120 Mikael Renberg, Phil. [Bronze] 5.00 .50
121 Chris Chelios, Chic. [Bronze] 10.00 1.00
122 Guy Hebert (G), Anah. [Bronze] 4.00 .35
123 Keith Tkachuk, Winn. [Gold] 40.00 15.00
124 Joé Juneau, Wash. [Silver] 10.00 2.50
125 R. Dvorak, Flor. [Silver] RC 30.00 12.00
126 Gary Suter, Chic. [Bronze] 4.00 .35
127 Ron Francis, Pitt. [Bronze] 10.00 1.00
128 Mike Modano, Dall. [Gold] 70.00 30.00
129 Tom Barrasso (G), Pitt. [Bronze] 5.00 .50
130 Pat LaFontaine, Buff. [Bronze] 10.00 1.00
131 Pat Verbeek, NYRa. [Bronze] 5.00 .50
132 Sean Burke (G), Hart. [Silver] 25.00 4.00
133 Rick Tocchet, Bost. [Bronze] 5.00 .50
134 P. Sykora, NJer. [Bronze] RC 20.00 5.00
135 Félix Potvin (G), Toro. [Bronze] 10.00 1.00
136 Scott Mellanby, Flor. [Bronze] 4.00 .35
137 Paul Coffey, Detr. [Bronze] 10.00 1.00
138 Aki Berg, LosA. [Gold] RC 30.00 20.00
139 Jason Arnott, Edmo. [Bronze] 5.00 .50
140 A. Mogilny, Vanc. [Gold] 30.00 10.00
141 Sandis Ozolinsh, Colo. [Bronze] 4.00 .35
142 Owen Nolan, SanJ. [Silver] 25.00 4.00
143 Brian Bradley, Tamp. [Bronze] 4.00 .35
144 Trevor Linden, Vanc. [Bronze] 5.00 .50
145 Patrick Roy (G), Colo. [Bronze] 60.00 6.00
146 Bertuzzi, NYIs. [Bronze] RC 80.00 20.00
147 Michal Pivonka, Wash. [Bronze] 4.00 .35
148 Kevin Hatcher, Dall. [Silver] 10.00 2.50
149 Chris Terreri (G), SanJ. [Bronze] 4.00 .35
150 Mario Lemieux, Pitt. [Bronze] 60.00 6.00
151 Alexei Yashin, Otta. [Silver] 25.00 4.00
152 Scott Stevens, NJer. [Silver] 15.00 2.50
153 Dale Hawerchuk, SLou. [Bronze] 10.00 1.00
154 Markus Näslund, Pitt. [Bronze] 20.00 2.00
155 Teemu Selänne, Winn. [Bronze] 15.00 1.50
156 Darcy Wakaluk, Dall. [Silver] 10.00 2.50
157 Vitali Yachmenev, LosA. [Bronze] 4.00 .35
158 Jason Dawe, Buff. [Bronze] 4.00 .35
159 Chris Osgood (G), Detr. [Bronze] 10.00 1.00
160 A. Mogilny, Vanc. [Bronze] 5.00 .50
161 Kirk McLean (G), Vanc. [Silver] 10.00 2.50
162 Steve Yzerman, Detr. [Gold] 175.00 70.00
163 Shean Donovan, SanJ. [Bronze] 4.00 .35
164 Valeri Kamensky, Colo. [Silver] 10.00 2.50
165 Paul Kariya, Anah. [Bronze] 25.00 2.50
166 Dmitri Khristich, LosA. [Silver] 10.00 2.50
167 Teppo Numminen, Winn. [Bronze] 5.00 .50
168 Joe Nieuwendyk, Dall. [Silver] 15.00 2.50
169 Mike Richter (G), NYRa. [Silver] 20.00 4.00
170 Doug Gilmour, Toro. [Bronze] 10.00 1.00
171 Sergei Zubov, Pitt. [Bronze] 4.00 .35
172 Michael Nylander, Calg. [Bronze] 4.00 .35
173 Geoff Sanderson, Hart. [Bronze] 4.00 .35
174 Éric Desjardins, Phil. [Silver] 10.00 2.50
175 Jeremy Roenick, Chic. [Bronze] 15.00 1.50
176 Ed Jovanovski, Flor. [Gold] 30.00 10.00
177 Mats Sundin, Toro. [Bronze] 20.00 2.00
178 M. Brodeur (G), NJer. [Bronze] 30.00 3.00
179 John LeClair, Phil. [Gold] 60.00 20.00
180 Wayne Gretzky, SLou. [Gold] 300.00 120.00
181 Theoren Fleury, Calg. [Bronze] 10.00 1.00
182 Pierre Turgeon, Mont. [Silver] 15.00 2.50
183 R. Svehla, Flor. [Bronze] RC 10.00 3.00
184 Brett Hull, SLou. [Gold] 70.00 30.00
185 Jaromir Jagr, Pitt. [Gold] 75.00 30.00
186 Sergei Fedorov, Detr. [Bronze] 20.00 2.00
187 Pavel Bure, Vanc. [Gold] 50.00 20.00
188 Vanbiesbrouck (G), Flor. [Bronze] 5.00 .50
189 Paul Kariya, Anah. [Bronze] 25.00 2.50
190 Mario Lemieux, Pitt. [Gold] 225.00 90.00
191 Checklist [Gold] 20.00 10.00

1995 - 96 TOPPS STADIUM CLUB

These cards have two versions: the regular card and a Members Only mail offer parallel.

	M.O.	TSC
Complete Set (227 cards):	-	**50.00**
Master Set (283 cards):	**525.00**	-
Common Player:	**.75**	**.20**

Player	M.O.	TSC
1 Alexander Mogilny, Vanc.	3.50	.20
2 Raymond Bourque, Bost.	8.00	.50
2 Bill Ranford (G), Edmo [Error: s/b card #20]	3.00	.20
3 Garry Galley, Buff.	.75	.20
4 Glen Wesley, Hart.	1.00	.20
5 Dave Andreychuk, Toro.	2.00	.20
6 Daren Puppa (G), Tamp.	1.50	.20
7 Shayne Corson, SLou.	2.00	.20
8 Kelly Hrudey (G), LosA.	2.00	.20
9 Russ Courtnall, Vanc.	1.50	.20
10 Chris Chelios, Chic.	4.00	.20
11 Ulf Samuelsson, NYRa.	1.00	.20
12 Mike Vernon (G), Detr.	3.00	.20
13 Al MacInnis, SLou.	3.00	.20
14 Joel Otto, Phil.	1.00	.20
15 Patrick Roy (G), Mont.	22.00	1.50
16 Steve Thomas, NJer.	1.50	.20
17 Pat Verbeek, NYRa.	2.00	.20
18 Joe Nieuwendyk, Calg.	3.00	.20
19 Todd Krygier, Anah.	.75	.20
20 Steve Yzerman, Detr.	18.00	1.50
22 Ron Francis, Pitt.	4.00	.20
23 Sylvain Côté, Wash.	1.00	.20
24 Grant Fuhr (G), SLou.	4.00	.20
25 Brendan Shanahan, Hart. [vs. M.Messier]	6.00	.50
26 John MacLean, NJer.	1.00	.20
27 Darren Turcotte, Winn.	1.00	.20
28 Bernie Nicholls, Chic.	1.50	.20
29 Sean Burke (G), Hart.	4.00	.20
30 Brian Leetch, NYRa.	4.00	.20
31 Dave Gagner, Dall.	1.00	.20
32 Rick Tocchet, LosA.	2.00	.20
33 Ron Hextall (G), Phil.	4.50	.20
34 Paul Coffey, Detr.	4.00	.20
35 John Vanbiesbrouck (G), Flor.	3.50	.20
36 Rod Brind'Amour, Phil. [vs. S.Lefebvre]	2.00	.20
37 Brian Savage, Mont.	2.00	.20
38 Nelson Emerson, Hart.	1.00	.20
39 Brian Bradley, Tamp.	.75	.20
40 Adam Oates, Bost.	3.00	.20
41 Kirk McLean (G), Vanc.	2.00	.20
42 Kevin Hatcher, Dall.	1.00	.20
43 Mike Keane, Mont.	1.00	.20
44 Don Beaupré (G), Otta.	1.00	.20
45 Scott Stevens, NJer.	3.00	.20
46 Dale Hawerchuk, SLou.	4.00	.20
47 Scott A. Young, Colo.	2.00	.20
48 Mark Recchi, Mont.	3.00	.20
49 Mike Richter (G), NYRa.	3.50	.20
50 Kevin Stevens, Bost.	1.50	.20
51 Mike Ridley, Vanc.	1.00	.20
52 Joe Murphy, Chic.	1.00	.20
53 Stéphane Fiset (G), Colo.	2.00	.20
54 Donald Audette, Buff.	3.00	.20
55 Ed Belfour (G), Chic.	6.00	.50
56 Rob Blake, LosA.	4.00	.20
57 Adam Graves, NYRa [vs. A.Semenov]	3.00	.20
58 Arturs Irbe (G), SanJ.	2.00	.20
59 Mathieu Schneider, NYIs.	1.50	.20
60 Dominik Hasek (G), Buff.	6.00	.50
61 Andrew Cassels, Hart.	1.50	.20
62 Johan Garpenlöv, Flor.	.75	.20
63 Kyle McLaren, Bost. RC	**4.00**	**1.00**
64 Petr Nedved, Pitt.	2.00	.20
65 Owen Nolan, SanJ.	4.00	.20
66 Keith Primeau, Detr.	3.00	.20
67 Mark Tinordi, Wash.	1.00	.20
68 Dmitri Khristich, LosA.	1.00	.20
69 Chris Pronger, SLou.	4.00	.20
70 Jaromir Jagr, Pitt.	6.00	.50
71 Mike Ricci, Colo.	2.00	.20
72 Trevor Kidd (G), Calg.	2.00	.20
73 Stu Barnes, Flor.	.75	.20
74 Doug Weight, Edmo.	4.00	.20
75 Mats Sundin, Toro.	6.00	.50
76 Scott Niedermayer, NJer.	2.00	.20
77 J. LeClair, Phil. [vs. JC.Bergeron]	6.00	.50
78 Derian Hatcher, Dall.	2.00	.20
79 Brad May, Buff.	1.00	.20
80 Félix Potvin (G), Toro.	4.00	.20
81 Derek King, NYIs.	1.00	.20
82 Guy Hebert (G), Anah.	1.50	.20
83 Shawn McEachern, Bost.	2.00	.20
84 Vyacheslav Kozlov, Detr.	1.50	.20
85 Martin Brodeur (G), NJer. [vs. D.Ciccarelli]	12.00	1.00
86 Ray Whitney, SanJ.	1.50	.20
87 Martin Straka, Otta.	2.00	.20
88 Keith Jones, Wash.	1.00	.20
89 Roman Hamrlik, Tamp.	1.50	.20
90 Keith Tkachuk, Winn.	4.00	.20
91 Jim Dowd, NJer. [vs. S.Podein]	.75	.20
92 Sergei Zubov, Pitt.	1.50	.20
93 Bryan McCabe, NYIs.	1.50	.20
94 Rob Niedermayer, Flor.	1.50	.20
95 Alexei Zhamnov, Winn.	2.00	.20
96 Zarley Zalapski, Calg.	.75	.20
97 Alexandre Daigle, Otta.	1.00	.20
98 Jocelyn Thibault (G), Colo.	3.00	.20
99 Zigmund Palffy, NYIs.	4.00	.20
100 Luc Robitaille, Pitt.	6.00	.50
101 Radek Bonk, Otta.	2.00	.20
102 Todd Marchant, Edmo.	1.50	.20
103 Todd Harvey, Dall.	1.50	.20
104 Blaine Lacher (G), Bost.	1.00	.20
105 Peter Forsberg, Colo.	10.00	.50
106 Jeff Friesen, SanJ.	2.00	.20
107 Kenny Jönsson, Toro.	1.50	.20
108 Brett Lindros, NYIs.	2.00	.20
109 David Oliver, Edmo.	.75	.20
110 Mikael Renberg, Phil.	2.00	.20
111 Alexander Selivanov, Tamp.	.75	.20
112 Stanislav Neckar, Otta.	1.00	.20
113 Oleg Tverdovsky, Anah.	1.00	.20
114 Shean Donovan, SanJ.	1.00	.20
115 Jim Carey (G), Wash.	1.00	.20
116 Tony Granato, LosA.	1.50	.20
117 Tony Amonte, Chic.	4.00	.20
118 Tomas Sandström, Pitt.	1.50	.20
119 Rick Tabaracci (G), Calg.	1.00	.20
120 R. Ferraro, NYRa. [vs. G.Wesley]	1.00	.20
121 Brian Noonan, SLou.	.75	.20
122 Miroslav Satan, Edmo. RC	**6.00**	**1.50**
123 Sergio Momesso, Toro.	.75	.20
124 Gary Suter, Chic.	1.50	.20
125 Éric Desjardins, Phil.	2.00	.20
126 Steve Duchesne, Otta.	1.50	.20
127 Zdeno Ciger, Edmo.	1.00	.20
128 Cliff Ronning, Vanc.	1.50	.20
129 Nicklas Lidström, Detr.	4.00	.20
130 Bill Guerin, NJer.	3.00	.20
131 Igor Korolev, Winn.	1.00	.20
132 Roman Oksiuta, Vanc.	.75	.20
133 Jesse Bélanger, Flor.	.75	.20
134 Chris Gratton, Tamp.	1.50	.20
135 Chris Osgood (G), Detr.	4.00	.20
136 Pat Peake, Wash.	.75	.20
137 Viktor Kozlov, SanJ.	2.00	.20
138 Aaron Gavey, Tamp.	.75	.20
139 Zdenek Nedved, Toro.	.75	.20
140 Rhett Warrener, Flor. RC	**2.00**	**.50**
141 Marko Kiprusoff, Mont.	.75	.20
142 Dan Quinn, Otta.	.75	.20
143 Alexei Zhitnik, Buff.	1.00	.20
144 Larry Murphy, Toro.	1.50	.20
145 Phil Housley, Calg.	2.00	.20
146 Don Sweeney, Bost.	1.00	.20
147 Jason Dawe, Buff.	.75	.20
148 Marcus Ragnarsson, SanJ. RC	**4.00**	**1.00**
149 Andrei Nikolishin, Hart.	1.00	.20
150 Dino Ciccarelli, Detr.	2.00	.20
151 Jari Kurri, LosA.	6.00	.50
152 Bob Probert, Chic.	2.00	.20
153 R. McKay, NJer. [vs. C.Huddy]	.75	.20
154 Michael Nylander, Calg.	1.50	.20
155 Wendel Clark, NYIs.	6.00	.50
156 Antti Törmänen, Otta. RC	**2.00**	**.50**
157 Nikolai Khabibulin (G), Winn.	3.00	.20
158 Tom Barrasso (G), Pitt.	3.00	.20
159 Vincent Damphousse, Mont.	4.00	.20
160 Trevor Linden, Vanc.	3.00	.20
161 Kamensky, Colo. [vs. McSorley]	2.00	.20
162 Mike Gartner, Toro.	6.00	.50
EC163 Cam Neely, Bost.	6.00	2.00
EC164 Pat LaFontaine, Buff.	4.00	1.00
EC165 Theoren Fleury, Calg.	4.00	1.00
EC166 Jeremy Roenick, Chic.	6.00	1.50
EC167 Joe Sakic, Colo.	12.00	3.00
EC168 Mike Modano, Dall.	6.00	2.00
EC169 Sergei Fedorov, Detr.	6.00	2.00
EC170 Scott Mellanby, Flor.	1.50	.50
EC171 Jason Arnott, Edmo.	2.00	.50
EC172 Geoff Sanderson, Hart.	1.50	.50
EC173 Wayne Gretzky, LosA.	30.00	8.00
EC174 Paul Kariya, Anah.	10.00	2.50
EC175 Pierre Turgeon, Mont.	3.00	.50
EC176 Stéphane Richer, NJer.	1.50	.50
EC177 Kirk Muller, NYIs.	2.00	.50
EC178 Mark Messier, NYRa.	6.00	2.00
EC179 Craig Janney, SanJ.	1.50	.50
EC180 Mario Lemieux, Pitt.	22.00	6.00
EC181 Eric Lindros, Phil.	6.00	2.00
EC182 Alexei Yashin, Otta.	4.00	1.00
EC183 Brett Hull, SLou.	6.00	2.00
EC184 Doug Gilmour, Toro.	4.00	1.00
EC185 Petr Klima, Tamp.	1.00	.50
EC186 Pavel Bure, Vanc.	6.00	1.50
EC187 Joé Juneau, Wash.	1.50	.50
EC188 Teemu Selänne, Winn.	6.00	1.50
EC189 Claude Lemieux, Colo.	2.00	.50
ER190 Vitali Yachmenev, LosA.	2.00	.50
ER191 Jason Bonsignore, Edmo.	1.50	.50
ER192 Jeff O'Neill, Hart.	6.00	1.50
ER193 Brendan Witt, Wash.	1.50	.50
ER194 Brian Holzinger, Buff. RC	**2.00**	**1.50**
ER195 Éric Dazé, Chic.	6.00	1.50
ER196 Ed Jovanovski, Flor.	6.00	1.50
ER197 Deron Quint, Winn.	2.00	.50
ER198 Marty Murray, Calg.	1.50	.50
ER199 Jere Lehtinen, Dall.	4.00	1.00
ER200 Radek Dvorak, Flor. RC	**4.00**	**2.00**
ER201 Aki Berg, LosA. RC	**2.00**	**1.50**
ER202 Chad Kilger, Anah. RC	**4.00**	**2.00**
ER203 Saku Koivu, Mont.	12.00	3.00
ER204 Todd Bertuzzi, NYIs. RC	**26.00**	**12.00**
ER205 Niklas Sundström, NYRa.	3.50	.50
ER206 D. Alfredsson, Otta. RC	**12.00**	**6.00**
ER207 Shane Doan, Winn. RC	**4.00**	**2.00**
208 Richard Park, Pitt.	.75	.20
209 Peter Bondra, Wash.	4.00	.20
210 Bryan Smolinski, Pitt.	1.00	.20
211 Tommy Salo (G), NYIs. RC	**8.00**	**2.00**
212 Patrick Poulin, Chic.	1.00	.20
213 Mathieu Dandenault, Detr. RC	**2.00**	**.50**
214 Steve Rucchin, Anah.	1.50	.20
215 Ray Sheppard, SanJ.	1.00	.20
216 Robert Svehla, Flor. RC	**4.00**	**1.00**
217 Olaf Kölzig (G), Wash.	4.00	.20
218 Alexei Kovalev, NYRa.	4.00	.20
219 Ian Moran, Pitt.	.75	.20
220 Valeri Bure, Mont.	2.00	.20
221 Dean Malkoc, Vanc. RC	**2.00**	**.50**
222 Jason Doig, Winn.	.75	.20
223 David Nemirovsky, Flor. RC	**2.00**	**.50**
224 Jamie Pushor, Detr.	.75	.20
225 Ricard Persson, NJer. RC	**2.00**	**.50**
1 Checklist	-	.20
2 Checklist	-	.20

MASTER PHOTOS

These cards were issued in Topps bubble packs. One 3" x 5" card was issued with a pack of Topps Series One and a Topps team set. Only Canadian team packs are known to exist. Other singles may exist.

Card Size: 3 1/2" x 5"

Player	MP
Complete Set (9 cards):	**5.00**
Jason Arnott, Edmo.	.75
Theoren Fleury, Calg.	1.00
Doug Gilmour, Toro.	1.00
Trevor Linden, Vanc.	.75
Kirk McLean (G), Vanc.	.75
Alexander Mogilny, Vanc.	.75
Félix Potvin (G), Toro.	1.00
Mats Sundin, Toro.	2.00
Alexei Yashin, Otta.	1.00

EXTREME NORTH

These cards have two versions: the regular card and a Members Only paralell.

Player	M.O.	EN
Insert Set (9 cards):		**45.00**
EN1 Pavel Bure, Vanc.	4.00	6.00
EN2 Teemu Selänne, Winn.	4.00	6.00
EN3 Félix Potvin (G), Toro.	2.00	4.00
EN4 Patrick Roy (G), Mont.	14.00	20.00
EN5 Theoren Fleury, Calg.	2.00	4.00
EN6 Bill Ranford (G), Edmo.	2.00	3.00
EN7 Pierre Turgeon, Mont.	2.00	3.00
EN8 Doug Gilmour, Toro.	2.00	4.00
EN9 Alexander Mogilny, Vanc.	2.00	3.00

FEARLESS

These inserts have two versions: the regular card and a Members Only parallel.

Player	M.O.	F
Insert Set (9 cards):		**35.00**
F1 B. Shanahan, Hart. [vs. P.Verbeek]	4.00	10.00
F2 Chris Chelios, Chic.	2.00	6.00
F3 Keith Primeau, Detr.	2.00	4.00
F4 S. Stevens, NJer. [vs. Mt.Naslund]	2.00	4.00
F5 Rick Tocchet, LosA.	.75	2.00
F6 Kevin Stevens, Bost.	.75	2.00
F7 U. Samuelsson, NYRa. [vs. Gartner]	.75	2.00
F8 Wendel Clark, NYIs.	4.00	8.00
F9 Keith Tkachuk, Winn.	2.00	6.00

GENERATION TSC

These inserts have two versions: the regular card and a Members Only parallel.

Insert Set (9 cards):		35.00
Player	M.O.	GT
GT1 Paul Kariya, Anah.	6.00	8.00
GT2 Teemu Selänne, Winn.	4.00	4.00
GT3 Jaromir Jagr, Pitt.	4.00	6.00
GT4 Peter Forsberg, Colo.	6.00	8.00
GT5 Martin Brodeur (G), NJer.	8.00	10.00
GT6 Jim Carey (G), Wash.	.75	2.00
GT7 Mikael Renberg, Phil.	.75	2.00
GT8 Scott Niedermayer, NJer.	.75	2.00
GT9 Ed Jovanovski, Flor.	2.00	2.00

METALIST

These laser-cut cards have two versions: the regular card and a Members Only parallel.

Insert Set (12 cards):		110.00
Player	M.O.	TSC
M1 Wayne Gretzky, LosA.	20.00	35.00
M2 Mario Lemieux, Pitt.	15.00	25.00
M3 Patrick Roy (G), Mont.	15.00	25.00
M4 Raymond Bourque, Bost.	6.00	10.00
M5 Ed Belfour (G), Chic.	4.00	8.00
M6 Tom Barrasso (G), Pitt.	2.00	2.00
M7 Joe Mullen, Bost.	2.00	2.00
M8 Brian Leetch, NYRa.	2.00	4.00
M9 Mark Messier, NYRa.	4.00	8.00
M10 Dominik Hasek (G), Buff.	4.00	8.00
M11 Paul Coffey, Detr.	2.00	4.00
M12 Guy Carbonneau, Dall.	.75	2.00

NEMESES

These cards have two versions: the regular card and a Members Only parallel.

Insert Set (9 cards):		120.00
Player	M.O.	N
N1 Eric Lindros/ Scott Stevens	6.00	10.00
N2 Wayne Gretzky/ Mario Lemieux	30.00	50.00
N3 Cam Neely/ Claude Lemieux	6.00	8.00
N4 Pavel Bure/ Mike Richter (G)	6.00	8.00
N5 Brian Leetch/ Raymond Bourque	8.00	12.00
N6 Brodeur (G)/ Dominik Hasek (G)	10.00	15.00
N7 Doug Gilmour/ Sergei Fedorov	8.00	12.00
N8 Mark Messier/ Joel Otto	4.00	8.00
N9 Paul Kariya/ Peter Forsberg	10.00	20.00

POWER STREAK

These cards have two versions: the regular card and a Members Only parallel.

Insert Set (10 cards):		20.00
Player	M.O.	PS
PS1 Pierre Turgeon, Mont.	2.00	2.00
PS2 Eric Lindros, Phil.	4.00	4.00
PS3 Ron Francis, Pitt.	2.00	2.00
PS4 Paul Coffey, Detr.	2.00	2.00
PS5 Mikael Renberg, Phil.	.75	2.00
PS6 John LeClair, Phil.	4.00	4.00
PS7 Dino Ciccarelli, Detr.	.75	2.00
PS8 Wendel Clark, NYIs.	4.00	4.00
PS9 Brett Hull, SLou.	4.00	4.00
PS10 Stéphane Richer, NJer.	.75	2.00

1995 - 96 TOPPS STADIUM CLUB MEMBERS ONLY

Complete Set (50 cards):	20.00
Player	TSCMO
1 Wayne Gretzky, All-Star '96	4.00
2 Paul Kariya, All-Star '96	1.00
3 Brett Hull, All-Star '96	1.00
4 Chris Chelios, All-Star '96	.50
5 Paul Coffey, All-Star '96	.50
6 Ed Belfour (G), All-Star '96	1.00
7 Theoren Fleury, All-Star '96	.50
8 Owen Nolan, All-Star '96	.50
9 Al MacInnis, All-Star '96	.25
10 Alexander Mogilny, All-Star '96	.25
11 Kevin Hatcher, All-Star '96	.25
12 Doug Weight, All-Star '96	.50
13 Félix Potvin (G), All-Star '96	.50
14 Teemu Selänne, All-Star '96	.50
15 Sergei Fedorov, All-Star '96	1.00
16 Larry Murphy, All-Star '96	.25
17 Joe Sakic, All-Star '96	1.50
18 Mats Sundin, All-Star '96	1.00
19 Nicklas Lidström, All-Star '96	.50
20 Peter Forsberg, All-Star '96	1.00
21 Chris Osgood (G), All-Star '96	.50
22 Mike Gartner, All-Star '96	.50
23 D. Savard / C. MacTavish	.25
24 Mario Lemieux, All-Star '96	3.00
25 Jaromir Jagr, All-Star '96	1.00
26 Brendan Shanahan, All-Star '96	1.00
27 Scott Stevens, All-Star '96	.25
28 Raymond Bourque, All-Star '96	1.00
29 Martin Brodeur (G), All-Star '96	1.50
30 Eric Lindros, All-Star '96	1.00
31 Peter Bondra, All-Star '96	.50
32 Scott Mellanby, All-Star '96	.25
33 Brian Leetch, All-Star '96	.50
34 John Vanbiesbrouck (G), All-Star '96	.25
35 Pat Verbeek, All-Star '96	.25
36 Cam Neely, All-Star '96	1.00
37 Roman Hamrlik, All-Star '96	.25
38 Daniel Alfredsson, All-Star '96	.50
39 Pierre Turgeon, All-Star '96	.25
40 Mark Messier, All-Star '96	1.00
41 Éric Desjardins, All-Star	.25
42 Dominik Hasek (G), All-Star '96	1.00
43 John LeClair, All-Star '96	.50
44 Mathieu Schneider, All-Star '96	.25
45 Ron Francis, All-Star	.50
46 Saku Koivu, Mont.	1.50
47 Ed Jovanovski, Flor.	.50
48 Vitali Yachmenev, LosA.	.25
49 Petr Sykora, NJer.	.50
50 Éric Dazé, Chic.	.50

1995 - 96 TOPPS SUPER SKILLS

These cards have two versions: the regular card and a Platinum parallel.

Complete Set (90 cards):	75.00	15.00
Common Player:	.50	.20
Player	Plat.	Reg.
1 Mario Lemieux, Pitt.	7.00	1.50
2 Adam Oates, Bost.	1.00	.20
3 Donald Audette, Buff.	1.00	.20
4 Andrew Cassels, Hart.	.50	.20
5 Pat LaFontaine, Buff.	1.50	.20
6 Mathieu Schneider, NYIs.	.50	.20
7 Scott Stevens, NJer.	1.00	.20
8 Mikael Renberg, Phil.	.50	.20
9 Pierre Turgeon, Mont.	1.00	.20
10 Steve Yzerman, Detr.	6.00	1.00
11 Russ Courtnall, Vanc.	.50	.20
12 Oleg Tverdovsky, Anah.	.50	.20
13 Craig Janney, SanJ.	.50	.20
14 Doug Gilmour, Toro.	1.50	.20
15 Wayne Gretzky, LosA.	10.00	2.00
16 Paul Kariya, Anah.	3.50	.50
17 Joe Sakic, Québ.	4.00	.50
18 Peter Forsberg, Québ.	3.50	.50
19 Brian Leetch, NYRa.	1.50	.20
20 Jaromir Jagr, Pitt.	2.50	.50
21 Geoff Sanderson, Hart.	.50	.20
22 Rob Niedermayer, Flor.	.50	.20
23 Ray Ferraro, NYIs.	.50	.20
24 Alexandre Daigle, Otta.	.50	.20
25 Joé Juneau, Wash.	.50	.20
26 Don Sweeney, Bost.	.50	.20
27 Scott Niedermayer, NJer.	.50	.20
28 Mike Gartner, Toro.	2.00	.20
29 Paul Coffey, Detr.	1.50	.20
30 Pavel Bure, Vanc.	2.00	.20
31 Teemu Selänne, Winn.	2.00	.20
32 Mats Sundin, Toro.	2.50	.50
33 Trevor Linden, Vanc.	1.00	.20
34 Sergei Fedorov, Detr.	2.50	.50
35 Theoren Fleury, Calg.	1.50	.20
36 Alexander Mogilny, Vanc.	1.00	.20
37 Garry Galley, Buff.	.50	.20
38 Stu Barnes, Flor.	.50	.20
39 Glen Wesley, Hart.	.50	.20
40 Eric Lindros, Phil.	2.50	.50
41 Stéphane Richer, NJer.	.50	.20
42 John LeClair, Phil.	2.00	.20
43 Pat Verbeek, NYRa.	.50	.20
44 Bill Guerin, NJer.	1.00	.20
45 Wendel Clark, Toro.	2.00	.20
46 Mike Modano, Dall.	2.50	.50
47 Keith Primeau, Detr.	1.00	.20
48 Brett Hull, SLou.	2.50	.50
49 Al MacInnis, SLou.	1.00	.20
50 Chris Chelios, Chic.	1.50	.20
51 Keith Tkachuk, Winn.	1.50	.20
52 Dave Andreychuk, Toro.	.50	.20
53 Kevin Hatcher, Dall.	.50	.20
54 Chris Pronger, SLou.	1.50	.20
55 Brendan Shanahan, Hart.	2.50	.50
56 Luc Robitaille, Pitt.	2.00	.20
57 Raymond Bourque, Bost.	3.00	.50
58 Mark Recchi, Mont.	1.00	.20
59 Brian Bradley, Tamp.	.50	.20
60 Mark Messier, NYRa.	2.50	.50
61 Kevin Stevens, Bost.	.50	.20
62 John MacLean, NJer.	.50	.20
63 Cam Neely, Bost.	2.50	.50
64 Rick Tocchet, LosA.	.50	.20
65 Jeremy Roenick, Chic.	2.00	.20
66 Phil Housley, Calg.	.50	.20
67 Jason Arnott, Edmo.	1.00	.20
68 Todd Harvey, Dall.	.50	.20
69 Jeff Friesen, SanJ.	.50	.20
70 Alexei Zhamnov, Winn.	.50	.20
71 David Oliver, Edmo.	.50	.20
72 Bernie Nicholls, Chic.	.50	.20
73 Jim Carey (G), Wash.	.50	.20
74 Mike Richter (G), NYRa.	1.00	.20
75 Dominik Hasek (G), Buff.	2.50	.50
76 Sean Burke (G), Hart.	1.50	.20
77 Ron Hextall (G), Phil.	1.50	.20
78 John Vanbiesbrouck (G), Flor.	1.00	.20
79 Tom Barrasso (G), Pitt. [b/ Wregget]	1.00	.20
80 Martin Brodeur (G), NJer.	4.00	.50
81 Patrick Roy (G), Mont.	7.00	1.50
82 Trevor Kidd (G), Calg.	.50	.20
83 Andy Moog (G), Dall.	1.00	.20
84 Mike Vernon (G), Detr.	1.00	.20
85 Félix Potvin (G), Toro.	1.50	.20
86 Bill Ranford (G), Edmo.	1.00	.20
87 Kelly Hrudey (G), LosA.	.50	.20
88 Grant Fuhr (G), SLou.	1.50	.20
89 Kirk McLean (G), Vanc.	.50	.20
90 Ed Belfour (G), Chic.	2.50	.50

SUPER ROOKIES

Insert Set (15 cards):	20.00
Insert (1:1)	SR
SR1 Ed Jovanovski, Flor.	2.00
SR2 Jason Bonsignore, Edmo.	.50
SR3 Jeff O'Neill, Hart.	2.00
SR4 Cory Stillman, Calg.	1.00
SR5 Chad Kilger, Anah.	1.00
SR6 Aki Berg, LosA.	.50
SR7 Todd Bertuzzi, NYIs.	6.00
SR8 Shane Doan, Winn.	1.00
SR9 Kyle McLaren, Bost.	1.00
SR10 Radek Dvorak, Flor.	1.00
SR11 Saku Koivu, Mont.	4.00
SR12 Daniel Alfredsson, Otta.	3.00
SR13 Antti Törmänen, Otta.	.50
SR14 Niklas Sundström, NYRa.	1.00
SR15 Vitali Yachmenev, LosA.	.50

1995 - 96 UPPER DECK

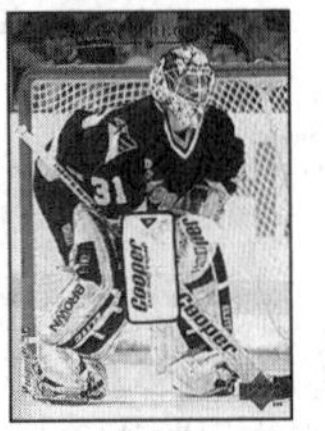

These cards have three versions: the regular card, an Electric Ice parallel and an Electric Ice Gold parallel.

Series One Set (270 cards):	2300.00	150.00	30.00
Series Two Set (300 cards):	2100.00	180.00	55.00
Common Player:	6.00	.50	.20
Player	EIG	EI	Reg.
1 Cam Neely, Bost.	35.00	3.50	.50
2 Donald Audette, Buff.	15.00	1.50	.20
3 Derian Hatcher, Dall.	10.00	1.00	.20
4 Mike Vernon (G), Detr.	15.00	1.50	.20
5 Darryl Sydor, LosA.	6.00	.50	.20
6 Patrice Brisebois, Mont.	6.00	.50	.20
7 John LeClair, Phil.	30.00	3.00	.50
8 Luc Robitaille, NYRa.	30.00	3.00	.50
9 Todd Krygier, Anah.	6.00	.50	.20
10 Steve Chiasson, Calg.	6.00	.50	.20
11 Sergei Krivokrasov, Chic.	6.00	.50	.20
12 M. Tuomainen, Edmo.	6.00	.50	.20
13 Paul Ranheim, Hart.	6.00	.50	.20
14 Brian Rolston, NJer.	10.00	1.00	.20
15 Alexei Yashin, Otta.	20.00	2.00	.20
16 Joe Mullen, Bost.	15.00	1.50	.20
17 Dallas Drake, Winn.	6.00	.50	.20
18 Tony Amonte, Chic.	20.00	2.00	.20
19 Gary Roberts, Calg.	15.00	1.50	.20
20 Geoff Sanderson, Hart.	6.00	.50	.20
21 Gord Murphy, Flor.	6.00	.50	.20
22 Dean Evason, Calg.	6.00	.50	.20
23 B. Myhres, Tamp. RC	**10.00**	**1.50**	**.50**
24 Sergei Makarov, SanJ.	15.00	1.50	.20
25 Joé Juneau, Wash.	6.00	.50	.20
26 Greg A. Adams, Dall.	6.00	.50	.20
27 Yuri Khmylev, Buff.	6.00	.50	.20
28 Yanic Perreault, LosA.	10.00	1.00	.20
29 Jason Arnott, Edmo.	15.00	1.50	.20
30 Glenn Healy (G), NYRa.	6.00	.50	.20
31 Sergei Brylin, NJer.	6.00	.50	.20
32 Ian Laperrière, SLou.	6.00	.50	.20
33 Trevor Linden, Vanc.	15.00	1.50	.20
34 Nicklas Lidström, Detr.	20.00	2.00	.20
35 Don Sweeney, Bost.	6.00	.50	.20
36 Brian Savage, Mont.	10.00	1.00	.20
37 Richard Matvichuk, Dall.	6.00	.50	.20
38 Dale Hawerchuk, SLou.	20.00	2.00	.20
39 P. Roy (G), Mont.	110.00	10.00	1.50
40 Alexander Semak, NYIs.	6.00	.50	.20
41 Kirk Maltby, Edmo.	6.00	.50	.20
42 Jiri Slégr, Edmo.	6.00	.50	.20
43 Joe Sacco, Anah.	6.00	.50	.20
44 C. Lemieux w/ Smythe	10.00	1.00	.20
45 Eric Weinrich, Chic.	6.00	.50	.20
46 Ron Francis, Pitt.	20.00	2.00	.20
47 Jamie Storr (G), LosA.	6.00	.50	.20
48 Félix Potvin (G), Toro.	20.00	2.00	.20
49 Steve Duchesne, Otta.	6.00	.50	.20
50 Jody Hull, Flor.	6.00	.50	.20
51 Dave Manson, Winn.	6.00	.50	.20
52 Marty McInnis, NYIs.	6.00	.50	.20
53 James Patrick, Calg.	6.00	.50	.20
54 Joe Sakic, Colo.	60.00	6.00	1.00
55 Andrei Nikolishin, Hart.	6.00	.50	.20
56 Adrian Aucoin, Vanc.	6.00	1.00	.20
57 W. Flaherty, SanJ. RC	**15.00**	**3.00**	**1.00**
58 Marek Malik, Hart.	6.00	.50	.20
59 Jason Allison, Wash.	20.00	2.00	.20
60 S. Matteau, NYRa.	6.00	.50	.20
61 Jason Dawe, Buff.	6.00	.50	.20
62 Ray Whitney, SanJ.	6.00	.50	.20
63 Bill Lindsay, Flor.	6.00	.50	.20
64 Alexei Zhamnov, Winn.	10.00	1.00	.20
65 Adam Deadmarsh, Colo.	10.00	1.00	.20
66 V. Damphousse, Mont.	20.00	2.00	.20
67 Josef Beranek, Vanc.	6.00	.50	.20
68 Stanislav Neckar, Otta.	6.00	.50	.20
69 Alexei Kasatonov, Bost.	6.00	.50	.20
70 Jon Casey (G), SLou.	6.00	.50	.20
71 Todd Marchant, Edmo.	6.00	.50	.20
72 Mike Sillinger, Anah.	6.00	.50	.20
73 Markus Näslund, Pitt.	35.00	3.50	.50
74 John MacLean, NJer.	6.00	.50	.20
75 Mike Ridley, Vanc.	6.00	.50	.20
76 Petr* Svoboda, Phil.	6.00	.50	.20
77 Milos Holan, Anah.	6.00	.50	.20
78 John Tucker, Tamp.	6.00	.50	.20
79 Doug Brown, Detr.	6.00	.50	.20
80 Ted Donato, Bost.	6.00	.50	.20
81 Dmitry Yushkevich, Phil.	6.00	.50	.20
82 Brett Lindros, NYIs.	10.00	1.00	.20
83 Brian Bradley, Tamp.	6.00	.50	.20
84 Mario Lemieux, Pitt.	110.00	10.00	1.50
85 N. Khabibulin (G), Winn.	15.00	1.50	.20
86 Larry Murphy, Toro.	6.00	.50	.20
87 Mike Donnelly, Dall.	6.00	.50	.20
88 B. Holzinger, Buff. RC	**15.00**	**3.00**	**1.00**
89 S. Larouche, Otta. RC	**10.00**	**1.50**	**.50**
90 Ray Ferraro, NYRa.	6.00	.50	.20
91 M. Shtalenkov, Anah.	6.00	.50	.20
92 Viktor Kozlov, SanJ.	10.00	1.00	.20
93 Jon Klemm, Colo. RC	**15.00**	**3.00**	**1.00**
94 Mark Tinordi, Wash.	6.00	.50	.20
95 Bret Hedican, Vanc.	6.00	.50	.20
96 Kevin Stevens, Bost.	6.00	.50	.20
97 Bernie Nicholls, Chic.	6.00	.50	.20
98 Pat Verbeek, NYRa.	10.00	1.00	.20
99 Wayne Gretzky, LosA.	150.00	15.00	2.50
100 René Corbet, Colo.	6.00	.50	.20
101 Shayne Corson, SLou.	10.00	1.00	.20
102 Cliff Ronning, Vanc.	6.00	.50	.20
103 Olaf Kölzig (G), Wash.	20.00	2.00	.20
104 D. Hasek (G), Buff.	35.00	3.50	.50
105 Corey Millen, Dall.	6.00	.50	.20
106 Patrick Flatley, NYIs.	6.00	.50	.20
107 Chris Therien, Phil.	6.00	.50	.20
108 Ken Wregget (G), Pitt.	6.00	.50	.20
109 Paul Ysebaert, Tamp.	6.00	.50	.20
110 Mike Gartner, Toro.	30.00	3.00	.50
111 Michal Grosek, Winn.	6.00	.50	.20
112 C. Billington (G), Bost.	6.00	.50	.20
113 Steve Yzerman, Detr.	90.00	9.00	1.50
114 Neal Broten, NJer.	6.00	.50	.20
115 T. Barrasso (G), Pitt.	15.00	1.50	.20
116 Brent Fedyk, Phil.	6.00	.50	.20
117 Todd Gill, Toro.	6.00	.50	.20
118 Petr Klima, Tamp.	6.00	.50	.20
119 Dave Karpa, Anah.	6.00	.50	.20
120 Geoff Courtnall, SLou.	6.00	.50	.20
121 Kelly Buchberger, Edmo.	6.00	.50	.20
122 Éric Lacroix, LosA.	6.00	.50	.20
123 Janne Laukkanen, Colo.	6.00	.50	.20
124 Radek Bonk, Otta.	10.00	1.00	.20
125 Sergio Momesso, Toro.	6.00	.50	.20
126 Esa Tikkanen, SLou.	6.00	.50	.20
127 Jon Rohloff, Bost.	6.00	.50	.20
128 Ken Klee, Wash. RC	**10.00**	**1.50**	**.50**
129 Johan Garpenlöv, Flor.	6.00	.50	.20
130 Sean Burke (G), Hart.	20.00	2.00	.20
131 Shean Donovan, SanJ.	6.00	.50	.20

1995 TOPPS STADIUM CLUB – BASEBALL

Topps Stadium Club	TSC
148 Larry Walker	.50

☐☐☐ 132 Alexei Kovalev, NYRa.	20.00	2.00	.20
☐☐☐ 133 Sylvain Côté, Wash.	6.00	.50	.20
☐☐☐ 134 Jeff Friesen, SanJ.	10.00	1.00	.20
☐☐☐ 135 Scott Pearson, Buff.	6.00	.50	.20
☐☐☐ 136 Kirk McLean (G), Vanc.	10.00	1.00	.20
☐☐☐ 137 Glen Wesley, Hart.	6.00	.50	.20
☐☐☐ 138 Bob Kudelski, Flor.	6.00	.50	.20
☐☐☐ 139 Craig Johnson, SLou.	6.00	.50	.20
☐☐☐ 140 Zigmund Palffy, NYIs.	20.00	2.00	.20
☐☐☐ 141 Kris King, Winn.	6.00	.50	.20
☐☐☐ **142 R. Fitzgerald, Pitt. RC**	**10.00**	**1.50**	**.50**
☐☐☐ 143 Trevor Kidd (G), Calg.	10.00	1.00	.20
☐☐☐ 144 Dave Ellett, Toro.	6.00	.50	.20
☐☐☐ 145 K. Hrudey (G), LosA.	10.00	1.00	.20
☐☐☐ 146 Igor Kravchuk, Edmo.	6.00	.50	.20
☐☐☐ 147 Mats Sundin, Toro.	35.00	3.50	.50
☐☐☐ 148 S. Chambers, NJer.	6.00	.50	.20
☐☐☐ 149 Bob Corkum, Anah.	6.00	.50	.20
☐☐☐ 150 Shjon Podein, Phil.	6.00	.50	.20
☐☐☐ 151 Murray Craven, Chic.	6.00	.50	.20
☐☐☐ 152 Roman Hamrlik, Tamp.	6.00	.50	.20
☐☐☐ 153 Lyle Odelein, Mont.	6.00	.50	.20
☐☐☐ 154 Vy. Kozlov, Detr.	6.00	.50	.20
☐☐☐ 155 David Emma, NJer.	6.00	.50	.20
☐☐☐ 156 Benoît Brunet, Mont.	6.00	.50	.20
☐☐☐ 157 Jozef Stumpel, Bost.	6.00	.50	.20
☐☐☐ 158 Darrin Madeley, Otta.	6.00	.50	.20
☐☐☐ 159 Keith Primeau, Detr.	15.00	1.50	.20
☐☐☐ 160 Jeff Norton, SLou.	6.00	.50	.20
☐☐☐ 161 M. Schneider, NYIs.	6.00	.50	.20
☐☐☐ 162 Trent Klatt, Dall.	6.00	.50	.20
☐☐☐ 163 Pat Peake, Wash.	6.00	.50	.20
☐☐☐ 164 Rob Gaudreau, Otta.	6.00	.50	.20
☐☐☐ 165 Doug Bodger, Buff.	6.00	.50	.20
☐☐☐ 166 S. Nemchinov, NYRa.	6.00	.50	.20
☐☐☐ 167 David Oliver, Edmo.	6.00	.50	.20
☐☐☐ 168 Sandis Ozolinsh, SanJ.	6.00	.50	.20
☐☐☐ 169 Mark Messier, NYRa.	35.00	3.50	.50
☐☐☐ 170 Chris Chelios, Chic.	20.00	2.00	.20
☐☐☐ 171 Teemu Selänne, Winn.	30.00	3.00	.50
☐☐☐ **172 R. Svehla, Flor. RC**	**25.00**	**4.50**	**1.50**
☐☐☐ 173 N. Borschevsky, Calg.	6.00	.50	.20
☐☐☐ 174 Chris Pronger, SLou.	20.00	2.00	.20
☐☐☐ 175 Dave Lowry, Flor.	6.00	.50	.20
☐☐☐ 176 Owen Nolan, Colo.	20.00	2.00	.20
☐☐☐ 177 Sylvain Turgeon, Otta.	6.00	.50	.20
☐☐☐ 178 Nelson Emerson, Winn.	6.00	.50	.20
☐☐☐ 179 Theoren Fleury, Calg.	20.00	2.00	.20
☐☐☐ 180 Patrik Carnbäck, Anah.	6.00	.50	.20
☐☐☐ 181 Kevin Smyth, Hart.	6.00	.50	.20
☐☐☐ 182 Jeff Shantz, Chic.	6.00	.50	.20
☐☐☐ 183 B. Carpenter, NJer.	6.00	.50	.20
☐☐☐ 184 B. Shanahan, Hart.	35.00	3.50	.50
☐☐☐ 185 Tomas Sandström, Pitt.	6.00	.50	.20
☐☐☐ 186 Éric Desjardins, Phil.	10.00	1.00	.20
☐☐☐ 187 Alexei Zhitnik, Buff.	6.00	.50	.20
☐☐☐ 188 A. Mogilny, Vanc.	15.00	1.50	.20
☐☐☐ 189 M. Czerkawski, Bost.	6.00	.50	.20
☐☐☐ 190 V. Konstantinov, Detr.	10.00	1.00	.20
☐☐☐ 191 Andy Moog (G), Dall.	15.00	1.50	.20
☐☐☐ 192 Peter Popovic, Mont.	6.00	.50	.20
☐☐☐ 193 Marty McSorley, LosA.	6.00	.50	.20
☐☐☐ 194 Mikael Renberg, Phil.	10.00	1.00	.20
☐☐☐ **195 A. Stojanov, Vanc. RC**	**10.00**	**1.50**	**.50**
☐☐☐ 196 R. Tabaracci (G), Calg.	6.00	.50	.20
☐☐☐ 197 Adam Oates, Bost.	15.00	1.50	.20
☐☐☐ 198 Garry Galley, Buff.	6.00	.50	.20
☐☐☐ 199 Todd Harvey, Dall.	6.00	.50	.20
☐☐☐ 200 Martin Lapointe, Detr.	15.00	1.50	.20
☐☐☐ 201 Tony Granato, LosA.	6.00	.50	.20
☐☐☐ 202 T. Stevenson, Mont.	6.00	.50	.20
☐☐☐ 203 J. Beukeboom, NYRa.	6.00	.50	.20
☐☐☐ 204 Adam Foote, Colo.	10.00	1.00	.20
☐☐☐ 205 D. Puppa (G), Tamp.	6.00	.50	.20
☐☐☐ 206 Paul Kariya, Anah.	50.00	5.00	.50
☐☐☐ 207 German Titov, Calg.	6.00	.50	.20
☐☐☐ 208 Patrick Poulin, Chic.	6.00	.50	.20
☐☐☐ 209 Jesse Bélanger, Flor.	6.00	.50	.20
☐☐☐ 210 Steven Rice, Hart.	6.00	.50	.20
☐☐☐ 211 Brodeur (G) w/ Cup	60.00	6.00	1.00
☐☐☐ 212 Rob Pearson, Wash.	6.00	.50	.20
☐☐☐ 213 Igor Larionov, SanJ.	20.00	2.00	.20
☐☐☐ 214 Pavel Bure, Vanc.	30.00	3.00	.20
☐☐☐ 215 Sergei Fedorov, Detr.	35.00	3.50	.50
☐☐☐ 216 Ed Belfour (G), Chi.	35.00	3.50	.50
☐☐☐ 217 Mark Messier, NYRa.	35.00	3.50	.50
☐☐☐ 218 Steve Yzerman, Detr.	90.00	9.00	1.00
☐☐☐ 219 Mats Sundin, Toro.	35.00	3.50	.50
☐☐☐ 220 Mike Modano, Dall.	35.00	3.50	.50
☐☐☐ 221 A. Mogilny, Vanc.	15.00	1.50	.20
☐☐☐ 222 W. Gretzky, LosA.	150.00	15.00	2.00
☐☐☐ 223 Keith Primeau, Detr.	15.00	1.50	.20
☐☐☐ 224 Adam Graves, NYRa.	15.00	1.50	.20
☐☐☐ 225 Owen Nolan, Col.	20.00	2.00	.20
☐☐☐ 226 Paul Coffey, Detr.	20.00	2.00	.20
☐☐☐ 227 Jeremy Roenick, Chi.	30.00	3.00	.20
☐☐☐ 228 Félix Potvin (G), Toro.	20.00	2.00	.20
☐☐☐ 229 Trevor Kidd (G), Calg.	10.00	1.00	.20
☐☐☐ 230 Ray Bourque, Bost.	45.00	4.50	.50
☐☐☐ 231 Mario Lemieux, Pitt.	110.00	10.00	1.50
☐☐☐ 232 Peter Bondra, Wash.	20.00	2.00	.20
☐☐☐ 233 Brett Hull, SLou.	35.00	3.50	.50
☐☐☐ 234 Alexei Zhamnov, Winn.	6.00	.50	.20
☐☐☐ 235 Theoren Fleury, Calg.	15.00	1.50	.20
☐☐☐ 236 Brian Leetch, NYRa.	15.00	1.50	.20
☐☐☐ 237 Cam Neely, Bost.	30.00	3.00	.50
☐☐☐ 238 Chris Chelios, Chic.	15.00	1.50	.20
☐☐☐ 239 Adam Graves, NYRa.	10.00	1.00	.20
☐☐☐ 240 Doug Gilmour, Toro.	15.00	1.50	.20
☐☐☐ 241 Jeremy Roenick, Chic.	20.00	2.00	.20
☐☐☐ 242 Joe Sakic, Colo.	45.00	4.50	.50
☐☐☐ 243 Keith Tkachuk, Winn.	15.00	1.50	.20
☐☐☐ 244 Luc Robitaille, NYRa.	20.00	2.00	.20
☐☐☐ 245 Paul Kariya, Anah.	40.00	4.00	.50
☐☐☐ 246 Owen Nolan, Colo.	15.00	1.50	.20
☐☐☐ 247 John LeClair, Phil.	20.00	2.00	.20
☐☐☐ 248 Paul Coffey, Detr.	15.00	1.50	.20
☐☐☐ 249 Peter Bondra, Wash.	15.00	1.50	.20
☐☐☐ 250 R. Bourque, Bost.	35.00	3.50	.50
☐☐☐ 251 Brett Hull, SLou.	30.00	3.00	.50
☐☐☐ 252 W. Gretzky, LosA.	120.00	12.00	2.00
☐☐☐ 253 T. Selänne, Winn.	20.00	2.00	.20
☐☐☐ 254 Ray Sheppard, Detr.	6.00	.50	.20
☐☐☐ 255 Ron Francis, Pitt.	15.00	1.50	.20
☐☐☐ 256 Kevin Hatcher, Dall.	6.00	.50	.20
☐☐☐ 257 Brett Lindros, NYIs.	6.00	.50	.20
☐☐☐ 258 Claude Lemieux, NJer.	6.00	.50	.20
☐☐☐ 259 Saku Koivu, Mont.	45.00	6.00	1.00
☐☐☐ **260 R. Dvorak, Flor. RC**	**25.00**	**4.50**	**1.50**
☐☐☐ 261 N. Sundström, NYRa.	10.00	1.50	.20
☐☐☐ **262 C. Kilger, Anah. RC**	**25.00**	**4.50**	**1.50**
☐☐☐ 263 V. Yachmenev, LosA.	6.00	1.00	.20
☐☐☐ 264 Jeff O'Neill, Hart.	20.00	3.00	.50
☐☐☐ 265 Brendan Witt, Wash.	6.00	.50	.20
☐☐☐ 266 J. Bonsignore, Edmo.	6.00	.50	.20
☐☐☐ **267 Aki Berg, LosA. RC**	**15.00**	**3.00**	**1.00**
☐☐☐ 268 Éric Dazé, Chic.	20.00	3.00	.50
☐☐☐ **269 S. Doan, Winn. RC**	**25.00**	**4.50**	**1.50**
☐☐☐ 270 D. Langkow, Tamp.	25.00	4.50	1.00
☐☐☐ 271 Alexandre Daigle, Otta.	6.00	.50	.20
☐☐☐ 272 Brian Noonan, SLou.	6.00	.50	.20
☐☐☐ 273 Guy Carbonneau, Dall.	10.00	1.00	.20
☐☐☐ 274 Rick Tocchet, LosA.	10.00	1.00	.20
☐☐☐ 275 T. Numminen, Winn.	10.00	1.00	.20
☐☐☐ 276 Brian Skrudland, Flor.	6.00	.50	.20
☐☐☐ 277 Andrei Trefilov, Buff.	6.00	.50	.20
☐☐☐ 278 Joe Murphy, Chic.	6.00	.50	.20
☐☐☐ 279 Sergei Fedorov, Detr.	35.00	3.50	.50
☐☐☐ 280 Doug Weight, Edmo.	20.00	2.00	.20
☐☐☐ 281 Robert Lang, LosA.	6.00	.50	.20
☐☐☐ 282 Darryl Shannon, Winn.	6.00	.50	.20
☐☐☐ 283 Cory Stillman, Calg.	6.00	.50	.20
☐☐☐ 284 Gary Suter, Chic.	6.00	.50	.20
☐☐☐ 285 Joe Nieuwendyk, Dall.	15.00	1.50	.20
☐☐☐ 286 Terry Carkner, Flor.	6.00	.50	.20
☐☐☐ 287 Dmitri Khristich, LosA.	6.00	.50	.20
☐☐☐ 288 A. Karpovtsev, NYRa.	6.00	.50	.20
☐☐☐ 289 Garth Snow (G), Phil.	10.00	1.00	.20
☐☐☐ 290 Al MacInnis, SLou.	15.00	1.50	.20
☐☐☐ 291 Doug Gilmour, Toro.	20.00	2.00	.20
☐☐☐ 292 Mike Eastwood, Winn.	6.00	.50	.20
☐☐☐ 293 Stephen Heinze, Bost.	6.00	.50	.20
☐☐☐ 294 Phil Housley, Calg.	10.00	1.00	.20
☐☐☐ 295 Tim Taylor, Detr.	6.00	.50	.20
☐☐☐ 296 Cu. Joseph (G), Edmo.	35.00	3.50	.50
☐☐☐ 297 P. Roy (G), Colo.	110.00	10.00	1.50
☐☐☐ 298 Ted Drury, Otta.	6.00	.50	.20
☐☐☐ 299 Igor Korolev, Winn.	6.00	.50	.20
☐☐☐ 300 R. Bourque, Bost.	45.00	4.50	.50
☐☐☐ 301 Darren McCarty, Detr.	10.00	1.00	.20
☐☐☐ **302 M. Satan, Edmo. RC**	**35.00**	**6.00**	**2.00**
☐☐☐ 303 Adam Burt, Hart.	6.00	.50	.20
☐☐☐ 304 Valeri Bure, Mont.	10.00	1.00	.20
☐☐☐ 305 Sergei Gonchar, Wash.	10.00	1.00	.20
☐☐☐ 306 Jason York, Anah.	6.00	.50	.20
☐☐☐ 307 Brent Grieve, Chic.	6.00	.50	.20
☐☐☐ 308 Craig Johnson, SLou.	6.00	.50	.20
☐☐☐ 309 Kevin Hatcher, Dall.	6.00	.50	.20
☐☐☐ 310 Rob Niedermayer, Flor.	6.00	.50	.20
☐☐☐ 311 Nelson Emerson, Hart.	6.00	.50	.20
☐☐☐ 312 Mark Janssens, Hart.	6.00	.50	.20
☐☐☐ 313 T. Söderström (G), NYIs.	6.00	.50	.20
☐☐☐ 314 Joey Kocur, NYRa.	6.00	.50	.20
☐☐☐ 315 Craig Janney, SanJ.	6.00	.50	.20
☐☐☐ 316 A. Selivanov, Tamp.	6.00	.50	.20
☐☐☐ 317 Russ Courtnall, Vanc.	6.00	.50	.20
☐☐☐ **318 P. Sykora, NJer. RC**	**45.00**	**7.00**	**2.50**
☐☐☐ 319 Rick Zombo, Bost.	6.00	.50	.20
☐☐☐ 320 Randy Burridge, Buff.	6.00	.50	.20
☐☐☐ 321 V'b'sbrouck (G), Flor.	15.00	1.50	.20
☐☐☐ 322 Dmitri Mironov, Pitt.	6.00	.50	.20
☐☐☐ 323 Sean Hill, Otta.	6.00	.50	.20
☐☐☐ 324 Rod Brind'Amour, Phil.	10.00	1.00	.20
☐☐☐ 325 Wendel Clark, Toro.	30.00	3.00	.50
☐☐☐ 326 Brent Gilchrist, Dall.	6.00	.50	.20
☐☐☐ 327 Tyler Wright, Edmo.	6.00	.50	.20
☐☐☐ **328 S. Daniels, Hart. RC**	**10.00**	**1.50**	**.50**
☐☐☐ 329 Adam Graves, NYRa.	15.00	1.50	.20
☐☐☐ **330 D. Malkoc, Vanc. RC**	**10.00**	**1.50**	**.50**
☐☐☐ 331 Jamie Macoun, Toro.	6.00	.50	.20
☐☐☐ **332 S. Moger, Bost. RC**	**10.00**	**1.50**	**.50**
☐☐☐ 333 Michael Peca, Buff.	15.00	1.50	.20
☐☐☐ 334 Greg Johnson, Detr.	6.00	.50	.20
☐☐☐ 335 Jason Woolley, Flor.	6.00	.50	.20
☐☐☐ 336 Rob DiMaio, Phil.	6.00	.50	.20
☐☐☐ 337 D. Rhodes (G), Otta.	6.00	.50	.20
☐☐☐ 338 Gino Odjick, Vanc.	6.00	.50	.20
☐☐☐ 339 Peter Bondra, Wash.	20.00	2.00	.20
☐☐☐ 340 Todd Ewen, Anah.	6.00	.50	.20
☐☐☐ 341 Matthew Barnaby, Buff.	6.00	.50	.20
☐☐☐ 342 Sylvain Lefebvre, Colo.	6.00	.50	.20
☐☐☐ 343 Oleg Petrov, Mont.	10.00	1.00	.20
☐☐☐ 344 Jim Carey (G), Wash.	6.00	.50	.20
☐☐☐ 345 Stu Barnes, Flor.	6.00	.50	.20
☐☐☐ 346 Kelly Miller, Wash.	6.00	.50	.20
☐☐☐ **347 Törmänen, Otta. RC**	**10.00**	**1.50**	**.50**
☐☐☐ 348 Ray Sheppard, SanJ.	6.00	.50	.20
☐☐☐ 349 Igor Larionov, Detr.	20.00	2.00	.20
☐☐☐ 350 Kjell Samuelsson, Phil.	6.00	.50	.20
☐☐☐ 351 Benoît Hogue, Toro.	6.00	.50	.20
☐☐☐ 352 Jeff R. Brown, Vanc.	6.00	.50	.20
☐☐☐ 353 N. Baumgartner, Wash.	6.00	.50	.20
☐☐☐ 354 Denis Pederson, NJer.	6.00	.50	.20
☐☐☐ 355 Shawn Burr, Tamp.	6.00	.50	.20
☐☐☐ 356 Jyrki Lumme, Vanc.	6.00	.50	.20
☐☐☐ 357 Kevin Haller, Phil.	6.00	.50	.20
☐☐☐ 358 John Cullen, Tamp.	6.00	.50	.20
☐☐☐ 359 Martin Gélinas, Vanc.	6.00	.50	.20
☐☐☐ 360 S. McEachern, Bost.	10.00	1.00	.20
☐☐☐ 361 Sandy McCarthy, Calg.	6.00	.50	.20
☐☐☐ **362 G. Marshall, Dall. RC**	**15.00**	**3.00**	**1.00**
☐☐☐ 363 D. McAmmond, Edmo.	6.00	.50	.20
☐☐☐ 364 Kevin Todd, LosA.	6.00	.50	.20
☐☐☐ 365 Bobby Holik, NJer.	10.00	1.00	.20
☐☐☐ 366 Joel Otto, Phil.	6.00	.50	.20
☐☐☐ 367 D. Andreychuk, Toro.	10.00	1.00	.20
☐☐☐ 368 Ronnie Stern, Calg.	6.00	.50	.20
☐☐☐ 369 J. Thibault (G), Mont.	15.00	1.50	.20
☐☐☐ 370 Dave Gagner, Dall.	6.00	.50	.20
☐☐☐ 371 Bryan Marchment, Edmo.	6.00	.50	.20
☐☐☐ 372 Jari Kurri, LosA.	35.00	3.50	.50
☐☐☐ 373 Bill Guerin, NJer.	15.00	1.50	.20
☐☐☐ 374 Eric Lindros, Phil.	35.00	3.50	.50
☐☐☐ 375 Adam Creighton, SLou.	6.00	.50	.20
☐☐☐ 376 D. Yushkevich, Toro.	6.00	.50	.20
☐☐☐ 377 Peter Zezel, SLou.	6.00	.50	.20
☐☐☐ 378 Valeri Karpov, Anah.	6.00	.50	.20
☐☐☐ **379 Labrecque, Mont. RC**	**10.00**	**1.50**	**.50**
☐☐☐ 380 Mick Vukota, NYIs.	6.00	.50	.20
☐☐☐ 381 Ulf Dahlén, SanJ.	6.00	.50	.20
☐☐☐ 382 Enrico Ciccone, Tamp.	6.00	.50	.20
☐☐☐ 383 S. Niedermayer, NJer.	10.00	1.00	.20
☐☐☐ 384 Ville Peltonen, SanJ.	6.00	.50	.20
☐☐☐ 385 B. Lacher (G), Bost.	6.00	.50	.20
☐☐☐ 386 P. LaFontaine, Buff.	20.00	2.00	.20
☐☐☐ 387 Jeff Hackett (G), Chic.	10.00	1.00	.20
☐☐☐ 388 Mike Keane, Colo.	6.00	.50	.20
☐☐☐ 389 Pierre Turgeon, Mont.	15.00	1.50	.20
☐☐☐ 390 Scott Lachance, NYIs.	6.00	.50	.20
☐☐☐ 391 Jason Wiemer, Tamp.	6.00	.50	.20
☐☐☐ 392 Michal Pivonka, Wash.	6.00	.50	.20
☐☐☐ **393 D. Bonvie, Edmo. RC**	**10.00**	**1.50**	**.50**
☐☐☐ 394 Glen Murray, Pitt.	15.00	1.50	.20
☐☐☐ 395 Bobby Dollas, Anah.	6.00	.50	.20
☐☐☐ 396 Paul Coffey, Detr.	20.00	2.00	.20
☐☐☐ 397 S. Fiset (G), Colo.	10.00	1.00	.20
☐☐☐ 398 Jere Lehtinen, Dall.	15.00	2.00	.20
☐☐☐ 399 Scott Mellanby, Flor.	6.00	.50	.20
☐☐☐ 400 Robert Kron, Hart.	6.00	.50	.20
☐☐☐ 401 Doug Lidster, NYRa.	6.00	.50	.20
☐☐☐ 402 Don Beaupré (G), Otta.	6.00	.50	.20
☐☐☐ 403 Arturs Irbe (G), SanJ.	15.00	1.50	.20
☐☐☐ 404 Brian Bellows, Tamp.	6.00	.50	.20
☐☐☐ 405 Corey Hirsch, Vanc.	6.00	.50	.20
☐☐☐ 406 Pavel Bure, Vanc.	30.00	3.00	.50
☐☐☐ 407 Chris Gratton, Tamp.	6.00	.50	.20
☐☐☐ 408 Oleg Tverdovsky, Winn.	6.00	.50	.20
☐☐☐ 409 Derek Plante, Buff.	6.00	.50	.20
☐☐☐ 410 Dan Keczmer, Calg.	6.00	.50	.20
☐☐☐ 411 Donald Brashear, Mont.	6.00	.50	.20
☐☐☐ **412 An. Vasilyev, NYIs. RC**	**10.00**	**1.50**	**.50**
☐☐☐ **413 T. Salo (G), NYIs. RC**	**45.00**	**7.00**	**2.50**
☐☐☐ 414 Kevin Lowe, NYRa.	10.00	1.00	.20
☐☐☐ 415 Dody Wood, SanJ.	6.00	.50	.20
☐☐☐ 416 Denis Chassé, SLou.	6.00	.50	.20
☐☐☐ 417 Aaron Gavey, Tamp.	6.00	.50	.20
☐☐☐ **418 S. Walker, Vanc. RC**	**25.00**	**4.50**	**1.50**
☐☐☐ 419 Richard Park, Pitt.	6.00	.50	.20
☐☐☐ 420 Mike Modano, Dall.	35.00	3.50	.50
☐☐☐ **421 McLaren, Bost. RC**	**25.00**	**4.50**	**1.50**
☐☐☐ 422 J. Roenick, Chic.	30.00	3.00	.50
☐☐☐ 423 M. Fitzpatrick (G), Flor.	6.00	.50	.20
☐☐☐ **424 L. Wilson, Colo. RC**	**15.00**	**3.00**	**1.00**
☐☐☐ 425 Steve Rucchin, Anah.	6.00	.50	.20
☐☐☐ 426 Stéphane Richer, NJer.	6.00	.50	.20
☐☐☐ 427 Martin Straka, Otta.	10.00	1.00	.20
☐☐☐ 428 Ron Hextall (G), Phil.	20.00	2.00	.20
☐☐☐ **429 J. Dziedzic, Pitt. RC**	**10.00**	**1.50**	**.50**
☐☐☐ 430 Peter Forsberg, Colo.	50.00	5.00	.50
☐☐☐ 431 Dino Ciccarelli, Detr.	10.00	1.00	.20
☐☐☐ 432 Robert Dirk, Anah.	6.00	.50	.20
☐☐☐ 433 Wayne Primeau, Buff.	15.00	3.00	.50
☐☐☐ 434 Denis Savard, Chic.	15.00	1.50	.20
☐☐☐ 435 Keith Carney, Chic.	6.00	.50	.20
☐☐☐ 436 Tom Fitzgerald, Flor.	6.00	.50	.20
☐☐☐ 437 Cale Hulse, NJer.	6.00	.50	.20
☐☐☐ 438 Mike Richter (G), NYRa.	15.00	1.50	.20
☐☐☐ **439 Ragnarsson, SanJ. RC**	**25.00**	**4.50**	**1.50**
☐☐☐ **440 R. Vopat, SLou. RC**	**10.00**	**1.50**	**.50**
☐☐☐ 441 Zdenek Nedved, Toro.	6.00	.50	.20
☐☐☐ 442 Dale Hunter, Wash.	10.00	1.00	.20
☐☐☐ 443 Bob Sweeney, NYIs.	6.00	.50	.20
☐☐☐ 444 Randy McKay, NJer.	6.00	.50	.20
☐☐☐ 445 C. Osgood (G), Detr.	20.00	2.00	.20
☐☐☐ 446 A. Kovalenko, Mont.	6.00	.50	.20
☐☐☐ 447 D. Kasparaitis, NYIs.	6.00	.50	.20
☐☐☐ 448 Ulf Samuelsson, Pitt.	6.00	.50	.20
☐☐☐ 449 Chris Joseph (G), Pitt.	6.00	.50	.20
☐☐☐ 450 Chris Terreri (G), SanJ.	6.00	.50	.20
☐☐☐ 451 Keith Jones, Wash.	6.00	.50	.20
☐☐☐ 452 T. Chevelade (G), Winn.	6.00	.50	.20
☐☐☐ 453 Stephen Leach, Bost.	6.00	.50	.20
☐☐☐ 454 M. Nylander, Calg.	6.00	.50	.20
☐☐☐ 455 Ed Belfour (G), Chic.	35.00	3.50	.50
☐☐☐ 456 Claude Lemieux, Colo.	10.00	1.00	.20
☐☐☐ 457 Mike Ricci, Colo.	10.00	1.00	.20
☐☐☐ 458 Shane Churla, Dall.	6.00	.50	.20
☐☐☐ 459 Kris Draper, Detr.	6.00	.50	.20
☐☐☐ 460 B. Dafoe (G), LosA.	15.00	1.50	.20
☐☐☐ 461 Troy Mallette, Otta.	6.00	.50	.20
☐☐☐ 462 Petr Nedved, Pitt.	10.00	1.00	.20
☐☐☐ 463 Kenny Jönsson, Toro.	6.00	.50	.20
☐☐☐ 464 Keith Tkachuk, Winn.	20.00	2.00	.20
☐☐☐ 465 Jaromir Jagr, Pitt.	35.00	3.50	.50
☐☐☐ 466 V. Malakhov, Mont.	6.00	.50	.20
☐☐☐ 467 Guy Hebert (G), Anah.	6.00	.50	.20
☐☐☐ 468 Brad May, Buff.	6.00	.50	.20
☐☐☐ 469 Bob Probert, Chic.	10.00	1.00	.20
☐☐☐ 470 Sandis Ozolinsh, Colo.	6.00	.50	.20
☐☐☐ **471 Mikulchik, Anah. RC**	**10.00**	**1.50**	**.50**
☐☐☐ 472 Steve Thomas, NJer.	6.00	.50	.20
☐☐☐ 473 Travis Green, NYIs.	6.00	.50	.20
☐☐☐ 474 Sergei Zubov, Pitt.	6.00	.50	.20
☐☐☐ 475 Bill Houlder, Tamp.	6.00	.50	.20
☐☐☐ 476 Roman Oksiuta, Vanc.	6.00	.50	.20
☐☐☐ 477 Jamie Rivers, SLou.	6.00	.50	.20
☐☐☐ 478 Rob Blake, LosA.	20.00	2.00	.20
☐☐☐ 479 Todd Elik, Bost.	6.00	.50	.20
☐☐☐ 480 Zarley Zalapski, Calg.	6.00	.50	.20
☐☐☐ 481 Darren Turcotte, Winn.	6.00	.50	.20
☐☐☐ 482 Scott Stevens, NJer.	15.00	1.50	.20
☐☐☐ 483 Pat Falloon, Phil.	6.00	.50	.20
☐☐☐ 484 Grant Fuhr (G), SLou.	20.00	2.00	.20
☐☐☐ 485 M. Rucinsky, Mont.	6.00	.50	.20
☐☐☐ 486 Brett Hull, SLou.	35.00	3.50	.50
☐☐☐ 487 Brian Leetch, NYRa.	20.00	2.00	.20
☐☐☐ 488 Shaun Van Allen, Anah.	6.00	.50	.20
☐☐☐ 489 Valeri Kamensky, Colo.	10.00	1.00	.20
☐☐☐ 490 Mark Recchi, Mont.	15.00	1.50	.20
☐☐☐ 491 Jason Muzzatti, Hart.	6.00	.50	.20
☐☐☐ 492 Andrew Cassels, Hart.	6.00	.50	.20
☐☐☐ 493 Nick Kypreos, NYRa.	6.00	.50	.20
☐☐☐ 494 Bryan Smolinski, Pitt.	6.00	.50	.20
☐☐☐ 495 Owen Nolan, SanJ.	20.00	2.00	.20
☐☐☐ 496 Bryan McCabe, NYIs.	10.00	1.50	.20
☐☐☐ **497 Dandenault, Detr. RC**	**15.00**	**3.00**	**1.00**
☐☐☐ 498 Deron Quint, Winn.	6.00	1.00	.20
☐☐☐ 499 Jason Doig, Winn.	6.00	.50	.20
☐☐☐ 500 Marty Murray, Calg.	6.00	.50	.20
☐☐☐ 501 Ed Jovanovski, Flor.	20.00	3.00	.50
☐☐☐ 502 Stefan Ustorf, Wash.	6.00	.50	.20
☐☐☐ 503 Langenbrunner, Dall.	10.00	1.50	.20
☐☐☐ **504 Alfredsson, Otta. RC**	**65.00**	**10.00**	**3.50**
☐☐☐ 505 D. Hendrickson, Toro.	6.00	1.00	.20
☐☐☐ **506 B. McLean, Cdn. RC**	**10.00**	**1.50**	**.50**
☐☐☐ **507 D. Cleary, Cdn. RC**	**35.00**	**6.00**	**2.00**
☐☐☐ **508 T. Robinson, Cdn. RC**	**10.00**	**1.50**	**.50**
☐☐☐ **509 A. Asham, Cdn. RC**	**10.00**	**1.50**	**.50**
☐☐☐ **510 D. Corso, Cdn. RC**	**15.00**	**3.00**	**1.00**
☐☐☐ **511 D. Van Oene, Cdn. RC**	**10.00**	**1.50**	**.50**
☐☐☐ **512 T. Wasyluk, Cdn. RC**	**10.00**	**1.50**	**.50**
☐☐☐ **513 J. Holden, Cdn. RC**	**15.00**	**3.00**	**1.00**
☐☐☐ **514 É. Drapeau, Cdn. RC**	**10.00**	**1.50**	**.50**
☐☐☐ **515 M. Osborne, Cdn. RC**	**10.00**	**1.50**	**.50**
☐☐☐ **516 Komarniski, Cdn. RC**	**10.00**	**1.50**	**.50**
☐☐☐ **517 C. Phillips, Cdn. RC**	**25.00**	**4.50**	**1.50**
☐☐☐ **518 C. Fleury, Cdn. RC**	**10.00**	**1.50**	**.50**
☐☐☐ **519 Cory Sarich, Cdn. RC**	**15.00**	**3.00**	**1.00**
☐☐☐ **520 G. Crawford, Cdn. RC**	**10.00**	**1.50**	**.50**
☐☐☐ **521 F. Méthot, Cdn. RC**	**10.00**	**1.50**	**.50**
☐☐☐ **522 Geoff Peters, Cdn. RC**	**10.00**	**1.50**	**.50**
☐☐☐ **523 J. Tetarenko, Cdn. RC**	**10.00**	**1.50**	**.50**
☐☐☐ **524 R. Petruk, Cdn. RC**	**10.00**	**1.50**	**.50**
☐☐☐ **525 M. Garon, Cdn. RC**	**45.00**	**7.00**	**5.00**

☐☐☐ 526 D. Langkow	10.00	1.50	.20
☐☐☐ **527 Craig Mills RC**	**10.00**	**1.50**	**.50**
☐☐☐ **528 R. Warrener RC**	**10.00**	**1.50**	**.50**
☐☐☐ **529 Marc Denis (G) RC**	**90.00**	**18.00**	**10.00**
☐☐☐ **530 Théodore (G) RC**	**250.00**	**65.00**	**30.00**
☐☐☐ **531 Curtis Brown RC**	**15.00**	**3.00**	**1.00**
☐☐☐ 532 Chad Allan	6.00	.50	.20
☐☐☐ **533 D. Gauthier RC**	**10.00**	**1.50**	**.50**
☐☐☐ 534 Brad Larsen	6.00	.50	.20
☐☐☐ **535 J. Wright RC**	**10.00**	**1.50**	**.50**
☐☐☐ **536 Mike Watt RC**	**10.00**	**1.50**	**.50**
☐☐☐ **537 J. Holland RC**	**10.00**	**1.50**	**.50**
☐☐☐ **538 R. Gordon RC**	**10.00**	**1.50**	**.50**
☐☐☐ **539 Domenichelli RC**	**15.00**	**3.00**	**1.00**
☐☐☐ **540 O. Kratena RC**	**10.00**	**1.50**	**.50**
☐☐☐ **541 M. Bros RC**	**10.00**	**1.50**	**.50**
☐☐☐ **542 Marek Posmyk RC**	**10.00**	**1.50**	**.50**
☐☐☐ **543 M. Melenovsky RC**	**10.00**	**1.50**	**.50**
☐☐☐ **544 Jan Tomajko RC**	**10.00**	**1.50**	**.50**
☐☐☐ **545 Ales Pisa RC**	**10.00**	**1.50**	**.50**
☐☐☐ 546 Miika Elomo	6.00	.50	.20
☐☐☐ 547 Timo Salonen	6.00	.50	.20
☐☐☐ **548 Teemu Riihijärvi RC**	**10.00**	**1.50**	**.50**
☐☐☐ **549 Antti-Jussi Niemi RC**	**10.00**	**1.50**	**.50**
☐☐☐ **550 Pasi Petriläinen RC**	**10.00**	**1.50**	**.50**
☐☐☐ **551 Toni Lydman RC**	**15.00**	**3.00**	**1.00**
☐☐☐ 552 Dimitri Nabokov	6.00	1.00	.20
☐☐☐ 553 Aleksey Morozov	10.00	1.50	.20
☐☐☐ 554 Sergei Samsonov	30.00	4.50	.50
☐☐☐ **555 Alexei Vasilyev RC**	**10.00**	**1.50**	**.50**
☐☐☐ 556 Andrei Petrunin	6.00	.50	.20
☐☐☐ **557 Dmitri Ryabykin RC**	**10.00**	**1.50**	**.50**
☐☐☐ **558 Sergei Zimakov RC**	**10.00**	**1.50**	**.50**
☐☐☐ **559 Peter Nylander RC**	**10.00**	**1.50**	**.50**
☐☐☐ **560 Marcus Nilson RC**	**15.00**	**3.00**	**1.00**
☐☐☐ **561 Niklas Anger RC**	**10.00**	**1.50**	**.50**
☐☐☐ **562 PA Lundström RC**	**10.00**	**1.50**	**.50**
☐☐☐ **563 Patrik Wallenberg RC**	**10.00**	**1.50**	**.50**
☐☐☐ **564 PR Bergkvist RC**	**10.00**	**1.50**	**.50**
☐☐☐ **565 Mike Sylvia RC**	**10.00**	**1.50**	**.50**
☐☐☐ 566 Marty Reasoner	10.00	1.50	.20
☐☐☐ **567 Reg Berg RC**	**10.00**	**1.50**	**.50**
☐☐☐ **568 Tom Poti RC**	**15.00**	**3.00**	**1.00**
☐☐☐ **569 Chris Drury RC**	**150.00**	**40.00**	**14.00**
☐☐☐ 570 Mike McBain	6.00	.50	.20

3 1/2" x 5" Electric Ice	**EIG**
☐ 26 Chris Chelios, Chic.	1.00
☐ 48 Félix Potvin (G), Toro.	1.00
☐ 99 Wayne Gretzky, LosA.	6.00
☐ 188 Alexander Mogilny, Vanc.	1.00

ALL-STARS

These cards have two versions: a 5" x 7" box insert and the standard size insert.

Series Two Insert Set (20 cards): 70.00 140.00

	Player	5x7	Insert
□ □	AS1 Ray Bourque/ Paul Coffey	4.00	8.00
□ □	AS2 Scott Stevens/ Chris Chelios	2.00	4.00
□ □	AS3 Jaromir Jagr/ Brett Hull	5.00	10.00
□ □	AS4 Brendan Shanahan/ Pavel Bure	4.00	8.00
□ □	AS5 Mario Lemieux/ Wayne Gretzky	20.00	40.00
□ □	AS6 Martin Brodeur (G)/ Ed Belfour (G)	5.00	10.00
□ □	AS7 Brian Leetch/ Nicklas Lidström	3.00	6.00
□ □	AS8 Roman Hamrlik/ Gary Suter	1.00	2.00
□ □	AS9 Eric Desjardins/ Al MacInnis	1.00	2.00
□ □	AS10 Cam Neely/ Alexander Mogilny	3.00	6.00
□ □	AS11 Peter Bondra/ Theoren Fleury	3.00	6.00
□ □	AS12 Alfredsson/ Selänne	3.00	6.00
□ □	AS13 Pat Verbeek/ Owen Nolan	2.00	4.00
□ □	AS14 John LeClair/ Paul Kariya	5.00	10.00
□ □	AS15 Pierre Turgeon/ Sergei Fedorov	3.00	6.00
□ □	AS16 Mark Messier/ Doug Weight	4.00	8.00
□ □	AS17 Eric Lindros/ Peter Forsberg	6.00	12.00
□ □	AS18 Ron Francis/ Mats Sundin	4.00	8.00
□ □	AS19 Vanbiesbrouck (G)/ Osgood (G)	2.00	4.00
□ □	AS20 Dominik Hasek (G)/ Félix Potvin (G)	4.00	8.00

FREEZE FRAME

These cards have two versions: a 5" x 7" box insert and the standard sized insert. The oversize cards were given out as promos.

	Player	5x7	Insert
	Series One Insert Set (20 cards):	**65.00**	**125.00**
□ □	F1 Peter Forsberg, Colo.	5.00	10.00
□ □	F2 Wayne Gretzky, LosA.	15.00	30.00
□ □	F3 Eric Lindros, Phil.	3.00	6.00
□ □	F4 Jaromir Jagr, Pitt.	3.00	6.00
□ □	F5 Cam Neely, Bost.	3.00	6.00
□ □	F6 Jeremy Roenick, Chic.	3.00	6.00
□ □	F7 Mark Messier, NYRa.	3.00	6.00
□ □	F8 Sergei Fedorov, Detr.	3.00	6.00
□ □	F9 Paul Kariya, Anah.	5.00	10.00
□ □	F10 Pavel Bure, Vanc.	3.00	6.00
□ □	F11 Dominik Hasek (G), Buff.	3.00	6.00
□ □	F12 Theoren Fleury, Calg.	2.00	4.00
□ □	F13 Alexei Zhamnov, Winn.	1.00	2.00
□ □	F14 Martin Brodeur (G), NJer.	6.00	12.00
□ □	F15 Brett Hull, SLou.	3.00	6.00
□ □	F16 Mario Lemieux, Pitt.	10.00	22.00
□ □	F17 Paul Coffey, Detr.	2.00	4.00
□ □	F18 Brian Leetch, NYRa.	2.00	4.00
□ □	F19 Raymond Bourque, Bost.	4.00	8.00
□ □	F20 Jim Carey (G), Wash.	1.00	2.00

AWARD PREDICTOR

If the depicted player finished first or second in his category, the card could be redeemed for a 10-card gold set. Redeemed Gold cards had the prefix "HR-". Hobby Predictors have bronze foil and a grey background on the card front. Redeemed cards have gold foil instead of the bronze or silver.

	Player	Gold	Silver
	Hart Set (H1-H10):	**25.00**	**60.00**
	Vezina Set (H11-H20):	**15.00**	**30.00**
	Calder Set (H21-H30):	**5.00**	**15.00**
	Norris Set (H31-H40):	**5.00**	**15.00**
□ □	H1 Eric Lindros, Phil.	2.00	4.00
□ □	H2 Jaromir Jagr, Pitt. [Hart]	2.00	4.00
□ □	H3 Paul Coffey, Detr. [Hart]	1.00	2.00
□ □	H4 Mario Lemieux, Pitt. [Hart; Win]	7.00	18.00
□ □	H5 Martin Brodeur (G), NJer. [Hart]	4.00	8.00
□ □	H6 Sergei Fedorov, Detr. [Hart]	2.00	4.00
□ □	H7 Wayne Gretzky, LosA. [Hart]	10.00	20.00
□ □	H8 Peter Forsberg, Colo. [Hart]	3.00	6.00
□ □	H9 Mark Messier, NYRa. [Hart; Win]	2.00	6.00
□ □	H10 Long Shot, [Hart]	.50	1.00
□ □	H11 M. Brodeur (G), NJer. [Vézina]	4.00	8.00
□ □	H12 Mike Richter (G), NYRa. [Vézina]	1.00	2.00
□ □	H13 D. Hasek (G), Buff. [Vézina]	2.00	4.00
□ □	H14 Patrick Roy (G), Mont. [Vézina]	7.00	14.00
□ □	H15 Blaine Lacher (G), Bost. [Vézina]	.50	1.00
□ □	H16 Carey (G), Wash. [Vézina; Win]	.50	1.00
□ □	H17 Félix Potvin (G), Toro. [Vézina]	1.00	2.00
□ □	H18 Ed Belfour (G), Chic. [Vézina]	2.00	4.00
□ □	H19 Vanbiesbrouck (G), Flor. [Vézina]	1.00	2.00
□ □	H20 Long Shot, [Vézina; Win]	.50	1.00
□ □	H21 Vitali Yachmenev, LosA. [Calder]	.50	1.00
□ □	H22 Saku Koivu, Mont. [Calder]	3.00	6.00
□ □	H23 D. Alfredsson, Otta. [Calder; Win]	2.00	6.00
□ □	H24 Ed Jovanovski, Flor. [Calder]	1.00	2.00
□ □	H25 Aki Berg, LosA. [Calder]	.50	1.00
□ □	H26 Radek Dvorak, Flor. [Calder]	.50	1.00
□ □	H27 Shane Doan, Winn. [Calder]	.50	1.00
□ □	H28 Niklas Sundström, NYRa. [Calder]	.50	1.00
□ □	H29 Éric Dazé, Chic. [Calder; Win]	1.00	2.00
□ □	H30 Long Shot, [Calder]	.50	1.00
□ □	H31 Paul Coffey, Detr. [Norris]	1.00	2.00
□ □	H32 R. Bourque, Bost. [Norris; Win]	3.00	6.00
□ □	H33 Brian Leetch, NYRa. [Norris]	1.00	2.00
□ □	H34 Chris Chelios, Chic. [Norris; Win]	1.00	2.00
□ □	H35 Scott Stevens, NJer. [Norris]	1.00	2.00
□ □	H36 Nicklas Lidström, Detr. [Norris]	1.00	2.00
□ □	H37 Sergei Zubov, Pitt. [Norris]	.50	1.00
□ □	H38 Larry Murphy, Toro. [Norris]	.50	1.00
□ □	H39 Roman Hamrlik, Tamp. [Norris]	.50	1.00
□ □	H40 Long Shot, [Norris]	.50	1.00

SCORING PREDICTOR

If the depicted player finished first or second in his category, the card could be redeemed for a 10-card gold set. Redeemed Gold cards had the prefix "RR-". Retail Predictors have silver foil and a burgandy background. Redeemed cards have gold foil instead of the bronze or silver.

	Player	Gold	Silver
	Assists (Goals) Set (R1-R10):	**10.00**	**25.00**
	Goals (Assists) Set (R11-R20):	**20.00**	**40.00**
	Points Set (R21-R30):	**20.00**	**45.00**
	Art Ross Set (R31-R40):	**25.00**	**60.00**
	Pearson Set (R41-R50):	**30.00**	**65.00**
	Conn Smythe Set (R51-R60):	**35.00**	**75.00**
□ □	R1 Cam Neely, Bost.	2.00	4.00
□ □	R2 Eric Lindros, Phil. [Assists]	2.00	4.00
□ □	R3 Jaromir Jagr, Pitt. [Assists; Win]	2.00	6.00
□ □	R4 Brendan Shanahan, Hart. [Assists]	2.00	4.00
□ □	R5 Brett Hull, SLou. [Assists]	2.00	4.00
□ □	R6 Alexander Mogilny, Vanc. [Assists]	1.00	2.00
□ □	R7 Owen Nolan, Colo. [Assists]	1.00	3.00
□ □	R8 Theoren Fleury, Calg. [Assists]	1.00	2.00
□ □	R9 Pavel Bure, Vanc. [Assists]	2.00	4.00
□ □	R10 Long Shot [Assists; Win]	.50	1.00
□ □	R11 Ron Francis, Pitt. [Goals; Win]	1.00	2.00
□ □	R12 Paul Coffey, Detr. [Goals]	1.00	2.00
□ □	R13 Wayne Gretzky, LosA. [Goals]	10.00	20.00
□ □	R14 Joe Sakic, Colo. [Goals]	4.00	8.00
□ □	R15 Steve Yzerman, Detr. [Goals]	6.00	12.00
□ □	R16 Adam Oates, Bost. [Goals]	1.00	2.00
□ □	R17 Joé Juneau, Wash. [Goals]	.50	1.00
□ □	R18 Brian Leetch, NYRa. [Goals]	1.00	2.00
□ □	R19 Pat LaFontaine, Buff. [Goals]	1.00	2.00
□ □	R20 Long Shot [Goals; Win]	.50	1.00
□ □	R21 Eric Lindros, Phil. [Playoff Points]	2.00	4.00
□ □	R22 J. Jagr, Pitt. [Playoff Points; Win]	2.00	6.00
□ □	R23 Gretzky, LosA. [Playoff Points]	10.00	20.00
□ □	R24 Fedorov, Detr. [Playoff Points]	2.00	4.00
□ □	R25 Forsberg, Colo. [Playoff Points]	3.00	6.00
□ □	R26 P. Bure, Vanc. [Playoff Points]	2.00	4.00
□ □	R27 Joe Sakic, Colo. [Playoff Points]	4.00	8.00
□ □	R28 Zhamnov, Winn. [Playoff Points]	.50	1.00
□ □	R29 LaFontaine, Buff. [Playoff Points]	1.00	2.00
□ □	R30 Long Shot [Playoff Points; Win]	.50	1.00
□ □	R31 Wayne Gretzky, LosA. [Ross]	10.00	20.00
□ □	R32 Mario Lemieux, Pitt. [Ross; Win]	7.00	18.00
□ □	R33 Eric Lindros, Phil. [Ross]	2.00	4.00
□ □	R34 Sergei Fedorov, Detr. [Ross]	2.00	4.00
□ □	R35 Alexander Mogilny, Vanc. [Ross]	1.00	2.00
□ □	R36 Joe Sakic, Colo. [Ross]	4.00	8.00
□ □	R37 Peter Forsberg, Colo. [Ross]	3.00	6.00
□ □	R38 Jaromir Jagr, Pitt. [Ross; Win]	2.00	6.00
□ □	R39 Mark Messier, NYRa. [Ross]	2.00	4.00
□ □	R40 Long Shot [Ross]	.50	1.00
□ □	R41 W. Gretzky, LosA. [Pearson]	10.00	20.00
□ □	R42 M. Lemieux, Pitt. [Pearson; Win]	7.00	18.00
□ □	R43 Paul Kariya, Anah. [Pearson]	3.00	6.00
□ □	R44 Sergei Fedorov, Detr. [Pearson]	2.00	4.00
□ □	R45 Joe Sakic, Colo. [Pearson]	4.00	8.00
□ □	R46 Jaromir Jagr, Pitt. [Pearson; Win]	2.00	6.00
□ □	R47 Jeremy Roenick, Chic. [Pearson]	2.00	4.00
□ □	R48 R. Bourque, Bost. [Pearson]	3.00	6.00
□ □	R49 Teemu Selänne, Winn. [Pearson]	2.00	4.00
□ □	R50 Long Shot [Pearson]	.50	1.00
□ □	R51 Wayne Gretzky, LosA. [Smythe]	10.00	20.00
□ □	R52 Eric Lindros, Phil. [Smythe]	2.00	4.00
□ □	R53 Mario Lemieux, Pitt. [Smythe]	7.00	14.00
□ □	R54 Peter Forsberg, Colo. [Smythe]	3.00	6.00
□ □	R55 P. Roy (G), Colo. [Smythe; Win]	7.00	18.00
□ □	R56 Mark Messier, NYRa. [Smythe]	2.00	4.00
□ □	R57 M. Brodeur (G), NJer. [Smythe]	4.00	8.00
□ □	R58 Steve Yzerman, Detr. [Smythe]	6.00	12.00
□ □	R59 Ron Francis, Pitt. [Smythe]	1.00	3.00
□ □	R60 Long Shot [Smythe; Win]	.50	1.00

SPECIAL EDITION

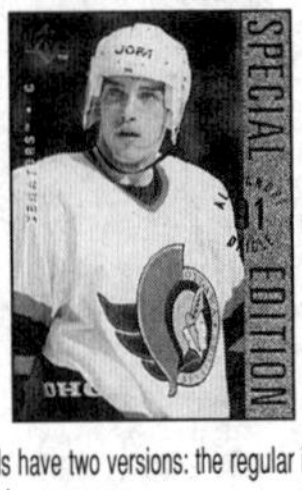

These cards have two versions: the regular insert and a Gold parallel

	Player	Gold	SE
	Series One Set (90 cards):	**400.00**	**30.00**
	Series Two Set (90 cards):	**475.00**	**40.00**
	Common Player:	**3.00**	**.30**
□ □	SE1 Paul Kariya, Anah.	25.00	2.00
□ □	SE2 Oleg Tverdovsky, Anah.	3.00	.30
□ □	SE3 Guy Hebert (G), Anah.	4.00	.30
□ □	SE4 Raymond Bourque, Bost.	20.00	2.00
□ □	SE5 Adam Oates, Bost.	8.00	.30
□ □	SE6 Mariusz Czerkawski, Bost.	4.00	.30
□ □	SE7 Blaine Lacher (G), Bost.	3.00	.30
□ □	SE8 Doug Bodger, Buff.	3.00	.30
□ □	SE9 Donald Audette, Buff.	8.00	.30
□ □	SE10 Pat LaFontaine, Buff.	12.00	1.00
□ □	SE11 Alexei Zhitnik, Buff.	3.00	.30
□ □	SE12 Joe Nieuwendyk, Calg.	8.00	.30
□ □	SE13 Phil Housley, Calg.	6.00	.30
□ □	SE14 German Titov, Calg.	3.00	.30
□ □	SE15 Trevor Kidd (G), Calg.	6.00	.30
□ □	SE16 Bernie Nicholls, Chic.	4.00	.30
□ □	SE17 Chris Chelios, Chic.	12.00	1.00
□ □	SE18 Tony Amonte, Chic.	12.00	1.00
□ □	SE19 Ed Belfour (G), Chic.	20.00	2.00
□ □	SE20 Jon Klemm, Colo.	3.00	.30
□ □	SE21 Peter Forsberg, Colo.	25.00	2.00
□ □	SE22 Adam Deadmarsh, Colo.	6.00	.30
□ □	SE23 Stéphane Fiset (G), Colo.	6.00	.30
□ □	SE24 Dave Gagner, Dall.	3.00	.30
□ □	SE25 Kevin Hatcher, Dall.	3.00	.30
□ □	SE26 Mike Modano, Dall.	20.00	2.00
□ □	SE27 Keith Primeau, Detr.	8.00	.30
□ □	SE28 Dino Ciccarelli, Detr.	6.00	.30
□ □	SE29 Nicklas Lidström, Detr.	12.00	1.00
□ □	SE30 Steve Yzerman, Detr.	45.00	4.00
□ □	SE31 Doug Weight, Edmo.	12.00	1.00
□ □	SE32 Bill Ranford (G), Edmo.	8.00	.30
□ □	SE33 Stu Barnes, Flor.	3.00	.30
□ □	SE34 Bob Kudelski, Flor.	3.00	.30
□ □	SE35 Rob Niedermayer, Flor.	4.00	.30
□ □	SE36 Andrew Cassels, Hart.	4.00	.30
□ □	SE37 Darren Turcotte, Hart.	3.00	.30
□ □	SE38 Andrei Nikolishin, Hart.	3.00	.30
□ □	SE39 Sean Burke (G), Hart.	12.00	1.00
□ □	SE40 Rick Tocchet, LosA.	6.00	.30
□ □	SE41 Jari Kurri, LosA.	20.00	2.00
□ □	SE42 Rob Blake, LosA.	12.00	1.00
□ □	SE43 Mark Recchi, Mont.	8.00	.30
□ □	SE44 Pierre Turgeon, Mont.	8.00	.30
□ □	SE45 Vladimir Malakhov, Mont.	3.00	.30
□ □	SE46 Valeri Bure, Mont.	6.00	.30
□ □	SE47 Stéphane Richer, NJer.	4.00	.30
□ □	SE48 Bill Guerin, NJer.	8.00	.30
□ □	SE49 Scott Stevens w/ Stanley Cup	8.00	.30
□ □	SE50 C. Lemieux w/ Cup, Smythe	6.00	.30
□ □	SE51 Zigmund Palffy, NYIs.	12.00	1.00
□ □	SE52 Kirk Muller, NYIs.	6.00	.30
□ □	SE53 Todd Bertuzzi, NYIs.	45.00	8.00
□ □	SE54 Brett Lindros, NYIs.	6.00	.30
□ □	SE55 Brian Leetch, NYRa.	12.00	1.00
□ □	SE56 Alexei Kovalev, NYRa.	12.00	1.00
□ □	SE57 Adam Graves, NYRa.	8.00	.30
□ □	SE58 Mike Richter (G), NYRa.	9.00	.30
□ □	SE59 Alexei Yashin, Otta.	12.00	1.00
□ □	SE60 Alexandre Daigle, Otta.	3.00	.30
□ □	SE61 Don Beaupré (G), Otta.	3.00	.30
□ □	SE62 Radek Bonk, Otta.	6.00	.30
□ □	SE63 John LeClair, Phil.	15.00	1.00
□ □	SE64 Rod Brind'Amour, Phil.	6.00	.30
□ □	SE65 Ron Hextall (G), Phil.	12.00	1.00
□ □	SE66 Ron Francis, Pitt.	12.00	1.00
□ □	SE67 Markus Näslund, Pitt.	20.00	2.00
□ □	SE68 Tom Barrasso (G), Pitt.	8.00	.30
□ □	SE69 Ian Laperrière, SLou.	3.00	.30
□ □	SE70 Esa Tikkanen, SLou.	3.00	.30
□ □	SE71 Al MacInnis, SLou.	8.00	.30
□ □	SE72 Ulf Dahlén, SanJ.	3.00	.30
□ □	SE73 Craig Janney, SanJ.	4.00	.30
□ □	SE74 Jeff Friesen, SanJ.	6.00	.30
□ □	SE75 Chris Gratton, Tamp.	4.00	.30
□ □	SE76 Roman Hamrlik, Tamp.	4.00	.30
□ □	SE77 Alexander Selivanov, Tamp.	3.00	.30
□ □	SE78 Daren Puppa (G), Tamp.	4.00	.30
□ □	SE79 Dave Andreychuk, Toro.	6.00	.30
□ □	SE80 Doug Gilmour, Toro.	12.00	1.00
□ □	SE81 Kenny Jönsson, Toro.	4.00	.30
□ □	SE82 Trevor Linden, Vanc.	8.00	.30
□ □	SE83 Kirk McLean (G), Vanc.	6.00	.30
□ □	SE84 Jeff R. Brown, Vanc.	3.00	.30
□ □	SE85 Keith Jones, Wash.	3.00	.30
□ □	SE86 Joé Juneau, Wash.	4.00	.30
□ □	SE87 Jim Carey (G), Wash.	3.00	.30
□ □	SE88 Keith Tkachuk, Winn.	10.00	1.00
□ □	SE89 Teemu Selänne, Winn.	15.00	1.00
□ □	SE90 Igor Korolev, Winn.	3.00	.30
□ □	SE91 Mike Sillinger, Anah.	3.00	.30
□ □	SE92 Steve Rucchin, Anah.	4.00	.30
□ □	SE93 Valeri Karpov, Anah.	3.00	.30
□ □	SE94 Cam Neely, Bost.	20.00	2.00
□ □	SE95 Shawn McEachern, Bost.	6.00	.30
□ □	SE96 Kevin Stevens, Bost.	4.00	.30
□ □	SE97 Ted Donato, Bost.	3.00	.30
□ □	SE98 Dominik Hasek (G), Buff.	20.00	2.00
□ □	SE99 Randy Burridge, Buff.	3.00	.30
□ □	SE100 Jason Dawe, Buff.	3.00	.30
□ □	SE101 Theoren Fleury, Calg.	10.00	1.00
□ □	SE102 Michael Nylander, Calg.	4.00	.30
□ □	SE103 Rick Tabaracci (G), Calg.	3.00	.30
□ □	SE104 Jeremy Roenick, Chic.	15.00	1.00
□ □	SE105 Bob Probert, Chic.	6.00	.30
□ □	SE106 Patrick Poulin, Chic.	3.00	.30
□ □	SE107 Gary Suter, Chic.	4.00	.30
□ □	SE108 Claude Lemieux, Colo.	6.00	.30
□ □	SE109 Sandis Ozolinsh, Colo.	4.00	.30
□ □	SE110 Patrick Roy (G), Colo.	60.00	6.00
□ □	SE111 Joe Sakic, Colo.	30.00	2.00
□ □	SE112 Derian Hatcher, Dall.	6.00	.30
□ □	SE113 Greg A. Adams, Dall.	3.00	.30
□ □	SE114 Todd Harvey, Dall.	4.00	.30
□ □	SE115 Sergei Fedorov, Detr.	20.00	2.00
□ □	SE116 Chris Osgood (G), Detr.	12.00	1.00
□ □	SE117 Vyacheslav Kozlov, Detr.	4.00	.30
□ □	SE118 Paul Coffey, Detr.	12.00	1.00
□ □	SE119 Jason Arnott, Edmo.	9.00	.30
□ □	SE120 David Oliver, Edmo.	3.00	.30
□ □	SE121 Todd Marchant, Edmo.	4.00	.30
□ □	SE122 John Vanbiesbrouck (G), Flor.	9.00	.30
□ □	SE123 Jody Hull, Flor.	3.00	.30
□ □	SE124 Jason Woolley, Flor.	3.00	.30
□ □	SE125 Brendan Shanahan, Hart.	20.00	2.00
□ □	SE126 Nelson Emerson, Hart.	3.00	.30
□ □	SE127 Geoff Sanderson, Hart.	4.00	.30
□ □	SE128 Wayne Gretzky, LosA.	80.00	8.00
□ □	SE129 Marty McSorley, LosA.	4.00	.30
□ □	SE130 Yanic Perreault, LosA.	6.00	.30
□ □	SE131 Jocelyn Thibault (G), Mont.	8.00	.30
□ □	SE132 Brian Savage, Mont.	6.00	.30
□ □	SE133 Vincent Damphousse, Mont.	12.00	1.00
□ □	SE134 John MacLean, NJer.	3.00	.30
□ □	SE135 Martin Brodeur (G), NJer.	30.00	3.00
□ □	SE136 Steve Thomas, NJer.	4.00	.30
□ □	SE137 Scott Niedermayer, NJer.	6.00	.30
□ □	SE138 Travis Green, NYIs.	4.00	.30
□ □	SE139 Wendel Clark, NYIs.	15.00	1.00
□ □	SE140 Tommy Söderström (G), NYIs.	3.00	.30
□ □	SE141 Mark Messier, NYRa.	20.00	2.00
□ □	SE142 Ulf Samuelsson, NYRa.	3.00	.30
□ □	SE143 Ray Ferraro, NYRa.	3.00	.30
□ □	SE144 Luc Robitaille, NYRa.	15.00	1.00
□ □	SE145 Daniel Alfredsson, Otta.	12.00	1.00
□ □	SE146 Martin Straka, Otta.	6.00	.30
□ □	SE147 Steve Duchesne, Otta.	4.00	.30
□ □	SE148 Eric Lindros, Phil.	20.00	2.00
□ □	SE149 Mikael Renberg, Phil.	6.00	.30
□ □	SE150 Éric Desjardins, Phil.	6.00	.30
□ □	SE151 Joel Otto, Phil.	3.00	.30
□ □	SE152 Mario Lemieux, Pitt.	60.00	6.00
□ □	SE153 Jaromir Jagr, Pitt.	20.00	2.00
□ □	SE154 Petr Nedved, Pitt.	6.00	.30
□ □	SE155 Sergei Zubov, Pitt.	4.00	.30
□ □	SE156 Tomas Sandström, Pitt.	4.00	.30
□ □	SE157 Brett Hull, SLou.	20.00	2.00
□ □	SE158 Grant Fuhr (G), SLou.	12.00	1.00
□ □	SE159 Shayne Corson, SLou.	6.00	.30
□ □	SE160 Chris Pronger, SLou.	12.00	1.00
□ □	SE161 Ray Sheppard, SanJ.	3.00	.30
□ □	SE162 Arturs Irbe (G), SanJ.	8.00	.30
□ □	SE163 Owen Nolan, SanJ.	12.00	1.00
□ □	SE164 Andrei Nazarov, SanJ.	3.00	.30
□ □	SE165 Paul Ysebaert, Tamp.	3.00	.30
□ □	SE166 Brian Bradley, Tamp.	3.00	.30
□ □	SE167 Petr Klima, Tamp.	3.00	.30
□ □	SE168 Félix Potvin (G), Toro.	12.00	1.00
□ □	SE169 Mats Sundin, Toro.	20.00	2.00
□ □	SE170 Larry Murphy, Toro.	4.00	.30
□ □	SE171 Benoît Hogue, Toro.	3.00	.30
□ □	SE172 Pavel Bure, Vanc.	15.00	1.00
□ □	SE173 Alexander Mogilny, Vanc.	9.00	.30
□ □	SE174 Cliff Ronning, Vanc.	4.00	.30
□ □	SE175 Pat Peake, Wash.	3.00	.30
□ □	SE176 Sylvain Côté, Wash.	3.00	.30
□ □	SE177 Peter Bondra, Wash.	12.00	1.00
□ □	SE178 Dallas Drake, Winn.	3.00	.30
□ □	SE179 Tim Cheveldae (G), Winn.	3.00	.30
□ □	SE180 Darren Turcotte, Winn.	3.00	.30

1995 - 96 UPPER DECK – BUYBACKS

	Buyback Autograph	UD
□	7 John LeClair, Phil. ✍ {#/2}	
□	113 Steve Yzerman, Detr. ✍ {#/2}	
□	247 John LeClair, Phil. ✍ {#/1}	
□	296 Curtis Joseph (G), SLou. ✍ {#/1}	
□	Raymond Bourque, Bost. ✍ {#/3}	
□	Mike Modano, Dall. ✍ {#/7}	
□	438 Mike Richter (G), NYRa. ✍ {#/2}	
□	Keith Tkachuk, Winn. ✍ {#/2}	
□	**530 José Théodore, Canada RC ✍ {#/3}**	
	Buyback Autograph • Electric Ice parallel	**UD**
□	**530 José Théodore, Canada RC ✍ {#/1}**	

1995 - 96 UPPER DECK ALL-STAR GAME PREDICTOR

These cards were handed out at the All-Star Game in Boston. Redeemed Gold cards have the prefix "MVP-R". The Silver Adam Oates card has not been confirmed to exist. Ray Bourque's Silver card was the winning card that could be redeemed for a 30-card Gold set.

	Player	Gold	Silver
	Complete Set (29 or 30 cards):	**1600.00**	**300.00**
□ □	MVP1 Wayne Gretzky, LosA.	250.00	50.00
□ □	MVP2 Sergei Fedorov, Detr.	60.00	12.00
□ □	MVP3 Brett Hull, SLou.	60.00	12.00
□ □	MVP4 Alexander Mogilny, Vanc.	30.00	6.00
□ □	MVP5 Joe Sakic, Colo.	100.00	20.00
□ □	MVP6 Paul Kariya, Anah.	85.00	15.00
□ □	MVP7 Teemu Selänne, Winn.	50.00	10.00
□ □	MVP8 Paul Coffey, Detr.	35.00	6.00
□ □	MVP9 Chris Chelios, Chic.	35.00	6.00
□ □	MVP10 Doug Gilmour, Toro.	35.00	6.00
□ □	MVP11 Peter Forsberg, Colo.	85.00	15.00
□ □	MVP12 Jeremy Roenick, Chic.	50.00	10.00
□ □	MVP13 Theoren Fleury, Calg.	35.00	6.00
□ □	MVP14 Mike Modano, Dall.	60.00	12.00
□ □	MVP15 Steve Yzerman, Detr.	150.00	30.00
□ □	MVP16 Mario Lemieux, Pitt.	180.00	30.00
□ □	MVP17 Jaromir Jagr, Pitt.	60.00	10.00
□ □	MVP18 Eric Lindros, Phil.	60.00	10.00
□ □	MVP19 Mark Messier, NYRa.	60.00	12.00
□ □	MVP20 Brendan Shanahan, Hart.	60.00	12.00
□ □	MVP21 Raymond Bourque, Bost. [Win]	75.00	15.00
□ □	MVP22 Cam Neely, Bost.	60.00	12.00
□ □	MVP23 Ron Francis, Pitt.	35.00	6.00
□ □	MVP24 John LeClair, Phil.	50.00	10.00
□ □	MVP25 Brian Leetch, NYRa.	35.00	6.00
□ □	MVP26 Peter Bondra, Wash.	35.00	6.00
□ □	MVP27 Scott Stevens, NJer.	25.00	4.00
□ □	MVP29 Martin Brodeur (G), NJer.	100.00	20.00
□ □	MVP30 Long Shot	5.00	2.00
□	MVPR28 Adam Oates, Bost.	20.00	-

1995 - 96 UPPER DECK BE A PLAYER

Complete Set (225 cards): 40.00
Common Player: .25

Player	BAP
1 Brett Hull, SLou.	1.50
2 Jyrki Lumme, Vanc.	.25
3 Shean Donovan Jrs. (SanJ.)	.25
4 Yuri Khmylev, Buff.	.25
5 Stéphane Matteau, NYRa. (SLou.)	.25
6 Basil McRae, SLou.	.25
7 Dmitry Yushkevich, Toro.	.25
8 Ron Francis, Pitt.	.50
9 Keith Carney, Chic.	.25
10 Brad Dalgarno, NYIs.	.25
11 Bob Carpenter, NJer.	.25
12 Kevin Stevens, Bost.	.25
13 Patrick Flatley, NYIs.	.25
14 Craig Muni, Buff.	.25
15 Travis Green, NYIs.	.25
16 Derek Plante, Buff.	.25
17 Mike Craig, Toro.	.25
18 Chris Pronger, NHLPA (SLou.)	.50
19 Bret Hedican, Vanc.	.25
20 Mathieu Schneider, NYIs.	.25
21 Chris Therien, Phil.	.25
22 Greg A. Adams, Dall.	.25
23 Arturs Irbe (G), SanJ.	.50
24 Zigmund Palffy, NYIs.	.50
25 Peter Douris, Anah.	.25
26 Bob Sweeney, NYIs.	.25
27 Chris Terreri (G), SanJ.	.25
28 Alexei Zhitnik, Buff.	.25
29 Jay Wells, SLou.	.25
30 Andrew Cassels, Hart.	.25
31 Radek Bonk, Otta.	.50
32 Brian Bellows, Tamp.	.25
33 Frantisek Kucera, Hart.	.25
34 Valeri Bure, Mont.	.50
35 Randy Wood, NHLPA (Dall.)	.25
36 Dmitri Khristich, LosA.	.25
37 Randy Ladouceur, Anah.	.25
38 Nelson Emerson, Hart.	.25
39 Bryan Marchment, Edmo.	.25
40 Kevin Lowe, NYRa.	.25
41 Trevor Linden, NHLPA (Vanc.)	.50
42 Neal Broten, NJer.	.25
43 Tom Chorske, Otta.	.25
44 Patrice Brisebois, Mont.	.25
45 Wayne Presley, NYRa.	.25
46 Murray Craven, Chic.	.25
47 Craig Janney, SanJ.	.25
48 Ken Daneyko, NJer.	.25
49 Dino Ciccarelli, Detr.	.50
50 Jason Dawe, Buff.	.25
51 Brad McCrimmon, Hart.	.25
52 Randy McKay, NJer.	.25
53 Rudy Poeschek, NHLPA (Tamp.)	.25
54 Calle Johansson, Wash.	.25
55 Wendel Clark, NYIs.	1.00
56 Rob Ray, Buff.	.25
57 Garth Snow (G), Phil.	.50
58 Joé Juneau, Wash. [Drums]	.25
59 Craig Wolanin, Colo.	.25
60 Ray Sheppard, SanJ.	.25
61 Oleg Tverdovsky, Anah. (Winn.)	.25
62 Geoff Sanderson, Hart.	.25
63 Mike Ridley, Vanc.	.25
64 David Oliver, Edmo.	.25
65 Russ Courtnall, Vanc.	.25
66 Joe Reekie, Wash.	.25
67 Ken Wregget (G), Pitt.	.25
68 Teppo Numminen, Winn.	.50
69 Mikhail Shtalenkov, Anah.	.25
70 Luke Richardson, Edmo.	.25
71 Brent Gilchrist, Dall.	.25
72 P. Housley, NHLPA-U.S.A. (NJer.)	.50
73 Greg Johnson, Detr.	.25
74 Sean Hill, Otta.	.25
75 Karl Dykhuis, Phil.	.25
76 Tim Chevelade (G), Winn.	.25
77 Shjon Podein, Phil.	.25
78 René Corbet, Colo.	.25
79 Ronnie Stern, Calg.	.25
80 Mike Donnelly, Dall.	.25
81 Randy Cunneyworth, Otta.	.25
82 Rick Tocchet, NHLPA (Bost.)	.50
83 Dallas Drake, Winn.	.25
84 Cam Russell, Chic.	.25
85 Daren Puppa (G), Tamp.	.25
86 Benoît Brunet, Mont.	.25
87 Paul Ranheim, Hart.	.25
88 Bob Rouse, Detr.	.25
89 Todd Elik, Bost.	.25
90 Darcy Wakaluk, Dall.	.25
91 Cliff Ronning, Vanc.	.25
92 Pat Conacher, LosA. (Calg.)	.25
93 Todd Krygier, Anah.	.25
94 Dave Babych, Vanc.	.25
95 Pat Falloon, Phil.	.25
96 Don Beaupré (G), Otta.	.25
97 Wayne Gretzky, LosA. (SLou.)	6.50
98 Chris Joseph (G), Pitt.	.25
99 Vyacheslav Kozlov, Detr.	.25
100 Brent Fedyk, Phil. (Dall.)	.25
101 Tim Taylor, Detr.	.25
102 Mike Eastwood, Winn.	.25
103 Mike Keane, Colo.	.25
104 Grant Ledyard, Dall.	.25
105 Rob DiMaio, Phil.	.25
106 Martin Straka, Otta. (NYIs.)	.50
107 Scott Young, Colo.	.50
108 Zarley Zalapski, Calg.	.25
109 Stephen Leach, Bost.	.25
110 Jody Hull, Flor.	.25
111 Lyle Odelein, Mont.	.25
112 Bob Corkum, NHLPA (Phil.)	.25
113 Rob Blake, NHLPA (LosA.)	.50
114 Randy Burridge, Buff.	.25
115 Keith Primeau, Detr.	.50
116 G. Wesley, NHLPA-Team West	.25
117 Brian Bradley, Tamp.	.25
118 Andrei Kovalenko, Mont.	.25
119 Patrik Juhlin, Phil.	.25
120 John Tucker, Tamp.	.25
121 Stéphane Fiset (G), Colo.	.50
122 Mike Hough, Flor.	.25
123 Steve Smith, NHLPA (Chic.)	.25
124 Tom Barrasso (G), Pitt.	.50
125 Ray Whitney, NHLPA (SanJ.)	.25
126 Benoît Hogue, Toro. (Dall.)	.25
127 Stu Barnes, Flor.	.25
128 Craig Ludwig, Dall.	.25
129 Curtis Leschyshyn, NHLPA (Colo.)	.25
130 John LeClair, Phil. [cameo: E.Lindros]	1.00
131 Dennis Vial, Otta.	.25
132 Cory Stillman, Calg.	.25
133 Roman Hamrlik, NHLPA (Tamp.)	.25
134 Al MacInnis, SLou.	.50
135 Igor Korolev, Winn.	.25
136 Rick Zombo, Bost.	.25
137 Zdeno Ciger, Edmo.	.25
138 Brian Savage, Mont.	.50
139 Paul Ysebaert, Tamp.	.25
140 Brent Sutter, Chic.	.25
141 Ed Olczyk, Winn.	.25
142 Adam Creighton, SLou.	.25
143 Jesse Bélanger, Flor.	.25
144 Glen Murray, Pitt.	.50
145 Alexander Selivanov, Tamp.	.25
146 Trent Yawney, Calg.	.25
147 Bruce Driver, NHLPA (NYRa.)	.25
148 Michael Nylander, Calg.	.25
149 Martin Gélinas, Vanc.	.25
150 Yanic Perreault, LosA.	.50
151 Craig Billington (G), Bost.	.50
152 Pierre Turgeon, Mont.	.50
153 Mike Modano, NHLPA (Dall.)	1.50
154 Joe Mullen, Bost.	.50
155 Todd Ewen, Anah.	.25
156 Petr Nedved, Pitt.	.50
157 Dominic Roussel, Phil.	.25
158 Murray Baron, SLou.	.25
159 Robert Dirk, Anah. (Mont.)	.25
160 Tomas Sandström, Pitt.	.25
161 Brian Holzinger, Buff.	1.00
162 Ken Klee, Wash.	.25
163 Radek Dvorak, Flor.	.25
164 Marcus Ragnarsson, SanJ.	1.50
165 Aaron Gavey, Tamp.	.25
166 Jeff O'Neill, NHLPA (Hart.)	.50
167 Chad Kilger, Anah. (Winn.)	1.50
168 Todd Bertuzzi, NYIs.	7.50
169 Robert Svehla, Flor.	1.50
170 Éric Dazé, Chic.	.50
171 Daniel Alfredsson, Otta.	3.50
172 S. Doan, NHLPA (Winn.)	1.50
173 K. McLaren, NHLPA (Bost.)	1.50
174 Saku Koivu, Mont.	1.00
175 Jere Lehtinen, Dall.	.50
176 Nikolai Khabibulin (G), USSR Jrs. (Winn.)	.50
177 Niklas Sundström, Sweden Jrs. (NYRa.)	.25
178 Ed Jovanovski, CanadaJrs. (Flor.)	.50
179 Jason Bonsignore, U.S.A. Jrs. (Edmo.)	.25
180 Kenny Jönsson, Sweden Jrs. (Toro.)	.25
181 Vitali Yachmenev, Russia Jrs. (LosA.)	.25
182 Alexei Kovalev, USSR Jrs. (NYRa.)	.50
183 Sandis Ozolinsh, USSR Jrs. (Colo.)	.25
184 Rob Niedermayer, Canada Jrs. (Flor.)	.25
185 Richard Park, U.S.A. Jrs. (Pitt.)	.25
186 Adam Deadmarsh, U.S.A. Jrs. (Colo.)	.50
187 Sergei Krivokrasov, USSR Jrs. (Chic.)	.25
188 Alexandre Daigle, Canada Jrs. (Otta.)	.25
189 Jim Carey (G), U.S.A. Nationals (Wash.)	.25
190 T. Marchant, U.S.A. Nationals (Edmo.)	.25
191 Mike Richter (G), NYRa. (NYRa.)	.50
192 Dominik Hasek (G), Buff.	1.50
193 Chris Osgood (G), Detr.	.50
194 Ed Belfour (G), Chic.	1.50
195 Félix Potvin (G), Toro.	.50
196 Grant Fuhr (G), SLou.	.50
197 Patrick Roy (G), Colo.	4.50
198 Ron Hextall (G), Phil.	.50
199 Jocelyn Thibault (G), NHLPA (Mont.)	.50
200 Kirk McLean (G), Vanc.	.50
201 Jari Kurri, NHLPA (LosA.)	1.50
202 Bobby Holik, NJer.	.50
203 Mats Sundin, Toro.	1.50
204 Alexander Mogilny, Vanc.	.50
205 Valeri Karpov, Anah.	.25
206 Igor Larionov, Detr.	.50
207 Valeri Zelepukin, NJer.	.25
208 Jozef Stumpel, Bost.	.25
209 Sergei Nemchinov, NYRa.	.25
210 Peter Bondra, Wash.	.50
211 Chris Chelios, Chic.	.50
212 A. Graves, NHLPA (NYRa.)	.50
213 Dale Hunter, Wash.	.50
214 Tony Twist, SLou.	.25
215 Keith Tkachuk, Winn.	.50
216 Vladimir Konstantinov, Detr.	.50
217 Sandy McCarthy, Calg.	.25
218 Jamie Macoun, Toro.	.25
219 Scott Stevens, NJer.	.50
220 Mark Tinordi, Wash.	.25
221 Bob Probert, Chic.	.50
222 Gino Odjick, Vanc.	.25
223 U. Samuelsson, NHLPA (NYRa.)	.25
224 Stu Grimson, Anah. (Detr.)	.25
225 Marty McSorley, LosA.	.25

AUTOGRAPHS

Autograph cards are seeded one per pack. Die-Cut autographs have a gold hologram as opposed to a silver hologram on the card back. Wayne Gretzky signed fewer autographs than any other player: 648 regular cards and 234 Die-Cut cards. Mike Richter (G)'s autographs were not inserted into packs. Instead, 3,000 regular autographs and 400 autographed Die-Cut cards were available by mail.

Complete Set (225 cards): 2685.00 1300.00
Common Player: 8.00 4.00

Player	D.C.	Auto.
S1 Brett Hull, SLou.	50.00	25.00
S2 Jyrki Lumme, Vanc.	12.00	6.00
S3 S. Donovan, Canada (SanJ.)	8.00	4.00
S4 Yuri Khmylev, Buff.	8.00	4.00
S5 S. Matteau, NYRa. (SLou.)	8.00	4.00
S6 Basil McRae, SLou.	8.00	4.00
S7 Dmitry Yushkevich, Toro.	12.00	6.00
S8 Ron Francis, Pitt.	30.00	16.00
S9 Keith Carney, Chic.	8.00	4.00
S10 Brad Dalgarno, NYIs.	8.00	4.00
S11 Bob Carpenter, NJer.	12.00	6.00
S12 Kevin Stevens, Bost.	12.00	6.00
S13 Patrick Flatley, NYIs.	8.00	4.00
S14 Craig Muni, Buff.	8.00	4.00
S15 Travis Green, NYIs.	12.00	6.00
S16 Derek Plante, Buff.	8.00	4.00
S17 Mike Craig, Toro.	8.00	4.00
S18 C. Pronger, NHLPA (SLou.)	30.00	16.00
S19 Bret Hedican, Vanc.	8.00	4.00
S20 Mathieu Schneider, NYIs.	12.00	6.00
S21 Chris Therien, Phil.	8.00	4.00
S22 Greg A. Adams, Dall.	8.00	4.00
S23 Arturs Irbe (G), SanJ.	20.00	10.00
S24 Zigmund Palffy, NYIs.	30.00	16.00
S25 Peter Douris, Anah.	8.00	4.00
S26 Bob Sweeney, NYIs.	8.00	4.00
S27 Chris Terreri (G), SanJ.	8.00	4.00
S28 Alexei Zhitnik, Buff.	8.00	4.00
S29 Jay Wells, SLou.	8.00	4.00
S30 Andrew Cassels, Hart.	12.00	6.00
S31 Radek Bonk, Otta.	16.00	8.00
S32 Brian Bellows, Tamp.	12.00	6.00
S33 Frantisek Kucera, Hart.	8.00	4.00
S34 Valeri Bure, Mont.	16.00	8.00
S35 Randy Wood, NHLPA (Dall.)	8.00	4.00
S36 Dmitri Khristich, LosA.	8.00	4.00
S37 Randy Ladouceur, Anah.	8.00	4.00
S38 Nelson Emerson, Hart.	8.00	4.00
S39 Bryan Marchment, Edmo.	8.00	4.00
S40 Kevin Lowe, NYRa.	16.00	8.00
S41 T. Linden, NHLPA (Vanc.)	20.00	10.00
S42 Neal Broten, NJer.	12.00	6.00
S43 Tom Chorske, Otta.	8.00	4.00
S44 Patrice Brisebois, Mont.	8.00	4.00
S45 Wayne Presley, NYRa.	8.00	4.00
S46 Murray Craven, Chic.	8.00	4.00
S47 Craig Janney, SanJ.	12.00	6.00
S48 Ken Daneyko, NJer.	12.00	6.00
S49 Dino Ciccarelli, Detr.	16.00	8.00
S50 Jason Dawe, Buff.	8.00	4.00
S51 Brad McCrimmon, Hart.	8.00	4.00
S52 Randy McKay, NJer.	8.00	4.00
S53 R. Poeschek, NHLPA (Tamp.)	8.00	4.00
S54 Calle Johansson, Wash.	12.00	6.00
S55 Wendel Clark, NYIs.	40.00	20.00
S56 Rob Ray, Buff.	12.00	6.00
S57 Garth Snow (G), Phil.	16.00	8.00
S58 Joé Juneau, Wash. [Drums]	12.00	6.00
S59 Craig Wolanin, Colo.	8.00	4.00
S60 Ray Sheppard, SanJ.	8.00	4.00
S61 O. Tverdovsky, Anah. (Winn.)	8.00	4.00
S62 Geoff Sanderson, Hart.	12.00	6.00
S63 Mike Ridley, Vanc.	8.00	4.00
S64 David Oliver, Edmo.	8.00	4.00
S65 Russ Courtnall, Vanc.	12.00	6.00
S66 Joe Reekie, Wash.	8.00	4.00
S67 Ken Wregget (G), Pitt.	12.00	6.00
S68 Teppo Numminen, Winn.	16.00	8.00
S69 Mikhail Shtalenkov, Anah.	8.00	4.00
S70 Luke Richardson, Edmo.	8.00	4.00
S71 Brent Gilchrist, Dall.	8.00	4.00
S72 Housley, NHLPA-USA. (NJer.)	16.00	8.00
S73 Greg Johnson, Detr.	8.00	4.00
S74 Sean Hill, Otta.	8.00	4.00
S75 Karl Dykhuis, Phil.	8.00	4.00
S76 Tim Chevelade (G), Winn.	8.00	4.00
S77 Shjon Podein, Phil.	12.00	6.00
S78 René Corbet, Colo.	8.00	4.00
S79 Ronnie Stern, Calg.	8.00	4.00
S80 Mike Donnelly, Dall.	8.00	4.00
S81 Randy Cunneyworth, Otta.	8.00	4.00
S82 R. Tocchet, NHLPA (Bost.)	16.00	8.00
S83 Dallas Drake, Winn.	8.00	4.00
S84 Cam Russell, Chic.	8.00	4.00
S85 Daren Puppa (G), Tamp.	12.00	6.00
S86 Benoît Brunet, Mont.	8.00	4.00
S87 Paul Ranheim, Hart.	8.00	4.00
S88 Bob Rouse, Detr.	8.00	4.00
S89 Todd Elik, Bost.	8.00	4.00
S90 Darcy Wakaluk, Dall.	8.00	4.00
S91 Cliff Ronning, Vanc.	12.00	6.00
S92 Pat Conacher, LosA. (Calg.)	8.00	4.00
S93 Todd Krygier, Anah.	8.00	4.00
S94 Dave Babych, Vanc.	8.00	4.00
S95 Pat Falloon, Phil.	8.00	4.00
S96 Don Beaupré (G), Otta.	8.00	4.00
S97 Gretzky, LosA. (SLou.)	1,400.00	550.00
S98 Chris Joseph (G), Pitt.	8.00	4.00
S99 Vyacheslav Kozlov, Detr.	12.00	6.00
S100 Brent Fedyk, Phil. (Dall.)	8.00	4.00
S101 Tim Taylor, Detr.	8.00	4.00
S102 Mike Eastwood, Winn.	8.00	4.00
S103 Mike Keane, Colo.	8.00	4.00
S104 Grant Ledyard, Dall.	8.00	4.00
S105 Rob DiMaio, Phil.	8.00	4.00
S106 Martin Straka, Otta. (NYIs.)	16.00	8.00
S107 Scott Young, Colo.	16.00	8.00
S108 Zarley Zalapski, Calg.	8.00	4.00
S109 Stephen Leach, Bost.	8.00	4.00
S110 Jody Hull, Flor.	8.00	4.00
S111 Lyle Odelein, Mont.	8.00	4.00
S112 B. Corkum, NHLPA (Phil.)	8.00	4.00
S113 R. Blake, NHLPA (LosA.)	30.00	16.00
S114 Randy Burridge, Buff.	8.00	4.00
S115 Keith Primeau, Detr.	20.00	10.00
S116 G. Wesley, NHLPA-West	8.00	4.00
S117 Brian Bradley, Tamp.	8.00	4.00
S118 Andrei Kovalenko, Mont.	8.00	4.00
S119 Patrik Juhlin, Phil.	8.00	4.00
S120 John Tucker, Tamp.	8.00	4.00
S121 Stéphane Fiset (G), Colo.	16.00	8.00
S122 Mike Hough, Flor.	8.00	4.00
S123 S. Smith, NHLPA (Chic.)	20.00	10.00
S124 Tom Barrasso (G), Pitt.	40.00	20.00
S125 R. Whitney, NHLPA (SanJ.)	12.00	6.00
S126 Benoît Hogue, Toro. (Dall.)	8.00	4.00
S127 Stu Barnes, Flor.	8.00	4.00
S128 Craig Ludwig, Dall.	8.00	4.00
S129 Leschyshyn, NHLPA (Colo.)	8.00	4.00
S130 J. LeClair, Phil.	40.00	20.00
S131 Dennis Vial, Otta.	8.00	4.00
S132 Cory Stillman, Calg.	12.00	6.00
S133 R. Hamrlik, NHLPA (Tamp.)	12.00	6.00
S134 Al MacInnis, SLou.	20.00	10.00
S135 Igor Korolev, Winn.	8.00	4.00
S136 Rick Zombo, Bost.	8.00	4.00
S137 Zdeno Ciger, Edmo.	8.00	4.00
S138 Brian Savage, Mont.	16.00	8.00
S139 Paul Ysebaert, Tamp.	8.00	4.00
S140 Brent Sutter, Chic.	12.00	6.00
S141 Ed Olczyk, Winn.	12.00	6.00
S142 Adam Creighton, SLou.	8.00	4.00
S143 Jesse Bélanger, Flor.	8.00	4.00
S144 Glen Murray, Pitt.	24.00	12.00
S145 A. Selivanov, Tamp.	8.00	4.00
S146 Trent Yawney, Calg.	8.00	4.00
S147 B. Driver, NHLPA (NYRa.)	8.00	4.00
S148 Michael Nylander, Calg.	12.00	6.00
S149 Martin Gélinas, Vanc.	12.00	6.00
S150 Yanic Perreault, LosA.	16.00	8.00
S151 Craig Billington (G), Bost.	8.00	4.00
S152 Pierre Turgeon, Mont.	20.00	10.00
S153 M. Modano, NHLPA (Dall.)	50.00	25.00
S154 Joe Mullen, Bost.	20.00	10.00
S155 Todd Ewen, Anah.	8.00	4.00
S156 Petr Nedved, Pitt.	16.00	8.00
S157 Dominic Roussel, Phil.	8.00	4.00
S158 Murray Baron, SLou.	8.00	4.00
S159 Robert Dirk, Anah. (Mont.)	8.00	4.00
S160 Tomas Sandström, Pitt.	12.00	6.00
S161 Brian Holzinger, Buff.	8.00	6.00
S162 Ken Klee, Wash.	8.00	4.00
S163 Radek Dvorak, Flor.	12.00	6.00
S164 Marcus Ragnarsson, SanJ.	14.00	8.00
S165 Aaron Gavey, Tamp.	8.00	4.00
S166 Jeff O'Neill, NHLPA (Hart.)	20.00	10.00
S167 C. Kilger, Anah. (Winn.)	14.00	8.00
S168 Todd Bertuzzi, NYIs.	70.00	45.00
S169 Robert Svehla, Flor.	14.00	8.00
S170 Éric Dazé, Chic.	20.00	10.00
S171 Daniel Alfredsson, Otta.	35.00	20.00
S172 S. Doan, NHLPA (Winn.)	14.00	8.00
S173 K. McLaren, NHLPA (Bost.)	14.00	8.00
S174 Saku Koivu, Mont.	40.00	20.00
S175 Jere Lehtinen, Dall.	16.00	8.00
S176 Khabibulin (G), USSR (Winn.)	20.00	10.00
S177 N. Sundström, Swe. (NYRa.)	12.00	6.00
S178 Jovanovski, Cdn. (Flor.)	24.00	16.00
S179 Bonsignore, U.S.A. (Edmo.)	8.00	4.00
S180 K. Jönsson, Swe. (Toro.)	10.00	4.00
S181 B. Yachmenev, Rus. (LosA.)	8.00	4.00
S182 Kovalev, USSR (NYRa.)	30.00	16.00
S183 S. Ozolinsh, USSR (Colo.)	12.00	6.00
S184 R. Niedermayer, Cdn. (Flor.)	12.00	6.00
S185 R. Park, U.S.A. (Pitt.)	8.00	4.00
S186 Deadmarsh, U.S.A. (Colo.)	16.00	8.00
S187 Krivokrasov, USSR (Chic.)	8.00	4.00
S188 Daigle, Canada (Otta.)	8.00	4.00
S189 Carey (G), U.S.A. (Wash.)	8.00	4.00
S190 T. Marchant, U.S.A. (Edmo.)	12.00	6.00
S191 Mike Richter (G) (NYRa.)	175.00	100.00
S192 Dominik Hasek (G), Buff.	50.00	25.00
S193 Chris Osgood (G), Detr.	30.00	16.00
S194 Ed Belfour (G), Chic.	50.00	25.00
S195 Félix Potvin (G), Toro.	30.00	16.00
S196 Grant Fuhr (G), SLou.	30.00	16.00
S197 Patrick Roy (G), Colo.	150.00	80.00
S198 Ron Hextall (G), Phil.	30.00	16.00
S199 Thibault (G), NHLPA (Mont.)	20.00	10.00
S200 Kirk McLean (G), Vanc.	16.00	8.00
S201 Jari Kurri, NHLPA (LosA.)	50.00	25.00
S202 Bobby Holik, NJer.	16.00	8.00
S203 Mats Sundin, Toro.	50.00	25.00
S204 Alexander Mogilny, Vanc.	24.00	12.00
S205 Valeri Karpov, Anah.	8.00	4.00
S206 Igor Larionov, Detr.	30.00	16.00
S207 Valeri Zelepukin, NJer.	8.00	4.00
S208 Jozef Stumpel, Bost.	12.00	6.00

S209 Sergei Nemchinov, NYRa. ✍	12.00	6.00
S210 Peter Bondra, Wash. ✍	30.00	16.00
S211 Chris Chelios, Chic. ✍	30.00	16.00
S212 A. Graves, NHLPA (NYRa.) ✍	20.00	10.00
S213 Dale Hunter, Wash. ✍	16.00	8.00
S214 Tony Twist, SLou. ✍	8.00	4.00
S215 Keith Tkachuk, Winn. ✍	30.00	15.00
S216 V. Konstantinov, Detr. ✍	90.00	65.00
S217 Sandy McCarthy, Calg. ✍	8.00	4.00
S218 Jamie Macoun, Toro. ✍	8.00	4.00
S219 Scott Stevens, NJer. ✍	20.00	10.00
S220 Mark Tinordi, Wash. ✍	8.00	4.00
S221 Bob Probert, Chic. ✍	16.00	8.00
S222 Gino Odjick, Vanc. ✍	8.00	4.00
S223 Samuelsson, NHLPA (NYRa.) ✍	8.00	4.00
S224 Stu Grimson, Anah. (Detr.) ✍	12.00	6.00
S225 Marty McSorley, LosA. ✍	12.00	6.00

GREAT MEMORIES

Singles sell at $8-10.

Insert Set (10 cards): 80.00

Player	Player
GM1 Wayne Gretzky	GM2 Wayne Gretzky
GM3 Wayne Gretzky	GM4 Wayne Gretzky
GM5 Wayne Gretzky	GM6 Wayne Gretzky
GM7 Wayne Gretzky	GM8 Wayne Gretzky
GM9 Wayne Gretzky	GM10 Wayne Gretzky

LETHAL LINES

Each set of three cards (LL1-LL3, LL4-LL6, etc.) connect to form a line.

Insert Set (15 cards): 75.00

Insert (1:7)	LL
LL1 Keith Tkachuk, Winn.	4.00
LL2 Wayne Gretzky, SLou.	20.00
LL3 Brett Hull, SLou.	4.00
LL4 Eric Dazé, Chic.	4.00
LL5 Saku Koivu, Mont.	8.00
LL6 Daniel Alfredsson, Otta.	6.00
LL7 Pavel Bure, Vanc.	4.00
LL8 Sergei Fedorov, Detr.	4.00
LL9 Alexander Mogilny, Vanc.	4.00
LL10 Paul Kariya, Anah.	6.00
LL11 Mario Lemieux, Pitt.	14.00
LL12 Jaromir Jagr, Pitt.	4.00
LL13 Brendan Shanahan, Hart.	4.00
LL14 Eric Lindros, Phil.	4.00
LL15 Alexei Kovalev, NYRa.	4.00

1995 - 96 UPPER DECK COLLECTOR'S CHOICE

Cards 1-396 have three versions: the regular card, a Player's Club parallel and a Platinum Player's Club parallel. A Young Guns trade card found in packs could be redeemed for a 15-card update set.

Complete Set (396 cards): 1875.00 190.00 55.00
Young Guns Set (15 cards): - - 10.00
Young Guns Expired Trade Card: .50
Common Player: 2.50 .30 .20

Player	PPC	PC	CC
1 Wayne Gretzky, LosA.	100.00	10.00	2.00
2 Darius Kasparaitis, NYIs.	5.00	.50	.20
3 S. Niedermayer, NJer.	5.00	.50	.20
4 Shanahan, SLou. (Hart.)	25.00	2.50	.50
5 Doug Gilmour, Toro.	15.00	1.50	.20
6 Lyle Odelein, Mont.	2.50	.30	.20
7 Dave Gagner, Dall.	2.50	.30	.20
8 Gary Suter, Chic.	5.00	.50	.20
9 Sandis Ozolinsh, SanJ.	5.00	.50	.20
10 Sergei Zubov, NYRa.	5.00	.50	.20
11 Don Beaupré (G), Otta.	2.50	.30	.20
12 Bill Lindsay, Flor.	2.50	.30	.20
13 David Oliver, Edmo.	2.50	.30	.20
14 Bob Corkum, Anah.	2.50	.30	.20
15 German Titov, Calg.	2.50	.30	.20
16 Jari Kurri, LosA.	25.00	2.50	.50
17 Cliff Ronning, Vanc.	5.00	.50	.20
18 Paul Coffey, Detr.	15.00	1.50	.20
19 Ian Laperrière, SLou.	2.50	.30	.20
20 Dave Andreychuk, Toro.	5.00	.50	.20
21 Andrei Nikolishin, Hart.	2.50	.30	.20
22 Blaine Lacher (G), Bost.	2.50	.30	.20
23 Yuri Khmylev, Buff.	2.50	.30	.20
24 Darren Turcotte, Hart.	2.50	.30	.20
25 Joe Mullen, Pitt.	10.00	1.00	.20
26 Peter Forsberg, Québ.	35.00	3.50	.50
27 Paul Ysebaert, Tamp.	2.50	.30	.20
28 T. Söderström (G), NYIs.	2.50	.30	.20
29 Rod Brind'Amour, Phil.	5.00	.50	.20
30 Jim Carey (G), Wash.	2.50	.30	.20
31 Geoff Courtnall, Vanc.	2.50	.30	.20
32 Vyacheslav Kozlov, Detr.	5.00	.50	.20
33 Ray Ferraro, NYIs.	2.50	.30	.20
34 John MacLean, NJer.	2.50	.30	.20
35 Benoît Brunet, Mont.	2.50	.30	.20
36 Trent Klatt, Dall.	2.50	.30	.20
37 Chris Chelios, Chic.	15.00	1.50	.20
38 Tom Pederson, SanJ.	2.50	.30	.20
39 Pat Elynuik, Otta.	2.50	.30	.20
40 Rob Niedermayer, Flor.	5.00	.50	.20
41 Jason Arnott, Edmo.	10.00	1.00	.20
42 Patrik Carnbäck, Anah.	2.50	.30	.20
43 Steve Chiasson, Calg.	2.50	.30	.20
44 Marty McSorley, LosA.	5.00	.50	.20
45 Pavel Bure, Vanc.	20.00	2.00	.20
46 Glenn Anderson, SLou.	5.00	.50	.20
47 Doug Brown, Detr.	2.50	.30	.20
48 M. Ridley, Toro. (Vanc.)	2.50	.30	.20
49 Alexei Zhamnov, Winn.	5.00	.50	.20
50 M. Czerkawski, Bost.	5.00	.50	.20
51 Derek Plante, Buff.	2.50	.30	.20
52 Andrew Cassels, Hart.	5.00	.50	.20
53 Tom Barrasso (G), Pitt.	10.00	1.00	.20
54 Andrei Kovalenko, Québ.	2.50	.30	.20
55 Pat Verbeek, NYRa.	5.00	.50	.20
56 Alexander Semak, Tamp.	2.50	.30	.20
57 Eric Lindros, Phil.	25.00	2.50	.50
58 Peter Bondra, Wash.	15.00	1.50	.20
59 Marty McInnis, NYIs.	2.50	.30	.20
60 Bill Guerin, NJer.	10.00	1.00	.20
61 Patrice Brisebois, Mont.	2.50	.30	.20
62 Andy Moog (G), Dall.	10.00	1.00	.20
63 Eric Weinrich, Chic.	2.50	.30	.20
64 Arturs Irbe (G), SanJ.	10.00	1.00	.20
65 Sean Hill, Otta.	2.50	.30	.20
66 Jesse Bélanger, Flor.	2.50	.30	.20
67 Bryan Marchment, Edmo.	2.50	.30	.20
68 Joe Sacco, Anah.	2.50	.30	.20
69 Trevor Kidd (G), Calg.	5.00	.50	.20
70 Dan Quinn, LosA. (Otta.)	2.50	.30	.20
71 Kirk McLean (G), Vanc.	5.00	.50	.20
72 Benoît Hogue, Toro.	2.50	.30	.20
73 Garry Galley, Buff.	2.50	.30	.20
74 Randy Wood, Toro.	2.50	.30	.20
75 N. Khabibulin (G), Winn.	10.00	1.00	.20
76 Ted Donato, Bost.	2.50	.30	.20
77 Doug Bodger, Buff.	2.50	.30	.20
78 Paul Ranheim, Hart.	2.50	.30	.20
79 Ulf Samuelsson, Pitt.	2.50	.30	.20
80 Uwe Krupp, Québ.	2.50	.30	.20
81 O. Tverdovsky, Anah.	2.50	.30	.20
82 Kelly Miller, Wash.	2.50	.30	.20
83 Darryl Sydor, LosA.	5.00	.50	.20
84 Brian Bellows, Mont.	5.00	.50	.20
85 Jeremy Roenick, Chic.	20.00	2.00	.20
86 Phil Bourque, Otta.	2.50	.30	.20
87 Louie DeBrusk, Edmo.	2.50	.30	.20
88 Joel Otto, Calg. (Phil.)	2.50	.30	.20
89 Dino Ciccarelli, Detr.	5.00	.50	.20
90 Mats Sundin, Toro.	25.00	2.50	.50
91 Don Sweeney, Bost.	2.50	.30	.20
92 Roman Hamrlik, Tamp.	5.00	.50	.20
93 Petr* Svoboda, Phil.	5.00	.50	.20
94 Zigmund Palffy, NYIs.	15.00	1.50	.20
95 Patrick Roy (G), Mont.	75.00	7.50	1.50
96 Sergei Krivokrasov, Chic.	2.50	.30	.20
97 W. Flaherty, SanJ. RC	**5.00**	**1.00**	**.50**
98 Fredrik Olausson, Edmo.	5.00	.50	.20
99 Momesso, Vanc. (Toro.)	2.50	.30	.20
100 Mike Vernon (G), Detr.	10.00	1.00	.20
101 Todd Gill, Toro.	2.50	.30	.20
102 Cam Neely, Bost.	25.00	2.50	.50
103 Wendel Clark, Québ.	20.00	2.00	.20
104 John Tucker, Tamp.	2.50	.30	.20
105 Éric Desjardins, Phil.	5.00	.50	.20
106 Ed Olczyk, Winn.	5.00	.50	.20
107 Bob Beers, NYIs.	2.50	.30	.20
108 Mark Recchi, Mont.	10.00	1.00	.20
109 Ed Belfour (G), Chic.	25.00	2.50	.50
110 Radek Bonk, Otta.	5.00	.50	.20
111 Cory Stillman, Calg.	5.00	.50	.20
112 Jeff Norton, SLou.	2.50	.30	.20
113 Terry Carkner, Detr.	2.50	.30	.20
114 Félix Potvin (G), Toro.	15.00	1.50	.20
115 Alexei Kasatonov, Bost.	5.00	.50	.20
116 Brian Noonan, NYRa.	2.50	.30	.20
117 D. Puppa (G), Tamp.	5.00	.50	.20
118 Joé Juneau, Wash.	5.00	.50	.20
119 Valeri Bure, Mont.	5.00	.50	.20
120 Murray Craven, Chic.	2.50	.30	.20
121 M. Tuomainen, Edmo.	5.00	.50	.20
122 Trevor Linden, Vanc.	10.00	1.00	.20
123 Zarley Zalapski, Calg.	2.50	.30	.20
124 Jeff Shantz, Chic.	2.50	.30	.20
125 Dmitri Mironov, Toro.	2.50	.30	.20
126 J. Huscroft, Bost. RC	**5.00**	**.50**	**.20**
127 Jaromir Jagr, Pitt.	25.00	2.50	.50
128 Brian Bradley, Tamp.	2.50	.30	.20
129 Brett Lindros, NYIs.	5.00	.50	.20
130 Calle Johansson, Wash.	5.00	.50	.20
131 Pierre Turgeon, Mont.	10.00	1.00	.20
132 Denis Savard, Chic.	10.00	1.00	.20
133 Joe Nieuwendyk, Calg.	10.00	1.00	.20
134 Petr Klima, Tamp.	2.50	.30	.20
135 John Druce, LosA.	2.50	.30	.20
136 C. Osgood (G), Detr.	15.00	1.50	.20
137 Kenny Jönsson, Toro.	5.00	.50	.20
138 Jocelyn Lemieux, Hart.	2.50	.30	.20
139 Tomas Sandström, Pitt.	5.00	.50	.20
140 Chris Gratton, Tamp.	5.00	.50	.20
141 Mark Tinordi, Wash.	2.50	.30	.20
142 Kirk Muller, NYIs.	5.00	.50	.20
143 V. Malakhov, Mont.	2.50	.30	.20
144 Jiri Slégr, Edmo.	2.50	.30	.20
145 McEachern, Pitt. (Bost.)	5.00	.50	.20
146 Corson, Edmo. (SLou.)	5.00	.50	.20
147 Kelly Hrudey (G), LosA.	5.00	.50	.20
148 Sergei Fedorov, Detr.	25.00	2.50	.50
149 Mike Gartner, Toro.	20.00	2.00	.20
150 S. Fiset (G), Québ.	5.00	.50	.20
151 L. Murphy, Pitt. (Toro.)	5.00	.50	.20
152 Enrico Ciccone, Tamp.	2.50	.30	.20
153 Mike Keane, Mont.	2.50	.30	.20
154 Steve Larmer, NYRa.	10.00	1.00	.20
155 Dale Hunter, Wash.	5.00	.50	.20
156 Joe Murphy, Chic.	2.50	.30	.20
157 Pat LaFontaine, Buff.	15.00	1.50	.20
158 Rob Gaudreau, Otta.	2.50	.30	.20
159 Paul Kariya, Anah.	35.00	3.50	.50
160 Rob Blake, LosA.	15.00	1.50	.20
161 Keith Primeau, Detr.	10.00	1.00	.20
162 Dave Ellett, Toro.	2.50	.30	.20
163 Mogilny, Buff. (Vanc.)	10.00	1.00	.20
164 Luc Robitaille, Pitt.	20.00	2.00	.20
165 A. Selivanov, Tamp.	2.50	.30	.20
166 Keith Jones, Wash.	2.50	.30	.20
167 T. Stevenson, Mont.	2.50	.30	.20
168 Keith Tkachuk, Winn.	15.00	1.50	.20
169 Bernie Nicholls, Chic.	5.00	.50	.20
170 Stanislav Neckar, Otta.	2.50	.30	.20
171 Scott Mellanby, Flor.	5.00	.50	.20
172 Doug Weight, Edmo.	15.00	1.50	.20
173 Shaun Van Allen, Anah.	2.50	.30	.20
174 Gary Roberts, Calg.	10.00	1.00	.20
175 Robert Lang, LosA.	5.00	.50	.20
176 Martin Gélinas, Vanc.	5.00	.50	.20
177 Ray Sheppard, Detr.	2.50	.30	.20
178 Smolinski, Bost. (Pitt.)	2.50	.30	.20
179 Wayne Presley, Buff.	2.50	.30	.20
180 Jimmy Carson, Hart.	2.50	.30	.20
181 John Cullen, Pitt.	5.00	.50	.20
182 M. Andersson, Tamp.	2.50	.30	.20
183 Khristich, Wash. (LosA.)	2.50	.30	.20
184 Chris Therien, Phil.	2.50	.30	.20
185 Bobby Holik, NJer.	5.00	.50	.20
186 Kevin Hatcher, Dall.	2.50	.30	.20
187 Patrick Poulin, Chic.	2.50	.30	.20
188 Pat Falloon, SanJ.	2.50	.30	.20
189 Alexei Yashin, Otta.	15.00	1.50	.20
190 Gord Murphy, Flor.	2.50	.30	.20
191 Kirk Maltby, Edmo.	5.00	.50	.20
192 Dave Karpa, Anah.	2.50	.30	.20
193 Kelly Kisio, Calg.	2.50	.30	.20
194 Tony Granato, LosA.	5.00	.50	.20
195 Al Iafrate, Bost.	5.00	.50	.20
196 Nelson Emerson, Winn.	2.50	.30	.20
197 Adam Oates, Bost.	10.00	1.00	.20
198 Rob Ray, Buff.	5.00	.50	.20
199 Sean Burke (G), Hart.	15.00	1.50	.20
200 Ron Francis, Pitt.	15.00	1.50	.20
201 Theoren Fleury, Calg.	15.00	1.50	.20
202 Patrick Flatley, NYIs.	2.50	.30	.20
203 Ron Hextall (G), Phil.	15.00	1.50	.20
204 M. Brodeur (G), NJer.	40.00	4.00	.50
205 Mike Kennedy, Dall.	2.50	.30	.20
206 Tony Amonte, Chic.	15.00	1.50	.20
207 S. Makarov, SanJ.	10.00	1.00	.20
208 Alexandre Daigle, Otta.	2.50	.30	.20
209 Stu Barnes, Flor.	2.50	.30	.20
210 Todd Marchant, Edmo.	5.00	.50	.20
211 Valeri Karpov, Anah.	2.50	.30	.20
212 Phil Housley, Calg.	5.00	.50	.20
213 Jamie Storr (G), LosA.	5.00	.50	.20
214 Brett Hull, SLou.	25.00	2.50	.50
215 Kris King, Winn.	2.50	.30	.20
216 R. Bourque, Bost.	30.00	3.00	.50
217 Donald Audette, Buff.	10.00	1.00	.20
218 Steven Rice, Hart.	2.50	.30	.20
219 K. Stevens, Pitt. (Bost.)	5.00	.50	.20
220 Mark Messier, NYRa.	25.00	2.50	.50
221 Valeri Kamensky, Québ.	5.00	.50	.20
222 Mikael Renberg, Phil.	5.00	.50	.20
223 Scott Stevens, NJer.	10.00	1.00	.20
224 Derian Hatcher, Dall.	5.00	.50	.20
225 Ray Whitney, SanJ.	5.00	.50	.20
226 Bob Kudelski, Flor.	2.50	.30	.20
227 M. Shtalenkov, Anah.	2.50	.30	.20
228 Nicklas Lidström, Detr.	15.00	1.50	.20
229 Creighton, SLou.(Wash.)	2.50	.30	.20
230 Dave Manson, Winn.	2.50	.30	.20
231 Craig Simpson, Buff.	2.50	.30	.20
232 Chris Pronger, Hart.	15.00	1.50	.20
233 Adrien Plavsic, Tamp.	2.50	.30	.20
234 Alexei Kovalev, NYRa.	15.00	1.50	.20
235 T. Salo (G), NYIs. RC	**20.00**	**3.00**	**1.50**
236 Patrik Juhlin, Phil.	2.50	.30	.20
237 Tom Chorske, NJer.	2.50	.30	.20
238 Mike Modano, Dall.	25.00	2.50	.50
239 Igor Larionov, Detr.	15.00	1.50	.20
240 Johan Garpenlöv, Flor.	2.50	.30	.20
241 Todd Krygier, Anah.	2.50	.30	.20
242 Tie Domi, Toro.	5.00	.50	.20
243 Houlder, SLou. (Tamp.)	2.50	.30	.20
244 T. Selänne, Winn.	20.00	2.00	.20
245 Hawerchuk, Buff. (SLou.)	15.00	1.50	.20
246 B. Ranford (G), Edmo.	10.00	1.00	.20
247 Brian Leetch, NYRa.	15.00	1.50	.20
248 Steve Thomas, NYIs.	5.00	.50	.20
249 Dmitry Yushkevich, Phil.	5.00	.50	.20
250 Stéphane Richer, NJer.	5.00	.50	.20
251 Todd Harvey, Dall.	5.00	.50	.20
252 Viktor Kozlov, SanJ.	5.00	.50	.20
253 Vanbiesbrouck (G), Flor.	10.00	1.00	.20
254 Rick Tocchet, LosA.	5.00	.50	.20
255 Bret Hedican, Vanc.	2.50	.30	.20
256 Mario Lemieux, Pitt.	75.00	7.50	1.50
257 Igor Korolev, Winn.	2.50	.30	.20
258 D. Hasek (G), Buff.	25.00	2.50	.50
259 Owen Nolan, Québ.	15.00	1.50	.20
260 Michal Pivonka, Wash.	2.50	.30	.20
261 John LeClair, Phil.	20.00	2.00	.20
262 Claude Lemieux, NJer.	5.00	.50	.20
263 Mike Donnelly, Dall.	2.50	.30	.20
264 Craig Janney, SanJ.	5.00	.50	.20
265 Milos Holan, Anah.	2.50	.30	.20
266 Steve Yzerman, Detr.	60.00	6.00	1.00
267 Russ Courtnall, Vanc.	5.00	.50	.20
268 Esa Tikkanen, SLou.	2.50	.30	.20
269 Dallas Drake, Winn.	2.50	.30	.20
270 Norm Maciver, Pitt.	2.50	.30	.20
271 Scott A. Young, Québ.	5.00	.50	.20
272 Glenn Healy (G), NYRa.	5.00	.50	.20
273 Brian Rolston, NJer.	5.00	.50	.20
274 Corey Millen, Dall.	2.50	.30	.20
275 Kevin Miller, SanJ.	2.50	.30	.20
276 Éric Lacroix, LosA.	2.50	.30	.20
277 Adam Graves, NYRa.	10.00	1.00	.20
278 Christian Ruuttu, Vanc.	2.50	.30	.20
279 Duchesne, SLou. (Otta.)	5.00	.50	.20
280 Quintal, Winn. (Mont.)	2.50	.30	.20
281 Brent Gretzky, Tamp.	2.50	.30	.20
282 Mike Ricci, Québ.	5.00	.50	.20
283 S. Nemchinov, NYRa.	5.00	.50	.20
284 Sylvain Côté, Wash.	2.50	.30	.20
285 Neal Broten, NJer.	5.00	.50	.20
286 Greg A. Adams, Dall.	2.50	.30	.20
287 Guy Hebert (G), Anah.	5.00	.50	.20
288 Joe Sakic, Québ.	40.00	4.00	.50
289 Bobby Dollas, Anah.	2.50	.30	.20
290 Gino Odjick, Vanc.	2.50	.30	.20
291 Joseph (G), SLou.(Edmo.)	25.00	2.50	.50
292 Teppo Numminen, Winn.	5.00	.50	.20
293 Geoff Sanderson, Hart.	5.00	.50	.20
294 Deadmarsh, Québ.	5.00	.50	.20
295 Haller, Phil. (Mont.)	2.50	.30	.20
296 Sergei Brylin, NJer.	2.50	.30	.20
297 Ulf Dahlén, SanJ.	2.50	.30	.20
298 Robert Kron, Hart.	2.50	.30	.20
299 Dave Lowry, Flor.	5.00	.50	.20
300 Borschevsky, Calg.	2.50	.30	.20
301 Jeff R. Brown, Vanc.	2.50	.30	.20
302 Guy Carbonneau, SLou.	5.00	.50	.20
303 Alexei Zhitnik, Buff.	2.50	.30	.20
304 Frantisek Kucera, Hart.	2.50	.30	.20
305 Leschyshyn, Québ.	2.50	.30	.20
306 Richter (G), NYRa.	10.00	1.00	.20
307 Dean Evason, Dall.	2.50	.30	.20
308 Jozef Stumpel, Bost.	5.00	.50	.20
309 Jeff Friesen, SanJ.	5.00	.50	.20
310 Buchberger, Edmo.	2.50	.30	.20
311 Michael Nylander, Calg.	5.00	.50	.20
312 Josef Beranek, Vanc.	2.50	.30	.20
313 Al MacInnis, SLou.	10.00	1.00	.20
314 Ken Wregget (G), Pitt.	5.00	.50	.20
315 Glen Wesley, Hart.	2.50	.30	.20
316 Thibault (G), Québ.	10.00	1.00	.20
317 Jeff Beukeboom, NYRa.	2.50	.30	.20
318 Konowalchuk, Wash.	5.00	.50	.20
319 Chevelade (G), Winn.	2.50	.30	.20
320 Damphousse, Mont.	15.00	1.50	.20
321 Mats Näslund, Bost.	5.00	.50	.20
322 Schneider, NYIs.	5.00	.50	.20
323 Petr Nedved, NYRa.	5.00	.50	.20
324 Brent Fedyk, Phil.	2.50	.30	.20
325 Jussi Tie RC	**5.00**	**.50**	**.50**
326 M. Markkanen RC	**5.00**	**.50**	**.50**
327 Timo Hakanen RC	**5.00**	**.50**	**.50**
328 Sami Salonen RC	**5.00**	**.50**	**.50**
329 J. Viinikainen RC	**5.00**	**.50**	**.50**
330 Jani Riihinen RC	**5.00**	**.50**	**.50**
331 T. Riihijärvi RC	**5.00**	**.50**	**.50**
332 J. Niskavaara RC	**5.00**	**.50**	**.50**
333 Miika Elomo	2.50	.30	.20
334 Tomi Kallio RC	**25.00**	**2.50**	**1.00**
335 Vesa Toskala RC	**5.00**	**.50**	**.50**
336 T. Reijonen RC	**5.00**	**.50**	**.50**
337 Aki Berg RC	**5.00**	**1.00**	**.50**
338 Tomi Hirvonen RC	**5.00**	**.50**	**.50**
339 Jussi Salminen RC	**5.00**	**.50**	**.50**
340 A. Sjolund RC	**5.00**	**.50**	**.50**
341 J. Ramstedt RC	**5.00**	**.50**	**.50**
342 B. Danielsson RC	**5.00**	**.50**	**.50**
343 P. Gustavsson RC	**5.00**	**.50**	**.50**
344 Niklas Anger RC	**5.00**	**.50**	**.50**
345 Marcus Nilson RC	**5.00**	**1.00**	**.50**
346 PA Lundström RC	**5.00**	**.50**	**.50**
347 H. Rehnberg RC	**5.00**	**.50**	**.50**
348 R. Borgqvist RC	**5.00**	**.50**	**.50**
349 T. Christensen RC	**5.00**	**.50**	**.50**
350 Sam. Påhlsson RC	**5.00**	**1.00**	**.50**
351 Fredrik Loven RC	**5.00**	**.50**	**.50**
352 P. Wallenberg RC	**5.00**	**.50**	**.50**
353 Jan Labraaten RC	**5.00**	**.50**	**.50**
354 Peter Wallin RC	**5.00**	**.50**	**.50**
355 Cam Neely, Bost.	25.00	2.50	.50
356 Keith Tkachuk, Winn.	15.00	1.50	.20
357 Chris Gratton, Tamp.	5.00	.50	.20
358 Adam Graves, NYRa.	10.00	1.00	.20
359 Doug Gilmour, Toro.	15.00	1.50	.20
360 Adam Deadmarsh, Québ.	5.00	.50	.20
361 Wayne Gretzky, LosA.	100.00	10.00	2.00
362 Joe Sakic, Québ.	40.00	4.00	.50
363 Paul Kariya, Anah.	35.00	3.50	.50
364 Brett Hull, SLou.	25.00	2.50	.50
365 Sergei Fedorov, Detr.	25.00	2.50	.50
366 Brian Rolston, NJer.	5.00	.50	.20
367 Dom. Hasek (G), Buff.	25.00	2.50	.50
368 V'b'sbrouck (G), Flor.	10.00	1.00	.20
369 Jim Carey (G), Wash.	2.50	.30	.20
370 Paul Kariya, Anah.	35.00	3.50	.50
371 Peter Forsberg, Québ.	35.00	3.50	.50
372 Jeff Friesen, SanJ.	5.00	.50	.20
373 Kenny Jönsson, Toro.	5.00	.50	.20
374 Chris Therien, Phil.	2.50	.30	.20
375 Jim Carey (G), Wash.	2.50	.30	.20
376 John LeClair, Phil.	20.00	2.00	.20
377 Eric Lindros, Phil.	25.00	2.50	.50

□□□	378 Jaromir Jagr, Pitt.	25.00	2.50	.50
□□□	379 Paul Coffey, Detr.	15.00	1.50	.20
□□□	380 Chris Chelios, Chic.	15.00	1.50	.20
□□□	381 Dom. Hasek (G), Buff.	25.00	2.50	.50
□□□	382 Keith Tkachuk, Winn.	15.00	1.50	.20
□□□	383 Alexei Zhamnov, Winn.	5.00	.50	.20
□□□	384 Theoren Fleury, Calg.	15.00	1.50	.20
□□□	385 R. Bourque, Bost.	30.00	3.00	.50
□□□	386 L. Murphy, Pitt. (Toro.)	5.00	.50	.20
□□□	387 Ed Belfour (G), Chic.	25.00	2.50	.50
□□□	388 Eric Lindros, Phil.	25.00	2.50	.50
□□□	389 Jaromir Jagr, Pitt.	25.00	2.50	.50
□□□	390 Paul Coffey, Detr.	15.00	1.50	.20
□□□	391 Peter Forsberg, Québ.	35.00	3.50	.50
□□□	392 Claude Lemieux, NJer.	5.00	.50	.20
□□□	393 Ron Francis, Pitt.	15.00	1.50	.20
□□□	394 D. Hasek (G), Buff.	25.00	2.50	.50
□□□	395 Checklist	2.50	.30	.20
□□□	396 Checklist	2.50	.30	.20
□	397 Saku Koivu, Mont. [YG]			2.00
□	**398 R. Dvorak, Flor. [YG] RC**			**1.50**
□	399 Ed Jovanovski, Flor. [YG]			1.00
□	400 Brendan Witt, Wash. [YG]			.50
□	401 Jeff O'Neill, Hart. [YG]			1.00
□	402 D. Langkow, Tamp. [YG]			1.50
□	**403 S. Doan, Winn. [YG] RC**			**1.50**
□	404 Bryan McCabe, NYIs. [YG]			.50
□	405 Marty Murray, Calg. [YG]			.50
□	**406 Alfredsson, Otta. [YG] RC**			**4.50**
□	407 Jason Doig, Winn. [YG]			.50
□	408 N. Sundström, NYRa. [YG]			.50
□	409 V. Yachmenev, LosA. [YG]			.50
□	410 Aki Berg, LosA. [YG]			.50
□	411 Éric Dazé, Chic. [YG]			1.00

YOU CRASH THE GAME

Each gold and silver version have three dates. If the player scored a goal on the specified date, the card could be exchanged for a 30-card "You Crash the Game" set plus a Bonus card of that player.

Insert Set (90 cards):		65.00
	Player	Silv.
□□□	C1 P. Bure (10-12; 12-17; 3-23)	1.00
□□□	C2 S. Fedorov (10-19; 12-31; 3-12)	1.50
□□□	C3 W. Gretzky (10-7; 12-21; 2-10)	6.00
□□□	C4 E. Lindros (11-12; 1-3; 3-3)	1.50
□□□	C5 B. Hull (10-10; 12-9; 3-24)	1.50
□□□	C6 M. Messier (11-8; 1-22; 3-31)	1.50
□□□	C7 J. Jagr (10-14; 12-17; 3-5)	1.50
□□□	C8 A. Zhamnov (10-9; 12-28; 2-21)	.50
□□□	C9 J. Sakic (10-6; 12-9; 2-3)	2.00
□□□	C10 P. Kariya (10-18; 12-19; 3-17)	2.00
□□□	C11 T. Fleury (10-27; 12-11; 2-6)	.50
□□□	C12 O. Nolan (11-1; 1-4; 3-17)	.50
□□□	C13 P. Bondra (10-13; 12-2; 3-12)	.50
□□□	C14 C. Neely (11-7; 1-11; 3-23)	1.50
□□□	C15 P. Turgeon (10-25; 12-23; 2-21)	.50
□□□	C16 M. Modano (11-1; 1-5; 2-22)	1.50
□□□	C17 B. Nicholls (10-10; 12-15; 3-24)	.50
□□□	C18 A. Yashin (11-4; 12-23; 2-21)	.50
□□□	C19 J. Arnott (10-27; 12-18; 2-28)	.50
□□□	C20 P. Forsberg (11-22; 2-15; 3-27)	2.00
□□□	C21 D. Gilmour (10-17; 12-16; 2-18)	.50
□□□	C22 G. Sanderson (10-11; 12-18; 3-6)	.50
□□□	C23 J. LeClair (10-15; 12-16; 2-19)	1.00
□□□	C24 R. Bourque (10-11; 12-16; 2-6)	1.50
□□□	C25 M. Lemieux (11-1; 12-1; 2-6)	4.50
□□□	C26 S. Yzerman (11-11; 1-24; 2-27)	3.50
□□□	C27 P. LaFontaine (10-20; 12-27; 2-17)	.50
□□□	C28 C. Lemieux (10-7; 12-15; 2-10)	.50
□□□	C29 P. Coffey (10-15; 12-5; 2-13)	.50
□□□	C30 M. Sundin (11-7; 1-3; 3-15)	1.50

YOU CRASH THE GAME GOLD

Insert Set (90 cards):		300.00
	Player	Gold
□□□	C1 P. Bure (10-12; 12-17; 3-23)	4.50
□□□	C2 S. Fedorov (10-19; 12-31; 3-12)	6.00
□□□	C3 W. Gretzky (10-7; 12-21; 2-10)	24.00
□□□	C4 E. Lindros (11-12; 1-3; 3-3)	6.00
□□□	C5 B. Hull (10-10; 12-9; 3-24)	6.00
□□□	C6 M. Messier (11-8; 1-22; 3-31)	6.00
□□□	C7 J. Jagr (10-14; 12-17; 3-5)	6.00
□□□	C8 A. Zhamnov (10-9; 12-28; 2-21)	2.00
□□□	C9 J. Sakic (10-6; 12-9; 2-3)	9.50
□□□	C10 P. Kariya (10-18; 12-19; 3-17)	8.00
□□□	C11 T. Fleury (10-27; 12-11; 2-6)	3.50
□□□	C12 O. Nolan (11-1; 1-4; 3-17)	3.50
□□□	C13 P. Bondra (10-13; 12-2; 3-12)	3.50
□□□	C14 C. Neely (11-7; 1-11; 3-23)	6.00
□□□	C15 P. Turgeon (10-25; 12-23; 2-21)	2.00
□□□	C16 M. Modano (11-1; 1-5; 2-22)	6.00
□□□	C17 B. Nicholls (10-10; 12-15; 3-24)	2.00
□□□	C18 A. Yashin (11-4; 12-23; 2-21)	3.50
□□□	C19 J. Arnott (10-27; 12-18; 2-28)	2.50
□□□	C20 P. Forsberg (11-22; 2-15; 3-27)	8.00
□□□	C21 D. Gilmour (10-17; 12-16; 2-18)	3.50
□□□	C22 G. Sanderson (10-11; 12-18; 3-6)	2.00
□□□	C23 J. LeClair (10-15; 12-16; 2-19)	4.50
□□□	C24 R. Bourque (10-11; 12-16; 2-6)	7.00
□□□	C25 M. Lemieux (11-1; 12-1; 2-6)	18.00
□□□	C26 S. Yzerman (11-11; 1-24; 2-27)	14.00
□□□	C27 P. LaFontaine (10-20; 12-27; 2-17)	3.50
□□□	C28 C. Lemieux (10-7; 12-15; 2-10)	2.00
□□□	C29 P. Coffey (10-15; 12-5; 2-13)	3.50
□□□	C30 M. Sundin (11-7; 1-3; 3-15)	6.00

YOU CRASH THE GAME WIN

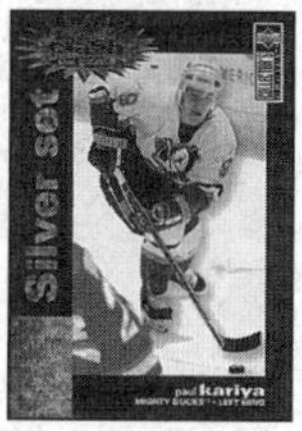

Winning cards have four versions: the silver winner, a silver bonus card, the gold winner and a gold bonus card. Loser cards do not have bonus versions. Cards C3,C4,C17, C18,C20,C22 and C27 did not win.

Redeemed Set (30 cards):		25.00	10.00
	Player	G-Win	S-Win
□□	C1 Pavel Bure, Vanc.	.75	.30
□□	C2 Sergei Fedorov, Detr.	1.00	.50
□□	C3 Wayne Gretzky, LosA.	4.00	2.00
□□	C4 Eric Lindros, Phil.	1.00	.50
□□	C5 Brett Hull, SLou.	1.00	.50
□□	C6 Mark Messier, NYRa.	1.00	.50
□□	C7 Jaromir Jagr, Pitt.	1.00	.50
□□	C8 Alexei Zhamnov, Winn.	.75	.30
□□	C9 Joe Sakic, Québ.	1.50	.50
□□	C10 Paul Kariya, Anah.	1.00	.50
□□	C11 Theoren Fleury, Calg.	.75	.30
□□	C12 Owen Nolan, Québ.	.75	.30
□□	C13 Peter Bondra, Wash.	.75	.30
□□	C14 Cam Neely, Bost.	1.00	.50
□□	C15 Pierre Turgeon, Mont.	.75	.30
□□	C16 Mike Modano, Dall.	1.00	.50
□□	C17 Bernie Nicholls, Chic.	.75	.30
□□	C18 Alexei Yashin, Otta.	.75	.30
□□	C19 Jason Arnott, Edmo.	.75	.30
□□	C20 Peter Forsberg, Québ.	1.00	.50
□□	C21 Doug Gilmour, Toro.	.75	.30
□□	C22 Geoff Sanderson, Hart.	.75	.30
□□	C23 John LeClair, Phil.	.75	.30
□□	C24 Raymond Bourque, Bost.	1.00	.50
□□	C25 Mario Lemieux, Pitt.	3.00	1.50
□□	C26 Steve Yzerman, Detr.	2.00	1.00
□□	C27 Pat LaFontaine, Buff.	.75	.30
□□	C28 Claude Lemieux, NJer.	.75	.30
□□	C29 Paul Coffey, Detr.	.75	.30
□□	C30 Mats Sundin, Toro.	1.00	.50

YOU CRASH THE GAME BONUS

Bonus Set (23 cards):		135.00	55.00
	Player	GB	SB
□□	C1 Pavel Bure, Vanc.	6.00	2.00
□□	C2 Sergei Fedorov, Detr.	6.00	2.00
□□	C5 Brett Hull, SLou.	6.00	2.00
□□	C6 Mark Messier, NYRa.	6.00	2.00
□□	C7 Jaromir Jagr, Pitt.	6.00	2.00
□□	C8 Alexei Zhamnov, Winn.	4.00	2.00
□□	C9 Joe Sakic, Québ.	12.00	6.00
□□	C10 Paul Kariya, Anah.	10.00	4.00
□□	C11 Theoren Fleury, Calg.	4.00	2.00
□□	C12 Owen Nolan, Québ.	4.00	2.00
□□	C13 Peter Bondra, Wash.	4.00	2.00
□□	C14 Cam Neely, Bost.	6.00	2.00
□□	C15 Pierre Turgeon, Mont.	4.00	2.00
□□	C16 Mike Modano, Dall.	6.00	2.00
□□	C19 Jason Arnott, Edmo.	4.00	2.00
□□	C21 Doug Gilmour, Toro.	4.00	2.00
□□	C23 John LeClair, Phil.	6.00	2.00
□□	C24 Raymond Bourque, Bost.	8.00	4.00
□□	C25 Mario Lemieux, Pitt.	22.00	10.00
□□	C26 Steve Yzerman, Detr.	18.00	8.00
□□	C28 Claude Lemieux, NJer.	4.00	2.00
□□	C29 Paul Coffey, Detr.	4.00	2.00
□□	C30 Mats Sundin, Toro.	6.00	2.00

1995 - 96 UPPER DECK ELITSERIEN

This set is licensed by the Swedish players' association, SICO. The most expensive singles are Johan Hedberg at $4-6, Peter Forsberg at $2-3 and Mats Sundin at $1-2. NHL stars sell at $0.50-1.50. All other singles sell between 20¢ and $1.00.

Complete Set (260 cards): 25.00

	Player		Player
□	1 Joakim Persson	□	2 Erik Hamalainen
□	3 Dick Tarnström	□	4 Ricard Franzen
□	5 Niclas Havelid	□	6 Tony Barthelsson
□	7 Tommy Hedlund	□	8 Patric Aberg
□	9 Stefan Gustavson	□	10 Anders Gozzi
□	11 David Engblom	□	12 Stefan Andersson
□	13 Tomas Stranberg	□	14 Mats Lindberg
□	15 Tommy Lehmann	□	16 Björn Ahlström
□	17 Patric Englund	□	18 Morgan Samuelsson
□	19 Michael Sundlov	□	20 Bedrich Scerban
□	21 Mikael Lindman	□	22 Mikael Wiklander
□	23 Tommy Melkersson	□	24 Stefan Klockare
□	25 Per Lofstrom	□	26 Jonas Johnsson
□	27 Roger Kyro	□	28 Jonas Lofstrom
□	29 Stefan Ketola	□	30 Mikael Wahlberg
□	31 Stefan Polla	□	32 Greg Parks
□	33 Ove Molin	□	34 Peter Larsson
□	35 Fredrik Modin	□	36 Andreas Dackell
□	37 Thomas Ostlund	□	38 Tommy Jakobsen
□	39 Christian Due-Boje	□	40 Thomas Johansson
□	41 Joakim Lundberg	□	42 Bjorn Nord
□	43 Mikael Magnusson	□	44 Erik Huusko
□	45 Anders Kuusko	□	46 Kristoffer Ottosson
□	47 Magnus Jansson	□	48 Nichlas Falk
□	49 Ola Josefsson	□	50 Per Eklund
□	51 Espen Knutsen	□	52 Jens Ohling
□	53 Patrik Kjellberg	□	54 Patrik Erickson
□	55 Jan Viktorsson	□	56 Markus Ketterer
□	57 Jesper Duus	□	58 Sergei Fokin
□	59 Per Lundell	□	60 Thomas Rhodin
□	61 Henrik Rehnberg	□	62 Roger Johansson
□	63 Leif Carlsson	□	64 Hakan Loob
□	65 Stefan Nilsson	□	66 Vitali Prokhorov
□	67 Magnus Arvedsson	□	68 Jonas Höglund
□	69 Mattias Johansson	□	70 Patrik Wallenberg
□	71 Clas Eriksson	□	72 Jörgen Jönsson
□	73 Peter Nordstrom	□	74 Peter Ottosson
□	75 Boo Ahl	□	76 Per Gustafsson
□	77 Niklas Rahm	□	78 Hans Abrahamsson
□	79 Kennth Kennholt	□	80 Daniel Johansson
□	81 Vesa Salo	□	82 Thomas Gustavsson
□	83 Stefan Ornskog	□	84 Stefan Falk
□	85 Peter Hammarstrom	□	86 Johan Davidsson
□	87 Peter Ekelund	□	88 Johan Lindbom
□	89 Esa Keskinen	□	90 Kai Nurminen
□	91 Magnus Eliasson	□	92 Marcus Thuresson
□	93 Johan Brummer	□	94 Johan Hedberg (G)
□	95 Tomas Jönsson	□	96 Torbjorn Johansson
□	97 Hans Lodin	□	98 Orjan Lindmark
□	99 Jan Huokko	□	100 Joakim Lidgren
□	101 Per-Erik Eklund	□	102 Anders Carlsson
□	103 Niklas Eriksson	□	104 Michael Karlberg
□	105 Jonas Bergqvist	□	106 Torgny Lowgren
□	107 Stefan Hellqvist	□	108 Markus Akerblom
□	109 Mikael Holmberg	□	110 Andreas Karlsson
□	111 Markus Eriksson	□	112 Tomas Forslund
□	113 Jarmo Myllys	□	114 Lars Modig
□	115 Patrik Höglund	□	116 Torbjorn Lindberg
□	117 Jan Mertzig	□	118 Petter Nilsson
□	119 Mattias Öhlund	□	120 Roger Åkerström
□	121 Stefan Jönsson	□	122 Stefan Nilsson
□	123 Thomas Holmstrom	□	124 Mikael Lindholm
□	125 Johan Stromwall	□	126 Jiri Kucera
□	127 Joakim Backlund	□	128 Robert Nordberg
□	129 Tomas Berglund	□	130 Fredrik Johansson
□	131 Lars Hurtig	□	132 Johan Rosen
□	133 R. Nordström (G)	□	134 Kim Johnsson
□	135 Peter Hasselblad	□	136 Ilja Byakin
□	137 Johan Salle	□	138 Peter Andersson
□	139 Roger Ohman	□	140 Marko Palo
□	141 Raimo Helminen	□	142 Mattias Bosson
□	143 Markus Magnertoft	□	144 Roger Hansson
□	145 Bo Svanberg	□	146 Patrik Sylvegard
□	147 Brian McReynolds	□	148 Hakan Ahlund
□	149 Robert Burakovski	□	150 Stefan Elvenes
□	151 Patrik Boij	□	152 Petter Ronnqvist
□	153 Mattias Timmander	□	154 Lars Jansson
□	155 Frantisek Kaberle	□	156 Hans Jönsson
□	157 Tomas Nanzen	□	158 Marcus Karlsson
□	159 Kristian Gahn	□	160 Magnus Wernblom
□	161 Anders Soderberg	□	162 Martin Hostak
□	163 Kyosti Karjalainen	□	164 Mikael Hakansson
□	165 Jan Larsson	□	166 Per Svartvadet
□	167 A. Salomonsson	□	168 Samuel Pahlsson
□	169 Lars Bystrom	□	170 Magnus Swardh
□	171 Anders Berglund	□	172 Pierre Johnsson
□	173 Johan Finnstrom	□	174 Arto Routanen
□	175 Daniel Tjarnqvist	□	176 Greg Brown
□	177 Peter Wallin	□	178 Peter Lundmark
□	179 Roger Elvenes	□	180 Michael Hjalm
□	181 Jens Hemstrom	□	182 Pelle Svensson
□	183 Harjis Vitolins	□	184 Jens Nielsen
□	185 Mats Loov	□	186 Mats Ytter
□	187 Lars Ivarsson	□	188 Edvin Frylen
□	189 Andrei Lyulin	□	190 Johan Tornberg
□	191 Mattias Olsson	□	192 Mats Lusth
□	193 Fredrik Oberg	□	194 Alexei Salomatin
□	195 Mishat Fahrutdinov	□	196 Mikael Pettersson
□	197 Andrei Korolev	□	198 Mattias Loof
□	199 Claes Lindblom	□	200 Paul Andersson
□	201 Roger Rosen	□	202 Hakan Algotsson
□	203 Par Djoos	□	204 Mikael Sandberg
□	205 Joacim Esbjors	□	206 Stefan Axelsson
□	207 Ronnie Sundin	□	208 Stefan Larsson
□	209 Petteri Nummelin	□	210 Christian Ruuttu
□	211 Marko Jantunen	□	212 Peter Strom
□	213 Peter Berndtsson	□	214 Lars Edstrom
□	215 Peter Hogardh	□	216 Par Edlund
□	217 L-G Wiklander	□	218 Henrik Nilsson
□	219 Rikard Franzen	□	220 F. Modin, Brynas
□	221 Anders Soderberg	□	222 Per Eklund
□	223 Hakan Loob	□	224 Markus Ketterer (G)
□	225 Esa Keskinen	□	226 Per Gustafsson
□	227 Tomas Jönsson	□	228 Per-Erik Eklund
□	229 Mattias Öhlund	□	230 Jarmo Myllys (G)
□	231 Peter Andersson	□	232 Raimo Helminen
□	233 Christian Ruuttu	□	234 Peter Forsberg
□	235 Mikael Renberg	□	236 Mats Sundin
□	237 Michael Nylander	□	238 T. Söderström (G)
□	239 Nicklas Lidström	□	240 Kenny Jönsson
□	241 Patrik Carnback	□	242 Johan Garpenlov
□	243 Magnus Svensson	□	244 Patrik Juhlin
□	245 Markus Näslund	□	246 Tommy Salo (G)
□	247 Fredrik Olausson	□	248 Tommy Albelin
□	249 Rikard Franzen	□	250 Jonas Johnsson
□	251 Thomas Ostlund	□	252 Hakan Loob
□	253 Per Gustafsson	□	254 Per-Erik Eklund
□	255 Tomas Jönsson	□	256 Mattias Öhlund
□	257 Peter Andersson	□	258 Christian Ruuttu
□	259 Checklist (1-150)	□	260 Checklist

FIRST DIVISION STARS

Singles sell at $1-2 each.

Insert Set (20 cards): 20.00

	Player		Player
□	DS1 Anders Huss	□	DS2 Igor Vlasov
□	DS3 Ulf Sandstrom	□	DS4 Hans Huczkowski
□	DS5 Johan Ramstedt	□	DS6 Anders Eldebrink
□	DS7 Niklas Brannstrom	□	DS8 Peter Nilsson
□	DS9 Sam Lindstahl	□	DS10 Tony Skopac
□	DS11 Jonas Eriksson	□	DS12 Anders Lonn
□	DS13 Peter Hagstrom	□	DS14 Magnus Roupe
□	DS15 Peter Pettersson	□	DS16 Peter Eriksson
□	DS17 Fredrik Bergqvist	□	DS18 Larry Pilut
□	DS19 Peter Olsson	□	DS20 Staffan Lundh

TICKET TO NORTH AMERICA

Stars sell at $4-6; singles start at $2.

Insert Set (20 cards): 40.00

	Player		Player
□	NA1 Joakim Persson	□	NA2 Dick Tarnström
□	NA3 Andreas Dackell	□	NA4 Fredrik Modin
□	NA5 Per Eklund	□	NA6 Espen Knutsen
□	NA7 Fredrik Lindqvist	□	NA8 Jonas Höglund
□	NA9 Jörgen Jönsson	□	NA10 Johan Davidsson
□	NA11 Per Gustafsson	□	NA12 Johan Lindbom
□	NA13 Markus Akerblom	□	NA14 Jan Huokko
□	NA15 T. Holmström	□	NA16 Mattias Öhlund
□	NA17 Johan Rosen	□	NA18 Frantisek Kaberle
□	NA19 Mattias Timander	□	NA20 M. Wernblom

1995 - 96 UPPER DECK / POST

One cellophane wrapped card per Post Honey Combs or Sugar Crisps cereal box.

Complete Set (24 cards):		20.00
□	Wayne Gretzky Autograph ✍ (#/500)	900.00
	Player	NRMT-MT
□	1 Ray Bourque	3.00
□	2 Martin Brodeur (G)	1.00
□	3 Steve Duchesne	1.00
□	4 Vincent Damphousse	1.50
□	5 Eric Desjardins	1.00
□	6 Eric Lindros	1.00
□	7 Joé Juneau	1.00
□	8 Luc Robitaille	2.00
□	9 Mark Recchi	1.00
□	10 Patrick Roy (G)	5.00
□	11 Brendan Shanahan	2.50
□	12 Scott Stevens	1.00
□	13 Jason Arnott	1.00
□	14 Trevor Linden	1.00
□	15 Chris Chelios	1.50
□	16 Paul Coffey	1.50
□	17 Wayne Gretzky	10.00
□	18 Doug Gilmour	1.50
□	19 Kelly Hrudey (G)	1.00
□	20 Paul Kariya	1.00
□	21 Larry Murphy	1.00
□	22 Félix Potvin (G)	1.50
□	23 Keith Tkachuk	1.50
□	24 Rob Blake	1.50

1995 - 96 UPPER DECK RECORD COLLECTION

These cross-brand inserts were included in packs of: Upper Deck Collector's Choice (G1-G9 plus header, 1:11 packs); Upper Deck series 1 (G10-G13 plus header, 1:29 packs); Upper Deck series 2 (G14-G17 plus header, 1:29 packs); and SP (G18-20 plus header, 1:45 packs). Oversize blow-ups exist for the Upper Deck Collector's Choice Record Collection cards (G1-G9 plus header).

Complete Set (24 cards):		50.00	165.00
	Player	Oversize	Insert
□□	G1 Wayne Gretzky, Edmo.	6.00	4.00
□□	G2 Wayne Gretzky, Edmo.	6.00	4.00
□□	G3 Wayne Gretzky, Edmo.	6.00	4.00
□□	G4 Wayne Gretzky, Edmo.	6.00	4.00
□□	G5 Wayne Gretzky, Edmo.	6.00	4.00
□□	G6 Wayne Gretzky, Edmo.	6.00	4.00
□□	G7 Wayne Gretzky, Edmo.	6.00	4.00
□□	G8 Wayne Gretzky, Edmo.	6.00	4.00
□□	G9 Wayne Gretzky, Edmo. [XCX-Kurri]	6.00	4.00
□	G10 Wayne Gretzky, Edmo.	-	8.00

☐	G11 Wayne Gretzky, Edmo.	-	8.00
☐	G12 Wayne Gretzky, Edmo.	-	8.00
☐	G13 Wayne Gretzky, Edmo.	-	8.00
☐	G14 Wayne Gretzky, LosA.	-	8.00
☐	G15 Wayne Gretzky, LosA.	-	8.00
☐	G16 Wayne Gretzky, NHL All-Star	-	8.00
☐	G17 Wayne Gretzky, NHL All-Star	-	8.00
☐	G18 Wayne Gretzky, LosA. [Most Goals]	-	25.00
☐	G19 Wayne Gretzky, LosA. [Most Assists]	-	25.00
☐	G20 Wayne Gretzky, LosA. [Most Points]	-	25.00
☐☐	Checklist [Gretzky UDCC]	6.00	4.00
☐	Checklist [Gretzky UD1]	-	8.00
☐	Checklist [Gretzky UD2]	-	8.00
☐	Checklist [Gretzky SP]	-	25.00

1995 - 96 ZELLERS MASTERS OF HOCKEY

Each set came with a certificate of authenticity. Each player signed 3,500 cards. Only a Signature Series was available this year.

Complete Set (8 cards): 200.00

	Player	NRMT-MT
☐	Mike Bossy, Zellers ✍	30.00
☐	Ed Giacomin, Zellers ✍	25.00
☐	Gordie Howe, Zellers ✍	70.00
☐	Jacques Laperrière, Zellers ✍	25.00
☐	Gilbert Perreault, Zellers ✍	25.00
☐	Serge Savard, Zellers ✍	25.00
☐	Steve Shutt, Zellers ✍	25.00
☐	Darryl Sittler, Zellers ✍	25.00

1996 SUPER MARIO

Each five-card set comes packaged in a tin "Super Mario" container. Singles sell at $5-7.

Imprint: CUI, Inc. Licensed by Mario Lemieux.

Complete Set (5 cards): 30.00

Tin Box (Mario Lemieux): 5.00

Player	Player
☐ 1 Mario Lemieux, Pitt.	☐ 2 Mario Lemieux, Pitt.
☐ 3 Mario Lemieux, Pitt.	☐ 4 Mario Lemieux, Pitt.
☐ 5 Mario Lemieux, Pitt.	

1996 QUÉBEC INTERNATIONAL PEE WEE

Complete Set (1470):

SAINTE-FOY GOUVERNEURS AA PEE WEE

The most expensive single is Daniel Boisclair at $2-3.

☐ 1 Martin Bricault ☐ 2 Samuel Demay
☐ 3 Mathieu Beauchesne ☐ 4 Alexandre Côté
☐ 5 Jean-Philippe Brière ☐ 6 Alexandre Blackburn
☐ 7 Frédéric Faucher ☐ 8 Jean-Philippe Côté
☐ 9 Simon Matte ☐ 10 Sébastien Gagnon
☐ 11 Frédéric Couet ☐ 12 Christian Barbeau
☐ 13 Sylvain Ruel ☐ 14 Dominic Brisson
☐ 15 Nicolas Pelletier ☐ 16 Daniel Boisclair
☐ 17 Instructeurs

TAMPA BAY PEE WEE

The most expensive single is Jesse Lane at $2-3.

☐ 18 Ryan Ahearn ☐ 19 Chris Brooks
☐ 20 Sean Cronin ☐ 21 Joey Dech
☐ 22 Chris Distefano ☐ 23 Bobby Goeppert
☐ 24 Shep Halsey ☐ 25 Michael Jayne
☐ 26 Christian* Jensen ☐ 27 Matthew Kroell
☐ 28 Jesse Lane ☐ 29 Michael Lionetti
☐ 30 Jame McKenna ☐ 31 Jimmy Merola
☐ 32 Ryan Shannon ☐ 33 Justin Solis
☐ 34 Matthew Thomas

CAMPUS ST-AUGUSTIN PEE WEE

☐ 35 Philippe Avard ☐ 36 Pierre-Olivier Martel
☐ 37 David Dubois ☐ 38 Jonathan Keays
☐ 39 Jean-Phylippe Côté ☐ 40 C. Châteauneuf
☐ 41 Martin Faucher ☐ 42 Louis-David Caron
☐ 43 Maxime Racette ☐ 44 Louis-Philippe Rioux
☐ 45 P. Dufour-Gaudreault ☐ 46 Nicolas Berthelot
☐ 47 Patrick Doré ☐ 48 Philippe Joncasz
☐ 49 Alexandre Turcotte ☐ 50 Romain Gaudreault
☐ 51 Instructeurs

VAL-BÉLAIR PEE WEE

☐ 52 Jean-Michel Bédard ☐ 53 Stéphane Bernier
☐ 54 Éric Bilodeau ☐ 55 Luc Blouin
☐ 56 Martin Blouin ☐ 57 Pascal Brulotte
☐ 58 Éric Descarreaux ☐ 59 Sébastien Girard
☐ 60 Alexandre Grenier ☐ 61 Jimmy Joannette
☐ 62 Sébastien Jolivet ☐ 63 Vincent Létourneau
☐ 64 Steve Lévesque ☐ 65 Gabriel Montminy
☐ 66 Olivier Pageau ☐ 67 Jonathan Robichaud
☐ 68 Olivier Roy ☐ 69 Nicolas* Savard
☐ 70 Instructeurs

CHARLESBOURG PEE WEE

☐ 71 Jean-François Drolet ☐ 72 Gabriel Dussault
☐ 73 François Gendron ☐ 74 Christian Plante
☐ 75 Christian Dorval ☐ 76 Philippe** Bourque
☐ 77 Jonathan Nadeau ☐ 78 Vincent Quirion
☐ 79 Pierre-Luc Leclair ☐ 80 Vincent Royer
☐ 81 J-M Thibodeau ☐ 82 Sébastien Guay
☐ 83 Sami Fekir ☐ 84 Guillaume Lefrançois
☐ 85 Éric Bédard ☐ 86 C-P Coulombe
☐ 87 Instructeurs

STE-ANNE DE LA PÉRADE PEE WEE

☐ 88 O. Gariépy-Dussault ☐ 89 Pascal Moisan
☐ 90 Maxime Trudel ☐ 91 J-F Saucier
☐ 92 Richard Tessier ☐ 93 Patrick Germain
☐ 94 Mathieu Leduc ☐ 95 David Mayrand
☐ 96 Guillaume Marcotte ☐ 97 Yannick Therrien
☐ 98 Marc-André Hamelin ☐ 99 Mario Leduc
☐ 100 Maxime Lefebvre ☐ 101 Danny* Naud
☐ 102 L-P Thibeault ☐ 103 Instructeurs

ST-HUBERT PEE WEE

☐ 104 Jonathan Émond ☐ 105 David Bazo
☐ 106 Éric Tremblay ☐ 107 Karl Harbec
☐ 108 J. Régimbald ☐ 109 Marc-André Sauvé
☐ 110 Mathieu Péladeau ☐ 111 Mathieu Deleau
☐ 112 Danny Boileau ☐ 113 Alexis Cloutier
☐ 114 Jonathan Pigeon ☐ 115 Pierre-Luc Geneau
☐ 116 J-M Bastien ☐ 117 S. Désaulniers
☐ 118 Pierre-Luc St-Louis ☐ 119 Sébastien Larivière
☐ 120 Mathieu Gladu ☐ 121 Instructeurs

BELLECHASSE PEE WEE

☐ 122 Nicolas Gagné ☐ 123 Maxime Couture
☐ 124 Samuel Pelletier ☐ 125 J-P Asselin
☐ 126 Maxime Michaud ☐ 127 Nicolas Mercier
☐ 128 Michaël Normand ☐ 129 Mathieu Morissette
☐ 130 Bryan Nadeau ☐ 131 Francis Tanguay
☐ 132 Jérôme Corriveau ☐ 133 Steeve Taylor
☐ 134 Jaeson Ruel ☐ 135 Jean-Simon Couture
☐ 136 Hugo Lapointe ☐ 137 Guillaume Ouellet
☐ 138 Instructeurs

HERSHEY PEE WEE

☐ 139 Adam Bonenberger ☐ 140 Justin Cassel
☐ 141 Chris Conner ☐ 143 Lowell Franko
☐ 144 Jason Harmony ☐ 145 Matt Healy (G)
☐ 146 Brendon Herr ☐ 147 Justin Hill
☐ 148 Greg Hooke ☐ 149 Matt Junkins
☐ 150 Nolan Meanor ☐ 151 Mike Patton
☐ 152 Joey Schmidt ☐ 153 A.J. Skinner
☐ 154 Chris Snavely ☐ 155 Bret Wilhite
☐ 156 Jordan Yingling ☐ 157 Instructeurs
☐ 1042 Jeff Fischl

CHICAGO PEE WEE BLACK HAWKS

☐ 158 Dov Grumet-Morris ☐ 159 Jeff Ronkoske
☐ 160 Jason Brush ☐ 161 Bobby Demola
☐ 162 Anthony Derosa ☐ 163 Clay Eastbrooke
☐ 165 Mike Kreger ☐ 166 Brett Lebda
☐ 167 Troy Lother ☐ 168 Sean Mirzabegian
☐ 169 Bobby Rankin ☐ 170 Ryan Roeder
☐ 171 Garrett Roth ☐ 172 Danny Schor
☐ 173 Éric Vesely ☐ 174 Instructeurs

SHERBROOKE PEE WEE

☐ 175 Daniel Beaupré (G) ☐ 176 Sébastien Bélanger
☐ 177 Martin Bellavance ☐ 178 Jason Boyer
☐ 179 David Chicoine ☐ 180 Ashley Conn
☐ 181 Pierre Crête ☐ 182 Mathieu Dumas
☐ 183 A. Duplessis ☐ 184 Carl Gagnon
☐ 185 Vincent Guay ☐ 186 Pascal Lafrenière
☐ 187 Louis-Philip Lemay ☐ 188 Olivier Martin
☐ 189 A. M.-Channon ☐ 190 Alexandre Ponton
☐ 191 Charles Trudeau ☐ 192 Instructeurs

BEAUCE-AMIANTE PEE WEE

The most expensive single is Jonathan Ferland at $2-3.

☐ 193 J-F Michaud ☐ 194 Martin Vachon
☐ 195 Vincent Doyon ☐ 196 J-F Duguay
☐ 197 Stéphane Hébert ☐ 198 Alexandre Cloutier
☐ 199 Dave Quirion ☐ 200 Sylvain Turmel
☐ 201 Olivier Spénard ☐ 202 J-F Gosselin
☐ 203 David** Gosselin ☐ 204 James Drouin
☐ 205 Jonathan Ferland ☐ 206 Alexandre Gilbert
☐ 207 Michael Parent ☐ 208 Sylvain Plante
☐ 209 Instructeurs

POINTE-LÉVY C PEE WEE

☐ 210 Jean-Michel Soucy ☐ 211 Jérôme Doré
☐ 212 Mathieu Lajoie ☐ 213 Philippe Guérin
☐ 214 Jean-Philippe Blais ☐ 215 Benjamin Pelletier
☐ 216 Sébastien Lacombe ☐ 217 J-P Lacombe
☐ 218 Dominic Bourassa ☐ 219 William Morrison
☐ 220 M. G-Pelletier ☐ 221 Guillaume Prévost
☐ 223 David Dufresne ☐ 224 Rony Bernard
☐ 225 Sébastien Guérard ☐ 226 Yan Maheux

DRUMMONDVILLE PEE WEE

The most expensive single is J-F Dufort at $2-3.

☐ 227 Guillaume Beaudry ☐ 228 Philippe Brouillard
☐ 229 David** Lessard ☐ 230 Nicolas Lemelin
☐ 231 J-C Parenteau ☐ 232 Martin Autotte
☐ 233 François Fillion ☐ 234 Didier Bochatay
☐ 235 Hugo Lafond ☐ 236 Maxime Charron
☐ 237 Yannick Beaulieu ☐ 238 Anthony Fontaine
☐ 239 Alexis Ricard ☐ 240 Carl Donais
☐ 241 J-F Dufort ☐ 242 Patrick** Gosselin
☐ 243 Instructeurs

CALGARY PEE WEE FLAMES

The most expensive single is Jared Aulin at $3-5.

☐ 244 Chris** Armstrong ☐ 245 Jared Aulin
☐ 246 Jye Carder ☐ 247 John Casagranda
☐ 248 Jordan Chomack ☐ 249 Matthew Jenkins
☐ 250 Tom Kinred ☐ 251 Shane Kuzek
☐ 252 James Logullo ☐ 253 Matthew McMahon
☐ 254 Curtis McRae ☐ 255 Jonathan Pittis
☐ 256 Pat Richards ☐ 257 Scott Serwa
☐ 258 Alex Thymaras ☐ 259 Cory Wright

CHARLEVOIS PEE WEE

☐ 260 Jean-Michel Néron ☐ 261 Jérôme Gagné
☐ 262 David Gagné ☐ 263 Keven Tremblay
☐ 264 Julien Lavoie ☐ 265 Jean-François Pilote
☐ 266 François Côté ☐ 267 Jean-Nicolas Pilote
☐ 268 Antoine Tremblay ☐ 269 Michaël Tremblay
☐ 270 Nicolas Boivin ☐ 271 Jonathan Côté
☐ 272 Simon Guay ☐ 273 Jean-Michel Dufour
☐ 274 Alexandre Routhier ☐ 275 Nicolas** Savard
☐ 276 Instructeurs

QUÉBEC CHAMPLAINS PEE WEE

☐ 277 Francis Allard ☐ 278 David Bergeron
☐ 279 S. Blouin-Fournier ☐ 280 J-F Bouchard
☐ 281 Olivier Bourque ☐ 282 Simon Chénard
☐ 283 Éric** Côté ☐ 284 Charles Faber
☐ 285 Simon Gagnon ☐ 286 Jonathan Jolette
☐ 287 Kevin Lachance ☐ 288 Julien Matte
☐ 289 Olivier St-Antoine ☐ 290 Guillaume Talbot
☐ 291 Benjamin Théberge ☐ 292 Pascal Turmel
☐ 293 Instructeurs

SAINTE-FOY C PEE WEE

☐ 294 Andreas Lafrenière ☐ 295 M. Lévesque-Landry
☐ 296 Mathieu Dumais ☐ 297 D. Jacob-Robitaille
☐ 298 Simon Fleury ☐ 299 F-O Côté
☐ 300 François Vallières ☐ 301 Pierre-Luc Girard
☐ 302 André Lessard ☐ 303 J-M Baillargeon
☐ 304 François Gosselin ☐ 305 François Genest
☐ 306 Éric L'Italien ☐ 307 François St-Laurent
☐ 308 J-F Gagné ☐ 309 Mathieu Cossette
☐ 310 Instructeurs

QUÉBEC PEE WEE FRONTENAC

☐ 311 Sylvain Cayer ☐ 312 Mikaël Cloutier
☐ 313 Steeve** Boucher ☐ 314 Simon Fradet
☐ 315 Marc-Antoine Motin ☐ 316 Charles Turgeon
☐ 317 M. Ferland-Lapointe ☐ 318 Joël Leroux
☐ 319 Pierre-Marc Paquet ☐ 320 Steve McKinnon
☐ 321 Stéphane Harvey ☐ 322 Lee Kiley
☐ 323 Nicolas Morin ☐ 324 J-F Léveillé
☐ 325 Mathieu Dion ☐ 326 Instructeurs

MONTRÉAL PEE WEE CANADIENS

The most expensive single is Pascal Leclaire at $6-10.

☐ 327 Éric Salvail ☐ 328 Pascal Leclaire
☐ 329 Marin Papillon ☐ 330 Pierre-Luc Bacon
☐ 331 Daniel Poliquin ☐ 332 Guillaume Ferland
☐ 333 Yanick Lehoux ☐ 334 Yannick Searles
☐ 335 Jason Pominville ☐ 336 Alexandre Lippé
☐ 337 Jonathan Walsh ☐ 338 Jean-René Labelle
☐ 339 Michel Beaupré (G) ☐ 340 Steve Arneault
☐ 341 C. Washipabano ☐ 342 Nicolas Duval
☐ 343 Instructeurs ☐ 1392 Team Photo

BEAUBOURG PEE WEE

☐ 344 Alexandre Asselin ☐ 345 Maxime Côté
☐ 346 Nicolas Dorval ☐ 347 Pierre-Luc Gosselin
☐ 348 Thierry Kaszap ☐ 349 Maxime Lachance
☐ 350 Martin Lanouette ☐ 351 Nicolas Lapointe
☐ 352 Simon Noël ☐ 353 Michael Pichette
☐ 354 Carl Simard ☐ 355 Pierre-Luc Xavier
☐ 356 Samuel Bouchard ☐ 357 J-P Hamel
☐ 358 Philippe St-Cyr ☐ 359 Carl Gauthier
☐ 360 Instructeurs

BEAUPORT PEE WEE MARINIERS

☐ 361 Dave Leclerc ☐ 362 P-A Vallée
☐ 363 David Norton ☐ 364 Louis Chabot
☐ 365 Stéphane Carrier ☐ 366 Patrick Beaumont
☐ 367 Martin Lahaye ☐ 368 J-P Pichette
☐ 369 David Bélanger ☐ 370 J-M Laroche
☐ 371 Philippe Powell ☐ 372 Patrick Roy (G)er
☐ 373 Mathieu Dufresne ☐ 374 Nicolas Valcourt
☐ 375 Anthony Fournier ☐ 376 Jean-Pierre Léveillé
☐ 377 S. Chouinard ☐ 378 Instructeurs

DETROIT PEE WEE FALCONS

☐ 379 Geoff Brethen ☐ 380 John Dipace
☐ 381 Ben Dunne ☐ 382 Scott Eovaldi
☐ 383 Frank Furdero ☐ 384 Joe Karam
☐ 385 Lenny Karam ☐ 386 Jonathan Katulski
☐ 387 Joey Kay ☐ 388 Mike Kinnie
☐ 389 Ryan Mechigian ☐ 390 Ryan** Murray
☐ 391 Joe Steenland ☐ 392 Tony Zancanaro
☐ 393 Brad Zancanaro ☐ 394 Instructeurs

WINDSOR PEE WEE

☐ 395 Matthew Thomas ☐ 396 Matthew Livingstone
☐ 397 Francis Dostie ☐ 398 Kevin Martel
☐ 399 Brian Kominar ☐ 400 David Renaud
☐ 401 Chris Dupuis ☐ 402 David Dubé
☐ 403 Bryan Dennison ☐ 404 Kevin Emery
☐ 405 Justin Stephen ☐ 406 Travis Stevenson
☐ 407 Jeff Soulière ☐ 408 Ryan Battagello
☐ 409 Marty Hogan ☐ 410 Mike James
☐ 411 Shawn Kelly ☐ 412 Instructeurs

BEAUCE-NORD PEE WEE

☐ 413 Denis Lehoux ☐ 414 Maxime Campagna
☐ 415 O. Bolduc-Cloutier ☐ 416 Martin Talbot
☐ 417 Tommy Vachon ☐ 418 Gino Deblois
☐ 419 Jérôme Ferland ☐ 420 Pascal Maheyx
☐ 421 Tony Lafontaine ☐ 422 Sébastien Vachon
☐ 423 Stéphane Rancourt ☐ 424 Louis Brousseau
☐ 425 V. Châteauneuf ☐ 426 Nicolas Bégin
☐ 427 Steeve Poulin ☐ 428 Nicolas Grenier
☐ 429 Éric Marcoux ☐ 430 Instructeurs

BOSTON PEE WEE BRUINS

☐ 431 Mark Vandam ☐ 432 Dominic Papile
☐ 433 Derek Nocera ☐ 434 Frank Curreri
☐ 435 Jeffrey Sousa ☐ 436 Daniel Connors
☐ 437 Daniel Kennedy ☐ 438 Ryan Doyle
☐ 439 Joseph Coffey ☐ 440 Robert Settana
☐ 441 Stephen Vettori ☐ 442 Robert Connolly
☐ 443 Andrew Cleary ☐ 444 Joseph Horgan
☐ 445 Joseph Wilkins ☐ 446 Matthew McCarthy
☐ 447 Brian Nutting ☐ 448 Éric Raymond
☐ 449 William Corcoran ☐ 450 Kevin Galvin
☐ 451 Instructeurs ☐ 452 Instructeurs
☐ 453 Instructeurs ☐ 454 Instructeurs
☐ 455 Instructeurs

BEAUPORT B PEE WEE

☐ 456 Patrick Bergeron ☐ 457 J-F Bourbeau
☐ 458 Olivier Cloutier ☐ 459 Benoît Daigle
☐ 460 Mathieu Gagné ☐ 461 Sébastien Garneau
☐ 462 Sébastien Hains ☐ 463 Stéphane Hébert
☐ 464 Philippe Labrecque ☐ 465 François Lépine
☐ 466 Thomas Ménard ☐ 467 Benjamin Moffet
☐ 468 André (Jr.) Morin ☐ 469 Dany Rancourt
☐ 470 Mathieu Roussy ☐ 471 Charles Simard
☐ 472 Instructeurs

LAKESHORE PEE WEE

☐ 473 Patrick Normand ☐ 474 Mark Conforti
☐ 475 Jason Belleville ☐ 476 Bryan Siciliani
☐ 477 Chris Depretis ☐ 478 Sean Walker
☐ 479 Frederik Tessier ☐ 480 Ryan Sicotte
☐ 481 Ludovic Dumas ☐ 482 Andrew Billinghurst
☐ 483 Jason Pratt-Tully ☐ 484 Jonathan Landry
☐ 485 Wilder Weir ☐ 486 Charles Konczarek
☐ 487 Chris Athams ☐ 488 Chris Brown

ROCHESTER PEE WEE

☐ 489 Marc Ferger ☐ 490 Dan Pike
☐ 491 Peter Borrelli ☐ 492 Kevin Allison
☐ 493 Marciano Chinappi ☐ 494 Patrick Jones
☐ 495 Anthony Leccese ☐ 496 Jeffrey Lovier
☐ 497 Dave McDermott ☐ 498 Ryan Nangreave
☐ 499 Justin Robertson ☐ 500 Scott Root
☐ 501 Dan Welch ☐ 502 Dylan Naumann
☐ 503 Brian May ☐ 504 Jason Vasas
☐ 505 Brian Bonn ☐ 506 Frank Burgio
☐ 507 Mike Pasley ☐ 508 Instructeurs

HOBBEMA PEE WEE

☐ 509 Adam Buffalo ☐ 510 Craig Potts
☐ 511 Ian Buffalo ☐ 512 M. (Spike) Johnson
☐ 513 Ryan* Johnson ☐ 514 Tyrone Ermineskin
☐ 515 O. Ermineskin ☐ 516 Owen Buffalo
☐ 517 Tyrus White ☐ 518 Thomas Soosay
☐ 519 Thomas Minde ☐ 520 Houston Buffalo
☐ 521 Mitchel Rattlesnake ☐ 522 Leonard Buffalo
☐ 523 Matthew Wildcat ☐ 524 Wayland Littlechild
☐ 1314 Todd Wharton

DETROIT PEE WEE RED WINGS

☐ 525 John* Bowers ☐ 526 Brian Boyes
☐ 527 Andrew Bozoian ☐ 528 Joshua Chambers
☐ 529 Adam Dunn ☐ 530 James Geldhof
☐ 531 Robert Globke ☐ 532 Chad Larose
☐ 533 Corey Leclair ☐ 534 James McNamara
☐ 535 Mark Nebus ☐ 536 Jared Newman
☐ 537 Larry Sterling ☐ 538 Stephen Swistak
☐ 539 Bryan Thompson ☐ 540 Ryan Webb
☐ 541 Instructeurs

WASHINGTON PEE WEE

The most expensive single is Peter Hafner at $2-3.

☐ 542 Joshua Baker ☐ 543 Thomas Carolan
☐ 544 James Fontana ☐ 545 Jason Farrell
☐ 546 Philip Giampietro ☐ 547 Peter Hafner
☐ 548 Nathaniel Jackson ☐ 549 Blair Kipp
☐ 550 Joel Lord ☐ 551 Jake Plattner
☐ 552 Kyle Rowland ☐ 553 Scott Seney
☐ 554 Patrick Schaeffer ☐ 555 Ryan Stuart
☐ 556 Gregory Windsor ☐ 557 Thomas Zlockie
☐ 558 Patrick Copettino

ACTON VALE PEE WEE

☐ 559 Jonthan Bluteau ☐ 560 J-F Racine
☐ 561 Rémi** Bergeron ☐ 562 Joël Dion
☐ 563 Olivier Bisaillon ☐ 564 Ian Asselin
☐ 565 Michael Morneau ☐ 566 François Ares
☐ 567 Jeremy Knight ☐ 568 Aniko Pelland
☐ 569 Pierre Morvan ☐ 570 Philippe Desautels
☐ 571 Alexandre Ouellet ☐ 572 J-F Touchette
☐ 573 Nicolas Dupuis ☐ 574 Instructeurs

NEW YORK PEE WEE RANGERS

The most expensive singles are Gregory Campbell and Ryan Murphy each at $2-3.

☐ 575 Anthony Balsamo ☐ 576 Jonathan Bria
☐ 577 Brian Burns ☐ 578 Gregory Campbell
☐ 579 Julie Chu ☐ 580 Brian D'Ambrosio
☐ 581 Timothy Donohue ☐ 582 Brian Escobedo
☐ 583 Nicolas Fata ☐ 584 Steven Lerner
☐ 585 Eric Morgan ☐ 586 Ryan** Murphy
☐ 587 Chris Pelak ☐ 588 Matthew Scanlan
☐ 589 Chris Uber ☐ 590 Gary Vorgity
☐ 591 J. David Yaros ☐ 592 Instructeurs

SYRACUSE PEE WEE

The most expensive single is Katherine Maglione at $2-3.

☐ 593 Jon Ames ☐ 594 Chris Balash
☐ 595 Chris Collins ☐ 596 Tom Ditzer
☐ 597 Mike Fish ☐ 598 S. Fouladgar-Mercer
☐ 599 G. Goodnough ☐ 600 J.R. Pakan
☐ 601 Justin McCutcheon ☐ 602 Brian Reese
☐ 603 Justin Riley ☐ 604 Zachary Wallace
☐ 605 Kyle Albright ☐ 606 Jeremy Downs
☐ 607 Chris Willis ☐ 608 Matthew Samure
☐ 609 Brad Roberts ☐ 610 Instructeurs
☐ 611 Instructeurs ☐ 612 Instructeurs
☐ 613 Instructeurs ☐ 1315 J. (Jr.) Saddleback
☐ 1316 Katharine Maglione

QUÉBEC PEE WEE CITADELLES

☐ 614 Guillaume Rodrigue ☐ 615 Pascal Pelletier
☐ 616 Randy Lemay ☐ 617 Nicolas Martin
☐ 618 C-J Massé ☐ 619 Guillaume Duval
☐ 620 Éric Courcy ☐ 621 Michael Garneau
☐ 622 Éric Roberge ☐ 623 Charls Veilleux
☐ 624 Mathieu Leclerc ☐ 625 Thierry Drapeau
☐ 626 Jessy Garneau ☐ 627 Éric McGee
☐ 628 Simon Tardif ☐ 629 Steve Côté
☐ 630 Instructeurs

CAMPUS CAP-ROUGE PEE WEE

☐ 631 David** Bernier ☐ 632 J-P Bonneau
☐ 633 Olivier** Gagnon ☐ 634 Guillaume Gignac
☐ 635 Pierre Laliberté ☐ 636 Simon Laliberté
☐ 637 J-M Lavertu ☐ 638 Philippe Lavigne
☐ 639 M-O Lefrançois ☐ 640 Luc Morissette
☐ 641 Jérôme Noël ☐ 642 Simon Plante

☐ 643 Nicolas Rivard ☐ 644 Simon Vaillancourt
☐ 645 Jeffrey Veilleux ☐ 646 Jérôme Villeneuve
☐ 647 Instructeurs

PETERBOROUGH PEE WEE

☐ 648 David Currie ☐ 649 Ryan Aschabar
☐ 650 Jeff Mackie ☐ 651 Jordan Houser
☐ 652 David Jones ☐ 653 Darren Doherty
☐ 654 Danny Growden ☐ 655 Derek Hennessey
☐ 656 Brandon Jutras ☐ 657 Brad Ormond
☐ 658 Graydon Crowley ☐ 659 Timothy Collins
☐ 660 Samuel McCullum ☐ 661 Michael Konieczny
☐ 662 Mike Craigen ☐ 663 Ryan Courtney
☐ 664 Curtis Hockaday ☐ 665 Instructeurs

DETROIT LITTLE CAESARS PEE WEE

The most expensive singles are Tim Gleason and Kris Vernasky at $2-3 each.

☐ 666 Michael Blackhurst ☐ 667 Brandon Davis
☐ 668 Timothy Gleason ☐ 669 Jared Hoffmeyer
☐ 670 Trevor Johnson ☐ 671 Nathan Kiser
☐ 672 Ryan McBroom ☐ 673 Matthew Migliaccio
☐ 674 Trevor Riebling ☐ 675 Matthew Rutkowski
☐ 676 Stephen Sabo ☐ 677 Joseph Simon
☐ 678 James Slater ☐ 679 James Tudor
☐ 680 Kris Vernarsky ☐ 681 Instructeurs

SAN JOSE PEE WEE

☐ 682 Phillip Smith ☐ 683 Andrew Smith
☐ 684 Sean Riley ☐ 685 Drew Sanders
☐ 686 Michael Romano ☐ 687 Daniel Lee
☐ 688 Willie Hodgson ☐ 689 B.J. Howe
☐ 690 Michael Kopinski ☐ 691 John Koch
☐ 692 Chris Lee ☐ 693 Aaron Schenone
☐ 694 Logan Hayden ☐ 695 Mikey Bergin
☐ 696 Glen Carlson ☐ 697 Ben Terwilliger
☐ 698 Instructeurs

POINTE-LÉVY PEE WEE FAUCONS

☐ 699 Jocelyn Auger ☐ 700 Dave Boucher
☐ 701 François Brisson ☐ 702 Pascal Caron
☐ 703 Stéphane Caron ☐ 704 J-F Carrignan
☐ 705 David Dechamplain ☐ 706 Dominique Dussault
☐ 707 J-P Fournier ☐ 708 Éric Lévesque
☐ 709 Marie-Claude Morin ☐ 710 Sébastien Nadeau
☐ 711 Martin Pellerin ☐ 712 Mathieu Roy
☐ 713 Nicolas Roy ☐ 714 Frédéric St-Pierre
☐ 715 Instructeurs

EDMONTON PEE WEE OILERS

The most expensive single is Jay Bouwmeester at $15-20.

☐ 716 James Hamilton ☐ 717 Robert Hadley
☐ 718 Adam Sopka ☐ 719 Richard Hamula
☐ 720 Jay Bouwmeester ☐ 721 Andy Coates
☐ 722 Joshua Podaima ☐ 723 Joel Amyotte
☐ 724 Tyler Cronk ☐ 725 Nicholas Rolheiser
☐ 726 Mark Smith ☐ 727 D. Auchenberg
☐ 728 C. McLeod ☐ 729 Nathan Hollands
☐ 730 Danny Covelli ☐ 731 Mateo Ferrari
☐ 732 Instructeurs

ST-JÉRÔME PEE WEE

☐ 733 Jonathan Labrèche ☐ 734 Maxime Lachance
☐ 735 Étienne Rolland ☐ 736 Jonathan Labelle
☐ 737 Nicolas Gagnon ☐ 738 A. Desormeaux
☐ 739 David Plouffe ☐ 740 H. Campbell-Ouellet
☐ 741 Olivier Forget ☐ 742 Éric Tessier
☐ 743 St-Denis Lalonde ☐ 744 Francis Robert
☐ 745 David Guenette ☐ 746 Jonathan Poirier
☐ 747 Éthienne Delcourt ☐ 748 Instructeurs
☐ 1393 Instructeurs

VANCOUVER PEE WEE CANUCKS

☐ 749 Maxwell Shaw ☐ 750 Kevin** Mackay
☐ 751 Dana Pretty ☐ 752 Simon Jones
☐ 753 Max Izen ☐ 754 Brandon Janes
☐ 755 T. Van Bemmelen ☐ 756 Derek Epp
☐ 757 Richard Mueller ☐ 758 Macey Ter Borg
☐ 759 Daniel Bustillo ☐ 760 Naudeep Dha
☐ 761 Kelly Neudore ☐ 762 James Raymond
☐ 763 Robbie MacGregor

ÉTOILE DE L'EST PEE WEE

☐ 764 Steven Brill ☐ 765 Stéphane Martin
☐ 766 Éric Boulerice ☐ 767 A-P Tremblay
☐ 768 Benoît Boisvert ☐ 769 François Cadrin
☐ 770 A. Delvecchio ☐ 771 Patrick Thouin
☐ 772 Éric Côté-Bouliane ☐ 773 Sébastien Urbain
☐ 774 B. Welsh-Morasse ☐ 775 Daniel Belzile
☐ 776 A. Martineau ☐ 777 Ian Liboiron
☐ 778 Jean-Marc Cyr ☐ 779 J-S De Cesare

JONQUIÈRE PEE WEE

☐ 780 Martin Rioux ☐ 781 Sean-Oak O'Connor
☐ 782 Hugo Villeneuve ☐ 783 Martin Gagnon
☐ 784 David** Lapointe ☐ 785 Éric Gareau
☐ 786 Dany Villeneuve ☐ 787 C-P Godin-Fortin
☐ 788 Jean-Luc Otis ☐ 789 Michel Bourgeois
☐ 790 Sébastien Gilbert ☐ 791 Jonathan Gauthier

☐ 792 Simon Blackburn ☐ 793 Alexandre Bédard
☐ 794 Daniel** Bouchard ☐ 795 Patrick* Boily
☐ 796 Anthony Jomphe ☐ 797 Instructeurs

HALIFAX PEE WEE MOOSEHEAD

☐ 798 Robbie Foster ☐ 799 Michael Couch
☐ 800 Matthew Nichol ☐ 801 Nicholas Binder
☐ 802 Thomas Drummey ☐ 803 Anthony Thomas
☐ 804 Regan Isenor ☐ 805 Christopher** Miller
☐ 806 Steven McDonald ☐ 807 Neil Lyons
☐ 808 Matthew Kerr ☐ 809 Bradley Bodnarchuk
☐ 810 Adam Rafuse ☐ 811 Bradley Manley
☐ 812 Steven Hazlehurst ☐ 813 Evan Bigney
☐ 814 Instructeurs

LOTBINIÈRE PEE WEE

☐ 815 S. Vaillancourt ☐ 816 Yanick Pothier
☐ 817 Simon Bédard ☐ 818 David Bergeron
☐ 819 Julien Bisson ☐ 820 Jimmy Blaney
☐ 821 Steve*** Boucher ☐ 822 Sébastien Côté
☐ 823 J. Desruisseaux ☐ 824 Matthieu Fillion
☐ 825 Nelson Fillion ☐ 826 Mathieu Fournier
☐ 827 Samuel Lemieux ☐ 828 Frédéric Moreau
☐ 829 Patrick Olivier ☐ 830 Nicolas Sylvain
☐ 831 Instructeurs

LAC MÉGANTIC PEE WEE

☐ 832 Dave*** Cameron ☐ 833 C. Plamondon
☐ 834 J-F Carrier ☐ 835 David** Morin
☐ 836 Mathieu Lacroix ☐ 837 Nicholas Lessard
☐ 838 François Béliveau ☐ 839 Éric Beaudoin
☐ 840 Keven Turmel ☐ 841 Marc-André Vachon
☐ 842 Maxime Roy ☐ 843 J-P Ménard
☐ 844 M-A Lavallée ☐ 845 Marie-Eve Lacroix
☐ 846 Nicolas Dulac ☐ 847 Mathieu Dostie
☐ 848 J-P Parent ☐ 849 Instructeurs

ST-ÉPHREM BEAUCE PEE WEE

☐ 850 Frédéric Roy ☐ 851 Francis Pomerleau
☐ 852 Johnny Duquet ☐ 853 Guillaume Plante
☐ 854 Gabriel Cloutier ☐ 855 Julien Roy
☐ 856 Mark Roy (G) ☐ 857 Jonathan Lessard
☐ 858 Mario** Lessard ☐ 859 Nicolas Léger
☐ 860 Yvan Busque ☐ 861 Alain Rodrigue
☐ 862 É. Champagne ☐ 863 Jérôme Baillargeon
☐ 864 Marco Veilleux ☐ 865 Myguel Couture
☐ 866 Kevin Boucher ☐ 867 Audrey Busque
☐ 868 Alain Bolduc ☐ 869 Instructeurs

SUISSE ITALIENNE PEE WEE

☐ 870 Mauro Campana ☐ 871 Lorenzo Croce
☐ 872 Luca Bigler ☐ 873 Enea Dell'Ambrogio
☐ 874 Pietro Ottini ☐ 875 Jonathan Pan
☐ 876 Filippo Schenker ☐ 877 Alan Belossi
☐ 878 Emanuele Snider ☐ 879 Manuel Beyeler
☐ 880 Davide Bianchi ☐ 881 Daniele Celio
☐ 882 Athos Cima ☐ 883 Moreno Della Santa
☐ 884 Massimo Gandolfi ☐ 885 Daniel Guidinetti
☐ 886 Roberto Jamusci ☐ 887 Demian Klöti
☐ 888 Dario Pancaldi ☐ 889 Frederico Rossini
☐ 890 Instructeurs

NEW YORK PEE WEE ISLANDERS

The most expensive single is Michael Komisarek at $4-6.

☐ 891 Matthew Anderson ☐ 892 Michael Brodsky
☐ 893 Reed Coleman ☐ 894 Scott Ferguson
☐ 895 Jordan Hart ☐ 896 Noël Henck
☐ 897 Marc Higgenbotham ☐ 898 Doug Hoffman
☐ 899 Michael Komisarek ☐ 900 James Lenz
☐ 901 Kevin Richardson ☐ 901 Ryan Sochacki
☐ 903 Bryan Stoothoff ☐ 904 Ryan Vesce
☐ 905 Jeff Wolski ☐ 906 Billy Zimmerman
☐ 908 Frank Barker ☐ 909 Instructeurs

CHAUDIÈRE-OUEST PEE WEE

☐ 910 Pierre-Yves Blondin ☐ 911 P-O Cloutier
☐ 912 Jonathan Doré ☐ 913 Nicolas Paquet
☐ 914 Patrick Brulé ☐ 915 J-F Fecteau
☐ 916 Simon Corriveau ☐ 917 Bruno Vandal
☐ 918 Sébastien** Paradis ☐ 919 P-L Montminy
☐ 920 François Leclerc ☐ 921 Stéphane Pouliot
☐ 922 Alexandre Landry ☐ 923 L-M Dubé
☐ 924 Benoît Blanchet ☐ 925 Instructeurs

TORONTO PEE WEE MAPLE LEAFS

☐ 926 Ryan Roberts ☐ 927 Robert* Turner
☐ 928 Scott Divier ☐ 929 Beau Llewelln
☐ 930 Christopher Yip ☐ 931 Jesse Rycroft
☐ 932 Ryan*** Stewart ☐ 933 Liam Bowen
☐ 934 Mike Taylor ☐ 935 Peter Mayer
☐ 936 Justin Turpin ☐ 937 Geo Eliopoulos
☐ 938 Ian Johnston ☐ 939 Cole Baron
☐ 940 Kevin Mair ☐ 941 Ryan Teitler

CHICOUTIMI PEE WEE SAGUENÉENS

☐ 942 C-O Potvin ☐ 943 Éric Bourbeau
☐ 944 Éric Verreault ☐ 945 Frédéric Laroche
☐ 946 Paul Houde ☐ 947 J-F Brassard
☐ 948 Patrice Marchand ☐ 949 Jean-Denis Charrest

☐ 950 J-M Gauthier ☐ 951 S-P Harvey
☐ 952 M-A Lefebvre ☐ 953 Sylvain Pedneault
☐ 954 Sébastien Lavoie ☐ 955 Pierre-Luc Laprise
☐ 956 Nicolas Harvey ☐ 957 Mathieu Gauthier
☐ 958 Yoan Boudreault ☐ 959 Instructeurs

WEXFORD PEE WEE

☐ 960 Davide Memme ☐ 961 John Walters
☐ 962 Scott Oldfield ☐ 963 Nathan Herrington
☐ 964 Jason Katsoras ☐ 965 Jordan Manganaro
☐ 966 Michael Lymer ☐ 967 Jason Wyles
☐ 968 Michael Firmani ☐ 969 Alex Kovechev
☐ 970 Vito Montesano ☐ 971 Steven Camerlengo
☐ 972 Jon Smyth ☐ 973 Michael** McKay
☐ 974 Joey Petsalis ☐ 975 Sean McMorrow

BEAUPORT PEE WEE HARFANGS

The most expensive single is Antoine Vermette at $2-3.

☐ 977 J-P Lessard ☐ 978 Jocelyn Guimond
☐ 979 Kevin Magher ☐ 980 Yannick Paré
☐ 981 David Audet ☐ 982 Jérôme Couture
☐ 983 Steve Vachon ☐ 984 L-P Lessard
☐ 985 Jean-François Cyr ☐ 986 Guillaume Fournier
☐ 987 Richard Pelchat ☐ 988 Pierre-Olivier Roy
☐ 989 Lucas Tanguay ☐ 990 D. Ouellet-Beaudry
☐ 991 Alexandre Roberge ☐ 992 Antoine Vermette
☐ 993 Instructeurs

KAMOURASKA PEE WEE

☐ 994 Sébastien Bélanger ☐ 995 Alexandre Lavoie
☐ 996 Olivier Labbé ☐ 997 Pierre-Luc Beaulieu
☐ 998 Marc-André Boutin ☐ 999 Philippe Langlois
☐ 1000 J-L Levasseur ☐ 1001 Lucas Daigle
☐ 1002 Maxime Bernier ☐ 1003 Alain Chénard
☐ 1004 Éliane Ouellet ☐ 1005 Pierre-Luc Pelletier
☐ 1006 G. Laverdière ☐ 1007 Philippe Pelletier
☐ 1008 Charles Morneau ☐ 1009 Yannick Morneau
☐ 1010 Adam Thériault ☐ 1011 Instructeurs

AMIANTE PEE WEE

☐ 1012 Dave Noël ☐ 1014 Louis Latulippe
☐ 1015 Dany Lévesque ☐ 1016 Yanick Doyon
☐ 1017 P-É Duclos ☐ 1018 Jonathan Bélisle
☐ 1019 G. Marchand ☐ 1020 Yoan Poulin
☐ 1021 A. Lessard ☐ 1022 Patrick Bolduc
☐ 1023 P-O Vachon ☐ 1024 Yannick Roy (G)
☐ 1025 Rock Boudreau ☐ 1026 Jason Grenier
☐ 1027 Toby Fortin ☐ 1913 G. Rousseau

PITTSBURGH PEE WEE PENGUINS

☐ 1028 Adam Boehm ☐ 1029 John Brausch
☐ 1030 Chip Crispino ☐ 1031 Justin Depretis
☐ 1032 David Donatelli ☐ 1033 Craig Hoolahan
☐ 1034 Shawn Keller ☐ 1035 Bobby Macwhinnie
☐ 1036 Todd Meehan ☐ 1037 Nick Mish
☐ 1038 Michael Necciai ☐ 1039 Chris Perry
☐ 1040 Carmen Posteraro ☐ 1041 R.J. Sirianni
☐ 1043 K. Trombetta ☐ 1044 Aaron Wassenaar
☐ 1045 Instructeurs

MOUNT-PEARL PEE WEE

☐ 1046 Jason Thorne ☐ 1047 Rodger Guy
☐ 1048 Colin Duffet ☐ 1049 Jerry Martin
☐ 1050 Preston Hickey ☐ 1051 B.J. Robart
☐ 1052 Chris King ☐ 1053 Jonathan Dawe
☐ 1054 Stephen Schell ☐ 1055 Brad Woolfrey
☐ 1056 Michael Halitzki ☐ 1057 Jeff Furlong
☐ 1058 Michael Lee ☐ 1059 Gerald Stamp
☐ 1060 Grant Kenny ☐ 1061 Justin Burrage
☐ 1062 Instructeurs

SEATTLE PEE WEE

☐ 1063 Radley Raven ☐ 1064 Brendon Nepon
☐ 1065 Antoine Dallain ☐ 1066 Clark McNees
☐ 1067 Jake Hall ☐ 1068 Nick Bartolo
☐ 1069 Tyler Carter ☐ 1070 Joey Matuszewski
☐ 1071 Wes Van Duine ☐ 1072 Brett Grandstrand
☐ 1073 Casey Russell ☐ 1074 Wes Scott
☐ 1075 Chris Krueger ☐ 1076 Erik Ellingson

PHILADELPHIA PEE WEE

The most expensive single is Dennis Packard at $2-3.

☐ 1077 Brett Landrum ☐ 1078 Buddy Anderson
☐ 1079 Joseph Ciocco ☐ 1080 Edwin Gardner
☐ 1081 Patrick* Hannigan ☐ 1082 Matt Herneisen
☐ 1083 Brian Holland ☐ 1084 Eric Kastner
☐ 1085 Chris Lawrence ☐ 1086 Steve Mead
☐ 1087 Nate Meyers ☐ 1088 Dennis Packard
☐ 1089 Chase Roth ☐ 1090 Dale Scherholz
☐ 1091 Joseph Sheridan ☐ 1092 Joseph Sidman
☐ 1093 Joseph Testh ☐ 1094 Chase Watson
☐ 1095 Brian Tetley ☐ 1096 Jonathan Ciocco
☐ 1097 Keith Krem

BOSTON PEE WEE TERRIERS

The most expensive singles are John Toffey and Michael Walsh each at $2-3.

☐ 1098 Eugene Binda ☐ 1099 Danile Brown
☐ 1100 James Byrnes ☐ 1101 Peter Cohen
☐ 1102 Patrick Conroy ☐ 1103 John Cronin
☐ 1104 Derek Kilduff ☐ 1105 Richard Labelle

☐ 1106 Ryan Lannon ☐ 1107 Kevin** Lyons
☐ 1108 Gregory Nicolls ☐ 1109 Sean Pero
☐ 1110 Joseph Rego ☐ 1111 Terence Sweeney
☐ 1112 John Toffey ☐ 1113 Michael Walsh
☐ 1114 Instructeurs

PAPINEAU PEE WEE

☐ 1115 A-M Lasalle ☐ 1116 Kevin Lawlis
☐ 1117 Martin Prévost ☐ 1118 Pierre-Luc Brunet
☐ 1119 J. Mageau-David ☐ 1120 Brett Dewey
☐ 1121 Karl Carrière ☐ 1122 J-F Maillé
☐ 1123 Michel Gauthier ☐ 1124 Pierre-Luc Chenier
☐ 1125 Martin Faubert ☐ 1126 Michel Ebacher
☐ 1127 Jonathan Laplante ☐ 1128 Pascal Boileau
☐ 1129 Bertrand Plouffe ☐ 1130 Adam Haramis
☐ 1131 G. Thibaudeau ☐ 1132 Instructeurs

RIMOUSKI PEE WEE

☐ 1133 Denis Bérubé ☐ 1134 J-F Boulet
☐ 1135 Louis-David Côté ☐ 1136 Guillaume Doucet
☐ 1137 Jimmy Fillion ☐ 1138 Sébastien Hébert
☐ 1139 G. Lafrance ☐ 1140 Dominic Langlois
☐ 1141 Sébastien Leblanc ☐ 1142 Philippe Lévesque
☐ 1143 Martin Ouellet ☐ 1144 Michel Ouellet
☐ 1145 Jérôme Pigeon ☐ 1146 Jérôme Rioux
☐ 1147 Jean-Michel Ross ☐ 1148 Vincent** Tremblay
☐ 1149 Instructeurs ☐ 1337 Christian Boudreau
☐ 1338 David Bellavance ☐ 1339 Billy Poirier

ROBERVAL PEE WEE

☐ 1150 Patrick** Boily ☐ 1151 S. Bonneau
☐ 1152 G. Bouchard ☐ 1153 Manuel Boudreault
☐ 1154 L-D Dallaire ☐ 1155 Mathieu Gagnon
☐ 1156 Sébastien Genest ☐ 1157 Brian Guay
☐ 1158 Daniel Hudon ☐ 1159 Dany Lepagne
☐ 1160 Yves Paul ☐ 1161 J-F Racine
☐ 1162 Luc St-Pierre ☐ 1163 M. Thibeault-Martel
☐ 1164 Julien Tremblay ☐ 1165 Instructeurs

TORONTO PEE WEE RED WINGS

The most expensive singles are Michael Cammalleri at $4-6 and Anthony Aquino at $2-3.

☐ 1166 Donald McMillan ☐ 1167 Cyril Philipps
☐ 1168 Mark Wires ☐ 1169 Chris Serre
☐ 1170 Greg Hogeboom ☐ 1171 Chris Godin
☐ 1172 Adam Paiement ☐ 1173 Bernie Scanlon
☐ 1174 M. Cammalleri ☐ 1175 Patrick Barbieri
☐ 1176 Joey MacKey ☐ 1177 John Dunphy
☐ 1178 Ryan Merriman ☐ 1179 Anthony Aquino
☐ 1180 Chris Davidson ☐ 1181 Frank Coccia

DON MILLS PEE WEE

The most expensive single is Marco Rosa at $2-3.

☐ 1182 Adam Ruzycki ☐ 1183 Jason Connors
☐ 1184 Ryan Taylor ☐ 1185 Ian Lauder
☐ 1186 Daniel Iliakis ☐ 1187 M. Stathopulos
☐ 1188 Chris Luck ☐ 1189 Michael Barrett
☐ 1190 James Kim ☐ 1191 Chris Scott
☐ 1192 Chris Black ☐ 1193 Marco Rosa
☐ 1194 Shaun Casement ☐ 1195 Mike Andreoff
☐ 1196 Instructeurs

AUSTRIA PEE WEE

☐ 1197 Gerd Gruber ☐ 1198 Peter Preis
☐ 1199 Daniel Schildrofer ☐ 1200 Christoph Allmaier
☐ 1201 Christian Ban ☐ 1202 Daniel Leiner
☐ 1203 Christoph Backer ☐ 1204 Markus Hausegger
☐ 1205 Benjamin Galler ☐ 1206 Johannes Reichel
☐ 1207 Jürgen Penker ☐ 1208 Marco Schwinger
☐ 1209 Michael Mana ☐ 1210 Harald Bischop
☐ 1211 Michael Pollross ☐ 1212 Thomas Müller
☐ 1213 M-P Schönberger ☐ 1214 Patrik Mössmer
☐ 1215 Wolfgang Zerza ☐ 1216 S. Hochenberger
☐ 1217 Stefan Wiedmaier ☐ 1218 Patrik Posch
☐ 1219 Martin Harkamp ☐ 1220 Manuel Aigner

ST-PROSPER PEE WEE

☐ 1221 Olivier Landry ☐ 1222 Keven Carrier
☐ 1223 Cédric Labonté ☐ 1224 Yannick** Poulin
☐ 1225 Mathieu Parent ☐ 1226 Jimmy Colgan
☐ 1227 M-A Pouliot ☐ 1228 Julien Maheux
☐ 1229 Mathieu Boulet ☐ 1230 Dave Lehoux
☐ 1231 David* Poulin ☐ 1232 Karl Morin
☐ 1233 F. Rouillard ☐ 1234 Alain Landry
☐ 1235 Cédric Dupont ☐ 1236 Simon Nadeau
☐ 1237 Miguel Nadeau ☐ 1238 René Gagné
☐ 1239 Instructeurs

SHAWINIGAN PEE WEE

☐ 1240 Dave Grenier ☐ 1241 Pierre-Luc O'Brien
☐ 1242 Jean-Simon Pépin ☐ 1243 David Jacob
☐ 1244 J-M Boisvert ☐ 1245 Rodrigue Boucher
☐ 1246 Yann Chrétien ☐ 1247 Frédérik** Martin
☐ 1248 Daniel Fontaine ☐ 1249 Dominic Bégin
☐ 1250 François Huard ☐ 1251 Hugo Lampron
☐ 1252 Steve Leblanc ☐ 1253 Pierre-Marc Vézina
☐ 1254 David Lachance ☐ 1255 J-F Caron
☐ 1256 Cédrick Lefebvre ☐ 1257 Instructeurs

SUISSE ROMAND PEE WEE

☐ 1258 Gilles Catella ☐ 1259 Sébastien Corthay
☐ 1260 Olivier Amadio ☐ 1261 Félicien Du Bois
☐ 1262 Lukas Gerber ☐ 1263 Julian Mauri
☐ 1264 Michael Ncgoy ☐ 1265 Patrick Pecon
☐ 1266 Didier Ruffieux ☐ 1267 Julien Spinelli
☐ 1268 Lionel Berra ☐ 1269 Nicolas Boserup
☐ 1270 Steven Clennon ☐ 1271 Thomas Deruns
☐ 1272 Fabrice Eisenring ☐ 1273 Philipp Fontana
☐ 1274 Cédric Metrailler ☐ 1275 Thibault Monnet
☐ 1276 Luc Oppenheim ☐ 1277 Paul Savary
☐ 1278 Lionel Schmid ☐ 1279 Julien Turler
☐ 1280 Instructeurs ☐ 1281 Instructeurs

SEIGNEURS DES MILLES ILES PEE WEE

The most expensive single is Charline Labonté at $4-8.

☐ 1282 Benoît Bibeau ☐ 1283 J-F David
☐ 1284 Maxime Bouchard ☐ 1285 Mathieu Dupont
☐ 1286 François Duquette ☐ 1287 Pascal Labelle
☐ 1288 C. Labonté (G) ☐ 1289 Dominic Labranche
☐ 1290 Francis Leroux ☐ 1291 M. Maisonneuve
☐ 1292 Étienne Plouffe ☐ 1293 F. Massicotte
☐ 1294 Jonathan Robert ☐ 1295 Ian Séguin
☐ 1296 J-F Touchette ☐ 1297 Jonathan Tremblay
☐ 1298 François Veilleux

NEW JERSEY PEE WEE DEVILS

☐ 1299 Joseph Aliseo ☐ 1300 Joseph Andrasko
☐ 1301 Brian Brauth ☐ 1302 Bill Caputo
☐ 1303 Michael Caputo ☐ 1304 Ryan Cullen
☐ 1305 John Feltz ☐ 1306 Bill Gardner
☐ 1307 Robert Heyrich ☐ 1308 Peter Haglund
☐ 1309 Michael Lagola ☐ 1310 C. McCallum
☐ 1311 Kellen Murphy ☐ 1312 Jason Ortolano
☐ 1313 Jason Sarno

ENGLAND PEE WEE

☐ 1318 James Morgan ☐ 1319 Adam White
☐ 1320 S. Greenwood ☐ 1321 Richard Thornton
☐ 1322 Jason Moses ☐ 1323 Paul Sample
☐ 1324 Paul Price ☐ 1325 Scott Parsons
☐ 1326 C. Acchione ☐ 1327 Dillan Leslie Rowe
☐ 1328 Tom Wilson ☐ 1329 Andrew Munroe
☐ 1330 Dale Taylor ☐ 1331 Stuart Brittal
☐ 1332 David Riapley ☐ 1333 Jonathan Philips
☐ 1334 Daniel Madge ☐ 1335 Richard Wojciak
☐ 1336 Simon Beere

BUFFALO PEE WEE REGALS

☐ 1340 Nick Iwanicki ☐ 1341 Jeff Lévesque
☐ 1342 Nick Watroba ☐ 1343 Michael Piepszny
☐ 1344 Richard Gioia ☐ 1345 Michael Piccillo
☐ 1346 Anthony Maritato ☐ 1347 Stephen Greco
☐ 1348 Erik Hlavaty ☐ 1349 Nick Buser
☐ 1350 Jeff Homewood ☐ 1351 Nick Schmitt
☐ 1352 Brad Rhéaume ☐ 1353 Rob Kossowsky
☐ 1354 Rob Lalonde ☐ 1355 Charles Giovino
☐ 1356 Eric Murtaugh ☐ 1357 Adam Zurowski

ZURICH PEE WEE

☐ 1358 Deny Bärtschi ☐ 1359 A. Camenzind
☐ 1360 Duri Carmichael ☐ 1361 Claudio Fontana
☐ 1362 Stefan Gaehler ☐ 1363 Claudio Gollman
☐ 1364 M. Gossweiler ☐ 1365 Sven Helfenstein
☐ 1366 Jonas Hiller ☐ 1367 Patrick Landolt
☐ 1368 Raeto Raffainer ☐ 1369 Fabio Saiani
☐ 1370 Patrick Schmid ☐ 1371 Stefan Schnyder
☐ 1372 Matthias Schoder ☐ 1373 Samuel Stalder
☐ 1374 Florian Trepp ☐ 1375 Thomas Walser
☐ 1376 Fabian Wassmer ☐ 1377 Instructeurs

NORTH YORK PEE WEE

☐ 1378 Chris Hrynyk ☐ 1379 Tom Gill
☐ 1380 Tyler Middlebrook ☐ 1381 M. Hennebury
☐ 1382 Vince Bellissimo ☐ 1383 Greg Jacina
☐ 1384 Jason Peyman ☐ 1385 Greg Chambers
☐ 1386 Barry Dyer ☐ 1387 Jason Young
☐ 1388 Glen Coyle ☐ 1389 Jonathan Kotyck
☐ 1390 Jeff McGee ☐ 1391 J-D Smithson
☐ 1392 Team Photo

FORT MCMURRAY PEE WEE

☐ 1394 Drew Campbell ☐ 1395 T.J. Campbell
☐ 1396 Beckie Sager ☐ 1397 Andrew Hoffman
☐ 1398 George Power ☐ 1399 Robert Law
☐ 1400 Michael Mellon ☐ 1401 Patrick Dupuis
☐ 1402 Bruce Gillis ☐ 1403 Mark Nolan
☐ 1404 Dustin Sheaves ☐ 1405 Justin White
☐ 1406 Scotie Ufshall ☐ 1407 A. Gniazdowsky
☐ 1408 Trevor Mortson ☐ 1409 Dustin Doucet
☐ 1410 P. (Rick) Deobald ☐ 1411 Curtis Johnston

MASSACHUSSETS PEE WEE FLAMES

The most expensive singles are Scott Horvath and Eddie Caron at $2-3 each.

☐ 1412 Scott Annan ☐ 1413 Collin Cook
☐ 1414 Kevin Brooks ☐ 1415 Gerard Burke

1416 Bobby Cardin	1417 Eddie Caron
1418 Brian Doherty	1419 Jonathan Goodwin
1420 Richard** Grenier	1421 Ned Havern
1422 Scott Horvath	1423 Matt** Macleod
1424 Billy Magnuson	1425 Adam Newell
1426 Kevin Pelkey	1427 K.C. Thomson
1428 Ryan Tuttle	1429 Steve Wenzel

COLLÈGE FRANÇAIS PEE WEE

1430 M-A Hubert	1431 Sébastien Laprise
1432 Patrice Michaud	1433 M-A Demers
1434 Étienne Germain	1435 Éric Chartrand
1436 Benoît Desrochers	1437 François Jean
1438 J-C Charette	1439 Sébastien Pruneau
1440 C. Guillemette	1441 R. Guillemette
1442 Patrick Simard	1443 Alexandre Turgeon
1444 J-F Lapolice	1445 Instructeurs

KUUJJUAQ PEE WEE

1448 Ahoyak Dupuis	1449 Ned Gordon
1450 Henri Saunders	1451 Barry Davies
1452 Daniel Gadbois	1453 Tunic Robertson
1454 Steven Terliluk	1455 Peter Baron
1456 Alex Ezekiel	1457 Alec Nassak
1458 Hughes Cloutier	1459 François Hardy
1460 Saima Mark	1461 Tivi Dupuis
1462 Instructeurs	

HARTFORD PEE WEE WHALERS

1463 S. Baldasarri	1464 Derek Swan
1466 Ryan Kelly	1467 Mark Kaufman
1468 Jonathan Foster	1469 Peter Alden
1470 Chris Wathey	1471 Nathan Cardoza
1472 Scott Davidson	1472 Jarod Simon
1473 Gary Nathanson	1475 Ryan Michalowski
1476 Joe Milot	1477 Hunter Kass
1478 Matt Norton	

1996 TOPPS FINEST BRONZE

These oversized cards were sold by Topps as a complete set.

Card Size: 2 3/4" x 3 3/4"

Series Three Set (8 cards): 115.00

Player	TFB
15 Mark Messier, NYRa.	15.00
16 Mario Lemieux, Pitt.	50.00
17 Peter Forsberg, Colo.	20.00
18 Félix Potvin (G), Toro.	10.00
19 Alexander Mogilny, Vanc.	8.00
20 Raymond Bourque, Bost.	20.00
21 Ed Jovanovski, Flor.	8.00
22 Mikael Renberg, Phil.	8.00

1996 WIEN

This World Championship set was produced by Semic Sports Cards.

Complete Set (240 cards): 30.00
Common Player: .20

Player	NRMT-MT
1 Jarmo Myllys (G), Fin.	.20
2 Marko Kiprusoff, Fin.	.20
3 Petteri Nummelin, Fin.	.20
4 Erik Hamalainen, Fin.	.20
5 Timo Jutila, Fin.	.20
6 Janne Niinimaa, Fin.	.20
7 Raimo Summanen, Fin.	.20
8 Janne Ojanen, Fin.	.20
9 Esa Keskinen, Fin.	.20
10 Ari Sulander, Fin.	.20
11 Saku Koivu, Fin.	1.00
12 Jukka Tammi, Fin.	.20
13 Marko Palo, Fin.	.20
14 Raimo Helminen, Fin.	.20
15 Anntti Törmänen, Fin.	.20
16 Ville Peltonen, Fin.	.20
17 Tero Lehterä, Fin.	.20
18 Mika Stromberg, Fin.	.20
19 Sami Kapanen, Fin.	.20
20 Jere Lehtinen, Fin.	.20
21 Juha Ylonen, Fin.	.20
22 Mika Nieminen, Fin.	.20
23 Hannu Virta, Fin.	.20
24 Jari Kurri, Fin.	1.00
25 Christian Ruuttu, Fin.	.20
26 Jyrki Lumme, Fin.	.20
27 Teppo Numminen, Fin.	.20
28 Esa Tikkanen, Fin.	.20
29 Janne Laukkanen, Fin.	.20
30 Aki Berg, Fin.	.20
31 Teemu Selänne, Fin.	1.00
32 Markus Ketterer (G), Fin.	.20
33 Joni Lehto, Fin.	.20
34 Juha Riihijarvi, Fin.	.20
35 Sakari Lindfors (G), Fin.	.50
36 Kai Nurminen, Fin.	.20
37 Ville Peltonen/ Saku Koivu/ Jere Lehtinen	1.00
38 Tommy Söderström (G), Swe.	.20
39 Tommy Salo (G), Swe.	.50
40 Thomas Ostlund, Swe.	.20
41 Boo Ahl, Swe.	.20
42 Calle Johansson, Swe.	.20
43 Tommy Albelin, Swe.	.20
44 Ulf Samuelsson, Swe.	.20
45 Nicklas Lidström, Swe.	.50
46 Magnus Svensson, Swe.	.20
47 Tomas Jönsson, Swe.	.20
48 Tommy Sjodin, Swe.	.20
49 Marcus Ragnarsson, Swe.	.20
50 Christer Olsson, Swe.	.20
51 Rikard Franzen, Swe.	.20
52 Mattias Öhlund, Swe.	.20
53 Kenny Jönsson, Swe.	.20
54 Roger Johansson, Swe.	.20
55 Anders Eriksson, Swe.	.20
56 Mats Sundin, Swe.	1.00
57 Peter Forsberg, Swe.	1.50
58 Mikael Renberg, Swe.	.20
59 Tomas Sandström, Swe.	.20
60 Ulf Dahlen, Swe.	.20
61 Michael Nylander, Swe.	.20
62 Patrik Juhlin, Swe.	.20
63 Patrick Carnback, Swe.	.20
64 Andreas Johansson, Swe.	.20
65 Mikael Johansson, Swe.	.20
66 Per-Erik Eklund, Swe.	.20
67 Tomas Forslund, Swe.	.20
68 Andreas Dackell, Swe.	.20
69 Per Eklund, Swe.	.20
70 Tomas Holmstrom, Swe.	.20
71 Jonas Bergvist, Swe.	.20
72 Daniel Alfredsson, Swe.	.50
73 Fredrik Modin, Swe.	.20
74 HL: Peter Forsberg, Swe.	1.50
75 Ed Belfour (G), Cdn.	1.00
76 Bill Ranford (G), Cdn.	.50
77 Sean Burke (G), Cdn.	.50
78 Ray Bourque, Cdn.	1.50
79 Paul Coffey, Cdn.	.50
80 Scott Stevens, Cdn.	.50
81 Al MacInnis, Cdn.	.50
82 Larry Murphy, Cdn.	.20
83 Eric Desjardins, Cdn.	.20
84 Steve Duchesne, Cdn.	.20
85 Mario Lemieux, Cdn.	.20
86 Mark Messier, Cdn.	1.00
87 Theoren Fleury, Cdn.	.50
88 Eric Lindros, Cdn.	1.00
89 Rick Tocchet, Cdn.	.20
90 Brendan Shanahan, Cdn.	1.00
91 Claude Lemieux, Cdn.	.20
92 Joé Juneau, Cdn.	.20
93 Luc Robitaille, Cdn.	1.00
94 Paul Kariya, Cdn.	1.50
95 Joe Sakic, Cdn.	2.00
96 Mark Recchi, Cdn.	.50
97 Jason Arnott, Cdn.	.50
98 Rod Brind'Amour, Cdn.	.20
99 Wayne Gretzky, Cdn.	5.00
100 Adam Graves, Cdn.	.50
101 Steve Yzerman, Cdn.	3.00
102 Roman Turek (G), Cze.	.50
103 Dominik Hasek (G), Cze.	1.00
104 Petr Briza (G), Cze.	.50
105 Antonin Stavjana, Cze.	.20
106 Frantisek Kucera, Cze.	.20
107 Jiri Vukoukal, Cze.	.20
108 Jan Vopat, Cze.	.20
109 Libor Prochazka, Cze.	.20
110 Petr Kuchyna, Cze.	.20
111 Frantisek Musil, Cze.	.20
112 Leo Gudas, Cze.	.20
113 Jiri Slegr, Cze.	.20
114 Pavel Patera, Cze.	.20
115 Otakar Vejvoda, Cze.	.20
116 Martin Prochazka, Cze.	.20
117 Jiri Kucera, Cze.	.20
118 Pavel Janku, Cze.	.20
119 Roman Meluzin, Cze.	.20
120 Richard Zemlicka, Cze.	.20
121 Martin Hostak, Cze.	.20
122 Jiri Dopita, Cze.	.20
123 Radek Belohlav, Cze.	.20
124 Roman Horak, Cze.	.20
125 Jaromir Jagr, Cze.	1.00
126 Michal Pivonka, Cze.	.20
127 Josef Beranek, Cze.	.20
128 Robert Reichel, Cze.	.20
129 Nikolai Khabibulin (G), Rus.	.50
130 Sergei Abramov, Rus.	.20
131 Evgeni Tarasov, Rus.	.20
132 Igor Kravchuk, Rus.	.20
133 Dmitri Mironov, Rus.	.20
134 Alexei Zhitnik, Rus.	.20
135 Vladimir Malakhov, Rus.	.20
136 Sergei Zubov, Rus.	.20
137 Dmitry Yushkevich, Rus.	.20
138 Ilya Byakin, Rus.	.20
139 Alexander Smirnov, Rus.	.20
140 Andrei Skopintsev, Rus.	.20
141 Sergei Fedorov, Rus.	1.00
142 Pavel Bure, Rus.	1.00
143 Alexei Zhamnov, Rus.	.20
144 Andrei Kovalenko, Rus.	.20
145 Igor Korolev, Rus.	.20
146 Vyacheslav Kozlov, Rus.	.20
147 Viktor Kozlov, Rus.	.20
148 Alexei Yashin, Rus.	.50
149 Valeri Kamensky, Rus.	.20
150 Stanislav Romanov, Rus.	.20
151 Vyacheslav Bykov, Rus.	.20
152 Andrei Khomutov, Rus.	.20
153 Sergei Berezin, Rus.	.20
154 German Titov, Rus.	.20
155 Dmitri Denisov, Rus.	.20
156 John Vanbiesbrouck (G), USA.	.50
157 Jim Carey (G), USA.	.20
158 Mike Richter (G), USA.	.50
159 Chris Chelios, USA.	.50
160 Brian Leetch, USA.	.50
161 Phil Housley, USA.	.20
162 Gary Suter, USA.	.20
163 Kevin Hatcher, USA.	.20
164 Brett Hull, USA.	1.00
165 Pat LaFontaine, USA.	.50
166 Mike Modano, USA.	1.00
167 Jeremy Roenick, USA.	1.00
168 Keith Tkachuk, USA.	.50
169 Joe Mullen, USA.	.50
170 Craig Janney, USA.	.20
171 Joel Otto, USA.	.20
172 Doug Weight, USA.	.50
173 Scott Young, USA.	.20
174 Michael Rosati (G), Ita.	.20
175 Bruno Campese (G), Ita.	.20
176 Robert Oberrauch, Ita.	.20
177 Robert Nardella, Ita.	.20
178 Stefano Figliuzzi, Ita.	.20
179 Maurizio Mansi, Ita.	.20
180 Gaetano Orlando, Ita.	.20
181 Mario Chitarroni, Ita.	.20
182 Martin Pavlu, Ita.	.20
183 Petri Ylonen (G), Fra.	.50
184 Michel Valliere, Fra.	.20
185 Serge Poudrier, Fra.	.20
186 Denis Perez, Fra.	.20
187 Antoine Richer, Fra.	.20
188 Philippe Bozon, Fra.	.20
189 Christian Pouget, Fra.	.20
190 Franck Pajonkowski, Fra.	.20
191 Stephane Barin, Fra.	.20
192 Klaus Merk (G), Ger.	.50
193 Marc Seliger (G), Ger.	.20
194 Mirco Ludemann, Ger.	.20
195 Jason Meyer, Ger.	.20
196 Benoît Doucet, Ger.	.20
197 Thomas Brandl, Ger.	.20
198 Dieter Hegen, Ger.	.20
199 Martin Reichel, Ger.	.20
200 Leo Stefan, Ger.	.20
201 Robert Schistad, Nor.	.20
202 Jim Marthinsen, Nor.	.20
203 Tommy Jakobsen, Nor.	.20
204 Petter Salsten, Nor.	.20
205 Svein E. Norstebo, Nor.	.20
206 Espen Knutsen, Nor.	.20
207 Trond Magnussen, Nor.	.20
208 Henrik Aaby, Nor.	.20
209 Marius Rath, Nor.	.20
210 Claus Dalpiaz (G), Aut.	.50
211 Michael Puschacher, Aut.	.20
212 Robin Doyle, Aut.	.20
213 James Burton, Aut.	.20
214 Herbert Hohenberger, Aut.	.20
215 Andreas Pusnik, Aut.	.20
216 Richard Nasheim, Aut.	.20
217 Dieter Kalt, Aut.	.20
218 Werner Kerth, Aut.	.20
219 Eduard Hartmann, Slo.	.20
220 Jaromir Dragan, Slo.	.20
221 Robert Svehla, Slo.	.20
222 Lubomir Sekeras, Slo.	.20
223 Marian Smerciak, Slo.	.20
224 Jergus Baca, Slo.	.20
225 Stanislav Medrik, Slo.	.20
226 Miroslav Marcinko, Slo.	.20
227 Peter Stastny, Slo.	.50
228 Peter Bondra, Slo.	.50
229 Zdeno Ciger, Slo.	.20
230 Jozef Stumpel, Slo.	.20
231 Miroslav Satan, Slo.	.50
232 Lubomir Kolnik, Slo.	.20
233 Robert Petrovicky, Slo.	.20
234 Zigmund Palffy, Slo.	.50
235 Oto Hascak, Slo.	.20
236 Jozef Dano, Slo.	.20
237 CL:M. Renberg/ S. Koivu	.50
238 CL:M. Renberg/ S. Koivu	.50
239 CL:M. Renberg/ S. Koivu	.50
240 CL:M. Renberg/ S. Koivu	.50

Players	NRMT-MT
Super Chase: Renberg / Koivu	40.00

HOCKEY LEGENDS

Insert Set (18 cards): 55.00

Player	NRMT-MT
HL1 Ken Dryden (G), Cdn.	8.00
HL2 Guy Lafleur, Cdn.	8.00
HL3 Mike Bossy, Cdn.	6.00
HL4 Valeri Vasiliev, USSR	3.00
HL5 Anatoli Firsov, USSR	3.00
HL6 Alexander Maltsev, USSR	3.00
HL7 Tony Esposito (G), Cdn.	4.00
HL8 Rod Langway, USA.	3.00
HL9 Bryan Trottier, USA.	4.00
HL10 Lennart Häggroth, Swe.	3.00
HL11 Ulf Nilsson, Swe.	3.00
HL12 Lars-Gunnar Lundberg, Swe.	3.00
HL13 Veli-Pekka Ketola, Fin.	3.00
HL14 Lasse Oksanen, Fin.	3.00
HL15 Pekka Rautakallio, Fin.	3.00
HL16 Jiri Holocek, Cze.	3.00
HL17 Jan Suchy, Cze.	3.00
HL18 Vaclav Nedomansky, Cze.	3.00

NORDIC STARS

Insert Set (6 cards): 40.00

Player	NRMT-MT
NS1 Peter Forsberg, Swe.	14.00
NS2 Teemu Selänne, Fin.	8.00
NS3 Mats Sundin, Swe.	10.00
NS4 Jari Kurri, Fin.	10.00
NS5 Nicklas Lidström, Swe.	6.00
NS6 Esa Tikkanen, Fin.	4.00

SUPER GOALIES

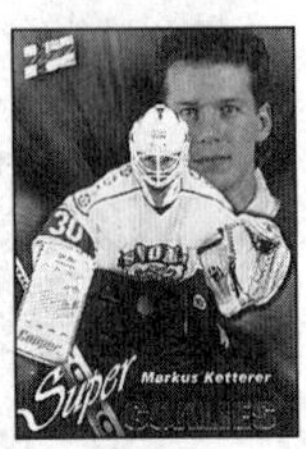

Insert Set (9 cards): 40.00

Player	NRMT-MT
SG1 Dominik Hasek (G), Cze.	6.00
SG2 Ed Belfour (G), Cdn.	6.00
SG3 Jarmo Myllys (G), Fin.	3.00
SG4 Tommy Söderström (G), Swe.	3.00
SG5 Jim Carey (G), USA.	3.00
SG6 Roman Turek (G), Cze.	3.00
SG7 Patrick Roy (G), Cdn.	18.00
SG8 Markus Ketterer (G), Fin.	3.00
SG9 Tommy Salo (G), Swe.	3.00

WORLD CHAMPIONSHIP 1995 ALL-STARS

Insert Set (6 cards): 20.00

Player	NRMT-MT
AS1 Roman Turek/ Jarmo Myllys	3.00
AS2 Timo Jutila/ Christer Olsson	3.00
AS3 Tommy Sjodin/ Marko Kiprusoff	3.00
AS4 Jere Lehtinen/ Sergei Berezin	3.00
AS5 Saku Koivu/ Per-Erik Eklund	10.00
AS6 Ville Peltonen/ Andrew McKim	3.00

1996 - 97 ALL-SPORT PPF

This 200-card multi-sport set features only 23 hockey players. There are two versions: the regular card and a gold parallel. A 200-card regular set sells for $20.

Player	Gold	AAP
71 Ed Jovanovski	3.00	.50
72 Chris Phillips	1.00	.25
73 Alexandre Volchkov	.75	.25
74 Adam Colagiacomo	1.00	.25
75 Johnathan Aitken	.75	.25
76 Rico Fata	1.00	.25
77 Andrei Zyuzin	1.00	.25
78 Josh Holden	1.00	.25
79 Boyd Devereaux	1.00	.25
97 Bryan Berard	2.00	.25
98 Dainius Zubrus	1.00	.25
99 Radek Dvorak	1.00	.25
170 Dainius Zubrus	1.00	.25
171 Joe Thornton	9.00	1.50
172 Daniel Brière	3.00	.50
173 Radek Dvorak	1.00	.25
174 Richard Jackman	1.00	.25
175 Robert Dome	1.00	.25
176 Sergei Samsonov	4.00	.50
177 Jarome Iginla	6.00	1.00
178 Chris Drury	2.00	.25
197 Andrei Zyuzin	1.00	.25
198 Ed Jovanovski	3.00	.50

1996 - 97 APS

It should be noted that since this product is not readibly available in North America, regional and NHL stars often sell at a premium (usually $1-2 each).

Complete Set (432 cards): 65.00

Player	NM-MT
1 Marek Sykora, Coach, Slavia Praha	.30
2 Vladimir Kolek (G), Coach, Slavia Praha	.30
3 Rudolf Pejchar (G), Slavia Praha	.30
4 Ladislav Kudrna (G), Slavia Praha	.30
5 Miloslav Horava, Slavia Praha	.50
6 Petr Kadlec, Slavia Praha	.30
7 Jaromir Latal, Slavia Praha	.30
8 Jiri Hes, Slavia Praha	.30
9 Andrei Jakovenko, Slavia Praha	.30
10 Martin Maskarinec, Slavia Praha	.30
11 Jaroslav Horacek, Slavia Praha	.30
12 Robert Kostka, Slavia Praha	.30
13 Jiri Dolezal, Slavia Praha	.30
14 Tomas Kucharcik, Slavia Praha	.30
15 Ivo Prorok, Slavia Praha	.30

☐ 16 Roman Kadera, Slavia Praha .50
☐ 17 Jiri Hlinka, Slavia Praha .30
☐ 18 Tomas Kupka, Slavia Praha .30
☐ 19 Viktor Ujcik, Slavia Praha .50
☐ 20 Vladimir Ruzicka, Slavia Praha 1.00
☐ 21 Ladislav Slizek, Slavia Praha .30
☐ 22 Jaroslav Bednar, Slavia Praha .50
☐ 23 Michal Sup, Slavia Praha .30
☐ 24 Radek Matejovsky, Slavia Praha .30
☐ 25 Horst Valasek, Coach, ZPS Zlin .30
☐ 26 Jiri Vodak, Coach, ZPS Zlin .30
☐ 27 Jaroslav Kames (G), ZPS Zlin .30
☐ 28 Petr Kubena (G), ZPS Zlin .30
☐ 29 Petr Kuchyna, ZPS Zlin .30
☐ 30 Jiri Marusak, ZPS Zlin .30
☐ 31 Radim Tesarik, ZPS Zlin .30
☐ 32 Vadim Podrezov, ZPS Zlin .30
☐ 33 Stanislav Medrik, ZPS Zlin .30
☐ 34 Jan Krajicek, ZPS Zlin .30
☐ 35 Pavel Kowalczyk, ZPS Zlin .30
☐ 36 David Bruk, ZPS Zlin .30
☐ 37 Tomas Nemcicky, ZPS Zlin .50
☐ 38 Zdenek Sedlak, ZPS Zlin .30
☐ 39 Ales Zima, ZPS Zlin .30
☐ 40 Zbynek Marak, ZPS Zlin .30
☐ 41 Ales Polcar, ZPS Zlin .30
☐ 42 Roman Meluzin, ZPS Zlin .30
☐ 43 Pavel Janku, ZPS Zlin .30
☐ 44 Miroslav Okal, ZPS Zlin .30
☐ 45 Petr Cajanek, ZPS Zlin .50
☐ 46 Martin Kotasek, ZPS Zlin .30
☐ 47 Petr Leska, ZPS Zlin .30
☐ 48 Alois Hadamczik, Coach, Trinec .30
☐ 49 Ales Mach, Coach, Trinec .30
☐ 50 Radovan Biegl (G), Trinec .30
☐ 51 Josef Lucak (G), Trinec .30
☐ 52 Petr Jancarik, Trinec .30
☐ 53 L'ubomir Sekeras, Trinec .50
☐ 54 Jiri Kuntos, Trinec .30
☐ 55 Stanislav Pavelec, Trinec .30
☐ 56 Patrik Hucko, Trinec .30
☐ 57 Miroslav Cihal, Trinec .30
☐ 58 Karel Pavlik, Trinec .30
☐ 59 Ondrej Zetek, Trinec .30
☐ 60 Richard Kral, Trinec .30
☐ 61 Petr Folta, Trinec .30
☐ 62 Josef Straub, Trinec .30
☐ 63 Petr Zajonc, Trinec .30
☐ 64 Roman Kontsek, Trinec .30
☐ 65 Marek Zadina, Trinec .30
☐ 66 Roman Blazek, Trinec .30
☐ 67 Michal Piskor, Trinec .30
☐ 68 Jozef Dano, Trinec .30
☐ 69 Vladimir Machulda, Trinec .30
☐ 70 Jiri Novotny, Trinec .30
☐ 71 Petr Lipina, Trinec .30
☐ 72 Jan Novotny, Coach, Kladno .30
☐ 73 Lubomir Bauer, Coach, Kladno .30
☐ 74 Milan Hnilicka (G), Kladno 1.00
☐ 75 Martin Chlad (G), Kladno .30
☐ 76 Petr Kasik, Kladno .30
☐ 77 Jan Krulis, Kladno .30
☐ 78 Libor Prochazka, Kladno .50
☐ 79 Jan Dlouhy, Kladno .30
☐ 80 Marek Zidlicky, Kladno .30
☐ 81 Tomas Kaberle, Kladno 1.50
☐ 82 Pavel Skrbek, Kladno .50
☐ 83 Tomas Trachta, Kladno .30
☐ 84 Zdenek Eichenmann, Kladno .30
☐ 85 Josef Zajic, Kladno .30
☐ 86 David Cermak, Kladno .30
☐ 87 Ladislav Svoboda, Kladno .30
☐ 88 Tomas Mikolasek, Kladno .30
☐ 89 Petr Ton, Kladno .30
☐ 90 Jiri Beranek, Kladno .30
☐ 91 Vaclav Eiselt, Kladno .30
☐ 92 Jiri Burger, Kladno .30
☐ 93 Petr Tenkrat, Kladno 1.50
☐ 94 Petr Vogeltanz, Kladno .30
☐ 95 Filip Klapac, Kladno .30
☐ 96 Karel Suchanek, Coach, Opava .30
☐ 97 Kamil Konecny, Coach, Opava .30
☐ 98 Rostislav Haas (G), Opava .30
☐ 99 Roman Slupina (G), Opava .30
☐ 100 Milos Hrubes, Opava .30
☐ 101 Petr Tejkl, Opava .30
☐ 102 Martin Bakula, Opava .30
☐ 103 Radek Mesicek, Opava .30
☐ 104 Karel Frydl, Opava .30
☐ 105 David Gavlas, Opava .30
☐ 106 Denis Tsygurov, Opava .50
☐ 107 Juraj Jurik, Opava .30
☐ 108 Petr Fabian, Opava .30
☐ 109 Radim Radevic, Opava .30
☐ 110 Jiri Zadrazil, Opava .30
☐ 111 Martin Filip, Opava .30
☐ 112 Karel Horny, Opava .30
☐ 113 Zdenek Pavelek, Opava .30
☐ 114 Eduard Gorbachev, Opava .30
☐ 115 Valeri Belov, Opava .30
☐ 116 Dalibor Rimsky, Opava .30
☐ 117 Marek Harazim, Opava .30
☐ 118 David Dostal, Opava .30
☐ 119 Slavomir Lener, Coach, Sparta Praha .30
☐ 120 Vaclav Sykora, Coach, Sparta Praha .30
☐ 121 Robert Schistad (G), Sparta Praha .30
☐ 122 Martin Cinibulk (G), Sparta Praha .30
☐ 123 Jiri Vykoukal, Sparta Praha .30
☐ 124 Jan Bohacek, Sparta Praha .30
☐ 125 Jaroslav Nedved, Sparta Praha .30
☐ 126 Jiri Krocak, Sparta Praha .30
☐ 127 Vaclav Burda, Sparta Praha .30
☐ 128 Radek Hamr, Sparta Praha .50
☐ 129 Frantisek Ptacek, Sparta Praha .30
☐ 130 Roman Horak, Sparta Praha .30
☐ 131 Pavel Geffert, Sparta Praha .30
☐ 132 Richard Zemlicka, Sparta Praha .30
☐ 133 Jiri Zelenka, Sparta Praha .30
☐ 134 Patrik Martinec, Sparta Praha .30
☐ 135 David Vyborny, Sparta Praha .50
☐ 136 Miroslav Hlinka, Sparta Praha .30
☐ 137 Martin Hostak, Sparta Praha .50
☐ 138 Jan Hlavac, Sparta Praha 1.00
☐ 139 Jaroslav Hlinka, Sparta Praha .30
☐ 140 Jan Benda, Sparta Praha .30
☐ 141 Milos Riha, Coach, Pardubice .30
☐ 142 Josef Palecek, Coach, Pardubice .30
☐ 143 Libor Barta (G), Pardubice .30
☐ 144 Dusan Salficky (G), Pardubice .30
☐ 145 Radomir Brazda, Pardubice .30
☐ 146 Pavel Augusta, Pardubice .30
☐ 147 Jiri Malinsky, Pardubice .30
☐ 148 Tomas Pacal, Pardubice .30
☐ 149 Ales Pisa, Pardubice 1.00
☐ 150 Pavel Kriz, Pardubice .30
☐ 151 Alexander Tsyplakov, Pardubice .30
☐ 152 Petr Mudroch, Pardubice .30
☐ 153 Ladislav Lubina, Pardubice .30
☐ 154 David Pospisil, Pardubice .30
☐ 155 Stanislav Prochazka, Pardubice .30
☐ 156 Tomas Blazek, Pardubice .50
☐ 157 Milan Hejduk, Pardubice 8.00
☐ 158 Tomas Martinec, Pardubice .30
☐ 159 Jiri Jantovsky, Pardubice .30
☐ 160 Martin Koudelka, Pardubice .30
☐ 161 Pavel Kabrt, Pardubice .30
☐ 162 Petr** Sykora, Pardubice .30
☐ 163 Milan Prochazka, Pardubice .30
☐ 164 Karel Plasek, Pardubice .30
☐ 165 J. Beranek, Coach, Chemopetrol Litvinov .50
☐ 166 V. Kyhos, Coach, Chemopetrol Litvinov .30
☐ 167 Zdenek Orct (G), Chemopetrol Litvinov .30
☐ 168 Richard Hrazdira (G), Chemopetrol Litvinov .30
☐ 169 Kamil Prachar, Chemopetrol Litvinov .30
☐ 170 Radek Mrazek, Chemopetrol Litvinov .30
☐ 171 Roman Cech, Chemopetrol Litvinov .30
☐ 172 Angel Nikolov, Chemopetrol Litvinov .30
☐ 173 Martin Stepanek, Chemopetrol Litvinov .30
☐ 174 Sergei Butko, Chemopetrol Litvinov .30
☐ 175 Normunds Sejejs, Chemopetrol Litvinov .30
☐ 176 Petr Kratky, Chemopetrol Litvinov .30
☐ 177 Vladimir Jerabek, Chemopetrol Litvinov .30
☐ 178 Kamil Kastak, Chemopetrol Litvinov .30
☐ 179 Robert Kysela, Chemopetrol Litvinov .30
☐ 180 Petr Hrbek, Chemopetrol Litvinov .30
☐ 181 Martin Rousek, Chemopetrol Litvinov .30
☐ 182 Tomas Krasny, Chemopetrol Litvinov .30
☐ 183 Tomas Vlasak, Chemopetrol Litvinov .50
☐ 184 David Balazs, Chemopetrol Litvinov .30
☐ 185 Jindrich Kotrla, Chemopetrol Litvinov .30
☐ 186 Josef Straka, Chemopetrol Litvinov .30
☐ 187 Jaroslav Buchal, Chemopetrol Litvinov .30
☐ 188 Kamil Piros, Chemopetrol Litvinov .50
☐ 189 Vladimir (Sr.) Vujtek, Coach, Vitkovice .30
☐ 190 Ladislav Svozil, Coach, Vitkovice .30
☐ 191 Martin Prusek (G), Vitkovice 3.00
☐ 192 Tomas Vasicek (G), Vitkovice .30
☐ 193 Jiri Jonak, Vitkovice .30
☐ 194 Ales Tomasek, Vitkovice .30
☐ 195 Daniel Kysela, Vitkovice .30
☐ 196 Vitezslav Skuta, Vitkovice .30
☐ 197 Tomas Kramny, Vitkovice .30
☐ 198 René Sevecek, Vitkovice .30
☐ 199 Dmitri Jerofejev, Vitkovice .30
☐ 200 Pavel Kumstat, Vitkovice .30
☐ 201 Roman Rysanek, Vitkovice .30
☐ 202 Roman Simicek, Vitkovice .50
☐ 203 Martin Smetak, Vitkovice .30
☐ 204 Tomas Chlubna, Vitkovice .30
☐ 205 Ludek Krayzel, Vitkovice .30
☐ 206 David Moravec, Vitkovice .50
☐ 207 Alexander Prokopjev, Vitkovice .30
☐ 208 Ales Kratoska, Vitkovice .30
☐ 209 Libor Pavlis, Vitkovice .30
☐ 210 Radek Klauda, Vitkovice .30
☐ 211 Libor Polasek, Vitkovice .30
☐ 212 Jan Neliba, Coach, Dadak Vsetin .30
☐ 213 Zdislav Tabara, Coach, Dadak Vsetin .30
☐ 214 Roman Cechmanek (G), Dadak Vsetin .50
☐ 215 Ivo Pesat (G), Dadak Vsetin .30
☐ 216 Antonin Stavjana, Dadak Vsetin .30
☐ 217 Bedrich Scerban, Dadak Vsetin .30
☐ 218 Jiri Veber, Dadak Vsetin .30
☐ 219 Alexei Jaskin, Dadak Vsetin .30
☐ 220 Jan Srdinko, Dadak Vsetin .30
☐ 221 Tomas Jakes, Dadak Vsetin .30
☐ 222 Petr Kubos, Dadak Vsetin .30
☐ 223 Michal Divisek, Dadak Vsetin .30
☐ 224 Rostislav Vlach, Dadak Vsetin .30
☐ 225 Michal Tomek, Dadak Vsetin .30
☐ 226 Oto Hascak, Dadak Vsetin .30
☐ 227 Tomas Kapusta, Dadak Vsetin .30
☐ 228 Tomas Srsen, Dadak Vsetin .30
☐ 229 Roman Stantien, Dadak Vsetin .30
☐ 230 Jiri Dopita, Dadak Vsetin .50
☐ 231 Ivan Padelek, Dadak Vsetin .30
☐ 232 Andrei Galkin, Dadak Vsetin .30
☐ 233 Ondrej Kratena, Dadak Vsetin .50
☐ 234 David Hruska, Dadak Vsetin .30
☐ 235 Daniel Tesarik, Dadak Vsetin .30
☐ 236 Lukas Duba, Dadak Vsetin .30
☐ 237 Vladimir Caldr, Coach, Ceske Budejovice .30
☐ 238 Jaroslav Liska, Coach, Ceske Budejovice .30
☐ 239 Oldrich Svoboda (G), Ceske Budejovice .30
☐ 240 Robert Slavik (G), Ceske Budejovice .30
☐ 241 Rudolf Suchanek, Ceske Budejovice .30
☐ 242 Karel Soudek, Ceske Budejovice .30
☐ 243 Milan Nedoma, Ceske Budejovice .30
☐ 244 Kamil Toupal, Ceske Budejovice .30
☐ 245 Petr Sedy, Ceske Budejovice .30
☐ 246 Lukas Zib, Ceske Budejovice .30
☐ 247 Martin Masak, Ceske Budejovice .30
☐ 248 Radek Martinek, Ceske Budejovice .50
☐ 249 Vladimir Antipin, Ceske Budejovice .30
☐ 250 Radek Toupal, Ceske Budejovice .30
☐ 251 Pavel Pycha, Ceske Budejovice .30
☐ 252 Lubos Rob, Ceske Budejovice .30
☐ 253 Filip Turek, Ceske Budejovice .30
☐ 254 Arpad Gyori, Ceske Budejovice .30
☐ 255 Radek Belohlav, Ceske Budejovice .30
☐ 256 Ondrej Vosta, Ceske Budejovice .30
☐ 257 Milan Navratil, Ceske Budejovice .30
☐ 258 Frantisek Sevcik, Ceske Budejovice .30
☐ 259 Petr Sailer, Ceske Budejovice .30
☐ 260 Michal Horak, Ceske Budejovice .30
☐ 261 Kamil Brabenec, Ceske Budejovice .30
☐ 262 Miroslav Barus, Ceske Budejovice .30
☐ 263 Jiri Latal, Coach, Olomouc .50
☐ 264 Miroslav Venkrbec, Coach, Olomouc .30
☐ 265 Ladislav Blazek (G), Olomouc .30
☐ 266 Robert Horyna (G), Olomouc .30
☐ 267 Petr Pavlas, Olomouc .30
☐ 268 Roman Veber, Olomouc .30
☐ 269 Marek Tichy, Olomouc .30
☐ 270 Jergus Baca, Olomouc .50
☐ 271 Ladislav Benysek, Olomouc .50
☐ 272 Jiri Polak, Olomouc .30
☐ 273 Marek Cernosek, Olomouc .30
☐ 274 Michal Slavik, Olomouc .30
☐ 275 Pavel Nohel, Olomouc .30
☐ 276 Radek Sip, Olomouc .30
☐ 277 Jan Tomajko, Olomouc .50
☐ 278 Michal Bros, Olomouc .50
☐ 279 Radek Prochazka, Olomouc .30
☐ 280 Radek Svoboda, Olomouc .30
☐ 281 Michal Dvorak, Olomouc .30
☐ 282 Ales Lipensky, Olomouc .30
☐ 283 Filip Dvorak, Olomouc .30
☐ 284 Milan Jurak, Olomouc .30
☐ 285 Adam Drabek, Olomouc .30
☐ 286 M. Ebermann, Coach, Interconex Plzen .30
☐ 287 Radim Rulik, Coach, Interconex Plzen .30
☐ 288 Martin Altrichter (G), Interconex Plzen .30
☐ 289 Michal Marik (G), Interconex Plzen .30
☐ 290 Ivan Vlcek, Interconex Plzen .30
☐ 291 Josef Reznicek, Interconex Plzen .30
☐ 292 Karel Smid, Interconex Plzen .30
☐ 293 Vaclav Ruprecht, Interconex Plzen .30
☐ 294 Jaroslav Spacek, Interconex Plzen .50
☐ 295 Jiri Hanzlik, Interconex Plzen .30
☐ 296 Robert Jindrich, Interconex Plzen .30
☐ 297 Tomas Jelinek, Interconex Plzen .50
☐ 298 Milan Volak, Interconex Plzen .30
☐ 299 Radek Kampf, Interconex Plzen .30
☐ 300 Miroslav Mach, Interconex Plzen .30
☐ 301 Petr Korinek, Interconex Plzen .30
☐ 302 Jiri Kucera, Interconex Plzen .30
☐ 303 Michal Straka, Interconex Plzen .30
☐ 304 Tomas Klimt, Interconex Plzen .50
☐ 305 Josef Rybar, Interconex Plzen .30
☐ 306 Dalibor Sanda, Interconex Plzen .30
☐ 307 Jiri Novotny, Interconex Plzen .30
☐ 308 Pavel Vostrak, Interconex Plzen .30
☐ 309 Frantisek Vorlicek, Coach, Dukla Jihlava .30
☐ 310 Jan Hrbaty, Coach, Dukla Jihlava .30
☐ 311 Ivo Capek (G), Dukla Jihlava .30
☐ 312 Marek Novotny (G), Dukla Jihlava .30
☐ 313 Roman Kankovsky, Dukla Jihlava .30
☐ 314 Miroslav Javin, Dukla Jihlava .30
☐ 315 Michael Vyhlidal, Dukla Jihlava .30
☐ 316 Zdenek Touzimsky, Dukla Jihlava .30
☐ 317 Martin Tupa, Dukla Jihlava .30
☐ 318 Marian Morava, Dukla Jihlava .30
☐ 319 Filip Vanecek, Dukla Jihlava .30
☐ 320 Marek Posmyk, Dukla Jihlava .50
☐ 321 Libor Dolana, Dukla Jihlava .30
☐ 322 Petr Vlk, Dukla Jihlava .30
☐ 323 Petr Kankovsky, Dukla Jihlava .30
☐ 324 Jaroslav Hub, Dukla Jihlava .30
☐ 325 Jiri Poukar, Dukla Jihlava .30
☐ 326 Leos Pipa, Dukla Jihlava .30
☐ 327 Ladislav Prokupek, Dukla Jihlava .50
☐ 328 Patrik Fink, Dukla Jihlava .30
☐ 329 Marek Melenovsky, Dukla Jihlava .30
☐ 330 Milan Antos, Dukla Jihlava .30
☐ 331 Jiri Holik, Dukla Jihlava 1.50
☐ 332 Miroslav Bruna, Dukla Jihlava .30
☐ 333 Michail Fadejev, Dukla Jihlava .30
☐ 334 Ludek Bukac, Coach, Czech Nationals .30
☐ 335 Slavomir Lener, Coach, Czech Nationals .30
☐ 336 Zdenek Uher (G), Czech Nationals .30
☐ 337 Roman Cechmanek (G), Czech Nationals .50
☐ 338 Roman Turek, Czech Nationals 2.50
☐ 339 Robert Kysela, Czech Nationals .30
☐ 340 Jiri Veber, Czech Nationals .30
☐ 341 Pavel Patera, Czech Nationals .50
☐ 342 Radek Bonk, Czech Nationals 1.50
☐ 343 Radek Belohlav, Czech Nationals .30
☐ 344 Drahomir Kadlec, Czech Nationals .30
☐ 345 Michal Sykora, Czech Nationals .50
☐ 346 Jiri Vykoukal, Czech Nationals .30
☐ 347 Viktor Ujcik, Czech Nationals .50
☐ 348 Stanislav Neckar, Czech Nationals .50
☐ 349 Robert Reichel, Czech Nationals 1.50
☐ 350 Roman Meluzin, Czech Nationals .30
☐ 351 Otakar Vejvoda, Czech Nationals .30
☐ 352 Martin Prochazka, Czech Nationals .50
☐ 353 Robert Lang, Czech Nationals 1.00
☐ 354 Antonin Stavjana, Czech Nationals .30
☐ 355 Jiri Dopita, Czech Nationals .50
☐ 356 Jiri Kucera, Czech Nationals .30
☐ 357 Frantisek* Kaberle, Czech Nationals .50
☐ 358 David Vyborny, Czech Nationals .50
☐ 359 Petr Briza (G), Czech Nationals .50
☐ 360 Roman Hamrlik, Czech Nationals 1.00
☐ 361 Martin Straka, Czech Nationals 1.50
☐ 362 Petr* Sykora, Czech Nationals 2.00
☐ 363 Tomas Vlasak, Czech Nationals .50
☐ 364 Jiri Dopita, Czech Nationals .50
☐ 365 Roman Cechmanek (G), Awards .50
☐ 366 Jaromir Jagr, Awards 6.00
☐ 367 Vladimir Jerabek, Awards .30
☐ 368 Ondrej Kratena, Awards .50
☐ 369 Vladimir Ruzicka, Awards 1.00
☐ 370 Viktor Ujcik, Awards .50
☐ 371 Libor Zabransky, Awards .50
☐ 372 Bohumil Modry (G), Czechoslovakia .30
☐ 373 Miroslav Dvorak, Czechoslovakia .30
☐ 374 Jiri Holecek (G), Czechoslovakia .30
☐ 375 Jaroslav Holik, Czechoslovakia 1.50
☐ 376 Frantisek** Kaberle, Czechoslovakia 1.00
☐ 377 Milan Novy, Czechoslovakia 1.00
☐ 379 Vladimir Hudacek (G), Vitkovice .30
☐ 380 Andrei Potaichuk, Sparta Praha .30
☐ 381 Vladimir Petrovka, Olomouc .30
☐ 382 Adam Svoboda, Sparta Praha .30
☐ 383 Robert Lang, Sparta Praha 1.00
☐ 384 Josef Beranek, Dadak Vsetin .50
☐ 385 Petr Nedved, Sparta Praha 1.50
☐ 386 Milan Hnilicka (G), All-Stars 1.00
☐ 387 Jiri Vykoukal, All-Stars .30
☐ 388 Radek Hamr, All Stars .50
☐ 389 Robert Lang, All-Stars 1.00
☐ 390 Jiri Kucera, All-Stars .30
☐ 391 Viktor Ujcik, All-Stars .50
☐ 392 Oldrich Svoboda (G), All-Stars .30
☐ 393 Vaclav Burda, All-Stars .30
☐ 394 Normunds Sejejs, All-Stars .30
☐ 395 Andrei Potaichuk, All-Stars .30
☐ 396 Ladislav Lubina, All-Stars .30
☐ 397 Vladimir Ruzicka, All-Stars 1.00
☐ 398 Libor Prochazka, All-Stars .50
☐ 399 Martin Stepanek, All-Stars .30
☐ 400 Milan Hejduk, All-Stars 8.00
☐ 401 Tomas Vlasak, All-Stars .50
☐ 402 Martin Rousek, All-Stars .30
☐ 403 Jaroslav Spacek, All-Stars .50
☐ 404 Milan Nedoma, All-Stars .30
☐ 405 Tomas Jelinek, All-Stars .50
☐ 406 Radek Toupal, All-Stars .30
☐ 407 Josef Beranek, All-Stars .30
☐ 407 Stanislav Berger, All-Stars .30
☐ 408 Team West All-Stars .30
☐ 409 Martin Prusek, All-Stars 3.00
☐ 410 Vitezslav Skuta, All-Stars .30
☐ 411 Jiri Veber, All-Stars .30
☐ 412 Josef Beranek, All-Stars .50
☐ 413 Jiri Dopita, All-Stars .50
☐ 414 Roman Meluzin, All-Stars .30
☐ 415 Roman Cechmanek, All-Stars .50
☐ 416 Dmitri Jerofejev, All-Stars .30
☐ 417 Radim Tesarik, All-Stars .30
☐ 418 David Moravec, All-Stars .50
☐ 419 Pavel Janku, All-Stars .30
☐ 420 Tomas Srsen, All-Stars .30
☐ 421 Jergus Baca, All-Stars .50
☐ 422 Petr Pavlas, All-Stars .30
☐ 423 Petr Kankovsky, All-Stars .30
☐ 424 Petr Fabian, All-Stars .30
☐ 425 Petr Vlk, All-Stars .30
☐ 426 Alexei Jaskin, All-Stars .30
☐ 427 Petr Tejkl, All-Stars .30
☐ 428 Josef Straub, All-Stars .30
☐ 429 Roman Simicek, All-Stars .50
☐ 430 Richard Kral, All-Stars .30
☐ 431 Horst Valasek, All-Stars .30
☐ 431 Vladimir (Jr.) Vujtek, All-Stars .30
☐ 432 Team East All-Stars .50

1996 - 97 AUTOGRAPH COLLECTION

This 50-card multi-sport set features only six hockey cards. A 50-card set sells for $15.

	Player	AC
☐	45 Joe Thornton	3.50
☐	46 Daniel Cleary	.25
☐	47 Robert Dome	.25
☐	48 Alexandre Volchkov	.25
☐	49 Adam Colagiacomo	.25
☐	50 Andrei Zyuzin	.25

AUTHENTIC AUTOGRAPH

Players signed both a regular card and a Gold parallel (#/350).

	Autograph	G350	Auto.
☐ ☐	Daniel Cleary ✍	16.00	8.00
☐ ☐	Adam Colagiacomo ✍	10.00	5.00
☐ ☐	Robert Dome ✍	10.00	5.00
☐ ☐	Sergei Samsonov ✍	45.00	20.00
☐ ☐	Joe Thornton ✍	90.00	45.00
☐ ☐	Dainius Zubrus ✍	12.00	6.00
☐ ☐	Andrei Zyuzin ✍	10.00	5.00

GAME BREAKERS

This 30-card set features only two hockey cards. There are two versions: the regular insert and a gold parallel.

	Insert	Gold	GB
☐ ☐	Joe Thornton	50.00	10.00
☐ ☐	Alexandre Volchkov	10.00	4.00

1996 - 97 BICYCLE SPORTS / ACES

There are two versions: the regular card and a Press Proof parallel (#/2000).

Complete Deck (55 cards): 6.00

	Player	NM-MT
☐	10-Club Pierre Turgeon, Mont.	.20
☐	10-Diamond Doug Weight, Edmo.	.20

☐	10-Heart Keith Tkachuk, Winn. (Phoe.)	.20
☐	10-Spade Chris Osgood (G), Detr.	.20
☐	2-Club Gary Roberts, Calg.	.20
☐	2-Diamond Alexei Yashin, Otta.	.20
☐	2-Heart Pavel Bure, Vanc.	.20
☐	2-Spade Travis Green, NYIs.	.20
☐	3-Club Ray Ferraro, LosA.	.20
☐	3-Diamond Jason Arnott, Edmo.	.20
☐	3-Heart Doug Gilmour, Toro.	.20
☐	3-Spade Roman Hamrlik, Tamp.	.20
☐	4-Club Owen Nolan, SanJ.	.20
☐	4-Diamond Mike Gartner, Toro. (Phoe.)	.20
☐	4-Heart Joé Juneau, Wash.	.20
☐	4-Spade Adam Oates, Bost.	.20
☐	5-Club Chris Chelios, Chic.	.20
☐	5-Diamond Jeremy Roenick, Chic.	.20
☐	5-Heart Raymond Bourque, Bost.	.50
☐	5-Spade Trevor Linden, Vanc.	.20
☐	6-Club Brendan Shanahan, Hart.	.50
☐	6-Diamond Mike Modano, Dall.	.50
☐	6-Heart Jocelyn Thibault (G), Mont.	.20
☐	6-Spade Daren Puppa (G), Tamp.	.20
☐	7-Club Daniel Alfredsson, Otta.	.20
☐	7-Diamond Pat LaFontaine, Buff.	.20
☐	7-Heart Steve Yzerman, Detr.	1.00
☐	7-Spade Éric Dazé, Chic.	.20
☐	8-Club Brian Leetch, NYRa.	.20
☐	8-Diamond Mats Sundin, Toro.	.50
☐	8-Heart Grant Fuhr, SLou.	.20
☐	8-Spade Rod Brind'Amour, Phil.	.20
☐	9-Club Martin Brodeur (G), NJer.	.50
☐	9-Diamond Brett Hull, SLou.	.50
☐	9-Heart Vincent Damphousse, Mont.	.20
☐	9-Spade Ron Francis, Pitt.	.20
☐	A-Club Wayne Gretzky, SLou. (NYRa.)	2.00
☐	A-Diamond Joe Sakic, Colo.	.50
☐	A-Heart Patrick Roy (G), Colo.	1.50
☐	A-Spade Mario Lemieux, Pitt.	1.50
☐	J-Club Alexander Mogilny, Vanc.	.20
☐	J-Diamond Theoren Fleury, Calg.	.20
☐	J-Heart Teemu Selänne, Anah.	.20
☐	J-Spade Jim Carey (G), Wash.	.20
☐	K-Club Jaromir Jagr, Pitt.	.50
☐	K-Diamond Paul Kariya, Anah.	.50
☐	K-Heart Peter Forsberg, Colo.	.50
☐	K-Spade Eric Lindros, Phil.	.50
☐	Q-Club John Vanbiesbrouck (G), Flor.	.20
☐	Q-Diamond Mark Messier, NYRa.	.50
☐	Q-Heart Sergei Fedorov, Detr.	.50
☐	Q-Spade Ed Jovanovski, Flor.	.20
☐	Checklist	.20
☐	Eastern Conference	.20
☐	Western Conference	.20

1996 - 97 DEL

It should be noted that since this product is not readibly available in North America, regional and NHL stars often sell at a premium (usually $1-2 each).

Complete Set (360 cards):		50.00
	Player	NM-MT
☐	1 Gary Prior, Coach	.30
☐	2 Bruno Campese (G)	.30
☐	3 Leonardo Conti	.30
☐	4 Scott Campbell	.30
☐	5 Rob Mendel	.30
☐	6 Serge Poudrier	.30
☐	7 Torsten Fendt	.30
☐	8 Shawn Rivers	.50
☐	9 Stefan Mayer	.30
☐	10 Michael Bakos	.30
☐	11 Tommy Jakobsen	.30
☐	12 Duanne Moeser	.30
☐	13 Tero Arkiomaa	.30
☐	14 Sven Zywitza	.30
☐	15 Craig Streu	.30
☐	16 Terence Campbell	.30
☐	17 Tim Ferguson	.30
☐	18 Yves Heroux	.30
☐	19 Max Boldt	.30
☐	20 André Faust	.50
☐	21 Rochus Schneider	.30
☐	22 Ron Kennedy, Coach	.30
☐	23 Barry Lewis, Asst. Coach	.30
☐	24 Mario Brunetta (G)	.50
☐	25 Udo Dohler	.30
☐	26 Dirk Perschau	.30
☐	27 Darren Durdle	.30
☐	28 Greg Andrusak	.50
☐	29 Leif Carlsson	.30
☐	30 Derek Mayer	.50
☐	31 Rob Leask	.30
☐	32 Chad Biafore	.30
☐	33 Thomas Steen	1.50
☐	34 Lorenz Funk	.30
☐	35 Florian Funk	.30
☐	36 Sven Felski	.30
☐	37 Peter Lee	.50
☐	38 Andrew McKim	.50
☐	39 Andrei Lomakin	.50
☐	40 Pelle Svensson	.30
☐	41 Jan Schertz	.30
☐	42 Kraig Nienhuis	.30
☐	43 Niklas Hede	.30
☐	44 Mario Chitaroni	.30
☐	45 Chris Govedaris	.50
☐	46 Pentti Matikainen, Coach	.30
☐	47 Jukka Tammi (G)	.30
☐	48 Rupert Meister	.30
☐	49 Florian Storf	.30
☐	50 Greg Thomson	.30
☐	51 Toni Porkka	.30
☐	52 Sergei Schendelev	.30
☐	53 Kai Rautio	.30
☐	54 Rudi Gorgenlander	.30
☐	55 Petr Kopta	.30
☐	56 Tony Virta	.50
☐	57 Ilja Vorobiev	.30
☐	58 Thomas Popiesch	.30
☐	59 François Sills	.30
☐	60 Iiro Järvi	.50
☐	61 Jurgen Schaal	.30
☐	62 Pavel Vit	.30
☐	63 Timo Peltomaa	.30
☐	64 Igor Schultz	.30
☐	65 Dave Archibald	.50
☐	66 Joni Lehto	.30
☐	67 Brad Jones	.50
☐	68 Miroslav Berek, Coach	.30
☐	69 Karel Lang	.30
☐	70 Peter Franke	.30
☐	71 Markus Krawinkel	.30
☐	72 Zdenek Trávnicek	.30
☐	73 Martin Gebel	.30
☐	74 Klaus Micheller	.30
☐	75 Earl Spry	.30
☐	76 Frantisek Frosch	.30
☐	77 Petri Liimatainen	.30
☐	78 André Grein	.30
☐	79 Ken Petrash	.30
☐	80 James Hanlon	.30
☐	81 Andrei Kovalev	.50
☐	82 Reemt Pyka	.30
☐	83 Chris Lindberg	.50
☐	84 Jay Luknowsky	.30
☐	85 Peter Ihnacak	.50
☐	86 Marek Strebnicki	.30
☐	87 Johnny Walker	.30
☐	88 Danton Cole	.50
☐	89 Michael Hreus	.30
☐	90 Damian Adamus	.30
☐	91 Bill Lochead, Coah	.50
☐	92 Joakim Persson (G)	.30
☐	93 Ian Wood	.30
☐	94 Pierre Jonsson	.30
☐	95 Juha Lampinen	.30
☐	96 Christian Schmitz	.30
☐	97 Cory Holden	.30
☐	98 Peter Lutter	.30
☐	99 Dieter Bloem	.30
☐	100 Maurizio Catenacci	.30
☐	101 Andrei Fuchs	.30
☐	102 Mark Montanari	.30
☐	103 Boris Fuchs	.30
☐	104 Andreas Salomonsson	1.00
☐	105 Robert Reynolds	.30
☐	106 Axel Kammerer	.30
☐	107 Jeff Lazaro	.50
☐	108 Olaf Scholz	.30
☐	109 Tony Cimellaro	.30
☐	110 Ken (Jr.) Hodge	.50
☐	111 Gregory Burke	.30
☐	112 Tom Coolen, Coach	.30
☐	113 Marc Pethke	.30
☐	114 Christian Künast	.30
☐	115 Drahomir Kadlec	.30
☐	116 Florian Kuhn	.30
☐	117 Erich Goldmann	1.00
☐	118 Jurgen Simon	.30
☐	119 Jeff Winstanley	.30
☐	120 Stefano Figliuzzi	.30
☐	121 Maurizio Mansi	.30
☐	122 Agostino Casale	.30
☐	123 Hans-Jörg Mayer	.30
☐	124 Dino Felicetti	.30
☐	125 Roland Timoschuk	.30
☐	126 Jim Hoffmann	.30
☐	127 John Porco	.30
☐	128 Rolf Hammer	.30
☐	129 Manuel Hess	.30
☐	130 Andy Rymsha	.30
☐	131 Wolfgang Kummer	.30
☐	132 Trevor Burgess	.30
☐	133 Daniel Kunce	.30
☐	134 Timo Sutinen, Coach	.30
☐	135 Petr Briza (G)	.50
☐	136 Markus Nachtmann	.30
☐	137 Markus Wieland	.30
☐	138 Michael Heidt	.30
☐	139 Peter Gulda	.30
☐	140 Jacek Plachta	.30
☐	141 Georg Franz	.30
☐	142 Stephan Retzer	.30
☐	143 Henry Marcoux	.30
☐	144 Mike Bullard	1.00
☐	145 José Charbonneau	.50
☐	146 Wally Schrieber	.50
☐	147 Jörg Handrick	.30
☐	148 Helmut Steiger	.30
☐	149 Marco Sturm	3.50
☐	150 Jonas Jönsson	.30
☐	151 Vesa Salo	.30
☐	152 Gino Cavallini	.50
☐	153 Lars Hurtig	.30
☐	154 Olli Kaski	.30
☐	155 Card	.30
☐	156 Lance Nethery, Coach	.30
☐	157 Ross Yates, A. Coach	.30
☐	158 Joachim Appel	.30
☐	159 Michael Rosati (G)	1.00
☐	160 Harold Kreis	.30
☐	161 Paul Stanton	.50
☐	162 Christian Lukes	.30
☐	163 Bob Nardella	.30
☐	164 Alexander Erdmann	.30
☐	165 Stéphane J.G. Richer	.50
☐	166 Martin Ulrich	.30
☐	167 Mike Pellegrims	.30
☐	168 Mario Gehrig	.30
☐	169 Pavel Gross	.30
☐	170 Dave Tomlinson	.50
☐	171 Daniel Korber	.30
☐	172 François Guay	.30
☐	173 Jochen Hecht	3.50
☐	174 Florian Keller	.30
☐	175 Till Feser	.30
☐	176 Alexander Serikov	.30
☐	177 Christian Pouget	.30
☐	178 Dieter Kalt	.30
☐	179 Paul Beraldo	.30
☐	180 Steven Thornton	.30
☐	181 Robert Cimetta	.50
☐	182 Gary Clark, Coach	.30
☐	183 Björn Leonhardt	.30
☐	184 Klaus Dalpiaz (G)	.30
☐	185 Jesper Duus	.30
☐	186 Manuel Hiemer	.30
☐	187 Markus Pottinger	.30
☐	188 Chris Bartolone	.30
☐	189 Christian Gegenfurth	.30
☐	190 Heinrich Schiffl	.30
☐	191 Per Lundell	.30
☐	192 Joel Savage	.50
☐	193 Josef Muller	.30
☐	194 Jari Torkki	.30
☐	195 Jim Hiller	.50
☐	196 Doug Derraugh	.30
☐	197 Pekka Tirkkonen	.30
☐	198 Martin Reichel	.30
☐	199 Raimond Hilger	.30
☐	200 Michael Schneidawind	.30
☐	201 Scott Beattie	.30
☐	202 Paris Proft	.30
☐	203 Kevin Gaudet, Coach	.30
☐	204 Wayne Cowley	.30
☐	205 Marco Herbst	.30
☐	206 Andreas Schubert	.30
☐	207 Stephan Sinner	.30
☐	208 Heinrich Synowietz	.30
☐	209 Paul Synowietz	.30
☐	210 Dmitri Frolov	.30
☐	211 Andrei Saposhnikov	.30
☐	212 Jedrzej Kasperczyk	.30
☐	213 Joseph West	.30
☐	214 Fabian Ahrens	.30
☐	215 Maurice Lemay	.30
☐	216 Mark Kosturik	.30
☐	217 Mark Jooris	.30
☐	218 Len Soccio	.30
☐	219 Mark Mahon	.30
☐	220 Frank LaScala	.30
☐	221 Jari Pasanen	.30
☐	222 Ralph Vos	.30
☐	223 Anthony Circelli	.30
☐	224 Emilio Iovio	.30
☐	225 Gerhard Brunner, Coach	.30
☐	226 Pavel Cagas	.30
☐	227 Jonas Eriksson	.30
☐	228 Alexander Engel	.30
☐	229 Greg Johnston	.50
☐	230 Alexander Wedl	.30
☐	231 Jouni Vento	.30
☐	232 Roger Öhman	.30
☐	233 Dave Morrison	.30
☐	234 Bruce Eakin	.30
☐	235 Mike Millar	.30
☐	236 Roger Hansson	.30
☐	237 Peter Kwasigroch	.30
☐	238 Branjo Heisig	.30
☐	239 Jukka Seppo	.30
☐	240 Greg Evtushevski	.30
☐	241 Falk Ozellis	.30
☐	242 Daniel Larin	.30
☐	243 Tino Boos	.30
☐	244 Toni Krinner	.30
☐	245 Milan Mokros	.30
☐	246 Peter Ustorf, Coach	.30
☐	247 Klaus Merk (G)	.30
☐	248 David Berge	.30
☐	249 Georg Holzmann	.30
☐	250 Tom O'Regan	.30
☐	251 Jochen Molling	.30
☐	252 Josef Lehner	.30
☐	253 Marco Rentzsch	.30
☐	254 Pekka Laksola	.30
☐	255 Petri Matikainen	.30
☐	256 Tony Tanti	.50
☐	257 Gaetan Malo	.30
☐	258 Thomas Schinko	.30
☐	259 Vitali Karamnov	.50
☐	260 Günter Oswald	.30
☐	261 Christian Brittig	.30
☐	262 Jürgen Rumrich	.30
☐	263 John Chabot	.50
☐	264 Andreas Dimbat	.30
☐	265 Mark Teevens	.30
☐	266 Veli-Pekka Kautonen	.30
☐	267 Jarmo-Sakari Peltonen	.30
☐	268 Hardy Nilsson, Coach	.30
☐	269 Martin Karlsson, A. Coach	.30
☐	270 Åke Lilljebjörn	.30
☐	271 Kai Fischer	.50
☐	272 Brad Bergen	.30
☐	273 Andreas Niederberger	.30
☐	274 Sergei Sorokin	.30
☐	275 Robert Sterflinger	.30
☐	276 Peter** Andersson	.50
☐	277 Viktor Gordiouk	.50
☐	278 Gord Sherven	.30
☐	279 Benoît Doucet	.30
☐	280 Bernd Kühnhauser	.30
☐	281 Dieter Hegen	.50
☐	282 Andreas Brockmann	.30
☐	283 Ernst Köpf	.50
☐	284 Alexei Kudashov	.50
☐	285 Bernd Truntschka	.30
☐	286 Mikko Mäkelä	.50
☐	287 Niki Mondt	.30
☐	288 Boris Lingemann	.30
☐	289 Thomas Brandl	.30
☐	290 Leo Stefan	.30
☐	291 Bob Burns, Coach	.30
☐	292 Carsten Solbach	.30
☐	293 Matthias Hoppe	.30
☐	294 Sascha Goc	1.50
☐	295 Gord Hynes	.50
☐	296 Thomas Gaus	.30
☐	297 Brian Tutt	.30
☐	298 Richard Trojan	.30
☐	299 Daniel Nowak	.30
☐	300 Andreas Renz	.30
☐	301 Sana Hassan	.30
☐	302 Alan Young	.30
☐	303 Mike Bader	.30
☐	304 Robert Brezina	.30
☐	305 Wayne Hynes	.30
☐	306 Mark Bassen	.30
☐	307 Andrew Clark	.30
☐	308 Grant Martin	.30
☐	309 Michael Lay	.30
☐	310 Jackson Penney	.30
☐	311 Rich Chernomaz	.30
☐	312 Mark MacKay	.30
☐	313 Vladimir Fedosov	.30
☐	314 Emanuel Viveiros	.30
☐	315 Jan Eysselt, Coach	.30
☐	316 Michel Vallière	.30
☐	317 Stefan Lahn	.30
☐	318 Christian Gerum	.30
☐	319 Heiko Smazal	.30
☐	320 Christian Curth	.30
☐	321 Miroslav Maly	.30
☐	322 Torsten Kienass	.30
☐	323 Thomas Sterflinger	.30
☐	324 Lars Brüggermann	.30
☐	325 Paul Geddes	.30
☐	326 Roland Ramoser	.30
☐	327 Martin Jiranek	.30
☐	328 Stefan Steinbock	.30
☐	329 Martin Ekrt	.30
☐	330 Jurgen Lechl	.30
☐	331 Dion Del Monte	.30
☐	332 Markus Welz	.30
☐	333 Henrik Holscher	.30
☐	334 Otto Sykora	.30
☐	335 Milos Vanik	.30
☐	336 Bob J. Murdoch, Coach	.50
☐	337 Bernd Haake, Coach	.30
☐	338 Josef Heiss (G)	.30
☐	339 Olaf Grundmann	.30
☐	340 Alexander Genze	.30
☐	341 Jörg Mayr	.30
☐	342 Mirco Lüdemann	.30
☐	343 Jayson Meyer	.30
☐	344 Karsten Mende	.30
☐	345 Herbert Hohenberger	.30
☐	346 Joe Cirella	.50
☐	347 Petter Nilsson	.30
☐	348 Jim Montgomery	.50
☐	349 Stefan Mann	.30
☐	350 Luciano Borsato	.50
☐	351 Dwayne Norris	.50
☐	352 Bruno Zarrillo	.30
☐	353 Peter Draisaitl	.30
☐	354 Joe Busillo	.30
☐	355 Andreas Lupzig	.30
☐	356 Rainer Zerwesz	.30
☐	357 Tomas Forslund	.50
☐	358 Tobias Abstreiter	.30
☐	359 Patrik Carnbäck	.50
☐	360 Franz Demmel	.30

1996 - 97 DONRUSS

There are two versions: the regular card and a Press Proof parallel (#/2000).

Complete Set (240 cards):		675.00	20.00
	Player	PP	Reg.
☐ ☐	1 Joe Sakic, Colo.	20.00	.50
☐ ☐	2 Jeremy Roenick, Chic.	10.00	.20
☐ ☐	3 Kirk McLean (G), Vanc.	4.00	.20
☐ ☐	4 Zarley Zalapski, Calg.	2.00	.20
☐ ☐	5 Jyrki Lumme, Vanc.	3.00	.20
☐ ☐	6 Owne Nolan, SanJ.	7.00	.20
☐ ☐	7 Luc Robitaille, NYRa.	10.00	.20
☐ ☐	8 Bob Probert, Chic.	4.00	.20
☐ ☐	9 Ken Baumgartner, Anah.	2.00	.20
☐ ☐	10 Rick Tabaracci (G), Calg.	2.00	.20
☐ ☐	11 Alexei Zhitnik, Buff.	2.00	.20
☐ ☐	12 Al MacInnis, SLou.	5.00	.20
☐ ☐	13 Brian Leetch, NYRa.	7.00	.20
☐ ☐	14 Valeri Kamensky, Col	4.00	.20
☐ ☐	15 Todd Gill, Toro.	2.00	.20
☐ ☐	16 Mark Messier, NYRa.	10.00	.50
☐ ☐	17 Pierre Turgeon, Mont.	5.00	.20
☐ ☐	18 Mathieu Schneider, Toro.	3.00	.20
☐ ☐	19 Vyacheslav Kozlov, Detr.	3.00	.20
☐ ☐	20 Milos Holan, Anah.	2.00	.20
☐ ☐	21 Yanic Perreault, LosA.	4.00	.20
☐ ☐	22 Mike Modano, Dall.	10.00	.50
☐ ☐	23 Claude Lemieux, Colo.	4.00	.20
☐ ☐	24 Rob Niedermayer, Flor.	3.00	.20
☐ ☐	25 Éric Desjardins, Phil.	4.00	.20
☐ ☐	26 Alexander Semak, NYIs.	2.00	.20
☐ ☐	27 Mark Recchi, Mont.	5.00	.20
☐ ☐	28 Viacheslav Fetisov, Detr.	7.00	.20
☐ ☐	29 Kevin Hatcher, Dall.	2.00	.20
☐ ☐	30 Mats Sundin, Toro.	10.00	.50
☐ ☐	31 Jeff Reese (G), Tamp.	2.00	.20
☐ ☐	32 Alexander Selivanov, Tamp.	2.00	.20
☐ ☐	33 Jim Carey (G), Wash.	2.00	.20

34 Daren Puppa (G), Tamp.	3.00	.20
35 Vincent Damphousse, Mont.	7.00	.20
36 John LeClair, Phil.	10.00	.20
37 Jon Casey (G), SLou.	2.00	.20
38 Chris Terreri (G), SanJ.	2.00	.20
39 Larry Murphy, Toro.	3.00	.20
40 Geoff Sanderson, Hart.	3.00	.20
41 Adam Oates, Bost.	5.00	.20
42 Sandy McCarthy, Detr.	2.00	.20
43 Jaromir Jagr, Pitt.	10.00	.50
44 Roman Oksiuta, Anah.	2.00	.20
45 Zigmund Palffy, NYIs.	7.00	.20
46 Doug Gilmour, Toro.	7.00	.20
47 Cliff Ronning, Vanc.	3.00	.20
48 Curtis Leschyshyn, Colo.	2.00	.20
49 Scott Mellanby, Flor.	3.00	.20
50 Sergei Fedorov, Detr.	10.00	.50
51 Denis Savard, Chic.	5.00	.20
52 Mike Vernon (G), Detr.	5.00	.20
53 Todd Marchant, Edmo.	3.00	.20
54 Geoff Courtnall, SLou.	2.00	.20
55 Shayne Corson, SLou.	4.00	.20
56 Dimitri Khristich, LosA.	2.00	.20
57 Scott Stevens, NJer.	5.00	.20
58 German Titov, Calg.	2.00	.20
59 Darren Turcotte, SanJ.	2.00	.20
60 Michal Pivonka, Wash.	2.00	.20
61 Ron Hextall (G), Phil.	7.00	.20
62 Ed Belfour (G), Chic.	10.00	.50
63 Chris Pronger, SLou.	7.00	.20
64 Brian Bellows, Tamp.	3.00	.20
65 Pavel Bure, Vanc.	10.00	.20
66 Adam Graves, NYRa.	5.00	.20
67 Tom Barrasso (G), Pitt.	5.00	.20
68 Stu Barnes, Flor.	2.00	.20
69 Norm Maciver, Winn.	2.00	.20
70 Jesse Belanger, Vanc.	2.00	.20
71 Chris Chelios, Chic.	7.00	.20
72 Tommy Söderström (G), NYIs.	2.00	.20
73 Nelson Emerson, Winn.	2.00	.20
74 Kenny Jönsson, NYIs.	2.00	.20
75 Bill Lindsay, Flor.	2.00	.20
76 Petr Nedved, Pitt.	4.00	.20
77 Robert Svehla, Flor.	3.00	.20
78 Tomas Sandström, Pitt.	3.00	.20
79 Jeff Friesen, SanJ.	4.00	.20
80 Tony Amonte, Chic.	7.00	.20
81 Sylvain Lefebvre, Colo.	2.00	.20
82 Greg Adams, Dall.	2.00	.20
83 Vladimir Konstantinov, Detr.	4.00	.20
84 Roman Hamrlik, Tamp.	3.00	.20
85 Doug Weight, Edmo.	5.00	.20
86 Shaun Van Allen, Anah.	2.00	.20
87 Bill Ranford (G), Bost.	5.00	.20
88 Jeff Hackett, Chic.	4.00	.20
89 Alexei Zhamnov, Winn.	4.00	.20
90 Dale Hawerchuk, Phil.	7.00	.20
91 Sergei Zubov, Pitt.	3.00	.20
92 Dan Quinn, Phil.	2.00	.20
93 Wayne Gretzky, SLou.	60.00	2.00
94 Todd Harvey, Dall.	3.00	.20
95 Chris Osgood (G), Detr.	5.00	.20
96 Félix Potvin (G), Toro.	7.00	.20
97 Richard Matvichuk, Dall.	3.00	.20
98 Wendel Clark, Toro.	10.00	.20
99 Bryan Smolinski, Pitt.	2.00	.20
100 Rob Blake, LosA.	7.00	.20
101 Jocelyn Thibault (G), Mont.	5.00	.20
102 Trevor Linden, Vanc.	5.00	.20
103 Craig MacTavish, Phil.	2.00	.20
104 Sandis Ozolinsh, Colo.	3.00	.20
105 Oleg Tverdovsky, Winn.	2.00	.20
106 Garry Galley, Buff.	2.00	.20
107 Derek Plante, Buff.	2.00	.20
108 Stéphane Richer, NJer.	3.00	.20
109 Dave Andreychuk, NJer.	4.00	.20
110 Curtis Joseph (G), Edmo.	10.00	.50
111 Greg Johnson, Detr.	2.00	.20
112 Patrick Roy (G), Colo.	45.00	1.50
113 Pat LaFontaine, Buff.	7.00	.20
114 Uwe Krupp, Colo.	2.00	.20
115 Ulf Dahlen, SanJ.	2.00	.20
116 Brian Bradley, Tamp.	2.00	.20
117 Grant Fuhr (G), SLou.	7.00	.20
118 Brian Skrudland, Flor.	2.00	.20
119 Nicklas Lidström, Detr.	7.00	.20
120 Steve Chiasson, Calg.	2.00	.20
121 Sean Burke (G), Hart.	7.00	.20
122 Rick Tocchet, Bost.	4.00	.20
123 Martin Rucinsky, Mont.	3.00	.20
124 Alexei Yashin, Otta.	7.00	.20
125 Mikael Renberg, Phil.	4.00	.20
126 Teppo Numminen, Winn.	4.00	.20
127 Randy Burridge, Buff.	2.00	.20
128 Radek Bonk, Otta.	4.00	.20
129 Scott Young, Colo.	4.00	.20
130 Gary Suter, Chic.	3.00	.20
131 Mario Lemieux, Pitt.	40.00	1.50
132 Raymond Bourque, Bost.	15.00	.50
133 Martin Gelinas, Vanc.	3.00	.20
134 Keith Tkachuk, Winn.	5.00	.20
135 Benoît Hogue, Dall.	2.00	.20
136 Ken Wregget (G), Pitt.	3.00	.20
137 Eric Lindros, Phil.	10.00	.50
138 Keith Primeau, Detr.	5.00	.20
139 Peter Forsberg, Colo.	20.00	.50
140 Paul Coffey, Detr.	5.00	.20
141 Mike Ridley, Vanc.	2.00	.20
142 Paul Kariya, Anah.	20.00	.50
143 Jason Arnott, Edmo.	6.00	.20
144 Joe Murphy, Chic.	2.00	.20
145 Adam Deadmarsh, Colo.	4.00	.20
146 John MacLean, NJer.	2.00	.20
147 Peter Bondra, Wash.	7.00	.20
148 Martin Brodeur (G), NJer.	20.00	.50
149 Ron Francis, Pitt.	7.00	.20
150 Dino Ciccarelli, Detr.	4.00	.20
151 Joé Juneau, Wash.	3.00	.20
152 Matthew Barnaby, Buff.	2.00	.20
153 Mark Tinordi, Wash.	2.00	.20
154 Craig Janney, Winn.	3.00	.20
155 Rod Brind'Amour, Phil.	4.00	.20
156 Damian Rhodes (G), Otta.	3.00	.20
157 Teemu Selänne, Anah.	10.00	.20
158 James Patrick, Calg.	2.00	.20
159 Theoren Fleury, Calg.	5.00	.20
160 Trevor Kidd (G), Calg.	4.00	.20
161 Kirk Muller, Toro.	4.00	.20
162 Andrew Cassels, Hart.	3.00	.20
163 Brent Fedyk, Dall.	2.00	.20
164 Guy Hebert (G), Anah.	3.00	.20
165 Jason Dawe, Buff.	2.00	.20
166 Andy Moog (G), Dall.	5.00	.20
167 Igor Larionov, Detr.	7.00	.20
168 Brian Savage, Mont.	4.00	.20
169 Kris Draper, Detr.	3.00	.20
170 Dave Gagner, Toro.	2.00	.20
171 Steve Yzerman, Detr.	30.00	1.00
172 Nikolai Khabibulin (G), Winn.	5.00	.20
173 Chris Gratton, Tamp.	3.00	.20
174 Dave Lowry, Flor.	3.00	.20
175 Travis Green, NYIs.	3.00	.20
176 Alexei Kovalev, NYRa.	7.00	.20
177 Mike Ricci, Colo.	4.00	.20
178 Brendan Shanahan, Hart.	10.00	.50
179 Corey Hirsch (G), Vanc.	2.00	.20
180 Bill Guerin, NJer.	5.00	.20
181 Alexander Mogilny, Vanc.	6.00	.20
182 Steve Duchesne, Otta.	3.00	.20
183 Ray Ferraro, LosA.	2.00	.20
184 Mike Richter (G), NYRa.	6.00	.20
185 Yuri Khmylev, SLou.	2.00	.20
186 Stéphane Fiset (G), Colo.	4.00	.20
187 John Vanbiesbrouck (G), Flor.	6.00	.20
188 Scott Niedermayer, NJer.	4.00	.20
189 Brad May, Buff.	2.00	.20
190 Shawn McEachern, Bost.	4.00	.20
191 Joe Mullen, Bost.	5.00	.20
192 Dominik Hasek (G), Buff.	10.00	.50
193 Steve Thomas, NJer.	3.00	.20
194 Russ Courtnall, Vanc.	3.00	.20
195 Joe Nieuwendyk, Dall.	5.00	.20
196 Petr Klima, Tamp.	2.00	.20
197 Brett Hull, SLou.	10.00	.50
198 Bernie Nicholls, Chic.	3.00	.20
199 Dale Hunter, Wash.	4.00	.20
200 Pat Verbeek, NYRa.	4.00	.20
201 Phil Housley, NJer.	4.00	.20
202 Todd Krygier, Anah.	2.00	.20
203 Zdeno Ciger, Edmo.	2.00	.20
204 Alexandre Daigle, Otta.	2.00	.20
205 Cam Neely, Bost.	10.00	.50
206 Mike Gartner, Toro.	10.00	.20
207 Garth Snow (G), Phil.	4.00	.20
208 Pat Falloon, Phil.	2.00	.20
209 Kelly Hrudey (G), LosA.	4.00	.20
210 Ray Sheppard, Flor.	2.00	.20
211 Ted Donato, Bost.	2.00	.20
212 Glenn Healy (G), NYRa.	3.00	.20
213 Radek Dvorak, Flor.	3.00	.20
214 Niclas Andersson, NYIs.	2.00	.20
215 Miroslav Satan, Edmo.	4.00	.20
216 R. Vopat, LosA., Err. (Jan Vopat)	2.00	.20
217 Bryan McCabe, NYIs.	3.00	.20
218 Jamie Langenbrunner, Dall.	3.00	.20
219 Kyle McLaren, Bost.	3.00	.20
220 Stéphane Yelle, Colo.	2.00	.20
221 Byron Dafoe (G), LosA.	5.00	.20
222 Grant Marshall, Dall.	2.00	.20
223 Ryan Smyth, Edmo.	6.00	.20
224 Ville Peltonen, SanJ.	2.00	.20
225 Deron Quint, Winn.	2.00	.20
226 Brian Holzinger, Buff.	2.00	.20
227 José Théodore, Mont.	15.00	1.00
228 Ethan Moreau, Chic.	2.00	.20
229 Steve Sullivan, NJer. RC	**10.00**	**1.00**
230 Kevin Hodson (G), Detr.	3.00	.20
231 Cory Stillman, Calg.	3.00	.20
232 Ralph Intranuovo, Edmo.	2.00	.20
233 Vital Yachmenev, LosA.	2.00	.20
234 Marcus Ragnarsson, SanJ.	3.00	.20
235 Nolan Baumgartner, Wash.	2.00	.20
236 Chad Kilger, Winn.	3.00	.20
237 Niklas Sundström, NYRa.	3.00	.20
238 CL: Paul Coffey, Detr.	4.00	.20
239 CL: Doug Gilmour, Toro.	4.00	.20
240 CL: Steve Yzerman, Detr.	15.00	.50

BETWEEN THE PIPES

Insert Set (10 cards):	125.00
Insert (#/4000)	BTP
1 Patrick Roy (G), Colo.	45.00
2 Martin Brodeur (G), NJer.	24.00
3 Jim Carey (G), Wash.	8.00
4 John Vanbiesbrouck (G), Flor.	8.00
5 Chris Osgood (G), Detr.	9.00
6 Ed Belfour (G), Chic.	15.00
7 Jocelyn Thibault (G), Mont.	8.00
8 Curtis Joseph (G), Edmo.	15.00
9 Nikolai Khabibulin (G), Winn. (Phoe.)	8.00
10 Félix Potvin (G), Toro.	9.00

DOMINATORS

Insert Set (10 cards):	95.00
Insert (#/5000)	Dom.
1 Brodeur (G) / Carey (G) / Vanbiesbrouck (G)	10.00
2 Khabibulin (G) / Osgood (G) / Thibault (G)	8.00
3 R. Bourque / C. Chelios / P. Coffey	10.00
4 R. Francis / J. Jagr / M. Lemieux	20.00
5 J. Arnott / W. Gretzky / E. Lindros	25.00
6 W. Clark / D. Gilmour / P. Turgeon	8.00
7 P. Bure / T. Linden / A. Mogilny	8.00
8 P. Kariya / T. Selänne / K. Tkachuk	10.00
9 S. Fedorov / J. Roenick / M. Modano	10.00
10 É. Dazé / E. Jovanovski / S. Koivu	8.00

ELITE SERIES

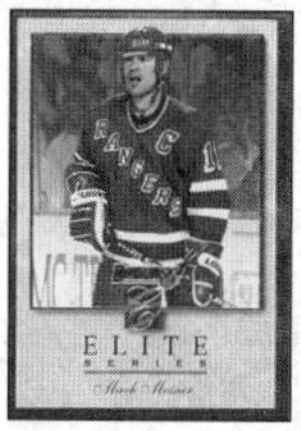

There are two versions: the silver insert (#/10,000) and the Gold insert (#/1,500).

Insert Set (10 cards):	235.00	80.00
Inserts	ESG	ES
1 Pavel Bure, Vanc.	15.00	6.00
2 Wayne Gretzky, SLou. (NYRa.)	75.00	25.00
3 Doug Weight, Edmo.	12.00	6.00
4 Brett Hull, SLou.	18.00	6.00
5 Mark Messier, NYRa.	18.00	6.00
6 Brendan Shanahan, Hart.	18.00	6.00
7 Joe Sakic, Colo.	30.00	10.00
8 Sergei Fedorov, Detr.	18.00	6.00
9 Eric Lindros, Phil.	18.00	6.00
10 Patrick Roy (G), Colo.	56.00	18.00

GO TOP SHELF

Insert Set (10 cards):	160.00
Insert (#/2000)	GTS
1 Mario Lemieux, Pitt.	45.00
2 Teemu Selänne, Anah.	12.00
3 Joe Sakic, Colo.	24.00
4 Alexander Mogilny, Vanc.	12.00
5 Jaromir Jagr, Pitt.	14.00
6 Brett Hull, SLou.	14.00
7 Mike Modano, Dall.	14.00
8 Paul Kariya, Anah.	20.00
9 Eric Lindros, Phil.	14.00
10 Peter Forsberg, Colo.	20.00

HIT LIST

Insert Set (20 cards):	80.00
Insert (#/10,000)	HL
1 Eric Lindros, Phil.	7.00
2 Wendel Clark, Toro.	6.00
3 Ed Jovanovski, Flor.	3.00
4 Jeremy Roenick, Chic.	6.00
5 Doug Weight, Edmo.	4.00
6 Chris Chelios, Chic.	4.00
7 Brendan Shanahan, Hart.	7.00
8 Mark Messier, NYRa.	7.00
9 Scott Stevens, NJer.	3.00
10 Keith Tkachuk, Winn.	4.00
11 Trevor Linden, Vanc.	3.00
12 Éric Dazé, Chic.	3.00
13 John LeClair, Phil.	6.00
14 Peter Forsberg, Colo.	10.00
15 Doug Gilmour, Toro.	4.00
16 Roman Hamrlik, Tamp.	2.00
17 Owen Nolan, SanJ.	4.00
18 Claude Lemieux, Colo.	2.00
19 Saku Koivu, Mont.	6.00
20 Theoren Fleury, Calg.	4.00

RATED ROOKIES

There are two versions: the regular card and a Press Proof parallel (not inserted into packs).

Insert Set (10 cards):	40.00
Inserts	RR
1 Éric Dazé, Chic.	4.00
2 Petr' Sykora, NJer.	4.00
3 Valeri Bure, Mont.	3.00
4 Jere Lehtinen, Dall.	3.00
5 Jeff O'Neill, Hart.	4.00
6 Saku Koivu, Mont.	8.00
7 Ed Jovanovski, Flor.	4.00
8 Éric Fichaud (G), NYIs.	2.00
9 Todd Bertuzzi, NYIs.	12.00
10 Daniel Alfredsson, Otta.	6.00

1996 - 97 DONRUSS CANADIAN ICE

There are three versions: the regular card, the Canadian Red parallel (#/750) and the Canadian Gold parallel (#/150). Promo versions with clipped versions also exist.

Complete Set (150 cards):	2400.00	725.00	35.00
Common Player:	6.00	3.00	.25
Player	CG150	CR750	DCI
1 Jaromir Jagr, Pitt.	50.00	15.00	1.00
2 J. Thibault (G), Mont.	20.00	5.00	.25
3 Paul Kariya, Anah.	70.00	25.00	1.00
4 Derian Hatcher, Dall.	15.00	5.00	.25
5 Wayne Gretzky, NYRa.	250.00	70.00	4.00
6 Peter Forsberg, Colo.	70.00	25.00	1.00
7 Eric Lindros, Phil.	50.00	15.00	1.00
8 Adam Oates, Bost.	20.00	5.00	.25
9 Paul Coffey, Hart.	30.00	10.00	.50
10 Chris Osgood (G), Detr.	30.00	10.00	.50
11 Pat LaFontaine, Buff.	30.00	10.00	.50
12 Mats Sundin, Toro.	50.00	15.00	1.00
13 Rob Niedermayer, Flor.	10.00	4.00	.25
14 Doug Weight, Edmo.	30.00	10.00	.50
15 Al MacInnis, SLou.	20.00	5.00	.25
16 D. Rhodes (G), Otta.	10.00	4.00	.25
17 S. Fiset (G), LosA.	15.00	6.00	.25
18 Mike Gartner, Phoe.	40.00	15.00	.50
19 P. Roy (G), Colo.	170.00	50.00	3.00
20 Eric Dazé, Chic.	20.00	7.00	.25
21 R. Bourque, Bost.	60.00	20.00	1.00
22 Keith Tkachuk, Phoe.	30.00	10.00	.50
23 Mark Recchi, Mont.	20.00	5.00	.25
24 Peter Bondra, Wash.	30.00	10.00	.50
25 Mike Modano, Dall.	50.00	15.00	1.00
26 Mike Richter (G), NYRa.	20.00	5.00	.25
27 Keith Primeau, Hart.	20.00	5.00	.25
28 Todd Bertuzzi, NYIs.	60.00	20.00	2.00
29 Wendel Clark, Toro.	40.00	15.00	.50
30 Scott Young, Colo.	15.00	5.00	.25
31 Mario Lemieux, Pitt.	170.00	50.00	3.00
32 Valeri Kamensky, Colo.	15.00	5.00	.25
33 Kirk McLean (G), Vanc.	15.00	5.00	.25
34 Daniel Alfredsson, Otta.	30.00	10.00	.50
35 Ed Jovanovski, Flor.	20.00	7.00	.25
36 Kelly Hrudey (G), SanJ.	15.00	5.00	.25
37 Trevor Kidd (G), Calg.	15.00	5.00	.25
38 Joé Juneau, Wash.	10.00	4.00	.25
39 Steve Yzerman, Detr.	120.00	45.00	2.00
40 Saku Koivu, Mont.	40.00	15.00	.50
41 Alexei Kovalev, NYRa.	30.00	10.00	.50
42 Rob Blake, LosA.	30.00	10.00	.50
43 Shayne Corson, SLou.	15.00	5.00	.25
44 Roman Hamrlik, Tamp.	10.00	4.00	.25
45 Stéphane Yelle, Colo.	8.00	3.00	.25
46 M. Brodeur (G), NJer.	80.00	30.00	1.50
47 Kirk Muller, Toro.	15.00	5.00	.25
48 Pat Verbeek, Dall.	15.00	5.00	.25
49 Jari Kurri, Anah.	50.00	15.00	1.00
50 Michal Pivonka, Wash.	6.00	3.00	.25
51 Ron Hextall (G), Phil.	30.00	10.00	.50
52 Trevor Linden, Vanc.	20.00	5.00	.25
53 V. Damphousse, Mont.	30.00	10.00	.50
54 Owen Nolan, SanJ.	30.00	10.00	.50
55 Sergei Fedorov, Detr.	50.00	15.00	1.00
56 Chris Chelios, Chic.	30.00	10.00	.50
57 Jeremy Roenick, Phoe.	40.00	15.00	.50
58 Zigmund Palffy, NYIs.	30.00	10.00	.50
59 Pavel Bure, Vanc.	40.00	15.00	.50
60 D. Hasek (G), Buff.	50.00	15.00	1.00
61 Alexei Yashin, Otta.	30.00	10.00	.50
62 Chris Gratton, Tamp.	10.00	4.00	.25
63 Joe Nieuwendyk, Dall.	20.00	5.00	.25
64 Luc Robitaille, NYRa.	40.00	15.00	.50
65 Brett Hull, SLou.	50.00	15.00	1.00
66 Sean Burke (G), Hart.	30.00	10.00	.50
67 Félix Potvin (G), Toro.	30.00	10.00	.50
68 Jason Arnott, Edmo.	20.00	5.00	.25
69 Valeri Bure, Mont.	15.00	5.00	.25
70 T. Barrasso (G), Pitt.	20.00	5.00	.25
71 Vy. Kozlov, Detr.	10.00	4.00	.25
72 Petr Sykora, NJer.	20.00	5.00	.25
73 Corey Hirsch (G), Vanc.	8.00	3.00	.25
74 Joe Sakic, Colo.	80.00	30.00	1.50
75 Bill Ranford (G), Bost.	20.00	5.00	.25
76 Yanic Perreault, LosA.	15.00	6.00	.25
77 Mikael Renberg, Phil.	15.00	5.00	.25
78 Theoren Fleury, Calg.	30.00	10.00	.50
79 Jim Carey (G), Wash.	6.00	3.00	.25
80 Vitali Yachmenev, LosA.	8.00	3.00	.25
81 Martin Rucinsky, Mont.	10.00	4.00	.25
82 Jeff O'Neill, Hart.	20.00	5.00	.25
83 M. Ragnarsson, SanJ.	10.00	4.00	.25
84 Vanbiesbrouck (G), Flor.	20.00	5.00	.25
85 Teemu Selänne, Anah.	40.00	15.00	.50
86 Larry Murphy, Toro.	10.00	4.00	.25
87 Mark Messier, NYRa.	50.00	15.00	1.00
88 Alexei Zhamnov, Chic.	15.00	5.00	.25
89 Ryan Smith, Edmo.	20.00	5.00	.25
90 Andy Moog (G), Dall.	20.00	5.00	.25
91 A. Mogilny, Vanc.	20.00	5.00	.25
92 Kris Draper, Detr.	12.00	4.00	.25
93 Ron Francis, Pitt.	30.00	10.00	.50
94 Mike Vernon (G), Detr.	20.00	5.00	.25
95 N. Khabibulin (G), Phoe.	20.00	5.00	.25
96 M. Czerkawski, Edmo.	10.00	4.00	.25
97 Mathieu Schneider, Toro.	10.00	4.00	.25
98 Stéphane Richer, Mont.	10.00	4.00	.25
99 Mike Ricci, Colo.	15.00	5.00	.25
100 John LeClair, Phil.	40.00	15.00	.50
101 B. Shanahan, Detr.	50.00	15.00	1.00
102 D. Puppa (G), Tamp.	10.00	4.00	.25
103 Scott Stevens, NJer.	20.00	5.00	.25
104 Alexandre Daigle, Otta.	8.00	3.00	.25
105 Dimitri Khristich, LosA.	8.00	3.00	.25
106 Bernie Nicholls, SanJ.	10.00	4.00	.25
107 Scott Mellanby, Flor.	10.00	4.00	.25
108 Brian Leetch, NYRa.	30.00	10.00	.50
109 Grant Fuhr (G), SLou.	30.00	10.00	.50
110 Pierre Turgeon, Mont.	20.00	5.00	.25

□□□ 111 Jere Lehtinen, Dal	15.00	5.00	.25
□□□ 112 Doug Gilmour, Toro.	30.00	10.00	.50
□□□ 113 Ed Belfour (G), Chic.	50.00	15.00	1.00
□□□ 114 Geoff Sanderson, Hart.	10.00	4.00	.25
□□□ 115 Claude Lemieux, Colo.	15.00	5.00	.25
□□□ 116 Cu. Joseph (G), Edmo.	50.00	15.00	1.00
□□□ 117 Igor Larionov, Detr.	30.00	10.00	.50
□□□ 118 Jamie Pushor, Detr.	6.00	3.00	.25
□□□ **119 S. Berezin, Toro. RC**	**20.00**	**5.00**	**1.50**
□□□ 120 Éric Fichaud (G), NYIs.	8.00	3.00	.25
□□□ 121 Wade Redden, Otta.	15.00	6.00	.50
□□□ 122 Domenichelli, Hart.	8.00	3.00	.25
□□□ **123 R. Murray, Edmo. RC**	**10.00**	**3.00**	**.50**
□□□ 124 Jarome Iginla, Calg.	40.00	15.00	1.50
□□□ **125 R. Zednik, Wash. RC**	**40.00**	**15.00**	**2.50**
□□□ **126 D. Goneau, NYRa. RC**	**6.00**	**3.00**	**.50**
□□□ 127 Ethan Moreau, Chic.	8.00	3.00	.25
□□□ 128 Janne Niinimaa, Phil.	10.00	4.00	.25
□□□ **129 Holmström, Detr. RC**	**20.00**	**5.00**	**1.50**
□□□ **130 Modin, Toro. RC**	**20.00**	**5.00**	**1.50**
□□□ 131 Bryan Berard, NYIs.	15.00	6.00	.50
□□□ 132 Jim Campbell, Stl	6.00	3.00	.25
□□□ 133 Chris O'Sullivan, Calg.	6.00	3.00	.25
□□□ **134 A. Dackell, Otta. RC**	**15.00**	**5.00**	**1.00**
□□□ 135 D. Langkow, Tamp.	10.00	4.00	.25
□□□ 136 K. Hodson (G), Detr.	12.00	4.00	.25
□□□ 137 Langenbrunner, Dall.	10.00	4.00	.25
□□□ **138 M.Timander, Bost. RC**	**10.00**	**3.00**	**.50**
□□□ 139 T. Grönman, Chic.	6.00	3.00	.25
□□□ 140 Jonas Hoglund, Calg.	8.00	3.00	.25
□□□ **141 M. Grier, Edmo. RC**	**20.00**	**5.00**	**1.50**
□□□ **142 T. Ryan, Mont. RC**	**10.00**	**3.00**	**.50**
□□□ 143 Darcy Tucker, Mont.	10.00	4.00	.25
□□□ 144 Brandon Convery, Toro.	6.00	3.00	.25
□□□ 145 Anders Eriksson, Detr.	6.00	3.00	.25
□□□ 146 Christian Dubé, NYRa.	8.00	3.00	.25
□□□ **147 D. Zubrus, Phil. RC**	**20.00**	**5.00**	**1.50**
□□□ 148 CL: Grant Fuhr, SLou.	15.00	5.00	.25
□□□ 149 CL: Paul Coffey, Hart.	15.00	5.00	.25
□□□ 150 CL: R. Bourque, Bost.	30.00	10.00	.50

LES GARDIENS

There are two versions: the insert (#/1500) and the promo version.

Complete Set (10 cards):	15.00	175.00
Player	Promo	Insert
□□ 1 Patrick Roy (G), Colo.	7.00	60.00
□□ 2 Jocelyn Thibault (G), Mont.	1.00	12.00
□□ 3 Félix Potvin (G), Toro.	1.00	12.00
□□ 4 Martin Brodeur (G), NJer.	4.00	30.00
□□ 5 Stéphane Fiset (G), LosA.	1.00	12.00
□□ 6 Éric Fichaud (G), NYIs.	1.00	12.00
□□ 7 Dominic Roussel, Phil.	1.00	12.00
□□ 8 Manny Fernandez, Dall.	1.00	12.00
□□ 9 Martin Biron, Buff.	1.00	12.00
□□ 10 José Théodore, Mont.	3.00	35.00

O CANADA

Insert Set (16 cards):	225.00
Insert (#/2000)	OC
□ 1 Joe Sakic, Colo.	24.00
□ 2 Paul Kariya, Anah.	20.00
□ 3 Mark Messier, NYRa.	15.00
□ 4 Jarome Iginla, Calg.	12.00
□ 5 Theoren Fleury, Calg.	9.00
□ 6 Ed Belfour (G), Chic.	15.00
□ 7 Wayne Gretzky, NYRa.	60.00
□ 8 Chris Gratton, Tamp.	6.00
□ 9 Doug Gilmour, Toro.	9.00
□ 10 Kirk Muller, Toro.	6.00
□ 11 Eric Lindros, Phil.	15.00
□ 12 Brendan Shanahan, Detr.	15.00
□ 13 Mario Lemieux, Pitt.	45.00
□ 14 Éric Dazé, Chic.	6.00
□ 15 Geoff Sanderson, Hart.	6.00
□ 16 Terry Ryan, Mont.	6.00

SCRAPBOOK

Complete Set (25 cards):	250.00
Framed Set:	250.00
Player	LS
□ 1 Mario Lemieux, Pitt. [10/11/1984]	12.00
□ 2 Mario Lemieux, Awards (Pitt.) [Calder]	12.00
□ 3 Mario Lemieux, All-Star '(Pitt.) [Sweater]	12.00
□ 4 Mario Lemieux, All-Star '(Pitt.) [Sweater]	12.00
□ 5 Mario Lemieux, Pitt. [w/ Stanley Cup]	12.00
□ 6 Mario Lemieux, All-Star (Pitt.) [Sweater]	12.00
□ 7 Mario Lemieux, Pitt.	12.00
□ 8 Mario Lemieux, NHL All-Star '	12.00
□ 9 Mario Lemieux, Pitt.	12.00
□ 10 Mario Lemieux, Pitt. [cameo: J.Jagr]	12.00
□ 11 Mario Lemieux, Pitt.	12.00
□ 12 Mario Lemieux, Pitt. [vs. M.Richter]	12.00
□ 13 Mario Lemieux, Pitt.	12.00
□ 14 Mario Lemieux, Pitt.	12.00
□ 15 Mario Lemieux, Pitt.	12.00
□ 16 Mario Lemieux, Pitt.	12.00
□ 17 Mario Lemieux, Pitt.	12.00
□ 18 Mario Lemieux, NHL All-Star '	12.00
□ 19 Mario Lemieux, Pitt. [cameo: R.Bourque]	12.00
□ 20 Mario Lemieux, NHL All-Star '	12.00
□ 21 Mario Lemieux, Pitt.	12.00
□ 22 Mario Lemieux, Pitt.	12.00
□ 23 Mario Lemieux, Pitt. [Sweaters]	12.00
□ 24 Mario Lemieux, Pitt.	12.00
□ 25 Mario Lemieux, Pitt.	12.00
□ Mario Lemieux ✍	250.00

1996 - 97 DONRUSS ELITE

There are two versions: the regular card and a Die-Cut parallel.

Complete Set (150 cards):	1200.00	35.00
Common Player:	5.00	.20
Player	DC	Elite
□□ 1 Paul Kariya, Anah.	30.00	1.00
□□ 2 Ron Hextall (G), Phil.	15.00	.50
□□ 3 Andy Moog (G), Dall.	10.00	.20
□□ 4 Brett Hull, SLou.	25.00	1.00
□□ 5 Félix Potvin (G), Toro.	15.00	.50
□□ 6 Jocelyn Thibault (G), Mont.	10.00	.20
□□ 7 Eric Lindros, Phil.	25.00	1.00
□□ 8 Jaromir Jagr, Pitt.	20.00	1.00
□□ 9 Sergei Fedorov, Detr.	25.00	1.00
□□ 10 Wayne Gretzky, NYRa.	100.00	4.00
□□ 11 Peter Bondra, Wash.	15.00	.50
□□ 12 Peter Forsberg, Colo.	35.00	1.00
□□ 13 Stéphane Fiset (G), LosA.	8.00	.20
□□ 14 Owen Nolan, SanJ.	15.00	.50
□□ 15 Rob Niedermayer, Flor.	6.00	.20
□□ 16 Martin Brodeur (G), NJer.	40.00	1.50
□□ 17 Raymond Bourque, Bost.	30.00	1.00
□□ 18 Todd Bertuzzi, NYIs.	30.00	2.00
□□ 19 Jim Carey (G), Wash.	5.00	.20
□□ 20 Chris Chelios, Chic.	15.00	.50
□□ 21 Chris Osgood (G), Detr.	15.00	.50
□□ 22 Mark Messier, NYRa.	25.00	1.00
□□ 23 Roman Hamrlik, Tamp.	6.00	.20
□□ 24 Kevin Hatcher, Pitt.	5.00	.20
□□ 25 Doug Weight, Edmo.	15.00	.50
□□ 26 Mark Recchi, Mont.	10.00	.20
□□ 27 Jeremy Roenick, Phoe.	20.00	.50
□□ 28 Derian Hatcher, Dall.	8.00	.20
□□ 29 Grant Fuhr (G), SLou.	15.00	.50
□□ 30 Scott Stevens, NJer.	10.00	.20
□□ 31 Adam Oates, Bost.	10.00	.20
□□ 32 Scott Mellanby, Flor.	6.00	.20
□□ 33 Mikael Renberg, Phil.	8.00	.20
□□ 34 Corey Hirsch (G), Vanc.	5.00	.20
□□ 35 Mikael Pivonka, Wash.	5.00	.20
□□ 36 Stéphane Richer, Mont.	6.00	.20
□□ 37 Dominik Hasek (G), Buff.	25.00	1.00
□□ 38 Steve Yzerman, Detr.	60.00	2.00
□□ 39 Jeff O'Neill, Hart.	10.00	.20
□□ 40 Ron Francis, Pitt.	15.00	.50
□□ 41 Alexei Yashin, Otta.	15.00	.50
□□ 42 Pat Verbeek, Dall.	8.00	.20
□□ 43 Geoff Courtnall, SLou.	5.00	.20
□□ 44 Doug Gilmour, Toro.	15.00	.50
□□ 45 Trevor Kidd (G), Calg.	8.00	.20
□□ 46 Jason Arnott, Edmo.	10.00	.20
□□ 47 Niklas Sundström, NYRa.	6.00	.20
□□ 48 Rob Blake, LosA.	15.00	.50
□□ 49 Nikolai Khabibulin (G), Phoe.	10.00	.20
□□ 50 Igor Larionov, Detr.	15.00	.50
□□ 51 Sean Burke (G), Hart.	15.00	.50
□□ 52 Zigmund Palffy, NYIs.	15.00	.50
□□ 53 Jeff Friesen, SanJ.	8.00	.20
□□ 54 Theoren Fleury, Calg.	15.00	.50
□□ 55 Mats Sundin, Toro.	25.00	1.00
□□ 56 Alexander Mogilny, Vanc.	10.00	.20
□□ 57 John LeClair, Phil.	20.00	.50
□□ 58 Shayne Corson, Mont.	8.00	.20
□□ 59 Teemu Selänne, Anah.	20.00	.50
□□ 60 Kelly Hrudey (G), SanJ.	8.00	.20
□□ 61 Keith Tkachuk, Phoe.	15.00	.50
□□ 62 Joe Nieuwendyk, Dall.	10.00	.20
□□ 63 Tom Barrasso (G), Pitt.	10.00	.20
□□ 64 Aaron Gavey, Calg.	5.00	.20
□□ 65 Alexei Zhamnov, Chic.	8.00	.20
□□ 66 Patrick Roy (G), Colo.	70.00	3.00
□□ 67 Al MacInnis, SLou.	10.00	.20
□□ 68 Trevor Linden,Vanc.	10.00	.20
□□ 69 Bill Guerin, NJer.	10.00	.20
□□ 70 Dimitri Khristich, LosA.	5.00	.20
□□ 71 Eric Dazé, Chic.	10.00	.20
□□ 72 Paul Coffey, Phil.	15.00	.50
□□ 73 Keith Primeau, Hart.	10.00	.20
□□ 74 John Vanbiesbrouck (G), Flor.	10.00	.20
□□ 75 Bernie Nicholls, SanJ.	6.00	.20
□□ 76 Yanic Perreault, LosA.	8.00	.20
□□ 77 Jere Lehtinen, Dall.	8.00	.20
□□ 78 Luc Robitaille, NYRa.	20.00	.50
□□ 79 Todd Gill, SanJ.	5.00	.20
□□ 80 Saku Koivu, Mont.	20.00	.50
□□ 81 Vyacheslav Kozlov, Detr.	6.00	.20
□□ 82 Ed Jovanovski, Flor.	10.00	.20
□□ 83 Brendan Witt, Wash.	5.00	.20
□□ 84 Alexandre Daigle, Otta.	5.00	.20
□□ 85 Jari Kurri, Anah.	25.00	1.00
□□ 86 Mike Vernon (G), Calg.	10.00	.20
□□ 87 Jeff Beukeboom, NYRa.	5.00	.20
□□ 88 Mathieu Schneider, Toro.	6.00	.20
□□ 89 Niklas Andersson, NYIs.	5.00	.20
□□ 90 Joé Juneau, Wash.	6.00	.20
□□ 91 Ed Belfour (G), SanJ.	25.00	1.00
□□ 92 Curtis Joseph (G), Edmo.	25.00	1.00
□□ 93 Rod Brind'Amour, Phil.	8.00	.20
□□ 94 Vitali Yachmenev, LosA.	5.00	.20
□□ 95 Alexander Selivanov, Tamp.	5.00	.20
□□ 96 Mike Richter (G), NYRa.	10.00	.20
□□ 97 Bill Ranford (G), Bost.	10.00	.20
□□ 98 Wendel Clark,Toro.	20.00	.50
□□ 99 Viacheslav Fetisov, Detr.	15.00	.50
□□ 100 Daniel Alfredsson, Otta.	15.00	.50
□□ 101 Pat LaFontaine, Buff.	15.00	.50
□□ 102 Joe Murphy, SLou.	5.00	.20
□□ 103 Pavel Bure, Vanc.	20.00	.50
□□ 104 Craig Janney, SanJ.	6.00	.20
□□ 105 Radek Dvorak, Flor.	6.00	.20
□□ 106 Cory Stillman, Calg.	6.00	.20
□□ 107 Adam Graves, NYRa.	10.00	.20
□□ 108 Aki Berg, LosA.	5.00	.20
□□ 109 Mario Lemieux, Pitt.	70.00	3.00
□□ 110 Claude Lemieux, Colo.	8.00	.20
□□ 111 Sergei Zubov, Dall.	6.00	.20
□□ 112 Pierre Turgeon, SLou.	10.00	.20
□□ 113 Damian Rhodes (G), Otta.	6.00	.20
□□ 114 Daren Puppa (G), Tamp.	6.00	.20
□□ 115 Alexei Zhitnik, Buff.	5.00	.20
□□ 116 Mike Modano, Dall.	25.00	1.00
□□ 117 Kenny Jönsson, NYIs.	5.00	.20
□□ 118 Valeri Kamensky, Colo.	8.00	.20
□□ 119 Valeri Bure, Mont.	8.00	.20
□□ 120 Joe Sakic, Colo.	40.00	1.50
□□ 121 Kirk McLean (G), Vanc.	8.00	.20
□□ 122 Petr Sykora, NJer.	10.00	.20
□□ 123 Mike Gartner, Phoe.	20.00	.50
□□ 124 Ryan Smyth, Edmo.	10.00	.20
□□ 125 Brian Leetch, NYRa.	15.00	.50
□□ 126 Brendan Shanahan, Detr.	25.00	1.00
□□ 127 Geoff Sanderson, Hart.	6.00	.20
□□ 128 Corey Schwab (G), Tamp.	5.00	.20
□□ 129 Anders Eriksson, Detr.	5.00	.20
□□ **130 Harry York, SLou. RC**	**5.00**	**.50**
□□ 131 Jarome Iginla, Calg.	20.00	1.50
□□ 132 Éric Fichaud (G), NYIs.	5.00	.20
□□ **133 Patrick Lalime (G), Pitt. RC**	**60.00**	**5.00**
□□ 134 Daymond Langkow, Tamp.	6.00	.20
□□ **135 Mattias Timander, Bost. RC**	**5.00**	**.50**
□□ 136 Ethan Moreau, Chic.	5.00	.20
□□ 137 Christian Dubé, NYRa.	5.00	.20
□□ **138 Sergei Berezin, Toro. RC**	**10.00**	**1.50**
□□ 139 José Théodore (G), Mont.	30.00	2.00
□□ 140 Wade Redden, Otta.	8.00	.50
□□ **141 Danius Zubrus, Phil. RC**	**10.00**	**1.50**
□□ 142 Jim Campbell, SLou.	5.00	.20
□□ 143 Daniel Goneau, NYRa.	5.00	.50
□□ 144 Jamie Langenbrunner, Dall.	6.00	.20
□□ **145 Rem Murray, Edmo. RC**	**5.00**	**.50**
□□ 146 Jonas Hoglund, Calg.	5.00	.20
□□ 147 Bryan Berard, NYIs.	8.00	.50
□□ 148 CL: Chris Osgood (G), Detr.	5.00	.20
□□ 149 CL: Eric Lindros, Phil.	10.00	.50
□□ 150 CL: Jason Arnott, Edmo.	5.00	.20

HART TO HART

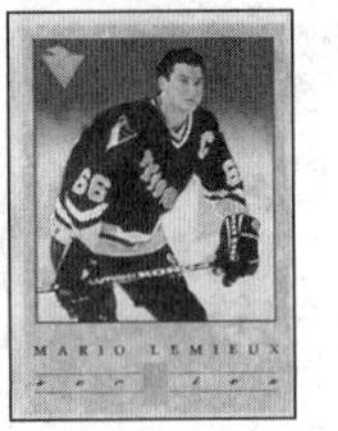

Lemieux Series (6 cards):	105.00
Lindros Series (6 cards):	220.00
Player	HtH
□ M. Lemieux ✍ / E. Lindros ✍	225.00
□ 1 Mario Lemieux, Pitt.	25.00
□ 2 Mario Lemieux, Pitt.	25.00
□ 3 Mario Lemieux, Pitt.	25.00
□ 4 Mario Lemieux, Pitt.	25.00
□ 5 Mario Lemieux, Pitt.	25.00
□ 6 Mario Lemieux, Pitt.	25.00
□ 1 Mario Lemieux, Pitt. ✍	185.00
□ 2 Mario Lemieux, Pitt. ✍	185.00
□ 3 Mario Lemieux, Pitt. ✍	185.00
□ 4 Mario Lemieux, Pitt. ✍	185.00
□ 5 Mario Lemieux, Pitt. ✍	185.00
□ 6 Mario Lemieux, Pitt. ✍	185.00
□ 1 Eric Lindros, Phil.	15.00
□ 2 Eric Lindros, Phil.	15.00
□ 3 Eric Lindros, Phil.	15.00
□ 4 Eric Lindros, Phil.	15.00
□ 5 Eric Lindros, Phil.	15.00
□ 6 Eric Lindros, Phil.	15.00
□ 1 Eric Lindros, Phil. ✍	85.00
□ 2 Eric Lindros, Phil. ✍	85.00
□ 3 Eric Lindros, Phil. ✍	85.00
□ 4 Eric Lindros, Phil. ✍	85.00
□ 5 Eric Lindros, Phil. ✍	85.00
□ 6 Eric Lindros, Phil. ✍	85.00

ASPIRATIONS

Insert Set (25 cards):	135.00
Insert (#/3000)	Asp
□ 1 Éric Dazé, Chic.	6.00
□ 2 Daniel Alfredsson, Otta.	10.00
□ 3 Petr* Sykora, NJer.	6.00
□ 4 Todd Bertuzzi, NYIs.	20.00
□ 5 Saku Koivu, Mont.	14.00
□ 6 Ed Jovanovski, Flor.	6.00
□ 7 Jim Campbell, SLou.	4.00
□ 8 Valeri Bure, Mont.	4.00
□ 9 Jeff O'Neill, Hart.	6.00
□ 10 Jere Lehtinen, Dall.	4.00
□ 11 Terry Ryan, Mont.	4.00
□ 12 Jonas Höglund, Calg.	4.00
□ 13 Daymond Langkow, Tamp.	4.00
□ 14 Éric Fichaud (G), NYIs.	4.00
□ 15 Dainius Zubrus, Phil.	8.00
□ 16 Janne Niinimaa, Phil.	8.00
□ 17 Sergei Berezin, Toro.	8.00
□ 18 Daniel Goneau, NYRa.	4.00
□ 19 Jarome Iginla, Calg.	14.00
□ 20 Ethan Moreau, Chic.	4.00
□ 21 Jamie Langenbrunner, Dall.	4.00
□ 22 Rem Murray, Edmo.	4.00
□ 23 Bryan Berard, NYIs.	4.00
□ 24 Wade Redden, Otta.	4.00
□ 25 Christian Dubé, NYRa.	4.00

PAINTED WARRIORS

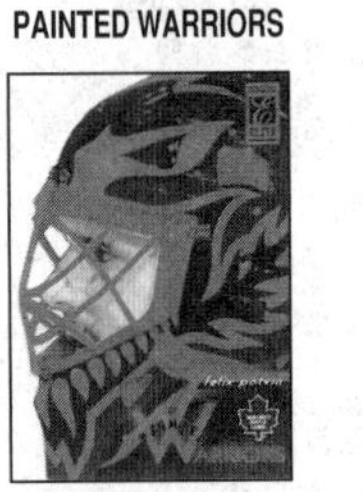

There are two versions: the insert (#/2500) and the promo card.

Complete Set (10 cards):	15.00	195.00
Player	Promo	Insert
□□ 1 Patrick Roy (G), Colo.	7.00	80.00
□□ 2 Mike Richter (G), NYRa.	1.00	12.00
□□ 3 Jim Carey (G), Wash.	1.00	12.00
□□ 4 John Vanbiesbrouck (G), Flor.	1.00	12.00
□□ 5 Jocelyn Thibault (G), Mont.	1.00	12.00
□□ 6 Félix Potvin (G), Toro.	1.00	15.00
□□ 7 Ed Belfour (G), Chic.	2.00	25.00
□□ 8 Martin Brodeur (G), NJer.	4.00	40.00
□□ 9 Nikolai Khabibulin (G), Phoe.	1.00	12.00
□□ 10 Stéphane Fiset (G), LosA.	1.00	12.00

PERSPECTIVES

Insert Set (12 cards):	425.00
Insert (#/500)	Persp.
□ 1 Wayne Gretzky, NYRa.	120.00
□ 2 Mark Messier, NYRa.	30.00
□ 3 Steve Yzerman, Detr.	70.00
□ 4 Mario Lemieux, Pitt.	90.00
□ 5 Paul Coffey, Phil.	20.00
□ 6 Doug Gilmour, Toro.	20.00
□ 7 Brendan Shanahan, Detr.	30.00
□ 8 Jaromir Jagr, Pitt.	30.00
□ 9 Brett Hull, SLou.	30.00
□ 10 Pat LaFontaine, Buff.	20.00
□ 11 Chris Chelios, Chic.	20.00
□ 12 Grant Fuhr, SLou.	20.00

STATUS

Insert Set (12 cards):	225.00
Insert (#/750)	Status
□ 1 Pavel Bure, Vanc.	20.00
□ 2 Keith Tkachuk, Phoe.	15.00
□ 3 Sergei Fedorov, Detr.	25.00
□ 4 Doug Weight, Edmo.	15.00
□ 5 Paul Kariya, Anah.	30.00
□ 6 Owen Nolan, SanJ.	15.00
□ 7 Peter Forsberg, Colo.	35.00
□ 8 Eric Lindros, Phil.	20.00
□ 9 Alexander Mogilny, Vanc.	15.00
□ 10 Teemu Selänne, Anah.	20.00
□ 11 Joe Sakic, Colo.	40.00
□ 12 Jeremy Roenick, Phoe.	20.00

1996 - 97 DS STICKERS

It should be noted that since this product is not readibly available in North America, regional and NHL stars often sell at a premium (usually $1-2 each).

	Complete Set (283 stickers):	40.00
	Player	NM-MT
☐	1 Roman Cechmanek, Dream Team	2.00
☐	2 Jiri Veber, Dream Team	.25
☐	3 Jiri Vykoukal, Dream Team	.25
☐	4 Miloslav Horava, Dream Team	.25
☐	5 Martin Stepanek, Dream Team	.25
☐	6 Antonin Stavjana, Dream Team	.25
☐	7 Bedrich Scerban, Dream Team	.25
☐	8 Radek Belohlav, Dream Team	.25
☐	9 Extraliga logo	.25
☐	10 Jiri Dopita, Dream Team	.50
☐	11 David Vyborny, Dream Team	.50
☐	12 Josef Beranek, Dream Team	.50
☐	13 Vladimir Jerabek, Dream Team	.25
☐	14 Viktor Ujcik, Dream Team	.50
☐	15 Roman Meluzin, Dream Team	.25
☐	16 Jiri Kucera, Dream Team	.25
☐	17 Robert Lang, Dream Team	1.00
☐	18 Roman Cechmanek, Vsetin	2.00
☐	19 Antonin Stavjana, Vsetin	.25
☐	20 Tomas Jakes, Vsetin	.25
☐	21 Alexei Jaskin, Vsetin	.25
☐	22 Jan Srdinko, Vsetin	.25
☐	23 Jiri Veber, Vsetin	.25
☐	24 Bedrich Scerban, Vsetin	.25
☐	25 Ivan Padelek, Vsetin	.25
☐	26 Vsetin Team Logo	.25
☐	27 Vsetin Team Photo	.25
☐	28 Vsetin Team Photo	.25
☐	29 Rostislav Vlach, Vsetin	.25
☐	30 Josef Beranek, Vsetin	.50
☐	31 Ondrej Kratena, Vsetin	.25
☐	32 Jiri Dopita, Vsetin	.50
☐	33 Tomas Kapusta, Vsetin	.25
☐	34 Tomas Srsen, Vsetin	.25
☐	35 Andrei Galkin, Vsetin	.25
☐	36 Otto Hascak, Vsetin	.25
☐	37 Zdenek Orct, Litvinov	.25
☐	38 Martin Stepanek, Litvinov	.25
☐	39 Normunds Sejejs, Litvinov	.25
☐	40 Sergei Butko, Litvinov	.25
☐	41 Roman Cech, Litvinov	.25
☐	42 Radek Mrazek, Litvinov	.25
☐	43 Angel Nikolov, Litvinov	.25
☐	44 Robert Kysela, Litvinov	.25
☐	45 Team Logo	.25
☐	46 Team Photo	.25
☐	47 Team Photo	.25
☐	48 Vladimir Jerabek, Litvinov	.25
☐	49 Martin Rousek, Litvinov	.25
☐	50 Jaroslav Buchal, Litvinov	.25
☐	51 Petr Hrbek, Litvinov	.25
☐	52 Tomas Vlasak, Litvinov	.25
☐	53 Tomas Krasny, Litvinov	.25
☐	54 Josef Straka, Litvinov	.25
☐	55 Kamil Kastak, Litvinov	.25
☐	56 Robert Schistad, Sparta Praha	.25
☐	57 Radek Hamr, Sparta Praha	.25
☐	58 Jaroslav Nedved, Sparta Praha	.25
☐	59 Jan Bohacek, Sparta Praha	.25
☐	60 Vaclav Burda, Sparta Praha	.25
☐	61 Jiri Vykoukal, Sparta Praha	.25
☐	62 Frantisek Ptacek, Sparta Praha	.25
☐	63 Jan Benda, Sparta Praha	.25
☐	64 Team Logo	.25
☐	65 Team Photo	.25
☐	66 Team Photo	.25
☐	67 Richard Zemlicka, Sparta Praha	.25
☐	68 Roman Horak, Sparta Praha	.25
☐	69 Patrik Martinec, Sparta Praha	.25
☐	70 Martin Hostak, Sparta Praha	.25
☐	71 David Vyborny, Sparta Praha	.50
☐	72 Pavel Geffert, Sparta Praha	.25
☐	73 Robert Lang, Sparta Praha	1.00
☐	74 Andrei Potajcuk, Sparta Praha	.25
☐	75 Oldrich Svoboda, Ceske Budejovice	.25
☐	76 Karel Soudek, Ceske Budejovice	.25
☐	77 Kamil Toupal, Ceske Budejovice	.25
☐	78 Milan Nedoma, Ceske Budejovice	.25
☐	79 Radek Martinek, Ceske Budejovice	.25
☐	80 Vladimir Antipin, Ceske Budejovice	.25
☐	81 Rudolf Suchanek, Ceske Budejovice	.25
☐	82 Pavel Pycha, Ceske Budejovice	.25
☐	83 Team Logo	.25
☐	84 Team Photo	.25
☐	85 Team Photo	.25
☐	86 Radek Toupal, Ceske Budejovice	.25
☐	87 Lubos Rob, Ceske Budejovice	.25
☐	88 Milan Navratil, Ceske Budejovice	.25
☐	89 Filip Turek, Ceske Budejovice	.25
☐	90 Radek Belohlav, Ceske Budejovice	.25
☐	91 Miroslav Barus, Ceske Budejovice	.25
☐	92 Frantisek Sevcik, Ceske Budejovice	.25
☐	93 Arpad Györi, Ceske Budejovice	.25
☐	94 Jaroslav Kames, Zlin	.25
☐	95 Petr Kuchyna, Zlin	.25
☐	96 Pavel Kowalczyk, Zlin	.25
☐	97 Stanislav Medrik, Zlin	.25
☐	98 Jan Krajicek, Zlin	.25
☐	99 Radim Tesarik, Zlin	.25
☐	100 Jiri Marusak, Zlin	.25
☐	101 Pavel Janku, Zlin	.25
☐	102 Team Logo	.25
☐	103 Team Photo	.25
☐	104 Team Photo	.25
☐	105 Ales Polcar, Zlin	.25
☐	106 David Bruk, Zlin	.25
☐	107 Zbynek Marak, Zlin	.25
☐	108 Ales Zima, Zlin	.25
☐	109 Roman Meluzin, Zlin	.25
☐	110 Miroslav Okal, Zlin	.25
☐	111 Petr Cajanek, Zlin	.25
☐	112 Tomas Nemicicky, Zlin	.25
☐	113 Rudolf Pejchar, Slavia Praha	.25
☐	114 Jaromir Latal, Slavia Praha	.25
☐	115 Robert Kostka, Slavia Praha	.25
☐	116 Jiri Hes, Slavia Praha	.25
☐	117 Petr Kadlec, Slavia Praha	.25
☐	118 Martin Maskarinec, Slavia Praha	.25
☐	119 Miloslav Horava, Slavia Praha	.25
☐	120 Roman Kadera, Slavia Praha	.25
☐	121 Team Logo	.25
☐	122 Team Photo	.25
☐	123 Team Photo	.25
☐	124 Tomas Kucharcik, Slavia Praha	.25
☐	125 Jiri Dolezal, Slavia Praha	.25
☐	126 Jaroslav Bednar, Slavia Praha	.50
☐	127 Ladislav Slizek, Slavia Praha	.25
☐	128 Tomas Kupka, Slavia Praha	.25
☐	129 Viktor Ujcik, Slavia Praha	.50
☐	130 Vladimir Ruzicka, Slavia Praha	1.00
☐	131 Ivo Prorok, Slavia Praha	.25
☐	132 Milan Hnilicka, Kladno	1.00
☐	133 Jan Krulis, Kladno	.25
☐	134 Jan Dlouhy, Kladno	.25
☐	135 Libor Prochazka, Kladno	.25
☐	136 Tomas Kaberle, Kladno	1.00
☐	137 Marek Zidlicky, Kladno	.25
☐	138 Petr Kasik, Kladno	.25
☐	139 Jiri Beranek, Kladno	.25
☐	140 Team Logo	.25
☐	141 Team Photo	.25
☐	142 Team Photo	.25
☐	143 Josef Zajic, Kladno	.25
☐	144 Tomas Mikolasek, Kladno	.25
☐	145 Ladislav Svoboda, Kladno	.25
☐	146 Zdenek Eichenmann, Kladno	.25
☐	147 Vaclav Eisett, Kladno	.25
☐	148 Petr Ton, Kladno	.25
☐	149 Jiri Burger, Kladno	.25
☐	150 David Cermak, Kladno	.25
☐	151 Ivo Capek, Jihlava	.25
☐	152 Marian Morava, Jihlava	.25
☐	153 Michael Vyhlidal, Jihlava	.25
☐	154 Roman Kankovsky, Jihlava	.25
☐	155 Zdenek Touzimsky, Jihlava	.25
☐	156 Marek Posmyk, Jihlava	.25
☐	157 Miroslav Javin, Jihlava	.25
☐	158 Miroslav Bruna, Jihlava	.25
☐	159 Team Logo	.25
☐	160 Team Photo	.25
☐	161 Team Photo	.25
☐	162 Jaroslav Hub, Jihlava	.25
☐	163 Petr Vlk, Jihlava	.25
☐	164 Jiri Poukar, Jihlava	.25
☐	165 Petr Kankovsky, Jihlava	.25
☐	166 Ladislav Prokupek, Jihlava	.25
☐	167 Milan Antos, Jihlava	.25
☐	168 Leos Pipa, Jihlava	.25
☐	169 Michail Fadejev, Jihlava	.25
☐	170 Ladislav Blazek, Olomouc	.25
☐	171 Petr Pavlas, Olomouc	.25
☐	172 Marek Cernosek, Olomouc	.25
☐	173 Ladislav Benysek, Olomouc	.25
☐	174 Jergus Baca, Olomouc	.25
☐	175 Marek Tichy, Olomouc	.25
☐	176 Roman Veber, Olomouc	.25
☐	177 Martin Streit, Olomouc	.25
☐	178 Team Logo	.25
☐	179 Team Photo	.25
☐	180 Team Photo	.25
☐	181 Michal Bros, Olomouc	.25
☐	182 Radek Svoboda, Olomouc	.25
☐	183 Pavel Nohel, Olomouc	.25
☐	184 Radek Prochazka, Olomouc	.25
☐	185 Jan Tomajko, Olomouc	.25
☐	186 Michal Slavik, Olomouc	.25
☐	187 Radek Sip, Olomouc	.25
☐	188 Filip Dvorak, Olomouc	.25
☐	189 Martin Prusek, Vitkovice	2.00
☐	190 Jiri Jonak, Vitkovice	.25
☐	191 Pavel Kumstat, Vitkovice	.25
☐	192 Vitezslav Skuta, Vitkovice	.25
☐	193 Dmitri Jerofejev, Vitkovice	.25
☐	194 Rene Sevecek, Vitkovice	.25
☐	195 Ales Tomasek, Vitkovice	.25
☐	196 Roman Simicek, Vitkovice	.25
☐	197 Team Logo	.25
☐	198 Team Photo	.25
☐	199 Team Photo	.25
☐	200 Alexander Prokopjev, Vitkovice	.25
☐	201 Jan Peterek, Vitkovice	.25
☐	202 David Moravec, Vitkovice	.25
☐	203 Tomas Chlubna, Vitkovice	.25
☐	204 Libor Polasek, Vitkovice	.25
☐	205 Ales Kratoska, Vitkovice	.25
☐	206 Roman Rysanek, Vitkovice	.25
☐	207 Martin Smetak, Vitkovice	.25
☐	208 Martin Altrichter, Plzen	.25
☐	209 Karel Smid, Plzen	.25
☐	210 Josef Reznicek, Plzen	.25
☐	211 Jaroslav Spacek, Plzen	.25
☐	212 Ivan Vlacek, Plzen	.25
☐	213 Jiri Hanzlik, Plzen	.25
☐	214 Robert Jindrich, Plzen	.25
☐	215 Milan Volak, Plzen	.25
☐	216 Team Logo	.25
☐	217 Team Photo	.25
☐	218 Team Photo	.25
☐	219 Jiri Kucera, Plzen	.25
☐	220 Tomas Klimt, Plzen	.25
☐	221 Tomas Jelinek, Plzen	.25
☐	222 Michal Straka, Plzen	.25
☐	223 Miroslav Mach, Plzen	.25
☐	224 Pavel Vostrak, Plzen	.25
☐	225 Petr Korinek, Plzen	.25
☐	226 Radek Kampf, Plzen	.25
☐	227 Radovan Biegl, Trinec	.25
☐	228 Jiri Kuntos, Trinec	.25
☐	229 Lubomir Sekeras, Trinec	.50
☐	230 Petr Jancarik, Trinec	.25
☐	231 Stanislav Pavelec, Trinec	.25
☐	232 Ondrej Zetek, Trinec	.25
☐	233 Patrik Hucko, Trinec	.25
☐	234 Vladimir Machulda, Trinec	.25
☐	235 Team Logo	.25
☐	236 Team Photo	.25
☐	237 Team Photo	.25
☐	238 Jozef Dano, Trinec	.25
☐	239 Roman Blazek, Trinec	.25
☐	240 Marek Zadina, Trinec	.25
☐	241 Richard Kral, Trinec	.25
☐	242 Petr Folta, Trinec	.25
☐	243 Michal Piskor, Trinec	.25
☐	244 Josef Straub, Trinec	.25
☐	245 Petr Zajonc, Trinec	.25
☐	246 Dusan Salficky, Pardubice	.25
☐	247 Pavel Augusta, Pardubice	.25
☐	248 Tomas Pacal, Pardubice	.25
☐	249 Jiri Malinsky, Pardubice	.25
☐	250 Pavel Kriz, Pardubice	.25
☐	251 Radomir Brazda, Pardubice	.25
☐	252 Ales Pisa, Pardubice	.50
☐	253 Ladislav Lubina, Pardubice	.25
☐	254 Team Logo	.25
☐	255 Team Photo	.25
☐	256 Team Photo	.25
☐	257 Tomas Blazek, Pardubice	.25
☐	258 Jiri Jantovsky, Pardubice	.25
☐	259 Milan Hejduk, Pardubice	7.00
☐	260 Tomas Martinec, Pardubice	.25
☐	261 David Pospisil, Pardubice	.25
☐	262 Stanislav Prochazka, Pardubice	.25
☐	263 Milan Prochazka, Pardubice	.25
☐	264 Milan Kastner, Pardubice	.25
☐	265 Rostislav Haas, Opava	.25
☐	266 Denis Tsygurov, Opava	.25
☐	267 Martin Bakula, Opava	.25
☐	268 David Galvas, Opava	.25
☐	269 Petr Tejkl, Opava	.25
☐	270 Radek Mesicek, Opava	.25
☐	271 Milos Hrubes, Opava	.25
☐	272 Eduard Gorbachev, Opava	.25
☐	273 Team Logo	.25
☐	274 Team Photo	.25
☐	275 Team Photo	.25
☐	276 Petr Fabian, Opava	.25
☐	277 Zdenek Pavelek, Opava	.25
☐	278 Karel Horny, Opava	.25
☐	279 Martin Filip, Opava	.25
☐	280 Juraj Jurik, Opava	.25
☐	281 Radim Radevic, Opava	.25
☐	282 Jan Zurek, Opava	.25
☐	283 Valeri Belov, Opava	.25

1996 - 97 DURACELL

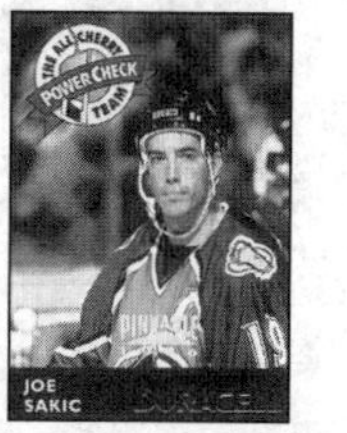

The statistics on the back are revealed when the black bards are heated lightly.

	Pinnacle All-Cherry Team Set (22 cards):	20.00
	Pinnacle All-Béliveau Team Set (22 cards):	25.00
	Player	DC
☐	DC1 Paul Coffey, Detr.	.50
☐	DC2 Lyle Odelein, Mont.	.50
☐	DC3 Joe Sakic, Colo.	2.00
☐	DC4 Curtis Joseph (G), Edmo.	1.50
☐	DC5 Brett Hull, SLou.	1.50
☐	DC6 Eric Lindros, Phil.	1.50
☐	DC7 Doug Gilmour, Toro.	.50
☐	DC8 Chris Chelios, Chic.	.50
☐	DC9 Marty McSorley, NYRa.	.50
☐	DC10 Kirk Muller, Toro.	.50
☐	DC11 Trevor Linden, Vanc.	.50
☐	DC12 Brendan Shanahan, Hart.	1.50
☐	DC13 Tie Domi, Toro.	.50
☐	DC14 Rick Tocchet, Bost.	.50
☐	DC15 Steve Yzerman, Detr.	3.50
☐	DC16 Scott Stevens, NJer.	.50
☐	DC17 Patrick Roy (G), Colo.	4.50
☐	DC18 Keith Tkachuk, Winn.	.50
☐	DC19 Owen Nolan, SanJ.	.50
☐	DC20 Dale Hunter, Wash.	.50
☐	DC21 Don Cherry, Bost. [Coach]	1.50
☐	DC22 Don Cherry, HNIC [w/ Dog Blue]	1.50
	Player	JB
☐	JB1 Paul Coffey, Detr.	.50
☐	JB2 Lyle Odelein, Mont.	.50
☐	JB3 Joe Sakic, Colo.	2.00
☐	JB4 Éric Dazé, Chic.	.50
☐	JB5 Brett Hull, SLou.	1.50
☐	JB6 Martin Brodeur (G), NJer.	2.00
☐	JB7 Doug Gilmour, Toro.	.50
☐	JB8 Peter Forsberg, Colo.	2.00
☐	JB9 Mike Gartner, Toro.	1.00
☐	JB10 Saku Koivu, Mont.	1.00
☐	JB11 Trevor Linden, Vanc.	.50
☐	JB12 Félix Potvin (G), Toro.	.50
☐	JB13 Mats Sundin, Toro.	1.50
☐	JB14 Pierre Turgeon, Mont.	.50
☐	JB15 Vincent Damphousse, Mont.	.50
☐	JB16 Scott Stevens, NJer.	.50
☐	JB17 Patrick Roy (G), Colo.	4.50
☐	JB18 Keith Tkachuk, Winn.	.50
☐	JB19 Raymond Bourque, Bost.	1.50
☐	JB20 Paul Kariya, Anah.	2.00
☐	JB21 Béliveau, Mont.	3.00
☐	JB22 Jean Béliveau, Mont.	3.00

1996 - 97 FLAIR

There are two versions: the regular card and a Blue Ice parallel (#/250, prefix B-).

	Complete Set (125 cards):	1600.00	100.00
	Shell Set (100 cards):	-	35.00
	Common Player:	5.00	.25
	Player	Bl250	Flair
☐ ☐	1 Guy Hebert, Anah.	5.00	.25
☐ ☐	2 Paul Kariya, Anah.	60.00	2.00
☐ ☐	3 Teemu Selänne, Anah.	30.00	1.00
☐ ☐	4 Raymond Bourque, Bost.	40.00	1.50
☐ ☐	5 Adam Oates, Bost.	15.00	.50
☐ ☐	6 Bill Ranford (G), Bost.	15.00	.50
☐ ☐	7 Jozef Stümpel, Bost.	5.00	.25
☐ ☐	8 Dominik Hasek (G), Buff.	30.00	1.50
☐ ☐	9 Pat LaFontaine, Buff.	20.00	.50
☐ ☐	10 Alexei Zhitnik, Buff.	5.00	.25
☐ ☐	11 Theoren Fleury, Calg.	20.00	.50
☐ ☐	12 Dave Gagner, Calg.	6.00	.25
☐ ☐	13 Trevor Kidd (G), Calg.	10.00	.25
☐ ☐	14 Tony Amonte, Chic.	20.00	.50
☐ ☐	15 Chris Chelios, Chic.	20.00	.50
☐ ☐	16 Eric Dazé, Chic.	15.00	.50
☐ ☐	17 Alexei Zhamnov, Chic.	10.00	.25
☐ ☐	18 Peter Forsberg, Colo.	50.00	2.00
☐ ☐	19 Sandis Ozolinsh, Colo.	5.00	.25
☐ ☐	20 Patrick Roy (G), Colo.	140.00	4.50
☐ ☐	21 Joe Sakic, Colo.	60.00	2.00
☐ ☐	22 Derian Hatcher, Dall.	10.00	.25
☐ ☐	23 Mike Modano, Dall.	35.00	1.50
☐ ☐	24 Andy Moog (G), Dall.	15.00	.50
☐ ☐	25 Pat Verbeek, Dall.	10.00	.25
☐ ☐	26 Sergei Fedorov, Detr.	35.00	1.50
☐ ☐	27 Viacheslav Fetisov Detr.	20.00	.50
☐ ☐	28 Nicklas Lidström, Detr.	20.00	.50
☐ ☐	29 Chris Osgood (G), Detr.	20.00	.50
☐ ☐	30 Brendan Shanahan, Detr.	30.00	1.50
☐ ☐	31 Steve Yzerman, Detr.	100.00	3.50
☐ ☐	32 Jason Arnott, Edmo.	15.00	.50
☐ ☐	33 Curtis Joseph (G), Edmo.	30.00	1.50
☐ ☐	34 Boris Mironov, Edmo.	5.00	.25
☐ ☐	35 Ryan Smyth, Edmo.	15.00	.50
☐ ☐	36 Doug Weight, Edmo.	20.00	.50
☐ ☐	37 Ed Jovanovski, Flor.	15.00	.50
☐ ☐	38 Ray Sheppard, Flor.	5.00	.25
☐ ☐	39 Robert Svehla, Flor.	5.00	.25
☐ ☐	40 John Vanbiesbrouck (G), Flor.	15.00	.50
☐ ☐	41 Andrew Cassels, Hart.	5.00	.25
☐ ☐	42 Jason Muzzatti (G), Hart.	5.00	.25
☐ ☐	43 Keith Primeau, Hart.	15.00	.50
☐ ☐	44 Geoff Sanderson, Hart.	5.00	.25
☐ ☐	45 Rob Blake, LosA.	20.00	.50
☐ ☐	46 Dimitri Khristich, LosA.	5.00	.25
☐ ☐	47 Vincent Damphousse, Mont.	20.00	.50
☐ ☐	48 Saku Koivu, Mont.	30.00	1.00
☐ ☐	49 Mark Recchi, Mont.	15.00	.50
☐ ☐	50 Martin Rucinsky, Mont.	5.00	.25
☐ ☐	51 Jocelyn Thibault (G), Mont.	15.00	.50
☐ ☐	52 Martin Brodeur (G), NJer.	60.00	2.00
☐ ☐	53 Bill Guerin, NJer.	15.00	.50
☐ ☐	54 Scott Stevens, NJer.	15.00	.50
☐ ☐	55 Scott Lachance, NYIs.	5.00	.25
☐ ☐	56 Zigmund Palffy, NYIs.	20.00	.50
☐ ☐	57 Tommy Salo (G), NYIs.	15.00	.50
☐ ☐	58 Brian Smolinski, NYIs.	5.00	.25
☐ ☐	59 Wayne Gretzky, NYRa.	200.00	6.00
☐ ☐	60 Brian Leetch, NYRa.	20.00	.50
☐ ☐	61 Mark Messier, NYRa.	35.00	1.50
☐ ☐	62 Mike Richter (G), NYRa.	15.00	.50
☐ ☐	63 Daniel Alfredsson, Otta.	20.00	.50
☐ ☐	64 Damian Rhodes (G), Otta.	5.00	.25
☐ ☐	65 Alexei Yashin, Otta.	20.00	.50
☐ ☐	66 Paul Coffey, Phil.	20.00	.50
☐ ☐	67 Dale Hawerchuk, Phil.	20.00	.50
☐ ☐	68 Ron Hextall (G), Phil.	20.00	.50
☐ ☐	69 John LeClair, Phil.	30.00	1.00
☐ ☐	70 Eric Lindros, Phil.	40.00	1.50
☐ ☐	71 Nikolai Khabibulin (G), Phoe.	15.00	.50
☐ ☐	72 Jeremy Roenick, Phoe.	30.00	1.00
☐ ☐	73 Keith Tkachuk, Phoe.	20.00	.50
☐ ☐	74 Oleg Tverdovsky, Phoe.	5.00	.25
☐ ☐	75 Ron Francis, Pitt.	20.00	.50
☐ ☐	76 Kevin Hatcher, Pitt.	5.00	.25
☐ ☐	77 Jaromir Jagr, Pitt.	40.00	1.50
☐ ☐	78 Mario Lemieux, Pitt.	140.00	4.50
☐ ☐	79 Peter Nedved, Pitt.	10.00	.25
☐ ☐	80 Grant Fuhr (G), SLou.	20.00	.50
☐ ☐	81 Brett Hull, SLou.	35.00	1.50
☐ ☐	82 Al MacInnis, SLou.	15.00	.50
☐ ☐	83 Ed Belfour (G), SanJ.	35.00	1.50
☐ ☐	84 Tony Granato, SanJ.	5.00	.25
☐ ☐	85 Owen Nolan, SanJ.	20.00	.50
☐ ☐	86 Dino Ciccarelli, Tamp.	10.00	.25
☐ ☐	87 John Cullen, Tamp.	5.00	.25
☐ ☐	88 Roman Hamrlik, Tamp.	5.00	.25
☐ ☐	89 Wendel Clark, Toro.	30.00	1.00
☐ ☐	90 Doug Gilmour, Toro.	20.00	.50
☐ ☐	91 Félix Potvin (G), Toro.	20.00	.50
☐ ☐	92 Mats Sundin, Toro.	35.00	1.50
☐ ☐	93 Pavel Bure, Vanc.	30.00	1.00
☐ ☐	94 Corey Hirsch (G), Vanc.	5.00	.25
☐ ☐	95 Trevor Linden, Vanc.	15.00	.50
☐ ☐	96 Alexander Mogilny, Vanc.	15.00	.50
☐ ☐	97 Peter Bondra, Wash.	20.00	.50
☐ ☐	98 Jim Carey (G), Wash.	5.00	.25
☐ ☐	99 Dale Hunter, Wash.	10.00	.25
☐ ☐	100 Chris Simon, Wash.	5.00	.25

WAVE OF THE FUTURE

Insert	BI250	Flair
101 Mattias Timander, Bost. RC	**5.00**	**2.00**
102 Vaclav Varada, Buff. RC	**10.00**	**6.00**
103 Jarome Iginla, Calg.	30.00	8.00
104 Ethan Moreau, Chic.	5.00	2.00
105 Jamie Langenbrunner, Dall.	5.00	2.00
106 Roman Turek (G), Dall. RC	**35.00**	**15.00**
107 Tomas Holmström, Detr. RC	**15.00**	**8.00**
108 Kevin Hodson (G), Detr.	9.00	2.00
109 Mats Lindgren, Edmo.	5.00	2.00
110 Mike Grier, Edmo. RC	**15.00**	**8.00**
111 Rem Murray, Edmo. RC	**5.00**	**2.00**
112 José Théodore (G), Mont.	45.00	12.00
113 David Wilkie, Mont.	5.00	2.00
114 Bryan Berard, NYIs.	10.00	2.00
115 Éric Fichaud (G), NYIs.	5.00	2.00
116 Daniel Goneau, NYRa.	7.00	2.00
117 Andreas Dackell, Otta. RC	**10.00**	**6.00**
118 Wade Redden, Otta.	10.00	2.00
119 Danius Zubrus, Phil. RC	**15.00**	**8.00**
120 Janne Niinimaa, Phil.	5.00	2.00
121 Patrick Lalime (G), Pitt. RC	**45.00**	**20.00**
122 Harry York, SLou. RC	**5.00**	**2.00**
123 Jim Campbell, SLou.	5.00	2.00
124 Sergei Berezin, Toro. RC	**15.00**	**8.00**
125 Jaroslav Svejkovsky, Wash.	10.00	4.00

CENTER ICE SPOTLIGHT

Insert Set (10 cards):	125.00
Insert (1:30)	CIS
1 Pavel Bure, Vanc.	10.00
2 Sergei Fedorov, Detr.	12.00
3 Peter Forsberg, Colo.	16.00
4 Brett Hull, SLou.	12.00
5 Jaromir Jagr, Pitt.	12.00
6 Paul Kariya, Anah.	16.00
7 Joe Sakic, Colo.	20.00
8 Teemu Selänne, Anah.	10.00
9 Mats Sundin, Toro.	12.00
10 Steve Yzerman, Detr.	30.00

HOT GLOVES

Insert Set (10 cards):	175.00
Insert (1:40)	HG
1 Ed Belfour (G), Chic.	20.00
2 Martin Brodeur (G), NJer.	30.00
3 Jim Carey (G), Wash.	8.00
4 Dominik Hasek (G), Buff.	20.00
5 Curtis Joseph (G), Edmo.	20.00
6 Patrick Lalime, Pitt.	20.00
7 Chris Osgood (G), Detr.	10.00
8 Félix Potvin (G), Toro.	10.00
9 Mike Richter (G), NYRa.	8.00
10 Patrick Roy (G), Colo.	60.00
11 Jocelyn Thibault (G), Mont.	8.00
12 John Vanbiesbrouck (G), Flor.	8.00

HOT NUMBERS

Insert Set (10 cards):	200.00
Insert (1:72)	HN
1 Raymond Bourque, Bost.	20.00
2 Paul Coffey, Phil.	10.00
3 Éric Dazé, Chic.	10.00
4 Wayne Gretzky, NYRa.	80.00
5 Ed Jovanovski, Flor.	10.00
6 Saku Koivu, Mont.	15.00
7 Mario Lemieux, Pitt.	60.00
8 Eric Lindros, Phil.	20.00
9 Mark Messier, NYRa.	20.00
10 Owen Nolan, SanJ.	10.00

NOW & THEN

Insert Set (3 cards):	275.00
Insert (1:720)	N&T
1 M. Gartner / W. Gretzky / M. Messier	125.00
2 M. Lemieux / K. Muller / P. Roy	125.00
3 P. Forsberg / S. Niedermayer / E. Lindros	75.00

1996 - 97 FLEER

Complete Set (150 cards):	20.00
Common Player:	.20
Player	Fleer
1 Guy Hebert (G), Anah.	.20
2 Paul Kariya, Anah.	.50
3 Teemu Selänne, Anah.	.50
4 Raymond Bourque, Bost.	.50
5 Kyle McLaren, Bost.	.20
6 Adam Oates, Bost.	.20
7 Bill Ranford (G), Bost.	.20
8 Rick Tocchet, Bost.	.20
9 Jason Dawe, Buff.	.20
10 Dominik Hasek (G), Buff.	.50
11 Pat LaFontaine, Buff.	.20
12 Theoren Fleury, Calg.	.20
13 Trevor Kidd (G), Calg.	.20
14 German Titov, Calg.	.20
15 Ed Belfour (G), Chic.	.50
16 Chris Chelios, Chic.	.20
17 Eric Dazé, Chic.	.20
18 Jeremy Roenick, Chic.	.50
19 Gary Suter, Chic.	.20
20 Peter Forsberg, Colo.	.50
21 Valeri Kamensky, Colo.	.20
22 Claude Lemieux, Colo.	.20
23 Sandis Ozolinsh, Colo.	.20
24 Patrick Roy (G), Colo.	1.50
25 Joe Sakic, Colo.	1.00
26 Derian Hatcher, Dall.	.20
27 Mike Modano, Dall.	.50
28 Sergei Zubov, Pitt. (Dall.)	.20
29 Paul Coffey, Detr.	.20
30 Sergei Fedorov, Detr.	.50
31 Vladimir Konstantinov, Detr.	.20
32 Vyacheslav Kozlov, Detr.	.20
33 Chis Osgood (G), Detr.	.20
34 Keith Primeau, Detr.	.20
35 Steve Yzerman, Detr.	1.50
36 Jason Arnott, Edmo.	.20
37 Curtis Joseph (G), Edmo.	.50
38 Doug Weight, Edmo.	.20
39 Ed Jovanovski, Flor.	.20
40 Scott Mellanby, Flor.	.20
41 Rob Niedermayer, Flor.	.20
42 Ray Sheppard, Flor.	.20
43 Robert Svehla, Flor.	.20
44 John Vanbiesbrouck (G), Flor.	.20
45 Sean Burke (G), Hart.	.20
46 Andrew Cassels, Hart.	.20
47 Geoff Sanderson, Hart.	.20
48 Brendan Shanahan, Hart.	.50
49 Ray Ferraro, LosA.	.20
50 Dimitri Khristich, LosA.	.20
51 Vitali Yachmenev, LosA.	.20
52 Valeri Bure, Mont.	.20
53 Vincent Damphousse, Mont.	.20
54 Saku Koivu, Mont.	.50
55 Mark Recchi, Mont.	.20
56 Jocelyn Thibault (G), Mont.	.20
57 Pierre Turgeon, Mont.	.20
58 Martin Brodeur (G), NJer.	1.00
59 Phil Housley, NJer.	.20
60 Scott Niedermayer, NJer.	.20
61 Scott Stevens, NJer.	.20
62 Steve Thomas, NJer.	.20
63 Todd Bertuzzi, NYIs.	1.50
65 Travis Green, NYIs.	.20
65 Kenny Jönsson, NYIs.	.20
66 Zigmund Palffy, NYIs.	.20
67 Adam Graves, NYRa.	.20
68 Wayne Gretzky, NYRa.	2.50
69 Alexei Kovalev, NYRa.	.20
70 Brian Leetch, NYRa.	.20
71 Mark Messier, NYRa.	.50
72 Niklas Sundström, NYRa.	.20
73 Daniel Alfredsson, Otta.	.20
74 Radek Bonk, Otta.	.20
75 Steve Duchesne, Otta.	.20
76 Damian Rhodes (G), Otta.	.20
77 Alexei Yashin, Otta.	.20
78 Rod Brind'Amour, Phil.	.20
79 Éric Desjardins, Phil.	.20
80 Ron Hextall (G), Phil.	.20
81 John LeClair, Phil.	.50
82 Eric Lindros, Phil.	.50
83 Mikael Renberg, Phil.	.20
84 Tom Barrasso (G), Pitt.	.20
85 Ron Francis, Pitt.	.20
86 Jaromir Jagr, Pitt.	.50
87 Mario Lemieux, Pitt.	1.50
88 Petr Nedved, Pitt.	.20
89 Bryan Smolinski, Pitt.	.20
90 Nikolai Khabibulin (G), Winn. (Phoe.)	.20
91 Teppo Numminen, Winn. (Phoe.)	.20
92 Keith Tkachuk, Winn. (Phoe.)	.20
93 Oleg Tverdovsky, Winn. (Phoe.)	.20
94 Alexei Zhamnov, Winn. (Phoe.)	.20
95 Shayne Corson, SLou.	.20
96 Grant Fuhr (G), SLou.	.20
97 Brett Hull, SLou.	.50
98 Al MacInnis, SLou.	.20
99 Chris Pronger, SLou.	.20
100 Owen Nolan, SanJ.	.20
101 Marcus Ragnarsson, SanJ.	.20
102 Chris Terreri (G), SanJ.	.20
103 Brian Bradley, Tamp.	.20
104 Roman Hamrlik, Tamp.	.20
105 Daren Puppa (G), Tamp.	.20
106 Alexander Selivanov, Tamp.	.20
107 D. Gilmour, Toro. (Photo is Dave Gagner)	.20
108 Larry Murphy, Toro.	.20
109 Félix Potvin (G), Toro.	.20
110 Mats Sundin, Toro.	.50
111 Pavel Bure, Vanc.	.50
112 Trevor Linden, Vanc.	.20
113 Kirk McLean (G), Vanc.	.20
114 Alexander Mogilny, Vanc.	.20
115 Peter Bondra, Wash.	.20
116 Jim Carey (G), Wash.	.20
117 Sergei Gonchar, Wash.	.20
118 Joé Juneau, Wash.	.20
119 Michael Pivonka, Wash.	.20
120 Brendan Witt, Wash.	.20
121 Nolan Baumgartner, Wash.	.20
122 Martin Biron (G), Buff.	.50
123 Jason Bonsignore, Edmo.	.20
124 Andrew Brunette, Wash. RC	**.50**
125 Jason Doig, Winn.	.20
126 Peter Ferraro, NYRa.	.20
127 Éric Fichaud (G), NYIs.	.20
128 Ladislav Kohn, Calg.	.20
129 Jamie Langenbrunner, Dall.	.20
130 Daymond Langkow, Tamp.	.20
131 Jay McKee, Buff. RC	**.20**
132 Wayne Primeau, Buff.	.20
133 Jamie Storr (G), LosA.	.20
134 José Théodore (G), Mont.	1.50
135 Roman Vopat, LosA.	.20
136 LL: Eric Dazé/ Alfredsson/ V. Bure/ Koivu	.20
137 LL: Mario Lemieux/ Jagr/ Sakic/ Francis	.50
138 LL: Mario Lemieux/ Jagr/ Mogilny/ Bondra	.50
139 LL: Ron Francis/ Lemieux/ Jagr/ Forsberg	.50
140 LL: Brian Leetch/ Coffey/ Bourque/ Chelios	.20
141 LL: Mario Lemieux/ Jagr/ Kariya/ Tkachuk	.50
142 LL: J. Jagr/ Fedorov/ LeClair/ C. Lemieux	.20
143 LL: Konstastinov/ Fedorov/ Fetisov/ Nedved	.20
144 LL: Ron Hextall (G)/ Osgood (G)/ Carey (G)/ Vernon (G)	.20
145 LL: Chris Osgood (G)/ Carey (G)/ Brodeur (G)/ Hextall (G)	.20
146 LL: Jim Carey (G)/ Brodeur (G)/ Osgood (G)/ Puppa (G)	.20
147 LL: D. Hasek (G)/ Puppa (G)/ Hackett (G)/ Hebert (G)	.20
148 Checklist	.20
149 Checklist	.20
150 Checklist	.20

ART ROSS TROPHY

Insert Set (25 cards):	50.00
Insert (1:6)	ART
1 Pavel Bure, Vanc.	2.00
2 Sergei Fedorov, Detr.	2.00
3 Theoren Fleury, Calg.	1.00
4 Peter Forsberg, Colo.	3.00
5 Ron Francis, Pitt.	1.00
6 Wayne Gretzky, SLou. (NYRa.)	10.00
7 Brett Hull, SLou.	2.00
8 Jaromir Jagr, Pitt.	2.00
9 Valeri Kamensky, Colo.	.75
10 Paul Kariya, Anah.	3.00
11 Pat LaFontaine, Buff.	1.00
12 John LeClair, Phil.	2.00
13 Mario Lemieux, Pitt.	7.00
14 Eric Lindros, Phil.	2.00
15 Mark Messier, NYRa.	2.00
16 Alexander Mogilny, Vanc.	1.00
17 Petr Nedved, Pitt.	.75
18 Adam Oates, Bost.	1.00
19 Jeremy Roenick, Chic.	2.00
20 Joe Sakic, Colo.	4.00
21 Selänne, Anah.	2.00
22 Keith Tkachuk, Winn. (Phoe.)	1.00
23 Pierre Turgeon, Mont.	1.00
24 Doug Weight, Edmo.	1.00
25 Steve Yzerman, Detr.	6.00

CALDER CANDIDATES

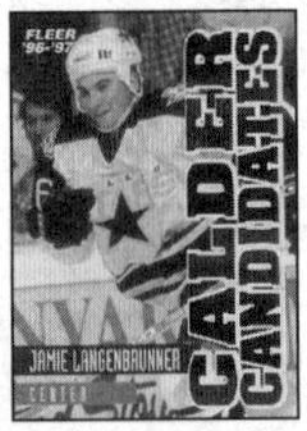

Insert Set (10 cards):	45.00
Insert (1:96)	CC
1 Andrew Brunette, Wash.	4.00
2 Jason Doig, Winn. (Phoe.)	4.00
3 Peter Ferraro, NYRa.	4.00
4 Éric Fichaud (G), NYIs.	4.00
5 Ladislav Kohn, Calg.	4.00
6 Jamie Langenbrunner, Dall.	4.00
7 Daymond Langkow, Tamp.	4.00
8 Jamie Storr, LosA.	4.00
9 José Théodore, Mont.	20.00
10 Roman Vopat, SLou. (LosA.)	4.00

NORRIS TROPHY

Insert Set (10 cards):	40.00
Insert (1:36)	NT
1 Raymond Bourque, Bost.	12.00
2 Chris Chelios, Chic.	6.00
3 Paul Coffey, Detr.	6.00
4 Éric Desjardins, Phil.	3.00
5 Phil Housley, NJer.	3.00
6 Vladimir Konstantinov, Detr.	3.00
7 Brian Leetch, NYRa.	6.00
8 Teppo Numminen, Winn. (Phoe.)	3.00
9 Larry Murphy, Toro.	3.00
10 Sandis Ozolinsh, Colo.	3.00

PEARSON AWARD

Insert Set (10 cards):	300.00
Insert (1:144)	PA
1 Pavel Bure, Vanc.	15.00
2 Sergei Fedorov, Detr.	20.00
3 Peter Forsberg, Colo.	25.00
4 Wayne Gretzky, SLou. (NYRa.)	80.00
5 Jaromir Jagr, Pitt.	20.00
6 Paul Kariya, Anah.	25.00
7 Mario Lemieux, Pitt.	60.00
8 Eric Lindros, Phil.	20.00
9 Patrick Roy (G), Colo.	60.00
10 Joe Sakic, Colo.	30.00

ROOKIE SENSATIONS

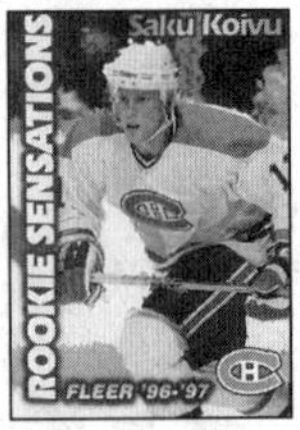

Insert Set (10 cards):	45.00
Insert (1:20 Hobby)	RS
1 Daniel Alfredsson, Otta.	6.00
2 Todd Bertuzzi, NYIs.	12.00
3 Valeri Bure, Mont.	4.00
4 Éric Dazé, Chic.	4.00
5 Sergei Gonchar, Wash.	4.00
6 Ed Jovanovski, Flor.	4.00
7 Saku Koivu, Mont.	8.00
8 Marcus Ragnarsson, SanJ.	4.00
9 Petr* Sykora, NJer.	4.00
10 Vitali Yachmenev, LosA.	4.00

VÉZINA TROPHY

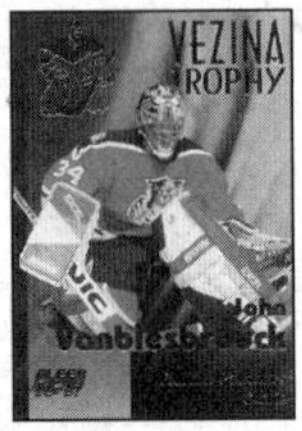

Insert Set (10 cards):	100.00
Insert (1:60)	VT
1 Ed Belfour (G), Chic.	14.00
2 Sean Burke, Hart.	8.00
3 Jim Carey (G), Wash.	6.00
4 Dominik Hasek (G), Buff.	15.00
5 Ron Hextall (G), Phil.	8.00
6 Chris Osgood (G), Detr.	8.00
7 Félix Potvin (G), Toro.	8.00
8 Daren Puppa (G), Tamp.	6.00
9 Patrick Roy (G), Colo.	45.00
10 John Vanbiesbrouck (G), Flor.	6.00

1996 - 97 FLEER PICKS

This series features even numbers only for cards 1-184. See Topps Picks for corresponding odd numbers.

Complete Set (92 cards):	10.00
Common Player:	.20
Player	FP
2 Joe Sakic, Colo.	1.00
4 Eric Lindros, Phil.	.50

	Player	Price
□	6 Paul Kariya, Anah.	1.00
□	8 Wayne Gretzky, SLou.	3.00
□	10 Chris Osgood (G), Detr.	.20
□	12 Brian Leetch, NYRa.	.20
□	14 Raymond Bourque, Bost.	.50
□	16 Ron Francis, Pitt.	.20
□	18 Keith Tkachuk, Winn.	.20
□	20 Paul Coffey, Detr.	.20
□	22 Phil Housley, Wash.	.20
□	24 Theoren Fleury, Calg.	.20
□	26 Sergei Zubov, Pitt.	.20
□	28 Adam Oates, Bost.	.20
□	30 John LeClair, Phil.	.50
□	32 Pierre Turgeon, Mont.	.20
□	34 Nicklas Lidström, Detr.	.20
□	36 Vincent Damphousse, Mont.	.20
□	38 Pat LaFontaine, Buff.	.20
□	40 Brendan Shanahan, Hart.	.50
□	42 Robert Svehla, Flor.	.20
□	44 Peter Bondra, Wash.	.20
□	46 Mikael Renberg, Phil.	.20
□	48 Alexei Yashin, Otta.	.20
□	50 Zigmund Palffy, NYIs.	.20
□	52 Larry Murphy, Toro.	.20
□	54 Rod Brind'Amour, Phil.	.20
□	56 Alexei Zhamnov, Winn.	.20
□	58 Jason Arnott, Edmo.	.20
□	60 Craig Janney, Winn.	.20
□	62 Jason Woolley, Flor.	.20
□	64 Jeff Brown, Hart.	.20
□	66 Tomas Sandström, Pitt.	.20
□	68 Doug Gilmour, Toro.	.20
□	70 Travis Green, NYIs.	.20
□	72 Teppo Numminen, Winn.	.20
□	74 Petr Sykora, NJer.	.20
□	76 Saku Koivu, Mont.	.50
□	78 Daniel Alfredsson, Otta.	.20
□	80 Ron Hextall (G), Phil.	.20
□	82 Jocelyn Thibault (G), Mont.	.20
□	84 Mike Richter (G), NYRa.	.20
□	86 Nikolai Khabibulin (G), Wpg	.20
□	88 John Vanbiesbrouck (G), Flor.	.20
□	90 Adam Graves, NYRa.	.20
□	92 Kenny Jönsson, NYIs.	.20
□	94 Jyrki Lumme, Vanc.	.20
□	96 Zdeno Ciger, Edmo.	.20
□	98 Ed Jovanovski, Flor.	.20
□	100 Greg Johnson, Detr.	.20
□	102 Pat Falloon, Phil.	.20
□	104 Andrew Cassels, Hart.	.20
□	106 German Titov, Calg.	.20
□	108 Joé Juneau, Wash.	.20
□	110 Igor Larionov, Detr.	.20
□	112 Norm Maciver, Winn.	.20
□	114 Chris Pronger, SLou.	.20
□	116 Scott Niedermayer, NJer.	.20
□	118 Vladimir Malakhov, Mont.	.20
□	120 Dale Hawerchuk, Phil.	.20
□	122 Jason Dawe, Buff.	.20
□	124 Valeri Bure, Mont.	.20
□	126 Marcus Ragnarsson, SanJ.	.20
□	128 Stéphane Richer, NJer.	.20
□	130 Wendel Clark, Toro.	.50
□	132 Bryan Smolinski, Pitt.	.20
□	134 Dimitri Khristich, LosA.	.20
□	136 Benoît Hogue, Dall.	.20
□	138 Kirk Muller, Toro.	.20
□	140 Ray Ferraro, LosA.	.20
□	142 Vitali Yachmenev, LosA.	.20
□	144 Jere Lehtinen, Dall.	.20
□	146 Brandon Convery, Toro.	.20
□	148 Darcy Tucker, Mont.	.20
□	150 Curtis Brown, Buff.	.20
□	152 Alexei Zhitnik, LosA.	.20
□	154 John Slaney, LosA.	.20
□	156 Bruce Driver, NJer.	.20
□	158 Jeff O'Neill, Hart.	.20
□	160 Patrice Brisebois, Mont.	.20
□	162 Gord Murphy, Flor.	.20
□	164 Doug Bodger, SanJ.	.20
□	166 Marty McSorley, NYRa.	.20
□	168 Nolan Baumgartner, Wash.	.20
□	170 Mike Gartner, Toro.	.50
□	172 Alexei Nikolishin, Hart.	.20
□	174 Alexei Yegorov, SanJ.	.20
□	176 Dave Reid, Dall.	.20
□	178 Marty Murray, Calg.	.20
□	180 Anders Eriksson, Detr.	.20
□	182 Checklist	.20
□	184 Checklist	.20

CAPTAIN'S CHOICE

	Player	Price
	Insert Set (10 cards):	**275.00**
	Insert (1:360)	**CC**
□	1 Eric Lindros, Phil.	20.00
□	2 Steve Yzerman, Detr.	50.00
□	3 Mario Lemieux, Pitt.	65.00
□	4 Wayne Gretzky, SLou.	90.00
□	5 Mark Messier, NYRa.	20.00
□	6 Joe Sakic, Colo.	35.00
□	7 Keith Tkachuk, Winn.	10.00
□	8 Doug Gilmour, Toro.	10.00
□	9 Trevor Linden, Vanc.	10.00
□	10 Brendan Shanahan, Hart.	20.00

FABULOUS FIFTY

	Player	Price
	Insert Set (50 cards):	**1085.00**
	Insert (1:1)	**Fab50**
□	1 Daniel Alfredsson, Otta.	.50
□	2 Peter Bondra, Wash.	.50
□	3 Raymond Bourque, Bost.	1.50
□	4 Martin Brodeur (G), NJer.	2.00
□	5 Pavel Bure, Vanc.	1.00
□	6 Jim Carey (G), Wash.	.35
□	7 Chris Chelios, Chic.	.50
□	8 Paul Coffey, Detr.	.50
□	9 Eric Dazé, Chic.	.50
□	10 Sergei Fedorov, Detr.	1.00
□	11 Theoren Fleury, Calg.	.50
□	12 Peter Forsberg, Colo.	1.50
□	13 Ron Francis, Pitt.	.50
□	14 Sergei Gonchar, Wash.	.35
□	15 Wayne Gretzky, SLou.	5.00
□	16 Roman Hamrlik, Tamp.	.35
□	17 Kevin Hatcher, Dall.	.35
□	18 Ron Hextall (G), Phil.	.50
□	19 Brett Hull, SLou.	1.00
□	20 Jaromir Jagr, Pitt.	1.00
□	21 Ed Jovanovski, Flor.	.50
□	22 Valeri Kamensky, Colo.	.35
□	23 Paul Kariya, Anah.	1.50
□	24 John LeClair, Phil.	1.00
□	25 Brian Leetch, NYRa.	.50
□	26 Mario Lemieux, Pitt.	3.50
□	27 Trevor Linden, Vanc.	.50
□	28 Eric Lindros, Phil.	1.00
□	29 Mark Messier, NYRa.	1.00
□	30 Mike Modano, Dall.	1.00
□	31 Alexander Mogilny, Vanc.	.50
□	32 Petr Nedved, Pitt.	.35
□	33 Joe Nieuwendyk, Dall.	.50
□	34 Owen Nolan, SanJ.	.50
□	35 Adam Oates, Bost.	.50
□	36 Chris Osgood (G), Detr.	.50
□	37 Sandis Ozolinsh, Colo.	.35
□	38 Zigmund Palffy, NYIs.	.50
□	39 Jeremy Roenick, Chic.	1.00
□	40 Patrick Roy (G), Colo.	3.50
□	41 Joe Sakic, Colo.	2.00
□	42 Teemu Selänne, Anah.	1.00
□	43 Brendan Shanahan, Hart.	1.00
□	44 Keith Tkachuk, Winn.	.50
□	45 Pierre Turgeon, Mont.	.50
□	46 John Vanbiesbrouck (G), Flor.	.50
□	47 Doug Weight, Edmo.	.50
□	48 Alexei Yashin, Otta.	.50
□	49 Steve Yzerman, Detr.	3.00
□	50 Alexei Zhamnov, Winn.	.35

DREAM LINE

	Player	Price
	Insert Set (10 cards):	**25.00**
	Insert (1:70)	**DL**
□	1 W. Gretzky / M. Lemieux / E. Lindros	30.00
□	2 C. Chelios / M. Richter / J. Roenick	6.00
□	3 D. Alfredsson / P. Forsberg / M. Brodeur	14.00
□	4 P. Bure / S. Fedorov / A. Mogilny	8.00
□	5 P. Kariya / T. Selänne / K. Tkachuk	10.00
□	6 D. Hasek / R. Hamrlik / J. Jagr	8.00
□	7 J. LeClair / M. Modano / B. Shanahan	10.00
□	8 E. Belfour / P. Roy / J. Vanbiesbrouck (G)	16.00
□	9 V. Kamensky / S. Ozolinsh / J. Sakic	8.00
□	10 Br. Hull / P. LaFontaine / P. Verbeek	6.00

FANTASY FORCE

	Player	Price
	Insert Set (10 cards):	**50.00**
	Insert (1:50)	**FF**
□	1 John LeClair, Phil.	8.00
□	2 Chris Osgood (G), Detr.	6.00
□	3 Ron Hextall (G), Phil.	6.00
□	4 Éric Dazé, Chic.	4.00
□	5 Jaromir Jagr, Pitt.	10.00
□	6 Brett Hull, SLou.	10.00
□	7 Ron Francis, Pitt.	6.00
□	8 Martin Brodeur (G), NJer.	16.00
□	9 Sergei Fedorov, Detr.	10.00
□	10 Petr Nedved, Pitt.	3.00

JAGGED EDGE

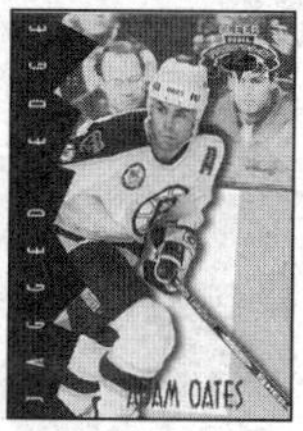

	Player	Price
	Insert Set (20 cards):	**50.00**
	Insert (1:18)	**JE**
□	1 Daniel Alfredsson, Otta.	4.00
□	2 Theoren Fleury, Calg.	4.00
□	3 Alexander Mogilny, Vanc.	3.00
□	4 Doug Weight, Edmo.	4.00
□	5 Alexei Yashin, Otta.	4.00
□	6 Paul Kariya, Anah.	10.00
□	7 Saku Koivu, Mont.	6.00
□	8 Sandis Ozolinsh, Colo.	2.00
□	9 Petr Nedved, Pitt.	2.00
□	10 Jeremy Roenick, Chic.	6.00
□	11 Mike Modano, Dall.	7.00
□	12 Jim Carey (G), Wash.	2.00
□	13 Ed Jovanovski, Flor.	3.00
□	14 Alexei Zhamnov, Winn.	2.00
□	15 Adam Oates, Bost.	3.00
□	16 Ron Francis, Pitt.	4.00
□	17 Brian Leetch, NYRa.	4.00
□	18 Paul Coffey, Detr.	4.00
□	19 Éric Dazé, Chic.	3.00
□	20 Zigmund Palffy, NYIs.	4.00

1996 - 97 FLEER ULTRA

There are two versions: the regular card and a Gold Medallion parallel (prefix G-)

	Player	GM	FU
	Complete Set (180 cards):	**160.00**	**40.00**
	Common Player:	**.35**	**.20**
□ □	1 Guy Hebert, Anah.	.35	.20
□ □	2 Paul Kariya, Anah.	5.00	1.00
□ □	3 Jari Kurri, Anah.	3.00	.50
□ □	4 Roman Oksiuta, Anah.	.35	.20
□ □	**5 Ruslan Salei, Anah. RC**	**.35**	**.50**
□ □	6 Teemu Selänne, Anah.	3.00	.50
□ □	7 Darren Van Impe, Anah.	.35	.20
□ □	8 Raymond Bourque, Bost.	4.00	.50
□ □	9 Kyle McLaren, Bost.	.35	.20
□ □	10 Adam Oates, Bost.	1.00	.20
□ □	11 Bill Ranford (G), Bost.	1.00	.20
□ □	12 Rick Tocchet, Bost.	1.00	.20
□ □	13 Donald Audette, Buff.	1.00	.20
□ □	14 Curtis Brown, Buff.	.35	.20
□ □	15 Jason Dawe, Buff.	.35	.20
□ □	16 Domonik Hasek (G), Buff.	3.00	.50
□ □	17 Pat LaFontaine, Buff.	2.00	.20
□ □	**18 Jay McKee, Buff. RC**	**.35**	**.50**
□ □	19 Derek Plante, Buff.	.35	.20
□ □	20 Wayne Primeau, Buff.	.35	.20
□ □	21 Theoren Fleury, Calg.	2.00	.20
□ □	22 Dave Gagner, Calg.	.35	.20
□ □	23 Jonas Hoglund, Calg.	.35	.20
□ □	24 Jarome Iginla, Calg.	3.00	1.00
□ □	25 Trevor Kidd (G), Calg.	1.00	.20
□ □	26 Robert Reichel, Calg.	1.00	.20
□ □	27 German Titov, Calg.	.35	.20
□ □	28 Tony Amonte, Chic.	2.00	.20
□ □	29 Ed Belfour (G), Chic.	3.00	.50
□ □	30 Chris Chelios, Chic.	2.00	.20
□ □	31 Eric Dazé, Chic.	1.00	.20
□ □	32 Ethan Moreau, Chic.	.35	.20
□ □	33 Gary Suter, Chic.	.35	.20
□ □	34 Adam Deadmarsh, Colo.	1.00	.20
□ □	35 Peter Forsberg, Colo.	5.00	1.00
□ □	36 Valeri Kamensky, Colo.	1.00	.20
□ □	37 Claude Lemieux, Colo.	1.00	.20
□ □	38 Sandis Ozolinsh, Colo.	.35	.20
□ □	39 Patrick Roy (G), Colo.	10.00	2.00
□ □	40 Joe Sakic, Colo.	6.00	1.00
□ □	41 Landon Wilson, Colo.	.35	.20
□ □	42 Derian Hatcher, Dall.	1.00	.20
□ □	43 Jamie Langenbrunner, Dall.	.35	.20
□ □	44 Mike Modano, Dall.	3.00	.50
□ □	45 Andy Moog (G), Dall.	1.00	.20
□ □	46 Joe Nieuwendyk, Dall.	1.00	.20
□ □	47 Pat Verbeek, Dall.	1.00	.20
□ □	48 Sergei Zubov, Dall.	.35	.20
□ □	49 Anders Eriksson, Detr.	.35	.20
□ □	50 Sergei Fedorov, Detr.	3.00	.50
□ □	51 Vladimir Konstantinov, Detr.	1.00	.20
□ □	52 Vyacheslav Kozlov, Detr.	.35	.20
□ □	53 Nicklas Lidström, Detr.	2.00	.20
□ □	54 Chris Osgood (G), Detr.	2.00	.20
□ □	55 Brendan Shanahan, Detr.	3.00	.50
□ □	56 Steve Yzerman, Detr.	5.00	1.50
□ □	57 Jason Arnott, Edmo.	1.00	.20
□ □	**58 Mike Grier, Edmo. RC**	**1.00**	**1.50**
□ □	59 Curtis Joseph (G), Edmo.	3.00	.50
□ □	**60 Rem Murray, Edmo. RC**	**.35**	**.50**
□ □	61 Jeff Norton, Edmo.	.35	.20
□ □	62 Miroslav Satan, Edmo.	1.00	.20
□ □	63 Doug Weight, Edmo.	2.00	.20
□ □	64 Radek Dvorak, Flor.	.35	.20
□ □	65 Ed Jovanovski, Flor.	1.00	.20
□ □	66 Scott Mellanby, Flor.	.35	.20
□ □	67 Rob Niedermayer, Flor.	.35	.20
□ □	68 Ray Sheppard, Flor.	.35	.20
□ □	69 Robert Svehla, Flor.	.35	.20
□ □	70 John Vanbiesbrouck (G), Flor.	1.00	.20
□ □	**71 Steve Washburn, Flor. RC**	**.35**	**.50**
□ □	72 Jeff Brown, Hart.	.35	.20
□ □	73 Sean Burke (G), Hart.	2.00	.20
□ □	74 Hnat Domenichelli, Hart.	.35	.20
□ □	75 Keith Primeau, Hart.	1.00	.20
□ □	76 Geoff Sanderson, Hart.	.35	.20
□ □	77 Rob Blake, LosA.	2.00	.20
□ □	78 Stéphane Fiset (G), LosA.	1.00	.20
□ □	79 Dimitri Khristich, LosA.	.35	.20
□ □	80 Mattias Norstrom, LosA.	.35	.20
□ □	81 Ed Olczyk, LosA.	.35	.20
□ □	82 Jamie Storr (G), LosA.	.35	.20
□ □	83 Jan Vopat, LosA.	.35	.20
□ □	84 Vitali Yachmenev, LosA.	.35	.20
□ □	85 Shayne Corson, Mont.	1.00	.20
□ □	86 Vincent Damphousse, Mont.	2.00	.20
□ □	87 Saku Koivu, Mont.	3.00	.50
□ □	88 Mark Recchi, Mont.	1.00	.20
□ □	89 Stéphane Richer, Mont.	.35	.20
□ □	90 Jocelyn Thibault (G), Mont.	1.00	.20
□ □	91 David Wilkie, Mont.	.35	.20
□ □	92 Dave Andreychuk, NJer.	1.00	.20
□ □	93 Martin Brodeur (G), NJer.	6.00	1.00
□ □	94 Scott Niedermayer, NJer.	1.00	.20
□ □	95 Scott Stevens, NJer.	1.00	.20
□ □	96 Petr Sykora, NJer.	1.00	.20
□ □	97 Steve Thomas, NJer.	.35	.20
□ □	98 Bryan Berard, NYIs.	1.00	.20
□ □	99 Todd Bertuzzi, NYIs.	4.00	1.50
□ □	100 Eric Fichaud (G), NYIs.	.35	.20
□ □	101 Travis Green, NYIs.	.35	.20
□ □	102 Kenny Jönsson, NYIs.	.35	.20
□ □	103 Zigmund Palffy, NYIs.	2.00	.20
□ □	104 Christian Dubé, NYRa.	.35	.20
□ □	105 Daniel Goneau, NYRa.	.35	.50
□ □	106 Wayne Gretzky, NYRa.	15.00	3.00
□ □	107 Alexei Kovalev, NYRa.	2.00	.20
□ □	108 Brian Leetch, NYRa.	2.00	.20
□ □	109 Mark Messier, NYRa.	3.00	.50
□ □	110 Mike Richter (G), NYRa.	1.00	.20
□ □	111 Luc Robitaille, NYRa.	3.00	.50
□ □	112 Niklas Sundström, NYRa.	.35	.20
□ □	113 Daniel Alfredsson, Otta.	2.00	.20
□ □	114 Radek Bonk, Otta.	1.00	.20
□ □	**115 Andreas Dackell, Otta. RC**	**1.00**	**1.00**
□ □	116 Alexandre Daigle, Otta.	.35	.20
□ □	117 Steve Duchesne, Otta.	.35	.20
□ □	118 Wade Redden, Otta.	1.00	.20
□ □	119 Damian Rhodes (G), Otta.	.35	.20
□ □	120 Alexei Yashin, Otta.	2.00	.20
□ □	121 Rod Brind'Amour, Phil.	1.00	.20
□ □	122 Paul Coffey, Phil.	2.00	.20
□ □	123 Éric Desjardins, Phil.	1.00	.20
□ □	124 Ron Hextall (G), Phil.	2.00	.20
□ □	125 John LeClair, Phil.	3.00	.50
□ □	126 Eric Lindros, Phil.	.35	.50
□ □	127 Janne Niinimaa, Phil.	.35	.20
□ □	128 Mikael Renberg, Phil.	1.00	.20
□ □	**129 Danius Zubrus, Phil. RC**	**1.00**	**1.50**
□ □	130 Mike Gartner, Phoe.	3.00	.50
□ □	131 Craig Janney, Phoe.	.35	.20
□ □	132 Nikolai Khabibulin (G), Phoe.	1.00	.20
□ □	133 Dave Manson, Phoe.	.35	.20
□ □	134 Teppo Numminen, Phoe.	1.00	.20
□ □	135 Jeremy Roenick, Phoe.	3.00	.50
□ □	136 Keith Tkachuk, Phoe.	2.00	.20
□ □	137 Oleg Tverdovsky, Phoe.	.35	.20
□ □	138 Tom Barrasso (G), Pitt.	1.00	.20
□ □	139 Ron Francis, Pitt.	2.00	.20
□ □	140 Kevin Hatcher, Pitt.	.35	.20
□ □	141 Jaromir Jagr, Pitt.	.35	.50
□ □	**142 Patrick Lalime (G), Pitt. RC**	**9.00**	**5.00**
□ □	143 Mario Lemieux, Pitt.	10.00	2.00
□ □	144 Jim Campbell, SLou.	.35	.20
□ □	145 Grant Fuhr (G), SLou.	2.00	.20
□ □	146 Brett Hull, SLou.	3.00	.50
□ □	147 Al MacInnis, SLou.	1.00	.20
□ □	148 Pierre Turgeon, SLou.	1.00	.20
□ □	**149 Harry York, SLou. RC**	**.35**	**.50**
□ □	150 Kelly Hrudey (G), SanJ.	1.00	.20
□ □	151 Al Iafrate, SanJ.	.35	.20
□ □	152 Bernie Nicholls, SanJ.	.35	.20
□ □	153 Owen Nolan, SanJ.	2.00	.20
□ □	154 Darren Turcotte, SanJ.	.35	.20
□ □	155 Brian Bradley, Tamp.	.35	.20
□ □	156 Dino Ciccarelli, Tamp.	1.00	.20
□ □	157 Roman Hamrlik, Tamp.	.35	.20
□ □	158 Daymond Langkow, Tamp.	.35	.20
□ □	159 Daren Puppa (G), Tamp.	.35	.20
□ □	160 Alexander Selivanov, Tamp.	.35	.20
□ □	**161 Sergei Berezin, Toro. RC**	**1.00**	**1.50**
□ □	162 Wendel Clark, Toro.	3.00	.50
□ □	163 Doug Gilmour, Toro.	2.00	.20
□ □	164 Larry Murphy, Toro.	.35	.20
□ □	165 Félix Potvin (G), Toro.	2.00	.20
□ □	166 Mats Sundin, Toro.	3.00	.50
□ □	167 Pavel Bure, Vanc.	3.00	.50
□ □	168 Trevor Linden, Vanc.	1.00	.20
□ □	169 Kirk McLean (G), Vanc.	1.00	.20
□ □	170 Alexander Mogilny, Vanc.	1.00	.20
□ □	171 Esa Tikkanen, Vanc.	.35	.20
□ □	172 Peter Bondra, Wash.	2.00	.20
□ □	**173 Andrew Brunette, Wash. RC**	**1.00**	**1.00**
□ □	174 Jim Carey (G), Wash.	.35	.20
□ □	175 Sergei Gonchar, Wash.	1.00	.20
□ □	176 Phil Housley, Wash.	1.00	.20
□ □	177 Joé Juneau, Wash.	.35	.20
□ □	178 Mikael Pivonka, Wash.	.35	.20
□ □	179 Checklist	3.00	.50
□ □	180 Checklist	3.00	.50

CLEAR THE ICE

	Player	Price
	Insert Set (10 cards):	**325.00**
	Insert (1:350)	**CTI**
□	1 Jim Carey (G), Wash.	15.00
□	2 Peter Forsberg, Colo.	50.00
□	3 Dominik Hasek (G), Buff.	35.00
□	4 Jaromir Jagr, Pitt.	35.00
□	5 John LeClair, Phil.	30.00
□	6 Eric Lindros, Phil.	35.00
□	7 Mark Messier, NYRa.	35.00

□ 8 Patrick Roy (G), Colo.	110.00
□ 9 Brendan Shanahan, Detr.	35.00
□ 10 Keith Tkachuk, Phoe.	20.00

MR. MOMENTUM

Insert Set (10 cards):	150.00
Insert (1:36 Retail)	MM
□ 1 Peter Bondra, Wash.	10.00
□ 2 Pavel Bure, Vanc.	15.00
□ 3 Ron Francis, Pitt.	10.00
□ 4 Brett Hull, SLou.	20.00
□ 5 Jaromir Jagr, Pitt.	20.00
□ 6 Pat LaFontaine, Buff.	10.00
□ 7 Eric Lindros, Phil.	20.00
□ 8 Mark Messier, NYRa.	20.00
□ 9 Mats Sundin, Toro.	20.00
□ 10 Steve Yzerman, Detr.	45.00

POWER BLUE LINE

Insert Set (8 cards):	50.00
Insert (#/1082)	PBL
□ 1 Raymond Bourque, Bost.	20.00
□ 2 Chris Chelios, Chic.	10.00
□ 3 Paul Coffey, Phil.	10.00
□ 4 Roman Hamrlik, Tamp.	5.00
□ 5 Ed Jovanovski, Flor.	5.00
□ 6 Vladimir Konstantinov, Detr.	5.00
□ 7 Brian Leetch, NYRa.	10.00
□ 8 Nicklas Lidström, Detr.	10.00

POWER RED LINE

Insert Set (10 cards):	150.00
Insert (#/1082)	PRL
□ 1 Sergei Fedorov, Detr.	15.00
□ 2 Wayne Gretzky, NYRa.	70.00
□ 3 Paul Kariya, Anah.	20.00
□ 4 Mario Lemieux, Pitt.	50.00
□ 5 Alexander Mogilny, Vanc.	5.00
□ 6 Adam Oates, Bost.	5.00
□ 7 Joe Sakic, Colo.	25.00
□ 8 Teemu Selänne, Anah.	10.00

ROOKIE

Insert Set (20 cards):	25.00
Insert (1:9)	R
□ 1 Bryan Berard, NYIs.	2.00
□ 2 Sergei Berezin, Toro.	4.00
□ 3 Curtis Brown, Buff.	2.00
□ 4 Jim Campbell, SLou.	2.00
□ 5 Christian Dubé, NYRa.	2.00
□ 6 Anders Eriksson, Detr.	2.00
□ 7 Éric Fichaud (G), NYIs.	2.00
□ 8 Daniel Goneau, NYRa.	2.00
□ 9 Mike Grier, Edmo.	4.00
□ 10 Jarome Iginla, Calg.	7.00
□ 11 Jamie Langenbrunner, Dall.	2.00
□ 12 Jay McKee, Buff.	2.00
□ 13 Ethan Moreau, Chic.	2.00
□ 14 Rem Murray, Edmo.	2.00
□ 15 Janne Niinimaa, Phil.	2.00
□ 16 Wayne Primeau, Buff.	2.00
□ 17 Wade Redden, Otta.	2.00
□ 18 Jamie Storr, LosA.	2.00
□ 19 David Wilkie, Mont.	2.00
□ 20 Landon Wilson, Colo.	2.00

ULTRA POWER

Insert Set (16 cards):	100.00
Insert	UP
□ 1 Raymond Bourque, Bost.	10.00
□ 2 Chris Chelios, Chic.	5.00
□ 3 Paul Coffey, Phil.	5.00
□ 4 Sergei Fedorov, Detr.	8.00
□ 5 Wayne Gretzky, NYRa.	35.00
□ 6 Roman Hamrlik, Tamp.	3.00
□ 7 Ed Jovanovski, Flor.	3.00
□ 8 Paul Kariya, Anah.	12.00
□ 9 Vladimir Konstantinov, Detr.	3.00
□ 10 Brian Leetch, NYRa.	5.00
□ 11 Mario Lemieux, Pitt.	25.00
□ 12 Nicklas Lidström, Detr.	5.00
□ 13 Alexander Mogilny, Vanc.	4.00
□ 14 Adam Oates, Bost.	3.00
□ 15 Joe Sakic, Colo.	14.00
□ 16 Teemu Selänne, Anah.	7.00

1996 - 97 GOT-UM / GREATS MEDALLIONS

These medallions have two versions: a regular "silver" medallion and a 24 kt. gold-plated parallel. While all 24 kt. gold-plated medallions are supposed to have the engraving "24 kt." on the edge, some gold medallions have come out of the packs without the engraving.

Complete Set (25 medallions):	450.00	50.00
Album:	4.00	
Medallion	Gold	Reg.
□□ Ed Belfour (G), NHLPA (Chic.)	30.00	2.00
□□ Sergei Berezin, NHLPA (Toro.)	10.00	1.00
□□ Raymond Bourque, NHLPA (Bost.)	30.00	3.00
□□ Pavel Bure, NHLPA (Vanc.)	20.00	2.00
□□ Jim Campbell, NHLPA (SLou.)	10.00	1.00
□□ Chris Chelios, NHLPA (Chic.)	15.00	1.00
□□ Vincent Damphousse, NHLPA (Mont.)	15.00	1.00
□□ Sergei Fedorov, NHLPA (Detr.)	30.00	2.00
□□ Theoren Fleury, NHLPA (Calg.)	10.00	1.00
□□ Doug Gilmour, NHLPA (Toro.)	15.00	1.00
□□ Wayne Gretzky, NHLPA	120.00	10.00
□□ Brett Hull, NHLPA (SLou.)	30.00	2.00
□□ Jarome Iginla, NHLPA (Calg.)	25.00	2.00
□□ Jaromir Jagr, NHLPA (Pitt.)	30.00	2.00
□□ Paul Kariya, NHLPA (Anah.)	40.00	3.00
□□ Mario Lemieux, NHLPA (Pitt.)	90.00	7.00
□□ Eric Lindros, NHLPA (Phil.)	30.00	2.00
□□ Mark Messier, NHLPA (NYRa.)	30.00	2.00
□□ Alexander Mogilny, NHLPA (Vanc.)	15.00	1.00
□□ Rem Murray, NHLPA (Edmo.)	10.00	1.00
□□ Jeremy Roenick, NHLPA	25.00	2.00
□□ Patrick Roy (G), NHLPA (Colo.)	90.00	7.00
□□ Joe Sakic, NHLPA (Colo.)	50.00	4.00
□□ David Wilkie, NHLPA	10.00	1.00
□□ Steve Yzerman, NHLPA (Detr.)	70.00	6.00

1996 - 97 KELLOGG'S

These pop-up cards were issued in specially-marked boxes of Kellogg's cereal. The team pop-ups featured a goalie mask with the team logo.

Player	Card
□ Curtis Joseph (G), Edmo.	5.00
□ Félix Potvin (G), Toro.	3.00
□ Canadiens	2.00
□ Canucks	2.00
□ Flames	2.00
□ Senators	2.00
□ Tony the Tiger	2.00

1996 - 97 KRAFT

Master Set (64 cards):	70.00
Kraft / Upper Deck Album:	35.00

JELL-O INSTANT PUDDING / ALL-STARS

One of six different cards was found on the back of specially-marked 102g JELL-O Instant Pudding boxes.

Card Size: 2 3/4" x 4"

Complete Set 6 cards):	10.00
Player	JELL-O
□ Raymond Bourque, Bost.	2.00
□ Chris Chelios, Chic.	1.00
□ Jaromir Jagr, Pitt.	2.00
□ Paul Kariya, Anah.	2.50
□ Mario Lemieux, Pitt.	6.00
□ Chris Osgood (G), Detr.	1.00

JELL-O JELLY POWDER / FAVOURITE PLAYER

One of five different cards was found on the back of specially-marked 85g JELL-O Jelly Powder boxes.

Complete Set (5 cards):	4.00
Player	JELL-O
□ Harvey Hound / D. Gagner, Calg.	1.00
□ San Jose Sharkie / M. McSorley, SanJ.	1.00
□ Stanley Panther / R. Niedermayer, Flor.	1.00
□ Carlton / Félix Potvin (G), Toro.	1.00
□ Wild Thing / T. Selänne, Anah.	1.50

JELL-O PUDDING SNACKS / CREASE KEEPERS

Two of 20 different cards were found on specially-marked 4x142g cups of JELL-O Pudding Snacks.

Complete Set (20 cards):	30.00
Player	JELL-O
□ Daniel Alfredsson, Otta.	1.00
□ Scotty Bowman, Detr.	1.00
□ Jim Carey (G), Wash.	1.00
□ Chris Chelios, Chic.	1.00
□ Marc Crawford, Colo.	1.00
□ Sergei Fedorov, Detr.	2.00
□ Peter Forsberg, Colo.	2.50
□ Ron Francis, Pitt.	1.00
□ Jarome Iginla, Calg.	1.50
□ Jagr / LeClair / Shanahan	1.50
□ Ed Jovanovski, Flor.	1.00
□ Paul Kariya, Anah.	2.50
□ Mario Lemieux, Pitt.	6.00
□ Mario Lemieux, Pitt.	6.00
□ Eric Lindros, Phil.	2.00
□ Adam Oates, Bost.	1.00
□ C. Osgood (G) / M. Vernon (G)	1.00
□ Mike Richter (G), NYRa.	1.00
□ Joe Sakic, Colo.	3.00
□ Jocelyn Thibault (G), Mont.	1.00

KRAFT DINNER / TEAM MVP

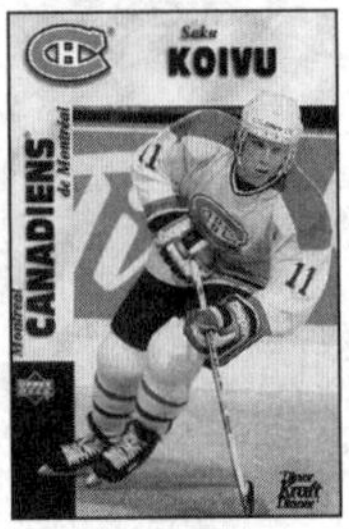

One of 20 different cards was found on the back of specially-marked Kraft Dinner Macaroni & Cheese boxes while one of six different cards was found on the back of Kraft Dinner specialty flavours.

Complete Set (26 cards):	35.00
Player	KD
□ Ed Belfour (G), Chic.	2.00
□ Martin Brodeur (G), NJer.	3.00
□ Sergei Fedorov, Detr.	2.00
□ Theoren Fleury, Calg.	1.00
□ Dominik Hasek (G), Buff.	2.00
□ Guy Hebert (G), Anah.	1.00
□ Brett Hull, SLou.	2.00
□ Saku Koivu, Mont.	1.50
□ Brian Leetch, NYRa.	1.00
□ Mario Lemieux, Pitt.	6.00
□ Eric Lindros, Phil.	2.00
□ Alexander Mogilny, Vanc.	1.00
□ Joe Nieuwendyk, Dall.	1.00
□ Owen Nolan, SanJ.	1.00
□ Adam Oates, Bost.	1.00
□ Zigmund Palffy, NYIs.	1.00
□ Yanic Perreault, LosA.	1.50
□ Michal Pivonka, Wash.	1.00
□ Daren Puppa (G), Tamp.	1.00
□ Patrick Roy (G), Colo.	6.00
□ Geoff Sanderson, Hart.	1.00
□ Mats Sundin, Toro.	2.00
□ Keith Tkachuk, Phoe.	1.00
□ John Vanbiesbrouck (G), Flor.	1.00
□ Doug Weight, Edmo.	1.00
□ Alexei Yashin, Otta.	1.00

PEANUT BUTTER / TEAM RIVALS

This set of seven disks was available through a redemption offer. Details were found on specially-marked 500g or 1kg Kraft Peanut Butter jars.

Complete Set (7 disks):	8.00
Player	NRMT-MT
□ Bondra / Dineen / Kariya / Neely	1.50
□ Bourque / Cunneyworth / Graves / LaFontaine	1.00
□ Buchberger / Fleury / King / Linden	1.00
□ Chelios / Palffy / S.Stevens / Yzerman	2.00
□ Damphousse / Gilmour / M.Lemieux / Lindros	2.50
□ MacInnis / Modano / Nolan / Ysebaert	1.00
□ J. Sakic / B. Skrudland	1.50

1996 - 97 KRAFT FLEX MAGNETS

One of eight different flex magnets was found in specially-marked Kraft Dinner 12-box cases.

Complete Set (8 magnets):	25.00
Player	Magnet
□ Theoren Fleury, Calg.	3.00
□ Saku Koivu, Mont.	3.00
□ Mario Lemieux, Pitt.	10.00
□ Eric Lindros, Phil.	3.00
□ Alexander Mogilny, Vanc.	3.00
□ Mats Sundin, Toro.	3.00
□ Doug Weight, Edmo.	3.00
□ Alexei Yashin, Otta.	3.00

1996 - 97 LEAF

There are two versions: the regular card and a Press Proof die-cut parallel.

Complete Set (240 cards):	1000.00	30.00
Common Player:	3.00	.20
Player	PP1500	Leaf
□□ 1 Sergei Fedorov, Det	20.00	1.00
□□ 2 Bill Ranford (G), Bost.	5.00	.20
□□ 3 Oleg Tverdovsky, Winn.	3.00	.20
□□ 4 Brad May, Buff.	3.00	.20
□□ 5 Chris Pronger, SLou.	10.00	.50
□□ 6 Martin Brodeur (G), NJer.	30.00	1.50
□□ 7 Yanic Perreault, LosA.	6.00	.20
□□ 8 Garry Galley, Buff.	3.00	.20
□□ 9 Shawn McEachern, Bost. (Otta.)	6.00	.20
□□ 10 Brian Bellows, Tamp.	4.00	.20
□□ 11 Ron Francis, Pitt.	10.00	.50
□□ 12 Mike Modano, Dall.	20.00	1.00
□□ 13 Steve Yzerman, Detr.	45.00	2.00
□□ 14 Joe Mullen, Bost.	5.00	.20
□□ 15 Pavel Bure, Vanc.	15.00	.50
□□ 16 Dino Ciccarelli, Tamp.	6.00	.20
□□ 17 Claude Lemieux, Colo.	6.00	.20
□□ 18 Stéphane Richer, NJer. (Mont.)	4.00	.20
□□ 19 Dominik Hasek (G), Buff.	20.00	1.00
□□ 20 Adam Graves, NYRa.	5.00	.20
□□ 21 Joé Juneau, Wash.	4.00	.20
□□ 22 Rob Niedermayer, Flor.	4.00	.20
□□ 23 Zigmund Palffy, NYIs.	10.00	.50
□□ 24 Dave Andreychuk, NJer.	6.00	.20
□□ 25 Steve Thomas, NJer.	4.00	.20
□□ 26 Tom Barrasso (G), Pitt.	5.00	.20
□□ 27 Éric Desjardins, Phil.	6.00	.20
□□ 28 Curtis Joseph (G), Edmo.	20.00	1.00
□□ 29 Russ Courtnall, Vanc.	4.00	.20
□□ 30 Stu Barnes, Flor.	3.00	.20
□□ 31 Mark Tinordi, Wash.	3.00	.20
□□ 32 Gary Suter, Chic.	4.00	.20
□□ 33 Greg Johnson, Detr.	3.00	.20
□□ 34 Joe Nieuwendyk, Dall.	5.00	.20
□□ 35 Norm Maciver, Winn.	3.00	.20
□□ 36 Craig Janney, Winn.	4.00	.20
□□ 37 Mark Recchi, Mont.	5.00	.20
□□ 38 Patrick Roy (G), Colo.	60.00	3.00
□□ 39 Petr Klima, Tamp.	3.00	.20
□□ 40 Ken Wregget (G), Pitt.	4.00	.20
□□ 41 Rod Brind'Amour, Phil.	6.00	.20
□□ 42 Viacheslav Fetisov, Detr.	10.00	.50
□□ 43 Kirk McLean (G), Vanc.	6.00	.20
□□ 44 Pat LaFontaine, Buff.	10.00	.50
□□ 45 Brett Hull, SLou.	20.00	1.00
□□ 46 Chris Chelios, Chic.	10.00	.50
□□ 47 Damian Rhodes (G), Otta.	4.00	.20
□□ 48 Kevin Hatcher, Pitt.	3.00	.20
□□ 49 Uwe Krupp, Colo.	3.00	.20
□□ 50 Bernie Nicholls, Chic.	4.00	.20
□□ 51 Tommy Söderström (G), NYIs.	3.00	.20
□□ 52 Teemu Selänne, Anah.	15.00	.50
□□ 53 Mats Sundin, Toro.	20.00	1.00
□□ 54 Jeff Hackett (G), Chic.	5.00	.20
□□ 55 Ulf Dahlen, SanJ.	3.00	.20
□□ 56 Dale Hunter, Wash.	6.00	.20
□□ 57 Robert Kron, Hart.	3.00	.20
□□ 58 Brian Bradley, Tamp.	3.00	.20
□□ 59 Pat Verbeek, NYRa.	6.00	.20
□□ 60 Kenny Jönsson, Toro.	4.00	.20
□□ 61 Theoren Fleury, Calg.	10.00	.50
□□ 62 Alexander Selivanov, Tamp.	3.00	.20
□□ 63 Nikolai Khabibulin (G), Winn.	5.00	.20
□□ 64 Grant Fuhr (G), SLou.	10.00	.50
□□ 65 Phil Housley, Wash.	6.00	.20
□□ 66 Bill Lindsay, Flor.	3.00	.20
□□ 67 Trevor Kidd (G), Calg.	6.00	.20
□□ 68 Jim Carey (G), Wash.	3.00	.20
□□ 69 Brian Skrudland, Flor.	3.00	.20
□□ 70 Todd Krygier, Wash.	3.00	.20
□□ 71 Petr Nedved, Pitt.	5.00	.20

☐☐	72 Kirk Muller, Toro.	6.00	.20
☐☐	73 Darren Puppa (G), Tamp.	4.00	.20
☐☐	74 Doug Gilmour, Toro.	10.00	.50
☐☐	75 Nicklas Lidström, Detr.	10.00	.50
☐☐	76 Zdeno Ciger, Edmo.	3.00	.20
☐☐	77 Robert Svehla, Flor.	4.00	.20
☐☐	78 Andrew Cassels, Hart.	4.00	.20
☐☐	79 Vincent Damphousse, Mont.	10.00	.50
☐☐	80 Alexandre Daigle, Otta.	3.00	.20
☐☐	81 Tomas Sandström, Pitt.	4.00	.20
☐☐	82 Brent Fedyk, Dall.	3.00	.20
☐☐	83 John LeClair, Phil.	15.00	.50
☐☐	84 Mario Lemieux, Pitt.	60.00	3.00
☐☐	85 Sean Burke (G), Hart.	10.00	.50
☐☐	86 Cam Neely, Bost.	20.00	1.00
☐☐	87 Jeff Friesen, SanJ.	6.00	.20
☐☐	88 Guy Hebert (G), Anah.	4.00	.20
☐☐	89 Jon Casey, SLou.	3.00	.20
☐☐	90 Rick Tocchet, Bost.	6.00	.20
☐☐	91 Mike Gartner, Toro. (Phoe.)	15.00	.50
☐☐	92 Tony Amonte, Chic.	10.00	.50
☐☐	93 Jason Dawe, Buff.	3.00	.20
☐☐	94 Chris Terreri (G), SanJ.	3.00	.20
☐☐	95 Zarley Zalapski, Calg.	3.00	.20
☐☐	96 Martin Rucinsky, Mont.	4.00	.20
☐☐	97 Garth Snow (G), Phil.	6.00	.20
☐☐	98 Sylvain Lefebvre, Toro.	3.00	.20
☐☐	99 Andy Moog (G), Dall.	5.00	.20
☐☐	100 Larry Murphy, Toro.	4.00	.20
☐☐	101 Alexei Yashin, Otta.	10.00	.50
☐☐	102 Pat Falloon, Phil.	3.00	.20
☐☐	103 Greg Adams, Dall.	3.00	.20
☐☐	104 Igor Larionov, Detr.	10.00	.50
☐☐	105 Geoff Sanderson, Hart.	4.00	.20
☐☐	106 Jaromir Jagr, Pitt.	20.00	1.00
☐☐	107 Alexei Zhamnov, Winn.	6.00	.20
☐☐	108 Mikael Renberg, Phil.	6.00	.20
☐☐	109 Kelly Hrudey (G), LosA.	6.00	.20
☐☐	110 Vladimir Konstantinov, Detr.	6.00	.20
☐☐	111 Brian Savage, Mont.	6.00	.20
☐☐	112 Adam Oates, Bost.	5.00	.20
☐☐	113 Teppo Numminen, Winn.	6.00	.20
☐☐	114 Ray Sheppard, Flor.	3.00	.20
☐☐	115 Michael Nylander, Calg.	4.00	.20
☐☐	116 Jozef Stümpel, Bost.	4.00	.20
☐☐	117 Ed Olczyk, LosA.	4.00	.20
☐☐	118 Roman Hamrlik, Tamp.	4.00	.20
☐☐	119 Kris Draper, Detr.	4.00	.20
☐☐	120 Chris Gratton, Tamp.	4.00	.20
☐☐	121 Randy Burridge, Wash.	3.00	.20
☐☐	122 Raymond Bourque, Bost.	20.00	1.00
☐☐	123 Jyrki Lumme, Vanc.	4.00	.20
☐☐	124 Dale Hawerchuk, Phil.	10.00	.50
☐☐	125 Dave Lowry, Flor.	4.00	.20
☐☐	126 Curtis Leschyshyn, Colo.	3.00	.20
☐☐	127 Martin Gelinas, Vanc.	4.00	.20
☐☐	128 Owen Nolan, SanJ.	10.00	.50
☐☐	129 Radek Bonk, Otta.	6.00	.20
☐☐	130 Sergei Zubov, Pitt.	4.00	.20
☐☐	131 Travis Green, NYIs.	4.00	.20
☐☐	132 Scott Mellanby, Flor.	4.00	.20
☐☐	133 Keith Tkachuk, Winn.	10.00	.50
☐☐	134 Luc Robitaille, NYRa.	15.00	.50
☐☐	135 Alexei Kovalev, NYRa.	10.00	.50
☐☐	136 Doug Weight, Edmo.	10.00	.50
☐☐	137 Benoît Hogue, Dall.	3.00	.20
☐☐	138 Cory Stillman, Calg.	4.00	.20
☐☐	139 Joe Sakic, Colo.	30.00	1.50
☐☐	140 Wayne Gretzky, SLou. (NYRa.)	80.00	4.00
☐☐	141 Mike Ricci, Colo.	6.00	.20
☐☐	142 Kyle McLaren, Bost.	4.00	.20
☐☐	143 Deron Quint, Winn.	3.00	.20
☐☐	144 Ville Peltonen, SanJ.	3.00	.20
☐☐	145 Todd Harvey, Dall.	4.00	.20
☐☐	146 B. Shanahan, Hart. (Detr.)	20.00	1.00
☐☐	147 Mike Vernon (G), Detr.	5.00	.20
☐☐	148 Eric Lindros, Phil.	20.00	1.00
☐☐	149 Rick Tabaracci (G), Tamp.	3.00	.20
☐☐	150 Stéphane Yelle, Colo.	3.00	.20
☐☐	151 Chris Osgood (G), Detr.	10.00	.50
☐☐	152 Corey Hirsch (G), Vanc.	3.00	.20
☐☐	153 Todd Marchant, Edmo.	4.00	.20
☐☐	154 Keith Primeau, Hart.	5.00	.20
☐☐	155 Alexei Zhitnik, LosA.	3.00	.20
☐☐	156 Félix Potvin (G), Toro.	10.00	.50
☐☐	157 Vitali Yachmenev, LosA.	3.00	.20
☐☐	158 Geoff Courtnall, SLou.	3.00	.20
☐☐	159 Peter Forsberg, Colo.	25.00	1.00
☐☐	160 Radek Dvorak, Flor.	4.00	.20
☐☐	161 Bryan McCabe, NYIs.	4.00	.20
☐☐	162 Alexander Mogilny, Vanc.	5.00	.20
☐☐	163 Shayne Corson, Mont.	6.00	.20
☐☐	164 Paul Coffey, Detr. (Hart.)	10.00	.50
☐☐	165 Brian Leetch, NYRa.	10.00	.50
☐☐	166 Wendel Clark, Toro.	15.00	.50
☐☐	167 Aaron Gavey, Tamp.	3.00	.20
☐☐	168 Dimitri Khristich, Wash.	3.00	.20
☐☐	169 Grant Marshall, Dall.	3.00	.20
☐☐	170 Valeri Kamensky, Colo.	6.00	.20
☐☐	171 Ryan Smyth, Edmo.	5.00	.20
☐☐	172 Niklas Sundström, NYRa.	4.00	.20
☐☐	173 Cliff Ronning, Vanc. (Phoe.)	4.00	.20
☐☐	174 Al MacInnis, SLou.	5.00	.20
☐☐	175 Scott Stevens, NJer.	5.00	.20
☐☐	176 Paul Kariya, Anah.	25.00	1.00
☐☐	177 Rob Blake, LosA.	10.00	.50
☐☐	178 Mike Richter (G), NYRa.	5.00	.20
☐☐	179 Jason Arnott, Edmo.	5.00	.20
☐☐	180 Mark Messier, NYRa.	20.00	1.00
☐☐	181 Scott Young, Colo.	6.00	.20
☐☐	182 Jocelyn Thibault (G), Mont.	5.00	.20
☐☐	183 Marcus Ragnarsson, SanJ.	4.00	.20
☐☐	184 Darren Turcotte, SanJ.	3.00	.20
☐☐	185 Joe Murphy, SLou.	3.00	.20
☐☐	186 Pierre Turgeon, SLou.	5.00	.20
☐☐	187 Trevor Linden, Vanc.	5.00	.20
☐☐	188 Stéphane Fiset (G), Colo.	6.00	.20
☐☐	189 Miroslav Satan, Edmo.	6.00	.20
☐☐	190 Mathieu Schneider, Toro.	4.00	.20
☐☐	191 Jeremy Roenick, Chic.	15.00	.50
☐☐	192 Craig MacTavish, Phil.	3.00	.20
☐☐	193 John Vanbiesbrouck (G), Flor.	5.00	.20
☐☐	194 Ron Hextall (G), Phil.	10.00	.50
☐☐	195 John MacLean, NJer.	3.00	.20
☐☐	196 Vyacheslav Kozlov, Detr.	4.00	.20
☐☐	197 Sandis Ozolinsh, Colo.	4.00	.20
☐☐	198 Scott Niedermayer, NJer.	6.00	.20
☐☐	199 Ed Belfour (G), Chic.	20.00	1.00
☐☐	200 Peter Bondra, Wash.	10.00	.50
☐☐	201 Jere Lehtinen, Dall.	6.00	.20
☐☐	202 Eric Dazé, Chic.	8.00	.20
☐☐	203 Chad Kilger, Winn.	4.00	.20
☐☐	204 Saku Koivu, Mont.	15.00	.50
☐☐	205 Todd Bertuzzi, NYIs.	24.00	2.00
☐☐	206 Petr Sykora, NJer.	5.00	.20
☐☐	207 Valeri Bure, Mont.	6.00	.20
☐☐	208 Ed Jovanovski, Flor.	8.00	.20
☐☐	209 Jeff O'Neill, Hart.	5.00	.20
☐☐	210 Daniel Alfredsson, Otta.	10.00	.50
☐☐	211 Byron Dafoe (G), LosA.	5.00	.20
☐☐	212 Brian Holzinger, Buff.	3.00	.20
☐☐	213 Martin Biron (G), Buff.	5.00	.50
☐☐	214 Anders Eriksson, Detr.	3.00	.20
☐☐	215 Landon Wilson, Colo.	3.00	.20
☐☐	**216 Alexei Yegorov, SanJ. RC**	**4.00**	**.50**
☐☐	**217 Jan Caloun, SanJ. RC**	**4.00**	**.50**
☐☐	218 David Sacco, Anah.	3.00	.20
☐☐	219 David Nemirovsky, Flor.	3.00	.20
☐☐	220 Anders Myrvold, Colo.	3.00	.20
☐☐	221 Tommy Salo (G), NYIs.	5.00	.50
☐☐	222 Jan Vopat, LosA.	3.00	.20
☐☐	**223 Steve Staios, Bost. RC**	**4.00**	**.50**
☐☐	224 Patrick Labrecque (G), Mont.	3.00	.20
☐☐	225 Jamie Langenbrunner, Dall.	4.00	.20
☐☐	226 Denis Pederson, NJer.	3.00	.20
☐☐	227 Marek Malik, Hart.	3.00	.20
☐☐	228 Geoff Sarjeant (G), SanJ.	3.00	.20
☐☐	229 Chris Ferraro, NYRa.	3.00	.20
☐☐	230 Zdenek Nedved, Toro.	3.00	.20
☐☐	231 Wayne Primeau, Buff.	3.00	.20
☐☐	232 Daymond Langkow, Tamp.	4.00	.20
☐☐	233 Marko Kiprusoff, Mont.	3.00	.20
☐☐	234 Niklas Sundblad, NYRa.	3.00	.20
☐☐	**235 Jamie Ram (G), NYRa. RC**	**6.00**	**1.00**
☐☐	236 Jamie Rivers, SLou.	3.00	.20
☐☐	**237 Steve Washburn, Flor. RC**	**4.00**	**.50**
☐☐	238 CL: Teemu Selänne, Anah.	5.00	.20
☐☐	239 CL: Steve Yzerman, Detr.	25.00	1.00
☐☐	240 CL: Eric Lindros, Phil.	10.00	.50

FIRE ON ICE

	Insert Set (15 cards):	400.00
	Insert (#/2500)	FOI
☐	1 Mario Lemieux, Pitt.	75.00
☐	2 Alexander Mogilny, Vanc.	12.00
☐	3 Joe Sakic, Colo.	40.00
☐	4 Paul Kariya, Anah.	35.00
☐	5 Wayne Gretzky, NYRa.	100.00
☐	6 Doug Weight, Edmo.	15.00
☐	7 Zigmund Palffy, NYIs.	15.00
☐	8 Eric Lindros, Phil.	25.00
☐	9 Teemu Selänne, Anah.	20.00
☐	10 Doug Gilmour, Toro.	15.00
☐	11 Jeremy Roenick, Chic.	20.00
☐	12 Steve Yzerman, Detr.	60.00
☐	13 Ed Jovanovski, Flor.	10.00
☐	14 Mike Modano, Dall.	25.00
☐	15 Mark Messier, NYRa.	25.00

GOLD LEAF ROOKIE

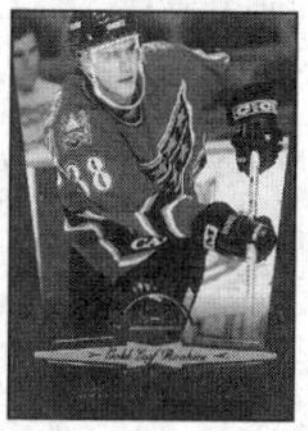

	Insert Set (10 cards):	25.00
	Insert	GLR
☐	1 Ethan Moreau, Chic.	3.00
☐	2 Kevin Hodson, Detr.	3.00
☐	3 José Théodore, Mont.	18.00
☐	4 Peter Ferraro, NYRa.	3.00
☐	5 Ralph Intranuovo, Toro.	3.00
☐	6 Nolan Baumgartner, Wash.	3.00
☐	7 Brandon Convery, Toro.	3.00
☐	8 Darcy Tucker, Mont.	4.00
☐	9 Éric Fichaud (G), NYIs.	3.00
☐	10 Steve Sullivan, NJer.	6.00

LEATHER & LACES

There are two versions: the promo card and the insert (#/5000).

	Complete Set (20 cards):	25.00	200.00
	Player	Promo	Insert
☐☐	1 Joe Sakic, Colo.	4.00	20.00
☐☐	2 Keith Tkachuk, Winn.	1.00	7.00
☐☐	3 Brett Hull, SLou.	2.00	12.00
☐☐	4 Paul Coffey, Detr.	1.00	7.00
☐☐	5 Jaromir Jagr, Pitt.	2.00	12.00
☐☐	6 Peter Forsberg, Colo.	3.00	17.00
☐☐	7 Zigmund Palffy, NYIs.	1.00	7.00
☐☐	8 Wayne Gretzky, NYRa.	10.00	50.00
☐☐	9 Pavel Bure, Vanc.	2.00	10.00
☐☐	10 Eric Lindros, Phil.	2.00	12.00
☐☐	11 Alexander Mogilny, Vanc.	1.00	6.00
☐☐	12 Trevor Linden, Vanc.	1.00	5.00
☐☐	13 Jeremy Roenick, Chic.	2.00	10.00
☐☐	14 Doug Gilmour, Toro.	1.00	7.00
☐☐	15 Mike Modano, Dall.	2.00	12.00
☐☐	16 Sergei Fedorov, Detr.	2.00	12.00
☐☐	17 Brendan Shanahan, Hart.	2.00	12.00
☐☐	18 Pierre Turgeon, SLou.	1.00	5.00
☐☐	19 Ed Jovanovski, Flor.	1.00	5.00
☐☐	20 Saku Koivu, Mont.	2.00	10.00

SHUT DOWN

	Insert Set (15 cards):	225.00
	Insert (#/2500)	SD
☐	1 Patrick Roy (G), Colo.	75.00
☐	2 John Vanbiesbrouck (G), Flor.	12.00
☐	3 Jocelyn Thibault (G), Mont.	10.00
☐	4 Ed Belfour (G), Chic.	25.00
☐	5 Curtis Joseph (G), Edmo.	25.00
☐	6 Martin Brodeur (G), NJer.	40.00
☐	7 Damian Rhodes (G), Otta.	8.00
☐	8 Félix Potvin (G), Toro.	15.00
☐	9 Nikolai Khabibulin (G), Winn.	10.00
☐	10 Jim Carey (G), Wash.	8.00
☐	11 Mike Richter (G), NYRa.	12.00
☐	12 Corey Hirsch (G), Vanc.	8.00
☐	13 Chris Osgood (G), Detr.	15.00
☐	14 Ron Hextall (G), Phil.	15.00
☐	15 Daren Puppa (G), Tamp.	8.00

SWEATERS

There are two versions: the Away card (#/5000) and the Home card (#/1000).

	Insert Set (15 cards):	525.00	150.00
	Player	Home	Away
☐☐	1 Mario Lemieux, Pitt.	110.00	35.00
☐☐	2 Patrick Roy (G), Colo.	110.00	35.00
☐☐	3 Eric Lindros, Phil.	35.00	10.00
☐☐	4 John Vanbiesbrouck (G), Flor.	15.00	5.00
☐☐	5 Paul Kariya, Anah.	50.00	15.00
☐☐	6 Martin Brodeur (G), NJer.	60.00	20.00
☐☐	7 Éric Dazé, Chic.	15.00	5.00
☐☐	8 Mark Messier, NYRa.	35.00	10.00
☐☐	9 Jim Carey (G), Wash.	10.00	4.00
☐☐	10 Brendan Shanahan, Detr.	35.00	10.00
☐☐	11 Sergei Fedorov, Detr.	35.00	10.00
☐☐	12 Brett Hull, SLou.	35.00	10.00
☐☐	13 Pavel Bure, Vanc.	30.00	10.00
☐☐	14 Daniel Alfredsson, Otta.	20.00	5.00
☐☐	15 Saku Koivu, Mont.	30.00	10.00

THE BEST OF...

	Insert Set (9 cards):	125.00
	Insert (#/1500)	TBO
☐	1 Jaromir Jagr, Pitt.	30.00
☐	2 Éric Dazé, Chic.	10.00
☐	3 Eric Lindros, Phil.	30.00
☐	4 Chris Osgood (G), Detr.	15.00
☐	5 Keith Tkachuk, Winn. (Phoe.)	15.00
☐	6 Nikolai Khabibulin (G), Winn. (Phoe.)	10.00
☐	7 Doug Weight, Edmo.	15.00
☐	8 Peter Forsberg, Colo.	40.00
☐	9 Jocelyn Thibault (G), Mont.	10.00

1996 - 97 LEAF LIMITED

There are two versions: the regular card and a Limited Gold parallel.

	Complete Set (90 cards):	850.00	60.00
	Common Player:	4.00	.35
	Player	LLG	LL
☐☐	1 Chris Chelios, Chic.	15.00	1.50
☐☐	2 Brendan Shanahan, Detr.	25.00	2.50
☐☐	3 Keith Tkachuk, Phoe.	15.00	1.50
☐☐	4 Roman Hamrlik, Tamp.	6.00	.50
☐☐	5 Adam Oates, Bost.	10.00	1.00
☐☐	6 Chris Osgood (G), Detr.	15.00	1.50
☐☐	7 Wayne Gretzky, NYRa.	100.00	10.00
☐☐	8 Alexander Mogilny, Vanc.	10.00	1.00
☐☐	9 Patrick Roy (G), Colo.	70.00	7.50
☐☐	10 Saku Koivu, Mont.	20.00	2.00
☐☐	11 Jaromir Jagr, Pitt.	25.00	2.50
☐☐	12 Wendel Clark, Toro.	20.00	2.00
☐☐	13 Mike Modano, Dall.	25.00	2.50
☐☐	14 Ed Jovanovski, Flor.	10.00	1.00
☐☐	15 John LeClair, Phil.	20.00	2.00
☐☐	16 Jim Carey (G), Wash.	4.00	.35
☐☐	17 Paul Kariya, Anah.	35.00	3.50
☐☐	18 Paul Coffey, Hart.	15.00	1.50
☐☐	19 Todd Bertuzzi, NYIs.	30.00	6.00
☐☐	20 Owen Nolan, SanJ.	15.00	1.50
☐☐	21 Dominik Hasek (G), Buff.	25.00	2.50
☐☐	22 Bill Ranford (G), Bost.	10.00	1.00
☐☐	23 Scott Stevens, NJer.	10.00	1.00
☐☐	24 Brett Hull, SLou.	25.00	2.50
☐☐	25 Trevor Kidd (G), Calg.	8.00	.50
☐☐	26 Viacheslav Fetisov, Detr.	15.00	1.50
☐☐	27 Luc Robitaille, NYRa.	20.00	2.00
☐☐	28 Mats Sundin, Toro.	25.00	2.50
☐☐	29 Peter Forsberg, Colo.	35.00	3.50
☐☐	30 John Vanbiesbrouck (G), Flor.	10.00	1.00
☐☐	31 Alexei Yashin, Otta.	15.00	1.50
☐☐	32 Pavel Bure, Vanc.	20.00	2.00
☐☐	33 Pat Verbeek, Dall.	8.00	.50
☐☐	34 Vitali Yachmenev, LosA.	4.00	.35
☐☐	35 Ron Hextall (G), Phil.	15.00	1.50
☐☐	36 Michal Pivonka, Wash.	4.00	.35
☐☐	37 Eric Dazé, Chic.	10.00	1.00
☐☐	38 Pierre Turgeon, Mont.	10.00	1.00
☐☐	39 Petr Nedved, Pitt.	8.00	.50
☐☐	40 Steve Yzerman, Detr.	60.00	6.00
☐☐	41 Mike Richter (G), NYRa.	10.00	1.00
☐☐	42 Marcus Ragnarsson, SanJ.	6.00	.50
☐☐	43 Jason Arnott, Edmo.	10.00	1.00
☐☐	44 Jocelyn Thibault (G), Mont.	10.00	1.00
☐☐	45 Alexander Selivanov, Tamp.	4.00	.35
☐☐	46 Claude Lemieux, Colo.	8.00	.50
☐☐	47 Eric Lindros, Phil.	25.00	2.50
☐☐	48 Grant Fuhr (G), SLou.	15.00	1.50
☐☐	49 Raymond Bourque, Bost.	30.00	3.00
☐☐	50 Scott Mellanby, Flor.	6.00	.50
☐☐	51 Craig Janney, Phoe.	6.00	.50
☐☐	52 Ron Francis, Pitt.	15.00	1.50
☐☐	53 Ed Belfour (G), Chic.	25.00	2.50
☐☐	54 Petr Sykora, NJer.	10.00	1.00
☐☐	55 Damian Rhodes (G), Otta.	6.00	.50
☐☐	56 Joe Sakic, Colo.	40.00	4.00
☐☐	57 Zigmund Palffy, NYIs.	15.00	1.50
☐☐	58 Daren Puppa (G), Tamp.	6.00	.50
☐☐	59 Pat LaFontaine, Buff.	15.00	1.50
☐☐	60 Nikolai Khabibulin (G), Phoe.	10.00	1.00
☐☐	61 Sergei Fedorov, Detr.	25.00	2.50
☐☐	62 Valeri Bure, Mont.	8.00	.50
☐☐	63 Peter Bondra, Wash.	15.00	1.50
☐☐	64 Teemu Selänne, Anah.	20.00	2.00
☐☐	65 Mark Messier, NYRa.	25.00	2.50
☐☐	66 Shayne Corson, SLou.	8.00	.50
☐☐	67 Theoren Fleury, Calg.	15.00	1.50
☐☐	68 Jeff O'Neill, Hart.	10.00	1.00
☐☐	69 Éric Fichaud (G), NYIs.	4.00	.35
☐☐	70 Doug Gilmour, Toro.	15.00	1.50
☐☐	71 Doug Weight, Edmo.	15.00	1.50
☐☐	72 Stéphane Fiset (G), LosA.	8.00	.50
☐☐	73 Daniel Alfredsson, Otta.	15.00	1.50
☐☐	74 Trevor Linden, Vanc.	10.00	1.00
☐☐	75 Joe Nieuwendyk, Dall.	10.00	1.00
☐☐	76 Brian Bradley, Tamp.	4.00	.35
☐☐	77 Jere Lehtinen, Dall.	8.00	.50
☐☐	78 Rob Niedermayer, Flor.	6.00	.50
☐☐	79 Mikael Renberg, Phil.	8.00	.50
☐☐	80 Félix Potvin (G), Toro.	15.00	1.50
☐☐	81 Valeri Kamensky, Colo.	8.00	.50
☐☐	82 Brian Leetch, NYRa.	15.00	1.50
☐☐	83 Jeff Friesen, SanJ.	8.00	.50
☐☐	84 Vincent Damphousse, Mont.	15.00	1.50
☐☐	85 Mario Lemieux, Pitt.	70.00	7.50
☐☐	86 Jeremy Roenick, Phoe. [Harley]	20.00	3.00
☐☐	87 Martin Brodeur (G), NJer.	40.00	4.00
☐☐	88 Vyacheslav Kozlov, Detr.	6.00	.50
☐☐	89 Corey Hirsch (G), Vanc.	4.00	.35
☐☐	90 Curtis Joseph (G), Edmo.	25.00	2.50
☐	Eric Lindros, Phil. [Checklist]		

BASH THE BOARDS

There are two versions: the regular card and a Press Proof parallel (#/2000).

	Insert Set (10 cards):	.00	325.00	100.00
	Player	Promo	LE350	BTB
☐☐☐	1 Eric Lindros, Phil.	2.00	55.00	15.00
☐☐☐	2 Mark Messier, NYRa.	2.00	55.00	15.00
☐☐☐	3 Owen Nolan, SanJ.	1.00	30.00	10.00
☐☐☐	4 Doug Gilmour, Toro.	1.00	30.00	10.00
☐☐☐	5 K. Tkachuk, Winn. (Phoe.)	1.00	30.00	10.00
☐☐☐	6 Claude Lemieux, Colo.	1.00	20.00	6.00
☐☐☐	7 Ed Jovanovski, Flor.	1.00	20.00	6.00
☐☐☐	8 Peter Forsberg, Colo.	3.00	75.00	25.00
☐☐☐	9 Brendan Shanahan, Hart.	2.00	55.00	15.00
☐☐☐	10 Éric Dazé, Chic.	1.00	20.00	6.00

LIMITED ROOKIES

A tough-to-find gold parallel (not inserted into packs) does exist.

Insert Set (10 cards): 50.00

Insert	LR
1 Ethan Moreau, Chic.	6.00
2 Jarome Iginla, Calg.	10.00
3 Bryan Berard, NYIs.	6.00
4 Hnat Domenichelli, Hart.	6.00
5 Wade Redden, Otta.	6.00
6 Dainius Zubrus, Phil. RC	**6.00**
7 Sergei Berezin, Toro. RC	**6.00**
8 Jamie Langenbrunner, Dall.	6.00
9 Tomas Holmström, Detr. RC	**6.00**
10 Jonas Höglund, Calg.	6.00

STUBBLE

Insert Set (20 cards):	625.00
Insert (#/1500)	S
1 Patrick Roy (G), Colo.	90.00
2 Eric Lindros, Phil.	30.00
3 Wayne Gretzky, NYRa.	120.00
4 Paul Coffey, Detr.	15.00
5 Jim Carey (G), Wash.	10.00
6 Ed Belfour (G), Chic.	30.00
7 Mario Lemieux, Pitt.	90.00
8 Mike Modano, Dall.	30.00
9 Todd Bertuzzi, NYIs.	50.00
10 Pavel Bure, Vanc.	20.00
11 Martin Brodeur (G), NJer.	45.00
12 Petr Nedved, Pitt.	10.00
13 Alexander Mogilny, Vanc.	10.00
14 Steve Yzerman, Detr.	70.00
15 Brett Hull, SLou.	30.00
16 Joe Sakic, Colo.	45.00
17 Scott Mellanby, Flor.	10.00
18 Trevor Linden, Vanc.	10.00
19 Rob Niedermayer, Flor.	10.00
20 Wendel Clark, Toro.	20.00

1996 - 97 LEAF PREFERRED

There are two versions: the regular card and a Press Proof parallel (limited to 250).

Complete Set (150 cards):	1800.00	30.00
Common Player:	5.00	.20
Player	PP250	LP
1 Patrick Roy (G), Colo.	120.00	3.00
2 Alexander Mogilny, Vanc.	15.00	.20
3 Bill Ranford (G), Bost.	15.00	.20
4 Jeremy Roenick, Chic.	30.00	.50
5 Travis Green, NYIs.	9.00	.20
6 Owen Nolan, SanJ.	20.00	.50
7 Paul Kariya, Anah.	50.00	1.00
8 Pat Verbeek, NYRa.	10.00	.20
9 Jeff O'Neill, Hart.	15.00	.20
10 Nikolai Khabibulin (G), Phoe.	15.00	.20
11 Pat LaFontaine, Buff.	20.00	.50
12 Rob Niedermayer, Flor.	9.00	.20
13 Luc Robitaille, NYRa.	30.00	.50
14 Mats Sundin, Toro.	40.00	1.00
15 Cory Stillman, Calg.	9.00	.20
16 Ray Ferraro, LosA.	6.00	.20
17 Alexei Yashin, Otta.	20.00	.50
18 Brian Bradley, Tamp.	5.00	.20
19 Chris Chelios, Chic.	20.00	.50
20 Jason Arnott, Edmo.	15.00	.20
21 Petr Sykora, NJer.	15.00	.20
22 Jaromir Jagr, Pitt.	40.00	1.00
23 Jim Carey (G), Wash.	6.00	.20
24 Claude Lemieux, Colo.	10.00	.20
25 Vincent Damphousse, Mont.	20.00	.50
26 Shayne Corson, Mont.	10.00	.20
27 Joe Nieuwendyk, Dall.	15.00	.20
28 Kenny Jönsson, NYIs.	8.00	.20
29 Peter Bondra, Wash.	20.00	.50
30 Ed Belfour (G), Chic.	40.00	1.00
31 Brendan Shanahan, Detr.	40.00	1.00
32 Éric Desjardins, Phil.	10.00	.20
33 Corey Hirsch (G), Vanc.	6.00	.20
34 Viacheslav Fetisov, Detr.	20.00	.50
35 Craig Janney, SanJ.	9.00	.20
36 Félix Potvin (G), Toro.	20.00	.50
37 Joe Sakic, Colo.	60.00	1.50
38 Scott Stevens, NJer.	15.00	.20
39 Kelly Hrudey (G), LosA.	10.00	.20
40 Adam Oates, Bost.	15.00	.20
41 John Vanbiesbrouck (G), Flor.	15.00	.20
42 Brian Leetch, NYRa.	20.00	.50
43 Alexander Selivanov, Tamp.	5.00	.20
44 Mike Modano, Dall.	40.00	1.00
45 Saku Koivu, Mont.	30.00	.50
46 Tom Barrasso (G), Pitt.	15.00	.20
47 Jere Lehtinen, Dall.	10.00	.20
48 Daniel Alfredsson, Otta.	20.00	.50
49 Joé Juneau, Wash.	9.00	.20
50 Chris Osgood (G), Detr.	20.00	.50
51 Dave Andreychuk, NJer.	10.00	.20
52 Marcus Ragnarsson, SanJ.	9.00	.20
53 Valeri Kamensky, Colo.	10.00	.20
54 Doug Weight, Edmo.	20.00	.50
55 Mike Richter (G), NYRa.	15.00	.20
56 Teemu Selänne, Anah.	30.00	.50
57 Stéphane Fiset (G), LosA.	10.00	.20
58 Mikael Renberg, Phil.	10.00	.20
59 Trevor Linden, Vanc.	15.00	.20
60 Bernie Nicholls, SanJ.	9.00	.20
61 Eric Dazé, Chic.	16.00	.20
62 Ron Francis, Pitt.	20.00	.50
63 Sergei Zubov, Dall.	9.00	.20
64 Rod Brind'Amour, Phil.	10.00	.20
65 Sergei Fedorov, Detr.	40.00	1.00
66 Mark Messier, NYRa.	40.00	1.00
67 Theoren Fleury, Calg.	20.00	.50
68 Ed Jovanovski, Flor.	16.00	.20
69 Daren Puppa (G), Tamp.	9.00	.20
70 Pierre Turgeon, SLou.	15.00	.20
71 Oleg Tverdovsky, Phoe.	6.00	.20
72 Ryan Smyth, Edmo.	15.00	.20
73 Jocelyn Thibault (G), Mont.	15.00	.20
74 Brendan Witt, Wash.	5.00	.20
75 Igor Larionov, Detr.	20.00	.50
76 Stéphane Richer, Mont.	9.00	.20
77 Ron Hextall (G), Phil.	20.00	.50
78 Mike Ricci, Colo.	10.00	.20
79 Dimitri Khristich, LosA.	6.00	.20
80 Derian Hatcher, Dall.	10.00	.20
81 Martin Brodeur (G), NJer.	60.00	1.50
82 Petr Nedved, Pitt.	10.00	.20
83 Raymond Bourque, Bost.	45.00	1.00
84 Keith Primeau, Hart.	15.00	.20
85 Sean Burke (G), Hart.	20.00	.50
86 Geoff Sanderson, Hart.	9.00	.20
87 Wendel Clark, Toro.	30.00	.50
88 Valeri Bure, Mont.	10.00	.20
89 Keith Tkachuk, Phoe.	20.00	.50
90 Roman Hamrlik, Tamp.	9.00	.20
91 Dominik Hasek (G), Buff.	40.00	1.00
92 Ray Sheppard, Flor.	6.00	.20
93 Todd Bertuzzi, NYIs.	45.00	2.00
94 Pavel Bure, Vanc.	30.00	.50
95 Alexei Zhamnov, Winn.	10.00	.20
96 Alexei Kovalev, NYRa.	20.00	.50
97 Jeff Friesen, SanJ.	10.00	.20
98 Scott Young, Colo.	10.00	.20
99 Vitali Yachmenev, LosA.	6.00	.20
100 Michal Pivonka, Wash.	5.00	.20
101 Paul Coffey, Hart.	20.00	.50
102 Steve Yzerman, Detr.	90.00	2.00
103 Zigmund Palffy, NYIs.	20.00	.50
104 Doug Gilmour, Toro.	20.00	.50
105 John LeClair, Phil.	30.00	.50
106 Brett Hull, SLou.	40.00	1.00
107 Yanic Perreault, LosA.	12.00	.20
108 Bill Guerin, NJer.	15.00	.20
109 Damian Rhodes (G), Otta.	9.00	.20
110 Peter Forsberg, Colo.	50.00	1.00
111 Scott Mellanby, Flor.	9.00	.20
112 Wayne Gretzky, NYRa.	160.00	4.00
113 Mario Lemieux, Pitt.	120.00	3.00
114 Todd Harvey, Dall.	9.00	.20
115 Mark Recchi, Mont.	15.00	.20
116 Trevor Kidd (G), Calg.	10.00	.20
117 Eric Lindros, Phil.	40.00	1.00
118 Jarome Iginla, Calg.	30.00	1.50
119 Éric Fichaud (G), NYIs.	6.00	.20
120 Mattias Timander, Bost. RC	**8.00**	**.50**
121 Hnat Domenichelli, Hart.	6.00	.20
122 Chris O'Sullivan, Calg.	5.00	.20
123 Sergei Berezin, Toro. RC	**15.00**	**1.50**
124 Jonas Hoglund, Calg.	6.00	.20
125 Anders Eriksson, Detr.	5.00	.20
126 Corey Schwab, Tamp.	6.00	.20
127 Janne Niinimaa, Phil.	9.00	.20
128 Dainius Zubrus, Phil. RC	**15.00**	**1.50**
129 Bryan Berard, NYIs.	10.00	.50
130 Wade Redden, Otta.	12.00	.50
131 Wayne Primeau, Buff.	6.00	.20
132 Brandon Convery, Toro.	5.00	.20
133 Richard Zednik, Wash. RC	**30.00**	**2.50**
134 Darcy Tucker, Mont.	9.00	.20
135 Christian Dubé, NYRa.	6.00	.20
136 Rem Murray, Edmo. RC	**8.00**	**.50**
137 Keven Hodson (G), Detr.	9.00	.20
138 Steve Washburn, Flor. RC	**8.00**	**.50**
139 Ethan Moreau, Chic.	6.00	.20
140 Daymond Langkow, Tamp.	9.00	.20
141 Terry Ryan, Mont. RC	**8.00**	**.50**
142 Curtis Brown, Buff.	6.00	.20
143 Steve Sullivan, NJer. RC	**25.00**	**2.00**
144 Jamie Langenbrunner, Dall.	9.00	.20
145 Daniel Goneau, NYRa.	8.00	.50
146 Anson Carter, Wash.	15.00	.50
147 Jim Campbell, SLou.	5.00	.20
148 CL: Keith Tkachuk, Phoe.	10.00	.20
149 CL: Eric Dazé, Chic.	10.00	.20
150 CL: Mike Modano, Dall.	20.00	.50

LEAF STEEL

There are two versions: the silver Steel card and the Gold Steel parallel.

Complete Set (63 cards):	425.00	85.00
Inserts	LSG	LS
1 Sergei Fedorov, Detr.	20.00	4.00
2 Martin Brodeur (G), NJer.	35.00	7.00
3 Corey Hirsch (G), Vanc.	5.00	1.00
4 Raymond Bourque, Bost.	25.00	5.00
5 Saku Koivu, Mont.	15.00	3.00
6 Ron Francis, Pitt.	10.00	2.00
7 Chris Chelios, Chic.	10.00	2.00
8 Scott Mellanby, Flor.	5.00	1.00
9 Ron Hextall (G), Phil.	10.00	2.00
10 Doug Gilmour, Toro.	10.00	2.00
11 Joe Sakic, Colo.	35.00	7.00
12 Petr Sykora, NJer.	5.00	1.00
13 Marcus Ragnarsson, SanJ.	5.00	1.00
14 Pat Verbeek, NYRa.	5.00	1.00
15 Stéphane Fiset (G), LosA.	5.00	1.00
16 Alexei Yashin, Otta.	10.00	2.00
17 Daren Puppa (G), Tamp.	5.00	1.00
18 Eric Lindros, Phil.	20.00	1.00
19 Jason Arnott, Edmo.	10.00	2.00
20 Todd Bertuzzi, NYIs.	25.00	8.00
21 Jim Carey (G), Wash.	5.00	1.00
22 Pat LaFontaine, Buff.	10.00	2.00
23 Brian Leetch, NYRa.	10.00	2.00
24 Trevor Linden, Vanc.	5.00	1.00
25 Eric Dazé, Chic.	5.00	1.00
26 Pierre Turgeon, SLou.	5.00	1.00
27 Tom Barrasso (G), Pitt.	5.00	1.00
28 Mike Modano, Dall.	20.00	4.00
29 Brendan Shanahan, Detr.	20.00	4.00
30 Nikolai Khabibulin (G), Phoe.	5.00	1.00
31 Claude Lemieux, Colo.	5.00	1.00
32 Zigmund Palffy, NYIs.	10.00	2.00
33 Mats Sundin, Toro.	20.00	4.00
34 Paul Kariya, Anah.	30.00	5.00
35 Daniel Alfredsson, Otta.	10.00	2.00
36 Patrick Roy (G), Colo.	60.00	10.00
37 Jaromir Jagr, Pitt.	20.00	1.00
38 Vyacheslav Kozlov, Detr.	5.00	1.00
39 John LeClair, Phil.	15.00	3.00
40 Bill Ranford (G), Bost.	5.00	1.00
41 Vitali Yachmenev, LosA.	5.00	1.00
42 Mark Messier, NYRa.	20.00	4.00
43 Valeri Bure, Mont.	5.00	1.00
44 Roman Hamrlik, Tamp.	5.00	1.00
45 Joe Nieuwendyk, Dall.	5.00	1.00
46 Mike Richter (G), NYRa.	10.00	2.00
47 Theoren Fleury, Calg.	10.00	2.00
48 Wendel Clark, Toro.	15.00	3.00
49 Doug Weight, Edmo.	10.00	2.00
50 Damian Rhodes (G), Otta.	5.00	1.00
51 Alexander Mogilny, Vanc.	10.00	2.00
52 Dominik Hasek (G), Buff.	20.00	4.00
53 Éric Fichaud (G), NYIs.	5.00	1.00
54 Adam Oates, Bost.	5.00	1.00
55 Jocelyn Thibault (G), Mont.	5.00	1.00
56 Petr Nedved, Pitt.	5.00	1.00
57 Mike Vernon (G), Detr.	5.00	1.00
58 Mikael Renberg, Phil.	5.00	1.00
59 Valeri Kamensky, Colo.	5.00	1.00
60 Peter Forsberg, Colo.	30.00	6.00
61 Rob Niedermayer, Flor.	5.00	1.00
62 Owen Nolan, SanJ.	10.00	2.00
63 Jere Lehtinen, SanJ.	5.00	1.00

MASKED MARAUDERS

Insert Set (12 cards):	225.00
Insert (#/2500)	MM
1 Jim Carey (G), Wash.	8.00
2 Martin Brodeur (G), NJer.	40.00
3 John Vanbiesbrouck (G), Flor.	12.00
4 Patrick Roy (G), Colo.	75.00
5 Félix Potvin (G), Toro.	15.00
6 Chris Osgood (G), Detr.	15.00
7 Dominik Hasek (G), Buff.	25.00
8 Jocelyn Thibault (G), Mont.	10.00
9 Nikolai Khabibulin (G), Phoe.	10.00
10 Curtis Joseph (G), Edmo.	25.00
11 Mike Richter (G), NYRa.	12.00
12 Ed Belfour (G), Chic.	25.00

STEEL POWER

Insert Set (12 cards):	150.00
Insert (#/5000)	SP
1 Joe Sakic, Colo.	20.00
2 Mario Lemieux, Pitt.	35.00
3 Pavel Bure, Vanc.	10.00
4 Mark Messier, NYRa.	10.00
5 Wayne Gretzky, NYRa.	50.00
6 Peter Forsberg, Colo.	15.00
7 Sergei Fedorov, Detr.	10.00
8 Jaromir Jagr, Pitt.	10.00
9 Brett Hull, SLou.	10.00
10 Teemu Selänne, Anah.	10.00
11 Paul Kariya, Anah.	15.00
12 Eric Lindros, Phil.	10.00

VANITY PLATES

There are two versions: the regular steel card and the gold parallel.

Insert Set (14 cards):	275.00	100.00
Insert	VPG	VP
1 Wayne Gretzky, NYRa.	75.00	35.00
2 John Vanbiesbrouck (G), Flor.	9.00	4.00
3 Chris Osgood (G), Detr.	10.00	5.00
4 Steve Yzerman, Detr.	45.00	20.00
5 Brett Hull, SLou.	18.00	5.00
6 Mario Lemieux, Pitt.	56.00	25.00
7 Eric Lindros, Phil.	18.00	5.00
8 Ed Jovanovski, Flor.	7.00	4.00
9 Pavel Bure, Vanc.	15.00	5.00
10 Félix Potvin (G), Toro.	10.00	5.00
11 Teemu Selänne, Anah.	15.00	5.00
12 Keith Tkachuk, Phoe.	10.00	5.00
13 Curtis Joseph (G), Edmo.	18.00	5.00
14 Ed Belfour (G), Chic.	18.00	5.00

1996 - 97 LEGENDS OF HOCKEY

Artwork by Doug West. The most expensive single is Bobby Hull at $12-15. Other singles sell between $8-12.

Card Size: 3 1/2" x 5 1/2"

Series Five Set (18 cards): 125.00

Player	Player
73 Terry Sawchuk (G)	74 Turk Broda (G)
75 Father David Bauer	76 George Armstrong
77 Marcel Pronovost	78 Bill Quackenbush
79 Harry Watson	80 Charlie Rayner
81 Keith Allen	82 Art Ross
83 Doug Bentley	84 Max Bentley
85 Charlie Drinkwater	86 Moose Goheen
87 Mike Bossy	88 Glenn Hall (G)
89 Bobby Hull	90 Sam Pollock

1996 - 97 MAGGERS

This series includes 24 short prints (*) and 12 double prints (**). The Hebert and Brodeur magnets have spelling mistakes while the Damphousse and Koivu magnets have their names switched.

It is believed this was to be the first of two series. There are no magnets of the Phoenix Coyotes or Washington Capitals in this series. There were also proof versions printed on light cardboard stock. Common magnets start at about $1 each while common proofs start at $2 each.

Magnet Size: 6" x 7 1/2"

Player	Maggers
1 Paul Kariya, Anah. (*)	
2 Teemu Selänne, Anah.	
5 Guy Hebert, Anah.	
12 Bill Ranford (G), Bost.	
13 Adam Oates, Bost.	
14 Rick Tocchet, Bost.	
15 Cam Neely, Bost. (*)	
17 Raymond Bourque, Bost.	
19 Theoren Fleury, Calg. (*)	
21 Trevor Kidd (G), Calg.	
22 Steve Chiasson, Calg.	
24 German Titov, Calg.	
25 Gary Roberts, Calg.	
26 Ed Belfour (G), Chic.	
27 Chris Chelios, Chic.	
28 Denis Savard, Chic. (*)	
29 Joe Murphy, Chic.	
30 Jeremy Roenick, Chic. (**)	
31 Gary Suter, Chic.	
32 Éric Dazé, Chic.	
34 Bernie Nicholls, Chic.	
35 Patrick Roy (G), Colo. (**)	
36 Peter Forsberg, Colo. (**)	
37 Joe Sakic, Colo. (*)	
39 Mike Ricci, Colo. (*)	
40 Claude Lemieux, Colo.	
42 Alexei Gusarov, Colo.	
43 Valeri Kamensky, Colo.	
44 Sandis Ozolinsh, Colo.	
45 Joe Nieuwendyk, Dall.	
47 Derian Hatcher, Dall.	
49 Mike Modano, Dall.	
50 Andy Moog, Dall.	
51 Sergei Fedorov, Detr.	
53 Vyacheslav Kozlov, Detr.	
54 Keith Primeau, Detr.	
55 Steve Yzerman, Detr.	
57 Dino Ciccarelli, Detr.	
58 Chris Osgood (G), Detr. (*)	
60 Mike Vernon (G), Detr.	
61 Igor Larionov, Detr.	
62 Paul Coffey, Detr. (*)	
65 Zdeno Ciger, Edmo.	
66 Jason Arnott, Edmo.	
68 John Vanbiesbrouck (G), Flor. (*)	

□ □ 71 Ed Jovanovski, Flor.
□ □ 73 Sean Burke (G), Hart.
□ □ 74 Brendan Shanahan, Hart.
□ □ 76 Kelly Hrudey (G), LosA.
□ □ 78 Kevin Stevens, LosA.
□ □ 80 Tony Granato, LosA.
□ □ 81 Yanic Perreault, LosA.
□ □ 82 Jocelyn Thibault (G), Mont. (*)
□ □ 83 Andrei Kovalenko, Mont.
□ □ 84 Benoît Brunet, Mont.
□ □ 85 Pierre Turgeon, Mont.
□ □ 86 Saku Koivu, Mont. [Error: Damphousse] (*)
□ □ 88 V.Damphousse, Mont. [Error: name Koivu] (*)
□ □ 91 Martin Brodeur (G), NJer. (*)
□ □ 92 Scott Stevens, NJer.
□ □ 93 Phil Housley, NJer.
□ □ 95 Zigmund Palffy, NYIs.
□ □ 97 Éric Fichaud (G), NYIs.
□ □ 99 Mark Messier, NYRa.
□ □ 101 Mike Richter (G), NYRa. (*)
□ □ 102 Brian Leetch, NYRa. (*)
□ □ 104 Luc Robitaille, NYRa.
□ □ 105 Pat Verbeek, NYRa.
□ □ 106 Adam Graves, NYRa.
□ □ 109 Alexei Yashin, Otta. (*)
□ □ 110 Alexandre Daigle, Otta. (*)
□ □ 111 Eric Lindros, Phil. (**)
□ □ 113 Ron Hextall (G), Phil.
□ □ 114 Dale Hawerchuk, Phil.
□ □ 115 Mikael Renberg, Phil.
□ □ 117 John LeClair, Phil. (*)
□ □ 119 Mario Lemieux, Pitt. (**)
□ □ 122 Tom Barrasso (G), Pitt.
□ □ 123 Petr Nedved, Pitt.
□ □ 124 Jaromir Jagr, Pitt. (**)
□ □ 126 Ron Francis, Pitt.
□ □ 127 Tomas Sandström, Pitt.
□ □ 129 Chris Terreri, SanJ.
□ □ 131 Owen Nolan, SanJ.
□ □ 133 Jeff Odgers, SanJ.
□ □ 135 Wayne Gretzky, SLou. (**)
□ □ 137 Brett Hull, SLou. (**)
□ □ 139 Grant Fuhr (G), SLou. (**)
□ □ 141 Chris Pronger, SLou.
□ □ 142 Al MacInnis, SLou.
□ □ 143 Shayne Corson, SLou.
□ □ 144 Daren Puppa (G), Tamp.
□ □ 145 Petr Klima, Tamp.
□ □ 146 Félix Potvin (G), Toro. (*)
□ □ 149 Doug Gilmour, Toro. (**)
□ □ 151 Mats Sundin, Toro. (*)
□ □ 152 Tie Domi, Toro. (*)
□ □ 153 Wendel Clark, Toro. (*)
□ □ 155 Corey Hirsch (G), Vanc.
□ □ 156 Pavel Bure, Vanc. (**)
□ □ 158 Trevor Linden, Vanc. (*)
□ □ 159 Alexander Mogilny, Vanc. (**)
□ □ 161 Esa Tikkanen, Vanc.
□ □ 162 Peter Bondra, Wash.
□ □ 164 Joé Juneau, Wash.
□ □ 165 Michal Pivonka, Wash.
□ □ 166 Sergei Gonchar, Wash.
□ □ 167 Jim Carey (G), Wash. (*)

1996 - 97 MCDONALD'S

Complete Set (40 cards):	25.00
Player	McD
□ McD-1 Paul Coffey, Hart. [Ice Breakers]	.50
□ McD-2 Teemu Selänne, Anah. [Ice Breakers]	1.00
□ McD-3 Éric Dazé, Chic. [Ice Breakers]	.50
□ McD-4 John LeClair, Phil. [Ice Breakers]	1.00
□ McD-5 Saku Koivu, Mont. [Ice Breakers]	1.00
□ McD-6 Ed Jovanovski, Flor. [Ice Breakers]	.50
□ McD-7 Chris Osgood (G), Detr. [Ice Breakers]	.50
□ McD-8 Chris Chelios, Chic. [Ice Breakers]	.50
□ McD-9 Daniel Alfredsson, Otta. [Ice Breakers]	.50
□ McD-10 Joe Sakic, Colo. [Ice Breakers]	2.00
□ McD-11 Alexander Mogilny, Vanc. [Ice Breakers]	.50
□ McD-12 Jeremy Roenick, Phoe. [Ice Breakers]	1.00
□ McD-13 Keith Tkachuk, Phoe. [Ice Breakers]	.50
□ McD-14 Doug Gilmour, Toro. [Ice Breakers]	.50
□ McD-15 Theoren Fleury, Calg. [Ice Breakers]	.50
□ McD-16 Doug Weight, Edmo. [Ice Breakers]	.50
□ McD-17 Steve Yzerman, Detr. [Ice Breakers]	3.00
□ McD-18 Zigmund Palffy, NYIs. [Ice Breakers]	.50
□ McD-19 Pierre Turgeon, Mont. [Ice Breakers]	.50
□ McD-20 Brian Leetch, NYRa. [Ice Breakers]	.50
□ McD-21 Lemieux, Pitt. [Premier]	3.50
□ McD-22 Mark Messier, NYRa. [Premier]	1.00
□ McD-23 Jaromir Jagr, Pitt. [Premier]	1.00
□ McD-24 Brett Hull, SLou. [Premier]	1.00
□ McD-25 Eric Lindros, Phil. [Premier]	1.00
□ McD-26 Sergei Fedorov, Detr. [Premier]	1.00
□ McD-27 Pavel Bure, Vanc. [Premier]	1.00
□ McD-28 Peter Forsberg, Colo. [Premier]	1.50
□ McD-29 Paul Kariya, Anah. [Premier]	1.50
□ McD-30 Patrick Roy (G), Colo. [Premier]	3.50
□ McD-31 Bourque, Bost. [Premier]	1.50
□ McD-32 Carey, Wash. [Caged]	.35
□ McD-33 Martin Brodeur (G), NJer. [Caged]	2.00
□ McD-34 Trevor Kidd, Calg. [Caged]	.35
□ McD-35 John Vanbiesbrouck (G), Flor. [Caged]	.50
□ McD-36 Jocelyn Thibault (G), Mont. [Caged]	.50
□ McD-37 Ed Belfour (G), Chic. [Caged]	1.00
□ McD-38 Félix Potvin (G), Toro. [Caged]	.50
□ McD-39 Damian Rhodes (G), Otta. [Caged]	.35
□ McD-40 Curtis Joseph (G), Edmo. [Caged]	1.00
□ Checklist	.35

1996 - 97 METAL UNIVERSE

Complete Set (200 cards):	20.00
Common Player:	.20
Player	MU
□ 1 Guy Hebert (G), Anah.	.20
□ 2 Paul Kariya, Anah.	1.00
□ 3 Jari Kurri, Anah.	.50
□ 4 Roman Oksiuta, Anah.	.20
□ 5 Steve Rucchin, Anah.	.20
□ 6 Teemu Selänne, Anah.	.50
□ 7 Raymond Bourque, Bost.	.50
□ 8 Kirk McLaren, Bost.	.20
□ 9 Adam Oates, Bost.	.20
□ 10 Bill Ranford (G), Bost.	.20
□ 11 Rick Tocchet, Bost.	.20
□ 12 Donald Audette, Buff.	.20
□ 13 Jason Dawe, Buff.	.20
□ 14 Dominik Hasek (G), Buff.	.50
□ 15 Pat LaFontaine, Buff.	.20
□ 16 Derek Plante, Buff.	.20
□ 17 Wayne Primeau, Buff.	.20
□ 18 Theoren Fleury, Calg.	.20
□ 19 Dave Gagner, Calg.	.20
□ 20 Trevor Kidd (G), Calg.	.20
□ 21 James Patrick, Calg.	.20
□ 22 Robert Reichel, Calg.	.20
□ 23 German Titov, Calg.	.20
□ 24 Tony Amonte, Chic.	.20
□ 25 Ed Belfour (G), Chic.	.50
□ 26 Chris Chelios, Chic.	.20
□ 27 Eric Dazé, Chic.	.20
□ 28 Gary Suter, Chic.	.20
□ 29 Alexei Zhamnov, Chic.	.20
□ 30 Adam Deadmarsh, Colo.	.20
□ 31 Adam Foote, Colo.	.20
□ 32 Peter Forsberg, Colo.	1.00
□ 33 Valeri Kamensky, Colo.	.20
□ 34 Uwe Krupp, Colo.	.20
□ 35 Claude Lemieux, Colo.	.20
□ 36 Sandis Ozolinsh, Colo.	.20
□ 37 Patrick Roy (G), Colo.	2.00
□ 38 Joe Sakic, Colo.	1.00
□ 39 Derian Hatcher, Dall.	.20
□ 40 Mike Modano, Dall.	.50
□ 41 Andy Moog (G), Dall.	.20
□ 42 Joe Nieuwendyk, Dall.	.20
□ 43 Pat Verbeek, Dall.	.20
□ 44 Sergei Zubov, Dall.	.20
□ 45 Sergei Fedorov, Detr.	.50
□ 46 Vladimir Konstantinov, Detr.	.20
□ 47 Vyacheslav Kozlov, Detr.	.20
□ 48 Nicklas Lidström, Detr.	.20
□ 49 Chris Osgood (G), Detr.	.20
□ 50 Brendan Shanahan, Detr.	.50
□ 51 Steve Yzerman, Detr.	1.50
□ 52 Jason Arnott, Edmo.	.20
□ 53 Curtis Joseph (G), Edmo.	.50
□ 54 Andrei Kovalenko, Edmo.	.20
□ 55 Miroslav Satan, Edmo.	.20
□ 56 Doug Weight, Edmo.	.20
□ 57 Radek Dvorak, Flor.	.20
□ 58 Per Gustafsson, Flor.	.20
□ 59 Ed Jovanovski, Flor.	.20
□ 60 Scott Mellanby, Flor.	.20
□ 61 Rob Niedermayer, Flor.	.20
□ 62 Ray Sheppard, Flor.	.20
□ 63 Robert Svehla, Flor.	.20
□ 64 John Vanbiesbrouck (G), Flor.	.20
□ 65 Jeff Brown, Hart.	.20
□ 66 Sean Burke (G), Hart.	.20
□ 67 Paul Coffey, Hart.	.20
□ 68 Nelson Emerson, Hart.	.20
□ 69 Jeff O'Neill, Hart.	.20
□ 70 Keith Primeau, Hart.	.20
□ 71 Geoff Sanderson, Hart.	.20
□ 72 Aki Berg, LosA.	.20
□ 73 Rob Blake, LosA.	.20
□ 74 Stéphane Fiset (G), LosA.	.20
□ 75 Dimitri Khristich, LosA.	.20
□ 76 Petr Klima, LosA.	.20
□ 77 Ed Olczyk, LosA.	.20
□ 78 Vitali Yachmenev, LosA.	.20
□ 79 Vincent Damphousse, Mont.	.20
□ 80 Saku Koivu, Mont.	.50
□ 81 Mark Recchi, Mont.	.20
□ 82 Stéphane Richer, Mont.	.20
□ 83 Jocelyn Thibault (G), Mont.	.20
□ 84 Pierre Turgeon, Mont.	.20
□ 85 Dave Andreychuk, NJer.	.20
□ 86 Martin Brodeur (G), NJer.	1.00
□ 87 Scott Niedermayer, NJer.	.20
□ 88 Scott Stevens, NJer.	.20
□ 89 Petr Sykora, NJer.	.20
□ 90 Steve Thomas, NJer.	.20
□ 91 Todd Bertuzzi, NYIs.	1.50
□ 92 Travis Green, NYIs.	.20
□ 93 Kenny Jönsson, NYIs.	.20
□ 94 Bryan McCabe, NYIs.	.20
□ 95 Zigmund Palffy, NYIs.	.20
□ 96 Wayne Gretzky, NYRa.	3.00
□ 97 Alexei Kovalev, NYRa.	.20
□ 98 Brian Leetch, NYRa.	.20
□ 99 Mark Messier, NYRa.	.50
□ 100 Mike Richter (G), NYRa.	.20
□ 101 Luc Robitaille, NYRa.	.50
□ 102 Niklas Sundström, NYRa.	.20
□ 103 Daniel Alfredsson, Otta.	.20
□ 104 Radek Bonk, Otta.	.20
□ 105 Alexandre Daigle, Otta.	.20
□ 106 Steve Duchesne, Otta.	.20
□ 107 Damian Rhodes (G), Otta.	.20
□ 108 Alexei Yashin, Otta.	.20
□ 109 Rod Brind'Amour, Phil.	.20
□ 110 Éric Desjardins, Phil.	.20
□ 111 Dale Hawerchuk, Phil.	.20
□ 112 Ron Hextall (G), Phil.	.20
□ 113 John LeClair, Phil.	.50
□ 114 Eric Lindros, Phil.	.50
□ 115 Mikael Renberg, Phil.	.20
□ 116 Mike Gartner, Phoe.	.50
□ 117 Craig Janney, Phoe.	.20
□ 118 Nikolai Khabibulin (G), Phoe.	.20
□ 119 Dave Manson, Phoe.	.20
□ 120 Teppo Numminen, Phoe.	.20
□ 121 Jeremy Roenick, Phoe.	.50
□ 122 Keith Tkachuk, Phoe.	.20
□ 123 Oleg Tverdovsky, Phoe.	.20
□ 124 Tom Barrasso (G), Pitt.	.20
□ 125 Ron Francis, Pitt.	.20
□ 126 Kevin Hatcher, Pitt.	.20
□ 127 Jaromir Jagr, Pitt.	.50
□ 128 Mario Lemieux, Pitt.	2.00
□ 129 Petr Nedved, Pitt.	.20
□ 130 Shayne Corson, SLou.	.20
□ 131 Grant Fuhr (G), SLou.	.20
□ 132 Brett Hull, SLou.	.50
□ 133 Al MacInnis, SLou.	.20
□ 134 Joe Murphy, SLou.	.20
□ 135 Chris Pronger, SLou.	.20
□ 136 Kelly Hrudey (G), SanJ.	.20
□ 137 Al Iafrate, SanJ.	.20
□ 138 Bernie Nicholls, SanJ.	.20
□ 139 Owen Nolan, SanJ.	.20
□ 140 Marcus Ragnarsson, SanJ.	.20
□ 141 Darren Turcotte, SanJ.	.20
□ 142 Bradley Bradley,Tamp.	.20
□ 143 Dino Ciccarelli, Tamp.	.20
□ 144 Chris Gratton, Tamp.	.20
□ 145 Roman Hamrlik, Tamp.	.20
□ 146 Daren Puppa (G), Tamp.	.20
□ 147 Alexander Selivanov, Tamp.	.20
□ 148 Wendel Clark, Toro.	.50
□ 149 Doug Gilmour, Toro.	.20
□ 150 Kirk Muller, Toro.	.20
□ 151 Larry Murphy, Toro.	.20
□ 152 Félix Potvin (G), Toro.	.20
□ 153 Mathieu Schneider, Toro.	.20
□ 154 Mats Sundin, Toro.	.50
□ 155 Pavel Bure, Vanc.	.50
□ 156 Russ Courtnall, Vanc.	.20
□ 157 Trevor Linden, Vanc.	.20
□ 158 Kirk McLean (G), Vanc.	.20
□ 159 Alexander Mogilny, Vanc.	.20
□ 160 Esa Tikkanen, Vanc.	.20
□ 161 Peter Bondra, Wash.	.20
□ 162 Jim Carey (G), Wash.	.20
□ 163 Sergei Gonchar, Wash.	.20
□ 164 Phil Housley, Wash.	.20
□ 165 Calle Johansson, Wash.	.20
□ 166 Joé Juneau, Wash.	.20
□ 167 Mikael Pivonka, Wash.	.20
□ 168 Brendan Witt, Wash.	.20
□ 169 Nolan Baumgartner, Wash.	.20
□ 170 Bryan Berard, NYIs.	.20
□ **171 Sergei Berezin, Toro. RC**	**1.50**
□ 172 Curtis Brown, Buff.	.20
□ **173 Jan Caloun, SanJ. RC**	**.50**
□ **174 Andreas Dackell, Otta. RC**	**1.00**
□ 175 Hnat Domenichelli, Hart.	.20
□ 176 Christian Dubé, NYRa.	.20
□ 177 Anders Eriksson, Detr.	.20
□ 178 Peter Ferraro, NYRa.	.20
□ 179 Éric Fichaud (G), NYIs.	.20
□ 180 Daniel Goneau, NYRa.	.50
□ **181 Mike Grier, Edmo. RC**	**1.50**
□ 182 Jarome Iginla, Calg.	1.00
□ **183 Steve Kelly, Edmo. RC**	**.50**
□ 184 Jamie Lagenbrunner, Dall.	.20
□ 185 Daymond Langkow, Tamp.	.20
□ **186 Jay McKee, Buff. RC**	**.50**
□ 187 Ethan Moreau, Chic.	.20
□ **188 Rem Murray, Edmo. RC**	**.50**
□ 189 Janne Niinimaa, Phil.	.20
□ 190 Wade Redden, Otta.	.20
□ **191 Ruslan Salei, Anah. RC**	**.50**
□ 192 Jamie Storr (G), Anah.	.20
□ 193 Darren Van Impe, LosA.	.20
□ 194 Roman Vopat, Anah.	.20
□ 195 David Wilkie, Mont.	.20
□ 196 Landon Wilson, Colo.	.20
□ **197 Richard Zednik, Wash. RC**	**2.50**
□ **198 Danius Zubrus, Phil. RC**	**1.50**
□ 199 Checklist	.20
□ 200 Checklist	.20

ARMOR PLATE

There are two versions: the regular insert (1:72) and the Super Power parallel (1:720).

Insert Set (12 cards):	375.00	125.00
Insert	Super	Insert
□ □ 1 Ed Belfour (G), Chic.	45.00	15.00
□ □ 2 Martin Brodeur (G), NJer.	70.00	24.00
□ □ 3 Jim Carey (G), Wash.	12.00	5.00
□ □ 4 Dominik Hasek (G), Buff.	45.00	14.00
□ □ 5 Ron Hextall (G), Phil.	25.00	9.00
□ □ 6 Chris Osgood (G), Detr.	25.00	8.00
□ □ 7 Félix Potvin (G), Toro.	25.00	8.00
□ □ 8 Daren Puppa (G), Tamp.	12.00	5.00
□ □ 9 Damian Rhodes (G), Otta.	12.00	5.00
□ □ 10 Mike Richter (G), NYRa.	20.00	6.00
□ □ 11 Patrick Roy (G), Colo.	135.00	45.00
□ □ 12 John Vanbiesbrouck (G), Flor.	20.00	6.00

COOL STEEL

There are two versions: the regular insert (1:48) and the Super Power parallel (1:480).

Insert Set (12 cards):	250.00	75.00
Insert	Super	Insert
□ □ 1 Chris Chelios, Chic.	15.00	6.00
□ □ 2 Peter Forsberg, Colo.	40.00	14.00
□ □ 3 Ron Francis, Pitt.	15.00	6.00
□ □ 4 Dominik Hasek (G), Buff.	30.00	10.00
□ □ 5 Ed Jovanovski, Flor.	10.00	4.00
□ □ 6 Vladimir Konstantinov, Detr.	8.00	3.00
□ □ 7 Eric Lindros, Phil.	30.00	10.00
□ □ 8 Mark Messier, NYRa.	30.00	10.00
□ □ 9 Patrick Roy (G), Colo.	90.00	30.00
□ □ 10 Brendan Shanahan, Detr.	30.00	10.00
□ □ 11 Keith Tkachuk, Phoe.	15.00	6.00
□ □ 12 John Vanbiesbrouck (G), Flor.	10.00	4.00

ICE CARVINGS

There are two versions: the regular insert (1:24) and the Super Power parallel (1:240).

Insert Set (12 cards):	175.00	50.00
Insert	Super	Insert
□ □ 1 Martin Brodeur (G), NJer.	30.00	10.00
□ □ 2 Pavel Bure, Vanc.	15.00	5.00
□ □ 3 Jim Carey (G), Wash.	8.00	2.00
□ □ 4 Paul Coffey, Hart.	10.00	3.00
□ □ 5 Sergei Fedorov, Detr.	15.00	6.00
□ □ 6 Jaromir Jagr, Pitt.	15.00	6.00
□ □ 7 Paul Kariya, Anah.	25.00	8.00
□ □ 8 Pat LaFontaine, Buff.	10.00	3.00
□ □ 9 Brian Leetch, NYRa.	10.00	3.00
□ □ 10 Mario Lemieux, Pitt.	55.00	18.00
□ □ 11 Alexander Mogilny, Vanc.	8.00	3.00
□ □ 12 Joe Sakic, Colo.	30.00	10.00

LETHAL WEAPONS

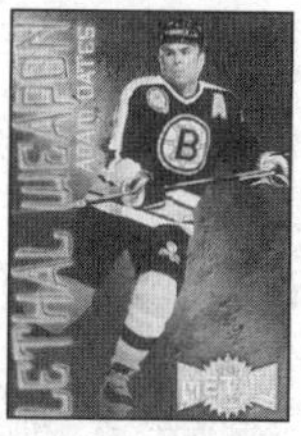

There are two versions: the regular insert (1:12) and the Super Power parallel (1:120).

Insert Set (20 cards):	175.00	50.00
Insert	Super	Insert
□ □ 1 Peter Bondra, Wash.	5.00	2.00
□ □ 2 Pavel Bure, Vanc.	5.00	3.00
□ □ 3 Sergei Fedorov, Detr.	10.00	3.00
□ □ 4 Peter Forsberg, Colo.	15.00	5.00
□ □ 5 Ron Francis, Pitt.	5.00	2.00
□ □ 6 Wayne Gretzky, NYRa.	45.00	15.00
□ □ 7 Brett Hull, SLou.	10.00	3.00
□ □ 8 Jaromir Jagr, Pitt.	10.00	3.00
□ □ 9 Paul Kariya, Anah.	15.00	5.00
□ □ 10 John LeClair, Phil.	5.00	3.00
□ □ 11 Mario Lemieux, Pitt.	30.00	10.00
□ □ 12 Eric Lindros, Phil.	10.00	3.00
□ □ 13 Mark Messier, NYRa.	10.00	3.00
□ □ 14 Alexander Mogilny, Vanc.	5.00	1.00
□ □ 15 Adam Oates, Bost.	3.00	1.00
□ □ 16 Joe Sakic, Colo.	15.00	6.00
□ □ 17 Teemu Selänne, Anah.	5.00	3.00
□ □ 18 Brendan Shanahan, Detr.	10.00	3.00
□ □ 19 Keith Tkachuk, Phoe.	5.00	2.00
□ □ 20 Doug Weight, Edmo.	5.00	2.00

1996 - 97 PANINI STICKERS

Complete Set (304 stickers):	50.00
Album:	3.00
Player	Panini
□ 1 Raymond Bourque, Bost.	1.50
□ 2 Bill Ranford (G), Bost.	.50
□ 3 Cam Neely, Bost.	1.00
□ 4 Adam Oates, Bost.	.50
□ 5 Kyle McLaren, Bost.	.20
□ 6 Rick Tocchet, Bost.	.20

	Player	Price
☐	7 Shawn McEachern, Bost.	.20
☐	8 Foil: Boston Bruins Logo	.20
☐	9 Jozef Stümpel, Bost.	.20
☐	10 Ted Donato, Bost.	.20
☐	11 Dave Reid, Bost.	.20
☐	12 Donald Audette, Buff.	.50
☐	13 Garry Galley, Buff.	.20
☐	14 Dominik Hasek (G), Buff.	1.00
☐	15 Pat LaFontaine, Buff.	.50
☐	16 Jason Dawe, Buff.	.20
☐	17 Alexei Zhitnik, Buff.	.20
☐	18 Brad May, Buff.	.20
☐	19 Foil: Buffalo Sabres Logo	.20
☐	20 Matthew Barnaby, Buff.	.20
☐	21 Darryl Shannon, Buff.	.20
☐	22 Derek Plante, Buff.	.20
☐	23 Geoff Sanderson, Hart.	.20
☐	24 Sean Burke (G), Hart.	.50
☐	25 Nelson Emerson, Hart.	.20
☐	26 Brendan Shanahan, Hart.	1.00
☐	27 Jeff Brown, Hart.	.20
☐	28 Andrew Cassels, Hart.	.20
☐	29 Foil: Hartford Whalers Logo	.20
☐	30 Jeff O'Neill, Hart.	.50
☐	31 Robert Kron, Hart.	.20
☐	32 Andrei Nikolishin, Hart.	.20
☐	33 Brad McCrimmon, Hart.	.20
☐	34 Valeri Bure, Mont.	.20
☐	35 Vincent Damphousse, Mont.	.50
☐	36 Jocelyn Thibault (G), Mont.	.50
☐	37 Saku Koivu, Mont.	1.00
☐	38 Mark Recchi, Mont.	.50
☐	39 Martin Rucinsky, Mont.	.20
☐	40 Pierre Turgeon, Mont.	.50
☐	41 Foil: Montréal Canadiens Logo	.20
☐	42 Andrei Kovalenko, Mont.	.20
☐	43 Peter Popovic, Mont.	.20
☐	44 Vladimir Malakhov, Mont.	.20
☐	45 Alexandre Daigle, Otta.	.20
☐	46 Daniel Alfredsson, Otta.	.50
☐	47 Damian Rhodes (G), Otta.	.20
☐	48 Alexei Yashin, Otta.	.50
☐	49 Radek Bonk, Otta.	.20
☐	50 Steve Duchesne, Otta.	.20
☐	51 Foil: Ottawa Senators Logo	.20
☐	52 Pavol Demitra, Otta.	.50
☐	53 Antti Törmänen, Otta.	.20
☐	54 Stanislav Neckar, Otta.	.20
☐	55 Randy Cunneyworth, Otta.	.20
☐	56 Petr Nedved, Pitt.	.20
☐	57 Ron Francis, Pitt.	.50
☐	58 Jaromir Jagr, Pitt.	1.00
☐	59 Mario Lemieux, Pitt.	3.50
☐	60 Tom Barrasso (G), Pitt.	.50
☐	61 Tomas Sandström, Pitt.	.20
☐	62 Bryan Smolinski, Pitt.	.20
☐	63 Foil: Pittsburgh Penguins Logo	.20
☐	64 Sergei Zubov, Pitt. (Dall.)	.20
☐	65 Dmitri Mironov, Pitt.	.20
☐	66 Kevin Miller, Pitt.	.20
☐	67 Scott Mellanby, Flor.	.20
☐	68 Ed Jovanovski, Flor.	.50
☐	69 Ray Sheppard, Flor.	.20
☐	70 John Vanbiesbrouck (G), Flor.	.50
☐	71 Radek Dvorak, Flor.	.20
☐	72 Rob Niedermayer, Flor.	.20
☐	73 Foil: Florida Panthers Logo	.20
☐	74 Robert Svehla, Flor.	.20
☐	75 Johan Garpenlov, Flor.	.20
☐	76 Martin Straka, Flor.	.20
☐	77 Paul Laus, Flor.	.20
☐	78 Steve Thomas, NJer.	.20
☐	79 Martin Brodeur (G), NJer.	2.00
☐	80 Scott Stevens, NJer.	.50
☐	81 Petr Sykora, NJer.	.50
☐	82 Dave Andreychuk, NJer.	.20
☐	83 Bill Guerin, NJer.	.50
☐	84 Foil: New Jersey Devils Logo	.20
☐	85 Phil Housley, NJer.	.20
☐	86 Scott Niedermayer, NJer.	.20
☐	87 Valeri Zelepukin, NJer.	.20
☐	88 John MacLean, NJer.	.20
☐	89 Todd Bertuzzi, NYIs.	1.50
☐	90 Éric Fichaud (G), NYIs.	.20
☐	91 Zigmund Palffy, NYIs.	.50
☐	92 Travis Green, NYIs.	.20
☐	93 Kenny Jönsson, NYIs.	.20
☐	94 Bryan McCabe, NYIs.	.20
☐	95 Marty McInnis, NYIs.	.20
☐	96 Foil: New York Islanders Logo	.20
☐	97 Alexander Semak, NYIs.	.20
☐	98 Niclas Andersson, NYIs.	.20
☐	99 Scott Lachance, NYIs.	.20
☐	100 Adam Graves, NYRa.	.50
☐	101 Mark Messier, NYRa.	1.00
☐	102 Brian Leetch, NYRa.	.50
☐	103 Mike Richter (G), NYRa.	.50
☐	104 Alexei Kovalev, NYRa.	.50
☐	105 Luc Robitaille, NYRa.	1.00
☐	106 Foil: New York Rangers Logo	.20
☐	107 Ulf Samuelsson, NYRa.	.20
☐	108 Niklas Sundström, NYRa.	.20
☐	109 Jari Kurri, NYRa. (Anah.)	1.00
☐	110 Sergei Nemchinov, NYRa.	.20
☐	111 Rod Brind'Amour, Phil.	.20
☐	112 John LeClair, Phil.	1.00
☐	113 Ron Hextall (G), Phil.	.50
☐	114 Eric Lindros, Phil.	1.00
☐	115 Éric Desjardins, Phil.	.20
☐	116 Dale Hawerchuk, Phil.	.50
☐	117 Foil: Philadelphia Flyers Logo	.20
☐	118 Mikael Renberg, Phil.	.20
☐	119 Joel Otto, Phil.	.20
☐	120 Petr Svoboda, Phil.	.20
☐	121 Karl Dykhuis, Phil.	.20
☐	122 Brian Bradley, Tamp.	.20
☐	123 Roman Hamrlik, Tamp.	.20
☐	124 Chris Gratton, Tamp.	.20
☐	125 Daren Puppa (G), Tamp.	.20
☐	126 Petr Klima, Tamp.	.20
☐	127 Alexander Semak, Tamp.	.20
☐	128 Foil: Tampa Bay Lightning Logo	.20
☐	129 Aaron Gavey, Tamp.	.20
☐	130 Brian Bellows, Tamp.	.20
☐	131 Rob Zamuner, Tamp.	.20
☐	132 Mikael Andersson, Tamp.	.20
☐	133 Peter Bondra, Wash.	.50
☐	134 Jim Carey (G), Wash.	.20
☐	135 Sergei Gonchar, Wash.	.20
☐	136 Brendan Witt, Wash.	.20
☐	137 Sylvain Côté, Wash.	.20
☐	138 Joé Juneau, Wash.	.20
☐	139 Michal Pivonka, Wash.	.20
☐	140 Foil: Washington Capitals Logo	.20
☐	141 Andrew Brunette, Wash.	.20
☐	142 Calle Johansson, Wash.	.20
☐	143 Stefan Ustorf, Wash.	.20
☐	144 LL: Mario Lemieux, Pitt.	3.50
☐	145 LL: Ron Francis, Pitt.	.50
☐	146 LL: Ron Hextall (G), Phil.	.50
☐	147 LL: Vladimir Konstantinov, Detr.	.20
☐	148 LL: Brian Leetch, NYRa.	.50
☐	149 LL: Gary Roberts, Calg.	.50
☐	150 LL: Mario Lemieux, Pitt.	3.50
☐	151 LL: Chris Chelios, Chic.	.50
☐	152 LL: Daniel Alfredsson, Otta.	.50
☐	153 LL: Paul Kariya, Anah.	1.50
☐	154 LL: Jim Carey (G), Wash.	.20
☐	155 LL: Joe Sakic, Colo.	2.00
☐	156 Ed Belfour (G), Chic.	1.00
☐	157 Chris Chelios, Chic.	.50
☐	158 Jeremy Roenick, Chic.	1.00
☐	159 Eric Dazé, Chic.	.50
☐	160 Tony Amonte, Chic.	.50
☐	161 Bernie Nicholls, Chic.	.20
☐	162 Foil: Chicago Blackhawks Logo	.20
☐	163 Gary Suter, Chic.	.20
☐	164 Denis Savard, Chic.	.50
☐	165 Brent Sutter, Chic.	.20
☐	166 Keith Carney, Chic.,	.20
☐	167 Derian Hatcher, Dall.	.20
☐	168 Mike Modano, Dall.	1.00
☐	169 Joe Nieuwendyk, Dall.	.50
☐	170 Kevin Hatcher, Dall. (Pitt.)	.20
☐	171 Benoît Hogue, Dall.	.20
☐	172 Grant Marshall, Dall.	.20
☐	173 Andy Moog (G), Dall.	.50
☐	174 Foil: Dallas Stars Logo	.20
☐	175 Jere Lehtinen, Dall.	.20
☐	176 Greg Adams, Dall.	.20
☐	177 Brent Gilchrist, Dall.	.20
☐	178 Sergei Fedorov, Detr.	1.00
☐	179 Paul Coffey, Detr.	.50
☐	180 Chris Osgood (G), Detr.	.50
☐	181 Steve Yzerman, Detr.	3.00
☐	182 Vladimir Konstantinov, Detr.	.20
☐	183 Vyacheslav Kozlov, Detr.	.20
☐	184 Foil: Detroit Red Wings Logo	.20
☐	185 Nicklas Lidström, Detr.	.50
☐	186 Keith Primeau, Detr.	.50
☐	187 Viacheslav Fetisov, Detr.	.50
☐	188 Igor Larionov, Detr.	.50
☐	189 Nikolai Khabibulin (G), Winn. (Phoe.)	.50
☐	190 Chad Kilger, Winn. (Phoe.)	.20
☐	191 Keith Tkachuk, Winn. (Phoe.)	.50
☐	192 Oleg Tverdovsky, Winn. (Phoe.)	.20
☐	193 Ed Olczyk, Winn. (Phoe.)	.20
☐	194 Teppo Numminen, Winn. (Phoe.)	.20
☐	195 Foil: Phoenix Coyotes Logo	.20
☐	196 Alexei Zhamnov, Winn. (Phoe.)	.20
☐	197 Dave Manson, Winn. (Phoe.)	.20
☐	198 Craig Janney, Winn. (Phoe.)	.20
☐	199 Igor Korolev, Winn. (Phoe.)	.20
☐	200 Wayne Gretzky, SLou.	5.00
☐	201 Chris Pronger, SLou.	.50
☐	202 Brett Hull, SLou.	1.00
☐	203 Grant Fuhr (G), SLou.	.50
☐	204 Shayne Corson, SLou.	.20
☐	205 Geoff Courtnall, SLou.	.20
☐	206 Foil: St. Louis Blues Logo	.20
☐	207 Al MacInnis, SLou.	.50
☐	208 Christer Olsson, SLou.	.20
☐	209 Adam Creighton, SLou.	.20
☐	210 Tony Twist, SLou.	.20
☐	211 Félix Potvin (G), Toro.	.50
☐	212 Kirk Muller, Toro.	.20
☐	213 Wendel Clark, Toro.	1.00
☐	214 Doug Gilmour, Toro.	.50
☐	215 Mike Gartner, Toro.	1.00
☐	216 Larry Murphy, Toro.	.20
☐	217 Foil: Toronto Maple Leafs Logo	.20
☐	218 Mats Sundin, Toro.	1.00
☐	219 Dave Gagner, Toro.	.20
☐	220 Mathieu Schneider, Toro.	.20
☐	221 Tie Domi, Toro.	.20
☐	222 Paul Kariya, Anah.	1.50
☐	223 Guy Hebert (G), Anah.	.20
☐	224 Roman Oksiuta, Anah.	.20
☐	225 Teemu Selänne, Anah.	1.00
☐	226 Steve Rucchin, Anah.	.20
☐	227 Bobby Dollas, Anah.	.20
☐	228 Foil: Anaheim Mighty Ducks Logo	.20
☐	229 Darren Van Impe, Anah.	.20
☐	230 Fredrik Olausson, Anah.	.20
☐	231 Shaun Van Allen, Anah.	.20
☐	232 Joe Sacco, Anah.	.20
☐	233 Trevor Kidd (G), Calg.	.20
☐	234 Theoren Fleury, Calg.	.50
☐	235 German Titov, Calg.	.20
☐	236 James Patrick, Calg.	.20
☐	237 Michael Nylander, Calg.	.20
☐	238 Cory Stillman, Calg.	.20
☐	239 Foil: Calgary Flames Logo	.20
☐	240 Gary Roberts, Calg.	.50
☐	241 Jamie Huscroft, Calg.	.20
☐	242 Tommy Albelin, Calg.	.20
☐	243 Zarley Zalapski, Calg.	.20
☐	244 Peter Forsberg, Colo.	1.50
☐	245 Joe Sakic, Colo.	2.00
☐	246 Claude Lemieux, Colo.	.20
☐	247 Patrick Roy (G), Colo.	3.50
☐	248 Valeri Kamensky, Colo.	.20
☐	249 Uwe Krupp, Colo.	.20
☐	250 Foil: Colorado Avalanche Logo	.20
☐	251 Sandis Ozolinsh, Colo.	.20
☐	252 Curtis Leschyshyn, Colo.	.20
☐	253 Scott Young, Colo.	.20
☐	254 Alexei Gusarov, Colo.	.20
☐	255 Curtis Joseph (G), Edmo.	1.00
☐	256 Bryan Marchment, Edmo.	.20
☐	257 Doug Weight, Edmo.	.50
☐	258 Jason Arnott, Edmo.	.50
☐	259 Zdeno Ciger, Edmo.	.20
☐	260 Miroslav Satan, Edmo.	.20
☐	261 Mariusz Czerkawski, Edmo.	.20
☐	262 Foil: Edmonton Oilers Logo	.20
☐	263 Jiri Slegr, Edmo.	.20
☐	264 Jeff Norton, Edmo.	.20
☐	265 Boris Mironov, Edmo.	.20
☐	266 Vitali Yachmenev, LosA.	.20
☐	267 Byron Dafoe (G), LosA.	.50
☐	268 Rob Blake, LosA.	.50
☐	269 Ray Ferraro, LosA.	.20
☐	270 Dimitri Khristich, LosA.	.20
☐	271 Kevin Todd, LosA.	.20
☐	272 Yanic Perreault, LosA.	.20
☐	273 Foil: Los Angeles Kings Logo	.20
☐	274 Tony Granato, LosA.	.20
☐	275 Jaroslav Modry, LosA.	.20
☐	276 Mattias Norstrom, LosA.	.20
☐	277 Owen Nolan, SanJ.	.50
☐	278 Jeff Friesen, SanJ.	.20
☐	279 Marcus Ragnarsson, SanJ.	.20
☐	280 Chris Terreri (G), SanJ.	.20
☐	281 Darren Turcotte, SanJ.	.20
☐	282 Viktor Kozlov, SanJ.	.20
☐	283 Ulf Dahlen, SanJ.	.20
☐	284 Foil: San Jose Sharks Logo	.20
☐	285 Michal Sykora, SanJ.	.20
☐	286 Ray Whitney, SanJ.	.20
☐	287 Shean Donovan, SanJ.	.20
☐	288 Alexander Mogilny, Vanc.	.50
☐	289 Pavel Bure, Vanc.	1.00
☐	290 Trevor Linden, Vanc.	.50
☐	291 Kirk McLean (G), Vanc.	.20
☐	292 Russ Courtnall, Vanc.	.20
☐	293 Jyrki Lumme, Vanc.	.20
☐	294 Foil: Vancouver Canucks Logo	.20
☐	295 Cliff Ronning, Vanc.	.20
☐	296 Markus Näslund, Vanc.	1.00
☐	297 Esa Tikkanen, Vanc.	.20
☐	298 Josef Beranek, Vanc.	.20
☐	299 Foil: Martin Biron (G), Buff.	1.00
☐	300 Foil: Peter Ferraro, NYRa.	.20
☐	301 Foil: Jason Bonsignore, Edmo.	.20
☐	302 Foil: Jamie Storr (G), LosA.	.20
☐	303 Foil: Éric Fichaud (G), NYIs.	.20
☐	304 Foil: Andrew Brunette, Wash.	.20

1996 - 97 PINNACLE

These cards have five versions: the regular card (gold bottom border), a foil card (magazine packs), a premium stock card (silver bottom border), a Rink Collection parallel (dufex technology) and an Artist's Proof parallel.

		PS	Foil	Pinn.
	Complete Set (250 cards):	**95.00**	**50.00**	**30.00**
	Common Player:	**.50**	**.35**	**.20**
	Player	**PS**	**Foil**	**Pinn.**
☐☐☐	1 Wayne Gretzky, NYRa.	8.00	4.00	3.00
☐☐☐	2 Mark Messier, NYRa.	2.00	1.00	.50
☐☐☐	3 Kevin Hatcher, Dall.	.50	.35	.20
☐☐☐	4 Scott Stevens, NJer.	.50	.35	.20
☐☐☐	5 Derek Plante, Buff.	.50	.35	.20
☐☐☐	6 Theoren Fleury, Calg.	1.00	.50	.20
☐☐☐	7 Brian Rolston, NJer.	.50	.35	.20
☐☐☐	8 Teppo Numminen, Winn.	.50	.35	.20
☐☐☐	9 Adam Graves, NYRa.	.50	.35	.20
☐☐☐	10 Jason Dawe, Buff.	.50	.35	.20
☐☐☐	11 Sergei Nemchinov, NYRa.	.50	.35	.20
☐☐☐	12 Jeff Brown, Hart.	.50	.35	.20
☐☐☐	13 Alexei Zhamnov, Winn.	.50	.35	.20
☐☐☐	14 Paul Coffey, Detr.	1.00	.50	.20
☐☐☐	15 Kevin Miller, Pitt.	.50	.35	.20
☐☐☐	16 Mike Vernon (G), Detr.	.50	.35	.20
☐☐☐	17 Brian Bradley, Tamp.	.50	.35	.20
☐☐☐	18 Jeff Friesen, SanJ.	.50	.35	.20
☐☐☐	19 Phil Housley, NJer.	.50	.35	.20
☐☐☐	20 Ray Whitney, SanJ.	.50	.35	.20
☐☐☐	21 Sergei Fedorov, Detr.	2.00	1.00	.50
☐☐☐	22 Pierre Turgeon, Mont.	.50	.35	.20
☐☐☐	23 Rick Tocchet, Bost.	.50	.35	.20
☐☐☐	24 Uwe Krupp, Colo.	.50	.35	.20
☐☐☐	25 Steve Yzerman, Detr.	4.50	2.00	1.50
☐☐☐	26 Tom Chorske, Otta.	.50	.35	.20
☐☐☐	27 Pat LaFontaine, Buff.	1.00	.50	.20
☐☐☐	28 Nicklas Lidström, Detr.	1.00	.50	.20
☐☐☐	29 Ray Ferraro, LosA.	.50	.35	.20
☐☐☐	30 Brian Noonan, SLou.	.50	.35	.20
☐☐☐	31 Dino Ciccarelli, Detr.	.50	.35	.20
☐☐☐	32 Rob Niedermayer, Flor.	.50	.35	.20
☐☐☐	33 Stéphane Richer, NJer.	.50	.35	.20
☐☐☐	34 Chris Chelios, Chic.	1.00	.50	.20
☐☐☐	35 Mike Gartner, Toro.	1.50	.50	.50
☐☐☐	36 German Titov, Calg.	.50	.35	.20
☐☐☐	37 Sean Burke (G), Hart.	1.00	.50	.20
☐☐☐	38 Robert Svehla, Flor.	.50	.35	.20
☐☐☐	39 Dave Gagner, Toro.	.50	.35	.20
☐☐☐	40 Sergei Gonchar, Wash.	.50	.35	.20
☐☐☐	41 Bernie Nicholls, Chic.	.50	.35	.20
☐☐☐	42 Yanic Perreault, LosA.	.50	.35	.20
☐☐☐	43 Adam Deadmarsh, Colo.	.50	.35	.20
☐☐☐	44 Dale Hawerchuk, Phil.	1.00	.50	.20
☐☐☐	45 A. Kovalev [Photo: Karpovtsev]	1.00	.50	.20
☐☐☐	46 Esa Tikkanen, Vanc.	.50	.35	.20
☐☐☐	47 Valeri Kamensky, Colo.	.50	.35	.20
☐☐☐	48 Craig Janney, Winn.	.50	.35	.20
☐☐☐	49 John LeClair, Phil.	1.50	.50	.50
☐☐☐	50 Radek Bonk, Otta.	.50	.35	.20
☐☐☐	51 David Oliver, Edmo.	.50	.35	.20
☐☐☐	52 Todd Harvey, Dall.	.50	.35	.20
☐☐☐	53 Steve Thomas, NJer.	.50	.35	.20
☐☐☐	54 Tony Amonte, Chic.	1.00	.50	.20
☐☐☐	55 Mikael Renberg, Phil.	.50	.35	.20
☐☐☐	56 Brendan Shanahan, Hart.	2.00	1.00	.50
☐☐☐	57 Tom Fitzgerald, Flor.	.50	.35	.20
☐☐☐	58 Chris Pronger, SLou.	1.00	.50	.20
☐☐☐	59 Donald Audette, Buff.	.50	.35	.20
☐☐☐	60 Nelson Emerson, Hart.	.50	.35	.20
☐☐☐	61 Joe Mullen , Bost.	.50	.35	.20
☐☐☐	62 Marty McInnis, NYIs.	.50	.35	.20
☐☐☐	63 Martin Rucinsky, Mont.	.50	.35	.20
☐☐☐	64 Mark Recchi, Mont.	.50	.35	.20
☐☐☐	65 V. Konstantinov, Detr.	.50	.35	.20
☐☐☐	66 Rick Tabaracci (G), Calg.	.50	.35	.20
☐☐☐	67 Marty McSorley, NYRa.	.50	.35	.20
☐☐☐	68 Pat Verbeek, NYRa.	.50	.35	.20
☐☐☐	69 Garry Galley, Buff.	.50	.35	.20
☐☐☐	70 Travis Green, NYIs.	.50	.35	.20
☐☐☐	71 Chris Tancill, SanJ.	.50	.35	.20
☐☐☐	72 V. Damphousse, Mont.	1.00	.50	.20
☐☐☐	73 Benoît Hogue, Dall.	.50	.35	.20
☐☐☐	74 Igor Larionov, Detr.	1.00	.50	.20
☐☐☐	75 Russ Courtnall, Vanc.	.50	.35	.20
☐☐☐	76 Mike Hough, Flor.	.50	.35	.20
☐☐☐	77 A. Selivanov, Tamp.	.50	.35	.20
☐☐☐	78 Peter Forsberg, Colo.	2.50	1.00	1.00
☐☐☐	79 Petr Klima, Tamp.	.50	.35	.20
☐☐☐	80 Adam Creighton, SLou.	.50	.35	.20
☐☐☐	81 Dave Lowry, Flor.	.50	.35	.20
☐☐☐	82 Andrew Cassels, Hart.	.50	.35	.20
☐☐☐	83 Martin Gelinas, Vanc.	.50	.35	.20
☐☐☐	84 Bob Probert, Chic.	.50	.35	.20
☐☐☐	85 Calle Johansson, Wash.	.50	.35	.20
☐☐☐	86 Mario Lemieux, Pitt.	6.00	3.00	2.00
☐☐☐	87 Alexander Mogilny, Vanc.	.50	.35	.20
☐☐☐	88 Guy Hebert (G), Anah.	.50	.35	.20
☐☐☐	89 Bill Ranford (G), Bost.	.50	.35	.20
☐☐☐	90 Kirk McLean (G), Vanc.	.50	.35	.20
☐☐☐	91 Kenny Jönsson, NYIs.	.50	.35	.20
☐☐☐	92 Martin Brodeur (G), NJer.	3.00	1.50	1.00
☐☐☐	93 Keith Jones, Wash.	.50	.35	.20
☐☐☐	94 Ed Belfour (G), Chic.	2.00	1.00	.50
☐☐☐	95 Tom Barrasso (G), Pitt.	.50	.35	.20
☐☐☐	96 Félix Potvin (G), Toro.	1.00	.50	.20
☐☐☐	97 Daren Puppa (G), Tamp.	.50	.35	.20
☐☐☐	98 Jeremy Roenick, Chic.	1.50	.50	.50
☐☐☐	99 Chris Osgood (G), Detr.	1.00	.50	.20
☐☐☐	100 Zigmund Palffy, NYIs.	1.00	.50	.20
☐☐☐	101 Ron Hextall (G), Phil.	1.00	.50	.20
☐☐☐	102 Jaromir Jagr, Pitt.	2.00	1.00	.50
☐☐☐	103 Chris Terreri (G), SanJ.	.50	.35	.20
☐☐☐	104 Shayne Corson, SLou.	.50	.35	.20
☐☐☐	105 Jim Carey (G), Wash.	.50	.35	.20
☐☐☐	106 D. Hasek (G), Buff.	2.00	1.00	.50
☐☐☐	107 Eric Lindros, Phil.	2.00	1.00	.50
☐☐☐	108 Petr Nedved, Pitt.	.50	.35	.20
☐☐☐	109 Peter Bondra, Wash.	1.00	.50	.20
☐☐☐	110 Jeff Hackett (G), Chic.	.50	.35	.20
☐☐☐	111 Trevor Linden, Vanc.	.50	.35	.20
☐☐☐	112 Mike Richter (G), NYRa.	.50	.35	.20
☐☐☐	113 Claude Lemieux, Colo.	.50	.35	.20
☐☐☐	114 Keith Tkachuk, Winn.	1.00	.50	.20
☐☐☐	115 Pat Falloon, Phil.	.50	.35	.20
☐☐☐	116 Brent Fedyk, Dall.	.50	.35	.20
☐☐☐	117 Todd Marchant, Edmo.	.50	.35	.20
☐☐☐	118 Jason Arnott, Edmo.	.50	.35	.20
☐☐☐	119 Zarley Zalapski, Calg.	.50	.35	.20
☐☐☐	120 Kelly Hrudey (G), LosA.	.50	.35	.20
☐☐☐	121 Alexei Yashin, Otta.	1.00	.50	.20
☐☐☐	122 Sergei Zubov, Pitt.	.50	.35	.20
☐☐☐	123 Rod Brind'Amour, Phil.	.50	.35	.20
☐☐☐	124 Mathieu Schneider, Toro.	.50	.35	.20
☐☐☐	125 Bryan Smolinski, Pitt.	.50	.35	.20
☐☐☐	126 Scott Mellanby, Flor.	.50	.35	.20
☐☐☐	127 Doug Gilmour, Toro.	1.00	.50	.20
☐☐☐	128 Brett Hull, SLou.	2.00	1.00	.50
☐☐☐	129 Vy. Kozlov, Detr.	.50	.35	.20
☐☐☐	130 Adam Oates, Bost.	.50	.35	.20
☐☐☐	131 S. Konowalchuk, Wash.	.50	.35	.20
☐☐☐	132 Robert Kron, Hart.	.50	.35	.20
☐☐☐	133 Alexandre Daigle, Otta.	.50	.35	.20
☐☐☐	134 Brian Savage, Mont.	.50	.35	.20
☐☐☐	135 Stu Barnes, Flor.	.50	.35	.20
☐☐☐	136 Cam Neely, Bost.	2.00	1.00	.50
☐☐☐	137 Steve Rucchin, Anah.	.50	.35	.20
☐☐☐	138 Patrick Roy (G), Colo.	6.00	3.00	2.00
☐☐☐	139 Roman Oksiuta, Anah.	.50	.35	.20
☐☐☐	140 Greg Johnson, Detr.	.50	.35	.20
☐☐☐	141 Chris Gratton, Tamp.	.50	.35	.20
☐☐☐	142 J. Thibault (G), Mont.	.50	.35	.20
☐☐☐	143 Ron Francis, Pitt.	1.00	.50	.20
☐☐☐	144 Mats Sundin, Toro.	2.00	1.00	.50
☐☐☐	145 Oleg Tverdovsky, Winn.	.50	.35	.20
☐☐☐	146 Geoff Courtnall, SLou.	.50	.35	.20
☐☐☐	147 Kirk Muller, Toro.	.50	.35	.20
☐☐☐	148 Zdeno Ciger, Edmo.	.50	.35	.20
☐☐☐	149 John MacLean, NJer.	.50	.35	.20
☐☐☐	150 Damian Rhodes (G), Otta.	.50	.35	.20
☐☐☐	151 Michael Nylander, Calg.	.50	.35	.20
☐☐☐	152 Andrei Kovalenko, Mont.	.50	.35	.20
☐☐☐	153 Al MacInnis, SLou.	.50	.35	.20

☐☐☐	154 Mike Modano, Dall.	2.00	1.00	.50
☐☐☐	155 Teemu Selänne, Anah.	1.50	.50	.50
☐☐☐	156 Tomas Sandström, Pitt.	.50	.35	.20
☐☐☐	157 Bobby Dollas, Anah.	.50	.35	.20
☐☐☐	158 Doug Weight, Edmo.	1.00	.50	.20
☐☐☐	159 Sandis Ozolinsh, Colo.	.50	.35	.20
☐☐☐	160 Joé Juneau, Wash.	.50	.35	.20
☐☐☐	161 N. Khabibulin (G), Winn.	.50	.35	.20
☐☐☐	162 Murray Craven, Chic.	.50	.35	.20
☐☐☐	163 Cliff Ronning, Vanc.	.50	.35	.20
☐☐☐	164 Curtis Joseph (G), Edmo.	2.00	1.00	.50
☐☐☐	165 Darren Turcotte, SanJ.	.50	.35	.20
☐☐☐	166 Andy Moog (G), Dall.	.50	.35	.20
☐☐☐	167 M. Czerkawski, Edmo.	.50	.35	.20
☐☐☐	168 Keith Primeau, Detr.	.50	.35	.20
☐☐☐	169 Éric Desjardins, Phil.	.50	.35	.20
☐☐☐	170 Bill Guerin, NJer.	.50	.35	.20
☐☐☐	171 Glenn Anderson, SLou.	.50	.35	.20
☐☐☐	172 Mike Ridley, Vanc.	.50	.35	.20
☐☐☐	173 Michal Pivonka, Wash.	.50	.35	.20
☐☐☐	174 Trevor Kidd (G), Calg.	.50	.35	.20
☐☐☐	175 Pavel Bure, Vanc.	1.50	.50	.50
☐☐☐	176 Todd Gill, Toro.	.50	.35	.20
☐☐☐	177 Dave Andreychuk, NJer.	.50	.35	.20
☐☐☐	178 Roman Hamrlik, Tamp.	.50	.35	.20
☐☐☐	179 Andrei Nikolishin, Hart.	.50	.35	.20
☐☐☐	180 Alexei Zhitnik, Buff.	.50	.35	.20
☐☐☐	181 Grant Fuhr (G), SLou.	1.00	.50	.20
☐☐☐	182 Dave Reid, Bost.	.50	.35	.20
☐☐☐	183 Joe Nieuwendyk, Dall.	.50	.35	.20
☐☐☐	184 Paul Kariya, Anah.	2.50	1.00	1.00
☐☐☐	185 Jyrki Lumme, Vanc.	.50	.35	.20
☐☐☐	186 Owen Nolan, SanJ.	1.00	.50	.20
☐☐☐	187 Geoff Sanderson, Hart.	.50	.35	.20
☐☐☐	188 Alexander Semak, NYIs.	.50	.35	.20
☐☐☐	189 Larry Murphy, Toro.	.50	.35	.20
☐☐☐	190 Dimitri Khristich, LosA.	.50	.35	.20
☐☐☐	191 Shane Churla, Dall.	.50	.35	.20
☐☐☐	192 Bill Lindsay, Flor.	.50	.35	.20
☐☐☐	193 Brian Leetch, NYRa.	1.00	.50	.20
☐☐☐	194 Greg Adams, Dall.	.50	.35	.20
☐☐☐	195 Gary Suter, Chic.	.50	.35	.20
☐☐☐	196 Wendel Clark, Toro.	1.50	.50	.50
☐☐☐	197 Scott Young, Colo.	.50	.35	.20
☐☐☐	198 Randy Burridge, Buff.	.50	.35	.20
☐☐☐	199 R. Bourque, Bost.	2.00	1.00	.50
☐☐☐	200 Joe Murphy, Chic.	.50	.35	.20
☐☐☐	201 Joe Sakic, Colo.	3.00	1.50	1.00
☐☐☐	202 Saku Koivu, Mont.	1.50	.50	.50
☐☐☐	203 Vanbiesbrouck (G), Flor.	.50	.35	.20
☐☐☐	204 Ed Jovanovski, Flor.	1.50	.50	.50
☐☐☐	205 Daniel Alfredsson, Otta.	2.00	1.00	.50
☐☐☐	206 Vitali Yachmenev, LosA.	.50	.35	.20
☐☐☐	207 M. Ragnarsson, SanJ.	.50	.35	.20
☐☐☐	208 Todd Bertuzzi, NYIs.	4.50	2.00	1.50
☐☐☐	209 Valeri Bure, Mont.	1.00	.50	.20
☐☐☐	210 Jeff O'Neill, Hart.	1.50	.50	.50
☐☐☐	211 Corey Hirsch (G), Vanc.	.50	.35	.20
☐☐☐	212 Eric Dazé, Chic.	1.50	.50	.50
☐☐☐	213 David Sacco, Anah.	.50	.35	.20
☐☐☐	214 Jan Vopat, LosA.	.50	.35	.20
☐☐☐	215 Scott Bailey (G), Bost.	.50	.35	.20
☐☐☐	216 Jamie Rivers, SLou.	.50	.35	.20
☐☐☐	217 J. Théodore (G), Mont.	4.50	2.00	1.50
☐☐☐	218 Peter Ferraro, NYRa.	.50	.35	.20
☐☐☐	219 Anders Eriksson, Detr.	.50	.35	.20
☐☐☐	220 Wayne Primeau, NJer.	.50	.35	.20
☐☐☐	221 Denis Pederson, NJer.	.50	.35	.20
☐☐☐	222 Jay McKee, Buff.	1.00	.50	.20
☐☐☐	223 Sean Pronger, Anah.	.50	.35	.20
☐☐☐	224 Martin Biron (G), Buff.	1.50	.50	.50
☐☐☐	225 Marek Malik, Hart.	.50	.35	.20
☐☐☐	**226 S. Sullivan, NJer. RC**	**3.00**	**1.50**	**1.50**
☐☐☐	227 Curtis Brown, Buff.	.50	.35	.20
☐☐☐	228 Éric Fichaud (G), NYIs.	.50	.35	.20
☐☐☐	**229 Jan Caloun, SanJ. RC**	**1.00**	**.50**	**.50**
☐☐☐	230 Niklas Sundblad, Calg.	.50	.35	.20
☐☐☐	**231 S. Staios, Bost. RC**	**1.00**	**.50**	**.50**
☐☐☐	**232 S. Washburn, Flor. RC**	**1.00**	**.50**	**.50**
☐☐☐	233 Chris Ferraro, NYRa.	.50	.35	.20
☐☐☐	234 Marko Kiprusoff, Mont.	.50	.35	.20
☐☐☐	235 Larry Courville, Vanc.	.50	.35	.20
☐☐☐	236 David Nemirovsky, Flor.	.50	.35	.20
☐☐☐	237 Ralph Intranuovo, Edmo.	.50	.35	.20
☐☐☐	238 Kevin Hodson (G), Detr.	.50	.35	.20
☐☐☐	239 Ethan Moreau, Chic.	.50	.35	.20
☐☐☐	240 Daymond Langkow, Tamp.	.50	.35	.20
☐☐☐	241 Brandon Convery, Toro.	.50	.35	.20
☐☐☐	242 Cale Hulse, Calg.	.50	.35	.20
☐☐☐	243 Zdenek Nedved, Toro.	.50	.35	.20
☐☐☐	244 Tommy Salo (G), NYIs.	1.50	.50	.50
☐☐☐	245 N. Baumgartner, Wash.	.50	.35	.20
☐☐☐	246 P. Labrecque (G), Mont.	.50	.35	.20
☐☐☐	247 J. Langenbrunner, Dall.	.50	.35	.20
☐☐☐	248 CL: Pavel Bure, Vanc.	.50	.35	.20
☐☐☐	249 CL: Peter Forsberg, Colo.	1.50	.50	.50
☐☐☐	250 CL: Teemu Selänne, Anah.	.50	.35	.20

PARALLELS

		AP	Rink
	Complete Set (250 cards):	**1500.00**	**275.00**
	Common Player:	**4.00**	**1.00**
	Player	**AP**	**Rink**
☐☐	1 Wayne Gretzky, NYRa.	180.00	30.00
☐☐	2 Mark Messier, NYRa.	35.00	5.00
☐☐	3 Kevin Hatcher, Dall.	5.00	1.00
☐☐	4 Scott Stevens, NJer.	15.00	3.00
☐☐	5 Derek Plante, Buff.	5.00	1.00
☐☐	6 Theoren Fleury, Calg.	20.00	1.00
☐☐	7 Brian Rolston, NJer.	10.00	2.00
☐☐	8 Teppo Numminen, Winn.	10.00	2.00
☐☐	9 Adam Graves, NYRa.	15.00	3.00
☐☐	10 Jason Dawe, Buff.	4.00	1.00
☐☐	11 Sergei Nemchinov, NYRa.	5.00	1.00
☐☐	12 Jeff Brown, Hart.	4.00	1.00
☐☐	13 Alexei Zhamnov, Winn.	10.00	2.00
☐☐	14 Paul Coffey, Detr.	20.00	4.00
☐☐	15 Kevin Miller, Pitt.	4.00	1.00
☐☐	16 Mike Vernon (G), Detr.	15.00	3.00
☐☐	17 Brian Bradley, Tamp.	4.00	1.00
☐☐	18 Jeff Friesen, SanJ.	10.00	2.00
☐☐	19 Phil Housley, NJer.	10.00	2.00
☐☐	20 Ray Whitney, SanJ.	5.00	1.00
☐☐	21 Sergei Fedorov, Detr.	35.00	5.00
☐☐	22 Pierre Turgeon, Mont.	15.00	3.00
☐☐	23 Rick Tocchet, Bost.	10.00	2.00
☐☐	24 Uwe Krupp, Colo.	4.00	1.00
☐☐	25 Steve Yzerman, Detr.	100.00	15.00
☐☐	26 Tom Chorske, Otta.	4.00	1.00
☐☐	27 Pat LaFontaine, Buff.	20.00	4.00
☐☐	28 Nicklas Lidström, Detr.	20.00	4.00
☐☐	29 Ray Ferraro, LosA.	5.00	1.00
☐☐	30 Brian Noonan, SLou.	4.00	1.00
☐☐	31 Dino Ciccarelli, Detr.	10.00	2.00
☐☐	32 Rob Niedermayer, Flor.	5.00	1.00
☐☐	33 Stéphane Richer, NJer.	5.00	1.00
☐☐	34 Chris Chelios, Chic.	20.00	4.00
☐☐	35 Mike Gartner, Toro.	30.00	6.00
☐☐	36 German Titov, Calg.	4.00	1.00
☐☐	37 Sean Burke (G), Hart.	20.00	4.00
☐☐	38 Robert Svehla, Flor.	5.00	1.00
☐☐	39 Dave Gagner, Toro.	5.00	1.00
☐☐	40 Sergei Gonchar, Wash.	10.00	2.00
☐☐	41 Bernie Nicholls, Chic.	5.00	1.00
☐☐	42 Yanic Perreault, LosA.	10.00	2.00
☐☐	43 Adam Deadmarsh, Colo.	10.00	2.00
☐☐	44 Dale Hawerchuk, Phil.	20.00	4.00
☐☐	45 A. Kovalev [Photo: Karpovtsev]	20.00	4.00
☐☐	46 Esa Tikkanen, Vanc.	5.00	1.00
☐☐	47 Valeri Kamensky, Colo.	10.00	2.00
☐☐	48 Craig Janney, Winn.	5.00	1.00
☐☐	49 John LeClair, Phil.	30.00	5.00
☐☐	50 Radek Bonk, Otta.	10.00	2.00
☐☐	51 David Oliver, Edmo.	4.00	1.00
☐☐	52 Todd Harvey, Dall.	5.00	1.00
☐☐	53 Steve Thomas, NJer.	5.00	1.00
☐☐	54 Tony Amonte, Chic.	20.00	4.00
☐☐	55 Mikael Renberg, Phil.	10.00	2.00
☐☐	56 Brendan Shanahan, Hart.	35.00	5.00
☐☐	57 Tom Fitzgerald, Flor.	4.00	1.00
☐☐	58 Chris Pronger, SLou.	20.00	4.00
☐☐	59 Donald Audette, Buff.	15.00	3.00
☐☐	60 Nelson Emerson, Hart.	5.00	1.00
☐☐	61 Joe Mullen , Bost.	15.00	3.00
☐☐	62 Marty McInnis, NYIs.	5.00	1.00
☐☐	63 Martin Rucinsky, Mont.	5.00	1.00
☐☐	64 Mark Recchi, Mont.	15.00	3.00
☐☐	65 Vladimir Konstantinov, Detr.	10.00	2.00
☐☐	66 Rick Tabaracci (G), Calg.	5.00	1.00
☐☐	67 Marty McSorley, NYRa.	5.00	1.00
☐☐	68 Pat Verbeek, NYRa.	10.00	2.00
☐☐	69 Garry Galley, Buff.	4.00	1.00
☐☐	70 Travis Green, NYIs.	5.00	1.00
☐☐	71 Chris Tancill, SanJ.	4.00	1.00
☐☐	72 Vincent Damphousse, Mont.	20.00	4.00
☐☐	73 Benoît Hogue, Dall.	5.00	1.00
☐☐	74 Igor Larionov, Detr.	20.00	4.00
☐☐	75 Russ Courtnall, Vanc.	5.00	1.00
☐☐	76 Mike Hough, Flor.	4.00	1.00
☐☐	77 Alexander Selivanov, Tamp.	4.00	1.00
☐☐	78 Peter Forsberg, Colo.	50.00	10.00
☐☐	79 Petr Klima, Tamp.	5.00	1.00
☐☐	80 Adam Creighton, SLou.	4.00	1.00
☐☐	81 Dave Lowry, Flor.	5.00	1.00
☐☐	82 Andrew Cassels, Hart.	5.00	1.00
☐☐	83 Martin Gelinas, Vanc.	5.00	1.00
☐☐	84 Bob Probert, Chic.	10.00	2.00
☐☐	85 Calle Johansson, Wash.	5.00	1.00
☐☐	86 Mario Lemieux, Pitt.	120.00	20.00
☐☐	87 Alexander Mogilny, Vanc.	15.00	3.00
☐☐	88 Guy Hebert (G), Anah.	5.00	1.00
☐☐	89 Bill Ranford (G), Bost.	15.00	3.00
☐☐	90 Kirk McLean (G), Vanc.	10.00	2.00
☐☐	91 Kenny Jönsson, NYIs.	5.00	1.00
☐☐	92 Martin Brodeur (G), NJer.	60.00	10.00
☐☐	93 Keith Jones, Wash.	5.00	1.00
☐☐	94 Ed Belfour (G), Chic.	35.00	5.00
☐☐	95 Tom Barrasso (G), Pitt.	15.00	3.00
☐☐	96 Félix Potvin (G), Toro.	20.00	4.00
☐☐	97 Daren Puppa (G), Tamp.	5.00	1.00
☐☐	98 Jeremy Roenick, Chic.	30.00	6.00
☐☐	99 Chris Osgood (G), Detr.	20.00	4.00
☐☐	100 Zigmund Palffy, NYIs.	20.00	4.00
☐☐	101 Ron Hextall (G), Phil.	20.00	4.00
☐☐	102 Jaromir Jagr, Pitt.	40.00	5.00
☐☐	103 Chris Terreri (G), SanJ.	5.00	1.00
☐☐	104 Shayne Corson, SLou.	10.00	2.00
☐☐	105 Jim Carey (G), Wash.	5.00	1.00
☐☐	106 Dominik Hasek (G), Buff.	30.00	5.00
☐☐	107 Eric Lindros, Phil.	40.00	5.00
☐☐	108 Petr Nedved, Pitt.	10.00	2.00
☐☐	109 Peter Bondra, Wash.	20.00	4.00
☐☐	110 Jeff Hackett (G), Chic.	10.00	2.00
☐☐	111 Trevor Linden, Vanc.	15.00	3.00
☐☐	112 Mike Richter (G), NYRa.	15.00	3.00
☐☐	113 Claude Lemieux, Colo.	10.00	2.00
☐☐	114 Keith Tkachuk, Winn.	20.00	4.00
☐☐	115 Pat Falloon, Phil.	5.00	1.00
☐☐	116 Brent Fedyk, Dall.	4.00	1.00
☐☐	117 Todd Marchant, Edmo.	5.00	1.00
☐☐	118 Jason Arnott, Edmo.	15.00	3.00
☐☐	119 Zarley Zalapski, Calg.	4.00	1.00
☐☐	120 Kelly Hrudey (G), LosA.	10.00	2.00
☐☐	121 Alexei Yashin, Otta.	20.00	4.00
☐☐	122 Sergei Zubov, Pitt.	5.00	1.00
☐☐	123 Rod Brind'Amour, Phil.	10.00	2.00
☐☐	124 Mathieu Schneider, Toro.	5.00	1.00
☐☐	125 Bryan Smolinski, Pitt.	5.00	1.00
☐☐	126 Scott Mellanby, Flor.	5.00	1.00
☐☐	127 Doug Gilmour, Toro.	20.00	4.00
☐☐	128 Brett Hull, SLou.	35.00	5.00
☐☐	129 Vyacheslav Kozlov, Detr.	5.00	1.00
☐☐	130 Adam Oates, Bost.	15.00	3.00
☐☐	131 Steve Konowalchuk, Wash.	5.00	1.00
☐☐	132 Robert Kron, Hart.	5.00	1.00
☐☐	133 Alexandre Daigle, Otta.	5.00	1.00
☐☐	134 Brian Savage, Mont.	10.00	2.00
☐☐	135 Stu Barnes, Flor.	4.00	1.00
☐☐	136 Cam Neely, Bost.	35.00	7.00
☐☐	137 Steve Rucchin, Anah.	5.00	1.00
☐☐	138 Patrick Roy (G), Colo.	120.00	20.00
☐☐	139 Roman Oksiuta, Anah.	4.00	1.00
☐☐	140 Greg Johnson, Detr.	5.00	1.00
☐☐	141 Chris Gratton, Tamp.	5.00	1.00
☐☐	142 Jocelyn Thibault (G), Mont.	15.00	3.00
☐☐	143 Ron Francis, Pitt.	20.00	4.00
☐☐	144 Mats Sundin, Toro.	35.00	5.00
☐☐	145 Oleg Tverdovsky, Winn.	5.00	1.00
☐☐	146 Geoff Courtnall, SLou.	5.00	1.00
☐☐	147 Kirk Muller, Toro.	10.00	2.00
☐☐	148 Zdeno Ciger, Edmo.	5.00	1.00
☐☐	149 John MacLean, NJer.	5.00	1.00
☐☐	150 Damian Rhodes (G), Otta.	5.00	1.00
☐☐	151 Michael Nylander, Calg.	5.00	1.00
☐☐	152 Andrei Kovalenko, Mont.	5.00	1.00
☐☐	153 Al MacInnis, SLou.	15.00	3.00
☐☐	154 Mike Modano, Dall.	35.00	5.00
☐☐	155 Teemu Selänne, Anah.	30.00	5.00
☐☐	156 Tomas Sandström, Pitt.	5.00	1.00
☐☐	157 Bobby Dollas, Anah.	4.00	1.00
☐☐	158 Doug Weight, Edmo.	20.00	4.00
☐☐	159 Sandis Ozolinsh, Colo.	5.00	1.00
☐☐	160 Joé Juneau, Wash.	5.00	1.00
☐☐	161 N. Khabibulin (G), Winn.	15.00	3.00
☐☐	162 Murray Craven, Chic.	5.00	1.00
☐☐	163 Cliff Ronning, Vanc.	5.00	1.00
☐☐	164 Curtis Joseph (G), Edmo.	35.00	5.00
☐☐	165 Darren Turcotte, SanJ.	5.00	1.00
☐☐	166 Andy Moog (G), Dall.	15.00	3.00
☐☐	167 Mariusz Czerkawski, Edmo.	5.00	1.00
☐☐	168 Keith Primeau, Detr.	15.00	3.00
☐☐	169 Éric Desjardins, Phil.	10.00	2.00
☐☐	170 Bill Guerin, NJer.	15.00	3.00
☐☐	171 Glenn Anderson, SLou.	10.00	2.00
☐☐	172 Mike Ridley, Vanc.	5.00	1.00
☐☐	173 Michal Pivonka, Wash.	4.00	1.00
☐☐	174 Trevor Kidd (G), Calg.	10.00	2.00
☐☐	175 Pavel Bure, Vanc.	30.00	5.00
☐☐	176 Todd Gill, Toro.	5.00	1.00
☐☐	177 Dave Andreychuk, NJer.	10.00	2.00
☐☐	178 Roman Hamrlik, Tamp.	5.00	1.00
☐☐	179 Andrei Nikolishin, Hart.	5.00	1.00
☐☐	180 Alexei Zhitnik, Buff.	5.00	1.00
☐☐	181 Grant Fuhr (G), SLou.	20.00	4.00
☐☐	182 Dave Reid, Bost.	5.00	1.00
☐☐	183 Joe Nieuwendyk, Dall.	15.00	3.00
☐☐	184 Paul Kariya, Anah.	60.00	10.00
☐☐	185 Jyrki Lumme, Vanc.	5.00	1.00
☐☐	186 Owen Nolan, SanJ.	20.00	4.00
☐☐	187 Geoff Sanderson, Hart.	5.00	1.00
☐☐	188 Alexander Semak, NYIs.	4.00	1.00
☐☐	189 Larry Murphy, Toro.	5.00	1.00
☐☐	190 Dimitri Khristich, LosA.	5.00	1.00
☐☐	191 Shane Churla, Dall.	4.00	1.00
☐☐	192 Bill Lindsay, Flor.	4.00	1.00
☐☐	193 Brian Leetch, NYRa.	20.00	4.00
☐☐	194 Greg Adams, Dall.	5.00	1.00
☐☐	195 Gary Suter, Chic.	5.00	1.00
☐☐	196 Wendel Clark, Toro.	30.00	6.00
☐☐	197 Scott Young, Colo.	10.00	2.00
☐☐	198 Randy Burridge, Buff.	5.00	1.00
☐☐	199 Raymond Bourque, Bost.	45.00	5.00
☐☐	200 Joe Murphy, Chic.	5.00	1.00
☐☐	201 Joe Sakic, Colo.	60.00	10.00
☐☐	202 Saku Koivu, Mont.	30.00	6.00
☐☐	203 J. Vanbiesbrouck (G), Flor.	15.00	3.00
☐☐	204 Ed Jovanovski, Flor.	15.00	3.00
☐☐	205 Daniel Alfredsson, Otta.	20.00	4.00
☐☐	206 Vitali Yachmenev, LosA.	5.00	1.00
☐☐	207 Marcus Ragnarsson, SanJ.	5.00	1.00
☐☐	208 Todd Bertuzzi, NYIs.	45.00	9.00
☐☐	209 Valeri Bure, Mont.	10.00	2.00
☐☐	210 Jeff O'Neill, Hart.	15.00	3.00
☐☐	211 Corey Hirsch (G), Vanc.	5.00	1.00
☐☐	212 Eric Dazé, Chic.	15.00	3.00
☐☐	213 David Sacco, Anah.	4.00	1.00
☐☐	214 Jan Vopat, LosA.	4.00	1.00
☐☐	215 Scott Bailey (G), Bost.	5.00	1.00
☐☐	216 Jamie Rivers, SLou.	4.00	1.00
☐☐	217 José Théodore (G), Mont.	45.00	9.00
☐☐	218 Peter Ferraro, NYRa.	5.00	1.00
☐☐	219 Anders Eriksson, Detr.	4.00	1.00
☐☐	220 Wayne Primeau, NJer.	5.00	1.00
☐☐	221 Denis Pederson, NJer.	4.00	1.00
☐☐	222 Jay McKee, Buff.	5.00	1.00
☐☐	223 Sean Pronger, Anah.	4.00	1.00
☐☐	224 Martin Biron (G), Buff.	15.00	3.00
☐☐	225 Marek Malik, Hart.	4.00	1.00
☐☐	**226 Steve Sullivan, NJer. RC**	**20.00**	**4.00**
☐☐	227 Curtis Brown, Buff.	5.00	1.00
☐☐	228 Éric Fichaud (G), NYIs.	5.00	1.00
☐☐	**229 Jan Caloun, SanJ. RC**	**5.00**	**1.00**
☐☐	230 Niklas Sundblad, Calg.	4.00	1.00
☐☐	**231 Steve Staios, Bost. RC**	**5.00**	**1.00**
☐☐	**232 S. Washburn, Flor. RC**	**5.00**	**1.00**
☐☐	233 Chris Ferraro, NYRa.	5.00	1.00
☐☐	234 Marko Kiprusoff, Mont.	4.00	1.00
☐☐	235 Larry Courville, Vanc.	4.00	1.00
☐☐	236 David Nemirovsky, Flor.	4.00	1.00
☐☐	237 Ralph Intranuovo, Edmo.	4.00	1.00
☐☐	238 Kevin Hodson (G), Detr.	5.00	1.00
☐☐	239 Ethan Moreau, Chic.	5.00	1.00
☐☐	240 Daymond Langkow, Tamp.	5.00	1.00
☐☐	241 Brandon Convery, Toro.	4.00	1.00
☐☐	242 Cale Hulse, Calg.	4.00	1.00
☐☐	243 Zdenek Nedved, Toro.	4.00	1.00
☐☐	244 Tommy Salo (G), NYIs.	15.00	3.00
☐☐	245 Nolan Baumgartner, Wash.	4.00	1.00
☐☐	246 P. Labrecque (G), Mont.	4.00	1.00
☐☐	247 Jamie Langenbrunner, Dall.	5.00	1.00
☐☐	248 CL: Pavel Bure, Vanc.	15.00	3.00
☐☐	249 CL: Peter Forsberg, Colo.	30.00	5.00
☐☐	250 CL: Teemu Selänne, Anah.	15.00	3.00

BY THE NUMBERS

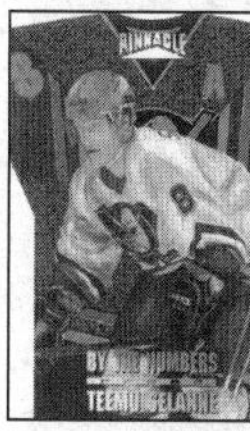

		Promo	PS	DC
	Insert Set (15 cards):	**25.00**	**200.00**	**100.00**
	Player	**Promo**	**PS**	**DC**
☐☐☐	1 Teemu Selänne, Anah.	2.00	14.00	7.00
☐☐☐	2 Brendan Shanahan, Hart.	2.00	17.00	8.00
☐☐☐	3 Sergei Fedorov, Detr.	2.00	17.00	8.00
☐☐☐	4 Ed Jovanovski, Flor.	1.00	7.00	4.00
☐☐☐	5 Doug Weight, Edmo.	1.00	10.00	5.00
☐☐☐	6 Brett Hull, SLou.	2.00	17.00	8.00
☐☐☐	7 Doug Gilmour, Toro.	1.00	10.00	5.00
☐☐☐	8 Jaromir Jagr, Pitt.	2.00	17.00	8.00
☐☐☐	9 Wayne Gretzky, NYRa.	10.00	70.00	35.00
☐☐☐	10 Daniel Alfredsson, Otta.	1.00	10.00	5.00
☐☐☐	11 Éric Dazé, Chic.	1.00	7.00	4.00
☐☐☐	12 Mark Messier, NYRa.	2.00	17.00	8.00
☐☐☐	13 Jocelyn Thibault (G), Mont.	1.00	7.00	4.00
☐☐☐	14 Eric Lindros, Phil.	2.00	17.00	8.00
☐☐☐	15 Pavel Bure, Vanc.	2.00	14.00	7.00

MASKS

		DC	Mask
	Insert Set (10 cards):	**175.00**	**125.00**
	Inserts	**DC**	**Mask**
☐☐	1 Patrick Roy (G), Colo.	135.00	90.00
☐☐	2 Jim Carey (G), Wash.	20.00	15.00
☐☐	3 John Vanbiesbrouck (G), Flor.	20.00	15.00
☐☐	4 Martin Brodeur (G), NJer.	70.00	45.00
☐☐	5 Jocelyn Thibault (G), Mont.	20.00	15.00
☐☐	6 Ron Hextall (G), Phil.	25.00	15.00
☐☐	7 Nikolai Khabibulin (G), Phoe.	20.00	15.00
☐☐	8 Stéphane Fiset (G), LosA.	20.00	15.00
☐☐	9 Mike Richter (G), NYRa.	20.00	15.00
☐☐	10 Kelly Hrudey, SanJ.	20.00	15.00

TEAM PINNACLE

		TP
	Insert Set (10 cards):	**250.00**
	Insert (1:90)	**TP**
☐	1 W. Gretzky / J. Sakic	70.00
☐	2 M. Lemieux / P. Forsberg	55.00
☐	3 E. Lindros / J. Roenick	20.00
☐	4 M. Messier / D. Weight	20.00
☐	5 B. Shanahan / P. Kariya	30.00
☐	6 J. Jagr / Br. Hull	25.00
☐	7 E. Jovanovski / P. Coffey	10.00
☐	8 J. Vanbiesbrouck (G) / P. Roy	40.00
☐	9 M. Brodeur / C. Osgood (G)	25.00
☐	10 S. Koivu / É. Dazé	15.00

TROPHIES

		T
	Insert Set (10 cards):	**200.00**
	Insert (1:33 Mag.)	**T**
☐	1 Mario Lemieux, Pitt.	75.00
☐	2 Paul Kariya, Anah.	35.00
☐	3 Sergei Fedorov, Detr.	25.00
☐	4 Daniel Alfredsson, Otta.	15.00
☐	5 Jim Carey (G), Wash.	8.00
☐	6 C. Osgood (G) / M. Vernon	15.00
☐	7 Kris King, Winn. (Phoe.)	8.00
☐	8 Chris Chelios, Chic.	15.00
☐	9 Joe Sakic, Colo.	40.00
☐	10 Avalanche , Colo.	8.00

1996 - 97 PINNACLE BE A PLAYER

These cards have at least three versions: the regular card, a one per pack autograph insert and an autographed foil card parallel. Promo cards likely exist for all regular cards and Link 2 History cards and have the same value as the regular card.

		BAP
	Complete Set (240 cards):	**60.00**
	Common Player:	**.25**
	Player	**BAP**
☐	1 Todd Gill, SanJ.	.25
☐	2 Dave Andreychuk, NJer.	.25
☐	3 Igor Kravchuk, SLou.	.25
☐	4 Tom Fitzgerald, Flor.	.25
☐☐	5 Jeremy Roenick, Phoe.	1.00
☐	6 Peter Popovic, Mont.	.25
☐☐	7 Andy Moog (G), Dall.	.50
☐	8 Steve Rice, Hart.	.25
☐	9 Darren Langdon, NYRa.	.25
☐	10 Mark Fitzpatrick (G), Flor.	.25
☐	11 Alexei Zhamnov, Chic.	.25
☐	12 Luc Robitaille, NYRa.	1.00

	Player	Price
□	13 Michal Pivonka, Wash.	.25
□	14 Kevin Hatcher, Pitt.	.25
□	15 Stéphane Yelle, Colo.	.25
□	16 Bill Ranford (G), Bost.	.50
□	17 Jamie Baker, Toro.	.25
□	18 Sean Burke (G), Hart.	.50
□□	19 Al Iafrate, SanJ.	.25
□	20 Mark Recchi, Mont.	.50
□	21 Rod Brind'Amour, Phil.	.25
□	22 Doug Gilmour, NJer.	.50
□	23 Mike Wilson, Buff.	.25
□	**24 Barry Potomski, LosA. RC**	**1.00**
□	25 Mike Gartner, Phoe.	1.00
□	26 Jason Wiemer, Tamp.	.25
□	27 Scott Lachance, NYIs.	.25
□	28 Joe Murphy, Chic.	.25
□	29 Bill Guerin, NJer.	.50
□	30 Byron Dafoe (G), LosA.	.50
□	31 Esa Tikkanen, NYRa.	.25
□	32 Ken Baumgartner, Anah.	.25
□	33 Valeri Kamensky, Colo.	.25
□	34 J.J. Daigneault, Pitt.	.25
□	35 Ulf Dahlen, Chic.	.25
□	36 Jason Allison, Wash.	.50
□	37 Ted Donato, Bost.	.25
□	38 Pat Verbeek, Dall.	.25
□	39 Miroslav Satan, Edmo.	.25
□	40 Éric Desjardins, Phil.	.25
□	41 Dave Karpa, Colo.	.25
□	42 Jeff Hackett (G), Chic.	.25
□	43 Doug Brown, Detr.	.25
□	44 Gord Murphy, Flor.	.25
□	45 Kelly Hrudey (G), SanJ.	.25
□	46 Kelly Miller, Wash.	.25
□	47 Tie Domi, Toro.	.25
□	48 Alexei Yashin, Otta.	.50
□□	49 German Titov, Calg.	.25
□	50 Stéphane Richer, NJer.	.25
□	51 Corey Hirsch (G), Vanc.	.25
□	52 Brad May, Buff.	.25
□	53 Joe Nieuwendyk, Dall.	.50
□	54 Sylvain Lefebvre, Toro.	.25
□□	55 Brian Leetch, NYRa.	.50
□	56 Petr Svoboda, Phil.	.25
□	57 Dave Manson, Phoe.	.25
□	58 Jason Woolley, Pitt.	.25
□	59 Scott Niedermayer, NJer.	.25
□□	60 Kelly Chase, Hart.	.25
□	61 Guy Hebert (G), Anah.	.25
□	62 Shayne Corson, Mont.	.25
□□	63 Jon Casey (G), SLou.	.25
□	64 Rob Zettler, Phil.	.25
□	65 Mikael Andersson, Tamp.	.25
□	66 Tony Amonte, Chic.	.50
□	67 Johan Garpenlov, Flor.	.25
□	68 Denny Lambert, Anah.	.25
□	69 Jim McKenzie, Phoe.	.25
□	70 Darren Turcotte, SanJ.	.25
□	71 Eric Weinrich, Chic.	.25
□□	72 Troy Mallette, Bost.	.25
□	73 Donald Audette, Buff.	.50
□	74 Philippe Boucher, LosA.	.25
□	75 Shawn Chambers, NJer.	.25
□	76 Joel Otto, Phil.	.25
□□	77 Tommy Salo (G), NYIs.	.50
□	78 Olaf Kölzig (G), Wash.	.50
□	79 Adrian Aucoin, Vanc.	.25
□	80 Alek Stojanov, Pitt.	.25
□	81 Robert Reichel, Calg.	.25
□	82 Marc Bureau, Mont.	.25
□	83 Alexei Godynyuk, Hart.	.25
□	84 Bill Berg, NYRa.	.25
□	85 Marc Bergevin, Detr.	.25
□	86 Kevin Kaminski, Wash.	.25
□	87 Uwe Krupp, Colo.	.25
□	88 Boris Mironov, Edmo.	.25
□	89 Bob Bassen, Dall.	.25
□	90 Darryl Shannon, Phoe.	.25
□	91 Mikael Renberg, Phil.	.25
□	92 Mike Stapleton, Phoe.	.25
□	93 Dave Roberts, Vanc.	.25
□	94 Peter Zezel, NJer.	.25
□	95 Mathieu Dandenault, Detr.	.25
□	96 Bobby Dollas, Anah.	.25
□	97 Don Sweeney, Bost.	.25
□	98 Niclas Andersson, NYIs.	.25
□	99 Pat Jablonski (G), Mont.	.25
□	100 John Slaney, LosA.	.25
□	101 Kevin Todd, LosA.	.25
□	102 Jamie Pushor, Detr.	.25
□	**103 Andreas Johansson, NYIs. RC**	**2.00**
□	104 Corey Schwab (G), Tamp.	.25
□□	**105 Todd Simpson, Calg.**	**1.00**
□	106 Landon Wilson, Colo.	.25
□	**107 Daniel Goneau, NYRa. RC**	**1.00**

	Player	Price
□	108 David Wilkie, Mont.	.25
□	**109 Andreas Dackell, Otta. RC**	**1.50**
□	110 Marek Malik, Hart.	.25
□	111 Mark Messier, NYRa.	1.50
□	112 François Leroux, Pitt.	.25
□	113 Michal Sykora, NJer.	.25
□	114 Rob Zamuner, Tamp.	.25
□	115 Craig Berube, Wash.	.25
□	116 Mike Ricci, Colo.	.25
□	117 Adam Burt, Hart.	.25
□	118 Alexander Karpovtsev, NYRa.	.25
□	119 Shawn McEachern, Otta.	.25
□	120 Shawn Antoski, Pitt.	.25
□	121 Dave Reid, Dall.	.25
□	122 Todd Warriner, Toro.	.25
□	123 Markus Näslund, Vanc.	1.50
□	124 Martin Rucinsky, Mont.	.25
□	125 Bob Carpenter, NJer.	.25
□	126 Dean McAmmond, Edmo.	.25
□	127 Trevor Kidd (G), Calg.	.25
□□	128 Martin Lapointe, Detr.	.50
□□	129 Enrico Ciccone, Chic.	.25
□	130 Dixon Ward, Buff.	.25
□	131 Jason Muzzatti (G), Hart.	.25
□	132 Bryan Smolinski, NYIs.	.25
□	133 Norm Maciver, Phoe.	.25
□	134 Fredrik Olausson, Phoe.	.25
□	135 Daniel Lacroix, Phil.	.25
□	136 Mike Peluso, SLou.	.25
□	137 Andrei Nikolishin, Hart.	.25
□	138 Rhett Warrener, Flor.	.25
□	139 Ray Ferraro, LosA.	.25
□	140 Glenn Healy (G), NYRa.	.25
□□	141 Steve Duchesne, Otta.	.25
□	142 Tony Granato, SanJ.	.25
□	143 Cory Cross, Tamp.	.25
□	144 Jon Klemm, Colo.	.25
□	145 Sami Kapanen, Hart.	.25
□	146 Grant Marshall, Dall.	.25
□	147 Matthew Barnaby, Buff.	.25
□	148 Lyle Odelein, NJer.	.25
□	149 Joe Dziedzic, Pitt.	.25
□	150 Sergei Gonchar, Wash.	.25
□	151 Doug Zmolek, LosA.	.25
□	**152 Sean O'Donnell, LosA. RC**	**1.00**
□	153 Scott Thornton, Mont.	.25
□	154 Steve Heinze, Bost.	.25
□	155 Gary Valk, Anah.	.25
□	156 Jeff Finley, Phoe.	.25
□□	157 Trent Klatt, Phil.	.25
□	158 Jeff Beukeboom, NYRa.	.25
□	159 Theoren Fleury, Calg.	.50
□	160 Dana Murzyn, Vanc.	.25
□□	161 Tommy Albelin, Calg.	.25
□	162 Bryan McCabe, NYIs.	.25
□	163 Shaun Van Allen, Otta.	.25
□	164 Rick Tabaracci (G), Tamp.	.25
□	165 Kevin Miller, Chic.	.25
□□	166 Mariusz Czerkawski, Edmo.	.25
□	167 Gerald Diduck, Hart.	.25
□	168 Brad McCrimmon, Phoe.	.25
□	169 Stéphane Matteau, SLou.	.25
□	170 Scott Daniels, Phil.	.25
□	171 Scott Mellanby, Flor.	.25
□	172 Sandy Moger, Bost.	.25
□	173 Steve Konowalchuk, Wash.	.25
□	174 Doug Weight, Edmo.	.50
□	175 Darren McCarty, Detr.	.25
□	176 Darryl Sydor, Dall.	.25
□	177 Dave Ellett, Toro. (NJer.)	.25
□	**178 Bob Boughner, Buff. RC**	**1.00**
□	179 Derek Armstrong, NYIs.	.25
□	180 Gary Suter, Chic.	.25
□	181 Donald Brashear, Vanc.	.25
□	182 Chris Tamer, Pitt.	.25
□	183 Darrin Shannon, Phoe.	.25
□	184 Stan Neckar, Otta.	.25
□	185 Brent Severyn, Colo.	.25
□	186 Steve Rucchin, Anah.	.25
□	187 Jeff Norton, Edmo.	.25
□	188 Steve Finn, LosA.	.25
□	189 Kjell Samuelsson, Phil.	.25
□	190 Jeff Friesen, SanJ.	.25
□	191 Shawn Burr, Detr.	.25
□	192 Paul Laus, Flor.	.25
□	193 Jeff Odgers, SanJ.	.25
□	194 Keith Jones, Colo.	.25
□	195 Rich Matvichuk, Dall.	.25
□	196 Adam Foote, Colo.	.25
□	197 Bob Errey, Detr.	.25
□	198 Ryan Smyth, Edmo.	.50
□□	199 Mark Janssens, Hart.	.25
□	200 Claude Lapointe, NYIs.	.25
□	201 Brian Noonan, Vanc.	.25
□	202 Damian Rhodes (G), Otta.	.25

	Player	Price
□	203 Dale Hawerchuk, Phil.	.50
□	204 Bill Lindsay, Flor.	.25
□□	205 Brian Skrudland, Flor.	.25
□	206 Curtis Joseph (G), Edmo.	1.50
□	207 Jon Rohloff, Bost.	.25
□	208 Doug Bodger, SanJ.	.25
□□	**209 Steve Sullivan, NJer. RC**	**3.00**
□	210 Ricard Persson, NJer.	.25
□	**211 D. Roloson (G), Calg. RC**	**1.50**
□	212 Mike Dunham (G), NJer.	1.00
□	**213 M. Cousineau (G), Toro. RC**	**1.00**
□	214 Éric Fichaud (G), NYIs.	.25
□	215 Matt Johnson, LosA.	.25
□	**216 Fredrik Modin, Toro. RC**	**2.00**
□	217 Denis Pederson, NJer.	.25
□□	218 Kevin Hodson (G), Detr.	.25
□	219 Drew Bannister, Tamp.	.25
□□	**220 Mike Grier, Edmo. RC**	**2.00**
□	LTH01A Jarome Iginla, Calg.	2.00
□	LTH01B Teemu Selänne, Anah.	1.00
□	**LTH2A Harry York, SLou. RC**	**1.00**
□	LTH02B Peter Forsberg, Colo.	2.00
□	**LTH03A Sergei Berezin, Toro.**	**2.00**
□	LTH03B Brendan Shanahan, Detr.	1.50
□□	LTH04A Ethan Moreau, Chic.	.25
□	LTH04B Pavel Bure, Vanc.	1.00
□□	**LTH5A Rem Murray, Edmo. RC**	**1.00**
□	LTH05B Rem Murray, Edmo.	.50
□	LTH06A Jamie Langenbrunner, Dall.	.25
□	LTH06B Paul Kariya, Anah.	2.00
□	LTH07A Jim Campbell, SLou.	.25
□□	LTH07B Eric Lindros, Phil.	1.50
□	LTH08A Jonas Höglund, Calg.	.25
□	LTH08B Pat LaFontaine, Buff.	.50
□	LTH09A Wade Redden, Otta.	.50
□	LTH09B Steve Yzerman, Detr.	3.50
□□	**LTH10A Patrick Lalime (G), Pitt.**	**6.00**
□□	LTH10B J. Vanbiesbrouck (G), Flor.	.50

AUTOGRAPHS

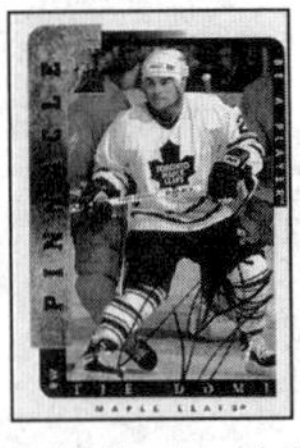

Alexei Zhamnov (#11) did not sign cards for this series.

Autograph Set (239 cards): 1800.00 1000.00

Common Player: 8.00 4.00

	Player	DC	Auto.
□□	1 Todd Gill, SanJ. ✍	8.00	4.00
□□	2 Dave Andreychuk, NJer. ✍	15.00	8.00
□□	3 Igor Kravchuk, SLou. ✍	8.00	4.00
□□	4 Tom Fitzgerald, Flor. ✍	8.00	4.00
□□	5 Jeremy Roenick, Phoe. ✍	40.00	22.00
□□	6 Peter Popovic, Mont. ✍	8.00	4.00
□□	7 Andy Moog (G), Dall. ✍	20.00	10.00
□□	8 Steve Rice, Hart. ✍	8.00	4.00
□□	9 Darren Langdon, NYRa. ✍	10.00	6.00
□□	10 Mark Fitzpatrick (G), Flor. ✍	8.00	4.00
□□	12 Luc Robitaille, NYRa. ✍	40.00	22.00
□□	13 Michal Pivonka, Wash. ✍	8.00	4.00
□□	14 Kevin Hatcher, Pitt. ✍	8.00	4.00
□□	15 Stéphane Yelle, Colo. ✍	8.00	4.00
□□	16 Bill Ranford (G), Bost. ✍	20.00	10.00
□□	17 Jamie Baker, Toro. ✍	8.00	4.00
□□	18 Sean Burke (G), Hart. ✍	30.00	16.00
□□	19 Al Iafrate, SanJ. ✍	10.00	6.00
□□	20 Mark Recchi, Mont. ✍	20.00	10.00
□□	21 Rod Brind'Amour, Phil. ✍	15.00	8.00
□□	22 Doug Gilmour, NJer. ✍	30.00	16.00
□□	23 Mike Wilson, Buff. ✍	8.00	4.00
□□	24 Barry Potomski, LosA. ✍ RC	8.00	4.00
□□	25 Mike Gartner, Phoe. ✍	40.00	22.00
□□	26 Jason Wiemer, Tamp. ✍	8.00	4.00
□□	27 Scott Lachance, NYIs. ✍	8.00	4.00
□□	28 Joe Murphy, Chic. ✍	8.00	4.00
□□	29 Bill Guerin, NJer. ✍	20.00	10.00
□□	30 Byron Dafoe (G), LosA. ✍	20.00	10.00
□□	31 Esa Tikkanen, NYRa. ✍	8.00	4.00
□□	32 Ken Baumgartner, Anah. ✍	8.00	4.00
□□	33 Valeri Kamensky, Colo. ✍	15.00	8.00
□□	34 J. ✍J. ✍ Daigneault, Pitt. ✍	8.00	4.00
□□	35 Ulf Dahlen, Chic. ✍	8.00	4.00
□□	36 Jason Allison, Wash. ✍	30.00	16.00
□□	37 Ted Donato, Bost. ✍	8.00	4.00
□□	38 Pat Verbeek, Dall. ✍	15.00	8.00
□□	39 Miroslav Satan, Edmo. ✍	15.00	8.00
□□	40 Éric Desjardins, Phil. ✍	15.00	8.00
□□	41 Dave Karpa, Colo. ✍	8.00	4.00
□□	42 Jeff Hackett (G), Chic. ✍	15.00	8.00
□□	43 Doug Brown, Detr. ✍	8.00	4.00
□□	44 Gord Murphy, Flor. ✍	8.00	4.00
□□	45 Kelly Hrudey (G), SanJ. ✍	15.00	8.00
□□	46 Kelly Miller, Wash. ✍	8.00	4.00
□□	47 Tie Domi, Toro. ✍	15.00	8.00
□□	48 Alexei Yashin, Otta. ✍	30.00	16.00
□□	49 German Titov, Calg. ✍	8.00	4.00
□□	50 Stéphane Richer, NJer. ✍	10.00	6.00
□□	51 Corey Hirsch (G), Vanc. ✍	8.00	4.00
□□	52 Brad May, Buff. ✍	8.00	4.00
□□	53 Joe Nieuwendyk, Dall. ✍	20.00	10.00
□□	54 Sylvain Lefebvre, Toro. ✍	8.00	4.00
□□	55 Brian Leetch, NYRa. ✍	30.00	16.00
□□	56 Petr Svoboda, Phil. ✍	10.00	6.00
□□	57 Dave Manson, Phoe. ✍	8.00	4.00
□□	58 Jason Woolley, Pitt. ✍	8.00	4.00
□□	59 Scott Niedermayer, NJer. ✍	15.00	8.00
□□	60 Kelly Chase, Hart. ✍	8.00	4.00
□□	61 Guy Hebert (G), Anah. ✍	10.00	6.00
□□	62 Shayne Corson, Mont. ✍	15.00	8.00
□□	63 Jon Casey (G), SLou. ✍	8.00	4.00
□□	64 Rob Zettler, Phil. ✍	8.00	4.00
□□	65 Mikael Andersson, Tamp. ✍	8.00	4.00
□□	66 Tony Amonte, Chic. ✍	30.00	16.00
□□	67 Johan Garpenlov, Flor. ✍	8.00	4.00
□□	68 Denny Lambert, Anah. ✍	8.00	4.00
□□	69 Jim McKenzie, Phoe. ✍	8.00	4.00
□□	70 Darren Turcotte, SanJ. ✍	8.00	4.00
□□	71 Eric Weinrich, Chic. ✍	8.00	4.00
□□	72 Troy Mallette, Bost. ✍	8.00	4.00
□□	73 Donald Audette, Buff. ✍	20.00	10.00
□□	74 Philippe Boucher, LosA. ✍	8.00	4.00
□□	75 Shawn Chambers, NJer. ✍	8.00	4.00
□□	76 Joel Otto, Phil. ✍	8.00	4.00
□□	77 Tommy Salo (G), NYIs. ✍	20.00	10.00
□□	78 Olaf Kölzig (G), Wash. ✍	30.00	16.00
□□	79 Adrian Aucoin, Vanc. ✍	8.00	4.00
□□	80 Alek Stojanov, Pitt. ✍	8.00	4.00
□□	81 Robert Reichel, Calg. ✍	15.00	8.00
□□	82 Marc Bureau, Mont. ✍	8.00	4.00
□□	83 Alexei Godynyuk, Hart. ✍	8.00	4.00
□□	84 Bill Berg, NYRa. ✍	8.00	4.00
□□	85 Marc Bergevin, Detr. ✍	8.00	4.00
□□	86 Kevin Kaminski, Wash. ✍	8.00	4.00
□□	87 Uwe Krupp, Colo. ✍	8.00	4.00
□□	88 Boris Mironov, Edmo. ✍	8.00	4.00
□□	89 Bob Bassen, Dall. ✍	8.00	4.00
□□	90 Darryl Shannon, Phoe. ✍	8.00	4.00
□□	91 Mikael Renberg, Phil. ✍	15.00	8.00
□□	92 Mike Stapleton, Phoe. ✍	8.00	4.00
□□	93 Dave Roberts, Vanc. ✍	8.00	4.00
□□	94 Peter Zezel, NJer. ✍	8.00	4.00
□□	95 Mathieu Dandenault, Detr. ✍	8.00	4.00
□□	96 Bobby Dollas, Anah. ✍	8.00	4.00
□□	97 Don Sweeney, Bost. ✍	8.00	4.00
□□	98 Niclas Andersson, NYIs. ✍	8.00	4.00
□□	99 Pat Jablonski (G), Mont. ✍	8.00	4.00
□□	100 John Slaney, LosA. ✍	8.00	4.00
□□	101 Kevin Todd, LosA. ✍	8.00	4.00
□□	102 Jamie Pushor, Detr. ✍	8.00	4.00
□□	103 A. Johansson, NYIs. ✍	10.00	6.00
□□	104 Corey Schwab (G), Tamp. ✍	8.00	4.00
□□	105 Todd Simpson, Calg. ✍	8.00	4.00
□□	106 Landon Wilson, Colo. ✍	8.00	4.00
□□	107 Daniel Goneau, NYRa. ✍	8.00	4.00
□□	108 David Wilkie, Mont. ✍	8.00	4.00
□□	109 Andreas Dackell, Otta. ✍	8.00	4.00
□□	110 Marek Malik, Hart. ✍	8.00	4.00
□□	111 Mark Messier, NYRa. ✍	120.00	60.00
□□	112 François Leroux, Pitt. ✍	8.00	4.00
□□	113 Michal Sykora, NJer. ✍	8.00	4.00
□□	114 Rob Zamuner, Tamp. ✍	10.00	6.00
□□	115 Craig Berube, Wash. ✍	8.00	4.00
□□	116 Mike Ricci, Colo. ✍	15.00	8.00
□□	117 Adam Burt, Hart. ✍	8.00	4.00
□□	118 Alexander Karpovtsev, NYRa. ✍	8.00	4.00
□□	119 Shawn McEachern, Otta. ✍	15.00	8.00
□□	120 Shawn Antoski, Pitt. ✍	8.00	4.00
□□	121 Dave Reid, Dall. ✍	8.00	4.00
□□	122 Todd Warriner, Toro. ✍	8.00	4.00
□□	123 Markus Näslund, Vanc. ✍	50.00	26.00
□□	124 Martin Rucinsky, Mont. ✍	10.00	6.00
□□	125 Bob Carpenter, NJer. ✍	10.00	6.00
□□	126 Dean McAmmond, Edmo. ✍	8.00	4.00
□□	127 Trevor Kidd (G), Calg. ✍	15.00	8.00
□□	128 Martin Lapointe, Detr. ✍	20.00	10.00
□□	129 Enrico Ciccone, Chic. ✍	8.00	4.00
□□	130 Dixon Ward, Buff. ✍	8.00	4.00
□□	131 Jason Muzzatti (G), Hart. ✍	8.00	4.00
□□	132 Bryan Smolinski, NYIs. ✍	8.00	4.00
□□	133 Norm Maciver, Phoe. ✍	8.00	4.00
□□	134 Fredrik Olausson, Phoe. ✍	10.00	6.00
□□	135 Daniel Lacroix, Phil. ✍	8.00	4.00
□□	136 Mike Peluso, SLou. ✍	8.00	4.00
□□	137 Andrei Nikolishin, Hart. ✍	8.00	4.00
□□	138 Rhett Warrener, Flor. ✍	8.00	4.00
□□	139 Ray Ferraro, LosA. ✍	8.00	4.00
□□	140 Glenn Healy (G), NYRa. ✍	10.00	6.00
□□	141 Steve Duchesne, Otta. ✍	10.00	6.00
□□	142 Tony Granato, SanJ. ✍	10.00	6.00
□□	143 Cory Cross, Tamp. ✍	8.00	4.00
□□	144 Jon Klemm, Colo. ✍	8.00	4.00
□□	145 Sami Kapanen, Hart. ✍	15.00	8.00
□□	146 Grant Marshall, Dall. ✍	8.00	4.00
□□	147 Matthew Barnaby, Buff. ✍	8.00	4.00
□□	148 Lyle Odelein, NJer. ✍	8.00	4.00
□□	149 Joe Dziedzic, Pitt. ✍	8.00	4.00
□□	150 Sergei Gonchar, Wash. ✍	15.00	8.00
□□	151 Doug Zmolek, LosA. ✍	8.00	4.00
□□	152 Sean O'Donnell, LosA. ✍	8.00	4.00
□□	153 Scott Thornton, Mont. ✍	8.00	4.00
□□	154 Steve Heinze, Bost. ✍	8.00	4.00
□□	155 Gary Valk, Anah. ✍	8.00	4.00
□□	156 Jeff Finley, Phoe. ✍	8.00	4.00
□□	157 Trent Klatt, Phil. ✍	8.00	4.00
□□	158 Jeff Beukeboom, NYRa. ✍	8.00	4.00
□□	159 Theoren Fleury, Calg. ✍	30.00	16.00
□□	160 Dana Murzyn, Vanc. ✍	8.00	4.00
□□	161 Tommy Albelin, Calg. ✍	8.00	4.00
□□	162 Bryan McCabe, NYIs. ✍	10.00	6.00
□□	163 Shaun Van Allen, Otta. ✍	8.00	4.00
□□	164 Rick Tabaracci (G), Tamp. ✍	8.00	4.00
□□	165 Kevin Miller, Chic. ✍	8.00	4.00
□□	166 Mariusz Czerkawski, Edmo. ✍	10.00	6.00
□□	167 Gerald Diduck, Hart. ✍	8.00	4.00
□□	168 Brad McCrimmon, Phoe. ✍	8.00	4.00
□□	169 Stéphane Matteau, SLou. ✍	8.00	4.00
□□	170 Scott Daniels, Phil. ✍	8.00	4.00
□□	171 Scott Mellanby, Flor. ✍	10.00	6.00
□□	172 Sandy Moger, Bost. ✍	8.00	4.00
□□	173 Steve Konowalchuk, Wash. ✍	10.00	6.00
□□	174 Doug Weight, Edmo. ✍	30.00	16.00
□□	175 Darren McCarty, Detr. ✍	15.00	8.00
□□	176 Darryl Sydor, Dall. ✍	10.00	6.00
□□	177 Dave Ellett, Toro. ✍ (NJer.)	8.00	4.00
□□	178 Bob Boughner, Buff. ✍	8.00	4.00
□□	179 Derek Armstrong, NYIs. ✍	8.00	4.00
□□	180 Gary Suter, Chic. ✍	10.00	6.00
□□	181 Donald Brashear, Vanc. ✍	10.00	6.00
□□	182 Chris Tamer, Pitt. ✍	8.00	4.00
□□	183 Darrin Shannon, Phoe. ✍	8.00	4.00
□□	184 Stan Neckar, Otta. ✍	8.00	4.00
□□	185 Brent Severyn, Colo. ✍	8.00	4.00
□□	186 Steve Rucchin, Anah. ✍	10.00	6.00
□□	187 Jeff Norton, Edmo. ✍	8.00	4.00
□□	188 Steve Finn, LosA. ✍	8.00	4.00
□□	189 Kjell Samuelsson, Phil. ✍	8.00	4.00
□□	190 Jeff Friesen, SanJ. ✍	15.00	8.00
□□	191 Shawn Burr, Detr. ✍	8.00	4.00
□□	192 Paul Laus, Flor. ✍	8.00	4.00
□□	193 Jeff Odgers, SanJ. ✍	8.00	4.00
□□	194 Keith Jones, Colo. ✍	8.00	4.00
□□	195 Rich Matvichuk, Dall. ✍	10.00	6.00
□□	196 Adam Foote, Colo. ✍	15.00	8.00
□□	197 Bob Errey, Detr. ✍	8.00	4.00
□□	198 Ryan Smyth, Edmo. ✍	20.00	12.00
□□	199 Mark Janssens, Hart. ✍	8.00	4.00
□□	200 Claude Lapointe, NYIs. ✍	8.00	4.00
□□	201 Brian Noonan, Vanc. ✍	8.00	4.00
□□	202 Damian Rhodes (G), Otta. ✍	10.00	6.00
□□	203 Dale Hawerchuk, Phil. ✍	30.00	16.00
□□	204 Bill Lindsay, Flor. ✍	8.00	4.00
□□	205 Brian Skrudland, Flor. ✍	8.00	4.00
□□	206 Curtis Joseph (G), Edmo. ✍	50.00	25.00
□□	207 Jon Rohloff, Bost. ✍	8.00	4.00
□□	208 Doug Bodger, SanJ. ✍	8.00	4.00
□□	209 Steve Sullivan, NJer. ✍	15.00	8.00
□□	210 Ricard Persson, NJer. ✍	8.00	4.00
□□	211 D. Roloson (G), Calg. ✍	8.00	4.00
□□	212 Mike Dunham (G), NJer. ✍	20.00	10.00
□□	213 M. Cousineau (G), Toro. ✍	8.00	4.00
□□	214 Éric Fichaud (G), NYIs. ✍	8.00	4.00
□□	215 Matt Johnson, LosA. ✍	8.00	4.00
□□	216 Fredrik Modin, Toro. ✍	10.00	6.00
□□	217 Denis Pederson, NJer. ✍	8.00	4.00
□□	218 Kevin Hodson (G), Detr. ✍	10.00	6.00
□□	219 Drew Bannister, Tamp. ✍	8.00	4.00
□□	220 Mike Grier, Edmo. ✍	10.00	6.00
□□	LTH1A Jarome Iginla, Calg. ✍	60.00	30.00
□□	LTH1B Teemu Selänne, Anah. ✍	50.00	30.00
□□	LTH2A Harry York, SLou. ✍	8.00	4.00
□□	LTH2B Peter Forsberg, Colo. ✍	80.00	50.00
□□	LTH3A Sergei Berezin, Toro. ✍	15.00	8.00
□□	LTH3B Brendan Shanahan, Detr. ✍	60.00	40.00
□□	LTH4A Ethan Moreau, Chic. ✍	10.00	6.00
□□	LTH4B Pavel Bure, Vanc. ✍	50.00	30.00
□□	LTH5A Rem Murray, Edmo. ✍	8.00	4.00
□□	LTH5B Jason Arnott, Edmo. ✍	30.00	18.00

□ □	LTH6A Jamie Langenbrunner, Dall. ✍	15.00	8.00
□ □	LTH6B Paul Kariya, Anah. ✍	80.00	50.00
□ □	LTH7A Jim Campbell, SLou. ✍	8.00	4.00
□ □	LTH7B Eric Lindros, Phil. ✍	60.00	40.00
□ □	LTH8A Jonas Höglund, Calg. ✍	10.00	6.00
□ □	LTH8B Pat LaFontaine, Buff. ✍	35.00	24.00
□ □	LTH9A Wade Redden, Otta. ✍	20.00	12.00
□ □	LTH9B Steve Yzerman, Detr. ✍	150.00	90.00
□ □	LTH10A Patrick Lalime (G), Pitt. ✍	45.00	24.00
□ □	LTH10B J. Vanbiesbrouck (G), Flor. ✍	30.00	18.00

BISCUIT IN THE BASKET

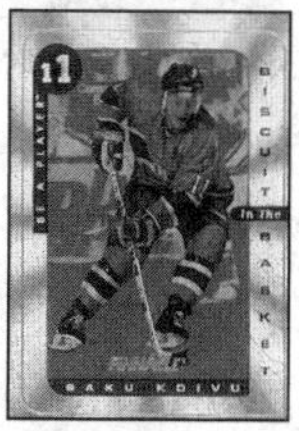

Insert Set (25 cards): 145.00

	Insert (1:17)	BitB
□	1 Wayne Gretzky, NYRa.	25.00
□	2 Mario Lemieux, Pitt.	18.00
□	3 Eric Lindros, Phil.	6.00
□	4 Theoren Fleury, Calg.	3.00
□	5 Peter Forsberg, Colo.	8.00
□	6 Keith Tkachuk, Phoe.	3.00
□	7 Sergei Fedorov, Detr.	6.00
□	8 Mike Modano, Dall.	6.00
□	9 Jaromir Jagr, Pitt.	6.00
□	10 Brendan Shanahan, Detr.	6.00
□	11 Teemu Selänne, Anah.	5.00
□	12 Mats Sundin, Toro.	6.00
□	13 Steve Yzerman, Detr.	15.00
□	14 Brett Hull, SLou.	6.00
□	15 Zigmund Palffy, NYIs.	3.00
□	16 Joe Sakic, Colo.	10.00
□	17 John LeClair, Phil.	5.00
□	18 Pavel Bure, Vanc.	5.00
□	19 Mark Messier, NHL All-Star	6.00
□	20 Paul Kariya, Anah.	8.00
□	21 Arnott, Edmo.	3.00
□	22 Saku Koivu, Mont.	5.00
□	23 Daniel Alfredsson, Otta.	3.00
□	24 Alexander Mogilny, Vanc.	3.00
□	25 Owen Nolan, SanJ.	3.00

DIE-CUT SERIES

	Insert	DC
□	1 Mario Lemieux, Pitt. {#/66}	600.00
□	2 Mario Lemieux, Pitt. {#/66}	600.00
□	1 Eric Lindros, Phil. ✍ {#/88}	700.00
□	1 Mark Messier, NYRa. ✍ {#/11}	1400.00
□	2 Eric Lindros, Phil. ✍ {#/88}	700.00
□	2 Mark Messier, NYRa. ✍ {#/11}	1400.00

STACKING THE PADS

Insert Set (15 cards): 135.00

	Insert (1:35)	StP
□	1 Patrick Lalime, Pitt.	15.00
□	2 Chris Osgood (G), Detr.	5.00
□	3 Ron Hextall (G), Phil.	5.00
□	4 John Vanbiesbrouck (G), Flor.	5.00
□	5 Martin Brodeur (G), NJer.	20.00
□	6 Félix Potvin (G), Toro.	5.00
□	7 Nikolai Khabibulin (G), Phoe.	5.00
□	8 Jim Carey (G), Wash.	5.00
□	9 Grant Fuhr, SLou.	5.00
□	10 Mike Richter (G), NYRa.	5.00
□	11 Dominik Hasek (G), Buff.	15.00
□	12 Andy Moog, Dall.	5.00
□	13 Patrick Roy (G), Colo.	45.00
□	14 Curtis Joseph (G), Edmo.	15.00
□	15 Jocelyn Thibault (G), Mont.	5.00

1996 - 97 PINNACLE FANTASY

These cards have four versions: a die-cut card (coin holder), a bronze team card, a silver team card and a gold team card (dufex technology).

Complete Set (21 cards): 60.00

	Player	Fantasy
□	Eric Lindros Promo	8.00
□	1 Raymond Bourque, Bost.	3.00
□	2 Paul Coffey, Hart.	1.00
□	3 Eric Lindros, Phil.	2.00
□	4 Mario Lemieux, Pitt.	7.00
□	5 Wayne Gretzky, NYRa.	10.00
□	6 Mark Messier, NYRa.	2.00
□	7 Jarome Iginla, Calg.	2.00
□	8 Brendan Shanahan, Detr.	2.00
□	9 John Vanbiesbrouck (G), Flor.	1.00
□	10 Mike Richter (G), NYRa.	1.00
□	11 Chris Chelios, Chic.	1.00
□	12 Nicklas Lidström, Detr.	1.00
□	13 Sergei Fedorov, Detr.	2.00
□	14 Pavel Bure, Vanc.	2.00
□	15 Peter Forsberg, Colo.	3.00
□	16 Brett Hull, SLou.	2.00
□	17 Joe Sakic, Colo.	4.00
□	18 Owen Nolan, SanJ.	1.00
□	19 Patrick Roy (G), Colo.	7.00
□	20 Ed Belfour (G), Chic.	2.00

□	Kelly Hrudey, SanJ.	20.00

1996 - 97 PINNACLE MARIO LEMIEUX MOMENTS

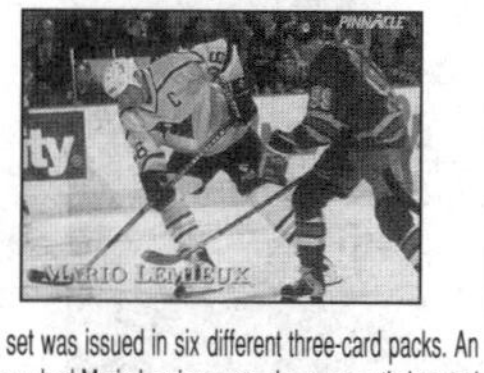

This set was issued in six different three-card packs. An autographed Mario Lemieux was also apparently inserted in the packs. Unsigned singles sell at $2-3.

Complete Set (18 cards): 18.00
Album: 3.00

□	1 Mario Lemieux	□	2 Lemieux (w/ Cup)
□	3 Mario Lemeiux	□	4 Lemieux (w/ Messier)
□	5 Mario Lemeiux	□	6 Mario Lemieux
□	7 Mario Lemieux	□	8 Mario Lemieux
□	9 Mario Lemieux	□	10 Lemieux (w/ Jagr)
□	11 Mario Lemieux	□	12 Mario Lemieux
□	13 Lemieux (CC'87)	□	14 Mario Lemieux
□	15 Mario Lemieux	□	16 Lemieux (w/ Gretzky)
□	17 Mario Lemieux	□	18 Mario Lemieux

1996 - 97 PINNACLE LEMIEUX 600 GOALS

This card was produced for Lemieux and his agent. Only 5,000 copies were produced.

	Player	Pinnacle
□	Mario Lemieux 600 goals	

1996 - 97 PINNACLE MINT COLLECTION

These cards have four versions: a die-cut card (coin holder), a bronze team card, a silver team card and a gold team card (dufex technology).

Complete Set (30 cards):	450.00	135.00	30.00
Player	GT	ST	BT
□□□□ 1 Mario Lemieux	55.00	15.00	3.00
□□□□ 2 Domink Hasek (G)	15.00	5.00	1.00
□□□□ 3 Eric Lindros	15.00	5.00	1.00
□□□□ 4 Jaromir Jagr	15.00	5.00	1.00
□□□□ 5 Paul Kariya	25.00	5.00	1.00
□□□□ 6 Peter Forsberg	25.00	5.00	1.00
□□□□ 7 Pavel Bure	15.00	5.00	1.00
□□□□ 8 Sergei Fedorov	15.00	5.00	1.00
□□□□ 9 Saku Koivu	15.00	5.00	1.00
□□□□ 10 Daniel Alfredsson	10.00	2.00	.75
□□□□ 11 Joe Sakic	30.00	10.00	2.00
□□□□ 12 Steve Yzerman	40.00	15.00	3.00
□□□□ 13 Teemu Selänne	15.00	5.00	1.00
□□□□ 14 Brett Hull	15.00	5.00	1.00
□□□□ 15 Jeremy Roenick	15.00	5.00	1.00
□□□□ 16 Mark Messier	15.00	5.00	1.00
□□□□ 17 Mats Sundin	15.00	5.00	1.00
□□□□ 18 Brendan Shanahan	15.00	5.00	1.00
□□□□ 19 Keith Tkachuk	10.00	2.00	.75
□□□□ 20 Paul Coffey	10.00	2.00	.75
□□□□ 21 Patrick Roy (G)	55.00	15.00	3.00
□□□□ 22 Chris Chelios	10.00	2.00	.75
□□□□ 23 Martin Brodeur (G)	30.00	10.00	2.00
□□□□ 24 Félix Potvin (G)	10.00	2.00	.75
□□□□ 25 Chris Osgood (G)	10.00	2.00	.75
□□□□ 26 J. Vanbiesbrouck (G)	5.00	2.00	.75
□□□□ 27 Jocelyn Thibault (G)	5.00	2.00	.75
□□□□ 28 Jim Carey (G)	5.00	2.00	.75
□□□□ 29 Jarome Iginla	15.00	5.00	1.00
□□□□ 30 Jim Campbell	5.00	2.00	.75

MEDALLIONS

These medallions had four versions that were readily available: the brass medallion, a nickel-silver medallion, a gold plated medallion and a fine silver medallion. A one of a kind solid gold medallion was also available.

Complete Set (30 medallions):	450.00	200.00	45.00
Player	GP	NS	Bro.
□□□ 01 Mario Lemieux	50.00	25.00	6.00
□□□ 02 Dominik Hasek (G)	15.00	5.00	2.00
□□□ 03 Eric Lindros	15.00	5.00	2.00
□□□ 04 Jaromir Jagr	15.00	5.00	2.00
□□□ 05 Paul Kariya	25.00	10.00	2.00
□□□ 06 Peter Forsberg	25.00	10.00	2.00
□□□ 07 Pavel Bure	15.00	5.00	1.00
□□□ 08 Sergei Fedorov	15.00	8.00	2.00
□□□ 09 Saku Koivu	15.00	7.00	1.00
□□□ 10 Daniel Alfredsson	10.00	5.00	1.00
□□□ 11 Joe Sakic	30.00	10.00	3.00
□□□ 12 Steve Yzerman	40.00	20.00	4.00
□□□ 13 Teemu Selänne	15.00	5.00	1.00
□□□ 14 Brett Hull	15.00	8.00	2.00
□□□ 15 Jeremy Roenick	15.00	7.00	1.00
□□□ 16 Mark Messier	15.00	8.00	2.00
□□□ 17 Mats Sundin	15.00	8.00	2.00
□□□ 18 Brendan Shanahan	15.00	8.00	2.00
□□□ 19 Keith Tkachuk	10.00	5.00	1.00
□□□ 20 Paul Coffey	10.00	5.00	1.00
□□□ 21 Patrick Roy (G)	55.00	25.00	6.00
□□□ 22 Chris Chelios	10.00	5.00	1.00
□□□ 23 Martin Brodeur (G)	30.00	10.00	3.00
□□□ 24 Félix Potvin (G)	10.00	5.00	1.00
□□□ 25 Chris Osgood (G)	10.00	5.00	1.00
□□□ 26 J. Vanbiesbrouck (G)	5.00	4.00	1.00
□□□ 27 Jocelyn Thibault (G)	5.00	3.00	1.00
□□□ 28 Jim Carey (G)	5.00	3.00	1.00
□□□ 29 Jarome Iginla	15.00	7.00	1.00
□□□ 30 Jim Campbell	5.00	3.00	1.00

FINE SILVER, SOLID GOLD

Complete Set (30 medallions):	2600.00
Player	Silver
□□ 01 Mario Lemieux	300.00
□□ 02 Dominik Hasek (G)	100.00
□□ 03 Eric Lindros	100.00
□□ 04 Jaromir Jagr	100.00
□□ 05 Paul Kariya	140.00
□□ 06 Peter Forsberg	140.00
□□ 07 Pavel Bure	80.00
□□ 08 Sergei Fedorov	100.00
□□ 09 Saku Koivu	80.00
□□ 10 Daniel Alfredsson	60.00
□□ 11 Joe Sakic	160.00
□□ 12 Steve Yzerman	240.00
□□ 13 Teemu Selänne	80.00
□□ 14 Brett Hull	100.00
□□ 15 Jeremy Roenick	80.00
□□ 16 Mark Messier	100.00
□□ 17 Mats Sundin	100.00
□□ 18 Brendan Shanahan	100.00
□□ 19 Keith Tkachuk	60.00
□□ 20 Paul Coffey	60.00
□□ 21 Patrick Roy (G)	300.00
□□ 22 Chris Chelios	60.00
□□ 23 Martin Brodeur (G)	160.00
□□ 24 Félix Potvin (G)	60.00
□□ 25 Chris Osgood (G)	60.00
□□ 26 J. Vanbiesbrouck (G)	40.00
□□ 27 Jocelyn Thibault (G)	40.00
□□ 28 Jim Carey (G)	20.00
□□ 29 Jarome Iginla	80.00
□□ 30 Jim Campbell	20.00

1996 - 97 PINNACLE SUMMIT

These cards have five versions: the regular card, a metal card (magazine packs), a Premium Stock card, a Summit Ice parallel card and an Artist Proof parallel. metal versions have a flat silver face while Premium Stock versions reflect light. Ice parallel cards reflect light on a patterned face and say "Summit Ice" on the back.

Complete Set (200 cards):	90.00	55.00	25.00
Common Player:	.65	.35	.20
Player	PS	Metal	Smmt.
□□□ 1 Joe Sakic, Colo.	3.00	2.00	1.00
□□□ 2 Dominik Hasek (G), Buff.	2.00	1.50	.50
□□□ 3 Paul Coffey, Detr.	1.00	.50	.20
□□□ 4 Todd Gill, Toro.	.65	.35	.20
□□□ 5 Pat Verbeek, NYRa.	.65	.35	.20
□□□ 6 John LeClair, Phil.	1.50	1.00	.50
□□□ 7 Joé Juneau, Wash.	.65	.35	.20
□□□ 8 Scott Mellanby, Flor.	.65	.35	.20
□□□ 9 Scott Stevens, NJer.	.65	.50	.20
□□□ 10 Ron Francis, Pitt.	1.00	.50	.20
□□□ 11 Larry Murphy, Toro.	.65	.35	.20
□□□ 12 Sandis Ozolinsh, Colo.	.65	.35	.20
□□□ 13 Luc Robitaille, NYRa.	1.50	1.00	.50
□□□ 14 Grant Fuhr (G), SLou.	1.00	.50	.20
□□□ 15 Adam Oates, Bost.	.65	.50	.20
□□□ 16 Keith Primeau, Detr.	.65	.50	.20
□□□ 17 Mark Recchi, Mont.	.65	.50	.20
□□□ 18 Brian Bradley, Tamp.	.65	.35	.20
□□□ 19 Zdeno Ciger, Edmo.	.65	.35	.20
□□□ 20 Zigmund Palffy, NYIs.	1.00	.50	.20
□□□ 21 Damian Rhodes (G), Otta.	.65	.35	.20
□□□ 22 Russ Courtnall, Vanc.	.65	.35	.20
□□□ 23 Mike Modano, Dall.	2.00	1.50	.50
□□□ 24 Geoff Sanderson, Hart.	.65	.35	.20
□□□ 25 Michal Pivonka, Wash.	.65	.35	.20
□□□ 26 Randy Burridge, Buff.	.65	.35	.20
□□□ 27 Dimitri Khristich, LosA.	.65	.35	.20
□□□ 28 Mike Gartner, Toro.	1.50	1.00	.50
□□□ 29 Cam Neely, Bost.	2.00	1.50	.50
□□□ 30 Mathieu Schneider, Toro.	.65	.35	.20
□□□ 31 Steve Thomas, NJer.	.65	.35	.20
□□□ 32 Mario Lemieux, Pitt.	6.00	4.50	2.00
□□□ 33 Darryl Sydor, Dal	.65	.35	.20
□□□ 34 Alexei Yashin, Otta.	1.00	.50	.20
□□□ 35 Brett Hull, SLou.	2.00	1.50	.50
□□□ 36 Trevor Kidd (G), Calg.	.65	.35	.20
□□□ 37 Alexei Zhamnov, Winn.	.65	.35	.20
□□□ 38 Uwe Krupp, Colo.	.65	.35	.20
□□□ 39 Brian Skrudland, Flor.	.65	.35	.20
□□□ 40 Igor Larionov, Detr.	1.00	.50	.20
□□□ 41 N. Khabibulin (G), Winn.	.65	.50	.20
□□□ 42 Pavel Bure, Vanc.	1.50	1.00	.50
□□□ 43 Chris Chelios, Chic.	1.00	.50	.20
□□□ 44 Andrew Cassels, Hart.	.65	.35	.20
□□□ 45 Owen Nolan, SanJ.	1.00	.50	.20
□□□ 46 Todd Harvey, Dall.	.65	.35	.20
□□□ 47 Jari Kurri, NYRa.	2.00	1.50	.50
□□□ 48 Olaf Kölzig (G), Wash.	1.00	.50	.20
□□□ 49 Greg Johnson, Detr.	.65	.35	.20
□□□ 50 Dominic Roussel (G), Phil.	.65	.35	.20
□□□ 51 Mats Sundin, Toro.	2.00	1.50	.50
□□□ 52 Robert Svehla, Flor.	.65	.35	.20
□□□ 53 Sandy Moger, Bost.	.65	.35	.20
□□□ 54 Darren Turcotte, SanJ.	.65	.35	.20
□□□ 55 Teppo Numminen, Winn.	.65	.35	.20
□□□ 56 Benoît Hogue, Dall.	.65	.35	.20
□□□ 57 Scott Niedermayer, NJer.	.65	.35	.20
□□□ 58 A. Selivanov, Tamp.	.65	.35	.20
□□□ 59 Valeri Kamensky, Colo.	.65	.35	.20
□□□ 60 Ken Wregget (G), Pitt.	.65	.35	.20
□□□ 61 Travis Green, NYIs.	.65	.35	.20
□□□ 62 Peter Bondra, Wash.	1.00	.50	.20
□□□ 63 V. Konstantinov, Detr.	.65	.35	.20
□□□ 64 Craig Janney, Winn.	.65	.35	.20
□□□ 65 Joe Nieuwendyk, Flor.	.65	.50	.20
□□□ 66 Vanbiesbrouck (G), Flor.	.65	.50	.20
□□□ 67 Wayne Gretzky, SLou.	8.00	6.00	3.00
□□□ 68 Kirk McLean (G), Vanc.	.65	.35	.20
□□□ 69 Alexei Zhitnik, Buff.	.65	.35	.20
□□□ 70 Mike Ricci, Colo.	.65	.35	.20
□□□ 71 Jeff Beukeboom, NYRa.	.65	.35	.20
□□□ 72 Félix Potvin (G), Toro.	1.00	.50	.20
□□□ 73 Mikael Renberg, Phil.	.65	.35	.20
□□□ 74 J. Baker, SanJ. (Toro.)	.65	.35	.20
□□□ 75 Guy Hebert (G), Anah.	.65	.35	.20
□□□ 76 Steve Yzerman, Detr.	4.50	3.50	1.50
□□□ 77 Daren Puppa (G), Tamp.	.65	.35	.20
□□□ 78 Scott Young, Colo.	.65	.35	.20
□□□ 79 Martin Gelinas, Vanc.	.65	.35	.20
□□□ 80 Dave Gagner, Dall. (Calg.)	.65	.35	.20
□□□ 81 Tomas Sandström, Pitt.	.65	.35	.20
□□□ 82 Alexei Kovalev, NYRa.	1.00	.50	.20
□□□ 83 Ray Whitney, SanJ.	.65	.35	.20
□□□ 84 Vyacheslav Kozlov, Detr.	.65	.35	.20
□□□ 85 Jaromir Jagr, Pitt.	2.00	1.50	.50
□□□ 86 Joe Murphy, Chic.	.65	.35	.20
□□□ 87 Patrick Roy (G), Colo.	6.00	4.50	2.00
□□□ 88 Ray Sheppard, Flor.	.65	.35	.20
□□□ 89 Chris Terreri (G), SanJ.	.65	.35	.20
□□□ 90 Pierre Turgeon, Mont.	.65	.50	.20
□□□ 91 Theoren Fleury, Calg.	1.00	.50	.20
□□□ 92 Doug Weight, Edmo.	1.00	.50	.20
□□□ 93 Tom Barrasso (G), Pitt.	.65	.50	.20
□□□ 94 Jim Carey (G), Wash.	.65	.35	.20
□□□ 95 Greg Adams, Dall.	.65	.35	.20
□□□ 96 Brian Leetch, NYRa.	1.00	.50	.20
□□□ 97 Ed Belfour (G), Chic.	2.00	1.50	.50
□□□ 98 Stéphane Fiset (G), Colo.	.65	.35	.20
□□□ 99 Stéphane Richer, NJer.	.65	.35	.20
□□□ 100 Ron Hextall (G), Pitt.	1.00	.50	.20
□□□ 101 Mike Vernon (G), Detr.	.65	.50	.20
□□□ 102 J. Thibault (G), Mont.	.65	.50	.20
□□□ 103 Jason Arnott, Edmo.	.65	.50	.20
□□□ 104 Keith Tkachuk, Winn.	1.00	.50	.20
□□□ 105 Sergei Fedorov, Detr.	2.00	1.50	.50
□□□ 106 Alexandre Daigle, Otta.	.65	.35	.20
□□□ 107 Alexander Mogilny, Vanc.	.65	.50	.20
□□□ 108 German Titov, Calg.	.65	.35	.20
□□□ 109 Sean Burke (G), Hart.	1.00	.50	.20
□□□ 110 Arturs Irbe (G), SanJ.	.65	.50	.20
□□□ 111 Mark Messier, NYRa.	2.00	1.50	.50
□□□ 112 Nicklas Lidström, Detr.	1.00	.50	.20
□□□ 113 Claude Lemieux, Colo.	.65	.35	.20
□□□ 114 M. Brodeur (G), NJer.	3.00	2.00	1.00
□□□ 115 Bernie Nicholls, Chic.	.65	.35	.20
□□□ 116 Paul Kariya, Anah.	2.50	2.00	1.00
□□□ 117 Eric Lindros, Phil.	2.00	1.50	.50
□□□ 118 Doug Gilmour, Toro.	1.00	.50	.20
□□□ 119 Sergei Zubov, Pitt.	.65	.35	.20
□□□ 120 Adam Graves, NYRa.	.65	.50	.20
□□□ 121 Phil Housley, NJer.	.65	.35	.20
□□□ 122 Bob Bassen, Dall.	.65	.35	.20
□□□ 123 Rod Brind'Amour, Pha	.65	.35	.20
□□□ 124 Dave Andreychuk, NJer.	.65	.35	.20
□□□ 125 Corey Hirsch (G), Vanc.	.65	.35	.20
□□□ 126 Kelly Hrudey (G), LosA.	.65	.35	.20
□□□ 127 Pat LaFontaine, Buff.	1.00	.50	.20
□□□ 128 V. Fetisov, Detr.	1.00	.50	.20
□□□ 129 OlegTverdovsky, Winn.	.65	.35	.20
□□□ 130 Andy Moog (G), Dall.	.65	.50	.20
□□□ 131 Stu Barnes, Flor.	.65	.35	.20
□□□ 132 Roman Hamrlik, Tamp.	.65	.35	.20

133 Teemu Selänne, Anah.	1.50	1.00	.50
134 Trevor Linden, Vanc.	.65	.50	.20
135 Chris Osgood (G), Detr.	1.00	.50	.20
136 V. Damphousse, Mont.	1.00	.50	.20
137 Shayne Corson, SLou.	.65	.35	.20
138 Jeremy Roenick, Chic.	1.50	1.00	.50
139 B. Shanahan, Hart.	2.00	1.50	.50
140 Wendel Clark, Toro.	1.50	1.00	.50
141 R. Bourque, Bost.	2.00	1.50	.50
142 Peter Forsberg, Colo.	2.50	2.00	1.00
143 John MacLean, NJer.	.65	.35	.20
144 Jeff Friesen, SanJ.	.65	.35	.20
145 Mike Richter (G), NYRa.	.65	.50	.20
146 Dave Reid, Bost.	.65	.35	.20
147 Rob Niedermayer, Flor.	.65	.35	.20
148 Petr Nedved, Pitt.	.65	.35	.20
149 Sylvain Lefebvre, Colo.	.65	.35	.20
150 Curtis Joseph (G), Edmo.	2.00	1.50	.50
151 Eric Dazé, Chic.	.65	.50	.20
152 Saku Koivu, Mont.	1.50	1.00	.50
153 Jere Lehtinen, Dall.	.65	.35	.20
154 Todd Bertuzzi, NYIs.	4.50	3.50	1.50
155 Chad Kilger, Winn.	.65	.35	.20
156 Stéphane Yelle, Colo.	.65	.35	.20
157 Bryan McCabe, NYIs.	.65	.35	.20
158 Aaron Gavey, Tamp.	.65	.35	.20
159 Kyle McLaren, Bost.	.65	.35	.20
160 Valeri Bure, Mont.	.65	.35	.20
161 Antti Törmänen, Otta.	.65	.35	.20
162 Brendan Witt, Wash.	.65	.35	.20
163 Ed Jovanovski, Flor.	.65	.50	.20
164 Aki Berg, LosA.	.65	.35	.20
165 M. Ragnarsson, SanJ.	.65	.35	.20
166 Miroslav Satan, Edmo.	.65	.35	.20
167 D. Alfredsson, Otta.	1.00	.50	.20
168 Jeff O'Neill, Hart.	.65	.50	.20
169 Radek Dvorak, Flor.	.65	.35	.20
170 Petr Sykora, NJer.	.65	.50	.20
171 Vitali Yachmenev, LosA.	.65	.35	.20
172 Niklas Andersson, NYIs.	.65	.35	.20
173 N. Baumgartner, Wash.	.65	.35	.20
174 Brandon Convery, Toro.	.65	.35	.20
175 Ralph Intranuovo, Edmo.	.65	.35	.20
176 Niklas Sundblad, Calg.	.65	.35	.20
177 P. Labrecque (G), Mont.	.65	.35	.20
178 Éric Fichaud (G), NYIs.	.65	.35	.20
179 Martin Biron (G), Buff.	1.50	1.00	.50
180 S. Sullivan, NJer. RC	**3.00**	**2.00**	**1.50**
181 Peter Ferraro, NYRa.	.65	.35	.20
182 J. Théodore (G), Mont.	4.50	3.50	1.50
183 Kevin Hodson (G), Detr.	.65	.35	.20
184 Ethan Moreau, Chic.	.65	.35	.20
185 Curtis Brown, Buff.	.65	.35	.20
186 D. Langkow, Tamp.	.65	.35	.20
187 Jan Caloun, SanJ. RC	**1.00**	**.50**	**.50**
188 Landon Wilson, Colo.	.65	.35	.20
189 Tommy Salo (G), NYIs.	.65	.50	.20
190 Anders Eriksson, Detr.	.65	.35	.20
191 David Nemirovsky, Flor.	.65	.35	.20
192 J. Langenbrunner, Dall.	.65	.35	.20
193 Zdenick Nedved, Toro.	.65	.35	.20
194 Todd Hlushko, Calg.	.65	.35	.20
195 A. Yegorov, SanJ. RC	**1.00**	**.50**	**.50**
196 Jamie Pushor, Detr.	.65	.35	.20
197 Anders Myrvold, Colo.	.65	.35	.20
198 CL: M. Messier, NYRa.	1.00	.50	.20
199 CL: Brett Hull, SLou.	1.00	.50	.20
200 CL: Pavel Bure, Vanc.	.65	.50	.20

PARALLELS

These cards have five versions: the regular card, a metal card (magazine packs), a Premium Stock card, a Summit Ice parallel card and an Artist Proof parallel. metal versions have a flat silver face while Premium Stock versions reflect light. Ice parallel cards reflect light on a patterned face and say "Summit Ice" on the back.

Complete Set (200 cards): 1385.00 185.00
Common Player: 4.00 1.00

Player	AP	Ice
1 Joe Sakic, Colo.	60.00	10.00
2 Dominik Hasek (G), Buff.	30.00	5.00
3 Paul Coffey, Detr.	20.00	1.00
4 Todd Gill, Toro.	5.00	1.00
5 Pat Verbeek, NYRa.	10.00	1.00
6 John LeClair, Phil.	30.00	5.00
7 Joé Juneau, Wash.	5.00	1.00
8 Scott Mellanby, Flor.	5.00	1.00
9 Scott Stevens, NJer.	15.00	1.00
10 Ron Francis, Pitt.	20.00	1.00
11 Larry Murphy, Toro.	5.00	1.00
12 Sandis Ozolinsh, Colo.	5.00	1.00
13 Luc Robitaille, NYRa.	30.00	5.00
14 Grant Fuhr (G), SLou.	20.00	1.00
15 Adam Oates, Bost.	15.00	1.00
16 Keith Primeau, Detr.	15.00	1.00
17 Mark Recchi, Mont.	15.00	1.00
18 Brian Bradley, Tamp.	4.00	1.00
19 Zdeno Ciger, Edmo.	5.00	1.00
20 Zigmund Palffy, NYIs.	20.00	1.00
21 Damian Rhodes (G), Otta.	5.00	1.00
22 Russ Courtnall, Vanc.	5.00	1.00
23 Mike Modano, Dall.	35.00	5.00
24 Geoff Sanderson, Hart.	5.00	1.00
25 Michal Pivonka, Wash.	4.00	1.00
26 Randy Burridge, Buff.	5.00	1.00
27 Dimitri Khristich, LosA.	5.00	1.00
28 Mike Gartner, Toro.	30.00	5.00
29 Cam Neely, Bost.	35.00	5.00
30 Mathieu Schneider, Toro.	5.00	1.00
31 Steve Thomas, NJer.	5.00	1.00
32 Mario Lemieux, Pitt.	110.00	20.00
33 Darryl Sydor, Dal	5.00	1.00
34 Alexei Yashin, Otta.	20.00	1.00
35 Brett Hull, SLou.	35.00	5.00
36 Trevor Kidd (G), Calg.	10.00	1.00
37 Alexei Zhamnov, Winn.	10.00	1.00
38 Uwe Krupp, Colo.	4.00	1.00
39 Brian Skrudland, Flor.	5.00	1.00
40 Igor Larionov, Detr.	20.00	1.00
41 Nikolai Khabibulin (G), Winn.	15.00	1.00
42 Pavel Bure, Vanc.	30.00	5.00
43 Chris Chelios, Chic.	20.00	1.00
44 Andrew Cassels, Hart.	5.00	1.00
45 Owen Nolan, SanJ.	20.00	1.00
46 Todd Harvey, Dall.	5.00	1.00
47 Jari Kurri, NYRa.	35.00	5.00
48 Olaf Kölzig (G), Wash.	20.00	1.00
49 Greg Johnson, Detr.	5.00	1.00
50 Dominic Roussel (G), Phil.	5.00	1.00
51 Mats Sundin, Toro.	35.00	5.00
52 Robert Svehla, Flor.	5.00	1.00
53 Sandy Moger, Bost.	4.00	1.00
54 Darren Turcotte, SanJ.	5.00	1.00
55 Teppo Numminen, Winn.	10.00	1.00
56 Benoît Hogue, Dall.	5.00	1.00
57 Scott Niedermayer, NJer.	10.00	1.00
58 Alexander Selivanov, Tamp.	4.00	1.00
59 Valeri Kamensky, Colo.	10.00	1.00
60 Ken Wregget (G), Pitt.	5.00	1.00
61 Travis Green, NYIs.	5.00	1.00
62 Peter Bondra, Wash.	20.00	1.00
63 Vladimir Konstantinov, Detr.	10.00	1.00
64 Craig Janney, Winn.	5.00	1.00
65 Joe Nieuwendyk, Flor.	15.00	1.00
66 J. Vanbiesbrouck (G), Flor.	15.00	1.00
67 Wayne Gretzky, SLou.	150.00	30.00
68 Kirk McLean (G), Vanc.	10.00	1.00
69 Alexei Zhitnik, Buff.	5.00	1.00
70 Mike Ricci, Colo.	10.00	1.00
71 Jeff Beukeboom, NYRa.	5.00	1.00
72 Félix Potvin (G), Toro.	20.00	1.00
73 Mikael Renberg, Phil.	10.00	1.00
74 Jamie Baker, SanJ. (Toro.)	4.00	1.00
75 Guy Hebert (G), Anah.	5.00	1.00
76 Steve Yzerman, Detr.	90.00	15.00
77 Daren Puppa (G), Tamp.	5.00	1.00
78 Scott Young, Colo.	10.00	1.00
79 Martin Gelinas, Vanc.	5.00	1.00
80 Dave Gagner, Dall. (Calg.)	5.00	1.00
81 Tomas Sandström, Pitt.	5.00	1.00
82 Alexei Kovalev, NYRa.	20.00	1.00
83 Ray Whitney, SanJ.	5.00	1.00
84 Vyacheslav Kozlov, Detr.	5.00	1.00
85 Jaromir Jagr, Pitt.	30.00	5.00
86 Joe Murphy, Chic.	5.00	1.00
87 Patrick Roy (G), Colo.	110.00	20.00
88 Ray Sheppard, Flor.	5.00	1.00
89 Chris Terreri (G), SanJ.	5.00	1.00
90 Pierre Turgeon, Mont.	15.00	1.00
91 Theoren Fleury, Calg.	20.00	1.00
92 Doug Weight, Edmo.	20.00	1.00
93 Tom Barrasso (G), Pitt.	15.00	1.00
94 Jim Carey (G), Wash.	5.00	1.00
95 Greg Adams, Dall.	5.00	1.00
96 Brian Leetch, NYRa.	20.00	1.00
97 Ed Belfour (G), Chic.	35.00	5.00
98 Stéphane Fiset (G), Colo.	10.00	1.00
99 Stéphane Richer, NJer.	5.00	1.00
100 Ron Hextall (G), Pitt.	20.00	1.00
101 Mike Vernon (G), Detr.	15.00	1.00
102 Jocelyn Thibault (G), Mont.	15.00	1.00
103 Jason Arnott, Edmo.	15.00	1.00
104 Keith Tkachuk, Winn.	20.00	1.00
105 Sergei Fedorov, Detr.	35.00	5.00
106 Alexandre Daigle, Otta.	5.00	1.00
107 Alexander Mogilny, Vanc.	15.00	1.00
108 German Titov, Calg.	4.00	1.00
109 Sean Burke (G), Hart.	20.00	1.00
110 Arturs Irbe (G), SanJ.	15.00	1.00
111 Mark Messier, NYRa.	35.00	5.00
112 Nicklas Lidström, Detr.	20.00	1.00
113 Claude Lemieux, Colo.	10.00	1.00
114 Martin Brodeur (G), NJer.	60.00	10.00
115 Bernie Nicholls, Chic.	5.00	1.00
116 Paul Kariya, Anah.	50.00	10.00
117 Eric Lindros, Phil.	30.00	5.00
118 Doug Gilmour, Toro.	20.00	1.00
119 Sergei Zubov, Pitt.	5.00	1.00
120 Adam Graves, NYRa.	15.00	1.00
121 Phil Housley, NJer.	10.00	1.00
122 Bob Bassen, Dall.	4.00	1.00
123 Rod Brind'Amour, Pha	10.00	1.00
124 Dave Andreychuk, NJer.	10.00	1.00
125 Corey Hirsch (G), Vanc.	5.00	1.00
126 Kelly Hrudey (G), LosA.	10.00	1.00
127 Pat LaFontaine, Buff.	20.00	1.00
128 Viacheslav Fetisov, Detr.	20.00	1.00
129 OlegTverdovsky, Winn.	5.00	1.00
130 Andy Moog (G), Dall.	15.00	1.00
131 Stu Barnes, Flor.	4.00	1.00
132 Roman Hamrlik, Tamp.	5.00	1.00
133 Teemu Selänne, Anah.	30.00	5.00
134 Trevor Linden, Vanc.	15.00	1.00
135 Chris Osgood (G), Detr.	20.00	1.00
136 Vincent Damphousse, Mont.	20.00	1.00
137 Shayne Corson, SLou.	10.00	1.00
138 Jeremy Roenick, Chic.	30.00	5.00
139 Brendan Shanahan, Hart.	35.00	5.00
140 Wendel Clark, Toro.	30.00	5.00
141 Raymond Bourque, Bost.	45.00	5.00
142 Peter Forsberg, Colo.	50.00	10.00
143 John MacLean, NJer.	5.00	1.00
144 Jeff Friesen, SanJ.	10.00	1.00
145 Mike Richter (G), NYRa.	15.00	1.00
146 Dave Reid, Bost.	5.00	1.00
147 Rob Niedermayer, Flor.	5.00	1.00
148 Petr Nedved, Pitt.	10.00	1.00
149 Sylvain Lefebvre, Colo.	5.00	1.00
150 Curtis Joseph (G), Edmo.	35.00	5.00
151 Eric Dazé, Chic.	15.00	1.00
152 Saku Koivu, Mont.	30.00	5.00
153 Jere Lehtinen, Dall.	10.00	1.00
154 Todd Bertuzzi, NYIs.	45.00	5.00
155 Chad Kilger, Winn.	5.00	1.00
156 Stéphane Yelle, Colo.	5.00	1.00
157 Bryan McCabe, NYIs.	5.00	1.00
158 Aaron Gavey, Tamp.	4.00	1.00
159 Kyle McLaren, Bost.	5.00	1.00
160 Valeri Bure, Mont.	10.00	1.00
161 Antti Törmänen, Otta.	4.00	1.00
162 Brendan Witt, Wash.	4.00	1.00
163 Ed Jovanovski, Flor.	15.00	1.00
164 Aki Berg, LosA.	5.00	1.00
165 Marcus Ragnarsson, SanJ.	5.00	1.00
166 Miroslav Satan, Edmo.	10.00	1.00
167 Daniel Alfredsson, Otta.	20.00	1.00
168 Jeff O'Neill, Hart.	15.00	1.00
169 Radek Dvorak, Flor.	5.00	1.00
170 Petr Sykora, NJer.	15.00	1.00
171 Vitali Yachmenev, LosA.	5.00	1.00
172 Niklas Andersson, NYIs.	4.00	1.00
173 Nolan Baumgartner, Wash.	4.00	1.00
174 Brandon Convery, Toro.	4.00	1.00
175 Ralph Intranuovo, Edmo.	4.00	1.00
176 Niklas Sundblad, Calg.	4.00	1.00
177 P. Labrecque (G), Mont.	4.00	1.00
178 Éric Fichaud (G), NYIs.	5.00	1.00
179 Martin Biron (G), Buff.	15.00	1.00
180 Steve Sullivan, NJer. RC	**10.00**	**1.00**
181 Peter Ferraro, NYRa.	5.00	1.00
182 José Théodore (G), Mont.	45.00	5.00
183 Kevin Hodson (G), Detr.	5.00	1.00
184 Ethan Moreau, Chic.	5.00	1.00
185 Curtis Brown, Buff.	5.00	1.00
186 Daymond Langkow, Tamp.	5.00	1.00
187 Jan Caloun, SanJ. RC	**4.00**	**1.00**
188 Landon Wilson, Colo.	5.00	1.00
189 Tommy Salo (G), NYIs.	15.00	1.00
190 Anders Eriksson, Detr.	4.00	1.00
191 David Nemirovsky, Flor.	4.00	1.00
192 Jamie Langenbrunner, Dall.	5.00	1.00
193 Zdenick Nedved, Toro.	4.00	1.00
194 Todd Hlushko, Calg.	4.00	1.00
195 A. Yegorov, SanJ. RC	**4.00**	**1.00**
196 Jamie Pushor, Detr.	5.00	1.00
197 Anders Myrvold, Colo.	5.00	1.00
198 CL: Mark Messier, NYRa.	20.00	1.00
199 CL: Brett Hull, SLou.	20.00	1.00
200 CL: Pavel Bure, Vanc.	15.00	1.00

HIGH VOLTAGE

There are two versions: the regular insert (#/1500) and the Mirage parallel (#/600).

Insert Set (16 cards): 600.00 275.00
Eric Lindros Promo 4.00

Inserts	M600	HV
1 Mark Messier, NYRa.	35.00	15.00
2 Joe Sakic, Colo.	60.00	30.00
3 Paul Kariya, Anah.	50.00	25.00
4 Daniel Alfredsson, Otta.	20.00	10.00
5 Wayne Gretzky, SLou.	150.00	75.00
6 Peter Forsberg, Colo.	50.00	25.00
7 Éric Dazé, Chic.	15.00	6.00
8 Mario Lemieux, Pitt.	110.00	55.00
9 Eric Lindros, Phil.	35.00	15.00
10 Jeremy Roenick, Chic.	30.00	15.00
11 Alexander Mogilny, Vanc.	15.00	6.00
12 Teemu Selänne, Anah.	30.00	15.00
13 Sergei Fedorov, Detr.	35.00	15.00
14 Saku Koivu, Mont.	30.00	15.00
15 Jaromir Jagr, Pitt.	35.00	15.00
16 Brett Hull, SLou.	35.00	15.00

IN THE CREASE

There are two versions: the regular insert (#/6,000) and the Premium Stock parallel (#/600).

Insert Set (16 cards): 475.00 150.00
Patrick Roy Promo 8.00

Inserts	PS600	ITC
1 Patrick Roy (G), Colo.	135.00	45.00
2 Mike Richter (G), NYRa.	20.00	8.00
3 Ed Belfour (G), Chic.	45.00	15.00
4 Daren Puppa (G), Tamp.	20.00	8.00
5 Curtis Joseph (G), Edmo.	45.00	15.00
6 Jim Carey (G), Wash.	20.00	8.00
7 Damian Rhodes (G), Otta.	20.00	8.00
8 Martin Brodeur (G), NJer.	70.00	20.00
9 Félix Potvin (G), Toro.	25.00	8.00
10 John Vanbiesbrouck (G), Flor.	20.00	8.00
11 Jocelyn Thibault (G), Mont.	20.00	8.00
12 Nikolai Khabibulin (G), Winn.	20.00	8.00
13 Chris Osgood (G), Detr.	25.00	8.00
14 Dominik Hasek (G), Buff.	45.00	15.00
15 Corey Hirsch (G), Vanc.	20.00	8.00
16 Ron Hextall (G), Phil.	25.00	8.00

UNTOUCHABLES

Insert Set (18 cards): 475.00
Mario Lemieux Promo 8.00

Insert (#/1000)	U1000
1 Mario Lemieux, Pitt.	75.00
3 Joe Sakic, Colo.	40.00
4 Ron Francis, Pitt.	15.00
5 Peter Forsberg, Colo.	35.00
6 Eric Lindros, Phil.	25.00
7 Paul Kariya, Anah.	35.00
8 Teemu Selänne, Anah.	20.00
9 Alexander Mogilny, Vanc.	12.00
10 Sergei Fedorov, Detr.	25.00
11 Doug Weight, Edmo.	15.00
12 Wayne Gretzky, SLou.	100.00
13 Chris Osgood (G), Detr.	15.00
14 Jim Carey (G), Wash.	8.00
15 Patrick Roy (G), Colo.	75.00
16 Martin Brodeur (G), NJer.	40.00
17 Félix Potvin (G), Toro.	15.00
18 Ron Hextall (G), Phil.	15.00

1996 - 97 PINNACLE ZENITH

There are two versions: the regular card and the Artist's Proof parallel.

Complete Set (150 cards): 1865.00 60.00
Common Player: 5.00 .25

Player	AP	PZ
1 Mike Modano, Dall.	45.00	1.50
2 Martin Brodeur (G), NJer.	70.00	2.00
3 Pavel Bure, Vanc.	30.00	1.00
4 Raymond Bourque, Bost.	50.00	1.50
5 Steve Yzerman, Detr.	100.00	3.50
6 Keith Tkachuk, Phoe.	25.00	.50
7 Jim Carey (G), Wash.	5.00	.25
8 Valeri Kamensky, Colo.	10.00	.25
9 Valeri Bure, Mont.	10.00	.25
10 Ron Francis, Pitt.	25.00	.50
11 Trevor Kidd (G), Calg.	10.00	.25
12 Doug Weight, Edmo.	25.00	.50
13 Wayne Gretzky, NYRa.	180.00	6.00
14 Todd Gill, SanJ.	5.00	.25
15 Dominik Hasek (G), Buff.	40.00	1.50
16 Scott Mellanby, Flor.	10.00	.25
17 John LeClair, Phil.	35.00	1.00
18 Al MacInnis, SLou.	15.00	.50
19 Derian Hatcher, Dall.	10.00	.25
20 Stéphane Fiset (G), LosA.	10.00	.25
21 Alexander Selivanov, Tamp.	5.00	.25
22 Vyacheslav Kozlov, Detr.	10.00	.25
23 Alexei Yashin, Otta.	25.00	.50
24 Wendel Clark, Toro.	35.00	1.00
25 Ed Belfour (G), Chic.	45.00	1.50
26 Travis Green, NYIs.	10.00	.25
27 Joé Juneau, Wash.	10.00	.25
28 Teemu Selänne, Anah.	30.00	1.00
29 Jeff O'Neill, Hart.	15.00	.50
30 Jeremy Roenick, Phoe.	35.00	1.00
31 Félix Potvin (G), Toro.	25.00	.50
32 Bernie Nicholls, SanJ.	10.00	.25
33 Steve Thomas, NJer.	10.00	.25
34 Alexander Mogilny, Vanc.	20.00	.50
35 Patrick Roy (G), Colo.	130.00	4.50
36 Luc Robitaille, NYRa.	35.00	1.00
37 Owen Nolan, SanJ.	25.00	.50
38 Sergei Zubov, Dall.	10.00	.25
39 Pierre Turgeon, SLou.	15.00	.50
40 Nikolai Khabibulin (G), Phoe.	15.00	.50
41 Adam Oates, Bost.	15.00	.50
42 Stéphane Richer, Mont.	10.00	.25
43 Daren Puppa (G), Tamp.	10.00	.25
44 Joe Sakic, Colo.	70.00	2.00
45 Ed Jovanovski, Flor.	15.00	.50
46 Ron Hextall (G), Phil.	25.00	.50
47 Doug Gilmour, Toro.	25.00	.50
48 Paul Coffey, Phil.	25.00	.50
49 Craig Janney, Phoe.	10.00	.25
50 Brendan Witt, Wash.	5.00	.25
51 Jere Lehtinen, Dall.	10.00	.25
52 Vitali Yachmenev, LosA.	5.00	.25
53 Damian Rhodes (G), Otta.	10.00	.25
54 Petr Nedved, Pitt.	10.00	.25
55 Theoren Fleury, Calg.	25.00	.50
56 Petr Sykora, NJer.	15.00	.50
57 Kelly Hrudey (G), SanJ.	10.00	.25
58 Saku Koivu, Mont.	35.00	1.00
59 Brian Bradley, Tamp.	5.00	.25
60 Arturs Irbe (G), Dall.	15.00	.50
61 Eric Lindros, Phil.	40.00	1.50
62 Michal Pivonka, Wash.	5.00	.25
63 Joe Nieuwendyk, Dall.	15.00	.50
64 Mats Sundin, Toro.	45.00	1.50
65 Jason Arnott, Edmo.	20.00	.50
66 Mike Richter (G), NYRa.	20.00	.50
67 Brett Hull, SLou.	45.00	1.50
68 Chris Chelios, Chic.	25.00	.50
69 Jocelyn Thibault (G), Mont.	15.00	.50
70 Oleg Tverdovsky, Phoe.	5.00	.25
71 Peter Bondra, Wash.	25.00	.50
72 Bill Ranford (G), Bost.	15.00	.50
73 Scott Stevens, NJer.	15.00	.50
74 Jaromir Jagr, Pitt.	40.00	1.50
75 Corey Hirsch (G), Vanc.	5.00	.25
76 Peter Forsberg, Colo.	60.00	2.00

□□	77 Brendan Shanahan, Detr.	45.00	1.50
□□	78 Antti Törmänen, Otta.	5.00	.25
□□	79 Marcus Ragnarsson, SanJ.	10.00	.25
□□	80 Sergei Fedorov, Detr.	45.00	1.50
□□	81 Todd Bertuzzi, NYIs.	50.00	3.50
□□	82 Grant Fuhr (G), Buff.	25.00	.50
□□	83 Pat LaFontaine, Buff.	25.00	.50
□□	84 Rob Niedermayer, Flor.	10.00	.25
□□	85 Brian Leetch, NYRa.	25.00	.50
□□	86 Yanic Perreault, LosA.	10.00	.25
□□	87 Dino Ciccarelli, Tamp.	10.00	.25
□□	88 Dimitri Khristich, LosA.	5.00	.25
□□	89 Jeff Friesen, SanJ.	10.00	.25
□□	90 Paul Kariya, Anah.	60.00	2.00
□□	91 John Vanbiesbrouck (G), Flor.	20.00	.50
□□	92 Roman Hamrlik, Tamp.	10.00	.25
□□	93 Pat Verbeek, Dall.	10.00	.25
□□	94 Mark Messier, NYRa.	45.00	1.50
□□	95 Trevor Linden, Vanc.	15.00	.50
□□	96 Igor Larionov, Detr.	25.00	.50
□□	97 Zigmund Palffy, NYIs.	25.00	.50
□□	98 Tom Barrasso (G), Pitt.	15.00	.50
□□	99 Eric Dazé, Chic.	15.00	.50
□□	100 Vincent Damphousse, Mont.	25.00	.50
□□	101 Keith Primeau, Hart.	15.00	.50
□□	102 Claude Lemieux, Colo.	10.00	.25
□□	103 Daniel Alfredsson, Otta.	25.00	.50
□□	104 Ryan Smyth, Edmo.	20.00	.50
□□	105 Chris Osgood (G), Detr.	25.00	.50
□□	106 Bill Guerin, NJer.	15.00	.50
□□	107 Shayne Corson, Mont.	10.00	.25
□□	108 Alexei Zhamnov, Chic.	10.00	.25
□□	109 Mikael Renberg, Phil.	10.00	.25
□□	110 Andy Moog (G), Dall.	15.00	.50
□□	111 Larry Murphy, Toro.	10.00	.25
□□	112 Curtis Joseph (G), Edmo.	40.00	1.50
□□	113 Cory Stillman, Calg.	10.00	.25
□□	114 Mario Lemieux, Pitt.	130.00	4.50
□□	115 Scott Young, Colo.	10.00	.25
□□	116 Éric Fichaud (G), NYIs.	5.00	.25
□□	117 Jonas Höglund, Calg.	5.00	.25
□□	**118 Tomas Holmström, Detr. RC**	**35.00**	**2.00**
□□	119 Jarome Iginla, Calg.	35.00	2.00
□□	**120 Richard Zednik, Wash. RC**	**60.00**	**4.00**
□□	**121 Andreas Dackell, Otta. RC**	**20.00**	**1.50**
□□	122 Anson Carter, Bost.	15.00	1.00
□□	**123 Dainius Zubrus, Phil. RC**	**35.00**	**2.00**
□□	124 Janne Niinimaa, Phil.	10.00	.50
□□	125 Jason Allison, Wash.	25.00	.50
□□	126 Bryan Berard, NYIs.	10.00	.50
□□	**127 Sergei Berezin, Toro. RC**	**35.00**	**2.00**
□□	128 Wade Redden, Otta.	10.00	.50
□□	129 Jim Campbell, SLou.	5.00	.25
□□	130 Darcy Tucker, Mont.	10.00	.50
□□	**131 Harry York, SLou. RC**	**15.00**	**1.00**
□□	132 Brandon Convery, Toro.	5.00	.25
□□	133 Ethan Moreau, Chic.	5.00	.25
□□	**134 Mattias Timander, Bost. RC**	**15.00**	**1.00**
□□	135 Christian Dubé, NYRa.	5.00	.25
□□	136 Kevin Hodson (G), Detr.	10.00	.25
□□	137 Anders Eriksson, Detr.	5.00	.25
□□	138 Chris O'Sullivan, Calg.	5.00	.25
□□	139 Jamie Langenbrunner, Dall.	10.00	.25
□□	**140 Steve Sullivan, NJer. RC**	**45.00**	**3.00**
□□	141 Daymond Langkow, Tamp.	10.00	.25
□□	142 Landon Wilson, Bost.	5.00	.25
□□	143 Scott Bailey (G), Bost.	5.00	.25
□□	**144 Terry Ryan, Mont. RC**	**15.00**	**1.00**
□□	145 Curtis Brown, Buff.	5.00	.25
□□	**146 Rem Murray, Edmo. RC**	**15.00**	**1.00**
□□	147 Jamie Pushor, Detr.	5.00	.25
□□	148 Daniel Goneau, NYRa.	15.00	1.00
□□	149 Mike Prokopec, Chic.	5.00	.25
□□	**150 Brad Smyth, LosA. RC**	**15.00**	**1.00**

ASSAILANTS

Insert Set (15 cards):		**45.00**
	Insert (1:10)	**A**
□	1 Alexei Yashin, Otta.	3.00
□	2 Mike Modano, Dall.	5.00
□	3 Jason Arnott, Edmo.	3.00
□	4 Mikael Renberg, Phil.	3.00
□	5 Saku Koivu, Mont.	5.00
□	6 Todd Bertuzzi, NYIs.	5.00
□	7 Zigmund Palffy, NYIs.	3.00
□	8 Eric Lindros, Phil.	5.00
□	9 Pat LaFontaine, Buff.	3.00
□	10 John LeClair, Phil.	5.00
□	11 Theoren Fleury, Calg.	3.00
□	12 Pierre Turgeon, SLou.	3.00
□	13 Petr Nedved, Pitt.	3.00
□	14 Owen Nolan, SanJ.	3.00
□	15 Valeri Bure, Mont.	3.00

CHAMPION SALUTE

There are three versions: the promo, the regular insert (1:23), and a Diamond Chip parallel.

Insert Set (15 cards):		**35.00**	**850.00**	**160.00**
	Inserts	**Promo**	**Chip**	**CS**
□□□	1 Mark Messier, NYRa.	2.00	50.00	10.00
□□□	2 Wayne Gretzky, NYRa.	10.00	200.00	40.00
□□□	3 Grant Fuhr, SLou.	1.00	30.00	5.00
□□□	4 Paul Coffey, Hart.	1.00	30.00	5.00
□□□	5 Mario Lemieux, Pitt.	7.00	150.00	30.00
□□□	6 Jaromir Jagr, Pitt.	2.00	50.00	10.00
□□□	7 Ron Francis, Pitt.	1.00	30.00	5.00
□□□	8 Joe Sakic, Colo.	4.00	80.00	15.00
□□□	9 Peter Forsberg, Colo.	3.00	70.00	10.00
□□□	10 Claude Lemieux, Colo.	1.00	15.00	3.00
□□□	11 Patrick Roy (G), Colo.	7.00	150.00	30.00
□□□	12 Chris Chelios, Chic.	1.00	30.00	5.00
□□□	13 Doug Gilmour, Toro.	1.00	30.00	5.00
□□□	14 Mike Richter (G), NYRa.	1.00	20.00	3.00
□□□	15 Martin Brodeur (G), NJer.	4.00	80.00	15.00

Z-TEAM

Insert Set (18 cards):		**450.00**
□	Promo Martin Brodeur	4.00
	Insert (1:71)	**ZT**
□	1 Eric LIndros, Phil.	40.00
□	2 Paul Kariya, Anah.	55.00
□	3 Teemu Selänne, Anah.	30.00
□	4 Brendan Shanahan, Detr.	40.00
□	5 Sergei Fedorov, Detr.	40.00
□	6 Steve Yzerman, Detr.	95.00
□	7 Brett Hull, SLou.	40.00
□	8 Pavel Bure, Vanc.	30.00
□	9 Alexander Mogilny, Vanc.	15.00
□	10 Jeremy Roenick, Phoe.	30.00
□	11 Jocelyn Thibault (G), Mont.	15.00
□	12 Keith Tkachuk, Phoe.	20.00
□	13 Daniel Alfredsson, Otta.	20.00
□	14 Éric Dazé, Chic.	15.00
□	15 Jim Carey (G), Wash.	15.00
□	16 Félix Potvin (G), Toro.	20.00
□	17 John Vanbiesbrouck (G), Flor.	15.00
□	18 Chris Osgood (G), Detr.	20.00

1996 - 97 PLAYOFF ONE-ON-ONE CHALLENGE

These cards have an orange border. Cards 405-427 are Rare (silver) and cards 428-440 are Ultra-Rare (gold).

Complete Set (110 cards):		**400.00**
Common Player:		**.20**
	Player	**Playoff**
□	331 Mike Sillinger, Vanc.	.20
□	332 Oleg Tverdovsky, Phoe.	.20
□	333 Kevin Stevens, LosA.	.20
□	334 Joe Nieuwendyk, Dall.	.20
□	335 Owen Nolan, SanJ.	.20
□	336 Jocelyn Thibault (G), Mont.	.20
□	337 Dave Gagner, Calg.	.20
□	338 Ray Sheppard, Flor.	.20
□	339 Jesse Belanger, Edmo.	.20
□	340 Tony Granato, SanJ.	.20
□	341 Daniel Alfredsson, Otta.	.20
□	342 Stéphane Richer, Mont.	.20
□	343 Mathieu Schneider, Toro.	.20
□	344 Kirk Muller, Toro.	.20
□	345 Arturs Irbe (G), Dall.	.20
□	346 Igor Larionov, Detr.	.20
□	347 Steve Duchesne, Otta.	.20
□	348 Dave Andreychuk, NJer.	.20
□	349 Mike Gartner, Phoe.	.50
□	350 Teppo Numminen, Phoe.	.20
□	351 Keith Tkachuk, Phoe.	.20
□	352 Mike Modano, Dall.	.50
□	353 Paul Kariya, Anah.	1.00
□	354 German Titov, Calg.	.20
□	355 Bernie Nicholls, SanJ.	.20
□	356 Doug Gilmour, Toro.	.20
□	357 Peter Forsberg, Colo.	1.00
□	358 David Oliver, Edmo.	.20
□	359 Pat Verbeek, Dall.	.20
□	360 Ron Francis, Pitt.	.20
□	361 Pat Falloon, Phil.	.20
□	362 Jeff Friesen, SanJ.	.20
□	363 Todd Krygier, Wash.	.20
□	364 Félix Potvin (G), Toro.	.20
□	365 Shane Churla, NYRa.	.20
□	366 Steve Yzerman, Detr.	1.50
□	367 Kelly Hrudey (G), SanJ.	.20
□	368 Mariusz Czerkawski, Edmo.	.20
□	369 Patrick Poulin, Tamp.	.20
□	370 Chris Chelios, Chic.	.20
□	371 Raymond Bourque, Bost.	.50
□	372 Igor Kravchuk, SLou.	.20
□	373 Kirk Maltby, Detr.	.20
□	374 Bill Ranford (G), Bost.	.20
□	375 Darryl Sydor, Dall.	.20
□	376 Rick Tocchet, Bost.	.20
□	377 J.J. Daigneault, Pitt.	.20
□	378 Chris Osgood (G), Detr.	.20
□	379 Zigmund Palffy, NYIs.	.20
□	380 Ray Ferraro, LosA.	.20
□	381 Don Beaupré (G), Toro.	.20
□	382 Andy Moog (G), Dall.	.20
□	383 Sergei Zubov, Dall.	.20
□	384 Craig Janney, Phoe.	.20
□	385 Sandis Ozolinsh, Colo.	.20
□	386 Dave Reid, Dall.	.20
□	387 Scott Mellanby, Flor.	.20
□	388 Saku Koivu, Mont.	.50
□	389 Bryan Smolinski, Pitt.	.20
□	390 Alexander Selivanov, Tamp.	.20
□	391 Peter Bondra, Wash.	.20
□	392 Esa Tikkanen, Vanc.	.20
□	393 Ken Baumgartner, Anah.	.20
□	394 Ed Belfour (G), Chic.	.50
□	395 Randy Wood, Dall.	.20
□	396 Jeff Brown, Hart.	.20
□	397 Roman Oksiuta, Anah.	.20
□	398 Cliff Ronning, Phoe.	.20
□	399 Mike Eastwood, Phoe.	.20
□	400 Nelson Emerson, Hart.	.20
□	401 Dave Manson, Phoe.	.20
□	402 Jamie Baker, Toro.	.20
□	403 Ian Laperrière, LosA.	.20
□	404 Petr Klima, LosA.	.20
□	405 Dallas Drake, Phoe.	.75
□	406 Tim Cheveldae (G), Bost.	.75
□	407 Igor Korolev, Phoe.	.75
□	408 Kevin Hatcher, Pitt.	.75
□	409 Dale Hawerchuk, Phil.	1.00
□	410 Martin Straka, Flor.	.75
□	411 Wendel Clark, Toro.	2.00
□	412 Jari Kurri, Anah.	2.00
□	413 Darren Turcotte, SanJ.	.75
□	414 Yuri Khmylev, SLou.	.75
□	415 Bob Corkum, Phil.	.75
□	416 Roman Hamrlik, Tamp.	.75
□	417 Jayson More, NYRa.	.75
□	418 Travis Green, NYIs.	.75
□	419 Dean McAmmond, Edmo.	.75
□	420 Valeri Kamensky, Edmo.	.75
□	421 Jason Dawe, Buff.	.75
□	422 Alexander Mogilny, Vanc.	1.00
□	423 Keith Jones, Wash.	.75
□	424 Mark Messier, NYRa.	2.00
□	425 John Vanbiesbrouck (G), Flor.	1.00
□	426 Jim Carey (G), Wash.	.75
□	427 Brett Hull, SLou.	2.00
□	428 Teemu Selänne, Anah.	30.00
□	429 Phil Housley, Wash.	12.00
□	430 Wayne Gretzky, NYRa.	150.00
□	431 Patrick Roy (G), Colo.	110.00
□	432 Joe Sakic, Colo.	60.00
□	433 Jaromir Jagr, Pitt.	30.00
□	434 Doug Weight, Edmo.	20.00
□	435 Rob Niedermayer, Flor.	12.00
□	436 Mario Lemieux, Pitt.	110.00
□	437 Sergei Fedorov, Detr.	35.00
□	438 Pavel Bure, Vanc.	30.00
□	439 Eric Lindros, Phil.	30.00
□	440 Martin Brodeur (G), NJer.	60.00

1996 - 97 SCORE

There are six versions to the Score set. Seeded in packs were regular cards, two different Golden Blades parallels and an Artist's Proof parallel.

A shaded area on the back of Golden Blades cards could be decoded to read "Special Artist's Proof" or "Sorry Try Again." The winner card could be redeemed for a special 24 point stock Artist's Proof card (the fifth version). If the cards were sent via a Pinnacle dealer, a "Dealer's Choice" Artist's Proof card was also redeemable (the sixth version).

Complete Set (275 cards):		**1100.00**	**175.00**	**25.00**
Common Player:		**3.00**	**.75**	**.20**
	Player	**AP**	**GB**	**Score**
□□□	1 Patrick Roy (G), Colo.	90.00	10.00	1.50
□□□	2 B. Shanahan, Hart.	30.00	4.00	.50
□□□	3 Rob Niedermayer, Flor.	5.00	1.00	.20
□□□	4 Jeff Friesen, SanJ.	5.00	1.00	.20
□□□	5 Teppo Numminen, Winn.	5.00	1.00	.20
□□□	6 Mario Lemieux, Pitt.	90.00	10.00	1.50
□□□	7 Eric Lindros, Phil.	30.00	4.00	.50
□□□	8 Paul Kariya, Anah.	40.00	5.00	.50
□□□	9 Joe Sakic, Colo.	45.00	7.00	.50
□□□	10 M. Brodeur (G), NJer.	45.00	7.00	.50
□□□	11 Mark Tinordi, Wash.	3.00	.75	.20
□□□	12 Theroren Fleury, Calg.	15.00	2.00	.20
□□□	13 Guy Hebert (G), Anah.	5.00	1.00	.20
□□□	14 D. Gagner, Toro. (Calg.)	3.00	.75	.20
□□□	15 Travis Green, NYIs.	5.00	1.00	.20
□□□	16 A. Mogilny, Vanc.	10.00	2.00	.20
□□□	17 S. Fiset (G), Colo.	5.00	1.00	.20
□□□	18 D. Hasek (G), Buff.	30.00	4.00	.50
□□□	19 Brett Hull, SLou.	30.00	4.00	.50
□□□	20 Zdeno Ciger, Edmo.	3.00	.75	.20
□□□	21 Pat Falloon, Phil.	3.00	.75	.20
□□□	22 Jyrki Lumme, Vanc.	5.00	1.00	.20
□□□	23 Rick Tabaracci (G), Calg.	3.00	.75	.20
□□□	24 Mark Messier, NYRa.	30.00	4.00	.50
□□□	25 Yanic Perreault, LosA.	5.00	1.00	.20
□□□	26 Mark Recchi, Mont.	10.00	1.00	.20
□□□	27 A. Selivanov, Tamp.	3.00	.75	.20
□□□	28 Chris Terreri (G), SanJ.	3.00	.75	.20
□□□	29 Jaromir Jagr, Pitt.	30.00	.75	.50
□□□	30 Ted Donato, Bost.	3.00	.75	.20
□□□	31 Scott Mellanby, Flor.	5.00	1.00	.20
□□□	32 Geoff Courtnall, SLou.	3.00	.75	.20
□□□	33 Michal Pivonka, Wash.	3.00	.75	.20
□□□	34 Glenn Healy (G), NYRa.	5.00	1.00	.20
□□□	35 Pavel Bure, Vanc.	20.00	3.00	.20
□□□	36 Chris Chelios, Chic.	15.00	2.00	.20
□□□	37 Nelson Emerson, Hart.	3.00	.75	.20
□□□	38 Petr Nedved, Phil.	5.00	1.00	.20
□□□	39 Greg Adams, Dall.	3.00	.75	.20
□□□	40 Bill Ranford (G), Edmo.	10.00	1.00	.20
□□□	41 W.yne Gretzky, SLou.	120.00	15.00	2.00
□□□	42 Wendel Clark, Toro.	20.00	3.00	.20
□□□	43 Sandis Ozolinsh, Colo.	5.00	1.00	.20
□□□	44 Dave Andreychuk, NJer.	5.00	1.00	.20
□□□	45 Brian Bradley, Tamp.	3.00	.75	.20
□□□	46 Sean Burke (G), Hart.	15.00	2.00	.20
□□□	47 Keith Tkachuk, Winn.	15.00	2.00	.20
□□□	48 Brad May, Buff.	3.00	.75	.20
□□□	49 Brent Gilchrist, Dall.	3.00	.75	.20
□□□	50 V. Damphousse, Mont.	15.00	2.00	.20
□□□	51 Dale Hawerchuk, Phil.	15.00	2.00	.20
□□□	52 Randy Burridge, Buff.	3.00	.75	.20
□□□	53 R. Bourque, Bost.	35.00	5.00	.50
□□□	54 Keith Primeau, Detr.	10.00	1.00	.20
□□□	55 Jason Arnott, Edmo.	10.00	2.00	.20
□□□	56 Ron Francis, Pitt.	15.00	2.00	.20
□□□	57 Craig Janney, Winn.	5.00	1.00	.20
□□□	58 Trevor Kidd (G), Calg.	5.00	1.00	.20
□□□	59 Jason Dawe, Buff.	3.00	.75	.20
□□□	60 Steve Yzerman, Detr.	70.00	10.00	1.00
□□□	61 Alexei Kovalev, NYRa.	15.00	2.00	.20
□□□	62 Steve Duchesne, Otta.	5.00	1.00	.20
□□□	63 Vanbiesbrouck (G), Flor.	10.00	2.00	.20
□□□	64 Steve Thomas, NJer.	5.00	1.00	.20
□□□	65 Bernie Nicholls, Chic.	5.00	1.00	.20
□□□	66 Alexandre Daigle, Otta.	3.00	.75	.20
□□□	67 Pat Peake, Wash.	3.00	.75	.20
□□□	68 Kelly Hrudey (G), LosA.	5.00	1.00	.20
□□□	69 Owen Nolan, SanJ.	15.00	2.00	.20
□□□	70 Alexei Zhitnik, Buff.	3.00	.75	.20
□□□	71 Pierre Turgeon, Mont.	10.00	1.00	.20
□□□	72 Mike Modano, Dall.	30.00	4.00	.50
□□□	73 V. Fetisov, Detr.	15.00	2.00	.20
□□□	74 Jim Carey (G), Wash.	3.00	.75	.20
□□□	75 Larry Murphy, Toro.	5.00	1.00	.20
□□□	76 Roman Oksiuta, Anah.	3.00	.75	.20
□□□	77 Sergei Fedorov, Detr.	30.00	4.00	.50
□□□	78 Shayne Corson, SLou.	5.00	1.00	.20
□□□	79 Michael Nylander, Calg.	5.00	1.00	.20
□□□	80 Ron Hextall (G), Phil.	15.00	2.00	.20
□□□	81 Adam Graves, NYRa.	10.00	1.00	.20
□□□	82 T. Söderström (G), NYIs.	3.00	.75	.20
□□□	83 Robert Svehla, Flor.	5.00	1.00	.20
□□□	84 V. Konstantinov, Detr.	5.00	1.00	.20
□□□	85 Jeff Hackett (G), Chic.	5.00	1.00	.20
□□□	86 Todd Harvey, Dall.	5.00	1.00	.20
□□□	87 Jeff Brown, Hart.	3.00	.75	.20
□□□	88 Bryan Smolinski, Pitt.	3.00	.75	.20
□□□	89 Oleg Tverdovsky, Winn.	3.00	.75	.20
□□□	90 Cu. Joseph (G), Edmo.	30.00	4.00	.50
□□□	91 Grant Fuhr (G), SLou.	15.00	2.00	.20
□□□	92 Rick Tocchet, Bost.	5.00	1.00	.20
□□□	93 Adam Deadmarsh, Colo.	5.00	1.00	.20
□□□	94 Pat Verbeek, NYRa.	5.00	1.00	.20
□□□	95 Doug Gilmour, Toro.	15.00	2.00	.20
□□□	96 J. Thibault (G), Mont.	10.00	1.00	.20
□□□	97 Radek Bonk, Otta.	5.00	1.00	.20
□□□	98 Martin Gelinas, Vanc.	5.00	1.00	.20
□□□	99 Peter Forsberg, Colo.	40.00	6.00	.50
□□□	100 Joe Murphy, Chic.	3.00	.75	.20
□□□	101 Dino Ciccarelli, Detr.	5.00	1.00	.20
□□□	102 Rod Brind'Amour, Phil.	5.00	1.00	.20
□□□	103 Kirk Muller, Toro.	5.00	1.00	.20
□□□	104 Andy Moog (G), Dall.	10.00	1.00	.20
□□□	105 Khabibulin (G), Winn.	10.00	1.00	.20
□□□	106 Mike Ricci, Colo.	5.00	1.00	.20
□□□	107 Ray Ferraro, LosA.	3.00	.75	.20
□□□	108 S. Niedermayer, NJer.	5.00	1.00	.20
□□□	109 Russ Courtnall, Vanc.	5.00	1.00	.20
□□□	110 Dale Hunter, Wash.	5.00	1.00	.20
□□□	111 Cam Neely, Bost.	30.00	4.00	.50
□□□	112 Ray Sheppard, Flor.	3.00	.75	.20
□□□	113 Luc Robitaille, NYRa.	20.00	3.00	.20
□□□	114 Al MacInnis, SLou.	10.00	1.00	.20
□□□	115 M. Schneider, Toro.	5.00	1.00	.20
□□□	116 Claude Lemieux, Colo.	5.00	1.00	.20
□□□	117 Kevin Hatcher, Dall.	3.00	.75	.20
□□□	118 D. Puppa (G), Tamp.	5.00	1.00	.20
□□□	119 Geoff Sanderson, Hart.	5.00	1.00	.20
□□□	120 Zigmund Palffy, NYIs.	15.00	2.00	.20
□□□	121 Denis Savard, Chic.	10.00	1.00	.20
□□□	122 Dimitri Khristich, LosA.	3.00	.75	.20
□□□	123 Ed Belfour (G), Chic.	30.00	4.00	.50
□□□	124 T. Barrasso (G), Pitt.	10.00	1.00	.20
□□□	125 Rob Rouse, Detr.	3.00	.75	.20
□□□	126 Tomas Sandström, Pitt.	5.00	1.00	.20
□□□	127 Roman Hamrlik, Tamp.	5.00	1.00	.20
□□□	128 Alexei Zhamnov, Winn.	5.00	1.00	.20
□□□	129 C. Osgood (G), Detr.	15.00	2.00	.20
□□□	130 Rob Blake, LosA.	15.00	2.00	.20
□□□	131 Garry Galley, Buff.	3.00	.75	.20
□□□	132 Greg Johnson, Detr.	3.00	.75	.20
□□□	133 Brian Skrudland, Flor.	3.00	.75	.20
□□□	134 Martin Rucinsky, Mont.	5.00	1.00	.20
□□□	135 S. Konowalchuk, Wash.	5.00	1.00	.20
□□□	136 D. Rhodes (G), Otta.	5.00	1.00	.20
□□□	137 Jeremy Roenick, Chic.	20.00	3.00	.20
□□□	138 Scott Stevens, NJer.	10.00	1.00	.20
□□□	139 Pat LaFontaine, Buff.	15.00	2.00	.20
□□□	140 Scott Young, Colo.	5.00	1.00	.20
□□□	141 Benoît Hogue, Dall.	3.00	.75	.20
□□□	142 Paul Coffey, Detr.	15.00	2.00	.20
□□□	143 John MacLean, NJer.	3.00	.75	.20
□□□	144 Joé Juneau, Wash.	5.00	1.00	.20
□□□	145 T. Selänne, Anah.	20.00	3.00	.20
□□□	146 Andrew Cassels, Hart.	5.00	1.00	.20
□□□	147 Brian Savage, Mont.	5.00	1.00	.20
□□□	148 Chris Gratton, Tamp.	5.00	1.00	.20
□□□	149 Corey Hirsch (G), Vanc.	3.00	.75	.20
□□□	150 Mike Richter (G), NYRa.	10.00	2.00	.20
□□□	151 S. McEachern, Bost.	5.00	1.00	.20
□□□	152 Joe Nieuwendyk, Dall.	10.00	1.00	.20
□□□	153 Phil Housley, NJer.	5.00	1.00	.20
□□□	154 Gartner, Toro. (Phoe.)	20.00	3.00	.20
□□□	155 Kirk McLean (G), Vanc.	5.00	1.00	.20
□□□	156 Bob Probert, Chic.	5.00	1.00	.20
□□□	157 Valeri Kamensky, Colo.	5.00	1.00	.20
□□□	158 V. Kozlov, Detr.	5.00	1.00	.20
□□□	159 Éric Desjardins, Phil.	5.00	1.00	.20
□□□	160 Mats Sundin, Toro.	30.00	4.00	.50
□□□	161 John LeClair, Phil.	20.00	3.00	.20
□□□	162 Adam Oates, Bost.	10.00	1.00	.20
□□□	163 Cliff Ronning, Vanc.	5.00	1.00	.20
□□□	164 Mike Vernon (G), Detr.	10.00	1.00	.20
□□□	165 German Titov, Calg.	3.00	.75	.20
□□□	166 Chris Pronger, SLou.	15.00	2.00	.20
□□□	167 Norm Maciver, Winn.	3.00	.75	.20
□□□	168 Kenny Jönsson, NYIs.	5.00	.75	.20
□□□	169 Tony Amonte, Chic.	15.00	2.00	.20
□□□	170 Doug Weight, Edmo.	15.00	2.00	.20
□□□	171 Sergei Zubov, Pitt.	5.00	1.00	.20
□□□	172 Félix Potvin (G), Toro.	15.00	2.00	.20
□□□	173 Trevor Linden, Vanc.	10.00	1.00	.20
□□□	174 Derek Plante, Buff.	3.00	.75	.20
□□□	175 Uwe Krupp, Colo.	3.00	.75	.20
□□□	176 Nicklas Lidström, Detr.	15.00	2.00	.20
□□□	177 Mikael Renberg, Phil.	5.00	1.00	.20
□□□	178 Igor Larionov, Detr.	15.00	2.00	.20
□□□	179 Brian Leetch, NYRa.	15.00	2.00	.20
□□□	180 Stu Barnes, Flor.	3.00	.75	.20
□□□	181 Alexei Yashin, Otta.	15.00	2.00	.20
□□□	182 Gary Suter, Chic.	5.00	1.00	.20
□□□	183 Ken Wregget (G), Pitt.	5.00	1.00	.20
□□□	184 Mike Ridley, Vanc.	3.00	.75	.20
□□□	185 Peter Bondra, Wash.	15.00	2.00	.20
□□□	186 Steve Rucchin, Anah.	5.00	1.00	.20
□□□	187 Jozef Stümpel, Bost.	5.00	1.00	.20
□□□	188 Matthew Barnaby, Buff.	3.00	.75	.20
□□□	189 James Patrick, Calg.	3.00	.75	.20
□□□	190 Chris Simon, Colo.	5.00	1.00	.20
□□□	191 Brent Fedyk, Dall.	3.00	.75	.20
□□□	192 Kris Draper, Detr.	5.00	1.00	.20
□□□	193 David Oliver, Edmo.	3.00	.75	.20
□□□	194 Dave Lowry, Flor.	5.00	1.00	.20
□□□	195 Robert Kron, Hart.	3.00	.75	.20
□□□	196 A. Kovalenko, Mont.	3.00	.75	.20
□□□	197 Bill Guerin, NJer.	10.00	1.00	.20

□□□	198 Ed Olczyk, Winn.	5.00	1.00	.20
□□□	199 Yuri Khmylev, SLou.	3.00	.75	.20
□□□	200 Rob Ray, Buff.	5.00	1.00	.20
□□□	201 Joe Mullen, Bost.	10.00	1.00	.20
□□□	202 Petr Klima, Tamp.	3.00	.75	.20
□□□	203 Todd Krygier, Anah.	3.00	.75	.20
□□□	204 Garth Snow (G), Phil.	5.00	1.00	.20
□□□	205 Zarley Zalapski, Calg.	3.00	.75	.20
□□□	206 K. Baumgartner, Anah.	3.00	.75	.20
□□□	207 Tony Twist, SLou.	3.00	.75	.20
□□□	208 Todd Gill, Toro. (SanJ.)	3.00	.75	.20
□□□	209 Michael Peca, Buff.	10.00	1.00	.20
□□□	210 D. Wakaluk (G), Dall.	3.00	.75	.20
□□□	211 Milos Holan, Anah.	3.00	.75	.20
□□□	212 A. Semak, NYIs.	3.00	.75	.20
□□□	213 Jeff Reese (G), Tamp.	3.00	.75	.20
□□□	214 Jon Casey (G), SLou.	3.00	.75	.20
□□□	215 Sandy McCarthy, Calg.	3.00	.75	.20
□□□	216 C. Leschyshyn, Colo.	3.00	.75	.20
□□□	217 Todd Marchant, Edmo.	5.00	1.00	.20
□□□	218 Bob Bassen, Dall.	3.00	.75	.20
□□□	219 Darren Turcotte, SanJ.	3.00	.75	.20
□□□	220 David Reid, Bost.	3.00	.75	.20
□□□	221 Brian Bellows, Tamp.	5.00	1.00	.20
□□□	222 Jesse Belanger, Vanc.	3.00	.75	.20
□□□	223 Bill Lindsay, Flor.	3.00	.75	.20
□□□	224 Lyle Odelein, Mont.	3.00	.75	.20
□□□	225 Keith Jones, Wash.	3.00	.75	.20
□□□	226 Sylvain Lefebvre, Colo.	3.00	.75	.20
□□□	227 Shaun Van Allen, Anah.	3.00	.75	.20
□□□	228 Dan Quinn, Phil.	3.00	.75	.20
□□□	229 R. Matvichuk, Dall.	5.00	1.00	.20
□□□	230 Craig MacTavish, SLou.	3.00	.75	.20
□□□	231 C. Billington (G), Bost.	3.00	.75	.20
□□□	232 Stéphane Richer, NJer.	5.00	1.00	.20
□□□	233 Donald Audette, Buff.	10.00	1.00	.20
□□□	234 Ulf Dahlen, SanJ.	3.00	.75	.20
□□□	235 Steve Chiasson, Calg.	3.00	.75	.20
□□□	236 Eric Dazé, Chic.	10.00	1.00	.20
□□□	237 Petr Sykora, NJer.	10.00	1.00	.20
□□□	238 Saku Koivu, Mont.	20.00	3.00	.20
□□□	239 Ed Jovanovski, Flor.	10.00	1.00	.20
□□□	240 D. Alfredsson, Otta.	15.00	2.00	.20
□□□	241 V. Yachmenov, LosA.	3.00	.75	.20
□□□	242 M. Ragnarsson, SanJ.	5.00	1.00	.20
□□□	243 Cory Stillman, Calg.	5.00	1.00	.20
□□□	244 Todd Bertuzzi, NYIs.	35.00	5.00	1.00
□□□	245 Valeri Bure, Mont.	5.00	1.00	.20
□□□	246 Jere Lehtinen, Dall.	5.00	1.00	.20
□□□	247 Radek Dvorak, Flor.	5.00	1.00	.20
□□□	248 Niclas Andersson, NYIs.	3.00	.75	.20
□□□	249 Miroslav Satan, Edmo.	5.00	1.00	.20
□□□	250 Jeff O'Neill, Hart.	10.00	1.00	.20
□□□	251 N. Baumgartner, Wash.	3.00	.75	.20
□□□	252 Roman Vopat, LosA.	3.00	.75	.20
□□□	253 Bryan McCabe, NYIs.	5.00	1.00	.20
□□□	254 J. Langenbrunner, Dall.	5.00	1.00	.20
□□□	255 C. Kilger, Winn. (Phoe.)	5.00	1.00	.20
□□□	256 Éric Fichaud (G), NYIs.	3.00	.75	.20
□□□	257 Landon Wilson, Colo.	3.00	.75	.20
□□□	258 Kyle McLaren, Bost.	5.00	1.00	.20
□□□	259 Aaron Gavey, Tamp.	3.00	.75	.20
□□□	260 B. Dafoe (G), LosA.	10.00	1.00	.20
□□□	261 Grant Marshall, Dall.	3.00	.75	.20
□□□	262 Shane Doan, Winn.	5.00	1.00	.20
□□□	263 R. Intranuovo, Edmo.	3.00	.75	.20
□□□	264 Aki Berg, LosA.	3.00	.75	.20
□□□	265 Antti Törmänen, Otta.	3.00	.75	.20
□□□	266 Brian Holzinger, Buff.	3.00	.75	.20
□□□	267 J. Théodore (G), Mont.	35.00	5.00	1.00
□□□	268 Ethan Moreau, Chic.	3.00	.75	.20
□□□	269 N. Sundström, NYRa.	5.00	1.00	.20
□□□	270 Brendan Witt, Wash.	3.00	.75	.20
□□□	271 Checklist 1-70	3.00	.75	.20
□□□	272 Checklist 71-140	3.00	.75	.20
□□□	273 Checklist 141-210	3.00	.75	.20
□□□	274 Checklist 211-275	3.00	.75	.20
□□□	275 Chase Checklist	3.00	.75	.20

PROMOTION

One Golden Blades card (a # 10 Martin Brodeur card) could be decoded for a trip for two to the 1997 NHL All-Star Fanfest Weekend. Since checklists did not have the decoder bar, there are no Special Artist's Proof, Dealer's Choice Artist's Proof or second Golden Blades versions for cards 271-275.

	Complete Set (270 cards):	1500.00	1400.00	200.00
	Common Player:	5.00	4.00	1.00
	Player	**DCAP**	**SAPGB-Win**	
□□□	1 Patrick Roy (G), Colo.	110.00	100.00	15.00
□□□	2 B. Shanahan, Hart.	35.00	35.00	6.00
□□□	3 Rob Niedermayer, Flor.	5.00	5.00	1.00
□□□	4 Jeff Friesen, SanJ.	10.00	10.00	2.00
□□□	5 Teppo Numminen, Winn.	10.00	10.00	2.00
□□□	6 Mario Lemieux, Pitt.	110.00	100.00	15.00
□□□	7 Eric Lindros, Phil.	30.00	30.00	5.00
□□□	8 Paul Kariya, Anah.	50.00	40.00	5.00
□□□	9 Joe Sakic, Colo.	60.00	55.00	10.00
□□□	10 M. Brodeur (G), NJer.	60.00	55.00	10.00
□□□	11 Mark Tinordi, Wash.	5.00	5.00	1.00
□□□	12 Theoren Fleury, Calg.	20.00	20.00	3.00
□□□	13 Guy Hebert (G), Anah.	5.00	5.00	1.00
□□□	14 D. Gagner, Toro. (Calg.)	5.00	5.00	1.00
□□□	15 Travis Green, NYIs.	5.00	5.00	1.00
□□□	16 A. Mogilny, Vanc.	15.00	15.00	3.00
□□□	17 S. Fiset (G), Colo.	10.00	10.00	2.00
□□□	18 D. Hasek (G), Buff.	35.00	35.00	6.00
□□□	19 Brett Hull, SLou.	35.00	35.00	6.00
□□□	20 Zdeno Ciger, Edmo.	5.00	5.00	1.00
□□□	21 Pat Falloon, Phil.	5.00	5.00	1.00
□□□	22 Jyrki Lumme, Vanc.	5.00	5.00	1.00
□□□	23 Rick Tabaracci (G), Calg.	5.00	5.00	1.00
□□□	24 Mark Messier, NYRa.	35.00	35.00	6.00
□□□	25 Yanic Perreault, LosA.	10.00	10.00	2.00
□□□	26 Mark Recchi, Mont.	15.00	10.00	2.00
□□□	27 A. Selivanov, Tamp.	5.00	4.00	1.00
□□□	28 Chris Terreri (G), SanJ.	5.00	5.00	1.00
□□□	29 Jaromir Jagr, Pitt.	30.00	30.00	5.00
□□□	30 Ted Donato, Bost.	5.00	4.00	1.00
□□□	31 Scott Mellanby, Flor.	5.00	5.00	1.00
□□□	32 Geoff Courtnall, SLou.	5.00	5.00	1.00
□□□	33 Michal Pivonka, Wash.	5.00	4.00	1.00
□□□	34 Glenn Healy (G), NYRa.	5.00	5.00	1.00
□□□	35 Pavel Bure, Vanc.	30.00	25.00	5.00
□□□	36 Chris Chelios, Chic.	20.00	20.00	3.00
□□□	37 Nelson Emerson, Hart.	5.00	5.00	1.00
□□□	38 Petr Nedved, Phil.	10.00	10.00	2.00
□□□	39 Greg Adams, Dall.	5.00	5.00	1.00
□□□	40 Bill Ranford (G), Edmo.	15.00	10.00	2.00
□□□	41 W.yne Gretzky, SLou.	150.00	140.00	25.00
□□□	42 Wendel Clark, Toro.	30.00	25.00	5.00
□□□	43 Sandis Ozolinsh, Colo.	5.00	5.00	1.00
□□□	44 Dave Andreychuk, NJer.	10.00	10.00	2.00
□□□	45 Brian Bradley, Tamp.	5.00	4.00	1.00
□□□	46 Sean Burke (G), Hart.	20.00	20.00	3.00
□□□	47 Keith Tkachuk, Winn.	20.00	20.00	3.00
□□□	48 Brad May, Buff.	5.00	5.00	1.00
□□□	49 Brent Gilchrist, Dall.	5.00	4.00	1.00
□□□	50 V. Damphousse, Mont.	20.00	20.00	3.00
□□□	51 Dale Hawerchuk, Phil.	20.00	20.00	3.00
□□□	52 Randy Burridge, Buff.	5.00	5.00	1.00
□□□	53 R. Bourque, Bost.	45.00	40.00	7.00
□□□	54 Keith Primeau, Detr.	15.00	10.00	2.00
□□□	55 Jason Arnott, Edmo.	15.00	15.00	3.00
□□□	56 Ron Francis, Pitt.	20.00	20.00	3.00
□□□	57 Craig Janney, Winn.	5.00	5.00	1.00
□□□	58 Trevor Kidd (G), Calg.	10.00	10.00	2.00
□□□	59 Jason Dawe, Buff.	5.00	4.00	1.00
□□□	60 Steve Yzerman, Detr.	90.00	80.00	15.00
□□□	61 Alexei Kovalev, NYRa.	20.00	20.00	3.00
□□□	62 Steve Duchesne, Otta.	5.00	5.00	1.00
□□□	63 Vanbiesbrouck (G), Flor.	15.00	15.00	3.00
□□□	64 Steve Thomas, NJer.	5.00	5.00	1.00
□□□	65 Bernie Nicholls, Chic.	5.00	5.00	1.00
□□□	66 Alexandre Daigle, Otta.	5.00	5.00	1.00
□□□	67 Pat Peake, Wash.	5.00	4.00	1.00
□□□	68 Kelly Hrudey (G), LosA.	10.00	10.00	2.00
□□□	69 Owen Nolan, SanJ.	20.00	20.00	3.00
□□□	70 Alexei Zhitnik, Buff.	5.00	5.00	1.00
□□□	71 Pierre Turgeon, Mont.	15.00	10.00	2.00
□□□	72 Mike Modano, Dall.	35.00	35.00	6.00
□□□	73 V. Fetisov, Detr.	20.00	20.00	3.00
□□□	74 Jim Carey (G), Wash.	5.00	5.00	1.00
□□□	75 Larry Murphy, Toro.	5.00	5.00	1.00
□□□	76 Roman Oksiuta, Anah.	5.00	4.00	1.00
□□□	77 Sergei Fedorov, Detr.	35.00	35.00	6.00
□□□	78 Shayne Corson, SLou.	10.00	10.00	2.00
□□□	79 Michael Nylander, Calg.	5.00	5.00	1.00
□□□	80 Ron Hextall (G), Phil.	20.00	20.00	3.00
□□□	81 Adam Graves, NYRa.	15.00	10.00	2.00
□□□	82 T. Söderström (G), NYIs.	5.00	5.00	1.00
□□□	83 Robert Svehla, Flor.	5.00	5.00	1.00
□□□	84 V. Konstantinov, Detr.	10.00	10.00	2.00
□□□	85 Jeff Hackett (G), Chic.	10.00	10.00	2.00
□□□	86 Todd Harvey, Dall.	5.00	5.00	1.00
□□□	87 Jeff Brown, Hart.	5.00	4.00	1.00
□□□	88 Bryan Smolinski, Pitt.	5.00	5.00	1.00
□□□	89 Oleg Tverdovsky, Winn.	5.00	5.00	1.00
□□□	90 Cu. Joseph (G), Edmo.	35.00	35.00	6.00
□□□	91 Grant Fuhr (G), SLou.	20.00	20.00	3.00
□□□	92 Rick Tocchet, Bost.	10.00	10.00	2.00
□□□	93 Adam Deadmarsh, Colo.	10.00	10.00	2.00
□□□	94 Pat Verbeek, NYRa.	10.00	10.00	2.00
□□□	95 Doug Gilmour, Toro.	20.00	20.00	3.00
□□□	96 J. Thibault (G), Mont.	15.00	10.00	2.00
□□□	97 Radek Bonk, Otta.	10.00	10.00	2.00
□□□	98 Martin Gelinas, Vanc.	5.00	5.00	1.00
□□□	99 Peter Forsberg, Colo.	50.00	45.00	5.00
□□□	100 Joe Murphy, Chic.	5.00	5.00	1.00
□□□	101 Dino Ciccarelli, Detr.	10.00	10.00	2.00
□□□	102 Rod Brind'Amour, Phil.	10.00	10.00	2.00
□□□	103 Kirk Muller, Toro.	10.00	10.00	2.00
□□□	104 Andy Moog (G), Dall.	15.00	10.00	2.00
□□□	105 Khabibulin (G), Winn.	15.00	10.00	2.00
□□□	106 Mike Ricci, Colo.	10.00	10.00	2.00
□□□	107 Ray Ferraro, LosA.	5.00	5.00	1.00
□□□	108 S. Niedermayer, NJer.	10.00	10.00	2.00
□□□	109 Russ Courtnall, Vanc.	5.00	5.00	1.00
□□□	110 Dale Hunter, Wash.	10.00	10.00	2.00
□□□	111 Cam Neely, Bost.	35.00	35.00	6.00
□□□	112 Ray Sheppard, Flor.	5.00	5.00	1.00
□□□	113 Luc Robitaille, NYRa.	30.00	25.00	5.00
□□□	114 Al MacInnis, SLou.	15.00	10.00	2.00
□□□	115 M. Schneider, Toro.	5.00	5.00	1.00
□□□	116 Claude Lemieux, Colo.	10.00	10.00	2.00
□□□	117 Kevin Hatcher, Dall.	5.00	5.00	1.00
□□□	118 D. Puppa (G), Tamp.	5.00	5.00	1.00
□□□	119 Geoff Sanderson, Hart.	5.00	5.00	1.00
□□□	120 Zigmund Palffy, NYIs.	20.00	20.00	3.00
□□□	121 Denis Savard, Chic.	15.00	10.00	2.00
□□□	122 Dimitri Khristich, LosA.	5.00	5.00	1.00
□□□	123 Ed Belfour (G), Chic.	35.00	35.00	6.00
□□□	124 T. Barrasso (G), Pitt.	15.00	10.00	2.00
□□□	125 Rob Rouse, Detr.	5.00	4.00	1.00
□□□	126 Tomas Sandström, Pitt.	5.00	5.00	1.00
□□□	127 Roman Hamrlik, Tamp.	5.00	5.00	1.00
□□□	128 Alexei Zhamnov, Winn.	10.00	10.00	2.00
□□□	129 C. Osgood (G), Detr.	20.00	20.00	3.00
□□□	130 Rob Blake, LosA.	20.00	20.00	3.00
□□□	131 Garry Galley, Buff.	5.00	4.00	1.00
□□□	132 Greg Johnson, Detr.	5.00	5.00	1.00
□□□	133 Brian Skrudland, Flor.	5.00	5.00	1.00
□□□	134 Martin Rucinsky, Mont.	5.00	5.00	1.00
□□□	135 S. Konowalchuk, Wash.	5.00	5.00	1.00
□□□	136 D. Rhodes (G), Otta.	5.00	5.00	1.00
□□□	137 Jeremy Roenick, Chic.	30.00	25.00	5.00
□□□	138 Scott Stevens, NJer.	15.00	10.00	2.00
□□□	139 Pat LaFontaine, Buff.	20.00	20.00	3.00
□□□	140 Scott Young, Colo.	10.00	10.00	2.00
□□□	141 Benoît Hogue, Dall.	5.00	5.00	1.00
□□□	142 Paul Coffey, Detr.	20.00	20.00	3.00
□□□	143 John MacLean, NJer.	5.00	5.00	1.00
□□□	144 Joé Juneau, Wash.	5.00	5.00	1.00
□□□	145 T. Selänne, Anah.	30.00	25.00	5.00
□□□	146 Andrew Cassels, Hart.	5.00	5.00	1.00
□□□	147 Brian Savage, Mont.	10.00	10.00	2.00
□□□	148 Chris Gratton, Tamp.	5.00	5.00	1.00
□□□	149 Corey Hirsch (G), Vanc.	5.00	5.00	1.00
□□□	150 Mike Richter (G), NYRa.	15.00	15.00	3.00
□□□	151 S. McEachern, Bost.	10.00	10.00	2.00
□□□	152 Joe Nieuwendyk, Dall.	15.00	10.00	2.00
□□□	153 Phil Housley, NJer.	10.00	10.00	2.00
□□□	154 Gartner, Toro. (Phoe.)	30.00	25.00	5.00
□□□	155 Kirk McLean (G), Vanc.	10.00	10.00	2.00
□□□	156 Bob Probert, Chic.	10.00	10.00	2.00
□□□	157 Valeri Kamensky, Colo.	10.00	10.00	2.00
□□□	158 V. Kozlov, Detr.	5.00	5.00	1.00
□□□	159 Éric Desjardins, Phil.	10.00	10.00	2.00
□□□	160 Mats Sundin, Toro.	35.00	35.00	6.00
□□□	161 John LeClair, Phil.	30.00	25.00	5.00
□□□	162 Adam Oates, Bost.	15.00	10.00	2.00
□□□	163 Cliff Ronning, Vanc.	5.00	5.00	1.00
□□□	164 Mike Vernon (G), Detr.	15.00	10.00	2.00
□□□	165 German Titov, Calg.	5.00	4.00	1.00
□□□	166 Chris Pronger, SLou.	20.00	20.00	3.00
□□□	167 Norm Maciver, Winn.	5.00	4.00	1.00
□□□	168 Kenny Jönsson, NYIs.	5.00	5.00	1.00
□□□	169 Tony Amonte, Chic.	20.00	20.00	3.00
□□□	170 Doug Weight, Edmo.	20.00	20.00	3.00
□□□	171 Sergei Zubov, Pitt.	5.00	5.00	1.00
□□□	172 Félix Potvin (G), Toro.	20.00	20.00	3.00
□□□	173 Trevor Linden, Vanc.	15.00	10.00	2.00
□□□	174 Derek Plante, Buff.	5.00	5.00	1.00
□□□	175 Uwe Krupp, Colo.	5.00	4.00	1.00
□□□	176 Nicklas Lidström, Detr.	20.00	20.00	3.00
□□□	177 Mikael Renberg, Phil.	10.00	10.00	2.00
□□□	178 Igor Larionov, Detr.	20.00	20.00	3.00
□□□	179 Brian Leetch, NYRa.	20.00	20.00	3.00
□□□	180 Stu Barnes, Flor.	5.00	4.00	1.00
□□□	181 Alexei Yashin, Otta.	20.00	20.00	3.00
□□□	182 Gary Suter, Chic.	5.00	5.00	1.00
□□□	183 Ken Wregget (G), Pitt.	5.00	5.00	1.00
□□□	184 Mike Ridley, Vanc.	5.00	5.00	1.00
□□□	185 Peter Bondra, Wash.	20.00	20.00	3.00
□□□	186 Steve Rucchin, Anah.	5.00	5.00	1.00
□□□	187 Jozef Stümpel, Bost.	5.00	5.00	1.00
□□□	188 Matthew Barnaby, Buff.	5.00	4.00	1.00
□□□	189 James Patrick, Calg.	5.00	4.00	1.00
□□□	190 Chris Simon, Colo.	5.00	5.00	1.00
□□□	191 Brent Fedyk, Dall.	5.00	4.00	1.00
□□□	192 Kris Draper, Detr.	5.00	5.00	1.00
□□□	193 David Oliver, Edmo.	5.00	4.00	1.00
□□□	194 Dave Lowry, Flor.	5.00	5.00	1.00
□□□	195 Robert Kron, Hart.	5.00	5.00	1.00
□□□	196 A. Kovalenko, Mont.	5.00	5.00	1.00
□□□	197 Bill Guerin, NJer.	15.00	10.00	2.00
□□□	198 Ed Olczyk, Winn.	5.00	5.00	1.00
□□□	199 Yuri Khmylev, SLou.	5.00	4.00	1.00
□□□	200 Rob Ray, Buff.	5.00	5.00	1.00
□□□	201 Joe Mullen, Bost.	15.00	10.00	2.00
□□□	202 Petr Klima, Tamp.	5.00	5.00	1.00
□□□	203 Todd Krygier, Anah.	5.00	4.00	1.00
□□□	204 Garth Snow (G), Phil.	10.00	10.00	2.00
□□□	205 Zarley Zalapski, Calg.	5.00	4.00	1.00
□□□	206 K. Baumgartner, Anah.	5.00	4.00	1.00
□□□	207 Tony Twist, SLou.	5.00	5.00	1.00
□□□	208 Todd Gill, Toro. (SanJ.)	5.00	5.00	1.00
□□□	209 Michael Peca, Buff.	15.00	10.00	2.00
□□□	210 D. Wakaluk (G), Dall.	5.00	5.00	1.00
□□□	211 Milos Holan, Anah.	5.00	4.00	1.00
□□□	212 A. Semak, NYIs.	5.00	4.00	1.00
□□□	213 Jeff Reese (G), Tamp.	5.00	5.00	1.00
□□□	214 Jon Casey (G), SLou.	5.00	5.00	1.00
□□□	215 Sandy McCarthy, Calg.	5.00	5.00	1.00
□□□	216 C. Leschyshyn, Colo.	5.00	5.00	1.00
□□□	217 Todd Marchant, Edmo.	5.00	5.00	1.00
□□□	218 Bob Bassen, Dall.	5.00	4.00	1.00
□□□	219 Darren Turcotte, SanJ.	5.00	5.00	1.00
□□□	220 David Reid, Bost.	5.00	5.00	1.00
□□□	221 Brian Bellows, Tamp.	5.00	5.00	1.00
□□□	222 Jesse Belanger, Vanc.	5.00	4.00	1.00
□□□	223 Bill Lindsay, Flor.	5.00	4.00	1.00
□□□	224 Lyle Odelein, Mont.	5.00	5.00	1.00
□□□	225 Keith Jones, Wash.	5.00	5.00	1.00
□□□	226 Sylvain Lefebvre, Colo.	5.00	5.00	1.00
□□□	227 Shaun Van Allen, Anah.	5.00	5.00	1.00
□□□	228 Dan Quinn, Phil.	5.00	4.00	1.00
□□□	229 R. Matvichuk, Dall.	5.00	5.00	1.00
□□□	230 Craig MacTavish, SLou.	5.00	5.00	1.00
□□□	231 C. Billington (G), Bost.	5.00	5.00	1.00
□□□	232 Stéphane Richer, NJer.	5.00	5.00	1.00
□□□	233 Donald Audette, Buff.	15.00	10.00	2.00
□□□	234 Ulf Dahlen, SanJ.	5.00	5.00	1.00
□□□	235 Steve Chiasson, Calg.	5.00	5.00	1.00
□□□	236 Eric Dazé, Chic.	15.00	10.00	2.00
□□□	237 Petr Sykora, NJer.	15.00	10.00	2.00
□□□	238 Saku Koivu, Mont.	30.00	25.00	5.00
□□□	239 Ed Jovanovski, Flor.	15.00	10.00	2.00
□□□	240 D. Alfredsson, Otta.	20.00	20.00	3.00
□□□	241 V. Yachmenov, LosA.	5.00	5.00	1.00
□□□	242 M. Ragnarsson, SanJ.	5.00	5.00	1.00
□□□	243 Cory Stillman, Calg.	5.00	5.00	1.00
□□□	244 Todd Bertuzzi, NYIs.	45.00	40.00	7.00
□□□	245 Valeri Bure, Mont.	10.00	10.00	2.00
□□□	246 Jere Lehtinen, Dall.	10.00	10.00	2.00
□□□	247 Radek Dvorak, Flor.	5.00	5.00	1.00
□□□	248 Niclas Andersson, NYIs.	5.00	4.00	1.00
□□□	249 Miroslav Satan, Edmo.	10.00	10.00	2.00
□□□	250 Jeff O'Neill, Hart.	15.00	10.00	2.00
□□□	251 N. Baumgartner, Wash.	5.00	4.00	1.00
□□□	252 Roman Vopat, LosA.	5.00	4.00	1.00
□□□	253 Bryan McCabe, NYIs.	5.00	5.00	1.00
□□□	254 J. Langenbrunner, Dall.	5.00	5.00	1.00
□□□	255 C. Kilger, Winn. (Phoe.)	5.00	5.00	1.00
□□□	256 Éric Fichaud (G), NYIs.	5.00	5.00	1.00
□□□	257 Landon Wilson, Colo.	5.00	5.00	1.00
□□□	258 Kyle McLaren, Bost.	5.00	5.00	1.00
□□□	259 Aaron Gavey, Tamp.	5.00	4.00	1.00
□□□	260 B. Dafoe (G), LosA.	15.00	10.00	2.00
□□□	261 Grant Marshall, Dall.	5.00	5.00	1.00
□□□	262 Shane Doan, Winn.	5.00	5.00	1.00
□□□	263 R. Intranuovo, Edmo.	5.00	4.00	1.00
□□□	264 Aki Berg, LosA.	5.00	5.00	1.00
□□□	265 Antti Törmänen, Otta.	5.00	4.00	1.00
□□□	266 Brian Holzinger, Buff.	5.00	5.00	1.00
□□□	267 J. Théodore (G), Mont.	45.00	40.00	7.00
□□□	268 Ethan Moreau, Chic.	5.00	5.00	1.00
□□□	269 N. Sundström, NYRa.	5.00	5.00	1.00
□□□	270 Brendan Witt, Wash.	5.00	4.00	1.00

CHECK IT

	Insert Set (16 cards):	**110.00**
	Insert (1:35 Jumbo packs)	**CI**
□	1 Eric Lindros, Phil. [vs. T.Taylor]	12.00
□	2 Peter Forsberg, Colo.	16.00
□	3 Keith Tkachuk, Winn. [vs. D.Bodger]	6.00
□	4 Cam Neely, Bost.	12.00
□	5 Jeremy Roenick, Chic. [cameo: P.Poulin]	10.00
□	6 Brendan Shanahan, Hart.	12.00
□	7 Wendel Clark, Toro. [vs. J.Murphy]	10.00
□	8 Owen Nolan, SanJ. [vs. P.Turgeon]	6.00
□	9 Doug Gilmour, Toro. [vs. Canadiens]	6.00
□	10 Trevor Linden, Vanc.	4.00
□	11 Saku Koivu, Mont.	10.00
□	12 Ed Jovanovski, Flor. [vs. K.Jönsson]	4.00
□	13 Theoren Fleury, Calg.	6.00
□	14 Doug Weight, Edmo.	6.00
□	15 Chris Chelios, Chic. [vs. D.Gilmour]	6.00
□	16 Éric Dazé, Chic. [vs. M.Osborne]	4.00

DREAM TEAM

	Insert Set (12 cards):	**95.00**
	Insert (1:35 packs)	**DT**
□	1 Eric Lindros, Phil.	6.00
□	2 Paul Kariya, Anah.	8.00
□	3 Joe Sakic, Colo.	10.00
□	4 Peter Forsberg, Colo.	8.00
□	5 Mark Messier, NYRa.	6.00
□	6 Mario Lemieux, Pitt.	18.00
□	7 Jaromir Jagr, Pitt.	6.00
□	8 Wayne Gretzky, SLou.	25.00
□	9 Alexander Mogilny, Vanc.	3.00
□	10 Pavel Bure, Vanc.	5.00
□	11 Sergei Fedorov, Detr.	6.00
□	12 Patrick Roy (G), Colo.	18.00

NET WORTH

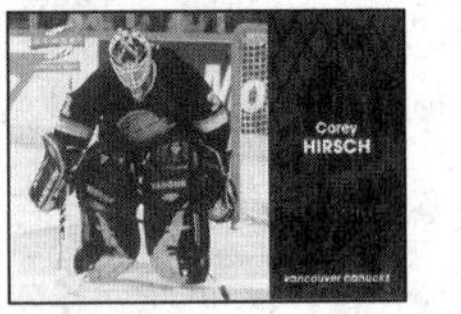

	Insert Set (18 cards):	**115.00**
	Insert (1:35 Retail packs)	**NW**
□	1 Patrick Roy (G), Colo.	35.00
□	2 Martin Brodeur (G), NJer.	20.00
□	3 Jim Carey (G), Wash.	4.00
□	4 Dominik Hasek (G), Buff.	10.00
□	5 Ed Belfour (G), Chic.	10.00
□	6 Chris Osgood (G), Detr.	5.00
□	7 Curtis Joseph (G), Edmo.	10.00
□	8 John Vanbiesbrouck (G), Flor.	5.00
□	9 Jocelyn Thibault (G), Mont.	5.00
□	10 Stéphane Fiset (G), Colo.	4.00
□	11 Ron Hextall (G), Phil.	5.00
□	12 Tom Barrasso (G), Pitt.	5.00
□	13 Daren Puppa (G), Tamp.	4.00
□	14 Mike Vernon (G), Detr.	5.00
□	15 Bill Ranford (G), Bost.	5.00
□	16 Corey Hirsch (G), Vanc.	4.00
□	17 Damian Rhodes (G), Otta.	4.00
□	18 Nikolai Khabibulin (G), Winn. (Phoe.)	5.00

SUDDEN DEATH

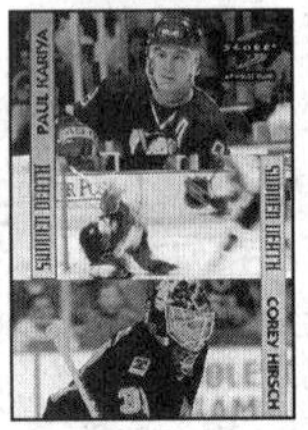

	Insert Set (15 cards):	**145.00**
	Insert (1:35 Hobby packs)	**SD**
□	1 M. Brodeur / P. Turgeon	10.00
□	2 J. Carey / S. Yzerman	12.00
□	3 D. Hasek / B. Shanahan	10.00
□	4 E. Belfour / Br. Hull	10.00
□	5 C. Osgood (G) / J. Roenick	6.00
□	6 Cu. Joseph / P. Bure	8.00
□	7 J. Vanbiesbrouck (G) / M. Lemieux	4.00
□	8 J. Thibault / A. Mogilny	4.00
□	9 M. Richter / J. Jagr	6.00
□	10 T. Barrasso (G) / M. Messier	6.00
□	11 D. Puppa (G) / J. Sakic	8.00
□	12 F. Potvin / W. Gretzky	22.00
□	13 C. Hirsch / P. Kariya	6.00
□	14 R. Hextall / S. Fedorov	8.00
□	15 N. Khabibulin (G) / T. Selänne	6.00

SUPERSTITIONS

	Insert Set (13 cards):	**20.00**
	Insert (1:19)	**SS**
□	1 Teemu Selänne, Anah.	3.00
□	2 Doug Weight, Edmo.	2.00

☐	3 Mats Sundin, Toro.	3.00
☐	4 Mike Modano, Dall.	3.00
☐	5 Félix Potvin (G), Toro.	2.00
☐	6 Paul Coffey, Detr.	2.00
☐	7 Raymond Bourque, Bost.	4.00
☐	8 Chris Chelios, Chic.	2.00
☐	9 Ron Hextall (G), Phil.	2.00
☐	10 Alexander Selivanov, Tamp.	.75
☐	11 Brett Hull, SLou.	3.00
☐	12 Mike Richter (G), NYRa.	1.00
☐	13 Scott Mellanby, Flor.	.75

GOLDEN BLADES PROMO

These Golden Blades promotional cards have two versions: one that deciphers the phrase Sorry Try Again on the back and the other version that deciphers Special Artist's Proof. These promo cards could not be redeemed as part of the promotion.

Complete Set (8 cards):		**4.00**
	Promo	**GB**
☐☐	Patrick Roy (G), Colo.	.75
☐☐	10 Martin Brodeur (G), NJer.	.75
☐☐	16 Alexander Mogilny, Vanc.	.75
☐☐	19 Brett Hull, Slou.	.75
☐☐	63 John Vanbiesbrouck (G), Flor.	.75
☐☐	77 Sergei Fedorov, Detr.	.75
☐☐	236 Eric Dazé, Chic.	.75
☐☐	238 Saku Koivu, Mont.	.75

1996 - 97 SELECT CERTIFIED EDITION

This series has seven versions: the regular card, a Certified Red, a Certifiede Blue, and Artist's Proof, a Mirror Red (60-75 copies), a Mirror Blue (30-40 copies) and a Mirror Gold (19-25 copies). The Certified Blue and the Artist's Proof have the same value; Mirror Red cards are valued at 50% more than Certified Blue and Artist's Proof cards. Artist's Proof cards mistakenly say "1 of 500" on the card face; there are in fact only 125-150 copies.

Complete Set (120 cards):		**1600.00**	**275.00**	**50.00**
Common Player:		**6.00**	**1.00**	**.35**
	Player	**AP**	**CR**	**SCE**
☐☐☐☐	1 Eric Lindros	40.00	5.00	1.50
☐☐☐☐	2 Mike Modano	45.00	7.00	1.50
☐☐☐☐	3 Jocelyn Thibault (G)	15.00	3.00	.50
☐☐☐☐	4 Wayne Gretzky	240.00	30.00	6.00
☐☐☐☐	5 Raymond Bourque	50.00	9.00	1.50
☐☐☐☐	6 Martin Brodeur (G)	70.00	10.00	2.00
☐☐☐☐	7 Rob Niedermayer	10.00	1.50	.35
☐☐☐☐	8 Stéphane Fiset (G)	10.00	2.00	.35
☐☐☐☐	9 Pat LaFontaine	25.00	4.00	.50
☐☐☐☐	10 Mario Lemieux	160.00	20.00	4.50
☐☐☐☐	11 Ed Belfour (G)	45.00	7.00	1.50
☐☐☐☐	12 Ron Francis	25.00	4.00	.50
☐☐☐☐	13 Luc Robitaille	35.00	6.00	1.00
☐☐☐☐	14 Paul Kariya	60.00	10.00	2.00
☐☐☐☐	15 Doug Gilmour	25.00	4.00	.50
☐☐☐☐	16 Joe Sakic, Col.	70.00	12.00	2.00
☐☐☐☐	17 Nikolai Khabibulin (G)	15.00	3.00	.50
☐☐☐☐	18 Valeri Bure	10.00	2.00	.35
☐☐☐☐	19 Brett Hull	45.00	7.00	1.50
☐☐☐☐	20 Chris Osgood (G)	25.00	4.00	.50
☐☐☐☐	21 Trevor Kidd (G)	10.00	2.00	.35
☐☐☐☐	22 Kirk McLean (G)	10.00	2.00	.35
☐☐☐☐	23 Zigmund Palffy	25.00	4.00	.50
☐☐☐☐	24 Keith Tkachuk	25.00	4.00	.50
☐☐☐☐	25 Andy Moog (G)	15.00	3.00	.50
☐☐☐☐	26 Bill Guerin	15.00	3.00	.50
☐☐☐☐	27 Chris Chelios	25.00	4.00	.50
☐☐☐☐	28 Damian Rhodes (G)	10.00	1.50	.35
☐☐☐☐	29 Jim Carey (G)	6.00	1.00	.35
☐☐☐☐	30 Ed Jovanovski	15.00	3.00	.50
☐☐☐☐	31 Félix Potvin (G)	25.00	4.00	.50
☐☐☐☐	32 Teemu Selänne	30.00	6.00	1.00
☐☐☐☐	33 John LeClair	35.00	6.00	1.00
☐☐☐☐	34 Pavel Bure	30.00	5.00	1.00
☐☐☐☐	35 Grant Fuhr	25.00	4.00	.50
☐☐☐☐	36 Mark Messier	45.00	7.00	1.50
☐☐☐☐	37 V. Damphousse	25.00	4.00	.50
☐☐☐☐	38 Jason Arnott	20.00	3.00	.50
☐☐☐☐	39 Mike Richter (G)	20.00	3.50	.50
☐☐☐☐	40 Keith Primeau	15.00	3.00	.50
☐☐☐☐	41 Steve Yzerman	110.00	15.00	3.50
☐☐☐☐	42 Trevor Linden	15.00	3.00	.50
☐☐☐☐	43 Jaromir Jagr	40.00	5.00	1.50
☐☐☐☐	44 Sean Burke (G)	25.00	4.00	.50
☐☐☐☐	45 Alexei Zhitnik	6.00	1.00	.35
☐☐☐☐	46 Dmitri Khristich	6.00	1.00	.35
☐☐☐☐	47 Daniel Alfredsson	25.00	4.00	.50
☐☐☐☐	48 Roman Hamrlik	10.00	1.50	.35
☐☐☐☐	49 Pat Verbeek	10.00	2.00	.35
☐☐☐☐	50 Doug Weight	25.00	4.00	.50
☐☐☐☐	51 Adam Graves	15.00	3.00	.50
☐☐☐☐	52 Michal Pivonka	6.00	1.00	.35
☐☐☐☐	53 Claude Lemieux	10.00	2.00	.35
☐☐☐☐	54 Scott Stevens	15.00	3.00	.50
☐☐☐☐	55 Sergei Fedorov	45.00	7.00	1.50
☐☐☐☐	56 Owen Nolan	25.00	4.00	.50
☐☐☐☐	57 Niclas Andersson	6.00	1.00	.35
☐☐☐☐	58 Cory Stillman	10.00	1.50	.35
☐☐☐☐	59 J.Vanbiesbrouck (G)	20.00	3.50	.50
☐☐☐☐	60 Craig Janney	10.00	1.50	.35
☐☐☐☐	61 Jeff Friesen	10.00	2.00	.35
☐☐☐☐	62 Igor Larionov	25.00	4.00	.50
☐☐☐☐	63 Ron Hextall (G)	25.00	4.50	.50
☐☐☐☐	64 Saku Koivu	35.00	6.00	1.00
☐☐☐☐	65 Wendel Clark	35.00	6.00	1.00
☐☐☐☐	66 Curtis Joseph (G)	40.00	7.00	1.50
☐☐☐☐	67 Valeri Kamensky	10.00	2.00	.35
☐☐☐☐	68 Adam Oates	15.00	3.00	.50
☐☐☐☐	69 Daren Puppa (G)	10.00	1.50	.35
☐☐☐☐	70 Alexander Mogilny	20.00	3.50	.50
☐☐☐☐	71 Corey Hirsch (G)	6.00	1.00	.35
☐☐☐☐	72 Brendan Shanahan	45.00	7.00	1.50
☐☐☐☐	73 Shayne Corson	10.00	2.00	.35
☐☐☐☐	74 Dominik Hasek (G)	40.00	5.00	1.50
☐☐☐☐	75 Theoren Fleury	25.00	4.00	.50
☐☐☐☐	76 Brian Leetch	25.00	4.00	.50
☐☐☐☐	77 Jeremy Roenick	35.00	6.00	1.00
☐☐☐☐	78 Peter Bondra	25.00	4.00	.50
☐☐☐☐	79 Eric Dazé	15.00	3.00	.50
☐☐☐☐	80 Todd Bertuzzi	50.00	9.00	3.50
☐☐☐☐	81 Patrick Roy (G)	140.00	20.00	4.50
☐☐☐☐	82 Pierre Turgeon	15.00	3.00	.50
☐☐☐☐	83 Alexei Yashin	25.00	4.00	.50
☐☐☐☐	84 Scott Mellanby	10.00	1.50	.35
☐☐☐☐	85 Mats Sundin	45.00	7.00	1.50
☐☐☐☐	86 Jari Kurri	45.00	7.00	1.50
☐☐☐☐	87 Kelly Hrudey (G)	10.00	2.00	.35
☐☐☐☐	88 Joe Nieuwendyk	15.00	3.00	.50
☐☐☐☐	89 Paul Coffey	25.00	4.00	.50
☐☐☐☐	90 Jeff O'Neill	15.00	3.00	.50
☐☐☐☐	**91 Kai Nurminen RC**	**6.00**	**1.50**	**1.00**
☐☐☐☐	92 Anders Eriksson	6.00	1.00	.35
☐☐☐☐	93 Jarome Iginla	35.00	6.00	2.00
☐☐☐☐	94 Anson Carter	15.00	3.00	1.00
☐☐☐☐	95 Christian Dubé	6.00	1.00	.35
☐☐☐☐	**96 Harry York RC**	**6.00**	**1.50**	**1.00**
☐☐☐☐	**97 T. Holmström RC**	**10.00**	**3.50**	**2.00**
☐☐☐☐	**98 S. Berezin RC**	**10.00**	**3.50**	**2.00**
☐☐☐☐	**99 M. Timander RC**	**6.00**	**1.50**	**1.00**
☐☐☐☐	100 Wade Redden	10.00	2.00	.50
☐☐☐☐	**101 Mike Grier RC**	**10.00**	**3.50**	**2.00**
☐☐☐☐	102 Jonas Höglund	6.00	1.00	.35
☐☐☐☐	103 Éric Fichaud (G)	6.00	1.00	.35
☐☐☐☐	104 Janne Niinimaa	10.00	1.50	.50
☐☐☐☐	105 Tomas Grönman	6.00	1.00	.35
☐☐☐☐	106 Jim Campbell	6.00	1.00	.35
☐☐☐☐	107 D. Goneau	6.00	1.50	1.00
☐☐☐☐	**108 P. Lalime (G) RC**	**25.00**	**9.00**	**6.00**
☐☐☐☐	**109 Ruslan Salei RC**	**6.00**	**1.50**	**1.00**
☐☐☐☐	**110 R. Zednik RC**	**15.00**	**6.00**	**4.00**
☐☐☐☐	111 Chris O'Sullivan	6.00	1.00	.35
☐☐☐☐	**112 Fredrik Modin RC**	**10.00**	**3.50**	**2.00**
☐☐☐☐	**113 Brad Smyth RC**	**6.00**	**1.50**	**1.00**
☐☐☐☐	114 Bryan Berard	10.00	2.00	.50
☐☐☐☐	115 J. Langenbrunner	10.00	1.50	.35
☐☐☐☐	116 Ethan Moreau	6.00	1.00	.35
☐☐☐☐	117 Daymond Langkow	10.00	1.50	.35
☐☐☐☐	**118 A. Dackell RC**	**6.00**	**2.00**	**1.50**
☐☐☐☐	**119 Rem Murray RC**	**6.00**	**1.50**	**1.00**
☐☐☐☐	**120 D. Zubrus RC**	**10.00**	**3.50**	**2.00**

MIRROR PARALLELS

Complete Set (120 cards):		**1200.00**	**500.00**	
Common Player:		**40.00**	**18.00**	**8.00**
	Player	**MG**	**MB**	**MR**
☐☐☐	1 Eric Lindros	350.00	150.00	70.00
☐☐☐	2 Mike Modano	375.00	150.00	75.00
☐☐☐	3 Jocelyn Thibault (G)	150.00	60.00	30.00
☐☐☐	4 Wayne Gretzky	2800.00	825.00	350.00
☐☐☐	5 Raymond Bourque	450.00	180.00	90.00
☐☐☐	6 Martin Brodeur (G)	600.00	225.00	120.00
☐☐☐	7 Rob Niedermayer	90.00	35.00	15.00
☐☐☐	8 Stéphane Fiset (G)	120.00	45.00	20.00
☐☐☐	9 Pat LaFontaine	225.00	90.00	45.00
☐☐☐	10 Mario Lemieux	1200.00	450.00	225.00
☐☐☐	11 Ed Belfour (G)	375.00	150.00	75.00
☐☐☐	12 Ron Francis	225.00	90.00	45.00
☐☐☐	13 Luc Robitaille	300.00	120.00	60.00
☐☐☐	14 Paul Kariya	500.00	200.00	105.00
☐☐☐	15 Doug Gilmour	225.00	90.00	45.00
☐☐☐	16 Joe Sakic, Col.	600.00	225.00	120.00
☐☐☐	17 Nikolai Khabibulin (G)	150.00	60.00	30.00
☐☐☐	18 Valeri Bure	120.00	45.00	20.00
☐☐☐	19 Brett Hull	375.00	150.00	75.00
☐☐☐	20 Chris Osgood (G)	225.00	90.00	45.00
☐☐☐	21 Trevor Kidd (G)	120.00	45.00	20.00
☐☐☐	22 Kirk McLean (G)	120.00	45.00	20.00
☐☐☐	23 Zigmund Palffy	225.00	90.00	45.00
☐☐☐	24 Keith Tkachuk	225.00	90.00	45.00
☐☐☐	25 Andy Moog (G)	150.00	60.00	30.00
☐☐☐	26 Bill Guerin	150.00	60.00	30.00
☐☐☐	27 Chris Chelios	225.00	90.00	45.00
☐☐☐	28 Damian Rhodes (G)	90.00	35.00	15.00
☐☐☐	29 Jim Carey (G)	60.00	20.00	10.00
☐☐☐	30 Ed Jovanovski	150.00	60.00	30.00
☐☐☐	31 Félix Potvin (G)	225.00	90.00	45.00
☐☐☐	32 Teemu Selänne	300.00	120.00	60.00
☐☐☐	33 John LeClair	300.00	120.00	60.00
☐☐☐	34 Pavel Bure	300.00	100.00	60.00
☐☐☐	35 Grant Fuhr	225.00	90.00	45.00
☐☐☐	36 Mark Messier	375.00	150.00	75.00
☐☐☐	37 V. Damphousse	225.00	90.00	45.00
☐☐☐	38 Jason Arnott	180.00	70.00	35.00
☐☐☐	39 Mike Richter (G)	180.00	70.00	35.00
☐☐☐	40 Keith Primeau	150.00	60.00	30.00
☐☐☐	41 Steve Yzerman	900.00	350.00	180.00
☐☐☐	42 Trevor Linden	150.00	60.00	30.00
☐☐☐	43 Jaromir Jagr	350.00	150.00	75.00
☐☐☐	44 Sean Burke (G)	225.00	90.00	45.00
☐☐☐	45 Alexei Zhitnik	60.00	20.00	10.00
☐☐☐	46 Dmitri Khristich	60.00	20.00	10.00
☐☐☐	47 Daniel Alfredsson	225.00	90.00	45.00
☐☐☐	48 Roman Hamrlik	90.00	35.00	15.00
☐☐☐	49 Pat Verbeek	120.00	45.00	20.00
☐☐☐	50 Doug Weight	225.00	90.00	45.00
☐☐☐	51 Adam Graves	150.00	60.00	30.00
☐☐☐	52 Michal Pivonka	40.00	18.00	8.00
☐☐☐	53 Claude Lemieux	120.00	45.00	20.00
☐☐☐	54 Scott Stevens	150.00	60.00	30.00
☐☐☐	55 Sergei Fedorov	375.00	150.00	75.00
☐☐☐	56 Owen Nolan	225.00	90.00	45.00
☐☐☐	57 Niclas Andersson	40.00	18.00	8.00
☐☐☐	58 Cory Stillman	90.00	35.00	15.00
☐☐☐	59 J.Vanbiesbrouck (G)	180.00	70.00	35.00
☐☐☐	60 Craig Janney	90.00	35.00	15.00
☐☐☐	61 Jeff Friesen	120.00	45.00	20.00
☐☐☐	62 Igor Larionov	225.00	90.00	45.00
☐☐☐	63 Ron Hextall (G)	225.00	90.00	45.00
☐☐☐	64 Saku Koivu	300.00	120.00	60.00
☐☐☐	65 Wendel Clark	300.00	120.00	60.00
☐☐☐	66 Curtis Joseph (G)	350.00	150.00	75.00
☐☐☐	67 Valeri Kamensky	120.00	45.00	20.00
☐☐☐	68 Adam Oates	150.00	60.00	30.00
☐☐☐	69 Daren Puppa (G)	90.00	35.00	15.00
☐☐☐	70 Alexander Mogilny	180.00	70.00	35.00
☐☐☐	71 Corey Hirsch (G)	60.00	20.00	10.00
☐☐☐	72 Brendan Shanahan	375.00	150.00	75.00
☐☐☐	73 Shayne Corson	120.00	45.00	20.00
☐☐☐	74 Dominik Hasek (G)	350.00	150.00	75.00
☐☐☐	75 Theoren Fleury	225.00	90.00	45.00
☐☐☐	76 Brian Leetch	225.00	90.00	45.00
☐☐☐	77 Jeremy Roenick	300.00	120.00	60.00
☐☐☐	78 Peter Bondra	225.00	90.00	45.00
☐☐☐	79 Eric Dazé	150.00	60.00	30.00
☐☐☐	80 Todd Bertuzzi	450.00	180.00	90.00
☐☐☐	81 Patrick Roy (G)	1350.00	450.00	225.00
☐☐☐	82 Pierre Turgeon	150.00	60.00	30.00
☐☐☐	83 Alexei Yashin	225.00	90.00	45.00
☐☐☐	84 Scott Mellanby	90.00	35.00	15.00
☐☐☐	85 Mats Sundin	375.00	150.00	75.00
☐☐☐	86 Jari Kurri	375.00	150.00	75.00
☐☐☐	87 Kelly Hrudey (G)	120.00	45.00	20.00
☐☐☐	88 Joe Nieuwendyk	150.00	60.00	30.00
☐☐☐	89 Paul Coffey	225.00	90.00	45.00
☐☐☐	90 Jeff O'Neill	150.00	60.00	30.00
☐☐☐	**91 Kai Nurminen RC**	**40.00**	**20.00**	**15.00**
☐☐☐	92 Anders Eriksson	40.00	18.00	10.00
☐☐☐	93 Jarome Iginla	300.00	130.00	80.00
☐☐☐	94 Anson Carter	150.00	65.00	40.00
☐☐☐	95 Christian Dubé	60.00	25.00	15.00
☐☐☐	**96 Harry York RC**	**40.00**	**20.00**	**15.00**
☐☐☐	**97 T. Holmström RC**	**90.00**	**50.00**	**35.00**
☐☐☐	**98 S. Berezin RC**	**90.00**	**50.00**	**35.00**
☐☐☐	**99 M. Timander RC**	**40.00**	**20.00**	**15.00**
☐☐☐	100 Wade Redden	120.00	50.00	30.00
☐☐☐	**101 Mike Grier RC**	**90.00**	**50.00**	**35.00**
☐☐☐	102 Jonas Höglund	60.00	25.00	15.00
☐☐☐	103 Éric Fichaud (G)	60.00	20.00	10.00
☐☐☐	104 Janne Niinimaa	90.00	35.00	20.00
☐☐☐	105 Tomas Grönman	40.00	18.00	10.00
☐☐☐	106 Jim Campbell	40.00	18.00	10.00
☐☐☐	**107 D. Goneau RC**	**40.00**	**20.00**	**15.00**
☐☐☐	**108 P. Lalime (G) RC**	**335.00**	**180.00**	**110.00**
☐☐☐	**109 Ruslan Salei RC**	**40.00**	**20.00**	**15.00**
☐☐☐	**110 R. Zednik RC**	**225.00**	**120.00**	**75.00**
☐☐☐	111 Chris O'Sullivan	40.00	18.00	10.00
☐☐☐	**112 Fredrik Modin RC**	**90.00**	**50.00**	**35.00**
☐☐☐	**113 Brad Smyth RC**	**40.00**	**20.00**	**15.00**
☐☐☐	114 Bryan Berard	120.00	50.00	30.00
☐☐☐	115 J. Langenbrunner	90.00	35.00	15.00
☐☐☐	116 Ethan Moreau	60.00	20.00	10.00
☐☐☐	117 Daymond Langkow	90.00	35.00	15.00
☐☐☐	**118 A. Dackell RC**	**60.00**	**35.00**	**20.00**
☐☐☐	**119 Rem Murray RC**	**40.00**	**20.00**	**15.00**
☐☐☐	**120 D. Zubrus RC**	**90.00**	**50.00**	**35.00**

SAMPLE

☐	Wendel Clark, Toro.	1.00

CORNERSTONE

Insert Set (15 cards):		**135.00**
	Insert (1:38)	**C**
☐	1 Eric Lindros, Phil.	7.00
☐	2 Mario Lemieux, Pitt.	22.00
☐	3 Jaromir Jagr, Pitt.	7.00
☐	4 Wayne Gretzky, NYRa.	30.00
☐	5 Mark Messier, NYRa.	7.00
☐	6 Brett Hull, SLou.	7.00
☐	7 Pavel Bure, Vanc.	6.00
☐	8 Saku Koivu, Mont.	6.00
☐	9 Joe Sakic, Colo.	12.00
☐	10 Keith Tkachuk, Phoe.	4.00
☐	11 Paul Kariya, Anah.	10.00
☐	12 Teemu Selänne, Anah.	6.00
☐	13 Sergei Fedorov, Detr.	7.00
☐	14 Steve Yzerman, Detr.	18.00
☐	15 Peter Forsberg, Colo.	10.00

FREEZERS

Insert Set (15 cards):		**70.00**
	Insert (1:41)	**F**
☐	1 Martin Brodeur (G), NJer.	12.00
☐	2 Patrick Roy (G), Colo.	22.00
☐	3 Jim Carey (G), Wash.	3.00
☐	4 John Vanbiesbrouck (G), Flor.	3.00
☐	5 Dominik Hasek (G), Buff.	7.00
☐	6 Ed Belfour (G), Chic.	7.00
☐	7 Curtis Joseph (G), Edmo.	7.00
☐	8 Félix Potvin (G), Toro.	4.00
☐	9 Daren Puppa (G), Tamp.	3.00
☐	10 Chris Osgood (G), Detr.	4.00
☐	11 Mike Richter (G), NYRa.	3.00
☐	12 Jocelyn Thibault (G), Mont.	3.00
☐	13 Ron Hextall (G), Phil.	4.00
☐	14 Nikolai Khabibulin (G), Phoe.	3.00
☐	15 Damian Rhodes (G), Otta.	3.00

1996 - 97 SCORE BOARD 7-ELEVEN PHONECARD

	15-min Phonecard	**Unused**	**Used**
☐	Daniel Alfredsson, Otta. {#/625}	30.00	15.00
☐	Paul Coffey, Detr.	15.00	5.00
☐	Vincent Damphousse, Mont.	15.00	5.00
☐	Doug Gilmour, Toro.	15.00	5.00
☐	Curtis Joseph (G), Edmo.	15.00	5.00
☐	Trevor Linden, Vanc.	15.00	5.00
☐	Joe Sakic, Colo.	20.00	10.00
☐	Brendan Shanahan, Detr.	15.00	5.00
☐	Pierre Turgeon, Mont.	15.00	5.00
☐	Doug Weight, Edmo.	15.00	5.00
	30-min Phonecard	**Unused**	**Used**
☐	Raymond Bourque, Bost.	35.00	15.00
☐	Pavel Bure, Flor.	35.00	15.00
☐	Theoren Fleury	35.00	15.00
☐	Peter Forsberg, Colo.	35.00	15.00
☐	Paul Kariya, Anah.	35.00	15.00
☐	John LeClair, Phil.	35.00	15.00
☐	Brian Leetch, NYRa.	35.00	15.00
☐	Eric Lindros, Phil.	35.00	15.00
☐	Mike Richter (G), NYRa.	35.00	15.00
☐	Steve Yzerman, Detr.	45.00	20.00

1996 - 97 SISU

There are two versions: the regular card and a Press Proof die-cut parallel.

Complete Set (240 cards):		**40.00**
Common Player:		**.30**
	Player	**Sisu**
☐	1 Checklist	.30
☐	2 Sakari Lindfors, HIFK Helsinki	.30
☐	3 Peter Ahola, HIFK Helsinki	.50
☐	4 Jere Karalahti, HIFK Helsinki	.50
☐	5 Pertti Lehtonen, HIFK Helsinki	.30
☐	6 Lauri Puolanne, HIFK Helsinki	.30
☐	7 Sami Laine, HIFK Helsinki	.30
☐	8 Tommy Kiviaho, HIFK Helsinki	.30
☐	9 Markku Hurme, HIFK Helsinki	.30
☐	10 Jari Laukkanen, HIFK Helsinki	.30
☐	11 Tero Nyman, HIFK Helsinki	.30
☐	12 Toni Sihvonen, HIFK Helsinki	.30
☐	13 Mika Kortelainen, HIFK Helsinki	.30
☐	14 Tero Hämäläinen, HIFK Helsinki	.30
☐	15 Mika Pietilä, HIFK Helsinki	.30
☐	16 Erik Kakko, HIFK Helsinki	.30
☐	17 Tom Koivisto, HIFK Helsinki	.30
☐	18 Jani Nikko, HIFK Helsinki	.30
☐	19 Risto Jalo, HIFK Helsinki	.30
☐	20 Alexander Andrijevski, HIFK Helsinki	.50
☐	21 Jari Kauppila, HIFK Helsinki	.30
☐	22 Jarkko Savijoki, HIFK Helsinki	.30
☐	23 Toni Mäkiaho, HIFK Helsinki	.30
☐	24 Mika Kannisto, HIFK Helsinki	.30
☐	25 Mika Puhakka, HIFK Helsinki	.30
☐	26 Toni Saarinen, HIFK Helsinki	.30
☐	27 Vesa Toskala, Ilves Tampere	.50
☐	28 Teemu Vuorinen, Ilves Tampere	.30
☐	29 Petri Kokko, Ilves Tampere	.30
☐	30 Pekka Kangasalusta, Ilves Tampere	.30
☐	31 Jarno Peltonen, Ilves Tampere	.30
☐	32 Jarno Peltonen, Ilves Tampere	.30
☐	33 Mika Arvaja, Ilves Tampere	.30
☐	34 Matti Kaipainen, Ilves Tampere	.30
☐	35 Hannu Mattila, Ilves Tampere	.30
☐	36 Tomi Hirvonen, Ilves Tampere	.30
☐	37 Jouni Lahtinen, Ilves Tampere	.30
☐	38 Jari Suorsa, Ilves Tampere	.30
☐	39 Juha Järvenpää, Ilves Tampere	.30
☐	40 Semi Pekki, Ilves Tampere	.30
☐	41 Ari Sulander, Jokerit Helsinki	.30
☐	42 Mika Strömberg, Jokerit Helsinki	.30
☐	43 Marko Tuulola, Jokerit Helsinki	.30
☐	44 Pasi Sormunen, Jokerit Helsinki	.30
☐	45 Waltteri Immonen, Jokerit Helsinki	.30
☐	46 Jukka Penttinen, Jokerit Helsinki	.30
☐	47 Petri Varis, Jokerit Helsinki	.30
☐	48 Keijo Säilynoja, Jokerit Helsinki	.30
☐	49 Tero Lehterä, Jokerit Helsinki	.30
☐	50 Checklist	.30
☐	51 Jari Lindroos, Jokerit Helsinki	.30
☐	52 Ismo Kuoppala, Jokerit Helsinki	.30
☐	53 Juha Ylönen, Jokerit Helsinki	.50
☐	54 Pasi Saarela, Jokerit Helsinki	.30
☐	55 Marko Leinonen, JyP HT Jyväskylä	.30
☐	56 Kalle Koskinen, JyP HT Jyväskylä	.30
☐	57 J.P. Laamanen, JyP HT Jyväskylä	.30
☐	58 Jouni Loponen, JyP HT Jyväskylä	.30
☐	59 Pekka Poikolainen, JyP HT Jyväskylä	.30
☐	60 Jan Latvala, JyP HT Jyväskylä	.30
☐	61 Timo Ahmaoja, JyP HT Jyväskylä	.30
☐	62 Mika Paananen, JyP HT Jyväskylä	.30
☐	63 Kimmo Salminen, JyP HT Jyväskylä	.30
☐	64 Lasse Jämsen, JyP HT Jyväskylä	.30
☐	65 Thomas Sjögren, JyP HT Jyväskylä	.30
☐	66 Juha Viinikainen, JyP HT Jyväskylä	.30
☐	67 Mikko Inkinen, JyP HT Jyväskylä	.30
☐	68 Toni Koivenen, JyP HT Jyväskylä	.30
☐	69 Pari Kuivalainen, Kiekko-Espoo	.30
☐	70 Tommi Kovanen, Kiekko-Espoo	.30
☐	71 Jermu Pisto, Kiekko-Espoo	.30
☐	72 Ivan Vlzek, Kiekko-Espoo	.30
☐	73 Mika Laaksonen, Kiekko-Espoo	.30
☐	74 Miikka Ruokonen, Kiekko-Espoo	.30
☐	75 Sami Simonen, Kiekko-Espoo	.30
☐	76 Mikko Honkonen, Kiekko-Espoo	.30
☐	77 Veli-Pekka Nutikka, Kiekko-Espoo	.30
☐	78 Arto Sirviö, Kiekko-Espoo	.30
☐	79 Janne Kekäläinen, Kiekko-Espoo	.30
☐	80 Jarno Levonen, Kiekko-Espoo	.30
☐	81 Jussi Tarvainen, Kiekko-Espoo	.30
☐	82 Iiro Itämies, Kiekko-Espoo	.30
☐	83 Tommi Nyyssänen, Kiekko-Espoo	.30
☐	84 Kari Haakana, Kiekko-Espoo	.30
☐	85 Jarmo Muukkonen, Kiekko-Espoo	.30
☐	86 Tero Nissinen, Kiekko-Espoo	.30
☐	87 Tero Tiainen, Kiekko-Espoo	.30
☐	88 Joonas Jääskeläinen, Kiekko-Espoo	.30
☐	89 Juha Ikonen, Kiekko-Espoo	.30
☐	90 Timo Norppa, Kiekko-Espoo	.30
☐	91 Teemu Riihijärvi, Kiekko-Espoo	.30

92 Mikko Koivunoro, Kiekko-Espoo	.30
93 Sergei Priakin, Kiekko-Espoo	.30
94 Timo Hirvonen, Kiekko-Espoo	.30
95 Boris Rousson, Lukko Rauma	.30
96 Kimmo Lotvonen, Lukko Rauma	.30
97 Riku Kallioniemi, Lukko Rauma	.30
98 Martti Järventie, Lukko Rauma	.50
99 Mikko Luori, Lukko Rauma	.30
100 Checklist	.30
101 Kalle Sahlstedt, Lukko Rauma	.30
102 Sakari Palsola, Lukko Rauma	.30
103 Tommi Turunen, Lukko Rauma	.30
104 Petri Lätti, Lukko Rauma	.30
105 Jonni Vauhkonea, Lukko Rauma	.30
106 Veli-Pekka Ahonen, Lukko Rauma	.30
107 Jari Torkki, Lukko Rauma	.30
108 Jarkko Varvio, Lukko Rauma	.30
109 Matti Viitakoski, Lukko Rauma	.30
110 Mikko Myllykoski, Lukko Rauma	.30
111 Petri Peronmoa, Lukko Rauma	.30
112 Vesa Ruotsalainen, Lukko Rauma	.30
113 Timo Lohko, Lukko Rauma	.30
114 Simo Liukka, Lukko Rauma	.30
115 Juha-Pekka Rinkinen, Lukko Rauma	.30
116 Timo Mäkinen, Lukko Rauma	.30
117 Marko Ek, Lukko Rauma	.30
118 Matti Nevalainen, Lukko Rauma	.30
119 Ari Santanen, Lukko Rauma	.30
120 Jonas Flemming, Lukko Rauma	.30
121 Mika Karapuu, Lukko Rauma	.30
122 Ilpo Kauhanen, Tappara Tampere	.30
123 Sami-Ville Salomaa, Tappara Tampere	.30
124 Antti Rahkonen, Tappara Tampere	.30
125 Harri Laurila, Tappara Tampere	.30
126 Sami Lehtonen, Tappara Tampere	.30
127 Pasi Petriläinen, Tappara Tampere	.30
128 Arto Kulmala, Tappara Tampere	.30
129 Jarkko Nikander, Tappara Tampere	.30
130 Timo Nurmberg, Tappara Tampere	.30
131 Tuomas Reijones, Tappara Tampere	.30
132 Alexander Barkov, Tappara Tampere	.30
133 Mika Niittymäki, Tappara Tampere	.30
134 Valeri Krykov, Tappara Tampere	.30
135 Fredrik Norrena, Tappara Tampere	.30
136 Mika Lehtinen, Tappara Tampere	.30
137 Sami Salo, Tappara Tampere	1.00
138 Riku-Petteri Lehtonen, Tappara Tampere	.30
139 Mikko Sokka, Tappara Tampere	.30
140 Manu Laapas, Tappara Tampere	.30
141 Hannes Hyvönen, Tappara Tampere	.30
142 Mikka Rousu, Tappara Tampere	.30
143 Simo Rouvali, Tappara Tampere	.30
144 Tommi Miettinen, Tappara Tampere	.30
145 Kimmo Rintanen, Tappara Tampere	.30
146 Tomi Kallio, Tappara Tampere	1.50
147 Antti Aalto, TPS Turku	.50
148 Miika Elomo, Tappara Tampere	.50
149 Kari Takko, Ässät Pori	.50
150 Checklist	.30
151 Tommi Rajamäki, Ässät Pori	.30
152 Pasi Peltonen, Ässät Pori	.30
153 Karri Kivi, Ässät Pori	.30
154 Jokke Heinänen, Ässät Pori	.30
155 Teppo Kivelä, Ässät Pori	.30
156 Vesa Goman, Ässät Pori	.30
157 Pekka Virta, Ässät Pori	.30
158 Pasi Tuominen, Ässät Pori	.30
159 Timo Hakanen, Ässät Pori	.30
160 Jari Levonen, Ässät Pori	.30
161 Jari Korpisalo, Ässät Pori	.30
162 Timo Salonen, Ässät Pori	.30
163 Jokerit , Jokerit Helsinki	.30
164 Action	.30
165 Action	.30
166 Action	.30
167 Action	.30
168 Action	.30
169 Action	.30
170 Action	.30
171 Action	.30
172 Action	.30
173 Action	.30
174 Action	.30
175 Ari Sulander, Jokerit Helsinki	.30
176 Joni Lehto	.30
177 Timo Jutila	.30
178 Mikko Peltola	.30
179 Juha Riihijärvi	.30
180 Petri Varis	.30
181 Boris Rousson	.30
182 Kimmo Timonen	.30
183 Mika Strömberg, Jokerit Helsinki	.30
184 Jari Korpisalo	.30
185 Otakar Janecky	.30
186 Juha Lind	.50
187 Aarne Honkavaara	.30
188 Esko Niemi	.30
189 Raimo Kilpiö	.30
190 Jarmo Wasama	.30
191 Talli Partinen	.30
192 Urpo Ylönen	.30
193 Ilpo Koskela	.30
194 Jorma Vehmanen	.30
195 Pekka Marjamäki	.30
196 Veli-Pekka Ketola	1.50
197 Matti Murto	.30
198 Juhani Tamminen	.30
199 Matti Hagman	.50
200 Checklist	.30

KEEPING IT GREEN

Insert Set (4 cards):	65.00
Player	KIG
1 Ari Sulander (G), Jokerit Helsinki	20.00
2 Jani Hurme (G)	20.00
3 Boris Rousson (G)	20.00
4 Mika Pietilä (G)	20.00

GOLDEN HELMET

Player	GH
Juha Riihijärvi	60.00

AT THE GALA

Insert Set (8 cards):	20.00
Player	ATG
1 Petri Varis	3.00
2 Juha Riihijärvi	3.00
3 Waltteri Immonen	3.00
4 Jani Hurme (G)	5.00
5 Pasi Kuivalainen (G)	3.00
6 Mika Strömberg, Jokerit Helsinki	3.00
7 Sakari Pietilä	3.00
8 Ari Sulander (G), Jokerit Helsinki	3.00

MIGHTY ADVERSARIES

Insert Set (9 cards):	65.00
Player	MA
1 Kari Takko (G) / Kimmon Rintanen	4.00
2 Boris Rousson (G) / Pasi Saarela	4.00
3 Ilpo Kauhanen (G) / Alexander Andrijevski	4.00
4 Ari Sulander (G) / Mika Kortelainen	4.00
5 Pasi Kuivalainen (G) / Thomas Sjögren	4.00
6 Vesa Toskala (G) / Janne Ojanen	4.00
7 Fredrik Norrena (G) / Otakar Janecky	4.00
8 Sakari Lindfors (G) / Jari Korpisalo	4.00
9 Ari-Pekka Siekkinen (G) / Jari Lindroos	4.00

ROOKIE ENERGY

Insert Set (9 cards):	25.00
Player	RE
1 Jani Hurme	7.00
2 Mikko Eloranta	3.00
3 Sami Salo	3.00
4 Tero Hämäläinen	3.00
5 Miika Elomo	3.00
6 Mika Pietilä	3.00
7 Arto Kuki	3.00
8 Vesa Toskalo (G)	3.00
9 Miikka Rousu	3.00

SISU SPECIAL

Player	SS
Kari Takko (G)	40.00

SLEDGEHAMMERS

Insert Set (9 cards):	30.00
Player	SH
1 Hannu Henriksson	4.00
2 Robert Nordmark	4.00
3 Pasi Sormunen	4.00
4 Tuomas Grönman	4.00
5 Derek Mayer	4.00
6 Toni Porkka	4.00
7 Timo Peltomaa	4.00
8 Iiro Järvi	4.00
9 Joni Lehto	4.00

1996 - 97 SKYBOX IMPACT

Complete Set (175 cards):	25.00
Common Player:	.20
Player	SBx
1 Guy Hebert (G), Anah.	.20
2 Paul Kariya, Anah.	1.00
3 Roman Oksiuta, Anah.	.20
4 Teemu Selänne, Anah.	.50
5 Raymond Bourque, Bost.	.50
6 Kyle McLaren, Bost.	.20
7 Adam Oates, Bost.	.20
8 Bill Ranford (G), Bost.	.20
9 Rick Tocchet, Bost.	.20
10 Dominik Hasek (G), Buff.	.50
11 Pat LaFontaine, Buff.	.20
12 Michael Peca, Buff.	.20
13 Theoren Fleury, Calg.	.20
14 Trevor Kidd (G), Calg.	.20
15 German Titov, Calg.	.20
16 Tony Amonte, Chic.	.20
17 Ed Belfour (G), Chic.	.50
18 Chris Chelios, Chic.	.20
19 Eric Dazé, Chic.	.20
20 Gary Suter, Chic.	.20
21 Alexei Zhamnov, Chic.	.20
22 Peter Forsberg, Colo.	1.00
23 Valeri Kamensky, Colo.	.20
24 Uwe Krupp, Colo.	.20
25 Claude Lemieux, Colo.	.20
26 Sandis Ozolinsh, Colo.	.20
27 Patrick Roy (G), Colo.	2.00
28 Joe Sakic, Colo.	1.00
29 Derian Hatcher, Dall.	.20
30 Mike Modano, Dall.	.50
31 Joe Nieuwendyk, Dall.	.20
32 Sergei Zubov, Pitt. (Dall.)	.20
33 Paul Coffey, Detr.	.20
34 Sergei Fedorov, Detr.	.50
35 Vladimir Konstantinov, Detr.	.20
36 Vyacheslav Kozlov, Detr.	.20
37 Nicklas Lidström, Detr.	.20
38 Chris Osgood (G), Detr.	.20
39 Keith Primeau, Detr.	.20
40 Steve Yzerman, Detr.	1.50
41 Jason Arnott, Edmo.	.20
42 Curtis Joseph (G), Edmo.	.50
43 Doug Weight, Edmo.	.20
44 Radek Dvorak, Flor.	.20
45 Ed Jovanovski, Flor.	.20
46 Scott Mellanby, Flor.	.20
47 Rob Niedermayer, Flor.	.20
48 Ray Sheppard, Flor.	.20
49 Robert Svehla, Flor.	.20
50 John Vanbiesbrouck (G), Flor.	.20
51 Jeff Brown, Hart.	.20
52 Sean Burke (G), Hart.	.20
53 Andrew Cassels, Hart.	.20
54 Geoff Sanderson, Hart.	.20
55 Brendan Shanahan, Hart.	.50
56 Byron Dafoe (G), LosA.	.20
57 Ray Ferraro, LosA.	.20
58 Dimitri Khristich, LosA.	.20
59 Vitali Yachmenev, LosA.	.20
60 Valeri Bure, Mont.	.20
61 Vincent Damphousse, Mont.	.20
62 Saku Koivu, Mont.	.50
63 Mark Recchi, Mont.	.20
64 Martin Rucinsky, Mont.	.20
65 Jocelyn Thibault (G), Mont.	.20
66 Pierre Turgeon, Mont.	.20
67 Dave Andreychuk, NJer.	.20
68 Martin Brodeur (G), NJer.	1.00
69 Bill Guerin, NJer.	.20
70 Scott Niedermayer, NJer.	.20
71 Scott Stevens, NJer.	.20
72 Petr Sykora, NJer.	.20
73 Steve Thomas, NJer.	.20
74 Todd Bertuzzi, NYIs.	1.50
75 Travis Green, NYIs.	.20
76 Kenny Jönsson, NYIs.	.20
77 Zigmund Palffy, NYIs.	.20
78 Adam Graves, NYIs.	.20
79 Wayne Gretzky, NYRa.	3.00
80 Alexei Kovalev, NYRa.	.20
81 Brian Leetch, NYRa.	.20
82 Mark Messier, NYRa.	.50
83 Mike Richter (G), NYRa.	.20
84 Ulf Samuelsson, NYRa.	.20
85 Niklas Sundström, NYRa.	.20
86 Daniel Alfredsson, Otta.	.20
87 Radek Bonk, Otta.	.20
88 Alexandre Daigle, Otta.	.20
89 Steve Duchesne, Otta.	.20
90 Damian Rhodes (G), Otta.	.20
91 Alexei Yashin, Otta.	.20
92 Rod Brind'Amour, Phil.	.20
93 Éric Desjardins, Phil.	.20
94 Dale Hawerchuk, Phil.	.20
95 Ron Hextall (G), Phil.	.20
96 John LeClair, Phil.	.50
97 Eric Lindros, Phil.	.50
98 Mikael Renberg, Phil.	.20
99 Tom Barrasso (G), Pitt.	.20
100 Ron Francis, Pitt.	.20
101 Jaromir Jagr, Pitt.	.50
102 Mario Lemieux, Pitt.	2.00
103 Petr Nedved, Pitt.	.20
104 Bryan Smolinski, Pitt.	.20
105 Nikolai Khabibulin (G), Phoe.	.20
106 Teppo Numminen, Phoe.	.20
107 Keith Tkachuk, Phoe.	.20
108 Jeremy Roenick, Chic.	.50
109 Oleg Tverdovsky, Phoe.	.20
110 Shayne Corson, SLou.	.20
111 Geoff Courtnall, SLou.	.20
112 Grant Fuhr (G), SLou.	.20
113 Brett Hull, SLou.	.50
114 Al MacInnis, SLou.	.20
115 Chris Pronger, SLou.	.20
116 Jeff Friesen, SLou.	.20
117 Owen Nolan, SanJ.	.20
118 Marcus Ragnarsson, SanJ.	.20
119 Chris Terreri (G), SanJ.	.20
120 Brian Bradley, SanJ.	.20
121 Chris Gratton, Tamp.	.20
122 Roman Hamrlik, Tamp.	.20
123 Daren Puppa (G), Tamp.	.20
124 Alexander Selivanov, Tamp.	.20
125 Wendel Clark, Toro.	.50
126 Doug Gilmour, Toro.	.20
127 Kirk Muller, Toro.	.20
128 Larry Murphy, Toro.	.20
129 Félix Potvin (G), Toro.	.50
130 Mats Sundin, Toro.	.50
131 Pavel Bure, Vanc.	.50
132 Russ Courtnall, Vanc.	.20
133 Trevor Linden, Vanc.	.20
134 Kirk McLean (G), Vanc.	.20
135 Alexander Mogilny, Vanc.	.20
136 Peter Bondra, Wash.	.20
137 Jim Carey (G), Wash.	.20
138 Sylvain Côté, Wash.	.20
139 Sergei Gonchar, Wash.	.20
140 Phil Housley, Wash.	.20
141 Joe Juneau, Wash.	.20
142 Michal Pivonka, Wash.	.20
143 Brendan Witt, Wash.	.20
144 Nolan Baumgartner, Wash.	.20
145 Martin Biron (G), Buff.	.50
146 Jason Bonsignore, Edmo.	.20
147 Andrew Brunette, Wash. RC	**.50**
148 Jason Doig, Winn.	.20
149 Peter Ferraro, NYRa.	.20
150 Éric Fichaud (G), NYIs.	.20
151 Ladislav Kohn, Calg.	.20
152 Jamie Langenbrunner, Dall.	.20
153 Daymond Langkow, Tamp.	.20
154 Jay McKee, Buff. RC	**.50**
155 Marty Murray, Calg.	.20
156 Wayne Primeau, Buff.	.20
157 Jamie Pushor, Detr.	.20
158 Jamie Rivers, SLou.	.20
159 Jamie Storr (G), LosA.	.20
160 Steve Sullivan, NJer. RC	**1.50**
161 José Théodore (G), Mont.	1.50
162 Roman Vopat, LosA.	.20
163 Alexei Yegorov, SanJ. RC	**.50**
164 Daniel Alfredsson, Otta.	.20
165 Niklas Andersson, NYIs.	.20
166 Todd Bertuzzi, NYIs.	.50
167 Valeri Bure, Mont.	.20
168 Eric Dazé, Chic.	.20
169 Saku Koivu, Mont.	.50
170 Miroslav Satan, Edmo.	.20
171 Petr Sykora, NJer.	.20
172 Cory Stillman, NJer.	.20
173 Vitali Yachmenev, LosA.	.20
174 Checklist (1 - 121)	.20
175 Checklist (120 -/ inserts)	.20

BLADERUNNERS

Insert Set (25 cards):	30.00
Insert (1:3)	BR
1 Brian Bradley, Tamp.	1.00
2 Chris Chelios, Chic.	2.00
3 Peter Forsberg, Colo.	5.00
4 Ron Francis, Pitt.	2.00
5 Mike Gartner, Toro.	3.00
6 Doug Gilmour, Toro.	2.00
7 Phil Housley, NJer.	1.00
8 Brett Hull, SLou.	4.00
9 Valeri Kamensky, Colo.	1.00
10 Pat LaFontaine, Buff.	2.00
11 John LeClair, Phil.	3.00
12 Claude Lemieux, Colo.	1.00
13 Nicklas Lidström, Detr.	2.00
14 Mark Messier, NYRa.	4.00
15 Alexander Mogilny, Vanc.	1.50
16 Petr Nedved, Pitt.	1.00
17 Adam Oates, Bost.	1.50
18 Zigmund Palffy, NYIs.	2.00
19 Jeremy Roenick, Chic.	3.00
20 Teemu Selänne, Anah.	3.00
21 Brendan Shanahan, Hart.	4.00
22 Keith Tkachuk, Phoe.	2.00
23 Pierre Turgeon, Mont.	1.50
24 Doug Weight, Edmo.	2.00
25 Steve Yzerman, Detr.	9.00

COUNTDOWN TO IMPACT

Insert Set (10 cards):	210.00
Insert (1:30)	CTI
1 Pavel Bure, Vanc.	10.00
2 Sergei Fedorov, Detr.	15.00
3 Wayne Gretzky, NYRa.	60.00
4 Jaromir Jagr, Pitt.	15.00
5 Ed Jovanovski, Flor.	6.00
6 Paul Kariya, Anah.	20.00
7 Mario Lemieux, Pitt.	45.00
8 Eric Lindros, Phil.	15.00
9 Patrick Roy (G), Colo.	45.00
10 Joe Sakic, Colo.	20.00

NHL ON FOX

Insert Set (20 cards):	85.00
Insert (1:10)	Fox
1 Daniel Alfredsson, Otta.	6.00
2 Todd Bertuzzi, NYIs.	18.00
3 Raymond Bourque, Bost.	12.00
4 Valeri Bure, Mont.	3.00
5 Chris Chelios, Chic.	6.00
6 Paul Coffey, Detr.	6.00
7 Éric Dazé, Chic.	4.00
8 Éric Desjardins, Phil.	3.00
9 Sergei Gonchar, Wash.	3.00
10 Phil Housley, NJer.	3.00
11 Ed Jovanovski, Flor.	4.00
12 Vladimir Konstantinov, Detr.	3.00
13 Saku Koivu, Mont.	8.00

☐ 14 Brian Leetch, NYRa. 6.00
☐ 15 Larry Murphy, Toro. 3.00
☐ 16 Teppo Numminen, Phoe. 3.00
☐ 17 Sandis Ozolinsh, Colo. 3.00
☐ 18 Marcus Ragnarsson, SanJ. 3.00
☐ 19 Petr' Sykora, NJer. 4.00
☐ 20 Vitali Yachmenev, LosA. 3.00

VERSA TEAM

Insert Set (10 cards): 275.00
Insert (1:120) VT
☐ 1 Pavel Bure, Vanc. 15.00
☐ 2 Sergei Fedorov, Detr. 20.00
☐ 3 Peter Forsberg, Colo. 30.00
☐ 4 Wayne Gretzky, NYRa. 90.00

☐ 5 Jaromir Jagr, Pitt. 20.00
☐ 6 Paul Kariya, Anah. 30.00
☐ 7 Mario Lemieux, Pitt. 65.00
☐ 8 Eric Lindros, Phil. 20.00
☐ 9 Joe Sakic, Colo. 35.00
☐ 10 Teemu Selänne, Anah. 15.00

ZERO HEROES

Insert Set (10 cards): 95.00
Insert (1:30) ZH
☐ 1 Ed Belfour (G), Chic. 14.00
☐ 2 Sean Burke, Hart. 8.00
☐ 3 Jim Carey (G), Wash. 8.00
☐ 4 Dominik Hasek (G), Buff. 14.00
☐ 5 Ron Hextall (G), Phil. 8.00
☐ 6 Chris Osgood (G), Detr. 8.00
☐ 7 Félix Potvin (G), Toro. 8.00
☐ 8 Daren Puppa (G), Tamp. 8.00
☐ 9 Patrick Roy (G), Colo. 45.00
☐ 10 John Vanbiesbrouck (G), Flor. 8.00

1996 - 97 SP

Complete Set (188 cards): 65.00
Common Player: .25
Player SP
☐ 1 Paul Kariya, Anah. 1.50
☐ 2 Teemu Selänne, Anah. 1.00
☐ 3 Jari Kurri, Anah. 1.00
☐ 4 Darren Van Impe, Anah. .25
☐ 5 Guy Hebert, Anah. .25
☐ 6 Steve Rucchin, Anah. .25
☐ 7 Raymond Bourque, Bost. 1.50
☐ 8 Kyle McLaren, Bost. .25
☐ 9 Bill Ranford (G), Bost. .50
☐ 10 Don Sweeney, Bost. .25
☐ 11 Adam Oates, Bost. .50
☐ 12 Rick Tocchet, Bost. .25
☐ 13 Ted Donato, Bost. .25
☐ 14 Curtis Brown, Buff. .25
☐ 15 Pat LaFontaine, Buff. .50
☐ 16 Derek Plante, Buff. .25
☐ 17 Dominik Hasek (G), Buff. 1.00
☐ 18 Brian Holzinger, Buff. .25
☐ 19 Alexei Zhitnik, Buff. .25
☐ 20 Theoren Fleury, Calg. .50
☐ 21 Trevor Kidd (G), Calg. .25
☐ 22 Steve Chiasson, Calg. .25
☐ 23 Jarome Iginla, Calg. 2.00
☐ 24 German Titov, Calg. .25
☐ 25 Zarley Zalapski, Calg. .25
☐ 26 Eric Dazé, Chic. .50
☐ 27 Chris Chelios, Chic. .50
☐ 28 Ed Belfour (G), Chic. 1.00
☐ 29 Gary Suter, Chic. .25
☐ 30 Alexei Zhamnov, Chic. .25
☐ 31 Ethan Moreau, Chic. .25
☐ 32 Tony Amonte, Chic. .50
☐ 33 Peter Forsberg, Colo. 1.50
☐ 34 Joe Sakic, Colo. 2.00
☐ 35 Patrick Roy (G), Colo. 3.50
☐ 36 Adam Deadmarsh, Colo. .25
☐ 37 Mike Ricci, Colo. .25
☐ 38 Adam Foote, Colo. .25
☐ 39 Claude Lemieux, Colo. .25
☐ 40 Mike Modano, Dall. 1.00
☐ 41 Pat Verbeek, Dall. .25
☐ 42 Todd Harvey, Dall. .25
☐ 43 Sergei Zubov, Dall. .25
☐ 44 Andy Moog (G), Dall. .50
☐ 45 Derian Hatcher, Dall. .25
☐ 46 Jamie Langenbrunner, Dall. .25
☐ 47 Steve Yzerman, Detr. 3.00
☐ 48 Sergei Fedorov, Detr. 1.00
☐ 49 Vyacheslav Kozlov, Detr. .25
☐ 50 Brendan Shanahan, Detr. 1.00
☐ 51 Chris Osgood (G), Detr. .50
☐ 52 Nicklas Lidström, Detr. .50
☐ 53 Vladimir Konstantinov, Detr. .25
☐ 54 Curtis Joseph (G), Edmo. 1.00
☐ 55 Jason Arnott, Edmo. .50
☐ 56 Ryan Smyth, Edmo. .50
☐ 57 Doug Weight, Edmo. .50
☐ 58 Andrei Kovalenko, Edmo. .25
☐ 59 Mariusz Czerkawski, Edmo. .25
☐ 60 Ed Jovanovski, Flor. .50
☐ 61 John Vanbiesbrouck (G), Flor. .50
☐ 62 Rob Niedermayer, Flor. .25
☐ 63 Robert Svehla, Flor. .25
☐ 64 Brian Skrudland, Flor. .25
☐ 65 Scott Mellanby, Flor. .25
☐ 66 Ray Sheppard, Flor. .25
☐ 67 Jeff O'Neill, Hart. .50
☐ 68 Keith Primeau, Hart. .50
☐ 69 Geoff Sanderson, Hart. .25
☐ 70 Sean Burke, Hart. .50
☐ 71 Kevin Dineen, Hart. .25
☐ 72 Andrew Cassels, Hart. .25
☐ 73 Kevin Stevens, LosA. .25
☐ 74 Rob Blake, LosA. .50
☐ 75 Ed Olczyk, LosA. .25
☐ 76 Mattias Norstrom, LosA. .25
☐ 77 Stéphane Fiset (G), LosA. .25
☐ 78 Vitali Yachmenev, LosA. .25
☐ 79 Saku Koivu, Mont. 1.00
☐ 80 Valeri Bure, Mont. .25
☐ 81 Jocelyn Thibault (G), Mont. .50
☐ 82 David Wilkie, Mont. .25
☐ 83 Stéphane Richer, Mont. .25
☐ 84 Shayne Corson, Mont. .25
☐ 85 Mark Recchi, Mont. .50
☐ 86 Martin Brodeur (G), NJer. 2.00
☐ 87 Bobby Holik, NJer. .25
☐ 88 Petr Sykora, NJer. .50
☐ 89 Scott Stevens, NJer. .50
☐ 90 Scott Niedermayer, NJer. .25
☐ 91 Bill Guerin, NJer. .50
☐ 92 Éric Fichaud (G), NYIs. .25
☐ 93 Kenny Jönsson, NYIs. .25
☐ 94 Travis Green, NYIs. .25
☐ 95 Derek King, NYIs. .25
☐ 96 Todd Bertuzzi, NYIs. 3.00
☐ 97 Zigmund Palffy, NYIs. .50
☐ 98 Mark Messier, NYRa. 1.00
☐ 99 Wayne Gretzky, NYRa. 5.00
☐ 100 Mike Richter (G), NYRa. .50
☐ 101 Brian Leetch, NYRa. .50
☐ 102 Luc Robitaille, NYRa. 1.00
☐ 103 Adam Graves, NYRa. .50
☐ 104 Alexei Kovalev, NYRa. .50
☐ 105 Radek Bonk, Otta. .25
☐ 106 Alexandre Daigle, Otta. .25
☐ 107 Daniel Alfredsson, Otta. .50
☐ 108 Alexei Yashin, Otta. .50
☐ **109 Andreas Dackell, Otta. RC 1.00**
☐ 110 Damian Rhodes (G), Otta. .25
☐ 111 Petr Svoboda, Phil. .25
☐ 112 John LeClair, Phil. 1.00
☐ 113 Éric Desjardins, Phil. .25
☐ 114 Eric Lindros, Phil. 1.00
☐ 115 Mikael Renberg, Phil. .25
☐ 116 Ron Hextall (G), Phil. .50
☐ **117 Danius Zubrus, Phil. RC 2.00**
☐ 118 Keith Tkachuk, Phoe. .50
☐ 119 Jeremy Roenick, Phoe. 1.00
☐ 120 Nikolai Khabibulin (G), Phoe. .50
☐ 121 Oleg Tverdovsky, Phoe. .25
☐ 122 Teppo Numminen, Phoe. .25
☐ 123 Mike Gartner, Phoe. 1.00
☐ 124 Cliff Ronning, Phoe. .25
☐ 125 Mario Lemieux, Pitt. 3.50
☐ 126 Jaromir Jagr, Pitt. 1.00
☐ 127 Ron Francis, Pitt. .50
☐ 128 Petr Nedved, Pitt. .25
☐ 129 Darius Kasparaitis, Pitt. .25
☐ 130 Kevin Hatcher, Pitt. .25
☐ 131 Joe Mullen, Pitt. .50
☐ 132 Joe Murphy, SLou. .25
☐ 133 Grant Fuhr (G), SLou. .50
☐ **134 Harry York, SLou. RC 1.00**
☐ 135 Chris Pronger, SLou. .50
☐ 136 Brett Hull, SLou. 1.00
☐ 137 Pierre Turgeon, SLou. .50
☐ 138 Owen Nolan, SanJ. .50
☐ 139 Bernie Nicholls, SanJ. .25
☐ 140 Tony Granato, SanJ. .25
☐ 141 Kelly Hrudey, SanJ. .25
☐ 142 Darren Turcotte, SanJ. .25
☐ 143 Jeff Friesen, SanJ. .25
☐ 144 Roman Hamrlik, Tamp. .25
☐ 145 Chris Gratton, Tamp. .25
☐ 146 Daymond Langkow, Tamp. .25
☐ 147 Dino Ciccarelli, Tamp. .25
☐ 148 Alexander Selivanov, Tamp. .25
☐ 149 Brian Bradley, Tamp. .25
☐ 150 Wendel Clark, Toro. 1.00
☐ 151 Mats Sundin, Toro. 1.00
☐ 152 Doug Gilmour, Toro. .50
☐ 153 Félix Potvin (G), Toro. .50
☐ 154 Larry Murphy, Toro. .25
☐ 155 Mathieu Schneider, Toro. .25
☐ 156 Kirk Muller, Toro. .25
☐ 157 Pavel Bure, Vanc. 1.00
☐ 158 Alexander Mogilny, Vanc. .50
☐ 159 Corey Hirsch (G), Vanc. .25
☐ 160 Jyrki Lumme, Vanc. .25
☐ 161 Russ Courtnall, Vanc. .25
☐ **162 Mike Fountain (G), Vanc. RC 1.00**
☐ 163 Peter Bondra, Wash. .50
☐ 164 Jim Carey (G), Wash. .25
☐ 165 Sergei Gonchar, Wash. .25
☐ 166 Joé Juneau, Wash. .25
☐ 167 Phil Housley, Wash. .25
☐ 168 Jason Allison, Wash. .50
☐ **169 Ruslan Salei, Anah. 1.00**
☐ **170 Mattias Timander, Bost. RC 1.00**
☐ **171 Vaclav Varada, Buff. RC 1.50**
☐ 172 Jonas Höglund, Calg. .25
☐ 173 Jason Podollan, Flor. .25
☐ 174 José Théodore (G), Mont. 3.00
☐ **175 Roman Turek (G), Dall. RC 6.50**
☐ 176 Anders Eriksson, Detr. .25
☐ **177 Mike Grier, Edmo. RC 2.00**
☐ **178 Rem Murray, Edmo. RC 1.00**
☐ **179 Per Gustafsson, Flor. 1.00**
☐ 180 Jay Pandolfo, NJer., Error (/b: Patrik Elias) 2.00
☐ **181 Kai Nurminen, LosA. RC 1.00**
☐ 182 Bryan Berard, NYIs. .50
☐ 183 Christian Dubé, NYRa. .25
☐ 184 Daniel Goneau, NYRa. .50
☐ 185 Wade Redden, Otta. .50
☐ 186 Janne Niinimaa, Phil. .50
☐ 187 Jim Campbell, SLou. .25
☐ **188 Sergei Berezin, Toro. RC 2.00**
Sample Promo
☐ Wayne Gretzky Promo 10.00

CLEARCUT WINNER

Insert Set (20 cards): 615.00
Insert (1:91) CW
☐ CW1 Wayne Gretzky, NYRa. 120.00
☐ CW2 Saku Koivu, Mont. 20.00
☐ CW3 Mario Lemieux, Pitt. 90.00
☐ CW4 Sergei Fedorov, Detr. 30.00
☐ CW5 Paul Kariya, Anah. 40.00
☐ CW6 Patrick Roy (G), Colo. 90.00
☐ CW7 Jeremy Roenick, Phoe. 20.00
☐ CW8 Brendan Shanahan, Detr. 30.00
☐ CW9 John Vanbiesbrouck (G), Flor. 10.00
☐ CW10 Doug Weight, Edmo. 15.00
☐ CW11 Mark Messier, NYRa. 30.00
☐ CW12 Mats Sundin, Toro. 30.00
☐ CW13 Paul Coffey, Phil. 15.00
☐ CW14 Theoren Fleury, Calg. 15.00
☐ CW15 Steve Yzerman, Detr. 70.00
☐ CW16 Pavel Bure, Vanc. 20.00
☐ CW17 Adam Deadmarsh, Colo. 10.00
☐ CW18 Chris Chelios, Chic. 15.00
☐ CW19 Joe Sakic, Colo. 45.00
☐ CW20 Eric Dazé, Chic. 10.00

GAME FILM

Insert Set (20 cards): 300.00
Insert (1:30) GF
☐ GF1 Wayne Gretzky, NYRa. 60.00
☐ GF2 Peter Forsberg, Colo. 20.00
☐ GF3 Patrick Roy (G), Colo. 45.00

☐ GF4 Brett Hull, SLou. 15.00
☐ GF5 Keith Tkachuk, Phoe. 5.00
☐ GF6 Eric Lindros, Phil. 15.00
☐ GF7 Félix Potvin (G), Toro. 5.00
☐ GF8 John Vanbiesbrouck (G), Flor. 5.00
☐ GF9 Paul Kariya, Anah. 20.00
☐ GF10 Mark Messier, NYRa. 15.00
☐ GF11 Ed Belfour (G), Chic. 15.00
☐ GF12 Alexander Mogilny, Vanc. 5.00
☐ GF13 Jim Carey (G), Wash. 5.00
☐ GF14 Ed Jovanovski, Flor. 5.00
☐ GF15 Theoren Fleury, Calg. 5.00
☐ GF16 Doug Gilmour, Toro. 5.00
☐ GF17 John LeClair, Phil. 10.00
☐ GF18 Pat LaFontaine, Buff. 5.00
☐ GF19 Paul Coffey, Hart. 5.00
☐ GF20 Daniel Alfredsson, Otta. 5.00

HOLOVIEW COLLECTION

Insert Set (30 cards): 85.00
Insert (1:9) HC
☐ HC1 Wayne Gretzky, NYRa. 30.00
☐ HC2 Eric Dazé, Chic. 2.00
☐ HC3 Doug Gilmour, Toro. 4.00
☐ HC4 Jason Arnott, Edmo. 2.00
☐ HC5 Sergei Fedorov, Detr. 6.00
☐ HC6 Chris Chelios, Chic. 4.00
☐ HC7 Alexei Kovalev, NYRa. 4.00
☐ HC8 Pat LaFontaine, Buff. 4.00
☐ HC9 Daniel Alfredsson, Otta. 4.00
☐ HC10 Chris Pronger, SLou. 4.00
☐ HC11 Jocelyn Thibault (G), Mont. 2.00
☐ HC12 Chris Gratton, Tamp. 2.00
☐ HC13 Alexei Yashin, Otta. 4.00
☐ HC14 Peter Bondra, Wash. 4.00
☐ HC15 Saku Koivu, Mont. 6.00
☐ HC16 Valeri Bure, Mont. 2.00
☐ HC17 Joé Juneau, Wash. 2.00
☐ HC18 Tony Amonte, Chic. 4.00
☐ HC19 Brian Holzinger, Buff. 2.00
☐ HC20 Mats Sundin, Toro. 6.00
☐ HC21 Chris Osgood (G), Detr. 4.00
☐ HC22 Roman Hamrlik, Tamp. 2.00
☐ HC23 Raymond Bourque, Bost. 8.00
☐ HC24 Doug Weight, Edmo. 4.00
☐ HC25 Mike Modano, Dall. 6.00
☐ HC26 Niklas Sundström, NYRa. 2.00
☐ HC27 Mike Richter (G), NYRa. 2.00
☐ HC28 Zigmund Palffy, NYIs. 4.00
☐ HC29 Adam Oates, Bost. 2.00
☐ HC30 Dominik Hasek (G), Buff. 6.00

INSIDE INFO

Insert Set (8 cards): 450.00 65.00
Inserts Gold Info
☐☐ Raymond Bourque, Bost. 50.00 5.00
☐☐ Wayne Gretzky, NYRa. 180.00 30.00
☐☐ Félix Potvin (G), Toro. 25.00 5.00
☐☐ Joe Sakic, Colo. 70.00 10.00
☐☐ Teemu Selänne, Anah. 35.00 5.00
☐☐ Brendan Shanahan, Detr. 45.00 5.00
☐☐ Keith Tkachuk, Phoe. 25.00 5.00
☐☐ Steve Yzerman, Detr. 100.00 15.00

SP^X FORCE

Insert Set (5 cards): 2175.00
Insert (1:360) SPxF
☐ 1 Forsberg / Lindros / Gretzky / Lemieux 115.00
☐ 2 P. Bure / Br. Hull / J. Jagr / T. Selänne 45.00
☐ 3 Hasek / Brodeur / Richter / Osgood (G) 45.00
☐ 4 Berard / Berezin / Eriksson / Iginla 30.00
☐ 5 M. Brodeur / J. Iginla / J. Jagr / W. Gretzky 90.00

SP^X FORCE SIGNED

Insert Set (4 cards): 925.00
Insert (#/100) Auto.
☐ 5 Martin Brodeur (G), NJer. ✍ 150.00
☐ 5 Wayne Gretzky, NYRa. ✍ 650.00
☐ 5 Jarome Iginla, Calg. ✍ 100.00
☐ 5 Jaromir Jagr, Pitt. ✍ 200.00

1996 - 97 SP – BUYBACKS

Buyback Autograph SP
☐ 40 Mike Modano, Dall. ✍ {#/5}
☐ 48 Steve Yzerman, Detr. ✍ {#/21}
☐ 48 Steve Yzerman, Detr. ✍ {#/9}
☐ 52 Nicklas Lidström, Detr. ✍ {#/14}
☐ 54 Curtis Joseph (G), Edmo. ✍ {#/29}
☐ 86 Martin Brodeur (G), NJer. ✍ {#/21}
☐ 97 Zigmund Palffy, NYIs. ✍ {#/36}
☐ 98 Mark Messier, NYRa. ✍ {#/3}
☐ 99 Wayne Gretzky, NYRa. ✍ {#/13}
☐ 99 Wayne Gretzky, NYRa. ✍ {#/2}
☐ 100 Mike Richter, NYRa. ✍ {#/21}
☐ 112 John LeClair, Phil. ✍ {#/138}
☐ 112 John LeClair, Phil. ✍ {#/14}
☐ 119 Jeremy Roenick, Phoe. ✍ {#/32}
☐ 125 Mario Lemieux, Pitt. ✍ {#/1}
☐ 153 Félix Potvin (G), Toro. ✍ {#/2}
☐ 157 Pavel Bure, Vanc. ✍ {#/16}
☐ 157 Pavel Bure, Vanc. ✍ {#/16}

1996 - 97 SP^X

There are two versions: the regular card (white lettering on back) and a gold parallel (black lettering on back).

Complete Set (50 cards): 200.00 65.00
Common Player: 3.00 1.00
Player
☐☐ 1 Paul Kariya, Anah. 12.00 4.00
☐☐ 2 Teemu Selänne, Anah. 6.00 2.00
☐☐ 3 Raymond Bourque, Bost. 10.00 3.50
☐☐ 4 Cam Neely, Bost. 8.00 3.00
☐☐ 5 Theoren Fleury, Calg. 4.00 1.50
☐☐ 6 Chris Chelios, Chic. 5.00 1.50
☐☐ 7 Jeremy Roenick, Chic. 7.00 2.00
☐☐ 8 Peter Forsberg, Colo. 12.00 4.00
☐☐ 9 Joe Sakic, Colo. 14.00 4.50
☐☐ 10 Patrick Roy (G), Colo. 25.00 5.00
☐☐ 11 Mike Modano, Dall. 8.00 3.00
☐☐ 12 Joe Nieuwendyk, Dall. 3.00 1.00
☐☐ 13 Sergei Fedorov, Detr. 8.00 3.00
☐☐ 14 Steve Yzerman, Detr. 20.00 7.00
☐☐ 15 Paul Coffey, Detr. 5.00 1.50
☐☐ 16 Chris Osgood (G), Detr. 5.00 1.50
☐☐ 17 Doug Weight, Edmo. 5.00 1.50
☐☐ 18 Pat LaFontaine, Buff. 5.00 1.50
☐☐ 19 Brendan Shanahan, Hart. 8.00 3.00
☐☐ 20 Vitali Yachmenev, LosA. 3.00 1.00
☐☐ 21 Saku Koivu, Mont. 7.00 2.00
☐☐ 22 Pierre Turgeon, Mont. 3.00 1.00
☐☐ 23 Petr' Sykora, NJer. 3.00 1.00
☐☐ 24 Scott Stevens, NJer. 3.00 1.00
☐☐ 25 Martin Brodeur (G), NJer. 14.00 4.50
☐☐ 26 Brian Leetch, NYRa. 5.00 1.50
☐☐ 27 Mark Messier, NYRa. 8.00 3.00
☐☐ 28 Mike Richter (G), NYRa. 4.00 1.00
☐☐ 29 Zigmund Palffy, NYIs. 5.00 1.50
☐☐ 30 Todd Bertuzzi, NYIs. 15.00 7.00
☐☐ 31 Alexei Yashin, Otta. [b/ white text] 5.00 1.50
☐☐ 32 D. Alfredsson, Otta. [b/ white text] 5.00 1.50
☐☐ 33 Eric Lindros, Phil. 8.00 3.00
☐☐ 34 John LeClair, Phil. 6.00 2.00
☐☐ 35 Keith Tkachuk, Winn. 5.00 1.50
☐☐ 36 Alexei Zhamnov, Winn. 3.00 1.00
☐☐ 37 Mario Lemieux, Pitt. 25.00 5.00
☐☐ 38 Jaromir Jagr, Pitt. 8.00 3.00
☐☐ 39 Wayne Gretzky, NYRa. 35.00 10.00
☐☐ 40 Brett Hull, SLou. 8.00 3.00
☐☐ 41 Owen Nolan, SanJ. 5.00 1.50
☐☐ 42 Roman Hamrlik, Tamp. 3.00 1.00
☐☐ 43 Mats Sundin, Toro. 8.00 3.00
☐☐ 44 Félix Potvin (G), Toro. 5.00 1.50
☐☐ 45 Doug Gilmour, Toro. 5.00 1.50
☐☐ 46 Pavel Bure, Vanc. 6.00 2.00
☐☐ 47 Alexander Mogilny, Vanc. 4.00 1.00
☐☐ 48 Jim Carey (G), Wash. 3.00 1.00
☐☐ 49 Peter Bondra, Wash. 5.00 1.50
☐☐ 50 Éric Dazé, Chic. 3.00 1.00
Great Futures GF
☐ GF1 W. Gretzky / É. Dazé / V. Yachmenev / S. Koivu / D. Alfredsson 17.00

Tribute	Trib.
☐ GT1 Wayne Gretzky, Edmo.	20.00
☐ GT1 Wayne Gretzky, Edmo. ✍	250.00

HOLOVIEW HEROES

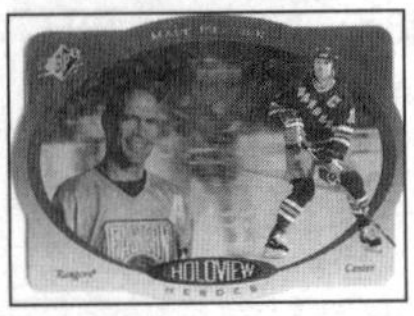

Insert Set (10 cards):	140.00
Insert (1:24)	HH
☐ HH1 Raymond Bourque, Bost.	10.00
☐ HH2 Patrick Roy (G), Colo.	30.00
☐ HH3 Steve Yzerman, Detr.	20.00
☐ HH4 Paul Coffey, Detr.	6.00
☐ HH5 Mark Messier, NYRa.	10.00
☐ HH6 Mario Lemieux, Pitt.	30.00
☐ HH7 Wayne Gretzky, NYRa.	40.00
☐ HH8 Brett Hull, SLou.	10.00
☐ HH9 Doug Gilmour, Toro.	6.00
☐ HH10 Grant Fuhr, SLou.	6.00

1996 - 97 SPORTS ILLUSTRATED FOR KIDS

These cards were distributed as part of nine-card perforated sheets included in *Sports Illustrated for Kids*. While these cards were intended for editorial purposes, they have made their way onto the secondary market. Cards issued in the 12 issues between June 1996 and June 1997 were numbered 487-594.

1996-97 Sports Illustrated for Kids	
☐ Aug. 1996 • 499 Joe Sakic, Colo.	3.00
☐ Nov. 1996 • 527 Cammi Granato, U.S.A.	3.00
☐ Dec. 1996 • 540 Ed Jovanovski, Flor.	1.00
☐ Jan. 1997 • 546 Daren Puppa (G), Tamp.	1.00
☐ Jan. 1997 • 547 Wayne Gretzky, NYRa.	8.00
☐ Feb. 1997 • 551 Erin Whitten (G), USA.	2.00
☐ Feb. 1997 • 557 Sergei Fedorov, Detr.	2.00
☐ Mar. 1997 • 559 Patrick Roy (G), Colo.	3.00
☐ May 1997 • 585 Chris Chelios, Chic.	2.00

1996 - 97 STARTING LINEUP

One SkyBox Impact card (1995 - 96 design) was packaged with each figure.

Complete Set (24 cards):	30.00
Player	Card
☐ 530440 Paul Kariya, Anah.	2.50
☐ Tom Barrasso (G), Pitt.	1.00
☐ Brian Bradley, Tamp.	1.00
☐ Jim Carey (G), Wash.	1.00
☐ Paul Coffey, Detr.	1.00
☐ Sergei Fedorov, Detr.	2.00
☐ Ron Francis, Pitt.	1.00
☐ Dominik Hasek (G), Buff.	2.00
☐ Pat LaFontaine, Buff.	1.00
☐ John LeClair, Phil.	1.50
☐ Brian Leetch, NYRa.	1.00
☐ Eric Lindros, Phil.	2.00
☐ Al MacInnis, SLou.	1.00
☐ Scott Mellanby, Flor.	1.00
☐ Mark Messier, NYRa.	2.00
☐ Mike Modano, Dall.	2.00
☐ Adam Oates, Wash.	1.00
☐ Mikael Renberg, Phil.	1.00
☐ Stéphane J.J. Richer, NJer.	1.00
☐ Jeremy Roenick, Phoe.	1.50
☐ Patrick Roy (G), Colo.	6.00
☐ Joe Sakic, Colo.	3.00
☐ Brendan Shanahan, Detr.	2.00
☐ Mats Sundin, Toro.	2.00

FIGURES

Figures were available in American (English text) and Canadian (bilingual text) packaging. The figures and cards in each type of package are the same. Priced below are retail selling prices for packaged figures (each package includes one card) and loose figures.

	US	CAN	Loose
Canadian Set (15 packages):	-	160.00	-
American Set (24 packages):	250.00	-	-
Figure Set (21 loose figures):	-	-	50.00
Player	US	CAN	Loose
☐ Tom Barrasso (G), Pitt.	30.00	-	5.00
☐ Brian Bradley, Tamp.	12.00	12.00	3.00
☐ Jim Carey (G), Wash.	20.00	20.00	5.00
☐ Paul Coffey, Detr.	20.00	-	4.00
☐ Sergei Fedorov, Detr.	12.00	12.00	3.00
☐ Ron Francis, Pitt.	12.00	12.00	3.00
☐ Dominik Hasek (G), Buff.	35.00	-	6.00
☐ Paul Kariya, Anah.	30.00	30.00	5.00
☐ Pat LaFontaine, Buff.	20.00	-	4.00
☐ John LeClair, Phil.	18.00	18.00	4.00
☐ Brian Leetch, NYRa.	12.00	12.00	3.00
☐ Eric Lindros, Phil.	18.00	18.00	4.00
☐ Al MacInnis, SLou.	12.00	12.00	3.00
☐ Scott Mellanby, Flor.	12.00	12.00	3.00
☐ Mark Messier, NYRa.	18.00	18.00	4.00
☐ Mike Modano, Dall.	12.00	-	3.00
☐ Adam Oates, Wash.	12.00	-	3.00
☐ Mikael Renberg, Phil.	12.00	12.00	3.00
☐ Stéphane J.J. Richer, NJer.	12.00	-	3.00
☐ Jeremy Roenick, Phoe.	12.00	-	3.00
☐ Patrick Roy (G), Colo.	75.00	75.00	10.00
☐ Joe Sakic, Colo.	20.00	20.00	5.00
☐ Brendan Shanahan, Detr.	15.00	-	3.00
☐ Mats Sundin, Toro.	12.00	12.00	3.00

1996 - 97 STARTING LINEUP TIMELESS LEGENDS

One card was packaged with each figure. There are just the two hockey figures in this multi-sport set.

Player	Card
☐ Tony Esposito (G), Chic.	2.00
☐ Maurice Richard, Mont.	5.00

FIGURES

Player	Pack.	Loose
☐ Tony Esposito (G), Chic.	15.00	3.00
☐ Maurice Richard, Mont.	25.00	5.00

1996 - 97 TEAM OUT!

Complete Set (89 cards):	25.00
Player	TO
☐ Daniel Alfredsson, Otta.	.50
☐ Jason Arnott, Edmo.	.50
☐ Ed Belfour (G), Chic.	1.00
☐ Rob Blake, LosA.	.50
☐ Peter Bondra, Wash.	.50
☐ Raymond Bourque, Bost.	1.50
☐ Martin Brodeur (G), NJer.	2.00
☐ Jeff Brown, Hart.	.20
☐ Pavel Bure, Vanc.	1.00
☐ Jim Carey (G), Wash.	.20
☐ Chris Chelios, Chic.	.50
☐ Paul Coffey, Hart.	.50
☐ Shayne Corson, SLou.	.20
☐ Murray Craven, Chic.	.20
☐ Eric Dazé, Chic.	.50
☐ Éric Desjardins, Phil.	.20
☐ Steve Duchesne, Otta.	.20
☐ Sergei Fedorov, Detr.	1.00
☐ Theoren Fleury, Calg.	.50
☐ Peter Forsberg, Colo.	1.50
☐ Grant Fuhr (G), SLou.	.50
☐ Mike Gartner, Phoe.	1.00
☐ Sergei Gonchar, Wash.	.20
☐ Chris Gratton, Tamp.	.20
☐ Adam Graves, NYRa.	.50
☐ Wayne Gretzky, NYRa.	5.00
☐ Roman Hamrlik, Tamp.	.20
☐ Dominik Hasek (G), Buff.	1.00
☐ Derian Hatcher, Dall.	.20
☐ Guy Hebert (G), Anah.	.20
☐ Ron Hextall (G), Phil.	.50
☐ Brett Hull, SLou.	1.00
☐ Jaromir Jagr, Pitt.	1.00
☐ Ed Jovanovski, Flor.	.50
☐ Joé Juneau, Wash.	.20
☐ Paul Kariya, Anah.	1.50
☐ Darius Kasparaitis, NYIs.	.20
☐ Nikolai Khabibulin (G), Phoe.	.50
☐ Trevor Kidd (G), Calg.	.20
☐ Saku Koivu, Mont.	1.00
☐ Vyacheslav Kozlov, Detr.	.20
☐ John LeClair, Phil.	1.00
☐ Brian Leetch, NYRa.	.50
☐ Mario Lemieux, Pitt.	.20
☐ Claude Lemieux, Colo.	3.50
☐ Nicklas Lidström, Detr.	.50
☐ Eric Lindros, Phi.	1.00
☐ Jyrki Lumme, Vanc.	.20
☐ Al MacInnis, SLou.	.50
☐ Vladimir Malakhov, Mtl,	.20
☐ Kirk McLean (G), Vanc.	.20
☐ Scott Mellanby, Flor.	.20
☐ Mark Messier, NYRa.	1.00
☐ Mike Modano, Dall.	1.00
☐ Alexander Mogilny, Vanc.	.50
☐ Larry Murphy, Toro.	.20
☐ Scott Niedermayer, NJer.	.20
☐ Owen Nolan, SanJ.	.50
☐ Adam Oates, Bost.	.50
☐ Chris Osgood (G), Detr.	.50
☐ Sandis Ozolinsh, Colo.	.20
☐ Zigmund Palffy, NYIs.	.50
☐ Félix Potvin (G), Toro.	.50
☐ Stéphane Quintal, Mont.	.20
☐ Marcus Ragnarsson, SanJ.	.20
☐ Mikael Renberg, Phil.	.20
☐ Stéphane Richer, Toro.	.20
☐ Mike Richter (G), NYRa.	.50
☐ Luc Robitaille, NYRa.	1.00
☐ Patrick Roy (G), Colo.	3.50
☐ Joe Sakic, Colo.	2.00
☐ Mathieu Schneider, Toro.	.20
☐ Teemu Selänne, Anah.	1.00
☐ Ryan Smyth, Edmo.	.50
☐ Scott Stevens, NJer.	.20
☐ Keven Stevens, LosA.	.50
☐ Mats Sundin, Toro.	1.00
☐ Gary Suter, Chic.	.20
☐ Robert Svehla, Flor.	.20
☐ Esa Tikkanen, Vanc.	.20
☐ Keith Tkachuk, Phoe.	.50
☐ Rick Tocchet, Bost.	.20
☐ Pierre Turgeon, Mont.	.50
☐ John Vanbiesbrouck (G), Flor.	.50
☐ Glen Wesley, Hart.	.20
☐ Alexei Yashin, Otta.	.50
☐ Steve Yzerman, Detr.	3.00
☐ Zarley Zalapski, Calg.	.20
☐ Alexei Zhitnik, Buff.	.20

1996 - 97 TOPPS PICKS

There are two versions: the regular card and an O-Pee-Chee parallel. See Fleer NHL Picks for corresponding even numbers.

Complete Set (91 cards):	75.00	14.00
Common Player:	.20	.20
Player	OPC	TP
☐☐ 1 Jaromir Jagr, Pitt.	3.00	.50
☐☐ 3 Mario Lemieux, Pgh	10.00	1.50
☐☐ 5 Peter Forsberg, Colo.	5.00	.50
☐☐ 7 Teemu Selänne, Anah.	3.00	.50
☐☐ 9 Alexander Mogilny, Vanc.	1.00	.20
☐☐ 11 Patrick Roy (G), Colo.	10.00	1.50
☐☐ 13 Jim Carey (G), Wash.	.50	.20
☐☐ 15 Pavel Bure, Vanc.	3.00	.50
☐☐ 17 Sergei Fedorov, Detr.	3.00	.50
☐☐ 19 Chris Chelios, Chic.	2.00	.20
☐☐ 21 Sandis Ozolinsh, Colo.	.50	.20
☐☐ 23 Doug Weight, Edmo.	2.00	.20
☐☐ 25 Mark Messier, NYRa.	3.00	.50
☐☐ 27 Martin Brodeur (G), NJer.	6.00	1.00
☐☐ 29 Brett Hull, SLou.	3.00	.50
☐☐ 31 Steve Yzerman, Detr.	9.00	1.50
☐☐ 33 Kevin Hatcher, Dall.	.50	.20
☐☐ 35 Roman Hamrlik, Tamp.	.50	.20
☐☐ 37 Petr Nedved, Pitt.	1.00	.20
☐☐ 39 Valeri Kamensky, Colo. [w/ Cup]	2.00	.20
☐☐ 41 Gary Suter, Chic.	.50	.20
☐☐ 43 Mats Sundin, Toro.	3.00	.50
☐☐ 45 Trevor Linden, Vanc.	1.00	.20
☐☐ 47 Jeremy Roenick, Chic.	3.00	.50
☐☐ 49 Al MacInnis, SLou.	1.00	.20
☐☐ 51 Mike Modano, Dall.	3.00	.50
☐☐ 53 Mathieu Schneider, NYIs.	.50	.20
☐☐ 55 Michal Pivonka, Wash.	.50	.20
☐☐ 57 Owen Nolan, SanJ.	2.00	.20
☐☐ 59 Martin Rucinsky, Mont.	.50	.20
☐☐ 61 Joe Nieuwendyk, Dall.	1.00	.20
☐☐ 63 Mark Recchi, Mont.	1.00	.20
☐☐ 65 Geoff Sanderson, Hart.	.50	.20
☐☐ 67 Vyacheslav Koslov, Detr.	.50	.20
☐☐ 69 Pat Verbeek, NYRa.	1.00	.20
☐☐ 71 Brian Bradley, Tamp.	.50	.20
☐☐ 73 Steve Duchesne, Otta.	.50	.20
☐☐ 75 Steve Thomas, NJer.	.50	.20
☐☐ 77 Eric Dazé, Chic.	1.00	.20
☐☐ 79 Alexei Kovalev, NYRa.	2.00	.20
☐☐ 81 Kevin Stevens, LosA.	.50	.20
☐☐ 83 Curtis Joseph (G), Edmo.	3.00	.50
☐☐ 85 Bill Ranford (G), Bost.	1.00	.20
☐☐ 87 Luc Robitaille, NYRa.	3.00	.50
☐☐ 89 Claude Lemieux, Colo.	1.00	.20
☐☐ 91 Sergei Gonchar, Wash.	1.00	.20
☐☐ 93 Éric Desjardins, Phil.	1.00	.20
☐☐ 95 Garry Galley, Phil.	.50	.20
☐☐ 97 Oleg Tverdovsky, Winn.	.50	.20
☐☐ 99 Rob Niedermayer, Flor.	.50	.20
☐☐ 101 Scott Mellanby, Flor.	.50	.20
☐☐ 103 Adam Deadmarsh, Colo.	1.00	.20
☐☐ 105 Cliff Ronning, Vanc.	.50	.20
☐☐ 107 Russ Courtnall, Vanc.	.50	.20
☐☐ 109 Keith Primeau, Detr.	1.00	.20
☐☐ 111 Rick Tocchet, Bost.	1.00	.20
☐☐ 113 Scott Young, Colo.	1.00	.20
☐☐ 115 Scott Stevens, NJer.	1.00	.20
☐☐ 117 Al Iafrate, Bost.	.50	.20
☐☐ 119 Ray Ferraro, LosA.	.50	.20
☐☐ 121 Todd Bertuzzi, NYIs.	4.00	1.50
☐☐ 123 Alexander Selivanov, Tamp.	.50	.20
☐☐ 125 Steve Chiasson, Calg.	.50	.20
☐☐ 127 Dave Andreychuk, NJer.	1.00	.20
☐☐ 129 Ray Sheppard, Flor.	.50	.20
☐☐ 131 Bernie Nicholls, Chic.	.50	.20
☐☐ 133 Tony Amonte, Chic.	2.00	.20
☐☐ 135 Nelson Emerson, Hart.	.50	.20
☐☐ 137 Cam Neely, Bost.	3.00	.50
☐☐ 139 Shayne Corson, SLou.	1.00	.20
☐☐ 141 Bill Guerin, NJer.	1.00	.20
☐☐ 143 Joe Murphy, Chic.	.50	.20
☐☐ 145 Cory Stillman, Calg.	.50	.20
☐☐ 147 Radik Bonk, Otta.	1.00	.20
☐☐ 149 Geoff Courtnall, Stl	.50	.20
☐☐ 151 Chad Kilger, Winn.	.50	.20
☐☐ 153 Sylvain Côté, Wash.	.50	.20
☐☐ 155 Glen Wesley, Hart.	.50	.20
☐☐ 157 Jeff Norton, Edmo.	.50	.20
☐☐ 159 Rob Blake, LosA.	2.00	.20
☐☐ 161 Calle Johansson, Wash.	.50	.20
☐☐ 163 Uwe Krupp, Colo.	.50	.20
☐☐ 165 James Patrick, Calg.	.50	.20
☐☐ 167 Dimitri Mironov, Pitt.	.50	.20
☐☐ 169 Vladimir Konstantinov, Detr.	1.00	.20
☐☐ 171 Mattias Norstrom, NYRa.	.50	.20
☐☐ 173 David Wilkie, Mont.	.50	.20
☐☐ 175 Bryan McCabe, NYIs.	.50	.20
☐☐ 177 Barry Richter, NYRa. (Bost.)	.50	.20
☐☐ 179 Ed Belfour (G), Chic.	3.00	.50
☐☐ Checklist	.50	.20

FANTASY TEAM

Insert Set (22 cards):	155.00
Insert (1:24)	FT
☐ FT1 Patrick Roy (G), Colo.	20.00
☐ FT2 Chris Osgood (G), Detr.	4.00
☐ FT3 Martin Brodeur (G), NJer.	12.00
☐ FT4 Raymond Bourque, Bost.	8.00
☐ FT5 Brian Leetch, NYRa.	4.00
☐ FT6 Chris Chelios, Chic.	4.00
☐ FT7 Paul Coffey, Detr.	4.00
☐ FT8 Ed Jovanovski, Flor.	2.00
☐ FT9 Roman Hamrlik, Tamp.	2.00
☐ FT10 Wayne Gretzky, NYRa.	30.00
☐ FT11 Paul Kariya, Anah.	10.00
☐ FT12 Brett Hull, SLou.	6.00
☐ FT13 Pavel Bure, Vanc.	6.00
☐ FT14 Jaromir Jagr, Pitt.	6.00
☐ FT15 Mario Lemieux, Pitt.	20.00
☐ FT16 Peter Forsberg, Colo.	10.00
☐ FT17 Sergei Fedorov, Detr.	6.00
☐ FT18 Jeremy Roenick, Chic.	6.00
☐ FT19 Alexander Mogilny, Vanc.	2.00
☐ FT20 Joe Sakic, Colo.	12.00
☐ FT21 Teemu Selänne, Anah.	6.00
☐ FT22 Eric Lindros, Phil.	6.00

FIVE HUNDRED CLUB

Insert Set (8 cards):	65.00
Insert (1:36)	FC
☐ FC1 Wayne Gretzky, SLou.	25.00
☐ FC2 Mike Gartner, Toro.	4.00
☐ FC3 Jari Kurri, NYRa.	6.00
☐ FC4 Dino Ciccarelli, Detr.	2.00
☐ FC5 Mario Lemieux, Pitt.	18.00
☐ FC6 Mark Messier, NYRa.	6.00
☐ FC7 Steve Yzerman, Detr.	14.00
☐ FC8 Dale Hawerchuk, Phil.	2.00

ICE D

Insert Set (15 cards):	65.00
Insert (1:24)	ID
☐ ID1 Brian Leetch, NYRa.	4.00
☐ ID2 Raymond Bourque, Bost.	8.00
☐ ID3 Chris Chelios, Chic.	4.00
☐ ID4 Scott Stevens, NJer.	2.00
☐ ID5 Ed Jovanovski, Flor.	2.00
☐ ID6 Martin Brodeur (G), NJer.	12.00
☐ ID7 Patrick Roy (G), Colo.	22.00
☐ ID8 Chris Osgood (G), Detr.	4.00
☐ ID9 Jim Carey (G), Wash.	2.00
☐ ID10 Dominik Hasek (G), Buff.	6.00
☐ ID11 Ron Hextall (G), Phil.	4.00
☐ ID12 John Vanbiesbrouck (G), Flor.	2.00
☐ ID13 Mike Richter (G), NYRa.	2.00
☐ ID14 Félix Potvin (G), Toro.	4.00
☐ ID15 Grant Fuhr (G), SLou.	4.00

ROOKIE STARS

There are two versions: the regular insert (1:1) and an O-Pee-Chee parallel.

Insert Set (18 cards):	55.00	14.00
Inserts	OPC	RS
☐☐ RS1 Daniel Alfredsson, Otta.	6.00	1.50
☐☐ RS2 Jere Lehtinen, Dall.	3.00	.50
☐☐ RS3 Vitali Yachmenev, LosA.	1.00	.50
☐☐ RS4 Éric Dazé, Chic.	4.00	1.00
☐☐ RS5 Saku Koivu, Mont.	9.00	2.00
☐☐ RS6 Petr Sykora, NJer.	4.00	1.00
☐☐ RS7 Marcus Ragnarsson, SanJ.	2.00	.50
☐☐ RS8 Valeri Bure, Mont.	3.00	.50
☐☐ RS9 Cory Stillman, Calg.	2.00	.50
☐☐ RS10 Todd Bertuzzi, NYIs.	13.00	3.50
☐☐ RS11 Ed Jovanovski, Flor.	4.00	1.00
☐☐ RS12 Miroslav Satan, Edmo.	3.00	.50
☐☐ RS13 Kyle McLaren, Bost.	2.00	.50
☐☐ RS14 Byron Dafoe (G), LosA.	4.00	1.00

□ □	RS15 Éric Fichaud (G), NYIs.	1.00	.50
□ □	RS16 Corey Hirsch (G), Vanc.	1.00	.50
□ □	RS17 Jeff O'Neill, Hart.	4.00	1.00
□ □	RS18 Niklas Sundström, NYRa.	2.00	.50

TOP SHELF

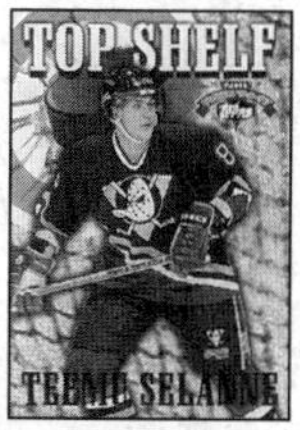

Insert Set (15 cards):		45.00
	Insert (1:12)	TS
□	TS1 John LeClair, Phil.	2.00
□	TS2 Wayne Gretzky, SLou.	14.00
□	TS3 Eric Lindros, Phil.	2.00
□	TS4 Paul Kariya, Anah.	4.00
□	TS5 Mark Messier, NYRa.	2.00
□	TS6 Jaromir Jagr, Pitt.	2.00
□	TS7 Peter Forsberg, Colo.	4.00
□	TS8 Teemu Selänne, Anah.	2.00
□	TS9 Alexander Mogilny, Vanc.	1.00
□	TS10 Brett Hull, SLou.	2.00
□	TS11 Sergei Fedorov, Detr.	2.00
□	TS12 Joe Sakic, Colo.	6.00
□	TS13 Mats Sundin, Toro.	2.00
□	TS14 Theoren Fleury, Calg.	2.00
□	TS15 Steve Yzerman, Detr.	8.00

1996 - 97 UPPER DECK

Series One Set (210 cards):		30.00
Series Two Set (180 cards):		50.00
Common Player:		.20
	Player	UD
□	1 Paul Kariya, Anah.	1.00
□	2 Guy Hebert (G), Anah.	.20
□	**3 J-F Jomphe, Anah.**	**.50**
□	4 Joe Sacco, Anah.	.20
□	5 Jason York, Anah.	.20
□	6 Alex Hicks, Anah.	.20
□	7 Mikhail Shtalenkov (G), Anah.	.20
□	8 Bill Ranford (G), Bost.	.20
□	9 Kyle McLaren, Bost.	.20
□	10 Rick Tocchet, Bost.	.20
□	11 Jon Rohloff, Bost.	.20
□	12 Jozef Stümpel, Bost.	.20
□	13 Cam Neely, Bost.	.50
□	14 Raymond Bourque, Bost.	.50
□	15 Pat LaFontaine, Buff.	.20
□	16 Brian Holzinger, Buff.	.20
□	17 Alexei Zhitnik, Buff.	.20
□	18 Donald Audette, Buff.	.20
□	19 Jason Dawe, Buff.	.20
□	20 Wayne Primeau, Buff.	.20
□	21 Michael Peca, Buff.	.20
□	22 Theoren Fleury, Calg.	.20
□	23 Sandy McCarthy, Calg.	.20
□	24 Zarley Zalapski, Calg.	.20
□	25 Trevor Kidd (G), Calg.	.20
□	26 Steve Chiasson, Calg.	.20
□	27 Michael Nylander, Calg.	.20
□	28 Ronnie Stern, Calg.	.20
□	29 Eric Dazé, Chic.	.20
□	30 Jeff Hackett (G), Chic.	.20
□	31 Chris Chelios, Chic.	.20
□	32 Tony Amonte, Chic.	.20
□	33 Bob Probert, Chic.	.20
□	34 Eric Weinrich, Chic.	.20
□	35 Jeremy Roenick, Chic.	.50
□	36 Mike Ricci, Colo.	.20
□	37 Sandis Ozolinsh, Colo.	.20
□	38 Patrick Roy (G), Colo.	2.00
□	39 Uwe Krupp, Colo.	.20
□	40 Stéphane Yelle, Colo.	.20
□	41 Adam Deadmarsh, Colo.	.20
□	42 Scott Young, Colo.	.20
□	43 Mike Modano, Dall.	.50
□	44 Derian Hatcher, Dall.	.20
□	45 Todd Harvey, Dall.	.20
□	46 Brent Fedyk, Dall.	.20
□	47 Grant Marshall, Dall.	.20
□	48 Jamie Langenbrunner, Dall.	.20
□	49 Jere Lehtinen, Dall.	.20
□	50 Steve Yzerman, Detr.	1.50
□	51 Igor Larionov, Detr.	.20
□	52 Vladimir Konstantinov, Detr.	.20
□	53 Chris Osgood (G), Detr.	.20
□	54 Jamie Pushor, Detr.	.20
□	55 Darren McCarty, Detr.	.20
□	56 Nicklas Lidström, Detr.	.20
□	57 Jason Arnott, Edmo.	.20
□	58 Doug Weight, Edmo.	.20
□	59 Todd Marchant, Edmo.	.20
□	60 David Oliver, Edmo.	.20
□	61 Luke Richardson, Edmo.	.20
□	62 Jason Bonsignore, Edmo.	.20
□	63 John Vanbiesbrouck (G), Flor.	.20
□	64 Stu Barnes, Flor.	.20
□	65 Martin Straka, Flor.	.20
□	66 Ed Jovanovski, Flor.	.20
□	67 Robert Svehla, Flor.	.20
□	68 Gord Murphy, Flor.	.20
□	69 Tom Fitzgerald, Flor.	.20
□	70 Jeff O'Neill, Hart.	.20
□	71 Jason Muzzatti (G), Hart.	.20
□	72 Sean Burke (G), Hart.	.20
□	73 Jeff Brown, Hart.	.20
□	74 Andrew Cassels, Hart.	.20
□	75 Geoff Sanderson, Hart.	.20
□	76 Dimitri Khristich, LosA.	.20
□	77 Vitali Yachmenev, LosA.	.20
□	78 Kevin Stevens, LosA.	.20
□	79 Yanic Perreault, LosA.	.20
□	80 Craig Johnson, LosA.	.20
□	81 John Slaney, LosA.	.20
□	82 Saku Koivu, Mont.	.50
□	83 Jocelyn Thibault (G), Mont.	.20
□	84 Vladimir Malakhou, Mont.	.20
□	85 Turner Stevenson, Mont.	.20
□	86 Vincent Damphousse, Mont.	.20
□	87 Mark Recchi, Mont.	.20
□	88 Patrick Brisebois, Mont.	.20
□	89 Dave Andreychuk, NJer.	.20
□	90 Bill Guerin, NJer.	.20
□	91 Martin Brodeur (G), NJer.	1.00
□	92 Scott Niedermayer, NJer.	.20
□	93 Petr Sykora, NJer.	.20
□	94 Stéphane Richer, NJer.	.20
□	95 John MacLean, NJer.	.20
□	96 Éric Fichaud (G), NYIs.	.20
□	97 Zigmund Palffy, NYIs.	.20
□	98 Alexander Semak, NYIs.	.20
□	99 Bryan McCabe, NYIs.	.20
□	100 Darley Hendrickson, NYIs.	.20
□	101 Kenny Jönsson, NYIs.	.20
□	102 Marty McInnis, NYIs.	.20
□	103 Alexei Kovalev, NYIs.	.20
□	104 Ulf Samuelsson, NYRa.	.20
□	105 Jeff Beukeboom, NYRa.	.20
□	106 Marty McSorley, NYRa.	.20
□	107 Niklas Sundström, NYRa.	.20
□	108 Wayne Gretzky, NYRa.	4.00
□	109 Mike Richter (G), NYRa.	.20
□	110 Alexei Yashin, Otta.	.20
□	111 Randy Cunneyworth, Otta.	.20
□	112 Damian Rhodes (G), Otta.	.20
□	113 Daniel Alfredsson, Otta.	.20
□	114 Antti Törmänen, Otta.	.20
□	115 Ted Drury, Otta.	.20
□	116 Janne Laukkanen, Otta.	.20
□	117 Sean Hill, Otta.	.20
□	118 John LeClair, Phil.	.50
□	119 Ron Hextall (G), Phil.	.20
□	120 Dale Hawerchuk, Phil.	.20
□	121 Rod Brind'Amour, Phil.	.20
□	122 Pat Falloon, Phil.	.20
□	123 Éric Desjardins, Phil.	.20
□	124 Joel Otto, Phil.	.20
□	125 Alexei Zhamnov, Winn.	.20
□	126 Nikolai Khabibulin (G), Winn.	.20
□	127 Craig Janney, Winn.	.20
□	128 Deron Quint, Winn.	.20
□	129 Oleg Tverdovsky, Winn.	.20
□	130 Chad Kilger, Winn.	.20
□	131 Teppo Numminen, Winn.	.20
□	132 Tom Barrasso (G), Winn.	.20
□	133 Ron Francis, Pitt.	.20
□	134 Petr Nedved, Pitt.	.20
□	135 Ken Wregget, Pitt.	.20
□	136 Joe Dziedgic, Pitt.	.20
□	137 Tomas Sandström, Pitt.	.20
□	138 Dmitri Mironov, Pitt.	.20
□	139 Shayne Corson, SLou.	.20
□	140 Grant Fuhr (G), SLou.	.20
□	141 Al MacInnis, SLou.	.20
□	142 Stephen Leach SLou.	.20
□	143 Murray Baron, SLou.	.20
□	144 Chris Pronger, SLou.	.20
□	145 Jamie Rivers, SLou.	.20
□	146 Owen Nolan, SanJ.	.20
□	147 Chris Terreri (G), SanJ.	.20
□	148 Marcus Ragnasson, SanJ.	.20
□	149 Shean Donovan, SanJ.	.20
□	150 Ray Whitney, SanJ.	.20
□	151 Michal Sykora, SanJ.	.20
□	152 Viktor Kozlov, SanJ.	.20
□	153 Roman Hamrlik, Tamp.	.20
□	154 Bill Houlder, Tamp.	.20
□	155 Mikael Andersson, Tamp.	.20
□	156 Petr Klima, Tamp.	.20
□	157 Jason Wiemer, Tamp.	.20
□	158 Rob Zamuner, Tamp.	.20
□	159 Paul Ysebaert, Tamp.	.20
□	160 Mats Sundin, Toro.	.50
□	161 Larry Murphy, Toro.	.20
□	162 Doug Gilmour, Toro.	.20
□	163 Todd Warriner, Toro.	.20
□	164 Dimitri Yushkevich, Toro.	.20
□	165 Kirk Muller, Toro.	.20
□	166 Jamie Macoun, Toro.	.20
□	167 Alexander Mogilny, Toro.	.20
□	168 Corey Hirsch (G), Vanc.	.20
□	169 Trevor Linden, Vanc.	.20
□	170 Markus Näslund, Vanc.	.50
□	171 Martin Gelinas, Vanc.	.20
□	172 Jyrki Lumme, Vanc.	.20
□	173 Bret Hedican, Vanc.	.20
□	174 Jim Carey (G), Wash.	.20
□	175 Sergei Gonchar, Wash.	.20
□	176 Joé Juneau, Wash.	.20
□	177 Brendan Witt, Wash.	.20
□	178 Dale Hunter, Wash.	.20
□	179 Steve Konowalchuk, Wash.	.20
□	180 Petr Bondra, Wash.	.20
□	181 Jarome Iginla, Calg.	1.00
□	182 Ralph Intranuovo, Edmo.	.20
□	183 Anders Eriksson, Detr.	.20
□	**184 Andrew Brunette, Wash. RC**	**1.00**
□	**185 Steve Sullivan, NJer. RC**	**2.00**
□	186 Brandon Convery, Toro.	.20
□	187 Ethan Moreau, Chic.	.20
□	188 Marko Kiprusoff, Mont.	.20
□	189 Jason McBain, Hart. RC	.20
□	190 Mark Kolesar, Toro. RC	.20
□	**191 Greg DeVries, Edmo. RC**	**1.00**
□	**192 Alexei Yegorov, SanJ. RC**	**.50**
□	**193 Sébastien Bordeleau, Mont. RC**	**.50**
□	194 Nick Stajduhar, Edmo.	.20
□	**195 Jan Caloun, SanJ. RC**	**.50**
□	196 Dino Ciccarelli, Detr.	.20
□	197 Ron Hextall (G), Phil.	.20
□	198 Murray Baron, SLou.	.20
□	199 Patrick Roy (G), Colo.	2.00
□	200 Scott Mellanby, Flor.	.20
□	201 Tie Domi, Toro.	.20
□	202 Glenn Healy, NYRa.	.20
□	203 Keith Primeau, Detr.	.20
□	204 Joe Sakic, Colo.	1.00
□	205 Jeremy Roenick, Chic.	.50
□	206 Sergei Fedorov, Detr.	.50
□	207 Claude Lemieux, Colo.	.20
□	208 Theoren Fleury, Calg.	.20
□	209 CL: Wayne Gretzky, NYRa.	.20
□	210 CL: Wayne Gretzky, NYRa.	.20
□	211 Teemu Selänne, Anah.	.50
□	212 Jari Kurri, Anah.	.50
□	213 Darren Van Impe, Anah.	.20
□	214 Steve Rucchin, Anah.	.20
□	**215 Ruslan Salei, Anah. RC**	**.50**
□	216 Adam Oates, Bost.	.20
□	217 Don Sweeney, Bost.	.20
□	**218 Steve Staios, Bost.**	**.50**
□	219 Barry Richter, Bost.	.20
□	**220 Mattias Timander, Bost. RC**	**.50**
□	221 Ted Donato, Bost.	.20
□	222 Dominik Hasek (G), Buff.	.50
□	223 Derek Plante, Buff.	.20
□	**224 Vaclav Varada, Buff. RC**	**1.00**
□	225 Andrei Trefilov (G), Buff.	.20
□	226 Curtis Brown, Buff.	.20
□	227 German Titov, Calg.	.20
□	228 Robert Reichel, Calg.	.20
□	229 Cory Stillman, Calg.	.20
□	230 Chris O'Sullivan, Calg.	.20
□	231 Corey Millen, Calg.	.20
□	232 Jonas Höglund, Calg.	.20
□	233 Alexei Zhamnov, Chic.	.20
□	234 Ed Belfour (G), Chic.	.50
□	235 Gary Suter, Chic.	.20
□	236 Kevin Miller, Chic.	.20
□	237 Tuomas Grönman, Chic.	.20
□	238 Enrico Ciccone, Chic.	.20
□	239 Peter Forsberg, Colo.	1.00
□	240 Joe Sakic, Colo.	1.00
□	241 Valeri Kamensky, Colo.	.20
□	242 Landon Wilson, Colo.	.20
□	243 Claude Lemieux, Colo.	.20
□	244 Eric Lacroix, Colo.	.20
□	245 Joe Nieuwendyk, Dall.	.20
□	246 Sergei Zubov, Dall.	.20
□	247 Benoît Hogue, Dall.	.20
□	248 Arturs Irbe (G), Dall.	.20
□	249 Pat Verbeek, Dall.	.20
□	250 Sergei Fedorov, Detr.	.50
□	251 Vyacheslav Kozlov, Detr.	.20
□	252 Brendan Shanahan, Detr.	.50
□	253 Kevin Hodson (G), Detr.	.20
□	254 Greg Johnson, Detr.	.20
□	**255 Tomas Holmström, Detr. RC**	**1.50**
□	256 Curtis Joseph (G), Edmo.	.50
□	257 Dean McAmmond, Edmo.	.20
□	258 Ryan Smyth, Edmo.	.20
□	**259 Mike Grier, Edmo. RC**	**1.50**
□	260 Miroslav Satan, Edmo.	.20
□	**261 Rem Murray, Edmo. RC**	**.50**
□	262 Rob Niedermayer, Flor.	.20
□	263 Ray Sheppard, Flor.	.20
□	264 Dave Lowry, Flor.	.20
□	265 Scott Mellanby, Flor.	.20
□	266 Rhett Warrener, Flor.	.20
□	**267 Per Gustafsson, Flor.**	**.50**
□	268 Paul Coffey, Hart.	.20
□	269 Nelson Emerson, Hart.	.20
□	270 Kevin Dineen, Hart.	.20
□	271 Keith Primeau, Hart.	.20
□	272 Hnat Domenichelli, Hart.	.20
□	273 Ray Ferraro, LosA.	.20
□	274 Stephane Fiset (G), LosA.	.20
□	**275 Kai Nurminen, LosA. RC**	**.50**
□	**276 Dan Bylsma, LosA. RC**	**.50**
□	277 Mattias Norstrom, LosA.	.20
□	278 Rob Blake, LosA.	.20
□	279 José Théodore (G), Mont.	2.50
□	280 Martin Ruchinsky, Mont.	.20
□	281 Darcy Tucker, Mont.	.20
□	282 David Wilkie, Mont.	.20
□	283 Valeri Bure, Mont.	.20
□	284 Steve Thomas, NJer.	.20
□	285 Brian Rolston, NJer.	.20
□	286 Scott Stevens, NJer.	.20
□	287 Shawn Chambers, NJer.	.20
□	288 Denis Pederson, NJer.	.20
□	289 Lyle Odelein, NJer.	.20
□	290 Travis Green, NYIs.	.20
□	291 Todd Bertuzzi, NYIs.	1.50
□	292 Niklas Andersson, NYIs.	.20
□	293 Darius Kasparaitis, NYIs.	.20
□	294 Bryan Berard, NYIs.	.20
□	295 Daniel Goneau, NYRa.	.50
□	296 Christian Dubé, NYRa.	.20
□	297 Adam Graves, NYRa.	.20
□	298 Sergei Nemchinov, NYRa.	.20
□	299 Mark Messier, NYRa.	.50
□	300 Brian Leetch, NYRa.	.20
□	301 Radek Bonk, Otta.	.20
□	302 Alexandre Daigle, Otta.	.20
□	**303 Andreas Dackell, Otta. RC**	**1.00**
□	304 Steve Duchesne, Otta.	.20
□	305 Wade Redden, Otta.	.20
□	306 Eric Lindros, Phil.	.50
□	307 Mikael Renberg, Phil.	.20
□	308 Shjon Podein, Phil.	.20
□	**309 Danius Zubrus, Phil. RC**	**1.50**
□	310 Janne Niinimaa, Phil.	.20
□	311 Karl Dykhuis, Phil.	.20
□	312 Jeremy Roenick, Phoe.	.50
□	313 Keith Tkachuk, Phoe.	.20
□	314 Shane Doan, Phoe.	.20
□	315 Cliff Ronning, Phoe.	.20
□	316 Mike Gartner, Phoe.	.50
□	317 Dave Manson, Phoe.	.20
□	318 Shawn Antoski, Pitt.	.20
□	319 Kevin Hatcher, Pitt.	.20
□	320 Jaromir Jagr, Pitt.	.50
□	321 Mario Lemieux, Pitt.	2.00
□	322 Bryan Smolinski, Pitt.	.20
□	**323 Stefan Bergkvist, Pitt. RC**	**.50**
□	324 Brett Hull, SLou.	.50
□	325 Joe Murphy, SLou.	.20
□	326 Stéphane Matteau, SLou.	.20
□	327 Geoff Courtnall, SLou.	.20
□	328 Jim Campbell, SLou.	.20
□	**329 Harry York, SLou. RC**	**.50**
□	330 Kelly Hrudey (G), SanJ.	.20
□	331 Al Iafrate, SanJ.	.20
□	332 Jeff Friesen, SanJ.	.20
□	333 Darren Turcotte, SanJ.	.20
□	334 Bernie Nicholls, SanJ.	.20
□	335 Ville Peltonen, SanJ.	.20
□	336 Dino Ciccarelli, Tamp.	.20
□	337 Chris Gratton, Tamp.	.20
□	338 Daren Puppa (G), Tamp.	.20
□	339 Alexander Selivanov, Tamp.	.20
□	340 Daymond Langkow, Tamp.	.20
□	341 Félix Potvin (G), Toro.	.20
□	342 Wendel Clark, Toro.	.50
□	343 Mathieu Schneider, Toro.	.20
□	344 Dave Ellett, Toro.	.20
□	**345 Fredrik Modin, Toro. RC**	**1.50**
□	**346 Sergei Berezin, Toro. RC**	**1.50**
□	347 Pavel Bure, Vanc.	.50
□	348 Kirk McLean (G), Vanc.	.20
□	349 Mike Sillinger, Vanc.	.20
□	350 Russ Courtnall, Vanc.	.20
□	351 Scott Walker, Vanc.	.20
□	352 Esa Tikkanen, Vanc.	.20
□	353 Pat Peake, Wash.	.20
□	354 Olaf Kölzig (G), Wash.	.20
□	355 Michal Pivonka, Wash.	.20
□	**356 Richard Zednik, Wash. RC**	**2.50**
□	357 Phil Housley, Wash.	.20
□	358 Anson Carter, Wash.	.50
□	359 Eric Dazé, Chic.	.20
□	360 Félix Potvin (G), Toro.	.20
□	361 Wayne Gretzky, NYRa.	3.00
□	362 Ed Jovanovski, Flor.	.20
□	363 Mike Modano, Dall.	.50
□	364 Peter Bondra, Wash.	.20
□	365 Patrick Roy (G), Colo.	2.00
□	366 Raymond Bourque, Bost.	.50
□	367 Roman Hamrlik, Tamp.	.20
□	368 John LeClair, Phil.	.50

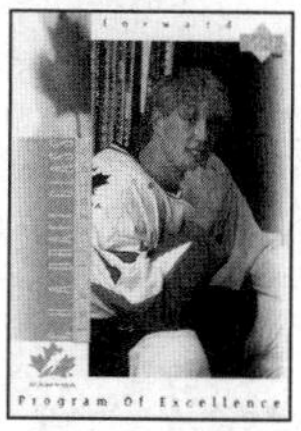

□	**369 Adam Colagiacomo, Cdn. RC**	**1.00**
□	**370 Joe Thornton, Cdn. RC**	**30.00**
□	**371 Patrick Desrochers, Cdn. RC**	**2.00**
□	**372 Pierre-Luc Therrien, Cdn. RC**	**1.00**
□	**373 Nick Boynton, Cdn. RC**	**1.50**
□	**374 Andrew Ference, Cdn. RC**	**2.00**
□	**375 Jean-François Fortin, Cdn. RC**	**1.00**
□	**376 Daniel Tétreault, Cdn. RC**	**1.00**
□	**377 Luc Theoret, Cdn. RC**	**1.00**
□	**378 Mike Van Ryn, Cdn. RC**	**3.00**
□	**379 Scott Barney, Cdn. RC**	**.50**
□	**380 Harold Druken, Cdn. RC**	**4.00**
□	**381 Dylan Gyori, Cdn. RC**	**1.00**
□	**382 Chris Heron, Cdn. RC**	**1.00**
□	**383 Chad Hinz, Cdn. RC**	**1.00**
□	**384 Patrick Marleau, Cdn. RC**	**6.50**
□	**385 Serge Payer, Cdn. RC**	**1.00**
□	**386 Jeremy Reich, Cdn. RC**	**1.00**
□	**387 Daniel Tkaczuk, Cdn. RC**	**1.50**
□	**388 Jason Ward, Cdn. RC**	**5.00**
□	389 CL: Wayne Gretzky, NYRa.	.20
□	390 CL: Wayne Gretzky, NYRa.	.20

GAME JERSEY

Insert Set (20 cards):		2,500.00
	Insert (1:2500)	GJ
□	Steve Yzerman, Detr. ✂	475.00
□	Doug Gilmour, Toro. ✂	125.00
□	Brett Hull, SLou. ✂	200.00
□	Raymond Bourque, Bost. ✂	225.00
□	Jaromir Jagr, Pitt. ✂	200.00
□	Mario Lemieux, Pitt. ✂	600.00
□	John Vanbiesbrouck (G), Flor. ✂	125.00
□	Eric Lindros, Phil. ✂	200.00
□	Mike Modano, Dall. ✂	200.00
□	Pavel Bure, Vanc. ✂	150.00
□	Mark Messier, NYRa. ✂	200.00
□	Theoren Fleury, Calg. ✂	125.00
□	Mats Sundin, Toro. ✂	200.00

GENERATION NEXT

	Series Two Insert Set (20 cards):	100.00
	Insert (1:4)	GN
☐	X1 W. Gretzky / P. Kariya	10.00
☐	X2 T. Linden / P. Forsberg	4.00
☐	X3 J. Sakic / R. Niedermayer	4.00
☐	X4 E. Weinrich / C. O'Sullivan	1.00
☐	X5 P. Roy / J. Thibault	8.00
☐	X6 Br. Hull / D. Alfredsson	4.00
☐	X7 J. Vanbiesbrouck (G) / C. Osgood (G)	2.00
☐	X8 R. Bourque / R. Hamrlik	3.00
☐	X9 P. Coffey / S. Ozolinsh	2.00
☐	X10 D. Gilmour / S. Fedorov	4.00
☐	X11 C. Chelios / E. Jovanovski	2.00
☐	X12 J. Roenick / J. Arnott	3.00
☐	X13 S. Yzerman / D. Weight	7.00
☐	X14 B. Shanahan / T. Bertuzzi	5.00
☐	X15 W. Clark / K. Tkachuk	3.00
☐	X16 T. Selänne / S. Koivu	4.00
☐	X17 J. Jagr / Z. Palffy	4.00
☐	X18 E. Belfour / M. Brodeur	6.00
☐	X19 O. Nolan / É. Dazé	2.00
☐	X20 V. Kamensky / V. Yachmenev	1.00
☐	X21 M. Modano / J. Iginla	4.00
☐	X22 N. Lidström / A. Eriksson	1.00
☐	X23 B. Leetch / B. Berard	2.00
☐	X24 J. Kurri / N. Sundström	3.00
☐	X25 S. Mellanby / A. Deadmarsh	1.00
☐	X26 P. Bondra / P. Sykora	2.00
☐	X27 Cu. Joseph / É. Fichaud (G)	2.00
☐	X28 D. Hasek / R. Turek	5.00
☐	X29 A. Mogilny / V. Bure	3.00
☐	X30 T. Fleury / D. Langkow	2.00
☐	X31 B. Nicholls / S. Berezin	1.00
☐	X32 R. Tocchet / C. Gratton	1.00
☐	X33 G. Fuhr / F. Potvin	3.00
☐	X34 K. Stevens / K. Primeau	1.00
☐	X35 R. Blake / W. Redden	2.00
☐	X36 S. Stevens / C. Pronger	2.00
☐	X37 G. Suter / K. McLaren	1.00
☐	X38 M. Sundin / J. Höglund	2.00
☐	X39 L. Murphy / S. Zubov	1.00
☐	X40 A. Oates / J. Juneau	1.00

HART HOPEFULS

There are three versions: a bronze insert (#/5000), a silver insert (#/1000) and a gold insert (#/100).

	Series Two Insert Set (20 cards):	1,500	250	125
	Player	G100	S1000	B5000
☐☐☐	HH1 Wayne Gretzky	350.00	60.00	30.00
☐☐☐	HH2 Mark Messier	75.00	15.00	6.00
☐☐☐	HH3 Eric Lindros	75.00	15.00	6.00
☐☐☐	HH4 Sergei Fedorov	75.00	15.00	6.00
☐☐☐	HH5 Saku Koivu	50.00	10.00	6.00
☐☐☐	HH6 Vanbiesbrouck (G)	25.00	6.00	4.00
☐☐☐	HH7 Peter Forsberg	125.00	20.00	10.00
☐☐☐	HH8 Keith Tkachuk	50.00	6.00	4.00
☐☐☐	HH9 Paul Kariya	125.00	20.00	10.00
☐☐☐	HH10 Martin Brodeur (G)	125.00	20.00	12.00
☐☐☐	HH11 Patrick Roy (G)	200.00	40.00	20.00
☐☐☐	HH12 Alexander Mogilny	40.00	6.00	4.00
☐☐☐	HH13 Brett Hull	75.00	15.00	6.00
☐☐☐	HH14 Pavel Bure	50.00	10.00	6.00
☐☐☐	HH15 Teemu Selänne	50.00	10.00	6.00
☐☐☐	HH16 Mario Lemieux	250.00	40.00	20.00
☐☐☐	HH17 Jeremy Roenick	50.00	10.00	6.00
☐☐☐	HH18 Jaromir Jagr	75.00	15.00	6.00
☐☐☐	HH19 Steve Yzerman	200.00	35.00	18.00
☐☐☐	HH20 Joe Sakic	125.00	20.00	12.00

1996 - 97 UPPER DECK

	Upper Deck	UD
☐	280 Steve Nash RC	3.00

LORD STANLEY'S HEROES

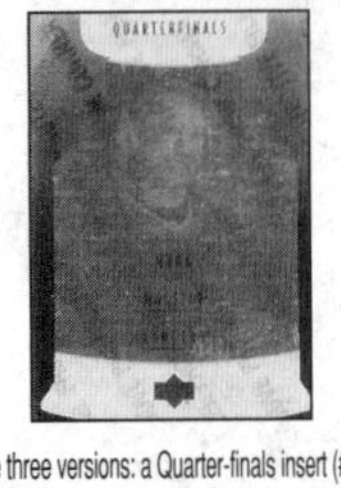

There are three versions: a Quarter-finals insert (#/5000), a Semi-finals insert (#/1000) and a Finals insert (#/100).

	Series One Insert Set (20 cards):	1,600	250	125
	Player	F100	S1000	Q5000
☐☐☐	LS1 Wayne Gretzky	350.00	60.00	30.00
☐☐☐	LS2 Mark Messier	75.00	15.00	6.00
☐☐☐	LS3 Mario Lemieux	250.00	40.00	20.00
☐☐☐	LS4 Jaromir Jagr	75.00	15.00	6.00
☐☐☐	LS5 Martin Brodeur (G)	125.00	20.00	12.00
☐☐☐	LS6 Patrick Roy (G)	200.00	40.00	20.00
☐☐☐	LS7 Joe Sakic	125.00	20.00	12.00
☐☐☐	LS8 Peter Forsberg	125.00	20.00	10.00
☐☐☐	LS9 Theoren Fleury	50.00	6.00	4.00
☐☐☐	LS10 Paul Coffey	50.00	6.00	4.00
☐☐☐	LS11 Doug Gilmour	50.00	6.00	4.00
☐☐☐	LS12 Paul Kariya	125.00	20.00	10.00
☐☐☐	LS13 Eric Lindros	75.00	15.00	6.00
☐☐☐	LS14 Sergei Fedorov	75.00	15.00	6.00
☐☐☐	LS15 Eric Dazé	35.00	6.00	4.00
☐☐☐	LS16 Teemu Selänne	50.00	10.00	6.00
☐☐☐	LS17 Keith Tkachuk	50.00	6.00	4.00
☐☐☐	LS18 Pavel Bure	50.00	10.00	6.00
☐☐☐	LS19 Mats Sundin	75.00	15.00	6.00
☐☐☐	LS20 Saku Koivu	50.00	10.00	6.00

POWER PERFORMERS

	Series Two Insert Set (20 cards):	85.00
	Insert (1:13)	PP
☐	P1 Brendan Shanahan, Detr.	7.00
☐	P2 Mikael Renberg, Phil.	2.00
☐	P3 John LeClair, Phil.	6.00
☐	P4 Keith Primeau, Hart.	3.00
☐	P5 Adam Graves, NYRa.	3.00
☐	P6 Jason Arnott, Edmo.	3.00
☐	P7 Todd Bertuzzi, NYIs.	10.00
☐	P8 Ed Jovanovski, Flor.	3.00
☐	P9 Scott Stevens, NJer.	3.00
☐	P10 Chris Gratton, Tamp.	2.00
☐	P11 Bill Guerin, NJer.	3.00
☐	P12 Vladimir Konstantinov, Detr.	2.00
☐	P13 Mike Grier, Edmo.	2.00
☐	P14 Theoren Fleury, Calg.	4.00
☐	P15 Chris Chelios, Chic.	4.00
☐	P16 Trevor Linden, Vanc.	3.00
☐	P17 Claude Lemieux, Colo.	2.00
☐	P18 Owen Nolan, SanJ.	4.00
☐	P19 Jarome Iginla, Calg.	6.00
☐	P20 Joe Nieuwendyk, Dall.	3.00
☐	P21 Kevin Hatcher, Pitt.	2.00
☐	P22 Dino Ciccarelli, Tamp.	2.00
☐	P23 Adam Deadmarsh, Colo.	2.00
☐	P24 Chris Pronger, SLou.	4.00
☐	P25 Mike Ricci, Colo.	2.00
☐	P26 Rod Brind'Amour, Phil.	2.00
☐	P27 Derian Hatcher, Dall.	2.00
☐	P28 Mats Sundin, Toro.	7.00
☐	P29 Doug Gilmour, Toro.	4.00
☐	P30 Todd Harvey, Dall.	2.00

SUPERSTAR SHOWDOWN

Series One Insert Set (20 cards): 155.00

	Insert (1:4)	SS
☐	SS1A Pavel Bure, Vanc.	3.00
☐	SS1B Paul Kariya, Anah.	5.00
☐	SS2A Patrick Roy (G), Colo.	10.00
☐	SS2B John Vanbiesbrouck (G), Flor.	2.00
☐	SS3A Eric Lindros, Phil.	2.00
☐	SS3B Ed Jovanovski, Flor.	2.00
☐	SS4A Theoren Fleury, Calg.	2.00
☐	SS4B Doug Gilmour, Toro.	2.00
☐	SS5A Wayne Gretzky, NYRa.	15.00
☐	SS5B Mario Lemieux, Pitt.	10.00
☐	SS6A Keith Tkachuk, Phoe.	2.00
☐	SS6B Brendan Shanahan, Hart.	3.00
☐	SS7A Raymond Bourque, Bost.	4.00
☐	SS7B Brian Leetch, NYRa.	2.00
☐	SS8A Peter Forsberg, Colo.	5.00
☐	SS8B Sergei Fedorov, Detr.	3.00
☐	SS9A Mark Messier, NYRa.	3.00
☐	SS9B Scott Stevens, NJer.	2.00
☐	SS10A Teemu Selänne, Anah.	3.00
☐	SS10B Alexander Mogilny, Vanc.	2.00
☐	SS11A Félix Potvin (G), Toro.	2.00
☐	SS11B Jocelyn Thibault (G), Mont.	2.00
☐	SS12A Martin Brodeur (G), NJer.	6.00
☐	SS12B Éric Fichaud (G), NYIs.	2.00
☐	SS13A Roman Hamrlik, Tamp.	2.00
☐	SS13B Jaromir Jagr, Pitt.	2.00
☐	SS14A Jim Carey (G), Wash.	2.00
☐	SS14B Saku Koivu, Mont.	3.00
☐	SS15A Jeremy Roenick, Chic.	3.00
☐	SS15B Brett Hull, SLou.	3.00
☐	SS16A Joe Sakic, Colo.	6.00
☐	SS16B Steve Yzerman, Detr.	8.00
☐	SS17A Doug Weight, Edmo.	2.00
☐	SS17B Pat LaFontaine, Buff.	2.00
☐	SS18A Daniel Alfredsson, Otta.	2.00
☐	SS18B Éric Dazé, Chic.	2.00
☐	SS19A Mike Modano, Dall.	3.00
☐	SS19B Jason Arnott, Edmo.	2.00
☐	SS20A Paul Coffey, Detr.	2.00
☐	SS20B Sandis Ozolinsh, Colo.	2.00
☐	SS21A Zigmund Palffy, NYIs.	2.00
☐	SS21B Petr Sykora, NJer.	2.00
☐	SS22A Ed Belfour (G), Chic.	3.00
☐	SS22B Ron Hextall (G), Phil.	2.00
☐	SS23A Mats Sundin, Toro.	3.00
☐	SS23B Mikael Renberg, Phil.	2.00
☐	SS24A Vitali Yachmenev, LosA.	2.00
☐	SS24B Alexei Zhamnov, Winn.	2.00
☐	SS25A Oleg Tverdovsky, Winn.	2.00
☐	SS25B Kyle McLaren, Bost.	2.00
☐	SS26A Dominik Hasek (G), Buff.	3.00
☐	SS26B Petr Nedved, Pitt.	2.00
☐	SS27A Chris Chelios, Chic.	2.00
☐	SS27B Chris Pronger, SLou.	2.00
☐	SS28A Rob Niedermayer, Flor.	2.00
☐	SS28B Scott Niedermayer, NJer.	2.00
☐	SS29A Keith Primeau, Detr.	2.00
☐	SS29B Bob Probert, Chic.	2.00
☐	SS30A Bill Ranford (G), Edmo.	2.00
☐	SS30B Chris Osgood (G), Detr.	2.00

1996 - 97 UPPER DECK – BUYBACKS

	Buyback Autograph	UD
☐	14 Raymond Bourque, Bost. ✍ {#/1}	
☐	43 Mike Modano, Dall. ✍ {#/3}	
☐	50 Steve Yzerman, Detr. ✍ {#/1}	
☐	91 Martin Brodeur (G), NJer. ✍ {#/1}	
☐	108 Wayne Gretzky, NYRa. ✍ {#/1}	
☐	109 Mike Richter (G), NYRa. ✍ {#/1}	
☐	118 John LeClair, Phil. ✍ {#/3}	
☐	363 Mike Modano, Dall. ✍ {#/39}	
☐	368 John LeClair, Phil. ✍ {#/2}	

1996 - 97 UD ALL-STAR GAME YOU CRASH THE GAME

Unnumbered blue cards were handed out at the 1997 All-Star Game in San Jose. Only ten Western Conference players, however, are confirmed to have been handed out. If the depicted player scored a goal, that card could be redeemed for a 20-card Gold set. The Gold cards are numbered AR1 to AR20.

	Complete Set (20 cards):		900.00
	Player	Blue	Gold
☐	AR1 Tony Amonte, Chic.		30.00
☐☐	AR2 Paul Kariya, Anah.	35.00	70.00
☐☐	AR3 Brett Hull, SLou.	30.00	50.00
☐☐	AR4 Teemu Selänne, Anah.	50.00	40.00
☐☐	AR5 Steve Yzerman, Detr.	60.00	120.00
☐☐	AR6 Owen Nolan, SanJ.	60.00	30.00
☐☐	AR7 Mats Sundin, Toro.	35.00	50.00
☐☐	AR8 Pavel Bure, Vanc.	150.00	40.00
☐☐	AR9 Brendan Shanahan, Detr.	35.00	50.00
☐☐	AR10 Sandis Ozolinsh, Colo.	35.00	20.00
☐☐	AR11 Keith Tkachuk, Phoe.	75.00	30.00
☐	AR12 Raymond Bourque, Bost.		60.00
☐	AR13 Eric Lindros, Phil.		50.00
☐	AR14 Mark Messier, NYRa.		50.00
☐	AR15 John LeClair, Phil.		40.00
☐	AR16 Jaromir Jagr, Pitt.		50.00
☐	AR17 Dino Ciccarelli, Tamp.		20.00
☐	AR18 Peter Bondra, Wash.		30.00
☐	AR19 Brian Leetch, NYRa.		30.00
☐	AR20 Wayne Gretzky, NYRa.		200.00

1996 - 97 UPPER DECK BLACK DIAMOND

There are two versions: the regular card and a gold parallel card. Cards have either one diamond (1-90), two diamonds (91-150) or three diamonds (151-180). There are 50 copies of each Triple Diamond Gold card.

	Complete Set (180 cards):	3400.00	1200.00
	Single Diamond Set (90 cards):		25.00
	Common Player:	2.00	.20
	Single	Gold	BD
☐☐	**1 Roman Turek (G), Dall. RC**	**12.00**	**6.50**
☐☐	2 Viacheslav Fetisov, Detr.	5.00	.50
☐☐	3 Mike Dunham (G), NJer.	3.00	1.00
☐☐	**4 Jean-François Fortin, Cdn. RC**	**2.00**	**1.00**
☐☐	5 Keith Primeau, Hart.	3.00	.50
☐☐	6 Zigmund Palffy, NYIs.	5.00	.50
☐☐	7 Curtis Leschyshyn, Hart.	2.00	.20
☐☐	8 Vladimir Tsyplakov, LosA.	2.00	.20
☐☐	9 Adam Graves, NYRa.	3.00	.50
☐☐	10 Ian Lapperière, LosA.	2.00	.20
☐☐	11 Bill Lindsay, Flor.	2.00	.20
☐☐	12 Brian Leetch, NYRa.	5.00	.50
☐☐	13 Martin Lapointe, Detr.	3.00	.50
☐☐	**14 Scott Barney, Cdn. RC**	**2.00**	**1.00**
☐☐	**15 Mike Grier, Edmo. RC**	**6.00**	**2.00**
☐☐	16 Vladimir Konstantinov, Detr.	2.00	.20
☐☐	**17 Rem Murray, Edmo. RC**	**2.00**	**1.00**
☐☐	18 Ed Jovanovski, Flor.	3.00	.50
☐☐	19 Chris O'Sullivan, Calg.	2.00	.20
☐☐	20 Steve Rucchin, Anah.	2.00	.20
☐☐	21 Jay Pandolfo, NJer.	2.00	.20
☐☐	**22 Nick Boynton, Cdn. RC**	**6.00**	**2.00**
☐☐	23 Greg Adams, Dall.	2.00	.20
☐☐	**24 Adam Colagiacomo, Cdn. RC**	**4.00**	**1.50**
☐☐	25 Vincent Damphousse, Mont.	5.00	.50
☐☐	**26 Shane Willis, Cdn. RC**	**6.00**	**3.00**
☐☐	27 Alexei Kovalev, NYRa.	5.00	.50
☐☐	28 Doug Gilmour, NJer.	5.00	.50
☐☐	29 Joel Otto, Phil.	2.00	.20
☐☐	30 Donald Audette, Buff.	3.00	.50
☐☐	31 Tommy Salo (G), NYIs.	3.00	.50
☐☐	32 Rob Ray, Buff.	2.00	.20
☐☐	33 Kris Draper, Detr.	2.00	.20
☐☐	34 Ed Belfour (G), SanJ.	8.00	1.00
☐☐	35 Mike Richter (G), NYRa.	4.00	.50
☐☐	36 Nikolai Khabibulin (G), Phoe.	3.00	.50
☐☐	37 Éric Desjardins, Phil.	2.00	.20
☐☐	**38 Daniel Tkaczuk, Cdn. RC**	**6.00**	**2.00**
☐☐	39 Keith Jones, Colo.	2.00	.20
☐☐	**40 Per Gustafsson, Flor.**	**2.00**	**1.00**
☐☐	41 Jocelyn Thibault (G), Mont.	3.00	.50
☐☐	42 Mike Gartner, Phoe.	7.00	1.00
☐☐	43 Vitali Yachmenev, LosA.	2.00	.20
☐☐	44 Jonas Höglund, Calg.	2.00	.20
☐☐	45 Craig Janney, Phoe.	2.00	.20
☐☐	46 Daymond Langkow, Tamp.	2.00	.20
☐☐	**47 Mattias Timander, Bost. RC**	**2.00**	**1.00**
☐☐	48 Scott Young, Colo.	2.00	.20
☐☐	49 Mikael Renberg, Phil.	2.00	.20
☐☐	50 Nicklas Lidström, Detr.	5.00	.50
☐☐	51 Andrei Kovalenko, Edmo.	2.00	.20
☐☐	52 Adam Foote, Colo.	2.00	.20
☐☐	53 Guy Hebert (G), Anah.	2.00	.20
☐☐	54 Kevin Hatcher, Pgh	2.00	.20
☐☐	55 Rick Tocchet, Wsh	2.00	.20
☐☐	56 Sergei Zubov, Dall.	2.00	.20
☐☐	57 Chris Phillips, Cdn.	2.00	.20
☐☐	58 Denis Savard, Chic.	3.00	.50
☐☐	59 Bernie Nicholls, SanJ.	2.00	.20
☐☐	60 Jozef Stümpel, Bost.	2.00	.20
☐☐	61 Darius Kasparaitis, Pitt.	2.00	.20
☐☐	62 Kelly Hrudey (G), SanJ.	2.00	.20
☐☐	**63 Marcel Cousineau (G), Toro. RC**	**2.00**	**1.00**
☐☐	64 Brian Skrudland, Flor.	2.00	.20
☐☐	65 Byron Dafoe (G), LosA.	3.00	.50
☐☐	66 Ray Sheppard, Flor.	2.00	.20
☐☐	67 Chris Simon, Wash.	2.00	.20
☐☐	**68 Dainius Zubrus, Phil. RC**	**6.00**	**2.00**
☐☐	69 Ethan Moreau, Chic.	2.00	.20
☐☐	70 Theoren Fleury, Calg.	5.00	.50
☐☐	71 Damian Rhodes (G), Otta.	2.00	.20
☐☐	72 Kevin Dineen, Hart.	2.00	.20
☐☐	73 Kenny Jönsson, NYIs.	2.00	.20
☐☐	74 Ray Ferraro, LosA.	2.00	.20
☐☐	75 Jaromir Jagr, Pitt.	5.00	1.00
☐☐	76 Wayne Primeau, Buff.	2.00	.20
☐☐	77 Chris Gratton, Tamp.	2.00	.20
☐☐	78 Alyn McCauley, Cdn.	2.00	.20
☐☐	79 Christian Dubé, NYRa.	2.00	.20
☐☐	80 Bill Ranford (G), Wash.	3.00	.50
☐☐	81 Adam Deadmarsh, Colo.	2.00	.20
☐☐	82 Dale Hunter, Wash.	2.00	.20
☐☐	83 Derek Plante, Buff.	2.00	.20
☐☐	84 Todd Bertuzzi, Buff.	10.00	3.00
☐☐	85 Stéphane Fiset (G), LosA.	2.00	.20
☐☐	86 Boyd Devereaux, Cdn.	6.00	1.50
☐☐	87 Jere Lehtinen, Dall.	2.00	.20
☐☐	**88 Peter Schaefer, Cdn. RC**	**4.00**	**1.50**
☐☐	89 Alexander Mogilny, Vanc.	4.00	.50
☐☐	90 Joé Juneau, Wash.	2.00	.20

DOUBLE DIAMOND

	Double	Gold	BD
☐☐	91 Alexandre Daigle, Ott	5.00	1.00
☐☐	92 Jeff O'Neill, Hart.	10.00	2.00
☐☐	93 Todd Warriner, Toro.	5.00	1.00
☐☐	**94 Sergei Berezin, Toro. RC**	**18.00**	**12.00**
☐☐	95 Petr Nedved, Pitt.	5.00	2.00
☐☐	96 Phil Housley, Wash.	5.00	2.00
☐☐	97 Jason Arnott, Edmo.	10.00	3.00
☐☐	98 Sandis Ozolinsh, Colo.	6.00	1.00
☐☐	99 Mike Modano, Dall.	25.00	6.00
☐☐	100 Mark Messier, NYRa.	25.00	6.00
☐☐	101 Ron Francis, Pitt.	15.00	3.00
☐☐	102 Oleg Tverdovsky, Phoe.	5.00	1.00
☐☐	**103 Patrick Marleau, Cdn. RC**	**125.00**	**100.00**
☐☐	104 Brian Bellows, Anah.	6.00	1.00
☐☐	105 Éric Fichaud (G), NYIs.	5.00	1.00
☐☐	106 Alexei Zhamnov, Chic.	5.00	2.00

□□ 107 Wendel Clark, Toro. 20.00 5.00
□□ 108 Dimitri Khristich, LosA. 5.00 1.00
□□ 109 Mike Ricci, Colo. 5.00 2.00
□□ 110 John LeClair, Phil. 20.00 5.00
□□ 111 Owen Nolan, SanJ. 15.00 3.00
□□ 112 Bill Guerin, NJer. 10.00 2.00
□□ 113 Vyacheslav Kozlov, Detr. 6.00 1.00
□□ 114 Brendan Shanahan, Detr. 25.00 6.00
□□ 115 Trevor Linden, Vanc. 10.00 2.00
□□ 116 José Théodore (G), Mont. 30.00 12.00
□□ 117 Rod Brind'Amour, Phil. 5.00 2.00
□□ 118 Brian Holzinger, Buff. 5.00 1.00
□□ 119 Shayne Corson, Mont. 5.00 2.00
□□ 120 Bryan Smolinski, NYIs. 5.00 1.00
□□ 121 Tony Granato, SanJ. 6.00 1.00
□□ 122 Mariusz Czerkawski, Edmo. 6.00 1.00
□□ 123 Andrew Cassels, Hart. 6.00 1.00
□□ 124 Scott Stevens, NJer. 10.00 2.00
□□ 125 Mike Ridley, Vanc. 5.00 1.00
□□ 126 Jamie Langenbrunner, Dall. 6.00 1.00
□□ 127 Scott Mellanby, Flor. 6.00 1.00
□□ 128 Grant Fuhr (G), SLou. 15.00 3.00
□□ 129 Félix Potvin (G), Toro. 15.00 3.00
□□ 130 Marc Denis (G), Colo. 10.00 6.00
□□ 131 Corey Hirsch (G), Vanc. 5.00 1.00
□□ 132 Chris Osgood (G), Detr. 15.00 3.00
□□ 133 Peter Bondra, Wash. 15.00 3.00
□□ 134 Martin Brodeur (G), NJer. 40.00 10.00
□□ 135 Pierre Turgeon, SLou. 10.00 2.00
□□ 136 Pat Verbeek, Dall. 5.00 2.00
□□ 137 Scott Niedermayer, NJer. 5.00 2.00
□□ 138 Geoff Sanderson, Hart. 6.00 1.00
□□ 139 Jason Dawe, Buff. 5.00 1.00
□□ 140 Rob Niedermayer, Flor. 6.00 1.00
□□ 141 Daniel Alfredsson, Otta. 15.00 3.00
□□ 142 Jim Campbell, SLou. 5.00 1.00
□□ 143 Roman Hamrlik, Tamp. 6.00 1.00
□□ 144 Rob Blake, LosA. 15.00 3.00
□□ 145 Chris Chelios, Chic. 15.00 3.00
□□ 146 Teemu Selänne, Anah. 20.00 5.00
□□ 147 Jim Carey (G), Bos 5.00 1.00
□□ 148 Dino Ciccarelli, Tamp. 5.00 2.00
□□ 149 Mark Recchi, Mont. 10.00 2.00
□□ 150 Chris Pronger, SLou. 15.00 3.00

TRIPLE DIAMOND

Triple	Gold	BD
□□ 151 Paul Coffey, Phil.	70.00	15.00
□□ 152 Adam Oates, Wash.	50.00	12.00
□□ 153 Keith Tkachuk, Phoe.	70.00	15.00
□□ 154 Janne Niinimaa, Phil.	30.00	12.00
□□ 155 Sergei Fedorov, Detr.	120.00	25.00
□□ 156 Dominik Hasek (G), Buff.	120.00	25.00
□□ 157 Eric Lindros, Phil.	120.00	25.00
□□ 158 Curtis Joseph (G), Edmo.	120.00	25.00
□□ 159 Alexei Yashin, Otta.	70.00	15.00
□□ **160 Joe Thornton, Cdn. RC**	**675.00**	**650.00**

♦ A Joe Thornton rookie card graded PSA-9 sold for $753.25 U.S. (approx. $1,130 Cdn.) at eBay.ca in Spring 2003.

□□ 161 Bryan Berard, NYIs.	40.00	15.00
□□ 162 Steve Yzerman, Detr.	300.00	60.00
□□ 163 Mats Sundin, Toro.	120.00	25.00
□□ 164 Jarome Iginla, Calg.	100.00	30.00
□□ 165 John Vanbiesbrouck (G), Flor.	60.00	12.00
□□ 166 Mario Lemieux, Pitt.	370.00	70.00
□□ 167 Jeremy Roenick, Phoe.	100.00	20.00
□□ **168 Patrick Lalime (G), Pitt. RC**	**300.00**	**250.00**
□□ 169 Joe Sakic, Colo.	200.00	40.00
□□ 170 Brett Hull, SLou.	120.00	25.00
□□ 171 Peter Forsberg, Colo.	170.00	35.00
□□ 172 Doug Weight, Edmo.	70.00	15.00
□□ 173 Tony Amonte, Chic.	70.00	15.00
□□ 174 Patrick Roy (G), Colo.	370.00	70.00
□□ 175 Paul Kariya, Anah.	170.00	30.00
□□ 176 Pavel Bure, Vanc.	100.00	20.00
□□ 177 Raymond Bourque, Bost.	150.00	30.00
□□ 178 Saku Koivu, Mont.	100.00	20.00
□□ 179 Wade Redden, Otta.	40.00	15.00
□□ 180 Wayne Gretzky, NYRa.	500.00	100.00
Promo		**Sample**
□ 180 Wayne Gretzky Sample		10.00

RUN FOR THE CUP

Complete Set (180 cards): 1200.00

Insert (#/100)	**RFTC**
□ RC1 Wayne Gretzky, NYRa.	350.00
□ RC2 Saku Koivu, Mont.	50.00
□ RC3 Mario Lemieux, Pitt.	250.00
□ RC4 Patrick Roy (G), Colo.	250.00
□ RC5 Jaromir Jagr, Pitt.	75.00
□ RC6 John Vanbiesbrouck (G), Flor.	25.00
□ RC7 Peter Forsberg, Colo.	100.00
□ RC8 Paul Kariya, Anah.	100.00
□ RC9 Steve Yzerman, Detr.	200.00
□ RC10 Joe Sakic, Colo.	125.00
□ RC11 Mark Messier, NYRa.	75.00
□ RC12 Sergei Fedorov, Detr.	75.00
□ RC13 Mats Sundin, Toro.	75.00
□ RC14 Pavel Bure, Vanc.	50.00
□ RC15 Ed Jovanovski, Flor.	35.00
□ RC16 Mike Modano, Dall.	75.00
□ RC17 Curtis Joseph (G), Edmo.	75.00
□ RC18 Teemu Selänne, Anah.	50.00
□ RC19 Jarome Iginla, Calg.	80.00
□ RC20 Eric Lindros, Phil.	75.00

1996 - 97 UPPER DECK COLLECTOR'S CHOICE

Complete Set (348 cards): 50.00
Young Guns Set (15 cards): 90.00
Common Player: .20

Player	UDCC
□ 1 Paul Kariya, Anah.	.50
□ 2 Teemu Selänne, Anah.	.20
□ 3 Steve Rucchin, Anah.	.20
□ 4 Mikael Shtalenkov (G), Anah.	.20
□ 5 Guy Hebert (G), Anah.	.20
□ 6 Shawn Van Allen, Anah.	.20
□ 7 Anatoli Semenov, Anah.	.20
□ **8 J.F. Jomphe, Anah. RC**	**.20**
□ 9 Alex Hicks, Anah.	.20
□ 10 Roman Oskiuta, Anah.	.20
□ 11 Todd Ewen, Anah.	.20
□ 12 Adam Oates, Bost.	.20
□ 13 Raymond Bourque, Bost.	.50
□ 14 Don Sweeney, Bost.	.20
□ 15 Kyle McLaren, Bost.	.20
□ 16 Cam Neely, Bost.	.50
□ 17 Bill Ranford (G), Bost.	.20
□ 18 Rick Tocchet, Bost.	.20
□ 19 Ted Donato, Bost.	.20
□ 20 Shawn McEachern, Bost. (Otta.)	.20
□ 21 Ron Rohloff, Bost.	.20
□ 22 Joe Mullen, Bost.	.20
□ 23 Pat LaFontaine, Buff.	.20
□ 24 Brian Holzinger, Buff.	.20
□ 25 Wayne Primeau, Buff.	.20
□ 26 Alexei Zhitnik, Buff.	.20
□ 27 Derek Plante, Buff.	.20
□ 28 Randy Burridge, Buff.	.20
□ 29 Brad May, Buff.	.20
□ 30 Dominik Hasek (G), Buff.	.50
□ 31 Jason Dawe, Buff.	.20
□ 32 Michael Peca, Buff.	.20
□ 33 Matthew Barnaby, Buff.	.20
□ 34 Trevor Kidd (G), Calg.	.20
□ 35 Theoren Fleury, Calg.	.20
□ 36 Cale Hulse, Calg.	.20
□ 37 Bob Sweeney, Calg.	.20
□ 38 Michael Nylander, Calg.	.20
□ 39 German Titov, Calg.	.20
□ 40 Cory Stillman, Cgy	.20
□ 41 Zarley Zalapski, Calg.	.20
□ 42 Jocelyn Lemieux, Calg.	.20
□ 43 Sandy McCarthy, Calg.	.20
□ 44 Steve Chiasson, Calg.	.20
□ 45 Eric Dazé, Chic.	.20
□ 46 Jeremy Roenick, Chic.	.20
□ 47 Chris Chelios, Chic.	.20
□ 48 Joe Murphy, Chic. (SLou.)	.20
□ 49 Tony Amonte, Chic.	.20
□ 50 Bernie Nicholls, Chic.	.20
□ 51 Eric Weinrich, Chic.	.20
□ 52 Gary Suter, Chic.	.20
□ 53 Jeff Shantz, Chic.	.20
□ 54 Jeff Hackett (G), Chic.	.20
□ 55 Ed Belfour (G), Chic.	.50
□ 56 Uwe Krupp, Colo.	.20
□ 57 Claude Lemieux, Colo.	.20
□ 58 Adam Deadmarsh, Colo.	.20
□ 59 Stéphane Fiset (G), Colo. (LosA.)	.20
□ 60 Sandis Ozolinsh, Colo.	.20
□ 61 Stéphane Yelle, Colo.	.20
□ 62 Valeri Kamensky, Colo.	.20
□ 63 Peter Forsberg, Colo.	.50
□ 64 Joe Sakic, Colo.	.50
□ 65 Patrick Roy (G), Colo.	1.50
□ 66 Chris Simon, Colo.	.20
□ 67 Todd Harvey, Dall.	.20
□ 68 Joe Nieuwendyk, Dall.	.20
□ 69 Mike Modano, Dall.	.50
□ 70 Derian Hatcher, Dall.	.20
□ 71 Kevin Hatcher, Dall. (Pitt.)	.20
□ 72 Benoît Hogue, Dall.	.20
□ 73 Guy Carbonneau, Dall.	.20
□ 74 Jamie Langenbrunner, Dall.	.20
□ 75 Jere Lehtinen, Dall.	.20
□ 76 Criag Ludwig, Dall.	.20
□ 77 Grant Marshall, Dall.	.20
□ 78 Greg Johnson, Detr.	.20
□ 79 Steve Yzerman, Detr.	1.00
□ 80 Sergei Fedorov, Detr.	.50
□ 81 Vyacheslav Kozlov, Detr.	.20
□ 82 Vladimir Konstantinov, Detr.	.20
□ 83 Igor Larionov, Detr.	.20
□ 84 Chris Osgood (G), Detr.	.20
□ 85 Paul Coffey, Detr.	.20
□ 86 Nicklas Lidström, Detr.	.20
□ 87 Keith Primeau, Detr.	.20
□ 88 Dino Ciccarelli, Detr.	.20
□ 89 Darren McCarty, Detr.	.20
□ 90 Curtis Joseph (G), Edmo.	.50
□ 91 Doug Weight, Edmo.	.20
□ 92 Jason Arnott, Edmo.	.20
□ 93 Mariusz Czerkawski, Edmo.	.20
□ 94 Kelly Buchberger, Edmo.	.20
□ 95 Zedeno Ciger, Edmo.	.20
□ 96 David Oliver, Edmo.	.20
□ 97 Todd Marchant, Edmo.	.20
□ 98 Miroslav Satan, Edmo.	.20
□ 99 Bryan Marchment, Edmo.	.20
□ 100 Louie DeBrusk, Edmo.	.20
□ 101 John Vanbiesbrouck (G), Flor.	.20
□ 102 Scott Mellanby, Flor.	.20
□ 103 Rob Niedermayer, Flor.	.20
□ 104 Robert Svehla, Flor.	.20
□ 105 Ed Jovanovski, Flor.	.20
□ 106 Joan Garpenlov, Flor.	.20
□ 107 Jody Hull, Flor.	.20
□ 108 Bill Lindsay, Flor.	.20
□ 109 Terry Carkner, Flor.	.20
□ 110 Stu Barnes, Flor.	.20
□ 111 Ray Sheppard, Flor.	.20
□ 112 Brendan Shanahan, Hart.	.50
□ 113 Geoff Sanderson, Hart.	.20
□ 114 Andrei Nikolishin, Hart.	.20
□ 115 Andrew Cassels, Hart.	.20
□ 116 Nelson Emerson, Hart.	.20
□ 117 Jason Muzzatti (G), Hart.	.20
□ 118 Marek Malik, Hart.	.20
□ 119 Sean Burke (G), Hart.	.20
□ 120 Jeff Brown, Hart.	.20
□ 121 Jeff O'Neill, Hart.	.20
□ 122 Kelly Chase, Hart.	.20
□ 123 Dimitri Khristich, LosA.	.20
□ 124 Kevin Stevens, LosA.	.20
□ 125 Vitali Yachmenev, LosA.	.20
□ 126 Yanic Perreault, LosA.	.20
□ 127 Kevin Todd, LosA.	.20
□ 128 Aki Berg, LosA.	.20
□ 129 Craig Johnson, LosA.	.20
□ 130 Mattias Norstrom, LosA.	.20
□ 131 Ray Ferraro, LosA.	.20
□ 132 Steve Finn, LosA.	.20
□ 133 Pierre Turgeon, Mont.	.20
□ 134 Saku Koivu, Mont.	.20
□ 135 Mark Recchi, Mont.	.20
□ 136 Jocelyn Thibault (G), Mont.	.20
□ 137 Andrei Kovalenko, Mont.	.20
□ 138 Vincent Damphousse, Mont.	.20
□ 139 Vladimir Malakhov, Mont.	.20
□ 140 Brian Savage, Mont.	.20
□ 141 Valeri Bure, Mont.	.20
□ 142 Patrice Brisebois, Mont.	.20
□ 143 Martin Rucinsky, Mont.	.20
□ 144 Martin Brodeur (G), NJer.	.50
□ 145 Steve Thomas, NJer.	.20
□ 146 Bill Guerin, NJer.	.20
□ 147 Petr Sykora, NJer.	.20
□ 148 Scott Stevens, NJer.	.20
□ 149 Scott Niedermayer, NJer.	.20
□ 150 Phil Housley, NJer.	.20
□ 151 Brian Rolston, NJer.	.20
□ 152 Neal Broten, NJer.	.20
□ 153 Dave Andreychuk, NJer.	.20
□ 154 Randy McKay, NJer.	.20
□ 155 Éric Fichaud (G), NYIs.	.20
□ 156 Zigmund Palffy, NYIs.	.20
□ 157 Travis Green, NYIs.	.20
□ 158 Darby Hendrickson, NYIs.	.20
□ 159 Kenny Jönsson, NYIs.	.20
□ 160 Marty McInnis, NYIs.	.20
□ 161 Bryan McCabe, NYIs.	.20
□ 162 Darius Kasparaitis, NYIs.	.20
□ 163 Alexander Semak, NYIs.	.20
□ 164 Todd Bertuzzi, NYIs.	1.00
□ 165 Niclas Andersson, NYIs.	.20
□ 166 Mark Messier, NYRa.	.50
□ 167 Mike Richter (G), NYRa.	.20
□ 168 Nicklas Lidström, NYRa.	.20
□ 169 Brian Leetch, NYRa.	.20
□ 170 Wayne Gretzky, NYRa.	2.00
□ 171 Luc Robitaille, NYRa.	.20
□ 172 Marty McSorley, NYRa.	.20
□ 173 Jari Kurri, NYRa.	.50
□ 174 Adam Graves, NYRa.	.20
□ 175 Sergei Nemchinov, NYRa.	.20
□ 176 Alexei Kovalev, NYRa.	.20
□ 177 Daniel Alfredsson, Otta.	.20
□ 178 Randy Cunneyworth, Otta.	.20
□ 179 Alexei Yashin, Otta.	.20
□ 180 Alexandre Daigle, Otta.	.20
□ 181 Radek Bonk, Otta.	.20
□ 182 Steve Duchesne, Otta.	.20
□ 183 Ted Drury, Otta.	.20
□ 184 Antti Törmänen, Otta.	.20
□ 185 Stanislav Neckar, Otta.	.20
□ 186 Damian Rhodes (G), Otta.	.20
□ 187 Janne Laukkanen, Otta.	.20
□ 188 Eric Lindros, Phil.	.50
□ 189 Mikael Renberg, Phil.	.20
□ 190 John LeClair, Phil.	.20
□ 191 Ron Hextall (G), Phil.	.20
□ 192 Rod Brind'Amour, Phil.	.20
□ 193 Joel Otto, Phil.	.20
□ 194 Pat Falloon, Phil.	.20
□ 195 Éric Desjardins, Phil.	.20
□ 196 Dale Hawerchuk, Phil.	.20
□ 197 Chris Therien, Phil.	.20
□ 198 Dan Quinn, Phil.	.20
□ 199 Oleg Tverdovsky, Winn.	.20
□ 200 Chad Kilger, Winn.	.20
□ 201 Keith Tkachuk, Winn.	.20
□ 202 Igor Korolev, Winn.	.20
□ 203 Alexei Zhamnov, Winn.	.20
□ 204 Nikolai Khabibulin (G), Winn.	.20
□ 205 Shane Doan, Winn.	.20
□ 206 Deron Quint, Winn.	.20
□ 207 Craig Janney, Winn.	.20
□ 208 Norm Maciver, Winn.	.20
□ 209 Teppo Numminen, Winn.	.20
□ 210 Mario Lemieux, Pitt.	1.50
□ 211 Jaromir Jagr, Pitt.	.50
□ 212 Ron Francis, Pitt.	.20
□ 213 Tom Barrasso (G), Pitt.	.20
□ 214 Sergei Zubov, Pitt.	.20
□ 215 Tomas Sandström, Pitt.	.20
□ 216 Joe Dziedzic, Pitt.	.20
□ 217 Richard Park, Pitt.	.20
□ 218 Bryan Smolinski, Pitt.	.20
□ 219 Petr Nedved, Pitt.	.20
□ 220 Ken Wregget (G), Pitt.	.20
□ 221 Dmitri Mironov, Pitt.	.20
□ 222 Peter Zezel, SLou.	.20
□ 223 Brett Hull, SLou.	.50
□ 224 Grant Fuhr (G), SLou.	.20
□ 225 Shayne Corson, SLou.	.20
□ 226 Chris Pronger, SLou.	.20
□ 227 Craig MacTavish, SLou.	.20
□ 228 Al MacInnis, SLou.	.20
□ 229 Geoff Courtnall, SLou.	.20
□ 230 Stéphane Matteau, SLou.	.20
□ 231 Tony Twist, SLou.	.20
□ 232 Brian Noonan, SLou.	.20
□ 233 Owen Nolan, SanJ.	.20
□ 234 Shean Donovan, SanJ.	.20
□ 235 Darren Turcotte, SanJ.	.20
□ 236 Marcus Ragnarsson, SanJ.	.20
□ 237 Viktor Kozlov, SanJ.	.20
□ 238 Jeff Friesen, SanJ.	.20
□ 239 Chris Terreri (G), SanJ.	.20
□ 240 Ray Whitney, SanJ.	.20
□ 241 Ville Peltonen, SanJ.	.20
□ 242 Andrei Nazarov, SanJ.	.20
□ 243 Ulf Dahlen, SanJ.	.20
□ 244 Roman Hamrlik, Tamp.	.20
□ 245 Chris Gratton, Tamp.	.20
□ 246 Petr Klima, Tamp.	.20
□ 247 Daren Puppa (G), Tamp.	.20
□ 248 Rob Zamuner, Tamp.	.20
□ 249 Aaron Gavey, Tamp.	.20
□ 250 Brian Bradley, Tamp.	.20
□ 251 Paul Ysebaert, Tamp.	.20
□ 252 Igor Ulanov, Tamp.	.20
□ 253 Alexander Selivanov, Tamp.	.20
□ 254 Shawn Burr, Tamp.	.20
□ 255 Mats Sundin, Toro.	.50
□ 256 Doug Gilmour, Toro.	.20
□ 257 Félix Potvin (G), Toro.	.20
□ 258 Wendel Clark, Toro.	.20
□ 259 Kirk Muller, Toro.	.20
□ 260 Dave Gagner, Toro.	.20
□ 261 Tie Domi, Toro.	.20
□ 262 Mathieu Schneider, Toro.	.20
□ 263 Dimitri Yushkevich, Toro.	.20
□ 264 Don Beaupré, Toro.	.20
□ 265 Larry Murphy, Toro.	.20
□ 266 Pavel Bure, Vanc.	.20
□ 267 Alexander Mogilny, Vanc.	.20
□ 268 Trevor Linden, Vanc.	.20
□ 269 Jyrki Lumme, Vanc.	.20
□ 270 Cliff Ronning, Vanc.	.20
□ 271 Kirk McLean (G), Vanc.	.20
□ 272 Corey Hirsch (G), Vanc.	.20
□ 273 Esa Tikkanen, Vanc.	.20
□ 274 Gino Odjick, Vanc.	.20
□ 275 Markus Näslund, Vanc.	.50
□ 276 Russ Courtnall, Vanc.	.20
□ 277 Joé Juneau, Wash.	.20
□ 278 Jim Carey (G), Wash.	.20
□ 279 Peter Bondra, Wash.	.20
□ 280 Michal Pivonka, Wash.	.20
□ 281 Steve Konowalchuk, Wash.	.20
□ 282 Pat Peake, Wash.	.20
□ 283 Brendan Witt, Wash.	.20
□ 284 Stefan Ustorf, Wash.	.20
□ 285 Keith Jones, Wash.	.20
□ 286 Sergei Gonchar, Wash.	.20
□ 287 Sylvain Côté, Wash.	.20
□ 288 Dale Hunter, Wash.	.20
□ 289 Paul Kariya, Anah.	.50
□ 290 Wayne Gretzky, NYRa.	2.00
□ 291 Eric Lindros, Phil.	.50
□ 292 Steve Yzerman, Detr.	1.00
□ 293 Mario Lemieux, Pitt.	1.50
□ 294 Jaromir Jagr, Pitt.	.50
□ 295 Keith Tkachuk, Winn.	.20
□ 296 Mark Messier, NYRa.	.50
□ 297 Jeremy Roenick, Chic.	.20
□ 298 Peter Forsberg, Colo.	.50
□ 299 Joe Sakic, Colo.	.50
□ 300 Theoren Fleury, Calg.	.20
□ 301 Chris Chelios, Chic.	.20
□ 302 Vladimir Konstantinov, Detr.	.20
□ 303 Brian Leetch, NYRa.	.20
□ 304 Raymond Bourque, Bost.	.50
□ 305 Scott Stevens, NJer.	.20
□ 306 Martin Brodeur (G), NJer.	.50
□ 307 Patrick Roy (G), Colo.	1.50
□ 308 Scotty Bowman, Detr.	.20
□ 309 P. Kariya, Anah. (G. Hebert/ T. Selänne)	.20
□ 310 R. Bourque, Bost. (C. Neely/ A. Oates)	.20
□ 311 P. LaFontaine, Buff. (Zhitnik/ Hasek (G))	.20
□ 312 T. Fleury, Calg. (T. Kidd/ M. Nylander)	.20
□ 313 J. Roenick, Chic. (E. Dazé/ C. Chelios)	.20
□ 314 J. Sakic, Colo. (P. Roy (G)/ P. Forsberg)	1.00
□ 315 M. Modano, Dall. (Harvey/ Nieuwendyk)	.20
□ 316 V. Konstantinov, Detr. (Coffey/ Fedorov)	.20
□ 317 D. Weight, Edmo. (C. Joseph (G)/ Arnott)	.20
□ 318 Vanbiesbrouck (G), Flor. (R. Niedermayer/ E. Jovanovski)	.20
□ 319 Shanahan, Hart. (Burke (G)/ Sanderson)	.20
□ 320 V. Yachmenev, LosA. (Khristich/ Ferraro)	.20
□ 321 S. Koivu, Mont. (Thibault (G)/ Turgeon)	.20
□ 322 M. Brodeur (G), NJer. (Stevens/ Thomas)	.20
□ 323 T. Bertuzzi, NYIs. (Fichaud (G)/ Palffy)	.20
□ 324 A. Yashin, Otta. (A. Daigle/ D. Rhodes (G))	.20
□ 325 A. Graves, NYRa. (Leetch/ Richter (G))	.20
□ 326 J. LeClair, Phil. (Renberg/ Hextall (G))	.20
□ 327 K. Tkachuk, Winn. (Zhamnov/ Tverdovsky)	.20
□ 328 J. Jagr, Pitt. (R. Francis/ P. Nedved)	.20
□ 329 W. Gretzky, SLou. (B. Hull/ A. MacInnis)	.50
□ 330 O. Nolan, SanJ. (Terreri (G)/ Turcotte)	.20
□ 331 R. Hamrlik, Tamp. (Puppa (G)/ Gratton)	.20
□ 332 M. Sundin, Toro. (Potvin (G)/ Gilmour)	.20
□ 333 A. Mogilny, Vanc. (T. Linden/ P. Bure)	.20
□ 334 J. Carey (G), Wash. (Juneau/ Bondra)	.20
□ 335 E. Lindros, East. (Messier/ Lemieux)	.50

336 J. Sakic, West. (W. Gretzky/ T. Selänne)	1.00
337 Chad Kilger, Winn.	.20
338 Todd Bertuzzi, NYIs.	.50
339 Petr Sykora, NJer.	.20
340 Ed Jovanovski, Flor.	.20
341 Kyle McLaren, Bost.	.20
342 Brian Holzinger, Buff.	.20
343 Jeff O'Neill, Hart.	.20
344 Daniel Alfredsson, Otta.	.20
345 Brendan Witt, Wash.	.20
346 Daymond Langkow, Tamp.	.20
347 CL: Roy (G)/ C. Lemieux	.20
348 CL: Vanbiesbrouck (G)/ Dvorak	.20
Young Guns	**YG**
349 Jarome Iginla, Calg.	3.00
350 Sergei Berezin, Toro. RC	**2.00**
351 José Théodore (G), Mont.	4.50
352 Rem Murray, Edmo.	.50
353 Daniel Goneau, NYRa.	.50
354 Ethan Moreau, Chic.	.50
355 Jonas Höglund, Calg.	.50
356 Anders Eriksson, Detr.	.50
357 Christian Dubé, NYRa.	.50
358 Roman Turek (G), Dall. RC	**4.50**
359 Bryan Berard, NYIs.	1.00
360 Jim Campbell, SLou.	.50
361 Janne Niinimaa, Phil.	.50
362 Wade Redden, Otta.	1.00
363 Marc Denis, Colo.	1.50

5X7 BLOW UP

Insert Set (18 oversize cards):	**15.00**
Oversize	**5x7**
13 Raymond Bourque, Bost.	3.00
23 Pat LaFontaine, Buff.	1.00
35 Theoren Fleury, Calg.	1.00
62 Valeri Kamensky, Colo.	1.00
69 Mike Modano, Dall.	2.00
84 Chris Osgood (G), Detr.	1.00
133 Pierre Turgeon, SLou.	1.00
170 Wayne Gretzky, SLou.	10.00
244 Roman Hamrlik, Tamp.	1.00
254 Félix Potvin (G), Toro.	1.00
1of8 Wayne Gretzky, NYRa.	10.00
2of8 Theoren Fleury, Calg.	1.00
3of8 Jason Arnott, Edmo.	1.00
4of8 Saku Koivu, Mont.	2.00
5of8 Pierre Turgeon, Mont.	1.00
6of8 Daniel Alfredsson, Otta.	1.00
7of8 Félix Potvin (G), Toro.	1.00
8of8 Alexander Mogilny, Vanc.	1.00

MVP

There are two versions: the silver insert (1:1) and the Gold parallel (1:35).

Insert Set (45 cards):	**125.00**	**12.00**
Inserts	**Gold**	**MVP**
UD1 Wayne Gretzky, SLou.	25.00	2.50
UD2 Ron Francis, Pitt.	3.00	.30
UD3 Peter Forsberg, Colo.	8.00	.50
UD4 Alexander Mogilny, Vanc.	3.00	.30
UD5 Joe Sakic, Colo.	10.00	1.00
UD6 Claude Lemieux, Colo.	2.00	.30
UD7 Teemu Selänne, Anah.	5.00	.50
UD8 John LeClair, Phil.	5.00	.50
UD9 Doug Weight, Edmo.	3.00	.30
UD10 Paul Kariya, Anah.	8.00	.50
UD11 Theoren Fleury, Calg.	3.00	.30
UD12 John Vanbiesbrouck (G), Flor.	3.00	.30
UD13 Sergei Fedorov, Detr.	6.00	.50
UD14 Steve Yzerman, Detr.	15.00	1.50
UD15 Adam Oates, Bost.	2.00	.30
UD16 Keith Tkachuk, Winn.	3.00	.30
UD17 Mike Modano, Dall.	6.00	.50
UD18 Jeremy Roenick, Chic.	5.00	.50
UD19 Patrick Roy (G), Colo.	18.00	1.50
UD20 Félix Potvin (G), Toro.	3.00	.30
UD21 Martin Brodeur (G), NJer.	10.00	1.00
UD22 Pavel Bure, Vanc.	5.00	.50
UD23 Peter Bondra, Wash.	3.00	.30
UD24 Zigmund Palffy, NYIs.	3.00	.30
UD25 Roman Hamrlik, Tamp.	2.00	.30
UD26 Brendan Shanahan, Hart.	6.00	.50
UD27 Raymond Bourque, Bost.	7.00	.50
UD28 Paul Coffey, Detr.	3.00	.30
UD29 Brett Hull, SLou.	6.00	.50
UD30 Pat LaFontaine, Buff.	3.00	.30
UD30 Brian Leetch, NYRa.	3.00	.30
UD31 Chris Chelios, Chic.	3.00	.30
UD32 Vitali Yachmenev, LosA.	2.00	.30
UD33 Nicklas Lidström, Detr.	3.00	.30
UD34 Ed Jovanovski, Flor.	2.00	.30
UD35 Sandis Ozolinsh, Colo.	2.00	.30
UD36 Scott Stevens, NJer.	2.00	.30
UD37 Éric Dazé, Chic.	2.00	.30
UD38 Saku Koivu, Mont.	5.00	.50
UD39 Daniel Alfredsson, Otta.	3.00	.30
UD41 Cam Neely, Bost.	6.00	.50
UD42 Owen Nolan, SanJ.	3.00	.30
UD43 Jaromir Jagr, Pitt.	6.00	.50
UD44 Mats Sundin, Toro.	6.00	.50
UD45 Doug Gilmour, Toro.	3.00	.30

STICK UM'S

Insert Set (30 stickers):	**30.00**
Insert	**SU**
S1 Wayne Gretzky, SLou.	5.00
S2 Brett Hull, SLou.	1.00
S3 Peter Forsberg, Colo.	1.50
S4 Patrick Roy (G), Colo.	3.50
S5 Cam Neely, Bost.	1.00
S6 Jeremy Roenick, Chic.	1.00
S7 Mario Lemieux, Pitt.	3.50
S8 Jaromir Jagr, Pitt.	1.00
S9 Eric Lindros, Phil.	1.00
S10 Mark Messier, NYRa.	1.00
S11 Félix Potvin (G), Toro.	.50
S12 Brendan Shanahan, Hart.	1.00
S13 Teemu Selänne, Anah.	1.00
S14 Paul Kariya, Anah.	1.50
S15 Mike Modano, Dall.	1.00
S16 Pavel Bure, Vanc.	1.00
S17 Jim Carey (G), Wash.	.50
S18 Roman Hamrlik, Tamp.	.50
S19 Pierre Turgeon, SLou.	.50
S20 Theoren Fleury, Calg.	.50
S21 Pat LaFontaine, Buff.	.50
S22 Steve Yzerman, Detr.	3.00
S23 Sergei Fedorov, Detr.	1.00
S24 Martin Brodeur (G), NJer.	2.00
S25 Owen Nolan, SanJ.	.50
S26 Ice Machine	.50
S27 Stanley Cup	1.00
S28 Snapshot	.50
S29 Stripes	.50
S30 Goal!	.50

YOU CRASH THE GAME

There are three versions for each player except Sakic (C7) and Oates (C21) of which there are only two versions. Each version has a Gold parallel.

Shell Set (30 cards):	**20.00**
Insert Set (88 cards):	**60.00**
Insert	**YCTG**
C1 Wayne Gretzky, NYRa.	4.00
C2 Doug Gilmour, Toro.	.50
C3 Alexander Mogilny, Vanc.	.30
C4 Peter Bondra, Wash.	.50
C5 Mario Lemieux, Pitt.	3.00
C6 Jaromir Jagr, Pitt.	1.00
C7 Joe Sakic, Colo.	1.50
C8 Vitali Yachmenev, LosA.	.30
C9 Doug Weight, Edmo.	.50
C10 Steve Yzerman, Detr.	2.00
C11 Alexei Zhamnov, Winn.	.30
C12 John LeClair, Phil.	.50
C13 Daniel Alfredsson, Otta.	.50
C14 Brendan Shanahan, Hart.	1.00
C15 Saku Koivu, Mont.	.50
C16 Steve Thomas, NJer.	.30
C17 Pavel Bure, Vanc.	.50
C18 Vyacheslav Kozlov, Detr.	.30
C19 Teemu Selänne, Anah.	.50
C20 Éric Dazé, Chic.	.30
C21 Adam Oates, Bost.	.30
C22 Raymond Bourque, Bost.	1.00
C23 Jason Arnott, Edmo.	.30
C24 Paul Kariya, Anah.	1.00
C25 Mikael Renberg, Phil.	.30
C26 Keith Tkachuk, Winn.	.50
C27 Brian Leetch, NYRa.	.50
C28 Eric Lindros, Phil.	1.00
C29 Mats Sundin, Toro.	1.00
C30 Mark Messier, NYRa.	1.00

YOU CRASH THE GAME GOLD

Insert Set (88 cards):	**275.00**
Insert	**Gold**
C1 Wayne Gretzky, NYRa.	16.00
C2 Doug Gilmour, Toro.	2.00
C3 Alexander Mogilny, Vanc.	1.00
C4 Peter Bondra, Wash.	2.00
C5 Mario Lemieux, Pitt.	12.00
C6 Jaromir Jagr, Pitt.	4.00
C7 Joe Sakic, Colo.	6.00
C8 Vitali Yachmenev, LosA.	1.00
C9 Doug Weight, Edmo.	2.00
C10 Steve Yzerman, Detr.	9.00
C11 Alexei Zhamnov, Winn.	1.00
C12 John LeClair, Phil.	3.00
C13 Daniel Alfredsson, Otta.	2.00
C14 Brendan Shanahan, Hart.	4.00
C15 Saku Koivu, Mont.	3.00
C16 Steve Thomas, NJer.	1.00
C17 Pavel Bure, Vanc.	3.00
C18 Vyacheslav Kozlov, Detr.	1.00
C19 Teemu Selänne, Anah.	3.00
C20 Éric Dazé, Chic.	1.00
C21 Adam Oates, Bost.	1.00
C22 Raymond Bourque, Bost.	4.00
C23 Jason Arnott, Edmo.	1.00
C24 Paul Kariya, Anah.	5.00
C25 Mikael Renberg, Phil.	1.00
C26 Keith Tkachuk, Winn.	2.00
C27 Brian Leetch, NYRa.	2.00
C28 Eric Lindros, Phil.	4.00
C29 Mats Sundin, Toro.	4.00
C30 Mark Messier, NYRa.	4.00

YOU CRASH THE GAME PRIZE

There are two versions: the silver redeemed card and the die-cut gold parallels. Cards 20 and 25 do not exist (C20 and C25 did not win prizes).

Complete Set (28 cards):	**200.00**	**75.00**
Redemption	**Gold**	**Silver**
CR1 Wayne Gretzky, NYRa.	40.00	20.00
CR2 Doug Gilmour, Toro.	6.00	3.00
CR3 Alexander Mogilny, Vanc.	5.00	2.00
CR4 Peter Bondra, Wash.	6.00	3.00
CR5 Mario Lemieux, Pitt.	30.00	15.00
CR6 Jaromir Jagr, Pitt.	10.00	5.00
CR7 Joe Sakic, Colo.	16.00	8.00
CR8 Vitali Yachmenev, LosA.	5.00	2.00
CR9 Doug Weight, Edmo.	6.00	3.00
CR10 Steve Yzerman, Detr.	24.00	12.00
CR11 Alexei Zhamnov, Winn.	5.00	2.00
CR12 John LeClair, Phil.	8.00	4.00
CR13 Daniel Alfredsson, Otta.	6.00	3.00
CR14 Brendan Shanahan, Hart.	10.00	5.00
CR15 Saku Koivu, Mont.	8.00	4.00
CR16 Steve Thomas, NJer.	5.00	2.00
CR17 Pavel Bure, Vanc.	8.00	4.00
CR18 Vyacheslav Kozlov, Detr.	5.00	2.00
CR19 Teemu Selänne, Anah.	8.00	4.00
CR21 Adam Oates, Bost.	5.00	2.00
CR22 Raymond Bourque, Bost.	12.00	6.00
CR23 Jason Arnott, Edmo.	5.00	2.00
CR24 Paul Kariya, Anah.	14.00	7.00
CR26 Keith Tkachuk, Winn.	6.00	3.00
CR27 Brian Leetch, NYRa.	6.00	3.00
CR28 Eric Lindros, Phil.	10.00	5.00
CR29 Mats Sundin, Toro.	10.00	5.00
CR30 Mark Messier, NYRa.	10.00	5.00

1996 - 97 UPPER DECK ICE

Cards 1-115 have two versions each. Numbers 1-75 have a bronze Performers parallel, 76-105 have silver Phenoms parallel and 106-115 have a gold Legends parallel.

Complete Set (150 cards):		**170.00**
Parallel Set (115 cards):	**1600.00**	
Common Player:	**5.00**	**.50**
Player	**Bro.**	**Ice**
1 Kevin Todd, Anah.	5.00	.50
2 Adam Oates, Bost.	6.00	1.00
3 Bill Ranford (G), Bost.	6.00	1.00
4 Rick Tocchet, Bost.	5.00	.50
5 Dominik Hasek (G), Buff.	10.00	3.00
6 Richard Smehlik, Buff.	5.00	.50
7 Derek Plante, Buff.	5.00	.50
8 Joel Bouchard, Calg.	5.00	.50
9 Theoren Fleury, Calg.	5.00	1.50
10 Chris Chelios, Chic.	9.00	1.50
11 Ed Belfour (G), Chic.	15.00	3.00
12 Eric Weinrich, Chic.	5.00	.50
13 Tony Amonte, Chic.	9.00	1.50
14 Greg Adams, Dall.	5.00	.50
15 Jamie Langenbrunner, Dall.	5.00	.50
16 Sergei Zubov, Dall.	5.00	.50
17 Pat Verbeek, Dall.	5.00	.50
18 Chris Osgood (G), Detr.	5.00	1.50
19 Rem Murray, Edmo. RC	**5.00**	**1.50**
20 Jason Arnott, Edmo.	7.00	1.00
21 Curtis Joseph (G), Edmo.	15.00	3.00
22 Bill Lindsay, Flor.	5.00	.50
23 Ray Sheppard, Flor.	5.00	.50
24 Martin Straka, Flor.	5.00	.50
25 J-S Giguère (G), Hart.	25.00	20.00
26 Sean Burke (G), Hart.	9.00	1.50
27 Keith Primeau, Hart.	6.00	1.00
28 Geoff Sanderson, Hart.	5.00	.50
29 Rob Blake, LosA.	9.00	1.50
30 Ian Laperrière, LosA.	5.00	.50
31 Byron Dafoe (G), LosA.	6.00	1.00
32 Vincent Damphousse, Mont.	9.00	1.50
33 Darcy Tucker, Mont.	5.00	1.00
34 Brian Savage, Mont.	5.00	.50
35 Bill Guerin, NJer.	6.00	1.00
36 Scott Niedermayer, NJer.	5.00	.50
37 Steve Thomas, NJer.	5.00	.50
38 Valeri Zelepukin, NJer.	5.00	.50
39 Bryan Smolinski, NYIs.	5.00	.50
40 Derek King, NYIs.	5.00	.50
41 Mike Richter (G), NYRa.	7.00	1.00
42 Daniel Goneau, NYRa.	5.00	1.00
43 Brian Leetch, NYRa.	9.00	1.50
44 Adam Graves, NYRa.	6.00	1.00
45 Damian Rhodes (G), Otta.	5.00	.50
46 Mikael Renberg, Phil.	5.00	.50
47 Éric Desjardins, Phil.	5.00	.50
48 Rod Brind'Amour, Phil.	5.00	.50
49 Janne Niinimaa, Phil.	5.00	1.00
50 Dale Hawerchuk, Phil.	9.00	1.50
51 Jeremy Roenick, Phoe.	10.00	2.00
52 Mike Gartner, Phoe.	10.00	2.00
53 Cliff Ronning, Phoe.	5.00	.50
54 Patrick Lalime (G), Pitt. RC	**15.00**	**10.00**
55 Ron Francis, Pitt.	9.00	1.50
56 Petr Nedved, Pitt.	5.00	.50
57 Bernie Nicholls, SanJ.	5.00	.50
58 Jeff Friesen, SanJ.	5.00	.50
59 Owen Nolan, SanJ.	9.00	1.50
60 Marty McSorley, SanJ.	5.00	.50
61 Pierre Turgeon, SLou.	6.00	1.00
62 Grant Fuhr (G), SLou.	9.00	1.50
63 Chris Pronger, SLou.	9.00	1.50
64 Jim Campbell, SLou.	5.00	.50
65 Chris Gratton, Tamp.	5.00	.50
66 Dino Ciccarelli, Tamp.	5.00	.50
67 Félix Potvin (G), Toro.	9.00	1.50
68 Tie Domi, Toro.	5.00	.50
69 Doug Gilmour, Toro.	9.00	1.50
70 Trevor Linden, Vanc.	6.00	1.00
71 Corey Hirsch (G), Vanc.	5.00	.50
72 Jim Carey (G), Wash.	5.00	.50
73 Chris Simon, Wash.	5.00	.50
74 Mark Tinordi, Wash.	5.00	.50
75 Sergei Gonchar, Wash.	5.00	.50
Player	**Sil.**	**Ice**
76 Paul Kariya, Anah.	40.00	4.00
77 Teemu Selänne, Anah.	20.00	2.00
78 Jarome Iginla, Calg.	20.00	4.50
79 Eric Dazé, Chic.	12.00	1.00
80 Sandis Ozolinsh, Colo.	8.00	.50
81 Peter Forsberg, Colo.	40.00	4.00
82 Mike Modano, Dall.	30.00	3.00
83 Anders Eriksson, Detr.	8.00	.50
84 Sergei Fedorov, Detr.	30.00	3.00
85 Brendan Shanahan, Detr.	30.00	3.00
86 Mike Grier Edmo. RC	**10.00**	**4.50**
87 Doug Weight, Edmo.	15.00	1.50
88 Ed Jovanovski, Flor.	12.00	1.00
89 Saku Koivu, Mont.	20.00	2.00
90 José Théodore (G), Mont.	35.00	7.00
91 Jocelyn Thibault (G), Mont.	10.00	1.00
92 Martin Brodeur (G), NJer.	45.00	4.50
93 Bryan Berard, NYIs.	8.00	1.50
94 Zigmund Palffy, NYIs.	15.00	1.50
95 Daniel Alfredsson, Otta.	15.00	1.50
96 Alexei Yashin, Otta.	15.00	1.50
97 Wade Redden, Otta.	9.00	1.50
98 John LeClair, Phil.	20.00	2.00
99 Oleg Tverdovsky, Phoe.	8.00	.50
100 Keith Tkachuk, Phoe.	15.00	1.50
101 Jaromir Jagr, Pitt.	30.00	3.00
102 Roman Hamrlik, Pitt.	8.00	.50
103 Sergei Berezin, Toro. RC	**10.00**	**4.50**
104 Alexander Mogilny, Vanc.	10.00	1.00
105 Pavel Bure, Vanc.	20.00	2.00
Player	**Gold**	**Ice**
106 Raymond Bourque, Bost.	125.00	3.50
107 Patrick Roy (G), Colo.	300.00	9.00
108 Joe Sakic, Colo.	150.00	4.50
109 Steve Yzerman, Detr.	250.00	7.00
110 John Vanbiesbrouck (G), Flor.	50.00	1.00
111 Mark Messier, NYRa.	100.00	3.00
112 Wayne Gretzky, NYRa.	400.00	10.00
113 Eric Lindros, Phil.	100.00	3.00
114 Mario Lemieux, Pitt.	300.00	5.00
115 Brett Hull, SLou.	100.00	3.00

WORLD JUNIORS

World Junior	**WJC**
116 Joe Thornton, Cdn. RC	**40.00**
117 Marc Denis (G), Cdn.	2.50
118 Martin Biron (G), Cdn.	7.00
119 Jason Doig, Cdn.	.50
120 Daniel Brière, Cdn.	5.00
121 Trevor Letowski, Cdn. RC	**3.50**
122 Boyd Devereaux, Cdn.	2.50
123 Dwayne Hay, Cdn. RC	**2.00**
124 Hugh Hamilton, Cdn.	.50
125 Brad Isbister, Cdn. RC	**5.00**
126 Shane Willis, Cdn. RC	**4.50**
127 Trent Whitfield, Cdn. RC	**3.50**
128 Jesse Wallin, Cdn.	1.00
129 Alyn McCauley, Cdn.	1.50
130 Cameron Mann, Cdn. RC	**3.50**
131 Jeff Ware, Cdn.	.50
132 Cory Sarich, Cdn.	1.50
133 Rick Jackman, Cdn. RC	**3.50**
134 Brad Larsen, Cdn.	.50
135 Peter Schaefer, Cdn. RC	**3.00**
136 Christian Dubé, Cdn.	.50
137 Chris Phillips, Cdn.	1.00
138 Sergei Samsonov, Rus.	3.50
139 Aleksey Morozov, Rus.	1.00
140 Sergei Fedotov, Rus. RC	**2.00**
141 Den. Khlopotnov (G), Rus. RC	**2.00**
142 Andrei Markov, Rus. RC	**3.50**
143 Andrei Petrunin, Rus.	.50
144 Roman Lyasenko, Rus. RC	**2.00**
145 Joe Corvo, USA. RC	**2.00**
146 Erik Rasmussen, USA.	1.00
147 Michael York, USA.	12.00
148 Brian Boucher (G), USA.	1.50
149 Paul Mara, USA. RC	**3.50**
150 Marty Reasoner, USA.	1.00

STANLEY CUP FOUNDATIONS

There are two versions: the regular insert (1:96) and a die-cut Dynasty parallel (1:960).

Insert Set (10 cards):		1100.00	325.00
	Inserts	SCD	SCF
☐☐	S1 W. Gretzky / M. Messier	275.00	90.00
☐☐	S2 B. Shanahan / S. Yzerman	175.00	60.00
☐☐	S3 Jovanovski / V'b'sbrouck (G)	40.00	12.00
☐☐	S4 S. Koivu / J. Thibault	50.00	20.00
☐☐	S5 P. Roy / J. Sakic	250.00	80.00
☐☐	S6 P. Kariya / T. Selänne	100.00	40.00
☐☐	S7 J. Jagr / M. Lemieux	225.00	70.00
☐☐	S8 J. Roenick / K. Tkachuk	75.00	20.00
☐☐	S9 J. Arnott / D. Weight	50.00	20.00
☐☐	S10 J. LeClair / E. Lindros	100.00	30.00

1996 - 97 UPPER DECK POST

Complete Set (24 cards):		45.00
	Player	Post
☐	Raymond Bourque, NHLPA	3.00
☐	Chris Chelios, NHLPA	1.50
☐	Paul Coffey, NHLPA	1.50
☐	Vincent Damphousse, NHLPA	1.50
☐	Steve Duchesne, NHLPA	1.00
☐	Theoren Fleury, NHLPA	1.50
☐	Doug Gilmour, NHLPA	1.50
☐	Wayne Gretzky, NHLPA	10.00
☐	Curtis Joseph (G), NHLPA	2.50
☐	Ed Jovanovski, NHLPA	1.00
☐	Paul Kariya, NHLPA	3.50
☐	Eric Lindros, NHLPA	2.50
☐	Al MacInnis, NHLPA	1.00
☐	Félix Potvin (G), NHLPA	1.50
☐	Mark Recchi, NHLPA	1.00
☐	Luc Robitaille, NHLPA	2.00
☐	Jeremy Roenick, NHLPA	2.00
☐	Patrick Roy (G), NHLPA	7.50
☐	Joe Sakic, NHLPA	4.00
☐	Mathieu Schneider, NHLPA	1.00
☐	Brendan Shanahan, NHLPA	2.50
☐	Scott Stevens, NHLPA	1.00
☐	John Vanbiesbrouck (G), NHLPA	1.00
☐	Alexei Yashin, NHLPA	1.50

STICK UM'S

Insert Set (4 stickers):		15.00
	Insert	SU
☐	1 V. Damphousse / D. Gilmour	3.00
☐	2 T. Fleury / Cu. Joseph (G)	4.00
☐	3 C. Chelios / B. Shanahan	4.00
☐	4 P. Kariya / J. Sakic	7.50

1996 - 97 VISIONS

This 150-card multi-sport set sells for $50. Other hockey singles exist.

	Player	
☐	94 Manon Rhéaume (G)	4.00

1996 - 97 VISIONS SIGNINGS

This 100-card multi-sport set sells for $50. Other hockey singles exist.

	Player	
☐	78 Manon Rhéaume (G)	4.00

1997 QUÉBEC INTERNATIONAL PEE WEE

Complete Set (1379):

SHERBROOKE PEE WEE

The most expensive single is Marc-André Roy at $2-3.

☐ 1 Martin Bellavance ☐ 2 Maxime Beaulieu
☐ 3 Nicolas Chapdelaine ☐ 4 Patrick Charpentier
☐ 5 Erik Desrosiers ☐ 6 Mathieu Dumas
☐ 7 David Gagnon ☐ 8 C-P Giguère
☐ 9 Jasmin Lessard ☐ 10 Pierre-André Moreau
☐ 11 J-P Ouellet ☐ 12 David Quirion
☐ 13 Marc-André Roy ☐ 14 Sébastien Roy
☐ 15 Kevin Simoneau ☐ 16 Dave St-Jean
☐ 17 Hugues Verpaelst ☐ 135 Instructeurs

DRUMMONDVILLE PEE WEE

☐ 18 David Bergeron ☐ 19 Jonathan Bluteau
☐ 20 Mathieu Duquette ☐ 21 Yan Brouillard
☐ 22 Dominic Fiset ☐ 23 Jonathan Guay
☐ 28 Pierre Morvan ☐ 29 Francis Trudel
☐ 24 J-F Touchette ☐ 25 Steven Bertrand
☐ 26 Benoît Duhamel ☐ 27 Christian Arpin
☐ 30 Didier Bochatay ☐ 31 Rémi Bergeron
☐ 32 Patrick Gosselin ☐ 33 David Auger
☐ 136 Instructeurs

BEAUCE-AMIANTE PEE WEE

☐ 34 Simon Nadeau ☐ 35 Pierre-André Bureau
☐ 36 J-P Ménard ☐ 37 Jonathan Ferland
☐ 38 Alexandre Cloutier ☐ 39 Olivier Cloutier
☐ 40 Maxime Roy ☐ 41 Yannick Roy
☐ 42 Nicolas Maheux ☐ 43 P-A Lessard
☐ 44 Martin Cabot ☐ 45 Dave Poulin
☐ 46 Olivier Landry ☐ 47 Martin Talbot
☐ 48 Yvan Busque ☐ 49 Mathieu Roy
☐ 137 Instructeurs

AMQUI PEE WEE

☐ 50 Rémi Leclerc ☐ 51 Mike Roy
☐ 52 Michel Dubé ☐ 53 Rémi Boulianne
☐ 54 Mathieu Pilote ☐ 55 Frédéric Chouinard
☐ 56 Jeff Boulianne ☐ 57 Pierre-Luc Coulombe
☐ 58 Olivier Gendron ☐ 59 Kevin Lavigne
☐ 60 Joël Boudreau ☐ 61 Yohan Boudreau
☐ 62 Jérôme McNicoll ☐ 63 J-F Saint-Amand
☐ 64 Francis Lussier ☐ 65 Sébastien Gagné
☐ 66 Jérémy Lafontaine ☐ 138 Instructeurs

BUCKINGHAM PEE WEE

☐ 67 Pascal Boileau ☐ 68 Jonathan Bourassa
☐ 69 Cyrille Cantin ☐ 70 Simon Hotte
☐ 71 Jimmy Houle ☐ 72 Mathieu Joanisse
☐ 73 J-M Lafrenière ☐ 74 Sébastien Lamarche
☐ 75 Jonathan Larivière ☐ 76 Philippe Lavallée
☐ 77 Kevin Lawlis ☐ 78 Nicholas Mayrand
☐ 79 Vincent Ouellet ☐ 80 Stéphane Pépin
☐ 81 Alexandre Valières ☐ 82 Patrick Viau
☐ 1395 J-M Cheenier

VICTORIAVILLE PEE WEE

The most expensive single is Mathieu Brunelle at $2-3.

☐ 84 Gaby Beaudet ☐ 85 Hugo Beaudet
☐ 86 Karl Bergeron ☐ 87 Joël Boissonneault
☐ 88 Mathieu Brunelle ☐ 89 Martin Chabot
☐ 90 Stéphane Côté ☐ 91 M. Desruisseaux
☐ 92 J-F Dugre ☐ 93 Sébastien Grégoire
☐ 94 Alain Labonté ☐ 96 Jérôme Mailhot
☐ 97 Paul-André Masson ☐ 98 David Mathieu
☐ 99 Thierry Poisson ☐ 100 Simon St-Pierre
☐ 101 Instructeur

CHARLEVOIX PEE WEE

☐ 102 Nicolas Boivin ☐ 103 Mario Chiasson
☐ 104 Jean-Michel Dufour ☐ 105 Jonathan Dufour
☐ 106 Kevin Dufour ☐ 107 David Gagné
☐ 108 Simon Guay ☐ 109 Simon Gaudreault
☐ 110 Éric Lavoie ☐ 111 Pierre-Luc Marcotte
☐ 112 Mathieu Perron ☐ 113 Frédéric Simard
☐ 114 Antoine Tremblay ☐ 115 David Tremblay
☐ 116 Michael Tremblay ☐ 117 Instructeurs

QUÉBEC PEE WEE CITADELLES

☐ 118 Stéphane Harvey ☐ 119 S. Blouin-Fournier
☐ 120 Julien Matte ☐ 121 Nicolas Marcotte
☐ 122 Pascal Pelletier ☐ 123 Charles Veilleux
☐ 124 Simon Chénard ☐ 125 Éric Bilodeau
☐ 126 Dominic Deblois ☐ 127 Olivier Gagné
☐ 128 P-M Paquet ☐ 129 Maxime Lamothe
☐ 130 Jonathan Arsenault ☐ 131 Jonathan Jolette
☐ 132 Sylvain Cayer ☐ 133 Kevin Lachance
☐ 134 Instructeurs

BELLECHASSE PEE WEE

☐ 139 Frédéric Laliberté ☐ 140 Benoît Therrien
☐ 141 François Auger ☐ 142 J-P Asselin
☐ 143 Francis Tanguay ☐ 144 Karl Gagné
☐ 145 Nicolas Mercier ☐ 146 Mathieu Morissette
☐ 147 J-P Bolduc ☐ 148 François Doiron
☐ 149 Jérôme Corriveau ☐ 150 Étienne Pomerleau
☐ 151 Alexandre Lavallée ☐ 152 Guillaume Labrie
☐ 153 Jeason Ruel ☐ 154 Hubert Chabot
☐ 155 Nicolas Fournier ☐ 156 Instructeurs

ÉTOILES PEE WEE DE L'EST

☐ 157 Stéphane Martin ☐ 158 François Bélair
☐ 159 Mathieu Garneau ☐ 160 Marc-André Roy
☐ 161 Nicholas Romano ☐ 162 M.A. Diaz-Lopez
☐ 163 François Leduc ☐ 164 Mathieu Fleurent
☐ 165 Anthony Orobello ☐ 166 Maurice Ghazi
☐ 167 Cédric Meloche ☐ 168 François Cantin
☐ 169 Gabriel Galarneau ☐ 170 P-A Bourgoin
☐ 171 J-F Poupart ☐ 172 Joey Gédéon
☐ 173 Jonathan Dorion ☐ 174 Instructeurs

BEAUPRÉ PEE WEE

☐ 175 Maxime Huot ☐ 176 Simon Gauthier
☐ 177 Simon Barrette ☐ 178 Francis Allaire
☐ 179 Maxime Lachance ☐ 180 Jean-Michel Caron
☐ 181 L-J Gravel ☐ 182 Jayson Audet
☐ 183 Patrick Guérin ☐ 184 Nicolas Tremblay
☐ 185 Garry Shields ☐ 186 Benoît Lavoie
☐ 187 Francis Labrecque ☐ 188 Vincent Boily
☐ 189 Steeve Racine ☐ 190 Sébastien Pichette
☐ 191 Sébastien Racine ☐ 192 Instructeurs

RICHMOND HILL PEE WEE

☐ 18 Instructeurs ☐ 193 Bryn Davies
☐ 194 Michael Fiume ☐ 195 James Gideon
☐ 196 Mark Giordano ☐ 197 Brian Hoffman
☐ 198 Will Hooper ☐ 199 Brian Hovnanian
☐ 200 Aiden Kennedy ☐ 201 Jonathan Kerr
☐ 202 Jamie Minchella ☐ 203 Anthony Minicucci
☐ 204 Jeff Mok ☐ 205 Loreto Pagnani
☐ 206 Matthew Ryan ☐ 207 Shawn Smith
☐ 208 Patrick Porretta ☐ 209 Louis (Jr.) Gabriele

HERSHEY PEE WEE

☐ 211 John Billiard ☐ 212 Jared Eberly
☐ 213 Chris Herr ☐ 214 Nolan Meanor
☐ 215 Adam Bonenberger ☐ 216 Brian Egan
☐ 217 Paul Hiester ☐ 218 Ryan Payne
☐ 219 David Cadoux ☐ 220 Jason Harmony
☐ 221 Zac Holmes ☐ 222 Marquise Prentice
☐ 223 Justin Cassel ☐ 224 Matt Healy
☐ 225 Greg Hooke ☐ 226 Danny Schwartz
☐ 227 Alex Delaney ☐ 228 Brendon Herr
☐ 229 Evan McLaren

JOLIETTE PEE WEE

☐ 232 Olivier Dupuis ☐ 233 Mathieu Whalen
☐ 234 Mathieu Dion ☐ 235 P-M Lauzière
☐ 236 J-P Bourgeois ☐ 237 Simon Perreault
☐ 238 Pascal Boucher ☐ 239 David Richard
☐ 240 Raphaël Laforest ☐ 241 Jonathan Payette
☐ 242 Éric Fortin ☐ 243 Pierre-André Malo
☐ 244 Mathieu Drainville ☐ 245 Éric Boulard
☐ 246 David Payette ☐ 247 Dominic Caron
☐ 248 Yanic Pelletier

BOSTON PEE WEE BRUINS

☐ 250 Shaun Flaherty ☐ 251 Daniel Aucoin
☐ 252 Robert Dashner ☐ 253 David Hynes
☐ 254 David Germain ☐ 255 Christopher Mellen
☐ 256 C. Cappadona ☐ 257 Charles Sorrento
☐ 258 Matthew Perry ☐ 259 James Balben
☐ 260 James Cashins ☐ 261 Sean Losier
☐ 262 Kevin Oakes ☐ 263 Kevin Patten
☐ 264 Daniel Markham ☐ 265 Timothy Byrnes
☐ 266 Beck Sloman ☐ 267 Patrick Watson
☐ 268 Instructeurs

WASHINGTON PEE WEE

☐ 269 Greg Vardy ☐ 270 David Eskridge
☐ 271 Ben Breiterman ☐ 272 Nathaniel Jackson
☐ 273 Ryan Stuart ☐ 274 Scott Seney
☐ 275 Mike Lorusso ☐ 276 Jonathan James
☐ 277 Henri Sanders ☐ 278 James Sixsmith
☐ 279 Chris Snappinger ☐ 280 Peter Hafner
☐ 281 Mike Masten ☐ 282 Mike Martyak
☐ 283 Scott Ohlschlager ☐ 284 Stephen Werner
☐ 285 Tom Carolan ☐ 286 Blair Kipp
☐ 287 Scott Falatach ☐ 288 Tom Zlockie
☐ 289 Patrick Copertino

FORT MCMURRAY PEE WEE

The most expensive single is Scottie Upshall at $5-7.

☐ 290 Scott Upshall ☐ 291 Justin Payne
☐ 292 Jarrett Lukin ☐ 293 Kyle Gladue
☐ 294 Corey Flynn ☐ 295 Colin Flynn
☐ 296 Stephen Young ☐ 297 Sean McDonnell
☐ 298 Gary Leblanc ☐ 299 T.J. Campbell
☐ 300 Chris Marchand ☐ 301 Ryan Gillis
☐ 302 Chris Odynski ☐ 303 Patrick Hudkins
☐ 304 Shawn Coolen ☐ 305 Justin Slade

AMIANTE PEE WEE

☐ 306 Jaeson Courchesne ☐ 307 Olivier St-Laurent
☐ 308 François Kenyon ☐ 309 Éric Gilbert
☐ 310 Steven Daigle ☐ 311 Vincent Lambert
☐ 312 J-P Lessard ☐ 313 P-O Vachon
☐ 314 Joël Lapointe ☐ 315 Xavier D. Landry
☐ 316 Mathieu Vachon ☐ 317 Jonathan Quirion
☐ 318 Mark Donovan ☐ 319 Éric Faucher
☐ 320 François Grenier ☐ 321 Olivier Turcotte
☐ 322 Instructeurs

BEAUBOURG PEE WEE

☐ 323 Sébastien Hains ☐ 324 Stéphane Hébert
☐ 325 Maxime Lachance ☐ 326 Stéphane Carrier
☐ 327 G. Lajeunesse ☐ 328 S. Guérin-St-Cyr
☐ 329 J-P Pichette ☐ 330 Pierre-Luc Gosselin
☐ 331 J-P Pichette ☐ 332 David Lévesque
☐ 334 François Gendron ☐ 335 Jean-Philippe Côté
☐ 336 Gabriel Grondines ☐ 337 Sébastien Hudon
☐ 338 Instructeurs ☐ 339 Guillaume Boudrias
☐ 340 Frédéric Lavoie ☐ 341 Jérémie Savard

BEAUCE-CENTRE PEE WEE

☐ 342 Alex Gagnon ☐ 343 Darrell Paré
☐ 344 J-F Pouliot ☐ 345 Marco Côté
☐ 346 Francis Dubreuil ☐ 347 Étienne Gilbert
☐ 348 Sébastien Cliche ☐ 349 Mathieu Gagné
☐ 350 Patrick Cyr ☐ 351 Maxim Cyr
☐ 352 Jérôme Gagnon ☐ 353 Maxim Rouleau
☐ 354 Enrico Thivierge ☐ 355 Pascal Vachon
☐ 356 Jonathan Vachon ☐ 357 Frédéric Labbé
☐ 358 Instructeurs

BEAUPORT PEE WEE VOILIERS

☐ 359 Kevin Allard ☐ 360 David Bergeron
☐ 361 David Bouchard ☐ 362 Simon Bouchard
☐ 363 C. Desormeaux ☐ 364 Pascal Desrochers
☐ 365 Alain Dorval ☐ 366 Simon Guérard
☐ 367 Nicolas Hébert ☐ 368 Pier-Luc Langevin
☐ 369 Martin Larochelle ☐ 370 J-F Lavigne
☐ 371 J-P Légaré ☐ 372 Nicolas Lévesque
☐ 373 Nicholas Lizotte ☐ 374 Guillaume Pageau
☐ 375 Dave Tondreau ☐ 376 Instructeurs

PHILADELPHIA PEE WEE

☐ 377 Josh Ciocco ☐ 378 Ben Orner
☐ 379 Steve Cohen ☐ 380 Rob Brougham
☐ 381 Brian Davis ☐ 382 Bryan Miller
☐ 383 Alex Bratice ☐ 384 Scott Foster
☐ 385 Anthony Nordo ☐ 386 John Garret Denise
☐ 387 Mike Gooch ☐ 388 Michael Becker
☐ 389 Geordan Murphy ☐ 390 Michael McMullen
☐ 391 Billy Sullivan ☐ 392 Jeff Rohland
☐ 393 Frankie McLaughlin ☐ 394 Jimmy Gehring
☐ 395 Christopher Wilson

POINTE-LÉVY C PEE WEE

☐ 396 T-L V.-Bouchard ☐ 397 Johnny Gamache
☐ 398 Sébastien Caron ☐ 399 Keven Patry
☐ 400 Mathieu Lavigne ☐ 401 Jean-Pierre Audet
☐ 402 Thomas Picard ☐ 403 G.-Benoît Bélanger
☐ 404 François Dussault ☐ 405 Anthony Dumas
☐ 406 Nicolas Langlois ☐ 407 Simon Fournier
☐ 408 Sylvain Faber ☐ 409 Jean-Philippe Blais
☐ 410 Dave Laverdière ☐ 411 Jérôme Doré
☐ 412 Christian Boucher ☐ 413 Instructeurs
☐ 414 Instructeurs

STE-FOY AA PEE WEE

☐ 415 Martin Bricault ☐ 416 Simon Laliberté
☐ 417 Pierre-Alexis Girard ☐ 418 Éric L'Italien
☐ 419 Samuel Demay ☐ 420 Nicolas Marier
☐ 421 C. B-Gagnon ☐ 422 J-M Baillargeon
☐ 423 Jonathan Keays ☐ 424 Vincent Penney
☐ 425 Charles Gauthier ☐ 426 Alexandre Garon
☐ 427 J-F B-Gagnon ☐ 428 Jeffrey Veilleux
☐ 429 Jérôme Voyer ☐ 430 Louis Bertrand
☐ 431 Instructeurs

CHICAGO PEE WEE BLACK HAWKS

☐ 432 Larry Amick ☐ 433 Jordon Black
☐ 434 Kevin Cooper ☐ 435 Joe Dovalina
☐ 436 Brandon Fenninger ☐ 437 Kevin Fetzer
☐ 438 Matt Fetzer ☐ 439 Brandon Lewe
☐ 440 Matt Monaghan ☐ 441 Matt Morrow
☐ 442 Brandon Mugford ☐ 443 Michael Salvi
☐ 444 Matt Schachman ☐ 445 Rob Sheppard
☐ 446 Michael Skalla ☐ 447 Alec Tessier
☐ 448 Jon Yermack ☐ 449 Instructeurs

MONTRÉAL PEE WEE CANADIENS

☐ 450 Jean-Robert Épinat ☐ 451 Steve Villeneuve
☐ 452 L-P Martin ☐ 453 D. Frac-Villeneuve
☐ 454 Mathieu Feizo ☐ 455 Mathieu Corbeil
☐ 456 Guillaume Rivest ☐ 457 Martin Maisonneuve
☐ 458 M-O Sarrazin ☐ 459 Dominic Benoît
☐ 460 S. Courcelles ☐ 461 M-A Normand
☐ 462 Joël Brault ☐ 463 Étienne Plouffe
☐ 464 Francis Walker ☐ 465 M-A Rocheleau
☐ 466 Patrice Cadieux ☐ 1063 Instructeurs
☐ 1064 Team Photo

STE-JULIE PEE WEE

☐ 467 M-A Fortin-Hudon ☐ 468 Sébastien Nolet
☐ 469 Alexandre Godère ☐ 470 Francis Lemieux
☐ 471 Nicolas Hugron ☐ 472 David Leroux
☐ 473 S. Ranger-Dubé ☐ 474 Jérémy Guilbault
☐ 475 Patrick Leroux ☐ 476 Pascal Gauthier
☐ 477 M-É Samson ☐ 478 Louis Chapdeleine
☐ 479 David Morin ☐ 480 Marc Gagnon
☐ 481 Mathieu Banville ☐ 482 Olivier Charpentier
☐ 483 Instructeurs

MONTRÉAL PEE WEE NOROIS

The most expensive single is François Caron at $2-3.

☐ 484 Joey Bucci ☐ 485 Mark Plenzich
☐ 486 François Caron ☐ 487 Joël Pajuelo
☐ 488 Mathieu Lapointe ☐ 489 Y. Verlaan-Lauzon
☐ 490 Marek Krasula ☐ 491 Mathieu Desnoyers
☐ 492 Guillaume Lavallée ☐ 493 Olivier Bertrand
☐ 494 Tommy Roger ☐ 495 Jonathan Charette
☐ 496 David Piché ☐ 497 Laurent Guimond
☐ 498 Michael Kosiuk ☐ 499 Marco Tesolin
☐ 500 Instructeurs ☐ 839 Mathew Medley

BEAUCE-NORD PEE WEE

☐ 501 Steve Poulin ☐ 502 Tommy Vachon
☐ 503 Mathieu Savoie ☐ 504 Étienne Jacques
☐ 505 Sébastien Larose ☐ 506 Joël Labrecque
☐ 507 Joël Nadeau ☐ 508 Kevin Larochelle
☐ 509 Nicolas Lapointe ☐ 510 J-F Vachon
☐ 511 Simon Gagné ☐ 512 Sonny Lehoux
☐ 513 Frédéric Lapierre ☐ 514 Olivier Desmeules
☐ 515 Stéphane Poulin ☐ 516 Daniel Turmel
☐ 517 Kevin Paré ☐ 518 Instructeurs

POINTE-LÉVY B PEE WEE

☐ 519 Yannick Dupont ☐ 520 C-F Carrier
☐ 525 Yan Maheux ☐ 526 Éric Vachon
☐ 527 J-F Carignan ☐ 528 S-P Moisan
☐ 529 Éric Lévesque ☐ 530 Bryan Nadeau
☐ 531 David Geneau ☐ 532 Benjamin Pelletier
☐ 533 Sébastien Nadeau ☐ 534 J-P Gagnon

BEAUPORT PEE WEE HARFANGS B

☐ 535 Stéphane Audet ☐ 536 Patrick Beaumont
☐ 537 Louis Chabot ☐ 538 Julien Chalifour
☐ 539 S. Chouinard ☐ 540 Mathieu Dufresne
☐ 541 Patrick Émond ☐ 542 François Gagnon
☐ 543 Jonathan Lachance ☐ 544 Mathieu Langevin
☐ 545 J.-Michel Laroche ☐ 546 Dave Leclerc
☐ 547 David Norton ☐ 548 Frédérick Picard
☐ 549 Danny Rancourt ☐ 550 Patrick Royer
☐ 551 Philippe St-Cyr

CHAUDIÈRE-ETCHEMIN PEE WEE

☐ 552 Frédérick Anctil ☐ 553 Éric Arsenault
☐ 554 S. Arsenault ☐ 555 Frédéric Boivin
☐ 556 P-É Cantin ☐ 557 Maxime Chevrier
☐ 558 Benoît Couturier ☐ 559 Guillaume Demers
☐ 560 Martin Dubé ☐ 561 François Dulac
☐ 562 G. Dumoulin ☐ 563 Mathieu Gosselin
☐ 564 L. Proulx-Dupéré ☐ 565 F. Riel-Roberge
☐ 566 Christian Rioux ☐ 567 Jean-Bastien Trudel
☐ 568 Instructeurs

ALMA PEE WEE

☐ 569 Simon Gagnon ☐ 570 Dominic Sherman
☐ 571 A. Tremblay ☐ 572 J-D Bouchard
☐ 573 Guillaume Gagnon ☐ 574 Pierre-Luc Fortin
☐ 575 Dane Blackburn ☐ 576 Carl Fortin
☐ 577 David Ouellet ☐ 578 David Côté
☐ 579 Simon Laplante ☐ 580 Mario Larouche
☐ 581 Jean-Benoît Côté ☐ 582 Dave Simard
☐ 583 Jean-Benoît Paillé ☐ 584 J-F Bouchard
☐ 585 Jean-François Perron

RIVE-SUD PEE WEE

The most expensive single is J-F Soucy at $2-3.

☐ 586 Simon Vallières ☐ 587 Stefan Thibault
☐ 588 Guillaume Joncas ☐ 589 Alain Chenard
☐ 590 Benoît Fortier ☐ 591 J-F Turcotte
☐ 592 Alexandre Landry ☐ 593 Jérôme Marceau
☐ 594 Mikael Aubé ☐ 595 Jean-François Cyr
☐ 596 Mathieu Deblois ☐ 597 J-F Fecteau
☐ 598 Kevin Magher ☐ 599 Kevin Dumont
☐ 600 J-F Soucy ☐ 601 Guillaume Fournier
☐ 602 Éric Morissette ☐ 603 Instructeurs

RIMOUSKI PEE WEE

☐ 604 Francis Lussier ☐ 605 Denis Bérubé
☐ 606 Stéphane Gagné ☐ 607 Patrick Gendron
☐ 608 L-C Harvey ☐ 609 Martin Sénéchal
☐ 610 J-F D'Amours ☐ 611 Sébastien Leblanc
☐ 612 David Boudreau ☐ 613 Christian Morneau
☐ 614 Bryan Buntic ☐ 615 Nicolas Mayrand
☐ 616 Michel Lévesque ☐ 617 Jimmy Fillion

☐ 618 Mathieu Pelletier ☐ 619 Alexandre Lavoie
☐ 620 Michel Dubé ☐ 621 Frédéric Gagnon
☐ 622 Robin Leblanc ☐ 623 Instructeurs

CHAUVEAU C PEE WEE

☐ 624 Mathieu Robitaille ☐ 625 Dany Proulx
☐ 626 Benoît Courchesne ☐ 627 Jean-Michel Bédard
☐ 628 Carl Labrecque ☐ 629 S. Boucher-Daigle
☐ 630 Guillaume D'Astous ☐ 631 Steeve Côté
☐ 632 Marc Jalbert ☐ 633 William Robitaille
☐ 634 Donald Dion ☐ 635 Nicolas Savard
☐ 636 Benoît Mayotte ☐ 637 C. M-Tremblay
☐ 638 P-Y Dagnault ☐ 639 Kevin Poulin
☐ 640 Instructeurs

DONNACONA PEE WEE

☐ 641 L-P Rioux ☐ 642 François Bonneau
☐ 643 Étienne Papillon ☐ 644 Maxime Racette
☐ 645 Guillaume Gignac ☐ 646 Sacha Goulet
☐ 647 Martin Faucher ☐ 648 Pierre-Luc Brière
☐ 649 William Ableson ☐ 650 S. Morissette
☐ 651 T. Gagné-Laplante ☐ 652 C. Châteauneuf
☐ 653 Olivier Gagnon ☐ 654 P-C Thibeault
☐ 655 Pierre-Luc Labbé ☐ 656 Frédéric Hamel
☐ 657 Instructeurs

BUFFALO PEE WEE REGALS

☐ 658 Andrew Brooken ☐ 659 Greg Busch
☐ 660 Trevor Calamel ☐ 661 Sam Cellino
☐ 662 Jason Ciesielski ☐ 663 Joseph Collien
☐ 664 Drew Dionne ☐ 665 Brandon Dziura
☐ 666 Ryan Huddy ☐ 667 Adam Koehn
☐ 668 Mike McCarriaghen ☐ 669 Mark McGuire
☐ 670 Matthew Montalbo ☐ 671 Matthew Neumann
☐ 672 Joseph Palmieri ☐ 673 Scott Santora
☐ 674 Daves Seegel ☐ 675 M. Syroczynski

BARRIE PEE WEE

☐ 676 Dan Boken ☐ 677 Nick Borton
☐ 678 Sean** Burke ☐ 679 Ryan Dolmage
☐ 680 Jonathan Dykstra ☐ 681 Chris Genier
☐ 682 Jeff Gilbert ☐ 683 Jay Griffiths
☐ 684 Mark Hunt ☐ 685 Nick Kemp
☐ 686 Blair Luck ☐ 687 Matt McKnight
☐ 688 Dan Miller ☐ 689 Alex Musso
☐ 690 Thomas Reid ☐ 691 Josh Schaap
☐ 692 Derek Smith ☐ 693 Instructeurs

JAPAN PEE WEE

☐ 694 Équipe du Japon

STE-FOY B PEE WEE

☐ 695 Louis Grégroire ☐ 696 F. Laurendeau
☐ 697 Daniel Leclerc ☐ 698 P-É Lebel-Morneau
☐ 699 Ian Boudreau ☐ 700 Nicolas Couët
☐ 701 François Vallières ☐ 702 Mathieu Cossette
☐ 703 André Vincent ☐ 704 Carl Cyr
☐ 705 Philippe Létourneau ☐ 706 C-A Marcoux
☐ 707 Félix Delaunay ☐ 708 Sébastien Dumas
☐ 709 Pierre-Luc Girard ☐ 710 O. B-Pearson
☐ 711 Instructeurs

CHAUVEAU PEE WEE AIGLES B

☐ 712 J-P Audet ☐ 713 Stéphane Bernier
☐ 714 Simon Bertrand ☐ 715 François Carrier
☐ 716 L-P Croussette ☐ 717 Dave Desjardins
☐ 718 David Drouin ☐ 719 J-P Gagné
☐ 720 Alexandre Grenier ☐ 721 Michael Hennessey
☐ 722 Sébastien Jolivet ☐ 723 D. Lamontagne-Roy
☐ 724 Jérôme Lapointe ☐ 725 Sébastien Racine
☐ 726 Nicolas Richard ☐ 727 Olivier Roy
☐ 728 Instructeurs

HALIFAX PEE WEE

☐ 729 Christopher Adams ☐ 730 Nicholas Binaer
☐ 731 Mark Theriault ☐ 732 Neil Lyons
☐ 733 Douglas Gelevan ☐ 734 Matthew Moore
☐ 735 Andrew Joudrey ☐ 736 Michael Couch
☐ 737 Justin Melnyk ☐ 738 Peter Dunbrack
☐ 739 Stephen O'Toole ☐ 740 Robbie Foster
☐ 741 Jared Greenlaw ☐ 742 Anthony Thomas
☐ 743 Christopher Miller ☐ 744 Michael McQueen
☐ 745 Instructeurs

ST-EPHREM PEE WEE

☐ 746 J-F Hamel ☐ 747 Francis Pomerleau
☐ 748 J-P Campeau ☐ 749 Serge Grondin
☐ 750 Jonathan Fecteau ☐ 751 Gabriel Cloutier
☐ 752 Guillaume Pouliot ☐ 753 Mark Roy
☐ 754 Bernard Poulin ☐ 755 Mario Lessard
☐ 756 Miguel St-Pierre ☐ 757 Philippe Couture
☐ 758 Alain Rodrique ☐ 759 Jean-Guy Beaudoin
☐ 760 Kevin Boucher ☐ 761 Jean-François Pépin
☐ 762 Myguel Couture ☐ 763 André** Roy
☐ 764 Benoît Talbot ☐ 765 Guillaume Poulin
☐ 766 Instructeurs

DETROIT PEE WEE RED WINGS

The most expensive single is Dwight Helminen at $2-3.

☐ 767 Marc Bowen ☐ 768 Jeremy Bronson
☐ 769 Troy Brummett ☐ 770 Joey Cigna
☐ 771 Justin Combs ☐ 772 Mark Fuqua
☐ 773 Joshua Griffith ☐ 774 Dwight Helminen
☐ 775 Jerrod Kuhn ☐ 776 Nikolas Lanq
☐ 777 Christopher Shea ☐ 778 Derek Smith
☐ 779 Kelly Sullivan ☐ 780 Justin Terry
☐ 781 Michael Walsh ☐ 782 Eric Werner
☐ 783 Instructeurs

CHAUDIÈRE-OUEST PEE WEE

☐ 784 Jérôme Auger ☐ 785 Dave Lapointe
☐ 786 Philippe Demers ☐ 787 Maxim Dufour
☐ 788 Julien Bérubé ☐ 789 C. Gaudreault
☐ 790 Jérôme Chabot ☐ 791 David Duquet
☐ 792 Simon Corriveau ☐ 793 Mathieu Lefrançois
☐ 794 Jason Lapointe ☐ 795 Guillaume Taillon
☐ 796 Christian Plante ☐ 797 Sébastien Couture
☐ 798 François Beaudoin ☐ 799 Instructeurs

DETROIT PEE WEE LITTLE CAESARS

The most expensive singles are Sean Collins and Lee Falardeau at $2-3 each.

☐ 800 Sean Collins ☐ 801 Lee Falardeau
☐ 802 Danny Knapp ☐ 803 Chris Conner
☐ 804 J. Krasnodemski ☐ 805 Jeff Lantz
☐ 806 Bobby Pruchnik ☐ 807 Cory Clements
☐ 808 Ryan Petty ☐ 809 Jason Moul
☐ 810 Art Mnatsakanov ☐ 811 Adam Krug
☐ 812 Kenny Jung ☐ 813 Ryan Wright
☐ 814 Brandon Pomish ☐ 815 Instructeurs
☐ 816 Instructeurs ☐ 817 Instructeurs
☐ 818 Instructeurs

NEW YORK PEE WEE ISLANDERS

The most expensive singles are Eric Nystrom at $4-5, Chris Higgins at $4-5, and Bobby Goeppert at $2-3.

☐ 819 Jordan Hart ☐ 820 Eric Nystrom
☐ 821 Patrick Dineen ☐ 822 Joseph Spitz
☐ 823 Douglas Kocis ☐ 824 Kyle Gabay
☐ 825 Aj Palkovich ☐ 826 Marc Mastropolo
☐ 827 Bryan Bendjy ☐ 828 Bryan Forero
☐ 829 Michael Midea ☐ 830 Ryan Farrell
☐ 831 Chris Higgins ☐ 832 Douglas Hoffman
☐ 833 Frank Schiavone ☐ 834 Jared Sternberg
☐ 835 Bobby Goeppert ☐ 836 Instructeurs
☐ 837 Instructeurs ☐ 838 Instructeurs

LAKESHORE PEE WEE B

☐ 840 Chris Brown ☐ 841 Aaron Graham
☐ 842 Ronald Smith ☐ 843 A. Courtemanche
☐ 844 Matthew Pearce ☐ 845 Jason Pratt-Tully
☐ 846 Bryan Wallwork ☐ 847 Wilder Weir
☐ 848 David Raymond ☐ 849 Chris O'Neil
☐ 850 Scott Stevenson ☐ 851 Paul Vannelli
☐ 852 Jonathan Landry ☐ 853 Christopher Tonkin
☐ 854 Anthony Kyriacou ☐ 855 Michael Boyarchuk

STE-FOY PEE WEE

☐ 856 François Vézina ☐ 857 Vincent Canuel
☐ 858 Simon Goulet ☐ 859 M-G Duduca
☐ 860 Francis Labrecque ☐ 861 Sébastien Cyr
☐ 862 Julien Cardinal ☐ 863 J-S Boîteau
☐ 864 Pascal Faubert ☐ 865 Benoît Lecompte
☐ 866 Michael Lavertu ☐ 867 P-L Nadeau
☐ 868 Daniel Gagnon ☐ 869 P-O Lachance
☐ 870 N. Dionne-Houde ☐ 871 Patrick Lecompte
☐ 872 F-P Monfet ☐ 873 Instructeurs

LAVAL PEE WEE

☐ 874 Martin Bourassa ☐ 876 Ian Mercier
☐ 877 Franco (Jr.) Narcisi ☐ 878 Richard Beauregard
☐ 879 Guillaume Bérubé ☐ 880 Guillaume Lessard
☐ 881 Benoît Beauchemin ☐ 882 Yann Locas
☐ 883 J-D Campeau ☐ 884 Jérémi Brunet
☐ 885 Laurent Lanoie ☐ 886 F-P Guénette
☐ 887 Anthony Dire ☐ 888 Martin St-Pierre
☐ 889 Daniel Barbeau ☐ 890 Louis-André Girard

CAP-ROUGE/ST-AUGUSTIN PEE WEE

☐ 891 Philippe Avard ☐ 892 Christian Boivin
☐ 893 J-S Massicotte ☐ 894 Louis-Olivier Guay
☐ 895 Olivier Langis ☐ 896 Philippe Lacroix
☐ 897 Y-A Chagnon ☐ 898 Martin-Pierre Jean
☐ 899 Jean-Philippe Côté ☐ 900 Philippe Gagnon
☐ 901 Nicolas Demers ☐ 902 Nicolas Simon
☐ 903 Olivier Bouchard ☐ 904 Richard Bazinet
☐ 905 Éric Simard ☐ 906 Alexandre Rivard

BEAUCE-SUD PEE WEE

☐ 907 Samuel Lachance ☐ 908 Alexandre Lacombe
☐ 909 Carl St-Pierre ☐ 910 David Giroux
☐ 911 Danny Gagné ☐ 912 Tim Lalomalec
☐ 913 Gilbert Lachance ☐ 914 David Tanguay
☐ 915 Bryan Paradis ☐ 916 Éric Tremblay
☐ 917 Bobby Thibodeau ☐ 918 P-A Drouin
☐ 919 Kevin Paradis ☐ 920 Jérôme Morin

☐ 921 L-A Lessard ☐ 922 Karl Boucher
☐ 923 David Carrier ☐ 924 Nicolas Laplante
☐ 925 Marc-Antoine Morin ☐ 926 Instructeurs

SAN JOSE PEE WEE

☐ 927 Steven Ackel ☐ 928 Ryan Castagna
☐ 929 Bobby Dippell ☐ 930 Derek Evjenth
☐ 931 Toby Fong ☐ 932 Jeff Hadley
☐ 933 Chris Hodgson ☐ 934 Brandon Howe
☐ 935 John Koch ☐ 936 Mathieu Leclair
☐ 937 Michael Popp ☐ 938 Drwe Sanders
☐ 939 Jordan Smith ☐ 940 Michael Tolibas
☐ 941 Logan Wellman ☐ 942 Andrew Whiteside
☐ 943 Steve Williason ☐ 944 Mark Lesar

KUUJJUAQ PEE WEE

☐ 945 Tuniq Robertson ☐ 946 Etua Jones
☐ 947 Saima Mark ☐ 948 Ronnie Gordon
☐ 949 Marden Tagoona ☐ 950 David Barrett
☐ 951 Hugues Cloutier ☐ 952 Chris Davies
☐ 953 Daniel Gadbois ☐ 954 Jake Chalmers
☐ 955 Étua Berthe ☐ 956 Norman Saunders
☐ 957 Matthew Lapage ☐ 958 Stephen Emeneau
☐ 960 Tiwi Dupuis ☐ 961 Ryan Makiuk
☐ 962 Instructeurs

KALAMAZOO PEE WEE

The most expensive single is Matthew Greene at $2-3.

☐ 963 B.J.Hungerford ☐ 964 Tony Campbell
☐ 965 Jeff Tejchma ☐ 966 Sean St-Peter
☐ 967 Jason Tejchma ☐ 968 Jonathan Saunders
☐ 969 Andrew Ruthkoski ☐ 970 Louis Johnson
☐ 971 Reese (II) Dobrick ☐ 972 Matthew Bobo
☐ 973 Kyle Field ☐ 974 Jordan Amendt
☐ 975 Matthew Greene ☐ 976 Martin Guerin
☐ 977 Chad Holthrop ☐ 978 Brent Palmer
☐ 979 Justin Horn

PITTSBURGH PEE WEE

☐ 980 Michael Handza ☐ 981 Randy Bauer
☐ 982 Ted Bartlett ☐ 983 Michael De Vita
☐ 984 Justin Lloyd ☐ 985 Derek Defelice
☐ 986 Casey Keefer ☐ 987 Lenny Blatnica
☐ 988 Colt Hileman ☐ 989 Boo White
☐ 990 Mike Monaco ☐ 991 Derek Elliott
☐ 992 Jeff Reich ☐ 993 Jason Schulz

LAKESHORE C PEE WEE

☐ 994 Patrick Post ☐ 995 David Barry
☐ 996 Jason Ryan ☐ 997 Chris Eagleton
☐ 998 Joe Ammendolea ☐ 999 Adam MacDonald
☐ 1000 Miguel Wilson ☐ 1001 Jamie Taraborelli
☐ 1002 Matt De Graff ☐ 1003 Ryan Bradford
☐ 1004 J-F Talbot ☐ 1005 Frédéric Gagnon
☐ 1006 Christian Laroche ☐ 1007 Michael Tomasetta
☐ 1008 Marc Barmash ☐ 1009 Instructeurs

HARTFORD PEE WEE WHALERS

☐ 1010 Gregory Cassista ☐ 1011 Ryan Trowbridge
☐ 1012 Ryan Keenan ☐ 1013 Jean-Paul Lefave
☐ 1014 Gregory Ledoux ☐ 1015 Christopher Schod
☐ 1016 Matthew Madalon ☐ 1017 Corey Winton
☐ 1018 Michael Lionetti ☐ 1019 Shannon Sturz
☐ 1020 Gregory Schena ☐ 1021 Adam Dann
☐ 1022 Keegan Rosenberger ☐ 1023 Jason Sayles
☐ 1024 Ryan** Johnson ☐ 1025 David Cannon
☐ 1026 Robert Giuliano ☐ 1027 Justin Laverdière

DETROIT PEE WEE FALCONS

☐ 1028 Grant Peace ☐ 1029 David Barrett
☐ 1030 Jim Bommarito ☐ 1031 Brandon Schnurr
☐ 1032 Ryan Blick ☐ 1033 Bobby Kukulka
☐ 1034 Shane Blismaster ☐ 1035 Brad Beloungea
☐ 1036 Sean Nappo ☐ 1037 Tony Wiseman
☐ 1038 Bryan Konkel ☐ 1039 Christian Moore
☐ 1040 Patrick McGrath ☐ 1041 Chris Ballach
☐ 1042 Alex White ☐ 1043 Brent Cooper

ROCHESTER PEE WEE

☐ 1044 Keith Cadwell ☐ 1045 Culhanee Williams
☐ 1046 Kevin Watters ☐ 1047 Ryan Woodworth
☐ 1048 Ryan Simmons ☐ 1049 Mark Langdon
☐ 1050 Stephen Glonta ☐ 1051 Anay Rice
☐ 1052 Brian Collins ☐ 1053 Chris Nealon
☐ 1054 Chris Collins ☐ 1055 Chris Barnard
☐ 1056 Mike Pasley ☐ 1057 Jeff Rasmussen
☐ 1058 Daniel Langlois ☐ 1059 Kevin Amborski
☐ 1060 Bill Burgio ☐ 1061 Frank Burgio
☐ 1062 Instructeurs

ENGLAND PEE WEE

☐ 1065 Marc Cornwell ☐ 1066 Elliott Baird
☐ 1067 Nathan Hunt ☐ 1068 Danny Meyers
☐ 1069 Chris Deacon ☐ 1070 Simon Greenwood
☐ 1071 Breit Kurby ☐ 1072 Tom Griffiths
☐ 1073 Kristian Lloyd ☐ 1074 Andrew Copping
☐ 1075 Lee Lansdowne ☐ 1076 Ross Jones
☐ 1077 Aaron Davies ☐ 1078 Paul Stanley
☐ 1079 Stuart Brittle ☐ 1080 Dan Hughes
☐ 1081 Adam Radmall ☐ 1082 Leon Morton

SHAWINIGAN PEE WEE CATARACTES

☐ 1083 Olivier Caron ☐ 1084 David Lacombe
☐ 1085 Michael Gerbeau ☐ 1086 Willy Yenegue
☐ 1087 J-F L'Hérault ☐ 1088 Marc-André Morel
☐ 1089 Michael Lafond ☐ 1090 Alexandre Grenier
☐ 1091 Tommy Boisvert ☐ 1092 Dave Grenier
☐ 1093 Joël Lapointe ☐ 1094 Benoît Grenier
☐ 1095 Mario Corriveau ☐ 1096 David Lachance
☐ 1097 M. Lafrenière ☐ 1098 Kevin Duval
☐ 1099 Luc Pilon ☐ 1100 Martin Sévigny
☐ 1101 Instructeurs

AUSTRIA PEE WEE

☐ 1102 Patrick Albl ☐ 1103 W. Bartholomäus
☐ 1104 Florian Berger ☐ 1105 M. Grabher-Meier
☐ 1106 Patrick Harand ☐ 1107 Markus Hofer
☐ 1108 Stefan Herzog ☐ 1109 Philippe Horsky
☐ 1110 J. Kassmannhuber ☐ 1111 Thomas Koch
☐ 1112 Patrick Preis ☐ 1113 Oliver Setzinger
☐ 1114 Emanuel Staudach ☐ 1115 Florian Stern
☐ 1116 Thomas Stadler ☐ 1117 R. Steinwender
☐ 1118 Thomas Vanek ☐ 1119 Daniel Wesler
☐ 1120 Diethard Winzig ☐ 1121 Philippe Winzig
☐ 1122 Markus Zebinger ☐ 1123 Markus Brugger
☐ 1124 Stefn Aschacher ☐ 1125 Georg Privoznik

ZURICH PEE WEE

The most expensive single is Beat Schiess at $2-3.

☐ 1126 Tobias Stephan ☐ 1127 Marco Carletta
☐ 1128 Yves Debus ☐ 1129 Marco Haldi
☐ 1130 M. Gossweiler ☐ 1131 Roman Hardmeier
☐ 1132 Fabio Schumacher ☐ 1133 Raphael Schoop
☐ 1134 Beat Schiess ☐ 1135 Ursin Conrad
☐ 1136 Andreas Ambühz ☐ 1137 S. Blindenbacher
☐ 1138 Stefan Schnyder ☐ 1139 Steve Gnädinger
☐ 1140 Roger Prinz ☐ 1141 Andreas Küng
☐ 1142 Andreas Furrer ☐ 1143 Daniel Boss
☐ 1144 Marco Grüber ☐ 1145 G-M Battaglia
☐ 1146 Roger Lüdi ☐ 1147 Instructeurs

SOUTH SHORE PEE WEE

The most expensive single is Ryan Whitney at $5-7. Other expensive singles are Robert Flynn, Brian McConnell and Mike Morris each at $2-3.

☐ 1148 Instructeurs ☐ 1149 John Barry
☐ 1150 Derek Boudreau ☐ 1151 Michael Boudreau
☐ 1152 Brendan Byrner ☐ 1153 Shawn Dooley
☐ 1154 Robert Flynn ☐ 1155 Jack Greeley
☐ 1156 Donald Grover ☐ 1157 Graham Johnson
☐ 1158 Brian McConnell ☐ 1159 Mike Morris
☐ 1160 Gerry Moffett ☐ 1161 Thomas Resor
☐ 1162 C. Rodday ☐ 1163 Ben Spitz
☐ 1164 Mark Thomas ☐ 1165 Ryan Whitney
☐ 1166 Brian Yandle ☐ 1167 John Binieris

RIGA PEE WEE

☐ 1168 Team Riga

SUISS ROMANDE PEE WEE

☐ 1169 Mickaël Luthi ☐ 1170 Daniel Manzato
☐ 1171 Steve Schaller ☐ 1172 S. Anthamatten
☐ 1173 Félicien DuBois ☐ 1174 Stéphane Gruber
☐ 1175 Ludovic Mano ☐ 1176 Lois Merz
☐ 1177 N. Schaller ☐ 1178 Nehdi Tedjani
☐ 1179 Steven Barkas ☐ 1180 Pascal Bruegger
☐ 1181 Grégory Christen ☐ 1182 Damien Eisenring
☐ 1183 Fabrice Gevisier ☐ 1184 Cédric Henry
☐ 1185 Marc Lambert ☐ 1186 Neuenschwander
☐ 1187 Christophe Rapit ☐ 1188 Martin Rex
☐ 1189 J. Scheidegger ☐ 1190 Patrick Schorderet
☐ 1191 Instructeurs ☐ 1192 Instructeurs

ROUEN PEE WEE

☐ 1193 Tristan Lemoine ☐ 1194 François DuBillot
☐ 1195 A. Lefebvre ☐ 1196 Xavier Guimard
☐ 1197 É. Picquenot ☐ 1198 B. Quessandier
☐ 1199 G. Damiens ☐ 1200 Julien Dequidt
☐ 1201 G. Charpentier ☐ 1202 Luc Tardif
☐ 1203 Thibault Geffroy ☐ 1204 Terry Prunier
☐ 1205 Guillaume Aubert ☐ 1206 Julien Dieu
☐ 1207 Quentin Robin ☐ 1208 Damien Raux
☐ 1209 Paul Rosant ☐ 1210 Bessard du Parc
☐ 1211 Jean-Baptiste Deffin

NORTH DELTA PEE WEE

The most expensive single is Brandon Segal at $2-3.

☐ 1212 Bobby Pryce ☐ 1213 Mark Bouchard
☐ 1214 Andrew Switzer ☐ 1215 Andrew Gondos
☐ 1216 David Young ☐ 1217 Richard Molenaar
☐ 1218 Brandon Segal ☐ 1219 John Crang
☐ 1220 Kevin Batchelor ☐ 1221 Kyle Jones
☐ 1222 Brandon Kazuta ☐ 1223 Brian Harris
☐ 1224 Tass Kanakos ☐ 1225 Nolan Neufeld
☐ 1226 Igor Agarunov ☐ 1227 Taylor Henshaw
☐ 1228 Blaine Kilmury

MIDDLESEX PEE WEE

The most expensive single is Dan Spang at $2-3.

☐ 1229 Rob Bergan ☐ 1230 Adam Bolduc
☐ 1232 Dan Boudreau ☐ 1233 Tony Brennan
☐ 1234 Sean Collins ☐ 1235 Bryan Conti
☐ 1236 Jared Coviello ☐ 1237 John Hurd
☐ 1238 Brendan Keefe ☐ 1239 Bill Leclerc
☐ 1240 Joe McCaig ☐ 1241 Billy McLucas
☐ 1242 James Morrissey ☐ 1243 Danny Murphy
☐ 1244 Ryan Murphy ☐ 1245 Rugo Santini
☐ 1246 Andrew Sironi ☐ 1247 Dan Spang
☐ 1248 Steve Therrien ☐ 1249 Tim Warner

ROUEN PEE WEE

☐ 1250 Delepine Benoît ☐ 1251 Guillaume Mahay
☐ 1252 Jérémy Leroux ☐ 1253 Thomas Fercoq
☐ 1254 Nicolas Meyer ☐ 1255 Cherif Mehdi
☐ 1256 Quentin Alléaume ☐ 1257 Romain Pedraut
☐ 1258 Florian Delcroix ☐ 1259 Aurélien Lefebvre
☐ 1260 Baptiste Sorin ☐ 1261 Thibault Pillet
☐ 1262 Adrian Cipel ☐ 1263 Vincent Denise
☐ 1264 Alexis Bauchain ☐ 1265 Florian Vavasseur
☐ 1266 J-C Offret ☐ 1267 Benoît Hauville
☐ 1268 Quentin Boutigny ☐ 1269 Schane Cauvin
☐ 1270 Patrick Goncalves ☐ 1271 Thibault Martin
☐ 1272 Nordine Mahdidi ☐ 1273 Romain Lamarque
☐ 1274 Maxime Tomulic ☐ 1275 Pierre Dalamarre
☐ 1276 Gregory Blanc ☐ 1277 Thomas Saadi
☐ 1278 Thibault Ricard ☐ 1279 Pierrick Leclerc
☐ 1280 Nicolas Hailly ☐ 1281 M-H Crevelle
☐ 1282 Axel Queffeulou ☐ 1283 Jeremie Poutrain
☐ 1284 Olivier Lamoureux ☐ 1285 Yann Auffret
☐ 1286 Fabien Gallot ☐ 1287 Vincent Thiebault

ROUEN PEE WEE

☐ 1288 Thomas Barralier ☐ 1289 Raphael Delcroix
☐ 1290 Thomas Kuypers ☐ 1291 G. Lenormand
☐ 1292 Alexandre Vieira ☐ 1293 M. Pyee-Marie
☐ 1294 Nicolas Duparc ☐ 1295 Renaud Aubin

PARIS PEE WEE

☐ 1296 Matthieu Duplant ☐ 1297 Bastien Mery
☐ 1298 Matthieu Heidet ☐ 1299 Romain Asfaux
☐ 1300 Nicolas Bussière ☐ 1301 Clément Dinay
☐ 1302 Q. Djeraouane ☐ 1303 O. Hannachi
☐ 1304 Cédric Poirot ☐ 1305 Thibaud Poujol
☐ 1306 Quentin Lamey ☐ 1307 Valentin Eudokinoff
☐ 1308 Instructeurs ☐ 1309 Instructeurs

NEW YORK PEE WEE RANGERS

☐ 1310 Kevin Hathway ☐ 1311 Justin Bodine
☐ 1312 A.J. Strait ☐ 1313 Brian Fage
☐ 1314 Matt Hughes ☐ 1315 Howard Jennings
☐ 1316 Greg Kemp ☐ 1317 Bryan Lane
☐ 1319 Gerard Miller ☐ 1320 Anthony Roman
☐ 1321 Mike Verdi ☐ 1322 Mark Yurkewecz
☐ 1323 Brian Mitchell ☐ 1324 Eric Lord
☐ 1325 Jake Schwan

MOUNT PEARL PEE WEE

☐ 1327 Matty Peddle ☐ 1328 Joseph Murphy
☐ 1329 Mark Lee ☐ 1330 Chris King
☐ 1331 Grant Kenny ☐ 1332 Mark Peddle
☐ 1333 Mike Halitzki ☐ 1334 Terry McCarthy
☐ 1335 Preston Hickey ☐ 1336 James Green
☐ 1337 Jeff Furlong ☐ 1338 Colin Power
☐ 1339 Josh Manning ☐ 1340 Geoff** Smith
☐ 1341 Pat Duke ☐ 1342 Ryan Gallivan
☐ 1343 Mark Garland ☐ 1344 Instructeurs

MEXICO PEE WEE

☐ 1345 Manuel Lopez ☐ 1346 Christopher Cullen
☐ 1347 Tyron Junge ☐ 1348 Fernando Rabago
☐ 1349 Kander Lopez ☐ 1350 J.P De Sayur
☐ 1351 Paul Medina ☐ 1352 Jesus Chavez
☐ 1353 J.P Bennlure ☐ 1354 Jose Bijteni
☐ 1355 Francisco Vargas ☐ 1356 Adrian Estrada
☐ 1357 Jaime Dominguez

ST. CATHARINES PEE WEE

☐ 1358 Robert Baerg ☐ 1359 Shayne Baylis
☐ 1360 David Bowman ☐ 1361 Andrew Burkholder
☐ 1362 Craig Conn ☐ 1363 Mark Cucciniello
☐ 1364 Michael De Listo ☐ 1365 Robert Hennigar
☐ 1366 Matt Kerling ☐ 1367 Matt Lostracco
☐ 1368 Arnaldo Magnotta ☐ 1369 Michael Melinko
☐ 1370 Kyle Neufeld ☐ 1371 Brian Palmieri
☐ 1372 Edward Pintwala ☐ 1373 Mark Uhryn

BADEN-WURTTENBERG PEE WEE

The most expensive single is Marcel Goc at $2-3.

☐ 1374 Sven Furgol ☐ 1375 Ron Howarth
☐ 1376 Simon Eisele ☐ 1377 Andreas Sarsenov
☐ 1378 Wayne Laub ☐ 1379 Manuel Weibler
☐ 1380 Andres Nowak ☐ 1381 S. Baumann
☐ 1382 Johannes Giel ☐ 1383 Axel Hackert
☐ 1384 Marcel Goc ☐ 1385 Kim Hauser
☐ 1386 Dirk Wrobel ☐ 1387 David Danner
☐ 1388 Mario Lavori ☐ 1389 Karsten Steinauser
☐ 1390 Marcus Zappe ☐ 1391 Yannic Seidenberg
☐ 1392 Peter Krejca ☐ 1393 Jimmy Hambrecht

CHAPTER FIVE

MODERN ISSUES 1997 TO 2004

1997 BOWMAN

Cards 1-160 have two versions: the regular card and an O-Pee-Chee parallel.

	OPC	Bowm.
Complete Set (160 cards):	175.00	40.00
Common Player:	.75	.20
Player	**OPC**	**Bowm.**
1 Jan Bulis, OHL	1.00	.20
2 Daniel Cleary, OHL	5.00	1.00
3 Dave Duerden, OHL	1.00	.20
4 Cameron Mann, OHL	2.00	.50
5 Alyn McCauley, OHL	5.00	1.00
6 Tyler Rennette, OHL	.75	.20
7 Marc Savard, OHL	3.00	.50
8 Daniel Tkaczuk, OHL	3.00	.50
9 John Tripp, OHL	.75	.20
10 Joel Trottier, OHL	.75	.20
11 Sean Venedam, OHL	.75	.20
12 Alexandre Volchkov, OHL	1.00	.20
13 Sean Blanchard, OHL	1.00	.20
14 Kevin Bolibruck, OHL	.75	.20
15 Nick Boynton, OHL	3.00	.50
16 Paul Mara, OHL	2.00	.50
17 Marc Moro, OHL	1.00	.20
18 Marty Wilford, OHL	.75	.20
19 Zac Bierk (G), OHL	3.00	.50
20 Kory Cooper (G), OHL	.75	.20
21 Richard Rochefort, OHL	.75	.20
22 Matt Cooke, OHL	2.00	.50
23 Boyd Devereaux, OHL	3.00	.50
24 Rico Fata, OHL	3.00	.50
25 Dwayne Hay, OHL	1.00	.20
26 Trevor Letowski, OHL	2.00	.50
27 Ryan Mougenel, OHL	.75	.20
28 Todd Norman, OHL	1.00	.20
29 Larry Paleczny, OHL	.75	.20
30 Colin Pepperall, OHL	.75	.20
31 Jonathan Sim, OHL	1.00	.20
32 Joe Thornton, OHL	20.00	6.00
33 Brian Wesenberg, OHL	1.00	.20
34 Andy Delmore, OHL	3.00	.50
35 Chris Hajt, OHL	1.00	.20
36 Richard Jackman, OHL	2.00	.50
37 Denis Smith, OHL	1.00	.20
38 Jamie Sokolsky, OHL	.75	.20
39 Paul Traynor, OHL	.75	.20
40 Patrick Desrochers (G), OHL	2.00	.50
41 Robert Esche (G), OHL	3.00	.50
42 Roberto Luongo (G), QMJHL	15.00	4.00
43 Frédéric Henry (G), QMJHL	.75	.20
44 Marc Olivier Roy, QMJHL	.75	.20
45 Samy Nasreddine, QMJHL	.75	.20
46 J.F. Fortin, QMJHL	1.00	.20
47 Martin Ethier, QMJHL	.75	.20
48 Jason Doig, QMJHL	1.00	.20
49 Dominic Perna, QMJHL	.75	.20
50 Daniel Brière, QMJHL	7.00	1.50
51 Pavel Rosa, QMJHL	2.00	.50
52 Philippe Audet, QMJHL	.75	.20
53 Gordie Dwyer, QMJHL	1.00	.20
54 Martin Menard, QMJHL	.75	.20
55 Jonathan Delisle, QMJHL	.75	.20
56 Peter Worrell, QMJHL	3.00	.50
57 François Methot, QMJHL	1.00	.20
58 Steve Bégin, QMJHL	3.00	.50
59 Karol Bartanus, QMJHL	.75	.20
60 J.P. Dumont, QMJHL	3.00	.50
61 Marc Denis (G), QMJHL	7.00	1.50
62 J-S Giguère (G), QMJHL	12.00	3.00
63 Jason Goneau, QMJHL	.75	.20
64 Radoslav Suchy, QMJHL	1.00	.20
65 Stéphane Robidas, QMJHL	1.00	.20
66 Marc-André Gaudet, QMJHL	.75	.20
67 Eric Drouin, QMJHL	.75	.20
68 Derrick Walser, QMJHL	1.00	.20
69 Vincent Lecavalier, QMJHL	20.00	5.00
70 Denis Hamel, QMJHL	1.00	.20
71 Daniel Corso, QMJHL	2.00	.50
72 Martin Moise, QMJHL	.75	.20
73 Eric Belanger, QMJHL	2.00	.50
74 Olivier Morin, QMJHL	.75	.20
75 Jérôme Tremblay, QMJHL	.75	.20
76 Jody Shelley, QMJHL	.75	.50
77 Eric Normandin, QMJHL	.75	.20
78 David Thibeault, QMJHL	.75	.20
79 Christian Daigle, QMJHL	.75	.20
80 Alexandre Jacques, QMJHL	.75	.20
81 Brian Boucher (G), WHL	5.00	1.00
82 Randy Petruk (G), WHL	1.00	.20
83 Hugh Hamilton, WHL	1.00	.20
84 Joel Kwiatkowski, WHL	1.00	.20
85 Zenith Komarniski, WHL	1.00	.20
86 Joey Tetarenko, WHL	1.00	.20
87 Tyler Willis, WHL	.75	.20
88 Patrick Marleau, WHL	7.00	1.50
89 Trent Whitfield, WHL	2.00	.50
90 Martin Cerven, WHL	.75	.20
91 Donnie Kinney, WHL	.75	.20
92 Brad Isbister, WHL	3.00	.50
93 Todd Robinson, WHL	1.00	.20
94 Greg Leeb, WHL	.75	.20
95 John Cirjak, WHL	.75	.20
96 Randy Perry, WHL	.75	.20
97 Derek Schutz, WHL	.75	.20
98 Brenden Morrow, WHL	5.00	1.00
99 Shawn McNeil, WHL	.75	.20
100 Brad Ference, WHL	2.00	.50
101 Ryan Hoople (G), WHL	.75	.20
102 Brian Elder (G), WHL	.75	.20
103 Mike McBain, WHL	1.00	.20
104 Jesse Wallin, WHL	1.00	.20
105 Chris Phillips, WHL	3.00	.50
106 Kelly Smart, WHL	.75	.20
107 Arron Asham, WHL	1.00	.20
108 Byron Ritchie, WHL	1.00	.20
109 Derek Morris, WHL	3.00	.50
110 Travis Brigley, WHL	1.00	.20
111 Justin Kurtz, WHL	1.00	.20
112 B.J. Young, WHL	.75	.20
113 Shane Willis, WHL	3.00	.50
114 Josh Holden, WHL	2.00	.50
115 Cory Sarich, WHL	2.00	.50
116 Brad Larsen, WHL	1.00	.20
117 Stefan Cherneski, WHL	1.00	.20
118 Peter Schaefer, WHL	2.00	.50
119 Dmitri Nabokov, WHL	2.00	.50
120 Sergei Varlamov, WHL	2.00	.50
121 Daniel Cleary, Team Cherry	5.00	1.00
122 Jarrett Smith, Team Cherry	.75	.20
123 Alexandre Mathieu, Team Cherry	.75	.20
124 Matt Elich, Team Cherry	2.00	.50
125 Joe Thornton, Team Cherry	20.00	6.00
126 Mike Brown, Team Cherry	2.00	.50
127 Derek Schutz, Team Cherry	.75	.20
128 Benoît Côté, Team Cherry	.75	.20
129 Jason Ward, Team Cherry	6.00	1.50
130 Karol Bartanus, Team Cherry	.75	.20
131 Tyler Rennette, Team Cherry	.75	.20
132 Matt Zultek, Team Cherry	1.00	.20
133 Brad Ference, Team Cherry	2.00	.50
134 Daniel Tetrault, Team Cherry	1.00	.20
135 Ray Bonni, Team Cherry	1.00	.20
136 Kevin Grimes, Team Cherry	.75	.20
137 Paul Mara, Team Cherry	2.00	.50
138 Nikos Tselios, Team Cherry	2.00	.50
139 C. Cruickshank (G), Tm Cherry	.75	.20
140 P-L Therrien (G), Tm Cherry	1.00	.20
141 Patrick Marleau, Team Orr	7.00	1.50
142 Ty Jones, Team Orr	1.00	.20
143 Jeremy Reich, Team Orr	1.00	.20
144 Adam Mair, Team Orr	2.00	.50
145 Adam Colagiacomo, Team Orr	2.00	.50
146 Harold Druken, Team Orr	5.00	1.00
147 Brenden Morrow, Team Orr	5.00	1.00
148 Jay Legault, Team Orr	.75	.20
149 Jeff Zehr, Team Orr	1.00	.20
150 Scott Barney, Team Orr	1.00	.20
151 Gregor Baumgartner, Team Orr	.75	.20
152 Daniel Tkaczuk, Team Orr	3.00	.50
153 Eric Brewer, Team Orr	6.00	1.50
154 Nick Boynton, Team Orr	3.00	.50
155 Vratislav Cech, Team Orr	.75	.20
156 Kyle Kos, Team Orr	.75	.20
157 J.F. Fortin, Team Orr	1.00	.20
158 Wes Jarvis, Team Orr	.75	.20
159 Roberto Luongo (G), Team Orr	15.00	4.00
160 J-F Damphousse (G), Team Orr	2.00	.50

BOWMAN'S BEST

There are three versions: the regular insert, the Refractor parallel and the Atomic Refractor parallel.

	Atomic	Refr.	BB
Insert Set (20 cards):	170.00	85.00	45.00
Insert	**Atomic**	**Refr.**	**BB**
1 Joe Thornton	60.00	30.00	15.00
2 Patrick Marleau	20.00	10.00	6.00
3 Paul Mara	10.00	5.00	3.00
4 Daniel Tkaczuk	10.00	6.00	3.00
5 Jason Ward	20.00	10.00	5.00
6 Nick Boynton	10.00	6.00	3.00
7 Daniel Cleary	15.00	8.00	4.00
8 Eric Brewer	20.00	10.00	5.00
9 Brad Ference	10.00	5.00	3.00
10 Stefan Cherneski	10.00	5.00	3.00
11 Ryan Bonni	10.00	5.00	3.00
12 Adam Colagiacomo	10.00	5.00	3.00
13 Mike Brown	10.00	5.00	3.00
14 Scott Barney	10.00	5.00	3.00
15 Jarrett Smith	10.00	5.00	3.00
16 Brenden Morrow	15.00	8.00	4.00
17 J.F. Fortin	10.00	5.00	3.00
18 Roberto Luongo (G)	40.00	20.00	10.00
19 Curtis Cruickshank (G)	10.00	5.00	3.00
20 Pierre-Luc Therrien	10.00	5.00	3.00

CERTIFIED AUTOGRAPH ISSUE

	Auto.
Insert Set (38 cards):	200.00
Autograph	**Auto.**
121 Daniel Cleary, Team Cherry ✍	16.00
122 Jarrett Smith, Team Cherry ✍	8.00
123 Alexandre Mathieu, Team Cherry ✍	8.00
124 Matt Elich, Team Cherry ✍	8.00
125 Joe Thornton, Team Cherry ✍	60.00
126 Mike Brown, Team Cherry ✍	8.00
127 Derek Schutz, Team Cherry ✍	8.00
128 Benoît Côté, Team Cherry ✍	8.00
129 Jason Ward, Team Cherry ✍	20.00
130 Karol Bartanus, Team Cherry ✍	8.00
131 Tyler Rennette, Team Cherry ✍	8.00
132 Matt Zultek, Team Cherry ✍	8.00
133 Brad Ference, Team Cherry ✍	8.00
134 Daniel Tetrault, Team Cherry ✍	8.00
135 Ray Bonni, Team Cherry ✍	8.00
136 Kevin Grimes, Team Cherry ✍	8.00
137 Paul Mara, Team Cherry ✍	8.00
138 Nikos Tselios, Team Cherry ✍	8.00
139 C. Cruickshank (G), Tm Cherry ✍	8.00
140 P-L Therrien (G), Tm Cherry ✍	8.00
142 Ty Jones, Team Orr ✍	8.00
143 Jeremy Reich, Team Orr ✍	8.00
144 Adam Mair, Team Orr ✍	8.00
145 Adam Colagiacomo, Team Orr ✍	8.00
146 Harold Druken, Team Orr ✍	16.00
147 Brenden Morrow, Team Orr ✍	16.00
148 Jay Legault, Team Orr ✍	8.00
149 Jeff Zehr, Team Orr ✍	8.00
150 Scott Barney, Team Orr ✍	8.00
151 Gregor Baumgartner, Team Orr ✍	8.00
152 Daniel Tkaczuk, Team Orr ✍	12.00
153 Eric Brewer, Team Orr ✍	20.00
154 Nick Boynton, Team Orr ✍	12.00
155 Vratislav Cech, Team Orr ✍	8.00
156 Kyle Kos, Team Orr ✍	8.00
157 J.F. Fortin, Team Orr ✍	8.00
158 Wes Jarvis, Team Orr ✍	8.00
160 J-F Damphousse (G), Team Orr ✍	8.00

1997 - 98 APS

NHL stars sometimes sell at a premium (usually $1-2).

	APS
Complete Set (380 cards):	100.00
Common Player:	.25
Player	**APS**
1 Slavomir Lener, Sparta Praha	.50
2 Vaclav Sykora, Sparta Praha	.25
3 Milan Hnilicka, Sparta Praha	1.50
4 Martin Cinibulk, Sparta Praha	.25
5 Frantisek Ptacek, Sparta Praha	.25
6 Frantisek Kucera, Sparta Praha	.50
7 Jaroslav Nedved, Sparta Praha	.25
8 Jirí Krocak, Sparta Praha	.25
9 Martin Holy, Sparta Praha	.25
10 Jaromir Kverka, Sparta Praha	.25
11 Jirí Zelenka, Sparta Praha	.25
12 Richard Zemlicka, Sparta Praha	.25
13 Jaroslav Hlinka, Sparta Praha	.25
14 Jaroslav Bednar, Sparta Praha	.50
15 Ivo Novotny, Sparta Praha	.25
16 Radek Duda, Sparta Praha	.25
17 Michal Sivek, Sparta Praha	2.00
18 Jan Hlavac, Sparta Praha	1.00
19 Miroslav Hlinka, Sparta Praha	.25
20 Patrik Stefan, Sparta Praha	4.00
21 Vaclav Burda, Sparta Praha	.25
22 Patrik Martinec, Sparta Praha	.25
23 Ladislav Benysek, Sparta Praha	.50
24 Jirí Vykoukal, Sparta Praha	.25
25 Petr Nedved, Sparta Praha	3.00
26 Jan Neliba, Dadak Vsetín	.25
27 Zdislav Tabara, Dadak Vsetín	.25
28 Roman Cechmanek, Dadak Vsetín	3.00
29 Ivo Pesat, Dadak Vsetín	.25
30 Radim Tesarík, Dadak Vsetín	.25
31 Antonín Stavjana, Dadak Vsetín	.25
32 Jirí Veber, Dadak Vsetín	.25
33 Michal Bros, Dadak Vsetín	.50
34 Alexei Jaskin, Dadak Vsetín	.25
35 Andrei Galkin, Dadak Vsetín	.25
36 Rostislav Vlach, Dadak Vsetín	.25
37 Ivan Padelek, Dadak Vsetín	.25
38 Tomas Srsen, Dadak Vsetín	.25
39 Jirí Dopita, Dadak Vsetín	.50
40 Ondrej Kratena, Dadak Vsetín	.50
41 Tomas Kapusta, Dadak Vsetín	.25
42 Pavel Zubícek, Dadak Vsetín	.25
43 Radek Belohlav, Dadak Vsetín	.25
44 Tomas Demel, Dadak Vsetín	.25
45 Michal Divísek, Dadak Vsetín	.25
46 Michal Safarik, Dadak Vsetín	.25
47 Josef Beranek, Dadak Vsetín	.50
48 Jan Tomajko, Dadak Vsetín	.50
49 Jan Srdinko, Dadak Vsetín	.25
50 Roman Stantien, Dadak Vsetín	.25
51 Eduard Novak, ZPS Zlín	.25
52 Zdenek Cech, ZPS Zlín	.25
53 Jaroslav Kames, ZPS Zlín	.25
54 Robert Hamrla, ZPS Zlín	.25
55 Pavel Kowalczyk, ZPS Zlín	.25
56 Jan Krajícek, ZPS Zlín	.25
57 Petr Kuchyna, ZPS Zlín	.25
58 Pavel Rajnoha, ZPS Zlín	.25
59 Pavel Hamrlík, ZPS Zlín	.25
60 Jirí Marusak, ZPS Zlín	.25
61 Karel Rachunek, ZPS Zlín	1.00
62 Roman Meluzin, ZPS Zlín	.25
63 Ales Zima, ZPS Zlín	.25
64 Pavel Janku, ZPS Zlín	.25
65 Tomas Nemcicky, ZPS Zlín	.50
66 Petr Cajanek, ZPS Zlín	.50
67 Miroslav Okal, ZPS Zlín	.25
68 Zdenek Sedlak, ZPS Zlín	.25
69 Ales Polcar, ZPS Zlín	.25
70 Petr Leska, ZPS Zlín	.25
71 Martin Spanhel, ZPS Zlín	.50
72 Branislav Janos, ZPS Zlín	.25
73 Marek Vorel, ZPS Zlín	.25
74 Tomas Zizka, ZPS Zlín	.50
75 Ondrej Weissmann, Chemopetrol Litvínov	.25
76 Vladimir Jerabek, Chemopetrol Litvínov	.25
77 Zdenek Orct, Chemopetrol Litvínov	.25
78 Richard Hrazdira, Chemopetrol Litvínov	.25
79 Angel Nikolov, Chemopetrol Litvínov	.25
80 Drahomir Kadlec, Chemopetrol Litvínov	.25
81 Frantisek Prochazka, Chemopetrol Litvínov	.25
82 Radek Mrazek, Chemopetrol Litvínov	.25
83 Petr Molnar, Chemopetrol Litvínov	.25
84 Martin Stepanek, Chemopetrol Litvínov	.25
85 Roman Cech, Chemopetrol Litvínov	.25
86 Vladimir Gyna, Chemopetrol Litvínov	.25
87 Tomas Vlasak, Chemopetrol Litvínov	.50
88 Robert Kysela, Chemopetrol Litvínov	.25
89 Martin Rousek, Chemopetrol Litvínov	.25
90 Petr Hrbek, Chemopetrol Litvínov	.25
91 Vladimir Petrovka, Chemopetrol Litvínov	.25
92 Ivo Prorok, Chemopetrol Litvínov	.25
93 Tomas Krasny, Chemopetrol Litvínov	.25
94 David Balazs, Chemopetrol Litvínov	.25
95 Josef Straka, Chemopetrol Litvínov	.25
96 Kamil Piros, Chemopetrol Litvínov	1.00
97 Denis Afinogenov, Chemopetrol Litvínov	.25
98 Rail Muftijev, Chemopetrol Litvínov	.25
99 Dmitri Denisov, Chemopetrol Litvínov	.25
100 Karel Franek, Opava	.25
101 Petr Pelucha, Opava	.25
102 Rostislav Haas, Opava	.25
103 Pavel Nestak, Opava	.25
104 Martin Maskarinec, Opava	.25
105 David Gavlas, Opava	.25
106 Milos Hrubes, Opava	.25
107 Pavel Sebesta, Opava	.25
108 Tomas Kramny, Opava	.25
109 Pavel Marecek, Opava	.25
110 Vaclav Slaby, Opava	.25
111 Petr Suchanek, Opava	.25
112 Zbynek Marak, Opava	.25
113 Michal Tomek, Opava	.25
114 Michal Piskor, Opava	.25
115 Juraj Jurik, Opava	.25
116 Karel Horny, Opava	.25
117 Jirí Zurek, Opava	.25
118 Michal Sychra, Opava	.25
119 Zdenek Pavelek, Opava	.25
120 Richard Brancik, Opava	.25
121 Milan Ministr, Opava	.25
122 Martin Sekera, Opava	.25
123 Vladimír (Sr.) Vujtek, Vítkovice	.25
124 Ladislav Svozil, Vítkovice	.25
125 Martin Prusek, Vítkovice	4.00
126 Zdenek Dobes, Vítkovice	.25
127 Jiri Jonak, Vítkovice	.25
128 Vitezslav Skuta, Vítkovice	.25
129 Dmitri Jerofejev, Vítkovice	.25
130 Petr Jurecka, Vítkovice	.25
131 Pavel Kumstat, Vítkovice	.25
132 Roman Simicek, Vítkovice	.50
133 Roman Rysanek, Vítkovice	.25

□ 134 David Moravec, Vítkovice .50
□ 135 Alexander Prokopjev, Vítkovice .25
□ 136 Alexander Cerbajev, Vítkovice .25
□ 137 Libor Pavlis, Vítkovice .25
□ 138 Jan Matejny, Vítkovice .25
□ 139 Libor Polasek, Vítkovice .25
□ 140 Martin Kotasek, Vítkovice .25
□ 141 Petr Zajonc, Vítkovice .25
□ 142 Martin Lamich, Vítkovice .25
□ 143 Daniel Vilasek, Vítkovice .25
□ 144 Martin Tomasek, Vítkovice .25
□ 145 Ales Kratoska, Vítkovice .25
□ 146 Richard Farda, Slavia Praha .25
□ 147 Ladislav Slizek, Slavia Praha .25
□ 148 Martin Altrichter, Slavia Praha .25
□ 149 Ladislav Blazek, Slavia Praha .25
□ 150 Robert Kostka, Slavia Praha .25
□ 151 Jirí Hes, Slavia Praha .25
□ 152 Andrei Jakovenko, Slavia Praha .25
□ 153 Pavel Kolarík, Slavia Praha .50
□ 154 Martin Bakula, Slavia Praha .25
□ 155 Petr Kadlec, Slavia Praha .25
□ 156 Jan Novak, Slavia Praha .25
□ 157 Jan Hejda, Slavia Praha .25
□ 158 Vladimír Ruzicka, Slavia Praha .50
□ 159 Viktor Ujcík, Slavia Praha .50
□ 160 Jirí Dolezal, Slavia Praha .25
□ 161 Jirí Poukar, Slavia Praha .25
□ 162 Tomas Kucharcík, Slavia Praha .25
□ 163 Michal Sup, Slavia Praha .25
□ 164 Jiri Hlinka, Slavia Praha .25
□ 165 Tomas Kupka, Slavia Praha .25
□ 166 Radek Matejovsky, Slavia Praha .25
□ 167 Robert Kucera, Slavia Praha .25
□ 168 Jan Fadrny, Slavia Praha .25
□ 169 Jan Sochor, Slavia Praha .25
□ 170 Marek Sykora, Interconex Plzen .25
□ 171 Radim Rulik, Interconex Plzen .25
□ 172 Michal Marík, Interconex Plzen .25
□ 173 Dusan Salficky, Interconex Plzen .25
□ 174 Josef Reznícek, Interconex Plzen .25
□ 175 Ivan Vlcek, Interconex Plzen .25
□ 176 Robert Jindrich, Interconex Plzen .25
□ 177 Jirí Hanzlík, Interconex Plzen .25
□ 178 Pavel Srek, Interconex Plzen .25
□ 179 Ondrej Zetek, Interconex Plzen .25
□ 180 Pavel Geffert, Interconex Plzen .25
□ 181 David Pospísil, Interconex Plzen .25
□ 182 Martin Filip, Interconex Plzen .25
□ 183 Tomas Jelínek, Interconex Plzen .50
□ 184 Michal Straka, Interconex Plzen .25
□ 185 Milan Volak, Interconex Plzen .25
□ 186 Pavel Vostrak, Interconex Plzen .25
□ 187 Dalibor Sanda, Interconex Plzen .25
□ 188 Milan Navratil, Interconex Plzen .25
□ 189 Mojmir Musil, Interconex Plzen .25
□ 190 Milan Kraft, Interconex Plzen 4.00
□ 191 Jirí Jelen, Interconex Plzen .25
□ 192 Martin Cech, Interconex Plzen .25
□ 193 Jan Novotny, Kladno .25
□ 194 Lubomir Bauer, Kladno .25
□ 195 Radek Tóth, Kladno .25
□ 196 Martin Bilek, Kladno .25
□ 197 Jan Krulis, Kladno .25
□ 198 Marek Zidlicky, Kladno .25
□ 199 Tomas Kaberle, Kladno 1.50
□ 200 Pavel Skrbek, Kladno .50
□ 201 Jan Penk, Kladno .25
□ 202 Jan Dlouhy, Kladno .25
□ 203 Jan Hranac, Kladno .25
□ 204 Josef Zajic, Kladno .25
□ 205 Zdenek Eichenmann, Kladno .25
□ 206 Petr Ton, Kladno .25
□ 207 Jirí Beranek, Kladno .25
□ 208 Ladislav Svoboda, Kladno .25
□ 209 Vaclav Eiselt, Kladno .25
□ 210 Jirí Burger, Kladno .25
□ 211 Petr Tenkrat, Kladno 1.00
□ 212 Jiri Kuchler, Kladno .25
□ 213 Tomas Trachta, Kladno .25
□ 214 Jiri Holsan, Kladno .25
□ 215 Milan Novy, Kladno 1.00
□ 216 Jiri Kloboucek, Kladno .25
□ 217 Tomas Mikolasek, Kladno .25
□ 218 Milan Kasparek, Karlovy Vary .25
□ 219 Karel Trachta, Karlovy Vary .25
□ 220 Vladimír Hudacek, Karlovy Vary .25
□ 221 Robert Horyna, Karlovy Vary .25
□ 222 Petr Pavlas, Karlovy Vary .25
□ 223 Petr Mainer, Karlovy Vary .25
□ 224 Ales Tomasek, Karlovy Vary .25
□ 225 Pavel Blaha, Karlovy Vary .25
□ 226 Jiri Polak, Karlovy Vary .25
□ 227 Martin Richter, Karlovy Vary .25
□ 228 Martin Rejthar, Karlovy Vary .25
□ 229 Michal Cerny, Karlovy Vary .50
□ 230 Zbynek Kukacka, Karlovy Vary .25
□ 231 Ondrej Steiner, Karlovy Vary .50
□ 232 Pavel Metlicka, Karlovy Vary .25
□ 233 Martin Streit, Karlovy Vary .25
□ 234 Radek Prochazka, Karlovy Vary .25
□ 235 Radek Svoboda, Karlovy Vary .25
□ 236 Michal Porak, Karlovy Vary .25
□ 237 Michal Horak, Karlovy Vary .25
□ 238 Jan Lipiansky, Karlovy Vary .25
□ 239 Jaroslav Buchal, Karlovy Vary .25
□ 240 Tomas Klimt, Karlovy Vary .50
□ 241 Petr Fical, Karlovy Vary .25
□ 242 Milos Riha, Pardubice .25
□ 243 Josef Palecek, Pardubice .25
□ 244 Libor Barta, Pardubice .25
□ 245 Adam Svoboda, Pardubice .25
□ 246 Patrik Rozsíval, Pardubice .25
□ 247 Jirí Malinsky, Pardubice .25
□ 248 Ales Písa, Pardubice .50
□ 249 Tomas Pacal, Pardubice .25
□ 250 Pavel Kríz, Pardubice .25
□ 251 Pavel Augusta, Pardubice .25
□ 252 Petr Mudroch, Pardubice .25
□ 253 Robert Pospísil, Pardubice .25
□ 254 Tomas Blazek, Pardubice .50
□ 255 Milan Hejduk, Pardubice 20.00
□ 256 Jirí Jantovsky, Pardubice .25
□ 257 Stanislav Prochazka, Pardubice .25
□ 258 Tomas Martinec, Pardubice .25
□ 259 Pavel Kabrt, Pardubice .25
□ 260 Jaroslav Kudrna, Pardubice .25
□ 261 Karel Plasek, Pardubice .25
□ 262 Petr** Sykora, Pardubice .50
□ 263 Lukas Palecek, Pardubice .25
□ 264 Vladimír Caldr, Ceske Budejovice .25
□ 265 Jaroslav Liska, Ceske Budejovice .25
□ 266 Oldrich Svoboda, Ceske Budejovice .25
□ 267 Robert Slavík, Ceske Budejovice .25
□ 268 Rudolf Suchanek, Ceske Budejovice .25
□ 269 Karel Soudek, Ceske Budejovice .25
□ 270 Milan Nedoma, Ceske Budejovice .25
□ 271 Kamil Toupal, Ceske Budejovice .25
□ 272 Lukas Zib, Ceske Budejovice .25
□ 273 Jan Bohacek, Ceske Budejovice .25
□ 274 Filip Vanecek, Ceske Budejovice .25
□ 275 Radek Martínek, Ceske Budejovice .50
□ 276 Radek Toupal, Ceske Budejovice .25
□ 277 Lubos Rob, Ceske Budejovice .25
□ 278 Pavel Pycha, Ceske Budejovice .25
□ 279 David Bruk, Ceske Budejovice .25
□ 280 Filip Turek, Ceske Budejovice .25
□ 281 Ondrej Vosta, Ceske Budejovice .25
□ 282 Arpad Gyori, Ceske Budejovice .25
□ 283 Petr Sailer, Ceske Budejovice .25
□ 284 Martin Strba, Ceske Budejovice .25
□ 285 Petr Sachl, Ceske Budejovice .25
□ 286 Miroslav Barus, Ceske Budejovice .25
□ 287 Vaclav Kral, Ceske Budejovice .25
□ 288 Ales Kotalik, Ceske Budejovice 3.00
□ 289 Josef Augusta, Dukla Jihlava .25
□ 290 Karel Dvorak, Dukla Jihlava .25
□ 291 Marek Novotny, Dukla Jihlava .25
□ 292 Lukas Sablik, Dukla Jihlava .25
□ 293 Michael Vyhlídal, Dukla Jihlava .25
□ 294 Miroslav Javín, Dukla Jihlava .25
□ 295 Martin Tupa, Dukla Jihlava .25
□ 296 Marian Morava, Dukla Jihlava .25
□ 297 Jaroslav Horacek, Dukla Jihlava .25
□ 298 Tomas Jakes, Dukla Jihlava .25
□ 299 Daniel Zapotocny, Dukla Jihlava .25
□ 300 Miroslav Duben, Dukla Jihlava .25
□ 301 Petr Vlk, Dukla Jihlava .25
□ 302 Roman Mejzlik, Dukla Jihlava .25
□ 303 Jiri Cihlar, Dukla Jihlava .25
□ 304 Jaroslav Hub, Dukla Jihlava .25
□ 305 Leos Pipa, Dukla Jihlava .25
□ 306 Ladislav Prokupek, Dukla Jihlava .50
□ 307 Marek Melenovsky, Dukla Jihlava .25
□ 308 Milan Antos, Dukla Jihlava .25
□ 309 Vaclav Adamec, Dukla Jihlava .25
□ 310 Ales Sochorec, Dukla Jihlava .25
□ 311 Ales Polcar, Dukla Jihlava .25
□ 312 Daniel Hodek, Dukla Jihlava .25
□ 313 Alois Hadamczik, Trinec .25
□ 314 Kamil Konecny, Trinec .25
□ 315 Radovan Biegl, Trinec .25
□ 316 Vlastimil Lakosil, Trinec .25
□ 317 L'ubomír Sekeras, Trinec .50
□ 318 Miroslav Cihal, Trinec .25
□ 319 Petr Jancarík, Trinec .25
□ 320 Stanislav Pavelec, Trinec .25
□ 321 Jiri Kuntos, Trinec .25
□ 322 Patrik Hucko, Trinec .25
□ 323 Petr Gregorek, Trinec .25
□ 324 Filip Stefanka, Trinec .25
□ 325 Vladimir Machulda, Trinec .25
□ 326 Marek Zadina, Trinec .25
□ 327 Richard Kral, Trinec .25
□ 328 Jozef Dano, Trinec .25
□ 329 Ladislav Lubina, Trinec .25
□ 330 Tomas Chlubna, Trinec .25
□ 331 Jan Peterek, Trinec .25
□ 332 Petr Folta, Trinec .25
□ 333 Josef Straub, Trinec .25
□ 334 Roman Kadera, Trinec .50
□ 335 Marian Kacir, Trinec .25
□ 336 Robert Kantor, Trinec .25
□ 337 Roman Kontsek, Trinec .25
□ 338 Miloslav Horava, Karlovy Vary .50
□ 339 Ladislav Kudrna, Dukla Jihlava .25
□ 340 Ivan Hlinka, Czech Republic Nationals 1.00
□ 341 Slavomir Lener, Czech Republic Nationals .50
□ 342 Roman Cechmanek, Czech Republic Nationals 3.00
□ 343 Milan Hnilicka, Czech Republic Nationals 1.00
□ 344 Martin Prusek, Czech Republic Nationals 4.00
□ 345 Frantisek* Kaberle, Czech Republic Nationals .50
□ 346 Jirí Slégr, Czech Republic Nationals .50
□ 347 Jirí Vykoukal, Czech Republic Nationals .50
□ 348 Jirí Veber, Czech Republic Nationals .50
□ 349 Ladislav Benysek, Czech Republic Nationals .50
□ 350 Frantisek Kucera, Czech Republic Nationals .50
□ 351 Libor Prochazka, Czech Republic Nationals .50
□ 352 Jaroslav Spacek, Czech Republic Nationals .50
□ 353 Vlastimil Kroupa, Czech Republic Nationals .50
□ 354 Robert Reichel, Czech Republic Nationals 1.50
□ 355 Robert Lang, Czech Republic Nationals 2.00
□ 356 Pavel Patera, Czech Republic Nationals .50
□ 357 Martin Prochazka, Czech Republic Nationals .50
□ 358 Jirí Dopita, Czech Republic Nationals .50
□ 359 Josef Beranek, Czech Republic Nationals .50
□ 360 Viktor Ujcík, Czech Republic Nationals .50
□ 361 David Vyborny, Czech Republic Nationals .50
□ 362 Vladimír (Jr.) Vujtek, Czech Republic Nationals .50
□ 363 Roman Simicek, Czech Republic Nationals .50
□ 364 Jan Alinic, Czech Republic Nationals .50
□ 365 Rostislav Vlach, Czech Republic Nationals .50
□ 366 Ondrej Kratena, Czech Republic Nationals .50
□ 367 Richard Zemlicka, Czech Republic Nationals .50
□ 368 Dominik Hasek, Awards 10.00
□ 369 Jirí Dopita, Awards .50
□ 370 Roman Cechmanek, Awards 3.00
□ 371 Roman Horak, Awards .50
□ 372 Richard Zemlicka, Awards .50
□ 373 Antonín Stavjana, Awards .50
□ 374 Ondrej Kratena, Awards .50
□ 375 Richard Farda, Czechoslovakia Nationals .50
□ 376 Frantisek Cernik, Czechoslovakia Nationals .50
□ 377 Ludek Cajka, Czechoslovakia Nationals .50
□ 378 Vlastimil Bubnik, Czechoslovakia Nationals .50
□ 379 Josef Mikolas, Czechoslovakia Nationals .50
□ 380 Stanislav Konopasek, Czechoslovakia Nationals .50

1997 - 98 AUTOGRAPHED COLLECTION

This multi-sport series includes a 50-card set that sells for $15. Other hockey singles may exist.

	Player	SPA
□	4 Joe Thornton	2.00
□	AE2 Joe Thornton	6.00
□	Joe Thornton Auto. ✍ {#/1950}	50.00

1997 - 98 BELL PHONECARDS

		150.00	75.00
	Complete Set (16 phonecards):	**150.00**	**75.00**
	$10 Phonecard (#/3500)	**Unused**	**Used**
□	Bryan Allen	15.00	8
□	Sean Blanchard	12.00	6
□	Curtis Cruickshank (G)	12.00	6
□	Patrick Desrochers (G)	12.00	6
□	Bryan Duce	12.00	6
□	Richard Jackman	12.00	6
□	Manny Malhotra	15.00	8
□	Mike Martone	12.00	6
□	Norm Milley	12.00	6
□	Larry Paleczny	12.00	6
□	Justin Papineau	12.00	6
□	Richard Pitirri	12.00	6
□	Tyler Rennette	12.00	6
□	Peter Sarno	12.00	6
□	Brian Simpson	12.00	6
□	Daniel Tkaczuk	15.00	8

1997 - 98 BICYCLE SPORTS / ACES

Complete Deck (55 cards): 6.00

	Player	Aces
□	10-Club Jaromir Jagr, Pitt.	.50
□	10-Diamond Saku Koivu, Mont.	.20
□	10-Heart Brendan Shanahan, Detr.	.50
□	10-Spade Sheldon Kennedy, Bost.	.20

□	2-Club Jere Lehtinen, Dall.	.20
□	2-Diamond Geoff Sanderson, Hart.	.20
□	2-Heart Mike Vernon, Detr.	.20
□	2-Spade Raymond Bourque, Bost.	.50
□	3-Club Trevor Linden, Vanc.	.20
□	3-Diamond Chris Chelios, Chic.	.20
□	3-Heart Doug Gilmour, NJer.	.20
□	3-Spade Ryan Smyth, Edmo.	.20
□	4-Club John LeClair, Phil.	.20
□	4-Diamond Félix Potvin, Toro.	.20
□	4-Heart Dmitri Khristich, LosA.	.20
□	4-Spade Jarome Iginla, Calg.	.20
□	5-Club Owen Nolan, SanJ.	.20
□	5-Diamond Adam Oates, Wash.	.20
□	5-Heart Mark Recchi, Mont.	.20
□	5-Spade Chris Gratton, Tamp.	.20
□	6-Club Pierre Turgeon, SLou.	.20
□	6-Diamond Roman Hamrlik, Tamp.	.20
□	6-Heart Daniel Alfredsson, Otta.	.20
□	6-Spade Jeremy Roenick, Chic.	.20
□	7-Club Tony Amonte, Chic.	.20
□	7-Diamond Theoren Fleury, Calg.	.20
□	7-Heart Eric Lindros, Phil.	.50
□	7-Spade Mike Modano, Dall.	.50
□	8-Club Alexei Yashin, Otta.	.20
□	8-Diamond Vincent Damphousse, Mont.	.20
□	8-Heart Keith Tkachuk, Phoe.	.20
□	8-Spade Doug Weight, Edmo.	.20
□	9-Club Mats Sundin, Toro.	.50
□	9-Diamond Zigmund Palffy, NYIs.	.20
□	9-Heart Pavel Bure, Vanc.	.20
□	9-Spade Jim Campbell, SLou.	.20
□	A-Club Michael Peca, Buff.	.20
□	A-Diamond Bryan Berard, NYIs.	.20
□	A-Heart Dominik Hasek, Buff.	.50
□	A-Spade Paul Kariya, Anah.	.50
□	J-Club Wayne Gretzky, NYRa.	2.00
□	J-Diamond Teemu Selänne, Anah.	.20
□	J-Heart Sandis Ozolinsh, Colo.	.20
□	J-Spade Jason Arnott, Edmo.	.20
□	K-Club Tony Granato, SanJ.	.20
□	K-Diamond Vladimir Konstantinov, Detr.	.20
□	K-Heart Patrick Roy, Colo.	1.50
□	K-Spade Brian Leetch, NYRa.	.20
□	Q-Club Martin Brodeur (G), NJer.	.50
□	Q-Diamond John Vanbiesbrouck (G), Flor.	.20
□	Q-Heart Mark Messier, NYRa.	.50
□	Q-Spade Peter Forsberg, Colo.	.50
□	Checklist	.20
□	Eastern Conference	.20
□	Western Conference	.20

1997 - 98 DONRUSS

There are three versions: the regular card, a Press Proof parallel (#/2000) and a Gold Press Proof parallel (#/500).

	Complete Set (230 cards):	**1410.00**	**675.00**	**25.00**
	Common Player:	**6.00**	**3.00**	**.20**
	Player	**PPG500**	**PP2000**	**Don.**
□□□	1 Peter Forsberg, Colo.	35.00	15.00	.50
□□□	2 Steve Yzerman, Detr.	60.00	30.00	1.50
□□□	3 Eric Lindros, Phil.	25.00	10.00	.50
□□□	4 Mark Messier, Vanc.	25.00	10.00	.50
□□□	5 Patrick Roy (G), Colo.	70.00	35.00	1.50
□□□	6 Jeremy Roenick, Phoe.	20.00	10.00	.50
□□□	7 Paul Kariya, Anah.	30.00	15.00	.50
□□□	8 Valeri Bure, Mont.	8.00	4.00	.20
□□□	9 Dominik Hasek (G), Buff.	25.00	10.00	.50
□□□	10 Doug Gilmour, NJer.	15.00	7.00	.20
□□□	11 Garth Snow (G), Phil.	8.00	4.00	.20
□□□	12 Todd Bertuzzi, NYIs.	30.00	15.00	.50
□□□	13 Chris Osgood (G), Detr.	15.00	5.00	.20

□□□	14 Jarome Iginla, Calg.	20.00	10.00	.50
□□□	15 Lonny Bohonos, Vanc.	6.00	3.00	.20
□□□	16 Jeff O'Neill, Hart.	10.00	5.00	.20
□□□	17 Daniel Alfredsson, Otta.	15.00	7.00	.20
□□□	18 Daymond Langkow, Tamp.	6.00	3.00	.20
□□□	19 Alexei Yashin, Otta.	15.00	7.00	.20
□□□	20 Byron Dafoe (G), LosA.	10.00	5.00	.20
□□□	21 Michael Peca, Buff.	10.00	5.00	.20
□□□	22 Jim Carey (G), Bost.	6.00	3.00	.20
□□□	23 Pat Verbeek, Dall.	8.00	4.00	.20
□□□	24 Terry Ryan, Mont.	6.00	3.00	.20
□□□	25 Adam Oates, Wash.	10.00	5.00	.20
□□□	26 Kevin Hatcher, Pitt.	6.00	3.00	.20
□□□	27 Ken Wregget (G), Pitt.	6.00	3.00	.20
□□□	28 Pierre Turgeon, SLou.	10.00	5.00	.20
□□□	29 John LeClair, Phil.	20.00	10.00	.50
□□□	30 Jere Lehtinen, Dall.	8.00	4.00	.20
□□□	31 Jamie Storr (G), LosA.	6.00	3.00	.20
□□□	32 Doug Weight, Edmo.	15.00	5.00	.20
□□□	33 Tommy Salo (G), NYIs.	10.00	5.00	.20
□□□	34 Bernie Nicholls, SanJ.	6.00	3.00	.20
□□□	35 Jocelyn Thibault (G), Mont.	10.00	5.00	.20
□□□	36 Dale Hawerchuk, Phil.	15.00	7.00	.20
□□□	37 Chris Chelios, Chic.	15.00	7.00	.20
□□□	38 Kirk Muller, Flor.	8.00	4.00	.20
□□□	39 Steve Sullivan, Toro.	8.00	4.00	.20
□□□	40 A. Moog (G), Dall. (Mont.)	10.00	5.00	.20
□□□	41 Martin Gelinas, Vanc.	6.00	3.00	.20
□□□	42 Shayne Corson, Mont.	8.00	4.00	.20
□□□	43 Curtis Joseph (G), Edmo.	25.00	10.00	.50
□□□	44 Donald Audette, Buff.	10.00	5.00	.20
□□□	45 Rick Tocchet, Wash. (Phoe.)	8.00	4.00	.20
□□□	46 Craig Janney, Phoe.	6.00	3.00	.20
□□□	47 Geoff Courtnall, SLou.	6.00	3.00	.20
□□□	48 Wade Redden, Otta.	8.00	4.00	.20
□□□	49 Steve Rucchin, Anah.	6.00	3.00	.20
□□□	50 Ethan Moreau, Chic.	6.00	3.00	.20
□□□	**51 Steve Shields (G), Buff. RC**	**10.00**	**6.00**	**1.00**
□□□	52 Jamie Pushor, Detr.	6.00	3.00	.20
□□□	53 Saku Koivu, Mont.	20.00	10.00	.50
□□□	54 Oleg Tverdovsky, Phoe.	6.00	3.00	.20
□□□	55 Jeff Friesen, SanJ.	8.00	4.00	.20
□□□	56 Chris Gratton, Tamp. (Phil.)	6.00	3.00	.20
□□□	57 Wendel Clark, Toro.	20.00	10.00	.50
□□□	58 John Vanbiesbrouck (G), Flor.	10.00	6.00	.20
□□□	59 Trevor Kidd (G), Calg.	8.00	4.00	.20
□□□	60 Sandis Ozolinsh, Colo.	6.00	3.00	.20
□□□	61 Dave Andreychuk, NJer.	8.00	4.00	.20
□□□	62 Travis Green, NYIs.	6.00	3.00	.20
□□□	63 Paul Coffey, Phil.	15.00	5.00	.20
□□□	64 Roman Turek (G), Dall.	10.00	6.00	.20
□□□	65 Vladimir Konstantinov, Detr.	8.00	4.00	.20
□□□	66 Raymond Bourque, Bost.	30.00	15.00	.50
□□□	67 Wayne Primeau, Buff.	6.00	3.00	.20
□□□	68 Todd Harvey, Dall.	6.00	3.00	.20
□□□	69 Derek King, Hart. (Toro.)	6.00	3.00	.20
□□□	70 Adam Graves, NYRa.	10.00	5.00	.20
□□□	71 Brett Hull, SLou.	25.00	10.00	.50
□□□	72 Scott Niedermayer, NJer.	8.00	4.00	.20
□□□	73 Mike Vernon (G), Detr. (SanJ.)	10.00	5.00	.20
□□□	74 Brian Holzinger, Buff.	6.00	3.00	.20
□□□	75 Dainius Zubrus, Phil.	6.00	3.00	.20
□□□	76 Patrick Lalime (G), Pitt.	15.00	7.00	.20
□□□	77 Corey Schwab (G), Tamp.	6.00	3.00	.20
□□□	78 Alexandre Daigle, Otta.	6.00	3.00	.20
□□□	79 Geoff Sanderson, Hart. (Caro.)	6.00	3.00	.20
□□□	80 Dave Gagner, Calg. (Flor.)	6.00	3.00	.20
□□□	81 José Théodore (G), Mont.	30.00	15.00	1.00
□□□	82 Sergei Fedorov, Detr.	25.00	10.00	.50
□□□	83 Keith Tkachuk, Phoe.	15.00	5.00	.20
□□□	84 Owen Nolan, SanJ.	15.00	7.00	.20
□□□	85 Brandon Convery, Toro.	6.00	3.00	.20
□□□	86 Trevor Linden, Vanc.	10.00	5.00	.20
□□□	87 Landon Wilson, Bost.	6.00	3.00	.20
□□□	88 Claude Lemieux, Colo.	8.00	4.00	.20
□□□	89 Dimitri Khristich, LosA.	6.00	3.00	.20
□□□	90 Luc Robitaille, NYRa.	20.00	10.00	.50
□□□	91 Todd Warriner, Toro.	6.00	3.00	.20
□□□	92 Kelly Hrudey, SanJ.	8.00	4.00	.20
□□□	93 Mike Dunham, NJer.	10.00	5.00	.20
□□□	94 Mike Grier, Edmo.	6.00	3.00	.20
□□□	95 Joé Juneau, Wash.	6.00	3.00	.20
□□□	96 Alexei Zhamnov, Chic.	8.00	4.00	.20
□□□	97 Jamie Langenbrunner, Dall.	6.00	3.00	.20
□□□	98 Sean Pronger, Anah.	6.00	3.00	.20
□□□	99 Janne Niinimaa, Phil.	6.00	3.00	.20
□□□	100 Chris Pronger, SLou.	15.00	7.00	.20
□□□	101 Ray Sheppard, Flor.	6.00	3.00	.20
□□□	102 Tony Amonte, Chic.	15.00	7.00	.20
□□□	103 Ron Tugnutt (G), Otta.	10.00	5.00	.20
□□□	104 Mike Modano, Dall.	25.00	10.00	.50
□□□	**105 Dan Trebil, Anah. RC**	**6.00**	**3.00**	**.50**
□□□	106 Alexander Mogilny, Vanc.	10.00	6.00	.20
□□□	107 Darren McCarty, Detr.	8.00	4.00	.20
□□□	108 Ted Donato, Bost.	6.00	3.00	.20
□□□	109 Brian Savage, Mont.	8.00	4.00	.20
□□□	110 Mike Gartner, Phoe.	20.00	10.00	.50
□□□	111 Jim Campbell, SLou.	6.00	3.00	.20
□□□	112 Roman Hamrlik, Tamp.	6.00	3.00	.20
□□□	113 Andreas Dackell, Otta.	6.00	3.00	.20
□□□	114 Ron Hextall (G), Phil.	15.00	7.00	.20
□□□	115 Steve Washburn, Flor.	6.00	3.00	.20
□□□	116 Jeff Hackett (G), Chic.	6.00	4.00	.20
□□□	117 Joe Sakic, Colo.	40.00	20.00	1.00
□□□	118 Anson Carter, Bost.	10.00	5.00	.20
□□□	119 Vyacheslav Kozlov, Detr.	6.00	3.00	.20
□□□	120 Nikolai Khabibulin (G), Phoe.	10.00	5.00	.20
□□□	121 Tony Granato, SanJ.	6.00	3.00	.20
□□□	122 Al MacInnis, SLou.	10.00	5.00	.20
□□□	123 Daren Puppa (G), Tamp.	6.00	3.00	.20
□□□	124 Mike Richter (G), NYRa.	10.00	6.00	.20
□□□	125 Zigmund Palffy, NYIs.	15.00	7.00	.20
□□□	126 Martin Brodeur (G), NJer.	40.00	20.00	1.00
□□□	127 Rem Murray, Edmo.	6.00	3.00	.20
□□□	128 Sean Burke (G), Hart. (Caro.)	15.00	7.00	.20
□□□	129 Aki Berg, LosA.	6.00	3.00	.20
□□□	130 Dmitri Mironov, Pitt.	6.00	3.00	.20
□□□	131 Jamie Allison, Calg.	15.00	5.00	.20
□□□	132 Valeri Kamensky, Colo.	8.00	4.00	.20
□□□	133 Pat LaFontaine, Buff.	15.00	7.00	.20
□□□	134 Jozef Stumpel, Bost.	6.00	3.00	.20
□□□	135 Peter Bondra, Wash.	15.00	7.00	.20
□□□	136 Mark Recchi, Mont.	10.00	5.00	.20
□□□	137 Ron Francis, Pitt.	15.00	7.00	.20
□□□	138 Harry York, SLou.	6.00	3.00	.20
□□□	139 Mats Sundin, Toro.	25.00	10.00	.50
□□□	140 Bobby Holik, NJer.	8.00	4.00	.20
□□□	141 Éric Desjardins, Phil.	8.00	4.00	.20
□□□	142 Scott Lachance, NYIs.	6.00	3.00	.20
□□□	143 Wayne Gretzky, NYRa.	100.00	50.00	2.50
□□□	144 Ed Jovanovski, Flor.	10.00	5.00	.20
□□□	145 Jason Arnott, Edmo.	10.00	6.00	.20
□□□	146 Andrew Cassels, Hart.	6.00	3.00	.20
□□□	147 Roman Vopat, LosA.	6.00	3.00	.20
□□□	148 Dwayne Roloson (G), Calg.	6.00	3.00	.20
□□□	149 Derek Plante, Buff.	6.00	3.00	.20
□□□	150 Phil Housley, Wash.	8.00	4.00	.20
□□□	151 Mikael Renberg, Phil.	8.00	4.00	.20
□□□	152 Petr Nedved, Pitt.	6.00	4.00	.20
□□□	153 Grant Fuhr (G), SLou.	15.00	7.00	.20
□□□	154 Félix Potvin (G), Toro.	15.00	7.00	.20
□□□	155 John MacLean, NJer.	6.00	3.00	.20
□□□	156 Brian Leetch, NYRa.	15.00	7.00	.20
□□□	157 Rod Brind'Amour, Phil.	8.00	4.00	.20
□□□	158 Ryan Smyth, Edmo.	10.00	6.00	.20
□□□	159 Teemu Selänne, Anah.	20.00	10.00	.50
□□□	160 Theoren Fleury, Calg.	15.00	5.00	.20
□□□	161 Adam Deadmarsh, Colo.	8.00	4.00	.20
□□□	162 Corey Hirsch (G), Vanc.	6.00	3.00	.20
□□□	163 Bryan Berard, NYIs.	8.00	4.00	.20
□□□	164 Ed Belfour (G), Dall.	25.00	10.00	.50
□□□	165 Sergei Berezin, Toro.	6.00	3.00	.20
□□□	166 Damian Rhodes (G), Otta.	6.00	3.00	.20
□□□	167 Guy Hebert (G), Anah.	6.00	3.00	.20
□□□	168 Derian Hatcher, Dall.	8.00	4.00	.20
□□□	169 Jonas Höglund, Calg.	6.00	3.00	.20
□□□	170 Matthew Barnaby, Buff.	6.00	3.00	.20
□□□	171 Scott Mellanby, Flor.	6.00	3.00	.20
□□□	172 Bill Ranford, Wash.	10.00	5.00	.20
□□□	173 Damphousse, Mont.	15.00	7.00	.20
□□□	174 Anders Eriksson, Detr.	6.00	3.00	.20
□□□	175 Chad Kilger, Phoe.	6.00	3.00	.20
□□□	176 Darren Turcotte, SanJ.	6.00	3.00	.20
□□□	177 Dino Ciccarelli, Tamp.	8.00	4.00	.20
□□□	178 Niklas Sundström, NYRa.	6.00	3.00	.20
□□□	179 Stéphane Fiset (G), LosA.	8.00	4.00	.20
□□□	180 Mike Ricci, Colo.	8.00	4.00	.20
□□□	181 Brendan Shanahan, Detr.	25.00	10.00	.50
□□□	182 Darcy Tucker, Mont.	6.00	3.00	.20
□□□	183 Éric Fichaud (G), NYIs.	6.00	3.00	.20
□□□	184 Todd Marchant, Edmo.	6.00	3.00	.20
□□□	185 Keith Primeau, Hart. (Caro.)	10.00	5.00	.20
□□□	186 Joe Nieuwendyk, Dall.	10.00	5.00	.20
□□□	187 Pavel Bure, Vanc.	20.00	10.00	.50
□□□	188 Jaromir Jagr, Pitt.	20.00	10.00	.50
□□□	189 Kirk McLean (G), Vanc.	8.00	4.00	.20
□□□	190 Daniel Goneau, NYRa.	6.00	3.00	.20
□□□	191 Rob Niedermayer, Flor., Err. (Barnes)	6.00	3.00	.20
□□□	192 Eric Dazé, Chic.	10.00	5.00	.20
□□□	193 Richard Matvichuk, Dall.	6.00	3.00	.20
□□□	194 Scott Stevens, NJer.	10.00	5.00	.20
□□□	195 Dale Hunter, Wash.	8.00	4.00	.20
□□□	196 Hnat Domenichelli, Calg.	6.00	3.00	.20
□□□	197 P. DeRouville (G), Pitt.	6.00	3.00	.20
□□□	198 M. Cousineau (G), Toro.	6.00	3.00	.20
□□□	199 Kevin Hodson (G), Detr.	6.00	3.00	.20
□□□	200 Giguère (G), Hart. (Caro.)	20.00	10.00	.50
□□□	**201 P. Schafer (G), Bost. RC**	**6.00**	**3.00**	**.50**
□□□	202 Marc Denis (G), Colo.	10.00	6.00	.20
□□□	**203 F. Banham, Anah. RC**	**6.00**	**3.00**	**.50**
□□□	204 Vadim Sharifjanov, NJer.	6.00	3.00	.20
□□□	**205 Paul Healey, Phil. RC**	**6.00**	**3.00**	**.50**
□□□	**206 D.J. Smith, Toro. RC**	**6.00**	**3.00**	**.50**
□□□	**207 C. Matte, Colo. RC**	**6.00**	**3.00**	**.50**
□□□	**208 Sean Brown, Edmo. RC**	**6.00**	**3.00**	**.50**
□□□	**209 T. Vokoun (G), Mont. RC**	**10.00**	**6.00**	**1.00**
□□□	**210 V. Vorobiev, NYRa. RC**	**6.00**	**3.00**	**.50**
□□□	**211 J-Y Leroux, Chic. RC**	**6.00**	**3.00**	**.50**
□□□	**212 Domenic Pittis, Pitt. RC**	**8.00**	**4.00**	**.50**
□□□	**213 Wilkinson (G), Tamp. RC**	**6.00**	**3.00**	**.50**
□□□	214 Jason Holland, NYIs.	6.00	3.00	.20
□□□	**215 P. Rhéaume, NJer. RC**	**6.00**	**3.00**	**.50**
□□□	216 Steve Kelly, Edmo.	6.00	3.00	.20
□□□	217 Vaclav Varada, Buff.	6.00	3.00	.20
□□□	218 Mike Fountain (G), Vanc.	6.00	3.00	.20
□□□	**219 Vaclav Prospal, Phil. RC**	**16.00**	**8.00**	**1.50**
□□□	220 Jaroslav Svejkovsky, Wash.	6.00	3.00	.20
□□□	221 Marty Murray, Calg.	6.00	3.00	.20
□□□	**222 Wade Belak, Colo. RC**	**6.00**	**3.00**	**.50**
□□□	**223 Jamal Mayers, SLou. RC**	**6.00**	**3.00**	**.50**
□□□	**224 S. Toporowski, Toro. RC**	**6.00**	**3.00**	**.50**
□□□	**225 Mike Knuble, Detr. RC**	**6.00**	**3.00**	**.50**
□□□	226 CL: Jarome Iginla, Calg.	11.00	5.00	.20
□□□	227 CL: Keith Tkachuk, Phoe.	6.00	4.00	.20
□□□	228 CL: Adam Oates, Wash.	6.00	3.00	.20
□□□	229 CL: John LeClair, Phil.	10.00	5.00	.20
□□□	230 CL: Brian Leetch, NYRa.	8.00	4.00	.20

BETWEEN THE PIPES

Insert Set (10 cards):		**90.00**
	Insert (#/3500)	**BTP**
□	1 Patrick Roy (G), Colo.	35.00
□	2 Martin Brodeur (G), NJer.	15.00
□	3 John Vanbiesbrouck (G), Flor.	6.00
□	4 Dominik Hasek (G), Buff.	10.00
□	5 Chris Osgood (G), Detr.	6.00
□	6 José Théodore (G), Mont.	15.00
□	7 Garth Snow (G), Phil.	6.00
□	8 Curtis Joseph (G), Edmo.	10.00
□	9 Félix Potvin (G), Toro.	6.00
□	10 Jocelyn Thibault (G), Mont.	6.00

ELITE SERIES

Insert Set (12 cards):		**165.00**
	Insert (#/2500)	**ES**
□	1 Wayne Gretzky, NYRa.	50.00
□	2 Jaromir Jagr, Pitt.	10.00
□	3 Eric Lindros, Phil.	10.00
□	4 Paul Kariya, Anah.	15.00
□	5 Patrick Roy (G), Colo.	35.00
□	6 Steve Yzerman, Detr.	30.00
□	7 Peter Forsberg, Colo.	15.00
□	8 John Vanbiesbrouck (G), Flor.	10.00
□	9 Brendan Shanahan, Detr.	10.00
□	10 Martin Brodeur (G), NJer.	15.00
□	11 Dominik Hasek (G), Buff.	10.00
□	12 Teemu Selänne, Anah.	10.00

LINE 2 LINE

Each Line 2 Line card has a regular insert and a die-cut parallel (serial numbered 1-250). Red cards (forwards) are serial numbered 251-4000 (3,750 total), blue cards (defencemen) are serial numbered 251-2000 (1,750 total) and gold cards are serial numbered 251-1000 (750 total).

Insert Set (24 cards):		**500.00**	**65.00**
	Inserts	**D.C.**	**L2L**
□□	1 Wayne Gretzky, NYRa. [Gold]	150.00	70.00
□□	2 Teemu Selänne, Anah. [Red]	30.00	6.00
□□	3 Brian Leetch, NYRa. [Blue]	20.00	6.00
□□	4 Peter Forsberg, Colo. [Red]	50.00	10.00
□□	5 Steve Yzerman, Detr. [Red]	90.00	15.00
□□	6 Oleg Tverdovsky, Phoe. [Blue]	8.00	3.00
□□	7 Doug Gilmour, NJer. [Red]	20.00	4.00
□□	8 Eric Lindros, Phil. [Gold]	30.00	15.00
□□	9 Bryan Berard, NYIs. [Blue]	10.00	3.00
□□	10 Brendan Shanahan, Detr. [Red]	35.00	6.00
□□	11 Pavel Bure, Vanc. [Red]	30.00	6.00
□□	12 Joe Sakic, Colo. [Red]	60.00	12.00
□□	13 Chris Chelios, Chic. [Blue]	20.00	6.00
□□	14 Mike Modano, Dall. [Red]	35.00	6.00
□□	15 Paul Coffey, Detr. [Blue]	20.00	6.00
□□	16 Jaromir Jagr, Pitt. [Gold]	30.00	10.00
□□	17 Jarome Iginla, Calg. [Red]	30.00	6.00
□□	18 Brett Hull, SLou. [Red]	35.00	6.00
□□	19 Wade Redden, Otta. [Blue]	10.00	3.00
□□	20 Paul Kariya, Anah. [Gold]	50.00	20.00
□□	21 Raymond Bourque, Bost. [Blue]	40.00	12.00
□□	22 Ryan Smyth, Edmo. [Red]	15.00	3.00
□□	23 Mark Messier, NYRa. [Red]	35.00	6.00
□□	24 Sandis Ozolinsh, Colo. [Blue]	8.00	3.00

RATED ROOKIES

There are two versions: the regular insert and a Medalists parallel.

Insert Set (10 cards):		**110.00**	**35.00**
	Inserts	**RRM**	**RR**
□□	1 Tomas Vokoun (G), Mont.	10.00	4.00
□□	2 Paxton Schafer, Bost.	8.00	2.00
□□	3 Vaclav Prospal, Phil.	16.00	6.00
□□	4 Marc Denis (G), Colo.	20.00	8.00
□□	5 Domenic Pittis, Pitt.	8.00	2.00
□□	6 Christian Matte, Colo.	8.00	2.00
□□	7 Marcel Cousineau (G), Toro.	8.00	2.00
□□	8 Steve Kelly, Edmo.	8.00	2.00
□□	9 Jaroslav Svejkovsky, Wash.	8.00	2.00
□□	10 Jean-Sébastien Giguère (G), Hart.	40.00	16.00

RED ALERT

Insert Set (10 cards):		**55.00**
	Insert (#/5000)	**RA**
□	1 Adam Deadmarsh, Colo.	3.00
□	2 Ryan Smyth, Edmo.	4.00
□	3 Sergei Fedorov, Detr.	10.00
□	4 Keith Tkachuk, Phoe.	6.00
□	5 Brett Hull, SLou.	10.00
□	6 Pavel Bure, Vanc.	5.00
□	7 John LeClair, Phil.	5.00
□	8 Zigmund Palffy, NYIs.	6.00
□	9 Mats Sundin, Toro.	10.00
□	10 Peter Bondra, Wash.	6.00

1997 - 98 DONRUSS CANADIAN ICE

There are three versions: the regular card, a Provincial Series (750 copies) and a Dominion Series (150 copies).

Complete Set (240 cards):		**2100.00**	**725.00**	**35.00**
Common Player:		**8.00**	**3.00**	**.20**
	Player	**DS150**	**PS750**	**DCI**
□□□	1 Patrick Roy (G), Colo.	150.00	50.00	3.00
□□□	2 Paul Kariya, Anah.	70.00	25.00	1.00
□□□	3 Eric Lindros, Phil.	50.00	15.00	1.00
□□□	4 Steve Yzerman, Detr.	120.00	45.00	2.00
□□□	5 Wayne Gretzky, NYRa.	200.00	70.00	4.00
□□□	6 Peter Forsberg, Colo.	70.00	25.00	1.00
□□□	7 John Vanbiesbrouck (G), Flor.	20.00	5.00	.20
□□□	8 Jaromir Jagr, Pitt.	50.00	15.00	1.00
□□□	9 Jim Campbell, SLou.	8.00	3.00	.20

10 Dominik Hasek (G), Buff.	50.00	15.00	1.00
11 Raymond Bourque, Bost.	60.00	20.00	1.00
12 Jarome Iginla, Calg.	40.00	15.00	.50
13 Mike Modano, Dall.	50.00	15.00	1.00
14 Ed Jovanovski, Flor.	20.00	7.00	.20
15 Jocelyn Thibault (G), Mont.	20.00	7.00	.20
16 Keith Tkachuk, Phoe.	30.00	10.00	.50
17 Brett Hull, SLou.	50.00	15.00	1.00
18 Pavel Bure, Vanc.	40.00	15.00	.50
19 Saku Koivu, Mont.	40.00	15.00	.50
20 Curtis Joseph (G), Edmo.	50.00	15.00	1.00
21 Eric Dazé, Chic.	20.00	7.00	.20
22 Keith Primeau, Hart. (Caro.)	20.00	7.00	.20
23 Theoren Fleury, Calg.	30.00	10.00	.50
24 Pierre Turgeon, SLou.	20.00	5.00	.20
25 Peter Bondra, Wash.	30.00	10.00	.50
26 Ed Belfour (G), SanJ.	50.00	15.00	1.00
27 Pat Verbeek, Dall.	15.00	6.00	.20
28 Chris Osgood (G), Detr.	30.00	10.00	.50
29 Ray Sheppard, Flor.	8.00	3.00	.20
30 Stéphane Fiset (G), LosA.	15.00	6.00	.20
31 Wade Redden, Otta.	15.00	6.00	.20
32 Trevor Linden, Vanc.	20.00	7.00	.20
33 Zigmund Palffy, NYIs.	30.00	10.00	.50
34 Tony Amonte, Chic.	30.00	10.00	.50
35 Derek Plante, Buff.	8.00	3.00	.20
36 Jonas Höglund, Calg.	8.00	3.00	.20
37 Guy Hebert (G), Anah.	10.00	4.00	.20
38 Garth Snow (G), Phil.	15.00	6.00	.20
39 Chris Gratton, Tamp.	10.00	4.00	.20
40 Mats Sundin, Toro.	50.00	15.00	1.00
41 G. Sanderson, Hart. (Caro.)	10.00	4.00	.20
42 Martin Brodeur (G), NJer.	80.00	30.00	1.50
43 Jozef Stumpel, Bost.	10.00	4.00	.20
44 Ron Francis, Pitt.	30.00	10.00	.50
45 A. Mogilny & P. Bure	20.00	5.00	.20
46 Bill Ranford (G), Wash.	20.00	7.00	.20
47 Kirk Muller, Flor.	15.00	6.00	.20
48 Ron Hextall (G), Phil.	30.00	11.00	.50
49 Doug Gilmour, NJer.	30.00	10.00	.50
50 Mark Messier, Vanc.	50.00	15.00	1.00
51 Joe Nieuwendyk, Dall.	20.00	7.00	.20
52 Ryan Smyth, Edmo.	20.00	9.00	.20
53 Mark Recchi, Mont.	20.00	7.00	.20
54 Mike Gartner, Phoe.	40.00	15.00	.50
55 Al MacInnis, SLou.	20.00	7.00	.20
56 Félix Potvin (G), Toro.	30.00	10.00	.50
57 Rob Blake, LosA.	30.00	10.00	.50
58 Dimitri Khristich, LosA.	8.00	3.00	.20
59 Jim Carey (G), Bost.	8.00	3.00	.20
60 Trevor Kidd (G), Calg.	15.00	6.00	.20
61 Martin Gelinas, Vanc.	10.00	4.00	.20
62 Oleg Tverdovsky, Phoe.	8.00	3.00	.20
63 Ron Tugnutt (G), Otta.	20.00	7.00	.20
64 Paul Coffey, Phil.	30.00	10.00	.50
65 Travis Green, NYIs.	10.00	4.00	.20
66 Andrew Cassels, Hart. (Caro.)	10.00	4.00	.20
67 Brendan Shanahan, Detr.	50.00	15.00	1.00
68 Luc Robitaille, NYRa.	40.00	15.00	.50
69 Pat LaFontaine, Buff.	30.00	10.00	.50
70 Daymond Langkow, Tamp.	10.00	4.00	.20
71 Petr Nedved, Pitt.	15.00	6.00	.20
72 Sergei Fedorov, Detr.	50.00	15.00	1.00
73 Anson Carter, Bost.	20.00	7.00	.20
74 Teemu Selänne, Anah.	40.00	15.00	.50
75 N. Khabibulin (G), Phoe.	20.00	7.00	.20
76 Ken Wregget (G), Pitt.	10.00	4.00	.20
77 Dino Ciccarelli, Tamp.	15.00	6.00	.20
78 Adam Oates, Wash.	20.00	7.00	.20
79 Kirk McLean (G), Vanc.	15.00	6.00	.20
80 Wendel Clark, Toro.	40.00	15.00	.50
81 Jeff Friesen, SanJ.	15.00	6.00	.20
82 Valeri Kamensky, Colo.	15.00	6.00	.20
83 Ethan Moreau, Chic.	8.00	3.00	.20
84 Matthew Barnaby, Buff.	8.00	3.00	.20
85 A. Moog (G), Dall. (Mont.)	20.00	7.00	.20
86 Doug Weight, Edmo.	30.00	10.00	.50
87 Mike Dunham (G), NJer.	20.00	5.00	.20
88 Brian Leetch, NYRa.	30.00	10.00	.50
89 Michael Peca, Buff.	20.00	7.00	.20
90 Chris Pronger, SLou.	30.00	10.00	.50
91 Alexei Zhamnov, Chic.	15.00	6.00	.20
92 Bryan Berard, NYIs.	15.00	6.00	.20
93 John LeClair, Phil.	40.00	15.00	.50
94 Steve Sullivan, Toro.	15.00	6.00	.20
95 Grant Fuhr (G), SLou.	30.00	10.00	.50
96 Mikael Renberg, Phil.	15.00	6.00	.20
97 Adam Graves, NYRa.	20.00	7.00	.20
98 Ray Ferraro, LosA.	8.00	3.00	.20
99 S. Burke (G), Hart. (Caro.)	30.00	11.00	.50
100 Jeremy Roenick, Phoe.	40.00	15.00	.50
101 Jeff Hackett (G), Chic.	15.00	6.00	.20
102 Joe Sakic, Colo.	80.00	30.00	1.50
103 J. Langenbrunner, Dall.	10.00	4.00	.20
104 Stéphane Richer, Mont.	10.00	4.00	.20
105 Dave Andreychuk, NJer.	15.00	6.00	.20
106 Tommy Salo, NYIs.	20.00	7.00	.20
107 Mike Richter (G), NYRa.	20.00	5.00	.20
108 Owen Nolan, SanJ.	30.00	10.00	.50
109 Corey Hirsch (G), Vanc.	8.00	3.00	.20
110 Daren Puppa (G), Tamp.	10.00	4.00	.20
111 Darcy Tucker, Mont.	10.00	4.00	.20
112 Daniel Alfredsson, Otta.	30.00	11.00	.50
113 Rod Brind'Amour, Phil.	15.00	6.00	.20
114 Scott Stevens, NJer.	20.00	7.00	.20
115 V. Damphousse, Mont.	30.00	11.00	.50
116 Mathieu Schneider, Toro.	10.00	4.00	.20
117 Jason Arnott, Edmo.	20.00	5.00	.20
118 Mike Vernon (G), Detr.	20.00	7.00	.20
119 Sandis Ozolinsh, Colo.	10.00	4.00	.20
120 Chris Chelios, Chic.	30.00	10.00	.50
121 Mike Grier, Edmo.	10.00	4.00	.20
122 Alexandre Daigle, Otta.	8.00	3.00	.20
123 Roman Hamrlik, Tamp.	10.00	4.00	.20
124 Derian Hatcher, Dall.	15.00	6.00	.20
125 Damian Rhodes (G), Otta.	10.00	4.00	.20
126 Adam Deadmarsh, Colo.	15.00	6.00	.20
127 Alexei Yashin, Otta.	30.00	10.00	.50
128 Terry Ryan, Mont.	8.00	3.00	.20
129 Jeff Ware, Toro.	8.00	3.00	.20
130 Steve Kelly, Edmo.	8.00	3.00	.20
131 Hnat Domenichelli, Calg.	8.00	3.00	.20
132 S. Shields (G), Buff. RC	**20.00**	**5.00**	**1.50**
133 P. Schafer (G), Bost. RC	**10.00**	**3.00**	**.50**
134 Vadim Sharifjanov, NJer.	8.00	3.00	.20
135 V. Prospal, Phil. RC	**30.00**	**12.00**	**2.00**
136 Mike Fountain (G), Vanc.	8.00	3.00	.20
137 C. Matte, Colo. RC	**10.00**	**3.00**	**.50**
138 T. Vokoun (G), Mont. RC	**20.00**	**5.00**	**1.50**
139 V. Vorobiev, NYRa. RC	**10.00**	**3.00**	**.50**
140 Domenic Pittis, Pitt. RC	**15.00**	**6.00**	**1.00**
141 Vaclav Varada, Buff.	**8.00**	**3.00**	**.20**
142 D.J. Smith, Toro. RC	**10.00**	**3.00**	**.50**
143 Jaroslav Svejkovsky, Wash.	8.00	3.00	.20
144 Jason Holland, NYIs.	8.00	3.00	.20
145 Marc Denis (G), Colo.	20.00	9.00	.50
146 Giguère (G), Hart. (Caro.)	40.00	15.00	1.50
147 M. Cousineau (G), Toro.	8.00	3.00	.20
148 CL: Dave Andreychuk, NJer.	10.00	3.00	.20
149 CL: Mike Gartner, Phoe.	20.00	8.00	.20
150 CL: Detroit Red Wings.	8.00	3.00	.20

LES GARDIENS

There are two versions: a promo card and the insert (serial numbered out of 1,500).

Complete Set (12 cards):	15.00	170.00
Goalie	Promo	LG
1 Patrick Roy (G), Colo.	6.00	60.00
2 Félix Potvin (G), Toro.	1.00	10.00
3 Martin Brodeur (G), NJer.	3.00	35.00
4 J.S. Giguère (G), Hart. (Caro.)	1.50	18.00
5 Stéphane Fiset (G), LosA.	1.00	7.00
6 José Théodore (G), Mont.	2.00	35.00
7 Jocelyn Thibault (G), Mont.	1.00	6.00
8 Éric Fichaud (G), NYIs.	1.00	6.00
9 Patrick Lalime (G), Pitt.	1.00	10.00
10 Marcel Cousineau (G), Toro.	1.00	6.00
11 Philippe DeRouville (G), Pitt.	1.00	6.00
12 Marc Denis (G), Colo.	1.00	10.00

NATIONAL PRIDE

Insert Set (30 cards):	200.00
Insert (#/1,997)	NP
1 Wayne Gretzky, NYRa.	40.00
2 Mark Messier, NYRa.	10.00
3 Paul Kariya, Anah.	14.00
4 Steve Yzerman, Detr.	20.00
5 Brendan Shanahan, Detr.	10.00
6 Chris Osgood (G), Detr.	6.00
7 Adam Oates, Wash.	4.00
8 Eric Lindros, Phil.	10.00
9 Doug Gilmour, NJer.	6.00
10 Ryan Smyth, Edmo.	4.00
11 Raymond Bourque, Bost.	12.00
12 Jason Arnott, Edmo.	4.00
13 Jarome Iginla, Calg.	8.00
14 Geoff Sanderson, Hart. (Caro.)	3.00
15 Alexandre Daigle, Otta.	3.00
16 Trevor Linden, Vanc.	4.00
17 Joe Sakic, Colo.	16.00
18 Mark Recchi, Phil.	4.00
19 Theoren Fleury, Calg.	6.00
20 Ron Francis, Pitt.	6.00
21 Daymond Langkow, Tamp.	3.00
22 Ed Belfour (G), SanJ.	10.00
23 Paul Coffey, Phil.	6.00
24 Pierre Turgeon, SLou.	4.00
25 Claude Lemieux, Colo.	3.00
26 Ron Hextall (G), Phil.	6.00
27 Curtis Joseph (G), Edmo.	10.00
28 Mike Vernon (G), Detr.	4.00
29 Vincent Damphousse, Mont.	6.00
30 Owen Nolan, SanJ.	6.00

STANLEY CUP SCRAPBOOK

Cards 1-16 (Bronze) are serial numbered out of 2,000; cards 17-24 (Silver) are serial numbered out of 1,500; cards 25-30 (Gold) are serial numbered out of 1,000; cards 31-32 are autographed and serial numbered out of 750; card 33 (Shanahan) is autographed and serial numbered out of 250.

Insert Set (33 cards):	500.00
Insert	SCC
1 Mike Modano, Dall.	10.00
2 Curtis Joseph (G), Edmo.	10.00
3 Joe Sakic, Colo.	16.00
4 Chris Chelios, Chic.	6.00
5 Chris Osgood (G), Detr.	6.00
6 Brett Hull, SLou.	10.00
7 Jeremy Roenick, Phoe.	8.00
8 Teemu Selänne, Anah.	8.00
9 Jaromir Jagr, Pitt.	10.00
10 Garth Snow (G), Phil.	4.00
11 Alexei Yashin, Otta.	6.00
12 Steve Shields (G), Buff.	4.00
13 Doug Gilmour, NJer.	6.00
14 José Théodore (G), Mont.	18.00
15 Mike Richter (G), NYRa.	4.00
16 John Vanbiesbrouck (G), Flor.	4.00
17 Ryan Smyth, Edmo.	6.00
18 Peter Forsberg, Colo.	20.00
19 Steve Yzerman, Detr.	35.00
20 Paul Kariya, Anah.	20.00
21 Janne Niinimaa, Phil.	6.00
22 Dominik Hasek (G), Buff.	15.00
23 Mark Messier, NYRa.	15.00
24 Martin Brodeur (G), NJer.	20.00
25 Vyacheslav Kozlov, Detr.	8.00
26 Sergei Fedorov, Detr.	20.00
27 Patrick Roy (G), Colo.	60.00
28 Wayne Gretzky, NYRa.	80.00
29 John LeClair, Phil.	15.00
30 Paul Coffey, Phil.	10.00
31 Mike Vernon (G), Detr. ✍	30.00
32 Eric Lindros, Phil. ✍	60.00
33 Brendan Shanahan, Detr. ✍	150.00

1997 - 98 DONRUSS ELITE

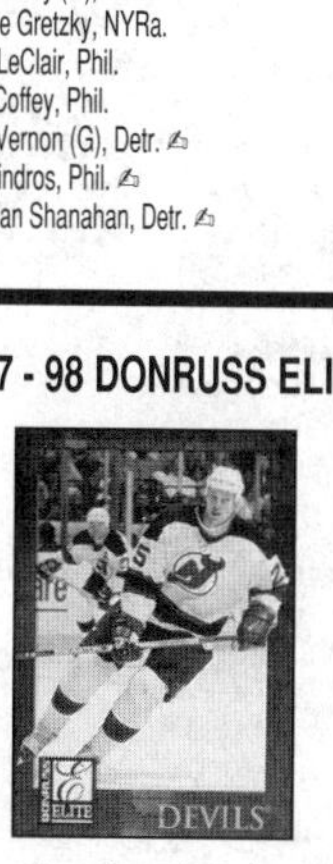

There are three versions: the regular card, an Elite Aspirations parallel (750 copies) and an Elite Status parallel (serial numbered out of 100).

Complete Set (150 cards):	**3100.00**	**400.00**	**40.00**
Common Player:	**10.00**	**2.00**	**.25**
Player	S100	A750	DE
1 Peter Forsberg, Colo.	80.00	15.00	1.50
2 Mike Modano, Dall.	60.00	10.00	1.00
3 John Vanbiesbrouck (G), Flor.	30.00	5.00	.50
4 Pavel Bure, Vanc.	50.00	5.00	1.00
5 Mark Messier, Vanc.	60.00	10.00	1.00
6 Joe Thornton, Bost.	75.00	10.00	2.00
7 Paul Kariya, Anah.	80.00	15.00	1.50
8 Martin Brodeur (G), NJer.	100.00	15.00	2.00
9 Wayne Gretzky, NYRa.	250.00	45.00	5.00
10 Eric Lindros, Phil.	60.00	10.00	1.00
11 Jaromir Jagr, Pitt.	60.00	10.00	1.00
12 Brett Hull, SLou.	60.00	10.00	1.00
13 Jarome Iginla, Calg.	50.00	9.00	1.00
14 Patrick Roy (G), Colo.	180.00	30.00	3.50
15 Steve Yzerman, Detr.	150.00	25.00	3.00
16 Sergei Samsonov, Bost.	35.00	5.00	1.50
17 Teemu Selänne, Anah.	50.00	5.00	1.00
18 Brendan Shanahan, Detr.	60.00	10.00	1.00
19 Curtis Joseph (G), Edmo.	60.00	10.00	1.00
20 Saku Koivu, Mont.	50.00	5.00	1.00
21 Raymond Bourque, Bost.	70.00	10.00	1.50
22 Jaroslav Svejkovsky, Wash.	10.00	2.00	.25
23 Keith Primeau, Caro.	25.00	4.00	.50
24 Alexandre Daigle, Otta.	10.00	2.00	.25
25 Vyacheslav Kozlov, Detr.	15.00	2.00	.25
26 Jozef Stumpel, Bost.	15.00	2.00	.25
27 Alexei Yashin, Otta.	35.00	6.00	.50
28 Marian Hossa, Otta. RC	**120.00**	**20.00**	**7.50**
29 Bryan Berard, NYIs.	20.00	3.00	.25
30 Dominik Hasek (G), Buff.	60.00	10.00	1.00
31 Chris Chelios, Chic.	35.00	6.00	.50
32 Derian Hatcher, Dall.	20.00	3.00	.25
33 Ed Jovanovski, Flor.	25.00	4.00	.50
34 Zigmund Palffy, NYIs.	35.00	6.00	.50
35 Ron Hextall (G), Phil.	35.00	6.00	.50
36 Daymond Langkow, Tamp.	15.00	2.00	.25
37 Daniel Cleary, Chic.	20.00	3.00	.50
38 Alyn McCauley, Toro.	20.00	3.00	.50
39 Sean Burke (G), Vanc.	35.00	6.00	.50
40 Brian Leetch, NYRa.	35.00	6.00	.50
41 Joé Juneau, Wash.	15.00	2.00	.25
42 Damian Rhodes (G), Otta.	15.00	2.00	.25
43 Dino Ciccarelli, Flor.	20.00	3.00	.25
44 Valeri Kamensky, Colo.	20.00	3.00	.25
45 Guy Hebert (G), Anah.	15.00	2.00	.25
46 Brad Isbister, Phoe.	15.00	2.00	.50
47 Adam Graves, NYRa.	25.00	4.00	.50
48 Andrew Cassels, Calg.	15.00	2.00	.25
49 Joe Sakic, Colo.	100.00	15.00	2.00
50 Dainius Zubrus, Phil.	15.00	2.00	.25
51 R. Luongo (G), NYIs. RC	**100.00**	**15.00**	**6.00**
52 Ethan Moreau, Chic.	10.00	2.00	.25
53 Chris Osgood (G), Detr.	35.00	5.00	.50
54 Stéphane Fiset (G), LosA.	20.00	3.00	.25
55 Sergei Berezin, Toro.	15.00	2.00	.25
56 Mike Richter (G), NYRa.	30.00	5.00	.50
57 Valeri Bure, Mont.	20.00	3.00	.25
58 Mats Sundin, Toro.	60.00	10.00	1.00
59 Mike Dunham (G), NJer.	25.00	4.00	.50
60 Byron Dafoe (G), Bost.	25.00	4.00	.50
61 Joe Nieuwendyk, Dall.	25.00	4.00	.50
62 Mike Grier, Edmo.	15.00	2.00	.25
63 Paul Coffey, Phil.	35.00	5.00	.50
64 Chris Phillips, Otta.	15.00	2.00	.50
65 Patrik Elias, NJer. RC	**100.00**	**15.00**	**6.00**
66 Andy Moog (G), Mont.	25.00	4.00	.50
67 Geoff Sanderson, Caro.	15.00	2.00	.25
68 Jere Lehtinen, Dall.	20.00	3.00	.25
69 Alexander Mogilny, Vanc.	30.00	5.00	.50
70 Ryan Smyth, Edmo.	30.00	5.00	.50
71 John LeClair, Phil.	50.00	5.00	1.00
72 Olli Jokinen, LosA. RC	**40.00**	**7.00**	**2.00**
73 Doug Gilmour, NJer.	35.00	6.00	.50
74 Theoren Fleury, Calg.	30.00	5.00	.50
75 Adam Deadmarsh, Colo.	20.00	3.00	.25
76 Scott Mellanby, Flor.	15.00	2.00	.25
77 Jeremy Roenick, Phoe.	50.00	5.00	1.00
78 Jim Campbell, SLou.	10.00	2.00	.25
79 Daren Puppa (G), Tamp.	15.00	2.00	.25
80 Vaclav Prospal, Phil. RC	**40.00**	**7.00**	**2.00**
81 Vincent Damphousse, Mont.	35.00	6.00	.50
82 Derek Plante, Buff.	10.00	2.00	.25
83 Sandis Ozolinsh, Colo.	15.00	2.00	.25
84 Darren McCarty, Detr.	20.00	3.00	.25
85 Luc Robitaille, LosA.	50.00	5.00	1.00
86 Wade Redden, Otta.	20.00	3.00	.25
87 Éric Fichaud (G), NYIs.	10.00	2.00	.25
88 Jocelyn Thibault (G), Mont.	25.00	4.00	.50
89 Trevor Linden, Vanc.	25.00	4.00	.50
90 Boyd Devereaux, Edmo.	15.00	2.00	.50
91 Chris Gratton, Phil.	15.00	2.00	.25
92 Janne Niinimaa, Phil.	15.00	2.00	.25
93 Jeff Friesen, SanJ.	20.00	3.00	.25
94 Roman Hamrlik, Edmo.	15.00	2.00	.25
95 Jason Arnott, NJer.	30.00	5.00	.50
96 Sergei Fedorov, Detr.	60.00	10.00	1.00

☐☐☐	97 Tony Amonte, Chic.	35.00	6.00	.50
☐☐☐	98 Mattias Öhlund, Vanc.	20.00	3.00	.50
☐☐☐	99 Patrick Marleau, SanJ.	30.00	5.00	1.00
☐☐☐	100 Félix Potvin (G), Toro.	35.00	6.00	.50
☐☐☐	101 Tommy Salo (G), NYIs.	25.00	4.00	.50
☐☐☐	102 Ed Belfour (G), Dall.	60.00	10.00	1.00
☐☐☐	103 Doug Weight, Edmo.	35.00	5.00	.50
☐☐☐	104 Daniel Alfredsson, Otta.	35.00	6.00	.50
☐☐☐	105 Pierre Turgeon, Mont.	25.00	4.00	.50
☐☐☐	**106 Espen Knutsen, Anah. RC**	**30.00**	**5.00**	**1.50**
☐☐☐	107 Trevor Kidd (G), Caro.	20.00	3.00	.25
☐☐☐	108 Alexei Morozov, Pitt.	15.00	2.00	.50
☐☐☐	109 Oleg Tverdovsky, Phoe.	10.00	2.00	.25
☐☐☐	110 Grant Fuhr (G), SLou.	35.00	6.00	.50
☐☐☐	111 Pat LaFontaine, NYRa.	35.00	6.00	.50
☐☐☐	112 Keith Tkachuk, Phoe.	35.00	5.00	.50
☐☐☐	113 Ron Francis, Pitt.	35.00	6.00	.50
☐☐☐	**114 Derek Morris, Calg. RC**	**30.00**	**5.00**	**1.50**
☐☐☐	115 Joe Sakic, Colo.	70.00	12.00	1.00
☐☐☐	116 Brian Leetch, NYRa.	25.00	4.00	.25
☐☐☐	117 Alyn McCauley, Toro.	10.00	2.00	.25
☐☐☐	118 Pavel Bure, Vanc.	30.00	5.00	.50
☐☐☐	119 Eric Lindros, Phil.	40.00	5.00	.50
☐☐☐	120 Teemu Selänne, Anah.	30.00	6.00	.50
☐☐☐	121 Jarome Iginla, Calg.	35.00	6.00	.50
☐☐☐	122 Steve Yzerman, Detr.	100.00	15.00	1.50
☐☐☐	123 Daniel Cleary, Chic.	10.00	2.00	.25
☐☐☐	124 Bryan Berard, NYIs.	10.00	2.00	.25
☐☐☐	125 Jaromir Jagr, Pitt.	40.00	5.00	.50
☐☐☐	126 Vanbiesbrouck (G), Flor.	20.00	3.00	.25
☐☐☐	127 Mark Messier, Vanc.	40.00	7.00	.50
☐☐☐	128 Patrick Marleau, SanJ.	20.00	3.00	.25
☐☐☐	129 Mike Modano, Dall.	40.00	7.00	.50
☐☐☐	130 Zigmund Palffy, NYIs.	25.00	4.00	.25
☐☐☐	131 Félix Potvin (G), Toro.	25.00	4.00	.25
☐☐☐	132 Derek Morris, Calg.	20.00	3.00	.25
☐☐☐	133 Brendan Shanahan, Detr.	40.00	7.00	.50
☐☐☐	134 Sergei Samsonov, Bost.	25.00	4.00	.25
☐☐☐	135 Dainius Zubrus, Phil.	10.00	2.00	.25
☐☐☐	136 Paul Kariya, Anah.	60.00	10.00	1.00
☐☐☐	137 Martin Brodeur (G), NJer.	70.00	10.00	1.00
☐☐☐	138 Joe Thornton, Bost.	50.00	9.00	.50
☐☐☐	139 Mattias Öhlund, Vanc.	10.00	2.00	.25
☐☐☐	140 Ryan Smyth, Edmo.	20.00	3.00	.25
☐☐☐	141 J. Svejkovsky, Wash.	10.00	2.00	.25
☐☐☐	142 Patrick Roy (G), Colo.	130.00	20.00	2.00
☐☐☐	143 Wayne Gretzky, NYRa.	170.00	30.00	3.00
☐☐☐	144 Espen Knutsen, Anah.	20.00	3.00	.25
☐☐☐	145 CL: Patrick Marleau, SanJ.	15.00	3.00	.25
☐☐☐	146 CL: Pat LaFontaine, NYRa.	20.00	3.00	.25
☐☐☐	147 CL: Mike Gartner, Phoe.	25.00	5.00	.50
☐☐☐	148 CL: Joe Thornton, Bost.	40.00	7.00	.50
☐☐☐	149 CL: Teemu Selänne, Anah.	25.00	5.00	.50
☐☐☐	150 CL: Mark Messier, Vanc.	30.00	6.00	.50

BACK TO THE FUTURE

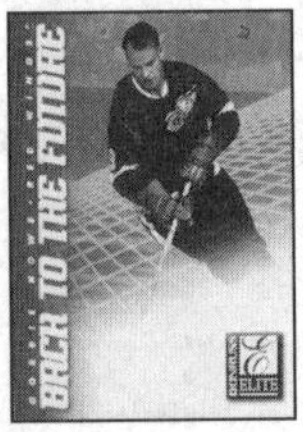

Insert Set (8 cards):		100.00
	Insert (#/1,500)	BttF
☐	1 E. Lindros / J. Thornton	20.00
☐	2 2. J. Thibault / M. Denis	8.00
☐	3 T. Selänne / P. Marleau	10.00
☐	4 J. Jagr / D. Cleary	10.00
☐	5 S. Fedorov / P. Forsberg	20.00
☐	6 Bo. Hull / Br. Hull	25.00
☐	7 M. Brodeur / R. Luongo	20.00
☐	8 G. Howe / S. Yzerman	40.00

BACK TO THE FUTURE AUTOGRAPH

Insert Set (8 cards):		1,500.00
	Autograph (#/100)	Auto.
☐	1 E. Lindros ✍ / J. Thornton ✍	225.00
☐	2 2. J. Thibault ✍ / M. Denis ✍	100.00
☐	3 T. Selänne ✍ / P. Marleau ✍	125.00
☐	4 J. Jagr ✍ / D. Cleary ✍	125.00
☐	5 S. Fedorov ✍ / P. Forsberg ✍	250.00
☐	6 Bo. Hull ✍ / Br. Hull ✍	225.00
☐	7 M. Brodeur ✍ / R. Luongo ✍	250.00
☐	8 G. Howe ✍ / S. Yzerman ✍	775.00

CRAFTSMEN & MASTER CRAFTSMEN

There are two versions: the regular Craftsmen insert (#/2400) and a Master Craftsmen parallel (#100).

Insert Set (30 cards): 1400.00 150.00

	Inserts	MC	Craft
☐☐	1 John Vanbiesbrouck (G), Flor.	25.00	3.00
☐☐	2 Eric Lindros, Phil.	60.00	6.00
☐☐	3 Joe Sakic, Colo.	90.00	12.00
☐☐	4 Mark Messier, Vanc.	60.00	6.00
☐☐	5 Jaroslav Svejkovsky, Wash.	20.00	3.00
☐☐	6 Dominik Hasek (G), Buff.	60.00	6.00
☐☐	7 Chris Osgood (G), Detr.	35.00	4.00
☐☐	8 Martin Brodeur (G), NJer.	90.00	12.00
☐☐	9 Sergei Fedorov, Detr.	60.00	6.00
☐☐	10 Daniel Cleary, Chic.	20.00	3.00
☐☐	11 Patrick Marleau, SanJ.	25.00	4.00
☐☐	12 Sergei Samsonov, Bost.	35.00	6.00
☐☐	13 Félix Potvin (G), Toro.	35.00	4.00
☐☐	14 Patrick Roy (G), Colo.	180.00	22.00
☐☐	15 Teemu Selänne, Anah.	40.00	6.00
☐☐	16 Steve Yzerman, Detr.	140.00	18.00
☐☐	17 Jarome Iginla, Calg.	45.00	6.00
☐☐	18 Mike Modano, Dall.	60.00	6.00
☐☐	19 Wayne Gretzky, NYRa.	240.00	30.00
☐☐	20 Pavel Bure, Vanc.	40.00	6.00
☐☐	21 Ryan Smyth, Edmo.	25.00	3.00
☐☐	22 Paul Kariya, Anah.	80.00	10.00
☐☐	23 Peter Forsberg, Colo.	80.00	10.00
☐☐	24 Joe Thornton, Bost.	70.00	12.00
☐☐	25 Jaromir Jagr, Pitt.	60.00	6.00
☐☐	26 Bryan Berard, NYIs.	20.00	3.00
☐☐	27 Brendan Shanahan, Detr.	60.00	6.00
☐☐	28 Keith Tkachuk, Phoe.	35.00	4.00
☐☐	29 Curtis Joseph (G), Edmo.	60.00	6.00
☐☐	30 Brian Leetch, NYRa.	35.00	4.00

PRIME NUMBERS

Each player has three different cards each with two versions: a regular insert and a die-cut insert. The three cards link together to highlight a significant statistic for the player (Roy's 349 career wins, for instance) and each card is sequentially numbered to that statistic.)

Actual realized pricing on scarce cards (10 copies or less) may vary considerably from listed pricing below. Please keep in mind that the below prices on scarce cards are only meant to act as a guide for potential pricing scenarios. Please email Canadian Sports Collector with details of actual realised sale results.

In the case of Roy's die-cut cards, the first 300 of his "3" a-card are die-cut, the first 40 of his "4" b-card are die-cut and the first 9 of his "9" c-card are die-cut. As such, the three toughest versions will always be the uncut a-card, the die-cut b-card and the die-cut c-card. The print runs for both versions are listed in parantheses after each player. In the case of Joe Sakic's "0" b-card, there is no die-cut card available.

	Inserts	PN	PNDC
☐☐	1a Peter Forsberg 2 (54+200)	135.00	70.00
☐☐	1b Peter Forsberg 5 (204+50)	70.00	140.00
☐☐	1c Peter Forsberg 4 (250+4)	50.00	525.00
☐☐	2a Patrick Roy 3 (G), (49+300)	300.00	90.00
☐☐	2b Patrick Roy 4 (G), (309+40)	90.00	335.00
☐☐	2c Patrick Roy 9 (G), (340+9)	80.00	1050.00
☐☐	3a Mark Messier 2 (95+200)	75.00	50.00
☐☐	3b Mark Messier 9 (205+90)	50.00	80.00
☐☐	3c Mark Messier 5 (290+5)	30.00	375.00
☐☐	4a Eric Lindros 4 (36+400)	115.00	25.00
☐☐	4b Eric Lindros 3 (406+30)	25.00	125.00
☐☐	4c Eric Lindros 6 (430+6)	20.00	350.00
☐☐	5a Paul Kariya 2 (46+200)	145.00	70.00
☐☐	5b Paul Kariya 4 (206+40)	70.00	155.00
☐☐	5c Paul Kariya 6 (240+6)	50.00	500.00
☐☐	6a Jaromir Jagr 2 (66+200)	90.00	50.00
☐☐	6b Jaromir Jagr 6 (206+60)	50.00	95.00
☐☐	6c Jaromir Jagr 6 (260+6)	35.00	350.00
☐☐	7a Teemu Selänne 2 (37+200)	95.00	40.00
☐☐	7b Teemu Selänne 3 (207+30)	40.00	100.00
☐☐	7c Teemu Selänne 7 (230+7)	35.00	275.00
☐☐	8a John Vanbiesbrouck (G) 2 (G), (88+200)	35.00	20.00
☐☐	8b John Vanbiesbrouck (G) 8 (G), (208+80)	20.00	40.00
☐☐	8c John Vanbiesbrouck (G) 8 (G). (280+8)	15.00	150.00
☐☐	9a Brendan Shanahan 3 (35+300)	115.00	30.00
☐☐	9b Brendan Shanahan 3 (305+30)	30.00	125.00
☐☐	9c Brendan Shanahan 5 (330+5)	25.00	375.00
☐☐	10a Steve Yzerman 5 (39+500)	270.00	50.00
☐☐	10b Steve Yzerman 3 (509+30)	50.00	300.00
☐☐	10c Steve Yzerman 9 (530+9)	50.00	825.00
☐☐	11a Joe Sakic 3 (7+300)	575.00	50.00
☐	11b Joe Sakic 0 (#/307)	50.00	10.00
☐☐	11c Joe Sakic 7 (300+7)	50.00	575.00
☐☐	12a Pavel Bure 3 (88+300)	60.00	25.00
☐☐	12b Pavel Bure 8 (308+80)	25.00	65.00
☐☐	12c Pavel Bure 8 (380+8)	20.00	275.00

1997 - 98 DONRUSS PREFERRED

There are two versions: the regular card and the Cut to the Chase parallel.

		CttC	Pref.
Complete Set (240 cards):		**1800.00**	**600.00**
Common Bronze:		**2.00**	**.35**
	Player	**CttC**	**Pref.**
☐☐	1 Dominik Hasek (G), Buff. [Gold]	30.00	15.00
☐☐	2 Peter Forsberg, Colo. [Gold]	50.00	20.00
☐☐	3 Brendan Shanahan, Detr. [Platinum]	70.00	30.00
☐☐	4 Wayne Gretzky, NYRa. [Platinum]	300.00	120.00
☐☐	5 Eric Lindros, Phil. [Platinum]	70.00	30.00
☐☐	6 Keith Tkachuk, Phoe. [Gold]	20.00	5.00
☐☐	7 Mark Messier, Vanc. [Platinum]	70.00	30.00
☐☐	8 Mike Modano, Dall. [Gold]	35.00	15.00
☐☐	9 John Vanbiesbrouck (G), Flor. [Platinum]	35.00	20.00
☐☐	10 Paul Kariya, Anah. [Platinum]	100.00	40.00
☐☐	11 Saku Koivu, Mont. [Gold]	30.00	10.00
☐☐	12 Paul Coffey, Phil. [Bronze]	6.00	.50
☐☐	13 Joé Juneau, Wash. [Bronze]	2.00	.35
☐☐	14 Jeff Friesen, SanJ. [Silver]	7.00	2.00
☐☐	15 Brett Hull, SLou. [Gold]	35.00	15.00
☐☐	16 Martin Brodeur (G), NJer. [Gold]	60.00	20.00
☐☐	17 Jarome Iginla, Calg. [Gold]	30.00	10.00
☐☐	18 Keith Primeau, Caro. [Silver]	9.00	3.00
☐☐	19 Ed Jovanovski, Flor. [Bronze]	4.00	.50
☐☐	20 Jamie Langenbrunner, Dall. [Bronze]	2.00	.35
☐☐	21 Derian Hatcher, Dall. [Silver]	7.00	2.00
☐☐	22 Brian Leetch, NYRa. [Gold]	20.00	5.00
☐☐	23 Daymond Langkow, Tamp. [Silver]	5.00	2.00
☐☐	24 Raymond Bourque, Bost. [Silver]	25.00	5.00
☐☐	25 Pavel Bure, Vanc. [Gold]	30.00	10.00
☐☐	26 Janne Niinimaa, Phil. [Silver]	5.00	2.00
☐☐	27 Jamie Storr (G), LosA. [Silver]	5.00	2.00
☐☐	28 Darcy Tucker, Mont. [Bronze]	2.00	.35
☐☐	29 Anson Carter, Bost. [Bronze]	4.00	.50
☐☐	30 Jeff O'Neill, Caro. [Bronze]	4.00	.50
☐☐	31 Jason Arnott, Edmo. [Gold]	15.00	5.00
☐☐	32 Tommy Salo (G), NYIs. [Bronze]	4.00	.50
☐☐	33 Petr Nedved, Pitt. [Bronze]	3.00	.35
☐☐	34 Michael Peca, Buff. [Bronze]	4.00	.50
☐☐	35 Ethan Moreau, Chic. [Silver]	5.00	2.00
☐☐	36 Ray Sheppard, Flor. [Bronze]	2.00	.35
☐☐	37 Damian Rhodes (G), Otta. [Bronze]	2.00	.35
☐☐	38 Mats Sundin, Toro. [Silver]	20.00	7.00
☐☐	39 Alexander Mogilny, Vanc. [Gold]	15.00	5.00
☐☐	40 Mike Dunham (G), NJer. [Silver]	5.00	3.00
☐☐	41 Steve Yzerman, Detr. [Platinum]	180.00	70.00
☐☐	42 Alexei Yashin, Otta. [Silver]	10.00	4.00
☐☐	43 Jim Carey (G), Bost. [Silver]	5.00	2.00
☐☐	44 Mike Grier, Edmo. [Silver]	5.00	2.00
☐☐	45 Steve Rucchin, Anah. [Bronze]	2.00	.35
☐☐	46 Mark Recchi, Mont. [Silver]	9.00	3.00
☐☐	47 Mike Gartner, Phoe. [Bronze]	8.00	1.00
☐☐	48 Alexandre Daigle, Otta. [Silver]	5.00	2.00
☐☐	49 Éric Fichaud (G), NYIs. [Gold]	9.00	5.00
☐☐	50 Harry York, SLou. [Bronze]	2.00	.35
☐☐	51 Dino Ciccarelli, Flor. [Bronze]	3.00	.35
☐☐	52 Bill Ranford (G), Wash. [Bronze]	4.00	.50
☐☐	53 Adam Deadmarsh, Colo. [Gold]	10.00	5.00
☐☐	54 Ed Belfour (G), Dall. [Bronze]	10.00	1.00
☐☐	55 Jozef Stumpel, LosA. [Silver]	5.00	2.00
☐☐	56 Rem Murray, Edmo. [Bronze]	2.00	.35
☐☐	57 Pat Verbeek, Dall. [Bronze]	3.00	.35
☐☐	58 Pat LaFontaine, NYRa. [Bronze]	6.00	.50
☐☐	59 Dainius Zubrus, Phil. [Bronze]	2.00	.35
☐☐	60 Grant Fuhr (G), SLou. [Bronze]	6.00	.50
☐☐	61 Rob Niedermayer, Flor. [Bronze]	2.00	.35
☐☐	62 Brian Savage, Mont. [Bronze]	3.00	.35
☐☐	63 Gary Roberts, Caro. [Bronze]	4.00	.50
☐☐	64 Tony Amonte, Chic. [Bronze]	6.00	.50
☐☐	65 Jere Lehtinen, Dall. [Bronze]	3.00	.35
☐☐	66 Dave Andreychuk, NJer. [Bronze]	3.00	.35
☐☐	67 Rod Brind'Amour, Phil. [Bronze]	3.00	.35
☐☐	68 Mikael Renberg, Tamp. [Bronze]	3.00	.35
☐☐	69 Doug Gilmour, NJer. [Silver]	10.00	4.00
☐☐	70 Kevin Hatcher, Pitt. [Bronze]	2.00	.35
☐☐	71 Byron Dafoe (G), Bost. [Bronze]	4.00	.50
☐☐	72 Derek Plante, Buff. [Silver]	5.00	2.00
☐☐	73 Trevor Kidd (G), Caro. [Bronze]	3.00	.35
☐☐	74 Doug Weight, Edmo. [Silver]	10.00	4.00
☐☐	75 Valeri Bure, Mont. [Bronze]	3.00	.35
☐☐	76 John LeClair, Phil. [Gold]	30.00	10.00
☐☐	77 Sergei Berezin, Toro. [Bronze]	2.00	.35
☐☐	78 Peter Bondra, Wash. [Silver]	10.00	4.00
☐☐	79 Bryan Berard, NYIs. [Gold]	10.00	5.00
☐☐	**80 Steve Shields (G), Buff. [Bronze] RC**	**4.00**	**2.00**
☐☐	81 Chris Osgood (G), Detr. [Gold]	20.00	5.00
☐☐	82 Mike Vernon (G), SanJ. [Bronze]	4.00	.50
☐☐	83 Martin Gélinas, Vanc. [Bronze]	2.00	.35
☐☐	84 Curtis Joseph (G), Edmo. [Silver]	20.00	5.00
☐☐	85 Geoff Sanderson, Caro. [Silver]	5.00	2.00
☐☐	86 Patrick Roy, Colo. [Platinum]	220.00	90.00
☐☐	87 Jocelyn Thibault (G), Mont. [Gold]	15.00	5.00
☐☐	88 Jeremy Roenick, Phoe. [Silver]	15.00	6.00
☐☐	89 Trevor Linden, Vanc. [Bronze]	4.00	.50
☐☐	90 Daniel Alfredsson, Otta. [Silver]	13.00	4.00
☐☐	91 Sergei Zubov, Dall. [Bronze]	2.00	.35
☐☐	92 Dmitri Khristich, Bost. [Silver]	5.00	2.00
☐☐	93 Brian Holzinger, Buff. [Bronze]	2.00	.35
☐☐	94 Andrew Cassels, Calg. [Bronze]	2.00	.35
☐☐	95 Teemu Selänne, Anah. [Gold]	30.00	10.00
☐☐	96 Ron Hextall (G), Phil. [Bronze]	6.00	.50
☐☐	97 Wade Redden, Otta. [Bronze]	3.00	.35
☐☐	98 Jim Campbell, SLou. [Bronze]	2.00	.35
☐☐	99 Félix Potvin (G), Toro. [Gold]	20.00	5.00
☐☐	100 Adam Oates, Wash. [Silver]	9.00	3.00
☐☐	101 Nikolai Khabibulin (G), Phoe. [Bronze]	4.00	.50
☐☐	102 José Théodore (G), Mont. [Silver]	27.00	9.00
☐☐	103 Sandis Ozolinsh, Colo. [Silver]	5.00	2.00
☐☐	104 Sean Burke (G), Caro. [Bronze]	6.00	.50
☐☐	**105 Vaclav Prospal, Phil. [Gold] RC**	**20.00**	**20.00**
☐☐	106 Zigmund Palffy, NYIs. [Gold]	20.00	5.00
☐☐	107 Kyle McLaren, Bost. [Bronze]	2.00	.35
☐☐	108 Owen Nolan, SanJ. [Silver]	10.00	4.00
☐☐	109 Chris Pronger, SLou. [Silver]	10.00	4.00
☐☐	110 Daren Puppa (G), Tamp. [Bronze]	2.00	.35
☐☐	111 Garth Snow (G), Phil. [Bronze]	3.00	.35
☐☐	112 Aki Berg, LosA. [Bronze]	2.00	.35
☐☐	113 Andy Moog (G), Mont. [Bronze]	4.00	.50
☐☐	114 Darren McCarty, Detr. [Bronze]	3.00	.35
☐☐	115 Joe Nieuwendyk, Dall. [Bronze]	4.00	.50
☐☐	116 Éric Dazé, Chic. [Silver]	9.00	3.00
☐☐	117 Pierre Turgeon, SLou. [Silver]	5.00	3.00
☐☐	118 Ken Wregget (G), Pitt. [Bronze]	2.00	.35
☐☐	119 Ryan Smyth, Edmo. [Gold]	15.00	5.00
☐☐	120 Kirk Muller, Flor. [Bronze]	3.00	.35
☐☐	121 Luc Robitaille, LosA. [Bronze]	8.00	1.00
☐☐	122 Sergei Fedorov, Detr. [Gold]	35.00	15.00
☐☐	123 Sean Pronger, Anah. [Bronze]	2.00	.35
☐☐	124 Mike Richter (G), NYRa. [Silver]	10.00	3.00
☐☐	125 Jaromir Jagr, Pitt. [Platinum]	70.00	30.00
☐☐	126 Claude Lemieux, Colo. [Bronze]	3.00	.35
☐☐	127 Chris Chelios, Chic. [Silver]	10.00	4.00
☐☐	128 Joe Sakic, Colo. [Platinum]	120.00	45.00
☐☐	129 Guy Hebert (G), Anah. [Silver]	5.00	2.00
☐☐	130 Chris Gratton, Phil. [Silver]	5.00	2.00
☐☐	131 Steve Sullivan, Toro. [Bronze]	3.00	.35
☐☐	132 Al MacInnis, SLou. [Bronze]	4.00	.50
☐☐	133 Adam Graves, NYRa. [Silver]	9.00	3.00
☐☐	134 Vyacheslav Kozlov, Detr. [Bronze]	2.00	.35
☐☐	135 Scott Mellanby, Flor. [Silver]	5.00	2.00
☐☐	136 Stéphane Fiset (G), LosA. [Bronze]	3.00	.35
☐☐	137 Oleg Tverdovsky, Phoe. [Silver]	5.00	2.00
☐☐	138 Theoren Fleury, Calg. [Silver]	10.00	4.00
☐☐	139 Jeff Hackett (G), Chic. [Bronze]	3.00	.35
☐☐	140 Vincent Damphousse, Mont. [Bronze]	6.00	.50
☐☐	141 Roman Hamrlik, Tamp. [Silver]	5.00	2.00
☐☐	142 Ron Francis, Pitt. [Silver]	10.00	4.00
☐☐	143 Scott Lachance, NYIs. [Bronze]	2.00	.35
☐☐	144 Todd Harvey, Dall. [Bronze]	2.00	.35
☐☐	145 Marc Denis (G), Colo. [Silver]	10.00	3.00
☐☐	146 Jaroslav Svejkovsky, Wash. [Gold]	9.00	5.00
☐☐	**147 Olli Jokinen, LosA. [Silver] RC**	**21.00**	**45.00**
☐☐	148 Sergei Samsonov, Bost. [Gold]	20.00	5.00
☐☐	149 Chris Phillips, Otta. [Gold]	9.00	5.00
☐☐	150 Patrick Marleau, SanJ. [Gold]	15.00	5.00
☐☐	151 Joe Thornton, Bost. [Gold]	45.00	25.00
☐☐	152 Daniel Cleary, Chic. [Silver]	7.00	4.00
☐☐	153 Alyn McCauley, Toro. [Gold]	12.00	5.00
☐☐	154 Brad Isbister, Phoe. [Silver]	5.00	3.00
☐☐	155 Aleksey Morozov, Pitt. [Silver]	5.00	3.00
☐☐	**156 Shawn Bates, Bost. [Bronze] RC**	**3.00**	**1.00**
☐☐	**157 Jean-Yves Leroux, Chic. [Bronze] RC**	**2.00**	**.50**
☐☐	158 Marcel Cousineau (G), Toro. [Bronze]	2.00	.35

□□	159 Vaclav Varada, Buff. [Bronze]	2.00	.35
□□	160 Jean-Sébastien Giguère (G), Calg. [Silver]	18.00	6.00
□□	**161 Espen Knutsen, Anah. [Bronze] RC**	**4.00**	**2.00**
□□	**162 Marian Hossa, Otta. [Silver] RC**	**150.00**	**125.00**

◆ A Marian Hossa basic rookie card graded PSA 9 sold for $102.50 U.S. (approx. $155 Cdn.) in an Internet auction at eBay in March 2003.

□□	**163 Robert Dome, Pitt. [Bronze] RC**	**3.00**	**1.00**
□□	**164 Juha Lind, Dall. [Bronze] RC**	**3.00**	**1.00**
□□	165 Sergei Fedorov, Detr. [Bronze]	10.00	1.00
□□	166 Jarome Iginla, Calg. [Bronze]	8.00	1.50
□□	167 Jaroslav Svejkovsky, Wash. [Bronze]	2.00	.35
□□	168 Patrick Roy (G), Colo. [Silver]	60.00	20.00
□□	169 Dominik Hasek (G), Buff. [Bronze]	10.00	1.00
□□	170 Alexander Mogilny, Vanc. [Bronze]	4.00	.50
□□	171 Chris Chelios, Chic. [Bronze]	6.00	.50
□□	172 Wayne Gretzky, NYRa. [Silver]	90.00	30.00
□□	173 Peter Forsberg, Colo. [Bronze]	10.00	1.50
□□	174 Raymond Bourque, Bost. [Bronze]	10.00	1.50
□□	175 Joe Sakic, Colo. [Silver]	35.00	10.00
□□	176 Mike Modano, Dall. [Bronze]	10.00	1.00
□□	177 Mark Messier, Vanc. [Bronze]	10.00	1.00
□□	178 Teemu Selänne, Anah. [Bronze]	5.00	1.00
□□	179 Steve Yzerman, Detr. [Silver]	50.00	15.00
□□	180 Eric Lindros, Phil. [Silver]	20.00	5.00
□□	181 Doug Weight, Edmo. [Bronze]	6.00	.50
□□	182 John Vanbiesbrouck (G), Flor. [Bronze]	4.00	.50
□□	183 Paul Kariya, Anah. [Silver]	30.00	10.00
□□	184 Brendan Shanahan, Detr. [Silver]	20.00	7.00
□□	185 Martin Brodeur (G), NJer. [Bronze]	15.00	2.00
□□	186 Bryan Berard, NYIs. [Bronze]	3.00	.35
□□	187 Marc Denis (G), Colo. [Bronze]	4.00	.50
□□	188 Brian Leetch, NYRa. [Bronze]	6.00	.50
□□	189 Ryan Smyth, Edmo. [Silver]	10.00	3.00
□□	190 Dainius Zubrus, Phil. [Bronze]	2.00	.35
□□	191 Keith Tkachuk, Phoe. [Bronze]	6.00	.50
□□	192 Jaromir Jagr, Pitt. [Silver]	20.00	5.00
□□	193 Brett Hull, SLou. [Bronze]	10.00	1.00
□□	194 Pavel Bure, Vanc. [Bronze]	5.00	1.00
□□	195 Sergei Samsonov, Bost. [Bronze] [Checklist]	3.00	.35
□□	196 Olli Jokinen, LosA. [Bronze] [Checklist]	4.00	.50
□□	197 Chris Phillips, Otta. [Bronze] [Checklist]	2.00	.35
□□	198 Patrick Marleau, SanJ. [Bronze] [Checklist]	2.00	.35
□□	199 Daniel Cleary, Chic. [Bronze] [Checklist]	2.00	.35
□□	200 Joe Thornton, Bost. [Bronze] [Checklist]	6.00	.50

COLOR GUARD

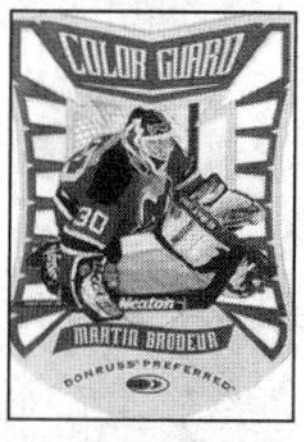

There are two versions: the insert (#/1500) and the Promo.

Complete Set (18 cards):		**25.00**	**225.00**
	Goalies	**Promo**	**Insert**
□□	1 Patrick Roy (G), Colo.	7.00	60.00
□□	2 Martin Brodeur (G), NJer.	4.00	35.00
□□	3 Curtis Joseph (G), Edmo.	2.00	20.00
□□	4 John Vanbiesbrouck (G), Flor.	1.00	10.00
□□	5 Félix Potvin (G), Toro.	1.00	10.00
□□	6 Dominik Hasek (G), Buff.	2.00	20.00
□□	7 Chris Osgood (G), Detr.	1.00	10.00
□□	8 Éric Fichaud (G), NYIs.	1.00	6.00
□□	9 Jocelyn Thibault (G), Mont.	1.00	6.00
□□	10 Marc Denis (G), Colo.	1.00	10.00
□□	11 José Théodore (G), Mont.	3.00	35.00
□□	12 Mike Vernon (G), SanJ.	1.00	6.00
□□	13 Jim Carey (G), Bost.	1.00	6.00
□□	14 Ron Hextall (G), Phil.	1.00	10.00
□□	15 Mike Richter (G), NYRa.	1.00	10.00
□□	16 Ed Belfour (G), Dall.	2.00	20.00
□□	17 Mike Dunham (G), NJer.	1.00	6.00
□□	18 Damian Rhodes (G), Otta.	1.00	6.00

LINE OF THE TIMES

Insert Set (24 cards):		**325.00**
	Insert (#/2,500)	**LotT**
□	1A Ryan Smyth, Edmo.	5.00
□	1B Sergei Fedorov, Detr.	15.00
□	1C Jaromir Jagr, Pitt.	15.00
□	2A Eric Lindros, Phil.	15.00
□	2B Joe Thornton, Bost.	20.00
□	2C Brendan Shanahan, Detr.	15.00
□	3A John LeClair, Phil.	10.00
□	3B Keith Tkachuk, Phoe.	10.00
□	3C Brett Hull, SLou.	15.00
□	4A Pavel Bure, Vanc.	10.00
□	4B Sergei Samsonov, Bost.	10.00
□	4C Paul Kariya, Anah.	20.00
□	5A Mike Modano, Dall.	15.00
□	5B Teemu Selänne, Anah.	10.00
□	5C Patrick Marleau, SanJ.	5.00
□	6A Wayne Gretzky, NYRa.	70.00
□	6B Steve Yzerman, Detr.	40.00
□	6C Daniel Cleary, Chic.	5.00
□	7A Jarome Iginla, Calg.	10.00
□	7B Peter Forsberg, Colo.	20.00
□	7C Mark Messier, Vanc.	15.00
□	8A Joe Sakic, Colo.	25.00
□	8B Jaroslav Svejkovsky, Wash.	5.00
□	8C Dainius Zubrus, Phil.	5.00

PRECIOUS METALS

Insert Set (15 cards):		**1700.00**
	Insert (#/100)	**PM**
□	1 Brendan Shanahan, Detr.	125.00
□	2 Joe Thornton, Bost.	150.00
□	3 Wayne Gretzky, NYRa.	525.00
□	4 Mark Messier, Vanc.	125.00
□	5 Patrick Roy (G), Colo.	375.00
□	6 Martin Brodeur (G), NJer.	200.00
□	7 Eric Lindros, Phil.	125.00
□	8 Paul Kariya, Anah.	175.00
□	9 Teemu Selänne, Anah.	100.00
□	10 Jaromir Jagr, Pitt.	125.00
□	11 Joe Sakic, Colo.	200.00
□	12 Peter Forsberg, Colo.	175.00
□	13 John Vanbiesbrouck (G), Flor.	75.00
□	14 Steve Yzerman, Detr.	300.00
□	15 Sergei Samsonov, Bost.	75.00

TIN PACKS

There are three colour variations for each tin pack: red, blue, and gold. Prices are the same for red or blue tin packs. Prices below are for opened tins.

Complete Set (24 tin packs):		**165.00**	**35.00**
	Tin Pack	**Gold**	**Reg.**
□□□	1 Eric Lindros, Phil.	6.00	1.00
□□□	2 Paul Kariya, Anah.	8.00	2.00
□□□	3 Wayne Gretzky, NYRa.	25.00	6.00
□□□	4 Teemu Selänne, Anah.	5.00	1.00
□□□	5 Patrick Roy (G), Colo.	18.00	4.00
□□□	6 John Vanbiesbrouck (G), Flor.	5.00	1.00
□□□	7 Mike Modano, Dall.	6.00	1.00
□□□	8 Joe Sakic, Colo.	10.00	2.00
□□□	9 Peter Forsberg, Colo.	8.00	2.00
□□□	10 Martin Brodeur (G), NJer.	10.00	2.00
□□□	11 Sergei Samsonov, Bost.	5.00	1.00
□□□	12 Brendan Shanahan, Detr.	6.00	1.00
□□□	13 Steve Yzerman, Detr.	15.00	3.00
□□□	14 Jaromir Jagr, Pitt.	6.00	1.00
□□□	15 Mark Messier, Vanc.	6.00	1.00
□□□	16 Joe Thornton, Bost.	7.00	1.00
□□□	17 Pavel Bure, Vanc.	5.00	1.00
□□□	18 Brett Hull, SLou.	6.00	1.00
□□□	19 Brendan Shanahan, Detr.	6.00	1.00
□□□	20 Jaromir Jagr, Pitt.	6.00	1.00
□□□	21 Eric Lindros, Phil.	6.00	1.00
□□□	22 Paul Kariya, Anah.	8.00	2.00
□□□	23 Wayne Gretzky, NYRa.	25.00	6.00
□□□	24 Patrick Roy (G), Colo.	18.00	4.00

TIN BOXES

There are two colour variations: red and blue. Prices below are for opened tins.

Complete Set (24 tins):		**125.00**
	Tin Pack	**Box**
□□	1 Eric Lindros, Phil.	4.00
□□	2 Paul Kariya, Anah.	6.00
□□	3 Wayne Gretzky, NYRa.	20.00
□□	4 Teemu Selänne, Anah.	4.00
□□	5 Patrick Roy (G), Colo.	14.00
□□	6 John Vanbiesbrouck (G), Flor.	4.00
□□	7 Mike Modano, Dall.	4.00
□□	8 Joe Sakic, Colo.	8.00
□□	9 Peter Forsberg, Colo.	6.00
□□	10 Martin Brodeur (G), NJer.	8.00
□□	11 Sergei Samsonov, Bost.	4.00
□□	12 Brendan Shanahan, Detr.	4.00
□□	13 Steve Yzerman, Detr.	12.00
□□	14 Jaromir Jagr, Pitt.	4.00
□□	15 Mark Messier, Vanc.	4.00
□□	16 Joe Thornton, Bost.	6.00
□□	17 Pavel Bure, Vanc.	4.00
□□	18 Brett Hull, SLou.	4.00
□□	19 Brendan Shanahan, Detr.	4.00
□□	20 Jaromir Jagr, Pitt.	4.00
□□	21 Eric Lindros, Phil.	4.00
□□	22 Paul Kariya, Anah.	6.00
□□	23 Wayne Gretzky, NYRa.	20.00
□□	24 Patrick Roy (G), Colo.	14.00

WIDE TIN PACKS

Prices below are for opened tins.

Complete Set (12 tins):		**30.00**
	Tin Pack	**Wide Tin**
□	1 Wayne Gretzky/ Joe Thornton	6.00
□	2 Paul Kariya/ Brett Hull	3.00
□	3 Eric Lindros/ Joe Sakic	3.00
□	4 Teemu Selänne/ Peter Forsberg	2.00
□	5 Pavel Bure/ Mike Modano	2.00
□	6 Sergei Samsonov/ Steve Yzerman	3.00
□	7 Jaromir Jagr/ Brendan Shanahan	2.00
□	8 Mark Messier/ John Vanbiesbrouck (G)	1.00
□	9 Patrick Roy (G)/ Martin Brodeur (G)	5.00
□	10 Brendan Shanahan/ Eric Lindros	2.00
□	11 Jaromir Jagr/ Paul Kariya	3.00
□	12 Wayne Gretzky/ Patrick Roy (G)	8.00

1997 - 98 DONRUSS PRIORITY

There are two versions: the regular card and a Stamp of Approval parallel (#/100). Odd numbers in the base set were short-printed.

Complete Set (220 cards):		**3300.00**	**65.00**
Common Odd Number:		**6.00**	**.30**
Common Even Number:		**6.00**	**.20**
	Player	**SoA100**	**DP**
□□	1 Patrick Roy (G), Colo.	150.00	3.50
□□	2 Eric Lindros, Phil.	50.00	.50
□□	3 Keith Tkachuk, Phil.	30.00	.50
□□	4 Steve Yzerman, Detr.	120.00	1.50
□□	5 John Vanbiesbrouck (G), Flor.	20.00	.50
□□	6 Teemu Selänne, Anah.	40.00	.50
□□	7 Martin Brodeur (G), NJer.	80.00	2.00
□□	8 Peter Forsberg, Colo.	70.00	1.00
□□	9 Brett Hull, SLou.	50.00	1.00
□□	10 Wayne Gretzky, NYRa.	200.00	3.00
□□	11 Mike Modano, Dall.	50.00	1.00
□□	12 Sergei Fedorov, Detr.	50.00	.50
□□	13 Paul Kariya, Anah.	70.00	1.50
□□	14 Saku Koivu, Mont.	40.00	.50
□□	15 Pavel Bure, Vanc.	40.00	1.00
□□	16 Mark Messier, Vanc.	50.00	.50
□□	17 Joe Sakic, Colo.	80.00	2.00
□□	18 Jaromir Jagr, Pitt.	50.00	.50
□□	19 Brendan Shanahan, Detr.	50.00	1.00
□□	20 Raymond Bourque, Bost.	60.00	.50
□□	21 Daymond Langkow, Tamp.	10.00	.30
□□	22 Alexandre Daigle, Otta. (Phil.)	6.00	.20
□□	23 Dainius Zubrus, Phil.	10.00	.30
□□	24 Ryan Smyth, Edmo.	20.00	.20
□□	25 Derek Plante, Buff.	6.00	.30
□□	26 Eric Dazé, Chic.	20.00	.20
□□	27 Ed Jovanovski, Flor.	20.00	.50
□□	28 Sergei Berezin, Toro.	10.00	.20
□□	29 Roman Turek (G), Dall.	20.00	.50
□□	30 Derian Hatcher, Dall.	15.00	.20
□□	31 Jarome Iginla, Calg.	40.00	1.50
□□	32 Luc Robitaille, LosA.	40.00	.50
□□	33 Rod Brind'Amour, Phil.	15.00	.30
□□	34 Mathieu Schneider, Toro.	10.00	.20
□□	35 Olaf Kölzig (G), Wash.	30.00	.50
□□	36 Nikolai Khabibulin (G), Phoe.	20.00	.20
□□	37 Scott Niedermayer, NJer.	15.00	.30
□□	38 Keith Primeau, Caro.	20.00	.20
□□	39 Dimitri Khristich, Bost.	6.00	.30
□□	40 Éric Fichaud (G), NYIs.	6.00	.20
□□	41 Pierre Turgeon, SLou.	20.00	.50
□□	42 Kevin Stevens, NYRa.	10.00	.20
□□	43 Nicklas Lidström, Detr.	30.00	.50
□□	44 Sean Burke (G), Vanc.	30.00	.20
□□	45 Sandis Ozolinsh, Colo.	10.00	.30
□□	46 Owen Nolan, SanJ.	30.00	.20
□□	47 Peter Bondra, Wash.	30.00	.50
□□	48 Ron Hextall (G), Phil.	30.00	.20
□□	49 Rob Blake, LosA.	30.00	.50
□□	50 Geoff Sanderson, Caro.	10.00	.20
□□	51 Sergei Zubov, Dall.	10.00	.30
□□	52 Doug Gilmour, NJer.	30.00	.20
□□	53 Oleg Tverdovsky, Phoe.	6.00	.30
□□	54 Bryan Berard, NYIs.	15.00	.20
□□	55 Bill Ranford (G), Wash.	20.00	.50
□□	56 Mats Sundin, Toro.	50.00	.50
□□	57 Damian Rhodes (G), Otta.	10.00	.30
□□	58 Zigmund Palffy, NYIs.	30.00	.20
□□	59 Mike Grier, Edmo.	10.00	.30
□□	60 Jozef Stumpel, LosA.	10.00	.20
□□	61 Mark Recchi, Mont.	20.00	.50
□□	62 Alexei Zhamnov, Chic.	15.00	.20
□□	63 Jere Lehtinen, Dall.	15.00	.30
□□	64 Andrew Cassels, Calg.	10.00	.20
□□	65 Kevin Hodson (G), Detr.	10.00	.30
□□	66 Dino Ciccarelli, Flor.	15.00	.20
□□	67 Niklas Sundström, NYRa.	10.00	.30
□□	68 Jeff Hackett (G), Chic.	15.00	.20
□□	69 Brian Holzinger, Buff.	6.00	.30
□□	70 Jeff Friesen, SanJ.	15.00	.20
□□	71 Ed Belfour (G), Dall.	50.00	1.00
□□	72 Wayne Primeau, Buff.	6.00	.20
□□	73 Sami Kapanen, Caro.	15.00	.30
□□	74 Brian Leetch, NYRa.	30.00	.20
□□	75 Mikael Renberg, Tamp.	15.00	.30
□□	76 Ron Tugnutt (G), Otta.	20.00	.20
□□	77 Ron Francis, Pitt.	30.00	.50
□□	78 Jocelyn Thibault (G), Mont.	20.00	.20
□□	79 Jamie Langenbrunner, Dall.	10.00	.30
□□	80 Dominik Hasek (G), Buff.	50.00	.50
□□	81 Chris Osgood (G), Detr.	30.00	.50
□□	82 Grant Fuhr (G), SLou.	30.00	.20
□□	83 Adam Graves, NYRa.	20.00	.50
□□	84 Janne Niinimaa, Phil.	10.00	.20
□□	85 Kelly Hrudey (G), S.J	15.00	.30
□□	86 Mike Dunham (G), NJer.	20.00	.20
□□	87 Valeri Kamensky, Colo.	15.00	.30
□□	88 Cory Stillman, Calg.	10.00	.20
□□	89 Anson Carter, Bost.	20.00	.50
□□	90 Igor Larionov, Detr.	30.00	.20
□□	91 Chris Pronger, SLou.	30.00	.50
□□	92 Steve Sullivan, Toro.	15.00	.20
□□	93 Mike Gartner, Phoe.	40.00	1.00
□□	94 Jim Campbell, SLou.	6.00	.20
□□	95 Valeri Bure, Mont.	15.00	.30
□□	96 Stéphane Fiset (G), LosA.	15.00	.20
□□	97 Jason Arnott, Edmo.	20.00	.50
□□	98 Trevor Kidd (G), Caro.	15.00	.20
□□	99 Chris Chelios, Chic.	30.00	.50
□□	100 Kevin Hatcher, Pitt.	6.00	.20
□□	101 Félix Potvin (G), Toro.	30.00	.50
□□	102 Travis Green, NYIs. (Anah.)	10.00	.20
□□	103 Dave Gagner, Flor.	6.00	.30
□□	104 Byron Dafoe (G), Bost.	20.00	.20
□□	105 Rick Tabaracci (G), Calg.	6.00	.30
□□	106 Gary Roberts, Caro.	20.00	.20
□□	107 Mike Ricci, SanJ.	15.00	.30
□□	108 Andy Moog (G), Mont.	20.00	.20
□□	109 Sean Pronger, Anah.	6.00	.30
□□	110 Paul Coffey, Phil.	30.00	.20
□□	111 Trevor Linden, Vanc.	20.00	.50
□□	112 Rob Zamuner, Tamp.	10.00	.20
□□	113 Daniel Alfredsson, Otta.	30.00	.50
□□	114 Ray Sheppard, Flor.	6.00	.20
□□	**115 Steve Shields (G), Buff. RC**	**20.00**	**1.50**
□□	116 Ethan Moreau, Chic.	6.00	.20
□□	117 Tomas Sandström, Anah.	10.00	.30
□□	118 Chris Gratton, Phil.	10.00	.20
□□	119 Alexander Mogilny, Vanc.	20.00	.50
□□	120 Roman Hamrlik, Edmo.	10.00	.20
□□	121 Tommy Salo (G), NYIs.	20.00	.50
□□	122 Jason Allison, Bost.	30.00	.20

□ □	123 Curtis Joseph (G), Edmo.	50.00	1.00
□ □	124 Guy Hebert (G), Anah.	10.00	.20
□ □	125 Jeff O'Neill, Caro.	20.00	.50
□ □	126 Donald Audette, Buff.	20.00	.20
□ □	127 Claude Lemieux, Colo.	15.00	.30
□ □	128 Brian Savage, Mont.	15.00	.20
□ □	129 Scott Mellanby, Flor.	10.00	.30
□ □	130 Vyacheslav Kozlov, Detr.	10.00	.20
□ □	131 Wade Redden, Otta.	15.00	.30
□ □	132 John LeClair, Phil.	40.00	.50
□ □	133 Jeremy Roenick, Phoe.	40.00	1.00
□ □	134 Andreas Johansson, Pitt.	10.00	.20
□ □	135 Nelson Emerson, Caro.	6.00	.30
□ □	136 Daren Puppa (G), Tamp.	10.00	.20
□ □	137 Joé Juneau, Wash.	10.00	.30
□ □	138 Garth Snow (G), Phil.	15.00	.20
□ □	139 Tom Barrasso (G), Pitt.	20.00	.50
□ □	140 Joe Nieuwendyk, Dall.	20.00	.20
□ □	141 Theoren Fleury, Calg.	30.00	.50
□ □	142 Yanic Perreault, LosA.	15.00	.20
□ □	143 Mike Richter (G), NYRa.	20.00	.50
□ □	144 Al MacInnis, SLou.	20.00	.20
□ □	145 Michael Peca, Buff.	20.00	.50
□ □	146 Darren McCarty, Detr.	15.00	.20
□ □	147 Alexei Yashin, Otta.	30.00	.50
□ □	148 Rick Tocchet, Phoe.	15.00	.20
□ □	149 Adam Oates, Wash.	20.00	.50
□ □	150 Wendel Clark, Toro.	40.00	.50
□ □	151 Tony Amonte, Chic.	30.00	.50
□ □	152 Dave Andreychuk, NJer.	15.00	.20
□ □	153 Jamie Storr (G), LosA.	10.00	.30
□ □	154 Craig Janney, Phoe.	10.00	.20
□ □	155 Todd Bertuzzi, NYIs.	60.00	1.50
□ □	156 Harry York, SLou.	6.00	.20
□ □	157 Todd Harvey, Dall.	10.00	.30
□ □	158 Bobby Holik, NJer.	15.00	.20
□ □	159 Mike Vernon (G), SanJ.	20.00	.50
□ □	160 Pat LaFontaine, NYRa.	30.00	.20
□ □	161 Doug Weight, Edmo.	30.00	.50
□ □	162 Kirk McLean (G), Caro.	15.00	.20
□ □	163 Adam Deadmarsh, Colo.	15.00	.30
□ □	164 Vincent Damphousse, Mont.	30.00	.20
□ □	**165 Vaclav Prospal, Phil. RC**	**30.00**	**2.00**
□ □	166 Daniel Cleary, Chic.	15.00	.20
□ □	167 Jaroslav Svejkovsky, Wash.	6.00	.30
□ □	**168 Marco Sturm, SanJ. RC**	**20.00**	**.50**
□ □	**169 Robert Dome, Pitt. RC**	**15.00**	**1.00**
□ □	**170 Patrik Elias, NJer. RC**	**80.00**	**3.00**
□ □	171 Mattias Öhlund, Vanc.	15.00	.50
□ □	**172 Espen Knutsen, Anah. RC**	**20.00**	**.50**
□ □	173 Joe Thornton, Bost.	60.00	3.00
□ □	**174 Jan Bulis, Wash. RC**	**6.00**	**.20**
□ □	175 Patrick Marleau, SanJ.	20.00	1.00
□ □	176 Brad Isbister, Phoe.	10.00	.20
□ □	**177 Kevin Weekes (G), Flor. RC**	**20.00**	**1.50**
□ □	178 Sergei Samsonov, Bost.	30.00	.50
□ □	**179 Tyler Moss (G), Calg. RC**	**15.00**	**1.00**
□ □	180 Chris Phillips, Otta.	10.00	.20
□ □	181 Alyn McCauley, Toro.	15.00	.50
□ □	**182 Derek Morris, Calg. RC**	**20.00**	**.50**
□ □	183 Alexei Morozov, Pitt.	10.00	.50
□ □	184 Boyd Devereaux, Edmo.	10.00	.20
□ □	185 Peter Forsberg, Colo.	70.00	1.00
□ □	186 Brendan Shanahan, Detr.	50.00	.50
□ □	187 Teemu Selänne, Anah.	40.00	.50
□ □	188 Eric Lindros, Phil.	50.00	.50
□ □	189 Mark Messier, Vanc.	50.00	.50
□ □	**190 Vaclav Prospal, Phil. RC**	**30.00**	**.50**
□ □	191 Jarome Iginla, Calg.	40.00	.50
□ □	192 Mike Modano, Dall.	50.00	.50
□ □	193 John Vanbiesbrouck (G), Flor.	20.00	.30
□ □	194 Bryan Berard, NYIs.	15.00	.20
□ □	195 Patrick Marleau, SanJ.	20.00	.30
□ □	196 Martin Brodeur (G), NJer.	80.00	.50
□ □	197 Patrick Roy (G), Colo.	150.00	2.50
□ □	198 Félix Potvin (G), Toro.	30.00	.20
□ □	199 Wayne Gretzky, NYRa.	200.00	3.50
□ □	200 Sergei Samsonov, Bost.	30.00	.20
□ □	201 Ryan Smyth, Edmo.	20.00	.30
□ □	202 Keith Tkachuk, Phoe.	30.00	.20
□ □	203 Chris Osgood (G), Detr.	30.00	.50
□ □	204 Paul Kariya, Anah.	70.00	.50
□ □	205 John LeClair, Phil.	40.00	.50
□ □	206 Alyn McCauley, Toro.	15.00	.20
□ □	207 Joe Thornton, Bost.	60.00	1.00
□ □	208 Joe Sakic, Colo.	80.00	.50
□ □	209 Steve Yzerman, Detr.	120.00	2.00
□ □	210 Saku Koivu, Mont.	40.00	.20
□ □	211 Pavel Bure, Vanc.	40.00	.50
□ □	212 Zigmund Palffy, NYIs.	30.00	.20
□ □	213 Alexei Yashin, Otta.	30.00	.50
□ □	214 Sergei Fedorov, Detr.	50.00	.50
□ □	215 CL: Joe Thornton, Bost.	30.00	.50
□ □	216 CL: Patrick Marleau, SanJ.	10.00	.20
□ □	217 CL: Daniel Cleary, Chic.	10.00	.30
□ □	218 CL: Sergei Samsonov, Detr.	15.00	.20
□ □	219 CL: Jaroslav Svejkovsky, Wash.	6.00	.30
□ □	220 CL: Alyn McCauley, Toro.	10.00	.20

DIRECT DEPOSIT

There are two versions:the insert (#/3000) and the promo. Other promos likely exist.

Insert Set (30 cards): 150.00

	Goalie	**Promo**	**DD**
□ □	1 Brendan Shanahan, Detr.	2.00	6.00
□	2 Steve Yzerman, Detr.		18.00
□	3 Pavel Bure, Vanc.		6.00
□	4 Jaromir Jagr, Pitt.		6.00
□	5 Ryan Smyth, Edmo.		2.00
□	6 Sergei Samsonov, Bost.		4.00
□	7 Mark Messier, Vanc.		6.00
□	8 Wayne Gretzky, NYRa.		30.00
□	9 Jarome Iginla, Calg.		6.00
□	10 Peter Forsberg, Colo.		10.00
□	11 Joe Sakic, Colo.		12.00
□	12 Sergei Fedorov, Detr.		6.00
□	13 Mike Modano, Dall.		6.00
□	14 Paul Kariya, Anah.		10.00
□	15 Teemu Selänne, Anah.		6.00
□	16 Eric Lindros, Phil.		6.00
□	17 Keith Tkachuk, Phoe.		4.00
□	18 Patrick Marleau, SanJ.		2.00
□	19 Jaroslav Svejkovsky, Wash.		2.00
□	20 Alyn McCauley, Toro.		2.00
□	21 Saku Koivu, Mont.		6.00
□	22 Zigmund Palffy, NYIs.		4.00
□	23 Brett Hull, SLou.		6.00
□	24 Patrik Elias, NJer.		12.00
□ □	25 Joe Thornton, Bost.	3.00	12.00
□ □	26 Espen Knutsen, Anah.	.50	2.00
□	27 Daniel Alfredsson, Otta.		4.00
□	28 John LeClair, Phil.		6.00
□ □	29 Dainius Zubrus, Phil.	.50	2.00
□	30 Jason Arnott, NJer.		2.00

OPENING DAY

Card size: 4" x 6"

Insert Set (30 cards): 340.00

	Insert (#/1,000)	**NRMT-MT**
□	1 Patrick Roy (G), Colo.	45.00
□	2 Eric Lindros, Phil.	15.00
□	3 Keith Tkachuk, Phil.	5.00
□	4 Steve Yzerman, Detr.	35.00
□	5 John Vanbiesbrouck (G), Flor.	5.00
□	6 Teemu Selänne, Anah.	10.00
□	7 Martin Brodeur (G), NJer.	20.00
□	8 Peter Forsberg, Colo.	20.00
□	9 Brett Hull, SLou.	15.00
□	10 Wayne Gretzky, NYRa.	60.00
□	11 Mike Modano, Dall.	15.00
□	12 Paul Kariya, Anah.	20.00
□	13 Pavel Bure, Vanc.	10.00
□	14 Mark Messier, Vanc.	15.00
□	15 Joe Sakic, Colo.	20.00
□	16 Jaromir Jagr, Pitt.	15.00
□	17 Brendan Shanahan, Detr.	15.00
□	18 Ryan Smyth, Edmo.	5.00
□	19 Jarome Iginla, Calg.	10.00
□	20 Bryan Berard, NYIs.	4.00
□	21 Jocelyn Thibault (G), Mont.	5.00
□	22 Dominik Hasek (G), Buff.	15.00
□	23 Chris Osgood (G), Detr.	5.00
□	24 Chris Chelios, Chic.	5.00
□	25 Félix Potvin (G), Toro.	5.00
□	26 John LeClair, Phil.	10.00
□	27 Saku Koivu, Mont.	10.00
□	28 Joe Thornton, Bost.	25.00
□	29 Patrick Marleau, SanJ.	5.00
□	30 Sergei Samsonov, Bost.	10.00

POSTCARDS

Card size: 4" x 6"

Complete Set (36 cards): 50.00

	Player	**4x6**
□	1 Patrick Roy (G)	6.00
□	2 Brendan Shanahan	2.00
□	3 Steve Yzerman	4.00
□	4 Jaromir Jagr	2.00
□	5 Pavel Bure	1.00
□	6 Mark Messier	2.00
□	7 Wayne Gretzky	8.00
□	8 Eric Lindros	2.00
□	9 Joe Sakic	3.00
□	10 Peter Forsberg	2.00
□	11 John Vanbiesbrouck (G)	1.00
□	12 Mike Modano	2.00
□	13 Paul Kariya	2.00
□	14 Teemu Selänne	1.00
□	15 Sergei Fedorov	2.00
□	16 Joe Thornton	3.00
□	17 Sergei Samsonov	1.00
□	18 Patrick Marleau	1.00
□	19 Ryan Smyth	1.00
□	20 Jarome Iginla	1.00
□	21 John LeClair	1.00
□	22 Brian Leetch	1.00
□	23 Chris Chelios	1.00
□	24 Martin Brodeur (G)	3.00
□	25 Bryan Berard	1.00
□	26 Keith Tkachuk	1.00
□	27 Saku Koivu	1.00
□	28 Brett Hull	2.00
□	29 Félix Potvin (G)	1.00
□	30 Chris Osgood (G)	1.00
□	31 Dominik Hasek (G)	2.00
□	32 Zigmund Palffy	1.00
□	33 Jeremy Roenick	1.00
□	34 Dainius Zubrus	1.00
□	35 Raymond Bourque	2.00
□	36 Jocelyn Thibault (G)	1.00

POSTMASTER GENERAL

Complete Set (20 cards):		**12.00**	**150.00**
	Insert (#/1,500)	**Promo**	**Insert**
□ □	1 Patrick Roy (G), Colo.	5.00	45.00
□ □	2 John Vanbiesbrouck (G), Flor.	.50	6.00
□ □	3 Félix Potvin (G), Toro.	.50	8.00
□ □	4 Curtis Joseph (G), Edmo.	.50	14.00
□ □	5 Mike Richter (G), NYRa.	.50	6.00
□ □	6 Jocelyn Thibault (G), Mont.	1.00	6.00
□ □	7 Ed Belfour (G), Dall.	.50	14.00
□ □	8 Chris Osgood (G), Detr.	.50	8.00
□ □	9 Ron Hextall (G), Phil.	1.00	9.00
□ □	10 Martin Brodeur (G), NJer.	.50	24.00
□ □	11 Mike Vernon (G), SanJ.	1.00	6.00
□ □	12 Éric Fichaud (G), NYIs.	.50	4.00
□ □	13 Dominik Hasek (G), Buff.	.50	14.00
□ □	14 Byron Dafoe (G), Bost.	1.00	6.00
□ □	15 Tommy Salo (G), NYIs.	1.00	6.00
□ □	16 Garth Snow (G), Phil.	.50	4.00
□ □	17 Tom Barrasso (G), Pitt.	1.00	6.00
□ □	18 Marc Denis (G), Colo.	1.00	7.00
□ □	19 Grant Fuhr (G), SLou.	.50	8.00
□ □	20 Guy Hebert (G), Anah.	.50	4.00

STAMPS

There are four stamp versions for each player in this series: the regular stamp, a bronze stamp, a silver stamp and a gold stamp.

Complete Set (36 cards):		**425.00**	**200.00**	**90.00**	**60.00**
	Player	**Gold**	**Silver**	**Bronze**	**Stamp**
□ □ □ □	1 Patrick Roy (G)	50.00	25.00	10.00	7.00
□ □ □ □	2 Brendan Shanahan	15.00	8.00	3.00	2.00
□ □ □ □	3 Steve Yzerman	40.00	20.00	9.00	6.00
□ □ □ □	4 Jaromir Jagr	15.00	5.00	3.00	2.00
□ □ □ □	5 Pavel Bure	10.00	5.00	3.00	2.00
□ □ □ □	6 Mark Messier	15.00	8.00	3.00	2.00
□ □ □ □	7 Wayne Gretzky	70.00	35.00	15.00	10.00
□ □ □ □	8 Eric Lindros	15.00	5.00	3.00	2.00
□ □ □ □	9 Joe Sakic	25.00	10.00	6.00	4.00
□ □ □ □	10 Peter Forsberg	20.00	10.00	5.00	3.00
□ □ □ □	11 Vanbiesbrouck (G)	5.00	4.00	1.00	1.00
□ □ □ □	12 Mike Modano	15.00	8.00	3.00	2.00
□ □ □ □	13 Paul Kariya	20.00	10.00	5.00	3.00
□ □ □ □	14 Teemu Selänne	10.00	5.00	3.00	2.00
□ □ □ □	15 Sergei Fedorov	15.00	8.00	3.00	2.00
□ □ □ □	16 Joe Thornton	20.00	10.00	4.00	4.00
□ □ □ □	17 Sergei Samsonov	10.00	5.00	2.00	1.00
□ □ □ □	18 Patrick Marleau	8.00	4.00	1.00	1.00
□ □ □ □	19 Ryan Smyth	8.00	4.00	1.00	1.00
□ □ □ □	20 Jarome Iginla	14.00	7.00	3.00	2.00
□ □ □ □	21 John LeClair	10.00	7.00	3.00	2.00
□ □ □ □	22 Brian Leetch	10.00	5.00	2.00	1.00
□ □ □ □	23 Chris Chelios	10.00	5.00	2.00	1.00
□ □ □ □	24 Brodeur (G)	25.00	10.00	6.00	4.00
□ □ □ □	25 Bryan Berard	5.00	2.00	1.00	.50
□ □ □ □	26 Keith Tkachuk	10.00	5.00	2.00	1.00
□ □ □ □	27 Saku Koivu	10.00	7.00	3.00	2.00
□ □ □ □	28 Brett Hull	15.00	8.00	3.00	2.00
□ □ □ □	29 Félix Potvin (G)	10.00	5.00	2.00	1.00
□ □ □ □	30 Chris Osgood (G)	10.00	5.00	2.00	1.00
□ □ □ □	31 Dominik Hasek (G)	15.00	5.00	3.00	2.00
□ □ □ □	32 Zigmund Palffy	10.00	5.00	2.00	1.00
□ □ □ □	33 Jeremy Roenick	10.00	7.00	3.00	2.00
□ □ □ □	34 Dainius Zubrus	4.00	2.00	1.00	.50
□ □ □ □	35 Raymond Bourque	20.00	10.00	4.00	3.00
□ □ □ □	36 Jocelyn Thibault (G)	7.00	3.00	1.00	1.00

1997 - 98 DONRUSS STUDIO

There are three versions: the regular card, a "Press Proof" parallel (1,000 copies) and a "Gold Press Proof" parallel (250 copies).

Complete Set (110 cards):		**1300.00**	**475.00**	**45.00**
Common Player:		**6.00**	**3.00**	**.20**
	Player	**PPG250**	**PPS1000**	**Studio**
□ □ □	1 Wayne Gretzky, NYRa.	150.00	60.00	4.00
□ □ □	2 Dominik Hasek (G), Buff.	30.00	15.00	1.00
□ □ □	3 Eric Lindros, Phil.	30.00	15.00	1.00
□ □ □	4 Paul Kariya, Anah.	50.00	20.00	1.00
□ □ □	5 Jaromir Jagr, Pitt.	30.00	15.00	1.00
□ □ □	6 Brendan Shanahan, Detr.	35.00	15.00	1.00
□ □ □	7 Patrick Roy (G), Colo.	110.00	40.00	3.00
□ □ □	8 Keith Tkachuk, Phoe.	20.00	5.00	.50
□ □ □	9 Mark Messier, Vanc.	35.00	15.00	1.00
□ □ □	10 Steve Yzerman, Detr.	90.00	35.00	2.00
□ □ □	11 Brett Hull, SLou.	35.00	15.00	1.00
□ □ □	12 Jarome Iginla, Calg.	30.00	10.00	.50
□ □ □	13 Mike Modano, Dall.	35.00	15.00	1.00
□ □ □	14 Pavel Bure, Vanc.	30.00	10.00	.50
□ □ □	15 Peter Forsberg, Colo.	50.00	20.00	1.00
□ □ □	16 Ryan Smyth, Edmo.	15.00	5.00	.20
□ □ □	17 Vanbiesbrouck (G), Flor.	15.00	5.00	.20
□ □ □	18 Teemu Selänne, Anah.	30.00	10.00	.50
□ □ □	19 Saku Koivu, Mont.	30.00	10.00	.50
□ □ □	20 Martin Brodeur (G), NJer.	60.00	20.00	1.50
□ □ □	21 Sergei Fedorov, Detr.	35.00	15.00	1.00
□ □ □	22 John LeClair, Phil.	30.00	10.00	.50
□ □ □	23 Joe Sakic, Colo.	60.00	20.00	1.50
□ □ □	24 José Théodore (G), Mont.	45.00	15.00	1.00
□ □ □	25 Marc Denis (G), Colo.	15.00	5.00	.20
□ □ □	26 Dainius Zubrus, Phil.	6.00	3.00	.20
□ □ □	27 Bryan Berard, NYIs.	10.00	3.00	.20
□ □ □	28 Raymond Bourque, Bost.	40.00	15.00	1.00
□ □ □	29 Curtis Joseph (G), Edmo.	30.00	15.00	1.00
□ □ □	30 Chris Chelios, Chic.	20.00	5.00	.50

☐☐☐	31 Alexei Yashin, Otta.	20.00	5.00	.50
☐☐☐	32 Adam Oates, Wash.	15.00	5.00	.20
☐☐☐	33 Anson Carter, Bost.	15.00	5.00	.20
☐☐☐	34 Jim Campbell, SLou.	6.00	3.00	.20
☐☐☐	35 Jason Arnott, Edmo.	15.00	5.00	.20
☐☐☐	36 Derek Plante, Buff.	6.00	3.00	.20
☐☐☐	37 Guy Hebert (G), Anah.	6.00	3.00	.20
☐☐☐	38 Oleg Tverdovsky, Phoe.	6.00	3.00	.20
☐☐☐	39 Ed Jovanovski, Flor.	15.00	5.00	.20
☐☐☐	40 Jeremy Roenick, Phoe.	30.00	10.00	.50
☐☐☐	41 Scott Mellanby, Flor.	6.00	3.00	.20
☐☐☐	42 Keith Primeau, Caro.	15.00	5.00	.20
☐☐☐	43 Ron Hextall (G), Phil.	20.00	5.00	.50
☐☐☐	44 Daren Puppa (G), Tamp.	6.00	3.00	.20
☐☐☐	45 Jim Carey (G), Bost.	6.00	3.00	.20
☐☐☐	46 Zigmund Palffy, NYIs.	20.00	5.00	.50
☐☐☐	47 Jaroslav Svejkovsky, Wash.	6.00	3.00	.20
☐☐☐	48 Daymond Langkow, Tamp.	6.00	3.00	.20
☐☐☐	49 Mikael Renberg, Tamp.	10.00	3.00	.20
☐☐☐	50 Pat LaFontaine, NYRa.	20.00	5.00	.50
☐☐☐	51 Mike Grier, Edmo.	6.00	3.00	.20
☐☐☐	52 Stéphane Fiset (G), LosA.	10.00	3.00	.20
☐☐☐	53 Luc Robitaille, LosA.	30.00	10.00	.50
☐☐☐	54 Joe Thornton, Bost.	45.00	15.00	2.00
☐☐☐	55 Joe Nieuwendyk, Das.	15.00	5.00	.20
☐☐☐	56 Mike Dunham (G), NJer.	15.00	5.00	.20
☐☐☐	57 Mark Recchi, Mont.	15.00	5.00	.20
☐☐☐	58 Ed Belfour (G), Dall.	35.00	15.00	1.00
☐☐☐	59 Mike Richter (G), NYRa.	15.00	5.00	.20
☐☐☐	60 Peter Bondra, Wash.	20.00	5.00	.50
☐☐☐	61 Trevor Kidd (G), Caro.	10.00	3.00	.20
☐☐☐	62 Sean Burke (G), Caro.	20.00	5.00	.50
☐☐☐	63 Khabibulin (G), Phoe.	15.00	5.00	.20
☐☐☐	64 Pierre Turgeon, SLou.	15.00	5.00	.20
☐☐☐	65 Dino Ciccarelli, Tamp.	10.00	3.00	.20
☐☐☐	66 Félix Potvin (G), Toro.	20.00	5.00	.50
☐☐☐	67 Mats Sundin, Toro.	35.00	15.00	1.00
☐☐☐	68 Joé Juneau, Wash.	6.00	3.00	.20
☐☐☐	69 Mike Vernon (G), SanJ.	15.00	5.00	.20
☐☐☐	70 Adam Deadmarsh, Colo.	10.00	3.00	.20
☐☐☐	71 Damian Rhodes (G), Otta.	6.00	3.00	.20
☐☐☐	72 Michael Peca, Buff.	15.00	5.00	.20
☐☐☐	73 J-S Giguère (G), Calg.	30.00	10.00	.50
☐☐☐	74 Ron Francis, Pitt.	20.00	5.00	.50
☐☐☐	75 Roman Hamrlik, Tamp.	6.00	3.00	.20
☐☐☐	76 V. Damphousse, Mont.	20.00	5.00	.50
☐☐☐	77 Jocelyn Thibault (G), Mont.	15.00	5.00	.20
☐☐☐	78 Claude Lemieux, Colo.	10.00	3.00	.20
☐☐☐	**79 S. Shields (G), Buff. RC**	**15.00**	**5.00**	**1.50**
☐☐☐	80 Dimitri Khristich, Bost.	6.00	3.00	.20
☐☐☐	81 Theoren Fleury, Calg.	20.00	5.00	.50
☐☐☐	82 Sandis Ozolinsh, Colo.	6.00	3.00	.20
☐☐☐	83 Ethan Moreau, Chic.	6.00	3.00	.20
☐☐☐	84 Geoff Sanderson, Caro.	6.00	3.00	.20
☐☐☐	85 Paul Coffey, Phil.	20.00	5.00	.50
☐☐☐	86 Brian Leetch, NYRa.	20.00	5.00	.50
☐☐☐	87 Chris Osgood (G), Detr.	20.00	5.00	.50
☐☐☐	88 Kirk McLean (G), Vanc.	10.00	3.00	.20
☐☐☐	89 Mike Gartner, Phoe.	30.00	10.00	.50
☐☐☐	90 Chris Gratton, Phil.	6.00	3.00	.20
☐☐☐	91 Éric Fichaud (G), NYIs.	6.00	3.00	.20
☐☐☐	92 Alexandre Daigle, Otta.	6.00	3.00	.20
☐☐☐	93 Doug Gilmour, NJer.	20.00	5.00	.50
☐☐☐	94 Daniel Alfredsson, Otta.	20.00	5.00	.50
☐☐☐	95 Doug Weight, Edmo.	20.00	5.00	.50
☐☐☐	96 Derian Hatcher, Dall.	10.00	3.00	.20
☐☐☐	97 Wade Redden, Otta.	10.00	3.00	.20
☐☐☐	98 Jeff Friesen, SanJ.	10.00	3.00	.20
☐☐☐	99 Tony Amonte, Chic.	20.00	5.00	.50
☐☐☐	100 Janne Niinimaa, Phil.	6.00	3.00	.20
☐☐☐	101 Trevor Linden, Vanc.	15.00	5.00	.20
☐☐☐	102 Grant Fuhr (G), SLou.	20.00	5.00	.50
☐☐☐	103 Chris Phillips, Otta.	6.00	3.00	.20
☐☐☐	104 Sergei Berezin, Toro.	6.00	3.00	.20
☐☐☐	105 CL: Shanahan, Detr.	20.00	5.00	.50
☐☐☐	106 CL: Yzerman, Detr.	40.00	15.00	1.00
☐☐☐	107 CL: Selänne, Anah.	15.00	5.00	.20
☐☐☐	108 CL: Eric Lindros, Phil.	20.00	5.00	.50
☐☐☐	109 CL: Gretzky, NYRa.	70.00	30.00	2.00
☐☐☐	110 CL: Patrick Roy (G), Colo.	50.00	20.00	1.50

PORTRAITS

Photo Size: 8" x 10"

Complete Set (36 cards): 40.00

	Insert	**8x10**
☐	1 Wayne Gretzky, NYRa.	6.00
☐	2 Dominik Hasek (G), Buff.	1.00
☐	3 Eric Lindros, Phil.	1.00
☐	4 Paul Kariya, Anah.	2.00
☐	5 Jaromir Jagr, Pitt.	1.00
☐	6 Brendan Shanahan, Detr.	1.00
☐	7 Patrick Roy (G), Colo.	4.00
☐	8 Keith Tkachuk, Phoe.	1.00
☐	9 Mark Messier, Vanc.	1.00
☐	10 Steve Yzerman, Detr.	3.00
☐	11 Brett Hull, SLou.	1.00
☐	12 Jarome Iginla, Calg.	1.00
☐	13 Mike Modano, Dall.	1.00
☐	14 Pavel Bure, Vanc.	1.00
☐	15 Peter Forsberg, Colo.	2.00
☐	16 Ryan Smyth, Edmo.	1.00
☐	17 John Vanbiesbrouck (G), Flor.	1.00
☐	18 Teemu Selänne, Anah.	1.00
☐	19 Saku Koivu, Mont.	1.00
☐	20 Martin Brodeur (G), NJer.	2.00
☐	21 Sergei Fedorov, Detr.	1.00
☐	22 Joe Thornton, Bost.	3.00
☐	23 Joe Sakic, Colo.	2.00
☐	24 Bryan Berard, NYIs.	1.00
☐	25 John LeClair, Phil.	1.00
☐	26 Marc Denis (G), Colo.	1.00
☐	27 Dainius Zubrus, Phil.	1.00
☐	28 Chris Chelios, Chic.	1.00
☐	29 Jason Arnott, Edmo.	1.00
☐	30 Jermey Roenick, Phoe.	1.00
☐	31 Zigmund Palffy, NYIs.	1.00
☐	32 Jaroslav Svejkovsky, Wash.	1.00
☐	33 Mike Richter (G), NYRa.	1.00
☐	34 Félix Potvin (G), Toro.	1.00
☐	35 Brian Leetch, NYRa.	1.00
☐	36 Chris Osgood (G), Detr.	1.00

PORTRAITS AUTOGRAPHED

Photo Size: 8" x 10"

	Autograph	**8x10**
☐	12 Jarome Iginla, Calg.	40.00
☐	16 Ryan Smyth, Edmo.	20.00
☐	20 Martin Brodeur (G), NJer.	100.00

HARD HATS

Insert Set (24 cards): 110.00

	Insert (#/3000)	**NRMT-MT**
☐	1 Wayne Gretzky, NYRa.	40.00
☐	2 Eric Lindros, Phil.	10.00
☐	3 Paul Kariya, Anah.	10.00
☐	4 Bryan Berard, NYIs.	3.00
☐	5 Dainius Zubrus, Phil.	3.00
☐	6 Daymond Langkow, Tamp.	3.00
☐	7 Keith Tkachuk, Phoe.	5.00
☐	8 Ryan Smyth, Edmo.	3.00
☐	9 Brendan Shanahan, Detr.	10.00
☐	10 Steve Yzerman, Detr.	20.00
☐	11 Teemu Selänne, Anah.	5.00
☐	12 Jarome Iginla, Calg.	5.00
☐	13 Zigmund Palffy, NYIs.	5.00
☐	14 Sergei Berezin, Toro.	3.00
☐	15 Saku Koivu, Mont.	5.00
☐	16 Peter Forsberg, Colo.	10.00
☐	17 Joe Sakic, Colo.	15.00
☐	18 Pavel Bure, Vanc.	5.00
☐	19 Jaromir Jagr, Pitt.	10.00
☐	20 Brett Hull, SLou.	10.00
☐	21 Sergei Fedorov, Detr.	10.00
☐	22 Mike Grier, Edmo.	3.00
☐	23 Ethan Moreau, Chic.	3.00
☐	24 Mats Sundin, Toro.	10.00

SILHOUETTES

Photo These laser-cut cards have two versions: the standard-sized insert (serial numbered out 1,500) and 8" x 10" parallels (serial numbered out of 3,000).

Insert Set (24 cards): 100.00 225.00

	Inserts	**8x10**	**Card**
☐☐	1 Wayne Gretzky, NYRa.	30.00	60.00
☐☐	2 Eric Lindros, Phil.	5.00	15.00
☐☐	3 Patrick Roy (G), Colo.	20.00	45.00
☐☐	4 Martin Brodeur (G), NJer.	10.00	20.00
☐☐	5 Paul Kariya, Anah.	10.00	20.00
☐☐	6 Mark Messier, Vanc.	5.00	15.00
☐☐	7 Dominik Hasek (G), Buff.	5.00	15.00
☐☐	8 Brett Hull, SLou.	5.00	15.00
☐☐	9 Pavel Bure, Vanc.	5.00	10.00
☐☐	10 Steve Yzerman, Detr.	15.00	35.00
☐☐	11 Brendan Shanahan, Detr.	5.00	15.00
☐☐	12 Joe Sakic, Colo.	10.00	20.00
☐☐	13 Peter Forsberg, Colo.	10.00	20.00
☐☐	14 Sergei Fedorov, Detr.	5.00	15.00
☐☐	15 John LeClair, Phil.	5.00	10.00
☐☐	16 John Vanbiesbrouck (G), Flor.	4.00	8.00
☐☐	17 Teemu Selänne, Anah.	5.00	10.00
☐☐	18 Keith Tkachuk, Phoe.	4.00	8.00
☐☐	19 Mike Modano, Dall.	5.00	15.00
☐☐	20 Félix Potvin (G), Toro.	4.00	8.00
☐☐	21 Ryan Smyth, Edmo.	4.00	8.00
☐☐	22 Jaromir Jagr, Pitt.	5.00	15.00
☐☐	23 Brian Leetch, NYRa.	4.00	8.00
☐☐	24 Jarome Iginla, Calg.	5.00	10.00

1997 - 98 DS

NHL stars sometimes sell at a premium (usually $1-2). Card one (gold) is seeded 1:48 packs; cards 2-12 are seeded 1:4 packs.

Complete Set (120 cards): 60.00

Common Player: .30

	Player	**DS**
☐	1 Roman Cechmanek, Dadak Vsetín	25.00
☐	2 Milan Hnilicka, Sparta Praha	6.00
☐	3 Josef Beranek, Dadak Vsetín	4.00
☐	4 Milan Nedoma, Ceske Budejovice	1.00
☐	5 L'ubomír Sekeras, Trinec	4.00
☐	6 Jirí Vykoukal, Sparta Praha	1.00
☐	7 Jirí Dopita, Dadak Vsetín	4.00
☐	8 Robert Kysela, Chemopetrol Litvínov	1.00
☐	9 Roman Meluzin, ZPS Zlín	1.00
☐	10 Roman Simicek, Vítkovice	2.50
☐	11 Petr Ton, Kladno	1.00
☐	12 Viktor Ujcík, Slavia Praha	4.00
☐	13 Vladimír Hudacek, Karlovy Vary	.30
☐	14 Petr Pavlas, Karlovy Vary	.30
☐	15 Ales Tomasek, Karlovy Vary	.30
☐	16 Pavel Blaha, Karlovy Vary	.30
☐	17 Pavel Nohel, Karlovy Vary	.30
☐	18 Tomas Klimt, Karlovy Vary	.30
☐	19 Radek Prochazka, Karlovy Vary	.30
☐	20 Rostislav Haas, Opava	.30
☐	21 Karel Smíd, Opava	.30
☐	22 Milos Hrubes, Opava	.30
☐	23 Martin Maskarinec, Opava	.30
☐	24 Zbynek Marak, Opava	.30
☐	25 Michal Tomek, Opava	.30
☐	26 Juraj Jurik, Opava	.30
☐	27 Oldrich Svoboda, Ceske Budejovice	.30
☐	28 Rudolf Suchanek, Ceske Budejovice	.30
☐	29 Karel Soudek, Ceske Budejovice	.30
☐	30 Radek Martínek, Ceske Budejovice	.30
☐	31 Radek Toupal, Ceske Budejovice	.30
☐	32 Lubos Rob, Ceske Budejovice	.30
☐	33 Pavel Pycha, Ceske Budejovice	.30
☐	34 Marek Novotny, Dukla Jihlava	.30
☐	35 Michael Vyhlídal, Dukla Jihlava	.30
☐	36 Petr Vlk, Dukla Jihlava	.30
☐	37 Roman Mejzlik, Dukla Jihlava	.30
☐	38 Jiri Cihlar, Dukla Jihlava	.30
☐	39 Jaroslav Hub, Dukla Jihlava	.30
☐	40 Marek Melenovsky, Dukla Jihlava	.30
☐	41 Zdenek Orct, Chemopetrol Litvínov	.30
☐	42 Angel Nikolov, Chemopetrol Litvínov	.30
☐	43 Frantisek Prochazka, Chemopetrol Litvínov	.30
☐	44 Martin Stepanek, Chemopetrol Litvínov	.30
☐	45 Tomas Vlasak, Chemopetrol Litvínov	.30
☐	46 Martin Rousek, Chemopetrol Litvínov	.30
☐	47 Petr Hrbek, Chemopetrol Litvínov	.30
☐	48 Ivo Prorok, Chemopetrol Litvínov	.30
☐	49 Dusan Salficky, Interconex Plzen	.30
☐	50 Josef Reznícek, Interconex Plzen	.30
☐	51 Ivan Vlcek, Interconex Plzen	.30
☐	52 Robert Jindrich, Interconex Plzen	.30
☐	53 Pavel Geffert, Interconex Plzen	.30
☐	54 Tomas Jelínek, Interconex Plzen	.30
☐	55 David Pospísil, Interconex Plzen	.30
☐	56 Milan Volak, Interconex Plzen	.30
☐	57 Antonín Stavjana, Dadak Vsetín	.30
☐	58 Radim Tesarík, Dadak Vsetín	.30
☐	59 Alexei Jaskin, Dadak Vsetín	.30
☐	60 Tomas Srsen, Dadak Vsetín	.30
☐	61 Tomas Kapusta, Dadak Vsetín	.30
☐	62 Radek Belohlav, Dadak Vsetín	.30
☐	63 Ondrej Kratena, Dadak Vsetín	.30
☐	64 Jan Tomajko, Dadak Vsetín	.30
☐	65 Michal Bros, Dadak Vsetín	.30
☐	66 Rostislav Vlach, Dadak Vsetín	.30
☐	67 Libor Barta, Pardubice	.30
☐	68 Pavel Augusta, Pardubice	.30
☐	69 Tomas Blazek, Pardubice	.30
☐	70 Milan Hejduk, Pardubice	15.00
☐	71 Stanislav Prochazka, Pardubice	.30
☐	72 Tomas Martinec, Pardubice	.30
☐	73 Jaroslav Kudrna, Pardubice	.30
☐	74 Ladislav Blazek, Slavia Praha	.30
☐	75 Martin Bakula, Slavia Praha	.30
☐	76 Vladimír Ruzicka, Slavia Praha	.50
☐	77 Jirí Dolezal, Slavia Praha	.30
☐	78 Jirí Poukar, Slavia Praha	.30
☐	79 Tomas Kucharcík, Slavia Praha	.30
☐	80 Frantisek Kucera, Sparta Praha	.30
☐	81 Vaclav Burda, Sparta Praha	.30
☐	82 Jaroslav Nedved, Sparta Praha	.30
☐	83 Richard Zemlicka, Sparta Praha	.30
☐	84 Jirí Zelenka, Sparta Praha	.30
☐	85 Patrik Martinec, Sparta Praha	.30
☐	86 Jan Hlavac, Sparta Praha	.50
☐	87 Patrik Stefan, Sparta Praha	5.00
☐	88 Jaroslav Bednar, Sparta Praha	.50
☐	89 Radek Tóth, Kladno	.30
☐	90 Jan Krulis, Kladno	.30
☐	91 Pavel Skrbek, Kladno	.30
☐	92 Josef Zajic, Kladno	.30
☐	93 Zdenek Eichenmann, Kladno	.30
☐	94 Ladislav Svoboda, Kladno	.30
☐	95 Martin Prusek, Vítkovice	5.00
☐	96 Jiri Jonak, Vítkovice	.30
☐	97 Vitezslav Skuta, Vítkovice	.30
☐	98 Dmitri Jerofejev, Vítkovice	.30
☐	99 Roman Rysanek, Vítkovice	.30
☐	100 David Moravec, Vítkovice	.30
☐	101 Alexander Prokopjev, Vítkovice	.30
☐	102 Jaroslav Kames, ZPS Zlín	.30
☐	103 Pavel Kowalczyk, ZPS Zlín	.30
☐	104 Petr Kuchyna, ZPS Zlín	.30
☐	105 Ales Zima, ZPS Zlín	.30
☐	106 Pavel Janku, ZPS Zlín	.30
☐	107 Tomas Nemcicky, ZPS Zlín	.30
☐	108 Petr Cajanek, ZPS Zlín	.30
☐	109 Branislav Janos, ZPS Zlín	.30
☐	110 Radovan Biegl, Trinec	.30
☐	111 Richard Kral, Trinec	.30
☐	112 Roman Kontsek, Trinec	.30
☐	113 Jozef Dano, Trinec	.30
☐	114 Ladislav Lubina, Trinec	.30
☐	115 Tomas Chlubna, Trinec	.30
☐	116 Josef Straub, Trinec	.30
☐	117 Roman Kadera, Trinec	.30
☐	118 Marek Zadina, Trinec	.30
☐	119 Checklist	.30
☐	120 Premium	.30

1997 - 98 DS STICKERS

NHL stars sometimes sell at a premium (usually $1-2). We do not have a complete checklist for this series. Any information that collectors can provide would be greatly appreciated.

	Player	**DS**
☐	1 HC Petra Vsetin Team Photo, Vsetin	
☐	2 HC Petra Vsetin Team Photo, Vsetin	

☐ 3 HC Petra Vsetin Team Photo, Vsetin
☐ 4 HC Petra Vsetin Team Photo, Vsetin
☐ 5 HC Petra Vsetin Team Photo, Vsetin
☐ 6 HC Petra Vsetin Team Photo, Vsetin
☐ 7 Bedrich Scerban
☐ 8 Roman Cechmanek
☐ 9
☐ 10 Antonin Stavjana
☐ 11 Milan Nedoma
☐ 12 Jiri Vykoukal
☐ 13
☐ 14 Martin Stepanek
☐ 15 Vitezslav Skuta
☐ 16 Jiri Zelenka
☐ 17 Robert Lang
☐ 18 Ondrej Kratena
☐ 19 Viktor Ujcik
☐ 20
☐ 21
☐ 22
☐ 23
☐ 24 Karlovy Vary Logo, Karlovy Vary
☐ 25 Karlovy Vary Photo, Karlovy Vary
☐ 26 Karlovy Vary Photo, Karlovy Vary
☐ 27 Vladimir Hudacek, Karlovy Vary
☐ 28 Robert Horyna, Karlovy Vary
☐ 29 Petr Pavlas, Karlovy Vary
☐ 30 Ales Tomasek, Karlovy Vary
☐ 31 Pavel Blaha, Karlovy Vary
☐ 32 Jiri Polak, Karlovy Vary
☐ 33 Martin Richter, Karlovy Vary
☐ 34 Marek Cernosek, Karlovy Vary
☐ 35 Pavel Nohel, Karlovy Vary
☐ 36 Michal Cerny, Karlovy Vary
☐ 37 Tomas Klimt, Karlovy Vary
☐ 38 Ondrej Steiner, Karlovy Vary
☐ 39 Zbynek Kukacka, Karlovy Vary
☐ 40 Martin Streit, Karlovy Vary
☐ 41 Radek Prochazka, Karlovy Vary
☐ 42 Radek Svoboda, Karlovy Vary
☐ 43 Jan Lipiansky, Karlovy Vary
☐ 44 Opava Logo, Opava
☐ 45 Opava Photo, Opava
☐ 46 Opava Photo, Opava
☐ 47 Rostislav Haas, Opava
☐ 48 Pavel Nestak, Opava
☐ 49 Martin Maskarinec, Opava
☐ 50 David Galvas, Opava
☐ 51 Milos Hrubes, Opava
☐ 52 Karel Smid, Opava
☐ 53 Tomas Kramny, Opava
☐ 54 Pavel Marecek, Opava
☐ 55 Zbynek Marak, Opava
☐ 56 Michal Tomek, Opava
☐ 57 Juraj Jurik, Opava
☐ 58 Michal Piskor, Opava
☐ 59 Karel Horny, Opava
☐ 60 Pavel Sebesta, Opava
☐ 61 Martin Sychra, Opava
☐ 62 Zdenek Pavelek, Opava
☐ 63 Milan Kubis, Opava
☐ 64 Ceske Budejovice Logo, Ceske Budejovice
☐ 65 Ceske Budejovice Photo, Ceske Budejovice
☐ 66 Ceske Budejovice Photo, Ceske Budejovice
☐ 67 Oldrich Svoboda, Ceske Budejovice
☐ 68 Rudolf Suchanek, Ceske Budejovice
☐ 69 Karel Soudek, Ceske Budejovice
☐ 70 Milan Nedoma, Ceske Budejovice
☐ 71 Radek Martinek, Ceske Budejovice
☐ 72 Jan Bohacek, Ceske Budejovice
☐ 73 Kamil Toupal, Ceske Budejovice
☐ 74 Radek Toupal, Ceske Budejovice
☐ 75 Lubos Rob, Ceske Budejovice
☐ 76 Pavel Pycha, Ceske Budejovice
☐ 77 Filip Turek, Ceske Budejovice
☐ 78 David Bruk, Ceske Budejovice
☐ 79 Ondrej Vosta, Ceske Budejovice
☐ 80 Arpad Györi, Ceske Budejovice
☐ 81 Miroslav Barus, Ceske Budejovice
☐ 82 Petr Sailer, Ceske Budejovice
☐ 83 Petr Sachl, Ceske Budejovice
☐ 84 Litvinov Logo, Litvinov
☐ 85 Litvinov Photo, Litvinov
☐ 86 Litvinov Photo, Litvinov
☐ 87 Zdenek Orct, Litvinov
☐ 88 Richard Hrazdira, Litvinov
☐ 89 Frantisek Prochazka, Litvinov
☐ 90 Angel Nikolov, Litvinov
☐ 91 Martin Stepanek, Litvinov
☐ 92 Roman Cech, Litvinov
☐ 93 Radek Mrazek, Litvinov
☐ 94 Robert Kysela, Litvinov
☐ 95 Tomas Vlasak, Litvinov
☐ 96 Martin Rousek, Litvinov
☐ 97 Petr Hrbek, Litvinov
☐ 98 Vladimir Petrovka, Litvinov
☐ 99 Ivo Prorok, Litvinov
☐ 100 Denis Afinogenov, Litvinov
☐ 101 Rail Muftijev, Litvinov
☐ 102 Dmitri Denisov, Litvinov
☐ 103 Kamil Piros, Litvinov
☐ 104 Jihlava Logo, Jihlava
☐ 105 Jihlava Photo, Jihlava
☐ 106 Jihlava Photo, Jihlava
☐ 107 Marek Novotny, Jihlava
☐ 108 Lukas Sablik, Jihlava
☐ 109 Michael Vyhlidal, Jihlava
☐ 110 Miroslav Javin, Jihlava
☐ 111 Martin Tupa, Jihlava
☐ 112 Marian Morava, Jihlava
☐ 113 Tomas Jakes, Jihlava
☐ 114 Miroslav Duben, Jihlava
☐ 115 Petr Vik, Jihlava
☐ 116 Roman Mejzlik, Jihlava
☐ 117 Jiri Cihlar, Jihlava
☐ 118 Jaroslav Hub, Jihlava
☐ 119 Leos Pipa, Jihlava
☐ 120 Ladislav Prokupek, Jihlava
☐ 121 Marek Melenovsky, Jihlava
☐ 122 Milan Antos, Jihlava
☐ 123 Miroslav Stavjana, Jihlava
☐ 124 Pardubice Logo, Pardubice
☐ 125 Pardubice Photo, Pardubice
☐ 126 Pardubice Photo, Pardubice
☐ 127 Libor Barta, Pardubice
☐ 128 Adam Svoboda, Pardubice
☐ 129 Michal Sykora, Pardubice
☐ 130 Pavel Augusta, Pardubice
☐ 131 Tomas Pascal, Pardubice
☐ 132 Ales Pisa, Pardubice
☐ 133 Petr Mudroch, Pardubice
☐ 134 Alexander Tsyplakov, Pardubice
☐ 135 Jiri Malinsky, Pardubice
☐ 136 Milan Hejduk, Pardubice
☐ 137 Tomas Blazek, Pardubice
☐ 138 Jaroslav Kudrna, Pardubice
☐ 139 Tomas Maskarinec, Pardubice
☐ 140 Stanislav Prochazka, Pardubice
☐ 141 Jiri Jantovsky, Pardubice
☐ 142 Pavel Kabrt, Pardubice
☐ 143 Martin Koudelka, Pardubice
☐ 144 Plzen Logo, Plzen
☐ 145 Plzen Photo, Plzen
☐ 146 Plzen Photo, Plzen
☐ 147 Dusan Marik, Plzen
☐ 148 Michal Marik, Plzen
☐ 149 Josef Reznicek, Plzen
☐ 150 Ivan Vlcek, Plzen
☐ 151 Robert Jindrich, Plzen
☐ 152 Martin Cech, Plzen
☐ 153 Jiri Hanzlik, Plzen
☐ 154 Pavel Srek, Plzen
☐ 155 Tomas Jelinek, Plzen
☐ 156 Pavel Geffert, Plzen
☐ 157 David Pospisil, Plzen
☐ 158 Martin Filip, Plzen
☐ 159 Milan Volak, Plzen
☐ 160 Michal Straka, Plzen
☐ 161 Milan Navratil, Plzen
☐ 162 Mojmir Musil, Plzen
☐ 163 Pavel Vostraka, Plzen
☐ 164 Vsetin Logo, Vsetin
☐ 165 Vsetin Photo, Vsetin
☐ 166 Vsetin Photo, Vsetin
☐ 167 Roman Cechmanek, Vsetin
☐ 168 Antonin Stavjana, Vsetin
☐ 169 Jan Srdinko, Vsetin
☐ 170 Radim Tesarik, Vsetin
☐ 171 Alexei Jaskin, Vsetin
☐ 172 Michal Divisek, Vsetin
☐ 173 Pavel Zubicek, Vsetin
☐ 174 Rostislav Vlach, Vsetin
☐ 175 Jiri Dopita, Vsetin
☐ 176 Tomas Srsen, Vsetin
☐ 177 Radek Belohlav, Vsetin
☐ 178 Tomas Kapusta, Vsetin
☐ 179 Ondrej Kratena, Vsetin
☐ 180 Michal Bros, Vsetin
☐ 181 Jan Tomajko, Vsetin
☐ 182 Andrei Galkin, Vsetin
☐ 183 Josef Beranek, Vsetin
☐ 184 Slavia Praha Logo, Slavia Praha
☐ 185 Slavia Praha Photo, Slavia Praha
☐ 186 Slavia Praha Photo, Slavia Praha
☐ 187 Ladislav Blazek, Slavia Praha
☐ 188 Martin Altrichter, Slavia Praha
☐ 189 Robert Kostka, Slavia Praha
☐ 190 Andrej Jakovenko, Slavia Praha
☐ 191 Pavel Kolarik, Slavia Praha
☐ 192 Martin Bakula, Slavia Praha
☐ 193 Petr Kadlec, Slavia Praha
☐ 194 Jan Hejda, Slavia Praha
☐ 195 Vladimir Ruzicka, Slavia Praha
☐ 196 Viktor Ujcik, Slavia Praha
☐ 197 Jiri Dolezal, Slavia Praha
☐ 198 Jiri Poukar, Slavia Praha
☐ 199 Tomas Kucharcik, Slavia Praha
☐ 200 Michal Sup, Slavia Praha
☐ 201 Jiri Hlinka, Slavia Praha
☐ 202 Tomas Kupka, Slavia Praha
☐ 203 Radek Matejovsky, Slavia Praha
☐ 204 Sparta Praha Logo, Sparta Praha
☐ 205 Sparta Praha Photo, Sparta Praha
☐ 206 Sparta Praha Photo, Sparta Praha
☐ 207 Milan Hnilicka, Sparta Praha
☐ 208 Martin Cinibulk, Sparta Praha
☐ 209 Jiri Vykoukal, Sparta Praha
☐ 210 Vaclav Burda, Sparta Praha
☐ 211 Frantisek Kucera, Sparta Praha
☐ 212 Jaroslav Nedved, Sparta Praha
☐ 213 Frantisek Ptacek, Sparta Praha
☐ 214 Richard Zemlicka, Sparta Praha
☐ 215 Jiri Zelenka, Sparta Praha
☐ 216 Patrik Martinec, Sparta Praha
☐ 217 Jaroslav Bednar, Sparta Praha
☐ 218 Jaromir Kverka, Sparta Praha
☐ 219 Jan Hlavac, Sparta Praha
☐ 220 Miroslav Hlinka, Sparta Praha
☐ 221 Jaroslav Hlinka, Sparta Praha
☐ 222 Patrik Stefan, Sparta Praha
☐ 223 Petr Nedved, Sparta Praha
☐ 224 Kladno Logo, Kladno
☐ 225 Kladno Photo, Kladno
☐ 226 Kladno Photo, Kladno
☐ 227 Radek Toth, Kladno
☐ 228 Martin Bilek, Kladno
☐ 229 Jan Krulis, Kladno
☐ 230 Marek Zidlicky, Kladno
☐ 231 Tomas Kaberle, Kladno
☐ 232 Pavel Skrbek, Kladno
☐ 233 Jan Penk, Kladno
☐ 234 Jan Dlouhy, Kladno
☐ 235 Josef Zajic, Kladno
☐ 236 Zdenek Eichenmann, Kladno
☐ 237 Petr Ton, Kladno
☐ 238 Jiri Beranek, Kladno
☐ 239 Tomas Mikolasek, Kladno
☐ 240 Ladislav Svoboda, Kladno
☐ 241 Vaclav Eiselt, Kladno
☐ 242 Jiri Burger, Kladno
☐ 243 Petr Tenkrat, Kladno
☐ 244 Vitkovice Logo, Vitkovice
☐ 245 Vitkovice Photo, Vitkovice
☐ 246 Vitkovice Photo, Vitkovice
☐ 247 Martin Prusek, Vitkovice
☐ 248 Zdenek Dobes, Vitkovice
☐ 249 Vitezslav Skuta, Vitkovice
☐ 250 Pavel Kumstat, Vitkovice
☐ 251 Jiri Jonak, Vitkovice
☐ 252 Rene Sevecek, Vitkovice
☐ 253 Dmitri Jerofejev, Vitkovice
☐ 254 Petr Jurecka, Vitkovice
☐ 255 Roman Simicek, Vitkovice
☐ 256 Roman Rysanek, Vitkovice
☐ 257 David Moravec, Vitkovice
☐ 258 Alexander Prokopjev, Vitkovice
☐ 259 Libor Polasek, Vitkovice
☐ 260 Martin Kotasek, Vitkovice
☐ 261 Alexander Cerbajev, Vitkovice
☐ 262 Libor Pavlis, Vitkovice
☐ 263 Petr Zajonc, Vitkovice
☐ 264 Trinec Logo, Trinec
☐ 265 Trinec Photo, Trinec
☐ 266 Trinec Photo, Trinec
☐ 267 Radovan Biegl, Trinec
☐ 268 Lubomir Sekeras, Trinec
☐ 269 Jiri Kuntos, Trinec
☐ 270 Stanislav Pavelec, Trinec
☐ 271 Patrik Hucko, Trinec
☐ 272 Petr Jancarik, Trinec
☐ 273 Robert Kantor, Trinec
☐ 274 Richard Kral, Trinec
☐ 275 Ladislav Lubina, Trinec
☐ 276 Tomas Chlubna, Trinec
☐ 277 Roman Kadera, Trinec
☐ 278 Josef Straub, Trinec
☐ 279 Jozef Dano, Trinec
☐ 280 Roman Kontsek, Trinec
☐ 281 Marek Zadina, Trinec
☐ 282 Petr Folta, Trinec
☐ 283 Jan Peterek, Trinec
☐ 284 Zlin Logo, Zlin
☐ 285 Zlin Photo, Zlin
☐ 286 Zlin Photo, Zlin
☐ 287 Jaroslav Kames, Zlin
☐ 288 Pavel Kowalczyk, Zlin
☐ 289 Jan Krajicek, Zlin
☐ 290 Petr Kuchyna, Zlin
☐ 291 Martin Hamrlik, Zlin
☐ 292 Pavel Rajnoha, Zlin
☐ 293 Jiri Marusak, Zlin
☐ 294 Roman Meluzin, Zlin
☐ 295 Pavel Janku, Zlin
☐ 296 Ales Zima, Zlin
☐ 297 Miroslav Okal, Zlin
☐ 298 Petr Cajanek, Zlin
☐ 299 Tomas Nemcicky, Zlin
☐ 300 Branislav Janos, Zlin
☐ 301 Ales Polcar, Zlin
☐ 302 Zdenek Sediak, Zlin
☐ 303 Petr Leska, Zlin

1997 - 98 ESSO OLYMPIC HEROES

One of six different 10-card packs was available each week for six weeks at Esso gas stations for only $2.99. An album and eight page dividers came with the first week's pack. There is both an English and French version available. Twenty Canadian players also signed 500 sheets each.

Page Size: 4 3/4" x 6 5/8"

	French	English
Complete Set (60 sheets):	**15.00**	**15.00**
Album:	**4.00**	**4.00**
Player	**French**	**English**
☐☐ 1 Table of Contents	.50	.50
☐☐ 2 Nagano Winter Games	.50	.50
☐☐ 3 CBC Olympic Schedule	.50	.50
☐☐ 4 Schedule	.50	.50
☐☐ 5 Canada	.50	.50
☐☐ 6 Eric Lindros, Canada	1.00	1.00
☐☐ 7 Joe Sakic, Canada	2.00	1.50
☐☐ 8 Trevor Linden, Canada	.50	.50
☐☐ 9 Paul Kariya, Canada	1.00	1.00
☐☐ 10 Brendan Shanahan, Canada	1.00	1.00
☐☐ 11 Rod Brind'Amour, Canada	.50	.50
☐☐ 12 Theoren Fleury, Canada	.50	.50
☐☐ 13 Éric Desjardins, Canada	.50	.50
☐☐ 14 Scott Niedermayer, Canada	.50	.50
☐☐ 15 Chris Pronger, Canada	.50	.50
☐☐ 16 Rob Blake, Canada	.50	.50
☐☐ 17 Patrick Roy, Canada	3.00	3.00
☐☐ 18 Curtis Joseph, Canada	1.00	1.00
☐☐ 19 Keith Primeau, Canada	.50	.50
☐☐ 20 Mark Messier, Canada	1.00	1.00
☐☐ 21 Adam Foote, Canada	.50	.50
☐☐ 22 U.S.A.	.50	.50
☐☐ 23 Keith Tkachuk, U.S.A.	.50	.50
☐☐ 24 Mike Modano, U.S.A.	1.00	1.00
☐☐ 25 John LeClair, U.S.A.	1.00	.50
☐☐ 26 Doug Weight, U.S.A.	.50	.50
☐☐ 27 Brett Hull, U.S.A.	1.00	1.00
☐☐ 28 Jeremy Roenick, U.S.A.	1.00	.50
☐☐ 29 Brian Leetch, U.S.A.	.50	.50
☐☐ 30 Chris Chelios, U.S.A.	.50	.50
☐☐ 31 Kevin Hatcher, U.S.A.	.50	.50
☐☐ 32 Derian Hatcher, U.S.A.	.50	.50
☐☐ 33 Mike Richter, U.S.A.	.50	.50
☐☐ 34 John Vanbiesbrouck (G), U.S.A.	.50	.50
☐☐ 35 Russia	.50	.50
☐☐ 36 Sergei Fedorov, Russia	1.00	1.00
☐☐ 37 Alexei Yashin, Russia	.50	.50
☐☐ 38 Pavel Bure, Russia	1.00	.50
☐☐ 39 Alexander Mogilny, Russia	.50	.50
☐☐ 40 Nikolai Khabibulin, Russia	.50	.50
☐☐ 41 Sweden	.50	.50
☐☐ 42 Mats Sundin, Sweden	1.00	1.00
☐☐ 43 Peter Forsberg, Sweden	1.00	1.00
☐☐ 44 Daniel Alfredsson, Sweden	.50	.50
☐☐ 45 Nicklas Lidström, Sweden	.50	.50
☐☐ 46 Kenny Jönsson, Sweden	.50	.50
☐☐ 47 Finland	.50	.50
☐☐ 48 Saku Koivu, Finland	1.00	.50
☐☐ 49 Esa Tikkanen, Finland	.50	.50
☐☐ 50 Teemu Selänne, Finland	1.00	.50
☐☐ 51 Czech Republic	.50	.50
☐☐ 52 Jaromir Jagr, Czech Republic	1.00	1.00
☐☐ 53 Roman Hamrlik, Czech Republic	.50	.50
☐☐ 54 Dominik Hasek, Czech Republic	1.00	1.00
☐☐ 55 Canada	.50	.50
☐☐ 56 Nancy Drolet, Canada	.50	.50

☐☐	57 Geraldine Heaney, Canada	.50	.50
☐☐	58 Hayley Wickenheiser, Canada	1.00	1.50
☐☐	59 Cassie Campbell, Canada	1.00	1.50
☐☐	60 Stacy Wilson, Canada	.50	.50

1997 - 98 ESSO OLYMPIC HEROES AUTOGRAPHED

Autograph Set (20 cards):

	Player	Autograph
☐	6 Eric Lindros, Canada ✍	100.00
☐	7 Joe Sakic, Canada ✍	175.00
☐	8 Trevor Linden, Canada ✍	30.00
☐	9 Paul Kariya, Canada ✍	150.00
☐	10 Brendan Shanahan, Canada ✍	100.00
☐	11 Rod Brind'Amour, Canada ✍	30.00
☐	12 Theoren Fleury, Canada ✍	50.00
☐	13 Éric Desjardins, Canada ✍	30.00
☐	14 Scott Niedermayer, Canada ✍	30.00
☐	15 Chris Pronger, Canada ✍	50.00
☐	16 Rob Blake, Canada ✍	50.00
☐	17 Patrick Roy, Canada ✍	375.00
☐	18 Curtis Joseph, Canada ✍	100.00
☐	19 Keith Primeau, Canada ✍	30.00
☐	21 Adam Foote, Canada ✍	30.00
☐	56 Nancy Drolet, Canada ✍	30.00
☐	57 Geraldine Heaney, Canada ✍	30.00
☐	58 Hayley Wickenheiser, Canada ✍	80.00
☐	59 Cassie Campbell, Canada ✍	80.00
☐	60 Stacy Wilson, Canada ✍	30.00

1997 - 98 EUROTEL

We do not have full information on the Czech and Slovak phonecard sets.

1997 - 98 GAME OF HER LIFE

This eight-card set features players from the 1998 Canadian Olympic team.

Complete Set (8 cards): 20.00

	Player	GoHL
☐	Cassie Campbell	6.00
☐	Angela James	3.00
☐	Luce Letendre	2.00
☐	Shannon Miller, Coach	2.00
☐	Manon Rhéaume (G)	9.00
☐	France St-Louis	2.00
☐	Vicky Sunohara	2.00
☐	Hayley Wickenheiser	6.00

1997 - 98 GENERAL MILLS

This nine-card multi-sport Olympic set features six hockey players. A complete 9-card set sells for $35.

	Player	GM
☐	Cassie Campbell	4.00
☐	Éric Desjardins	2.00
☐	Nancy Drolet	2.00
☐	Geraldine Heaney	2.00
☐	Brendan Shanahan	3.00
☐	Vicky Sunohara	2.00

1997- 98 HOCKEY-BOX

These cards are odd-shaped. We have no pricing information on this series.

Kuvasarjat-1	**Kuvasarjat-1**
☐ Aho	☐ Jan Caloun
☐ Högardh	☐ Kimmo Kapanen
☐ Kalle Koskinen	☐ Allan Measures
☐ Nieminen	☐ Semi Pekki
☐ Pasi Petriläinen	☐ Joel Salonen
☐ Suursoo	☐ Pekka Virta
☐ SaiPa	☐
Kuvasarjat-2	**Kuvasarjat-2**
☐ Ackerström	☐ Juha Hautamaa
☐ Jere Karalahti	☐ Niko Kapanen
☐ Joonas Jääskeläinen	☐ Alexei Kudashov
☐ Krykov	☐ Korhonen
☐ Ässät Pori	
☐ Alexander Matsijevski	☐ Vesa Salo
☐ Toni Koivunen	☐ Markus Ketterer
☐ Kuoppala	☐ Mika Kortelainen
☐ Miska Kangasniemi	☐ Tomi Kallio
☐ Raimo Helminen	☐ Juha Ikonen
☐ Aigars Cipruss	☐ Hassinen
Kuvasarjat-3	**Kuvasarjat-3**
☐ Kokko	☐ Mika Noronen
☐ Kai Rautio	☐ Svedberg
☐ Kiekko-Espoo Blues	
Kuvasarjat-4	**Kuvasarjat-4**
☐ Hascak	☐ Erik Kakko
☐ Patrik Juhlin	☐ Koivunen
☐ Lehtonen	☐ Toni Lydman
☐ Palo	☐ Pekka Poikolainen
☐ Määttänen	☐ Markkanen
Kuvasarjat-5	**Kuvasarjat-5**
☐ Tappara Tampere	
☐ Vesa Toskala	☐ Marko Tuomainen
☐ Håkan Åhlund	☐ Peter Ahola
☐ Alexander Barkov	☐ Mikko Haapakoski
☐ Jokke Heinänen	☐ Yuri Kuznetsov
☐ Sami Nuutinen	☐ Peietilä
☐ Christian Ruuttu	☐ Sami Simonen
☐ HPK Hämeenlinna	
☐ Antti Törmänen	☐ Tshervjakov
Kuvasarjat-6	**Kuvasarjat-6**
☐ Kautonen	☐ Otakar Janecky
☐ Sami Lehtonen	☐ Dale McTavish
☐ Tommi Miettinen	☐ Niko Mikkola
☐ Jarkko Nikander	☐ Marko Ojanen
☐ Andrei Potaichuk	☐ Jarkko Ruutu
☐ Jaakko Uhlbäck	☐ Varvio
☐ Ilves Tampere	
Kuvasarjat-7	**Kuvasarjat-7**
☐ Ville Hämäläinen	☐ Kercs
☐ Jari Levonen	☐ Sakari Lindfors
☐ Toni Mäkiaho	☐ Jukka Mattila
☐ Sakari Palsola	☐ Jermu Pisto
☐ Sergei Priakin	☐ Kimmo Rintanen
☐ Pasi Saarela	☐ Kevin Wortman
☐ Lukko Rauma	
Kuvasarjat-8	**Kuvasarjat-8**
☐ Johan Davidsson	☐ Nils Ekman
☐ Mikko Eloranta	☐ Waltteri Immonen
☐ Kauppila	☐ Mikko Myllykoski
☐ Norrena	☐ Pikkarainen
☐ Timo Salonen	☐ Simonton
☐ Jussi Tarvainen	☐ Vesa Viitakoski
Kuvasarjat-9	**Kuvasarjat-9**
☐ TPS Turku	
☐ Jan Alinic	☐ Bouchard
☐ Markku Hurme	☐ Timo Jutila
☐ Arto Kuki	☐ Leinonen
☐ Loney	☐ Rantanen
☐ Timo Saarikoski	☐ Ari Saarinen
☐ Kalle Sahlstedt	☐ Wahlsten
☐ KalPa Kuopio	
Kuvasarjat-10	**Kuvasarjat-10**
☐ Kim Ahlroos	☐ Kaminsky
☐ Lasse Jämsen	☐ Pasi Kuivalainen
☐ Tom Koivisto	☐ Peter Larsson
☐ Lasse Pirjetä	☐ Teemu Sillanpää
☐ Pasi Sormunen	☐ Tommi Sova
☐ Sundblad	☐ Kimmo Timonen
☐ HIFK Helsinki	
Kuvasarjat-11	**Kuvasarjat-11**
☐ Sami Ahlberg	☐ Alexander Andrijevski
☐ Kuzminski	☐ Jarmo Kuusisto
☐ Jan Latvala	☐ Kimmo Lecklin
☐ Tero Lehterä	☐ Jani Nikko
☐ Ari Santanen	☐ Ari Sulander
☐ Tiilikainen	☐ Juha Vuorivirta
☐ JyP HT Jyväskylä	
Kuvasarjat-12	**Kuvasarjat-12**
☐ Viacheslav Fandul	☐ Hannes Hyvönen
☐ Kauhanen	☐ Riku Kallioniemi
☐ Juha Järvenpää	☐ Mikko Konttila
☐ Petri Lätti	☐ Lasse Nieminen
☐ Brian Rafalski	☐ Ari-Pekka Siekkinen
☐ Mika Strömberg	☐ Antti Virtanen
☐ Jokerit Helsinki	

1997 - 98 KRAFT

Complete Set (58 cards / disks): 100.00

JELL-O JELLY POWDER / JUNIORS TO PROS OF CANADA

One of six different cards was found on specially-marked boxes of JELL-O Instant Pudding (4-serving size).

Complete Set (6 cards): 15.00

	Player	JELL-O
☐	Wayne Gretzky, NYRa.	8.00
☐	Paul Kariya,Anah.	2.00
☐	Eric Lindros, Phil.	2.00

☐	Mark Messier, Vanc.	2.00
☐	Patrick Roy (G), Colo.	6.00
☐	Joe Sakic, Colo.	3.00

JELL-O JELLY POWDER / JUNIORS TO PROS OF THE WORLD

One of six different cards was found on specially-marked boxes of JELL-O Jelly Powder (85g).

Complete Set (6 cards): 5.00

	Player	JELL-O
☐	Chris Chelios, Chic.	1.00
☐	Sergei Fedorov, Detr.	2.00
☐	Jaromir Jagr, Pitt.	2.00
☐	Saku Koivu, Mont.	1.00
☐	Zigmund Palffy, NYIs.	1.00
☐	Mats Sundin, Toro.	2.00

KRAFT DINNER / WORLD'S BEST PLAYERS

One of 26 different cards was found on the back of specially marked boxes of Kraft Dinner.

Complete Set (26 cards): 35.00

	Player	WBP
☐	Peter Bondra, Wash.	1.00
☐	Vincent Damphousse, Mont.	1.00
☐	Sergei Fedorov, Detr.	2.00
☐	Theoren Fleury, Calg.	1.00
☐	Peter Forsberg, Colo.	2.00
☐	Ron Francis, Pitt.	1.00
☐	Wayne Gretzky, NYRa.	8.00
☐	Brett Hull, SLou.	2.00
☐	Jaromir Jagr, Pitt.	2.00
☐	Paul Kariya,Anah.	2.00
☐	Saku Koivu, Mont.	1.00
☐	Uwe Krupp, Colo.	1.00
☐	John LeClair, Phil.	1.00
☐	Eric Lindros, Phil.	2.00
☐	Mark Messier, Vanc.	2.00
☐	Mike Modano, Dall.	2.00
☐	Adam Oates, Wash.	1.00
☐	Zigmund Palffy, NYIs.	1.00
☐	Mikael Renberg, Phil.	1.00
☐	Teemu Selänne, Anah.	1.00
☐	Jozef Stümpel, LosA.	1.00
☐	Mats Sundin, Toro.	2.00
☐	Keith Tkachuk, Phoe.	1.00
☐	Doug Weight, Edmo.	1.00
☐	Alexei Yashin, Otta.	1.00
☐	Steve Yzerman, Detr.	4.00

KRAFT DINNER / CASE CARDS

One of eight different cards was found in specially-marked 12-box cases of Kraft Dinner.

Complete Set (8 cards): 20.00

	Player	Case
☐	Vincent Damphousse, Mont.	3.00
☐	Theoren Fleury, Calg.	3.00
☐	Paul Kariya, Anah.	5.00
☐	Saku Koivu, Mont.	3.00
☐	Mark Messier, Vanc.	3.00
☐	Mats Sundin, Toro.	3.00
☐	Doug Weight, Edmo.	3.00
☐	Alexei Yashin, Otta.	3.00

PEANUT BUTTER / TEAM CANADA

A 12-disk set was available via a redemption offer.

Complete Set (12 disks): 40.00

	Canada	TC
☐	Rob Blake / Joe Nieuwendyk	3.00
☐	Raymond Bourque / Shayne Corson	3.00
☐	Rod Brind'Amour / Paul Kariya	3.00
☐	Martin Brodeur (G) / Joe Sakic	6.00
☐	Marc Crawford / Eric Lindros	3.00
☐	Éric Desjardins / Adam Foote	3.00
☐	Theoren Fleury / Al MacInnis	3.00
☐	Wayne Gretzky / Brendan Shanahan	8.00
☐	Curtis Joseph (G) / Patrick Roy (G)	6.00
☐	Trevor Linden / Keith Primeau	3.00
☐	Chris Pronger / Steve Yzerman	4.00
☐	Scott Stevens / Rob Zamuner	3.00

1997 - 98 LEAF

Each card has three versions in the regular packaging: the regular card, a coloured parallel (Bronze, Silver or Gold) and a coloured die-cut parallel (X-Axis, Y-Axis or Z-Axis). Cards 148-197 in the regular series are short printed.

Bronze cards are limited to 1,800 copies: 73 players are bronze-X (1,400 uncut, 400 die-cut), 20 players are bronze-Y (1,600, 200) and 5 players are bronze-Z (1,700, 100).

Silver cards are limited to 900 copies: 19 players are silver-X (500, 400), 33 players are silver-Y (700, 200) and 11 players are silver-Z (800, 100).

Gold cards are limited to 450 copies: 4 players are gold-X (50, 400), 25 players are gold-Y (250, 200) and 10 players are gold-Z (350, 100).

Two additional parallels for cards 1-147 and 198-200 are found in Leaf International: a regular card and a Universal Ice parallel (250 copies). Cards 198-200 are renumbered 148-150 in this series.

		DC	FM	Leaf
	Leaf Set (200 cards):	2200.00	1300.00	120.00
	Common Player:	-	-	.20
	Player	**DC**	**FM**	**Leaf**
☐☐☐	1 Eric Lindros [GX]	20.00	80.00	1.00
☐☐☐	2 Dominik Hasek (G) [GZ]	60.00	25.00	1.00
☐☐☐	3 Peter Forsberg [GZ]	80.00	35.00	1.00
☐☐☐	4 Steve Yzerman [GZ]	150.00	60.00	2.00
☐☐☐	5 John Vanbiesbrouck (G) [GZ]	30.00	10.00	.20
☐☐☐	6 Paul Kariya [GX]	30.00	120.00	1.00
☐☐☐	7 Martin Brodeur (G) [GZ]	100.00	40.00	1.50
☐☐☐	8 Wayne Gretzky [GX]	90.00	350.00	4.00
☐☐☐	9 Mark Messier [GY]	40.00	35.00	1.00
☐☐☐	10 Jaromir Jagr [GZ]	60.00	20.00	1.00
☐☐☐	11 Brett Hull [GY]	40.00	35.00	1.00
☐☐☐	12 Brendan Shanahan [GZ]	60.00	25.00	1.00
☐☐☐	13 Raymond Bourque [GY]	50.00	45.00	1.00
☐☐☐	14 Jarome Iginla [GY]	35.00	30.00	.50
☐☐☐	15 Mike Modano [GY]	40.00	35.00	1.00
☐☐☐	16 Curtis Joseph (G) [GY]	40.00	35.00	1.00
☐☐☐	17 Ed Jovanovski [SX]	5.00	5.00	.20
☐☐☐	18 Teemu Selänne [GZ]	50.00	20.00	.50
☐☐☐	19 Saku Koivu [GY]	35.00	30.00	.50
☐☐☐	20 Éric Fichaud (G) [SZ]	10.00	2.00	.20
☐☐☐	21 Paul Coffey [SX]	10.00	10.00	.50
☐☐☐	22 Jeremy Roenick [SX]	15.00	15.00	.50
☐☐☐	23 Owen Nolan [BX]	10.00	5.00	.50
☐☐☐	24 Félix Potvin (G) [GY]	25.00	20.00	.50
☐☐☐	25 Alexander Mogilny [SZ]	30.00	5.00	.20
☐☐☐	26 Alexandre Daigle [SX]	4.00	2.00	.20
☐☐☐	27 Chris Gratton [SX]	5.00	2.00	.20
☐☐☐	28 Geoff Sanderson [SX]	5.00	2.00	.20
☐☐☐	29 Dimitri Khristich [SX]	4.00	2.00	.20
☐☐☐	30 Bryan Berard [GY]	10.00	10.00	.20
☐☐☐	31 Vyacheslav Kozlov [BX]	5.00	1.00	.20
☐☐☐	32 Jeff Hackett (G) [BY]	10.00	1.00	.20
☐☐☐	33 Bill Ranford (G) [BY]	15.00	1.00	.20
☐☐☐	34 Pat LaFontaine [SY]	25.00	5.00	.50
☐☐☐	35 Joe Sakic [GY]	70.00	60.00	1.50
☐☐☐	36 Niklas Sundström [BX]	5.00	1.00	.20
☐☐☐	37 Martin Gelinas [BX]	5.00	1.00	.20
☐☐☐	38 Mikael Renberg [BX]	5.00	1.00	.20
☐☐☐	39 Trevor Linden [BX]	5.00	5.00	.20
☐☐☐	40 Jozef Stumpel [BY]	10.00	1.00	.20
☐☐☐	41 CL: Joe Thornton [SZ]	75.00	15.00	2.00
☐☐☐	42 Jocelyn Thibault (G) [GY]	15.00	15.00	.20
☐☐☐	43 Pierre Turgeon [BX]	5.00	5.00	.20
☐☐☐	44 Ron Francis [BX]	10.00	5.00	.50
☐☐☐	45 Damian Rhodes (G) [SY]	10.00	2.00	.20
☐☐☐	46 Jamie Langenbrunner [SY]	10.00	2.00	.20
☐☐☐	47 Chris Osgood (G) [SZ]	35.00	5.00	.50
☐☐☐	48 Vaclav Varada [SY]	5.00	2.00	.20
☐☐☐	49 Ryan Smyth [GZ]	30.00	10.00	.20
☐☐☐	50 Daren Puppa (G) [BX]	5.00	1.00	.20

51 Petr Nedved [BX]	5.00	1.00	.20
52 Ron Hextall (G) [BX]	10.00	5.00	.50
53 Joé Juneau [BX]	5.00	1.00	.20
54 Jim Campbell [SY]	5.00	2.00	.20
55 Zigmund Palffy [SZ]	35.00	5.00	.50
56 Roman Turek (G) [BX]	10.00	5.00	.20
57 Adam Deadmarsh [GY]	10.00	10.00	.20
58 Rob Niedermayer [BX]	5.00	1.00	.20
59 Alexei Yashin [GY]	25.00	20.00	.50
60 Pavel Bure [GY]	30.00	30.00	.50
61 Jason Arnott [GY]	20.00	15.00	.20
62 N. Khabibulin (G) [SY]	15.00	5.00	.20
63 Sean Burke (G) [SY]	25.00	5.00	.50
64 Chris Chelios [SX]	10.00	10.00	.50
65 Mike Ricci [BX]	5.00	1.00	.20
66 Sergei Berezin [SY]	10.00	2.00	.20
67 Jaroslav Svejkovsky [GY]	5.00	5.00	.20
68 Brian Savage [BX]	5.00	1.00	.20
69 Roman Vopat [BX]	4.00	1.00	.20
70 Mike Richter (G) [SX]	10.00	5.00	.20
71 Jim Carey (G) [SY]	5.00	2.00	.20
72 Guy Hebert (G) [BY]	10.00	1.00	.20
73 Keith Tkachuk [GY]	25.00	20.00	.50
74 Kirk McLean (G) [BX]	5.00	1.00	.20
75 Janne Niinimaa [SY]	10.00	2.00	.20
76 Roman Hamrlik [SY]	10.00	2.00	.20
77 Darcy Tucker [SY]	10.00	2.00	.20
78 Pat Verbeek [BX]	5.00	1.00	.20
79 Hnat Domenichelli [BX]	4.00	1.00	.20
80 Doug Gilmour [SY]	25.00	5.00	.50
81 Mike Grier [GY]	10.00	5.00	.20
82 Ken Wregget (G) [BX]	5.00	1.00	.20
83 Dino Ciccarelli [BX]	5.00	1.00	.20
84 Steve Sullivan [BX]	5.00	1.00	.20
85 Anson Carter [SX]	5.00	5.00	.20
86 S. Shields (G) [BY] RC	**20.00**	**5.00**	**1.00**
87 Ed Belfour (G) [SY]	40.00	15.00	1.00
88 Darren McCarty [BX]	5.00	1.00	.20
89 Adam Graves [BX]	5.00	5.00	.20
90 Chris Pronger [BX]	10.00	5.00	.50
91 Peter Bondra [SY]	25.00	5.00	.50
92 Oleg Tverdovsky [SY]	5.00	2.00	.20
93 Stéphane Fiset (G) [BX]	5.00	1.00	.20
94 Mike Vernon (G) [BY]	15.00	1.00	.20
95 Scott Lachance [BX]	4.00	1.00	.20
96 Corey Schwab (G) [BX]	4.00	1.00	.20
97 Eric Dazé [BY]	15.00	1.00	.20
98 Jere Lehtinen [BX]	5.00	1.00	.20
99 Donald Audette [BX]	5.00	5.00	.20
100 John LeClair [GY]	35.00	30.00	.50
101 Steve Rucchin [BX]	5.00	1.00	.20
102 Jeff Friesen [SX]	5.00	5.00	.20
103 Daymond Langkow [SX]	5.00	2.00	.20
104 Mike Dunham (G) [SY]	15.00	5.00	.20
105 CL: Marc Denis (G) [BZ]	30.00	1.00	.20
106 Andrew Cassels [BX]	5.00	1.00	.20
107 Michael Peca [BX]	5.00	5.00	.20
108 Joe Nieuwendyk [BX]	5.00	5.00	.20
109 V. Damphousse [BX]	10.00	5.00	.50
110 Scott Mellanby [BX]	5.00	1.00	.20
111 Patrick Lalime (G) [BX]	10.00	5.00	.50
112 Derek Plante [SY]	5.00	2.00	.20
113 Wade Redden [SY]	10.00	5.00	.20
114 Marcel Cousineau (G) [SY]	5.00	2.00	.20
115 Ray Sheppard [BX]	4.00	1.00	.20
116 Dave Andreychuk [BX]	5.00	1.00	.20
117 Brian Leetch [GY]	25.00	20.00	.50
118 Sandis Ozolinsh [BY]	10.00	1.00	.20
119 Keith Primeau [BX]	5.00	5.00	.20
120 Brian Holzinger [BX]	4.00	1.00	.20
121 Luc Robitaille [BX]	15.00	10.00	.50
122 José Théodore (G) [SX]	35.00	30.00	2.00
123 Grant Fuhr (G) [SY]	25.00	5.00	.50
124 Dainius Zubrus [GY]	10.00	5.00	.20
125 Rod Brind'Amour [BZ]	20.00	1.00	.20
126 Trevor Kidd (G) [SY]	10.00	5.00	.20
127 Mark Recchi [BX]	5.00	5.00	.20
128 Patrick Roy (G) [GY]	130.00	110.00	3.00
129 Kevin Hatcher [BX]	4.00	1.00	.20
130 Adam Oates [SY]	15.00	5.00	.20
131 Doug Weight [SX]	10.00	10.00	.50
132 V. Prospal [SX] RC	**10.00**	**10.00**	**1.50**
133 Harry York [SY]	5.00	2.00	.20
134 Todd Bertuzzi [BX]	25.00	15.00	1.00
135 Sergei Fedorov [GY]	40.00	35.00	1.00
136 Theoren Fleury [SX]	10.00	10.00	.50
137 Chad Kilger [BY]	10.00	1.00	.20
138 Jamie Storr (G) [SX]	5.00	2.00	.20
139 Tony Amonte [BY]	25.00	5.00	.50
140 Rem Murray [BY]	5.00	1.00	.20
141 Chris O'Sullivan [BX]	4.00	1.00	.20
142 Mats Sundin [SZ]	60.00	15.00	1.00
143 Ethan Moreau [SZ]	10.00	2.00	.20
144 Derian Hatcher [SY]	10.00	5.00	.20
145 Daniel Alfredsson [SY]	25.00	5.00	.50
146 Corey Hirsch (G) [BX]	4.00	1.00	.20
147 Landon Wilson [BX]	4.00	1.00	.20
148 Marc Denis (G) [GY]	20.00	15.00	3.50
149 Boyd Devereaux [BX]	5.00	1.00	1.50
150 Joe Thornton [GX]	25.00	100.00	9.00
151 Sergei Samsonov [GZ]	35.00	15.00	4.50
152 Alyn McCauley [SY]	10.00	10.00	2.00
153 Erik Rasmussen [SZ]	15.00	2.00	1.50
154 Patrick Marleau [SX]	10.00	5.00	3.50
155 Olli Jokinen [SY] RC	**25.00**	**10.00**	**7.00**
156 Chris Phillips [SZ]	15.00	2.00	1.50
157 Tomas Vokoun [SZ] RC	**30.00**	**5.00**	**5.00**
158 Chris Dingman [SZ] RC	**20.00**	**2.00**	**3.50**
159 Daniel Cleary [GY]	10.00	10.00	2.00
160 Juha Lind [BX] RC	**5.00**	**1.00**	**3.50**
161 J-Y Leroux [BY] RC	**5.00**	**1.00**	**2.00**
162 Brad Isbister [SY]	10.00	2.00	1.50
163 Vadim Sharifjanov [BX]	4.00	1.00	.50
164 Alexei Morozov [SX]	5.00	2.00	1.50
165 Vaclav Prospal [BX]	10.00	5.00	2.00
166 Vaclav Varada [BY]	5.00	1.00	1.00
167 Jaroslav Svejkovsky [BZ]	10.00	1.00	1.00
168 Eric Lindros [SY]	40.00	15.00	3.50
169 Dominik Hasek (G) [BY]	40.00	10.00	3.50
170 Peter Forsberg [BY]	60.00	15.00	5.00
171 Steve Yzerman [SY]	100.00	35.00	9.00
172 J. Vanbiesbrouck (G) [BX]	10.00	5.00	1.50
173 Paul Kariya [SY]	60.00	20.00	5.00
174 Martin Brodeur (G) [BZ]	100.00	15.00	6.00
175 Wayne Gretzky [SY]	170.00	60.00	15.00
176 Mark Messier [BX]	20.00	10.00	3.50
177 Jaromir Jagr [BZ]	60.00	10.00	3.50
178 Brett Hull [BX]	20.00	10.00	3.50
179 Brendan Shanahan [BY]	40.00	10.00	3.50
180 Jarome Iginla [BX]	15.00	10.00	3.00
181 Mike Modano [BX]	40.00	10.00	3.50
182 Teemu Selänne [BY]	30.00	5.00	3.00
183 Bryan Berard [BY]	10.00	1.00	1.00
184 Ryan Smyth [SY]	20.00	5.00	1.50
185 Keith Tkachuk [BX]	10.00	5.00	2.00
186 Dainius Zubrus [BX]	5.00	1.00	.50
187 Patrick Roy (G) [BX]	60.00	35.00	11.00
188 Trevor Linden [BX]	5.00	5.00	1.00
189 Trevor Linden [BX]	5.00	5.00	1.00
190 Trevor Linden [BX]	5.00	5.00	1.00
191 Trevor Linden [BX]	5.00	5.00	1.00
192 Trevor Linden [BX]	5.00	5.00	1.00
193 Trevor Linden [BX]	5.00	5.00	1.00
194 Trevor Linden [BX]	5.00	5.00	1.00
195 Trevor Linden [BX]	5.00	5.00	1.00
196 Trevor Linden [BX]	5.00	5.00	1.00
197 Trevor Linden [BX]	5.00	5.00	1.00
198 CL: Chris Phillips [BX]	4.00	1.00	.20
199 CL: Sergei Samsonov [BX]	5.00	1.00	.20
200 CL: Daniel Cleary [BX]	4.00	1.00	.20

BANNER SEASON

Insert Set (24 cards):	100.00
Insert (#/3,500)	BS
1 Paul Kariya, Anah.	10.00
2 Eric Lindros, Phil.	5.00
3 Wayne Gretzky, NYRa.	30.00
4 Jaromir Jagr, Pitt.	5.00
5 Steve Yzerman, Detr.	15.00
6 Brendan Shanahan, Detr.	5.00
7 John LeClair, Phil.	5.00
8 Teemu Selänne, Anah.	5.00
9 Mike Modano, Dall.	5.00
10 Ryan Smyth, Edmo.	3.00
11 Brett Hull, SLou.	5.00
12 Zigmund Palffy, NYIs.	3.00
13 Peter Forsberg, Colo.	10.00
14 Keith Tkachuk, Phoe.	3.00
15 Saku Koivu, Mont.	5.00
16 Sergei Fedorov, Detr.	5.00
17 Brian Leetch, NYRa.	3.00
18 Bryan Berard, NYIs.	3.00
19 Mats Sundin, Toro.	5.00
20 Jarome Iginla, Calg.	5.00
21 Sergei Berezin, Toro.	3.00
22 Dainius Zubrus, Phil.	3.00
23 Mike Grier, Edmo.	3.00
24 Joe Sakic, Colo.	10.00

FIRE ON ICE

Insert Set (16 cards):	300.00
Insert (#/1,000)	FOI
1 Wayne Gretzky, NYRa.	80.00
2 Eric Lindros, Phil.	20.00
3 Jaromir Jagr, Pitt.	20.00
4 Steve Yzerman, Detr.	40.00
5 Brendan Shanahan, Detr.	20.00
6 Mike Modano, Dall.	20.00
7 Joe Sakic, Colo.	30.00
8 Pavel Bure, Vanc.	15.00
9 Ryan Smyth, Edmo.	6.00
10 Teemu Selänne, Anah.	15.00
11 Mark Messier, Vanc.	20.00
12 Peter Forsberg, Colo.	25.00
13 Dainius Zubrus, Phil.	9.00
14 Joe Thornton, Bost.	20.00
15 Sergei Samsonov, Bost.	10.00
16 Paul Kariya, Anah.	20.00

LEAF COLLECTION

Insert Set (5 cards):	600.00
Insert	
Eric Lindros, Phil. ✂ Home Jersey	200.00
Eric Lindros, Phil. ✂ Away Jersey	200.00
Eric Lindros, Phil. ✂ Stick	125.00
Eric Lindros, Phil. ✂ Gloves	125.00
Eric Lindros, Phil. ✂ Stirrups	125.00

PIPE DREAMS

Promo versions exist for some, if not all, singles.

Insert Set (16 cards):	100.00
Insert (#/2500)	Insert
1 Dominik Hasek (G), Buff.	20.00
2 John Vanbiesbrouck (G), Flor.	6.00
3 Patrick Roy (G), Colo.	60.00
4 Curtis Joseph (G), Edmo.	20.00
5 Félix Potvin (G), Toro.	10.00
6 Martin Brodeur (G), NJer.	30.00
7 Guy Hebert (G), Anah.	6.00
8 Mike Richter (G), NYRa.	6.00
9 José Théodore (G), Mont.	30.00
10 Jim Carey (G), Bost.	6.00
11 Damian Rhodes (G), Otta.	6.00
12 Jocelyn Thibault (G), Mont.	6.00
13 Nikolai Khabibulin (G), Phoe.	6.00
14 Chris Osgood (G), Detr.	10.00
15 Éric Fichaud (G), NYIs.	6.00
16 Mike Dunham (G), NJer.	6.00

1997 - 98 LEAF INTERNATIONAL

There are two versions: the regular card and a Universal Ice parallel (#/250).

International Set (150 cards):	1200.00	50.00
Common Player:	4.00	.30
Player	UI250	Int.
1 Eric Lindros, Phil.	30.00	1.00
2 Dominik Hasek, Buff.	30.00	1.00
3 Peter Forsberg, Colo.	40.00	1.50
4 Steve Yzerman, Detr.	75.00	3.00
5 John Vanbiesbrouck, Flor.	15.00	.50
6 Paul Kariya, Anah.	40.00	1.50
7 Martin Brodeur, NJer.	50.00	2.00
8 Wayne Gretzky, NYRa.	125.00	5.00
9 Mark Messier, Vanc.	30.00	1.00
10 Jaromir Jagr, Pitt.	30.00	1.00
11 Brett Hull, SLou.	30.00	1.00
12 Brendan Shanahan, Detr.	30.00	1.00
13 Raymond Bourque, Bost.	35.00	1.50
14 Jarome Iginla, Calg.	25.00	1.00
15 Mike Modano, Dall.	30.00	1.00
16 Curtis Joseph, Edmo.	30.00	1.00
17 Ed Jovanovski, Flor.	10.00	.50
18 Teemu Selänne, Anah.	25.00	1.00
19 Saku Koivu, Mont.	25.00	1.00
20 Éric Fichaud, NYIs.	5.00	.30
21 Paul Coffey, Phil.	15.00	.50
22 Jeremy Roenick, Phoe.	25.00	1.00
23 Owen Nolan, SanJ.	15.00	.50
24 Félix Potvin, Toro.	15.00	.50
25 Alexander Mogilny, Vanc.	15.00	.50
26 Alexandre Daigle, Otta.	5.00	.30
27 Chris Gratton, Phil.	5.00	.30
28 Geoff Sanderson, Caro.	5.00	.30
29 Dmitri Khristich, Bost.	5.00	.30
30 Bryan Berard, NYIs.	10.00	.30
31 Vyacheslav (Slava) Kozlov, Detr.	5.00	.30
32 Jeff Hackett, Chic.	10.00	.30
33 Bill Ranford, Wash.	10.00	.50
34 Pat LaFontaine, NYRa.	15.00	.50
35 Joe Sakic, Colo.	50.00	2.00
36 Niklas Sundström, NYRa.	5.00	.30
37 Martin Gélinas, Vanc.	5.00	.30
38 Mikael Renberg, Tamp.	10.00	.30
39 Trevor Linden, Vanc.	10.00	.50
40 Jozef Stümpel, LosA.	5.00	.30
41 Joe Thornton, Bost.	35.00	3.00
42 Jocelyn Thibault, Mont.	10.00	.50
43 Pierre Turgeon, SLou.	10.00	.50
44 Ron Francis, Pitt.	15.00	.50
45 Damian Rhodes, Otta.	5.00	.30
46 Jamie Langenbrunner, Dall.	5.00	.30
47 Chris Osgood, Detr.	15.00	.50
48 Vaclav Varada, Buff.	5.00	.30
49 Ryan Smyth, Edmo.	15.00	.50
50 Daren Puppa, Tamp.	5.00	.30
51 Petr Nedved, Pitt.	10.00	.30
52 Ron Hextall, Phil.	15.00	.50
53 Joé Juneau, Wash.	5.00	.30
54 Jim Campbell, SLou.	4.00	.30
55 Zigmund Palffy, NYIs.	15.00	.50
56 Roman Turek, Dall.	15.00	.50
57 Adam Deadmarsh, Colo.	10.00	.30
58 Rob Niedermayer, Flor.	5.00	.30
59 Alexei Yashin, Otta.	15.00	.50
60 Pavel Bure, Vanc.	25.00	1.00
61 Jason Arnott, Edmo.	15.00	.50
62 Nikolai Khabibulin, Phoe.	10.00	.50
63 Sean Burke, Caro.	15.00	.50
64 Chris Chelios, Chic.	15.00	.50
65 Mike Ricci, Colo.	10.00	.30
66 Sergei Berezin, Toro.	5.00	.30
67 Jaroslav (Yogi) Svejkovsky, Wash.	5.00	.30
68 Brian Savage, Mont.	10.00	.30
69 Roman Vopat, LosA.	4.00	.30
70 Mike Richter, NYRa.	15.00	.50
71 Jim Carey, Bost.	5.00	.30
72 Guy Hebert, Anah.	5.00	.30
73 Keith Tkachuk, Phoe.	15.00	.50
74 Kirk McLean, Vanc.	10.00	.30
75 Janne Niinimaa, Phil.	5.00	.30
76 Roman Hamrlik, Tamp.	5.00	.30
77 Darcy Tucker, Mont.	5.00	.30
78 Pat Verbeek, Dall.	10.00	.30
79 Hnat Domenichelli, Calg.	5.00	.30
80 Doug Gilmour, NJer.	15.00	.50
81 Mike Grier, Edmo.	5.00	.30
82 Ken Wregget, Pitt.	5.00	.30
83 Dino Ciccarelli, Tamp.	10.00	.30
84 Steve Sullivan, Toro.	10.00	.30
85 Anson Carter, Bost.	10.00	.50
86 Steve Shields, Buff. RC	**15.00**	**1.50**
87 Ed Belfour, Dall.	30.00	1.00
88 Darren McCarty, Detr.	10.00	.30
89 Adam Graves, NYRa.	10.00	.50
90 Chris Pronger, SLou.	15.00	.50
91 Peter Bondra, Wash.	15.00	.50
92 Oleg Tverdovsky, Phoe.	5.00	.30
93 Stéphane Fiset, LosA.	10.00	.30
94 Mike Vernon, SanJ.	10.00	.50
95 Scott Lachance, NYIs.	5.00	.30
96 Corey Schwab, Tamp.	5.00	.30
97 Éric Dazé, Chic.	10.00	.50
98 Jere Lehtinen, Dall.	10.00	.30
99 Donald Audette, Buff.	10.00	.50
100 John LeClair, Phil.	25.00	1.00
101 Steve Rucchin, Anah.	5.00	.30
102 Jeff Friesen, SanJ.	10.00	.30
103 Daymond Langkow, Tamp.	5.00	.30
104 Mike Dunham, NJer.	10.00	.50
105 Marc Denis, Colo.	15.00	.50
106 Andrew Cassels, Calg.	5.00	.30
107 Michael Peca, Buff.	10.00	.50
108 Joe Nieuwendyk, Dall.	10.00	.50
109 Vincent Damphousse, Mont.	15.00	.50
110 Scott Mellanby, Flor.	5.00	.30
111 Patrick Lalime, Pitt.	15.00	.50

☐☐ 112 Derek Plante, Buff.	5.00	.30
☐☐ 113 Wade Redden, Otta.	10.00	.30
☐☐ 114 Marcel Cousineau, Toro.	4.00	.30
☐☐ 115 Ray Sheppard, Flor.	5.00	.30
☐☐ 116 Dave Andreychuk, NJer.	10.00	.30
☐☐ 117 Brian Leetch, NYRa.	15.00	.50
☐☐ 118 Sandis Ozolinsh, Colo.	5.00	.30
☐☐ 119 Keith Primeau, Caro.	10.00	.50
☐☐ 120 Brian Holzinger, Buff.	5.00	.30
☐☐ 121 Luc Robitaille, LosA.	25.00	1.00
☐☐ 122 José Théodore, Mont.	35.00	3.00
☐☐ 123 Grant Fuhr, SLou.	15.00	.50
☐☐ 124 Dainius Zubrus, Phil.	5.00	.30
☐☐ 125 Rod Brind'Amour, Phil.	10.00	.30
☐☐ 126 Trevor Kidd, Caro.	10.00	.30
☐☐ 127 Mark Recchi, Mont.	10.00	.50
☐☐ 128 Patrick Roy, Colo.	90.00	3.50
☐☐ 129 Kevin Hatcher, Pitt.	5.00	.30
☐☐ 130 Adam Oates, Wash.	10.00	.50
☐☐ 131 Doug Weight, Edmo.	15.00	.50
☐☐ **132 Vaclav Prospal, Phil. RC**	**20.00**	**2.00**
☐☐ 133 Harry York, SLou.	4.00	.30
☐☐ 134 Todd Bertuzzi, NYIs.	35.00	1.50
☐☐ 135 Sergei Fedorov, Detr.	30.00	1.00
☐☐ 136 Theoren Fleury, Calg.	15.00	.50
☐☐ 137 Chad Kilger, Phoe.	5.00	.30
☐☐ 138 Jamie Storr, LosA.	5.00	.30
☐☐ 139 Tony Amonte, Chic.	15.00	.50
☐☐ 140 Rem Murray, Edmo.	4.00	.30
☐☐ 141 Chris O'Sullivan, Calg.	4.00	.30
☐☐ 142 Mats Sundin, Toro.	30.00	1.00
☐☐ 143 Ethan Moreau, Chic.	5.00	.30
☐☐ 144 Derian Hatcher, Dall.	10.00	.30
☐☐ 145 Daniel Alfredsson, Otta.	15.00	.50
☐☐ 146 Corey Hirsch, Vanc.	5.00	.30
☐☐ 147 Landon Wilson, Bost.	5.00	.30
☐☐ 148 Chris Phillips, Otta.	5.00	.30
☐☐ 149 Sergei Samsonov, Bost.	10.00	.30
☐☐ 150 Dan Cleary, Chic.	5.00	.30

1997 - 98 LIMITED

There are two versions: the regular card and a Press Proof parallel (#/2000).

Complete Set (200 cards): 7400.00 1200.00

Players	LE	Ltd.
☐☐ 1 C: B. Shanahan / H. York	10.00	1.00
☐☐ 2 C: P. Forsberg / M. Knuble	15.00	1.50
☐☐ 3 C: K. McLean / C. Osgood (G)	5.00	1.00
☐☐ 4 S: Wayne Gretzky, NYRa.	800.00	160.00
☐☐ 5 D: J. Vanbiesbrouck (G) / E. Jovanovski	35.00	5.00
☐☐ 6 C: P. Coffey / D. Sydor	5.00	1.00
☐☐ 7 C: P. Bure / V. Bure	10.00	1.00
☐☐ 8 P: J. Jagr / S. Berezin	70.00	15.00
☐☐ 9 C: M. Sundin / S. Koivu	15.00	2.00
☐☐ 10 C: T. Kidd / C. Hirsch	3.00	.50
☐☐ 11 S: Teemu Selänne, Anah.	160.00	30.00
☐☐ 12 C: R. Bonk / Z. Palffy	5.00	1.00
☐☐ 13 D: M. Sundin / S. Berezin	50.00	5.00
☐☐ 14 C: B. Ranford / J. Carey	5.00	.50
☐☐ 15 C: C. Lemieux / J. LeClair	10.00	1.00
☐☐ 16 P: C. Chelios / J. Niinimaa	50.00	10.00
☐☐ 17 D: M. Knuble / K. Hodson	15.00	2.00
☐☐ 18 C: A. Graves / K. Jones	5.00	.50
☐☐ 19 C: M. Modano / T. Linden	10.00	1.50
☐☐ 20 S: Brett Hull, SLou.	200.00	40.00
☐☐ 21 C: K. Hatcher / D. Hatcher	3.00	.50
☐☐ 22 C: D. Andreychuk / D. Alfredsson	5.00	1.00
☐☐ 23 D: S. Shields / V. Varada	15.00	3.00
☐☐ 24 C: G. Courtnall / T. Fleury	5.00	.50
☐☐ 25 C: M. Messier / D. Ciccarelli	10.00	1.50
☐☐ 26 S: Ryan Smyth, Edmo.	90.00	15.00
☐☐ 27 D: J. Arnott / M. Grier	30.00	5.00
☐☐ 28 C: A. Moog / E. Belfour	10.00	1.50
☐☐ 29 P: F. Potvin / JS. Giguère	80.00	16.00
☐☐ 30 C: E. Lindros / T. Bertuzzi	20.00	2.50
☐☐ 31 C: D. Langkow / D. Roberts	3.00	.35
☐☐ 32 C: G. Fuhr / M. Richter	10.00	1.00
☐☐ 32 D: A. Oates / J. Svejkovsky	25.00	4.00
☐☐ 34 D: D. Tucker / S. Koivu	40.00	5.00
☐☐ 35 S: Paul Kariya, Anah.	280.00	50.00
☐☐ 36 C: B. Nicholls / J. Sakic	15.00	2.00
☐☐ 37 C: E. Jovanovski / D. Smith	5.00	.50
☐☐ 38 P: B. Shanahan / V. Prospal	80.00	16.00
☐☐ 39 C: M. Peca / M. Murray	5.00	.50
☐☐ 40 C: M. Gartner / W. Clark	15.00	2.00
☐☐ 41 S: Steve Yzerman, Detr.	480.00	90.00
☐☐ 42 D: M. Modano / R. Turek	60.00	10.00
☐☐ 43 C: J. Nieuwendyk / J. Iginla	10.00	1.50
☐☐ 44 C: P. Roy / J. Thibault	30.00	4.00
☐☐ 45 C: A. Cassels / H. Domenichelli	3.00	.50
☐☐ 46 C: S. Sullivan / C. Dubé	3.00	.50
☐☐ 47 D: V. Kamensky / M. Denis	35.00	5.00
☐☐ 48 S: Peter Forsberg, Colo.	280.00	50.00
☐☐ 49 C: T. Harvey / D. Plante	3.00	.50
☐☐ 50 P: E. Lindros / M. Grier	70.00	15.00
☐☐ 51 D: Br. Hull / J. Campbell	40.00	5.00
☐☐ 52 C: M. Recchi / L. Wilson	5.00	.50
☐☐ 53 C: D. Tucker / P. Rhéaume	3.00	.35
☐☐ 54 C: A. Eriksson / C. O'Sullivan	3.00	.35
☐☐ 55 S: Jaromir Jagr, Pitt.	200.00	40.00
☐☐ 56 D: T. Selänne / P. Kariya	90.00	15.00
☐☐ 57 C: D. Rhodes / F. Potvin	5.00	1.00
☐☐ 58 C: M. Ricci / B. Holzinger	3.00	.50
☐☐ 59 D: T. Green / É. Fichaud	15.00	3.00
☐☐ 60 C: J. MacLean / E. Moreau	3.00	.35
☐☐ 61 C: J. Juneau / J. O'Neill	5.00	.50
☐☐ 62 S: John Vanbiesbrouck (G), Flor.	90.00	15.00
☐☐ 63 C: S. Shields / B. Dafoe	5.00	.50
☐☐ 64 C: M. Renberg / N. Sundström	5.00	.50
☐☐ 65 C: R. Smyth / É. Dazé	5.00	1.00
☐☐ 66 D: D. Gilmour / P. Rhéaume	30.00	5.00
☐☐ 67 C: C. Janney / J. Campbell	3.00	.35
☐☐ 68 C: A. Mogilny / M. Barnaby	5.00	.50
☐☐ 69 S: Alexei Yashin, Otta.	120.00	20.00
☐☐ 70 P: B. Leetch / B. Berard	50.00	10.00
☐☐ 71 C: A. Yashin / B. Savage	5.00	1.00
☐☐ 72 C: D. McCarty / J. Friesen	5.00	.50
☐☐ 73 C: D. Khristich / C. Kilger	3.00	.50
☐☐ 74 D: D. Andreychuk / M. Brodeur	80.00	10.00
☐☐ 75 C: P. Verbeek / L. Robitaille	10.00	1.00
☐☐ 76 C: D. Hasek / J. Storr	10.00	1.50
☐☐ 77 S: Félix Potvin (G), Toro.	120.00	20.00
☐☐ 78 D: M. Dunham / V. Sharifijanov	20.00	2.00
☐☐ 79 C: R. Niedermayer / J. Arnott	5.00	.50
☐☐ 80 C: C. Phillips / É. Desjardins	5.00	.50
☐☐ 81 C: J. Théodore / Cu. Joseph	20.00	3.50
☐☐ 82 C: D. Gilmour / R. Brind'Amour	5.00	1.00
☐☐ 83 C: R. Tocchet / K. Tkachuk	5.00	1.00
☐☐ 84 S: Mark Messier, NYRa.	200.00	40.00
☐☐ 85 C: C. Pronger / A. Berg	5.00	.50
☐☐ 86 P: D. Hasek / M. Cousineau	60.00	12.00
☐☐ 87 D: C. Chelios / E. Moreau	30.00	5.00
☐☐ 88 C: R. Zamuner / J. Höglund	3.00	.50
☐☐ 89 C: R. Hextall / K. Hodson	5.00	1.00
☐☐ 90 S: John LeClair, Phil.	160.00	30.00
☐☐ 91 C: Vy. Kozlov / V. Prospal	5.00	.50
☐☐ 92 D: R. Bourque / J. Thornton	100.00	15.00
☐☐ 93 C: O. Tverdovsky / S. Zubov	3.00	.50
☐☐ 94 P: E. Moreau / J. LeClair	60.00	12.00
☐☐ 95 S: Adam Deadmarsh, Colo.	60.00	12.00
☐☐ 96 C: J. Svejkovsky / J. Stumpel	3.00	.50
☐☐ 97 D: W. Gretzky / V. Vorobiev	180.00	30.00
☐☐ 98 S: Sergei Fedorov, Detr.	200.00	40.00
☐☐ 99 P: R. Smyth / J. Campbell	35.00	6.00
☐☐ 100 D: P. Coffey / V. Prospal	40.00	5.00
☐☐ 101 C: W. Primeau / S. Pronger	3.00	.35
☐☐ 102 C: G. Hebert / JS. Giguère	10.00	1.00
☐☐ 103 S: Curtis Joseph (G), Edmo.	200.00	40.00
☐☐ 104 D: A. Mogilny / P. Bure	50.00	5.00
☐☐ 105 C: J. Roenick / T. Amonte	10.00	1.50
☐☐ 106 C: K. McLaren / S. Ozolinsh	3.00	.50
☐☐ 107 C: A. Carter / S. Kelly	5.00	.50
☐☐ 108 S: Paul Coffey, Phil.	120.00	20.00
☐☐ 109 P: P. Forsberg / D. Zubrus	100.00	20.00
☐☐ 110 C: S. Mellanby / T. Green	3.00	.50
☐☐ 111 C: P. LaFontaine / V. Kamensky	5.00	1.00
☐☐ 112 S: Adam Oates, Wash.	80.00	15.00
☐☐ 113 C: J. Vanbiesbrouck (G) / R. Turek	5.00	1.00
☐☐ 114 P: P. Kariya / J. Iginla	130.00	25.00
☐☐ 115 D: S. Yzmeran / C. Osgood (G)	130.00	20.00
☐☐ 116 D: S. Sullivan / M. Cousineau	15.00	3.00
☐☐ 117 C: S. Rucchin / O. Nolan	5.00	1.00
☐☐ 118 C: T. Donato / D. Audette	5.00	.50
☐☐ 119 D: G. Sanderson / S. Burke	35.00	6.00
☐☐ 120 S: Jeremy Roenick, Phoe.	160.00	30.00
☐☐ 121 C: A. Johansson / V. Vorobiev	3.00	.35
☐☐ 122 S: Alexander Mogilny, Vanc.	90.00	15.00
☐☐ 123 D: J. Thibault / T. Ryan	20.00	3.00
☐☐ 124 C: É. Fichaud / N. Khabibulin	5.00	.50
☐☐ 125 C: R. Bourque / É. Messier	10.00	1.50
☐☐ 126 C: S. Fedorov / K. Primeau	10.00	1.50
☐☐ 127 P: M. Brodeur / M. Denis	130.00	25.00
☐☐ 128 S: Mats Sundin, Toro.	200.00	40.00
☐☐ 129 C: P. Bondra / R. Vopat	5.00	.50
☐☐ 130 C: T. Salo / C. Schwab	5.00	.50
☐☐ 131 D: S. Samsonov / J. Carey	30.00	5.00
☐☐ 132 D: J. Sakic / A. Deadmarsh	80.00	10.00
☐☐ 133 P: K. Tkachuk / D. Langkow	50.00	10.00
☐☐ 134 S: Mike Richter (G), NYRa.	90.00	15.00
☐☐ 135 C: G. Sanderson / J. Lehtinen	5.00	.50
☐☐ 136 C: J. Pushor / J. Niinimaa	3.00	.35
☐☐ 137 C: V. Damphousse / A. Dackell	5.00	.50
☐☐ 138 S: Keith Tkachuk, Phoe.	120.00	20.00
☐☐ 139 S: Raymond Bourque, Bost.	240.00	40.00
☐☐ 140 D: K. Tkachuk / J. Roenick	60.00	10.00
☐☐ 141 C: R. Sheppard / R. Murray	3.00	.35
☐☐ 142 C: P. Schafer / P. Lalime	5.00	.50
☐☐ 143 P: T. Selänne / J. Svejkovsky	60.00	12.00
☐☐ 144 C: T. Granato / T. Marchant	3.00	.50
☐☐ 145 S: Sandis Ozolinsh, Colo.	45.00	12.00
☐☐ 146 C: N. Lidström / R. Hamrlik	5.00	1.00
☐☐ 147 S: Dominik Hasek (G), Buff.	200.00	40.00
☐☐ 148 C: C. Gratton / D. Goneau	3.00	.35
☐☐ 149 S: Martin Brodeur (G), NJer.	320.00	60.00
☐☐ 150 C: S. Fiset / M. Brodeur	15.00	2.00
☐☐ 151 P: P. Roy / J. Théodore	260.00	65.00
☐☐ 152 D: M. Recchi / J. Théodore	70.00	15.00
☐☐ 153 S: Pavel Bure, Vanc.	160.00	30.00
☐☐ 154 C: D. Pederson / S. Berezin	3.00	.35
☐☐ 155 S: Doug Gilmour, NJer.	120.00	20.00
☐☐ 156 C: P. Nedved / K. Muller	5.00	.50
☐☐ 157 S: Theoren Fleury, Calg.	120.00	20.00
☐☐ 158 D: H. York / P. Turgeon	20.00	2.00
☐☐ 159 D: A. Johansson / P. Lalime	35.00	6.00
☐☐ 160 C: J. Hackett / M. Cousineau	3.00	.50
☐☐ 161 C: A. Deadmarsh / A. Daigle	3.00	.50
☐☐ 162 C: A. Oates / T. Warriner	5.00	.50
☐☐ 163 S: Zigmund Palffy, NYIs.	120.00	20.00
☐☐ 164 S: Ed Belfour (G), Dall.	200.00	40.00
☐☐ 165 P: S. Yzerman / S. Koivu	200.00	40.00
☐☐ 166 C: C. Chelios / S. Lachance	5.00	.50
☐☐ 167 C: J. Langenbrunner / B. Convery	3.00	.35
☐☐ 168 D: J. LeClair / J. Niinimaa	40.00	5.00
☐☐ 169 S: Brendan Shanahan, Detr.	200.00	40.00
☐☐ 170 C: G. Snow / D. Puppa	5.00	.50
☐☐ 171 S: Chris Osgood (G), Detr.	120.00	20.00
☐☐ 172 C: P. Turgeon / S. Corson	5.00	.50
☐☐ 173 D: D. Weight / R. Murray	30.00	5.00
☐☐ 174 P: Cu. Joseph / É. Fichaud	70.00	14.00
☐☐ 175 S: Chris Chelios, Chic.	120.00	20.00
☐☐ 176 C: S. Stevens / W. Redden	5.00	.50
☐☐ 177 D: J. Iginla / T. Fleury	60.00	10.00
☐☐ 178 C: I. Larionov / V. Varada	5.00	.50
☐☐ 179 S: Brian Leetch, NYRa.	120.00	20.00
☐☐ 180 D: S. Fiset / R. Vopat	15.00	3.00
☐☐ 181 D: Z. Palffy / B. Berard	40.00	5.00
☐☐ 182 C: B. Leetch / B. Berard	5.00	1.00
☐☐ 183 S: Eric Lindros, Phil.	200.00	40.00
☐☐ 184 D: D. Plante / B. Holzinger	10.00	2.00
☐☐ 185 C: Br. Hull / M. Gélinas	10.00	1.50
☐☐ 186 D: D. Rhodes / D. Alfredsson	35.00	6.00
☐☐ 187 P: M. Messier / J. Thornton	130.00	25.00
☐☐ 188 C: M. Vernon / K. Wregget	5.00	.50
☐☐ 189 D: A. Yashin / W. Redden	40.00	5.00
☐☐ 190 S: Joe Sakic, Colo.	320.00	60.00
☐☐ 191 C: D. Weight / D. Turcotte	5.00	.50
☐☐ 192 D: D. Puppa / D. Langkow	20.00	3.00
☐☐ 193 S: Mike Modano, Dall.	200.00	40.00
☐☐ 194 C: S. Burke / M. Dunham	10.00	1.00
☐☐ 195 C: S. Bordeleau / D. Zubrus	3.00	.35
☐☐ 196 D: O. Nolan / J. Friesen	40.00	5.00
☐☐ 197 P: S. Fedorov / V. Vorobiev	60.00	12.00
☐☐ 198 S: Patrick Roy (G), Colo.	600.00	120.00
☐☐ 199 C: R. Francis / M. Grier	5.00	1.00
☐☐ 200 P: W. Gretzky / P. Marleau	280.00	70.00

FABRIC OF THE GAME

This 72-card set contains five levels of difficulty: Major Material (21 cards, sequentially numbered to 1,000), Star Material (18 cards, sequentially numbered to 750), Superstar Material (12 cards, sequentially numbered to 500), Hall of Fame material (12 cards, sequentially numbered to 250) and Legendary Material (9 cards, sequentially numbered to 100). Each level is divided into three subsets featuring a different fabric: Goals-Nylon, Wins-Canvas and Assists-Wood.

Insert Set (72 cards): 1600.00

Player	FotG
☐ 1 Wayne Gretzky, NYRa., Goals (#/250)	180.00
☐ 2 Martin Brodeur (G), NJer. (#/750)	40.00
☐ 3 Dainius Zubrus, Phil., Goals (#/1000)	4.00
☐ 4 Joe Sakic, Colo., Assists (#/500)	55.00
☐ 5 Joe Sakic, Colo., Goals (#/250)	70.00
☐ 6 Sergei Fedorov, Detr., Assists (#/750)	25.00
☐ 7 John Vanbiesbrouck (G), Flor. (#/250)	20.00
☐ 8 Saku Koivu, Mont., Assists (#/1000)	15.00
☐ 9 J.S. Giguère (G), Calg. (#/1000)	15.00
☐ 10 Paul Kariya, Anah., Goals (#/750)	30.00
☐ 11 Mike Richter (G), NYRa. (#/500)	15.00
☐ 12 Paul Coffey, Phil., Assists (#/100)	40.00
☐ 13 Brendan Shanahan, Detr., Goals (#/100)	75.00
☐ 14 Jaromir Jagr, Pitt., Assists (#/500)	35.00
☐ 15 Félix Potvin (G), Toro. (#/500)	20.00
☐ 16 Mats Sundin, Toro., Goals (#/500)	35.00
☐ 17 Mike Vernon (G), SanJ. (#/250)	15.00
☐ 18 Keith Tkachuk, Phoe., Goals (#/750)	15.00
☐ 19 Doug Gilmour, NJer., Assists (#/250)	25.00
☐ 20 Patrick Roy (G), Colo. (#/100)	225.00
☐ 21 Sergei Samsonov, Bost., Goals (#/1000)	10.00
☐ 22 Mike Grier, Edmo., Assists (#/1000)	4.00
☐ 23 Curtis Joseph (G), Edmo. (#/500)	35.00
☐ 24 Zigmund Palffy, NYIs., Goals (#/750)	15.00
☐ 25 Chris Osgood (G), Detr. (#/750)	15.00
☐ 26 Mats Sundin, Toro., Assists (#/750)	25.00
☐ 27 Kelly Hrudey (G), SanJ. (#/250)	10.00
☐ 28 Brett Hull, SLou., Assists (#/500)	75.00
☐ 29 Raymond Bourque, Bost., Assists (#/250)	50.00
☐ 30 Nikolai Khabibulin (G), Phoe. (#/750)	10.00
☐ 31 Bryan Berard, NYIs., Assists (#/1000)	5.00
☐ 32 Jaroslav Svejkovsky, Wash., Goals (#/1000)	4.00
☐ 33 Ed Belfour (G), Dall. (#/500)	35.00
☐ 34 Wayne Gretzky, NYRa., Assists (#/100)	325.00
☐ 35 Jeremy Roenick, Phoe., Goals (#/500)	25.00
☐ 36 Andy Moog (G), Mont. (#/100)	30.00
☐ 37 Eric Lindros, Phil., Goals (#/750)	20.00
☐ 38 Brett Hull, SLou., Goals (#/100)	35.00
☐ 39 Marcel Cousineau (G), Toro. (#/1000)	4.00
☐ 40 Paul Kariya, Anah., Assists (#/1000)	25.00
☐ 41 Mike Dunham (G), NJer. (#/1000)	5.00
☐ 42 Chris Phillips, Otta., Assists (#/1000)	4.00
☐ 43 Teemu Selänne, Anah., Goals (#/500)	25.00
☐ 44 Mark Messier, Vanc., Assists (#/100)	75.00
☐ 45 Grant Fuhr (G), SLou. (#/100)	25.00
☐ 46 Daniel Alfredsson, Otta., Goals (#/1000)	10.00
☐ 47 Marc Denis (G), Colo. (#/1000)	5.00
☐ 48 Daymond Langkow, Tamp., Goals (#/1000)	4.00
☐ 49 Steve Yzerman, Detr., Assists (#/250)	100.00
☐ 50 Ryan Smyth, Edmo., Goals (#/750)	10.00
☐ 51 Alexander Mogilny, Vanc., Goals (#/250)	20.00
☐ 52 Ron Hextall (G), Phil. (#/250)	25.00
☐ 53 Brendan Shanahan, Detr., Assists (#/750)	25.00
☐ 54 Jim Carey (G), Bost. (#/750)	5.00
☐ 55 Eric Lindros, Phil., Assists (#/750)	20.00
☐ 56 Éric Fichaud (G), NYIs. (#/1000)	4.00
☐ 57 Sergei Berezin, Toro., Goals (#/1000)	4.00
☐ 58 Chris Chelios, Chic., Assists (#/250)	25.00
☐ 59 Mark Messier, Vanc., Goals (#/250)	45.00
☐ 60 Damian Rhodes (G), Otta. (#/1000)	4.00
☐ 61 Jarome Iginla, Calg., Assists (#/1000)	15.00
☐ 62 Jocelyn Thibault (G), Mont. (#/750)	10.00
☐ 63 John LeClair, Phil., Goals (#/750)	20.00
☐ 64 Brian Leetch, NYRa., Assists (#/500)	20.00
☐ 65 Dominik Hasek (G), Buff. (#/750)	25.00
☐ 66 Pavel Bure, Vanc., Goals (#/500)	25.00
☐ 67 Mike Modano, Dall., Assists (#/750)	25.00
☐ 68 Daniel Cleary, Chic., Goals (#/1000)	10.00
☐ 69 Janne Niinimaa, Phil., Assists (#/1000)	4.00
☐ 70 Steve Yzerman, Detr., Goals (#/100)	175.00
☐ 71 José Théodore (G), Mont. (#/1000)	25.00
☐ 72 Peter Forsberg, Colo., Assists (#/750)	35.00

1997 - 98 MCDONALD'S

Cards McD23-McD32 are "Caged Ice" subsets and cards McD33-McD40 are "Ice Breakers" subsets. McDonald's was released in late December, 1997.

Complete Set (42 cards): 25.00

Player	McD
☐ McD1 Wayne Gretzky, NYRa.	5.00
☐ McD2 Theoren Fleury, Calg.	.50
☐ McD3 Pavel Bure, Vanc.	1.00
☐ McD4 Saku Koivu, Mont.	1.00
☐ McD5 Joe Sakic, Colo.	2.00
☐ McD6 Wade Redden, Otta.	.35
☐ McD7 Keith Tkachuk, Phoe.	.50
☐ McD8 Eric Lindros, Phil.	1.00
☐ McD9 Paul Kariya, Anah.	1.50
☐ McD10 Bryan Berard, NYIs.	.35

□	McD11 Teemu Selänne, Anah.	1.00
□	McD12 Jarome Iginla, Calg.	1.00
□	McD13 Mats Sundin, Toro.	1.00
□	McD14 Brendan Shanahan, Detr.	1.00
□	McD15 Peter Forsberg, Colo.	1.50
□	McD16 Brett Hull, SLou.	1.00
□	McD17 Raymond Bourque, Bost.	1.50
□	McD18 Doug Weight, Edmo.	.50
□	McD19 Steve Yzerman, Detr.	3.00
□	McD20 Jaromir Jagr, Pitt.	1.00
□	McD21 Vincent Damphousse, Mont.	.50
□	McD22 Trevor Linden, Vanc.	.50
□	McD23 Patrick Roy (G), Colo.	3.50
□	McD24 John Vanbiesbrouck (G), Flor.	.50
□	McD25 Martin Brodeur (G), NJer.	2.00
□	McD26 Dominik Hasek (G), Buff.	1.00
□	McD27 Curtis Joseph (G), Edmo.	1.00
□	McD28 Andy Moog (G), Mont.	.50
□	McD29 Mike Richter (G), NYRa.	.50
□	McD30 Damian Rhodes (G), Otta.	.35
□	McD31 Félix Potvin (G), Toro.	.50
□	McD32 Chris Osgood (G), Detr.	.50
□	McD33 Joe Thornton, Bost.	3.00
□	McD34 Patrick Marleau, SanJ.	1.00
□	McD35 Jaroslav Svejkovsky, Wash.	.35
□	McD36 Daniel Cleary, Chic.	.50
□	McD37 Chris Phillips, Otta.	.50
□	McD38 Alexei Morozov, Pitt.	.50
□	McD39 Vaclav Prospal, Phil.	.50
□	McD40 Sergei Samsonov, Bost.	1.50

GAME FILM

Insert Set (10 cards): 95.00

	Player	GF
□	F1 Wayne Gretzky, NYRa.	30.00
□	F2 Alexander Mogilny, Vanc.	3.00
□	F3 Steve Yzerman, Detr.	18.00
□	F4 Eric Lindros, Phil.	6.00
□	F5 Patrick Roy (G), Colo.	22.00
□	F6 Paul Kariya, Anah.	10.00
□	F7 Raymond Bourque, Bost.	8.00
□	F8 Saku Koivu, Mont.	6.00
□	F9 Theoren Fleury, Calg.	4.00
□	F10 Mats Sundin, Toro.	6.00
□	Wayne Gretzky Jersey ✂	

PRIZE INSERTS

	Player	GF
□	Wayne Gretzky 5x7	25.00

1997 - 98 OMEGA

These cards have six versions: the regular silver card, a Gold parallel (retail), a Dark Grey parallel (Canadian retail), a Copper parallel (hobby), an Emerald Green parallel (Canadian hobby) and an Ice Blue parallel (limited to 67 copies).

Complete Set (250 cards): 3100.00 40.00
Common Player: 6.00 .20

	Player	IB67	Omega
□ □	1 Matt Cullen, Anah.	10.00	.50
□ □	2 Guy Hebert (G), Anah.	10.00	.20
□ □	3 Paul Kariya, Anah.	70.00	1.00
□ □	4 Dmitri Mironov, Anah.	6.00	.20
□ □	5 Steve Rucchin, Anah.	10.00	.20
□ □	6 Tomas Sandström, Anah.	10.00	.20
□ □	7 Teemu Selänne, Anah.	40.00	.50
□ □	8 Mikhail Shtalenkov (G), Anah.	6.00	.20
□ □	**9 Pavel Trnka, Anah. RC**	**6.00**	**.50**
□ □	10 Jason Allison, Bost.	30.00	.20
□ □	11 Per Axelsson, Bost.	6.00	.20
□ □	12 Raymond Bourque, Bost.	60.00	.50
□ □	13 Anson Carter, Bost.	20.00	.20
□ □	14 Byron Dafoe (G), Bost.	20.00	.20
□ □	15 Ted Donato, Bost.	6.00	.20
□ □	**16 Hal Gill, Bost. RC**	**6.00**	**.50**
□ □	17 Dmitri Khristich, Bost.	6.00	.20
□ □	18 Sergei Samsonov, Bost.	30.00	.50
□ □	19 Joe Thornton, Bost.	60.00	1.50
□ □	20 Jason Dawe, Buff.	6.00	.20
□ □	21 Michal Grosek, Buff.	6.00	.20
□ □	22 Dominik Hasek (G), Buff.	50.00	.50
□ □	23 Brian Holzinger, Buff.	6.00	.20
□ □	24 Michael Peca, Buff.	20.00	.20
□ □	25 Derek Plante, Buff.	6.00	.20
□ □	26 Miroslav Satan, Buff.	15.00	.20
□ □	**27 Steve Shields (G), Buff. RC**	**10.00**	**1.00**
□ □	28 Andrew Cassels, Calg.	10.00	.20
□ □	29 Theoren Fleury, Calg.	30.00	.20
□ □	30 Jarome Iginla, Calg.	40.00	.50
□ □	**31 Derek Morris, Calg. RC**	**10.00**	**1.00**
□ □	**32 Tyler Moss (G), Calg. RC**	**6.00**	**.50**
□ □	33 Michael Nylander, Calg.	10.00	.20
□ □	34 Dwayne Roloson (G), Calg.	6.00	.20
□ □	35 Cory Stillman, Calg.	10.00	.20
□ □	36 Rick Tabaracci (G), Calg.	6.00	.20
□ □	37 German Titov, Calg.	6.00	.20
□ □	**38 Jon (Bates) Battaglia, Caro. RC**	**10.00**	**4.00**
□ □	39 Nelson Emerson, Caro.	6.00	.20
□ □	40 Martin Gélinas, Caro.	10.00	.20
□ □	41 Sami Kapanen, Caro.	15.00	.20
□ □	42 Trevor Kidd (G), Caro.	15.00	.20
□ □	43 Kirk McLean (G), Caro.	15.00	.20
□ □	44 Keith Primeau, Caro.	20.00	.20
□ □	45 Gary Roberts, Caro.	20.00	.20
□ □	46 Tony Amonte, Chic.	30.00	.20
□ □	47 Keith Carney, Chic.	6.00	.20
□ □	48 Chris Chelios, Chic.	30.00	.20
□ □	49 Éric Dazé, Chic.	20.00	.20
□ □	**50 Brian Felsner, Chic. RC**	**6.00**	**.50**
□ □	51 Jeff Hackett (G), Chic.	15.00	.20
□ □	**52 Christian Laflamme, Chic. RC**	**6.00**	**.50**
□ □	53 Alexei Zhamnov, Chic.	15.00	.20
□ □	54 Craig Billington (G), Colo.	6.00	.20
□ □	55 Adam Deadmarsh, Colo.	15.00	.20
□ □	56 Peter Forsberg, Colo.	70.00	1.00
□ □	57 Valeri Kamensky, Colo.	15.00	.20
□ □	58 Uwe Krupp, Colo.	6.00	.20
□ □	59 Jari Kurri, Colo.	50.00	.50
□ □	60 Claude Lemieux, Colo.	15.00	.20
□ □	**61 Éric Messier, Colo. RC**	**6.00**	**.50**
□ □	62 Jeff Odgers, Colo.	6.00	.20
□ □	63 Sandis Ozolinsh, Colo.	10.00	.20
□ □	64 Patrick Roy (G), Colo.	150.00	2.00
□ □	65 Joe Sakic, Colo.	80.00	1.00
□ □	66 Greg A.	6.00	.20
□ □	67 Ed Belfour (G), Dall.	50.00	.50
□ □	68 Manny Fernandez (G), Dall.	20.00	.20
□ □	69 Derian Hatcher, Dall.	15.00	.20
□ □	70 Jamie Langenbrunner, Dall.	10.00	.20
□ □	71 Jere Lehtinen, Dall.	15.00	.20
□ □	**72 Juha Lind, Dall. RC**	**6.00**	**.50**
□ □	73 Mike Modano, Dall.	50.00	.50
□ □	74 Joe Nieuwendyk, Dall.	20.00	.20
□ □	75 Darryl Sydor, Dall.	10.00	.20
□ □	76 Pat Verbeek, Dall.	15.00	.20
□ □	77 Sergei Zubov, Dall.	10.00	.20
□ □	78 Viacheslav Fetisov, Detr.	30.00	.20
□ □	79 Brent Gilchrist, Detr.	6.00	.20
□ □	80 Kevin Hodson (G), Detr.	10.00	.20
□ □	81 Vyacheslav (Slava) Kozlov, Detr.	10.00	.20
□ □	82 Igor Larionov, Detr.	30.00	.20
□ □	83 Nicklas Lidström, Detr.	30.00	.20
□ □	84 Darren McCarty, Detr.	15.00	.20
□ □	85 Larry Murphy, Detr.	10.00	.20
□ □	86 Chris Osgood (G), Detr.	30.00	.20
□ □	87 Brendan Shanahan, Detr.	50.00	.50
□ □	88 Steve Yzerman, Detr.	120.00	1.50
□ □	89 Kelly Buchberger, Edmo.	6.00	.20
□ □	90 Mike Grier, Edmo.	10.00	.20
□ □	91 Bill Guerin, Edmo.	20.00	.20
□ □	92 Roman Hamrlik, Edmo.	10.00	.20
□ □	93 Curtis Joseph (G), Edmo.	50.00	.50
□ □	94 Boris Mironov, Edmo.	6.00	.20
□ □	95 Ryan Smyth, Edmo.	20.00	.20
□ □	96 Doug Weight, Edmo.	30.00	.20
□ □	97 Dino Ciccarelli, Flor.	15.00	.20
□ □	98 Dave Gagner, Flor.	6.00	.20
□ □	99 Ed Jovanovski, Flor.	20.00	.20
□ □	100 Scott Mellanby, Flor.	10.00	.20
□ □	101 Robert Svehla, Flor.	10.00	.20
□ □	102 John Vanbiesbrouck (G), Flor.	20.00	.20
□ □	103 Steve Washburn, Flor.	6.00	.20
□ □	**104 Kevin Weekes (G), Flor. RC**	**10.00**	**1.50**
□ □	105 Ray Whitney, Flor.	10.00	.20
□ □	106 Rob Blake, LosA.	30.00	.20
□ □	107 Stéphane Fiset (G), LosA.	15.00	.20
□ □	108 Garry Galley, LosA.	6.00	.20
□ □	**109 Steve McKenna, LosA. RC**	**6.00**	**.50**
□ □	110 Glen Murray, LosA.	20.00	.20
□ □	111 Yanic Perreault, LosA.	15.00	.20
□ □	112 Luc Robitaille, LosA.	40.00	.50
□ □	113 Jamie Storr (G), LosA.	10.00	.20
□ □	114 Jozef Stümpel, LosA.	10.00	.20
□ □	115 Vladimir Tsyplakov, LosA.	6.00	.20
□ □	116 Shayne Corson, Mont.	15.00	.20
□ □	117 Vincent Damphousse, Mont.	30.00	.20
□ □	118 Saku Koivu, Mont.	40.00	.50
□ □	119 Vladimir Malakhov, Mont.	6.00	.20
□ □	120 Andy Moog (G), Mont.	20.00	.20
□ □	121 Mark Recchi, Mont.	20.00	.20
□ □	122 Martin Rucinsky, Mont.	10.00	.20
□ □	123 Brian Savage, Mont.	15.00	.20
□ □	124 Jocelyn Thibault (G), Mont.	20.00	.20
□ □	125 Jason Arnott, NJer.	20.00	.20
□ □	**126 Brad Bombardir, NJer. RC**	**6.00**	**.50**
□ □	127 Martin Brodeur (G), NJer.	80.00	1.00
□ □	**128 Patrik Elias, NJer. RC**	**40.00**	**4.00**
□ □	129 Doug Gilmour, NJer.	30.00	.20
□ □	130 Bobby Holik, NJer.	15.00	.20
□ □	131 Randy McKay, NJer.	6.00	.20
□ □	132 Scott Niedermayer, NJer.	15.00	.20
□ □	**133 Krzysztof Oliwa, NJer. RC**	**10.00**	**1.00**
□ □	134 Scott Stevens, NJer.	20.00	.20
□ □	135 Petr* Sykora, NJer.	20.00	.20
□ □	136 Bryan Berard, NYIs.	15.00	.20
□ □	137 Travis Green, NYIs.	10.00	.20
□ □	138 Bryan McCabe, Vanc.	10.00	.20
□ □	139 Sergei Nemchinov, NYIs.	10.00	.20
□ □	140 Zigmund Palffy, NYIs.	30.00	.20
□ □	141 Robert Reichel, NYIs.	15.00	.20
□ □	142 Tommy Salo (G), NYIs.	20.00	.20
□ □	143 Bryan Smolinski, NYIs.	6.00	.20
□ □	144 Adam Graves, NYRa.	20.00	.20
□ □	145 Wayne Gretzky, NYRa.	200.00	3.00
□ □	146 Pat LaFontaine, NYRa.	30.00	.20
□ □	147 Brian Leetch, NYRa.	30.00	.20
□ □	148 Mike Richter (G), NYRa.	20.00	.20
□ □	149 Kevin Stevens, NYRa.	10.00	.20
□ □	150 Niklas Sundström, NYRa.	10.00	.20
□ □	151 Tim Sweeney, NYRa.	6.00	.20
□ □	152 Daniel Alfredsson, Otta.	30.00	.20
□ □	**153 Magnus Arvedson, Otta. RC**	**6.00**	**.50**
□ □	154 Andreas Dackell, Otta.	6.00	.20
□ □	155 Igor Kravchuk, Otta.	6.00	.20
□ □	156 Shawn McEachern, Otta.	15.00	.20
□ □	157 Damian Rhodes (G), Otta.	10.00	.20
□ □	158 Ron Tugnutt (G), Otta.	20.00	.20
□ □	159 Alexei Yashin, Otta.	30.00	.20
□ □	160 Rod Brind'Amour, Phil.	15.00	.20
□ □	161 Paul Coffey, Phil.	30.00	.20
□ □	162 Éric Desjardins, Phil.	15.00	.20
□ □	**163 Colin Forbes, Phil. RC**	**6.00**	**.50**
□ □	164 Chris Gratton, Phil.	10.00	.20
□ □	165 Ron Hextall (G), Phil.	30.00	.20
□ □	166 Trent Klatt, Phil.	6.00	.20
□ □	167 John LeClair, Phil.	40.00	.50
□ □	168 Eric Lindros, Phil.	50.00	.50
□ □	169 Joel Otto, Phil.	6.00	.20
□ □	170 Garth Snow (G), Phil.	15.00	.20
□ □	171 Dainius Zubrus, Phil.	10.00	.20
□ □	172 Dallas Drake, Phoe.	6.00	.20
□ □	173 Mike Gartner, Phoe.	40.00	.50
□ □	174 Nikolai Khabibulin (G), Phoe.	20.00	.20
□ □	175 Teppo Numminen, Phoe.	15.00	.20
□ □	176 Jeremy Roenick, Phoe.	40.00	.50
□ □	177 Keith Tkachuk, Phoe.	30.00	.20
□ □	178 Rick Tocchet, Phoe.	15.00	.20
□ □	179 Oleg Tverdovsky, Phoe.	6.00	.20
□ □	180 Juha Ylönen, Phoe.	6.00	.20
□ □	181 Stu Barnes, Pitt.	6.00	.20
□ □	182 Tom Barrasso (G), Pitt.	20.00	.20
□ □	183 Rob (Jr.	6.00	.20
□ □	184 Ron Francis, Pitt.	30.00	.20
□ □	185 Kevin Hatcher, Pitt.	6.00	.20
□ □	186 Jaromir Jagr, Pitt.	50.00	.50
□ □	187 Aleksey Morozov, Pitt.	10.00	.20
□ □	188 Ed Olczyk, Pitt.	10.00	.20
□ □	189 Jim Campbell, SLou.	6.00	.20
□ □	190 Geoff Courtnall, SLou.	6.00	.20
□ □	191 Pavol Demitra, SLou.	20.00	.20
□ □	192 Steve Duchesne, SLou.	10.00	.20
□ □	193 Grant Fuhr (G), SLou.	30.00	.20
□ □	194 Brett Hull, SLou.	50.00	.50
□ □	195 Al MacInnis, SLou.	20.00	.20
□ □	196 Chris Pronger, SLou.	30.00	.20
□ □	**197 Pascal Rhéaume, SLou. RC**	**6.00**	**.50**
□ □	198 Jamie Rivers, SLou.	6.00	.20
□ □	199 Pierre Turgeon, SLou.	20.00	.20
□ □	200 Jeff Friesen, SanJ.	15.00	.20
□ □	201 Tony Granato, SanJ.	10.00	.20
□ □	202 John MacLean, SanJ.	6.00	.20
□ □	203 Patrick Marleau, SanJ.	20.00	.50
□ □	204 Marty McSorley, SanJ.	10.00	.20
□ □	205 Owen Nolan, SanJ.	30.00	.20
□ □	**206 Marco Sturm, SanJ. RC**	**10.00**	**1.00**
□ □	207 Mike Vernon (G), SanJ.	20.00	.20
□ □	**208 Andrei Zyuzin, SanJ. RC**	**6.00**	**.50**
□ □	209 Karl Dykhuis, Tamp.	6.00	.20
□ □	210 Daymond Langkow, Tamp.	10.00	.20
□ □	211 Bryan Marchment, Tamp.	6.00	.20
□ □	212 Daren Puppa (G), Tamp.	10.00	.20
□ □	213 Mikael Renberg, Tamp.	15.00	.20
□ □	214 Alexander Selivanov, Tamp.	6.00	.20
□ □	215 Paul Ysebaert, Tamp.	6.00	.20
□ □	216 Rob Zamuner, Tamp.	10.00	.20
□ □	217 Sergei Berezin, Toro.	10.00	.20
□ □	218 Wendel Clark, Toro.	40.00	.50
□ □	219 Marcel Cousineau, Toro.	6.00	.20
□ □	220 Tie Domi, Toro.	15.00	.20
□ □	**221 Mike Johnson, Toro. RC**	**10.00**	**1.00**
□ □	222 Igor Korolev, Toro.	6.00	.20
□ □	223 Félix Potvin (G), Toro.	30.00	.20
□ □	224 Mathieu Schneider, Toro.	10.00	.20
□ □	225 Mats Sundin, Toro.	50.00	.50
□ □	**226 Yannick Tremblay, Toro. RC**	**6.00**	**.50**
□ □	227 Donald Brashear, Vanc.	10.00	.20
□ □	228 Pavel Bure, Vanc.	40.00	.50
□ □	229 Sean Burke (G), Vanc.	30.00	.20
□ □	230 Trevor Linden, Vanc.	20.00	.20
□ □	231 Mark Messier, Vanc.	50.00	.50
□ □	232 Alexander Mogilny, Vanc.	20.00	.20
□ □	233 Markus Näslund, Vanc.	50.00	.50
□ □	234 Mattias Öhlund, Vanc.	15.00	.20
□ □	**235 Dave Scatchard, Vanc. RC**	**6.00**	**.50**
□ □	236 Peter Bondra, Wash.	30.00	.20
□ □	237 Andrew Brunette, Wash.	6.00	.20
□ □	238 Phil Housley, Wash.	15.00	.20
□ □	239 Dale Hunter, Wash.	15.00	.20
□ □	240 Calle Johansson, Wash.	10.00	.20
□ □	241 Joé Juneau, Wash.	10.00	.20
□ □	242 Olaf Kölzig (G), Wash.	30.00	.20
□ □	243 Adam Oates, Wash.	20.00	.20
□ □	244 Richard Zedník, Wash.	20.00	.20
□ □	245 C. Chelios / K. Tkachuk	30.00	.20
□ □	246 E. Belfour (G) / M. Modano	50.00	.50
□ □	247 S. Koivu / T. Selänne	40.00	.50
□ □	248 S. Corson / E. Lindros	30.00	.20
□ □	249 M. Brodeur (G) / P. Roy (G)	110.00	1.50
□ □	250 W. Gretzky / M. Messier	120.00	1.50

ONE-PER-PACK PARALLELS

One-per-pack parallels are Gold (US retail), Copper (US hobby), Emerald (Cdn. hobby), and Dark Grey (Cdn. retail). Dealers may sell some parallels for more or less depending on their supply.

Complete Set (250 cards): 100.00
Common Player: .50

	Player	Para.
□ □ □ □	1 Matt Cullen, Anah.	1.50
□ □ □ □	2 Guy Hebert (G), Anah.	.50
□ □ □ □	3 Paul Kariya, Anah.	3.50
□ □ □ □	4 Dmitri Mironov, Anah.	.50
□ □ □ □	5 Steve Rucchin, Anah.	.50
□ □ □ □	6 Tomas Sandström, Anah.	.50
□ □ □ □	7 Teemu Selänne, Anah.	2.00
□ □ □ □	8 Mikhail Shtalenkov (G), Anah.	.50
□ □ □ □	**9 Pavel Trnka, Anah. RC**	**.50**
□ □ □ □	10 Jason Allison, Bost.	1.50
□ □ □ □	11 Per Axelsson, Bost.	.50
□ □ □ □	12 Raymond Bourque, Bost.	3.00
□ □ □ □	13 Anson Carter, Bost.	1.00
□ □ □ □	14 Byron Dafoe (G), Bost.	1.00
□ □ □ □	15 Ted Donato, Bost.	.50
□ □ □ □	**16 Hal Gill, Bost. RC**	**.50**
□ □ □ □	17 Dmitri Khristich, Bost.	.50
□ □ □ □	18 Sergei Samsonov, Bost.	2.00
□ □ □ □	19 Joe Thornton, Bost.	4.50
□ □ □ □	20 Jason Dawe, Buff.	.50
□ □ □ □	21 Michal Grosek, Buff.	.50
□ □ □ □	22 Dominik Hasek (G), Buff.	2.50
□ □ □ □	23 Brian Holzinger, Buff.	.50
□ □ □ □	24 Michael Peca, Buff.	1.00
□ □ □ □	25 Derek Plante, Buff.	.50
□ □ □ □	26 Miroslav Satan, Buff.	.50
□ □ □ □	**27 Steve Shields (G), Buff. RC**	**1.50**
□ □ □ □	28 Andrew Cassels, Calg.	.50
□ □ □ □	29 Theoren Fleury, Calg.	1.50
□ □ □ □	30 Jarome Iginla, Calg.	2.00
□ □ □ □	**31 Derek Morris, Calg. RC**	**1.50**
□ □ □ □	**32 Tyler Moss (G), Calg. RC**	**1.00**
□ □ □ □	33 Michael Nylander, Calg.	.50
□ □ □ □	34 Dwayne Roloson (G), Calg.	.50
□ □ □ □	35 Cory Stillman, Calg.	.50
□ □ □ □	36 Rick Tabaracci (G), Calg.	.50
□ □ □ □	37 German Titov, Calg.	.50
□ □ □ □	**38 Jon (Bates) Battaglia, Caro. RC**	**5.00**
□ □ □ □	39 Nelson Emerson, Caro.	.50
□ □ □ □	40 Martin Gélinas, Caro.	.50
□ □ □ □	41 Sami Kapanen, Caro.	.50
□ □ □ □	42 Trevor Kidd (G), Caro.	.50
□ □ □ □	43 Kirk McLean (G), Caro.	.50
□ □ □ □	44 Keith Primeau, Caro.	1.00

□□□□	45 Gary Roberts, Caro.	1.00
□□□□	46 Tony Amonte, Chic.	1.50
□□□□	47 Keith Carney, Chic.	.50
□□□□	48 Chris Chelios, Chic.	1.50
□□□□	49 Éric Dazé, Chic.	1.00
□□□□	**50 Brian Felsner, Chic. RC**	**.50**
□□□□	51 Jeff Hackett (G), Chic.	.50
□□□□	**52 Christian Laflamme, Chic. RC**	**.50**
□□□□	53 Alexei Zhamnov, Chic.	.50
□□□□	54 Craig Billington (G), Colo.	.50
□□□□	55 Adam Deadmarsh, Colo.	.50
□□□□	56 Peter Forsberg, Colo.	3.50
□□□□	57 Valeri Kamensky, Colo.	.50
□□□□	58 Uwe Krupp, Colo.	.50
□□□□	59 Jari Kurri, Colo.	2.50
□□□□	60 Claude Lemieux, Colo.	.50
□□□□	**61 Éric Messier, Colo. RC**	**1.00**
□□□□	62 Jeff Odgers, Colo.	.50
□□□□	63 Sandis Ozolinsh, Colo.	.50
□□□□	64 Patrick Roy (G), Colo.	7.50
□□□□	65 Joe Sakic, Colo.	4.00
□□□□	66 Greg A.	.50
□□□□	67 Ed Belfour (G), Dall.	2.50
□□□□	68 Manny Fernandez (G), Dall.	1.00
□□□□	69 Derian Hatcher, Dall.	.50
□□□□	70 Jamie Langenbrunner, Dall.	.50
□□□□	71 Jere Lehtinen, Dall.	.50
□□□□	**72 Juha Lind, Dall. RC**	**1.00**
□□□□	73 Mike Modano, Dall.	2.50
□□□□	74 Joe Nieuwendyk, Dall.	1.00
□□□□	75 Darryl Sydor, Dall.	.50
□□□□	76 Pat Verbeek, Dall.	.50
□□□□	77 Sergei Zubov, Dall.	.50
□□□□	78 Viacheslav Fetisov, Detr.	1.50
□□□□	79 Brent Gilchrist, Detr.	.50
□□□□	80 Kevin Hodson (G), Detr.	.50
□□□□	81 Vyacheslav (Slava) Kozlov, Detr.	.50
□□□□	82 Igor Larionov, Detr.	1.50
□□□□	83 Nicklas Lidström, Detr.	1.50
□□□□	84 Darren McCarty, Detr.	.50
□□□□	85 Larry Murphy, Detr.	.50
□□□□	86 Chris Osgood (G), Detr.	1.50
□□□□	87 Brendan Shanahan, Detr.	2.50
□□□□	88 Steve Yzerman, Detr.	6.00
□□□□	89 Kelly Buchberger, Edmo.	.50
□□□□	90 Mike Grier, Edmo.	.50
□□□□	91 Bill Guerin, Edmo.	1.00
□□□□	92 Roman Hamrlik, Edmo.	.50
□□□□	93 Curtis Joseph (G), Edmo.	2.50
□□□□	94 Boris Mironov, Edmo.	.50
□□□□	95 Ryan Smyth, Edmo.	1.00
□□□□	96 Doug Weight, Edmo.	1.50
□□□□	97 Dino Ciccarelli, Flor.	.50
□□□□	98 Dave Gagner, Flor.	.50
□□□□	99 Ed Jovanovski, Flor.	1.00
□□□□	100 Scott Mellanby, Flor.	.50
□□□□	101 Robert Svehla, Flor.	.50
□□□□	102 John Vanbiesbrouck (G), Flor.	1.00
□□□□	103 Steve Washburn, Flor.	.50
□□□□	**104 Kevin Weekes (G), Flor. RC**	**4.00**
□□□□	105 Ray Whitney, Flor.	.50
□□□□	106 Rob Blake, LosA.	1.50
□□□□	107 Stéphane Fiset (G), LosA.	.50
□□□□	108 Garry Galley, LosA.	.50
□□□□	**109 Steve McKenna, LosA. RC**	**.50**
□□□□	110 Glen Murray, LosA.	1.00
□□□□	111 Yanic Perreault, LosA.	.50
□□□□	112 Luc Robitaille, LosA.	2.00
□□□□	113 Jamie Storr (G), LosA.	.50
□□□□	114 Jozef Stümpel, LosA.	.50
□□□□	115 Vladimir Tsyplakov, LosA.	.50
□□□□	116 Shayne Corson, Mont.	.50
□□□□	117 Vincent Damphousse, Mont.	1.50
□□□□	118 Saku Koivu, Mont.	2.00
□□□□	119 Vladimir Malakhov, Mont.	.50
□□□□	120 Andy Moog (G), Mont.	1.00
□□□□	121 Mark Recchi, Mont.	1.00
□□□□	122 Martin Rucinsky, Mont.	.50
□□□□	123 Brian Savage, Mont.	.50
□□□□	124 Jocelyn Thibault (G), Mont.	1.00
□□□□	125 Jason Arnott, NJer.	1.00
□□□□	**126 Brad Bombardir, NJer. RC**	**.50**
□□□□	127 Martin Brodeur (G), NJer.	4.00
□□□□	**128 Patrik Elias, NJer. RC**	**6.00**
□□□□	129 Doug Gilmour, NJer.	1.50
□□□□	130 Bobby Holik, NJer.	.50
□□□□	131 Randy McKay, NJer.	.50
□□□□	132 Scott Niedermayer, NJer.	.50
□□□□	**133 Krzysztof Oliwa, NJer. RC**	**1.50**
□□□□	134 Scott Stevens, NJer.	1.00
□□□□	135 Petr* Sykora, NJer.	1.00
□□□□	136 Bryan Berard, NYIs.	.50
□□□□	137 Travis Green, NYIs.	.50
□□□□	138 Bryan McCabe, Vanc.	.50
□□□□	139 Sergei Nemchinov, NYIs.	.50
□□□□	140 Zigmund Palffy, NYIs.	1.50
□□□□	141 Robert Reichel, NYIs.	.50
□□□□	142 Tommy Salo (G), NYIs.	1.00
□□□□	143 Bryan Smolinski, NYIs.	.50
□□□□	144 Adam Graves, NYRa.	1.00
□□□□	145 Wayne Gretzky, NYRa.	10.00
□□□□	146 Pat LaFontaine, NYRa.	1.50
□□□□	147 Brian Leetch, NYRa.	1.50
□□□□	148 Mike Richter (G), NYRa.	1.00
□□□□	149 Kevin Stevens, NYRa.	.50
□□□□	150 Niklas Sundström, NYRa.	.50
□□□□	151 Tim Sweeney, NYRa.	.50
□□□□	152 Daniel Alfredsson, Otta.	1.50
□□□□	**153 Magnus Arvedson, Otta. RC**	**1.00**
□□□□	154 Andreas Dackell, Otta.	.50
□□□□	155 Igor Kravchuk, Otta.	.50
□□□□	156 Shawn McEachern, Otta.	.50
□□□□	157 Damian Rhodes (G), Otta.	.50
□□□□	158 Ron Tugnutt (G), Otta.	1.00
□□□□	159 Alexei Yashin, Otta.	1.50
□□□□	160 Rod Brind'Amour, Phil.	.50
□□□□	161 Paul Coffey, Phil.	1.50
□□□□	162 Éric Desjardins, Phil.	.50
□□□□	**163 Colin Forbes, Phil. RC**	**.50**
□□□□	164 Chris Gratton, Phil.	.50
□□□□	165 Ron Hextall (G), Phil.	1.50
□□□□	166 Trent Klatt, Phil.	.50
□□□□	167 John LeClair, Phil.	2.00
□□□□	168 Eric Lindros, Phil.	2.50
□□□□	169 Joel Otto, Phil.	.50
□□□□	170 Garth Snow (G), Phil.	.50
□□□□	171 Dainius Zubrus, Phil.	.50
□□□□	172 Dallas Drake, Phoe.	.50
□□□□	173 Mike Gartner, Phoe.	2.00
□□□□	174 Nikolai Khabibulin (G), Phoe.	1.00
□□□□	175 Teppo Numminen, Phoe.	.50
□□□□	176 Jeremy Roenick, Phoe.	2.00
□□□□	177 Keith Tkachuk, Phoe.	1.50
□□□□	178 Rick Tocchet, Phoe.	.50
□□□□	179 Oleg Tverdovsky, Phoe.	.50
□□□□	180 Juha Ylönen, Phoe.	.50
□□□□	181 Stu Barnes, Pitt.	.50
□□□□	182 Tom Barrasso (G), Pitt.	1.00
□□□□	183 Rob (Jr.	.50
□□□□	184 Ron Francis, Pitt.	1.50
□□□□	185 Kevin Hatcher, Pitt.	.50
□□□□	186 Jaromir Jagr, Pitt.	2.50
□□□□	187 Aleksey Morozov, Pitt.	.50
□□□□	188 Ed Olczyk, Pitt.	.50
□□□□	189 Jim Campbell, SLou.	.50
□□□□	190 Geoff Courtnall, SLou.	.50
□□□□	191 Pavol Demitra, SLou.	1.00
□□□□	192 Steve Duchesne, SLou.	.50
□□□□	193 Grant Fuhr (G), SLou.	1.50
□□□□	194 Brett Hull, SLou.	2.50
□□□□	195 Al MacInnis, SLou.	1.00
□□□□	196 Chris Pronger, SLou.	1.50
□□□□	**197 Pascal Rhéaume, SLou. RC**	**.50**
□□□□	198 Jamie Rivers, SLou.	.50
□□□□	199 Pierre Turgeon, SLou.	1.00
□□□□	200 Jeff Friesen, SanJ.	.50
□□□□	201 Tony Granato, SanJ.	.50
□□□□	202 John MacLean, SanJ.	.50
□□□□	203 Patrick Marleau, SanJ.	1.50
□□□□	204 Marty McSorley, SanJ.	.50
□□□□	205 Owen Nolan, SanJ.	1.50
□□□□	**206 Marco Sturm, SanJ. RC**	**1.50**
□□□□	207 Mike Vernon (G), SanJ.	1.00
□□□□	**208 Andrei Zyuzin, SanJ. RC**	**1.00**
□□□□	209 Karl Dykhuis, Tamp.	.50
□□□□	210 Daymond Langkow, Tamp.	.50
□□□□	211 Bryan Marchment, Tamp.	.50
□□□□	212 Daren Puppa (G), Tamp.	.50
□□□□	213 Mikael Renberg, Tamp.	.50
□□□□	214 Alexander Selivanov, Tamp.	.50
□□□□	215 Paul Ysebaert, Tamp.	.50
□□□□	216 Rob Zamuner, Tamp.	.50
□□□□	217 Sergei Berezin, Toro.	.50
□□□□	218 Wendel Clark, Toro.	2.00
□□□□	219 Marcel Cousineau, Toro.	.50
□□□□	220 Tie Domi, Toro.	.50
□□□□	**221 Mike Johnson, Toro. RC**	**1.50**
□□□□	222 Igor Korolev, Toro.	.50
□□□□	223 Félix Potvin (G), Toro.	1.50
□□□□	224 Mathieu Schneider, Toro.	.50
□□□□	225 Mats Sundin, Toro.	2.50
□□□□	**226 Yannick Tremblay, Toro. RC**	**.50**
□□□□	227 Donald Brashear, Vanc.	.50
□□□□	228 Pavel Bure, Vanc.	2.00
□□□□	229 Sean Burke (G), Vanc.	1.50
□□□□	230 Trevor Linden, Vanc.	1.00
□□□□	231 Mark Messier, Vanc.	2.50
□□□□	232 Alexander Mogilny, Vanc.	1.00
□□□□	233 Markus Näslund, Vanc.	2.50
□□□□	234 Mattias Öhlund, Vanc.	1.00
□□□□	**235 Dave Scatchard, Vanc. RC**	**.50**
□□□□	236 Peter Bondra, Wash.	1.50
□□□□	237 Andrew Brunette, Wash.	.50
□□□□	238 Phil Housley, Wash.	.50
□□□□	239 Dale Hunter, Wash.	.50
□□□□	240 Calle Johansson, Wash.	.50
□□□□	241 Joé Juneau, Wash.	.50
□□□□	242 Olaf Kölzig (G), Wash.	1.50
□□□□	243 Adam Oates, Wash.	1.00
□□□□	244 Richard Zednik, Wash.	1.00
□□□□	245 C. Chelios / K. Tkachuk	1.50
□□□□	246 E. Belfour / M. Modano	2.50
□□□□	247 S. Koivu / T. Selänne	2.00
□□□□	248 S. Corson / E. Lindros	1.50
□□□□	249 M. Brodeur / P. Roy	5.50
□□□□	250 W. Gretzky / M. Messier	6.00
	Sample	**Promo**
□	Mike Modano, Dall.	2.00

GAME FACE

Insert Set (20 cards):		**170.00**
	Insert (1:37)	**GF**
□	1 Paul Kariya, Anah.	10.00
□	2 Teemu Selänne, Anah.	5.00
□	3 Peter Forsberg, Colo.	10.00
□	4 Joe Sakic, Colo.	15.00
□	5 Mike Modano, Dall.	10.00
□	6 Nicklas Lidström, Detr.	5.00
□	7 Brendan Shanahan, Detr.	10.00
□	8 Steve Yzerman, Detr.	20.00
□	9 Ryan Smyth, Edmo.	5.00
□	10 Saku Koivu, Mont.	5.00
□	11 Wayne Gretzky, NYRa.	40.00
□	12 John LeClair, Phil.	5.00
□	13 Eric Lindros, Phil.	10.00
□	14 Dainius Zubrus, Phil.	5.00
□	15 Keith Tkachuk, Phoe.	5.00
□	16 Jaromir Jagr, Pitt.	10.00
□	17 Brett Hull, SLou.	10.00
□	18 Pavel Bure, Vanc.	5.00
□	19 Mark Messier, Vanc.	10.00
□	20 Peter Bondra, Wash.	5.00

NO SCORING ZONE

Insert Set (10 cards):		**35.00**
	Insert (2:37)	**NSZ**
□	1 Dominik Hasek (G), Buff.	4.00
□	2 Patrick Roy (G), Colo.	15.00
□	3 Ed Belfour (G), Dall.	4.00
□	4 Chris Osgood (G), Detr.	2.00
□	5 John Vanbiesbrouck (G), Flor.	2.00
□	6 Andy Moog (G), Mont.	2.00
□	7 Martin Brodeur (G), NJer.	8.00
□	8 Mike Richter (G), NYRa.	2.00
□	9 Ron Hextall (G), Phil.	2.00
□	10 Félix Potvin (G), Toro.	2.00

SILKS

Silk Size: 3 3/8" x 5"

Insert Set (12 silks):		**175.00**
	Insert (1:73)	**Silk**
□	1 Paul Kariya, Anah.	15.00
□	2 Teemu Selänne, Anah.	10.00
□	3 Peter Forsberg, Colo.	15.00
□	4 Patrick Roy (G), Colo.	35.00
□	5 Joe Sakic, Colo.	20.00
□	6 Steve Yzerman, Detr.	30.00
□	7 Martin Brodeur (G), NJer.	20.00
□	8 Wayne Gretzky, NYRa.	50.00
□	9 Eric Lindros, Phil.	10.00
□	10 Jaromir Jagr, Pitt.	10.00
□	11 Pavel Bure, Vanc.	10.00
□	12 Mark Messier, Vanc.	10.00

STICK HANDLE LASER CUTS

Insert Set (20 cards):		**350.00**
	Insert (1:145)	**SHLC**
□	1 Paul Kariya, Anah.	25.00
□	2 Teemu Selänne, Anah.	15.00
□	3 Theoren Fleury, Calg.	10.00
□	4 Chris Chelios, Chic.	10.00
□	5 Peter Forsberg, Colo.	25.00
□	6 Joe Sakic, Colo.	30.00
□	7 Mike Modano, Dall.	15.00
□	8 Brendan Shanahan, Detr.	15.00
□	9 Steve Yzerman, Detr.	45.00
□	10 Saku Koivu, Mont.	15.00
□	11 Doug Gilmour, NJer.	10.00
□	12 Zigmund Palffy, NYIs.	10.00
□	13 Wayne Gretzky, NYRa.	80.00
□	14 Pat LaFontaine, NYRa.	10.00
□	15 John LeClair, Phil.	15.00
□	16 Eric Lindros, Phil.	20.00
□	17 Jaromir Jagr, Pitt.	20.00
□	18 Mats Sundin, Toro.	15.00
□	19 Pavel Bure, Vanc.	15.00
□	20 Mark Messier, Vanc.	15.00

TEAM LEADERS

Insert Set (20 cards):		**180.00**
	Insert (2:48)	**TL**
□	1 Paul Kariya, Anah.	10.00
□	2 Raymond Bourque, Bost.	10.00
□	3 Theoren Fleury, Calg.	5.00
□	4 Patrick Roy (G), Colo.	30.00
□	5 Joe Sakic, Colo.	10.00
□	6 Ed Belfour, Dall.	10.00
□	7 Joe Niewendyk, Dall.	4.00
□	8 Brendan Shanahan, Detr.	10.00
□	9 Steve Yzerman, Detr.	20.00
□	10 Ryan Smyth, Edmo.	4.00
□	11 Shayne Corson, Mont.	4.00
□	12 Mark Recchi, Mont.	4.00
□	13 Martin Brodeur (G), NJer.	15.00
□	14 Wayne Gretzky, NYRa.	40.00
□	15 Rod Brind'Amour, Phi.	4.00
□	16 Eric Lindros, Phil.	10.00
□	17 Chris Pronger, SLou.	5.00
□	18 Félix Potvin, Toro.	5.00
□	19 Pavel Bure, Flor.	5.00
□	20 Mark Messier, Vanc.	10.00

1997 - 98 PACIFIC CROWN COLLECTION

These cards have six versions: the regular card, an Emerald Green (Canadian) parallel, a Copper (Hobby) parallel, a Silver (Retail) parallel, a Red parallel and an Ice Blue (limited to 67 copies) parallel. The Green, Copper and Silver parallels all sell at approximately the same price. There is no card #66 in this set. It was retired in recognition of Mario Lemieux.

Complete Set (350 cards):	**3000.00**	**50.00**
Common Player:	**6.00**	**.20**

Player	IB67	PCC
1 Raymond Bourque, Bost.	60.00	1.00
2 Brian Leetch, NYRa.	30.00	.50
3 Claude Lemieux, Colo.	15.00	.20
4 Mike Modano, Dall.	50.00	1.00
5 Zigmund Palffy, NYIs.	30.00	.50
6 Nikolai Khabibulin (G), Phoe.	20.00	.20
7 Chris Chelios, Chic.	30.00	.50
8 Teemu Selänne, Anah.	40.00	.50
9 Paul Kariya, Anah.	70.00	1.00
10 John LeClair, Phil.	40.00	.50
11 Mark Messier, NYRa.	50.00	1.00
12 Jarome Iginla, Calg.	40.00	.50
13 Petr Nedved, Pitt.	15.00	.20
14 Brendan Shanahan, Detr.	50.00	1.00
15 Dino Ciccarelli, Tamp.	15.00	.20
16 Brett Hull, SLou.	50.00	1.00
17 Wendel Clark, Toro.	40.00	.50
18 Peter Bondra, Wash.	30.00	.50
19 Steve Yzerman, Detr.	120.00	2.00
20 Ed Belfour (G), SanJ.	50.00	1.00
21 Peter Forsberg, Colo.	70.00	1.00
22 Mike Gartner, Phoe.	40.00	.50
23 Jim Carey (G), Bost.	6.00	.20
24 Mike Vernon (G), Detr.	20.00	.20
25 Vincent Damphousse, Mont.	30.00	.50
26 Adam Graves, NYRa.	20.00	.20
27 Ron Hextall (G), Phil.	30.00	.50
28 Keith Tkachuk, Phoe.	30.00	.50
29 Félix Potvin (G), Toro.	30.00	.50
30 Martin Brodeur (G), NJer.	80.00	1.50
31 Rod Brind'Amour, Phil.	15.00	.20
32 Pierre Turgeon, SLou.	20.00	.20
33 Patrick Roy (G), Colo.	150.00	3.00
34 J. Vanbiesbrouck (G), Flor.	20.00	.20
35 Andy Moog (G), Dall.	20.00	.20
36 Sergei Berezin, Toro.	10.00	.20
37 Adam Oates, Wash.	20.00	.20
38 Joe Sakic, Colo.	80.00	1.50
39 Dominik Hasek (G), Buff.	50.00	1.00
40 Patrick Lalime (G), Pitt.	30.00	.50
41 Bobby Dollas, Anah.	6.00	.20
42 Kyle McLaren, Bost.	10.00	.20
43 Wayne Primeau, Buff.	6.00	.20
44 Stéphane Richer, Mont.	10.00	.20
45 Theoren Fleury, Calg.	30.00	.50
46 Kevin Miller, Chic.	6.00	.20
47 Adam Deadmarsh, Colo.	15.00	.20
48 Darryl Sydor, Dall.	10.00	.20
49 Igor Larionov, Detr.	30.00	.50
50 Radek Dvorak, Flor.	10.00	.20
51 Andrei Kovalenko, Edmo.	6.00	.20
52 Keith Primeau, Hart.	20.00	.20
53 Ray Ferraro, LosA.	6.00	.20
54 David Wilkie, Mont.	6.00	.20
55 Bobby Holik, NJer.	15.00	.20
56 Tommy Salo (G), NYIs.	20.00	.20
57 Jeff Beukeboom, NYRa.	6.00	.20
58 Daniel Alfredsson, Otta.	30.00	.50
59 Mikael Renberg, Phil.	15.00	.20
60 Norm Maciver, Phoe.	6.00	.20
61 Darius Kasparaitis, Pitt.	10.00	.20
62 Geoff Courtnall, SLou.	6.00	.20
63 Jeff Friesen, SanJ.	15.00	.20
64 Brian Bradley, Tamp.	6.00	.20
65 Tie Domi, Toro.	15.00	.20
67 Martin Gelinas, Vanc.	10.00	.20
68 Jaromir Jagr, Pitt.	50.00	1.00
69 Steve Konowalchuk, Wash.	10.00	.20
70 Brian Bellows, Anah.	10.00	.20
71 Jozef Stumpel, Bost.	10.00	.20
72 Darryl Shannon, Buff.	6.00	.20
73 Todd Simpson, Calg.	6.00	.20
74 Ulf Dahlen, Chic.	6.00	.20
75 Sandis Ozolinsh, Colo.	10.00	.20
76 Sergei Zubov, Dall.	10.00	.20
77 Paul Coffey, Phil.	30.00	.50
78 Nicklas Lidström, Detr.	30.00	.50
79 Jason Arnott, Edmo.	20.00	.20
80 Ray Sheppard, Flor.	6.00	.20
81 Sean Burke (G), Hart.	30.00	.50
82 Vladimir Tsyplakov, LosA.	6.00	.20
83 Darcy Tucker, Mont.	10.00	.20
84 Dave Andreychuk, NJer.	15.00	.20
85 Scott Lachance, NYIs.	6.00	.20
86 Niklas Sundström, NYRa.	10.00	.20
87 Ron Tugnutt (G), Otta.	20.00	.20
88 Eric Lindros, Phil.	50.00	1.00
89 Alexander Mogilny, Vanc.	20.00	.20
90 Kris King, Phoe.	6.00	.20
91 Sergei Fedorov, Detr.	50.00	1.00
92 Ed Olczyk, Pitt.	10.00	.20
93 Doug Gilmour, NJer.	30.00	.50
94 Ryan Smyth, Edmo.	20.00	.20
95 Scott Pellerin, SLou.	6.00	.20
96 Pavel Bure, Vanc.	40.00	.50
97 Jeremy Roenick, Phoe.	40.00	.50
98 Todd Gill, SanJ.	6.00	.20
99 Wayne Gretzky, NYRa.	200.00	4.00
100 Roman Hamrlik, Tamp.	10.00	.20
101 Rob Zettler, Toro.	6.00	.20
102 Sergei Nemchinov, Vanc.	10.00	.20
103 Sergei Gonchar, Wash.	15.00	.20
104 Steve Rucchin, Anah.	10.00	.20
105 Landon Wilson, Bost.	6.00	.20
106 Anatoli Semenov, Buff.	6.00	.20
107 Corey Millen, Calg.	6.00	.20
108 Eric Dazé, Chic.	20.00	.20
109 Mike Ricci, Colo.	15.00	.20
110 Jamie Langenbrunner, Dall.	10.00	.20
111 Viacheslav Fetisov, Detr.	30.00	.50
112 Rem Murray, Edmo.	6.00	.20
113 Tom Fitzgerald, Flor.	6.00	.20
114 Robert Kron, Hart.	6.00	.20
115 Kevin Stevens, LosA.	10.00	.20
116 Valeri Bure, Mont.	15.00	.20
117 Bill Guerin, NJer.	20.00	.20
118 Bryan McCabe, NYIs.	10.00	.20
119 Alex Kovalev, NYRa.	30.00	.50
120 Alexei Yashin, Otta.	30.00	.50
121 Éric Desjardins, Phil.	15.00	.20
122 Teppo Numminen, Phoe.	15.00	.20
123 Ron Francis, Pitt.	30.00	.50
124 Chris Pronger, SLou.	30.00	.50
125 Viktor Kozlov, SanJ.	15.00	.20
126 Corey Schwab (G), Tamp.	6.00	.20
127 Fredrik Modin, Toro.	10.00	.20
128 Markus Näslund, Vanc.	50.00	1.00
129 Dale Hunter, Wash.	15.00	.20
130 Warren Rychel, Anah.	6.00	.20
131 Anson Carter, Bost.	20.00	.20
132 Miroslav Satan, Buff.	15.00	.20
133 Trevor Kidd (G), Calg.	15.00	.20
134 Sergei Krivokrasov, Chic.	6.00	.20
135 Adam Foote, Colo.	15.00	.20
136 Brent Gilchrist, Dall.	6.00	.20
137 Chris Osgood (G), Detr.	30.00	.50
138 Doug Weight, Edmo.	30.00	.50
139 Martin Straka, Flor.	15.00	.20
140 Jeff O'Neill, Hart.	20.00	.20
141 Byron Dafoe, LosA.	20.00	.20
142 Brian Savage, Mont.	15.00	.20
143 Lyle Odelein, NJer.	6.00	.20
144 Niklas Andersson, NYIs.	6.00	.20
145 Luc Robitaille, NYRa.	40.00	.50
146 Damian Rhodes (G), Otta.	10.00	.20
147 Garth Snow (G), Phil.	15.00	.20
148 Craig Janney, Phoe.	10.00	.20
149 Fredrik Olausson, Pitt.	10.00	.20
150 Joe Murphy, SLou.	6.00	.20
151 Owen Nolan, SanJ.	30.00	.50
152 Shawn Burr, Tamp.	6.00	.20
153 Dimitri Yushkevich, Toro.	10.00	.20
154 Trevor Linden, Vanc.	20.00	.20
155 Joé Juneau, Wash.	10.00	.20
156 Sean Pronger, Anah.	6.00	.20
157 Jeff Odgers, Bost.	6.00	.20
158 Brian Holzinger, Buff.	6.00	.20
159 Dave Gagner, Calg.	6.00	.20
160 Jeff Hackett (G), Chic.	15.00	.20
161 Eric Lacroix, Colo.	6.00	.20
162 Pat Verbeek, Dall.	15.00	.20
163 Darren McCarty, Detr.	15.00	.20
164 Mike Grier, Edmo.	10.00	.20
165 Per Gustafsson, Flor.	6.00	.20
166 Andrew Cassels, Hart.	10.00	.20
167 Vitali Yachmenev, LosA.	6.00	.20
168 Jocelyn Thibault (G), Mont.	20.00	.20
169 John MacLean, NJer.	6.00	.20
170 Travis Green, NYIs.	10.00	.20
171 Ulf Samuelsson, NYRa.	6.00	.20
172 Bruce Gardiner, Otta. RC	**6.00**	**.50**
173 Janne Niinimaa, Phil.	10.00	.20
174 Jim Johnson, Phoe.	6.00	.20
175 Stu Barnes, Pitt.	6.00	.20
176 Harry York, SLou.	6.00	.20
177 Al Iafrate, SanJ.	10.00	.20
178 Paul Ysebaert, Tamp.	6.00	.20
179 Mathieu Schneider, Toro.	10.00	.20
180 Corey Hirsch (G), Vanc.	6.00	.20
181 Mark Tinordi, Wash.	6.00	.20
182 Kevin Todd, Anah.	6.00	.20
183 Tim Sweeney, Bost.	6.00	.20
184 Donald Audette, Buff.	20.00	.20
185 Jonas Höglund, Calg.	6.00	.20
186 Brent Sutter, Chic.	10.00	.20
187 Scott Young, Colo.	15.00	.20
188 Arturs Irbe (G), Dall.	20.00	.20
189 Vladimir Konstantinov, Detr.	15.00	.20
190 Mats Lindgren, Edmo.	6.00	.20
191 Dave Nemirovsky, Flor.	6.00	.20
192 Sami Kapanen, Hart.	15.00	.20
193 Rob Blake, LosA.	30.00	.50
194 Sébastien Bordeleau, Mont.	6.00	.20
195 Steve Thomas, NJer.	10.00	.20
196 Bryan Smolinski, NYIs.	6.00	.20
197 Mike Richter (G), NYRa.	20.00	.20
198 Randy Cunneyworth, Otta.	6.00	.20
199 Pat Falloon, Phil.	6.00	.20
200 Cliff Ronning, Phoe.	10.00	.20
201 Ken Wregget (G), Pitt.	10.00	.20
202 Al MacInnis, SLou.	20.00	.20
203 Tony Granato, SanJ.	10.00	.20
204 Rob Zamuner, Tamp.	10.00	.20
205 Mats Sundin, Toro.	50.00	1.00
206 Mike Ridley, Vanc.	6.00	.20
207 Sylvain Côté, Wash.	6.00	.20
208 Joe Sacco, Anah.	6.00	.20
209 Ted Donato, Bost.	6.00	.20
210 Matthew Barnaby, Buff.	6.00	.20
211 Cory Stillman, Calg.	10.00	.20
212 Gary Suter, Chic.	10.00	.20
213 Valeri Kamensky, Colo.	15.00	.20
214 Derian Hatcher, Dall.	15.00	.20
215 Jamie Pushor, Detr.	6.00	.20
216 Mariusz Czerkawski, Edmo.	10.00	.20
217 Kirk Muller, Flor.	15.00	.20
218 Kevin Dineen, Hart.	6.00	.20
219 Dimitri Khristich, LosA.	6.00	.20
220 Martin Rucinsky, Mont.	10.00	.20
221 Denis Pederson, NJer.	6.00	.20
222 Bryan Berard, NYIs.	15.00	.20
223 A. Karpovtsev, NYRa.	6.00	.20
224 Shawn McEachern, Otta.	15.00	.20
225 Dale Hawerchuk, Phil.	30.00	.50
226 Bob Corkum, Phoe.	6.00	.20
227 Kevin Hatcher, Pitt.	6.00	.20
228 Grant Fuhr (G), SLou.	30.00	.50
229 Darren Turcotte, SanJ.	6.00	.20
230 Patrick Poulin, Tamp.	6.00	.20
231 Jamie Macoun, Toro.	6.00	.20
232 Jyrki Lumme, Vanc.	10.00	.20
233 Bill Ranford (G), Wash.	20.00	.20
234 Dmitri Mironov, Anah.	6.00	.20
235 Mattias Timander, Bost.	6.00	.20
236 Alexei Zhitnik, Buff.	6.00	.20
237 Hnat Domenichelli, Calg.	6.00	.20
238 Murray Craven, Chic.	6.00	.20
239 Mike Keane, Colo.	6.00	.20
240 Benoît Hogue, Dall.	6.00	.20
241 Martin Lapointe, Detr.	20.00	.20
242 Curtis Joseph (G), Edmo.	50.00	1.00
243 Robert Svehla, Flor.	10.00	.20
244 Glen Wesley, Hart.	6.00	.20
245 Stéphane Fiset (G), LosA.	15.00	.20
246 Shayne Corson, Mont.	15.00	.20
247 Scott Niedermayer, NJer.	15.00	.20
248 Steve Webb, NYIs. RC	**6.00**	**.50**
249 Esa Tikkanen, NYRa.	6.00	.20
250 Alexandre Daigle, Otta.	6.00	.20
251 Trent Klatt, Phil.	6.00	.20
252 Oleg Tverdovsky, Phoe.	6.00	.20
253 Dave Roche, Pitt.	6.00	.20
254 Tony Twist, SLou.	6.00	.20
255 Bernie Nicholls, SanJ.	10.00	.20
256 Rick Tabaracci (G), Tamp.	6.00	.20
258 Kirk McLean (G), Vanc.	6.00	.20
257 Todd Warriner, Toro.	15.00	.20
259 Phil Housley, Wash.	15.00	.20
260 Guy Hebert (G), Anah.	10.00	.20
261 Steve Heinze, Bost.	6.00	.20
262 Derek Plante, Buff.	6.00	.20
263 German Titov, Calg.	6.00	.20
264 Tony Amonte, Chic.	30.00	.50
265 Uwe Krupp, Colo.	6.00	.20
266 Joe Nieuwendyk, Dall.	20.00	.20
267 Vyacheslav Kozlov, Detr.	10.00	.20
268 Kelly Buchberger, Edmo.	6.00	.20
269 Rob Niedermayer, Flor.	10.00	.20
270 Geoff Sanderson, Hart.	10.00	.20
271 Jan Vopat, LosA.	6.00	.20
272 Saku Koivu, Mont.	40.00	.50
273 Scott Stevens, NJer.	20.00	.20
274 Éric Fichaud (G), NYIs.	6.00	.20
275 Russ Courtnall, NYRa.	10.00	.20
276 Wade Redden, Otta.	15.00	.20
277 Petr Svoboda, Phil.	10.00	.20
278 Andreas Dackell, Otta.	6.00	.20
279 Jason Woolley, Pitt.	6.00	.20
280 Stéphane Matteau, SLou.	6.00	.20
281 S. Guolla, SanJ. RC	**6.00**	**.50**
282 John Cullen, Tamp.	10.00	.20
283 Steve Sullivan, Toro.	15.00	.20
284 Bret Hedican, Vanc.	6.00	.20
285 Michal Pivonka, Wash.	6.00	.20
286 Darren Van Impe, Anah.	6.00	.20
287 Rob DiMaio, Bost.	6.00	.20
288 Garry Galley, Buff.	6.00	.20
289 Kent Manderville, Calg.	6.00	.20
290 Bob Probert, Chic.	15.00	.20
291 Keith Jones, Colo.	6.00	.20
292 Guy Carbonneau, Dall.	15.00	.20
293 Tomas Sandström, Detr.	10.00	.20
294 D. McGillis, Edmo. RC	**6.00**	**1.00**
295 Brian Skrudland, Flor.	6.00	.20
296 Stu Grimson, Hart.	10.00	.20
297 Doug Zmolek, Bost.	6.00	.20
298 Mark Recchi, Mont.	20.00	.20
299 Valeri Zelepukin, NJer.	6.00	.20
300 Derek Armstrong, NYIs.	6.00	.20
301 Eric Cairns, NYRa. RC	**6.00**	**.50**
302 Steve Duchesne, Otta.	10.00	.20
303 Dainius Zubrus, Phil.	10.00	.20
304 Deron Quint, Phoe.	6.00	.20
305 Joe Dziedzic, Pitt.	6.00	.20
306 Mike Peluso, SLou.	6.00	.20
307 Andrei Nazarov, SanJ.	6.00	.20
308 Chris Gratton, Tamp.	10.00	.20
309 Mike Craig, Toro.	6.00	.20
310 Lonny Bohonos, Vanc.	6.00	.20
311 Rick Tocchet, Wash.	15.00	.20
312 Ted Drury, Anah.	6.00	.20
313 Jean-Yves Roy, Bost.	6.00	.20
314 Jason Dawe, Buff.	6.00	.20
315 Jamie Allison, Calg.	6.00	.20
316 Alexei Zhamnov, Chic.	15.00	.20
317 Aaron Miller, Colo. RC	**6.00**	**.50**
318 Todd Krygier, Wash.	6.00	.20
319 Tomas Holmström, Detr.	10.00	.20
320 Todd Marchant, Edmo.	10.00	.20
321 Scott Mellanby, Flor.	10.00	.20
322 Marek Malik, Hart.	6.00	.20
323 Dan Bylsma, LosA.	6.00	.20
324 Stéphane Quintal, Mont.	6.00	.20
325 Ken Daneyko, NJer.	10.00	.20
326 Robert Reichel, NYIs.	15.00	.20
327 Daniel Goneau, NYRa.	6.00	.20
328 Sergei Zholtok, Otta.	6.00	.20
329 Kjell Samuelsson, Phil.	6.00	.20
330 Shane Doan, Phoe.	10.00	.20
331 Radek Bonk, Otta.	15.00	.20
332 Jim Campbell, SLou.	6.00	.20
333 Marty McSorley, SanJ.	10.00	.20
334 Brantt Myhres, Tamp.	6.00	.20
335 Mike Johnson, Toro. RC	**10.00**	**1.00**
336 Mike Sillinger, Vanc.	6.00	.20
337 Kelly Hrudey (G), SanJ.	15.00	.20
338 Joel Bouchard, Calg.	6.00	.20
339 Brian Noonan, Vanc.	6.00	.20
340 Dean Chynoweth, Bost.	6.00	.20
341 Michael Peca, Buff.	20.00	.20
342 Jeff Toms, Tamp. RC	**6.00**	**.50**
343 Denis Savard, Chic.	20.00	.20
344 Stéphane Yelle, Colo.	6.00	.20
345 Grant Ledyard, Dall.	6.00	.20
346 Ronnie Stern, Calg.	6.00	.20
347 Petr Klima, Edmo.	6.00	.20
348 Johan Garpenlov, Flor.	6.00	.20
349 Nelson Emerson, Hart.	6.00	.20
350 Matt Johnson, LosA.	6.00	.20
351 Ken Belanger, NYIs. RC	**6.00**	**.50**

ONE-PER-PACK PARALLELS

One-per-pack parallels are Copper (US hobby), Silver (US retail), Emerald (Cdn. hobby), and Red (Treat packs). Dealers may sell some parallels for more or less depending on their supply.

Complete Set (350 cards):	**575.00**	**275.00**
Common Player:	**.75**	**.50**
Player	**Red**	**Par.**
1 Raymond Bourque, Bost.	12.00	6.00
2 Brian Leetch, NYRa.	6.00	3.00
3 Claude Lemieux, Colo.	3.00	1.00
4 Mike Modano, Dall.	10.00	5.00
5 Zigmund Palffy, NYIs.	6.00	3.00
6 Nikolai Khabibulin (G), Phoe.	4.00	2.00
7 Chris Chelios, Chic.	6.00	3.00
8 Teemu Selänne, Anah.	8.00	4.00
9 Paul Kariya, Anah.	10.00	5.00
10 John LeClair, Phil.	8.00	4.00

□□□□ 11 Mark Messier, NYRa.	10.00	5.00
□□□□ 12 Jarome Iginla, Calg.	8.00	4.00
□□□□ 13 Petr Nedved, Pitt.	3.00	1.00
□□□□ 14 Brendan Shanahan, Detr.	10.00	5.00
□□□□ 15 Dino Ciccarelli, Tamp.	3.00	1.00
□□□□ 16 Brett Hull, SLou.	10.00	5.00
□□□□ 17 Wendel Clark, Toro.	8.00	4.00
□□□□ 18 Peter Bondra, Wash.	6.00	3.00
□□□□ 19 Steve Yzerman, Detr.	20.00	10.00
□□□□ 20 Ed Belfour (G), SanJ.	10.00	5.00
□□□□ 21 Peter Forsberg, Colo.	14.00	7.00
□□□□ 22 Mike Gartner, Phoe.	8.00	4.00
□□□□ 23 Jim Carey (G), Bost.	1.00	.50
□□□□ 24 Mike Vernon (G), Detr.	4.00	2.00
□□□□ 25 Vincent Damphousse, Mont.	6.00	3.00
□□□□ 26 Adam Graves, NYRa.	4.00	2.00
□□□□ 27 Ron Hextall (G), Phil.	6.00	3.00
□□□□ 28 Keith Tkachuk, Phoe.	6.00	3.00
□□□□ 29 Félix Potvin (G), Toro.	6.00	3.00
□□□□ 30 Martin Brodeur (G), NJer.	16.00	8.00
□□□□ 31 Rod Brind'Amour, Phil.	3.00	1.00
□□□□ 32 Pierre Turgeon, SLou.	4.00	2.00
□□□□ 33 Patrick Roy (G), Colo.	30.00	15.00
□□□□ 34 J. Vanbiesbrouck (G), Flor.	4.00	2.00
□□□□ 35 Andy Moog (G), Dall.	4.00	2.00
□□□□ 36 Sergei Berezin, Toro.	2.00	1.00
□□□□ 37 Adam Oates, Wash.	4.00	2.00
□□□□ 38 Joe Sakic, Colo.	16.00	8.00
□□□□ 39 Dominik Hasek (G), Buff.	10.00	5.00
□□□□ 40 Patrick Lalime (G), Pitt.	6.00	3.00
□□□□ 41 Bobby Dollas, Anah.	1.00	.50
□□□□ 42 Kyle McLaren, Bost.	2.00	1.00
□□□□ 43 Wayne Primeau, Buff.	1.00	.50
□□□□ 44 Stéphane Richer, Mont.	2.00	1.00
□□□□ 45 Theoren Fleury, Calg.	6.00	3.00
□□□□ 46 Kevin Miller, Chic.	1.00	.50
□□□□ 47 Adam Deadmarsh, Colo.	3.00	1.00
□□□□ 48 Darryl Sydor, Dall.	2.00	1.00
□□□□ 49 Igor Larionov, Detr.	6.00	3.00
□□□□ 50 Radek Dvorak, Flor.	2.00	1.00
□□□□ 51 Andrei Kovalenko, Edmo.	1.00	.50
□□□□ 52 Keith Primeau, Hart.	4.00	2.00
□□□□ 53 Ray Ferraro, LosA.	1.00	.50
□□□□ 54 David Wilkie, Mont.	1.00	.50
□□□□ 55 Bobby Holik, NJer.	3.00	1.00
□□□□ 56 Tommy Salo (G), NYIs.	4.00	2.00
□□□□ 57 Jeff Beukeboom, NYRa.	1.00	.50
□□□□ 58 Daniel Alfredsson, Otta.	6.00	3.00
□□□□ 59 Mikael Renberg, Phil.	3.00	1.00
□□□□ 60 Norm Maciver, Phoe.	1.00	.50
□□□□ 61 Darius Kasparaitis, Pitt.	2.00	1.00
□□□□ 62 Geoff Courtnall, SLou.	1.00	.50
□□□□ 63 Jeff Friesen, SanJ.	3.00	1.00
□□□□ 64 Brian Bradley, Tamp.	1.00	.50
□□□□ 65 Tie Domi, Toro.	3.00	1.00
□□□□ 67 Martin Gelinas, Vanc.	2.00	1.00
□□□□ 68 Jaromir Jagr, Pitt.	10.00	5.00
□□□□ 69 Steve Konowalchuk, Wash.	2.00	1.00
□□□□ 70 Brian Bellows, Anah.	2.00	1.00
□□□□ 71 Jozef Stumpel, Bost.	2.00	1.00
□□□□ 72 Darryl Shannon, Buff.	1.00	.50
□□□□ 73 Todd Simpson, Calg.	1.00	.50
□□□□ 74 Ulf Dahlen, Chic.	1.00	.50
□□□□ 75 Sandis Ozolinsh, Colo.	2.00	1.00
□□□□ 76 Sergei Zubov, Dall.	2.00	1.00
□□□□ 77 Paul Coffey, Phil.	6.00	3.00
□□□□ 78 Nicklas Lidström, Detr.	6.00	3.00
□□□□ 79 Jason Arnott, Edmo.	4.00	2.00
□□□□ 80 Ray Sheppard, Flor.	1.00	.50
□□□□ 81 Sean Burke (G), Hart.	6.00	3.00
□□□□ 82 Vladimir Tsyplakov, LosA.	1.00	.50
□□□□ 83 Darcy Tucker, Mont.	2.00	1.00
□□□□ 84 Dave Andreychuk, NJer.	3.00	1.00
□□□□ 85 Scott Lachance, NYIs.	1.00	.50
□□□□ 86 Niklas Sundström, NYRa.	2.00	1.00
□□□□ 87 Ron Tugnutt (G), Otta.	4.00	2.00
□□□□ 88 Eric Lindros, Phil.	10.00	5.00
□□□□ 89 Alexander Mogilny, Vanc.	4.00	2.00
□□□□ 90 Kris King, Phoe.	1.00	.50
□□□□ 91 Sergei Fedorov, Detr.	10.00	5.00
□□□□ 92 Ed Olczyk, Pitt.	2.00	1.00
□□□□ 93 Doug Gilmour, NJer.	6.00	3.00
□□□□ 94 Ryan Smyth, Edmo.	4.00	2.00
□□□□ 95 Scott Pellerin, SLou.	1.00	.50
□□□□ 96 Pavel Bure, Vanc.	8.00	4.00
□□□□ 97 Jeremy Roenick, Phoe.	8.00	4.00
□□□□ 98 Todd Gill, SanJ.	1.00	.50
□□□□ 99 Wayne Gretzky, NYRa.	40.00	20.00
□□□□ 100 Roman Hamrlik, Tamp.	2.00	1.00
□□□□ 101 Rob Zettler, Toro.	1.00	.50
□□□□ 102 Sergei Nemchinov, Vanc.	2.00	1.00
□□□□ 103 Sergei Gonchar, Wash.	3.00	1.00
□□□□ 104 Steve Rucchin, Anah.	2.00	1.00
□□□□ 105 Landon Wilson, Bost.	1.00	.50
□□□□ 106 Anatoli Semenov, Buff.	1.00	.50
□□□□ 107 Corey Millen, Calg.	1.00	.50
□□□□ 108 Eric Dazé, Chic.	4.00	2.00
□□□□ 109 Mike Ricci, Colo.	3.00	1.00
□□□□ 110 Jamie Langenbrunner, Dall.	2.00	1.00
□□□□ 111 Viacheslav Fetisov, Detr.	6.00	3.00
□□□□ 112 Rem Murray, Edmo.	1.00	.50
□□□□ 113 Tom Fitzgerald, Flor.	1.00	.50
□□□□ 114 Robert Kron, Hart.	1.00	.50
□□□□ 115 Kevin Stevens, LosA.	2.00	1.00
□□□□ 116 Valeri Bure, Mont.	3.00	1.00
□□□□ 117 Bill Guerin, NJer.	4.00	2.00
□□□□ 118 Bryan McCabe, NYIs.	2.00	1.00
□□□□ 119 Alex Kovalev, NYRa.	6.00	3.00
□□□□ 120 Alexei Yashin, Otta.	6.00	3.00
□□□□ 121 Éric Desjardins, Phil.	3.00	1.00
□□□□ 122 Teppo Numminen, Phoe.	3.00	1.00
□□□□ 123 Ron Francis, Pitt.	6.00	3.00
□□□□ 124 Chris Pronger, SLou.	6.00	3.00
□□□□ 125 Viktor Kozlov, SanJ.	3.00	1.00
□□□□ 126 Corey Schwab (G), Tamp.	1.00	.50
□□□□ 127 Fredrik Modin, Toro.	2.00	1.00
□□□□ 128 Markus Näslund, Vanc.	10.00	5.00
□□□□ 129 Dale Hunter, Wash.	3.00	1.00
□□□□ 130 Warren Rychel, Anah.	1.00	.50
□□□□ 131 Anson Carter, Bost.	4.00	2.00
□□□□ 132 Miroslav Satan, Buff.	3.00	1.00
□□□□ 133 Trevor Kidd (G), Calg.	3.00	1.00
□□□□ 134 Sergei Krivokrasov, Chic.	1.00	.50
□□□□ 135 Adam Foote, Colo.	3.00	1.00
□□□□ 136 Brent Gilchrist, Dall.	1.00	.50
□□□□ 137 Chris Osgood (G), Detr.	6.00	3.00
□□□□ 138 Doug Weight, Edmo.	6.00	3.00
□□□□ 139 Martin Straka, Flor.	3.00	1.00
□□□□ 140 Jeff O'Neill, Hart.	4.00	2.00
□□□□ 141 Byron Dafoe, LosA.	4.00	2.00
□□□□ 142 Brian Savage, Mont.	3.00	1.00
□□□□ 143 Lyle Odelein, NJer.	1.00	.50
□□□□ 144 Niklas Andersson, NYIs.	1.00	.50
□□□□ 145 Luc Robitaille, NYRa.	8.00	4.00
□□□□ 146 Damian Rhodes (G), Otta.	2.00	1.00
□□□□ 147 Garth Snow (G), Phil.	3.00	1.00
□□□□ 148 Craig Janney, Phoe.	2.00	1.00
□□□□ 149 Fredrik Olausson, Pitt.	2.00	1.00
□□□□ 150 Joe Murphy, SLou.	1.00	.50
□□□□ 151 Owen Nolan, SanJ.	6.00	3.00
□□□□ 152 Shawn Burr, Tamp.	1.00	.50
□□□□ 153 Dimitri Yushkevich, Toro.	2.00	1.00
□□□□ 154 Trevor Linden, Vanc.	4.00	2.00
□□□□ 155 Joé Juneau, Wash.	2.00	1.00
□□□□ 156 Sean Pronger, Anah.	1.00	.50
□□□□ 157 Jeff Odgers, Bost.	1.00	.50
□□□□ 158 Brian Holzinger, Buff.	1.00	.50
□□□□ 159 Dave Gagner, Calg.	1.00	.50
□□□□ 160 Jeff Hackett (G), Chic.	3.00	1.00
□□□□ 161 Eric Lacroix, Colo.	1.00	.50
□□□□ 162 Pat Verbeek, Dall.	3.00	1.00
□□□□ 163 Darren McCarty, Detr.	3.00	1.00
□□□□ 164 Mike Grier, Edmo.	2.00	1.00
□□□□ 165 Per Gustafsson, Flor.	1.00	.50
□□□□ 166 Andrew Cassels, Hart.	2.00	1.00
□□□□ 167 Vitali Yachmenev, LosA.	1.00	.50
□□□□ 168 Jocelyn Thibault (G), Mont.	4.00	2.00
□□□□ 169 John MacLean, NJer.	1.00	.50
□□□□ 170 Travis Green, NYIs.	2.00	1.00
□□□□ 171 Ulf Samuelsson, NYRa.	1.00	.50
□□□□ **172 Bruce Gardiner, Otta. RC**	**2.00**	**1.00**
□□□□ 173 Janne Niinimaa, Phil.	2.00	1.00
□□□□ 174 Jim Johnson, Phoe.	1.00	.50
□□□□ 175 Stu Barnes, Pitt.	1.00	.50
□□□□ 176 Harry York, SLou.	1.00	.50
□□□□ 177 Al Iafrate, SanJ.	2.00	1.00
□□□□ 178 Paul Ysebaert, Tamp.	1.00	.50
□□□□ 179 Mathieu Schneider, Toro.	2.00	1.00
□□□□ 180 Corey Hirsch (G), Vanc.	1.00	.50
□□□□ 181 Mark Tinordi, Wash.	1.00	.50
□□□□ 182 Kevin Todd, Anah.	1.00	.50
□□□□ 183 Tim Sweeney, Bost.	1.00	.50
□□□□ 184 Donald Audette, Buff.	4.00	2.00
□□□□ 185 Jonas Höglund, Calg.	1.00	.50
□□□□ 186 Brent Sutter, Chic.	2.00	1.00
□□□□ 187 Scott Young, Colo.	3.00	1.00
□□□□ 188 Arturs Irbe (G), Dall.	4.00	2.00
□□□□ 189 Vladimir Konstantinov, Detr.	3.00	1.00
□□□□ 190 Mats Lindgren, Edmo.	1.00	.50
□□□□ 191 Dave Nemirovsky, Flor.	1.00	.50
□□□□ 192 Sami Kapanen, Hart.	3.00	1.00
□□□□ 193 Rob Blake, LosA.	6.00	3.00
□□□□ 194 Sébastien Bordeleau, Mont.	1.00	.50
□□□□ 195 Steve Thomas, NJer.	2.00	1.00
□□□□ 196 Bryan Smolinski, NYIs.	1.00	.50
□□□□ 197 Mike Richter (G), NYRa.	4.00	2.00
□□□□ 198 Randy Cunneyworth, Otta.	1.00	.50
□□□□ 199 Pat Falloon, Phil.	1.00	.50
□□□□ 200 Cliff Ronning, Phoe.	2.00	1.00
□□□□ 201 Ken Wregget (G), Pitt.	2.00	1.00
□□□□ 202 Al MacInnis, SLou.	4.00	2.00
□□□□ 203 Tony Granato, SanJ.	2.00	1.00
□□□□ 204 Rob Zamuner, Tamp.	2.00	1.00
□□□□ 205 Mats Sundin, Toro.	10.00	5.00
□□□□ 206 Mike Ridley, Vanc.	1.00	.50
□□□□ 207 Sylvain Côté, Wash.	1.00	.50
□□□□ 208 Joe Sacco, Anah.	1.00	.50
□□□□ 209 Ted Donato, Bost.	1.00	.50
□□□□ 210 Matthew Barnaby, Buff.	1.00	.50
□□□□ 211 Cory Stillman, Calg.	2.00	1.00
□□□□ 212 Gary Suter, Chic.	2.00	1.00
□□□□ 213 Valeri Kamensky, Colo.	3.00	1.00
□□□□ 214 Derian Hatcher, Dall.	3.00	1.00
□□□□ 215 Jamie Pushor, Detr.	1.00	.50
□□□□ 216 Mariusz Czerkawski, Edmo.	2.00	1.00
□□□□ 217 Kirk Muller, Flor.	3.00	1.00
□□□□ 218 Kevin Dineen, Hart.	1.00	.50
□□□□ 219 Dimitri Khristich, LosA.	1.00	.50
□□□□ 220 Martin Rucinsky, Mont.	2.00	1.00
□□□□ 221 Denis Pederson, NJer.	1.00	.50
□□□□ 222 Bryan Berard, NYIs.	3.00	1.00
□□□□ 223 A. Karpovtsev, NYRa.	1.00	.50
□□□□ 224 Shawn McEachern, Otta.	3.00	1.00
□□□□ 225 Dale Hawerchuk, Phil.	6.00	3.00
□□□□ 226 Bob Corkum, Phoe.	1.00	.50
□□□□ 227 Kevin Hatcher, Pitt.	1.00	.50
□□□□ 228 Grant Fuhr (G), SLou.	6.00	3.00
□□□□ 229 Darren Turcotte, SanJ.	1.00	.50
□□□□ 230 Patrick Poulin, Tamp.	1.00	.50
□□□□ 231 Jamie Macoun, Toro.	1.00	.50
□□□□ 232 Jyrki Lumme, Vanc.	2.00	1.00
□□□□ 233 Bill Ranford (G), Wash.	4.00	2.00
□□□□ 234 Dmitri Mironov, Anah.	1.00	.50
□□□□ 235 Mattias Timander, Bost.	1.00	.50
□□□□ 236 Alexei Zhitnik, Buff.	1.00	.50
□□□□ 237 Hnat Domenichelli, Calg.	1.00	.50
□□□□ 238 Murray Craven, Chic.	1.00	.50
□□□□ 239 Mike Keane, Colo.	1.00	.50
□□□□ 240 Benoît Hogue, Dall.	1.00	.50
□□□□ 241 Martin Lapointe, Detr.	4.00	2.00
□□□□ 242 Curtis Joseph (G), Edmo.	10.00	5.00
□□□□ 243 Robert Svehla, Flor.	2.00	1.00
□□□□ 244 Glen Wesley, Hart.	1.00	.50
□□□□ 245 Stéphane Fiset (G), LosA.	3.00	1.00
□□□□ 246 Shayne Corson, Mont.	3.00	1.00
□□□□ 247 Scott Niedermayer, NJer.	3.00	1.00
□□□□ **248 Steve Webb, NYIs. RC**	**2.00**	**1.00**
□□□□ 249 Esa Tikkanen, NYRa.	1.00	.50
□□□□ 250 Alexandre Daigle, Otta.	1.00	.50
□□□□ 251 Trent Klatt, Phil.	1.00	.50
□□□□ 252 Oleg Tverdovsky, Phoe.	1.00	.50
□□□□ 253 Dave Roche, Pitt.	1.00	.50
□□□□ 254 Tony Twist, SLou.	1.00	.50
□□□□ 255 Bernie Nicholls, SanJ.	2.00	1.00
□□□□ 256 Rick Tabaracci (G), Tamp.	1.00	.50
□□□□ 258 Kirk McLean (G), Vanc.	1.00	.50
□□□□ 257 Todd Warriner, Toro.	3.00	1.00
□□□□ 259 Phil Housley, Wash.	3.00	1.00
□□□□ 260 Guy Hebert (G), Anah.	2.00	1.00
□□□□ 261 Steve Heinze, Bost.	1.00	.50
□□□□ 262 Derek Plante, Buff.	1.00	.50
□□□□ 263 German Titov, Calg.	1.00	.50
□□□□ 264 Tony Amonte, Chic.	6.00	3.00
□□□□ 265 Uwe Krupp, Colo.	1.00	.50
□□□□ 266 Joe Nieuwendyk, Dall.	4.00	2.00
□□□□ 267 Vyacheslav Kozlov, Detr.	2.00	1.00
□□□□ 268 Kelly Buchberger, Edmo.	1.00	.50
□□□□ 269 Rob Niedermayer, Flor.	2.00	1.00
□□□□ 270 Geoff Sanderson, Hart.	2.00	1.00
□□□□ 271 Jan Vopat, LosA.	1.00	.50
□□□□ 272 Saku Koivu, Mont.	8.00	4.00
□□□□ 273 Scott Stevens, NJer.	4.00	2.00
□□□□ 274 Éric Fichaud (G), NYIs.	1.00	.50
□□□□ 275 Russ Courtnall, NYRa.	2.00	1.00
□□□□ 276 Wade Redden, Otta.	3.00	1.00
□□□□ 277 Petr Svoboda, Phil.	2.00	1.00
□□□□ 278 Andreas Dackell, Otta.	1.00	.50
□□□□ 279 Jason Woolley, Pitt.	1.00	.50
□□□□ 280 Stéphane Matteau, SLou.	1.00	.50
□□□□ **281 S. Guolla, SanJ. RC**	**2.00**	**1.00**
□□□□ 282 John Cullen, Tamp.	2.00	1.00
□□□□ 283 Steve Sullivan, Toro.	3.00	1.00
□□□□ 284 Bret Hedican, Vanc.	1.00	.50
□□□□ 285 Michal Pivonka, Wash.	1.00	.50
□□□□ 286 Darren Van Impe, Anah.	1.00	.50
□□□□ 287 Rob DiMaio, Bost.	1.00	.50
□□□□ 288 Garry Galley, Buff.	1.00	.50
□□□□ 289 Kent Manderville, Calg.	1.00	.50
□□□□ 290 Bob Probert, Chic.	3.00	1.00
□□□□ 291 Keith Jones, Colo.	1.00	.50
□□□□ 292 Guy Carbonneau, Dall.	3.00	1.00
□□□□ 293 Tomas Sandström, Detr.	2.00	1.00
□□□□ **294 D. McGillis, Edmo. RC**	**3.00**	**1.00**
□□□□ 295 Brian Skrudland, Flor.	1.00	.50
□□□□ 296 Stu Grimson, Hart.	2.00	1.00
□□□□ 297 Doug Zmolek, Bost.	1.00	.50
□□□□ 298 Mark Recchi, Mont.	4.00	2.00
□□□□ 299 Valeri Zelepukin, NJer.	1.00	.50
□□□□ 300 Derek Armstrong, NYIs.	1.00	.50
□□□□ **301 Eric Cairns, NYRa. RC**	**2.00**	**1.00**
□□□□ 302 Steve Duchesne, Otta.	2.00	1.00
□□□□ 303 Dainius Zubrus, Phil.	2.00	1.00
□□□□ 304 Deron Quint, Phoe.	1.00	.50
□□□□ 305 Joe Dziedzic, Pitt.	1.00	.50
□□□□ 306 Mike Peluso, SLou.	1.00	.50
□□□□ 307 Andrei Nazarov, SanJ.	1.00	.50
□□□□ 308 Chris Gratton, Tamp.	2.00	1.00
□□□□ 309 Mike Craig, Toro.	1.00	.50
□□□□ 310 Lonny Bohonos, Vanc.	1.00	.50
□□□□ 311 Rick Tocchet, Wash.	3.00	1.00
□□□□ 312 Ted Drury, Anah.	1.00	.50
□□□□ 313 Jean-Yves Roy, Bost.	1.00	.50
□□□□ 314 Jason Dawe, Buff.	1.00	.50
□□□□ 315 Jamie Allison, Calg.	1.00	.50
□□□□ 316 Alexei Zhamnov, Chic.	3.00	1.00
□□□□ **317 Aaron Miller, Colo. RC**	**2.00**	**1.00**
□□□□ 318 Todd Krygier, Wash.	1.00	.50
□□□□ 319 Tomas Holmström, Detr.	2.00	1.00
□□□□ 320 Todd Marchant, Edmo.	2.00	1.00
□□□□ 321 Scott Mellanby, Flor.	2.00	1.00
□□□□ 322 Marek Malik, Hart.	1.00	.50
□□□□ 323 Dan Bylsma, LosA.	1.00	.50
□□□□ 324 Stéphane Quintal, Mont.	1.00	.50
□□□□ 325 Ken Daneyko, NJer.	2.00	1.00
□□□□ 326 Robert Reichel, NYIs.	3.00	1.00
□□□□ 327 Daniel Goneau, NYRa.	1.00	.50
□□□□ 328 Sergei Zholtok, Otta.	1.00	.50
□□□□ 329 Kjell Samuelsson, Phil.	1.00	.50
□□□□ 330 Shane Doan, Phoe.	2.00	1.00
□□□□ 331 Radek Bonk, Otta.	3.00	1.00
□□□□ 332 Jim Campbell, SLou.	1.00	.50
□□□□ 333 Marty McSorley, SanJ.	2.00	1.00
□□□□ 334 Brantt Myhres, Tamp.	1.00	.50
□□□□ **335 Mike Johnson, Toro. RC**	**4.00**	**2.00**
□□□□ 336 Mike Sillinger, Vanc.	1.00	.50
□□□□ 337 Kelly Hrudey (G), SanJ.	3.00	1.00
□□□□ 338 Joel Bouchard, Calg.	1.00	.50
□□□□ 339 Brian Noonan, Vanc.	1.00	.50
□□□□ 340 Dean Chynoweth, Bost.	1.00	.50
□□□□ 341 Michael Peca, Buff.	4.00	2.00
□□□□ **342 Jeff Toms, Tamp. RC**	**2.00**	**1.00**
□□□□ 343 Denis Savard, Chic.	4.00	2.00
□□□□ 344 Stéphane Yelle, Colo.	1.00	.50
□□□□ 345 Grant Ledyard, Dall.	1.00	.50
□□□□ 346 Ronnie Stern, Calg.	1.00	.50
□□□□ 347 Petr Klima, Edmo.	1.00	.50
□□□□ 348 Johan Garpenlov, Flor.	1.00	.50
□□□□ 349 Nelson Emerson, Hart.	1.00	.50
□□□□ 350 Matt Johnson, LosA.	1.00	.50
□□□□ **351 Ken Belanger, NYIs. RC**	**2.00**	**1.00**

Sample	**Promo**
□ Mike Modano, Dall.	2.00

CARD SUPIALS

Insert Set (20 mini + 20 standard-sized cards): 180.00

Inserts (together 1:37)	**Mini**	
□□ 1 Paul Kariya, Anah.	5.00	10.00
□□ 2 Teemu Selänne, Anah.	3.00	5.00
□□ 3 Jarome Iginla, Calg.	3.00	5.00
□□ 4 Peter Forsberg, Colo.	5.00	10.00
□□ 5 Mike Modano, Dall.	3.00	5.00
□□ 6 Sergei Fedorov, Detr.	3.00	5.00
□□ 7 Vladimir Konstantinov, Detr.	1.00	3.00
□□ 8 Steve Yzerman, Detr.	5.00	15.00
□□ 9 John Vanbiesbrouck (G), Flor.	1.00	3.00
□□ 10 Martin Brodeur (G), NJer.	6.00	10.00
□□ 11 Doug Gilmour, NJer.	2.00	3.00
□□ 12 Wayne Gretzky, NYRa.	15.00	30.00
□□ 13 Mark Messier, NYRa.	3.00	5.00
□□ 14 John LeClair, Phil.	3.00	5.00
□□ 15 Eric Lindros, Phil.	1.00	5.00
□□ 16 Jeremy Roenick, Phoe.	3.00	5.00
□□ 17 Keith Tkachuk, Phoe.	2.00	3.00
□□ 18 Brett Hull, SLou.	3.00	5.00
□□ 19 Félix Potvin (G), Toro.	2.00	3.00
□□ 20 Pavel Bure, Vanc.	3.00	5.00

CAREER MOVES

	Career Moves	CM
☐	1 Mark Messier, Vanc.	6.00

CRAMER'S CHOICE AWARDS

	Insert Set (10 cards):	700.00
	Insert (1:721)	CCA
☐	1 Paul Kariya, Anah.	70.00
☐	2 Dominik Hasek (G), Buff.	50.00
☐	3 Jarome Iginla, Calg.	40.00
☐	4 Peter Forsberg, Colo.	70.00
☐	5 Patrick Roy (G), Colo.	150.00
☐	6 Steve Yzerman, Detr.	120.00
☐	7 Wayne Gretzky, NYRa.	200.00
☐	8 Mark Messier, NYRa.	50.00
☐	9 Eric Lindros, Phil.	50.00
☐	10 Jaromir Jagr, Pitt.	50.00

GOLD CROWN DIE CUTS

	Insert Set (20 cards):	195.00
	Insert (1:37)	GCDC
☐	1 Paul Kariya, Anah.	10.00
☐	2 Teemu Selänne, Anah.	5.00
☐	3 Dominik Hasek (G), Buff.	10.00
☐	4 Michael Peca, Buff.	4.00
☐	5 Jarome Iginla, Calg.	5.00
☐	6 Chris Chelios, Chic.	5.00
☐	7 Peter Forsberg, Colo.	10.00
☐	8 Patrick Roy (G), Colo.	30.00
☐	9 Joe Sakic, Colo.	15.00
☐	10 Brendan Shanahan, Detr.	10.00
☐	11 Steve Yzerman, Detr.	20.00
☐	12 Ryan Smyth, Edmo.	4.00
☐	13 John Vanbiesbrouck (G), Flor.	4.00
☐	14 Martin Brodeur (G), NJer.	15.00
☐	15 Wayne Gretzky, NYRa.	40.00
☐	16 Mark Messier, NYRa.	10.00
☐	17 Eric Lindros, Phil.	10.00
☐	18 Jaromir Jagr, Pitt.	10.00
☐	19 Brett Hull, SLou.	10.00
☐	20 Pavel Bure, Vanc.	5.00

IN THE CREASE

	Insert Set (20 cards):	290.00
	Insert (1:145)	ITC
☐	1 Guy Hebert (G), Anah.	8.00
☐	2 Dominik Hasek (G), Buff.	25.00
☐	3 Trevor Kidd (G), Calg.	8.00
☐	4 Jeff Hackett (G), Chic.	8.00
☐	5 Patrick Roy (G), Colo.	70.00
☐	6 Andy Moog (G), Dall.	10.00
☐	7 Chris Osgood (G), Detr.	15.00
☐	8 Mike Vernon (G), Detr.	10.00
☐	9 Curtis Joseph (G), Edmo.	25.00
☐	10 John Vanbiesbrouck (G), Flor.	10.00
☐	11 Jocelyn Thibault (G), Mont.	10.00
☐	12 Martin Brodeur (G), NJer.	40.00
☐	13 Mike Richter (G), NYRa.	10.00
☐	14 Ron Hextall (G), Phil.	15.00
☐	15 Garth Snow (G), Phil.	8.00
☐	16 Nikolai Khabibulin (G), Phoe.	10.00
☐	17 Patrick Lalime (G), Pitt.	15.00
☐	18 Grant Fuhr (G), SLou.	15.00
☐	19 Ed Belfour (G), SanJ.	20.00
☐	20 Félix Potvin (G), Toro.	15.00

SLAP SHOT DIE CUTS

	Insert Set (36 cards):	405.00
	Insert (1:73)	SSDC
☐	1A Paul Kariya, Anah.	20.00
☐	1B Jari Kurri, Anah.	15.00
☐	1C Teemu Selänne, Anah.	10.00
☐	2A Peter Forsberg, Colo.	20.00
☐	2B Joe Sakic, Colo.	25.00
☐	2C Claude Lemieux, Colo.	6.00
☐	3A Brendan Shanahan, Detr.	15.00
☐	3B Sergei Fedorov, Detr.	15.00
☐	3C Steve Yzerman, Detr.	40.00
☐	4A Mark Recchi, Mont.	6.00
☐	4B Vincent Damphousse, Mont.	10.00
☐	4C Stéphane Richer, Mont.	6.00
☐	5A Wayne Gretzky, NYRa.	70.00
☐	5B Mark Messier, NYRa.	15.00
☐	5C Brian Leetch, NYRa.	10.00
☐	6A Rod Brind'Amour, Phil.	6.00
☐	6B Eric Lindros, Phil.	15.00
☐	6C John LeClair, Phil.	10.00
☐	7A Keith Tkachuk, Phoe.	10.00
☐	7B Jeremy Roenick, Phoe.	10.00
☐	7C Mike Gartner, Phoe.	10.00
☐	8A Petr Nedved, Pitt.	6.00
☐	8B Ron Francis, Pitt.	10.00
☐	8C Jaromir Jagr, Pgh	15.00
☐	9A Geoff Courtnall, SLou.	6.00
☐	9B Pierre Turgeon, SLou.	6.00
☐	9C Brett Hull, SLou.	15.00
☐	10A Wendel Clark, Toro.	10.00
☐	10B Mats Sundin, Toro.	15.00
☐	10C Sergei Berezin, Toro.	6.00
☐	11A Pavel Bure, Vanc.	10.00
☐	11B Trevor Linden, Vanc.	6.00
☐	11C Alexander Mogilny, Can.	6.00
☐	12A Joé Juneau, Wash.	6.00
☐	12B Adam Oates, Wash.	6.00
☐	12C Peter Bondra, Wash.	10.00

TEAM CHECKLISTS

	Insert Set (26 cards):	300.00
	Insert (1:73)	TC
☐	1 Teemu Selänne, Anah.	10.00
☐	2 Raymond Bourque, Bost.	15.00
☐	3 Dominik Hasek (G), Buff.	10.00
☐	4 Jarome Iginla, Calg.	10.00
☐	5 Keith Primeau, Hart. (Caro.)	5.00
☐	6 Chris Chelios, Chic.	5.00
☐	7 Patrick Roy (G), Colo.	45.00
☐	8 Mike Modano, Dall.	15.00
☐	9 Steve Yzerman, Detr.	35.00
☐	10 Curtis Joseph (G), Edmo.	15.00
☐	11 John Vanbiesbrouck (G), Flor.	5.00
☐	12 Rob Blake, LosA.	5.00
☐	13 Stéphane Richer, Mont.	5.00
☐	14 Martin Brodeur (G), NJer.	20.00
☐	15 Zigmund Palffy, NYIs.	5.00
☐	16 Wayne Gretzky, NYRa.	60.00
☐	17 Alexandre Daigle, Otta.	5.00
☐	18 Eric Lindros, Phil.	15.00
☐	19 Jeremy Roenick, Phoe.	10.00
☐	20 Jaromir Jagr, Pitt.	15.00
☐	21 Brett Hull, SLou.	15.00
☐	22 Owen Nolan, SanJ.	5.00
☐	23 Dino Ciccarelli, Tamp.	5.00
☐	24 Félix Potvin (G), Toro.	5.00
☐	25 Pavel Bure, Vanc.	10.00
☐	26 Peter Bondra, Wash.	5.00

1997 - 98 PACIFIC CROWN ROYALE

These die-cut cards have four versions: the regular card, a Silver parallel (U.S packs), an Emerald Green parallel (Canadian packs) and an Ice Blue parallel.

		Ice Blue	Si/Em	CR
	Complete Set (144 cards):	2200.00	550.00	115.00
	Common Player:	8.00	1.50	.50
	Player	Ice Blue	Si/Em	CR
☐☐☐☐	1 Guy Hebert (G), Anah.	10.00	3.00	.50
☐☐☐☐	2 Paul Kariya, Anah.	70.00	15.00	3.00
☐☐☐☐	3 Steve Rucchin, Anah.	10.00	3.00	.50
☐☐☐☐	4 Tomas Sandström, Anah.	10.00	3.00	.50
☐☐☐☐	5 Teemu Selänne, Anah.	40.00	10.00	2.00
☐☐☐☐	6 Jason Allison, Bost.	30.00	5.00	1.00
☐☐☐☐	7 Raymond Bourque, Bost.	60.00	15.00	3.00
☐☐☐☐	8 Anson Carter, Bost.	20.00	5.00	1.00
☐☐☐☐	9 Byron Dafoe (G), Bost.	20.00	5.00	1.00
☐☐☐☐	10 Ted Donato, Bost.	8.00	1.50	.50
☐☐☐☐	11 Joe Thornton, Bost.	60.00	15.00	6.00
☐☐☐☐	12 Jason Dawe, Buff.	8.00	1.50	.50
☐☐☐☐	13 Michal Grosek, Buff.	8.00	1.50	.50
☐☐☐☐	14 Dominik Hasek (G), Buff.	50.00	10.00	2.00
☐☐☐☐	15 Michael Peca, Buff.	20.00	5.00	1.00
☐☐☐☐	16 Miroslav Satan, Buff.	15.00	4.00	.50
☐☐☐☐	**17 Chris Dingman, Calg. RC**	**8.00**	**4.00**	**2.00**
☐☐☐☐	18 Theoren Fleury, Calg.	30.00	5.00	1.00
☐☐☐☐	19 Jarome Iginla, Calg.	40.00	10.00	2.00
☐☐☐☐	**20 Tyler Moss (G), Calg. RC**	**8.00**	**4.00**	**2.00**
☐☐☐☐	21 Cory Stillman, Calg.	10.00	3.00	.50
☐☐☐☐	22 Kevin Dineen, Caro.	8.00	2.00	.50
☐☐☐☐	23 Nelson Emerson, Caro.	8.00	2.00	.50
☐☐☐☐	24 Trevor Kidd (G), Caro.	15.00	4.00	.50
☐☐☐☐	25 Keith Primeau, Caro.	20.00	5.00	1.00
☐☐☐☐	26 Geoff Sanderson, Caro.	10.00	3.00	.50
☐☐☐☐	27 Tony Amonte, Chic.	30.00	7.00	1.00
☐☐☐☐	28 Chris Chelios, Chic.	30.00	7.00	1.00
☐☐☐☐	29 Eric Dazé, Chic.	20.00	5.00	1.00
☐☐☐☐	30 Jeff Hackett (G), Chic.	15.00	4.00	.50
☐☐☐☐	31 Chris Terreri (G), Chic.	8.00	2.00	.50
☐☐☐☐	32 Adam Deadmarsh, Colo.	15.00	4.00	.50
☐☐☐☐	33 Peter Forsberg, Colo.	70.00	15.00	3.00
☐☐☐☐	34 Valeri Kamensky, Colo.	15.00	4.00	.50
☐☐☐☐	35 Jari Kurri, Colo.	50.00	10.00	2.00
☐☐☐☐	36 Claude Lemieux, Colo.	15.00	4.00	.50
☐☐☐☐	37 Patrick Roy (G), Colo.	150.00	35.00	7.00
☐☐☐☐	38 Joe Sakic, Colo.	80.00	20.00	4.00
☐☐☐☐	39 Ed Belfour (G), Dall.	50.00	10.00	2.00
☐☐☐☐	40 Derian Hatcher, Dall.	15.00	4.00	.50
☐☐☐☐	41 Mike Modano, Dall.	50.00	10.00	2.00
☐☐☐☐	42 Joe Nieuwendyk, Dall.	20.00	5.00	1.00
☐☐☐☐	43 Pat Verbeek, Dall.	15.00	4.00	.50
☐☐☐☐	44 Sergei Zubov, Dall.	10.00	3.00	.50
☐☐☐☐	45 Sergei Fedorov, Detr.	50.00	10.00	2.00
☐☐☐☐	46 Vyacheslav Kozlov, Detr.	10.00	3.00	.50
☐☐☐☐	47 Nicklas Lidström, Detr.	30.00	7.00	1.00
☐☐☐☐	48 Darren McCarty, Detr.	15.00	4.00	.50
☐☐☐☐	49 Chris Osgood (G), Detr.	30.00	5.00	1.00
☐☐☐☐	50 Brendan Shanahan, Detr.	50.00	10.00	2.00
☐☐☐☐	51 Steve Yzerman, Detr.	120.00	30.00	6.00
☐☐☐☐	52 Jason Arnott, Edmo.	20.00	6.00	1.00
☐☐☐☐	53 Curtis Joseph (G), Edmo.	50.00	10.00	2.00
☐☐☐☐	54 Ryan Smyth, Edmo.	20.00	6.00	1.00
☐☐☐☐	55 Doug Weight, Edmo.	30.00	5.00	1.00
☐☐☐☐	56 Dave Gagner, Flor.	8.00	2.00	.50
☐☐☐☐	57 Ed Jovanovski, Flor.	20.00	5.00	1.00
☐☐☐☐	58 Viktor Kozlov, Flor.	15.00	4.00	.50
☐☐☐☐	59 Scott Mellanby, Flor.	10.00	3.00	.50
☐☐☐☐	60 J. Vanbiesbrouck (G), Flor.	20.00	6.00	1.00
☐☐☐☐	**61 K. Weekes (G), Flor. RC**	**10.00**	**6.00**	**4.00**
☐☐☐☐	62 Rob Blake, LosA.	30.00	7.00	1.00
☐☐☐☐	**63 D. MacLean, LosA. RC**	**8.00**	**2.00**	**1.00**
☐☐☐☐	64 Yanic Perreault, LosA.	15.00	4.00	.50
☐☐☐☐	65 Luc Robitaille, LosA.	40.00	10.00	2.00
☐☐☐☐	66 Jozef Stumpel, LosA.	10.00	3.00	.50
☐☐☐☐	67 Shayne Corson, Mont.	15.00	4.00	.50
☐☐☐☐	68 Vincent Damphousse, Mont.	30.00	7.00	1.00
☐☐☐☐	69 Saku Koivu, Mont.	40.00	10.00	2.00
☐☐☐☐	70 Andy Moog (G), Mont.	20.00	5.00	1.00
☐☐☐☐	71 Mark Recchi, Mont.	20.00	5.00	1.00
☐☐☐☐	72 Stéphane Richer, Mont.	10.00	3.00	.50
☐☐☐☐	73 Martin Brodeur (G), NJer.	80.00	20.00	4.00
☐☐☐☐	**74 Patrik Elias, NJer. RC**	**40.00**	**20.00**	**10.00**
☐☐☐☐	75 Doug Gilmour, NJer.	30.00	7.00	1.00
☐☐☐☐	76 Bobby Holik, NJer.	15.00	4.00	.50
☐☐☐☐	77 Scott Stevens, NJer.	20.00	5.00	1.00
☐☐☐☐	78 Bryan Berard, NYIs.	15.00	4.00	.50
☐☐☐☐	79 Zigmund Palffy, NYIs.	30.00	7.00	1.00
☐☐☐☐	80 Robert Reichel, NYIs.	15.00	4.00	.50
☐☐☐☐	81 Tommy Salo (G), NYIs.	20.00	5.00	1.00
☐☐☐☐	82 Bryan Smolinski, NYIs.	8.00	2.00	.50
☐☐☐☐	83 Adam Graves, NYRa.	20.00	5.00	1.00
☐☐☐☐	84 Wayne Gretzky, NYRa.	200.00	50.00	10.00
☐☐☐☐	85 Pat LaFontaine, NYRa.	30.00	7.00	1.00
☐☐☐☐	86 Brian Leetch, NYRa.	30.00	7.00	1.00
☐☐☐☐	87 Mike Richter (G), NYRa.	20.00	6.00	1.00
☐☐☐☐	88 Niklas Sundström, NYRa.	10.00	3.00	.50
☐☐☐☐	89 Daniel Alfredsson, Otta.	30.00	7.00	1.00
☐☐☐☐	90 Alexandre Daigle, Otta.	8.00	2.00	.50
☐☐☐☐	91 Shawn McEachern, Otta.	15.00	4.00	.50
☐☐☐☐	92 Chris Phillips, Otta.	10.00	3.00	1.00
☐☐☐☐	93 Ron Tugnutt (G), Otta.	20.00	5.00	1.00
☐☐☐☐	94 Alexei Yashin, Otta.	30.00	7.00	1.00
☐☐☐☐	95 Rod Brind'Amour, Phil.	15.00	4.00	.50
☐☐☐☐	96 Chris Gratton, Phil.	10.00	3.00	.50
☐☐☐☐	97 Ron Hextall (G), Phil.	30.00	7.00	1.00
☐☐☐☐	98 John LeClair, Phil.	40.00	10.00	2.00
☐☐☐☐	99 Eric Lindros, Phil.	50.00	10.00	2.00
☐☐☐☐	**100 Vaclav Prospal, Phil. RC**	**15.00**	**8.00**	**4.00**
☐☐☐☐	101 Dainius Zubrus, Phil.	10.00	3.00	.50
☐☐☐☐	102 Mike Gartner, Phoe.	40.00	10.00	2.00
☐☐☐☐	103 Brad Isbister, Phoe.	10.00	3.00	1.00
☐☐☐☐	104 Nikolai Khabibulin (G), Phoe.	20.00	5.00	1.00
☐☐☐☐	105 Jeremy Roenick, Phoe.	40.00	10.00	2.00
☐☐☐☐	106 Cliff Ronning, Phoe.	10.00	3.00	.50
☐☐☐☐	107 Keith Tkachuk, Phoe.	30.00	5.00	1.00
☐☐☐☐	108 Tom Barrasso (G), Pitt.	20.00	5.00	1.00
☐☐☐☐	109 Ron Francis, Pitt.	30.00	7.00	1.00
☐☐☐☐	110 Jaromir Jagr, Pitt.	50.00	10.00	2.00
☐☐☐☐	111 Alexei Morozov, Pitt.	10.00	3.00	1.00
☐☐☐☐	112 Ed Olczyk, Pitt.	10.00	3.00	.50
☐☐☐☐	113 Jim Campbell, SLou.	8.00	1.50	.50
☐☐☐☐	114 Pavol Demitra, SLou.	20.00	5.00	1.00
☐☐☐☐	115 Steve Duchesne, SLou.	10.00	3.00	.50
☐☐☐☐	116 Grant Fuhr (G), SLou.	30.00	7.00	1.00
☐☐☐☐	117 Brett Hull, SLou.	50.00	10.00	2.00
☐☐☐☐	118 Pierre Turgeon, SLou.	20.00	5.00	1.00
☐☐☐☐	119 Jeff Friesen, SanJ.	15.00	4.00	.50
☐☐☐☐	120 Patrick Marleau, SanJ.	20.00	6.00	2.00
☐☐☐☐	121 Owen Nolan, SanJ.	30.00	7.00	1.00
☐☐☐☐	**122 Marco Sturm, SanJ. RC**	**10.00**	**6.00**	**3.00**
☐☐☐☐	123 Mike Vernon, SanJ.	20.00	5.00	1.00
☐☐☐☐	124 Dino Ciccarelli, Tamp.	15.00	4.00	.50
☐☐☐☐	125 Roman Hamrlik, Tamp.	10.00	3.00	.50
☐☐☐☐	126 Daren Puppa (G), Tamp.	10.00	3.00	.50
☐☐☐☐	127 Paul Ysebaert, Tamp.	8.00	1.50	.50
☐☐☐☐	128 Sergei Berezin, Toro.	10.00	3.00	.50
☐☐☐☐	129 Wendel Clark, Toro.	40.00	10.00	2.00
☐☐☐☐	130 Alyn McCauley, Toro.	15.00	4.00	1.00
☐☐☐☐	131 Félix Potvin (G), Toro.	30.00	7.00	1.00
☐☐☐☐	132 Mats Sundin, Toro.	50.00	10.00	2.00
☐☐☐☐	133 Pavel Bure, Vanc.	40.00	10.00	2.00
☐☐☐☐	134 Martin Gelinas, Vanc.	10.00	3.00	.50
☐☐☐☐	135 Trevor Linden, Vanc.	20.00	5.00	1.00
☐☐☐☐	136 Mark Messier, Vanc.	50.00	10.00	2.00
☐☐☐☐	137 Alexander Mogilny, Vanc.	20.00	6.00	1.00
☐☐☐☐	138 Peter Bondra, Wash.	30.00	7.00	1.00
☐☐☐☐	139 Dale Hunter, Wash.	15.00	4.00	.50
☐☐☐☐	140 Joé Juneau, Wash.	10.00	3.00	.50
☐☐☐☐	141 Olaf Kölzig, Wash.	30.00	7.00	1.00
☐☐☐☐	142 Adam Oates, Wash.	20.00	5.00	1.00
☐☐☐☐	143 Jaroslav Svejkovsky, Wash.	8.00	2.00	.50
☐☐☐☐	144 Richard Zednik, Wash.	20.00	5.00	1.00

	Sample	Promo
☐	Mike Modano, Dall.	2.00

CRAMER'S CHOICE AWARDS

Cramer's Choice Awards oversized cards are inserted one per box. A parallel version limited to 10 copies each and signed by Michael Cramer also exists.

	Insert Set (10 cards):	5,000.00	85.00
	Insert	CCAS	CCA
☐☐	1 Paul Kariya, Anah.	475.00	8.00
☐☐	2 Teemu Selänne, Anah.	275.00	6.00
☐☐	3 Joe Thornton, Bost.	400.00	6.00
☐☐	4 Peter Forsberg, Colo.	475.00	8.00
☐☐	5 Patrick Roy (G), Colo.	1000.00	18.00
☐☐	6 Steve Yzerman, Detr.	825.00	14.00
☐☐	7 Wayne Gretzky, NYRa.	1400.00	25.00
☐☐	8 Eric Lindros, Phil.	350.00	6.00
☐☐	9 Jaromir Jagr, Pitt.	350.00	6.00
☐☐	10 Pavel Bure, Vanc.	275.00	6.00

BLADES OF STEEL

Insert Set (20 cards): 300.00

	Player	BoS
	Insert (1:49)	BoS
☐	1 Paul Kariya, Anah.	20.00
☐	2 Teemu Selänne, Anah.	10.00
☐	3 Joe Thornton, Bost.	25.00
☐	4 Chris Chelios, Chic.	6.00
☐	5 Peter Forsberg, Colo.	20.00
☐	6 Patrick Roy (G), Colo.	45.00
☐	7 Mike Modano, Dall.	15.00
☐	8 Sergei Fedorov, Detr.	15.00
☐	9 Brendan Shanahan, Detr.	15.00
☐	10 Steve Yzerman, Detr.	35.00
☐	11 Ryan Smyth, Edmo.	6.00
☐	12 Saku Koivu, Mont.	10.00
☐	13 Bryan Berard, NYIs.	6.00
☐	14 Wayne Gretzky, NYRa.	60.00
☐	15 Brian Leetch, NYRa.	6.00
☐	16 Eric Lindros, Phil.	15.00
☐	17 Jaromir Jagr, Pitt.	15.00
☐	18 Brett Hull, SLou.	15.00
☐	19 Pavel Bure, Vanc.	10.00
☐	20 Mark Messier, Vanc.	15.00

FREEZE OUT

	Player	Price
	Insert Set (20 cards):	150.00
	Insert (1:25)	FO
☐	1 Guy Hebert (G), Anah.	6.00
☐	2 Byron Dafoe (G), Bost.	6.00
☐	3 Dominik Hasek (G), Buff.	10.00
☐	4 Tyler Moss (G), Calg.	6.00
☐	5 Patrick Roy (G), Colo.	40.00
☐	6 Ed Belfour (G), Dall.	10.00
☐	7 Chris Osgood (G), Detr.	6.00
☐	8 Curtis Joseph (G), Edmo.	10.00
☐	9 John Vanbiesbrouck (G), Flor.	6.00
☐	10 Andy Moog (G), Mont.	6.00
☐	11 Martin Brodeur (G), NJer.	20.00
☐	12 Mike Richter (G), NYRa.	6.00
☐	13 Ron Hextall (G), Phil.	6.00
☐	14 Garth Snow (G), Phil.	6.00
☐	15 Nikolai Khabibulin (G), Phoe.	6.00
☐	16 Tom Barrasso (G), Pitt.	6.00
☐	17 Grant Fuhr (G), SLou.	6.00
☐	18 Mike Vernon (G), SanJ.	6.00
☐	19 Félix Potvin (G), Toro.	6.00
☐	20 Olaf Kölzig (G), Wash.	6.00

HAT TRICKS

	Player	Price
	Insert Set (20 cards):	225.00
	Insert (1:25)	HT
☐	1 Paul Kariya, Anah.	15.00
☐	2 Teemu Selänne, Anah.	10.00
☐	3 Joe Thornton, Bost.	20.00
☐	4 Peter Forsberg, Colo.	15.00
☐	5 Joe Sakic, Colo.	20.00
☐	6 Mike Modano, Dall.	10.00
☐	7 Brendan Shanahan, Detr.	10.00
☐	8 Steve Yzerman, Detr.	30.00
☐	9 Ryan Smyth, Edmo.	5.00
☐	10 Zigmund Palffy, NYIs.	5.00
☐	11 Wayne Gretzky, NYRa.	50.00
☐	12 John LeClair, Phil.	10.00
☐	13 Eric Lindros, Phil.	10.00
☐	14 Keith Tkachuk, Phoe.	5.00
☐	15 Jaromir Jagr, Pitt.	10.00
☐	16 Brett Hull, SLou.	10.00
☐	17 Mats Sundin, Toro.	10.00
☐	18 Pavel Bure, Vanc.	10.00
☐	19 Mark Messier, Vanc.	10.00
☐	20 Peter Bondra, Wash.	5.00

LAMPLIGHTERS

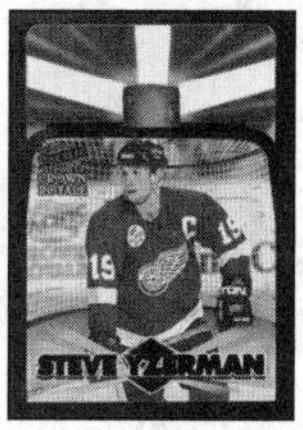

	Player	Price
	Insert Set (20 cards):	495.00
	Insert (1:73)	LL
☐	1 Paul Kariya, Anah.	30.00
☐	2 Teemu Selänne, Anah.	20.00
☐	3 Joe Thornton, Bost.	45.00
☐	4 Michael Peca, Buff.	10.00
☐	5 Peter Forsberg, Colo.	35.00
☐	6 Joe Sakic, Colo.	40.00
☐	7 Mike Modano, Dall.	25.00
☐	8 Brendan Shanahan, Detr.	25.00
☐	9 Steve Yzerman, Detr.	60.00
☐	10 Saku Koivu, Mont.	20.00
☐	11 Wayne Gretzky, NYRa.	100.00
☐	12 Pat LaFontaine, NYRa.	15.00
☐	13 John LeClair, Phil.	20.00
☐	14 Eric Lindros, Phil.	25.00
☐	15 Dainius Zubrus, Phil.	8.00
☐	16 Keith Tkachuk, Phoe.	15.00
☐	17 Jaromir Jagr, Pitt.	20.00
☐	18 Brett Hull, SLou.	25.00
☐	19 Pavel Bure, Vanc.	20.00
☐	20 Mark Messier, Vanc.	25.00

1997 - 98 PACIFIC DYNAGON

These cards have seven versions: the regular Gold card, an Emerald Green parallel (Canadian hobby), a Dark Grey (Canadian retail), a Copper parallel (Hobby), a Silver parallel (Retail), a Red parallel and an Ice Blue parallel.

	Player	IB67	Dyn.
	Complete Set (156 cards):	2100.00	100.00
	Common Player:	6.00	.50
	Player	IB67	Dyn.
☐☐	1 Brian Bellows	10.00	.50
☐☐	2 Guy Hebert (G)	10.00	.50
☐☐	3 Paul Kariya	70.00	3.00
☐☐	4 Steve Rucchin	10.00	.50
☐☐	5 Teemu Selänne	40.00	2.00
☐☐	6 Jason Allison	30.00	1.00
☐☐	7 Raymond Bourque	60.00	3.00
☐☐	8 Jim Carey (G)	6.00	.50
☐☐	9 Jozef Stumpel	10.00	.50
☐☐	10 Dominik Hasek (G)	50.00	2.00
☐☐	11 Brian Holzinger	6.00	.50
☐☐	12 Michael Peca	20.00	1.00
☐☐	13 Derek Plante	6.00	.50
☐☐	14 Miroslav Satan	15.00	.50
☐☐	15 Theoren Fleury	30.00	1.00
☐☐	16 Jonas Höglund	6.00	.50
☐☐	17 Jarome Iginla	40.00	2.00
☐☐	18 Trevor Kidd (G)	15.00	.50
☐☐	19 German Titov	6.00	.50
☐☐	20 Sean Burke (G)	30.00	1.00
☐☐	21 Andrew Cassels	10.00	.50
☐☐	22 Keith Primeau	20.00	1.00
☐☐	23 Geoff Sanderson	10.00	.50
☐☐	24 Tony Amonte	30.00	1.00
☐☐	25 Chris Chelios	30.00	1.00
☐☐	26 Éric Dazé	20.00	1.00
☐☐	27 Jeff Hackett (G)	15.00	.50
☐☐	28 Ethan Moreau	6.00	.50
☐☐	29 Peter Forsberg	70.00	3.00
☐☐	30 Valeri Kamensky	15.00	.50
☐☐	31 Claude Lemieux	15.00	.50
☐☐	32 Sandis Ozolinsh	10.00	.50
☐☐	33 Patrick Roy (G)	150.00	7.00
☐☐	34 Joe Sakic	80.00	4.00
☐☐	35 Derian Hatcher	15.00	.50
☐☐	36 Jamie Langenbrunner	10.00	.50
☐☐	37 Mike Modano	50.00	2.00
☐☐	38 Joe Nieuwendyk	20.00	1.00
☐☐	39 Darryl Sydor	10.00	.50
☐☐	40 Sergei Zubov	10.00	.50
☐☐	41 Sergei Fedorov	50.00	2.00
☐☐	42 Vladimir Konstantinov	15.00	.50
☐☐	43 Chris Osgood (G)	30.00	1.00
☐☐	44 Brendan Shanahan	50.00	2.00
☐☐	45 Mike Vernon (G)	20.00	1.00
☐☐	46 Steve Yzerman	120.00	6.00
☐☐	47 Kelly Buchberger	6.00	.50
☐☐	48 Mike Grier	10.00	.50
☐☐	49 Curtis Joseph (G)	50.00	2.00
☐☐	50 Rem Murray	6.00	.50
☐☐	51 Ryan Smyth	20.00	1.00
☐☐	52 Doug Weight	30.00	1.00
☐☐	53 Ed Jovanovski	20.00	1.00
☐☐	54 Scott Mellanby	10.00	.50
☐☐	55 Ray Sheppard	6.00	.50
☐☐	56 Robert Svehla	10.00	.50
☐☐	57 John Vanbiesbrouck (G)	20.00	1.00
☐☐	58 Rob Blake	30.00	1.00
☐☐	59 Ray Ferraro	6.00	.50
☐☐	60 Dmitri Khristich	6.00	.50
☐☐	61 Vladimir Tsyplakov	6.00	.50
☐☐	62 Vincent Damphousse	30.00	1.00
☐☐	63 Saku Koivu	40.00	2.00
☐☐	64 Mark Recchi	20.00	1.00
☐☐	65 Stéphane Richer	10.00	.50
☐☐	66 Jocelyn Thibault (G)	20.00	1.00
☐☐	67 Dave Andreychuk	15.00	.50
☐☐	68 Martin Brodeur (G)	80.00	4.00
☐☐	69 Doug Gilmour	30.00	1.00
☐☐	70 Bobby Holik	15.00	.50
☐☐	71 John MacLean	6.00	.50
☐☐	72 Bryan Berard	15.00	.50
☐☐	73 Travis Green	10.00	.50
☐☐	74 Zigmund Palffy	30.00	1.00
☐☐	75 Tommy Salo (G)	20.00	1.00
☐☐	76 Bryan Smolinski	6.00	.50
☐☐	77 Adam Graves	20.00	1.00
☐☐	78 Wayne Gretzky	200.00	10.00
☐☐	79 Alex Kovalev	30.00	1.00
☐☐	80 Brian Leetch	30.00	1.00
☐☐	81 Mark Messier	50.00	2.00
☐☐	82 Mike Richter (G)	20.00	1.00
☐☐	83 Daniel Alfredsson	30.00	1.00
☐☐	84 Alexandre Daigle	6.00	.50
☐☐	85 Wade Redden	15.00	.50
☐☐	86 Damian Rhodes (G)	10.00	.50
☐☐	87 Alexei Yashin	30.00	1.00
☐☐	88 Rod Brind'Amour	15.00	.50
☐☐	89 Ron Hextall (G)	30.00	1.00
☐☐	90 John LeClair	40.00	2.00
☐☐	91 Eric Lindros	50.00	2.00
☐☐	92 Janne Niinimaa	10.00	.50
☐☐	93 Garth Snow (G)	15.00	.50
☐☐	94 Dainius Zubrus	10.00	.50
☐☐	95 Mike Gartner	40.00	2.00
☐☐	96 Nikolai Khabibulin (G)	20.00	1.00
☐☐	97 Jeremy Roenick	40.00	2.00
☐☐	98 Keith Tkachuk	30.00	1.00
☐☐	99 Oleg Tverdovsky	6.00	.50
☐☐	100 Ron Francis	30.00	1.00
☐☐	101 Kevin Hatcher	6.00	.50
☐☐	102 Jaromir Jagr	50.00	2.00
☐☐	103 Patrick Lalime (G)	30.00	1.00
☐☐	104 Petr Nedved	15.00	.50
☐☐	105 Jim Campbell	6.00	.50
☐☐	106 Grant Fuhr (G)	30.00	1.00
☐☐	107 Brett Hull	50.00	2.00
☐☐	108 Pierre Turgeon	20.00	1.00
☐☐	109 Harry York	6.00	.50
☐☐	110 Jeff Friesen	15.00	.50
☐☐	111 Tony Granato	10.00	.50
☐☐	**112 Stephen Guolla RC**	**6.00**	**1.00**
☐☐	113 Viktor Kozlov	15.00	.50
☐☐	114 Owen Nolan	30.00	1.00
☐☐	115 Dino Ciccarelli	15.00	.50
☐☐	116 John Cullen	10.00	.50
☐☐	117 Chris Gratton	10.00	.50
☐☐	118 Roman Hamrlik	10.00	.50
☐☐	119 Daymond Langkow	10.00	.50
☐☐	120 Sergei Berezin	10.00	.50
☐☐	121 Wendel Clark	40.00	2.00
☐☐	122 Félix Potvin (G)	30.00	1.00
☐☐	123 Steve Sullivan	15.00	.50
☐☐	124 Mats Sundin	50.00	2.00
☐☐	125 Pavel Bure	40.00	2.00
☐☐	126 Martin Gélinas	10.00	.50
☐☐	127 Trevor Linden	20.00	1.00
☐☐	128 Kirk McLean (G)	15.00	.50
☐☐	129 Alexander Mogilny	20.00	1.00
☐☐	130 Peter Bondra	30.00	1.00
☐☐	131 Joé Juneau	10.00	.50
☐☐	132 Steve Konowalchuk	10.00	.50
☐☐	133 Adam Oates	20.00	1.00
☐☐	134 Bill Ranford	20.00	1.00
☐☐	135 P. Kariya / T. Selänne	50.00	2.00
☐☐	136 D. Hasek / M. Peca	30.00	1.00
☐☐	137 T. Fleury / J. Iginla	30.00	1.00
☐☐	138 P. Forsberg / P. Roy	110.00	5.00
☐☐	139 B. Shanahan / S. Yzerman	80.00	4.00
☐☐	140 W. Gretzky / M. Messier	120.00	6.00
☐☐	141 J. LeClair / E. Lindros	40.00	2.00
☐☐	142 J. Jagr / P. Lalime	40.00	2.00
☐☐	143 Br. Hull / J. Campbell	25.00	1.00
☐☐	144 M. Sundin / S. Berezin	30.00	1.00
☐☐	**Shawn Bates RC**	**8.00**	**3.00**
☐☐	Daniel Cleary	15.00	1.00
☐☐	**Marian Hossa RC**	**100.00**	**20.00**
☐☐	**Olli Jokinen RC**	**15.00**	**7.00**
☐☐	**Espen Knutsen RC**	**10.00**	**5.00**
☐☐	Patrick Marleau	20.00	2.00
☐☐	Alyn McCauley	15.00	1.00
☐☐	Mattias Öhlund	15.00	1.00
☐☐	Chris Phillips	10.00	1.00
☐☐	Erik Rasmussen	10.00	1.00
☐☐	Sergei Samsonov	30.00	3.00
☐☐	Joe Thornton	60.00	7.00

TWO-PER-BOX PARALLELS

Two-per-box parallels are Copper (US hobby), Silver (US retail), Emerald (Cdn. hobby), Dark Grey (Cdn. retail), and Red (Treat packs). Dealers may sell some parallels for more or less depending on their supply.

	Player	Parallel
	Complete Set (156 cards):	625.00
	Common Player:	2.00
	Player	Parallel
☐☐☐☐☐	1 Brian Bellows	2.00
☐☐☐☐☐	2 Guy Hebert (G)	2.00
☐☐☐☐☐	3 Paul Kariya	20.00
☐☐☐☐☐	4 Steve Rucchin	2.00
☐☐☐☐☐	5 Teemu Selänne	12.00
☐☐☐☐☐	6 Jason Allison	8.00
☐☐☐☐☐	7 Raymond Bourque	18.00
☐☐☐☐☐	8 Jim Carey (G)	2.00
☐☐☐☐☐	9 Jozef Stumpel	2.00
☐☐☐☐☐	10 Dominik Hasek (G)	14.00
☐☐☐☐☐	11 Brian Holzinger	2.00
☐☐☐☐☐	12 Michael Peca	6.00
☐☐☐☐☐	13 Derek Plante	2.00
☐☐☐☐☐	14 Miroslav Satan	4.00
☐☐☐☐☐	15 Theoren Fleury	8.00
☐☐☐☐☐	16 Jonas Höglund	2.00
☐☐☐☐☐	17 Jarome Iginla	12.00
☐☐☐☐☐	18 Trevor Kidd (G)	4.00
☐☐☐☐☐	19 German Titov	2.00
☐☐☐☐☐	20 Sean Burke (G)	8.00
☐☐☐☐☐	21 Andrew Cassels	2.00
☐☐☐☐☐	22 Keith Primeau	6.00
☐☐☐☐☐	23 Geoff Sanderson	2.00
☐☐☐☐☐	24 Tony Amonte	8.00
☐☐☐☐☐	25 Chris Chelios	8.00
☐☐☐☐☐	26 Éric Dazé	6.00
☐☐☐☐☐	27 Jeff Hackett (G)	4.00
☐☐☐☐☐	28 Ethan Moreau	2.00
☐☐☐☐☐	29 Peter Forsberg	20.00
☐☐☐☐☐	30 Valeri Kamensky	4.00
☐☐☐☐☐	31 Claude Lemieux	4.00
☐☐☐☐☐	32 Sandis Ozolinsh	2.00
☐☐☐☐☐	33 Patrick Roy (G)	45.00
☐☐☐☐☐	34 Joe Sakic	24.00
☐☐☐☐☐	35 Derian Hatcher	4.00
☐☐☐☐☐	36 Jamie Langenbrunner	2.00
☐☐☐☐☐	37 Mike Modano	14.00
☐☐☐☐☐	38 Joe Nieuwendyk	6.00
☐☐☐☐☐	39 Darryl Sydor	2.00
☐☐☐☐☐	40 Sergei Zubov	2.00
☐☐☐☐☐	41 Sergei Fedorov	14.00
☐☐☐☐☐	42 Vladimir Konstantinov	4.00
☐☐☐☐☐	43 Chris Osgood (G)	8.00
☐☐☐☐☐	44 Brendan Shanahan	14.00
☐☐☐☐☐	45 Mike Vernon (G)	6.00
☐☐☐☐☐	46 Steve Yzerman	35.00
☐☐☐☐☐	47 Kelly Buchberger	2.00
☐☐☐☐☐	48 Mike Grier	2.00
☐☐☐☐☐	49 Curtis Joseph (G)	14.00
☐☐☐☐☐	50 Rem Murray	2.00
☐☐☐☐☐	51 Ryan Smyth	6.00
☐☐☐☐☐	52 Doug Weight	8.00
☐☐☐☐☐	53 Ed Jovanovski	6.00
☐☐☐☐☐	54 Scott Mellanby	2.00
☐☐☐☐☐	55 Ray Sheppard	2.00
☐☐☐☐☐	56 Robert Svehla	2.00
☐☐☐☐☐	57 John Vanbiesbrouck (G)	6.00
☐☐☐☐☐	58 Rob Blake	8.00
☐☐☐☐☐	59 Ray Ferraro	2.00
☐☐☐☐☐	60 Dmitri Khristich	2.00
☐☐☐☐☐	61 Vladimir Tsyplakov	2.00
☐☐☐☐☐	62 Vincent Damphousse	8.00
☐☐☐☐☐	63 Saku Koivu	12.00

□□□□□	64 Mark Recchi	6.00
□□□□□	65 Stéphane Richer	2.00
□□□□□	66 Jocelyn Thibault (G)	6.00
□□□□□	67 Dave Andreychuk	4.00
□□□□□	68 Martin Brodeur (G)	24.00
□□□□□	69 Doug Gilmour	8.00
□□□□□	70 Bobby Holik	4.00
□□□□□	71 John MacLean	2.00
□□□□□	72 Bryan Berard	4.00
□□□□□	73 Travis Green	2.00
□□□□□	74 Zigmund Palffy	8.00
□□□□□	75 Tommy Salo (G)	6.00
□□□□□	76 Bryan Smolinski	2.00
□□□□□	77 Adam Graves	6.00
□□□□□	78 Wayne Gretzky	60.00
□□□□□	79 Alex Kovalev	8.00
□□□□□	80 Brian Leetch	8.00
□□□□□	81 Mark Messier	14.00
□□□□□	82 Mike Richter (G)	6.00
□□□□□	83 Daniel Alfredsson	8.00
□□□□□	84 Alexandre Daigle	2.00
□□□□□	85 Wade Redden	4.00
□□□□□	86 Damian Rhodes (G)	2.00
□□□□□	87 Alexei Yashin	8.00
□□□□□	88 Rod Brind'Amour	4.00
□□□□□	89 Ron Hextall (G)	8.00
□□□□□	90 John LeClair	12.00
□□□□□	91 Eric Lindros	14.00
□□□□□	92 Janne Niinimaa	2.00
□□□□□	93 Garth Snow (G)	4.00
□□□□□	94 Dainius Zubrus	2.00
□□□□□	95 Mike Gartner	12.00
□□□□□	96 Nikolai Khabibulin (G)	6.00
□□□□□	97 Jeremy Roenick	12.00
□□□□□	98 Keith Tkachuk	8.00
□□□□□	99 Oleg Tverdovsky	2.00
□□□□□	100 Ron Francis	8.00
□□□□□	101 Kevin Hatcher	2.00
□□□□□	102 Jaromir Jagr	14.00
□□□□□	103 Patrick Lalime (G)	8.00
□□□□□	104 Petr Nedved	4.00
□□□□□	105 Jim Campbell	2.00
□□□□□	106 Grant Fuhr (G)	8.00
□□□□□	107 Brett Hull	14.00
□□□□□	108 Pierre Turgeon	6.00
□□□□□	109 Harry York	2.00
□□□□□	110 Jeff Friesen	4.00
□□□□□	111 Tony Granato	2.00
□□□□□	**112 Stephen Guolla RC**	**2.00**
□□□□□	113 Viktor Kozlov	4.00
□□□□□	114 Owen Nolan	8.00
□□□□□	115 Dino Ciccarelli	4.00
□□□□□	116 John Cullen	2.00
□□□□□	117 Chris Gratton	2.00
□□□□□	118 Roman Hamrlik	2.00
□□□□□	119 Daymond Langkow	2.00
□□□□□	120 Sergei Berezin	2.00
□□□□□	121 Wendel Clark	12.00
□□□□□	122 Félix Potvin (G)	8.00
□□□□□	123 Steve Sullivan	4.00
□□□□□	124 Mats Sundin	14.00
□□□□□	125 Pavel Bure	12.00
□□□□□	126 Martin Gélinas	2.00
□□□□□	127 Trevor Linden	6.00
□□□□□	128 Kirk McLean (G)	4.00
□□□□□	129 Alexander Mogilny	6.00
□□□□□	130 Peter Bondra	8.00
□□□□□	131 Joé Juneau	2.00
□□□□□	132 Steve Konowalchuk	2.00
□□□□□	133 Adam Oates	6.00
□□□□□	134 Bill Ranford	6.00
□□□□□	135 P. Kariya / T. Selänne	16.00
□□□□□	136 D. Hasek / M. Peca	10.00
□□□□□	137 T. Fleury / J. Iginla	10.00
□□□□□	138 P. Forsberg / P. Roy	30.00
□□□□□	139 B. Shanahan / S. Yzerman	24.00
□□□□□	140 W. Gretzky / M. Messier	35.00
□□□□□	141 J. LeClair / E. Lindros	12.00
□□□□□	142 J. Jagr / P. Lalime	12.00
□□□□□	143 Br. Hull / J. Campbell	8.00
□□□□□	144 M. Sundin / S. Berezin	8.00
□□□□□	**Shawn Bates RC**	**8.00**
□□□□□	Daniel Cleary	8.00
□□□□□	**Marian Hossa RC**	**60.00**
□□□□□	**Olli Jokinen RC**	**8.00**
□□□□□	**Espen Knutsen RC**	**6.00**
□□□□□	Patrick Marleau	14.00
□□□□□	Alyn McCauley	8.00
□□□□□	Mattias Öhlund	8.00
□□□□□	Chris Phillips	6.00
□□□□□	Erik Rasmussen	6.00
□□□□□	Sergei Samsonov	18.00
□□□□□	Joe Thornton	35.00

	Sample	**Promo**
□	Mike Modano, Dall.	2.00

DYANMIC DUOS

Insert Set (30 cards):		**275.00**
	Insert (1:37)	**DD**
□	1A Paul Kariya, Anah.	15.00
□	1B Teemu Selänne, Anah.	10.00
□	2A Raymond Bourque, Bost.	15.00
□	2B Jim Carey (G), Bost.	5.00
□	3A Dominik Hasek (G), Buff.	10.00
□	3B Michael Peca, Buff.	5.00
□	4A Theoren Fleury, Calg.	5.00
□	4B Jarome Iginla, Calg.	10.00
□	5A Peter Forsberg, Colo.	15.00
□	5B Claude Lemieux, Colo.	5.00
□	6A Patrick Roy (G), Colo.	35.00
□	6B Joe Sakic, Colo.	20.00
□	7A Sergei Fedorov, Detr.	10.00
□	7B Vladimir Konstantinov, Detr.	5.00
□	8A Brendan Shanahan, Detr.	10.00
□	8B Steve Yzerman, Detr.	30.00
□	9A Bryan Berard, NYIs.	5.00
□	9B Zigmund Palffy, NYIs.	5.00
□	10A Wayne Gretzky, NYRa.	50.00
□	10B Brian Leetch, NYRa.	5.00
□	11A Eric Lindros, Phil.	10.00
□	11B Dainius Zubrus, Phil.	5.00
□	12A Jeremy Roenick, Phoe.	10.00
□	12B Keith Tkachuk, Phoe.	5.00
□	13A Jaromir Jagr, Pitt.	10.00
□	13B Patrick Lalime (G), Pitt.	5.00
□	14A Jim Campbell, SLou.	5.00
□	14B Brett Hull, SLou.	10.00
□	15A Pavel Bure, Vanc.	5.00
□	15B Alexander Mogilny, Vanc.	5.00

KINGS OF THE NHL

Insert Set (10 cards):		**650.00**
	Insert (1:361)	**KotN**
□	1 Paul Kariya, Anah.	70.00
□	2 Peter Forsberg, Colo.	70.00
□	3 Patrick Roy (G), Colo.	150.00
□	4 Joe Sakic, Colo.	80.00
□	5 John Vanbiesbrouck (G), Flor.	20.00
□	6 Wayne Gretzky, NYRa.	200.00
□	7 Mark Messier, NYRa.	50.00
□	8 Eric Lindros, Phil.	50.00
□	9 Jaromir Jagr, Pitt.	50.00
□	10 Pavel Bure, Vanc.	40.00

STONEWALLERS

Insert Set (20 cards):		**140.00**
	Insert (1:37)	**SW**
□	1 Guy Hebert (G), Anah.	6.00
□	2 Jim Carey (G), Bost.	6.00
□	3 Dominik Hasek (G), Buff.	10.00
□	4 Trevor Kidd (G), Calg.	6.00
□	5 Jeff Hackett (G), Chic.	6.00
□	6 Patrick Roy (G), Colo.	40.00
□	7 Chris Osgood (G), Detr.	6.00
□	8 Mike Vernon (G), Detr.	6.00
□	9 Curtis Joseph (G), Edmo.	10.00
□	10 John Vanbiesbrouck (G), Flor.	6.00
□	11 Jocelyn Thibault (G), Mont.	6.00
□	12 Martin Brodeur (G), NJer.	20.00
□	13 Tommy Salo (G), NYIs.	6.00
□	14 Mike Richter (G), NYRa.	6.00
□	15 Ron Hextall (G), Phil.	6.00
□	16 Garth Snow (G), Phil.	6.00
□	17 Nikolai Khabibulin (G), Phoe.	6.00
□	18 Patrick Lalime (G), Pitt.	6.00
□	19 Grant Fuhr (G), SLou.	6.00
□	20 Félix Potvin (G), Toro.	6.00

TANDEMS

Insert Set (72 cards):		**500.00**
Common Player:		**5.00**
	Double-Sided Insert (1:37)	**Insert**
□	1 W. Gretzky / E. Lindros	60.00
□	2 J. Sakic / P. Kariya	30.00
□	3 M. Messier / J. Iginla	20.00
□	4 D. Hasek / P. Roy	50.00
□	5 J. Jagr / P. Forsberg	30.00
□	6 B. Shanahan / K. Tkachuk	20.00
□	7 S. Yzerman / T. Selänne	40.00
□	8 Br. Hull / S. Fedorov	25.00
□	9 D. Zubrus / P. Lalime	10.00
□	10 S. Berezin / M. Grier	5.00
□	11 Cu. Joseph / Z. Palffy	20.00
□	12 M. Brodeur / C. Osgood (G)	20.00
□	13 J. Vanbiesbrouck (G) / J. Thibault	10.00
□	14 P. Bure / S. Koivu	20.00
□	15 P. Bondra / J. LeClair	15.00
□	16 M. Sundin / J. Niinimaa	15.00
□	17 F. Potvin / J. Carey	5.00
□	18 G. Fuhr / J. Campbell / Br. Hull	15.00
□	19 W. Gretzky / A. Kovalev / B. Leetch	40.00
□	20 R. Brind'Amour / J. LeClair / E. Lindros	10.00
□	21 D. Hasek / M. Peca / M. Satan	15.00
□	22 J. Jagr / P. Lalime / P. Nedved	10.00
□	23 T. Fleury / J. Iginla / T. Kidd	15.00
□	24 G. Hebert / P. Kariya / T. Selänne	20.00
□	25 P. Forsberg / C. Lemieux / P. Roy	40.00
□	26 V. Konstantinov / B. Shanahan / S. Yzerman	30.00
□	27 S. Berezin / W. Clark / M. Sundin	15.00
□	28 R. Bourque / D. Plante	15.00
□	29 B. Bellows / J. Allison	10.00
□	30 K. Primeau / S. Rucchin	5.00
□	31 É. Dazé / J. Stümpel	5.00
□	32 B. Holzinger / J. Langenbrunner	5.00
□	33 T. Amonte / M. Peca	10.00
□	34 D. Sydor / G. Titov	5.00
□	35 C. Chelios / T. Fleury	15.00
□	36 J. Höglund / D. Khristich	5.00
□	37 S. Burke / D. Andreychuk	10.00
□	38 D. Hatcher / G. Sanderson	5.00
□	39 A. Cassels / J. Hackett	5.00
□	40 E. Moreau / R. Ferraro	5.00
□	41 D. Gilmour / S. Ozolinsh	10.00
□	42 V. Kamensky / M. Modano	15.00
□	43 J. Nieuwendyk / V. Tsyplakov	5.00
□	44 M. Vernon / S. Zubov	5.00
□	45 R. Blake / B. Holik	10.00
□	46 V. Damphousse / D. Weight	15.00
□	47 M. Recchi / R. Smyth	10.00
□	48 J. MacLean / S. Richer	5.00
□	49 K. Buchberger / E. Jovanovski	5.00
□	50 O. Nolan / R. Murray	5.00
□	51 B. Ranford / R. Svehla	5.00
□	52 R. Sheppard / S. Sullivan	5.00
□	53 J. Cullen / S. Mellanby	5.00
□	54 A. Daigle / G. Snow	5.00
□	55 R. Hextall / A. Mogilny	10.00
□	56 K. McLean / A. Oates	5.00
□	57 D. Ciccarelli / J. Juneau	5.00
□	58 J. Campbell / S. Konowalchuk	5.00
□	59 T. Linden / P. Turgeon	10.00
□	60 J. Friesen / M. Gélinas	5.00
□	61 R. Hamrlik / H. York	5.00
□	62 C. Gratton / K. Hatcher	5.00
□	63 R. Francis / J. Roenick	15.00
□	64 N. Khabibulin / Vi. Kozlov	5.00
□	65 M. Gartner / D. Langkow	10.00
□	66 S. Guolla / O. Tverdovsky	5.00
□	67 T. Granato / T. Salo	5.00
□	68 W. Redden / B. Smolinski	5.00
□	69 A. Graves / D. Rhodes	5.00
□	70 M. Richter / A. Yashin	10.00
□	71 D. Alfredsson / B. Berard	10.00
□	72 T. Green / A. Kovalev	10.00

BEST KEPT SECRETS

Bonus Set (110 cards):		**25.00**
Common Player:		**.25**
	Bonus Card (1:1)	**BKS**
□	1 J-J Daigneault, Anah.	.25
□	2 Paul Kariya, Anah.	1.00
□	3 Dave Karpa, Anah.	.25
□	4 Teemu Selänne, Anah.	.50
□	5 Raymond Bourque, Bost.	1.00
□	6 Jim Carey (G), Bost.	.25
□	**7 Davis Payne, Bost. RC**	**.50**
□	**8 Paxton Schafer (G), Bost. RC**	**.50**
□	9 Bob Boughner, Buff.	.25
□	10 Dominik Hasek (G), Buff.	1.00
□	11 Brad May, Buff.	.25
□	12 Cale Hulse, Calg.	.25
□	13 Jarome Iginla, Calg.	.50
□	14 James Patrick, Calg.	.25
□	15 Zarley Zalapski, Calg.	.25
□	16 Jeff Brown, Hart. (Caro.)	.25
□	17 Keith Primeau, Hart. (Caro.)	.25
□	18 Steven Rice, Hart. (Caro.)	.25
□	19 James Black, Chic.	.25
□	20 Chris Chelios, Chic.	.50
□	21 Steve Dubinsky, Chic.	.25
□	22 Steve Smith, Chic.	.25
□	23 Craig Billington (G), Colo.	.25
□	24 Peter Forsberg, Colo.	1.00
□	25 Jon Klemm, Colo.	.25
□	26 Patrick Roy (G), Colo.	3.00
□	27 Joe Sakic, Colo.	1.50
□	28 Neal Broten, Dall.	.25
□	29 Richard Matvichuk, Dall.	.25
□	30 Mike Modano, Dall.	1.00
□	31 Andy Moog (G), Dall.	.25
□	32 Sergei Fedorov, Detr.	1.00
□	33 Kirk Maltby, Detr.	.25
□	34 Brendan Shanahan, Detr.	1.00
□	35 Tim Taylor, Detr.	.25
□	36 Steve Yzerman, Detr.	2.00
□	37 Louie DeBrusk, Edmo.	.25
□	**38 Joe Hulbig, Edmo. RC**	**.50**
□	39 Ryan Smyth, Edmo.	.25
□	40 Mike Hough, Flor.	.25
□	41 Jody Hull, Flor.	.25
□	42 Paul Laus, Flor.	.25
□	43 John Vanbiesbrouck (G), Flor.	.25
□	44 Aki Berg, LosA.	.25
□	45 Ray Ferraro, LosA.	.25
□	46 Craig Johnson, LosA.	.25
□	47 Ian Laperrière, LosA.	.25
□	48 Vincent Damphousse, Mont.	.50
□	49 Dave Manson, Mont.	.25
□	50 Stéphane Richer, Mont.	.25
□	51 Craig Rivet, Mont.	.25
□	52 Martin Brodeur (G), NJer.	1.50
□	53 Jay Pandolfo, NJer.	.25
□	54 Brian Rolston, NJer.	.25
□	55 Doug Houda, NYIs.	.25
□	56 Brent Hughes, NYIs.	.25
□	57 Zigmund Palffy, NYIs.	.50
□	58 Adam Graves, NYRa.	.25
□	59 Wayne Gretzky, NYRa.	4.00
□	60 Chris Ferraro, NYRa.	.25
□	61 Glenn Healy (G), NYRa.	.25
□	62 Brian Leetch, NYRa.	.50
□	63 Mark Messier, NYRa.	1.00
□	64 Radim Bicanek, Otta.	.25
□	65 Philip Crowe, Otta.	.25
□	**66 Christer Olssen, Otta. RC**	**.50**
□	67 Jason York, Otta.	.25
□	68 Rod Brind'Amour, Phil.	.25
□	69 John Druce, Phil.	.25
□	70 Daniel Lacroix, Phil.	.25
□	71 John LeClair, Phil.	.50
□	72 Eric Lindros, Phil.	1.00
□	73 Murray Baron, Phoe.	.25
□	74 Mike Gartner, Phoe.	.50
□	75 Brad McCrimmon, Phoe.	.25
□	76 Keith Tkachuk, Phoe.	.50
□	77 Jaromir Jagr, Pitt.	1.00
□	78 Patrick Lalime (G), Pitt.	.50
□	79 Ian Moran, Pitt.	.25
□	80 Petr Nedved, Pitt.	.25
□	81 Brett Hull, SLou.	1.00
□	82 Robert Petrovicky, SLou.	.25
□	83 Pierre Turgeon, SLou.	.25
□	84 Trent Yawney, SLou.	.25
□	85 Tim Hunter, SanJ.	.25
□	86 Marcus Ragnarsson, SanJ.	.25
□	87 Dody Wood, SanJ.	.25
□	88 Dino Ciccarelli, Tamp.	.25
□	89 Alexander Selivanov, Tamp.	.25
□	90 Jason Wiemer, Tamp.	.25
□	91 Sergei Berezin, Toro.	.25
□	92 Félix Potvin (G), Toro.	.50
□	93 Mats Sundin, Toro.	1.00
□	94 Craig Wolanin, Toro.	.25
□	95 Pavel Bure, Vanc.	.50
□	96 Troy Crowder, Vanc.	.25
□	97 Dana Murzyn, Vanc.	.25
□	98 Gino Odjick, Vanc.	.25
□	99 Craig Berube, Wash.	.25
□	100 Peter Bondra, Wash.	.50
□	101 Mike Eagles, Wash.	.25
□	102 Andrei Nikolishin, Wash.	.25
□	103 AW: Paul Kariya, Anah.	1.00
□	104 AW: Dominik Hasek (G), Buff.	1.00
□	105 AW: Michael Peca, Buff.	.25
□	106 AW: M. Brodeur (G)/ M. Dunham (G)	1.00
□	107 AW: Bryan Berard, NYIs.	.25
□	108 AW: Brian Leetch, NYRa.	.50
□	109 AW: Tony Granato, SanJ.	.25
□	110 AW: Trevor Linden, Vanc.	.25

1997 - 98 PACIFIC INVINCIBLE

These cards have six versions: a one-per-pack regular card, an Emerald Green (Canadian) parallel, a Copper (Hobby) parallel, a Silver (Retail) parallel, a Red parallel and an Ice Blue parallel.

Complete Set (150 cards): 2000.00 140.00
Common Player: 8.00 .75

	Player	Red	Para.
☐☐	1 Brian Bellows	10.00	.75
☐☐	2 Guy Hebert (G)	10.00	.75
☐☐	3 Paul Kariya	70.00	4.00
☐☐	4 Teemu Selänne	40.00	3.00
☐☐	5 Darren Van Impe	8.00	.75
☐☐	6 Jason Allison	30.00	2.00
☐☐	7 Raymond Bourque	60.00	4.50
☐☐	8 Jim Carey (G)	8.00	.75
☐☐	9 Ted Donato	8.00	.75
☐☐	10 Jozef Stumpel	10.00	.75
☐☐	11 Jason Dawe	8.00	.75
☐☐	12 Dominik Hasek (G)	50.00	3.50
☐☐	13 Michael Peca	20.00	1.50
☐☐	14 Derek Plante	8.00	.75
☐☐	15 Miroslav Satan	15.00	1.00
☐☐	16 Theoren Fleury	30.00	2.00
☐☐	17 Dave Gagner	8.00	.75
☐☐	18 Jonas Höglund	8.00	.75
☐☐	19 Jarome Iginla	40.00	3.00
☐☐	20 Trevor Kidd (G)	15.00	1.00
☐☐	21 German Titov	8.00	.75
☐☐	22 Sean Burke (G)	30.00	2.00
☐☐	23 Andrew Cassels	10.00	.75
☐☐	24 Derek King	8.00	.75
☐☐	25 Keith Primeau	20.00	1.50
☐☐	26 G. Sanderson	10.00	.75
☐☐	27 Tony Amonte	30.00	2.00
☐☐	28 Chris Chelios	30.00	2.00
☐☐	29 Eric Dazé	20.00	1.50
☐☐	30 Jeff Hackett (G)	15.00	1.00
☐☐	31 Ethan Moreau	8.00	.75
☐☐	32 Alexei Zhamnov	15.00	1.00
☐☐	33 Adam Deadmarsh	15.00	1.00
☐☐	34 Peter Forsberg	70.00	5.00
☐☐	35 Valeri Kamensky	15.00	1.00
☐☐	36 Claude Lemieux	15.00	1.00
☐☐	37 Sandis Ozolinsh	10.00	.75
☐☐	38 Patrick Roy (G)	150.00	10.00
☐☐	39 Joe Sakic	80.00	6.00
☐☐	40 Jamie Langenbrunner	10.00	.75
☐☐	41 Mike Modano	50.00	3.50
☐☐	42 Andy Moog (G)	20.00	1.50
☐☐	43 Joe Nieuwendyk	20.00	1.50
☐☐	44 Pat Verbeek	15.00	1.00
☐☐	45 Sergei Zubov	10.00	.75
☐☐	46 Sergei Fedorov	50.00	3.50
☐☐	47 Vladimir Konstantinov	15.00	1.00
☐☐	48 Vyacheslav Kozlov	10.00	.75
☐☐	49 Nicklas Lidström	30.00	2.00
☐☐	50 Chris Osgood (G)	30.00	2.00
☐☐	51 Brendan Shanahan	50.00	3.50
☐☐	52 Mike Vernon (G)	20.00	1.50
☐☐	53 Steve Yzerman	120.00	8.00
☐☐	54 Jason Arnott	20.00	1.50
☐☐	55 Mike Grier	10.00	.75
☐☐	56 Curtis Joseph (G)	50.00	3.50
☐☐	57 Rem Murray	8.00	.75
☐☐	58 Ryan Smyth	20.00	1.50
☐☐	59 Doug Weight	30.00	2.00
☐☐	60 Ed Jovanovski	20.00	1.50
☐☐	61 Scott Mellanby	10.00	.75
☐☐	62 Kirk Muller	15.00	1.00
☐☐	63 Ray Sheppard	8.00	.75
☐☐	64 J. Vanbiesbrouck (G)	20.00	1.50
☐☐	65 Rob Blake	30.00	2.00
☐☐	66 Ray Ferraro	8.00	.75
☐☐	67 Stéphane Fiset (G)	15.00	1.00
☐☐	68 Dimitri Khristich	8.00	.75
☐☐	69 Vladimir Tsyplakov	8.00	.75
☐☐	70 V. Damphousse	30.00	2.00
☐☐	71 Saku Koivu	40.00	3.00
☐☐	72 Mark Recchi	20.00	1.50
☐☐	73 Stéphane Richer	10.00	.75
☐☐	74 Jocelyn Thibault (G)	20.00	1.50
☐☐	75 Dave Andreychuk	15.00	1.00
☐☐	76 Martin Brodeur (G)	80.00	6.00
☐☐	77 Doug Gilmour	30.00	2.00
☐☐	78 Bobby Holik	15.00	1.00
☐☐	79 Denis Pederson	8.00	.75
☐☐	80 Bryan Berard	15.00	1.00
☐☐	81 Travis Green	10.00	.75
☐☐	82 Zigmund Palffy	30.00	2.00
☐☐	83 Tommy Salo (G)	20.00	1.50
☐☐	84 Bryan Smolinski	8.00	.75
☐☐	85 Adam Graves	20.00	1.50
☐☐	86 Wayne Gretzky	200.00	15.00
☐☐	87 Alex Kovalev	30.00	2.00
☐☐	88 Brian Leetch	30.00	2.00
☐☐	89 Mark Messier	50.00	3.50
☐☐	90 Mike Richter (G)	20.00	1.50
☐☐	91 Luc Robitaille	40.00	3.00
☐☐	92 Daniel Alfredsson	30.00	2.00
☐☐	93 Alexandre Daigle	8.00	.75
☐☐	94 Steve Duchesne	10.00	.75
☐☐	95 Wade Redden	15.00	1.00
☐☐	96 Ron Tugnutt (G)	20.00	1.50
☐☐	97 Alexei Yashin	30.00	2.00
☐☐	98 Rod Brind'Amour	15.00	1.00
☐☐	99 Paul Coffey	30.00	2.00
☐☐	100 Ron Hextall (G)	30.00	2.00
☐☐	101 John LeClair	40.00	3.00
☐☐	102 Eric Lindros	50.00	3.50
☐☐	103 Janne Niinimaa	10.00	.75
☐☐	104 Mikael Renberg	15.00	1.00
☐☐	105 Dainius Zubrus	10.00	.75
☐☐	106 Mike Gartner	40.00	3.00
☐☐	107 N. Khabibulin (G)	20.00	1.50
☐☐	108 Jeremy Roenick	40.00	3.00
☐☐	109 Keith Tkachuk	30.00	2.00
☐☐	110 Oleg Tverdovsky	8.00	.75
☐☐	111 Ron Francis	30.00	2.00
☐☐	112 Kevin Hatcher	8.00	.75
☐☐	113 Jaromir Jagr	50.00	2.00
☐☐	114 Patrick Lalime (G)	30.00	2.00
☐☐	115 Petr Nedved	15.00	1.00
☐☐	116 Ed Olczyk	10.00	.75
☐☐	117 Jim Campbell	8.00	.75
☐☐	118 Geoff Courtnall	8.00	.75
☐☐	119 Grant Fuhr (G)	30.00	2.00
☐☐	120 Brett Hull	50.00	3.50
☐☐	121 Sergio Momesso	8.00	.75
☐☐	122 Pierre Turgeon	20.00	1.50
☐☐	123 Ed Belfour (G)	50.00	3.50
☐☐	124 Jeff Friesen	15.00	1.00
☐☐	125 Tony Granato	10.00	.75
☐☐	**126 Stephen Guolla RC**	**8.00**	**1.50**
☐☐	127 Bernie Nicholls	10.00	.75
☐☐	128 Owen Nolan	30.00	2.00
☐☐	129 Dino Ciccarelli	15.00	1.00
☐☐	130 John Cullen	10.00	.75
☐☐	131 Chris Gratton	10.00	.75
☐☐	132 Roman Hamrlik	10.00	.75
☐☐	133 Daymond Langkow	10.00	.75
☐☐	134 Paul Ysebaert	8.00	.75
☐☐	135 Sergei Berezin	10.00	.75
☐☐	136 Wendel Clark	40.00	3.00
☐☐	137 Félix Potvin (G)	30.00	2.00
☐☐	138 Steve Sullivan	15.00	1.00
☐☐	139 Mats Sundin	50.00	3.50
☐☐	140 Pavel Bure	40.00	3.00
☐☐	141 Martin Gelinas	10.00	.75
☐☐	142 Trevor Linden	20.00	1.50
☐☐	143 Kirk McLean (G)	15.00	1.00
☐☐	144 Alexander Mogilny	20.00	1.50
☐☐	145 Peter Bondra	30.00	2.00
☐☐	146 Dale Hunter	15.00	1.00
☐☐	147 Joé Juneau	10.00	.75
☐☐	148 Steve Konowalchuk	10.00	.75
☐☐	149 Adam Oates	20.00	1.50
☐☐	150 Bill Ranford (G)	20.00	1.50

TWO-PER-BOX PARALLELS

Two-per-box parallels are Copper (US hobby), Silver (US retail), Emerald (Cdn. hobby), and Red (Treat packs). Dealers may sell some parallels for more or less depending on their supply.

Complete Set (150 cards): 1500.00 825.00
Common Player: 5.00 3.00

	Player	Red	Para.
☐☐☐☐☐☐	1 Brian Bellows	8.00	4.00
☐☐☐☐☐☐	2 Guy Hebert (G)	8.00	4.00
☐☐☐☐☐☐	3 Paul Kariya	50.00	30.00
☐☐☐☐☐☐	4 Teemu Selänne	30.00	15.00
☐☐☐☐☐☐	5 Darren Van Impe	5.00	3.00
☐☐☐☐☐☐	6 Jason Allison	22.00	12.00
☐☐☐☐☐☐	7 Raymond Bourque	45.00	25.00
☐☐☐☐☐☐	8 Jim Carey (G)	6.00	3.00
☐☐☐☐☐☐	9 Ted Donato	5.00	3.00
☐☐☐☐☐☐	10 Jozef Stumpel	8.00	4.00
☐☐☐☐☐☐	11 Jason Dawe	5.00	3.00
☐☐☐☐☐☐	12 Dominik Hasek (G)	35.00	20.00
☐☐☐☐☐☐	13 Michael Peca	14.00	8.00
☐☐☐☐☐☐	14 Derek Plante	6.00	3.00
☐☐☐☐☐☐	15 Miroslav Satan	12.00	6.00
☐☐☐☐☐☐	16 Theoren Fleury	20.00	10.00
☐☐☐☐☐☐	17 Dave Gagner	6.00	3.00
☐☐☐☐☐☐	18 Jonas Höglund	6.00	3.00
☐☐☐☐☐☐	19 Jarome Iginla	30.00	15.00
☐☐☐☐☐☐	20 Trevor Kidd (G)	12.00	6.00
☐☐☐☐☐☐	21 German Titov	5.00	3.00
☐☐☐☐☐☐	22 Sean Burke (G)	22.00	12.00
☐☐☐☐☐☐	23 Andrew Cassels	8.00	4.00
☐☐☐☐☐☐	24 Derek King	6.00	3.00
☐☐☐☐☐☐	25 Keith Primeau	14.00	8.00
☐☐☐☐☐☐	26 G. Sanderson	8.00	4.00
☐☐☐☐☐☐	27 Tony Amonte	22.00	12.00
☐☐☐☐☐☐	28 Chris Chelios	22.00	12.00
☐☐☐☐☐☐	29 Eric Dazé	14.00	8.00
☐☐☐☐☐☐	30 Jeff Hackett (G)	12.00	6.00
☐☐☐☐☐☐	31 Ethan Moreau	6.00	3.00
☐☐☐☐☐☐	32 Alexei Zhamnov	12.00	6.00
☐☐☐☐☐☐	33 Adam Deadmarsh	12.00	6.00
☐☐☐☐☐☐	34 Peter Forsberg	50.00	30.00
☐☐☐☐☐☐	35 Valeri Kamensky	12.00	6.00
☐☐☐☐☐☐	36 Claude Lemieux	12.00	6.00
☐☐☐☐☐☐	37 Sandis Ozolinsh	8.00	4.00
☐☐☐☐☐☐	38 Patrick Roy (G)	110.00	65.00
☐☐☐☐☐☐	39 Joe Sakic	60.00	35.00
☐☐☐☐☐☐	40 Jamie Langenbrunner	8.00	4.00
☐☐☐☐☐☐	41 Mike Modano	35.00	20.00
☐☐☐☐☐☐	42 Andy Moog (G)	14.00	8.00
☐☐☐☐☐☐	43 Joe Nieuwendyk	14.00	8.00
☐☐☐☐☐☐	44 Pat Verbeek	12.00	6.00
☐☐☐☐☐☐	45 Sergei Zubov	8.00	4.00
☐☐☐☐☐☐	46 Sergei Fedorov	35.00	20.00
☐☐☐☐☐☐	47 Vladimir Konstantinov	12.00	6.00
☐☐☐☐☐☐	48 Vyacheslav Kozlov	8.00	4.00
☐☐☐☐☐☐	49 Nicklas Lidström	22.00	12.00
☐☐☐☐☐☐	50 Chris Osgood (G)	22.00	12.00
☐☐☐☐☐☐	51 Brendan Shanahan	35.00	20.00
☐☐☐☐☐☐	52 Mike Vernon (G)	14.00	8.00
☐☐☐☐☐☐	53 Steve Yzerman	90.00	50.00
☐☐☐☐☐☐	54 Jason Arnott	18.00	10.00
☐☐☐☐☐☐	55 Mike Grier	8.00	4.00
☐☐☐☐☐☐	56 Curtis Joseph (G)	35.00	20.00
☐☐☐☐☐☐	57 Rem Murray	5.00	3.00
☐☐☐☐☐☐	58 Ryan Smyth	18.00	10.00
☐☐☐☐☐☐	59 Doug Weight	22.00	12.00
☐☐☐☐☐☐	60 Ed Jovanovski	14.00	8.00
☐☐☐☐☐☐	61 Scott Mellanby	8.00	4.00
☐☐☐☐☐☐	62 Kirk Muller	12.00	6.00
☐☐☐☐☐☐	63 Ray Sheppard	6.00	3.00
☐☐☐☐☐☐	64 J. Vanbiesbrouck (G)	18.00	10.00
☐☐☐☐☐☐	65 Rob Blake	22.00	12.00
☐☐☐☐☐☐	66 Ray Ferraro	6.00	3.00
☐☐☐☐☐☐	67 Stéphane Fiset (G)	12.00	6.00
☐☐☐☐☐☐	68 Dimitri Khristich	6.00	3.00
☐☐☐☐☐☐	69 Vladimir Tsyplakov	5.00	3.00
☐☐☐☐☐☐	70 V. Damphousse	22.00	12.00
☐☐☐☐☐☐	71 Saku Koivu	30.00	15.00
☐☐☐☐☐☐	72 Mark Recchi	14.00	8.00
☐☐☐☐☐☐	73 Stéphane Richer	8.00	4.00
☐☐☐☐☐☐	74 Jocelyn Thibault (G)	14.00	8.00
☐☐☐☐☐☐	75 Dave Andreychuk	12.00	6.00
☐☐☐☐☐☐	76 Martin Brodeur (G)	60.00	35.00
☐☐☐☐☐☐	77 Doug Gilmour	22.00	12.00
☐☐☐☐☐☐	78 Bobby Holik	12.00	6.00
☐☐☐☐☐☐	79 Denis Pederson	5.00	3.00
☐☐☐☐☐☐	80 Bryan Berard	12.00	6.00
☐☐☐☐☐☐	81 Travis Green	8.00	4.00
☐☐☐☐☐☐	82 Zigmund Palffy	22.00	12.00
☐☐☐☐☐☐	83 Tommy Salo (G)	14.00	8.00
☐☐☐☐☐☐	84 Bryan Smolinski	6.00	3.00
☐☐☐☐☐☐	85 Adam Graves	14.00	8.00
☐☐☐☐☐☐	86 Wayne Gretzky	150.00	90.00
☐☐☐☐☐☐	87 Alex Kovalev	22.00	12.00
☐☐☐☐☐☐	88 Brian Leetch	22.00	12.00
☐☐☐☐☐☐	89 Mark Messier	35.00	20.00
☐☐☐☐☐☐	90 Mike Richter (G)	18.00	10.00
☐☐☐☐☐☐	91 Luc Robitaille	30.00	15.00
☐☐☐☐☐☐	92 Daniel Alfredsson	22.00	12.00
☐☐☐☐☐☐	93 Alexandre Daigle	6.00	3.00
☐☐☐☐☐☐	94 Steve Duchesne	8.00	4.00
☐☐☐☐☐☐	95 Wade Redden	12.00	6.00
☐☐☐☐☐☐	96 Ron Tugnutt (G)	14.00	8.00
☐☐☐☐☐☐	97 Alexei Yashin	22.00	12.00
☐☐☐☐☐☐	98 Rod Brind'Amour	12.00	6.00
☐☐☐☐☐☐	99 Paul Coffey	22.00	12.00
☐☐☐☐☐☐	100 Ron Hextall (G)	22.00	12.00
☐☐☐☐☐☐	101 John LeClair	30.00	15.00
☐☐☐☐☐☐	102 Eric Lindros	35.00	20.00
☐☐☐☐☐☐	103 Janne Niinimaa	8.00	4.00
☐☐☐☐☐☐	104 Mikael Renberg	12.00	6.00
☐☐☐☐☐☐	105 Dainius Zubrus	8.00	4.00
☐☐☐☐☐☐	106 Mike Gartner	30.00	15.00
☐☐☐☐☐☐	107 N. Khabibulin (G)	14.00	8.00
☐☐☐☐☐☐	108 Jeremy Roenick	30.00	15.00
☐☐☐☐☐☐	109 Keith Tkachuk	20.00	10.00
☐☐☐☐☐☐	110 Oleg Tverdovsky	6.00	3.00
☐☐☐☐☐☐	111 Ron Francis	22.00	12.00
☐☐☐☐☐☐	112 Kevin Hatcher	6.00	3.00
☐☐☐☐☐☐	113 Jaromir Jagr	35.00	20.00
☐☐☐☐☐☐	114 Patrick Lalime (G)	22.00	12.00
☐☐☐☐☐☐	115 Petr Nedved	12.00	6.00
☐☐☐☐☐☐	116 Ed Olczyk	8.00	4.00
☐☐☐☐☐☐	117 Jim Campbell	5.00	3.00
☐☐☐☐☐☐	118 Geoff Courtnall	6.00	3.00
☐☐☐☐☐☐	119 Grant Fuhr (G)	22.00	12.00
☐☐☐☐☐☐	120 Brett Hull	35.00	20.00
☐☐☐☐☐☐	121 Sergio Momesso	5.00	3.00
☐☐☐☐☐☐	122 Pierre Turgeon	14.00	8.00
☐☐☐☐☐☐	123 Ed Belfour (G)	35.00	20.00
☐☐☐☐☐☐	124 Jeff Friesen	12.00	6.00
☐☐☐☐☐☐	125 Tony Granato	8.00	4.00
☐☐☐☐☐☐	**126 Stephen Guolla RC**	**5.00**	**4.00**
☐☐☐☐☐☐	127 Bernie Nicholls	8.00	4.00
☐☐☐☐☐☐	128 Owen Nolan	22.00	12.00
☐☐☐☐☐☐	129 Dino Ciccarelli	12.00	6.00
☐☐☐☐☐☐	130 John Cullen	8.00	4.00
☐☐☐☐☐☐	131 Chris Gratton	8.00	4.00
☐☐☐☐☐☐	132 Roman Hamrlik	8.00	4.00
☐☐☐☐☐☐	133 Daymond Langkow	8.00	4.00
☐☐☐☐☐☐	134 Paul Ysebaert	5.00	3.00
☐☐☐☐☐☐	135 Sergei Berezin	8.00	4.00
☐☐☐☐☐☐	136 Wendel Clark	30.00	15.00
☐☐☐☐☐☐	137 Félix Potvin (G)	22.00	12.00
☐☐☐☐☐☐	138 Steve Sullivan	12.00	6.00
☐☐☐☐☐☐	139 Mats Sundin	35.00	20.00
☐☐☐☐☐☐	140 Pavel Bure	30.00	15.00
☐☐☐☐☐☐	141 Martin Gelinas	8.00	4.00
☐☐☐☐☐☐	142 Trevor Linden	14.00	8.00
☐☐☐☐☐☐	143 Kirk McLean (G)	12.00	6.00
☐☐☐☐☐☐	144 Alexander Mogilny	18.00	10.00
☐☐☐☐☐☐	145 Peter Bondra	22.00	12.00
☐☐☐☐☐☐	146 Dale Hunter	12.00	6.00
☐☐☐☐☐☐	147 Joé Juneau	8.00	4.00
☐☐☐☐☐☐	148 Steve Konowalchuk	8.00	4.00
☐☐☐☐☐☐	149 Adam Oates	14.00	8.00
☐☐☐☐☐☐	150 Bill Ranford (G)	14.00	8.00

	Sample	Promo
☐	Mike Modano, Dall.	2.00

ATTACK ZONE

Insert Set (24 cards): 275.00

	Insert (1:37)	AZ
☐	1 Paul Kariya, Anah.	20.00
☐	2 Teemu Selänne, Anah.	10.00
☐	3 Michael Peca, Buff.	5.00
☐	4 Jarome Iginla, Calg.	10.00
☐	5 Peter Forsberg, Colo.	20.00
☐	6 Claude Lemieux, Colo.	5.00
☐	7 Joe Sakic, Colo.	20.00
☐	8 Mike Modano, Dall.	15.00
☐	9 Sergei Fedorov, Detr.	15.00
☐	10 Brendan Shanahan, Detr.	15.00
☐	11 Steve Yzerman, Detr.	35.00
☐	12 Bryan Berard, NYIs.	5.00
☐	13 Zigmund Palffy, NYIs.	5.00
☐	14 Wayne Gretzky, NYRa.	60.00
☐	15 Brian Leetch, NYRa.	5.00
☐	16 Mark Messier, NYRa.	15.00
☐	17 John LeClair, Phil.	10.00
☐	18 Eric Lindros, Phil.	15.00
☐	19 Ron Francis, Pitt.	5.00
☐	20 Jaromir Jagr, Pitt.	15.00
☐	21 Brett Hull, SLou.	15.00
☐	22 Dino Ciccarelli, Tamp.	5.00
☐	23 Pavel Bure, Vanc.	10.00
☐	24 Alexander Mogilny, Vanc.	5.00

FEATURE PERFORMERS

Insert Set (36 cards): 210.00

	Insert (2:37)	FP
☐	1 Paul Kariya, Anah.	10.00
☐	2 Teemu Selänne, Anah.	5.00

☐ 3 Raymond Bourque, Bost. 10.00
☐ 4 Dominik Hasek (G), Buff. 5.00
☐ 5 Jarome Iginla, Calg. 5.00
☐ 6 Chris Chelios, Chic. 5.00
☐ 7 Peter Forsberg, Colo. 10.00
☐ 8 Claude Lemieux, Colo. 3.00
☐ 9 Patrick Roy (G), Colo. 25.00
☐ 10 Joe Sakic, Colo. 10.00
☐ 11 Mike Modano, Dall. 5.00
☐ 12 Sergei Fedorov, Detr. 5.00
☐ 13 Vladimir Konstantinov, Detr. 3.00
☐ 14 Brendan Shanahan, Detr. 5.00
☐ 15 Mike Vernon (G), Detr. 3.00
☐ 16 Steve Yzerman, Detr. 20.00
☐ 17 John Vanbiesbrouck (G), Flor. 3.00
☐ 18 Saku Koivu, Mont. 5.00
☐ 19 Martin Brodeur (G), NJer. 10.00
☐ 20 Zigmund Palffy, NYIs. 5.00
☐ 21 Wayne Gretzky, NYRa. 35.00
☐ 22 Mark Messier, NYRa. 5.00
☐ 23 Alexandre Daigle, Ott. 3.00
☐ 24 John LeClair, Phil. 5.00
☐ 25 Eric Lindros, Phil. 5.00
☐ 26 Janne Niinimaa, Phil. 3.00
☐ 27 Jeremy Roenick, Phoe. 5.00
☐ 28 Jaromir Jagr, Pitt. 5.00
☐ 29 Patrick Lalime (G), Pitt. 5.00
☐ 30 Jim Campbell, SLou. 3.00
☐ 31 Brett Hull, SLou. 5.00
☐ 32 Sergei Berezin, Toro. 3.00
☐ 33 Félix Potvin (G), Toro. 5.00
☐ 34 Mats Sundin, Toro. 5.00
☐ 35 Alexander Mogilny, Vanc. 3.00
☐ 36 Peter Bondra, Wash. 5.00

OFF THE GLASS CEL-FUSIONS

Insert Set (20 cards): 350.00

Insert (1:73)	OTGCF
☐ 1 Paul Kariya, Anah.	25.00
☐ 2 Teemu Selänne, Anah.	15.00
☐ 3 Michael Peca, Buff.	6.00
☐ 4 Jarome Iginla, Calg.	15.00
☐ 5 Peter Forsberg, Colo.	25.00
☐ 6 Joe Sakic, Colo.	30.00
☐ 7 Sergei Fedorov, Detr.	20.00
☐ 8 Brendan Shanahan, Detr.	20.00
☐ 9 Steve Yzerman, Detr.	45.00
☐ 10 Mike Grier, Edmo.	6.00
☐ 11 Saku Koivu, Mont.	15.00
☐ 12 Wayne Gretzky, NYRa.	80.00
☐ 13 Mark Messier, NYRa.	20.00
☐ 14 Eric Lindros, Phil.	20.00
☐ 15 Dainius Zubrus, Phil.	6.00
☐ 16 Keith Tkachuk, Phoe.	10.00
☐ 17 Jaromir Jagr, Pitt.	20.00
☐ 18 Brett Hull, SLou.	20.00
☐ 19 Sergei Berezin, Toro.	6.00
☐ 20 Pavel Bure, Vanc.	15.00

REGIME

Bonus Set (220 cards): 50.00
Common Player: .25

Insert (1:1)	Regime
☐ 1 Ken Baumgartner, Anah.	.25
☐ 2 Mark Janssens, Anah.	.25
☐ 3 Jean-François Jomphe, Anah.	.25
☐ 4 Paul Kariya, Anah.	1.00
☐ 5 Jason Marshall, Anah.	.25
☐ 6 Richard Park, Anah.	.25
☐ 7 Teemu Selänne, Anah.	.50
☐ 8 Mikhail Shtalenkov (G), Anah.	.25
☐ 9 Bob Beers, Bost.	.25
☐ 10 Raymond Bourque, Bost.	1.00
☐ 11 Jim Carey (G), Bost.	.25
☐ 12 Brett Harkins, Bost.	.25
☐ 13 Sheldon Kennedy, Bost.	.25
☐ 14 Troy Mallette, Bost.	.25
☐ 15 Sandy Moger, Bost.	.25
☐ 16 Jon Rohloff, Bost.	.25
☐ 17 Don Sweeney, Bost.	.25
☐ 18 Randy Burridge, Buff.	.25
☐ 19 Michal Grosek, Buff.	.25
☐ 20 Dominik Hasek (G), Buff.	1.00
☐ 21 Rob Ray, Buff.	.25
☐ **22 Steve Shields (G), Buff. RC**	**1.00**
☐ 23 Richard Smehlik, Buff.	.25
☐ 24 Dixon Ward, Buff.	.25
☐ 25 Mike Wilson, Buff.	.25
☐ 26 Tommy Albelin, Calg.	.25
☐ 27 Aaron Gavey, Calg.	.25
☐ 28 Todd Hlushko, Calg.	.25
☐ 29 Jarome Iginla, Calg.	.50
☐ 30 Yves Racine, Calg.	.25
☐ 31 Dwayne Roloson (G), Calg.	.25
☐ 32 Mike Sullivan, Calg.	.25
☐ 33 Ed Ward, Calg.	.25
☐ 34 Adam Burt, Hart. (Caro.)	.25
☐ 35 Nelson Emerson, Hart. (Caro.)	.25
☐ 36 Kevin Haller, Hart. (Caro.)	.25
☐ 37 Derek King, Hart. (Caro.)	.25
☐ 38 Curtis Leschyshyn, Hart. (Caro.)	.25
☐ **39 Chris Murray, Hart. (Caro.) RC**	**.50**
☐ 40 Jason Muzzatti (G), Hart. (Caro.)	.25
☐ 41 Keith Carney, Chic.	.25
☐ 42 Chris Chelios, Chic.	.50
☐ 43 Enrico Ciccone, Chic.	.25
☐ 44 Jim Cummins, Chic.	.25
☐ 45 Cam Russell, Chic.	.25
☐ 46 Jeff Shantz, Chic.	.25
☐ 47 Michal Sykora, Chic.	.25
☐ 48 Chris Terreri (G), Chic.	.25
☐ 49 Eric Weinrich, Chic.	.25
☐ 50 René Corbet, Colo.	.25
☐ 51 Peter Forsberg, Colo.	1.00
☐ 52 Alexei Gusarov, Colo.	.25
☐ 53 Uwe Krupp, Colo.	.25
☐ 54 Sylvain Lefebvre, Colo.	.25
☐ **55 Eric Messier, Colo. RC**	**.50**
☐ 56 Patrick Roy (G), Colo.	3.00
☐ 57 Joe Sakic, Colo.	1.50
☐ 58 Brent Severyn, Colo.	.25
☐ 59 Greg Adams, Dall.	.25
☐ 60 Todd Harvey, Dall.	.25
☐ 61 Jere Lehtinen, Dall.	.25
☐ 62 Craig Ludwig, Dall.	.25
☐ 63 Mike Modano, Dall.	1.00
☐ 64 Andy Moog (G), Dall.	.25
☐ 65 Dave Reid, Dall.	.25
☐ 66 Roman Turek (G), Dall.	.25
☐ 67 Doug Brown, Detr.	.25
☐ 68 Kris Draper, Detr.	.25
☐ 69 Sergei Fedorov, Detr.	1.00
☐ 70 Joey Kocur, Detr.	.25
☐ 71 Kirk Maltby, Detr.	.25
☐ 72 Bob Rouse, Detr.	.25
☐ 73 Brendan Shanahan, Detr.	1.00
☐ 74 Aaron Ward, Detr.	.25
☐ 75 Steve Yzerman, Detr.	2.00
☐ 76 Greg de Vries, Edmo.	.25
☐ 77 Bob Essensa (G), Edmo.	.25
☐ 78 Kevin Lowe, Edmo.	.25
☐ 79 Bryan Marchment, Edmo.	.25
☐ 80 Dean McAmmond, Edmo.	.25
☐ 81 Boris Mironov, Edmo.	.25
☐ 82 Luke Richardson, Edmo.	.25
☐ 83 Ryan Smyth, Edmo.	.25
☐ 84 Terry Carkner, Flor.	.25
☐ 85 Ed Jovanovski, Flor.	.25
☐ 86 Bill Lindsay, Flor.	.25
☐ 87 Dave Lowry, Flor.	.25
☐ 88 Gord Murphy, Flor.	.25
☐ 89 John Vanbiesbrouck (G), Flor.	.25
☐ 90 Steve Washburn, Flor.	.25
☐ 91 Chris Wells, Flor.	.25
☐ 92 Philippe Boucher, LosA.	.25
☐ 93 Steve Finn, LosA.	.25
☐ 94 Mattias Norstrom, LosA.	.25
☐ 95 Kai Nurminen, LosA.	.25
☐ 96 Sean O'Donnell, LosA.	.25
☐ 97 Yanic Perreault, LosA.	.25
☐ **98 Jeff Shevalier, LosA. RC**	**.50**
☐ 99 Brad Smyth, LosA.	.25
☐ **100 Brad Brown, Mont. RC**	**.50**
☐ 101 Jassen Cullimore, Mont.	.25
☐ 102 Vincent Damphousse, Mont.	.50
☐ 103 Vladimir Malakhov, Mont.	.25
☐ 104 Peter Popovic, Mont.	.25
☐ 105 Stéphane Richer, Mont.	.25
☐ 106 Turner Stevenson, Mont.	.25
☐ 107 José Théodore (G), Mont.	1.00
☐ 108 Martin Brodeur (G), NJer.	1.50
☐ 109 Bob Carpenter, NJer.	.25
☐ 110 Mike Dunham (G), NJer.	.25
☐ **111 Patrik Elias, NJer. RC**	**4.00**
☐ 112 Dave Ellett, NJer.	.25
☐ 113 Doug Gilmour, NJer.	.50
☐ 114 Randy McKay, NJer.	.25
☐ 115 Todd Bertuzzi, NYIs.	1.00
☐ 116 Kenny Jönsson, NYIs.	.25
☐ 117 Paul Kruse, NYIs.	.25
☐ 118 Claude Lapointe, NYIs.	.25
☐ 119 Zigmund Palffy, NYIs.	.50
☐ 120 Richard Pilon, NYIs.	.25
☐ 121 Dan Plante, NYIs.	.25
☐ 122 Dennis Vaske, NYIs.	.25
☐ 123 Shane Churla, NYRa.	.25
☐ 124 Bruce Driver, NYRa.	.25
☐ 125 Mike Eastwood, NYRa.	.25
☐ 126 Patrick Flatley, NYRa.	.25
☐ 127 Adam Graves, NYRa.	.25
☐ 128 Wayne Gretzky, NYRa.	4.00
☐ 129 Brian Leetch, NYRa.	.50
☐ 130 Doug Lidster, NYRa.	.25
☐ 131 Mark Messier, NYRa.	1.00
☐ 132 Tom Chorske, Ott.	.25
☐ 133 Sean Hill, Ott.	.25
☐ 134 Denny Lambert, Ott.	.25
☐ 135 Janne Laukkanen, Ott.	.25
☐ 136 Frank Musil, Ott.	.25
☐ **137 Lance Pitlick, Ott. RC**	**.50**
☐ 138 Shaun VanAllen, Ott.	.25
☐ 139 Rod Brind'Amour, Phil.	.25
☐ 140 Paul Coffey, Phil.	.50
☐ 141 Karl Dykhuis, Phil.	.25
☐ 142 Dan Kordic, Phil.	.25
☐ 143 Daniel Lacroix, Phil.	.25
☐ 144 John LeClair, Phil.	.50
☐ 145 Eric Lindros, Phil.	1.00
☐ 146 Joel Otto, Phil.	.25
☐ 147 Shjon Podein, Phil.	.25
☐ 148 Chris Therien, Phil.	.25
☐ 149 Shane Doan, Phoe.	.25
☐ 150 Dallas Drake, Phoe.	.25
☐ 151 Jeff Finley, Phoe.	.25
☐ 152 Mike Gartner, Phoe.	.50
☐ 153 Nikolai Khabibulin (G), Phoe.	.25
☐ 154 Darrin Shannon, Phoe.	.25
☐ 155 Mike Stapleton, Phoe.	.25
☐ 156 Keith Tkachuk, Phoe.	.50
☐ 157 Tom Barrasso (G), Pitt.	.25
☐ 158 Josef Beranek, Pitt.	.25
☐ 159 Alex Hicks, Pitt.	.25
☐ 160 Jaromir Jagr, Pitt.	1.00
☐ 161 Patrick Lalime (G), Pitt.	.50
☐ 162 François Leroux, Pitt.	.25
☐ 163 Petr Nedved, Pitt.	.25
☐ 164 Roman Oksiuta, Pitt.	.25
☐ 165 Chris Tamer, Pitt.	.25
☐ 166 Marc Bergevin, SLou.	.25
☐ 167 Jon Casey, SLou.	.25
☐ 168 Craig Conroy, SLou.	.25
☐ 169 Brett Hull, SLou.	1.00
☐ 170 Igor Kravchuk, SLou.	.25
☐ 171 Stephen Leach, SLou.	.25
☐ 172 Ricard Persson, SLou.	.25
☐ 173 Pierre Turgeon, SLou.	.25
☐ 174 Ed Belfour (G), SanJ.	1.00
☐ 175 Doug Bodger, SanJ.	.25
☐ 176 Shean Donovan, SanJ.	.25
☐ 177 Bob Errey, SanJ.	.25
☐ 178 Todd Ewen, SanJ.	.25
☐ 179 Wade Flaherty (G), SanJ.	.25
☐ 180 Mike Rathje, SanJ.	.25
☐ 181 Ron Sutter, SanJ.	.25
☐ 182 Mikael Andersson, Tamp.	.25
☐ 183 Dino Ciccarelli, Tamp.	.25
☐ 184 Cory Cross, Tamp.	.25
☐ 185 Jamie Huscroft, Tamp.	.25
☐ 186 Rudy Poeschek, Tamp.	.25
☐ 187 Daren Puppa (G), Tamp.	.25
☐ 188 David Shaw, Tamp.	.25
☐ 189 Jay Wells, Tamp.	.25
☐ 190 Jamie Baker, Toro.	.25
☐ 191 Sergei Berezin, Toro.	.25
☐ 192 Brandon Convery, Toro.	.25
☐ 193 Darby Hendrickson, Toro.	.25
☐ 194 Matt Martin, Toro.	.25
☐ 195 Félix Potvin (G), Toro.	.50
☐ 196 Jason Smith, Toro.	.25
☐ 197 Craig Wolanin, Toro.	.25
☐ 198 Adrian Aucoin, Vanc.	.25
☐ 199 Dave Babych, Vanc.	.25
☐ 200 Donald Brashear, Vanc.	.25
☐ 201 Pavel Bure, Vanc.	.50
☐ 202 Chris Joseph, Vanc.	.25
☐ 203 Alexander Mogilny, Vanc.	.25
☐ 204 David Roberts, Vanc.	.25
☐ 205 Scott Walker, Vanc.	.25
☐ 206 Peter Bondra, Wash.	.50
☐ 207 Andrew Brunette, Wash.	.25
☐ 208 Calle Johansson, Wash.	.25
☐ 209 Ken Klee, Wash.	.25
☐ 210 Olaf Kölzig (G), Wash.	.50
☐ 211 Kelly Miller, Wash.	.25
☐ 212 Joe Reekie, Wash.	.25
☐ 213 Chris Simon, Wash.	.25
☐ 214 Brendan Witt, Wash.	.25
☐ 215 Paul Kariya, Anah.	1.00
☐ 216 Peter Forsberg, Colo.	1.00
☐ 217 Patrick Roy (G), Colo.	3.00
☐ 218 Wayne Gretzky, NYRa.	4.00
☐ 219 Eric Lindros, Phil.	1.00
☐ 220 Jaromir Jagr, Pitt.	1.00

1997 - 98 PACIFIC PARAMOUNT

These cards have seven versions: the regular card, an Emerald Green parallel (Canadian), a Copper parallel (Hobby), a Silver parallel (Retail), a Dark Grey parallel, a Red parallel and an Ice Blue parallel.

	IB67	Param.
Complete Set (200 cards):	**2300.00**	**35.00**
Common Player:	**6.00**	**.20**
Player	**IB67**	**Param.**
☐☐ 1 Guy Hebert (G), Anah.	10.00	.20
☐☐ 2 Paul Kariya, Anah.	70.00	1.00
☐☐ **3 Espen Knutsen, Anah. RC**	**10.00**	**1.00**
☐☐ 4 Dmitri Mironov, Anah.	6.00	.20
☐☐ 5 Steve Rucchin, Anah.	10.00	.20
☐☐ 6 Tomas Sandström, Anah.	10.00	.20
☐☐ 7 Teemu Selänne, Anah.	40.00	.50
☐☐ 8 Scott Young, Anah.	15.00	.20
☐☐ 9 Raymond Bourque, Bost.	60.00	.50
☐☐ 10 Jim Carey (G), Bost.	6.00	.20
☐☐ 11 Anson Carter, Bost.	20.00	.20
☐☐ 12 Ted Donato, Bost.	6.00	.20
☐☐ 13 Dave Ellett, Bost.	6.00	.20
☐☐ 14 Dimitri Khristich, Bost.	6.00	.20
☐☐ 15 Sergei Samsonov, Bost.	30.00	.50
☐☐ 16 Joe Thornton, Bost.	60.00	1.50
☐☐ 17 Matthew Barnaby, Buff.	6.00	.20
☐☐ 18 Jason Dawe, Buff.	6.00	.20
☐☐ 19 Dominik Hasek (G), Buff.	50.00	.50
☐☐ 20 Brian Holzinger, Buff.	6.00	.20
☐☐ 21 Michael Peca, Buff.	20.00	.20
☐☐ 22 Derek Plante, Buff.	6.00	.20
☐☐ 23 Erik Rasmussen, Buff.	10.00	.20
☐☐ 24 Miroslav Satan, Buff.	15.00	.20
☐☐ **25 Steve Bégin, Calg. RC**	**10.00**	**1.00**
☐☐ 26 Andrew Cassels, Calg.	10.00	.20
☐☐ **27 Chris Dingman, Calg. RC**	**6.00**	**.50**
☐☐ 28 Theoren Fleury, Calg.	30.00	.20
☐☐ 29 Jonas Höglund, Calg.	6.00	.20
☐☐ 30 Jarome Iginla, Calg.	40.00	.50
☐☐ 31 Rick Tabaracci (G), Calg.	6.00	.20
☐☐ 32 German Titov, Calg.	6.00	.20
☐☐ 33 Kevin Dineen, Caro.	6.00	.20
☐☐ 34 Nelson Emerson, Caro.	6.00	.20
☐☐ 35 Trevor Kidd (G), Caro.	15.00	.20
☐☐ 36 Stephen Leach, Caro.	6.00	.20
☐☐ 37 Keith Primeau, Caro.	20.00	.20
☐☐ 38 Steven Rice, Caro.	6.00	.20
☐☐ 39 Gary Roberts, Caro.	20.00	.20
☐☐ 40 Tony Amonte, Chic.	30.00	.20
☐☐ 41 Chris Chelios, Chic.	30.00	.20
☐☐ 42 Dan Cleary, Chic.	15.00	.20
☐☐ 43 Eric Dazé, Chic.	20.00	.20
☐☐ 44 Jeff Hackett (G), Chic.	15.00	.20
☐☐ 45 Sergei Krivokrasov, Chic.	6.00	.20
☐☐ 46 Ethan Moreau, Chic.	6.00	.20
☐☐ 47 Alexei Zhamnov, Chic.	15.00	.20
☐☐ 48 Adam Deadmarsh, Colo.	15.00	.20
☐☐ 49 Peter Forsberg, Colo.	70.00	1.00
☐☐ 50 Valeri Kamensky, Colo.	15.00	.20
☐☐ 51 Jari Kurri, Colo.	50.00	.50
☐☐ 52 Claude Lemieux, Colo.	15.00	.20
☐☐ 53 Sandis Ozolinsh, Colo.	10.00	.20
☐☐ 54 Patrick Roy (G), Colo.	150.00	2.00
☐☐ 55 Joe Sakic, Colo.	80.00	1.00
☐☐ 56 Ed Belfour (G), Dall.	50.00	.50
☐☐ 57 Derian Hatcher, Dall.	15.00	.20
☐☐ 58 Jamie Langenbrunner, Dall.	10.00	.20

□□ 59 Jere Lehtinen, Dall.	15.00	.20
□□ 60 Mike Modano, Dall.	50.00	.50
□□ 61 Joe Nieuwendyk, Dall.	20.00	.20
□□ 62 Darryl Sydor, Dall.	10.00	.20
□□ 63 Pat Verbeek, Dall.	15.00	.20
□□ 64 Anders Eriksson, Detr.	6.00	.20
□□ 65 Sergei Fedorov, Detr.	50.00	.50
□□ 66 Vyacheslav Kozlov, Detr.	10.00	.20
□□ 67 Nicklas Lidström, Detr.	30.00	.20
□□ 68 Darren McCarty, Detr.	15.00	.20
□□ 69 Chris Osgood (G), Detr.	30.00	.20
□□ 70 Brendan Shanahan, Detr.	50.00	.50
□□ 71 Steve Yzerman, Detr.	120.00	1.50
□□ 72 Jason Arnott, Edmo.	20.00	.20
□□ 73 Boyd Devereaux, Edmo.	10.00	.20
□□ 74 Mike Grier, Edmo.	10.00	.20
□□ 75 Curtis Joseph (G), Edmo.	50.00	.50
□□ 76 Andrei Kovalenko, Edmo.	6.00	.20
□□ 77 Ryan Smyth, Edmo.	20.00	.20
□□ 78 Doug Weight, Edmo.	30.00	.20
□□ 79 Dave Gagner, Flor.	6.00	.20
□□ 80 Ed Jovanovski, Flor.	20.00	.20
□□ 81 Scott Mellanby, Flor.	10.00	.20
□□ 82 Kirk Muller, Flor.	15.00	.20
□□ 83 Rob Niedermayer, Flor.	10.00	.20
□□ 84 Ray Sheppard, Flor.	6.00	.20
□□ 85 Esa Tikkanen, Flor.	6.00	.20
□□ 86 J. Vanbiesbrouck (G), Flor.	20.00	.20
□□ 87 Rob Blake, LosA.	30.00	.20
□□ 88 Stéphane Fiset (G), LosA.	15.00	.20
□□ 89 Garry Galley, LosA.	6.00	.20
□□ **90 Olli Jokinen, LosA. RC**	**15.00**	**1.50**
□□ 91 Luc Robitaille, LosA.	40.00	.50
□□ 92 Jozef Stumpel, LosA.	10.00	.20
□□ 93 Shayne Corson, Mont.	15.00	.20
□□ 94 Vincent Damphousse, Mont.	30.00	.20
□□ 95 Saku Koivu, Mont.	40.00	.50
□□ 96 Andy Moog (G), Mont.	20.00	.20
□□ 97 Mark Recchi, Mont.	20.00	.20
□□ 98 Stéphane Richer, Mont.	10.00	.20
□□ 99 Brian Savage, Mont.	15.00	.20
□□ 100 Dave Andreychuk, NJer.	15.00	.20
□□ 101 Martin Brodeur (G), NJer.	80.00	1.00
□□ 102 Doug Gilmour, NJer.	30.00	.20
□□ 103 Bobby Holik, NJer.	15.00	.20
□□ 104 John MacLean, NJer.	6.00	.20
□□ 105 Brian Rolston, NJer.	15.00	.20
□□ 106 Bryan Berard, NYIs.	15.00	.20
□□ 107 Todd Bertuzzi, NYIs.	60.00	.50
□□ 108 Travis Green, NYIs.	10.00	.20
□□ 109 Zigmund Palffy, NYIs.	30.00	.20
□□ 110 Robert Reichel, NYIs.	15.00	.20
□□ 111 Tommy Salo (G), NYIs.	20.00	.20
□□ 112 Bryan Smolinski, NYIs.	6.00	.20
□□ 113 Christian Dubé, NYRa.	6.00	.20
□□ 114 Adam Graves, NYRa.	20.00	.20
□□ 115 Wayne Gretzky, NYRa.	200.00	3.00
□□ 116 Alex Kovalev, NYRa.	30.00	.20
□□ 117 Pat LaFontaine, NYRa.	30.00	.20
□□ 118 Brian Leetch, NYRa.	30.00	.20
□□ 119 Mike Richter, NYRa.	20.00	.20
□□ 120 Brian Skrudland, NYRa.	6.00	.20
□□ 121 Kevin Stevens, NYRa.	10.00	.20
□□ 122 Daniel Alfredsson, Ott.	30.00	.20
□□ 123 Radek Bonk, Ott.	15.00	.20
□□ 124 Alexandre Daigle, Ott.	6.00	.20
□□ **125 Marian Hossa, Ott. RC**	**50.00**	**5.00**
□□ 126 Igor Kravchuk, Ott.	6.00	.20
□□ 127 Chris Phillips, Ott.	10.00	.20
□□ 128 Damian Rhodes (G), Ott.	10.00	.20
□□ 129 Alexei Yashin, Ott.	30.00	.20
□□ 130 Rod Brind'Amour, Phil.	15.00	.20
□□ 131 Chris Gratton, Phil.	10.00	.20
□□ 132 Ron Hextall (G), Phil.	30.00	.20
□□ 133 John LeClair, Phil.	40.00	.50
□□ 134 Eric Lindros, Phil.	50.00	.50
□□ 135 Janne Niinimaa, Phil.	10.00	.20
□□ **136 Vaclav Prospal, Phil. RC**	**15.00**	**1.50**
□□ 137 Garth Snow (G), Phil.	15.00	.20
□□ 138 Dainius Zubrus, Phil.	10.00	.20
□□ 139 Mike Gartner, Phoe.	40.00	.50
□□ 140 Brad Isbister, Phoe.	10.00	.20
□□ 141 Nikolai Khabibulin (G), Phoe.	20.00	.20
□□ 142 Jeremy Roenick, Phoe.	40.00	.50
□□ 143 Cliff Ronning, Phoe.	10.00	.20
□□ 144 Keith Tkachuk, Phoe.	30.00	.20
□□ 145 Rick Tocchet, Phoe.	15.00	.20
□□ 146 Oleg Tverdovsky, Phoe.	6.00	.20
□□ 147 Tom Barrasso (G), Phoe.	20.00	.20
□□ 148 Ron Francis, Pitt.	30.00	.20
□□ 149 Kevin Hatcher, Pitt.	6.00	.20
□□ 150 Jaromir Jagr, Pitt.	50.00	.50
□□ 151 Darius Kasparaitis, Pitt.	10.00	.20
□□ 152 Alexei Morozov, Pitt.	10.00	.20
□□ 153 Petr Nedved, Pitt.	15.00	.20
□□ 154 Ed Olczyk, Pitt.	10.00	.20
□□ 155 Jim Campbell, SLou.	6.00	.20
□□ 156 Kelly Chase, SLou.	6.00	.20
□□ 157 Geoff Courtnall, SLou.	6.00	.20
□□ 158 Grant Fuhr (G), SLou.	30.00	.20
□□ 159 Brett Hull, SLou.	50.00	.50
□□ 160 Joe Murphy, SLou.	6.00	.20
□□ 161 Pierre Turgeon, SLou.	20.00	.20
□□ 162 Tony Twist, SLou.	6.00	.20
□□ 163 Shawn Burr, SanJ.	6.00	.20
□□ 164 Jeff Friesen, SanJ.	15.00	.20
□□ 165 Tony Granato, SanJ.	10.00	.20
□□ 166 Viktor Kozlov, SanJ.	15.00	.20
□□ 167 Patrick Marleau, SanJ.	20.00	.50
□□ 168 Stéphane Matteau, SanJ.	6.00	.20
□□ 169 Owen Nolan, SanJ.	30.00	.20
□□ 170 Mike Vernon (G), SanJ.	20.00	.20
□□ 171 Dino Ciccarelli, Tamp.	15.00	.20
□□ 172 Karl Dykhuis, Tamp.	6.00	.20
□□ 173 Roman Hamrlik, Tamp.	10.00	.20
□□ 174 Daymond Langkow, Tamp.	10.00	.20
□□ 175 Mikael Renberg, Tamp.	15.00	.20
□□ 176 Alexander Selivanov, Tamp.	6.00	.20
□□ 177 Paul Ysebaert, Tamp.	6.00	.20
□□ 178 Sergei Berezin, Toro.	10.00	.20
□□ 179 Wendel Clark, Toro.	40.00	.50
□□ 180 Glenn Healy (G), Toro.	10.00	.20
□□ 181 Derek King, Toro.	6.00	.20
□□ 182 Alyn McCauley, Toro.	15.00	.20
□□ 183 Félix Potvin (G), Toro.	30.00	.20
□□ **184 Martin Prochazka, Toro. RC**	**6.00**	**.50**
□□ 185 Mats Sundin, Toro.	50.00	.50
□□ 186 Pavel Bure, Vanc.	40.00	.50
□□ 187 Martin Gelinas, Vanc.	10.00	.20
□□ 188 Trevor Linden, Vanc.	20.00	.20
□□ 189 Kirk McLean (G), Vanc.	15.00	.20
□□ 190 Mark Messier, Vanc.	50.00	.50
□□ **191 Lubomir Vaic, Vanc. RC**	**6.00**	**.50**
□□ 192 Mattias Öhlund, Vanc.	15.00	.20
□□ 193 Peter Bondra, Wash.	30.00	.20
□□ 194 Dale Hunter, Wash.	15.00	.20
□□ 195 Joé Juneau, Wash.	10.00	.20
□□ 196 Olaf Kölzig (G), Wash.	30.00	.20
□□ 197 Steve Konowalchuk, Wash.	10.00	.20
□□ 198 Adam Oates, Wash.	20.00	.20
□□ 199 Bill Ranford (G), Wash.	20.00	.20
□□ 200 Jaroslav Svejkovsky, Wash.	6.00	.20

ONE-PER-PACK PARALLELS

One-per-pack parallels are Copper (US hobby), Silver (US retail), Emerald (Cdn. hobby), Dark Grey (Cdn. retail), and Red (Treat packs). Dealers may sell some parallels for more or less depending on their supply.

Complete Set (200 cards):	**300.00**	**125.00**
Common Player:	**.75**	**.50**
Player	**Red**	**Paral.**
□□□□□ 1 Guy Hebert (G), Anah.	1.00	.50
□□□□□ 2 Paul Kariya, Anah.	8.00	4.00
□□□□□ **3 Espen Knutsen, Anah. RC**	**4.00**	**2.00**
□□□□□ 4 Dmitri Mironov, Anah.	1.00	.50
□□□□□ 5 Steve Rucchin, Anah.	1.00	.50
□□□□□ 6 Tomas Sandström, Anah.	1.00	.50
□□□□□ 7 Teemu Selänne, Anah.	5.00	2.00
□□□□□ 8 Scott Young, Anah.	2.00	.50
□□□□□ 9 Raymond Bourque, Bost.	7.00	3.50
□□□□□ 10 Jim Carey (G), Bost.	1.00	.50
□□□□□ 11 Anson Carter, Bost.	2.00	1.00
□□□□□ 12 Ted Donato, Bost.	.75	.50
□□□□□ 13 Dave Ellett, Bost.	1.00	.50
□□□□□ 14 Dimitri Khristich, Bost.	1.00	.50
□□□□□ 15 Sergei Samsonov, Bost.	5.00	2.50
□□□□□ 16 Joe Thornton, Bost.	11.00	5.00
□□□□□ 17 Matthew Barnaby, Buff.	.75	.50
□□□□□ 18 Jason Dawe, Buff.	.75	.50
□□□□□ 19 Dominik Hasek (G), Buff.	6.00	3.00
□□□□□ 20 Brian Holzinger, Buff.	1.00	.50
□□□□□ 21 Michael Peca, Buff.	2.00	1.00
□□□□□ 22 Derek Plante, Buff.	1.00	.50
□□□□□ 23 Erik Rasmussen, Buff.	2.00	1.00
□□□□□ 24 Miroslav Satan, Buff.	2.00	.50
□□□□□ **25 Steve Bégin, Calg. RC**	**4.00**	**2.00**
□□□□□ 26 Andrew Cassels, Calg.	1.00	.50
□□□□□ **27 Chris Dingman, Calg. RC**	**3.00**	**1.00**
□□□□□ 28 Theoren Fleury, Calg.	3.00	1.50
□□□□□ 29 Jonas Höglund, Calg.	1.00	.50
□□□□□ 30 Jarome Iginla, Calg.	5.00	2.00
□□□□□ 31 Rick Tabaracci (G), Calg.	1.00	.50
□□□□□ 32 German Titov, Calg.	.75	.50
□□□□□ 33 Kevin Dineen, Caro.	1.00	.50
□□□□□ 34 Nelson Emerson, Caro.	1.00	.50
□□□□□ 35 Trevor Kidd (G), Caro.	2.00	.50
□□□□□ 36 Stephen Leach, Caro.	.75	.50
□□□□□ 37 Keith Primeau, Caro.	2.00	1.00
□□□□□ 38 Steven Rice, Caro.	.75	.50
□□□□□ 39 Gary Roberts, Caro.	2.00	1.00
□□□□□ 40 Tony Amonte, Chic.	3.00	1.50
□□□□□ 41 Chris Chelios, Chic.	3.00	1.50
□□□□□ 42 Dan Cleary, Chic.	3.00	1.00
□□□□□ 43 Eric Dazé, Chic.	2.00	1.00
□□□□□ 44 Jeff Hackett (G), Chic.	2.00	.50
□□□□□ 45 Sergei Krivokrasov, Chic.	1.00	.50
□□□□□ 46 Ethan Moreau, Chic.	1.00	.50
□□□□□ 47 Alexei Zhamnov, Chic.	2.00	.50
□□□□□ 48 Adam Deadmarsh, Colo.	2.00	.50
□□□□□ 49 Peter Forsberg, Colo.	8.00	4.00
□□□□□ 50 Valeri Kamensky, Colo.	2.00	.50
□□□□□ 51 Jari Kurri, Colo.	6.00	3.00
□□□□□ 52 Claude Lemieux, Colo.	2.00	.50
□□□□□ 53 Sandis Ozolinsh, Colo.	1.00	.50
□□□□□ 54 Patrick Roy (G), Colo.	18.00	9.00
□□□□□ 55 Joe Sakic, Colo.	10.00	4.50
□□□□□ 56 Ed Belfour (G), Dall.	6.00	3.00
□□□□□ 57 Derian Hatcher, Dall.	2.00	.50
□□□□□ 58 Jamie Langenbrunner, Dall.	1.00	.50
□□□□□ 59 Jere Lehtinen, Dall.	2.00	.50
□□□□□ 60 Mike Modano, Dall.	6.00	3.00
□□□□□ 61 Joe Nieuwendyk, Dall.	2.00	1.00
□□□□□ 62 Darryl Sydor, Dall.	1.00	.50
□□□□□ 63 Pat Verbeek, Dall.	2.00	.50
□□□□□ 64 Anders Eriksson, Detr.	.75	.50
□□□□□ 65 Sergei Fedorov, Detr.	6.00	3.00
□□□□□ 66 Vyacheslav Kozlov, Detr.	1.00	.50
□□□□□ 67 Nicklas Lidström, Detr.	3.00	1.50
□□□□□ 68 Darren McCarty, Detr.	2.00	.50
□□□□□ 69 Chris Osgood (G), Detr.	3.00	1.50
□□□□□ 70 Brendan Shanahan, Detr.	6.00	3.00
□□□□□ 71 Steve Yzerman, Detr.	15.00	7.00
□□□□□ 72 Jason Arnott, Edmo.	3.00	1.00
□□□□□ 73 Boyd Devereaux, Edmo.	2.00	1.00
□□□□□ 74 Mike Grier, Edmo.	1.00	.50
□□□□□ 75 Curtis Joseph (G), Edmo.	6.00	3.00
□□□□□ 76 Andrei Kovalenko, Edmo.	1.00	.50
□□□□□ 77 Ryan Smyth, Edmo.	3.00	1.00
□□□□□ 78 Doug Weight, Edmo.	3.00	1.50
□□□□□ 79 Dave Gagner, Flor.	1.00	.50
□□□□□ 80 Ed Jovanovski, Flor.	2.00	1.00
□□□□□ 81 Scott Mellanby, Flor.	1.00	.50
□□□□□ 82 Kirk Muller, Flor.	2.00	.50
□□□□□ 83 Rob Niedermayer, Flor.	1.00	.50
□□□□□ 84 Ray Sheppard, Flor.	1.00	.50
□□□□□ 85 Esa Tikkanen, Flor.	1.00	.50
□□□□□ 86 J. Vanbiesbrouck (G), Flor.	3.00	1.00
□□□□□ 87 Rob Blake, LosA.	3.00	1.50
□□□□□ 88 Stéphane Fiset (G), LosA.	2.00	.50
□□□□□ 89 Garry Galley, LosA.	.75	.50
□□□□□ **90 Olli Jokinen, LosA. RC**	**6.00**	**2.50**
□□□□□ 91 Luc Robitaille, LosA.	5.00	2.00
□□□□□ 92 Jozef Stumpel, LosA.	1.00	.50
□□□□□ 93 Shayne Corson, Mont.	2.00	.50
□□□□□ 94 Vincent Damphousse, Mont.	3.00	1.50
□□□□□ 95 Saku Koivu, Mont.	5.00	2.00
□□□□□ 96 Andy Moog (G), Mont.	2.00	1.00
□□□□□ 97 Mark Recchi, Mont.	2.00	1.00
□□□□□ 98 Stéphane Richer, Mont.	1.00	.50
□□□□□ 99 Brian Savage, Mont.	2.00	.50
□□□□□ 100 Dave Andreychuk, NJer.	2.00	.50
□□□□□ 101 Martin Brodeur (G), NJer.	10.00	4.50
□□□□□ 102 Doug Gilmour, NJer.	3.00	1.50
□□□□□ 103 Bobby Holik, NJer.	2.00	.50
□□□□□ 104 John MacLean, NJer.	1.00	.50
□□□□□ 105 Brian Rolston, NJer.	2.00	.50
□□□□□ 106 Bryan Berard, NYIs.	2.00	.50
□□□□□ 107 Todd Bertuzzi, NYIs.	7.00	3.50
□□□□□ 108 Travis Green, NYIs.	1.00	.50
□□□□□ 109 Zigmund Palffy, NYIs.	3.00	1.50
□□□□□ 110 Robert Reichel, NYIs.	2.00	.50
□□□□□ 111 Tommy Salo (G), NYIs.	2.00	1.00
□□□□□ 112 Bryan Smolinski, NYIs.	1.00	.50
□□□□□ 113 Christian Dubé, NYRa.	1.00	.50
□□□□□ 114 Adam Graves, NYRa.	2.00	1.00
□□□□□ 115 Wayne Gretzky, NYRa.	25.00	12.00
□□□□□ 116 Alex Kovalev, NYRa.	3.00	1.50
□□□□□ 117 Pat LaFontaine, NYRa.	3.00	1.50
□□□□□ 118 Brian Leetch, NYRa.	3.00	1.50
□□□□□ 119 Mike Richter, NYRa.	3.00	1.00
□□□□□ 120 Brian Skrudland, NYRa.	1.00	.50
□□□□□ 121 Kevin Stevens, NYRa.	1.00	.50
□□□□□ 122 Daniel Alfredsson, Ott.	3.00	1.50
□□□□□ 123 Radek Bonk, Ott.	2.00	.50
□□□□□ 124 Alexandre Daigle, Ott.	1.00	.50
□□□□□ **125 Marian Hossa, Ott. RC**	**18.00**	**9.00**
□□□□□ 126 Igor Kravchuk, Ott.	1.00	.50
□□□□□ 127 Chris Phillips, Ott.	2.00	1.00
□□□□□ 128 Damian Rhodes (G), Ott.	1.00	.50
□□□□□ 129 Alexei Yashin, Ott.	3.00	1.50
□□□□□ 130 Rod Brind'Amour, Phil.	2.00	.50
□□□□□ 131 Chris Gratton, Phil.	1.00	.50
□□□□□ 132 Ron Hextall (G), Phil.	3.00	1.50
□□□□□ 133 John LeClair, Phil.	5.00	2.00
□□□□□ 134 Eric Lindros, Phil.	6.00	3.00
□□□□□ 135 Janne Niinimaa, Phil.	1.00	.50
□□□□□ **136 Vaclav Prospal, Phil. RC**	**6.00**	**2.50**
□□□□□ 137 Garth Snow (G), Phil.	2.00	.50
□□□□□ 138 Dainius Zubrus, Phil.	1.00	.50
□□□□□ 139 Mike Gartner, Phoe.	5.00	2.00
□□□□□ 140 Brad Isbister, Phoe.	2.00	1.00
□□□□□ 141 Nikolai Khabibulin (G), Phoe.	2.00	1.00
□□□□□ 142 Jeremy Roenick, Phoe.	5.00	2.00
□□□□□ 143 Cliff Ronning, Phoe.	1.00	.50
□□□□□ 144 Keith Tkachuk, Phoe.	3.00	1.50
□□□□□ 145 Rick Tocchet, Phoe.	2.00	.50
□□□□□ 146 Oleg Tverdovsky, Phoe.	1.00	.50
□□□□□ 147 Tom Barrasso (G), Phoe.	2.00	1.00
□□□□□ 148 Ron Francis, Pitt.	3.00	1.50
□□□□□ 149 Kevin Hatcher, Pitt.	1.00	.50
□□□□□ 150 Jaromir Jagr, Pitt.	6.00	3.00
□□□□□ 151 Darius Kasparaitis, Pitt.	1.00	.50
□□□□□ 152 Alexei Morozov, Pitt.	2.00	1.00
□□□□□ 153 Petr Nedved, Pitt.	2.00	.50
□□□□□ 154 Ed Olczyk, Pitt.	1.00	.50
□□□□□ 155 Jim Campbell, SLou.	.75	.50
□□□□□ 156 Kelly Chase, SLou.	1.00	.50
□□□□□ 157 Geoff Courtnall, SLou.	1.00	.50
□□□□□ 158 Grant Fuhr (G), SLou.	3.00	1.50
□□□□□ 159 Brett Hull, SLou.	6.00	3.00
□□□□□ 160 Joe Murphy, SLou.	1.00	.50
□□□□□ 161 Pierre Turgeon, SLou.	2.00	1.00
□□□□□ 162 Tony Twist, SLou.	1.00	.50
□□□□□ 163 Shawn Burr, SanJ.	.75	.50
□□□□□ 164 Jeff Friesen, SanJ.	2.00	.50
□□□□□ 165 Tony Granato, SanJ.	1.00	.50
□□□□□ 166 Viktor Kozlov, SanJ.	2.00	.50
□□□□□ 167 Patrick Marleau, SanJ.	4.00	2.00
□□□□□ 168 Stéphane Matteau, SanJ.	1.00	.50
□□□□□ 169 Owen Nolan, SanJ.	3.00	1.50
□□□□□ 170 Mike Vernon (G), SanJ.	2.00	1.00
□□□□□ 171 Dino Ciccarelli, Tamp.	2.00	.50
□□□□□ 172 Karl Dykhuis, Tamp.	.75	.50
□□□□□ 173 Roman Hamrlik, Tamp.	1.00	.50
□□□□□ 174 Daymond Langkow, Tamp.	1.00	.50
□□□□□ 175 Mikael Renberg, Tamp.	2.00	.50
□□□□□ 176 Alexander Selivanov, Tamp.	.75	.50
□□□□□ 177 Paul Ysebaert, Tamp.	.75	.50
□□□□□ 178 Sergei Berezin, Toro.	1.00	.50
□□□□□ 179 Wendel Clark, Toro.	5.00	2.00
□□□□□ 180 Glenn Healy (G), Toro.	1.00	.50
□□□□□ 181 Derek King, Toro.	1.00	.50
□□□□□ 182 Alyn McCauley, Toro.	3.00	1.00
□□□□□ 183 Félix Potvin (G), Toro.	3.00	1.50
□□□□□ **184 Martin Prochazka, Toro. RC**	**3.00**	**1.00**
□□□□□ 185 Mats Sundin, Toro.	6.00	3.00
□□□□□ 186 Pavel Bure, Vanc.	5.00	2.00
□□□□□ 187 Martin Gelinas, Vanc.	1.00	.50
□□□□□ 188 Trevor Linden, Vanc.	2.00	1.00
□□□□□ 189 Kirk McLean (G), Vanc.	2.00	.50
□□□□□ 190 Mark Messier, Vanc.	6.00	3.00
□□□□□ **191 Lubomir Vaic, Vanc. RC**	**1.00**	**.50**
□□□□□ 192 Mattias Öhlund, Vanc.	3.00	1.00
□□□□□ 193 Peter Bondra, Wash.	3.00	1.50
□□□□□ 194 Dale Hunter, Wash.	2.00	.50
□□□□□ 195 Joé Juneau, Wash.	1.00	.50
□□□□□ 196 Olaf Kölzig (G), Wash.	3.00	1.50
□□□□□ 197 Steve Konowalchuk, Wash.	1.00	.50
□□□□□ 198 Adam Oates, Wash.	2.00	1.00
□□□□□ 199 Bill Ranford (G), Wash.	2.00	1.00
□□□□□ 200 Jaroslav Svejkovsky, Wash.	1.00	.50

Sample	**Promo**
□ Mike Modano	2.00

BIG NUMBERS

Insert Set (20 cards):	**200.00**
Insert (1:37)	**BN**
□ 1 Paul Kariya, Anah.	10.00
□ 2 Teemu Selänne, Anah.	5.00
□ 3 Joe Thornton, Bost.	15.00
□ 4 Dominik Hasek (G), Buff.	10.00
□ 5 Peter Forsberg, Colo.	10.00
□ 6 Patrick Roy (G), Colo.	30.00
□ 7 Joe Sakic, Colo.	15.00
□ 8 Sergei Fedorov, Detr.	10.00
□ 9 Brendan Shanahan, Detr.	10.00
□ 10 Steve Yzerman, Detr.	20.00
□ 11 John Vanbiesbrouck (G), Flor.	4.00
□ 12 Martin Brodeur (G), NJer.	15.00
□ 13 Doug Gilmour, NJer.	5.00
□ 14 Wayne Gretzky, NYRa.	40.00
□ 15 Eric Lindros, Phil.	10.00
□ 16 Keith Tkachuk, Phoe.	5.00
□ 17 Jaromir Jagr, Pitt.	10.00
□ 18 Brett Hull, SLou.	10.00
□ 19 Pavel Bure, Vanc.	5.00
□ 20 Mark Messier, Vanc.	10.00

CANADIAN GREATS

	Insert Set (12 cards):	**120.00**
	Insert (1:24 Cdn Retail)	**CG**
□	1 Paul Kariya, Anah.	10.00
□	2 Joe Thornton, Bost.	12.00
□	3 Jarome Iginla, Calg.	6.00
□	4 Patrick Roy (G), Colo.	22.00
□	5 Joe Sakic, Colo.	12.00
□	6 Brendan Shanahan, Detr.	6.00
□	7 Steve Yzerman, Detr.	18.00
□	8 Ryan Smyth, Edmo.	3.00
□	9 Martin Brodeur (G), NJer.	12.00
□	10 Wayne Gretzky, NYRa.	30.00
□	11 Eric Lindros, Phil.	6.00
□	12 Mark Messier, Vanc.	6.00

GLOVE SIDE LASER CUTS

	Insert Set (10 cards):	**225.00**
	Insert (1:73)	**GSLC**
□	1 Guy Hebert (G), Anah.	8.00
□	2 Dominik Hasek (G), Buff.	20.00
□	3 Trevor Kidd (G), Caro.	8.00
□	4 Jeff Hackett (G), Chic.	8.00
□	5 Patrick Roy (G), Colo.	60.00
□	6 Ed Belfour (G), Dall.	20.00
□	7 Chris Osgood (G), Detr.	10.00
□	8 Curtis Joseph (G), Edmo.	20.00
□	9 John Vanbiesbrouck (G), Flor.	8.00
□	10 Andy Moog (G), Mont.	8.00
□	11 Martin Brodeur (G), NJer.	30.00
□	12 Tommy Salo (G), NYIs.	8.00
□	13 Mike Richter (G), NYRa.	8.00
□	14 Ron Hextall (G), Phil.	10.00
□	15 Garth Snow (G), Phil.	8.00
□	16 Nikolai Khabibulin (G), Phoe.	8.00
□	17 Tom Barrasso (G), Pitt.	8.00
□	18 Grant Fuhr (G), SLou.	10.00
□	19 Mike Vernon (G), SanJ.	8.00
□	20 Félix Potvin (G), Toro.	10.00

PHOTOENGRAVINGS

	Insert Set (20 cards):	**150.00**
	Insert (2:37)	**PE**
□	1 Paul Kariya, Anah.	10.00
□	2 Teemu Selänne, Anah.	6.00
□	3 Joe Thornton, Bost.	12.00
□	4 Dominik Hasek (G), Buff.	6.00
□	5 Peter Forsberg, Colo.	10.00
□	6 Patrick Roy (G), Colo.	22.00
□	7 Joe Sakic, Colo.	12.00
□	8 Mike Modano, Dall.	6.00
□	9 Brendan Shanahan, Detr.	6.00
□	10 Steve Yzerman, Detr.	18.00
□	11 John Vanbiesbrouck (G), Flor.	3.00
□	12 Saku Koivu, Mont.	6.00
□	13 Wayne Gretzky, NYRa.	30.00
□	14 John LeClair, Phil.	6.00
□	15 Eric Lindros, Phil.	6.00
□	16 Keith Tkachuk, Phoe.	4.00
□	17 Jaromir Jagr, Pitt.	6.00
□	18 Brett Hull, SLou.	6.00
□	19 Pavel Bure, Vanc.	6.00
□	20 Mark Messier, Vanc.	6.00

1997 - 98 PACIFIC REVOLUTION

These cards have five versions: the regular card, an Emerald Green parallel (Canadian), a Copper parallel (Hobby), a Silver parallel (Retail) and an Ice Blue parallel.

	Complete Set (150 cards):	**2300.00**	**650.00**	**125.00**
	Common Player:	**8.00**	**2.00**	**.50**
	Player	**IB67**	**Para.**	**Revo.**
□□□□□	1 Guy Hebert (G)	10.00	3.00	.50
□□□□□	2 Paul Kariya	70.00	20.00	3.50
□□□□□	3 Dmitri Mironov	8.00	2.00	.50
□□□□□	4 Ruslan Salei	8.00	2.00	.50
□□□□□	5 Teemu Selänne	40.00	10.00	2.00
□□□□□	6 Jason Allison	30.00	5.00	1.50
□□□□□	7 Raymond Bourque	60.00	15.00	3.00
□□□□□	8 Byron Dafoe (G)	20.00	6.00	1.00
□□□□□	9 Ted Donato	8.00	2.00	.50
□□□□□	10 Dimitri Khristich	8.00	2.00	.50
□□□□□	11 Joe Thornton	60.00	15.00	6.00
□□□□□	12 Matthew Barnaby	8.00	2.00	.50
□□□□□	13 Jason Dawe	8.00	2.00	.50
□□□□□	14 Dominik Hasek (G)	50.00	15.00	2.50
□□□□□	15 Michael Peca	20.00	6.00	1.00
□□□□□	16 Miroslav Satan	15.00	4.00	.50
□□□□□	17 Theoren Fleury	30.00	5.00	1.50
□□□□□	18 Jarome Iginla	40.00	12.00	2.00
□□□□□	19 Marty McInnis	8.00	2.00	.50
□□□□□	20 Cory Stillman	10.00	3.00	.50
□□□□□	21 Rick Tabaracci (G)	8.00	2.00	.50
□□□□□	22 Martin Gelinas	10.00	3.00	.50
□□□□□	23 Sami Kapanen	15.00	4.00	.50
□□□□□	24 Trevor Kidd (G)	15.00	4.00	.50
□□□□□	25 Keith Primeau	20.00	6.00	1.00
□□□□□	26 Gary Roberts	20.00	6.00	1.00
□□□□□	27 Tony Amonte	30.00	9.00	1.50
□□□□□	28 Chris Chelios	30.00	9.00	1.50
□□□□□	29 Eric Dazé	20.00	6.00	1.00
□□□□□	30 Jeff Hackett (G)	15.00	4.00	.50
□□□□□	31 Dmitri Nabokov	8.00	2.00	.50
□□□□□	32 Peter Forsberg	70.00	20.00	3.50
□□□□□	33 Valeri Kamensky	15.00	4.00	.50
□□□□□	34 Jari Kurri	50.00	15.00	2.50
□□□□□	35 Claude Lemieux	15.00	4.00	.50
□□□□□	**36 Eric Messier RC**	**15.00**	**4.00**	**2.00**
□□□□□	37 Sandis Ozolinsh	10.00	3.00	.50
□□□□□	38 Patrick Roy (G)	150.00	45.00	7.50
□□□□□	39 Joe Sakic	80.00	20.00	4.00
□□□□□	40 Ed Belfour (G)	50.00	15.00	2.50
□□□□□	41 Jamie Langenbrunner	10.00	3.00	.50
□□□□□	42 Jere Lehtinen	15.00	4.00	.50
□□□□□	43 Mike Modano	50.00	15.00	2.50
□□□□□	44 Joe Nieuwendyk	20.00	6.00	1.00
□□□□□	45 Sergei Zubov	10.00	3.00	.50
□□□□□	46 Viacheslav Fetisov	30.00	9.00	1.50
□□□□□	47 Nicklas Lidström	30.00	9.00	1.50
□□□□□	48 Darren McCarty	15.00	4.00	.50
□□□□□	49 Larry Murphy	10.00	3.00	.50
□□□□□	50 Chris Osgood (G)	30.00	5.00	1.50
□□□□□	51 Brendan Shanahan	50.00	15.00	2.50
□□□□□	52 Steve Yzerman	120.00	35.00	6.00
□□□□□	53 Roman Hamrlik	10.00	3.00	.50
□□□□□	54 Bill Guerin	20.00	6.00	1.00
□□□□□	55 Curtis Joseph (G)	50.00	15.00	2.50
□□□□□	56 Ryan Smyth	20.00	7.00	1.00
□□□□□	57 Doug Weight	30.00	5.00	1.50
□□□□□	58 Dino Ciccarelli	15.00	4.00	.50
□□□□□	59 Dave Gagner	8.00	2.00	.50
□□□□□	60 Ed Jovanovski	20.00	6.00	1.00
□□□□□	61 Paul Laus	8.00	2.00	.50
□□□□□	62 John Vanbiesbrouck (G)	20.00	7.00	1.00
□□□□□	63 Ray Whitney	10.00	3.00	.50
□□□□□	64 Russ Courtnall	10.00	3.00	.50
□□□□□	65 Yanic Perreault	15.00	4.00	.50
□□□□□	66 Luc Robitaille	40.00	10.00	2.00
□□□□□	67 Jozef Stumpel	10.00	3.00	.50
□□□□□	68 Vladimir Tsyplakov	8.00	2.00	.50
□□□□□	69 Shayne Corson	15.00	4.00	.50
□□□□□	70 Vincent Damphousse	30.00	9.00	1.50
□□□□□	71 Saku Koivu	40.00	10.00	2.00
□□□□□	72 Andy Moog (G)	20.00	6.00	1.00
□□□□□	73 Mark Recchi	20.00	6.00	1.00
□□□□□	74 Jocelyn Thibault (G)	20.00	6.00	1.00
□□□□□	75 Martin Brodeur (G)	80.00	20.00	4.00
□□□□□	**76 Patrik Elias RC**	**80.00**	**20.00**	**10.00**
□□□□□	77 Doug Gilmour	30.00	9.00	1.50
□□□□□	78 Bobby Holik	15.00	4.00	.50
□□□□□	79 Scott Niedermayer	15.00	4.00	.50
□□□□□	80 Bryan Berard	15.00	4.00	.50
□□□□□	81 Travis Green	10.00	3.00	.50
□□□□□	82 Zigmund Palffy	30.00	9.00	1.50
□□□□□	83 Robert Reichel	15.00	4.00	.50
□□□□□	84 Tommy Salo (G)	20.00	6.00	1.00
□□□□□	85 Dan Cloutier (G)	20.00	6.00	2.00
□□□□□	86 Adam Graves	20.00	6.00	1.00
□□□□□	87 Wayne Gretzky	200.00	60.00	10.00
□□□□□	88 Pat LaFontaine	30.00	9.00	1.50
□□□□□	89 Brian Leetch	30.00	9.00	1.50
□□□□□	90 Mike Richter (G)	20.00	7.00	1.00
□□□□□	91 Kevin Stevens	10.00	3.00	.50
□□□□□	92 Daniel Alfredsson	30.00	9.00	1.50
□□□□□	93 Shawn McEachern	15.00	4.00	.50
□□□□□	94 Damian Rhodes (G)	10.00	3.00	.50
□□□□□	95 Ron Tugnutt (G)	20.00	6.00	1.00
□□□□□	96 Alexei Yashin	30.00	9.00	1.50
□□□□□	97 Rod Brind'Amour	15.00	4.00	.50
□□□□□	98 Paul Coffey	30.00	5.00	1.50
□□□□□	99 Alexandre Daigle	8.00	2.00	.50
□□□□□	100 Chris Gratton	10.00	3.00	.50
□□□□□	101 Ron Hextall (G)	30.00	9.00	1.50
□□□□□	102 John LeClair	40.00	10.00	2.00
□□□□□	103 Eric Lindros	50.00	15.00	2.50
□□□□□	104 Dainius Zubrus	10.00	3.00	.50
□□□□□	105 Mike Gartner	40.00	10.00	2.00
□□□□□	106 Craig Janney	10.00	3.00	.50
□□□□□	107 Nikolai Khabibulin (G)	20.00	6.00	1.00
□□□□□	108 Jeremy Roenick	40.00	10.00	2.00
□□□□□	109 Keith Tkachuk	30.00	5.00	1.50
□□□□□	110 Stu Barnes	8.00	2.00	.50
□□□□□	111 Tom Barrasso (G)	20.00	6.00	1.00
□□□□□	112 Ron Francis	30.00	9.00	1.50
□□□□□	113 Jaromir Jagr	50.00	15.00	2.50
□□□□□	**114 P. Skudra (G) RC**	**15.00**	**4.00**	**2.00**
□□□□□	115 Martin Straka	15.00	4.00	.50
□□□□□	**116 B. Atcheynum RC**	**10.00**	**3.00**	**1.50**
□□□□□	117 Jim Campbell	8.00	2.00	.50
□□□□□	118 Geoff Courtnall	8.00	2.00	.50
□□□□□	119 Steve Duchesne	10.00	3.00	.50
□□□□□	120 Grant Fuhr (G)	30.00	9.00	1.50
□□□□□	121 Brett Hull	50.00	15.00	2.50
□□□□□	122 Pierre Turgeon	20.00	6.00	1.00
□□□□□	123 Jeff Friesen	15.00	4.00	.50
□□□□□	124 John MacLean	8.00	2.00	.50
□□□□□	125 Patrick Marleau	20.00	7.00	2.00
□□□□□	126 Owen Nolan	30.00	9.00	1.50
□□□□□	**127 Marco Sturm RC**	**10.00**	**3.00**	**3.50**
□□□□□	128 Mike Vernon (G)	20.00	6.00	1.00
□□□□□	129 Daren Puppa (G)	10.00	3.00	.50
□□□□□	130 Mikael Renberg	15.00	4.00	.50
□□□□□	131 Paul Ysebaert	8.00	2.00	.50
□□□□□	132 Rob Zamuner	10.00	3.00	.50
□□□□□	133 Wendel Clark	40.00	12.00	2.00
□□□□□	134 Tie Domi	15.00	4.00	.50
□□□□□	135 Igor Korolev	8.00	2.00	.50
□□□□□	136 Félix Potvin (G)	30.00	9.00	1.50
□□□□□	137 Mats Sundin	50.00	15.00	2.50
□□□□□	138 Donald Brashear	10.00	3.00	.50
□□□□□	139 Pavel Bure	40.00	10.00	2.00
□□□□□	140 Sean Burke (G)	30.00	9.00	1.50
□□□□□	141 Trevor Linden	20.00	6.00	1.00
□□□□□	142 Mark Messier	50.00	15.00	2.50
□□□□□	143 Alexander Mogilny	20.00	7.00	1.00
□□□□□	144 Mattias Öhlund	15.00	4.00	1.50
□□□□□	145 Peter Bondra	30.00	9.00	1.50
□□□□□	146 Phil Housley	15.00	4.00	.50
□□□□□	147 Dale Hunter	15.00	4.00	.50
□□□□□	148 Joé Juneau	10.00	3.00	.50
□□□□□	149 Olaf Kölzig (G)	30.00	9.00	1.50
□□□□□	150 Adam Oates	20.00	6.00	1.00

	Sample	**Promo**
□	Mike Modano, Dall.	2.00

ALL-STAR GAME

	Insert Set (20 cards):	**275.00**
	Insert (1:49)	**ASG**
□	1 Teemu Selänne, Anah.	10.00
□	2 Raymond Bourque, Bost.	15.00
□	3 Dominik Hasek (G), Buff.	10.00
□	4 Theoren Fleury, Calg.	8.00
□	5 Chris Chelios, Chic.	8.00
□	6 Peter Forsberg, Colo.	20.00
□	7 Patrick Roy (G), Colo.	45.00
□	8 Joe Sakic, Colo.	20.00
□	9 Ed Belfour (G), Dall.	15.00
□	10 Mike Modano, Dall.	15.00
□	11 Brendan Shanahan, Detr.	15.00
□	12 Saku Koivu, Mont.	10.00
□	13 Martin Brodeur (G), NJer.	20.00
□	14 Wayne Gretzky, NYRa.	60.00
□	15 John LeClair, Phil.	10.00
□	16 Eric Lindros, Phil.	15.00
□	17 Jaromir Jagr, Pitt.	15.00
□	18 Pavel Bure, Vanc.	10.00
□	19 Mark Messier, Vanc.	15.00
□	20 Peter Bondra, Wash.	8.00

ICONS

	Insert Set (10 cards):	**355.00**
	Insert (1:121)	**Icons**
□	1 Paul Kariya, Anah.	30.00
□	2 Teemu Selänne, Anah.	20.00
□	3 Peter Forsberg, Colo.	35.00
□	4 Patrick Roy (G), Colo.	70.00
□	5 Steve Yzerman, Detr.	60.00
□	6 Martin Brodeur (G), NJer.	40.00
□	7 Wayne Gretzky, NYRa.	100.00
□	8 Eric Lindros, Phil.	25.00
□	9 Jaromir Jagr, Pitt.	20.00
□	10 Pavel Bure, Vanc.	20.00

RETURN TO SENDER

	Insert Set (20 cards):	**200.00**
	Insert (1:25)	**RTS**
□	1 Guy Hebert (G), Anah.	6.00
□	2 Byron Dafoe (G), Bost.	6.00
□	3 Dominik Hasek (G), Buff.	16.00
□	4 Jeff Hackett (G), Chic.	6.00
□	5 Patrick Roy (G), Colo.	50.00
□	6 Ed Belfour (G), Dall.	16.00
□	7 Chris Osgood (G), Detr.	10.00
□	8 Curtis Joseph (G), Edmo.	16.00
□	9 John Vanbiesbrouck (G), Flor.	8.00
□	10 Andy Moog (G), Mont.	6.00
□	11 Martin Brodeur (G), NJer.	25.00
□	12 Tommy Salo (G), NYIs.	6.00
□	13 Mike Richter (G), NYRa.	8.00
□	14 Ron Hextall (G), Phil.	10.00
□	15 Nikolai Khabibulin (G), Phoe.	6.00
□	16 Tom Barrasso (G), Pitt.	6.00
□	17 Grant Fuhr (G), SLou.	10.00
□	18 Mike Vernon (G), SanJ.	6.00
□	19 Félix Potvin (G), Toro.	10.00
□	20 Olaf Kölzig (G), Wash.	10.00

TEAM CHECKLIST

	Insert Set (26 cards):	**275.00**
	Insert (1:25)	**TC**
□	1 Paul Kariya, Anah.	16.00
□	2 Joe Thornton, Bost.	22.00
□	3 Michael Peca, Buff.	5.00
□	4 Theoren Fleury, Calg.	6.00
□	5 Keith Primeau, Caro.	5.00
□	6 Chris Chelios, Chic.	6.00
□	7 Patrick Roy (G), Colo.	35.00
□	8 Mike Modano, Dall.	12.00
□	9 Steve Yzerman, Detr.	30.00

	Player	Price
☐	10 Ryan Smyth, Edmo.	6.00
☐	11 John Vanbiesbrouck (G), Flor.	6.00
☐	12 Jozef Stumpel, LosA.	5.00
☐	13 Saku Koivu, Mont.	10.00
☐	14 Martin Brodeur (G), NJer.	20.00
☐	15 Zigmund Palffy, NYIs.	6.00
☐	16 Wayne Gretzky, NYRa.	50.00
☐	17 Daniel Alfredsson, Otta.	6.00
☐	18 Eric Lindros, Phil.	12.00
☐	19 Keith Tkachuk, Phoe.	6.00
☐	20 Jaromir Jagr, Pitt.	12.00
☐	21 Brett Hull, SLou.	12.00
☐	22 Mike Vernon (G), SanJ.	5.00
☐	23 Rob Zamuner, Tamp.	5.00
☐	24 Mats Sundin, Toro.	12.00
☐	25 Pavel Bure, Vanc.	10.00
☐	26 Peter Bondra, Wash.	6.00

1997 - 98 PANINI STICKERS

This series was issued for European distribution only.

Sticker Size: 2 1/8" x 3"

Complete Set (252 stickers): 65.00

	Player	Panini
☐	1 Rob DiMaio, Bost.	.25
☐	2 Jeff Odgers, Bost.	.25
☐	3 Jozef Stumpel, Bost.	.25
☐	4 Ted Donato, Bost.	.25
☐	5 Mattias Timander, Bost.	.25
☐	6 Boston Bruins logo	.25
☐	7 Don Sweeney, Bost.	.25
☐	8 Jim Carey (G), Bost.	.25
☐	9 Raymond Bourque, Bost.	1.50
☐	10 Dominik Hasek (G), Buff.	1.50
☐	11 Alexei Zhitnik, Buff.	.25
☐	12 Derek Plante, Buff.	.25
☐	13 Michael Peca, Buff.	.50
☐	14 Darryl Shannon, Buff.	.25
☐	15 Buffalo Sabres logo	.25
☐	16 Donald Audette, Buff.	.50
☐	17 Michal Grosek, Buff.	.25
☐	18 Miroslav Satan, Buff.	.25
☐	19 Robert Kron, Caro.	.25
☐	20 Geoff Sanderson, Caro.	.25
☐	21 Andrew Cassels, Caro.	.25
☐	22 Marek Malik, Caro.	.25
☐	23 Derek King, Caro.	.25
☐	24 Carolina Hurricanes logo	.25
☐	25 Sami Kapanen, Caro.	.25
☐	26 Alexander Godynyuk, Caro.	.25
☐	27 Keith Primeau, Caro.	.50
☐	28 Saku Koivu, Mont.	1.00
☐	29 Vincent Damphousse, Mont.	.50
☐	30 Brian Savage, Mont.	.25
☐	31 Valeri Bure, Mont.	.25
☐	32 Mark Recchi, Mont.	.50
☐	33 Montréal Canadiens logo	.25
☐	34 Vladimir Malakhov, Mont.	.25
☐	35 Peter Popovic, Mont.	.25
☐	36 Martin Rucinsky, Mont.	.25
☐	37 Radek Bonk, Ott.	.25
☐	38 Alexandre Daigle, Ott.	.25
☐	39 Sergei Zholtok, Ott.	.25
☐	40 Janne Laukkanen, Ott.	.25
☐	41 Daniel Alfredsson, Ott.	.50
☐	42 Ottawa Senators logo	.25
☐	43 Alexei Yashin, Ott.	.50
☐	44 Frank Musil, Ott.	.25
☐	45 Steve Duchesne, Ott.	.25
☐	46 Darius Kasparaitis, Pitt.	.25
☐	47 Jaromir Jagr, Pitt.	1.50
☐	48 Roman Oksiuta, Pitt.	.25
☐	49 Kevin Hatcher, Pitt.	.25
☐	50 Ron Francis, Pitt.	.50
☐	51 Pittsburgh Penguins logo	.25
☐	52 Petr Nedved, Pitt.	.25
☐	53 Andreas Johansson, Pitt.	.25
☐	54 Fredrik Olausson, Pitt.	.25
☐	55 Robert Svehla, Flor.	.25
☐	56 Radek Dvorak, Flor.	.25
☐	57 Martin Straka, Flor.	.25
☐	58 Kirk Muller, Flor.	.25
☐	59 Per Gustafsson, Flor.	.25
☐	60 Florida Panthers logo	.25
☐	61 Ray Sheppard, Flor.	.25
☐	62 Johan Garpenlov, Flor.	.25
☐	63 Scott Mellanby, Flor.	.25
☐	64 Martin Brodeur (G), NJer.	2.00
☐	65 Bobby Holik, NJer.	.25
☐	66 Doug Gilmour, NJer.	.50
☐	67 Valeri Zelepukin, NJer.	.25
☐	68 Petr Sykora, NJer.	.50
☐	69 New Jersey Devils logo	.25
☐	70 John MacLean, NJer.	.25
☐	71 Dave Andreychuk, NJer.	.25
☐	72 Scott Niedermayer, NJer.	.25
☐	73 Zigmund Palffy, NYIs.	.50
☐	74 Tommy Salo (G), NYIs.	.50
☐	75 Niklas Andersson, NYIs.	.25
☐	76 Kenny Jönsson, NYIs.	.25
☐	77 Robert Reichel, NYIs.	.25
☐	78 New York Islanders logo	.25
☐	79 Travis Green, NYIs.	.25
☐	80 Bryan Berard, NYIs.	.25
☐	81 Bryan Smolinski, NYIs.	.25
☐	82 Wayne Gretzky, NYRa.	6.00
☐	83 Mark Messier, NYRa.	1.50
☐	84 Brian Leetch, NYRa.	.50
☐	85 Alex Kovalev, NYRa.	.50
☐	86 Esa Tikkanen, NYRa.	.25
☐	87 New York Rangers logo	.25
☐	88 Ulf Samuelsson, NYRa.	.25
☐	89 Niklas Sundström, NYRa.	.25
☐	90 Alexander Karpovtsev, NYRa.	.25
☐	91 Ron Hextall (G), Phil.	.50
☐	92 Eric Lindros, Phil.	1.50
☐	93 Rod Brind'Amour, Phil.	.25
☐	94 Janne Niinimaa, Phil.	.25
☐	95 Dainius Zubrus, Phil.	.25
☐	96 Philadelphia Flyers logo	.25
☐	97 Petr Svoboda, Phil.	.25
☐	98 John LeClair, Phil.	1.00
☐	99 Mikael Renberg, Phil.	.25
☐	100 Dino Ciccarelli, Tamp.	.25
☐	101 Roman Hamrlik, Tamp.	.25
☐	102 Alexander Selivanov, Tamp.	.25
☐	103 Chris Gratton, Tamp.	.25
☐	104 Mikael Andersson, Tamp.	.25
☐	105 Tampa Bay Lightning logo	.25
☐	106 Igor Ulanov, Tamp.	.25
☐	107 John Cullen, Tamp.	.25
☐	108 Rob Zamuner, Tamp.	.25
☐	109 Peter Bondra, Wash.	.50
☐	110 Bill Ranford (G), Wash.	.50
☐	111 Michal Pivonka, Wash.	.25
☐	112 Sergei Gonchar, Wash.	.25
☐	113 Calle Johansson, Wash.	.25
☐	114 Washington Capitals logo	.25
☐	115 Dale Hunter, Wash.	.25
☐	116 Adam Oates, Wash.	.50
☐	117 Andrei Nikolishin, Wash.	.25
☐	118 LL: Dominik Hasek (G), Buff.	1.50
☐	119 LL: Bryan Berard, NYIs.	.25
☐	120 LL: Brian Leetch, NYRa.	.50
☐	121 LL: Paul Kariya, Anah.	2.00
☐	122 LL: Michael Peca, Buff.	.50
☐	123 LL: Keith Tkachuk, Phoe.	.50
☐	124 LL: Martin Brodeur (G), NJer.	2.00
☐	125 LL: John LeClair, Phil.	1.00
☐	126 LL: Miroslav Satan, Buff.	.25
☐	127 LL: Patrick Roy (G), Colo.	4.50
☐	128 Alexei Zhamnov, Chic.	.25
☐	129 Chris Chelios, Chic.	.50
☐	130 Ulf Dahlen, Chic.	.25
☐	131 Tony Amonte, Chic.	.50
☐	132 Michal Sykora, Chic.	.25
☐	133 Chicago Blackhawks logo	.25
☐	134 Eric Weinrich, Chic.	.25
☐	135 Sergei Krivokrasov, Chic.	.25
☐	136 Eric Dazé, Chic.	.50
☐	137 Pat Verbeek, Dall.	.50
☐	138 Sergei Zubov, Dall.	.25
☐	139 Mike Modano, Dall.	1.50
☐	140 Darryl Sydor, Dall.	.25
☐	141 Dave Reid, Dall.	.25
☐	142 Dallas Stars logo	.25
☐	143 Benoît Hogue, Dall.	.25
☐	144 Joe Nieuwendyk, Dall.	.50
☐	145 Jere Lehtinen, Dall.	.25
☐	146 Nicklas Lidström, Detr.	.50
☐	147 Vladimir Konstantinov, Detr.	.25
☐	148 Sergei Fedorov, Detr.	1.50
☐	149 Steve Yzerman, Detr.	3.50
☐	150 Tomas Sandström, Detr.	.25
☐	151 Detroit Red Wings logo	.25
☐	152 Igor Larionov, Detr.	.50
☐	153 Vyacheslav Kozlov, Detr.	.25
☐	154 Brendan Shanahan, Detr.	1.50
☐	155 Nikolai Khabibulin (G), Phoe.	.50
☐	156 Teppo Numminen, Phoe.	.25
☐	157 Jeremy Roenick, Phoe.	1.00
☐	158 Mike Gartner, Phoe.	1.00
☐	159 Igor Korolev, Phoe.	.25
☐	160 Phoenix Coyotes logo	.25
☐	161 Craig Janney, Phoe.	.25
☐	162 Keith Tkachuk, Phoe.	.50
☐	163 Oleg Tverdovsky, Phoe.	.25
☐	164 Pierre Turgeon, SLou.	.50
☐	165 Igor Kravchuk, SLou.	.25
☐	166 Robert Petrovicky, SLou.	.25
☐	167 Geoff Courtnall, SLou.	.25
☐	168 Brett Hull, SLou.	1.50
☐	169 St. Louis Blues logo	.25
☐	170 Chris Pronger, SLou.	.50
☐	171 Joe Murphy, SLou.	.25
☐	172 Grant Fuhr (G), SLou.	.50
☐	173 Dimitri Yushkevich, Toro.	.25
☐	174 Wendel Clark, Toro.	1.00
☐	175 Steve Sullivan, Toro.	.25
☐	176 Tie Domi, Toro.	.25
☐	177 Todd Warriner, Toro.	.25
☐	178 Toronto Maple Leafs logo	.25
☐	179 Mats Sundin, Toro.	1.50
☐	180 Sergei Berezin, Toro.	.25
☐	181 Fredrik Modin, Toro.	.25
☐	182 Dmitri Mironov, Anah.	.25
☐	183 Paul Kariya, Anah.	2.00
☐	184 Steve Rucchin, Anah.	.25
☐	185 Darren Van Impe, Anah.	.25
☐	186 Joe Sacco, Anah.	.25
☐	187 Anaheim Mighty Ducks logo	.25
☐	188 Teemu Selänne, Anah.	1.00
☐	189 Jari Kurri, Anah.	1.50
☐	190 Brian Bellows, Anah.	.25
☐	191 Dave Gagner, Calg.	.25
☐	192 German Titov, Calg.	.25
☐	193 Marty McInnis, Calg.	.25
☐	194 Jarome Iginla, Calg.	1.00
☐	195 Tommy Albelin, Calg.	.25
☐	196 Calgary Flames logo	.25
☐	197 Joel Bouchard, Calg.	.25
☐	198 Jonas Höglund, Calg.	.25
☐	199 Theoren Fleury, Calg.	.50
☐	200 Uwe Krupp, Colo.	.25
☐	201 Peter Forsberg, Colo.	2.00
☐	202 Adam Foote, Colo.	.25
☐	203 Valeri Kamensky, Colo.	.25
☐	204 Joe Sakic, Colo.	2.00
☐	205 Colorado Avalanche logo	.25
☐	206 Sandis Ozolinsh, Colo.	.25
☐	207 Alexei Gusarov, Colo.	.25
☐	208 Patrick Roy (G), Colo.	4.50
☐	209 Andrei Kovalenko, Edmo.	.25
☐	210 Jason Arnott, Edmo.	.50
☐	211 Mariusz Czerkawski, Edmo.	.25
☐	212 Ryan Smyth, Edmo.	.50
☐	213 Mats Lindgren, Edmo.	.25
☐	214 Edmonton Oilers logo	.25
☐	215 Doug Weight, Edmo.	.50
☐	216 Boris Mironov, Edmo.	.25
☐	217 Petr Klima, Edmo.	.25
☐	218 Vladimir Tsyplakov, LosA.	.25
☐	219 Mattias Norstrom, LosA.	.25
☐	220 Rob Blake, LosA.	.50
☐	221 Kai Nurminen, LosA.	.25
☐	222 Vitali Yachmenev, LosA.	.25
☐	223 Los Angeles Kings logo.	.25
☐	224 Ray Ferraro, LosA.	.25
☐	225 Kevin Stevens, LosA.	.25
☐	226 Dimitri Khristich, LosA.	.25
☐	227 Tony Granato, SanJ.	.25
☐	228 Bernie Nicholls, SanJ.	.25
☐	229 Doug Bodger, SanJ.	.25
☐	230 Owen Nolan, SanJ.	.50
☐	231 Viktor Kozlov, SanJ.	.25
☐	232 San Jose Sharks logo	.25
☐	233 Jeff Friesen, SanJ.	.25
☐	234 Marcus Ragnarsson, SanJ.	.25
☐	235 Andrei Nazarov, SanJ.	.25
☐	236 Pavel Bure, Vanc.	1.00
☐	237 Alexander Mogilny, Vanc.	.50
☐	238 Martin Gelinas, Vanc.	.25
☐	239 Markus Näslund, Vanc.	1.50
☐	240 David Roberts, Vanc.	.25
☐	241 Vancouver Canucks logo	.25
☐	242 Trevor Linden, Vanc.	.50
☐	243 Mike Ridley, Vanc.	.25
☐	244 Jyrki Lumme, Vanc.	.25
☐	245 Janne Niinimaa, Phil.	.25
☐	246 Patrick Lalime (G), Pitt.	.50
☐	247 Bryan Berard, NYIs.	.25
☐	248 Jim Campbell, SLou.	.25
☐	249 Dainius Zubrus, Phil.	.25
☐	250 Sergei Berezin, Toro.	.25
☐	251 Jarome Iginla, Calg.	1.00
☐	252 Jarome Iginla, Calg.	1.00

1997 - 98 PINNACLE

Cards 1-100 have a second Rink Collection parallel and a third Artist's Proof parallel. One-of-one Press Plates exist (Black, Cyan, Magenta and Yellow for front and back).

		AP	Rink	Pinn.
	Complete Set (200 cards):	-	-	40.00
	Parallel Set (100 cards):	1300.00	375.00	-
	Common Player:	4.00	1.50	.20
	Player	AP	Rink	Pinn.
☐☐☐	**1 Espen Knutsen, Anah. RC**	**5.00**	**4.00**	**1.50**
☐☐☐	**2 Juha Lind, Dall. RC**	**5.00**	**3.00**	**1.00**
☐☐☐	3 Erik Rasmussen, Buff.	5.00	2.00	.20
☐☐☐	**4 Olli Jokinen, LosA. RC**	**10.00**	**6.00**	**2.00**
☐☐☐	5 Chris Phillips, Ott.	5.00	2.00	.20
☐☐☐	6 Alexei Morozov, Pitt.	5.00	2.00	.20
☐☐☐	**7 Chris Dingman, Calg. RC**	**5.00**	**3.00**	**1.00**
☐☐☐	8 Mattias Öhlund, Vanc.	10.00	3.00	.50
☐☐☐	9 Sergei Samsonov, Bost.	20.00	5.00	1.00
☐☐☐	10 Daniel Cleary, Chic.	10.00	3.00	.50
☐☐☐	11 Terry Ryan, Mont.	4.00	1.50	.20
☐☐☐	12 Patrick Marleau, SanJ.	15.00	4.00	.50
☐☐☐	13 Boyd Devereaux, Edmo.	5.00	2.00	.20
☐☐☐	**14 D. MacLean, LosA. RC**	**4.00**	**2.00**	**.50**
☐☐☐	15 Marc Savard, NYRa.	5.00	2.00	.20
☐☐☐	**16 M. Arvedson, Ott. RC**	**5.00**	**3.00**	**1.00**
☐☐☐	**17 Marian Hossa, Ott. RC**	**35.00**	**20.00**	**6.00**
☐☐☐	18 Alyn McCauley, Toro.	10.00	3.00	.50
☐☐☐	**19 Vaclav Prospal, Phil. RC**	**10.00**	**6.00**	**2.00**
☐☐☐	20 Brad Isbister, Phoe.	5.00	2.00	.20
☐☐☐	**21 Robert Dome, Pitt. RC**	**5.00**	**3.00**	**1.00**
☐☐☐	22 Kevyn Adams, Toro.	5.00	1.50	.20
☐☐☐	23 Joe Thornton, Bost.	45.00	10.00	2.00
☐☐☐	**24 Jan Bulis, Wash. RC**	**4.00**	**2.00**	**.50**
☐☐☐	25 J. Svejkovsky, Wash.	5.00	1.50	.20
☐☐☐	26 Saku Koivu, Mont.	30.00	5.00	.50
☐☐☐	27 Mark Messier, Vanc.	35.00	10.00	1.00
☐☐☐	28 Dominik Hasek (G), Buff.	30.00	10.00	1.00
☐☐☐	29 Patrick Roy (G), Colo.	110.00	30.00	3.00
☐☐☐	30 Jaromir Jagr, Pitt.	30.00	10.00	1.00
☐☐☐	31 Jarome Iginla, Calg.	30.00	8.00	.50
☐☐☐	32 Joe Sakic, Colo.	60.00	15.00	1.50
☐☐☐	33 Jeremy Roenick, Phoe.	30.00	5.00	.50
☐☐☐	34 Chris Osgood (G), Detr.	20.00	5.00	.50
☐☐☐	35 Brett Hull, SLou.	35.00	10.00	1.00
☐☐☐	36 Mike Vernon (G), SanJ.	15.00	4.00	.20
☐☐☐	37 J. Vanbiesbrouck (G), Flor.	15.00	4.00	.20
☐☐☐	38 Raymond Bourque, Bost.	40.00	10.00	1.00
☐☐☐	39 Doug Gilmour, NJer.	20.00	6.00	.50
☐☐☐	40 Keith Tkachuk, Phoe.	20.00	5.00	.50
☐☐☐	41 Pavel Bure, Vanc.	30.00	5.00	.50
☐☐☐	42 Sean Burke (G), Hart.	20.00	6.00	.50
☐☐☐	43 Martin Brodeur (G), NJer.	60.00	15.00	1.50
☐☐☐	44 Damian Rhodes (G), Ott.	5.00	2.00	.20
☐☐☐	45 Geoff Sanderson, Caro.	5.00	2.00	.20
☐☐☐	46 Bill Ranford (G), Wash.	15.00	4.00	.20
☐☐☐	47 Kevin Hodson (G), Detr.	5.00	2.00	.20
☐☐☐	48 Eric Lindros, Phil.	30.00	10.00	1.00
☐☐☐	49 Owen Nolan, SanJ.	20.00	6.00	.50
☐☐☐	50 Mats Sundin, Toro.	35.00	10.00	1.00
☐☐☐	51 Ed Belfour (G), SanJ.	35.00	10.00	1.00
☐☐☐	52 Stéphane Fiset (G), LosA.	10.00	3.00	.20
☐☐☐	53 Paul Kariya, Anah.	50.00	10.00	1.00
☐☐☐	54 Doug Weight, Edmo.	20.00	5.00	.50
☐☐☐	55 Mike Richter (G), NYRa.	15.00	4.00	.20
☐☐☐	56 Zigmund Palffy, NYIs.	20.00	6.00	.50
☐☐☐	57 John LeClair, Phil.	30.00	5.00	.50
☐☐☐	58 Alexander Mogilny, Vanc.	15.00	4.00	.20
☐☐☐	59 Tommy Salo (G), NYIs.	15.00	4.00	.20
☐☐☐	60 Trevor Kidd (G), Caro.	10.00	3.00	.20
☐☐☐	61 Jason Arnott, Edmo.	15.00	4.00	.20
☐☐☐	62 Adam Oates, Wash.	15.00	4.00	.20
☐☐☐	63 Garth Snow (G), Phil.	10.00	3.00	.20
☐☐☐	64 Rob Blake, LosA.	20.00	6.00	.50
☐☐☐	65 Chris Chelios, Chic.	20.00	6.00	.50
☐☐☐	66 Éric Fichaud (G), NYIs.	5.00	1.50	.20
☐☐☐	67 Wayne Gretzky, NYRa.	150.00	40.00	4.00
☐☐☐	68 Dino Ciccarelli, Tamp.	10.00	3.00	.20
☐☐☐	69 Pat LaFontaine, NYRa.	20.00	6.00	.50
☐☐☐	70 Andy Moog (G), Mont.	15.00	4.00	.20
☐☐☐	71 Steve Yzerman, Detr.	90.00	20.00	2.00
☐☐☐	72 Jeff Hackett (G), Chic.	10.00	3.00	.20
☐☐☐	73 Peter Forsberg, Colo.	50.00	10.00	1.00
☐☐☐	74 Arturs Irbe (G), Vanc.	15.00	4.00	.20
☐☐☐	75 Pierre Turgeon, Mont.	15.00	4.00	.20
☐☐☐	76 Tom Barrasso (G), Pitt.	15.00	4.00	.20

□□□	77 Sergei Fedorov, Detr.	35.00	10.00	1.00
□□□	78 Ron Francis, Pitt.	20.00	6.00	.50
□□□	79 Mike Dunham (G), NJer.	15.00	4.00	.20
□□□	80 Brendan Shanahan, Detr.	35.00	10.00	1.00
□□□	81 Grant Fuhr (G), SLou.	20.00	6.00	.50
□□□	82 Jamie Storr (G), LosA.	5.00	2.00	.20
□□□	83 Jim Carey (G), Bost.	5.00	1.50	.20
□□□	84 Daren Puppa (G), Tamp.	5.00	2.00	.20
□□□	85 V. Damphousse, Mont.	20.00	6.00	.50
□□□	86 Teemu Selänne, Anah.	30.00	5.00	.50
□□□	87 Dwayne Roloson (G), Calg.	5.00	1.50	.20
□□□	88 Kirk McLean (G), Vanc.	10.00	3.00	.20
□□□	89 Olaf Kölzig (G), Wash.	20.00	6.00	.50
□□□	90 Guy Hebert (G), Anah.	5.00	2.00	.20
□□□	91 Mike Modano, Dall.	35.00	10.00	1.00
□□□	92 Brian Leetch, NYRa.	20.00	6.00	.50
□□□	93 Curtis Joseph (G), Edmo.	30.00	10.00	1.00
□□□	94 N. Khabibulin (G), Phoe.	15.00	4.00	.20
□□□	95 Félix Potvin (G), Toro.	20.00	6.00	.50
□□□	96 Ken Wregget (G), Pitt.	5.00	2.00	.20
□□□	**97 S. Shields (G), Buff. RC**	**5.00**	**4.00**	**1.50**
□□□	98 Jocelyn Thibault (G), Mont.	15.00	4.00	.20
□□□	99 Ron Tugnutt (G), Ott.	15.00	4.00	.20
□□□	100 Ron Hextall (G), Phil.	20.00	6.00	.50

□	101 Michael Peca, Buff.	.20
□	102 Donald Audette, Buff.	.20
□	103 Theoren Fleury, Calg.	.50
□	104 Mark Recchi, Mont.	.20
□	105 Dainius Zubrus, Phil.	.20
□	106 Trevor Linden, Vanc.	.20
□	107 Joé Juneau, Wash.	.20
□	108 Matthew Barnaby, Buff.	.20
□	109 Keith Primeau, Caro.	.20
□	110 Joe Nieuwendyk, Dall.	.20
□	111 Rod Brind'Amour, Phil.	.20
□	112 Daymond Langkow, Tamp.	.20
□	113 Ed Jovanovski, Flor.	.20
□	114 Adam Deadmarsh, Colo.	.20
□	115 Scott Niedermayer, NJer.	.20
□	116 Al MacInnis, SLou.	.20
□	117 Vyacheslav Kozlov, Detr.	.20
□	118 Jere Lehtinen, Dall.	.20
□	119 Jeff Friesen, SanJ.	.20
□	120 Alex Kovalev, NYRa.	.50
□	121 Eric Dazé, Chic.	.20
□	122 Mariusz Czerkawski, Edmo.	.20
□	123 Alexei Zhamnov, Chic.	.20
□	124 Petr Nedved, Pitt.	.20
□	125 Dmitri Mironov, Anah.	.20
□	126 Alexei Yashin, Ott.	.50
□	127 Todd Marchant, Edmo.	.20
□	128 Sandis Ozolinsh, Colo.	.20
□	129 Igor Larionov, Detr.	.50
□	130 Jim Campbell, SLou.	.20
□	131 Dave Andreychuk, NJer.	.20
□	132 Glen Wesley, Caro.	.20
□	133 Rem Murray, Edmo.	.20
□	134 Steve Sullivan, Toro.	.20
□	135 Miroslav Satan, Buff.	.20
□	136 Bill Guerin, NJer.	.20
□	137 Mike Gartner, Phoe.	.50
□	138 Jozef Stumpel, LosA.	.20
□	139 Darryl Sydor, Dall.	.20
□	140 Darcy Tucker, Mont.	.20
□	141 Robert Svehla, Flor.	.20
□	142 Steve Duchesne, Ott.	.20
□	143 Kevin Stevens, NYRa.	.20
□	144 Mikael Renberg, Tamp.	.20
□	145 Bryan Berard, NYIs.	.20
□	146 Ray Ferraro, LosA.	.20
□	147 Jason Allison, Bost.	.50
□	148 Tony Amonte, Chic.	.50
□	149 Luc Robitaille, LosA.	.50
□	150 Mathieu Schneider, Toro.	.20
□	151 Steve Rucchin, Anah.	.20
□	152 Brian Savage, Mont..	.20
□	153 Paul Coffey, Phil.	.50
□	154 Jeff O'Neill, Caro.	.20
□	155 Daniel Alfredsson, Ott.	.50
□	156 Dave Gagner, Flor.	.20
□	157 Rob Niedermayer, Flor.	.20
□	158 Scott Stevens, NJer.	.20
□	159 Alexandre Daigle, Ott.	.20
□	160 Stéphane Richer, Mont.	.20
□	161 Harry York, SLou.	.20
□	162 Sergei Berezin, Toro.	.20
□	163 Claude Lemieux, Colo.	.20
□	164 Ray Sheppard, Flor.	.20
□	165 Bernie Nicholls, SanJ.	.20
□	166 Oleg Tverdovsky, Phoe.	.20
□	167 Travis Green, NYIs.	.20
□	168 Martin Gelinas, Vanc.	.20
□	169 Derek Plante, Buff.	.20
□	170 Gary Roberts, Caro.	.20
□	171 Kevin Hatcher, Pitt.	.20
□	172 Martin Rucinsky, Mont.	.20
□	173 Pat Verbeek, Dall.	.20
□	174 Adam Graves, NYRa.	.20
□	175 Roman Hamrlik, Tamp.	.20
□	176 Darren McCarty, Detr.	.20
□	177 Mike Grier, Edmo.	.20
□	178 Andrew Cassels, Calg.	.20
□	179 Dimitri Khristich, LosA.	.20
□	180 Tomas Sandström, Anah.	.20
□	181 Peter Bondra, Wash.	.50
□	182 Derian Hatcher, Dall.	.20
□	183 Chris Gratton, Phil.	.20
□	184 John MacLean, NJer.	.20
□	185 Wendel Clark, Toro.	.50
□	186 Valeri Kamensky, Colo.	.20
□	187 Tony Granato, SanJ.	.20
□	**188 Vladimir Vorobiev, NYRa. RC**	**.50**
□	189 Ethan Moreau, Chic.	.20
□	190 Kirk Muller, Flor.	.20
□	191 Peter Forsberg, Colo.	1.00
□	192 Wayne Gretzky, NYRa.	4.00
□	193 Jaromir Jagr, Pitt.	1.00
□	194 Mark Messier, Vanc.	1.00
□	195 Brian Leetch, NYRa.	.50
□	196 John LeClair, Phil.	.50
□	197 Jeremy Roenick, Phoe.	.50
□	198 Checklist	.20
□	199 Checklist	.20
□	200 Checklist	.20

MASKS

There are up to three versions for each card: the regular insert (1:89), a Die-Cut parallel (1:299), and a Promo version. We have not confirmed the existence of promo variations for cards 9 and 10.

	Insert Set (10 cards):		175.00	130.00
	Inserts	Promo	DC	Mask
□□□	1 John Vanbiesbrouck (G), Flor.	2.00	20.00	15.00
□□□	2 Mike Richter (G), NYRa.	2.00	20.00	15.00
□□□	3 Martin Brodeur (G), NJer.	4.00	60.00	40.00
□□□	4 Curtis Joseph (G), Edmo.	2.00	30.00	25.00
□□□	5 Patrick Roy (G), Colo.	7.00	110.00	70.00
□□□	6 Guy Hebert (G), Anah.	2.00	20.00	15.00
□□□	7 Jeff Hackett (G), Chic.	2.00	20.00	15.00
□□□	8 Garth Snow (G), Phil.	2.00	20.00	15.00
□□	9 Nikolai Khabibulin (G), Phoe.		20.00	15.00
□□	10 Grant Fuhr (G), SLou.		20.00	15.00

TEAM PINNACLE

There are four versions: the regular insert, a Mirror Gold parallel, a white-front insert and a white-front Mirror Gold insert.

	Insert Set (10 cards):	1600.00	155.00
	Inserts		TPMG
□□□□	1 P. Roy / M. Brodeur	575.00	55.00
□□□□	2 Cu. Joseph / D.Hasek	250.00	25.00
□□□□	3 C. Chelios / B. Leetch	150.00	15.00
□□□□	4 P. Kariya / W. Gretzky	675.00	60.00
□□□□	5 M. Messier / E. Lindros	250.00	25.00
□□□□	6 K. Tkachuk / J. Jagr	200.00	20.00
□□□□	7 P. Forsberg / S. Koivu	270.00	25.00
□□□□	8 B. Shanahan / J. LeClair	220.00	20.00
□□□□	9 S. Yzerman / D. Gilmour	370.00	35.00
□□□□	10 Osgood (G) / Vanbiesbrouck (G)	130.00	10.00

TIN MASKS

Tin Size: 3 3/4" x 4 3/8"

	Complete Set (10 opened tins):	8.00
	Inserts	Opened
□	1 Martin Brodeur (G), NJer.	2.50
□	2 Grant Fuhr (G), SLou.	1.00
□	3 Jeff Hackett (G), Chic.	1.00
□	4 Guy Hebert (G), Anah.	1.00
□	5 Curtis Joseph (G), Edmo.	1.50
□	6 Nikolai Khabibulin (G), Phoe.	1.00
□	7 Mike Richter (G), NYRa.	1.00
□	8 Patrick Roy (G), Colo.	5.00
□	9 Garth Snow (G), Phil.	1.00
□	10 John Vanbiesbrouck (G), Flor.	1.00

OVERSIZE

	Insert Set (24 cards):	20.00
□	13 J. Vanbiesbrouck Promo	1.00
	Inserts (1:1 Power)	Power
□	1 Eric Lindros, Phil.	1.00
□	2 Paul Kariya, Anah.	2.00
□	3 Joe Thornton, Bost.	1.00
□	4 Dominik Hasek (G), Buff.	1.00
□	5 Patrick Roy (G), Colo.	4.00
□	6 Keith Tkachuk, Phoe.	1.00
□	7 Martin Brodeur (G), NJer.	2.00
□	8 Brett Hull, SLou.	1.00
□	9 Mark Messier, Vanc.	1.00
□	10 Saku Koivu, Mont.	1.00
□	11 Jaromir Jagr, Pitt.	1.00
□	12 Joe Sakic	2.00
□	13 John Vanbiesbrouck (G), Flor.	1.00
□	14 Pavel Bure, Vanc.	1.00
□	15 Jarome Iginla, Calg.	1.00
□	16 Mats Sundin, Toro.	1.00
□	17 Wayne Gretzky, NYRa.	6.00
□	18 Steve Yzerman, Detr.	3.00
□	19 Peter Forsberg, Colo.	2.00
□	20 Brendan Shanahan, Detr.	1.00
□	21 Sergei Fedorov, Detr.	1.00
□	22 Curtis Joseph (G), Edmo.	1.00
□	23 John LeClair, Phil.	1.00
□	24 Teemu Selänne, Anah.	1.00

1997 - 98 PINNACLE BE A PLAYER

	Complete Set (250 cards):	45.00
	Common Player:	.25
	Player	BAP
□	1 Eric Lindros, Phil.	1.00
□	2 Martin Brodeur (G), NJer.	2.00
□	3 Saku Koivu, Mont.	1.00
□	4 Félix Potvin (G), Toro.	.50
□	5 Adam Oates, Wash.	.50
□	6 Rob DiMaio, Bost.	.25
□	7 Jari Kurri, Colo.	1.00
□	8 Andrew Cassels, Calg.	.25
□	9 Trevor Linden, Vanc.	.50
□	10 Jocelyn Thibault (G), Mont.	.50
□	11 Chris Chelios, Chic.	.50
□	12 Paul Coffey, Phil.	.50
□	13 Nikolai Khabibulin (G), Phoe.	.50
□	14 Robert Lang, Pitt.	.25
□	15 Brett Hull, SLou.	1.00
□	16 Mike Sillinger, Vanc.	.25
□	17 Lyle Odelein, NJer.	.25
□	18 Bryan Berard, NYIs.	.25
□	19 Craig Muni, Dall.	.25
□	20 Kris Draper, Detr.	.25
□	21 Ed Jovanovski, Flor.	.50
□	22 Keith Tkachuk, Phoe.	.50
□	23 Dean Malkoc, Bost.	.25
□	24 Cory Stillman, Calg.	.25
□	25 Chris Osgood (G), Detr.	.50
□	26 Dainius Zubrus, Phil.	.25
□	27 Yves Racine, Tamp.	.25
□	**28 Eric Cairns, NYRa. RC**	**.50**
□	29 Dan Bylsma, LosA.	.25
□	30 Chris Terreri (G), Chic.	.25
□	31 Bill Huard, Edmo.	.25
□	32 Warren Rychel, Anah.	.25
□	33 Scott Walker, Vanc.	.25
□	34 Brian Holzinger, Buff.	.25
□	35 Roman Turek (G), Dall.	.50
□	36 Ron Tugnutt (G), Ott.	.50
□	37 Mike Richter (G), NYRa.	.50
□	38 Mattias Norstrom, LosA.	.25
□	39 Joe Sacco, Anah.	.25
□	40 Derek King, Toro.	.25
□	41 Brad Werenka, Pitt.	.25
□	42 Paul Kruse, NYIs.	.25
□	**43 Mike Knuble, Detr. RC**	**.50**
□	44 Michael Peca, Buff.	.50
□	**45 J-Y Leroux, Chic. RC**	**.50**
□	46 Ray Sheppard, Flor.	.25
□	**47 Reid Simpson, NJer. RC**	**.50**
□	48 Rob Brown, Pitt.	.25
□	49 Dave Babych, Vanc.	.25
□	50 Scott Pellerin, SLou.	.25
□	**51 Bruce Gardiner, Ott. RC**	**.50**
□	52 Adam Deadmarsh, Colo.	.25
□	53 Curtis Brown, Buff.	.25
□	54 Jason Marshall, Anah.	.25
□	55 Gerald Diduck, Phoe.	.25
□	56 Mick Vukota, Tamp.	.25
□	57 Kevin Dean, NJer.	.25
□	58 Adam Graves, NYRa.	.50
□	59 Craig Conroy, SLou.	.25
□	60 Cale Hulse, Calg.	.25
□	61 Dimitri Khristich, Bost.	.25
□	62 Chris Wells, Flor.	.25
□	63 Travis Green, NYIs.	.25
□	64 Tyler Wright, Pitt.	.25
□	65 Chris Simon, Wash.	.25
□	66 Mikhail Shtalenkov (G), Anah.	.25
□	67 Anson Carter, Bost.	.50
□	68 Zarley Zalapski, Calg.	.25
□	69 Per Gustafsson, Toro.	.25
□	70 Jayson More, Phoe.	.25
□	71 Steve Thomas, NJer.	.25
□	72 Todd Marchant, Edmo.	.25
□	73 Gary Roberts, Caro.	.50
□	74 Richard Smehlik, Buff.	.25
□	**75 Aaron Miller, Colo. RC**	**.50**
□	76 Daren Puppa (G), Tamp.	.25
□	77 Garth Snow (G), Phil.	.25
□	78 Greg deVries, Edmo.	.25
□	79 Randy Burridge, Buff.	.25
□	80 Jim Cummins, Chic.	.25
□	81 Richard Pilon, NYIs.	.25
□	82 Chris McAlpine, SLou.	.25
□	83 Joe Sakic, Colo.	2.00
□	84 Ted Drury, Anah.	.25
□	85 Brent Gilchrist, Dall.	.25
□	**86 Dallas Eakins, Flor. RC**	**.50**
□	87 Bruce Driver, NYRa.	.25
□	88 Jamie Huscroft, Tamp.	.25
□	89 Jeff Brown, Toro.	.25
□	90 Janne Laukkanen, Ott.	.25
□	91 Ken Klee, Wash.	.25
□	92 Peter Bondra, Wash.	.50
□	93 Ian Moran, Pitt.	.25
□	94 Stéphane Quintal, Mont.	.25
□	95 Jason York, Ott.	.25
□	96 Todd Harvey, Dall.	.25
□	97 Vyacheslav Kozlov, Detr.	.25
□	98 Kevin Haller, Caro.	.25
□	99 Alexei Zhamnov, Chic.	.25
□	100 Craig Johnson, LosA.	.25
□	101 Mike Keane, NYRa.	.25
□	102 Craig Rivet, Mont.	.25
□	103 Roman Vopat, LosA.	.25
□	104 Jim Johnson, Phoe.	.25
□	105 Ray Whitney, Flor.	.25
□	106 Ron Sutter, SanJ.	.25
□	107 J. McLennan (G), SLou.	.25
□	108 Kris King, Toro.	.25
□	**109 Lance Pitlick, Ott. RC**	**.50**
□	110 Mike Dunham (G), NJer.	.50
□	111 Jim Dowd, Calg.	.25
□	112 Geoff Sanderson, Hart.	.25
□	113 Vladimir Vujtek, Tamp.	.25
□	114 Tim Taylor, Bost.	.25
□	115 Sandis Ozolinsh, Colo.	.25
□	116 Scott Daniels, NJer.	.25
□	117 Bob Corkum, Phoe.	.25
□	118 Kirk McLean (G), Caro.	.25
□	119 Darcy Tucker, Mont.	.25
□	120 Dennis Vaske, NYIs.	.25
□	121 Kirk Muller, Flor.	.25
□	122 Jay McKee, Buff.	.25
□	123 Jere Lehtinen, Dall.	.25
□	124 Ruslan Salei, Anah.	.25
□	125 Al MacInnis, SLou.	.50
□	126 Ulf Samuelsson, NYRa.	.25

	Card	Price
☐	127 Rick Tocchet, Phoe.	.25
☐	128 Nick Kypreos, Toro.	.25
☐	129 Joel Bouchard, Calg.	.25
☐	130 Jeff O'Neill, Caro.	.50
☐	**131 D. McGillis, Edmo. RC**	**1.00**
☐	132 Sean Pronger, Anah.	.25
☐	133 Vladimir Malakhov, Mont.	.25
☐	134 Petr Sykora, NJer.	.50
☐	135 Zigmund Palffy, NYIs.	.50
☐	136 Joe Reekie, Wash.	.25
☐	137 Chris Gratton, Phil.	.25
☐	138 Craig Billington (G), Colo.	.25
☐	139 Steve Washburn, Flor.	.25
☐	140 Robert Kron, Caro.	.25
☐	141 Larry Murphy, Detr.	.25
☐	142 Shean Donovan, Colo.	.25
☐	143 Scott Young, Colo.	.25
☐	144 Janne Niinimaa, Phil.	.25
☐	**145 Ken Belanger, NYIs. RC**	**.50**
☐	146 Pavol Demitra, SLou.	.50
☐	147 Roman Hamrlik, Edmo.	.25
☐	148 Lonny Bohonos, Vanc.	.25
☐	149 Mike Eagles, Wash.	.25
☐	150 Kelly Buchberger, Edmo.	.25
☐	151 Mattias Timander, Bost.	.25
☐	152 Benoît Hogue, Dall.	.25
☐	153 Joey Kocur, Detr.	.25
☐	154 Mats Lindgren, Edmo.	.25
☐	155 Aki Berg, LosA.	.25
☐	156 Tim Sweeney, NYRa.	.25
☐	157 V. Damphousse, Mont.	.50
☐	158 Dan Kordic, Phil.	.25
☐	159 Darius Kasparaitis, Pitt.	.25
☐	160 Randy McKay, NJer.	.25
☐	161 Steve Staios, Vanc.	.25
☐	162 Brendan Witt, Wash.	.25
☐	163 Paul Ysebaert, Tamp.	.25
☐	164 Greg Adams, Dall.	.25
☐	165 Kent Manderville, Caro.	.25
☐	166 Steve Dubinsky, Chic.	.25
☐	167 David Nemirovsky, Flor.	.25
☐	168 Todd Bertuzzi, NYIs.	1.50
☐	**169 F. Chabot, LosA. RC**	**1.00**
☐	170 Dmitri Mironov, Anah.	.25
☐	171 Pat Peake, Wash.	.25
☐	172 Ed Ward, Calg.	.25
☐	173 Jeff Shantz, Chic.	.25
☐	174 Dave Gagner, Flor.	.25
☐	175 Randy Cunneyworth, Ott.	.25
☐	176 D. Langkow, Tamp.	.25
☐	177 Alex Hicks, Pitt.	.25
☐	178 D. Hendrickson, Toro.	.25
☐	179 Mike Sullivan, Bost.	.25
☐	180 Anders Eriksson, Detr.	.25
☐	181 Turner Stevenson, Mont.	.25
☐	182 Shane Churla, NYRa.	.25
☐	183 Dave Lowry, SanJ.	.25
☐	184 Joé Juneau, Wash.	.25
☐	185 Bob Essensa, Edmo.	.25
☐	186 James Black, Chic.	.25
☐	187 Michal Grosek, Buff.	.25
☐	188 Tomas Holmström, Detr.	.25
☐	189 Ian Laperrière, LosA.	.25
☐	190 Terry Yake, SLou.	.25
☐	191 Jason Smith, Toro.	.25
☐	192 Sergei Zholtok, Ott.	.25
☐	193 Doug Houda, NYIs.	.25
☐	194 Guy Carbonneau, Mont.	.25
☐	195 Terry Carkner, Flor.	.25
☐	196 Alexei Gusarov, Colo.	.25
☐	197 Vladimir Tsyplakov, LosA.	.25
☐	198 Jarrod Skalde, Chic.	.25
☐	199 Marty Murray, Calg.	.25
☐	200 Aaron Ward, Detr.	.25
☐	201 Bobby Holik, NJer.	.25
☐	202 Steve Chiasson, Caro.	.25
☐	203 Brantt Myhres, Phil.	.25
☐	**204 Eric Messier, Colo. RC**	**1.00**
☐	205 René Corbet, Colo.	.25
☐	206 Mathieu Schneider, Toro.	.25
☐	207 Tom Chorske, NYIs.	.25
☐	208 Doug Lidster, NYRa.	.25
☐	209 Igor Ulanov, Tamp.	.25
☐	**210 B. Atcheynum, SLou. RC**	**.50**
☐	211 Sébastien Bordeleau, Mont.	.25
☐	212 Alexei Morozov, Pitt.	.50
☐	**213 V. Prospal, Phil. RC**	**2.00**
☐	**214 B. Bombardir, NJer. RC**	**.50**
☐	215 Mattias Öhlund, Vanc.	.50
☐	**216 C. Dingman, Calg. RC**	**1.00**
☐	217 Erik Rasmussen, Buff.	.50
☐	**218 M. Johnson, Toro. RC**	**1.50**
☐	219 Chris Phillips, Ott.	.50
☐	220 Sergei Samsonov, Bost.	1.50
☐	221 Patrick Marleau, SanJ.	1.00
☐	222 Alyn McCauley, Toro.	.50
☐	**223 VandenBussche RC**	**.50**
☐	224 Daniel Cleary, Chic.	.50
☐	**225 M. Arvedsson, Ott. RC**	**1.00**
☐	226 Brad Isbister, Phoe.	.50
☐	**227 P. Rhéaume, S.H. RC**	**.50**
☐	**228 Patrik Elias, NJer. RC**	**6.00**
☐	**229 K. Oliwa, NJer. RC**	**1.50**
☐	**230 Tyler Moss (G), Calg. RC**	**1.00**
☐	231 Jamie Rivers, SLou.	.25
☐	232 Joe Thornton, Bost.	3.00
☐	**233 S. Shields (G), Buff. RC**	**1.50**
☐	**234 D. Scatchard, Vanc. RC**	**.50**
☐	**235 Patrick Côté, Dall. RC**	**.50**
☐	**236 Rich Brennan, SanJ. RC**	**.50**
☐	237 Boyd Devereaux, Edmo.	.50
☐	238 Per-Johan Axelsson, Bost.	.25
☐	**239 Craig Millar, Edmo. RC**	**.50**
☐	240 Juha Ylönen, Phoe.	.25
☐	**241 D. MacLean, LosA. RC**	**.50**
☐	242 J. Svejkovsky, Wash.	.25
☐	**243 Marco Sturm, SanJ. RC**	**1.50**
☐	**244 S. McKenna, LosA. RC**	**.50**
☐	**245 Derek Morris, Calg. RC**	**1.50**
☐	246 Dean Chynoweth, Bost.	.25
☐	247 A. Mogilny, Vanc.	.50
☐	248 R. Bourque, Bost.	1.50
☐	249 Ed Belfour (G), Dall.	1.00
☐	250 John LeClair, Phil.	1.00

AUTOGRAPHS

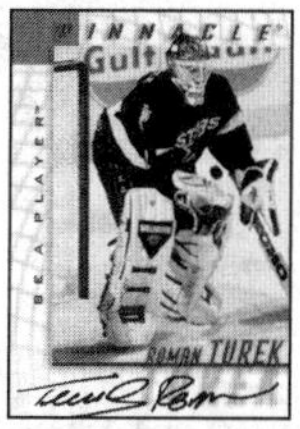

These autographed cards have three versions: the regular autographed card (3,500 copies), a foil die-cut autographed card (400 copies) and a foil-prismatic die-cut autographed card (100 copies). Eight cards are short-printed (*) in the autographed foil die-cut autographed and prismatic die-cut autographed parallel versions. There are no Eric Lindros regular autographs, only foil die-cut (44 copies) and prismatic die-cut (44 copies) autographs. There are no Bryan Berard autographed cards.

Autograph Set (248 cards): -1300.00

Autograph Parallel Set (249 cards): 4400.00 2500.00

Autograph: 12.00 8.00 4.00

	Player	Prism.	DC	Auto.
☐☐	1 Eric Lindros, Phil. ✍ (*)	180.00	180.00	-
☐☐☐	2 M. Brodeur (G), NJer. ✍ (*)	400.00	225.00	150.00
☐☐☐	3 Saku Koivu, Mont. ✍	80.00	40.00	20.00
☐☐☐	4 Félix Potvin (G), Toro. ✍	60.00	30.00	16.00
☐☐☐	5 Adam Oates, Wash. ✍	40.00	20.00	10.00
☐☐☐	6 Rob DiMaio, Bost. ✍	15.00	8.00	4.00
☐☐☐	7 Jari Kurri, Colo. ✍	100.00	50.00	25.00
☐☐☐	8 Andrew Cassels, Calg. ✍	20.00	10.00	6.00
☐☐☐	9 Trevor Linden, Vanc. ✍	40.00	20.00	10.00
☐☐☐	10 J. Thibault (G), Mont. ✍	40.00	20.00	10.00
☐☐☐	11 Chris Chelios, Chic. ✍	60.00	30.00	16.00
☐☐☐	12 Paul Coffey, Phil. ✍	60.00	30.00	16.00
☐☐☐	13 Khabibulin (G), Phoe. ✍	40.00	20.00	10.00
☐☐☐	14 Robert Lang, Pitt. ✍	20.00	10.00	6.00
☐☐☐	15 Brett Hull, SLou. ✍ (*)	175.00	100.00	90.00
☐☐☐	16 Mike Sillinger, Vanc. ✍	15.00	8.00	4.00
☐☐☐	17 Lyle Odelein, NJer. ✍	15.00	8.00	4.00
☐☐☐	19 Craig Muni, Dall. ✍	12.00	8.00	4.00
☐☐☐	20 Kris Draper, Detr. ✍	20.00	10.00	6.00
☐☐☐	21 Ed Jovanovski, Flor. ✍	40.00	20.00	10.00
☐☐☐	22 Keith Tkachuk, Phoe. ✍	60.00	30.00	15.00
☐☐☐	23 Dean Malkoc, Bost. ✍	12.00	8.00	4.00
☐☐☐	24 Cory Stillman, Calg. ✍	20.00	10.00	6.00
☐☐☐	25 Chris Osgood (G), Detr. ✍	60.00	30.00	16.00
☐☐☐	26 Dainius Zubrus, Phil. ✍	20.00	10.00	6.00
☐☐☐	27 Yves Racine, Tamp. ✍	12.00	8.00	4.00
☐☐☐	28 Eric Cairns, NYRa. ✍	12.00	8.00	4.00
☐☐☐	29 Dan Bylsma, LosA. ✍	12.00	8.00	4.00
☐☐☐	30 Chris Terreri (G), Chic. ✍	15.00	8.00	4.00
☐☐☐	31 Bill Huard, Edmo. ✍	12.00	8.00	4.00
☐☐☐	32 Warren Rychel, Anah. ✍	12.00	8.00	4.00
☐☐☐	33 Scott Walker, Vanc. ✍	20.00	10.00	6.00
☐☐☐	34 Brian Holzinger, Buff. ✍	15.00	8.00	4.00
☐☐☐	35 Roman Turek (G), Dall. ✍	45.00	20.00	12.00
☐☐☐	36 Ron Tugnutt (G), Ott. ✍	40.00	20.00	10.00
☐☐☐	37 M. Hichter (G), NYRa. ✍	40.00	20.00	12.00
☐☐☐	38 M. Norstrom, LosA. ✍	20.00	10.00	6.00
☐☐☐	39 Joe Sacco, Anah. ✍	12.00	8.00	4.00
☐☐☐	40 Derek King, Toro. ✍	15.00	8.00	4.00
☐☐☐	41 Brad Werenka, Pitt. ✍	12.00	8.00	4.00
☐☐☐	42 Paul Kruse, NYIs. ✍	12.00	8.00	4.00
☐☐☐	43 Mike Knuble, Detr. ✍	12.00	8.00	4.00
☐☐☐	44 Michael Peca, Buff. ✍	40.00	20.00	10.00
☐☐☐	45 J-Y Leroux, Chic. ✍	12.00	8.00	4.00
☐☐☐	46 Ray Sheppard, Flor. ✍	15.00	8.00	4.00
☐☐☐	47 Reid Simpson, NJer. ✍	12.00	8.00	4.00
☐☐☐	48 Rob Brown, Pitt. ✍	15.00	8.00	4.00
☐☐☐	49 Dave Babych, Vanc. ✍	15.00	8.00	4.00
☐☐☐	50 Scott Pellerin, SLou. ✍	15.00	8.00	4.00
☐☐☐	51 Bruce Gardiner, Ott. ✍	12.00	8.00	4.00
☐☐☐	52 A. Deadmarsh, Colo. ✍	30.00	15.00	8.00
☐☐☐	53 Curtis Brown, Buff. ✍	15.00	8.00	4.00
☐☐☐	54 Jason Marshall, Anah. ✍	12.00	8.00	4.00
☐☐☐	55 Gerald Diduck, Phoe. ✍	12.00	8.00	4.00
☐☐☐	56 Mick Vukota, Tamp. ✍	12.00	8.00	4.00
☐☐☐	57 Kevin Dean, NJer. ✍	12.00	8.00	4.00
☐☐☐	58 Adam Graves, NYRa. ✍	40.00	20.00	10.00
☐☐☐	59 Craig Conroy, SLou. ✍	30.00	15.00	8.00
☐☐☐	60 Cale Hulse, Calg. ✍	12.00	8.00	4.00
☐☐☐	61 Dimitri Khristich, Bost. ✍	15.00	8.00	4.00
☐☐☐	62 Chris Wells, Flor. ✍	12.00	8.00	4.00
☐☐☐	63 Travis Green, NYIs. ✍	20.00	10.00	6.00
☐☐☐	64 Tyler Wright, Pitt. ✍	12.00	8.00	4.00
☐☐☐	65 Chris Simon, Wash. ✍	20.00	10.00	6.00
☐☐☐	66 Shtalenkov (G), Anah. ✍	15.00	8.00	4.00
☐☐☐	67 Anson Carter, Bost. ✍	40.00	20.00	10.00
☐☐☐	68 Zarley Zalapski, Calg. ✍	12.00	8.00	4.00
☐☐☐	69 Per Gustafsson, Toro. ✍	12.00	8.00	4.00
☐☐☐	70 Jayson More, Phoe. ✍	12.00	8.00	4.00
☐☐☐	71 Steve Thomas, NJer. ✍	20.00	10.00	6.00
☐☐☐	72 Todd Marchant, Edmo. ✍	20.00	10.00	6.00
☐☐☐	73 Gary Roberts, Caro. ✍	40.00	20.00	10.00
☐☐☐	74 Richard Smehlik, Buff. ✍	12.00	8.00	4.00
☐☐☐	75 Aaron Miller, Colo. ✍	12.00	8.00	4.00
☐☐☐	76 D. Puppa (G), Tamp. ✍	20.00	10.00	6.00
☐☐☐	77 Garth Snow (G), Phil. ✍	30.00	15.00	8.00
☐☐☐	78 Greg deVries, Edmo. ✍	15.00	8.00	4.00
☐☐☐	79 Randy Burridge, Buff. ✍	15.00	8.00	4.00
☐☐☐	80 Jim Cummins, Chic. ✍	12.00	8.00	4.00
☐☐☐	81 Richard Pilon, NYIs. ✍	12.00	8.00	4.00
☐☐☐	82 Chris McAlpine, SLou. ✍	12.00	8.00	4.00
☐☐☐	83 Joe Sakic, Colo. ✍ (*)	400.00	225.00	130.00
☐☐☐	84 Ted Drury, Anah. ✍	12.00	8.00	4.00
☐☐☐	85 Brent Gilchrist, Dall. ✍	12.00	8.00	4.00
☐☐☐	86 Dallas Eakins, Flor. ✍	12.00	8.00	4.00
☐☐☐	87 Bruce Driver, NYRa. ✍	12.00	8.00	4.00
☐☐☐	88 Jamie Huscroft, Tamp. ✍	12.00	8.00	4.00
☐☐☐	89 Jeff Brown, Toro. ✍	12.00	8.00	4.00
☐☐☐	90 Janne Laukkanen, Ott. ✍	12.00	8.00	4.00
☐☐☐	91 Ken Klee, Wash. ✍	12.00	8.00	4.00
☐☐☐	92 Peter Bondra, Wash. ✍	60.00	30.00	16.00
☐☐☐	93 Ian Moran, Pitt. ✍	12.00	8.00	4.00
☐☐☐	94 S. Quintal, Mont. ✍	15.00	8.00	4.00
☐☐☐	95 Jason York, Ott. ✍	15.00	8.00	4.00
☐☐☐	96 Todd Harvey, Dall. ✍	20.00	10.00	6.00
☐☐☐	97 Vy. Kozlov, Detr. ✍	20.00	10.00	6.00
☐☐☐	98 Kevin Haller, Caro. ✍	12.00	8.00	4.00
☐☐☐	99 Alexei Zhamnov, Chic. ✍	30.00	15.00	8.00
☐☐☐	100 Craig Johnson, LosA. ✍	12.00	8.00	4.00
☐☐☐	101 Mike Keane, NYRa. ✍	15.00	8.00	4.00
☐☐☐	102 Craig Rivet, Mont. ✍	12.00	8.00	4.00
☐☐☐	103 Roman Vopat, LosA. ✍	12.00	8.00	4.00
☐☐☐	104 Jim Johnson, Phoe. ✍	12.00	8.00	4.00
☐☐☐	105 Ray Whitney, Flor. ✍	20.00	10.00	6.00
☐☐☐	106 Ron Sutter, SanJ. ✍	20.00	10.00	6.00
☐☐☐	107 McLennan (G), SLou. ✍	15.00	8.00	4.00
☐☐☐	108 Kris King, Toro. ✍	15.00	8.00	4.00
☐☐☐	109 Lance Pitlick, Ott. ✍	12.00	8.00	4.00
☐☐☐	110 M. Dunham (G), NJer. ✍	40.00	20.00	10.00
☐☐☐	111 Jim Dowd, Calg. ✍	12.00	8.00	4.00
☐☐☐	112 G. Sanderson, Hart. ✍	20.00	10.00	6.00
☐☐☐	113 Vladimir Vujtek, Tamp. ✍	12.00	8.00	4.00
☐☐☐	114 Tim Taylor, Bost. ✍	12.00	8.00	4.00
☐☐☐	115 S. Ozolinsh, Colo. ✍	20.00	10.00	6.00
☐☐☐	116 Scott Daniels, NJer. ✍	12.00	8.00	4.00
☐☐☐	117 Bob Corkum, Phoe. ✍	12.00	8.00	4.00
☐☐☐	118 K. McLean (G), Caro. ✍	30.00	15.00	8.00
☐☐☐	119 Darcy Tucker, Mont. ✍	20.00	10.00	6.00
☐☐☐	120 Dennis Vaske, NYIs. ✍	12.00	8.00	4.00
☐☐☐	121 Kirk Muller, Flor. ✍	30.00	15.00	8.00
☐☐☐	122 Jay McKee, Buff. ✍	12.00	8.00	4.00
☐☐☐	123 Jere Lehtinen, Dall. ✍	30.00	15.00	8.00
☐☐☐	124 Ruslan Salei, Anah. ✍	12.00	8.00	4.00
☐☐☐	125 Al MacInnis, SLou. ✍ (*)	100.00	60.00	35.00
☐☐☐	126 U.Samuelsson, NYRa. ✍	15.00	8.00	4.00
☐☐☐	127 Rick Tocchet, Phoe. ✍	30.00	15.00	8.00
☐☐☐	128 Nick Kypreos, Toro. ✍	20.00	10.00	6.00
☐☐☐	129 Joel Bouchard, Calg. ✍	12.00	8.00	4.00
☐☐☐	130 Jeff O'Neill, Caro. ✍	40.00	20.00	10.00
☐☐☐	131 D. McGillis, Edmo. ✍	15.00	8.00	6.00
☐☐☐	132 Sean Pronger, Anah. ✍	12.00	8.00	4.00
☐☐☐	133 V. Malakhov, Mont. ✍	15.00	8.00	4.00
☐☐☐	134 Petr Sykora, NJer. ✍	40.00	20.00	10.00
☐☐☐	135 Zigmund Palffy, NYIs. ✍	60.00	30.00	16.00
☐☐☐	136 Joe Reekie, Wash. ✍	12.00	8.00	4.00
☐☐☐	137 Chris Gratton, Phil. ✍	20.00	10.00	6.00
☐☐☐	138 C. Billington (G), Colo. ✍	15.00	8.00	4.00
☐☐☐	139 Steve Washburn, Flor. ✍	12.00	8.00	4.00
☐☐☐	140 Robert Kron, Caro. ✍	15.00	8.00	4.00
☐☐☐	141 Larry Murphy, Detr. ✍	20.00	10.00	6.00
☐☐☐	142 Shean Donovan, Colo. ✍	15.00	8.00	4.00
☐☐☐	143 Scott Young, Colo. ✍	30.00	15.00	8.00
☐☐☐	144 Janne Niinimaa, Phil. ✍	20.00	10.00	6.00
☐☐☐	145 Ken Belanger, NYIs. ✍	12.00	8.00	4.00
☐☐☐	146 Pavol Demitra, SLou. ✍	40.00	20.00	10.00
☐☐☐	147 R. Hamrlik, Edmo. ✍	20.00	10.00	6.00
☐☐☐	148 L. Bohonos, Vanc. ✍	12.00	8.00	4.00
☐☐☐	149 Mike Eagles, Wash. ✍	12.00	8.00	4.00
☐☐☐	150 K. Buchberger, Edmo. ✍	15.00	8.00	4.00
☐☐☐	151 M. Timander, Bost. ✍	12.00	8.00	4.00
☐☐☐	152 Benoît Hogue, Dall. ✍	15.00	8.00	4.00
☐☐☐	153 Joey Kocur, Detr. ✍	15.00	8.00	4.00
☐☐☐	154 Mats Lindgren, Edmo. ✍	15.00	8.00	4.00
☐☐☐	155 Aki Berg, LosA. ✍	15.00	8.00	4.00
☐☐☐	156 Tim Sweeney, NYRa. ✍	12.00	8.00	4.00
☐☐☐	157 Damphousse, Mont. ✍	60.00	30.00	16.00
☐☐☐	158 Dan Kordic, Phil. ✍	12.00	8.00	4.00
☐☐☐	159 D. Kasparaitis, Pitt. ✍	20.00	10.00	6.00
☐☐☐	160 Randy McKay, NJer. ✍	12.00	8.00	4.00
☐☐☐	161 Steve Staios, Vanc. ✍	12.00	8.00	4.00
☐☐☐	162 Brendan Witt, Wash. ✍	12.00	8.00	4.00
☐☐☐	163 Paul Ysebaert, Tamp. ✍	12.00	8.00	4.00
☐☐☐	164 Greg Adams, Dall. ✍	15.00	8.00	4.00
☐☐☐	165 K. Manderville, Caro. ✍	12.00	8.00	4.00
☐☐☐	166 Steve Dubinsky, Chic. ✍	12.00	8.00	4.00
☐☐☐	167 D. Nemirovsky, Flor. ✍	12.00	8.00	4.00
☐☐☐	168 Todd Bertuzzi, NYIs. ✍	120.00	60.00	30.00
☐☐☐	169 F. Chabot, LosA. ✍	15.00	8.00	6.00
☐☐☐	170 Dmitri Mironov, Anah. ✍	15.00	8.00	4.00
☐☐☐	171 Pat Peake, Wash. ✍	12.00	8.00	4.00
☐☐☐	172 Ed Ward, Calg. ✍	12.00	8.00	4.00
☐☐☐	173 Jeff Shantz, Chic. ✍	12.00	8.00	4.00
☐☐☐	174 Dave Gagner, Flor. ✍	15.00	8.00	4.00
☐☐☐	175 R. Cunneyworth, Ott. ✍	15.00	8.00	4.00
☐☐☐	176 D. Langkow, Tamp. ✍	20.00	10.00	6.00
☐☐☐	177 Alex Hicks, Pitt. ✍	12.00	8.00	4.00
☐☐☐	178 D. Hendrickson, Toro. ✍	15.00	8.00	4.00
☐☐☐	179 Mike Sullivan, Bost. ✍	12.00	8.00	4.00
☐☐☐	180 Anders Eriksson, Detr. ✍	12.00	8.00	4.00
☐☐☐	181 T. Stevenson, Mont. ✍	15.00	8.00	4.00
☐☐☐	182 Shane Churla, NYRa. ✍	12.00	8.00	4.00
☐☐☐	183 Dave Lowry, SanJ. ✍	20.00	10.00	6.00
☐☐☐	184 Joé Juneau, Wash. ✍	20.00	10.00	6.00
☐☐☐	185 Bob Essensa, Edmo. ✍	20.00	10.00	6.00
☐☐☐	186 James Black, Chic. ✍	12.00	8.00	4.00
☐☐☐	187 Michal Grosek, Buff. ✍	12.00	8.00	4.00
☐☐☐	188 T. Holmström, Detr. ✍	20.00	10.00	6.00
☐☐☐	189 Ian Laperrière, LosA. ✍	15.00	8.00	4.00
☐☐☐	190 Terry Yake, SLou. ✍	12.00	8.00	4.00
☐☐☐	191 Jason Smith, Toro. ✍	15.00	8.00	4.00
☐☐☐	192 Sergei Zholtok, Ott. ✍	15.00	8.00	4.00
☐☐☐	193 Doug Houda, NYIs. ✍	12.00	8.00	4.00
☐☐☐	194 G. Carbonneau, Mont. ✍	30.00	15.00	8.00
☐☐☐	195 Terry Carkner, Flor. ✍	12.00	8.00	4.00
☐☐☐	196 Alexei Gusarov, Colo. ✍	15.00	8.00	4.00
☐☐☐	197 V. Tsyplakov, LosA. ✍	12.00	8.00	4.00
☐☐☐	198 Jarrod Skalde, Chic. ✍	12.00	8.00	4.00
☐☐☐	199 Marty Murray, Calg. ✍	12.00	8.00	4.00
☐☐☐	200 Aaron Ward, Detr. ✍	15.00	8.00	4.00
☐☐☐	201 Bobby Holik, NJer. ✍	30.00	15.00	8.00
☐☐☐	202 S. Chiasson, Caro. ✍	60.00	30.00	16.00
☐☐☐	203 Brantt Myhres, Phil. ✍	12.00	8.00	4.00
☐☐☐	204 Eric Messier, Colo. ✍	15.00	8.00	6.00
☐☐☐	205 René Corbet, Colo. ✍	15.00	8.00	4.00
☐☐☐	206 M. Schneider, Toro. ✍	20.00	10.00	6.00
☐☐☐	207 Tom Chorske, NYIs. ✍	12.00	8.00	4.00
☐☐☐	208 Doug Lidster, NYRa. ✍	12.00	8.00	4.00
☐☐☐	209 Igor Ulanov, Tamp. ✍	15.00	8.00	4.00
☐☐☐	210 Atcheynum, SLou. ✍	12.00	8.00	4.00
☐☐☐	211 S. Bordeleau, Mont. ✍	12.00	8.00	4.00
☐☐☐	212 Alexei Morozov, Pitt. ✍	20.00	10.00	6.00
☐☐☐	213 V. Prospal, Phil. ✍	30.00	15.00	12.00
☐☐☐	214 B. Bombardir, NJer. ✍	12.00	8.00	4.00
☐☐☐	215 M. Öhlund, Vanc. ✍	30.00	15.00	12.00
☐☐☐	216 C. Dingman, Calg. ✍	15.00	8.00	6.00
☐☐☐	217 Erik Rasmussen, Buff. ✍	20.00	10.00	6.00
☐☐☐	218 M. Johnson, Toro. ✍	20.00	10.00	8.00
☐☐☐	219 Chris Phillips, Ott. ✍	20.00	10.00	6.00
☐☐☐	220 S. Samsonov, Bost. ✍	60.00	30.00	16.00
☐☐☐	221 P. Marleau, SanJ. ✍	45.00	20.00	18.00
☐☐☐	222 Alyn McCauley, Toro. ✍	30.00	15.00	12.00
☐☐☐	223 VandenBussche ✍	12.00	8.00	4.00
☐☐☐	224 Daniel Cleary, Chic. ✍	30.00	15.00	8.00
☐☐☐	225 M. Arvedsson, Ott. ✍	15.00	8.00	6.00
☐☐☐	226 Brad Isbister, Phoe. ✍	20.00	10.00	6.00
☐☐☐	227 P. Rhéaume, S.H. ✍	12.00	8.00	4.00
☐☐☐	228 Patrik Elias, NJer. ✍	80.00	40.00	30.00
☐☐☐	229 K. Oliwa, NJer. ✍	20.00	10.00	8.00
☐☐☐	230 T. Moss (G), Calg. ✍	15.00	8.00	6.00
☐☐☐	231 Jamie Rivers, SLou. ✍	12.00	8.00	4.00
☐☐☐	232 Joe Thornton, Bost. ✍	120.00	60.00	30.00
☐☐☐	233 S. Shields (G), Buff. ✍	20.00	10.00	8.00
☐☐☐	234 D. Scatchard, Vanc. ✍	12.00	8.00	4.00
☐☐☐	235 Patrick Côté, Dall. ✍	12.00	8.00	4.00
☐☐☐	236 Rich Brennan, SanJ. ✍	12.00	8.00	4.00
☐☐☐	237 B. Devereaux, Edmo. ✍	20.00	10.00	6.00
☐☐☐	238 P-J Axelsson, Bost. ✍	15.00	8.00	4.00

□□□	239 Craig Millar, Edmo. ✍	12.00	8.00	4.00
□□□	240 Juha Ylönen, Phoe. ✍	15.00	8.00	4.00
□□□	241 D. MacLean, LosA. ✍	12.00	8.00	4.00
□□□	242 J. Svejkovsky, Wash. ✍	15.00	8.00	4.00
□□□	243 Marco Sturm, SanJ. ✍	20.00	10.00	8.00
□□□	244 S. McKenna, LosA. ✍	12.00	8.00	4.00
□□□	245 Derek Morris, Calg. ✍	20.00	10.00	8.00
□□□	246 D. Chynoweth, Bost. ✍	12.00	8.00	4.00
□□□	247 A. Mogilny, Vanc. ✍ (*)	120.00	70.00	45.00
□□□	248 R. Bourque, Bost. ✍ (*)	300.00	180.00	110.00
□□□	249 Belfour (G), Dall. ✍ (*)	250.00	150.00	90.00
□□□	250 J. LeClair, Phil. ✍ (*)	200.00	120.00	70.00

ONE TIMERS

Insert Set (20 cards):		55.00
	Insert (1:7)	OT
□	1 Wayne Gretzky, NYRa.	15.00
□	2 Keith Tkachuk, Phoe.	2.00
□	3 Eric Lindros, Phil.	2.00
□	4 Brendan Shanahan, Detr.	2.00
□	5 Paul Kariya, Anah.	4.00
□	6 Brett Hull, SLou.	2.00
□	7 Jaromir Jagr, Pitt.	2.00
□	8 Teemu Selänne, Anah.	2.00
□	9 John LeClair, Phil.	2.00
□	10 Mike Modano, Dall.	2.00
□	11 Peter Forsberg, Colo.	4.00
□	12 Pavel Bure, Vanc.	2.00
□	13 Peter Bondra, Wash.	2.00
□	14 Saku Koivu, Mont.	2.00
□	15 Pat LaFontaine, NYRa.	2.00
□	16 Patrik Elias, NJer.	6.00
□	17 Richard Zednik, Wash.	2.00
□	18 Mike Johnson, Toro.	1.00
□	19 Marco Sturm, SanJ.	1.00
□	20 Joe Thornton, Bost.	8.00

STACKING THE PADS

Insert Set (15 cards):		100.00
	Insert (1:15)	STP
□	1 Guy Hebert (G), Anah.	3.00
□	2 Dominik Hasek (G), Buff.	10.00
□	3 Félix Potvin (G), Toro.	6.00
□	4 Patrick Roy (G), Colo.	30.00
□	5 Ed Belfour (G), Dall.	10.00
□	6 Chris Osgood (G), Detr.	6.00
□	7 Curtis Joseph (G), Edmo.	10.00
□	8 John Vanbiesbrouck (G), Flor.	4.00
□	9 Jocelyn Thibault (G), Mont.	4.00
□	10 Mike Richter (G), NYRa.	4.00
□	11 Martin Brodeur (G), NJer.	16.00
□	12 Garth Snow (G), Phil.	3.00
□	13 Nikolai Khabibulin (G), Phoe.	4.00
□	14 Tommy Salo (G), NYIs.	4.00
□	15 Byron Dafoe (G), Bost.	4.00

TAKE A NUMBER

Insert Set (20 cards):		170.00
	Insert (1:15)	TN
□	TN1 Raymond Bourque, Bost.	12.00
□	TN2 Éric Dazé, Chic.	4.00
□	TN3 Ed Belfour (G), Dall.	10.00
□	TN4 Patrick Roy (G), Colo.	30.00
□	TN5 Sergei Fedorov, Detr.	10.00
□	TN6 John Vanbiesbrouck (G), Flor.	4.00
□	TN7 Doug Gilmour, NJer.	6.00
□	TN8 Wayne Gretzky, NYRa.	40.00
□	TN9 Bryan Berard, NYIs.	3.00
□	TN10 Eric Lindros, Phil.	10.00
□	TN11 Paul Coffey, Phil.	6.00
□	TN12 Jeremy Roenick, Phoe.	8.00
□	TN13 Brett Hull, SLou.	10.00
□	TN14 Pierre Turgeon, SLou.	4.00
□	TN15 Keith Primeau, Caro.	4.00
□	TN16 Daren Puppa (G), Tamp.	3.00
□	TN17 Mark Messier, Vanc.	10.00
□	TN18 Alexander Mogilny, Vanc.	4.00
□	TN19 Joe Sakic, Colo.	16.00
□	TN20 Jaromir Jagr, Pitt.	10.00

1997 - 98 PINNACLE BEEHIVES

These cards have two versions: the regular card and a Golden Portraits parallel [1:3]. Cards 51-75 have a third autographed parallel. Autographed cards 54 and 55 were available through a redemption offer only.

Card Size: 5" x 7"

	Complete Set (75 cards):	**100.00**	**65.00**
	Common Player:	**1.00**	**.60**
	Player	**Gold**	**Reg.**
□□	1 Eric Lindros, Phil.	3.00	1.50
□□	2 Teemu Selänne, Anah.	2.00	1.00
□□	3 Brendan Shanahan, Detr.	3.00	1.50
□□	4 Joe Sakic, Colo.	4.00	2.00
□□	5 John LeClair, Phil.	2.00	1.00
□□	6 Brett Hull, SLou.	3.00	1.50
□□	7 Jaromir Jagr, Pitt.	3.00	1.50
□□	8 Bryan Berard, NYIs.	1.00	.50
□□	9 Peter Forsberg, Colo.	4.00	2.00
□□	10 Ed Belfour (G), Dall.	3.00	1.50
□□	11 Steve Yzerman, Detr.	7.00	3.50
□□	12 Curtis Joseph (G), Edmo.	3.00	1.50
□□	13 Saku Koivu, Mont.	2.00	1.00
□□	14 Keith Tkachuk, Phoe.	1.00	.50
□□	15 Pavel Bure, Vanc.	2.00	1.00
□□	16 Félix Potvin (G), Toro.	1.00	.50
□□	17 Raymond Bourque, Bost.	3.00	1.50
□□	18 Theoren Fleury, Calg.	1.00	.50
□□	19 Patrick Roy (G), Colo.	9.00	4.50
□□	20 Joe Nieuwendyk, Dall.	1.00	.50
□□	21 Alexei Yashin, Otta.	1.00	.50
□□	22 Owen Nolan, SanJ.	1.00	.50
□□	23 Mark Recchi, Mont.	1.00	.50
□□	24 Dominik Hasek (G), Buff.	3.00	1.50
□□	25 Chris Chelios, Chic.	1.00	.50
□□	26 Mike Modano, Dall.	3.00	1.50
□□	27 John Vanbiesbrouck (G), Flor.	1.00	.50
□□	28 Brian Leetch, NYRa.	1.00	.50
□□	29 Dino Ciccarelli, Flor.	1.00	.50
□□	30 Mark Messier, Vanc.	3.00	1.50
□□	31 Paul Kariya, Anah.	4.00	2.00
□□	32 Jocelyn Thibault (G), Mont.	1.00	.50
□□	33 Wayne Gretzky, NYRa.	10.00	6.00
□□	34 Doug Weight, Edmo.	1.00	.50
□□	35 Yanic Perreault, LosA.	1.00	.50
□□	36 Luc Robitaille, LosA.	2.00	1.00
□□	37 Chris Osgood (G), Detr.	1.00	.50
□□	38 Adam Oates, Wash.	1.00	.50
□□	39 Mats Sundin, Toro.	3.00	1.50
□□	40 Trevor Linden, Vanc. (NYIs.)	1.00	.50
□□	41 Mike Richter (G), NYRa.	1.00	.50
□□	42 Zigmund Palffy, NYIs.	1.00	.50
□□	43 Pat LaFontaine, NYRa.	1.00	.50
□□	44 Grant Fuhr (G), SLou.	1.00	.50
□□	45 Martin Brodeur (G), NJer.	4.00	2.00
□□	46 Sergei Fedorov, Detr.	3.00	1.50
□□	47 Doug Gilmour, NJer.	1.00	.50
□□	48 Daniel Alfredsson, Otta.	1.00	.50
□□	49 Ron Francis, Pitt.	1.00	.50
□□	50 Geoff Sanderson, Vanc.	1.00	.50
□□	51 Joe Thornton, Bost.	7.00	3.50
□□	**52 Vaclav Prospal, Phil. RC**	**2.00**	**3.00**
□□	**53 Patrik Elias, NJer. RC**	**7.00**	**8.00**
□□	**54 Mike Johnson, Toro. RC**	**1.00**	**2.00**
□□	55 Alyn McCauley, Toro.	1.00	.50
□□	**56 Brendan Morrison, NJer. RC**	**1.00**	**3.00**
□□	57 J. Bower (G), Toro. [Golden Originals]	2.00	1.00
□□	58 Johnny Bucyk, Bost. [Golden Originals]	1.00	.50
□□	59 Stan Mikita, Chic. [Golden Originals]	2.00	1.00
□□	60 Ted Lindsay, Detr. [Golden Originals]	3.00	1.50
□□	61 M. Richard, Mont. [Golden Originals]	8.00	4.00
□□	62 Andy Bathgate, NYRa. [Golden Originals]	1.00	.50
□□	**63 Stefan Cherneski, Brandon RC**	**1.00**	**1.00**
□□	64 Craig Hillier (G), Ottawa	1.00	.50
□□	65 Daniel Tkaczuk, Barrie	1.00	.50
□□	66 Josh Holden, Regina	1.00	.50
□□	**67 Marian Cisar, Spokane RC**	**1.00**	**1.50**
□□	68 Jean-Pierre Dumont, Val d'Or	2.00	2.00
□□	**69 Roberto Luongo (G), Val d'Or RC**	**7.00**	**8.00**
□□	**70 Aren Miller (G), Spokane RC**	**1.00**	**1.00**
□□	71 Mathieu Garon (G), Victoriaville	2.00	1.00
□□	**72 Charlie Stephens, Toronto RC**	**1.00**	**1.00**
□□	**73 Sergei Varlamov, Swift Current RC**	**1.00**	**1.50**
□□	**74 Pierre Dagenais, Rouyn-Noranda RC**	**1.00**	**1.50**
□□	**75 Willie O'Ree, Bost. RC**	**3.00**	**4.00**

AUTOGRAPHS

Autographed cards 54 and 55 were available through a redemption offer only.

Card Size: 5" x 7"

Autograph Set (25 cards):		250.00
	Player	Auto.
□	51 Joe Thornton, Bost. ✍	45.00
□	52 Vaclav Prospal, Phil. ✍	10.00
□	53 Patrik Elias, NJer. ✍	30.00
□	54 Mike Johnson, Toro. ✍	10.00
□	55 Alyn McCauley, Toro. ✍	10.00
□	56 Brendan Morrison, NJer. ✍	10.00
□	57 Johnny Bower (G), Toro. ✍	20.00
□	58 Johnny Bucyk, Bost. ✍	20.00
□	59 Stan Mikita, Chic. ✍	30.00
□	60 Ted Lindsay, Detr. ✍	35.00
□	61 Maurice Richard, Mont. ✍ •	90.00
□	62 Andy Bathgate, NYRa. ✍	15.00
□	63 Stefan Cherneski, Brandon ✍	10.00
□	64 Craig Hillier (G), Ottawa ✍	10.00
□	65 Daniel Tkaczuk, Barrie ✍	10.00
□	66 Josh Holden, Regina ✍	10.00
□	67 Marian Cisar, Spokane ✍	10.00
□	68 Jean-Pierre Dumont, Val d'Or ✍	10.00
□	69 Roberto Luongo (G), Val d'Or ✍	30.00
□	70 Aren Miller (G), Spokane ✍	10.00
□	71 Mathieu Garon (G), Victoriaville ✍	15.00
□	72 Charlie Stephens, Toronto ✍	10.00
□	73 Sergei Varlamov, Swift Current ✍	10.00
□	74 Pierre Dagenais, Rouyn-Noranda ✍	10.00
□	75 Willie O'Ree, Bost. ✍	20.00

BEEHIVE TEAM

These cards have two versions: the regular insert [1:11] and a Golden parallel [1:49].

	Insert Set (25 cards):	465.00	230.00
	Player	Golden	Team
□□	1 Paul Kariya, Anah.	25.00	10.00
□□	2 Mark Messier, Vanc.	20.00	10.00
□□	3 Mike Modano, Dall.	20.00	10.00
□□	4 Brendan Shanahan, Detr.	20.00	10.00
□□	5 John Vanbiesbrouck (G), Flor.	6.00	4.00
□□	6 Martin Brodeur (G), NJer.	30.00	15.00
□□	7 Wayne Gretzky, NYRa.	80.00	40.00
□□	8 Eric Lindros, Phil.	20.00	10.00
□□	9 Peter Forsberg, Colo.	25.00	10.00
□□	10 Jaromir Jagr, Pitt.	20.00	10.00
□□	11 Teemu Selänne, Anah.	15.00	5.00
□□	12 John LeClair, Phil.	15.00	5.00
□□	13 Saku Koivu, Mont.	15.00	8.00
□□	14 Brett Hull, SLou.	20.00	10.00
□□	15 Patrick Roy (G), Colo.	60.00	30.00
□□	16 Steve Yzerman, Detr.	45.00	20.00
□□	17 Keith Tkachuk, Phoe.	10.00	6.00
□□	18 Pat LaFontaine, NYRa.	10.00	6.00
□□	19 Joe Sakic, Colo.	30.00	15.00
□□	20 Patrik Elias, NJer.	15.00	10.00
□□	21 Vaclav Prospal, Phil.	6.00	4.00
□□	22 Joe Thornton, Bost.	20.00	15.00
□□	23 Sergei Samsonov, Bost.	10.00	5.00
□□	24 Alexei Morozov, Pitt.	6.00	4.00
□□	25 Marco Sturm, SanJ.	6.00	4.00

1997 - 98 PINNACLE CBC SPORTS

Complete Set (13 cards):	
	CBC Sports
□	Steve Armitage
□	Don Cherry
□	Bob Cole
□	Chris Cuthbert
□	John Garrett
□	Dick Irvin
□	Ron MacLean
□	Greg Millen
□	Harry Neale
□	Scott Oake
□	Scott Russell
□	John Shannon
□	Don Whittman

1997 - 98 PINNACLE CERTIFIED

These cards have five versions: the regular card, a Certified Red parallel, a Mirror Red parallel, a Mirror Blue parallel and a Mirror Gold parallel. Regular card goalies (1-30) are short printed and inserted one per pack.

	Complete Set (130 cards):	**325.00**	**50.00**
	Common Player:	**1.50**	**.35**
	Player	**CR**	**PC**
□□	1 Dominik Hasek (G), Buff.	10.00	2.00
□□	2 Patrick Roy (G), Colo.	30.00	6.00
□□	3 Martin Brodeur (G), NJer.	15.00	3.00
□□	4 Chris Osgood (G), Detr.	6.00	1.00
□□	5 Andy Moog (G), Dall.	4.00	.50
□□	6 J. Vanbiesbrouck (G), Flor.	4.00	.50
□□	**7 S. Shields (G), Buff. RC**	**4.00**	**2.50**
□□	8 Mike Vernon (G), Detr.	4.00	.50
□□	9 Ed Belfour (G), SanJ.	10.00	2.00
□□	10 Grant Fuhr (G), SLou.	6.00	1.00
□□	11 Félix Potvin (G), Toro.	6.00	1.00
□□	12 Bill Ranford (G), Wash.	4.00	.50
□□	13 Mike Richter (G), NYRa.	4.00	.50
□□	14 Stéphane Fiset (G), LosA.	3.00	.50
□□	15 Jim Carey (G), Bost.	1.50	.50

□□	16 Nikolai Khabibulin (G), Phoe.	4.00	.50
□□	17 Ken Wregget (G), Pitt.	2.00	.50
□□	18 Curtis Joseph (G), Edmo.	10.00	2.00
□□	19 Guy Hebert (G), Anah.	2.00	.50
□□	20 Damian Rhodes (G), Ott.	2.00	.50
□□	21 Trevor Kidd (G), Calg.	3.00	.50
□□	22 Daren Puppa (G), Tamp.	2.00	.50
□□	23 Patrick Lalime (G), Pitt.	6.00	1.00
□□	24 Tommy Salo (G), NYIs.	4.00	.50
□□	25 Sean Burke (G), Hart.	6.00	1.00
□□	26 Jocelyn Thibault (G), Mont.	4.00	.50
□□	27 Kirk McLean (G), Vanc.	3.00	.50
□□	28 Garth Snow (G), Phil.	3.00	.50
□□	29 Ron Tugnutt (G), Ott.	4.00	.50
□□	30 Jeff Hackett (G), Chic.	3.00	.50
□□	31 Eric Lindros, Phil.	5.00	1.50
□□	32 Peter Forsberg, Colo.	10.00	2.00
□□	33 Mike Modano, Dall.	7.00	1.50
□□	34 Paul Kariya, Anah.	10.00	2.00
□□	35 Jaromir Jagr, Pitt.	5.00	1.50
□□	36 Brian Leetch, NYRa.	4.00	.35
□□	37 Keith Tkachuk, Phoe.	4.00	.35
□□	38 Steve Yzerman, Detr.	15.00	3.50
□□	39 Teemu Selänne, Anah.	6.00	1.00
□□	40 Bryan Berard, NYIs.	2.00	.35
□□	41 Raymond Bourque, Bost.	9.00	1.50
□□	42 Theoren Fleury, Calg.	4.00	.35
□□	43 Mark Messier, NYRa.	7.00	1.50
□□	44 Saku Koivu, Mont.	6.00	1.00
□□	45 Pavel Bure, Vanc.	5.00	1.00
□□	46 Peter Bondra, Wash.	4.00	.35
□□	47 Dave Gagner, Calg.	1.50	.35
□□	48 Ed Jovanovski, Flor.	3.00	.35
□□	49 Adam Oates, Wash.	3.00	.35
□□	50 Joe Sakic, Colo.	12.00	2.00
□□	51 Doug Gilmour, NJer.	4.00	.35
□□	52 Jim Campbell, SLou.	1.50	.35
□□	53 Mats Sundin, Toro.	7.00	1.50
□□	54 Derian Hatcher, Dall.	2.00	.35
□□	55 Jarome Iginla, Calg.	6.00	1.00
□□	56 Sergei Fedorov, Detr.	7.00	1.50
□□	57 Keith Primeau, Hart.	3.00	.35
□□	58 Mark Recchi, Mont.	3.00	.35
□□	59 Owen Nolan, SanJ.	4.00	.35
□□	60 Alexander Mogilny, Vanc.	3.00	.35
□□	61 Brendan Shanahan, Detr.	7.00	1.50
□□	62 Pierre Turgeon, SLou.	3.00	.35
□□	63 Joe Juneau, Wash.	1.50	.35
□□	64 Steve Rucchin, Anah.	1.50	.35
□□	65 Jeremy Roenick, Phoe.	6.00	1.00
□□	66 Doug Weight, Edmo.	4.00	.35
□□	67 Valeri Kamensky, Colo.	2.00	.35
□□	68 Tony Amonte, Chic.	4.00	.35
□□	69 Dave Andreychuk, NJer.	2.00	.35
□□	70 Brett Hull, SLou.	7.00	1.50
□□	71 Wendel Clark, Toro.	6.00	1.00
□□	72 V. Damphousse, Mont.	4.00	.35
□□	73 Mike Grier, Edmo.	1.50	.35
□□	74 Chris Chelios, Chic.	4.00	.35
□□	75 Nicklas Lidström, Detr.	4.00	.35
□□	76 Joe Nieuwendyk, Dall.	3.00	.35
□□	77 Rob Blake, LosA.	4.00	.35
□□	78 Alexei Yashin, Ott.	4.00	.35
□□	79 Ryan Smyth, Edmo.	3.00	.35
□□	80 Pat LaFontaine, Buff.	4.00	.35
□□	81 Jeff Friesen, SanJ.	2.00	.35
□□	82 Ray Ferraro, LosA.	1.50	.35
□□	83 Steve Sullivan, Toro.	2.00	.35
□□	84 Chris Gratton, Tamp.	1.50	.35
□□	85 Mike Gartner, Phoe.	6.00	1.00
□□	86 Kevin Hatcher, Pitt.	1.50	.35
□□	87 Ted Donato, Bost.	1.50	.35
□□	88 German Titov, Calg.	1.50	.35
□□	89 Sandis Ozolinsh, Colo.	1.50	.35
□□	90 Ray Sheppard, Flor.	1.50	.35
□□	91 John MacLean, NJer.	1.50	.35
□□	92 Luc Robitaille, LosA.	6.00	1.00
□□	93 Rod Brind'Amour, Phil.	2.00	.35
□□	94 Zigmund Palffy, NYIs.	4.00	.35
□□	95 Peter Nedved, Pitt.	2.00	.35
□□	96 Adam Graves, NYRa.	3.00	.35
□□	97 Jozef Stumpel, Bost.	1.50	.35
□□	98 Alexandre Daigle, Ott.	1.50	.35
□□	99 Michael Peca, Buff.	3.00	.35
□□	100 Wayne Gretzky, NYRa.	30.00	6.00
□□	101 Alexei Zhamnov, Chic.	2.00	.35
□□	102 Paul Coffey, Phil.	4.00	.35
□□	103 Oleg Tverdovsky, Phoe.	1.50	.35
□□	104 Trevor Linden, Vanc.	3.00	.35
□□	105 Dino Ciccarelli, Tamp.	2.00	.35
□□	106 Andrei Kovalenko, Edmo.	1.50	.35
□□	107 Scott Mellanby, Flor.	1.50	.35
□□	108 Bryan Smolinski, NYIs.	1.50	.35
□□	109 Bernie Nicholls, SanJ.	1.50	.35
□□	110 Derek Plante, Buff.	1.50	.35
□□	111 Pat Verbeek, Dall.	2.00	.35
□□	112 Adam Deadmarsh, Colo.	2.00	.35
□□	113 Martin Gelinas, Vanc.	1.50	.35
□□	114 Daniel Alfredsson, Ott.	4.00	.35
□□	115 Scott Stevens, NJer.	3.00	.35
□□	116 Dainius Zubrus, Phil.	1.50	.35
□□	117 Kirk Muller, Flor.	2.00	.35
□□	118 Brian Holzinger, Buff.	1.50	.35
□□	119 John LeClair, Phil.	6.00	1.00
□□	120 Al MacInnis, SLou.	3.00	.35
□□	121 Ron Francis, Pitt.	4.00	.35
□□	122 Eric Dazé, Chic.	3.00	.35
□□	123 Travis Green, NYIs.	1.50	.35
□□	124 Jason Arnott, Edmo.	3.00	.35
□□	125 Geoff Sanderson, Hart.	1.50	.35
□□	126 Dimitri Khristich, LosA.	1.50	.35
□□	127 Sergei Berezin, Toro.	1.50	.35
□□	128 Jeff O'Neill, Hart.	3.00	.35
□□	129 Claude Lemieux, Colo.	2.00	.35
□□	130 Andrew Cassels, Hart.	1.50	.35

MIRROR PARALLELS

These cards have five versions: the regular card, a Certified Red parallel, a Mirror Red parallel, a Mirror Blue parallel and a Mirror Gold parallel. Regular card goalies (1-30) are short printed and inserted one per pack.

Complete Set (130 cards):		**15500.00**	**7400.00**	**3600.00**
Common Player:		**30.00**	**15.00**	**8.00**
	Player	**MG**	**MB**	**MR**
□□□	1 Dominik Hasek (G), Buff.	375.00	200.00	100.00
□□□	2 Patrick Roy (G), Colo.	1125.00	600.00	300.00
□□□	3 Martin Brodeur (G), NJer.	600.00	300.00	160.00
□□□	4 Chris Osgood (G), Detr.	220.00	120.00	60.00
□□□	5 Andy Moog (G), Dall.	150.00	80.00	40.00
□□□	6 J. Vanbiesbrouck (G), Flor.	180.00	90.00	40.00
□□□	**7 S. Shields (G), Buff. RC**	**180.00**	**90.00**	**45.00**
□□□	8 Mike Vernon (G), Detr.	150.00	80.00	40.00
□□□	9 Ed Belfour (G), SanJ.	370.00	200.00	100.00
□□□	10 Grant Fuhr (G), SLou.	220.00	120.00	60.00
□□□	11 Félix Potvin (G), Toro.	220.00	120.00	60.00
□□□	12 Bill Ranford (G), Wash.	150.00	80.00	40.00
□□□	13 Mike Richter (G), NYRa.	180.00	90.00	40.00
□□□	14 Stéphane Fiset (G), LosA.	120.00	60.00	30.00
□□□	15 Jim Carey (G), Bost.	60.00	30.00	15.00
□□□	16 N. Khabibulin (G), Phoe.	150.00	80.00	40.00
□□□	17 Ken Wregget (G), Pitt.	90.00	45.00	20.00
□□□	18 Cu. Joseph (G), Edmo.	375.00	200.00	100.00
□□□	19 Guy Hebert (G), Anah.	90.00	40.00	20.00
□□□	20 Damian Rhodes (G), Ott.	90.00	45.00	20.00
□□□	21 Trevor Kidd (G), Calg.	120.00	60.00	30.00
□□□	22 Daren Puppa (G), Tamp.	90.00	45.00	20.00
□□□	23 Patrick Lalime (G), Pitt.	220.00	120.00	60.00
□□□	24 Tommy Salo (G), NYIs.	150.00	80.00	40.00
□□□	25 Sean Burke (G), Hart.	220.00	120.00	60.00
□□□	26 J. Thibault (G), Mont.	150.00	80.00	40.00
□□□	27 Kirk McLean (G), Vanc.	120.00	60.00	30.00
□□□	28 Garth Snow (G), Phil.	120.00	60.00	30.00
□□□	29 Ron Tugnutt (G), Ott.	150.00	80.00	40.00
□□□	30 Jeff Hackett (G), Chic.	120.00	60.00	30.00
□□□	31 Eric Lindros, Phil.	300.00	150.00	70.00
□□□	32 Peter Forsberg, Colo.	400.00	200.00	100.00
□□□	33 Mike Modano, Dall.	300.00	150.00	70.00
□□□	34 Paul Kariya, Anah.	400.00	200.00	100.00
□□□	35 Jaromir Jagr, Pitt.	300.00	150.00	70.00
□□□	36 Brian Leetch, NYRa.	180.00	90.00	45.00
□□□	37 Keith Tkachuk, Phoe.	180.00	90.00	40.00
□□□	38 Steve Yzerman, Detr.	700.00	350.00	180.00
□□□	39 Teemu Selänne, Anah.	240.00	120.00	60.00
□□□	40 Bryan Berard, NYIs.	95.00	45.00	20.00
□□□	41 Raymond Bourque, Bost.	350.00	175.00	90.00
□□□	42 Theoren Fleury, Calg.	180.00	90.00	40.00
□□□	43 Mark Messier, NYRa.	300.00	150.00	70.00
□□□	44 Saku Koivu, Mont.	240.00	120.00	60.00
□□□	45 Pavel Bure, Vanc.	225.00	100.00	60.00
□□□	46 Peter Bondra, Wash.	180.00	90.00	45.00
□□□	47 Dave Gagner, Calg.	45.00	20.00	10.00
□□□	48 Ed Jovanovski, Flor.	120.00	60.00	30.00
□□□	49 Adam Oates, Wash.	120.00	60.00	30.00
□□□	50 Joe Sakic, Colo.	475.00	225.00	120.00
□□□	51 Doug Gilmour, NJer.	180.00	90.00	45.00
□□□	52 Jim Campbell, SLou.	30.00	15.00	8.00
□□□	53 Mats Sundin, Toro.	300.00	150.00	70.00
□□□	54 Derian Hatcher, Dall.	95.00	45.00	20.00
□□□	55 Jarome Iginla, Calg.	240.00	120.00	60.00
□□□	56 Sergei Fedorov, Detr.	300.00	150.00	70.00
□□□	57 Keith Primeau, Hart.	120.00	60.00	30.00
□□□	58 Mark Recchi, Mont.	120.00	60.00	30.00
□□□	59 Owen Nolan, SanJ.	180.00	90.00	45.00
□□□	60 Alexander Mogilny, Vanc.	140.00	70.00	35.00
□□□	61 Brendan Shanahan, Detr.	300.00	150.00	70.00
□□□	62 Pierre Turgeon, SLou.	120.00	60.00	30.00
□□□	63 Joe Juneau, Wash.	70.00	35.00	15.00
□□□	64 Steve Rucchin, Anah.	70.00	35.00	15.00
□□□	65 Jeremy Roenick, Phoe.	240.00	120.00	60.00
□□□	66 Doug Weight, Edmo.	180.00	90.00	40.00
□□□	67 Valeri Kamensky, Colo.	95.00	45.00	20.00
□□□	68 Tony Amonte, Chic.	180.00	90.00	45.00
□□□	69 Dave Andreychuk, NJer.	95.00	45.00	20.00
□□□	70 Brett Hull, SLou.	300.00	150.00	70.00
□□□	71 Wendel Clark, Toro.	240.00	120.00	60.00
□□□	72 V. Damphousse, Mont.	180.00	90.00	45.00
□□□	73 Mike Grier, Edmo.	70.00	35.00	15.00
□□□	74 Chris Chelios, Chic.	180.00	90.00	45.00
□□□	75 Nicklas Lidström, Detr.	180.00	90.00	45.00
□□□	76 Joe Nieuwendyk, Dall.	120.00	60.00	30.00
□□□	77 Rob Blake, LosA.	180.00	90.00	45.00
□□□	78 Alexei Yashin, Ott.	180.00	90.00	45.00
□□□	79 Ryan Smyth, Edmo.	140.00	70.00	35.00
□□□	80 Pat LaFontaine, Buff.	180.00	90.00	45.00
□□□	81 Jeff Friesen, SanJ.	95.00	45.00	20.00
□□□	82 Ray Ferraro, LosA.	45.00	20.00	10.00
□□□	83 Steve Sullivan, Toro.	95.00	45.00	20.00
□□□	84 Chris Gratton, Tamp.	70.00	35.00	15.00
□□□	85 Mike Gartner, Phoe.	240.00	120.00	60.00
□□□	86 Kevin Hatcher, Pitt.	45.00	20.00	10.00
□□□	87 Ted Donato, Bost.	30.00	15.00	8.00
□□□	88 German Titov, Calg.	30.00	15.00	8.00
□□□	89 Sandis Ozolinsh, Colo.	70.00	35.00	15.00
□□□	90 Ray Sheppard, Flor.	45.00	20.00	10.00
□□□	91 John MacLean, NJer.	45.00	20.00	10.00
□□□	92 Luc Robitaille, LosA.	240.00	120.00	60.00
□□□	93 Rod Brind'Amour, Phil.	95.00	45.00	20.00
□□□	94 Zigmund Palffy, NYIs.	180.00	90.00	45.00
□□□	95 Peter Nedved, Pitt.	90.00	40.00	20.00
□□□	96 Adam Graves, NYRa.	120.00	60.00	30.00
□□□	97 Jozef Stumpel, Bost.	70.00	35.00	15.00
□□□	98 Alexandre Daigle, Ott.	45.00	20.00	10.00
□□□	99 Michael Peca, Buff.	120.00	60.00	30.00
□□□	100 Wayne Gretzky, NYRa.	1200.00	600.00	300.00
□□□	101 Alexei Zhamnov, Chic.	95.00	45.00	20.00
□□□	102 Paul Coffey, Phil.	180.00	90.00	40.00
□□□	103 Oleg Tverdovsky, Phoe.	45.00	20.00	10.00
□□□	104 Trevor Linden, Vanc.	120.00	60.00	30.00
□□□	105 Dino Ciccarelli, Tamp.	95.00	45.00	20.00
□□□	106 Andrei Kovalenko, Edmo.	45.00	20.00	10.00
□□□	107 Scott Mellanby, Flor.	70.00	35.00	15.00
□□□	108 Bryan Smolinski, NYIs.	45.00	20.00	10.00
□□□	109 Bernie Nicholls, SanJ.	70.00	35.00	15.00
□□□	110 Derek Plante, Buff.	45.00	20.00	10.00
□□□	111 Pat Verbeek, Dall.	95.00	45.00	20.00
□□□	112 Adam Deadmarsh, Colo.	95.00	45.00	20.00
□□□	113 Martin Gelinas, Vanc.	70.00	35.00	15.00
□□□	114 Daniel Alfredsson, Ott.	180.00	90.00	45.00
□□□	115 Scott Stevens, NJer.	120.00	60.00	30.00
□□□	116 Dainius Zubrus, Phil.	70.00	35.00	15.00
□□□	117 Kirk Muller, Flor.	95.00	45.00	20.00
□□□	118 Brian Holzinger, Buff.	45.00	20.00	10.00
□□□	119 John LeClair, Phil.	240.00	120.00	60.00
□□□	120 Al MacInnis, SLou.	120.00	60.00	30.00
□□□	121 Ron Francis, Pitt.	180.00	90.00	45.00
□□□	122 Eric Dazé, Chic.	120.00	60.00	30.00
□□□	123 Travis Green, NYIs.	70.00	35.00	15.00
□□□	124 Jason Arnott, Edmo.	140.00	70.00	35.00
□□□	125 Geoff Sanderson, Hart.	70.00	35.00	15.00
□□□	126 Dimitri Khristich, LosA.	45.00	20.00	10.00
□□□	127 Sergei Berezin, Toro.	70.00	35.00	15.00
□□□	128 Jeff O'Neill, Hart.	120.00	60.00	30.00
□□□	129 Claude Lemieux, Colo.	95.00	45.00	20.00
□□□	130 Andrew Cassels, Hart.	70.00	35.00	15.00

CERTIFIED TEAM

These cards have two versions: the regular insert and a Gold (#/300) parallel. A third Mirror Gold version also exists.

Insert Set (20 cards):		**750.00**	**140.00**
□	Steve Yzerman Promo		3.00
	Inserts	**G300**	**CT**
□□□	1 Martin Brodeur (G), NJer.	60.00	10.00
□□□	2 Patrick Roy (G), Colo.	110.00	20.00
□□□	3 John Vanbiesbrouck (G), Flor.	15.00	3.00
□□□	4 Dominik Hasek (G), Buff.	30.00	5.00
□□□	5 Chris Chelios, Chic.	20.00	4.00
□□□	6 Brian Leetch, NYRa.	20.00	4.00
□□□	7 Wayne Gretzky, NYRa.	150.00	30.00
□□□	8 Eric Lindros, Phil.	30.00	5.00
□□□	9 Paul Kariya, Anah.	50.00	10.00
□□□	10 Peter Forsberg, Colo.	50.00	10.00
□□□	11 Keith Tkachuk, Phoe.	20.00	4.00
□□□	12 Mark Messier, Vanc.	35.00	7.00
□□□	13 Steve Yzerman, Detr.	90.00	15.00
□□□	14 Jaromir Jagr, Pitt.	30.00	5.00
□□□	15 Mats Sundin, Toro.	35.00	7.00
□□□	16 Teemu Selänne, Anah.	30.00	5.00
□□□	17 Brendan Shanahan, Detr.	35.00	7.00
□□□	18 Saku Koivu, Mont.	30.00	6.00
□□□	19 Brett Hull, SLou.	35.00	7.00
□□□	20 John LeClair, Phil.	30.00	6.00

ROOKIE

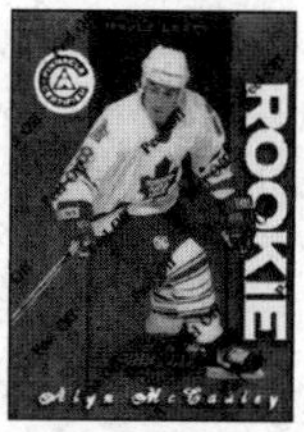

These cards have two versions: the regular insert and a Gold (#/250) parallel. A third Mirror Gold version also exists.

Insert Set (12 cards):		**125.00**	**50.00**
	Inserts	**G250**	**R**
□□□	A Joe Thornton, Bost.	45.00	18.00
□□□	B Chris Phillips, Otta.	8.00	3.00
□□□	C Patrick Marleau, SanJ.	15.00	6.00
□□□	D Sergei Samsonov, Bost.	20.00	8.00
□□□	E Daniel Cleary, Chic.	10.00	4.00
□□□	**F Olli Jokinen, LosA. RC**	**10.00**	**4.00**
□□□	G Alyn McCauley, Toro.	10.00	4.00
□□□	H Aleksey Morozov, Pitt.	8.00	3.00
□□□	I Brad Isbister, Phoe.	8.00	3.00
□□□	J Boyd Devereaux, Edmo.	8.00	3.00
□□□	**K Espen Knutsen, Anah. RC**	**8.00**	**3.00**
□□□	L Marc Savard, NYRa.	8.00	3.00

SUMMIT

The last card was signed in Black ink (700 copies), Silver ink (200 copies) and Gold ink (100 copies).

Insert Set (4 cards):		**40.00**
	Insert	**Summit**
□	S1 Paul Henderson	12.00
□	S2 Paul Henderson	12.00
□	S3 Paul Henderson	12.00
□	S4 Paul Henderson	12.00
□	Paul Henderson Black ✍ {#/700}	60.00
□	Paul Henderson Gold ✍ {#/100}	300.00
□	Paul Henderson Silver ✍ {#/200}	125.00

1997 - 98 PINNACLE EPIX

This 24-player set was inserted into 1997 - 98 Pinnacle products: Pinnacle Certified, Score, Pinnacle and Pinnacle Zenith. Each player has one of four cards (Game, Season, Moment or Play) inserted into each product. In turn, each card (Game, Season, Moment or Play) is available in three colours: emerald, orange or violet. So while Gretzky has a total of 12 Epix cards, only three Epix cards are available in any one product.

PLAY

Play cards E1-E6 were available in Pinnacle Certified, E7-E12 were available in Score, E13-E18 were available in Pinnacle and E19-E24 were available in Pinnacle Zenith.

Insert Set (24 cards):		**350.00**	**175.00**	**120.00**
	Insert	**Emer.**	**Pur.**	**Ora.**
□□□	E1 Wayne Gretzky, NYRa.	60.00	30.00	20.00
□□□	E2 John Vanbiesbrouck (G), Flor.	6.00	3.00	2.00
□□□	E3 Joe Sakic, Colo.	20.00	12.00	8.00
□□□	E4 Alexei Yashin, Otta.	8.00	4.00	3.00
□□□	E5 Sergei Fedorov, Detr.	14.00	7.00	5.00
□□□	E6 Keith Tkachuk, Phoe.	8.00	4.00	3.00
□□□	E7 Patrick Roy (G), Colo.	45.00	22.00	15.00
□□□	E8 Martin Brodeur (G), NJer.	20.00	12.00	8.00
□□□	E9 Steve Yzerman, Detr.	35.00	18.00	12.00

E10 Saku Koivu, Mont.	12.00	6.00	4.00
E11 Félix Potvin (G), Toro.	8.00	4.00	3.00
E12 Mark Messier, NYRa.	15.00	7.00	5.00
E13 Eric Lindros, Phil.	15.00	7.00	5.00
E14 Peter Forsberg, Colo.	20.00	10.00	7.00
E15 Teemu Selänne, Anah.	10.00	6.00	4.00
E16 Brendan Shanahan, Detr.	15.00	7.00	5.00
E17 Curtis Joseph (G), Edmo.	15.00	7.00	5.00
E18 Brett Hull, SLou.	15.00	7.00	5.00
E19 Paul Kariya, Anah.	20.00	10.00	7.00
E20 Jaromir Jagr, Pitt.	15.00	7.00	5.00
E21 Pavel Bure, Vanc.	10.00	6.00	4.00
E22 Dominik Hasek (G), Buff.	15.00	7.00	5.00
E23 John LeClair, Phil.	12.00	6.00	4.00
E24 Doug Gilmour, NJer.	8.00	4.00	3.00

GAME

Game cards E1-E6 were available in Score, E7-E12 were available in Pinnacle, E13-E18 were available in Zenith and E19-E24 were available in Pinancle Certified.

Insert Set (24 cards):	700.00	275.00	140.00
Insert	Emer.	Pur.	Ora.
E1 Wayne Gretzky, NYRa.	120.00	50.00	25.00
E2 J. Vanbiesbrouck (G), Flor.	10.00	6.00	2.50
E3 Joe Sakic, Colo.	45.00	20.00	10.00
E4 Alexei Yashin, Otta.	15.00	6.00	2.50
E5 Sergei Fedorov, Detr.	30.00	12.00	6.00
E6 Keith Tkachuk, Phoe.	15.00	6.00	2.50
E7 Patrick Roy (G), Colo.	90.00	35.00	15.00
E8 Martin Brodeur (G), NJer.	45.00	20.00	10.00
E9 Steve Yzerman, Detr.	70.00	30.00	15.00
E10 Saku Koivu, Mont.	20.00	10.00	4.00
E11 Félix Potvin (G), Toro.	15.00	6.00	2.50
E12 Mark Messier, NYRa.	30.00	12.00	6.00
E13 Eric Lindros, Phil.	30.00	12.00	6.00
E14 Peter Forsberg, Colo.	40.00	16.00	8.00
E15 Teemu Selänne, Anah.	20.00	10.00	4.00
E16 Brendan Shanahan, Detr.	30.00	12.00	6.00
E17 Curtis Joseph (G), Edmo.	30.00	12.00	6.00
E18 Brett Hull, SLou.	30.00	12.00	6.00
E19 Paul Kariya, Anah.	40.00	15.00	8.00
E20 Jaromir Jagr, Pitt.	30.00	10.00	6.00
E21 Pavel Bure, Vanc.	20.00	10.00	4.00
E22 Dominik Hasek (G), Buff.	30.00	10.00	6.00
E23 John LeClair, Phil.	20.00	10.00	4.00
E24 Doug Gilmour, NJer.	15.00	6.00	2.50

SEASON

Season cards E1-E6 were available in Pinnacle, E7-E12 were available in Zenith, E13-E18 were available in Pinancle Certified and E19-E24 were available in Score.

Insert Set (24 cards):	1500.00	600.00	275.00
Insert	Emer.	Pur.	Ora.
E1 Wayne Gretzky, NYRa.	250.00	100.00	50.00
E2 J. Vanbiesbrouck (G), Flor.	30.00	10.00	6.00
E3 Joe Sakic, Colo.	100.00	40.00	20.00
E4 Alexei Yashin, Otta.	35.00	15.00	6.00
E5 Sergei Fedorov, Detr.	60.00	25.00	12.00
E6 Keith Tkachuk, Phoe.	35.00	15.00	6.00
E7 Patrick Roy (G), Colo.	180.00	70.00	35.00
E8 Martin Brodeur (G), NJer.	100.00	40.00	20.00
E9 Steve Yzerman, Detr.	150.00	60.00	30.00
E10 Saku Koivu, Mont.	50.00	20.00	10.00
E11 Félix Potvin (G), Toro.	35.00	15.00	6.00
E12 Mark Messier, NYRa.	60.00	25.00	12.00
E13 Eric Lindros, Phil.	60.00	25.00	10.00
E14 Peter Forsberg, Colo.	80.00	35.00	15.00
E15 Teemu Selänne, Anah.	50.00	20.00	10.00
E16 Brendan Shanahan, Detr.	60.00	25.00	12.00
E17 Curtis Joseph (G), Edmo.	60.00	25.00	10.00
E18 Brett Hull, SLou.	60.00	25.00	12.00
E19 Paul Kariya, Anah.	80.00	30.00	15.00
E20 Jaromir Jagr, Pitt.	60.00	20.00	10.00
E21 Pavel Bure, Vanc.	50.00	20.00	10.00
E22 Dominik Hasek (G), Buff.	60.00	25.00	10.00
E23 John LeClair, Phil.	50.00	20.00	10.00
E24 Doug Gilmour, NJer.	35.00	15.00	6.00

MOMENT

Moment cards E1-E6 were available in Zenith, E7-E12 were available in Pinnacle Certified, E13-E18 were available in Score and E19-E24 were available in Pinnacle.

Insert Set (24 cards):	3700.00	1500.00	700.00
Insert	Emer.	Pur.	Ora.
E1 Wayne Gretzky, NYRa.	600.00	250.00	120.00
E2 J. Vanbiesbrouck (G), Flor.	70.00	30.00	10.00
E3 Joe Sakic, Colo.	240.00	100.00	45.00
E4 Alexei Yashin, Otta.	90.00	35.00	15.00
E5 Sergei Fedorov, Detr.	150.00	60.00	30.00
E6 Keith Tkachuk, Phoe.	90.00	35.00	15.00
E7 Patrick Roy (G), Colo.	450.00	180.00	90.00
E8 Martin Brodeur (G), NJer.	230.00	100.00	45.00
E9 Steve Yzerman, Detr.	360.00	150.00	70.00
E10 Saku Koivu, Mont.	120.00	50.00	20.00
E11 Félix Potvin (G), Toro.	90.00	35.00	15.00
E12 Mark Messier, NYRa.	150.00	60.00	30.00
E13 Eric Lindros, Phil.	150.00	60.00	30.00
E14 Peter Forsberg, Colo.	210.00	80.00	40.00
E15 Teemu Selänne, Anah.	120.00	50.00	20.00
E16 Brendan Shanahan, Detr.	150.00	60.00	30.00
E17 Cu. Joseph (G), Edmo.	150.00	60.00	30.00
E18 Brett Hull, SLou.	150.00	60.00	30.00
E19 Paul Kariya, Anah.	210.00	80.00	40.00
E20 Jaromir Jagr, Pitt.	150.00	60.00	30.00
E21 Pavel Bure, Vanc.	110.00	50.00	20.00
E22 D. Hasek (G), Buff.	140.00	60.00	30.00
E23 John LeClair, Phil.	120.00	50.00	20.00
E24 Doug Gilmour, NJer.	90.00	35.00	15.00

1997 - 98 PINNACLE INSIDE

Cards 1-90 have three versions: the regular card, a Coach's Collection parallel and an Executive Collection parallel. A fourth promo version also exist; promo cards have the same value as the regular card.

Complete Set (190 cards):	-		60.00
Parallel Set (90 cards):	2,000	275	
Common Player:	8.00	2.00	.25
Player	EC	PC	PI
1 Brendan Shanahan, Detr.	60.00	10.00	1.50
2 Dominik Hasek (G), Buff.	60.00	10.00	1.50
3 Wayne Gretzky, NYRa.	250.00	40.00	6.00
4 Eric Lindros, Phil.	60.00	10.00	1.50
5 Keith Tkachuk, Phoe.	35.00	5.00	.50
6 Jaromir Jagr, Pitt.	60.00	10.00	1.50
7 Martin Brodeur (G), NJer.	100.00	15.00	2.00
8 Peter Forsberg, Colo.	80.00	10.00	2.00
9 Chris Osgood (G), Detr.	35.00	5.00	.50
10 Paul Kariya, Anah.	80.00	10.00	2.00
11 Pavel Bure, Vanc.	50.00	5.00	1.00
12 Brett Hull, SLou.	60.00	10.00	1.50
13 Saku Koivu, Mont.	50.00	5.00	1.00
14 Zigmund Palffy, NYIs.	35.00	5.00	.50
15 Mike Modano, Dall.	60.00	10.00	1.50
16 Raymond Bourque, Bost.	70.00	10.00	1.50
17 Jarome Iginla, Calg.	50.00	5.00	1.00
18 Chris Chelios, Chic.	35.00	5.00	.50
19 J. Vanbiesbrouck (G), Flor.	30.00	2.00	.50
20 Brian Leetch, NYRa.	35.00	5.00	.50
21 Mats Sundin, Toro.	60.00	10.00	1.50
22 Ron Hextall (G), Phil.	35.00	5.00	.50
23 Stéphane Fiset (G), LosA.	20.00	2.00	.25
24 Steve Yzerman, Detr.	150.00	20.00	3.50
25 Curtis Joseph (G), Edmo.	60.00	10.00	1.50
26 Daniel Alfredsson, Ott.	35.00	5.00	.50
27 Owen Nolan, SanJ.	35.00	5.00	.50
28 Adam Oates, Wash.	25.00	2.00	.50
29 Corey Hirsch (G), Vanc.	10.00	2.00	.25
30 Sean Burke (G), Hart.	35.00	5.00	.50
31 Éric Fichaud (G), NYIs.	10.00	2.00	.25
32 Ken Wregget (G), Pitt.	15.00	2.00	.25
33 Dainius Zubrus, Phil.	15.00	2.00	.25
34 Alexander Mogilny, Vanc.	30.00	2.00	.50
35 Bill Ranford (G), Wash.	25.00	2.00	.50
36 V. Damphousse, Mont.	35.00	5.00	.50
37 Patrick Roy (G), Colo.	180.00	30.00	4.50
38 Teemu Selänne, Anah.	50.00	5.00	1.00
39 Pat LaFontaine, Buff.	35.00	5.00	.50
40 Theoren Fleury, Calg.	30.00	5.00	.50
41 Jeff Hackett (G), Chic.	20.00	2.00	.25
42 Sergei Fedorov, Detr.	60.00	10.00	1.50
43 Jocelyn Thibault (G), Mont.	25.00	2.00	.50
44 N. Khabibulin (G), Phoe.	25.00	2.00	.50
45 Daren Puppa (G), Tamp.	15.00	2.00	.25
46 Félix Potvin (G), Toro.	35.00	5.00	.50
47 Andy Moog (G), Dall.	25.00	2.00	.50
48 Doug Weight, Edmo.	35.00	5.00	.50
49 Tommy Salo (G), NYIs.	25.00	2.00	.50
50 Mark Messier, NYRa.	60.00	10.00	1.50
51 Grant Fuhr (G), SLou.	35.00	5.00	.50
52 Ron Francis, Pitt.	35.00	5.00	.50
53 Tony Amonte, Chic.	35.00	5.00	.50
54 Joe Sakic, Colo.	100.00	15.00	2.00
55 Jason Arnott, Edmo.	30.00	2.00	.50
56 José Théodore (G), Mont.	75.00	10.00	1.50
57 Alexei Yashin, Ott.	35.00	5.00	.50
58 John LeClair, Phil.	50.00	5.00	1.00
59 Jeremy Roenick, Phoe.	50.00	5.00	1.00
60 Kirk McLean (G), Vanc.	20.00	2.00	.25
61 Arturs Irbe (G), Dall.	25.00	2.00	.50
62 Jim Carey (G), Bost.	10.00	2.00	.25
63 J.S. Giguère (G), Hart.	50.00	5.00	1.00
64 Marc Denis (G), Colo.	30.00	2.00	.50
65 Damian Rhodes (G), Ott.	15.00	2.00	.25
66 Jim Campbell, SLou.	8.00	2.00	.25
67 Patrick Lalime (G), Pitt.	35.00	5.00	.50
68 Garth Snow (G), Phil.	20.00	2.00	.25
69 M. Cousineau (G), Toro.	8.00	2.00	.25
70 Guy Hebert (G), Anah.	15.00	2.00	.25
71 Rob Blake, LosA.	35.00	5.00	.50
72 T. Vokoun (G), Mont. RC	**15.00**	**2.00**	**2.00**
73 Doug Gilmour, Toro.	35.00	5.00	.50
74 Ed Belfour (G), SanJ.	60.00	10.00	1.50
75 P. Duffus (G), Phoe. RC	**10.00**	**2.00**	**1.50**
76 Mike Fountain (G), Vanc.	8.00	2.00	.25
77 S. Shields (G), Buff. RC	**15.00**	**2.00**	**2.00**
78 Geoff Sanderson, Hart.	15.00	2.00	.25
79 Roman Turek (G), Dall.	30.00	2.00	.50
80 Bryan Berard, NYIs.	20.00	2.00	.25
81 Mike Richter (G), NYRa.	30.00	2.00	.50
82 Ron Tugnutt (G), Ott.	25.00	2.00	.50
83 Peter Bondra, Wash.	35.00	5.00	.50
84 Mike Vernon (G), Detr.	25.00	2.00	.50
85 Mike Grier, Edmo.	15.00	2.00	.25
86 Ed Jovanovski, Flor.	25.00	2.00	.50
87 Trevor Kidd (G), Calg.	20.00	2.00	.25
88 Eric Dazé, Chic.	25.00	2.00	.50
89 Wendel Clark, Toro.	50.00	5.00	1.00
90 Checklist	8.00	2.00	.25
91 Nicklas Lidström, Detr.			.50
92 Rod Brind'Amour, Phil.			.25
93 Hnat Domenichelli, Calg.			.25
94 Rem Murray, Edmo.			.25
95 Scott Niedermayer, NJer.			.25
96 Martin Rucinsky, Mont.			.25
97 Mike Gartner, Phoe.			1.00
98 Kevin Hatcher, Pitt.			.25
99 Daymond Langkow, Tamp.			.25
100 Jamie Langenbrunner, Dall.			.25
101 Ted Donato, Bost.			.25
102 Steve Sullivan, Toro.			.25
103 Martin Gelinas, Vanc.			.25
104 Adam Graves, NYRa.			.50
105 Donald Audette, Buff.			.50
106 Andrew Cassels, Hart.			.25
107 Alexei Zhamnov, Chic.			.25
108 Kirk Muller, Flor.			.25
109 Alexandre Daigle, Ott.			.25
110 Chris Gratton, Tamp.			.25
111 Andrew Brunette, Wash.			.25
112 Mark Recchi, Mont.			.50
113 Jari Kurri, Anah.			1.50
114 Valeri Kamensky, Colo.			.25
115 Joe Nieuwendyk, Dall.			.50
116 Vyacheslav Kozlov, Detr.			.25
117 Steve Kelly, Edmo.			.25
118 Dave Andreychuk, NJer.			.25
119 Mikael Renberg, Phil.			.25
120 Sergei Berezin, Toro.			.25
121 Jeff Friesen, SanJ.			.25
122 Pierre Turgeon, SLou.			.50
123 Vladimir Vorobiev, NYRa. RC			**1.00**
124 Dimitri Khristich, LosA.			.25
125 Jaroslav Svejkovsky, Wash.			.25
126 Vladimir Konstantinov, Detr.			.25
127 Jozef Stumpel, Bost.			.25
128 Michael Peca, Buff.			.50
129 Jonas Höglund, Calg.			.25
130 Travis Green, NYIs.			.25
131 Bill Guerin, NJer.			.50
132 Oleg Tverdovsky, Phoe.			.25
133 Petr Nedved, Pitt.			.25
134 Dino Ciccarelli, Tamp.			.25
135 Brian Savage, Mont.			.25
136 Steve Duchesne, Ott.			.25
137 Sandis Ozolinsh, Colo.			.25
138 Derian Hatcher, Dall.			.25
139 Ray Sheppard, Flor.			.25
140 Brian Bellows, Anah.			.25
141 Paul Brousseau, Tamp. RC			**1.00**
142 Tony Granato, LosA.			.25
143 Vaclav Prospal, Phil. RC			**3.00**
144 Vitali Yachmenev, LosA.			.25
145 John MacLean, NJer.			.25
146 Igor Larionov, Detr.			.50
147 Jason Allison, Bost.			.50
148 Derek Plante, Buff.			.25
149 Jeff O'Neill, Hart.			.50
150 Trevor Linden, Vanc.			.50
151 Joé Juneau, Wash.			.25
152 Brandon Convery, Toro.			.25
153 Kevin Stevens, LosA.			.25
154 Scott Stevens, NJer.			.50
155 Niklas Sundström, NYRa.			.25
156 Claude Lemieux, Colo.			.25
157 Pat Verbeek, Dall.			.25
158 Mariusz Czerkawski, Edmo.			.25
159 Robert Svehla, Flor.			.25
160 Paul Coffey, Phil.			.50
161 Al MacInnis, SLou.			.50
162 Roman Hamrlik, Tamp.			.25
163 Brian Holzinger, Buff.			.25
164 Cory Stillman, Detr.			.25
165 Scott Mellanby, Flor.			.25
166 Todd Warriner, Toro.			.25
167 Terry Ryan, Mont.			.25
168 Luc Robitaille, NYRa.			1.00
169 Ed Olczyk, Pitt.			.25
170 Adam Deadmarsh, Colo.			.25
171 Anson Carter, Bost.			.50
172 Mike Knuble, Detr. RC			**1.00**
173 Cliff Ronning, Phoe.			.25
174 Rick Tocchet, Wash.			.25
175 Chris Pronger, SLou.			.50
176 Matthew Barnaby, Buff.			.25
177 Andrei Kovalenko, Edmo.			.25
178 Bryan Smolinski, NYIs.			.25
179 Janne Niinimaa, Phil.			.25
180 Ray Ferraro, LosA.			.25
181 Dave Gagner, Calg.			.25
182 Rob Niedermayer, Flor.			.25
183 Vadim Sharifjanov, NJer.			.25
184 Ethan Moreau, Chic.			.25
185 Bernie Nicholls, SanJ.			.25
186 Jean-Yves Leroux, Chic. RC			**1.00**
187 Jere Lehtinen, Dall.			.25
188 Steve Rucchin, Anah.			.25
189 Keith Primeau, Hart.			.50
190 Checklist			.25

INSIDE TRACK

Insert Set (30 cards):	375.00
Insert (1:23)	IT
1 Wayne Gretzky, NYRa.	60.00
2 Patrick Roy (G), Colo.	45.00
3 Eric Lindros, Phil.	15.00
4 Paul Kariya, Anah.	20.00
5 Peter Forsberg, Colo.	20.00
6 Martin Brodeur (G), NJer.	20.00
7 John Vanbiesbrouck (G), Flor.	5.00
8 Joe Sakic, Colo.	20.00
9 Steve Yzerman, Detr.	35.00
10 Jaromir Jagr, Pitt.	15.00
11 Teemu Selänne, Anah.	10.00
12 Pavel Bure, Vanc.	10.00
13 Sergei Fedorov, Detr.	15.00
14 Brendan Shanahan, Detr.	15.00
15 Dominik Hasek (G), Buff.	15.00
16 Saku Koivu, Mont.	10.00
17 Jocelyn Thibault (G), Mont.	5.00
18 Mark Messier, NYRa.	15.00
19 Brett Hull, SLou.	15.00
20 Félix Potvin (G), Toro.	5.00
21 Curtis Joseph (G), Edmo.	15.00
22 Zigmund Palffy, NYIs.	5.00
23 Mats Sundin, Toro.	15.00
24 Keith Tkachuk, Phoe.	5.00
25 John LeClair, Phil.	10.00
26 Mike Richter (G), NYRa.	5.00
27 Alexander Mogilny, Vanc.	5.00
28 Jarome Iginla, Calg.	10.00
29 Mike Grier, Edm	5.00
30 Dainius Zubrus, Phil.	5.00

STAND-UP GUYS

Insert Set (20 cards):	20.00
Insert (1:1 Large Can)	SUG
1A/B T. Barrasso / M. Vernon	1.00
1C/D T. Barrasso / M. Vernon	1.00

2A/B M. Brodeur / J. Vanbiesbrouck (G)	3.00
2C/D M. Brodeur / J. Vanbiesbrouck (G)	3.00
3A/B J. Carey / J. Thibault	.50
3C/D J. Carey / J. Thibault	.50
4A/B M. Cousineau / G. Snow	.50
4C/D M. Cousineau / G. Snow	.50
5A/B É. Fichaud / P. Roy	4.50
5C/D É. Fichaud / P. Roy	4.50
6A/B G. Fuhr / P. Lalime	1.50
6C/D G. Fuhr / P. Lalime	1.50
7A/B J. Hackett / O. Kölzig	1.00
7C/D J. Hackett / O. Kölzig	1.00
8A/B G. Hebert / T. Kidd	.50
8C/D G. Hebert / T. Kidd	.50
9A/B C. Hirsch / N. Khabibulin	.50
9C/D C. Hirsch / N. Khabibulin	.50
10A/B K. Hrudey / Cu. Joseph	1.50
10C/D K. Hrudey / Cu. Joseph	1.50

STOPPERS

Disk Diametre: 2 1/2"

Insert Set (24 disks):	**165.00**
Insert (1:7)	**Stop.**
1 Patrick Roy (G), Colo.	35.00
2 John Vanbiesbrouck (G), Flor.	6.00
3 Dominik Hasek (G), Buff.	12.00
4 Martin Brodeur (G), NJer.	20.00
5 Mike Richter (G), NYRa.	6.00
6 Guy Hebert (G), Anah.	4.00
7 Jim Carey (G), Bost.	4.00
8 Jeff Hackett (G), Chic.	4.00
9 Roman Turek (G), Dall.	6.00
10 Kevin Hodson (G), Detr.	4.00
11 Mike Vernon (G), Detr.	4.00
12 Curtis Joseph (G), Edmo.	12.00
13 J.S. Giguère (G), Hart.	10.00
14 José Théodore (G), Mont.	18.00
15 Jocelyn Thibault (G), Mont.	4.00
16 Nikolai Khabibulin (G), Phoe.	4.00
17 Garth Snow (G), Phil.	4.00
18 Ron Hextall (G), Phil.	6.00
19 Steve Shields (G), Buff.	4.00
20 Grant Fuhr (G), Buff.	6.00
21 Félix Potvin (G), Toro.	6.00
22 Marcel Cousineau (G), Toro.	4.00
23 Bill Ranford (G), Wash.	4.00
24 Ed Belfour (G), SanJ.	12.00

CANS

There are two versions for each can: the regular can and the Gold parallel card. Prices below are for opened tins.

Insert Set (24 opened cans):	**95.00**	**20.00**
Tin Can	**Gold**	**Can**
1 Patrick Roy (G), Colo.	12.00	3.00
2 Martin Brodeur (G), NJer.	6.00	1.50
3 John Vanbiesbrouck (G), Flor.	2.00	.75
4 Curtis Joseph (G), Edmo.	4.00	1.00
5 Mike Richter (G), NYRa.	2.00	.75
6 Jocelyn Thibault (G), Mont.	2.00	.75
7 Guy Hebert (G), Anah.	2.00	.75
8 Mike Vernon (G), Detr.	2.00	.75
9 Wayne Gretzky, NYRa.	16.00	4.00
10 Paul Kariya, Anah.	5.50	1.00
11 Peter Forsberg, Colo.	5.50	1.00
12 Eric Lindros, Phil.	4.00	1.00
13 Jaromir Jagr, Pitt.	4.00	1.00
14 Steve Yzerman, Detr.	9.50	2.00
15 Joe Sakic, Colo.	6.00	1.50
16 Saku Koivu, Mont.	3.00	.75
17 John LeClair, Phil.	3.00	.75
18 Keith Tkachuk, Phoe.	2.00	.75
19 Teemu Selänne, Anah.	3.00	.75
20 Pavel Bure, Vanc.	3.00	.75
21 Brendan Shanahan, Detr.	4.00	1.00
22 Mark Messier, NYRa.	4.00	1.00
23 Mats Sundin, Toro.	4.00	1.00
24 Brett Hull, SLou.	4.00	1.00

LARGE CANS

There are two versions for each can: the regular can and the Gold parallel card. Prices below are for opened tins.

Insert Set (8 opened cans):	**35.00**	**5.00**
Tin Can	**Gold**	**Can**
Martin Brodeur (G), NJer.	8.00	2.00
Guy Hebert (G), Anah.	3.00	1.00
Curtis Joseph (G), Edmo.	5.00	1.00
Mike Richter (G), NYRa.	3.00	1.00
Patrick Roy (G), Colo.	15.00	3.50
Garth Snow (G), Phil.	3.00	1.00
Jocelyn Thibault (G), Mont.	3.00	1.00
2 John Vanbiesbrouck (G), Fla	3.00	1.00

1997 - 98 MINT COLLECTION

There are four versions for each card: a die-cut coin-holder card, a Bronze Mint Team card, a Silver Mint Team card and a Gold Mint Team card.

Complete Set (30 cards):	**450.00**	**200.00**	**30.00**	**15.00**
Player	**Gold**	**Silv.**	**Bro.**	**DC**
1 Eric Lindros	20.00	10.00	1.00	.50
2 Paul Kariya	25.00	10.00	2.00	1.00
3 Peter Forsberg	25.00	10.00	2.00	1.00
4 Vanbiesbrouck (G)	5.00	2.00	.50	.25
5 Steve Yzerman	45.00	20.00	3.00	1.50
6 B. Shanahan	20.00	10.00	1.00	.50
7 Teemu Selänne	15.00	5.00	1.00	.50
8 Dominik Hasek (G)	20.00	10.00	1.00	.50
9 Jarome Iginla	15.00	5.00	1.00	.50
10 Mats Sundin	20.00	10.00	1.00	.50
11 Patrick Roy (G)	60.00	30.00	4.00	2.00
12 Joe Sakic	30.00	15.00	2.00	1.00
13 Mark Messier	20.00	10.00	1.00	.50
14 Sergei Fedorov	20.00	10.00	1.00	.50
15 Saku Koivu	15.00	5.00	1.00	.50
16 M. Brodeur (G)	30.00	15.00	2.00	1.00
17 Pavel Bure	15.00	5.00	1.00	.50
18 Wayne Gretzky	80.00	40.00	6.00	3.00
19 Brian Leetch	10.00	5.00	.50	.25
20 John LeClair	15.00	5.00	1.00	.50
21 Keith Tkachuk	10.00	5.00	.50	.25
22 Jaromir Jagr	20.00	10.00	1.00	.50
23 Brett Hull	20.00	10.00	1.00	.50
24 Curtis Joseph (G)	20.00	10.00	1.00	.50
25 J. Svejkovsky	4.00	2.00	.50	.25
26 Sergei Samsonov	10.00	5.00	.50	.25
27 Alexei Morozov	4.00	2.00	.50	.25
28 Alyn McCauley	5.00	2.00	.50	.25
29 Joe Thornton	20.00	10.00	1.00	.50
30 V. Prospal RC	**10.00**	**5.00**	**1.50**	**1.00**

MINTERNATIONAL

Each player in this series has both a card and an oversized medallion.

Insert Set (6 cards or medallions):	**30.00**	**20.00**
Player	**Medal.**	**Card**
1 Eric Lindros, Phil.	10.00	6.00
2 Peter Forsberg, Colo.	14.00	10.00
3 Brett Hull, SLou.	10.00	6.00
4 Teemu Selänne, Anah.	8.00	6.00
5 Dominik Hasek (G), Buff.	10.00	6.00
6 Pavel Bure, Vanc.	8.00	6.00

MEDALLIONS

There are six versions of each medallion: a brass medallion, a brass Artist's Proof medallion, a nickel medallion, a nickel Artist's Proof medallion, a gold-plated medallion and a gold-plated Artist's Proof medallion (100 copies). The Gold-Plated and Nickel Artist's Proof medallions are priced similarly.

Complete Set (30 medallions):	**1225.00**	**210.00**	**40.00**
Medallion	**Gold**	**NS**	**Brass**
1 Eric Lindros	50.00	10.00	2.00
2 Paul Kariya	70.00	10.00	2.50
3 Peter Forsberg	70.00	10.00	2.50
4 John Vanbiesbrouck (G)	20.00	1.50	.75
5 Steve Yzerman	120.00	20.00	4.50
6 Brendan Shanahan	50.00	10.00	2.00
7 Teemu Selänne	40.00	5.00	1.50
8 Dominik Hasek (G)	50.00	10.00	2.00
9 Jarome Iginla	40.00	5.00	1.50
10 Mats Sundin	50.00	10.00	2.00
11 Patrick Roy (G)	150.00	30.00	6.00
12 Joe Sakic	80.00	15.00	3.00
13 Mark Messier	50.00	10.00	2.00
14 Sergei Fedorov	50.00	10.00	2.00
15 Saku Koivu	40.00	5.00	1.50
16 Martin Brodeur (G)	80.00	15.00	3.00
17 Pavel Bure	40.00	5.00	1.50
18 Wayne Gretzky	200.00	40.00	8.00
19 Brian Leetch	30.00	5.00	1.00
20 John LeClair	40.00	5.00	1.50
21 Keith Tkachuk	30.00	5.00	1.00
22 Jaromir Jagr	50.00	10.00	2.00
23 Brett Hull	50.00	10.00	2.00
24 Curtis Joseph (G)	50.00	10.00	2.00
25 Jaroslav Svejkovsky	6.00	1.50	.75
26 Sergei Samsonov	30.00	5.00	1.00
27 Alexei Morozov	10.00	1.50	.75
28 Alyn McCauley	15.00	1.50	.75
29 Joe Thornton	60.00	10.00	2.00
30 Vaclav Prospal	15.00	1.50	.75

MEDALLIONS

Complete Set (30 medallions):	**2400.00**	**1225.00**	**675.00**
Medallion	**Gold**	**NS**	**Brass**
1 Eric Lindros	100.00	50.00	30.00
2 Paul Kariya	140.00	70.00	40.00
3 Peter Forsberg	140.00	70.00	40.00
4 John Vanbiesbrouck (G)	45.00	20.00	10.00
5 Steve Yzerman	240.00	120.00	70.00
6 Brendan Shanahan	100.00	50.00	30.00
7 Teemu Selänne	80.00	40.00	20.00
8 Dominik Hasek (G)	100.00	50.00	30.00
9 Jarome Iginla	80.00	40.00	20.00
10 Mats Sundin	100.00	50.00	30.00
11 Patrick Roy (G)	300.00	150.00	90.00
12 Joe Sakic	160.00	80.00	45.00
13 Mark Messier	100.00	50.00	30.00
14 Sergei Fedorov	100.00	50.00	30.00
15 Saku Koivu	80.00	40.00	20.00
16 Martin Brodeur (G)	160.00	80.00	45.00
17 Pavel Bure	80.00	40.00	20.00
18 Wayne Gretzky	400.00	200.00	120.00
19 Brian Leetch	60.00	30.00	15.00
20 John LeClair	80.00	40.00	20.00
21 Keith Tkachuk	60.00	30.00	15.00
22 Jaromir Jagr	100.00	50.00	30.00
23 Brett Hull	100.00	50.00	30.00
24 Curtis Joseph (G)	100.00	50.00	30.00
25 Jaroslav Svejkovsky	15.00	6.00	4.00
26 Sergei Samsonov	60.00	30.00	15.00
27 Alexei Morozov	20.00	10.00	5.00
28 Alyn McCauley	30.00	15.00	5.00
29 Joe Thornton	120.00	60.00	35.00
30 Vaclav Prospal	30.00	15.00	5.00

1997 - 98 PINNACLE TOTALLY CERTIFIED

While these cards have the same checklist as Pinnacle Certified, they have different photography and are all serial numbered on the card back. Goalies (1-30) are shortprinted throughout the set. The four versions are Platinum Red (goalies numbered out 4,299, skaters numbered out of 6,199), Platinum Blue (goalies numbered out of 2,599, skaters numbered out of 3,099), Platinum Gold (goalies numbered out of 59, skaters numbered out of 69) and Platinum Mirror Gold (skaters numbered out of 30, goalies numbered out of 25). The Platinum Mirror Gold cards were available with the redemption of a Mirror Gold card only (Platinum Mirror Gold cards sell at approximately 2X the value of the Mirror Gold cards). Promo cards for this series also exist.

Complete Set (130 cards):	**6000.00**	**500.00**	**300.00**
Common Goalie:	**40.00**	**6.00**	**3.00**
Common Player:	**30.00**	**4.00**	**2.00**
Player	**Gold**	**Blue**	**Red**
1 Dominik Hasek (G), Buff.	160.00	10.00	10.00
2 Patrick Roy (G), Colo.	480.00	45.00	30.00
3 Martin Brodeur (G), NJer.	260.00	20.00	15.00
4 Chris Osgood (G), Detr.	90.00	6.00	6.00
5 Andy Moog (G), Dall.	60.00	6.00	4.00
6 J. Vanbiesbrouck (G), Flor.	70.00	6.00	4.00
7 S. Shields (G), Buff. RC	**70.00**	**10.00**	**12.00**
8 Mike Vernon (G), Detr.	60.00	6.00	4.00
9 Ed Belfour (G), SanJ.	160.00	15.00	10.00
10 Grant Fuhr (G), SLou.	90.00	6.00	6.00
11 Félix Potvin (G), Toro.	90.00	6.00	6.00
12 Bill Ranford (G), Wash.	60.00	6.00	4.00
13 Mike Richter (G), NYRa.	70.00	6.00	4.00
14 Stéphane Fiset (G), LosA.	50.00	6.00	3.00
15 Jim Carey (G), Bost.	40.00	6.00	3.00
16 Nikolai Khabibulin (G), Phoe.	60.00	6.00	4.00
17 Ken Wregget (G), Pitt.	40.00	6.00	3.00
18 Curtis Joseph (G), Edmo.	160.00	15.00	10.00
19 Guy Hebert (G), Anah.	40.00	6.00	3.00
20 Damian Rhodes (G), Ott.	40.00	6.00	3.00
21 Trevor Kidd (G), Calg.	50.00	6.00	3.00
22 Daren Puppa (G), Tamp.	40.00	6.00	3.00
23 Patrick Lalime (G), Pitt.	90.00	6.00	6.00
24 Tommy Salo (G), NYIs.	60.00	6.00	4.00
25 Sean Burke (G), Hart.	90.00	6.00	6.00
26 Jocelyn Thibault (G), Mont.	60.00	6.00	4.00
27 Kirk McLean (G), Vanc.	50.00	6.00	3.00
28 Garth Snow (G), Phil.	50.00	6.00	3.00
29 Ron Tugnutt (G), Ott.	60.00	6.00	4.00
30 Jeff Hackett (G), Chic.	50.00	6.00	3.00
31 Eric Lindros, Phil.	150.00	10.00	6.00
32 Peter Forsberg, Colo.	210.00	15.00	10.00
33 Mike Modano, Dall.	150.00	10.00	6.00
34 Paul Kariya, Anah.	210.00	15.00	10.00
35 Jaromir Jagr, Pitt.	150.00	10.00	6.00
36 Brian Leetch, NYRa.	90.00	5.00	4.00
37 Keith Tkachuk, Phoe.	90.00	5.00	4.00
38 Steve Yzerman, Detr.	360.00	30.00	15.00
39 Teemu Selänne, Anah.	120.00	10.00	6.00
40 Bryan Berard, NYIs.	45.00	4.00	2.00
41 Raymond Bourque, Bost.	180.00	15.00	8.00
42 Theoren Fleury, Calg.	90.00	5.00	4.00
43 Mark Messier, NYRa.	150.00	10.00	6.00
44 Saku Koivu, Mont.	120.00	10.00	6.00
45 Pavel Bure, Vanc.	110.00	10.00	6.00
46 Peter Bondra, Wash.	90.00	5.00	4.00
47 Dave Gagner, Calg. (Flor.)	30.00	4.00	2.00
48 Ed Jovanovski, Flor.	60.00	5.00	2.00
49 Adam Oates, Wash.	60.00	5.00	2.00
50 Joe Sakic, Colo.	240.00	20.00	12.00
51 Doug Gilmour, NJer.	90.00	5.00	4.00
52 Jim Campbell, SLou.	30.00	4.00	2.00
53 Mats Sundin, Toro.	150.00	10.00	6.00
54 Derian Hatcher, Dall.	45.00	4.00	2.00
55 Jarome Iginla, Calg.	120.00	10.00	6.00
56 Sergei Fedorov, Detr.	150.00	10.00	6.00
57 Keith Primeau, Hart.	60.00	5.00	2.00
58 Mark Recchi, Mont.	60.00	5.00	2.00
59 Owen Nolan, SanJ.	90.00	5.00	4.00
60 Alexander Mogilny, Vanc.	70.00	5.00	2.00
61 Brendan Shanahan, Detr.	150.00	10.00	6.00
62 Pierre Turgeon, SLou.	60.00	5.00	2.00
63 Joé Juneau, Wash.	35.00	4.00	2.00
64 Steve Rucchin, Anah.	35.00	4.00	2.00
65 Jeremy Roenick, Phoe.	120.00	10.00	6.00
66 Doug Weight, Edmo.	90.00	5.00	4.00
67 Valeri Kamensky, Colo.	45.00	4.00	2.00
68 Tony Amonte, Chic.	90.00	5.00	4.00
69 Dave Andreychuk, NJer.	45.00	4.00	2.00
70 Brett Hull, SLou.	150.00	10.00	6.00
71 Wendel Clark, Toro.	120.00	10.00	6.00
72 Vincent Damphousse, Mont.	90.00	5.00	4.00
73 Mike Grier, Edmo.	35.00	4.00	2.00
74 Chris Chelios, Chic.	90.00	5.00	4.00
75 Nicklas Lidström, Detr.	90.00	5.00	4.00
76 Joe Nieuwendyk, Dall.	60.00	5.00	2.00
77 Rob Blake, LosA.	90.00	5.00	4.00
78 Alexei Yashin, Ott.	90.00	5.00	4.00
79 Ryan Smyth, Edmo.	70.00	5.00	2.00
80 Pat LaFontaine, Buff.	90.00	5.00	4.00
81 Jeff Friesen, SanJ.	45.00	4.00	2.00
82 Ray Ferraro, LosA.	30.00	4.00	2.00
83 Steve Sullivan, Toro.	45.00	4.00	2.00
84 Chris Gratton, Tamp.	35.00	4.00	2.00
85 Mike Gartner, Phoe.	120.00	10.00	6.00
86 Kevin Hatcher, Pitt.	30.00	4.00	2.00
87 Ted Donato, Bost.	30.00	4.00	2.00
88 German Titov, Calg.	30.00	4.00	2.00
89 Sandis Ozolinsh, Colo.	35.00	4.00	2.00
90 Ray Sheppard, Flor.	30.00	4.00	2.00
91 John MacLean, NJer.	30.00	4.00	2.00
92 Luc Robitaille, LosA.	120.00	10.00	6.00
93 Rod Brind'Amour, Phil.	45.00	4.00	2.00
94 Zigmund Palffy, NYIs.	90.00	5.00	4.00
95 Peter Nedved, Pitt.	40.00	4.00	2.00
96 Adam Graves, NYRa.	60.00	5.00	2.00

97 Jozef Stumpel, Bost.	35.00	4.00	2.00
98 Alexandre Daigle, Ott.	30.00	4.00	2.00
99 Michael Peca, Buff.	60.00	5.00	2.00
100 Wayne Gretzky, NYRa.	600.00	50.00	30.00
101 Alexei Zhamnov, Chic.	45.00	4.00	2.00
102 Paul Coffey, Phil.	90.00	5.00	4.00
103 Oleg Tverdovsky, Phoe.	30.00	4.00	2.00
104 Trevor Linden, Vanc.	60.00	5.00	2.00
105 Dino Ciccarelli, Tamp.	45.00	4.00	2.00
106 Andrei Kovalenko, Edmo.	30.00	4.00	2.00
107 Scott Mellanby, Flor.	35.00	4.00	2.00
108 Bryan Smolinski, NYIs.	30.00	4.00	2.00
109 Bernie Nicholls, SanJ.	35.00	4.00	2.00
110 Derek Plante, Buff.	30.00	4.00	2.00
111 Pat Verbeek, Dall.	45.00	4.00	2.00
112 Adam Deadmarsh, Colo.	45.00	4.00	2.00
113 Martin Gelinas, Vanc.	35.00	4.00	2.00
114 Daniel Alfredsson, Ott.	90.00	5.00	4.00
115 Scott Stevens, NJer.	60.00	5.00	2.00
116 Dainius Zubrus, Phil.	35.00	4.00	2.00
117 Kirk Muller, Flor.	45.00	4.00	2.00
118 Brian Holzinger, Buff.	30.00	4.00	2.00
119 John LeClair, Phil.	120.00	10.00	6.00
120 Al MacInnis, SLou.	60.00	5.00	2.00
121 Ron Francis, Pitt.	90.00	5.00	4.00
122 Eric Dazé, Chic.	60.00	5.00	2.00
123 Travis Green, NYIs.	35.00	4.00	2.00
124 Jason Arnott, Edmo.	70.00	5.00	2.00
125 Geoff Sanderson, Hart.	35.00	4.00	2.00
126 Dimitri Khristich, LosA.	30.00	4.00	2.00
127 Sergei Berezin, Toro.	35.00	4.00	2.00
128 Jeff O'Neill, Hart.	60.00	5.00	2.00
129 Claude Lemieux, Colo.	45.00	4.00	2.00
130 Andrew Cassels, Hart.	35.00	4.00	2.00

4 Brian Leetch, NYRa.	1.50
5 Mark Messier, Vanc.	3.00
6 Jason Arnott, Edmo.	1.00
7 Paul Kariya, Anah.	4.00
8 Martin Brodeur (G), NJer.	4.50
9 Vincent Damphousse, Mont.	1.50
10 Steve Yzerman, Detr.	7.00
11 Brett Hull, SLou.	3.00
12 Chris Chelios, Chic.	1.50
13 Sergei Fedorov, Detr.	3.00
14 Nicklas Lidström, Detr.	1.50
15 Sergei Berezin, Toro.	1.00
16 Dominik Hasek, Buff.	3.00
17 Pavel Bure, Vanc.	2.00
18 Saku Koivu, Mont.	2.00
19 Teemu Selänne, Anah.	2.00
20 Peter Forsberg, Colo.	4.00
21 Jaromir Jagr, Pitt.	3.00
22 Peter Bondra, Wash.	1.50
23 Alexei Yashin, Otta.	1.50
24 Viacheslav Fetisov, Detr.	1.50
Player	**Auto.**
1 Eric Lindros, Phil. ✍ Black Ink	
1 Eric Lindros, Phil. ✍ Blue Ink	

WORLD'S BEST

Complete Set (6 cards):	**20.00**
Player	**Foil**
F1 Eric Lindros, Phil.	2.00
F2 Patrick Roy, Colo.	10.00
F3 Mark Messier, Vanc.	2.00
F4 Jason Arnott, Edmo.	.25
F5 Joe Sakic, Colo.	6.00
F6 Paul Kariya, Anah.	4.00

1997 - 98 PINNACLE UNCUT

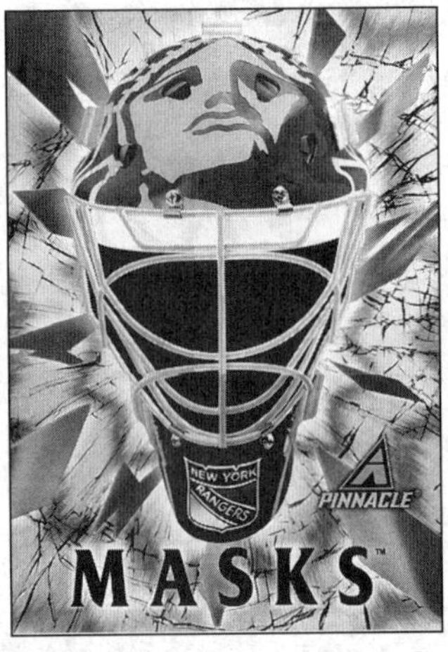

Size: 13 3/8" x 18 3/4"

Complete Set (7 cards):	**95.00**
Player	**Mask**
1 Martin Brodeur (G), NJer.	15.00
7 Garth Snow (G), Phil.	15.00
2 Mike Richter (G), NYRa.	15.00
3 Guy Hebert (G), Anah.	15.00
4 Curtis Joseph (G), Edmo.	15.00
5 Patrick Roy (G), Colo.	30.00
6 John Vanbiesbrouck (G), Flor.	15.00

1997 - 98 PINNACLE POST

These cards were inserted into specially-marked boxes of Post Cereals.

Complete Set (24 cards):	**55.00**
Common Player:	**1.00**
Player	**Post**
1 Eric Lindros, Phil.	3.00
2 Patrick Roy, Colo.	9.00
3 Joe Sakic, Colo.	4.50

1997 - 98 SCORE

Cards 1-160 have three versions: the regular card, a Golden Blades parallel (1:7) and an Artist's Proofs (1:35) parallel. Six players also have a promo card.

Complete Set (270 cards):	-	-	**35.00**
Parallel Set (160 cards):	**1100.00**	**215.00**	-
Common Player:	**3.00**	**.75**	**.20**
Player	**A.P.**	**G.B.**	**Score**
1 Sean Burke (G), Caro.	15.00	3.00	.20
2 Chris Osgood (G), Detr.	15.00	3.00	.20
3 Garth Snow (G), Phil.	8.00	1.00	.20
4 Mike Vernon (G), SanJ.	10.00	2.00	.20
5 Grant Fuhr (G), SLou.	15.00	3.00	.20
6 Guy Hebert (G), Anah.	6.00	1.00	.20
7 Arturs Irbe (G), Vanc.	10.00	2.00	.20
8 Andy Moog (G), Mont.	10.00	2.00	.20
9 Tommy Salo (G), NYIs.	10.00	2.00	.20
10 Nikolai Khabibulin (G), Phoe.	10.00	2.00	.20
11 Mike Richter (G), NYRa.	10.00	2.00	.20
12 Corey Hirsch (G), Vanc.	4.00	.75	.20
13 Bill Ranford (G), Wash.	10.00	2.00	.20
14 Jim Carey (G), Bost.	4.00	.75	.20
15 Jeff Hackett (G), Chic.	5.00	1.00	.20
16 Damian Rhodes (G), Ott.	6.00	1.00	.20
17 Tom Barrasso (G), Pitt.	10.00	2.00	.20
18 Daren Puppa (G), Tamp.	6.00	1.00	.20
19 Craig Billington (G), Colo.	4.00	.75	.20
20 Ed Belfour (G), Dall.	25.00	5.00	.50
21 M. Shtalenkov (G), Anah.	4.00	.75	.20
22 Glenn Healy (G), Toro.	6.00	1.00	.20
23 Marcel Cousineau (G), Toro.	3.00	.75	.20
24 Kevin Hodson (G), Detr.	6.00	1.00	.20
25 Olaf Kölzig (G), Wash.	15.00	3.00	.20
26 Éric Fichaud (G), NYIs.	4.00	.75	.20
27 Ron Hextall (G), Phil.	15.00	3.00	.20
28 Rick Tabaracci (G), Calg.	4.00	.75	.20
29 Félix Potvin (G), Toro.	15.00	3.00	.20
30 Martin Brodeur (G), NJer.	40.00	8.00	.50
31 Curtis Joseph (G), Edmo.	25.00	5.00	.50
32 Ken Wregget (G), Pitt.	6.00	1.00	.20
33 Patrick Roy (G), Colo.	70.00	15.00	1.50
34 Vanbiesbrouck (G), Flor.	10.00	2.00	.20
35 Stéphane Fiset (G), LosA.	8.00	1.00	.20
36 Roman Turek (G), Dall.	10.00	2.00	.20
37 Trevor Kidd (G), Caro.	8.00	1.00	.20
38 Dwayne Roloson (G), Calg.	4.00	.75	.20
39 Dominik Hasek (G), Buff.	25.00	5.00	.50
40 Patrick Lalime (G), Pitt.	15.00	3.00	.20
41 Jocelyn Thibault (G), Mont.	10.00	2.00	.20
42 José Théodore (G), Mont.	30.00	6.00	.50
43 Kirk McLean (G), Vanc.	8.00	1.00	.20
44 S. Shields (G), Buff. RC	**6.00**	**2.00**	**.50**
45 Mike Dunham (G), NJer.	10.00	2.00	.20
46 Jamie Storr (G), LosA.	6.00	1.00	.20
47 Byron Dafoe (G), Bost.	10.00	2.00	.20
48 Chris Terreri (G), Chic.	4.00	.75	.20
49 Ron Tugnutt (G), Ott.	10.00	2.00	.20
50 Kelly Hrudey (G), SanJ.	8.00	1.00	.20
51 Vaclav Prospal, Phil. RC	**8.00**	**3.00**	**1.00**
52 Alyn McCauley, Toro.	8.00	1.00	.20
53 Jaroslav Svejkovsky, Bost.	4.00	.75	.20
54 Joe Thornton, Bost.	30.00	6.00	1.00
55 Chris Dingman, Calg. RC	**4.00**	**1.00**	**.50**
56 Vadim Sharifjanov, NJer.	3.00	.75	.20
57 Larry Courville, Vanc.	3.00	.75	.20
58 Erik Rasmussen, Buff.	6.00	1.00	.20
59 Sergei Samsonov, Bost.	15.00	3.00	.50
60 Kevyn Adams, Toro.	4.00	.75	.20
61 Daniel Cleary, Chic.	8.00	1.00	.20
62 M. Prochazka, Toro. RC	**4.00**	**1.00**	**.50**
63 Mattias Öhlund, Vanc.	8.00	1.00	.20
64 Juha Lind, Dall. RC	**4.00**	**1.00**	**.50**
65 Olli Jokinen, LosA. RC	**8.00**	**3.00**	**1.00**
66 E. Knutsen, Anah. RC	**6.00**	**2.00**	**.50**
67 Marc Savard, NYRa.	6.00	1.00	.20
68 Hnat Domenichelli, Calg.	4.00	.75	.20
69 W. Luhning, NYIs. RC	**3.00**	**1.00**	**.20**
70 M. Arvedsson, Ott. RC	**4.00**	**1.00**	**.50**
71 Chris Phillips, Ott.	6.00	1.00	.20
72 Brad Isbister, Phoe.	6.00	1.00	.20
73 Boyd Devereaux, Edmo.	6.00	1.00	.20
74 Alexei Morozov, Pitt.	6.00	1.00	.20
75 V. Vorobiev, NYRa. RC	**3.00**	**1.00**	**.20**
76 Steve Rice, Caro.	3.00	.75	.20
77 Tony Granato, SanJ.	6.00	1.00	.20
78 Lonny Bohonos, Vanc.	3.00	.75	.20
79 Dave Gagner, Flor.	4.00	.75	.20
80 Brendan Shanahan, Detr.	25.00	5.00	.50
81 Brett Hull, SLou.	25.00	5.00	.50
82 Jaromir Jagr, Pitt.	20.00	5.00	.50
83 Peter Forsberg, Colo.	35.00	7.00	.50
84 Paul Kariya, Anah.	30.00	5.00	.50
85 Mark Messier, Vanc.	25.00	5.00	.50
86 Steve Yzerman, Detr.	60.00	10.00	1.00
87 Keith Tkachuk, Phoe.	15.00	3.00	.20
88 Eric Lindros, Phil.	25.00	5.00	.50
89 Raymond Bourque, Bost.	30.00	6.00	.50
90 Chris Chelios, Chic.	15.00	3.00	.20
91 Sergei Fedorov, Detr.	25.00	5.00	.50
92 Mike Modano, Dall.	25.00	5.00	.50
93 Doug Gilmour, NJer.	15.00	3.00	.20
94 Saku Koivu, Mont.	20.00	4.00	.20
95 Mats Sundin, Toro.	25.00	5.00	.50
96 Pavel Bure, Vanc.	20.00	4.00	.20
97 Theoren Fleury, Calg.	15.00	3.00	.20
98 Keith Primeau, Caro.	10.00	2.00	.20
99 Wayne Gretzky, NYRa.	100.00	20.00	2.00
100 Doug Weight, Edmo.	15.00	3.00	.20
101 Alexandre Daigle, Ott.	4.00	.75	.20
102 Owen Nolan, SanJ.	15.00	3.00	.20
103 Peter Bondra, Wash.	15.00	3.00	.20
104 Pat LaFontaine, NYRa.	15.00	3.00	.20
105 Kirk Muller, Flor.	8.00	1.00	.20
106 Zigmund Palffy, NYIs.	15.00	3.00	.20
107 Jeremy Roenick, Phoe.	20.00	4.00	.20
108 John LeClair, Phil.	20.00	4.00	.20
109 Derek Plante, Buff.	4.00	.75	.20
110 Geoff Sanderson, Caro.	6.00	1.00	.20
111 Dimitri Khristich, Bost.	4.00	.75	.20
112 V. Damphousse, Mont.	15.00	3.00	.20
113 Teemu Selänne, Anah.	20.00	4.00	.20
114 Tony Amonte, Chic.	15.00	3.00	.20
115 Dave Andreychuk, NJer.	8.00	1.00	.20
116 Alexei Yashin, Ott.	15.00	3.00	.20
117 Adam Oates, Wash.	10.00	2.00	.20
118 Pierre Turgeon, SLou.	10.00	2.00	.20
119 Dino Ciccarelli, Tamp.	8.00	1.00	.20
120 Ryan Smyth, Edmo.	10.00	2.00	.20
121 Ray Sheppard, Flor.	4.00	.75	.20
122 Jozef Stumpel, LosA.	6.00	1.00	.20
123 Jarome Iginla, Calg.	20.00	4.00	.20
124 Pat Verbeek, Dall.	8.00	1.00	.20
125 Joe Sakic, Colo.	40.00	8.00	.50
126 Brian Leetch, NYRa.	15.00	3.00	.20
127 Rod Brind'Amour, Phil.	8.00	1.00	.20
128 Wendel Clark, Toro.	20.00	4.00	.20
129 Alexander Mogilny, Vanc.	10.00	2.00	.20
130 Mark Recchi, Phil.	10.00	2.00	.20
131 Daniel Alfredsson, Ott.	15.00	3.00	.20
132 Ron Francis, Pitt.	15.00	3.00	.20
133 Martin Gelinas, Vanc.	6.00	1.00	.20
134 Andrew Cassels, Caro.	6.00	1.00	.20
135 Joe Nieuwendyk, Dall.	10.00	2.00	.20
136 Jason Arnott, Edmo.	10.00	2.00	.20
137 Bryan Berard, NYIs.	8.00	1.00	.20
138 Mikael Renberg, Tamp.	8.00	1.00	.20
139 Mike Gartner, Phoe.	20.00	4.00	.20
140 Joé Juneau, Wash.	6.00	1.00	.20
141 John MacLean, NJer.	4.00	.75	.20
142 Adam Graves, NYRa.	10.00	2.00	.20
143 Petr Nedved, Pitt.	5.00	1.00	.20
144 Trevor Linden, Vanc.	10.00	2.00	.20
145 Sergei Berezin, Toro.	6.00	1.00	.20
146 Adam Deadmarsh, Colo.	8.00	1.00	.20
147 Jeff O'Neill, Hart.	10.00	2.00	.20
148 Rob Blake, LosA.	15.00	3.00	.20
149 Robitaille, NYRa. (LosA.)	20.00	4.00	.20
150 Markus Näslund, Vanc.	25.00	5.00	.50
151 Ethan Moreau, Chic.	4.00	.75	.20
152 Martin Rucinsky, Mont.	6.00	1.00	.20
153 Mike Grier, Edmo.	6.00	1.00	.20
154 Craig Janney, Phoe.	6.00	1.00	.20
155 John Cullen, Tamp.	6.00	1.00	.20
156 Alex Kovalev, NYRa.	15.00	3.00	.20
157 Tony Twist, SLou.	4.00	.75	.20
158 Claude Lemieux, Colo.	8.00	1.00	.20
159 Kevin Stevens, NYRa.	6.00	1.00	.20
160 Mathieu Schneider, Toro.	6.00	1.00	.20
161 Randy Cunneyworth, Ott.			.20
162 Darius Kasparaitis, Pitt.			.20
163 Joe Murphy, SLou.			.20
164 Brandon Convery, Toro.			.20
165 Janne Niinimaa, Phil.			.20
166 Paul Coffey, Phil.			.20
167 Daymond Langkow, Tamp.			.20
168 Chris Gratton, Phil.			.20
169 Ray Ferraro, LosA.			.20
170 Jeff Friesen, SanJ.			.20
171 Ted Donato, Bost.			.20
172 Brian Holzinger, Buff.			.20
173 Travis Green, NYIs.			.20
174 Sandis Ozolinsh, Colo.			.20
175 Alexei Zhamnov, Chic.			.20
176 Steve Rucchin, Anah.			.20
177 Scott Mellanby, Flor.			.20
178 Andrei Kovalenko, Edmo.			.20
179 Donald Audette, Buff.			.20
180 Bernie Nicholls, SanJ.			.20
181 Jonas Höglund, Calg.			.20
182 Nicklas Lidström, Detr.			.20
183 Bobby Holik, NJer.			.20
184 Geoff Courtnall, SLou.			.20
185 Steve Sullivan, Toro.			.20
186 Valeri Kamensky, Colo.			.20
187 Michael Peca, Buff.			.20
188 Jere Lehtinen, Dall.			.20
189 Robert Svehla, Flor.			.20
190 Darren McCarty, Detr.			.20
191 Brian Savage, Mont.			.20
192 Harry York, SLou.			.20
193 Eric Dazé, Chic.			.20
194 Niklas Sundström, NYRa.			.20
195 Oleg Tverdovsky, Phoe.			.20
196 Éric Desjardins, Phil.			.20
197 German Titov, Calg.			.20
198 Derian Hatcher, Dall.			.20
199 Bill Guerin, NJer.			.20
200 Rob Zamuner, Tamp.			.20
201 Dale Hunter, Wash.			.20
202 Darcy Tucker, Mont.			.20
203 Andreas Dackell, Ott.			.20
204 Jason Dawe, Buff.			.20
205 Brian Rolston, NJer.			.20
206 Ed Olczyk, Pitt.			.20
207 Todd Warriner, Toro.			.20
208 Mariusz Czerkawski, NYIs.			.20
209 Vyacheslav Kozlov, Detr.			.20
210 Marty MacInnis, Calg.			.20
211 Jamie Langenbrunner, Dall.			.20
212 Vitali Yachmenev, LosA.			.20
213 Stéphane Richer, Mont.			.20
214 Roman Hamrlik, Tamp.			.20
215 Jim Campbell, SLou.			.20
216 Matthew Barnaby, Buff.			.20
217 Benoît Hogue, Dall.			.20
218 Robert Reichel, NYIs.			.20
219 Tie Domi, Toro.			.20
220 Steve Konowalchuk, Wash.			.20
221 Radek Dvorak, Flor.			.20
222 Kevin Hatcher, Pitt.			.20
223 Viktor Kozlov, SanJ.			.20
224 Scott Stevens, NJer.			.20
225 Cory Stillman, Calg.			.20
226 Anson Carter, Bost.			.20
227 Rem Murray, Edmo.			.20
228 Vladimir Konstantinov, Detr.			.20
229 Scott Niedermayer, NJer.			.20
230 Steve Duchesne, SLou.			.20
231 Valeri Bure, Mont.			.20
232 Miroslav Satan, Buff.			.20
233 Jason Allison, Bost.			.20

☐	234 Mark Fitzpatrick (G), Flor.	.20
☐	235 Ed Jovanovski, Flor.	.20
☐	236 Esa Tikkanen, Flor.	.20
☐	237 Stu Barnes, Pitt.	.20
☐	238 Darryl Sydor, Dall.	.20
☐	239 Ulf Samuelsson, NYRa.	.20
☐	240 Dmitri Mironov, Anah.	.20
☐	241 Bryan Smolinski, NYIs.	.20
☐	242 Rob Ray, Buff.	.20
☐	243 Todd Marchant, Edmo.	.20
☐	244 Cliff Ronning, Phoe.	.20
☐	245 Alexander Selivanov, Tamp.	.20
☐	246 Rick Tocchet, Phoe.	.20
☐	247 Vladimir Malakhov, Mont.	.20
☐	248 Al MacInnis, SLou.	.20
☐	249 Dainius Zubrus, Phil.	.20
☐	250 Keith Jones, Colo.	.20
☐	251 Darren Turcotte, SLou.	.20
☐	252 Ulf Dahlen, Chic.	.20
☐	253 Rob Niedermayer, Flor.	.20
☐	254 J.J. Daigneault, Anah.	.20
☐	255 Michal Grosek, Buff.	.20
☐	256 Chris Therien, Phil.	.20
☐	257 Adam Foote, Colo.	.20
☐	258 Tomas Sandström, Anah.	.20
☐	259 Scott Lachance, NYIs.	.20
☐	260 Paul Kariya, Anah.	.50
☐	261 Pavel Bure, Vanc.	.20
☐	262 Mike Modano, Dall.	.50
☐	263 Steve Yzerman, Detr.	1.00
☐	264 Sergei Fedorov, Detr.	.50
☐	265 Eric Lindros, Phil.	.50
☐	266 CL: Dominik Hasek (G), Buff.	.20
☐	267 CL: Bryan Berard, NYIs.	.20
☐	268 CL: Michael Peca, Buff.	.20
☐	269 CL: Brodeur (G)/ Dunham (G)	.20
☐	270 CL: Paul Kariya, Anah.	.20

CHECK IT

Insert Set (18 cards):		30.00
	Insert (1:18)	CI
☐	1 Eric Lindros, Phil. [vs. J.McKee]	3.00
☐	2 Mark Recchi, Mont.	2.00
☐	3 Brendan Shanahan, Detr. [vs. R.Dvorak]	3.00
☐	4 Keith Tkachuk, Phoe.	2.00
☐	5 John LeClair, Phil. [vs. D.Murzyn]	3.00
☐	6 Doug Gilmour, NJer. [vs. T.Green]	2.00
☐	7 Jarome Iginla, Calg. [vs. D.Reid]	3.00
☐	8 Ryan Smyth, Edmo.	2.00
☐	9 Chris Chelios, Chic. [vs. B.Holik]	2.00
☐	10 Mike Grier, Edmo. [vs. Flames]	2.00
☐	11 Vincent Damphousse, Mont. [vs. D.Gagner]	2.00
☐	12 Bryan Berard, NYIs. [vs. J.Dawe]	2.00
☐	13 Jaromir Jagr, Pitt. [vs. T.Green]	3.00
☐	14 Michael Peca, Buff. [vs. E.Desjardins]	2.00
☐	15 Dino Ciccarelli, Tamp.	2.00
☐	16 Rod Brind'Amour, Phil. [vs. B.Holik]	2.00
☐	17 Owen Nolan, SanJ. [vs. I.Moran]	2.00
☐	18 Pat Verbeek, Dall. [vs. D.McGillis]	2.00

NET WORTH

Insert Set (18 cards):		120.00
	Insert (1:35)	NW
☐	1 Guy Hebert (G), Anah.	3.00
☐	2 Jim Carey (G), Bost.	3.00
☐	3 Trevor Kidd (G), Calg.	4.00
☐	4 Chris Osgood (G), Detr.	6.00
☐	5 Curtis Joseph (G), Edmo.	10.00
☐	6 Mike Richter (G), NYRa.	6.00
☐	7 Damian Rhodes (G), Otta.	3.00
☐	8 Garth Snow (G), Phil.	4.00
☐	9 Nikolai Khabibulin (G), Phoe.	4.00
☐	10 Grant Fuhr (G), SLou.	6.00
☐	11 Jocelyn Thibault (G), Mont.	4.00
☐	12 Tommy Salo (G), NYIs.	4.00
☐	13 Patrick Roy (G), Colo.	35.00
☐	14 Martin Brodeur (G), NJer.	20.00
☐	15 John Vanbiesbrouck (G), Flor.	6.00
☐	16 Félix Potvin (G), Toro.	6.00
☐	17 Dominik Hasek (G), Buff.	10.00
☐	18 Ed Belfour (G), SanJ.	12.00

1997 - 98 SCORE TEAM SETS

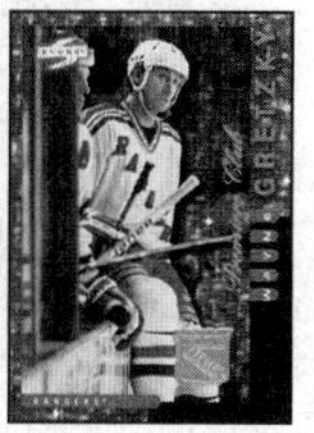

These cards have three versions: a regular card, a Platinum Team parallel [1:6] and a Premiere Club parallel [1:31].

Common Player:		3.00	1.00	0.30
	Player	PC	PT	Team
Mighty Ducks Set (20 cards):		80.00	25.00	10.00
☐☐☐	1 Paul Kariya	25.00	10.00	3.50
☐☐☐	2 Teemu Selänne	15.00	6.00	2.00
☐☐☐	3 Steve Rucchin	4.00	1.00	.50
☐☐☐	4 Dmitri Mironov	4.00	1.00	.30
☐☐☐	5 Matt Cullen	4.00	1.00	.50
☐☐☐	6 Kevin Todd	4.00	1.00	.30
☐☐☐	7 Joe Sacco	4.00	1.00	.30
☐☐☐	8 J.J. Daigneault	4.00	1.00	.30
☐☐☐	9 Darren Van Impe	4.00	1.00	.30
☐☐☐	10 Scott A. Young	5.00	2.00	.50
☐☐☐	11 Ted Drury	4.00	1.00	.30
☐☐☐	12 Tomas Sandström	4.00	1.00	.50
☐☐☐	13 Warren Rychel	4.00	1.00	.30
☐☐☐	14 Guy Hebert (G)	4.00	1.00	.50
☐☐☐	15 Shawn Antoski	4.00	1.00	.30
☐☐☐	16 Mikhail Shtalenkov (G)	4.00	1.00	.30
☐☐☐	17 Peter LeBoutillier	4.00	1.00	1.00
☐☐☐	18 Sean Pronger	4.00	1.00	.30
☐☐☐	19 Dave Karpa	4.00	1.00	.30
☐☐☐	20 Espen Knutsen	4.00	1.00	.50
Bruins Set (20 cards):		510.00	170.00	100.00
☐☐☐	1 Shawn Bates	4.00	1.00	.30
☐☐☐	2 Jim Carey (G)	4.00	1.00	.30
☐☐☐	3 Robbie Tallas (G) [Photo: Bailey]	4.00	1.00	.30
☐☐☐	4 Raymond Bourque	20.00	9.00	3.00
☐☐☐	5 Dmitri Khristich	4.00	1.00	.30
☐☐☐	6 Ted Donato	4.00	1.00	.30
☐☐☐	7 Jason Allison	10.00	4.00	1.50
☐☐☐	8 Anson Carter	5.00	3.00	1.00
☐☐☐	9 Rob DiMaio	4.00	1.00	.30
☐☐☐	10 Stephen Heinze	4.00	1.00	.30
☐☐☐	11 Jean-Yves Roy	4.00	1.00	.30
☐☐☐	12 Randy Robitaille	4.00	1.00	.30
☐☐☐	13 Byron Dafoe (G)	5.00	3.00	1.00
☐☐☐	14 Sergei Samsonov	10.00	4.00	1.50
☐☐☐	15 Ken Baumgartner	4.00	1.00	.30
☐☐☐	16 Dave Ellett	4.00	1.00	.30
☐☐☐	17 Joe Thornton	20.00	9.00	6.00
☐☐☐	18 Jeff Odgers	4.00	1.00	.30
☐☐☐	19 Kyle McLaren	4.00	1.00	.50
☐☐☐	20 Don Sweeney	4.00	1.00	.30
Sabres Set (20 cards):		530.00	175.00	98.00
☐☐☐	1 Dominik Hasek (G)	20.00	5.00	2.50
☐☐☐	2 Steve Shields (G)	4.00	1.00	.50
☐☐☐	3 Dixon Ward	4.00	1.00	.30
☐☐☐	4 Donald Audette	5.00	3.00	1.00
☐☐☐	5 Matthew Barnaby	4.00	1.00	.30
☐☐☐	6 Randy Burridge	4.00	1.00	.30
☐☐☐	7 Jason Dawe	4.00	1.00	.30
☐☐☐	8 Michal Grosek	4.00	1.00	.30
☐☐☐	9 Brian Holzinger	4.00	1.00	.30
☐☐☐	10 Brad May	4.00	1.00	.30
☐☐☐	11 Michael Peca	5.00	3.00	1.00
☐☐☐	12 Derek Plante	4.00	1.00	.30
☐☐☐	13 Wayne Primeau	4.00	1.00	.30
☐☐☐	14 Rob Ray	4.00	1.00	.50
☐☐☐	15 Miroslav Satan	5.00	2.00	.50
☐☐☐	16 Erik Rasmussen	4.00	1.00	.50
☐☐☐	17 Jason Woolley	4.00	1.00	.30
☐☐☐	18 Alexei Zhitnik	4.00	1.00	.30
☐☐☐	19 Darryl Shannon	4.00	1.00	.30
☐☐☐	20 Mike Wilson	4.00	1.00	.30
Avalanche Set (20 cards):		545.00	185.00	98.00
☐☐☐	1 Patrick Roy (G)	60.00	20.00	7.50
☐☐☐	2 Craig Billington (G)	4.00	1.00	.30
☐☐☐	3 Marc Denis (G)	5.00	3.00	1.00
☐☐☐	4 Peter Forsberg	25.00	10.00	3.50
☐☐☐	5 Jari Kurri	20.00	7.00	2.50
☐☐☐	6 Sandis Ozolinsh	4.00	1.00	.50
☐☐☐	7 Valeri Kamensky	5.00	2.00	.50
☐☐☐	8 Adam Deadmarsh	5.00	2.00	.50
☐☐☐	9 Keith Jones	4.00	1.00	.30
☐☐☐	10 Josef Marha	4.00	1.00	.30
☐☐☐	11 Claude Lemieux	5.00	2.00	.50
☐☐☐	12 Adam Foote	5.00	2.00	.50
☐☐☐	13 Éric Lacroix	4.00	1.00	.30
☐☐☐	14 René Corbet	4.00	1.00	.30
☐☐☐	15 Uwe Krupp	4.00	1.00	.30
☐☐☐	16 Sylvain Lefebvre	4.00	1.00	.30
☐☐☐	17 Mike Ricci	5.00	2.00	.50
☐☐☐	18 Joe Sakic	30.00	12.00	4.00
☐☐☐	19 Stéphane Yelle	4.00	1.00	.30
☐☐☐	20 Yves Sarault	4.00	1.00	.50
Red Wings Set (20 cards):		460.00	155.00	84.00
☐☐☐	1 Brendan Shanahan	20.00	7.00	2.50
☐☐☐	2 Steve Yzerman	45.00	15.00	6.00
☐☐☐	3 Sergei Fedorov	20.00	7.00	2.50
☐☐☐	4 Nicklas Lidström	10.00	4.00	1.50
☐☐☐	5 Igor Larionov	10.00	4.00	1.50
☐☐☐	6 Darren McCarty	5.00	2.00	.50
☐☐☐	7 Vyacheslav Kozlov	4.00	1.00	.50
☐☐☐	8 Larry Murphy	4.00	1.00	.50
☐☐☐	9 Vladimir Konstantinov	5.00	2.00	.50
☐☐☐	10 Martin Lapointe	5.00	3.00	1.00
☐☐☐	11 Viacheslav Fetisov	10.00	4.00	1.50
☐☐☐	12 Kris Draper	4.00	1.00	.50
☐☐☐	13 Doug Brown	4.00	1.00	.30
☐☐☐	14 Brent Gilchrist	4.00	1.00	.30
☐☐☐	15 Kirk Maltby	4.00	1.00	.50
☐☐☐	16 Tomas Holmström	4.00	1.00	.50
☐☐☐	17 Chris Osgood (G)	10.00	4.00	1.50
☐☐☐	18 Kevin Hodson (G)	4.00	1.00	.50
☐☐☐	19 Jamie Pushor	4.00	1.00	.30
☐☐☐	20 Mike Knuble	4.00	1.00	.30
Canadiens Set (20 cards):		425.00	140.00	74.00
☐☐☐	1 Andy Moog (G)	5.00	3.00	1.00
☐☐☐	2 Jocelyn Thibault (G)	5.00	3.00	1.00
☐☐☐	3 José Théodore (G)	20.00	9.00	3.00
☐☐☐	4 Vincent Damphousse	10.00	4.00	1.50
☐☐☐	5 Mark Recchi	5.00	3.00	1.00
☐☐☐	6 Brian Savage	5.00	2.00	.50
☐☐☐	7 Saku Koivu	15.00	6.00	2.00
☐☐☐	8 Stéphane J.J. Richer	4.00	1.00	.50
☐☐☐	9 Martin Rucinsky	4.00	1.00	.50
☐☐☐	10 Valeri Bure	5.00	2.00	.50
☐☐☐	11 Vladimir Malakhov	4.00	1.00	.30
☐☐☐	12 Shayne Corson	5.00	2.00	.50
☐☐☐	13 Darcy Tucker	4.00	1.00	.50
☐☐☐	14 Sébastien Bordeleau	4.00	1.00	.30
☐☐☐	15 Terry Ryan	4.00	1.00	.30
☐☐☐	16 David Ling	4.00	1.00	.50
☐☐☐	17 Dave Manson	4.00	1.00	.30
☐☐☐	18 Benoît Brunet	4.00	1.00	.30
☐☐☐	19 Marc Bureau	4.00	1.00	.30
☐☐☐	20 Patrice Brisebois	4.00	1.00	.30
Devils Set (20 cards):		435.00	140.00	70.00
☐☐☐	1 Doug Gilmour	10.00	4.00	1.50
☐☐☐	2 Bobby Holik	5.00	2.00	.50
☐☐☐	3 Dave Andreychuk	5.00	2.00	.50
☐☐☐	4 John MacLean	4.00	1.00	.30
☐☐☐	5 Bill Guerin	5.00	3.00	1.00
☐☐☐	6 Brian Rolston	5.00	2.00	.50
☐☐☐	7 Scott Niedermayer	5.00	2.00	.50
☐☐☐	8 Scott Stevens	5.00	3.00	1.00
☐☐☐	9 Valeri Zelepukin	4.00	1.00	.30
☐☐☐	10 Steve Thomas	4.00	1.00	.50
☐☐☐	11 Denis Pederson	4.00	1.00	.30
☐☐☐	12 Randy McKay	4.00	1.00	.30
☐☐☐	13 Mike Dunham (G)	5.00	3.00	1.00
☐☐☐	14 Petr Sykora	5.00	3.00	1.00
☐☐☐	15 Lyle Odelein	4.00	1.00	.30
☐☐☐	16 Martin Brodeur (G)	30.00	10.00	4.00
☐☐☐	17 Vadim Sharifijanov	4.00	1.00	.30
☐☐☐	18 Bob Carpenter	4.00	1.00	.50
☐☐☐	19 Sergei Brylin	4.00	1.00	.30
☐☐☐	20 Ken Daneyko	4.00	1.00	.50
Rangers Set (20 cards):		375.00	115.00	56.00
☐☐☐	1 Wayne Gretzky	80.00	30.00	10.00
☐☐☐	2 Brian Leetch	10.00	4.00	1.50
☐☐☐	3 Mike Keane	4.00	1.00	.30
☐☐☐	4 Adam Graves	5.00	3.00	1.00
☐☐☐	5 Niklas Sundström	4.00	1.00	.50
☐☐☐	6 Kevin Stevens	4.00	1.00	.50
☐☐☐	7 Alex Kovalev	10.00	4.00	1.50
☐☐☐	8 Alexander Karpovtsev	4.00	1.00	.30
☐☐☐	9 Bill Berg	4.00	1.00	.30
☐☐☐	10 Pat LaFontaine	10.00	4.00	1.50
☐☐☐	11 Bruce Driver	4.00	1.00	.30
☐☐☐	12 Patrick Flatley	4.00	1.00	.30
☐☐☐	13 Vladimir Vorobiev	4.00	1.00	.30
☐☐☐	14 Christian Dubé	4.00	1.00	.30
☐☐☐	15 Ulf Samuelsson	4.00	1.00	.30
☐☐☐	16 Mike Richter (G)	5.00	3.00	1.00
☐☐☐	17 Jason Muzzatti (G)	4.00	1.00	.30
☐☐☐	18 Daniel Goneau	4.00	1.00	.30
☐☐☐	19 Marc Savard	4.00	1.00	.50
☐☐☐	20 Jeff Beukeboom	4.00	1.00	.30
Flyers Set (20 cards):		310.00	90.00	44.00
☐☐☐	1 Ron Hextall (G)	10.00	4.00	1.50
☐☐☐	2 Garth Snow (G)	5.00	2.00	.50
☐☐☐	3 Eric Lindros	20.00	5.00	2.50
☐☐☐	4 John LeClair	15.00	6.00	2.00
☐☐☐	5 Rod Brind'Amour	5.00	2.00	.50
☐☐☐	6 Chris Gratton	4.00	1.00	.50
☐☐☐	7 Éric Desjardins	5.00	2.00	.50
☐☐☐	8 Trent Klatt	4.00	1.00	.30
☐☐☐	9 Janne Niinimaa	4.00	1.00	.50
☐☐☐	10 Luke Richardson	4.00	1.00	.30
☐☐☐	11 Paul Coffey	10.00	4.00	1.50
☐☐☐	12 Dainius Zubrus	4.00	1.00	.50
☐☐☐	13 Shjon Podein	4.00	1.00	.50
☐☐☐	14 Joel Otto	4.00	1.00	.30
☐☐☐	15 Chris Therien	4.00	1.00	.30
☐☐☐	16 Pat Falloon	4.00	1.00	.30
☐☐☐	17 Petr* Svoboda	4.00	1.00	.50
☐☐☐	18 Vaclav Prospal	5.00	2.00	.50
☐☐☐	19 John Druce	4.00	1.00	.30
☐☐☐	20 Daniel Lacroix	4.00	1.00	.30
Penguins Set (20 cards):		285.00	80.00	38.00
☐☐☐	1 Tom Barrasso (G)	5.00	3.00	1.00
☐☐☐	2 Ken Wregget (G)	4.00	1.00	.50
☐☐☐	3 Patrick Lalime (G)	10.00	4.00	1.50
☐☐☐	4 Jaromir Jagr	20.00	5.00	2.50
☐☐☐	5 Ron Francis	10.00	4.00	1.50
☐☐☐	6 Petr Nedved	5.00	2.00	.50
☐☐☐	7 Ed Olczyk	4.00	1.00	.50
☐☐☐	8 Kevin Hatcher	4.00	1.00	.30
☐☐☐	9 Stu Barnes	4.00	1.00	.30
☐☐☐	10 Darius Kasparaitis	4.00	1.00	.50
☐☐☐	11 Greg Johnson	4.00	1.00	.30
☐☐☐	12 Garry Valk	4.00	1.00	.30
☐☐☐	13 Roman Oksiuta	4.00	1.00	.30
☐☐☐	14 Dan Quinn	4.00	1.00	.30
☐☐☐	15 Alex Hicks	4.00	1.00	.30
☐☐☐	16 Robert Dome	4.00	1.00	.30
☐☐☐	17 Dave Roche	4.00	1.00	.30
☐☐☐	18 Aleksey Morozov	4.00	1.00	.50
☐☐☐	19 Rob (Jr.) Brown	4.00	1.00	.30
☐☐☐	20 Domenic Pittis	4.00	1.00	.30
Blues Set (20 cards):		250.00	70.00	30.00
☐☐☐	1 Brett Hull	20.00	7.00	2.50
☐☐☐	2 Pierre Turgeon	5.00	3.00	1.00
☐☐☐	3 Joe Murphy	4.00	1.00	.30
☐☐☐	4 Jim Campbell	4.00	1.00	.30
☐☐☐	5 Harry York	4.00	1.00	.30
☐☐☐	6 Al MacInnis	5.00	3.00	1.00
☐☐☐	7 Chris Pronger	10.00	4.00	1.50
☐☐☐	8 Darren Turcotte	4.00	1.00	.30
☐☐☐	9 Robert Petrovicky	4.00	1.00	.30
☐☐☐	10 Tony Twist	4.00	1.00	.30
☐☐☐	11 Grant Fuhr (G)	10.00	4.00	1.50
☐☐☐	12 Scott Pellerin	4.00	1.00	.30
☐☐☐	13 Jamie Rivers	4.00	1.00	.30
☐☐☐	14 Chris McAlpine	4.00	1.00	.30
☐☐☐	15 Geoff Courtnall	4.00	1.00	.30
☐☐☐	16 Steve Duchesne	4.00	1.00	.50
☐☐☐	17 Libor Zabransky	4.00	1.00	.30
☐☐☐	18 Pavol Demitra	5.00	3.00	1.00
☐☐☐	19 Marc Bergevin	4.00	1.00	.30
☐☐☐	20 Jamie McLennan (G)	4.00	1.00	.30
Maple Leafs Set (20 cards):		210.00	55.00	20.00
☐☐☐	1 Félix Potvin (G)	10.00	4.00	1.50
☐☐☐	2 Glenn Healy (G)	4.00	1.00	.50
☐☐☐	3 Marcel Cousineau (G)	4.00	1.00	.30
☐☐☐	4 Mats Sundin	20.00	7.00	2.50
☐☐☐	5 Wendel Clark	15.00	6.00	2.00
☐☐☐	6 Sergei Berezin	4.00	1.00	.50
☐☐☐	7 Steve Sullivan	5.00	2.00	.50
☐☐☐	8 Tie Domi	5.00	2.00	.50
☐☐☐	9 Todd Warriner	4.00	1.00	.30
☐☐☐	10 Mathieu Schneider	4.00	1.00	.50
☐☐☐	11 Mike Craig	4.00	1.00	.30
☐☐☐	12 Darby Hendrickson	4.00	1.00	.30
☐☐☐	13 Fredrik Modin	4.00	1.00	.50
☐☐☐	14 Brandon Convery	4.00	1.00	.30
☐☐☐	15 Kevyn Adams	4.00	1.00	.30
☐☐☐	16 Dmitry Yushkevich	4.00	1.00	.50
☐☐☐	17 Alyn McCauley	5.00	2.00	.50
☐☐☐	18 Derek King	4.00	1.00	.30
☐☐☐	19 Jamie Baker	4.00	1.00	.30
☐☐☐	20 Martin Prochazka	4.00	1.00	.30
Canucks Set (20 cards):		150.00	30.00	12.00
☐☐☐	1 Pavel Bure	15.00	5.00	2.00
☐☐☐	2 Alexander Mogilny	5.00	3.00	1.00
☐☐☐	3 Mark Messier	20.00	7.00	2.50
☐☐☐	4 Trevor Linden	5.00	3.00	1.00
☐☐☐	5 Martin Gélinas	4.00	1.00	.50
☐☐☐	6 Mattias Öhlund	5.00	2.00	.50
☐☐☐	7 Markus Näslund	20.00	7.00	2.50
☐☐☐	8 Jyrki Lumme	4.00	1.00	.50
☐☐☐	9 Lonny Bohonos	4.00	1.00	.30
☐☐☐	10 Kirk McLean (G)	5.00	2.00	.50
☐☐☐	11 Corey Hirsch (G)	4.00	1.00	.30
☐☐☐	12 Arturs Irbe (G)	5.00	3.00	1.00

☐☐☐	13 Larry Courville	4.00	1.00	.30
☐☐☐	14 Adrian Aucoin	4.00	1.00	.30
☐☐☐	15 Grant Ledyard	4.00	1.00	.30
☐☐☐	16 Gino Odjick	4.00	1.00	.30
☐☐☐	17 Donald Brashear	4.00	1.00	.50
☐☐☐	18 Brian Noonan	4.00	1.00	.30
☐☐☐	19 David Roberts	4.00	1.00	.30
☐☐☐	20 Dave Babych	4.00	1.00	.30

1997 - 98 SP AUTHENTIC

Complete Set (198 cards): 75.00
Common Player: .25

	Player	SPA
☐	1 Teemu Selänne, Anah.	1.00
☐	2 Sean Pronger, Anah.	.25
☐	3 Joe Sacco, Anah.	.25
☐	4 Tomas Sandström, Anah.	.25
☐	5 Steve Rucchin, Anah.	.25
☐	6 Paul Kariya, Anah.	1.50
☐	7 Ted Donato, Anah.	.25
☐	8 Raymond Bourque, Bost.	1.50
☐	9 Tim Taylor, Bost.	.25
☐	10 Jason Allison, Bost.	.50
☐	11 Kyle McLaren, Bost.	.25
☐	12 Dimitri Khristich, Bost.	.25
☐	13 Jason Dawe, Buff.	.25
☐	14 Dominik Hasek (G), Buff.	1.00
☐	15 Miroslav Satan, Buff.	.25
☐	16 Brian Holzinger, Buff.	.25
☐	17 Alexei Zhitnik, Buff.	.25
☐	18 Theoren Fleury, Calg.	.50
☐	19 Cory Stillman, Calg.	.25
☐	20 Jarome Iginla, Calg.	1.00
☐	21 Sandy McCarthy, Calg.	.25
☐	22 German Titov, Calg.	.25
☐	23 Glen Wesley, Caro.	.25
☐	24 Keith Primeau, Caro.	.50
☐	25 Geoff Sanderson, Caro.	.25
☐	26 Gary Roberts, Caro.	.50
☐	27 Sami Kapanen, Caro.	.25
☐	28 Jeff O'Neill, Caro.	.50
☐	29 Tony Amonte, Chic.	.50
☐	30 Chris Chelios, Chic.	.50
☐	31 Eric Dazé, Chic.	.50
☐	32 Alexei Zhamnov, Chic.	.25
☐	33 Chris Terreri (G), Chic.	.25
☐	34 Sergei Krivokrasov, Chic.	.25
☐	35 Joe Sakic, Colo.	2.00
☐	36 Peter Forsberg, Colo.	1.50
☐	37 Patrick Roy (G), Colo.	3.50
☐	38 Claude Lemieux, Colo.	.25
☐	39 Valeri Kamensky, Colo.	.25
☐	40 Adam Deadmarsh, Colo.	.25
☐	41 Sandis Ozolinsh, Colo.	.25
☐	42 Jari Kurri, Colo.	1.00
☐	43 Mike Modano, Dall.	1.00
☐	44 Ed Belfour, Dall.	1.00
☐	45 Derian Hatcher, Dall.	.25
☐	46 Sergei Zubov, Dall.	.25
☐	47 Jamie Langenbrunner, Dall.	.25
☐	48 Jere Lehtinen, Dall.	.25
☐	49 Joe Nieuwendyk, Dall.	.50
☐	50 Vyacheslav Kozlov, Detr.	.25
☐	51 Chris Osgood (G), Detr.	.50
☐	52 Steve Yzerman, Detr.	3.00
☐	53 Nicklas Lidström, Detr.	.50
☐	54 Igor Larionov, Detr.	.50
☐	55 Brendan Shanahan, Detr.	1.00
☐	56 Anders Eriksson, Detr.	.25
☐	57 Darren McCarty, Detr.	.25
☐	58 Doug Weight, Edmo.	.50
☐	59 Jason Arnott, Edmo.	.50
☐	60 Curtis Joseph (G), Edmo.	1.00
☐	61 Ryan Smyth, Edmo.	.50
☐	62 Dean McAmmond, Edmo.	.25
☐	63 Mike Grier, Edmo.	.25
☐	64 Kelly Buchberger, Edmo.	.25
☐	65 Ed Jovanovski, Flor.	.50
☐	66 Ray Whitney, Flor.	.25
☐	67 Rob Niedermayer, Flor.	.25
☐	68 Scott Mellanby, Flor.	.25
☐	69 John Vanbiesbrouck (G), Flor.	.50
☐	70 Viktor Kozlov, Flor.	.25
☐	71 Jozef Stumpel, LosA.	.25
☐	72 Rob Blake, LosA.	.50
☐	73 Garry Galley, LosA.	.25
☐	74 Vladimir Tsyplakov, LosA.	.25
☐	75 Yanic Perreault, LosA.	.25
☐	76 Stéphane Fiset (G), LosA.	.25
☐	77 Luc Robitaille, LosA.	1.00
☐	78 Valeri Bure, Mont.	.25
☐	79 Mark Recchi, Mont.	.50
☐	80 Saku Koivu, Mont.	1.00
☐	81 Andy Moog, Mont.	.50
☐	82 Vincent Damphousse, Mont.	.50
☐	83 Vladmir Malakhov, Mont.	.25
☐	84 Shayne Corson, Mont.	.25
☐	85 Scott Stevens, NJer.	.50
☐	86 Bill Guerin, NJer.	.50
☐	87 Martin Brodeur (G), NJer.	2.00
☐	88 Doug Gilmour, NJer.	.50
☐	89 Bobby Holik, NJer.	.25
☐	90 Petr Sykora, NJer.	.50
☐	91 Zigmund Palffy, NYIs.	.50
☐	92 Bryan Berard, NYIs.	.25
☐	93 Tommy Salo, NYIs.	.50
☐	94 Travis Green, NYIs.	.25
☐	95 Kenny Jönsson, NYIs.	.25
☐	96 Todd Bertuzzi, NYIs.	1.50
☐	97 Robert Reichel, NYIs.	.25
☐	98 Pat LaFontaine, NYRa.	.50
☐	99 Wayne Gretzky, NYRa.	5.00
☐	100 Brian Leetch, NYRa.	.50
☐	101 Mike Richter (G), NYRa.	.50
☐	102 Alex Kovalev, NYRa.	.50
☐	103 Adam Graves, NYRa.	.50
☐	104 Niklas Sundström, NYRa.	.25
☐	105 Alexei Yashin, Ott.	.50
☐	106 Daniel Alfredsson, Ott.	.50
☐	107 Alexandre Daigle, Ott.	.25
☐	108 Wade Redden, Ott.	.25
☐	109 Andreas Dackell, Ott.	.25
☐	110 Shawn McEachern, Ott.	.25
☐	111 Eric Lindros, Phil.	1.00
☐	112 Chris Gratton, Phil.	.25
☐	113 Paul Coffey, Phil.	.50
☐	114 John LeClair, Phil.	1.00
☐	115 Rod Brind'Amour, Phil.	.25
☐	116 Ron Hextall (G), Phil.	.50
☐	117 Dainius Zubrus, Phil.	.25
☐	118 Jeremy Roenick, Phoe.	1.00
☐	119 Keith Tkachuk, Phoe.	.50
☐	120 Nikolai Khabibulin (G), Phoe.	.50
☐	121 Rick Tocchet, Phoe.	.25
☐	122 Teppo Numminen, Phoe.	.25
☐	123 Craig Janney, Phoe.	.25
☐	124 Mike Gartner, Phoe.	1.00
☐	125 Jaromir Jagr, Pitt.	1.00
☐	126 Ron Francis, Pitt.	.50
☐	127 Kevin Hatcher, Pitt.	.25
☐	**128 Robert Dome, Pitt. RC**	**2.00**
☐	129 Martin Straka, Pitt.	.25
☐	**130 Petr Skudra (G), Pitt. RC**	**2.00**
☐	131 Owen Nolan, SanJ.	.50
☐	132 Bernie Nicholls, SanJ.	.25
☐	133 Mike Vernon (G), SanJ.	.50
☐	134 Jeff Friesen, SanJ.	.25
☐	135 Tony Granato, SanJ.	.25
☐	136 Mike Ricci, SanJ.	.25
☐	137 Jim Campbell, SLou.	.25
☐	138 Brett Hull, SLou.	1.00
☐	139 Chris Pronger, SLou.	.50
☐	140 Al MacInnis, SLou.	.50
☐	141 Pierre Turgeon, SLou.	.50
☐	142 Pavol Demitra, SLou.	.50
☐	143 Grant Fuhr (G), SLou.	.50
☐	144 Steve Duchesne, SLou.	.25
☐	145 Daymond Langkow, Tamp.	.25
☐	146 Alexander Selivanov, Tamp.	.25
☐	147 Daren Puppa (G), Tamp.	.25
☐	148 Dino Ciccarelli, Tamp.	.25
☐	149 Roman Hamrlik, Tamp.	.25
☐	150 Mats Sundin, Toro.	1.00
☐	151 Félix Potvin (G), Toro.	.50
☐	152 Wendel Clark, Toro.	1.00
☐	153 Sergei Berezin, Toro.	.25
☐	154 Steve Sullivan, Toro.	.25
☐	155 Alexander Mogilny, Vanc.	.50
☐	156 Pavel Bure, Vanc.	1.00
☐	157 Mark Messier, Vanc.	1.00
☐	158 Bret Hedican, Vanc.	.25
☐	159 Kirk McLean (G), Vanc.	.25
☐	160 Trevor Linden, Vanc.	.50
☐	**161 Dave Scatchard, Vanc. RC**	**1.00**
☐	162 Adam Oates, Wash.	.50
☐	163 Joé Juneau, Wash.	.25
☐	164 Peter Bondra, Wash.	.50
☐	165 Bill Ranford (G), Wash.	.50
☐	166 Sergei Gonchar, Wash.	.25
☐	167 Calle Johansson, Wash.	.25
☐	168 Phil Housley, Wash.	.25
☐	**169 Espen Knutsen, Anah. RC**	**3.00**
☐	**170 Pavel Trnka, Anah. RC**	**1.00**
☐	171 Joe Thornton, Bost.	3.00
☐	172 Sergei Samsonov, Bost.	1.50
☐	173 Erik Rasmussen, Buff.	.50
☐	**174 Tyler Moss (G), Calg. RC**	**2.00**
☐	**175 Derek Morris, Calg. RC**	**3.00**
☐	176 Craig Mills, Chic.	.25
☐	177 Daniel Cleary, Chic.	.50
☐	**178 Eric Messier, Colo. RC**	**2.00**
☐	179 Kevin Hodson (G), Detr.	.50
☐	**180 Mike Knuble, Detr. RC**	**1.00**
☐	181 Boyd Devereaux, Edmo.	.50
☐	**182 Craig Millar, Edmo. RC**	**1.00**
☐	**183 Kevin Weekes (G), Fla RC**	**4.00**
☐	**184 Donald MacLean, LosA. RC**	**1.00**
☐	**185 Patrik Elias, NJer. RC**	**10.00**
☐	**186 Zdeno Chara, NYIs. RC**	**6.00**
☐	187 Chris Phillips, Ott.	.50
☐	**188 Vaclav Prospal, Phil. RC**	**5.00**
☐	189 Brad Isbister, Phoe.	.50
☐	190 Alexei Morozov, Pitt.	.50
☐	191 Patrick Marleau, SanJ.	1.00
☐	**192 Marco Sturm, SanJ. RC**	**3.00**
☐	**193 Brendan Morrison, NJer. RC**	**4.50**
☐	**194 Mike Johnson, Toro. RC**	**2.50**
☐	195 Alyn McCauley, Toro.	.50
☐	196 Mattias Öhlund, Vanc.	.50
☐	197 Richard Zednik, Wash.	1.00
☐	**198 Jan Bulis, Wash. RC**	**1.00**

ICONS

These inserts have three versions. The regular insert (1:5), an embossed insert (1:12) and a die-cut insert (numbered out of 100).

Insert Set (40 cards):		**1900.00**	**125.00**	**95.00**
	Player	**D.C.**	**Emb.**	**Icon**
☐☐☐	I1 Pat LaFontaine, Buff.	40.00	1.50	2.00
☐☐☐	I2 Brett Hull, SLou.	70.00	5.00	3.00
☐☐☐	I3 Chris Chelios, Chic.	40.00	1.50	2.00
☐☐☐	I4 Joe Sakic, Colo.	120.00	10.00	6.00
☐☐☐	I5 Vanbiesbrouck (G), Flor.	30.00	1.50	1.00
☐☐☐	I6 Patrik Elias, NJer.	120.00	10.00	6.00
☐☐☐	I7 Eric Lindros, Phil.	70.00	5.00	3.00
☐☐☐	I8 Jaromir Jagr, Pitt.	70.00	5.00	3.00
☐☐☐	I9 Joe Thornton, Bost.	90.00	5.00	6.00
☐☐☐	I10 Brendan Shanahan, Detr.	70.00	5.00	3.00
☐☐☐	I11 Paul Kariya, Anah.	100.00	5.00	5.00
☐☐☐	I12 Peter Forsberg, Colo.	100.00	5.00	5.00
☐☐☐	I13 Ed Belfour (G), Dall.	70.00	5.00	3.00
☐☐☐	I14 Martin Brodeur (G), NJer.	120.00	10.00	6.00
☐☐☐	I15 Alexei Morozov, Pitt.	15.00	1.50	1.00
☐☐☐	I16 Mark Messier, Vanc.	70.00	5.00	3.00
☐☐☐	I17 John LeClair, Phil.	60.00	5.00	3.00
☐☐☐	I18 Luc Robitaille, LosA.	60.00	5.00	3.00
☐☐☐	I19 Teemu Selänne, Anah.	60.00	5.00	3.00
☐☐☐	I20 Theoren Fleury, Calg.	40.00	1.50	2.00
☐☐☐	I21 Steve Yzerman, Detr.	180.00	15.00	9.00
☐☐☐	I22 Chris Phillips, Ott.	15.00	1.50	1.00
☐☐☐	I23 Keith Tkachuk, Phoe.	40.00	1.50	2.00
☐☐☐	I24 Patrick Roy (G), Colo.	220.00	15.00	10.00
☐☐☐	I25 Mark Recchi, Mont.	30.00	1.50	1.00
☐☐☐	I26 Wayne Gretzky, NYRa.	300.00	25.00	15.00
☐☐☐	I27 Dino Ciccarelli, Tamp.	20.00	1.50	1.00
☐☐☐	I28 Raymond Bourque, Bost.	90.00	5.00	4.00
☐☐☐	I29 Tony Amonte, Chic.	40.00	1.50	2.00
☐☐☐	I30 Daniel Alfredsson, Ott.	45.00	1.50	2.00
☐☐☐	I31 Saku Koivu, Mont.	60.00	5.00	3.00
☐☐☐	I32 Doug Weight, Edmo.	40.00	1.50	2.00
☐☐☐	I33 Mats Sundin, Toro.	70.00	5.00	3.00
☐☐☐	I34 Dominik Hasek (G), Buff.	70.00	5.00	3.00
☐☐☐	I35 Scott Stevens, NJer.	30.00	1.50	1.00
☐☐☐	I36 Pavel Bure, Vanc.	60.00	5.00	3.00
☐☐☐	I37 Mike Modano, Dall.	70.00	5.00	3.00
☐☐☐	I38 Zigmund Palffy, NYIs.	40.00	1.50	2.00
☐☐☐	I39 Brian Leetch, NYRa.	40.00	1.50	2.00
☐☐☐	I40 Marco Sturm, SanJ.	35.00	1.50	1.00

MARK OF A LEGEND

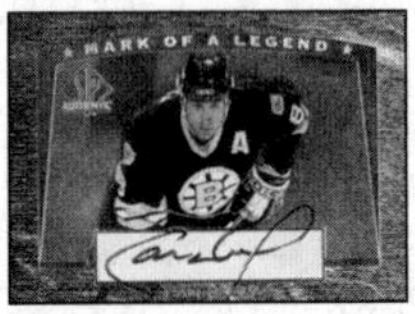

Insert Set (6 cards):		**675.00**
	Autograph	**Auto.**
☐	M1 Gordie Howe, Detr. ✍ {#/112}	310.00
☐	M2 Billy Smith ✍ (G), NYIs. ✍ {#/560}	40.00
☐	M3 Cam Neely, Bost. ✍ {#/560}	50.00
☐	M4 Bryan Trottier, NYIs. ✍ {#/560}	50.00
☐	M5 Bobby Hull, Chic. ✍ {#/560}	50.00
☐	M6 Wayne Gretzky, NYRa. ✍ {#/560}	300.00

SIGN OF THE TIMES

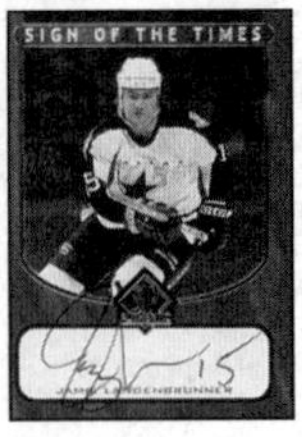

Insert Set (29 cards):		**1,000.00**
	Autograph (1:23)	**Auto.**
☐	Bryan Berard, NYIs. ✍	15.00
☐	Brian Holzinger, Buff. ✍	15.00
☐	Brett Hull, SLou. ✍	50.00
☐	Chris Chelios, Chic. ✍	30.00
☐	Darren McCarty, Detr. ✍	15.00
☐	Doug Weight, Edmo. ✍	30.00
☐	Dainius Zubrus, Phil. ✍	15.00
☐	Grant Fuhr (G), SLou. ✍	30.00
☐	Guy Hebert (G), Anah. ✍	15.00
☐	Jarome Iginla, Calg. ✍	40.00
☐	Jamie Langenbrunner, Dall. ✍	15.00
☐	Jaroslav Svejkovsky, Wash. ✍	15.00
☐	José Théodore, Mont. ✍	60.00
☐	Joe Thornton, Bost. ✍	50.00
☐	Martin Brodeur (G), NJer. ✍	80.00
☐	Mike Grier, Edmo. ✍	15.00
☐	Mats Sundin, Toro. ✍	50.00
☐	Nikolai Khabibulin (G), Phoe. ✍	20.00
☐	Nicklas Lidström, Detr. ✍	30.00
☐	Peter Bondra, Wash. ✍	30.00
☐	Patrick Roy (G), Colo. ✍	150.00
☐	Raymond Bourque, Bost. ✍	70.00
☐	Rob Niedermayer, Flor. ✍	15.00
☐	Sergei Berezin, Toro. ✍	15.00
☐	Sergei Samsonov, Bost. ✍	30.00
☐	Steve Yzerman, Detr. ✍	120.00
☐	Tony Amonte, Chic. ✍	30.00
☐	Wayne Gretzky, NYRa. ✍	275.00
☐	Yanic Perreault, LosA. ✍	15.00

TRADITION

Insert Set (6 cards):		**1400.00**
	Autograph (1:340)	**T**
☐	T1 Wayne Gretzky ✍ / Gordie Howe ✍	950.00
☐	T2 Patrick Roy (G) ✍ / Billy Smith (G) ✍	225.00
☐	T3 Joe Thornton ✍ / Cam Neely ✍	100.00
☐	T4 Bryan Berard ✍ / Bryan Trottier ✍	50.00
☐	T5 Brett Hull ✍ / Bobby Hull ✍	100.00
☐	T6 Raymond Bourque ✍ / Cam Neely ✍	225.00

1997 - 98 SP AUTHENTIC – BUYBACKS

Photo Photo-need

	Buyback Autograph	**SPA**
☐	15 Miroslav Satan, Buff. ✍ {#/3}	
☐	43 Mike Modano, Dall. ✍ {#/2}	
☐	53 Nicklas Lidström, Detr. ✍ {#/1}	

◆ The one-of-one Nicklas Lidström buyback autograph sold for $185.83 U.S. (approx. $278.75 Cdn.) in an Internet auction at eBay in March 2003.

☐	77 Luc Robitaille, LosA. ✍ {#/6}	
☐	91 Zigmund Palffy, NYIs. ✍ {#/13}	
☐	93 Tommy Salo, NYIs. ✍ {#/12}	
☐	99 Wayne Gretzky, NYRa. ✍ {#/2}	
☐	101 Mike Richter (G), NYRa. ✍ {#/8}	
☐	114 John LeClair, Phil. ✍ {#/10}	
☐	138 Brett Hull, SLou. ✍ {#/4}	
☐	138 Brett Hull, SLou. ✍ {#/3}	
☐	151 Félix Potvin (G), Toro. ✍ {#/5}	
☐	156 Pavel Bure, Vanc. ✍ {#/6}	
☐	157 Mark Messier, Vanc. ✍ {#/10}	
☐	172 Sergei Samsonov, Bost. ✍ {#/3}	
☐	**185 Patrik Elias, NJer. RC** ✍ {#/1}	
☐	**194 Mike Johnson, Toro. RC** ✍ {#/26}	
	Buyback Autograph • Icons	**SPA**
☐	I2 Brett Hull, SLou. ✍ {#/2}	
☐	I2 Brett Hull, SLou. ✍ {#/1}	

□	I17 John LeClair, Phil. ✍ {#/6}	
□	I18 Luc Robitaille, LosA. ✍ {#/6}	
□	I36 Pavel Bure, Vanc. ✍ {#/2}	
	Buyback Autograph • Icons Embossed	**SPA**
□	I36 Pavel Bure, Vanc. ✍ {#/3}	

1997 - 98 SP^X

These cards have six versions: the regular card, a Steel parallel, a Bronze parallel, a Silver parallel, a Gold parallel and a Grand Finale parallel (50 copies).

	Complete Set (50 cards):	**3800.00**	**100.00**	**50.00**
	Common Player:	**30.00**	**1.00**	**.50**
	Player	**GF50**	**Steel**	**SPx**
□□□	1 Paul Kariya	190.00	5.00	2.50
□□□	2 Teemu Selänne	110.00	3.00	1.50
□□□	3 Raymond Bourque	165.00	4.50	2.00
□□□	4 Dominik Hasek (G)	135.00	3.50	2.00
□□□	5 Pat LaFontaine	80.00	2.00	1.00
□□□	6 Theoren Fleury	80.00	2.00	1.00
□□□	7 Jarome Iginla	110.00	3.00	1.50
□□□	8 Tony Amonte	80.00	2.00	1.00
□□□	9 Chris Chelios	80.00	2.00	1.00
□□□	10 Patrick Roy (G)	410.00	10.00	6.00
□□□	11 Peter Forsberg	190.00	5.00	2.50
□□□	12 Joe Sakic	220.00	6.00	3.00
□□□	13 Mike Modano	135.00	3.50	2.00
□□□	14 Steve Yzerman	330.00	9.00	4.50
□□□	15 Sergei Fedorov	135.00	3.50	2.00
□□□	16 Brendan Shanahan	135.00	3.50	2.00
□□□	17 Doug Weight	80.00	2.00	1.00
□□□	18 Jason Arnott	65.00	1.50	.50
□□□	19 Curtis Joseph (G)	135.00	3.50	2.00
□□□	20 J.Vanbiesbrouck (G)	65.00	1.50	.50
□□□	21 Ed Jovanovski	55.00	1.50	.50
□□□	22 Geoff Sanderson	30.00	1.00	.50
□□□	23 Rob Blake	80.00	2.00	1.00
□□□	24 Saku Koivu	110.00	3.00	1.50
□□□	25 Doug Gilmour	80.00	2.00	1.00
□□□	26 Scott Stevens	55.00	1.50	.50
□□□	27 Martin Brodeur (G)	220.00	6.00	3.00
□□□	28 Zigmund Palffy	80.00	2.00	1.00
□□□	29 Bryan Berard	40.00	1.00	.50
□□□	30 Wayne Gretzky	550.00	15.00	8.00
□□□	31 Mike Richter (G)	65.00	1.50	.50
□□□	32 Mark Messier	135.00	3.50	2.00
□□□	33 Brian Leetch	80.00	2.00	1.00
□□□	34 Daniel Alfredsson	80.00	2.00	1.00
□□□	35 Alexei Yashin	80.00	2.00	1.00
□□□	36 Eric Lindros	135.00	3.50	2.00
□□□	37 Janne Niinimaa	30.00	1.00	.50
□□□	38 John LeClair	110.00	3.00	1.50
□□□	39 Jeremy Roenick	110.00	3.00	1.50
□□□	40 Keith Tkachuk	80.00	2.00	1.00
□□□	41 Ron Francis	80.00	2.00	1.00
□□□	42 Jaromir Jagr	135.00	3.50	2.00
□□□	43 Brett Hull	135.00	3.50	2.00
□□□	44 Owen Nolan	80.00	2.00	1.00
□□□	45 Chris Gratton	30.00	1.00	.50
□□□	46 Mats Sundin	135.00	3.50	2.00
□□□	47 Pavel Bure	110.00	3.00	1.50
□□□	48 Adam Oates	55.00	1.50	.50
□□□	49 Joé Juneau	30.00	1.00	.50
□□□	50 Peter Bondra	80.00	2.00	1.00

BRONZE, SILVER & GOLD PARALLELS

	Complete Set (50 cards):	**400.00**	**175.00**	**120.00**
	Player	**Gold**	**Silv.**	**Bro.**
□□□	1 Paul Kariya	20.00	10.00	6.00
□□□	2 Teemu Selänne	12.00	6.00	4.00
□□□	3 Raymond Bourque	18.00	8.00	6.00
□□□	4 Dominik Hasek (G)	14.00	6.00	4.00
□□□	5 Pat LaFontaine	8.00	4.00	2.00
□□□	6 Theoren Fleury	8.00	4.00	2.00
□□□	7 Jarome Iginla	12.00	6.00	4.00
□□□	8 Tony Amonte	8.00	4.00	2.00
□□□	9 Chris Chelios	8.00	4.00	2.00
□□□	10 Patrick Roy (G)	44.00	22.00	14.00
□□□	11 Peter Forsberg	20.00	10.00	6.00
□□□	12 Joe Sakic	24.00	12.00	8.00
□□□	13 Mike Modano	14.00	6.00	4.00
□□□	14 Steve Yzerman	36.00	18.00	12.00
□□□	15 Sergei Fedorov	14.00	6.00	4.00
□□□	16 Brendan Shanahan	14.00	6.00	4.00
□□□	17 Doug Weight	8.00	4.00	2.00
□□□	18 Jason Arnott	6.00	2.00	2.00
□□□	19 Curtis Joseph (G)	14.00	6.00	4.00
□□□	20 J.Vanbiesbrouck (G)	6.00	2.00	2.00
□□□	21 Ed Jovanovski	6.00	2.00	2.00
□□□	22 Geoff Sanderson	4.00	2.00	1.50
□□□	23 Rob Blake	8.00	4.00	2.00
□□□	24 Saku Koivu	12.00	6.00	4.00
□□□	25 Doug Gilmour	8.00	4.00	2.00
□□□	26 Scott Stevens	6.00	2.00	2.00
□□□	27 Martin Brodeur (G)	24.00	12.00	8.00
□□□	28 Zigmund Palffy	8.00	4.00	2.00
□□□	29 Bryan Berard	4.00	2.00	1.50
□□□	30 Wayne Gretzky	60.00	30.00	20.00
□□□	31 Mike Richter (G)	6.00	2.00	2.00
□□□	32 Mark Messier	14.00	6.00	4.00
□□□	33 Brian Leetch	8.00	4.00	2.00
□□□	34 Daniel Alfredsson	8.00	4.00	2.00
□□□	35 Alexei Yashin	8.00	4.00	2.00
□□□	36 Eric Lindros	14.00	6.00	4.00
□□□	37 Janne Niinimaa	4.00	2.00	1.50
□□□	38 John LeClair	12.00	6.00	4.00
□□□	39 Jeremy Roenick	12.00	6.00	4.00
□□□	40 Keith Tkachuk	8.00	4.00	2.00
□□□	41 Ron Francis	8.00	4.00	2.00
□□□	42 Jaromir Jagr	14.00	6.00	4.00
□□□	43 Brett Hull	14.00	6.00	4.00
□□□	44 Owen Nolan	8.00	4.00	2.00
□□□	45 Chris Gratton	4.00	2.00	1.50
□□□	46 Mats Sundin	14.00	6.00	4.00
□□□	47 Pavel Bure	12.00	6.00	4.00
□□□	48 Adam Oates	6.00	2.00	2.00
□□□	49 Joé Juneau	4.00	2.00	1.50
□□□	50 Peter Bondra	8.00	4.00	2.00

DIMENSION

	Insert Set (20 cards):	**575.00**
	Insert (1:54)	**SPXD**
□	SPX1 Wayne Gretzky, NYRa.	150.00
□	SPX2 Jeremy Roenick, Phoe.	30.00
□	SPX3 Mark Messier, NYRa.	35.00
□	SPX4 Eric Lindros, Phil.	30.00
□	SPX5 Doug Gilmour, NJer.	20.00
□	SPX6 Pavel Bure, Vanc.	30.00
□	SPX7 Brendan Shanahan, Detr.	35.00
□	SPX8 Bryan Berard, NYIs.	10.00
□	SPX9 Curtis Joseph (G), Edmo.	30.00
□	SPX10 Chris Chelios, Chic.	20.00
□	SPX11 Sergei Fedorov, Detr.	35.00
□	SPX12 Adam Oates, Wash.	15.00
□	SPX13 Zigmund Palffy, NYIs.	20.00
□	SPX14 Theoren Fleury, Calg.	20.00
□	SPX15 Keith Tkachuk, Phoe.	20.00
□	SPX16 Peter Forsberg, Colo.	50.00
□	SPX17 Mats Sundin, Toro.	35.00
□	SPX18 Teemu Selänne, Anah.	30.00
□	SPX19 Paul Kariya, Anah.	50.00
□	SPX20 Brett Hull, SLou.	35.00

DUOVIEW

	Insert Set (10 cards):	**850.00**
	Insert (1:252)	**DV**
□□	DV1 Wayne Gretzky, NYRa.	250.00
□□	Martin Brodeur (G), NJer.	100.00
□	Dominik Hasek (G), Buff.	60.00
□□	Jarome Iginla, Calg.	50.00
□□	Jaromir Jagr, Pitt.	60.00
□□	Patrick Roy (G), Colo.	180.00
□	Joe Sakic, Colo.	100.00
□	John Vanbiesbrouck (G), Flor.	30.00
□□	Doug Weight, Edmo.	35.00
□	Steve Yzerman, Detr.	150.00

DUOVIEW AUTOGRAPH

	Autograph Set (6 cards):	**1300.00**
	Inserts	**Auto.**
□□	Wayne Gretzky, NYRa. ✍	550.00
□□	Martin Brodeur (G), NJer. ✍	200.00
□□	Jarome Iginla, Calg. ✍	100.00
□□	Jaromir Jagr, Pitt. ✍	250.00
□□	Patrick Roy (G), Colo. ✍	375.00
□□	Doug Weight, Edmo. ✍	75.00

1997 - 98 STARTING LINEUP

One Fleer card (1996 - 97 design) was packaged with each figure. The Lemieux All-Star package included a special All-Star Lemieux card (not produced or resembling 1996 - 97 Fleer).

	Complete Set (22 cards):	**30.00**
	Player	**SLU**
□	7 Zigmund Palffy, NYIs.	1.00
□	Daniel Alfredsson, Otta.	1.00
□	Jason Arnott, Edmo.	1.00
□	Peter Bondra, Wash.	1.00
□	Martin Brodeur (G), NJer.	3.00
□	Chris Chelios, Chic.	1.00
□	Paul Coffey, Phil.	1.00
□	Peter Forsberg, Colo.	2.00
□	Wayne Gretzky, NYRa.	8.00
□	Ron Hextall (G), Phil.	1.00
□	Jaromir Jagr, Pitt.	2.00
□	Patrick Lalime (G), Pitt.	1.00
□	Eric Lindros, Phil.	2.00
□	Mark Messier, NYRa.	2.00
□	Chris Osgood (G), Detr.	1.00
□	Sandis Ozolinsh, SanJ.	1.00
□	Daren Puppa (G), Tamp.	1.00
□	Mark Recchi, Mont.	1.00
□	Teemu Selänne, Anah.	1.00
□	Keith Tkachuk, Phoe.	1.00
□	John Vanbiesbrouck (G), Flor.	1.00
□	Mario Lemieux, Pitt. (All-Star)	6.00

FIGURES

Figures were available in American (English text) and Canadian (bilingual text) packaging. The figures and cards in each type of package are the same. Priced below are retail selling prices for packaged figures (each package includes one card) and loose figures.

	Complete Set (22 packages):	**400.00**	**-**
	Complete Set (22 loose figures):	**-**	**75.00**
□	**Player**	**Pack.**	**Loose**
□	Daniel Alfredsson, Otta.	20.00	4.00
□	Jason Arnott, Edmo.	15.00	3.00
□	Peter Bondra, Wash.	15.00	3.00
□	Martin Brodeur (G), NJer.	25.00	5.00
□	Chris Chelios, Chic.	15.00	3.00
□	Paul Coffey, Phil.	20.00	4.00
□	Peter Forsberg, Colo.	20.00	4.00
□	Wayne Gretzky, NYRa.	50.00	10.00
□	Ron Hextall (G), Phil.	25.00	5.00
□	Jaromir Jagr, Pitt.	20.00	4.00
□	Patrick Lalime (G), Pitt.	25.00	5.00
□	Eric Lindros, Phil.	15.00	3.00
□	Mark Messier, NYRa.	15.00	3.00
□	Chris Osgood (G), Detr.	25.00	5.00
□	Sandis Ozolinsh, SanJ.	15.00	3.00
□	Zigmund Palffy, NYIs.	15.00	3.00
□	Daren Puppa (G), Tamp.	35.00	5.00
□	Mark Recchi, Mont.	15.00	3.00
□	Teemu Selänne, Anah.	15.00	3.00
□	Keith Tkachuk, Phoe.	15.00	3.00
□	John Vanbiesbrouck (G), Flor.	30.00	5.00
□	Mario Lemieux, Pitt. (All-Star)	35.00	6.00

1997 - 98 SLU CANADIAN LEGENDS

One card was packaged with each figure.

	Complete Set (20 cards):	**10.00**
	Player	**SLU**
□	Jean Béliveau, Mont.	4.00
□	Mike Bossy, NYIs.	3.00
□	Marcel Dionne, LosA.	2.00
□	Phil Esposito, Bost.	2.00
□	Glenn Hall, Chic.	2.00
□	Bernie Parent, Phil.	1.00

FIGURES

Figures were available in American (English text) and Canadian (bilingual text) packaging. The figures and cards in each type of package are the same. Priced below are retail selling prices for packaged figures (each package includes one card) and loose figures.

	Canadian Set (6 packages):	**75.00**	**-**
	Figure Set (6 loose figures):	**-**	**15.00**
	Player	**Pack.**	**Loose**
□	Jean Béliveau, Mont.	15.00	3.00
□	Mike Bossy, NYIs.	15.00	3.00
□	Marcel Dionne, LosA.	15.00	3.00
□	Phil Esposito, Bost.	15.00	3.00
□	Glenn Hall, Chic.	25.00	4.00
□	Bernie Parent, Phil.	25.00	4.00

1997 - 98 UPPER DECK

Thirty cards from each series have a Game-Dated foil parallel (seeded 1:1,500 packs). The Willie O'Ree promo card was handed out at the 1998 NHL All-Star Fanfest in Vancouver.

Series One Set (210 cards):	**-**	**35.00**
Series Two Set (210 cards):	**-**	**60.00**
Game-Dated Foil Set (60 cards):	**3100.00**	**-**

	Common Player:	**30.00**	**.20**
	Player	**Foil**	
□□	1 4/9/97: Teemu Selänne, Anah.	75.00	.50
□	2 Steve Rucchin, Anah.		.20
□	3 Kevin Todd, Anah.		.20
□	4 Darren Van Impe, Anah.		.20
□	5 Mark Janssens, Anah.		.20
□	6 Guy Hebert (G), Anah.		.20
□	7 Sean Pronger, Anah.		.20
□	8 Jason Allison, Bost.		.50
□□	9 3/27/97: Raymond Bourque, Bost.	125.00	1.00
□	10 Landon Wilson, Bost.		.20
□	11 Anson Carter, Bost.		.20
□	12 Jean-Yves Roy, Bost.		.20
□	13 Kyle McLaren, Bost.		.20
□	14 Don Sweeney, Bost.		.20
□	15 Brian Holzinger, Buff.		.20
□	16 Matthew Barnaby, Buff.		.20
□	17 Wayne Primeau, Buff.		.20
□	**18 Steve Shields (G), Buff. RC**		**1.50**
□	19 Jason Dawe, Buff.		.20
□	20 Donald Audette, Buff.		.20
□	21 Dixon Ward, Buff.		.20
□	22 Hnat Domenichelli, Calg.		.20
□	23 Trevor Kidd (G), Calg.		.20
□	24 Jarome Iginla, Calg.		.50
□	25 Sandy McCarthy, Calg.		.20
□	26 Marty McInnis, Calg.		.20
□	27 Jonas Höglund, Calg.		.20
□	28 Aaron Gavey, Calg.		.20
□	29 Keith Primeau, Hart. (Caro.)		.20
□□	30 1/18/97: Geoff Sanderson, Hart. (Caro.)	30.00	.20
□	31 Sean Burke (G), Hart. (Caro.)		.50
□	32 Steve Rice, Hart. (Caro.)		.20
□	33 Stu Grimson, Hart. (Caro.)		.20
□	34 Jeff O'Neill, Hart. (Caro.)		.20
□	35 Curtis Leschyshyn, Hart.		.20
□	36 Chris Chelios, Chic.		.50
□	37 Sergei Krivokrasov, Chic.		.20
□	38 Jeff Hackett (G), Chic.		.20
□	39 Bob Probert, Chic.		.20
□	40 Chris Terreri (G), Chic.		.20
□	41 Eric Dazé, Chic.		.20
□	42 Alexei Zhamnov, Chic.		.20
□□	43 5/24/97: Patrick Roy (G), Colo.	325.00	3.00
□	44 Sandis Ozolinsh, Colo.		.20
□	**45 Eric Messier, Colo. RC**		**1.00**
□	46 Adam Deadmarsh, Colo.		.20
□□	47 5/24/97: Claude Lemieux, Colo.	35.00	.20
□	48 Mike Ricci, Colo.		.20
□	49 Stéphane Yelle, Colo.		.20
□	50 Joe Nieuwendyk, Dall.		.20
□	51 Derian Hatcher, Dall.		.20
□	52 Jere Lehtinen, Dall.		.20
□	53 Roman Turek (G), Dall.		.20
□	54 Darryl Sydor, Dall.		.20
□	55 Todd Harvey, Dall.		.20
□	56 Mike Modano, Dall.		1.00
□□	57 6/7/97: Steve Yzerman, Detr.	250.00	2.00
□	58 Martin Lapointe, Detr.		.20
□□	59 6/7/97: Darren McCarty, Detr.	35.00	.20
□□	60 6/7/97: Mike Vernon (G), Detr.	45.00	.20
□	61 Kirk Maltby, Detr.		.20
□	62 Kris Draper, Detr.		.20
□□	63 6/7/97: Vladimir Konstantinov, Detr.	35.00	.20
□□	64 4/29/97: Todd Marchant, Edmo.	30.00	.20
□	65 Doug Weight, Edmo.		.50
□	66 Jason Arnott, Edmo.		.20
□	67 Mike Grier, Edmo.		.20
□	68 Mats Lindgren, Edmo.		.20
□	69 Bryan Marchment, Edmo.		.20
□	70 Rem Murray, Edmo.		.20
□	71 Radek Dvorak, Flor.		.20
□□	72 4/17/97: John Vanbiesbrouck (G), Flor.	50.00	.20
□	73 Robert Svehla, Flor.		.20
□	74 Bill Lindsay, Flor.		.20
□	75 Paul Laus, Flor.		.20
□	76 Kirk Muller, Flor.		.20
□	77 Dave Nemirovsky, Flor.		.20
□	78 Roman Vopat, LosA.		.20
□	79 Jan Vopat, LosA.		.20
□	80 Dimitri Khristich, LosA.		.20
□	81 Glen Murray, LosA.		.20
□	82 Mattias Norstrom, LosA.		.20
□	83 Ian Laperrière, LosA.		.20
□□	84 1/18/97: Mark Recchi, Mont.	45.00	.20

□ □ 85 11/6/96: José Théodore (G), Mont. 135.00 1.00
□ 86 Vincent Damphousse, Mont. .50
□ 87 Sébastien Bordeleau, Mont. .20
□ 88 Darcy Tucker, Mont. .20
□ 89 Martin Rucinsky, Mont. .20
□ 90 Jocelyn Thibault (G), Mont. .20
□ □ 91 2/26/97: Doug Gilmour, NJer. 50.00 .50
□ 92 Brian Rolston, NJer. .20
□ 93 Jay Pandolfo, NJer. .20
□ 94 John MacLean, NJer. .20
□ 95 Scott Stevens, NJer. .20
□ 96 Dave Andreychuk, NJer. .20
□ 97 Denis Pederson, NJer. .20
□ □ 98 6/19/97: Bryan Berard, NYIs. 35.00 .20
□ 99 Zigmund Palffy, NYIs. .50
□ 100 Bryan McCabe, NYIs. .20
□ 101 Rich Pilon, NYIs. .20
□ 102 Éric Fichaud (G), NYIs. .20
□ 103 Todd Bertuzzi, NYIs. 1.00
□ 104 Robert Reichel, NYIs. .20
□ □ 105 10/16/96: Christian Dubé, NYRa. 30.00 .20
□ 106 Niklas Sundström, NYRa. .20
□ □ 107 5/4/97: Mike Richter (G), NYRa. 50.00 .20
□ 108 Adam Graves, NYRa. .20
□ □ 109 5/18/97: Wayne Gretzky, NYRa. 450.00 4.00
□ 110 Bruce Driver, NYRa. .20
□ 111 Esa Tikkanen, NYRa. .20
□ □ 112 4/17/97: Daniel Alfredsson, Ott. 65.00 .50
□ 113 Ron Tugnutt (G), Ott. .20
□ 114 Steve Duchesne, Ott. .20
□ **115 Bruce Gardiner, Ott. RC** **.50**
□ 116 Sergei Zholtok, Ott. .20
□ 117 Alexandre Daigle, Ott. .20
□ □ 118 4/11/97: Wade Redden, Ott. 35.00 .20
□ 119 Mikael Renberg, Phil. .20
□ 120 Trent Klatt, Phil. .20
□ □ 121 5/25/97: Rod Brind'Amour, Phil. 35.00 .20
□ 122 Dainius Zubrus, Phil. .20
□ 123 John LeClair, Phil. .50
□ □ 124 5/16/97: Janne Niinimaa, Phil. 30.00 .20
□ **125 Vaclav Prospal, Phil. RC** **2.00**
□ □ 126 1/18/97: Keith Tkachuk, Phoe. 50.00 .50
□ 127 Jeremy Roenick, Phoe. .50
□ 128 Mike Gartner, Phoe. .50
□ 129 Nikolai Khabibulin (G), Phoe. .20
□ 130 Chad Kilger, Phoe. .20
□ 131 Shane Doan, Phoe. .20
□ 132 Cliff Ronning, Phoe. .20
□ □ 133 1/15/97: Patrick Lalime (G), Pitt. 65.00 .50
□ 134 Greg Johnson, Pitt. .20
□ □ 135 11/30/96: Ron Francis, Pitt. 50.00 .50
□ 136 Darius Kasparaitis, Pitt. .20
□ 137 Petr Nedved, Pitt. .20
□ 138 Jason Woolley, Pitt. .20
□ 139 Fredrik Olausson, Pitt. .20
□ 140 Harry York, SLou. .20
□ □ 141 12/22/96: Brett Hull, SLou. 100.00 1.00
□ 142 Chris Pronger, SLou. .50
□ □ 143 11/1/96: Jim Campbell, SLou. 30.00 .20
□ **144 Libor Zabransky, SLou. RC** **1.00**
□ 145 Grant Fuhr (G), SLou. .50
□ 146 Pavol Demitra, SLou. .20
□ □ 147 1/18/97: Owen Nolan, SanJ. 50.00 .50
□ **148 Stephen Guolla, SanJ. RC** **.50**
□ 149 Marcus Ragnarsson, SanJ. .20
□ 150 Bernie Nicholls, SanJ. .20
□ 151 Todd Gill, SanJ. .20
□ 152 Shean Donovan, SanJ. .20
□ 153 Corey Schwab (G), Tamp. .20
□ □ 154 2/20/97: Dino Ciccarelli, Tamp. 35.00 .20
□ 155 Chris Gratton, Tamp. .20
□ 156 Alexander Selivanov, Tamp. .20
□ 157 Roman Hamrlik, Tamp. .20
□ 158 Daymond Langkow, Tamp. .20
□ 159 Paul Ysebaert, Tamp. .20
□ 160 Steve Sullivan, Toro. .20
□ 161 Sergei Berezin, Toro. .20
□ 162 Fredrik Modin, Toro. .20
□ 163 Todd Warriner, Toro. .20
□ 164 Wendel Clark, Toro. .50
□ 165 Jason Podollan, Toro. .20
□ 166 Darby Hendrickson, Toro. .20
□ 167 Martin Gelinas, Vanc. .20
□ □ 168 1/18/97: Pavel Bure, Vanc. 75.00 .50
□ 169 Trevor Linden, Vanc. .20
□ 170 Mike Sillinger, Vanc. .20
□ 171 Corey Hirsch (G), Vanc. .20
□ 172 Lonny Bohonos, Vanc. .20
□ 173 Markus Näslund, Vanc. 1.00
□ 174 Steve Konowalchuk, Wash. .20
□ 175 Dale Hunter, Wash. .20
□ 176 Joé Juneau, Wash. .20
□ 177 Adam Oates, Wash. .20
□ 178 Bill Ranford (G), Wash. .20
□ 179 Pat Peake, Wash. .20
□ 180 Sergei Gonchar, Wash. .20
□ **181 Mike Leclerc, Anah. RC** **1.00**
□ **182 Randy Robitaille, Bost. RC** **2.00**
□ **183 Paxton Schafer (G), Bost. RC** **.50**
□ **184 Rumun Ndur, Buff. RC** **1.00**
□ **185 Christian Laflamme, Chic. RC** **.50**
□ **186 Wade Belak, Colo., RC** **.50**
□ **187 Mike Knuble, Detr. RC** **.50**
□ 188 Steve Kelly, Edmo. .20
□ **189 Patrik Elias, NJer. RC** **5.00**
□ **190 Ken Belanger, NYIs. RC** **.50**
□ **191 Colin Forbes, Phil. RC** **.50**
□ 192 Juha Ylönen, Phoe. .20
□ **193 David Cooper, Toro., RC** **1.00**
□ **194 D.J. Smith, Toro., RC** **.50**
□ 195 Jaroslav Svejkovsky, Wash. .20
□ 196 Tie Domi, Toro. .20
□ 197 Bob Probert, Chic. .20
□ 198 Doug Gilmour, NJer. .50
□ 199 Dino Ciccarelli, Tamp. .20
□ 200 Martin Gelinas, Vanc. .20
□ 201 Tony Twist, SLou. .20
□ 202 Claude Lemieux, Colo. .20
□ 203 Vladimir Konstantinov, Detr. .20
□ 204 Ulf Samuelsson, NYRa. .20
□ 205 Chris Simon, Wash. .20
□ 206 Gino Odjick, Vanc. .20
□ 207 Mike Grier, Edmo. .20
□ 208 Tony Amonte, Chic. .50
□ 209 CL: Wayne Gretzky, NYRa. .20
□ 210 CL: Patrick Roy (G), Colo. .20
□ □ 211 4/16/97: Paul Kariya, Anah. 150.00 1.00
□ 212 J.J. Daigneault, Anah. .20
□ 213 Dmitri Mironov, Anah. .20
□ 214 Joe Sacco, Anah. .20
□ 215 Richard Park, Anah. .20
□ **216 Espen Knutsen, Anah. RC** **1.50**
□ 217 Dave Karpa, Anah. .20
□ □ 218 6/21/97: Joe Thornton, Bost. 125.00 2.00
□ □ 219 6/21/97: Sergei Samsonov, Bost. 50.00 1.00
□ 220 P.J. Axelsson, Bost. .20
□ 221 Ted Donato, Bost. .20
□ 222 Dean Chynoweth, Bost. .20
□ **223 Rob Tallas (G), Bost. RC** **1.00**
□ 224 Mattias Timander, Bost. .20
□ □ 225 Dominik Hasek (G), Buff. 100.00 1.00
□ 226 Erik Rasmussen, Buff. .20
□ □ 227 6/19/97: Michael Peca, Buff. 45.00 .20
□ 228 Rob Ray, Buff. .20
□ 229 Vaclav Varada, Buff. .20
□ 230 Curtis Brown, Buff. .20
□ 231 Jay McKee, Buff. .20
□ □ 232 2/3/97: Theoren Fleury, Calg. 50.00 .50
□ **233 Derek Morris, Calg. RC** **1.50**
□ **234 Chris Dingman, Calg. RC** **1.00**
□ 235 Chris O'Sullivan, Calg. .20
□ 236 Rick Tabaracci (G), Calg. .20
□ 237 Tommy Albelin, Calg. .20
□ 238 Todd Simpson, Calg. .20
□ 239 Sami Kapanen, Caro. .20
□ □ 240 10/1/97: Gary Roberts, Caro. 45.00 .20
□ 241 Kevin Dineen, Caro. .20
□ 242 Kevin Haller, Caro. .20
□ 243 Nelson Emerson, Caro. .20
□ 244 Glen Wesley, Caro. .20
□ □ 245 1/18/97: Tony Amonte, Chic. 50.00 .50
□ 246 Eric Weinrich, Chic. .20
□ 247 Daniel Cleary, Chic. .50
□ 248 Jeff Shantz, Chic. .20
□ **249 Jean-Yves Leroux, Chic. RC** **.50**
□ 250 Ethan Moreau, Chic. .20
□ 251 Craig Mills, Chic. .20
□ □ 252 5/2/97: Peter Forsberg, Colo. 150.00 1.00
□ □ 253 10/15/96: Joe Sakic, Colo. 175.00 1.50
□ 254 Valeri Kamensky, Colo. .20
□ 255 Adam Foote, Colo. .20
□ 256 Josef Marha, Colo. .20
□ **257 Christian Matte, Colo. RC** **.50**
□ **258 Aaron Miller, Colo. RC** **.50**
□ 259 Ed Belfour (G), Dall. 1.00
□ 260 Jamie Langenbrunner, Dall. .20
□ **261 Juha Lind, Dall. RC** **1.00**
□ 262 Pat Verbeek, Dall. .20
□ 263 Sergei Zubov, Dall. .20
□ 264 Dave Reid, Dall. .20
□ 265 Greg Adams, Dall. .20
□ □ 266 6/7/97: Sergei Fedorov, Detr. 100.00 1.00
□ □ 267 6/7/97: Nicklas Lidström, Detr. 50.00 .50
□ □ 268 Brendan Shanahan, Detr. 100.00 1.00
□ 269 Chris Osgood (G), Detr. .50
□ 270 Aaron Ward, Detr. .20
□ □ 271 6/7/97: Vyacheslav Kozlov, Detr. 30.00 .20
□ 272 Kevin Hodson (G), Detr. .20
□ □ 273 4/29/97: Curtis Joseph (G), Edmo. 100.00 1.00
□ □ 274 4/25/97: Ryan Smyth, Edmo. 50.00 .20
□ 275 Dean McAmmond, Edmo. .20
□ 276 Boris Mironov, Edmo. .20
□ 277 Dennis Bonvie, Edmo. .20
□ 278 Kelly Buchberger, Edmo. .20
□ 279 Kevin Lowe, Edmo. .20
□ 280 Ray Sheppard, Flor. .20
□ 281 Rob Niedermayer, Flor. .20
□ □ 282 10/27/96: Scott Mellanby, Flor. 30.00 .20
□ 283 Terry Carkner, Flor. .20
□ 284 Ed Jovanovski, Flor. .20
□ 285 Gord Murphy, Flor. .20
□ 286 Tom Fitzgerald, Flor. .20
□ 287 Jamie Storr (G), LosA. .20
□ **288 Olli Jokinen, LosA. RC** **2.00**
□ 289 Vladimir Tsyplakov, LosA. .20
□ □ 290 10/12/97: Luc Robitaille, LosA. 75.00 .50
□ 291 Vitali Yachmenev, LosA. .20
□ **292 Donald MacLean, LosA. RC** **.50**
□ 293 Saku Koivu, Mont. .50
□ 294 Andy Moog (G), Mont. .20
□ 295 Patrice Brisebois, Mont. .20
□ **296 Brad Brown, Mont. RC** **.50**
□ 297 Turner Stevenson, Mont. .20
□ 298 Shayne Corson, Mont. .20
□ 299 Brian Savage, Mont. .20
□ □ 300 4/497: Martin Brodeur (G), NJer. 175.00 1.50
□ 301 Scott Niedermayer, NJer. .20
□ **302 Krzysztof Oliwa, NJer. RC** **1.50**
□ 303 Valeri Zelepukin, NJer. .20
□ 304 Bobby Holik, NJer. .20
□ 305 Ken Daneyko, NJer. .20
□ 306 Lyle Odelein, NJer. .20
□ 307 Travis Green, NYIs. .20
□ **308 Steve Webb, NYIs. RC** **.50**
□ 309 Dan Plante, NYIs. .20
□ 310 Bryan Smolinski, NYIs. .20
□ 311 Claude Lapointe, NYIs. .20
□ 312 Kenny Jönsson, NYIs. .20
□ 313 Ulf Samuelsson, NYRa. .20
□ 314 Jeff Beukeboom, NYRa. .20
□ 315 Mike Keane, NYRa. .20
□ □ 316 1/27/97: Brian Leetch, NYRa. 50.00 .50
□ 317 Shane Churla, NYRa. .20
□ 318 Pat LaFontaine, NYRa. .50
□ 319 Alex Kovalev, NYRa. .50
□ 320 Radek Bonk, Ott. .20
□ 321 Alexei Yashin, Ott. .50
□ 322 Damian Rhodes (G), Ott. .20
□ 323 Andreas Dackell, Ott. .20
□ **324 Magnus Arvedsson, Ott., RC** **1.00**
□ □ 325 6/22/96: Chris Phillips, Ott. 30.00 .20
□ **326 Marian Hossa, Ott. RC** **6.00**
□ 327 Chris Gratton, Phil. .20
□ 328 Shjon Podein, Phil. .20
□ □ 329 12/19/96: Paul Coffey, Phil. 50.00 .50
□ 330 Luke Richardson, Phil. .20
□ □ 331 1/18/97: Eric Lindros, Phil. 100.00 1.00
□ 332 Éric Desjardins, Phil. .20
□ 333 Joel Otto, Phil. .20
□ 334 Craig Janney, Phoe. .20
□ □ 335 1/18/97: Oleg Tverdovsky, Phoe. 30.00 .20
□ 336 Teppo Numminen, Phoe. .20
□ 337 Jim McKenzie, Phoe. .20
□ 338 Dallas Drake, Phoe. .20
□ 339 Rick Tocchet, Phoe. .20
□ 340 Brad Isbister, Phoe. .20
□ 341 Alexei Morozov, Pitt. .20
□ □ 342 11/30/96: Jaromir Jagr, Pitt. 100.00 1.00
□ 343 Kevin Hatcher, Pitt. .20
□ 344 Ken Wregget (G), Pitt. .20
□ 345 Chris Tamer, Pitt. .20
□ **346 Robert Dome, Pitt. RC** **1.00**
□ 347 Neil Wilkinson, Pitt. .20
□ 348 Chris McAlpine, SLou. .20
□ 349 Joe Murphy, SLou. .20
□ 350 Robert Petrovicky, SLou. .20
□ 351 Marc Bergevin, SLou. .20
□ 352 Al MacInnis, SLou. .20
□ □ 353 12/22/96: Pierre Turgeon, SLou. 30.00 .20
□ □ 354 6/21/97: Patrick Marleau, SanJ. 50.00 .50
□ **355 Marco Sturm, SanJ. RC** **1.50**
□ 356 Mike Vernon (G), SanJ. .20
□ 357 Al Iafrate, SanJ. .20
□ 358 Jeff Friesen, SanJ. .20
□ 359 Viktor Kozlov, SanJ. .20
□ □ 360 1/18/97: Tony Granato, SanJ. 30.00 .20
□ 361 Mikael Renberg, Tamp. .20
□ 362 Daren Puppa (G), Tamp. .20
□ 363 Roman Hamrlik, Tamp. .20
□ 364 Rob Zamuner, Tamp. .20
□ 365 Cory Cross, Tamp. .20
□ 366 Patrick Poulin, Tamp. .20
□ 367 Félix Potvin (G), Toro. .50
□ 368 Tie Domi, Toro. .20
□ □ 369 10/31/96: Mats Sundin, Toro. 100.00 1.00
□ 370 Jeff Ware, Toro. .20
□ 371 Alyn McCauley, Toro. .50
□ 372 Mathieu Schneider, Toro. .20
□ 373 Craig Wolanin, Toro. .20
□ □ 374 7/28/97: Mark Messier, Vanc. 100.00 1.00
□ 375 Kirk McLean (G), Vanc. .20
□ 376 Donald Brashear, Vanc. .20
□ 377 Arturs Irbe (G), Vanc. .20
□ 378 Jyrki Lumme, Vanc. .20
□ 379 Gino Odjick, Vanc. .20
□ 380 Mattias Öhlund, Vanc. .50
□ **381 Jan Bulis, Wash. RC** **.50**
□ 382 Andrew Brunette, Wash. .20
□ 383 Calle Johansson, Wash. .20
□ 384 Brendan Witt, Wash. .20
□ 385 Mark Tinordi, Wash. .20
□ 386 Ken Klee, Wash. .20
□ 387 Chris Simon, Wash. .20
□ 388 Richard Zednick, Wash. .20
□ 389 Ed Jovanovski, Flor. .20
□ 390 Darren McCarty, Detr. .20
□ 391 Darius Kasparaitis, Pitt. .20
□ 392 Bryan Marchment, Edmo. .20
□ 393 Matthew Barnaby, Buff. .20
□ 394 Chris Chelios, Chic. .50
□ 395 Ulf Samuelsson, NYRa. .20
□ 396 Scott Stevens, NJer. .20
□ 397 Derian Hatcher, Dall. .20
□ 398 Chris Pronger, SLou. .50
□ **399 Mathieu Chouinard (G), Cdn. RC** **2.00**
□ **400 Jake McCracken (G), Cdn. RC** **1.00**
□ **401 Bryan Allen, Cdn. RC** **2.00**
□ **402 Christian Chartier, Cdn. RC** **1.00**
□ **403 Jonathan Girard, Cdn. RC** **1.00**
□ **404 Abe Herbst, Cdn. RC** **1.00**
□ **405 Stephen Peat, Cdn., RC** **1.00**
□ **406 Robyn Regehr, Cdn. RC** **2.00**
□ **407 Blair Betts, Cdn. RC** **2.00**
□ **408 Éric Chouinard (G), Cdn. RC** **3.00**
□ **409 Brett DeCecco, Cdn. RC** **1.00**
□ **410 Rico Fata, Cdn., RC** **3.00**
□ **411 Simon Gagné, Cdn. RC** **15.00**
□ **412 Vincent Lecavalier, Cdn. RC** **6.00**
□ **413 Manny Malhotra, Cdn., RC** **1.50**
□ **414 Norm Milley, Cdn. RC** **2.00**
□ **415 Justin Papineau, Cdn. RC** **2.00**
□ **416 Garrett Prosofsky, Cdn. RC** **1.00**
□ **417 Mike Ribeiro, Cdn. RC** **4.00**
□ **418 Brad Richards, Cdn. RC** **6.00**
□ 419 CL: Wayne Gretzky, NYRa. .20
□ 420 CL: Patrick Roy (G), Colo. .20

GAME JERSEY

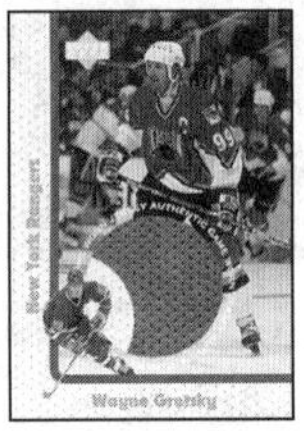

Insert Set (13 cards): **3200.00**

Goalie **GJ**

□ GJ1 Patrick Roy, Colo. ✂ 600.00
□ GJ2 Patrick Roy, Colo. ✂ 600.00
□ GJ3 Dominik Hasek, Buff. ✂ 200.00
□ GJ4 Jarome Iginla, Calg. ✂ 150.00
□ GJ5 Sergei Fedorov, Detr. ✂ 200.00
□ GJ6 Tony Amonte, Chic. ✂ 100.00
□ GJ7 Joe Sakic, Colo. ✂ 300.00
□ GJ8 Wayne Gretzky, NYRa. ✂ 1000.00
□ GJ9 Saku Koivu, Mont. ✂ 150.00
□ GJ11 Mike Richter, NYRa. ✂ 100.00
□ GJ12 Doug Weight, Edmo. ✂ 100.00
□ GJ13 Brendan Shanahan, Detr. ✂ 200.00
□ GJ14 Brian Leetch, NYRa. ✂ 100.00
□ Wayne Gretzky, NYRa. ✍ ✂ {#/99} 1200.00
□ Patrick Roy, Colo. ✍ ✂ {#/33} 1500.00

SIXTH SENSE

These Series Two cards have two versions: a Masters insert (#/2000) and a Wizards insert (#/100).

Insert Set (30 cards): **1900.00 375.00**

Inserts **W100 SS2000**

□ □ SS1 Wayne Gretzky, NYRa. 300.00 60.00
□ □ SS2 Jaromir Jagr, Pitt. 70.00 15.00
□ □ SS3 Sergei Fedorov, Detr. 70.00 15.00

☐☐	SS4 Brett Hull, SLou.	70.00	15.00
☐☐	SS5 Brian Leetch, NYRa.	40.00	6.00
☐☐	SS6 Joe Thornton, Bost.	90.00	25.00
☐☐	SS7 Raymond Bourque, Bost.	90.00	15.00
☐☐	SS8 Teemu Selänne, Anah.	60.00	10.00
☐☐	SS9 Paul Kariya, Anah.	100.00	20.00
☐☐	SS10 Doug Weight, Edmo.	40.00	6.00
☐☐	SS11 Mark Messier, Vanc.	70.00	15.00
☐☐	SS12 Adam Oates, Wash.	30.00	6.00
☐☐	SS13 Mats Sundin, Toro.	70.00	15.00
☐☐	SS14 Brendan Shanahan, Detr.	70.00	15.00
☐☐	SS15 Saku Koivu, Mont.	60.00	10.00
☐☐	SS16 Doug Gilmour, NJer.	40.00	6.00
☐☐	SS17 Eric Lindros, Phil.	70.00	15.00
☐☐	SS18 Tony Amonte, Chic.	40.00	6.00
☐☐	SS19 Joe Sakic, Colo.	120.00	20.00
☐☐	SS20 Steve Yzerman, Detr.	180.00	35.00
☐☐	SS21 Peter Forsberg, Colo.	100.00	20.00
☐☐	SS22 Geoff Sanderson, Hart.	20.00	6.00
☐☐	SS23 Keith Tkachuk, Phoe.	40.00	6.00
☐☐	SS24 Pavel Bure, Vanc.	60.00	10.00
☐☐	SS25 Ron Francis, Pitt.	45.00	6.00
☐☐	SS26 Zigmund Palffy, NYIs.	40.00	6.00
☐☐	SS27 Daniel Alfredsson, Ott.	45.00	6.00
☐☐	SS28 Bryan Berard, NYIs.	20.00	6.00
☐☐	SS29 Mike Modano, Dall.	70.00	15.00
☐☐	SS30 Patrick Roy (G), Colo.	220.00	45.00

SMOOTH GROOVES

Insert Set (60 cards):		**75.00**
	Insert (1:4)	**SG**
☐	SG1 Wayne Gretzky, NYRa.	12.00
☐	SG2 Patrick Roy (G), Colo.	8.00
☐	SG3 Patrick Marleau, SanJ.	.75
☐	SG4 Martin Brodeur (G), NJer.	4.00
☐	SG5 Zigmund Palffy, NYIs.	.75
☐	SG6 Joe Thornton, Bost.	2.00
☐	SG7 Chris Chelios, Chic.	.75
☐	SG8 Teemu Selänne, Anah.	2.00
☐	SG9 Paul Kariya, Anah.	4.00
☐	SG10 Tony Amonte, Chic.	.75
☐	SG11 Mark Messier, Vanc.	2.00
☐	SG12 Jarome Iginla, Calg.	2.00
☐	SG13 Mats Sundin, Toro.	2.00
☐	SG14 Brendan Shanahan,Detr.	2.00
☐	SG15 Ed Jovanovski, Flor.	.75
☐	SG16 Brett Hull, SLou.	2.00
☐	SG17 Brian Rolston, NJer.	.75
☐	SG18 Saku Koivu, Mont.	2.00
☐	SG19 Steve Yzerman, Detr.	6.00
☐	SG20 Doug Weight, Edmo.	.75
☐	SG21 Peter Forsberg, Colo.	4.00
☐	SG22 Brian Leetch, NYRa.	.75
☐	SG23 Alexei Yashin, Ott.	.75
☐	SG24 Owen Nolan, SanJ.	.75
☐	SG25 Mike Grier, Edmo.	.75
☐	SG26 Jere Lehtinen, Dall.	.75
☐	SG27 Vaclav Prospal, Phil.	.75
☐	SG28 Sandis Ozolinsh, Colo.	.75
☐	SG29 Mike Modano, Dall.	2.00
☐	SG30 Sergei Samsonov, Bost.	.75
☐	SG31 Curtis Joseph (G), Edmo.	2.00
☐	SG32 Daymond Langkow, Tamp.	.75
☐	SG33 Doug Gilmour, NJer.	.75
☐	SG34 Bryan Berard, NYIs.	.75
☐	SG35 Joe Sakic, Colo.	4.00
☐	SG36 Wade Redden, Ott.	.75
☐	SG37 Keith Tkachuk, Phoe.	.75
☐	SG38 Jaromir Jagr, Pitt.	2.00
☐	SG39 Dominik Hasek (G), Buff.	2.00
☐	SG40 Patrick Lalime (G), Pitt.	.75
☐	SG41 Janne Niinimaa, Phil.	.75
☐	SG42 Oleg Tverdovsky, Phoe.	.75
☐	SG43 Vitali Yachmenev, LosA.	.75
☐	SG44 Rob Niedermayer, Flor.	.75
☐	SG45 Nicklas Lidström, Detr.	.75
☐	SG46 Jim Campbell, SLou.	.75
☐	SG47 Roman Hamrlik, Tamp.	.75
☐	SG48 Eric Lindros, Phil.	2.00
☐	SG49 Brian Holzinger, Buff.	.75
☐	SG50 John LeClair, Phil.	2.00
☐	SG51 Sergei Berezin, Toro.	.75
☐	SG52 Jaroslav Svejkovsky, Wash.	.75
☐	SG53 Mike Richter (G), NYRa.	.75
☐	SG54 John Vanbiesbrouck (G), Flor.	.75
☐	SG55 Keith Primeau, Caro.	.75
☐	SG56 Adam Oates, Wash.	.75
☐	SG57 Jeremy Roenick, Phoe.	2.00
☐	SG58 Pavel Bure, Vanc.	2.00
☐	SG59 Dainius Zubrus, Phil.	.75
☐	SG60 José Théodore (G), Mont.	4.00

THE SPECIALISTS

These cards have two versions: a Level 1 insert (limited to 4,000 copies) and a Level 2 parallel (serial numbered from 1 to 100).

Insert Set (30 cards):		**2,000.00**	**250.00**
	Inserts	**S100**	**S4000**
☐☐	S1 Wayne Gretzky, NYRa.	300.00	40.00
☐☐	S2 Patrick Roy (G), Colo.	220.00	30.00
☐☐	S3 Jaromir Jagr, Pitt.	70.00	10.00
☐☐	S4 Joe Sakic, Colo.	120.00	15.00
☐☐	S5 Mark Messier, NYRa.	70.00	10.00
☐☐	S6 Eric Lindros, Phil.	70.00	10.00
☐☐	S7 John Vanbiesbrouck (G), Flor.	30.00	4.00
☐☐	S8 Teemu Selänne, Anah.	60.00	5.00
☐☐	S9 Paul Kariya, Anah.	100.00	10.00
☐☐	S10 Pavel Bure, Vanc.	60.00	5.00
☐☐	S11 Sergei Fedorov, Detr.	70.00	10.00
☐☐	S12 Peter Bondra, Wash.	40.00	5.00
☐☐	S13 Mats Sundin, Toro.	70.00	10.00
☐☐	S14 Brendan Shanahan, Detr.	70.00	10.00
☐☐	S15 Keith Tkachuk, Phoe.	40.00	5.00
☐☐	S16 Brett Hull, SLou.	70.00	10.00
☐☐	S17 Jeremy Roenick, Phoe.	60.00	5.00
☐☐	S18 Dominik Hasek (G), Buff.	70.00	10.00
☐☐	S19 Steve Yzerman, Detr.	180.00	20.00
☐☐	S20 John LeClair, Phil.	60.00	5.00
☐☐	S21 Peter Forsberg, Colo.	100.00	10.00
☐☐	S22 Zigmund Palffy, NYIs.	40.00	5.00
☐☐	S23 Tony Amonte, Chic.	40.00	5.00
☐☐	S24 Jarome Iginla, Calg.	60.00	5.00
☐☐	S25 Curtis Joseph (G), Edmo.	70.00	10.00
☐☐	S26 Mike Modano, Dall.	70.00	10.00
☐☐	S27 Raymond Bourque, Bost.	90.00	10.00
☐☐	S28 Brian Leetch, NYRa.	40.00	5.00
☐☐	S29 Bryan Berard, NYIs.	20.00	4.00
☐☐	S30 Martin Brodeur (G), NJer.	120.00	15.00

THREE-STAR SELECTS

Insert Set (60 cards):		**75.00**
	Insert (1:4)	**TSS**
☐	T1A Eric Lindros, Phil.	2.00
☐	T1B Wayne Gretzky, NYRa.	12.00
☐	T1C Peter Forsberg, Colo.	4.00
☐	T2A Dominik Hasek (G), Chic.	2.00
☐	T2B Patrick Roy (G), Colo.	8.00
☐	T2C John Vanbiesbrouck (G), Flor.	.75
☐	T3A Joe Sakic, Colo.	4.00
☐	T3B Steve Yzerman, Detr.	6.00
☐	T3C Paul Kariya, Anah.	4.00
☐	T4A Bryan Berard, NYIs.	.75
☐	T4B Brian Leetch, NYRa.	.75
☐	T4C Chris Chelios, Chic.	.75
☐	T5A Teemu Selänne, Anah.	2.00
☐	T5B Jaromir Jagr, Pitt.	2.00
☐	T5C Pavel Bure, Vanc.	2.00
☐	T6A Owen Nolan, SanJ.	.75
☐	T6B Brendan Shanahan, Detr.	2.00
☐	T6C Keith Tkachuk, Phoe.	.75
☐	T7A Sergei Fedorov, Detr.	2.00
☐	T7B Niklas Sundström, NYRa.	.75
☐	T7C Michael Peca, Buff.	.75
☐	T8A Janne Niinimaa, Phil.	.75
☐	T8B Saku Koivu, Mont.	2.00
☐	T8C Jere Lehtinen, Dall.	.75
☐	T9A Tony Amonte, Chic.	.75
☐	T9B John LeClair, Phil.	2.00
☐	T9C Brett Hull, SLou.	2.00
☐	T10A Martin Brodeur (G), NJer.	4.00
☐	T10B Curtis Joseph (G), Edmo.	2.00
☐	T10C Mike Richter (G), NYRa.	.75
☐	T11A Raymond Bourque, Bost.	2.00
☐	T11B Mark Messier, Vanc.	2.00
☐	T11C Scott Stevens, NJer.	.75
☐	T12A Patrick Lalime (G), Pitt.	.75
☐	T12B Marc Denis (G), Colo.	.75
☐	T12C José Théodore (G), Mont.	4.00
☐	T13A Adam Deadmarsh, Colo.	.75
☐	T13B Doug Weight, Edmo.	.75
☐	T13C Bill Guerin, NJer.	.75
☐	T14A Daniel Alfredsson, Ott.	.75
☐	T14B Mats Sundin, Toro.	2.00
☐	T14C Nicklas Lidström, Detr.	.75
☐	T15A Jim Campbell, SLou.	.75
☐	T15B Dainius Zubrus, Phil.	.75
☐	T15C Daymond Langkow, Tamp.	.75
☐	T16A Mike Grier, Edmo.	.75
☐	T16B Mike Modano, Dall.	2.00
☐	T16C Jeremy Roenick, Phoe.	2.00
☐	T17A Jason Arnott, Edmo.	.75
☐	T17B Trevor Linden, Vanc.	.75
☐	T17C Rod Brind'Amour, Phil.	.75
☐	T18A Adam Oates, Wash.	.75
☐	T18B Doug Gilmour, NJer.	.75
☐	T18C Joé Juneau, Wash.	.75
☐	T19A Sergei Berezin, Toro.	.75
☐	T19B Alexander Mogilny, Vanc.	.75
☐	T19C Alexei Zhamnov, Chic.	.75
☐	T20A Derian Hatcher, Dall.	.75
☐	T20B Wade Redden, Ott.	.75
☐	T20C Sandis Ozolinsh, Colo.	.75

1997 - 98 UPPER DECK – BUYBACKS

	Buyback Autograph	**SPA**
☐	9 Raymond Bourque, Bost. ✍ {#/1}	
☐	57 Steve Yzerman, Detr. ✍ {#/1}	
☐	85 José Théodore, Mont. ✍ {#/4}	
☐	107 Mike Richter (G), NYRa. ✍ {#/1}	
☐	109 Wayne Gretzky, NYRa. ✍ {#/1}	
☐	123 John LeClair, Phil. ✍ {#/7}	
☐	126 Keith Tkachuk, Phoe. ✍ {#/1}	
☐	273 Curtis Joseph (G), Edmo. ✍ {#/1}	
☐	300 Martin Brodeur (G), NJer. ✍ {#/7}	
☐	417 Mike Ribeiro, Canada RC ✍ {#/52}	

1997 - 98 UPPER DECK BLACK DIAMOND

These cards have four versions: a Single diamond, a Double diamond parallel, a Triple diamond parallel and a Quadruple diamond parallel. The Quadruple diamond parallel is limited to 50 copies.

Complete Set (150 cards):		**8400.00**	**475.00**	**200.00**	**125.00**
Common Player:		**20.00**	**1.50**	**.35**	**.20**
	Player	**Q50**	**TD**	**DD**	**BD**
☐☐☐☐	1 Alexei Zhitnik	20.00	1.50	.35	.20
☐☐☐☐	2 Adam Graves	50.00	1.50	1.00	.50
☐☐☐☐	3 Keith Primeau	50.00	1.50	1.00	.50
☐☐☐☐	4 Mike Richter (G)	60.00	1.50	1.00	.50
☐☐☐☐	5 Félix Potvin (G)	70.00	1.50	1.50	.50
☐☐☐☐	6 Valeri Bure	40.00	1.50	.50	.20
☐☐☐☐	7 Mark Messier	120.00	5.00	2.50	1.00
☐☐☐☐	8 Dainius Zubrus	30.00	1.50	.50	.20
☐☐☐☐	9 Owen Nolan	70.00	1.50	1.50	.50
☐☐☐☐	10 Kenny Jönsson	25.00	1.50	.50	.20
☐☐☐☐	11 Ron Francis	70.00	1.50	1.50	.50
☐☐☐☐	12 Bryan Berard	40.00	1.50	.50	.20
☐☐☐☐	**13 Éric Messier RC**	**20.00**	**1.50**	**2.00**	**1.50**
☐☐☐☐	14 Paul Kariya	170.00	10.00	3.50	1.50
☐☐☐☐	**15 T. Elomo RC**	**20.00**	**1.50**	**1.00**	**1.50**
☐☐☐☐	16 Joe Nieuwendyk	50.00	1.50	1.00	.50
☐☐☐☐	17 Scott Stevens	50.00	1.50	1.00	.50
☐☐☐☐	18 Zigmund Palffy	70.00	1.50	1.50	.50
☐☐☐☐	19 Brett Hull	120.00	5.00	2.50	1.00
☐☐☐☐	20 D. Hasek (G)	120.00	5.00	2.50	1.00
☐☐☐☐	21 Dino Ciccarelli	40.00	1.50	.50	.20
☐☐☐☐	22 R. Niedermayer	30.00	1.50	.50	.20
☐☐☐☐	23 Mark Recchi	50.00	1.50	1.00	.50
☐☐☐☐	24 Brad Isbister	30.00	1.50	1.00	.50
☐☐☐☐	**25 Timo Vertala RC**	**20.00**	**1.50**	**1.00**	**1.50**
☐☐☐☐	**26 Noronen (G) RC**	**75.00**	**20.00**	**10.00**	**8.00**
☐☐☐☐	27 Sandis Ozolinsh	30.00	1.50	.50	.20
☐☐☐☐	28 Chris Phillips	30.00	1.50	1.00	.50
☐☐☐☐	29 Chris Chelios	70.00	1.50	1.50	.50
☐☐☐☐	30 Jason Dawe	20.00	1.50	.35	.20
☐☐☐☐	31 Kirk McLean (G)	40.00	1.50	.50	.20
☐☐☐☐	32 Jason Allison	70.00	1.50	1.50	.50
☐☐☐☐	33 Brian Leetch	70.00	1.50	1.50	.50
☐☐☐☐	34 Guy Hebert (G)	30.00	1.50	.50	.20
☐☐☐☐	**35 D. Legwand RC**	**70.00**	**15.00**	**8.00**	**6.00**
☐☐☐☐	**36 Pierre Hedin RC**	**20.00**	**1.50**	**1.00**	**1.50**
☐☐☐☐	37 Sergei Samsonov	70.00	5.00	3.00	1.50
☐☐☐☐	38 Bill Guerin	50.00	1.50	1.00	.50
☐☐☐☐	39 Chris Osgood (G)	70.00	1.50	1.50	.50
☐☐☐☐	40 Jere Lehtinen	40.00	1.50	.50	.20
☐☐☐☐	41 Patrick Roy (G)	370.00	20.00	7.50	3.50
☐☐☐☐	42 Vanbiesbrouck (G)	60.00	1.50	1.00	.50
☐☐☐☐	**43 Afinogenov RC**	**70.00**	**20.00**	**10.00**	**6.00**
☐☐☐☐	**44 Patrik Elias RC**	**150.00**	**15.00**	**10.00**	**8.00**
☐☐☐☐	45 Josh Holden	20.00	1.50	.35	.20
☐☐☐☐	46 Saku Koivu	100.00	5.00	2.00	1.00
☐☐☐☐	**47 Bal'khnykh RC**	**30.00**	**5.00**	**3.00**	**2.00**
☐☐☐☐	48 Pasi Petriläinen	20.00	1.50	.35	.20
☐☐☐☐	49 Robert Reichel	40.00	1.50	.50	.20
☐☐☐☐	50 Wade Redden	40.00	1.50	.50	.20
☐☐☐☐	51 Richard Zednik	50.00	1.50	1.00	.50
☐☐☐☐	**52 Ty Jones RC**	**20.00**	**1.50**	**1.00**	**1.50**
☐☐☐☐	53 N. Khabibulin (G)	50.00	1.50	1.00	.50
☐☐☐☐	54 Kyle McLaren	30.00	1.50	.50	.20
☐☐☐☐	55 Daniel Tkaczuk	30.00	1.50	.50	.20
☐☐☐☐	56 Alexei Zhamnov	40.00	1.50	.50	.20
☐☐☐☐	**57 D. MacLean RC**	**20.00**	**1.50**	**1.00**	**1.00**
☐☐☐☐	58 Dave Gagner	20.00	1.50	.35	.20
☐☐☐☐	59 Jeremy Roenick	100.00	5.00	2.00	1.00
☐☐☐☐	60 R. Bourque	150.00	5.00	3.00	1.50
☐☐☐☐	61 Rod Brind'Amour	40.00	1.50	.50	.20
☐☐☐☐	62 Miroslav Satan	40.00	1.50	.50	.20
☐☐☐☐	63 Eric Dazé	50.00	1.50	1.00	.50
☐☐☐☐	64 Mike Ricci	40.00	1.50	.50	.20
☐☐☐☐	65 John LeClair	100.00	5.00	2.00	1.00
☐☐☐☐	66 Bryan Marchment	20.00	1.50	.35	.20
☐☐☐☐	**67 Henrik Petré RC**	**20.00**	**1.50**	**1.00**	**1.50**
☐☐☐☐	68 John MacLean	20.00	1.50	.35	.20
☐☐☐☐	**69 A. Chubarov RC**	**30.00**	**5.00**	**3.00**	**2.00**
☐☐☐☐	70 Doug Gilmour	70.00	1.50	1.50	.50
☐☐☐☐	**71 Marco Sturm RC**	**45.00**	**5.00**	**3.00**	**2.00**
☐☐☐☐	72 Jaromir Jagr	120.00	5.00	2.50	1.00
☐☐☐☐	73 Daniel Alfredsson	75.00	1.50	1.50	.50
☐☐☐☐	74 Daren Puppa (G)	30.00	1.50	.50	.20
☐☐☐☐	75 Adam Deadmarsh	40.00	1.50	.50	.20
☐☐☐☐	76 Luc Robitaille	100.00	5.00	2.00	1.00
☐☐☐☐	77 Mats Sundin	120.00	5.00	2.50	1.00
☐☐☐☐	78 Dan Cloutier (G)	50.00	1.50	2.00	1.00
☐☐☐☐	**79 M. Malhotra RC**	**45.00**	**5.00**	**3.00**	**2.00**
☐☐☐☐	80 Mike Modano	120.00	5.00	2.50	1.00
☐☐☐☐	**81 E. Knutsen RC**	**45.00**	**5.00**	**3.00**	**2.00**
☐☐☐☐	82 Sergei Fedorov	120.00	5.00	2.50	1.00
☐☐☐☐	83 Chris Pronger	70.00	1.50	1.50	.50
☐☐☐☐	84 Doug Weight	70.00	1.50	1.50	.50
☐☐☐☐	85 Dmitri Nabakov	20.00	1.50	.50	.20
☐☐☐☐	86 Gary Roberts	50.00	1.50	1.00	.50
☐☐☐☐	87 Peter Bondra	70.00	1.50	1.50	.50
☐☐☐☐	**88 Robert Dome RC**	**20.00**	**1.50**	**2.00**	**1.50**
☐☐☐☐	**89 Jan Bulis RC**	**20.00**	**1.50**	**1.00**	**1.00**
☐☐☐☐	**90 Eric Brewer RC**	**75.00**	**15.00**	**7.00**	**6.00**
☐☐☐☐	**91 Nikos Tselios RC**	**30.00**	**1.50**	**2.00**	**2.00**
☐☐☐☐	92 Scott Mellanby	30.00	1.50	.50	.20
☐☐☐☐	**93 V. Vishnevski RC**	**45.00**	**5.00**	**3.00**	**3.50**
☐☐☐☐	94 Derian Hatcher	40.00	1.50	.50	.20
☐☐☐☐	95 Teemu Selänne	100.00	5.00	2.00	1.00
☐☐☐☐	96 Joe Sakic	200.00	10.00	4.00	2.00
☐☐☐☐	97 A. Mogilny	60.00	1.50	1.00	.50
☐☐☐☐	**98 J. Boulerice RC**	**20.00**	**1.50**	**1.00**	**1.50**
☐☐☐☐	**99 J. Forsander RC**	**20.00**	**1.50**	**1.00**	**1.50**
☐☐☐☐	100 Pierre Turgeon	50.00	1.50	1.00	.50
☐☐☐☐	101 Tony Amonte	70.00	1.50	1.50	.50
☐☐☐☐	**102 T. Ahmaoja RC**	**20.00**	**1.50**	**1.00**	**1.50**
☐☐☐☐	103 Rob Blake	70.00	1.50	1.50	.50
☐☐☐☐	**104 Derek Morris RC**	**30.00**	**5.00**	**3.00**	**2.00**
☐☐☐☐	**105 A. Tanguay RC**	**110.00**	**30.00**	**15.00**	**8.00**
☐☐☐☐	106 Peter Forsberg	170.00	10.00	3.50	1.50
☐☐☐☐	107 Shayne Corson	40.00	1.50	.50	.20
☐☐☐☐	**108 T. Moss (G) RC**	**20.00**	**1.50**	**2.00**	**1.50**
☐☐☐☐	109 Adam Oates	50.00	1.50	1.00	.50
☐☐☐☐	110 Keith Tkachuk	70.00	1.50	1.50	.50
☐☐☐☐	111 Alexei Yashin	70.00	1.50	1.50	.50
☐☐☐☐	112 Joe Thornton	150.00	10.00	6.00	3.00
☐☐☐☐	113 Andy Moog (G)	50.00	1.50	1.00	.50
☐☐☐☐	**114 Daniel Sedin RC**	**70.00**	**20.00**	**10.00**	**9.00**
☐☐☐☐	115 Pavel Bure	100.00	5.00	2.00	1.00
☐☐☐☐	**116 D. Shvidki RC**	**45.00**	**10.00**	**4.50**	**5.00**
☐☐☐☐	117 Jason Arnott	60.00	1.50	1.00	.50
☐☐☐☐	**118 Mi. Johnson RC**	**35.00**	**1.50**	**2.50**	**2.00**
☐☐☐☐	119 Nicklas Lidström	70.00	1.50	1.50	.50
☐☐☐☐	120 Mattias Öhlund	40.00	1.50	1.50	.50

121 A. Selivanov	20.00	1.50	.35	.20
122 M. Brodeur (G)	200.00	10.00	4.00	2.00
123 Steve Yzerman	300.00	15.00	6.00	3.00
124 Vlasenkov RC	**20.00**	**1.50**	**1.00**	**1.50**
125 Jeff Farkas	45.00	5.00	3.00	2.00
126 Cu. Joseph (G)	120.00	5.00	2.50	1.00
127 Yanic Perreault	40.00	1.50	.50	.20
128 Alyn McCauley	40.00	1.50	1.50	.50
129 Vy. Kozlov	30.00	1.50	.50	.20
130 Aleksey Morozov	30.00	1.50	1.00	.50
131 Luongo (G) RC	**150.00**	**15.00**	**10.00**	**10.00**
132 Jarome Iginla	100.00	5.00	2.00	1.00
133 Pat LaFontaine	70.00	1.50	1.50	.50
134 Ed Belfour (G)	120.00	5.00	2.50	1.00
135 T. Petersen RC	**20.00**	**5.00**	**3.00**	**3.50**
136 H. Sedin RC	**70.00**	**20.00**	**10.00**	**9.00**
137 Marcus Nilsson	20.00	1.50	.35	.20
138 Cameron Mann	20.00	1.50	.35	.20
139 Somervuori RC	**20.00**	**1.50**	**1.00**	**1.50**
140 Patrick Marleau	60.00	5.00	2.00	1.00
141 Ed Jovanovski	50.00	1.50	1.00	.50
142 Roman Hamrlik	30.00	1.50	.50	.20
143 Theoren Fleury	70.00	1.50	1.50	.50
144 Wayne Gretzky	500.00	30.00	10.00	5.00
145 Eric Lindros	120.00	5.00	2.50	1.00
146 Boyd Devereaux	30.00	1.50	1.00	.50
147 Sami Kapanen	40.00	1.50	.50	.20
148 Grant Fuhr (G)	70.00	1.50	1.50	.50
149 B. Shanahan	120.00	5.00	2.50	1.00
150 Lecavalier RC	**180.00**	**45.00**	**20.00**	**10.00**

PREMIUM CUT

These cards have five versions: a Single diamond (1:17), a Double diamond parallel (1:15), a Triple diamond parallel (1:30), a Quadruple diamond parallel (1:180) and a Quadruple diamond horizontals (different odds).

Insert Set (30 cards):	**500.00**	**285.00**	**170.00**
Player	**TPC**	**DPC**	**PC**
PC1 Wayne Gretzky, NYRa.	80.00	40.00	25.00
PC2 Patrick Roy (G), Colo.	60.00	30.00	18.00
PC3 Brendan Shanahan, Detr.	20.00	10.00	6.00
PC4 Raymond Bourque, Bost.	20.00	12.00	6.00
PC5 Alexei Morozov, Pitt.	4.00	4.00	3.00
PC6 John LeClair, Phil.	15.00	8.00	4.00
PC7 Steve Yzerman, Detr.	45.00	24.00	14.00
PC8 Patrik Elias, NJer.	15.00	12.00	10.00
PC9 Pavel Bure, Vanc.	15.00	8.00	4.00
PC10 Brian Leetch, NYRa.	10.00	6.00	3.00
PC11 Peter Forsberg, Colo.	25.00	14.00	8.00
PC12 Marco Sturm, SanJ.	4.00	4.00	3.00
PC13 Eric Lindros, Phil.	20.00	10.00	6.00
PC14 Keith Tkachuk, Phoe.	10.00	6.00	3.00
PC15 Teemu Selänne, Anah.	15.00	8.00	4.00
PC16 Bryan Berard, NYIs.	5.00	4.00	3.00
PC17 Joe Thornton, Bost.	20.00	12.00	6.00
PC18 Brett Hull, SLou.	20.00	10.00	6.00
PC19 Nicklas Lidström, Detr.	10.00	6.00	3.00
PC20 Jaromir Jagr, Pitt.	20.00	10.00	6.00
PC21 Vaclav Prospal, Phil.	5.00	4.00	4.00
PC22 Pat LaFontaine, NYRa.	10.00	6.00	3.00
PC23 Mark Messier, Vanc.	20.00	10.00	6.00
PC24 Martin Brodeur (G), NJer.	30.00	16.00	10.00
PC25 Mike Modano, Dall.	20.00	10.00	6.00
PC26 Paul Kariya, Anah.	25.00	14.00	8.00
PC27 Mike Johnson, Toro.	4.00	4.00	3.00
PC28 Sergei Samsonov, Bost.	10.00	8.00	6.00
PC29 Joe Sakic, Colo.	30.00	16.00	10.00
PC30 Mats Sundin, Toro.	20.00	10.00	6.00

PREMIUM CUT QUADRUPLE

Insert Set (30 cards):	**3300.00**	**2000.00**
Player	**Q_Hor.**	**QPC**
PC1 Wayne Gretzky, NYRa.	1400.00	300.00
PC2 Patrick Roy (G), Colo.	1000.00	225.00
PC3 Brendan Shanahan, Detr.	250.00	75.00
PC4 Raymond Bourque, Bost.	20.00	90.00
PC5 Alexei Morozov, Pitt.	6.00	15.00
PC6 John LeClair, Phil.	100.00	60.00
PC7 Steve Yzerman, Detr.	45.00	175.00
PC8 Patrik Elias, NJer.	15.00	70.00
PC9 Pavel Bure, Vanc.	100.00	60.00
PC10 Brian Leetch, NYRa.	5.00	45.00
PC11 Peter Forsberg, Colo.	175.00	100.00
PC12 Marco Sturm, SanJ.	6.00	15.00
PC13 Eric Lindros, Phil.	250.00	70.00
PC14 Keith Tkachuk, Phoe.	10.00	45.00
PC15 Teemu Selänne, Anah.	15.00	60.00
PC16 Bryan Berard, NYIs.	4.00	20.00
PC17 Joe Thornton, Bost.	15.00	90.00
PC18 Brett Hull, SLou.	10.00	75.00
PC19 Nicklas Lidström, Detr.	5.00	45.00
PC20 Jaromir Jagr, Pitt.	125.00	70.00
PC21 Vaclav Prospal, Phil.	6.00	20.00
PC22 Pat LaFontaine, NYRa.	10.00	45.00
PC23 Mark Messier, Vanc.	10.00	75.00
PC24 Martin Brodeur (G), NJer.	200.00	120.00
PC25 Mike Modano, Dall.	20.00	75.00
PC26 Paul Kariya, Anah.	25.00	100.00
PC27 Mike Johnson, Toro.	4.00	15.00
PC28 Sergei Samsonov, Bost.	75.00	45.00
PC29 Joe Sakic, Colo.	15.00	120.00
PC30 Mats Sundin, Toro.	10.00	75.00

1997 - 98 UPPER DECK COLLECTOR'S CHOICE

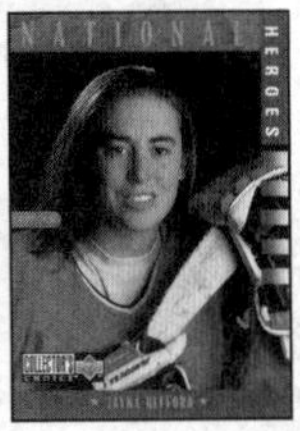

Complete Set (320 cards):	**30.00**
Common Player:	**.20**
Player	**UD CC**
1 Guy Hebert (G), Anah.	.20
2 Sean Pronger, Anah.	.20
3 Dmitri Mironov, Anah.	.20
4 Darren Van Impe, Anah.	.20
5 Joe Sacco, Anah.	.20
6 Ted Drury, Anah.	.20
7 Steve Rucchin, Anah.	.20
8 Teemu Selänne, Anah.	.20
9 Paul Kariya, Anah.	.50
10 Jari Kurri, Anah.	.50
11 Kevin Todd, Anah.	.20
12 Raymond Bourque, Bost.	.50
13 Anson Carter, Bost.	.20
14 Ted Donato, Bost.	.20
15 Kyle McLaren, Bost.	.20
16 Jason Allison, Bost.	.20
17 Jim Carey (G), Bost.	.20
18 Jozef Stumpel, Bost.	.20
19 Jean-Yves Roy, Bost.	.20
20 Steve Heinze, Bost.	.20
21 Sheldon Kennedy, Bost.	.20
22 Dominik Hasek (G), Buff.	.50
23 Rob Ray, Buff.	.20
24 Derek Plante, Buff.	.20
25 Brian Holzinger, Buff.	.20
26 Michael Peca, Buff.	.20
27 Matthew Barnaby, Buff.	.20
28 Donald Audette, Buff.	.20
29 Alexei Zhitnik, Buff.	.20
30 Garry Galley, Buff.	.20
31 Pat LaFontaine, Buff.	.20
32 Jason Dawe, Buff.	.20
33 Hnat Domenichelli, Calg.	.20
34 Jarome Iginla, Calg.	.20
35 Chris O'Sullivan, Calg.	.20
36 Todd Simpson, Calg.	.20
37 Trevor Kidd (G), Calg.	.20
38 Dave Gagner, Calg.	.20
39 German Titov, Calg.	.20
40 Theoren Fleury, Calg.	.20
41 Dwayne Roloson, Calg.	.20
42 Marty McInnis, Calg.	.20
43 Jonas Höglund, Calg.	.20
44 Tony Amonte, Chic.	.20
45 Gary Suter, Chic.	.20
46 Chris Chelios, Chic.	.20
47 Jeff Hackett (G), Chic.	.20
48 Ulf Dahlen, Chic.	.20
49 Bob Probert, Chic.	.20
50 Kevin Miller, Chic.	.20
51 Ethan Moreau, Chic.	.20
52 Eric Weinrich, Chic.	.20
53 Eric Dazé, Chic.	.20
54 Peter Forsberg, Colo.	.50
55 Joe Sakic, Colo.	.50
56 Patrick Roy (G), Colo.	1.50
57 Adam Deadmarsh, Colo.	.20
58 Valeri Kamensky, Colo.	.20
59 Keith Jones, Colo.	.20
60 Sandis Ozolinsh, Colo.	.20
61 Mike Ricci, Colo.	.20
62 Claude Lemieux, Colo.	.20
63 Mike Keane, Colo.	.20
64 Adam Foote, Colo.	.20
65 Mike Modano, Dall.	.50
66 Pat Verbeek, Dall.	.20
67 Andy Moog (G), Dall.	.20
68 Joe Nieuwendyk, Dall.	.20
69 Jamie Langenbrunner, Dall.	.20
70 Derian Hatcher, Dall.	.20
71 Greg Adams, Dall.	.20
72 Darryl Sydor, Dall.	.20
73 Dave Reid, Dall.	.20
74 Jere Lehtinen, Dall.	.20
75 Todd Harvey, Dall.	.20
76 Brendan Shanahan, Detr.	.50
77 Mike Vernon, Detr.	.20
78 Steve Yzerman, Detr.	1.00
79 Sergei Fedorov, Detr.	.50
80 Chris Osgood (G), Detr.	.20
81 Nicklas Lidström, Detr.	.20
82 Vladimir Konstantinov, Detr.	.20
83 Darren McCarty, Detr.	.20
84 Kirk Maltby, Detr.	.20
85 Vyacheslav Kozlov, Detr.	.20
86 Martin Lapointe, Detr.	.20
87 Doug Weight, Edmo.	.20
88 Mike Grier, Edmo.	.20
89 Curtis Joseph (G), Edmo.	.50
90 Andrei Kovalenko, Edmo.	.20
91 Rem Murray, Edmo.	.20
92 Ryan Smyth, Edmo.	.20
93 Mariusz Czerkawski, Edmo.	.20
94 Drew Bannister, Edmo. RC	**.20**
95 Jason Arnott, Edmo.	.20
96 Luke Richardson, Edmo.	.20
97 Dean McAmmond, Edmo.	.20
98 Kirk Muller, Flor.	.20
99 Ray Sheppard, Flor.	.20
100 Scott Mellanby, Flor.	.20
101 Ed Jovanovski, Flor.	.20
102 John Vanbiesbrouck (G), Flor.	.20
103 Radek Dvorak, Flor.	.20
104 Robert Svehla, Flor.	.20
105 Rob Niedermayer, Flor.	.20
106 Dave Nemirovsky, Flor.	.20
107 Steve Washburn, Flor.	.20
108 Bill Lindsay, Flor.	.20
109 Kevin Dineen, Hart.	.20
110 Keith Primeau, Hart.	.20
111 Sean Burke (G), Hart.	.20
112 Derek King, Hart.	.20
113 Andrew Cassels, Hart.	.20
114 Glen Wesley, Hart.	.20
115 Nelson Emerson, Hart.	.20
116 Geoff Sanderson, Hart.	.20
117 Jeff O'Neill, Hart.	.20
118 Kent Manderville, Hart.	.20
119 Dimitri Khristich, LosA.	.20
120 Ian Laperrière, LosA.	.20
121 Aki Berg, LosA.	.20
122 Vladimir Tsyplakov, LosA.	.20
123 Vitali Yachmenev, LosA.	.20
124 Roman Vopat, LosA.	.20
125 Rob Blake, LosA.	.20
126 Jan Vopat, LosA.	.20
127 Jeff Shevalier, LosA. RC	**.20**
128 Jeff Shevalier, LosA. RC	**.20**
129 Saku Koivu, Mont.	.20
130 Vincent Damphousse, Mont.	.20
131 Brian Savage, Mont.	.20
132 Valeri Bure, Mont.	.20
133 Mark Recchi, Mont.	.20
134 Jocelyn Thibault (G), Mont.	.20
135 José Théodore (G), Mont.	.50
136 Dave Manson, Mont.	.20
137 Shayne Corson, Mont.	.20
138 Stéphane Richer, Mont.	.20
139 Doug Gilmour, NJer.	.20
140 Scott Stevens, NJer.	.20
141 Martin Brodeur (G), NJer.	.50
142 Dave Andreychuk, NJer.	.20
143 Bobby Holik, NJer.	.20
144 Brian Rolston, NJer.	.20
145 Jay Pandolfo, NJer.	.20
146 John MacLean, NJer.	.20
147 Bill Guerin, NJer.	.20
148 Scott Niedermayer, NJer.	.20
149 Denis Pederson, NJer.	.20
150 Zigmund Palffy, NYIs.	.20
151 Robert Reichel, NYIs.	.20
152 Bryan Smolinski, NYIs.	.20
153 Éric Fichaud (G), NYIs.	.20
154 Todd Bertuzzi, NYIs.	.50
155 Bryan Berard, NYIs.	.20
156 Niklas Andersson, NYIs.	.20
157 Bryan McCabe, NYIs.	.20
158 Tommy Salo, NYIs.	.20
159 Kenny Jönsson, NYIs.	.20
160 Travis Green, NYIs.	.20
161 Mike Richter (G), NYRa.	.20
162 Brian Leetch, NYRa.	.20
163 Adam Graves, NYRa.	.20
164 Vladimir Vorobiev, NYRa. RC	**.20**
165 Niklas Sundström, NYRa.	.20
166 Russ Courtnall, NYRa.	.20
167 Wayne Gretzky, NYRa.	2.00
168 Mark Messier, NYRa.	.50
169 Alexander Karpovtsev, NYRa.	.20
170 Luc Robitaille, NYRa.	.20
171 Ulf Samuelsson, NYRa.	.20
172 Daniel Alfredsson, Ott.	.20
173 Alexei Yashin, Ott.	.20
174 Alexandre Daigle, Ott.	.20
175 Andreas Dackell, Ott.	.20
176 Wade Redden, Ott.	.20
177 Sergei Zholtok, Ott.	.20
178 Damian Rhodes (G), Ott.	.20
179 Steve Duchesne, Ott.	.20
180 Shawn McEachern, Ott.	.20
181 Ron Tugnutt (G), Ott.	.20
182 John LeClair, Phil.	.20
183 Janne Niinimaa, Phil.	.20
184 Mikael Renberg, Phil.	.20
185 Vaclav Prospal, Phil. RC	**1.00**
186 Eric Lindros, Phil.	.50
187 Dainius Zubrus, Phil.	.20
188 Ron Hextall (G), Phil.	.20
189 Paul Coffey, Phil.	.20
190 Dale Hawerchuk, Phil.	.20
191 Trent Klatt, Phil.	.20
192 Rod Brind'Amour, Phil.	.20
193 Nikolai Khabibulin (G), Phoe.	.20
194 Keith Tkachuk, Phoe.	.20
195 Jeremy Roenick, Phoe.	.20
196 Mike Gartner, Phoe.	.20
197 Dallas Drake, Phoe.	.20
198 Oleg Tverdovsky, Phoe.	.20
199 Cliff Ronning, Phoe.	.20
200 Teppo Numminen, Phoe.	.20
201 Craig Janney, Phoe.	.20
202 Deron Quint, Phoe.	.20
203 Jason Woolley, Pitt.	.20
204 Ron Francis, Pitt.	.20
205 Jaromir Jagr, Pitt.	.50
206 Greg Johnson, Pitt.	.20
207 Kevin Hatcher, Pitt.	.20
208 Patrick Lalime (G), Pitt.	.20
209 Petr Nedved, Pitt.	.20
210 Ken Wregget (G), Pitt.	.20
211 Darius Kasparaitis, Pitt.	.20
212 Stu Barnes, Pitt.	.20
213 Joe Dziedzic, Pitt.	.20
214 Owen Nolan, SanJ.	.20
215 Jeff Friesen, SanJ.	.20
216 Ed Belfour (G), SanJ.	.50
217 Viktor Kozlov, SanJ.	.20
218 Tony Granato, SanJ.	.20
219 Darren Turcotte, SanJ.	.20
220 Stephen Guolla, SanJ. RC	**.20**
221 Marty McSorley, SanJ.	.20
222 Marcus Ragnarsson, SanJ.	.20
223 Al Iafrate, SanJ.	.20
224 Brett Hull, SLou.	.50
225 Grant Fuhr (G), SLou.	.20
226 Pierre Turgeon, SLou.	.20
227 Geoff Courtnall, SLou.	.20
228 Jim Campbell, SLou.	.20
229 Harry York, SLou.	.20
230 Tony Twist, SLou.	.20
231 Joe Murphy, SLou.	.20
232 Pavol Demitra, SLou.	.20
233 Chris Pronger, SLou.	.20
234 Al MacInnis, SLou.	.20
235 Daren Puppa (G), Tamp.	.20
236 Chris Gratton, Tamp.	.20
237 Dino Ciccarelli, Tamp.	.20
238 Rob Zamuner, Tamp.	.20
239 Igor Ulanov, Tamp.	.20
240 Roman Hamrlik, Tamp.	.20
241 Alexander Selivanov, Tamp.	.20
242 Patrick Poulin, Tamp.	.20
243 Daymond Langkow, Tamp.	.20
244 Corey Schwab (G), Tamp.	.20
245 Mats Sundin, Toro.	.50
246 Wendel Clark, Toro.	.20
247 Sergei Berezin, Toro.	.20
248 Steve Sullivan, Toro.	.20
249 Fredrik Modin, Toro.	.20
250 Darby Hendrickson, Toro.	.20
251 Jason Podollan, Toro.	.20
252 Félix Potvin (G), Toro.	.20

☐ 253 Tie Domi, Toro. .20
☐ 254 Todd Warriner, Toro. .20
☐ 255 Pavel Bure, Vanc. .20
☐ 256 Alexander Mogilny, Vanc. .20
☐ 257 Martin Gelinas, Vanc. .20
☐ 258 Corey Hirsch (G), Vanc. .20
☐ 259 Trevor Linden, Vanc. .20
☐ 260 Mike Sillinger, Vanc. .20
☐ 261 Markus Näslund, Vanc. .50
☐ 262 Jyrki Lumme, Vanc. .20
☐ 263 Gino Odjick, Vanc. .20
☐ 264 Mike Ridley, Vanc. .20
☐ 265 Dave Roberts, Vanc. .20
☐ 266 Adam Oates, Wash. .20
☐ 267 Bill Ranford (G), Wash. .20
☐ 268 Joé Juneau, Wash. .20
☐ 269 Chris Simon, Wash. .20
☐ 270 Peter Bondra, Wash. .20
☐ 271 Dale Hunter, Wash. .20
☐ 272 Jaroslav Svejkovsky, Wash. .20
☐ 273 Sergei Gonchar, Wash. .20
☐ 274 Steve Konowalchuk, Wash. .20
☐ 275 Phil Housley, Wash. .20
☐ 276 Angela James, Cdn. 2.00
☐ 277 Nancy Drolet, Cdn. 1.00
☐ 278 Lesley Reddon (G), Cdn. .50
☐ 279 Hayley Wickenheiser, Cdn. 4.00
☐ **280 Vicki Sunohara, Cdn. RC 1.50**
☐ 281 Cassie Campbell, Cdn. 4.00
☐ 282 Geraldine Heaney, Cdn. 1.00
☐ 283 Judy Diduck, Cdn. .50
☐ 284 France St-Louis, Cdn. 1.00
☐ 285 Danielle Goyette, Cdn. 1.00
☐ 286 Thérèse Brisson, Cdn. .50
☐ 287 Stacy Wilson, Cdn. .50
☐ **288 Danielle Dubé, Cdn. RC 1.00**
☐ **289 Jayna Hefford, Cdn. RC 2.50**
☐ **290 Luce Letendre, Cdn. RC 1.00**
☐ **291 Lori Dupuis, Cdn. RC .50**
☐ **292 Rebecca Fahey, Cdn. RC 1.00**
☐ **293 Fiona Smith, Cdn. RC 1.00**
☐ **294 Laura Schuler, Cdn. RC .50**
☐ 295 Karen Nystrom, Cdn. .50
☐ 296 Joe Thornton, Cdn. 1.00
☐ 297 Peter Schaefer, Cdn. .20
☐ 298 Daniel Tkaczuk, Cdn. .20
☐ 299 Alyn McCauley, Cdn. .20
☐ 300 Shane Willis, Cdn. .20
☐ 301 Chris Phillips, Cdn. .20
☐ 302 Marc Denis (G), Cdn. .20
☐ 303 Jason Ward, Cdn. .20
☐ 304 Patrick Marleau, Cdn. .20
☐ 305 Brad Isbister, Cdn. .20
☐ 306 Cameron Mann, Cdn. .20
☐ 307 Dan Cleary, Cdn. .20
☐ 308 Brad Larsen, Cdn. .20
☐ 309 Nick Boynton, Cdn. .20
☐ 310 Scott Barney, Cdn. .20
☐ 311 Boyd Devereaux, Cdn. .20
☐ 312 CL: Wayne Gretzky, NYRa. 1.00
☐ 313 CL: Steve Yzerman, Detr. .50
☐ 314 CL: Jaromir Jagr, Pitt. .20
☐ 315 CL: Jarome Iginla, Calg. .20
☐ 316 CL: Patrick Roy (G), Colo. .50
☐ 317 CL: John Vanbiesbrouck (G), Flor. .20
☐ 318 CL: Paul Kariya, Anah. .20
☐ 319 CL: Doug Weight, Edmo. .20
☐ 320 CL: Mats Sundin, Toro. .20

5X7 CARDS

Insert Set (5 cards): 8.00
Insert 5x7
☐ 1 Theoren Fleury, Calg. 1.50
☐ 2 Curtis Joseph (G), Edmo. 2.50
☐ 3 José Théodore (G), Mont. 3.00
☐ 4 Wade Redden, Otta. 1.00
☐ 5 Mats Sundin, Toro. 2.50

MAGIC MEN

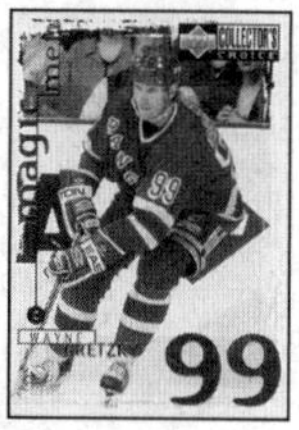

Insert Set (10 cards): 55.00
Insert MM
☐ MM1 Wayne Gretzky, NYRa. 8.00
☐ MM2 Wayne Gretzky, NYRa. 8.00
☐ MM3 Wayne Gretzky, NYRa. 8.00
☐ MM4 Wayne Gretzky, NYRa. 8.00
☐ MM5 Wayne Gretzky, NYRa. 8.00
☐ MM6 Patrick Roy (G), Colo. 5.00
☐ MM7 Patrick Roy (G), Colo. 5.00
☐ MM8 Patrick Roy (G), Colo. 5.00
☐ MM9 Patrick Roy (G), Colo. 5.00
☐ MM10 Patrick Roy (G), Colo. 5.00

STARQUEST

StarQuest cards are inserted at four levels of difficulty: StarQuest 1 cards (1-45) are inserted one per pack; StarQuest 2 cards (46-65) are inserted one per 21 packs; StarQuest 3 cards (66-80) are inserted one per 71 packs; and StarQuest 4 (81-90) are inserted one per 145 packs.

Shell Set (45 cards): 12.00
Insert Set (90 cards): 325.00
Insert SQ
☐ SQ1 Bryan Berard, NYIs. .30
☐ SQ2 Robert Svehla, Flor. .30
☐ SQ3 Peter Nedved, Pitt. .30
☐ SQ4 Steve Sullivan, Toro. .30
☐ SQ5 Nicklas Lidström, Detr. .50
☐ SQ6 Wade Redden, Ott. .30
☐ SQ7 Jason Arnott, Edmo. .30
☐ SQ8 Martin Gelinas, Vanc. .30
☐ SQ9 Mikael Renberg, Phil. .30
☐ SQ10 Jeff Friesen, SanJ. .30
☐ SQ11 Chris Chelios, Chic. .50
☐ SQ12 Jarome Iginla, Calg. .50
☐ SQ13 Vyacheslav Kozlov, Detr. .30
☐ SQ14 Brian Holzinger, Buff. .30
☐ SQ15 Eric Dazé, Chic. .30
☐ SQ16 Pat Verbeek, Dall. .30
☐ SQ17 Jozef Stumpel, Bost. .30
☐ SQ18 Rob Niedermayer, Flor. .30
☐ SQ19 Sergei Fedorov, Detr. 1.00
☐ SQ20 Brian Leetch, NYRa. .50
☐ SQ21 Bill Guerin, NJer. .30
☐ SQ22 Dino Ciccarelli, Tamp. .30
☐ SQ23 Adam Oates, Wash. .30
☐ SQ24 Mike Grier, Edmo. .30
☐ SQ25 Alexandre Daigle, Ott. .30
☐ SQ26 Janne Niinimaa, Phil. .30
☐ SQ27 Dimitri Khristich, LosA. .30
☐ SQ28 Oleg Tverdovsky, Phoe. .30
☐ SQ29 Félix Potvin (G), Toro. .50
☐ SQ30 Mike Richter (G), NYRa. .30
☐ SQ31 Curtis Joseph (G), Edmo. 1.00
☐ SQ32 Vincent Damphousse, Mont. .50
☐ SQ33 Vladimir Konstantinov, Detr. .30
☐ SQ34 Andy Moog (G), Dall. .30
☐ SQ35 Nikolai Khabibulin (G), Phoe. .30
☐ SQ36 Ed Belfour (G), SanJ. 1.00
☐ SQ37 Scott Mellanby, Flor. .30
☐ SQ38 Sandis Ozolinsh, Colo. .30
☐ SQ38 Travis Green, NYIs. .30
☐ SQ40 Patrick Lalime (G), Pitt. .50
☐ SQ41 Niklas Sundström, NYRa. .30
☐ SQ42 Guy Hebert (G), Anah. .30
☐ SQ43 Vitali Yachmenev, LosA. .30
☐ SQ44 Roman Hamrlik, Tamp. .30
☐ SQ45 Adam Deadmarsh, Colo. .30
☐ SQ46 Alexei Zhamnov, Chic. 1.00
☐ SQ47 Saku Koivu, Mont. 3.00
☐ SQ48 Sergei Berezin, Toro. 1.00
☐ SQ49 Mark Messier, NYRa. 3.00
☐ SQ50 Martin Brodeur (G), NJer. 6.00
☐ SQ51 Daniel Alfredsson, Ott. 2.00
☐ SQ52 John LeClair, Phil. 3.00
☐ SQ53 Mike Vernon (G), Detr. 1.00
☐ SQ54 Ron Francis, Pitt. 2.00
☐ SQ55 Keith Primeau, Hart. 1.00
☐ SQ56 Pierre Turgeon, SLou. 1.00
☐ SQ57 Jim Carey (G), Bost. 1.00
☐ SQ58 Peter Bondra, Wash. 2.00
☐ SQ59 Pavel Bure, Vanc. 3.00
☐ SQ60 Ray Sheppard, Flor. 1.00
☐ SQ61 Chris Gratton, Tamp. 1.00
☐ SQ62 Derek Plante, Buff. 1.00
☐ SQ63 Joe Sakic, Colo. 6.00
☐ SQ64 Theoren Fleury, Calg. 2.00
☐ SQ65 Tony Amonte, Chic. 2.00
☐ SQ66 Zigmund Palffy, NYIs. 6.00
☐ SQ67 Steve Yzerman, Detr. 20.00
☐ SQ68 Doug Weight, Edmo. 6.00
☐ SQ69 Alexander Mogilny, Vanc. 4.00
☐ SQ70 Doug Gilmour, NJer. 6.00
☐ SQ71 Peter Forsberg, Colo. 10.00
☐ SQ72 Alexei Yashin, Ott. 6.00
☐ SQ73 Geoff Sanderson, Hart. 4.00
☐ SQ74 Brendan Shanahan, Detr. 10.00
☐ SQ75 Mark Recchi, Mont. 4.00
☐ SQ76 Brett Hull, SLou. 10.00
☐ SQ77 Raymond Bourque, Bost. 10.00
☐ SQ78 Owen Nolan, SanJ. 6.00
☐ SQ79 Jeremy Roenick, Phoe. 8.00
☐ SQ80 Teemu Selänne, Anah. 5.00
☐ SQ81 Dominik Hasek (G), Buff. 15.00
☐ SQ82 Mike Modano, Dall. 20.00
☐ SQ83 Mats Sundin, Toro. 20.00
☐ SQ84 John Vanbiesbrouck (G), Flor. 8.00
☐ SQ85 Paul Kariya, Anah. 25.00
☐ SQ86 Patrick Roy (G), Colo. 60.00
☐ SQ87 Keith Tkachuk, Phoe. 10.00
☐ SQ88 Eric Lindros, Phil. 20.00
☐ SQ89 Jaromir Jagr, Pitt. 20.00
☐ SQ90 Wayne Gretzky, NYRa. 80.00

STICK UM'S

Insert Set (30 stickers): 30.00
Insert (1:3) SU
☐ S1 Wayne Gretzky, NYRa. 5.00
☐ S2 John Vanbiesbrouck (G), Flor. .50
☐ S3 Martin Brodeur (G), NJer. 2.00
☐ S4 Rob Blake, LosA. .50
☐ S5 Saku Koivu, Mont. 1.00
☐ S6 Curtis Joseph (G), Edmo. 1.00
☐ S7 Chris Chelios, Chic. .50
☐ S8 Mike Modano, Dall. 1.00
☐ S9 Paul Kariya, Anah. 1.00
☐ S10 Eric Lindros, Phil. 1.00
☐ S11 Daniel Alfredsson, Ott. .50
☐ S12 Jarome Iginla, Calg. 1.00
☐ S13 Jeremy Roenick, Phoe. 1.00
☐ S14 Brendan Shanahan, Detr. 1.00
☐ S15 Jaromir Jagr, Pitt. 1.00
☐ S16 Zigmund Palffy, NYIs. .50
☐ S17 Mats Sundin, Toro. 1.00
☐ S18 Teemu Selänne, Anah. 1.00
☐ S19 Joe Sakic, Colo. 2.00
☐ S20 Ed Belfour (G), SanJ. 1.00
☐ S21 Peter Forsberg, Colo. 1.00
☐ S22 Dino Ciccarelli, Tamp. .50
☐ S23 Patrick Roy (G), Colo. 3.00
☐ S24 Doug Gilmour, NJer. .50
☐ S25 Pavel Bure, Vanc. 1.00
☐ S26 Brett Hull, SLou. 1.00
☐ S27 Raymond Bourque, Bost. 1.00
☐ S28 Adam Oates, Wash. .50
☐ S29 Steve Yzerman, Detr. 3.00
☐ S30 Dominik Hasek (G), Buff. 1.00

WORLD DOMINATION

Insert Set (20 cards): 40.00
Insert (1:4 Canadian) WD
☐ W1 Wayne Gretzky, NYRa. 10.00
☐ W2 Mark Messier, Vanc. 2.00
☐ W3 Steve Yzerman, Detr. 6.00
☐ W4 Brendan Shanahan, Detr. 2.00
☐ W5 Paul Kariya, Anah. 3.00
☐ W6 Joe Sakic, Colo. 4.00
☐ W7 Eric Lindros, Phil. 2.00
☐ W8 Rod Brind'Armour, Phil. 1.00
☐ W9 Keith Primeau, Caro. 1.00
☐ W10 Trevor Linden, Vanc. 1.00
☐ W11 Theoren Fleury, Calg. 1.00
☐ W12 Scott Niedermayer, NJer. 1.00
☐ W13 Rob Blake, LosA. 1.00
☐ W14 Chris Pronger, SLou. 1.00
☐ W15 Éric Desjardins, Phil. 1.00
☐ W16 Adam Foote, Colo. 1.00
☐ W17 Scott Stevens, NJer. 1.00
☐ W18 Patrick Roy (G), Colo. 7.00
☐ W19 Curtis Joseph (G), Edmo. 2.00
☐ W20 Martin Brodeur (G), NJer. 4.00

YOU CRASH THE GAME

Insert Set (90 cards): 65.00
Insert (1:5) YCTG
☐☐☐ C1 Wayne Gretzky, NYRa. 5.00
☐☐☐ C2 Mike Modano, Dall. 1.00
☐☐☐ C3 Doug Weight, Edmo. .50
☐☐☐ C4 Brendan Shanahan, Detr. 1.00
☐☐☐ C5 Ray Sheppard, Flor. .50
☐☐☐ C6 Keith Primeau, Hart. .50
☐☐☐ C7 Raymond Bourque, Bost. 1.00
☐☐☐ C8 Teemu Selänne, Anah. 1.00
☐☐☐ C9 Paul Kariya, Anah. 1.00
☐☐☐ C10 Tony Amonte, Chic. .50
☐☐☐ C11 Saku Koivu, Mont. 1.00
☐☐☐ C12 Donald Audette, Buff. .50
☐☐☐ C13 Doug Gilmour, NJer. .50
☐☐☐ C14 Theoren Fleury, Calg. .50
☐☐☐ C15 Alexei Yashin, Otta. .50
☐☐☐ C16 Zigmund Palffy, NYIs. .50
☐☐☐ C17 Dmitri Khristich, LosA. .50
☐☐☐ C18 Joe Sakic, Colo. 2.00
☐☐☐ C19 Steve Yzerman, Detr. 3.00
☐☐☐ C20 Eric Lindros, Phil. 1.00
☐☐☐ C21 Peter Forsberg, Colo. 1.00
☐☐☐ C22 Dino Ciccarelli, Tamp. .50
☐☐☐ C23 Mats Sundin, Toro. 1.00
☐☐☐ C24 Pavel Bure, Vanc. 1.00
☐☐☐ C25 Peter Bondra, Wash. .50
☐☐☐ C26 Brett Hull, SLou. 1.00
☐☐☐ C27 Keith Tkachuk, Phoe. .50
☐☐☐ C28 Jaromir Jagr, Pitt. 1.00
☐☐☐ C29 Jarome Iginla, Calg. 1.00
☐☐☐ C30 Owen Nolan, SanJ. .50

YOU CRASH THE GAME REDEEMED

These cards were redeemed.

Complete Set (30 cards): 50.00
Player YCTG
☐ CR1 Wayne Gretzky, NYRa. 12.00
☐ CR2 Mike Modano, Dall. 3.00
☐ CR3 Doug Weight, Edmo. 1.50
☐ CR4 Brendan Shanahan, Detr. 3.00
☐ CR5 Ray Sheppard, Flor. .50
☐ CR6 Keith Primeau, Hart. 1.00
☐ CR7 Raymond Bourque, Bost. 3.50
☐ CR8 Teemu Selänne, Anah. 2.00
☐ CR9 Paul Kariya, Anah. 4.00
☐ CR10 Tony Amonte, Chic. 1.50
☐ CR11 Saku Koivu, Mont. 2.00
☐ CR12 Donald Audette, Buff. 1.00
☐ CR13 Doug Gilmour, NJer. 1.50
☐ CR14 Theoren Fleury, Calg. 1.50
☐ CR15 Alexei Yashin, Otta. 1.50
☐ CR16 Zigmund Palffy, NYIs. 1.50
☐ CR17 Dmitri Khristich, LosA. .50
☐ CR18 Joe Sakic, Colo. 4.50
☐ CR19 Steve Yzerman, Detr. 7.00
☐ CR20 Eric Lindros, Phil. 3.00
☐ CR21 Peter Forsberg, Colo. 4.00
☐ CR22 Dino Ciccarelli, Tamp. .50
☐ CR23 Mats Sundin, Toro. 3.00
☐ CR24 Pavel Bure, Vanc. 2.00
☐ CR25 Peter Bondra, Wash. 1.50
☐ CR26 Brett Hull, SLou. 3.00
☐ CR27 Keith Tkachuk, Phoe. 1.50
☐ CR28 Jaromir Jagr, Pitt. 3.00
☐ CR29 Jarome Iginla, Calg. 2.00
☐ CR30 Owen Nolan, SanJ. 1.50

1997 - 98 UPPER DECK DIAMOND VISION

These cards have two versions: the regular card and a Signature Moves [1:5] parallel.

		SM	DV
Complete Set (25 cards):		**150.00**	**80.00**
	Player	**SM**	**DV**
☐☐	1 Wayne Gretzky, NYRa.	40.00	25.00
☐☐	2 Patrick Roy, Colo.	30.00	15.00
☐☐	3 Jaromir Jagr, Pitt.	10.00	5.00

□ □	4 Steve Yzerman, Detr.	20.00	15.00
□ □	5 Martin Brodeur (G), NJer.	15.00	10.00
□ □	6 Paul Kariya, Anah.	10.00	5.00
□ □	7 John Vanbiesbrouck (G), Flor.	4.00	2.00
□ □	8 Raymond Bourque, Bost.	10.00	5.00
□ □	9 Theoren Fleury, Calg.	5.00	2.00
□ □	10 Pavel Bure, Vanc.	5.00	5.00
□ □	11 Brendan Shanahan, Detr.	10.00	5.00
□ □	12 Brian Leetch, NYRa.	5.00	2.00
□ □	13 Owen Nolan, SanJ.	5.00	2.00
□ □	14 Peter Forsberg, Colo.	10.00	5.00
□ □	15 Doug Weight, Edmo.	5.00	2.00
□ □	16 Teemu Selänne, Anah.	5.00	5.00
□ □	17 Mats Sundin, Toro.	10.00	5.00
□ □	18 Keith Tkachuk, Phoe.	5.00	2.00
□ □	19 Tony Amonte, Chic.	5.00	2.00
□ □	20 Joe Sakic, Colo.	15.00	10.00
□ □	21 Zigmund Palffy, NYIs.	5.00	2.00
□ □	22 Eric Lindros, Phil.	10.00	5.00
□ □	23 Sergei Fedorov, Detr.	10.00	5.00
□ □	24 Dominik Hasek, Buff.	10.00	5.00
□ □	25 Brett Hull, SLou.	10.00	5.00

DEFINING MOMENTS

Insert Set (10 cards):		200.00
	Goalie	DM
□	DM1 Wayne Gretzky, NYRa.	80.00
□	DM2 Patrick Roy, Colo.	60.00
□	DM3 Steve Yzerman, Detr.	40.00
□	DM4 Jaromir Jagr, Pitt.	20.00
□	DM5 Joe Sakic, Colo.	30.00
□	DM6 Brendan Shanahan, Detr.	20.00

REEL TIME

	Insert (1:500)	RT
□	RT1 Wayne Gretzky, NYRa.	275.00

1997 - 98 UPPER DECK ELITSERIEN

NHL stars sometimes sell at a premium (usually $1-2).

Complete Set (225 cards):		45.00
Common Player:		.25
	Player	UDE
□	1 Miikka Kiprusoff, AIK Stockholm	2.00
□	2 Karri Kivi, AIK Stockholm	.25
□	3 Erik Hämäläinen, AIK Stockholm	.25
□	4 Libor Prochazka, AIK Stockholm	.50
□	5 Dick Tarnstrom, AIK Stockholm	1.00
□	6 Niclas Hävelid, AIK Stockholm	.50
□	7 Tomas Strandberg, AIK Stockholm	.25
□	8 Stefan Gustavson, AIK Stockholm	.25
□	9 Anders Gozzi, AIK Stockholm	.25
□	10 Pavel Patera, AIK Stockholm	.50
□	11 David Engblom, AIK Stockholm	.25
□	12 Peter Hammarström, AIK Stockholm	.25
□	13 Mats Lindberg, AIK Stockholm	.25
□	14 Fredrik Krekula, AIK Stockholm	.25
□	15 Otakar Vejboda, AIK Stockholm	.25
□	16 Björn Ahlström, AIK Stockholm	.25
□	17 Michael Sundlöv, Brynäs Gavle	.25
□	18 Per Djoos, Brynäs Gavle	.50
□	19 Tommy Melkersson, Brynäs Gavle	.25
□	20 Stefan Klockare, Brynäs Gavle	.25
□	21 Johan Hansson, Brynas Gävle	.25
□	22 Per Löfström, Brynäs Gavle	.25
□	23 Tommy Westlund, Brynäs Gavle	.50
□	24 Teppo Kivelä, Brynäs Gavle	.25
□	25 Niclas Wallin, Brynäs Gavle	.50
□	26 Roger Kyrö, Brynäs Gavle	.25
□	27 Ove Molin, Brynäs Gavle	.25
□	28 Mikko Luovi, Brynäs Gavle	.25
□	29 Evgeny (Gene) Davydov, Brynäs Gavle	.50
□	30 Anders Huss, Brynäs Gavle	.25
□	31 Peter Nylander, Brynäs Gavle	.25
□	32 Jan Larsson, Brynäs Gavle	.25
□	33 Tommy Söderström, Djurgården Stockholm	.50
□	34 Marcus Matthiason, Djurgården Stockholm	.25
□	35 Daniel Carlsson, Djurgården Stockholm	.25
□	36 Ronnie Pettersson, Djurgården Stockholm	.25
□	37 Kenneth Kennholt, Djurgården Stockholm	.25
□	38 Björn Nord, Djurgården Stockholm	.25
□	39 Mikael Johansson, Djurgården Stockholm	.25
□	40 Daniel Tjärnqvist, Djurgården Stockholm	.50
□	41 Charles Berglund, Djurgården Stockholm	.25
□	42 Mikael Johansson, Djurgården Stockholm	.25
□	43 Marcus Nilson, Djurgården Stockholm	.50
□	44 Niklas Falk, Djurgården Stockholm	.25
□	45 Fredrik Lindquist, Djurgården Stockholm	.50
□	46 Patric Kjellberg, Djurgården Stockholm	.50
□	47 Patrik Erickson, Djurgården Stockholm	.25
□	48 Jan Viktorsson, Djurgården Stockholm	.25
□	49 Niklas Anger, Djurgården Stockholm	.25
□	50 Boris Rousson, Färjestad Karlstad	.25
□	51 Peter Jakobsson, Färjestad Karlstad	.25
□	52 Peter Nordström, Färjestad Karlstad	.50
□	53 Sergei Fokin, Färjestad Karlstad	.25
□	54 Niklas Sjökvist, Färjestad Karlstad	.25
□	55 Jaroslav Sprachek, Färjestad Karlstad	.25
□	56 Greger Arvedsson, Färjestad Karlstad	.25
□	57 Roger Johansson, Färjestad Karlstad	.50
□	58 Stefan Nilsson, Färjestad Karlstad	.25
□	59 Pelle Prestberg, Färjestad Karlstad	.25
□	60 Kristian Huselius, Färjestad Karlstad	4.00
□	61 Mattias Johansson, Färjestad Karlstad	.50
□	62 Trond Magnussen, Färjestad Karlstad	.25
□	63 Clas Eriksson, Färjestad Karlstad	.25
□	64 Jörgen Jönsson, Färjestad Karlstad	1.00
□	65 Atle Olson, Färjestad Karlstad	.25
□	66 Patrik Wallenberg, Färjestad Karlstad	.25
□	67 Lars-Göran Wiklander, Vastra Frölunda Goteborg	.25
□	68 Mikael Sandberg, Vastra Frölunda Goteborg	.25
□	69 Christer Olsson, Vastra Frölunda Goteborg	.50
□	70 Joacim Esbjörs, Vastra Frölunda Goteborg	.25
□	71 Henrik Nilsson, Vastra Frölunda Goteborg	.25
□	72 Arto Blomsten, Vastra Frölunda Goteborg	.25
□	73 Magnus Johansson, Vastra Frölunda Goteborg	.25
□	74 Stefan Larsson, Vastra Frölunda Goteborg	.25
□	75 Par Edlund, Vastra Frölunda Goteborg	.25
□	76 Marko Jantunen, Vastra Frölunda Goteborg	.25
□	77 Joni Lius, Vastra Frolunda Goteborg	.25
□	78 Patrik Carnbäck, Vastra Frölunda Goteborg	.50
□	79 Ville Peltonen, Vastra Frölunda Goteborg	.50
□	80 Peter Berndtsson, Vastra Frölunda Goteborg	.25
□	81 Kai Nurminen, Vastra Frölunda Goteborg	.50
□	82 Jonas Esbjörs, Vastra Frölunda Goteborg	.25
□	83 Peter Ström, Vastra Frölunda Goteborg	.25
□	84 Kari Takko, HV 71 Jonkoping	.50
□	85 Johan Forsander, HV 71 Jonkoping	.25
□	86 Jouni Loponen, HV 71 Jonkoping	.25
□	87 David Petrasek, HV 71 Jonkoping	.25
□	88 Daniel Johansson, HV 71 Jonkoping	.50
□	89 Fredrik Stillman, HV 71 Jonkoping	.25
□	90 Anatoli Fedotov, HV 71 Jonkoping	.25
□	91 Stefan Örnskog, HV 71 Jonkoping	.25
□	92 Stefan Falk, HV 71 Jonkoping	.25
□	93 Peter Ekelund, HV 71 Jonkoping	.25
□	94 Esa Keskinen, HV 71 Jonkoping	.25
□	95 Patrik Lundback, HV 71 Jonkoping	.25
□	96 Anders Huusko, HV 71 Jonkoping	.25
□	97 Magnus Svensson, HV 71 Jonkoping	.50
□	98 Alexei Salomatin, HV 71 Jonkoping	.25
□	99 Patric Englund, HV 71 Jonkoping	.25
□	100 Åke Lilljebjörn, Leksand	.25
□	101 Tomas Jonsson, Leksand	.50
□	102 Torbjörn Johansson, Leksand	.25
□	103 Hans Lodin, Leksand	.25
□	104 Magnus Svensson, Leksand	.50
□	105 Andreas Karlsson, Leksand	.50
□	106 Joakim Lidgren, Leksand	.25
□	107 Fredrik Jönsson, Leksand	.25
□	108 Per-Erik (Pelle) Eklund, Leksand	.50
□	109 Anders Carlsson, Leksand	.25
□	110 Johan Witehall, Leksand	.50
□	111 Jens Nielsen, Leksand	.25
□	112 Niklas Eriksson, Leksand	.25
□	113 Jonas Bergkvist, Leksand	.25
□	114 Stefan Hellkvist, Leksand	.25
□	115 Markus Akerblom, Leksand	.25
□	116 Anders Lönn, Leksand	.25
□	117 Jarmo Myllys, Luleå	.50
□	118 Johan Finnström, Lulea	.25
□	119 Sergei Bautin, Luleå	.50
□	120 Jan Mertzig, Luleå	.25
□	121 Osmo Soutokorva, Luleå	.25
□	122 Roger Kerstrom, Luleå	.25
□	123 Stefan Jönsson, Luleå	.25
□	124 Stefan Nilsson, Luleå	.25
□	125 Jonas Rönnqvist, Luleå	.50
□	126 Joakim Backlund, Luleå	.25
□	127 Robert Nordberg, Luleå	.25
□	128 Mikael Lövgren, Luleå	.25
□	129 Anders Burström, Luleå	.25
□	130 Fredrik Johansson, Luleå	.50
□	131 Mika Alatalo, Luleå	.50
□	132 Fredrik Nilsson, Luleå	.25
□	133 Roger Nordström, Malmö	.25
□	134 Andrew Verner, Malmö	.50
□	135 Marko Kiprusoff, Malmo	.50
□	136 Kim Johnsson, Malmö	.50
□	137 Marcus Nilson, Malmö	.50
□	138 Jesper Damgaard, Malmö	.25
□	139 Marek Malík, Malmö	.50
□	140 Mats Lusth, Malmö	.25
□	141 Janne Ojanen, Malmö	.50
□	142 Mikko Peltola, Malmö	.25
□	143 Mathias Bosson, Malmö	.25
□	144 Daniel Rydmark, Malmö	.25
□	145 Patrik Sylvegård, Malmö	.25
□	146 Juha Riihijärvi, Malmö	.25
□	147 Fredrik Öberg, Malmö	.25
□	148 Mikael Burakovsky, Malmö	.25
□	149 Petter Rönnqvist, MoDo Hockey	.25
□	150 Pierre Hedin, MoDo Hockey	.25
□	151 Jan-Axel Alavaara, MoDo Hockey	.25
□	152 Frantisek* Kaberle, MoDo Hockey	.50
□	153 Hans Jonsson, MoDo Hockey	.50
□	154 Jonas Junkka, MoDo Hockey	.25
□	155 Marcus Karlsson, MoDo Hockey	.25
□	156 Kristian Gahn, MoDo Hockey	.25
□	157 Magnus Wernblom, MoDo Hockey	.25
□	158 Anders Söderberg, MoDo Hockey	.25
□	159 Daniel Sedin, MoDo Hockey	5.00
□	160 Henrik Sedin, MoDo Hockey	5.00
□	161 Samuel Påhlsson, MoDo Hockey	.50
□	162 Per Svartvadet, MoDo Hockey	.50
□	163 Andreas Salomonsson, MoDo Hockey	.50
□	164 Ravil Yakubov, MoDo Hockey	.25
□	165 David Vyborny, MoDo Hockey	.50
□	166 Magnus Lindvist, Sodertalje	.25
□	167 Anders Eldebrink, Sodertalje	.25
□	168 Johan Nordgren, Sodertalje	.25
□	169 Christian Due-Boje, Sodertalje	.25
□	170 Jonas Heed, Sodertalje	.25
□	171 Josef Boumedienne, Sodertalje	.50
□	172 Marko Virtanen, Sodertalje	.25
□	173 Kyosti Karjalainen, Sodertalje	.50
□	174 Jörgen Bemström, Sodertalje	.25
□	175 Joakim Eriksson, Sodertalje	.25
□	176 Jens Öhling, Sodertalje	.25
□	177 Martin Hostak, Sodertalje	.25
□	178 Lars Dahlström, Sodertalje	.25
□	179 Niklas Brännström, Sodertalje	.25
□	180 Mikko Mäkelä, Sodertalje	.50
□	181 Petr Korínek, Sodertalje	.25
□	182 Joakim Persson, Västerås	.25
□	183 Tobias Lilja, Västerås	.25
□	184 Edvin Frylén, Västerås	.25
□	185 Jakob Karlsson, Västerås	.50
□	186 Johan Tornberg, Västerås	.25
□	187 Patrik Höglund, Västerås	.25
□	188 Mattias Lööf, Västerås	.25
□	189 Mikael Pettersson, Västerås	.25
□	190 Johan Modin, Västerås	.25
□	191 Fredrik Eriksson, Västerås	.25
□	192 Henrik Nordfeldt, Västerås	.25
□	193 Jonas Olsson, Västerås	.25
□	194 Roger Jönsson, Västerås	.25
□	195 Roger Rosén, Västerås	.25
□	196 Henric Bjorkman, Västerås	.25
□	197 Harri Sillgren, Västerås	.25
□	198 P.A. Everberg, Västerås	.25
□	199 Tommy Söderström, Djurgården Stockholm	.50
□	200 Stefan Nilsson, Luleå	.25
□	201 Tomas Jonsson, Leksand	.50
□	202 Jonas Bergkvist, Leksands	.25
□	203 Christer Olsson, Vastra Frölunda Goteborg	.50
□	204 Per Svartvadet, MoDo Hockey	.50
□	205 Anders Huss, Brynäs Gavle	.25
□	206 Roger Johansson, Färjestad Karlstad	.50
□	207 Stefan Örnskog, HV 71 Jonkoping	.25
□	208 Anders Eldebrink, Sodertalje	.25
□	209 Niclas Hävelid, AIK Stockholm	.50
□	210 Charles Berglund, Djurgården Stockholm	.25
□	211 Kai Nurminen, Vastra Frölunda Goteborg	.50
□	212 Stefan Nilsson, Luleå	.25
□	213 Per-Erik (Pelle) Eklund, Leksand	.50
□	214 Janne Ojanen, Malmö	.50
□	215 Per Svartvadet, MoDo Hockey	.50
□	216 Michael Sundlöv, Brynäs Gavle	.25
□	217 Roger Johansson, Färjestad Karlstad	.50
□	218 Stefan Örnskog, HV 71 Jonkoping	.25
□	219 Kyosti Karjalainen, Sodertalje	.50
□	220 Roger Rosén, Västerås	.25
□	221 Jonas Bergkvist, Leksands	.25
□	222 Esa Keskinen, HV 71 Jonkoping	.25
□	223 Christer Olsson, Vastra Frölunda Goteborg	.50
□	224 Checklist	.25
□	225 Checklist	.25

SELECTS

Insert Set (15 cards):		40.00
	Insert (1:8)	UDS
□	UDS1 Peter Forsberg, V75 ATG	12.00
□	UDS2 Daniel Sedin, MoDo Hockey	6.00
□	UDS3 Nichlas Falk, Djurgården Stockholm	2.00
□	UDS4 Marko Jantunen, Vastra Frölunda Goteborg	2.00
□	UDS5 Ville Peltonen, Vastra Frölunda Goteborg	2.00
□	UDS6 Jörgen Jönsson, Färjestad Karlstad	3.00
□	UDS7 Roger Johansson, Färjestad Karlstad	2.00
□	UDS8 Stefan Örnskog, HV 71 Jonkoping	2.00
□	UDS9 Henrik Sedin, MoDo Hockey	6.00
□	UDS10 Jonas Bergkvist, Leksands	2.00
□	UDS11 Tomas Jonsson, Leksand	2.00
□	UDS12 Stefan Nilsson, Luleå	2.00
□	UDS13 Janne Ojanen, Malmö	2.00
□	UDS14 Magnus Wernblom, MoDo Hockey	2.00
□	UDS15 Edvin Frylén, Västerås	2.00

STICK UM'S

Insert Set (15 stickers):		14.00
	Insert (1:3)	SU
□	S1 Miikka Kiprusoff, AIK Stockholm	1.00
□	S2 Marcus Nilson, Djurgården Stockholm	1.00
□	S3 Christer Olsson, Vastra Frölunda Goteborg	1.00
□	S4 Jörgen Jönsson, Färjestad Karlstad	1.00
□	S5 Fredrik Stillman, HV 71 Jonkoping	1.00
□	S6 Per-Erik (Pelle) Eklund, Leksand	1.00
□	S7 Jarmo Myllys, Luleå	1.00
□	S8 Daniel Rydmark, Malmö	1.00
□	S9 Henric Bjorkman, Västerås	1.00
□	S10 Henrik Sedin, MoDo Hockey	2.00
□	S11 Daniel Sedin, MoDo Hockey	2.00
□	S12 Anders Huss, Brynäs Gavle	1.00
□	S13 Patrik Carnbäck, Vastra Frölunda Goteborg	1.00
□	S14 Daniel Tjärnqvist, Djurgården Stockholm	1.00
□	S15 Jonas Bergkvist, Leksands	1.00

YOU CRASH THE GAME

Insert Set (30 cards):		85.00
	Insert (1:12)	YCTG
□	C01 Patric Kjellberg, Djurgården Stockholm	3.00
□	C02 Mikael Johansson, Djurgården Stockholm	3.00
□	C03 Daniel Tjärnqvist, Djurgården Stockholm	3.00
□	C04 Christer Olsson, Vastra Frölunda Goteborg	3.00
□	C05 Ville Peltonen, Vastra Frölunda Goteborg	3.00
□	C06 Kai Nurminen, Vastra Frölunda Goteborg	3.00
□	C07 Stefan Nilsson, Luleå	3.00
□	C08 Jan Mertzig, Luleå	3.00
□	C09 Anders Carlsson, Leksand	3.00
□	C10 Jonas Bergkvist, Leksands	3.00
□	C11 Magnus Svensson,	3.00
□	C12 Janne Ojanen, Malmö	3.00
□	C13 Marko Kiprusoff, Malmo	3.00
□	C14 Juha Riihijärvi, Malmö	3.00

□	C15 Daniel Sedin, MoDo Hockey	8.00
□	C16 Henrik Sedin, MoDo Hockey	8.00
□	C17 Evgeny (Gene) Davydov, Brynäs Gavle	3.00
□	C18 Anders Huss, Brynäs Gavle	3.00
□	C19 Jan Larsson, Brynäs Gavle	3.00
□	C20 Roger Johansson, Färjestad Karlstad	3.00
□	C21 Jörgen Jönsson, Färjestad Karlstad	4.00
□	C22 Kristian Huselius, Färjestad Karlstad	6.00
□	C23 Stefan Örnskog, HV 71 Jonkoping	3.00
□	C24 Anders Huusko, HV 71 Jonkoping	3.00
□	C25 Esa Keskinen, HV 71 Jonkoping	3.00
□	C26 Joakim Eriksson, Sodertalje	3.00
□	C27 Anders Eldebrink, Sodertalje	3.00
□	C28 Mikko Mäkelä, Sodertalje	3.00
□	C29 Henric Bjorkman, Västerås	3.00
□	C30 Roger Rosén, Västerås	3.00

1997 - 98 UPPER DECK ICE

Each card has three versions: the regular card, a gold Power Shift parallel [1:23] and a third coloured parallel. Cards 1-30 have a red Ice Performers parallel [1:2], cards 31-60 have a blue Ice Phenoms parallel [1:3] and cards 61-90 have a green Ice Legends parallel [1:11].

Complete Set (90 cards):		1100.00	-	100.00
Ice Performers Set (30 cards):		-	25.00	-
Ice Phenoms Set (30 cards):		-	45.00	-
Ice Legends Set (30 cards):		-	225.00	-
Common Player:		5.00	.75	.50
	Player	**Gold**	**Para.**	**Ice**
□□□	1 Nelson Emerson (G), Caro.	5.00	.75	.50
□□□	2 Derian Hatcher, Dall.	10.00	1.00	.50
□□□	3 Mike Richter (G), NYRa.	15.00	1.00	1.00
□□□	4 Sergei Berezin, Toro.	5.00	.75	.50
□□□	5 Nicklas Lidström, Detr.	15.00	2.00	1.50
□□□	6 Ryan Smyth, Edmo.	15.00	1.00	1.00
□□□	7 Martin Brodeur (G), NJer.	50.00	6.00	4.00
□□□	8 Geoff Sanderson, Caro.	5.00	.75	.50
□□□	9 Doug Weight, Edmo.	15.00	2.00	1.50
□□□	10 Owen Nolan, SanJ.	15.00	2.00	1.50
□□□	11 Daniel Alfredsson, Ott.	15.00	2.00	1.50
□□□	12 Peter Bondra, Wash.	15.00	2.00	1.50
□□□	13 Jim Campbell, SLou.	5.00	.75	.50
□□□	14 Rob Niedermayer, Flor.	5.00	.75	.50
□□□	15 Daymond Langkow, Tamp.	5.00	.75	.50
□□□	16 Zigmund Palffy, NYIs.	15.00	2.00	1.50
□□□	17 Adam Oates, Wash.	10.00	1.00	1.00
□□□	18 Adam Deadmarsh, Colo.	10.00	1.00	.50
□□□	19 Brian Holzinger, Buff.	5.00	.75	.50
□□□	20 Jarome Iginla, Calg.	25.00	3.00	2.00
□□□	21 Janne Niinimaa, Phil.	5.00	.75	.50
□□□	22 Dino Ciccarelli, Flor.	10.00	1.00	.50
□□□	23 Mark Recchi, Mont.	10.00	1.00	1.00
□□□	24 Sandis Ozolinsh, Colo.	5.00	.75	.50
□□□	25 Keith Primeau, Caro.	10.00	1.00	1.00
□□□	26 Ed Jovanovski, Flor.	10.00	1.00	1.00
□□□	27 Jeremy Roenick, Phoe.	25.00	3.00	2.00
□□□	28 Alexei Yashin, Ott.	15.00	2.00	1.50
□□□	29 Félix Potvin (G), Toro.	15.00	2.00	1.50
□□□	30 Chris Osgood (G), Detr.	15.00	2.00	1.50
□□□	31 Marc Denis (G), Colo.	15.00	3.00	2.00
□□□	**32 Tyler Moss (G), Calg. RC**	**5.00**	**2.00**	**2.00**
□□□	33 Kevin Hodson (G), Detr.	5.00	1.50	1.00
□□□	34 Jamie Storr (G), LosA.	5.00	1.50	1.00
□□□	35 Roman Turek (G), Dall.	15.00	3.00	2.00
□□□	36 José Théodore (G), Mont.	35.00	7.00	6.00
□□□	**37 Magnus Arvedsson, Ott. RC**	**5.00**	**2.00**	**2.00**
□□□	38 Daniel Cleary, Chic.	10.00	2.00	1.50
□□□	**39 Mike Knuble, Detr. RC**	**5.00**	**1.50**	**1.50**
□□□	40 Jaroslav Svejkovsky, Wash.	5.00	1.50	.50
□□□	41 Patrick Marleau, SanJ.	15.00	3.00	2.00
□□□	42 Mattias Öhlund, Vanc.	10.00	2.00	1.50
□□□	43 Sergei Samsonov, Bost.	15.00	3.00	3.00
□□□	**44 Espen Knutsen, Anah. RC**	**10.00**	**3.00**	**3.50**
□□□	**45 Vaclav Prospal, Phil. RC**	**15.00**	**4.00**	**4.50**
□□□	46 Joe Thornton, Bost.	35.00	7.00	6.00
□□□	47 Chris Phillips, Ott.	5.00	1.50	1.00
□□□	**48 Mike Johnson, Toro. RC**	**5.00**	**2.00**	**3.00**
□□□	49 Dainius Zubrus, Phil.	5.00	1.50	1.00
□□□	50 Wade Redden, Ott.	10.00	2.00	1.50
□□□	**51 Derek Morris, Calg. RC**	**10.00**	**3.00**	**3.50**
□□□	**52 Marco Sturm, SanJ. RC**	**10.00**	**3.00**	**3.50**
□□□	**53 Donald MacLean, LosA. RC**	**5.00**	**1.50**	**1.50**
□□□	54 Bryan Berard, NYIs.	10.00	2.00	1.50
□□□	55 Richard Zednik, Wash.	10.00	2.00	2.00
□□□	56 Alexei Morozov, Pitt.	5.00	1.50	1.00
□□□	57 Erik Rasmussen, Buff.	5.00	1.50	1.00
□□□	**58 Olli Jokinen, LosA. RC**	**15.00**	**4.00**	**4.50**
□□□	**59 Jan Bulis, Wash. RC**	**5.00**	**1.50**	**1.50**
□□□	**60 Patrik Elias, NJer. RC**	**35.00**	**10.00**	**12.00**
□□□	61 Peter Forsberg, Colo.	40.00	15.00	3.50
□□□	62 Mike Modano, Dall.	30.00	10.00	2.50
□□□	63 Tony Amonte, Chic.	15.00	5.00	1.50
□□□	64 Theoren Fleury, Calg.	15.00	5.00	1.50
□□□	65 Ron Francis, Pitt.	15.00	5.00	1.50
□□□	66 Brett Hull, SLou.	30.00	10.00	2.50
□□□	67 Chris Chelios, Chic.	15.00	5.00	1.50
□□□	68 Jaromir Jagr, Pitt.	30.00	10.00	2.50
□□□	69 Sergei Fedorov, Detr.	30.00	10.00	2.50
□□□	70 Keith Tkachuk, Phoe.	15.00	5.00	1.50
□□□	71 Mark Messier, Vanc.	30.00	10.00	2.50
□□□	72 Pat LaFontaine, NYRa.	15.00	5.00	1.50
□□□	73 Mats Sundin, Toro.	30.00	10.00	2.50
□□□	74 John Vanbiesbrouck (G), Flor.	15.00	5.00	1.00
□□□	75 John LeClair, Phil.	25.00	10.00	2.00
□□□	76 Brian Leetch, NYRa.	15.00	5.00	1.50
□□□	77 Raymond Bourque, Bost.	35.00	15.00	3.00
□□□	78 Saku Koivu, Mont.	25.00	10.00	2.00
□□□	79 Joe Sakic, Colo.	50.00	20.00	4.00
□□□	80 Teemu Selänne, Anah.	25.00	10.00	2.00
□□□	81 Curtis Joseph (G), Edmo.	30.00	10.00	2.50
□□□	82 Doug Gilmour, NJer.	15.00	5.00	1.50
□□□	83 Patrick Roy (G), Colo.	90.00	35.00	7.50
□□□	84 Brendan Shanahan, Detr.	30.00	10.00	2.50
□□□	85 Paul Kariya, Anah.	40.00	15.00	3.50
□□□	86 Pavel Bure, Vanc.	20.00	10.00	2.00
□□□	87 Dominik Hasek (G), Buff.	30.00	10.00	2.50
□□□	88 Eric Lindros, Phil.	30.00	10.00	2.50
□□□	89 Steve Yzerman, Detr.	70.00	30.00	6.00
□□□	90 Wayne Gretzky, NYRa.	120.00	50.00	10.00

ICE CHAMPIONS

These cards have two versions: the regular insert (1:47) and an Ice Champions 2 parallel (#/100).

Insert Set (20 cards):		1600.00	325.00
	Player	**L2-100**	**IC**
□□	IC1 Wayne Gretzky, NYRa.	300.00	60.00
□□	IC2 Patrick Roy (G), Colo.	220.00	45.00
□□	IC3 Eric Lindros, Phil.	70.00	15.00
□□	IC4 Saku Koivu, Mont.	60.00	10.00
□□	IC5 Dominik Hasek (G), Buff.	70.00	15.00
□□	IC6 Joe Thornton, Bost.	90.00	25.00
□□	IC7 Martin Brodeur (G), NJer.	120.00	20.00
□□	IC8 Teemu Selänne, Anah.	60.00	10.00
□□	IC9 Paul Kariya, Anah.	100.00	20.00
□□	IC10 Joe Sakic, Colo.	120.00	20.00
□□	IC11 Mark Messier, Vanc.	70.00	15.00
□□	IC12 Peter Forsberg, Colo.	100.00	20.00
□□	IC13 Mats Sundin, Toro.	70.00	15.00
□□	IC14 Brendan Shanahan, Detr.	70.00	15.00
□□	IC15 Keith Tkachuk, Phoe.	40.00	5.00
□□	IC16 Brett Hull, SLou.	70.00	15.00
□□	IC17 John Vanbiesbrouck (G), Flor.	30.00	5.00
□□	IC18 Jaromir Jagr, Pitt.	70.00	15.00
□□	IC19 Steve Yzerman, Detr.	180.00	35.00
□□	IC20 Sergei Samsonov, Bost.	40.00	5.00

LETHAL LINES

These cards have two versions: the regular insert (1:8) and a Gold parallel (1:120).

Insert Set (10 cards):		11150.00	
	Inserts	**Gold**	**LL**
□□	L1A Paul Kariya, Anah.	50.00	12.00
□□	L1B Wayne Gretzky, NYRa.	150.00	35.00
□□	L1C Joe Thornton, Bost.	45.00	14.00
□□	L2A Brendan Shanahan, Detr.	35.00	8.00
□□	L2B Eric Lindros, Phil.	30.00	8.00
□□	L2C Jaromir Jagr, Pitt.	30.00	8.00
□□	L3A Keith Tkachuk, Phoe.	20.00	4.00
□□	L3B Mark Messier, Vanc.	35.00	8.00
□□	L3C Owen Nolan, SanJ.	20.00	4.00
□□	L4A Daniel Alfredsson, Ott.	20.00	4.00
□□	L4B Peter Forsberg, Colo.	50.00	12.00
□□	L4C Mats Sundin, Toro.	35.00	8.00
□□	L5A Ryan Smyth, Edmo.	15.00	4.00
□□	L5B Steve Yzerman, Detr.	90.00	20.00
□□	L5C Jarome Iginla, Calg.	30.00	6.00
□□	L6A Sergei Samsonov, Bost.	20.00	4.00
□□	L6B Igor Larionov, Detr.	20.00	4.00
□□	L6C Sergei Fedorov, Detr.	35.00	8.00
□□	L7A Patrik Elias, NJer.	60.00	14.00
□□	L7B Alexei Morozov, Pitt.	6.00	3.00
□□	L7C Vaclav Prospal, Phil.	20.00	4.00
□□	L8A John LeClair, Phil.	30.00	6.00
□□	L8B Mike Modano, Dall.	35.00	8.00
□□	L8C Brett Hull, SLou.	35.00	8.00
□□	L9A Olli Jokinen, LosA.	20.00	4.00
□□	L9B Saku Koivu, Mont.	30.00	6.00
□□	L9C Teemu Selänne, Anah.	30.00	6.00
□□	L10A Brian Leetch, NYRa.	20.00	4.00
□□	L10B Patrick Roy (G), Colo.	110.00	25.00
□□	L10C Nicklas Lidström, Detr.	20.00	4.00

1997 - 98 UPPER DECK O'REE PROMO

	Player	**UD**
□	22 Willie O'Ree, Bost.	4.00

1997 - 98 VALU-NET

Complete Set (24 phonecards):		35.00
	Player	**Unused**
□	Rob Blake	2.00
□	Raymond Bourque	3.00
□	Rod Brind'Amour	2.00
□	Martin Brodeur (G)	4.00
□	Shayne Corson	2.00
□	Marc Crawford, Coach	2.00
□	Éric Desjardins	2.00
□	Theoren Fleury	2.00
□	Adam Foote	2.00
□	Wayne Gretzky	10.00
□	Curtis Joseph (G)	2.00
□	Paul Kariya	3.00
□	Trevor Linden	2.00
□	Eric Lindros	2.00
□	Al MacInnis	2.00
□	Joe Nieuwendyk	2.00
□	Keith Primeau	2.00
□	Chris Pronger	2.00
□	Patrick Roy (G)	7.00
□	Joe Sakic	4.00
□	Brendan Shanahan	2.00
□	Scott Stevens	2.00
□	Steve Yzerman	6.00
□	Rob Zamuner	2.00

ASK ME ABOUT VALU-NET BUTTONS

These badges were available in French and English.

Complete Set (6 buttons):

	Player
□□	Éric Desjardins
□□	Paul Kariya
□□	Eric Lindros
□□	Patrick Roy (G)
□□	Joe Sakic
□□	Brendan Shanahan

SIGNED PHONECARDS

While these autographed phonecards do exist, there has been next to no market activity on these phonecards. The autographs were distributed in sets. Most sets were distributed without the Gretzky or Kariya signatures.

Autographed Set (24 phonecards):

Shell Set (22 phonecards):

	Player
□	Rob Blake ✍
□	Raymond Bourque ✍
□	Rod Brind'Amour ✍
□	Martin Brodeur (G) ✍
□	Shayne Corson ✍
□	Marc Crawford, Coach ✍
□	Éric Desjardins ✍
□	Theoren Fleury ✍
□	Adam Foote ✍
□	Wayne Gretzky ✍
□	Curtis Joseph (G) ✍
□	Paul Kariya ✍
□	Trevor Linden ✍
□	Eric Lindros ✍
□	Al MacInnis ✍
□	Joe Nieuwendyk ✍
□	Keith Primeau ✍
□	Chris Pronger ✍
□	Patrick Roy (G) ✍
□	Joe Sakic ✍
□	Brendan Shanahan ✍
□	Scott Stevens ✍
□	Steve Yzerman ✍
□	Rob Zamuner ✍

1997 - 98 VISIONS SIGNINGS

This series includes a 50-card base set that sells for $20 and a 50-card Gold set that sells for $60. A 20-card Artistry's insert set sells for $100. Other hockey singles may exist.

	Player	**Gold**	**Reg.**
□□	40 Dainius Zubrus	2.00	.50
□□	41 Joe Thornton	6.00	2.00
□□	42 Daniel Cleary	2.00	.50
□□	43 Sergei Samsonov, Detroit-IHL	4.00	1.50
□	A20 Dainius Zubrus		5.00
	Autograph		**Auto.**
□	Dainius Zubrus ✍		20.00
□	Joe Thornton ✍		40.00
□	Sergei Samsonov, Detroit-IHL ✍		25.00
□	A20 Dainius Zubrus ✍		30.00

1997 - 98 ZENITH

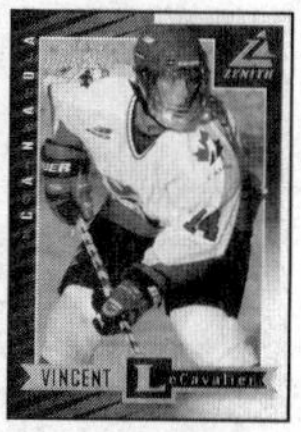

These cards have three versions: the regular card, a Silver parallel and a Gold parallel. At least four cards also have a promo version.

Complete Set (100 cards):		3500.00	650.00	300.00
Common Player:		8.00	2.00	.50
	Player	**Z-G**	**Z-S**	**Zen.**
□□□	1 Jarome Iginla, Calg.	60.00	8.00	2.00
□□□	2 Peter Forsberg, Colo.	100.00	14.00	3.50
□□□	3 Brendan Shanahan, Detr.	70.00	10.00	2.50
□□□	4 Wayne Gretzky, NYRa.	300.00	40.00	10.00
□□□	5 Steve Yzerman, Detr.	180.00	24.00	6.00
□□□□	6 Eric Lindros, Phil.	70.00	10.00	2.50
□□□	7 Keith Tkachuk, Phoe.	40.00	6.00	1.50
□□□	8 John LeClair, Phil.	60.00	8.00	2.00
□□□□	9 John Vanbiesbrouck (G), Flor.	30.00	4.00	1.00
□□□	10 Patrick Roy (G), Colo.	220.00	30.00	7.50
□□□	11 Raymond Bourque, Bost.	90.00	12.00	3.00
□□□	12 Theoren Fleury, Calg.	40.00	6.00	1.50

13 Brian Leetch, NYRa.	40.00	6.00	1.50
14 Chris Chelios, Chic.	40.00	6.00	1.50
15 Paul Kariya, Anah.	100.00	14.00	3.50
16 Mark Messier, Vanc.	70.00	10.00	2.50
17 Curtis Joseph (G), Edmo.	70.00	10.00	2.50
18 Mike Richter (G), NYRa.	30.00	4.00	1.00
19 Jeremy Roenick, Phoe.	60.00	8.00	2.00
20 Dominik Hasek (G), Buff.	70.00	10.00	2.50
21 Martin Brodeur (G), NJer.	120.00	16.00	4.00
22 Sergei Fedorov, Detr.	70.00	10.00	2.50
23 Pierre Turgeon, SLou.	30.00	4.00	1.00
24 Teemu Selänne, Anah.	60.00	8.00	2.00
25 Brett Hull, SLou.	70.00	10.00	2.50
26 Saku Koivu, Mont.	60.00	8.00	2.00
27 Owen Nolan, SanJ.	40.00	6.00	1.50
28 Jozef Stumpel, LosA.	15.00	2.00	.50
29 Joe Sakic, Colo.	120.00	16.00	4.00
30 Zigmund Palffy, NYIs.	40.00	6.00	1.50
31 Jaromir Jagr, Pitt.	70.00	10.00	2.50
32 Adam Oates, Wash.	30.00	4.00	1.00
33 Jeff Friesen, SanJ.	20.00	2.00	.50
34 Pavel Bure, Vanc.	60.00	8.00	2.00
35 Chris Osgood (G), Detr.	40.00	6.00	1.50
36 Mark Recchi, Mont.	30.00	4.00	1.00
37 Mike Modano, Dall.	70.00	10.00	2.50
38 Félix Potvin (G), Toro.	40.00	6.00	1.50
39 Vincent Damphousse, Mont.	45.00	6.00	1.50
40 Byron Dafoe (G), Bost.	30.00	4.00	1.00
41 Luc Robitaille, LosA.	60.00	8.00	2.00
42 Peter Bondra, Wash.	40.00	6.00	1.50
43 Daniel Alfredsson, Ott.	45.00	6.00	1.50
44 Pat LaFontaine, NYRa.	40.00	6.00	1.50
45 Mikael Renberg, Tamp.	20.00	2.00	.50
46 Doug Gilmour, NJer.	40.00	6.00	1.50
47 Dino Ciccarelli, Flor.	20.00	2.00	.50
48 Mats Sundin, Toro.	70.00	10.00	2.50
49 Ed Belfour (G), Dall.	70.00	10.00	2.50
50 Ron Francis, Pitt.	45.00	6.00	1.50
51 Miroslav Satan, Buff.	20.00	2.00	.50
52 Cory Stillman, Calg.	15.00	2.00	.50
53 Bryan Berard, NYIs.	20.00	2.00	.50
54 Keith Primeau, Caro.	30.00	4.00	1.00
55 Eric Dazé, Chic.	30.00	4.00	1.00
56 Chris Gratton, Phil.	15.00	2.00	.50
57 Claude Lemieux, Colo.	20.00	2.00	.50
58 Nicklas Lidström, Detr.	40.00	6.00	1.50
59 Olaf Kölzig (G), Wash.	40.00	6.00	1.50
60 Grant Fuhr (G), SLou.	40.00	6.00	1.50
61 Jamie Langenbrunner, Dall.	15.00	2.00	.50
62 Doug Weight, Edmo.	40.00	6.00	1.50
63 Joe Nieuwendyk, Dall.	30.00	4.00	1.00
64 Yanic Perreault, LosA.	20.00	2.00	.50
65 Jocelyn Thibault (G), Mont.	30.00	4.00	1.00
66 Guy Hebert (G), Anah.	15.00	2.00	.50
67 Shayne Corson, Mont.	20.00	2.00	.50
68 Bobby Holik, NJer.	20.00	2.00	.50
69 Sami Kapanen, Caro.	20.00	2.00	.50
70 Robert Reichel, NYIs.	20.00	2.00	.50
71 Ryan Smyth, Edmo.	35.00	4.00	1.00
72 Alexei Yashin, Ott.	40.00	6.00	1.50
73 Trevor Linden, Vanc.	30.00	4.00	1.00
74 Rod Brind'Amour, Phil.	20.00	2.00	.50
75 Dave Gagner, Flor.	10.00	2.00	.50
76 Nikolai Khabibulin (G), Phoe.	30.00	4.00	1.00
77 Tom Barrasso (G), Pitt.	30.00	4.00	1.00
78 Tony Amonte, Chic.	40.00	6.00	1.50
79 Alexander Mogilny, Vanc.	35.00	4.00	1.00
80 Jason Allison, Bost.	40.00	6.00	1.50
81 Patrik Elias, NJer. RC	**100.00**	**60.00**	**40.00**
82 Mike Johnson, Toro. RC	**30.00**	**8.00**	**5.00**
83 Richard Zednik, Wash.	30.00	4.00	1.00
84 Patrick Marleau, SanJ.	35.00	4.00	2.00
85 Mattias Öhlund, Vanc.	20.00	2.00	1.50
86 Sergei Samsonov, Bost.	40.00	6.00	3.00
87 Marco Sturm, SanJ. RC	**40.00**	**12.00**	**6.00**
88 Alyn McCauley, Toro.	20.00	2.00	1.50
89 Chris Phillips, Ott.	15.00	2.00	1.00
90 B. Morrison, NJer. RC	**60.00**	**30.00**	**25.00**
91 Vaclav Prospal, Phil. RC	**60.00**	**12.00**	**8.00**
92 Joe Thornton, Bost.	90.00	12.00	6.00
93 Boyd Devereaux, Edmo.	15.00	2.00	1.00
94 Alexei Morozov, Pitt.	15.00	2.00	1.00
95 Vincent Lecavalier RC	**175.00**	**120.00**	**100.00**
96 Manny Malhotra RC	**40.00**	**15.00**	**9.00**
97 Roberto Luongo (G) RC	**150.00**	**95.00**	**80.00**
98 Mathieu Garon (G)	30.00	4.00	2.00
99 Alex Tanguay RC	**100.00**	**70.00**	**50.00**
100 Josh Holden	10.00	2.00	.50

CHASING THE CUP

Insert Set (15 cards):	**175.00**
Insert (1:25)	**CTC**
1 Patrick Roy (G), Colo.	30.00
2 Wayne Gretzky, NYRa.	40.00
3 Jaromir Jagr, Pitt.	10.00
4 Eric Lindros, Phil.	10.00
5 Mike Modano, Dall.	10.00
6 Brendan Shanahan, Detr.	10.00
7 Brett Hull, SLou.	10.00
8 John LeClair, Phil.	8.00
9 Jocelyn Thibault (G), Mont.	4.00
10 Ed Belfour (G), SanJ.	10.00
11 Martin Brodeur (G), NJer.	16.00
12 Peter Forsberg, Colo.	14.00
13 Saku Koivu, Mont.	8.00
14 Pat LaFontaine, NYRa.	6.00
15 Steve Yzerman, Detr.	20.00

ROOKIE REIGN

Insert Set (15 cards):	**95.00**
Insert (1:25)	**RR**
1 Sergei Samsonov, Bost.	12.00
2 Joe Thornton, Bost.	24.00
3 Erik Rasmussen, Buff.	4.00
4 Brendan Morrison, NJer.	6.00
5 Magnus Arvedson, Otta.	4.00
6 Vaclav Prospal, Phil.	6.00
7 Brad Isbister, Phoe.	4.00
8 Aleksey Morozov, Pitt.	4.00
9 Marco Sturm, SanJ.	4.00
10 Patrick Marleau, SanJ.	8.00
11 Alyn McCauley, Toro.	6.00
12 Mike Johnson, Toro.	4.00
13 Mattias Öhlund, Vanc.	6.00
14 Patrik Elias, NJer.	16.00
15 Richard Zednik, Wash.	8.00

Z-TEAM

These cards have up to three versions: the regular insert, the Gold parallel and a 5"x7" card (1-9 only).

Insert Set (18 cards):	**-**	**775.00**	**350.00**
Insert Set (9 cards):	**175.00**	**-**	**-**
Insert	**5x7**	**GZT**	**ZT**
1 Teemu Selänne, Anah.	10.00	30.00	15.00
2 Wayne Gretzky, NYRa.	70.00	180.00	80.00
3 Patrick Roy (G), Colo.	50.00	130.00	60.00
4 Eric Lindros, Phil.	15.00	40.00	20.00
5 Peter Forsberg, Colo.	20.00	60.00	25.00
6 Paul Kariya, Anah.	20.00	60.00	25.00
7 John LeClair, Phil.	10.00	35.00	15.00
8 Martin Brodeur (G), NJer.	25.00	70.00	30.00
9 Brendan Shanahan, Detr.	15.00	45.00	20.00
10 Joe Thornton, Bost.		80.00	45.00
11 Mattias Öhlund, Vanc.		20.00	10.00
12 Mike Johnson, Toro.		10.00	6.00
13 Vaclav Prospal, Phil.		20.00	10.00
14 Sergei Samsonov, Bost.		40.00	20.00
15 Marco Sturm, SanJ.		15.00	6.00
16 Patrik Elias, NJer.		50.00	30.00
17 Richard Zednik, Wash.		25.00	15.00
18 Aleksey Morozov, Pitt.		15.00	6.00

DARE TO TEAR

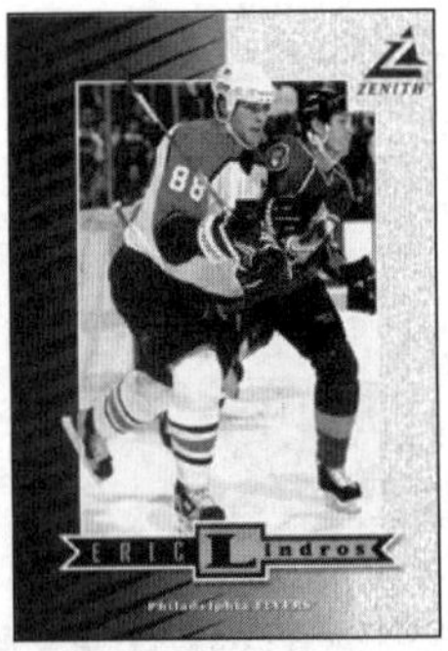

These cards have three versions: the regular card, an Impulse parallel and a Golden Impulse parallel (serial numbered out of 100). One standard-sized card came packaged inside each 5" x 7" card. Collectors could either keep the 5" x 7" card or tear the oversized card to see which card was inside. Oversize cards do not have the same photos as the smaller cards. Nine different 5" x 7" promo cards exist; each promo card has the same value as the regular card.

Card Size: 5" x 7"

Complete Set (80 cards):	**2600.00**	**350.00**	**165.00**
Common Player:	**10.00**	**3.00**	**1.00**
5x7 Card (Sealed)	**GI**	**SI**	**5x7**
Z1 Wayne Gretzky, NYRa.	250.00	30.00	10.00
Z2 Eric Lindros, Phil.	60.00	6.00	2.50
Z3 Patrick Roy (G), Colo.	180.00	22.00	7.50
Z4 Vanbiesbrouck (G), Flor.	30.00	3.00	1.00
Z5 Martin Brodeur (G), NJer.	100.00	12.00	4.00
Z6 Teemu Selänne, Anah.	50.00	6.00	2.00
Z7 Joe Sakic, Colo.	100.00	12.00	4.00
Z8 Jaromir Jagr, Pitt.	60.00	6.00	2.50
Z9 Brendan Shanahan, Detr.	60.00	6.00	2.50
Z10 Ed Belfour (G), Dall.	60.00	6.00	2.50
Z11 Guy Hebert (G), Anah.	15.00	3.00	1.00
Z12 Doug Gilmour, NJer.	35.00	4.00	1.50
Z13 Keith Primeau, Caro.	25.00	3.00	1.00
Z14 Grant Fuhr (G), SLou.	35.00	4.00	1.50
Z15 Joe Nieuwendyk, Dall.	25.00	3.00	1.00
Z16 Ryan Smyth, Edmo.	30.00	3.00	1.00
Z17 Chris Osgood (G), Detr.	30.00	4.00	1.50
Z18 Keith Tkachuk, Phoe.	30.00	4.00	1.50
Z19 Peter Forsberg, Colo.	80.00	10.00	3.50
Z20 Jarome Iginla, Calg.	50.00	6.00	2.00
Z21 Steve Yzerman, Detr.	150.00	18.00	6.00
Z22 Jeremy Roenick, Phoe.	50.00	6.00	2.00
Z23 Jozef Stumpel, LosA.	15.00	3.00	1.00
Z24 Mark Recchi, Mont.	25.00	3.00	1.00
Z25 Daniel Alfredsson, Ott.	35.00	4.00	1.50
Z26 Pat LaFontaine, NYRa.	35.00	4.00	1.50
Z27 Zigmund Palffy, NYIs.	35.00	4.00	1.50
Z28 Jason Allison, Bost.	30.00	4.00	1.50
Z29 Yanic Perreault, LosA.	20.00	3.00	1.00
Z30 Olaf Kölzig (G), Wash.	35.00	4.00	1.50
Z31 Mikael Renberg, Tamp.	20.00	3.00	1.00
Z32 Bryan Berard, NYIs.	20.00	3.00	1.00
Z33 Jocelyn Thibault (G), Mont.	25.00	3.00	1.00
Z34 Shayne Corson, Mont.	20.00	3.00	1.00
Z35 Dave Gagner, Flor.	10.00	3.00	1.00
Z36 Claude Lemieux, Colo.	20.00	3.00	1.00
Z37 Saku Koivu, Mont.	50.00	6.00	2.00
Z38 Curtis Joseph (G), Edmo.	60.00	6.00	2.50
Z39 Chris Chelios, Chic.	35.00	4.00	1.50
Z40 Raymond Bourque, Bost.	70.00	8.00	3.00
Z41 Adam Oates, Wash.	25.00	3.00	1.00
Z42 Félix Potvin (G), Toro.	35.00	4.00	1.50
Z43 Peter Bondra, Wash.	35.00	4.00	1.50
Z44 Sergei Fedorov, Detr.	60.00	6.00	2.50
Z45 Paul Kariya, Anah.	80.00	10.00	3.50
Z46 Theoren Fleury, Calg.	30.00	4.00	1.50
Z47 John LeClair, Phil.	50.00	6.00	2.00
Z48 Brett Hull, SLou.	60.00	6.00	2.50
Z49 Rod Brind'Amour, Phil.	20.00	3.00	1.00
Z50 Doug Weight, Edmo.	30.00	4.00	1.50
Z51 J. Langenbrunner, Dall.	15.00	3.00	1.00
Z52 Mats Sundin, Toro.	60.00	6.00	2.50
Z53 Ron Francis, Pitt.	35.00	4.00	1.50
Z54 Eric Dazé, Chic.	25.00	3.00	1.00
Z55 Nicklas Lidström, Detr.	35.00	4.00	1.50
Z56 Luc Robitaille, LosA.	50.00	6.00	2.00
Z57 V. Damphousse, Mont.	35.00	4.00	1.50
Z58 Mike Modano, Dall.	60.00	6.00	2.50
Z59 Pavel Bure, Vanc.	50.00	6.00	2.00
Z60 Owen Nolan, SanJ.	35.00	4.00	1.50
Z61 Pierre Turgeon, Mont.	25.00	3.00	1.00
Z62 Dominik Hasek (G), Buff.	60.00	6.00	2.50
Z63 Mike Richter (G), NYRa.	30.00	3.00	1.00
Z64 Mark Messier, Vanc.	60.00	6.00	2.50
Z65 Brian Leetch, NYRa.	35.00	4.00	1.50
Z66 Sergei Samsonov, Bost.	30.00	4.00	3.00
Z67 Alexei Morozov, Pitt.	15.00	3.00	1.00
Z68 Marco Sturm, SanJ. RC	**30.00**	**8.00**	**3.00**
Z69 Patrik Elias, NJer. RC	**100.00**	**30.00**	**20.00**
Z70 Alyn McCauley, Toro.	20.00	3.00	1.50
Z71 Mi. Johnson, Toro. RC	**25.00**	**4.00**	**2.50**
Z72 Richard Zednik, Wash.	25.00	3.00	2.00
Z73 Mattias Öhlund, Vanc.	20.00	3.00	1.50
Z74 Joe Thornton, Bost.	70.00	12.00	6.00
Z75 Vincent Lecavalier RC	**120.00**	**35.00**	**25.00**
Z76 Manny Malhotra, RC	**30.00**	**6.00**	**4.50**
Z77 R. Luongo (G) RC	**100.00**	**30.00**	**20.00**
Z78 Mathieu Garon (G)	25.00	3.00	2.00
Z79 Alex Tanguay RC	**70.00**	**22.00**	**15.00**
Z80 Josh Holden	10.00	3.00	1.00

1998 BONAPARTE

Complete Deck (32 cards):	**30.00**
Player	**B**
1A Martin Prochazka	.50
1B Robert Reichel	1.00
1C Robert Lang	.50
1D Milan Hejduk	3.00
2A Martin Rucinsky	.50
2B Jaromir Jagr	3.00
2C Richard Smehlik	.50
2D Dominik Hasek	3.00
3A Josef Beranek	.50
3B Jaroslav Spacek	.50
3C Jaromir Jagr	3.00
3D Jiri Slegr	.50
4A Vladimir Ruzicka	.50
4B Roman Cechmanek (G)	1.50
4C Jan Caloun	.50
4D Milan Hnilicka (G)	.50
5A Jiri Dopita	.50
5B Frantisek Kucera	.50
5C Jaromir Jagr	3.00
5D Petr Svoboda	.50
6A Petr Svoboda	.50
6B Ivan Hlinka	.50
6C Slavomir Lener	.50
6D Jaromir Jagr	3.00
7A Jiri Slegr	.50
7B Martin Straka	1.00
7C Pavel Patera	.50
7D David Moravec	.50
8A Vladimir Ruzicka	.50
8A Libor Procazka	.50
8C Roman Hamrlik	.50
8D Dominik Hasek (G)	3.00

1998 BONAPARTE PEXESO

These cards were available as a perforated sheet.

Complete Deck (28 cards):	**25.00**
Player	**B**
1 Martin Prochazka	.50
2 Robert Reichel	1.00
3 Robert Lang	.50
4 Milan Hejduk	3.00
5 Martin Rucinsky	.50
6 Richard Smehlik	.50
7 Dominik Hasek (G)	3.50
8 Josef Beranek	.50
9 Jaroslav Spacek	.50
10 Jaromir Jagr	3.50
11 Roman Cechmanek (G)	1.50
12 Vladimir Ruzicka	.50
13 Jiri Slegr	.50
14 Jan Caloun	.50
15 Milan Hnilicka	.50
16 Jiri Dopita	.50
17 Frantisek Kucera	.50
18 Jaromir Jagr	3.50
19 Petr Svoboda	.50
20 Ivan Hlinka	.50
21 Slavomir Lener	.50
22 Jiri Slegr	.50
23 Martin Straka	1.00
24 Pavel Patera	.50
25 David Moravec	.50
26 Libor Prochazka	.50
27 Roman Hamrlik	.50
28 Dominik Hasek (G)	3.50

1998 McDONALD'S NAGANO

This card was available in Japan.

Olympics

Wayne Gretzky, Canada

1998 QUÉBEC INTERNATIONAL PEE WEE

Only 200 sets were produced for the 1998 tournament Common players start at 50¢.

Complete Set (1424): **175.00**

PITTSBURGH PEE WEE

1 P. Bates	10 R. Nolte
2 M. Brinton	11 C. Payne
3 C. Cummings	12 J. Plass-Meyer
4 M. Cox	13 D. Pomerico
5 Z. Flora	14 J. Romano
6 A. Fodor	15 N. Rua

☐ 7 A. Freyer
☐ 8 M. Frame
☐ 9 A. Mercurio
☐ 16 T. Tripadi
☐ 17 Instructeurs

MOUNT-PEARL PEE WEE
☐ 18 M. Acreman
☐ 19 Z. Attwood
☐ 20 N. Roberts
☐ 21 B. Norris
☐ 22 G. Smith
☐ 23 J. Manning
☐ 24 J. Burrage
☐ 25 B. Grant
☐ 26 M. Lee
☐ 27 J. Anthony
☐ 28 M. O'Brien
☐ 29 M. Fagan
☐ 30 J. Cashin
☐ 31 G. Aylward
☐ 32 C. Power
☐ 33 Instructeurs

HERSHEY PEE WEE
☐ 34 J. Kullman
☐ 35 J. Eberly
☐ 36 J. Eberly
☐ 37 B. Kemmerer
☐ 38 A. Helms
☐ 39 M. Hoffman
☐ 40 D. Lutz
☐ 41 J. Cassel
☐ 42 D. Fahnestock
☐ 43 E. Mc Laren
☐ 44 C. Zarefoss
☐ 45 C. Herr
☐ 46 J. Rich
☐ 47 B. Egan
☐ 48 J. Freeman
☐ 49 R. Tiburtini
☐ 50 S. Hartley
☐ 51 C. Holroyd
☐ 52 J. Hastings
☐ 53 T. Hanks
☐ 54 B. Bungey
☐ 55 B. Henry
☐ 56 Instructeurs

NEWMARKET PEE WEE
☐ 57 S. Burns
☐ 58 J. Dickson
☐ 59 S. Downing
☐ 60 D. Duscharm
☐ 61 T. Fraser
☐ 62 D. Halls
☐ 63 C. Koneczny
☐ 64 Y. Laporte
☐ 65 P. Lehnan
☐ 66 C. Nutter
☐ 67 M. O'Connor
☐ 68 M. Pacione
☐ 69 R. Peymen
☐ 70 T. Reid
☐ 71 C. Simone
☐ 72 B. Stefiuk
☐ 73 M. Whitehead
☐ 74 Instructeurs

PHILADELPHIA FLYERS PEE WEE
☐ 75 N. Silvestri
☐ 76 C. Lefever
☐ 77 B. Berger
☐ 78 M. Curran
☐ 79 T. Wochok
☐ 80 M. Ciccaglione
☐ 81 J. Giacobbo
☐ 82 T. Procida
☐ 83 S. Bruch
☐ 84 M. Mould
☐ 85 J. Beck
☐ 86 A. Francks
☐ 87 A. Zaccaria
☐ 88 D. Baratta
☐ 89 M. Corey
☐ 90 B. Verdecchio
☐ 91 T. Barron
☐ 92 E. Mackey
☐ 93 C. Grunther
☐ 94 M. Potacco
☐ 95 Instructeurs

STE-FOY AA PEE WEE
☐ 96 D. Drouin
☐ 97 L. Grégoire
☐ 98 P. Lacroix
☐ 99 S. Goulet
☐ 100 B. Couchesne
☐ 101 P. Brière
☐ 102 P. Létourneau
☐ 103 A. Vincent
☐ 104 J. Landry
☐ 105 Gagné-Laplante
☐ 106 K. Vigneault
☐ 107 J. Boiteau
☐ 108 A. Garon
☐ 109 P. Bergeron
☐ 110 D. Leclerc
☐ 111 Bergeron-Pearson
☐ 112 Instructeurs

MATANE PEE WEE
☐ 113 J. Lavigne
☐ 114 J. Turbide
☐ 115 R. Banville
☐ 116 K. Gagné
☐ 117 É. Lévesque
☐ 118 G. Coulombe
☐ 119 P. Tremblay
☐ 120 J. Lavoie
☐ 121 B. Arsenault
☐ 122 P. Gauthier
☐ 123 J. Boudreau
☐ 124 J. Cloutier
☐ 125 R. Godbout
☐ 126 P. Blais
☐ 127 P. Turbide
☐ 128 P. Bouchard
☐ 129 Instructeurs

BLAINVILLE PEE WEE
☐ 130 P. Boudreau
☐ 131 J. Guindon
☐ 132 A. Nobert-Roy
☐ 133 A. Lamarche
☐ 134 I. Jones
☐ 135 J. Girard
☐ 136 S. Séguin
☐ 137 F. Lapointe
☐ 138 S. Brisson
☐ 139 M. Rousseau
☐ 140 S. Lagacé
☐ 141 B. Metcalfe
☐ 142 J. Carreau
☐ 143 J. Bourgeois
☐ 144 P. Tétreault
☐ 145 M. Trottier
☐ 146 Instructeurs

DETROIT LITTLE CAESARS PEE WEE
☐ 147 B. Lukas
☐ 148 C. Trick
☐ 149 D. Shencopp
☐ 150 C. Lewis
☐ 151 J. Dest
☐ 152 J. Mass
☐ 153 K. Voss
☐ 154 J. Cappelli
☐ 155 J. Milam
☐ 156 Z. Pearson
☐ 157 R. Kesler
☐ 158 J. Coules
☐ 159 M. Lee
☐ 160 N. Pomponio
☐ 161 D. Vicari
☐ 162 Instructeurs

BEAUCE-NORD PEE WEE
☐ 163 J. Vachon
☐ 164 M. Vachon
☐ 165 M. Savoie
☐ 166 F. Marcoux
☐ 167 É. Savoie
☐ 172 J. Labbé
☐ 173 D. Rousseau
☐ 174 G. Bety
☐ 175 S. Rhéaume
☐ 176 R. Langevin
☐ 168 M. Mercier
☐ 169 S. Gagné
☐ 170 S. Larose
☐ 171 P. Turmel
☐ 177 N. Blais
☐ 178 F. Therrien
☐ 179 Instructeurs

CÔTE-DE-BEAUPRÉ, ILE D'ORLÉANS PEE-WEE
☐ 180 J. Caron
☐ 181 V. Coulombe
☐ 182 K. Cauchon
☐ 183 É. Brown
☐ 184 S. Racine
☐ 185 J. Dupont
☐ 186 S. Barrette
☐ 187 G. Shields
☐ 188 S. Trépanier
☐ 189 S. Racine
☐ 190 K. Deschênes
☐ 191 A. Bourget
☐ 192 S. Pichette
☐ 193 L. Gravel
☐ 194 B. Lavoie
☐ 195 F. Fortin G. Rémi
☐ 196 D. Brown
☐ 197 É. Dion
☐ 198 N. Mariage
☐ 199 B. Goulet
☐ 200 S. St-Gelais
☐ 201 Instructeurs

VICTORIAVILLE PEE-WEE
☐ 202 D. Morin
☐ 203 K. Daigle
☐ 204 M. Desruisseaux
☐ 205 C. Laroche
☐ 206 J. B.-Lebel
☐ 207 M. Raby-Goyette
☐ 208 T. Poudrier
☐ 209 A. Carignan
☐ 210 M. Melançon
☐ 211 T. Lafontaine
☐ 212 M. Jalbert
☐ 213 R. Morissette
☐ 214 K. Dion
☐ 215 T. Bellemare
☐ 216 J. Marcoux
☐ 217 Instructeurs

ASBESTOS PEE-WEE
☐ 218 H. Leclerc
☐ 219 K. Daigle
☐ 220 M. Gagnon
☐ 221 F. Ducharme
☐ 222 F. Perreault
☐ 223 W. éliveau
☐ 224 G. Moreau
☐ 225 M. Gagnière
☐ 226 A. Daigle
☐ 227 A. Deslauriers
☐ 228 L. Pépin
☐ 229 Y. Comtois
☐ 230 K. Ducharme
☐ 231 A. Francoeur
☐ 232 A. Savoie
☐ 233 J. Fontaine
☐ 234 C. Bachand
☐ 235 Instructeurs

DRUMMONDVILLE PEE-WEE
One of the more expensive singles is Maxime Boisclair ($1-2).

☐ 236 K. Asselin
☐ 237 J. Beaudoin
☐ 238 M. Boisclair
☐ 239 R. Chamberland
☐ 240 F. Donais
☐ 241 F. Duhamel
☐ 242 P. Gallant
☐ 243 P. Hamel
☐ 244 T. Hamel
☐ 245 É. Lemaire
☐ 246 A. Lussier
☐ 247 C. Masse
☐ 248 F. Nault
☐ 249 P. Sarrazin
☐ 250 M. Tardif
☐ 251 D. Tessier
☐ 252 Instructeurs

PROSPER ETCHEMIN PEE-WEE
☐ 253 K. Morin
☐ 254 O. Poulin
☐ 255 M. Turcotte
☐ 256 S. Thompson
☐ 257 D. Poulin
☐ 258 J. Poulin
☐ 259 O. Deblois
☐ 260 A. Boily
☐ 261 S. Bourque
☐ 262 N. Nadeau-Ouellet
☐ 263 J. Tanguay
☐ 264 K. Fortin
☐ 265 F. Chabot
☐ 266 P. Chabot
☐ 267 P. Audet
☐ 268 Instructeurs

NEW-JERSEY DEVILS PEE-WEE
☐ 269 S. Burton
☐ 270 S. Eberenz
☐ 271 M. Gershon
☐ 272 M. Gilroy
☐ 273 H. Jessiman
☐ 274 B. Liamero
☐ 275 S. Lunav
☐ 276 A. Minicucci
☐ 277 G. Overlock
☐ 278 A. Reison
☐ 279 V. Rinaldi
☐ 280 T. Roth
☐ 281 K. Schaeffer
☐ 282 T. Sheridan
☐ 283 P. Tocicki
☐ 284 Instructeurs

QUINTE PEE-WEE
☐ 285 É. Tobia
☐ 286 A. Beare
☐ 287 D. Van Egmond
☐ 288 J. Miller
☐ 289 R. Desjardins
☐ 290 J. Sparling
☐ 291 J. Freeland
☐ 292 D. Smith
☐ 293 M. Simpson
☐ 294 R. Card
☐ 295 M. Simmons
☐ 296 B. Fiorini
☐ 297 T. Pope
☐ 298 B. Richardson
☐ 299 S. Bowen
☐ 300 S. Turner
☐ 301 M. Campbell
☐ 302 J. Clarke
☐ 303 T. Pigden
☐ 304 A. Hamilton
☐ 305 Instructeurs

BOSTON BRUINS PEE-WEE
☐ 306 P. Greer
☐ 307 N. Lucia
☐ 308 R. Carolan
☐ 309 B. O'Hanley
☐ 310 C. Diozzi
☐ 311 M. Doe
☐ 312 S. McClellan
☐ 313 G. Wieschhoff
☐ 314 S. Semenchuk
☐ 315 D. Warren
☐ 316 J. Patriquin
☐ 317 S. McDougall
☐ 318 J. Polsen
☐ 319 J. Marcus
☐ 320 M. Toscano
☐ 321 R. Donahue
☐ 322 D. Gallup
☐ 323 H. Horgan Robbie
☐ 324 Team photo

MONTMAGNY PEE-WEE
☐ 325 P. Daigle
☐ 326 S. Boulet
☐ 327 M. Poitras
☐ 334 D. Gaudreau
☐ 335 É. Thibault
☐ 336 J. Vaillancourt
☐ 328 P. Huot
☐ 329 G. Proulx
☐ 330 T. Dugal
☐ 331 T. Beaumont
☐ 332 S. Cloutier
☐ 333 P. Gagnon
☐ 337 J. Latouche
☐ 338 V. Côté
☐ 339 R. Dupont
☐ 340 M. Morin
☐ 341 C. Vézina
☐ 342 Instructeurs

RIVE-SUD PEE-WEE
☐ 343 A. Lehouillier
☐ 344 J. Lemieux-Walsh
☐ 345 C. Rioux
☐ 346 P. Bélanger
☐ 347 M. Morin
☐ 348 C. Paquet
☐ 349 B. Blondin
☐ 350 J. Marceau
☐ 351 M. Aubé
☐ 352 K. Gagné
☐ 353 F. Beaudoin
☐ 354 J. Grégoire
☐ 355 D. Duquet
☐ 356 É. Albert
☐ 357 K. Dumont
☐ 358 D. Soucy
☐ 359 Instructeurs

CHARLEVOIX PEE-WEE
☐ 360 F. Rochette
☐ 361 D. Jean
☐ 362 Y. Bergeron
☐ 363 G. Dufour
☐ 364 J. Dufour
☐ 365 P. Gagné
☐ 366 É. Marinoff
☐ 367 G. Lavoie
☐ 368 S. Dufour
☐ 369 H. Harvey. Manuel
☐ 370 J. Turcotte
☐ 371 E. Carrier
☐ 372 S. Chamberland
☐ 373 D. Tremblay
☐ 374 J. Marcoux
☐ 375 F. Turcotte
☐ 376 Instructeurs

BADEN-WURTTEMBERG PEE-WEE
☐ 377 M. Koch
☐ 378 P. Zehrlaut
☐ 379 B. Stehle
☐ 380 D. Roztocil
☐ 381 M. Muller
☐ 382 R. Baumann
☐ 383 M. Schwierz
☐ 384 T. Thieringer
☐ 385 B. Gross
☐ 386 S. Schmitt
☐ 387 S. Milovanovic
☐ 388 A. Elter
☐ 389 B. Jarosch
☐ 390 M. Metz
☐ 391 D. Walther
☐ 392 P. Braun
☐ 393 M. Hemmerich
☐ 394 P. Gorel
☐ 395 Y. Seidenberg
☐ 396 A. Hackert

ST-GÉDÉON PEE-WEE
☐ 397 S. Lachance
☐ 398 S. Pépin
☐ 399 P. Poulin
☐ 400 D. Quirion
☐ 401 F. Poulin
☐ 402 I. Mathieu-Girard
☐ 403 S. Lachance
☐ 404 B. Thibodeau
☐ 405 J. Fecteau
☐ 406 B. Lachance
☐ 407 P. Poulin
☐ 408 D. Bégin
☐ 409 P. Paradis
☐ 410 M. Therrien
☐ 411 B. Roy
☐ 412 Instructeurs

CHAUVEAU AIGLES PEE-WEE
☐ 413 Y. Gauvin
☐ 414 Carrier- François
☐ 415 M. Jalbert
☐ 416 J. Bédard
☐ 417 J. Audet
☐ 418 K. Poulin
☐ 419 C. Labrecque
☐ 420 F. Brassard
☐ 421 B. Mayotte
☐ 422 M. Bernier
☐ 423 D. Proulx
☐ 424 O. Pouliot
☐ 425 F. Giroux
☐ 426 S. Côté
☐ 427 W. Robitaille
☐ 428 J. Lapointe
☐ 429 Instructeurs

POINTE-LÉVY C PEE-WEE
☐ 430 K. Carrier
☐ 431 T. Carrier
☐ 432 A. Baillargeon
☐ 433 G. Côté
☐ 434 D. Boudreault
☐ 435 N. Rodrigue
☐ 436 S. Marceau
☐ 437 M. Nolet
☐ 438 Lavallée-Lecours
☐ 439 C. Morin
☐ 440 J. Pichette
☐ 441 Camiré-Tremblay
☐ 442 M. Daigle
☐ 443 H. Deroy
☐ 444 C. Savoie
☐ 445 J. Langlois
☐ 446 M. Patry
☐ 447 Instructeurs

LAC MÉGANTIC PEE-WEE
☐ 448 F. Gilbert
☐ 449 N. Bellegarde
☐ 450 S. Turgeon
☐ 451 J. Therrien
☐ 452 O. Paradis
☐ 453 F. Therrien
☐ 454 M. Proteau
☐ 455 M. Lacroix
☐ 456 M. Béliveau
☐ 457 L. Nadeau
☐ 458 G. Hallée
☐ 459 J. Jacques
☐ 460 D. Hallé
☐ 461 R. Lavoie
☐ 462 J. Baillargeon
☐ 463 F. Gagnon
☐ 464 J. Roy

CHICAGO BLACK HAWKS PEE-WEE
☐ 465 B. Kirby
☐ 466 D. Switalla
☐ 467 É. Hanek
☐ 468 B. Vacala
☐ 469 C. Parrilli
☐ 470 M. Borden
☐ 471 L. Bruno
☐ 472 B. Duvoney
☐ 473 J. Stone
☐ 474 G. Shaw
☐ 475 K. Sheehan
☐ 476 K. Pink
☐ 477 R. Merz
☐ 478 M. Tylka
☐ 479 J. Barr
☐ 480 M. Degeorge
☐ 481 Instructeurs

BUDAPEST PEE-WEE
☐ 482 A. Nagy
☐ 483 Z. Szëkely Madai
☐ 484 R. Budai
☐ 485 T. Galgoczi
☐ 492 A. Koszeghy
☐ 493 L. Subely-Madai
☐ 494 L. Nyerges
☐ 495 Z. Gergely
☐ 486 G. Haznagy
☐ 487 L. Miski
☐ 488 A. Vegh
☐ 489 G. Incze
☐ 490 B. Vigh
☐ 491 N. Fekecs
☐ 496 M. Haragos
☐ 497 A. Schleicher
☐ 498 K. Illyes
☐ 499 O. Kiss
☐ 500 Instructeurs
☐ 501 Instructeurs

WASHINGTON CAPITALS PEE-WEE
☐ 502 T. Carolan
☐ 503 B. Coleman
☐ 504 C. Merrill
☐ 505 S. Bowles
☐ 505 A. Robinson
☐ 506 C. Varoy
☐ 507 J. Sixsmith
☐ 508 S. Werner
☐ 510 G. Costa
☐ 511 J. Fritsch
☐ 512 D. Hunter
☐ 513 R. Keravuori
☐ 514 K. Laughlin
☐ 515 T. Nussbaum
☐ 516 E. Waryas
☐ 517 M. Weber
☐ 518 A. White
☐ 519 J. Young
☐ 520 C. Cashen
☐ 521 B. Forino
☐ 522 G. Rando
☐ 523 N. Staal
☐ 524 M. Tildh
☐ 525 C. Donovan

BEAUCE-SUD PEE-WEE
☐ 526 A. Lacombe
☐ 527 G. Courtemanche
☐ 528 É. Veilleux-Poulin
☐ 529 M. Poulin-Grenier
☐ 530 G. Blais
☐ 531 D. Carrier
☐ 532 J. Lehoux
☐ 533 G. Fortier
☐ 534 D. Giroux
☐ 535 É. Tremblay
☐ 536 J. Morin
☐ 537 M. Champagne
☐ 538 F. Bougie
☐ 539 S. Pomerleau
☐ 540 G. Isabelle
☐ 541 P. Boies
☐ 542 Instructeurs

TEAM ILLINOIS PEE-WEE
☐ 543 E. Pfligler
☐ 544 D. Richmond
☐ 545 T. Edwardson
☐ 546 D. Rankin
☐ 547 J. Elzinga
☐ 548 A. Murray
☐ 549 J. Friedman
☐ 550 S. Nicholson
☐ 551 D. Hunt
☐ 552 D. Charleston
☐ 553 C. Solberg
☐ 554 M. Giangreco
☐ 555 D. Bayer
☐ 556 M. Mannina
☐ 557 A. Park
☐ 558 M. Gluck

POINTE-LÉVY B PEE-WEE
☐ 559 D. McNeil
☐ 560 D. Geneau
☐ 561 T. Veilleux
☐ 562 C. Carrier
☐ 563 M. Marois
☐ 564 K. Patry
☐ 565 S. Caron
☐ 566 F. Vincent
☐ 567 Y. Bourque
☐ 568 P. Rancourt
☐ 569 J. Pouliot
☐ 570 C. Dumas
☐ 571 J. Lemelin
☐ 572 P. Soucy
☐ 573 P. Leblond
☐ 574 K. Ouellet
☐ 575 É. Boulanger
☐ 576 Instructeurs

CAMPUS CAP ROUGE ST-AUGUSTIN PEE-WEE
☐ 577 S. Lessard
☐ 578 A. Beaudoin
☐ 579 J. Croteau
☐ 580 J. Delisle
☐ 581 M. Fortin
☐ 582 D. Gagnon
☐ 583 P. Gagnon
☐ 584 P. Labbé
☐ 585 G. Magher
☐ 586 J. Massicotte
☐ 587 D. Plante
☐ 588 A. Rivard
☐ 589 V. Tardif
☐ 590 P. Thibeault
☐ 591 R. Robitaille
☐ 592 R. Teasdale
☐ 593 Instructeurs

STE-FOY B PEE-WEE
☐ 594 J. Côté
☐ 595 B. Lecompte
☐ 596 M. Castonguay
☐ 597 P. Dionne
☐ 598 I. Boudreau
☐ 599 S. Goulet
☐ 600 K. Raymond
☐ 601 G. Bédard-Pagé
☐ 602 L. Ratté
☐ 603 A. Lagacé
☐ 604 C. Marcoux
☐ 605 L. Gendron
☐ 606 R. Bazinet
☐ 607 S. Agostini-Cayer
☐ 608 P. Nadeau
☐ 609 V. Tardif
☐ 610 B. Mailloux
☐ 611 Instructeurs

DÉTROIT RED WINGS PEE-WEE
☐ 612 J. Archer
☐ 613 D. Booth
☐ 614 B. Boyes
☐ 615 P. Mannino
☐ 616 R. Overfield
☐ 617 D. Miller
☐ 618 J. Paige
☐ 619 C. Potter
☐ 620 D. Punches
☐ 621 D. Pszenyczny
☐ 622 E. Sargent
☐ 623 D. Storm
☐ 624 L. Schmidt
☐ 625 J. Tracy
☐ 626 M. Trevino
☐ 627 C. Wright
☐ 628 Instructeurs

WEST ISLAND PEE-WEE
☐ 629 V. Barrucco
☐ 630 M. Bernier
☐ 631 M. Davies
☐ 632 K. Demers
☐ 633 C. De Sa
☐ 634 J. Dion
☐ 635 S. Duckett
☐ 636 M. Faccone
☐ 637 A. Fares
☐ 638 B. Gager
☐ 639 T. Kuchiran
☐ 640 L. Richard
☐ 641 P. Schetagne
☐ 642 T. Smith
☐ 643 C. Tisdall
☐ 644 M. Labelle
☐ 645 Instructeurs

MIDDLESEX ISLANDERS PEE-WEE
☐ 646 J. Butler
☐ 647 B. Caldarelli
☐ 655 A. Martignetti
☐ 656 G. McDonnell

□ 648 K. Colwell
□ 649 P. Forshner
□ 650 C. Green Halgh
□ 651 J. Halverson
□ 652 J. Henry
□ 653 M. Hines
□ 654 T. O'Rourke
□ 657 M. Ottariana
□ 658 D. Shribman
□ 659 A. Stanieich
□ 660 S. Tomes
□ 661 D. Ward
□ 662 Instructeurs

BOSTON TERRIERS PEE-WEE

□ 663 M. Aylward
□ 664 D. Balcom
□ 665 C. Carr
□ 666 P. Connors
□ 667 J. Fraser
□ 668 G. Gallagher
□ 669 N. Joyal
□ 670 B. Keane
□ 671 B. Kneeland
□ 672 B. Le Clerc
□ 673 P. Mignosa
□ 674 A. Millman
□ 675 R. Ortiz
□ 676 K. Regan
□ 677 M. Rosen
□ 678 A. Sherr
□ 679 S. Sullivan
□ 680 Instructeurs

CENTRAL ONTARIO PEE-WEE

□ 681 T. Barton
□ 682 S. Burns
□ 683 P. Callaghan
□ 684 A. Dankiw
□ 685 C. Dean
□ 686 S. Dell
□ 687 T. Fitzpatrick
□ 688 B. Garringer
□ 689 B. Hill
□ 690 C. Huntley
□ 691 M. Imrie
□ 692 J. Magee
□ 693 J. Moffatt
□ 694 A. Sachs
□ 695 C. Sturge
□ 696 B. Welsh
□ 697 J. Wilson
□ 698 Instructeurs

CHAUDIÈRE OUEST C PEE-WEE

□ 699 M. Pelletier
□ 700 G. Collard-Simard
□ 701 De la Sablonnière
□ 702 J. Paradis
□ 703 G. Royer
□ 704 J. Gosselin
□ 705 O. St-Cyr
□ 706 A. Desruisseaux
□ 707 D. Golden
□ 708 A. Prud'Homme
□ 709 F. Lachapelle
□ 710 V. Boulay
□ 711 J. Bolduc
□ 712 É. Gauthier
□ 713 G. Belleau
□ 714 Instructeurs

SHAWINIGAN PEE-WEE

□ 715 J. Guay
□ 716 P. Beaulieu
□ 717 D. Gélinas
□ 718 P. Lévesque
□ 719 N. Parr
□ 720 M. Lefrançois
□ 721 M. Montplaisir
□ 722 N. Gervais
□ 723 M. Huard
□ 724 G. Manseau
□ 725 M. Gélinas
□ 726 M. Gignac
□ 727 G. Trudel
□ 728 S. Hélie
□ 729 S. L'Heureux
□ 730 M. Thibodeau
□ 731 M. Lanciault
□ 732 M. Robert
□ 733 P. Bédard
□ 734 Instructeurs

CHAUDIÈRE OUEST B PEE-WEE

□ 735 M. Welsh
□ 736 É. Lepage
□ 737 N. Desrochers
□ 738 C. Benjamin
□ 739 Turcotte-Tremblay
□ 740 J. Lapierre
□ 741 J. Chabot
□ 742 L. Leblanc
□ 841 J. Pinel
□ 743 G. Robert
□ 744 L. Meillleur
□ 745 F. Paradis
□ 746 R. Rochette
□ 747 J. Martel
□ 748 S. Ouellet
□ 749 L. Duchesne
□ 750 Instructeurs

BELLECHASSE PEE-WEE

□ 751 A. Couture
□ 752 L. Asselin
□ 753 D. Labonté
□ 754 M. Boissonneault
□ 755 J. Bélanger
□ 756 F. Boutin
□ 757 É. Thibault
□ 758 P. Turgeon
□ 759 A. Lamontagne
□ 760 J. Buteau
□ 761 J. Mercier
□ 762 G. Labrie
□ 763 J. Gilbert
□ 764 M. Bélanger
□ 765 M. Pouliot
□ 766 J. Gagnon
□ 767 J. Labrecque
□ 768 Instructeurs

BEAUCE-AMIANTE PEE-WEE

□ 769 M. Vachon
□ 770 P. Bureau
□ 771 A. Beaudoin
□ 772 J. Morin
□ 773 J. Fecteau
□ 774 G. Durand
□ 775 G. Bédard
□ 776 D. Poulin
□ 777 M. Rouleau
□ 778 A. Gagnon
□ 779 F. Lapierre
□ 780 P. Bouffard
□ 781 É. Lessard
□ 782 S. Poulin
□ 783 S. Godin
□ 784 N. Laplante
□ 785 P. Couture
□ 786 I. Instructreurs

NEW-YORK ISLANDERS PEE-WEE

□ 787 J. Ames
□ 788 M. Arcieri
□ 789 R. Cruthers
□ 790 B. Dobler
□ 791 M. Dowling
□ 792 E. Falcone
□ 793 J. Fischer
□ 794 A. Gartman
□ 795 R. Goldman
□ 796 M. Holstman
□ 797 P. Martin
□ 798 B. Murray
□ 799 K. Poulos
□ 800 R. Scimone
□ 801 P. Taglia
□ 802 D. Valente
□ 803 M. Wax
□ 804 B. Rizzo
□ 805 C. Molinaro

BEAUPORT MARINIERS PEE-WEE

□ 806 G. Samson
□ 807 M. Pichette
□ 808 S. Robitaille
□ 815 K. Mathieu
□ 816 K. White
□ 817 M. Joncas
□ 809 M. Leblond
□ 810 J. Thomassin
□ 811 J. Morency
□ 812 J. Laflamme
□ 813 L. Fournier
□ 814 J. Lafrance
□ 818 K. Émond
□ 819 J. Rioux
□ 820 S. Picard
□ 821 S. Morency
□ 822 R. Roy
□ 823 Instructeurs

BEAUBOURG PEE-WEE

□ 824 G. Boudrias
□ 825 C. Daigle
□ 826 P. Desrochers
□ 827 A. Dorval
□ 828 S. Guérard
□ 829 F. Labrecque
□ 830 J. Lachance
□ 831 G. Lajeunesse
□ 832 M. Larochelle
□ 833 M. Lefaivre
□ 834 J. Légaré
□ 835 V. Lemoine
□ 836 D. Lévesque
□ 837 F. Picard
□ 838 J. Savard
□ 839 G. Turgeon
□ 840 Instructeurs

ÉTOILES DE L'EST PEE-WEE

□ 842 P. Fleming
□ 843 J. Gauvreau
□ 844 F. Hernandez
□ 845 K. Murray
□ 846 É. McCarthy
□ 847 M. Carrière
□ 848 K. Di Cesare
□ 849 J. Charrette
□ 850 M. Beaulieu
□ 851 É. Fournier
□ 852 M. Foucher - G
□ 853 M. Garneau
□ 854 É. Delisle
□ 855 P. Bourgouin
□ 856 N. Romano
□ 857 J. Boucher
□ 858 N. Cadrin-Alpin
□ 859 Instructeurs

ST-LOUIS BLUES PEE-WEE

□ 860 A. Calcaterra
□ 861 A. Crohn
□ 862 J. Dietl
□ 863 D. Dileo
□ 864 J. Fox
□ 865 C. Garcia
□ 866 M. Kern
□ 867 S. Kunst
□ 868 J. Leiendecker
□ 869 J. Mantovani
□ 870 B. Mongey
□ 871 D. Mueller
□ 872 B. Prest
□ 873 L. Privett
□ 874 J. Sales
□ 875 A. Thompson
□ 876 C. Vitale
□ 877 Instructeurs

VANCOUVER PEE-WEE

□ 878 W. Shaw
□ 879 A. Sollitt
□ 880 J. Vickers
□ 881 B. Steele
□ 882 T. Wheat
□ 883 D. Norman
□ 884 S. Carmichael
□ 885 A. Ritchie
□ 886 A. Burgoyne
□ 887 A. Mitchell
□ 888 B. Palin
□ 889 M. Grondin
□ 890 C. McLachlan
□ 891 B. Appleton
□ 892 M. Noir
□ 893 W. Dewitt
□ 894 A. Riddell

QUÉBEC CITADELLES PEE-WEE

More expensive singles are Steve Bernier ($2-4), Marc-André Pouliot ($2-4) and Dany Roussin ($2-3).

□ 895 F. Laverdière
□ 896 L. Beaulieu
□ 897 S. Boutet
□ 898 K. Glode
□ 899 D. Roussin
□ 900 P. Bilodeau
□ 901 J. Lachance
□ 902 A. Bucchino
□ 903 O. Roland-Bouchard
□ 904 S. Dufour
□ 905 S. Moisan
□ 906 M. Trudel
□ 907 S. Bernier
□ 908 D. Deblois
□ 909 N. Marcotte
□ 910 M. Pouliot
□ 911 Instructeurs

BEAUPORT HARFANGS PEE-WEE

□ 912 C. Bernier
□ 913 J. Bernier
□ 914 S. Bernier
□ 915 Y. Bernier
□ 916 D. Bouchard
□ 917 S. Bouchard
□ 918 V. Couture
□ 919 P. Émond
□ 920 F. Gagnon
□ 921 M. Garneau
□ 922 M. Grenier
□ 923 F. Hébert
□ 924 O. Jeffrey
□ 925 V. Paquet
□ 926 J. Parent
□ 927 S. Roy
□ 928 K. Thibeault
□ 929 Instructeurs

NORTH DELTA PEE-WEE

□ 930 K. Batchelor
□ 931 M. Bodnar
□ 932 T. Brouwer
□ 933 T. Dietrich
□ 934 B. Harris
□ 935 D. Hofer
□ 936 C. Jensen
□ 937 S. Johnson
□ 938 T. Kanakos
□ 939 C. Koch
□ 940 M. Levangie
□ 941 S. Leyden
□ 942 W. Long
□ 943 N. Macdonald
□ 944 T. Mulock
□ 945 D. Pinder
□ 946 T. Williams
□ 947 Instructeurs

SHERBROOKE PEE-WEE

□ 948 M. Beaudoin
□ 949 J. Chicoine
□ 950 A. Gagné
□ 951 T. Lacroix
□ 952 M. Pedneault
□ 953 C. Giguère
□ 954 H. Verpaelst
□ 955 K. Simoneau
□ 956 M. Roy
□ 957 S. Jean
□ 958 D. Beaudoin
□ 959 L. Longpré
□ 960 D. Marcoux
□ 961 A. Bouchard
□ 962 D. Doyon
□ 963 P. Lyonnais
□ 964 M. Lapointe
□ 965 Instructeurs

SAN JOSE SHARKS PEE-WEE

□ 966 P. Angeles
□ 967 B. Dale
□ 968 R. Fish
□ 974 B. Nguyent
□ 975 J. Pors
□ 976 L. Sanny
□ 969 R. Hazelwood
□ 970 J. Hornig
□ 971 L. Jensen
□ 972 A. Lee
□ 973 S. Mickelson
□ 977 C. Sheppard
□ 978 A. Shklyarevsky
□ 979 M. Sullivan
□ 980 D. Wood
□ 981 C. Zaldain

ST-HUBERT PEE-WEE

□ 982 M. Trépanier
□ 983 M. Loiseau
□ 984 K. Pépin
□ 985 D. Loiseau
□ 986 M. Tremblay
□ 987 N. Rhéaume
□ 988 L. Lacasse
□ 989 J. Gorce
□ 990 M. Lettera
□ 991 M. Joyal
□ 992 G. Comeau
□ 993 R. Turgeon
□ 994 S. Harbec
□ 995 W. Huet
□ 996 S. Daoust
□ 997 É. Schumann
□ 998 Instructeurs

CHAUVEAU FAUCONS PEE-WEE

□ 999 M. Robitaille
□ 1000 G. Tailleur
□ 1001 S. Jalbert
□ 1002 A. Harvey
□ 1003 M. Houde
□ 1004 M. Giguère
□ 1005 D. Montgomery
□ 1006 T. Moisan
□ 1007 F. Robitaille
□ 1008 J. Parent
□ 1009 A. Pageau
□ 1010 M. Fournier
□ 1011 S. Pelletier
□ 1012 F. Tremblay
□ 1013 G. Faucher
□ 1014 J. Deblois
□ 1015 D. Bédard
□ 1016 Instructeurs

MOSCOW DYNAMOS PEE-WEE

More expensive cards include Dmitri Kazionov ($1-2) and Evgeni Tunik ($1-2).

□ 1017 Y. Nikolayev
□ 1018 S. Chiline
□ 1019 Badiaoutdinov
□ 1020 I. Korotkov
□ 1021 N. Duvarov
□ 1022 D. Yerchov
□ 1023 E. Tunik
□ 1024 A. Tikhomirov
□ 1025 D. Grinine
□ 1026 V. Evseev
□ 1027 V. Skripitsine
□ 1028 A. Kojeunikov
□ 1029 A. Fadeev
□ 1030 S. Karpov
□ 1031 A. Porkov
□ 1032 I. Mirnov
□ 1033 A. Yakhine
□ 1034 D. Saveliev
□ 1035 D. Kazionov
□ 1036 A. Kononov

MONTRÉAL CANADIENS PEE-WEE

□ 1037 J. Épinat
□ 1038 C. De Petrillo
□ 1039 K. Sellan
□ 1040 C. Séguin
□ 1041 V. Lambert
□ 1042 O. Labelle
□ 1043 J. Brière
□ 1044 M. Labelle
□ 1045 M. Lalande
□ 1046 S. Courcelles
□ 1372 Team photo
□ 1047 B. Langevin
□ 1048 Franc-Villeneuve
□ 1049 F. Raymond
□ 1050 L. Martin
□ 1051 G. Glazer
□ 1052 F. Harland
□ 1053 Instructeurs
□ 1054 Instructeurs
□ 1055 Instructeurs
□ 1056 Instructeurs

AUTRICHE PEE-WEE

□ 1057 A. Binner
□ 1058 M. Dobner
□ 1059 M. Fehringer
□ 1060 M. Fuchs
□ 1061 C. Gielg
□ 1062 M. Hollenstein
□ 1063 R. Kasprian
□ 1064 G. Khrenn
□ 1065 M. Lange
□ 1066 M. Latusa
□ 1067 M. Oraze
□ 1068 N. Petrik
□ 1069 S. Poelzl
□ 1070 F. Redeczy
□ 1071 R. Ritter
□ 1072 C. Rud
□ 1073 C. Sommer
□ 1074 S. Sommweber
□ 1075 E. Staudach
□ 1076 M. Thorineg
□ 1077 D. Usubelli
□ 1078 T. Vanek
□ 1079 S. Pittl
□ 1080 B. Berger

BEAUPORT VOILIERS PEE-WEE

□ 1081 A. Bilodeau
□ 1082 J. Maheux
□ 1083 J. Drolet
□ 1084 Racine-Gauthier
□ 1085 D. Walsh
□ 1086 V. Marcon
□ 1087 D. Dufour
□ 1088 D. Boucher
□ 1089 M. Smith
□ 1090 A. Gauthier
□ 1091 A. St-Hilaire
□ 1092 P. Tremblay
□ 1093 N. Bell
□ 1094 G. Turgeon
□ 1095 S. Lachance
□ 1096 J. Auger
□ 1097 A. Breton
□ 1098 Instructeurs

QUÉBEC CHAMPLAINS PEE-WEE

□ 1099 V. Guay
□ 1100 É. Lachance
□ 1101 J. Argouin
□ 1102 M. Dufour
□ 1103 B. Deschênes
□ 1104 P. Lemay
□ 1105 J. Lizotte
□ 1106 T. Gariépy
□ 1107 P. Lefebvre
□ 1108 S. Grenon
□ 1109 K. Ruel
□ 1110 N. Garneau
□ 1111 J. Lemay
□ 1112 P. St-Pierre
□ 1113 J. Prémont
□ 1114 Instructeurs

HALIFAX PEE-WEE

□ 1115 C. Adams
□ 1116 M. Adams
□ 1117 A. Archibald
□ 1118 J. Hayes
□ 1119 R. Hyson
□ 1120 B. Irvine
□ 1121 A. Joudrey
□ 1122 C. Maccormack
□ 1123 J. Melnyk
□ 1124 M. Moore
□ 1125 A. Muir
□ 1126 S. O'Toole
□ 1127 S. Robar
□ 1128 R. Rogers
□ 1129 M. Russell
□ 1130 M. Theriault
□ 1131 B. Verge
□ 1132 Instructeurs

ZURICH PEE-WEE

□ 1133 P. Bärtschi
□ 1134 P. Bigliel
□ 1135 F. Blatter
□ 1136 S. Bruderer
□ 1137 A. Brunold
□ 1138 O. Eglauf
□ 1139 L. Grauwiler
□ 1140 M. Huber
□ 1141 R. Lemm
□ 1142 T. Stephan
□ 1143 G. Vivalda
□ 1144 A. Wegmüller
□ 1145 M. Wichser
□ 1146 T. Ramholt
□ 1147 E. Peter
□ 1148 P. Wohlgemuth
□ 1149 R. Nötzli
□ 1150 B. Riedner
□ 1151 L. Baumgartner
□ 1152 G. Ehrensperger
□ 1153 S. Haas
□ 1154 Instructeurs

CHAUVEAU ÉPERVIERS PEE-WEE

□ 1155 D. Ashini
□ 1156 D. Chabot
□ 1157 S. Deroy
□ 1158 K. Gauthier
□ 1159 J. Hallé
□ 1160 M. Jalbert
□ 1161 D. Lajoie
□ 1162 K. Lamothe
□ 1163 N. Langlois
□ 1164 F. Lapierre
□ 1165 J. Laroque
□ 1166 N. Montgomery
□ 1167 V. Pagé
□ 1168 N. Paquet
□ 1169 M. Picard
□ 1170 S. Savard
□ 1171 D. Goran
□ 1172 Instructeurs

LAKESHORE PEE-WEE

□ 1173 S. Ackad
□ 1174 J. Ammendolea
□ 1175 M. Barmash
□ 1176 D. Barry
□ 1177 P. Cullen
□ 1178 F. Gagnon
□ 1179 A. Graham
□ 1180 P. Laurin
□ 1181 A. MacDonald
□ 1182 K. Mowat
□ 1183 C. Oles
□ 1184 M. Ricci
□ 1185 R. Ruggeri
□ 1186 R. Smith
□ 1187 M. Tomaseta
□ 1188 J. Tordjman
□ 1189 Instructeurs

MISSISSAUGA REBELS PEE-WEE

□ 1190 M. Tanel
□ 1191 Z. Brown
□ 1192 I. Starkman
□ 1193 J. Bell
□ 1194 N. Macinnis
□ 1195 P. Gibson
□ 1196 C. Clarkson
□ 1197 T. Leeb
□ 1198 B. Wilkieson
□ 1199 T. Trevelyan
□ 1200 M. Sirman
□ 1201 N. Kerhoulas
□ 1202 R. Roger
□ 1203 B. Turner
□ 1204 D. Knowles
□ 1205 Instructeurs

SAINT-ALBERT PEE-WEE

□ 1206 J. Baker
□ 1207 S. Belland
□ 1208 R. Chappell
□ 1209 J. Cherewyk
□ 1210 J. Chwedoruk
□ 1211 J. Doucette
□ 1212 D. Ewart
□ 1213 P. Gayler
□ 1214 C. Gloweski
□ 1215 B. Graham
□ 1216 M. Ireland
□ 1217 S. Kinsey
□ 1218 D. May
□ 1219 K. Roberge
□ 1220 L. St-Arnaud
□ 1221 B. Steeter
□ 1222 G. Whitenect

RICHMOND HILL PEE-WEE

□ 1223 C. Aquino
□ 1224 Beckford-Tseu
□ 1225 B. Burgio
□ 1226 C. Campoli
□ 1227 B. Cescon
□ 1228 M. Christie
□ 1229 C. Collins
□ 1230 M. Dibiase
□ 1231 G. Goodnough
□ 1232 A. Keefe
□ 1233 P. Magagna
□ 1234 R. Martynowski
□ 1235 D. Rowe
□ 1236 C. Trull
□ 1237 W. Wheeler
□ 1238 P. Zylbergerg
□ 1239 Instructeurs

NEW-YORK RANGERS PEE-WEE

□ 1240 B. Blair
□ 1241 R. Fuld
□ 1242 B. Kandora
□ 1243 B. Kelly
□ 1244 G. Kelly
□ 1245 S. Kiviat
□ 1246 B. McLaughlin
□ 1247 J. Orsen
□ 1248 M. Ovittore
□ 1249 D. Riley
□ 1250 M. Russel
□ 1251 T. Russell
□ 1252 G. Schultz
□ 1253 A. Strait
□ 1254 M. Verderame
□ 1255 R. Wisnowski

SUISSE ROMANDE PEE-WEE

□ 1256 A. Leuthardt
□ 1257 D. Manzato
□ 1258 S. Romerio
□ 1259 S. Anthamatten
□ 1260 N. Bernasconi
□ 1261 L. Emery
□ 1262 M. Ftacsek
□ 1263 Y. Leoni
□ 1264 J. Locorotondo
□ 1265 L. Mano
□ 1266 M. Schupbach
□ 1267 Y. Benoît
□ 1268 K. Casarico
□ 1269 G. Clivaz
□ 1270 N. Clopt
□ 1271 F. Conz
□ 1272 D. Eisenring
□ 1273 O. Moret
□ 1274 Neuenschwander
□ 1275 K. Romy
□ 1276 T. Schmid
□ 1277 S. Sollberger
□ 1278 Instructeurs
□ 1279 Instructeurs
□ 1280 Instructeurs
□ 1281 Instructeurs
□ 1282 Instructeurs
□ 1283 Instructeurs

MOSCOU KRYSTAL PEE-WEE

Some of the more expensive cards are Igor Ignatushkin ($2-5) and Ilia Krikunov ($2-5).

□ 1284 V. Khijniakov
□ 1285 A. Nikonorov
□ 1286 A. Chkotov
□ 1287 A. Koulmanov
□ 1293 S. Matreev
□ 1294 D. Naoumov
□ 1295 M. Chtcheviev
□ 1296 L. Artemenkov

1288 D. Smirnov	1297 A. Spiridonov
1289 N. Lapine	1298 S. Popov
1290 I. Ignatushkin	1299 A. Tikhonov
1291 I. Krikunov	1300 D. Samarin
1292 D. Kostiouk	1301 P. Salomatine

LAVAL TITANS PEE-WEE

One of the more expensive singles is M-A Bernier ($1-2).

1302 D. Crispino	1311 Y. Turcotte
1303 F. Guenette	1312 Y. Gaudette
1304 B.-Vacchinao	1313 M. Bernier
1305 É. Beaudin	1314 C. Dagenais
1306 S. Picard	1315 M. Morin-Atwill
1307 G. Macdonald	1316 Y. Boutin
1308 K. Maurice	1317 J. Daigneault
1309 E. Lajoie	1318 V. Di Caprio
1310 A. Neven	

KUUJJUAQ PEE-WEE

1319 J. Robertson	1329 W. Koneak
1320 D. Bentley	1330 J. Ookpik
1321 C. Davies	1331 B. Alaku
1322 W. Cain jr	1332 K. Oumaaluk
1323 M. Tagoona	1333 P. Cain
1324 J. Cloutier	1334 K. Gordon
1325 E. Jones	1335 M. Ningiruvik
1326 D. Barrett	1336 T. Dupuis
1327 R. Makiuk	1337 Instructeurs
1328 M. Lapage	

DÉTROIT COMPUWARE PEE-WEE

1338 P. Barnertt	1348 T. Sarnovski
1339 C. Common	1349 M. Stempky
1340 C. Craig	1350 P. Switaj
1341 D. Gardner	1351 J. Tobe
1342 É. Giosa	1352 C. Podsiad
1343 A. Linard	1353 J. Wisniewski
1344 S. O'Malley	1354 J. Wollak
1345 D. Peace	1355 Instructeurs
1346 F. Rediker	1356 Instructeurs
1347 D. Rohlfs	1373 A. Foster
1374 J. Samson	

TORONTO MAPLE LEAFS PEE-WEE

One of the more expensive singles is Rick Nash ($10-25).

1357 K. Arruda	1365 A. Henrich
1358 M. Caprara	1366 R. Janco
1359 S. Clarke	1367 R. Nash
1360 D. Clarkson	1368 M. Nicoletti
1361 D. Cumbertach	1369 R. Power
1362 J. Dickson	1370 S. Simmons
1363 A. Efthimiou	1371 Instructeurs
1364 R. Flood	

COLLÈGE FRANÇAIS PEE-WEE

More expensive singles are Pierre-Marc Bouchard ($5-10) and Marc-André Fleury ($7-15).

1375 S. Beauchemin	1384 C. Lecours
1376 PM. Bouchard	1385 M. Mandeville
1377 R. Briggs	1386 A. Martel
1378 L. Chapdeleine	1387 K. Rainville
1379 B. Cournoyer	1388 M. St-Jean
1380 C. Duhamel	1389 J. Savage
1381 M. Fleury	1390 P. Séguin
1382 F. Kennedy	1391 J. Synnott
1383 P. Lambert	1392 Instructeurs

ANGLETERRE PEE-WEE

1393 A. Levers	1403 M. Stratford
1394 S. Wallace	1404 L. Slade
1395 J. Eley	1405 D. Thomas
1396 A. Keeble	1406 D. Hughes
1397 A. Carr	1407 A. Radmall
1398 M. Towalski	1408 J. McGrath
1399 A. Brittle	1409 R. Evans
1400 B. Grier	1410 A. Stanton
1401 A. Smith	1411 L. Ross
1402 A. Green	

MISSISSAUGA SENATORS PEE-WEE

1412 A. Armstrong	1419 P. Lovisek
1413 R. Arnaldo	1420 M. Mc Isaac
1414 A. Butera	1421 T. Nisbe
1415 T. Cann	1422 D. Pegoraro
1416 K. Couture	1423 A. Peplow
1417 S. Halford	1425 A. Vinelli
1418 J. Lehun	

1998 ZATKOVY PASTA

Two cards were found on the backs of Czech pasta boxes Zatkovy Pasta. Unlike several other unlicensed sets, these cards are licensed by the National Hockey League Players' Association as well as the Czech federation. Cards pairs are as follows: Beranek-Slegr; Hamrlik-Svoboda; Hasek-Lang; Jagr-Rucinsky; Prochazka-Reichel; Smehlik-Straka.

Complete Deck (32 cards):	**25.00**
Player	**B**
1 Jaromir Jagr	8.00
2 Dominik Hasek (G)	8.00
3 Josef Beranek	1.00
4 Roman Hamrlik	1.50
5 Robert Lang	1.50
6 Martin Straka	2.50
7 Robert Reichel	2.50
8 Martin Rucinsky	1.50
9 Jiri Slegr	1.00
10 Petr Svoboda	1.50
11 Richard Smehlik	1.00
12 Martin Prochazka	1.00

1998 BOWMAN

These cards have three versions: the regular card, an O-Pee-Chee parallel and a 50th Anniversary parallel (#/50). Prices vary considerably for regional stars.

Complete Set (165 cards):	**2200.00**	**70.00**	**40.00**
Common Player:	**8.00**	**.35**	**.20**
Player	**50A**	**OPC**	**Bowm.**
1 Robert Esche (G), OHL	30.00	1.50	1.00
2 Chris Hajt, OHL	12.00	.50	.50
3 Mark McMahon, OHL	8.00	.35	.20
4 Jeff Brown, OHL	8.00	.35	.20
5 Richard Jackman, OHL	20.00	1.00	.50
6 Greg Labenski, OHL	8.00	.35	.20
7 Marek Posmyk, OHL	12.00	.50	.50
8 Brian Willsie, OHL	12.00	.50	.50
9 Jason Ward, OHL	50.00	3.00	2.00
10 Manny Malhotra, OHL	30.00	1.50	1.00
11 Matt Cooke, OHL	20.00	1.00	.50
12 Mike Gorman (G), OHL	8.00	.35	.20
13 Rodney Richard, OHL	8.00	.35	.20
14 David Legwand, OHL	50.00	3.00	2.00
15 Jon Sim, OHL	12.00	.50	.50
16 Peter Sarno, OHL	8.00	.35	.20
17 Andrew Long, OHL	8.00	.35	.20
18 Peter Cava, OHL	8.00	.35	.20
19 Colin Pepperall, OHL	8.00	.35	.20
20 Jay Legault, OHL	8.00	.35	.20
21 Brian Finley (G), OHL	25.00	1.50	1.00
22 Martin Skoula, OHL	30.00	1.50	1.00
23 Brian Campbell, OHL	12.00	.50	.50
24 Sean Blanchard, OHL	12.00	.50	.50
25 Bryan Allen, OHL	20.00	1.00	.50
26 Peter Hogan, OHL	8.00	.35	.20
27 Nick Boynton, OHL	30.00	1.50	1.00
28 Matt Bradley, OHL	20.00	1.00	.50
29 Jeremy Adduono, OHL	8.00	.35	.20
30 Mike Henrich, OHL	20.00	1.00	.50
31 Justin Papineau, OHL	20.00	1.00	.50
32 Bujar Amidovski (G), OHL	12.00	.50	.50
33 Robert Mailloux, OHL	8.00	.35	.20
34 Daniel Tkaczuk, OHL	30.00	1.50	1.00
35 Sean Avery, OHL	20.00	1.00	.50
36 Mark Bell, OHL	30.00	1.50	1.00
37 Kevin Colley, OHL	8.00	.35	.20
38 Norm Milley, OHL	20.00	1.00	.50
39 Scott Barney, OHL	12.00	.50	.50
40 Joel Trottier, OHL	8.00	.35	.20
41 Brent Belecki (G), WHL	8.00	.35	.20
42 Randy Petruk (G), WHL	12.00	.50	.50
43 Brad Ference, WHL	20.00	1.00	.50
44 Perry Johnson, WHL	8.00	.35	.20
45 Joel Kwiatkowski, WHL	12.00	.50	.50
46 Zenith Komarniski, WHL	12.00	.50	.50
47 Greg Kuznik, WHL	12.00	.50	.50
48 Andrew Ference, WHL	20.00	1.00	.50
49 Jason Deleurme, WHL	8.00	.35	.20
50 Trent Whitfield, WHL	20.00	1.00	.50
51 Dylan Gyori, WHL	12.00	.50	.50
52 Todd Robinson, WHL	12.00	.50	.50
53 Marian Hossa, WHL	130.00	7.50	5.00
54 Mike Hurley, WHL	8.00	.35	.20
55 Greg Leeb, WHL	8.00	.35	.20
56 Andrei Podkonicky, WHL	20.00	1.00	.50
57 Quinn Hancock, WHL	8.00	.35	.20
58 Marian Cisar, WHL	20.00	1.00	.50
59 Bret DeCecco, WHL	12.00	.50	.50
60 Brenden Morrow, WHL	40.00	2.00	1.50
61 Evan Lindsay (G), WHL	8.00	.35	.20
62 Terry Friesen (G), WHL	8.00	.35	.20
63 Ryan Shannon, WHL	8.00	.35	.20
64 Michal Rozsival, WHL	12.00	.50	.50
65 Luc Théoret, WHL	12.00	.50	.50
66 Brad Stuart, WHL	50.00	3.00	2.00
67 Burke Henry, WHL	8.00	.35	.20
68 Cory Sarich, WHL	20.00	1.00	.50
69 Martin Sonnenberg, WHL	12.00	.50	.50
70 Mark Smith, WHL	12.00	.50	.50
71 Shawn McNeil, WHL	8.00	.35	.20
72 Brad Moran, WHL	12.00	.50	.50
73 Josh Holden, WHL	20.00	1.00	.50
74 Cory Cyrenne, WHL	8.00	.35	.20
75 Shane Willis, WHL	30.00	1.50	1.00
76 Stefan Cherneski, WHL	12.00	.50	.50
77 Jay Henderson, WHL	12.00	.50	.50
78 Ronald Petrovicky, WHL	20.00	1.00	.50
79 Sergei Varlamov, WHL	20.00	1.00	.50
80 Chad Hinz, WHL	12.00	.50	.50
81 M. Garon (G), QMJHL	50.00	3.00	2.00
82 M. Chouinard (G), QMJHL	20.00	1.00	.50
83 Dominic Perna, QMJHL	8.00	.35	.20
84 Didier Tremblay, QMJHL	8.00	.35	.20
85 Mike Ribeiro, QMJHL	40.00	2.00	1.50
86 Marty Johnston, QMJHL	8.00	.35	.20
87 Rémi Royer, QMJHL	12.00	.50	.50
88 Patrick Pelchat, QMJHL	8.00	.35	.20
89 Daniel Corso, QMJHL	20.00	1.00	.50
90 François Fortier, QMJHL	8.00	.35	.20
91 M-A Gaudet, QMJHL	8.00	.35	.20
92 F. Beauchemin, QMJHL	8.00	.35	.20
93 Michel Tremblay, QMJHL	8.00	.35	.20
94 Jean-Philippe Pare, QMJHL	8.00	.35	.20
95 François Methot, QMJHL	12.00	.50	.50
96 David Thibeault, QMJHL	8.00	.35	.20
97 Jonathan Girard, QMJHL	12.00	.50	.50
98 Karol Bartanus, QMJHL	12.00	.50	.50
99 Peter Ratchuk, QMJHL	12.00	.50	.50
100 Pierre Dagenais, QMJHL	20.00	1.00	.50
101 P. Sauvé (G), QMJHL	30.00	1.50	1.00
102 R. Bergeron (G), QMJHL	8.00	.35	.20
103 V. Lecavalier, QMJHL	130.00	7.50	5.00
104 Eric Chouinard, QMJHL	30.00	1.50	1.00
105 Oleg Timchenko, QMJHL	8.00	.35	.20
106 Sébastien Roger, QMJHL	12.00	.50	.50
107 Simon Gagné, QMJHL	100.00	6.00	4.00
108 Alex Tanguay, QMJHL	70.00	4.50	3.00
109 David Gosselin, QMJHL	12.00	.50	.50
110 Ramzi Abid, QMJHL	30.00	1.50	1.00
111 Eric Drouin, QMJHL	8.00	.35	.20
112 Dominic Auger, QMJHL	8.00	.35	.20
113 Martin Moise, QMJHL	8.00	.35	.20
114 Randy Cooper, QMJHL	8.00	.35	.20
115 A. Mathieu, QMJHL	8.00	.35	.20
116 Brad Richards, QMJHL	60.00	3.50	2.00
117 Dmitri Tolkunov, QMJHL	8.00	.35	.20
118 Alexei Tezikov, QMJHL	12.00	.50	.50
119 Derrick Walser, QMJHL	12.00	.50	.50
120 Adam Borzecki, QMJHL	8.00	.35	.20
121 Ramzi Abid, CHL	30.00	1.50	1.00
122 Brett Allan, CHL	8.00	.35	.20
123 Mark Bell, CHL	30.00	1.50	1.00
124 Blair Betts, CHL	20.00	1.00	.50
125 Randy Copley, CHL	8.00	.35	.20
126 Simon Gagné, CHL	100.00	6.00	4.00
127 Michael Henrich, CHL	20.00	1.00	.50
128 Vincent Lecavalier, CHL	130.00	7.50	5.00
129 Norm Milley, CHL	20.00	1.00	.50
130 Chris Nielsen, CHL	20.00	1.00	.50
131 Rico Fata, CHL	30.00	1.50	1.00
132 Mike Ribeiro, CHL	40.00	2.00	1.50
133 Bryan Allen, CHL	20.00	1.00	.50
134 John Erksine, CHL	12.00	.50	.50
135 Jonathan Girard, CHL	12.00	.50	.50
136 Stephen Peat, CHL	12.00	.50	.50
137 Robyn Regehr, CHL	20.00	1.00	.50
138 Brad Stuart, CHL	50.00	3.00	2.00
139 P. DesRochers (G), CHL	20.00	1.00	.50
140 J. LaBarbera (G), CHL	20.00	1.00	.50
141 David Cameron, CHL	8.00	.35	.20
142 J. Cheechoo, CHL	40.00	2.00	1.50
143 Eric Chouinard, CHL	30.00	1.50	1.00
144 Brent Gauvreau, CHL	8.00	.35	.20
145 Scott Gomez, CHL	50.00	3.00	2.00
146 Jeff Heerema, CHL	20.00	1.00	.50
147 David Legwand, CHL	50.00	3.00	2.00
148 Manny Malhotra, CHL	30.00	1.50	1.00
149 Justin Papineau, CHL	20.00	1.00	.50
150 Andrew Peters, CHL	8.00	.35	.20
151 Michael Rupp, CHL	40.00	2.00	1.50
152 Alex Tanguay, CHL	70.00	4.50	3.00
153 F. Beauchemin, CHL	8.00	.35	.20
154 Mathieu Biron, CHL	20.00	1.00	.50
155 Jiri Fischer, CHL	30.00	1.50	1.00
156 Alex Henry, CHL	8.00	.35	.20
157 Kyle Rossiter, CHL	12.00	.50	.50
158 Martin Skoula, CHL	30.00	1.50	1.00
159 M. Chouinard (G), CHL	20.00	1.00	.50
160 P. Sauvé (G), CHL	30.00	1.50	1.00
161 MVP: Finley (G), OHL	25.00	1.50	1.00
162 MVP: Belecki (G), WHL	8.00	.35	.20
163 MVP: Perna, WHL	8.00	.35	.20
164 MVP: Cheechoo, CHL	40.00	2.00	1.50
165 Checklist	12.00	.50	.50

CERTIFIED AUTOGRAPH

There are three versions: a blue foil card (1:39), a silver foil card (1:157, approx. 75 copies of each) and a gold foil card (1:470, approx. 25 copies of each). Prices vary for regional stars.

Insert Set (40 cards):	**2000.00**	**900.00**	**500.00**
Autographs	**Gold**	**Silver**	**Blue**
A1 Justin Papineau ✍	40.00	20.00	10.00
A2 Jason Labarbera (G) ✍	40.00	20.00	10.00
A3 Michael Rupp ✍	80.00	40.00	20.00
A4 Stephen Peat ✍	30.00	12.00	8.00
A5 Manny Malhotra ✍	60.00	30.00	15.00
A6 Michael Henrich ✍	40.00	20.00	10.00
A7 Kyle Rossiter ✍	30.00	12.00	8.00
A8 Mark Bell ✍	60.00	30.00	15.00
A9 Mathieu Chouinard (G) ✍	40.00	20.00	10.00
A10 Vincent Lecavalier ✍	250.00	120.00	75.00
A11 David Legwand ✍	100.00	50.00	30.00
A12 Bryan Allen ✍	40.00	20.00	10.00
A13 François Beauchemin ✍	30.00	12.00	8.00
A14 Robyn Regehr ✍	40.00	20.00	10.00
A15 Eric Chouinard ✍	60.00	30.00	15.00
A16 Norm Milley ✍	40.00	20.00	10.00
A17 Alex Henry ✍	30.00	12.00	8.00
A18 Ramzi Abid ✍	60.00	30.00	15.00
A19 Jiri Fischer ✍	60.00	30.00	15.00
A20 P. DesRochers (G) ✍	40.00	20.00	10.00
A21 Mathieu Biron ✍	40.00	20.00	10.00
A22 Brad Stuart ✍	100.00	50.00	30.00
A23 Philippe Sauvé (G) ✍	60.00	30.00	15.00
A24 John Erskine ✍	30.00	12.00	8.00
A25 Jonathan Cheechoo ✍	80.00	40.00	20.00
A26 Brett Allan ✍	30.00	12.00	8.00
A27 Scott Gomez ✍	100.00	50.00	30.00
A28 Chris Neilsen ✍	40.00	20.00	10.00
A29 David Cameron ✍	30.00	12.00	8.00
A30 Jonathan Girard ✍	30.00	12.00	8.00
A31 Jeff Heerema ✍	40.00	20.00	10.00
A32 Blair Betts ✍	40.00	20.00	10.00
A33 Andrew Peters ✍	30.00	12.00	8.00
A34 Randy Copley ✍	30.00	12.00	8.00
A35 Alex Tanguay ✍	150.00	70.00	45.00
A36 Simon Gagné ✍	200.00	100.00	60.00
A37 Brent Gauvreau ✍	30.00	12.00	8.00
A38 Mike Ribeiro ✍	80.00	40.00	20.00
A39 Martin Skoula ✍	60.00	30.00	15.00
A40 Rico Fata ✍	60.00	30.00	15.00

SCOUT'S CHOICE

Insert Set (21 cards):	**50.00**
Insert (1:12)	**SC**
SC1 Bryan Allen	1.50
SC2 Manny Malhotra	2.00
SC3 Daniel Tkaczuk	2.00
SC4 Bujar Amidovski (G)	1.50
SC5 Patrick DesRochers (G)	1.50
SC6 Brad Ference	1.50
SC7 Marian Hossa	10.00
SC8 Brad Stuart	4.00
SC9 Sergei Varlamov	1.50
SC10 Randy Petruk (G)	1.50
SC11 Karol Bartanus	1.50
SC12 Vincent Lecavalier	10.00
SC13 Jonathan Girard	1.50
SC14 Peter Ratchuk	1.50
SC15 Alex Tanguay	6.00
SC16 Rico Fata	2.00
SC17 Brian Finley (G)	2.00
SC18 Jonathan Cheechoo	3.00
SC19 Scott Gomez	4.00
SC20 Michal Rozsival	1.50
SC21 Mathieu Garon (G)	4.00

1998 BOWMAN CHROME

The first three versions in this series are: the Chrome card, the O-Pee-Chee Chrome parallel, and the 50th Anniversary Chrome parallel (#/50).

	50A	OPC	Bowm.
Complete Set (165 cards):	2100.00	115.00	65.00
Common Player:	8.00	.75	.50
Bowman Chrome	**50A**	**OPC**	**Bowm.**
1 Robert Esche (G), OHL	30.00	2.50	1.50
2 Chris Hajt, OHL	10.00	1.00	.50
3 Mark McMahon, OHL	8.00	.75	.50
4 Jeff Brown, OHL	8.00	.75	.50
5 Richard Jackman, OHL	20.00	1.50	1.00
6 Greg Labenski, OHL	8.00	.75	.50
7 Marek Posmyk, OHL	10.00	1.00	.50
8 Brian Willsie, OHL	10.00	1.00	.50
9 Jason Ward, OHL	50.00	4.50	3.00
10 Manny Malhotra, OHL	30.00	2.50	1.50
11 Matt Cooke, OHL	20.00	1.50	1.00
12 Mike Gorman (G), OHL	8.00	.75	.50
13 Rodney Richard, OHL	8.00	.75	.50
14 David Legwand, OHL	50.00	4.50	3.00
15 Jon Sim, OHL	10.00	1.00	.50
16 Peter Sarno, OHL	8.00	.75	.50
17 Andrew Long, OHL	8.00	.75	.50
18 Peter Cava, OHL	8.00	.75	.50
19 Colin Pepperall, OHL	8.00	.75	.50
20 Jay Legault, OHL	8.00	.75	.50
21 Brian Finley (G), OHL	25.00	2.00	1.50
22 Martin Skoula, OHL	30.00	2.50	1.50
23 Brian Campbell, OHL	10.00	1.00	.50
24 Sean Blanchard, OHL	10.00	1.00	.50
25 Bryan Allen, OHL	20.00	1.50	1.00
26 Peter Hogan, OHL	8.00	.75	.50
27 Nick Boynton, OHL	30.00	2.50	1.50
28 Matt Bradley, OHL	20.00	1.50	1.00
29 Jeremy Adduono, OHL	8.00	.75	.50
30 Mike Henrich, OHL	20.00	1.50	1.00
31 Justin Papineau, OHL	20.00	1.50	1.00
32 Bujar Amidovski (G), OHL	10.00	1.00	.50
33 Robert Mailloux, OHL	8.00	.75	.50
34 Daniel Tkaczuk, OHL	30.00	2.50	1.50
35 Sean Avery, OHL	20.00	1.50	1.00
36 Mark Bell, OHL	30.00	2.50	1.50
37 Kevin Colley, OHL	8.00	.75	.50
38 Norm Milley, OHL	20.00	1.50	1.00
39 Scott Barney, OHL	10.00	1.00	.50
40 Joel Trottier, OHL	8.00	.75	.50
41 Brent Belecki (G), WHL	8.00	.75	.50
42 Randy Petruk (G), WHL	10.00	1.00	.50
43 Brad Ference, WHL	20.00	1.50	1.00
44 Perry Johnson, WHL	8.00	.75	.50
45 Joel Kwiatkowski, WHL	10.00	1.00	.50
46 Zenith Komarniski, WHL	10.00	1.00	.50
47 Greg Kuznik, WHL	10.00	1.00	.50
48 Andrew Ference, WHL	20.00	1.50	1.00
49 Jason Deleurme, WHL	8.00	.75	.50
50 Trent Whitfield, WHL	20.00	1.50	1.00
51 Dylan Gyori, WHL	10.00	1.00	.50
52 Todd Robinson, WHL	10.00	1.00	.50
53 Marian Hossa, WHL	130.00	12.00	8.00
54 Mike Hurley, WHL	8.00	.75	.50
55 Greg Leeb, WHL	8.00	.75	.50
56 Andrej Podkonicky, WHL	8.00	.75	.50
57 Quinn Hancock, WHL	8.00	.75	.50
58 Marian Cisar, WHL	20.00	1.50	1.00
59 Bret DeCecco, WHL	10.00	1.00	.50
60 Brenden Morrow, WHL	40.00	3.50	2.50
61 Evan Lindsay (G), WHL	8.00	.75	.50
62 Terry Friesen (G), WHL	8.00	.75	.50
63 Ryan Shannon, WHL	8.00	.75	.50
64 Michal Rozsival, WHL	10.00	1.00	.50
65 Luc Théoret, WHL	10.00	1.00	.50
66 Brad Stuart, WHL	50.00	4.50	3.00
67 Burke Henry, WHL	8.00	.75	.50
68 Cory Sarich, WHL	20.00	1.50	1.00
69 Martin Sonnenberg, WHL	10.00	1.00	.50
70 Mark Smith, WHL	10.00	1.00	.50
71 Shawn McNeil, WHL	8.00	.75	.50
72 Brad Moran, WHL	10.00	1.00	.50
73 Josh Holden, WHL	20.00	1.50	1.00
74 Cory Cyrenne, WHL	8.00	.75	.50
75 Shane Willis, WHL	30.00	2.50	1.50
76 Stefan Cherneski, WHL	10.00	1.00	.50
77 Jay Henderson, WHL	10.00	1.00	.50
78 Ronald Petrovicky, WHL	20.00	1.50	1.00
79 Sergei Varlamov, WHL	20.00	1.50	1.00
80 Chad Hinz, WHL	10.00	1.00	.50
81 M. Garon (G), QMJHL	50.00	4.50	3.00
82 M. Chouinard (G), QMJHL	20.00	1.50	1.00
83 Dominic Perna, QMJHL	8.00	.75	.50
84 Didier Tremblay, QMJHL	8.00	.75	.50
85 Mike Ribiero, QMJHL	40.00	3.50	2.50
86 Marty Johnston, QMJHL	8.00	.75	.50
87 Rémi Royer, QMJHL	10.00	1.00	.50
88 Patrick Pelchat, QMJHL	8.00	.75	.50
89 Daniel Corso, QMJHL	20.00	1.50	1.00
90 François Fortier, QMJHL	8.00	.75	.50
91 M-A Gaudet, QMJHL	8.00	.75	.50
92 F. Beauchemin, QMJHL	8.00	.75	.50
93 Michel Tremblay, QMJHL	8.00	.75	.50
94 Jean-Philippe Pare, QMJHL	8.00	.75	.50
95 François Methot, QMJHL	10.00	1.00	.50
96 David Thibeault, QMJHL	8.00	.75	.50
97 Jonathan Girard, QMJHL	10.00	1.00	.50
98 Karol Bartanus, QMJHL	10.00	1.00	.50
99 Peter Ratchuk, QMJHL	10.00	1.00	.50
100 Pierre Dagenais, QMJHL	20.00	1.50	1.00
101 P. Sauvé (G), QMJHL	30.00	2.50	1.50
102 R. Bergeron (G), QMJHL	8.00	.75	.50
103 V. Lecavalier, QMJHL	130.00	12.00	8.00
104 Eric Chouinard, QMJHL	30.00	2.50	1.50
105 Oleg Timchenko, QMJHL	8.00	.75	.50
106 Sébastien Roger, QMJHL	10.00	1.00	.50
107 Simon Gagné, QMJHL	100.00	9.50	6.00
108 Alex Tanguay, QMJHL	70.00	7.00	4.50
109 David Gosselin, QMJHL	10.00	1.00	.50
110 Ramzi Abid, QMJHL	30.00	2.50	1.50
111 Eric Drouin, QMJHL	8.00	.75	.50
112 Dominic Auger, QMJHL	8.00	.75	.50
113 Martin Moise, QMJHL	8.00	.75	.50
114 Randy Cooper, QMJHL	8.00	.75	.50
115 A. Mathieu, QMJHL	8.00	.75	.50
116 Brad Richards, QMJHL	60.00	5.50	3.50
117 Dmitri Tolkunov, QMJHL	8.00	.75	.50
118 Alexei Tezikov, QMJHL	10.00	1.00	.50
119 Derrick Walser, QMJHL	10.00	1.00	.50
120 Adam Borzecki, QMJHL	8.00	.75	.50
121 Ramzi Abid, CHL	30.00	2.50	1.50
122 Brett Allan, CHL	8.00	.75	.50
123 Mark Bell, CHL	30.00	2.50	1.50
124 Blair Betts, CHL	20.00	1.50	1.00
125 Randy Copley, CHL	8.00	.75	.50
126 Simon Gagné, CHL	100.00	9.50	6.00
127 Michael Henrich, CHL	20.00	1.50	1.00
128 Vincent Lecavalier, CHL	130.00	12.00	8.00
129 Norm Milley, CHL	20.00	1.50	1.00
130 Chris Nielsen, CHL	20.00	1.50	1.00
131 Rico Fata, CHL	30.00	2.50	1.50
132 Mike Ribeiro, CHL	40.00	3.50	2.50
133 Bryan Allen, CHL	20.00	1.50	1.00
134 John Erskine, CHL	10.00	1.00	.50
135 Jonathan Girard, CHL	10.00	1.00	.50
136 Stephen Peat, CHL	10.00	1.00	.50
137 Robyn Regehr, CHL	20.00	1.50	1.00
138 Brad Stuart, CHL	50.00	4.50	3.00
139 P. DesRochers (G), CHL	20.00	1.50	1.00
140 J. LaBarbera (G), CHL	20.00	1.50	1.00
141 David Cameron, CHL	8.00	.75	.50
142 J. Cheechoo, CHL	40.00	3.50	2.50
143 Eric Chouinard, CHL	30.00	2.50	1.50
144 Brent Gauvreau, CHL	8.00	.75	.50
145 Scott Gomez, CHL	50.00	4.50	3.00
146 Jeff Heerema, CHL	20.00	1.50	1.00
147 David Legwand, CHL	50.00	4.50	3.00
148 Manny Malhotra, CHL	30.00	2.50	1.50
149 Justin Papineau, CHL	20.00	1.50	1.00
150 Andrew Peters, CHL	8.00	.75	.50
151 Michael Rupp, CHL	40.00	3.50	2.50
152 Alex Tanguay, CHL	70.00	7.00	4.50
153 F. Beauchemin, CHL	8.00	.75	.50
154 Mathieu Biron, CHL	20.00	1.50	1.00
155 Jiri Fischer, CHL	30.00	2.50	1.50
156 Alex Henry, CHL	8.00	.75	.50
157 Kyle Rossiter, CHL	10.00	1.00	.50
158 Martin Skoula, CHL	30.00	2.50	1.50
159 M. Chouinard (G), CHL	20.00	1.50	1.00
160 P. Sauvé (G), CHL	30.00	2.50	1.50
161 MVP: Finley (G), OHL	25.00	2.00	1.50
162 MVP: Belecki (G), WHL	8.00	.75	.50
163 MVP: Perna, WHL	8.00	.75	.50
164 MVP: Cheechoo, CHL	40.00	3.50	2.50
165 Checklist	10.00	1.00	.50

REFRACTORS

The three Refractor parallels are: Chrome Refractor, O-Pee-Chee Chrome Refractor, and 50th Anniversary Refractor (#/5). Actual realized sales on the scarce 50th Anniversary Refractor cards may vary considerably from the prices listed below.

	50A	OPC	Refr.
Complete Set (165 cards):		1000.00	450.00
Common Player:	40.00	4.00	2.00
Player	**50A**	**OPC**	**Refr.**
1 Robert Esche (G), OHL	90.00	15.00	5.00
2 Chris Hajt, OHL	40.00	5.00	3.00
3 Mark McMahon, OHL	40.00	4.00	2.00
4 Jeff Brown, OHL	40.00	4.00	2.00
5 Richard Jackman, OHL	60.00	10.00	5.00
6 Greg Labenski, OHL	40.00	4.00	2.00
7 Marek Posmyk, OHL	40.00	5.00	3.00
8 Brian Willsie, OHL	40.00	5.00	3.00
9 Jason Ward, OHL	150.00	25.00	10.00
10 Manny Malhotra, OHL	90.00	15.00	5.00
11 Matt Cooke, OHL	60.00	10.00	5.00
12 Mike Gorman (G), OHL	40.00	4.00	2.00
13 Rodney Richard, OHL	40.00	4.00	2.00
14 David Legwand, OHL	150.00	25.00	10.00
15 Jon Sim, OHL	40.00	5.00	3.00
16 Peter Sarno, OHL	40.00	4.00	2.00
17 Andrew Long, OHL	40.00	4.00	2.00
18 Peter Cava, OHL	40.00	4.00	2.00
19 Colin Pepperall, OHL	40.00	4.00	2.00
20 Jay Legault, OHL	40.00	4.00	2.00
21 Brian Finley (G), OHL	75.00	10.00	5.00
22 Martin Skoula, OHL	90.00	15.00	5.00
23 Brian Campbell, OHL	40.00	5.00	3.00
24 Sean Blanchard, OHL	40.00	5.00	3.00
25 Bryan Allen, OHL	60.00	10.00	5.00
26 Peter Hogan, OHL	40.00	4.00	2.00
27 Nick Boynton, OHL	90.00	15.00	5.00
28 Matt Bradley, OHL	60.00	10.00	5.00
29 Jeremy Adduono, OHL	40.00	4.00	2.00
30 Mike Henrich, OHL	60.00	10.00	5.00
31 Justin Papineau, OHL	60.00	10.00	5.00
32 Bujar Amidovski (G), OHL	40.00	5.00	3.00
33 Robert Mailloux, OHL	40.00	4.00	2.00
34 Daniel Tkaczuk, OHL	90.00	15.00	5.00
35 Sean Avery, OHL	60.00	10.00	5.00
36 Mark Bell, OHL	90.00	15.00	5.00
37 Kevin Colley, OHL	40.00	4.00	2.00
38 Norm Milley, OHL	60.00	10.00	5.00
39 Scott Barney, OHL	40.00	5.00	3.00
40 Joel Trottier, OHL	40.00	4.00	2.00
41 Brent Belecki (G), WHL	40.00	4.00	2.00
42 Randy Petruk (G), WHL	40.00	5.00	3.00
43 Brad Ference, WHL	60.00	10.00	5.00
44 Perry Johnson, WHL	40.00	4.00	2.00
45 Joel Kwiatkowski, WHL	40.00	5.00	3.00
46 Zenith Komarniski, WHL	40.00	5.00	3.00
47 Greg Kuznik, WHL	40.00	5.00	3.00
48 Andrew Ference, WHL	60.00	10.00	5.00
49 Jason Deleurme, WHL	40.00	4.00	2.00
50 Trent Whitfield, WHL	60.00	10.00	5.00
51 Dylan Gyori, WHL	40.00	5.00	3.00
52 Todd Robinson, WHL	40.00	5.00	3.00
53 Marian Hossa, WHL	370.00	60.00	30.00
54 Mike Hurley, WHL	40.00	4.00	2.00
55 Greg Leeb, WHL	40.00	4.00	2.00
56 Andrej Podkonicky, WHL	40.00	4.00	2.00
57 Quinn Hancock, WHL	40.00	4.00	2.00
58 Marian Cisar, WHL	60.00	10.00	5.00
59 Bret DeCecco, WHL	40.00	5.00	3.00
60 Brenden Morrow, WHL	120.00	20.00	10.00
61 Evan Lindsay (G), WHL	40.00	4.00	2.00
62 Terry Friesen (G), WHL	40.00	4.00	2.00
63 Ryan Shannon, WHL	40.00	4.00	2.00
64 Michal Rozsival, WHL	40.00	5.00	2.00
65 Luc Théoret, WHL	40.00	5.00	3.00
66 Brad Stuart, WHL	150.00	25.00	10.00
67 Burke Henry, WHL	40.00	4.00	2.00
68 Cory Sarich, WHL	60.00	10.00	5.00
69 Martin Sonnenberg, WHL	40.00	5.00	3.00
70 Mark Smith, WHL	40.00	5.00	3.00
71 Shawn McNeil, WHL	40.00	4.00	2.00
72 Brad Moran, WHL	40.00	5.00	3.00
73 Josh Holden, WHL	60.00	10.00	5.00
74 Cory Cyrenne, WHL	40.00	4.00	2.00
75 Shane Willis, WHL	90.00	15.00	5.00
76 Stefan Cherneski, WHL	40.00	5.00	3.00
77 Jay Henderson, WHL	40.00	5.00	3.00
78 Ronald Petrovicky, WHL	60.00	10.00	5.00
79 Sergei Varlamov, WHL	60.00	10.00	5.00
80 Chad Hinz, WHL	40.00	5.00	3.00
81 M. Garon (G), QMJHL	150.00	25.00	10.00
82 M. Chouinard (G), QMJHL	60.00	10.00	5.00
83 Dominic Perna, QMJHL	40.00	4.00	2.00
84 Didier Tremblay, QMJHL	40.00	4.00	2.00
85 Mike Ribiero, QMJHL	120.00	20.00	10.00
86 Marty Johnston, QMJHL	40.00	4.00	2.00
87 Rémi Royer, QMJHL	40.00	5.00	3.00
88 Patrick Pelchat, QMJHL	40.00	4.00	2.00
89 Daniel Corso, QMJHL	60.00	10.00	5.00
90 François Fortier, QMJHL	40.00	4.00	2.00
91 M-A Gaudet, QMJHL	40.00	4.00	2.00
92 F. Beauchemin, QMJHL	40.00	4.00	2.00
93 Michel Tremblay, QMJHL	40.00	4.00	2.00
94 Jean-Philippe Pare, QMJHL	40.00	4.00	2.00
95 François Methot, QMJHL	40.00	5.00	3.00
96 David Thibeault, QMJHL	40.00	4.00	2.00
97 Jonathan Girard, QMJHL	40.00	5.00	3.00
98 Karol Bartanus, QMJHL	40.00	5.00	2.00
99 Peter Ratchuk, QMJHL	40.00	5.00	3.00
100 Pierre Dagenais, QMJHL	60.00	10.00	5.00
101 P. Sauvé (G), QMJHL	90.00	15.00	5.00
102 R. Bergeron (G), QMJHL	40.00	4.00	2.00
103 V. Lecavalier, QMJHL	375.00	60.00	30.00
104 Eric Chouinard, QMJHL	90.00	15.00	5.00
105 Oleg Timchenko, QMJHL	40.00	4.00	2.00
106 Sébastien Roger, QMJHL	40.00	5.00	3.00
107 Simon Gagné, QMJHL	300.00	50.00	25.00
108 Alex Tanguay, QMJHL	225.00	35.00	20.00
109 David Gosselin, QMJHL	40.00	5.00	3.00
110 Ramzi Abid, QMJHL	90.00	15.00	5.00
111 Eric Drouin, QMJHL	40.00	4.00	2.00
112 Dominic Auger, QMJHL	40.00	4.00	2.00
113 Martin Moise, QMJHL	40.00	4.00	2.00
114 Randy Cooper, QMJHL	40.00	4.00	2.00
115 A. Mathieu, QMJHL	40.00	4.00	2.00
116 Brad Richards, QMJHL	180.00	30.00	15.00
117 Dmitri Tolkunov, QMJHL	40.00	4.00	2.00
118 Alexei Tezikov, QMJHL	40.00	5.00	3.00
119 Derrick Walser, QMJHL	40.00	5.00	3.00
120 Adam Borzecki, QMJHL	40.00	4.00	2.00
121 Ramzi Abid, CHL	90.00	15.00	5.00
122 Brett Allan, CHL	40.00	4.00	2.00
123 Mark Bell, CHL	90.00	15.00	5.00
124 Blair Betts, CHL	60.00	10.00	5.00
125 Randy Copley, CHL	40.00	4.00	2.00
126 Simon Gagné, CHL	300.00	50.00	25.00
127 Michael Henrich, CHL	60.00	10.00	5.00
128 Vincent Lecavalier, CHL	375.00	60.00	30.00
129 Norm Milley, CHL	60.00	10.00	5.00
130 Chris Nielsen, CHL	60.00	10.00	5.00
131 Rico Fata, CHL	90.00	15.00	5.00
132 Mike Ribeiro, CHL	120.00	20.00	10.00
133 Bryan Allen, CHL	60.00	10.00	5.00
134 John Erksine, CHL	40.00	5.00	2.00
135 Jonathan Girard, CHL	40.00	5.00	3.00
136 Stephen Peat, CHL	40.00	5.00	3.00
137 Robyn Regehr, CHL	60.00	10.00	5.00
138 Brad Stuart, CHL	150.00	25.00	10.00
139 P. DesRochers (G), CHL	60.00	10.00	5.00
140 J. LaBarbera (G), CHL	60.00	10.00	5.00
141 David Cameron, CHL	40.00	4.00	2.00
142 J. Cheechoo, CHL	120.00	20.00	10.00
143 Eric Chouinard, CHL	90.00	15.00	5.00
144 Brent Gauvreau, CHL	40.00	4.00	2.00
145 Scott Gomez, CHL	150.00	20.00	10.00
146 Jeff Heerema, CHL	60.00	10.00	5.00
147 David Legwand, CHL	150.00	25.00	10.00
148 Manny Malhotra, CHL	90.00	15.00	5.00
149 Justin Papineau, CHL	60.00	10.00	5.00
150 Andrew Peters, CHL	40.00	4.00	2.00
151 Michael Rupp, CHL	120.00	20.00	10.00
152 Alex Tanguay, CHL	225.00	35.00	20.00
153 F. Beauchemin, CHL	40.00	4.00	2.00
154 Mathieu Biron, CHL	60.00	10.00	5.00
155 Jiri Fischer, CHL	90.00	15.00	5.00
156 Alex Henry, CHL	40.00	4.00	2.00
157 Kyle Rossiter, CHL	40.00	5.00	2.00
158 Martin Skoula, CHL	90.00	15.00	5.00
159 M. Chouinard (G), CHL	60.00	10.00	5.00
160 P. Sauvé (G), CHL	90.00	15.00	5.00
161 MVP: Finley (G), OHL	75.00	10.00	5.00
162 MVP: Belecki (G), WHL	40.00	4.00	2.00
163 MVP: Perna, WHL	40.00	4.00	2.00
164 MVP: Cheechoo, CHL	120.00	20.00	10.00
165 Checklist	40.00	5.00	3.00

1998 - 99 AURORA

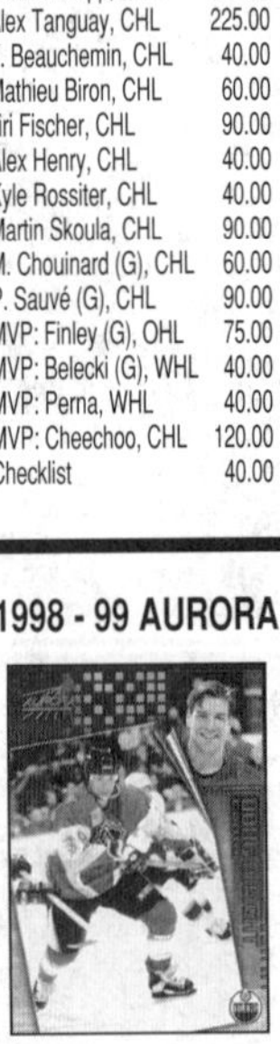

	Aurora
Complete Set (200 cards):	40.00
Common Player:	.25
Player	**Aurora**
1 Travis Green, Anah.	.25
2 Guy Hebert (G), Anah.	.25
3 Paul Kariya, Anah.	1.00
4 Steve Rucchin, Anah.	.25
5 Tomas Sandström, Anah.	.25
6 Teemu Selänne, Anah.	.50
7 Jason Allison, Bost.	.50
8 Raymond Bourque, Bost.	1.00
9 Anson Carter, Bost.	.25

☐	10 Byron Dafoe (G), Bost.	.25
☐	11 Ted Donato, Bost.	.25
☐	12 Dave Ellett, Bost.	.25
☐	13 Dimitri Khristich, Bost.	.25
☐	14 Sergei Samsonov, Bost.	.50
☐	15 Matthew Barnaby, Buff.	.25
☐	16 Michal Grosek, Buff.	.25
☐	17 Dominik Hasek (G), Buff.	1.00
☐	18 Brian Holzinger, Buff.	.25
☐	19 Michael Peca, Buff.	.25
☐	20 Miroslav Satan, Buff.	.25
☐	21 Dixon Ward, Buff.	.25
☐	22 Alexei Zhitnik, Buff.	.25
☐	23 Andrew Cassels, Calg.	.25
☐	24 Theoren Fleury, Calg.	.50
☐	25 Jarome Iginla, Calg.	.50
☐	26 Marty McInnis, Calg.	.25
☐	27 Derek Morris, Calg.	.25
☐	28 Michael Nylander, Calg.	.25
☐	29 Cory Stillman, Calg.	.25
☐	30 Kevin Dineen, Caro.	.25
☐	31 Nelson Emerson, Caro.	.25
☐	32 Martin Gélinas, Caro.	.25
☐	33 Sami Kapanen, Caro.	.25
☐	34 Trevor Kidd (G), Caro.	.25
☐	35 Robert Kron, Caro.	.25
☐	36 Jeff O'Neill, Caro.	.25
☐	37 Keith Primeau, Caro.	.25
☐	38 Tony Amonte, Chic.	.50
☐	39 Chris Chelios, Chic.	.50
☐	40 Éric Dazé, Chic.	.25
☐	41 Jeff Hackett (G), Chic.	.25
☐	42 Jean-Yves Leroux, Chic.	.25
☐	43 Jeff Shantz, Chic.	.25
☐	44 Alexei Zhamnov, Chic.	.25
☐	45 Adam Deadmarsh, Colo.	.25
☐	46 Peter Forsberg, Colo.	1.00
☐	47 Valeri Kamensky, Colo.	.25
☐	48 Claude Lemieux, Colo.	.25
☐	49 Éric Messier, Colo.	.25
☐	50 Sandis Ozolinsh, Colo.	.25
☐	51 Patrick Roy (G), Colo.	3.00
☐	52 Joe Sakic, Colo.	1.50
☐	53 Ed Belfour (G), Dall.	1.00
☐	54 Derian Hatcher, Dall.	.25
☐	55 Brett Hull, Dall.	1.00
☐	56 Jamie Langenbrunner, Dall.	.25
☐	57 Jere Lehtinen, Dall.	.25
☐	58 Mike Modano, Dall.	1.00
☐	59 Joe Nieuwendyk, Dall.	.25
☐	60 Darryl Sydor, Dall.	.25
☐	61 Sergei Zubov, Dall.	.25
☐	62 Sergei Fedorov, Detr.	1.00
☐	63 Vyacheslav Kozlov, Detr.	.25
☐	64 Igor Larionov, Detr.	.50
☐	65 Nicklas Lidström, Detr.	.50
☐	66 Darren McCarty, Detr.	.25
☐	67 Chris Osgood (G), Detr.	.50
☐	68 Brendan Shanahan, Detr.	1.00
☐	69 Steve Yzerman, Detr.	2.00
☐	70 Kelly Buchberger, Edmo.	.25
☐	71 Mike Grier, Edmo.	.25
☐	72 Bill Guerin, Edmo.	.25
☐	73 Roman Hamrlik, Edmo.	.25
☐	74 Boris Mironov, Edmo.	.25
☐	75 Janne Niinimaa, Edmo.	.25
☐	76 Ryan Smyth, Edmo.	.25
☐	77 Doug Weight, Edmo.	.50
☐	78 Dino Ciccarelli, Flor.	.25
☐	79 Dave Gagner, Flor.	.25
☐	80 Ed Jovanovski, Flor.	.25
☐	81 Viktor Kozlov, Flor.	.25
☐	82 Paul Laus, Flor.	.25
☐	83 Scott Mellanby, Flor.	.25
☐	84 Ray Whitney, Flor.	.25
☐	85 Rob Blake, LosA.	.50
☐	86 Stéphane Fiset (G), LosA.	.25
☐	87 Yanic Perreault, LosA.	.25
☐	88 Luc Robitaille, LosA.	.50
☐	89 Jamie Storr (G), LosA.	.25
☐	90 Jozef Stümpel, LosA.	.25
☐	91 Vladimir Tsyplakov, LosA.	.25
☐	92 Shayne Corson, Mont.	.25
☐	93 Vincent Damphousse, Mont.	.50
☐	94 Saku Koivu, Mont.	.50
☐	95 Mark Recchi, Mont.	.25
☐	96 Martin Rucinsky, Mont.	.25
☐	97 Brian Savage, Mont.	.25
☐	98 Jocelyn Thibault (G), Mont.	.25
☐	99 Andrew Brunette, Wash. (Nash.)	.25
☐	100 Mike Dunham (G), NJer. (Nash.)	.25
☐	101 Tom Fitzgerald, Colo. (Nash.)	.25
☐	102 Sergei Krivokrasov, Chic. (Nash.)	.25
☐	103 Denny Lambert, Ott. (Nash.)	.25
☐	104 Mikhail Shtalenkov (G), Anah. (Nash.)	.25
☐	105 Darren Turcotte, SLou. (Nash.)	.25
☐	106 Dave Andreychuk, NJer.	.25
☐	107 Jason Arnott, NJer.	.25
☐	108 Martin Brodeur (G), NJer.	1.50
☐	109 Patrik Elias, NJer.	.50
☐	110 Bobby Holik, NJer.	.25
☐	111 Randy McKay, NJer.	.25
☐	112 Scott Niedermayer, NJer.	.25
☐	113 Scott Stevens, NJer.	.25
☐	114 Bryan Berard, NYIs.	.25
☐	115 Jason Dawe, NYIs.	.25
☐	116 Trevor Linden, NYIs.	.25
☐	117 Zigmund Palffy, NYIs.	.50
☐	118 Robert Reichel, NYIs.	.25
☐	119 Tommy Salo (G), NYIs.	.25
☐	120 Bryan Smolinski, NYIs.	.25
☐	121 Adam Graves, NYRa.	.25
☐	122 Wayne Gretzky, NYRa.	4.00
☐	123 Alexei Kovalev, NYRa.	.50
☐	124 Brian Leetch, NYRa.	.50
☐	125 Mike Richter (G), NYRa.	.25
☐	126 Ulf Samuelsson, NYRa.	.25
☐	127 Kevin Stevens, NYRa.	.25
☐	128 Daniel Alfredsson, Ott.	.50
☐	129 Andreas Dackell, Ott.	.25
☐	130 Igor Kravchuk, Ott.	.25
☐	131 Shawn McEachern, Ott.	.25
☐	132 Chris Phillips, Ott.	.25
☐	133 Damian Rhodes (G), Ott.	.25
☐	134 Alexei Yashin, Ott.	.50
☐	135 Rod Brind'Amour, Phil.	.25
☐	136 Alexandre Daigle, Phil.	.25
☐	137 Éric Desjardins, Phil.	.25
☐	138 Chris Gratton, Phil.	.25
☐	139 Ron Hextall (G), Phil.	.50
☐	140 John LeClair, Phil.	.50
☐	141 Eric Lindros, Phil.	1.00
☐	142 John Vanbiesbrouck (G), Phil.	.25
☐	143 Dainius Zubrus, Phil.	.25
☐	144 Brad Isbister, Phoe.	.25
☐	145 Nikolai Khabibulin (G), Phoe.	.25
☐	146 Jeremy Roenick, Phoe.	.50
☐	147 Cliff Ronning, Phoe.	.25
☐	148 Keith Tkachuk, Phoe.	.50
☐	149 Rick Tocchet, Phoe.	.25
☐	150 Oleg Tverdovsky, Phoe.	.25
☐	151 Stu Barnes, Pitt.	.25
☐	152 Tom Barrasso (G), Pitt.	.25
☐	153 Kevin Hatcher, Pitt.	.25
☐	154 Jaromir Jagr, Pitt.	1.00
☐	155 Darius Kasparaitis, Pitt.	.25
☐	156 Alexei Morozov, Pitt.	.25
☐	157 Martin Straka, Pitt.	.25
☐	158 Jim Campbell, SLou.	.25
☐	159 Geoff Courtnall, SLou.	.25
☐	160 Grant Fuhr (G), SLou.	.50
☐	161 Al MacInnis, SLou.	.25
☐	162 Jamie McLennan, SLou.	.25
☐	163 Chris Pronger, SLou.	.50
☐	164 Pierre Turgeon, SLou.	.25
☐	165 Tony Twist, SLou.	.25
☐	166 Jeff Friesen, SanJ.	.25
☐	167 Tony Granato, SanJ.	.25
☐	168 Patrick Marleau, SanJ.	.25
☐	169 Marty McSorley, SanJ.	.25
☐	170 Owen Nolan, SanJ.	.50
☐	171 Marco Sturm, SanJ.	.25
☐	172 Mike Vernon (G), SanJ.	.25
☐	173 Karl Dykhuis, Tamp.	.25
☐	174 Mikael Renberg, Tamp.	.25
☐	175 Stéphane Richer, Tamp.	.25
☐	176 Alexander Selivanov, Tamp.	.25
☐	177 Paul Ysebaert, Tamp.	.25
☐	178 Rob Zamuner, Tamp.	.25
☐	179 Sergei Berezin, Toro.	.25
☐	180 Tie Domi, Toro.	.25
☐	181 Mike Johnson, Toro.	.25
☐	182 Curtis Joseph (G), Toro.	1.00
☐	183 Igor Korolev, Toro.	.25
☐	184 Mathieu Schneider, Toro.	.25
☐	185 Mats Sundin, Toro.	1.00
☐	186 Todd Bertuzzi, Vanc.	1.00
☐	187 Donald Brashear, Vanc.	.25
☐	188 Pavel Bure, Vanc.	.50
☐	189 Mark Messier, Vanc.	1.00
☐	190 Alexander Mogilny, Vanc.	.25
☐	191 Mattias Öhlund, Vanc.	.25
☐	192 Garth Snow (G), Vanc.	.25
☐	193 Brian Bellows, Wash.	.25
☐	194 Peter Bondra, Wash.	.50
☐	195 Sergei Gonchar, Wash.	.25
☐	196 Calle Johansson, Wash.	.25
☐	197 Joé Juneau, Wash.	.25
☐	198 Olaf Kölzig (G), Wash.	.50
☐	199 Adam Oates, Wash.	.25
☐	200 Richard Zednik, Wash.	.25
	Player	**Sample**
☐	Martin Brodeur (G), NJer.	2.00

ATOMIC LASER CUTS

Insert Set (20 cards):		55.00
	Insert (4:37)	**ALC**
☐	1 Paul Kariya, Anah.	4.00
☐	2 Teemu Selänne, Anah.	2.00
☐	3 Sergei Samsonov, Bost.	2.00
☐	4 Dominik Hasek (G), Buff.	2.00
☐	5 Peter Forsberg, Colo.	4.00
☐	6 Patrick Roy (G), Colo.	8.00
☐	7 Joe Sakic, Colo.	4.00
☐	8 Mike Modano, Dall.	2.00
☐	9 Sergei Fedorov, Detr.	2.00
☐	10 Brendan Shanahan, Detr.	2.00
☐	11 Steve Yzerman, Detr.	6.00
☐	12 Martin Brodeur (G), NJer.	4.00
☐	13 Wayne Gretzky, NYRa.	12.00
☐	14 John LeClair, Phil.	2.00
☐	15 Eric Lindros, Phil.	2.00
☐	16 Jaromir Jagr, Pitt.	2.00
☐	17 Mats Sundin, Toro.	2.00
☐	18 Pavel Bure, Vanc.	2.00
☐	19 Mark Messier, Vanc.	2.00
☐	20 Peter Bondra, Wash.	2.00

CHAMPIONSHIP FEVER

There are five versions: the regular insert (1:1), the Red parallel, the Silver parallel (#/250), an Ice Blue parallel (#/100) and a Copper parallel (#/20). There are four versions of the Brodeur autograph card: the regular autograph (97 copies), a Silver card (1 copy), an Ice Blue card (1 copy) and a Copper card (1 copy).

Insert Set (50 cards):		2200.00	900.00	100.00	30.00
	Insert	**IB100**	**S250**	**Red**	**CF**
☐☐☐☐	1 Paul Kariya	80.00	30.00	5.00	1.50
☐☐☐☐	2 Teemu Selänne	50.00	20.00	3.00	1.00
☐☐☐☐	3 Raymond Bourque	70.00	30.00	4.50	1.50
☐☐☐☐	4 Byron Dafoe (G)	25.00	10.00	1.50	.50
☐☐☐☐	5 Sergei Samsonov	35.00	15.00	2.00	.50
☐☐☐☐	6 Dominik Hasek (G)	60.00	25.00	3.50	1.00
☐☐☐☐	7 Michael Peca	25.00	10.00	1.50	.50
☐☐☐☐	8 Theoren Fleury	30.00	15.00	2.00	.50
☐☐☐☐	9 Keith Primeau	25.00	10.00	1.50	.50
☐☐☐☐	10 Chris Chelios	35.00	15.00	2.00	.50
☐☐☐☐	11 Peter Forsberg	80.00	35.00	5.00	1.50
☐☐☐☐	12 Patrick Roy (G)	180.00	70.00	11.00	3.50
☐☐☐☐	13 Joe Sakic	100.00	40.00	6.00	2.00
☐☐☐☐	14 Ed Belfour (G)	60.00	25.00	3.50	1.00
☐☐☐☐	15 Mike Modano	60.00	25.00	3.50	1.00
☐☐☐☐	16 Sergei Fedorov	60.00	25.00	3.50	1.00
☐☐☐☐	17 Nicklas Lidström	35.00	15.00	2.00	.50
☐☐☐☐	18 Chris Osgood (G)	35.00	15.00	2.00	.50
☐☐☐☐	19 Brendan Shanahan	60.00	25.00	3.50	1.00
☐☐☐☐	20 Steve Yzerman	150.00	60.00	9.00	3.00
☐☐☐☐	21 Doug Weight	35.00	15.00	2.00	.50
☐☐☐☐	22 Dino Ciccarelli	20.00	8.00	1.00	.50
☐☐☐☐	23 Rob Blake	35.00	15.00	2.00	.50
☐☐☐☐	24 Saku Koivu	50.00	20.00	3.00	1.00
☐☐☐☐	25 Mark Recchi	25.00	10.00	1.50	.50
☐☐☐☐	26 Martin Brodeur (G)	100.00	40.00	6.00	2.00
☐☐☐☐	27 Patrik Elias	50.00	20.00	3.00	1.00
☐☐☐☐	28 Trevor Linden	25.00	10.00	1.50	.50
☐☐☐☐	29 Zigmund Palffy	35.00	15.00	2.00	.50
☐☐☐☐	30 Wayne Gretzky	250.00	100.00	15.00	5.00
☐☐☐☐	31 Mike Richter (G)	30.00	10.00	1.50	.50
☐☐☐☐	32 Daniel Alfredsson	35.00	15.00	2.00	.50
☐☐☐☐	33 D. Rhodes (G)	15.00	8.00	1.00	.50
☐☐☐☐	34 Alexei Yashin	35.00	15.00	2.00	.50
☐☐☐☐	35 John LeClair	50.00	20.00	3.00	1.00
☐☐☐☐	36 Eric Lindros	60.00	25.00	3.50	1.00
☐☐☐☐	37 Dainius Zubrus	15.00	8.00	1.00	.50
☐☐☐☐	38 Keith Tkachuk	35.00	15.00	2.00	.50
☐☐☐☐	39 Tom Barrasso (G)	25.00	10.00	1.50	.50
☐☐☐☐	40 Jaromir Jagr	60.00	20.00	3.50	1.00
☐☐☐☐	41 Grant Fuhr (G)	35.00	15.00	2.00	.50
☐☐☐☐	42 Pierre Turgeon	25.00	10.00	1.50	.50
☐☐☐☐	43 Patrick Marleau	30.00	10.00	1.50	.50
☐☐☐☐	44 Mike Vernon (G)	25.00	10.00	1.50	.50
☐☐☐☐	45 Rob Zamuner	15.00	8.00	1.00	.50
☐☐☐☐	46 Mats Sundin	60.00	25.00	3.50	1.00
☐☐☐☐	47 Pavel Bure	50.00	20.00	3.00	1.00
☐☐☐☐	48 Mark Messier	60.00	25.00	3.50	1.00
☐☐☐☐	49 Peter Bondra	35.00	15.00	2.00	.50
☐☐☐☐	50 Olaf Kölzig (G)	35.00	15.00	2.00	.50
	Autographs	**C1**	**IB1**	**S1**	**CF97**
☐☐☐☐	26 Martin Brodeur (G)				175

CHAMPIONSHIP FEVER COPPER

Copper Set (50 cards):		8200.00
	Insert	**C20**
☐	1 Paul Kariya	315.00
☐	2 Teemu Selänne	180.00
☐	3 Raymond Bourque	270.00
☐	4 Byron Dafoe (G)	90.00
☐	5 Sergei Samsonov	135.00
☐	6 Dominik Hasek (G)	225.00
☐	7 Michael Peca	90.00
☐	8 Theoren Fleury	135.00
☐	9 Keith Primeau	90.00
☐	10 Chris Chelios	135.00
☐	11 Peter Forsberg	315.00
☐	12 Patrick Roy (G)	675.00
☐	13 Joe Sakic	360.00
☐	14 Ed Belfour (G)	225.00
☐	15 Mike Modano	225.00
☐	16 Sergei Fedorov	225.00
☐	17 Nicklas Lidström	135.00
☐	18 Chris Osgood (G)	135.00
☐	19 Brendan Shanahan	225.00
☐	20 Steve Yzerman	540.00
☐	21 Doug Weight	135.00
☐	22 Dino Ciccarelli	70.00
☐	23 Rob Blake	135.00
☐	24 Saku Koivu	180.00
☐	25 Mark Recchi	90.00
☐	26 Martin Brodeur (G)	360.00
☐	27 Patrik Elias	180.00
☐	28 Trevor Linden	90.00
☐	29 Zigmund Palffy	135.00
☐	30 Wayne Gretzky	900.00
☐	31 Mike Richter (G)	105.00
☐	32 Daniel Alfredsson	135.00
☐	33 Damian Rhodes (G)	50.00
☐	34 Alexei Yashin	135.00
☐	35 John LeClair	180.00
☐	36 Eric Lindros	225.00
☐	37 Dainius Zubrus	50.00
☐	38 Keith Tkachuk	135.00
☐	39 Tom Barrasso (G)	90.00
☐	40 Jaromir Jagr	225.00
☐	41 Grant Fuhr (G)	135.00
☐	42 Pierre Turgeon	90.00
☐	43 Patrick Marleau	105.00
☐	44 Mike Vernon (G)	90.00
☐	45 Rob Zamuner	50.00
☐	46 Mats Sundin	225.00
☐	47 Pavel Bure	180.00
☐	48 Mark Messier	225.00
☐	49 Peter Bondra	135.00
☐	50 Olaf Kölzig (G)	135.00

FRONT LINE

This series has three versions: a copper card (#/80), an Ice Blue card (#/15) and a Red card (#/5). Red cards are too scarce to be priced.

Insert Set (10 cards):				1000.00
	Player	**R5**	**IB15**	**C80**
☐☐☐	1 Dominik Hasek (G), Buff.	500.00	300.00	70.00
☐☐☐	2 Peter Forsberg, Colo.	700.00	420.00	100.00
☐☐☐	3 Patrick Roy (G), Colo.	1500.00	900.00	220.00
☐☐☐	4 Joe Sakic, Colo.	800.00	480.00	120.00
☐☐☐	5 Steve Yzerman, Detr.	1200.00	720.00	180.00
☐☐☐	6 Daniel Alfredsson, Ott.	300.00	180.00	40.00
☐☐☐	7 Eric Lindros, Phil.	500.00	300.00	70.00
☐☐☐	8 Jaromir Jagr, Pitt.	500.00	300.00	70.00
☐☐☐	9 Wayne Gretzky, NYRa.	2000.00	1200.00	300.00
☐☐☐	10 Tie Domi, Toro.	160.00	90.00	20.00

MAN ADVANTAGE CEL-FUSIONS

Insert Set (20 cards):		235.00
	Insert (1:73)	**MACF**
☐	1 Paul Kariya, Anah.	16.00
☐	2 Teemu Selänne, Anah.	10.00
☐	3 Raymond Bourque, Bost.	14.00
☐	4 Michael Peca, Buff.	6.00

☐ 5 Peter Forsberg, Colo.	16.00
☐ 6 Joe Sakic, Colo.	20.00
☐ 7 Mike Modano, Dall.	12.00
☐ 8 Joe Nieuwendyk, Dall.	6.00
☐ 9 Brendan Shanahan, Detr.	12.00
☐ 10 Steve Yzerman, Detr.	30.00
☐ 11 Shayne Corson, Mont.	6.00
☐ 12 Zigmund Palffy, NYIs.	6.00
☐ 13 Wayne Gretzky, NYRa.	50.00
☐ 14 John LeClair, Phil.	10.00
☐ 15 Eric Lindros, Phil.	12.00
☐ 16 Jaromir Jagr, Pitt.	12.00
☐ 17 Mats Sundin, Toro.	12.00
☐ 18 Pavel Bure, Vanc.	10.00
☐ 19 Mark Messier, Vanc.	12.00
☐ 20 Peter Bondra, Wash.	6.00

NHL COMMAND

Insert Set (10 cards):	**620.00**
Insert (1:361)	**NC**
☐ 1 Teemu Selänne, Anah.	30.00
☐ 2 Dominik Hasek (G), Buff.	40.00
☐ 3 Peter Forsberg, Colo.	60.00
☐ 4 Patrick Roy (G), Colo.	130.00
☐ 5 Mike Modano, Dall.	40.00
☐ 6 Steve Yzerman, Detr.	100.00
☐ 7 Martin Brodeur (G), NJer.	70.00
☐ 8 Wayne Gretzky, NYRa.	180.00
☐ 9 Eric Lindros, Phil.	40.00
☐ 10 Jaromir Jagr, Pitt.	40.00

CUBES

Insert Set (30 cubes):	**205.00**
Insert (1:box)	**Cube**
☐ 1 Paul Kariya, Anah.	4.00
☐ 2 Teemu Selänne, Anah.	4.00
☐ 3 Dominik Hasek (G), Buff.	4.00
☐ 4 Peter Forsberg, Colo.	4.00
☐ 5 Patrick Roy (G), Colo.	10.00
☐ 6 Joe Sakic, Colo.	6.00
☐ 7 Mike Modano, Dall.	4.00
☐ 8 Sergei Fedorov, Detr.	4.00
☐ 9 Brendan Shanahan, Detr.	4.00
☐ 10 Steve Yzerman, Detr.	8.00
☐ 11 Martin Brodeur (G), NJer.	6.00
☐ 12 Wayne Gretzky, NYRa.	14.00
☐ 13 John LeClair, Phil.	4.00
☐ 14 Eric Lindros, Phil.	4.00
☐ 15 Jaromir Jagr, Pitt.	4.00
☐ 16 Mats Sundin, Toro.	4.00
☐ 17 Pavel Bure, Vanc.	4.00
☐ 18 Mark Messier, Vanc.	4.00
☐ 19 Peter Bondra, Wash.	4.00
☐ 20 Olaf Kölzig (G), Wash.	4.00

1998 - 99 BE A PLAYER

There are two versions of each base card: the silver card and the gold parallel.

Show-stamped wrapper-redemption parallels include: All-Star Fantasy '99 (cards 1-150, each #/50), Toronto Spring Expo '99 (151-300, each #/25), National '99 (cards 1-300, each #/10) and Toronto Fall Expo '99 (cards 1-300, each #/5).

Complete Set (300 cards):	**425.00**	**150.00**
Common Player:	**1.00**	**.50**
Insert	**Gold**	**Reg.**
☐☐ 1 Jason Marshall	1.50	.50
☐☐ 2 Paul Kariya	10.00	3.50
☐☐ 3 Teemu Selänne	5.00	2.00
☐☐ 4 Guy Hebert (G)	1.50	.50
☐☐ 5 Ted Drury	1.50	.50
☐☐ 6 Byron Dafoe (G)	3.00	1.00
☐☐ 7 Rob DiMaio	1.50	.50
☐☐ 8 Raymond Bourque	5.00	3.00
☐☐ 9 Joe Thornton	9.00	3.00
☐☐ 10 Sergei Samsonov	4.00	1.50
☐☐ 11 Dimitri Khristich	1.50	.50
☐☐ 12 Michael Peca	3.00	1.00
☐☐ 13 Jason Woolley	1.50	.50
☐☐ 14 Matthew Barnaby	1.50	.50
☐☐ 15 Brian Holzinger	1.50	.50
☐☐ 16 Dixon Ward	1.50	.50
☐☐ 17 Tyler Moss (G)	1.50	.50
☐☐ 18 Jarome Iginla	6.00	2.00
☐☐ 19 Marty McInnis	1.50	.50
☐☐ 20 Andrew Cassels	1.50	.50
☐☐ 21 Jason Wiemer	1.50	.50
☐☐ 22 Trevor Kidd (G)	2.00	.50
☐☐ 23 Keith Primeau	3.00	1.00
☐☐ 24 Sami Kapanen	2.00	.50
☐☐ 25 Robert Kron	1.50	.50
☐☐ 26 Glen Wesley	1.50	.50
☐☐ 27 Jeff Hackett (G)	2.00	.50
☐☐ 28 Tony Amonte	4.00	1.50
☐☐ 29 Alexei Zhamnov	2.00	.50
☐☐ 30 Eric Weinrich	1.50	.50
☐☐ 31 Jeff Shantz	1.50	.50
☐☐ 32 Christian Laflamme	1.50	.50
☐☐ 33 Adam Foote	2.00	.50
☐☐ 34 Patrick Roy (G)	20.00	7.50
☐☐ 35 Peter Forsberg	10.00	3.50
☐☐ 36 Adam Deadmarsh	2.00	.50
☐☐ 37 Joe Sakic	10.00	4.00
☐☐ 38 Éric Lacroix	1.50	.50
☐☐ 39 Guy Carbonneau	2.00	.50
☐☐ 40 Mike Modano	7.00	2.50
☐☐ 41 Roman Turek (G)	3.00	1.00
☐☐ 42 Mike Keane	1.50	.50
☐☐ 43 Sergei Zubov	1.50	.50
☐☐ 44 Jere Lehtinen	2.00	.50
☐☐ 45 Sergei Fedorov	7.00	2.50
☐☐ 46 Steve Yzerman	15.00	6.00
☐☐ 47 Chris Osgood (G)	4.00	1.50
☐☐ 48 Larry Murphy	1.50	.50
☐☐ 49 Vyacheslav Kozlov	1.50	.50
☐☐ 50 Darren McCarty	2.00	.50
☐☐ 51 Boris Mironov	1.50	.50
☐☐ 52 Roman Hamrlik	1.50	.50
☐☐ 53 Bill Guerin	3.00	1.00
☐☐ 54 Mike Grier	1.50	.50
☐☐ 55 Todd Marchant	1.50	.50
☐☐ 56 Ray Whitney	1.50	.50
☐☐ 57 Dave Gagner	1.50	.50
☐☐ 58 Scott Mellanby	1.50	.50
☐☐ 59 Robert Svehla	1.50	.50
☐☐ 60 Viktor Kozlov	2.00	.50
☐☐ 61 Luc Robitaille	6.00	2.00
☐☐ 62 Yanic Perreault	2.00	.50
☐☐ 63 Jozef Stümpel	1.50	.50
☐☐ 64 Sandy Moger	1.50	.50
☐☐ 65 Ian Laperrière	1.50	.50
☐☐ 66 Jocelyn Thibault (G)	3.00	1.00
☐☐ 67 Dave Manson	1.50	.50
☐☐ 68 Mark Recchi	3.00	1.00
☐☐ 69 Patrick Poulin	1.50	.50
☐☐ 70 Benoît Brunet	1.50	.50
☐☐ 71 Turner Stevenson	1.50	.50
☐☐ 72 Mike Dunham (G)	3.00	1.00
☐☐ 73 Tom Fitzgerald	1.50	.50
☐☐ 74 Darren Turcotte	1.50	.50
☐☐ 75 Brad Smyth	1.50	.50
☐☐ 76 J.J. Daigneault	1.50	.50
☐☐ 77 Dave Andreychuk	2.00	.50
☐☐ 78 Jason Arnott	3.00	1.00
☐☐ 79 Martin Brodeur (G)	10.00	4.00
☐☐ 80 Randy McKay	1.50	.50
☐☐ 81 Patrik Elias	6.00	2.00
☐☐ 82 Kevin Dean	1.50	.50
☐☐ 83 Tommy Salo (G)	3.00	1.00
☐☐ 84 Scott Lachance	1.50	.50
☐☐ 85 Bryan Berard	2.00	.50
☐☐ 86 Robert Reichel	2.00	.50
☐☐ 87 Kenny Jönsson	1.50	.50
☐☐ 88 Kevin Stevens	1.50	.50
☐☐ 89 Mike Richter (G)	3.00	1.00
☐☐ 90 Wayne Gretzky (X-LTD)	30.00	10.00
☐☐ 91 Adam Graves	3.00	1.00
☐☐ 92 Alexei Kovalev	4.00	1.50
☐☐ 93 Ulf Samuelsson	1.50	.50
☐☐ 94 Radek Bonk	2.00	.50
☐☐ 95 Wade Redden	2.00	.50
☐☐ 96 Damian Rhodes (G)	1.50	.50
☐☐ 97 Bruce Gardiner	1.50	.50
☐☐ 98 Daniel Alfredsson	4.00	1.50
☐☐ 99 Ron Hextall (G)	4.00	1.50
☐☐ 100 Eric Lindros	5.00	2.50
☐☐ 101 Chris Gratton	1.50	.50
☐☐ 102 Dainius Zubrus	1.50	.50
☐☐ 103 Luke Richardson	1.50	.50
☐☐ 104 Petr Svoboda	1.50	.50
☐☐ 105 Rick Tocchet	2.00	.50
☐☐ 106 Teppo Numminen	2.00	.50
☐☐ 107 Jeremy Roenick	6.00	2.00
☐☐ 108 Nikolai Khabibulin (G)	3.00	1.00
☐☐ 109 Brad Isbister	1.50	.50
☐☐ 110 Peter Skudra (G)	1.50	.50
☐☐ 111 Alexei Morozov	1.50	.50
☐☐ 112 Kevin Hatcher	1.50	.50
☐☐ 113 Darius Kasparaitis	1.50	.50
☐☐ 114 Stu Barnes	1.50	.50
☐☐ 115 Martin Straka	2.00	.50
☐☐ 116 Andrei Zyuzin	1.50	.50
☐☐ 117 Marcus Ragnarsson	1.50	.50
☐☐ 118 Murray Craven	1.50	.50
☐☐ 119 Marco Sturm	1.50	.50
☐☐ 120 Patrick Marleau	3.00	1.00
☐☐ 121 Shawn Burr	1.50	.50
☐☐ 122 Grant Fuhr (G)	4.00	1.50
☐☐ 123 Chris Pronger	4.00	1.50
☐☐ 124 Geoff Courtnall	1.50	.50
☐☐ 125 Jim Campbell	1.50	.50
☐☐ 126 Pavol Demitra	3.00	1.00
☐☐ 127 Todd Gill	1.50	.50
☐☐ 128 Cory Cross	1.50	.50
☐☐ 129 Daymond Langkow	1.50	.50
☐☐ 130 Alexander Selivanov	1.50	.50
☐☐ 131 Mikael Renberg	2.00	.50
☐☐ 132 Rob Zamuner	1.50	.50
☐☐ 133 Stéphane Richer	1.50	.50
☐☐ 134 Fredrik Modin	1.50	.50
☐☐ 135 Derek King	1.50	.50
☐☐ 136 Mats Sundin	7.00	2.50
☐☐ 137 Mike Johnson	1.50	.50
☐☐ 138 Alyn McCauley	2.00	.50
☐☐ 139 Jason Smith	1.50	.50
☐☐ 140 Markus Näslund	7.00	2.50
☐☐ 141 Alexander Mogilny	3.00	1.00
☐☐ 142 Mattias Öhlund	2.00	.50
☐☐ 143 Donald Brashear	1.50	.50
☐☐ 144 Garth Snow (G)	2.00	.50
☐☐ 145 Brian Bellows	1.50	.50
☐☐ 146 Peter Bondra	4.00	1.50
☐☐ 147 Joé Juneau	1.50	.50
☐☐ 148 Steve Konowalchuk	1.50	.50
☐☐ 149 Ken Klee	1.50	.50
☐☐ 150 Michal Pivonka	1.50	.50
☐☐ 151 Steve Rucchin	1.50	.50
☐☐ 152 Stu Grimson	1.50	.50
☐☐ 153 Tomas Sandström	1.50	.50
☐☐ 154 Fredrik Olausson	1.50	.50
☐☐ 155 Travis Green	1.50	.50
☐☐ 156 Jason Allison	4.00	1.50
☐☐ 157 Steve Heinze	1.50	.50
☐☐ 158 Rob Tallas	1.50	.50
☐☐ 159 Darren Van Impe	1.50	.50
☐☐ 160 Ken Baumgartner	1.50	.50
☐☐ 161 Peter Ferraro	1.50	.50
☐☐ 162 Dominik Hasek (G)	5.00	2.50
☐☐ 163 Geoff Sanderson	1.50	.50
☐☐ 164 Miroslav Satan	2.00	.50
☐☐ 165 Rob Ray	1.50	.50
☐☐ 166 Alexei Zhitnik	1.50	.50
☐☐ 167 Phil Housley	2.00	.50
☐☐ 168 Theoren Fleury	4.00	1.50
☐☐ 169 Ken Wregget (G)	1.50	.50
☐☐ 170 Valeri Bure	2.00	.50
☐☐ 171 Rico Fata	1.50	.50
☐☐ 172 Arturs Irbe (G)	3.00	1.00
☐☐ 173 Sean Hill	1.50	.50
☐☐ 174 Ron Francis	4.00	1.50
☐☐ 175 Jeff O'Neill	3.00	1.00
☐☐ 176 Paul Ranheim	1.50	.50
☐☐ 177 Paul Coffey	4.00	1.50
☐☐ 178 Doug Gilmour	4.00	1.50
☐☐ 179 Éric Dazé	3.00	1.00
☐☐ 180 Chris Chelios	4.00	1.50
☐☐ 181 Bob Probert	2.00	.50
☐☐ 182 Mark Fitzpatrick (G)	1.50	.50
☐☐ 183 Alexei Gusarov	1.50	.50
☐☐ 184 Sylvain Lefebvre	1.50	.50
☐☐ 185 Craig Billington (G)	1.50	.50
☐☐ 186 Valeri Kamensky	2.00	.50
☐☐ **187 Milan Hejduk RC**	**15.00**	**10.00**
☐☐ 188 Sandis Ozolinsh	1.50	.50
☐☐ 189 Brett Hull	7.00	2.50
☐☐ 190 Ed Belfour (G)	7.00	2.50
☐☐ 191 Darryl Sydor	1.50	.50
☐☐ **192 Sergei Gusev RC**	**1.50**	**1.50**
☐☐ 193 Joe Nieuwendyk	3.00	1.00
☐☐ 194 Derian Hatcher	2.00	.50
☐☐ 195 Brendan Shanahan	7.00	2.50
☐☐ 196 Tomas Holmström	1.50	.50
☐☐ 197 Nicklas Lidström	4.00	1.50
☐☐ 198 Martin Lapointe	3.00	1.00
☐☐ 199 Igor Larionov	4.00	1.50
☐☐ 200 Kris Draper	1.50	.50
☐☐ 201 Kelly Buchberger	1.50	.50
☐☐ 202 Andrei Kovalenko	1.50	.50
☐☐ 203 Josef Beranek	1.50	.50
☐☐ 204 Mikhail Shtalenkov (G)	1.50	.50
☐☐ 205 Pat Falloon	1.50	.50
☐☐ 206 Mark Parrish	6.00	6.00
☐☐ 207 Terry Carkner	1.50	.50
☐☐ 208 Rob Niedermayer	1.50	.50
☐☐ 209 Sean Burke (G)	4.00	1.50
☐☐ **210 Oleg Kvasha RC**	**2.00**	**3.00**
☐☐ 211 Pavel Bure	5.00	2.00
☐☐ 212 Rob Blake	4.00	1.50
☐☐ 213 Vladimir Tsyplakov	1.50	.50
☐☐ 214 Stéphane Fiset (G)	2.00	.50
☐☐ 215 Steve Duchesne	1.50	.50
☐☐ 216 Patrice Brisebois	1.50	.50
☐☐ 217 Vincent Damphousse	4.00	1.50
☐☐ 218 Saku Koivu	6.00	2.00
☐☐ 219 José Théodore (G)	9.00	3.00
☐☐ **220 Brett Clark RC**	**1.50**	**1.50**
☐☐ 221 Martin Rucinsky	1.50	.50
☐☐ 222 Vladimir Malakhov	1.50	.50
☐☐ 223 Sergei Krivokrasov	1.50	.50
☐☐ 224 Scott Walker	1.50	.50
☐☐ 225 Greg Johnson	1.50	.50
☐☐ 226 Cliff Ronning	1.50	.50
☐☐ 227 Éric Fichaud (G)	1.50	.50
☐☐ 228 Bob Carpenter	1.50	.50
☐☐ 229 Scott Daniels	1.50	.50
☐☐ 230 Brian Rolston	2.00	.50
☐☐ 231 Sergei Brylin	1.50	.50
☐☐ 232 Scott Niedermayer	2.00	.50
☐☐ 233 Bryan Smolinski	1.50	.50
☐☐ 234 Trevor Linden	3.00	1.00
☐☐ 235 Eric Brewer	3.00	2.00
☐☐ 236 Zigmund Palffy	4.00	1.50
☐☐ 237 Sergei Nemchinov	1.50	.50
☐☐ 238 Brian Leetch	4.00	1.50
☐☐ 239 Mathieu Schneider	1.50	.50
☐☐ 240 Niklas Sundström	1.50	.50
☐☐ 241 Manny Malhotra	1.50	1.00
☐☐ 242 Jeff Beukeboom	1.50	.50
☐☐ 243 Peter Nedved	2.00	.50
☐☐ 244 Ron Tugnutt (G)	3.00	1.00
☐☐ 245 Shaun Van Allen	1.50	.50
☐☐ 246 Alexei Yashin	4.00	1.50
☐☐ 247 Jason York	1.50	.50
☐☐ 248 Shawn McEachern	2.00	.50
☐☐ 249 Marian Hossa	7.00	2.50
☐☐ 250 John LeClair	6.00	2.00
☐☐ 251 Rod Brind'Amour	2.00	.50
☐☐ 252 John Vanbiesbrouck (G)	3.00	1.00
☐☐ 253 Éric Desjardins	2.00	.50
☐☐ 254 Valeri Zelepukin	1.50	.50
☐☐ 255 Karl Dykhuis	1.50	.50
☐☐ 256 Keith Tkachuk	4.00	1.50
☐☐ 257 Dallas Drake	1.50	.50
☐☐ 258 Oleg Tverdovsky	1.50	.50
☐☐ 259 Jyrki Lumme	1.50	.50
☐☐ 260 Jimmy Waite (G)	1.50	.50
☐☐ 261 Jaromir Jagr	5.00	2.50
☐☐ 262 German Titov	1.50	.50
☐☐ 263 Robert Lang	1.50	.50
☐☐ 264 Brad Werenka	1.50	.50
☐☐ 265 Rob Brown	1.50	.50
☐☐ 266 Bobby Dollas	1.50	.50
☐☐ 267 Jeff Friesen	2.00	.50
☐☐ **268 Andy Sutton RC**	**1.50**	**1.50**
☐☐ 269 Steve Shields (G)	1.50	.50
☐☐ 270 Mike Ricci	2.00	.50
☐☐ 271 Joe Murphy	1.50	.50
☐☐ 272 Tony Granato	1.50	.50
☐☐ 273 Jamie McLennan	1.50	.50
☐☐ 274 Al MacInnis	3.00	1.00
☐☐ 275 Pierre Turgeon	3.00	1.00
☐☐ 276 Kelly Chase	1.50	.50
☐☐ 277 Craig Conroy	2.00	.50
☐☐ 278 Scott Young	2.00	.50
☐☐ 279 Vincent Lecavalier	7.00	5.00
☐☐ 280 Wendel Clark	6.00	2.00
☐☐ 281 Daren Puppa (G)	1.50	.50
☐☐ 282 Sandy McCarthy	1.50	.50
☐☐ **283 Danny Markov RC**	**2.00**	**3.00**
☐☐ 284 Curtis Joseph (G)	5.00	2.50
☐☐ 285 Sergei Berezin	1.50	.50
☐☐ 286 Steve Sullivan	2.00	.50
☐☐ **287 Tomas Kaberle RC**	**6.00**	**6.00**
☐☐ 288 Kris King	1.50	.50
☐☐ 289 Igor Korolev	1.50	.50
☐☐ 290 Mark Messier	7.00	2.50
☐☐ **291 Bill Muckalt RC**	**3.00**	**3.00**
☐☐ 292 Todd Bertuzzi	9.00	3.00
☐☐ 293 Brad May	1.50	.50
☐☐ 294 Peter Zezel	1.50	.50
☐☐ 295 Dmitri Mironov	1.50	.50
☐☐ 296 Adam Oates	3.00	1.00
☐☐ 297 Calle Johansson	1.50	.50
☐☐ 298 Craig Berube	1.50	.50
☐☐ 299 Sergei Gonchar	2.00	.50
☐☐ 300 Andrei Nikolishin	1.50	.50

AUTOGRAPH

There are two versions: the silver Autograph card (1:1) and the gold Autograph card (500 copies). A number of players were short-printed in the silver (450 copies) and gold (50 copies) autograph versions. Players with limited-run autographs are marked LTD below.

		AutoG	Auto
	Complete Set (300 cards):	**7300.00**	**2800.00**
	Common Player:	**8.00**	**5.00**
	Insert	**AutoG**	**Auto**
☐ ☐	1 Jason Marshall ✍	8.00	5.00
☐ ☐	2 Paul Kariya (LTD) ✍	210.00	70.00
☐ ☐	3 Teemu Selänne (LTD) ✍	120.00	40.00
☐ ☐	4 Guy Hebert (G) ✍	8.00	5.00
☐ ☐	5 Ted Drury ✍	8.00	5.00
☐ ☐	6 Byron Dafoe (G) ✍	15.00	6.00
☐ ☐	7 Rob DiMaio ✍	8.00	5.00
☐ ☐	8 Raymond Bourque (LTD) ✍	180.00	60.00
☐ ☐	9 Joe Thornton ✍	45.00	20.00
☐ ☐	10 Sergei Samsonov ✍	20.00	10.00
☐ ☐	11 Dimitri Khristich ✍	8.00	5.00
☐ ☐	12 Michael Peca ✍	15.00	6.00
☐ ☐	13 Jason Woolley ✍	8.00	5.00
☐ ☐	14 Matthew Barnaby ✍	8.00	5.00
☐ ☐	15 Brian Holzinger ✍	8.00	5.00
☐ ☐	16 Dixon Ward ✍	8.00	5.00
☐ ☐	17 Tyler Moss (G) ✍	8.00	5.00
☐ ☐	18 Jarome Iginla ✍	30.00	15.00
☐ ☐	19 Marty McInnis ✍	8.00	5.00
☐ ☐	20 Andrew Cassels ✍	8.00	5.00
☐ ☐	21 Jason Wiemer ✍	8.00	5.00
☐ ☐	22 Trevor Kidd (G) ✍	10.00	6.00
☐ ☐	23 Keith Primeau ✍	15.00	6.00
☐ ☐	24 Sami Kapanen ✍	10.00	6.00
☐ ☐	25 Robert Kron ✍	8.00	5.00
☐ ☐	26 Glen Wesley ✍	8.00	5.00
☐ ☐	27 Jeff Hackett (G) ✍	10.00	6.00
☐ ☐	28 Tony Amonte (LTD) ✍	90.00	30.00
☐ ☐	29 Alexei Zhamnov ✍	10.00	6.00
☐ ☐	30 Eric Weinrich ✍	8.00	5.00
☐ ☐	31 Jeff Shantz ✍	8.00	5.00
☐ ☐	32 Christian Laflamme ✍	8.00	5.00
☐ ☐	33 Adam Foote ✍	10.00	6.00
☐ ☐	34 Patrick Roy (G) (LTD) ✍	450.00	150.00
☐ ☐	35 Peter Forsberg (LTD) ✍	200.00	70.00
☐ ☐	36 Adam Deadmarsh ✍	10.00	6.00
☐ ☐	37 Joe Sakic (LTD) ✍	240.00	80.00
☐ ☐	38 Éric Lacroix ✍	8.00	5.00
☐ ☐	39 Guy Carbonneau ✍	10.00	6.00
☐ ☐	40 Mike Modano (LTD) ✍	150.00	50.00
☐ ☐	41 Roman Turek (G) ✍	15.00	8.00
☐ ☐	42 Mike Keane ✍	8.00	5.00
☐ ☐	43 Sergei Zubov ✍	8.00	5.00
☐ ☐	44 Jere Lehtinen ✍	10.00	6.00
☐ ☐	45 Sergei Fedorov (LTD) ✍	150.00	50.00
☐ ☐	46 Steve Yzerman (LTD) ✍	360.00	120.00
☐ ☐	47 Chris Osgood (G) ✍	20.00	10.00
☐ ☐	48 Larry Murphy ✍	8.00	5.00
☐ ☐	49 Vyacheslav Kozlov ✍	8.00	5.00
☐ ☐	50 Darren McCarty ✍	10.00	6.00
☐ ☐	51 Boris Mironov ✍	8.00	5.00
☐ ☐	52 Roman Hamrlik ✍	8.00	5.00
☐ ☐	53 Bill Guerin ✍	15.00	6.00
☐ ☐	54 Mike Grier ✍	8.00	5.00
☐ ☐	55 Todd Marchant ✍	8.00	5.00
☐ ☐	56 Ray Whitney ✍	8.00	5.00
☐ ☐	57 Dave Gagner ✍	8.00	5.00
☐ ☐	58 Scott Mellanby ✍	8.00	5.00
☐ ☐	59 Robert Svehla ✍	8.00	5.00
☐ ☐	60 Viktor Kozlov ✍	10.00	6.00
☐ ☐	61 Luc Robitaille (LTD) ✍	120.00	40.00
☐ ☐	62 Yanic Perreault ✍	10.00	6.00
☐ ☐	63 Jozef Stümpel ✍	8.00	5.00
☐ ☐	64 Sandy Moger ✍	8.00	5.00
☐ ☐	65 Ian Laperrière ✍	8.00	5.00
☐ ☐	66 Jocelyn Thibault (G) ✍	15.00	6.00
☐ ☐	67 Dave Manson ✍	8.00	5.00
☐ ☐	68 Mark Recchi (LTD) ✍	60.00	20.00
☐ ☐	69 Patrick Poulin ✍	8.00	5.00
☐ ☐	70 Benoît Brunet ✍	8.00	5.00
☐ ☐	71 Turner Stevenson ✍	8.00	5.00
☐ ☐	72 Mike Dunham (G) ✍	15.00	6.00
☐ ☐	73 Tom Fitzgerald ✍	8.00	5.00
☐ ☐	74 Darren Turcotte ✍	8.00	5.00
☐ ☐	75 Brad Smyth ✍	8.00	5.00
☐ ☐	76 J.J. Daigneault ✍	8.00	5.00
☐ ☐	77 Dave Andreychuk ✍	10.00	6.00
☐ ☐	78 Jason Arnott ✍	15.00	8.00
☐ ☐	79 Martin Brodeur (G) ✍	60.00	30.00
☐ ☐	80 Randy McKay ✍	8.00	5.00
☐ ☐	81 Patrik Elias ✍	30.00	15.00
☐ ☐	82 Kevin Dean ✍	8.00	5.00
☐ ☐	83 Tommy Salo (G) ✍	15.00	6.00
☐ ☐	84 Scott Lachance ✍	8.00	5.00
☐ ☐	85 Bryan Berard ✍	10.00	6.00
☐ ☐	86 Robert Reichel ✍	10.00	6.00
☐ ☐	87 Kenny Jönsson ✍	8.00	5.00
☐ ☐	88 Kevin Stevens ✍	8.00	5.00
☐ ☐	89 Mike Richter (G) (LTD) ✍	70.00	20.00
☐ ☐	90 Wayne Gretzky (X-LTD) ✍	3300.00	1000.00
☐ ☐	91 Adam Graves (LTD) ✍	60.00	20.00
☐ ☐	92 Alexei Kovalev ✍	20.00	10.00
☐ ☐	93 Ulf Samuelsson ✍	8.00	5.00
☐ ☐	94 Radek Bonk ✍	10.00	6.00
☐ ☐	95 Wade Redden ✍	10.00	6.00
☐ ☐	96 Damian Rhodes (G) ✍	8.00	5.00
☐ ☐	97 Bruce Gardiner ✍	8.00	5.00
☐ ☐	98 Daniel Alfredsson ✍	20.00	10.00
☐ ☐	99 Ron Hextall (G) ✍	20.00	10.00
☐ ☐	100 Eric Lindros (LTD) ✍	150.00	50.00
☐ ☐	101 Chris Gratton ✍	8.00	5.00
☐ ☐	102 Dainius Zubrus ✍	8.00	5.00
☐ ☐	103 Luke Richardson ✍	8.00	5.00
☐ ☐	104 Petr Svoboda ✍	8.00	5.00
☐ ☐	105 Rick Tocchet ✍	10.00	6.00
☐ ☐	106 Teppo Numminen ✍	10.00	6.00
☐ ☐	107 Jeremy Roenick (LTD) ✍	120.00	40.00
☐ ☐	108 Nikolai Khabibulin (G) ✍	15.00	6.00
☐ ☐	109 Brad Isbister ✍	8.00	5.00
☐ ☐	110 Peter Skudra (G) ✍	8.00	5.00
☐ ☐	111 Alexei Morozov ✍	8.00	5.00
☐ ☐	112 Kevin Hatcher ✍	8.00	5.00
☐ ☐	113 Darius Kasparaitis ✍	8.00	5.00
☐ ☐	114 Stu Barnes ✍	8.00	5.00
☐ ☐	115 Martin Straka ✍	10.00	6.00
☐ ☐	116 Andrei Zyuzin ✍	8.00	5.00
☐ ☐	117 Marcus Ragnarsson ✍	8.00	5.00
☐ ☐	118 Murray Craven ✍	8.00	5.00
☐ ☐	119 Marco Sturm ✍	8.00	5.00
☐ ☐	120 Patrick Marleau ✍	15.00	8.00
☐ ☐	121 Shawn Burr ✍	8.00	5.00
☐ ☐	122 Grant Fuhr (G) ✍	20.00	10.00
☐ ☐	123 Chris Pronger ✍	20.00	10.00
☐ ☐	124 Geoff Courtnall ✍	8.00	5.00
☐ ☐	125 Jim Campbell ✍	8.00	5.00
☐ ☐	126 Pavol Demitra ✍	15.00	6.00
☐ ☐	127 Todd Gill ✍	8.00	5.00
☐ ☐	128 Cory Cross ✍	8.00	5.00
☐ ☐	129 Daymond Langkow ✍	8.00	5.00
☐ ☐	130 Alexander Selivanov ✍	8.00	5.00
☐ ☐	131 Mikael Renberg ✍	10.00	6.00
☐ ☐	132 Rob Zamuner ✍	8.00	5.00
☐ ☐	133 Stéphane Richer ✍	8.00	5.00
☐ ☐	134 Fredrik Modin ✍	8.00	5.00
☐ ☐	135 Derek King ✍	8.00	5.00
☐ ☐	136 Mats Sundin (LTD) ✍	150.00	50.00
☐ ☐	137 Mike Johnson ✍	8.00	5.00
☐ ☐	138 Alyn McCauley ✍	10.00	6.00
☐ ☐	139 Jason Smith ✍	8.00	5.00
☐ ☐	140 Markus Näslund ✍	35.00	15.00
☐ ☐	141 Alexander Mogilny (LTD) ✍	70.00	20.00
☐ ☐	142 Mattias Öhlund ✍	10.00	6.00
☐ ☐	143 Donald Brashear ✍	8.00	5.00
☐ ☐	144 Garth Snow (G) ✍	10.00	6.00
☐ ☐	145 Brian Bellows ✍	8.00	5.00
☐ ☐	146 Peter Bondra (LTD) ✍	90.00	30.00
☐ ☐	147 Joé Juneau ✍	8.00	5.00
☐ ☐	148 Steve Konowalchuk ✍	8.00	5.00
☐ ☐	149 Ken Klee ✍	8.00	5.00
☐ ☐	150 Michal Pivonka ✍	8.00	5.00
☐ ☐	151 Steve Rucchin ✍	8.00	5.00
☐ ☐	152 Stu Grimson ✍	8.00	5.00
☐ ☐	153 Tomas Sandström ✍	8.00	5.00
☐ ☐	154 Fredrik Olausson ✍	8.00	5.00
☐ ☐	155 Travis Green ✍	8.00	5.00
☐ ☐	156 Jason Allison ✍	20.00	10.00
☐ ☐	157 Steve Heinze ✍	8.00	5.00
☐ ☐	158 Rob Tallas ✍	8.00	5.00
☐ ☐	159 Darren Van Impe ✍	8.00	5.00
☐ ☐	160 Ken Baumgartner ✍	8.00	5.00
☐ ☐	161 Peter Ferraro ✍	8.00	5.00
☐ ☐	162 Dominik Hasek (G) (LTD) ✍	150.00	50.00
☐ ☐	163 Geoff Sanderson ✍	8.00	5.00
☐ ☐	164 Miroslav Satan ✍	10.00	6.00
☐ ☐	165 Rob Ray ✍	8.00	5.00
☐ ☐	166 Alexei Zhitnik ✍	8.00	5.00
☐ ☐	167 Phil Housley ✍	10.00	6.00
☐ ☐	168 Theoren Fleury (LTD) ✍	90.00	30.00
☐ ☐	169 Ken Wregget (G) ✍	8.00	5.00
☐ ☐	170 Valeri Bure ✍	10.00	6.00
☐ ☐	171 Rico Fata ✍	8.00	5.00
☐ ☐	172 Arturs Irbe (G) ✍	15.00	6.00
☐ ☐	173 Sean Hill ✍	8.00	5.00
☐ ☐	174 Ron Francis (LTD) ✍	90.00	30.00
☐ ☐	175 Jeff O'Neill ✍	15.00	6.00
☐ ☐	176 Paul Ranheim ✍	8.00	5.00
☐ ☐	177 Paul Coffey (LTD) ✍	90.00	30.00
☐ ☐	178 Doug Gilmour ✍	20.00	10.00
☐ ☐	179 Éric Dazé ✍	15.00	6.00
☐ ☐	180 Chris Chelios (LTD) ✍	90.00	30.00
☐ ☐	181 Bob Probert ✍	10.00	6.00
☐ ☐	182 Mark Fitzpatrick (G) ✍	8.00	5.00
☐ ☐	183 Alexei Gusarov ✍	8.00	5.00
☐ ☐	184 Sylvain Lefebvre ✍	8.00	5.00
☐ ☐	185 Craig Billington (G) ✍	8.00	5.00
☐ ☐	186 Valeri Kamensky ✍	10.00	6.00
☐ ☐	187 Milan Hejduk ✍	40.00	30.00
☐ ☐	188 Sandis Ozolinsh ✍	8.00	5.00
☐ ☐	189 Brett Hull (LTD) ✍	150.00	50.00
☐ ☐	190 Ed Belfour (G) (LTD) ✍	150.00	50.00
☐ ☐	191 Darryl Sydor ✍	8.00	5.00
☐ ☐	192 Sergei Gusev ✍	8.00	5.00
☐ ☐	193 Joe Nieuwendyk (LTD) ✍	60.00	20.00
☐ ☐	194 Derian Hatcher ✍	10.00	6.00
☐ ☐	195 Brendan Shanahan (LTD) ✍	150.00	50.00
☐ ☐	196 Tomas Holmström ✍	8.00	5.00
☐ ☐	197 Nicklas Lidström ✍	20.00	10.00
☐ ☐	198 Martin Lapointe ✍	15.00	6.00
☐ ☐	199 Igor Larionov ✍	20.00	10.00
☐ ☐	200 Kris Draper ✍	8.00	5.00
☐ ☐	201 Kelly Buchberger ✍	8.00	5.00
☐ ☐	202 Andrei Kovalenko ✍	8.00	5.00
☐ ☐	203 Josef Beranek ✍	8.00	5.00
☐ ☐	204 Mikhail Shtalenkov (G) ✍	8.00	5.00
☐ ☐	205 Pat Falloon ✍	8.00	5.00
☐ ☐	206 Mark Parrish ✍	15.00	8.00
☐ ☐	207 Terry Carkner ✍	8.00	5.00
☐ ☐	208 Rob Niedermayer ✍	8.00	5.00
☐ ☐	209 Sean Burke (G) ✍	20.00	10.00
☐ ☐	210 Oleg Kvasha ✍	8.00	5.00
☐ ☐	211 Pavel Bure (LTD) ✍	120.00	40.00
☐ ☐	212 Rob Blake ✍	20.00	10.00
☐ ☐	213 Vladimir Tsyplakov ✍	8.00	5.00
☐ ☐	214 Stéphane Fiset (G) ✍	10.00	6.00
☐ ☐	215 Steve Duchesne ✍	8.00	5.00
☐ ☐	216 Patrice Brisebois ✍	8.00	5.00
☐ ☐	217 Vincent Damphousse ✍	20.00	10.00
☐ ☐	218 Saku Koivu ✍	30.00	15.00
☐ ☐	219 José Théodore (G) ✍	45.00	20.00
☐ ☐	220 Brett Clark ✍	8.00	5.00
☐ ☐	221 Martin Rucinsky ✍	8.00	5.00
☐ ☐	222 Vladimir Malakhov ✍	8.00	5.00
☐ ☐	223 Sergei Krivokrasov ✍	8.00	5.00
☐ ☐	224 Scott Walker ✍	8.00	5.00
☐ ☐	225 Greg Johnson ✍	8.00	5.00
☐ ☐	226 Cliff Ronning ✍	8.00	5.00
☐ ☐	227 Éric Fichaud (G) ✍	8.00	5.00
☐ ☐	228 Bob Carpenter ✍	8.00	5.00
☐ ☐	229 Scott Daniels ✍	8.00	5.00
☐ ☐	230 Brian Rolston ✍	10.00	6.00
☐ ☐	231 Sergei Brylin ✍	8.00	5.00
☐ ☐	232 Scott Niedermayer ✍	10.00	6.00
☐ ☐	233 Bryan Smolinski ✍	8.00	5.00
☐ ☐	234 Trevor Linden ✍	15.00	6.00
☐ ☐	235 Eric Brewer ✍	15.00	8.00
☐ ☐	236 Zigmund Palffy (LTD) ✍	90.00	30.00
☐ ☐	237 Sergei Nemchinov ✍	8.00	5.00
☐ ☐	238 Brian Leetch (LTD) ✍	90.00	30.00
☐ ☐	239 Mathieu Schneider ✍	8.00	5.00
☐ ☐	240 Niklas Sundström ✍	8.00	5.00
☐ ☐	241 Manny Malhotra ✍	8.00	5.00
☐ ☐	242 Jeff Beukeboom ✍	8.00	5.00
☐ ☐	243 Peter Nedved ✍	10.00	6.00
☐ ☐	244 Ron Tugnutt (G) ✍	15.00	6.00
☐ ☐	245 Shaun Van Allen ✍	8.00	5.00
☐ ☐	246 Alexei Yashin ✍	20.00	10.00
☐ ☐	247 Jason York ✍	8.00	5.00
☐ ☐	248 Shawn McEachern ✍	10.00	6.00
☐ ☐	249 Marian Hossa ✍	35.00	15.00
☐ ☐	250 John LeClair (LTD) ✍	120.00	40.00
☐ ☐	251 Rod Brind'Amour ✍	10.00	6.00
☐ ☐	252 John Vanbiesbrouck (G) ✍	15.00	8.00
☐ ☐	253 Eric Desjardins ✍	10.00	6.00
☐ ☐	254 Valeri Zelepukin ✍	8.00	5.00
☐ ☐	255 Karl Dykhuis ✍	8.00	5.00
☐ ☐	256 Keith Tkachuk (LTD) ✍	90.00	30.00
☐ ☐	257 Dallas Drake ✍	8.00	5.00
☐ ☐	258 Oleg Tverdovsky ✍	8.00	5.00
☐ ☐	259 Jyrki Lumme ✍	8.00	5.00
☐ ☐	260 Jimmy Waite (G) ✍	8.00	5.00
☐ ☐	261 Jaromir Jagr (LTD) ✍	150.00	100.00
☐ ☐	262 German Titov ✍	8.00	5.00
☐ ☐	263 Robert Lang ✍	8.00	5.00
☐ ☐	264 Brad Werenka ✍	8.00	5.00
☐ ☐	265 Rob Brown ✍	8.00	5.00
☐ ☐	266 Bobby Dollas ✍	8.00	5.00
☐ ☐	267 Jeff Friesen ✍	10.00	6.00
☐ ☐	268 Andy Sutton ✍	8.00	5.00
☐ ☐	269 Steve Shields (G) ✍	8.00	5.00
☐ ☐	270 Mike Ricci ✍	10.00	6.00
☐ ☐	271 Joe Murphy ✍	8.00	5.00
☐ ☐	272 Tony Granato ✍	8.00	5.00
☐ ☐	273 Jamie McLennan ✍	8.00	5.00
☐ ☐	274 Al MacInnis (LTD) ✍	60.00	20.00
☐ ☐	275 Pierre Turgeon ✍	15.00	6.00
☐ ☐	276 Kelly Chase ✍	8.00	5.00
☐ ☐	277 Craig Conroy ✍	10.00	6.00
☐ ☐	278 Scott Young ✍	10.00	6.00
☐ ☐	279 Vincent Lecavalier ✍	30.00	15.00
☐ ☐	280 Wendel Clark ✍	30.00	15.00
☐ ☐	281 Daren Puppa (G) ✍	8.00	5.00
☐ ☐	282 Sandy McCarthy ✍	8.00	5.00
☐ ☐	283 Danny Markov ✍	8.00	5.00
☐ ☐	284 Curtis Joseph (G) (LTD) ✍	150.00	50.00
☐ ☐	285 Sergei Berezin ✍	8.00	5.00
☐ ☐	286 Steve Sullivan ✍	10.00	6.00
☐ ☐	287 Tomas Kaberle ✍	10.00	6.00
☐ ☐	288 Kris King ✍	8.00	5.00
☐ ☐	289 Igor Korolev ✍	8.00	5.00
☐ ☐	290 Mark Messier (LTD) ✍	150.00	60.00
☐ ☐	291 Bill Muckalt ✍	8.00	5.00
☐ ☐	292 Todd Bertuzzi ✍	45.00	22.00
☐ ☐	293 Brad May ✍	8.00	5.00
☐ ☐	294 Peter Zezel ✍	8.00	5.00
☐ ☐	295 Dmitri Mironov ✍	8.00	5.00
☐ ☐	296 Adam Oates (LTD) ✍	60.00	20.00
☐ ☐	297 Calle Johansson ✍	8.00	5.00
☐ ☐	298 Craig Berube ✍	8.00	5.00
☐ ☐	299 Sergei Gonchar ✍	10.00	6.00
☐ ☐	300 Andrei Nikolishin ✍	8.00	5.00

BE A PLAYER LEGEND

The Lemieux Legend inserts are limited to just 66 copies.

	Insert	**Legend**
☐	GH1 Gordie Howe Jersey ✍ Aut. ✂	1000.00
☐	GH2 Gordie Howe Jersey ✂	300.00
☐	L-1 Mario Lemieux Jersey ✂	800.00
☐	L-2 Mario Lemieux AS Jersey ✂	800.00
☐	L-3 M. Lemieux Jersey ✂ Stick ✂ Auto. ✍	1200.00
☐	L-3 M. Lemieux AS Jersey ✂ Stick ✂ Auto. ✍	1200.00

AUTHENTIC GAME-USED JERSEY

		GJ
	Playoff Insert Set (24 cards):	**2,400.00**
	Insert	**GJ**
☐	Tony Amonte, Chic. ✂	50.00
☐	Ed Belfour (G), Dall. ✂	100.00
☐	Raymond Bourque, Bost. ✂	100.00
☐	Martin Brodeur (G), NJer. ✂	150.00
☐	Pavel Bure, Flor. ✂	75.00
☐	Sergei Fedorov, Detr. ✂	100.00
☐	Peter Forsberg, Colo. ✂	125.00
☐	Wayne Gretzky, Edmo. ✂	425.00
☐	Brett Hull, Dall. ✂	100.00
☐	Jaromir Jagr, Pitt. ✂	100.00
☐	Paul Kariya, Anah. ✂	125.00
☐	John LeClair, Phil. ✂	75.00
☐	Eric Lindros, Phil. ✂	100.00
☐	Mark Messier, Vanc. ✂	100.00
☐	Mike Modano, Dall. ✂	100.00
☐	Alexander Mogilny, Vanc. ✂	50.00
☐	Jeremy Roenick, Phoe. ✂	75.00
☐	Patrick Roy (G), Colo. ✂	225.00
☐	Joe Sakic, Colo. ✂	150.00
☐	Teemu Selänne, Anah. ✂	75.00
☐	Brendan Shanahan, Detr. ✂	100.00
☐	Mats Sundin, Toro. ✂	100.00
☐	Alexei Yashin, Ott. ✂	50.00
☐	Steve Yzerman, Detr. ✂	225.00

AUTHENTIC GAME-USED JERSEY AUTOGRAPH

		GJA10
	Autograph Set (14 cards):	**14200**
	Insert (#/10)	**GJA10**
☐	Martin Brodeur (G), NJer. ✍ ✂	1100.00
☐	Pavel Bure, Flor. ✍ ✂	500.00
☐	Sergei Fedorov, Detr. ✍ ✂	700.00
☐	Wayne Gretzky, Edmo. ✍ ✂	4200.00
☐	Paul Kariya, Anah. ✍ ✂	900.00
☐	John LeClair, Phil. ✍ ✂	500.00
☐	Eric Lindros, Phil. ✍ ✂	700.00
☐	Patrick Roy (G), Colo. ✍ ✂	2100.00
☐	Joe Sakic, Colo. ✍ ✂	1100.00
☐	Teemu Selänne, Anah. ✍ ✂	500.00
☐	Brendan Shanahan, Detr. ✍ ✂	700.00
☐	Mats Sundin, Toro. ✍ ✂	700.00
☐	Alexei Yashin, Ott. ✍ ✂	400.00
☐	Steve Yzerman, Detr. ✍ ✂	1600.00

AUTHENTIC MEMORABILIA / JERSEY

		ASJ
	All-Star Insert Set (25 cards):	**2,500.00**
	Insert	**ASJ**
☐	Ed Belfour (G), AS '96 ✂	100.00
☐	Raymond Bourque, AS '98 ✂	100.00
☐	Martin Brodeur (G), AS '97 ✂	150.00
☐	Pavel Bure, AS '98 ✂	75.00
☐	Chris Chelios, AS '96 ✂	60.00

□	Paul Coffey, AS '97 ✂	60.00
□	Sergei Fedorov, AS '94 ✂	100.00
□	Peter Forsberg, AS '98 ✂	125.00
□	Wayne Gretzky, AS '98 ✂	400.00
□	Dominik Hasek (G), AS '98 ✂	100.00
□	Brett Hull, AS '96 ✂	100.00
□	Jaromir Jagr, AS '98 ✂	100.00
□	Paul Kariya, AS '97 ✂	125.00
□	John LeClair, AS '97 ✂	75.00
□	Eric Lindros, AS '98 ✂	100.00
□	Mark Messier, AS '94 ✂	100.00
□	Mike Modano, AS '98 ✂	100.00
□	Alexander Mogilny, AS '96 ✂	60.00
□	Jeremy Roenick, AS '94 ✂	75.00
□	Patrick Roy (G), AS '94 ✂	300.00
□	Joe Sakic, AS '98 ✂	150.00
□	Teemu Selänne, AS '94 ✂	75.00
□	Brendan Shanahan, AS '96 ✂	100.00
□	Mats Sundin, AS '97 ✂	100.00
□	Steve Yzerman, AS '97 ✂	225.00

AUTHENTIC MEMORABILIA / STICK

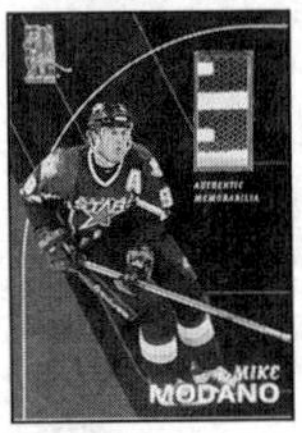

All-Star Insert Set (23 cards):		**2,500.00**
	Insert	**Stick**
□	Eric Lindros Stick ✂	100.00
□	Peter Forsberg Stick ✂	150.00
□	Teemu Selänne Stick ✂	75.00
□	Mike Modano Stick ✂	100.00
□	Mats Sundin Stick ✂	100.00
□	Patrick Roy (G) Stick ✂	325.00
□	Paul Kariya Stick ✂	150.00
□	Martin Brodeur (G) Stick ✂	175.00
□	Steve Yzerman Stick ✂	250.00
□	Mark Messier Stick ✂	100.00
□	Brett Hull Stick ✂	100.00
□	Joe Sakic Stick ✂	175.00
□	Alexander Mogilny Stick ✂	50.00
□	Sergei Fedorov Stick ✂	100.00
□	Raymond Bourque Stick ✂	125.00
□	Jeremy Roenick Stick ✂	75.00
□	Jaromir Jagr Stick ✂	100.00
□	Dominik Hasek (G) Stick ✂	100.00
□	Chris Chelios Stick ✂	50.00
□	John LeClair Stick ✂	75.00
□	Brendan Shanahan Stick ✂	100.00
□	Ed Belfour (G) Stick ✂	100.00
□	Wayne Gretzky Stick ✂	450.00

MILESTONES

All-Star Insert Set (22 cards):		**135.00**
	Player	**M**
□	M1 Wayne Gretzky, Edmo.	30.00
□	M2 Mark Messier, NYRa.	6.00
□	M3 Dino Ciccarelli, Detr.	3.00
□	M4 Steve Yzerman, Detr.	15.00
□	M5 Dave Andreychuk, NJer.	3.00
□	M6 Brett Hull, SLou.	6.00
□	M7 Wayne Gretzky, Edmo.	30.00
□	M8 Mark Messier, Edmo.	6.00
□	M9 Dino Ciccarelli, Detr.	3.00
□	M10 Steve Yzerman, Detr.	15.00
□	M11 Bernie Nicholls, NJer.	3.00
□	M12 Ron Francis, Pitt.	4.00
□	M13 Raymond Bourque, Bost.	8.00
□	M14 Paul Coffey, Pitt.	4.00
□	M15 Adam Oates, Wash.	3.00
□	M16 Phil Housley, Wash.	3.00
□	M17 Dale Hunter, Wash.	3.00
□	M18 Luc Robitaille, LosA.	6.00
□	M19 Doug Gilmour, Toro.	4.00
□	M20 Larry Murphy, Toro.	3.00
□	M21 Dave Andreychuk, NJer.	3.00
□	M22 Al MacInnis, SLou.	3.00

PLAYOFF HIGHLIGHTS

Playoff Insert Set (18 cards):		**55.00**
	Player	**PH**
□	H-1 Mark Messier, NYRa.	3.00
□	H-2 Peter Forsberg, Colo.	4.00
□	H-3 Wayne Gretzky, Edmo.	12.00
□	H-4 Martin Brodeur (G), NJer.	4.00
□	H-5 Jaromir Jagr, Pitt.	3.00
□	H-6 Mike Richter, NYRa.	2.00
□	H-7 Steve Yzerman, Detr.	7.00
□	H-8 Patrick Roy (G), Mont.	9.00
□	H-9 Paul Coffey, Edmo.	2.00
□	H-10 Joe Sakic, Colo.	4.00
□	H-11 John Vanbiesbrouck (G), Phil.	2.00
□	H-12 Pavel Bure, Vanc.	2.00
□	H-13 Chris Osgood (G), Detr.	2.00
□	H-14 Chris Chelios, Mont.	2.00
□	H-15 Curtis Joseph (G), Edmo.	3.00
□	H-16 Brian Leetch, NYRa.	2.00
□	H-17 Sergei Fedorov, Detr.	3.00
□	H-18 Doug Gilmour, Calg.	2.00

PRACTICE-USED JERSEY

Playoff Insert Set (24 cards):		**1,800.00**
	Insert	**PJ**
□	Tony Amonte, Chic.	35.00
□	Ed Belfour (G), Dall.	75.00
□	Raymond Bourque, Bost.	75.00
□	Martin Brodeur (G), NJer.	100.00
□	Pavel Bure, Flor.	50.00
□	Sergei Fedorov, Detr.	75.00
□	Peter Forsberg, Colo.	100.00
□	Wayne Gretzky, NYRa.	300.00
□	Brett Hull, Dall.	75.00
□	Jaromir Jagr, Pitt.	75.00
□	Paul Kariya, Anah.	100.00
□	John LeClair, Phil.	50.00
□	Eric Lindros, Phil.	75.00
□	Mark Messier, Vanc.	75.00
□	Mike Modano, Dall.	75.00
□	Alexander Mogilny, Vanc.	35.00
□	Jeremy Roenick, Phoe.	50.00
□	Patrick Roy (G), Colo.	225.00
□	Joe Sakic, Colo.	100.00
□	Teemu Selänne, Anah.	50.00
□	Brendan Shanahan, Detr.	75.00
□	Mats Sundin, Toro.	75.00
□	Alexei Yashin, Otta.	35.00
□	Steve Yzerman, Detr.	175.00

1998 - 99 BICYCLE SPORTS / ACES

These disks measure 3" in diameter.

Complete Deck (54 cards):		**6.00**
Common Player:		**.20**
	Insert	**Disk**
□	10-Club Daren Puppa (G), Tamp.	.20
□	10-Diamond Nikolai Khabibulin (G), Phoe.	.20
□	10-Heart Grant Fuhr (G), SLou.	.20
□	10-Spade Jeff Hackett (G), Chic.	.20
□	2-Club Ken Wregget (G), Pitt. (Calg.)	.20
□	2-Diamond Robbie Tallas (G), Bost.	.20
□	2-Heart Marcel Cousineau (G), Toro. (NYIs.)	.20
□	2-Spade Glenn Healy (G), Toro.	.20
□	3-Club Bill Ranford (G), Wash. (Tamp.)	.20
□	3-Diamond Kirk McLean (G), Flor.	.20
□	3-Heart Corey Schwab (G), Tamp.	.20
□	3-Spade Mike Dunham (G), NJer.	.20
□	4-Club Jamie Storr (G), LosA.	.20
□	4-Diamond Peter Skudra (G), Pitt.	.20
□	4-Heart Dwayne Roloson (G), Calg. (Buff.)	.20
□	4-Spade Roman Turek (G), Dall.	.20
□	5-Club Chris Terreri (G), Chic.	.20
□	5-Diamond Éric Fichaud (G), NYIs. (Edmo.)	.20
□	5-Heart Mark Fitzpatrick (G), Tamp. (Chic.)	.20
□	5-Spade Steve Shields (G), Buff. (SanJ.)	.20
□	6-Club Kelly Hrudey (G), SanJ.	.20
□	6-Diamond Bob Essensa (G), Edmo.	.20
□	6-Heart Guy Hebert (G), Anah.	.20
□	6-Spade Garth Snow (G), Vanc.	.20
□	7-Club Ron Tugnutt (G), Otta.	.20
□	7-Diamond Sean Burke (G), Phil.	.20
□	7-Heart Jamie McLennan (G), SLou.	.20
□	7-Spade Kevin Hodson (G), Detr.	.20
□	8-Club Mike Vernon (G), SanJ.	.20
□	8-Diamond Jocelyn Thibault (G), Mont.	.20
□	8-Heart Rick Tabaracci (G), Calg.	.20
□	8-Spade Craig Billington (G), Colo.	.20
□	9-Club Mikhail Shtalenkov (G), Anah.	.20
□	9-Diamond Ron Hextall (G), Phil.	.20
□	9-Heart José Théodore (G), Mont.	.50
□	9-Spade Trevor Kidd (G), Caro.	.20
□	A-Club Patrick Roy (G), Colo.	1.50
□	A-Diamond Dominik Hasek (G), Buff.	.50
□	A-Heart Olaf Kölzig (G), Wash.	.20
□	A-Spade Curtis Joseph (G), Edmo. (Toro.)	.50
□	J-Club Byron Dafoe (G), Bost.	.20
□	J-Club Stéphane Fiset (G), LosA.	.20
□	J-Diamond Mike Richter (G), NYRa.	.20
□	J-Heart Ed Belfour (G), Dall.	.50
□	K-Club Chris Osgood (G), Detr.	.20
□	K-Diamond John Vanbiesbrouck (G), Flor. (Phil.)	.20
□	K-Heart Damian Rhodes (G), Otta.	.20
□	K-Spade Martin Brodeur (G), NJer.	.50
□	Q-Club Arturs Irbe (G), Vanc.	.20
□	Q-Diamond Tommy Salo (G), NYIs.	.20
□	Q-Heart Félix Potvin (G), Toro.	.20
□	Q-Spade Tom Barrasso (G), Pitt.	.20
□	Eastern Conference	.20
□	Western Conference Logo	.20

1998 - 99 BOWMAN'S BEST

These cards have three versions: the regular card, a Refractor parallel (#/400) and an Atomic Refractor parallel (#/100). Base cards 101-150 are short-printed.

Complete Set (150 cards):		**3100.00**	**800.00**	**120.00**
Common Player:		**12.00**	**4.00**	**.20**
	Player	**AR100**	**R400**	**BB**
□□□	1 Steve Yzerman, Detr.	180.00	45.00	3.00
□□□	2 Paul Kariya, Anah.	100.00	25.00	1.00
□□□	3 Wayne Gretzky, NYRa.	300.00	70.00	5.00
□□□	4 Jaromir Jagr, Pitt.	70.00	15.00	1.00
□□□	5 Mark Messier, Vanc.	70.00	18.00	1.00
□□□	6 Keith Tkachuk, Phoe.	40.00	10.00	.20
□□□	7 John LeClair, Phil.	60.00	14.00	1.00
□□□	8 Martin Brodeur (G), NJer.	120.00	30.00	2.00
□□□	9 Rob Blake, LosA.	45.00	10.00	.20
□□□	10 Brett Hull, Dall.	70.00	18.00	1.00
□□□	11 Dominik Hasek (G), Buff.	70.00	15.00	1.00
□□□	12 Peter Forsberg, Colo.	100.00	25.00	1.00
□□□	13 Doug Gilmour, Chic.	45.00	10.00	.20
□□□	14 V. Damphousse, Mont.	45.00	10.00	.20
□□□	15 Zigmund Palffy, NYIs.	45.00	10.00	.20
□□□	16 Daniel Alfredsson, Ott.	45.00	10.00	.20
□□□	17 Mike Vernon (G), SanJ.	30.00	6.00	.20
□□□	18 Chris Pronger, SLou.	45.00	10.00	.20
□□□	19 Wendel Clark, Tamp.	60.00	14.00	1.00
□□□	20 Curtis Joseph (G), Toro.	70.00	15.00	1.00
□□□	21 Peter Bondra, Wash.	45.00	10.00	.20
□□□	22 Grant Fuhr (G), SLou.	45.00	10.00	.20
□□□	23 N. Khabibulin (G), Phoe.	30.00	6.00	.20
□□□	24 Kevin Hatcher, Pitt.	12.00	4.00	.20
□□□	25 Brian Leetch, NYRa.	45.00	10.00	.20
□□□	26 Patrik Elias, NJer.	60.00	14.00	1.00
□□□	27 Chris Osgood (G), Detr.	40.00	10.00	.20
□□□	28 Patrick Roy (G), Colo.	220.00	55.00	3.00
□□□	29 Chris Chelios, Chic.	45.00	10.00	.20
□□□	30 Trevor Kidd (G), Caro.	20.00	6.00	.20
□□□	31 Theoren Fleury, Calg.	40.00	10.00	.20
□□□	32 Michael Peca, Buff.	30.00	6.00	.20
□□□	33 Raymond Bourque, Bost.	90.00	20.00	1.00
□□□	34 Ed Belfour (G), Dall.	70.00	18.00	1.00
□□□	35 Sergei Fedorov, Detr.	70.00	18.00	1.00
□□□	36 Adrian Aucoin, Vanc.	12.00	4.00	.20
□□□	37 Alexei Yashin, Ott.	45.00	10.00	.20
□□□	38 Rick Tocchet, Phoe.	20.00	6.00	.20
□□□	39 Mats Sundin, Toro.	70.00	18.00	1.00
□□□	40 Alexander Mogilny, Vanc.	35.00	8.00	.20
□□□	41 Jeff Friesen, SanJ.	20.00	6.00	.20
□□□	42 Eric Lindros, Phil.	70.00	15.00	1.00
□□□	43 Mike Richter (G), NYRa.	35.00	8.00	.20
□□□	44 Saku Koivu, Mont.	60.00	14.00	1.00
□□□	45 Teemu Selänne, Anah.	60.00	14.00	1.00
□□□	46 Doug Weight, Edmo.	40.00	10.00	.20
□□□	47 Nicklas Lidström, Detr.	45.00	10.00	.20
□□□	48 Mike Modano, Dall.	70.00	18.00	1.00
□□□	49 Joe Sakic, Colo.	120.00	30.00	2.00
□□□	50 Ron Francis, Caro.	45.00	10.00	.20
□□□	51 Jason Allison, Bost.	40.00	10.00	.20
□□□	52 Brendan Shanahan, Detr.	70.00	18.00	1.00
□□□	53 Bobby Holik, NJer.	20.00	6.00	.20
□□□	54 Damian Rhodes (G), Ott.	15.00	4.00	.20
□□□	55 Jeremy Roenick, Phoe.	60.00	14.00	1.00
□□□	56 Tom Barrasso (G), Pitt.	30.00	6.00	.20
□□□	57 Al MacInnis, SLou.	30.00	6.00	.20
□□□	58 Pavel Bure, Vanc.	60.00	15.00	1.00
□□□	59 Olaf Kölzig (G), Wash.	45.00	10.00	.20
□□□	60 Patrick Marleau, SanJ.	35.00	8.00	.20
□□□	61 Cliff Ronning, Phoe.	15.00	4.00	.20
□□□	62 Joe Nieuwendyk, Dall.	30.00	6.00	.20
□□□	63 Jeff Hackett (G), Mont.	20.00	6.00	.20
□□□	64 Keith Primeau, Caro.	30.00	6.00	.20
□□□	65 Jarome Iginla, Calg.	60.00	14.00	1.00
□□□	66 Sergei Samsonov, Bost.	40.00	10.00	.20
□□□	67 Rod Brind'Amour, Phil.	20.00	6.00	.20
□□□	68 Dino Ciccarelli, Flor.	20.00	6.00	.20
□□□	69 Ryan Smyth, Edmo.	35.00	8.00	.20
□□□	70 Owen Nolan, SanJ.	45.00	10.00	.20
□□□	71 Mike Johnson, Toro.	15.00	4.00	.20
□□□	72 Adam Oates, Wash.	30.00	6.00	.20
□□□	73 Mattias Öhlund, Vanc.	20.00	6.00	.20
□□□	74 Jamie Heward, Nash.	12.00	4.00	.20
□□□	75 Mike Dunham (G), Nash.	30.00	6.00	.20
□□□	76 Jere Lehtinen, Dall.	20.00	6.00	.20
□□□	77 Tony Amonte, Chic.	45.00	10.00	.20
□□□	78 Derek Morris, Calg.	15.00	4.00	.20
□□□	79 Darren McCarty, Detr.	20.00	6.00	.20
□□□	80 Bryan Berard, NYIs.	20.00	6.00	.20
□□□	81 Adam Graves, NYRa.	30.00	6.00	.20
□□□	82 J. Vanbiesbrouck (G), Phil.	35.00	8.00	.20
□□□	83 Marco Sturm, SanJ.	15.00	4.00	.20
□□□	84 Joe Thornton, Bost.	90.00	22.00	1.00
□□□	85 Wade Redden, Ott.	20.00	6.00	.20
□□□	86 Pierre Turgeon, SLou.	30.00	6.00	.20
□□□	87 Bill Ranford (G), Tamp.	30.00	6.00	.20
□□□	88 Alexei Zhitnik, Buff.	12.00	4.00	.20
□□□	89 Valeri Kamensky, Colo.	20.00	6.00	.20
□□□	90 Dean McAmmond, Edmo.	12.00	4.00	.20
□□□	91 Jozef Stümpel, LosA.	15.00	4.00	.20
□□□	92 Jocelyn Thibault (G), Chic.	30.00	6.00	.20
□□□	93 Joé Juneau, Wash.	15.00	4.00	.20
□□□	94 Craig Janney, Tamp.	15.00	4.00	.20
□□□	95 Robert Reichel, NYIs.	20.00	6.00	.20
□□□	96 Mark Recchi, Mont.	30.00	6.00	.20
□□□	97 Sami Kapanen, Caro.	20.00	6.00	.20
□□□	98 Shayne Corson, Mont.	20.00	6.00	.20
□□□	99 Scott Niedermayer, NJer.	20.00	6.00	.20
□□□	100 Trevor Linden, NYIs.	30.00	6.00	.20
□□□	101 Olli Jokinen, LosA.	20.00	6.00	2.00
□□□	102 Chris Drury, Colo.	45.00	10.00	4.00
□□□	103 Daniel Cleary, Chic.	20.00	6.00	2.00
□□□	**104 Golubovsky, Detr. RC**	**12.00**	**4.00**	**2.00**
□□□	105 Brendan Morrison, NJer.	20.00	6.00	2.00
□□□	106 Manny Malhotra, NYRa.	15.00	4.00	1.50
□□□	107 Marian Hossa, Ott.	70.00	18.00	7.00
□□□	108 Daniel Brière, Phoe.	35.00	8.00	3.00
□□□	109 Lecavalier, Tamp.	70.00	18.00	7.00
□□□	**110 Hejduk, Colo. RC**	**60.00**	**30.00**	**20.00**
□□□	111 Tom Poti, Edmo.	12.00	4.00	1.50
□□□	**112 Mike Maneluk, Phil. RC**	**12.00**	**4.00**	**2.00**
□□□	113 Marty Reasoner, SLou.	15.00	4.00	1.50
□□□	114 Rico Fata, Calg.	15.00	4.00	1.50
□□□	115 Eric Brewer, NYIs.	30.00	6.00	3.00
□□□	116 Dan Cloutier (G), NYRa.	30.00	6.00	3.00
□□□	117 Mike Leclerc, Anah.	12.00	4.00	1.50
□□□	**118 Tertyshny, Phil. RC**	**12.00**	**4.00**	**2.00**
□□□	119 Josh Green, LosA.	12.00	6.00	2.00
□□□	120 Mark Parrish, Flor.	30.00	14.00	7.00
□□□	121 Jamie Wright, Dall.	12.00	4.00	1.50
□□□	**122 Lindquist, Edmo. RC**	**12.00**	**4.00**	**2.00**
□□□	**123 D. Markov, Toro. RC**	**12.00**	**6.00**	**4.00**
□□□	**124 Bill Muckalt, Vanc. RC**	**12.00**	**6.00**	**4.00**
□□□	125 Johan Davidsson, Anah.	12.00	4.00	1.50
□□□	**126 Oleg Kvasha, Flor. RC**	**12.00**	**6.00**	**4.00**
□□□	127 Cameron Mann, Bost.	12.00	4.00	1.50
□□□	**128 Trépanier, Colo. RC**	**12.00**	**4.00**	**2.00**
□□□	**129 Clarke Wilm, Calg. RC**	**12.00**	**4.00**	**2.00**
□□□	**130 Nasreddine, Mont. RC**	**12.00**	**4.00**	**2.00**
□□□	**131 Helmer, Phoe. RC**	**12.00**	**4.00**	**2.00**
□□□	**132 Handzus, SLou. RC**	**15.00**	**8.00**	**6.00**
□□□	**133 Kubina, Tamp. RC**	**12.00**	**6.00**	**4.00**
□□□	**134 Matt Cooke, Vanc. RC**	**12.00**	**6.00**	**4.00**
□□□	**135 Matt Higgins, Mont. RC**	**12.00**	**4.00**	**2.00**
□□□	136 David Legwand	30.00	6.00	3.00
□□□	**137 Brad Stuart RC**	**60.00**	**14.00**	**10.00**
□□□	**138 Mark Bell RC**	**15.00**	**8.00**	**6.00**
□□□	139 Éric Chouinard	15.00	4.00	1.50
□□□	140 Simon Gagné	60.00	14.00	6.00
□□□	**141 Ramzi Abid RC**	**15.00**	**8.00**	**6.00**
□□□	142 Sergei Varlamov	12.00	4.00	1.50
□□□	143 Mike Ribeiro	20.00	6.00	2.00

☐☐☐	**144 Derrick Walser RC**	**12.00**	**4.00**	**2.00**
☐☐☐	145 Mathieu Garon (G)	30.00	6.00	3.00
☐☐☐	146 Daniel Tkaczuk	15.00	4.00	1.50
☐☐☐	**147 Jeff Heerema RC**	**12.00**	**6.00**	**4.00**
☐☐☐	**148 Sébastien Roger RC**	**12.00**	**4.00**	**2.00**
☐☐☐	149 Brett DeCecco	12.00	4.00	1.50
☐☐☐	150 Checklist	12.00	4.00	.20

BEST PERFORMERS

These cards have three versions: the regular card (1:12), a Refractor parallel (1:387, #/200) and an Atomic Refractor parallel (1:1,549, #/50).

Insert Set (10 cards):		**415.00**	**140.00**	**45.00**
	Insert	**AR50**	**R200**	**BP**
☐☐☐	BP1 Mike Johnson, Toro.	20.00	6.00	2.00
☐☐☐	BP2 Sergei Samsonov, Bost.	60.00	20.00	6.00
☐☐☐	BP3 Patrik Elias, NJer.	80.00	30.00	10.00
☐☐☐	BP4 Patrick Marleau, SanJ.	45.00	15.00	6.00
☐☐☐	BP5 Mattias Öhlund, Vanc.	30.00	10.00	4.00
☐☐☐	BP6 Manny Malhotra, NYRa.	20.00	6.00	2.00
☐☐☐	BP7 Chris Drury, Colo.	60.00	20.00	6.00
☐☐☐	BP8 Daniel Brière, Phoe.	45.00	15.00	6.00
☐☐☐	BP9 Brendan Morrison, NJer.	30.00	10.00	4.00
☐☐☐	BP10 Vincent Lecavalier, Tamp.	100.00	35.00	12.00

CERTIFIED AUTOGRAPH

These cards have three versions: the regular card (1:97), a Refractor parallel (1:516) and an Atomic Refractor parallel (1:1,549).

Insert Set (10 cards):		**1700.00**	**800.00**	**450.00**
	Insert	**AR50**	**R200**	**CAI**
☐☐☐	A1A D. Hasek (G), Buff. ✍	150.00	70.00	35.00
☐☐☐	A1B D. Hasek (G), Buff. ✍	150.00	70.00	35.00
☐☐☐	A2A Jaromir Jagr, Pitt. ✍	150.00	75.00	35.00
☐☐☐	A2B Jaromir Jagr, Pitt. ✍	150.00	75.00	35.00
☐☐☐	A3A Peter Bondra, Wash. ✍	90.00	45.00	20.00
☐☐☐	A3B Peter Bondra, Wash. ✍	90.00	45.00	20.00
☐☐☐	A4A S. Fedorov, Detr. ✍	150.00	75.00	35.00
☐☐☐	A4B S. Fedorov, Detr. ✍	150.00	75.00	35.00
☐☐☐	A5A R. Bourque, Bost. ✍	200.00	100.00	50.00
☐☐☐	A5B R. Bourque, Bost. ✍	200.00	100.00	50.00
☐☐☐	A6A Bill Muckalt, Vanc. ✍	30.00	20.00	15.00
☐☐☐	A6B Bill Muckalt, Vanc. ✍	30.00	20.00	15.00
☐☐☐	A7A B. Morrison, NJer. ✍	45.00	20.00	15.00
☐☐☐	A7B B. Morrison, NJer. ✍	45.00	20.00	15.00
☐☐☐	A8A Chris Drury, Colo. ✍	90.00	45.00	30.00
☐☐☐	A8B Chris Drury, Colo. ✍	90.00	45.00	30.00
☐☐☐	A9A Mark Parrish, Flor. ✍	60.00	30.00	20.00
☐☐☐	A9B Mark Parrish, Flor. ✍	60.00	30.00	20.00
☐☐☐	A10A M. Malhotra, NYRa. ✍	35.00	20.00	15.00
☐☐☐	A10B M. Malhotra, NYRa. ✍	35.00	20.00	15.00

FUSION

These cards have three versions: the regular card (1:12), a Refractor parallel (1:387)and an Atomic Refractor parallel (1:1,549).

Insert Set (10 cards):		**635.00**	**225.00**	**30.00**
	Insert	**AR25**	**R100**	**MIF**
☐☐☐	F1 J. LeClair / B. Battaglia	100.00	35.00	6.00
☐☐☐	F2 P. Kariya / J. Leclerc	150.00	50.00	8.00
☐☐☐	F3 J. Jagr / M. Parrish	125.00	50.00	8.00
☐☐☐	F4 T. Selänne / F. Lindquist	175.00	60.00	4.00
☐☐☐	F5 E. Lindros / V. Lecavalier	200.00	70.00	12.00
☐☐☐	F6 P. Forsberg / O. Jokinen	170.00	60.00	10.00
☐☐☐	F7 B. Leetch / D. Markov	70.00	25.00	4.00
☐☐☐	F8 Lidström / Golubovsky	140.00	50.00	4.00
☐☐☐	F9 D. Hasek / D. Cloutier	140.00	50.00	8.00
☐☐☐	F10 P. Roy / T. Moss	300.00	110.00	18.00
☐☐☐	F11 S. Samsonov / M. Watt	70.00	25.00	4.00
☐☐☐	F12 K.Tkachuk / J. Wright	70.00	25.00	4.00
☐☐☐	F13 P. Bondra / M. Hossa	160.00	60.00	10.00
☐☐☐	F14 P. Bure / B. Muckalt	90.00	30.00	6.00
☐☐☐	F15 W. Gretzky / B. Morrison	425.00	160.00	25.00
☐☐☐	F16 Fedorov / Reasoner	120.00	45.00	6.00
☐☐☐	F17 R. Bourque / E. Brewer	160.00	60.00	10.00
☐☐☐	F18 C. Pronger / T. Poti	70.00	25.00	4.00
☐☐☐	F19 Brodeur / Théodore	275.00	100.00	16.00
☐☐☐	F20 C. Osgood / J. Storr	80.00	30.00	4.00

SCOTTY BOWMAN'S BEST

Photo These cards have three versions: the regular card (1:6), a Refractor parallel (1:704, #/200) and an Atomic Refractor parallel (1:2,816, #/50).

Insert Set (10 cards):		**490.00**	**175.00**	**25.00**
	Insert	**AR50**	**R100**	**SBB**
☐☐☐	SB1 D. Hasek (G), Buff.	120.00	45.00	6.00
☐☐☐	SB2 M. Brodeur (G), NJer.	160.00	60.00	10.00
☐☐☐	SB3 Chris Osgood (G), Detr.	90.00	30.00	4.00
☐☐☐	SB4 Nicklas Lidström, Detr.	90.00	30.00	4.00
☐☐☐	SB5 Eric Lindros, Phil.	120.00	45.00	6.00
☐☐☐	SB6 Jaromir Jagr, Pitt.	120.00	40.00	6.00
☐☐☐	SB7 Steve Yzerman, Detr.	220.00	80.00	14.00
☐☐☐	SB8 Peter Forsberg, Colo.	150.00	55.00	8.00
☐☐☐	SB9 Paul Kariya, Anah.	150.00	50.00	8.00
☐☐☐	SB10 R. Bourque, Bost.	130.00	50.00	8.00
☐☐☐	SB11 S. Bowman, Detr.	120.00	45.00	6.00
	Autograph			**Auto.**
☐	SB11 Scotty Bowman ✍ (#/100)			150.00

1998 - 99 CARDSET

NHL stars sometimes sell at a premium (usually $1-2).

Complete Set (270 cards):		**60.00**
Common Player:		**.30**
	Player	**Card**
☐	1 Jari Kurri, Jokerit Helsinki	2.50
☐	2 Esa Tikkanen, HIFK Helsinki	.50
☐	3 Janne Laukkanen	.50
☐	4 Ari Sulander	.50
☐	5 Kimmo Timonen	.50
☐	6 Jarmo Myllys	.50
☐	7 Ari-Pekka Siekkinen, Kiekko-Espoo Blues	.30
☐	8 Jani Riihinen, Kiekko-Espoo Blues	.30
☐	9 Riku Varjamo, Kiekko-Espoo Blues	.30
☐	10 Jiri Vykoukal, Kiekko-Espoo Blues	.30
☐	11 Jonas Andersson-Junkka, Kiekko-Espoo Blues	.30
☐	12 Riku-Petteri Lehtonen, Kiekko-Espoo Blues	.30
☐	13 Pasi Sromunen, Kiekko-Espoo Blues	.30
☐	14 Robert Salo, Kiekko-Espoo Blues	.30
☐	15 Juha Gustafsson, Kiekko-Espoo Blues	.30
☐	16 Christian Ruuttu, Kiekko-Espoo Blues	.50
☐	17 Tero Hämäläinen, Kiekko-Espoo Blues	.30
☐	18 Juha Ikonen, Kiekko-Espoo Blues	.30
☐	19 Hannes Hyvönen, Kiekko-Espoo Blues	.30
☐	20 Timo Hirvonen, Kiekko-Espoo Blues	.30
☐	21 Petr Ton, Kiekko-Espoo Blues	.30
☐	22 Nils Ekman, Kiekko-Espoo Blues	.50
☐	23 Joonas Jääskeläinen, Kiekko-Espoo Blues	.30
☐	24 Tommy Kiviaho, Kiekko-Espoo Blues	.30
☐	25 Tomas Kapusta, Kiekko-Espoo Blues	.30
☐	26 Tero Tiainen, Kiekko-Espoo Blues	.30
☐	27 Teemu Riihijärvi, Kiekko-Espoo Blues	.30
☐	28 Jan Lundell, HIFK Helsinki	.30
☐	29 Niklas Bäckström, HIFK Helsinki	.30
☐	30 Ville Siren, HIFK Helsinki	.30
☐	31 Marko From, HIFK Helsinki	.30
☐	32 Brian Rafalski, HIFK Helsinki	1.00
☐	33 Jarno Kultanen, HIFK Helsinki	.30
☐	34 Toni Lydman, HIFK Helsinki	.50
☐	35 Jani Nikko, HIFK Helsinki	.30
☐	36 Jere Karalahti, HIFK Helsinki	.50
☐	37 Kari Rajala, HIFK Helsinki	.30
☐	38 Kari Kalto, HIFK Helsinki	.30
☐	39 Kimmo Kuhta, HIFK Helsinki	.30
☐	40 Jan Caloun, HIFK Helsinki	.50
☐	41 Markku Hurme, HIFK Helsinki	.30
☐	42 Tom Laaksonen, HIFK Helsinki	.30
☐	43 Niklas Hagman, HIFK Helsinki	2.00
☐	44 Luciano Borsato, HIFK Helsinki	.30
☐	45 Toni Sihvonen, HIFK Helsinki	.30
☐	46 Mika Kortelainen, HIFK Helsinki	.30
☐	47 Toni Mäkiaho, HIFK Helsinki	.30
☐	48 Mika Nieminen, HIFK Helsinki	.30
☐	49 Jarkko Ruutu, HIFK Helsinki	2.00
☐	50 Marko Tuomainen, HIFK Helsinki	.50
☐	51 Pasi Nurminen, HPK Hämeenlinna	3.00
☐	52 Kari Rosenberg, HPK Hämeenlinna	.30
☐	53 Aki Heino, HPK Hämeenlinna	.30
☐	54 Erik Kakko, HPK Hämeenlinna	.30
☐	55 Tom Koivisto, HPK Hämeenlinna	.30
☐	56 Ari Vallin, HPK Hämeenlinna	.30
☐	57 Tomi Källarsson, HPK Hämeenlinna	.30
☐	58 Jaroslav Nedved, HPK Hämeenlinna	.30
☐	59 Kai Rautio, HPK Hämeenlinna	.30
☐	60 Mikko Kuparinen, HPK Hämeenlinna	.30
☐	61 Mike Kannisto, HPK Hämeenlinna	.30
☐	62 Juha Virtanen, HPK Hämeenlinna	.30
☐	63 Jani Keinänen, HPK Hämeenlinna	.30
☐	64 Jyrki Louhi, HPK Hämeenlinna	.30
☐	65 Roman Simicek, HPK Hämeenlinna	.50
☐	66 Semi Pekki, HPK Hämeenlinna	.30
☐	67 Timo Pärssinen, HPK Hämeenlinna	.50
☐	68 Jarkko Savijoki, HPK Hämeenlinna	.30
☐	69 Marko Palo, HPK Hämeenlinna	.30
☐	70 Antti Virtanen, HPK Hämeenlinna	.30
☐	71 Niko Kapanen, HPK Hämeenlinna	3.00
☐	72 Tomas Vlasak, HPK Hämeenlinna	.50
☐	73 Riku Hahl, HPK Hämeenlinna	2.00
☐	74 Vesa Toskala, Ilves Tampere	.30
☐	75 Markus Korhonen, Ilves Tampere	.30
☐	76 Timo Willman, Ilves Tampere	.30
☐	77 Veli-Pekka Hård, Ilves Tampere	.30
☐	78 Pekka Kangasalusta, Ilves Tampere	.30
☐	79 Oscar Ackerström, Ilves Tampere	.30
☐	80 Allan Measures, Ilves Tampere	.30
☐	81 Pasi Puistola, Ilves Tampere	.30
☐	82 Pasi Saarinen, Ilves Tampere	.30
☐	83 Mikko Haapakoski, Ilves Tampere	.30
☐	84 Martti Järventie, Ilves Tampere	.50
☐	85 Mika Arvaja, Ilves Tampere	.30
☐	86 Juha Hautamaa, Ilves Tampere	.30
☐	87 Raimo Helminen, Ilves Tampere	.50
☐	88 Tomi Hirvonen, Ilves Tampere	.30
☐	89 Matti Kaipainen, Ilves Tampere	.30
☐	90 Peter Larsson, Ilves Tampere	.30
☐	91 Vesa Viitakoski, Ilves Tampere	.30
☐	92 Mikko Peltola, Ilves Tampere	.30
☐	93 Timo Peltomaa, Ilves Tampere	.30
☐	94 Hannu Mattila, Ilves Tampere	.30
☐	95 Sami Ahlberg, Ilves Tampere	.30
☐	96 Juha Järvenpää, Ilves Tampere	.30
☐	97 Markus Ketterer, Jokerit Helsinki	.50
☐	98 Ari Kumpula, Jokerit Helsinki	.30
☐	99 Waltteri Immonen, Jokerit Helsinki	.30
☐	100 Antti-Jussi Niemi, Jokerit Helsinki	.50
☐	101 Sami Nuutinen, Jokerit Helsinki	.30
☐	102 Yves Racine, Jokerit Helsinki	.50
☐	103 Rami Alanko, Jokerit Helsinki	.30
☐	104 Mika Strömberg, Jokerit Helsinki	.30
☐	105 Ossi Väänänen, Jokerit Helsinki	.50
☐	106 Jani Rita, Jokerit Helsinki	4.00
☐	107 Sami Mettovaara, Jokerit Helsinki	.30
☐	108 Fredrik Nilsson, Jokerit Helsinki	.30
☐	109 Kimmo Rintanen, Jokerit Helsinki	.30
☐	110 Jari Kauppila, Jokerit Helsinki	.30
☐	111 Pasi Saarela, Jokerit Helsinki	.30
☐	112 Timo Saarikoski, Jokerit Helsinki	.30
☐	113 Eero Somervuori, Jokerit Helsinki	.30
☐	114 Jukka Tiilikainen, Jokerit Helsinki	.30
☐	115 Jarkko Väänänen, Jokerit Helsinki	.30
☐	116 Otakar Janecky, Jokerit Helsinki	.30
☐	117 Patrik Juhlin, Jokerit Helsinki	.50
☐	118 Juha Lind, Jokerit Helsinki	.50
☐	119 Marko Leinonen, JyP HT Jyväskylä	.30
☐	120 Tommi Satosaari, JyP HT Jyväskylä	.30
☐	121 Mikko Luoma, JyP HT Jyväskylä	.30
☐	122 Jan Latvala, JyP HT Jyväskylä	.30
☐	123 Kevin Wortman, JyP HT Jyväskylä	.30
☐	124 Kalle Koskinen, JyP HT Jyväskylä	.30
☐	125 Jyrki Välivaara, JyP HT Jyväskylä	.30
☐	126 Markus Kankaanperä, JyP HT Jyväskylä	.30
☐	127 Jarkko Glad, JyP HT Jyväskylä	.30
☐	128 Marko Kauppinen, JyP HT Jyväskylä	.30
☐	129 Robert Nordberg, JyP HT Jyväskylä	.30
☐	130 Juha Viinikainen, JyP HT Jyväskylä	.30
☐	131 Marko Ojanen, JyP HT Jyväskylä	.30
☐	132 Toni Koivunen, JyP HT Jyväskylä	.30
☐	133 Mikko Rantala, JyP HT Jyväskylä	.30
☐	134 Jussi Tarvainen, JyP HT Jyväskylä	.30
☐	135 Tommi Turunen, JyP HT Jyväskylä	.30
☐	136 Timo Vertala, JyP HT Jyväskylä	.30
☐	137 Veli-Pekka Nutikka, JyP HT Jyväskylä	.30
☐	138 Stefan Örnskog, JyP HT Jyväskylä	.30
☐	139 Marko Virtanen, JyP HT Jyväskylä	.30
☐	140 Lasse Jämsen, JyP HT Jyväskylä	.30
☐	141 Kimmo Kapanen (G), KalPa Kuopio	.30
☐	142 Ari Luostarinen, KalPa Kuopio	.30
☐	143 Tobias Åblad, KalPa Kuopio	.30
☐	144 Derry Menard, KalPa Kuopio	.30
☐	145 Jermu Pisto, KalPa Kuopio	.30
☐	146 Sebastien Sulku, KalPa Kuopio	.30
☐	147 Timo Ahmaoja, KalPa Kuopio	.30
☐	148 Teemu* Tuomainen, KalPa Kuopio	.30
☐	149 Pekka Poikolainen, KalPa Kuopio	.30
☐	150 Aki Korhonen, KalPa Kuopio	.30
☐	151 Pekka Tirkkonen, KalPa Kuopio	.30
☐	152 Petro Koivunen, KalPa Kuopio	.30
☐	153 Marko Leväinen, KalPa Kuopio	.30
☐	154 Janne Kekäläinen, KalPa Kuopio	.30
☐	155 Anntti Riekkinen, KalPa Kuopio	.30
☐	156 Mikko Honkonen, KalPa Kuopio	.30
☐	157 Timo Seikkula, KalPa Kuopio	.30
☐	158 Sami Simonen, KalPa Kuopio	.30
☐	159 Mikko Knottila, KalPa Kuopio	.30
☐	160 Jaakko Uhlbäck, KalPa Kuopio	.30
☐	161 Lubos Rob, KalPa Kuopio	.30
☐	162 Kimmo Vesa, Lukko Rauma	.30
☐	163 Sinuhe Wallinheimo, Lukko Rauma	.30
☐	164 Jaakko Harikkala, Lukko Rauma	.30
☐	165 Atvars Tribuntsovs, Lukko Rauma	.30
☐	166 Ismo Kuoppala, Lukko Rauma	.30
☐	167 Kimmo Lotvonen, Lukko Rauma	.30
☐	168 Emarko Toivonen, Lukko Rauma	.30
☐	169 Erik Hämäläinen, Lukko Rauma	.30
☐	170 Mikael Tjällden, Lukko Rauma	.30
☐	171 Roland Carlsson, Lukko Rauma	.30
☐	172 Niko Halttunen, Lukko Rauma	.30
☐	173 Jonni Vauhkonen, Lukko Rauma	.30
☐	174 Matti Raunio, Lukko Rauma	.30
☐	175 Ville Mikkonen, Lukko Rauma	.30
☐	176 Petri Pakaslahti, Lukko Rauma	.30
☐	177 Janne Seva, Lukko Rauma	.30
☐	178 Harri Sillgren, Lukko Rauma	.30
☐	179 Leonids Tambijevs, Lukko Rauma	.30
☐	180 Jari Hyvärinen, Lukko Rauma	.30
☐	181 Patrik Wallenberg, Lukko Rauma	.30
☐	182 Jarkko Nikander, Lukko Rauma	.30
☐	183 Aigars Cipruss, Lukko Rauma	.30
☐	184 Jussi Markkanen, SaiPa	.50
☐	185 Pasi Häkkinen, SaiPa	.30
☐	186 Harri Tikkanen, SaiPa	.30
☐	187 Yuri Kuznetsov, SaiPa	.30
☐	188 Riku Kallioniemi, SaiPa	.30
☐	189 Jussi Pekkala, SaiPa	.30
☐	190 Mikko Myllykoski, SaiPa	.30
☐	191 Vesa Ruotsalainen, SaiPa	.30
☐	192 Tommi Sova, SaiPa	.30
☐	193 Dale McTavish, SaiPa	.30
☐	194 Pasi Määttänen, SaiPa	.30
☐	194 Alexander Matsijevski, SaiPa	.30
☐	196 Sami Kaartinen, SaiPa	.30
☐	197 Ari Saarinen, SaiPa	.30
☐	198 Joel Salonen, SaiPa	.30
☐	199 Ari Santanen, SaiPa	.30
☐	200 Mika Skyttä, SaiPa	.30
☐	201 Mika Kauppinen, SaiPa	.30
☐	202 Keijo Säilynoja, SaiPa	.30
☐	203 Eric Weilleux, SaiPa	.30
☐	204 Ville Immonen, SaiPa	.30
☐	205 Mika Noronen, Tappara Tampere	5.00
☐	206 Iiro Itämies, Tappara Tampere	.30
☐	207 Josef Boumedienne, Tappara Tampere	.50
☐	208 Miska Kangasniemi, Tappara Tampere	.30
☐	209 Mikko Tamminen, Tappara Tampere	.30
☐	210 Timo Jutila, Tappara Tampere	1.00
☐	211 Janne Grönvall, Tappara Tampere	.50
☐	212 Sami-Ville Salomaa, Tappara Tampere	.30
☐	213 Janne Vuorela, Tappara Tampere	.30
☐	214 Pasi Petriläinen, Tappara Tampere	.30
☐	215 Pasi Tuominen, Tappara Tampere	.30
☐	216 Jani Hassinen, Tappara Tampere	.30
☐	217 Valeri Krykov, Tappara Tampere	.30
☐	218 Juha Vuorivirta, Tappara Tampere	.30
☐	219 Alexander Barkov, Tappara Tampere	.30
☐	220 Harri Lönnberg, Tappara Tampere	.30
☐	221 Arto Kulmala, Tappara Tampere	.30
☐	222 Janne Ojanen, Tappara Tampere	.30
☐	223 Lasse Pirjetä, Tappara Tampere	.50
☐	224 Sami Salonen, Tappara Tampere	.30
☐	225 Johannes Alanen, Tappara Tampere	.30
☐	226 Mikko Mäkelä, Tappara Tampere	.50
☐	227 Fredrik Norrena, TPS Turku	.30
☐	228 Miikka Kiprusoff, TPS Turku	1.50
☐	229 Kimmo Eronen, TPS Turku	.30
☐	230 Marko Kiprusoff, TPS Turku	.50
☐	231 Jouni Loponen, TPS Turku	.30
☐	232 Ilkka Mikkola, TPS Turku	.30
☐	233 Aki Berg, TPS Turku	.50
☐	234 Tommi Rajamäki, TPS Turku	.30
☐	235 Peter Ahola, TPS Turku	.50
☐	236 Mika Lehtinen, TPS Turku	.30

☐	237 Tony Virta, TPS Turku	.30
☐	238 Joni Lius, TPS Turku	.30
☐	239 Mikko Eloranta, TPS Turku	.30
☐	240 Marco Tuokko, TPS Turku	.30
☐	241 Juho Jokinen, TPS Turku	.30
☐	242 Tomi Kallio, TPS Turku	.50
☐	243 Mikko Rautee, TPS Turku	.30
☐	244 Jani Kiviharju, TPS Turku	.30
☐	245 Tommi Miettinen, TPS Turku	.30
☐	246 Simo Rouvali, TPS Turku	.30
☐	247 Kalle Sahlstedt, TPS Turku	.30
☐	248 Teemu Elomo, TPS Turku	.30
☐	249 Mika Alatalo, TPS Turku	.50
☐	250 Miika Elomo, TPS Turku	.30
☐	251 Pasi Kuivalainen, Ässät Pori	.30
☐	252 Mika Lehto, Ässät Pori	.30
☐	253 Joacim Esbjörs, Ässät Pori	.30
☐	254 Mikko Sokka, Ässät Pori	.30
☐	255 Pasi Peltonen, Ässät Pori	.30
☐	256 Vesa Salo, Ässät Pori	.30
☐	257 Mika Laaksonen, Ässät Pori	.30
☐	258 Santeri Immonen, Ässät Pori	.30
☐	259 Jonas Esbjörs, Ässät Pori	.30
☐	260 Viacheslav Fandul, Ässät Pori	.30
☐	261 Kimmo Salminen, Ässät Pori	.30
☐	262 Jokke Heinänen, Ässät Pori	.30
☐	263 Jari Levonen, Ässät Pori	.30
☐	264 Niko Mikkola, Ässät Pori	.30
☐	265 Andrei Potaichuk, Ässät Pori	.30
☐	266 Rauli Raitanen, Ässät Pori	.30
☐	267 Timo Hakanen, Ässät Pori	.30
☐	268 Jan Benda, Ässät Pori	.30
☐	269 Tero Arkiomaa, Ässät Pori	.30
☐	270 Marko Kivenmäki, Ässät Pori	.30

90S TOP 12

	Insert Set (12 cards):	35.00
	Insert	top12
☐	1 Jere Lehtinen	4.00
☐	2 Pertti Lehtonen	2.00
☐	3 Janne Laukkanen	2.00
☐	4 Jukka Tammi	2.00
☐	5 Teemu Selänne	10.00
☐	6 Jari Lindroos	2.00
☐	7 Sami Kapanen	4.00
☐	8 Jarmo Kuusisto	2.00
☐	9 Ari Santanen	2.00
☐	10 Timo Jutila	3.00
☐	11 Saku Koivu	10.00
☐	12 Kari Takko	2.00

DREAM TEAM

	Insert Set (7 cards):	35.00
	Insert	DT
☐	1 Jari Kurri	12.00
☐	2 Ari Sulander	2.00
☐	3 Jyrki Lumme	3.00
☐	4 Janne Niinimaa	3.00
☐	5 Jere Lehtinen	4.00
☐	6 Saku Koivu	10.00
☐	7 Teemu Selänne	10.00

LEIJONAT

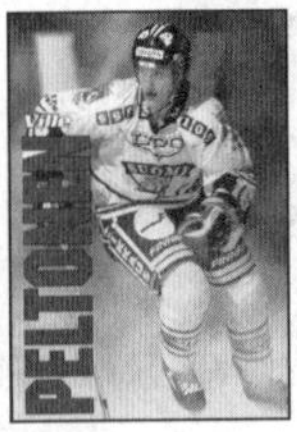

	Insert Set (47 cards):	55.00
	Insert	L
☐	1 Markus Ketterer	2.00
☐	2 Jarmo Myllys	2.00
☐	3 Jukka Tammi	.75
☐	4 Peter Ahola	1.00
☐	5 Tero Hämäläinen	.75
☐	6 Timo Jutila	3.00
☐	7 Jere Karalahti	1.00
☐	8 Marko Kiprusoff	1.00
☐	9 Janne Laukkanen	1.00
☐	10 Mika Lehto	.75
☐	11 Kaj Linna	.75
☐	12 Jouni Loponen	.75
☐	13 Toni Lydman	2.00
☐	14 Antti-Jussi Niemi	1.00
☐	15 Petteri Nummelin	2.00
☐	16 Mika Strömberg	.75
☐	17 Kimmo Timonen	2.00
☐	18 Hannu Virta	.75
☐	19 Mika Alatalo	2.00
☐	20 Mikko Eloranta	1.00
☐	21 Raimo Helminen	3.00
☐	22 Juha Ikonen	.75
☐	23 Marko Jantunen	.75
☐	24 Olli Jokinen	4.00
☐	25 Joonas Jääskeläinen	.75
☐	26 Sami Kapanen	4.00
☐	27 Esa Keskinen	.75
☐	28 Jari Korpisalo	.75
☐	29 Tero Lehterä	.75
☐	30 Juha Lind	2.00
☐	31 Joni Lius	.75
☐	32 Toni Mäkiaho	1.00
☐	33 Mika Nieminen	.75
☐	34 Janne Ojanen	1.00
☐	35 Marko Palo	.75
☐	36 Ville Peltonen	1.00
☐	37 Juha Riihijärvi	.75
☐	38 Kimmo Rintanen	1.00
☐	39 Christian Ruuttu	2.00
☐	40 Jarkko Ruutu	2.00
☐	41 Jukka Seppo	.75
☐	42 Raimo Summanen	.75
☐	43 Esa Tikkanen	2.00
☐	44 Marko Tuomainen	1.00
☐	45 Antti Törmänen	1.00
☐	46 Jarkko Varvio	3.00
☐	47 Juha Ylönen	2.00

MAD MASKS

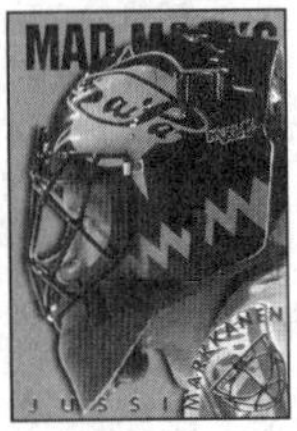

	Insert Set (12 cards):	50.00
	Insert	MM
☐	1 Ari-Pekka Siekkinen	4.00
☐	2 Jan Lundell	4.00
☐	3 Pasi Nurminen	8.00
☐	4 Vesa Toskala	4.00
☐	5 Markus Ketterer	4.00
☐	6 Marko Leinonen	4.00
☐	7 Kimmo Kapanen (G)	4.00
☐	8 Sinuhe Wallinheimo	4.00
☐	9 Jussi Markkanen	4.00
☐	10 Mika Noronen	15.00
☐	11 Fredrik Norrena	4.00
☐	12 Pasi Kuivalainen	4.00

OFF DUTY

	Insert Set (12 cards):	20.00
	Insert	OD
☐	1 Juha Ikonen	2.00
☐	2 Toni Sihvonen	2.00
☐	3 Tom Koivisto	2.00
☐	4 Juha Hautamaa	2.00
☐	5 Kimmo Rintanen	2.00
☐	6 Marko Leinonen	2.00
☐	7 Sami Simonen	2.00
☐	8 Sinuhe Wallinheimo	2.00
☐	9 Jussi Markkanen	2.00
☐	10 Arto Kulmala	2.00
☐	11 Marko Kiprusoff	2.00
☐	12 Pasi Kuivalainen	2.00

1998 - 99 COLLECTION SOUVENIR

	Complete Set (30 cards):	
	Common Player:	
	Player	Card
☐	01 Brad Park, Scarborough Pee-Wee	
☐	02 Guy Chouinard, Coach	
☐	03 Manon Rhéaume, Charlesbourg Pee-Wee	
☐	04 Patrick Roy (G), Montréal Pee-Wee	
☐	05 Joé Juneau, Pont-Rouge Pee-Wee	
☐	06 Sergei Samsonov, Moscow Pee-Wee	
☐	07 Dainius Zubrus, Kharkov Pee-Wee	
☐	08 Robert Dome, Slovensko Pee-Wee	
☐	09 Daniel Tkaczuk, Toronto Pee-Wee Red Wings	
☐	10 Alex Tanguay, Beauce-Amiante Pee-Wee	
☐	11 Jean-Marc Pelletier (G), Champlain-Richelieu Pee-Wee	
☐	12 Oleg Kvasha, Moscow Pee-Wee	
☐	13 Steve Bégin, Francheville Pee-Wee	
☐	14 Daniel Corso, Champlain-Richelieu Pee-Wee	
☐	15 Sascha Goc, Germany Pee-Wee	
☐	16 Marian Hossa, Slovak Pee-Wee	
☐	17 Paul Mara, South Shore Pee-Wee	
☐	18 Jean-François Damphousse (G), Ste-Foy Pee-Wee	
☐	19 Philippe Sauvé (G), Milles-Îles Pee-Wee	
☐	20 Gregor Baumgarnter, Austria Pee-Wee	
☐	21 Ladislav Nagy, Slovak Pee-Wee	
☐	22 Vincent Lecavalier, North Shore Pee Wee	
☐	23 David Legwand, Detroit Pee-Wee	
☐	24 Rico Fata, Sault Ste. Marie Pee-Wee	
☐	25 Mathieu Chouinard, Milles-Îles Pee-Wee	
☐	26 Éric Chouinard, Sherbrooke Pee-Wee	
☐	27 Mathieu Biron, Charlesbourg Pee-Wee	
☐	28 Simon Gagné, Ste-Foy Pee-Wee	
☐	29 Mike Ribeiro, Hochelaga Pee-Wee	
☐	30 Jonathan Girard, Montréal Pee-Wee Canadiens	

1998 - 99 DEL

NHL and regional stars sometimes sell at a premium (usually $1-2).

	Complete Set (341 cards):	65.00
	Common Player:	.30
	Player	Card
☐	1 Burke Murphy, Revier Lowe	.30
☐	2 Marc Seliger, Revier Lowen	.50
☐	3 Jason Clark, Revier Lowen	.30
☐	4 Mike McNeill, Revier Lowe	.30
☐	5 Norm Batherson, Revier Lowen	.30
☐	6 Jeff Sebastian, Revier Lowen	.30
☐	7 Phil Huber, Revier Lowen	.30
☐	8 Todd Wetzel, Revier Lowen	.30
☐	9 Jesper Morin, Revier Lowe	.30
☐	10 Marc Pethke, Revier Lowen	.30
☐	11 Jacek Plachta, Revier Lowen	.30
☐	12 Marcus Adolfson, Revier Lowen	.30
☐	13 Christian Scmitz, Revier Lowen	.30
☐	14 Bob Marshall, Revier Lowen	.30
☐	15 Peter Lutter, Revier Lowen	.30
☐	16 Stefan Mayer, Revier Lowen	.30
☐	17 Daniel Körber, Revier Lowen	.30
☐	18 Carsten Gosdeck, Revier Lowen	.30
☐	19 Jiri Kochta, Revier Lowen	.30
☐	20 Petri Liimtainen, Krefeld Pinguine	.30
☐	21 Thomas Brandl, Krefeld Pinguine	.30
☐	22 Andrei Kovalev, Krefeld Pinguine	.50
☐	23 Johnny Walker, Krefeld Pinguine	.30
☐	24 Neil Eisanhut, Krefeld Pinguine	.30
☐	25 Karel Lang, Krefeld Pinguine	.30
☐	26 Marek Stebnicki, Krefeld Pinguine	.30
☐	27 Chris Bartolone, Krefeld Pinguine	.30
☐	28 John van Kessel, Krefeld Pinguine	.30
☐	29 Lars Brüggemann, Krefeld Pinguine	.30
☐	30 Jayson Meyer, Krefeld Pinguine	.30
☐	31 Reemt Pyka, Krefeld Pinguine	.30
☐	32 Mark Pederson, Krefeld Pinguine	.50
☐	33 Veli-Pekka Kautonen, Krefeld Pinguine	.30
☐	34 Tommie Hartogs, Krefeld Pinguine	.30
☐	35 Frantisek Frosch, Krefeld Pinguine	.30
☐	36 Leo van den Thillart, Krefeld Pinguine	.30
☐	37 Vitali Karamnov, Krefeld Pinguine	.50
☐	38 Stéphane Barin, Krefeld Pinguine	.30
☐	39 Roger Nordström, Krefeld Pinguine	.30
☐	40 Robert Ouellet, Krefeld Pinguine	.30
☐	41 Doug Mason, Krefeld Pinguine	.30
☐	42 François Guay, Kassel Huskies	.30
☐	43 Greg* Johnston, Kassel Huskies	.30
☐	44 Greg Evtushevski, Kassel Huskies	.30
☐	45 Shane Peacock, Kassel Huskies	.30
☐	46 Chris Rogles, Kassel Huskies	.30
☐	47 Günter Oswald, Kassel Huskies	.30
☐	48 Jukka Seppo, Kassel Huskies	.30
☐	49 Jürgen Rumrich, Kassel Huskies	.30
☐	50 Roger Hansson, Kassel Huskies	.30
☐	51 Stéphane Robitaille, Kassel Huskies	.30
☐	52 Örjan Lindmark, Kassel Huskies	.30
☐	53 Jeff McLeod, Kassel Huskies	.30
☐	54 Alexander Wedl, Kassel Huskies	.30
☐	55 Jochen Molling, Kassel Huskies	.30
☐	56 Paul Cohen, Kassel Huskies	.30
☐	57 Daniel Kreutzer, Kassel Huskies	.30
☐	58 Nikolaus Mondt, Kassel Huskies	.30
☐	59 John Lilley, Kassel Huskies	.50
☐	60 Roland Ramoser, Kassel Huskies	.30
☐	61 Thomas Dolak, Kassel Huskies	.30
☐	62 Tino Boos, Kassel Huskies	.30
☐	63 Tobias Abstreiter, KasselHuskies	.30
☐	64 Hans Zach, Kassel Huskies	.30
☐	65 Petr Briza, EV Landshut	.30
☐	66 Wally Schreiber, EV Landshut	.30
☐	67 Chris Luongo, EV Landshut	.50
☐	68 Dean Evason, EV Landshut	.50
☐	69 David Bruce, EV Landshut	.50
☐	70 Peter Douris, EV Landshut	.50
☐	71 Jason Herter, EV Landshut	.50
☐	72 Jörg Handrick, EV Landshut	.30
☐	73 Rob Murphy, EV Landshut	.50
☐	74 Mike Casselman, EV Landshut	.30
☐	76 Steve Junker, EV Landshut	.50
☐	76 Zbynek Kukacka, EV Landshut	.30
☐	77 Mark Krys, EV Landshut	.30
☐	78 Markus Wieland, EV Landshut	.30
☐	79 Evan Marble, EV Landshut	.30
☐	80 Jari Korpisalo, EV Landshut	.30
☐	81 Peter Guida, EV Landshut	.30
☐	82 Bob Joyce, EV Landshut	.50
☐	83 Johan Rosén, EV Landshut	.30
☐	84 Christian Künast, EV Landshut	.30
☐	85 Olli Kaski, EV Landshut	.30
☐	86 Chris Valentine, EV Landshut	.50
☐	87 Corey Millen, Kolner Haie	.50
☐	88 Tomas Forslund, Kolner Haie	.50
☐	89 Bruno Zarrillo, Kolner Haie	.30
☐	90 Igor Alexandrov, Kölner Haie	.50
☐	92 Petri Varis, Kolner Haie	.30
☐	93 Joseph Heib, Kolner Haie	.30
☐	94 Greg Brown, Kölner Haie	.50
☐	95 Dwayne Norris, Kolner Haie	.50
☐	96 Mirko Lüdermann, Kolner Haie	.30
☐	97 John Miner, Kolner Haie	.30
☐	98 Boris Rousson, Kolner Haie	.50
☐	99 Craig Woodcroft, Kolner Haie	.50
☐	100 Jörg Mayr, Kolner Haie	.30
☐	101 Steve Wilson, Kolner Haie	.30
☐	102 Rainer Zerwesz, Kolner Haie	.30
☐	103 Brian McReynolds, Kolner Haie	.50
☐	104 Andreas Lupzig, Kolner Haie	.30
☐	105 Giuseppe Busillo, Kolner Haie	.30
☐	106 Jeff Ricciardi, Kolner Haie	.30
☐	107 Mike Hartman, Kolner Haie	.50
☐	108 Timo Lahtinen, Kolner Haie	.30
☐	109 Stéphane Morin, Berlin Capitals	.50
☐	110 Paul Broten, Berlin Capitals	.50
☐	111 Robert Guillet, Berlin Capitals	.30
☐	112 Clayton Beddoes, Berlin Capitals	.50
☐	113 Robert Cimetta, Berlin Capitals	.50
☐	114 Dave MacIntyre, Berlin Capitals	.30
☐	115 Johan Norgren, Berlin Capitals	.50
☐	116 Todd Nelson, Berlin Capitals	.50
☐	117 Guy Philips, Berlin Capitals	.30
☐	118 Craig Martin, Berlin Capitals	.50
☐	119 Parris Duffus, Berlin Capitals	.50
☐	120 Christian Brittig, Berlin Capitals	.30
☐	121 Thomas Schinko, Berlin Capitals	.30
☐	122 Mario Gehrig, Berlin Capitals	.30
☐	123 Fredrik Ytfeldt, Berlin Capitals	.30
☐	124 Lawrence Rucchin, Berlin Capitals	.30
☐	125 Heinz Ehlers, Berlin Capitals	.30
☐	126 Heinrich Schifft, Berlin Capitals	.30

☐ 127 Sylvain Couturier, Berlin Capitals .50
☐ 128 Hakan Gattamoutsas, Berlin Capitals .30
☐ 129 David Berge, Berlin Capitals .30
☐ 130 Marc Savard, Berlin Capitals .30
☐ 131 Dale McCourt, Berlin Capitals 1.00
☐ 132 Jukka Tammi, Frankfort Lions .30
☐ 133 Chris Snell, Frankfort Lions .50
☐ 134 John Chabot, Frankfurt Lions .50
☐ 135 Len Barrie, Frankfurt Lions .50
☐ 136 Ilja Vorobiev, Frankfort Lions .30
☐ 137 Steve Palmer, Frankfort Lions .30
☐ 138 Fabrice Lhenry, Frankfort Lions .30
☐ 139 Rob Doyle, Frankfort Lions .30
☐ 140 Victor Gervais, Frankfort Lions .30
☐ 141 José Charbonneau, Frankfurt Lions .50
☐ 142 Thorsten Apel, Frankfurt Lions .30
☐ 143 Michael Bresagk, Frankfurt Lions .30
☐ 144 Rick Hayward, Frankfort Lions .30
☐ 145 Phil von Steffenelli, Frankfort Lions .50
☐ 146 Martin Williams, Frankfort Lions .30
☐ 147 Toni Porkka, Frankfort Lions .30
☐ 148 Jean-Marc Richard, Frankfort Lions .30
☐ 149 Douglas Kirton, Frankfort Lions .30
☐ 150 Joel Savage, Frankfort Lions .50
☐ 151 Ralf Hantschke, Frankfort Lions .30
☐ 152 Ken Quinney, Frankfort Lions .50
☐ 153 Marcus Bleicher, Frankfurt Lions .30
☐ 154 Bob Manno, Frankfort Lions .50
☐ 155 Rob Crowie, Eisbaren Berlin .30
☐ 156 Mike Bullard, Eisbaren Berlin 1.00
☐ 157 Maren Valenti, Eisbaren Berlin .30
☐ 158 Sven Felski, Eisbaren Berlin .30
☐ 159 Andrew McKim, Eisbaren Berlin .50
☐ 160 Derek Mayer, Eisbaren Berlin .50
☐ 161 Niklas Hede, Eisbaren Berlin .30
☐ 162 Thomas Steen, Eisbaren Berlin .50
☐ 163 Mario Brunetta (G), Eisbaren Berlin .50
☐ 164 Marc Fortier, Eisbaren Berlin .50
☐ 165 Thomas Rhodin, Eisbaren Berlin .30
☐ 166 Nico Pyka, Eisbaren Berlin .30
☐ 167 Chris Govedaris, Eisbaren Berlin .50
☐ 168 Lorenz Funk, Eisbaren Berlin .30
☐ 169 Florian Funk, Eisbaren Berlin .30
☐ 170 Yvon Corriveau, Eisbaren Berlin .50
☐ 171 Mikael Wahlberg, Eisbaren Berlin .30
☐ 172 Darren Durdle, Eisbaren Berlin .30
☐ 173 Pelle Svensson, Eisbaren Berlin .30
☐ 174 Greg Andrusak, Schwenninger Wild Wings .50
☐ 175 Leif Carlsson, Eisbaren Berlin .30
☐ 176 Andreas Brockmann, Eisbaren Berlin .30
☐ 177 Robert Leask, Eisbaren Berlin .30
☐ 178 Mario Chitaroni, Eisbaren Berlin .30
☐ 179 Chad Biafore, Eisbaren Berlin .30
☐ 180 Peter John Lee, Eisbaren Berlin .30
☐ 181 Len Soccio, Hannover Scorpions .30
☐ 182 Jason Lafrenière, Hanover .50
☐ 183 Joe West, Hanover .30
☐ 184 Brent Tully, Hanover .50
☐ 185 Mark Kosturik, Hanover .30
☐ 186 David Haas, Hanover .30
☐ 187 Darcy Martini, Hanover .30
☐ 188 Gary Leeman, Hanover .50
☐ 189 Lee Davidson, Hanover .30
☐ 190 Scott Metcalfe, Hannover Scorpions .30
☐ 191 Tom Pederson, Hanover .50
☐ 192 François Gravel, Hanover .30
☐ 193 Björn Leonhardt, Hanover .30
☐ 194 Michael* Johnson, Hanover .30
☐ 195 Claudio Scremin, Hanover .30
☐ 196 Mike Ware, Hanover .30
☐ 197 Jürgen Trattner, Hanover .30
☐ 198 Dan Currie, Hanover .50
☐ 199 Patrick Curcio, Hanover .30
☐ 200 Patrick Senger, Hanover .30
☐ 201 Frank Di Muzio, Hanover .30
☐ 202 Kevin Gaudet, Hanover .30
☐ 203 Mark MacKay, Schwenningen Wild Wings .30
☐ 204 Claude Vilgrain, Schwenninger Wild Wings .50
☐ 205 Rich Chernomaz, Schwenninger Wild Wings .30
☐ 206 Daniel Laperrière, Schwenningen Wild Wings .50
☐ 207 Wayne Hynes, Schwenningen Wild Wings .30
☐ 208 Todd Harkins, Schwenningen Wild Wings .50
☐ 209 Scott McCrory, Schwenninger Wild Wings .30
☐ 210 Andrew Rymsha, Schwenninger Wild Wings .30
☐ 211 Daniel Nowak, Schwenningen Wild Wings .30
☐ 212 Andy Schneider, Schwenningen Wild Wings .50
☐ 213 Dave Marcinyshyn, Schwenningen Wild Wings .50
☐ 214 Marc Laniel, Schwenningen Wild Wings .30
☐ 215 Guy Lehoux, Schwenninger Wild Wings .30
☐ 216 Matthias Vater, Schwenninger Wild Wings .30
☐ 217 Jens Stramkowski, Schwenningen Wild Wings .30
☐ 218 Alexander Dexheimer, Schwenningen Wild Wings .30
☐ 219 Mark Bassen, Schwenninger Wild Wings .30
☐ 220 Steffen Karg, Schwenninger Wild Wings .30
☐ 221 Randy Perry, Schwenningen Wild Wings .30
☐ 222 Robert Schistad, Schwenningen Wild Wings .30
☐ 223 Andreas Renz, Schwenningen Wild Wings .30
☐ 224 Matthias Hoppe, Schwenningen Wild Wings .30
☐ 225 Ron Ivany, Schwenninger Wild Wings .30
☐ 226 Philippe Bozon, Adler Mannheim .50
☐ 227 Dave Tomlinson, Adler Manheim .50
☐ 228 Stéphane J.G. Richer, Adler Manheim .50
☐ 229 Paul Stanton, Adler Manheim .50
☐ 230 Pavel Gross, Adler Manheim .30
☐ 231 Christian Pouget, Adler Manheim .30
☐ 232 Jackson Penney, Adler Manheim .30
☐ 233 Gord Hynes, Adler Manheim .50
☐ 234 Jason Young, Adler Manheim .30
☐ 235 Alexander Serikow, Adler Manheim .30
☐ 236 Mike Stevens, Adler Manheim .30
☐ 237 Mike Pellegrims, Adler Manheim .30
☐ 238 Reid Simonton, Adler Manheim .30
☐ 239 Christian Lukes, Adler Manheim .30
☐ 240 Ron Pasco, Adler Manheim .30
☐ 241 Mike Hudson, Adler Manheim .50
☐ 242 Denis Perez, Adler Manheim .30
☐ 243 Sven Rampf, Adler Manheim .30
☐ 244 Danny Lorenz, Adler Manheim .50
☐ 245 Brian Tutt, Adler Manheim .30
☐ 246 Jan Alston, Adler Mannheim .30
☐ 247 Lance Nethery, Adler Manheim .30
☐ 248 Sergio Momesso, Nurnberg Ice Tigers .50
☐ 249 Andrei Mezin (G), Nurnberg Ice Tigers .30
☐ 250 Jarno Peltonen, Nurnberg Ice Tigers .30
☐ 251 Martin Feichel, Nuremberg Ice Tigers .30
☐ 252 Sergei Stas, Nuremberg Ice Tigers .30
☐ 253 Martin Jiranek, Nuremberg Ice Tigers .30
☐ 254 Jason Miller, Nurnberg Ice Tigers .50
☐ 255 Jozef Cierny, Nurnberg Ice Tigers .50
☐ 256 Liam Garvey, Nuremberg Ice Tigers .30
☐ 257 Kevin Grant, Nuremberg Ice Tigers .30
☐ 258 Chris Straube, Nuremberg Ice Tigers .30
☐ 259 Heiko Smazal, Nuremberg Ice Tigers .30
☐ 260 Vadim Shakhraichuk, Nuremberg Ice Tigers .30
☐ 261 Leszek Lasxklewicz, Nuremberg Ice Tigers .30
☐ 262 Sven Valenti, Nürnberg Ice Tigers .30
☐ 263 Michel Vallière, Nürnberg Ice Tigers .30
☐ 264 Per Lundell, Nurnberg Ice Tigers .30
☐ 265 Dimitri Dudik, Nuremberg Ice Tigers .30
☐ 266 Daniel Kunce, Nuremberg Ice Tigers .30
☐ 267 Ivan Droppa, Nuremberg Ice Tigers .50
☐ 268 Peter Ihnacak, Nuremberg Ice Tigers .50
☐ 269 Harald Birk, Augsburger Panther .30
☐ 270 Bradley Bergen, Augsburger Panther .30
☐ 271 Pierre Rioux, Augsburg Panthers .30
☐ 272 Jim Camazzola, Augsburg Panthers .30
☐ 273 Klaus Merk, Augsburg Panthers .30
☐ 274 Rick Girard, Augsburg Panthers .50
☐ 275 André Faust, Augsburg Panthers .50
☐ 276 Håkan Åhlund, Augsburger Panther .30
☐ 277 Kyösti Karjalainen, Augsburg Panther .30
☐ 278 Leonardo Conti, Augsburg Panthers .30
☐ 279 Leo Gudas, Augsburg Panthers .30
☐ 280 Mathias Ahxner, Augsburger Panther .30
☐ 281 François Groleau, Augsburg Panthers .50
☐ 282 Michael Bakos, Augsburger Panther .30
☐ 283 Alan Reader, Augsburg Panthers .30
☐ 284 Nordin Harfaoui, Augsburg Panthers .30
☐ 285 Dale Craigwell, Augsburg Panthers .50
☐ 286 Dimitri Grömling, Augsburg Panthers .30
☐ 287 Duanne Moeser, Augsburg Panthers .30
☐ 288 Tommy Jakobsen, Augsburg Panther .30
☐ 289 Patrik Degerstedt, Augsburg Panthers .30
☐ 290 Greg Bullock, Augsburg Panthers .30
☐ 291 GÜnnar Leidborg, Augsburg Panthers .30
☐ 292 Dieter Hegen, Rosenheim Star Bulls .50
☐ 293 Derek Cormier, Rosenheim Star Bulls .30
☐ 294 Jim Hiller, Rosenheim Star Bulls .50
☐ 295 Gord Sherven, Rosenheim Star Bulls .30
☐ 296 Eric Murano, Rosenheim Star Bulls .30
☐ 297 Robert Müller, Rosenheim Star Bulls .30
☐ 298 Klaus Kathan, Rosenheim Star Bulls .30
☐ 299 Raimond Hilger, Rosenheim Star Bulls .30
☐ 300 Christian Due-Boje, Rosenheim Star Bulls .30
☐ 301 Jesper Duus, Rosenheim Star Bulls .30
☐ 302 Michael Pohl, Rosenheim Star Bulls .30
☐ 303 Bernd Kühnhauser, Rosenheim Star Bulls .30
☐ 304 Frank Hohenadl, Rosenheim Star Bulls .30
☐ 305 Alexander Jansen, Rosenheim Star Bulls .30
☐ 306 Teemu Siilanpää, Rosenheim Star Bulls .30
☐ 307 Hans Abrahamsson, Rosenheim Star Bulls .30
☐ 308 Klaus Dalpiaz, Rosenheim Star Bulls .30
☐ 309 Kari Haakana, Rosenheim Star Bulls .30
☐ 310 Christian Gegenfurtner, Rosenheim Star Bulls .30
☐ 311 Peter Ottosson, Rosenheim Star Bulls .30
☐ 312 Wolfgang Kummer, Rosenheim Star Bulls .30
☐ 313 Beppi Eckmaier, Rosenheim Star Bulls .30
☐ 314 Gerhard Brunner, Star Bulls Rosenheim .30
☐ 315 Mirko Lüdemann, Germany Nationals .30
☐ 316 Sven Felski, Germany Nationals .30
☐ 317 Reemt Pyka, Germany Nationals .30
☐ 318 Jörg Mayr, Germany Nationals .30
☐ 319 Michael Bresagk, Germany Nationals .30
☐ 320 Andreas Lupzig, Germany Nationals .30
☐ 321 Jürgen Rumrich, Germany Nationals .30
☐ 322 Josef Lehner, Germany Nationals .30
☐ 323 Peter Draisaitl, Germany Nationals .30
☐ 324 Leo Stefan, Germany Nationals .30
☐ 325 Joseph Haib, Germany Nationals .30
☐ 326 Klaus Kathan, Germany Nationals .30
☐ 327 Klaus Merk, Germany Nationals .30
☐ 328 Peter Gulda, Germany Nationals .30
☐ 329 Daniel Nowak, Germany Nationals .30
☐ 330 Bradley Bergen, Germany Nationals .30
☐ 331 Thomas Dolak, Germany Nationals .30
☐ 332 Martin Reichel, Germany Nationals .30
☐ 333 Alexander Serikow, Germany Nationals .30
☐ 334 Harald Birk, Germany Nationals .30
☐ 335 Michael Bakos, Germany Nationals .30
☐ 336 Mario Gehrig, Germany Nationals .30
☐ 337 Mark MacKay, Germany Nationals .30
☐ 338 Dieter Hegen, Germany Nationals .30
☐ 339 Hans Zach, Germany Nationals .30
☐ 340 Erich Kühnhacki, Germany Nationals .30
☐ 341 Ernst Höfner, Germany Nationals .30
☐ Rick Amann
☐ Gerhard Leinauer
☐ Ernst Müller

1998 - 99 DONRUSS

This series was cancelled when Pinnacle Brands and Donruss Trading Cards lost their hockey license for the 1998-99 season. This promo was for the Elite Series insert. Some cards are easier to find than others, particularly the Dominik Hasek and Sergei Samsonov cards.

Donruss

☐ 1 John LeClair, Phil. 20.00
☐ 2 Brett Hull, SLou. 10.00
☐ 3 Saku Koivu, Mont. 30.00
☐ 4 Mark Messier, NYRa. 25.00
☐ 5 Keith Tkachuk, Phoe. 10.00
☐ 6 Teemu Selänne, Anah. 20.00
☐ 7 Sergei Samsonov, Bost. 5.00
☐ 8 Pavel Bure, Vanc. 20.00
☐ 9 Brendan Shanahan, Detr. 25.00
☐ 10 Dominik Hasek (G), Buff. 5.00
☐ 11 Joe Thornton, Bost. 30.00
☐ 12 Joe Sakic, Colo. 40.00
☐ 13 Martin Brodeur (G), NJer. 40.00
☐ 14 Peter Forsberg, Colo. 35.00
☐ 15 Steve Yzerman, Detr. 60.00
☐ 16 Patrick Roy (G), Colo. 60.00
☐ 17 Jaromir Jagr, Pitt. 25.00
☐ 18 Paul Kariya, Anah. 35.00
☐ 19 Eric Lindros, Phil. 25.00
☐ 20 Wayne Gretzky, NYRa. 100.00

1998 - 99 DS

NHL stars sometimes sell at a premium (usually $1-2). Card 1 (Gold) is seeded 1:125 packs; cards 2-11 (Dream Team) are seeded 1:30 packs; cards 12-25 (Goalies) are seeded 1:30 packs.

Complete Set (125 cards): 150.00
Common Player: .30

Player	Card
☐ 1 Jiri Dopita	20.00
☐ 2 Pavel Patera	8.00
☐ 3 Martin Prochazka	8.00
☐ 4 Martin Rucinsky	8.00
☐ 5 Vladimir (Jr.) Vujtek	8.00
☐ 6 David Moravec	8.00
☐ 7 Libor Prochazka	8.00
☐ 8 Viktor Ujcik	8.00
☐ 9 Vladimir Ruzicka	8.00
☐ 10 Frantisek Kucera	8.00
☐ 11 David Vyborny	8.00
☐ 12 Rudolf Pejchar (G)	8.00
☐ 13 Oldrich Svoboda (G)	8.00
☐ 14 Marek Novotny (G)	8.00
☐ 15 Zdenek Orct (G)	8.00
☐ 16 Libor Barta (G)	8.00
☐ 17 Dusan Salficky (G)	8.00
☐ 18 Pavel Cagas (G)	8.00
☐ 19 Ladislav Blazek (G)	8.00
☐ 20 Roman Cechmanek (G)	12.00
☐ 21 Milan Hnilicka (G)	8.00
☐ 22 Martin Cinibulk (G)	8.00
☐ 23 Martin Prusek (G)	14.00
☐ 24 Jaroslav Kames (G)	8.00
☐ 25 Radovan Biegl (G)	8.00
☐ 26 Petr Pavlas, Karlovy Vary	.30
☐ 27 Ondrej Steiner, Karlovy Vary	.50
☐ 28 Pavel Janku, Karlovy Vary	.30
☐ 29 Jaromir Kverka, Karlovy Vary	.30
☐ 30 Martin Rousek, Karlovy Vary	.30
☐ 31 Milan Nedoma, Ceske Budejovice	.30
☐ 32 Radek Martinek, Ceske Budejovice	.50
☐ 33 Rudolf Suchanek, Ceske Budejovice	.30
☐ 34 Radek Toupal, Ceske Budejovice	.30
☐ 35 Filip Turek, Ceske Budejovice	.30
☐ 36 Miroslav Barus, Ceske Budejovice	.30
☐ 37 Miroslav Duben, Dukla Jihlava	.30
☐ 38 Petr Vlk, Dukla Jihlava	.30
☐ 39 Marek Melenovsky, Dukla Jihlava	.30
☐ 40 Jiri Cihlar, Dukla Jihlava	.30
☐ 41 Roman Mejzlik, Dukla Jihlava	.30
☐ 42 Ales Polcar, Dukla Jihlava	.30
☐ 43 Angel Nikolov, Chemopetrol Litvinov	.30
☐ 44 Martin Stepanek, Chemopetrol Litvinov	.30
☐ 45 Petr Hrbek, Chemopetrol Litvinov	.30
☐ 46 Ivo Prorok, Chemopetrol Litvinov	.30
☐ 47 Vladimir Petrovka, Chemopetrol Litvinov	.30
☐ 48 Robert Kysela, Chemopetrol Litvinov	.30
☐ 49 Josef Straka, Chemopetrol Litvinov	.30
☐ 50 Ales Pisa, Pardubice	.50
☐ 51 Pavel Kriz, Pardubice	.30
☐ 52 Tomas Blazek, Pardubice	.50
☐ 53 Tomas Martinec, Pardubice	.30
☐ 54 Jiri Jantovsky, Pardubice	.30
☐ 55 Stanislav Prochazka, Pardubice	.30
☐ 56 Jaroslav Kudrna, Pardubice	.30
☐ 57 Josef Reznicek, Interconex Plzen	.30
☐ 58 Pavel Geffert, Interconex Plzen	.30
☐ 59 Petr Korinek, Interconex Plzen	.30
☐ 60 Pavel Vostrak, Interconex Plzen	.30
☐ 61 Michal Straka, Interconex Plzen	.30
☐ 62 David Pospisil, Interconex Plzen	.30
☐ 63 Milan Volak, Interconex Plzen	.30
☐ 64 Milan Navratil, Interconex Plzen	.30
☐ 65 Vitezslav Skuta, Opava	.30
☐ 66 Michael Vyhlidal, Opava	.30
☐ 67 Petr Kuchyna, Opava	.30
☐ 68 Drahomir Kadlec, Opava	.30
☐ 69 Petr Kadlec, Slavia Praha	.30
☐ 70 Martin Bakula, Slavia Praha	.30
☐ 71 Andrei Jakovenko, Slavia Praha	.30
☐ 72 Marian Kacir, Slavia Praha	.30
☐ 73 Vladimir Machulda, Slavia Praha	.30
☐ 74 Michal Sup, Slavia Praha	.30
☐ 75 Jiri Dolezal, Slavia Praha	.30
☐ 76 Tomas Kucharcik, Slavia Praha	.30
☐ 77 Jiri Veber, Dadak Vsetin	.30
☐ 78 Jan Srdinko, Dadak Vsetin	.30
☐ 79 Radim Tesarik, Dadak Vsetin	.30
☐ 80 Ondrej Kratena, Dadak Vsetin	.50
☐ 81 Michal Bros, Dadak Vsetin	.50
☐ 82 Jan Tomajko, Dadak Vsetin	.50
☐ 83 Tomas Srsen, Dadak Vsetin	.30
☐ 84 Zbynek Marak, Dadak Vsetin	.30
☐ 85 Radek Belohlav, Dadak Vsetin	.30
☐ 86 Roman Stantien, Dadak Vsetin	.30
☐ 87 Alexei Jaskin, Dadak Vsetin	.30
☐ 88 Vaclav Burda, Sparta Praha	.30
☐ 89 Ladislav Benysek, Sparta Praha	.50
☐ 90 Frantisek Ptacek, Sparta Praha	.30
☐ 91 Roman Horak, Sparta Praha	.30
☐ 92 Richard Zemlicka, Sparta Praha	.30
☐ 93 Jan Hlavac, Sparta Praha	1.00
☐ 94 Jiri Zelenka, Sparta Praha	.30
☐ 95 Patrik Martinec, Sparta Praha	.30
☐ 96 Jaroslav Bednar, Sparta Praha	.50
☐ 97 Marek Zidlicky, Kladno	.30
☐ 98 Ladislav Svoboda, Kladno	.30
☐ 99 Vaclav Eiselt, Kladno	.30
☐ 100 Zdenek Eichenmann, Kladno	.30
☐ 101 Jiri Burger, Kladno	.30
☐ 102 Ales Tomasek, Vitkovice	.30
☐ 103 Tomas Jelinek, Vitkovice	.50
☐ 104 René Sevecek, Vitkovice	.30
☐ 105 Pavel Kowalczyk, Vitkovice	.30
☐ 106 Alexander Cerbajev, Vitkovice	.30
☐ 107 Martin Kotasek, Vitkovice	.30
☐ 108 Ales Kratoska, Vitkovice	.30
☐ 109 Martin Hamrlik, ZPS Zlin	.30
☐ 110 Roman Meluzin, ZPS Zlin	.30
☐ 111 Petr Cajanek, ZPS Zlin	.50
☐ 112 Tomas Nemcicky, ZPS Zlin	.50
☐ 113 Josef Straub, ZPS Zlin	.30
☐ 114 Miroslav Okal, ZPS Zlin	.30
☐ 115 L'ubomir Sekeras, Trinec	.50

116 Jiri Kuntos, Trinec	.30
117 Stanislav Pavelec, Trinec	.30
118 Richard Kral, Trinec	.30
119 Ladislav Lubina, Trinec	.30
120 Roman Kadera, Trinec	.50
121 Jozef Dano, Trinec	.30
122 Tomas Chlubna, Trinec	.30
123 Ales Zima, Trinec	.30
124 Branislav Janos, Trinec	.30
125 Checklist	.30

1998 - 99 DYNAGON ICE

These cards have three versions: the regular card, a red parallel (treat packs) and an Ice Blue parallel (67 copies).

Complete Set (200 cards):	**2525.00**	**350.00**	**45.00**
Common Player:	**8.00**	**1.00**	**.25**
Player	**Ice Blue**	**Red**	**Reg.**
1 Travis Green, Anah.	10.00	1.00	.25
2 Guy Hebert (G), Anah.	10.00	1.00	.25
3 Paul Kariya, Anah.	70.00	10.00	1.00
4 Steve Rucchin, Anah.	10.00	1.00	.25
5 Tomas Sandström, Anah.	10.00	1.00	.25
6 Teemu Selänne, Anah.	40.00	6.00	.50
7 Jason Allison, Bost.	30.00	4.00	.50
8 Raymond Bourque, Bost.	60.00	8.00	1.00
9 Byron Dafoe (G), Bost.	20.00	3.00	.25
10 Anson Carter, Bost.	20.00	3.00	.25
11 Dimitri Khristich, Bost.	8.00	1.00	.25
12 A. Laaksonen, Bost. RC	**8.00**	**1.00**	**.50**
13 P. Nordström, Bost. RC	**8.00**	**1.00**	**.50**
14 Sergei Samsonov, Bost.	30.00	4.00	.50
15 Joe Thornton, Bost.	60.00	9.00	1.00
16 Matthew Barnaby, Buff.	8.00	1.00	.25
17 Michal Grosek, Buff.	8.00	1.00	.25
18 Dominik Hasek (G), Buff.	50.00	6.00	1.00
19 Brian Holzinger, Buff.	8.00	1.00	.25
20 Michael Peca, Buff.	20.00	3.00	.25
21 Miroslav Satan, Buff.	15.00	2.00	.25
22 Vaclav Varada, Buff.	8.00	1.00	.25
23 Andrew Cassels, Calg.	10.00	1.00	.25
24 Rico Fata, Calg.	10.00	1.00	.25
25 Theoren Fleury, Calg.	30.00	4.00	.50
26 Phil Housley, Calg.	15.00	2.00	.25
27 Jarome Iginla, Cgy	40.00	6.00	.50
28 M. St-Louis, Calg. RC	**20.00**	**7.00**	**3.50**
29 Ken Wregget (G), Calg.	10.00	1.00	.25
30 Kevin Dineen, Caro.	8.00	1.00	.25
31 Ron Francis, Caro.	30.00	4.00	.50
32 Martin Gélinas, Caro.	10.00	1.00	.25
33 Arturs Irbe (G), Caro.	20.00	3.00	.25
34 Sami Kapanen, Caro.	15.00	2.00	.25
35 Trevor Kidd (G), Caro.	15.00	2.00	.25
36 Robert Kron, Caro.	8.00	1.00	.25
37 Keith Primeau, Caro.	20.00	3.00	.25
38 Tony Amonte, Chic.	30.00	4.00	.50
39 Chris Chelios, Chic.	30.00	4.00	.50
40 Éric Dazé, Chic.	20.00	3.00	.25
41 Doug Gilmour, Chic.	30.00	4.00	.50
42 Jeff Hackett (G), Chic.	15.00	2.00	.25
43 Ty Jones, Chic.	8.00	1.00	.25
44 Bob Probert, Chic.	15.00	2.00	.25
45 Adam Deadmarsh, Colo.	15.00	2.00	.25
46 Chris Drury, Colo.	30.00	4.00	1.00
47 Peter Forsberg, Colo.	70.00	10.00	1.00
48 Milan Hejduk, Colo. RC	**80.00**	**12.00**	**7.00**
49 Valeri Kamensky, Colo.	15.00	2.00	.25
50 Claude Lemieux, Colo.	15.00	2.00	.25
51 Patrick Roy (G), Colo.	150.00	22.00	3.00
52 Joe Sakic, Colo.	80.00	12.00	1.50
53 Ed Belfour (G), Dall.	50.00	7.00	1.00
54 Sergey Gusev, Dall. RC	**8.00**	**1.00**	**.50**
55 Derian Hatcher, Dall.	15.00	2.00	.25
56 Brett Hull, Dall.	50.00	7.00	1.00
57 J. Langenbrunner, Dall.	10.00	1.00	.25
58 Jere Lehtinen, Dall.	15.00	2.00	.25
59 Mike Modano, Dall.	50.00	7.00	1.00
60 Joe Nieuwendyk, Dall.	20.00	3.00	.25
61 Sergei Zubov, Dall.	10.00	1.00	.25
62 Sergei Fedorov, Detr.	50.00	7.00	1.00
63 Vyacheslav Kozlov, Detr.	10.00	1.00	.25
64 Uwe Krupp, Detr.	8.00	1.00	.25
65 Nicklas Lidström, Detr.	30.00	4.00	.50
66 Darren McCarty, Detr.	15.00	2.00	.25
67 Chris Osgood (G), Detr.	30.00	4.00	.50
68 Brendan Shanahan, Detr.	50.00	7.00	1.00
69 Steve Yzerman, Detr.	120.00	18.00	2.00
70 Bob Essensa (G), Edmo.	10.00	1.00	.25
71 Mike Grier, Edmo.	10.00	1.00	.25
72 Bill Guerin, Edmo.	20.00	3.00	.25
73 Roman Hamrlik, Edmo.	10.00	1.00	.25
74 Janne Niinimaa, Edmo.	10.00	1.00	.25
75 Tom Poti, Edmo.	8.00	1.00	.25
76 Ryan Smyth, Edmo.	20.00	3.00	.25
77 Doug Weight, Edmo.	30.00	4.00	.50
78 Sean Burke (G), Flor.	30.00	4.00	.50
79 Dino Ciccarelli, Flor.	15.00	2.00	.25
80 Dave Gagner, Flor.	8.00	1.00	.25
81 Ed Jovanovski, Flor.	20.00	3.00	.25
82 Viktor Kozlov, Flor.	15.00	2.00	.25
83 Oleg Kvasha, Flor. RC	**8.00**	**2.00**	**1.00**
84 Paul Laus, Flor.	8.00	1.00	.25
85 Mark Parrish, Flor.	20.00	6.00	2.00
86 Rob Blake, LosA.	30.00	4.00	.50
87 Stéphane Fiset (G), LosA.	15.00	2.00	.25
88 Josh Green, LosA.	8.00	2.00	.50
89 Yanic Perreault, LosA.	15.00	2.00	.25
90 Luc Robitaille, LosA.	40.00	6.00	.50
91 Jozef Stümpel, LosA.	10.00	1.00	.25
92 Vladimir Tsyplakov, LosA.	8.00	1.00	.25
93 Brad Brown, Mont.	8.00	1.00	.25
94 Shayne Corson, Mont.	15.00	2.00	.25
95 V. Damphousse, Mont.	30.00	4.00	.50
96 Saku Koivu, Mont.	40.00	6.00	.50
97 Mark Recchi, Mont.	20.00	3.00	.25
98 J. Thibault (G), Mont.	20.00	3.00	.25
99 Sergei Zholtok, Mont.	8.00	1.00	.25
100 Andrew Brunette, Nash.	8.00	1.00	.25
101 Mike Dunham, Nash.	20.00	3.00	.25
102 Tom Fitzgerald, Nash.	8.00	1.00	.25
103 Patric Kjellberg, Nash.	8.00	1.00	.25
104 Sergei Krivokrasov, Nash.	8.00	1.00	.25
105 Darren Turcotte, Nash.	8.00	1.00	.25
106 Dave Andreychuk, NJer.	15.00	2.00	.25
107 Jason Arnott, NJer.	20.00	3.00	.25
108 Martin Brodeur (G), NJer.	80.00	12.00	1.50
109 Patrik Elias, NJer.	40.00	6.00	.50
110 Bobby Holik, NJer.	15.00	2.00	.25
111 Brendan Morrison, NJer.	15.00	2.00	.25
112 Scott Stevens, NJer.	20.00	3.00	.25
113 Bryan Berard, NYIs.	15.00	2.00	.25
114 Eric Brewer, NYIs.	20.00	3.00	.50
115 Trevor Linden, NYIs.	20.00	3.00	.25
116 Zigmund Palffy, NYIs.	30.00	4.00	.50
117 Robert Reichel, NYIs.	15.00	2.00	.25
118 Tommy Salo (G), NYIs.	20.00	3.00	.25
119 Bryan Smolinski, NYIs.	8.00	1.00	.25
120 Adam Graves, NYRa.	20.00	3.00	.25
121 Wayne Gretzky, NYRa.	200.00	30.00	4.00
122 Alexei Kovalev, NYRa.	30.00	4.00	.50
123 Brian Leetch, NYRa.	30.00	4.00	.50
124 Manny Malhotra, NYRa.	10.00	1.00	.25
125 Mike Richter (G), NYRa.	20.00	3.00	.25
126 Daniel Alfredsson, Ott.	30.00	4.00	.50
127 Igor Kravchuk, Ott.	8.00	1.00	.25
128 Shawn McEachern, Ott.	15.00	2.00	.25
129 Vaclav Prospal, Ott.	15.00	2.00	.25
130 Damian Rhodes (G), Ott.	10.00	1.00	.25
131 Sami Salo, Ott. RC	**8.00**	**1.00**	**.50**
132 Alexei Yashin, Ott.	30.00	4.00	.50
133 Rod Brind'Amour, Phil.	15.00	2.00	.25
134 Alexandre Daigle, Phil.	8.00	1.00	.25
135 Chris Gratton, Phil.	10.00	1.00	.25
136 Ron Hextall (G), Phil.	30.00	4.00	.50
137 John LeClair, Phil.	40.00	6.00	.50
138 Eric Lindros, Phil.	50.00	6.00	1.00
139 Mike Maneluk, Phil. RC	**8.00**	**1.00**	**.50**
140 Vanbiesbrouck (G), Phil.	20.00	3.00	.25
141 Dainius Zubrus, Phil.	10.00	1.00	.25
142 Brad Isbister, Phoe.	10.00	1.00	.25
143 N. Khabibulin (G), Phoe.	20.00	3.00	.25
144 Jeremy Roenick, Phoe.	40.00	6.00	.50
145 Keith Tkachuk, Phoe.	30.00	4.00	.50
146 Rick Tocchet, Phoe.	15.00	2.00	.25
147 Oleg Tverdovsky, Phoe.	8.00	1.00	.25
148 Tom Barrasso (G), Pitt.	20.00	3.00	.25
149 Kevin Hatcher, Pitt.	8.00	1.00	.25
150 Jan Hrdina, Pitt. RC	**10.00**	**3.00**	**1.50**
151 Jaromir Jagr, Pitt.	50.00	6.00	1.00
152 Alexei Morozov, Pitt.	10.00	1.00	.25
153 Jiri Slegr, Pitt.	8.00	1.00	.25
154 Martin Straka, Pitt.	15.00	2.00	.25
155 Jim Campbell, SLou.	8.00	1.00	.25
156 Geoff Courtnall, SLou.	8.00	1.00	.25
157 Grant Fuhr (G), SLou.	30.00	4.00	.50
158 M. Handzus, SLou. RC	**10.00**	**3.00**	**1.50**
159 Al MacInnis, SLou.	20.00	3.00	.25
160 Jamie McLennan, SLou.	8.00	1.00	.25
161 Chris Pronger, SLou.	30.00	4.00	.50
162 Marty Reasoner, SLou.	10.00	1.00	.25
163 Pierre Turgeon, SLou.	20.00	3.00	.25
164 Jeff Friesen, SanJ.	15.00	2.00	.25
165 Tony Granato, SanJ.	10.00	1.00	.25
166 Scott Hannan, SanJ. RC	**8.00**	**1.00**	**.50**
167 Patrick Marleau, SanJ.	20.00	3.00	.25
168 Owen Nolan, SanJ.	30.00	4.00	.50
169 Marco Sturm, SanJ.	10.00	1.00	.25
170 Mike Vernon (G), SanJ.	20.00	3.00	.25
171 Wendel Clark, Tamp.	40.00	6.00	.50
172 John Cullen, Tamp.	10.00	1.00	.25
173 V. Lecavalier, Tamp.	50.00	7.00	2.00
174 Stéphane Richer, Tamp.	10.00	1.00	.25
175 Paul Ysebaert, Tamp.	8.00	1.00	.25
176 Rob Zamuner, Tamp.	10.00	1.00	.25
177 Sergei Berezin, Toro.	10.00	1.00	.25
178 Tie Domi, Toro.	15.00	2.00	.25
179 Mike Johnson, Toro.	10.00	1.00	.25
180 Curtis Joseph (G), Toro.	50.00	6.00	1.00
181 T. Kaberle, Toro. RC	**15.00**	**4.00**	**2.00**
182 Igor Korolev, Toro.	8.00	1.00	.25
183 Alyn McCauley, Toro.	15.00	2.00	.25
184 Mats Sundin, Toro.	50.00	7.00	1.00
185 Todd Bertuzzi, Vanc.	60.00	9.00	1.00
186 Donald Brashear, Vanc.	10.00	1.00	.25
187 Pavel Bure, Vanc.	40.00	6.00	.50
188 Matt Cooke, Vanc. RC	**8.00**	**2.00**	**1.00**
189 Mark Messier, Vanc.	50.00	7.00	1.00
190 Alexander Mogilny, Vanc.	20.00	3.00	.25
191 Mattias Öhlund, Vanc.	15.00	2.00	.25
192 Garth Snow (G), Vanc.	15.00	2.00	.25
193 Peter Bondra, Wash.	30.00	4.00	.50
194 Matt Herr, Wash.	8.00	1.00	.50
195 Calle Johansson, Wash.	10.00	1.00	.25
196 Joé Juneau, Wash.	10.00	1.00	.25
197 Olaf Kölzig (G), Wash.	30.00	4.00	.50
198 Adam Oates, Wash.	20.00	3.00	.25
199 J. Svejkovsky, Wash.	8.00	1.00	.25
200 Richard Zednik, Wash.	20.00	3.00	.25

Player	**Sample**
Martin Brodeur (G), NJer.	2.00

ADRENALINE RUSH

There are four versions: a Bronze parallel (#/180), a Silver parallel (#/120), a Red parallel (#/79) and an Ice Blue parallel (#/10).

Insert Set (10 cards):	**3740.00**	**745.00**	**535.00**	**440.00**
Insert	**IB10**	**R79**	**S120**	**B180**
1 Paul Kariya	350.00	70.00	50.00	40.00
2 Teemu Selänne	200.00	40.00	30.00	20.00
3 D. Hasek (G)	250.00	50.00	30.00	30.00
4 Peter Forsberg	350.00	70.00	50.00	40.00
5 Patrick Roy (G).	750.00	150.00	110.00	90.00
6 Joe Sakic	400.00	80.00	60.00	50.00
7 Steve Yzerman	600.00	120.00	90.00	70.00
8 Wayne Gretzky	1000.00	200.00	150.00	120.00
9 Eric Lindros	250.00	50.00	30.00	30.00
10 Jaromir Jagr	250.00	50.00	30.00	30.00

FORWARD THINKING

Insert Set (20 cards):	**135.00**
Insert (1:37)	**FT**
1 Paul Kariya, Anah.	10.00
2 Teemu Selänne, Anah.	6.00
3 Michael Peca, Buff.	3.00
4 Doug Gilmour, Chic.	4.00
5 Peter Forsberg, Colo.	10.00
6 Joe Sakic, Colo.	12.00
7 Brett Hull, Dall.	6.00
8 Mike Modano, Dall.	6.00
9 Sergei Fedorov, Detr.	6.00
10 Brendan Shanahan, Detr.	6.00
11 Steve Yzerman, Detr.	18.00
12 Saku Koivu, Mont.	6.00
13 Wayne Gretzky, NYRa.	30.00
14 John LeClair, Phil.	6.00
15 Eric Lindros, Phil.	6.00
16 Jaromir Jagr, Pitt.	6.00
17 Vincent Lecavalier, Tamp.	6.00
18 Mats Sundin, Toro.	6.00
19 Mark Messier, Vanc.	6.00
20 Peter Bondra, Wash.	4.00

ICE ROOKIES

Insert Set (10 cards):	**90.00**
Insert (1:73)	**IR**
1 Chris Drury, Colo.	15.00
2 Milan Hejduk, Colo.	20.00
3 Mark Parrish, Flor.	10.00
4 Brendan Morrison, NJer.	8.00
5 Mike Maneluk, Phil.	8.00
6 Jan Hrdina, Pitt.	8.00
7 Marty Reasoner, SLou.	8.00
8 Vincent Lecavalier, Tamp.	25.00
9 Tomas Kaberle, Toro.	8.00
10 Bill Muckalt, Vanc.	8.00

ICE WATCHMEN

Insert Set (10 cards):	**140.00**
Insert (1:73)	**IW**
1 Dominik Hasek (G), Buff.	15.00
2 Patrick Roy (G), Colo.	50.00
3 Ed Belfour (G), Dall.	15.00
4 Chris Osgood (G), Detr.	10.00
5 Martin Brodeur (G), NJer.	25.00
6 Mike Richter (G), NYRa.	8.00
7 John Vanbiesbrouck (G), Phil.	8.00
8 Grant Fuhr (G), SLou.	10.00
9 Curtis Joseph (G), Toro.	15.00
10 Olaf Kölzig (G), Wash.	10.00

PREEMINENT PLAYERS

Insert Set (10 cards):	**375.00**
Insert (1:181)	**PP**
1 Paul Kariya, Anah.	35.00
2 Dominik Hasek (G), Buff.	25.00
3 Peter Forsberg, Colo.	35.00
4 Patrick Roy (G), Colo.	75.00
5 Mike Modano, Dall.	25.00
6 Steve Yzerman, Detr.	60.00
7 Martin Brodeur (G), NJer.	40.00
8 Wayne Gretzky, NYRa.	100.00
9 Eric Lindros, Phil.	25.00
10 Jaromir Jagr, Pitt.	25.00

TEAM CHECKLISTS

Insert Set (27 cards):	**115.00**
Insert (2:37)	**TC**
1 Paul Kariya, Anah.	6.00
2 Raymond Bourque, Bost.	6.00
3 Dominik Hasek (G), Buff.	4.00
4 Theoren Fleury, Calg.	3.00
5 Keith Primeau, Caro.	3.00

☐	6 Chris Chelios, Chic.	3.00
☐	7 Patrick Roy (G), Colo.	14.00
☐	8 Mike Modano, Dall.	4.00
☐	9 Steve Yzerman, Detr.	12.00
☐	10 Ryan Smyth, Edmo.	3.00
☐	11 Dino Ciccarelli, Flor.	3.00
☐	12 Rob Blake, LosA.	3.00
☐	13 Saku Koivu, Mont.	4.00
☐	14 Mike Dunham, Nash.	3.00
☐	15 Martin Brodeur (G), NJer.	8.00
☐	16 Trevor Linden, NYIs.	3.00
☐	17 Wayne Gretzky, NYRa.	20.00
☐	18 Alexei Yashin, Ott.	3.00
☐	19 Eric Lindros, Phil.	4.00
☐	20 Keith Tkachuk, Phoe.	3.00
☐	21 Jaromir Jagr, Pitt.	4.00
☐	22 Grant Fuhr (G), SLou.	3.00
☐	23 Mike Vernon (G), SanJ.	3.00
☐	24 Vincent Lecavalier, Tamp.	4.00
☐	25 Mats Sundin, Toro.	4.00
☐	26 Mark Messier, Vanc.	4.00
☐	27 Peter Bondra, Wsh	3.00

1998 - 99 EBK SPORTS / ECHL ALL-STARS

These cards were issued as two 20-card team sets.

Northern Set (21 cards): 10.00
Southern Set (21 cards): 10.00

Northern	Northern
☐ 1 Tom O'Connor	☐ 2 Duane Harmer
☐ 3 Jamie Ling	☐ 4 Darren Maloney
☐ 5 Bret Meyers	☐ 6 Jim Bermingham
☐ 7 Jamie Thompson	☐ 8 Andrew Williamson
☐ 9 Marc Tropper	☐ 10 Bobby* Brown
☐ 11 Jakub Ficenec	☐ 12 Arturs Kupaks
☐ 13 Dru Burgess	☐ 14 Dan Ceman
☐ 15 Ryan Kraft	☐ 16 Joe Blaznek
☐ 17 Casey Kesselring	☐ 18 Matt Mullin
☐ 19 Maxime Gingras	☐ 20 Karl Infanger
☐ Checklist	
Southern	**Southern**
☐ 1 Jaroslav Obsut	☐ 2 Terry Lindgren
☐ 3 Kelly Hurd	☐ 4 Dana Mulvihill
☐ 5 Jonas Soling	☐ 6 Jamey Hicks
☐ 7 Patrick Rochon	☐ 8 John Varga
☐ 9 David Seitz	☐ 10 Jason Elders
☐ 11 Cail MacLean	☐ 12 Allan Sirois
☐ 13 Shane Calder	☐ 14 Chris Valicevic
☐ 15 J-F Aubé	☐ 16 Luke Curtin
☐ 17 Jan Kobezda	☐ 18 Bujar Amidovski (G)
☐ 19 Chris Hynnes	☐ 20 Chris Wickenheiser
☐ Checklist	

1998 - 99 EBK SPORTS / IHL ALL-STARS

Eastern Set (24 cards): 15.00
Western Set (23 cards): 10.00

Eastern	Eastern
☐ 1 Guy Dupuis	☐ 2 Viacheslav Butsayev
☐ 3 Zac Bierk (G)	☐ 4 Brian Noonan
☐ 5 David Hymovitz	☐ 6 Marty Turco (G)
☐ 7 Jonathan Sim	☐ 8 Brad Shaw
☐ 9 Pat Neaton	☐ 10 Peter Ciavaglia
☐ 11 Mike Prokopec	☐ 12 Stan Drulia
☐ 13 Steve Walker	☐ 14 Todd Richards
☐ 15 Maxim Spiridonov	☐ 16 Robert Petrovicky
☐ 17 Curtis Murphy	☐ 18 Mark Beaufait
☐ 19 Gilbert Dionne	☐ 20 Brad Lukowich
☐ 21 Bruce Cassidy	☐ 22 S. Ludzik, Coach
☐ 23 Keith Aldridge	☐ 24 Checklist
Western	**Western**
☐ 1 R. Shulmistra (G)	☐ 2 Brett Hauer
☐ 3 Bill Bowler	☐ 4 Pat Jablonski (G)
☐ 5 Niklas Andersson	☐ 6 Steve Maltais
☐ 7 Tom Tilley	☐ 8 Dan Ratushny
☐ 9 Andy Roach	☐ 10 Robert Valicevic
☐ 11 Jeff Tory	☐ 12 Patrik Augusta
☐ 13 Kimmo Timonen	☐ 14 Mark Mowers
☐ 15 Patrice Lefebvre	☐ 16 Cam Stewart
☐ 17 Brian Wiseman	☐ 18 Greg Hawgood
☐ 19 John Purves	☐ 20 Scott Thomas
☐ 21 Randy Carlyle	☐ 22 Dave Tippett
☐ 23 Checklist	

1998 - 99 KRAFT / POST COLLECTION

Complete Set (51 cards / disks): 50.00

KRAFT DINNER / FEARLESS FORWARDS

One of 13 different cards was found on the back of specially marked boxes of Kraft Dinner.

Card Size: 3 3/16" x 4 15/16"

Complete Set (13 cards): 20.00

	Player	FF
☐	Peter Bondra, Wash.	1.50
☐	Pavel Bure, Vanc.	2.00
☐	Vincent Damphousse, Mont.	1.50
☐	Jaromir Jagr, Wash.	3.00
☐	Paul Kariya, Anah.	4.00
☐	John LeClair, Phil.	2.00
☐	Claude Lemieux, Colo.	1.00
☐	Mike Modano, Dall.	3.00
☐	Brendan Shanahan, Detr.	3.00
☐	Cory Stillman, Calg.	1.00
☐	Mats Sundin, Toro.	3.00
☐	Doug Weight, Edmo.	1.50
☐	Alexei Yashin, Ott.	1.50

OSCAR MAYER LUNCHABLES / GOALIE GREATS

One of eight different panels (two cards per panel) were found on the back of specially marked boxes of Oscar Mayer Lunchables.

Card Size: 2 13/16" x 5 11/16"

Complete Set (8 panels): 20.00

	Player	GG
☐	Ed Belfour (G), Dall.	2.00
☐	Martin Brodeur (G), NJer.	6.00
☐	Dominik Hasek (G), Buff.	2.00
☐	Olaf Kölzig (G), Wash.	2.00
☐	Chris Osgood (G), Detr.	2.00
☐	Damian Rhodes (G), Otta.	2.00
☐	Mike Richter (G), NYRa.	2.00
☐	Patrick Roy (G), Colo.	10.00

PEANUT BUTTER / DYNAMITE DEFENDERS

A set of eight disks was available via a redemption offer.

Disk Size: 2 3/4"

Complete Set (8 disks): 20.00

	Player	DD
☐	Rob Blake, LosA. / Larry Murphy, Detr.	3.00
☐	Raymond Bourque, Bost. / Boris Mironov, Chic.	4.00
☐	Patrice Brisebois, Mont. / Scott Niedermayer, NJer.	3.00
☐	Chris Chelios, Chic. / Teppo Numminen, Phoe.	3.00
☐	Brian Leetch, NYRa. / Robert Svehla, Flor.	3.00
☐	Nicklas Lidström, Detr. / Mathieu Schneider, Toro.	3.00
☐	Al MacInnis, SLou. / Alexei Zhitnik, Buff.	3.00
☐	Vladimir Malakhov, Mont. / Darryl Sydor, Dall.	3.00

POST / HOME TEAM FAVOURITES

One of 22 different cards was found in Post cereal boxes.

Complete Set (22 cards): 45.00

	Player	HTF
☐	1 Wayne Gretzky, NYRa.	12.00
☐	2 Martin Brodeur (G), NJer.	4.50
☐	3 Joe Nieuwendyk, Dall.	1.00
☐	4 Rick Tocchet, Phoe.	1.00
☐	5 Theoren Fleury, Calg.	1.50
☐	6 Adam Oates, Wash.	1.00
☐	7 Mark Recchi, Mont.	1.00
☐	8 Eric Lindros, Phil.	3.00
☐	9 Steve Yzerman, Detr.	7.00
☐	10 Wade Redden, Otta.	1.00
☐	11 Glen Murray, LosA.	1.00
☐	12 Mike Johnson, Toro.	1.00
☐	13 Kelly Buchberger, Edmo.	1.00
☐	14 Joe Sakic, Colo.	4.50
☐	15 Mark Messier, Vanc.	3.00
☐	16 Keith Primeau, Caro.	1.00
☐	17 Mike Vernon (G), SanJ.	1.00
☐	18 Chris Pronger, SLou.	1.50
☐	19 Michael Peca, Buff.	1.00
☐	20 Dave Gagner, Flor.	1.00
☐	21 Rob Zamuner, Tamp.	1.00
☐	22 Chris Chelios, Chic.	1.50

1998 - 99 MCDONALD'S

Complete Set (30 cards): 25.00

	Player	McD
☐	McD1 Wayne Gretzky, NYRa.	5.00
☐	McD2 Theoren Fleury, Calg.	.50
☐	McD3 Joe Sakic, Colo.	2.00
☐	McD4 Saku Koivu, Mont.	1.00
☐	McD5 Brendan Shanahan, Detr.	1.00
☐	McD6 Steve Yzerman, Detr.	3.00
☐	McD7 Peter Forsberg, Colo.	1.50
☐	McD8 Paul Kariya, Anah.	1.50
☐	McD9 Alexei Yashin, Otta.	.50
☐	McD10 Eric Lindros, Phil.	1.00
☐	McD11 Jaromir Jagr, Pitt.	1.00
☐	McD12 Mats Sundin, Toro.	1.00
☐	McD13 Sergei Samsonov, Bost.	.50
☐	McD14 Pavel Bure, Vanc.	1.00
☐	McD15 Patrick Roy (G), Colo.	3.50
☐	McD16 Dominik Hasek (G), Buff.	1.00
☐	McD17 Martin Brodeur (G), NJer.	2.00
☐	McD18 Curtis Joseph (G), Toro.	1.00
☐	McD19 Jocelyn Thibault, Mont.	.50
☐	McD20 Chris Osgood (G), Detr.	.50
☐	McD21 Ed Belfour (G), Dall.	1.00
☐	McD22 Mattias Öhlund, Vanc.	.35
☐	McD23 Marian Hossa, Otta.	1.00
☐	McD24 Brendan Morrison, NJer.	.35
☐	McD25 Jason Botterill, Dall.	.35
☐	McD26 Cameron Mann, Bost.	.35
☐	McD27 Daniel Brière, Phoe.	.50
☐	McD28 Terry Ryan, Mont.	.35
☐	Checklist	.35
☐	Insert Checklist	.35

GAME JERSEY

	Insert (#/199)	GJ
☐	Wayne Gretzky, Edmo.	550.00

GRAND MOMENTS

Insert Set (9 cards): 65.00

	Player	McD
☐	M1 Wayne Gretzky, Edmo. [10/14/1979]	10.00
☐	M2 Wayne Gretzky, Edmo. [02/24/1982]	10.00
☐	M3 Wayne Gretzky, Edmo. [w/ Cup; 05/19/1984]	10.00
☐	M4 Wayne Gretzky, Edmo. [w/ Cup; 05/30/985]	10.00
☐	M5 Wayne Gretzky, Edmo. [w/ Cup; 05/31/1987]	10.00
☐	M6 Wayne Gretzky, Edmo. [03/01/1988]	10.00
☐	M7 Wayne Gretzky, LosA. [10/15/1989]	10.00
☐	M8 Wayne Gretzky, LosA. [03/23/1994]	10.00
☐	M9 Wayne Gretzky, NYRa. [10/26/1997]	10.00
	Player	**5x7**
☐	Wayne Gretzky 5x7	25.00

1998 - 99 MCDONALD'S

Insert Set (13 cards): 10.00

	Player	McD
☐	T1 Walter Gretzky, [w/ Wayne Gretzky]	2.00
☐	T2 Gordie Howe, New England [w/ Gretzky]	2.00
☐	T3 Marty McSorley, Edmo. [w/ Gretzky]	1.00
☐	T4 Brian Leetch, NYRa. [w/ Gretzky]	1.00
☐	T5 Brett Hull, SLou. [w/ Gretzky]	1.50
☐	T6 Esa Tikkanen, Edmo. [w/ Gretzky]	1.00
☐	T7 Grant Fuhr (G), Edmo. [w/ Gretzky]	1.00
☐	T8 Mike Richter, NYRa. [w/ Gretzky]	1.00
☐	T9 Jari Kurri, Edmo. [w/ Gretzky]	1.50
☐	T10 Paul Coffey, Edmo. [w/ Gretzky]	1.00
☐	T11 Rob Blake, LosA. [w/ Gretzky]	1.00
☐	T12 Mario Lemieux, Cdn. [w/ Gretzky]	2.00
☐	T13 Luc Robitaille, LosA. [w/ Gretzky]	1.50

1998 - 99 MIR

NHL stars sometimes sell at a premium (usually $1-2).

Complete Set (167 cards): 40.00
Common Player: .30

	Player	Card
☐	1 Sergei Gomolyako, Magnitogorsk	.30
☐	2 Sergei Zemchenok, Magnitogorsk	.30
☐	3 Oleg Mikulchik, Magnitogorsk	.30
☐	4 Evgeni Koreshkov, Magnitogorsk	.30
☐	5 Andrei Razin, Magnitogorsk	.30
☐	6 Ravil Gusmanov, Magnitogorsk	.50
☐	7 Dmitri Popov, Magnitogorsk	.30
☐	8 Valeri Karpov, Magnitogorsk	.50
☐	9 Andrei Sokolov, Magnitogorsk	.30
☐	10 Mikhail Borodulin, Magnitogorsk	.30
☐	11 Konstantin Shafranov, Magnitogorsk	.30
☐	12 Vladimir Antipin, Magnitogorsk	.30
☐	13 Igor Zemlyanoi, Magnitogorsk	.30
☐	14 Sergei Tertyshny, Magnitogorsk	.30
☐	15 Vadim Glovatski, Magnitogorsk	.30
☐	16 Alexander Goltz, Magnitogorsk	.30
☐	17 Alexander Koreshkov, Magnitogorsk	.30
☐	18 Boris Tortunov, Magnitogorsk	.30
☐	19 Valeri Nikulin, Magnitogorsk	.30
☐	20 Andrei Sapoznikov, Magnitogorsk	.30
☐	21 Dmitri Maksimov, Magnitogorsk	.30
☐	22 Dmitri Mylnikov, Krylja Sovetov Moscow	.30
☐	23 Maxim Sushinsky, Avangard	.50
☐	24 Yuri Panov, Avangard	.30
☐	25 Alexander Terekhov, Krylja Sovetov Moscow	.30
☐	26 Vladimir Zorkin, Krylja Sovetov Moscow	.30
☐	27 Eduard Gorbachev, Krylja Sovetov Moscow	.30
☐	28 Leonid Kanarekin, Krylja Sovetov Moscow	.30
☐	29 Alexander Savchenkov, Krylja Sovetov Moscow	.30
☐	30 Maxim Chukanov, Krylja Sovetov Moscow	.30
☐	31 Evgeni Fedorov, Krylja Sovetov Moscow	.30
☐	32 Yaroslav Lyuzenkov, Krylja Sovetov Moscow	.30
☐	33 Oleg Leontiev, Magnitogorsk	.30
☐	34 Sergei Osipov, Magnitogorsk	.30
☐	35 Andrei Kudinov, Magnitogorsk	.30
☐	36 Dmitri Krasotkin, Torpedo Y	.30
☐	37 Ravil Yakubov, Avangard	.30
☐	38 Dmitri Zatonski, Avangard	.30
☐	39 Konstantin Maslyukov, Avangard	.30
☐	40 Andrei Subbotin, Avangard	.30
☐	41 Pavel Kamentsev, Avangard	.30
☐	42 Evgeny Tarasov, Avangard	.30
☐	43 Oleg Kryazhev, Avangard	.30
☐	44 Igor Nikitin, Avangard	.30
☐	45 Denis Arkhipov, AkBars	3.00
☐	46 Albert Loginov, Avangard	.30
☐	47 Andrei Samokhvalov, Avangard	.30
☐	48 Igor Dorofeyev, Avangard	.30
☐	49 Sergei Bautin, AkBars	.50
☐	50 Evgeni Varlamov, AkBars	.30
☐	51 Sergei Korobkin, Avangard	.30
☐	52 Rafik Yakubov, AkBars	.30
☐	53 Alexei Chupin, AkBars	.30
☐	54 Dmitri Ryabikin, Avangard	.30
☐	55 Alexei Kudashov, Akbars	.50
☐	56 Alexander Trofimov, AkBars	.30
☐	57 Igor Andryushenko, Amur	.30
☐	58 Igor Gorbenko, Amur	.30
☐	59 Dmitri Gorenko, Amur	.30
☐	60 Alexander Kazakov, Amur	.30
☐	61 Evgeni Kuveko, Amur	.30
☐	62 Igor Nikolaev, Amur	.30
☐	63 Mikhail Pereyaslov, Amur	.30
☐	64 Alexander Filippov, Amur	.30
☐	65 Igor Mikhailov, CSKA Moscow	.30
☐	66 Roman Shipulin, Amur	.30
☐	67 Dmitri Shpakovski, Amur	.30
☐	68 Dmitri Shulakov, Amur	.30
☐	69 Konstantin Golokhvastov, Avangard	.30
☐	70 Yuri Fimin, Amur	.30
☐	71 Sergei Yasakov, Amur	.30
☐	72 Oleg Filimonov, Amur	.30
☐	73 Anatoli Ustyugov, Amur	.30
☐	74 Andrei Skabelka, AkBars	.30
☐	75 Sergei Zolotov, AkBars	.30

76 Dmitri Bezrukov, AkBars	.30
77 Dmitri Vanyasov, Neftikhimik	.30
78 Evgeni Zakharov, Neftikhimik	.30
79 Arat Kadyekin, Neftikhimik	.30
80 Evgeni Mlinchenko, Neftikhimik	.30
81 Leonid Labzov, Neftikhimik	.30
82 Andrei Mazhugin, Neftikhimik	.30
83 Vladislav Makarov, Neftikhimik	.30
84 Remir Khaidarov, Neftikhimik	.30
85 Pavel Agarkov, Novokuznetsk	.30
86 Igor Belyavski, Novokuznetsk	.30
87 Dmitri Dubrovski, Novokuznetsk	.30
88 Vyacheslav Zavalnyuk, Novokuznetsk	.30
89 Yuri Zuev, Novokuznetsk	.30
90 Andrei Evstafiev, Novokuznetsk	.30
91 Vadim Epanchinsev, Novokuznetsk	.30
92 Igor Zelenchev, Novokuznetsk	.30
93 Dmitri Klevakin, Novokuznetsk	.30
94 Alexei Koledaev, Novokuznetsk	.30
95 Nikolai Kurochkin, Novokuznetsk	.30
96 Boris Kuzmin, Novokuznetsk	.30
97 Roman Kukhtinov, Novokuznetsk	.30
98 Sergei Moskalev, Novokuznetsk	.30
99 Evgeni Pupkov, Novokuznetsk	.30
100 Alexei Tkachuk, Novokuznetsk	.30
101 Rinat Khasanov, Novokuznetsk	.30
102 Sergei Shalamai, Novokuznetsk	.30
103 Vadim Tarasov (G), Novokuznetsk	4.00
104 Vladislav Morozov, Novokuznetsk	.30
105 Almaz Garifullin, Akbars	.30
106 Ilnur Gizatullin, AkBars	.30
107 Alexander Zavyalov, AkBars	.30
108 Oleg Vevcherenko, Avangard	.30
109 Alexander Savitski, AkBars	.30
110 Mikhail Sarmatin, AkBars	.30
111 Igor Stepanov, AkBars	.30
112 Konstantin Butsenko, Neftikhimik	.30
113 Alexei Murzin, Neftikhimik	.30
114 Andrei Nikolaev, Neftikhimik	.30
115 Dmitri Plekhanov, Neftikhimik	.30
116 Roman Salnikov, Neftikhimik	.30
117 Vyacheslav Timchenko, Neftikhimik	.30
118 Anitoli Stepanishev, Neftikhimik	.30
119 Roman Baranov, Akbars	.30
120 Artem Anisimov, Akbars	.30
121 Yuri Guniko, Akbars	.30
122 Eduard Kudermetov, Akbars	.30
123 Dmitri Balmin, AkBars	.30
124 Igor Dyakiv, Avangard	.30
125 Ramil Saifullin, Avangard	.30
126 Alexander Vyukhin, Avangard	.30
127 Oleg Leontiev, Magnitogorsk	.30
128 Evgeni Koreshkov, Magnitogorsk	.30
129 Sergei Gomolyako, Magnitogorsk	.30
130 Oleg Mikylchuk, Magnitogorsk	.50
131 Andrei Petrakov, Magnitogorsk	.30
132 Alexei Stepanov, Magnitogorsk	.30
133 Dmitri Verzhinin, CSKA Moscow	.30
134 Artem Ostroushko, CSKA Moscow	.30
135 Sergei Berdnikov, Severstal	.30
136 Konstantin Koltsov, Severstal	.30
137 Vladimir Tarasov, Severstal	.30
138 Sergei Shimkovski, Severstal	.30
139 Oleg Pchelyakov, Severstal	.30
140 Oleg Burlutski, Severstal	.30
141 Oleg Bratash, Krylja Sovetov Moscow	.30
142 Sergei Voronov, Dynamo Moscow	.30
143 Ildar Mukhometov, Dynamo Moscow	.30
144 Alexei Egorov, Dynamo Moscow	.30
145 Vladimir Kopat, Severstal	.30
146 Vladimir Kochin, Severstal	.30
147 Alexei Putilin, Severstal	.30
148 Andrei Rasolko, Severstal	.30
149 Vadim Molotilov, Severstal	.30
150 Dmitri Nazarov, Severstal	.30
151 Igor Vyazmikin, Severstal	.30
152 Alexei Kalyukhny, Dynamo Moscow	.30
153 Denis Kartsev, Dynamo Moscow	.30
154 Alexander Kuvaldin, Dynamo Moscow	.30
155 Alexei Troshinski, Dynamo Moscow	.30
156 Alexander Kharitonov, Dynamo Moscow	1.00
157 Valeri Cherny, Dynamo Moscow	.30
158 Yuri Dobrishkin, Krylja Sovetov Moscow	.30
159 Evgeni Pavlov, Severstal	.30
160 Nikolai Antropov, Dynamo Moscow	6.00
161 Alexander Zhurik, Dynamo Moscow	.30
162 Valeri Belousov, Magnitogorsk	.30
163 Artem Chubarov, Dynamo Moscow	2.00
164 Boris Zelenko, Dynamo Moscow	.30
165 Dmitri Frolov, Avangard	.30
166 Vladimir Kirik, Avangard	.30
167 Alexei Danilov, Severstal	.30

1998 - 99 NHC

We do not have a full checklist for this Danish set.

1998 - 1999 NHL-NHLPA / POWER PLAY

These cards were included as magazine inserts distributed exclusivesly at games around the NHL. We do not know the players for a few cards on our checklist.

Player / Series	MT
ANA1 Paul Kariya, Anah.	7.00
ANA2 Steve Rucchin, Anah.	1.00
ANA3 Guy Hebert (G), Anah.	1.00
ANA4 Teemu Selänne, Anah.	4.00
BOS1	1.00
BOS2	1.00
BOS3 Sergei Samsonov, Bost.	3.00
BOS4 Joe Thornton, Bost.	6.00
BUF1 Miroslav Satan, Buff.	1.50
BUF2 Brian Holzinger, Buff.	1.00
BUF3 Dominik Hasek (G), Buff.	5.00
BUF4 Michael Peca, Buff.	2.00
CAL1 Valeri Bure, Calg.	1.50
CAL2 Theoren Fleury, Calg.	4.50
CAL3 Jarome Iginla, Calg.	4.00
CAL4 Theoren Fleury, Calg.	1.00
CAR Sami Kapanen, Caro.	2.00
CAR Keith Primeau, Caro.	3.00
CAR Kevin Dineen, Caro.	1.00
CAR Gary Roberts, Caro.	3.00
CHI2 Bob Probert, Chic.	1.50
CHI1 Chris Chelios, Chic.	3.00
CHI3 Tony Amonte, Chic.	3.00
CHI4 Doug Gilmour, Chic.	3.00
COL1 Patrick Roy (G), Colo.	15.00
COL2 Adam Deadmarsh, Colo.	1.50
COL3 Peter Forsberg, Colo.	7.00
COL4 Joe Sakic, Colo.	8.00
DAL1 Ed Belfour (G), Dall.	5.00
DAL2 Joe Nieuwendyk, Dall.	2.00
DAL3 Mike Modano, Dall.	5.00
DAL4 Brett Hull, Dall.	5.00
DET1 Steve Yzerman, Detr.	12.00
DET2 Sergei Fedorov, Detr.	5.00
DET3 Nicklas Lidström, Detr.	3.00
DET4 Brendan Shanahan, Detr.	5.00
EDM1 Kelly Buchberger, Edmo.	1.00
EDM2 Doug Weight, Edmo.	3.00
EDM3 Bill Guerin, Edmo.	2.00
EDM4 Mike Grier, Edmo.	1.00
FLA1 Rob Niedermayer, Flor.	1.00
FLA2 Viktor Kozlov, Flor.	1.50
FLA3 Pavel Bure, Flor.	4.00
FLA4 Scott Mellanby, Flor.	1.00
LAK1 Rob Blake, LosA.	3.00
LAK2 Jozef Stümpel, LosA.	1.00
LAK3 Luc Robitaille, LosA.	4.00
LAK4 Yanic Perreault, LosA.	1.50
MON1 Vincent Damphousse, Mont.	3.00
MON2 Mark Recchi, Mont.	2.00
MON3 Saku Koivu, Mont.	4.00
MON4 Martin Rucinsky, Mont.	1.00
NSH1	1.00
NSH2	1.00
NSH3 Mike Dunham, Nash.	2.00
NSH4 Sergei Krivokrasov, Nash.	1.00
NJD1 Scott Niedermayer, NJer.	1.50
NJD2 Scott Stevens, NJer.	2.00
NJD3 Martin Brodeur, NJer.	8.00
NJD4 Bobby Holik, NJer.	1.50
NYI1 Trevor Linden, NYIs.	2.00
NYI2 Bryan Smolinski, NYIs.	1.00
NYI3 Zigmund Palffy, NYIs.	3.00
NYI4 Mike Watt, NYIs.	1.00
NYR1 Wayne Gretzky, NYRa.	20.00
NYR2 Todd Harvey, NYRa.	1.00
NYR3 Brian Leetch, NYRa.	3.00
NYR4 Mike Richter (G), NYRa.	2.00
OTT1 Alexei Yashin, Otta.	3.00
OTT2 Marian Hossa, Otta.	5.00
OTT3 Daniel Alfredsson, Otta.	3.00
OTT4 Wade Redden, Otta.	1.50
PHI1 Eric Lindros, Phil.	5.00
PHI2 John Vanbiesbrouck, Phil.	2.00
PHI3 Rod Brind'Amour, Phil.	1.50
PHI4 John LeClair, Phil.	4.00
PHX1 Jeremy Roenick, Phoe.	4.00
PHX2 Rick Tocchet, Phoe.	1.50
PHX3 Keith Tkachuk, Phoe.	3.00
PHX4 Nikolai Khabibulin, Phoe.	2.00
PIT1 Martin Straka, Pitt.	1.50
PIT2 Stu Barnes, Pitt.	1.00
PIT3 Tom Barrasso (G), Pitt.	2.00
PIT4 Jaromir Jagr, Pitt.	5.00
SJS1 Owen Nolan, SanJ.	3.00
SJS2 Marco Sturm, SanJ.	1.00
SJS3 Jeff Friesen, SanJ.	1.50
SJS4 Patrick Marleau, SanJ.	2.00
STL1 Pavol Demitra, SLou.	2.00
STL2 Chris Pronger, SLou.	3.00
STL3 Grant Fuhr, SLou.	3.00
STL4 Al MacInnis, SLou.	2.00
TBL1 Rob Zamuner, Tamp.	1.00
TBL2 Darcy Tucker, Tamp.	1.00
TBL3 Vincent Lecavalier, Tamp.	5.00
TBL4 Wendel Clark, Tamp.	4.00
TOR1 Curtis Joseph (G), Toro.	5.00
TOR2 Tie Domi, Toro.	1.50
TOR3 Mike Johnson, Toro.	1.00
TOR4 Mats Sundin, Toro.	5.00
VAN1 Mattias Öhlund, Vanc.	1.50
VAN2 Alexander Mogilny, Vanc.	2.00
VAN3 Mark Messier, Vanc.	5.00
VAN4 Markus Näslund, Vanc.	5.00
WAS1 Olaf Kölzig, Wash.	4.50
WAS2 Adam Oates, Wash.	3.00
WAS3 Peter Bondra, Wash.	4.50
WAS4 Dale Hunter, Wash.	2.00

1998 - 99 O-PEE-CHEE CHROME

Please see listing under 1998 - 99 Topps & O-Pee-Chee Chrome

1998 - 99 OFS

NHL stars sometimes sell at a premium (usually $1-2).

Complete Set (498 cards): 100.00
Common Player: .30

Player	Card
1 Ondrej Weissmann, Chemopetrol Litvinov	.30
2 Zdenek Orct, Chemopetrol Litvinov	.30
3 Angel Nikolov, Chemopetrol Litvinov	.30
4 Radek Mrazek, Chemopetrol Litvinov	.30
5 Martin Stepanek, Chemopetrol Litvinov	.30
6 Sergei Butko, Chemopetrol Litvinov	.30
7 Oleg Romanov, Chemopetrol Litvinov	.30
8 Marian Menhart, Chemopetrol Litvinov	.30
9 Vladimir Petrovka, Chemopetrol Litvinov	.30
10 Ivo Prorok, Chemopetrol Litvinov	.30
11 Jindrich Kotrla, Chemopetrol Litvinov	.30
12 Josef Straka, Chemopetrol Litvinov	.30
13 Vadim Bekbulatov, Chemopetrol Litvinov	.30
14 Daniel Branda, Chemopetrol Litvinov	.30
15 Vojtech Kubincak, Chemopetrol Litvinov	.30
16 Mikhail Travnicek, Chemopetrol Litvinov	.30
17 Zdenek Venera, ZPS Zlin	.30
18 Jaroslav Kames, ZPS Zlin	.30
19 Pavel Augusta, ZPS Zlin	.30
20 Patrik Hucko, ZPS Zlin	.30
21 Martin Hamrlik, ZPS Zlin	.30
22 Jiri Marusak, ZPS Zlin	.30
23 Pavel Mojzis, ZPS Zlin	.30
24 Tomas Zizka, ZPS Zlin	.30
25 Roman Meluzin, ZPS Zlin	.30
26 Michal Tomek, ZPS Zlin	.30
27 Josef Straub, ZPS Zlin	.30
28 Tomas Nemcicky, ZPS Zlin	.30
29 Petr Cajanek, ZPS Zlin	.30
30 Miroslav Okal, ZPS Zlin	.30
31 Petr Leska, ZPS Zlin	.30
32 Petr Vala, ZPS Zlin	.30
33 Radim Rulik, Interconex Plzen	.30
34 Dusan Salficky, Interconex Plzen	.30
35 Josef Reznicek, Interconex Plzen	.30
36 Robert Jindrich, Interconex Plzen	.30
37 Jiri Hanzlik, Interconex Plzen	.30
38 Ondrej Kriz, Interconex Plzen	.30
39 Vladimir Zajic, Interconex Plzen	.30
40 Pavel Geffert, Interconex Plzen	.30
41 David Pospisil, Interconex Plzen	.30
42 Milan Antos, Interconex Plzen	.30
43 Petr Korinek, Interconex Plzen	.30
44 Michal Straka, Interconex Plzen	.30
45 Milan Volak, Interconex Plzen	.30
46 Pavel Vostrak, Interconex Plzen	.30
47 Milan Navratil, Interconex Plzen	.30
48 Martin Spanhel, Interconex Plzen	.50
49 Josef Augusta, Dukla Jihlava	.30
50 Jaroslav Suchan, Dukla Jihlava	.30
51 Martin Tupa, Dukla Jihlava	.30
52 Marian Morava, Dukla Jihlava	.30
53 Michal Divisek, Dukla Jihlava	.30
54 Petr** Svoboda, Dukla Jihlava	2.00
55 Zdenek Fuksa, Dukla Jihlava	.30
56 Petr Vlk, Dukla Jihlava	.30
57 Jiri Cihlar, Dukla Jihlava	.30
58 Leos Pipa, Dukla Jihlava	.30
59 Marek Melenovsky, Dukla Jihlava	.30
60 Miroslav Bruna, Dukla Jihlava	.30
61 Petr Mokrejs, Dukla Jihlava	.30
62 Vaclav Adamec, Dukla Jihlava	.30
63 Richard Cachnin, Dukla Jihlava	.30
64 Jan Kloboucek, Dukla Jihlava	.30
65 Stanislav Nevesely, Opava	.30
66 Radek Masny, Opava	.30
67 Jan Krajicek, Opava	.30
68 Ales Tomasek, Opava	.30
69 Vladimir Holik, Opava	.30
70 Tomas Jelinek, Opava	.30
71 Pavel Nohel, Opava	.30
72 Jaroslav Hub, Opava	.30
73 Robert Kucera, Opava	.30
74 Andrei Galkin, Opava	.30
75 Pavel Selingr, Opava	.30
76 Pavel Bacho, Opava	.30
77 Jiri Zurek, Opava	.30
78 Pavel Zdrahal, Opava	.30
79 Bogdan Savenko, Opava	.30
80 Zdenek Sedlak, Opava	.30
81 Karel Trachta, Karlovy Vary	.30
82 Rudolf Pejchar, Karlovy Vary	.30
83 Petr Pavlas, Karlovy Vary	.30
84 Pavel Blaha, Karlovy Vary	.30
85 Martin Richter, Karlovy Vary	.30
86 Jan Snopek, Karlovy Vary	.30
87 Martin Filip, Karlovy Vary	.30
88 Jaromir Kverka, Karlovy Vary	.30
89 Pavel Janku, Karlovy Vary	.30
90 Martin Rousek, Karlovy Vary	.30
91 Ondrej Steiner, Karlovy Vary	.30
92 Pavel Metlicka, Karlovy Vary	.30
93 Streit Martin, Karlovy Vary	.30
94 Ladislav Prokupek, Karlovy Vary	.30
95 Richard Richter, Karlovy Vary	.30
96 Martin Maskarinec, Karlovy Vary	.30
97 Zdislav Tabara, Dadak Vsetin	.30
98 Miroslav Venkrbec, Dadak Vsetin	.30
99 Roman Cechmanek, Dadak Vsetin	4.00
100 Jiri Veber, Dadak Vsetin	.30
101 Radim Tesarik, Dadak Vsetin	.30
102 Jan Srdinko, Dadak Vsetin	.30
103 Alexei Jaskin, Dadak Vsetin	.30
104 Pavel Zubicek, Dadak Vsetin	.30
105 Jiri Dopita, Dadak Vsetin	.50
106 Martin Prochazka, Dadak Vsetin	.50
107 Pavel Patera, Dadak Vsetin	.50
108 Radek Belohlav, Dadak Vsetin	.30
109 Ondrej Kratena, Dadak Vsetin	.30
110 Michal Bros, Dadak Vsetin	.30
111 Jan Tomajko, Dadak Vsetin	.30
112 Roman Stantien, Dadak Vsetin	.30
113 Ladislav Svozil, Vitkovice	.30
114 Jiri Trvaj, Vitkovice	.30
115 René Sevecek, Vitkovice	.30
116 Vitezslav Skuta, Vitkovice	.30
117 Pavel Kowalczyk, Vitkovice	.30
118 Radek Philipp, Vitkovice	.30
119 Vladimir (Jr.) Vujtek, Vitkovice	.50
120 Alexander Cerbajev, Vitkovice	.30
121 Libor Pavlis, Vitkovice	.30
122 Libor Polasek, Vitkovice	.30
123 Martin Kotasek, Vitkovice	.30
124 Zdenek Pavelek, Vitkovice	.30
125 Martin Lamich, Vitkovice	.30
126 Igor Varickij, Vitkovice	.30
127 Petr Hubacek, Vitkovice	.30
128 Zbynek Irgl, Vitkovice	.30
129 Julius Supler, Sparta Praha	.30
130 Milan Hnilicka (G), Sparta Praha	2.00
131 Frantisek Ptacek, Sparta Praha	.30
132 Ladislav Benysek, Sparta Praha	.30
133 Richard Adam, Sparta Praha	.30
134 Frantisek Kucera, Sparta Praha	.50
135 Pavel Srek, Sparta Praha	.30
136 Jiri Zelenka, Sparta Praha	.30

☐ 137 David Vyborny, Sparta Praha .30
☐ 138 Patrik Martinec, Sparta Praha .30
☐ 139 Jaroslav Bednar, Sparta Praha .50
☐ 140 Jan Hlavac, Sparta Praha 1.00
☐ 141 Miroslav Hlinka, Sparta Praha .30
☐ 142 Jaroslav Hlinka, Sparta Praha .30
☐ 143 Martin Chabada, Sparta Praha .30
☐ 144 Vaclav Novak, Sparta Praha .30
☐ 145 Milan Chalupa, Pardubice .30
☐ 146 Adam Svoboda, Pardubice .30
☐ 147 Jiri Malinsky, Pardubice .30
☐ 148 Ales Pisa, Pardubice 1.00
☐ 149 Tomas Pacal, Pardubice .30
☐ 150 Pavel Kriz, Pardubice .30
☐ 151 Petr Jancarik, Pardubice .30
☐ 152 Petr Mudroch, Pardubice .30
☐ 153 Tomas Blazek, Pardubice .30
☐ 154 Jiri Jantovsky, Pardubice .30
☐ 155 Stanislav Prochazka, Pardubice .30
☐ 156 Tomas Martinec, Pardubice .30
☐ 157 Pavel Kabrt, Pardubice .30
☐ 158 Jaroslav Kudrna, Pardubice .30
☐ 159 Karel Plasek, Pardubice .30
☐ 160 Michal Mikeska, Pardubice .30
☐ 161 Zdenek Sindler, Kladno .30
☐ 162 Martin Cinibulk, Kladno .30
☐ 163 Marek Zidlicky, Kladno .30
☐ 164 Jan Dlouhy, Kladno .30
☐ 165 Pavel Taborsky, Kladno .30
☐ 166 Michal Madl, Kladno .30
☐ 167 Jiri Jelinek, Kladno .30
☐ 168 Tomas Mikolasek, Kladno .30
☐ 169 Ladislav Svoboda, Kladno .30
☐ 170 Jiri Burger, Kladno .30
☐ 171 Petr Tenkrat, Kladno .50
☐ 172 Tomas Kupka, Kladno .30
☐ 173 Marek Vorel, Kladno .30
☐ 174 Michal Kanka, Kladno .30
☐ 175 Tomas Horna, Kladno .30
☐ 176 Zdenek Mraz, Kladno .30
☐ 177 Kamil Konecny, Trinec .30
☐ 178 Radovan Biegl, Trinec .30
☐ 179 Stanislav Pavelec, Trinec .30
☐ 180 Jiri Kuntos, Trinec .30
☐ 181 Petr Gregorek, Trinec .30
☐ 182 Miroslav Cihal, Trinec .30
☐ 183 Robert Prochazka, Trinec .30
☐ 184 Viktor Ujcik, Trinec .30
☐ 185 Ladislav Lubina, Trinec .30
☐ 186 Jan Peterek, Trinec .30
☐ 187 Petr Folta, Trinec .30
☐ 188 Ales Zima, Trinec .30
☐ 189 Roman Kadera, Trinec .30
☐ 190 Vaclav Pletka, Trinec .30
☐ 191 Patrik Moskal, Trinec .30
☐ 192 David Appel, Trinec .30
☐ 193 Jaroslav Parizek, Ceske Budejovice .30
☐ 194 Michal Marik, Ceske Budejovice .30
☐ 195 Rudolf Suchanek, Ceske Budejovice .30
☐ 196 Milan Nedoma, Ceske Budejovice .30
☐ 197 Kamil Toupal, Ceske Budejovice .30
☐ 198 Roman Cech, Ceske Budejovice .30
☐ 199 Radek Martinek, Ceske Budejovice .50
☐ 200 Vladimir Sicak, Ceske Budejovice .30
☐ 201 Radek Toupal, Ceske Budejovice .30
☐ 202 Filip Turek, Ceske Budejovice .30
☐ 203 Petr Sailer, Ceske Budejovice .30
☐ 204 Martin Strba, Ceske Budejovice .30
☐ 205 Miroslav Barus, Ceske Budejovice .30
☐ 206 Vaclav Kral, Ceske Budejovice .30
☐ 207 Milan Filipi, Ceske Budejovice .30
☐ 208 Peter Bartos, Ceske Budejovice .50
☐ 209 Richard Farda, Slavia Praha .30
☐ 210 Roman Malek, Slavia Praha .30
☐ 211 Robert Kostka, Slavia Praha .30
☐ 212 Pavel Kolarik, Slavia Praha .50
☐ 213 Martin Bakula, Slavia Praha .30
☐ 214 Petr Kadlec, Slavia Praha .30
☐ 215 Jan Novak, Slavia Praha .30
☐ 216 Vladimir Ruzicka, Slavia Praha 1.00
☐ 217 Jiri Dolezal, Slavia Praha .30
☐ 218 Tomas Kucharcik, Slavia Praha .30
☐ 219 Michal Sup, Slavia Praha .30
☐ 220 Vladimir Machulda, Slavia Praha .30
☐ 221 Petr Mika, Slavia Praha .50
☐ 222 Tomas Divisek, Slavia Praha 1.00
☐ 223 Jan Kopecky, Slavia Praha .30
☐ 224 Jiri Polak, Slavia Praha .30
☐ 225 Ivan Hlinka, Czech Republic Nationals 1.50
☐ 226 Slavomir Lener, Czech Republic Nationals .75
☐ 227 Dominik Hasek (G), Czech Republic Nationals 10.00
☐ 228 Roman Cechmanek, Czech Republic Nationals 4.00
☐ 229 Milan Hnilicka (G), Czech Republic Nationals 1.50
☐ 230 Richard Smehlik, Czech Republic Nationals .75
☐ 231 Petr* Svoboda, Czech Republic Nationals 1.50
☐ 232 Roman Hamrlik, Czech Republic Nationals 1.50
☐ 233 Jiri Slégr, Czech Republic Nationals 1.00
☐ 234 Frantisek Kucera, Czech Republic Nationals .75
☐ 235 Libor Prochazka, Czech Republic Nationals .75
☐ 236 Jaroslav Spacek, Czech Republic Nationals .75
☐ 237 Robert Reichel, Czech Republic Nationals 2.00
☐ 238 Robert Lang, Czech Republic Nationals 1.50
☐ 239 Pavel Patera, Czech Republic Nationals .75
☐ 240 Martin Prochazka, Czech Republic Nationals 1.00
☐ 241 Jiri Dopita, Czech Republic Nationals 1.00
☐ 242 Josef Beranek, Czech Republic Nationals 1.00
☐ 243 David Moravec, Czech Republic Nationals .75
☐ 244 Jan Caloun, Czech Republic Nationals .75
☐ 245 Martin Rucinsky, Czech Republic Nationals 1.50
☐ 246 Martin Straka, Czech Republic Nationals 2.00
☐ 247 Jaromir Jagr, Czech Republic Nationals 10.00
☐ 248 Vladimir Ruzicka, Czech Republic Nationals 1.50
☐ 249 Milan Hejduk, Czech Republic Nationals 20.00
☐ 250 Ladislav Slizek, Slavia Praha .30
☐ 251 Ladislav Blazek, Slavia Praha .30
☐ 252 Andrei Jakovenko, Slavia Praha .30
☐ 253 Jan Hejda, Slavia Praha .30
☐ 254 Marian Kacir, Slavia Praha .30
☐ 255 Robin Bacul, Slavia Praha .30
☐ 256 Jan Sochor, Slavia Praha .30
☐ 257 Petr Hrbek, Slavia Praha .30
☐ 258 Jan Sebor, Slavia Praha .30
☐ 259 Michal Slavik, Slavia Praha .30
☐ 260 Vladimir Jerabek, Chemopetrol Litvinov .30
☐ 261 Marek Pinc, Chemopetrol Litvinov .30
☐ 262 Vladimir Gyna, Chemopetrol Litvinov .30
☐ 263 Martin Znojemsky, Chemopetrol Litvinov .30
☐ 264 Robert Kysela, Chemopetrol Litvinov .30
☐ 265 Petr Hrbek, Chemopetrol Litvinov .30
☐ 266 Kamil Piros, Chemopetrol Litvinov 2.00
☐ 267 Viktor Hubl, Chemopetrol Litvinov .30
☐ 268 Marian Kacir, Chemopetrol Litvinov .30
☐ 269 Miloslav Horava, Chemopetrol Litvinov .50
☐ 270 Michal Pinc, Chemopetrol Litvinov .30
☐ 271 Zdenek Skorepa, Chemopetrol Litvinov .30
☐ 272 Vaclav Sykora, Chemopetrol Litvinov .30
☐ 273 Antonin Stavjana, ZPS Zlin .30
☐ 274 Richard Hrazdira, ZPS Zlin .30
☐ 275 Karel Rachunek, ZPS Zlin 2.00
☐ 276 David Brezik, ZPS Zlin .30
☐ 277 Marek Zadina, ZPS Zlin .30
☐ 278 Jaroslav Balastik, ZPS Zlin .30
☐ 279 Martin Ambruz, ZPS Zlin .30
☐ 280 Ondrej Vesely, ZPS Zlin .30
☐ 281 Tomas Kapusta, ZPS Zlin .30
☐ 282 Tomas Martinak, ZPS Zlin .30
☐ 283 Ivan Rachunek, ZPS Zlin .30
☐ 284 Karel Sefcik, ZPS Zlin .30
☐ 285 Marek Sykora, Interconex Plzen .30
☐ 286 Vladimir Hudacek (G), Interconex Plzen .30
☐ 287 Ivan Vlcek, Interconex Plzen .30
☐ 288 Martin Cech, Interconex Plzen .30
☐ 289 Michal Vasicek, Interconex Plzen .30
☐ 290 Michal Jeslinek, Interconex Plzen .30
☐ 291 Vladimir Bednar, Interconex Plzen .30
☐ 292 Pavel Augusta, Interconex Plzen .30
☐ 293 Ladislav Slizek, Interconex Plzen .30
☐ 294 Karel Dvorak, Dukla Jihlava .30
☐ 295 Marek Novotny, Dukla Jihlava .30
☐ 296 Lukas Sablik, Dukla Jihlava .30
☐ 297 Daniel Zapotocny, Dukla Jihlava .30
☐ 298 Miroslav Duben, Dukla Jihlava .30
☐ 299 Ales Polcar, Dukla Jihlava .30
☐ 300 Roman Mejzlik, Dukla Jihlava .30
☐ 301 Radek Matejovsky, Dukla Jihlava .30
☐ 302 Daniel Hodek, Dukla Jihlava .30
☐ 303 Ales Padelek, Dukla Jihlava .30
☐ 304 Ivan Padelek, Dukla Jihlava .30
☐ 305 Pavel Rajnoha, Dukla Jihlava .30
☐ 306 Richard Adam, Dukla Jihlava .30
☐ 307 Vladimir Caldr, Dukla Jihlava .30
☐ 308 Jiri Dobrovolny, Dukla Jihlava .30
☐ 309 Lukas Novak, Dukla Jihlava .30
☐ 310 Ivo Novotny, Dukla Jihlava .30
☐ 311 Jan Smarda, Dukla Jihlava .30
☐ 312 Lubomir Oslizlo, Opava .30
☐ 313 Pavel Cagas, Opava .30
☐ 314 Petr Kuchyna, Opava .30
☐ 315 Drahomir Kadlec, Opava .30
☐ 316 Michael Vyhlidal, Opava .30
☐ 317 Miroslav Javin, Opava .30
☐ 318 Petr Suchanek, Opava .30
☐ 319 Vitezslav Skuta, Opava .30
☐ 320 Libor Polasek, Opava .30
☐ 321 Jiri Poukar, Opava .30
☐ 322 Michal Cech, Opava .30
☐ 323 Lukas Fiala, Opava .30
☐ 324 Milota Florian, Opava .30
☐ 325 Milan Kubis, Opava .30
☐ 326 Jiri Latal, Opava .50
☐ 327 Libor Pavlis, Opava .30
☐ 328 Ivan Puncochar, Opava .30
☐ 329 Rostislav Vlach, Opava .30
☐ 330 Tomas Zapletal, Opava .30
☐ 331 Josef Beranek, Karlovy Vary .50
☐ 332 Robert Hamrla, Karlovy Vary .30
☐ 333 Marek Cernosek, Karlovy Vary .30
☐ 334 Normunds Sejejs, Karlovy Vary .30
☐ 335 Tomas Klimt, Karlovy Vary .30
☐ 336 Radek Prochazka, Karlovy Vary .30
☐ 337 Radek Svoboda, Karlovy Vary .30
☐ 338 Michal Horak, Karlovy Vary .30
☐ 339 Jakub Kraus, Karlovy Vary .30
☐ 340 Ivo Pesat, Dadak Vsetin .30
☐ 341 Tomas Jakes, Dadak Vsetin .30
☐ 342 Michal Safarik, Dadak Vsetin .30
☐ 343 Tomas Srsen, Dadak Vsetin .30
☐ 344 Zbynek Marak, Dadak Vsetin .30
☐ 345 Tomas Demel, Dadak Vsetin .30
☐ 346 Ondrej Kavulic, Dadak Vsetin .30
☐ 347 Petr Suchy, Dadak Vsetin .30
☐ 348 Libor Zabransky, Dadak Vsetin .50
☐ 349 Vladimir (Jr.) Vujtek, Vitkovice .50
☐ 350 Martin Prusek (G), Vitkovice 4.00
☐ 351 Lukas Galvas, Vitkovice .30
☐ 352 Petr Jurecka, Vitkovice .30
☐ 353 Vadim Brezgunov, Vitkovice .30
☐ 354 Lukas Zatopek, Vitkovice .30
☐ 355 David Moravec, Vitkovice .50
☐ 356 Ludek Krayzel, Vitkovice .30
☐ 357 Ales Kratoska, Vitkovice .30
☐ 358 Ales Tomasek, Vitkovice .30
☐ 359 Milos Holan, Vitkovice .50
☐ 360 Roman Kelner, Vitkovice .30
☐ 361 Frantisek Vyborny, Sparta Praha .30
☐ 362 Petr Prikryl, Sparta Praha .30
☐ 363 Zdenek Touzimsky, Sparta Praha .30
☐ 364 Vaclav Burda, Sparta Praha .30
☐ 365 Vaclav Benak, Sparta Praha .30
☐ 366 Michal Dobron, Sparta Praha .30
☐ 367 Richard Zemlicka, Sparta Praha .30
☐ 368 Roman Horak, Sparta Praha .30
☐ 369 Michal Sivek, Sparta Praha 2.00
☐ 370 Jaroslav Kalla, Sparta Praha .30
☐ 371 Pavel Richter, Sparta Praha .30
☐ 372 Jaroslav Roubik, Sparta Praha .30
☐ 373 Michal Sykora, Sparta Praha .50
☐ 374 Milos Riha, Pardubice .30
☐ 375 Libor Barta, Pardubice .30
☐ 376 Alexander Cypljakov, Pardubice .30
☐ 377 Robert Pospisil, Pardubice .30
☐ 378 Petr Caslava, Pardubice .30
☐ 379 Martin Koudelka, Pardubice .30
☐ 380 Patrik Rozsival, Pardubice .30
☐ 381 Michal Tvrdik, Pardubice .30
☐ 382 Tomas Vak, Pardubice .30
☐ 383 Alois Hadamczik, Trinec .30
☐ 384 Vlastimil Lakosil, Trinec .30
☐ 385 L'ubomir Sekeras, Trinec .50
☐ 386 Libor Prochazka, Trinec .50
☐ 387 Robert Kantor, Trinec .30
☐ 388 Mario Cartelli, Trinec .30
☐ 389 Richard Kral, Trinec .30
☐ 390 Jozef Dano, Trinec .30
☐ 391 Branislav Janos, Trinec .30
☐ 392 Tomas Chlubna, Trinec .30
☐ 393 Martin Havlat, Trinec 30.00
☐ 394 Jaroslav Jagr, Trinec .30
☐ 395 Lubomir Bauer, Kladno .30
☐ 396 Martin Bilek, Kladno .30
☐ 397 Lubos Horcinka, Kladno .30
☐ 398 Jiri Krocak, Kladno .30
☐ 399 Martin Taborsky, Kladno .30
☐ 400 Zdenek Eichenmann, Kladno .30
☐ 401 Vaclav Eiselt, Kladno .30
☐ 402 Premysl Sedlak, Kladno .30
☐ 403 Jiri Holsan, Kladno .30
☐ 404 Jiri Kames, Kladno .30
☐ 405 Jiri Hubacek, Kladno .30
☐ 406 Stanislav Lapacek, Kladno .30
☐ 407 Lukas Poznik, Kladno .30
☐ 408 Otakar Vejvoda, Kladno .30
☐ 409 Jaroslav Liska, Ceske Budejovice .30
☐ 410 Oldrich Svoboda, Ceske Budejovice .30
☐ 411 Lukas Zib, Ceske Budejovice .30
☐ 412 Michal Klimes, Ceske Budejovice .30
☐ 413 Kamil Brabenec, Ceske Budejovice .30
☐ 414 Ales Kotalik, Ceske Budejovice 2.00
☐ 415 Jiri Broz, Ceske Budejovice .30
☐ 416 Zdenek Kutlak, Ceske Budejovice .50
☐ 417 Vaclav Nedorost, Ceske Budejovice 12.00
☐ 418 Lubos Rob, Ceske Budejovice .30
☐ 419 Martin Prusek (G), Czech Republic Nationals 4.00
☐ 420 Frantisek* Kaberle, Czech Republic Nationals .50
☐ 421 Jiri Vykoukal, Czech Republic Nationals .50
☐ 422 Jiri Veber, Czech Republic Nationals .50
☐ 423 Ladislav Benysek, Czech Republic Nationals .50
☐ 424 Martin Stepanek, Czech Republic Nationals .50
☐ 425 Jan Srdinko, Czech Republic Nationals .50
☐ 426 Radek Belohlav, Czech Republic Nationals .50
☐ 427 David Vyborny, Czech Republic Nationals .50
☐ 428 Viktor Ujcik, Czech Republic Nationals .50
☐ 429 Roman Meluzin, Czech Republic Nationals .50
☐ 430 Vladimir (Jr.) Vujtek, Czech Republic Nationals .50
☐ 431 Ondrej Kratena, Czech Republic Nationals .50
☐ 432 Michal Bros, Czech Republic Nationals .50
☐ 433 Marian Kacir, Czech Republic Nationals .50
☐ 434 Jan Hlavac, Czech Republic Nationals 1.00
☐ 435 Richard Kral, Czech Republic Nationals .50
☐ 436 Roman Kadera, Czech Republic Nationals .50
☐ 437 Ivan Hlinka, Czech Republic Nationals 1.00
☐ 438 Roman Cechmanek, Czech Republic Nationals 4.00
☐ 439 Milan Hnilicka (G), Czech Republic Nationals 1.00
☐ 440 Libor Prochazka, Czech Republic Nationals .50
☐ 441 Pavel Patera, Czech Republic Nationals .50
☐ 442 Martin Prochazka, Czech Republic Nationals .50
☐ 443 Josef Augusta, Czech Republic Nationals .50
☐ 444 Pavel Richter, All-Star West .50
☐ 445 Marek Sykora, All-Star West .50
☐ 446 Milan Hnilicka (G), All-Star West 1.00
☐ 447 Dusan Salficky, All-Star West .50
☐ 448 Frantisek Kucera, All-Star West .50
☐ 449 Ladislav Benysek, All-Star West .50
☐ 450 Josef Reznicek, All-Star West .50
☐ 451 Martin Richter, All-Star West .50
☐ 452 Ales Pisa, All-Star West .50
☐ 453 Ivan Vlcek, All-Star West .50
☐ 454 Martin Stepanek, All-Star West .50
☐ 455 Petr Jancarik, All-Star West .50
☐ 456 David Vyborny, All-Star West .50
☐ 457 Jan Hlavac, All-Star West 1.00
☐ 458 Jiri Zelenka, All-Star West .50
☐ 459 Petr Tenkrat, All-Star West .50
☐ 460 Vaclav Kral, All-Star West .50
☐ 461 David Pospisil, All-Star West .50
☐ 462 Vaclav Eiselt, All-Star West .50
☐ 463 Tomas Kucharcik, All-Star West .50
☐ 464 Petr Korinek, All-Star West .50
☐ 465 Pavel Janku, All-Star West .50
☐ 466 Radek Toupal, All-Star West .50
☐ 467 Ivo Prorok, All-Star West .50
☐ 468 Zdislav Tabara, All-Star East .50
☐ 469 Jaroslav Jagr, All-Star East .50
☐ 470 Roman Cechmanek, All-Star East 4.00
☐ 471 Libor Prochazka, All-Star East .50
☐ 472 Jiri Veber, All-Star East .50
☐ 473 Milos Holan, All-Star East .50
☐ 474 Jan Srdinko, All-Star East .50
☐ 475 Robert Kantor, All-Star East .50
☐ 476 Ales Tomasek, All-Star East .50
☐ 477 Miroslav Duben, All-Star East .50
☐ 478 Jiri Dopita, All-Star East .50
☐ 479 Martin Prochazka, All-Star East .50
☐ 480 Pavel Patera, All-Star East .50
☐ 481 Radek Belohlav, All-Star East .50
☐ 482 David Moravec, All-Star East .50
☐ 483 Roman Meluzin, All-Star East .50
☐ 484 Jiri Poukar, All-Star East .50
☐ 485 Andrei Galkin, All-Star East .50
☐ 486 Ivan Padelek, All-Star East .50
☐ 487 Marek Zadina, All-Star East .50
☐ 488 Petr Cajanek, All-Star East .50
☐ 489 Miroslav Javin, All-Star East .50
☐ 490 Ondrej Kratena, All-Star East .50
☐ Checklist 1 .30
☐ Checklist 2 .30
☐ Checklist 3 .30
☐ Checklist 4 .30
☐ Checklist 5 .30
☐ Checklist 6 .30
☐ Checklist 7 .30
☐ Checklist 8 .30

LEGENDS

Insert Set (20 cards): 55.00

Czech Nationals — **Legends**

☐ 1 Vaclav Nedomansky 3.00
☐ 2 Miloslav Horava 3.00
☐ 3 Peter Stastny 9.00
☐ 4 Jiri Sejba 3.00
☐ 5 Ivan Hlinka 3.00
☐ 6 Vladimir Martinec 3.00
☐ 7 Jaroslav Pouzar 3.00
☐ 8 Jiri Holecek 3.00
☐ 9 Ludek Cajka 3.00
☐ 10 Ludek Bukac 3.00
☐ 11 Milan Novy 3.00
☐ 12 Jiri Kralic 3.00
☐ 13 Jiri Hrdina 3.00
☐ 14 Frantisek Cernik 3.00
☐ 15 Frantisek Pospisil 3.00
☐ 16 Jiri Lala 3.00
☐ 17 Antonin Stavjana 3.00
☐ 18 Jaromir Sindel 3.00
☐ 19 Vincent Lukac 3.00
☐ 20 Dusan Pasek 3.00

LOGOS

Insert Set (14 cards):	15.00
OFS	Logos
☐ 1 Slavia Praha	1.50
☐ 2 Litvinov	1.50
☐ 3 Zlin	1.50
☐ 4 Plzen	1.50
☐ 5 Jihlava	1.50
☐ 6 Opava	1.50
☐ 7 Karlovy Kary	1.50
☐ 8 Vsetin	1.50
☐ 9 Vitkovice	1.50
☐ 10 Sparta Praha	1.50
☐ 11 Pardubice	1.50
☐ 12 Trinec	1.50
☐ 13 Kladno	1.50
☐ 14 Budejovice	1.50

NAGANO

Insert Set (4 cards):	20.00
OFS	Nagano
☐ 1 Nagano	6.00
☐ 2 Nagano	6.00
☐ 3 Nagano	6.00
☐ 4 Nagano	6.00
☐ 5 Nagano	6.00

STARS OF NAGANO

Insert Set (20 cards):	80.00
Czech Olympians	Nagano
☐ 1 Jiri Dopita	4.00
☐ 2 Dominik Hasek (G)	14.00
☐ 3 Jaromir Jagr	14.00
☐ 4 Frantisek Kucera	4.00
☐ 5 Pavel Patera	4.00
☐ 6 Robert Reichel	6.00
☐ 7 Martin Rucinsky	4.00
☐ 8 Vladimir Ruzicka	4.00
☐ 9 Jiri Slégr	4.00
☐ 10 Petr* Svoboda	4.00
☐ 11 David Moravec	4.00
☐ 12 Richard Smehlik	4.00
☐ 13 Jaroslav Spacek	4.00
☐ 14 Martin Prochazka	4.00
☐ 15 Roman Hamrlik	4.00
☐ 16 Ivan Hlinka	4.00
☐ 17 Roman Cechmanek (G)	8.00
☐ 18 Josef Beranek	4.00
☐ 19 Robert Lang	4.00
☐ 20 Martin Straka	6.00

1998 - 99 OMEGA

These cards have three versions: the regular card, a Red parallel (4:25) and an Opening Day parallel (#/56).

	OD56	Red	Omega
Complete Set (252 cards):	-	-	**70.00**
Parallel Set (250 cards):	**3600.00**	**160.00**	-
Common Player:	**8.00**	**.50**	**.20**
Player	**OD56**	**Red**	**Omega**
☐☐☐ 1 Travis Green, Anah.	15.00	.50	.20
☐☐☐ 2 Stu Grimson, Anah.	15.00	.50	.20
☐☐☐ 3 Guy Hebert (G), Anah.	15.00	.50	.20
☐☐☐ 4 Paul Kariya, Anah.	80.00	4.00	1.00
☐☐☐ 5 Marty McInnis, Anah.	10.00	.50	.20
☐☐☐ 6 Fredrik Olausson, Anah.	15.00	.50	.20
☐☐☐ 7 Steve Rucchin, Anah.	15.00	.50	.20
☐☐☐ 8 Teemu Selänne, Anah.	50.00	2.00	.50
☐☐☐ 9 A. Aalto / J. Davidsson	8.00	.50	.20
☐☐☐ 10 Jason Allison, Bost.	35.00	1.50	.20
☐☐☐ 11 Ken Belanger, Bost.	8.00	.50	.20
☐☐☐ 12 Raymond Bourque, Bost.	70.00	3.50	.50
☐☐☐ 13 Anson Carter, Bost.	25.00	1.00	.20
☐☐☐ 14 Byron Dafoe (G), Bost.	25.00	1.00	.20
☐☐☐ 15 Stephen Heinze, Bost.	10.00	.50	.20
☐☐☐ 16 Dmitri Khristich, Bost.	10.00	.50	.20
☐☐☐ 17 Sergei Samsonov, Bost.	35.00	1.50	.20
☐☐☐ 18 Robbie Tallas, Bost.	10.00	.50	.20
☐☐☐ 19 Joe Thornton, Bost.	75.00	3.50	.50
☐☐☐ 20 Matthew Barnaby, Buff.	8.00	.50	.20
☐☐☐ 21 Curtis Brown, Buff.	10.00	.50	.20
☐☐☐ 22 Michal Grosek, Buff.	8.00	.50	.20
☐☐☐ 23 Dominik Hasek (G), Buff.	60.00	3.00	.50
☐☐☐ 24 Brian Holzinger, Buff.	10.00	.50	.20
☐☐☐ 25 Michael Peca, Buff.	25.00	1.00	.20
☐☐☐ 26 Rob Ray, Buff.	15.00	.50	.20
☐☐☐ 27 Geoff Sanderson, Buff.	15.00	.50	.20
☐☐☐ 28 Miroslav Satan, Buff.	20.00	.50	.20
☐☐☐ 29 Dixon Ward, Buff.	8.00	.50	.20
☐☐☐ 30 Valeri Bure, Calg.	20.00	.50	.20
☐☐☐ 31 Theoren Fleury, Calg.	30.00	1.50	.20
☐☐☐ 32 J-S Giguère (G), Calg.	50.00	2.00	.50
☐☐☐ 33 Jarome Iginla, Calg.	50.00	2.00	.50
☐☐☐ 34 Tyler Moss, Calg.	10.00	.50	.20
☐☐☐ 35 Cory Stillman, Calg.	15.00	.50	.20
☐☐☐ 36 Jason Wiemer, Calg.	8.00	.50	.20
☐☐☐ **37 Clarke Wilm, Calg. RC**	**8.00**	**1.00**	**.50**
☐☐☐ **38 M. St-Louis RC / R. Fata**	**20.00**	**3.00**	**2.00**
☐☐☐ 39 Paul Coffey, Caro.	35.00	1.50	.20
☐☐☐ 40 Ron Francis, Caro.	35.00	1.50	.20
☐☐☐ 41 Martin Gélinas, Caro.	15.00	.50	.20
☐☐☐ 42 Arturs Irbe (G), Caro.	25.00	1.00	.20
☐☐☐ 43 Sami Kapanen, Caro.	20.00	.50	.20
☐☐☐ 44 Trevor Kidd (G), Caro.	20.00	.50	.20
☐☐☐ 45 Keith Primeau, Caro.	25.00	1.00	.20
☐☐☐ 46 Gary Roberts, Caro.	25.00	1.00	.20
☐☐☐ 47 Ray Sheppard, Caro.	10.00	.50	.20
☐☐☐ 48 Tony Amonte, Chic.	35.00	1.50	.20
☐☐☐ 49 Chris Chelios, Chic.	35.00	1.50	.20
☐☐☐ 50 Éric Dazé, Chic.	25.00	1.00	.20
☐☐☐ 51 Nelson Emerson, Chic.	10.00	.50	.20
☐☐☐ 52 Doug Gilmour, Chic.	35.00	1.50	.20
☐☐☐ **53 Mike Maneluk, Chic. RC**	**8.00**	**1.00**	**.50**
☐☐☐ 54 Bob Probert, Chic.	20.00	.50	.20
☐☐☐ 55 Jocelyn Thibault (G), Chic.	25.00	1.00	.20
☐☐☐ 56 Alexei Zhamnov, Chic.	20.00	.50	.20
☐☐☐ **57 T. White RC / B. Brown**	**8.00**	**1.00**	**.50**
☐☐☐ 58 Adam Deadmarsh, Colo.	20.00	.50	.20
☐☐☐ 59 Marc Denis (G), Colo.	30.00	1.00	.20
☐☐☐ 60 Peter Forsberg, Colo.	80.00	4.00	1.00
☐☐☐ 61 Claude Lemieux, Colo.	20.00	.50	.20
☐☐☐ 62 Jeff Odgers, Colo.	10.00	.50	.20
☐☐☐ 63 Sandis Ozolinsh, Colo.	15.00	.50	.20
☐☐☐ 64 Patrick Roy (G), Colo.	180.00	9.00	2.00
☐☐☐ 65 Joe Sakic (G), Colo.	100.00	4.50	1.00
☐☐☐ **66 S. Parker RC / W. Belak**	**8.00**	**1.00**	**.50**
☐☐☐ **67 M. Hejduk RC / C. Drury**	**130.00**	**14.00**	**9.00**
☐☐☐ 68 Ed Belfour (G), Dall.	60.00	3.00	.50
☐☐☐ 69 Derian Hatcher, Dall.	20.00	.50	.20
☐☐☐ 70 Brett Hull, Dall.	60.00	3.00	.50
☐☐☐ 71 Jamie Langenbrunner, Dall.	15.00	.50	.20
☐☐☐ 72 Jere Lehtinen, Dall.	20.00	.50	.20
☐☐☐ 73 Mike Modano, Dall.	60.00	3.00	.50
☐☐☐ 74 Joe Nieuwendyk, Dall.	25.00	1.00	.20
☐☐☐ 75 Darryl Sydor, Dall.	15.00	.50	.20
☐☐☐ 76 Roman Turek (G), Dall.	30.00	1.00	.20
☐☐☐ 77 Sergei Zubov, Dall.	15.00	.50	.20
☐☐☐ **78 S. Gusev RC / J. Wright**	**8.00**	**1.00**	**.50**
☐☐☐ 79 Sergei Fedorov, Detr.	60.00	3.00	.50
☐☐☐ 80 Joey Kocur, Detr.	10.00	.50	.20
☐☐☐ 81 Martin Lapointe, Detr.	25.00	1.00	.20
☐☐☐ 82 Igor Larionov, Detr.	35.00	1.50	.20
☐☐☐ 83 Nicklas Lidström, Detr.	35.00	1.50	.20
☐☐☐ 84 Darren McCarty, Detr.	20.00	.50	.20
☐☐☐ 85 Larry Murphy, Detr.	15.00	.50	.20
☐☐☐ 86 Chris Osgood (G), Detr.	35.00	1.50	.20
☐☐☐ 87 Brendan Shanahan, Detr.	60.00	3.00	.50
☐☐☐ 88 Steve Yzerman, Detr.	150.00	7.00	1.50
☐☐☐ **89 Maracle RC / Roest RC**	**10.00**	**2.00**	**1.00**
☐☐☐ 90 Josef Beranek, Edmo.	10.00	.50	.20
☐☐☐ 91 Sean Brown, Edmo.	8.00	.50	.20
☐☐☐ 92 Bill Guerin, Edmo.	25.00	1.00	.20
☐☐☐ 93 Roman Hamrlik, Edmo.	15.00	.50	.20
☐☐☐ 94 Janne Niinimaa, Edmo.	15.00	.50	.20
☐☐☐ 95 M. Shtalenkov (G), Edmo.	10.00	.50	.20
☐☐☐ 96 Ryan Smyth, Edmo.	30.00	1.00	.20
☐☐☐ 97 Doug Weight, Edmo.	35.00	1.50	.20
☐☐☐ 98 C. Millar / T. Poti	8.00	.50	.20
☐☐☐ 99 Pavel Bure, Flor.	50.00	2.00	.50
☐☐☐ 100 Sean Burke, Flor.	35.00	1.50	.20
☐☐☐ 101 Dino Ciccarelli, Flor.	20.00	.50	.20
☐☐☐ 102 Bret Hedican, Flor.	8.00	.50	.20
☐☐☐ 103 Viktor Kozlov, Flor.	20.00	.50	.20
☐☐☐ 104 Paul Laus, Flor.	8.00	.50	.20
☐☐☐ 105 Rob Niedermayer, Flor.	15.00	.50	.20
☐☐☐ 106 Mark Parrish, Flor.	25.00	2.00	3.00
☐☐☐ 107 Ray Whitney, Flor.	15.00	.50	.20
☐☐☐ **108 Kvasha RC / Worrell RC**	**10.00**	**2.00**	**1.50**
☐☐☐ 109 Rob Blake, LosA.	35.00	1.50	.20
☐☐☐ 110 Stéphane Fiset (G), LosA.	20.00	.50	.20
☐☐☐ 111 Glen Murray, LosA.	30.00	1.00	.20
☐☐☐ 112 Luc Robitaille, LosA.	50.00	2.00	.50
☐☐☐ 113 Jamie Storr (G), LosA.	15.00	.50	.20
☐☐☐ 114 Jozef Stümpel, LosA.	15.00	.50	.20
☐☐☐ 115 Vladimir Tsyplakov, LosA.	8.00	.50	.20
☐☐☐ **116 J. Green / M. Visheau RC**	**8.00**	**1.00**	**.50**
☐☐☐ **117 P. Rosa RC / O. Jokinen**	**15.00**	**2.00**	**1.00**
☐☐☐ 118 Benoît Brunet, Mont.	8.00	.50	.20
☐☐☐ 119 Shayne Corson, Mont.	20.00	.50	.20
☐☐☐ 120 V. Damphousse, Mont.	35.00	1.50	.20
☐☐☐ 121 Jeff Hackett (G), Mont.	20.00	.50	.20
☐☐☐ **122 Matt Higgins, Mont. RC**	**8.00**	**.50**	**.50**
☐☐☐ 123 Saku Koivu, Mont.	50.00	2.00	.50
☐☐☐ 124 Mark Recchi, Mont.	25.00	1.00	.20
☐☐☐ 125 Martin Rucinsky, Mont.	15.00	.50	.20
☐☐☐ 126 Brian Savage, Mont.	20.00	.50	.20
☐☐☐ 127 Andrew Brunette, Nash.	10.00	.50	.20
☐☐☐ 128 Mike Dunham (G), Nash.	25.00	1.00	.20
☐☐☐ 129 Greg Johnson, Nash.	10.00	.50	.20
☐☐☐ 130 Sergei Krivokrasov, Nash.	10.00	.50	.20
☐☐☐ 131 Denny Lambert, Nash.	8.00	.50	.20
☐☐☐ 132 Cliff Ronning, Nash.	15.00	.50	.20
☐☐☐ 133 T. Vokoun (G), Nash.	15.00	.50	.20
☐☐☐ 134 P. Côté / K. Timonen	8.00	.50	.20
☐☐☐ 135 Jason Arnott, NJer.	30.00	1.00	.20
☐☐☐ 136 M. Brodeur (G), NJer.	100.00	4.50	1.00
☐☐☐ 137 Patrik Elias, NJer.	50.00	2.00	.50
☐☐☐ 138 Bobby Holik, NJer.	20.00	.50	.20
☐☐☐ 139 Brendan Morrison, NJer.	20.00	.50	.20
☐☐☐ 140 Krzysztof Oliwa, NJer.	15.00	.50	.20
☐☐☐ 141 Brian Rolston, NJer.	20.00	.50	.20
☐☐☐ 142 Vadim Sharifijanov, NJer.	8.00	.50	.20
☐☐☐ 143 Scott Stevens, NJer.	25.00	1.00	.20
☐☐☐ 144 Petr* Sykora, NJer.	25.00	1.00	.20
☐☐☐ 145 Ted Donato, NYIs.	8.00	.50	.20
☐☐☐ 146 Kenny Jönsson, NYIs.	10.00	.50	.20
☐☐☐ 147 Trevor Linden, NYIs.	25.00	1.00	.20
☐☐☐ 148 Gino Odjick, NYIs.	10.00	.50	.20
☐☐☐ 149 Zigmund Palffy, NYIs.	35.00	1.50	.20
☐☐☐ 150 Félix Potvin (G), NYIs.	35.00	1.50	.20
☐☐☐ 151 Robert Reichel, NYIs.	20.00	.50	.20
☐☐☐ 152 Tommy Salo (G), NYIs.	25.00	1.00	.20
☐☐☐ 154 E. Brewer / M. Watt	15.00	.50	.20
☐☐☐ 154 Dan Cloutier (G), NYRa.	25.00	1.00	.20
☐☐☐ 155 Adam Graves, NYRa.	25.00	1.00	.20
☐☐☐ 156 Wayne Gretzky, NYRa.	250.00	12.00	3.00
☐☐☐ 157 Todd Harvey, NYRa.	15.00	.50	.20
☐☐☐ 158 Brian Leetch, NYRa.	35.00	1.50	.20
☐☐☐ 159 Manny Malhotra, NYRa.	15.00	.50	.20
☐☐☐ 160 Petr Nedved, NYRa.	20.00	.50	.20
☐☐☐ 161 Mike Richter (G), NYRa.	30.00	1.00	.20
☐☐☐ 162 Esa Tikkanen, NYRa.	10.00	.50	.20
☐☐☐ 163 Daniel Alfredsson, Otta.	35.00	1.50	.20
☐☐☐ 164 Marian Hossa, Otta.	60.00	3.00	.50
☐☐☐ 165 Andreas Johansson, Otta.	15.00	.50	.20
☐☐☐ 166 Shawn McEachern, Otta.	20.00	.50	.20
☐☐☐ 167 Wade Redden, Otta.	20.00	.50	.20
☐☐☐ 168 Damian Rhodes (G), Otta.	15.00	.50	.20
☐☐☐ 169 Ron Tugnutt (G), Otta.	25.00	1.00	.20
☐☐☐ 170 Alexei Yashin, Otta.	35.00	1.50	.20
☐☐☐ **171 Salo RC / Traverse RC**	**8.00**	**1.50**	**1.00**
☐☐☐ 172 Rod Brind'Amour, Phil.	20.00	.50	.20
☐☐☐ 173 Éric Desjardins, Phil.	20.00	.50	.20
☐☐☐ 174 Ron Hextall (G), Phil.	35.00	1.50	.20
☐☐☐ 175 Keith Jones, Phil.	10.00	.50	.20
☐☐☐ 176 John LeClair, Phil.	50.00	2.00	.50
☐☐☐ 177 Eric Lindros, Phil.	60.00	3.00	.50
☐☐☐ 178 Mikael Renberg, Phil.	20.00	.50	.20
☐☐☐ **179 D. Tertyshny, Phil. RC**	**8.00**	**1.00**	**.50**
☐☐☐ 180 Vanbiesbrouck (G), Phil.	30.00	1.00	.20
☐☐☐ 181 Dainius Zubrus, Phil.	15.00	.50	.20
☐☐☐ 182 Daniel Brière, Phoe.	30.00	1.00	.50
☐☐☐ 183 Dallas Drake, Phoe.	10.00	.50	.20
☐☐☐ 184 N. Khabibulin (G), Phoe.	25.00	1.00	.20
☐☐☐ 185 Jyrki Lumme, Phoe.	15.00	.50	.20
☐☐☐ 186 Teppo Numminen, Phoe.	20.00	.50	.20
☐☐☐ 187 Jeremy Roenick, Phoe.	50.00	2.00	.50
☐☐☐ 188 Keith Tkachuk, Phoe.	35.00	1.50	.20
☐☐☐ 189 Rick Tocchet, Phoe.	20.00	.50	.20
☐☐☐ 190 Oleg Tverdovsky, Phoe.	10.00	.50	.20
☐☐☐ 191 Jimmy Waite (G), Phoe.	10.00	.50	.20
☐☐☐ **192 J-S Aubin (G), Pitt. RC**	**15.00**	**1.00**	**1.50**
☐☐☐ 193 Stu Barnes, Pitt.	8.00	.50	.20
☐☐☐ 194 Tom Barrasso (G), Pitt.	25.00	1.00	.20
☐☐☐ 195 Jaromir Jagr, Pitt.	60.00	3.00	.50
☐☐☐ 196 Alexei Kovalev, Pitt.	35.00	1.50	.20
☐☐☐ 197 Robert Lang, Pitt.	15.00	.50	.20
☐☐☐ 198 Aleksey Morozov, Pitt.	15.00	.50	.20
☐☐☐ 199 Martin Straka, Pitt.	20.00	.50	.20
☐☐☐ **200 Hrdina RC / Galanov**	**10.00**	**1.50**	**1.00**
☐☐☐ 201 Pavol Demitra, SLou.	25.00	1.00	.20
☐☐☐ 202 Grant Fuhr (G), SLou.	35.00	1.50	.20
☐☐☐ 203 Al MacInnis, SLou.	25.00	1.00	.20
☐☐☐ 204 J. McLennan (G), SLou.	10.00	.50	.20
☐☐☐ 205 Chris Pronger, SLou.	35.00	1.50	.20
☐☐☐ 206 Pierre Turgeon, SLou.	25.00	1.00	.20
☐☐☐ 207 Tony Twist, SLou.	10.00	.50	.20
☐☐☐ **208 Bartecko RC / Reasoner**	**10.00**	**1.50**	**1.00**
☐☐☐ 209 Jeff Friesen, SanJ.	20.00	.50	.20
☐☐☐ 210 Bryan Marchment, SanJ.	10.00	.50	.20
☐☐☐ 211 Patrick Marleau, SanJ.	30.00	1.00	.20
☐☐☐ 212 Owen Nolan, SanJ.	35.00	1.50	.20
☐☐☐ 213 Mike Ricci, SanJ.	20.00	.50	.20
☐☐☐ 214 Steve Shields (G), SanJ.	15.00	.50	.20
☐☐☐ 215 Marco Sturm, SanJ.	15.00	.50	.20
☐☐☐ 216 Mike Vernon (G), SanJ.	25.00	1.00	.20
☐☐☐ 217 Wendel Clark, Tamp.	50.00	2.00	.50
☐☐☐ 218 Chris Gratton, Tamp.	15.00	.50	.20
☐☐☐ 219 Vincent Lecavalier, Tamp.	60.00	3.00	1.50
☐☐☐ 220 Sandy McCarthy, Tamp.	10.00	.50	.20
☐☐☐ 221 Stéphane Richer, Tamp.	15.00	.50	.20
☐☐☐ 222 Darcy Tucker, Tamp.	15.00	.50	.20
☐☐☐ 223 Rob Zamuner, Tamp.	15.00	.50	.20
☐☐☐ **224 Bierk RC / Kubina RC**	**10.00**	**2.00**	**1.50**
☐☐☐ 225 Bryan Berard, Toro.	20.00	.50	.20
☐☐☐ 226 Tie Domi, Toro.	20.00	.50	.20
☐☐☐ 227 Mike Johnson, Toro.	10.00	.50	.20
☐☐☐ 228 Curtis Joseph (G), Toro.	60.00	3.00	.50
☐☐☐ 229 Igor Korolev, Toro.	10.00	.50	.20
☐☐☐ 230 Alyn McCauley, Toro.	20.00	.50	.20
☐☐☐ 231 Mats Sundin, Toro.	60.00	3.00	.50
☐☐☐ 232 Steve Thomas, Toro.	15.00	.50	.20
☐☐☐ **233 Kaberle RC / Markov RC**	**15.00**	**2.00**	**1.50**
☐☐☐ 234 Adrian Aucoin, Vanc.	10.00	.50	.20
☐☐☐ 235 Corey Hirsch (G), Vanc.	10.00	.50	.20
☐☐☐ 236 Mark Messier, Vanc.	60.00	3.00	.50
☐☐☐ 237 Alexander Mogilny, Vanc.	30.00	1.00	.20
☐☐☐ **238 Bill Muckalt, Vanc. RC**	**10.00**	**1.50**	**1.00**
☐☐☐ 239 Markus Näslund, Vanc.	60.00	3.00	.50
☐☐☐ 240 Mattias Öhlund, Vanc.	20.00	.50	.20
☐☐☐ 241 Garth Snow (G), Vanc.	20.00	.50	.20
☐☐☐ **242 Cooke RC / Schaefer**	**10.00**	**1.00**	**.50**
☐☐☐ 243 Brian Bellows, Wash.	15.00	.50	.20
☐☐☐ 244 Craig Berube, Wash.	10.00	.50	.20
☐☐☐ 245 Peter Bondra, Wash.	35.00	1.50	.20
☐☐☐ 246 Matt Herr, Wash.	8.00	1.00	.50
☐☐☐ 247 Joé Juneau, Wash.	15.00	.50	.20
☐☐☐ 248 Olaf Kölzig (G), Wash.	35.00	1.50	.20
☐☐☐ 249 Adam Oates, Wash.	25.00	1.00	.20
☐☐☐ 250 Richard Zednik, Wash.	25.00	1.00	.20
☐☐☐ 251 Maple Leaf Gardens	-	-	20.00
☐☐☐ 252 Air Canada Centre	-	-	15.00

Player	Sample
☐ Martin Brodeur (G), NJer.	2.00

CHAMPIONSHIP SPOTLIGHT

These cards have four versions: the regular card (1:49), a green parallel (#/50), a red parallel (#/10) and a one-of-one gold parallel. The gold cards are too scarce to be priced.

Insert Set (10 cards):	3600.00	800.00	150.00
Insert	R10	G50	CS
☐☐☐☐ 1 Paul Kariya, Anah.	350.00	80.00	15.00
☐☐☐☐ 2 Dominik Hasek (G), Buff.	250.00	60.00	10.00
☐☐☐☐ 3 Patrick Roy (G), Colo.	750.00	180.00	35.00
☐☐☐☐ 4 Steve Yzerman, Detr.	600.00	150.00	30.00
☐☐☐☐ 5 Pavel Bure, Flor.	200.00	50.00	10.00
☐☐☐☐ 6 Martin Brodeur (G), NJer.	400.00	100.00	20.00
☐☐☐☐ 7 Wayne Gretzky, NYRa.	1000.00	250.00	50.00
☐☐☐☐ 8 Eric Lindros, Phil.	250.00	60.00	10.00
☐☐☐☐ 9 Jaromir Jagr, Pitt.	250.00	60.00	10.00
☐☐☐☐ 10 Curtis Joseph (G), Toro.	250.00	60.00	10.00

EO PORTRAITS

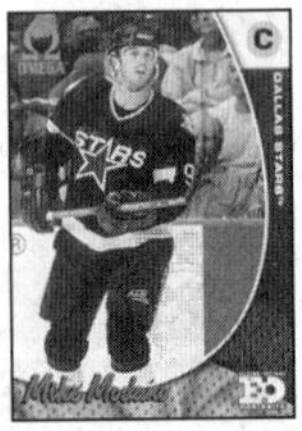

These cards have two versions: the regular insert (1:73) and a one-of-one parallel. The one-of-one parallels are too scarce to be priced.

Insert Set (20 cards):	250.00
Insert (1:73)	EOP
☐☐ 1 Paul Kariya, Anah.	15.00
☐☐ 2 Teemu Selänne, Anah.	10.00
☐☐ 3 Dominik Hasek (G), Buff.	10.00
☐☐ 4 Peter Forsberg, Colo.	15.00
☐☐ 5 Patrick Roy (G), Colo.	35.00
☐☐ 6 Joe Sakic, Colo.	20.00
☐☐ 7 Brett Hull, Dall.	10.00
☐☐ 8 Mike Modano, Dall.	10.00
☐☐ 9 Sergei Fedorov, Detr.	10.00
☐☐ 10 Brendan Shanahan, Detr.	10.00
☐☐ 11 Steve Yzerman, Detr.	30.00
☐☐ 12 Pavel Bure, Flor.	10.00
☐☐ 13 Martin Brodeur (G), NJer.	20.00
☐☐ 14 Wayne Gretzky, NYRa.	50.00
☐☐ 15 John LeClair, Phil.	10.00
☐☐ 16 Eric Lindros, Phil.	10.00
☐☐ 17 Keith Tkachuk, Phoe.	8.00
☐☐ 18 Jaromir Jagr, Pitt.	10.00
☐☐ 19 Mats Sundin, Toro.	10.00
☐☐ 20 Mark Messier, Vanc.	10.00

FACE TO FACE

Insert Set (10 cards):	375.00
Insert (1:145)	FTF
☐ 1 M. Brodeur / P. Roy	80.00
☐ 2 W. Gretzky / P. Kariya	100.00

☐	3 D. Hasek / J. Jagr	30.00
☐	4 P. Bure / S. Fedorov	30.00
☐	5 B. Shanahan / K. Tkachuk	30.00
☐	6 S. Yzerman / J. Sakic	70.00
☐	7 S. Koivu / T. Selänne	30.00
☐	8 P. Forsberg / M. Sundin	40.00
☐	9 J. LeClair / M. Modano	30.00
☐	10 M. Messier / E. Lindros	30.00

ONLINE

	Insert Set (36 cards):	270.00
	Insert (4:37)	Online
☐	1 Paul Kariya, Anah.	3.50
☐	2 Teemu Selänne, Anah.	2.00
☐	3 Raymond Bourque, Bost.	3.00
☐	4 Dominik Hasek (G), Buff.	2.50
☐	5 Theoren Fleury, Calg.	1.50
☐	6 Chris Chelios, Chic.	1.50
☐	7 Doug Gilmour, Chic.	1.50
☐	8 Peter Forsberg, Colo.	3.50
☐	9 Patrick Roy (G), Colo.	7.50
☐	10 Joe Sakic, Colo.	4.00
☐	11 Ed Belfour (G), Dall.	2.50
☐	12 Brett Hull, Dall.	2.50
☐	13 Mike Modano, Dall.	2.50
☐	14 Sergei Fedorov, Detr.	2.50
☐	15 Brendan Shanahan, Detr.	2.50
☐	16 Steve Yzerman, Detr.	6.00
☐	17 Pavel Bure, Flor.	2.00
☐	18 Saku Koivu, Mont.	2.00
☐	19 Martin Brodeur (G), NJer.	4.00
☐	20 Brendan Morrison, NJer.	1.50
☐	21 Zigmund Palffy, NYIs.	1.50
☐	22 Félix Potvin (G), NYIs.	1.50
☐	23 Wayne Gretzky, NYRa.	10.00
☐	24 Alexei Yashin, Otta.	1.50
☐	25 John LeClair, Phil.	2.00
☐	26 Eric Lindros, Phil.	2.50
☐	27 John Vanbiesbrouck (G), Phil.	1.00
☐	28 Nikolai Khabibulin (G), Phoe.	1.00
☐	29 Keith Tkachuk, Phoe.	1.50
☐	30 Jaromir Jagr, Pitt.	2.50
☐	31 Vincent Lecavalier, Tamp.	5.00
☐	32 Curtis Joseph (G), Toro.	2.50
☐	33 Mats Sundin, Toro.	2.50
☐	34 Mark Messier, Vanc.	2.50
☐	35 Bill Muckalt, Vanc.	1.00
☐	36 Peter Bondra, Wash.	1.50

PLANET ICE

These cards have two versions: a regular insert (4:37) and a coloured parallel. The gold parallels (26-30) are too scarce to be priced.

	Insert Set (30 cards):	-	15.00
	Insert	Para.	Insert
☐☐	1 Raymond Bourque, Bost.	60.00	3.00
☐☐	2 Chris Chelios, Chic.	30.00	1.00
☐☐	3 Vincent Lecavalier, Tamp.	50.00	5.00
☐☐	4 Mark Parrish, Flor.	20.00	1.00
☐☐	5 Félix Potvin (G), NYIs.	30.00	1.00
☐☐	6 Alexei Yashin, Otta.	30.00	1.00
☐☐	7 Ed Belfour (G), Dall.	50.00	2.00
☐☐	8 Peter Bondra, Wash.	30.00	1.00
☐☐	9 Brett Hull, Dall.	50.00	2.00
☐☐	10 Mark Messier, Vanc.	50.00	2.00
☐☐	11 Mats Sundin, Toro.	50.00	2.00
☐☐	12 John Vanbiesbrouck (G), Flor.	20.00	1.00
☐☐	13 Sergei Fedorov, Detr.	50.00	2.00
☐☐	14 Curtis Joseph (G), Toro.	50.00	2.00
☐☐	15 John LeClair, Phil.	40.00	2.00
☐☐	16 Mike Modano, Dall.	50.00	2.00
☐☐	17 Brendan Shanahan, Detr.	50.00	2.00
☐☐	18 Keith Tkachuk, Phoe.	30.00	1.00
☐☐	19 Martin Brodeur (G), NJer.	275.00	4.00
☐☐	20 Pavel Bure, Flor.	125.00	2.00
☐☐	21 Dominik Hasek (G), Buff.	175.00	2.00
☐☐	22 Joe Sakic, Colo.	275.00	4.00
☐☐	23 Teemu Selänne, Anah.	125.00	2.00
☐☐	24 Steve Yzerman, Detr.	400.00	6.00
☐☐	25 Peter Forsberg, Colo.		3.00
☐☐	26 Wayne Gretzky, NYRa.		10.00
☐☐	27 Jaromir Jagr, Pitt.		2.00
☐☐	28 Paul Kariya, Anah.		3.00
☐☐	29 Eric Lindros, Phil.		2.00
☐☐	30 Patrick Roy (G), Colo.		7.00

PRISM

	Insert Set (20 cards):	160.00
	Insert (1:37)	Prism
☐	1 Paul Kariya, Anah.	10.00
☐	2 Teemu Selänne, Anah.	6.00
☐	3 Dominik Hasek (G), Buff.	6.00
☐	4 Peter Forsberg, Colo.	10.00
☐	5 Patrick Roy (G), Colo.	22.00
☐	6 Joe Sakic, Colo.	12.00
☐	7 Mike Modano, Dall.	6.00
☐	8 Sergei Fedorov, Detr.	6.00
☐	9 Brendan Shanahan, Detr.	6.00
☐	10 Steve Yzerman, Detr.	18.00
☐	11 Pavel Bure, Flor.	6.00
☐	12 Martin Brodeur (G), NJer.	12.00
☐	13 Wayne Gretzky, NYRa.	30.00
☐	14 Alexei Yashin, Otta.	6.00
☐	15 John LeClair, Phil.	6.00
☐	16 Eric Lindros, Phil.	6.00
☐	17 Keith Tkachuk, Phoe.	6.00
☐	18 Jaromir Jagr, Pitt.	6.00
☐	19 Mats Sundin, Toro.	6.00
☐	20 Mark Messier, Vanc.	6.00

1998 - 99 PACIFIC

These cards have three versions: the regular card, a Red parallel (1:1 treat packs) and an Ice Blue parallel (1:73). There is no card #66; the number was retired in recognition of Mario Lemieux.

	Complete Set (450 cards):	4800.00	225.00	60.00
	Common Player:	8.00	.75	.20
	Player	IB67	Red	Pac.
☐☐☐	1 Damian Rhodes (G), Ott.	15.00	.75	.20
☐☐☐	2 Mattias Öhlund, Vanc.	20.00	.75	.20
☐☐☐	3 Craig Ludwig, Dall.	10.00	.75	.20
☐☐☐	4 Rob Blake, LosA.	35.00	1.00	.50
☐☐☐	5 Nicklas Lidström, Detr.	35.00	1.00	.50
☐☐☐	6 Calle Johansson, Wash.	15.00	.75	.20
☐☐☐	7 Chris Chelios, Chic.	35.00	1.00	.50
☐☐☐	8 Teemu Selänne, Anah.	50.00	2.00	.50
☐☐☐	9 Paul Kariya, Anah.	80.00	4.00	1.00
☐☐☐	10 Pavel Bure, Vanc.	50.00	2.00	.50
☐☐☐	11 Mark Messier, Vanc.	60.00	3.00	1.00
☐☐☐	12 Peter Bondra, Wash.	35.00	1.00	.50
☐☐☐	13 Mats Sundin, Toro.	60.00	3.00	1.00
☐☐☐	14 Brendan Shanahan, Detr.	60.00	3.00	1.00
☐☐☐	15 Jamie Langenbrunner, Dall.	15.00	.75	.20
☐☐☐	16 Brett Hull, SLou.	60.00	3.00	1.00
☐☐☐	17 Rod Brind'Amour, Phil.	20.00	.75	.20
☐☐☐	18 Adam Deadmarsh, Colo.	20.00	.75	.20
☐☐☐	19 Steve Yzerman, Detr.	150.00	7.00	2.00
☐☐☐	20 Ed Belfour (G), Dall.	60.00	3.00	1.00
☐☐☐	21 Peter Forsberg, Colo.	80.00	4.00	1.00
☐☐☐	22 Dino Ciccarelli, Detr.	20.00	.75	.20
☐☐☐	23 Brian Bellows, Wash.	15.00	.75	.20
☐☐☐	24 Janne Niinimaa, Edmo.	15.00	.75	.20
☐☐☐	25 Joe Nieuwendyk, Dall.	25.00	1.00	.20
☐☐☐	26 Patrik Elias, NJer.	50.00	2.00	.50
☐☐☐	27 Michael Peca, Buff.	25.00	1.00	.20
☐☐☐	28 Tie Domi, Toro.	20.00	.75	.20
☐☐☐	29 Félix Potvin (G), Toro.	35.00	1.00	.50
☐☐☐	30 Martin Brodeur (G), NJer.	100.00	4.00	1.50
☐☐☐	31 Grant Fuhr (G), SLou.	35.00	1.00	.50
☐☐☐	32 Trevor Linden, NYIs.	25.00	1.00	.20
☐☐☐	33 Patrick Roy (G), Colo.	180.00	9.00	3.00
☐☐☐	34 J. Vanbiesbrouck (G), Flor.	30.00	1.00	.20
☐☐☐	35 Tom Barrasso (G), Pitt.	25.00	1.00	.20
☐☐☐	36 Matthew Barnaby, Buff.	8.00	.75	.20
☐☐☐	37 Olaf Kölzig (G), Wash.	35.00	1.00	.50
☐☐☐	38 Pavol Demitra, SLou.	25.00	1.00	.20
☐☐☐	39 Dominik Hasek (G), Buff.	60.00	3.00	1.00
☐☐☐	40 Chris Terreri (G), SanJ.	10.00	.75	.20
☐☐☐	41 Jason Allison, Bost.	35.00	1.00	.50
☐☐☐	42 Richard Smehlik, Buff.	8.00	.75	.20
☐☐☐	43 Frank Banham, Anah.	8.00	.75	.20
☐☐☐	44 Chris Pronger, SLou.	35.00	1.00	.50
☐☐☐	45 Matt Cullen, Anah.	15.00	.75	.20
☐☐☐	**46 Mike Rucinski, Anah. RC**	**8.00**	**.75**	**.50**
☐☐☐	**47 Mike Crowley, Anah. RC**	**8.00**	**.75**	**.50**
☐☐☐	48 Scott Young, Anah.	20.00	.75	.20
☐☐☐	49 Brian Savage, Mont.	20.00	.75	.20
☐☐☐	50 Travis Green, Anah.	15.00	.75	.20
☐☐☐	51 John LeClair, Phil.	50.00	2.00	.50
☐☐☐	52 Adam Foote, Colo.	20.00	.75	.20
☐☐☐	53 Derek Morris, Calg.	15.00	.75	.20
☐☐☐	54 Guy Hebert (G), Anah.	15.00	.75	.20
☐☐☐	55 Chris Gratton, Phil.	15.00	.75	.20
☐☐☐	56 Sergei Zubov, Dall.	15.00	.75	.20
☐☐☐	57 Dave Karpa, Anah.	8.00	.75	.20
☐☐☐	58 Sergei Varlamov, Calg.	10.00	.75	.20
☐☐☐	59 Josef Marha, Anah.	8.00	.75	.20
☐☐☐	60 Jason Marshall, Dall.	8.00	.75	.20
☐☐☐	**61 Jeff Nielsen, Anah. RC**	**8.00**	**.75**	**.50**
☐☐☐	62 Steve Rucchin, Anah.	15.00	.75	.20
☐☐☐	63 Tomas Sandström, Anah.	15.00	.75	.20
☐☐☐	64 Jason Bonsignore, Tamp.	8.00	.75	.20
☐☐☐	65 M. Shtalenkov (G), Anah.	10.00	.75	.20
☐☐☐	**67 Tom Askey (G), Anah. RC**	**10.00**	**.75**	**1.00**
☐☐☐	68 Jaromir Jagr, Pitt.	60.00	3.00	1.00
☐☐☐	69 Per Axelsson, Bost.	10.00	.75	.20
☐☐☐	70 Ken Baumgartner, Bost.	8.00	.75	.20
☐☐☐	71 Jiri Slegr, Pitt.	10.00	.75	.20
☐☐☐	72 Mathieu Schneider, Toro.	15.00	.75	.20
☐☐☐	73 Anson Carter, Bost.	25.00	1.00	.20
☐☐☐	74 Byron Dafoe (G), Bost.	25.00	1.00	.20
☐☐☐	75 Rob DiMaio, Bost.	10.00	.75	.20
☐☐☐	76 Ted Donato, Bost.	8.00	.75	.20
☐☐☐	77 Raymond Bourque, Bost.	70.00	3.00	1.00
☐☐☐	78 Dave Ellett, Bost.	10.00	.75	.20
☐☐☐	79 Steve Heinze, Bost.	10.00	.75	.20
☐☐☐	80 Geoff Sanderson, Buff.	15.00	.75	.20
☐☐☐	81 Miroslav Satan, Buff.	20.00	.75	.20
☐☐☐	82 Martin Straka, Flor.	20.00	.75	.20
☐☐☐	83 Dimitri Khristich, Bost.	10.00	.75	.20
☐☐☐	84 Grant Ledyard, Bost.	8.00	.75	.20
☐☐☐	85 Cameron Mann, Bost.	10.00	.75	.20
☐☐☐	86 Kyle McLaren, Bost.	15.00	.75	.20
☐☐☐	87 Sergei Samsonov, Bost.	35.00	1.00	.50
☐☐☐	88 Eric Lindros, Phil.	60.00	3.00	1.00
☐☐☐	89 Alexander Mogilny, Vanc.	30.00	1.00	.20
☐☐☐	90 Joé Juneau, Wash.	15.00	.75	.20
☐☐☐	91 Sergei Fedorov, Detr.	60.00	3.00	1.00
☐☐☐	92 Rick Tocchet, Phoe.	20.00	.75	.20
☐☐☐	93 Doug Gilmour, NJer.	35.00	1.00	.50
☐☐☐	94 Ryan Smyth, Edmo.	30.00	1.00	.20
☐☐☐	95 Alexei Morozov, Pitt.	15.00	.75	.20
☐☐☐	96 Phil Housley, Wash.	20.00	.75	.20
☐☐☐	97 Jeremy Roenick, Phoe.	50.00	2.00	.50
☐☐☐	98 Jay More, Phoe.	8.00	.75	.20
☐☐☐	99 Wayne Gretzky, NYRa.	250.00	10.00	4.00
☐☐☐	100 Rob Tallas (G), Bost.	10.00	.75	.20
☐☐☐	101 Tim Taylor, Bost.	8.00	.75	.20
☐☐☐	102 Joe Thornton, Bost.	75.00	3.00	1.00
☐☐☐	103 Donald Audette, Buff.	25.00	1.00	.20
☐☐☐	104 Curtis Brown, Buff.	10.00	.75	.20
☐☐☐	105 Michal Grosek, Buff.	8.00	.75	.20
☐☐☐	106 Brian Holzinger, Buff.	10.00	.75	.20
☐☐☐	107 Derek Plante, Buff.	10.00	.75	.20
☐☐☐	108 Rob Ray, Buff.	15.00	.75	.20
☐☐☐	109 Darryl Shannon, Buff.	8.00	.75	.20
☐☐☐	110 Steve Shields (G), Buff.	15.00	.75	.20
☐☐☐	111 Vaclav Varada, Buff.	10.00	.75	.20
☐☐☐	112 Dixon Ward, Buff.	8.00	.75	.20
☐☐☐	113 Jason Woolley, Buff.	8.00	.75	.20
☐☐☐	114 Alexei Zhitnik, Buff.	10.00	.75	.20
☐☐☐	115 Andrew Cassels, Calg.	15.00	.75	.20
☐☐☐	116 Hnat Domenichelli, Calg.	10.00	.75	.20
☐☐☐	117 Theoren Fleury, Calg.	30.00	1.00	.50
☐☐☐	118 Denis Gauthier, Calg.	8.00	.75	.20
☐☐☐	119 Cale Hulse, Calg.	8.00	.75	.20
☐☐☐	120 Jarome Iginla, Calg.	50.00	2.00	.50
☐☐☐	121 Marty McInnis, Calg.	10.00	.75	.20
☐☐☐	122 Tyler Moss (G), Calg.	10.00	.75	.20
☐☐☐	123 Michael Nylander, Calg.	15.00	.75	.20
☐☐☐	124 D. Roloson (G), Calg.	10.00	.75	.20
☐☐☐	125 Cory Stillman, Calg.	15.00	.75	.20
☐☐☐	126 Rick Tabaracci (G), Calg.	10.00	.75	.20
☐☐☐	127 German Titov, Calg.	8.00	.75	.20
☐☐☐	128 Jason Wiemer, Calg.	8.00	.75	.20
☐☐☐	129 Steve Chaisson, Calg.	10.00	.75	.20
☐☐☐	130 Kevin Dineen, Caro.	10.00	.75	.20
☐☐☐	131 Nelson Emerson, Caro.	10.00	.75	.20
☐☐☐	132 Martin Gelinas, Caro.	15.00	.75	.20
☐☐☐	133 Stu Grimson, Caro.	15.00	.75	.20
☐☐☐	134 Sami Kapanen, Caro.	20.00	.75	.20
☐☐☐	135 Trevor Kidd (G), Caro.	20.00	.75	.20
☐☐☐	136 Robert Kron, Caro.	10.00	.75	.20
☐☐☐	137 Jeff O'Neill, Caro.	25.00	1.00	.20
☐☐☐	138 Keith Primeau, Caro.	25.00	1.00	.20
☐☐☐	139 Paul Ranheim, Caro.	10.00	.75	.20
☐☐☐	140 Gary Roberts, Caro.	25.00	1.00	.20
☐☐☐	141 Glen Wesley, Caro.	10.00	.75	.20
☐☐☐	142 Tony Amonte, Chic.	35.00	1.00	.50
☐☐☐	143 Eric Dazé, Chic.	25.00	1.00	.20
☐☐☐	144 Jeff Hackett (G), Chic.	20.00	.75	.20
☐☐☐	145 Greg Johnson, Chic.	10.00	.75	.20
☐☐☐	146 Chad Kilger, Chic.	15.00	.75	.20
☐☐☐	147 Sergei Krivokrasov, Chic.	10.00	.75	.20
☐☐☐	148 Christian LaFlamme, Chic.	8.00	.75	.20
☐☐☐	149 Jean-Yves Leroux, Chic.	8.00	.75	.20
☐☐☐	150 Dmitri Nabokov, Chic.	10.00	.75	.20
☐☐☐	151 Jeff Shantz, Chic.	8.00	.75	.20
☐☐☐	152 Gary Suter, Chic.	15.00	.75	.20
☐☐☐	153 Eric Weinrich, Chic.	8.00	.75	.20
☐☐☐	**154 Todd White, Chic. RC**	**8.00**	**.75**	**.50**
☐☐☐	155 Alexei Zhamnov, Chic.	20.00	.75	.20
☐☐☐	156 Wade Belak, Colo.	10.00	.75	.20
☐☐☐	157 Craig Billington (G), Colo.	8.00	.75	.20
☐☐☐	158 René Corbet, Colo.	10.00	.75	.20
☐☐☐	159 Shean Donovan, Colo.	10.00	.75	.20
☐☐☐	160 Valeri Kamensky, Colo.	20.00	.75	.20
☐☐☐	161 Uwe Krupp, Colo.	8.00	.75	.20
☐☐☐	162 Jari Kurri, Colo.	60.00	3.00	1.00
☐☐☐	163 Eric Lacroix, Colo.	8.00	.75	.20
☐☐☐	164 Claude Lemieux, Colo.	20.00	.75	.20
☐☐☐	165 Eric Messier, Colo.	10.00	.75	.20
☐☐☐	166 Jeff Odgers, Colo.	10.00	.75	.20
☐☐☐	167 Sandis Ozolinsh, Colo.	15.00	.75	.20
☐☐☐	168 Warren Rychel, Colo.	8.00	.75	.20
☐☐☐	169 Joe Sakic, Colo.	100.00	4.00	1.50
☐☐☐	170 Stéphane Yelle, Colo.	10.00	.75	.20
☐☐☐	171 Greg Adams, Dall.	10.00	.75	.20
☐☐☐	172 Jason Botterill, Dall.	8.00	.75	.20
☐☐☐	173 Guy Carbonneau, Dall.	20.00	.75	.20
☐☐☐	174 Shawn Chambers, Dall.	8.00	.75	.20
☐☐☐	175 Manny Fernandez (G), Dall.	25.00	1.00	.20
☐☐☐	176 Derian Hatcher, Dall.	20.00	.75	.20
☐☐☐	177 Benoît Hogue, Dall.	10.00	.75	.20
☐☐☐	178 Mike Keane, Dall.	10.00	.75	.20
☐☐☐	179 Jere Lehtinen, Dall.	20.00	.75	.20
☐☐☐	180 Juha Lind, Dall.	10.00	.75	.20
☐☐☐	181 Mike Modano, Dall.	60.00	3.00	1.00
☐☐☐	182 Brian Skrudland, Dall.	10.00	.75	.20
☐☐☐	183 Darryl Sydor, Dall.	15.00	.75	.20
☐☐☐	184 Roman Turek (G), Dall.	30.00	1.00	.20
☐☐☐	185 Pat Verbeek, Dall.	20.00	.75	.20
☐☐☐	186 Jamie Wright, Dall.	8.00	.75	.20
☐☐☐	187 Doug Brown, Detr.	8.00	.75	.20
☐☐☐	188 Kris Draper, Detr.	15.00	.75	.20
☐☐☐	189 Anders Eriksson, Detr.	8.00	.75	.20
☐☐☐	190 Viacheslav Fetisov, Detr.	35.00	1.00	.50
☐☐☐	191 Brent Gilchrist, Detr.	8.00	.75	.20
☐☐☐	192 Kevin Hodson (G), Detr.	15.00	.75	.20
☐☐☐	193 Tomas Holmström, Detr.	15.00	.75	.20
☐☐☐	194 Mike Knuble, Detr.	8.00	.75	.20
☐☐☐	195 Joey Kocur, Detr.	10.00	.75	.20
☐☐☐	196 Vyacheslav Kozlov, Detr.	15.00	.75	.20
☐☐☐	197 Martin Lapointe, Detr.	25.00	1.00	.20
☐☐☐	198 Igor Larionov, Detr.	35.00	1.00	.50
☐☐☐	199 Kirk Maltby, Detr.	15.00	.75	.20
☐☐☐	**200 N. Maracle (G), Detr. RC**	**10.00**	**.75**	**1.00**
☐☐☐	201 Darren McCarty, Detr.	20.00	.75	.20
☐☐☐	202 Dmitri Mironov, Detr.	10.00	.75	.20
☐☐☐	203 Larry Murphy, Detr.	15.00	.75	.20
☐☐☐	204 Chris Osgood (G), Detr.	35.00	1.00	.50
☐☐☐	205 Kelly Buchberger, Edmo.	10.00	.75	.20
☐☐☐	206 Bob Essensa (G), Edmo.	15.00	.75	.20
☐☐☐	**207 Scott Fraser, Edmo. RC**	**8.00**	**.75**	**.50**
☐☐☐	208 Mike Grier, Edmo.	15.00	.75	.20
☐☐☐	209 Bill Guerin, Edmo.	25.00	1.00	.20
☐☐☐	210 Tony Hrkac, Edmo.	10.00	.75	.20
☐☐☐	211 Curtis Joseph (G), Edmo.	60.00	3.00	1.00
☐☐☐	212 Mats Lindgren, Edmo.	10.00	.75	.20
☐☐☐	213 Todd Marchant, Edmo.	15.00	.75	.20
☐☐☐	214 Dean McAmmond, Edmo.	10.00	.75	.20
☐☐☐	215 Craig Millar, Edmo.	8.00	.75	.20
☐☐☐	216 Boris Mironov, Edmo.	10.00	.75	.20
☐☐☐	217 Doug Weight, Edmo.	35.00	1.00	.50
☐☐☐	218 Valeri Zelepukin, Edmo.	8.00	.75	.20
☐☐☐	219 Roman Hamrlik, Edmo.	15.00	.75	.20
☐☐☐	220 Radek Dvorak, Flor.	15.00	.75	.20
☐☐☐	221 Dave Gagner, Flor.	10.00	.75	.20
☐☐☐	222 Ed Jovanovski, Flor.	25.00	1.00	.20
☐☐☐	223 Viktor Kozlov, Flor.	20.00	.75	.20
☐☐☐	224 Paul Laus, Flor.	8.00	.75	.20
☐☐☐	225 Kirk McLean (G), Flor.	20.00	.75	.20
☐☐☐	226 Scott Mellanby, Flor.	15.00	.75	.20
☐☐☐	227 Kirk Muller, Flor.	20.00	.75	.20

228 Robert Svehla, Flor.	15.00	.75	.20
229 Steve Washburn, Flor.	8.00	.75	.20
230 Kevin Weekes (G), Flor.	15.00	.75	.20
231 Ray Whitney, Flor.	15.00	.75	.20
232 Peter Worrell, Flor. RC	**15.00**	**1.00**	**1.50**
233 Russ Courtnall, LosA.	15.00	.75	.20
234 S. Fiset (G), LosA.	20.00	.75	.20
235 Garry Galley, LosA.	8.00	.75	.20
236 Craig Johnson, LosA.	8.00	.75	.20
237 Ian Laperrière, LosA.	10.00	.75	.20
238 Donald MacLean, LosA.	8.00	.75	.20
239 Steve McKenna, LosA.	8.00	.75	.20
240 Sandy Moger, LosA.	8.00	.75	.20
241 Glen Murray, LosA.	30.00	1.00	.20
242 Sean O'Donnell, LosA.	8.00	.75	.20
243 Yanic Perreault, LosA.	20.00	.75	.20
244 Luc Robitaille, LosA.	50.00	2.00	.50
245 Jamie Storr (G), LosA.	15.00	.75	.20
246 Jozef Stümpel, LosA.	15.00	.75	.20
247 Vladimir Tsyplakov, LosA.	8.00	.75	.20
248 Benoît Brunet, Mont.	8.00	.75	.20
249 Shayne Corson, Mont.	20.00	.75	.20
250 V. Damphousse, Mont.	35.00	1.00	.50
251 Éric Houde, Mont. RC	**8.00**	**.75**	**.50**
252 Saku Koivu, Mont.	50.00	2.00	.50
253 Vladimir Malakhov, Mont.	10.00	.75	.20
254 Dave Manson, Mont.	10.00	.75	.20
255 Andy Moog (G), Mont.	25.00	1.00	.20
256 Mark Recchi, Mont.	25.00	1.00	.20
257 Martin Rucinsky, Mont.	15.00	.75	.20
258 J. Thibault (G), Mont.	25.00	1.00	.20
259 Mick Vukota, Mont.	8.00	.75	.20
260 D. Andreychuck, NJer.	20.00	.75	.20
261 Jason Arnott, NJer.	30.00	1.00	.20
262 Mike Dunham (G), NJer.	25.00	1.00	.20
263 Bobby Holik, NJer.	20.00	.75	.20
264 Randy McKay, NJer.	8.00	.75	.20
265 Brendan Morrison, NJer.	20.00	.75	.20
266 Scott Niedermayer, NJer.	20.00	.75	.20
267 Lyle Odelein, NJer.	10.00	.75	.20
268 Krzysztof Oliwa, NJer.	15.00	.75	.20
269 Denis Pederson, NJer.	8.00	.75	.20
270 Brian Rolston, NJer.	20.00	.75	.20
271 S. Souray, NJer. RC	**8.00**	**.75**	**.50**
272 Scott Stevens, NJer.	25.00	1.00	.20
273 Petr Sykora, NJer.	25.00	1.00	.20
274 Steve Thomas, NJer.	15.00	.75	.20
275 Bryan Berard, NYIs.	20.00	.75	.20
276 Zdeno Chara, NYIs.	15.00	.75	.20
277 Chebaturkin, NYIs. RC	**8.00**	**.75**	**.50**
278 Tom Chorske, NYIs.	8.00	.75	.20
279 M. Czerkawski, NYIs.	15.00	.75	.20
280 Jason Dawe, NYIs.	8.00	.75	.20
281 Wade Flaherty (G), NYIs.	10.00	.75	.20
282 Kenny Jönsson, NYIs.	10.00	.75	.20
283 Sergei Nemchinov, NYIs.	15.00	.75	.20
284 Zigmund Palffy, NYIs.	35.00	1.00	.50
285 Richard Pilon, NYIs.	8.00	.75	.20
286 Robert Reichel, NYIs.	20.00	.75	.20
287 Joe Sacco, NYIs.	8.00	.75	.20
288 Tommy Salo (G), NYIs.	25.00	1.00	.20
289 Bryan Smolinski, NYIs.	10.00	.75	.20
290 Jeff Beukeboom, NYRa.	10.00	.75	.20
291 Dan Cloutier (G), NYRa.	25.00	1.00	.20
292 Bruce Driver, NYRa.	8.00	.75	.20
293 Adam Graves, NYRa.	25.00	1.00	.20
294 Alexei Kovalev, NYRa.	35.00	1.00	.50
295 Pat LaFontaine, NYRa.	35.00	1.00	.50
296 Darren Langdon, NYRa.	15.00	.75	.20
297 Brian Leetch, NYRa.	35.00	1.00	.50
298 Mike Richter (G), NYRa.	30.00	1.00	.20
299 Ulf Samuelsson, NYRa.	10.00	.75	.20
300 Marc Savard, NYRa.	15.00	.75	.20
301 Kevin Stevens, NYRa.	15.00	.75	.20
302 Niklas Sundström, NYRa.	15.00	.75	.20
303 Tim Sweeney, NYRa.	8.00	.75	.20
304 Vladimir Vorobiev, NYRa.	8.00	.75	.20
305 Daniel Alfredsson, Ott.	35.00	1.00	.50
306 Magnus Arvedsson, Ott.	10.00	.75	.20
307 Radek Bonk, Ott.	20.00	.75	.20
308 Andreas Dackell, Ott.	10.00	.75	.20
309 Bruce Gardiner, Ott.	8.00	.75	.20
310 Igor Kravchuk, Ott.	10.00	.75	.20
311 Denny Lambert, Ott.	8.00	.75	.20
312 Janne Laukkanen, Ott.	8.00	.75	.20
313 Shawn McEachern, Ott.	20.00	.75	.20
314 Chris Phillips, Ott.	15.00	.75	.20
315 Wade Redden, Ott.	20.00	.75	.20
316 Ron Tugnutt (G), Ott.	25.00	1.00	.20
317 Shaun Van Allen, Ott.	10.00	.75	.20
318 Alexei Yashin, Ott.	35.00	1.00	.50
319 Jason York, Ott.	10.00	.75	.20
320 Sergei Zholtok, Ott.	10.00	.75	.20
321 Sean Burke (G), Phil.	35.00	1.00	.50
322 Paul Coffey, Phil.	35.00	1.00	.50
323 Alexandre Daigle, Phil.	10.00	.75	.20
324 Éric Desjardins, Phil.	20.00	.75	.20
325 Colin Forbes, Phil.	8.00	.75	.20
326 Ron Hextall (G), Phil.	35.00	1.00	.50
327 Trent Klatt, Phil.	10.00	.75	.20
328 Dan McGillis, Phil.	10.00	.75	.20
329 Joel Otto, Phil.	10.00	.75	.20
330 Shjon Podein, Phil.	15.00	.75	.20
331 Mike Sillinger, Phil.	10.00	.75	.20
332 Chris Therien, Phil.	8.00	.75	.20
333 Dainius Zubrus, Phil.	15.00	.75	.20
334 Bob Corkum, Phoe.	8.00	.75	.20
335 Jim Cummins, Phoe.	8.00	.75	.20
336 Jason Doig, Phoe.	8.00	.75	.20
337 Dallas Drake, Phoe.	10.00	.75	.20
338 Mike Gartner, Phoe.	50.00	2.00	.50
339 Brad Isbister, Phoe.	15.00	.75	.20
340 Craig Janney, Phoe.	15.00	.75	.20
341 N. Khabibulin (G), Phoe.	25.00	1.00	.20
342 Teppo Numminen, Phoe.	20.00	.75	.20
343 Cliff Ronning, Phoe.	15.00	.75	.20
344 Keith Tkachuk, Phoe.	35.00	1.00	.50
345 Oleg Tverdovsky, Phoe.	10.00	.75	.20
346 Jim Waite (G), Phoe.	10.00	.75	.20
347 Juha Ylönen, Phoe.	10.00	.75	.20
348 Stu Barnes, Pitt.	8.00	.75	.20
349 Rob Brown, Pitt.	10.00	.75	.20
350 Robert Dome, Pitt.	10.00	.75	.20
351 Ron Francis, Pitt.	35.00	1.00	.50
352 Kevin Hatcher, Pitt.	10.00	.75	.20
353 Alex Hicks, Pitt.	8.00	.75	.20
354 Darius Kasparaitis, Pitt.	15.00	.75	.20
355 Robert Lang, Pitt.	15.00	.75	.20
356 Fredrik Olausson, Pitt.	15.00	.75	.20
357 Ed Olczyk, Pitt.	15.00	.75	.20
358 Petr Skudra (G), Pitt.	10.00	.75	.20
359 Chris Tamer, Pitt.	8.00	.75	.20
360 Ken Wregget (G), Pitt.	15.00	.75	.20
361 Blair Atcheynum, SLou.	8.00	.75	.20
362 Jim Campbell, SLou.	8.00	.75	.20
363 Kelly Chase, SLou.	10.00	.75	.20
364 Craig Conroy, SLou.	20.00	.75	.20
365 Geoff Courtnall, SLou.	10.00	.75	.20
366 Steve Duchesne, SLou.	15.00	.75	.20
367 Todd Gill, SLou.	10.00	.75	.20
368 Al MacInnis, SLou.	25.00	1.00	.20
369 J. McLennan (G), SLou.	10.00	.75	.20
370 Scott Pellerin, SLou.	10.00	.75	.20
371 Pascal Rhéaume, SLou.	8.00	.75	.20
372 Jamie Rivers, SLou.	8.00	.75	.20
373 Darren Turcotte, SLou.	10.00	.75	.20
374 Pierre Turgeon, SLou.	25.00	1.00	.20
375 Tony Twist, SLou.	10.00	.75	.20
376 Terry Yake, SLou.	8.00	.75	.20
377 Richard Brennan, SanJ.	8.00	.75	.20
378 Murray Craven, SanJ.	10.00	.75	.20
379 Jeff Friesen, SanJ.	20.00	.75	.20
380 Tony Granato, SanJ.	15.00	.75	.20
381 Bill Houlder, SanJ.	8.00	.75	.20
382 Kelly Hrudey (G), SanJ.	20.00	.75	.20
383 Alexander Korolyuk, SanJ.	8.00	.75	.20
384 John MacLean, SanJ.	10.00	.75	.20
385 Bryan Marchment, SanJ.	10.00	.75	.20
386 Patrick Marleau, SanJ.	30.00	1.00	.20
387 Stéphane Matteau, SanJ.	10.00	.75	.20
388 Marty McSorley, SanJ.	15.00	.75	.20
389 Bernie Nicholls, SanJ.	15.00	.75	.20
390 Owen Nolan, SanJ.	35.00	1.00	.50
391 Mike Ricci, SanJ.	20.00	.75	.20
392 Marco Sturm, SanJ.	15.00	.75	.20
393 Mike Vernon (G), SanJ.	25.00	1.00	.20
394 Andrei Zyuzin, SanJ.	10.00	.75	.20
395 Mikael Andersson, Tamp.	8.00	.75	.20
396 Z. Bierk (G), Tamp. RC	**15.00**	**1.00**	**1.50**
397 Enrico Ciccone, Tamp.	10.00	.75	.20
398 Louis DeBrusk, Tamp.	8.00	.75	.20
399 Karl Dykhuis, Tamp.	8.00	.75	.20
400 D. Langkow, Tamp.	15.00	.75	.20
401 Mike McBain, Tamp.	8.00	.75	.20
402 Sandy McCarthy, Tamp.	10.00	.75	.20
403 Daren Puppa (G), Tamp.	15.00	.75	.20
404 Mikael Renberg, Tamp.	20.00	.75	.20
405 Stéphane Richer, Tamp.	15.00	.75	.20
406 A. Selivanov, Tamp.	8.00	.75	.20
407 Darcy Tucker, Tamp.	15.00	.75	.20
408 Paul Ysebaert, Tamp.	8.00	.75	.20
409 Rob Zamuner, Tamp.	15.00	.75	.20
410 Sergei Berezin, Toro.	15.00	.75	.20
411 Wendal Clark, Toro.	50.00	2.00	.50
412 Sylvain Côté, Toro.	10.00	.75	.20
413 Mike Johnson, Toro.	10.00	.75	.20
414 Derek King, Toro.	10.00	.75	.20
415 Kris King, Toro.	10.00	.75	.20
416 Igor Korolev, Toro.	10.00	.75	.20
417 D. Markov, Toro. RC	**10.00**	**.75**	**1.00**
418 Alyn McCauley, Toro.	20.00	.75	.20
419 Fredrik Modin, Toro.	15.00	.75	.20
420 Martin Prochazka, Toro.	10.00	.75	.20
421 Jason Smith, Toro.	10.00	.75	.20
422 Steve Sullivan, Toro.	20.00	.75	.20
423 Yannick Tremblay, Toro.	8.00	.75	.20
424 Todd Bertuzzi, Vanc.	75.00	3.00	1.00
425 Donald Brashear, Vanc.	15.00	.75	.20
426 Bret Hedican, Vanc.	8.00	.75	.20
427 Arturs Irbe (G), Vanc.	25.00	1.00	.20
428 Jyrki Lumme, Vanc.	15.00	.75	.20
429 Brad May, Vanc.	10.00	.75	.20
430 Bryan McCabe, Vanc.	15.00	.75	.20
431 Markus Näslund, Vanc.	60.00	3.00	1.00
432 Brian Noonan, Vanc.	8.00	.75	.20
433 Dave Scatchard, Vanc.	8.00	.75	.20
434 Garth Snow (G), Vanc.	20.00	.75	.20
435 Lubomir Vaic, Vanc.	15.00	.75	.20
436 Peter Zezel, Vanc.	10.00	.75	.20
437 Craig Berube, Wash.	10.00	.75	.20
438 Jeff Brown, Wash.	8.00	.75	.20
439 Andrew Brunette, Wsh	10.00	.75	.20
440 Jan Bulis, Wash.	8.00	.75	.20
441 Sergei Gonchar, Wash.	20.00	.75	.20
442 Dale Hunter, Wash.	20.00	.75	.20
443 S. Konowalchuk, Wash.	15.00	.75	.20
444 Kelly Miller, Wash.	10.00	.75	.20
445 Adam Oates, Wash.	25.00	1.00	.20
446 Bill Ranford (G), Wash.	25.00	1.00	.20
447 J. Svejkovsky, Wash.	10.00	.75	.20
448 Esa Tikkanen, Wash.	10.00	.75	.20
449 Mark Tinordi, Wash.	10.00	.75	.20
450 Brendan Witt, Wash.	8.00	.75	.20
451 Richard Zednik, Wash.	25.00	1.00	.20

Player	**Sample**
Mike Modano, Dall.	2.00

CRAMER'S CHOICE AWARD

Insert Set (10 cards):	**790.00**
Insert (1:721)	**CCA**
1 Sergei Samsonov, Bost.	35.00
2 Dominik Hasek (G), Buff.	60.00
3 Peter Forsberg, Colo.	80.00
4 Patrick Roy (G), Colo.	180.00
5 Mike Modano, Dall.	60.00
6 Martin Brodeur (G), NJer.	100.00
7 Wayne Gretzky, NYRa.	250.00
8 Eric Lindros, Phil.	60.00
9 Jaromir Jagr, Pitt.	60.00
10 Pavel Bure, Vanc.	50.00

DYNAGON ICE

This series has two versions: an insert card (4:37) and a Titanium parallel (#/99).

Insert Set (20 cards):	**1350.00**	**35.00**
Insert	**T99**	**DI**
1 Paul Kariya, Anah.	80.00	2.00
2 Teemu Selänne, Anah.	50.00	1.00
3 Sergei Samsonov, Bost.	30.00	1.00
4 Dominik Hasek (G), Buff.	60.00	2.00
5 Peter Forsberg, Colo.	80.00	2.00
6 Patrick Roy (G), Colo.	180.00	6.00
7 Joe Sakic, Colo.	100.00	3.00
8 Mike Modano, Dall.	60.00	2.00
9 Sergei Fedorov, Detr.	60.00	2.00
10 Steve Yzerman, Detr.	150.00	4.00
11 Saku Koivu, Mont.	50.00	1.00
12 Martin Brodeur (G), NJer.	100.00	3.00
13 Wayne Gretzky, NYRa.	250.00	8.00
14 John LeClair, Phil.	50.00	1.00
15 Eric Lindros, Phil.	60.00	2.00
16 Jaromir Jagr, Pitt.	60.00	2.00
17 Pavel Bure, Vanc.	50.00	1.00
18 Mark Messier, Vanc.	60.00	2.00
19 Peter Bondra, Wash.	30.00	1.00
20 Olaf Kölzig (G), Wash.	30.00	1.00

GOLD CROWN DIE-CUTS

Insert Set (36 cards):	**250.00**
Insert (1:37)	**GCDC**
1 Paul Kariya, Anah.	12.00
2 Teemu Selänne, Anah.	6.00
3 Sergei Samsonov, Bost.	5.00
4 Dominik Hasek (G), Buff.	8.00
5 Michael Peca, Buff.	5.00
6 Theoren Fleury, Calg.	5.00
7 Chris Chelios, Chic.	5.00
8 Peter Forsberg, Colo.	12.00
9 Patrick Roy (G), Colo.	25.00
10 Joe Sakic, Colo.	14.00
11 Ed Belfour (G), Dall.	8.00
12 Mike Modano, Dall.	8.00
13 Sergei Fedorov, Detr.	8.00
14 Chris Osgood (G), Detr.	5.00
15 Brendan Shanahan, Detr.	8.00
16 Steve Yzerman, Detr.	20.00
17 Saku Koivu, Mont.	7.00
18 Martin Brodeur (G), NJer.	14.00
19 Patrik Elias, NJer.	7.00
20 Doug Gilmour, NJer.	5.00
21 Trevor Linden, NYIs.	5.00
22 Zigmund Palffy, NYIs.	5.00
23 Wayne Gretzky, NYRa.	35.00
24 John LeClair, Phil.	6.00
25 Eric Lindros, Phil.	8.00
26 Dainius Zubrus, Phil.	5.00
27 Keith Tkachuk, Phoe.	5.00
28 Tom Barrasso (G), Pitt.	5.00
29 Jaromir Jagr, Pitt.	8.00
30 Brett Hull, SLou.	8.00
31 Félix Potvin (G), Toro.	5.00
32 Mats Sundin, Toro.	8.00
33 Pavel Bure, Vanc.	6.00
34 Mark Messier, Vanc.	8.00
35 Peter Bondra, Wash.	5.00
36 Olaf Kölzig (G), Wash.	5.00

TEAM CHECKLISTS

Insert Set (30 cards):	**80.00**
Insert (2:37)	**TC**
1 Paul Kariya, Anah.	4.00
2 Sergei Samsonov, Bost.	2.00
3 Dominik Hasek (G), Buff.	2.00
4 Theoren Fleury, Calg.	2.00
5 Keith Primeau, Caro.	2.00
6 Chris Chelios, Chic.	2.00
7 Patrick Roy (G), Colo.	10.00
8 Mike Modano, Dall.	3.00
9 Steve Yzerman, Detr.	8.00
10 Ryan Smyth, Edmo.	2.00
11 John Vanbiesbrouck (G), Flor.	2.00
12 Jozef Stümpel, LosA.	2.00
13 Saku Koivu, Mont.	3.00
14 Predators	2.00
15 Martin Brodeur (G), NJer.	6.00
16 Zigmund Palffy, NYIs.	2.00
17 Wayne Gretzky, NYRa.	15.00
18 Alexei Yashin, Otta.	2.00
19 Eric Lindros, Phil.	2.00
20 Keith Tkachuk, Phoe.	2.00
21 Jaromir Jagr, Pitt.	2.00
22 Brett Hull, SLou.	3.00
23 Patrick Marleau, SanJ.	2.00
24 Rob Zamuner, Tamp.	2.00
25 Mats Sundin, Toro.	3.00
26 Pavel Bure, Vanc.	2.00
27 Olaf Kölzig (G), Wash.	2.00
28 Thrashers	2.00
29 Wild	2.00
30 Blue Jackets	2.00

TIMELINES

Insert Set (20 cards):	**525.00**

Insert (1:181)	Time
1 Teemu Selänne, Anah./Winn.	20.00
2 Dominik Hasek (G), Buff.	25.00
3 Peter Forsberg, Colo.	35.00
4 Patrick Roy (G), Colo./Mont.	75.00
5 Joe Sakic, Colo. / Québ.	40.00
6 Ed Belfour (G), Dall./SanJ./Chic.	25.00
7 Brendan Shanahan, Detr./Hart./SLou./NJer.	25.00
8 Steve Yzerman, Detr. [w/ Cup]	60.00
9 Mike Modano, Dall./Minn.	25.00
10 Doug Gilmour, NJer./Toro./Calg.	15.00
11 Wayne Gretzky, NYRa.	100.00
12 Pat LaFontaine, NYRa./Buff./NYIs.	15.00
13 John LeClair, Phil./Mont.	20.00
14 Eric Lindros, Phil.	25.00
15 Keith Tkachuk, Phoe./Winn.	15.00
16 Jaromir Jagr, Pitt.	25.00
17 Brett Hull, SLou./Calg.	25.00
18 Mats Sundin, Toro./Québ.	25.00
19 Pavel Bure, Vanc.	20.00
20 Mark Messier, Vanc./NYRa./Edmo.	25.00

TROPHY WINNERS

Insert Set (10 cards):	100.00
Insert (1:37 Canadian)	TW
1 Martin Brodeur (G), Awards	20.00
2 Dominik Hasek (G), Awards	10.00
3 Jaromir Jagr, Awards	10.00
4 Sergei Samsonov, Awards	5.00
5 Sergei Fedorov with Stanley Cup	10.00
6 Niklas Lidstrom with Stanley Cup	8.00
7 Darren McCarty with Stanley Cup	8.00
8 Chris Osggod with Stanley Cup	8.00
9 Brendan Shanahan with Stanley Cup	10.00
10 Steve Yzerman with Stanley Cup	30.00

1998 - 99 PACIFIC CROWN ROYALE

There are two versions: the regular card and a Limited Series parallel (#/99).

Complete Set (144 cards):	1700.00	100.00
Common Player:	6.00	.50
Insert	LS99	CR
1 Travis Green, Anah.	10.00	.50
2 Guy Hebert (G), Anah.	10.00	.50
3 Paul Kariya, Anah.	70.00	4.00
4 Tomas Sandström, Anah.	10.00	.50
5 Teemu Selänne, Anah.	40.00	2.00
6 Jason Allison, Bost.	30.00	1.50
7 Raymond Bourque, Bost.	60.00	3.50
8 Byron Dafoe (G), Bost.	20.00	1.00
9 Dimitri Khristich, Bost.	6.00	.50
10 Sergei Samsonov, Bost.	30.00	1.50
11 Matthew Barnaby, Buff.	6.00	.50
12 Michal Grosek, Buff.	6.00	.50
13 Dominik Hasek (G), Buff.	50.00	3.00
14 Michael Peca, Buff.	20.00	1.00
15 Miroslav Satan, Buff.	15.00	.50
16 Andrew Cassels, Calg.	10.00	.50
17 Rico Fata, Calg.	10.00	1.00
18 Theoren Fleury, Calg.	30.00	1.50
19 Jarome Iginla, Calg.	40.00	2.00
20 Martin St-Louis, Calg. RC	**45.00**	**9.00**
21 Ken Wregget (G), Calg.	10.00	.50
22 Ron Francis, Caro.	30.00	1.50
23 Arturs Irbe (G), Caro.	20.00	1.00
24 Sami Kapanen, Caro.	15.00	.50
25 Trevor Kidd (G), Caro.	15.00	.50
26 Keith Primeau, Caro.	20.00	1.00
27 Tony Amonte, Chic.	30.00	1.50
28 Chris Chelios, Chic.	30.00	1.50
29 Éric Dazé, Chic.	20.00	1.00
30 Doug Gilmour, Chic.	30.00	1.50
31 Jocelyn Thibault (G), Chic.	20.00	1.00
32 Chris Drury, Colo.	30.00	3.50
33 Peter Forsberg, Colo.	70.00	4.00
34 Milan Hejduk, Colo. RC	**80.00**	**14.00**
35 Patrick Roy (G), Colo.	150.00	9.00
36 Joe Sakic, Colo.	80.00	4.50
37 Ed Belfour (G), Dall.	50.00	3.00
38 Brett Hull, Dall.	50.00	3.00
39 Jamie Langenbrunner, Dall.	10.00	.50
40 Jere Lehtinen, Dall.	15.00	.50
41 Mike Modano, Dall.	50.00	3.00
42 Joe Nieuwendyk, Dall.	20.00	1.00
43 Darryl Sydor, Dall.	10.00	.50
44 Sergei Fedorov, Detr.	50.00	3.00
45 Nicklas Lidström, Detr.	30.00	1.50
46 Darren McCarty, Detr.	15.00	.50
47 Chris Osgood (G), Detr.	30.00	1.50
48 Brendan Shanahan, Detr.	50.00	3.00
49 Steve Yzerman, Detr.	120.00	7.00
50 Bob Essensa (G), Edmo.	10.00	.50
51 Bill Guerin, Edmo.	20.00	1.00
52 Janne Niinimaa, Edmo.	10.00	.50
53 Tom Poti, Edmo.	6.00	.50
54 Ryan Smyth, Edmo.	20.00	1.00
55 Doug Weight, Edmo.	30.00	1.50
56 Sean Burke (G), Flor.	30.00	1.50
57 Dino Ciccarelli, Flor.	15.00	.50
58 Ed Jovanovski, Flor.	20.00	1.00
59 Viktor Kozlov, Flor.	15.00	.50
60 Oleg Kvasha, Flor. RC	**15.00**	**3.00**
61 Mark Parrish, Flor.	40.00	6.00
62 Rob Blake, LosA.	30.00	1.50
63 Manny Legace (G), LosA.	15.00	1.50
64 Yanic Perreault, LosA.	15.00	.50
65 Luc Robitaille, LosA.	40.00	2.00
66 Jozef Stümpel, LosA.	10.00	.50
67 Shayne Corson, Mont.	15.00	.50
68 Vincent Damphousse, Mont.	30.00	1.50
69 Jeff Hackett (G), Mont.	15.00	.50
70 Saku Koivu, Mont.	40.00	2.00
71 Mark Recchi, Mont.	20.00	1.00
72 Andrew Brunette, Nash.	6.00	.50
73 Mike Dunham, Nash.	20.00	1.00
74 Tom Fitzgerald, Nash.	6.00	.50
75 Greg Johnson, Nash.	6.00	.50
76 Sergei Krivokrasov, Nash.	6.00	.50
77 Jason Arnott, NJer.	20.00	1.00
78 Martin Brodeur (G), NJer.	80.00	4.50
79 Patrik Elias, NJer.	40.00	2.00
80 Bobby Holik, NJer.	15.00	.50
81 Brendan Morrison, NJer.	15.00	.50
82 Bryan Berard, NYIs.	15.00	.50
83 Trevor Linden, NYIs.	20.00	1.00
84 Zigmund Palffy, NYIs.	30.00	1.50
85 Robert Reichel, NYIs.	15.00	.50
86 Tommy Salo (G), NYIs.	20.00	1.00
87 Adam Graves, NYRa.	20.00	1.00
88 Wayne Gretzky, NYRa.	200.00	12.00
89 Brian Leetch, NYRa.	30.00	1.50
90 Manny Malhotra, NYRa.	10.00	1.00
91 Mike Richter (G), NYRa.	20.00	1.00
92 Daniel Alfredsson, Ott.	30.00	1.50
93 Igor Kravchuk, Ott.	6.00	.50
94 Shawn McEachern, Ott.	15.00	.50
95 Damian Rhodes (G), Ott.	10.00	.50
96 Alexei Yashin, Ott.	30.00	1.50
97 Rod Brind'Amour, Phil.	15.00	.50
98 Ron Hextall (G), Phil.	30.00	1.50
99 John LeClair, Phil.	40.00	2.00
100 Eric Lindros, Phil.	50.00	3.00
101 John Vanbiesbrouck (G), Phil.	20.00	1.00
102 Dainius Zubrus, Phil.	10.00	.50
103 Nikolai Khabibulin (G), Phoe.	20.00	1.00
104 Jeremy Roenick, Phoe.	40.00	2.00
105 Keith Tkachuk, Phoe.	30.00	1.50
106 Rick Tocchet, Phoe.	15.00	.50
107 Oleg Tverdovsky, Phoe.	6.00	.50
108 Tom Barrasso (G), Pitt.	20.00	1.00
109 Jan Hrdina, Pitt. RC	**20.00**	**4.50**
110 Jaromir Jagr, Pitt.	50.00	3.00
111 Alexei Morozov, Pitt.	10.00	.50
112 German Titov, Pitt.	6.00	.50
113 Jim Campbell, SLou.	6.00	.50
114 Grant Fuhr (G), SLou.	30.00	1.50
115 Al MacInnis, SLou.	20.00	1.00
116 Chris Pronger, SLou.	30.00	1.50
117 Pierre Turgeon, SLou.	20.00	1.00
118 Jeff Friesen, SanJ.	15.00	.50
119 Patrick Marleau, SanJ.	20.00	1.00
120 Owen Nolan, SanJ.	30.00	1.50
121 Marco Sturm, SanJ.	10.00	.50
122 Mike Vernon (G), SanJ.	20.00	1.00
123 Wendel Clark, Tamp.	40.00	2.00
124 Vincent Lecavalier, Tamp.	50.00	6.00
125 Bill Ranford (G), Tamp.	20.00	1.00
126 Stéphane Richer, Tamp.	10.00	.50
127 Rob Zamuner, Tamp.	10.00	.50
128 Sergei Berezin, Toro.	10.00	.50
129 Tie Domi, Toro.	15.00	.50
130 Mike Johnson, Toro.	10.00	.50
131 Curtis Joseph (G), Toro.	50.00	3.00
132 Mats Sundin, Toro.	50.00	3.00
133 Donald Brashear, Vanc.	10.00	.50
134 Pavel Bure, Vanc.	40.00	2.00
135 Mark Messier, Vanc.	50.00	3.00
136 Alexander Mogilny, Vanc.	20.00	1.00
137 Bill Muckalt, Vanc. RC	**15.00**	**3.00**
138 Mattias Öhlund, Vanc.	15.00	.50
139 Garth Snow (G), Vanc.	15.00	.50
140 Peter Bondra, Wash.	30.00	1.50
141 Matt Herr, Wash.	10.00	1.50
142 Joé Juneau, Wash.	10.00	.50
143 Olaf Kölzig (G), Wash.	30.00	1.50
144 Adam Oates, Wash.	20.00	1.00

Player	Sample
Martin Brodeur (G), NJer.	2.00

CRAMER'S CHOICE AWARD

These cards have seven versions: the regular card, a Dark Blue parallel (#/35), a Green parallel (#/30), a Red parallel (#/25), a Light Blue parallel (#/20), a Gold parallel (#/10) and a Purple parallel (1 copy).

Card Size: 4" x 5 9/16"

Insert Set (10 cards):			65.00
Green / Dark Blue / Insert	Gr30	DB35	CCA
1 Paul Kariya	225.00	200.00	6.00
2 Teemu Selänne	125.00	100.00	5.00
3 Dominik Hasek (G)	150.00	150.00	5.00
4 Peter Forsberg	225.00	200.00	6.00
5 Patrick Roy (G)	475.00	450.00	14.00
6 Steve Yzerman	375.00	350.00	12.00
7 Martin Brodeur (G)	250.00	225.00	8.00
8 Wayne Gretzky	650.00	600.00	20.00
9 Eric Lindros	150.00	150.00	5.00
10 Jaromir Jagr	150.00	150.00	5.00
Gold / Light Blue / Red	Go10	LB20	R25
1 Paul Kariya	350.00	275.00	240.00
2 Teemu Selänne	200.00	150.00	140.00
3 Dominik Hasek (G)	250.00	200.00	170.00
4 Peter Forsberg	350.00	275.00	240.00
5 Patrick Roy (G)	750.00	600.00	520.00
6 Steve Yzerman	600.00	475.00	420.00
7 Martin Brodeur (G)	400.00	300.00	280.00
8 Wayne Gretzky	1000.00	800.00	700.00
9 Eric Lindros	250.00	200.00	170.00
10 Jaromir Jagr	250.00	200.00	170.00

LIVING LEGENDS

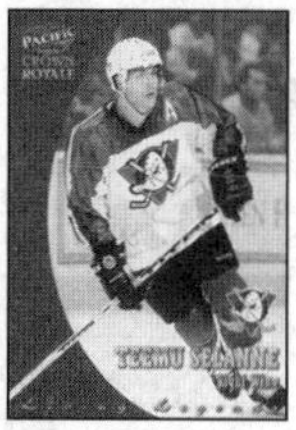

Insert Set (10 cards):	160.00
Insert (1:73)	LL
1 Paul Kariya, Anah.	15.00
2 Teemu Selänne, Anah.	10.00
3 Dominik Hasek (G), Buff.	10.00
4 Peter Forsberg, Colo.	15.00
5 Patrick Roy (G), Colo.	35.00
6 Steve Yzerman, Detr.	30.00
7 Martin Brodeur (G), NJer.	20.00
8 Wayne Gretzky, NYRa.	50.00
9 Eric Lindros, Phil.	10.00
10 Jaromir Jagr, Pitt.	10.00

MASTER PERFORMERS

Insert Set (20 cards):	65.00
Insert (2:25)	MP
1 Paul Kariya, Anah.	4.00
2 Teemu Selänne, Anah.	2.00
3 Dominik Hasek (G), Buff.	2.00
4 Peter Forsberg, Colo.	4.00
5 Patrick Roy (G), Colo.	10.00
6 Joe Sakic, Colo.	6.00
7 Brett Hull, Dall.	2.00
8 Mike Modano, Dall.	2.00
9 Sergei Fedorov, Detr.	2.00
10 Brendan Shanahan, Detr.	2.00
11 Steve Yzerman, Detr.	8.00
12 Saku Koivu, Mont.	2.00
13 Martin Brodeur (G), NJer.	6.00
14 Wayne Gretzky, NYRa.	15.00
15 John LeClair, Phil.	2.00
16 Eric Lindros, Phil.	2.00
17 Jaromir Jagr, Pitt.	2.00
18 Mats Sundin, Toro.	2.00
19 Mark Messier, Vanc.	2.00
20 Peter Bondra, Wash.	2.00

PILLARS OF THE GAME

Insert Set (25 cards):	25.00
Insert (1:1)	PotG
1 Teemu Selänne, Anah.	1.00
2 Raymond Bourque, Bost.	1.50
3 Michael Peca, Buff.	.50
4 Theoren Fleury, Calg.	.50
5 Chris Chelios, Chic.	.50
6 Doug Gilmour, Chic.	.50
7 Patrick Roy (G), Colo.	4.50
8 Joe Sakic, Colo.	2.00
9 Ed Belfour (G), Dall.	1.50
10 Brett Hull, Dall.	1.50
11 Mike Modano, Dall.	1.50
12 Sergei Fedorov, Detr.	1.50
13 Brendan Shanahan, Detr.	1.50
14 Steve Yzerman, Detr.	3.50
15 Saku Koivu, Mont.	1.00
16 Martin Brodeur (G), NJer.	2.00
17 John LeClair, Phil.	1.00
18 Eric Lindros, Phil.	1.50
19 John Vanbiesbrouck (G), Phil.	.50
20 Keith Tkachuk, Phoe.	.50
21 Jaromir Jagr, Pitt.	1.50
22 Curtis Joseph (G), Toro.	1.50
23 Mats Sundin, Toro.	1.50
24 Mark Messier, Vanc.	1.50
25 Peter Bondra, Wash.	.50

PIVOTAL PLAYERS

Insert Set (25 cards):	25.00
Insert (1:1)	PP
1 Paul Kariya, Anah.	2.00
2 Dominik Hasek (G), Buff.	1.50
3 Michael Peca, Buff.	.50

4 Peter Forsberg, Colo.	2.00
5 Joe Sakic, Colo.	2.00
6 Brett Hull, Dall.	1.50
7 Mike Modano, Dall.	1.50
8 Sergei Fedorov, Detr.	1.50
9 Chris Osgood (G), Detr.	.50
10 Brendan Shanahan, Detr.	1.50
11 Ryan Smyth, Edmo.	.50
12 Mark Parrish, Flor.	.50
13 Saku Koivu, Mont.	1.00
14 Martin Brodeur (G), NJer.	2.00
15 Trevor Linden, NYIs.	.50
16 Wayne Gretzky, NYRa.	6.00
17 Alexei Yashin, Ott.	.50
18 John LeClair, Phil.	1.00
19 John Vanbiesbrouck (G), Phil.	.50
20 Keith Tkachuk, Phoe.	.50
21 Vincent Lecavalier, Tamp.	3.00
22 Mats Sundin, Toro.	1.50
23 Mark Messier, Vanc.	1.50
24 Peter Bondra, Wash.	.50
25 Olaf Kölzig (G), Wash.	.50

ROOKIE CLASS

Insert Set (10 cards): 75.00

Insert (1:25)	Rookie
1 Chris Drury, Colo.	12.00
2 Milan Hejduk, Colo.	16.00
3 Mark Parrish, Flor.	8.00
4 Manny Legace, LosA.	6.00
5 Brendan Morrison, NJer.	6.00
6 Manny Malhotra, NYRa.	6.00
7 Daniel Brière, Phoe.	8.00
8 Vincent Lecavalier, Tamp.	20.00
9 Tomas Kaberle, Toro.	6.00
10 Bill Muckalt, Vanc.	6.00

1998 - 99 PACIFIC PARAMOUNT

These cards have six versions: the regular card, an Emerald Green parallel (1:1 Cdn), a Silver parallel (1:1 Retail), a Copper parallel (1:1 Hobby), an Ice Blue parallel (1:73) and a Holoelectric parallel (#/99). The one-per-pack Emerald, Silver, and Copper parallels have the same pricing below.

Complete Set (250 cards): 3300.00 2500.00 25.00
Common Player: 6.00 5.00 0.20

Player	IB67	HE99	Reg.
1 Travis Green	15.00	10.00	.20
2 Guy Hebert (G)	15.00	10.00	.20
3 Paul Kariya	80.00	70.00	1.00
4 Josef Marha	6.00	5.00	.20
5 Steve Rucchin	15.00	10.00	.20
6 Tomas Sandström	15.00	10.00	.20
7 Teemu Selänne	50.00	40.00	.50
8 Jason Allison	35.00	30.00	.20
9 Per Axelsson	10.00	5.00	.20
10 Raymond Bourque	70.00	60.00	.50
11 Anson Carter	25.00	20.00	.20
12 Byron Dafoe (G)	25.00	20.00	.20
13 Ted Donato	6.00	5.00	.20
14 Dave Ellett	10.00	5.00	.20
15 Dimitri Khristich	10.00	5.00	.20
16 Sergei Samsonov	35.00	30.00	.20
17 Matthew Barnaby	6.00	5.00	.20
18 Michal Grosek	6.00	5.00	.20
19 Dominik Hasek (G)	60.00	50.00	.50
20 Brian Holzinger	10.00	5.00	.20
21 Michael Peca	25.00	20.00	.20
22 Miroslav Satan	20.00	15.00	.20
23 Vaclav Varada	10.00	5.00	.20
24 Dixon Ward	6.00	5.00	.20
25 Alexei Zhitnik	10.00	5.00	.20
26 Andrew Cassels	15.00	10.00	.20
27 Theoren Fleury	30.00	30.00	.20
28 Jarome Iginla	50.00	40.00	.50
29 Marty McInnis	10.00	5.00	.20
30 Derek Morris	15.00	10.00	.20
31 Michael Nylander	15.00	10.00	.20
32 Cory Stillman	15.00	10.00	.20
33 Rick Tabaracci (G)	10.00	5.00	.20
34 Kevin Dineen	10.00	5.00	.20
35 Nelson Emerson	10.00	5.00	.20
36 Martin Gelinas	15.00	10.00	.20
37 Sami Kapanen	20.00	15.00	.20
38 Trevor Kidd (G)	20.00	15.00	.20
39 Robert Kron	10.00	5.00	.20
40 Jeff O'Neill	25.00	20.00	.20
41 Keith Primeau	25.00	20.00	.20
42 Gary Roberts	25.00	20.00	.20
43 Tony Amonte	35.00	30.00	.20
44 Chris Chelios	35.00	30.00	.20
45 Paul Coffey	35.00	30.00	.20
46 Eric Dazé	25.00	20.00	.20
47 Doug Gilmour	35.00	30.00	.20
48 Jeff Hackett (G)	20.00	15.00	.20
49 Jean-Yves Leroux	6.00	5.00	.20
50 Eric Weinrich	6.00	5.00	.20
51 Alexei Zhamnov	20.00	15.00	.20
52 Craig Billington (G)	10.00	5.00	.20
53 Adam Deadmarsh	20.00	15.00	.20
54 Adam Foote	20.00	15.00	.20
55 Peter Forsberg	80.00	70.00	1.00
56 Valeri Kamensky	20.00	15.00	.20
57 Claude Lemieux	20.00	15.00	.20
58 Eric Messier	10.00	5.00	.20
59 Sandis Ozolinsh	15.00	10.00	.20
60 Patrick Roy (G)	180.00	150.00	2.00
61 Joe Sakic	100.00	80.00	1.00
62 Ed Belfour (G)	60.00	50.00	.50
63 Derian Hatcher	20.00	15.00	.20
64 Brett Hull	60.00	50.00	.50
65 Jamie Langenbrunner	15.00	10.00	.20
66 Jere Lehtinen	20.00	15.00	.20
67 Juha Lind	10.00	5.00	.20
68 Mike Modano	60.00	50.00	.50
69 Joe Nieuwendyk	25.00	20.00	.20
70 Darryl Sydor	15.00	10.00	.20
71 Roman Turek (G)	30.00	20.00	.20
72 Sergei Zubov	15.00	10.00	.20
73 Anders Eriksson	6.00	5.00	.20
74 Sergei Fedorov	60.00	50.00	.50
75 Kevin Hodson (G)	15.00	10.00	.20
76 Vyacheslav Kozlov	15.00	10.00	.20
77 Igor Larionov	35.00	30.00	.20
78 Nicklas Lidström	35.00	30.00	.20
79 Darren McCarty	20.00	15.00	.20
80 Larry Murphy	15.00	10.00	.20
81 Chris Osgood (G)	35.00	30.00	.20
82 Brendan Shanahan	60.00	50.00	.50
83 Steve Yzerman	150.00	120.00	1.50
84 Kelly Buchberger	10.00	5.00	.20
85 Mike Grier	15.00	10.00	.20
86 Bill Guerin	25.00	20.00	.20
87 Roman Hamrlik	15.00	10.00	.20
88 Todd Marchant	15.00	10.00	.20
89 Dean McAmmond	10.00	5.00	.20
90 Boris Mironov	10.00	5.00	.20
91 Janne Niinimaa	15.00	10.00	.20
92 Ryan Smyth	30.00	20.00	.20
93 Doug Weight	35.00	30.00	.20
94 Dino Ciccarelli	20.00	15.00	.20
95 Dave Gagner	10.00	5.00	.20
96 Ed Jovanovski	25.00	20.00	.20
97 Viktor Kozlov	20.00	15.00	.20
98 Paul Laus	6.00	5.00	.20
99 Scott Mellanby	15.00	10.00	.20
100 Robert Svehla	15.00	10.00	.20
101 Ray Whitney	15.00	10.00	.20
102 Rob Blake	35.00	30.00	.20
103 Russ Courtnall	15.00	10.00	.20
104 Stéphane Fiset (G)	20.00	15.00	.20
105 Glen Murray	30.00	20.00	.20
106 Yanic Perreault	20.00	15.00	.20
107 Luc Robitaille	50.00	40.00	.50
108 Jamie Storr (G)	15.00	10.00	.20
109 Jozef Stümpel	15.00	10.00	.20
110 Vladimir Tsyplakov	6.00	5.00	.20
111 Shayne Corson	20.00	15.00	.20
112 Vincent Damphousse	35.00	30.00	.20
113 Saku Koivu	50.00	40.00	.50
114 Vladimir Malakhov	10.00	5.00	.20
115 Dave Manson	10.00	5.00	.20
116 Mark Recchi	25.00	20.00	.20
117 Martin Rucinsky	15.00	10.00	.20
118 Brian Savage	20.00	15.00	.20
119 Jocelyn Thibault (G)	25.00	20.00	.20
120 Blair Atcheynum	6.00	5.00	.20
121 Andrew Brunette	10.00	5.00	.20
122 Mike Dunham (G)	25.00	20.00	.20
123 Tom Fitzgerald	6.00	5.00	.20
124 Sergei Krivokrasov	10.00	5.00	.20
125 Denny Lambert	6.00	5.00	.20
126 Jay More	6.00	5.00	.20
127 Mikhail Shtalenkov (G)	10.00	5.00	.20
128 Darren Turcotte	10.00	5.00	.20
129 Scott Walker	15.00	10.00	.20
130 Dave Andreychuk	20.00	15.00	.20
131 Jason Arnott	30.00	20.00	.20
132 Martin Brodeur (G)	100.00	80.00	1.00
133 Patrik Elias	50.00	40.00	.50
134 Bobby Holik	20.00	15.00	.20
135 Randy McKay	6.00	5.00	.20
136 Scott Niedermayer	20.00	15.00	.20
137 Krzysztof Oliwa	15.00	10.00	.20
138 Sheldon Souray RC	**6.00**	**5.00**	**.50**
139 Scott Stevens	25.00	20.00	.20
140 Bryan Berard	20.00	15.00	.20
141 Mariusz Czerkawski	15.00	10.00	.20
142 Jason Dawe	6.00	5.00	.20
143 Kenny Jönsson	10.00	10.00	.20
144 Trevor Linden	25.00	20.00	.20
145 Zigmund Palffy	35.00	30.00	.20
146 Richard Pilon	6.00	5.00	.20
147 Robert Reichel	20.00	15.00	.20
148 Tommy Salo (G)	25.00	20.00	.20
149 Bryan Smolinski	10.00	5.00	.20
150 Dan Cloutier (G)	25.00	20.00	.20
151 Adam Graves	25.00	20.00	.20
152 Wayne Gretzky	250.00	200.00	3.00
153 Alexei Kovalev	35.00	30.00	.20
154 Pat LaFontaine	35.00	30.00	.20
155 Brian Leetch	35.00	30.00	.20
156 Mike Richter (G)	30.00	20.00	.20
157 Ulf Samuelsson	10.00	5.00	.20
158 Kevin Stevens	15.00	10.00	.20
159 Niklas Sundström	15.00	10.00	.20
160 Daniel Alfredsson	35.00	30.00	.20
161 Magnus Arvedsson	10.00	5.00	.20
162 Andreas Dackell	10.00	5.00	.20
163 Igor Kravchuk	10.00	5.00	.20
164 Shawn McEachern	20.00	15.00	.20
165 Chris Phillips	15.00	10.00	.20
166 Damian Rhodes (G)	15.00	10.00	.20
167 Ron Tugnutt (G)	25.00	20.00	.20
168 Alexei Yashin	35.00	30.00	.20
169 Ron Brind'Amour	20.00	15.00	.20
170 Alexandre Daigle	10.00	5.00	.20
171 Éric Desjardins	20.00	15.00	.20
172 Colin Forbes	6.00	5.00	.20
173 Chris Gratton	15.00	10.00	.20
174 Ron Hextall (G)	35.00	30.00	.20
175 Trent Klatt	10.00	5.00	.20
176 John LeClair	50.00	40.00	.50
177 Eric Lindros	60.00	50.00	.50
178 John Vanbiesbrouck (G)	30.00	20.00	.20
179 Dainius Zubrus	15.00	10.00	.20
180 Dallas Drake	10.00	5.00	.20
181 Brad Isbister	15.00	10.00	.20
182 Nikolai Khabibulin (G)	25.00	20.00	.20
183 Teppo Nemminen	20.00	15.00	.20
184 Jeremy Roenick	50.00	40.00	.50
185 Cliff Ronning	15.00	10.00	.20
186 Keith Tkachuk	35.00	30.00	.20
187 Rick Tocchet	20.00	15.00	.20
188 Oleg Tverdovsky	10.00	5.00	.20
189 Stu Barnes	6.00	5.00	.20
190 Tom Barrasso (G)	25.00	20.00	.20
191 Kevin Hatcher	10.00	5.00	.20
192 Jaromir Jagr	60.00	50.00	.50
193 Darius Kasparaitis	15.00	10.00	.20
194 Alexei Morozov	15.00	10.00	.20
195 Fredrik Olausson	15.00	10.00	.20
196 Jiri Slegr	10.00	5.00	.20
197 Martin Straka	20.00	15.00	.20
198 Jim Campbell	6.00	5.00	.20
199 Kelly Chase	10.00	5.00	.20
200 Craig Conroy	20.00	15.00	.20
201 Geoff Courtnall	10.00	5.00	.20
202 Pavol Demitra	25.00	20.00	.20
203 Grant Fuhr (G)	35.00	30.00	.20
204 Al MacInnis	25.00	20.00	.20
205 Jamie McLennan	10.00	5.00	.20
206 Chris Pronger	35.00	30.00	.20
207 Pierre Turgeon	25.00	20.00	.20
208 Tony Twist	10.00	5.00	.20
209 Jeff Friesen	20.00	15.00	.20
210 Tony Granato	15.00	10.00	.20
211 Patrick Marleau	30.00	20.00	.20
212 Stéphane Matteau	10.00	5.00	.20
213 Marty McSorley	15.00	10.00	.20
214 Owen Nolan	35.00	30.00	.20
215 Marco Sturm	15.00	10.00	.20
216 Mike Vernon (G)	25.00	20.00	.20
217 Karl Dykhuis	6.00	5.00	.20
218 Sandy McCarthy	10.00	5.00	.20
219 Mikael Renberg	20.00	15.00	.20
220 Stéphane Richer	15.00	10.00	.20
221 Alexander Selivanov	6.00	5.00	.20
222 Paul Ysebaert	6.00	5.00	.20
223 Rob Zamuner	15.00	10.00	.20
224 Sergei Berezin	15.00	10.00	.20
225 Tie Domi	20.00	15.00	.20
226 Mike Johnson	10.00	10.00	.20
227 Curtis Joseph (G)	60.00	50.00	.50
228 Derek King	10.00	5.00	.20
229 Igor Korolev	10.00	5.00	.20
230 Mathieu Schneider	15.00	10.00	.20
231 Mats Sundin	60.00	50.00	.50
232 Todd Bertuzzi	75.00	60.00	.50
233 Donald Brashear	15.00	10.00	.20
234 Pavel Bure	50.00	40.00	.50
235 Arturs Irbe (G)	25.00	20.00	.20
236 Mark Messier	60.00	50.00	.50
237 Alexander Mogilny	30.00	20.00	.20
238 Mattias Öhlund	20.00	15.00	.20
239 Dave Scatchard	6.00	5.00	.20
240 Garth Snow (G)	20.00	15.00	.20
241 Brian Bellows	15.00	10.00	.20
242 Peter Bondra	35.00	30.00	.20
243 Jeff Brown	6.00	5.00	.20
244 Sergei Gonchar	20.00	15.00	.20
245 Calle Johansson	15.00	10.00	.20
246 Joé Juneau	15.00	10.00	.20
247 Olaf Kölzig (G)	35.00	30.00	.20
248 Steve Konowalchuk	15.00	10.00	.20
249 Adam Oates	25.00	20.00	.20
250 Richard Zednik	25.00	20.00	.20

ONE-PER-PACK PARALLELS

The one-per-pack Emerald, Silver, and Copper parallels have the same pricing below.

Complete Set (250 cards): 100.00
Common Player: .50

Player	Parallel
1 Travis Green	.50
2 Guy Hebert (G)	.50
3 Paul Kariya	2.50
4 Josef Marha	.50
5 Steve Rucchin	.50
6 Tomas Sandström	.50
7 Teemu Selänne	1.50
8 Jason Allison	1.00
9 Per Axelsson	.50
10 Raymond Bourque	2.00
11 Anson Carter	.50
12 Byron Dafoe (G)	.50
13 Ted Donato	.50
14 Dave Ellett	.50
15 Dimitri Khristich	.50
16 Sergei Samsonov	1.00
17 Matthew Barnaby	.50
18 Michal Grosek	.50
19 Dominik Hasek (G)	2.00
20 Brian Holzinger	.50
21 Michael Peca	.50
22 Miroslav Satan	.50
23 Vaclav Varada	.50
24 Dixon Ward	.50
25 Alexei Zhitnik	.50
26 Andrew Cassels	.50
27 Theoren Fleury	1.00
28 Jarome Iginla	1.50
29 Marty McInnis	.50
30 Derek Morris	.50
31 Michael Nylander	.50
32 Cory Stillman	.50
33 Rick Tabaracci (G)	.50
34 Kevin Dineen	.50
35 Nelson Emerson	.50
36 Martin Gelinas	.50
37 Sami Kapanen	.50
38 Trevor Kidd (G)	.50
39 Robert Kron	.50
40 Jeff O'Neill	.50
41 Keith Primeau	.50
42 Gary Roberts	.50
43 Tony Amonte	1.00
44 Chris Chelios	1.00
45 Paul Coffey	1.00
46 Eric Dazé	.50
47 Doug Gilmour	1.00
48 Jeff Hackett (G)	.50
49 Jean-Yves Leroux	.50
50 Eric Weinrich	.50
51 Alexei Zhamnov	.50
52 Craig Billington (G)	.50
53 Adam Deadmarsh	.50
54 Adam Foote	.50
55 Peter Forsberg	2.50
56 Valeri Kamensky	.50
57 Claude Lemieux	.50
58 Eric Messier	.50

☐☐☐	59 Sandis Ozolinsh	.50
☐☐☐	60 Patrick Roy (G)	6.00
☐☐☐	61 Joe Sakic	3.00
☐☐☐	62 Ed Belfour (G)	2.00
☐☐☐	63 Derian Hatcher	.50
☐☐☐	64 Brett Hull	2.00
☐☐☐	65 Jamie Langenbrunner	.50
☐☐☐	66 Jere Lehtinen	.50
☐☐☐	67 Juha Lind	.50
☐☐☐	68 Mike Modano	2.00
☐☐☐	69 Joe Nieuwendyk	.50
☐☐☐	70 Darryl Sydor	.50
☐☐☐	71 Roman Turek (G)	.50
☐☐☐	72 Sergei Zubov	.50
☐☐☐	73 Anders Eriksson	.50
☐☐☐	74 Sergei Fedorov	2.00
☐☐☐	75 Kevin Hodson (G)	.50
☐☐☐	76 Vyacheslav Kozlov	.50
☐☐☐	77 Igor Larionov	1.00
☐☐☐	78 Nicklas Lidström	1.00
☐☐☐	79 Darren McCarty	.50
☐☐☐	80 Larry Murphy	.50
☐☐☐	81 Chris Osgood (G)	1.00
☐☐☐	82 Brendan Shanahan	2.00
☐☐☐	83 Steve Yzerman	4.50
☐☐☐	84 Kelly Buchberger	.50
☐☐☐	85 Mike Grier	.50
☐☐☐	86 Bill Guerin	.50
☐☐☐	87 Roman Hamrlik	.50
☐☐☐	88 Todd Marchant	.50
☐☐☐	89 Dean McAmmond	.50
☐☐☐	90 Boris Mironov	.50
☐☐☐	91 Janne Niinimaa	.50
☐☐☐	92 Ryan Smyth	.50
☐☐☐	93 Doug Weight	1.00
☐☐☐	94 Dino Ciccarelli	.50
☐☐☐	95 Dave Gagner	.50
☐☐☐	96 Ed Jovanovski	.50
☐☐☐	97 Viktor Kozlov	.50
☐☐☐	98 Paul Laus	.50
☐☐☐	99 Scott Mellanby	.50
☐☐☐	100 Robert Svehla	.50
☐☐☐	101 Ray Whitney	.50
☐☐☐	102 Rob Blake	1.00
☐☐☐	103 Russ Courtnall	.50
☐☐☐	104 Stéphane Fiset (G)	.50
☐☐☐	105 Glen Murray	.50
☐☐☐	106 Yanic Perreault	.50
☐☐☐	107 Luc Robitaille	1.50
☐☐☐	108 Jamie Storr (G)	.50
☐☐☐	109 Jozef Stümpel	.50
☐☐☐	110 Vladimir Tsyplakov	.50
☐☐☐	111 Shayne Corson	.50
☐☐☐	112 Vincent Damphousse	1.00
☐☐☐	113 Saku Koivu	1.50
☐☐☐	114 Vladimir Malakhov	.50
☐☐☐	115 Dave Manson	.50
☐☐☐	116 Mark Recchi	.50
☐☐☐	117 Martin Rucinsky	.50
☐☐☐	118 Brian Savage	.50
☐☐☐	119 Jocelyn Thibault (G)	.50
☐☐☐	120 Blair Atcheynum	.50
☐☐☐	121 Andrew Brunette	.50
☐☐☐	122 Mike Dunham (G)	.50
☐☐☐	123 Tom Fitzgerald	.50
☐☐☐	124 Sergei Krivokrasov	.50
☐☐☐	125 Denny Lambert	.50
☐☐☐	126 Jay More	.50
☐☐☐	127 Mikhail Shtalenkov (G)	.50
☐☐☐	128 Darren Turcotte	.50
☐☐☐	129 Scott Walker	.50
☐☐☐	130 Dave Andreychuk	.50
☐☐☐	131 Jason Arnott	.50
☐☐☐	132 Martin Brodeur (G)	3.00
☐☐☐	133 Patrik Elias	1.50
☐☐☐	134 Bobby Holik	.50
☐☐☐	135 Randy McKay	.50
☐☐☐	136 Scott Niedermayer	.50
☐☐☐	137 Krzysztof Oliwa	.50
☐☐☐	**138 Sheldon Souray RC**	**1.00**
☐☐☐	139 Scott Stevens	.50
☐☐☐	140 Bryan Berard	.50
☐☐☐	141 Mariusz Czerkawski	.50
☐☐☐	142 Jason Dawe	.50
☐☐☐	143 Kenny Jönsson	.50
☐☐☐	144 Trevor Linden	.50
☐☐☐	145 Zigmund Palffy	1.00
☐☐☐	146 Richard Pilon	.50
☐☐☐	147 Robert Reichel	.50
☐☐☐	148 Tommy Salo (G)	.50
☐☐☐	149 Bryan Smolinski	.50
☐☐☐	150 Dan Cloutier (G)	.50
☐☐☐	151 Adam Graves	.50
☐☐☐	152 Wayne Gretzky	8.00
☐☐☐	153 Alexei Kovalev	1.00
☐☐☐	154 Pat LaFontaine	1.00
☐☐☐	155 Brian Leetch	1.00
☐☐☐	156 Mike Richter (G)	.50
☐☐☐	157 Ulf Samuelsson	.50
☐☐☐	158 Kevin Stevens	.50
☐☐☐	159 Niklas Sundström	.50
☐☐☐	160 Daniel Alfredsson	1.00
☐☐☐	161 Magnus Arvedsson	.50
☐☐☐	162 Andreas Dackell	.50
☐☐☐	163 Igor Kravchuk	.50
☐☐☐	164 Shawn McEachern	.50
☐☐☐	165 Chris Phillips	.50
☐☐☐	166 Damian Rhodes (G)	.50
☐☐☐	167 Ron Tugnutt (G)	.50
☐☐☐	168 Alexei Yashin	1.00
☐☐☐	169 Ron Brind'Amour	.50
☐☐☐	170 Alexandre Daigle	.50
☐☐☐	171 Éric Desjardins	.50
☐☐☐	172 Colin Forbes	.50
☐☐☐	173 Chris Gratton	.50
☐☐☐	174 Ron Hextall (G)	1.00
☐☐☐	175 Trent Klatt	.50
☐☐☐	176 John LeClair	1.50
☐☐☐	177 Eric Lindros	2.00
☐☐☐	178 John Vanbiesbrouck (G)	.50
☐☐☐	179 Dainius Zubrus	.50
☐☐☐	180 Dallas Drake	.50
☐☐☐	181 Brad Isbister	.50
☐☐☐	182 Nikolai Khabibulin (G)	.50
☐☐☐	183 Teppo Nemminen	.50
☐☐☐	184 Jeremy Roenick	1.50
☐☐☐	185 Cliff Ronning	.50
☐☐☐	186 Keith Tkachuk	1.00
☐☐☐	187 Rick Tocchet	.50
☐☐☐	188 Oleg Tverdovsky	.50
☐☐☐	189 Stu Barnes	.50
☐☐☐	190 Tom Barrasso (G)	.50
☐☐☐	191 Kevin Hatcher	.50
☐☐☐	192 Jaromir Jagr	2.00
☐☐☐	193 Darius Kasparaitis	.50
☐☐☐	194 Alexei Morozov	.50
☐☐☐	195 Fredrik Olausson	.50
☐☐☐	196 Jiri Slegr	.50
☐☐☐	197 Martin Straka	.50
☐☐☐	198 Jim Campbell	.50
☐☐☐	199 Kelly Chase	.50
☐☐☐	200 Craig Conroy	.50
☐☐☐	201 Geoff Courtnall	.50
☐☐☐	202 Pavol Demitra	.50
☐☐☐	203 Grant Fuhr (G)	1.00
☐☐☐	204 Al MacInnis	.50
☐☐☐	205 Jamie McLennan	.50
☐☐☐	206 Chris Pronger	1.00
☐☐☐	207 Pierre Turgeon	.50
☐☐☐	208 Tony Twist	.50
☐☐☐	209 Jeff Friesen	.50
☐☐☐	210 Tony Granato	.50
☐☐☐	211 Patrick Marleau	.50
☐☐☐	212 Stéphane Matteau	.50
☐☐☐	213 Marty McSorley	.50
☐☐☐	214 Owen Nolan	1.00
☐☐☐	215 Marco Sturm	.50
☐☐☐	216 Mike Vernon (G)	.50
☐☐☐	217 Karl Dykhuis	.50
☐☐☐	218 Sandy McCarthy	.50
☐☐☐	219 Mikael Renberg	.50
☐☐☐	220 Stéphane Richer	.50
☐☐☐	221 Alexander Selivanov	.50
☐☐☐	222 Paul Ysebaert	.50
☐☐☐	223 Rob Zamuner	.50
☐☐☐	224 Sergei Berezin	.50
☐☐☐	225 Tie Domi	.50
☐☐☐	226 Mike Johnson	.50
☐☐☐	227 Curtis Joseph (G)	2.00
☐☐☐	228 Derek King	.50
☐☐☐	229 Igor Korolev	.50
☐☐☐	230 Mathieu Schneider	.50
☐☐☐	231 Mats Sundin	2.00
☐☐☐	232 Todd Bertuzzi	2.00
☐☐☐	233 Donald Brashear	.50
☐☐☐	234 Pavel Bure	1.50
☐☐☐	235 Arturs Irbe (G)	.50
☐☐☐	236 Mark Messier	2.00
☐☐☐	237 Alexander Mogilny	.50
☐☐☐	238 Mattias Öhlund	.50
☐☐☐	239 Dave Scatchard	.50
☐☐☐	240 Garth Snow (G)	.50
☐☐☐	241 Brian Bellows	.50
☐☐☐	242 Peter Bondra	1.00
☐☐☐	243 Jeff Brown	.50
☐☐☐	244 Sergei Gonchar	.50
☐☐☐	245 Calle Johansson	.50
☐☐☐	246 Joé Juneau	.50
☐☐☐	247 Olaf Kölzig (G)	1.00
☐☐☐	248 Steve Konowalchuk	.50
☐☐☐	249 Adam Oates	.50
☐☐☐	250 Richard Zednik	.50
	Player	**Sample**
☐	Martin Brodeur (G), NJer.	2.00

GLOVE SIDE LASER CUTS

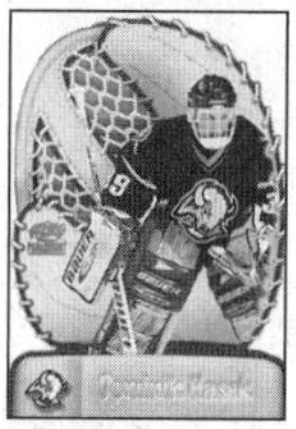

	Insert Set (20 cards):	**205.00**
	Insert (1:73)	**GSLC**
☐	1 Guy Hebert (G), Anah.	5.00
☐	2 Byron Dafoe (G), Bost.	5.00
☐	3 Dominik Hasek (G), Buff.	20.00
☐	4 Trevor Kidd (G), Caro.	5.00
☐	5 Jeff Hackett (G), Chic.	5.00
☐	6 Patrick Roy (G), Colo.	60.00
☐	7 Ed Belfour (G), Dall.	20.00
☐	8 Chris Osgood (G), Detr.	10.00
☐	9 Mike Dunham (G), Nash.	5.00
☐	10 Martin Brodeur (G), NJer.	30.00
☐	11 Tommy Salo (G), NYIs.	5.00
☐	12 Mike Richter (G), NYRa.	5.00
☐	13 Damian Rhodes (G), Ott.	5.00
☐	14 Ron Hextall (G), Phil.	10.00
☐	15 Nikolai Khabibulin (G), Phoe.	5.00
☐	16 Tom Barrasso (G), Pitt.	5.00
☐	17 Grant Fuhr (G), SLou.	10.00
☐	18 Mike Vernon (G), SanJ.	5.00
☐	19 Curtis Joseph (G), Toro.	20.00
☐	20 Olaf Kölzig (G), Wash.	10.00

HALL OF FAME BOUND

There are two versions: the regular insert (1:361) and the Proof parallel (#/20).

	Insert Set (10 cards):	**3200.00**	**525.00**
	Insert	**P20**	**HOFB**
☐☐	1 Teemu Selänne, Anah.	175.00	30.00
☐☐	2 Dominik Hasek (G), Buff.	225.00	35.00
☐☐	3 Peter Forsberg, Colo.	300.00	50.00
☐☐	4 Patrick Roy (G), Colo.	675.00	110.00
☐☐	5 Steve Yzerman, Detr.	525.00	90.00
☐☐	6 Martin Brodeur (G), NJer.	350.00	60.00
☐☐	7 Wayne Gretzky, NYRa.	900.00	150.00
☐☐	8 Eric Lindros, Phil.	225.00	35.00
☐☐	9 Jaromir Jagr, Pitt.	225.00	35.00
☐☐	10 Mark Messier, Vanc.	225.00	35.00

ICE GALAXY

These cards have three versions: the bronze parallel (1:97 Cdn), a silver parallel (#/50) and a gold parallel (#/10).

	Insert Set (10 cards):	**4500.00**	**1500.00**	**875.00**
	Insert	**IG10**	**IG50**	**IG140**
☐☐☐	1 Paul Kariya, Anah.	420.00	140.00	85.00
☐☐☐	2 Peter Forsberg, Colo.	420.00	140.00	85.00
☐☐☐	3 Patrick Roy (G), Colo.	900.00	300.00	185.00
☐☐☐	4 Joe Sakic, Colo.	480.00	160.00	100.00
☐☐☐	5 Steve Yzerman, Detr.	720.00	240.00	150.00
☐☐☐	6 Martin Brodeur (G), NJer.	480.00	160.00	100.00
☐☐☐	7 Wayne Gretzky, NYRa.	1200.00	400.00	250.00
☐☐☐	8 Alexei Yashin, Ott.	180.00	60.00	35.00
☐☐☐	9 Eric Lindros, Phil.	300.00	100.00	60.00
☐☐☐	10 Curtis Joseph (G), Toro.	300.00	100.00	60.00

SPECIAL DELIVERY DIE CUTS

	Insert Set (20 cards):	**115.00**
	Insert (1:37)	**SD**
☐	1 Paul Kariya	8.00
☐	2 Teemu Selänne	4.00
☐	3 Sergei Samsonov	4.00
☐	4 Peter Forsberg	8.00
☐	5 Joe Sakic	10.00
☐	6 Mike Modano	6.00
☐	7 Sergei Fedorov	6.00
☐	8 Brendan Shanahan	6.00
☐	9 Steve Yzerman	15.00
☐	10 Saku Koivu	4.00
☐	11 Zigmund Palffy	4.00
☐	12 Wayne Gretzky	25.00
☐	13 John LeClair	4.00
☐	14 Eric Lindros	6.00
☐	15 Keith Tkachuk	4.00
☐	16 Jaromir Jagr	6.00
☐	17 Mats Sundin	6.00
☐	18 Pavel Bure	4.00
☐	19 Mark Messier	6.00
☐	20 Peter Bondra	4.00

TEAM CHECKLISTS

	Insert Set (27 cards):	**90.00**
	Insert (2:37)	**TC**
☐	1 Teemu Selänne, Ana	4.00
☐	2 Sergei Samsonov, Bost.	2.00
☐	3 Dominik Hasek (G), Buff.	4.00
☐	4 Theoren Fleury, Cal.	2.00
☐	5 Keith Primeau, Caro.	2.00
☐	6 Chris Chelios, Chic.	2.00
☐	7 Patrick Roy (G), Colo.	14.00
☐	8 Mike Modano, Dall.	4.00
☐	9 Steve Yzerman, Detr.	12.00
☐	10 Ryan Smith, Edmo.	2.00
☐	11 Dino Ciccarelli, Flor.	2.00
☐	12 Rob Blake, LosA.	2.00
☐	13 Saku Koivu, Mont.	4.00
☐	14 Tom Fitzgerald, Nas.	2.00
☐	15 Martin Brodeur (G), NJer.	8.00
☐	16 Zigmund Palffy, NYIs.	2.00
☐	17 Wayne Gretzky, NYRa.	20.00
☐	18 Alexei Yashin, Ott.	2.00
☐	19 Eric Lindros, Phil.	4.00
☐	20 Keith Tkachuk, Phe.	2.00
☐	21 Jaromir Jagr, Pitt.	4.00
☐	22 Grant Fuhr (G), SLou.	2.00
☐	23 Patrick Marleau, SanJ.	2.00
☐	24 Rob Zamuner, Tamp.	2.00
☐	25 Mats Sundin, Toro.	4.00
☐	26 Mark Messier, Vanc.	4.00
☐	27 Peter Bondra, Wash.	2.00

1998 - 99 PACIFIC REVOLUTION

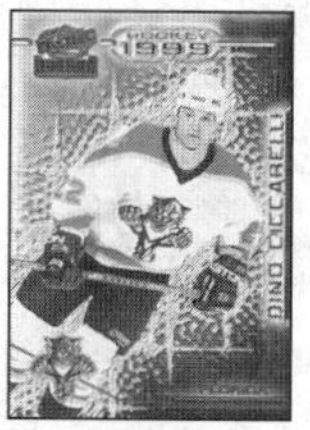

These cards have three versions: the regular card, a red parallel (#/299) and an Ice Shadow parallel (#/99).

	Complete Set (150 cards):	**2200.00**	**325.00**	**95.00**
	Common Player:	**6.00**	**2.00**	**.50**
	Player	**IS99**	**R299**	**PR**
☐☐☐	1 Guy Hebert (G), Anah.	10.00	2.00	.50
☐☐☐	2 Paul Kariya, Anah.	70.00	10.00	2.50
☐☐☐	3 Marty McInnis, Anah.	6.00	2.00	.50
☐☐☐	4 Steve Rucchin, Anah.	10.00	2.00	.50
☐☐☐	5 Teemu Selänne, Anah.	40.00	5.00	1.50

6 Jason Allison, Bost.	30.00	4.00	1.00
7 Raymond Bourque, Bost.	60.00	5.00	2.00
8 Anson Carter, Bost.	20.00	3.00	.50
9 Byron Dafoe (G), Bost.	20.00	3.00	.50
10 Dmitri Khristich, Bost.	6.00	2.00	.50
11 Sergei Samsonov, Bost.	30.00	4.00	1.00
12 Matthew Barnaby, Buff.	6.00	2.00	.50
13 Michal Grosek, Buff.	6.00	2.00	.50
14 Dominik Hasek (G), Buff.	50.00	5.00	2.00
15 Michael Peca, Buff.	20.00	3.00	.50
16 Miroslav Satan, Buff.	15.00	2.00	.50
17 Dixon Ward, Buff.	6.00	2.00	.50
18 Theoren Fleury, Calg.	30.00	4.00	1.00
19 J-S Giguère (G), Calg.	40.00	6.00	1.50
20 Jarome Iginla, Calg.	40.00	6.00	1.50
21 Tyler Moss (G), Calg.	6.00	2.00	.50
22 Cory Stillman, Calg.	10.00	2.00	.50
23 Ron Francis, Caro.	30.00	4.00	1.00
24 Arturs Irbe (G), Caro.	20.00	3.00	.50
25 Trevor Kidd (G), Caro.	15.00	2.00	.50
26 Keith Primeau, Caro.	20.00	3.00	.50
27 Ray Sheppard, Caro.	6.00	2.00	.50
28 Tony Amonte, Chic.	30.00	4.00	1.00
29 Chris Chelios, Chic.	30.00	4.00	1.00
30 Éric Dazé, Chic.	20.00	3.00	.50
31 Doug Gilmour, Chic.	30.00	4.00	1.00
32 Jocelyn Thibault (G), Chic.	20.00	3.00	.50
33 Adam Deadmarsh, Colo.	15.00	2.00	.50
34 Chris Drury, Colo.	30.00	4.00	2.00
35 Peter Forsberg, Colo.	70.00	10.00	2.50
36 Milan Hejduk, Colo. RC	**80.00**	**20.00**	**15.00**
37 Claude Lemieux, Colo.	15.00	2.00	.50
38 Patrick Roy (G), Colo.	150.00	20.00	6.00
39 Joe Sakic, Colo.	80.00	10.00	3.00
40 Ed Belfour (G), Dall.	50.00	7.00	2.00
41 Brett Hull, Dall.	50.00	7.00	2.00
42 Jamie Langenbrunner, Dall.	10.00	2.00	.50
43 Jere Lehtinen, Dall.	15.00	2.00	.50
44 Mike Modano, Dall.	50.00	7.00	2.00
45 Joe Nieuwendyk, Dall.	20.00	3.00	.50
46 Darryl Sydor, Dall.	10.00	2.00	.50
47 Sergei Fedorov, Detr.	50.00	7.00	2.00
48 Nicklas Lidström, Detr.	30.00	4.00	1.00
49 N. Maracle (G), Detr. RC	**6.00**	**2.00**	**2.00**
50 Darren McCarty, Detr.	15.00	2.00	.50
51 Chris Osgood (G), Detr.	30.00	4.00	1.00
52 Brendan Shanahan, Detr.	50.00	7.00	2.00
53 Steve Yzerman, Detr.	120.00	15.00	4.50
54 Bill Guerin, Edmo.	20.00	3.00	.50
55 Andrei Kovalenko, Edmo.	6.00	2.00	.50
56 M. Shtalenkov (G), Edmo.	6.00	2.00	.50
57 Ryan Smyth, Edmo.	20.00	3.00	.50
58 Doug Weight, Edmo.	30.00	4.00	1.00
59 Pavel Bure, Flor.	40.00	5.00	1.50
60 Sean Burke, Flor.	30.00	4.00	1.00
61 Dino Ciccarelli, Flor.	15.00	2.00	.50
62 Viktor Kozlov, Flor.	15.00	2.00	.50
63 Rob Niedermayer, Flor.	10.00	2.00	.50
64 Mark Parrish, Flor.	20.00	6.00	6.00
65 Rob Blake, LosA.	30.00	4.00	1.00
66 Stéphane Fiset (G), LosA.	15.00	2.00	.50
67 Olli Jokinen, LosA.	15.00	2.00	.50
68 Luc Robitaille, LosA.	40.00	6.00	1.50
69 Pavel Rosa, LosA. RC	**6.00**	**2.00**	**2.00**
70 Jozef Stümpel, LosA.	10.00	2.00	.50
71 Shayne Corson, Mont.	15.00	2.00	.50
72 V. Damphousse, Mont.	30.00	4.00	1.00
73 Jeff Hackett (G), Mont.	15.00	2.00	.50
74 Saku Koivu, Mont.	40.00	6.00	1.50
75 Mark Recchi, Mont.	20.00	3.00	.50
76 Brian Savage, Mont.	15.00	2.00	.50
77 Andrew Brunette, Nash.	6.00	2.00	.50
78 Mike Dunham (G), Nash.	20.00	3.00	.50
79 Sergei Krivokrasov, Nash.	6.00	2.00	.50
80 Cliff Ronning, Nash.	10.00	2.00	.50
81 Tomas Vokoun, Nash.	10.00	2.00	.50
82 Jason Arnott, NJer.	20.00	3.00	.50
83 Martin Brodeur (G), NJer.	80.00	10.00	3.00
84 Patrik Elias, NJer.	40.00	6.00	1.50
85 Bobby Holik, NJer.	15.00	2.00	.50
86 Brendan Morrison, NJer.	15.00	2.00	.50
87 Kenny Jönsson, NYIs.	10.00	2.00	.50
88 Trevor Linden, NYIs.	20.00	3.00	.50
89 Zigmund Palffy, NYIs.	30.00	4.00	1.00
90 Tommy Salo (G), NYIs.	20.00	3.00	.50
91 Mike Watt, NYIs.	6.00	2.00	.50
92 Wayne Gretzky, NYRa.	200.00	30.00	8.00
93 Todd Harvey, NYRa.	10.00	2.00	.50
94 Brian Leetch, NYRa.	30.00	4.00	1.00
95 Manny Malhotra, NYRa.	10.00	2.00	.50
96 Petr Nedved, NYRa.	15.00	2.00	.50
97 Mike Richter (G), NYRa.	20.00	3.00	.50
98 Daniel Alfredsson, Otta.	30.00	4.00	1.00
99 Marian Hossa, Otta.	50.00	7.00	2.00
100 Shawn McEachern, Otta.	15.00	2.00	.50
101 Damian Rhodes (G), Otta.	10.00	2.00	.50
102 Alexei Yashin, Otta.	30.00	4.00	1.00
103 Rod Brind'Amour, Phil.	15.00	2.00	.50
104 Ron Hextall (G), Phil.	30.00	4.00	1.00
105 John LeClair, Phil.	40.00	6.00	1.50
106 Eric Lindros, Phil.	50.00	5.00	2.00
107 Vanbiesbrouck (G), Phil.	20.00	3.00	.50
108 Dainius Zubrus, Phil.	10.00	2.00	.50
109 Daniel Brière, Phoe.	20.00	3.00	1.50
110 N. Khabibulin (G), Phoe.	20.00	3.00	.50
111 Jeremy Roenick, Phoe.	40.00	6.00	1.50
112 Keith Tkachuk, Phoe.	30.00	4.00	1.00
113 Rick Tocchet, Phoe.	15.00	2.00	.50
114 Jimmy Waite (G), Phoe.	6.00	2.00	.50
115 J-S Aubin (G), Pitt. RC	**10.00**	**3.00**	**3.50**
116 Stu Barnes, Pitt.	6.00	2.00	.50
117 Tom Barrasso (G), Pitt.	20.00	3.00	.50
118 Jaromir Jagr, Pitt.	50.00	5.00	2.00
119 Alexei Kovalev, Pitt.	30.00	4.00	1.00
120 Martin Straka, Pitt.	15.00	2.00	.50
121 Pavol Demitra, SLou.	20.00	3.00	.50
122 Grant Fuhr (G), SLou.	30.00	4.00	1.00
123 Al MacInnis, SLou.	20.00	3.00	.50
124 Chris Pronger, SLou.	30.00	4.00	1.00
125 Pierre Turgeon, SLou.	20.00	3.00	.50
126 Jeff Friesen, SanJ.	15.00	2.00	.50
127 Patrick Marleau, SanJ.	20.00	3.00	.50
128 Owen Nolan, SanJ.	30.00	4.00	1.00
129 Marco Sturm, SanJ.	10.00	2.00	.50
130 Mike Vernon (G), SanJ.	20.00	3.00	.50
131 Wendel Clark, Tamp.	40.00	6.00	1.50
132 Daren Puppa (G), Tamp.	10.00	2.00	.50
133 Vincent Lecavalier, Tamp.	50.00	7.00	4.00
134 Stéphane Richer, Tamp.	10.00	2.00	.50
135 Rob Zamuner, Tamp.	10.00	2.00	.50
136 Tie Domi, Toro.	15.00	2.00	.50
137 Mike Johnson, Toro.	10.00	2.00	.50
138 Curtis Joseph (G), Toro.	50.00	5.00	2.00
139 T. Kaberle, Toro. RC	**15.00**	**4.00**	**4.50**
140 Mats Sundin, Toro.	50.00	7.00	2.00
141 Mark Messier, Vanc.	50.00	7.00	2.00
142 Alexander Mogilny, Vanc.	20.00	3.00	.50
143 Bill Muckalt, Vanc. RC	**6.00**	**2.00**	**2.00**
144 Mattias Öhlund, Vanc.	15.00	2.00	.50
145 Garth Snow (G), Vanc.	15.00	2.00	.50
146 Peter Bondra, Wash.	30.00	4.00	1.00
147 Joé Juneau, Wash.	10.00	2.00	.50
148 Olaf Kölzig (G), Wash.	30.00	4.00	1.00
149 Adam Oates, Wash.	20.00	3.00	.50
150 Richard Zednik, Wash.	20.00	3.00	.50

Player	Sample
Martin Brodeur (G), NJer.	2.00

ALL-STAR GAME

Insert Set (30 cards):	260.00
Insert (1:25)	ASG
1 Tony Amonte	6.00
2 Ed Belfour (G)	12.00
3 Peter Bondra	6.00
4 Raymond Bourque	14.00
5 Martin Brodeur (G)	20.00
6 Theoren Fleury	6.00
7 Peter Forsberg	16.00
8 Wayne Gretzky	50.00
9 Dominik Hasek (G)	12.00
10 Bobby Holik	5.00
11 Arturs Irbe (G)	5.00
12 Jaromir Jagr	10.00
13 Paul Kariya	15.00
14 Nikolai Khabibulin (G)	5.00
15 Sergei Krivokrasov	5.00
16 John LeClair	10.00
17 Nicklas Lidström	6.00
18 Eric Lindros	12.00
19 Al MacInnis	5.00
20 Mike Modano	12.00
21 Mattias Öhlund	5.00
22 Keith Primeau	5.00
23 Chris Pronger	6.00
24 Mark Recchi	5.00
25 Jeremy Roenick	10.00
26 Teemu Selänne	10.00
27 Brendan Shanahan	12.00
28 Mats Sundin	12.00
29 Keith Tkachuk	6.00
30 Steve Yzerman	6.00

THREE-PRONGED ATTACK

These cards have two versions: the regular insert and a parallel. Parallels are limited to 99 (cards 1-10), 199 (cards 11-20), or 299 (cards 21-30).

Insert Set (30 cards):	825.00	85.00
Insert	P99	Insert
1 Matthew Barnaby, Buff.	15.00	1.50
2 Theoren Fleury, Calg.	30.00	2.00
3 Chris Chelios, Chic.	30.00	2.00
4 Darren McCarty, Detr.	15.00	1.50
5 Brendan Shanahan, Detr.	50.00	3.00
6 Eric Lindros, Phil.	50.00	3.00
7 Keith Tkachuk, Phoe.	30.00	2.00
8 Tony Twist, SLou.	15.00	1.50
9 Tie Domi, Toro.	15.00	1.50
10 Donald Brashear, Vanc.	15.00	1.50
Insert	P199	Insert
11 Dominik Hasek (G), Buff.	30.00	3.00
12 Patrick Roy (G), Colo.	110.00	10.00
13 Ed Belfour (G), Dall.	35.00	3.00
14 Chris Osgood (G), Detr.	20.00	2.00
15 Martin Brodeur (G), NJer.	60.00	6.00
16 Mike Richter (G), NYRa.	15.00	1.50
17 John Vanbiesbrouck (G), Phil.	15.00	1.50
18 Nikolai Khabibulin (G), Phoe.	15.00	1.50
19 Curtis Joseph (G), Toro.	35.00	3.00
20 Olaf Kölzig (G), Wash.	20.00	2.00
Insert	P299	Insert
21 Paul Kariya, Anah.	30.00	4.00
22 Teemu Selänne, Anah.	20.00	3.00
23 Peter Forsberg, Colo.	35.00	5.00
24 Joe Sakic, Colo.	40.00	6.00
25 Mike Modano, Dall.	25.00	3.00
26 Steve Yzerman, Detr.	60.00	8.00
27 Wayne Gretzky, NYRa.	100.00	15.00
28 John LeClair, Phil.	20.00	3.00
29 Jaromir Jagr, Pitt.	20.00	2.00
30 Pavel Bure, Flor.	20.00	3.00

CHALK TALK LASER CUTS

Insert Set (20 cards):	110.00
Insert (1:49)	CTLC
1 Paul Kariya, Anah.	10.00
2 Teemu Selänne, Anah.	6.00
3 Theoren Fleury, Calg.	4.00
4 Peter Forsberg, Colo.	10.00
5 Joe Sakic, Colo.	12.00
6 Brett Hull, Dall.	7.00
7 Mike Modano, Dall.	7.00
8 Sergei Fedorov, Detr.	7.00
9 Brendan Shanahan, Detr.	7.00
10 Steve Yzerman, Detr.	18.00
11 Wayne Gretzky, NYRa.	30.00
12 Alexei Yashin, Ott.	4.00
13 John LeClair, Phil.	6.00
14 Eric Lindros, Phil.	6.00
15 Keith Tkachuk, Phoe.	4.00
16 Jaromir Jagr, Pitt.	6.00
17 Vincent Lecavalier, Tamp.	7.00
18 Mats Sundin, Toro.	7.00
19 Mark Messier, Vanc.	7.00
20 Peter Bondra, Wash.	4.00

NHL ICONS

Insert Set (10 cards):	375.00
Insert (1:121)	NI
1 Paul Kariya, Anah.	35.00
2 Dominik Hasek (G), Buff.	25.00
3 Peter Forsberg, Colo.	35.00
4 Patrick Roy (G), Colo.	75.00
5 Mike Modano, Dall.	25.00
6 Steve Yzerman, Detr.	60.00
7 Martin Brodeur (G), NJer.	40.00
8 Wayne Gretzky, NYRa.	100.00
9 Eric Lindros, Phil.	25.00
10 Jaromir Jagr, Pitt.	25.00

SHOWSTOPPERS

Insert Set (36 cards):	185.00
Insert (2:25)	Show.
1 Paul Kariya, Anah.	5.00
2 Teemu Selänne, Anah.	5.00
3 Raymond Bourque, Bost.	7.00
4 Dominik Hasek (G), Buff.	5.00
5 Michael Peca, Buff.	2.00
6 Theoren Fleury, Calg.	3.00
7 Tony Amonte, Chic.	3.00
8 Chris Chelios, Chic.	3.00
9 Doug Gilmour, Chic.	3.00
10 Peter Forsberg, Colo.	5.00
11 Patrick Roy (G), Colo.	15.00
12 Joe Sakic, Colo.	10.00
13 Ed Belfour (G), Dall.	6.00
14 Brett Hull, Dall.	6.00
15 Mike Modano, Dall.	6.00
16 Sergei Fedorov, Detr.	6.00
17 Brendan Shanahan, Detr.	6.00
18 Steve Yzerman, Detr.	15.00
19 Mark Parrish, Flor.	2.00
20 Saku Koivu, Mont.	5.00
21 Martin Brodeur (G), NJer.	10.00
22 Zigmund Palffy, NYIs.	3.00
23 Wayne Gretzky, NYRa.	25.00
24 Alexei Yashin, Ott.	3.00
25 John LeClair, Phil.	5.00
26 Eric Lindros, Phil.	5.00
27 John Vanbiesbrouck (G), Phil.	3.00
28 Nikolai Khabibulin (G), Phoe.	2.00
29 Jeremy Roenick, Phoe.	5.00
30 Keith Tkachuk, Phoe.	3.00
31 Jaromir Jagr, Pitt.	5.00
32 Vincent Lecavalier, Tamp.	12.00
33 Curtis Joseph (G), Toro.	6.00
34 Mats Sundin, Toro.	6.00
35 Mark Messier, Vanc.	6.00
36 Peter Bondra, Wash.	3.00

1998 -99 PANINI PHOTOCARDS

Card Size: 3 7/8" x 5 7/8"

Complete Set (108 cards):	70.00
Common Player:	.75
Player	Panini
Paul Kariya, Anah.	2.00
Teemu Selänne, Anah.	1.00
Jason Allison, Bost.	.75
Raymond Bourque, Bost.	1.50
Sergei Samsonov, Bost.	.75
Joe Thornton, Bost.	1.50
Michal Grosek, Buff.	.75
Dominik Hasek (G), Buff.	1.50
Michael Peca, Buff.	.75

☐ Geoff Sanderson, Buff.	.75
☐ Theoren Fleury, Calg.	.75
☐ Cory Stillman, Calg.	.75
☐ Ron Francis, Caro.	.75
☐ Keith Primeau, Caro.	.75
☐ Tony Amonte, Chic.	.75
☐ Chris Chelios, Chic.	.75
☐ Éric Dazé, Chic.	.75
☐ Doug Gilmour, Chic.	.75
☐ Peter Forsberg, Colo.	2.00
☐ Claude Lemieux, Colo.	.75
☐ Patrick Roy (G), Colo.	4.50
☐ Joe Sakic, Colo.	2.00
☐ Ed Belfour (G), Dall.	1.50
☐ Brett Hull, Dall.	1.50
☐ Mike Modano, Dall.	1.50
☐ Joe Nieuwendyk, Dall.	.75
☐ Red Wings	.75
☐ Sergei Fedorov, Detr.	1.50
☐ Chris Osgood (G), Detr.	.75
☐ Brendan Shanahan, Detr.	1.50
☐ Steve Yzerman, Detr. [w/ Stanley Cup]	3.50
☐ Steve Yzerman, Detr.	3.50
☐ Ryan Smyth, Edmo.	.75
☐ Doug Weight, Edmo.	.75
☐ **Oleg Kvasha, Flor. RC**	**1.00**
☐ Mark Parrish, Flor.	3.00
☐ Rob Blake, LosA.	.75
☐ Stéphane Fiset, LosA.	.75
☐ Yanic Perreault, LosA.	.75
☐ Luc Robitaille, LosA.	1.00
☐ Vincent Damphousse, Mont.	.75
☐ Saku Koivu, Mont.	1.00
☐ Mark Recchi, Mont.	.75
☐ Jocelyn Thibault (G), Mont.	.75
☐ Andrew Brunette, Nash.	.75
☐ Mike Dunham (G), Nash.	.75
☐ Jason Arnott, NJer.	.75
☐ Martin Brodeur (G), NJer.	2.00
☐ Brendan Morrison, NJer.	.75
☐ Scott Niedermayer, NJer.	.75
☐ Bryan Berard, NYIs.	.75
☐ Trevor Linden, NYIs.	.75
☐ Zigmund Palffy, NYIs.	.75
☐ Tommy Salo (G), NYIs.	.75
☐ Adam Graves, NYRa.	.75
☐ Wayne Gretzky, NYRa.	6.00
☐ Brian Leetch, NYRa.	.75
☐ Mike Richter, NYRa.	.75
☐ Daniel Alfredsson, Otta.	.75
☐ Alexei Yashin, Otta.	.75
☐ Rod Brind'Amour, Phil.	.75
☐ John LeClair, Phil.	1.00
☐ Eric Lindros, Phil.	1.50
☐ John Vanbiesbrouck (G), Phil.	.75
☐ Nikolai Khabibulin (G), Phoe.	.75
☐ Jeremy Roenick, Phoe.	1.00
☐ Keith Tkachuk, Phoe.	.75
☐ Oleg Tverdovsky, Phoe.	.75
☐ Stu Barnes, Pitt.	.75
☐ Tom Barrasso (G), Pitt.	.75
☐ Kevin Hatcher, Pitt.	.75
☐ Jaromir Jagr, Pitt.	1.50
☐ Jeff Friesen, SanJ.	.75
☐ Mike Vernon (G), SanJ.	.75
☐ Grant Fuhr (G), SLou.	.75
☐ Al MacInnis, SLou.	.75
☐ Chris Pronger, SLou.	.75
☐ Pierre Turgeon, SLou.	.75
☐ Vincent Lecavalier, Tamp.	3.00
☐ Daren Puppa (G), Tamp.	.75
☐ Mike Johnson, Toro.	.75
☐ Curtis Joseph (G), Toro.	1.50
☐ Félix Potvin (G), Toro.	.75
☐ Mats Sundin, Toro.	1.50
☐ Pavel Bure, Vanc.	1.00
☐ Mark Messier, Vanc.	1.50
☐ Alexander Mogilny, Vanc.	.75
☐ Garth Snow (G), Vanc.	.75
☐ Peter Bondra, Wash.	.75
☐ Joé Juneau, Wash.	.75
☐ Olaf Kölzig (G), Wash.	.75
☐ Adam Oates, Wash.	.75
☐ Peter Bondra, NHL All-Star '98 (Wash.) [All-Star]	.75
☐ Raymond Bourque, NHL All-Star '98 (Bost.) [All-Star]	1.50
☐ Peter Forsberg, NHL All-Star '98 (Colo.) [All-Star]	2.00
☐ Wayne Gretzky, NHL All-Star (NYRa.) [All-Star]	6.00
☐ Saku Koivu, NHL All-Star '98 (Mont.) [All-Star]	1.00
☐ Eric Lindros, NHL All-Star '98 (Phil.) [All-Star]	1.50
☐ Mark Messier, NHL All-Star '98 (Vanc.) [All-Star]	1.50
☐ Patrick Roy (G), NHL All-Star '98 (Colo.) [All-Star]	4.50
☐ Teemu Selänne, NHL All-Star '98 (Anah.) [All-Star]	1.00
☐ Mats Sundin, NHL All-Star '98 (Toro.) [All-Star]	1.50
☐ Rob Blake, NHL Awards (LosA.) [Norris Trophy]	.75
☐ Brodeur (G), NHL Awards (NJer.) [Jennings Trophy]	2.00
☐ Ron Francis, NHL Awards (Pitt.) [Selke Trophy]	.75
☐ Hasek (G), NHL Awards (Buff.) [Vézina Trophy]	1.50
☐ Jaromir Jagr, NHL Awards (Pitt.) [Art Ross Trophy]	1.50
☐ Samsonov, NHL Awards (Bost.) [Calder Trophy]	.75

1998 - 99 PANINI STICKERS

Complete Set (228 stickers): **60.00**
Album: **3.00**
Common Player: **.20**

Sticker	Panini
☐ 1 Teemu Selänne, Anah.	1.00
☐ 2 Peter Bondra, Wash.	.50
☐ 3 Wayne Gretzky, NYRa.	6.00
☐ 4 Jaromir Jagr, Pitt.	1.50
☐ 5 Chris Pronger, SLou.	.50
☐ 6 Ed Belfour (G), Dall.	1.50
☐ 7 Boston Bruins Logo	.20
☐ 8 Dmitri Khristich, Bost.	.20
☐ 9 Per Axelsson, Bost.	.20
☐ 10 Byron Dafoe (G), Bost.	.50
☐ 11 Ted Donato, Bost.	.20
☐ 12 Raymond Bourque, Bost.	1.50
☐ 13 Sergei Samsonov, Bost.	.50
☐ 14 Jason Allison, Bost.	.50
☐ 15 Buffalo Sabres Logo	.20
☐ 16 Miroslav Satan, Buff.	.20
☐ 17 Donald Audette, Buff.	.50
☐ 18 Michal Grosek, Buff.	.20
☐ 19 Dominik Hasek (G), Buff.	1.50
☐ 20 Richard Smehlik, Buff.	.20
☐ 21 Michael Peca, Buff.	.50
☐ 22 Alexei Zhitnik, Buff.	.20
☐ 23 Carolina Hurricanes Logo	.20
☐ 24 Trevor Kidd (G), Caro.	.20
☐ 25 Nelson Emerson, Caro.	.20
☐ 26 Curtis Leschyshyn, Caro.	.20
☐ 27 Robert Kron, Caro.	.20
☐ 28 Gary Roberts, Caro.	.50
☐ 29 Sami Kapanen, Caro.	.20
☐ 30 Keith Primeau, Caro.	.50
☐ 31 Montréal Canadiens Logo	.20
☐ 32 Saku Koivu, Mont.	1.00
☐ 33 Vladimir Malakhov, Mont.	.20
☐ 34 Mark Recchi, Mont.	.50
☐ 35 Jocelyn Thibault (G), Mont.	.50
☐ 36 Peter Popovic, Mont.	.20
☐ 37 Martin Rucinsky, Mont.	.20
☐ 38 Jonas Höglund, Mont.	.20
☐ 39 Ottawa Senators Logo	.20
☐ 40 Damian Rhodes (G), Otta.	.20
☐ 41 Radek Bonk, Otta.	.20
☐ 42 Daniel Alfredsson, Otta.	.50
☐ 43 Alexei Yashin, Otta.	.50
☐ 44 Magnus Arvedson, Otta.	.20
☐ 45 Janne Laukkanen, Otta.	.20
☐ 46 Igor Kravchuk, Otta.	.20
☐ 47 Pittsburgh Penguins Logo	.20
☐ 48 Jaromir Jagr, Pitt.	1.50
☐ 49 Ron Francis, Pitt.	.50
☐ 50 Darius Kasparaitis, Pitt.	.20
☐ 51 Tom Barrasso (G), Pitt.	.50
☐ 52 Martin Straka, Pitt.	.20
☐ 53 Alexei Morozov, Pitt.	.20
☐ 54 Fredrik Olausson, Pitt.	.20
☐ 55 Florida Panthers Logo	.20
☐ 56 Radek Dvorak, Flor.	.20
☐ 57 Robert Svehla, Flor.	.20
☐ 58 Ray Whitney, Flor.	.20
☐ 59 Dave Gagner, Flor.	.20
☐ 60 John Vanbiesbrouck (G), Flor.	.50
☐ 61 Ed Jovanovski, Flor.	.50
☐ 62 Viktor Kozlov, Flor.	.20
☐ 63 New Jersey Devils Logo	.20
☐ 64 Petr Sykora, NJer.	.50
☐ 65 Scott Niedermayer, NJer.	.20
☐ 66 Dave Andreychuk, NJer.	.20
☐ 67 Martin Brodeur (G), NJer.	2.00
☐ 68 Bobby Holik, NJer.	.20
☐ 69 Doug Gilmour, NJer.	.50
☐ 70 Patrik Elias, NJer.	1.00
☐ 71 New York Islanders Logo	.20
☐ 72 Tommy Salo (G), NYIs.	.50
☐ 73 Zigmund Palffy, NYIs.	.50
☐ 74 Bryan Smolinski, NYIs.	.20
☐ 75 Robert Reichel, NYIs.	.20
☐ 76 Sergei Nemchinov, NYIs.	.20
☐ 77 Kenny Jönsson, NYIs.	.20
☐ 78 Bryan Berard, NYIs.	.20
☐ 79 New York Rangers Logo	.20
☐ 80 Wayne Gretzky, NYRa.	6.00
☐ 81 Adam Graves, NYRa.	.50
☐ 82 Mike Richter (G), NYRa.	.50
☐ 83 Brian Leetch, NYRa.	.50
☐ 84 Alexei Kovalev, NYRa.	.50
☐ 85 Ulf Samuelsson, NYRa.	.20
☐ 86 Niklas Sundström, NYRa.	.20
☐ 87 Philadelphia Flyers Logo	.20
☐ 88 John LeClair, Phil.	1.00
☐ 89 Petr Svoboda, Phil.	.20
☐ 90 Rod Brind'Amour, Phil.	.20
☐ 91 Sean Burke (G), Phil.	.50
☐ 92 Dainius Zubrus, Phil.	.20
☐ 93 Alexandre Daigle, Phil.	.20
☐ 94 Eric Lindros, Phil.	1.50
☐ 95 Tampa Bay Lightning Logo	.20
☐ 96 Mark Fitzpatrick (G), Tamp.	.20
☐ 97 Alexander Selivanov, Tamp.	.20
☐ 98 Mikael Renberg, Tamp.	.20
☐ 99 Rob Zamuner, Tamp.	.20
☐ 100 Karl Dykhuis, Tamp.	.20
☐ 101 Paul Ysebaert, Tamp.	.20
☐ 102 Mikael Andersson, Tamp.	.20
☐ 103 Washington Capitals Logo	.20
☐ 104 Peter Bondra, Wash.	.50
☐ 105 Sergei Gonchar, Wash.	.20
☐ 106 Adam Oates, Wash.	.50
☐ 107 Calle Johansson, Wash.	.20
☐ 108 Olaf Kölzig (G), Wash.	.50
☐ 109 Esa Tikkanen, Wash.	.20
☐ 110 Andrei Nikolishin, Wash.	.20
☐ 111 Chicago Blackhawks Logo	.20
☐ 112 Alexei Zhamnov, Chic.	.20
☐ 113 Éric Dazé, Chic.	.50
☐ 114 Chris Chelios, Chic.	.50
☐ 115 Jeff Hackett (G), Chic.	.20
☐ 116 Gary Suter, Chic.	.20
☐ 117 Eric Weinrich, Chic.	.20
☐ 118 Tony Amonte, Chic.	.50
☐ 119 Dallas Stars Logo	.20
☐ 120 Jere Lehtinen, Dall.	.20
☐ 121 Joe Nieuwendyk, Dall.	.50
☐ 122 Ed Belfour (G), Dall.	1.50
☐ 123 Mike Modano, Dall.	1.50
☐ 124 Sergei Zubov, Dall.	.20
☐ 125 Darryl Sydor, Dall.	.20
☐ 126 Pat Verbeek, Dall.	.20
☐ 127 Detroit Red Wings Logo	.20
☐ 128 Chris Osgood (G), Detr.	.50
☐ 129 Sergei Fedorov, Detr.	1.50
☐ 130 Stanley Cup	.20
☐ 131 Igor Larionov, Detr.	.50
☐ 132 Vyacheslav Kozlov, Detr.	.20
☐ 133 Brendan Shanahan, Detr.	1.50
☐ 134 Nicklas Lidström, Detr.	.50
☐ 135 Steve Yzerman, Detr.	3.50
☐ 136 Nashville Predators Logo	.20
☐ 137 Jan Vopat, Nash.	.20
☐ 138 Sergei Krivokrasov, Nash.	.20
☐ 139 Darren Turcotte, Nash.	.20
☐ 140 Tom Fitzgerald, Nash.	.20
☐ 141 Joël Bouchard, Nash.	.20
☐ 142 Scott Walker, Vanc. Nash.	.20
☐ 143 Phoenix Coyotes Logo.	.20
☐ 144 Keith Tkachuk, Phoe.	.50
☐ 145 Craig Janney, Phoe.	.20
☐ 146 Oleg Tverdovsky, Phoe.	.20
☐ 147 Nikolai Khabibulin (G), Phoe.	.50
☐ 148 Teppo Numminen, Phoe.	.20
☐ 149 Cliff Ronning, Phoe.	.20
☐ 150 Jeremy Roenick, Phoe.	1.00
☐ 151 St. Louis Blues Logo.	.20
☐ 152 Brett Hull, SLou.	1.50
☐ 153 Chris Pronger, SLou.	.50
☐ 154 Pierre Turgeon, SLou.	.50
☐ 155 Grant Fuhr (G), SLou.	.50
☐ 156 Geoff Courtnall, SLou.	.20
☐ 157 Pavol Demitra, SLou.	.50
☐ 158 Steve Duchesne, SLou.	.20
☐ 159 Toronto Maple Leafs Logo.	.20
☐ 160 Fredrik Modin, Toro.	.20
☐ 161 Dimitri Yushkevich, Toro.	.20
☐ 162 Tie Domi, Toro.	.20
☐ 163 Igor Korolev, Toro.	.20
☐ 164 Mats Sundin, Toro.	1.50
☐ 165 Félix Potvin (G), Toro.	.50
☐ 166 Sergei Berezin, Toro.	.20
☐ 167 Anaheim Mighty Ducks Logo	.20
☐ 168 Guy Hebert (G), Anah.	.20
☐ 169 Teemu Selänne, Anah.	1.00
☐ 170 Paul Kariya, Anah.	2.00
☐ 171 Steve Rucchin, Anah.	.20
☐ 172 Tomas Sandström, Anah.	.20
☐ 173 Josef Marha, Anah.	.20
☐ 174 Ruslan Salei, Anah.	.20
☐ 175 Calgary Flames Logo	.20
☐ 176 Theoren Fleury, Calg.	.50
☐ 177 Michael Nylander, Calg.	.20
☐ 178 German Titov, Calg.	.20
☐ 179 Rick Tabaracci (G), Calg.	.20
☐ 180 Cory Stillman, Calg.	.20
☐ 181 Jarome Iginla, Calg.	1.00
☐ 182 Tommy Albelin, Calg.	.20
☐ 183 Colorado Avalanche Logo	.20
☐ 184 Patrick Roy (G), Colo.	4.50
☐ 185 Peter Forsberg, Colo.	2.00
☐ 186 Alexei Gusarov, Colo.	.20
☐ 187 Uwe Krupp, Colo.	.20
☐ 188 Valeri Kamensky, Colo.	.20
☐ 189 Joe Sakic, Colo.	2.00
☐ 190 Sandis Ozolinsh, Colo.	.20
☐ 191 Edmonton Oilers Logo	.20
☐ 192 Boris Mironov, Edmo.	.20
☐ 193 Mats Lindgren, Edmo.	.20
☐ 194 Andrei Kovalenko, Edmo.	.20
☐ 195 Curtis Joseph (G), Edmo.	1.50
☐ 196 Roman Hamrlik, Edmo.	.20
☐ 197 Doug Weight, Edmo.	.50
☐ 198 Janne Niinimaa, Edmo.	.20
☐ 199 Los Angeles Kings Logo	.20
☐ 200 Stéphane Fiset (G), LosA.	.20
☐ 201 Jozef Stümpel, LosA.	.20
☐ 202 Aki Berg, LosA.	.20
☐ 203 Glen Murray, LosA.	.50
☐ 204 Vladimir Tsyplakov, LosA.	.20
☐ 205 Rob Blake, LosA.	.50
☐ 206 Mattias Norström, LosA.	.20
☐ 207 San Jose Sharks Logo	.20
☐ 208 Marcus Ragnarsson, SanJ.	.20
☐ 209 Jeff Friesen, SanJ.	.20
☐ 210 Owen Nolan, SanJ.	.50
☐ 211 Mike Vernon (G), SanJ.	.50
☐ 212 John MacLean, SanJ.	.20
☐ 213 Andrei Zyuzin, SanJ.	.20
☐ 214 Marco Sturm, SanJ.	.20
☐ 215 Vancouver Canucks Logo	.20
☐ 216 Pavel Bure, Vanc.	1.00
☐ 217 Alexander Mogilny, Vanc.	.50
☐ 218 Arturs Irbe (G), Vanc.	.50
☐ 219 Mark Messier, Vanc.	1.50
☐ 220 Markus Näslund, Vanc.	1.50
☐ 221 Mattias Öhlund, Vanc.	.20
☐ 222 Jyrki Lumme, Vanc.	.20
☐ 223 Dominik Hasek (G), Buff.	1.50
☐ 224 Rob Blake, LosA.	.50
☐ 225 Sergei Samsonov, Bost.	.50
☐ 226 Jere Lehtinen, Dall.	.20
☐ 227 Ron Francis, Pitt.	.50
☐ 228 Jamie McLennan, SLou.	.20

1998 - 99 SP AUTHENTIC

There are two versions: the regular card and a Power Shift parallel (#/500).

Shell Set (90 cards):	**-**	**35.00**
Complete Set (135 cards):	**1000.00**	**500.00**
Common Player:	**2.00**	**.25**
Insert	**PS500**	**SPA**
☐☐ 1 Paul Kariya, Anah.	20.00	1.50
☐☐ 2 Teemu Selänne, Anah.	10.00	1.00
☐☐ 3 Guy Hebert (G), Anah.	2.00	.25
☐☐ 4 Sergei Samsonov, Bost.	5.00	.50
☐☐ 5 Joe Thornton, Bost.	15.00	1.50
☐☐ 6 Jason Allison, Bost.	5.00	.50
☐☐ 7 Raymond Bourque, Bost.	15.00	1.50
☐☐ 8 Dominik Hasek (G), Buff.	15.00	1.00
☐☐ 9 Michael Peca, Buff.	5.00	.50
☐☐ 10 Michal Grosek, Buff.	2.00	.25
☐☐ 11 Derek Morris, Calg.	2.00	.25
☐☐ 12 Theoren Fleury, Calg.	5.00	.50
☐☐ 13 Jarome Iginla, Calg.	10.00	1.00
☐☐ 14 Ron Francis, Caro.	5.00	.50
☐☐ 15 Keith Primeau, Caro.	5.00	.50
☐☐ 16 Sami Kapanen, Caro.	2.00	.25
☐☐ 17 Tony Amonte, Chic.	5.00	.50
☐☐ 18 Doug Gilmour, Chic.	5.00	.50
☐☐ 19 Chris Chelios, Chic.	5.00	.50
☐☐ 20 Peter Forsberg, Colo.	20.00	1.50

☐☐	21 Patrick Roy (G), Colo.	45.00	3.50
☐☐	22 Joe Sakic, Colo.	20.00	2.00
☐☐	23 Adam Deadmarsh, Colo.	2.00	.25
☐☐	24 Brett Hull, Dall.	15.00	1.00
☐☐	25 Mike Modano, Dall.	15.00	1.00
☐☐	26 Ed Belfour (G), Dall.	15.00	1.00
☐☐	27 Jere Lehtinen, Dall.	2.00	.25
☐☐	28 Sergei Fedorov, Detr.	15.00	1.00
☐☐	29 Brendan Shanahan, Detr.	15.00	1.00
☐☐	30 Chris Osgood (G), Detr.	5.00	.50
☐☐	31 Steve Yzerman, Detr.	35.00	3.00
☐☐	32 Nicklas Lidström, Detr.	5.00	.50
☐☐	33 Doug Weight, Edmo.	5.00	.50
☐☐	34 Bill Guerin, Edmo.	5.00	.50
☐☐	35 Tom Poti, Edmo.	2.00	.25
☐☐	36 Rob Niedermayer, Flor.	2.00	.25
☐☐	37 Ed Jovanovski, Flor.	5.00	.50
☐☐	38 Luc Robitaille, LosA.	10.00	1.00
☐☐	39 Rob Blake, LosA.	5.00	.50
☐☐	40 Glen Murray, LosA.	5.00	.50
☐☐	41 Saku Koivu, Mont.	10.00	1.00
☐☐	42 Mark Recchi, Mont.	5.00	.50
☐☐	43 Vincent Damphousse, Mont.	5.00	.50
☐☐	44 Mike Dunham (G), Nash.	5.00	.50
☐☐	45 Sergei Krivokrasov, Nash.	2.00	.25
☐☐	46 Andrew Brunette, Nash.	2.00	.25
☐☐	47 Brendan Morrison, NJer.	2.00	.25
☐☐	48 Martin Brodeur (G), NJer.	20.00	2.00
☐☐	49 Scott Stevens, NJer.	5.00	.50
☐☐	50 Patrik Elias, NJer.	10.00	1.00
☐☐	51 Trevor Linden, NYIs.	5.00	.50
☐☐	52 Zigmund Palffy, NYIs.	5.00	.50
☐☐	53 Bryan Berard, NYIs.	2.00	.25
☐☐	54 Robert Reichel, NYIs.	2.00	.25
☐☐	55 Mike Richter, NYRa.	5.00	.50
☐☐	56 Wayne Gretzky, NYRa.	60.00	5.00
☐☐	57 Brian Leetch, NYRa.	5.00	.50
☐☐	58 Wade Redden, Otta.	2.00	.25
☐☐	59 Alexei Yashin, Otta.	5.00	.50
☐☐	60 Daniel Alfredsson, Otta.	5.00	.50
☐☐	61 Eric Lindros, Phil.	15.00	1.00
☐☐	62 John Vanbiesbrouck (G), Phil.	5.00	.50
☐☐	63 John LeClair, Phil.	10.00	1.00
☐☐	64 Rod Brind'Amour, Phil.	2.00	.25
☐☐	65 Jeremy Roenick, Phoe.	10.00	1.00
☐☐	66 Keith Tkachuk, Phoe.	5.00	.50
☐☐	67 Nikolai Khabibulin (G), Phoe.	5.00	.50
☐☐	68 German Titov, Pitt.	2.00	.25
☐☐	69 Martin Straka, Pitt.	2.00	.25
☐☐	70 Jaromir Jagr, Pitt.	15.00	1.00
☐☐	71 Chris Pronger, SLou.	5.00	.50
☐☐	72 Al MacInnis, SLou.	5.00	.50
☐☐	73 Pierre Turgeon, SLou.	5.00	.50
☐☐	74 Pavol Demitra, SLou.	5.00	.50
☐☐	75 Patrick Marleau, SanJ.	5.00	.50
☐☐	76 Jeff Friesen, SanJ.	2.00	.25
☐☐	77 Owen Nolan, SanJ.	5.00	.50
☐☐	78 Bill Ranford (G), Tamp.	5.00	.50
☐☐	79 Wendel Clark, Tamp.	10.00	1.00
☐☐	80 Craig Janney, Tamp.	2.00	.25
☐☐	81 Mike Johnson, Toro.	2.00	.25
☐☐	82 Curtis Joseph (G), Toro.	15.00	1.00
☐☐	83 Mats Sundin, Toro.	15.00	1.00
☐☐	84 Mattias Öhlund, Vanc.	2.00	.25
☐☐	85 Mark Messier, Vanc.	15.00	1.00
☐☐	86 Pavel Bure, Vanc.	10.00	1.00
☐☐	87 Olaf Kölzig (G), Wash.	5.00	.50
☐☐	88 Peter Bondra, Wash.	5.00	.50
☐☐	89 Joé Juneau, Wash.	2.00	.25
☐☐	90 Adam Oates, Wash.	5.00	.50

FUTURE WATCH

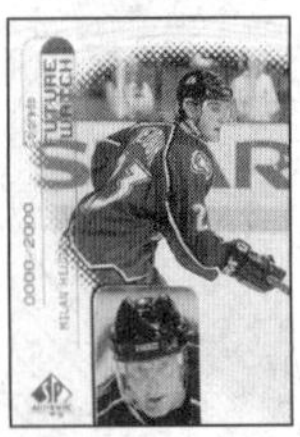

	Insert (#/2000)	PS	FW
☐☐	91 Johan Davidsson, Anah.	8.00	4.00
☐☐	92 Rico Fata, Calg.	8.00	4.00
☐☐	**93 Mike Maneluk, Chic. RC**	**12.00**	**10.00**
☐☐	94 Jean-Pierre Dumont, Chic.	8.00	4.00
☐☐	**95 Milan Hejduk, Colo. RC**	**240.00**	**200.00**
☐☐	96 Chris Drury, Colo.	18.00	12.00
☐☐	97 Mark Parrish, Flor.	24.00	20.00
☐☐	**98 Oleg Kvasha, Flor. RC**	**18.00**	**16.00**
☐☐	99 Josh Green, LosA.	18.00	8.00
☐☐	100 Olli Jokinen, LosA.	8.00	6.00
☐☐	101 Manny Malhotra, NYRa.	8.00	4.00
☐☐	102 Eric Brewer, NYIs.	12.00	8.00
☐☐	103 Mike Watt, NYIs.	8.00	4.00
☐☐	104 Daniel Brière, Phoe.	14.00	8.00
☐☐	**105 Jean-Sébastien Aubin (G), Pitt. RC**	**28.00**	**20.00**
☐☐	**106 Jan Hrdina, Pitt. RC**	**28.00**	**20.00**
☐☐	107 Marty Reasoner, SLou.	8.00	4.00
☐☐	**108 Michal Handzus, SLou. RC**	**28.00**	**20.00**
☐☐	109 Vincent Lecavalier, Tamp.	30.00	20.00
☐☐	**110 Tomas Kaberle, Toro. RC**	**35.00**	**30.00**
☐☐	**111 Bill Muckalt, Vanc. RC**	**18.00**	**16.00**
☐☐	112 Josh Holden, Vanc.	8.00	4.00
☐☐	113 Matt Herr, Wash.	12.00	4.00
☐☐	**114 Brian Finley (G), Cdn. RC**	**24.00**	**20.00**
☐☐	**115 Maxime Ouellet (G), Cdn. RC**	**45.00**	**40.00**
☐☐	**116 Kurtis Foster, Cdn. RC**	**12.00**	**10.00**
☐☐	**117 Barret Jackman, Cdn. RC**	**45.00**	**40.00**
☐☐	**118 Ross Lupaschuk, Cdn. RC**	**18.00**	**16.00**
☐☐	**119 Steven McCarthy, Cdn. RC**	**18.00**	**16.00**
☐☐	**120 Peter Reynolds, Cdn. RC**	**12.00**	**10.00**
☐☐	**121 Bart Rushmer, Cdn. RC**	**12.00**	**10.00**
☐☐	**122 Jonathon Zion, Cdn. RC**	**12.00**	**10.00**
☐☐	**123 Kris Beech, Cdn. RC**	**60.00**	**50.00**
☐☐	**124 Brandin Cote, Cdn. RC**	**12.00**	**10.00**
☐☐	**125 Scott Kelman, Cdn. RC**	**18.00**	**16.00**
☐☐	**126 Jamie Lundmark, Cdn. RC**	**60.00**	**50.00**
☐☐	**127 Derek MacKenzie, Cdn. RC**	**12.00**	**10.00**
☐☐	**128 Rory McDade, Cdn. RC**	**12.00**	**10.00**
☐☐	**129 David Morisset, Cdn. RC**	**18.00**	**16.00**
☐☐	**130 Mirko Murovic, Cdn. RC**	**12.00**	**10.00**
☐☐	**131 Taylor Pyatt, Cdn. RC**	**28.00**	**20.00**
☐☐	132 Charlie Stephens, Cdn.	8.00	4.00
☐☐	**133 Kyle Wanvig, Cdn. RC**	**18.00**	**16.00**
☐☐	**134 Krzystof Wieckowski, Cdn. RC**	**12.00**	**10.00**
☐☐	**135 Michael Zigomanis, Cdn. RC**	**18.00**	**16.00**

SIGN OF THE TIMES

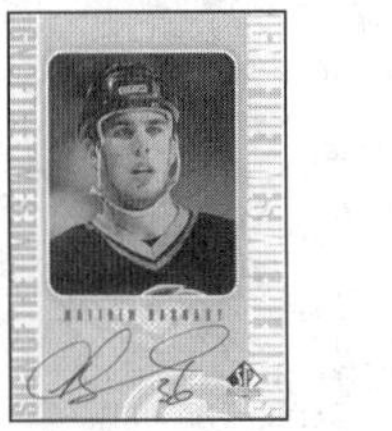

These cards have two versions: an autographed regular card and an autographed serial-numbered parallel card. Gold parallel autographed cards of NHL players are serial-numbered to the player's sweater number (with a minimum of 10 copies). Gold parallels of Canadian juniors are limited to 100 copies.

	Insert Set (50 cards):	6300.00	1000.00
	Insert	Gold	SotT
☐☐	Adam Deadmarsh, Colo. ✍	80.00	10.00
☐☐	Alexander Mogilny, Vanc. ✍	60.00	15.00
☐☐	Alexander Selivanov, Tamp. ✍	20.00	10.00
☐☐	Bates Battaglia, Caro. ✍	40.00	10.00
☐☐	Byron Dafoe (G), Bost. ✍	80.00	15.00
☐☐	Brett Hull, Dall. ✍	300.00	35.00
☐☐	Curtis Joseph (G), Toro. ✍	210.00	35.00
☐☐	Daniel Alfredsson, Otta. ✍	220.00	20.00
☐☐	Doug Weight, Edmo. ✍	110.00	20.00
☐☐	Ed Jovanovski, Flor. ✍	70.00	15.00
☐☐	Jason Allison, Bost. ✍	110.00	20.00
☐☐	Joé Juneau, Wash. ✍	40.00	10.00
☐☐	Jozef Stümpel, LosA. ✍	70.00	10.00
☐☐	Joe Thornton, Bost. ✍	480.00	45.00
☐☐	Keith Tkachuk, Phoe. ✍	240.00	20.00
☐☐	Matthew Barnaby, Buff. ✍	20.00	10.00
☐☐	Marian Hossa, Otta. ✍	250.00	35.00
☐☐	Manny Malhotra, NYRa. ✍	90.00	10.00
☐☐	Marty McSorley, Edmo. ✍	50.00	10.00
☐☐	Mattias Öhlund, Vanc. ✍	120.00	10.00
☐☐	Mats Sundin, Toro. ✍	340.00	35.00
☐☐	Nicklas Lidström, Detr. ✍	240.00	20.00
☐☐	Owen Nolan, SanJ. ✍	220.00	20.00
☐☐	Pavel Bure, Vanc. ✍	300.00	30.00
☐☐	Peter Bondra, Wash. ✍	210.00	20.00
☐☐	Patrick Roy (G), Colo. ✍	600.00	125.00
☐☐	Rob Blake, LosA. ✍	240.00	20.00
☐☐	Rumun Ndur, Buff. ✍	20.00	10.00
☐☐	Ryan Smyth, Edmo. ✍	60.00	15.00
☐☐	Sergei Gonchar, Wash. ✍	50.00	10.00
☐☐	Steve Yzerman, Detr. ✍	600.00	100.00
☐☐	Tomas Holmström, Detr. ✍	30.00	10.00
☐☐	Vincent Lecavalier, Tamp. ✍	320.00	35.00
☐☐	Wayne Gretzky, NYRa. ✍	1000.00	200.00
☐☐	Brian Finley, Cdn. ✍	30.00	20.00
☐☐	Barret Jackman, Cdn. ✍	70.00	40.00
☐☐	Charlie Stephens, Cdn. ✍	20.00	10.00
☐☐	David Morisset, Cdn. ✍	30.00	15.00
☐☐	Derek Mackenzie, Cdn. ✍	20.00	10.00
☐☐	Kris Beech, Cdn. ✍	60.00	30.00
☐☐	Kurtis Foster, Cdn. ✍	20.00	10.00
☐☐	Maxime Ouellet, Cdn. ✍	70.00	40.00
☐☐	Mirko Murovic, Cdn. ✍	20.00	10.00
☐☐	Michael Zigomanis, Cdn. ✍	30.00	15.00
☐☐	Peter Reynolds, Cdn. ✍	20.00	10.00
☐☐	Ross Lupaschuk, Cdn. ✍	30.00	15.00
☐☐	Rory McDade, Cdn. ✍	20.00	10.00
☐☐	Scott Kelman, Cdn. ✍	30.00	15.00
☐☐	Steven McCarthy, Cdn. ✍	30.00	15.00
☐☐	Taylor Pyatt, Cdn. ✍	40.00	20.00

SNAPSHOTS

	Insert Set (30 cards):	80.00
	Insert (1:11)	SS
☐	SS1 Wayne Gretzky, NYRa.	15.00
☐	SS2 Patrick Roy (G), Colo.	10.00
☐	SS3 Steve Yzerman, Detr.	8.00
☐	SS4 Brett Hull, Dall.	2.00
☐	SS5 Jaromir Jagr, Pitt.	2.00
☐	SS6 Peter Forsberg, Colo.	4.00
☐	SS7 Dominik Hasek (G), Buff.	2.00
☐	SS8 Paul Kariya, Anah.	4.00
☐	SS9 Eric Lindros, Phil.	2.00
☐	SS10 Teemu Selänne, Anah.	2.00
☐	SS11 John LeClair, Phil.	2.00
☐	SS12 Mike Modano, Dall.	2.00
☐	SS13 Martin Brodeur (G), NJer.	6.00
☐	SS14 Brendan Shanahan, Detr.	2.00
☐	SS15 Raymond Bourque, Bost.	4.00
☐	SS16 John Vanbiesbrouck (G), Flor.	1.00
☐	SS17 Brian Leetch, NYRa.	2.00
☐	SS18 Vincent Lecavalier, Tamp.	2.00
☐	SS19 Joe Sakic, Colo.	6.00
☐	SS20 Chris Drury, Colo.	2.00
☐	SS21 Eric Brewer, NYIs.	1.00
☐	SS22 Jeremy Roenick, Phoe.	2.00
☐	SS23 Mats Sundin, Toro.	2.00
☐	SS24 Zigmund Palffy, NYIs.	2.00
☐	SS25 Keith Tkachuk, Phoe.	2.00
☐	SS26 Sergei Samsonov, Bost.	2.00
☐	SS27 Curtis Joseph (G), Toro.	2.00
☐	SS28 Peter Bondra, Wash.	2.00
☐	SS29 Sergei Fedorov, Detr.	2.00
☐	SS30 Doug Gilmour, Chic.	2.00

STAT MASTERS

	Insert Set (30 cards):	850.00
	Insert	SM
☐	S1 Brendan Shanahan, Detr. {#/400}	20.00
☐	S2 Brett Hull, Dall. {#/1000}	6.00
☐	S3 Dominik Hasek (G), Buff. {#/200}	35.00
☐	S4 Doug Gilmour, Chic. {#/1200}	6.00
☐	S5 Doug Weight, Edmo. {#/500}	8.00
☐	S6 Eric Lindros, Phil. {#/115}	75.00
☐	S7 Jaromir Jagr, Pitt. {#/301}	25.00
☐	S8 Joe Sakic, Colo. {#/900}	15.00
☐	S9 John LeClair, Phil. {#/500}	10.00
☐	S10 John Vanbiesbrouck (G), Phil. {#/306}	15.00
☐	S11 Keith Tkachuk, Phoe. {#/250}	15.00
☐	S12 Mark Messier, Vanc. {#/600}	10.00
☐	S13 Martin Brodeur (G), NJer. {#/200}	55.00
☐	S14 Mike Modano, Dall. {#/650}	10.00
☐	S15 Patrick Roy (G), Colo. {#/400}	60.00
☐	S16 Paul Kariya, Anah. {#/108}	105.00
☐	S17 Pavel Bure, Vanc. {#/500}	10.00
☐	S18 Peter Bondra, Wash. {#/300}	15.00
☐	S19 Peter Forsberg, Colo. {#/400}	25.00
☐	S20 Raymond Bourque, Bost. {#/1500}	6.00
☐	S21 Ron Francis, Caro. {#/1500}	6.00
☐	S22 Sergei Fedorov, Detr. {#/600}	10.00
☐	S23 Steve Yzerman, Detr. {#/1500}	15.00
☐	S24 Steve Yzerman, Detr. {#/900}	20.00
☐	S25 Steve Yzerman, Detr. {#/500}	35.00
☐	S26 Teemu Selänne, Anah. {#/300}	20.00
☐	S27 Vincent Lecavalier, Tamp. {#/1998}	6.00
☐	S28 Wayne Gretzky, NYRa. {#/92}	300.00
☐	S29 Wayne Gretzky, NYRa. {#/900}	40.00
☐	S30 Wayne Gretzky, NYRa. {#/2000}	25.00

1998 - 99 SP AUTHENTIC – BUYBACKS

These signed cards were inserted into packs of either 1999-2000 or 2000-01 SP Authentic.

	Autograph	SPA
☐	4 S. Samsonov, Bost. ✍ (#/20, 00-01 SPA)	50.00
☐	4 S. Samsonov, Bost. ✍ (#/255, 99-00 SPA)	20.00
☐	7 R. Bourque, Bost. ✍ (#/24, 00-01 SPA)	100.00
☐	24 Br. Hull, Dall. ✍ (#/16, 00-01 SPA)	100.00
☐	24 Br. Hull, Dall. ✍ (#/100, 99-00 SPA)	60.00
☐	25 M. Modano, Dall. ✍ (#/40, 00-01 SPA)	75.00
☐	31 S. Yzerman, Detr. ✍ (#/5, 00-01 SPA)	325.00
☐	31 S. Yzerman, Detr. ✍ (#/77, 99-00 SPA)	150.00
☐	32 N. Lidström, Detr. ✍ (#/19, 00-01 SPA)	50.00
☐	38 L. Robitaille, LosA. ✍ (#/65, 99-00 SPA)	50.00
☐	48 M. Brodeur (G), NJer. ✍ (#/5, 00-01 SPA)	200.00
☐	50 P. Elias, NJer. ✍ (#/43, 00-01 SPA)	50.00
☐	52 Z. Palffy, NYIs. ✍ (#/100, 99-00 SPA)	30.00
☐	55 M. Richter (G), NYRa. ✍ (#/48, 00-01 SPA)	25.00
☐	56 W. Gretzky, NYRa. ✍ (#/4, 00-01 SPA)	575.00
☐	56 W. Gretzky, NYRa. ✍ (#/100, 99-00 SPA)	250.00
☐	63 J. LeClair, Phil. ✍ (#/100, 99-00 SPA)	50.00
☐	63 J. LeClair, Phil. ✍ (#/22, 00-01 SPA)	75.00
☐	65 J. Roenick, Phoe. ✍ (#/100, 99-00 SPA)	50.00
☐	81 M. Johnson, Toro. ✍ (#/300, 99-00 SPA)	15.00
☐	82 Cu. Joseph (G), Toro. ✍ (#/14, 00-01 SPA)	100.00
☐	82 Cu. Joseph (G), Toro. ✍ (#/200, 99-00 SPA)	40.00
☐	85 M. Messier, NYRa. ✍ (#/26, 00-01 SPA)	75.00
☐	86 Pavel Bure, Vanc. ✍ (#/1, 00-01 SPA)	125.00
☐	86 P. Bure, Vanc. ✍ (#/30, 99-00 SPA)	50.00
	Autograph	SPA
☐	S14 M. Modano, Dall. ✍ (#/1, 00-01 SPA)	175.00
	Autograph	SPA
☐	SS3 S. Yzerman, Detr. ✍ (#/1, 00-01 SPA)	400.00
☐	SS15 R. Bourque, Bost. ✍ (#/1, 00-01 SPA)	200.00

1998 - 99 SPx FINITE

There are three versions: the regular card, a Radiance parallel and a Spectrum parallel.

	Shell Set (90 cards):	**-**	**-**	**70.00**
	Complete Set (180 cards):	**-**	**550.00**	**325.00**
	Common Player:	**6.00**	**1.00**	**.50**
	Player	**S300**	**R4750**	**F9500**
☐☐☐	1 Teemu Selänne, Anah.	20.00	3.50	2.00
☐☐☐	2 Guy Hebert (G), Anah.	6.00	1.00	.50
☐☐☐	3 Josef Marha, Anah.	6.00	1.00	.50
☐☐☐	4 Travis Green, Anah.	6.00	1.00	.50
☐☐☐	5 Sergei Samsonov, Bost.	15.00	2.50	1.50
☐☐☐	6 Jason Allison, Bost.	15.00	2.50	1.50
☐☐☐	7 Byron Dafoe (G), Bost.	10.00	1.50	1.00
☐☐☐	8 Dominik Hasek (G), Buff.	25.00	4.50	3.00
☐☐☐	9 Michael Peca, Buff.	10.00	1.50	1.00
☐☐☐	10 Erik Rasmussen, Buff.	6.00	1.00	.50
☐☐☐	11 Matthew Barnaby, Buff.	6.00	1.00	.50
☐☐☐	12 Theoren Fleury, Calg.	15.00	2.50	1.50
☐☐☐	13 Derek Morris, Calg.	6.00	1.00	.50
☐☐☐	14 Valeri Bure, Calg.	6.00	1.00	.50
☐☐☐	15 Trevor Kidd (G), Caro.	6.00	1.00	.50
☐☐☐	16 Sami Kapanen, Caro.	6.00	1.00	.50
☐☐☐	17 Bates Battaglia, Caro.	6.00	1.00	.50
☐☐☐	18 Tony Amonte, Chic.	15.00	2.50	1.50
☐☐☐	19 Dmitri Nabokov, Chic.	6.00	1.00	.50
☐☐☐	20 Daniel Cleary, Chic.	6.00	1.00	.50
☐☐☐	21 Jeff Hackett (G), Chic.	6.00	1.00	.50
☐☐☐	22 Joe Sakic, Colo.	40.00	7.00	4.50
☐☐☐	23 Valeri Kamensky, Colo.	6.00	1.00	.50
☐☐☐	24 Patrick Roy (G), Colo.	70.00	12.00	9.00
☐☐☐	25 Wade Belak, Colo.	6.00	1.00	.50
☐☐☐	26 Joe Nieuwendyk, Dall.	10.00	1.50	1.00
☐☐☐	27 Mike Keane, Dall.	6.00	1.00	.50
☐☐☐	28 Jere Lehtinen, Dall.	6.00	1.00	.50
☐☐☐	29 Ed Belfour (G), Dall.	25.00	4.50	3.00
☐☐☐	30 Steve Yzerman, Detr.	60.00	10.00	7.00
☐☐☐	31 Dmitri Mironov, Detr.	6.00	1.00	.50
☐☐☐	32 Brendan Shanahan, Detr.	25.00	4.50	3.00
☐☐☐	33 Nicklas Lidström, Detr.	15.00	2.50	1.50
☐☐☐	34 Doug Weight, Edmo.	15.00	2.50	1.50
☐☐☐	35 Janne Niinimaa, Edmo.	6.00	1.00	.50
☐☐☐	36 Bill Guerin, Edmo.	10.00	1.50	1.00
☐☐☐	37 Ray Whitney, Flor.	6.00	1.00	.50
☐☐☐	38 Robert Svehla, Flor.	6.00	1.00	.50
☐☐☐	39 Ed Jovanovski, Flor.	10.00	1.50	1.00
☐☐☐	40 Vladimir Tsyplakov, LosA.	6.00	1.00	.50
☐☐☐	41 Jozef Stümpel, LosA.	6.00	1.00	.50
☐☐☐	42 Rob Blake, LosA.	15.00	2.50	1.50
☐☐☐	43 Mark Recchi, Mont.	10.00	1.50	1.00
☐☐☐	44 Andy Moog (G), Mont.	10.00	1.50	1.00
☐☐☐	**45 Matt Higgins, Mont. RC**	**6.00**	**1.50**	**1.50**
☐☐☐	46 Martin Brodeur (G), NJer.	40.00	7.00	4.50
☐☐☐	47 Doug Gilmour, NJer.	15.00	2.50	1.50
☐☐☐	48 Brendan Morrison, NJer.	6.00	1.00	.50
☐☐☐	49 Patrik Elias, NJer.	20.00	3.50	2.00
☐☐☐	50 Trevor Linden, NYIs.	10.00	1.50	1.00
☐☐☐	51 Bryan Berard, NYIs.	6.00	1.00	.50

☐☐☐	52 Zdeno Chara, NYIs.	6.00	1.00	.50
☐☐☐	53 Wayne Gretzky, NYRa.	100.00	18.00	12.00
☐☐☐	54 Marc Savard, NYRa.	6.00	1.00	.50
☐☐☐	55 Daniel Goneau, NYRa.	6.00	1.00	.50
☐☐☐	56 Pat LaFontaine, NYRa.	15.00	2.50	1.50
☐☐☐	57 Alexei Yashin, Otta.	15.00	2.50	1.50
☐☐☐	58 Marian Hossa, Otta.	25.00	4.50	3.00
☐☐☐	59 Wade Redden, Otta.	8.00	1.00	.50
☐☐☐	60 John LeClair, Phil.	20.00	3.50	2.00
☐☐☐	61 Alexandre Daigle, Phil.	6.00	1.00	.50
☐☐☐	62 Rod Brind'Amour, Phil.	6.00	1.00	.50
☐☐☐	63 Chris Therien, Phil.	6.00	1.00	.50
☐☐☐	64 Keith Tkachuk, Phoe.	15.00	2.50	1.50
☐☐☐	65 Brad Isbister, Phoe.	6.00	1.00	.50
☐☐☐	66 N. Khabibulin (G), Phoe.	10.00	1.50	1.00
☐☐☐	67 Robert Dome, Pitt.	6.00	1.00	.50
☐☐☐	68 Alexei Morozov, Pitt.	6.00	1.00	.50
☐☐☐	69 Stu Barnes, Pitt.	6.00	1.00	.50
☐☐☐	70 Tom Barrasso (G), Pitt.	10.00	1.50	1.00
☐☐☐	71 Owen Nolan, SanJ.	15.00	2.50	1.50
☐☐☐	72 Marco Sturm, SanJ.	6.00	1.00	.50
☐☐☐	73 Patrick Marleau, SanJ.	10.00	2.00	1.00
☐☐☐	74 Pierre Turgeon, SLou.	10.00	1.50	1.00
☐☐☐	75 Chris Pronger, SLou.	15.00	2.50	1.50
☐☐☐	76 Pavol Demitra, SLou.	10.00	1.50	1.00
☐☐☐	77 Grant Fuhr (G), SLou.	15.00	2.50	1.50
☐☐☐	78 Stéphane Richer, Tamp.	6.00	1.00	.50
☐☐☐	**79 Zac Bierk (G), Tamp.**	**10.00**	**4.00**	**4.00**
☐☐☐	80 Alexander Selivanov, Tamp.	6.00	1.00	.50
☐☐☐	81 Mike Johnson, Toro.	6.00	1.00	.50
☐☐☐	82 Mats Sundin, Toro.	25.00	4.50	3.00
☐☐☐	83 Alyn McAuley, Toro.	8.00	1.00	.50
☐☐☐	84 Pavel Bure, Vanc.	20.00	3.50	2.00
☐☐☐	85 Todd Bertuzzi, Vanc.	30.00	5.00	3.50
☐☐☐	86 Garth Snow (G), Vanc.	6.00	1.00	.50
☐☐☐	87 Peter Bondra, Wash.	15.00	2.50	1.50
☐☐☐	88 Olaf Kölzig (G), Wash.	15.00	2.50	1.50
☐☐☐	89 Jan Bulis, Wash.	6.00	1.00	.50
☐☐☐	90 Sergei Gonchar, Wash.	8.00	1.00	.50

GLOBAL IMPACT

	Insert	S225	R3475	G6950
☐☐☐	91 Pavel Bure, Vanc.	30.00	4.00	2.00
☐☐☐	92 Joe Sakic, Colo.	60.00	8.00	6.00
☐☐☐	93 Steve Yzerman, Detr.	90.00	10.00	8.00
☐☐☐	94 Jaromir Jagr, Pitt.	30.00	5.00	2.00
☐☐☐	95 Peter Forsberg, Colo.	50.00	7.00	4.00
☐☐☐	96 Brendan Shanahan, Detr.	35.00	5.00	2.00
☐☐☐	97 Brett Hull, SLou.	35.00	5.00	2.00
☐☐☐	98 Alexei Yashin, Otta.	20.00	3.00	2.00
☐☐☐	99 Wayne Gretzky, NYR	150.00	20.00	15.00
☐☐☐	100 Eric Lindros, Phil.	30.00	5.00	2.00
☐☐☐	101 Sergei Samsonov, Bost.	20.00	3.00	2.00
☐☐☐	102 John LeClair, Phil.	30.00	4.00	2.00
☐☐☐	103 Dominik Hasek (G), Buff.	30.00	5.00	2.00
☐☐☐	104 Teemu Selänne, Anah.	30.00	4.00	2.00
☐☐☐	105 Martin Brodeur (G), NJer.	60.00	8.00	6.00
☐☐☐	106 Tony Amonte, Chic.	20.00	3.00	2.00
☐☐☐	107 Theoren Fleury, Calg.	20.00	3.00	2.00
☐☐☐	108 Rob Blake, LosA.	20.00	3.00	2.00
☐☐☐	109 Mike Modano, Dall.	35.00	5.00	2.00
☐☐☐	110 Peter Bondra, Wash.	20.00	3.00	2.00
☐☐☐	111 Brian Leetch, NYRa.	20.00	3.00	2.00
☐☐☐	112 Nicklas Lidström, Detr.	20.00	3.00	2.00
☐☐☐	113 Doug Weight, Edmo.	20.00	3.00	2.00
☐☐☐	114 Zigmund Palffy, NYIs.	20.00	3.00	2.00
☐☐☐	115 Saku Koivu, Mont.	30.00	4.00	2.00
☐☐☐	116 Paul Kariya, Anah.	50.00	5.00	4.00
☐☐☐	117 Raymond Bourque, Bost.	45.00	6.00	4.00
☐☐☐	118 Mats Sundin, Toro.	35.00	5.00	2.00
☐☐☐	119 Patrick Roy (G), Colo.	110.00	15.00	10.00
☐☐☐	120 Chris Chelios, Chic.	20.00	3.00	2.00

SURE SHOTS

	Sure Shots	S75	R1300	SS3900
☐☐☐	121 Sergei Samsonov, Bost.	60.00	5.00	6.00
☐☐☐	122 Mike Johnson, Toro.	20.00	4.00	2.00
☐☐☐	123 Patrik Elias, NJer.	80.00	10.00	8.00
☐☐☐	124 Josef Marha, Anah.	10.00	4.00	1.50
☐☐☐	125 Dan Cloutier (G), NYRa.	40.00	6.00	4.00
☐☐☐	126 Cameron Mann, Bost.	15.00	4.00	1.50
☐☐☐	127 Mattias Öhlund, Vanc.	30.00	4.00	3.00
☐☐☐	128 Daniel Cleary, Chic.	30.00	4.00	3.00
☐☐☐	129 Anders Eriksson, Detr.	10.00	4.00	1.50
☐☐☐	130 Patrick Marleau, SanJ.	45.00	7.00	4.00
☐☐☐	131 Jan Bulis, Wash.	10.00	4.00	1.50
☐☐☐	132 Alyn McAuley, Toro.	30.00	4.00	3.00
☐☐☐	133 Joe Thornton, Bost.	120.00	15.00	12.00
☐☐☐	134 Andrei Zyuzin, SanJ.	15.00	4.00	1.50
☐☐☐	135 Richard Zednik, Wash.	40.00	6.00	4.00
☐☐☐	136 Derek Morris, Calg.	20.00	4.00	2.00
☐☐☐	137 Bates Battaglia, Caro.	20.00	4.00	2.00
☐☐☐	138 Mike Watt, Edmo.	10.00	4.00	1.50
☐☐☐	139 Dmitri Nabokov, Chic.	15.00	4.00	1.50
☐☐☐	140 Marian Hossa, Otta.	100.00	15.00	10.00
☐☐☐	141 Daniel Goneau, NYRa.	10.00	4.00	1.50
☐☐☐	142 Erik Rasmussen, Buff.	20.00	4.00	2.00
☐☐☐	143 Daniel Brière, Phoe.	45.00	7.00	4.00
☐☐☐	**144 Norm Maracle (G), Detr.**	**30.00**	**4.00**	**4.00**
☐☐☐	145 Brendan Morrison, NJer.	30.00	4.00	3.00
☐☐☐	146 Brad Isbister, Phoe.	20.00	4.00	2.00
☐☐☐	147 Brian Boucher (G), Phil.	15.00	4.00	1.50
☐☐☐	148 Zac Bierk (G), Tamp.	45.00	4.00	2.00
☐☐☐	149 Alexei Morozov, Pitt.	20.00	4.00	2.00
☐☐☐	150 Marco Sturm, SanJ.	20.00	4.00	2.00

MARQUEE PERFORMERS

	Marquee Performers	S25	R875	M2625
☐☐☐	151 Wayne Gretzky, NYRa.	800.00	40.00	25.00
☐☐☐	152 Eric Lindros, Phil.	200.00	10.00	6.00
☐☐☐	153 Paul Kariya, Anah.	275.00	10.00	8.00
☐☐☐	154 Patrick Roy (G), Colo.	600.00	30.00	18.00
☐☐☐	155 Sergei Samsonov, Bost.	100.00	6.00	2.00
☐☐☐	156 Steve Yzerman, Detr.	475.00	20.00	14.00
☐☐☐	157 Teemu Selänne, Anah.	150.00	5.00	4.00
☐☐☐	158 B. Shanahan, Detr.	225.00	10.00	6.00
☐☐☐	159 D. Hasek (G), Buff.	200.00	10.00	6.00
☐☐☐	160 Mark Messier, Vanc.	200.00	10.00	6.00
☐☐☐	161 M. Brodeur (G), NJer.	300.00	15.00	10.00
☐☐☐	162 Mats Sundin, Toro.	200.00	10.00	6.00
☐☐☐	163 Joe Sakic, Colo.	300.00	15.00	10.00
☐☐☐	164 John LeClair, Phil.	150.00	5.00	4.00
☐☐☐	165 Jaromir Jagr, Pitt.	200.00	10.00	6.00
☐☐☐	166 Peter Forsberg, Colo.	275.00	10.00	8.00
☐☐☐	167 Theoren Fleury, Calg.	100.00	5.00	2.00
☐☐☐	168 Peter Bondra, Wash.	100.00	6.00	2.00
☐☐☐	169 Mike Modano, Dall.	200.00	10.00	6.00
☐☐☐	170 Pavel Bure, Vanc.	150.00	5.00	4.00

LIVING LEGENDS

	Living Legends	S1	R540	LL1620
☐☐☐	171 Patrick Roy (G), Colo.		45.00	22.00
☐☐☐	172 Eric Lindros, Phil.		15.00	6.00
☐☐☐	173 Dominik Hasek (G), Buff.		10.00	6.00
☐☐☐	174 Jaromir Jagr, Pitt.		15.00	6.00
☐☐☐	175 Steve Yzerman, Detr.		35.00	18.00
☐☐☐	176 Martin Brodeur (G), NJer.		20.00	12.00
☐☐☐	177 Raymond Bourque, Bost.		15.00	8.00
☐☐☐	178 Peter Forsberg, Colo.		20.00	10.00
☐☐☐	179 Paul Kariya, Anah.		20.00	10.00
☐☐☐	180 Wayne Gretzky, NYRa.		60.00	30.00

	Player	Sample
☐	Wayne Gretzky, NYRa.	5.00

1998 - 99 SP^{X} PROSPECTS

Each card has three versions: the regular card, a Radiance parallel and a Spectrum parallel. Spectrum cards (1 copy of each) are too scarce to be priced. The Sedin base cards (but not the parallels) are autographed.

Shell Set (60 cards):		**75.00**
Complete Set (90 cards):	**2400.00**	**300.00**
Common Player:	**8.00**	**.35**

	Player	R100	Reg.
☐☐☐	1 Paul Kariya, Anah.	100.00	3.50
☐☐☐	2 Teemu Selänne, Anah.	60.00	2.00
☐☐☐	3 Raymond Bourque, Bost.	90.00	3.00
☐☐☐	4 Sergei Samsonov, Bost.	40.00	1.50
☐☐☐	5 Joe Thornton, Bost.	90.00	3.00
☐☐☐	6 Dominik Hasek (G), Buff.	70.00	2.50
☐☐☐	7 Theoren Fleury, Calg.	40.00	1.50
☐☐☐	8 Keith Primeau, Caro.	30.00	1.00
☐☐☐	9 Tony Amonte, Chic.	45.00	1.50
☐☐☐	10 Doug Gilmour, Chic.	45.00	1.50
☐☐☐	11 Jean-Pierre Dumont, Chic.	15.00	.50
☐☐☐	12 Chris Chelios, Chic.	45.00	1.50
☐☐☐	13 Peter Forsberg, Colo.	100.00	3.50
☐☐☐	14 Patrick Roy (G), Colo.	220.00	7.50
☐☐☐	15 Joe Sakic, Colo.	120.00	4.00
☐☐☐	**16 Milan Hejduk, Colo. RC**	**90.00**	**10.00**
☐☐☐	17 Chris Drury, Colo.	45.00	1.50
☐☐☐	18 Mike Modano, Dall.	70.00	2.50
☐☐☐	19 Brett Hull, Dall.	70.00	2.50
☐☐☐	20 Ed Belfour (G), Dall.	70.00	2.50
☐☐☐	21 Steve Yzerman, Detr.	180.00	6.00
☐☐☐	22 Brendan Shanahan, Detr.	70.00	2.50
☐☐☐	23 Sergei Fedorov, Detr.	70.00	2.50
☐☐☐	24 Chris Osgood (G), Detr.	40.00	1.50
☐☐☐	25 Nicklas Lidström, Detr.	45.00	1.50
☐☐☐	26 Bill Guerin, Edmo.	30.00	1.00
☐☐☐	27 Doug Weight, Edmo.	40.00	1.50
☐☐☐	28 Tom Poti, Edmo.	10.00	.35
☐☐☐	29 Mark Parrish, Flor.	45.00	5.00
☐☐☐	30 Rob Blake, LosA.	45.00	1.50
☐☐☐	**31 Pavel Rosa, LosA. RC**	**15.00**	**2.00**
☐☐☐	32 Vincent Damphousse, Mont.	45.00	1.50
☐☐☐	33 Saku Koivu, Mont.	60.00	2.00
☐☐☐	34 Mike Dunham (G), Nash.	30.00	1.00
☐☐☐	35 Martin Brodeur (G), NJer.	120.00	4.00
☐☐☐	36 Zigmund Palffy, NYIs.	45.00	1.50
☐☐☐	37 Eric Brewer, NYIs.	30.00	1.00
☐☐☐	38 Wayne Gretzky, NYRa.	300.00	10.00
☐☐☐	39 Brian Leetch, NYRa.	45.00	1.50
☐☐☐	40 Manny Malhotra, NYRa.	15.00	.50
☐☐☐	41 Petr Nedved, NYRa.	20.00	.50
☐☐☐	42 Alexei Yashin, Otta.	45.00	1.50
☐☐☐	43 Eric Lindros, Phil.	70.00	2.50
☐☐☐	44 John LeClair, Phil.	60.00	2.00
☐☐☐	45 John Vanbiesbrouck (G), Phil.	35.00	1.00
☐☐☐	46 Keith Tkachuk, Phoe.	40.00	1.50
☐☐☐	47 Jeremy Roenick, Phoe.	60.00	2.00
☐☐☐	48 Daniel Brière, Phoe.	35.00	1.00
☐☐☐	49 Jaromir Jagr, Pitt.	70.00	2.50
☐☐☐	50 Patrick Marleau, SanJ.	35.00	1.00
☐☐☐	51 Al MacInnis, SLou.	30.00	1.00
☐☐☐	52 Chris Pronger, SLou.	45.00	1.50
☐☐☐	53 Vincent Lecavalier, Tamp.	70.00	2.50
☐☐☐	54 Curtis Joseph (G), Toro.	70.00	2.50
☐☐☐	55 Mats Sundin, Toro.	70.00	2.50
☐☐☐	**56 Tomas Kaberle, Toro. RC**	**35.00**	**4.00**
☐☐☐	57 Mark Messier, Vanc.	70.00	2.50
☐☐☐	58 Pavel Bure, Flor.	60.00	2.00
☐☐☐	**59 Bill Muckalt, Vanc. RC**	**15.00**	**2.00**
☐☐☐	60 Peter Bondra, Wash.	45.00	1.50

ROOKIE

	Insert	R100	R1999
☐☐☐	**61 Brian Finley (G), Cdn. RC**	**30.00**	**14.00**
☐☐☐	62 Roberto Luongo (G), Cdn.	60.00	8.00
☐☐☐	63 Mike Van Ryn, Cdn.	15.00	3.00
☐☐☐	64 Harold Druken, Cdn.	20.00	3.00
☐☐☐	65 Daniel Tkaczuk, Cdn.	15.00	3.00
☐☐☐	**66 Brenden Morrow, Cdn. RC**	**45.00**	**35.00**
☐☐☐	**67 Jani Rita, Fin. RC**	**45.00**	**35.00**
☐☐☐	**68 Tommi Santala, Fin. RC**	**15.00**	**8.00**
☐☐☐	**69 Teemu Virkkunen, Fin. RC**	**15.00**	**8.00**
☐☐☐	**70 Arto Laatikainen, Fin. RC**	**15.00**	**8.00**
☐☐☐	**71 Ilkka Mikkola, Fin. RC**	**15.00**	**8.00**
☐☐☐	**72 Miko Jokela, Fin. RC**	**20.00**	**12.00**
☐☐☐	**73 Kirill Safronov, Rus. RC**	**20.00**	**12.00**
☐☐☐	74 Denis Shvidky, Rus.	15.00	3.00
☐☐☐	**75 Denis Arkhipov, Rus. RC**	**35.00**	**18.00**
☐☐☐	76 Maxim Afinogenov, Rus.	30.00	4.00
☐☐☐	**77 Alexander Zevakhin, Rus. RC**	**15.00**	**8.00**
☐☐☐	**78 Alexei Volkov (G), Rus. RC**	**35.00**	**18.00**
☐	79 Daniel Sedin, Swe. ✍	-	30.00
☐☐	79 Daniel Sedin, Swe.	30.00	-
☐	80 Henrik Sedin, Swe. ✍	-	30.00
☐☐	80 Henrik Sedin, Swe.	30.00	-
☐☐☐	**81 Jimmie Ölvestad, Swe. RC**	**15.00**	**8.00**
☐☐☐	**82 Mattias Weinhandl, Swe. RC**	**15.00**	**8.00**
☐☐☐	**83 Mathias Tjarnqvist, Swe. RC**	**15.00**	**8.00**
☐☐☐	**84 Jakob Johansson, Swe. RC**	**15.00**	**8.00**
☐☐☐	**85 Barrett Heisten, USA. RC**	**35.00**	**18.00**
☐☐☐	**86 Tim Connolly, USA. RC**	**60.00**	**40.00**
☐☐☐	**87 Andy Hilbert, USA. RC**	**35.00**	**25.00**
☐☐☐	88 David Legwand, USA.	30.00	4.00
☐☐☐	**89 Joe Blackburn (G), USA. RC**	**20.00**	**12.00**
☐☐☐	**90 Dave Tanabe, USA. RC**	**20.00**	**15.00**

HIGHLIGHT HEROES

Insert Set (30 cards):		**140.00**
	Insert (1:8)	**HH**
☐	H1 Paul Kariya, Anah.	5.00
☐	H2 Teemu Selänne, Anah.	4.00
☐	H3 Raymond Bourque, Bost.	6.00
☐	H4 Sergei Samsonov, Bost.	3.00
☐	H5 Dominik Hasek (G), Buff.	5.00
☐	H6 Theoren Fleury, Calg.	3.00
☐	H7 Doug Gilmour, Chic.	3.00
☐	H8 Joe Sakic, Colo.	8.00
☐	H9 Patrick Roy (G), Colo.	15.00
☐	H10 Peter Forsberg, Colo.	7.00
☐	H11 Mike Modano, Dall.	5.00
☐	H12 Brett Hull, Dall.	5.00
☐	H13 Brendan Shanahan, Detr.	5.00
☐	H14 Steve Yzerman, Detr.	10.00
☐	H15 Sergei Fedorov, Detr.	5.00
☐	H16 Saku Koivu, Mont.	4.00
☐	H17 Martin Brodeur (G), NJer.	8.00
☐	H18 Wayne Gretzky, NYRa.	20.00
☐	H19 Zigmund Palffy, NYIs.	3.00
☐	H20 John Vanbiesbrouck (G), Phil.	2.00
☐	H21 Eric Lindros, Phil.	5.00
☐	H22 John LeClair, Phil.	4.00
☐	H23 Keith Tkachuk, Phoe.	3.00
☐	H24 Jeremy Roenick, Phoe.	4.00
☐	H25 Jaromir Jagr, Pitt.	5.00
☐	H26 Vincent Lecavalier, Tamp.	5.00
☐	H27 Mats Sundin, Toro.	5.00
☐	H28 Curtis Joseph (G), Toro.	5.00
☐	H29 Pavel Bure, Flor.	4.00
☐	H30 Peter Bondra, Wash.	3.00

LASTING IMPRESSIONS

Insert Set (30 cards):		**65.00**
	Insert (1:3)	**LI**
☐	L1 Vincent Lecavalier, Tamp.	5.00
☐	L2 John Vanbiesbrouck (G), Phil.	1.00
☐	L3 Paul Kariya, Anah.	3.00
☐	L4 Keith Tkachuk, Phoe.	1.00
☐	L5 Mike Modano, Dall.	2.00
☐	L6 Dominik Hasek (G), Buff.	2.00
☐	L7 Teemu Selänne, Anah.	2.00
☐	L8 Mats Sundin, Toro.	2.00
☐	L9 Brendan Morrison, NJer.	2.00
☐	L10 Pavel Bure, Flor.	2.00
☐	L11 Theoren Fleury, Calg.	1.00
☐	L12 Curtis Joseph (G), Toro.	2.00
☐	L13 Joe Sakic, Colo.	4.00
☐	L14 Eric Lindros, Phil.	2.00
☐	L15 Peter Bondra, Wash.	1.00
☐	L16 Brett Hull, Dall.	2.00
☐	L17 Raymond Bourque, Bost.	3.00
☐	L18 Jaromir Jagr, Pitt.	2.00
☐	L19 Steve Yzerman, Detr.	6.00
☐	L20 Jeremy Roenick, Phoe.	2.00
☐	L21 Martin Brodeur (G), NJer.	4.00
☐	L22 Saku Koivu, Mont.	2.00
☐	L23 Patrick Roy (G), Colo.	7.00
☐	L24 John LeClair, Phil.	2.00

L25 Doug Gilmour, Chic.	1.00
L26 Sergei Fedorov, Detr.	2.00
L27 Wayne Gretzky, NYRa.	10.00
L28 Peter Forsberg, Colo.	3.00
L29 Zigmund Palffy, NYIs.	1.00
L30 Sergei Samsonov, Bost.	1.00

PREMIER STARS

Insert Set (30 cards): 300.00

Insert (1:17)	PS
PS1 Wayne Gretzky, NYRa.	40.00
PS2 Sergei Samsonov, Bost.	6.00
PS3 Raymond Bourque, Bost.	10.00
PS4 Dominik Hasek (G), Buff.	10.00
PS5 Martin Brodeur (G), NJer.	15.00
PS6 Brian Leetch, NYRa.	6.00
PS7 Mike Richter (G), NYRa.	4.00
PS8 Eric Lindros, Phil.	10.00
PS9 John LeClair, Phil.	5.00
PS10 John Vanbiesbrouck (G), Phil.	4.00
PS11 Jaromir Jagr, Pitt.	10.00
PS12 Vincent Lecavalier, Tamp.	15.00
PS13 Mats Sundin, Toro.	10.00
PS14 Curtis Joseph (G), Toro.	10.00
PS15 Peter Bondra, Wash.	6.00
PS16 Wayne Gretzky, NYRa.	40.00
PS17 Teemu Selänne, Anah.	5.00
PS18 Paul Kariya, Anah.	10.00
PS19 Theoren Fleury, Calg.	5.00
PS20 Tony Amonte, Chic.	6.00
PS21 Patrick Roy (G), Colo.	30.00
PS22 Joe Sakic, Colo.	15.00
PS23 Peter Forsberg, Colo.	10.00
PS24 Mike Modano, Dall.	10.00
PS25 Brett Hull, Dall.	10.00
PS26 Steve Yzerman, Detr.	20.00
PS27 Brendan Shanahan, Detr.	10.00
PS28 Doug Weight, Edmo.	6.00
PS29 Keith Tkachuk, Phoe.	6.00
PS30 Mark Messier, Vanc.	10.00

WINNING MATERIALS

Insert Set (12 cards): 700.00

Insert	WM
Raymond Bourque, Bost. ✂	75.00
Jaromir Jagr, Cze. ✂	75.00
Curtis Joseph (G), SLou. ✂	75.00
John LeClair, Phil. ✂	50.00
Eric Lindros, Phil. ✂	75.00
Chris Osgood (G), Detr. ✂	30.00
Félix Potvin (G), Toro. ✂	30.00
Mike Richter (G), NYRa. ✂	30.00
Patrick Roy (G), Colo. ✂	225.00
Joe Sakic, Que. ✂	100.00
Mats Sundin, Toro. ✂	75.00
John Vanbiesbrouck (G), NYRa. ✂	30.00

YEAR OF THE GREAT ONE QUOTABLES

Insert Set (30 cards): 350.00
Gretzky Card: 15.00

Insert	Insert
WG1 Wayne Gretzky	WG2 Wayne Gretzky
WG3 Wayne Gretzky	WG4 Wayne Gretzky
WG5 Wayne Gretzky	WG6 Wayne Gretzky
WG7 Wayne Gretzky	WG8 Wayne Gretzky
WG9 Wayne Gretzky	WG10 Wayne Gretzky
WG11 Wayne Gretzky	WG12 Wayne Gretzky
WG13 Wayne Gretzky	WG14 Wayne Gretzky
WG15 Wayne Gretzky	WG16 Wayne Gretzky
WG17 Wayne Gretzky	WG18 Wayne Gretzky
WG19 Wayne Gretzky	WG20 Wayne Gretzky
WG21 Wayne Gretzky	WG22 Wayne Gretzky
WG23 Wayne Gretzky	WG24 Wayne Gretzky
WG25 Wayne Gretzky	WG26 Wayne Gretzky
WG27 Wayne Gretzky	WG28 Wayne Gretzky
WG29 Wayne Gretzky	WG30 Wayne Gretzky

1998 - 99 STARTING LINEUP

An Upper Deck card was packaged with first series figures while a Pacific card was packaged with extended figures.

Upper Deck Set (23 cards): 40.00
Pacific Set (10 cards): 8.00

Player	NRMT-MT
SL1 Wayne Gretzky, NYRa.	8.00
SL2 Tony Amonte, Chic.	1.00
SL3 Ed Belfour (G), Dall.	2.00
SL4 Bryan Berard, NYIs.	1.00
SL5 Martin Brodeur (G), NJer.	3.00
SL6 Jim Campbell, SLou.	1.00
SL7 Vincent Damphousse, Mont.	1.00
SL8 Dominik Hasek (G), Buff.	2.00
SL9 Jaromir Jagr, Pitt.	2.00
SL10 Paul Kariya, Anah.	2.00
SL11 Brian Leetch, NYRa.	1.00
SL12 Eric Lindros, Phil.	2.00
SL13 Kirk McLean (G), Vanc. (Flor.)	1.00
SL14 Mark Messier, Vanc.	2.00
SL15 Rob Niedermayer, Flor.	1.00
SL16 Chris Osgood (G), Detr.	1.00
SL17 Félix Potvin (G), Toro.	1.00
SL18 Jeremy Roenick, Phoe.	1.00
SL19 Patrick Roy (G), Colo.	6.00
SL20 Joe Sakic, Colo.	3.00
SL21 Joe Thornton, Bost.	2.00
SL22 Alexei Yashin, Otta.	1.00
SL23 Steve Yzerman, Detr.	4.00
1 Peter Bondra, Wash.	1.00
2 Theoren Fleury, Calg.	1.00
3 Grant Fuhr (G), SLou.	1.00
4 Doug Gilmour, Chic.	1.00
5 Nikolai Khabibulin (G), Phoe.	1.00
6 Trevor Kidd (G), Caro.	1.00
7 Olaf Kölzig (G), Wash.	1.00
8 Daren Puppa (G), Tamp.	1.00
9 Brendan Shanahan, Detr.	2.00
10 John Vanbiesbrouck (G), Phil.	1.00

FIGURES

Figures were available in American (English text) and Canadian (bilingual text) packaging. The figures and cards in each type of package are the same. Priced below are retail selling prices for packaged figures (each package includes one card) and loose figures.

	Pack.	Loose
Packaged Set (33 packages):	**425.00**	**-**
Figure Set (33 loose figures):	**-**	**105.00**
Player	Pack.	Loose
Tony Amonte, Chic.	15.00	4.00
Ed Belfour (G), Dall.	20.00	4.00
Bryan Berard, NYIs.	12.00	3.00
Peter Bondra, Wash.	12.00	3.00
Martin Brodeur (G), NJer.	20.00	4.00
Jim Campbell, SLou.	12.00	3.00
Vincent Damphousse, Mont.	12.00	3.00
Theoren Fleury, Calg.	12.00	3.00
Grant Fuhr (G), SLou.	15.00	4.00
Doug Gilmour, Chic.	12.00	4.00
Wayne Gretzky, NYRa.	25.00	6.00
Dominik Hasek (G), Buff.	20.00	4.00
Jaromir Jagr, Pitt.	15.00	4.00
Paul Kariya, Anah.	15.00	4.00
Nikolai Khabibulin (G), Phoe.	15.00	4.00
Trevor Kidd (G), Caro.	15.00	4.00
Olaf Kölzig (G), Wash.	15.00	4.00
Brian Leetch, NYRa.	12.00	3.00
Eric Lindros, Phil.	15.00	4.00
Kirk McLean (G), Vanc. (Flor.)	20.00	4.00
Mark Messier, Vanc.	12.00	4.00
Rob Niedermayer, Flor.	15.00	3.00
Chris Osgood (G), Detr.	20.00	4.00
Félix Potvin (G), Toro.	20.00	4.00
Daren Puppa (G), Tamp.	15.00	4.00
Jeremy Roenick, Phoe.	12.00	3.00
Patrick Roy (G), Colo.	25.00	5.00
Joe Sakic, Colo.	15.00	4.00
Brendan Shanahan, Detr.	12.00	3.00
Joe Thornton, Bost.	15.00	4.00
John Vanbiesbrouck (G), Phil.	15.00	4.00
Alexei Yashin, Otta.	15.00	3.00
Steve Yzerman, Detr.	20.00	4.00

1998 - 99 STARTING LINEUP CANADIAN LEGENDS

One card was packaged with each figure.

Complete Set (4 cards): 6.00

Player	NRMT-MT
Mike Bossy	3.00
Bobby Clarke	1.00
Marcel Dionne	2.00
Glenn Hall (G)	2.00

FIGURES

	CAN	Loose
Canadian Set (4 packages):	**45.00**	**-**
Figure Set (4 loose figures):	**-**	**10.00**
Player	CAN	Loose
Mike Bossy	12.00	3.00
Bobby Clarke	12.00	3.00
Marcel Dionne	12.00	3.00
Glenn Hall (G)	20.00	4.00

1998 - 99 TOPPS & O-PEE-CHEE CHROME

There are two versions is the Topps series: the regular Topps card and the O-Pee-Chee parallel. There are two versions in the O-Pee-Chee Chrome series: the regular O-Pee-Chee Chrome card and the Refractor parallel.

	OPCCR	OPCC	OPC	Topps
Complete Set (242 cards):	**1000.00**	**175.00**	**250.00**	**35.00**
Common Player:	**3.00**	**.50**	**.75**	**.20**
Player	OPCCR	OPCC	OPC	Topps
1 P. Forsberg, Colo.	25.00	3.50	7.00	1.00
2 P. Sykora, NJer.	5.00	1.00	2.00	.20
3 B. Dafoe (G), Bost.	5.00	1.00	2.00	.20
4 Ron Francis, Caro.	10.00	1.50	3.00	.50
5 Alexei Yashin, Otta.	10.00	1.50	3.00	.50
6 Dave Ellett, Bost.	3.00	.50	.75	.20
7 Langenbrunner, Dall.	3.00	.50	1.00	.20
8 D. Weight, Edmo.	10.00	1.50	3.00	.50
9 Jason Woolley, Buff.	3.00	.50	.75	.20
10 Paul Coffey, Chic.	10.00	1.50	3.00	.50
11 Uwe Krupp, Detr.	3.00	.50	.75	.20
12 Sandström, Anah.	3.00	.50	1.00	.20
13 Scott Mellanby, Flor.	3.00	.50	1.00	.20
14 V. Tsyplakov, LosA.	3.00	.50	.75	.20
15 M. Rucinsky, Mont.	3.00	.50	1.00	.20
16 M. Renberg, Tamp.	5.00	.50	1.00	.20
17 Marco Sturm, SanJ.	3.00	.50	1.00	.20
18 Eric Lindros, Phil.	20.00	2.50	5.00	1.00
19 Sean Burke, Phil.	10.00	1.50	3.00	.50
20 Brodeur (G), NJer.	30.00	4.00	8.00	1.50
21 B. Devereaux, Edmo.	3.00	.50	1.00	.20
22 K. Buchberger, Edmo.	3.00	.50	.75	.20
23 Scott Stevens, NJer.	5.00	1.00	2.00	.20
24 Jamie Storr (G), LosA.	3.00	.50	1.00	.20
25 Anders Eriksson, Detr.	3.00	.50	.75	.20
26 Gary Suter, SanJ.	3.00	.50	1.00	.20
27 T. Fleury, Calg.	10.00	1.50	3.00	.50
28 Steve Leach, Caro.	3.00	.50	.75	.20
29 F. Potvin (G), Toro.	10.00	1.50	3.00	.50
30 Brett Hull, Dall.	20.00	2.50	5.00	1.00
31 Mike Grier, Edmo.	3.00	.50	1.00	.20
32 Cale Hulse, Calg.	3.00	.50	.75	.20
33 Larry Murphy, Detr.	3.00	.50	1.00	.20
34 Rick Tocchet, Phoe.	5.00	.50	1.00	.20
35 Éric Desjardins, Phil.	5.00	.50	1.00	.20
36 Igor Kravchuk, Otta.	3.00	.50	.75	.20
37 R. Niedermayer, Flor.	3.00	.50	1.00	.20
38 B. Smolinski, NYIs.	3.00	.50	.75	.20
39 V. Kamensky, Colo.	5.00	.50	1.00	.20
40 Ryan Smyth, Edmo.	5.00	1.00	2.00	.20
41 Bruce Driver, NYRa.	3.00	.50	.75	.20
42 Mike Johnson, Toro.	3.00	.50	1.00	.20
43 Rob Zamuner, Tamp.	3.00	.50	1.00	.20
44 S. Duchesne, LosA.	3.00	.50	1.00	.20
45 Martin Straka, Pitt.	5.00	.50	1.00	.20
46 Bill Houlder, SanJ.	3.00	.50	.75	.20
47 Craig Conroy, SLou.	5.00	.50	1.00	.20
48 G. Hebert (G), Anah.	3.00	.50	1.00	.20
49 Colin Forbes, Phil.	3.00	.50	.75	.20
50 Mike Modano, Dall.	20.00	2.50	5.00	1.00
51 Jamie Pushor, Anah.	3.00	.50	.75	.20
52 Jarome Iginla, Calg.	15.00	2.00	4.00	.50
53 Paul Kariya, Anah.	25.00	3.50	5.00	1.00
54 Mattias Öhlund, Vanc.	5.00	.50	1.00	.20
55 Sergei Berezin, Toro.	3.00	.50	1.00	.20
56 Peter Zezel, Vanc.	3.00	.50	.75	.20
57 T. Numminen, Phoe.	5.00	.50	1.00	.20
58 Dale Hunter, Wash.	5.00	.50	1.00	.20
59 Sandy Moger, LosA.	3.00	.50	.75	.20
60 John LeClair, Phil.	15.00	2.00	4.00	.50
61 Wade Redden, Otta.	5.00	.50	1.00	.20
62 Patrik Elias, NJer.	15.00	2.00	4.00	.50
63 Rob Blake, LosA.	10.00	1.50	3.00	.50
64 T. Marchant, Edmo.	3.00	.50	1.00	.20
65 C. Lemieux, Colo.	5.00	.50	1.00	.20
66 T. Kidd (G), Caro.	5.00	.50	1.00	.20
67 S. Fedorov, Detr.	20.00	2.50	5.00	1.00
68 Joe Sakic, Colo.	30.00	4.00	8.00	1.50
69 Derek Morris, Calg.	3.00	.50	1.00	.20
70 Alexei Morozov, Pitt.	3.00	.50	1.00	.20
71 Mats Sundin, Toro.	20.00	2.50	5.00	1.00
72 D. Langkow, Tamp.	3.00	.50	1.00	.20
73 Kevin Hatcher, Pitt.	3.00	.50	.75	.20
74 D. Rhodes (G), Otta.	3.00	.50	1.00	.20
75 Brian Leetch, NYRa.	10.00	1.50	3.00	.50
76 Saku Koivu, Mont.	15.00	2.00	4.00	.50
77 Tabaracci (G), Wash.	3.00	.50	.75	.20
78 Bernie Nicholls, SanJ.	3.00	.50	1.00	.20
79 Alyn McCauley, Toro.	5.00	.50	1.00	.20
80 P. Brisebois, Mont.	3.00	.50	.75	.20
81 Bret Hedican, Vanc.	3.00	.50	.75	.20
82 S. McCarthy, Tamp.	3.00	.50	.75	.20
83 Viktor Kozlov, Flor.	5.00	.50	1.00	.20
84 Derek King, Toro.	3.00	.50	.75	.20
85 A. Selivanov, Tamp.	3.00	.50	.75	.20
86 M. Vernon (G), SanJ.	5.00	1.00	2.00	.20
87 J. Beukeboom, NYRa.	3.00	.50	.75	.20
88 T. Salo (G), NYIs.	5.00	1.00	2.00	.20
89 Adam Graves, NYRa.	5.00	1.00	2.00	.20
90 Randy McKay, NJer.	3.00	.50	.75	.20
91 Richard Pilon, NYIs.	3.00	.50	.75	.20
92 R. Zednik, Wash.	5.00	1.00	2.00	.20
93 Jeff Hackett (G), Chic.	5.00	.50	1.00	.20
94 Michael Peca, Buff.	5.00	1.00	2.00	.20
95 Brent Gilchrist, Detr.	3.00	.50	.75	.20
96 Stu Grimson, Anah.	3.00	.50	1.00	.20
97 Bob Probert, Chic.	5.00	.50	1.00	.20
98 Stu Barnes, Pitt.	3.00	.50	.75	.20
99 Ruslan Salei, Anah.	3.00	.50	.75	.20
100 Al MacInnis, SLou.	5.00	1.00	2.00	.20
101 Ken Daneyko, NJer.	3.00	.50	1.00	.20
102 Paul Ranheim, Caro.	3.00	.50	.75	.20
103 Marty McInnis, Calg.	3.00	.50	.75	.20
104 Marian Hossa, Otta.	20.00	2.50	5.00	1.00
105 D. McCarty, Detr.	5.00	.50	1.00	.20
106 G. Carbonneau, Dall.	5.00	.50	1.00	.20
107 Dallas Drake, Phoe.	3.00	.50	.75	.20
108 S. Samsonov, Bost.	10.00	1.50	3.00	.50
109 T. Selänne, Anah.	15.00	2.00	4.00	.50
110 Checklist	3.00	.50	.75	.20
111 Jaromir Jagr, Pitt.	20.00	2.50	5.00	1.00
112 Joe Thornton, Bost.	20.00	3.00	6.00	1.00
113 Jon Klemm, Colo.	3.00	.50	.75	.20
114 G. Fuhr (G), SLou.	10.00	1.50	3.00	.50
115 Khabibulin (G), Phoe.	5.00	1.00	2.00	.20
116 R. Brind'Amour, Phil.	5.00	.50	1.00	.20
117 Trevor Linden, NYIs.	5.00	1.00	2.00	.20
118 Damphousse, Mont.	10.00	1.50	3.00	.50
119 Dino Ciccarelli, Flor.	5.00	.50	1.00	.20
120 Pat Verbeek, Dall.	5.00	.50	1.00	.20
121 S. Ozolinsh, Colo.	3.00	.50	1.00	.20
122 G. Snow (G), Vanc.	5.00	.50	1.00	.20
123 E. Belfour (G), Dall.	20.00	2.50	5.00	1.00
124 K. Primeau, Caro.	5.00	1.00	2.00	.20
125 J. Allison, Bost.	10.00	1.50	3.00	.50
126 P. Bondra, Wash.	10.00	1.50	3.00	.50
127 U.Samuelsson, NYRa.	3.00	.50	.75	.20
128 Jeff Friesen, SanJ.	5.00	.50	1.00	.20
129 J. Bonsignore, Tamp.	3.00	.50	.75	.20
130 D. Alfredsson, Otta.	10.00	1.50	3.00	.50
131 Bobby Holik, NJer.	5.00	.50	1.00	.20
132 J. Stümpel, LosA.	3.00	.50	1.00	.20
133 B. Bellows, Wash.	3.00	.50	1.00	.20
134 C. Osgood (G), Detr.	10.00	1.50	3.00	.50
135 A. Zhamnov, Chic.	5.00	.50	1.00	.20
136 M. Norstrom, LosA.	3.00	.50	1.00	.20
137 Berehowsky, Edmo.	3.00	.50	.75	.20
138 M. Messier, Vanc.	20.00	2.50	5.00	1.00
139 G. Courtnall, SLou.	3.00	.50	.75	.20
140 Marc Bureau, Phil.	3.00	.50	.75	.20
141 Don Sweeney, Bost.	3.00	.50	.75	.20
142 W. Clark, Tamp.	15.00	2.00	4.00	.50
143 S Niedermayer, NJer.	5.00	.50	1.00	.20
144 Chris Therien, Phil.	3.00	.50	.75	.20
145 Kirk Muller, Flor.	5.00	.50	1.00	.20
146 W. Primeau, Buff.	3.00	.50	.75	.20

□□□□	147 T. Granato, SanJ.	3.00	.50	1.00	.20
□□□□	148 Derian Hatcher, Dall.	5.00	.50	1.00	.20
□□□□	149 Daniel Brière, Phoe.	5.00	2.00	2.00	.50
□□□□	150 F. Olausson, Pitt.	3.00	.50	1.00	.20
□□□□	151 Joé Juneau, Wash.	3.00	.50	1.00	.20
□□□□	152 M. Grosek, Buff.	3.00	.50	.75	.20
□□□□	153 J. Laukkanen, Otta.	3.00	.50	.75	.20
□□□□	154 K. Tkachuk, Phoe.	10.00	1.50	3.00	.50
□□□□	155 M. McSorley, SanJ.	3.00	.50	1.00	.20
□□□□	156 Owen Nolan, SanJ.	10.00	1.50	3.00	.50
□□□□	157 Mark Tinordi, Wash.	3.00	.50	.75	.20
□□□□	158 S. Washburn, Flor.	3.00	.50	.75	.20
□□□□	159 L. Richardson, Phil.	3.00	.50	.75	.20
□□□□	160 Kris King, Toro.	3.00	.50	.75	.20
□□□□	161 Nieuwendyk, Dall.	5.00	1.00	2.00	.20
□□□□	162 Travis Green, Anah.	3.00	.50	1.00	.20
□□□□	163 D. Hasek (G), Buff.	20.00	2.50	5.00	1.00
□□□□	164 D. Khristich, Bost.	3.00	.50	.75	.20
□□□□	165 Dave Manson, Mont.	3.00	.50	.75	.20
□□□□	166 Chris Chelios, Chic.	10.00	1.50	3.00	.50
□□□□	167 C. Lapointe, NYIs.	3.00	.50	.75	.20
□□□□	168 Kris Draper, Detr.	3.00	.50	1.00	.20
□□□□	169 Brad Isbister, Phoe.	3.00	.50	1.00	.20
□□□□	170 P. Marleau, SanJ.	5.00	1.00	2.00	.20
□□□□	171 J. Roenick, Phoe.	15.00	2.00	4.00	.50
□□□□	172 D. Langdon, NYRa.	3.00	.50	1.00	.20
□□□□	173 Kevin Dineen, Caro.	3.00	.50	.75	.20
□□□□	174 L. Robitaille, LosA.	15.00	2.00	4.00	.50
□□□□	175 S. Yzerman, Detr.	45.00	6.00	10.00	2.00
□□□□	176 Sergei Zubov, Dall.	3.00	.50	1.00	.20
□□□□	177 Ed Jovanovski, Flor.	5.00	1.00	2.00	.20
□□□□	178 S. Kapanen, Caro.	5.00	.50	1.00	.20
□□□□	179 Adam Oates, Wash.	5.00	1.00	2.00	.20
□□□□	180 Pavel Bure, Vanc.	15.00	2.00	4.00	.50
□□□□	181 C. Pronger, SLou.	10.00	1.50	3.00	.50
□□□□	182 Pat Falloon, Otta.	3.00	.50	.75	.20
□□□□	183 D. Tucker, Tamp.	3.00	.50	1.00	.20
□□□□	184 Z. Palffy, NYIs.	10.00	1.50	3.00	.50
□□□□	185 Curtis Brown, Buff.	3.00	.50	.75	.20
□□□□	186 Cu.Joseph (G), Toro.	20.00	2.50	5.00	1.00
□□□□	187 V. Zelepukin, Edmo.	3.00	.50	.75	.20
□□□□	188 R. Courtnall, LosA.	3.00	.50	1.00	.20
□□□□	189 Adam Foote, Colo.	5.00	.50	1.00	.20
□□□□	190 P. Roy (G), Colo.	60.00	7.50	15.00	3.00
□□□□	191 Cory Stillman, Calg.	3.00	.50	1.00	.20
□□□□	192 Alexei Zhitnik, Buff.	3.00	.50	.75	.20
□□□□	193 O. Kölzig (G), Wash.	10.00	1.50	3.00	.50
□□□□	194 Fitzpatrick (G), Chic.	3.00	.50	.75	.20
□□□□	195 Eric Dazé, Chic.	5.00	1.00	2.00	.20
□□□□	196 Z. Zalapski, Mont.	3.00	.50	.75	.20
□□□□	197 N. Sundström, NYRa.	3.00	.50	1.00	.20
□□□□	198 Bryan Berard, NYIs.	5.00	.50	1.00	.20
□□□□	199 Jason Arnott, NJer.	5.00	1.00	2.00	.20
□□□□	200 Mike Richter, NYRa.	5.00	1.00	2.00	.20
□□□□	201 Baumgartner, Bost.	3.00	.50	.75	.20
□□□□	202 Jason Dawe, NYIs.	3.00	.50	.75	.20
□□□□	203 N. Lidström, Detr.	10.00	1.50	3.00	.50
□□□□	204 Tony Amonte, Chic.	10.00	1.50	3.00	.50
□□□□	205 K. Samuelsson, Phil.	3.00	.50	.75	.20
□□□□	206 R. Bourque, Bost.	20.00	3.00	6.00	1.00
□□□□	207 A. Mogilny, Vanc.	5.00	1.00	2.00	.20
□□□□	208 P. Turgeon, SLou.	5.00	1.00	2.00	.20
□□□□	209 T. Barrasso (G), Pitt.	5.00	1.00	2.00	.20
□□□□	210 R. Matvichuk, Dall.	3.00	.50	1.00	.20
□□□□	211 S. Krivokrasov, Nas.	3.00	.50	.75	.20
□□□□	212 Ted Drury, Anah.	3.00	.50	.75	.20
□□□□	213 M. Barnaby, Buff.	3.00	.50	.75	.20
□□□□	214 D. Pederson, NJer.	3.00	.50	.75	.20
□□□□	215 V'biesbrouck(G), Phil.	5.00	1.00	2.00	.20
□□□□	216 B. Shanahan, Detr.	20.00	2.50	5.00	1.00
□□□□	217 Thibault (G), Mont.	5.00	1.00	2.00	.20
□□□□	218 N. Emerson, Caro.	3.00	.50	.75	.20
□□□□	219 W. Gretzky, NYRa.	80.00	10.00	20.00	4.00
□□□□	220 Checklist	3.00	.50	.75	.20
□□□□	**221 Ramzi Abid RC**	**10.00**	**6.00**	**2.00**	**1.50**
□□□□	**222 Mark BellRC**	**15.00**	**8.00**	**2.00**	**1.50**
□□□□	**223 M. Henrich RC**	**5.00**	**4.00**	**1.00**	**1.00**
□□□□	224 Vincent Lecavalier	25.00	12.00	5.00	2.00
□□□□	225 Rico Fata	5.00	2.00	1.00	.20
□□□□	226 Bryan Allen	3.00	2.00	.75	.20
□□□□	227 Daniel Tkaczuk	5.00	2.00	1.00	.20
□□□□	**228 Brad Stuart RC**	**30.00**	**14.00**	**4.00**	**3.00**
□□□□	**229 Derrick Walser RC**	**5.00**	**2.00**	**1.00**	**.50**
□□□□	**230 J. Cheechoo RC**	**15.00**	**10.00**	**3.00**	**2.00**
□□□□	231 Sergei Varlamov	3.00	2.00	.75	.20
□□□□	**232 Scott Gomez RC**	**65.00**	**30.00**	**4.00**	**4.00**
□□□□	**233 Jeff Heerema RC**	**5.00**	**4.00**	**1.00**	**1.00**
□□□□	234 David Legwand	10.00	4.00	2.00	.20
□□□□	235 Manny Malhotra	5.00	2.00	1.00	.20
□□□□	**236 Michael Rupp RC**	**15.00**	**10.00**	**3.00**	**2.00**
□□□□	237 Alex Tanguay	15.00	6.00	3.00	.50
□□□□	**238 Mathieu Biron RC**	**5.00**	**4.00**	**1.00**	**1.00**
□□□□	**239 B. Amidovski (G)RC**	**5.00**	**2.00**	**1.00**	**.50**
□□□□	**240 B. Finley (G) RC**	**10.00**	**6.00**	**2.00**	**1.50**
□□□□	**241 P. Sauvé (G)RC**	**10.00**	**6.00**	**2.00**	**1.50**
□□□□	**242 Jiri Fischer RC**	**15.00**	**8.00**	**2.00**	**1.50**

BOARD MEMBERS

These cards were inserted into packs of Topps (1:36) and O-Pee-Chee Chrome (1:12; Refractor 1:36).

Insert Set (15 cards):		60.00	25.00	25.00
	Insert (1:36)	OPCCR	OPCC	Topps
□□□	B1 Chris Pronger, SLou.	6.00	2.00	3.00
□□□	B2 Chris Chelios, Chic.	6.00	2.00	3.00
□□□	B3 Brian Leetch, NYRa.	6.00	2.00	3.00
□□□	B4 Raymond Bourque, Bost.	10.00	2.00	6.00
□□□	B5 Mattias Öhlund, Vanc.	4.00	2.00	1.00
□□□	B6 Nicklas Lidström, Detr.	6.00	2.00	3.00
□□□	B7 Sergei Zubov, Dall.	4.00	2.00	1.00
□□□	B8 Scott Niedermayer, NJer.	4.00	2.00	1.00
□□□	B9 Larry Murphy, Detr.	4.00	2.00	1.00
□□□	B10 Sandis Ozolinsh, Colo.	4.00	2.00	1.00
□□□	B11 Rob Blake, LosA.	6.00	2.00	3.00
□□□	B12 Scott Stevens, NJer.	4.00	2.00	2.00
□□□	B13 Derian Hatcher, Dall.	4.00	2.00	1.00
□□□	B14 Kevin Hatcher, Pitt.	4.00	2.00	1.00
□□□	B15 Wade Redden, Otta.	4.00	2.00	1.00

CERTIFIED AUTOGRAPH ISSUE

Insert Set (9 cards):		270.00
	Insert (1:209)	CAI
□	A1 Jason Allison, Bost.	30.00
□	A2 Sergei Samsonov, Bost.	30.00
□	A3 John LeClair, Phil.	40.00
□	A4 Mattias Öhlund, Vanc.	20.00
□	A5 Jaromir Jagr, Pitt.	50.00
□	A6 Keith Tkachuk, Phoe.	30.00
□	A7 Patrik Elias, NJer.	40.00
□	A8 Dominik Hasek (G), Buff.	50.00
□	A9 Brian Leetch, NYRa.	30.00

ICE AGE 2000

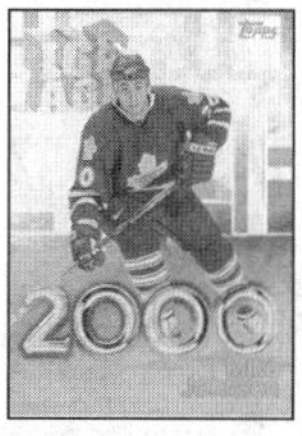

Topps Insert Set (15 cards):		25.00
	Insert (1:12)	IA
□	I1 Paul Kariya, Anah.	6.00
□	I2 Marco Sturm, SanJ.	.75
□	I3 Jarome Iginla, Calg.	2.00
□	I4 Denis Pederson, NJer.	.75
□	I5 Wade Redden, Otta.	.75
□	I6 Jason Allison, Bost.	2.00
□	I7 Chris Pronger, SLou.	2.00
□	I8 Peter Forsberg, Colo.	6.00
□	I9 Saku Koivu, Mont.	2.00
□	I10 Eric Lindros, Phil.	4.00
□	I11 Sergei Samsonov, Bost.	2.00
□	I12 Mattias Öhlund, Vanc.	.75
□	I13 Joe Thornton, Bost.	4.00
□	I14 Mike Johnson, Toro.	.75
□	I15 Nikolai Khabibulin (G), Phoe.	.75

LOCAL LEGENDS

Insert Set (15 cards):		95.00
	Insert (1:18)	LL
□	L1 Peter Forsberg, Colo.	5.00
□	L2 Mats Sundin, Toro.	6.00
□	L3 Zigmund Palffy, NYIs.	3.00
□	L4 Jaromir Jagr, Pitt.	5.00
□	L5 Dominik Hasek (G), Buff.	5.00
□	L6 Martin Brodeur (G), NJer.	10.00
□	L7 Wayne Gretzky, NYRa.	25.00
□	L8 Patrick Roy (G), Colo.	15.00
□	L9 Eric Lindros, Phil.	5.00
□	L10 Joe Sakic, Colo.	10.00
□	L11 Mark Messier, Vanc.	6.00
□	L12 Mike Modano, Dall.	6.00
□	L13 Sergei Fedorov, Detr.	6.00
□	L14 Pavel Bure, Vanc.	5.00
□	L15 Teemu Selänne, Anah.	5.00

MYSTERY FINEST

There are six versions: Bronze, Bronze Refractor, Silver, Silver Refractor, Gold and Gold Refractor. The Silver cards are valued at 50% more than the Bronze cards.

Insert Set (20 cards):		250.00	175.00	125.00
	Insert	Gold	Silv.	Bron.
□□□	M1 Teemu Selänne	12.00	5.00	6.00
□□□	M2 Olaf Kölzig (G)	8.00	5.00	4.00
□□□	M3 Pavel Bure	10.00	5.00	6.00
□□□	M4 Wayne Gretzky	50.00	45.00	30.00
□□□	M5 Mike Modano	14.00	10.00	6.00
□□□	M6 Jaromir Jagr	15.00	10.00	6.00
□□□	M7 Dominik Hasek (G)	15.00	10.00	6.00
□□□	M8 Peter Forsberg	20.00	15.00	10.00
□□□	M9 Eric Lindros	15.00	10.00	6.00
□□□	M10 John LeClair	12.00	5.00	6.00
□□□	M11 Zigmund Palffy	8.00	5.00	4.00
□□□	M12 Martin Brodeur (G)	20.00	15.00	12.00
□□□	M13 Keith Tkachuk	8.00	5.00	4.00
□□□	M14 Peter Bondra	8.00	5.00	4.00
□□□	M15 Nicklas Lidström	8.00	5.00	4.00
□□□	M16 Patrick Roy (G)	45.00	30.00	22.00
□□□	M17 Chris Chelios	8.00	5.00	4.00
□□□	M18 Saku Koivu	12.00	5.00	6.00
□□□	M19 Mark Messier	14.00	10.00	6.00
□□□	M20 Joe Sakic	20.00	15.00	12.00

MYSTERY FINEST REFRACTOR

Insert Set (20 cards):		575.00	400.00	250.00
	Insert	GR	SR	BR
□□□	M1 Teemu Selänne	25.00	15.00	12.00
□□□	M2 Olaf Kölzig (G)	15.00	10.00	8.00
□□□	M3 Pavel Bure	25.00	15.00	12.00
□□□	M4 Wayne Gretzky	125.00	90.00	50.00
□□□	M5 Mike Modano	30.00	20.00	14.00
□□□	M6 Jaromir Jagr	30.00	20.00	15.00
□□□	M7 Dominik Hasek (G)	30.00	20.00	14.00
□□□	M8 Peter Forsberg	40.00	30.00	20.00
□□□	M9 Eric Lindros	30.00	20.00	14.00
□□□	M10 John LeClair	25.00	15.00	12.00
□□□	M11 Zigmund Palffy	15.00	10.00	8.00
□□□	M12 Martin Brodeur (G)	50.00	35.00	20.00
□□□	M13 Keith Tkachuk	15.00	10.00	8.00
□□□	M14 Peter Bondra	15.00	10.00	8.00
□□□	M15 Nicklas Lidström	15.00	10.00	8.00
□□□	M16 Patrick Roy (G)	90.00	65.00	45.00
□□□	M17 Chris Chelios	15.00	10.00	8.00
□□□	M18 Saku Koivu	25.00	15.00	12.00
□□□	M19 Mark Messier	30.00	20.00	14.00
□□□	M20 Joe Sakic	50.00	35.00	20.00

ROOKIE REPRINTS

These cards were inserted into packs of Topps (1:24) and O-Pee-Chee Chrome (1:28, Refractor 1:112). The Howe, Hull and Esposito autographs were inserted 1:1878 packs while the Mikita autographs were inserted 1:3756 packs.

Insert Set (10 cards):		135.00	65.00	50.00
	Insert	OPCCR	OPCC	Topps
□□□	1 W. Gretzky, Edmo.'79-80	40.00	20.00	15.00
□□□	2 M. Messier, Edmo.'80-81	10.00	5.00	3.00
□□□	3 R. Bourque, Bost.'80-81	10.00	6.00	4.00
□□□	4 P. Roy (G), Mont.'86-87	30.00	15.00	10.00
□□□	5 G. Fuhr (G), Edmo. '82-83	6.00	3.00	2.00
□□□	6 Br. Hull, SLou. '88-89	10.00	5.00	3.00
□□□	7 Gordie Howe '54-55	25.00	10.00	10.00
□□□	8 Stan Mikita '60-61	8.00	4.00	3.00
□□□	9 Bobby Hull '58-59	15.00	5.00	5.00
□□□	10 Phil Esposito '65-66	10.00	6.00	4.00

ROOKIE REPRINTS AUTOGRAPHED

Autograph Set (4 cards):		425.00
	Insert	Auto.
□	7 Gordie Howe ✍	240.00
□	8 Stan Mikita ✍	80.00
□	9 Bobby Hull ✍	100.00
□	10 Phil Esposito ✍	100.00

SEASON'S BEST

These cards were inserted into packs of Topps (1:8) and O-Pee-Chee Chrome (1:8, Refractor 1:24).

Insert Set (30 cards):		175.00	95.00	60.00
	Insert	OPCCR	OPCC	Topps
□□□	SB1 Dominik Hasek (G), Buff.	10.00	5.00	3.00
□□□	SB2 Martin Brodeur (G), NJer.	15.00	8.00	6.00
□□□	SB3 Ed Belfour (G), Dall.	10.00	5.00	3.00
□□□	SB4 Curtis Joseph (G), Edmo.	10.00	5.00	3.00
□□□	SB5 Jeff Hackett (G), Chic.	3.00	1.50	1.00
□□□	SB6 Tom Barrasso (G), Pitt.	4.00	2.00	1.00
□□□	SB7 Mike Johnson, Toro.	3.00	1.50	1.00
□□□	SB8 Sergei Samsonov, Bost.	6.00	3.00	2.00
□□□	SB9 Patrik Elias, NJer.	8.00	4.00	3.00
□□□	SB10 Patrick Marleau, SanJ.	4.00	2.00	1.00
□□□	SB11 Mattias Öhlund, Vanc.	3.00	1.50	1.00
□□□	SB12 Marco Sturm, SanJ.	3.00	1.50	1.00
□□□	SB13 Teemu Selänne, Anah.	5.00	4.00	3.00
□□□	SB14 Peter Bondra, Wash.	6.00	3.00	2.00
□□□	SB15 Pavel Bure, Vanc.	5.00	4.00	3.00
□□□	SB16 John LeClair, Phil.	5.00	4.00	3.00
□□□	SB17 Zigmund Palffy, NYIs.	6.00	3.00	2.00
□□□	SB18 Keith Tkachuk, Phoe.	6.00	3.00	2.00
□□□	SB19 Jaromir Jagr, Pitt.	10.00	5.00	1.00
□□□	SB20 Wayne Gretzky, NYRa.	40.00	20.00	15.00
□□□	SB21 Peter Forsberg, Colo.	10.00	5.00	5.00
□□□	SB22 Ron Francis, Pitt.	6.00	3.00	2.00
□□□	SB23 Adam Oates, Wash.	4.00	2.00	1.00
□□□	SB24 Jozef Stümpel, LosA.	3.00	1.50	1.00
□□□	SB25 Chris Pronger, SLou.	6.00	3.00	2.00
□□□	SB26 Larry Murphy, Detr.	3.00	1.50	1.00
□□□	SB27 Jason Allison, Bost.	6.00	3.00	2.00
□□□	SB28 John LeClair, Phil.	5.00	4.00	3.00
□□□	SB29 Randy McKay, NJer.	3.00	1.50	1.00
□□□	SB30 Dainius Zubrus, Phil.	3.00	1.50	1.00

1998 - 99 TOPPS FINEST

These cards have four versions: the regular card, a Refractor parallel, a No-Protector parallel and a No-Protector Refractor parallel.

Complete Set (150 cards):		1,000.00	485.00	100.00	45.00
Common Player:		3.00	1.50	.75	.35
	Player	NPR	TFR	NP	TF
□□□□	1 T. Selänne, Anah.	20.00	10.00	2.00	1.00
□□□□	2 T. Fleury, Calg.	15.00	5.00	1.00	.35

3 Ed Belfour (G), Dall.	25.00	10.00	3.00	1.00
4 D. Hasek (G), Buff.	25.00	10.00	3.00	1.00
5 Dino Ciccarelli, Flor.	8.00	4.00	.75	.35
6 Peter Forsberg, Colo.	35.00	15.00	4.00	2.00
7 Rob Blake, LosA.	15.00	7.00	1.00	.35
8 Martin Gélinas, Caro.	6.00	3.00	.75	.35
9 Damphousse, Mont.	15.00	7.00	1.00	.35
10 Doug Brown, Detr.	3.00	1.50	.75	.35
11 Andreychuk, NJer.	8.00	4.00	.75	.35
12 Bill Guerin, Edmo.	10.00	5.00	1.00	.35
13 D. Alfredsson, Otta.	15.00	7.00	1.00	.35
14 Dainius Zubrus, Phil.	6.00	3.00	.75	.35
15 Khabibulin (G), Phoe.	10.00	5.00	1.00	.35
16 S. Nemchinov, NYIs.	6.00	3.00	.75	.35
17 R. Brind'Amour, Phil.	8.00	4.00	.75	.35
18 P. Marleau, SanJ.	10.00	6.00	1.00	.35
19 Brett Hull, Dall.	25.00	10.00	3.00	1.00
20 Rob Zamuner, Tamp.	6.00	3.00	.75	.35
21 Anson Carter, Bost.	10.00	5.00	1.00	.35
22 Chris Pronger, SLou.	15.00	7.00	1.00	.35
23 Owen Nolan, SanJ.	15.00	7.00	1.00	.35
24 Alexandre Daigle, Phil.	4.00	2.00	.75	.35
25 D. Kasparaitis, Pitt.	6.00	3.00	.75	.35
26 Steve Rucchin, Anah.	6.00	3.00	.75	.35
27 G. Fuhr (G), SLou.	15.00	7.00	1.00	.35
28 Mike Sillinger, Phil.	4.00	2.00	.75	.35
29 Tony Amonte, Chic.	15.00	7.00	1.00	.35
30 J. Roenick, Phoe.	20.00	10.00	2.00	1.00
31 Garry Galley, LosA.	3.00	1.50	.75	.35
32 Jeff Friesen, SanJ.	8.00	4.00	.75	.35
33 Alexei Zhitnik, Buff.	4.00	2.00	.75	.35
34 Sergei Fedorov, Detr.	25.00	10.00	3.00	1.00
35 Brodeur (G), NJer.	40.00	20.00	4.00	2.00
36 C. Joseph (G), Toro.	25.00	10.00	3.00	1.00
37 Mike Johnson, Toro.	5.00	2.00	.75	.35
38 Mattias Öhlund, Vanc.	8.00	4.00	.75	.35
39 Derian Hatcher, Dall.	8.00	4.00	.75	.35
40 Z. Palffy, NYIs.	15.00	7.00	1.00	.35
41 R.Niedermayer, Flor.	6.00	3.00	.75	.35
42 Keith Primeau, Caro.	10.00	5.00	1.00	.35
43 V. Kamensky, Colo.	8.00	4.00	.75	.35
44 Cliff Ronning, Phoe.	6.00	3.00	.75	.35
45 Saku Koivu, Mont.	20.00	10.00	2.00	1.00
46 Jiri Slegr, Pitt.	4.00	2.00	.75	.35
47 Igor Korolev, Toro.	4.00	2.00	.75	.35
48 S. Samsonov, Bost.	15.00	5.00	1.00	.35
49 Vaclav Prospal, Otta.	8.00	4.00	.75	.35
50 Ron Francis, Caro.	15.00	7.00	1.00	.35
51 John LeClair, Phil.	20.00	10.00	2.00	1.00
52 Peter Bondra, Wash.	15.00	7.00	1.00	.35
53 Matt Cullen, Anah.	6.00	3.00	.75	.35
54 Doug Gilmour, Chic.	15.00	7.00	1.00	.35
55 V'sbrouck (G), Flor.	10.00	6.00	1.00	.35
56 K. Stevens, NYRa.	6.00	3.00	.75	.35
57 V. Malakhov, Mont.	4.00	2.00	.75	.35
58 G. Hebert (G), Anah.	6.00	3.00	.75	.35
59 Patrik Elias, NJer.	20.00	10.00	2.00	1.00
60 Boris Mironov, Edmo.	4.00	2.00	.75	.35
61 Rob DiMaio, Bost.	4.00	2.00	.75	.35
62 P. Demitra, SLou.	10.00	5.00	1.00	.35
63 M. Nylander, Calg.	6.00	3.00	.75	.35
64 W. Gretzky, NYRa.	100.00	50.00	10.00	6.00
65 Miroslav Satan, Buff.	8.00	4.00	.75	.35
66 Éric Dazé, Chic.	10.00	5.00	1.00	.35
67 Jozef Stümpel, LosA.	6.00	3.00	.75	.35
68 M. Messier, Vanc.	25.00	10.00	3.00	1.00
69 Pat Verbeek, Dall.	8.00	4.00	.75	.35
70 F. Potvin (G), Toro.	15.00	7.00	1.00	.35
71 Ethan Moreau, Chic.	4.00	2.00	.75	.35
72 S. Yzerman, Detr.	60.00	30.00	7.00	3.00
73 Paul Ysebaert, Tamp.	3.00	1.50	.75	.35
74 Jaromir Jagr, Pitt.	20.00	10.00	3.00	1.00
75 Mike Modano, Dall.	25.00	10.00	3.00	1.00
76 C. Osgood (G), Detr.	15.00	5.00	1.00	.35
77 Robert Svehla, Flor.	6.00	3.00	.75	.35
78 Joé Juneau, Wash.	6.00	3.00	.75	.35
79 A. Deadmarsh, Colo.	8.00	4.00	.75	.35
80 K. Tkachuk, Phoe.	15.00	5.00	1.00	.35
81 Mark Recchi, Mont.	10.00	5.00	1.00	.35
82 A. Cassels, Calg.	6.00	3.00	.75	.35
83 Mike Hough, NYIs.	3.00	1.50	.75	.35
84 Rem Murray, Edmo.	3.00	1.50	.75	.35
85 Trevor Kidd (G), Caro.	8.00	4.00	.75	.35
86 J. Hackett (G), Chic.	5.00	4.00	.75	.35
87 M. Renberg, Tamp.	8.00	4.00	.75	.35
88 Al MacInnis, SLou.	10.00	5.00	1.00	.35
89 M. Richter (G), NYRa.	10.00	6.00	1.00	.35
90 M. Näslund, Vanc.	25.00	12.00	3.00	1.00
91 Joe Sakic, Colo.	40.00	20.00	4.00	2.00
92 Michael Peca, Buff.	10.00	5.00	1.00	.35
93 Scott Thornton, Mont.	3.00	1.50	.75	.35
94 Vy. Kozlov, Detr.	6.00	3.00	.75	.35
95 Bobby Holik, NJer.	8.00	4.00	.75	.35
96 Alexei Yashin, Otta.	15.00	7.00	1.00	.35
97 Robert Kron, Caro.	4.00	2.00	.75	.35
98 Adam Oates, Wash.	10.00	5.00	1.00	.35
99 Chris Simon, Wash.	6.00	3.00	.75	.35
100 Paul Kariya, Anah.	30.00	15.00	4.00	2.00
101 R. Bourque, Bost.	30.00	15.00	3.00	1.00
102 Éric Desjardins, Phil.	8.00	4.00	.75	.35
103 Glen Murray, LosA.	12.00	6.00	1.00	.35
104 Tverdovsky, Phoe.	4.00	2.00	.75	.35
105 Pavel Bure, Vanc.	20.00	10.00	2.00	1.00
106 Mats Sundin, Toro.	25.00	10.00	3.00	1.00
107 Bryan Berard, NYIs.	8.00	4.00	.75	.35
108 J. Niinimaa, Edmo.	6.00	3.00	.75	.35
109 Wade Redden, Otta.	8.00	4.00	.75	.35
110 T. Linden, NYIs.	10.00	5.00	1.00	.35
111 J. Iginla, Calg.	20.00	10.00	2.00	1.00
112 J. Nieuwendyk, Dall.	10.00	5.00	1.00	.35
113 A. Kovalev, NYRa.	15.00	7.00	1.00	.35
114 Dave Gagner, Flor.	4.00	2.00	.75	.35
115 D. Yushkevich, Toro.	6.00	3.00	.75	.35
116 S. Ozolinsh, Colo.	6.00	3.00	.75	.35
117 D. Khristich, Bost.	4.00	2.00	.75	.35
118 Jim Campbell, SLou.	3.00	1.50	.75	.35
119 N. Lidström, Detr.	15.00	7.00	1.00	.35
120 S.Niedermayer, Flor.	8.00	4.00	.75	.35
121 N.Sundström, NYRa.	6.00	3.00	.75	.35
122 Karl Dykhuis, Tamp.	3.00	1.50	.75	.35
123 B. Shanahan, Detr.	25.00	10.00	3.00	1.00
124 S. McCarthy, Tamp.	4.00	2.00	.75	.35
125 P. Turgeon, SLou.	10.00	5.00	1.00	.35
126 O. Kölzig (G), Wash.	15.00	7.00	1.00	.35
127 C. Chelios, Chic.	15.00	7.00	1.00	.35
128 L. Robitaille, LosA.	20.00	10.00	2.00	1.00
129 A. Mogilny, Vanc.	10.00	6.00	1.00	.35
130 S. Kapanen, Caro.	8.00	4.00	.75	.35
131 Stu Barnes, Pitt.	3.00	1.50	.75	.35
132 S. Stevens, NJer.	10.00	5.00	1.00	.35
133 D. Weight, Edmo.	15.00	5.00	1.00	.35
134 A. Zhamnov, Chic.	8.00	4.00	.75	.35
135 M. Vernon (G), SanJ.	10.00	5.00	1.00	.35
136 Derek Morris, Calg.	6.00	3.00	.75	.35
137 B. Leetch, NYRa.	15.00	7.00	1.00	.35
138 Ray Whitney, Flor.	6.00	3.00	.75	.35
139 Chris Gratton, Phil.	6.00	3.00	.75	.35
140 P. Roy (G), Colo.	70.00	35.00	9.00	4.00
141 Jason Allison, Bost.	15.00	5.00	1.00	.35
142 Barrasso (G), Pitt.	10.00	5.00	1.00	.35
143 Derek Plante, Buff.	4.00	2.00	.75	.35
144 D. Pederson, NJer.	3.00	1.50	.75	.35
145 Mike Ricci, SanJ.	8.00	4.00	.75	.35
146 D. Rhodes (G), Otta.	6.00	3.00	.75	.35
147 Marco Sturm, SanJ.	6.00	3.00	.75	.35
148 Darryl Sydor, Dall.	6.00	3.00	.75	.35
149 Eric Lindros, Phil.	20.00	10.00	3.00	1.00
150 Checklist	3.00	1.50	.75	.35

CENTURIONS

These cards have two versions: the regular card and a Refractor parallel (#/75).

Insert Set (20 cards):	620.00	135.00
Insert	CR75	C500
C1 Patrik Elias, NJer.	40.00	10.00
C2 Bryan Berard, NYIs.	15.00	4.00
C3 Chris Osgood (G), Detr.	30.00	5.00
C4 Saku Koivu, Mont.	40.00	10.00
C5 Alexei Yashin, Otta.	30.00	5.00
C6 Zigmund Palffy, NYIs.	30.00	5.00
C7 Peter Forsberg, Colo.	70.00	15.00
C8 Jason Allison, Bost.	30.00	5.00
C9 Wade Redden, Otta.	15.00	4.00
C10 Paul Kariya, Anah.	70.00	15.00
C11 Martin Brodeur (G), NJer.	80.00	20.00
C12 Patrick Marleau, SanJ.	20.00	5.00
C13 Jaromir Jagr, Pitt.	50.00	10.00
C14 Mattias Öhlund, Vanc.	15.00	4.00
C15 Teemu Selänne, Anah.	40.00	10.00
C16 Mike Johnson, Toro.	15.00	4.00
C17 Joe Thornton, Bost.	60.00	15.00
C18 Jocelyn Thibault (G), Mont.	20.00	5.00
C19 Daniel Alfredsson, Otta.	30.00	5.00
C20 Sergei Samsonov, Bost.	30.00	5.00

FUTURE'S FINEST

These cards have two versions: the regular card and a Refractor parallel.

Insert Set (20 cards):	215.00	180.00
Insert	FR150	F500
F1 David Legwand, CHL Prospect	15.00	12.00
F2 Manny Malhotra, NYRa.	8.00	6.00
F3 Vincent Lecavalier, Tamp.	30.00	30.00
F4 Brad Stuart, WHL All-Star RC	**15.00**	**18.00**
F5 Bryan Allen, OHL All-Star	8.00	4.00
F6 Rico Fata, CHL Prospect	8.00	6.00
F7 Mark Bell, OHL All-Star RC	**10.00**	**10.00**
F8 Michael Rupp, CHL Prospect RC	**15.00**	**14.00**
F9 Jeff Heerema, CHL Prospect RC	**8.00**	**6.00**
F10 Alex Tanguay, QMJHL All-Star	20.00	18.00
F11 Patrick Desrochers (G), CHL Prospect	8.00	4.00
F12 Mathieu Chouinard (G), CHL Prospect	8.00	4.00
F13 Éric Chouinard, CHL Prospect	8.00	6.00
F14 Martin Skoula, CHL Prospect RC	**15.00**	**14.00**
F15 Robyn Regehr, CHL Prospect	8.00	4.00
F16 Marian Hossa, Otta.	35.00	30.00
F17 Daniel Cleary, Chic.	10.00	8.00
F18 Olli Jokinen, LosA.	10.00	8.00
F19 Brendan Morrison, NJer.	10.00	8.00
F20 Erik Rasmussen, Buff.	8.00	6.00

MYSTERY FINEST

These cards have two versions: the regular card and a Refractor parallel (1:144).

Insert Set (50 cards):	1900.00	650.00
Insert	MFR	MF
M1 W. Gretzky / J. Jagr	90.00	30.00
M2 D. Hasek / J. Jagr	30.00	10.00
M3 J. Jagr / E. Lindros	30.00	10.00
M4 Jaromir Jagr, Pitt.	30.00	10.00
M5 W. Gretzky / D. Hasek	90.00	30.00
M6 E. Lindros / D. Hasek	30.00	10.00
M7 Dominik Hasek (G), Buff.	30.00	10.00
M8 W. Gretzky / E. Lindros	90.00	30.00
M9 Wayne Gretzky, NYRa.	150.00	50.00
M10 Eric Lindros, Phil.	30.00	10.00
M11 P. Kariya / T. Selänne	40.00	10.00
M12 R. Bourque / P. Kariya	40.00	15.00
M13 P. Kariya / S. Samsonov	30.00	10.00
M14 Paul Kariya, Anah.	50.00	15.00
M15 R. Bourque / T. Selänne	30.00	10.00
M16 S. Samsonov / T. Selänne	20.00	10.00
M17 Teemu Selänne, Anah.	30.00	10.00
M18 R. Bourque / S. Samsonov	30.00	10.00
M19 Raymond Bourque, Bost.	40.00	15.00
M20 Sergei Samsonov, Bost.	20.00	10.00
M21 P. Forsberg / M. Brodeur	50.00	15.00
M22 P. Roy / M. Brodeur	80.00	25.00
M23 M. Brodeur / J. Sakic	60.00	20.00
M24 Martin Brodeur (G), NJer.	60.00	20.00
M25 P. Forsberg / P. Roy	80.00	25.00
M26 P. Forsberg / J. Sakic	50.00	15.00
M27 Peter Forsberg, Colo.	50.00	15.00
M28 P. Roy / J. Sakic	80.00	25.00
M29 Patrick Roy (G), Colo.	110.00	35.00
M30 Joe Sakic, Colo.	60.00	20.00
M31 M. Modano / S. Yzerman	60.00	20.00
M32 S. Fedorov / M. Modano	30.00	10.00
M33 M. Modano / B. Shanahan	30.00	10.00
M34 Mike Modano, Dall.	30.00	10.00
M35 S. Fedorov / S. Yzerman	60.00	20.00
M36 B. Shanahan / S. Yzerman	60.00	20.00
M37 Steve Yzerman, Detr.	90.00	30.00
M38 S. Fedorov / B. Shanahan	30.00	10.00
M39 Sergei Fedorov, Detr.	30.00	10.00
M40 Brendan Shanahan, Detr.	30.00	10.00
M41 M. Messier / J. LeClair	30.00	10.00
M42 M. Messier / K. Tkachuk	30.00	10.00
M43 M. Messier / P. Bure	30.00	10.00
M44 Mark Messier, Vanc.	30.00	10.00
M45 J. LeClair / K. Tkachuk	20.00	10.00
M46 P. Bure / J. LeClair	30.00	10.00
M47 John LeClair, Phil.	30.00	10.00
M48 P. Bure / K. Tkachuk	20.00	10.00
M49 Pavel Bure, Vanc.	30.00	10.00
M50 Keith Tkachuk, Phoe.	20.00	10.00

RED LIGHTERS

These cards have two versions: the regular card and a Refractor parallel.

Insert Set (20 cards):	260.00	90.00
Insert	RLR	RL
R1 Jaromir Jagr, Pitt.	15.00	5.00
R2 Mike Modano, Dall.	15.00	5.00
R3 Paul Kariya, Anah.	20.00	5.00
R4 Pavel Bure, Vanc.	10.00	4.00
R5 Peter Bondra, Wash.	6.00	3.00
R6 Sergei Fedorov, Detr.	15.00	5.00
R7 Steve Yzerman, Detr.	35.00	10.00
R8 Teemu Selänne, Anah.	10.00	4.00
R9 Wayne Gretzky, NYRa.	60.00	20.00
R10 Brendan Shanahan, Detr.	15.00	5.00
R11 Eric Lindros, Phil.	15.00	5.00
R12 Alexei Yashin, Otta.	6.00	3.00
R13 Jason Allison, Bost.	6.00	3.00
R14 Joe Nieuwendyk, Dall.	6.00	3.00
R15 Joe Sakic, Colo.	20.00	8.00
R16 John LeClair, Phil.	10.00	4.00
R17 Keith Tkachuk, Phoe.	6.00	3.00
R18 Mark Messier, Vanc.	15.00	5.00
R19 Mats Sundin, Toro.	15.00	5.00
R20 Zigmund Palffy, NYIs.	6.00	3.00

OVERSIZE

These cards have two versions: the regular card and a Refractor parallel.

Insert Set (7 cards):	65.00	20.00
Insert	OR	O
1 Teemu Selänne, Anah.	8.00	3.00
2 Dominik Hasek (G), Buff.	8.00	3.00
3 Martin Brodeur (G), NJer.	10.00	3.00
4 Wayne Gretzky, NYRa.	25.00	8.00
5 Steve Yzerman, Detr.	15.00	4.00
6 Jaromir Jagr, Pitt.	8.00	3.00
7 Eric Lindros, Phil.	8.00	3.00

1998 - 99 TOPPS GOLD LABEL

There are three versions per Class: Gold, Black and Red. There are also nine one-of-one parallels for each version.

Complete Set (100 cards):	2100.00	375.00	85.00
Common Player:	8.00	3.00	.50
Class One	RL100	BL	GL
1 B. Shanahan, Detr.	60.00	10.00	2.00
2 M. Modano, Dall.	60.00	10.00	2.00
3 C. Chelios, Chic.	35.00	5.00	1.00
4 W. Gretzky, NYRa.	250.00	50.00	10.00
5 J. Jagr, Pitt.	60.00	10.00	2.00
6 M. Messier, Vanc.	60.00	10.00	2.00
7 T. Selänne, Anah.	50.00	10.00	2.00
8 T. Fleury, Calg.	35.00	5.00	1.00
9 R. Bourque, Bost.	75.00	15.00	3.00
10 M. Brodeur, NJer.	100.00	20.00	4.00
11 A. Yashin, Otta.	35.00	5.00	1.00
12 K. Tkachuk, Phoe.	35.00	5.00	1.00
13 E. Lindros, Phil.	60.00	10.00	2.00
14 O. Nolan, SanJ.	35.00	5.00	1.00
15 A. MacInnis, SLou.	25.00	5.00	1.00
16 P. Bondra, Wash.	35.00	5.00	1.00
17 S. Koivu, Mont.	50.00	10.00	2.00
18 D. Weight, Edmo.	35.00	5.00	1.00
19 R. Reichel, NYIs.	20.00	4.00	.50
20 S. Fedorov, Detr.	60.00	10.00	2.00
21 P. Forsberg, Colo.	85.00	15.00	3.00
22 R. Francis, Caro.	35.00	5.00	1.00
23 D. Khristich, Bost.	10.00	3.00	.50
24 E. Belfour, Dall.	60.00	10.00	2.00
25 O. Kvasha, Flor.	10.00	3.00	2.00
26 R. Whitney, Flor.	15.00	3.00	.50
27 K. Jönsson, NYIs.	10.00	3.00	.50
28 R. McKay, NJer.	8.00	3.00	.50
29 P. Demitra, SLou.	25.00	5.00	1.00
30 P. Turgeon, SLou.	25.00	5.00	1.00
31 S. Yzerman, Detr.	150.00	30.00	6.00
32 R. Smyth, Edmo.	30.00	6.00	1.00
33 T. Amonte, Chic.	35.00	5.00	1.00
34 D. Hasek, Buff.	60.00	10.00	2.00
35 J. Iginla, Calg.	50.00	10.00	2.00
36 S. Kapanen, Caro.	20.00	4.00	.50

37 P. Elias, NJer.	50.00	10.00	2.00
38 D. Cleary, Chic.	20.00	4.00	.50
39 C. Joseph, Toro.	60.00	10.00	2.00
40 J. Juneau, Wash.	15.00	3.00	.50
41 A. Graves, NYRa.	25.00	5.00	1.00
42 T. Linden, NYIs.	25.00	5.00	1.00
43 O. Jokinen, LosA.	20.00	4.00	.50
44 J. Nieuwendyk, Dall.	25.00	5.00	1.00
45 S. Samsonov, Bost.	35.00	5.00	1.00
46 R. Fata, Calg.	15.00	3.00	1.00
47 M. Recchi, Mont.	25.00	5.00	1.00
48 R. Tocchet, Phoe.	20.00	4.00	.50
49 C. Pronger, SLou.	35.00	5.00	1.00
50 J. Allison, Bost.	35.00	5.00	1.00
51 P. Kariya, Anah.	85.00	15.00	3.00
52 S. Barnes, Pitt.	8.00	3.00	.50
53 M. Sundin, Toro.	60.00	10.00	2.00
54 M. Richter, NYRa.	30.00	5.00	1.00
55 C. Ronning, Nash.	15.00	3.00	.50
56 K. Primeau, Caro.	25.00	5.00	1.00
57 G. Hebert, Anah.	15.00	3.00	.50
58 N. Lidström, Detr.	35.00	5.00	1.00
59 J. Vanbiesbrouck, Flor.	30.00	5.00	1.00
60 J. Friesen, SanJ.	20.00	4.00	.50
61 V. Lecavalier, Tamp.	60.00	10.00	5.00
62 A. Mogilny, Vanc.	30.00	5.00	1.00
63 O. Kölzig, Wash.	35.00	5.00	1.00
64 D. Gilmour, Chic.	35.00	5.00	1.00
65 J. Sakic, Colo.	100.00	20.00	4.00
66 M. Johnson, Toro.	10.00	3.00	.50
67 V. Damphousse, Mont.	35.00	7.00	1.00
68 E. Brewer, NYIs.	25.00	5.00	2.00
69 D. Alfredsson, Otta.	35.00	7.00	1.00
70 N. Khabibulin, Phoe.	25.00	5.00	1.00
71 M. Sturm, SanJ.	15.00	3.00	.50
72 M. Reasoner, SLou.	15.00	3.00	1.00
73 Muckalt, Vanc. RC	**10.00**	**3.00**	**2.00**
74 P. Bure, Vanc.	50.00	10.00	2.00
75 B. Guerin, Edmo.	25.00	5.00	1.00
76 C. Osgood, Detr.	35.00	5.00	1.00
77 P. Roy, Colo.	185.00	30.00	7.00
78 T. Barrasso, Pitt.	25.00	5.00	1.00
79 A. McCauley, Toro.	20.00	4.00	.50
80 A. Oates, Wash.	25.00	5.00	1.00
81 J. Thornton, Bost.	75.00	15.00	3.00
82 B. Morrison, NJer.	20.00	4.00	.50
83 M. Dunham, Nash.	25.00	5.00	1.00
84 J. Roenick, Phoe.	50.00	10.00	2.00
85 B. Leetch, NYRa.	35.00	5.00	1.00
86 J. LeClair, Phil.	50.00	10.00	2.00
87 M. Öhlund, Vanc.	20.00	4.00	.50
88 W. Redden, Otta.	20.00	4.00	.50
89 M. Parrish, Flor.	25.00	5.00	5.00
90 Hejduk, Colo. RC	**50.00**	**10.00**	**10.00**
91 M. Peca, Buff.	25.00	5.00	1.00
92 B. Hull, Dall.	60.00	10.00	2.00
93 M. Malhotra, NYRa.	15.00	3.00	1.00
94 P. Marleau, SanJ.	30.00	6.00	1.00
95 G. Fuhr, SLou.	35.00	5.00	1.00
96 R. Blake, LosA.	35.00	5.00	1.00
97 D. Rhodes, Otta.	15.00	3.00	.50
98 É. Dazé, Chic.	25.00	5.00	1.00
99 R. Brind'Amour, Phil.	20.00	4.00	.50
100 S. Stevens, NJer.	25.00	5.00	1.00

CLASS TWO

Complete Set (100 cards):	**3500.00**	**1200.00**	**250.00**
Class Two	**RL50**	**BL**	**GL**
1 B. Shanahan, Detr.	100.00	35.00	7.00
2 M. Modano, Dall.	100.00	35.00	7.00
3 C. Chelios, Chic.	60.00	20.00	4.00
4 W. Gretzky, NYRa.	400.00	150.00	30.00
5 J. Jagr, Pitt.	100.00	30.00	5.00
6 M. Messier, Vanc.	100.00	35.00	7.00
7 T. Selänne, Anah.	80.00	30.00	5.00
8 T. Fleury, Calg.	60.00	20.00	4.00
9 R. Bourque, Bost.	120.00	45.00	5.00
10 M. Brodeur, NJer.	160.00	60.00	10.00
11 A. Yashin, Otta.	60.00	20.00	4.00
12 K. Tkachuk, Phoe.	60.00	20.00	4.00
13 E. Lindros, Phil.	100.00	30.00	5.00
14 O. Nolan, SanJ.	60.00	20.00	4.00
15 A. MacInnis, SLou.	40.00	15.00	3.00
16 P. Bondra, Wash.	60.00	20.00	4.00
17 S. Koivu, Mont.	80.00	30.00	6.00
18 D. Weight, Edmo.	60.00	20.00	4.00
19 R. Reichel, NYIs.	30.00	10.00	2.00
20 S. Fedorov, Detr.	100.00	35.00	7.00
21 P. Forsberg, Colo.	140.00	50.00	10.00
22 R. Francis, Caro.	60.00	20.00	4.00
23 D. Khristich, Bost.	15.00	6.00	2.00
24 E. Belfour, Dall.	100.00	35.00	7.00
25 O. Kvasha, Flor.	15.00	6.00	3.00
26 R. Whitney, Flor.	20.00	6.00	2.00
27 K. Jönsson, NYIs.	20.00	6.00	2.00
28 R. McKay, NJer.	15.00	6.00	2.00
29 P. Demitra, SLou.	40.00	15.00	3.00
30 P. Turgeon, SLou.	40.00	15.00	3.00
31 S. Yzerman, Detr.	240.00	90.00	15.00
32 R. Smyth, Edmo.	45.00	15.00	3.00
33 T. Amonte, Chic.	60.00	20.00	4.00
34 D. Hasek, Buff.	100.00	30.00	5.00
35 J. Iginla, Calg.	80.00	30.00	6.00
36 S. Kapanen, Caro.	30.00	10.00	2.00
37 P. Elias, NJer.	80.00	30.00	6.00
38 D. Cleary, Chic.	30.00	10.00	2.00
39 C. Joseph, Toro.	100.00	35.00	5.00
40 J. Juneau, Wash.	20.00	6.00	2.00
41 A. Graves, NYRa.	40.00	15.00	3.00
42 T. Linden, NYIs.	40.00	15.00	3.00
43 O. Jokinen, LosA.	30.00	12.00	2.00
44 J. Nieuwendyk, Dall.	40.00	15.00	3.00
45 S. Samsonov, Bost.	60.00	20.00	4.00
46 R. Fata, Calg.	20.00	6.00	2.00
47 M. Recchi, Mont.	40.00	15.00	3.00
48 R. Tocchet, Phoe.	30.00	10.00	2.00
49 C. Pronger, SLou.	60.00	20.00	4.00
50 J. Allison, Bost.	60.00	20.00	4.00
51 P. Kariya, Anah.	140.00	50.00	10.00
52 S. Barnes, Pitt.	15.00	6.00	2.00
53 M. Sundin, Toro.	100.00	35.00	7.00
54 M. Richter, NYRa.	40.00	15.00	3.00
55 C. Ronning, Nash.	20.00	6.00	2.00
56 K. Primeau, Caro.	40.00	15.00	3.00
57 G. Hebert, Anah.	20.00	6.00	2.00
58 N. Lidström, Detr.	60.00	20.00	4.00
59 J. Vanbiesbrouck, Flor.	40.00	15.00	3.00
60 J. Friesen, SanJ.	30.00	10.00	2.00
61 V. Lecavalier, Tamp.	100.00	35.00	7.00
62 A. Mogilny, Vanc.	40.00	15.00	3.00
63 O. Kölzig, Wash.	60.00	20.00	4.00
64 D. Gilmour, Chic.	60.00	20.00	4.00
65 J. Sakic, Colo.	160.00	60.00	10.00
66 M. Johnson, Toro.	20.00	6.00	2.00
67 V. Damphousse, Mont.	60.00	20.00	4.00
68 E. Brewer, NYIs.	40.00	15.00	3.00
69 D. Alfredsson, Otta.	60.00	20.00	4.00
70 N. Khabibulin, Phoe.	40.00	15.00	3.00
71 M. Sturm, SanJ.	20.00	6.00	2.00
72 M. Reasoner, SLou.	20.00	6.00	2.00
73 Muckalt, Vanc. RC	**15.00**	**6.00**	**3.00**
74 P. Bure, Vanc.	80.00	30.00	5.00
75 B. Guerin, Edmo.	40.00	15.00	3.00
76 C. Osgood, Detr.	60.00	20.00	4.00
77 P. Roy, Colo.	300.00	110.00	20.00
78 T. Barrasso, Pitt.	40.00	15.00	3.00
79 A. McCauley, Toro.	30.00	10.00	2.00
80 A. Oates, Wash.	40.00	15.00	3.00
81 J. Thornton, Bost.	120.00	45.00	9.00
82 B. Morrison, NJer.	30.00	10.00	2.00
83 M. Dunham, Nash.	40.00	15.00	3.00
84 J. Roenick, Phoe.	80.00	30.00	6.00
85 B. Leetch, NYRa.	60.00	20.00	4.00
86 J. LeClair, Phil.	80.00	30.00	6.00
87 M. Öhlund, Vanc.	30.00	10.00	2.00
88 W. Redden, Otta.	30.00	10.00	2.00
89 M. Parrish, Flor.	40.00	15.00	9.00
90 Hejduk, Colo. RC	**80.00**	**30.00**	**15.00**
91 M. Peca, Buff.	40.00	15.00	3.00
92 B. Hull, Dall.	100.00	35.00	7.00
93 M. Malhotra, NYRa.	20.00	6.00	2.00
94 P. Marleau, SanJ.	45.00	15.00	3.00
95 G. Fuhr, SLou.	60.00	20.00	4.00
96 R. Blake, LosA.	60.00	20.00	4.00
97 D. Rhodes, Otta.	20.00	6.00	2.00
98 É. Dazé, Chic.	40.00	15.00	3.00
99 R. Brind'Amour, Phil.	30.00	10.00	2.00
100 S. Stevens, NJer.	40.00	15.00	3.00

CLASS THREE

Complete Set (100 cards):	**6500.00**	**2100.00**	**400.00**
Class Three	**RL25**	**BL**	**GL**
1 B. Shanahan, Detr.	180.00	60.00	10.00
2 M. Modano, Dall.	180.00	60.00	10.00
3 C. Chelios, Chic.	110.00	35.00	5.00
4 W. Gretzky, NYRa.	750.00	250.00	50.00
5 J. Jagr, Pitt.	180.00	60.00	10.00
6 M. Messier, Vanc.	180.00	60.00	10.00
7 T. Selänne, Anah.	150.00	50.00	10.00
8 T. Fleury, Calg.	110.00	30.00	5.00
9 R. Bourque, Bost.	220.00	70.00	15.00
10 M. Brodeur, NJer.	300.00	100.00	15.00
11 A. Yashin, Otta.	110.00	35.00	5.00
12 K. Tkachuk, Phoe.	110.00	30.00	5.00
13 E. Lindros, Phil.	180.00	60.00	10.00
14 O. Nolan, SanJ.	110.00	35.00	5.00
15 A. MacInnis, SLou.	70.00	25.00	5.00
16 P. Bondra, Wash.	110.00	35.00	5.00
17 S. Koivu, Mont.	150.00	50.00	10.00
18 D. Weight, Edmo.	110.00	30.00	5.00
19 R. Reichel, NYIs.	60.00	20.00	4.00
20 S. Fedorov, Detr.	180.00	60.00	10.00
21 P. Forsberg, Colo.	260.00	80.00	15.00
22 R. Francis, Caro.	110.00	35.00	7.00
23 D. Khristich, Bost.	30.00	10.00	3.00
24 E. Belfour, Dall.	180.00	60.00	10.00
25 O. Kvasha, Flor.	30.00	10.00	6.00
26 R. Whitney, Flor.	45.00	15.00	3.00
27 K. Jönsson, NYIs.	35.00	10.00	3.00
28 R. McKay, NJer.	20.00	8.00	3.00
29 P. Demitra, SLou.	75.00	25.00	5.00
30 P. Turgeon, SLou.	70.00	25.00	5.00
31 S. Yzerman, Detr.	450.00	150.00	30.00
32 R. Smyth, Edmo.	90.00	30.00	6.00
33 T. Amonte, Chic.	110.00	35.00	5.00
34 D. Hasek, Buff.	180.00	60.00	10.00
35 J. Iginla, Calg.	150.00	50.00	10.00
36 S. Kapanen, Caro.	60.00	20.00	4.00
37 P. Elias, NJer.	150.00	50.00	10.00
38 D. Cleary, Chic.	60.00	20.00	4.00
39 C. Joseph, Toro.	180.00	60.00	10.00
40 J. Juneau, Wash.	45.00	15.00	3.00
41 A. Graves, NYRa.	70.00	25.00	5.00
42 T. Linden, NYIs.	70.00	25.00	5.00
43 O. Jokinen, LosA.	60.00	20.00	4.00
44 J. Nieuwendyk, Dall.	70.00	25.00	5.00
45 S. Samsonov, Bost.	110.00	30.00	5.00
46 R. Fata, Calg.	45.00	15.00	3.00
47 M. Recchi, Mont.	70.00	25.00	5.00
48 R. Tocchet, Phoe.	60.00	20.00	4.00
49 C. Pronger, SLou.	110.00	35.00	5.00
50 J. Allison, Bost.	110.00	30.00	5.00
51 P. Kariya, Anah.	260.00	80.00	15.00
52 S. Barnes, Pitt.	20.00	8.00	3.00
53 M. Sundin, Toro.	180.00	60.00	10.00
54 M. Richter, NYRa.	90.00	30.00	5.00
55 C. Ronning, Nash.	45.00	15.00	3.00
56 K. Primeau, Caro.	70.00	25.00	5.00
57 G. Hebert, Anah.	40.00	15.00	3.00
58 N. Lidström, Detr.	110.00	35.00	5.00
59 J. Vanbiesbrouck, Flor.	90.00	30.00	5.00
60 J. Friesen, SanJ.	60.00	20.00	4.00
61 V. Lecavalier, Tamp.	180.00	60.00	10.00
62 A. Mogilny, Vanc.	90.00	30.00	6.00
63 O. Kölzig, Wash.	110.00	35.00	5.00
64 D. Gilmour, Chic.	110.00	35.00	5.00
65 J. Sakic, Colo.	300.00	100.00	20.00
66 M. Johnson, Toro.	35.00	10.00	3.00
67 V. Damphousse, Mont.	110.00	35.00	7.00
68 E. Brewer, NYIs.	75.00	25.00	5.00
69 D. Alfredsson, Otta.	110.00	35.00	7.00
70 N. Khabibulin, Phoe.	70.00	25.00	5.00
71 M. Sturm, SanJ.	45.00	15.00	3.00
72 M. Reasoner, SLou.	45.00	15.00	3.00
73 Muckalt, Vanc. RC	**30.00**	**10.00**	**6.00**
74 P. Bure, Vanc.	150.00	50.00	5.00
75 B. Guerin, Edmo.	70.00	25.00	5.00
76 C. Osgood, Detr.	110.00	30.00	5.00
77 P. Roy, Colo.	560.00	180.00	35.00
78 T. Barrasso, Pitt.	70.00	25.00	5.00
79 A. McCauley, Toro.	60.00	20.00	4.00
80 A. Oates, Wash.	70.00	25.00	5.00
81 J. Thornton, Bost.	220.00	70.00	15.00
82 B. Morrison, NJer.	60.00	20.00	4.00
83 M. Dunham, Nash.	70.00	25.00	5.00
84 J. Roenick, Phoe.	150.00	50.00	10.00
85 B. Leetch, NYRa.	110.00	35.00	5.00
86 J. LeClair, Phil.	150.00	50.00	10.00
87 M. Öhlund, Vanc.	60.00	20.00	4.00
88 W. Redden, Otta.	60.00	20.00	4.00
89 M. Parrish, Flor.	75.00	25.00	15.00
90 Hejduk, Colo. RC	**150.00**	**50.00**	**30.00**
91 M. Peca, Buff.	70.00	25.00	5.00
92 B. Hull, Dall.	180.00	60.00	10.00
93 M. Malhotra, NYRa.	45.00	15.00	3.00
94 P. Marleau, SanJ.	90.00	30.00	6.00
95 G. Fuhr, SLou.	110.00	35.00	5.00
96 R. Blake, LosA.	110.00	35.00	5.00
97 D. Rhodes, Otta.	45.00	15.00	3.00
98 É. Dazé, Chic.	75.00	25.00	5.00
99 R. Brind'Amour, Phil.	60.00	20.00	4.00
100 S. Stevens, NJer.	70.00	25.00	5.00

Checklist	**CL**
Checklist	.25

GOAL RACE

These cards have three versions: a Gold, a Black and a Red (#/92). One-of-one parallels exist for each colour.

Insert Set (10 cards):	**450.00**	**140.00**	**65.00**
Insert	**GRR92**	**GRB**	**GRG**
GR1 E. Lindros, Phil.	60.00	20.00	10.00
GR2 J. LeClair, Phil.	50.00	15.00	5.00
GR3 T. Selänne, Anah.	50.00	15.00	5.00
GR4 P. Kariya, Anah.	80.00	20.00	10.00
GR5 J. Jagr, Pitt.	60.00	20.00	10.00
GR6 K. Tkachuk, Phoe.	30.00	10.00	5.00
GR7 T. Fleury, Calg.	30.00	10.00	5.00
GR8 B. Shanahan, Detr.	60.00	20.00	10.00
GR9 T. Amonte, Chic.	35.00	10.00	6.00
GR10 J. Sakic, Colo.	100.00	30.00	15.00

1998 - 99 TOPPS PEARSON AWARD

Jaromir Jagr, Pitt.	20.00

1998 - 99 TOPPS WENDY'S

00 Dave Thomas, Wendy's

1998 - 99 UD CHOICE

These cards have three versions: the regular card, a Choice Reserve parallel and a Prime Choice Reserve parallel (#/100). Sixty cards have a fourth Preview version. Preview cards have the same value as the regular cards. Oversize cards (5" x 7") exist for at least five players.

Complete Set (310 cards):	**2,400.00**	**120.00**	**20.00**
Preview Set (60 cards):			**8.00**
Common Player:	**8.00**	**.50**	**.20**
Player	**PCR**	**CR**	**Reg.**
1 Guy Hebert (G), Anah.	15.00	.50	.20
2 Mikail Shtalenkov (G), Anah.	10.00	.50	.20
3 Josef Marha, Anah.	8.00	.50	.20
4 Paul Kariya, Anah.	80.00	5.00	.50
5 Travis Green, Anah.	15.00	.50	.20
6 Steve Rucchin, Anah.	15.00	.50	.20
7 Matt Cullen, Anah.	15.00	.50	.20
8 Teemu Selänne, Anah.	50.00	3.00	.20
9 Antti Aalto, Anah.	8.00	.50	.20
10 Byron Dafoe (G), Bost.	25.00	1.00	.20
11 Ted Donato, Bost.	8.00	.50	.20
12 Dimitri Khristich, Bost.	10.00	.50	.20
13 Sergei Samsonov, Bost.	35.00	2.00	.20
14 Jason Allison, Bost.	35.00	2.00	.20
15 Raymond Bourque, Bost.	70.00	4.00	.50
16 Kyle McLaren, Bost.	15.00	.50	.20
17 Cameron Mann, Bost.	10.00	.50	.20
18 Shawn Bates, Bost.	10.00	.50	.20
19 Joe Thornton, Bost.	75.00	4.00	.50
20 Vaclav Varada, Buff.	10.00	.50	.20
21 Brian Holzinger, Buff.	10.00	.50	.20
22 Miroslav Satan, Buff.	20.00	1.00	.20
23 Dominik Hasek (G), Buff.	60.00	3.00	.50
24 Michael Peca, Buff.	25.00	1.00	.20
25 Erik Rasmussen, Buff.	15.00	.50	.20
26 Alexei Zhitnik, Buff.	10.00	.50	.20
27 Geoff Sanderson, Buff.	15.00	.50	.20
28 Donald Audette, Buff.	25.00	1.00	.20
29 Derek Morris, Calg.	15.00	.50	.20
30 German Titov, Calg.	8.00	.50	.20
31 Valeri Bure, Calg.	20.00	1.00	.20
32 Michael Nylander, Calg.	15.00	.50	.20
33 Cory Stillman, Calg.	15.00	.50	.20
34 Theoren Fleury, Calg.	30.00	2.00	.20
35 Jarome Iginla, Calg.	50.00	3.00	.20
36 Gary Roberts, Caro.	25.00	1.00	.20
37 Jeff O'Neill, Caro.	25.00	1.00	.20
38 Bates Battaglia, Caro.	15.00	.50	.20
39 Keith Primeau, Caro.	25.00	1.00	.20
40 Sami Kapanen, Caro.	20.00	1.00	.20
41 Glen Wesley, Caro.	10.00	.50	.20
42 Trevor Kidd (G), Caro.	20.00	1.00	.20

□□□□	43 Nelson Emerson, Caro.	10.00	.50	.20
□□□	44 Daniel Cleary, Chic.	20.00	1.00	.20
□□□□	45 Eric Dazé, Chic.	25.00	1.00	.20
□□□	46 Chris Chelios, Chic.	35.00	2.00	.20
□□□	47 Gary Suter, Chic.	15.00	.50	.20
□□□	48 Alexei Zhamnov, Chic.	20.00	1.00	.20
□□□	49 Jeff Hackett (G), Chic.	20.00	1.00	.20
□□□	50 Dimitri Nabokov, Chic.	10.00	.50	.20
□□□□	51 Tony Amonte, Chic.	35.00	2.00	.20
□□□	52 Jean-Yves Leroux, Chic.	8.00	.50	.20
□□□□	53 Eric Messier, Colo.	10.00	.50	.20
□□□	54 Patrick Roy (G), Col	180.00	10.00	1.50
□□□□	55 Claude Lemieux, Colo.	20.00	1.00	.20
□□□	56 Peter Forsberg, Colo.	80.00	5.00	.50
□□□	57 Adam Deadmarsh, Colo.	20.00	1.00	.20
□□□	58 Valeri Kamensky, Colo.	20.00	1.00	.20
□□□	59 Joe Sakic, Colo.	100.00	6.00	.50
□□□	60 Sandis Ozolinsh, Colo.	15.00	.50	.20
□□□□	61 J. Langenbrunner, Dall.	15.00	.50	.20
□□□	62 Joe Nieuwendyk, Dall.	25.00	1.00	.20
□□□□	63 Ed Belfour (G), Dall.	60.00	3.00	.50
□□□	64 Juha Lind, Dall.	10.00	.50	.20
□□□□	65 Derian Hatcher, Dall.	20.00	1.00	.20
□□□	66 Sergei Zubov, Dall.	15.00	.50	.20
□□□	67 Darryl Sydor, Dall.	15.00	.50	.20
□□□	68 Jere Lehtinen, Dall.	20.00	1.00	.20
□□□	69 Mike Modano, Dall.	60.00	3.00	.50
□□□	70 Larry Murphy, Detr.	15.00	.50	.20
□□□□	71 Igor Larionov, Detr.	35.00	2.00	.20
□□□	72 Darren McCarty, Detr.	20.00	1.00	.20
□□□□	73 Steve Yzerman, Detr.	150.00	5.00	1.00
□□□	74 Chris Osgood (G), Detr.	35.00	2.00	.20
□□□□	75 Sergei Fedorov, Detr.	60.00	3.00	.50
□□□	76 Brendan Shanahan, Detr.	60.00	3.00	.50
□□□	77 Nicklas Lidström, Detr.	35.00	2.00	.20
□□□□	78 Vyacheslav Kozlov, Detr.	15.00	.50	.20
□□□	79 Dean McAmmond, Edmo.	10.00	.50	.20
□□□	80 Roman Hamrlik, Edmo.	15.00	.50	.20
□□□□	81 Curtis Joseph (G), Edmo.	60.00	3.00	.50
□□□	82 Ryan Smyth, Edmo.	30.00	1.00	.20
□□□□	83 Boris Mironov, Edmo.	10.00	.50	.20
□□□	84 Bill Guerin, Edmo.	25.00	1.00	.20
□□□□	85 Doug Weight, Edmo.	35.00	2.00	.20
□□□	86 Janne Niinimaa, Edmo.	15.00	.50	.20
□□□	87 Ray Whitney, Flor.	15.00	.50	.20
□□□	88 Robert Svehla, Flor.	15.00	.50	.20
□□□	89 J. Vanbiesbrouck (G), Flor.	30.00	1.00	.20
□□□□	90 Scott Mellanby, Flor.	15.00	.50	.20
□□□□	91 Ed Jovanovski, Flor.	25.00	1.00	.20
□□□	92 Dave Gagner, Flor.	10.00	.50	.20
□□□□	93 Dino Ciccarelli, Flor.	20.00	1.00	.20
□□□	94 Rob Niedermayer, Flor.	15.00	.50	.20
□□□□	95 Rob Blake, LosA.	35.00	2.00	.20
□□□	96 Yanic Perrault, LosA.	20.00	1.00	.20
□□□	97 Stéphane Fiset (G), LosA.	20.00	1.00	.20
□□□	98 Luc Robitaille, LosA.	50.00	3.00	.20
□□□	99 Glen Murray, LosA.	30.00	1.00	.20
□□□	100 Jozef Stümpel, LosA.	15.00	.50	.20
□□□□	101 Vladimir Tsyplakov, LosA.	8.00	.50	.20
□□□	102 Donald MacLean, LosA.	8.00	.50	.20
□□□□	103 Shayne Corson, Mont.	20.00	1.00	.20
□□□	104 Vladimir Malakhov, Mont.	10.00	.50	.20
□□□□	105 Saku Koivu, Mont.	50.00	3.00	.20
□□□	106 Andy Moog (G), Mont.	25.00	1.00	.20
□□□	107 Matt Higgins, Mont.	8.00	.50	.50
□□□	108 Dave Manson, Mont.	10.00	.50	.20
□□□	109 Mark Recchi, Mont.	25.00	1.00	.20
□□□	110 V. Damphousse, Mont.	35.00	2.00	.20
□□□□	111 Brian Savage, Mont.	20.00	1.00	.20
□□□	112 Petr Sykora, NJer.	25.00	1.00	.20
□□□□	113 Scott Stevens, NJer.	25.00	1.00	.20
□□□	114 Patrik Elias, NJer.	50.00	3.00	.20
□□□□	115 Bobby Holik, NJer.	20.00	1.00	.20
□□□	116 M. Brodeur (G), NJer.	100.00	6.00	.50
□□□	117 Doug Gilmour, NJer.	35.00	2.00	.20
□□□	118 Jason Arnott, NJer.	30.00	1.00	.20
□□□	119 Scott Niedermayer, NJer.	20.00	1.00	.20
□□□	120 Brendan Morrison, NJer.	20.00	1.00	.20
□□□□	121 Zigmund Palffy, NYIs.	35.00	2.00	.20
□□□	122 Trevor Linden, NYIs.	25.00	1.00	.20
□□□□	123 Bryan Berard, NYIs.	20.00	1.00	.20
□□□	124 Zdeno Chara, NYIs.	15.00	.50	.20
□□□□	125 Kenny Jönsson, NYIs.	10.00	.50	.20
□□□	126 Robert Reichel, NYIs.	20.00	1.00	.20
□□□	127 Bryan Smolinski, NYIs.	10.00	.50	.20
□□□	128 Wayne Gretzky, NYRa.	250.00	15.00	2.00
□□□	129 Brian Leetch, NYRa.	35.00	2.00	.20
□□□	130 Pat LaFontaine, NYRa.	35.00	2.00	.20
□□□□	131 Dan Cloutier (G), NYRa.	25.00	1.00	.20
□□□	132 Niklas Sundström, NYRa.	15.00	.50	.20
□□□□	133 Marc Savard, NYRa.	15.00	.50	.20
□□□	134 Adam Graves, NYRa.	25.00	1.00	.20
□□□□	135 Mike Richter (G), NYRa.	30.00	1.00	.20
□□□	136 Jeff Beukeboom, NYRa.	10.00	.50	.20
□□□	137 Daniel Goneau, NYRa.	8.00	.50	.20
□□□	138 Shawn McEachern, Otta.	20.00	1.00	.20
□□□	139 Damian Rhodes (G), Otta.	15.00	.50	.20
□□□	140 Wade Redden, Otta.	20.00	1.00	.20
□□□□	141 Alexei Yashin, Otta.	35.00	2.00	.20
□□□	142 Marian Hossa, Otta.	60.00	3.00	.50
□□□□	143 Chris Phillips, Otta.	15.00	.50	.20
□□□	144 Daniel Alfredsson, Otta.	35.00	2.00	.20
□□□	145 Vaclav Prospal, Otta.	20.00	1.00	.20
□□□	146 Andreas Dackell, Otta.	10.00	.50	.20
□□□	147 Sean Burke (G), Phil.	35.00	2.00	.20
□□□	148 Alexandre Daigle, Phil.	10.00	.50	.20
□□□	149 Rod Brind'Amour, Phil.	20.00	1.00	.20
□□□	150 Chris Gratton, Phil.	15.00	.50	.20
□□□□	151 Paul Coffey, Phil.	35.00	2.00	.20
□□□	152 Eric Lindros, Phil.	60.00	3.00	.50
□□□□	153 John LeClair, Phil.	50.00	3.00	.20
□□□	154 Chris Therien, Phil.	8.00	.50	.20
□□□	155 Keith Carney, Phoe.	10.00	.50	.20
□□□	156 Craig Janney, Phoe.	15.00	.50	.20
□□□	157 Teppo Numminen, Phoe.	20.00	1.00	.20
□□□	158 Jeremy Roenick, Phoe.	50.00	3.00	.20
□□□	159 Oleg Tverdovsky, Phoe.	10.00	.50	.20
□□□	160 Keith Tkachuk, Phoe.	35.00	2.00	.20
□□□□	161 Brad Isbister, Phoe.	15.00	.50	.20
□□□	162 N. Khabibulin (G), Phoe.	25.00	1.00	.20
□□□□	163 Daniel Brière, Phoe.	30.00	1.00	.20
□□□	164 Juha Ylönen, Phoe.	10.00	.50	.20
□□□	165 Tom Barrasso (G), Pitt.	25.00	1.00	.20
□□□	166 Alexei Morozov, Pitt.	15.00	.50	.20
□□□	167 Stu Barnes, Pitt.	8.00	.50	.20
□□□	168 Jaromir Jagr, Pitt.	60.00	.50	.50
□□□	169 Ron Francis, Pitt.	35.00	2.00	.20
□□□	170 Peter Skudra (G), Pitt.	10.00	.50	.20
□□□□	171 Robert Dome, Pitt.	10.00	.50	.20
□□□	172 Kevin Hatcher, Pitt.	10.00	.50	.20
□□□□	173 Patrick Marleau, SanJ.	30.00	1.00	.20
□□□	174 Jeff Friesen, SanJ.	20.00	1.00	.20
□□□	175 Owen Nolan, SanJ.	35.00	2.00	.20
□□□	176 John MacLean, SanJ.	10.00	.50	.20
□□□	177 Mike Vernon (G), SanJ.	25.00	1.00	.20
□□□	178 M. Ragnarsson, SanJ.	15.00	.50	.20
□□□	179 Andrei Zyuzin, SanJ.	10.00	.50	.20
□□□	180 Mike Ricci, SanJ.	20.00	1.00	.20
□□□□	181 Marco Sturm, SanJ.	15.00	.50	.20
□□□	182 Steve Duchesne, SLou.	15.00	.50	.20
□□□□	183 Brett Hull, SLou.	60.00	3.00	.50
□□□	184 Pierre Turgeon, SLou.	25.00	1.00	.20
□□□	185 Chris Pronger, SLou.	35.00	2.00	.20
□□□	186 Pavol Demitra, SLou.	25.00	1.00	.20
□□□	187 J. McLennan (G), SLou.	10.00	.50	.20
□□□	188 Al MacInnis, SLou.	25.00	1.00	.20
□□□	189 Jim Campbell, SLou.	8.00	.50	.20
□□□□	190 Geoff Courtnall, SLou.	10.00	.50	.20
□□□	191 Daren Puppa (G), Tamp.	15.00	.50	.20
□□□	192 Daymond Langkow, Tamp.	15.00	.50	.20
□□□□	193 Stéphane Richer, Tamp.	15.00	.50	.20
□□□	194 Paul Ysebaert, Tamp.	8.00	.50	.20
□□□	195 A. Selivanov, Tamp.	8.00	.50	.20
□□□	196 Rob Zamuner, Tamp.	15.00	.50	.20
□□□	197 Mikael Renberg, Tamp.	20.00	1.00	.20
□□□	198 Mathieu Schneider, Toro.	15.00	.50	.20
□□□	199 Mike Johnson, Toro.	10.00	.50	.20
□□□	200 Alyn McAuley, Toro.	20.00	1.00	.20
□□□□	201 Sergei Berezin, Toro.	15.00	.50	.20
□□□	202 Wendel Clark, Toro.	50.00	3.00	.20
□□□□	203 Mats Sundin, Toro.	60.00	3.00	.50
□□□	204 Tie Domi, Toro.	20.00	1.00	.20
□□□	205 Jyrki Lumme, Vanc.	15.00	.50	.20
□□□	206 Mattias Öhlund, Vanc.	20.00	1.00	.20
□□□	207 Garth Snow (G), Vanc.	20.00	1.00	.20
□□□	208 Pavel Bure, Vanc.	50.00	3.00	.20
□□□	209 Dave Scatchard, Vanc.	8.00	.50	.20
□□□	210 Alexander Mogilny, Vanc.	30.00	1.00	.20
□□□□	211 Mark Messier, Vanc.	60.00	3.00	.50
□□□	212 Todd Bertuzzi, Vanc.	75.00	4.00	.50
□□□□	213 Peter Bondra, Wash.	35.00	2.00	.20
□□□	214 Joé Juneau, Wash.	15.00	.50	.20
□□□	215 Olaf Kölzig (G), Wash.	35.00	2.00	.20
□□□	216 Jan Bulis, Wsh,.	8.00	.50	.20
□□□	217 Adam Oates, Wash.	25.00	1.00	.20
□□□	218 Richard Zednik, Wash.	25.00	1.00	.20
□□□	219 Calle Johansson, Wash.	15.00	.50	.20
□□□	220 Phil Housley, Wash.	20.00	1.00	.20
□□□	221 Dominik Hasek (G), Buff.	60.00	3.00	.50
□□□	222 Raymond Bourque, Bost.	70.00	4.00	.50
□□□	223 Chris Chelios, Chic.	35.00	2.00	.20
□□□	224 Paul Kariya, Anah.	80.00	5.00	.50
□□□	225 Wayne Gretzky, NYRa.	250.00	15.00	2.00
□□□	226 Jaromir Jagr, Pitt.	60.00	.50	.50
□□□	227 Rob Blake, LosA.	35.00	2.00	.20
□□□	228 Adam Foote, Colo.	20.00	1.00	.20
□□□	229 Peter Forsberg, Colo.	80.00	5.00	.50
□□□	230 Joe Sakic, Colo.	100.00	6.00	.50
□□□	231 Mark Recchi, Mont.	25.00	1.00	.20
□□□	232 Patrick Roy (G), Colo.	180.00	10.00	1.50
□□□	233 Nicklas Lidström, Detr.	35.00	2.00	.20
□□□	234 Rob Blake, LosA.	35.00	2.00	.20
□□□	235 John LeClair, Phil.	50.00	3.00	.20
□□□	236 Wayne Gretzky, NYRa.	250.00	15.00	2.00
□□□	237 Eric Lindros, Phil.	60.00	3.00	.50
□□□	238 Brian Leetch, NYRa.	35.00	2.00	.20
□□□	239 Scott Stevens, NJer.	25.00	1.00	.20
□□□	240 Paul Kariya, Anah.	80.00	5.00	.50
□□□	241 Peter Forsberg, Colo.	80.00	5.00	.50
□□□	242 Teemu Selänne, Anah.	50.00	3.00	.20
□□□	243 Patrick Roy (G), Colo.	180.00	10.00	1.50
□□□	244 Dominik Hasek (G), Buff.	60.00	3.00	.50
□□□	245 Martin Brodeur (G), NJer.	100.00	6.00	.50
□□□	246 Mike Richter (G), NYRa.	30.00	1.00	.20
□□□	247 Vanbiesbrouck (G), Flor.	30.00	1.00	.20
□□□	248 Chris Osgood (G), Detr.	35.00	2.00	.20
□□□	249 Ed Belfour (G), Dall.	60.00	3.00	.50
□□□	250 Tom Barrasso (G), Pitt.	25.00	1.00	.20
□□□	251 Curtis Joseph (G), Edmo.	60.00	3.00	.50
□□□	252 Sean Burke (G), Phil.	35.00	2.00	.20
□□□	253 Josh Holden, Cdn.	10.00	1.00	.20
□□□	254 Daniel Tkaczuk, Cdn.	15.00	1.00	.20
□□□	255 Manny Malhotra, Cdn.	15.00	1.00	.20
□□□	256 Eric Brewer, Cdn.	25.00	1.00	.20
□□□	257 Alex Tanguay, Cdn.	35.00	1.00	.50
□□□	258 Roberto Luongo (G), Cdn.	50.00	1.00	.50
□□□	259 Vincent Lecavalier, Cdn.	60.00	1.00	1.00
□□□	260 Mathieu Garon (G), Cdn.	25.00	1.00	.20
□□□	**261 B. Ference, Cdn. RC**	**20.00**	**2.00**	**1.50**
□□□	262 Jesse Wallin, Cdn.	8.00	1.00	.20
□□□	263 Zenith Komarniski, Cdn.	8.00	1.00	.20
□□□	**264 S. Blanchard, Cdn. RC**	**10.00**	**2.00**	**1.00**
□□□	265 Cory Sarich, Cdn.	10.00	1.00	.20
□□□	266 Mike Van Ryn, Cdn.	15.00	1.00	.20
□□□	267 Steve Bégin, Cdn.	15.00	1.00	.20
□□□	**268 Matt Cooke, Cdn. RC**	**20.00**	**2.00**	**.50**
□□□	269 Daniel Corso, Cdn.	10.00	1.00	.20
□□□	270 Brett McLean, Cdn.	8.00	1.00	.20
□□□	271 J-P Dumont, Cdn.	15.00	1.00	.20
□□□	272 Jason Ward, Cdn.	10.00	1.00	.20
□□□	**273 Brian Willsie, Cdn. RC**	**10.00**	**2.00**	**1.00**
□□□	274 Matt Bradley, Cdn.	10.00	2.00	.50
□□□	275 Olli Jokinen, Fin.	20.00	1.00	.20
□□□	276 Teemu Elomo, Fin.	8.00	1.00	.20
□□□	277 Timo Vertala, Fin.	8.00	1.00	.20
□□□	278 Mika Noronen (G), Fin.	25.00	1.00	.20
□□□	279 Pasi Petriläinen, Fin.	8.00	1.00	.20
□□□	280 Timo Ahmaoja, Fin.	8.00	1.00	.20
□□□	281 Eero Somervuori, Fin.	8.00	1.00	.20
□□□	282 Maxim Afinogenov, Rus.	25.00	1.00	.20
□□□	283 M. Balmochnykh, Rus.	10.00	1.00	.20
□□□	284 Artem Chubarov, Rus.	10.00	1.00	.20
□□□	285 Vitaly Vishnevski, Rus.	15.00	1.00	.20
□□□	286 Denis Shvidky, Rus.	15.00	1.00	.20
□□□	287 Dmitri Vlasenkov, Rus.	8.00	1.00	.20
□□□	288 Magnus Nilsson, Swe.	8.00	1.00	.20
□□□	**289 M. Homqvist, Swe. RC**	**10.00**	**2.00**	**1.00**
□□□	**290 M. Karlin, Swe. RC**	**10.00**	**2.00**	**1.00**
□□□	291 Pierre Hedin, Swe.	8.00	1.00	.20
□□□	292 Henrik Petré, Swe.	8.00	1.00	.20
□□□	293 Johan Forsander, Swe.	8.00	1.00	.20
□□□	294 Daniel Sedin, Swe.	25.00	1.00	.20
□□□	295 Henrik Sedin, Swe.	25.00	1.00	.20
□□□	296 Markus Nilsson, Swe.	10.00	1.00	.20
□□□	297 Paul Mara, USA.	10.00	1.00	.20
□□□	**298 Brian Gionta, USA. RC**	**30.00**	**2.00**	**2.00**
□□□	299 Chris Hajt, USA.	8.00	2.00	.50
□□□	**300 Mike Mottau, USA. RC**	**20.00**	**2.00**	**1.50**
□□□	**301 J-M Pelletier, USA. RC**	**20.00**	**2.00**	**1.50**
□□□	302 David Legwand, USA.	25.00	1.00	.20
□□□	303 Ty Jones, USA.	8.00	1.00	.20
□□□	304 Nikos Tselios, USA.	10.00	1.00	.20
□□□	305 Jesse Boulerice, USA.	8.00	1.00	.20
□□□	306 Jeff Farkas, USA.	15.00	1.00	.20
□□□	307 Toby Petersen, USA.	10.00	1.00	.20
□□□	308 CL: W. Gretzky, NYRa.	150.00	5.00	1.00
□□□	309 CL: P. Roy (G), Colo.	110.00	5.00	.50
□□□	310 CL: S. Yzerman, Detr.	90.00	5.00	.50

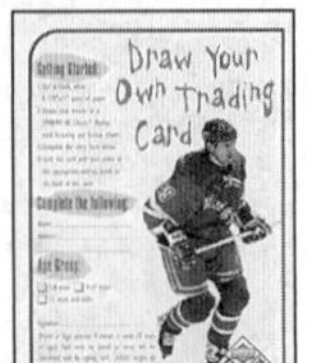

Draw Your Own Card	**DYOC**
□ Wayne Gretzky, NYRa.	.20

BOBBING HEADS

Insert Set (30 cards):	**30.00**
Insert (1:4)	**BH**
□ BH1 Wayne Gretzky	5.00
□ BH2 Keith Tkachuk	.50
□ BH3 Raymond Bourque	1.50
□ BH4 Brett Hull	1.00
□ BH5 Jaromir Jagr	1.00

□ BH6 John LeClair	1.00
□ BH7 Martin Brodeur (G)	2.00
□ BH8 Eric Lindros	1.00
□ BH9 Mark Messier	1.00
□ BH10 John Vanbiesbrouck (G)	.50
□ BH11 Paul Kariya	1.50
□ BH12 Luc Robitaille	1.00
□ BH13 Zigmund Palffy	.50
□ BH14 Peter Forsberg	1.50
□ BH15 Teemu Selänne	1.00
□ BH16 Mike Modano	1.00
□ BH17 Mats Sundin	1.00
□ BH18 Dominik Hasek (G)	1.00
□ BH19 Joe Sakic	2.00
□ BH20 Rob Blake	.50
□ BH21 Patrick Roy (G)	3.50
□ BH22 Sergei Samsonov	.50
□ BH23 Chris Chelios	.50
□ BH24 Brendan Shanahan	1.00
□ BH25 Theoren Fleury	.50
□ BH26 Ed Belfour (G)	1.00
□ BH27 Steve Yzerman	3.00
□ BH28 Saku Koivu	1.00
□ BH29 Brian Leetch	.50
□ BH30 Pavel Bure	1.00

HOMETEAM HEROES

Insert Set (20 cards):	**20.00**
Insert	**RW**
□ RW1 Steve Yzerman, Detr.	7.00
□ RW2 Sergei Fedorov, Detr.	3.00
□ RW3 Nicklas Lidström, Detr.	1.50
□ RW4 Vyacheslav Kozlov, Detr.	.50
□ RW5 Chris Osgood (G), Detr.	1.50
□ RW6 Darren McCarty, Detr.	.50
□ RW7 Brendan Shanahan, Detr.	3.00
□ RW8 Igor Larionov, Detr.	1.50
□ RW9 Martin Lapointe, Detr.	1.00
□ RW10 Doug Brown, Detr.	.50
□ RW11 Kirk Maltby, Detr.	.50
□ RW12 Kris Draper, Detr.	.50
□ RW13 Tomas Holmström, Detr.	.50
□ RW14 Larry Murphy, Detr.	.50
□ RW15 Viacheslav Fetisov, Detr.	1.50
□ RW16 Anders Eriksson, Detr.	.50
□ RW17 Brent Gilchrist, Detr.	.50
□ RW18 Joey Kocur, Detr.	.50
□ RW19 Mike Knuble, Detr.	.50
□ RW20 Kevin Hodson (G), Detr.	.50

STARQUEST

This series has four versions: a Blue insert, a Green insert, a Red insert and a Gold insert (#/100).

Insert Set (30 cards):	**1700.00**	**160.00**	**40.00**	**25.00**
Player	**G100**	**Red**	**Green**	**Blue**
□□□□ SQ1 W. Gretzky	250.00	25.00	6.00	4.00
□□□□ SQ2 Pavel Bure	50.00	5.00	1.00	.50
□□□□ SQ3 Patrick Roy (G)	180.00	15.00	4.50	3.00
□□□□ SQ4 D. Hasek (G)	60.00	5.00	1.50	1.00
□□□□ SQ5 T. Selänne	50.00	5.00	1.00	.50
□□□□ SQ6 S. Samsonov	30.00	3.00	.75	.50
□□□□ SQ7 Brian Leetch	35.00	3.00	.75	.50
□□□□ SQ8 Saku Koivu	50.00	5.00	1.00	.50
□□□□ SQ9 B. Shanahan	60.00	6.00	1.50	1.00
□□□□ SQ10 Alexei Yashin	35.00	3.00	.75	.50
□□□□ SQ11 Joe Sakic	100.00	10.00	2.00	1.50
□□□□ SQ12 Patrik Elias	50.00	5.00	1.00	.50
□□□□ SQ13 T. Fleury	30.00	3.00	.75	.50
□□□□ SQ14 Peter Bondra	35.00	3.00	.75	.50
□□□□ SQ15 John LeClair	50.00	5.00	1.00	.50
□□□□ SQ16 Jaromir Jagr	60.00	5.00	1.50	1.00
□□□□ SQ17 Ed Belfour (G)	60.00	6.00	1.50	1.00
□□□□ SQ18 S. Yzerman	150.00	15.00	3.50	2.00
□□□□ SQ19 Mats Sundin	60.00	6.00	1.50	1.00
□□□□ SQ20 P. Forsberg	80.00	5.00	2.00	1.00
□□□□ SQ21 R. Bourque	70.00	7.00	1.50	1.00

□□□□ SQ22 Brett Hull	60.00	6.00	1.50	1.00
□□□□ SQ23 Brodeur (G)	100.00	10.00	2.00	1.50
□□□□ SQ24 Mike Modano	60.00	6.00	1.50	1.00
□□□□ SQ25 Paul Kariya	80.00	5.00	2.00	1.00
□□□□ SQ26 Tony Amonte	35.00	3.00	.75	.50
□□□□ SQ27 Mike Johnson	10.00	2.00	.75	.50
□□□□ SQ28 Eric Lindros	60.00	5.00	1.50	1.00
□□□□ SQ29 Mark Messier	60.00	6.00	1.50	1.00
□□□□ SQ30 Keith Tkachuk	30.00	3.00	.75	.50

1998 - 99 UD^3

These cards have two versions: the regular card and a Die-Cut parallel (#/200). Die-Cut parallels for cards 31-60 (1 copy each) are too scarceto price.

Complete Set (180 cards): 80.00

Insert	DC	UD3
□□ 1 Sergei Samsonov, Bost.	15.00	.20
□□ 2 Ryan Johnson, Flor. RC	6.00	.20
□□ 3 Josef Marha, Anah.	4.00	.20
□□ 4 Patrick Marleau, SanJ.	15.00	.20
□□ 5 Derek Morris, Calg.	5.00	.20
□□ 6 Jamie Storr, LosA.	5.00	.20
□□ 7 Richard Zednik, Wash.	12.00	.20
□□ 8 Alyn McCauley, Toro.	10.00	.20
□□ 9 Robert Dome, Pitt.	5.00	.20
□□ 10 Patrik Elias, NJer.	25.00	1.00
□□ 11 Olli Jokinen, LosA.	10.00	.20
□□ 12 Peter Skudra (G), Pitt.	5.00	.20
□□ 13 Chris Phillips, Otta.	7.00	.20
□□ 14 Mattias Öhlund, Vanc.	10.00	.20
□□ 15 Joe Thornton, Bost.	35.00	1.00
□□ 16 Matt Cullen, Anah.	7.00	.20
□□ 17 Bates Battaglia, Caro.	7.00	.20
□□ 18 Andrei Zyuzin, SanJ.	5.00	.20
□□ 19 Cameron Mann, Bost.	5.00	.20
□□ 20 Zdeno Chara, NYIs.	5.00	.20
□□ 21 Marc Savard, NYRa.	5.00	.20
□□ 22 Alexei Morozov, Pitt.	7.00	.20
□□ 23 Mike Johnson, Toro.	5.00	.20
□□ 24 Vaclav Varada, Buff.	5.00	.20
□□ 25 Dan Cloutier (G), NYRa.	10.00	.20
□□ 26 Brad Isbister, Phoe.	7.00	.20
□□ 27 Marco Sturm, SanJ.	5.00	.20
□□ 28 Anders Eriksson, Detr.	4.00	.20
□□ 29 Jan Bulis, Wash.	4.00	.20
□□ 30 Brendan Morrison, NJer.	10.00	.20
□□ 31 Wayne Gretzky, NYRa.		6.00
□□ 32 Jaromir Jagr, Pitt.		1.00
□□ 33 Peter Forsberg, Colo.		2.00
□□ 34 Paul Kariya, Anah.		2.00
□□ 35 Brett Hull, SLou.		1.00
□□ 36 Martin Brodeur (G), NJer.		2.00
□□ 37 Eric Lindros, Phil.		1.00
□□ 38 Peter Bondra, Wash.		.20
□□ 39 Mike Modano, Dall.		1.00
□□ 40 Theoren Fleury, Calg.		.20
□□ 41 Curtis Joseph (G), Toro.		1.00
□□ 42 Sergei Fedorov, Detr.		1.00
□□ 43 Saku Koivu, Mont.		1.00
□□ 44 Zigmund Palffy, NYIs.		.20
□□ 45 Ed Belfour (G), Dall.		1.00
□□ 46 Patrick Roy (G), Colo.		4.00
□□ 47 Brendan Shanahan, Detr.		1.00
□□ 48 Mats Sundin, Toro.		1.00
□□ 49 Alexei Yashin, Otta.		.20
□□ 50 Doug Gilmour, NJer.		.20
□□ 51 Chris Osgood (G), Detr.		.20
□□ 52 Keith Tkachuk, Phoe.		.20
□□ 53 Mark Messier, Vanc.		1.00
□□ 54 John Vanbiesbrouck (G), Flor.		.20
□□ 55 Raymond Bourque, Bost.		1.00
□□ 56 John LeClair, Phil.		1.00
□□ 57 Dominik Hasek (G), Buff.		1.00
□□ 58 Teemu Selänne, Anah.		1.00
□□ 59 Joe Sakic, Colo.		2.00
□□ 60 Steve Yzerman, Detr.		3.00
□□ 61 Sergei Samsonov, Bost.	4.00	.20
□□ 62 Ryan Johnson, Flor.	2.00	.20
□□ 63 Josef Marha, Anah.	2.00	.20
□□ 64 Patrick Marleau, SanJ.	3.00	.20
□□ 65 Derek Morris, Calg.	2.00	.20
□□ 66 Jamie Storr (G), LosA.	2.00	.20
□□ 67 Richard Zednik, Wash.	3.00	.20
□□ 68 Alyn McCauley, Toro.	2.00	.20
□□ 69 Robert Dome, Pitt.	2.00	.20
□□ 70 Patrik Elias, NJer.	6.00	1.00
□□ 71 Olli Jokinen, LosA.	2.00	.20
□□ 72 Peter Skudra (G), Pitt.	2.00	.20
□□ 73 Chris Phillips, Otta.	2.00	.20
□□ 74 Mattias Öhlund, Vanc.	2.00	.20
□□ 75 Joe Thornton, Bost.	9.00	1.00
□□ 76 Matt Cullen, Anah.	2.00	.20
□□ 77 Bates Battaglia, Caro.	2.00	.20
□□ 78 Andrei Zyuzin, SanJ.	2.00	.20
□□ 79 Cameron Mann, Bost.	2.00	.20
□□ 80 Zdeno Chara, NYIs.	2.00	.20
□□ 81 Marc Savard, NYRa.	2.00	.20
□□ 82 Alexei Morozov, Pitt.	2.00	.20
□□ 83 Mike Johnson, Toro.	2.00	.20
□□ 84 Vaclav Varada, Buff.	2.00	.20
□□ 85 Dan Cloutier (G), NYRa.	3.00	.20
□□ 86 Brad Isbister, Phoe.	2.00	.20
□□ 87 Marco Sturm, SanJ.	2.00	.20
□□ 88 Anders Eriksson, Detr.	2.00	.20
□□ 89 Jan Bulis, Wash.	2.00	.20
□□ 90 Brendan Morrison, NJer.	2.00	.20
□□ 91 Wayne Gretzky, NYRa.	30.00	10.00
□□ 92 Jaromir Jagr, Pitt.	5.00	2.00
□□ 93 Peter Forsberg, Colo.	10.00	3.00
□□ 94 Paul Kariya, Anah.	10.00	3.00
□□ 95 Brett Hull, SLou.	7.00	2.00
□□ 96 Martin Brodeur (G), NJer.	10.00	4.00
□□ 97 Eric Lindros, Phil.	5.00	2.00
□□ 98 Peter Bondra, Wash.	4.00	1.00
□□ 99 Mike Modano, Dall.	7.00	2.00
□□ 100 Theoren Fleury, Calg.	4.00	1.00
□□ 101 Curtis Joseph (G), Toro.	5.00	2.00
□□ 102 Sergei Fedorov, Detr.	7.00	2.00
□□ 103 Saku Koivu, Mont.	6.00	2.00
□□ 104 Zigmund Palffy, NYIs.	4.00	1.00
□□ 105 Ed Belfour (G), Dall.	7.00	2.00
□□ 106 Patrick Roy (G), Colo.	20.00	7.00
□□ 107 Brendan Shanahan, Detr.	7.00	2.00
□□ 108 Mats Sundin, Toro.	7.00	2.00
□□ 109 Alexei Yashin, Otta.	4.00	1.00
□□ 110 Doug Gilmour, NJer.	4.00	1.00
□□ 111 Chris Osgood (G), Detr.	4.00	1.00
□□ 112 Keith Tkachuk, Phoe.	4.00	1.00
□□ 113 Mark Messier, Vanc.	7.00	2.00
□□ 114 John Vanbiesbrouck (G), Flor.	3.00	1.00
□□ 115 Raymond Bourque, Bost.	5.00	3.00
□□ 116 John LeClair, Phil.	6.00	2.00
□□ 117 Dominik Hasek (G), Buff.	5.00	2.00
□□ 118 Teemu Selänne, Anah.	5.00	2.00
□□ 119 Joe Sakic, Colo.	10.00	4.00
□□ 120 Steve Yzerman, Detr.	15.00	6.00
□□ 121 Sergei Samsonov, Bost.	60.00	2.00
□□ 122 Ryan Johnson, Flor.	20.00	1.00
□□ 123 Josef Marha, Anah.	15.00	1.00
□□ 124 Patrick Marleau, SanJ.	45.00	1.00
□□ 125 Derek Morris, Calg.	20.00	1.00
□□ 126 Jamie Storr (G), LosA.	20.00	1.00
□□ 127 Richard Zednik, Wash.	40.00	1.00
□□ 128 Alyn McCauley, Toro.	30.00	1.00
□□ 129 Robert Dome, Pitt.	15.00	1.00
□□ 130 Patrik Elias, NJer.	80.00	3.00
□□ 131 Olli Jokinen, LosA.	30.00	1.00
□□ 132 Peter Skudra (G), Pitt.	15.00	1.00
□□ 133 Chris Phillips, Otta.	20.00	1.00
□□ 134 Mattias Öhlund, Vanc.	30.00	1.00
□□ 135 Joe Thornton, Bost.	120.00	4.00
□□ 136 Matt Cullen, Anah.	20.00	1.00
□□ 137 Bates Battaglia, Caro.	20.00	1.00
□□ 138 Andrei Zyuzin, SanJ.	15.00	1.00
□□ 139 Cameron Mann, Bost.	15.00	1.00
□□ 140 Zdeno Chara, NYIs.	20.00	1.00
□□ 141 Marc Savard, NYRa.	20.00	1.00
□□ 142 Alexei Morozov, Pitt.	20.00	1.00
□□ 143 Mike Johnson, Toro.	20.00	1.00
□□ 144 Vaclav Varada, Buff.	15.00	1.00
□□ 145 Dan Cloutier (G), NYRa.	40.00	1.00
□□ 146 Brad Isbister, Phoe.	20.00	1.00
□□ 147 Marco Sturm, SanJ.	20.00	1.00
□□ 148 Anders Eriksson, Detr.	15.00	1.00
□□ 149 Jan Bulis, Wash.	15.00	1.00
□□ 150 Brendan Morrison, NJer.	30.00	1.00
□□ 151 Wayne Gretzky, NYRa.	250.00	40.00
□□ 152 Jaromir Jagr, Pitt.	60.00	10.00
□□ 153 Peter Forsberg, Colo.	80.00	10.00
□□ 154 Paul Kariya, Anah.	80.00	10.00
□□ 155 Brett Hull, SLou.	60.00	10.00
□□ 156 Martin Brodeur (G), NJer.	100.00	15.00
□□ 157 Eric Lindros, Phil.	60.00	10.00
□□ 158 Peter Bondra, Wash.	35.00	6.00
□□ 159 Mike Modano, Dall.	60.00	10.00
□□ 160 Theoren Fleury, Calg.	30.00	5.00
□□ 161 Curtis Joseph (G), Toro.	60.00	10.00
□□ 162 Sergei Fedorov, Detr.	60.00	10.00
□□ 163 Saku Koivu, Mont.	50.00	8.00
□□ 164 Zigmund Palffy, NYIs.	35.00	6.00
□□ 165 Ed Belfour (G), Dall.	60.00	10.00
□□ 166 Patrick Roy (G), Colo.	180.00	30.00
□□ 167 Brendan Shanahan, Detr.	60.00	10.00
□□ 168 Mats Sundin, Toro.	60.00	10.00
□□ 169 Alexei Yashin, Otta.	35.00	6.00
□□ 170 Doug Gilmour, NJer.	35.00	6.00
□□ 171 Chris Osgood (G), Detr.	30.00	6.00
□□ 172 Keith Tkachuk, Phoe.	30.00	6.00
□□ 173 Mark Messier, Vanc.	60.00	10.00
□□ 174 John Vanbiesbrouck (G), Flor.	30.00	4.00
□□ 175 Raymond Bourque, Bost.	70.00	10.00
□□ 176 John LeClair, Phil.	50.00	5.00
□□ 177 Dominik Hasek (G), Buff.	60.00	10.00
□□ 178 Teemu Selänne, Anah.	50.00	5.00
□□ 179 Joe Sakic, Colo.	100.00	15.00
□□ 180 Steve Yzerman, Detr.	150.00	20.00

1998 - 99 UPPER DECK & UPPER DECK GOLD RESERVE

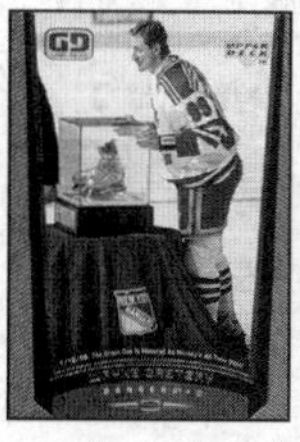

There are three versions in the Upper Deck series: the regular card, a UD Exclusive parallel (#100) and a one-of-one parallel (too scarce to price). The Upper Deck Gold Reserve series was a separate release. The high-number cards (381-420) were short-printed in the regular Upper Deck Series Two, but not short-printed in the Upper Deck Gold Reserve Update series.

Series One Set (210 cards):	**150.00**	**5000.00**	**90.00**
Series Two Set (210 cards):	**100.00**	**3700.00**	**125.00**
Common Player:	**.30**	**8.00**	**.20**

Player	UDGR	UD100	UD
□□□□ 1 Antti Aalto, Anah.	2.00	8.00	1.50
□□□□ 2 Cameron Mann, Bost.	2.00	10.00	1.50
□□□□ **3 Norm Maracle, Detr. RC**	**3.50**	**20.00**	**3.00**
□□□□ 4 Daniel Cleary, Chic.	2.50	20.00	1.50
□□□□ 5 Brendan Morrison, NJer.	2.50	20.00	1.50
□□□□ 6 Marian Hossa, Otta.	5.00	70.00	6.00
□□□□ 7 Daniel Brière, Phoe.	4.00	35.00	2.50
□□□□ **8 Mike Crowley, Anah. RC**	**2.00**	**15.00**	**1.50**
□□□□ **9 Darryl Laplante, Detr. RC**	**2.00**	**15.00**	**1.50**
□□□□ **10 Sven Butscheon, Pitt. RC**	**2.00**	**15.00**	**1.50**
□□□□ **11 Yan Golubovsky, Detr. RC**	**2.00**	**15.00**	**1.50**
□□□□ 12 Olli Jokinen, LosA.	2.50	20.00	1.50
□□□□ 13 J-S Giguère (G), Calg.	7.00	60.00	4.50
□□□□ 14 Mike Watt, NYIs.	2.00	8.00	1.50
□□□□ **15 Ryan Johnson, Flor. RC**	**2.00**	**15.00**	**1.50**
□□□□ 16 Teemu Selänne, Anah.	3.50	60.00	2.00
□□□□ 17 Paul Kariya, Anah.	5.00	100.00	4.00
□□□□ 18 Pavel Bure, Vanc.	2.00	60.00	2.00
□□□□ 19 Joe Thornton, Bost.	5.00	90.00	3.50
□□□□ 20 Dominik Hasek (G), Buff.	2.00	70.00	3.00
□□□□ 21 Bryan Berard, NYIs.	2.00	20.00	1.50
□□□□ 22 Chris Phillips, Otta.	2.00	15.00	1.50
□□□□ 23 Sergei Fedorov, Detr.	4.50	70.00	3.00
□□□□ 24 Sergei Samsonov, Bost.	2.50	40.00	1.50
□□□□ 25 Marc Denis, Colo.	2.00	35.00	1.50
□□□□ 26 Patrick Marleau, SanJ.	2.00	35.00	1.50
□□□□ 27 Jaromir Jagr, Pitt.	2.00	70.00	3.00
□□□□ 28 Saku Koivu, Mont.	3.50	60.00	2.00
□□□□ 29 Peter Forsberg, Colo.	5.00	100.00	4.00
□□□□ 30 Mike Modano, Dall.	4.50	70.00	3.00
□□□□ 31 Paul Kariya, Anah.	2.00	100.00	1.00
□□□□ 32 Matt Cullen, Anah.	.30	15.00	.20
□□□□ 33 Josef Marha, Anah.	.30	8.00	.20
□□□□ 34 Teemu Selänne, Anah.	1.00	60.00	.50
□□□□ 35 Pavel Trnka, Anah.	.30	8.00	.20
□□□□ **36 Tom Askey (G), Anah. RC**	**1.00**	**20.00**	**1.00**
□□□□ 37 Tim Taylor, Bost.	.30	8.00	.20
□□□□ 38 Raymond Bourque, Bost.	1.50	90.00	1.00
□□□□ 39 Sergei Samsonov, Bost.	.50	40.00	.50
□□□□ 40 Don Sweeney, Bost.	.30	10.00	.20
□□□□ 41 Jason Allison, Bost.	.50	40.00	.50
□□□□ 42 Steve Heinze, Bost.	.30	10.00	.20
□□□□ 43 Erik Rasmussen, Buff.	.30	15.00	.20
□□□□ 44 Dominik Hasek (G), Buff.	1.50	70.00	1.00
□□□□ 45 Geoff Sanderson, Buff.	.30	15.00	.20
□□□□ 46 Michael Peca, Buff.	.50	30.00	.20
□□□□ 47 Brian Holzinger, Buff.	.30	10.00	.20
□□□□ 48 Vaclav Varada, Buff.	.30	10.00	.20
□□□□ 49 Steve Bégin, Calg.	.30	15.00	.20
□□□□ 50 Denis Gauthier, Calg.	.30	8.00	.20
□□□□ 51 Derek Morris, Calg.	.30	15.00	.20
□□□□ 52 Valeri Bure, Calg.	.30	20.00	.20
□□□□ 53 Hnat Domenichelli, Calg.	.30	10.00	.20
□□□□ 54 Cory Stillman, Calg.	.30	15.00	.20
□□□□ 55 Jarome Iginla, Calg.	1.00	60.00	.50
□□□□ 56 Tyler Moss, Calg.	.30	10.00	.20
□□□□ 57 Sami Kapanen, Caro.	.30	20.00	.20
□□□□ 58 Trevor Kidd (G), Caro.	.30	20.00	.20
□□□□ 59 Glen Wesley, Caro.	.30	10.00	.20
□□□□ 60 Nelson Emerson, Caro.	.30	10.00	.20
□□□□ 61 Jeff O'Neill, Caro.	.50	30.00	.20
□□□□ 62 Bates Battaglia, Caro.	.30	15.00	.20
□□□□ 63 Doug Gilmour, Chic.	.50	45.00	.50
□□□□ 64 Christian Laflamme, Chic.	.30	8.00	.20
□□□□ 65 Chris Chelios, Chic.	.50	45.00	.50
□□□□ 66 Paul Coffey, Chic.	.50	40.00	.50
□□□□ 67 Eric Weinrich, Chic.	.30	8.00	.20
□□□□ 68 Éric Dazé, Chic.	.50	30.00	.20
□□□□ 69 Peter Forsberg, Colo.	2.00	100.00	1.00
□□□□ 70 Éric Messier, Colo.	.30	10.00	.20
□□□□ 71 Éric Lacroix, Colo.	.30	8.00	.20
□□□□ 72 Adam Deadmarsh, Colo.	.30	20.00	.20
□□□□ 73 Claude Lemieux, Colo.	.30	20.00	.20
□□□□ 74 Patrick Roy (G), Colo.	4.50	220.00	3.00
□□□□ 75 Marc Denis, Colo.	.50	35.00	.20
□□□□ 76 Brett Hull, Dall.	1.50	70.00	1.00
□□□□ 77 Mike Keane, Dall.	.30	10.00	.20
□□□□ 78 Joe Nieuwendyk, Dall.	.50	30.00	.20
□□□□ 79 Darryl Sydor, Dall.	.30	15.00	.20
□□□□ 80 Ed Belfour (G), Dall.	1.50	70.00	1.00
□□□□ 81 Jamie Langenbrunner, Dall.	.30	15.00	.20
□□□□ 82 Petr Buzek, Dall.	.30	8.00	.20
□□□□ 83 Nicklas Lidström, Detr.	.50	45.00	.50
□□□□ 84 Mathieu Dandenault, Detr.	.30	10.00	.20
□□□□ 85 Steve Yzerman, Detr.	3.50	180.00	2.00
□□□□ 86 Martin Lapointe, Detr.	.50	30.00	.20
□□□□ 87 Brendan Shanahan, Detr.	1.50	70.00	1.00
□□□□ 88 Anders Eriksson, Detr.	.30	8.00	.20
□□□□ 89 Tomas Holmström, Detr.	.30	15.00	.20
□□□□ 90 Doug Weight, Edmo.	.50	40.00	.50
□□□□ 91 Janne Niinimaa, Edmo.	.30	15.00	.20
□□□□ 92 Bill Guerin, Edmo.	.50	30.00	.20
□□□□ 93 Kelly Buchberger, Edmo.	.30	10.00	.20
□□□□ 94 Mike Grier, Edmo.	.30	15.00	.20
□□□□ 95 Craig Millar, Edmo.	.30	8.00	.20
□□□□ 96 Roman Hamrlik, Edmo.	.30	15.00	.20
□□□□ 97 Ray Whitney, Flor.	.30	15.00	.20
□□□□ 98 Viktor Kozlov, Flor.	.30	20.00	.20
□□□□ **99 Peter Worrell, Flor. RC**	**1.50**	**35.00**	**1.50**
□□□□ 100 Kevin Weekes, Flor.	.30	15.00	.20
□□□□ 101 Ed Jovanovski, Flor.	.50	30.00	.20
□□□□ 102 Bill Lindsay, Flor.	.30	8.00	.20
□□□□ 103 Jozef Stümpel, LosA.	.30	15.00	.20
□□□□ 104 Luc Robitaille, LosA.	1.00	60.00	.50
□□□□ 105 Yanic Perreault, LosA.	.30	20.00	.20
□□□□ 106 Donald MacLean, LosA.	.30	8.00	.20
□□□□ 107 Jamie Storr (G), LosA.	.30	15.00	.20
□□□□ 108 Ian Laperrière, LosA.	.30	10.00	.20
□□□□ **109 Jason Morgan, LosA. RC**	**1.50**	**20.00**	**1.50**
□□□□ 110 Vincent Damphousse, Mont.	.50	45.00	.50
□□□□ 111 Mark Recchi, Mont.	.50	30.00	.20
□□□□ 112 Vladimir Malakhov, Mont.	.30	10.00	.20
□□□□ 113 Dave Manson, Mont.	.30	10.00	.20
□□□□ 114 José Théodore (G), Mont.	1.50	90.00	1.00
□□□□ 115 Brian Savage, Mont.	.30	20.00	.20
□□□□ 116 Jonas Höglund, Mont.	.30	10.00	.20
□□□□ 117 Krzysztof Oliwa, NJer.	.30	15.00	.20
□□□□ 118 Martin Brodeur (G), NJer.	2.00	120.00	1.50
□□□□ 119 Patrik Elias, NJer.	1.00	60.00	.50
□□□□ 120 Jason Arnott, NJer.	.50	35.00	.20
□□□□ 121 Scott Stevens, NJer.	.50	30.00	.20
□□□□ **122 Sheldon Souray, NJer. RC**	**.50**	**15.00**	**.50**
□□□□ 123 Brian Rolston, NJer.	.30	20.00	.20
□□□□ 124 Trevor Linden, NYIs.	.50	30.00	.20
□□□□ 125 Warren Luhning, NYIs.	.30	8.00	.20
□□□□ 126 Zdeno Chara, NYIs.	.30	15.00	.20
□□□□ 127 Bryan Berard, NYIs.	.30	20.00	.20
□□□□ 128 Bryan Smolinski, NYIs.	.30	10.00	.20
□□□□ 129 Jason Dawe, NYIs.	.30	8.00	.20
□□□□ 130 Kevin Stevens, NYRa.	.30	15.00	.20
□□□□ **131 P.J. Stock, NYRa. RC**	**2.00**	**45.00**	**2.00**
□□□□ 132 Marc Savard, NYRa.	.30	15.00	.20
□□□□ 133 Pat LaFontaine, NYRa.	.50	45.00	.50
□□□□ 134 Dan Cloutier (G), NYRa.	.50	30.00	.20
□□□□ 135 Wayne Gretzky, NYRa.	6.00	300.00	4.00
□□□□ 136 Niklas Sundström, NYRa.	.30	15.00	.20
□□□□ 137 Damian Rhodes (G), Otta.	.30	15.00	.20
□□□□ 138 Magnus Arvedson, Otta.	.30	10.00	.20
□□□□ 139 Alexei Yashin, Otta.	.50	45.00	.50
□□□□ 140 Chris Phillips, Otta.	.30	15.00	.20
□□□□ 141 Janne Laukkanen, Otta.	.30	8.00	.20
□□□□ 142 Shawn McEachern, Otta.	.30	20.00	.20
□□□□ 143 John LeClair, Phil.	1.00	60.00	.50
□□□□ 144 Alexandre Daigle, Phil.	.30	10.00	.20
□□□□ 145 Dainius Zubrus, Phil.	.30	15.00	.20
□□□□ 146 Joel Otto, Phil.	.30	10.00	.20
□□□□ 147 Mike Sillinger, Phil.	.30	10.00	.20
□□□□ 148 J. Vanbiesbrouck (G), Phil.	.50	35.00	.20
□□□□ 149 Chris Gratton, Phil.	.30	15.00	.20
□□□□ 150 Éric Desjardins, Phil.	.30	20.00	.20
□□□□ 151 Juha Ylönen, Phoe.	.30	10.00	.20
□□□□ 152 Brad Isbister, Phoe.	.30	15.00	.20

□□□□	153 Oleg Tverdovsky, Phoe.	.30	10.00	.20
□□□□	154 Keith Tkachuk, Phoe.	.50	40.00	.50
□□□□	155 Teppo Numminen, Phoe.	.30	20.00	.20
□□□□	156 Cliff Ronning, Phoe.	.30	15.00	.20
□□□□	157 Nikolai Khabibulin (G), Phoe.	.50	30.00	.20
□□□□	158 Alexei Morozov, Pitt.	.30	15.00	.20
□□□□	159 Kevin Hatcher, Pitt.	.30	10.00	.20
□□□□	160 Darius Kasparaitis, Pitt.	.30	15.00	.20
□□□□	161 Jaromir Jagr, Pitt.	1.50	70.00	1.00
□□□□	162 Tom Barrasso (G), Pitt.	.50	30.00	.20
□□□□	163 Tuomas Grönman, Pitt.	.30	8.00	.20
□□□□	164 Robert Dome, Pitt.	.30	10.00	.20
□□□□	165 Peter Skudra (G), Pitt.	.30	10.00	.20
□□□□	166 Marcus Ragnarsson, SanJ.	.30	15.00	.20
□□□□	167 Mike Vernon (G), SanJ.	.50	30.00	.20
□□□□	168 Andrei Zyuzin, SanJ.	.30	10.00	.20
□□□□	169 Marco Sturm, SanJ.	.30	15.00	.20
□□□□	170 Mike Ricci, SanJ.	.30	20.00	.20
□□□□	171 Patrick Marleau, SanJ.	.50	35.00	.20
□□□□	172 Pierre Turgeon, SLou.	.50	30.00	.20
□□□□	173 Pavol Demitra, SLou.	.50	30.00	.20
□□□□	174 Chris Pronger, SLou.	.50	45.00	.50
□□□□	175 Pascal Rhéaume, SLou.	.30	8.00	.20
□□□□	176 Al MacInnis, SLou.	.50	30.00	.20
□□□□	177 Tony Twist, SLou.	.30	10.00	.20
□□□□	178 Jim Campbell, SLou.	.30	8.00	.20
□□□□	179 Mikael Renberg, Tamp.	.30	20.00	.20
□□□□	180 Jason Bonsignore, Tamp.	.30	8.00	.20
□□□□	**181 Zac Bierk, Tamp. RC**	**1.50**	**35.00**	**1.50**
□□□□	182 Alexander Selivanov, Tamp.	.30	8.00	.20
□□□□	183 Stéphane J.J. Richer, Tamp.	.30	15.00	.20
□□□□	184 Sandy McCarthy, Tamp.	.30	10.00	.20
□□□□	185 Alyn McCauley, Toro.	.30	20.00	.20
□□□□	186 Sergei Berezin, Toro.	.30	15.00	.20
□□□□	187 Mike Johnson, Toro.	.30	15.00	.20
□□□□	188 Wendel Clark, Toro.	1.00	60.00	.50
□□□□	189 Tie Domi, Toro.	.30	20.00	.20
□□□□	190 Yannick Tremblay, Toro.	.30	8.00	.20
□□□□	191 Curtis Joseph (G), Toro.	1.50	70.00	1.00
□□□□	192 Fredrik Modin, Toro.	.30	15.00	.20
□□□□	193 Pavel Bure, Vanc.	1.00	60.00	.50
□□□□	194 Todd Bertuzzi, Vanc.	1.50	90.00	1.00
□□□□	195 Mark Messier, Vanc.	1.50	70.00	1.00
□□□□	196 Bret Hedican, Vanc.	.30	8.00	.20
□□□□	197 Mattias Öhlund, Vanc.	.30	20.00	.20
□□□□	198 Garth Snow (G), Vanc.	.30	20.00	.20
□□□□	199 Adam Oates, Wash.	.50	30.00	.20
□□□□	200 Peter Bondra, Wash.	.50	45.00	.50
□□□□	201 Sergei Gonchar, Wash.	.30	20.00	.20
□□□□	202 Jan Bulis, Wash.	.30	8.00	.20
□□□□	203 Joé Juneau, Wash.	.30	15.00	.20
□□□□	204 Brian Bellows, Wash.	.30	15.00	.20
□□□□	205 Olaf Kölzig (G), Wash.	.50	45.00	.50
□□□□	206 Richard Zednik, Wash.	.50	30.00	.20
□□□□	207 CL: Wayne Gretzky, NYRa.	3.50	150.00	2.00
□□□□	208 CL: Patrick Roy (G), Colo.	2.50	110.00	1.50
□□□□	209 CL: Steve Yzerman, Detr.	2.00	90.00	1.00
□□□□	210 Mike Dunham (G), Nash.	.50	30.00	.20
□□□□	211 Johan Davidsson, Anah.	.30	8.00	.20
□□□□	212 Guy Hebert (G), Anah.	.30	15.00	.20
□□□□	213 Mike Leclerc, Anah.	.30	10.00	.20
□□□□	214 Steve Rucchin, Anah.	.30	15.00	.20
□□□□	215 Travis Green, Anah.	.30	15.00	.20
□□□□	216 Josef Marha, Anah.	.30	8.00	.20
□□□□	217 Ted Donato, Bost.	.30	8.00	.20
□□□□	218 Joe Thornton, Bost.	1.50	90.00	1.00
□□□□	219 Kyle McLaren, Bost.	.30	15.00	.20
□□□□	**220 P. Nordström, Bost. RC**	**.50**	**15.00**	**.50**
□□□□	221 Byron Dafoe (G), Bost.	.50	30.00	.20
□□□□	222 Jonathan Girard, Bost.	.30	8.00	.20
□□□□	**223 A. Laaksonen, Bost. RC**	**.50**	**15.00**	**.50**
□□□□	224 Jason Holland, Buff. RC	.30	8.00	.20
□□□□	225 Miroslav Satan, Buff.	.30	20.00	.20
□□□□	226 Alexei Zhitnik, Buff.	.30	10.00	.20
□□□□	227 Donald Audette, Buff.	.50	30.00	.20
□□□□	228 Matthew Barnaby, Buff.	.30	8.00	.20
□□□□	229 Rumun Ndur, Buff.	.30	8.00	.20
□□□□	230 Ken Wreggett (G), Calg.	.30	15.00	.20
□□□□	231 Andrew Cassels, Calg.	.30	15.00	.20
□□□□	232 Theoren Fleury, Calg.	.50	40.00	.50
□□□□	233 Phil Housley, Calg.	.30	20.00	.20
□□□□	**234 M. St-Louis, Calg. RC**	**7.00**	**70.00**	**6.00**
□□□□	**235 Mike Rucinski, Caro. RC**	**.50**	**15.00**	**.50**
□□□□	236 Gary Roberts, Caro.	.50	30.00	.20
□□□□	237 Keith Primeau, Caro.	.50	30.00	.20
□□□□	238 Martin Gélinas, Caro.	.30	15.00	.20
□□□□	**239 Nolan Pratt, Caro. RC**	**.50**	**15.00**	**.50**
□□□□	240 Ray Sheppard, Caro.	.30	10.00	.20
□□□□	241 Ron Francis, Caro.	.50	45.00	.50
□□□□	242 Ty Jones, Chic.	.30	8.00	.20
□□□□	243 Tony Amonte, Chic.	.50	45.00	.50
□□□□	244 Chad Kilger, Chic.	.30	15.00	.20
□□□□	245 Alexei Zhamnov, Chic.	.30	20.00	.20
□□□□	246 Rémi Royer, Chic.	.30	15.00	.50
□□□□	**247 Milan Hejduk, Colo. RC**	**6.00**	**120.00**	**5.00**
□□□□	248 Joe Sakic, Colo.	2.00	120.00	1.50
□□□□	249 Valeri Kamensky, Colo.	.30	20.00	.20
□□□□	250 Sandis Ozolinsh, Colo.	.30	15.00	.20
□□□□	251 Shean Donovan, Colo.	.30	10.00	.20
□□□□	252 Wade Belak, Colo.	.30	8.00	.20
□□□□	253 Jamie Wright, Dall.	.30	8.00	.20
□□□□	254 Sergei Zubov, Dall.	.30	15.00	.20
□□□□	255 Richard Matvichuk, Dall.	.30	15.00	.20
□□□□	256 Mike Modano, Dall.	1.50	70.00	1.00
□□□□	257 Pat Verbeek, Dall.	.30	20.00	.20
□□□□	258 Jere Lehtinen, Dall.	.30	20.00	.20
□□□□	259 Derian Hatcher, Dall.	.30	20.00	.20
□□□□	260 Jason Botterill, Dall.	.30	8.00	.20
□□□□	261 Igor Larionov, Detr.	.50	45.00	.50
□□□□	262 Sergei Fedorov, Detr.	1.50	70.00	1.00
□□□□	263 Chris Osgood (G), Detr.	.50	40.00	.50
□□□□	264 Vyacheslav Kozlov, Detr.	.30	15.00	.20
□□□□	265 Larry Murphy, Detr.	.30	15.00	.20
□□□□	266 Darren McCarty, Detr.	.30	20.00	.20
□□□□	267 Doug Brown, Detr.	.30	8.00	.20
□□□□	268 Kris Draper, Detr.	.30	15.00	.20
□□□□	269 Uwe Krupp, Detr.	.30	8.00	.20
□□□□	**270 F. Lindquist, Edmo. RC**	**.50**	**15.00**	**.50**
□□□□	271 Dean McAmmond, Edmo.	.30	10.00	.20
□□□□	272 Ryan Smyth, Edmo.	.50	35.00	.20
□□□□	273 Boris Mironov, Edmo.	.30	10.00	.20
□□□□	274 Tom Poti, Edmo.	.30	10.00	.20
□□□□	275 Todd Marchant, Edmo.	.30	15.00	.20
□□□□	276 Sean Brown, Edmo.	.30	8.00	.20
□□□□	277 Rob Niedermayer, Flor.	.30	15.00	.20
□□□□	278 Robert Svehla, Flor.	.30	15.00	.20
□□□□	279 Scott Mellanby, Flor.	.30	15.00	.20
□□□□	280 Radek Dvorak, Flor.	.30	15.00	.20
□□□□	**281 Jaroslav Spacek, Flor. RC**	**.50**	**15.00**	**.50**
□□□□	282 Mark Parrish, Flor.	3.00	150.00	.50
□□□□	283 Ryan Johnson, Flor.	.30	15.00	.20
□□□□	284 Glen Murray, LosA.	.50	35.00	.20
□□□□	285 Rob Blake, LosA.	.50	45.00	.50
□□□□	286 Steve Duchesne, LosA.	.30	15.00	.20
□□□□	287 Vladimir Tsyplakov, LosA.	.30	8.00	.20
□□□□	288 Stéphane Fiset, LosA.	.30	20.00	.20
□□□□	289 Mattias Norström, LosA.	.30	15.00	.20
□□□□	290 Saku Koivu, Mont.	1.00	60.00	.50
□□□□	291 Shayne Corson, Mont.	.30	20.00	.20
□□□□	292 Brad Brown, Mont.	.30	8.00	.20
□□□□	293 Patrice Brisebois, Mont.	.30	10.00	.20
□□□□	294 Terry Ryan, Mont.	.30	8.00	.20
□□□□	295 Jocelyn Thibault (G), Mont.	.50	30.00	.20
□□□□	296 Miroslav Guren, Mont.	.30	8.00	.20
□□□□	297 Darren Turcotte, Nash.	.30	10.00	.20
□□□□	298 Sébastien Bordeleau, Nash.	.30	8.00	.20
□□□□	299 Jan Vopat, Nash.	.30	8.00	.20
□□□□	300 Blair Atcheynum, Nash (Photo Tom Fitzgerald)	.30	8.00	.20
□□□□	301 Andrew Brunette, Nash.	.30	10.00	.20
□□□□	302 Sergei Krivokrasov, Nash.	.30	10.00	.20
□□□□	303 Marian Cisar, Nash.	.30	10.00	.20
□□□□	304 Patrick Côté, Nash.	.30	8.00	.20
□□□□	305 J.J. Daigneault, Nash.	.30	10.00	.20
□□□□	306 Greg Johnson, Nash.	.30	10.00	.20
□□□□	307 Chris Terreri, NJer.	.30	10.00	.20
□□□□	308 Scott Niedermayer, NJer.	.30	20.00	.20
□□□□	309 Vadim Sharifijanov, NJer.	.30	8.00	.20
□□□□	310 Petr Sykora, NJer.	.50	30.00	.20
□□□□	311 Sergei Brylin, NJer.	.30	10.00	.20
□□□□	312 Denis Pederson, NJer.	.30	8.00	.20
□□□□	313 Bobby Holik, NJer.	.30	20.00	.20
□□□□	**314 Bryan Muir, NJer. RC**	**.50**	**15.00**	**.50**
□□□□	315 Zigmund Palffy, NYIs.	.50	45.00	.50
□□□□	316 Mike Watt, NYIs.	.30	8.00	.20
□□□□	317 Tommy Salo (G), NYIs.	.50	30.00	.20
□□□□	318 Kenny Jönsson, NYIs.	.30	15.00	.20
□□□□	319 Dmitri Nabokov, NYIs.	.30	10.00	.20
□□□□	320 John MacLean, NYRa.	.30	10.00	.20
□□□□	321 Zarley Zalapski, NYRa.	.30	8.00	.20
□□□□	322 Brian Leetch, NYRa.	.50	45.00	.50
□□□□	323 Todd Harvey, NYRa.	.30	15.00	.20
□□□□	324 Mike Richter (G), NYRa.	.50	35.00	.20
□□□□	325 Mike Knuble, NYRa.	.30	8.00	.20
□□□□	326 Jeff Beukeboom, NYRa.	.30	10.00	.20
□□□□	327 Daniel Alfredsson, Otta.	.50	45.00	.50
□□□□	328 Vaclav Prospal, Otta.	.30	20.00	.20
□□□□	329 Wade Redden, Otta.	.30	20.00	.20
□□□□	330 Igor Kravchuk, Otta.	.30	10.00	.20
□□□□	331 Andreas Dackell, Otta.	.30	10.00	.20
□□□□	**332 Maneluk, Phil. (Chic.) RC**	**.50**	**15.00**	**.50**
□□□□	333 Eric Lindros, Phil.	1.50	70.00	1.00
□□□□	334 Rod Brind'Amour, Phil.	.30	20.00	.20
□□□□	335 Colin Forbes, Phil.	.30	8.00	.20
□□□□	**336 D. Tertyshny, Phil. RC**	**.50**	**15.00**	**.50**
□□□□	337 Shjon Podein, Phil.	.30	15.00	.20
□□□□	338 Chris Therien, Phil.	.30	8.00	.20
□□□□	339 Jeremy Roenick, Phoe.	1.00	60.00	.50
□□□□	340 Jyrki Lumme, Phoe.	.30	15.00	.20
□□□□	341 Rick Tocchet, Phoe.	.30	20.00	.20
□□□□	342 Dallas Drake, Phoe.	.30	10.00	.20
□□□□	343 Keith Carney, Phoe.	.30	10.00	.20
□□□□	344 Greg Adams, Phoe.	.30	10.00	.20
□□□□	**345 Jan Hrdina, Pitt. RC**	**1.50**	**35.00**	**1.50**
□□□□	346 German Titov, Pitt.	.30	8.00	.20
□□□□	347 Stu Barnes, Pitt.	.30	8.00	.20
□□□□	348 Kevin Hatcher, Pitt.	.30	10.00	.20
□□□□	349 Martin Straka, Pitt.	.30	20.00	.20
□□□□	**350 J-S Aubin (G), Pitt. RC**	**1.50**	**35.00**	**1.50**
□□□□	351 Jeff Friesen, SanJ.	.30	20.00	.20
□□□□	352 Tony Granato, SanJ.	.30	15.00	.20
□□□□	**353 Scott Hannan, SanJ. RC**	**.50**	**15.00**	**.50**
□□□□	354 Owen Nolan, SanJ.	.50	45.00	.50
□□□□	355 Stéphane Matteau, SanJ.	.30	10.00	.20
□□□□	356 Bryan Marchment, SanJ.	.30	10.00	.20
□□□□	357 Geoff Courtnall, SLou.	.30	10.00	.20
□□□□	**358 Brent Johnson, SLou. RC**	**3.00**	**60.00**	**4.50**
□□□□	359 Jamie Rivers, SLou.	.30	8.00	.20
□□□□	360 Terry Yake, SLou.	.30	8.00	.20
□□□□	361 Jamie McLennan (G), SLou.	.30	10.00	.20
□□□□	362 Grant Fuhr (G), SLou.	.50	45.00	.50
□□□□	**363 Michal Handzus, SLou. RC**	**1.50**	**35.00**	**1.50**
□□□□	364 Bill Ranford, Tamp.	.50	30.00	.20
□□□□	365 John Cullen, Tamp.	.30	15.00	.20
□□□□	366 Craig Janney, Tamp.	.30	15.00	.20
□□□□	367 Daren Puppa (G), Tamp.	.30	15.00	.20
□□□□	**368 Pavel Kubina, Tamp. RC**	**1.00**	**20.00**	**1.00**
□□□□	369 Wendel Clark, Tamp.	1.00	60.00	.50
□□□□	370 Mats Sundin, Toro.	1.50	70.00	1.00
□□□□	371 Félix Potvin (G), Toro.	.50	45.00	.50
□□□□	**372 Danny Markov, Toro. RC**	**1.00**	**20.00**	**1.00**
□□□□	373 Derek King, Toro.	.30	10.00	.20
□□□□	374 Steve Thomas, Toro.	.30	15.00	.20
□□□□	**375 Tomas Kaberle, Toro. RC**	**2.00**	**45.00**	**2.00**
□□□□	376 Alexander Mogilny, Vanc.	.50	35.00	.20
□□□□	**377 Bill Muckalt, Vanc. RC**	**1.00**	**20.00**	**1.00**
□□□□	378 Brian Noonan, Vanc.	.30	8.00	.20
□□□□	379 Markus Näslund, Vanc.	1.50	75.00	1.00
□□□□	380 Brad May, Vanc.	.30	10.00	.20
□□□□	**381 Matt Cooke, Vanc. RC**	**1.00**	**20.00**	**1.00**
□□□□	382 Calle Johansson, Wash.	.30	15.00	.20
□□□□	383 Dale Hunter, Wash.	.30	20.00	.20
□□□□	384 Jaroslav Svejkovsky, Wash.	.30	10.00	.20
□□□□	385 Dmitri Mironov, Wash.	.30	10.00	.20
□□□□	386 Matt Herr, Wash.	.50	15.00	.50
□□□□	387 Nolan Baumgartner, Wash.	.30	8.00	.20
□□□□	388 Wayne Gretzky, NYRa.	3.00	180.00	4.00
□□□□	389 Steve Yzerman, Detr.	1.50	50.00	1.00
□□□□	390 Wayne Gretzky, NYRa.	3.00	90.00	2.00
□□□□	**391 Brian Finley (G) RC**	**1.50**	**30.00**	**3.50**
□□□□	**392 Maxime Ouellet (G) RC**	**3.00**	**60.00**	**7.50**
□□□□	**393 Kurtis Foster RC**	**1.00**	**15.00**	**1.50**
□□□□	**394 Barret Jackman RC**	**3.00**	**60.00**	**7.50**
□□□□	**395 Ross Lupaschuk RC**	**1.00**	**20.00**	**3.00**
□□□□	**396 Steven McCarthy RC**	**1.00**	**20.00**	**3.00**
□□□□	**397 Peter Reynolds RC**	**1.00**	**15.00**	**1.50**
□□□□	**398 Bart Rushmer RC**	**1.00**	**15.00**	**1.50**
□□□□	**399 Jonathon Zion RC**	**1.00**	**15.00**	**1.50**
□□□□	**400 Kris Beech RC**	**2.00**	**45.00**	**6.00**
□□□□	**401 Brandin Cote RC**	**1.00**	**15.00**	**1.50**
□□□□	**402 Scott Kelman RC**	**1.00**	**20.00**	**3.00**
□□□□	**403 Jamie Lundmark RC**	**2.00**	**45.00**	**6.00**
□□□□	**404 Derek MacKenzie RC**	**1.00**	**15.00**	**1.50**
□□□□	**405 Rory McDade RC**	**1.00**	**15.00**	**1.50**
□□□□	**406 David Morisset RC**	**1.00**	**20.00**	**3.00**
□□□□	**407 Mirko Murovic RC**	**1.00**	**15.00**	**1.50**
□□□□	**408 Taylor Pyatt RC**	**1.50**	**35.00**	**4.50**
□□□□	409 Charlie Stephens	1.00	8.00	1.50
□□□□	**410 Kyle Wanvig RC**	**1.00**	**20.00**	**3.00**
□□□□	**411 Krzystof Wieckowski RC**	**1.00**	**15.00**	**1.50**
□□□□	**412 Michael Zigomanis RC**	**1.00**	**20.00**	**3.00**
□□□□	413 Rico Fata, Calg.	1.00	15.00	1.50
□□□□	414 Vincent Lecavalier, Tamp.	3.00	70.00	6.00
□□□□	415 Chris Drury, Colo.	1.50	45.00	3.50
□□□□	**416 Oleg Kvasha, Flor. RC**	**1.00**	**20.00**	**3.00**
□□□□	417 Eric Brewer, NYIs.	1.00	30.00	2.00
□□□□	418 Josh Green, LosA.	1.00	20.00	3.00
□□□□	419 Marty Reasoner, SLou.	1.00	15.00	1.50
□□□□	420 Manny Malhotra, NYRa.	1.00	15.00	1.50

FANTASTIC FINISHERS

These inserts have three versions: the regular insert, a Quantum 1 parallel (#/1,500), a Quantum 2 parallel (#/50) and a one-of-one Quantum 3 parallel, too scarce to be priced.

Insert Set (30 cards):		**2900.00**	**135.00**	**80.00**
	Insert	**Q50**	**Q1500**	**FF**
□□□□	FF1 Wayne Gretzky, NYRa.	500.00	25.00	15.00
□□□□	FF2 Peter Bondra, Wash.	70.00	3.00	2.00
□□□□	FF3 Sergei Samsonov, Bost.	70.00	3.00	2.00
□□□□	FF4 Jaromir Jagr, Pitt.	120.00	5.00	3.00
□□□□	FF5 Brendan Shanahan, Detr.	120.00	6.00	3.00
□□□□	FF6 Joe Sakic, Colo.	200.00	10.00	6.00
□□□□	FF7 Brett Hull, Dall.	120.00	6.00	3.00
□□□□	FF8 Paul Kariya, Anah.	170.00	5.00	5.00
□□□□	FF9 Keith Tkachuk, Phoe.	70.00	3.00	2.00
□□□□	FF10 Zigmund Palffy, NYIs.	70.00	3.00	2.00
□□□□	FF11 Eric Lindros, Phil.	120.00	5.00	3.00
□□□□	FF12 Mike Modano, Dall.	120.00	6.00	3.00
□□□□	FF13 Pavel Bure, Vanc.	100.00	5.00	3.00
□□□□	FF14 Mats Sundin, Toro.	120.00	6.00	3.00
□□□□	FF15 Patrik Elias, NJer.	100.00	5.00	3.00
□□□□	FF16 Tony Amonte, Chic.	70.00	3.00	2.00
□□□□	FF17 Peter Forsberg, Colo.	170.00	5.00	5.00
□□□□	FF18 Alexei Yashin, Otta.	70.00	3.00	2.00
□□□□	FF19 Mark Recchi, Mont.	50.00	2.50	1.50
□□□□	FF20 Steve Yzerman, Detr.	300.00	15.00	9.00
□□□□	FF21 Doug Weight, Edmo.	70.00	3.00	2.00
□□□□	FF22 Jeremy Roenick, Phoe.	100.00	5.00	3.00
□□□□	FF23 Teemu Selänne, Anah.	100.00	5.00	3.00
□□□□	FF24 Owen Nolan, SanJ.	70.00	3.00	2.00
□□□□	FF25 John LeClair, Phil.	100.00	5.00	3.00
□□□□	FF26 Jason Allison, Bost.	70.00	3.00	2.00
□□□□	FF27 Mike Johnson, Toro.	25.00	2.50	1.50
□□□□	FF28 Theoren Fleury, Calg.	70.00	3.00	2.00
□□□□	FF29 Nicklas Lidström, Detr.	70.00	3.00	2.00
□□□□	FF30 Joe Nieuwendyk, Dall.	50.00	2.50	1.50

FROZEN IN TIME

These inserts have three versions: the regular insert, a Quantum 1 parallel (#/1,000), a Quantum 2 insert and a one-of-one Quantum 3 parallel, too scarce to be priced.

Insert Set (30 cards):		**5510.00**	**180.00**	**135.00**
	Player	**Q25**	**Q1000**	**FT**
□□□□	FT1 Steve Yzerman, Detr.	480.00	15.00	10.00
□□□□	FT2 Peter Forsberg, Colo.	280.00	10.00	7.00
□□□□	FT3 Sergei Samsonov, Bost.	120.00	4.00	3.00
□□□□	FT4 Martin Brodeur (G), NJer.	320.00	10.00	8.00
□□□□	FT5 Theoren Fleury, Calg.	120.00	4.00	3.00
□□□□	FT6 Paul Kariya, Anah.	280.00	10.00	5.00
□□□□	FT7 Rob Blake, LosA.	120.00	4.00	3.00
□□□□	FT8 Jari Kurri, Colo.	200.00	7.00	5.00
□□□□	FT9 Eric Lindros, Phil.	200.00	5.00	5.00
□□□□	FT10 Dominik Hasek (G), Buff.	200.00	5.00	5.00
□□□□	FT11 Patrick Roy (G), Colo.	600.00	20.00	15.00
□□□□	FT12 Saku Koivu, Mont.	160.00	6.00	4.00
□□□□	FT13 Mike Modano, Dall.	200.00	7.00	5.00
□□□□	FT14 Alexei Morozov, Pitt.	45.00	3.00	2.00
□□□□	FT15 Chris Osgood (G), Detr.	120.00	4.00	3.00
□□□□	FT16 Doug Gilmour, NJer.	120.00	4.00	3.00
□□□□	FT17 Owen Nolan, SanJ.	120.00	4.00	3.00
□□□□	FT18 Mike Johnson, Toro.	40.00	3.00	2.00
□□□□	FT19 Keith Tkachuk, AS	120.00	4.00	3.00
□□□□	FT20 Adam Oates, Wash.	80.00	3.00	2.00
□□□□	FT21 Chris Chelios, Chic.	120.00	4.00	3.00
□□□□	FT22 Brendan Shanahan, Detr.	200.00	7.00	5.00
□□□□	FT23 Joe Sakic, Colo.	320.00	10.00	8.00
□□□□	FT24 Pavel Bure, Vanc.	160.00	5.00	4.00
□□□□	FT25 Raymond Bourque, Bost.	240.00	5.00	6.00
□□□□	FT26 Ed Belfour (G), Dall.	200.00	7.00	5.00
□□□□	FT27 John LeClair, Phil.	160.00	6.00	4.00
□□□□	FT28 Teemu Selänne, Anah.	160.00	5.00	4.00
□□□□	FT29 Jaromir Jagr, AS	200.00	5.00	5.00
□□□□	FT30 Wayne Gretzky, NYRa.	800.00	30.00	20.00

GAME JERSEY

Insert Set (24 cards):		**1200.00**
	Insert	**GJ**
□	Ed Belfour (G), Chic. ✂	70.00
□	Eric Brewer, Canada ✂	30.00
□	Martin Brodeur (G), NJer. ✂	120.00
□	Doug Gilmour, Chic. ✂	40.00
□	Wayne Gretzky, NYRa. ✂	300.00
□	Dominik Hasek (G), Buff. ✂	70.00
□	Derian Hatcher, Dall. ✂	30.00
□	Bobby Hull, Chic. ✂	130.00
□	Jaromir Jagr, Pitt. ✂	70.00
□	Curtis Joseph (G) ✂	70.00
□	Darius Kasparaitis, Pitt. ✂	30.00

☐	Vincent Lecavalier ✂	70.00
☐	Roberto Luongo (G), Canada ✂	60.00
☐	Al MacInnis, Calg. ✂	30.00
☐	Manny Malhotra, Canada ✂	30.00
☐	Joe Nieuwendyk, Dall. ✂	30.00
☐	Chris Osgood (G), Detr. ✂	40.00
☐	Brendan Shanahan, Detr. ✂	70.00
☐	Mats Sundin, Toro. ✂	70.00
☐	Darryl Sydor, Dall. ✂	30.00
☐	Alex Tanguay, Canada ✂	40.00
☐	Chris Therien, Phil. ✂	30.00
☐	Daniel Tkaczuk, Canada ✂	30.00
☐	Alexei Zhamnov, Chic. ✂	30.00

GAME JERSEY SIGNED

	Insert	Auto.
☐	GJA2 Wayne Gretzky, NYRa. ✍ ✂ {#/99}	1400.00
☐	GJA Wayne Gretzky (Double Jersey)	1600.00
☐	GJA1 Bobby Hull, Winn. ✍ ✂ {#/9}	2400.00
☐	GJA3 Vincent Lecavalier, Canada ✍ ✂ {#/99}	450.00

GENERATION NEXT

These inserts have three versions: the regular insert, a Quantum 1 parallel (#/1,000), a Quantum 2 insert and a one-of-one Quantum 3 parallel, too scarce to be priced.

Insert Set (30 cards):	5200.00	440.00	115.00
Insert	Q2	Q1	GN
☐☐☐☐ GN1 Gretzky / S. Samsonov	225.00	15.00	10.00
☐☐☐☐ GN2 Gretzky / M. Hossa	500.00	35.00	10.00
☐☐☐☐ GN3 Gretzky / V. Lecavalier	750.00	70.00	10.00
☐☐☐☐ GN4 Yzerman / B. Morrison	125.00	10.00	6.00
☐☐☐☐ GN5 Yzerman / M. Reasoner	250.00	15.00	6.00
☐☐☐☐ GN6 Yzerman / M. Malhotra	375.00	40.00	6.00
☐☐☐☐ GN7 Roy / JS. Giguère	175.00	10.00	9.00
☐☐☐☐ GN8 Roy / J. Théodore	400.00	30.00	10.00
☐☐☐☐ GN9 Roy / M. Denis	500.00	50.00	8.00
☐☐☐☐ GN10 Lindros / P. Marleau	50.00	5.00	3.00
☐☐☐☐ GN11 Lindros / B. Isbister	100.00	5.00	3.00
☐☐☐☐ GN12 Lindros / J. Thornton	325.00	30.00	5.00
☐☐☐☐ GN13 Shanahan / J. Green	50.00	4.00	2.00
☐☐☐☐ GN14 Shanahan / T. Jones	100.00	5.00	2.00
☐☐☐☐ GN15 Shanahan / M. Watt	150.00	15.00	2.00
☐☐☐☐ GN16 Bourque / M. Öhlund	75.00	5.00	3.00
☐☐☐☐ GN17 Bourque / T. Poti	125.00	10.00	3.00
☐☐☐☐ GN18 Bourque / E. Brewer	225.00	25.00	4.00
☐☐☐☐ GN19 Kariya / D. Brière	75.00	5.00	4.00
☐☐☐☐ GN20 Kariya / R. Fata	150.00	10.00	4.00
☐☐☐☐ GN21 Kariya / C. Drury	300.00	30.00	5.00
☐☐☐☐ GN22 Jagr / R. Dome	50.00	3.00	2.00
☐☐☐☐ GN23 Jagr / R. Zednik	125.00	10.00	3.00
☐☐☐☐ GN24 Jagr / O. Kvasha	150.00	15.00	2.00
☐☐☐☐ GN25 Forsberg / O. Jokinen	75.00	6.00	4.00
☐☐☐☐ GN26 Forsberg / Sundström	150.00	10.00	4.00
☐☐☐☐ GN27 Forsberg / B. Morrison	250.00	25.00	4.00
☐☐☐☐ GN28 Bure / V. Sharifijanov	25.00	3.00	2.00
☐☐☐☐ GN29 Bure / D. Nabokov	75.00	5.00	2.00
☐☐☐☐ GN30 Bure / S. Samsonov	200.00	20.00	3.00

LORD STANLEY'S HEROES

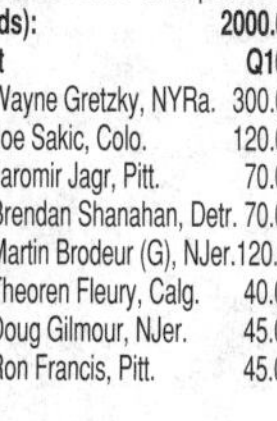

These inserts have four versions: the regular insert, a Quantum 1 parallel (#/2,000), a Quantum 2 parallel (#/100) and a one-of-one Quantum 3 parallel, too scarce to be priced.

Insert Set (30 cards):	2000.00	140.00	75.00
Insert	Q100	Q2000	LS
☐☐☐☐ LS1 Wayne Gretzky, NYRa.	300.00	20.00	12.00
☐☐☐☐ LS2 Joe Sakic, Colo.	120.00	8.00	4.00
☐☐☐☐ LS3 Jaromir Jagr, Pitt.	70.00	5.00	3.00
☐☐☐☐ LS4 Brendan Shanahan, Detr.	70.00	5.00	3.00
☐☐☐☐ LS5 Martin Brodeur (G), NJer.	120.00	8.00	4.00
☐☐☐☐ LS6 Theoren Fleury, Calg.	40.00	3.00	1.00
☐☐☐☐ LS7 Doug Gilmour, NJer.	45.00	3.00	1.00
☐☐☐☐ LS8 Ron Francis, Pitt.	45.00	3.00	1.00
☐☐☐☐ LS9 Sergei Fedorov, Detr.	70.00	5.00	3.00
☐☐☐☐ LS10 Patrick Roy (G), Colo.	220.00	15.00	9.00
☐☐☐☐ LS11 Mark Messier, NHL AS	70.00	5.00	3.00
☐☐☐☐ LS12 Peter Forsberg, Colo.	100.00	7.00	4.00
☐☐☐☐ LS13 Brian Leetch, NYRa.	45.00	3.00	1.00
☐☐☐☐ LS14 Steve Yzerman, Detr.	180.00	10.00	7.00
☐☐☐☐ LS15 Sergei Samsonov, Bost.	40.00	3.00	1.00
☐☐☐☐ LS16 Eric Lindros, Phil.	70.00	5.00	3.00
☐☐☐☐ LS17 Paul Kariya, Anah.	100.00	5.00	4.00
☐☐☐☐ LS18 Saku Koivu, Mont.	60.00	4.00	2.00
☐☐☐☐ LS19 Bryan Berard, NYIs.	20.00	2.00	1.00
☐☐☐☐ LS20 Chris Pronger, SLou.	45.00	3.00	1.00
☐☐☐☐ LS21 Keith Tkachuk, Phoe.	40.00	3.00	1.00
☐☐☐☐ LS22 Doug Weight, Edmo.	40.00	3.00	1.00
☐☐☐☐ LS23 Ed Belfour (G), Dall.	70.00	5.00	3.00
☐☐☐☐ LS24 Mats Sundin, Toro.	70.00	5.00	3.00
☐☐☐☐ LS25 John LeClair, Phil.	60.00	4.00	2.00
☐☐☐☐ LS26 Pavel Bure, Vanc.	60.00	4.00	2.00
☐☐☐☐ LS27 D. Hasek (G), Buff.	70.00	5.00	3.00
☐☐☐☐ LS28 Mike Modano, Dall.	70.00	5.00	3.00
☐☐☐☐ LS29 Curtis Joseph (G), Edmo.	70.00	5.00	3.00
☐☐☐☐ LS30 Teemu Selänne, Anah.	60.00	4.00	2.00

PROFILES

These inserts have four versions: the regular insert, a Quantum 1 parallel (#/1,500), a Quantum 2 parallel (#/50) and a one-of-one Quantum 3 parallel, too scarce to be priced.

Insert Set (30 cards):	3300.00	150.00	90.00
Insert	Q50	Q1500	P
☐☐☐☐ P1 Marty Reasoner, SLou.	30.00	2.50	1.50
☐☐☐☐ P2 Brett Hull, Dall.	120.00	6.00	3.00
☐☐☐☐ P3 Steve Yzerman, Detr.	300.00	15.00	8.00
☐☐☐☐ P4 Eric Lindros, Phil.	120.00	5.00	3.00
☐☐☐☐ P5 Eric Brewer, NYIs.	50.00	2.50	1.50
☐☐☐☐ P6 M. Brodeur (G), NJer.	200.00	10.00	6.00
☐☐☐☐ P7 Vanbiesbrouck (G), Phil.	60.00	3.00	1.50
☐☐☐☐ P8 Teemu Selänne, Anah.	100.00	5.00	3.00
☐☐☐☐ P9 Wayne Gretzky, NYRa.	500.00	25.00	15.00
☐☐☐☐ P10 Jaromir Jagr, Pitt.	120.00	5.00	2.00
☐☐☐☐ P11 Peter Forsberg, Colo.	170.00	5.00	5.00
☐☐☐☐ P12 Manny Malhotra, NYRa.	30.00	2.50	1.50
☐☐☐☐ P13 Sergei Samsonov, Bost.	70.00	3.00	2.00
☐☐☐☐ P14 Brendan Shanahan, Detr.	120.00	6.00	3.00
☐☐☐☐ P15 Doug Gilmour, Chic.	70.00	3.00	2.00
☐☐☐☐ P16 V. Lecavalier, Tamp.	120.00	6.00	3.00
☐☐☐☐ P17 D. Hasek (G), Buff.	120.00	5.00	3.00
☐☐☐☐ P18 Mike Modano, Dall.	120.00	6.00	3.00
☐☐☐☐ P19 Saku Koivu, Mont.	100.00	5.00	3.00
☐☐☐☐ P20 Curtis Joseph (G), Toro.	120.00	6.00	3.00
☐☐☐☐ P21 Paul Kariya, Anah.	170.00	5.00	4.00
☐☐☐☐ P22 Doug Weight, Edmo.	70.00	3.00	2.00
☐☐☐☐ P23 R. Bourque, Bost.	150.00	7.00	4.00
☐☐☐☐ P24 Patrick Roy (G), Colo.	370.00	15.00	10.00
☐☐☐☐ P25 John LeClair, Phil.	100.00	5.00	3.00
☐☐☐☐ P26 Chris Drury, Colo.	70.00	3.00	2.00
☐☐☐☐ P27 Theoren Fleury, Calg.	70.00	3.00	2.00
☐☐☐☐ P28 Mats Sundin, Toro.	120.00	6.00	3.00
☐☐☐☐ P29 Sergei Fedorov, Detr.	120.00	6.00	3.00
☐☐☐☐ P30 Rico Fata, Calg.	30.00	2.50	1.50

YEAR OF THE GREAT ONE

These inserts have four versions: the regular insert, a Quantum 1 parallel (#/1,999), a Quantum 2 parallel (#/99) and a one-of-one Quantum 3 parallel, too scarce to be priced. Regular cards start at $5, Quantum One singles start at $20 and Quantum Two singles start at $300.

Insert Set (30 cards):	5100.00	500.00	50.00
Gretzky Card:	200.00	20.00	2.00

☐☐☐☐ 1 Wayne Gretzky	☐☐☐☐ 2 Wayne Gretzky
☐☐☐☐ 3 Wayne Gretzky	☐☐☐☐ 4 Wayne Gretzky
☐☐☐☐ 5 Wayne Gretzky	☐☐☐☐ 6 Wayne Gretzky
☐☐☐☐ 7 Wayne Gretzky	☐☐☐☐ 8 Wayne Gretzky
☐☐☐☐ 9 Wayne Gretzky	☐☐☐☐ 10 Wayne Gretzky
☐☐☐☐ 11 Wayne Gretzky	☐☐☐☐ 12 Wayne Gretzky
☐☐☐☐ 13 Wayne Gretzky	☐☐☐☐ 14 Wayne Gretzky
☐☐☐☐ 15 Wayne Gretzky	☐☐☐☐ 16 Wayne Gretzky
☐☐☐☐ 17 Wayne Gretzky	☐☐☐☐ 18 Wayne Gretzky
☐☐☐☐ 19 Wayne Gretzky	☐☐☐☐ 20 Wayne Gretzky
☐☐☐☐ 21 Wayne Gretzky	☐☐☐☐ 22 Wayne Gretzky
☐☐☐☐ 23 Wayne Gretzky	☐☐☐☐ 24 Wayne Gretzky
☐☐☐☐ 25 Wayne Gretzky	☐☐☐☐ 26 Wayne Gretzky
☐☐☐☐ 27 Wayne Gretzky	☐☐☐☐ 28 Wayne Gretzky
☐☐☐☐ 29 Wayne Gretzky	☐☐☐☐ 30 Wayne Gretzky

1998 - 99 UPPER DECK – BUYBACKS

These signed cards were inserted into packs of 2000-01 UD Reserve.

	Buyback Autograph	UD
☐	30 Mike Modano ✍ {#/1}	
☐	38 Raymond Bourque ✍ {#/1}	
☐	104 Luc Robitaille ✍ {#/6}	
☐	135 Wayne Gretzky ✍ {#/1}	
☐	143 John LeClair ✍ {#/3}	
☐	191 Curtis Joseph (G) ✍ {#/1}	
☐	256 Mike Modano ✍ {#/8}	
☐	324 Mike Richter (G), NYRa. ✍ {#/1}	
☐	389 Steve Yzerman ✍ {#/1}	
☐	390 Wayne Gretzky ✍ {#/1}	

1998 - 99 UPPER DECK BLACK DIAMOND

These cards have four versions: the regular card, a Double Diamond parallel (#/2,000), a Triple Diamond parallel (#/1,000) and a Quadruple Diamond parallel (#/100).

Shell Set (90 cards):				35.00
Complete Set (240 cards):	3,600.00	650.00	350.00	175.00
Common Player:	8.00	2.00	.75	.25
Player	Q100	T1000	D2000	UD BD
☐☐☐☐ 1 P. Kariya, Anah.	100.00	15.00	5.00	1.50
☐☐☐☐ 2 T. Selänne, Anah.	60.00	10.00	4.00	1.00
☐☐☐☐ 3 J. Davidsson, Anah.	8.00	2.00	.75	.25
☐☐☐☐ 4 R. Bourque, Bost.	90.00	15.00	6.00	1.50
☐☐☐☐ 5 S. Samsonov, Bost.	40.00	5.00	3.00	.50
☐☐☐☐ 6 J. Allison, Bost.	40.00	5.00	3.00	.50
☐☐☐☐ 7 J. Thornton, Bost.	90.00	15.00	6.00	1.50
☐☐☐☐ 8 M. Satan, Buff.	20.00	2.00	1.50	.25
☐☐☐☐ 9 B. Holzinger, Buff.	10.00	2.00	.75	.25
☐☐☐☐ 10 D. Hasek, Buff.	70.00	10.00	5.00	1.00
☐☐☐☐ 11 R. Fata, Calg.	10.00	2.00	1.00	.25
☐☐☐☐ 12 J. Iginla, Calg.	60.00	10.00	4.00	1.00
☐☐☐☐ 13 T. Fleury, Calg.	40.00	5.00	3.00	.50
☐☐☐☐ 14 R. Francis, Caro.	40.00	5.00	3.00	.50
☐☐☐☐ 15 G. Roberts, Caro.	30.00	5.00	2.00	.50
☐☐☐☐ 16 K. Primeau, Caro.	30.00	5.00	2.00	.50
☐☐☐☐ 17 S. Kapanen, Caro.	20.00	2.00	1.50	.25
☐☐☐☐ 18 D. Gilmour, Chic.	40.00	5.00	3.00	.50
☐☐☐☐ 19 C. Chelios, Chic.	40.00	5.00	3.00	.50
☐☐☐☐ 20 T. Amonte, Chic.	40.00	5.00	3.00	.50
☐☐☐☐ 21 P. Forsberg, Colo.	100.00	15.00	7.00	1.50
☐☐☐☐ 22 P. Roy, Colo.	220.00	35.00	15.00	3.50
☐☐☐☐ 23 J. Sakic, Colo.	120.00	20.00	8.00	2.00
☐☐☐☐ 24 C. Drury, Colo.	40.00	5.00	3.00	1.50
☐☐☐☐ 25 B. Hull, Dall.	70.00	10.00	5.00	1.00
☐☐☐☐ 26 E. Belfour, Dall.	70.00	10.00	5.00	1.00
☐☐☐☐ 27 M. Modano, Dall.	70.00	10.00	5.00	1.00
☐☐☐☐ 28 D. Sydor, Dall.	10.00	2.00	1.00	.25
☐☐☐☐ 29 S. Fedorov, Detr.	70.00	10.00	5.00	1.00
☐☐☐☐ 30 S. Yzerman, Detr.	180.00	30.00	10.00	3.00
☐☐☐☐ 31 N. Lidström, Detr.	40.00	5.00	3.00	.50
☐☐☐☐ 32 C. Osgood, Detr.	40.00	5.00	3.00	.50
☐☐☐☐ 33 B. Shanahan, Detr.	70.00	10.00	5.00	1.00
☐☐☐☐ 34 D. Weight, Edmo.	40.00	5.00	3.00	.50
☐☐☐☐ 35 B. Guerin, Edmo.	30.00	5.00	2.00	.50
☐☐☐☐ 36 T. Poti, Edmo.	10.00	2.00	.75	.25
☐☐☐☐ 37 P. Bure, Flor.	60.00	10.00	4.00	1.00
☐☐☐☐ 38 M. Parrish, Flor.	60.00	10.00	4.00	2.50
☐☐☐☐ 39 Niedermayer, Flor.	10.00	2.00	1.00	.25
☐☐☐☐ **40 Rosa, LosA. RC**	**20.00**	**5.00**	**2.00**	**1.00**
☐☐☐☐ 41 R. Blake, LosA.	40.00	5.00	3.00	.50
☐☐☐☐ 42 O. Jokinen, LosA.	20.00	2.00	1.50	.25
☐☐☐☐ 43 Damphousse, Mont.	40.00	5.00	3.00	.50
☐☐☐☐ 44 M. Recchi, Mont.	30.00	5.00	2.00	.50
☐☐☐☐ 45 T. Ryan, Mont.	8.00	2.00	.75	.25
☐☐☐☐ 46 S. Koivu, Mont.	60.00	10.00	4.00	1.00
☐☐☐☐ 47 M. Dunham, Nash.	30.00	5.00	2.00	.50
☐☐☐☐ 48 Krivokrasov, Nash.	10.00	2.00	.75	.25
☐☐☐☐ 49 S. Stevens, NJer.	30.00	5.00	2.00	.50
☐☐☐☐ 50 M. Brodeur, NJer.	120.00	20.00	8.00	2.00
☐☐☐☐ 51 B. Morrison, NJer.	20.00	2.00	1.50	.25
☐☐☐☐ 52 E. Brewer, NYIs.	30.00	5.00	2.00	1.00
☐☐☐☐ 53 Z. Palffy, NYIs.	40.00	5.00	3.00	.50
☐☐☐☐ 54 F. Potvin, NYIs.	40.00	5.00	3.00	.50
☐☐☐☐ 55 Gretzky, NYRa.	300.00	50.00	20.00	5.00
☐☐☐☐ 56 B. Leetch, NYRa.	40.00	5.00	3.00	.50
☐☐☐☐ 57 M. Malhotra, NYRa.	10.00	2.00	1.00	.50
☐☐☐☐ 58 M. Richter, NYRa.	30.00	5.00	2.00	.50
☐☐☐☐ 59 A. Yashin, Otta.	40.00	5.00	3.00	.50
☐☐☐☐ 60 W. Redden, Otta.	20.00	2.00	1.50	.25
☐☐☐☐ 61 D. Alfredsson, Otta.	40.00	5.00	3.00	.50
☐☐☐☐ 62 E. Lindros, Phil.	70.00	10.00	5.00	1.00
☐☐☐☐ 63 J. LeClair, Phil.	60.00	10.00	4.00	1.00
☐☐☐☐ 64 Vanbiesbrouck, Phil.	30.00	5.00	2.00	.50
☐☐☐☐ 65 Brind'Amour, Phil.	20.00	2.00	1.50	.25
☐☐☐☐ 66 K. Tkachuk, Phoe.	40.00	5.00	3.00	.50
☐☐☐☐ 67 D. Brière, Phoe.	30.00	5.00	2.00	1.00
☐☐☐☐ 68 J. Roenick, Phoe.	60.00	10.00	4.00	1.00
☐☐☐☐ 69 J. Jagr, Pitt.	70.00	10.00	5.00	1.00
☐☐☐☐ 70 G. Titov, Pitt.	8.00	2.00	.75	.25
☐☐☐☐ 71 A. Morozov, Pitt.	10.00	2.00	1.00	.25
☐☐☐☐ 72 P. Marleau, SanJ.	30.00	5.00	2.00	.50
☐☐☐☐ 73 A. Zyuzin, SanJ.	10.00	2.00	.75	.25
☐☐☐☐ 74 M. Vernon, SanJ.	30.00	5.00	2.00	.50
☐☐☐☐ 75 O. Nolan, SanJ.	40.00	5.00	3.00	.50
☐☐☐☐ 76 Reasoner, SLou.	10.00	2.00	1.00	.50
☐☐☐☐ 77 A. MacInnis, SLou.	30.00	5.00	2.00	.50
☐☐☐☐ 78 C. Pronger, SLou.	40.00	5.00	3.00	.50
☐☐☐☐ 79 W. Clark, Tamp.	60.00	10.00	4.00	1.00
☐☐☐☐ 80 Lecavalier, Tamp.	70.00	10.00	5.00	2.50
☐☐☐☐ 81 C. Janney, Tamp.	10.00	2.00	1.00	.25
☐☐☐☐ **82 Kaberle, Toro. RC**	**40.00**	**10.00**	**4.50**	**2.00**
☐☐☐☐ 83 C. Joseph, Toro.	70.00	10.00	5.00	1.00
☐☐☐☐ 84 M. Sundin, Toro.	70.00	10.00	5.00	1.00
☐☐☐☐ 85 M. Messier, Vanc.	70.00	10.00	5.00	1.00
☐☐☐☐ **86 Muckalt, Vanc. RC**	**20.00**	**5.00**	**2.00**	**1.00**
☐☐☐☐ 87 M. Öhlund, Vanc.	20.00	2.00	1.50	.25
☐☐☐☐ 88 P. Bondra, Wash.	40.00	5.00	3.00	.50
☐☐☐☐ 89 O. Kölzig, Wash.	40.00	5.00	3.00	.50
☐☐☐☐ 90 R. Zednik, Wash.	30.00	5.00	2.00	.50

ROOKIE

Insert	Q100	T1000	D2000	UD BD
☐☐☐☐ 91 Harold Druken	20.00	3.00	3.00	2.00
☐☐☐☐ 92 R. Luongo (G)	60.00	10.00	8.00	6.00
☐☐☐☐ 93 Daniel Tkaczuk	10.00	3.00	2.50	2.00
☐☐☐☐ **94 B. Morrow RC**	**30.00**	**15.00**	**8.00**	**8.00**
☐☐☐☐ 95 Mike Van Ryn	10.00	3.00	2.50	2.00
☐☐☐☐ **96 Brian Finley RC**	**20.00**	**10.00**	**5.00**	**4.00**
☐☐☐☐ **97 Jani Rita RC**	**30.00**	**15.00**	**8.00**	**8.00**
☐☐☐☐ **98 Ilkka Mikkola RC**	**10.00**	**5.00**	**4.50**	**4.00**
☐☐☐☐ **99 Mikko Jokela RC**	**10.00**	**5.00**	**4.50**	**4.00**
☐☐☐☐ **100 T. Santala RC**	**10.00**	**5.00**	**4.50**	**4.00**
☐☐☐☐ **101 T. Virkkunen RC**	**10.00**	**5.00**	**4.50**	**4.00**
☐☐☐☐ **102 Laatikainen RC**	**10.00**	**5.00**	**4.50**	**4.00**
☐☐☐☐ **103 K. Safronov RC**	**10.00**	**5.00**	**4.50**	**4.00**
☐☐☐☐ **104 A. Volkov (G) RC**	**20.00**	**10.00**	**6.00**	**6.00**
☐☐☐☐ **105 D. Arkhipov RC**	**20.00**	**10.00**	**6.00**	**6.00**
☐☐☐☐ **106 A. Zevakhin RC**	**10.00**	**5.00**	**4.50**	**4.00**
☐☐☐☐ 107 Denis Shvidky	10.00	3.00	2.50	2.00
☐☐☐☐ 108 M. Afinogenov	30.00	5.00	4.00	3.00
☐☐☐☐ 109 Daniel Sedin	30.00	5.00	4.00	5.00
☐☐☐☐ 110 Henrik Sedin	30.00	5.00	4.00	5.00
☐☐☐☐ **111 J. Ölvestad RC**	**10.00**	**5.00**	**4.50**	**4.00**
☐☐☐☐ **112 M. Weinhandl RC**	**10.00**	**5.00**	**4.50**	**4.00**
☐☐☐☐ **113 M. Tjarnqvist RC**	**10.00**	**5.00**	**4.50**	**4.00**
☐☐☐☐ **114 J. Johansson RC**	**10.00**	**5.00**	**4.50**	**4.00**
☐☐☐☐ 115 David Legwand	30.00	5.00	4.00	3.00
☐☐☐☐ **116 B. Heisten RC**	**20.00**	**10.00**	**6.00**	**6.00**
☐☐☐☐ **117 T. Connolly RC**	**40.00**	**20.00**	**10.00**	**10.00**
☐☐☐☐ **118 A. Hilbert RC**	**20.00**	**10.00**	**6.00**	**6.00**
☐☐☐☐ **119 J. Blackburn RC**	**10.00**	**5.00**	**4.50**	**4.00**
☐☐☐☐ **120 D. Tanabe RC**	**10.00**	**5.00**	**4.50**	**4.00**

MYRIAD

These cards have a Myriad II one-of-one parallel (too scarce to be priced).

Insert Set (30 cards):	#REF!
Insert (#/1500)	M
☐☐ M1 Vincent Lecavalier, Tamp.	8.00
☐☐ M2 John Vanbiesbrouck (G), Flor.	4.00

☐ ☐	M3 Paul Kariya, Anah.	12.00
☐ ☐	M4 Keith Tkachuk, Phoe.	4.00
☐ ☐	M5 Mike Modano, Dall.	8.00
☐ ☐	M6 Dominik Hasek (G), Buff.	8.00
☐ ☐	M7 Teemu Selänne, Anah.	6.00
☐ ☐	M8 Manny Malhotra, NYRa.	4.00
☐ ☐	M9 Brendan Shanahan, Detr.	8.00
☐ ☐	M10 Pavel Bure, Flor.	6.00
☐ ☐	M11 Chris Drury, Colo.	4.00
☐ ☐	M12 Curtis Joseph (G), Toro.	8.00
☐ ☐	M13 Joe Sakic, Colo.	14.00
☐ ☐	M14 Eric Lindros, Phil.	8.00
☐ ☐	M15 Peter Bondra, Wash.	4.00
☐ ☐	M16 Brett Hull, Dall.	8.00
☐ ☐	M17 Raymond Bourque, Bost.	10.00
☐ ☐	M18 Jaromir Jagr, Pitt.	8.00
☐ ☐	M19 Steve Yzerman, Detr.	20.00
☐ ☐	M20 Mark Parrish, Flor.	4.00
☐ ☐	M21 Martin Brodeur (G), NJer.	14.00
☐ ☐	M22 Saku Koivu, Mont.	6.00
☐ ☐	M23 Patrick Roy (G), Colo.	25.00
☐ ☐	M24 John LeClair, Phil.	6.00
☐ ☐	M25 Doug Gilmour, Chic.	4.00
☐ ☐	M26 Sergei Fedorov, Detr.	8.00
☐ ☐	M27 Wayne Gretzky, NYRa.	35.00
☐ ☐	M28 Peter Forsberg, Colo.	12.00
☐ ☐	M29 Eric Brewer, NYIs.	4.00
☐ ☐	M30 Sergei Samsonov, Bost.	4.00

WINNING FORMULA

These cards have two versions: a gold card and a platinum parallel.

Insert Set (30 cards):

	Insert	WFG
☐ ☐	WF1 Paul Kariya, Anah. {#/17; #/850}	20.00
☐ ☐	WF2 Teemu Selänne, Anah. {#/52; #/2600}	4.00
☐ ☐	WF3 Sergei Samsonov, Bost. {#/22; #/1100}	8.00
☐ ☐	WF4 Dominik Hasek (G), Buff. {#/1650}	8.00
☐ ☐	WF5 Vincent Lecavalier, Tamp. {#/2200}	6.00
☐ ☐	WF6 Patrick Roy (G), Colo. {#/1550}	28.00
☐ ☐	WF7 Peter Forsberg, Colo. {#/1250}	16.00
☐ ☐	WF8 Joe Sakic, Colo. {#/1350}	18.00
☐ ☐	WF9 Ed Belfour (G), Dall. {#/1850}	8.00
☐ ☐	WF10 Brendan Shanahan, Detr. {#/1400}	10.00
☐ ☐	WF11 Steve Yzerman, Detr. {#/1200}	30.00
☐ ☐	WF12 Chris Osgood (G), Detr. {#/1650}	4.00
☐ ☐	WF13 Curtis Joseph (G), Toro. {#/1450}	10.00
☐ ☐	WF14 Manny Malhotra, NYRa. {#/800}	6.00
☐ ☐	WF15 Martin Brodeur (G), NJer. {#/2150}	10.00
☐ ☐	WF16 Chris Drury, Colo. {#/1400}	6.00
☐ ☐	WF17 Zigmund Palffy, NYIs. {#/2250}	3.00
☐ ☐	WF18 Wayne Gretzky, NYRa. {#/1150}	50.00
☐ ☐	WF19 Theoren Fleury, Calg. {#/1350}	6.00
☐ ☐	WF20 Alexei Yashin, Otta. {#/1650}	4.00
☐ ☐	WF21 Eric Lindros, Phil. {#/1500}	10.00
☐ ☐	WF22 John LeClair, Phil. {#/2550}	4.00
☐ ☐	WF23 Keith Tkachuk, Phoe. {#/2000}	4.00
☐ ☐	WF24 Mark Messier, Vanc. {#/1100}	14.00
☐ ☐	WF25 Jaromir Jagr, Pitt. {#/1750}	8.00
☐ ☐	WF26 Brett Hull, Dall. {#/1350}	10.00
☐ ☐	WF27 Mats Sundin, Toro. {#/1650}	8.00
☐ ☐	WF28 Pavel Bure, Flor. {#/2550}	4.00
☐ ☐	WF29 Peter Bondra, Wash. {#/2600}	3.00
☐ ☐	WF30 Mike Modano, Dall. {#/1050}	14.00

WINNING FORMULA PLATINUM

These cards have two versions: a gold card and a platinum parallel.

Insert Set (30 cards): 6400.00

	Platinum	WFP
☐	WF1 Paul Kariya, Anah. {#/17}	475.00
☐	WF2 Teemu Selänne, Anah. {#/52}	100.00
☐	WF3 Sergei Samsonov, Bost. {#/22; #/22}	175.00
☐	WF4 Dominik Hasek (G), Buff. {#/33}	200.00
☐	WF5 Vincent Lecavalier, Tamp. {#/44}	175.00
☐	WF6 Patrick Roy (G), Colo. {#/31}	675.00
☐	WF7 Peter Forsberg, Colo. {#/25}	350.00
☐	WF8 Joe Sakic, Colo. {#/27}	400.00
☐	WF9 Ed Belfour (G), Dall. {#/37}	200.00
☐	WF10 Brendan Shanahan, Detr. {#/28}	225.00
☐	WF11 Steve Yzerman, Detr. {#/24}	600.00
☐	WF12 Chris Osgood (G), Detr. {#/33}	100.00
☐	WF13 Curtis Joseph (G), Toro. {#/29}	225.00
☐	WF14 Manny Malhotra, NYRa. {#/16}	100.00
☐	WF15 Martin Brodeur (G), NJer. {#/43}	275.00
☐	WF16 Chris Drury, Colo. {#/28}	125.00
☐	WF17 Zigmund Palffy, NYIs. {#/45}	100.00
☐	WF18 Wayne Gretzky, NYRa. {#/23}	1000.00
☐	WF19 Theoren Fleury, Calg. {#/27}	150.00
☐	WF20 Alexei Yashin, Otta. {#/33}	100.00
☐	WF21 Eric Lindros, Phil. {#/30}	225.00
☐	WF22 John LeClair, Phil. {#/51}	100.00
☐	WF23 Keith Tkachuk, Phoe. {#/40}	100.00
☐	WF24 Mark Messier, Vanc. {#/22}	300.00
☐	WF25 Jaromir Jagr, Pitt. {#/35}	200.00
☐	WF26 Brett Hull, Dall. {#/27}	250.00
☐	WF27 Mats Sundin, Toro. {#/33}	200.00
☐	WF28 Pavel Bure, Flor. {#/51}	100.00
☐	WF29 Peter Bondra, Wash. {#/52}	75.00
☐	WF30 Mike Modano, Dall. {#/21}	300.00

YEAR OF THE GREAT ONE

Gretzky Card: 300.00

☐	1 W. Gretzky	☐	2 W. Gretzky
☐	3 W. Gretzky	☐	4 W. Gretzky
☐	5 W. Gretzky	☐	6 W. Gretzky
☐	7 W. Gretzky	☐	8 W. Gretzky
☐	9 W. Gretzky	☐	10 W. Gretzky
☐	11 W. Gretzky	☐	12 W. Gretzky
☐	13 W. Gretzky	☐	14 W. Gretzky
☐	15 W. Gretzky	☐	16 W. Gretzky
☐	17 W. Gretzky	☐	18 W. Gretzky
☐	19 W. Gretzky	☐	20 W. Gretzky
☐	21 W. Gretzky	☐	22 W. Gretzky
☐	23 W. Gretzky	☐	24 W. Gretzky
☐	25 W. Gretzky	☐	26 W. Gretzky
☐	27 W. Gretzky	☐	28 W. Gretzky
☐	29 W. Gretzky	☐	30 W. Gretzky
☐	31 W. Gretzky	☐	32 W. Gretzky
☐	33 W. Gretzky	☐	34 W. Gretzky
☐	35 W. Gretzky	☐	36 W. Gretzky
☐	37 W. Gretzky	☐	38 W. Gretzky
☐	39 W. Gretzky	☐	40 W. Gretzky
☐	41 W. Gretzky	☐	42 W. Gretzky
☐	43 W. Gretzky	☐	44 W. Gretzky
☐	45 W. Gretzky	☐	46 W. Gretzky
☐	47 W. Gretzky	☐	48 W. Gretzky
☐	49 W. Gretzky	☐	50 W. Gretzky
☐	51 W. Gretzky	☐	52 W. Gretzky
☐	53 W. Gretzky	☐	54 W. Gretzky
☐	55 W. Gretzky	☐	56 W. Gretzky
☐	57 W. Gretzky	☐	58 W. Gretzky
☐	59 W. Gretzky	☐	60 W. Gretzky
☐	61 W. Gretzky	☐	62 W. Gretzky
☐	63 W. Gretzky	☐	64 W. Gretzky
☐	65 W. Gretzky	☐	66 W. Gretzky
☐	67 W. Gretzky	☐	68 W. Gretzky
☐	69 W. Gretzky	☐	70 W. Gretzky
☐	71 W. Gretzky	☐	72 W. Gretzky
☐	73 W. Gretzky	☐	74 W. Gretzky
☐	75 W. Gretzky	☐	76 W. Gretzky
☐	77 W. Gretzky	☐	78 W. Gretzky
☐	79 W. Gretzky	☐	80 W. Gretzky
☐	81 W. Gretzky	☐	82 W. Gretzky
☐	83 W. Gretzky	☐	84 W. Gretzky
☐	85 W. Gretzky	☐	86 W. Gretzky
☐	87 W. Gretzky	☐	88 W. Gretzky
☐	89 W. Gretzky	☐	90 W. Gretzky
☐	91 W. Gretzky	☐	92 W. Gretzky
☐	93 W. Gretzky	☐	94 W. Gretzky
☐	95 W. Gretzky	☐	96 W. Gretzky
☐	97 W. Gretzky	☐	98 W. Gretzky
☐	99 W. Gretzky		

1998 - 99 UPPER DECK ELITSERIEN

NHL and regional stars sometimes sell at a premium (usually $1-2).

Complete Set (225 cards): 40.00

Common Player: .30

	Player	Card
☐	1 Jonas Forsberg (G), AIK Stockholm	.50
☐	2 Rikard Franzén, AIK Stockholm	.30
☐	3 Mathias Svedberg, AIK Stockholm	.30
☐	4 Dick Tärnström, AIK Stockholm	.30
☐	5 Jan Sandström, AIK Stockholm	.30
☐	6 Johan Silfwerplatz, AIK Stockholm	.30
☐	7 Henrik Tallinder, AIK Stockholm	.50
☐	8 Stefan Gustavson, AIK Stockholm	.30
☐	9 Kristian Gahn, AIK Stockholm	.30
☐	10 Björn Ahlström, AIK Stockholm	.30
☐	11 Peter Hammarström, AIK Stockholm	.30
☐	12 Anders Gozzi, AIK Stockholm	.30
☐	13 Fredrik Krekula, AIK Stockholm	.30
☐	14 Erik Norbäck, AIK Stockholm	.30
☐	15 Niklas Anger, AIK Stockholm	.30
☐	16 Mats Lindberg, AIK Stockholm	.30
☐	17 Jörgen Wikström, Björklöven	.30
☐	18 Per-Anton Lundström, Björklöven	.30
☐	19 Mattias Hedlund, Björklöven	.30
☐	20 Jörgen Hermansson, Björklöven	.30
☐	21 Fredrik Bergqvist, Björklöven	.30
☐	22 Joakim Lidgren, Björklöven	.30
☐	23 Robert Karlsson, Björklöven	.30
☐	24 Christian Lechtaler, Björklöven	.30
☐	25 Aleksandrs Belyavski, Björklöven	.30
☐	26 Jens Öhman, Björklöven	.30
☐	27 Stefan Öhman, Björklöven	.30
☐	28 Martin Wiita, Björklöven	.30
☐	29 Johan Ramstedt, Björklöven	.30
☐	30 Per Ledin, Björklöven	.30
☐	31 Jukka Penttinen, Björklöven	.30
☐	32 Aleksandrs Semjonovs, Björklöven	.30
☐	33 Johan Holmqvist (G), Brynäs Gavle	4.00
☐	34 Tommy Melkersson, Brynäs Gavle	.30
☐	35 Marko Tuulola, Brynäs Gavle	.30
☐	36 Johan Hansson, Brynäs Gavle	.30
☐	37 Pår Djoos, Brynäs Gavle	.30
☐	38 Per Löfström, Brynäs Gavle	.30
☐	39 Niclas Wallin, Brynäs Gavle	1.00
☐	40 Roger Kyrö, Brynäs Gavle	.30
☐	41 Ove Molin, Brynäs Gavle	.30
☐	42 Stefan Lundqvist, Brynäs Gavle	.30
☐	43 Peter Nylander, Brynäs Gavle	.30
☐	44 Jan Larsson, Brynäs Gavle	.30
☐	45 Teppo Kivelä, Brynäs Gavle	.30
☐	46 Tom Bissett, Brynäs Gavle	.30
☐	47 Anders Huss, Brynäs Gavle	.30
☐	48 Mikko Luovi, Brynäs Gavle	.30
☐	49 Tommy Söderström, Djugårdens	.50
☐	50 Björn Nord, Djugårdens	.30
☐	51 Ronnie Pettersson, Djugårdens	.30
☐	52 Thomas Johansson, Djugårdens	.30
☐	53 Daniel Tjärnqvist, Djugårdens	.50
☐	54 Anders Myrvold, Djugårdens	.50
☐	55 Mikael Magnusson, Djugårdens	.30
☐	56 Mikael Johansson, Djugårdens	.30
☐	57 Nichlas Falk, Djugårdens	.30
☐	58 Mikael Håkansson, Djurgården	.30
☐	59 Charles Berglund, Djugårdens	.30
☐	60 Lars-Göran Wiklander, Djugårdens	.30
☐	61 Per Eklund, Djugårdens	.30
☐	62 Jan Viktorsson, Djugårdens	.30
☐	63 Patrik Erickson, Djugårdens	.30
☐	64 Espen (Shampoo) Knutsen, Djugårdens	.30
☐	65 Jimmie Ölvestad, Djugårdens	1.00
☐	66 Mikael Sandberg, Vastra Frölunda	.30
☐	67 Christer Olsson, Vastra Frölunda	.50
☐	68 Petter Nilsson, Vastra Frölunda	.30
☐	69 Magnus Johansson, Vastra Frölunda	.30
☐	70 Ronnie Sundin, Vastra Frölunda	.30
☐	71 Radek Hamr, Vastra Frölunda	.50
☐	72 Stefan Larsson, Vastra Frölunda	.30
☐	73 Mattias Nilimaa, Vastra Frölunda	.30
☐	74 Linus Fagemo, Vastra Frölunda	.30
☐	75 Marko Jantunen, Vastra Frölunda	.30
☐	76 Patrik Carnbäck, Vastra Frölunda	.50
☐	77 Peter Berndtsson, Vastra Frölunda	.30
☐	78 Mikael Samuelsson, Vastra Frölunda	1.00
☐	79 Peter Ström, Vastra Frölunda	.30
☐	80 Pår Edlund, Vastra Frölunda	.30
☐	81 Henrik Nilsson, Vastra Frölunda	.30
☐	82 Jonas Johnsson, Vastra Frölunda	.30
☐	83 Kimmo Lecklin, Färjestads	.30
☐	84 Roger Johansson, Färjestads	.50
☐	85 Sergei Fokin, Färjestads	.30
☐	86 Greger Artursson, Färjestads	.30
☐	87 Jonas Elofsson, Färjestads	.30
☐	88 Peter Jakobsson, Färjestads	.30
☐	89 Dimitri Erofeev, Färjestads	.30
☐	90 Patrik Zetterberg, Färjestads	.30
☐	91 Niklas Sjökvist, Färjestads	.30
☐	92 Trond Magnussen, Färjestads	.30
☐	93 Peter Hagström, Färjestads	.30
☐	94 Pelle Prestberg, Färjestads	.30
☐	95 Mathias Johansson, Färjestads	.30
☐	96 Mikael Holmqvist, Färjestads	.30
☐	97 Clas Eriksson, Färjestads	.30
☐	98 Kristian Huselius, Färjestads	8.00
☐	99 Jörgen Jönsson, Färjestads	1.00
☐	100 Kari Takko, HV 71 Jonkoping	.50
☐	101 David Petrasek, HV 71 Jonkoping	.30
☐	102 Daniel Johansson, HV 71 Jonkoping	.50
☐	103 Per* Gustafsson, HV 71 Jonkoping	.50
☐	104 Fredrik Stillman, HV 71 Jonkoping	.30
☐	105 Niklas Rahm, HV 71 Jonkoping	.30
☐	106 Mikael Lindman, HV 71 Jonkoping	.30
☐	107 Jerry Persson, HV 71 Jonkoping	.30
☐	108 Esa Keskinen, HV 71 Jonkoping	.30
☐	109 Peter Ekelund, HV 71 Jonkoping	.30
☐	110 Antti Törmänen, HV 71 Jonkoping	.50
☐	111 Marcus Kristoffersson, HV 71 Jonkoping	.30
☐	112 Anders Huusko, HV 71 Jonkoping	.30
☐	113 Erik Huusko, HV 71 Jonkoping	.30
☐	114 Johan Lindbom, HV 71 Jonkoping	.30
☐	115 Jarkko Varvio, HV 71 Jonkoping	1.00
☐	116 Ulf Dahlén, HV 71 Jonkoping	.50
☐	117 Johan Hedberg (G), Leksand	5.00
☐	118 Jan Huokko, Leksand	.30
☐	119 Torbjörn Johansson, Leksand	.30
☐	120 Hans Lodin, Leksand	.30
☐	121 Nicklas Nordquist, Leksand	.30
☐	122 Stefan Bergkvist, Leksand	.50
☐	123 Magnus Svensson, Leksand	.50
☐	124 Andreas Karlsson, Leksand	.50
☐	125 Per-Erik (Pelle) Eklund, Leksand	.50
☐	126 Anders Carlsson, Leksand	.30
☐	127 Niklas Eriksson, Leksand	.30
☐	128 Stefan Hellkvist, Leksand	.30
☐	129 Jens Nielsen, Leksand	.30
☐	130 Anders Lönn, Leksand	.30
☐	131 Markus Åkerblom, Leksand	.30
☐	132 Mikael Karlberg, Leksand	.30
☐	133 Jarmo Myllys, Luleå	.50
☐	134 Stefan Jönsson, Luleå	.30
☐	135 Osmo Soutukorva, Luleå	.30
☐	136 Johan Finnström, Luleå	.30
☐	137 Roger Åkerström, Luleå	.30
☐	138 Igor Matushkin, Luleå	.30
☐	139 Jonas Rönnqvist, Luleå	.50
☐	140 Thomas Sjögren, Luleå	.30
☐	141 Tomas Berglund, Luleå	.30
☐	142 Mikael Lövgren, Luleå	.30
☐	143 Anders Burström, Luleå	.30
☐	144 Jörgen Bemström, Luleå	.30
☐	145 Martin Hostak, Luleå	.50
☐	146 Bert-Olav Karlsson, Luleå	.30
☐	147 Lars Edström, Luleå	.30
☐	148 Jiri Kucera, Luleå	.30
☐	149 Andrew Verner, Malmö Redhawks	.50
☐	150 Kim Johnsson, Malmö Redhawks	.50
☐	151 Kari Harila, Malmö Redhawks	.30
☐	152 Niclas Hävelid, Malmö Redhawks	.50
☐	153 Jesper Damgaard, Malmö Redhawks	.30
☐	154 Johan Tornberg, Malmö Redhawks	.30
☐	155 Mats Lusth, Malmö Redhawks	.30
☐	156 Jan Hammar, Malmö Redhawks	.30
☐	157 Marcus Magnertoft, Malmö Redhawks	.30
☐	158 Marcus Thuresson, Malmö Redhawks	.30
☐	159 Magnus Nilsson, Malmö Redhawks	.30
☐	160 Mikael Lindholm, Malmö Redhawks	.30
☐	161 Patrik Sylvegård, Malmö Redhawks	.30
☐	162 Juha Riihijärvi, Malmö Redhawks	.30
☐	163 Jesper Mattsson, Malmö Redhawks	.50
☐	164 Niklas Sundblad, Malmö Redhawks	.50
☐	165 Toivo Suursoo, Malmö Redhawks	.30
☐	166 Petter Rönnquist, MoDo Hockey	.30
☐	167 Pierre Hedin, MoDo Hockey	.30
☐	168 Per Hållberg, MoDo Hockey	.30
☐	169 Jan-Axel Alavaara, MoDo Hockey	.30
☐	170 Hans Jonsson, MoDo Hockey	.50
☐	171 Lars Jansson, MoDo Hockey	.30
☐	172 Frantisek* Kaberle, MoDo Hockey	.50
☐	173 Andreas Salomonsson, MoDo Hockey	.50
☐	174 Magnus Wernblom, MoDo Hockey	.30
☐	175 Mikael Pettersson, MoDo Hockey	.30
☐	176 Per Svartvadet, MoDo Hockey	.50
☐	177 Daniel Sedin, MoDo Hockey	2.00
☐	178 Henrik Sedin, MoDo Hockey	2.00
☐	179 Jan Alinic, MoDo Hockey	.30
☐	180 Samuel Påhlsson, MoDo Hockey	.50
☐	181 Anders Söderberg, MoDo Hockey	.50
☐	182 Magnus Eriksson, Västerås	.30
☐	183 Andrei Lulin, Västerås	.30
☐	184 Jakob Karlsson, Västerås	.50
☐	185 Patrik Höglund, Västerås	.30
☐	186 Joakim Lundberg, Västerås	.30
☐	187 Arto Blomsten, Västerås	.30
☐	188 Mattias Lööf, Västerås	.30
☐	189 Mikael Pettersson, Västerås	.30
☐	190 Joakim Backlund, Västerås	.30
☐	191 Daniel Rydmark, Västerås	.30
☐	192 Johan Molin, Västerås	.30
☐	193 Paul Andersson-Everberg, Västerås	.30
☐	194 Henrik Nordfeldt, Västerås	.30
☐	195 Jonas Olsson, Västerås	.30
☐	196 Fredrik Öberg, Västerås	.30
☐	197 Roger Rosén, Västerås	.30
☐	198 Roland Stoltz	.30
☐	199 Lars Björn	.30
☐	200 Ulf Sterner	.30
☐	201 Leif Holmqvist	.30
☐	202 Hans Mild	.30
☐	203 Bert-Ola Nordlander	.30

☐	204 Eilert Määttä	.30
☐	205 Ronnie Pettersson	.30
☐	206 Tord Lundström	.30
☐	207 Lennart (Lill-Strimma) Svedberg	.30
☐	208 Roland Stoltz	.30
☐	209 Eilert Määttä	.30
☐	210 Lennart (Lill-Strimma) Svedberg	.30
☐	211 Tord Lundström	.30
☐	212 Leif Holmqvist	.30
☐	213 Magnus Nilsson, Sweden Juniors	.30
☐	214 Mikael Holmqvist, Sweden Juniors	.30
☐	215 Mattias Karlin, Sweden Juniors	.30
☐	216 Pierre Hedin, Sweden Juniors	.30
☐	217 Henrik Petré, Sweden Juniors	.30
☐	218 Johan Forsander, Sweden Juniors	.30
☐	219 Daniel Sedin, Sweden Juniors	2.00
☐	220 Henrik Sedin, Sweden Juniors	2.00
☐	221 Marcus Nilson, Sweden Juniors	.50
☐	222 Checklist	.30
☐	223 Checklist	.30
☐	224 Checklist	.30
☐	225 Checklist	.30

GAME JERSEY

☐	GJ1 Daniel Sedin ✂ / Henrik Sedin ✂	150.00
☐	GJ1 Daniel Sedin ✂ ✍ / Henrik Sedin ✂ ✍	500.00

A DAY IN THE LIFE

We have no pricing information on these singles.

	Player	NRMT-MT
☐	DL01 Rikard Franzén	1.00
☐	DL02 Pår Djoos	2.00
☐	DL03 Tommy Söderström (G)	2.00
☐	DL04 Pelle Prestberg	1.00
☐	DL05 Esa Keskinen	1.00
☐	DL06 Johan Hedberg (G)	6.00
☐	DL07 Jarmo Myllys (G)	2.00
☐	DL08 Marcus Thuresson	1.00
☐	DL09 Samuel Påhlsson	2.00
☐	DL10 Christer Olsson	1.00

1998 - 99 UPPER DECK GOLD RESERVE

Please see 1998 - 99 Upper Deck & Upper Deck Gold Reserve for base checklist and price guide.

INSERTS

	Player	Insert
☐	Wayne Gretzky Autograph ✍	1000.00
☐	Steve Yzerman Autograph ✍	600.00
☐	Wayne Gretzky Stick ✂	600.00
☐	Steve Yzerman Stick ✂	400.00
☐	Wayne Gretzky Stick ✂ Signed ✍ {#/99}	1400.00
☐	Steve Yzerman Stick ✂ Signed ✍ {#/19}	2000.00

1998 - 99 UPPER DECK GRETZKY RETIREMENT

Complete Set (16 cards):		25.00
	Player	3.5x5
☐	D1 Wayne Gretzky	3.00
☐	D2 Wayne Gretzky	3.00
☐	D3 Wayne Gretzky	3.00
☐	D4 Wayne Gretzky	3.00
☐	D5 Wayne Gretzky	3.00
☐	D6 Wayne Gretzky	3.00
☐	D7 Wayne Gretzky	3.00
☐	D8 Wayne Gretzky	3.00
☐	D9 Wayne Gretzky	3.00
☐	D10 Wayne Gretzky	3.00
☐	D11 Wayne Gretzky	3.00
☐	D12 Wayne Gretzky	3.00
☐	D13 Wayne Gretzky	3.00
☐	D14 Wayne Gretzky	3.00
☐	D15 Wayne Gretzky	3.00
☐	D16 Wayne Gretzky	4.00

1998 - 99 UPPER DECK MVP

These cards have four versions: the regular card, a Silver Script parallel (1:6), a Gold script parallel (#/100) and a Super Script parallel (#/25).

		SS25	GS100	Sil.	Reg.
Complete Set (220 cards):		**1200.00**	**500.00**	**.00**	**.00**
Common Player:		**15.00**	**8.00**	**.50**	**.20**
	Player	**SS25**	**GS100**	**Sil.**	**Reg.**
☐☐☐☐	1 P. Kariya, Anah.	170.00	80.00	1.50	.50
☐☐☐☐	2 T. Selänne, Anah.	100.00	50.00	1.00	.50
☐☐☐☐	3 T. Sandström, Anah.	30.00	15.00	.50	.20
☐☐☐☐	4 J. Davidsson, Anah.	15.00	8.00	.50	.20
☐☐☐☐	**5 Crowley, Anah. RC**	**15.00**	**8.00**	**.50**	**.50**
☐☐☐☐	6 G. Hebert, Anah.	30.00	15.00	.50	.20
☐☐☐☐	7 M. McInnis, Anah.	20.00	10.00	.50	.20
☐☐☐☐	8 S. Rucchin, Anah.	30.00	15.00	.50	.20
☐☐☐☐	9 R. Bourque, Bost.	150.00	70.00	1.50	.50
☐☐☐☐	10 S. Samsonov, Bost.	70.00	35.00	.50	.20
☐☐☐☐	11 C. Mann, Bost.	20.00	10.00	.50	.20
☐☐☐☐	12 J. Thornton, Bost.	150.00	75.00	1.50	.50
☐☐☐☐	13 J. Allison, Bost.	70.00	35.00	.50	.20
☐☐☐☐	14 B. Dafoe, Bost.	50.00	25.00	.50	.20
☐☐☐☐	15 K. McLaren, Bost.	30.00	15.00	.50	.20
☐☐☐☐	16 D. Khristich, Bost.	20.00	10.00	.50	.20
☐☐☐☐	17 H. Gill, Bost.	15.00	8.00	.50	.20
☐☐☐☐	18 A. Carter, Bost.	50.00	25.00	.50	.20
☐☐☐☐	19 M. Satan, Buff.	40.00	20.00	.50	.20
☐☐☐☐	20 B. Holzinger, Buff.	20.00	10.00	.50	.20
☐☐☐☐	21 D. Hasek, Buff.	120.00	60.00	1.00	.50
☐☐☐☐	22 M. Barnaby, Buff.	15.00	8.00	.50	.20
☐☐☐☐	23 E. Rasmussen, Buff.	30.00	15.00	.50	.20
☐☐☐☐	24 G. Sanderson, Buff.	30.00	15.00	.50	.20
☐☐☐☐	25 M. Grosek, Buff.	15.00	8.00	.50	.20
☐☐☐☐	26 M. Peca, Buff.	50.00	25.00	.50	.20
☐☐☐☐	27 R. Fata, Calg.	30.00	15.00	.50	.20
☐☐☐☐	28 D. Morris, Calg.	30.00	15.00	.50	.20
☐☐☐☐	29 P. Housley, Calg.	40.00	20.00	.50	.20
☐☐☐☐	30 V. Bure, Calg.	40.00	20.00	.50	.20
☐☐☐☐	31 E. Ward, Calg.	15.00	8.00	.50	.20
☐☐☐☐	32 J. Giguère, Calg.	100.00	50.00	1.00	.50
☐☐☐☐	33 J. Shantz, Calg.	15.00	8.00	.50	.20
☐☐☐☐	34 J. Iginla, Calg.	100.00	50.00	1.00	.50
☐☐☐☐	35 R. Francis, Caro.	70.00	35.00	.50	.20
☐☐☐☐	36 T. Kidd, Caro.	40.00	20.00	.50	.20
☐☐☐☐	37 K. Primeau, Caro.	50.00	25.00	.50	.20
☐☐☐☐	38 S. Kapanen, Caro.	40.00	20.00	.50	.20
☐☐☐☐	39 M. Gélinas, Caro.	30.00	15.00	.50	.20
☐☐☐☐	40 J. O'Neill, Caro.	50.00	25.00	.50	.20
☐☐☐☐	41 G. Roberts, Caro.	50.00	25.00	.50	.20
☐☐☐☐	42 J. Thibault, Chic.	50.00	25.00	.50	.20
☐☐☐☐	43 D. Gilmour, Chic.	70.00	35.00	.50	.20
☐☐☐☐	44 C. Chelios, Chic.	70.00	35.00	.50	.20
☐☐☐☐	45 T. Amonte, Chic.	70.00	35.00	.50	.20
☐☐☐☐	46 B. Probert, Chic.	40.00	20.00	.50	.20
☐☐☐☐	47 D. Cleary, Chic.	40.00	20.00	.50	.20
☐☐☐☐	48 É. Dazé, Chic.	50.00	25.00	.50	.20
☐☐☐☐	**49 Maneluk, Chic. RC**	**15.00**	**8.00**	**.50**	**.50**
☐☐☐☐	50 R. Royer, Chic.	15.00	8.00	.50	.20
☐☐☐☐	51 P. Forsberg, Colo.	170.00	80.00	1.50	.50
☐☐☐☐	52 P. Roy, Colo.	370.00	180.00	3.50	1.50
☐☐☐☐	53 J. Sakic, Colo.	200.00	100.00	2.00	1.00
☐☐☐☐	54 C. Drury, Colo.	70.00	35.00	1.00	.50
☐☐☐☐	**55 Hejduk, Colo. RC**	**100.00**	**50.00**	**4.00**	**4.00**
☐☐☐☐	56 G. de Vries, Colo.	20.00	10.00	.50	.20
☐☐☐☐	57 T. Fleury, Colo.	70.00	30.00	.50	.20
☐☐☐☐	58 A. Deadmarsh, Colo.	40.00	20.00	.50	.20
☐☐☐☐	59 B. Hull, Dall.	120.00	60.00	1.00	.50
☐☐☐☐	60 E. Belfour, Dall.	120.00	60.00	1.00	.50
☐☐☐☐	61 M. Modano, Dall.	120.00	60.00	1.00	.50
☐☐☐☐	62 D. Sydor, Dall.	30.00	15.00	.50	.20
☐☐☐☐	63 J. Nieuwendyk, Dall.	50.00	25.00	.50	.20
☐☐☐☐	64 G. Marshall, Dall.	20.00	10.00	.50	.20
☐☐☐☐	65 S. Zubov, Dall.	30.00	15.00	.50	.20
☐☐☐☐	66 D. Hatcher, Dall.	40.00	20.00	.50	.20
☐☐☐☐	67 J. Lehtinen, Dall.	40.00	20.00	.50	.20
☐☐☐☐	68 S. Fedorov, Detr.	120.00	60.00	1.00	.50
☐☐☐☐	69 S. Yzerman, Detr.	300.00	150.00	3.00	1.50
☐☐☐☐	70 N. Lidström, Detr.	70.00	35.00	.50	.20
☐☐☐☐	71 C. Osgood, Detr.	70.00	35.00	.50	.20
☐☐☐☐	72 B. Shanahan, Detr.	120.00	60.00	1.00	.50
☐☐☐☐	73 D. McCarty, Detr.	40.00	20.00	.50	.20
☐☐☐☐	74 T. Holmström, Detr.	30.00	15.00	.50	.20
☐☐☐☐	**75 Maracle, Detr. RC**	**20.00**	**10.00**	**.50**	**.50**
☐☐☐☐	76 D. Brown, Detr.	15.00	8.00	.50	.20
☐☐☐☐	77 D. Weight, Edmo.	70.00	35.00	.50	.20
☐☐☐☐	78 J. Niinimaa, Edmo.	30.00	15.00	.50	.20
☐☐☐☐	79 T. Poti, Edmo.	20.00	10.00	.50	.20
☐☐☐☐	80 B. Guerin, Edmo.	50.00	25.00	.50	.20
☐☐☐☐	81 M. Grier, Edmo.	30.00	15.00	.50	.20
☐☐☐☐	82 R. Smyth, Edmo.	60.00	30.00	.50	.20
☐☐☐☐	83 R. Hamrlik, Edmo.	30.00	15.00	.50	.20
☐☐☐☐	84 K. Brown, Edmo.	15.00	8.00	.50	.20
☐☐☐☐	85 P. Bure, Flor.	100.00	50.00	1.00	.50
☐☐☐☐	**86 Spacek, Flor. RC**	**15.00**	**8.00**	**.50**	**.50**
☐☐☐☐	87 Niedermayer, Flor.	30.00	15.00	.50	.20
☐☐☐☐	88 R. Svehla, Flor.	30.00	15.00	.50	.20
☐☐☐☐	89 R. Whitney, Flor.	30.00	15.00	.50	.20
☐☐☐☐	**90 P. Worrell, Flor. RC**	**30.00**	**15.00**	**1.00**	**1.00**
☐☐☐☐	91 M. Parrish, Flor.	50.00	25.00	2.00	1.00
☐☐☐☐	**92 Kvasha, Flor. RC**	**20.00**	**10.00**	**.50**	**.50**
☐☐☐☐	93 S. Duchesne, LosA.	30.00	15.00	.50	.20
☐☐☐☐	94 R. Blake, LosA.	70.00	35.00	.50	.20
☐☐☐☐	95 O. Jokinen, LosA.	40.00	20.00	.50	.20
☐☐☐☐	96 D. Audette, LosA.	50.00	25.00	.50	.20
☐☐☐☐	97 L. Robitaille, LosA.	100.00	50.00	1.00	.50
☐☐☐☐	98 J. Green, LosA.	20.00	10.00	.50	.50
☐☐☐☐	99 P. Boucher, LosA.	15.00	8.00	.50	.20
☐☐☐☐	100 M. Johnson, LosA.	15.00	8.00	.50	.20
☐☐☐☐	101 Damphousse, Mont.	70.00	35.00	.50	.20
☐☐☐☐	102 D. Zubrus, Mont.	30.00	15.00	.50	.20
☐☐☐☐	103 T. Ryan, Mont.	15.00	8.00	.50	.20
☐☐☐☐	104 S. Koivu, Mont.	100.00	50.00	1.00	.50
☐☐☐☐	**105 B. Clark, Mont. RC**	**15.00**	**8.00**	**.50**	**.50**
☐☐☐☐	**106 Morissette, Mont. RC**	**15.00**	**8.00**	**.50**	**.50**
☐☐☐☐	107 E. Weinrich, Mont.	15.00	8.00	.50	.20
☐☐☐☐	108 B. Savage, Mont.	40.00	20.00	.50	.20
☐☐☐☐	109 S. Corson, Mont.	40.00	20.00	.50	.20
☐☐☐☐	110 M. Dunham, Nash.	50.00	25.00	.50	.20
☐☐☐☐	111 G. Johnson, Nash.	20.00	10.00	.50	.20
☐☐☐☐	112 C. Ronning, Nash.	30.00	15.00	.50	.20
☐☐☐☐	113 A. Brunette, Nash.	20.00	10.00	.50	.20
☐☐☐☐	114 Krivokrasov, Nash.	20.00	10.00	.50	.20
☐☐☐☐	115 S. Bordeleau, Nash.	15.00	8.00	.50	.20
☐☐☐☐	116 S. Stevens, NJer.	50.00	25.00	.50	.20
☐☐☐☐	117 Brodeur, NJer.	200.00	100.00	2.00	1.00
☐☐☐☐	118 B. Morrison, NJer.	40.00	20.00	.50	.20
☐☐☐☐	119 P. Elias, NJer.	100.00	50.00	1.00	.50
☐☐☐☐	120 Niedermayer, NJer.	40.00	20.00	.50	.20
☐☐☐☐	121 B. Holik, NJer.	40.00	20.00	.50	.20
☐☐☐☐	122 J. Arnott, NJer.	60.00	30.00	.50	.20
☐☐☐☐	123 J. Pandolfo, NJer.	20.00	10.00	.50	.20
☐☐☐☐	124 E. Brewer, NYIs.	50.00	25.00	.50	.50
☐☐☐☐	125 Z. Palffy, NYIs.	70.00	35.00	.50	.20
☐☐☐☐	126 F. Potvin, NYIs.	70.00	35.00	.50	.20
☐☐☐☐	127 R. Reichel, NYIs.	40.00	20.00	.50	.20
☐☐☐☐	128 M. Watt, NYIs.	15.00	8.00	.50	.20
☐☐☐☐	129 T. Salo, NYIs.	50.00	25.00	.50	.20
☐☐☐☐	130 K. Jönsson, NYIs.	20.00	10.00	.50	.20
☐☐☐☐	131 T. Linden, NYIs.	50.00	25.00	.50	.20
☐☐☐☐	132 Gretzky, NYRa.	500.00	250.00	5.00	2.50
☐☐☐☐	133 B. Leetch, NYRa.	70.00	35.00	.50	.20
☐☐☐☐	134 M. Malhotra, NYRa.	30.00	15.00	.50	.20
☐☐☐☐	135 M. Richter, NYRa.	60.00	30.00	.50	.20
☐☐☐☐	136 M. Knuble, NYRa.	15.00	8.00	.50	.20
☐☐☐☐	137 Sundström, NYRa.	30.00	15.00	.50	.20
☐☐☐☐	138 T. Harvey, NYRa.	30.00	15.00	.50	.20
☐☐☐☐	139 A. Yashin, Otta.	70.00	35.00	.50	.20
☐☐☐☐	140 D. Rhodes, Otta.	30.00	15.00	.50	.20
☐☐☐☐	141 Alfredsson, Otta.	70.00	35.00	.50	.20
☐☐☐☐	142 M. Arvedson, Otta.	20.00	10.00	.50	.20
☐☐☐☐	143 McEachern, Otta.	40.00	20.00	.50	.20
☐☐☐☐	144 C. Phillips, Otta.	30.00	15.00	.50	.20
☐☐☐☐	145 V. Prospal, Otta.	40.00	20.00	.50	.20
☐☐☐☐	146 W. Redden, Otta.	40.00	20.00	.50	.20
☐☐☐☐	147 E. Lindros, Phil.	120.00	60.00	1.00	.50
☐☐☐☐	148 J. LeClair, Phil.	100.00	50.00	1.00	.50
☐☐☐☐	149 Vanbiesbrouck, Phil.	60.00	30.00	.50	.20
☐☐☐☐	150 K. Jones, Phil.	20.00	10.00	.50	.20
☐☐☐☐	151 C. Forbes, Phil.	15.00	8.00	.50	.20
☐☐☐☐	152 M. Recchi, Phil.	50.00	25.00	.50	.20
☐☐☐☐	153 D. McGillis, Phil.	20.00	10.00	.50	.20
☐☐☐☐	154 É. Desjardins, Phil.	40.00	20.00	.50	.20
☐☐☐☐	155 Brind'Amour, Phil.	40.00	20.00	.50	.20
☐☐☐☐	156 K. Tkachuk, Phoe.	70.00	35.00	.50	.20
☐☐☐☐	157 D. Brière, Phoe.	60.00	30.00	.50	.50
☐☐☐☐	158 Khabibulin, Phoe.	50.00	25.00	.50	.20
☐☐☐☐	159 B. Isbister, Phoe.	30.00	15.00	.50	.20
☐☐☐☐	160 J. Roenick, Phoe.	100.00	50.00	1.00	.50
☐☐☐☐	161 Tverdovsky, Phoe.	20.00	10.00	.50	.20
☐☐☐☐	162 R. Tocchet, Phoe.	40.00	20.00	.50	.20
☐☐☐☐	163 J. Jagr, Pitt.	120.00	60.00	1.00	.50
☐☐☐☐	164 T. Barrasso, Pitt.	50.00	25.00	.50	.20
☐☐☐☐	165 A. Morozov, Pitt.	30.00	15.00	.50	.20
☐☐☐☐	166 R. Dome, Pitt.	20.00	10.00	.50	.20
☐☐☐☐	167 S. Barnes, Pitt.	15.00	8.00	.50	.20
☐☐☐☐	168 M. Straka, Pitt.	40.00	20.00	.50	.20
☐☐☐☐	169 G. Titov, Pitt.	15.00	8.00	.50	.20
☐☐☐☐	170 P. Marleau, SanJ.	60.00	30.00	.50	.20
☐☐☐☐	171 A. Zyuzin, SanJ.	20.00	10.00	.50	.20
☐☐☐☐	172 M. Sturm, SanJ.	30.00	15.00	.50	.20
☐☐☐☐	173 O. Nolan, SanJ.	70.00	35.00	.50	.20
☐☐☐☐	174 J. Friesen, SanJ.	40.00	20.00	.50	.20
☐☐☐☐	175 B. Rouse, SanJ.	15.00	8.00	.50	.20
☐☐☐☐	176 M. Vernon, SanJ.	50.00	25.00	.50	.20
☐☐☐☐	177 M. Ricci, SanJ.	40.00	20.00	.50	.20
☐☐☐☐	178 Reasoner, SLou.	30.00	15.00	.50	.20
☐☐☐☐	179 A. MacInnis, SLou.	50.00	25.00	.50	.20
☐☐☐☐	180 C. Pronger, SLou.	70.00	35.00	.50	.20
☐☐☐☐	181 P. Turgeon, SLou.	50.00	25.00	.50	.20
☐☐☐☐	**182 Handzus, SLou. RC**	**30.00**	**15.00**	**1.00**	**1.00**
☐☐☐☐	183 J. Campbell, SLou.	15.00	8.00	.50	.20
☐☐☐☐	184 T. Twist, SLou.	20.00	10.00	.50	.20
☐☐☐☐	185 P. Demitra, SLou.	50.00	25.00	.50	.20
☐☐☐☐	186 D. Puppa, Tamp.	30.00	15.00	.50	.20
☐☐☐☐	187 Lecavalier, Tamp.	120.00	60.00	1.50	1.00
☐☐☐☐	188 B. Ranford, Tamp.	50.00	25.00	.50	.20
☐☐☐☐	189 A. Daigle, Tamp.	20.00	10.00	.50	.20
☐☐☐☐	190 W. Clark, Tamp.	100.00	50.00	1.00	.50
☐☐☐☐	191 R. Zamuner, Tamp.	30.00	15.00	.50	.20
☐☐☐☐	192 C. Gratton, Tamp.	30.00	15.00	.50	.20
☐☐☐☐	193 F. Modin, Toro.	30.00	15.00	.50	.20
☐☐☐☐	194 C. Joseph, Toro.	120.00	60.00	1.00	.50
☐☐☐☐	195 M. Sundin, Toro.	120.00	60.00	1.00	.50
☐☐☐☐	196 S. Thomas, Toro.	30.00	15.00	.50	.20
☐☐☐☐	**197 Kaberle, Toro. RC**	**40.00**	**20.00**	**1.50**	**1.50**
☐☐☐☐	198 A. McCauley, Toro.	40.00	20.00	.50	.20
☐☐☐☐	199 M. Johnson, Toro.	20.00	10.00	.50	.20
☐☐☐☐	200 B. Berard, Toro.	40.00	20.00	.50	.20
☐☐☐☐	201 M. Messier, Vanc.	120.00	60.00	1.00	.50
☐☐☐☐	**202 Strudwick, Vanc. RC**	**15.00**	**8.00**	**.50**	**.50**
☐☐☐☐	203 M. Öhlund, Vanc.	40.00	20.00	.50	.20
☐☐☐☐	204 A. Mogilny, Vanc.	60.00	30.00	.50	.20
☐☐☐☐	**205 Muckalt, Vanc. RC**	**20.00**	**10.00**	**.50**	**.50**
☐☐☐☐	206 E. Jovanovski, Vanc.	50.00	25.00	.50	.20
☐☐☐☐	207 J. Holden, Vanc.	20.00	10.00	.50	.20
☐☐☐☐	208 P. Schaefer, Vanc.	20.00	10.00	.50	.20
☐☐☐☐	209 P. Bondra, Wash.	70.00	35.00	.50	.20
☐☐☐☐	210 O. Kölzig, Wash.	70.00	35.00	.50	.20
☐☐☐☐	211 S. Gonchar, Wash.	40.00	20.00	.50	.20
☐☐☐☐	212 A. Oates, Wash.	50.00	25.00	.50	.20
☐☐☐☐	213 B. Bellows, Wash.	30.00	15.00	.50	.20
☐☐☐☐	214 M. Herr, Wash.	15.00	8.00	.50	.20
☐☐☐☐	215 R. Zednik, Wash.	50.00	25.00	.50	.20
☐☐☐☐	216 J. Juneau, Wash.	30.00	15.00	.50	.20
☐☐☐☐	217 Svejkovsky, Wash.	20.00	10.00	.50	.20
☐☐☐☐	218 W. Gretzky	250.00	120.00	2.50	1.00
☐☐☐☐	219 W. Gretzky	250.00	120.00	2.50	1.00
☐☐☐☐	220 W. Gretzky	250.00	120.00	2.50	1.00

DYNAMICS

These cards start at $12.

Insert Set (15 cards): 150.00

	Player		Player
☐	D1 Wayne Gretzky	☐	D2 Wayne Gretzky
☐	D3 Wayne Gretzky	☐	D4 Wayne Gretzky
☐	D5 Wayne Gretzky	☐	D6 Wayne Gretzky
☐	D7 Wayne Gretzky	☐	D8 Wayne Gretzky
☐	D9 Wayne Gretzky	☐	D10 Wayne Gretzky
☐	D11 Wayne Gretzky	☐	D12 Wayne Gretzky
☐	D13 Wayne Gretzky	☐	D14 Wayne Gretzky
☐	D15 Wayne Gretzky		

GAME-USED SOUVENIR

Insert Set (12 cards):		**555.00**
	Insert	**GUS**
☐	Brett Hull, Dall.	35.00
☐	Brendan Shanahan, Detr.	35.00
☐	Eric Lindros, Phil.	35.00
☐	John LeClair, Phil.	30.00
☐	Mike Modano, Dall.	35.00
☐	Patrick Roy (G), Colo.	110.00
☐	Raymond Bourque, Bost.	45.00
☐	Sergei Fedorov, Detr.	35.00
☐	Sergei Samsonov, Bost.	20.00
☐	Steve Yzerman, Detr.	90.00
☐	Vincent Lecavalier, Tamp.	35.00
☐	Wayne Gretzky, NYRa.	150.00

GAME-USED SOUVENIR SIGNED

PhotoHOR	Photo-need
Insert	**Auto.**
□ Steve Yzerman, Detr. ✍ {#/19}	800.00
□ Vincent Lecavalier, Tamp. ✍ {#/14}	500.00

OT HEROES

Insert Set (15 cards):	60.00
Insert (1:9)	**OTH**
□ OT1 Steve Yzerman, Detr.	8.00
□ OT2 Patrick Roy (G), Colo.	10.00
□ OT3 Jaromir Jagr, Pitt.	2.00
□ OT4 Raymond Bourque, Bost.	4.00
□ OT5 Wayne Gretzky, NYRa.	14.00
□ OT6 Sergei Samsonov, Bost.	2.00
□ OT7 Dominik Hasek (G), Buff.	3.00
□ OT8 Peter Forsberg, Colo.	5.00
□ OT9 Paul Kariya, Anah.	4.00
□ OT10 Eric Lindros, Phil.	3.00
□ OT11 Pavel Bure, Flor.	3.00
□ OT12 Keith Tkachuk, Phoe.	2.00
□ OT13 Brendan Shanahan, Detr.	3.00
□ OT14 John LeClair, Phil.	3.00
□ OT15 Joe Sakic, Colo.	6.00

POWER GAME

Insert Set (15 cards):	30.00
Insert (1:9)	**PG**
□ PG1 Brendan Shanahan, Detr.	3.00
□ PG2 Keith Tkachuk, Phoe.	2.00
□ PG3 Eric Lindros, Phil.	3.00
□ PG4 Mike Modano, Dall.	3.00
□ PG5 Vincent Lecavalier, Tamp.	3.00
□ PG6 John LeClair, Phil.	3.00
□ PG7 Mark Messier, Vanc.	3.00
□ PG8 Mats Sundin, Toro.	3.00
□ PG9 Peter Forsberg, Colo.	5.00
□ PG10 Jaromir Jagr, Pitt.	2.00
□ PG11 Keith Primeau, Caro.	1.00
□ PG12 Mark Parrish, Flor.	1.00
□ PG13 Patrick Marleau, SanJ.	1.00
□ PG14 Bill Guerin, Edmo.	1.00
□ PG15 Jeremy Roenick, Phoe.	3.00

PROSIGN

Insert Set (23 cards):	280.00
Autograph	**NRMT-MT**
□ Alyn McCauley, Toro. ✍	15.00
□ Brian Bellows, Wash. ✍	10.00
□ Brendan Morrison, NJer. ✍	15.00
□ Chris Drury, Colo. ✍	30.00
□ Dimitri Nabokov, NYIs. ✍	10.00
□ Doug Weight, Edmo. ✍	30.00
□ Eric Brewer, NYIs. ✍	20.00
□ Erik Rasmussen, Buff. ✍	10.00
□ Jason Allison, Bost. ✍	30.00
□ Jason Arnott, NJer. ✍	25.00
□ Jarome Iginla, Calg. ✍	45.00
□ José Théodore (G), Mont. ✍	65.00
□ Mike Dunham (G), Nash. ✍	20.00
□ Mike Johnson, Toro. ✍	10.00
□ Manny Malhotra, NYRa. ✍	10.00
□ Mark Parrish, Flor. ✍	20.00
□ Oleg Tverdovsky, Phoe. ✍	10.00
□ Rico Fata, Calg. ✍	10.00
□ Rob Niedermayer, Flor. ✍	10.00
□ Steve Yzerman, Detr. ✍	160.00
□ Vincent Lecavalier, Tamp. ✍	55.00
□ Wayne Gretzky, NYRa. ✍	500.00
□ Wade Redden, Otta. ✍	15.00

SNIPERS

Insert Set (12 cards):	25.00
Insert (1:6)	**S**
□ S1 Vincent Lecavalier, Tamp.	5.00
□ S2 Wayne Gretzky, NYRa.	10.00
□ S3 Sergei Samsonov, Bost.	1.00
□ S4 Teemu Selänne, Anah.	2.00
□ S5 Peter Forsberg, Colo.	3.00
□ S6 Paul Kariya, Anah.	3.00
□ S7 Eric Lindros, Phil.	2.00
□ S8 Pavel Bure, Vanc.	2.00
□ S9 Peter Bondra, Wash.	1.00
□ S10 Joe Sakic, Colo.	4.00
□ S11 Steve Yzerman, Detr.	6.00
□ S12 Sergei Fedorov, Detr.	2.00

SPECIAL FORCES

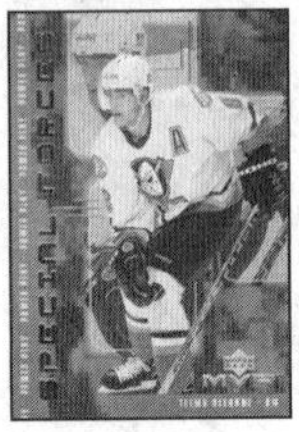

Insert Set (15 cards):	25.00
Insert (1:14)	**SF**
□ F1 Brett Hull, Dall.	6.00
□ F2 Sergei Samsonov, Bost.	3.00
□ F3 Vincent Lecavalier, Tamp.	6.00
□ F4 Dominik Hasek (G), Buff.	5.00
□ F5 Eric Lindros, Phil.	5.00
□ F6 Paul Kariya, Anah.	5.00
□ F7 Steve Yzerman, Detr.	15.00
□ F8 Brendan Shanahan, Detr.	6.00
□ F9 Martin Brodeur (G), NJer.	10.00
□ F10 Teemu Selänne, Anah.	5.00
□ F11 Jaromir Jagr, Pitt.	5.00
□ F12 Wayne Gretzky, NYRa.	25.00
□ F13 Patrick Roy (G), Colo.	15.00
□ F14 Peter Forsberg, Colo.	5.00
□ F15 Joe Sakic, Colo.	10.00

1998 - 99 UPPER DECK MVP – BUYBACKS

These signed cards were inserted into packs of 2000-01 UD Reserve.

Buyback Autograph	UDMVP
□ 97 Luc Robitaille ✍ {#/1}	

1999 QUÉBEC INTERNATIONAL PEE WEE

Complete Set (1364): 175.00

There are 200 copies of each card. Commons start at 50¢.

BADEN-WURTTEMBERG PEE-WEE

□ 1 D. Wrobel	□ 11 M. Bruns
□ 2 T. Ower	□ 12 C. Basham
□ 3 T. Exner	□ 13 M. Koch
□ 4 R. Herbst	□ 14 R. Schoofs
□ 5 N. Goc	□ 15 D. Riedlinger
□ 6 P. Braun	□ 16 M. Schmerda
□ 7 D. Unger	□ 17 M. Schzitz
□ 8 A. Haffner	□ 18 A. Achziger
□ 9 M. Hocker	□ 19 S. Danner
□ 10 C. Scholl	□ 20 P. Bomba

DRUMMONDVILLE PEE-WEE

Kevin Asselin and Maxime Boisclair are two of the more expensive cards.

□ 21 S. Bédard	□ 30 M. Bélanger
□ 22 M. Corriveau	□ 31 G. Morin
□ 23 A. Bourret	□ 32 T. Parenteau
□ 24 K. Duchaine	□ 33 D. Chabot
□ 25 K. Asselin	□ 34 M. Simoneau
□ 26 O. Charpentier	□ 35 N. Leduc
□ 27 M. Beaudet	□ 36 M. Boisclair
□ 28 J. Leclerc	□ 37 J. Doyon
□ 29 O. Beaulieu	□ 38 Instructeurs

BOSTON BRUINS PEE-WEE

□ 39 M. Leahy	□ 49 C. Flaherty
□ 40 C. Yablonski	□ 50 G. O'Brien
□ 41 J. Moran	□ 51 S. Kelley
□ 42 R. Feldhoff	□ 52 S. Butler
□ 43 M. Rosata	□ 53 M. Lentini
□ 44 A. Snickenberger	□ 54 B. Ortiz
□ 45 J. Grzetyck	□ 55 M. Davis
□ 46 A. Pellecchia	□ 56 J. Hubbard
□ 47 P. Welch	□ 57 Photo d'équipe
□ 48 J. Balben	

PITTSBURGH PENGUINS PEE-WEE

□ 58 S. Shimaek	□ 68 T. Senchur
□ 59 J. Poorman	□ 69 L. Delorenzo
□ 60 P. Supan	□ 70 B. Meyers
□ 61 R. McGrath	□ 71 M. Gigliotti
□ 62 E. Holzer	□ 72 C. Zach
□ 63 B. Hanley	□ 73 J. Trimble
□ 64 B. Spence	□ 74 Instructeurs
□ 65 A. Wroblewski	□ 75 Instructeurs
□ 66 J. Sanderson	□ 76 Instructeurs
□ 67 N. Signet	

HAMILTON PEE-WEE

□ 77 B. Roshko	□ 86 A. Kenderic
□ 78 B. Webster	□ 87 M. Chrysler
□ 79 J. Thomson	□ 88 G. Longe
□ 80 M. Szpiech	□ 89 C. Trdin
□ 81 S. Campbell	□ 90 K. Hagel
□ 82 D. Petkoff	□ 91 K. Barker
□ 83 M. Higson	□ 92 M. Whalen
□ 84 M. Ouzas	□ 93 D. Prodeus
□ 85 D. Brown	

SHERBROOKE PEE-WEE

Philippe Lacroix is one of the more expensive cards.

□ 94 L. Allaire	□ 104 R. Marion
□ 95 C. Bertrand	□ 105 G. Ouellette
□ 96 A. Bouchard	□ 106 P. Perron
□ 97 A. Gagné	□ 107 A. Poulin
□ 98 S. Gaudreau	□ 108 P. Renaud
□ 98 D. Grenier	□ 109 M. Sylvain
□ 100 P. Lacroix	□ 110 J. Trudeau
□ 101 G. Levasseur	□ 111 Instructeurs
□ 102 A. Lord	□ 112 Instructeurs
□ 103 O. Magnan	

LAVAL-NORD PEE-WEE

□ 113 P. Beauregard	□ 122 A. Fournier
□ 114 Boyer-Beaucage	□ 123 S. Frenette
□ 115 L. Champagne	□ 124 S. Gagné
□ 116 M. Cousineau	□ 125 C. Labonté
□ 117 M. Gagné	□ 126 C. Robitaille
□ 118 M. Labelle	□ 127 O. Tétrault
□ 119 D. Pereira	□ 128 J. Vadnais
□ 120 O. Beaulieu	□ 129 Viens-Chouinard
□ 121 C. Brault	□ 130 Instructeurs

HALIFAX PEE-WEE

□ 131 A. Archibald	□ 140 C. MacCormack
□ 132 M. Adams	□ 141 I. McIsaac
□ 133 S. Carr	□ 142 R. Moore
□ 134 J. Drinkwater	□ 143 B. Pasha
□ 135 L. Gallant	□ 144 C. Tang
□ 136 J. Giffin	□ 145 T. Whitehead
□ 137 D. Harper	□ 146 M. Youden
□ 138 C. Henman	□ 147 D. Sellers
□ 139 E. King	□ 148 Instructeurs

BOSTON JR EAGLES PEE-WEE

John Hennessey is one of the more expensive cards.

□ 149 D. Bailey	□ 157 N. Monroe
□ 150 I. Eiland	□ 158 A. Pineault
□ 151 J. Grant	□ 159 K. Plant
□ 152 T. Hawley	□ 160 J. Perus
□ 153 J. Hennessey	□ 161 M. Reynolds
□ 154 E. Lane	□ 162 J. Rocchio
□ 155 K. Longo	□ 163 B. Tyler
□ 156 J. Mearn	

VICTORIAVILLE PEE-WEE

□ 164 K. Messervier	□ 174 F. Tousignant
□ 165 K. Daigle	□ 175 F. Roux
□ 166 M. Bilodeau	□ 176 K. Dumont
□ 167 K. Daigle	□ 177 A. Francoeur
□ 168 M. Héon	□ 178 M. Chaperon
□ 169 F. Pilon	□ 179 D. Létourneau
□ 170 J. Girouard	□ 180 A. Savoie
□ 171 W. Béliveau	□ 181 P. Asselin
□ 172 P. Faucher	□ 182 Instructeurs
□ 173 S. Fortier	

MONTRÉAL NOROIS PEE-WEE

Éric Tétrault and Derrick Jasmin-Riel are two of the more expensive cards.

□ 183 É. Tétrault	□ 192 D. Jasmin-Riel
□ 184 M. Charbonneau	□ 193 B. Petit
□ 185 M. Bélisle	□ 194 T. Caimassidis
□ 186 M. Bocchichio	□ 195 J. Tahan
□ 187 S. Marin	□ 196 J. Lortie
□ 188 J. Gagnon	□ 197 P. Gagnon
□ 189 J. Ayoub	□ 198 M. Coursol-Tellier
□ 190 O. Plouffe	□ 199 F. Prud'homme
□ 191 P. Girard	□ 200 Instructeurs

NEW-YORK ISLANDERS PEE-WEE

□ 201 M. Arcieri	□ 210 L. Liotti
□ 202 A. Belknap	□ 211 C. Molinaro
□ 203 J. Colford	□ 212 A. Monforte
□ 204 M. Collette	□ 213 E. Neville
□ 205 W. Copp	□ 214 S. Rios
□ 206 M. Coppola	□ 215 F. Rizzo
□ 207 R. Crockett	□ 216 G. Vassel
□ 208 E. Falcone	□ 217 Instructeurs
□ 209 M. Karwoski	□ 218 Instructeurs

BEAUBOURG PEE-WEE

□ 219 J. Thomassin	□ 228 S. Lachance
□ 220 K. Lajoie	□ 229 C. Daigle
□ 221 V. Lemoine	□ 230 J. Lafrance
□ 222 M. Pichette	□ 231 J. Lessard
□ 223 M. Garneau	□ 232 M. Grenier
□ 224 P. Gagné	□ 233 A. Breton
□ 225 S. Roy	□ 234 G. Turgeon
□ 226 G. Samson	□ 235 Instructeurs
□ 227 A. Dubois	

LANAUDIÈRE PEE-WEE

Jean-François, Maxim Lapierre and Sylvain Michaud are three of the more expensive cards.

□ 236 J. Arkinson	□ 245 J. Jacques
□ 237 M. Bédard	□ 246 F. Jodoin
□ 238 M. Bourgeault	□ 247 M. Lapierre
□ 239 K. Bourgeois	□ 248 F. Lavallée
□ 240 A. Brousseau	□ 249 S. Michaud
□ 241 S. Cantin	□ 250 P. Renaud
□ 242 T. Côté-Bienvenu	□ 251 A. Sévigny
□ 243 S. Gauthier	□ 252 Instructeurs
□ 244 S. Haas	

BROSSARD PEE-WEE

□ 253 M. Trudeau	□ 262 M. Sauvé
□ 254 A. Pelletier	□ 263 J. Berthiaume
□ 255 M. Wallus	□ 264 J. Watier
□ 256 R. Chainey	□ 265 É. Bégin
□ 257 K. Sylvia	□ 266 E. Leclerc
□ 258 M. Bourgeois	□ 267 J. Dubois
□ 259 M. Duguay	□ 268 A. Sandoval
□ 260 Brault-Bertrand	□ 269 Instructeurs
□ 261 A. Massé	

QUÉBEC CHAMPLAIN PEE-WEE

Jonathan Duchesneau is one of the more expensive cards.

□ 270 J. Tremblay	□ 280 J. Leclerc
□ 271 J. Duchesneau	□ 281 L. Ringuette
□ 272 É. Lorrain	□ 282 D. Roy
□ 273 M. Nolet	□ 283 J. Rioux
□ 274 L. Lemieux	□ 284 A. Dupuis
□ 275 T. Element	□ 285 J. Lajeunesse
□ 276 J. Durand	□ 286 V. Duchesneau
□ 277 B. Morin	□ 287 Instructeurs
□ 278 J. Demers	□ 288 Instructeurs
□ 279 É. Paradis	

REPENTIGNY PEE-WEE

□ 289 R. Lajeunesse	□ 297 É. Duval
□ 290 J. Côté	□ 298 S. Bélanger
□ 291 A. Rousseau	□ 299 J. Miron
□ 292 M. Chouinard	□ 300 M. Turner
□ 293 S. Désautels	□ 301 M. Venne
□ 294 P. Veillette	□ 302 T. Gratton
□ 295 J. Marcil	□ 303 M. St-Aubin
□ 296 M. Mercier	□ 304 P. Searless

STE-THÉRÈSE PEE-WEE

□ 305 R. Fréchette	□ 313 N. Desrosiers
□ 306 S. Bernier	□ 314 D. Simard
□ 307 C. Dufault	□ 315 J. Ronci
□ 308 P. Provencher	□ 316 W. Gilbert
□ 309 J. Hogues	□ 317 M. Durocher
□ 310 P. Turbide	□ 318 V. Michaud
□ 311 L. Horky	□ 319 S. Daneault
□ 312 J. Charron	□ 320 G. Martineau

STE-FOY AA PEE-WEE

□ 321 Y. Gauvin	□ 330 K. Raymond
□ 322 A. Beaudoin	□ 331 P. Bertrand
□ 323 M. Castonguay	□ 332 M. Noël
□ 324 J. Côté	□ 333 Poulin-Robitaille
□ 325 G. Bédard-Pagé	□ 334 D. Plante

☐ 326 J. Landry
☐ 327 A. Couët
☐ 328 P. Bergeron
☐ 329 J. Godin
☐ 335 V. Bricault
☐ 336 J. Beaupré
☐ 337 Instructeurs

PHILADELPHIE FLYERS PEE-WEE

☐ 338 B. Watson
☐ 339 R. Campbell
☐ 340 D. Wiedmann
☐ 341 D. Reinhardt
☐ 342 J. Beck
☐ 343 S. Kohler
☐ 344 J. McDonald
☐ 345 J. Fetscher
☐ 346 D. Baratta
☐ 347 B. Berger
☐ 348 B. Kuper
☐ 349 S. Bruch
☐ 350 D. Sloane
☐ 351 G. Herneisen
☐ 352 M. Finnegan
☐ 353 H. Edwards
☐ 354 M. Martinelli
☐ 355 J. McCabe
☐ 356 R. Jordan
☐ 357 D. Pencinger

DÉTROIT COMPUWARE PEE-WEE

☐ 358 A. Balaze
☐ 359 D. Brownlee
☐ 360 J. Harris
☐ 361 L. Helminen
☐ 362 N. Kiser
☐ 363 P. Kozak
☐ 364 M. McNamara
☐ 365 B. Naurato
☐ 366 S. Niederriter
☐ 367 D. Pszencyzny
☐ 368 C. Skrzypek
☐ 369 D. Stoinski
☐ 370 J. Vigilante
☐ 371 C. Walsh
☐ 372 R. Wells
☐ 373 B. White

RICHELIEU PEE-WEE

Martin Houle is one of the more expensive cards.

☐ 374 S. Bellefleur
☐ 375 G. Brillon
☐ 376 J. Cloutier
☐ 377 J. Côté
☐ 378 S. D'Aoust
☐ 379 S. Harbec
☐ 380 M. Houle
☐ 381 M. Lamoureux
☐ 382 F. Lebrun
☐ 383 M. Lettera
☐ 384 D. Loiseau
☐ 385 J. Morin
☐ 386 J. Petit
☐ 387 N. Rhéaume
☐ 388 H. St-Pierre
☐ 389 M. Tremblay
☐ 390 M. Villalobos
☐ 391 Instructeurs

STE-FOY B PEE-WEE

☐ 392 J. Cyr
☐ 393 P. Laverdière
☐ 394 P. Lapierre
☐ 395 B. L'Italien
☐ 396 P. Savard
☐ 397 S. Simard
☐ 398 J. Beaulieu
☐ 399 P. Tardif
☐ 400 M. Béland
☐ 401 V. Zaoré-Vanié
☐ 402 S. Cantin
☐ 403 S. Richard
☐ 404 É. Julien
☐ 405 S. Vallières
☐ 406 B. Mailloux
☐ 407 J. Côté
☐ 408 Instructeurs

NEW-JERSEY DEVILS PEE-WEE

☐ 409 M. Atkinson
☐ 410 R. Collis
☐ 411 J. Cucci
☐ 412 V. De Antonio
☐ 413 C. Giblin
☐ 414 Z. Kalemba
☐ 415 C. Lefever
☐ 416 W. Lou
☐ 417 D. Lunau
☐ 418 T. Maldonado
☐ 419 M. McKenna
☐ 420 R. Mero
☐ 421 B. O'Donnell
☐ 422 P. Percella
☐ 423 T. Peskin
☐ 424 K. Shattenkirk
☐ 425 T. Tam
☐ 426 J. Zuck
☐ 427 Instructeurs

MARKHAM WAXERS PEE-WEE

☐ 428 B. Anderson
☐ 429 S. Badali
☐ 430 M. Brown
☐ 431 A. Buckstein
☐ 432 D. Falbo
☐ 433 D. French
☐ 434 G. Griffiths
☐ 435 D. Levy
☐ 436 E. Kleine
☐ 437 B. Napier
☐ 438 B. Patton
☐ 439 N. Rothwell
☐ 440 J. Rothwell
☐ 441 S. Routledge
☐ 442 G. Therens
☐ 443 T. Townsend
☐ 444 Instructeurs

AUTRICHE PEE-WEE

☐ 445 Y. Bodeman
☐ 446 M. Colleoni
☐ 447 C. Frei
☐ 448 C. Gielg
☐ 449 B. Grafschafter
☐ 450 C. Hehle
☐ 451 M. Iberer
☐ 452 C. Ibounig
☐ 453 P. Kink
☐ 454 J. Kirisits
☐ 455 A. Künz
☐ 1015 S. Kales
☐ 456 M. Lange
☐ 457 V. Lindgren
☐ 458 H. Nachbauer
☐ 459 C. Quantschnig
☐ 460 A. Pfeiffer
☐ 461 T. Teppert
☐ 462 M. Unger
☐ 463 F. Wilfan
☐ 464 M. Zechner
☐ 465 R. Fradler
☐ 466 C. Haas

AMIANTE B PEE-WEE

☐ 467 D. Wechselberger
☐ 468 K. Lemay
☐ 469 S. Argouin
☐ 470 S. Rousseau
☐ 471 J. Faucher
☐ 472 F. Labrecque
☐ 473 D. Chandonnet
☐ 474 B. Beaudoin
☐ 475 J. Dallaire
☐ 476 K. Doyon
☐ 477 C. Bergeron
☐ 478 P. Beaudoin
☐ 479 F. Guay
☐ 480 P. Turcotte
☐ 481 M. Couture
☐ 482 S. Thivierge
☐ 483 A. Jacques
☐ 484 Instructeurs

HERSHEY PEE-WEE

☐ 485 R. Albright
☐ 486 A. Allatt
☐ 487 B. Beck
☐ 488 C. Brogan
☐ 489 J. Devaney
☐ 490 J. Freeman
☐ 491 S. Gervais
☐ 492 T. Hanks
☐ 493 S. Haubert
☐ 494 J. Hastings
☐ 495 B. Henry
☐ 496 C. Herr
☐ 497 A. Jaffe
☐ 498 B. Kemmerer
☐ 499 D. Lutz
☐ 500 K. McKillips
☐ 501 J. Rich
☐ 502 W. Seidel
☐ 503 D. Smith
☐ 504 A. Wert
☐ 505 Instructeurs

CHARLEVOIX PEE-WEE

☐ 506 M. Bouchard
☐ 507 T. Racine
☐ 508 M. Duchesne
☐ 509 S. Lavoie
☐ 510 D. Belley
☐ 511 M. Harvey
☐ 512 P. Bilodeau
☐ 513 C. Dufour
☐ 514 F. Pilote
☐ 515 J. Ouellet
☐ 516 J. Dufour
☐ 517 M. Imbeault
☐ 518 G. Dufour
☐ 519 S. Chamberland
☐ 520 F. Rochette
☐ 521 F. Belley
☐ 522 J. Temblay
☐ 523 Instructeurs

ZURICH PEE-WEE

☐ 524 R. Alegre-Basarte
☐ 525 C. Bentele
☐ 526 D. Brunner
☐ 527 A. Brunold
☐ 528 R. Capaul
☐ 529 F. Collenberg
☐ 530 K. Egli
☐ 531 G. Ehrensperger
☐ 532 A. Meier
☐ 533 A. Rizzello
☐ 534 R. Schuppisser
☐ 535 V. Stancescu
☐ 536 C. Wäger
☐ 537 R. Wick
☐ 538 D. Schynder
☐ 539 C. Menghini
☐ 540 M. Trepp
☐ 541 F. Colura
☐ 542 M. Tobler
☐ 543 A. Schläffer
☐ 544 Instructeurs

CHICAGO BLACK HAWKS PEE-WEE

☐ 545 M. Bartlett
☐ 546 M. Brown
☐ 547 A. Cosmano
☐ 548 C. Fetzer
☐ 549 A. Gobersetin
☐ 550 J. Herderman
☐ 551 J. Heller
☐ 552 S. Lafrenier
☐ 553 J. Liang
☐ 554 J. Likens
☐ 555 M. Mclluane
☐ 556 A. Montayo
☐ 557 J. Pace
☐ 558 C. Palmer
☐ 559 R. Pettygrove
☐ 560 S. Prudden
☐ 561 A. Ruprecht
☐ 562 Instructeurs

BEAUPORT VOILIERS PEE-WEE

☐ 563 S. Laliberté
☐ 564 S. Côté
☐ 565 S. St-Germain
☐ 566 V. Marcon
☐ 567 M. Charbonneau
☐ 568 D. Dufour
☐ 569 M. Leblond
☐ 570 K. Thibeault
☐ 571 K. Émond
☐ 572 K. Mathieu
☐ 573 J. Drolet
☐ 574 L. Fournier
☐ 575 A. Gauthier
☐ 576 A. Bilodeau
☐ 577 D. Walsh
☐ 578 Instructeurs

DALLAS PEE-WEE

☐ 579 R. Moreau
☐ 580 T. Lugwig
☐ 581 A. Miller
☐ 582 T. Ludwing
☐ 583 R. Morgan
☐ 584 M. Damiano
☐ 585 J. Boeing
☐ 586 C. Cyrus
☐ 587 S. McCauley
☐ 588 J. Sparks
☐ 589 J. Shoemaker
☐ 590 W. Watterson
☐ 591 R. Sablotny
☐ 592 C. Nugent
☐ 593 J. upar
☐ 594 M. Barber
☐ 595 Instructeurs
☐ 596 A. Jones
☐ 597 R. Staub
☐ 598 M. Burzon
☐ 599 J. Nisbet

BEAUPORT MARINIERS PEE-WEE

☐ 600 F. Maheux
☐ 601 S. Keough
☐ 602 R. Duchesne
☐ 603 J. Labonté
☐ 604 M. Tanguay
☐ 605 K. Girard-Houle
☐ 606 V. Ouellet
☐ 607 É. Laliberté
☐ 608 D. Bouffard
☐ 609 P. Lachance
☐ 610 H. Harvey
☐ 611 M. Lortie
☐ 612 S. Doiron
☐ 613 M. Leclerc
☐ 614 M. Bertrand
☐ 615 V. Dubé
☐ 616 J. Gélinas
☐ 617 Instructeurs

ANCHORAGE PEE-WEE

☐ 618 G. Bundy
☐ 619 D. Lehe
☐ 620 B. Bales
☐ 621 B. Dubinsky
☐ 622 J. Sorenson
☐ 623 R. Rider
☐ 624 K. Francione
☐ 625 R. Masek
☐ 626 B. Martin
☐ 627 T. Hyatt
☐ 628 P. Duffy
☐ 629 R. Edmunds
☐ 630 J. Kovacevich
☐ 631 M. Johnson
☐ 632 C. Lambernakis
☐ 633 M. Bishop
☐ 634 J. Pearce
☐ 635 B. Lundeby
☐ 636 G. McManamin
☐ 637 E. Woelber

ST-GÉDÉON PEE-WEE

☐ 638 M. Hamel
☐ 639 B. Roy
☐ 640 P. Mathieu
☐ 647 P. Paradis
☐ 648 D. Bégin
☐ 649 K. Roy

☐ 641 K. Lachance
☐ 642 P. Poulin
☐ 643 M. Tanguay
☐ 644 S. Bélanger
☐ 645 P. Poulin
☐ 646 D. Quirion
☐ 650 M. Poulin
☐ 651 S. Cliche
☐ 652 J. Poulin
☐ 653 É. Demers
☐ 654 K. Drouin
☐ 655 Instructeurs

QUÉBEC REMPARTS PEE-WEE

Dany Roussin, Marc-Antoine Pouliot, Alexandre Picard, and Steve Bernier are four of the more expensive cards.

☐ 656 J. Zrudlo
☐ 657 L. Beaulieu
☐ 658 K. Ruel
☐ 659 V. Guay
☐ 660 D. Roussin
☐ 661 P. Lefebvre
☐ 662 J. Bilodeau
☐ 663 M. Pouliot
☐ 664 M. Sansfaçon
☐ 665 F. Giroux
☐ 666 O. Bédard
☐ 667 F. Palladini
☐ 668 J. Lemay
☐ 669 A. Picard
☐ 670 J. Lizotte
☐ 671 S. Bernier
☐ 672 Instructeurs

CÔTE DE BEAUPRÉ - ILE D'ORLÉANS PEE-WEE

☐ 673 M. Laberge
☐ 674 É. Brown
☐ 675 J. Dupont
☐ 676 N. Mariage
☐ 677 G. Caron
☐ 678 É. Dion
☐ 679 K. Deschênes
☐ 680 S. St-Gelais
☐ 681 M. Penney
☐ 682 M. Picard
☐ 683 M. Hamelin
☐ 684 D. Drouin-Belley
☐ 685 A. Bourget
☐ 686 T. Goulet
☐ 687 S. Trépanier
☐ 688 R. Fortin
☐ 689 F. Harvey-Asselin
☐ 690 R. Watson
☐ 691 J. Watson
☐ 692 A. Penny
☐ 693 Instructeurs

SHERMONT PEE-WEE

☐ 694 S. Vaillancourt
☐ 695 P. Lachance
☐ 696 D. Chicoine
☐ 697 D. Guay
☐ 698 M. Marcotte
☐ 699 K. Young
☐ 700 S. Thérriault
☐ 701 J. Aubé
☐ 702 P. Trudel
☐ 703 J. Roy
☐ 704 M. Fréchette
☐ 705 C. Croisetière
☐ 706 A. Fréchette
☐ 707 V. Fillion
☐ 708 C. James
☐ 709 P. Lauzon
☐ 710 F. Cabana
☐ 711 Instructeurs
☐ 712 Instructeurs
☐ 713 Instructeurs
☐ 714 Instructeurs
☐ 715 Instructeurs

LAJEMMERAIS PEE-WEE

☐ 716 G. Bouthillette
☐ 717 M. Cerutti
☐ 718 S. Choquet
☐ 719 B. Doucet
☐ 720 F. DuTilly
☐ 721 Y. Gendron
☐ 722 J. Laliberté
☐ 723 C. Lecours
☐ 724 M. Lussier
☐ 725 S. Palardy
☐ 726 D. Paradis
☐ 727 M. Phaneuf
☐ 728 M. Phaneuf
☐ 729 J. Synnott
☐ 730 J. Thibault
☐ 731 J. Rodrigue
☐ 732 A. Imbault

MONTRÉAL CANADIENS PEE-WEE

☐ 733 M. Dionne
☐ 734 M. Lalande
☐ 735 F. Ouimet
☐ 736 O. Labelle
☐ 737 D. Bouchard
☐ 738 J. Boucher
☐ 739 S. Landry
☐ 740 S. Courcelles
☐ 741 A. Sayasen
☐ 742 S. Gray
☐ 743 P. Marineau
☐ 744 V. Lambert
☐ 745 S. Forget
☐ 746 Fortier-Gaudreault
☐ 747 M. Aubut
☐ 748 A. Lanthier
☐ 749 Instructeurs
☐ 750 Instructeurs
☐ 751 Instructeurs
☐ 752 Instructeurs
☐ 753 Photo d'équipe

CHAUDIÈRE-OUEST PEE-WEE

☐ 754 J. Lefrançois
☐ 755 B. Noël
☐ 756 H. Meilleur
☐ 757 G. Royer
☐ 758 L. Leblanc
☐ 759 P. Baron
☐ 760 M. Bouchard
☐ 761 O. St-Cyr
☐ 762 J. Tanguay
☐ 763 J. Baron
☐ 764 J. Paradis
☐ 765 A. Desruisseaux
☐ 766 J. Bolduc
☐ 767 J. Gosselin
☐ 768 D. Proulx
☐ 769 M. Boissonneault
☐ 770 Instructeurs

RIVE-SUD PEE-WEE

Guillaume Desbiens is one of the more expensive cards.

☐ 771 J. Walsh
☐ 772 P. Langlois
☐ 773 L. Godbout
☐ 774 M. Labbé
☐ 775 M. Marois
☐ 776 S. Goulet
☐ 777 G. Desbiens
☐ 778 M. Pelletier
☐ 779 A. Blais
☐ 780 T. Dugal
☐ 781 J. Dulac-Lemelin
☐ 782 W. Demers
☐ 783 S. Faucher
☐ 784 B. Blondin
☐ 785 J. Bélanger
☐ 786 N. Constantin
☐ 787 Instructeurs

POINTE-LÉVY B PEE-WEE

☐ 788 M. Gagnon
☐ 789 G. Côté
☐ 790 A. Dulac-Lemelin
☐ 791 K. Lecours
☐ 798 J. Pouliot
☐ 799 A. Veilleux
☐ 800 C. Savoie
☐ 801 M. Guay

☐ 792 M. Carrier
☐ 793 P. Leblond
☐ 794 F. Lachance
☐ 795 D. McNeil
☐ 796 P. L'Hébreux
☐ 797 P. Rancourt
☐ 802 M. Poulin
☐ 803 K. Ouellet
☐ 804 J. Mercier
☐ 805 Instructeurs
☐ 806 Instructeurs
☐ 807 Instructeurs

CHARLESBOURG B PEE-WEE

☐ 808 U. Bélanger
☐ 809 A. Sarasin
☐ 810 D. Jetté
☐ 811 C. Mathieu
☐ 812 J. Paradis
☐ 813 P. Vear
☐ 814 Ch.-Parent
☐ 815 B. Lizotte
☐ 816 K. Tendland
☐ 817 J. Bouchard
☐ 818 M. Plante
☐ 819 M. Fleury
☐ 820 G. Dufour
☐ 821 J. Poulin
☐ 822 G. Fortin
☐ 823 J. Bluteau-Milot
☐ 824 Instructeurs

ST-PROSPER-ETCHEMIN PEE-WEE

☐ 825 M. Hébert
☐ 826 J. Tanguay
☐ 827 D. Loignon
☐ 828 M. Carrier
☐ 829 F. Turcotte
☐ 830 S. Gagné
☐ 831 S. Jacques
☐ 832 D. Parent
☐ 833 S. Bergeron
☐ 834 O. Deblois
☐ 835 P. Bussière
☐ 836 A. Nadeau
☐ 837 A. Bernier
☐ 838 D. Gagnon
☐ 839 Instructeurs

TORONTO WEXFORD PEE-WEE

☐ 840 G. Mak
☐ 841 M. Fini
☐ 842 M. Pawlak
☐ 843 F. Turano
☐ 844 M. Horyn
☐ 845 P. McFarland
☐ 846 G. Palka
☐ 847 D. Habibullah
☐ 848 C. Anderson
☐ 849 R. Ganswich
☐ 850 M. Tuomi
☐ 851 B. Cottreau
☐ 852 R. Hastings
☐ 853 S. Bozzo
☐ 854 C. Amodeo
☐ 855 Instructeurs

BEAUCE-AMIANTE PEE-WEE

☐ 856 É. Lessard
☐ 857 J. Lachance
☐ 858 F. Therrien
☐ 859 K. Hamel
☐ 860 D. Pomerleau
☐ 861 J. Drouin
☐ 862 A. Beaudoin
☐ 863 M. Rodrigue
☐ 864 P. Daigle
☐ 865 I. Mathieu-Girard
☐ 866 E. Bouchard
☐ 867 K. Gilbert
☐ 868 F. Champagne
☐ 869 L. Cloutier
☐ 870 M. Poulin-Grenier
☐ 871 G. Béty
☐ 872 Instructeurs

NICOLET-BÉCANCOUR PEE-WEE

Nicolas Désilets is one of the more expensive cards.

☐ 873 K. Martin
☐ 874 P. Lupien
☐ 875 K. Hébert
☐ 876 B.-Morrissette
☐ 877 M. Rousseau
☐ 878 É. Lampron
☐ 879 G. Boudreau
☐ 880 D. Brazeau
☐ 881 A. Daneau
☐ 882 S. Girard
☐ 883 P. Lanciault
☐ 884 B. Leblanc
☐ 885 H. Brisson
☐ 886 M. Castonguay
☐ 887 N. Désilets
☐ 888 G. Paquet-Poirier
☐ 889 Y. Plourde
☐ 890 Instructeurs

QUÉBEC CARTIER PEE-WEE

☐ 891 J. Dufour-Gravel
☐ 892 P. Fortin
☐ 893 M. Houde
☐ 894 F. Larue
☐ 895 M. Bédard
☐ 896 P. Giroux
☐ 897 M. Tétrault
☐ 898 M. Lacroix
☐ 899 A. Lecours
☐ 900 S. Lessard
☐ 901 S. Girard
☐ 902 P. Cliche
☐ 903 Y. Jomphe
☐ 904 N. Petit
☐ 905 St-Pierre-Gagnon
☐ 906 M. St-Laurent
☐ 907 Instructeurs

DÉTROIT LITTLE CAESARS PEE-WEE

☐ 908 M. Baehr
☐ 909 J. Dunn
☐ 910 J. Dunne
☐ 911 C. Elkins
☐ 912 R. Enmark
☐ 913 M. Kowalczyk
☐ 914 D. Miller
☐ 915 T. Paluszek
☐ 916 T. Sapiro
☐ 917 M. Schepke
☐ 918 D. Schmale
☐ 919 A. Smith
☐ 920 C. Swartz
☐ 921 J. Washchuk
☐ 922 G. White
☐ 923 C. Zarb

AMIENS PEE-WEE

☐ 924 P. Caudron
☐ 925 M. Caron
☐ 926 G. Derivière
☐ 927 C. Lecrypt
☐ 928 B. Henderson
☐ 929 L. Wiotte
☐ 930 V. Wiotte
☐ 931 A. Grossemy
☐ 932 J. Vasseur
☐ 933 A. Brison
☐ 934 F. Vives
☐ 935 A. Cozette
☐ 936 G. Magne
☐ 937 V. Troupin
☐ 938 B. Petit
☐ 939 C. Teixfira
☐ 940 J. Petigny
☐ 941 T. Roussel
☐ 942 A. Florin

BAY STATE SHARKS PEE-WEE

☐ 943 A. Baird
☐ 944 T. Brzek
☐ 945 J. Burns
☐ 946 N. Burns
☐ 952 G. Goldman
☐ 953 M. Greene
☐ 954 R. Hollstein
☐ 955 M. Leazott

☐ 947 J. Chandler ☐ 956 P. McDavitt
☐ 948 T. Daniels ☐ 957 J. Russo
☐ 949 D. Evans ☐ 958 J. Sheehy
☐ 950 J. Galvin ☐ 959 M. Skrzyniarz
☐ 951 R. Ginand ☐ 960 Instructeurs

BEAUCE-NORD PEE-WEE

☐ 961 M. Marcoux ☐ 969 É. Grégoire
☐ 962 J. Chabot ☐ 970 H. Turgeon
☐ 963 Y. Marcil ☐ 971 F. Berthiaume
☐ 964 S. Labrecque ☐ 972 D. Drouin-Allen
☐ 965 S. Turgeon ☐ 973 J. Roy
☐ 966 A. Grondin ☐ 974 D. Talbot
☐ 967 D. Guillemette ☐ 975 P. Turmel
☐ 968 É. Marcoux ☐ 976 Instructeurs

LAVAL PEE-WEE

Marc-André Bernier is one of the more expensive cards.

☐ 977 B. Lamarier ☐ 987 G. Labrecque
☐ 978 L. Laforce ☐ 988 C. Gariépy
☐ 979 M. Alfieri ☐ 989 D. Poncelet
☐ 980 K. Maurice ☐ 990 M. Bernier
☐ 981 B. Demchuk ☐ 991 J. Lemay
☐ 982 M. Schafhauser ☐ 992 G. MacDonald
☐ 983 S. Lepage ☐ 993 B. O'Shea
☐ 984 A. Fréchette ☐ 994 Instructeurs
☐ 985 A. Ouimet ☐ 995 Instructeurs
☐ 986 A. Neven

AMIANTE C PEE-WEE

☐ 996 F. Laroche ☐ 1006 F. McCutcheon
☐ 997 S. Delisle ☐ 1007 M. Pomerleau
☐ 998 D. Poulin ☐ 1008 J. Langlois
☐ 999 F. Langlois ☐ 1009 K. Fortin
☐ 1000 J. Roberge ☐ 1010 L. Doucet-Proulx
☐ 1001 M. Paré ☐ 1011 J. Vachon
☐ 1002 D. Goulet ☐ 1012 Instructeurs
☐ 1003 P. Boucher ☐ 1013 Instructeurs
☐ 1004 M. Camiré ☐ 1014 Instructeurs
☐ 1005 F. Jalbert

CHARLOTTETOWN PEE-WEE

Kyle Murnaghan is one of the more expensive cards.

☐ 1016 S. Quinn ☐ 1025 C. Kenny
☐ 1017 M. Large ☐ 1026 D. Carr
☐ 1018 L. Beck ☐ 1027 A. Hayes
☐ 1019 M. Dolan ☐ 1028 B. Vessy
☐ 1020 B. Hennessey ☐ 1029 D. Turner
☐ 1021 B. Murphy ☐ 1030 C. Hughes
☐ 1022 M. Roberts ☐ 1031 K. Murnaghan
☐ 1023 J. Waddell ☐ 1032 Instructeurs
☐ 1024 T. Cudmore

LANGLEY PEE-WEE

☐ 1033 G. Butler ☐ 1044 J. Orban
☐ 1034 T. Dakers ☐ 1045 P. Redmond
☐ 1035 D'F'cesantonio ☐ 1046 L. Reid
☐ 1036 T. Eckford ☐ 1047 T. Stewart
☐ 1037 B. MacDonald ☐ 1048 D. Yacboski
☐ 1038 B. Martin ☐ 1049 T. Moulton
☐ 1039 R. Mensing ☐ 1050 Instructeurs
☐ 1040 R. Mikan ☐ 1051 Instructeurs
☐ 1041 T. Mulock ☐ 1052 Instructeurs
☐ 1042 R. Noren ☐ 1053 Instructeurs
☐ 1043 D. O'Krane ☐ 1054 Instructeurs

WASHINGTON CAPITALS PEE-WEE

☐ 1055 R. Plant ☐ 1065 B. Forino
☐ 1056 T. Harrison ☐ 1066 K. Keller
☐ 1057 J. Cash ☐ 1067 A. Davis
☐ 1058 D. Hunter ☐ 1068 J. Sexton
☐ 1059 G. Costa ☐ 1069 C. Donovan
☐ 1060 F. Jean ☐ 1070 K. Norbo
☐ 1061 M. Fairchild ☐ 1071 R. Keravuori
☐ 1062 S. Bowles ☐ 1072 D. Parisian
☐ 1063 J. Fritsch ☐ 1073 A. Bronson
☐ 1064 M. Tilch

SUISSE ROMANDE PEE-WEE

☐ 1074 M. Aubert ☐ 1093 . Langel
☐ 1075 Y. Benoît ☐ 1094 Y. Lopez
☐ 1076 A. Birbaum ☐ 1095 J. Mercier
☐ 1077 J. Bonnet ☐ 1096 A. Posse
☐ 1078 C. Botter ☐ 1097 G. Praplan
☐ 1079 J. Collon ☐ 1098 G. Rey
☐ 1080 J. Conti ☐ 1099 K. Romy
☐ 1081 D. Dancourt ☐ 1100 G. Roth
☐ 1082 V. Dubois ☐ 1101 M. Rothenmund
☐ 1083 M. Duc ☐ 1102 A. Ruffiner
☐ 1084 R. Ducret ☐ 1103 B. Siegrist
☐ 1085 B. Ecabert ☐ 1104 J. Sprunger
☐ 1086 V. Ermacora ☐ 1105 T. Spicher
☐ 1087 J. Hauert ☐ 1106 L. Tacchini
☐ 1088 G. Hauptli ☐ 1107 T. Vauclair
☐ 1089 F. Hecquet ☐ 1108 G. Venthey
☐ 1090 D. Imsand ☐ 1109 V. Villard
☐ 1091 Y. Issad ☐ 1110 T. Wermeille
☐ 1092 V. Jaccard

WESTCHESTER PEE-WEE

☐ 1111 M. Arciero ☐ 1119 C. Irwin
☐ 1112 J. Coiro ☐ 1120 M. Kass
☐ 1113 K. Connolly ☐ 1121 J. Manchso
☐ 1114 K. Cooke ☐ 1122 W. Peltz
☐ 1115 A. Edge ☐ 1123 C. Post
☐ 1116 P. Ferraro ☐ 1124 G. Razouk
☐ 1117 J. Fischer ☐ 1125 M. Rofofsky
☐ 1118 M. Friedman ☐ 1126 A. Heller
☐ 1369 T. Sullivan

CHARLESBOURG C PEE-WEE

☐ 1127 S. Aubé ☐ 1136 P. Laforest
☐ 1128 S. Bernier ☐ 1137 A. L'Hérault
☐ 1129 D. Blais ☐ 1138 A. Martin
☐ 1130 S. Côté ☐ 1139 M. Rhéaume
☐ 1131 V. Dechamps ☐ 1140 D. Tremblay
☐ 1132 G. Gauthier ☐ 1141 M. Trottier
☐ 1133 S. Guérin ☐ 1142 M. Vallée
☐ 1134 C. Kelly ☐ 1143 Instructeurs
☐ 1135 D. Lafond

ST-LAURENT PEE-WEE

☐ 1144 J. Chartrand ☐ 1153 P. Mouton
☐ 1145 J. Minogue ☐ 1154 J. Pomerleau
☐ 1146 N. Giroux ☐ 1155 F. Cardinal
☐ 1147 A. McInnis ☐ 1156 A. Émard
☐ 1148 M. Talarico ☐ 1157 M. Cassivi
☐ 1149 M. Jardel ☐ 1158 N. Robillard
☐ 1150 M. Anctil ☐ 1159 É. Langlois
☐ 1151 B. Langlois ☐ 1160 Instructeurs
☐ 1152 C. Arbuthnot

CHAUVEAU PEE-WEE

☐ 1161 M. Picard ☐ 1170 S. Savard
☐ 1162 V. Robitaille ☐ 1171 F. Lepage
☐ 1163 G. Tailleur ☐ 1172 M. Bédard
☐ 1164 J. Dufresne ☐ 1173 A. Harvey
☐ 1165 S. Jalbert ☐ 1174 F. Bilodeau
☐ 1166 F. Robitaille ☐ 1175 D. Montgomery
☐ 1167 N. Paquet ☐ 1176 D. Bédard
☐ 1168 K. Lamothe ☐ 1177 Instructeurs
☐ 1169 M. Houde

ROCHESTER PEE-WEE

☐ 1178 C. Smith ☐ 1188 A. Lehmann
☐ 1179 N. Guzylak ☐ 1189 N. Gordon
☐ 1180 M. Leusch ☐ 1190 R. Lamontagne
☐ 1181 M. Milgate ☐ 1191 M. Bessette
☐ 1182 J. Burgio ☐ 1192 B. Muller
☐ 1183 D. Amborski ☐ 1193 M. Brown
☐ 1184 S. Bartlett ☐ 1194 B. Fournelle
☐ 1185 R. Callahan ☐ 1195 S. Mayor
☐ 1186 P. Kiefer ☐ 1196 R. Schremp
☐ 1187 B. Christman ☐ 1197 Instructeurs

KUUJJUAQ PEE-WEE

☐ 1198 T. Dupuis ☐ 1207 B. Saunders
☐ 1199 Gordon-Koneak ☐ 1208 J. Berthe
☐ 1200 J. Gordon ☐ 1209 D. Watkins
☐ 1201 K. Gordon ☐ 1210 J. Gadbois
☐ 1202 J. Saunders ☐ 1211 C. Snowball
☐ 1203 R. Bédard ☐ 1212 B. Grey
☐ 1204 D. Barrett ☐ 1213 B. York
☐ 1205 J. Cloutier ☐ 1214 Instructeurs
☐ 1206 F. Mercier

MARKHAM ISLANDERS PEE-WEE

☐ 1215 O. Eizenmen ☐ 1222 D. Pandovski
☐ 1216 M. McKeown ☐ 1223 M. Root
☐ 1217 R. Meloche ☐ 1224 J. Russell
☐ 1218 S. Mole ☐ 1225 J. Steidl
☐ 1219 A. Onorati ☐ 1226 K. Smith
☐ 1220 R. Oulahen ☐ 1227 A. Stein
☐ 1221 V. Oreskovich ☐ 1228 K. Zoon

ST-EPHREM PEE-WEE

☐ 1229 M. Drouin ☐ 1237 J. Loignon
☐ 1230 J. Plante ☐ 1238 S. Lambert
☐ 1231 S. Bédard ☐ 1239 J. Longchamps
☐ 1232 C. Busque ☐ 1240 S. Rodrigue
☐ 1233 M. Labonté ☐ 1241 G. Pagé
☐ 1234 R. Fecteau ☐ 1242 D. Roy
☐ 1235 C. Bolduc ☐ 1243 É. Lavoie
☐ 1236 S. St-Pierre ☐ 1244 C. Plante

TORONTO YOUNG NATS PEE-WEE

☐ 1249 M. Dibiase ☐ 1258 D. Templeton
☐ 1250 Z. Diluca ☐ 1259 C. Black
☐ 1251 D. Johnson ☐ 1260 A. Dennis
☐ 1252 J. Sawyer ☐ 1261 A. Willock
☐ 1253 C. Priolo ☐ 1262 M. Silva
☐ 1254 B. Marshall ☐ 1263 K. Sit
☐ 1255 C. Black ☐ 1264 A. Evans
☐ 1256 R. Bilski ☐ 1265 Instructeurs
☐ 1257 R. Rosati

POINTE-LÉVY C PEE-WEE

☐ 1266 J. Sirois ☐ 1276 M. Gagnon
☐ 1267 J. Labrie ☐ 1277 P. Séguin
☐ 1268 Turgeon-Mercier ☐ 1278 M. Marceau
☐ 1269 C. Cantin ☐ 1279 M. Dupont
☐ 1270 J. Métivier ☐ 1280 K. Laverdière
☐ 1271 C.-Leclerc ☐ 1281 D. Gagnon
☐ 1272 J. Guay ☐ 1282 Instructeurs
☐ 1273 J. Bélanger ☐ 1283 Instructeurs
☐ 1274 J. Vallières ☐ 1284 Instructeurs
☐ 1275 S. Boulanger

VALLEYFIELD-BEAUHARNOIS PEE-WEE

☐ 1285 P. Bordeleau ☐ 1293 J. Bertrand
☐ 1286 G. St-Aubin ☐ 1294 K. Plante
☐ 1287 I. Leduc ☐ 1295 B. Daoust
☐ 1288 D. Reddick ☐ 1296 P. Tardif
☐ 1289 J. Pharand ☐ 1297 A. Numainville
☐ 1290 S. Lacoste ☐ 1298 S. Bruneau
☐ 1291 É. Glaude ☐ 1299 K. Turgeon
☐ 1292 D. McSween

NEW-YORK RANGERS PEE-WEE

☐ 1300 E. Baran ☐ 1307 B. French
☐ 1301 J. Cooper ☐ 1308 G. Giannattasio
☐ 1302 A. Daigh ☐ 1309 T. Gregor
☐ 1303 Z. Dehm ☐ 1310 B. Kapteina
☐ 1304 A. Dimarzo ☐ 1311 D. Melançon
☐ 1305 C. Dowd ☐ 1312 T. Trocchia
☐ 1306 P. Forselius ☐ 1313 M. Walter

DÉTROIT RED-WINGS PEE-WEE

☐ 1314 J. Sciba ☐ 1323 J. Harris
☐ 1315 R. Maki ☐ 1324 B. Genrich
☐ 1316 R. Mahrle ☐ 1325 D. Vanbuskirk
☐ 1317 M. Fritz ☐ 1326 N. Dobrowski
☐ 1318 A. Spézia ☐ 1327 R. Cianfarani
☐ 1319 M. Hunwick ☐ 1328 D. Larman
☐ 1320 G. Barrett ☐ 1329 B. Cahill
☐ 1321 M. Waskerwitz ☐ 1330 T. Mullen
☐ 1322 B. Hensick

BUCKINGHAM PEE-WEE

☐ 1331 S. Neveu ☐ 1340 J. Lanthier
☐ 1332 J. Fairfield ☐ 1341 S. Trottier
☐ 1333 M. Jonanisse ☐ 1342 M. Levasseur
☐ 1334 M. Legault ☐ 1343 P. Lauriault
☐ 1335 C. Tourangeau ☐ 1344 F. Beaudoin
☐ 1336 S. Morin ☐ 1345 Y. Leblanc
☐ 1337 S. Guindon ☐ 1346 M. Artelle
☐ 1338 D. Trottier ☐ 1347 N. Pilon
☐ 1339 J. Rizk ☐ 1348 Instructeurs

ST-LOUIS BLUES PEE-WEE

The most expensive cards are Paul Stastny and the father-and-son duo card of Peter & Paul Stastny.

☐ 1349 B. Moran ☐ 1359 J. Ellrich
☐ 1350 J. Lovecchio ☐ 1360 J. Devine
☐ 1351 S. Muncy ☐ 1361 K. Rickerman
☐ 1352 E. Slais ☐ 1362 J. Ditch
☐ 1353 M. Buha ☐ 1363 D. Longrie
☐ 1354 Paul Stastny ☐ 1364 B. Yanics
☐ 1355 M. Sansone ☐ 1366 J. Vitale
☐ 1356 A. Switzer ☐ 1367 Stastny dad, son
☐ 1357 W. Gale ☐ 1368 Photo d'équipe
☐ 1358 A. Graves

1999 UPPER DECK YEAR OF THE GREAT ONE

	Insert (#/40) / Series	YOTGO
☐	Gretzky ✍ ✂ / 1998-99 SP Authentic	1000.00
☐	Gretzky ✍ ✂ / 1998-99 SPx Prospects	1000.00
☐	Gretzky ✍ ✂ / 1998-99 UD Black Diamond	1000.00
☐	Gretzky ✍ ✂ / 1998-99 Upper Deck MVP	1000.00
☐	Gretzky ✍ ✂ / 1999-00 SP Authentic	1000.00
☐	Gretzky ✍ ✂ / 1999-00 UD Century Legends	1000.00
☐	Gretzky ✍ ✂ / 1999-00 Upper Deck MVP	1000.00

1999 BOWMAN

This series was released in 1999. There are three versions: the regular card, an O-Pee-Chee parallel (1:1 packs) and a Golden parallel (#/50).

	G50	OPC	Bowm.
Complete Set (165 cards):	1,600.00	95.00	40.00
Common Player:	5.00	.50	.25

	Player	G50	OPC	Bowm.
☐☐☐	1 Alex Auld (G), CHL	25.00	1.00	.50
☐☐☐	2 Maxime Ouellet (G), CHL	45.00	3.00	1.50
☐☐☐	3 Nolan Yonkman, CHL	5.00	.50	.25
☐☐☐	4 Jeff Beatch, CHL	5.00	.50	.25
☐☐☐	5 Pavel Brendl, CHL	35.00	2.00	1.00
☐☐☐	6 Jamie Chamberlain, CHL	5.00	.50	.25
☐☐☐	7 Kyle Wanvig, CHL	5.00	.50	.25
☐☐☐	8 Chris Kelly, CHL	5.00	.50	.25
☐☐☐	9 Scott Kelman, CHL	5.00	.50	.25
☐☐☐	10 Derek MacKenzie, CHL	5.00	.50	.25
☐☐☐	11 Tim Connolly, CHL	45.00	3.00	1.50
☐☐☐	12 Alexandre Giroux, CHL	5.00	.50	.25
☐☐☐	13 Oleg Saprykin, CHL	25.00	1.00	.50
☐☐☐	14 Sheldon Keefe, CHL	10.00	.50	.25
☐☐☐	15 Branislav Mezei, CHL	5.00	.50	.25
☐☐☐	16 Brett Lysak, CHL	5.00	.50	.25
☐☐☐	17 Peter Reynolds, CHL	5.00	.50	.25
☐☐☐	18 Ross Lupaschuk, CHL	5.00	.50	.25
☐☐☐	19 Mirko Murovic, CHL	5.00	.50	.25
☐☐☐	20 Steve McCarthy, CHL	5.00	.50	.25
☐☐☐	21 Radim Vrbata, CHL	55.00	3.00	1.50
☐☐☐	22 Dusty Jamieson, CHL	5.00	.50	.25
☐☐☐	23 Matt Carkner, CHL	5.00	.50	.25
☐☐☐	24 Denis Shvidki, CHL	10.00	.50	.25
☐☐☐	25 Jonathan Fauteux, CHL	5.00	.50	.25
☐☐☐	26 Martin Grenier, CHL	5.00	.50	.25
☐☐☐	27 Marc-André Thinel, CHL	5.00	.50	.25
☐☐☐	28 Luke Sellars, CHL	5.00	.50	.25
☐☐☐	29 Brad Ralph, CHL	5.00	.50	.25
☐☐☐	30 Scott Cameron, CHL	5.00	.50	.25
☐☐☐	31 Charlie Stephens, CHL	5.00	.50	.25
☐☐☐	32 Jamie Lundmark, CHL	35.00	2.00	1.00
☐☐☐	33 Justin Mapletoft, CHL	5.00	.50	.25
☐☐☐	34 Kris Beech, CHL	35.00	2.00	1.00
☐☐☐	35 Taylor Pyatt, CHL	25.00	1.00	.50
☐☐☐	36 Michael Zigomanis, CHL	5.00	.50	.25
☐☐☐	37 Edward Hill, CHL	5.00	.50	.25
☐☐☐	38 Barret Jackman, CHL	45.00	3.00	1.50
☐☐☐	39 Simon Lajeunesse (G), CHL	20.00	1.00	.50
☐☐☐	40 Brian Finley (G), CHL	20.00	1.00	.50
☐☐☐	41 M. Ouellet (G), QMJHL	45.00	3.00	1.50
☐☐☐	42 Alexei Volkov (G), QMJHL	25.00	1.00	.50
☐☐☐	43 R. Luongo (G), QMJHL	120.00	8.00	3.00
☐☐☐	44 Chris Lyness, QMJHL	5.00	.50	.25
☐☐☐	45 Simon Tremblay, QMJHL	5.00	.50	.25
☐☐☐	46 Éric Tremblay, QMJHL	5.00	.50	.25
☐☐☐	47 Jonathan Girard, QMJHL	10.00	.50	.25
☐☐☐	48 Dimitri Tolkunov, QMJHL	5.00	.50	.25
☐☐☐	49 Philippe Plante, QMJHL	5.00	.50	.25
☐☐☐	50 Éric Chouinard, QMJHL	25.00	1.00	.50
☐☐☐	51 Wesley Scanzano, QMJHL	5.00	.50	.25
☐☐☐	52 Vincent Dionne, QMJHL	5.00	.50	.25
☐☐☐	53 Sébastien Roger, QMJHL	5.00	.50	.25
☐☐☐	54 Ladislav Nagy, QMJHL	25.00	1.00	.50
☐☐☐	55 Alex Tanguay, QMJHL	70.00	4.00	2.00
☐☐☐	56 Martin Moise, QMJHL	5.00	.50	.25
☐☐☐	57 Brad Richards, QMJHL	55.00	3.00	1.50
☐☐☐	58 Juraj Kolnik, QMJHL	15.00	1.00	.50
☐☐☐	59 Simon Gagné, QMJHL	120.00	8.00	3.00
☐☐☐	60 G. Baumgartner, QMJHL	5.00	.50	.25
☐☐☐	61 Mathieu Benoit, QMJHL	5.00	.50	.25
☐☐☐	62 P-L Therrien, QMJHL	5.00	.50	.25
☐☐☐	63 Danny Lavoie, QMJHL	5.00	.50	.25
☐☐☐	64 M. Chouinard (G), QMJHL	5.00	.50	.25
☐☐☐	65 Andrew Carver, QMJHL	5.00	.50	.25
☐☐☐	66 Jiri Fischer, QMJHL	25.00	1.00	.50
☐☐☐	67 A. Ryazantsev, QMJHL	5.00	.50	.25
☐☐☐	68 Didier Tremblay, QMJHL	5.00	.50	.25
☐☐☐	69 Mathieu Biron, QMJHL	15.00	1.00	.50
☐☐☐	70 Michel Périard, QMJHL	5.00	.50	.25
☐☐☐	71 Mike Ribeiro, QMJHL	35.00	2.00	1.00
☐☐☐	72 François* Fortier, QMJHL	5.00	.50	.25
☐☐☐	73 Benoît Dusablon, QMJHL	5.00	.50	.25
☐☐☐	74 Jérôme Tremblay, QMJHL	5.00	.50	.25
☐☐☐	75 Samuel St. Pierre, QMJHL	5.00	.50	.25
☐☐☐	76 Marc-André Thinel, QMJHL	5.00	.50	.25
☐☐☐	77 A. Tremblay, QMJHL	5.00	.50	.25
☐☐☐	78 P. Grandmaître, QMJHL	5.00	.50	.25
☐☐☐	79 Christian Daigle	5.00	.50	.25
☐☐☐	80 David Thibeault	5.00	.50	.25
☐☐☐	81 Dominic Forget	5.00	.50	.25
☐☐☐	82 James Desmarais	5.00	.50	.25
☐☐☐	83 Pavel Brendl, WHL	35.00	2.00	1.00
☐☐☐	84 Kyle Calder, WHL	10.00	.50	.25
☐☐☐	85 Jason Chimera, WHL	5.00	.50	.25
☐☐☐	86 Chad Hinz, WHL	5.00	.50	.25
☐☐☐	87 Curtis Huppe, WHL	5.00	.50	.25
☐☐☐	88 Milan Kraft, WHL	35.00	2.00	1.00
☐☐☐	89 Brad Leeb, WHL	5.00	.50	.25
☐☐☐	90 Jamie Lundmark, WHL	35.00	2.00	1.00
☐☐☐	91 Brett Lysak, WHL	5.00	.50	.25
☐☐☐	92 Brad Moran, WHL	10.00	.50	.25
☐☐☐	93 Frantisek Mrazek, WHL	5.00	.50	.25
☐☐☐	94 Brad Twordik, WHL	5.00	.50	.25
☐☐☐	95 Kurt Drummond, WHL	5.00	.50	.25
☐☐☐	96 Burke Henry, WHL	5.00	.50	.25

☐☐☐	97 Steve McCarthy, WHL	15.00	1.00	.50
☐☐☐	98 Richard Seeley, WHL	5.00	.50	.25
☐☐☐	99 Brad Stuart, WHL	45.00	3.00	1.50
☐☐☐	100 Luc Théoret, WHL	5.00	.50	.25
☐☐☐	101 A. Fomitchev, WHL	5.00	.50	.25
☐☐☐	102 Brady Block, WHL	5.00	.50	.25
☐☐☐	103 Ajay Baines, WHL	5.00	.50	.25
☐☐☐	104 Blair Betts, WHL	5.00	.50	.25
☐☐☐	105 Tyler Bouck, WHL	15.00	1.00	.50
☐☐☐	106 Mike Brown, WHL	15.00	1.00	.50
☐☐☐	107 Brett DeCecco, WHL	5.00	.50	.25
☐☐☐	108 Scott Gomez, WHL	45.00	3.00	1.50
☐☐☐	109 Dylan Gyori, WHL	5.00	.50	.25
☐☐☐	110 Donnie Kinney, WHL	5.00	.50	.25
☐☐☐	111 Ken McKay, WHL	5.00	.50	.25
☐☐☐	112 Brett McLean, WHL	5.00	.50	.25
☐☐☐	113 Brenden Morrow, WHL	35.00	2.00	1.00
☐☐☐	114 Marty Standish, WHL	5.00	.50	.25
☐☐☐	115 Andrew Ference, WHL	15.00	1.00	.50
☐☐☐	116 Brad Ference, WHL	15.00	1.00	.50
☐☐☐	117 Scott Hannan, WHL	5.00	.50	.25
☐☐☐	118 Darrell Hay, WHL	5.00	.50	.25
☐☐☐	119 Robyn Regehr, WHL	15.00	1.00	.50
☐☐☐	120 Chris St. Croix	5.00	.50	.25
☐☐☐	121 Kenric Exner	5.00	.50	.25
☐☐☐	122 Cody Rudkowsky	5.00	.50	.25
☐☐☐	123 Scott Barney, OHL	5.00	.50	.25
☐☐☐	124 Kevin Colley, OHL	5.00	.50	.25
☐☐☐	125 Sheldon Keefe, OHL	20.00	1.00	.50
☐☐☐	126 Norm Milley, OHL	5.00	.50	.25
☐☐☐	127 Scott Page, OHL	5.00	.50	.25
☐☐☐	128 Justin Papineau, OHL	15.00	1.00	.50
☐☐☐	129 Ryan Ready, OHL	5.00	.50	.25
☐☐☐	130 Denis Shvidki, OHL	10.00	.50	.25
☐☐☐	131 Chris Stanley, OHL	5.00	.50	.25
☐☐☐	132 Dan Tessier, OHL	5.00	.50	.25
☐☐☐	133 Daniel Tkaczuk, OHL	25.00	1.00	.50
☐☐☐	134 Michael Zigomanis, OHL	5.00	.50	.25
☐☐☐	135 Jim Baxter, OHL	5.00	.50	.25
☐☐☐	136 Branislav Mezei, OHL	15.00	1.00	.50
☐☐☐	137 Brian Campbell, OHL	5.00	.50	.25
☐☐☐	138 Greg Labenski, OHL	5.00	.50	.25
☐☐☐	139 Jeff McKercher, OHL	5.00	.50	.25
☐☐☐	140 Martin Skoula, OHL	25.00	1.00	.50
☐☐☐	141 Brian Finley (G), OHL	20.00	1.00	.50
☐☐☐	142 Seamus Kotyk (G), OHL	5.00	.50	.25
☐☐☐	143 Adam Colagiacomo, OHL	5.00	.50	.25
☐☐☐	144 Tim Connolly, OHL	45.00	3.00	1.50
☐☐☐	145 Harold Druken, OHL	35.00	2.00	1.00
☐☐☐	146 Rico Fata, OHL	25.00	1.00	.50
☐☐☐	147 David Legwand, OHL	45.00	3.00	1.50
☐☐☐	148 Adam Mair, OHL	15.00	1.00	.50
☐☐☐	149 Kent McDonell, OHL	5.00	.50	.25
☐☐☐	150 Ivan Novoseltsev, OHL	20.00	1.00	.50
☐☐☐	151 Peter Sarno, OHL	5.00	.50	.25
☐☐☐	152 Dan Snyder, OHL	5.00	.50	.25
☐☐☐	153 Jason Spezza, OHL	90.00	9.00	4.00
☐☐☐	154 Jason Ward, OHL	45.00	3.00	1.50
☐☐☐	155 Alex Henry, OHL	5.00	.50	.25
☐☐☐	156 Wes Jarvis, OHL	5.00	.50	.25
☐☐☐	157 Paul Mara, OHL	15.00	1.00	.50
☐☐☐	158 Kevin Mitchell, OHL	5.00	.50	.25
☐☐☐	159 Dan Passero, OHL	5.00	.50	.25
☐☐☐	160 Dan Watson, OHL	5.00	.50	.25
☐☐☐	161 Gene Chiarello, OHL	5.00	.50	.25
☐☐☐	162 Chris Madden (G), OHL	5.00	.50	.25
☐☐☐	163 DeCecco / Ouellet (G)	15.00	1.00	0.50
☐☐☐	164 Barney / Thinel	5.00	.50	.25
☐☐☐	165 Checklist	5.00	.50	.25

CERTIFIED AUTOGRAPH ISSUE

There are three versions: the regular autograph (1:16 packs), the silver-foil autograph and the gold-foil autograph.

Insert Set (40 cards):		**1,600.00**	**800.00**	**520.00**
	Autographs	**GF**	**SF**	**BA**
☐☐☐	BA1 Brian Finley (G) ✍	50.00	25.00	16.00
☐☐☐	BA2 Simon Lajeunesse (G) ✍	50.00	25.00	16.00
☐☐☐	BA3 Barret Jackman ✍	100.00	50.00	34.00
☐☐☐	BA4 Edward Hill ✍	35.00	15.00	8.00
☐☐☐	BA5 Michael Zigomanis ✍	40.00	20.00	14.00
☐☐☐	BA6 Taylor Pyatt ✍	60.00	30.00	20.00
☐☐☐	BA7 Kris Beech ✍	80.00	40.00	28.00
☐☐☐	BA8 Justin Mapletoft ✍	40.00	20.00	14.00
☐☐☐	BA9 Jamie Lundmark ✍	80.00	40.00	28.00
☐☐☐	BA10 Charlie Stephens ✍	35.00	15.00	8.00
☐☐☐	BA11 Scott Cameron ✍	35.00	15.00	8.00
☐☐☐	BA12 Brad Ralph ✍	40.00	20.00	14.00
☐☐☐	BA13 Luke Sellars ✍	40.00	20.00	14.00
☐☐☐	BA14 Marc-André Thinel ✍	40.00	20.00	14.00
☐☐☐	BA15 Martin Grenier ✍	35.00	15.00	8.00
☐☐☐	BA16 Jonathan Fauteux ✍	35.00	15.00	8.00
☐☐☐	BA17 Denis Shvidki ✍	60.00	30.00	20.00
☐☐☐	BA18 Matt Carkner ✍	35.00	15.00	8.00
☐☐☐	BA19 Dusty Jamieson ✍	35.00	15.00	8.00
☐☐☐	BA20 Radim Vrbata ✍	100.00	50.00	35.00
☐☐☐	BA21 Alex Auld (G) ✍	60.00	30.00	20.00
☐☐☐	BA22 Maxime Ouellet (G) ✍	100.00	50.00	35.00
☐☐☐	BA23 Nolan Yonkman ✍	35.00	15.00	8.00
☐☐☐	BA24 Jeff Beatch ✍	35.00	15.00	8.00
☐☐☐	BA25 Pavel Brendl ✍	80.00	40.00	28.00
☐☐☐	BA26 Jamie Chamberlain ✍	35.00	15.00	8.00
☐☐☐	BA27 Kyle Wanvig ✍	40.00	20.00	14.00
☐☐☐	BA28 Chris Kelly ✍	35.00	15.00	8.00
☐☐☐	BA29 Scott Kelman ✍	40.00	20.00	14.00
☐☐☐	BA30 Derek MacKenzie ✍	35.00	15.00	8.00
☐☐☐	BA31 Tim Connolly ✍	100.00	50.00	35.00
☐☐☐	BA32 Alexandre Giroux ✍	35.00	15.00	8.00
☐☐☐	BA33 Oleg Saprykin ✍	60.00	30.00	20.00
☐☐☐	BA34 Sheldon Keefe ✍	50.00	25.00	16.00
☐☐☐	BA35 Branislav Mezei ✍	40.00	20.00	14.00
☐☐☐	BA36 Brett Lysak ✍	35.00	15.00	8.00
☐☐☐	BA37 Peter Reynolds ✍	35.00	15.00	8.00
☐☐☐	BA38 Ross Lupaschuk ✍	40.00	20.00	14.00
☐☐☐	BA39 Mirko Murovic ✍	35.00	15.00	8.00
☐☐☐	BA40 Steve McCarthy ✍	40.00	20.00	14.00

SCOUT'S CHOICE

Insert Set (21 cards):		**80.00**
	Insert (1:12 packs)	**SC**
☐	SC1 Tim Connolly	5.00
☐	SC2 Scott Kelman	2.00
☐	SC3 Pavel Brendl	4.00
☐	SC4 Maxime Ouellet (G)	5.00
☐	SC5 Brian Finley (G)	2.00
☐	SC6 Denis Shvidki	3.00
☐	SC7 Michael Zigomanis	2.00
☐	SC8 Taylor Pyatt	3.00
☐	SC9 Kris Beech	4.00
☐	SC10 Jamie Lundmark	4.00
☐	SC11 Jason Spezza	10.00
☐	SC12 Rico Fata	3.00
☐	SC13 David Legwand	5.00
☐	SC14 Daniel Tkaczuk	3.00
☐	SC15 Brad Stuart	5.00
☐	SC16 Jiri Fischer	3.00
☐	SC17 Simon Gagné	10.00
☐	SC18 Alex Tanguay	7.00
☐	SC19 Scott Gomez	5.00
☐	SC20 Ladislav Nagy	3.00
☐	SC21 Roberto Luongo (G)	10.00

1999 - 2000 AURORA

This series was issued in September 1999. All 200 base cards (regular and Striped) have a Premiere Date parallel (#/50).

Complete Set (200 cards):		**3700.00**	**55.00**
Common Player:		**8.00**	**.25**
	Player	**PD50**	**Reg.**
☐☐	1 Guy Hebert (G), Anah.	8.00	.25
☐☐	2 Paul Kariya, Anah.	55.00	1.00
☐☐	3 Marty McInnis, Anah.	8.00	.25
☐☐	4 Steve Rucchin, Anah.	8.00	.25
☐☐	5 Teemu Selänne, Anah.	30.00	.50
☐☐	6 Andrew Brunette, Nash.	8.00	.25
☐☐	7 Kelly Buchberger, Edmo.	8.00	.25
☐☐	8 Damian Rhodes (G), Otta.	8.00	.25
☐☐	9 Jason Allison, Bost.	20.00	.50
☐☐	10 Raymond Bourque, Bost.	45.00	1.00
☐☐	11 Anson Carter, Bost.	15.00	.25
☐☐	12 Byron Dafoe (G), Bost.	15.00	.25
☐☐	13 Sergei Samsonov, Bost.	20.00	.50
☐☐	14 Joe Thornton, Bost.	45.00	1.00
☐☐	15 Curtis Brown, Buff.	8.00	.25
☐☐	16 Dominik Hasek (G), Buff.	40.00	1.00
☐☐	17 Joé Juneau, Buff.	8.00	.25
☐☐	18 Michael Peca, Buff.	15.00	.25
☐☐	19 Miroslav Satan, Buff.	10.00	.25
☐☐	20 Valeri Bure, Calg.	10.00	.25
☐☐	21 Jean-Sébastien Giguère (G), Calg.	30.00	.50
☐☐	22 Phil Housley, Calg.	10.00	.25
☐☐	23 Jarome Iginla, Calg.	30.00	.50
☐☐	24 Cory Stillman, Calg.	8.00	.25
☐☐	25 Ron Francis, Caro.	20.00	.50
☐☐	26 Arturs Irbe (G), Caro.	15.00	.25
☐☐	27 Sami Kapanen, Caro.	10.00	.25
☐☐	28 Keith Primeau, Caro.	15.00	.25
☐☐	29 Ray Sheppard, Caro.	8.00	.25
☐☐	30 Tony Amonte, Chic.	20.00	.50
☐☐	31 Jean-Pierre Dumont, Chic.	8.00	.25
☐☐	32 Doug Gilmour, Chic.	20.00	.50
☐☐	33 Jocelyn Thibault (G), Chic.	15.00	.25
☐☐	34 Alexei Zhamnov, Chic.	10.00	.25
☐☐	35 Adam Deadmarsh, Colo.	10.00	.25
☐☐	36 Chris Drury, Colo.	20.00	.50
☐☐	37 Theoren Fleury, Colo.	20.00	.50
☐☐	38 Peter Forsberg, Colo.	55.00	1.00
☐☐	39 Milan Hejduk, Colo.	30.00	.50
☐☐	40 Claude Lemieux, Colo.	10.00	.25
☐☐	41 Patrick Roy (G), Colo.	120.00	3.00
☐☐	42 Joe Sakic, Colo.	60.00	1.50
☐☐	43 Ed Belfour (G), Dall.	40.00	1.00
☐☐	44 Brett Hull, Dall.	40.00	1.00
☐☐	45 Jamie Langenbrunner, Dall.	8.00	.25
☐☐	46 Jere Lehtinen, Dall.	10.00	.25
☐☐	47 Mike Modano, Dall.	40.00	1.00
☐☐	48 Joe Nieuwendyk, Dall.	15.00	.25
☐☐	49 Chris Chelios, Detr.	20.00	.50
☐☐	50 Sergei Fedorov, Detr.	40.00	1.00
☐☐	51 Nicklas Lidström, Detr.	20.00	.50
☐☐	52 Darren McCarty, Detr.	10.00	.25
☐☐	53 Chris Osgood (G), Detr.	20.00	.50
☐☐	54 Brendan Shanahan, Detr.	40.00	1.00
☐☐	55 Steve Yzerman, Detr.	95.00	2.00
☐☐	56 Bill Guerin, Edmo.	15.00	.25
☐☐	57 Mike Grier, Edmo.	8.00	.25
☐☐	58 Tommy Salo (G), Edmo.	15.00	.25
☐☐	59 Ryan Smyth, Edmo.	15.00	.25
☐☐	60 Doug Weight, Edmo.	20.00	.50
☐☐	61 Pavel Bure, Flor.	30.00	.50
☐☐	62 Sean Burke (G), Flor.	20.00	.50
☐☐	63 Viktor Kozlov, Flor.	10.00	.25
☐☐	64 Rob Niedermayer, Flor.	8.00	.25
☐☐	65 Mark Parrish, Flor.	15.00	.25
☐☐	66 Ray Whitney, Flor.	8.00	.25
☐☐	67 Donald Audette, LosA.	15.00	.25
☐☐	68 Rob Blake, LosA.	20.00	.50
☐☐	69 Zigmund Palffy, All-Star '99	20.00	.50
☐☐	70 Luc Robitaille, LosA.	30.00	.50
☐☐	71 Jamie Storr (G), LosA.	8.00	.25
☐☐	72 Jozef Stumpel, LosA.	8.00	.25
☐☐	73 Shayne Corson, Mont.	10.00	.25
☐☐	74 Jeff Hackett (G), Mont.	10.00	.25
☐☐	75 Saku Koivu, Mont.	30.00	.50
☐☐	76 Martin Rucinsky, Mont.	8.00	.25
☐☐	77 Brian Savage, Mont.	10.00	.25
☐☐	78 Mike Dunham (G), Nash.	15.00	.25
☐☐	79 Sergei Krivokrasov, Nash.	8.00	.25
☐☐	80 David Legwand, Nash.	15.00	.50
☐☐	81 Cliff Ronning, Nash.	8.00	.25
☐☐	82 Scott Walker, Nash.	8.00	.25
☐☐	83 Jason Arnott, NJer.	15.00	.25
☐☐	84 Martin Brodeur (G), NJer.	60.00	1.50
☐☐	85 Patrik Elias, NJer.	30.00	.50
☐☐	86 Bobby Holik, NJer.	10.00	.25
☐☐	87 Brendan Morrison, NJer.	10.00	.25
☐☐	88 Petr* Sykora, NJer.	15.00	.25
☐☐	89 Mariusz Czerkawski, NYIs.	8.00	.25
☐☐	90 Kenny Jönsson, NYIs.	8.00	.25
☐☐	91 Félix Potvin (G), NYIs.	20.00	.50
☐☐	92 Mike Watt, NYIs.	8.00	.25
☐☐	93 Adam Graves, NYRa.	15.00	.25
☐☐	94 Brian Leetch, NYRa.	20.00	.50
☐☐	95 John MacLean, NYRa.	8.00	.25
☐☐	96 Petr Nedved, NYRa.	10.00	.25
☐☐	97 Mike Richter (G), NYRa.	15.00	.25
☐☐	98 Magnus Arvedson, Otta.	8.00	.25
☐☐	99 Marian Hossa, Otta.	40.00	1.00
☐☐	100 Shawn McEachern, Otta.	10.00	.25
☐☐	101 Ron Tugnutt (G), Otta.	15.00	.25
☐☐	102 Alexei Yashin, Otta.	20.00	.50
☐☐	103 Rod Brind'Amour, Phil.	10.00	.25
☐☐	104 Éric Desjardins, Phil.	10.00	.25
☐☐	105 John LeClair, Phil.	30.00	.50
☐☐	106 Eric Lindros, Phil.	40.00	1.00
☐☐	107 Mark Recchi, Phil.	15.00	.25
☐☐	108 John Vanbiesbrouck (G), Phil.	15.00	.25
☐☐	109 Nikolai Khabibulin (G), Phoe.	15.00	.25
☐☐	110 Teppo Numminen, Phoe.	10.00	.25
☐☐	111 Jeremy Roenick, Phoe.	30.00	.50
☐☐	112 Rick Tocchet, Phoe.	10.00	.25
☐☐	113 Keith Tkachuk, Phoe.	20.00	.50
☐☐	114 Matthew Barnaby, Pitt.	8.00	.25
☐☐	115 Tom Barrasso (G), Pitt.	15.00	.25
☐☐	116 Jaromir Jagr, Pitt.	40.00	1.00
☐☐	117 Alexei Kovalev, Pitt.	20.00	.50
☐☐	118 Martin Straka, Pitt.	10.00	.25
☐☐	119 Vincent Damphousse, SanJ.	20.00	.50
☐☐	120 Jeff Friesen, SanJ.	10.00	.25
☐☐	121 Patrick Marleau, SanJ.	15.00	.25
☐☐	122 Steve Shields (G), SanJ.	8.00	.25
☐☐	123 Mike Vernon (G), SanJ.	15.00	.25
☐☐	124 Pavol Demitra, SLou.	15.00	.25
☐☐	125 Grant Fuhr (G), SLou.	20.00	.50
☐☐	126 Al MacInnis, SLou.	15.00	.25
☐☐	127 Chris Pronger, SLou.	20.00	.50
☐☐	128 Pierre Turgeon, SLou.	15.00	.25
☐☐	129 Chris Gratton, Tamp.	8.00	.25
☐☐	130 Kevin Hodson (G), Tamp.	8.00	.25
☐☐	131 Vincent Lecavalier, Tamp.	40.00	1.00
☐☐	132 Paul Mara, Tamp.	8.00	.25
☐☐	133 Darcy Tucker, Tamp.	8.00	.25
☐☐	134 Sergei Berezin, Toro.	8.00	.25
☐☐	135 Mike Johnson, Toro.	8.00	.25
☐☐	136 Curtis Joseph (G), Toro.	40.00	1.00
☐☐	137 Yanic Perreault, Toro.	10.00	.25
☐☐	138 Mats Sundin, Toro.	40.00	1.00
☐☐	139 Steve Thomas, Toro.	8.00	.25
☐☐	140 Mark Messier, Vanc.	40.00	1.00
☐☐	141 Bill Muckalt, Vanc.	8.00	.25
☐☐	142 Alexander Mogilny, Vanc.	15.00	.25
☐☐	143 Markus Näslund, Vanc.	40.00	1.00
☐☐	144 Mattias Öhlund, Vanc.	10.00	.25
☐☐	145 Garth Snow (G), Vanc.	10.00	.25
☐☐	146 Peter Bondra, Wash.	20.00	.50
☐☐	147 Sergei Gonchar, Wash.	10.00	.25
☐☐	**148 Benoît Gratton, Wash.**	**8.00**	**.50**
☐☐	149 Olaf Kölzig (G), Wash.	20.00	.50
☐☐	150 Adam Oates, Wash.	15.00	.25

STRIPED

These cards parallel the regular base cards. All 50 Striped cards have a Premiere Date parallel (#/50).

Complete Set (50 cards):		**1225.00**	**25.00**
	Player	**PD50**	**Reg.**
☐☐	2 Paul Kariya, Anah.	55.00	1.00
☐☐	5 Teemy Selänne, Anah.	30.00	.50
☐☐	10 Raymond Bourque, Bost.	45.00	1.00
☐☐	12 Byron Dafoe (G), Bost.	15.00	.50
☐☐	16 Dominik Hasek (G), Buff.	40.00	1.00
☐☐	18 Michael Peca, Buff.	15.00	.50
☐☐	23 Jarome Iginla, Calg.	30.00	.50
☐☐	26 Arturs Irbe (G), Caro.	15.00	.50
☐☐	28 Keith Primeau, Caro.	15.00	.50
☐☐	30 Tony Amonte, Chic.	20.00	.50
☐☐	32 Doug Gilmour, Chic.	20.00	.50
☐☐	36 Chris Drury, Colo.	20.00	.50
☐☐	37 Theoren Fleury, Colo.	20.00	.50
☐☐	38 Peter Forsberg, Colo.	55.00	1.00
☐☐	41 Patrick Roy (G), Colo.	120.00	3.00
☐☐	42 Joe Sakic, Colo.	60.00	1.50
☐☐	43 Ed Belfour (G), Dall.	40.00	1.00
☐☐	44 Brett Hull, Dall.	40.00	1.00
☐☐	47 Mike Modano, Dall.	40.00	1.00
☐☐	49 Chris Chelios, Detr.	20.00	.50
☐☐	50 Sergei Fedorov, Detr.	40.00	1.00
☐☐	54 Brendan Shanahan, Detr.	40.00	1.00
☐☐	55 Steve Yzerman, Detr.	95.00	2.00
☐☐	60 Doug Weight, Edmo.	20.00	.50
☐☐	61 Pavel Bure, Flor.	30.00	.50
☐☐	65 Mark Parrish, Flor.	15.00	.50
☐☐	69 Zigmund Palffy, LosA.	20.00	.50
☐☐	70 Luc Robitaille, LosA.	30.00	.50
☐☐	75 Saku Koivu, Mont.	30.00	.50
☐☐	84 Martin Brodeur (G), NJer.	60.00	1.50
☐☐	91 Félix Potvin (G), NYIs.	20.00	.50
☐☐	94 Brian Leetch, NYRa.	20.00	.50
☐☐	97 Mike Richter (G), NYRa.	15.00	.50
☐☐	99 Marian Hossa, Otta.	40.00	1.00

□□ 102 Alexei Yashin, Otta.	20.00	.50
□□ 105 John LeClair, Phil.	30.00	.50
□□ 106 Eric Lindros, Phil.	40.00	1.00
□□ 107 Mark Recchi, Phil.	15.00	.50
□□ 108 John Vanbiesbrouck (G), Phil.	15.00	.50
□□ 111 Jeremy Roenick, Phoe.	30.00	.50
□□ 113 Keith Tkachuk, Phoe.	20.00	.50
□□ 116 Jaromir Jagr, Pitt.	40.00	1.00
□□ 119 Vincent Lecavalier, Tamp.	20.00	.50
□□ 125 Grant Fuhr (G), Slou.	20.00	.50
□□ 126 Al MacInnis, Slou.	15.00	.50
□□ 131 Vincent Lecavalier, Tamp.	40.00	1.00
□□ 136 Curtis Joseph (G), Toro.	40.00	1.00
□□ 138 Mats Sundin, Toro.	40.00	1.00
□□ 140 Mark Messier, Vanc.	40.00	1.00
□□ 146 Peter Bondra, Wash.	20.00	.50

CANVAS CREATIONS

Insert Set (10 cards):	425.00
Insert (1:193 packs)	CC
□ 1 Paul Kariya, Anah.	50.00
□ 2 Teemu Selänne, Anah.	30.00
□ 3 Dominik Hasek (G), Buff.	35.00
□ 4 Peter Forsberg, Colo.	50.00
□ 5 Patrick Roy (G), Colo.	90.00
□ 6 Steve Yzerman, Detr.	90.00
□ 7 Pavel Bure, Flor.	30.00
□ 8 John LeClair, Phil.	30.00
□ 9 Eric Lindros, Phil.	35.00
□ 10 Jaromir Jagr, Pitt.	35.00

CHAMPIONSHIP FEVER

There are four versions: the regular card, a Silver parallel (#/250), an Ice Blue parallel (#/100) and a Copper parallel (#/20).

Insert Set (20 cards):	2800.00	550.00	300.00	45.00
Inserts	C20	IB100	S250	Reg.
□□□□ 1 P. Kariya, Anah.	200.00	40.00	25.00	4.00
□□□□ 2 T. Selänne, Anah.	100.00	20.00	10.00	2.00
□□□□ 3 R. Bourque, Bost.	175.00	35.00	20.00	2.00
□□□□ 4 Hasek (G), Buff.	150.00	30.00	15.00	2.00
□□□□ 5 M. Peca, Buff.	50.00	10.00	5.00	1.00
□□□□ 6 T. Fleury, Colo.	75.00	15.00	10.00	.75
□□□□ 7 P. Forsberg, Colo.	200.00	40.00	25.00	4.00
□□□□ 8 P. Roy (G), Colo.	350.00	70.00	50.00	8.00
□□□□ 9 J. Sakic, Colo.	225.00	45.00	25.00	4.00
□□□□ 10 Belfour (G), Dall.	150.00	30.00	15.00	2.00
□□□□ 11 Modano, Dall.	150.00	30.00	15.00	2.00
□□□□ 12 Shanahan, Detr.	150.00	30.00	15.00	2.00
□□□□ 13 Yzerman, Detr.	350.00	70.00	40.00	6.00
□□□□ 14 P. Bure, Flor.	100.00	20.00	10.00	2.00
□□□□ 15 Brodeur (G), NJer.	225.00	45.00	25.00	4.00
□□□□ 16 J. LeClair, Phil.	100.00	20.00	10.00	2.00
□□□□ 17 E. Lindros, Phil.	150.00	30.00	15.00	2.00
□□□□ 18 J. Jagr, Pitt.	150.00	30.00	15.00	2.00
□□□□ 19 Joseph (G), Toro.	150.00	30.00	15.00	2.00
□□□□ 20 M. Sundin, Toro.	150.00	30.00	15.00	2.00

COMPLETE PLAYERS

There are four versions: a hobby-pack Silver insert (#/299), a hobby-pack Silver Variation insert (#/25), a retail-pack Gold insert (#/299) and a retail-pack Gold Variation insert (#/25). The Silver and Gold cards are priced similarly as are the Silver Variation and Gold Variation cards.

Insert Set (10 cards):	1400.00	290.00
Inserts	V25	CP299
□□□□ 1 Paul Kariya, Anah.	175.00	35.00
□□□□ 2 Teemu Selänne, Anah.	100.00	20.00
□□□□ 3 Dominik Hasek (G), Buff.	125.00	25.00
□□□□ 4 Peter Forsberg, Colo.	175.00	35.00
□□□□ 5 Patrick Roy (G), Colo.	300.00	75.00
□□□□ 6 Mike Modano, Dall.	125.00	25.00
□□□□ 7 Steve Yzerman, Detr.	300.00	60.00
□□□□ 8 John LeClair, Phil.	100.00	20.00
□□□□ 9 Eric Lindros, Phil.	125.00	25.00
□□□□ 10 Jaromir Jagr, Pitt.	125.00	25.00

GLOVE UNLIMITED

Insert Set (20 cards):	105.00
Insert (2:25 packs)	GU
□ 1 Guy Hebert (G), Anah.	4.00
□ 2 Byron Dafoe (G), Bost.	4.00
□ 3 Dominik Hasek (G), Buff.	8.00
□ 4 Arturs Irbe (G), Caro.	4.00
□ 5 Jocelyn Thibault (G), Chic.	4.00
□ 6 Patrick Roy (G), Colo.	25.00
□ 7 Ed Belfour (G), Dall.	8.00
□ 8 Chris Osgood (G), Detr.	5.00
□ 9 Tommy Salo (G), Edmo.	4.00
□ 10 Jeff Hackett (G), Mont.	4.00
□ 11 Martin Brodeur (G), NJer.	14.00
□ 12 Félix Potvin (G), NYIs.	5.00
□ 13 Mike Richter (G), NYRa.	4.00
□ 14 Ron Tugnutt (G), Otta.	4.00
□ 15 John Vanbiesbrouck (G), Phil.	4.00
□ 16 Nikolai Khabibulin (G), Phoe.	4.00
□ 17 Grant Fuhr (G), SLou.	5.00
□ 18 Steve Shields (G), SanJ.	4.00
□ 19 Curtis Joseph (G), Toro.	8.00
□ 20 Olaf Kölzig (G), Wash.	5.00

STYROTECHS

Insert Set (20 cards):	230.00
Insert (1:25 packs)	ST
□ 1 Paul Kariya, Anah.	16.00
□ 2 Teemu Selänne, Anah.	10.00
□ 3 Dominik Hasek (G), Buff.	12.00
□ 4 Theoren Fleury, Colo.	6.00
□ 5 Peter Forsberg, Colo.	16.00
□ 6 Patrick Roy (G), Colo.	35.00
□ 7 Ed Belfour (G), Dall.	12.00
□ 8 Mike Modano, Dall.	12.00
□ 9 Brendan Shanahan, Detr.	12.00
□ 10 Steve Yzerman, Detr.	30.00
□ 11 Pavel Bure, Flor.	10.00
□ 12 Martin Brodeur (G), NJer.	20.00
□ 13 Alexei Yashin, Otta.	6.00
□ 14 John LeClair, Phil.	10.00
□ 15 Eric Lindros, Phil.	12.00
□ 16 Keith Tkachuk, Phoe.	6.00
□ 17 Jaromir Jagr, Pitt.	12.00
□ 18 Curtis Joseph (G), Toro.	12.00
□ 19 Mats Sundin, Toro.	12.00
□ 20 Mark Messier, Vanc.	12.00

MONTRÉAL SHOW

These cards were available via a wrapper-redemption program.

Complete Set (20 cards):	170.00
Player (#/20)	MT
□ 2 Paul Kariya, Anah.	10.00
□ 5 Teemu Selänne, Anah.	5.00
□ 10 Raymond Bourque, Bost.	10.00
□ 13 Sergei Samsonov, Bost.	5.00
□ 16 Dominik Hasek (G), Buff.	10.00
□ 38 Peter Forsberg, Colo.	10.00
□ 41 Patrick Roy (G), Colo.	30.00
□ 43 Ed Belfour (G), Dall.	10.00
□ 47 Mike Modano, Dall.	10.00
□ 53 Chris Osgood (G), Detr.	5.00
□ 55 Steve Yzerman, Detr.	20.00
□ 70 Luc Robitaille, LosA.	5.00
□ 75 Saku Koivu, Mont.	5.00
□ 84 Martin Brodeur (G), NJer.	15.00
□ 105 John LeClair, Phil.	5.00
□ 106 Eric Lindros, Phil.	10.00
□ 108 John Vanbiesbrouck (G), Phil.	5.00
□ 116 Jaromir Jagr, Pitt.	10.00
□ 131 Vincent Lecavalier, Tamp.	10.00
□ 138 Mats Sundin, Toro.	10.00

1999 - 2000 BE A PLAYER MEMORABILIA

This series was distributed in two releases: the original series in 1999 and a Rookie & Traded Update in 2000. There are three versions: a regular cards, a Silver card (#/1000) and a Gold card (#/100). Wrapper-redemption cards from the 1999 Toronto Fall Expo (#/10) also exist.

Complete Set (400 cards):	2500.00	375.00	130.00
Common Player:	5.00	1.00	.25
Player	G100	S1000	Reg.
□□□ **1 Patrik Stefan, Atla. RC**	**20.00**	**4.00**	**3.00**
□□□ 2 Glen Murray, LosA.	14.00	2.00	.50
□□□ 3 Nicklas Lidström, Detr.	15.00	2.00	.50
□□□ 4 Arturs Irbe (G), Caro.	10.00	1.00	.50
□□□ 5 Viktor Kozlov, Flor.	8.00	1.00	.25
□□□ 6 Dmitry Yushkevich, Toro.	6.00	1.00	.25
□□□ **7 Byron Ritchie, Caro. RC**	**6.00**	**1.00**	**.50**
□□□ 8 Robert Svehla, Flor.	6.00	1.00	.25
□□□ 9 Jeremy Roenick, Phoe.	20.00	3.00	1.00
□□□ 10 Ron Francis, Caro.	15.00	2.00	.50
□□□ 11 Oleg Kvasha, Flor.	5.00	1.00	.25
□□□ 12 Marian Hossa, Otta.	30.00	4.00	1.00
□□□ 13 Mark Recchi, Phil.	12.00	1.00	.50
□□□ 14 Scott Mellanby, Flor.	6.00	1.00	.25
□□□ 15 Adam Graves, NYRa.	12.00	1.00	.50
□□□ 16 Boris Mironov, Chic.	5.00	1.00	.25
□□□ 17 Derian Hatcher, Dall.	8.00	1.00	.25
□□□ 18 Brian Leetch, NYRa.	15.00	2.00	.50
□□□ 19 Mattias Öhlund, Vanc.	8.00	1.00	.25
□□□ 20 Ray Whitney, Flor.	6.00	1.00	.25
□□□ 21 Mike Richter (G), NYRa.	14.00	2.00	.50
□□□ 22 Paul Mara, Tamp.	5.00	1.00	.25
□□□ 23 Todd Bertuzzi, Vanc.	35.00	5.00	1.50
□□□ 24 Sergei Zubov, Dall.	6.00	1.00	.25
□□□ 25 Cliff Ronning, Nash.	6.00	1.00	.25
□□□ 26 Anson Carter, Bost.	12.00	1.00	.50
□□□ 27 Dmitri Mironov, Wash.	5.00	1.00	.25
□□□ 28 Shane Willis, Caro.	6.00	1.00	.50
□□□ 29 Shayne Corson, Mont.	8.00	1.00	.25
□□□ 30 Chris Chelios, Detr.	15.00	2.00	.50
□□□ 31 Pavel Kubina, Tamp.	5.00	1.00	.25
□□□ 32 Michal Grosek, Buff.	5.00	1.00	.25
□□□ 33 Gary Suter, SanJ.	6.00	1.00	.25
□□□ 34 Greg A. Adams, Phoe.	5.00	1.00	.25
□□□ 35 Joe Thornton, Bost.	35.00	5.00	1.50
□□□ 36 Matt Higgins, Mont.	5.00	1.00	.25
□□□ 37 Chris Gratton, Tamp.	6.00	1.00	.25
□□□ 38 Raymond Bourque, Bost.	35.00	5.00	1.50
□□□ 39 Tommy Salo (G), Edmo.	12.00	1.00	.50
□□□ 40 Igor Kravchuk, Otta.	5.00	1.00	.25
□□□ 41 Byron Dafoe (G), Bost.	12.00	1.00	.50
□□□ 42 Larry Murphy, Detr.	6.00	1.00	.25
□□□ 43 Bryan McCabe, Chic.	6.00	1.00	.25
□□□ 44 Vanbiesbrouck (G), Phil.	14.00	2.00	.50
□□□ 45 Brett Hull, Dall.	30.00	4.00	1.00
□□□ 46 Christian Dubé, NYRa.	5.00	1.00	.25
□□□ 47 Kyle McLaren, Bost.	6.00	1.00	.25
□□□ 48 Jere Lehtinen, Dall.	8.00	1.00	.25
□□□ 49 Petr Nedved, NYRa.	8.00	1.00	.25
□□□ 50 Jason Allison, Bost.	15.00	2.00	.50
□□□ **51 Brad Lukowich, Dall. RC**	**10.00**	**2.00**	**1.50**
□□□ 52 Scott Stevens, NJer.	12.00	1.00	.50
□□□ 53 Sergei Krivokrasov, Nash.	5.00	1.00	.25
□□□ 54 Olaf Kölzig (G), Wash.	15.00	2.00	.50
□□□ 55 Sami Kapanen, Caro.	8.00	1.00	.25
□□□ 56 Sami Salo, Otta.	5.00	1.00	.25
□□□ 57 Cory Stillman, Calg.	6.00	1.00	.25
□□□ 58 Darcy Tucker, Tamp.	6.00	1.00	.25
□□□ 59 Rod Brind'Amour, Phil.	8.00	1.00	.25
□□□ **60 John Jakopin, Flor. RC**	**6.00**	**1.00**	**1.00**
□□□ 61 Martin Brodeur (G), NJer.	45.00	7.00	2.00
□□□ 62 Jiri Slégr, Pitt.	5.00	1.00	.25
□□□ 63 Rem Murray, Edmo.	5.00	1.00	.25
□□□ 64 Jason Arnott, NJer.	10.00	2.00	.50
□□□ **65 Jonathan Sim, Dall. RC**	**6.00**	**1.00**	**1.00**
□□□ 66 Cory Sarich, Buff.	5.00	1.00	.25
□□□ **67 Brian Rafalski, NJer. RC**	**15.00**	**3.00**	**2.00**
□□□ 68 Kevin Hatcher, Pitt.	5.00	1.00	.25
□□□ 69 Ted Donato, Anah.	5.00	1.00	.25
□□□ 70 Dan LaCouture, Edmo.	5.00	1.00	.25
□□□ 71 Alexei Kovalev, Pitt.	15.00	2.00	.50
□□□ 72 Peter Bondra, Wash.	15.00	2.00	.50
□□□ 73 John LeClair, Phil.	20.00	3.00	1.00
□□□ 74 Matthew Barnaby, Pitt.	5.00	1.00	.25
□□□ 75 Adam Oates, Wash.	12.00	1.00	.50
□□□ 76 Janne Niinimaa, Edmo.	6.00	1.00	.25
□□□ 77 Tom Barrasso (G), Pitt.	12.00	1.00	.50
□□□ 78 Sergei Gonchar, Wash.	8.00	1.00	.25
□□□ 79 Alex Tanguay, Colo.	15.00	3.00	1.50
□□□ **80 J-L Grand-Pierre, Buff. RC**	**6.00**	**1.00**	**1.00**
□□□ **81 Alexei Tezikov, Wash. RC**	**6.00**	**1.00**	**1.00**
□□□ 82 Doug Gilmour, Chic.	15.00	2.00	.50
□□□ 83 Sergei Brylin, NJer.	5.00	1.00	.25
□□□ 84 Ron Tugnutt (G), Otta.	12.00	1.00	.50
□□□ 85 Stéphane Richer, Tamp.	6.00	1.00	.25
□□□ 86 Marc Denis (G), Colo.	14.00	2.00	.50
□□□ 87 Sergei Fedorov, Detr.	30.00	4.00	1.00
□□□ 88 Brian Rolston, NJer.	8.00	1.00	.25
□□□ 89 Chris Pronger, SLou.	15.00	2.00	.50
□□□ 90 Dan Cloutier (G), Tamp.	12.00	1.00	.50
□□□ 91 Anders Eriksson, Chic.	5.00	1.00	.25
□□□ 92 Donald Audette, LosA.	12.00	1.00	.50
□□□ 93 Ed Jovanovski, Vanc.	12.00	1.00	.50
□□□ 94 Tony Amonte, Chic.	15.00	2.00	.50
□□□ 95 Jamie Storr (G), LosA.	6.00	1.00	.25
□□□ 96 German Titov, Pitt.	5.00	1.00	.25
□□□ 97 Éric Dazé, Chic.	12.00	1.00	.50
□□□ 98 Zigmund Palffy, LosA.	15.00	2.00	.50
□□□ 99 Dan McGillis, Phil.	5.00	1.00	.25
□□□ 100 N. Khabibulin (G), Phoe.	12.00	1.00	.50
□□□ 101 Mathieu Schneider, NYRa.	6.00	1.00	.25
□□□ 102 Magnus Arvedson, Otta.	5.00	1.00	.25
□□□ 103 Joe Sakic, Colo.	45.00	7.00	2.00
□□□ **104 B. Campbell, Buff. RC**	**6.00**	**1.00**	**1.00**
□□□ 105 Wade Redden, Otta.	8.00	1.00	.25
□□□ 106 Andrei Nikolishin, Wash.	5.00	1.00	.25
□□□ 107 Steve Rucchin, Anah.	6.00	1.00	.25
□□□ 108 Shawn McEachern, Otta.	8.00	1.00	.25
□□□ 109 A. Karpovtsev, Toro.	5.00	1.00	.25
□□□ 110 Miroslav Satan, Buff.	8.00	1.00	.25
□□□ 111 Andreas Dackell, Otta.	5.00	1.00	.25
□□□ 112 Niklas Sundström, SanJ.	6.00	1.00	.25
□□□ 113 Scott Niedermayer, NJer.	8.00	1.00	.25
□□□ 114 Ken Wregget (G), Detr.	6.00	1.00	.25
□□□ 115 Olli Jokinen, NYIs.	8.00	1.00	.25
□□□ 116 Vincent Lecavalier, Tamp.	30.00	4.00	1.00
□□□ 117 Paul Kariya, Anah.	40.00	6.00	1.50
□□□ 118 Alexei Zhamnov, Chic.	8.00	1.00	.25
□□□ 119 Martin Rucinsky, Mont.	6.00	1.00	.25
□□□ 120 Daniel Cleary, Edmo.	8.00	1.00	.25
□□□ 121 Yanic Perreault, Toro.	8.00	1.00	.25
□□□ 122 Alexei Zhitnik, Buff.	5.00	1.00	.25
□□□ 123 Vadim Sharifijanov, NJer.	5.00	1.00	.25
□□□ 124 Derek King, Toro.	5.00	1.00	.25
□□□ 125 Jason Woolley, Buff.	5.00	1.00	.25
□□□ 126 Pavel Bure, Flor.	20.00	3.00	1.00
□□□ 127 Darius Kasparaitis, Pitt.	6.00	1.00	.25
□□□ 128 Stu Barnes, Buff.	5.00	1.00	.25
□□□ 129 Josef Beranek, Edmo.	5.00	1.00	.25
□□□ 130 Milan Hejduk, Colo.	20.00	3.00	1.00
□□□ 131 Michael Peca, Buff.	12.00	1.00	.50
□□□ 132 Tomas Holmström, Detr.	6.00	1.00	.25
□□□ 133 Patrick Marleau, SanJ.	14.00	2.00	.50
□□□ 134 Dominik Hasek (G), Buff.	30.00	4.00	1.00
□□□ 135 Chris Osgood (G), Detr.	15.00	2.00	.50
□□□ 136 Radek Bonk, Otta.	8.00	1.00	.25
□□□ 137 Martin Biron (G), Buff.	14.00	2.00	.50
□□□ 138 Igor Larionov, Detr.	15.00	2.00	.50
□□□ 139 Félix Potvin (G), NYIs.	15.00	2.00	.50
□□□ 140 Oleg Tverdovsky, Anah.	5.00	1.00	.25
□□□ 141 Steve Yzerman, Detr.	70.00	10.00	3.00
□□□ 142 Bobby Holik, NJer.	8.00	1.00	.25
□□□ 143 Landon Wilson, Bost.	5.00	1.00	.25
□□□ 144 Marty McInnis, Anah.	5.00	1.00	.25
□□□ 145 Rémi Royer, Chic.	5.00	1.00	.25
□□□ 146 Brendan Morrison, NJer.	8.00	1.00	.25
□□□ 147 Jaromir Jagr, Pitt.	30.00	4.00	1.00
□□□ 148 Steve Thomas, Toro.	6.00	1.00	.25
□□□ 149 Rico Fata, Calg.	6.00	1.00	.25
□□□ **150 John Madden, NJer. RC**	**20.00**	**4.00**	**3.00**
□□□ 151 Miloslav Guren, Mont.	5.00	1.00	.25
□□□ **152 Jochen Hecht, SLou. RC**	**20.00**	**4.00**	**2.50**
□□□ 153 Gary Roberts, Caro.	12.00	1.00	.50
□□□ 154 Patrik Elias, NJer.	20.00	3.00	1.00
□□□ 155 Al MacInnis, SLou.	12.00	1.00	.50
□□□ 156 Jonathan Girard, Bost.	5.00	1.00	.25
□□□ 157 Jan Hlavac, NYRa.	6.00	1.00	.50
□□□ 158 Pierre Turgeon, SLou.	12.00	1.00	.50
□□□ 159 Matt Cullen, Anah.	6.00	1.00	.25
□□□ 160 Trevor Letowski, Phoe.	5.00	1.00	.25
□□□ 161 Roman Turek (G), SLou.	10.00	2.00	.50
□□□ 162 Luc Robitaille, LosA.	20.00	3.00	1.00
□□□ 163 Marcus Nilson, Flor.	5.00	1.00	.25
□□□ 164 Pavol Demitra, SLou.	12.00	1.00	.50
□□□ 165 Fredrik Olausson, Anah.	6.00	1.00	.25
□□□ 166 Blake Sloan, Dall.	5.00	1.00	.25
□□□ 167 Eric Lindros, Phil.	30.00	4.00	1.00
□□□ 168 Guy Hebert (G), Anah.	6.00	1.00	.25
□□□ 169 Adam Deadmarsh, Colo.	8.00	1.00	.25
□□□ 170 Mike Leclerc, Anah.	5.00	1.00	.25

☐☐☐	171 Teemu Selänne, Anah.	20.00	3.00	1.00
☐☐☐	172 Ty Jones, Chic.	5.00	1.00	.25
☐☐☐	173 Calle Johansson, Wash.	6.00	1.00	.25
☐☐☐	174 Ed Belfour (G), Dall.	30.00	4.00	1.00
☐☐☐	**175 C. MacDonald, Caro. RC**	**6.00**	**1.00**	**1.00**
☐☐☐	176 Todd Harvey, NYRa.	6.00	1.00	.25
☐☐☐	177 Martin Straka, Pitt.	8.00	1.00	.25
☐☐☐	178 Mariusz Czerkawski, NYIs.	6.00	1.00	.25
☐☐☐	179 Grant Fuhr (G), SLou.	15.00	2.00	.50
☐☐☐	180 Mark Parrish, Flor.	12.00	1.00	.50
☐☐☐	181 Sandis Ozolinsh, Colo.	6.00	1.00	.25
☐☐☐	182 Patrice Brisebois, Mont.	5.00	1.00	.25
☐☐☐	183 Geoff Courtnall, SLou.	5.00	1.00	.25
☐☐☐	184 Chris Drury, Colo.	15.00	2.00	.50
☐☐☐	185 Saku Koivu, Mont.	20.00	3.00	1.00
☐☐☐	186 Teppo Numminen, Phoe.	8.00	1.00	.25
☐☐☐	187 Aleksey Morozov, Pitt.	6.00	1.00	.25
☐☐☐	188 Stéphane Quintal, NYRa.	5.00	1.00	.25
☐☐☐	189 Éric Desjardins, Phil.	8.00	1.00	.25
☐☐☐	**190 Pavel Patera, Dall. RC**	**6.00**	**1.00**	**1.00**
☐☐☐	191 Vladimir Malakhov, Mont.	5.00	1.00	.25
☐☐☐	192 J-S Giguère (G), Calg.	24.00	3.00	1.00
☐☐☐	**193 Niclas Hävelid, Anah. RC**	**6.00**	**1.00**	**1.00**
☐☐☐	194 Trevor Linden, Mont.	12.00	1.00	.50
☐☐☐	195 Simon Gagné, Phil.	25.00	5.00	2.00
☐☐☐	196 Kevin Weekes (G), Vanc.	6.00	1.00	.25
☐☐☐	197 Joe Nieuwendyk, Dall.	12.00	1.00	.50
☐☐☐	198 Cameron Mann, Bost.	5.00	1.00	.25
☐☐☐	**199 Adam Mair, Toro. RC**	**10.00**	**2.00**	**1.50**
☐☐☐	**200 K. Johnsson, NYRa. RC**	**10.00**	**2.00**	**1.50**
☐☐☐	201 Mikael Renberg, Phil.	8.00	1.00	.25
☐☐☐	202 Curtis Joseph (G), Toro.	30.00	4.00	1.00
☐☐☐	203 Juha Lind, Dall.	5.00	1.00	.25
☐☐☐	204 Doug Weight, Edmo.	15.00	2.00	.50
☐☐☐	205 Mats Lindgren, NYIs.	5.00	1.00	.25
☐☐☐	206 Marcus Ragnarsson, SanJ.	6.00	1.00	.25
☐☐☐	207 Igor Korolev, Toro.	5.00	1.00	.25
☐☐☐	208 Claude Lemieux, Colo.	8.00	1.00	.25
☐☐☐	209 Jeff Hackett (G), Mont.	8.00	1.00	.25
☐☐☐	210 Brendan Witt, Wash.	5.00	1.00	.25
☐☐☐	**211 Steve Kariya, Vanc. RC**	**15.00**	**3.00**	**2.00**
☐☐☐	212 Jarome Iginla, Calg.	20.00	3.00	1.00
☐☐☐	213 Pavel Rosa, LosA.	5.00	1.00	.25
☐☐☐	214 Andrei Zyuzin, Tamp.	5.00	1.00	.25
☐☐☐	**215 Oleg Saprykin, Calg. RC**	**15.00**	**3.00**	**2.00**
☐☐☐	216 Sean Burke (G), Flor.	15.00	2.00	.50
☐☐☐	217 Mike Modano, Dall.	30.00	4.00	1.00
☐☐☐	218 Phil Housley, Calg.	8.00	1.00	.25
☐☐☐	219 Ryan Smyth, Edmo.	10.00	2.00	.50
☐☐☐	220 Daren Puppa (G), Tamp.	6.00	1.00	.25
☐☐☐	221 Aki Berg, LosA.	5.00	1.00	.25
☐☐☐	222 Mike Grier, Edmo.	6.00	1.00	.25
☐☐☐	223 Keith Jones, Phil.	5.00	1.00	.25
☐☐☐	224 Marc* Savard, Calg.	6.00	1.00	.25
☐☐☐	225 Bill Guerin, Edmo.	12.00	1.00	.50
☐☐☐	226 Theoren Fleury, NYRa.	15.00	2.00	.50
☐☐☐	**227 Shawn Heins, SanJ. RC**	**6.00**	**1.00**	**1.00**
☐☐☐	228 Tom Poti, Edmo.	5.00	1.00	.25
☐☐☐	229 Tim Connolly, NYIs.	12.00	2.00	1.00
☐☐☐	230 Glen Wesley, Caro.	5.00	1.00	.25
☐☐☐	231 Brendan Shanahan, Detr.	30.00	4.00	1.00
☐☐☐	232 Kenny Jönsson, NYIs.	6.00	1.00	.25
☐☐☐	233 Mats Sundin, Toro.	30.00	4.00	1.00
☐☐☐	234 Damian Rhodes (G), Atla.	6.00	1.00	.25
☐☐☐	235 Martin Lapointe, Detr.	12.00	1.00	.50
☐☐☐	236 David Legwand, Nash.	12.00	1.00	.50
☐☐☐	237 Rob Niedermayer, Flor.	6.00	1.00	.25
☐☐☐	238 Bill Muckalt, Vanc.	5.00	1.00	.25
☐☐☐	239 Valeri Bure, Calg.	8.00	1.00	.25
☐☐☐	240 Manny Malhotra, NYRa.	6.00	1.00	.25
☐☐☐	241 Jozef Stumpel, LosA.	6.00	1.00	.25
☐☐☐	242 Brad Stuart, SanJ.	12.00	2.00	1.00
☐☐☐	243 Curtis Brown, Buff.	5.00	1.00	.25
☐☐☐	244 Alexei Yashin, Otta.	15.00	2.00	.50
☐☐☐	245 Owen Nolan, SanJ.	15.00	2.00	.50
☐☐☐	246 Shawn Bates, Bost.	5.00	1.00	.25
☐☐☐	247 Jan Hrdina, Pitt.	6.00	1.00	.25
☐☐☐	248 Marco Sturm, SanJ.	6.00	1.00	.25
☐☐☐	249 Nelson Emerson, Atla.	5.00	1.00	.25
☐☐☐	250 Stéphane Fiset (G), LosA.	8.00	1.00	.25
☐☐☐	251 Mike Vernon (G), SanJ.	12.00	1.00	.50
☐☐☐	252 Jason Botterill, Atla.	5.00	1.00	.25
☐☐☐	253 Marty Reasoner, SLou.	6.00	1.00	.25
☐☐☐	254 Roman Hamrlik, Edmo.	6.00	1.00	.25
☐☐☐	255 Ray Ferraro, Atla.	5.00	1.00	.25
☐☐☐	256 J. Langenbrunner, Dall.	6.00	1.00	.25
☐☐☐	257 Brian Holzinger, Buff.	5.00	1.00	.25
☐☐☐	258 Andrew Brunette, Atla.	5.00	1.00	.25
☐☐☐	259 Peter Forsberg, Colo.	40.00	6.00	1.50
☐☐☐	260 Jyrki Lumme, Phoe.	6.00	1.00	.25
☐☐☐	261 Keith Primeau, Caro.	12.00	1.00	.50
☐☐☐	262 Patrick Roy (G), Colo.	90.00	13.00	3.50
☐☐☐	263 Dimitri Nabokov, NYIs.	5.00	1.00	.25
☐☐☐	264 Darryl Laplante, Detr.	5.00	1.00	.25
☐☐☐	265 Mark Messier, Vanc.	30.00	4.00	1.00
☐☐☐	**266 Benoît Gratton, Calg. RC**	**6.00**	**1.00**	**1.00**
☐☐☐	267 Bryan Berard, Toro.	8.00	1.00	.25

☐☐☐	268 Wendel Clark, Chic.	20.00	3.00	1.00
☐☐☐	269 V. Damphousse, SanJ.	15.00	2.00	.50
☐☐☐	270 Jean-Pierre Dumont, Chic.	6.00	1.00	.25
☐☐☐	271 Darryl Sydor, Dall.	6.00	1.00	.25
☐☐☐	272 Darren Turcotte, Nash.	5.00	1.00	.25
☐☐☐	273 Sergei Berezin, Toro.	6.00	1.00	.25
☐☐☐	274 Jeff Friesen, SanJ.	8.00	1.00	.25
☐☐☐	275 Ville Peltonen, Nash.	5.00	1.00	.25
☐☐☐	276 Rick Tocchet, Phoe.	8.00	1.00	.25
☐☐☐	277 Darren McCarty, Detr.	8.00	1.00	.25
☐☐☐	278 Greg Johnson, Nash.	5.00	1.00	.25
☐☐☐	**279 Dan Smith, Colo. RC**	**6.00**	**1.00**	**1.00**
☐☐☐	280 Sergei Samsonov, Bost.	15.00	2.00	.50
☐☐☐	281 Petr* Sykora, NJer.	12.00	1.00	.50
☐☐☐	282 Dallas Drake, Phoe.	5.00	1.00	.25
☐☐☐	283 Yan Golubovsky, Detr.	5.00	1.00	.25
☐☐☐	283 Steve Konowalchuk, Wash.	6.00	1.00	.25
☐☐☐	**285 Dan Boyle, Flor. RC**	**14.00**	**3.00**	**2.00**
☐☐☐	286 Alexander Mogilny, Vanc.	14.00	2.00	.50
☐☐☐	287 Daniel Alfredsson, Otta.	15.00	2.00	.50
☐☐☐	288 Steve Shields (G), SanJ.	6.00	1.00	.25
☐☐☐	289 Markus Näslund, Vanc.	30.00	4.00	1.00
☐☐☐	290 Vyacheslav Kozlov, Detr.	6.00	1.00	.25
☐☐☐	291 Keith Tkachuk, Phoe.	15.00	2.00	.50
☐☐☐	292 Adrian Aucoin, Vanc.	5.00	1.00	.25
☐☐☐	293 Jocelyn Thibault (G), Chic.	12.00	1.00	.50
☐☐☐	294 Kevin Stevens, NYRa.	6.00	1.00	.25
☐☐☐	295 John MacLean, NYRa.	5.00	1.00	.25
☐☐☐	296 Mike Ricci, SanJ.	8.00	1.00	.25
☐☐☐	297 Rob Blake, LosA.	15.00	2.00	.50
☐☐☐	298 Radek Dvorak, Flor.	6.00	1.00	.25
☐☐☐	299 Mike Dunham (G), Nash.	12.00	1.00	.50
☐☐☐	300 Richard Matvichuk, Dall.	6.00	1.00	.25
☐☐☐	301 Scott Gomez, NJer.	12.00	2.00	1.00
☐☐☐	**302 N. Antropov, Toro. RC**	**15.00**	**3.00**	**2.00**
☐☐☐	**303 G. Metropolit, Wash. RC**	**10.00**	**2.00**	**1.50**
☐☐☐	304 Robyn Regehr, Calg.	5.00	1.00	.25
☐☐☐	305 Mathieu Biron, NYIs.	5.00	1.00	.25
☐☐☐	**306 N. Dempsey, Toro. RC**	**10.00**	**2.00**	**1.50**
☐☐☐	307 Roberto Luongo (G), NYIs.	20.00	3.00	1.00
☐☐☐	**308 A. Karlsson, Atla. RC**	**6.00**	**1.00**	**1.00**
☐☐☐	309 Raymond Bourque, Colo.	35.00	5.00	1.50
☐☐☐	310 Artem Chubarov, Vanc.	5.00	1.00	.25
☐☐☐	**311 Mike Fisher, Otta. RC**	**14.00**	**3.00**	**2.00**
☐☐☐	312 Andrew Ference, Pitt.	5.00	1.00	.25
☐☐☐	**313 Todd Reirden, SLou. RC**	**6.00**	**1.00**	**1.00**
☐☐☐	314 Martin Skoula, Colo.	6.00	1.00	.50
☐☐☐	**315 R. Suchy, Phoe. RC**	**6.00**	**1.00**	**1.00**
☐☐☐	**316 Joel Prpic, Bost. RC**	**6.00**	**1.00**	**1.00**
☐☐☐	**317 Yuri Butsayev, Detr. RC**	**6.00**	**1.00**	**1.00**
☐☐☐	**318 Andy Delmore, Phil. RC**	**14.00**	**3.00**	**2.00**
☐☐☐	319 Steven McCarthy, Chic.	5.00	1.00	.25
☐☐☐	320 Brian Rolston, Bost.	8.00	1.00	.25
☐☐☐	**321 Dimitri Kalinin, Buff. RC**	**6.00**	**1.00**	**1.00**
☐☐☐	322 Brenden Morrow, Dall.	10.00	2.00	.50
☐☐☐	323 Mike Vernon (G), Flor.	12.00	1.00	.50
☐☐☐	**324 Nils Ekman, Tamp. RC**	**10.00**	**2.00**	**1.50**
☐☐☐	325 Félix Potvin (G), Vanc.	15.00	2.00	.50
☐☐☐	**326 Jan Nemecek, LosA. RC**	**6.00**	**1.00**	**1.00**
☐☐☐	327 Mike York, NYRa.	10.00	2.00	.50
☐☐☐	**328 Nabokov (G), SanJ. RC**	**80.00**	**15.00**	**12.00**
☐☐☐	329 Rick Tocchet, Phil.	8.00	1.00	.25
☐☐☐	330 Vitali Vishnevski, Anah.	6.00	1.00	.50
☐☐☐	**331 F. Bouillon, Mont. RC**	**6.00**	**1.00**	**1.00**
☐☐☐	**332 R. Esche (G), Phoe. RC**	**14.00**	**3.00**	**2.00**
☐☐☐	**333 R. Giroux, NYIs. RC**	**6.00**	**1.00**	**1.00**
☐☐☐	334 Per Svartvadet, Atla.	5.00	1.00	.25
☐☐☐	**335 Kyle Calder, Chic. RC**	**20.00**	**4.00**	**2.50**
☐☐☐	336 Brian Boucher (G), Phil.	10.00	2.00	.50
☐☐☐	**337 Dan Hinote, Colo. RC**	**12.00**	**2.00**	**2.00**
☐☐☐	**338 Darrel Scoville, Calg. RC**	**6.00**	**1.00**	**1.00**
☐☐☐	**339 I. Novoseltsev, Flor. RC**	**10.00**	**2.00**	**2.00**
☐☐☐	**340 P. Schastlivy, Otta. RC**	**15.00**	**3.00**	**2.00**
☐☐☐	**341 André Savage, Bost. RC**	**6.00**	**1.00**	**1.00**
☐☐☐	342 Michal Grosek, Chic.	5.00	1.00	.25
☐☐☐	**343 R. Lintner, Nash. RC**	**6.00**	**1.00**	**1.00**
☐☐☐	**344 Tyson Nash, SLou. RC**	**10.00**	**2.00**	**1.50**
☐☐☐	**345 T. Westlund, Caro. RC**	**6.00**	**1.00**	**1.00**
☐☐☐	**346 Jason Krog, NYIs. RC**	**14.00**	**3.00**	**2.00**
☐☐☐	**347 J. Ruutu, Vanc. RC**	**10.00**	**2.00**	**1.50**
☐☐☐	348 Mike Ribeiro, Mont.	10.00	2.00	.50
☐☐☐	349 Alexander Mogilny, NJer.	14.00	2.00	.50
☐☐☐	350 Maxim Afinogenov, Buff.	12.00	2.00	1.00
☐☐☐	351 Ron Tugnutt (G), Pitt.	12.00	1.00	.50
☐☐☐	352 Jaroslav Spacek, Flor.	5.00	1.00	.25
☐☐☐	353 Petr Buzek, Atla.	5.00	1.00	.25
☐☐☐	**354 Sami Helenius, Colo. RC**	**6.00**	**1.00**	**1.00**
☐☐☐	355 Peter Schaefer, Vanc.	5.00	1.00	.25
☐☐☐	**356 Alan Letang, Dall. RC**	**6.00**	**1.00**	**1.00**
☐☐☐	357 Keith Primeau, Phil.	12.00	1.00	.50
☐☐☐	**358 J. Henderson, Bost. RC**	**6.00**	**1.00**	**1.00**
☐☐☐	359 David Tanabe, Caro.	5.00	1.00	.25
☐☐☐	360 Fred Brathwaite (G), Calg.	8.00	1.00	.25
☐☐☐	361 Chris Gratton, Buff.	6.00	1.00	.25
☐☐☐	**362 Denis Hamel, Buff. RC**	**6.00**	**1.00**	**1.00**
☐☐☐	362 M. Balmochnykh, Anah.	5.00	1.00	.25
☐☐☐	363 John Emmons, Otta.	5.00	1.00	.25

☐☐☐	**364 Mark Eaton, Phil. RC**	**6.00**	**1.00**	**1.00**
☐☐☐	365 Kevyn Adams, Toro.	5.00	1.00	.25
☐☐☐	**366 A. Michaud (G), Vanc. RC**	**10.00**	**2.00**	**1.50**
☐☐☐	**367 C. Herperger, Chic. RC**	**6.00**	**1.00**	**1.00**
☐☐☐	**368 S. Langkow (G), Atla. RC**	**10.00**	**2.00**	**1.50**
☐☐☐	**369 M. Mathieu, Bost. RC**	**6.00**	**1.00**	**1.00**
☐☐☐	**370 M. Hnilicka (G), NYRa. RC**	**15.00**	**3.00**	**2.00**
☐☐☐	**371 M. Rozsival, Pitt. RC**	**6.00**	**1.00**	**1.00**
☐☐☐	372 Sergei Krivokrasov, Calg.	5.00	1.00	.25
☐☐☐	**373 B. Chartrand, LosA. RC**	**6.00**	**1.00**	**1.00**
☐☐☐	**374 Ryan Bonni, Vanc. RC**	**6.00**	**1.00**	**1.00**
☐☐☐	375 Roman Lyashenko, Dall.	5.00	1.00	.25
☐☐☐	**377 S. Robidas, Mont. RC**	**6.00**	**1.00**	**1.00**
☐☐☐	**378 Jeff Halpern, Wash. RC**	**15.00**	**3.00**	**2.00**
☐☐☐	**379 K. Skrastins, Nash. RC**	**6.00**	**1.00**	**1.00**
☐☐☐	**380 Jeff Zehr, Bost. RC**	**6.00**	**1.00**	**1.00**
☐☐☐	381 Brian Holzinger, Tamp.	5.00	1.00	.25
☐☐☐	382 Josef Beranek, Pitt.	5.00	1.00	.25
☐☐☐	383 Harold Druken, Vanc.	10.00	2.00	.50
☐☐☐	384 Doug Gilmour, Buff.	15.00	2.00	.50
☐☐☐	**385 L. Nagy, SLou. RC**	**14.00**	**3.00**	**2.00**
☐☐☐	**386 Robertsson, Edmo. RC**	**6.00**	**1.00**	**1.00**
☐☐☐	**387 Fankhouser (G), Atla. RC**	**10.00**	**2.00**	**1.50**
☐☐☐	388 Brian Willsie, Colo.	5.00	1.00	.25
☐☐☐	**389 E. Boguniecki, Flor. RC**	**20.00**	**5.50**	**5.00**
☐☐☐	**390 D. Yakushin, Toro. RC**	**6.00**	**1.00**	**1.00**
☐☐☐	**391 Chris Clark, Calg. RC**	**6.00**	**1.00**	**1.00**
☐☐☐	**392 P. Comrie, Edmo. RC**	**10.00**	**2.00**	**1.50**
☐☐☐	**393 Grahame (G), Bost. RC**	**15.00**	**3.00**	**2.00**
☐☐☐	394 Rod Brind'Amour, Caro.	8.00	1.00	.25
☐☐☐	395 Vladimir Malakhov, NJer.	5.00	1.00	.25
☐☐☐	396 Jiri Fischer, Detr.	6.00	1.00	.50
☐☐☐	397 Kimmo Timonen, Nash.	5.00	1.00	.25
☐☐☐	398 Brad Ference, Flor.	5.00	1.00	.25
☐☐☐	**399 M. Lamothe (G), Chic. RC**	**6.00**	**1.00**	**1.00**
☐☐☐	400 Radek Dvorak, NYRa.	6.00	1.00	.25

	Tribute	**T**
☐	DT-5 Dmitri Tertyshny, Phil.	.50
☐	SC-3 Steve Chiasson, Caro.	.50

ALL-STAR JERSEY, ETC.

There are four versions: the Jersey card (1:250 packs, prefix J-), the Jersey & Stick card (1:999 packs, prefix S-), the In The Numbers card (1:999 packs, prefix I-) and the Emblem card (1:999 packs, prefix E-).

Insert Set (28 cards):		**4000**	**3250**	**2500**	**750**
	Player	**E**	**I**	**JS**	**J**
☐☐☐☐	E. Lindros, AS'96	150.00	125.00	100.00	25.00
☐☐☐☐	P. Forsberg, AS'96	150.00	125.00	100.00	50.00
☐☐☐☐	T. Selänne, AS'97	150.00	125.00	100.00	25.00
☐☐☐☐	M. Modano, AS'99	150.00	125.00	100.00	25.00
☐☐☐☐	Mats Sundin, AS'99	150.00	125.00	100.00	25.00
☐☐☐☐	P. Roy (G), AS'98	200.00	175.00	100.00	100.00
☐☐☐☐	Paul Kariya, AS'99	150.00	125.00	100.00	50.00
☐☐☐☐	Brodeur (G), AS'96	150.00	125.00	100.00	50.00
☐☐☐☐	R. Bourque, AS'97	150.00	125.00	100.00	50.00
☐☐☐☐	M. Messier, AS'96	150.00	125.00	100.00	25.00
☐☐☐☐	Joseph (G), AS'94	150.00	125.00	100.00	25.00
☐☐☐☐	Brett Hull, AS'94	150.00	125.00	100.00	25.00
☐☐☐☐	Al MacInnis, AS'94	150.00	125.00	100.00	25.00
☐☐☐☐	T. Fleury, AS'97	150.00	125.00	100.00	25.00
☐☐☐☐	S. Fedorov, AS'96	150.00	125.00	100.00	25.00
☐☐☐☐	Brian Leetch, AS'98	150.00	125.00	100.00	25.00
☐☐☐☐	A. Yashin, AS'94	150.00	125.00	100.00	25.00
☐☐☐☐	Jaromir Jagr, AS'96	150.00	125.00	100.00	25.00
☐☐☐☐	Pavel Bure, AS'97	150.00	125.00	100.00	25.00
☐☐☐☐	D. Hasek (G), AS'97	150.00	125.00	100.00	25.00
☐☐☐☐	Chris Chelios, AS'98	150.00	125.00	100.00	25.00
☐☐☐☐	John LeClair, AS'98	150.00	125.00	100.00	25.00
☐☐☐☐	Shanahan, AS'94	150.00	125.00	100.00	25.00
☐☐☐☐	Belfour (G), AS'98	150.00	125.00	100.00	25.00
☐☐☐☐	W. Gretzky, AS'94	350.00	300.00	200.00	200.00
☐☐☐☐	Saku Koivu, AS'98	150.00	125.00	100.00	25.00
☐☐☐☐	T. Amonte, AS'99	150.00	125.00	100.00	25.00
☐☐☐☐	P. Bondra, AS'97	150.00	125.00	100.00	25.00

ALL-STAR SELECTS

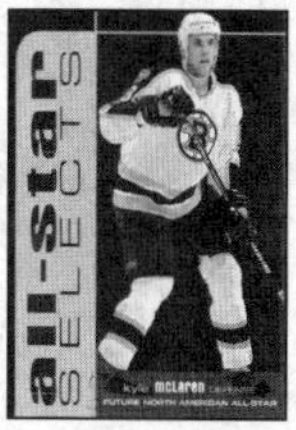

There are two versions: the regular insert [1:25] and a Gold parallel [1:250].

Insert Set (24 cards):		**245.00**	**50.00**
	Player	**Gold**	**Silver**
☐☐	SL-1 Peter Forsberg, Colo.	25.00	5.00
☐☐	SL-2 Pavol Demitra, SLou.	8.00	2.00
☐☐	SL-3 Jaromir Jagr, Pitt.	15.00	3.00
☐☐	SL-4 Sandis Ozolinsh, Colo.	8.00	2.00
☐☐	SL-5 Nicklas Lidström, Detr.	10.00	2.00
☐☐	SL-6 Dominik Hasek (G), Buff.	15.00	3.00
☐☐	SL-7 Eric Lindros, Phil.	15.00	3.00
☐☐	SL-8 Paul Kariya, Anah.	25.00	5.00
☐☐	SL-9 Tony Amonte, Chic.	10.00	2.00
☐☐	SL-10 Brian Leetch, NYRa.	10.00	2.00
☐☐	SL-11 Al MacInnis, SLou.	8.00	2.00
☐☐	SL-12 Martin Brodeur (G), NJer.	30.00	6.00
☐☐	SL-13 Petr* Sykora, NJer.	8.00	2.00
☐☐	SL-14 Sergei Samsonov, Bost.	10.00	2.00
☐☐	SL-15 Marian Hossa, Otta.	15.00	3.00
☐☐	SL-16 Andrei Zyuzin, Tamp.	8.00	2.00
☐☐	SL-17 Sami Salo, Otta.	8.00	2.00
☐☐	SL-18 Roman Turek (G), SLou.	8.00	2.00
☐☐	SL-19 Chris Drury, Colo.	10.00	2.00
☐☐	SL-20 Vincent Lecavalier, Tamp.	15.00	3.00
☐☐	SL-21 Jean-Pierre Dumont, Chic.	8.00	2.00
☐☐	SL-22 Kyle McLaren, Bost.	8.00	2.00
☐☐	SL-23 Adrian Aucoin, Vanc.	8.00	2.00
☐☐	SL-24 Marc Denis (G), Colo.	8.00	2.00

DOUBLE ALL-STAR JERSEY

These inserts were seeded in boxes [1:5 boxes] of Be A Player Memorabilia Rookie & Traded.

Insert Set (20 cards):		**2100.00**
	Player	**DASJ**
☐	D-1 Jaromir Jagr, All-Star	100.00
☐	D-2 Eric Lindros, All-Star	100.00
☐	D-3 Peter Forsberg, All-Star	125.00
☐	D-4 Patrick Roy (G), All-Star	225.00
☐	D-5 Paul Kariya, All-Star	125.00
☐	D-6 Mats Sundin, All-Star	100.00
☐	D-7 Raymond Bourque, All-Star	100.00
☐	D-8 Ed Belfour (G), All-Star	100.00
☐	D-9 Wayne Gretzky, All-Star	400.00
☐	D-10 Teemu Selänne, All-Star	75.00
☐	D-11 Brendan Shanahan, All-Star	100.00
☐	D-12 Dominik Hasek (G), All-Star	100.00
☐	D-13 Pavel Bure, All-Star	75.00
☐	D-14 John LeClair, All-Star	75.00
☐	D-15 Al MacInnis, All-Star	60.00
☐	D-16 Brett Hull, All-Star	100.00
☐	D-17 Brian Leetch, All-Star	60.00
☐	D-18 Mark Messier, All-Star	100.00
☐	D-19 Martin Brodeur (G), All-Star	150.00
☐	D-20 Sergei Fedorov, All-Star	100.00

HERITAGE SERIES

There are two versions: a Ruby insert (1000 copies), a Sapphire insert (100 copies) and a Emerald insert (10 copies). Please note that

Insert Set (24 cards):		**4600.00**	**900.00**	**100.00**
	Player	**E10**	**S100**	**R1000**
☐☐☐	H-1 B. Shanahan, NJer. / Detr.	250	50	6
☐☐☐	H-2 J. LeClair, Mont. / Phil.	200	40	5
☐☐☐	H-3 J. Roenick, Chic. / Phoe.	200	40	5
☐☐☐	H-4 V'sbrouck (G), NYRa. / Flor.	120	20	3
☐☐☐	H-5 D. Hasek (G), Chic. / Buff.	250	50	6
☐☐☐	H-6 A. Oates, Detr. / Wash.	100	20	2
☐☐☐	H-7 T. Selänne, Winn. / Anah.	200	40	5
☐☐☐	H-8 R. Francis, Hart. / Caro.	150	30	3
☐☐☐	H-9 A. MacInnis, Calg. / SLou.	100	20	2
☐☐☐	H-10 P. Roy (G), Mont. / Colo.	600	120	18
☐☐☐	H-11 D. Gilmour, SLou. / Chic.	150	30	3
☐☐☐	H-12 B. Hull, Calg. / Dall.	250	50	6
☐☐☐	H-13 Joseph (G), SLou. / Toro.	250	50	6
☐☐☐	H-14 M. Messier, Edmo. / Vanc.	250	50	6
☐☐☐	H-15 P. Coffey, Edmo. / Caro.	150	30	3
☐☐☐	H-16 Dafoe (G), Wash. / Bost.	100	20	2
☐☐☐	H-17 Belfour (G), Chic. / Dall.	250	50	6
☐☐☐	H-18 Gretzky, Edmo. / NYRa.	1000	200	25
☐☐☐	H-19 P. Bure, Vanc. / Flor.	200	40	5
☐☐☐	H-20 C. Chelios, Mont. / Detr.	150	30	3
☐☐☐	H-21 M. Sundin, Québ. / Toro.	250	50	6
☐☐☐	H-22 Nieuwendyk, Calg. / Dall.	100	20	2
☐☐☐	H-23 P. Demitra, Otta. / SLou.	100	20	2
☐☐☐	H-24 Fuhr (G), Edmo. / SLou.	150	30	3

ORIGINAL SIX

These inserts were found either in American Hobby packs (AH-prefix), Canadian Hobby packs (CH- prefix) or Retail packs (R-prefix).

Insert Set (36 cards): **110.00**

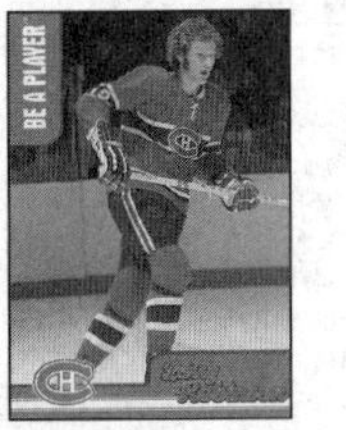

Player	Reg.
☐ AH-1 Ken Hodge, Bost.	3.00
☐ AH-2 Cam Neely, Bost.	6.00
☐ AH-3 Derek Sanderson, Bost.	3.00
☐ AH-4 Gerry Cheevers (G), Bost.	4.00
☐ AH-5 Johnny Bucyk, Bost.	3.00
☐ AH-6 Wayne Cashman, Bost.	3.00
☐ AH-7 Vic Hadfield, NYRa.	3.00
☐ AH-8 Andy Bathgate, NYRa.	3.00
☐ AH-9 Brad Park, NYRa.	3.00
☐ AH-10 Ed Giacomin (G), NYRa.	4.00
☐ AH-11 John Davidson (G), NYRa.	3.00
☐ AH-12 Rod Gilbert, NYRa.	3.00
☐ CH-1 Börje Salming, Toro.	4.00
☐ CH-2 Dave Keon, Toro.	4.00
☐ CH-3 Darryl Sittler, Toro.	4.00
☐ CH-4 Frank Mahovlich, Toro.	6.00
☐ CH-5 Johnny Bower, Toro.	4.00
☐ CH-6 Lanny McDonald, Toro.	4.00
☐ CH-7 Bob Gainey, Mont.	3.00
☐ CH-8 Dickie Moore, Mont.	3.00
☐ CH-9 John Ferguson, Mont.	3.00
☐ CH-10 Larry Robinson, Mont.	3.00
☐ CH-11 Yvan Cournoyer, Mont.	3.00
☐ CH-12 Serge Savard, Mont.	3.00
☐ R-1 Bobby Hull, Chic.	10.00
☐ R-2 Dennis Hull, Chic.	3.00
☐ R-3 Denis Savard, Chic.	3.00
☐ R-4 Pierre Pilote, Chic.	3.00
☐ R-5 Stan Mikita, Chic.	4.00
☐ R-6 Tony Esposito (G), Chic.	6.00
☐ R-7 Alex Delvecchio, Detr.	3.00
☐ R-8 Bill Gadsby, Detr.	3.00
☐ R-9 Mickey Redmond, Detr.	3.00
☐ R-10 Norm Ullman, Detr.	3.00
☐ R-11 Leonard (Red) Kelly, Detr.	3.00
☐ R-12 Ted Lindsay, Detr.	6.00

ORIGINAL SIX AUTOGRAPH

These autographed inserts were found either in American Hobby packs (AH- prefix), Canadian Hobby packs (CH- prefix) or Retail packs (R- prefix).

Insert Set (36 cards): **1400.00**

Player	Auto.
☐ AH-1 Ken Hodge, Bost. ✍	35.00
☐ AH-2 Cam Neely, Bost. ✍	75.00
☐ AH-3 Derek Sanderson, Bost. ✍	35.00
☐ AH-4 Gerry Cheevers (G), Bost. ✍	60.00
☐ AH-5 Johnny Bucyk, Bost. ✍	45.00
☐ AH-6 Wayne Cashman, Bost. ✍	35.00
☐ AH-7 Vic Hadfield, NYRa. ✍	35.00
☐ AH-8 Andy Bathgate, NYRa. ✍	35.00
☐ AH-9 Brad Park, NYRa. ✍	45.00
☐ AH-10 Ed Giacomin (G), NYRa. ✍	60.00
☐ AH-11 John Davidson (G), NYRa. ✍	35.00
☐ AH-12 Rod Gilbert, NYRa. ✍	35.00
☐ CH-1 Börje Salming, Toro. ✍	60.00
☐ CH-2 Dave Keon, Toro. ✍	60.00
☐ CH-3 Darryl Sittler, Toro. ✍	60.00
☐ CH-4 Frank Mahovlich, Toro. ✍	75.00
☐ CH-5 Johnny Bower, Toro. ✍	60.00
☐ CH-6 Lanny McDonald, Toro. ✍	60.00
☐ CH-7 Bob Gainey, Mont. ✍	45.00
☐ CH-8 Dickie Moore, Mont. ✍	45.00
☐ CH-9 John Ferguson, Mont. ✍	35.00
☐ CH-10 Larry Robinson, Mont. ✍	45.00
☐ CH-11 Yvan Cournoyer, Mont. ✍	45.00
☐ CH-12 Serge Savard, Mont. ✍	35.00
☐ R-1 Bobby Hull, Chic. ✍	75.00
☐ R-2 Dennis Hull, Chic. ✍	35.00
☐ R-3 Denis Savard, Chic. ✍	35.00
☐ R-4 Pierre Pilote, Chic. ✍	35.00
☐ R-5 Stan Mikita, Chic. ✍	60.00
☐ R-6 Tony Esposito (G), Chic. ✍	75.00
☐ R-7 Alex Delvecchio, Detr. ✍	35.00
☐ R-8 Bill Gadsby, Detr. ✍	35.00
☐ R-9 Mickey Redmond, Detr. ✍	35.00
☐ R-10 Norm Ullman, Detr. ✍	35.00
☐ R-11 Leonard (Red) Kelly, Detr. ✍	45.00
☐ R-12 Ted Lindsay, Detr. ✍	60.00

TEAMMATES JERSEY

These inserts were seeded in boxes (1:5 boxes) of Be A Player Memorabilia Rookie & Traded Update.

Insert Set (50 cards): **3500.00**

Players	TJ
☐ TM-1 Cu. Joseph (G) / J. Roenick	75.00
☐ TM-2 R. Blake / W. Gretzky	200.00
☐ TM-3 M. Messier / P. Roy	125.00
☐ TM-4 Br. Hull / T. Selänne	75.00
☐ TM-5 S. Fedorov / B. Shanahan	75.00
☐ TM-6 R. Bourque / B. Leetch	75.00
☐ TM-7 J. LeClair / E. Lindros	75.00
☐ TM-8 J. Jagr / M. Messier	75.00
☐ TM-9 M. Brodeur / B. Shanahan	100.00
☐ TM-10 P. Forsberg / P. Kariya	100.00
☐ TM-11 E. Belfour (G) / C. Chelios	50.00
☐ TM-12 P. Kariya / T. Selänne	75.00
☐ TM-13 P. Bondra / D. Hasek	50.00
☐ TM-14 P. Bure / S. Yzerman	125.00
☐ TM-15 R. Bourque / J. LeClair	75.00
☐ TM-16 T. Fleury / O. Nolan	50.00
☐ TM-17 M. Brodeur / P. Coffey	75.00
☐ TM-18 J. LeClair / E. Lindros	75.00
☐ TM-19 P. Bure / J. Jagr	75.00
☐ TM-20 D. Hasek / N. Khabibulin	50.00
☐ TM-21 B. Leetch / P. Roy	125.00
☐ TM-22 W. Gretzky / M. Modano	250.00
☐ TM-23 P. Forsberg / S. Ozolinsh	50.00
☐ TM-24 R. Bourque / C. Chelios	75.00
☐ TM-25 N. Lidström / M. Sundin	50.00
☐ TM-26 P. Kariya / M. Modano	100.00
☐ TM-27 T. Amonte / T. Fleury	50.00
☐ TM-28 P. Forsberg / T. Selänne	75.00
☐ TM-29 E. Lindros / D. Sydor	50.00
☐ TM-30 P. Bure / M. Sundin	75.00
☐ TM-31 J. Roenick / S. Stevens	50.00
☐ TM-32 J. Jagr / O. Kölzig	50.00
☐ TM-33 T. Amonte / M. Richter	40.00
☐ TM-34 A. MacInnis / C. Pronger	40.00
☐ TM-35 M. Brodeur / B. Shanahan	100.00
☐ TM-36 M. Messier / A. Mogilny	50.00
☐ TM-37 S. Fedorov / S. Yzerman	150.00
☐ TM-38 S. Fedorov / B. Shanahan	75.00
☐ TM-39 C. Chelios / S. Yzerman	125.00
☐ TM-40 B. Shanahan / S. Yzerman	125.00
☐ TM-41 Cu. Joseph (G) / M. Sundin	75.00
☐ TM-42 P. Forsberg / P. Roy	150.00
☐ TM-43 P. Forsberg / J. Sakic	125.00
☐ TM-44 P. Roy / J. Sakic	175.00
☐ TM-45 P. Kariya / T. Selänne	100.00
☐ TM-46 Br. Hull / M. Modano	75.00
☐ TM-47 E. Belfour (G) / Br. Hull	75.00
☐ TM-48 E. Belfour (G) / M. Modano	75.00
☐ TM-49 J. LeClair / E. Lindros	75.00
☐ TM-50 T. Fleury / B. Leetch	50.00

1999 - 2000 CANADA POST

Complete Set (6):

Player

☐☐ Gordie Howe, Detr.
☐☐ Wayne Gretzky, NYRa.
☐☐ Doug Harvey, Mont.
☐☐ Bobby Orr, Bost.
☐☐ Jacques Plante (G), Mont.
☐☐ Maurice Richard, Mont.

1999 - 2000 BICYCLE SPORTS / ACES

We do not have a full checklist for this series. This series does not feature any players, but team logos and stadiums instead.

1999 - 2000 CARDSET

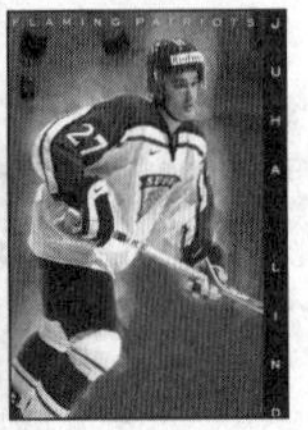

Cards of NHL stars and prospects usually sell at a premium (usually $1-$2).

Complete Set (346 cards): **45.00**
Common Player: **.30**

Player	Cardset
☐ 1 Miikka Kiprusoff (G), TPS Turku	1.50
☐ 2 Brian Rafalski, HIFK Helsinki	.50
☐ 3 Marko Kiprusoff, TPS Turku	.50
☐ 4 Jan Caloun, HIFK Helsinki	.50
☐ 5 Raimo Helminen, Ilves Tampere	.50
☐ 6 Tomas Vlasak, HPK Hämeenlinna	.50
☐ 7 Ari-Pekka Siekkinen, Kiekko-Espoo Blues	.30
☐ 8 Jiri Vykoukal, Kiekko-Espoo Blues	.30
☐ 9 Riku Varjamo, Kiekko-Espoo Blues	.30
☐ 10 Riku-Petteri Lehtonen, Kiekko-Espoo Blues	.30
☐ 11 Juha Gustafsson, Kiekko-Espoo Blues	.30
☐ 12 Arto Laatikainen, Kiekko-Espoo Blues	.50
☐ 13 Hannes Hyvönen, Kiekko-Espoo Blues	.30
☐ 14 Timo Hirvonen, Kiekko-Espoo Blues	.30
☐ 15 Tommy Kiviaho, Kiekko-Espoo Blues	.30
☐ 16 Tero Tiainen, Kiekko-Espoo Blues	.30
☐ 17 Joonas Jääskeläinen, Kiekko-Espoo Blues	.30
☐ 18 Teemu Riihijärvi, Kiekko-Espoo Blues	.50
☐ 19 Olli Ahonen, HIFK Helsinki	.30
☐ 20 Santeri Heiskanen, HIFK Helsinki	.30
☐ 21 Jarno Kultanen, HIFK Helsinki	.50
☐ 22 Marko From, HIFK Helsinki	.30
☐ 23 Kimmo Kuhta, HIFK Helsinki	.30
☐ 24 Tom Laaksonen, HIFK Helsinki	.30
☐ 25 Kari Kalto, HIFK Helsinki	.30
☐ 26 Jan Caloun, HIFK Helsinki	.50
☐ 27 Markku Hurme, HIFK Helsinki	.30
☐ 28 Toni Mäkiaho, HIFK Helsinki	.30
☐ 29 Mika Nieminen, HIFK Helsinki	.30
☐ 30 Luciano Borsato, HIFK Helsinki	.30
☐ 31 Aki Heino, HPK Hämeenlinna	.30
☐ 32 Jonas Andersson-Junkka, HPK Hämeenlinna	.50
☐ 33 Tomi Källarsson, HPK Hämeenlinna	.30
☐ 34 Roman Simicek, HPK Hämeenlinna	.50
☐ 35 Juha Virtanen, HPK Hämeenlinna	.30
☐ 36 Antti Virtanen, HPK Hämeenlinna	.30
☐ 37 Jyrki Louhi, HPK Hämeenlinna	.30
☐ 38 Jarkko Savijoki, HPK Hämeenlinna	.30
☐ 39 Jukka Hentunen, HPK Hämeenlinna	.50
☐ 40 Timo Pärssinen, HPK Hämeenlinna	.50
☐ 41 Niko Kapanen, HPK Hämeenlinna	1.00
☐ 42 Tomas Vlasak, HPK Hämeenlinna	.50
☐ 43 Kristian Antila, Ilves Tampere	.30
☐ 44 Pasi Puistola, Ilves Tampere	.30
☐ 45 Pasi Saarinen, Ilves Tampere	.30
☐ 46 Pekka Kangasalusta, Ilves Tampere	.30
☐ 47 Martti Järventie, Ilves Tampere	.50
☐ 48 Sami Karjalainen, Ilves Tampere	.30
☐ 49 Riku Niemelä, Ilves Tampere	.30
☐ 50 Mikko Peltola, Ilves Tampere	.30
☐ 51 Juha Hautamaa, Ilves Tampere	.30
☐ 52 Raimo Helminen, Ilves Tampere	1.00
☐ 53 Tomi Hirvonen, Ilves Tampere	.50
☐ 54 Sami Ahlberg, Ilves Tampere	.30
☐ 55 Vesa Viitakoski, Ilves Tampere	.50
☐ 56 Mika Arvaja, Ilves Tampere	.30
☐ 57 Rami Alanko, Jokerit Helsinki	.30
☐ 58 Antti-Jussi Niemi, Jokerit Helsinki	.50
☐ 59 Antti Hulkkonen, Jokerit Helsinki	.30
☐ 60 Jani Rita, Jokerit Helsinki	4.00
☐ 61 Jarkko Väänänen, Jokerit Helsinki	.30
☐ 62 Fredrik Nilsson, Jokerit Helsinki	.30
☐ 63 Jari Kauppila, Jokerit Helsinki	.30
☐ 64 Eero Somervuori, Jokerit Helsinki	.30
☐ 65 Jukka Tiilikainen, Jokerit Helsinki	.30
☐ 66 Patrik Juhlin, Jokerit Helsinki	.30
☐ 67 Tommi Satosaari, JyP HT Jyväskylä	.30
☐ 68 Jarkko Glad, JyP HT Jyväskylä	.30
☐ 69 Jyrki Välivaara, JyP HT Jyväskylä	.30
☐ 70 Markus Kankaanperä, JyP HT Jyväskylä	.30
☐ 71 Kalle Koskinen, JyP HT Jyväskylä	.30
☐ 72 Juha Viinikainen, JyP HT Jyväskylä	.30
☐ 73 Marko Ojanen, JyP HT Jyväskylä	.30
☐ 74 Toni Koivunen, JyP HT Jyväskylä	.30
☐ 75 Veli-Pekka Nutikka, JyP HT Jyväskylä	.30
☐ 76 Stefan Örnskog, JyP HT Jyväskylä	.30
☐ 77 Marko Virtanen, JyP HT Jyväskylä	.30
☐ 78 Lasse Jämsen, JyP HT Jyväskylä	.30
☐ 79 Petri Vehanen, Lukko Rauma	.30
☐ 80 Kimmo Lotvonen, Lukko Rauma	.30
☐ 81 Jaakko Harikkala, Lukko Rauma	.30
☐ 82 Ismo Kuoppala, Lukko Rauma	.30
☐ 83 Erik Hämäläinen, Lukko Rauma	.30
☐ 84 Zdenek Nedved, Lukko Rauma	.30
☐ 85 Harri Suvanto, Lukko Rauma	.30
☐ 86 Jonni Vauhkonen, Lukko Rauma	.30
☐ 87 Ville Mikkonen, Lukko Rauma	.30
☐ 88 Janne Seva, Lukko Rauma	.30
☐ 89 Petri Lätti, Lukko Rauma	.30
☐ 90 Harri Sillgren, Lukko Rauma	.30
☐ 91 Leonids Tambijevs, Lukko Rauma	.30
☐ 92 Sami Lehtinen, Pelicans	.30
☐ 93 Antti-Jussi Reimari, Pelicans	.30
☐ 94 Marko Ahonen, Pelicans	.30
☐ 95 Veli-Pekka Laitinen, Pelicans	.30
☐ 96 Mika Niskanen, Pelicans	.30
☐ 97 Jan Latvala, Pelicans	.30
☐ 98 Mika Asikainen, Pelicans	.30
☐ 99 Aigars Cipruss, Pelicans	.30
☐ 100 Michael Johansson, Pelicans	.30
☐ 101 Tomi-Pekka Kolu, Pelicans	.30
☐ 102 Jarkko Ollikainen, Pelicans	.30
☐ 103 Toni Saarinen, Pelicans	.30
☐ 104 Jussi Vienonen, Pelicans	.30
☐ 105 Jouko Myrrä, Pelicans	.30
☐ 106 Jussi Markkanen, SaiPa	.30
☐ 107 Harri Tikkanen, SaiPa	.30
☐ 108 Riku Kallioniemi, SaiPa	.30
☐ 109 Jussi Pekkala, SaiPa	.30
☐ 110 Mikko Myllykoski, SaiPa	.30
☐ 111 Vesa Ruotsalainen, SaiPa	.30
☐ 112 Tommi Sova, SaiPa	.30
☐ 113 Ari Santanen, SaiPa	.30
☐ 114 Pasi Määttänen, SaiPa	.30
☐ 115 Tero Hämäläinen, SaiPa	.30
☐ 116 Mika Skyttä, SaiPa	.30
☐ 117 Ville Immonen, SaiPa	.30
☐ 118 Keijo Säilynoja, SaiPa	.30
☐ 119 Miska Kangasniemi, Tappara Tampere	.30
☐ 120 Josef Boumedienne, Tappara Tampere	.50
☐ 121 Janne Vuorela, Tappara Tampere	.30
☐ 122 Janne Grönvall, Tappara Tampere	.30
☐ 123 Valeri Krykov, Tappara Tampere	.30
☐ 124 Arto Kulmala, Tappara Tampere	.30
☐ 125 Alexander Barkov, Tappara Tampere	.30
☐ 126 Johannes Alanen, Tappara Tampere	.30
☐ 127 Jani Hassinen, Tappara Tampere	.30
☐ 128 Janne Ojanen, Tappara Tampere	.30
☐ 129 Tuomas Reijonen, Tappara Tampere	.30
☐ 130 Sami Salonen, Tappara Tampere	.30
☐ 131 Fredrik Norrena, TPS Turku	.30
☐ 132 Kimmo Eronen, TPS Turku	.30
☐ 133 Marko Kiprusoff, TPS Turku	.50
☐ 134 Jouni Loponen, TPS Turku	.30
☐ 135 Ilkka Mikkola, TPS Turku	.30
☐ 136 Jani Kiviharju, TPS Turku	.30
☐ 137 Tony Virta, TPS Turku	.50
☐ 138 Kalle Sahlstedt, TPS Turku	.30
☐ 139 Tomi Kallio, TPS Turku	.50
☐ 140 Joni Lius, TPS Turku	.30
☐ 141 Teemu Elomo, TPS Turku	.30
☐ 142 Ville Vahalahti, TPS Turku	.30
☐ 143 Marco Tuokko, TPS Turku	.30
☐ 144 Kai Nurminen, TPS Turku	.50
☐ 145 Petr Kuchyna, Ässät Pori	.30
☐ 146 Tuomo Kyhä, Ässät Pori	.30
☐ 147 Pasi Peltonen, Ässät Pori	.30
☐ 148 Santeri Immonen, Ässät Pori	.30
☐ 149 Pauli Levokari, Ässät Pori	.30
☐ 150 Vesa Salo, Ässät Pori	.30
☐ 151 Timo Salonen, Ässät Pori	.30
☐ 152 Marko Kivenmäki, Ässät Pori	.30
☐ 153 Niko Mikkola, Ässät Pori	.30
☐ 154 Andrei Potaichuk, Ässät Pori	.30
☐ 155 Tero Arkiomaa, Ässät Pori	.30
☐ 156 Timo Hakanen, Ässät Pori	.30
☐ 157 Jan Peterek, Ässät Pori	.30
☐ 158 Jan Caloun, HIFK Helsinki	.50
☐ 159 Pasi Saarela, Jokerit Helsinki	.30
☐ 160 Tomas Vlasak, HPK Hämeenlinna	.50
☐ 161 Brian Rafalski, HPK Hämeenlinna	1.00
☐ 162 Peter Larsson, Ilves Tampere	.30
☐ 163 Roman Simicek, HPK Hämeenlinna	.50
☐ 164 Raimo Helminen, Ilves Tampere	1.00
☐ 165 Leonids Tambijevs, Lukko Rauma	.30
☐ 166 Mika Nieminen, HIFK Helsinki	.30
☐ 167 Janne Ojanen, Tappara Tampere	.50
☐ 168 Otakar Janecky, Jokerit Helsinki	.30
☐ 169 Juha Ikonen, Kiekko-Espoo Blues	.30
☐ 170 Jari Kauppila, Jokerit Helsinki	.30
☐ 171 Jan Benda, Ässät Pori	.30
☐ 172 Tony Virta, TPS Turku	.50
☐ 173 Niko Kapanen, HPK Hämeenlinna	1.00
☐ 174 Alexander Barkov, Tappara Tampere	.30
☐ 175 Hannes Hyvönen, Kiekko-Espoo Blues	.30
☐ 176 Lasse Pirjetä, Tappara Tampere	.30
☐ 177 Jussi Tarvainen, JyP HT Jyväskylä	.30
☐ 178 Miikka Kiprusoff (G), Finland	1.50
☐ 179 Ari Sulander (G), Finland	.50
☐ 180 Vesa Toskala (G), Finland	.50
☐ 181 Aki Berg, Finland	.50
☐ 182 Jere Karalahti, Finland	.50
☐ 183 Marko Kiprusoff, Finland	.50
☐ 184 Toni Lydman, Finland	.50
☐ 185 Kari Martikainen, Finland	.50
☐ 186 Antti-Jussi Niemi, Finland	.50
☐ 187 Petteri Nummelin, Finland	.50
☐ 188 Kimmo Timonen, Finland	.50
☐ 189 Mikko Eloranta, Finland	.50
☐ 190 Raimo Helminen, Finland	1.00
☐ 191 Olli Jokinen, Finland	1.50
☐ 192 Tomi Kallio, Finland	.50
☐ 193 Saku Koivu, Finland	4.00
☐ 194 Juha Lind, Finland	.50
☐ 195 Ville Peltonen, Finland	.50
☐ 196 Kimmo Rintanen, Finland	.50
☐ 197 Teemu Selänne, Finland	4.00
☐ 198 Toni Sihvonen, Finland	.50
☐ 199 Marko Tuomainen, Finland	.50
☐ 200 Antti Törmänen, Finland	.50

☐	201 Tom Draper, Lukko Rauma	.50
☐	202 Timo Leinonen, Ässät Pori	.30
☐	203 Pasi Nurminen, Jokerit Helsinki	3.00
☐	204 Tommi Satosaari, JyP HT Jyväskylä	.30
☐	205 Mika Oksa, Kiekko-Espoo Blues	.30
☐	206 Jermu Pisto, Kiekko-Espoo Blues	.30
☐	207 Niclas Hedberg, Kiekko-Espoo Blues	.30
☐	208 Peter Ahola, Kiekko-Espoo Blues	.50
☐	209 Aki Korhonen, Kiekko-Espoo Blues	.30
☐	210 Mikko Kaukokari, Kiekko-Espoo Blues	.30
☐	211 Esa Pirnes, Kiekko-Espoo Blues	.30
☐	212 Arto Kuki, Kiekko-Espoo Blues	.30
☐	213 Dale McTavish, Kiekko-Espoo Blues	.30
☐	214 Ari Katavisto, Kiekko-Espoo Blues	.30
☐	215 Teemu Siren, Kiekko-Espoo Blues	.30
☐	216 Mikael Jämsänen, Kiekko-Espoo Blues	.30
☐	217 Otakar Janecky, Kiekko-Espoo Blues	.30
☐	218 Niklas Bäckström, HIFK Helsinki	.30
☐	219 Ari Ahonen, HIFK Helsinki	3.00
☐	220 Jere Karalahti, HIFK Helsinki	.50
☐	221 Marek Zidlicky, HIFK Helsinki	.30
☐	222 Toni Lydman, HIFK Helsinki	.50
☐	223 Pekka Kangasalusta, HIFK Helsinki	.30
☐	224 Kari Rajala, HIFK Helsinki	.30
☐	225 Mike Gaffney, HIFK Helsinki	.30
☐	226 Timo Ahmaoja, HIFK Helsinki	.30
☐	227 Aki Tuominen, HIFK Helsinki	.30
☐	228 Aki Uusikartano, HIFK Helsinki	.30
☐	229 Mika Kortelainen, HIFK Helsinki	.30
☐	230 Toni Sihvonen, HIFK Helsinki	.30
☐	231 Pasi Nielikäinen, HIFK Helsinki	.30
☐	232 Lasse Pirjetä, HIFK Helsinki	.50
☐	233 Kimmo Kapanen (G), HPK Hämeenlinna	.30
☐	234 Ari Kumpula, HPK Hämeenlinna	.30
☐	235 Kimmo Peltonen, HPK Hämeenlinna	.30
☐	236 Sebastian Sulku, HPK Hämeenlinna	.30
☐	237 Harri Laurila, HPK Hämeenlinna	.30
☐	238 Teemu Aalto, HPK Hämeenlinna	.30
☐	239 Oscar Ackerström, HPK Hämeenlinna	.30
☐	240 Antti Miettinen, HPK Hämeenlinna	.30
☐	241 Marko Palo, HPK Hämeenlinna	.30
☐	242 Riku Hahl, HPK Hämeenlinna	2.00
☐	243 Petr Tenkrat, HPK Hämeenlinna	.50
☐	244 Pasi Kuivalainen, Ilves Tampere	.30
☐	245 Arto Tukio, Ilves Tampere	.30
☐	246 Hannu Henriksson, Ilves Tampere	.30
☐	247 Teemu Kesä, Ilves Tampere	.30
☐	248 Antti Bruun, Ilves Tampere	.30
☐	249 Tomi Pettinen, Ilves Tampere	.30
☐	250 Tapio Sammalkangas, Ilves Tampere	.30
☐	251 Rodrigo Lavins, Ilves Tampere	.30
☐	252 Ilkka Laitinen, Ilves Tampere	.30
☐	253 Tommi Miettinen, Ilves Tampere	.30
☐	254 Jarkko Nikander, Ilves Tampere	.30
☐	255 Daniel Marois, Ilves Tampere	.30
☐	256 Antti Hilden, Ilves Tampere	.30
☐	257 Kimmo Vesa, Jokerit Helsinki	.30
☐	258 Pasi Nurminen, Jokerit Helsinki	3.00
☐	259 Ossi Väänänen, Jokerit Helsinki	.30
☐	260 Sean Gagnon, Jokerit Helsinki	.30
☐	261 Marko Kauppinen, Jokerit Helsinki	.30
☐	262 Tuomas Grönman, Jokerit Helsinki	.30
☐	263 Tom Koivisto, Jokerit Helsinki	.30
☐	264 Tomek Valtonen, Jokerit Helsinki	.30
☐	265 Esa Tikkanen, Jokerit Helsinki	.50
☐	266 Jan Benda, Jokerit Helsinki	.30
☐	267 Tommi Santala, Jokerit Helsinki	.30
☐	268 Petri Varis, Jokerit Helsinki	.30
☐	269 Tuomas Eskelinen, Jokerit Helsinki	.30
☐	270 Tero Lehterä, Jokerit Helsinki	.30
☐	271 Markus Hätinen, JyP HT Jyväskylä	.30
☐	272 Pekka Poikolainen, JyP HT Jyväskylä	.30
☐	273 Mikko Luoma, JyP HT Jyväskylä	.30
☐	274 Vesa Ponto, JyP HT Jyväskylä	.30
☐	275 Nik Zupancic, JyP HT Jyväskylä	.30
☐	276 Pasi Kangas, JyP HT Jyväskylä	.30
☐	277 Topi Riutta, JyP HT Jyväskylä	.30
☐	278 Jussi Pesonen, JyP HT Jyväskylä	.30
☐	279 Petr Ton, JyP HT Jyväskylä	.30
☐	280 Jaroslav Bednar, JyP HT Jyväskylä	.50
☐	281 Tom Draper, Lukko Rauma	.50
☐	282 Mika Laaksonen, Lukko Rauma	.30
☐	283 Allan Measures, Lukko Rauma	.30
☐	284 Martin Stepanek, Lukko Rauma	.30
☐	285 Marko Toivonen, Lukko Rauma	.30
☐	286 Petteri Lotila, Lukko Rauma	.30
☐	287 Jari Hyvärinen, Lukko Rauma	.30
☐	288 Timo Peltomaa, Lukko Rauma	.30
☐	289 Petri Pakaslahti, Lukko Rauma	.30
☐	290 Jokke Heinänen, Lukko Rauma	.30
☐	291 Matti Kaipainen, Lukko Rauma	.30
☐	292 Ville Koivula, Pelicans	.30
☐	293 Veli-Pekka Kautonen, Pelicans	.30
☐	294 Daniel Johansson, Pelicans	.30
☐	295 Tommi Kovanen, Pelicans	.30
☐	296 Roland Carlsson, Pelicans	.30
☐	297 Jani Keinänen, Pelicans	.30
☐	298 Mikko Juutilainen, Pelicans	.30
☐	299 Aki Kaskinen, Pelicans	.30
☐	300 Tommi Turunen, Pelicans	.30
☐	301 Mathias Bosson, Pelicans	.30
☐	302 Teemu Riihijärvi, Pelicans	.30
☐	303 Pasi Häkkinen, SaiPa	.30
☐	304 Jani-Matti Loikala, SaiPa	.30
☐	305 Juri Kuznetsov, SaiPa	.30
☐	306 Mikko Jokela, SaiPa	.50
☐	307 Ville Hämäläinen, SaiPa	.30
☐	308 Joel Salonen, SaiPa	.30
☐	309 Timo Saarikoski, SaiPa	.30
☐	310 Pekka Tirkkonen, SaiPa	.30
☐	311 Mika Kauppinen, SaiPa	.30
☐	312 Sami Kaartinen, SaiPa	.30
☐	313 Timo Järvinen, Tappara Tampere	.30
☐	314 Jason Muzzatti, Tappara Tampere	.50
☐	315 Per Löfström, Tappara Tampere	.30
☐	316 Ari Vallin, Tappara Tampere	.30
☐	317 Asko Rantanen, Tappara Tampere	.30
☐	318 Tuukka Mäntylä, Tappara Tampere	.30
☐	319 Pasi Petriläinen, Tappara Tampere	.30
☐	320 Pasi Tuominen, Tappara Tampere	.30
☐	321 Roman Meluzin, Tappara Tampere	.30
☐	322 Miikka Männikkö, Tappara Tampere	.30
☐	323 Jussi Tarvainen, Tappara Tampere	.30
☐	324 Timo Vertala, Tappara Tampere	.50
☐	325 Jaakko Uhlbäck, Tappara Tampere	.30
☐	326 Antero Niittymäki, TPS Turku	.30
☐	327 Kimmo Lecklin, TPS Turku	.30
☐	328 Tommi Rajamäki, TPS Turku	.30
☐	329 Mika Lehtinen, TPS Turku	.30
☐	330 Kari Harila, TPS Turku	.30
☐	331 Petri Tähtisalo, TPS Turku	.30
☐	332 Esa Keskinen, TPS Turku	.30
☐	333 Kimmo Rintanen, TPS Turku	.30
☐	334 Mikael Holmqvist, TPS Turku	.50
☐	335 Mikko Rautee, TPS Turku	.30
☐	336 Mika Lehto, Ässät Pori	.30
☐	337 Timo Leinonen, Ässät Pori	.30
☐	338 Timo Willman, Ässät Pori	.30
☐	339 Olli Kaski, Ässät Pori	.30
☐	340 Samu Wesslin, Ässät Pori	.30
☐	341 Mika Kannisto, Ässät Pori	.30
☐	342 Ales Kratoska, Ässät Pori	.30
☐	343 Marko Luomala, Ässät Pori	.30
☐	344 Jaakko Mäkelä, Ässät Pori	.30
☐	345 Ondrej Steiner, Ässät Pori	.30
☐	346 Markku Tähtinen, Ässät Pori	.30
	Insert (#/100)	**MT**
☐	Jere Lehtinen (Triple Threat)	25.00
☐	Teemu Selänne (Global Glory)	60.00

ACES HIGH

Series Two Insert Set (54 cards):		**50.00**
	Insert	**AH**
☐	10-hertta Jarkko Varvio	1.00
☐	10-pata Christian Ruuttu	1.00
☐	10-risti Michael Nylander	1.00
☐	10-ruutu Sami Kapanen	1.50
☐	2-hertta Hannu Virta	1.00
☐	2-pata Reijo Ruotsalainen	1.50
☐	2-risti Peter Ahola	1.00
☐	2-ruutu Timo Blomqvist	1.00
☐	3-hertta Tuomas Grönman	1.00
☐	3-pata Janne Niinimaa	1.00
☐	3-risti Teppo Numminen	1.50
☐	3-ruutu Sami Salo	1.00
☐	4-hertta Timo Jutila	1.00
☐	4-pata Brian Rafalski	1.00
☐	4-risti Janne Laukkanen	1.00
☐	4-ruutu Marko Kiprusoff	1.00
☐	5-hertta Jyrki Lumme	1.00
☐	5-pata Kimmo Timonen	1.00
☐	5-risti Risto Siltanen	1.00
☐	5-ruutu Aki Berg	1.00
☐	6-hertta Juha Ylönen	1.00
☐	6-pata Kai Nurminen	1.00
☐	6-risti Iiro Järvi	1.00
☐	6-ruutu Jan Caloun	1.00
☐	7-hertta Janne Ojanen	1.00
☐	7-pata Raimo Helminen	1.00
☐	7-risti Antti Aalto	1.00
☐	7-ruutu Olli Jokinen	1.50
☐	8-hertta Juha Lind	1.00
☐	8-pata Raimo Summanen	1.00
☐	8-risti Theoren Fleury	3.00
☐	8-ruutu Patrik Juhlin	1.00
☐	9-hertta Antti Törmänen	1.00
☐	9-pata Petri Varis	1.00
☐	9-risti Ilkka Sinisalo	1.00
☐	9-ruutu Dale McTavish	1.00
☐	A-hertta Boris Rousson (G)	1.00
☐	A-pata Kari Takko	1.00
☐	A-risti Jani Hurme (G)	2.00
☐	A-ruutu Jarmo Myllys (G)	1.00
☐	J-hertta Jan Benda	1.00
☐	J-pata Marko Tuomainen	1.00
☐	J-risti Mika Alatalo	1.00
☐	J-ruutu Mikko Eloranta	1.00
☐	Joker Jari Kurri	5.00
☐	Joker Teemu Selänne	4.00
☐	K-hertta Saku Koivu	4.00
☐	K-pata Esa Tikkanen	1.00
☐	K-risti Ville Peltonen	1.00
☐	K-ruutu Jere Lehtinen	1.50
☐	Q-hertta Ann Björklöf	1.00
☐	Q-pata Satu Jokinen	1.00
☐	Q-risti Päivi Ylitie	1.00
☐	Q-ruutu Carissa Chan	1.00

BLAZING PATRIOTS

Series One Insert Set (6 cards):		**25.00**
	Insert (1:10 packs)	**BP**
☐	1 Miikka Kiprusoff (G)	6.00
☐	2 Jere Karalahti	3.00
☐	3 Kimmo Timonen	3.00
☐	4 Teemu Selänne	8.00
☐	5 Saku Koivu	8.00
☐	6 Marko Tuomainen	3.00

MOST WANTED

Series Two Insert Set (12 cards):		**25.00**
	Insert (1:4 packs)	**MW**
☐	1 Aki Berg	2.00
☐	2 Olli Jokinen	2.00
☐	3 Teemu Selänne	6.00
☐	4 Teemu Riihijärvi	2.00
☐	5 Jani Rita	2.00
☐	6 Saku Koivu	6.00
☐	7 Mika Noronen (G)	3.00
☐	8 Miika Elomo	2.00
☐	9 Jukka Seppo	2.00
☐	10 Ari Ahonen (G)	2.00
☐	11 Tuomas Grönman	2.00
☐	12 Ville Siren	2.00

PAR AVION

Series One Insert Set (12 cards):		**25.00**
	Insert (1:4 packs)	**PA**
☐	1 Mika Alatalo	2.00
☐	2 Toni Lydman	2.00
☐	3 Brian Rafalski	2.00
☐	4 Jere Karalahti	2.00
☐	5 Juha Lind	2.00
☐	6 Mikko Kuparinen	2.00
☐	7 Marko Tuomainen	2.00
☐	8 Miikka Kiprusoff (G)	4.00
☐	9 Mika Noronen (G)	6.00
☐	10 Vesa Toskala (G)	2.00
☐	11 Mikko Eloranta	2.00
☐	12 Jarkko Ruutu	2.00

PUCKSTOPPERS

Series Two Insert Set (6 cards):		**15.00**
	Insert (1:10 packs)	**Puck.**
☐	1 Antero Niitymäki (G), TPS	3.00
☐	2 Ari-Pekka Siekkinen (G), Blues	3.00
☐	3 Pasi Kuivalainen (G), Ilves	3.00
☐	4 Sami Lehtinen (G), Pelicans	3.00
☐	5 Jason Muzzatti (G), Tappara	3.00
☐	6 Kimmo Kapanen (G), HPK	3.00

1999 - 2000 CHALLENGER ENERGY BAR

These cards were issued in Europe and are not licensed by either the National Hockey League or National Hockey League Players' Association. We do not have a full checklist for this series. Other cards exist. Each card measures 1 3/4" x 2 3/4".

Complete Set (30 cards): **15.00**

	Player	**CEB**
☐	1 Rob Niedermayer, Flor.	.50
☐	2 Robert Svehla, Flor.	.50
☐	3 Richard Zednik, Wash.	1.00
☐	4 Steve Sullivan, Toro.	.50
☐	5 Alexei Yashin, Otta.	1.50
☐	6 Alexander Mogilny, NJer.	1.00
☐	7 Zigmund Palffy, LosA.	1.50
☐	8 Martin Brodeur (G), NJer.	4.00
☐	9 Sandis Ozolinsh, Colo.	.50
☐	10 Adam Deadmarsh, Colo.	.50
☐	11 Peter Forsberg, Colo.	3.50
☐	12 Martin Rucinsky, Mont.	.50
☐	13 Shayne Corson, Mont.	.50
☐	14 Grant Fuhr (G), SLou.	1.50
☐	15 Al MacInnis, SLou.	1.00
☐	16 Paul Kariya, Anah.	3.50
☐	17 Teemu Selänne, Anah.	2.00
☐	18 Steve Yzerman, Detr.	6.00
☐	19 Chris Osgood (G), Detr.	1.50
☐	20 Brendan Shanahan, Detr.	2.50
☐	21 Vaclav Varada, Buff.	.50
☐	22 Brian Holzinger, Buff.	.50
☐	23 Dominik Hasek (G), Buff.	2.50
☐	24 Michael Peca, Buff.	1.00
☐	25 Ed Belfour (G), Dall.	2.50
☐	26 Jere Lehtinen, Dall.	.50
☐	27 Jaromir Jagr, Pitt.	2.50
☐	28 Kevin Hatcher, Pitt.	.50
☐	29 John LeClair, Phil.	2.00
☐	30 Alexei Zhamnov, Chic.	.50

1999 - 2000 CHOICE AHL ALL-STARS

Complete Set (12 cards):		**20.00**
Common Player:		**.50**
	Player	**AS**
☐	1 Martin Brochu (G), Portland Pirates	1.00
☐	2 Craig Ferguson, Louisville Panthers	.50
☐	3 Peter Ferraro, Providence Bruins	1.00
☐	4 Michael Gaul, Hershey Bears	.50
☐	5 Miikka Kiprusoff (G), Kentucky Thoroughblades	7.00
☐	6 Christian Matte, Hershey Bears	.50
☐	7 Chris O'Sullivan, Syracuse Crunch	.50
☐	8 Martin St-Louis, Saint John Flames	12.00
☐	9 Brad Tiley, Springfield Falcons	.50
☐	10 Dan Trebil, Cincinnati Mighty Ducks	.50
☐	11 Alexandre Volchkov, Portland Pirates	.50
☐	12 Bob Wren, Cincinnati Mighty Ducks	.50

1999 - 2000 CROWN ROYALE

This series was released in 2000. There are three versions: the regular card, a Premiere Date parallel (#/73) and a Limited Series parallel (#/99). The rookie-subset cards (skip numbered) in the base set are limited to 450 copies.

Complete Set (144 cards):		**33,000**	**17,000**	**175.00**
Common Player:		**6.00**	**5.00**	**.50**
	Player	**PD73**	**LS99**	**Reg.**
☐☐☐	1 Guy Hebert (G), Anah.	10.00	5.00	.50
☐☐☐	2 Paul Kariya, Anah.	70.00	40.00	3.50
☐☐☐	3 Steve Rucchin, Anah.	10.00	5.00	.50
☐☐☐	4 Teemu Selänne, Anah.	40.00	20.00	2.00
☐☐☐	5 Andrew Brunette, Atla.	6.00	5.00	.50

6 ankhouser (G), Atla. RC (*)	**10.00**	**5.00**	**2.50**
7 A. Karlsson, Atla. RC (*)	**6.00**	**5.00**	**2.00**
8 Damian Rhodes (G), Atla.	10.00	5.00	.50
9 Patrik Stefan, Atla. RC (*)	**30.00**	**15.00**	**5.00**
10 Jason Allison, Bost.	30.00	15.00	1.50
11 Raymond Bourque, Bost.	60.00	35.00	3.00
12 Byron Dafoe (G), Bost.	20.00	10.00	1.00
13 Mikko Eloranta, Bost. RC	**6.00**	**5.00**	**1.00**
14 Sergei Samsonov, Bost.	30.00	15.00	1.50
15 Joe Thornton, Bost.	60.00	35.00	3.00
16 M. Afinogenov, Buff. (*)	20.00	10.00	2.50
17 Martin Biron (G), Buff. (*)	20.00	10.00	3.00
18 Dominik Hasek (G), Buff.	50.00	30.00	2.50
19 Michael Peca, Buff.	20.00	10.00	1.00
20 Miroslav Satan, Buff.	15.00	5.00	.50
21 Valeri Bure, Calg.	15.00	5.00	.50
22 Grant Fuhr (G), Calg.	30.00	15.00	1.50
23 Jarome Iginla, Calg.	40.00	20.00	2.00
24 Robyn Regehr, Calg. (*)	6.00	5.00	2.00
25 O. Saprykin, Calg. RC (*)	**20.00**	**10.00**	**4.00**
26 Ron Francis, Caro.	30.00	15.00	1.50
27 Arturs Irbe (G), Caro.	20.00	10.00	1.00
28 Sami Kapanen, Caro.	15.00	5.00	.50
29 Jeff O'Neill, Caro.	20.00	10.00	1.00
30 Tony Amonte, Chic.	30.00	15.00	1.50
31 Kyle Calder, Chic. RC (*)	**20.00**	**10.00**	**4.00**
32 Éric Dazé, Chic.	20.00	10.00	1.00
33 Doug Gilmour, Chic.	30.00	15.00	1.50
34 Jocelyn Thibault (G), Chic.	20.00	10.00	1.00
35 Marc Denis (G), Colo. (*)	20.00	10.00	3.00
36 Chris Drury, Colo.	30.00	15.00	1.50
37 Peter Forsberg, Colo.	70.00	40.00	3.50
38 Milan Hejduk, Colo.	40.00	20.00	2.00
39 Patrick Roy (G), Colo.	120.00	70.00	7.50
40 Joe Sakic, Colo.	80.00	45.00	4.00
41 Alex Tanguay, Colo. (*)	30.00	15.00	4.00
42 Ed Belfour (G), Dall.	50.00	30.00	2.50
43 R. Christie, Dall. RC (*)	**6.00**	**5.00**	**2.00**
44 Brett Hull, Dall.	50.00	30.00	2.50
45 Jere Lehtinen, Dall.	15.00	5.00	.50
46 Mike Modano, Dall.	50.00	30.00	2.50
47 Joe Nieuwendyk, Dall.	20.00	10.00	1.00
48 Chris Chelios, Detr.	30.00	15.00	1.50
49 Sergei Fedorov, Detr.	50.00	30.00	2.50
50 Nicklas Lidström, Detr.	30.00	15.00	1.50
51 Chris Osgood (G), Detr.	30.00	15.00	1.50
52 Brendan Shanahan, Detr.	50.00	30.00	2.50
53 Steve Yzerman, Detr.	120.00	70.00	6.00
54 Bill Guerin, Edmo.	20.00	10.00	1.00
55 Tommy Salo (G), Edmo.	20.00	10.00	1.00
56 A. Selivanov, Edmo.	6.00	5.00	.50
57 Ryan Smyth, Edmo.	20.00	10.00	1.00
58 Doug Weight, Edmo.	30.00	15.00	1.50
59 Pavel Bure, Flor.	40.00	20.00	2.00
60 Trevor Kidd (G), Flor.	15.00	5.00	.50
61 I. Novoseltsev, Flor. RC (*)	**15.00**	**5.00**	**3.00**
62 Ray Whitney, Flor.	10.00	5.00	.50
63 Mike Vernon (G), Flor.	20.00	10.00	1.00
64 Rob Blake, LosA.	30.00	15.00	1.50
65 Stéphane Fiset (G), LosA.	15.00	5.00	.50
66 Zigmund Palffy, LosA.	30.00	15.00	1.50
67 Luc Robitaille, LosA.	40.00	20.00	2.00
68 Bryan Smolinski, LosA.	6.00	5.00	.50
69 Jeff Hackett (G), Mont.	15.00	5.00	.50
70 Saku Koivu, Mont.	40.00	20.00	2.00
71 Trevor Linden, Mont.	20.00	10.00	1.00
72 Brian Savage, Mont.	15.00	5.00	.50
73 José Théodore (G), Mont.	60.00	35.00	3.00
74 Mike Dunham (G), Nash.	20.00	10.00	1.00
75 Sergei Krivokrasov, Nash.	6.00	5.00	.50
76 David Legwand, Nash. (*)	20.00	10.00	2.50
77 Cliff Ronning, Nash.	10.00	5.00	.50
78 Martin Brodeur (G), NJer.	80.00	45.00	4.00
79 Patrik Elias, NJer.	40.00	20.00	2.00
80 Scott Gomez, NJer. (*)	20.00	10.00	2.50
81 Bobby Holik, NJer.	15.00	5.00	.50
82 Claude Lemieux, NJer.	15.00	5.00	.50
83 Petr* Sykora, NJer.	20.00	10.00	1.00
84 Tim Connolly, NYIs. (*)	20.00	10.00	2.50
85 Mariusz Czerkawski, NYIs.	10.00	5.00	.50
86 Brad Isbister, NYIs.	10.00	5.00	.50
87 Kenny Jönsson, NYIs.	10.00	5.00	.50
88 R. Luongo (G), NYIs. (*)	40.00	20.00	5.00
89 Theoren Fleury, NYRa.	30.00	15.00	1.50
90 M. Hnilicka (G), NYRa. RC	**20.00**	**10.00**	**3.00**
91 Brian Leetch, NYRa.	30.00	15.00	1.50
92 Mike Richter (G), NYRa.	20.00	10.00	1.00
93 Mike York, NYRa. (*)	15.00	5.00	2.00
94 Daniel Alfredsson, Otta.	30.00	15.00	1.50
95 Radek Bonk, Otta.	15.00	5.00	.50
96 Mike Fisher, Otta. RC (*)	**20.00**	**10.00**	**4.00**
97 Marian Hossa, Otta.	50.00	30.00	2.50
98 Joé Juneau, Otta.	10.00	5.00	.50
99 Ron Tugnutt (G), Otta.	20.00	10.00	1.00
100 Alexei Yashin, Otta.	30.00	15.00	1.50
101 Simon Gagné, Phil. (*)	40.00	20.00	5.00
102 John LeClair, Phil.	40.00	20.00	2.00
103 Eric Lindros, Phil.	50.00	30.00	2.50
104 Keith Primeau, Phil.	20.00	10.00	1.00
105 Mark Recchi, Phil.	20.00	10.00	1.00
106 Vanbiesbrouck (G), Phil.	20.00	10.00	1.00
107 Travis Green, Phoe.	10.00	5.00	.50
108 N. Khabibulin (G), Phoe.	20.00	10.00	1.00
109 Jeremy Roenick, Phoe.	40.00	20.00	2.00
110 Keith Tkachuk, Phoe.	30.00	15.00	1.50
111 Tom Barrasso (G), Pitt.	20.00	10.00	1.00
112 Jaromir Jagr, Pitt.	50.00	30.00	2.50
113 Alexei Kovalev, Pitt.	30.00	15.00	1.50
114 Robert Lang, Pitt.	10.00	5.00	.50
115 Pavol Demitra, SLou.	20.00	10.00	1.00
116 J. Hecht, SLou. RC (*)	**20.00**	**10.00**	**4.00**
117 Al MacInnis, SLou.	20.00	10.00	1.00
118 L. Nagy, SLou. RC (*)	**15.00**	**10.00**	**4.00**
119 Chris Pronger, SLou.	30.00	15.00	1.50
120 Roman Turek (G), SLou.	20.00	10.00	1.00
121 Pierre Turgeon, SLou.	20.00	10.00	1.00
122 V. Damphousse, SanJ.	30.00	15.00	1.50
123 Jeff Friesen, SanJ.	15.00	5.00	.50
124 Patrick Marleau, SanJ.	20.00	10.00	1.00
125 Owen Nolan, SanJ.	30.00	15.00	1.50
126 Steve Shields (G), SanJ.	10.00	5.00	.50
127 Dan Cloutier (G), Tamp.	20.00	10.00	1.00
128 Chris Gratton, Tamp.	10.00	5.00	.50
129 Vincent Lecavalier, Tamp.	50.00	30.00	2.50
130 Mike Sillinger, Tamp.	6.00	5.00	.50
131 N. Antropov, Toro. RC (*)	**20.00**	**10.00**	**4.00**
132 Sergei Berezin, Toro.	10.00	5.00	.50
133 Tie Domi, Toro.	15.00	5.00	.50
134 Curtis Joseph (G), Toro.	50.00	30.00	2.50
135 Mats Sundin, Toro.	50.00	30.00	2.50
136 S. Kariya, Vanc. RC (*)	**20.00**	**10.00**	**4.00**
137 Mark Messier, Vanc.	50.00	30.00	2.50
138 Markus Näslund, Vanc.	50.00	30.00	2.50
139 Peter Schaefer, Vanc. (*)	6.00	5.00	2.00
140 Garth Snow (G), Vanc.	15.00	5.00	.50
141 Peter Bondra, Wash.	30.00	15.00	1.50
142 Jan Bulis, Wash.	6.00	5.00	.50
143 Olaf Kölzig (G), Wash.	30.00	15.00	1.50
144 Adam Oates, Wash.	20.00	10.00	1.00

ICE ELITE

There are two versions: the regular insert (1 per pack) and the Variation (#/10).

Insert Set (25 cards):	**5950.00**	**25.00**
Inserts	**IE10**	**IE**
1 Paul Kariya, Anah.	400.00	2.00
2 Teemu Selänne, Anah.	225.00	1.00
3 Joe Thornton, Bost.	350.00	1.50
4 Dominik Hasek (G), Buff.	300.00	1.50
5 Tony Amonte, Chic.	175.00	.75
6 Milan Hejduk, Colo.	225.00	1.00
7 Patrick Roy (G), Colo.	900.00	4.50
8 Joe Sakic, Colo.	475.00	2.00
9 Ed Belfour (G), Dall.	300.00	1.50
10 Brett Hull, Dall.	300.00	1.50
11 Brendan Shanahan, Detr.	300.00	1.50
12 Steve Yzerman, Detr.	700.00	3.50
13 Luc Robitaille, LosA.	225.00	1.00
14 Trevor Linden, Mont.	100.00	.75
15 David Legwand, Nash.	100.00	.75
16 Martin Brodeur (G), NJer.	475.00	2.00
17 Theoren Fleury, NYRa.	175.00	.75
18 Marian Hossa, Otta.	300.00	1.50
19 John LeClair, Phil.	225.00	1.00
20 Mark Recchi, Phil.	100.00	.75
21 Jeremy Roenick, Phoe.	225.00	1.00
22 Owen Nolan, SanJ.	175.00	.75
23 Vincent Lecavalier, Tamp.	300.00	1.50
24 Curtis Joseph (G), Toro.	300.00	1.50
25 Steve Kariya, Vanc.	50.00	.75

INTERNATIONAL GLORY

There are two versions: the regular insert (1 per pack) and the Passport to Glory variation (#/20).

Insert Set (25 cards):	**3890.00**	**20.00**
Inserts	**PG20**	**IG**
1 Teemu Selänne, Anah.	180.00	1.00
2 Patrik Stefan, Atla.	72.00	.75
3 Dominik Hasek (G), Buff.	225.00	1.50
4 Arturs Irbe (G), Caro.	90.00	.75
5 Chris Drury, Colo.	135.00	.75
6 Peter Forsberg, Colo.	315.00	2.00
7 Patrick Roy (G), Colo.	675.00	4.50
8 Mike Modano, Dall.	225.00	1.50
9 Sergei Fedorov, Detr.	225.00	1.50
10 Brendan Shanahan, Detr.	225.00	1.50
11 Pavel Bure, Flor.	180.00	1.00
12 Zigmund Palffy, LosA.	135.00	.75
13 Saku Koivu, Mont.	180.00	1.00
14 Martin Brodeur (G), NJer.	360.00	2.00
15 Scott Gomez, NJer.	90.00	.75
16 Theoren Fleury, NYRa.	135.00	.75
17 Simon Gagné, Phil.	180.00	1.00
18 Eric Lindros, Phil.	225.00	1.50
19 John Vanbiesbrouck (G), Phil.	108.00	.75
20 Keith Tkachuk, Phoe.	135.00	.75
21 Jaromir Jagr, Pitt.	225.00	1.50
22 Pavol Demitra, SLou.	90.00	.75
23 Jochen Hecht, SLou.	54.00	.75
24 Jeff Friesen, SanJ.	72.00	.75
25 Mats Sundin, Toro.	225.00	1.50

CARD-SUPIALS

There are two versions: the standard-size card and the miniature pocket-size card.

Insert Set (20 cards + 20 mini cards):		**8.00**
Insert (2:25 packs)	**Mini**	**CS**
1 Paul Kariya, Anah.	3.00	7.00
2 Teemu Selänne, Anah.	2.00	4.00
3 Patrik Stefan, Atla.	1.00	3.00
4 Joe Thornton, Bost.	3.00	6.00
5 Dominik Hasek (G), Buff.	2.00	5.00
6 Peter Forsberg, Colo.	3.00	7.00
7 Patrick Roy (G), Colo.	7.00	15.00
8 Alex Tanguay, Colo.	1.00	3.00
9 Mike Modano, Dall.	2.00	5.00
10 Brendan Shanahan, Detr.	2.00	5.00
11 Steve Yzerman, Detr.	6.00	12.00
12 Pavel Bure, Flor.	2.00	4.00
13 Martin Brodeur (G), NJer.	4.00	8.00
14 Scott Gomez, NJer.	1.00	4.00
15 Roberto Luongo (G), NYIs.	2.00	4.00
16 Eric Lindros, Phil.	2.00	5.00
17 John Vanbiesbrouck (G), Phil.	1.00	2.00
18 Jaromir Jagr, Pitt.	2.00	5.00
19 Mats Sundin, Toro.	2.00	5.00
20 Steve Kariya, Vanc.	1.00	2.00

CENTURY 21

Insert Set (10 cards):	**85.00**
Insert (#/375)	**C21**
1 Paul Kariya, Anah.	15.00
2 Patrik Stefan, Atla.	7.00
3 Chris Drury, Colo.	6.00
4 Peter Forsberg, Colo.	15.00
5 Pavel Bure, Flor.	9.00
6 Scott Gomez, NJer.	6.00
7 Roberto Luongo (G), NYIs.	13.00
8 Marian Hossa, Otta.	11.00
9 Jaromir Jagr, Pitt.	11.00
10 Vincent Lecavalier, Tamp.	11.00

CRAMER'S CHOICE AWARD

There are seven versions to these oversize cards: the regular insert, a Dark Blue parallel (#/35), a Green parallel (#/30), a Red parallel (#/25), a Light Blue parallel (#/20), a Gold parallel (#/10) and a Purple parallel (#/1).

Insert Set (10 cards):	**2000.00**	**1700.00**	**50.00**
Inserts	**C30**	**C35**	**CCA**
1 Paul Kariya, Anah.	225.00	200.00	7.00
2 Teemu Selänne, Anah.	125.00	100.00	5.00
3 Peter Forsberg, Colo.	225.00	200.00	7.00
4 Patrick Roy (G), Colo.	525.00	450.00	15.00
5 Mike Modano, Dall.	175.00	150.00	5.00
6 Steve Yzerman, Detr.	400.00	350.00	12.00
7 Pavel Bure, Flor.	125.00	100.00	5.00
8 Martin Brodeur (G), NJer.	275.00	225.00	8.00
9 Eric Lindros, Phil.	175.00	150.00	5.00
10 Jaromir Jagr, Pitt.	175.00	150.00	5.00

CRAMER'S CHOICE AWARD

Insert Set (10 cards):	**3500.00**	**2600.00**	**2400.00**
Inserts	**C10**	**C20**	**C25**
1 Paul Kariya, Anah.	400.00	300.00	275.00
2 Teemu Selänne, Anah.	225.00	175.00	150.00
3 Peter Forsberg, Colo.	400.00	300.00	275.00
4 Patrick Roy (G), Colo.	900.00	675.00	600.00
5 Mike Modano, Dall.	300.00	225.00	200.00
6 Steve Yzerman, Detr.	700.00	525.00	475.00
7 Pavel Bure, Flor.	225.00	175.00	150.00
8 Martin Brodeur (G), NJer.	475.00	350.00	300.00
9 Eric Lindros, Phil.	300.00	225.00	200.00
10 Jaromir Jagr, Pitt.	300.00	225.00	200.00

GOLD CROWN DIE-CUTS

Insert Set (6 cards):	**60.00**
Insert	**GCDC**
1 Teemu Selänne, Anah.	6.00
2 Dominik Hasek (G), Buff.	7.00
3 Patrick Roy (G), Colo.	22.00
4 Steve Yzerman, Detr.	18.00
5 Martin Brodeur (G), NJer.	12.00
6 John LeClair, Phil.	6.00

TEAM CAPTAINS DIE-CUTS

Insert Set (10 cards):	**55.00**
Inser (1:25)	**TC**
1 Paul Kariya, Anah.	8.00
2 Raymond Bourque, Bost.	7.00
3 Joe Sakic, Colo.	10.00
4 Steve Yzerman, Detr.	15.00
5 Eric Lindros, Phil.	6.00
6 Keith Tkachuk, Phoe.	3.00
7 Jaromir Jagr, Pitt.	6.00
8 Owen Nolan, SanJ.	3.00
9 Mats Sundin, Toro.	6.00
10 Mark Messier, Vanc.	6.00

1999 - 2000 DS

Cards of NHL stars and prospects usually sell at a premium ($1-$2).

Complete Set (198 cards):	**50.00**
Common Player:	**.30**
Player	**DS**
1 Richard Hrazdira, ZPS Zlin	.30
2 Vladimir Hudacek (G), ZPS Zlin	.30
3 Roman Hamrlik, ZPS Zlin	1.00
4 Martin Hamrlik, ZPS Zlin	.30
5 Jiri Marusak, ZPS Zlin	.30
6 Tomas Zizka, ZPS Zlin	.30
7 Petr Cajanek, ZPS Zlin	.30
8 Miroslav Okal, ZPS Zlin	.30
9 Josef Straub, ZPS Zlin	.30
10 Petr Leska, ZPS Zlin	.30
11 Michal Tomek, ZPS Zlin	.30
12 Martin Kotasek, ZPS Zlin	.30
13 Ondrej Vesely, ZPS Zlin	.30
14 Petr Vala, ZPS Zlin	.30
15 Rudolf Pejchar, Karlovy Vary	.30
16 Zdenek Smid, Karlovy Vary	.30
17 Martin Richter, Karlovy Vary	.30
18 Petr Pavlas, Karlovy Vary	.30
19 Martin Maskarinec, Karlovy Vary	.30
20 Jan Snopek, Karlovy Vary	.30
21 Michal Divisek, Karlovy Vary	.30
22 Pavel Janku, Karlovy Vary	.30
23 Jaromir Kverka, Karlovy Vary	.30
24 Martin Rousek, Karlovy Vary	.30
25 Miroslav Barus, Karlovy Vary	.30
26 Martin Streit, Karlovy Vary	.30
27 Martin Filip, Karlovy Vary	.30
28 Radek Prochazka, Karlovy Vary	.30
29 Ivo Capek, Ceske Budejovice	.30
30 Michal Marik, Ceske Budejovice	.30
31 Milan Nedoma, Ceske Budejovice	.30
32 Radek Martinek, Ceske Budejovice	.50
33 Rudolf Suchanek, Ceske Budejovice	.30
34 Roman Cech, Ceske Budejovice	.30
35 Vaclav Kral, Ceske Budejovice	.30
36 Filip Turek, Ceske Budejovice	.30
37 Peter Bartos, Ceske Budejovice	.50
38 Radek Toupal, Ceske Budejovice	.30
39 Lubos Rob, Ceske Budejovice	.30
40 Martin Strba, Ceske Budejovice	.30
41 Petr Sailer, Ceske Budejovice	.30
42 Kamil Brabenec, Ceske Budejovice	.30
43 Pavel Cagas, Havirov	.30
44 Robert Horyna, Havirov	.30
45 Michael Vyhlidal, Havirov	.30
46 Miroslav Javin, Havirov	.30
47 Libor Pivko, Havirov	.30
48 Ales Tomasek, Havirov	.30
49 Roman Horak, Havirov	.30
50 Pavel Nohel, Havirov	.30
51 Ales Zima, Havicov	.30
52 Marek Melanovsky, Havirov	.30
53 Jaroslav Hub, Havirov	.30
54 Pavel Zdrahal, Havicov	.30
55 Bogdan Savenko, Havinov	.30
56 Robert Kantor, Havirov	.30
57 Zdenek Orct, Chemopetrol Litvinov	.30
58 Marek Pinc, Chemopetrol Litvinov	.30
59 Miloslav Horava, Chemopetrol Litvinov	.50
60 Angel Nikolov, Chemopetrol Litvinov	.30
61 Petr Kratky, Chemopetrol Litvinov	.30
62 Radek Mrazek, Chemopetrol Litvinov	.30
63 Robert Reichel, Chemopetrol Litvinov	1.50
64 Robert Kysela, Chemopetrol Litvinov	.30
65 Ivo Prorok, Chemopetrol Litvinov	.30
66 Jan Alinic, Chemopetrol Litvinov	.30
67 Jindrich Kotrla, Chemopetrol Litvinov	.30
68 Zdenek Skorepa, Chemopetrol Litvinov	.30

☐	69 Josef Straka, Chemopetrol Litvinov	.30
☐	70 Mikhail Travnicek, Chemopetrol Litvinov	.30
☐	71 Libor Barta, Pardubice	.30
☐	72 Adam Svoboda, Pardubice	.30
☐	73 Ales Pisa, Pardubice	.50
☐	74 Tomas Pacal, Pardubice	.30
☐	75 Jiri Malinsky, Pardubice	.30
☐	76 Petr Jancarik, Pardubice	.30
☐	77 Patrik Elias, Pardubice	4.00
☐	78 Brendan Morrison, Pardubice	1.50
☐	79 Radek Bonk, Pardubice	1.50
☐	80 Jaroslav Kudrna, Pardubice	.30
☐	81 Tomas Blazek, Pardubice	.30
☐	82 Ladislav Lubina, Pardubice	.30
☐	83 Stanislav Prochazka, Pardubice	.30
☐	84 Jiri Jantovsky, Pardubice	.30
☐	85 Dusan Salficky, Interconex Plzen	.30
☐	86 Radek Masny, Interconex Plzen	.30
☐	87 Josef Reznicek, Interconex Plzen	.30
☐	88 Ivan Vlcek, Interconex Plzen	.30
☐	89 Martin Cech, Interconex Plzen	.30
☐	90 Jiri Hanzlik, Interconex Plzen	.30
☐	91 Martin Spanhel, Interconex Plzen	.50
☐	92 Michal Straka, Interconex Plzen	.30
☐	93 Zdenek Sedlak, Interconex Plzen	.30
☐	94 Pavel Vostrak, Interconex Plzen	.30
☐	95 Petr Korinek, Interconex Plzen	.30
☐	96 Pavel Geffert, Interconex Plzen	.30
☐	97 David Pospisil, Interconex Plzen	.30
☐	98 Milan Volak, Interconex Plzen	.30
☐	99 Vlastimil Lakosil, Trinec	.30
☐	100 Marek Novotny, Trinec	.30
☐	101 Jiri Kuntos, Trinec	.30
☐	102 Petr Gregorek, Trinec	.30
☐	103 Milos Holan, Trinec	.50
☐	104 L'ubomir Sekeras, Trinec	.50
☐	105 Richard Kral, Trinec	.30
☐	106 Marek Zadina, Trinec	.30
☐	107 Martin Havlat, Trinec	22.50
☐	108 Roman Kadera, Trinec	.30
☐	109 Tomas Chlubna, Trinec	.30
☐	110 Petr Folta, Trinec	.30
☐	111 Ondrej Zetek, Trinec	.30
☐	112 Branislav Janos, Trinec	.30
☐	113 Ladislav Blazek, Slavia Praha	.30
☐	114 Roman Malek, Slavia Praha	.30
☐	115 Vitezslav Skuta, Slavia Praha	.30
☐	116 Jan Krajicek, Slavia Praha	.30
☐	117 Pavel Kolarik, Slavia Praha	.50
☐	118 Martin Bakula, Slavia Praha	.30
☐	119 Vladimir Ruzicka, Slavia Praha	1.00
☐	120 Tomas Kucharcik, Slavia Praha	.30
☐	121 Michal Sup, Slavia Praha	.30
☐	122 Jiri Dolezal, Slavia Praha	.30
☐	123 Jan Kopecky, Slavia Praha	.30
☐	124 Petr Hrbek, Slavia Praha	.30
☐	125 Radek Matejovsky, Slavia Praha	.30
☐	126 Vladimir Machulda, Slavia Praha	.30
☐	127 Roman Cechmanek, Dadak Vsetin	2.00
☐	128 Ivo Pesat, Dadak Vsetin	.30
☐	129 Jan Srdinko, Dadak Vsetin	.30
☐	130 Libor Zabransky, Dadak Vsetin	.30
☐	131 Jiri Veber, Dadak Vsetin	.30
☐	132 Radim Tesarik, Dadak Vsetin	.30
☐	133 Jiri Dopita, Dadak Vsetin	.50
☐	134 Radek Belohlav, Dadak Vsetin	.30
☐	135 Jan Tomajko, Dadak Vsetin	.30
☐	136 Jan Pardavy, Dadak Vsetin	.30
☐	137 Roman Stantien, Dadak Vsetin	.30
☐	138 Zbynek Marak, Dadak Vsetin	.30
☐	139 Alexei Jaskin, Dadak Vsetin	.30
☐	140 Pavel Zubicek, Dadak Vsetin	.30
☐	141 Petr Briza, Sparta Praha	.30
☐	142 Petr Prikryl, Sparta Praha	.30
☐	143 Frantisek Kucera, Sparta Praha	.50
☐	144 Ladislav Benysek, Sparta Praha	.30
☐	145 Michal Sykora, Sparta Praha	.50
☐	146 Jaroslav Nedved, Sparta Praha	.30
☐	147 David Vyborny, Sparta Praha	.50
☐	148 Patrik Martinec, Sparta Praha	.30
☐	149 Jaroslav Hlinka, Sparta Praha	.30
☐	150 Ondrej Kratena, Sparta Praha	.30
☐	151 Michal Bros, Sparta Praha	.30
☐	152 Richard Zemlicka, Sparta Praha	.30
☐	153 Jiri Zelenka, Sparta Praha	.30
☐	154 Vaclav Eiselt, Sparta Praha	.30
☐	155 Martin Bilek, Kladno	.30
☐	156 Lubos Horcinka, Kladno	.30
☐	157 Michal Madl, Kladno	.30
☐	158 Jan Krulis, Kladno	.30
☐	159 Jiri Krocak, Kladno	.30
☐	160 Jan Dlouhy, Kladno	.30
☐	161 Tomas Horna, Kladno	.30
☐	162 Ladislav Svoboda, Kladno	.30
☐	163 Zdenek Eichenmann, Kladno	.30
☐	164 Jiri Burger, Kladno	.30
☐	165 Tomas Kupka, Kladno	.30
☐	166 Jiri Kames, Kladno	.30
☐	167 Jiri Holsan, Kladno	.30
☐	168 Ondrej Kriz, Kladno	.30
☐	169 Martin Prusek, Vitkovice	4.00
☐	170 Jiri Trvaj, Vitkovice	.30
☐	171 Dmitri Jerofejev, Vitkovice	.30
☐	172 Lukas Galvas, Vitkovice	.30
☐	173 Pavel Kowalczyk, Vitkovice	.30
☐	174 Petr Jurecka, Vitkovice	.30
☐	175 Ludek Krayzel, Vitkovice	.30
☐	176 Libor Polasek, Vitkovice	.30
☐	177 Martin Lamich, Vitkovice	.30
☐	178 Petr Hubacek, Vitkovice	.50
☐	179 Sergei Petrenko, Vitkovice	.30
☐	180 Zdenek Pavelek, Vitkovice	.30
☐	181 Martin Tomasek, Vitkovice	.30
☐	182 Zbynek Irgl, Vitkovice	.30
☐	183 Ladislav Kudrna, Znojmo	.30
☐	184 Pavol Rybar, Znojmo	.30
☐	185 Pavel Kumstat, Znojmo	.30
☐	186 Tomas Jakes, Znojmo	.30
☐	187 Karel Soudek, Znojmo	.30
☐	188 Jiri Hes, Znojmo	.30
☐	189 Petr Kankovsky, Znojmo	.30
☐	190 Milan Kastner, Znojmo	.30
☐	191 Jiri Poukar, Znojmo	.30
☐	192 Peter Pucher, Znojmo	.30
☐	193 Marek Vorel, Znojmo	.30
☐	194 Radek Haman, Znojmo	.30
☐	195 Karel Plasek, Znojmo	.30
☐	196 Milan Prochazka, Znojmo	.30
☐	197 Checklist	.30
☐	198 Checklist	.30
	Insert	**MT**
☐	GC Jaromir Jagr (Gold Card)	30.00

GOALIE

Insert Set (14 cards): 30.00

	Insert (1:5 packs)	**MT**
☐	G1 Richard Hrazdira (G)	2.00
☐	G2 Rudolf Pejchar (G)	2.00
☐	G3 Ivo Capek (G)	2.00
☐	G4 Pavel Cagas (G)	2.00
☐	G5 Zdenek Orct (G)	2.00
☐	G6 Libor Barta (G)	2.00
☐	G7 Dusan Salficky (G)	2.00
☐	G8 Vlastimil Lakosil (G)	2.00
☐	G9 Ladislav Blazek (G)	2.00
☐	G10 Roman Cechmanek (G)	5.00
☐	G11 Petr Briza (G)	2.00
☐	G12 Martin Bilek (G)	2.00
☐	G13 Martin Prusek (G)	7.00
☐	G14 Pavol Rybar (G)	2.00

NATIONAL STARS

Insert Set (23 cards): 45.00

	Insert (1:3 packs)	**MT**
☐	NS1 Dominik Hasek (G)	6.00
☐	NS2 Milan Hnilicka (G)	2.00
☐	NS3 Jaromir Jagr	6.00
☐	NS4 Jiri Slégr	2.00
☐	NS5 Jaroslav Spacek	2.00
☐	NS6 Frantisek Kucera	2.00
☐	NS7 Roman Hamrlik	2.00
☐	NS8 Petr* Svoboda	2.00
☐	NS9 Viktor Ujcik	2.00
☐	NS10 Frantisek Kaberle	2.00
☐	NS11 Libor Prochazka	2.00
☐	NS12 Robert Reichel	2.00
☐	NS13 Martin Rucinsky	2.00
☐	NS14 Martin Straka	2.00
☐	NS15 Martin Prochazka	2.00
☐	NS16 Pavel Patera	2.00
☐	NS17 Vladimir Ruzicka	2.00
☐	NS18 Josef Beranek	2.00
☐	NS19 David Moravec	2.00
☐	NS20 Jan Hlavac	2.00
☐	NS21 David Vyborny	2.00
☐	NS22 Jiri Dopita	2.00
☐	NS23 Petr* Sykora	2.00

PREMIUM

Complete Set (12 cards): 85.00

	Redeemed	**MT**
☐	P1 Dominik Hasek (G)	12.00
☐	P2 Roman Turek (G)	8.00
☐	P3 Roman Cechmanek (G)	8.00
☐	P4 Milan Hnilicka (G)	8.00
☐	P5 Martin Prochazka	8.00
☐	P6 Jaromir Jagr	12.00
☐	P7 Jiri Slégr	8.00
☐	P8 Jaroslav Spacek	8.00
☐	P9 Pavel Patera	8.00
☐	P10 Jiri Dopita	8.00
☐	P11 Robert Reichel	8.00
☐	P12 Martin Rucinsky	8.00

1999 - 2000 DYNAGON ICE

This series was released in 1999. There are five versions: the regular card, a Gold parallel (#/199), a Copper parallel (#/99), an Ice Blue parallel (#/67) and a Premiere Date parallel (#/63). The Ice Blue and Premiere Date parallels are priced similarly below.

Complete Set (206 cards): 2250.00 1500.00 600.00 90.00

Common Player: 8.00 6.00 3.00 .25

	Player	IB67	C99	G199	Reg.
☐☐☐☐☐	**1 S. Kariya RC (*)**	**10.00**	**10.00**	**5.00**	**7.50**
☐☐☐☐☐	2 S. Gagné (*)	30.00	25.00	20.00	6.00
☐☐☐☐☐	**3 M. Fisher RC (*)**	**10.00**	**10.00**	**5.00**	**7.50**
☐☐☐☐☐	4 Mike Ribeiro (*)	10.00	10.00	5.00	2.00
☐☐☐☐☐	**5 O. Saprykin RC (*)**	**10.00**	**10.00**	**5.00**	**7.50**
☐☐☐☐☐	**6 P. Stefan RC (*)**	**25.00**	**20.00**	**10.00**	**10.00**
☐☐☐☐☐	7 Ted Donato	8.00	5.00	2.00	.25
☐☐☐☐☐	**8 N. Hävelid RC**	**8.00**	**5.00**	**2.00**	**.50**
☐☐☐☐☐	9 Guy Hebert (G)	8.00	5.00	2.00	.25
☐☐☐☐☐	10 Paul Kariya	55.00	40.00	15.00	1.50
☐☐☐☐☐	11 Steve Rucchin	8.00	5.00	2.00	.25
☐☐☐☐☐	12 T. Selänne	30.00	25.00	10.00	1.00
☐☐☐☐☐	13 O. Tverdovsky	8.00	5.00	2.00	.25
☐☐☐☐☐	14 K. Buchberger	8.00	5.00	2.00	.25
☐☐☐☐☐	15 N. Emerson	8.00	5.00	2.00	.25
☐☐☐☐☐	16 Ray Ferraro	8.00	5.00	2.00	.25
☐☐☐☐☐	17 N. Maracle (G)	8.00	5.00	2.00	.25
☐☐☐☐☐	18 D. Rhodes (G)	8.00	5.00	2.00	.25
☐☐☐☐☐	19 Per Svartvadet	8.00	5.00	2.00	.25
☐☐☐☐☐	20 Jason Allison	20.00	15.00	5.00	.50
☐☐☐☐☐	21 R. Bourque	45.00	35.00	15.00	1.50
☐☐☐☐☐	22 Anson Carter	15.00	10.00	5.00	.50
☐☐☐☐☐	23 B. Dafoe (G)	15.00	10.00	5.00	.50
☐☐☐☐☐	**24 Grahame (G) RC**	**14.00**	**10.00**	**5.00**	**1.50**
☐☐☐☐☐	25 Sergei Samsonov	20.00	15.00	5.00	.50
☐☐☐☐☐	26 Joe Thornton	45.00	35.00	15.00	1.50
☐☐☐☐☐	27 Stu Barnes	8.00	5.00	2.00	.25
☐☐☐☐☐	28 Martin Biron (G)	15.00	15.00	5.00	.50
☐☐☐☐☐	29 Curtis Brown	8.00	5.00	2.00	.25
☐☐☐☐☐	30 Michal Grosek	8.00	5.00	2.00	.25
☐☐☐☐☐	31 D. Hasek (G)	40.00	30.00	10.00	1.00
☐☐☐☐☐	32 Michael Peca	15.00	10.00	5.00	.50
☐☐☐☐☐	33 Miroslav Satan	10.00	10.00	2.00	.25
☐☐☐☐☐	34 Valeri Bure	10.00	10.00	2.00	.25
☐☐☐☐☐	35 Grant Fuhr (G)	20.00	15.00	5.00	.50
☐☐☐☐☐	36 Jarome Iginla	30.00	25.00	10.00	1.00
☐☐☐☐☐	37 Derek Morris	8.00	5.00	2.00	.25
☐☐☐☐☐	38 Marc* Savard	8.00	5.00	2.00	.25
☐☐☐☐☐	39 Cory Stillman	8.00	5.00	2.00	.25
☐☐☐☐☐	40 Ron Francis	20.00	15.00	5.00	.50
☐☐☐☐☐	41 Arturs Irbe (G)	15.00	10.00	5.00	.50
☐☐☐☐☐	42 Sami Kapanen	10.00	10.00	2.00	.25
☐☐☐☐☐	43 Keith Primeau	15.00	10.00	5.00	.50
☐☐☐☐☐	44 David Tanabe	8.00	5.00	2.00	.25
☐☐☐☐☐	**45 T. Westlund RC**	**8.00**	**5.00**	**2.00**	**.50**
☐☐☐☐☐	46 Tony Amonte	20.00	15.00	5.00	.50
☐☐☐☐☐	47 Wendel Clark	30.00	25.00	10.00	1.00
☐☐☐☐☐	48 Éric Dazé	15.00	10.00	5.00	.50
☐☐☐☐☐	49 J-P Dumont	8.00	5.00	2.00	.25
☐☐☐☐☐	50 Doug Gilmour	20.00	15.00	5.00	.50
☐☐☐☐☐	51 Steven McCarthy	8.00	5.00	2.00	.25
☐☐☐☐☐	52 J. Thibault (G)	15.00	10.00	5.00	.50
☐☐☐☐☐	53 Alexei Zhamnov	10.00	10.00	2.00	.25
☐☐☐☐☐	54 Adam Deadmarsh	10.00	10.00	2.00	.25
☐☐☐☐☐	55 Chris Drury	20.00	15.00	5.00	.50
☐☐☐☐☐	56 Peter Forsberg	55.00	40.00	15.00	1.50
☐☐☐☐☐	57 Milan Hejduk	30.00	25.00	10.00	1.00
☐☐☐☐☐	**58 Dan Hinote RC**	**12.00**	**8.00**	**5.00**	**1.50**
☐☐☐☐☐	59 Patrick Roy (G)	95.00	75.00	35.00	3.50
☐☐☐☐☐	60 Joe Sakic	60.00	50.00	20.00	2.00
☐☐☐☐☐	61 Martin Skoula	8.00	5.00	2.00	.50
☐☐☐☐☐	62 Alex Tanguay	20.00	15.00	5.00	1.50
☐☐☐☐☐	63 Ed Belfour (G)	40.00	30.00	10.00	1.00
☐☐☐☐☐	64 Derian Hatcher	10.00	10.00	2.00	.25
☐☐☐☐☐	65 Brett Hull	40.00	30.00	10.00	1.00
☐☐☐☐☐	66 J. Langenbrunner	8.00	5.00	2.00	.25
☐☐☐☐☐	67 Jere Lehtinen	10.00	10.00	2.00	.25
☐☐☐☐☐	68 Mike Modano	40.00	30.00	10.00	1.00
☐☐☐☐☐	69 Joe Nieuwendyk	15.00	10.00	5.00	.50
☐☐☐☐☐	**70 Pavel Patera RC**	**8.00**	**5.00**	**2.00**	**.50**
☐☐☐☐☐	**71 Yuri Butsayev RC**	**8.00**	**5.00**	**2.00**	**.50**
☐☐☐☐☐	72 Chris Chelios	20.00	15.00	5.00	.50
☐☐☐☐☐	73 Sergei Fedorov	40.00	30.00	10.00	1.00
☐☐☐☐☐	74 Vy. Kozlov	8.00	5.00	2.00	.25
☐☐☐☐☐	75 Nicklas Lidström	20.00	15.00	5.00	.50
☐☐☐☐☐	76 Darren McCarty	10.00	10.00	2.00	.25
☐☐☐☐☐	77 Chris Osgood (G)	20.00	15.00	5.00	.50
☐☐☐☐☐	78 B. Shanahan	40.00	30.00	10.00	1.00
☐☐☐☐☐	79 Steve Yzerman	95.00	75.00	30.00	3.00
☐☐☐☐☐	**80 Paul Comrie RC**	**8.00**	**6.00**	**2.00**	**1.00**
☐☐☐☐☐	81 Mike Grier	8.00	5.00	2.00	.25
☐☐☐☐☐	82 Tom Poti	8.00	5.00	2.00	.25
☐☐☐☐☐	83 Bill Ranford (G)	15.00	10.00	5.00	.50
☐☐☐☐☐	84 Tommy Salo (G)	15.00	10.00	5.00	.50
☐☐☐☐☐	85 Ryan Smyth	15.00	15.00	5.00	.50
☐☐☐☐☐	86 Doug Weight	20.00	15.00	5.00	.50
☐☐☐☐☐	87 Pavel Bure	30.00	25.00	10.00	1.00
☐☐☐☐☐	88 Sean Burke (G)	20.00	15.00	5.00	.50
☐☐☐☐☐	89 Trevor Kidd (G)	10.00	10.00	2.00	.25
☐☐☐☐☐	90 Viktor Kozlov	10.00	10.00	2.00	.25
☐☐☐☐☐	**91 Novoseltsev RC**	**12.00**	**8.00**	**5.00**	**1.50**
☐☐☐☐☐	92 Mark Parrish	15.00	10.00	5.00	.50
☐☐☐☐☐	93 Ray Whitney	8.00	5.00	2.00	.25
☐☐☐☐☐	**94 Jason Blake RC**	**14.00**	**10.00**	**5.00**	**1.50**
☐☐☐☐☐	95 Rob Blake	20.00	15.00	5.00	.50
☐☐☐☐☐	96 S. Fiset (G)	10.00	10.00	2.00	.25
☐☐☐☐☐	97 Zigmund Palffy	20.00	15.00	5.00	.50
☐☐☐☐☐	98 Luc Robitaille	30.00	25.00	10.00	1.00
☐☐☐☐☐	99 Jozef Stumpel	8.00	5.00	2.00	.25
☐☐☐☐☐	100 Shayne Corson	10.00	10.00	2.00	.25
☐☐☐☐☐	101 Jeff Hackett (G)	10.00	10.00	2.00	.25
☐☐☐☐☐	102 Saku Koivu	30.00	25.00	10.00	1.00
☐☐☐☐☐	103 Trevor Linden	15.00	10.00	5.00	.50
☐☐☐☐☐	104 Martin Rucinsky	8.00	5.00	2.00	.25
☐☐☐☐☐	105 Brian Savage	10.00	10.00	2.00	.25
☐☐☐☐☐	106 M. Dunham (G)	15.00	10.00	5.00	.50
☐☐☐☐☐	107 Greg Johnson	8.00	5.00	2.00	.25
☐☐☐☐☐	108 S. Krivokrasov	8.00	5.00	2.00	.25
☐☐☐☐☐	109 David Legwand	15.00	10.00	5.00	.50
☐☐☐☐☐	110 Ville Peltonen	8.00	5.00	2.00	.25
☐☐☐☐☐	111 Cliff Ronning	8.00	5.00	2.00	.25
☐☐☐☐☐	112 Scott Walker	8.00	5.00	2.00	.25
☐☐☐☐☐	113 Jason Arnott	15.00	15.00	5.00	.50
☐☐☐☐☐	114 M. Brodeur (G)	60.00	50.00	20.00	2.00
☐☐☐☐☐	115 Patrik Elias	30.00	25.00	10.00	1.00
☐☐☐☐☐	116 Scott Gomez	15.00	10.00	5.00	1.00
☐☐☐☐☐	117 Bobby Holik	10.00	10.00	2.00	.25
☐☐☐☐☐	118 S. Niedermayer	10.00	10.00	2.00	.25
☐☐☐☐☐	**119 B. Rafalski RC**	**14.00**	**10.00**	**5.00**	**1.50**
☐☐☐☐☐	120 Petr* Sykora	15.00	10.00	5.00	.50
☐☐☐☐☐	121 Mathieu Biron	8.00	5.00	2.00	.25
☐☐☐☐☐	122 Tim Connolly	15.00	10.00	5.00	1.00
☐☐☐☐☐	123 M. Czerkawski	8.00	5.00	2.00	.25
☐☐☐☐☐	124 Olli Jokinen	10.00	10.00	2.00	.25
☐☐☐☐☐	**125 J. Jönsson RC**	**12.00**	**8.00**	**5.00**	**1.50**
☐☐☐☐☐	126 Kenny Jönsson	8.00	5.00	2.00	.25
☐☐☐☐☐	127 Félix Potvin (G)	20.00	15.00	5.00	.50
☐☐☐☐☐	128 Theoren Fleury	20.00	15.00	5.00	.50
☐☐☐☐☐	129 Adam Graves	15.00	10.00	5.00	.50
☐☐☐☐☐	**130 Kim Johnsson RC**	**8.00**	**6.00**	**2.00**	**1.00**
☐☐☐☐☐	131 Valeri Kamensky	10.00	10.00	2.00	.25
☐☐☐☐☐	132 Brian Leetch	20.00	15.00	5.00	.50
☐☐☐☐☐	133 Petr Nedved	10.00	10.00	2.00	.25
☐☐☐☐☐	134 Mike Richter (G)	15.00	15.00	5.00	.50
☐☐☐☐☐	135 Mike York	10.00	10.00	2.00	.50
☐☐☐☐☐	136 D. Alfredsson	20.00	15.00	5.00	.50
☐☐☐☐☐	137 M. Arvedson	8.00	5.00	2.00	.25
☐☐☐☐☐	138 Radek Bonk	10.00	10.00	2.00	.25
☐☐☐☐☐	139 Marian Hossa	40.00	30.00	10.00	1.00
☐☐☐☐☐	140 P. Lalime (G)	20.00	15.00	5.00	.50
☐☐☐☐☐	141 Ron Tugnutt (G)	15.00	10.00	5.00	.50
☐☐☐☐☐	142 Alexei Yashin	20.00	15.00	5.00	.50
☐☐☐☐☐	143 Rob Zamuner	8.00	5.00	2.00	.25
☐☐☐☐☐	144 B. Boucher (G)	10.00	10.00	2.00	.50
☐☐☐☐☐	145 R. Brind'Amour	10.00	10.00	2.00	.25
☐☐☐☐☐	**146 Mark Eaton RC**	**8.00**	**5.00**	**2.00**	**.50**
☐☐☐☐☐	147 John LeClair	30.00	25.00	10.00	1.00
☐☐☐☐☐	148 Eric Lindros	40.00	30.00	10.00	1.00
☐☐☐☐☐	149 Mark Recchi	15.00	10.00	5.00	.50
☐☐☐☐☐	150 Vanbiesbrouck (G)	15.00	15.00	5.00	.50
☐☐☐☐☐	151 Travis Green	8.00	5.00	2.00	.25
☐☐☐☐☐	152 N. Khabibulin (G)	15.00	10.00	5.00	.50
☐☐☐☐☐	153 Jeremy Roenick	30.00	25.00	10.00	1.00
☐☐☐☐☐	154 M. Shtalenkov	8.00	5.00	2.00	.25
☐☐☐☐☐	155 Keith Tkachuk	20.00	15.00	5.00	.50
☐☐☐☐☐	156 Rick Tocchet	10.00	10.00	2.00	.25
☐☐☐☐☐	157 M. Barnaby	8.00	5.00	2.00	.25
☐☐☐☐☐	158 Tom Barrasso (G)	15.00	10.00	5.00	.50
☐☐☐☐☐	159 Jaromir Jagr	40.00	30.00	10.00	1.00
☐☐☐☐☐	160 Alexei Kovalev	20.00	15.00	5.00	.50
☐☐☐☐☐	161 Aleksey Morozov	8.00	5.00	2.00	.25
☐☐☐☐☐	**162 M. Rozsival RC**	**8.00**	**5.00**	**2.00**	**.50**
☐☐☐☐☐	163 Martin Straka	10.00	10.00	2.00	.25
☐☐☐☐☐	164 German Titov	8.00	5.00	2.00	.25
☐☐☐☐☐	165 Pavol Demitra	15.00	10.00	5.00	.50
☐☐☐☐☐	166 Al MacInnis	15.00	10.00	5.00	.50
☐☐☐☐☐	167 Chris Pronger	20.00	15.00	5.00	.50
☐☐☐☐☐	168 R. Turek (G)	15.00	15.00	5.00	.50
☐☐☐☐☐	169 Pierre Turgeon	15.00	10.00	5.00	.50
☐☐☐☐☐	170 Scott A. Young	10.00	10.00	2.00	.25
☐☐☐☐☐	171 V. Damphousse	20.00	15.00	5.00	.50
☐☐☐☐☐	172 Jeff Friesen	10.00	10.00	2.00	.25
☐☐☐☐☐	173 Patrick Marleau	15.00	15.00	5.00	.50

□□□□□	174 Owen Nolan	20.00	15.00	5.00	.50
□□□□□	175 Steve Shields (G)	8.00	5.00	2.00	.25
□□□□□	176 Brad Stuart	15.00	10.00	5.00	1.00
□□□□□	177 Niklas Sundström	8.00	5.00	2.00	.25
□□□□□	178 Mike Vernon (G)	15.00	10.00	5.00	.50
□□□□□	179 Dan Cloutier (G)	15.00	10.00	5.00	.50
□□□□□	180 Chris Gratton	8.00	5.00	2.00	.25
□□□□□	181 V. Lecavalier	40.00	30.00	10.00	1.00
□□□□□	182 Fredrik Modin	8.00	5.00	2.00	.25
□□□□□	183 Darcy Tucker	8.00	5.00	2.00	.25
□□□□□	**184 N. Antropov RC**	**14.00**	**10.00**	**5.00**	**1.50**
□□□□□	185 Sergei Berezin	8.00	5.00	2.00	.25
□□□□□	186 Tie Domi	10.00	10.00	2.00	.25
□□□□□	187 Markus Näslund	40.00	30.00	10.00	1.00
□□□□□	187 Jonas Höglund	8.00	5.00	2.00	.25
□□□□□	188 Mike Johnson	8.00	5.00	2.00	.25
□□□□□	189 C. Joseph (G)	40.00	30.00	10.00	1.00
□□□□□	190 Mats Sundin	40.00	30.00	10.00	1.00
□□□□□	191 Steve Thomas	8.00	5.00	2.00	.25
□□□□□	192 Andrew Cassels	8.00	5.00	2.00	.25
□□□□□	193 Artem Chubarov	8.00	5.00	2.00	.25
□□□□□	194 Mark Messier	40.00	30.00	10.00	1.00
□□□□□	195 A. Mogilny	15.00	15.00	5.00	.50
□□□□□	196 Bill Muckalt	8.00	5.00	2.00	.25
□□□□□	198 K. Weekes (G)	8.00	5.00	2.00	.25
□□□□□	199 Peter Bondra	20.00	15.00	5.00	.50
□□□□□	200 Jan Bulis	8.00	5.00	2.00	.25
□□□□□	**201 J. Halpern RC**	**14.00**	**10.00**	**5.00**	**1.50**
□□□□□	202 Olaf Kölzig (G)	20.00	15.00	5.00	.50
□□□□□	203 Adam Oates	15.00	10.00	5.00	.50
□□□□□	204 Chris Simon	8.00	5.00	2.00	.25
□□□□□	**205 A. Volchkov RC**	**8.00**	**5.00**	**2.00**	**.50**
□□□□□	206 Richard Zednik	15.00	10.00	5.00	.50
	Sample				**Reg.**
□	Martin Brodeur (G)				1.00

2000 ALL-STAR PREVIEW

Insert Set (20 cards):		**115.00**
	Insert (2:37 packs)	**ASP**
□	1 Paul Kariya, Anah.	8.00
□	2 Teemu Selänne, Anah.	5.00
□	3 Raymond Bourque, Bost.	7.00
□	4 Dominik Hasek (G), Buff.	6.00
□	5 Patrick Roy (G), Colo.	18.00
□	6 Joe Sakic, Colo.	10.00
□	7 Nicklas Lidström, Detr.	3.00
□	8 Steve Yzerman, Detr.	15.00
□	9 Ed Belfour (G), Dall.	6.00
□	10 Jere Lehtinen, Dall.	2.00
□	11 Mike Modano, Dall.	6.00
□	12 Pavel Bure, Flor.	5.00
□	13 Martin Brodeur (G), NJer.	10.00
□	14 John LeClair, Phil.	5.00
□	15 Eric Lindros, Phil.	6.00
□	16 Jaromir Jagr, Pitt.	6.00
□	17 Keith Tkachuk, Phoe.	3.00
□	18 Curtis Joseph (G), Toro.	6.00
□	19 Mats Sundin, Toro.	6.00
□	20 Peter Bondra, Wash.	3.00

CHECKMATES

Insert Set (30 cards):		**105.00**
	Insert (2:37 packs)	**Check.**
□	1 Steve Kariya, Vanc.	2.00
□	2 Brendan Shanahan, Detr.	5.00
□	3 Eric Lindros, Phil.	5.00
□	4 Chris Pronger, SLou.	3.00
□	5 Peter Forsberg, Colo.	7.00
□	6 Theoren Fleury, NYRa.	3.00
□	7 Chris Chelios, Detr.	3.00
□	8 Michael Peca, Buff.	2.00
□	9 Derian Hatcher, Dall.	2.00
□	10 Raymond Bourque, Bost.	6.00
□	11 Keith Tkachuk, Phoe.	3.00
□	12 John LeClair, Phil.	4.00
□	13 Matthew Barnaby, Pitt.	2.00
□	14 Owen Nolan, SanJ.	3.00
□	15 Tie Domi, Toro.	2.00
□	16 Paul Kariya, Anah.	7.00
□	17 Teemu Selänne, Anah.	4.00
□	18 Patrik Stefan, Atla.	3.00
□	19 Tony Amonte, Chic.	3.00
□	20 Chris Drury, Colo.	3.00
□	21 Joe Sakic, Colo.	8.00
□	22 Steve Yzerman, Detr.	12.00
□	23 Brett Hull, Dall.	5.00
□	24 Mike Modano, Dall.	5.00
□	25 Pavel Bure, Flor.	4.00
□	26 Zigmund Palffy, LosA.	3.00
□	27 Marian Hossa, Otta.	5.00
□	28 Jaromir Jagr, Pitt.	5.00
□	29 Patrick Marleau, SanJ.	2.00
□	30 Mats Sundin, Toro.	5.00

GOALIE MASKS

There are three versions: the regular insert, a Holographic Gold parallel (#/99), a Holographic Blue parallel (#/67) and a Holographic Purple parallel (#/1).

Insert Set (10 cards):		**50.00**	**35.00**	**30.00**
	Inserts	**HB67**	**HG99**	**GM**
□□□□	1 Patrick Roy (G), Colo.	150.00	112.00	35.00
□□□□	2 Martin Brodeur (G), NJer.	80.00	60.00	20.00
□□□□	3 Mike Richter (G), NYRa.	24.00	18.00	6.00
□□□□	4 John Vanbiesbrouck (G), Phil.	24.00	18.00	6.00
□□□□	5 Curtis Joseph (G), Toro.	50.00	37.00	10.00
□□□□	6 Patrick Roy (G), Colo.	150.00	112.00	35.00
□□□□	7 Martin Brodeur (G), NJer.	80.00	60.00	20.00
□□□□	8 Mike Richter (G), NYRa.	24.00	18.00	6.00
□□□□	9 John Vanbiesbrouck (G), Phil.	24.00	18.00	6.00
□□□□	10 Curtis Joseph (G), Toro.	50.00	37.00	10.00

LAMPLIGHTER NET-FUSIONS

Insert Set (10 cards):		**230.00**
	Insert (1:73 packs)	**Lamp.**
□	1 Paul Kariya, Anah.	35.00
□	2 Teemu Selänne, Anah.	20.00
□	3 Patrik Stefan, Atla.	15.00
□	4 Joe Sakic, Colo.	40.00
□	5 Steve Yzerman, Detr.	60.00
□	6 Pavel Bure, Flor.	20.00
□	7 Theoren Fleury, NYRa.	15.00
□	8 John LeClair, Phil.	20.00
□	9 Eric Lindros, Phil.	25.00
□	10 Jaromir Jagr, Pitt.	25.00

LORDS OF THE RINK

Insert Set (10 cards):		**410.00**
	Insert (1:181 packs)	**LotR**
□	1 Paul Kariya, Anah.	45.00
□	2 Teemu Selänne, Anah.	25.00
□	3 Dominik Hasek (G), Buff.	30.00
□	4 Peter Forsberg, Colo.	45.00
□	5 Patrick Roy (G), Colo.	100.00
□	6 Joe Sakic, Colo.	50.00
□	7 Steve Yzerman, Detr.	80.00
□	8 Martin Brodeur (G), NJer.	50.00
□	9 Eric Lindros, Phil.	30.00
□	10 Jaromir Jagr, Pitt.	30.00

TORONTO FANTASY REDEMPTION

These wrapper-redemption parallel cards are limited to 20 copies. Other singles exist.

	Redemption (#/20)	**Show20**
□	63 Ed Belfour (G), Dall.	

1999 - 2000 EISHOCKEY NEWS

These cards were issued in Germany and feature players from the Deutschen Eishockey Liga. Other cards may exist.

Complete Set (434 cards):		**80.00**
	Player	**DEL**
□	1 Mannheim	.30
□	2 Gord Hynes, Mannheim	.50
□	3 Paul Stanton, Mannheim	.50
□	4 Christian Lukes, Mannheim	.30
□	5 Clayton Beddoes, Mannheim	.50
□	6 Shawn McCosh, Mannheim	.30
□	7 Dave Tomlinson, Mannheim	.50
□	8 Patrice Lefebvre, Mannheim	.30
□	9 Steve Junker, Mannheim	.50
□	10 Ralph Intranuovo, Mannheim	.50
□	11 Joel Savage, Mannheim	.50
□	12 Stéphane_JG Richer, Mannheim	.50
□	13 Rainer Zerwesz, Mannheim	.30
□	14 Yves Racine, Mannheim	.50
□	15 Mike Stevens, Mannheim	.30
□	16 Markus Weiland, Mannheim	.30
□	17 Bjorn Leonhardt, Mannheim	.30
□	18 Mike Rosati, Mannheim	.30
□	19 Philip Schumacher, Mannheim	.30
□	20 Jan Alston, Mannheim	.30
□	21 Kevin Grant, Mannheim	.30
□	22 Chris Straube, Mannheim	.30
□	23 Dennis Seidenberg, Mannheim	2.00
□	24 Chris Valentine, Mannheim	.50
□	25 Nürnberg	.30
□	26 Stefan Mann, Nürnberg	.30
□	27 Vadim Shakhraichuk, Nürnberg	.30
□	28 Roland Ramoser, Nürnberg	.30
□	29 Martin Jiranek, Nürnberg	.30
□	30 Hannes Körber, Nürnberg	.30
□	31 Jarno Peltonen, Nürnberg	.30
□	32 Dmitri Dudik, Nürnberg	.30
□	33 Viktor Ignatjevs, Nürnberg	.30
□	34 Alexander Cherbayev, Nürnberg	.50
□	35 Martin Reichel, Nürnberg	.30
□	36 Russ Romaniuk, Nürnberg	.50
□	37 Jason Miller, Nürnberg	.50
□	38 Sergei Bautin, Nürnberg	.50
□	39 Jozef Cierny, Nürnberg	.50
□	40 Marc Seliger, Nürnberg	.50
□	41 Daniel Kunce, Nürnberg	.30
□	42 Pasi Sormunen, Nürnberg	.30
□	43 Christian Schönmoser, Nürnberg	.30
□	44 Stefan Mayer, Nürnberg	.30
□	45 Alain_G Côté, Nürnberg	.50
□	46 Liam Garvey, Nürnberg	.30
□	47 John Craighead, Nürnberg	.30
□	48 Petr Franek, Nürnberg	.30
□	49 Peter Ihnacak, Nürnberg	.50
□	50 Eisbären	.30
□	51 Nico Pyka, Eisbären	.30
□	52 Robert Leask, Eisbären	.30
□	53 Alexander Godynyuk, Eisbären	.50
□	54 Lorenz Funk, Eisbären	.30
□	55 Sven Felski, Eisbären	.30
□	56 Giuseppe Busillo, Eisbären	.30
□	57 Yvon Corriveau, Eisbären	.50
□	58 Mikael Wahlberg, Eisbären	.30
□	59 Udo Dohler, Eisbären	.30
□	60 Sandy Smith, Eisbären	.30
□	61 Jaroslav Kames, Eisbären	.30
□	62 Rob Murphy, Eisbären	.50
□	63 Marc Fortier, Eisbären	.50
□	64 Mario Chitaroni, Eisbären	.30
□	65 Leif Carlsson, Eisbären	.30
□	66 Derek Mayer, Eisbären	.50
□	67 Sébastien Elwing, Eisbären	.30
□	68 Thomas Schinko, Eisbären	.30
□	69 Rob Cowie, Eisbären	.30
□	70 Thomas Rhodin, Eisbären	.30
□	71 Peter Hammarstrom, Eisbären	.30
□	72 Chris Govedaris, Eisbären	.50
□	73 Mike Bullard, Eisbären	1.00
□	74 Peter_John Lee, Eisbären	.30
□	75 Frankfurt	.30
□	76 Michael Bresagk, Frankfurt	.30
□	77 Joachim Appel, Frankfurt	.30
□	78 Rick Hayward, Frankfurt	.30
□	79 Robin Doyle, Frankfurt	.30
□	80 Christian Langer, Frankfurt	.30
□	81 Bob Bassen, Frankfurt	.50
□	82 John Chabot, Frankfurt	.50
□	83 Devin Edgerton, Frankfurt	.30
□	84 Toni Porkka, Frankfurt	.30
□	85 Jean-Marc Richard, Frankfurt	.30
□	86 José Charbonneau, Frankfurt	.50
□	87 Doug Kirton, Frankfurt	.30
□	88 Andrei Vasilyev, Frankfurt	.30
□	89 Ralf Hantschke, Frankfurt	.30
□	90 Steve Palmer, Frankfurt	.30
□	91 Jason Ruff, Frankfurt	.50
□	92 Bastian Niedermeier, Frankfurt	.30
□	93 Chris Hynes, Frankfurt	.30
□	94 Victor Gervais, Frankfurt	.30
□	95 Ken Quinney, Frankfurt	.50
□	96 Mark Bassen, Frankfurt	.30
□	97 Chris Snell, Frankfurt	.50
□	98 Pokey Reddick (G), Frankfurt	.30
□	99 Peter Obresa, Frankfurt	.30
□	100 Koln	.30
□	101 Joseph Heiss, Koln	.30
□	102 Steve Wilson, Koln	.30
□	103 Mario Doyon, Koln	.50
□	104 Jorg Mayer, Koln	.30
□	105 Marty Murray, Koln	.50
□	106 Mirko Lüdemann, Koln	.30
□	107 Dwayne Norris, Koln	.50
□	108 Christoph Paepke, Koln	.30
□	109 Bruno Zarrillo, Koln	.30
□	110 Dan Lambert, Koln	.50
□	111 Anders Huusko, Koln	.30
□	112 George Zajankala, Koln	.30
□	113 Andreas Lupzig, Koln	.30
□	114 Jean-Yves Roy, Koln	.50
□	115 Tomas Forslund, Koln	.50
□	116 Jason Young, Koln	.30
□	117 Todd Hlushko, Koln	.50
□	118 Andrew Verner, Koln	.50
□	119 Corey Millen, Koln	.50
□	120 Greg Brown, Koln	.50
□	121 John Miner, Koln	.30
□	122 Sergio Momesso, Koln	.50
□	123 Lance Nethery, Koln	.30
□	124 Krefeld	.30
□	125 Karel Lang, Krefeld	.30
□	126 Andy Roach, Krefeld	.30
□	127 Tomas Brandl, Krefeld	.30
□	128 Neil Eisenhut, Krefeld	.50
□	129 Ilya Vorobiev, Krefeld	.30
□	130 Andrei Kovalev, Krefeld	.50
□	131 Mark Pederson, Krefeld	.50
□	132 Shayne Wright, Krefeld	.30
□	133 Reemt Pyka, Krefeld	.30
□	134 Andrew Rymsha, Krefeld	.30
□	135 Lars Bruggemann, Krefeld	.30
□	136 Tommie Hartogs, Krefeld	.30
□	137 Marek Stebnicki, Krefeld	.30
□	138 Johnny Walker, Krefeld	.30
□	139 Chris Bartolone, Krefeld	.30
□	140 Stéphane Barin, Krefeld	.30
□	141 Mickey Elick, Krefeld	.30
□	142 Phil von Stefenelli, Krefeld	.30
□	143 Jean-François Jomphe, Krefeld	.50
□	144 Robert Ouellet, Krefeld	.30
□	145 Roger Nordström, Krefeld	.30
□	146 Martin Lindman, Krefeld	.30
□	147 Doug Mason, Krefeld	.30
□	148 Augsburg	.30
□	149 Vladislav Boulin, Augsburg	.50
□	150 Leo Gudas, Augsburg	.30
□	151 Duane Moeser, Augsburg	.30
□	152 Sergei Vostrikov, Augsburg	.50
□	153 Igor Maslennikov, Augsburg	.50
□	154 Kyosti Karjalainen, Augsburg	.50
□	155 Kurtis Miller, Augsburg	.30
□	156 Bradley Bergen, Augsburg	.30
□	157 Scott Allison, Augsburg	.50
□	158 Håkan Åhlund, Augsburg	.30
□	159 Peter Larsson, Augsburg	.30
□	160 Brian Loney, Augsburg	.50
□	161 Michael Bakos, Augsburg	.30
□	162 Sven Rampf, Augsburg	.30
□	163 Jim Camazzola, Augsburg	.30
□	164 Andre Faust, Augsburg	.30
□	165 Harald Birk, Augsburg	.30
□	166 Tommy Jakobsen, Augsburg	.30
□	167 Sergei Klimovich, Augsburg	.50
□	168 Klaus Merk, Augsburg	.30
□	169 Bob Manno, Augsburg	.50
□	170 Kassel	.30
□	171 Jochen Molling, Kassel	.30
□	172 David Cooper, Kassel	.50
□	173 Thomas Dolak, Kassel	.30
□	174 Stéphane Robitaille, Kassel	.30
□	175 Jeff MacLeod, Kassel	.30
□	176 Roger Hansson, Kassel	.30
□	177 François Guay, Kassel	.30
□	178 Nikolaus Mondt, Kassel	.30
□	179 Andreas Loth, Kassel	.30
□	180 Ron Pasco, Kassel	.30
□	181 Jurgen Rumrich, Kassel	.30
□	182 Greg Evtushevski, Kassel	.30
□	183 Daniel Kreutzer, Kassel	.30
□	184 Brent Tully, Kassel	.50
□	185 Ivan Droppa, Kassel	.50
□	186 Tobias Abstreiter, Kassel	.30
□	187 Sylvain Turgeon, Kassel	.50
□	188 Chris Rogles, Kassel	.30
□	189 Leonardo Conti, Kassel	.30
□	190 Tino Boos, Kassel	.30
□	191 Benjamin Hinterstocker, Kassel	.30
□	192 Craig Woodcroft, Kassel	.50
□	193 Orjan Lindmark, Kassel	.30
□	194 Hans Zach, Kassel	.30
□	195 Schwenningen Wild Wings	.30
□	196 Kevin Wortman, Schwenningen	.30
□	197 Marc Laniel, Schwenningen	.30
□	198 Daniel Laperrière, Schwenningen	.50
□	199 Marcel Goc, Schwenningen	.30
□	200 Guy Lehoux, Schwenningen	.30
□	201 Steffen Oder, Schwenningen	.30
□	202 Jens Stramkowski, Schwenningen	.30
□	203 Mark Kolesar, Schwenningen	.50
□	204 Scott McCrory, Schwenningen	.30
□	205 John Lilley, Schwenningen	.50
□	206 Patrik Augusta, Schwenningen	.30
□	207 Randy Perry, Schwenningen	.30
□	208 Daniel Nowak, Schwenningen	.30
□	209 Todd Harkins, Schwenningen	.50
□	210 Robert Schistad, Schwenningen	.30
□	211 Andreas Renz, Schwenningen	.30
□	212 Stéphane Beauregard, Schwenningen	.50
□	213 Rick Girard, Schwenningen	.50
□	214 Iain Fraser, Schwenningen	.50
□	215 Andy Schneider, Schwenningen	.50
□	216 Mark MacKay, Schwenningen	.30
□	217 Rich Chernomaz, Schwenningen	.30
□	218 Hannover	.30
□	219 Lars Janssen, Hannover	.30
□	220 Tom Pederson, Hannover	.50
□	221 Yuri Ginko, Hannover	.30
□	222 Mattias Lööf, Hannover	.30

	Card	Price
☐	223 Joseph West, Hannover	.30
☐	224 Egor Bashkatov, Hannover	.30
☐	225 Grigori Panteleyev, Hannover	.30
☐	226 Mark Kosturik, Hannover	.30
☐	227 Len Soccio, Hannover	.30
☐	228 Dominic Lavoie, Hannover	.50
☐	229 Peter Willmann, Hannover	.30
☐	230 Wally Schreiber, Hannover	.30
☐	231 Scott Metcalfe, Hannover	.30
☐	232 David Haas, Hannover	.30
☐	233 Ildar Mukhometov, Hannover	.30
☐	234 Igor Chibirev, Hannover	.50
☐	235 Michael Thurner, Hannover	.30
☐	236 Jan Munster, Hannover	.30
☐	237 Jacob Karlsson, Hannover	.30
☐	238 David Sulkovsky, Hannover	.30
☐	239 Brian Tutt, Hannover	.30
☐	240 Igor Alexandrov, Hannover	.50
☐	241 Kevin Gaudet, Hannover	.30
☐	242 Rosenheim Star Bulls	.30
☐	243 Håkan Algotsson, Rosenheim Star Bulls	.30
☐	244 Trevor Burgess, Rosenheim Star Bulls	.30
☐	245 Christian Due-Boje, Rosenheim Star Bulls	.30
☐	246 Teemu Sillanpaa, Rosenheim Star Bulls	.30
☐	247 Curtis Fry, Rosenheim Star Bulls	.30
☐	248 Gord Sherven, Rosenheim Star Bulls	.30
☐	249 Frank Hohenadl, Rosenheim Star Bulls	.30
☐	250 Bernd Kuhnhauser, Rosenheim Star Bulls	.30
☐	251 Michael Pohl, Rosenheim Star Bulls	.30
☐	252 Derek Cormier, Rosenheim Star Bulls	.30
☐	253 Jean-François Quintin, Rosenheim Star Bulls	.50
☐	254 Dieter Hegen, Rosenheim Star Bulls	.50
☐	255 Peter Ottosson, Rosenheim Star Bulls	.30
☐	256 Raimond Hilger, Rosenheim Star Bulls	.30
☐	257 Niklas Brannstrom, Rosenheim Star Bulls	.30
☐	258 Wolfgang Kummer, Rosenheim Star Bulls	.30
☐	259 Kari Haakana, Rosenheim Star Bulls	.50
☐	260 Paul Weismann, Rosenheim Star Bulls	.30
☐	261 Klaus Kathan, Rosenheim Star Bulls	.30
☐	262 Sami Nuutinen, Rosenheim Star Bulls	.30
☐	263 Patrik Hucko, Rosenheim Star Bulls	.30
☐	264 Robert Muller, Rosenheim Star Bulls	.30
☐	265 Gerhard Brunner, Rosenheim Star Bulls	.30
☐	266 Berlin	.30
☐	267 Andrei Mezin, Berlin	2.00
☐	268 Fredrik Stillman, Berlin	.30
☐	269 Fredrik Ytfeldt, Berlin	.30
☐	270 Markus Pottinger, Berlin	.30
☐	271 Niklas Hede, Berlin	.30
☐	272 Alexander Kuzminski, Berlin	.30
☐	273 Thomas Sjogren, Berlin	.30
☐	274 Dennis Meyer, Berlin	.30
☐	275 Robert Cimetta, Berlin	.50
☐	276 Jim Hiller, Berlin	.50
☐	277 Doug Derraugh, Berlin	.30
☐	278 Patrick Senger, Berlin	.30
☐	279 Pavel Gross, Berlin	.30
☐	280 Robert Guillet, Berlin	.30
☐	281 Sylvain Couturier, Berlin	.50
☐	282 Heinrich Schiffl, Berlin	.30
☐	283 Heinz Ehlers, Berlin	.30
☐	284 Larry Rucchin, Berlin	.30
☐	285 Greg Johnston, Berlin	.50
☐	286 David Berge, Berlin	.30
☐	287 Johan Norgren, Berlin	.50
☐	288 Martin Ulrich, Berlin	.30
☐	289 Benjamin Hecker, Berlin	.30
☐	290 Mike Pellegrims, Berlin	.30
☐	291 Michael Komma, Berlin	.30
☐	292 Oberhausen	.30
☐	293 Peter Gulda, Oberhausen	.30
☐	294 Jergus Baca, Oberhausen	.50
☐	295 Bob Marshall, Oberhausen	.30
☐	296 Mike Sullivan, Oberhausen	.50
☐	297 Jacek Plachta, Oberhausen	.30
☐	298 Andrej Fuchs, Oberhausen	.30
☐	299 Mike McNeill, Oberhausen	.50
☐	300 Aleksandrs Kerch, Oberhausen	.30
☐	301 Robert Hock, Oberhausen	.30
☐	302 Albert Malgin, Oberhausen	.50
☐	303 Kai Fischer, Oberhausen	.30
☐	304 Burke Murphy, Oberhausen	.30
☐	305 Jeff Sebastien, Oberhausen	.30
☐	306 Sergei Stas, Oberhausen	.30
☐	307 Sebastian Klenner, Oberhausen	.30
☐	308 Boris Fuchs, Oberhausen	.30
☐	309 Ivo Jan, Oberhausen	.30
☐	310 François Gravel, Oberhausen	.30
☐	311 Alexander Makritzky, Oberhausen	.30
☐	312 Viktor Karatchun, Oberhausen	.30
☐	313 Gunnar Leidborg, Oberhausen	.30
☐	314 Munchen	.30
☐	315 Boris Rousson, Munchen	.50
☐	316 Hans Lodin, Munchen	.30
☐	317 Chris Luongo, Munchen	.50
☐	318 Mike Casselman, Munchen	.30
☐	319 Heiko Smazal, Munchen	.30
☐	320 Peter Abstreiter, Munchen	.30
☐	321 Simon Wheeldon, Munchen	.30
☐	322 Phil Huber, Munchen	.30
☐	323 Peter Douris, Munchen	.50
☐	324 Jari Korpisalo, Munchen	.30
☐	325 Kent Fearns, Munchen	.30
☐	326 Markus Jocher, Munchen	.30
☐	327 Pelle Svensson, Munchen	.30
☐	328 Sven Wiele, Munchen	.30
☐	329 Wayne Hynes, Munchen	.30
☐	330 Bill McDougall, Munchen	.50
☐	331 Alexander Serikow, Munchen	.30
☐	332 Bob Joyce, Munchen	.50
☐	333 Jorg Handrick, Munchen	.30
☐	334 Jason Herter, Munchen	.50
☐	335 Johan Rosen, Munchen	.30
☐	336 Mike Kennedy, Munchen	.50
☐	337 Christian Kunast, Munchen	.30
☐	338 Shane Peacock, Munchen	.30
☐	339 Sean Simpson, Munchen	.30
☐	340 Essen	.30
☐	341 Oldrich Svoboda, Essen	.30
☐	342 Bodo Mueller-Boenigk, Essen	.30
☐	343 Vlastimil Kroupa, Essen	.50
☐	344 Zdenek Touzimsky, Essen	.30
☐	345 Pavel Augusta, Essen	.30
☐	346 Christian Kohmann, Essen	.30
☐	347 Martin Sychra, Essen	.30
☐	348 Torsten Kienass, Essen	.30
☐	349 Peter Draisaitl, Essen	.30
☐	350 Marian Kacir, Essen	.30
☐	351 Terry Campbell, Essen	.30
☐	352 Roland Verwey, Essen	.30
☐	353 Radek Toth, Essen	.30
☐	354 Josef Zajic, Essen	.30
☐	355 Jochen Vollmer, Essen	.30
☐	356 Jiri Sejba, Essen	.50
☐	357 Jukka Seppo, Essen	.30
☐	358 Marc** Savard, Essen	.30
☐	359 Enrico Ciccone, Essen	.50
☐	360 Michael Dvorak, Essen	.30
☐	361 Tomas Nemcicky, Essen	.50
☐	362 Andrej Nedorost, Essen	.50
☐	363 Tomas Srsen, Essen	.30
☐	364 Bedrich Scerban, Essen	.30
☐	365 Jan Benda, Essen	.30
☐	366 Germany	.30
☐	367 Robert Muller, Germany	.30
☐	368 Torsten Kienass, Germany	.30
☐	369 Markus Pottinger, Germany	.30
☐	370 Lorenz Funk, Germany	.30
☐	371 Nico Pyka, Germany	.30
☐	372 Sven Felski, Germany	.30
☐	373 Jochen Molling, Germany	.30
☐	374 Christian Langer, Germany	.30
☐	375 Nikolaus Mondt, Germany	.30
☐	376 Bernd Kuhnhauser, Germany	.30
☐	377 Jürgen Rumrich, Germany	.30
☐	378 Lars Bruggermann, Germany	.30
☐	379 Alexander Serikow, Germany	.30
☐	380 Klaus Kathan, Germany	.30
☐	381 Terry Campbell, Germany	.30
☐	382 Tino Boos, Germany	.30
☐	383 Michael Bresagk, Germany	.30
☐	384 Christian Lukes, Germany	.30
☐	385 Heiko Smazal, Germany	.30
☐	386 Tobias Abstreiter, Germany	.30
☐	387 Thoimas Dolak, Germany	.30
☐	388 Udo Dohler, Germany	.30
☐	389 Andreas Loth, Germany	.30
☐	390 David Berge, Germany	.30
☐	391 Mark MacKay, Germany	.30
☐	392 Hans Zach, Germany	.30
☐	393 Moderatoren	.30
☐	394 Marc Hindelang	.30
☐	395 Peter Kohl	.30
☐	396 Sven Kukulies	.30
☐	397 Claus Muller	.30
☐	398 Gerhard Leinauer	.30
☐	399 Michael Leopold	.30
☐	400 Rick Amann	.30
☐	401 Schiris	.30
☐	402 Holger Gerstberger	.30
☐	403 Ralph Dimmers	.30
☐	404 Harald Deubert	.30
☐	405 Petr Chvatal	.30
☐	406 Frank Awizus	.30
☐	407 Axel Rademaker	.30
☐	408 Wolfgang Hellwig	.30
☐	409 Gerhard Muller	.30
☐	410 Gerhard Lichtnecker	.30
☐	411 Rainer Kluge	.30
☐	412 Coach Stefan	.30
☐	413 Richard Schütz	.30
☐	414 Willi Schimm	.30
☐	415 Peter Slapke	.30
☐	416 Action	.30
☐	417 Action	.30
☐	418 Action	.30
☐	419 Action	.30
☐	420 Action	.30
☐	421 Action	.30
☐	422 Action	.30
☐	423 Action	.30
☐	424 Action	.30
☐	425 Action	.30
☐	426 Action	.30
☐	427 Action	.30
☐	428 Action	.30
☐	429 Action	.30
☐	430 Action	.30
☐	431 Action	.30
☐	432 Action	.30
☐	433 Action	.30
☐	434 Action	.30

1999 - 2000 HOLOGRFX

This series was released in 1999. There are two versions: the regular card and an AUsome parallel (1:17 packs). The AUsome cards have an AU suffix.

		AU	Reg.
	Complete Set (60 cards):	**425.00**	**40.00**
	Common Player:	**2.00**	**.50**
	Player	**AU**	**Reg.**
☐ ☐	1 Teemu Selänne, Anah.	12.00	1.00
☐ ☐	2 Paul Kariya, Anah.	20.00	1.50
☐ ☐	**3 Patrik Stefan, Atla. RC**	**8.00**	**3.00**
☐ ☐	4 Sergei Samsonov, Bost.	8.00	.50
☐ ☐	5 Raymond Bourque, Bost.	15.00	1.50
☐ ☐	6 Dominik Hasek (G), Buff.	15.00	1.00
☐ ☐	**7 Brian Campbell, Buff. RC**	**2.00**	**1.00**
☐ ☐	8 Marc Savard, Calg.	2.00	.50
☐ ☐	**9 Oleg Saprykin, Calg. RC**	**6.00**	**2.00**
☐ ☐	10 Sami Kapanen, Caro.	4.00	.50
☐ ☐	11 Keith Primeau, Caro.	6.00	.50
☐ ☐	12 Tony Amonte, Chic.	8.00	.50
☐ ☐	13 Jean-Pierre Dumont, Chic.	2.00	.50
☐ ☐	14 Peter Forsberg, Colo.	20.00	1.50
☐ ☐	15 Joe Sakic, Colo.	20.00	2.00
☐ ☐	16 Chris Drury, Colo.	8.00	.50
☐ ☐	17 Patrick Roy (G), Colo.	45.00	3.50
☐ ☐	18 Brett Hull, Dall.	15.00	1.00
☐ ☐	19 Mike Modano, Dall.	15.00	1.00
☐ ☐	20 Ed Belfour (G), Dall.	15.00	1.00
☐ ☐	21 Steve Yzerman, Detr.	35.00	3.00
☐ ☐	22 Brendan Shanahan, Detr.	15.00	1.00
☐ ☐	23 Sergei Fedorov, Detr.	15.00	1.00
☐ ☐	24 Doug Weight, Edmo.	8.00	.50
☐ ☐	25 Bill Guerin, Edmo.	6.00	.50
☐ ☐	26 Pavel Bure, Flor.	10.00	1.00
☐ ☐	27 Mark Parrish, Flor.	6.00	.50
☐ ☐	28 Luc Robitaille, LosA.	12.00	1.00
☐ ☐	29 Zigmund Palffy, LosA.	8.00	.50
☐ ☐	30 Mike Ribeiro, Mont.	4.00	.50
☐ ☐	31 David Legwand, Nash.	6.00	.50
☐ ☐	32 Scott Gomez, NJer.	6.00	1.00
☐ ☐	33 Martin Brodeur (G), NJer.	20.00	2.00
☐ ☐	34 Vadim Sharifijanov, NJer.	2.00	.50
☐ ☐	**35 Jörgen Jönsson, NYIs. RC**	**6.00**	**2.00**
☐ ☐	36 Eric Brewer, NYIs.	6.00	.50
☐ ☐	37 Tim Connolly, NYIs.	6.00	1.00
☐ ☐	38 Theoren Fleury, NYRa.	8.00	.50
☐ ☐	39 Brian Leetch, NYRa.	8.00	.50
☐ ☐	40 Mike Richter (G), NYRa.	6.00	.50
☐ ☐	41 Marian Hossa, Otta.	15.00	1.00
☐ ☐	42 Simon Gagné, Phil.	12.00	2.00
☐ ☐	43 Eric Lindros, Phil.	15.00	1.00
☐ ☐	44 John LeClair, Phil.	12.00	1.00
☐ ☐	45 Keith Tkachuk, Phoe.	8.00	.50
☐ ☐	46 Jeremy Roenick, Phoe.	12.00	1.00
☐ ☐	47 Jaromir Jagr, Pitt.	15.00	1.00
☐ ☐	48 Niklas Sundström, SanJ.	2.00	.50
☐ ☐	49 Jeff Friesen, SanJ.	4.00	.50
☐ ☐	50 Brad Stuart, SanJ.	6.00	1.00
☐ ☐	51 Pavol Demitra, SLou.	6.00	.50
☐ ☐	52 Al MacInnis, SLou.	6.00	.50
☐ ☐	53 Paul Mara, Tamp.	2.00	.50
☐ ☐	54 Vincent Lecavalier, Tamp.	15.00	1.00
☐ ☐	55 Mats Sundin, Toro.	15.00	1.00
☐ ☐	56 Sergei Berezin, Toro.	2.00	.50
☐ ☐	57 Curtis Joseph (G), Toro.	15.00	1.00
☐ ☐	**58 Steve Kariya, Vanc. RC**	**6.00**	**2.00**
☐ ☐	59 Peter Bondra, Wash.	8.00	.50
☐ ☐	60 Olaf Kölzig (G), Wash.	8.00	.50

GRETZKY GRFX

There are two versions: the regular insert (1:3 packs) and the AUsome parallel (1:105 packs).

		AU	GG
	Insert Set (15 cards):	**315.00**	**50.00**
	Inserts	**AU**	**GG**
☐ ☐	GG1 Wayne Gretzky, Edmo.	25.00	4.00
☐ ☐	GG2 Wayne Gretzky, NYRa.	25.00	4.00
☐ ☐	GG3 Wayne Gretzky, NYRa.	25.00	4.00
☐ ☐	GG4 Wayne Gretzky, LosA.	25.00	4.00
☐ ☐	GG5 Wayne Gretzky, SLou.	25.00	4.00
☐ ☐	GG6 Wayne Gretzky, Edmo.	25.00	4.00
☐ ☐	GG7 Wayne Gretzky, NYRa.	25.00	4.00
☐ ☐	GG8 Wayne Gretzky, LosA.	25.00	4.00
☐ ☐	GG9 Wayne Gretzky, Edmo.	25.00	4.00
☐ ☐	GG10 Wayne Gretzky, SLou.	25.00	4.00
☐ ☐	GG11 Wayne Gretzky, SLou.	25.00	4.00
☐ ☐	GG12 Wayne Gretzky, NYRa.	25.00	4.00
☐ ☐	GG13 Wayne Gretzky, LosA.	25.00	4.00
☐ ☐	GG14 Wayne Gretzky, Edmo.	25.00	4.00
☐ ☐	GG15 Wayne Gretzky, LosA.	25.00	4.00

IMPACT ZONE

There are two versions: the regular insert (1:34 packs) and the AUsome parallel (1:431 packs).

		AU	IZ
	Insert Set (6 cards):	**220.00**	**40.00**
	Inserts	**AU**	**IZ**
☐ ☐	IZ1 Dominik Hasek (G), Buff.	30.00	6.00
☐ ☐	IZ2 Jaromir Jagr, Pitt.	30.00	6.00
☐ ☐	IZ3 Eric Lindros, Phil.	30.00	6.00
☐ ☐	IZ4 Patrick Roy (G), Colo.	90.00	18.00
☐ ☐	IZ5 Paul Kariya, Anah.	40.00	8.00
☐ ☐	IZ6 Peter Forsberg, Colo.	40.00	8.00

PURE SKILL

There are two versions: the regular insert (1:17 packs) and the AUsome parallel (1:210 packs).

		AU	PS
	Insert Set (9 cards):	**160.00**	**30.00**
	Inserts	**AU**	**PS**
☐ ☐	PS1 Paul Kariya, Anah.	25.00	5.00
☐ ☐	PS2 Peter Forsberg, Colo.	25.00	5.00
☐ ☐	PS3 Dominik Hasek (G), Buff.	15.00	3.00
☐ ☐	PS4 Sergei Samsonov, Bost.	10.00	2.00
☐ ☐	PS5 Teemu Selänne, Anah.	15.00	3.00
☐ ☐	PS6 Patrick Roy (G), Colo.	55.00	10.00
☐ ☐	PS7 Brett Hull, Dall.	15.00	3.00
☐ ☐	PS8 Eric Lindros, Phil.	15.00	3.00
☐ ☐	PS9 Jaromir Jagr, Pitt.	15.00	3.00

UD AUTHENTICS

		UDA
	Insert Set (7 cards):	**480.00**
	Autograph	**UDA**
☐	Brett Hull, Dall. ✍	50.00
☐	Chris Drury, Colo. ✍	30.00
☐	David Legwand, Nash. ✍	20.00
☐	Pavel Bure, Flor. ✍	40.00
☐	Patrik Stefan, Atla. ✍	30.00
☐	Raymond Bourque, Bost. ✍	70.00
☐	Wayne Gretzky, NYRa. ✍	325.00

1999 - 2000 KRAFT

These cards were issued across several different Kraft products.

Complete Set (76): 140.00

JELL-O INSTANT PUDDING / GOALIE COLLECTION

		GC
	Complete Set (6 cards):	**12.00**
	Player	**GC**
☐	Martin Brodeur (G), NJer.	3.00
☐	Byron Dafoe (G), Bost.	1.00
☐	Dominik Hasek (G), Buff.	2.00
☐	Curtis Joseph (G), Toro.	2.00
☐	Patrick Roy (G), Colo.	6.00
☐	Ron Tugnutt (G), Otta.	1.00

JELL-O JELLY POWDER / PARTNERS OF POWER

		PP
	Complete Set (6 cards):	**10.00**
	Player	**PP**
☐	Ed Belfour (G) / Derian Hatcher	1.00
☐	Guy Hebert (G) / Paul Kariya	1.00
☐	Owen Nolan / Mike Vernon (G)	3.00
☐	Chris Osgood (G) / Steve Yzerman	3.00
☐	Patrick Roy (G) / Joe Sakic	4.00
☐	Tommy Salo (G) / Doug Weight	1.00

KRAFT DINNER / ALL-STAR SELECTS

Complete Set (15 cards): 20.00

	Player	ASS
☐	Shayne Corson, Mont.	1.00
☐	Jaromir Jagr, Pitt.	2.00
☐	Curtis Joseph (G), Toro.	2.00
☐	Paul Kariya, Anah.	2.00
☐	Saku Koivu, Mont.	1.00
☐	Eric Lindros, Phil.	2.00
☐	Mike Modano, Dall.	2.00
☐	Mattias Öhlund, Vanc.	1.00
☐	Chris Pronger, SLou.	1.00
☐	Joe Sakic, Colo.	3.00
☐	Brendan Shanahan, Detr.	2.00
☐	Scott Stevens, NJer.	1.00
☐	Mats Sundin, Toro.	2.00
☐	Alexei Yashin, Otta.	1.00
☐	Steve Yzerman, Detr.	4.00

KRAFT DINNER / GRETZKY RETIREMENT

Complete Set (4 cards):		25.00
	Player	GR
☐	Wayne Gretzky	8.00
☐	Wayne Gretzky	8.00
☐	Wayne Gretzky	8.00
☐	Wayne Gretzky	8.00

KRAFT DINNER / STANLEY CUP

Complete Set (15 cards):		20.00
	Player	SC
☐	1 Bill Ranford (G), Edmo.	1.00
☐	2 Theoren Fleury, Calg.	1.00
☐	3 Jaromir Jagr, Pitt.	2.00
☐	4 Éric Desjardins, Phil.	1.00
☐	5 Mark Messier, NYRa.	2.00
☐	6 Dominik Hasek (G), Buff.	2.00
☐	7 Claude Lemieux, NJer.	1.00
☐	8 Steve Yzerman, Detr.	4.00
☐	9 Joe Sakic, Colo.	3.00
☐	10 Paul Kariya, Anah.	1.00
☐	11 Eric Lindros, Phil.	2.00
☐	12 Michael Peca, Buff.	1.00
☐	13 Sergei Fedorov, Detr.	2.00
☐	14 Mats Sundin, Toro.	2.00
☐	15 Brett Hull, Dall.	2.00

OSCAR MAYER LUNCHABLES / GLOBAL SUPER HEROES

Complete Set (12 cards):		55.00
	Player	GSH
☐	Raymond Bourque, Bost.	2.00
☐	Pavel Bure, Flor.	1.00
☐	Dominik Hasek (G), Buff.	2.00
☐	Jaromir Jagr, Pitt.	2.00
☐	Curtis Joseph (G), Toro.	2.00
☐	Paul Kariya, Anah.	2.00
☐	Saku Koivu, Mont.	1.00
☐	Eric Lindros, Phil.	2.00
☐	Al MacInnis, SLou.	1.00
☐	Mark Messier, Vanc.	2.00
☐	Mats Sundin, Toro.	2.00
☐	Alexei Yashin, Otta.	1.00

PEANUT BUTTER / ALL-STAR LINEUP

Complete Set (12 disks):		35.00
	Player	MT
☐	Raymond Bourque, Bost.	4.00
☐	Martin Brodeur (G), NJer.	6.00
☐	Peter Forsberg, Colo.	5.00
☐	Dominik Hasek (G), Buff.	3.00
☐	Jaromir Jagr, Pitt.	3.00
☐	Paul Kariya, Anah.	5.00
☐	Nicklas Lidström, Detr.	3.00
☐	Eric Lindros, Phil.	3.00
☐	Al MacInnis, SLou.	3.00
☐	Teppo Numminen, Phoe.	3.00
☐	Teemu Selänne, Anah.	3.00
☐	Brendan Shanahan, Detr.	3.00

PEANUT BUTTER / FACE-OFF RIVALS

Complete Set (6 disks):		15.00
	Player	MT
☐	Stu Barnes / Mats Sundin	3.00
☐	Curtis Brown / Yanic Perreault	3.00
☐	Guy Carbonneau / Pierre Turgeon	3.00
☐	Mike Modano / Mike Eastwood	3.00
☐	Theoren Fleury / Joe Nieuwendyk	3.00
☐	Claude Lemieux / Steve Yzerman	3.00

1999 - 2000 MCDONALD'S / UPPER DECK FOR THE RECORD

Complete Set (15 cards):		15.00
	Player	MT
☐	1 Wayne Gretzky, NYRa.	1.50
☐	2 Wayne Gretzky, Edmo.	1.50
☐	3 Wayne Gretzky, NYRa.	1.50
☐	4 Wayne Gretzky, Edmo.	1.50
☐	5 Wayne Gretzky, NYRa.	1.50
☐	6 Wayne Gretzky, NYRa.	1.50
☐	7 Wayne Gretzky, NYRa.	1.50
☐	8 Wayne Gretzky, NYRa.	1.50
☐	9 Wayne Gretzky, Edmo.	1.50
☐	10 Wayne Gretzky, NYRa.	1.50
☐	11 Wayne Gretzky, Edmo.	1.50
☐	12 Wayne Gretzky, NYRa.	1.50
☐	13 Wayne Gretzky, NYRa.	1.50
☐	14 Wayne Gretzky, Edmo.	1.50
☐	15 Wayne Gretzky, Edmo.	1.50

CHECKLIST

Checklist Set (9 cards):		10.00
	Player	MT
☐	1 Wayne Gretzky, NYRa.	1.50
☐	2 Wayne Gretzky, NYRa.	1.50
☐	3 Wayne Gretzky, NYRa.	1.50
☐	4 Wayne Gretzky, NYRa.	1.50
☐	5 Wayne Gretzky, NYRa.	1.50
☐	6 Wayne Gretzky, NYRa.	1.50
☐	7 Wayne Gretzky, NYRa.	1.50
☐	8 Wayne Gretzky, NYRa.	1.50
☐	9 Wayne Gretzky, NYRa.	1.50

1999 - 2000 MCDONALD'S / UPPER DECK RETRO

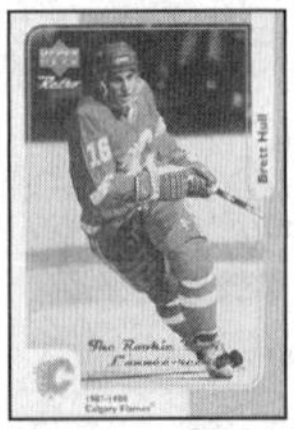

Complete Set (36 cards):		20.00
	Player	McD
☐	McD-1 Paul Kariya, Anah.	1.00
☐	McD-1R Paul Kariya, Anah. [The Rookie Year]	1.00
☐	McD-2 Eric Lindros, Phil.	.50
☐	McD-2R Eric Lindros, Phil. [The Rookie Year]	.50
☐	McD-3 Dominik Hasek (G), Buff.	.50
☐	McD-3R Dominik Hasek (G), Chic. [The Rookie Year]	.50
☐	McD-4 Steve Yzerman, Detr.	1.50
☐	McD-4R Steve Yzerman, Detr. [The Rookie Year]	1.50
☐	McD-5 Jarome Iginla, Calg.	.50
☐	McD-5R Jarome Iginla, Calg. [The Rookie Year]	.50
☐	McD-6 Jaromir Jagr, Pitt.	.50
☐	McD-6R Jaromir Jagr, Pitt. [The Rookie Year]	.50
☐	McD-7 Brett Hull, Dall.	.50
☐	McD-7R Brett Hull, Calg. [The Rookie Year]	.50
☐	McD-8 Ed Belfour (G), Dall.	.50
☐	McD-8R Ed Belfour (G), Chic. [The Rookie Year]	.50
☐	McD-9 Mats Sundin, Toro.	.50
☐	McD-9R Mats Sundin, Québ. [The Rookie Year]	.50
☐	McD-10 Peter Forsberg, Colo.	1.00
☐	McD-10R Peter Forsberg, Québ. [The Rookie Year]	1.00
☐	McD-11 Doug Weight, Edmo.	.35
☐	McD-11R Doug Weight, NYRa. [The Rookie Year]	.35
☐	McD-12 Curtis Joseph (G), Toro.	.50
☐	McD-12R Curtis Joseph (G), SLou. [The Rookie Year]	.50
☐	McD-13 Michael Peca, Buff.	.35
☐	McD-13R Michael Peca, Vanc. [The Rookie Year]	.35
☐	McD-14 Saku Koivu, Mont.	.50
☐	McD-14R Saku Koivu, Mont. [The Rookie Year]	.50
☐	McD-15 Patrick Roy (G), Colo.	2.00
☐	McD-15R Patrick Roy (G), Mont. [The Rookie Year]	2.00
☐	McD-16 José Théodore (G), Mont. [Today's Rookies]	2.50
☐	McD-17 David Legwand, Nash. [Today's Rookies]	.50
☐	McD-18 Chris Drury, Colo. [Today's Rookies]	1.00
☐	McD-19 Milan Hejduk, Colo. [Today's Rookies]	1.50
☐	McD-20 Marian Hossa, Otta. [Today's Rookies]	2.00
☐	Checklist	.35

GAME JERSEY

Insert Set (11 cards):		2000.00
	Player	MT
☐	Tony Amonte, All-Star '99	120.00
☐	Peter Bondra, Wash.	120.00
☐	Peter Forsberg, Colo.	280.00
☐	Grant Fuhr (G), SLou.	120.00
☐	Wayne Gretzky, All-Star '99	800.00
☐	Jaromir Jagr, All-Star '99	200.00
☐	Eric Lindros, All-Star '99	200.00
☐	Mike Modano, Dall.	200.00
☐	Chris Pronger, SLou.	120.00
☐	Scott Stevens, All-Star '99	80.00
☐	Darryl Sydor, All-Star '99	75.00
	Autograph	MT
☐	Wayne Gretzky ✍ ✂ All-Star '99	1650.00

SIGNATURE SERIES

Insert Set (16 cards):		2000.00
	Player	Aut99
☐	Tony Amonte, Chic.	50.00
☐	Ed Belfour (G), Dall.	85.00
☐	Raymond Bourque, Bost.	120.00
☐	Tie Domi, Toro.	45.00
☐	Grant Fuhr (G), SLou.	50.00
☐	Wayne Gretzky, NYRa.	1100.00
☐	Brett Hull, Dall.	85.00
☐	Curtis Joseph (G), Toro.	80.00
☐	Saku Koivu, Mont.	70.00
☐	John LeClair, Phil.	70.00
☐	Chris Osgood (G), Detr.	50.00
☐	Luc Robitaille, LosA.	70.00
☐	José Théodore (G), Mont.	100.00
☐	Steve Thomas, Toro.	45.00
☐	Alexei Yashin, Otta.	50.00
☐	Steve Yzerman, Detr.	200.00

THE GREAT ONE

Insert Set (5 cards):		15.00
	Player	MT
☐	GR81-1 Wayne Gretzky, Edmo.	4.00
☐	GR81-2 Wayne Gretzky, Edmo.	4.00
☐	GR81-3 Wayne Gretzky, LosA.	4.00
☐	GR81-4 Wayne Gretzky, Edmo.	4.00
☐	GR81-5 Wayne Gretzky, NYRa.	4.00

1999 - 2000 MILLENNIUM SIGNATURE

This series was released in February 2000. An autographed insert (listed below after the regular series) was included in every pack. There are four unsigned versions for cards 1-250: the regular card, a Ruby parallel (#/1000), a Sapphire parallel (#/100) and an Emerald parallel (#/10).

A number of wrapper-redemption unsigned parallels exist. These wrapper-redemption cards were available at: the 2000 All-Star Fantasy (Gold, Ruby, Sapphire and Silver versions limited to 10 copies each); the 2000 Toronto Spring Expo (Gold, Ruby, Sapphire versions each limited to 10 copies each); the 2000 Chicago Times show (Gold, Ruby and Sapphire versions limited to 10 copies each); and the 2000 Anaheim National (Emerald, Gold, Ruby and Sapphire versions limited to 10 copies each).

Complete Set (250 cards):		4000.00	525.00	225.00
Common Player:		4.00	1.00	.50
	Player	S100	R1000	Reg.
☐☐☐☐	1 Paul Kariya, Anah.	70.00	8.00	3.00
☐☐☐☐	2 Teemu Selänne, Anah.	40.00	5.00	2.00
☐☐☐☐	3 Oleg Tverdovsky, Anah.	5.00	1.00	.50
☐☐☐☐	**4 Niclas Hävelid, Anah. RC**	**10.00**	**2.00**	**1.50**
☐☐☐☐	5 Guy Hebert (G), Anah.	10.00	1.00	.50
☐☐☐☐	6 Stu Grimson, Anah.	10.00	1.00	.50
☐☐☐☐	7 Pavel Trnka, Anah.	5.00	1.00	.50
☐☐☐☐	8 Ladislav Kohn, Anah.	5.00	1.00	.50
☐☐☐☐	9 Matt Cullen, Anah.	10.00	1.00	.50
☐☐☐☐	10 Steve Rucchin, Anah.	10.00	1.00	.50
☐☐☐☐	11 Dominic Roussel (G), Anah.	5.00	1.00	.50
☐☐☐☐	**12 Patrik Stefan, Atla. RC**	**30.00**	**8.00**	**5.00**
☐☐☐☐	13 Damian Rhodes (G), Atla.	10.00	1.00	.50
☐☐☐☐	14 Ray Ferraro, Atla.	5.00	1.00	.50
☐☐☐☐	15 Andrew Brunette, Atla.	5.00	1.00	.50
☐☐☐☐	16 Johan Garpenlöv, Atla.	5.00	1.00	.50
☐☐☐☐	17 Nelson Emerson, Atla.	5.00	1.00	.50
☐☐☐☐	18 Jason Botterill, Atla.	5.00	1.00	.50
☐☐☐☐	19 Kelly Buchberger, Atla.	5.00	1.00	.50
☐☐☐☐	20 Raymond Bourque, Bost.	60.00	7.00	3.00
☐☐☐☐	21 Ken Belanger, Bost.	5.00	1.00	.50
☐☐☐☐	22 Sergei Samsonov, Bost.	30.00	3.00	1.50
☐☐☐☐	23 Byron Dafoe (G), Bost.	20.00	2.00	1.00
☐☐☐☐	24 Joe Thornton, Bost.	60.00	7.00	3.00
☐☐☐☐	25 Kyle McLaren, Bost.	10.00	1.00	.50
☐☐☐☐	26 Cameron Mann, Bost.	5.00	1.00	.50
☐☐☐☐	**27 Mikko Eloranta, Bost. RC**	**10.00**	**2.00**	**1.50**
☐☐☐☐	28 Jonathan Girard, Bost.	5.00	1.00	.50
☐☐☐☐	29 Dominik Hasek (G), Buff.	50.00	6.00	2.00
☐☐☐☐	30 Michael Peca, Buff.	20.00	2.00	1.00
☐☐☐☐	31 Erik Rasmussen, Buff.	10.00	1.00	.50
☐☐☐☐	**32 Brian Campbell, Buff. RC**	**10.00**	**2.00**	**1.50**
☐☐☐☐	33 Miroslav Satan, Buff.	15.00	2.00	.50
☐☐☐☐	34 Vaclav Varada, Buff.	5.00	1.00	.50
☐☐☐☐	35 Martin Biron (G), Buff.	20.00	3.00	1.00
☐☐☐☐	36 Dixon Ward, Buff.	5.00	1.00	.50
☐☐☐☐	37 Cory Sarich, Buff.	5.00	1.00	.50
☐☐☐☐	38 Grant Fuhr (G), Calg.	30.00	3.00	1.50
☐☐☐☐	39 Jarome Iginla, Calg.	40.00	5.00	2.00
☐☐☐☐	40 Valeri Bure, Calg.	15.00	2.00	.50
☐☐☐☐	**41 Oleg Saprykin, Calg. RC**	**25.00**	**5.50**	**4.00**
☐☐☐☐	42 René Corbet, Calg.	5.00	1.00	.50
☐☐☐☐	43 Cory Stillman, Calg.	10.00	1.00	.50
☐☐☐☐	44 Denis Gauthier, Calg.	5.00	1.00	.50
☐☐☐☐	45 Steve Dubinsky, Calg.	5.00	1.00	.50
☐☐☐☐	46 Rico Fata, Calg.	10.00	1.00	.50
☐☐☐☐	**47 Stevenn Halko, Caro. RC**	**10.00**	**2.00**	**1.50**
☐☐☐☐	48 Keith Primeau, Caro.	20.00	2.00	1.00
☐☐☐☐	49 Sami Kapanen, Caro.	15.00	2.00	.50
☐☐☐☐	50 Arturs Irbe (G), Caro.	20.00	2.00	1.00
☐☐☐☐	51 Jeff O'Neill, Caro.	20.00	2.00	1.00
☐☐☐☐	52 Kent Manderville, Caro.	5.00	1.00	.50
☐☐☐☐	53 Gary Roberts, Caro.	20.00	2.00	1.00
☐☐☐☐	54 Nolan Pratt, Caro.	5.00	1.00	.50
☐☐☐☐	55 Brad Brown, Chic.	5.00	1.00	.50
☐☐☐☐	56 Tony Amonte, Chic.	30.00	3.00	1.50
☐☐☐☐	57 Jean-Pierre Dumont, Chic.	10.00	1.00	.50
☐☐☐☐	58 Anders Eriksson, Chic.	5.00	1.00	.50
☐☐☐☐	59 Bryan Muir, Chic.	5.00	1.00	.50
☐☐☐☐	60 Dean McAmmond, Chic.	5.00	1.00	.50
☐☐☐☐	61 Jocelyn Thibault (G), Chic.	20.00	2.00	1.00
☐☐☐☐	62 Éric Dazé, Chic.	20.00	2.00	1.00
☐☐☐☐	63 Shean Donovan, Colo.	5.00	1.00	.50
☐☐☐☐	64 Scott Parker, Colo.	5.00	1.00	.50
☐☐☐☐	65 Peter Forsberg, Colo.	70.00	8.00	3.00
☐☐☐☐	66 Patrick Roy (G), Colo.	150.00	18.00	7.00
☐☐☐☐	67 Joe Sakic, Colo.	80.00	10.00	4.00
☐☐☐☐	68 Sandis Ozolinsh, Colo.	10.00	1.00	.50
☐☐☐☐	69 Chris Drury, Colo.	30.00	3.00	1.50
☐☐☐☐	70 Milan Hejduk, Colo.	40.00	5.00	2.00
☐☐☐☐	71 Shjon Podein, Colo.	10.00	1.00	.50
☐☐☐☐	72 Marc Denis (G), Colo.	20.00	3.00	1.00
☐☐☐☐	73 Alex Tanguay, Colo.	30.00	4.50	3.00
☐☐☐☐	74 Blake Sloan, Dall.	5.00	1.00	.50
☐☐☐☐	75 Jamie Langenbrunner, Dall.	10.00	1.00	.50
☐☐☐☐	76 Mike Modano, Dall.	50.00	6.00	2.50
☐☐☐☐	77 Derian Hatcher, Dall.	15.00	2.00	.50
☐☐☐☐	78 Joe Nieuwendyk, Dall.	20.00	2.00	1.00
☐☐☐☐	79 Ed Belfour (G), Dall.	50.00	6.00	2.50
☐☐☐☐	**80 Brad Lukowich, Dall. RC**	**15.00**	**3.50**	**3.00**
☐☐☐☐	81 Jere Lehtinen, Dall.	15.00	2.00	.50
☐☐☐☐	82 Brett Hull, Dall.	50.00	6.00	2.50
☐☐☐☐	83 Shawn Chambers, Dall.	5.00	1.00	.50
☐☐☐☐	**84 Pavel Patera, Dall. RC**	**10.00**	**2.00**	**1.50**
☐☐☐☐	85 Darryl Sydor, Dall.	10.00	1.00	.50
☐☐☐☐	86 Jiri Fischer, Detr.	10.00	1.50	1.00
☐☐☐☐	87 Nicklas Lidström, Detr.	30.00	3.00	1.50
☐☐☐☐	88 Steve Yzerman, Detr.	120.00	15.00	6.00
☐☐☐☐	89 Sergei Fedorov, Detr.	50.00	6.00	2.50
☐☐☐☐	90 Brendan Shanahan, Detr.	50.00	6.00	2.50
☐☐☐☐	91 Chris Chelios, Detr.	30.00	3.00	1.50

□□□□	92 Aaron Ward, Detr.	5.00	1.00	.50
□□□□	93 Kirk Maltby, Detr.	10.00	1.00	.50
□□□□	**94 Yuri Butsayev, Detr. RC**	**10.00**	**2.00**	**1.50**
□□□□	95 Mathieu Dandenault, Detr.	5.00	1.00	.50
□□□□	96 Doug Weight, Edmo.	30.00	3.00	1.50
□□□□	97 Bill Guerin, Edmo.	20.00	2.00	1.00
□□□□	98 Tom Poti, Edmo.	5.00	1.00	.50
□□□□	99 Wayne Gretzky, Edmo.	200.00	25.00	10.00
□□□□	**100 G. Laraque, Edmo. RC**	**15.00**	**3.50**	**3.00**
□□□□	101 Sean Brown, Edmo.	5.00	1.00	.50
□□□□	102 Mike Grier, Edmo.	10.00	1.00	.50
□□□□	103 Tommy Salo (G), Edmo.	20.00	2.00	1.00
□□□□	104 Rem Murray, Edmo.	5.00	1.00	.50
□□□□	**105 Paul Comrie, Edmo. RC**	**15.00**	**3.50**	**3.00**
□□□□	106 Pavel Bure, Flor.	40.00	5.00	2.00
□□□□	107 Rob Niedermayer, Flor.	10.00	1.00	.50
□□□□	108 Oleg Kvasha, Flor.	5.00	1.00	.50
□□□□	**109 Filip Kuba, Flor. RC**	**15.00**	**3.50**	**3.00**
□□□□	110 Viktor Kozlov, Flor.	15.00	2.00	.50
□□□□	111 Radek Dvorak, Flor.	10.00	1.00	.50
□□□□	112 Ray Whitney, Flor.	10.00	1.00	.50
□□□□	113 Mark Parrish, Flor.	20.00	2.00	1.00
□□□□	**114 Dan Boyle, Flor. RC**	**25.00**	**5.50**	**4.50**
□□□□	115 Marcus Nilson, Flor.	5.00	1.00	.50
□□□□	116 Lance Pitlick, Flor.	5.00	1.00	.50
□□□□	117 Paul Laus, Flor.	5.00	1.00	.50
□□□□	118 Rob Blake, LosA.	30.00	3.00	1.50
□□□□	119 Stéphane Fiset (G), LosA.	15.00	2.00	.50
□□□□	120 Zigmund Palffy, LosA.	30.00	3.00	1.50
□□□□	121 Donald Audette, LosA.	20.00	2.00	1.00
□□□□	122 Luc Robitaille, LosA.	40.00	5.00	2.00
□□□□	123 Jamie Storr (G), LosA.	10.00	1.00	.50
□□□□	124 Dan Bylsma, LosA.	5.00	1.00	.50
□□□□	125 Pavel Rosa, LosA.	5.00	1.00	.50
□□□□	**126 Jason Blake, LosA. RC**	**25.00**	**5.50**	**4.50**
□□□□	127 Mattias Norström, LosA.	10.00	1.00	.50
□□□□	128 Saku Koivu, Mont.	40.00	5.00	2.00
□□□□	129 Trevor Linden, Mont.	20.00	2.00	1.00
□□□□	130 Arron Asham, Mont.	5.00	1.00	.50
□□□□	131 Matt Higgins, Mont.	5.00	1.00	.50
□□□□	132 Martin Rucinsky, Mont.	10.00	1.00	.50
□□□□	133 Brian Savage, Mont.	15.00	2.00	.50
□□□□	134 Jeff Hackett (G), Mont.	15.00	2.00	.50
□□□□	135 Scott Thornton, Mont.	5.00	1.00	.50
□□□□	136 David Legwand, Nash.	20.00	2.00	1.00
□□□□	137 Cliff Ronning, Nash.	10.00	1.00	.50
□□□□	138 Ville Peltonen, Nash.	5.00	1.00	.50
□□□□	139 Tomas Vokoun (G), Nash.	10.00	1.00	.50
□□□□	140 Sergei Krivokrasov, Nash.	5.00	1.00	.50
□□□□	141 Greg Johnson, Nash.	5.00	1.00	.50
□□□□	142 Mike Dunham (G), Nash.	20.00	2.00	1.00
□□□□	143 Martin Brodeur (G), NJer.	80.00	10.00	4.00
□□□□	144 Scott Niedermayer, NJer.	15.00	2.00	.50
□□□□	145 Petr* Sykora, NJer.	20.00	2.00	1.00
□□□□	146 Vadim Sharifijanov, NJer.	5.00	1.00	.50
□□□□	147 Denis Pederson, NJer.	5.00	1.00	.50
□□□□	148 Jason Arnott, NJer.	20.00	3.00	1.00
□□□□	149 Brendan Morrison, NJer.	15.00	2.00	.50
□□□□	150 Bobby Holik, NJer.	15.00	2.00	.50
□□□□	**151 B. Rafalski, NJer. RC**	**25.00**	**5.50**	**4.00**
□□□□	152 Olli Jokinen, NYIs.	15.00	2.00	.50
□□□□	153 Tim Connolly, NYIs.	20.00	3.00	2.00
□□□□	154 Gino Odjick, NYIs.	5.00	1.00	.50
□□□□	155 Zdeno Chara, NYIs.	10.00	1.00	.50
□□□□	156 Kenny Jönsson, NYIs.	10.00	1.00	.50
□□□□	157 Mariusz Czerkawski, NYIs.	10.00	1.00	.50
□□□□	**158 K. Johnsson, NYRa. RC**	**15.00**	**3.50**	**3.00**
□□□□	159 Brian Leetch, NYRa.	30.00	3.00	1.50
□□□□	160 Theoren Fleury, NYRa.	30.00	3.00	1.50
□□□□	161 Petr Nedved, NYRa.	15.00	2.00	.50
□□□□	162 John MacLean, NYRa.	5.00	1.00	.50
□□□□	163 Manny Malhotra, NYRa.	10.00	1.00	.50
□□□□	164 Jan Hlavac, NYRa.	10.00	1.50	1.00
□□□□	165 Valeri Kamensky, NYRa.	15.00	2.00	.50
□□□□	166 Adam Graves, NYRa.	20.00	2.00	1.00
□□□□	167 Mike York, NYRa.	15.00	2.00	.50
□□□□	168 Mike Richter (G), NYRa.	20.00	3.00	1.00
□□□□	169 Chris Phillips, Otta.	10.00	1.00	.50
□□□□	170 Marian Hossa, Otta.	50.00	6.00	2.50
□□□□	171 Magnus Arvedson, Otta.	5.00	1.00	.50
□□□□	172 Ron Tugnutt (G), Otta.	20.00	2.00	1.00
□□□□	173 Vaclav Prospal, Otta.	15.00	2.00	.50
□□□□	174 Sami Salo, Otta.	5.00	1.00	.50
□□□□	175 Jason York, Otta.	5.00	1.00	.50
□□□□	176 Shawn McEachern, Otta.	15.00	2.00	.50
□□□□	177 Rob Zamuner, Otta.	10.00	1.00	.50
□□□□	178 Eric Lindros, Phil.	50.00	6.00	2.00
□□□□	179 John LeClair, Phil.	40.00	5.00	2.00
□□□□	180 Éric Desjardins, Phil.	15.00	2.00	.50
□□□□	181 Rod Brind'Amour, Phil.	15.00	2.00	.50
□□□□	182 Mark Recchi, Phil.	20.00	2.00	1.00
□□□□	183 Simon Gagné, Phil.	40.00	6.00	4.00
□□□□	184 Sandy McCarthy, Phil.	5.00	1.00	.50
□□□□	185 Vanbiesbrouck (G), Phil.	20.00	3.00	1.00
□□□□	186 Dan McGillis, Phil.	5.00	1.00	.50
□□□□	187 Keith Jones, Phil.	5.00	1.00	.50
□□□□	188 Keith Tkachuk, Phoe.	30.00	3.00	1.50
□□□□	189 Teppo Numminen, Phoe.	15.00	2.00	.50
□□□□	190 Jeremy Roenick, Phoe.	40.00	5.00	2.00
□□□□	191 Khabibulin (G), Phoe.	20.00	2.00	1.00
□□□□	192 Deron Quint, Phoe.	5.00	1.00	.50
□□□□	193 Trevor Letowski, Phoe.	5.00	1.00	.50
□□□□	194 Jaromir Jagr, Pitt.	50.00	6.00	2.00
□□□□	195 Jan Hrdina, Pitt.	10.00	1.00	.50
□□□□	196 Andrew Ference, Pitt.	5.00	1.00	.50
□□□□	197 Alexei Kovalev, Pitt.	30.00	3.00	1.50
□□□□	198 Martin Straka, Pitt.	15.00	2.00	.50
□□□□	199 Kip Miller, Pitt.	5.00	1.00	.50
□□□□	**200 Martin Sonnenberg, Pitt. RC**	**10.00**	**2.00**	**1.50**
□□□□	201 Aleksey Morozov, Pitt.	10.00	1.00	.50
□□□□	202 Chris Pronger, SLou.	30.00	3.00	1.50
□□□□	203 Al MacInnis, SLou.	20.00	2.00	1.00
□□□□	204 Pavol Demitra, SLou.	20.00	2.00	1.00
□□□□	205 Pierre Turgeon, SLou.	20.00	2.00	1.00
□□□□	206 Jamal Mayers, SLou.	5.00	1.00	.50
□□□□	207 Chris McAlpine, SLou.	5.00	1.00	.50
□□□□	208 Ron Sutter, SanJ.	10.00	1.00	.50
□□□□	209 Mike Rathje, SanJ.	5.00	1.00	.50
□□□□	210 Patrick Marleau, SanJ.	20.00	3.00	1.00
□□□□	211 Jeff Friesen, SanJ.	15.00	2.00	.50
□□□□	212 Niklas Sundström, SanJ.	10.00	1.00	.50
□□□□	213 Steve Shields (G), SanJ.	10.00	1.00	.50
□□□□	214 Brad Stuart, SanJ.	20.00	3.00	2.00
□□□□	215 Alexander Korolyuk, SanJ.	5.00	1.00	.50
□□□□	216 Mike Ricci, SanJ.	15.00	2.00	.50
□□□□	217 Paul Mara, Tamp.	5.00	1.00	.50
□□□□	218 Fredrik Modin, Tamp.	10.00	1.00	.50
□□□□	219 Dan Cloutier (G), Tamp.	20.00	2.00	1.00
□□□□	220 Vincent Lecavalier, Tamp.	50.00	6.00	2.50
□□□□	221 Pavel Kubina, Tamp.	5.00	1.00	.50
□□□□	222 Chris Gratton, Tamp.	10.00	1.00	.50
□□□□	223 Mike Sillinger, Tamp.	5.00	1.00	.50
□□□□	**224 Antropov, Toro. RC**	**25.00**	**5.50**	**4.00**
□□□□	225 Todd Warriner, Toro.	5.00	1.00	.50
□□□□	226 Mats Sundin, Toro.	50.00	6.00	2.50
□□□□	227 Curtis Joseph (G), Toro.	50.00	6.00	2.50
□□□□	**228 McAllister, Toro. RC**	**10.00**	**2.00**	**1.50**
□□□□	229 Bryan Berard, Toro.	15.00	2.00	.50
□□□□	230 Tomas Kaberle, Toro.	15.00	2.00	.50
□□□□	231 Igor Korolev, Toro.	5.00	1.00	.50
□□□□	232 Sergei Berezin, Toro.	10.00	1.00	.50
□□□□	233 Artem Chubarov, Vanc.	5.00	1.00	.50
□□□□	234 Ed Jovanovski, Vanc.	20.00	2.00	1.00
□□□□	235 Mark Messier, Vanc.	50.00	6.00	2.50
□□□□	236 Bill Muckalt, Vanc.	5.00	1.00	.50
□□□□	237 Brad May, Vanc.	5.00	1.00	.50
□□□□	238 Adrian Aucoin, Vanc.	5.00	1.00	.50
□□□□	239 Mattias Öhlund, Vanc.	15.00	2.00	.50
□□□□	240 Greg Hawgood, Vanc.	5.00	1.00	.50
□□□□	**241 Steve Kariya, Vanc. RC**	**25.00**	**5.50**	**4.00**
□□□□	242 Markus Näslund, Vanc.	50.00	6.00	2.50
□□□□	243 Alexander Mogilny, Vanc.	20.00	3.00	1.00
□□□□	244 Jamie Huscroft, Wash.	5.00	1.00	.50
□□□□	245 Peter Bondra, Wash.	30.00	3.00	1.50
□□□□	246 Olaf Kölzig (G), Wash.	30.00	3.00	1.50
□□□□	247 Brendan Witt, Wash.	5.00	1.00	.50
□□□□	248 Adam Oates, Wash.	20.00	2.00	1.00
□□□□	249 Sergei Gonchar, Wash.	15.00	2.00	.50
□□□□	250 Jan Bulis, Wash.	5.00	1.00	.50

AUTOGRAPHS

There are two versions: the Silver Autograph (silver-foil board, roughly 1500 copies) and the Gold Autograph (gold-foil board, roughly 500 copies). Most short-print autographs are limited to 450 Silver copies and 50 Gold copies. The Wayne Gretzky and Dominik Hasek (G) short-print autographs are the most limited cards. Both Limited cards (LTD) and First Signature Cards are marked below (FSC).

Complete Set (250 cards): 6200.00 3500.00
Common Autograph: 8.00 5.00

	Autograph	**Gold**	**Silver**
□□	1 Paul Kariya, Anah. ✍ (LTD)	175.00	70.00
□□	2 Teemu Selänne, Anah. ✍ (LTD)	100.00	40.00
□□	3 Oleg Tverdovsky, Anah. ✍	8.00	5.00
□□	4 Niclas Hävelid, Anah. ✍[FSC]	10.00	8.00
□□	5 Guy Hebert (G), Anah. ✍	8.00	6.00
□□	6 Stu Grimson, Anah. ✍	8.00	6.00
□□	7 Pavel Trnka, Anah. ✍[FSC]	10.00	8.00
□□	8 Ladislav Kohn, Anah. ✍[FSC]	10.00	8.00
□□	9 Matt Cullen, Anah. ✍[FSC]	10.00	8.00
□□	10 Steve Rucchin, Anah. ✍	8.00	6.00
□□	11 Dominic Roussel (G), Anah. ✍	8.00	5.00
□□	12 Patrik Stefan, Atla. ✍[FSC]	10.00	12.00
□□	13 Damian Rhodes (G), Atla. ✍	8.00	6.00
□□	14 Ray Ferraro, Atla. ✍	8.00	5.00
□□	15 Andrew Brunette, Atla. ✍[FSC]	10.00	8.00
□□	16 Johan Garpenlöv, Atla. ✍	8.00	5.00
□□	17 Nelson Emerson, Atla. ✍	8.00	5.00
□□	18 Jason Botterill, Atla. ✍[FSC]	10.00	8.00
□□	19 Kelly Buchberger, Atla. ✍	8.00	5.00
□□	20 Raymond Bourque, Bost. ✍	150.00	75.00
□□	21 Ken Belanger, Bost. ✍	8.00	5.00
□□	22 Sergei Samsonov, Bost. ✍ (LTD)	75.00	30.00
□□	23 Byron Dafoe (G), Bost. ✍ (LTD)	50.00	25.00
□□	24 Joe Thornton, Bost. ✍	45.00	30.00
□□	25 Kyle McLaren, Bost. ✍	8.00	6.00
□□	26 Cameron Mann, Bost. ✍[FSC]	10.00	8.00
□□	27 Mikko Eloranta, Bost. ✍[FSC]	10.00	8.00
□□	28 Jonathan Girard, Bost. ✍[FSC]	10.00	8.00
□□	29 Dominik Hasek (G), Buff. ✍ (X-LTD)	700.00	
□□	30 Michael Peca, Buff. ✍	50.00	25.00
□□	31 Erik Rasmussen, Buff. ✍	8.00	6.00
□□	32 Brian Campbell, Buff. ✍[FSC]	10.00	8.00
□□	33 Miroslav Satan, Buff. ✍	10.00	8.00
□□	34 Vaclav Varada, Buff. ✍[FSC]	10.00	8.00
□□	35 Martin Biron (G), Buff. ✍[FSC]	20.00	18.00
□□	36 Dixon Ward, Buff. ✍	8.00	5.00
□□	37 Cory Sarich, Buff. ✍[FSC]	10.00	8.00
□□	38 Grant Fuhr (G), Calg. ✍ (LTD)	75.00	30.00
□□	39 Jarome Iginla, Calg. ✍	30.00	20.00
□□	40 Valeri Bure, Calg. ✍	10.00	8.00
□□	41 Oleg Saprykin, Calg. ✍[FSC]	10.00	8.00
□□	42 René Corbet, Calg. ✍	8.00	5.00
□□	43 Cory Stillman, Calg. ✍	8.00	6.00
□□	44 Denis Gauthier, Calg. ✍[FSC]	10.00	8.00
□□	45 Steve Dubinsky, Calg. ✍	8.00	5.00
□□	46 Rico Fata, Calg. ✍	8.00	6.00
□□	47 Stevenn Halko, Caro. ✍[FSC]	10.00	8.00
□□	48 Keith Primeau, Caro. ✍ (LTD)	50.00	25.00
□□	49 Sami Kapanen, Caro. ✍	10.00	8.00
□□	50 Arturs Irbe (G), Caro. ✍	15.00	10.00
□□	51 Jeff O'Neill, Caro. ✍	15.00	10.00
□□	52 Kent Manderville, Caro. ✍	8.00	5.00
□□	53 Gary Roberts, Caro. ✍	15.00	10.00
□□	54 Nolan Pratt, Caro. ✍[FSC]	10.00	8.00
□□	55 Brad Brown, Chic. ✍[FSC]	10.00	8.00
□□	56 Tony Amonte, Chic. ✍ (LTD)	75.00	30.00
□□	57 Jean-Pierre Dumont, Chic. ✍[FSC]	10.00	8.00
□□	58 Anders Eriksson, Chic. ✍	8.00	5.00
□□	59 Bryan Muir, Chic. ✍[FSC]	10.00	8.00
□□	60 Dean McAmmond, Chic. ✍	8.00	5.00
□□	61 Jocelyn Thibault (G), Chic. ✍	15.00	10.00
□□	62 Éric Dazé, Chic. ✍	15.00	10.00
□□	63 Shean Donovan, Colo. ✍	8.00	5.00
□□	64 Scott Parker, Colo. ✍[FSC]	10.00	8.00
□□	65 Peter Forsberg, Colo. ✍ (LTD)	175.00	70.00
□□	66 Patrick Roy (G), Colo. ✍ (LTD)	375.00	160.00
□□	67 Joe Sakic, Colo. ✍ (LTD)	200.00	80.00
□□	68 Sandis Ozolinsh, Colo. ✍ (LTD)	8.00	6.00
□□	69 Chris Drury, Colo. ✍[FSC]	25.00	20.00
□□	70 Milan Hejduk, Colo. ✍	30.00	20.00
□□	71 Shjon Podein, Colo. ✍	8.00	6.00
□□	72 Marc Denis (G), Colo. ✍[FSC]	20.00	18.00
□□	73 Alex Tanguay, Colo. ✍[FSC]	25.00	20.00
□□	74 Blake Sloan, Dall. ✍[FSC]	10.00	8.00
□□	75 Jamie Langenbrunner, Dall. ✍	8.00	6.00
□□	76 Mike Modano, Dall. ✍ (LTD)	125.00	50.00
□□	77 Derian Hatcher, Dall. ✍	10.00	8.00
□□	78 Joe Nieuwendyk, Dall. ✍ (LTD)	50.00	25.00
□□	79 Ed Belfour (G), Dall. ✍ (LTD)	125.00	50.00
□□	80 Brad Lukowich, Dall. ✍[FSC]	10.00	8.00
□□	81 Jere Lehtinen, Dall. ✍	10.00	8.00
□□	82 Brett Hull, Dall. ✍ (LTD)	125.00	55.00
□□	83 Shawn Chambers, Dall. ✍	8.00	5.00
□□	84 Pavel Patera, Dall. ✍[FSC]	10.00	8.00
□□	85 Darryl Sydor, Dall. ✍	8.00	6.00
□□	86 Jiri Fischer, Detr. ✍[FSC]	10.00	8.00
□□	87 Nicklas Lidström, Detr. ✍	20.00	14.00
□□	88 Steve Yzerman, Detr. ✍ (LTD)	300.00	135.00
□□	89 Sergei Fedorov, Detr. ✍ (LTD)	125.00	55.00
□□	90 Brendan Shanahan, Detr. ✍ (LTD)	125.00	50.00
□□	91 Chris Chelios, Detr. ✍ (LTD)	75.00	30.00
□□	92 Aaron Ward, Detr. ✍	8.00	5.00
□□	93 Kirk Maltby, Detr. ✍	8.00	6.00
□□	94 Yuri Butsayev, Detr. ✍[FSC]	10.00	8.00
□□	95 Mathieu Dandenault, Detr. ✍	8.00	5.00
□□	96 Doug Weight, Edmo. ✍ (LTD)	75.00	30.00
□□	97 Bill Guerin, Edmo. ✍	15.00	10.00
□□	98 Tom Poti, Edmo. ✍[FSC]	10.00	8.00
□□	99 Wayne Gretzky, Edmo. ✍ (X-LTD)	2500.00	900.00
□□	100 Georges Laraque, Edmo. ✍[FSC]	10.00	8.00
□□	101 Sean Brown, Edmo. ✍[FSC]	10.00	8.00
□□	102 Mike Grier, Edmo. ✍	8.00	6.00
□□	103 Tommy Salo (G), Edmo. ✍	15.00	10.00
□□	104 Rem Murray, Edmo. ✍	8.00	5.00
□□	105 Paul Comrie, Edmo. ✍[FSC]	10.00	8.00
□□	106 Pavel Bure, Flor. ✍ (LTD)	100.00	40.00
□□	107 Rob Niedermayer, Flor. ✍	8.00	6.00
□□	108 Oleg Kvasha, Flor. ✍	8.00	5.00
□□	109 Filip Kuba, Flor. ✍[FSC]	10.00	8.00
□□	110 Viktor Kozlov, Flor. ✍	10.00	8.00
□□	111 Radek Dvorak, Flor. ✍	8.00	6.00
□□	112 Ray Whitney, Flor. ✍	8.00	6.00
□□	113 Mark Parrish, Flor. ✍	15.00	10.00
□□	114 Dan Boyle, Flor. ✍[FSC]	10.00	8.00
□□	115 Marcus Nilson, Flor. ✍[FSC]	10.00	8.00
□□	116 Lance Pitlick, Flor. ✍	8.00	5.00
□□	117 Paul Laus, Flor. ✍	8.00	5.00
□□	118 Rob Blake, LosA. ✍	20.00	14.00
□□	119 Stéphane Fiset (G), LosA. ✍	10.00	8.00
□□	120 Zigmund Palffy, LosA. ✍ (LTD)	75.00	30.00
□□	121 Donald Audette, LosA. ✍	15.00	10.00
□□	122 Luc Robitaille, LosA. ✍	30.00	20.00
□□	123 Jamie Storr (G), LosA. ✍[FSC]	10.00	8.00
□□	124 Dan Bylsma, LosA. ✍	8.00	5.00
□□	125 Pavel Rosa, LosA. ✍[FSC]	10.00	8.00
□□	126 Jason Blake, LosA. ✍[FSC]	10.00	8.00
□□	127 Mattias Norström, LosA. ✍	8.00	6.00
□□	128 Saku Koivu, Mont. ✍ (LTD)	100.00	40.00
□□	129 Trevor Linden, Mont. ✍	15.00	10.00
□□	130 Arron Asham, Mont. ✍[FSC]	10.00	8.00
□□	131 Matt Higgins, Mont. ✍[FSC]	10.00	8.00
□□	132 Martin Rucinsky, Mont. ✍	8.00	6.00
□□	133 Brian Savage, Mont. ✍	10.00	8.00
□□	134 Jeff Hackett (G), Mont. ✍	10.00	8.00
□□	135 Scott Thornton, Mont. ✍	8.00	5.00
□□	136 David Legwand, Nash. ✍[FSC]	15.00	14.00
□□	137 Cliff Ronning, Nash. ✍	8.00	6.00
□□	138 Ville Peltonen, Nash. ✍[FSC]	10.00	8.00
□□	139 Tomas Vokoun (G), Nash. ✍[FSC]	10.00	8.00
□□	140 Sergei Krivokrasov, Nash. ✍	8.00	5.00
□□	141 Greg Johnson, Nash. ✍	8.00	5.00
□□	142 Mike Dunham (G), Nash. ✍	15.00	10.00
□□	143 Martin Brodeur (G), NJer. ✍ (LTD)	200.00	80.00
□□	144 Scott Niedermayer, NJer. ✍ (LTD)	40.00	25.00
□□	145 Petr* Sykora, NJer. ✍	15.00	10.00
□□	146 Vadim Sharifijanov, NJer. ✍[FSC]	10.00	8.00
□□	147 Denis Pederson, NJer. ✍	8.00	5.00
□□	148 Jason Arnott, NJer. ✍ (LTD)	60.00	25.00
□□	149 Brendan Morrison, NJer. ✍[FSC]	10.00	12.00
□□	150 Bobby Holik, NJer. ✍	10.00	8.00
□□	151 Brian Rafalski, NJer. ✍[FSC]	10.00	8.00
□□	152 Olli Jokinen, NYIs. ✍[FSC]	10.00	12.00
□□	153 Tim Connolly, NYIs. ✍[FSC]	15.00	14.00
□□	154 Gino Odjick, NYIs. ✍	8.00	5.00
□□	155 Zdeno Chara, NYIs. ✍[FSC]	10.00	8.00
□□	156 Kenny Jönsson, NYIs. ✍	8.00	5.00
□□	157 Mariusz Czerkawski, NYIs. ✍	8.00	6.00
□□	158 Kim Johnsson, NYRa. ✍[FSC]	10.00	8.00
□□	159 Brian Leetch, NYRa. ✍ (LTD)	75.00	30.00
□□	160 Theoren Fleury, NYRa. ✍ (LTD)	75.00	30.00
□□	161 Petr Nedved, NYRa. ✍	10.00	8.00
□□	162 John MacLean, NYRa. ✍	8.00	5.00
□□	163 Manny Malhotra, NYRa. ✍	8.00	6.00
□□	164 Jan Hlavac, NYRa. ✍[FSC]	10.00	8.00
□□	165 Valeri Kamensky, NYRa. ✍	10.00	8.00
□□	166 Adam Graves, NYRa. ✍	15.00	10.00
□□	167 Mike York, NYRa. ✍[FSC]	10.00	12.00
□□	168 Mike Richter (G), NYRa. ✍ (LTD)	60.00	25.00
□□	169 Chris Phillips, Otta. ✍	8.00	6.00
□□	170 Marian Hossa, Otta. ✍	35.00	25.00
□□	171 Magnus Arvedson, Otta. ✍	8.00	5.00
□□	172 Ron Tugnutt (G), Otta. ✍	15.00	10.00
□□	173 Vaclav Prospal, Otta. ✍	10.00	8.00
□□	174 Sami Salo, Otta. ✍[FSC]	10.00	8.00
□□	175 Jason York, Otta. ✍	8.00	5.00
□□	176 Shawn McEachern, Otta. ✍	10.00	8.00
□□	177 Rob Zamuner, Otta. ✍	8.00	6.00
□□	178 Eric Lindros, Phil. ✍ (LTD)	125.00	50.00
□□	179 John LeClair, Phil. ✍ (LTD)	100.00	40.00
□□	180 Éric Desjardins, Phil. ✍	10.00	8.00
□□	181 Rod Brind'Amour, Phil. ✍	10.00	8.00
□□	182 Mark Recchi, Phil. ✍	15.00	10.00
□□	183 Simon Gagné, Phil. ✍[FSC]	35.00	30.00
□□	184 Sandy McCarthy, Phil. ✍	8.00	5.00
□□	185 John Vanbiesbrouck (G), Phil. ✍ (LTD)	60.00	25.00
□□	186 Dan McGillis, Phil. ✍	8.00	5.00
□□	187 Keith Jones, Phil. ✍	8.00	5.00
□□	188 Keith Tkachuk, Phoe. ✍ (LTD)	75.00	30.00
□□	189 Teppo Numminen, Phoe. ✍	10.00	8.00
□□	190 Jeremy Roenick, Phoe. ✍ (LTD)	100.00	40.00
□□	191 Nikolai Khabibulin (G), Phoe. ✍	15.00	10.00
□□	192 Deron Quint, Phoe. ✍[FSC]	10.00	8.00
□□	193 Trevor Letowski, Phoe. ✍[FSC]	10.00	8.00
□□	194 Jaromir Jagr, Pitt. ✍ (LTD)	125.00	110.00
□□	195 Jan Hrdina, Pitt. ✍[FSC]	10.00	8.00
□□	196 Andrew Ference, Pitt. ✍[FSC]	10.00	8.00
□□	197 Alexei Kovalev, Pitt. ✍	20.00	14.00
□□	198 Martin Straka, Pitt. ✍	10.00	8.00
□□	199 Kip Miller, Pitt. ✍[FSC]	10.00	8.00
□□	200 Martin Sonnenberg, Pitt. ✍[FSC]	10.00	8.00
□□	201 Aleksey Morozov, Pitt. ✍	8.00	6.00
□□	202 Chris Pronger, SLou. ✍ (LTD)	75.00	30.00
□□	203 Al MacInnis, SLou. ✍ (LTD)	50.00	25.00
□□	204 Pavol Demitra, SLou. ✍	15.00	10.00

□ □	205 Pierre Turgeon, SLou. ✍	15.00	10.00
□ □	206 Jamal Mayers, SLou. ✍[FSC]	10.00	8.00
□ □	207 Chris McAlpine, SLou. ✍	8.00	5.00
□ □	208 Ron Sutter, SanJ. ✍	8.00	6.00
□ □	209 Mike Rathje, SanJ. ✍[FSC]	10.00	8.00
□ □	210 Patrick Marleau, SanJ. ✍	15.00	12.00
□ □	211 Jeff Friesen, SanJ. ✍ (LTD)	40.00	25.00
□ □	212 Niklas Sundström, SanJ. ✍	8.00	6.00
□ □	213 Steve Shields (G), SanJ. ✍	8.00	6.00
□ □	214 Brad Stuart, SanJ. ✍[FSC]	15.00	14.00
□ □	215 Alexander Korolyuk, SanJ. ✍[FSC]	10.00	8.00
□ □	216 Mike Ricci, SanJ. ✍	10.00	8.00
□ □	217 Paul Mara, Tamp. ✍[FSC]	10.00	8.00
□ □	218 Fredrik Modin, Tamp. ✍	8.00	6.00
□ □	219 Dan Cloutier (G), Tamp. ✍[FSC]	15.00	14.00
□ □	220 Vincent Lecavalier, Tamp. ✍	35.00	25.00
□ □	221 Pavel Kubina, Tamp. ✍[FSC]	10.00	8.00
□ □	222 Chris Gratton, Tamp. ✍ (LTD)	40.00	25.00
□ □	223 Mike Sillinger, Tamp. ✍	8.00	5.00
□ □	224 Nikolai Antropov, Toro. ✍[FSC]	10.00	8.00
□ □	225 Todd Warriner, Toro. ✍	8.00	5.00
□ □	226 Mats Sundin, Toro. ✍ (LTD)	125.00	50.00
□ □	227 Curtis Joseph (G), Toro. ✍ (LTD)	125.00	50.00
□ □	228 Chris McAllister, Toro. ✍[FSC]	10.00	8.00
□ □	229 Bryan Berard, Toro. ✍ (LTD)	40.00	25.00
□ □	230 Tomas Kaberle, Toro. ✍	10.00	8.00
□ □	231 Igor Korolev, Toro. ✍	8.00	5.00
□ □	232 Sergei Berezin, Toro. ✍	8.00	6.00
□ □	233 Artem Chubarov, Vanc. ✍[FSC]	10.00	8.00
□ □	234 Ed Jovanovski, Vanc. ✍	15.00	10.00
□ □	235 Mark Messier, Vanc. ✍ (LTD)	150.00	60.00
□ □	236 Bill Muckalt, Vanc. ✍	8.00	5.00
□ □	237 Brad May, Vanc. ✍	8.00	5.00
□ □	238 Adrian Aucoin, Vanc. ✍	8.00	5.00
□ □	239 Mattias Öhlund, Vanc. ✍	10.00	8.00
□ □	240 Greg Hawgood, Vanc. ✍[FSC]	10.00	8.00
□ □	241 Steve Kariya, Vanc. ✍[FSC]	10.00	8.00
□ □	242 Markus Näslund, Vanc. ✍	35.00	25.00
□ □	243 Alexander Mogilny, Vanc. ✍ (LTD)	60.00	25.00
□ □	244 Jamie Huscroft, Wash. ✍	8.00	5.00
□ □	245 Peter Bondra, Wash. ✍ (LTD)	75.00	30.00
□ □	246 Olaf Kölzig (G), Wash. ✍ (LTD)	75.00	30.00
□ □	247 Brendan Witt, Wash. ✍	8.00	5.00
□ □	248 Adam Oates, Wash. ✍ (LTD)	50.00	25.00
□ □	249 Sergei Gonchar, Wash. ✍	10.00	8.00
□ □	250 Jan Bulis, Wash. ✍[FSC]	10.00	8.00

CALDER CANDIDATES

There are three versions: the Ruby insert (1000 copies), the Sapphire insert (100 copies) and the Emerald insert (10 copies).

Insert Set (50 cards):		2800.00	500.00	225.00
	Player	E10	S100	R1000
□ □ □	C-1 Alex Tanguay, Colo.	180.00	30.00	10.00
□ □ □	C-2 Simon Gagné, Phil.	240.00	40.00	15.00
□ □ □	C-3 Kyle Calder, Chic.	70.00	10.00	6.00
□ □ □	C-4 Ryan Johnson, Flor.	40.00	10.00	6.00
□ □ □	C-5 David Tanabe, Caro.	45.00	10.00	6.00
□ □ □	C-6 Scott Gomez, NJer.	120.00	20.00	6.00
□ □ □	C-7 Patrik Stefan, Atla.	95.00	15.00	6.00
□ □ □	C-8 Jiri Fischer, Detr.	70.00	10.00	6.00
□ □ □	C-9 Blake Sloan, Dall.	45.00	10.00	6.00
□ □ □	C-10 Trevor Letowski, Phoe.	45.00	10.00	6.00
□ □ □	C-11 Mike York, NYRa.	95.00	15.00	6.00
□ □ □	C-12 Mike Ribeiro, Mont.	95.00	15.00	6.00
□ □ □	C-13 Ladislav Kohn, Anah.	45.00	10.00	6.00
□ □ □	C-14 Martin Skoula, Colo.	70.00	10.00	6.00
□ □ □	C-15 Steve Kariya, Vanc.	70.00	10.00	6.00
□ □ □	C-16 Nikolai Antropov, Toro.	70.00	10.00	6.00
□ □ □	C-17 David Legwand, Nash.	120.00	20.00	6.00
□ □ □	C-18 J-P Dumont, Chic.	70.00	10.00	6.00
□ □ □	C-19 Filip Kuba, Flor.	45.00	10.00	6.00
□ □ □	C-20 Mike Fisher, Otta.	70.00	10.00	6.00
□ □ □	C-21 Tim Connolly, NYIs.	120.00	20.00	6.00
□ □ □	C-22 Martin Biron (G), Buff.	140.00	20.00	8.00
□ □ □	C-23 Oleg Saprykin, Calg.	70.00	10.00	6.00
□ □ □	C-24 M. Afinogenov, Buff.	120.00	20.00	6.00
□ □ □	C-25 Petr Buzek, Atla.	40.00	10.00	6.00
□ □ □	C-26 Paul Comrie, Edmo.	45.00	10.00	6.00
□ □ □	C-27 Brian Boucher (G), Phil.	95.00	15.00	6.00
□ □ □	C-28 Peter Schaefer, Vanc.	45.00	10.00	6.00
□ □ □	C-29 Alexei Tezikov, Wash.	40.00	10.00	6.00
□ □ □	C-30 M. Hnilicka (G), NYRa.	70.00	10.00	6.00
□ □ □	C-31 Brian Rafalski, NJer.	70.00	10.00	6.00
□ □ □	C-32 Sami Helenius, Colo.	40.00	10.00	6.00
□ □ □	C-33 F. Kaberle, LosA.	45.00	10.00	6.00
□ □ □	C-34 Jochen Hecht, SLou.	70.00	10.00	6.00
□ □ □	C-35 Mathieu Biron, NYIs.	45.00	10.00	6.00
□ □ □	C-36 Randy Robitaille, Nash.	45.00	10.00	6.00
□ □ □	C-37 R. Luongo (G), NYIs.	240.00	40.00	15.00
□ □ □	C-38 Steven McCarthy, Chic.	45.00	10.00	6.00
□ □ □	C-39 Brad Lukowich, Dall.	45.00	10.00	6.00
□ □ □	C-40 Kim Johnsson, NYRa.	45.00	10.00	6.00
□ □ □	C-41 Brad Stuart, SanJ.	120.00	20.00	6.00
□ □ □	C-42 Glen Metropolit, Wash.	45.00	10.00	6.00
□ □ □	C-43 Marc Denis (G), Colo.	140.00	20.00	8.00
□ □ □	C-44 Robyn Regehr, Calg.	45.00	10.00	6.00
□ □ □	C-45 Per Svartvadet, Atla.	40.00	10.00	6.00
□ □ □	C-46 Jonathan Girard, Bost.	40.00	10.00	6.00
□ □ □	C-47 Mark Eaton, Phil.	40.00	10.00	6.00
□ □ □	C-48 Ivan Novoseltsev, Flor.	60.00	10.00	6.00
□ □ □	C-49 Jan Hlavac, NYRa.	70.00	10.00	6.00
□ □ □	C-50 Richard Jackman, Dall.	45.00	10.00	6.00

GAME JERSEY

Jersey Set (32 cards):		1500.00
	Insert (*100)	J100
□	J-1 Theoren Fleury, NYRa. ✂	40.00
□	J-2 Brendan Shanahan, Detr. ✂	50.00
□	J-3 Curtis Joseph (G), Toro. ✂	50.00
□	J-4 Saku Koivu, Mont. ✂	50.00
□	J-5 Dominik Hasek (G), Buff. ✂	50.00
□	J-6 Al MacInnis, SLou. ✂	40.00
□	J-7 John LeClair, Phil. ✂	50.00
□	J-8 Teemu Selänne, Anah. ✂	50.00
□	J-9 Wayne Gretzky, Edmo. ✂	300.00
□	J-10 Pavel Bure, Flor. ✂	50.00
□	J-11 Mark Messier, Vanc. ✂	50.00
□	J-12 Jaromir Jagr, Pitt. ✂	50.00
□	J-13 Raymond Bourque, Bost. ✂	75.00
□	J-14 Chris Chelios, Detr. ✂	40.00
□	J-15 Mats Sundin, Toro. ✂	50.00
□	J-16 Paul Kariya, Anah. ✂	75.00
□	J-17 Peter Bondra, Wash. ✂	40.00
□	J-18 Eric Lindros, Phil. ✂	50.00
□	J-19 Sergei Fedorov, Detr. ✂	50.00
□	J-20 Peter Forsberg, Colo. ✂	75.00
□	J-21 Brett Hull, Dall. ✂	50.00
□	J-22 Tony Amonte, Chic. ✂	40.00
□	J-23 Patrick Roy (G), Colo. ✂	150.00
□	J-24 Ed Belfour (G), Dall. ✂	50.00
□	J-25 Martin Brodeur (G), NJer. ✂	100.00
□	J-26 Brian Leetch, NYRa. ✂	40.00
□	J-27 Mike Modano, Dall. ✂	50.00
□	J-28 Joe Sakic, Colo. ✂	100.00
□	J-29 Jeremy Roenick, Phoe. ✂	50.00
□	J-30 Steve Yzerman, Detr. ✂	150.00
□	J-31 Alexander Mogilny, Vanc. ✂	40.00
□	J-32 Paul Coffey, Caro. ✂	40.00

GAME JERSEY AUTOGRAPH

Autographed Set (22 cards):		14500.00
	Player	Aut10
□	J-1 Theoren Fleury, NYRa. ✍ ✂	400.00
□	J-2 Brendan Shanahan, Detr. ✍ ✂	700.00
□	J-3 Curtis Joseph (G), Toro. ✍ ✂	700.00
□	J-5 Dominik Hasek (G), Buff. ✍ ✂	100.00
□	J-6 Al MacInnis, SLou. ✍ ✂	300.00
□	J-7 John LeClair, Phil. ✍ ✂	600.00
□	J-8 Teemu Selänne, Anah. ✍ ✂	600.00
□	J-10 Pavel Bure, Flor. ✍ ✂	600.00
□	J-15 Mats Sundin, Toro. ✍ ✂	700.00
□	J-17 Peter Bondra, Wash. ✍ ✂	400.00
□	J-18 Eric Lindros, Phil. ✍ ✂	700.00
□	J-19 Sergei Fedorov, Detr. ✍ ✂	700.00
□	J-20 Peter Forsberg, Colo. ✍ ✂	1000.00
□	J-21 Brett Hull, Dall. ✍ ✂	700.00
□	J-23 Patrick Roy (G), Colo. ✍ ✂	1800.00
□	J-24 Ed Belfour (G), Dall. ✍ ✂	700.00
□	J-25 Martin Brodeur (G), NJer. ✍ ✂	1200.00
□	J-26 Brian Leetch, NYRa. ✍ ✂	400.00
□	J-27 Mike Modano, Dall. ✍ ✂	700.00
□	J-28 Joe Sakic, Colo. ✍ ✂	1200.00
□	J-30 Steve Yzerman, Detr. ✍ ✂	1800.00
□	J-32 Paul Coffey, Caro. ✍ ✂	400.00

GAME JERSEY ETC.

Priced below are Jersey & Stick cards (#/40, prefix JS-), In The Numbers cards (#/30, prefix N-) and Team Emblem cards (#/20, prefix E-).

Insert Set (32 cards):		3500.00	3200.00	2500.00
	Player	E20	N30	JS40
□ □ □	1 Theoren Fleury, NYRa. ✂	85.00	75.00	65.00
□ □ □	2 B. Shanahan, Detr. ✂	100.00	100.00	75.00
□ □ □	3 Curtis Joseph (G), Toro. ✂	100.00	100.00	75.00
□ □ □	4 Saku Koivu, Mont. ✂	85.00	75.00	65.00
□ □ □	5 Dominik Hasek (G), Buff. ✂	100.00	100.00	75.00
□ □ □	6 Al MacInnis, SLou. ✂	85.00	75.00	65.00
□ □ □	7 John LeClair, Phil. ✂	85.00	75.00	65.00
□ □ □	8 Teemu Selänne, Anah. ✂	85.00	75.00	65.00
□ □ □	9 Wayne Gretzky, Edmo. ✂	450.00	400.00	300.00
□ □ □	10 Pavel Bure, Flor. ✂	85.00	75.00	65.00
□ □ □	11 Mark Messier, Vanc. ✂	100.00	100.00	75.00
□ □ □	12 Jaromir Jagr, Pitt. ✂	100.00	100.00	75.00
□ □ □	13 R. Bourque, Bost. ✂	125.00	100.00	75.00
□ □ □	14 Chris Chelios, Detr. ✂	85.00	75.00	65.00
□ □ □	15 Mats Sundin, Toro. ✂	100.00	100.00	75.00
□ □ □	16 Paul Kariya, Anah. ✂	150.00	125.00	100.00
□ □ □	17 Peter Bondra, Wash. ✂	85.00	75.00	65.00
□ □ □	18 Eric Lindros, Phil. ✂	100.00	100.00	75.00
□ □ □	19 Sergei Fedorov, Detr. ✂	100.00	100.00	75.00
□ □ □	20 Peter Forsberg, Colo. ✂	150.00	125.00	100.00
□ □ □	21 Brett Hull, Dall. ✂	100.00	100.00	75.00
□ □ □	22 Tony Amonte, Chic. ✂	85.00	75.00	65.00
□ □ □	23 Patrick Roy (G), Colo. ✂	250.00	225.00	175.00
□ □ □	24 Ed Belfour (G), Dall. ✂	100.00	100.00	75.00
□ □ □	25 M. Brodeur (G), NJer. ✂	175.00	150.00	100.00
□ □ □	26 Brian Leetch, NYRa. ✂	85.00	75.00	65.00
□ □ □	27 Mike Modano, Dall. ✂	100.00	100.00	75.00
□ □ □	28 Joe Sakic, Colo. ✂	175.00	150.00	100.00
□ □ □	29 Jeremy Roenick, Phoe. ✂	85.00	75.00	65.00
□ □ □	30 Steve Yzerman, Detr. ✂	250.00	225.00	175.00
□ □ □	31 A. Mogilny, Vanc. ✂	85.00	75.00	65.00
□ □ □	32 Paul Coffey, Caro. ✂	85.00	75.00	65.00

GOALIE MEMORABILIA

These cards featured affixed pieces of goalie memorabilia (blocker or catcher).

Insert Set (8 cards):		1550.00
	Player	GM
□	G-1 Curtis Joseph (G), Toro. ✂	250.00
□	G-2 Patrick Roy (G), Colo. ✂	475.00
□	G-3 Grant Fuhr (G), Calg. ✂	150.00
□	G-4 Garth Snow (G), Vanc. ✂	150.00
□	G-5 Jeff Hackett (G), Mont. ✂	150.00
□	G-6 Chris Osgood (G), Detr. ✂	150.00
□	G-7 Dominik Hasek (G), Buff. ✂	250.00
□	G-8 Arturs Irbe (G), Caro. ✂	150.00

PEARSON 30

Each player signed 30 of the 300 cards.

Insert Set (16 cards):		325.00
	Insert (#/300)	LBP
□	P-1 Jaromir Jagr, Pitt.	10.00
□	P-2 Dominik Hasek (G), Buff.	10.00
□	P-3 Mario Lemieux, Pitt.	50.00
□	P-4 Eric Lindros, Phil.	10.00
□	P-5 Sergei Fedorov, Detr.	10.00
□	P-6 Mark Messier, Edmo.	10.00
□	P-7 Brett Hull, SLou.	10.00
□	P-8 Steve Yzerman, Detr.	40.00
□	P-9 Wayne Gretzky, Edmo.	70.00
□	P-10 Mike Liut, SLou.	8.00
□	P-11 Marcel Dionne, LosA.	10.00
□	P-12 Guy Lafleur, Mont.	20.00
□	P-13 Bobby Orr, Bost.	70.00
□	P-14 Phil Esposito, Bost.	20.00
□	P-15 Bobby Clarke, Phil.	10.00
□	P-16 Jean Ratelle, NYRa.	8.00

PEARSON 30 AUTOGRAPH

Insert Set (16 cards):		4600.00
	Autograph	Auto.
□	P-1 Jaromir Jagr, Pitt. ✍	400.00
□	P-2 Dominik Hasek (G), Buff. ✍	275.00
□	P-3 Mario Lemieux, Pitt. ✍	600.00
□	P-4 Eric Lindros, Phil. ✍	200.00
□	P-5 Sergei Fedorov, Detr. ✍	200.00
□	P-6 Mark Messier, Edmo. ✍	225.00
□	P-7 Brett Hull, SLou. ✍	200.00
□	P-8 Steve Yzerman, Detr. ✍	475.00
□	P-9 Wayne Gretzky, Edmo. ✍	1000.00
□	P-10 Mike Liut, SLou. ✍	75.00
□	P-11 Marcel Dionne, LosA. ✍	150.00
□	P-12 Guy Lafleur, Mont. ✍	200.00
□	P-13 Bobby Orr, Bost. ✍	800.00
□	P-14 Phil Esposito, Bost. ✍	200.00
□	P-15 Bobby Clarke, Phil. ✍	100.00
□	P-16 Jean Ratelle, NYRa. ✍	75.00

PLAYERS OF THE DECADE

Each player signed 90 of the 1000 cards.

Insert Set (10 cards):		125.00
	Insert (#/1000)	PotD
□	D-1 Wayne Gretzky, LosA.	40.00
□	D-2 Mark Messier, NYRa.	10.00
□	D-3 Patrick Roy (G), Colo.	30.00
□	D-4 Dominik Hasek (G), Buff.	10.00
□	D-5 Jaromir Jagr, Pitt.	10.00
□	D-6 Eric Lindros, Phil.	10.00
□	D-7 Sergei Fedorov, Detr.	10.00
□	D-8 Brett Hull, Dall.	10.00
□	D-9 Raymond Bourque, Bost.	10.00
□	D-10 Steve Yzerman, Detr.	20.00

PLAYERS OF THE DECADE AUTOGRAPH

There are two versions: the insert and the autographed parallel (#/30).

Insert Set (10 cards):		2100.00
	Player	Auto.
□	D-1 Wayne Gretzky, LosA. ✍	700.00
□	D-2 Mark Messier, NYRa. ✍	150.00
□	D-3 Patrick Roy (G), Colo. ✍	375.00
□	D-4 Dominik Hasek (G), Buff. ✍	175.00
□	D-5 Jaromir Jagr, Pitt. ✍	250.00
□	D-6 Eric Lindros, Phil. ✍	125.00
□	D-7 Sergei Fedorov, Detr. ✍	125.00
□	D-8 Brett Hull, Dall. ✍	125.00
□	D-9 Raymond Bourque, Bost. ✍	175.00
□	D-10 Steve Yzerman, Detr. ✍	300.00

GAME JERSEY SPECIAL

This card was sent with early redemptions for the Jaromir Jagr autographed card.

	Game Jersey Special	MT
□	Jaromir Jagr, Pitt. ✂	300.00

1999 - 2000 MIR

Cards of NHL stars and prospects do sell at a premium (usually $1-$2 for the regular cards).

Complete Set (270 cards):		135.00
	Player	Mir
□	1 Valeri Karpov	.50
□	2 Igor Zemlyanol	.30
□	3 Mikhail Borodulin	.30
□	4 Vladimir Antipin	.30
□	5 Vadim Glovatskin	.30
□	6 Alexei Stepanov	.30
□	7 Sergei Gomolyako	.30
□	8 Andrei Sokolov	.30
□	9 Andrei Razin	.30
□	10 Dmitri Popov	.30
□	11 Valeri Nikulin	.30
□	12 Andrei Petrakov	.30
□	13 Evgeni Koreshkov	.30
□	14 Alexander Koreshkov	.30
□	15 Andrei Sapozhnikov	.30
□	16 Oleg Mikulchik	.50
□	17 Ravil Gusmanov	.50
□	18 Viltai Prokhov	.30
□	19 Boris Tortunov	.30
□	20 Sergei Zemchenok	.30
□	21 Sergei Tertyshny	.30
□	22 Yuri Kuznetsov	.50
□	23 Maxim Bets	.50
□	24 Sergei Osipov	.30
□	25 Oleg Leontiev	.30
□	26 Andrei Kudinov	.30
□	27 Konstantin Bezborodov	.30
□	28 Maxim Stepanov	.30
□	29 Alexei Lazarenko	.30
□	30 Vladimir Tyurikov	.30
□	31 Alexei Komarov	.30
□	32 Oleg Poikovinkov	.30
□	33 Dmitri Vershinin	.30
□	34 Vladimir Dumnov	.30
□	35 Oleg Smirnov	.30
□	36 Denis Ivanov	.30
□	37 Alexander Grishin	.30
□	38 Sergei Luchinkin	.30
□	39 Sergei Reshetnikov	.30
□	40 Denis Martinyuk	.30
□	41 Igor Boldin	.30
□	42 Nikolai Semin	.50
□	43 Alexander Zhdan	.30
□	44 Denis Metlyuk	.50
□	45 Sergei Zolotov	.30
□	46 Yuri Dobryshkin	.30
□	47 Sergei Mylnikov (G)	1.00
□	48 Anton Ulyanov	.30
□	49 Yakov Deev	.30
□	50 Dmitri Bykov	3.00
□	51 Dmitri Milnikov	.30
□	52 Rinat Kacyanov	.30
□	53 Dmitri Balmin	.30
□	54 Alexei Chupin	.30
□	55 Artem Anisimov	.30
□	56 Sergei Smirnov	.30
□	57 Ivan Andriyashev	.30

☐	58 Sergei Shilov	.30
☐	59 Vladislav Makarov	.30
☐	60 Dmitri & Sergei Mylnikov	1.00
☐	61 Rafik Yakubov	.30
☐	62 Dmitri Shandurov	.30
☐	63 Vladimir Pozdnyakov	.30
☐	64 Alexei Ivashkin	.30
☐	65 Valeri Ivannikov	.30
☐	66 Egor Mikhailov	.30
☐	67 Alexander Zibin	.30
☐	68 Igor Averchenkov	.30
☐	69 Alexei Sherblanov	.30
☐	70 Dmitri Yachanov	.30
☐	71 Oleg Romanov	.30
☐	72 Denis Arkhipov	3.00
☐	73 Almaz Garifullin	.30
☐	74 Evgeni Varlamov	.30
☐	75 Igor Stepanov	.30
☐	76 Alexander Zavyalov	.30
☐	77 Ilnur Gizatullin	.30
☐	78 Alexander Trofimov	.30
☐	79 Eduard Kudemetov	.30
☐	80 Remir Khaidarov	.30
☐	81 Nikolai Pronin	.30
☐	82 Andrei Glebov	.30
☐	83 Andrei Savchenko	.30
☐	84 Andrei Mukhachev	.30
☐	85 Maxim Osipov	.30
☐	86 Sergei Mozyakin	.30
☐	87 Alexei Gubarev	.30
☐	88 Oleg Filimonov	.30
☐	89 Igor Nikolaev	.30
☐	90 Eduard Polyakov	.30
☐	91 Konstantin Tatarintsev	.30
☐	92 Anatoli Ustyugov	.30
☐	93 Victor Dronov	.30
☐	94 Sergei Yasakov	.30
☐	95 Oleg Gorbenko	.30
☐	96 Igor Andryushenko	.30
☐	97 Alexei Plotinkov	.30
☐	98 Igor Bakhmutov	.30
☐	99 Dmitri Shandurov	.30
☐	100 Dmitri Bezrukov	.30
☐	101 Airat Kadeikin	.30
☐	102 Leonid Labzov	.30
☐	103 Alexei Vakhrushev	.30
☐	104 Denis Tsygurov	.50
☐	105 Roman Baranov	.30
☐	106 Vladimir Zorkin	.30
☐	107 Dmitri Maksimov	.30
☐	108 Dmitri Kulikov	.30
☐	109 Alexander Guskov	.30
☐	110 Dmitri Khomutov	.30
☐	111 Alexander Skugarev	.30
☐	112 Mikhail Pereyaslov	.30
☐	113 Artem Argokov	.30
☐	114 Alexei Strakhov	.30
☐	115 Dmitri Shulakov	.30
☐	116 Oleg Vevcherenko	.30
☐	117 Yuri Fimin	.30
☐	118 Ruslan Bernikov	.30
☐	119 Alexander Titov	.30
☐	120 Dmitri Gorenko	.30
☐	121 Alexander Filippov	.30
☐	122 Konstantin Mitroshkin	.30
☐	123 Alexander Zevakhin	.50
☐	124 Steve Pluff	.30
☐	125 Nikolai Tsulygin	.50
☐	126 Alexei Tertyshny	.30
☐	127 Nikolai Zavarykhin	.30
☐	128 Evgeni Zakharov	.30
☐	129 Sergei Klimentiev	.30
☐	130 Pavel Duma	.30
☐	131 Maxim Vasyuchkov	.30
☐	132 Rustem Amirov	.30
☐	133 Matvei Belousov	.30
☐	134 Alexander Schev	.30
☐	135 Evgeni Muratov	.30
☐	136 Andrei Buldakov	.30
☐	137 Andrei Tsarev	.30
☐	138 Vladimir Zavyakov	.30
☐	139 Andrei Pchelyakov	.30
☐	140 Igor Knyazev	.30
☐	141 Ilya Kovalchuk	100.00
☐	142 Alexei Chervyakov	.30
☐	143 Vladimir Kulikov	.30
☐	144 Andrei Bushan	.30
☐	145 Ravil Yakubov	.50
☐	146 Sergei Shitkovski	.30
☐	147 Sergei Berdnikov	.30
☐	148 Ramil Saifullin	.30
☐	149 Konstantin Golokhvastov	.30
☐	150 Konstantin Maslyukov	.30
☐	151 Alexei Bulatov	.30
☐	152 Dmitri Kirilenko	.30
☐	153 Sergei Makarov	.30
☐	154 Rustem Kamalatdinov	.30
☐	155 Maxim Mikhailovski (G)	.30
☐	156 Denis Khlopotnov (G)	.50
☐	157 Albert Loginov	.30
☐	158 Dmitri Nazarov	.30
☐	159 Alexei Miroshnikov	.30
☐	160 Sergei Zimakov	.50
☐	161 Valeri Belov	.30
☐	162 Alexei Kochegarov	.30
☐	163 Alexei Pogonin	.30
☐	164 Andrei Rasolko	.30
☐	165 Dmitri Denisov	.30
☐	166 Dmitri Tarasov	.30
☐	167 Vadim Pokotilo	.30
☐	168 Evgeni Fedorov	.30
☐	169 Maxim Sushinki	.30
☐	170 Alexander Popov	.30
☐	171 Dmitri Parkhomenko	.30
☐	172 Oleg Kryazhev	.30
☐	173 Vitali Lyutkevich	.30
☐	174 Dmitri Zatonski	.30
☐	175 Oleg Ugolnikov	.30
☐	176 Alexander Svitov	16.00
☐	177 Dmitri Ryabkin	.30
☐	178 Nikolai Babenko	.30
☐	179 Yuri Panov	.30
☐	180 Andrei Samokhvalov	.30
☐	181 Alexander Ermakov	.30
☐	182 Sergei Kagaikin	.30
☐	183 Anvar Gatiyatullin	.30
☐	184 Vladimir Tarasov	.30
☐	185 Igor Varitskin	.30
☐	186 Oleg Bolkov	.30
☐	187 Rail Muftiev	.30
☐	188 Vitali Yeremeyev (G)	1.00
☐	189 Vladislav Brizgalov	.30
☐	190 Dmitri Teplyakov	.30
☐	191 Vladimir Kopat	.30
☐	192 Denis Kuzmenko	.30
☐	193 Yevgeny Petrochinin	.30
☐	194 Sergei Arekaeb	.30
☐	195 Pavel Agarkov	.30
☐	196 Evgeni Pupkov	.30
☐	197 Vadim Tarasov (G)	3.00
☐	198 Andrei Smironov	.30
☐	199 Alexander Maksimov	.30
☐	200 Vitali Valui	.30
☐	201 Sergei Petrenko	.50
☐	202 Alexei Chistyakov	.30
☐	203 Alexei Murzin	.30
☐	204 Oleg Komissarov	.30
☐	205 Mikhail Buturlin	.30
☐	206 Konstantin Frolov	.30
☐	207 Igor Zelenchev	.30
☐	208 Oleg Shargorodski	.30
☐	209 Sergei Selyutin	.30
☐	210 Alexei Kupreenkov	.30
☐	211 Roman Kukhtinov	.30
☐	212 Vladislav Morozov	.30
☐	213 Igor Belyavski	.30
☐	214 Sergei Moskalev	.30
☐	215 Alexei Tkachuk	.30
☐	216 Sergei Chernyavski	.30
☐	217 Vitali Kabanov	.30
☐	218 Dmitri Klevakin	.50
☐	219 Alexei Koledaeev	.30
☐	220 Oleg Glebov	.30
☐	221 Georgi Evtyukhin	.30
☐	222 Alexei Koznev	.30
☐	223 Alexei Rubov	.30
☐	224 Sergei Zinoviev	.30
☐	225 Yevgeny Petrochinin	.30
☐	226 Valeri Pokrovski	.30
☐	227 Sergei Fedotov	.50
☐	228 Vyacheslav Kurochkin	.30
☐	229 Oleg Boltunov	.30
☐	230 Alexei Baranov	.30
☐	231 Igor Emeleev	.30
☐	232 Roman Kribomazov	.30
☐	233 Sergei Tikhonov	.30
☐	234 Vladislav Brizgalov	.30
☐	235 Dmitri Dubrovski	.30
☐	236 Stepan Mokhov	.30
☐	237 Dmitri Gogolev	.30
☐	238 Evgeni Filinov	.30
☐	239 Alexander Yudin	.50
☐	240 Alexander Drozdetskin	.30
☐	241 Sergei Shalamai	.30
☐	242 Timofei Shishkanov	.30
☐	243 Alexander Sivov	.30
☐	244 Vadim Musatov	.30
☐	245 Andrei Chernoskutov	.30
☐	246 Ruslan Shafikov	.30
☐	247 Maxim Sokolov	.30
☐	248 Alexander Matvichuk	.30
☐	249 Andrei Evstafiev	.30
☐	250 Vyacheslav Zavalnyuk	.30
☐	251 Andrei Korolev	.30
☐	252 Alexander Yudin	.50
☐	253 Dmitri Mikhailov	.30
☐	254 Artem Ostroushko	.30
☐	255 Rinat Khasanov	.30
☐	256 Vadim Epanchintsev	.30
☐	257 Pavel Komarov	.30
☐	258 Alexander Vyukhin	.30
☐	259 Alfred Fatkullin	.30
☐	260 Danis Zaripov	.30
☐	261 Andrei Zubkov	.30
☐	262 Marat Askarov	.30
☐	263 Alexei Myagkikh	.30
☐	264 Alexander Yudin	.50
☐	265 Eduard Dmitriev	.30
☐	266 Oleg Salitkov	.30
☐	267 Oleg Grachev	.30
☐	268 Valeri Oleinik	.30
☐	269 Konstantin Koltsov	.30
☐	270 Andrei Raiski	.30

1999 - 2000 NHC

We do not have a full checklist for this Danish set.

1999 - 2000 NHL-NHLPA / 2T0R0NT0 FANTASY

	Player / Series	MT
☐	1 Darryl Sittler, Toro. [Pacific Prism]	3.00
☐	2 Darryl Sittler, Toro. [Topps]	4.00
☐	3 Darryl Sittler, Toro. [Upper Deck]	3.00

1999 - 2000 NHL-NHLPA / POWER PLAY

These cards were included as magazine inserts distributed exclusively at games around the NHL.

	Player / Series	MT
☐	1 Matt Cullen, Anah. [Pacific Paramount]	1.00
☐	451 Ladislav Kohn, Anah. [Pacific]	1.00
☐	AM1 Ladislav Kohn, Anah. [Upper Deck]	1.00
☐	AM2 Mike Leclerc, Anah. [Upper Deck]	1.00
☐	ANA-LK Ladislav Kohn, Anah. [Topps]	1.00
☐	ANA-OT Oleg Tverdovsky, Anah. [Topps]	1.00
☐	251 Patrik Stefan, Atla. [Pacific Paramount]	1.50
☐	452 Petr Buzek, Atla. [Pacific]	1.00
☐	AT1 Patrik Stefan, Atla. [Upper Deck]	1.50
☐	AT2 Shean Donovan, Atla. [Upper Deck]	1.00
☐	ATL-MJ Matt Johnson, Atla. [Topps]	1.00
☐	ATL-PS Patrik Stefan, Atla. [Topps]	1.50
☐	27 Kyle McLaren, Bost. [Pacific]	1.00
☐	252 Jonathan Girard, Bost. [Pacific Paramount]	1.00
☐	BB1 Jonathan Girard, Bost. [Upper Deck]	1.00
☐	BB2 Sergei Samsonov, Bost. [Upper Deck]	3.00
☐	BOS-JG Jonathan Girard, Bost. [Topps]	1.00
☐	BOS-JT Joe Thornton, Bost. [Topps]	6.00
☐	42 Erik Rasmussen, Buff. [Pacific]	1.00
☐	253 Maxim Afinogenov, Buff. [Pacific Paramount]	2.00
☐	BS1 Maxim Afinogenov, Buff. [Upper Deck]	2.00
☐	BS2 Cory Sarich, Buff. [Upper Deck]	1.00
☐	BUF-MA Maxim Afinogenov, Buff. [Topps]	2.00
☐	BUF-MB Martin Biron (G), Buff. [Topps]	2.00
☐	40 Jarome Iginla, Calg. [Pacific Paramount]	4.00
☐	453 Robyn Regehr, Calg. [Pacific]	1.00
☐	CAL-DG Denis Gauthier, Calg. [Topps]	1.00
☐	CAL-RR Robyn Regehr, Calg. [Topps]	1.00
☐	CF1 Robyn Regehr, Calg. [Upper Deck]	1.00
☐	CF2 Derek Morris, Calg. [Upper Deck]	1.00
☐	254 Byron Ritchie, Caro. [Pacific Paramount]	1.00
☐	454 David Tanabe, Caro. [Pacific]	1.00
☐	CAR-BB Bates Battaglia, Caro. [Topps]	1.00
☐	CAR-DT David Tanabe, Caro. [Topps]	1.00
☐	CH1 David Tanabe, Caro. [Upper Deck]	1.00
☐	CH2 Jeff O'Neill, Caro. [Upper Deck]	2.00
☐	58 Jocelyn Thibault (G), Chic. [Pacific Paramount]	2.00
☐	86 Jean-Pierre Dumont, Chic. [Pacific]	1.00
☐	CB1 Jean-Pierre Dumont, Chic. [Upper Deck]	1.00
☐	CB2 Bryan McCabe, Chic. [Upper Deck]	1.00
☐	CHI-ED Éric Dazé, Chic. [Topps]	2.00
☐	CHI-JP Jean-Pierre Dumont, Chic. [Topps]	1.00
☐	106 Milan Hejduk, Colo. [Pacific]	4.00
☐	255 Alex Tanguay, Colo. [Pacific Paramount]	3.00
☐	CA1 Alex Tanguay, Colo. [Upper Deck]	3.00
☐	CA2 Chris Drury, Colo. [Upper Deck]	3.00
☐	COL-AT Alex Tanguay, Colo. [Topps]	3.00
☐	COL-MD Marc Denis (G), Colo. [Topps]	2.00
☐	124 Brad Lukowich, Dall. [Pacific]	1.00
☐	256 Brenden Morrow, Dall. [Pacific Paramount]	1.50
☐	DAL-BM Brenden Morrow, Dall. [Topps]	1.50
☐	DAL-JS Jonathan Sim, Dall. [Topps]	1.00
☐	DS1 Brenden Morrow, Dall. [Upper Deck]	1.50
☐	DS2 Jamie Langenbrunner, Dall. [Upper Deck]	1.00
☐	257 Yuri Butsayev, Detr. [Pacific Paramount]	1.00
☐	455 Jiri Fischer, Detr. [Pacific]	1.00
☐	DET-JF Jiri Fischer, Detr. [Topps]	1.00
☐	DET-MD Mathieu Dandenault, Detr. [Topps]	1.00
☐	DR1 Jiri Fischer, Detr. [Upper Deck]	1.00
☐	DR2 Darryl Laplante, Detr. [Upper Deck]	1.00
☐	94 Tom Poti, Edmo. [Pacific Paramount]	1.00
☐	456 Paul Comrie, Edmo. [Pacific]	1.00
☐	EDM-GL Georges Laraque, Edmo. [Topps]	1.00
☐	EDM-PC Paul Comrie, Edmo. [Topps]	1.00
☐	EO1 Paul Comrie, Edmo. [Upper Deck]	1.00
☐	EO2 Boyd Devereaux, Edmo. [Upper Deck]	1.00
☐	184 Peter Worrell, Flor. [Pacific]	1.00
☐	258 Ivan Novoseltsev, Flor. [Pacific Paramount]	1.00
☐	FLO-IN Ivan Novoseltsev, Flor. [Topps]	1.00
☐	FLO-OK Oleg Kvasha, Flor. [Topps]	1.00
☐	FP1 Ivan Novoseltsev, Flor. [Upper Deck]	1.00
☐	FP2 Mark Parrish, Flor. [Upper Deck]	2.00
☐	259 Frantisek* Kaberle, LosA. [Pacific Paramount]	1.00
☐	457 Brad Chartrand, LosA. [Pacific]	1.00
☐	LA-FK Frantisek* Kaberle, LosA. [Topps]	1.00
☐	LA-JS Jamie Storr (G), LosA. [Topps]	1.00
☐	LK1 Frantisek* Kaberle, LosA. [Upper Deck]	1.00
☐	LK2 Aki Berg, LosA. [Upper Deck]	1.00
☐	229 David Legwand, Nash. [Pacific]	2.00
☐	260 Richard Lintner, Nash. [Pacific Paramount]	1.00
☐	NAS-DL David Legwand, Nash. [Topps]	2.00
☐	NAS-TV Tomas Vokoun (G), Nash. [Topps]	1.00
☐	NP1 David Legwand, Nash. [Upper Deck]	2.00
☐	NP2 Randy Robitaille, Nash. [Upper Deck]	1.00
☐	139 Petr* Sykora, NJer. [Pacific Paramount]	2.00
☐	458 Scott Gomez, NJer. [Pacific]	2.00
☐	ND1 Scott Gomez, NJer. [Upper Deck]	2.00
☐	ND2 Sheldon Souray, NJer. [Upper Deck]	1.00
☐	NJ-PE Patrik Elias, NJer. [Topps]	4.00
☐	NJ-SG Scott Gomez, NJer. [Topps]	2.00
☐	261 Tim Connolly, NYIs. [Pacific Paramount]	2.00
☐	459 Roberto Luongo (G), NYIs. [Pacific]	4.00
☐	NI1 Roberto Luongo (G), NYIs. [Upper Deck]	4.00
☐	NI2 Tim Connolly, NYIs. [Upper Deck]	2.00
☐	NYI-OJ Olli Jokinen, NYIs. [Topps]	1.50
☐	NYI-RL Roberto Luongo (G), NYIs. [Topps]	4.00
☐	263 Jason Doig, NYRa. [Pacific Paramount]	1.00
☐	460 Mike York, NYRa. [Pacific]	1.50
☐	NR1 Mike York, NYRa. [Upper Deck]	1.50
☐	NR2 Manny Malhotra, NYRa. [Upper Deck]	1.00
☐	NYR-KJ Kim Johnsson, NYRa. [Topps]	1.00
☐	NYR-MY Mike York, NYRa. [Topps]	1.50
☐	264 Mike Fisher, Otta. [Pacific Paramount]	1.00
☐	293 Wade Redden, Otta. [Pacific]	1.50
☐	OS1 Mike Fisher, Otta. [Upper Deck]	1.00
☐	OS2 Chris Phillips, Otta. [Upper Deck]	1.00
☐	OTT-MF Mike Fisher, Otta. [Topps]	1.00
☐	OTT-MH Marian Hossa, Otta. [Topps]	5.00
☐	266 Stanislav Neckar, Phoe. [Pacific Paramount]	1.00
☐	462 Trevor Letowski, Phoe. [Pacific]	1.00
☐	PC1 Trevor Letowski, Phoe. [Upper Deck]	1.00
☐	PC2 Shane Doan, Phoe. [Upper Deck]	1.00
☐	PHO-RS Radoslav Suchy, Phoe. [Topps]	1.00
☐	PHO-TL Trevor Letowski, Phoe. [Topps]	1.00
☐	267 Andrew Ference, Pitt. [Pacific Paramount]	1.00
☐	344 Aleksey Morozov, Pitt. [Pacific]	1.00
☐	PIT-AF Andrew Ference, Pitt. [Topps]	1.00
☐	PIT-JH Jan Hrdina, Pitt. [Topps]	1.00
☐	PP1 Andrew Ference, Pitt. [Upper Deck]	1.00
☐	PP2 Michal Rozsival, Pitt. [Upper Deck]	1.00
☐	206 Patrick Marleau, SanJ. [Pacific Paramount]	2.00
☐	463 Brad Stuart, SanJ. [Pacific]	2.00
☐	SJ-BS Brad Stuart, SanJ. [Topps]	2.00
☐	SJ-MS Marco Sturm, SanJ. [Topps]	1.00
☐	SS1 Brad Stuart, SanJ. [Upper Deck]	2.00
☐	SS2 Jeff Friesen, SanJ. [Upper Deck]	1.50
☐	197 Jochen Hecht, SLou. [Pacific Paramount]	1.00
☐	352 Lubos Bartecko, SLou. [Pacific]	1.00
☐	SB1 Jochen Hecht, SLou. [Upper Deck]	1.00
☐	SB2 Michal Handzus, SLou. [Upper Deck]	1.00
☐	STL-JH Jochen Hecht, SLou. [Topps]	1.00
☐	STL-TN Tyson Nash, SLou. [Topps]	1.00
☐	268 Paul Mara, Tamp. [Pacific Paramount]	1.00
☐	464 Ben Clymer, Tamp. [Pacific]	1.00
☐	TB-PM Paul Mara, Tamp. [Topps]	1.00

□	TB-VL Vincent Lecavalier, Tamp. [Topps]	5.00
□	TL1 Paul Mara, Tamp. [Upper Deck]	1.00
□	TL2 Andrei Zyuzin, Tamp. [Upper Deck]	1.00
□	221 Bryan Berard, Toro. [Pacific Paramount]	1.50
□	465 Nikolai Antropov, Toro. [Pacific]	1.00
□	TM1 Nikolai Antropov, Toro. [Upper Deck]	1.00
□	TM2 Danny Markov, Toro. [Upper Deck]	1.00
□	TOR-NA Nikolai Antropov, Toro. [Topps]	1.00
□	TOR-TK Tomas Kaberle, Toro. [Topps]	1.50
□	269 Steve Kariya, Vanc. [Pacific Paramount]	1.00
□	430 Mattias Öhlund, Vanc. [Pacific]	1.50
□	VAN-EJ Ed Jovanovski, Vanc. [Topps]	2.00
□	VAN-SK Steve Kariya, Vanc. [Topps]	1.00
□	VC1 Steve Kariya, Vanc. [Upper Deck]	1.00
□	VC2 Peter Schaefer, Vanc. [Upper Deck]	1.00
□	243 Jan Bulis, Wash. [Pacific Paramount]	1.00
□	466 Jeff Halpern, Wash. [Pacific]	1.00
□	WAS-JH Jeff Halpern, Wash. [Topps]	1.00
□	WAS-RZ Richard Zednik, Wash. [Topps]	2.00
□	WC1 Jeff Halpern, Wash. [Upper Deck]	1.00
□	WC2 Alexei Tezikov, Wash. [Upper Deck]	1.00
□	Header	.20

1999 - 2000 OFS

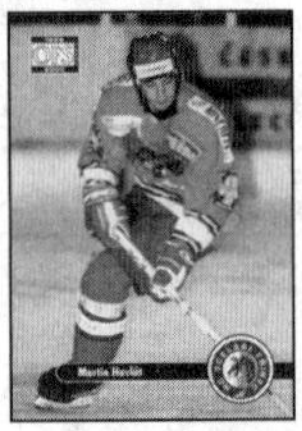

The following cards have two versions: cards 1-15 (Goalies) have a Die-Cut parallel, cards 16-40 (Jagr Team) have an Embossed parallel and cards 487-530 (All-Star Game) have an Embossed parallel. Cards of NHL stars and prospects do sell at a premium (usually $1-$2 for the regular cards).

Complete Set (552 cards): **140.00**
Common Player: **.30**

	Player	OFS
□ □	1 Libor Barta, Brankari	.30
□ □	2 Martin Bilek, Brankari	.30
□ □	3 Ladislav Blazek, Brankari	.30
□ □	4 Petr Briza, Brankari	.30
□ □	5 Ivo Capek, Brankari	.30
□ □	6 Roman Cechmanek, Brankari	2.00
□ □	7 Robert Horyna, Brankari	.30
□ □	8 Vladimir Hudacek (G), Brankari	.30
□ □	9 Ladislav Kudrna, Brankari	.30
□ □	10 Vlastimil Lakosil, Brankari	.30
□ □	11 Michal Marik, Brankari	.30
□ □	12 Zdenek Orct, Brankari	.30
□ □	13 Rudolf Pejchar, Brankari	.30
□ □	14 Martin Prusek, Brankari	1.00
□ □	15 Dusan Salficky, Brankaci	.30
□ □	16 Richard Farda, Jagr Team	.30
□ □	17 Marian Jelinek, Jagr Team	.30
□ □	18 Josef Beranek, Jagr Team	.30
□ □	19 Leo Gudas, Jagr Team	.30
□ □	20 Milan Hnilicka (G), Jagr Team	1.00
□ □	21 Milos Holan, Jagr Team	.30
□ □	22 Jan Hrdina, Jagr Team	1.00
□ □	23 Jaromir Jagr, Jagr Team	5.00
□ □	24 Frantisek* Kaberle, Jagr Team	1.00
□ □	25 Tomas Kaberle, Jagr Team	1.00
□ □	26 Pavel Kubina, Jagr Team	.30
□ □	27 Marek Malik, Jagr Team	.30
□ □	28 Pavel Patera, Jagr Team	.30
□ □	29 Martin Prochazka, Jagr Team	.30
□ □	30 Vaclav Prospal, Jagr Team	1.00
□ □	31 Robert Reichel, Jagr Team	1.00
□ □	32 Martin Rucinsky, Jagr Team	1.00
□ □	33 Vladimir Ruzicka, Jagr Team	1.00
□ □	34 Pavel Skrbek, Jagr Team	.30
□ □	35 Jiri Slégr, Jagr Team	.30
□ □	36 Jaroslav Spacek, Jagr Team	.30
□ □	37 Martin Straka, Jagr Team	1.00
□ □	38 Vaclav Varada, Jagr Team	.30
□ □	39 David Volek, Jagr Team	.30
□ □	40 Jan Vopat, Jagr Team	.30
□	41 Vladimir Caldr, Slavia Praha	.30
□	42 Martin Bakula, Slavia Praha	.30
□	43 Miroslav Hajek, Slavia Praha	.30
□	44 Petr Hrbek, Slavia Praha	.30
□	45 Petr Kadlec, Slavia Praha	.30
□	46 Jan Kopecky, Slavia Praha	.30
□	47 Jan Krajicek, Slavia Praha	.30
□	48 Angel Krstev, Slavia Praha	.30
□	49 Radek Matejovsky, Slavia Praha	.30
□	50 Jan Novak, Slavia Praha	.30
□	51 Vladimir Pojkar, Slavia Praha	.30
□	52 Vladimir Ruzicka, Slavia Praha	1.00
□	53 Jan Slavik, Slavia Praha	.30
□	54 Jan Sochor, Slavia Praha	.30
□	55 Michal Sup, Slavia Praha	.30
□	56 Zdislav Tabara, Dadak Vsetin	.30
□	57 Jiri Dopita, Dadak Vsetin	.30
□	58 Ondrej Kavulic, Dadak Vsetin	.30
□	59 Petr Kubos, Dadak Vsetin	.30
□	60 Radim Kucharczyk, Dadak Vsetin	.30
□	61 Marko Palo, Dadak Vsetin	.30
□	62 Jukka Seppo, Dadak Vsetin	.30
□	63 Lukas Slaby, Dadak Vsetin	.30
□	64 Roman Stantien, Dadak Vsetin	.30
□	65 Petr Suchy, Dadak Vsetin	.30
□	66 Radim Tesarik, Dadak Vsetin	.30
□	67 Jan Tomajko, Dadak Vsetin	.30
□	68 Martin Vozdecky, Dadak Vsetin	.30
□	69 Petr Zajgla, Dadak Vsetin	.30
□	70 Pavel Zubicek, Dadak Vsetin	.30
□	71 Pavel Pazourek, Znojmo	.30
□	72 Petr Belohlavek, Znojmo	.30
□	73 Radim Freibauer, Znojmo	.30
□	74 Radek Haman, Znojmo	.30
□	75 David Havir, Znojmo	.30
□	76 Jiri Hes, Znojmo	.30
□	77 Jiri Hradecky, Znojmo	.30
□	78 Jan Kloboucek, Znojmo	.30
□	79 David Pazourek, Znojmo	.30
□	80 David Petlak, Znojmo	.30
□	81 Karel Plasek, Znojmo	.30
□	82 Jiri Poukar, Znojmo	.30
□	83 Milan Prochazka, Znojmo	.30
□	84 Peter Pucher, Znojmo	.30
□	85 Marek Vorel, Znojmo	.30
□	86 Pavel Marek, Pardubice	.30
□	87 Martin Barek, Pardubice	.30
□	88 Tomas Blazek, Pardubice	.30
□	89 Jan Dusanek, Pardubice	.30
□	90 Patrik Elias, Pardubice	4.00
□	91 Petr Jancarik, Pardubice	.30
□	92 Jaroslav Kudrna, Pardubice	.30
□	93 Tomas Martinec, Pardubice	.30
□	94 Brendan Morrison, Pardubice	1.00
□	95 Andrej Novotny, Pardubice	.30
□	96 Tomas Pacal, Pardubice	.30
□	97 Rastislav Pal'ov, Pardubice	.30
□	98 Patrik Rozsival, Pardubice	.30
□	99 Michal Tvrdik, Pardubice	.30
□	100 Tomas Vak, Pardubice	.30
□	101 Pavel Richter, Sparta Praha	.30
□	102 Michal Bros, Sparta Praha	.30
□	103 Vaclav Eiselt, Sparta Praha	.30
□	104 Petr Havelka, Sparta Praha	.30
□	105 Martin Holy, Sparta Praha	.30
□	106 Pavel Kasparik, Sparta Praha	.30
□	107 Ondrej Kratena, Sparta Praha	.30
□	108 Frantisek Kucera, Sparta Praha	.30
□	109 Jaroslav Nedved, Sparta Praha	.30
□	110 Frantisek Ptacek, Sparta Praha	.30
□	111 Miha Rebolj, Sparta Praha	.30
□	112 Pavel Srek, Sparta Praha	.30
□	113 David Vyborny, Sparta Praha	.30
□	114 Jiri Zelenka, Sparta Praha	.30
□	115 Richard Zemlicka, Sparta Praha	.30
□	116 Marek Sykora, Interconex Plzen	.30
□	117 Milan Antos, Interconex Plzen	.30
□	118 Martin Cech, Interconex Plzen	.30
□	119 Marek Cernosek, Interconex Plzen	.30
□	120 Petr Chvojka, Interconex Plzen	.30
□	121 Pavel Geffert, Interconex Plzen	.30
□	122 Jiri Hanzlik, Interconex Plzen	.30
□	123 Jiri Jelen, Interconex Plzen	.30
□	124 Michal Jeslinek, Interconex Plzen	.30
□	125 Petr Korinek, Interconex Plzen	.30
□	126 Josef Reznicek, Interconex Plzen	.30
□	127 Radek Svoboda, Interconex Plzen	.30
□	128 Petr Úlehla, Interconex Plzen	.30
□	129 Ivan Vlcek, Interconex Plzen	.30
□	130 Pavel Vostrak, Interconex Plzen	.30
□	131 Martin Pesout, Karlovy Vary	.30
□	132 Michal Dobron, Karlovy Vary	.30
□	133 Martin Filip, Karlovy Vary	.30
□	134 Pavel Janku, Karlovy Vary	.30
□	135 Jaroslav Kalla, Karlovy Vary	.30
□	136 Jan Kostal, Karlovy Vary	.30
□	137 Jaromir Kverka, Karlovy Vary	.30
□	138 Petr Macek, Karlovy Vary	.30
□	139 Martin Maskarinec, Karlovy Vary	.30
□	140 Petr Pavlas, Karlovy Vary	.30
□	141 Josef Podlaha, Karlovy Vary	.30
□	142 Michal Porak, Karlovy Vary	.30
□	143 Martin Richter, Karlovy Vary	.30
□	144 Jan Snopek, Karlovy Vary	.30
□	145 Martin Streit, Litvinov	.30
□	146 Vaclav Sykora, Litvinov	.30
□	147 David Balazs, Litvinov	.30
□	148 Viktor Hubl, Litvinov	.30
□	149 Petr Kratky, Litvinov	.30
□	150 Vojtech Kubincak, Litvinov	.30
□	151 Robert Kysela, Litvinov	.30
□	152 Marian Menhart, Litvinov	.30
□	153 Radek Mrazek, Litvinov	.30
□	154 Angel Nikolov, Litvinov	.30
□	155 Karel Pilar, Litvinov	.30
□	156 Ivo Prorok, Litvinov	.30
□	157 Robert Reichel, Litvinov	.30
□	158 Zdenek Skorepa, Litvinov	.30
□	159 Josef Straka, Litvinov	.30
□	160 Martin Strbak, Litvinov	.30
□	161 Otakar Vejvoda, Kladno	.30
□	162 Jan Dlouhy, Kladno	.30
□	163 Zdenek Eichenmann, Kladno	.30
□	164 Jiri Holsan, Kladno	.30
□	165 Tomas Horna, Kladno	.30
□	166 Ondrej Kriz, Kladno	.30
□	167 Jiri Krocak, Kladno	.30
□	168 Tomas Kupka, Kladno	.30
□	169 Michal Madl, Kladno	.30
□	170 Milan Novy, Kladno	.30
□	171 Tomas Polansky, Kladno	.30
□	172 Lukas Poznik, Kladno	.30
□	173 Ladislav Svoboda, Kladno	.30
□	174 Tomas Ullrych, Kladno	.30
□	175 Martin Vejvoda, Kladno	.30
□	176 Jaroslav Liska, Ceske Budejovice	.30
□	177 Kamil Brabenec, Ceske Budejovice	.30
□	178 Roman Cech, Ceske Budejovice	.30
□	179 Milan Filipi, Ceske Budejovice	.30
□	180 Stanislav Jasecko, Ceske Budejovice	.30
□	181 Josef Jindra, Ceske Budejovice	.30
□	182 Michal Klimes, Ceske Budejovice	.30
□	183 Zdenek Kutlak, Ceske Budejovice	.30
□	184 Milan Nedoma, Ceske Budejovice	.30
□	185 David Nedorost, Ceske Budejovice	.30
□	186 Lubos Rob, Ceske Budejovice	.30
□	187 Petr Sailer, Ceske Budejovice	.30
□	188 Jiri Simanek, Ceske Budejovice	.30
□	189 Rudolf Suchanek, Ceske Budejovice	.30
□	190 Radek Toupal, Ceske Budejovice	.30
□	191 Alois Hadamczik, Trinec	.30
□	192 Mario Cartelli, Trinec	.30
□	193 Petr Gregorek, Trinec	.30
□	194 Martin Havlat, Trinec	15.00
□	195 Branislav Janos, Trinec	.30
□	196 Roman Kadera, Trinec	.30
□	197 Richard Kral, Trinec	.30
□	198 Jiri Kuntos, Trinec	.30
□	199 David Nosek, Trinec	.30
□	200 Vaclav Pletka, Trinec	.30
□	201 Pavel Selingr, Trinec	.30
□	202 Petr** Svoboda, Trinec	.30
□	203 Viktor Ujcik, Trinec	.30
□	204 Marek Zadina, Trinec	.30
□	205 Jiri Zurek, Trinec	.30
□	206 Antonin Stavjana, ZPS Zlin	.30
□	207 Jaroslav Balastik, ZPS Zlin	.30
□	208 Roman Hamrlik, ZPS Zlin	1.00
□	209 Lubomir Korhon, ZPS Zlin	.30
□	210 Martin Kotasek, ZPS Zlin	.30
□	211 Petr Leska, ZPS Zlin	.30
□	212 Patrik Luza, ZPS Zlin	.30
□	213 Jiri Marusak, ZPS Zlin	.30
□	214 Pavel Mojzis, ZPS Zlin	.30
□	215 Milan Navratil, ZPS Zlin	.30
□	216 Miroslav Okal, ZPS Zlin	.30
□	217 Michal Tomek, ZPS Zlin	.30
□	218 Petr Vala, ZPS Zlin	.30
□	219 Pavol Valko, ZPS Zlin	.30
□	220 Tomas Zizka, ZPS Zlin	.30
□	221 Vladimir (Sr.) Vujtek, Vitkovice	.30
□	222 Lukas Galvas, Vitkovice	.30
□	223 Dmitrij Gogolev, Vitkovice	.30
□	224 Zbynek Irgl, Vitkovice	.30
□	225 Dmitri Jerofejev, Vitkovice	.30
□	226 Petr Jurecka, Vitkovice	.30
□	227 Ludek Krayzel, Vitkovice	.30
□	228 Daniel Kysela, Vitkovice	.30
□	229 Zdenek Pavelek, Vitkovice	.30
□	230 Sergei Petrenko, Vitkovice	.30
□	231 Daniel Seman, Vitkovice	.30
□	232 Lukas Smolka, Vitkovice	.30
□	233 Vaclav Varada, Vitkovice	.30
□	234 Jan Vytisk, Vitkovice	.30
□	235 Lukas Zatopek, Vitkovice	.30
□	236 Richard Farda, Havirov	.30
□	237 Michal Cech, Havirov	.30
□	238 Vladimir Holik, Havirov	.30
□	239 Andrei Jakovenko, Havirov	.30
□	240 Marek Melenovsky, Havirov	.30
□	241 Martin Miklik, Havirov	.30
□	242 Pavel Nohel, Havirov	.30
□	243 Libor Pivko, Havirov	.30
□	244 Bogdan Savenko, Havinov	.30
□	245 Petr Suchanek, Havirov	.30
□	246 Kamil Suchanek, Havirov	.30
□	247 Petr Tejkl, Havirov	.30
□	248 Petr Vlasanek, Havirov	.30
□	249 Michael Vyhlidal, Havirov	.30
□	250 Tomas Zapletal, Havicov	.30
□	251 Josef Augusta, Czech Republic Nationals	.30
□	252 Ivan Hlinka, Czech Republic Nationals	1.00
□	253 Vladimir Martinec, Czech Republic Nationals	.30
□	254 Roman Cechmanek (G, Czech Republic	2.00
□	255 Martin Prusek, Czech Republic Nationals	4.00
□	256 Radek Belohlav, Czech Republic Nationals	.30
□	257 Ladislav Benysek, Czech Republic Nationals	.30
□	258 Petr Cajanek, Czech Republic Nationals	.30
□	259 Jan Caloun, Czech Republic Nationals	.30
□	260 Jiri Dopita, Czech Republic Nationals	.30
□	261 Vaclav Kral, Czech Republic Nationals	.30
□	262 Frantisek Kucera, Czech Republic Nationals	.30
□	263 Tomas Kucharcik, Czech Republic Nationals	.30
□	264 Radek Martinek, Czech Republic Nationals	.30
□	265 Ales Pisa, Czech Republic Nationals	.30
□	266 Robert Reichel, Czech Republic Nationals	1.00
□	267 Martin Richter, Czech Republic Nationals	.30
□	268 Roman Simicek, Czech Republic Nationals	.30
□	269 Jan Srdinko, Czech Republic Nationals	.30
□	270 Martin Stepanek, Czech Republic Nationals	.30
□	271 Petr Tenkrat, Czech Republic Nationals	.30
□	272 Jan Tomajko, Czech Republic Nationals	.30
□	273 Viktor Ujcik, Czech Republic Nationals	.30
□	274 Tomas Vlasak, Czech Republic Nationals	.30
□	275 David Vyborny, Czech Republic Nationals	.30
□	276 Jiri Vykoukal, Czech Republic Nationals	.30
□	277 Jaroslav Parizek, Ceske Budejovice	.30
□	278 Peter Bartos, Ceske Budejovice	.30
□	279 Jiri Broz, Ceske Budejovice	.30
□	280 Ales Kotalik, Ceske Budejovice	2.00
□	281 Lukas Zib, Ceske Budejovice	.30
□	282 Vaclav Kral, Ceske Budejovice	.30
□	283 Radek Martinek, Ceske Budejovice	.30
□	284 Vaclav Nedorost, Ceske Budejovice	6.00
□	285 Martin Strba, Ceske Budejovice	.30
□	286 Filip Turek, Ceske Budejovice	.30
□	287 Ivo Pestuka, Havirov	.30
□	288 Jaroslav Hub, Havirov	.30
□	289 Miroslav Javin, Havirov	.30
□	290 Roman Kontsek, Havirov	.30
□	291 Rostislav Pilavka, Havirov	.30
□	292 Ivan Puncochar, Havirov	.30
□	293 Roman Rysanek, Havirov	.30
□	294 Petr Sikora, Havirov	.30
□	295 Ales Tomasek, Havirov	.30
□	296 Daniel Vilasek, Havirov	.30
□	297 David Kriz, Havirov	.30
□	298 Michal Mikeska, Havirov	.30
□	299 Pavol Pekarik, Havirov	.30
□	300 Jan Peterek, Havirov	.30
□	301 Radek Philipp, Havirov	.30
□	302 Pavel Zdrahal, Havirov	.30
□	303 Ales Zima, Havirov	.30
□	304 Filip Stefanka, Havirov	.30
□	305 Tomas Sykora, Havirov	.30
□	306 Marcel Hanzal, Havirov	.30
□	307 Roman Horak, Havirov	.30
□	308 Milos Riha, Karlovy Vary	.30
□	309 Ladislav Prokupek, Karlovy Vary	.30
□	310 Roman Prosek, Karlovy Vary	.30
□	311 Martin Rousek, Karlovy Vary	.30
□	312 Miroslav Barus, Karlovy Vary	.30
□	313 Michal Divisek, Karlovy Vary	.30
□	314 David Hruska, Karlovy Vary	.30
□	315 Pavel Metlicka, Karlovy Vary	.30
□	316 Radek Prochazka, Karlovy Vary	.30
□	317 Tomas Martinec, Karlovy Vary	.30
□	318 Zdenek Pavelek, Karlovy Vary	.30
□	319 Jiri Polak, Karlovy Vary	.30
□	320 Tomas Chlubna, Karlovy Vary	.30
□	321 Jiri Malinsky, Karlovy Vary	.30
□	322 Petr Fiala, Karlovy Vary	.30
□	323 Eduard Novak, Kladno	.30
□	324 Lubomir Bauer, Kladno	.30
□	325 Petr Bohunicky, Kladno	.30
□	326 Jiri Burger, Kladno	.30
□	327 Jiri Hubacek, Kladno	.30
□	328 Jiri Kames, Kladno	.30
□	329 Michal Kanka, Kladno	.30
□	330 Petr Kounovsky, Kladno	.30
□	331 Jan Krulis, Kladno	.30
□	332 Radim Skuhrovec, Kladno	.30
□	333 Martin Taborsky, Kladno	.30
□	334 Ladislav Vlcek, Kladno	.30
□	335 Radek Gardon, Kladno	.30
□	336 Vladimir Jerabek, Litvinov	.30
□	337 Jan Alinc, Litvinov	.30
□	338 Vladimir Gyna, Litvinov	.30
□	339 Jindrich Kotrla, Litvinov	.30
□	340 Mikhail Travnicek, Litvinov	.30
□	341 Lukas Bednarik, Litvinov	.30

	Player	Price
☐	342 Daniel Branda, Litvinov	.30
☐	343 Marek Cernosek, Litvinov	.30
☐	344 Jan Liska, Litvinov	.30
☐	345 Marek Piros, Litvinov	.30
☐	346 Petr Rosol, Litvinov	.30
☐	347 Josef Palecek, Pardubice	.30
☐	348 Petr Hemsky, Pardubice	.30
☐	349 Milan Chalupa, Pardubice	.30
☐	350 Ales Hemsky, Pardubice	6.00
☐	351 Jiri Jantovsky, Pardubice	.30
☐	352 Robert Kantor, Pardubice	.30
☐	353 Ladislav Lubina, Pardubice	.30
☐	354 Jiri Malinsky, Pardubice	.30
☐	355 Miroslav Mosnar, Pardubice	.30
☐	356 Ales Pisa, Pardubice	.30
☐	357 Stanislav Prochazka, Pardubice	.30
☐	358 Petr Sykora, Pardubice	.30
☐	359 Jan Archalous, Pardubice	.30
☐	360 Martin Filip, Pardubice	.30
☐	361 Pavel Kabrt, Pardubice	.30
☐	362 Jan Kolar, Pardubice	.30
☐	363 Martin Koudelka, Pardubice	.30
☐	364 Radek Matejovsky, Pardubice	.30
☐	365 Michal Mikeska, Pardubice	.30
☐	366 Petr Mudroch, Pardubice	.30
☐	367 Petr Caslava, Pardubice	.30
☐	368 Radim Rulik, Plzen	.30
☐	369 Jiri Dobrovolny, Plzen	.30
☐	370 Mojmir Musil, Plzen	.30
☐	371 David Pospisil, Plzen	.30
☐	372 Martin Spanhel, Plzen	.30
☐	373 Jaroslav Spelda, Plzen	.30
☐	374 Michal Straka, Plzen	.30
☐	375 Milan Volek, Plzen	.30
☐	376 Zdenek Sedlak, Plzen	.30
☐	377 Jan Fiala, Plzen	.30
☐	378 Petr Kadlec, Plzen	.30
☐	379 Josef Straka, Plzen	.30
☐	380 Jiri Kalous, Slavia Praha	.30
☐	381 Josef Beranek, Slavia Praha	.30
☐	382 Jiri Dolezal, Slavia Praha	.30
☐	383 Jan Hejda, Slavia Praha	.30
☐	384 Pavel Kolarik, Slavia Praha	.30
☐	385 Tomas Kucharcik, Slavia Praha	.30
☐	386 Vladimir Machulda, Slavia Praha	.30
☐	387 Jan Bohac, Slavia Praha	.30
☐	388 Pavel Geffert, Slavia Praha	.30
☐	389 Jiri Jantovsky, Slavia Praha	.30
☐	390 Zdenek Skorepa, Slavia Praha	.30
☐	391 Vitezslav Skuta, Slavia Praha	.30
☐	392 Robin Bacul, Slavia Praha	.30
☐	393 Marek Tomica, Slavia Praha	.30
☐	394 Frantisek Vyborny, Sparta Praha	.30
☐	395 Ladislav Benysek, Sparta Praha	.30
☐	396 Jaroslav Hlinka, Sparta Praha	.30
☐	397 Martin Chabada, Sparta Praha	.30
☐	398 Patrik Martinec, Sparta Praha	.30
☐	399 Vaclav Novak, Sparta Praha	.30
☐	400 Josef Slanec, Sparta Praha	.30
☐	401 Michal Sykora, Sparta Praha	.30
☐	402 Vladimir Vujtek, Sparta Praha	.30
☐	403 Kamil Konecny, Trinec	.30
☐	404 Jozef Dano, Trinec	.30
☐	405 Petr Folta, Trinec	.30
☐	406 Tomas Chlubna, Trinec	.30
☐	407 Robert Kantor, Trinec	.30
☐	408 Jan Marek, Trinec	.30
☐	409 Lubomir Sekeras, Trinec	.30
☐	410 Ondrej Zetek, Trinec	.30
☐	411 David Appel, Trinec	.30
☐	412 Pavel Janku, Trinec	.30
☐	413 Dmitri Jerofejev, Trinec	.30
☐	414 David Nosek, Trinec	.30
☐	415 Vladimir Vlk, Trinec	.30
☐	416 Kamil Konecny, Trinec	.30
☐	417 Jan Sterbak, Vitkovice	.30
☐	418 Mojmir Trlicik, Vitkovice	.30
☐	419 Pavel Bacho, Vitkovice	.30
☐	420 Ondrej Zetek, Vitkovice	.30
☐	421 Roman Kadera, Vitkovice	.30
☐	422 Petr Hubacek, Vitkovice	.30
☐	423 Roman Kelner, Vitkovice	.30
☐	424 Pavel Kowalczyk, Vitkovice	.30
☐	425 Martin Lamich, Vitkovice	.30
☐	426 Jan Matejny, Vitkovice	.30
☐	427 Libor Pavlis, Vitkovice	.30
☐	428 Radek Philipp, Vitkovice	.30
☐	429 Libor Polasek, Vitkovice	.30
☐	430 Martin Tomasek, Vitkovice	.30
☐	431 Libor Gelacek, Vitkovice	.30
☐	432 Martin Louzek, Vitkovice	.30
☐	433 Martin Maskarinec, Vitkovice	.30
☐	434 David Moravec, Vitkovice	.30
☐	435 Ivan Padelek, Vitkovice	.30
☐	436 Martin Streit, Vsetin	.30
☐	437 Miroslav Venkrbec, Vsetin	.30
☐	438 Radek Belohlav, Vsetin	.30
☐	439 Alexei Jaskin, Vsetin	.30
☐	440 Zbynek Marak, Vsetin	.30
☐	441 Oleg Antonenko, Vsetin	.30
☐	442 Josef Mikes, Vsetin	.30
☐	443 Jan Pardavy, Vsetin	.30
☐	444 Jan Srdinko, Vsetin	.30
☐	445 Jiri Veber, Vsetin	.30
☐	446 Libor Zabransky, Vsetin	.30
☐	447 Pavel Patera, Vsetin	.30
☐	448 Martin Prochazka, Vsetin	.30
☐	449 Zbynek Spitzer, Vsetin	.30
☐	450 Stanislav Prikryl, Zlin	.30
☐	451 Petr Cajanek, Zlin	.30
☐	452 Jiri David, Zlin	.30
☐	453 Martin Hamrlik, Zlin	.30
☐	454 Marek Ivan, Zlin	.30
☐	455 Josef Straub, Zlin	.30
☐	456 Ondrej Vesely, Zlin	.30
☐	457 Martin Ambruz, Zlin	.30
☐	458 Jan Homer, Zlin	.30
☐	459 Rostislav Malena, Zlin	.30
☐	460 Stanislav Barada, Znojmo	.30
☐	461 Pavol Valko, Znojmo	.30
☐	462 Marek Uram, Znojmo	.30
☐	463 Patrik Fink, Znojmo	.30
☐	464 Tomas Hradecky, Znojmo	.30
☐	465 Tomas Jakes, Znojmo	.30
☐	466 Petr Kankovsky, Znojmo	.30
☐	467 Milan Kastner, Znojmo	.30
☐	468 David Kudelka, Znojmo	.30
☐	469 Pavel Kumstat, Znojmo	.30
☐	470 Karel Soudek, Znojmo	.30
☐	471 Jan Kopecky	.30
☐	472 Michal Bros	.30
☐	473 Martin Cech	.30
☐	474 Petr Gregorek	.30
☐	475 Jiri Hanzlik	.30
☐	476 Jaroslav Hlinka	.30
☐	477 Petr Korinek	.30
☐	478 Ludek Krayzel	.30
☐	479 David Moravec	.30
☐	480 Angel Nikolov	.30
☐	481 Pavel Patera	.30
☐	482 Kamil Piros	.30
☐	483 Vaclav Pletka	.30
☐	484 Martin Spanhel	.30
☐	485 Radim Tesarik	.30
☐	486 Libor Zabransky	.30
☐☐	487 Petr Briza	.30
☐☐	488 Dusan Salficky	.30
☐☐	489 Roman Cechmanek	2.00
☐☐	490 Vladimir Hudacek (G)	.30
☐☐	491 Peter Bartos	.30
☐☐	492 Vladimir (Jr.) Vujtek	.30
☐☐	493 David Vyborny	.30
☐☐	494 Ladislav Benysek	.30
☐☐	495 Tomas Blazek	.30
☐☐	496 Frantisek (Jr.) Kucera	.30
☐☐	497 Jiri Burger	.30
☐☐	498 Jan Kopecky	.30
☐☐	499 Vaclav Kral	.30
☐☐	500 Jan Krulis	.30
☐☐	501 Ivo Prorok	.30
☐☐	502 Radek Martinek	.30
☐☐	503 Jaroslav Nedved	.30
☐☐	504 Petr Pavlas	.30
☐☐	505 Ales Pisa	.30
☐☐	506 Michal Sykora	.30
☐☐	507 Robert Reichel	1.00
☐☐	508 Miroslav Buras	.30
☐☐	509 Martin Spanhel	.30
☐☐	510 Michal Sup	.30
☐☐	511 Petr Cajanek	.30
☐☐	512 Jiri Dopita	.30
☐☐	513 Martin Hamrlik	.30
☐☐	514 Roman Horak	.30
☐☐	515 Zbynek Irgl	.30
☐☐	516 Tomas Jakes	.30
☐☐	517 Ludek Krayzel	.30
☐☐	518 Jiri Kuntos	.30
☐☐	519 Petr Leska	.30
☐☐	520 Jiri Marusak	.30
☐☐	521 David Moravec	.30
☐☐	522 Jan Pardavy	.30
☐☐	523 Pavel Patera	.30
☐☐	524 Jan Peterek	.30
☐☐	525 Martin Prochazka	.30
☐☐	526 Karel Soudek	.30
☐☐	527 Jan Srdinko	.30
☐☐	528 Radim Tesarik	.30
☐☐	529 Viktor Ujcik	.30
☐☐	530 Libor Zabransky	.30
☐	531 Pavel Cagas, Havirov	.30
☐	532 Zdenek Smid, Karlovy Vary	.30
☐	533 Lubos Horcicka, Kladno	.30
☐	534 Pavel Krizek, Kladno	.30
☐	535 Marek Pinc,	.30
☐	536 Petr Jez, Plzen	.30
☐	537 Radek Masny,	.30
☐	538 Roman Malek, Slavia Praha	.30
☐	539 Tomas Duba, Sparta Praha	.30
☐	540 Petr Prikryl, Sparta Praha	.30
☐	541 Jiri Kratochvil,	.30
☐	542 Marek Novotny,	.30
☐	543 Jiri Trvaj, Vitkovice	.30
☐	544 Ivo Pesat, Vsetin	.30
☐	545 Richard Hrazdira,	.30
☐	546 Petr Kubena,	.30
☐	547 Pavol Rybar, Znojmo	.30
☐	548 Adam Svoboda, Pardubice	.30
☐	549 Radek Masny,	.30
☐	550 Petr Tucek,	.30
☐	551 Vladimir Hudacek (G), Znojmo	.30
☐	552 Dusan Salficky, Plzen	.50

CHECKLIST

Insert Set (8 cards): 9.00

	Player	CL
☐	Ladislav Blazek (G)	1.00
☐	Petr Briza (G)	1.00
☐	Roman Cechmanek (G)	2.00
☐	Vladimir Hudacek (G)	1.00
☐	Zdenek Orct (G)	1.00
☐	Rudolf Pejchar (G)	1.00
☐	Martin Prusek (G)	3.00
☐	Dusan Salficky (G)	1.00

1999 - 2000 OMEGA

This series was released in April 2000. There are five versions: a regular card, a Gold parallel (#/299), a Copper parallel (#/99), an Ice Blue parallel (#/75) and a Premiere Date parallel (#/68). Ice Blue and Premiere Date parallels are priced similarly below.

Complete Set (250 cards): 3590.00 2630.00 755.00 70.00

Common Player: 6.00 5.00 2.00 .20

	Player	IB75	C99	G299	Reg.
☐☐☐☐☐	1 Matt Cullen	10.00	5.00	2.00	.20
☐☐☐☐☐	2 Guy Hebert (G)	10.00	5.00	2.00	.20
☐☐☐☐☐	3 Paul Kariya	70.00	55.00	14.00	1.00
☐☐☐☐☐	4 Marty McInnis	6.00	5.00	2.00	.20
☐☐☐☐☐	5 Steve Rucchin	10.00	5.00	2.00	.20
☐☐☐☐☐	6 Teemu Selänne	40.00	30.00	8.00	.50
☐☐☐☐☐	7 Pascal Trépanier	6.00	5.00	2.00	.20
☐☐☐☐☐	8 L. Kohn / V. Vishnevski	10.00	5.00	2.00	.20
☐☐☐☐☐	9 Andrew Brunette	6.00	5.00	2.00	.20
☐☐☐☐☐	10 N. Emerson	6.00	5.00	2.00	.20
☐☐☐☐☐	11 Ray Ferraro	6.00	5.00	2.00	.20
☐☐☐☐☐	12 Rhodes (G)	10.00	5.00	2.00	.20
☐☐☐☐☐	**13 P. Stefan RC**	**24.00**	**18.00**	**5.00**	**1.50**
☐☐☐☐☐	**14 D. Sylvester RC**	**6.00**	**5.00**	**2.00**	**.50**
☐☐☐☐☐	**15 Buzek / Fankhouser RC**	**6.00**	**5.00**	**2.00**	**.50**
☐☐☐☐☐	16 Jason Allison	30.00	20.00	6.00	.50
☐☐☐☐☐	17 Andreychuk	15.00	10.00	3.00	.20
☐☐☐☐☐	18 Bourque	60.00	45.00	12.00	1.00
☐☐☐☐☐	19 Anson Carter	20.00	15.00	4.00	.20
☐☐☐☐☐	20 Byron Dafoe (G)	20.00	15.00	4.00	.20
☐☐☐☐☐	21 Samsonov	30.00	20.00	6.00	.50
☐☐☐☐☐	22 Joe Thornton	60.00	45.00	12.00	1.00
☐☐☐☐☐	**23 Grahame RC / Henderson RC**	**12.00**	**10.00**	**2.00**	**.50**
☐☐☐☐☐	24 M. Afinogenov	20.00	15.00	4.00	.50
☐☐☐☐☐	25 Martin Biron (G)	20.00	15.00	4.00	.20
☐☐☐☐☐	26 Curtis Brown	6.00	5.00	2.00	.20
☐☐☐☐☐	**27 B. Campbell RC**	**6.00**	**6.00**	**2.00**	**.50**
☐☐☐☐☐	28 D. Hasek (G)	50.00	40.00	10.00	1.00
☐☐☐☐☐	**29 D. Kalinin RC**	**6.00**	**6.00**	**2.00**	**.50**
☐☐☐☐☐	30 Michael Peca	20.00	15.00	4.00	.20
☐☐☐☐☐	31 Miroslav Satan	15.00	10.00	3.00	.20
☐☐☐☐☐	32 Rhett Warrener	6.00	5.00	2.00	.20
☐☐☐☐☐	**33 Grand-Pierre RC / Moravec RC**	**6.00**	**6.00**	**2.00**	**.50**
☐☐☐☐☐	34 F. Brathwaite (G)	15.00	10.00	3.00	.20
☐☐☐☐☐	35 Valeri Bure	15.00	10.00	3.00	.20
☐☐☐☐☐	36 Grant Fuhr (G)	30.00	20.00	6.00	.50
☐☐☐☐☐	37 Phil Housley	15.00	10.00	3.00	.20
☐☐☐☐☐	38 Jarome Iginla	40.00	30.00	8.00	.50
☐☐☐☐☐	**39 O. Saprykin RC**	**18.00**	**14.00**	**4.00**	**1.00**
☐☐☐☐☐	40 Marc Savard	10.00	5.00	2.00	.20
☐☐☐☐☐	41 Cory Stillman	10.00	5.00	2.00	.20
☐☐☐☐☐	**42 Brigley RC / Regehr**	**8.00**	**6.00**	**2.00**	**.50**
☐☐☐☐☐	43 Ron Francis	30.00	20.00	6.00	.50
☐☐☐☐☐	44 Sean Hill	6.00	5.00	2.00	.20
☐☐☐☐☐	45 Arturs Irbe (G)	20.00	15.00	4.00	.20
☐☐☐☐☐	46 Sami Kapanen	15.00	10.00	3.00	.20
☐☐☐☐☐	47 C. Leschyshyn	6.00	5.00	2.00	.20
☐☐☐☐☐	48 Jeff O'Neill	20.00	15.00	4.00	.20
☐☐☐☐☐	49 Gary Roberts	20.00	15.00	4.00	.20
☐☐☐☐☐	**50 Westlund RC / Tanabe**	**8.00**	**6.00**	**2.00**	**.50**
☐☐☐☐☐	51 Tony Amonte	30.00	20.00	6.00	.50
☐☐☐☐☐	52 Éric Dazé	20.00	15.00	4.00	.20
☐☐☐☐☐	53 Doug Gilmour	30.00	20.00	6.00	.50
☐☐☐☐☐	54 Michael Nylander	10.00	5.00	2.00	.20
☐☐☐☐☐	55 Steve Sullivan	15.00	10.00	3.00	.20
☐☐☐☐☐	56 J. Thibault (G)	20.00	15.00	4.00	.20
☐☐☐☐☐	57 Alexei Zhamnov	15.00	10.00	3.00	.20
☐☐☐☐☐	**58 Lamothe RC / Dumont**	**12.00**	**10.00**	**2.00**	**.50**
☐☐☐☐☐	**59 Herperger RC / McCarthy**	**8.00**	**6.00**	**2.00**	**.50**
☐☐☐☐☐	60 A. Deadmarsh	15.00	10.00	3.00	.20
☐☐☐☐☐	61 Chris Drury	30.00	20.00	6.00	.50
☐☐☐☐☐	62 Peter Forsberg	70.00	55.00	14.00	1.00
☐☐☐☐☐	63 Milan Hejduk	40.00	30.00	8.00	.50
☐☐☐☐☐	64 Sandis Ozolinsh	10.00	5.00	2.00	.20
☐☐☐☐☐	65 Patrick Roy (G)	120.00	95.00	30.00	3.00
☐☐☐☐☐	66 Joe Sakic	80.00	60.00	16.00	1.50
☐☐☐☐☐	67 Alex Tanguay	30.00	20.00	6.00	1.00
☐☐☐☐☐	68 Denis / Skoula	15.00	10.00	3.00	.50
☐☐☐☐☐	**69 Helenius RC / Willsie**	**6.00**	**6.00**	**2.00**	**.50**
☐☐☐☐☐	70 Ed Belfour (G)	50.00	40.00	10.00	1.00
☐☐☐☐☐	71 Fernandez (G)	20.00	15.00	4.00	.20
☐☐☐☐☐	72 Brett Hull	50.00	40.00	10.00	1.00
☐☐☐☐☐	73 Jere Lehtinen	15.00	10.00	3.00	.20
☐☐☐☐☐	74 Mike Modano	50.00	40.00	10.00	1.00
☐☐☐☐☐	75 Brenden Morrow	15.00	10.00	3.00	.50
☐☐☐☐☐	76 Joe Nieuwendyk	20.00	15.00	4.00	.20
☐☐☐☐☐	77 Sergei Zubov	10.00	5.00	2.00	.20
☐☐☐☐☐	**78 Christie RC / Lyashenko**	**6.00**	**6.00**	**2.00**	**.20**
☐☐☐☐☐	**79 Letang RC / R. Jackman**	**8.00**	**6.00**	**2.00**	**.50**
☐☐☐☐☐	80 Chris Chelios	30.00	20.00	6.00	.50
☐☐☐☐☐	81 Sergei Fedorov	50.00	40.00	10.00	1.00
☐☐☐☐☐	82 Igor Larionov	30.00	20.00	6.00	.50
☐☐☐☐☐	83 Nicklas Lidström	30.00	20.00	6.00	.50
☐☐☐☐☐	84 C. Osgood (G)	30.00	20.00	6.00	.50
☐☐☐☐☐	85 B. Shanahan	50.00	40.00	10.00	1.00
☐☐☐☐☐	86 Pat Verbeek	15.00	10.00	3.00	.20
☐☐☐☐☐	87 Ken Wregget (G)	10.00	5.00	2.00	.20
☐☐☐☐☐	88 Steve Yzerman	120.00	95.00	24.00	2.00
☐☐☐☐☐	**89 P. Comrie RC**	**12.00**	**8.00**	**2.00**	**.50**
☐☐☐☐☐	90 Bill Guerin	20.00	15.00	4.00	.20
☐☐☐☐☐	91 Tom Poti	6.00	5.00	2.00	.20
☐☐☐☐☐	**92 Robertsson RC**	**6.00**	**6.00**	**2.00**	**.50**
☐☐☐☐☐	93 Tommy Salo (G)	20.00	15.00	4.00	.20
☐☐☐☐☐	94 A. Selivanov	6.00	5.00	2.00	.20
☐☐☐☐☐	95 Ryan Smyth	20.00	15.00	4.00	.20
☐☐☐☐☐	96 Doug Weight	30.00	20.00	6.00	.50
☐☐☐☐☐	97 Pavel Bure	40.00	30.00	8.00	.50
☐☐☐☐☐	98 Viktor Kozlov	15.00	10.00	3.00	.20
☐☐☐☐☐	99 Mark Parrish	20.00	15.00	4.00	.20
☐☐☐☐☐	100 M. Shtalenkov	6.00	5.00	2.00	.20
☐☐☐☐☐	101 Robert Svehla	10.00	5.00	2.00	.20
☐☐☐☐☐	102 Mike Vernon (G)	20.00	15.00	4.00	.20
☐☐☐☐☐	103 Ray Whitney	10.00	5.00	2.00	.20
☐☐☐☐☐	**104 Duerden RC / Novoseltsev RC**	**10.00**	**8.00**	**2.00**	**.50**
☐☐☐☐☐	**105 Jakopin RC / Kuba RC**	**8.00**	**6.00**	**2.00**	**.50**
☐☐☐☐☐	106 Rob Blake	30.00	20.00	6.00	.50
☐☐☐☐☐	107 S. Fiset (G)	15.00	10.00	3.00	.20
☐☐☐☐☐	108 Jaroslav Modry	6.00	5.00	2.00	.20
☐☐☐☐☐	109 Glen Murray	20.00	15.00	4.00	.20
☐☐☐☐☐	110 Zigmund Palffy	30.00	20.00	6.00	.50
☐☐☐☐☐	111 Luc Robitaille	40.00	30.00	8.00	.50
☐☐☐☐☐	112 Bryan Smolinski	6.00	5.00	2.00	.20
☐☐☐☐☐	113 Jamie Storr (G)	10.00	5.00	2.00	.20
☐☐☐☐☐	114 M. Tuomainen	6.00	5.00	2.00	.20
☐☐☐☐☐	**115 Chartrand RC / Kaberle**	**8.00**	**6.00**	**2.00**	**.50**
☐☐☐☐☐	116 Shayne Corson	15.00	10.00	3.00	.20
☐☐☐☐☐	117 Craig Darby	6.00	5.00	2.00	.20
☐☐☐☐☐	118 J. Hackett (G)	15.00	10.00	3.00	.20
☐☐☐☐☐	119 Saku Koivu	40.00	30.00	8.00	.50
☐☐☐☐☐	120 Trevor Linden	20.00	15.00	4.00	.20
☐☐☐☐☐	121 Martin Rucinsky	10.00	5.00	2.00	.20
☐☐☐☐☐	122 Brian Savage	15.00	10.00	3.00	.20
☐☐☐☐☐	123 J. Théodore (G)	60.00	45.00	12.00	1.00
☐☐☐☐☐	**124 Bouillon / Robidas RCs**	**6.00**	**6.00**	**2.00**	**.50**
☐☐☐☐☐	125 Ribeiro / Ward	15.00	10.00	3.00	.50
☐☐☐☐☐	126 M. Dunham (G)	20.00	15.00	4.00	.20

□□□□□	127 Patric Kjellberg	6.00	5.00	2.00	.20
□□□□□	128 Cliff Ronning	10.00	5.00	2.00	.20
□□□□□	129 T. Vokoun (G)	10.00	5.00	2.00	.20
□□□□□	130 Legwand Robitaille	10.00	10.00	2.00	.50
□□□□□	**131 Lintner / Skrastins RCs**	**6.00**	**6.00**	**2.00**	**.50**
□□□□□	132 Jason Arnott	20.00	15.00	4.00	.20
□□□□□	133 M. Brodeur (G)	80.00	60.00	16.00	1.50
□□□□□	134 Patrik Elias	40.00	30.00	8.00	.50
□□□□□	135 Scott Gomez	20.00	15.00	4.00	.50
□□□□□	136 Bobby Holik	15.00	10.00	3.00	.20
□□□□□	137 Claude Lemieux	15.00	10.00	3.00	.20
□□□□□	138 Petr* Sykora	20.00	15.00	4.00	.20
□□□□□	**139 Madden / Rafalski RCs**	**20.00**	**16.00**	**4.00**	**1.50**
□□□□□	140 M. Czerkawski	10.00	5.00	2.00	.20
□□□□□	141 Brad Isbister	10.00	5.00	2.00	.20
□□□□□	**142 J. Jönsson RC**	**14.00**	**12.00**	**3.00**	**1.00**
□□□□□	143 R. Luongo (G)	40.00	30.00	8.00	.50
□□□□□	144 Bill Muckalt	6.00	5.00	2.00	.20
□□□□□	145 K. Weekes (G)	10.00	5.00	2.00	.20
□□□□□	**146 Korolev RC / Connolly**	**12.00**	**10.00**	**2.00**	**1.00**
□□□□□	147 Alexandre Daigle	6.00	5.00	2.00	.20
□□□□□	148 Radek Dvorak	10.00	5.00	2.00	.20
□□□□□	149 Theoren Fleury	30.00	20.00	6.00	.50
□□□□□	150 Adam Graves	20.00	15.00	4.00	.20
□□□□□	151 Brian Leetch	30.00	20.00	6.00	.50
□□□□□	152 Petr Nedved	15.00	10.00	3.00	.20
□□□□□	153 M. Richter (G)	20.00	15.00	4.00	.20
□□□□□	154 Mike York	15.00	10.00	3.00	.50
□□□□□	**155 K. Johnsson RC / Hlavac**	**14.00**	**12.00**	**3.00**	**.50**
□□□□□	156 D. Alfredsson	30.00	20.00	6.00	.50
□□□□□	157 M. Arvedson	6.00	5.00	2.00	.20
□□□□□	158 Radek Bonk	15.00	10.00	3.00	.20
□□□□□	159 Marian Hossa	50.00	40.00	10.00	1.00
□□□□□	160 P. Lalime (G)	30.00	20.00	6.00	.50
□□□□□	161 S. McEachern	15.00	10.00	3.00	.20
□□□□□	**162 Schastlivy RC**	**18.00**	**14.00**	**4.00**	**1.00**
□□□□□	163 R. Tugnutt (G)	20.00	15.00	4.00	.20
□□□□□	164 S. Van Allen	6.00	5.00	2.00	.20
□□□□□	165 Alexei Yashin	30.00	20.00	6.00	.50
□□□□□	**166 Fisher RC / Roy RC**	**14.00**	**12.00**	**3.00**	**1.00**
□□□□□	167 B. Boucher (G)	15.00	10.00	3.00	.50
□□□□□	168 Éric Desjardins	15.00	10.00	3.00	.20
□□□□□	169 Simon Gagné	40.00	30.00	8.00	1.50
□□□□□	170 D. Langkow	10.00	5.00	2.00	.20
□□□□□	171 John LeClair	40.00	30.00	8.00	.50
□□□□□	172 Eric Lindros	50.00	40.00	10.00	1.00
□□□□□	173 Keith Primeau	20.00	15.00	4.00	.20
□□□□□	174 Mark Recchi	20.00	15.00	4.00	.20
□□□□□	175 M. Renberg	15.00	10.00	3.00	.20
□□□□□	176 V'sbrouck (G)	20.00	15.00	4.00	.20
□□□□□	**177 Delmore RC / Eaton RC**	**12.00**	**10.00**	**2.00**	**.50**
□□□□□	178 Shane Doan	10.00	5.00	2.00	.20
□□□□□	179 Dallas Drake	6.00	5.00	2.00	.20
□□□□□	**180 Esche (G) RC**	**18.00**	**14.00**	**4.00**	**1.00**
□□□□□	181 Travis Green	10.00	5.00	2.00	.20
□□□□□	182 Khabibulin (G)	20.00	15.00	4.00	.20
□□□□□	183 T. Numminen	15.00	10.00	3.00	.20
□□□□□	184 J. Roenick	40.00	30.00	8.00	.50
□□□□□	185 Keith Tkachuk	30.00	20.00	6.00	.50
□□□□□	**186 R. Suchy RC / Letowski**	**8.00**	**6.00**	**2.00**	**.50**
□□□□□	187 Jan Hrdina	10.00	5.00	2.00	.20
□□□□□	188 Jaromir Jagr	50.00	40.00	10.00	1.00
□□□□□	**189 H. Jonsson RC**	**6.00**	**6.00**	**2.00**	**.50**
□□□□□	190 Alexei Kovalev	30.00	20.00	6.00	.50
□□□□□	191 Martin Straka	15.00	10.00	3.00	.20
□□□□□	192 German Titov	6.00	5.00	2.00	.20
□□□□□	193 Tyler Wright	6.00	5.00	2.00	.20
□□□□□	**194 Rozsival RC / Aubin (G)**	**12.00**	**10.00**	**2.00**	**.50**
□□□□□	195 Pavol Demitra	20.00	15.00	4.00	.20
□□□□□	196 Al MacInnis	20.00	15.00	4.00	.20
□□□□□	197 J. McLennan (G)	6.00	5.00	2.00	.20
□□□□□	**198 T. Nash RC**	**12.00**	**8.00**	**2.00**	**.50**
□□□□□	199 Chris Pronger	30.00	20.00	6.00	.50
□□□□□	**200 T. Reirden RC**	**6.00**	**6.00**	**2.00**	**.50**
□□□□□	201 R. Turek (G)	20.00	15.00	4.00	.20
□□□□□	202 Pierre Turgeon	20.00	15.00	4.00	.20
□□□□□	**203 Hecht RC / Nagy RC**	**18.00**	**14.00**	**4.00**	**1.50**
□□□□□	204 V. Damphousse	30.00	20.00	6.00	.50
□□□□□	205 Jeff Friesen	15.00	10.00	3.00	.20
□□□□□	206 Todd Harvey	10.00	5.00	2.00	.20
□□□□□	207 A. Korolyuk	6.00	5.00	2.00	.20
□□□□□	208 Patrick Marleau	20.00	15.00	4.00	.20
□□□□□	209 Owen Nolan	30.00	20.00	6.00	.50
□□□□□	210 S. Shields (G)	10.00	5.00	2.00	.20
□□□□□	211 Gary Suter	10.00	5.00	2.00	.20
□□□□□	**212 Nabokov RC / Stuart**	**60.00**	**50.00**	**20.00**	**10.00**
□□□□□	213 D. Cloutier (G)	20.00	15.00	4.00	.20
□□□□□	214 Stan Drulia	6.00	5.00	2.00	.20
□□□□□	215 Chris Gratton	10.00	5.00	2.00	.20
□□□□□	216 V. Lecavalier	50.00	40.00	10.00	1.00
□□□□□	**217 S. Martins RC**	**6.00**	**6.00**	**2.00**	**.50**
□□□□□	218 Fredrik Modin	10.00	5.00	2.00	.20
□□□□□	219 Mike Sillinger	6.00	5.00	2.00	.20
□□□□□	**220 N. Ekman RC / B. Clymer**	**8.00**	**6.00**	**2.00**	**.50**
□□□□□	**221 Antropov RC**	**18.00**	**14.00**	**4.00**	**1.00**
□□□□□	222 Sergei Berezin	10.00	5.00	2.00	.20
□□□□□	223 Tie Domi	15.00	10.00	3.00	.20
□□□□□	224 Jonas Höglund	6.00	5.00	2.00	.20
□□□□□	225 C. Joseph (G)	50.00	40.00	10.00	1.00
□□□□□	226 Tomas Kaberle	15.00	10.00	3.00	.20
□□□□□	227 Dmitri Khristich	6.00	5.00	2.00	.20
□□□□□	228 Mats Sundin	50.00	40.00	10.00	1.00
□□□□□	229 Steve Thomas	10.00	5.00	2.00	.20
□□□□□	**230 Yakushin RC / Mair RC**	**8.00**	**6.00**	**2.00**	**.50**
□□□□□	231 Todd Bertuzzi	60.00	45.00	12.00	1.00
□□□□□	232 A. Cassels	10.00	5.00	2.00	.20
□□□□□	**233 S. Kariya RC**	**18.00**	**14.00**	**4.00**	**1.00**
□□□□□	234 Mark Messier	50.00	40.00	10.00	1.00
□□□□□	235 A. Mogilny	20.00	15.00	4.00	.20
□□□□□	236 M. Näslund	50.00	40.00	10.00	1.00
□□□□□	237 Félix Potvin (G)	30.00	20.00	6.00	.50
□□□□□	**238 Bonni RC / Komarniski**	**6.00**	**6.00**	**2.00**	**.20**
□□□□□	239 H. Druken / P. Schaefer	15.00	10.00	4.00	.20
□□□□□	**240 Leeb RC / Michaud RC**	**8.00**	**6.00**	**2.00**	**.50**
□□□□□	241 Jan Bulis	6.00	5.00	2.00	.20
□□□□□	242 Peter Bondra	30.00	20.00	6.00	.50
□□□□□	243 Olaf Kölzig (G)	30.00	20.00	6.00	.50
□□□□□	244 S. Konowalchuk	10.00	5.00	2.00	.20
□□□□□	245 Adam Oates	20.00	15.00	4.00	.20
□□□□□	**246 Halpern RC / Metropolit RC**	**14.00**	**12.00**	**3.00**	**1.00**
□□□□□	**247 Tezikov RC / Volchkov RC**	**6.00**	**6.00**	**2.00**	**.50**
□□□□□	248 N.A All-Stars	6.00	5.00	2.00	.50
□□□□□	249 World All-Stars	6.00	5.00	2.00	.50
□□□□□	250 Bure brothers	25.00	20.00	5.00	.50

SAMPLE

□	Martin Brodeur (G), NJer.	2.00

5-STAR TALENT

There are two versions: the regular insert and a variation parallel.

	Insert Set (30 cards):	-	15.00
	Inserts	**Var.**	**Insert**
□□	1 Patrik Stefan, Atla. [Rookies]	15.00	2.00
□□	2 Alex Tanguay, Colo. [Rookies]	20.00	3.00
□□	3 David Legwand, Phil. [Rookies]	15.00	2.00
□□	4 Scott Gomez, NJer. [Rookies]	15.00	2.00
□□	5 Roberto Luongo (G), NYIs. [Rookies]	30.00	4.00
□□	6 Steve Kariya, Vanc. [Rookies]	10.00	1.50
□□	7 Brendan Shanahan, Detr. [Power Game]	50.00	2.50
□□	8 John LeClair, Phil. [Power Game]	40.00	2.00
□□	9 Eric Lindros, Phil. [Power Game]	50.00	2.50
□□	10 Keith Tkachuk, Phoe. [Power Game]	30.00	1.50
□□	11 Owen Nolan, SanJ. [Power Game]	30.00	1.50
□□	12 Mark Messier, Vanc. [Power Game]	50.00	2.50
□□	13 Paul Kariya, Anah. [Speed Merchants]	85.00	3.50
□□	14 T. Selänne, Anah. [Speed Merchants]	50.00	2.00
□□	15 Pavel Bure, Flor. [Speed Merchants]	50.00	2.00
□□	16 T. Fleury, NYRa. [Speed Merchants]	35.00	1.50
□□	17 Marian Hossa, Otta. [Speed Merchants]	60.00	2.50
□□	18 Jaromir Jagr, Pitt. [Speed Merchants]	60.00	2.50
□□	19 Peter Forsberg, Colo. [Playmakers]	175.00	3.50
□□	20 Mike Modano, Dall. [Playmakers]	125.00	2.50
□□	21 Steve Yzerman, Detr. [Playmakers]	300.00	6.00
□□	22 Mark Recchi, Phil. [Playmakers]	50.00	1.00
□□	23 Vincent Lecavalier, Tamp. [Playmakers]	125.00	2.50
□□	24 Mats Sundin, Toro. [Playmakers]	125.00	2.50
□□	25 Dominik Hasek (G), Buff. [Netminders]	-	2.50
□□	26 Patrick Roy (G), Colo. [Netminders]	-	7.50
□□	27 Ed Belfour (G), Dall. [Netminders]	-	2.50
□□	28 Martin Brodeur (G), NJer. [Netminders]	-	4.00
□□	29 John Vanbiesbrouck (G), Phil. [Netminders]	-	1.00
□□	30 Curtis Joseph (G), Toro. [Netminders]	-	2.50

CUP CONTENDERS

	Insert Set (20 cards):	**140.00**
	Insert (1:37 packs)	**CC**
□	1 Paul Kariya, Anah.	10.00
□	2 Dominik Hasek (G), Buff.	7.00
□	3 Peter Forsberg, Colo.	10.00
□	4 Patrick Roy (G), Colo.	22.00
□	5 Joe Sakic, Colo.	12.00
□	6 Brett Hull, Dall.	7.00
□	7 Mike Modano, Dall.	7.00
□	8 Sergei Fedorov, Detr.	7.00
□	9 Brendan Shanahan, Detr.	7.00
□	10 Steve Yzerman, Detr.	18.00
□	11 Pavel Bure, Flor.	6.00
□	12 Martin Brodeur (G), NJer.	12.00
□	13 Theoren Fleury, NYRa.	4.00
□	14 Mike Richter (G), NYRa.	3.00
□	15 John LeClair, Phil.	6.00
□	16 Jeremy Roenick, Phoe.	6.00
□	17 Jaromir Jagr, Pitt.	7.00
□	18 Al MacInnis, SLou.	3.00
□	19 Curtis Joseph (G), Toro.	7.00
□	20 Mark Messier, Vanc.	7.00

EO PORTRAITS

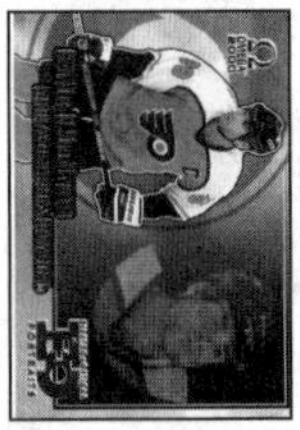

There are two versions: the insert (1:73 packs) and a one-of-one parallel (#/1).

	Insert Set (20 cards):	**160.00**
	Insert (1:37 packs)	**EOP**
□□	1 Paul Kariya, Anah.	12.00
□□	2 Teemu Selänne, Anah.	7.00
□□	3 Patrik Stefan, Atla.	5.00
□□	4 Dominik Hasek (G), Buff.	8.00
□□	5 Peter Forsberg, Colo.	12.00
□□	6 Patrick Roy (G), Colo.	25.00
□□	7 Mike Modano, Dall.	8.00
□□	8 Brendan Shanahan, Detr.	8.00
□□	9 Steve Yzerman, Detr.	20.00
□□	10 Pavel Bure, Flor.	7.00
□□	11 Martin Brodeur (G), NJer.	14.00
□□	12 Scott Gomez, NJer.	7.00
□□	13 Eric Lindros, Phil.	8.00
□□	14 John Vanbiesbrouck (G), Phil.	4.00
□□	15 Keith Tkachuk, Phoe.	5.00
□□	16 Jaromir Jagr, Pitt.	8.00
□□	17 Vincent Lecavalier, Tamp.	8.00
□□	18 Curtis Joseph (G), Toro.	8.00
□□	19 Mats Sundin, Toro.	8.00
□□	20 Mark Messier, Vanc.	8.00

GAME-WORN JERSEYS

These cards have a cut-piece of memorabilia affixed to the card front.

	Insert Set (10 cards):	**275.00**
	Insert (1:180 packs)	**GWJ**
□	1 Teemu Selänne, Anah. ✂	25.00
□	2 Mike Modano, Dall. ✂	30.00
□	3 Steve Yzerman, Detr. ✂	75.00
□	4 Martin Brodeur (G), NJer. ✂	50.00
□	5 Patrick Roy (G), Colo. ✂	20.00
□	6 John LeClair, Phil. ✂	25.00
□	7 Eric Lindros, Phil. ✂	30.00
□	8 John Vanbiesbrouck (G), Phil. ✂	20.00
□	9 Jaromir Jagr, Pitt. ✂	30.00
□	10 Mats Sundin, Toro. ✂	30.00

GENERATIONS

	Insert Set (10 cards):	**200.00**
	Insert (1:145 packs)	**Gen.**
□	1 P. Kariya / S. Kariya	20.00
□	2 T. Selänne / M. Hejduk	20.00
□	3 P. Forsberg / C. Drury	25.00
□	4 P. Roy / R. Luongo	45.00
□	5 M. Modano / D. Legwand	15.00
□	6 S. Yzerman / S. Gomez	35.00
□	7 P. Bure / M. Hossa	20.00
□	8 J. LeClair / S. Gagné	20.00
□	9 E. Lindros / V. Lecavalier	25.00
□	10 J. Jagr / P. Stefan	15.00

NORTH AMERICA ALL-STARS

	Insert Set (10 cards):	**35.00**
	Insert (2:37 packs)	**NA AS**
□	1 Paul Kariya, All-Star '00	5.00
□	2 Raymond Bourque, All-Star '00	4.00
□	3 Joe Sakic, All-Star '00	6.00
□	4 Mike Modano, All-Star '00	3.00
□	5 Brendan Shanahan, All-Star '00	3.00
□	6 Steve Yzerman, All-Star '00	9.00
□	7 Martin Brodeur (G), All-Star '00	6.00
□	8 Scott Gomez, All-Star '00	2.00
□	9 Curtis Joseph (G), All-Star '00	3.00
□	10 Mark Messier, All-Star '00	3.00

WORLD ALL-STARS

	Insert Set (10 cards):	**20.00**
	Insert (2:37 packs)	**W AS**
□	1 Teemu Selänne, All-Star '00	3.00
□	2 Valeri Bure, All-Star '00	2.00
□	3 Nicklas Lidström, All-Star '00	2.00
□	4 Pavel Bure, All-Star '00	3.00
□	5 Viktor Kozlov, All-Star '00	2.00
□	6 Jaromir Jagr, All-Star '00	3.00
□	7 Pavol Demitra, All-Star '00	2.00
□	8 Roman Turek (G), All-Star '00	2.00
□	9 Mats Sundin, All-Star '00	3.00
□	10 Olaf Kölzig (G), All-Star '00	2.00

TORONTO FALL EXPO REDEMPTION

These wrapper-redemption parallel cards are limited to 20 copies.

	Complete Set (20 cards):	**165.00**
	Redemption (#/20)	**Show20**
□	3 Paul Kariya, Ana.	10.00
□	6 Teemu Selänne, Anah.	5.00
□	13 Patrik Stefan, Atla.	2.00
□	28 Dominik Hasek (G), Buff.	10.00
□	62 Peter Forsberg, Colo.	10.00
□	65 Patrick Roy (G), Colo.	30.00
□	66 Joe Sakic, Colo.	15.00
□	85 Brendan Shanahan, Detr.	10.00
□	88 Steve Yzerman, Detr.	20.00
□	119 Saku Koivu, Mont.	5.00
□	133 Martin Brodeur (G), NJer.	15.00
□	135 Scott Gomez, NJer.	2.00
□	149 Theoren Fleury, NYRa.	5.00
□	171 John LeClair, Phil.	5.00
□	172 Eric Lindros, Phil.	10.00
□	188 Jaromir Jagr, Pitt.	10.00
□	216 Vincent Lecavalier, Tamp.	10.00
□	221 Nikolai Antropov, Toro.	2.00
□	225 Curtis Joseph (G), Toro.	10.00
□	228 Mats Sundin, Toro.	10.00

1999 - 2000 PACIFIC

This series was released in August 1999. There are five versions: the regular card, a Gold parallel (#/199), a Copper parallel (#/99), an Ice Blue parallel (#/75) and a Premiere Date parallel (#/47). Ice Blue cards are valued slightly more than the Copper cards. The Pacific Jewel Collection cards (Ruby and Emerald parallel) are listed after the first 450-card listing.

Complete Set (450 cards): 3600.00 2600.00 1100.00 55.00
Common Player: 6.00 5.00 2.00 .20

Player	PD68	C99	G199	Pac.
1 Matt Cullen	6.00	6.00	2.00	.20
2 Johan Davidsson	6.00	5.00	2.00	.20
3 Scott Ferguson RC	**6.00**	**5.00**	**2.00**	**.50**
4 Travis Green	6.00	6.00	2.00	.20
5 Stu Grimson	6.00	6.00	2.00	.20
6 Kevin Haller	6.00	5.00	2.00	.20
7 Guy Hebert (G)	6.00	6.00	2.00	.20
8 Paul Kariya	55.00	35.00	20.00	1.00
9 Marty McInnis	6.00	5.00	2.00	.20
10 Jim McKenzie	6.00	5.00	2.00	.20
11 Fredrik Olausson	6.00	6.00	2.00	.20
12 Dominic Roussel (G)	6.00	5.00	2.00	.20
13 Steve Rucchin	6.00	6.00	2.00	.20
14 Ruslan Salei	6.00	5.00	2.00	.20
15 Tomas Sandström	6.00	6.00	2.00	.20
16 Teemu Selänne	32.00	20.00	10.00	.50
17 Jason Allison	24.00	14.00	5.00	.50
18 Per Axelsson	6.00	5.00	2.00	.20
19 Shawn Bates	6.00	5.00	2.00	.20
20 Raymond Bourque	48.00	30.00	15.00	1.00
21 Anson Carter	15.00	10.00	5.00	.20
22 Byron Dafoe (G)	15.00	10.00	5.00	.20
23 Hal Gill	6.00	5.00	2.00	.20
24 Stephen Heinze	6.00	5.00	2.00	.20
25 Dmitri Khristich	6.00	5.00	2.00	.20
26 Cameron Mann	6.00	5.00	2.00	.20
27 Kyle McLaren	6.00	6.00	2.00	.20
28 Sergei Samsonov	24.00	14.00	5.00	.50
29 Robbie Tallas (G)	6.00	5.00	2.00	.20
30 Joe Thornton	45.00	30.00	15.00	1.00
31 Landon Wilson	6.00	5.00	2.00	.20
32 A. Savage RC / J. Girard	**6.00**	**5.00**	**2.00**	**.20**
33 Stu Barnes	6.00	5.00	2.00	.20
34 Martin Biron (G)	15.00	12.00	5.00	.20
35 Curtis Brown	6.00	5.00	2.00	.20
36 Michal Grosek	6.00	5.00	2.00	.20
37 Dominik Hasek (G)	40.00	25.00	15.00	1.00
38 Brian Holzinger	6.00	5.00	2.00	.20
39 Joé Juneau	6.00	6.00	2.00	.20
40 Jay McKee	6.00	5.00	2.00	.20
41 Michael Peca	15.00	10.00	5.00	.20
42 Erik Rasmussen	6.00	6.00	2.00	.20
43 Rob Ray	6.00	6.00	2.00	.20
44 Geoff Sanderson	6.00	6.00	2.00	.20
45 Miroslav Satan	10.00	8.00	2.00	.20
46 Darryl Shannon	6.00	5.00	2.00	.20
47 Vaclav Varada	6.00	5.00	2.00	.20
48 Dixon Ward	6.00	5.00	2.00	.20
49 Jason Woolley	6.00	5.00	2.00	.20
50 Alexei Zhitnik	6.00	5.00	2.00	.20
51 Fred Brathwaite (G)	10.00	8.00	2.00	.20
52 Valeri Bure	10.00	8.00	2.00	.20
53 Andrew Cassels	6.00	6.00	2.00	.20
54 René Corbet	6.00	5.00	2.00	.20
55 J-S Giguère (G)	30.00	20.00	10.00	.50
56 Phil Housley	10.00	8.00	2.00	.20
57 Jarome Iginla	32.00	20.00	10.00	.50
58 Derek Morris	6.00	6.00	2.00	.20
59 Andrei Nazarov	6.00	5.00	2.00	.20
60 Jeff Shantz	6.00	5.00	2.00	.20
61 Todd Simpson	6.00	5.00	2.00	.20
62 Cory Stillman	6.00	6.00	2.00	.20
63 Jason Wiemer	6.00	5.00	2.00	.20
64 Clarke Wilm	6.00	5.00	2.00	.20
65 Ken Wregget (G)	6.00	6.00	2.00	.20
66 Garner RC / Fata	**10.00**	**6.00**	**5.00**	**.50**
67 Bates Battaglia	6.00	6.00	2.00	.20
68 Paul Coffey	24.00	14.00	5.00	.50
69 Kevin Dineen	6.00	5.00	2.00	.20
70 Ron Francis	24.00	14.00	5.00	.50
71 Martin Gélinas	6.00	6.00	2.00	.20
72 Arturs Irbe (G)	16.00	10.00	5.00	.20
73 Sami Kapanen	10.00	8.00	2.00	.20
74 Trevor Kidd (G)	10.00	8.00	2.00	.20
75 Andrei Kovalenko	6.00	5.00	2.00	.20
76 Robert Kron	6.00	5.00	2.00	.20
77 Kent Manderville	6.00	5.00	2.00	.20
78 Jeff O'Neill	15.00	10.00	5.00	.20
79 Keith Primeau	15.00	10.00	5.00	.20
80 Gary Roberts	15.00	10.00	5.00	.20
81 Ray Sheppard	6.00	5.00	2.00	.20
82 Glen Wesley	6.00	5.00	2.00	.20
83 MacDonald RC / Ritchie RC	**6.00**	**5.00**	**2.00**	**.50**
84 Tony Amonte	24.00	14.00	5.00	.50
85 Eric Dazé	15.00	10.00	5.00	.20
86 Jean-Pierre Dumont	6.00	6.00	2.00	.20
87 Anders Eriksson	6.00	5.00	2.00	.20
88 Mark Fitzpatrick (G)	6.00	5.00	2.00	.20
89 Doug Gilmour	24.00	14.00	5.00	.50
90 Jean-Yves Leroux	6.00	5.00	2.00	.20
91 Dave Manson	6.00	5.00	2.00	.20
92 Josef Marha	6.00	5.00	2.00	.20
93 Dean McAmmond	6.00	5.00	2.00	.20
94 Boris Mironov	6.00	5.00	2.00	.20
95 Ed Olczyk	6.00	6.00	2.00	.20
96 Bob Probert	10.00	8.00	2.00	.20
97 Jocelyn Thibault (G)	15.00	10.00	5.00	.20
98 Alexei Zhamnov	10.00	8.00	2.00	.20
99 T. Jones / R. Royer	6.00	5.00	2.00	.20
100 Craig Billington (G)	6.00	5.00	2.00	.20
101 Adam Deadmarsh	10.00	8.00	2.00	.20
102 Chris Drury	24.00	14.00	5.00	.50
103 Theoren Fleury	24.00	15.00	5.00	.50
104 Adam Foote	10.00	8.00	2.00	.20
105 Peter Forsberg	55.00	35.00	20.00	1.00
106 Milan Hejduk	32.00	20.00	10.00	.50
107 Dale Hunter	10.00	8.00	2.00	.20
108 Valeri Kamensky	10.00	8.00	2.00	.20
109 Sylvain Lefebvre	6.00	5.00	2.00	.20
110 Claude Lemieux	10.00	8.00	2.00	.20
111 Aaron Miller	6.00	5.00	2.00	.20
112 Jeff Odgers	6.00	5.00	2.00	.20
113 Sandis Ozolinsh	6.00	6.00	2.00	.20
114 Patrick Roy (G)	100.00	60.00	35.00	3.00
115 Joe Sakic	60.00	40.00	20.00	1.50
116 Stéphane Yelle	6.00	5.00	2.00	.20
117 Ed Belfour (G)	40.00	25.00	15.00	1.00
118 Derian Hatcher	10.00	8.00	2.00	.20
119 Benoît Hogue	6.00	5.00	2.00	.20
120 Brett Hull	40.00	25.00	15.00	1.00
121 Mike Keane	6.00	5.00	2.00	.20
122 J. Langenbrunner	6.00	6.00	2.00	.20
123 Jere Lehtinen	10.00	8.00	2.00	.20
124 Brad Lukowich RC	**6.00**	**6.00**	**2.00**	**.50**
125 Grant Marshall	6.00	5.00	2.00	.20
126 Mike Modano	40.00	25.00	15.00	1.00
127 Joe Nieuwendyk	15.00	10.00	5.00	.20
128 Derek Plante	6.00	5.00	2.00	.20
129 Darryl Sydor	6.00	6.00	2.00	.20
130 Roman Turek (G)	20.00	12.00	5.00	.20
131 Pat Verbeek	10.00	8.00	2.00	.20
132 Sergei Zubov	6.00	6.00	2.00	.20
133 Sim RC / Sloan	**6.00**	**5.00**	**2.00**	**.50**
134 Doug Brown	6.00	5.00	2.00	.20
135 Chris Chelios	24.00	14.00	5.00	.50
136 Wendel Clark	30.000	20.00	10.00	.50
137 Kris Draper	6.00	6.00	2.00	.20
138 Sergei Fedorov	40.00	25.00	15.00	1.00
139 Tomas Holmström	6.00	6.00	2.00	.20
140 Vyacheslav Kozlov	6.00	6.00	2.00	.20
141 Martin Lapointe	15.00	10.00	5.00	.20
142 Igor Larionov	24.00	14.00	5.00	.50
143 Nicklas Lidström	24.00	14.00	5.00	.50
144 Darren McCarty	10.00	8.00	2.00	.20
145 Larry Murphy	6.00	6.00	2.00	.20
146 Chris Osgood (G)	24.00	14.00	5.00	.50
147 Bill Ranford (G)	15.00	10.00	5.00	.20
148 Ulf Samuelsson	6.00	5.00	2.00	.20
149 B. Shanahan	40.00	25.00	15.00	1.00
150 Aaron Ward	6.00	5.00	2.00	.20
151 Steve Yzerman	100.00	60.00	35.00	2.00
152 Josef Beranek	6.00	5.00	2.00	.20
153 Pat Falloon	6.00	5.00	2.00	.20
154 Mike Grier	6.00	6.00	2.00	.20
155 Bill Guerin	15.00	10.00	5.00	.20
156 Roman Hamrlik	6.00	6.00	2.00	.20
157 Chad Kilger	6.00	6.00	2.00	.20
158 G. Laraque RC	**6.00**	**6.00**	**2.00**	**.50**
159 Todd Marchant	6.00	6.00	2.00	.20
160 Ethan Moreau	6.00	5.00	2.00	.20
161 Rem Murray	6.00	5.00	2.00	.20
162 Janne Niinimaa	6.00	6.00	2.00	.20
163 Tom Poti	6.00	5.00	2.00	.20
164 Tommy Salo (G)	15.00	10.00	5.00	.20
165 A. Selivanov	6.00	5.00	2.00	.20
166 Ryan Smyth	19.00	12.00	5.00	.20
167 Doug Weight	24.00	14.00	5.00	.50
168 S.Passmore(G) RC	**6.00**	**6.00**	**2.00**	**.50**
169 Pavel Bure	32.00	20.00	10.00	.50
170 Sean Burke (G)	24.00	14.00	5.00	.50
171 Dino Ciccarelli	10.00	8.00	2.00	.20
172 Radek Dvorak	6.00	6.00	2.00	.20
173 Viktor Kozlov	10.00	8.00	2.00	.20
174 Oleg Kvasha	6.00	5.00	2.00	.20
175 Paul Laus	6.00	5.00	2.00	.20
176 Bill Lindsay	6.00	5.00	2.00	.20
177 Kirk McLean (G)	10.00	8.00	2.00	.20
178 Scott Mellanby	6.00	6.00	2.00	.20
179 Rob Niedermayer	6.00	6.00	2.00	.20
180 Mark Parrish	15.00	10.00	5.00	.20
181 Jaroslav Spacek	6.00	5.00	2.00	.20
182 Robert Svehla	6.00	6.00	2.00	.20
183 Ray Whitney	6.00	6.00	2.00	.20
184 Peter Worrell	6.00	6.00	2.00	.20
185 Boyle RC / Nilson	**10.00**	**6.00**	**5.00**	**1.00**
186 Donald Audette	15.00	10.00	5.00	.20
187 Rob Blake	24.00	14.00	5.00	.50
188 Russ Courtnall	6.00	6.00	2.00	.20
189 Ray Ferraro	6.00	5.00	2.00	.20
190 Stéphane Fiset (G)	10.00	8.00	2.00	.20
191 Craig Johnson	6.00	5.00	2.00	.20
192 Olli Jokinen	10.00	8.00	2.00	.20
193 Glen Murray	15.00	12.00	5.00	.20
194 Mattias Norström	6.00	6.00	2.00	.20
195 Sean O'Donnell	6.00	5.00	2.00	.20
196 Luc Robitaille	32.00	20.00	10.00	.50
197 Pavel Rosa	6.00	5.00	2.00	.20
198 Jamie Storr (G)	6.00	6.00	2.00	.20
199 Jozef Stumpel	6.00	6.00	2.00	.20
200 Vladimir Tsyplakov	6.00	5.00	2.00	.20
201 Benoît Brunet	6.00	5.00	2.00	.20
202 Shayne Corson	10.00	8.00	2.00	.20
203 Jeff Hackett (G)	10.00	8.00	2.00	.20
204 Matt Higgins	6.00	5.00	2.00	.20
205 Saku Koivu	32.00	20.00	10.00	.50
206 Vladimir Malakhov	6.00	5.00	2.00	.20
207 Patrick Poulin	6.00	5.00	2.00	.20
208 Stéphane Quintal	6.00	5.00	2.00	.20
209 Martin Rucinsky	6.00	6.00	2.00	.20
210 Brian Savage	10.00	8.00	2.00	.20
211 Turner Stevenson	6.00	5.00	2.00	.20
212 José Théodore (G)	45.00	30.00	15.00	1.00
213 Eric Weinrich	6.00	5.00	2.00	.20
214 Sergei Zholtok	6.00	5.00	2.00	.20
215 Dainius Zubrus	6.00	6.00	2.00	.20
216 M. Guren / T. Ryan	6.00	5.00	2.00	.20
217 Drake Berehowsky	6.00	5.00	2.00	.20
218 S. Bordeleau	6.00	5.00	2.00	.20
219 Bob Boughner	6.00	5.00	2.00	.20
220 Andrew Brunette	6.00	5.00	2.00	.20
221 Patrick* Côté	6.00	5.00	2.00	.20
222 Mike Dunham (G)	15.00	10.00	5.00	.20
223 Tom Fitzgerald	6.00	5.00	2.00	.20
224 Jamie Heward	6.00	5.00	2.00	.20
225 Greg Johnson	6.00	5.00	2.00	.20
226 Patric Kjellberg	6.00	5.00	2.00	.20
227 Sergei Krivokrasov	6.00	5.00	2.00	.20
228 Denny Lambert	6.00	5.00	2.00	.20
229 David Legwand	15.00	10.00	5.00	.20
230 Mark Mowers RC	**6.00**	**5.00**	**2.00**	**.50**
231 Cliff Ronning	6.00	6.00	2.00	.20
232 Tomas Vokoun (G)	6.00	6.00	2.00	.20
233 Scott Walker	6.00	6.00	2.00	.20
234 Jason Arnott	19.00	12.00	5.00	.20
235 Martin Brodeur (G)	60.00	40.00	20.00	1.50
236 Ken Daneyko	6.00	6.00	2.00	.20
237 Patrik Elias	30.00	20.00	10.00	.50
238 Bobby Holik	10.00	8.00	2.00	.20
239 John Madden RC	**15.00**	**12.00**	**5.00**	**1.50**
240 Randy McKay	6.00	5.00	2.00	.20
241 Brendan Morrison	10.00	8.00	2.00	.20
242 Scott Niedermayer	10.00	8.00	2.00	.20
243 Lyle Odelein	6.00	5.00	2.00	.20
244 Krzysztof Oliwa	6.00	6.00	2.00	.20
245 Jay Pandolfo	6.00	5.00	2.00	.20
246 Brian Rolston	10.00	8.00	2.00	.20
247 Vadim Sharifijanov	6.00	5.00	2.00	.20
248 Petr* Sykora	15.00	10.00	5.00	.20
249 Chris Terreri (G)	6.00	5.00	2.00	.20
250 Scott Stevens	15.00	10.00	5.00	.20
251 Eric Brewer	15.00	10.00	5.00	.20
252 Zdeno Chara	6.00	6.00	2.00	.20
253 Mariusz Czerkawski	6.00	6.00	2.00	.20
254 Wade Flaherty (G)	6.00	5.00	2.00	.20
255 Kenny Jönsson	6.00	5.00	2.00	.20
256 Claude Lapointe	6.00	5.00	2.00	.20
257 Mark Lawrence	6.00	5.00	2.00	.20
258 Trevor Linden	15.00	10.00	5.00	.20
259 Mats Lindgren	6.00	5.00	2.00	.20
260 Warren Luhning	6.00	5.00	2.00	.20
261 Zigmund Palffy	24.00	14.00	5.00	.50
262 Richard Pilon	6.00	5.00	2.00	.20
263 Félix Potvin (G)	24.00	14.00	5.00	.50
264 Barry Richter	6.00	5.00	2.00	.20
265 Bryan Smolinski	6.00	5.00	2.00	.20
266 Mike Watt	6.00	5.00	2.00	.20
267 Dan Cloutier (G)	15.00	10.00	5.00	.20
268 Brent Fedyk	6.00	5.00	2.00	.20
269 Adam Graves	15.00	10.00	5.00	.20
270 Todd Harvey	6.00	6.00	2.00	.20
271 Mike Knuble	6.00	5.00	2.00	.20
272 Brian Leetch	24.00	14.00	5.00	.50
273 John MacLean	6.00	5.00	2.00	.20
274 Manny Malhotra	6.00	6.00	2.00	.20
275 Rumun Ndur	6.00	5.00	2.00	.20
276 Petr Nedved	10.00	8.00	2.00	.20
277 Peter Popovic	6.00	5.00	2.00	.20
278 Mike Richter (G)	15.00	12.00	5.00	.20
279 Marc* Savard	6.00	6.00	2.00	.20
280 Mathieu Schneider	6.00	6.00	2.00	.20
281 Kevin Stevens	6.00	6.00	2.00	.20
282 Niklas Sundström	6.00	6.00	2.00	.20
283 Daniel Alfredsson	24.00	14.00	5.00	.50
284 Magnus Arvedson	6.00	5.00	2.00	.20
285 Radek Bonk	10.00	8.00	2.00	.20
286 Andreas Dackell	6.00	5.00	2.00	.20
287 Bruce Gardiner	6.00	5.00	2.00	.20
288 Marian Hossa	40.00	25.00	15.00	1.00
289 A. Johansson	6.00	6.00	2.00	.20
290 Igor Kravchuk	6.00	5.00	2.00	.20
291 S. McEachern	10.00	8.00	2.00	.20
292 Vaclav Prospal	10.00	8.00	2.00	.20
293 Wade Redden	10.00	8.00	2.00	.20
294 D. Rhodes (G)	6.00	6.00	2.00	.20
295 Sami Salo	6.00	5.00	2.00	.20
296 Ron Tugnutt (G)	15.00	10.00	5.00	.20
297 Alexei Yashin	24.00	14.00	5.00	.50
298 Jason York	6.00	5.00	2.00	.20
299 Rod Brind'Amour	10.00	8.00	2.00	.20
300 Adam Burt	6.00	5.00	2.00	.20
301 Éric Desjardins	10.00	8.00	2.00	.20
302 Ron Hextall (G)	20.00	14.00	5.00	.50
303 Jody Hull	6.00	5.00	2.00	.20
304 Keith Jones	6.00	5.00	2.00	.20
305 Daymond Langkow	6.00	6.00	2.00	.20
306 John LeClair	30.00	20.00	10.00	.50
307 Eric Lindros	40.00	25.00	15.00	1.00
308 Sandy McCarthy	6.00	5.00	2.00	.20
309 Dan McGillis	6.00	5.00	2.00	.20
310 Mark Recchi	15.00	10.00	5.00	.20
311 Mikael Renberg	10.00	8.00	2.00	.20
312 Chris Therien	6.00	5.00	2.00	.20
313 Vanbiesbrouck (G)	15.00	12.00	5.00	.20
314 Valeri Zelepukin	6.00	5.00	2.00	.20
315 Greg A. Adams	6.00	5.00	2.00	.20
316 Keith Carney	6.00	5.00	2.00	.20
317 Bob Corkum	6.00	5.00	2.00	.20
318 Jim Cummins	6.00	5.00	2.00	.20
319 Shane Doan	6.00	6.00	2.00	.20
320 Dallas Drake	6.00	5.00	2.00	.20
321 N. Khabibulin (G)	15.00	10.00	5.00	.20
322 Jyrki Lumme	6.00	6.00	2.00	.20
323 Teppo Numminen	10.00	8.00	2.00	.20
324 Robert Reichel	10.00	8.00	2.00	.20
325 Jeremy Roenick	32.00	20.00	10.00	.50
326 Mikhail Shtalenkov	6.00	5.00	2.00	.20
327 Mike Stapleton	6.00	5.00	2.00	.20
328 Keith Tkachuk	24.00	14.00	5.00	.50
329 Rick Tocchet	10.00	8.00	2.00	.20
330 Oleg Tverdovsky	6.00	5.00	2.00	.20
331 Juha Ylönen	6.00	5.00	2.00	.20
332 Esche RC / S. Langkow RC	**10.00**	**8.00**	**5.00**	**1.00**
333 Matthew Barnaby	6.00	5.00	2.00	.20
334 Tom Barrasso (G)	15.00	10.00	5.00	.20
335 Rob (Jr.) Brown	6.00	5.00	2.00	.20
336 Kevin Hatcher	6.00	5.00	2.00	.20
337 Jan Hrdina	6.00	6.00	2.00	.20
338 Jaromir Jagr	40.00	25.00	15.00	1.00
339 Darius Kasparaitis	6.00	6.00	2.00	.20
340 Dan Kesa	6.00	5.00	2.00	.20
341 Alexei Kovalev	24.00	14.00	5.00	.50
342 Robert Lang	6.00	6.00	2.00	.20
343 Kip Miller	6.00	5.00	2.00	.20
344 Aleksey Morozov	6.00	6.00	2.00	.20
345 Peter Skudra (G)	6.00	5.00	2.00	.20
346 Jiri Slégr	6.00	5.00	2.00	.20
347 Martin Straka	10.00	8.00	2.00	.20
348 German Titov	6.00	5.00	2.00	.20
349 Brad Werenka	6.00	5.00	2.00	.20
350 Bonin RC / Aubin (G)	**10.00**	**6.00**	**2.00**	**.50**
351 Blair Atcheynum	6.00	5.00	2.00	.20
352 Lubos Bartecko	6.00	5.00	2.00	.20
353 Craig Conroy	10.00	8.00	2.00	.20
354 Geoff Courtnall	6.00	5.00	2.00	.20
355 Pavol Demitra	15.00	10.00	5.00	.20
356 Grant Fuhr (G)	24.00	14.00	5.00	.50
357 Michal Handzus	6.00	6.00	2.00	.20
358 Al MacInnis	15.00	10.00	5.00	.20
359 Jamal Mayers	6.00	5.00	2.00	.20
360 J. McLennan (G)	6.00	5.00	2.00	.20
361 Scott Pellerin	6.00	5.00	2.00	.20

□□□□□	362 Chris Pronger	24.00	14.00	5.00	.50
□□□□□	363 Pascal Rhéaume	6.00	5.00	2.00	.20
□□□□□	364 Pierre Turgeon	15.00	10.00	5.00	.20
□□□□□	365 Tony Twist	6.00	5.00	2.00	.20
□□□□□	366 Scott A. Young	10.00	8.00	2.00	.20
□□□□□	**367 Hecht RC / Johnson (G)**	**15.00**	**12.00**	**5.00**	**1.50**
□□□□□	**368 Nash RC / Reasoner**	**10.00**	**6.00**	**5.00**	**.50**
□□□□□	369 V. Damphousse	24.00	14.00	5.00	.50
□□□□□	370 Jeff Friesen	10.00	8.00	2.00	.20
□□□□□	371 Tony Granato	6.00	6.00	2.00	.20
□□□□□	372 Bill Houlder	6.00	5.00	2.00	.20
□□□□□	373 Alexander Korolyuk	6.00	5.00	2.00	.20
□□□□□	374 Bryan Marchment	6.00	5.00	2.00	.20
□□□□□	375 Patrick Marleau	15.00	12.00	5.00	.20
□□□□□	376 Stéphane Matteau	6.00	5.00	2.00	.20
□□□□□	377 Joe Murphy	6.00	5.00	2.00	.20
□□□□□	378 Owen Nolan	24.00	14.00	5.00	.50
□□□□□	379 Mike Rathje	6.00	5.00	2.00	.20
□□□□□	380 Mike Ricci	10.00	8.00	2.00	.20
□□□□□	381 Steve Shields (G)	6.00	6.00	2.00	.20
□□□□□	382 Ronnie Stern	6.00	5.00	2.00	.20
□□□□□	383 Marco Sturm	6.00	6.00	2.00	.20
□□□□□	384 Mike Vernon (G)	15.00	10.00	5.00	.20
□□□□□	**385 Heins RC / S. Hannan**	**6.00**	**5.00**	**2.00**	**.20**
□□□□□	386 Cory Cross	6.00	5.00	2.00	.20
□□□□□	387 Alexandre Daigle	6.00	5.00	2.00	.20
□□□□□	388 Colin Forbes	6.00	5.00	2.00	.20
□□□□□	389 Chris Gratton	6.00	6.00	2.00	.20
□□□□□	390 Kevin Hodson (G)	6.00	6.00	2.00	.20
□□□□□	391 Pavel Kubina	6.00	5.00	2.00	.20
□□□□□	392 V. Lecavalier	40.00	25.00	15.00	1.00
□□□□□	393 Michael Nylander	6.00	6.00	2.00	.20
□□□□□	394 Stéphane Richer	6.00	6.00	2.00	.20
□□□□□	395 Corey Schwab (G)	6.00	5.00	2.00	.20
□□□□□	396 Mike Sillinger	6.00	5.00	2.00	.20
□□□□□	397 Petr* Svoboda	6.00	6.00	2.00	.20
□□□□□	398 Darcy Tucker	6.00	6.00	2.00	.20
□□□□□	399 Rob Zamuner	6.00	6.00	2.00	.20
□□□□□	400 Larocque / Mara	6.00	5.00	2.00	.20
□□□□□	401 Bryan Berard	10.00	8.00	2.00	.20
□□□□□	402 Sergei Berezin	6.00	6.00	2.00	.20
□□□□□	403 Lonny Bohonos	6.00	5.00	2.00	.20
□□□□□	404 Sylvain Côté	6.00	5.00	2.00	.20
□□□□□	405 Tie Domi	10.00	8.00	2.00	.20
□□□□□	406 Mike Johnson	6.00	5.00	2.00	.20
□□□□□	407 Curtis Joseph (G)	40.00	25.00	15.00	1.00
□□□□□	408 Tomas Kaberle	10.00	8.00	2.00	.20
□□□□□	409 A. Karpovtsev	6.00	5.00	2.00	.20
□□□□□	410 Derek King	6.00	5.00	2.00	.20
□□□□□	411 Igor Korolev	6.00	5.00	2.00	.20
□□□□□	**412 Adam Mair RC**	**6.00**	**6.00**	**2.00**	**.50**
□□□□□	413 Alyn McCauley	10.00	8.00	2.00	.20
□□□□□	414 Yanic Perreault	10.00	8.00	2.00	.20
□□□□□	415 Steve Sullivan	10.00	8.00	2.00	.20
□□□□□	416 Mats Sundin	40.00	25.00	15.00	1.00
□□□□□	417 Steve Thomas	6.00	6.00	2.00	.20
□□□□□	418 Garry Valk	6.00	5.00	2.00	.20
□□□□□	419 Adrian Aucoin	6.00	5.00	2.00	.20
□□□□□	420 Todd Bertuzzi	45.00	30.00	15.00	1.00
□□□□□	421 Donald Brashear	6.00	6.00	2.00	.20
□□□□□	422 Dave Gagner	6.00	5.00	2.00	.20
□□□□□	423 Josh Holden	6.00	5.00	2.00	.20
□□□□□	424 Ed Jovanovski	15.00	10.00	5.00	.20
□□□□□	425 Bryan McCabe	6.00	6.00	2.00	.20
□□□□□	426 Mark Messier	40.00	25.00	15.00	1.00
□□□□□	427 Alexander Mogilny	15.00	12.00	5.00	.20
□□□□□	428 Bill Muckalt	6.00	5.00	2.00	.20
□□□□□	429 Markus Näslund	40.00	25.00	15.00	1.00
□□□□□	430 Mattias Öhlund	10.00	8.00	2.00	.20
□□□□□	431 Dave Scatchard	6.00	5.00	2.00	.20
□□□□□	432 Peter Schaefer	6.00	5.00	2.00	.20
□□□□□	433 Garth Snow (G)	10.00	8.00	2.00	.20
□□□□□	434 Kevin Weekes (G)	6.00	6.00	2.00	.20
□□□□□	435 Brian Bellows	6.00	6.00	2.00	.20
□□□□□	436 James H. Black	6.00	5.00	2.00	.20
□□□□□	437 Peter Bondra	24.00	14.00	5.00	.50
□□□□□	438 Jan Bulis	6.00	5.00	2.00	.20
□□□□□	439 Sergei Gonchar	10.00	8.00	2.00	.20
□□□□□	**440 B. Gratton RC**	**6.00**	**5.00**	**2.00**	**.50**
□□□□□	441 Calle Johansson	6.00	6.00	2.00	.20
□□□□□	442 Ken Klee	6.00	5.00	2.00	.20
□□□□□	443 Olaf Kölzig (G)	24.00	14.00	5.00	.50
□□□□□	444 Steve Konowalchuk	6.00	6.00	2.00	.20
□□□□□	445 Andrei Nikolishin	6.00	5.00	2.00	.20
□□□□□	446 Adam Oates	15.00	10.00	5.00	.20
□□□□□	447 J. Svejkovsky	6.00	5.00	2.00	.20
□□□□□	448 Rick Tabaracci (G)	6.00	5.00	2.00	.20
□□□□□	449 Richard Zednik	15.00	10.00	5.00	.20
□□□□□	**450 Tezikov RC / Baumgartner**	**6.00**	**5.00**	**2.00**	**.20**

CENTER ICE

There are two versions: the regular insert and a Proof parallel (#10).

	Insert Set (20 cards):	**3700.00**	**65.00**
	Inserts	**CIP10**	**CI**
□□	1 Paul Kariya, Anah.	280.00	4.00
□□	2 Teemu Selänne, Anah.	160.00	2.00
□□	3 Dominik Hasek (G), Buff.	200.00	4.00
□□	4 Jarome Iginla, Calg.	160.00	2.00
□□	5 Theoren Fleury, Calg.	120.00	2.00
□□	6 Peter Forsberg, Colo.	280.00	4.00
□□	7 Patrick Roy (G), Colo.	600.00	12.00
□□	8 Joe Sakic, Colo.	320.00	6.00
□□	9 Mike Modano, Dall.	200.00	4.00
□□	10 Brendan Shanahan, Detr.	200.00	4.00
□□	11 Steve Yzerman, Detr.	480.00	8.00
□□	12 Doug Weight, Edmo.	120.00	2.00
□□	13 Trevor Linden, NYIs.	80.00	1.00
□□	14 Martin Brodeur (G), NJer.	320.00	6.00
□□	15 Alexei Yashin, Otta.	120.00	2.00
□□	16 Eric Lindros, Phil.	200.00	4.00
□□	17 Jaromir Jagr, Pitt.	200.00	4.00
□□	18 Curtis Joseph (G), Toro.	200.00	4.00
□□	19 Mats Sundin, Toro.	200.00	4.00
□□	20 Mark Messier, Vanc.	200.00	4.00

CRAMER'S CHOICE AWARD

	Insert Set (10 cards):	**450.00**
	Insert (#/299)	**CCA**
□	1 Paul Kariya, Anah.	50.00
□	2 Dominik Hasek (G), Buff.	35.00
□	3 Peter Forsberg, Colo.	50.00
□	4 Patrick Roy (G), Colo.	110.00
□	5 Joe Sakic, Colo.	60.00
□	6 Mike Modano, Dall.	35.00
□	7 Steve Yzerman, Detr.	90.00
□	8 Eric Lindros, Phil.	35.00
□	9 Jaromir Jagr, Pitt.	35.00
□	10 Curtis Joseph (G), Toro.	35.00

GOLD-CROWN DIE-CUTS

	Insert Set (36 cards):	**235.00**
	Insert (1:25 packs)	**GCDC**
□	1 Paul Kariya, Anah.	12.00
□	2 Teemu Selänne, Anah.	6.00
□	3 Raymond Bourque, Bost.	10.00
□	4 Byron Dafoe (G), Bost.	4.00
□	5 Dominik Hasek (G), Buff.	8.00
□	6 Michael Peca, Buff.	4.00
□	7 Chris Drury, Colo.	4.00
□	8 Theoren Fleury, Colo.	4.00
□	9 Peter Forsberg, Colo.	12.00
□	10 Milan Hejduk, Colo.	6.00
□	11 Patrick Roy (G), Colo.	25.00
□	12 Joe Sakic, Colo.	14.00
□	13 Ed Belfour (G), Dall.	8.00
□	14 Brett Hull, Dall.	8.00
□	15 Mike Modano, Dall.	8.00
□	16 Chris Chelios, Detr.	4.00
□	17 Brendan Shanahan, Detr.	8.00
□	18 Steve Yzerman, Detr.	20.00
□	19 Pavel Bure, Flor.	6.00
□	20 David Legwand, Nash.	4.00
□	21 Martin Brodeur (G), NJer.	14.00
□	22 Félix Potvin (G), NYIs.	4.00
□	23 Mike Richter (G), NYRa.	4.00
□	24 Alexei Yashin, Otta.	4.00
□	25 John LeClair, Phil.	6.00
□	26 Eric Lindros, Phil.	8.00
□	27 Mark Recchi, Phil.	4.00
□	28 John Vanbiesbrouck (G), Phil.	4.00
□	29 Jeremy Roenick, Phoe.	6.00
□	30 Keith Tkachuk, Phoe.	4.00
□	31 Jaromir Jagr, Pitt.	8.00
□	32 Vincent Lecavalier, Tamp.	8.00
□	33 Sergei Berezin, Toro.	4.00
□	34 Curtis Joseph (G), Toro.	8.00
□	35 Mats Sundin, Toro.	8.00
□	36 Mark Messier, Vanc.	8.00

HOME AND AWAY

Home cards (1-10) were seeded in Retail packs while Away cards (11-20) were seeded in Hobby packs.

	Insert Set (20 cards):	**115.00**
	Insert (2:25 packs)	**HAA**
□	1 Paul Kariya, Anah. [Home]	7.00
□	2 Teemu Selänne, Anah. [Home]	4.00
□	3 Dominik Hasek (G), Buff. [Home]	5.00
□	4 Peter Forsberg, Colo. [Home]	7.00
□	5 Patrick Roy (G), Colo. [Home]	15.00
□	6 Mike Modano, Dall. [Home]	5.00
□	7 Steve Yzerman, Detr. [Home]	12.00
□	8 John LeClair, Phil. [Home]	4.00
□	9 Eric Lindros, Phil. [Home]	5.00
□	10 Jaromir Jagr, Pitt. [Home]	5.00
□	11 Paul Kariya, Anah. [Away]	7.00
□	12 Teemu Selänne, Anah. [Away]	4.00
□	13 Dominik Hasek (G), Buff. [Away]	5.00
□	14 Peter Forsberg, Colo. [Away]	7.00
□	15 Patrick Roy (G), Colo. [Away]	15.00
□	16 Mike Modano, Dall. [Away]	5.00
□	17 Steve Yzerman, Detr. [Away]	12.00
□	18 John LeClair, Phil. [Away]	4.00
□	19 Eric Lindros, Phil. [Away]	5.00
□	20 Jaromir Jagr, Pitt. [Away]	5.00

IN THE CREASE NET-FUSIONS

	Insert Set (20 cards):	**300.00**
	Insert (1:97 packs)	**ITCNF**
□	1 Guy Hebert (G), Anah.	10.00
□	2 Byron Dafoe (G), Bost.	10.00
□	3 Dominik Hasek (G), Buff.	25.00
□	4 Arturs Irbe (G), Caro.	10.00
□	5 Patrick Roy (G), Colo.	75.00
□	6 Ed Belfour (G), Dall.	25.00
□	7 Chris Osgood (G), Detr.	15.00
□	8 Tommy Salo (G), Edmo.	10.00
□	9 Jeff Hackett (G), Mont.	10.00
□	10 Martin Brodeur (G), NJer.	40.00
□	11 Félix Potvin (G), NYIs.	15.00
□	12 Mike Richter (G), NYRa.	12.00
□	13 Ron Tugnutt (G), Otta.	10.00
□	14 John Vanbiesbrouck (G), Phil.	12.00
□	15 Nikolai Khabibulin (G), Phoe.	10.00
□	16 Tom Barrasso (G), Pitt.	10.00
□	17 Grant Fuhr (G), SLou.	15.00
□	18 Mike Vernon (G), SanJ.	10.00
□	19 Curtis Joseph (G), Toro.	25.00
□	20 Olaf Kölzig (G), Wash.	15.00

PAST AND PRESENT

	Insert Set (20 cards):	**245.00**
	Insert (1:49 Hobby packs)	**PAA**
□	1 Paul Kariya, Anah.	16.00
□	2 Teemu Selänne, Anah.	10.00
□	3 Raymond Bourque, Bost.	14.00
□	4 Dominik Hasek (G), Buff.	12.00
□	5 Theoren Fleury, Colo.	6.00
□	6 Peter Forsberg, Colo.	16.00
□	7 Patrick Roy (G), Colo.	35.00
□	8 Joe Sakic, Colo.	20.00
□	9 Ed Belfour (G), Dall.	12.00
□	10 Brett Hull, Dall.	12.00
□	11 Mike Modano, Dall.	12.00
□	12 Brendan Shanahan, Detr.	12.00
□	13 Steve Yzerman, Detr.	30.00
□	14 Pavel Bure, Flor.	10.00
□	15 Martin Brodeur (G), NJer.	20.00
□	16 John LeClair, Phil.	10.00
□	17 Eric Lindros, Phil.	12.00
□	18 John Vanbiesbrouck (G), Phil.	6.00
□	19 Jaromir Jagr, Pitt.	12.00
□	20 Curtis Joseph (G), Toro.	12.00

TEAM LEADERS

	Insert Set (28 cards):	**100.00**
	Insert (2:25 packs)	**TL**
□	1 Paul Kariya, Anah.	7.00
□	2 Thrashers , Atla.	2.00
□	3 Raymond Bourque, Bost.	6.00
□	4 Dominik Hasek (G), Buff.	5.00
□	5 Jarome Iginla, Calg.	4.00
□	6 Arturs Irbe (G), Caro.	2.00
□	7 Doug Gilmour, Chic.	3.00
□	8 Patrick Roy (G), Colo.	15.00
□	9 Mike Modano, Dall.	5.00
□	10 Steve Yzerman, Detr.	12.00
□	11 Bill Guerin, Edmo.	2.00
□	12 Pavel Bure, Flor.	4.00
□	13 Luc Robitaille, LosA.	4.00
□	14 Saku Koivu, Mont.	4.00
□	15 Mike Dunham (G), Nash.	2.00
□	16 Martin Brodeur (G), NJer.	8.00
□	17 Zigmund Palffy, NYIs.	3.00
□	18 Mike Richter (G), NYRa.	2.00
□	19 Alexei Yashin, Otta.	3.00
□	20 Eric Lindros, Phil.	5.00
□	21 Keith Tkachuk, Phoe.	3.00
□	22 Jaromir Jagr, Pitt.	5.00
□	23 Grant Fuhr (G), SLou.	3.00
□	24 Mike Vernon (G), SanJ.	2.00
□	25 Vincent Lecavalier, Tamp.	5.00
□	26 Curtis Joseph (G), Toro.	5.00
□	27 Mark Messier, Vanc.	5.00
□	28 Peter Bondra, Wash.	3.00

JEWEL COLLECTION

There are two versions: the Ruby card and an Emerald parallel.

	Complete Set (450 cards):	**1000.00**	**130.00**
	Player	**Emer.**	**Ruby**
□□	1 Matt Cullen, Anah.	2.00	.35
□□	2 Johan Davidsson, Anah.	2.00	.35
□□	3 Scott Ferguson, Anah.	2.00	.35
□□	4 Travis Green, Anah.	2.00	.35
□□	5 Stu Grimson, Anah.	2.00	.35
□□	6 Kevin Haller, Anah.	2.00	.35
□□	7 Guy Hebert (G), Anah.	2.00	.35
□□	8 Paul Kariya, Anah.	14.00	2.00
□□	9 Marty McInnis, Anah.	2.00	.35
□□	10 Jim McKenzie, Anah.	2.00	.35
□□	11 Fredrik Olausson, Anah.	2.00	.35
□□	12 Dominic Roussel (G), Anah.	2.00	.35
□□	13 Steve Rucchin, Anah.	2.00	.35
□□	14 Ruslan Salei, Anah.	2.00	.35
□□	15 Tomas Sandström, Anah.	2.00	.35
□□	16 Teemu Selänne, Anah.	8.00	1.00
□□	17 Jason Allison, Bost.	6.00	.35
□□	18 Per Axelsson, Bost.	2.00	.35
□□	19 Shawn Bates, Bost.	2.00	.35
□□	20 Raymond Bourque, Bost.	12.00	1.00
□□	21 Anson Carter, Bost.	4.00	.35
□□	22 Byron Dafoe (G), Bost.	4.00	.35
□□	23 Hal Gill, Bost.	2.00	.35
□□	24 Stephen Heinze, Bost.	2.00	.35
□□	25 Dmitri Khristich, Bost.	2.00	.35
□□	26 Cameron Mann, Bost.	2.00	.35
□□	27 Kyle McLaren, Bost.	2.00	.35
□□	28 Sergei Samsonov, Bost.	6.00	.35
□□	29 Robbie Tallas (G), Bost.	2.00	.35
□□	30 Joe Thornton, Bost.	12.00	1.00
□□	31 Landon Wilson, Bost.	2.00	.35
□□	**32 A. Savage RC / J. Girard**	**2.00**	**.35**
□□	33 Stu Barnes, Buff.	2.00	.35
□□	34 Martin Biron (G), Buff.	4.00	.35
□□	35 Curtis Brown, Buff.	2.00	.35
□□	36 Michal Grosek, Buff.	2.00	.35
□□	37 Dominik Hasek (G), Buff.	10.00	1.00
□□	38 Brian Holzinger, Buff.	2.00	.35
□□	39 Joé Juneau, Buff.	2.00	.35
□□	40 Jay McKee, Buff.	2.00	.35
□□	41 Michael Peca, Buff.	4.00	.35
□□	42 Erik Rasmussen, Buff.	2.00	.35
□□	43 Rob Ray, Buff.	2.00	.35
□□	44 Geoff Sanderson, Buff.	2.00	.35
□□	45 Miroslav Satan, Buff.	3.00	.35
□□	46 Darryl Shannon, Buff.	2.00	.35
□□	47 Vaclav Varada, Buff.	2.00	.35
□□	48 Dixon Ward, Buff.	2.00	.35
□□	49 Jason Woolley, Buff.	2.00	.35
□□	50 Alexei Zhitnik, Buff.	2.00	.35
□□	51 Fred Brathwaite (G), Calg.	3.00	.35
□□	52 Valeri Bure, Calg.	3.00	.35
□□	53 Andrew Cassels, Calg.	2.00	.35
□□	54 René Corbet, Calg.	2.00	.35
□□	55 Jean-Sébastien Giguère (G), Calg.	8.00	1.00
□□	56 Phil Housley, Calg.	3.00	.35
□□	57 Jarome Iginla, Calg.	8.00	1.00
□□	58 Derek Morris, Calg.	2.00	.35
□□	59 Andrei Nazarov, Calg.	2.00	.35
□□	60 Jeff Shantz, Calg.	2.00	.35
□□	61 Todd Simpson, Calg.	2.00	.35
□□	62 Cory Stillman, Calg.	2.00	.35
□□	63 Jason Wiemer, Calg.	2.00	.35

☐☐ 64 Clarke Wilm, Calg.	2.00	.35
☐☐ 65 Ken Wregget (G), Calg.	2.00	.35
☐☐ **66 T. Garner RC / R. Fata**	**3.00**	**.35**
☐☐ 67 Bates Battaglia, Caro.	2.00	.35
☐☐ 68 Paul Coffey, Caro.	6.00	.35
☐☐ 69 Kevin Dineen, Caro.	2.00	.35
☐☐ 70 Ron Francis, Caro.	6.00	.35
☐☐ 71 Martin Gélinas, Caro.	2.00	.35
☐☐ 72 Arturs Irbe (G), Caro.	4.00	.35
☐☐ 73 Sami Kapanen, Caro.	3.00	.35
☐☐ 74 Trevor Kidd (G), Caro.	3.00	.35
☐☐ 75 Andrei Kovalenko, Caro.	2.00	.35
☐☐ 76 Robert Kron, Caro.	2.00	.35
☐☐ 77 Kent Manderville, Caro.	2.00	.35
☐☐ 78 Jeff O'Neill, Caro.	4.00	.35
☐☐ 79 Keith Primeau, Caro.	4.00	.35
☐☐ 80 Gary Roberts, Caro.	4.00	.35
☐☐ 81 Ray Sheppard, Caro.	2.00	.35
☐☐ 82 Glen Wesley, Caro.	2.00	.35
☐☐ **83 C. MacDonald RC / B. Ritchie RC**	**2.00**	**.35**
☐☐ 84 Tony Amonte, Chic.	6.00	.35
☐☐ 85 Éric Dazé, Chic.	4.00	.35
☐☐ 86 Jean-Pierre Dumont, Chic.	2.00	.35
☐☐ 87 Anders Eriksson, Chic.	2.00	.35
☐☐ 88 Mark Fitzpatrick (G), Chic.	2.00	.35
☐☐ 89 Doug Gilmour, Chic.	6.00	.35
☐☐ 90 Jean-Yves Leroux, Chic.	2.00	.35
☐☐ 91 Dave Manson, Chic.	2.00	.35
☐☐ 92 Josef Marha, Chic.	2.00	.35
☐☐ 93 Dean McAmmond, Chic.	2.00	.35
☐☐ 94 Boris Mironov, Chic.	2.00	.35
☐☐ 95 Ed Olczyk, Chic.	2.00	.35
☐☐ 96 Bob Probert, Chic.	3.00	.35
☐☐ 97 Jocelyn Thibault (G), Chic.	4.00	.35
☐☐ 98 Alexei Zhamnov, Chic.	3.00	.35
☐☐ 99 T. Jones / R. Royer	2.00	.35
☐☐ 100 Craig Billington (G), Colo.	2.00	.35
☐☐ 101 Adam Deadmarsh, Colo.	3.00	.35
☐☐ 102 Chris Drury, Colo.	6.00	.35
☐☐ 103 Theoren Fleury, Colo.	6.00	.35
☐☐ 104 Adam Foote, Colo.	3.00	.35
☐☐ 105 Peter Forsberg, Colo.	14.00	2.00
☐☐ 106 Milan Hejduk, Colo.	8.00	1.00
☐☐ 107 Dale Hunter, Colo.	3.00	.35
☐☐ 108 Valeri Kamensky, Colo.	3.00	.35
☐☐ 109 Sylvain Lefebvre, Colo.	2.00	.35
☐☐ 110 Claude Lemieux, Colo.	3.00	.35
☐☐ 111 Aaron Miller, Colo.	2.00	.35
☐☐ 112 Jeff Odgers, Colo.	2.00	.35
☐☐ 113 Sandis Ozolinsh, Colo.	2.00	.35
☐☐ 114 Patrick Roy (G), Colo.	30.00	4.00
☐☐ 115 Joe Sakic, Colo.	16.00	2.00
☐☐ 116 Stéphane Yelle, Colo.	2.00	.35
☐☐ 117 Ed Belfour (G), Dall.	10.00	1.00
☐☐ 118 Derian Hatcher, Dall.	3.00	.35
☐☐ 119 Benoît Hogue, Dall.	2.00	.35
☐☐ 120 Brett Hull, Dall.	10.00	1.00
☐☐ 121 Mike Keane, Dall.	2.00	.35
☐☐ 122 Jamie Langenbrunner, Dall.	2.00	.35
☐☐ 123 Jere Lehtinen, Dall.	3.00	.35
☐☐ **124 Brad Lukowich, Dall. RC**	**2.00**	**.35**
☐☐ 125 Grant Marshall, Dall.	2.00	.35
☐☐ 126 Mike Modano, Dall.	10.00	1.00
☐☐ 127 Joe Nieuwendyk, Dall.	4.00	.35
☐☐ 128 Derek Plante, Dall.	2.00	.35
☐☐ 129 Darryl Sydor, Dall.	2.00	.35
☐☐ 130 Roman Turek (G), Dall.	4.00	.35
☐☐ 131 Pat Verbeek, Dall.	3.00	.35
☐☐ 132 Sergei Zubov, Dall.	2.00	.35
☐☐ **133 J. Sim RC / B. Sloan**	**2.00**	**.35**
☐☐ 134 Doug Brown, Detr.	2.00	.35
☐☐ 135 Chris Chelios, Detr.	6.00	.35
☐☐ 136 Wendel Clark, Detr.	8.00	1.00
☐☐ 137 Kris Draper, Detr.	2.00	.35
☐☐ 138 Sergei Fedorov, Detr.	10.00	1.00
☐☐ 139 Tomas Holmström, Detr.	2.00	.35
☐☐ 140 Vyacheslav Kozlov, Detr.	2.00	.35
☐☐ 141 Martin Lapointe, Detr.	4.00	.35
☐☐ 142 Igor Larionov, Detr.	6.00	.35
☐☐ 143 Nicklas Lidström, Detr.	6.00	.35
☐☐ 144 Darren McCarty, Detr.	3.00	.35
☐☐ 145 Larry Murphy, Detr.	2.00	.35
☐☐ 146 Chris Osgood (G), Detr.	6.00	.35
☐☐ 147 Bill Ranford (G), Detr.	4.00	.35
☐☐ 148 Ulf Samuelsson, Detr.	2.00	.35
☐☐ 149 Brendan Shanahan, Detr.	10.00	1.00
☐☐ 150 Aaron Ward, Detr.	2.00	.35
☐☐ 151 Steve Yzerman, Detr.	24.00	3.00
☐☐ 152 Josef Beranek, Edmo.	2.00	.35
☐☐ 153 Pat Falloon, Edmo.	2.00	.35
☐☐ 154 Mike Grier, Edmo.	2.00	.35
☐☐ 155 Bill Guerin, Edmo.	4.00	.35
☐☐ 156 Roman Hamrlik, Edmo.	2.00	.35
☐☐ 157 Chad Kilger, Edmo.	2.00	.35
☐☐ **158 Georges Laraque, Edmo. RC**	**2.00**	**.35**
☐☐ 159 Todd Marchant, Edmo.	2.00	.35
☐☐ 160 Ethan Moreau, Edmo.	2.00	.35
☐☐ 161 Rem Murray, Edmo.	2.00	.35
☐☐ 162 Janne Niinimaa, Edmo.	2.00	.35
☐☐ 163 Tom Poti, Edmo.	2.00	.35
☐☐ 164 Tommy Salo (G), Edmo.	4.00	.35
☐☐ 165 Alexander Selivanov, Edmo.	2.00	.35
☐☐ 166 Ryan Smyth, Edmo.	4.00	.35
☐☐ 167 Doug Weight, Edmo.	6.00	.35
☐☐ **168 Steve Passmore (G), Edmo. RC**	**2.00**	**.35**
☐☐ 169 Pavel Bure, Flor.	8.00	1.00
☐☐ 170 Sean Burke (G), Flor.	6.00	.35
☐☐ 171 Dino Ciccarelli, Flor.	3.00	.35
☐☐ 172 Radek Dvorak, Flor.	2.00	.35
☐☐ 173 Viktor Kozlov, Flor.	3.00	.35
☐☐ 174 Oleg Kvasha, Flor.	2.00	.35
☐☐ 175 Paul Laus, Flor.	2.00	.35
☐☐ 176 Bill Lindsay, Flor.	2.00	.35
☐☐ 177 Kirk McLean (G), Flor.	3.00	.35
☐☐ 178 Scott Mellanby, Flor.	2.00	.35
☐☐ 179 Rob Niedermayer, Flor.	2.00	.35
☐☐ 180 Mark Parrish, Flor.	4.00	.35
☐☐ 181 Jaroslav Spacek, Flor.	2.00	.35
☐☐ 182 Robert Svehla, Flor.	2.00	.35
☐☐ 183 Ray Whitney, Flor.	2.00	.35
☐☐ 184 Peter Worrell, Flor.	2.00	.35
☐☐ **185 D. Boyle RC / M. Nilson**	**3.00**	**.35**
☐☐ 186 Donald Audette, LosA.	4.00	.35
☐☐ 187 Rob Blake, LosA.	6.00	.35
☐☐ 188 Russ Courtnall, LosA.	2.00	.35
☐☐ 189 Ray Ferraro, LosA.	2.00	.35
☐☐ 190 Stéphane Fiset (G), LosA.	3.00	.35
☐☐ 191 Craig Johnson, LosA.	2.00	.35
☐☐ 192 Olli Jokinen, LosA.	3.00	.35
☐☐ 193 Glen Murray, LosA.	4.00	.35
☐☐ 194 Mattias Norström, LosA.	2.00	.35
☐☐ 195 Sean O'Donnell, LosA.	2.00	.35
☐☐ 196 Luc Robitaille, LosA.	8.00	1.00
☐☐ 197 Pavel Rosa, LosA.	2.00	.35
☐☐ 198 Jamie Storr (G), LosA.	2.00	.35
☐☐ 199 Jozef Stumpel, LosA.	2.00	.35
☐☐ 200 Vladimir Tsyplakov, LosA.	2.00	.35
☐☐ 201 Benoît Brunet, Mont.	2.00	.35
☐☐ 202 Shayne Corson, Mont.	3.00	.35
☐☐ 203 Jeff Hackett (G), Mont.	3.00	.35
☐☐ 204 Matt Higgins, Mont.	2.00	.35
☐☐ 205 Saku Koivu, Mont.	8.00	1.00
☐☐ 206 Vladimir Malakhov, Mont.	2.00	.35
☐☐ 207 Patrick Poulin, Mont.	2.00	.35
☐☐ 208 Stéphane Quintal, Mont.	2.00	.35
☐☐ 209 Martin Rucinsky, Mont.	2.00	.35
☐☐ 210 Brian Savage, Mont.	3.00	.35
☐☐ 211 Turner Stevenson, Mont.	2.00	.35
☐☐ 212 José Théodore (G), Mont.	12.00	1.00
☐☐ 213 Eric Weinrich, Mont.	2.00	.35
☐☐ 214 Sergei Zholtok, Mont.	2.00	.35
☐☐ 215 Dainius Zubrus, Mont.	2.00	.35
☐☐ 216 M. Guren / T. Ryan	2.00	.35
☐☐ 217 Drake Berehowsky, Nash.	2.00	.35
☐☐ 218 Sébastien Bordeleau, Nash.	2.00	.35
☐☐ 219 Bob Boughner, Nash.	2.00	.35
☐☐ 220 Andrew Brunette, Nash.	2.00	.35
☐☐ 221 Patrick* Côté, Nash.	2.00	.35
☐☐ 222 Mike Dunham (G), Nash.	4.00	.35
☐☐ 223 Tom Fitzgerald, Nash.	2.00	.35
☐☐ 224 Jamie Heward, Nash.	2.00	.35
☐☐ 225 Greg Johnson, Nash.	2.00	.35
☐☐ 226 Patric Kjellberg, Nash.	2.00	.35
☐☐ 227 Sergei Krivokrasov, Nash.	2.00	.35
☐☐ 228 Denny Lambert, Nash.	2.00	.35
☐☐ 229 David Legwand, Nash.	4.00	.35
☐☐ **230 Mark Mowers, Nash. RC**	**2.00**	**.35**
☐☐ 231 Cliff Ronning, Nash.	2.00	.35
☐☐ 232 Tomas Vokoun (G), Nash.	2.00	.35
☐☐ 233 Scott Walker, Nash.	2.00	.35
☐☐ 234 Jason Arnott, NJer.	4.00	.35
☐☐ 235 Martin Brodeur (G), NJer.	16.00	2.00
☐☐ 236 Ken Daneyko, NJer.	2.00	.35
☐☐ 237 Patrik Elias, NJer.	8.00	1.00
☐☐ 238 Bobby Holik, NJer.	3.00	.35
☐☐ **239 John Madden, NJer. RC**	**5.00**	**.35**
☐☐ 240 Randy McKay, NJer.	2.00	.35
☐☐ 241 Brendan Morrison, NJer.	3.00	.35
☐☐ 242 Scott Niedermayer, NJer.	3.00	.35
☐☐ 243 Lyle Odelein, NJer.	2.00	.35
☐☐ 244 Krzysztof Oliwa, NJer.	2.00	.35
☐☐ 245 Jay Pandolfo, NJer.	2.00	.35
☐☐ 246 Brian Rolston, NJer.	3.00	.35
☐☐ 247 Vadim Sharifijanov, NJer.	2.00	.35
☐☐ 248 Petr* Sykora, NJer.	4.00	.35
☐☐ 249 Chris Terreri (G), NJer.	2.00	.35
☐☐ 250 Scott Stevens, NJer.	4.00	.35
☐☐ 251 Eric Brewer, NYIs.	4.00	.35
☐☐ 252 Zdeno Chara, NYIs.	2.00	.35
☐☐ 253 Mariusz Czerkawski, NYIs.	2.00	.35
☐☐ 254 Wade Flaherty (G), NYIs.	2.00	.35
☐☐ 255 Kenny Jönsson, NYIs.	2.00	.35
☐☐ 256 Claude Lapointe, NYIs.	2.00	.35
☐☐ 257 Mark Lawrence, NYIs.	2.00	.35
☐☐ 258 Trevor Linden, NYIs.	4.00	.35
☐☐ 259 Mats Lindgren, NYIs.	2.00	.35
☐☐ 260 Warren Luhning, NYIs.	2.00	.35
☐☐ 261 Zigmund Palffy, NYIs.	6.00	.35
☐☐ 262 Richard Pilon, NYIs.	2.00	.35
☐☐ 263 Félix Potvin (G), NYIs.	6.00	.35
☐☐ 264 Barry Richter, NYIs.	2.00	.35
☐☐ 265 Bryan Smolinski, NYIs.	2.00	.35
☐☐ 266 Mike Watt, NYIs.	2.00	.35
☐☐ 267 Dan Cloutier (G), NYRa.	4.00	.35
☐☐ 268 Brent Fedyk, NYRa.	2.00	.35
☐☐ 269 Adam Graves, NYRa.	4.00	.35
☐☐ 270 Todd Harvey, NYRa.	2.00	.35
☐☐ 271 Mike Knuble, NYRa.	2.00	.35
☐☐ 272 Brian Leetch, NYRa.	6.00	.35
☐☐ 273 John MacLean, NYRa.	2.00	.35
☐☐ 274 Manny Malhotra, NYRa.	2.00	.35
☐☐ 275 Rumun Ndur, NYRa.	2.00	.35
☐☐ 276 Petr Nedved, NYRa.	3.00	.35
☐☐ 277 Peter Popovic, NYRa.	2.00	.35
☐☐ 278 Mike Richter (G), NYRa.	4.00	.35
☐☐ 279 Marc* Savard, NYRa.	2.00	.35
☐☐ 280 Mathieu Schneider, NYRa.	2.00	.35
☐☐ 281 Kevin Stevens, NYRa.	2.00	.35
☐☐ 282 Niklas Sundström, NYRa.	2.00	.35
☐☐ 283 Daniel Alfredsson, Otta.	6.00	.35
☐☐ 284 Magnus Arvedson, Otta.	2.00	.35
☐☐ 285 Radek Bonk, Otta.	3.00	.35
☐☐ 286 Andreas Dackell, Otta.	2.00	.35
☐☐ 287 Bruce Gardiner, Otta.	2.00	.35
☐☐ 288 Marian Hossa, Otta.	10.00	1.00
☐☐ 289 Andreas Johansson, Otta.	2.00	.35
☐☐ 290 Igor Kravchuk, Otta.	2.00	.35
☐☐ 291 Shawn McEachern, Otta.	3.00	.35
☐☐ 292 Vaclav Prospal, Otta.	3.00	.35
☐☐ 293 Wade Redden, Otta.	3.00	.35
☐☐ 294 Damian Rhodes (G), Otta.	2.00	.35
☐☐ 295 Sami Salo, Otta.	2.00	.35
☐☐ 296 Ron Tugnutt (G), Otta.	4.00	.35
☐☐ 297 Alexei Yashin, Otta.	6.00	.35
☐☐ 298 Jason York, Otta.	2.00	.35
☐☐ 299 Rod Brind'Amour, Phil.	3.00	.35
☐☐ 300 Adam Burt, Phil.	2.00	.35
☐☐ 301 Éric Desjardins, Phil.	3.00	.35
☐☐ 302 Ron Hextall (G), Phil.	6.00	.35
☐☐ 303 Jody Hull, Phil.	2.00	.35
☐☐ 304 Keith Jones, Phil.	2.00	.35
☐☐ 305 Daymond Langkow, Phil.	2.00	.35
☐☐ 306 John LeClair, Phil.	8.00	1.00
☐☐ 307 Eric Lindros, Phil.	10.00	1.00
☐☐ 308 Sandy McCarthy, Phil.	2.00	.35
☐☐ 309 Dan McGillis, Phil.	2.00	.35
☐☐ 310 Mark Recchi, Phil.	4.00	.35
☐☐ 311 Mikael Renberg, Phil.	3.00	.35
☐☐ 312 Chris Therien, Phil.	2.00	.35
☐☐ 313 John Vanbiesbrouck (G), Phil.	4.00	.35
☐☐ 314 Valeri Zelepukin, Phil.	2.00	.35
☐☐ 315 Greg A. Adams, Phoe.	2.00	.35
☐☐ 316 Keith Carney, Phoe.	2.00	.35
☐☐ 317 Bob Corkum, Phoe.	2.00	.35
☐☐ 318 Jim Cummins, Phoe.	2.00	.35
☐☐ 319 Shane Doan, Phoe.	2.00	.35
☐☐ 320 Dallas Drake, Phoe.	2.00	.35
☐☐ 321 Nikolai Khabibulin (G), Phoe.	4.00	.35
☐☐ 322 Jyrki Lumme, Phoe.	2.00	.35
☐☐ 323 Teppo Numminen, Phoe.	3.00	.35
☐☐ 324 Robert Reichel, Phoe.	3.00	.35
☐☐ 325 Jeremy Roenick, Phoe.	8.00	1.00
☐☐ 326 Mikhail Shtalenkov, Phoe.	2.00	.35
☐☐ 327 Mike Stapleton, Phoe.	2.00	.35
☐☐ 328 Keith Tkachuk, Phoe.	6.00	.35
☐☐ 329 Rick Tocchet, Phoe.	3.00	.35
☐☐ 330 Oleg Tverdovsky, Phoe.	2.00	.35
☐☐ 331 Juha Ylönen, Phoe.	2.00	.35
☐☐ **332 R. Esche RC / S. Langkow RC**	**3.00**	**.35**
☐☐ 333 Matthew Barnaby, Pitt.	2.00	.35
☐☐ 334 Tom Barrasso (G), Pitt.	4.00	.35
☐☐ 335 Rob (Jr.) Brown, Pitt.	2.00	.35
☐☐ 336 Kevin Hatcher, Pitt.	2.00	.35
☐☐ 337 Jan Hrdina, Pitt.	2.00	.35
☐☐ 338 Jaromir Jagr, Pitt.	10.00	1.00
☐☐ 339 Darius Kasparaitis, Pitt.	2.00	.35
☐☐ 340 Dan Kesa, Pitt.	2.00	.35
☐☐ 341 Alexei Kovalev, Pitt.	6.00	.35
☐☐ 342 Robert Lang, Pitt.	2.00	.35
☐☐ 343 Kip Miller, Pitt.	2.00	.35
☐☐ 344 Aleksey Morozov, Pitt.	2.00	.35
☐☐ 345 Peter Skudra (G), Pitt.	2.00	.35
☐☐ 346 Jiri Slégr, Pitt.	2.00	.35
☐☐ 347 Martin Straka, Pitt.	3.00	.35
☐☐ 348 German Titov, Pitt.	2.00	.35
☐☐ 349 Brad Werenka, Pitt.	2.00	.35
☐☐ **350 B. Bonin RC / JS. Aubin (G)**	**2.00**	**.35**
☐☐ 351 Blair Atcheynum, SLou.	2.00	.35
☐☐ 352 Lubos Bartecko, SLou.	2.00	.35
☐☐ 353 Craig Conroy, SLou.	3.00	.35
☐☐ 354 Geoff Courtnall, SLou.	2.00	.35
☐☐ 355 Pavol Demitra, SLou.	4.00	.35
☐☐ 356 Grant Fuhr (G), SLou.	6.00	.35
☐☐ 357 Michal Handzus, SLou.	2.00	.35
☐☐ 358 Al MacInnis, SLou.	4.00	.35
☐☐ 359 Jamal Mayers, SLou.	2.00	.35
☐☐ 360 Jamie McLennan (G), SLou.	2.00	.35
☐☐ 361 Scott Pellerin, SLou.	2.00	.35
☐☐ 362 Chris Pronger, SLou.	6.00	.35
☐☐ 363 Pascal Rhéaume, SLou.	2.00	.35
☐☐ 364 Pierre Turgeon, SLou.	4.00	.35
☐☐ 365 Tony Twist, SLou.	2.00	.35
☐☐ 366 Scott A. Young, SLou.	3.00	.35
☐☐ **367 J. Hecht RC / B. Johnson**	**4.00**	**1.00**
☐☐ **368 T. Nash RC / M. Reasoner**	**3.00**	**.35**
☐☐ 369 Vincent Damphousse, SanJ.	6.00	.35
☐☐ 370 Jeff Friesen, SanJ.	3.00	.35
☐☐ 371 Tony Granato, SanJ.	2.00	.35
☐☐ 372 Bill Houlder, SanJ.	2.00	.35
☐☐ 373 Alexander Korolyuk, SanJ.	2.00	.35
☐☐ 374 Bryan Marchment, SanJ.	2.00	.35
☐☐ 375 Patrick Marleau, SanJ.	4.00	.35
☐☐ 376 Stéphane Matteau, SanJ.	2.00	.35
☐☐ 377 Joe Murphy, SanJ.	2.00	.35
☐☐ 378 Owen Nolan, SanJ.	6.00	.35
☐☐ 379 Mike Rathje, SanJ.	2.00	.35
☐☐ 380 Mike Ricci, SanJ.	3.00	.35
☐☐ 381 Steve Shields (G), SanJ.	2.00	.35
☐☐ 382 Ronnie Stern, SanJ.	2.00	.35
☐☐ 383 Marco Sturm, SanJ.	2.00	.35
☐☐ 384 Mike Vernon (G), SanJ.	4.00	.35
☐☐ **385 S. Heins RC / S. Heins**	**2.00**	**.35**
☐☐ 386 Cory Cross, Tamp.	2.00	.35
☐☐ 387 Alexandre Daigle, Tamp.	2.00	.35
☐☐ 388 Colin Forbes, Tamp.	2.00	.35
☐☐ 389 Chris Gratton, Tamp.	2.00	.35
☐☐ 390 Kevin Hodson (G), Tamp.	2.00	.35
☐☐ 391 Pavel Kubina, Tamp.	2.00	.35
☐☐ 392 Vincent Lecavalier, Tamp.	10.00	1.00
☐☐ 393 Michael Nylander, Tamp.	2.00	.35
☐☐ 394 Stéphane Richer, Tamp.	2.00	.35
☐☐ 395 Corey Schwab (G), Tamp.	2.00	.35
☐☐ 396 Mike Sillinger, Tamp.	2.00	.35
☐☐ 397 Petr* Svoboda, Tamp.	2.00	.35
☐☐ 398 Darcy Tucker, Tamp.	2.00	.35
☐☐ 399 Rob Zamuner, Tamp.	2.00	.35
☐☐ **400 M. Larocque RC / P. Mara**	**2.00**	**.35**
☐☐ 401 Bryan Berard, Toro.	3.00	.35
☐☐ 402 Sergei Berezin, Toro.	2.00	.35
☐☐ 403 Lonny Bohonos, Toro.	2.00	.35
☐☐ 404 Sylvain Côté, Toro.	2.00	.35
☐☐ 405 Tie Domi, Toro.	3.00	.35
☐☐ 406 Mike Johnson, Toro.	2.00	.35
☐☐ 407 Curtis Joseph (G), Toro.	10.00	1.00
☐☐ 408 Tomas Kaberle, Toro.	3.00	.35
☐☐ 409 Alexander Karpovtsev, Toro.	2.00	.35
☐☐ 410 Derek King, Toro.	2.00	.35
☐☐ 411 Igor Korolev, Toro.	2.00	.35
☐☐ **412 Adam Mair, Toro. RC**	**2.00**	**.35**
☐☐ 413 Alyn McCauley, Toro.	3.00	.35
☐☐ 414 Yanic Perreault, Toro.	3.00	.35
☐☐ 415 Steve Sullivan, Toro.	3.00	.35
☐☐ 416 Mats Sundin, Toro.	10.00	1.00
☐☐ 417 Steve Thomas, Toro.	2.00	.35
☐☐ 418 Garry Valk, Toro.	2.00	.35
☐☐ 419 Adrian Aucoin, Vanc.	2.00	.35
☐☐ 420 Todd Bertuzzi, Vanc.	12.00	1.00
☐☐ 421 Donald Brashear, Vanc.	2.00	.35
☐☐ 422 Dave Gagner, Vanc.	2.00	.35
☐☐ 423 Josh Holden, Vanc.	2.00	.35
☐☐ 424 Ed Jovanovski, Vanc.	4.00	.35
☐☐ 425 Bryan McCabe, Vanc.	2.00	.35
☐☐ 426 Mark Messier, Vanc.	10.00	1.00
☐☐ 427 Alexander Mogilny, Vanc.	4.00	.35
☐☐ 428 Bill Muckalt, Vanc.	2.00	.35
☐☐ 429 Markus Näslund, Vanc.	10.00	1.00
☐☐ 430 Mattias Öhlund, Vanc.	3.00	.35
☐☐ 431 Dave Scatchard, Vanc.	2.00	.35
☐☐ 432 Peter Schaefer, Vanc.	2.00	.35
☐☐ 433 Garth Snow (G), Vanc.	3.00	.35
☐☐ 434 Kevin Weekes (G), Vanc.	2.00	.35
☐☐ 435 Brian Bellows, Wash.	2.00	.35
☐☐ 436 James H. Black, Wash.	2.00	.35
☐☐ 437 Peter Bondra, Wash.	6.00	.35
☐☐ 438 Jan Bulis, Wash.	2.00	.35
☐☐ 439 Sergei Gonchar, Wash.	3.00	.35
☐☐ **440 Benoît Gratton, Wash. RC**	**2.00**	**.35**
☐☐ 441 Calle Johansson, Wash.	2.00	.35
☐☐ 442 Ken Klee, Wash.	2.00	.35
☐☐ 443 Olaf Kölzig (G), Wash.	6.00	.35
☐☐ 444 Steve Konowalchuk, Wash.	2.00	.35
☐☐ 445 Andrei Nikolishin, Wash.	2.00	.35
☐☐ 446 Adam Oates, Wash.	4.00	.35
☐☐ 447 Jaroslav Svejkovsky, Wash.	2.00	.35
☐☐ 448 Rick Tabaracci (G), Wash.	2.00	.35
☐☐ 449 Richard Zednik, Wash.	4.00	.35
☐☐ 450 N. Baumgartner / A. Tezikov	2.00	.35

1999 - 2000 PACIFIC PARAMOUNT

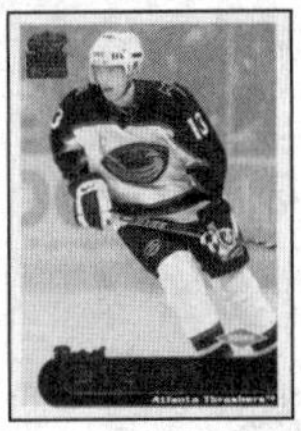

This series was released in October 1999. There are seven versions: the regular card, a Copper parallel (1:1 packs), a Gold parallel (1:1 packs), a Holo-Gold parallel (#/199), a Holo-Silver parallel (#/99), an Ice Blue parallel (1:73 packs) and a Premiere Date parallel (#/50). The Copper and Gold cards are priced similarly below. Premiere Date cards sell at 10-20% more than the Ice Blue cards. The Pacific Paramount Jewel Collection cards (Ruby, Emerald, Holo-Emerald) are listed after the first 251-card listing.

Complete Set (251 cards): 2395.00 175.00 45.00
Common Player: 5.00 .50 .20

	Player	IB	G/C	Param.
□□□□	1 Matt Cullen	5.00	.50	.20
□□□□	2 Guy Hebert (G)	5.00	.50	.20
□□□□	3 Paul Kariya	50.00	4.00	1.00
□□□□	4 Marty McInnis	5.00	.50	.20
□□□□	5 Fredrik Olausson	5.00	.50	.20
□□□□	6 Steve Rucchin	5.00	.50	.20
□□□□	7 Ruslan Salei	5.00	.50	.20
□□□□	8 Teemu Selänne	30.00	2.00	.50
□□□□	9 Jason Botterill	5.00	.50	.20
□□□□	10 Andrew Brunette	5.00	.50	.20
□□□□	11 Kelly Buchberger	5.00	.50	.20
□□□□	12 Matt Johnson	5.00	.50	.20
□□□□	13 Norm Maracle (G)	5.00	.50	.20
□□□□	14 Damian Rhodes (G)	5.00	.50	.20
□□□□	15 Steve Staios	5.00	.50	.20
□□□□	16 Jason Allison	20.00	1.00	.20
□□□□	17 Raymond Bourque	45.00	3.00	.50
□□□□	18 Anson Carter	15.00	1.00	.20
□□□□	19 Byron Dafoe (G)	15.00	1.00	.20
□□□□	20 Jonathan Girard	5.00	.50	.20
□□□□	21 Stephen Heinze	5.00	.50	.20
□□□□	22 Dmitri Khristich	5.00	.50	.20
□□□□	23 Sergei Samsonov	20.00	1.00	.20
□□□□	24 Joe Thornton	45.00	3.00	.50
□□□□	25 Stu Barnes	5.00	.50	.20
□□□□	26 Curtis Brown	5.00	.50	.20
□□□□	27 Michal Grosek	5.00	.50	.20
□□□□	28 Dominik Hasek (G)	35.00	3.00	.50
□□□□	29 Michael Peca	15.00	1.00	.20
□□□□	30 Geoff Sanderson	5.00	.50	.20
□□□□	31 Miroslav Satan	10.00	.50	.20
□□□□	32 Dixon Ward	5.00	.50	.20
□□□□	33 Jason Woolley	5.00	.50	.20
□□□□	34 Alexei Zhitnik	5.00	.50	.20
□□□□	35 Valeri Bure	10.00	.50	.20
□□□□	36 René Corbet	5.00	.50	.20
□□□□	37 Rico Fata	5.00	.50	.20
□□□□	38 J-S Giguère (G)	30.00	2.00	.50
□□□□	39 Phil Housley	10.00	.50	.20
□□□□	40 Jarome Iginla	30.00	2.00	.50
□□□□	41 Derek Morris	5.00	.50	.20
□□□□	42 J. Steve Smith	5.00	.50	.20
□□□□	43 Cory Stillman	5.00	.50	.20
□□□□	44 Ron Francis	20.00	1.00	.20
□□□□	45 Martin Gélinas	5.00	.50	.20
□□□□	46 Arturs Irbe (G)	15.00	1.00	.20
□□□□	47 Sami Kapanen	10.00	.50	.20
□□□□	48 Jeff O'Neill	15.00	1.00	.20
□□□□	49 Keith Primeau	15.00	1.00	.20
□□□□	50 Gary Roberts	15.00	1.00	.20
□□□□	51 Shane Willis	5.00	.50	.20
□□□□	52 Tony Amonte	20.00	1.00	.20
□□□□	53 Éric Dazé	15.00	1.00	.20
□□□□	54 Jean-Pierre Dumont	5.00	.50	.20
□□□□	55 Doug Gilmour	20.00	1.00	.20
□□□□	56 Dean McAmmond	5.00	.50	.20
□□□□	57 Boris Mironov	5.00	.50	.20
□□□□	58 Jocelyn Thibault (G)	15.00	1.00	.20
□□□□	59 Alexei Zhamnov	10.00	.50	.20
□□□□	60 Adam Deadmarsh	10.00	.50	.20
□□□□	61 Marc Denis (G)	15.00	1.00	.20
□□□□	62 Chris Drury	20.00	1.00	.20
□□□□	63 Peter Forsberg	50.00	4.00	1.00
□□□□	64 Milan Hejduk	30.00	2.00	.50
□□□□	65 Claude Lemieux	10.00	.50	.20
□□□□	66 Sandis Ozolinsh	5.00	.50	.20
□□□□	67 Patrick Roy (G)	110.00	9.00	2.00
□□□□	68 Joe Sakic	60.00	4.00	1.00
□□□□	69 Ed Belfour (G)	35.00	3.00	.50
□□□□	70 Guy Carbonneau	10.00	.50	.20
□□□□	71 Derian Hatcher	10.00	.50	.20
□□□□	72 Brett Hull	35.00	3.00	.50
□□□□	73 Jamie Langenbrunner	5.00	.50	.20
□□□□	74 Jere Lehtinen	10.00	.50	.20
□□□□	75 Mike Modano	35.00	3.00	.50
□□□□	76 Joe Nieuwendyk	15.00	1.00	.20
□□□□	77 Darryl Sydor	5.00	.50	.20
□□□□	78 Sergei Zubov	5.00	.50	.20
□□□□	79 Chris Chelios	20.00	1.00	.20
□□□□	80 Sergei Fedorov	35.00	3.00	.50
□□□□	81 Vyacheslav Kozlov	5.00	.50	.20
□□□□	82 Igor Larionov	20.00	1.00	.20
□□□□	83 Nicklas Lidström	20.00	1.00	.20
□□□□	84 Darren McCarty	10.00	.50	.20
□□□□	85 Larry Murphy	5.00	.50	.20
□□□□	86 Chris Osgood (G)	20.00	1.00	.20
□□□□	87 Brendan Shanahan	35.00	3.00	.50
□□□□	88 Steve Yzerman	90.00	7.00	1.50
□□□□	89 Josef Beranek	5.00	.50	.20
□□□□	90 Pat Falloon	5.00	.50	.20
□□□□	91 Mike Grier	5.00	.50	.20
□□□□	92 Bill Guerin	15.00	1.00	.20
□□□□	93 Rem Murray	5.00	.50	.20
□□□□	94 Tom Poti	5.00	.50	.20
□□□□	95 Tommy Salo (G)	15.00	1.00	.20
□□□□	96 Ryan Smyth	15.00	1.00	.20
□□□□	97 Doug Weight	20.00	1.00	.20
□□□□	98 Pavel Bure	30.00	2.00	.50
□□□□	99 Sean Burke (G)	20.00	1.00	.20
□□□□	100 Viktor Kozlov	10.00	.50	.20
□□□□	101 Oleg Kvasha	5.00	.50	.20
□□□□	102 Scott Mellanby	5.00	.50	.20
□□□□	103 Rob Niedermayer	5.00	.50	.20
□□□□	104 Marcus Nilson	5.00	.50	.20
□□□□	105 Mark Parrish	15.00	1.00	.20
□□□□	106 Ray Whitney	5.00	.50	.20
□□□□	107 Donald Audette	15.00	1.00	.20
□□□□	108 Rob Blake	20.00	1.00	.20
□□□□	109 Stéphane Fiset (G)	10.00	.50	.20
□□□□	110 Glen Murray	15.00	1.00	.20
□□□□	111 Zigmund Palffy	20.00	1.00	.20
□□□□	112 Jamie Storr (G)	5.00	.50	.20
□□□□	113 Jozef Stumpel	5.00	.50	.20
□□□□	114 Benoît Brunet	5.00	.50	.20
□□□□	115 Shayne Corson	10.00	.50	.20
□□□□	116 Jeff Hackett (G)	10.00	.50	.20
□□□□	117 Saku Koivu	30.00	2.00	.50
□□□□	118 Trevor Linden	15.00	1.00	.20
□□□□	119 Vladimir Malakhov	5.00	.50	.20
□□□□	120 Martin Rucinsky	5.00	.50	.20
□□□□	121 Igor Ulanov	5.00	.50	.20
□□□□	122 Dainius Zubrus	5.00	.50	.20
□□□□	123 Mike Dunham (G)	15.00	1.00	.20
□□□□	124 Tom Fitzgerald	5.00	.50	.20
□□□□	125 Greg Johnson	5.00	.50	.20
□□□□	126 Sergei Krivokrasov	5.00	.50	.20
□□□□	127 David Legwand	15.00	1.00	.20
□□□□	128 Cliff Ronning	5.00	.50	.20
□□□□	129 Scott Walker	5.00	.50	.20
□□□□	130 Jason Arnott	15.00	1.00	.20
□□□□	131 Martin Brodeur (G)	60.00	4.00	1.00
□□□□	132 Patrik Elias	30.00	2.00	.50
□□□□	133 Bobby Holik	10.00	.50	.20
□□□□	**134 John Madden RC**	**20.00**	**3.00**	**1.00**
□□□□	135 Randy McKay	5.00	.50	.20
□□□□	136 Brendan Morrison	10.00	.50	.20
□□□□	137 Scott Niedermayer	10.00	.50	.20
□□□□	138 Brian Rolston	10.00	.50	.20
□□□□	139 Petr* Sykora	15.00	1.00	.20
□□□□	140 Eric Brewer	15.00	1.00	.20
□□□□	141 Mariusz Czerkawski	5.00	.50	.20
□□□□	142 Kenny Jönsson	5.00	.50	.20
□□□□	143 Claude Lapointe	5.00	.50	.20
□□□□	144 Mats Lindgren	5.00	.50	.20
□□□□	**145 Vladimir Orszagh RC**	**10.00**	**1.00**	**.50**
□□□□	146 Félix Potvin (G)	20.00	1.00	.20
□□□□	147 Mike Watt	5.00	.50	.20
□□□□	148 Theoren Fleury	20.00	1.00	.20
□□□□	149 Adam Graves	15.00	1.00	.20
□□□□	150 Todd Harvey	5.00	.50	.20
□□□□	151 Valeri Kamensky	10.00	.50	.20
□□□□	152 Brian Leetch	20.00	1.00	.20
□□□□	153 John MacLean	5.00	.50	.20
□□□□	154 Manny Malhotra	5.00	.50	.20
□□□□	155 Petr Nedved	10.00	.50	.20
□□□□	156 Mike Richter (G)	15.00	1.00	.20
□□□□	157 Kevin Stevens	5.00	.50	.20
□□□□	158 Daniel Alfredsson	20.00	1.00	.20
□□□□	159 Magnus Arvedson	5.00	.50	.20
□□□□	160 Radek Bonk	10.00	.50	.20
□□□□	161 Andreas Dackell	5.00	.50	.20
□□□□	162 Marian Hossa	35.00	3.00	.50
□□□□	163 Shawn McEachern	10.00	.50	.20
□□□□	164 Wade Redden	10.00	.50	.20
□□□□	165 Sami Salo	5.00	.50	.20
□□□□	166 Ron Tugnutt (G)	15.00	1.00	.20
□□□□	167 Alexei Yashin	20.00	1.00	.20
□□□□	168 Rod Brind'Amour	10.00	.50	.20
□□□□	169 Éric Desjardins	10.00	.50	.20
□□□□	170 Keith Jones	5.00	.50	.20
□□□□	171 Daymond Langkow	5.00	.50	.20
□□□□	172 John LeClair	30.00	2.00	.50
□□□□	173 Eric Lindros	35.00	3.00	.50
□□□□	174 Mark Recchi	15.00	1.00	.20
□□□□	175 Mikael Renberg	10.00	.50	.20
□□□□	176 John Vanbiesbrouck (G)	15.00	1.00	.20
□□□□	177 Greg A. Adams	5.00	.50	.20
□□□□	178 Dallas Drake	5.00	.50	.20
□□□□	179 Nikolai Khabibulin (G)	15.00	1.00	.20
□□□□	180 Jyrki Lumme	5.00	.50	.20
□□□□	181 Teppo Numminen	10.00	.50	.20
□□□□	182 Jeremy Roenick	30.00	2.00	.50
□□□□	183 Mike Sullivan	5.00	.50	.20
□□□□	184 Keith Tkachuk	20.00	1.00	.20
□□□□	185 Rick Tocchet	10.00	.50	.20
□□□□	186 Matthew Barnaby	5.00	.50	.20
□□□□	187 Tom Barrasso (G)	15.00	1.00	.20
□□□□	188 Jan Hrdina	5.00	.50	.20
□□□□	189 Jaromir Jagr	35.00	3.00	.50
□□□□	190 Alexei Kovalev	20.00	1.00	.20
□□□□	191 Ian Moran	5.00	.50	.20
□□□□	192 Martin Straka	10.00	.50	.20
□□□□	193 German Titov	5.00	.50	.20
□□□□	194 Craig Conroy	10.00	.50	.20
□□□□	195 Pavol Demitra	15.00	1.00	.20
□□□□	196 Grant Fuhr (G)	20.00	1.00	.20
□□□□	**197 Jochen Hecht RC**	**15.00**	**2.00**	**1.00**
□□□□	198 Al MacInnis	15.00	1.00	.20
□□□□	199 Ricard Persson	5.00	.50	.20
□□□□	200 Chris Pronger	20.00	1.00	.20
□□□□	201 Pierre Turgeon	15.00	1.00	.20
□□□□	202 Scott A. Young	10.00	.50	.20
□□□□	203 Vincent Damphousse	20.00	1.00	.20
□□□□	204 Jeff Friesen	10.00	.50	.20
□□□□	205 Alexander Korolyuk	5.00	.50	.20
□□□□	206 Patrick Marleau	15.00	1.00	.20
□□□□	207 Owen Nolan	20.00	1.00	.20
□□□□	208 Mike Ricci	10.00	.50	.20
□□□□	209 Steve Shields (G)	5.00	.50	.20
□□□□	210 Marco Sturm	5.00	.50	.20
□□□□	211 Ron Sutter	5.00	.50	.20
□□□□	212 Mike Vernon (G)	15.00	1.00	.20
□□□□	**213 Karel Betik RC**	**5.00**	**1.00**	**.20**
□□□□	214 Dan Cloutier (G)	15.00	1.00	.20
□□□□	215 Jassen Cullimore	5.00	.50	.20
□□□□	216 Colin Forbes	5.00	.50	.20
□□□□	217 Chris Gratton	5.00	.50	.20
□□□□	218 Pavel Kubina	5.00	.50	.20
□□□□	219 Vincent Lecavalier	35.00	3.00	.50
□□□□	220 Darcy Tucker	5.00	.50	.20
□□□□	221 Bryan Berard	10.00	.50	.20
□□□□	222 Sergei Berezin	5.00	.50	.20
□□□□	223 Tie Domi	10.00	.50	.20
□□□□	224 Mike Johnson	5.00	.50	.20
□□□□	225 Curtis Joseph (G)	35.00	3.00	.50
□□□□	226 Derek King	5.00	.50	.20
□□□□	227 Igor Korolev	5.00	.50	.20
□□□□	228 Yanic Perreault	10.00	.50	.20
□□□□	229 Steve Sullivan	10.00	.50	.20
□□□□	230 Mats Sundin	35.00	3.00	.50
□□□□	231 Steve Thomas	5.00	.50	.20
□□□□	232 Adrian Aucoin	5.00	.50	.20
□□□□	233 Donald Brashear	5.00	.50	.20
□□□□	234 Ed Jovanovski	15.00	1.00	.20
□□□□	235 Mark Messier	35.00	3.00	.50
□□□□	236 Alexander Mogilny	15.00	1.00	.20
□□□□	237 Bill Muckalt	5.00	.50	.20
□□□□	238 Markus Näslund	35.00	3.00	.50
□□□□	239 Mattias Öhlund	10.00	.50	.20
□□□□	240 Garth Snow (G)	10.00	.50	.20
□□□□	241 Brian Bellows	5.00	.50	.20
□□□□	242 Peter Bondra	20.00	1.00	.20
□□□□	243 Jan Bulis	5.00	.50	.20
□□□□	244 Sergei Gonchar	10.00	.50	.20
□□□□	245 Olaf Kölzig (G)	20.00	1.00	.20
□□□□	246 Steve Konowalchuk	5.00	.50	.20
□□□□	247 Andrei Nikolishin	5.00	.50	.20
□□□□	248 Adam Oates	15.00	1.00	.20
□□□□	**249 Alexei Tezikov RC**	**5.00**	**1.00**	**.20**
□□□□	250 Richard Zednik	15.00	1.00	.20
□□□□	**251 Patrik Stefan RC**	**20.00**	**6.00**	**4.00**

SERIAL-NUMBERED PARALLELS

This series was released in October 1999. There are seven versions: the regular card, a Copper parallel (1:1 packs), a Gold parallel (1:1 packs), a Holo-Gold parallel (#/199), a Holo-Silver parallel (#/99), an Ice Blue parallel (1:73 packs) and a Premiere Date parallel (#/50). The Copper and Gold cards are priced similarly below. Premiere Date cards sell at 10-20% more than the Ice Blue cards. The Pacific Paramount Jewel Collection cards (Ruby, Emerald, Holo-Emerald) are listed after the first 251-card listing.

Complete Set (251 cards): 2,600 1,800 800.00

	Player	PD50	HS99	HG199
□□□	1 Matt Cullen	8.00	5.00	2.00
□□□	2 Guy Hebert (G)	8.00	5.00	2.00
□□□	3 Paul Kariya	50.00	40.00	20.00
□□□	4 Marty McInnis	8.00	5.00	2.00
□□□	5 Fredrik Olausson	8.00	5.00	2.00
□□□	6 Steve Rucchin	8.00	5.00	2.00
□□□	7 Ruslan Salei	8.00	5.00	2.00
□□□	8 Teemu Selänne	30.00	20.00	10.00
□□□	9 Jason Botterill	8.00	5.00	2.00
□□□	10 Andrew Brunette	8.00	5.00	2.00
□□□	11 Kelly Buchberger	8.00	5.00	2.00
□□□	12 Matt Johnson	8.00	5.00	2.00
□□□	13 Norm Maracle (G)	8.00	5.00	2.00
□□□	14 Damian Rhodes (G)	8.00	5.00	2.00
□□□	15 Steve Staios	8.00	5.00	2.00
□□□	16 Jason Allison	20.00	15.00	5.00
□□□	17 Raymond Bourque	45.00	35.00	15.00
□□□	18 Anson Carter	15.00	10.00	5.00
□□□	19 Byron Dafoe (G)	15.00	10.00	5.00
□□□	20 Jonathan Girard	8.00	5.00	2.00
□□□	21 Stephen Heinze	8.00	5.00	2.00
□□□	22 Dmitri Khristich	8.00	5.00	2.00
□□□	23 Sergei Samsonov	20.00	15.00	5.00
□□□	24 Joe Thornton	45.00	35.00	15.00
□□□	25 Stu Barnes	8.00	5.00	2.00
□□□	26 Curtis Brown	8.00	5.00	2.00
□□□	27 Michal Grosek	8.00	5.00	2.00
□□□	28 Dominik Hasek (G)	35.00	30.00	15.00
□□□	29 Michael Peca	15.00	10.00	5.00
□□□	30 Geoff Sanderson	8.00	5.00	2.00
□□□	31 Miroslav Satan	10.00	5.00	2.00
□□□	32 Dixon Ward	8.00	5.00	2.00
□□□	33 Jason Woolley	8.00	5.00	2.00
□□□	34 Alexei Zhitnik	8.00	5.00	2.00
□□□	35 Valeri Bure	10.00	5.00	2.00
□□□	36 René Corbet	8.00	5.00	2.00
□□□	37 Rico Fata	8.00	5.00	2.00
□□□	38 J-S Giguère (G)	30.00	20.00	10.00
□□□	39 Phil Housley	10.00	5.00	2.00
□□□	40 Jarome Iginla	30.00	20.00	10.00
□□□	41 Derek Morris	8.00	5.00	2.00
□□□	42 J. Steve Smith	8.00	5.00	2.00
□□□	43 Cory Stillman	8.00	5.00	2.00
□□□	44 Ron Francis	20.00	15.00	5.00
□□□	45 Martin Gélinas	8.00	5.00	2.00
□□□	46 Arturs Irbe (G)	15.00	10.00	5.00
□□□	47 Sami Kapanen	10.00	5.00	2.00
□□□	48 Jeff O'Neill	15.00	10.00	5.00
□□□	49 Keith Primeau	15.00	10.00	5.00
□□□	50 Gary Roberts	15.00	10.00	5.00
□□□	51 Shane Willis	8.00	5.00	2.00
□□□	52 Tony Amonte	20.00	15.00	5.00
□□□	53 Éric Dazé	15.00	10.00	5.00
□□□	54 Jean-Pierre Dumont	8.00	5.00	2.00
□□□	55 Doug Gilmour	20.00	15.00	5.00
□□□	56 Dean McAmmond	8.00	5.00	2.00
□□□	57 Boris Mironov	8.00	5.00	2.00
□□□	58 Jocelyn Thibault (G)	15.00	10.00	5.00
□□□	59 Alexei Zhamnov	10.00	5.00	2.00
□□□	60 Adam Deadmarsh	10.00	5.00	2.00
□□□	61 Marc Denis (G)	15.00	10.00	5.00
□□□	62 Chris Drury	20.00	15.00	5.00
□□□	63 Peter Forsberg	50.00	40.00	20.00
□□□	64 Milan Hejduk	30.00	20.00	10.00
□□□	65 Claude Lemieux	10.00	5.00	2.00
□□□	66 Sandis Ozolinsh	8.00	5.00	2.00
□□□	67 Patrick Roy (G)	110.00	90.00	45.00
□□□	68 Joe Sakic	60.00	45.00	20.00
□□□	69 Ed Belfour (G)	35.00	30.00	15.00
□□□	70 Guy Carbonneau	10.00	5.00	2.00
□□□	71 Derian Hatcher	10.00	5.00	2.00
□□□	72 Brett Hull	35.00	30.00	15.00
□□□	73 Jamie Langenbrunner	8.00	5.00	2.00
□□□	74 Jere Lehtinen	10.00	5.00	2.00
□□□	75 Mike Modano	35.00	30.00	15.00
□□□	76 Joe Nieuwendyk	15.00	10.00	5.00
□□□	77 Darryl Sydor	8.00	5.00	2.00
□□□	78 Sergei Zubov	8.00	5.00	2.00
□□□	79 Chris Chelios	20.00	15.00	5.00
□□□	80 Sergei Fedorov	35.00	30.00	15.00
□□□	81 Vyacheslav Kozlov	8.00	5.00	2.00
□□□	82 Igor Larionov	20.00	15.00	5.00
□□□	83 Nicklas Lidström	20.00	15.00	5.00
□□□	84 Darren McCarty	10.00	5.00	2.00
□□□	85 Larry Murphy	8.00	5.00	2.00
□□□	86 Chris Osgood (G)	20.00	15.00	5.00
□□□	87 Brendan Shanahan	35.00	30.00	15.00
□□□	88 Steve Yzerman	90.00	70.00	35.00
□□□	89 Josef Beranek	8.00	5.00	2.00
□□□	90 Pat Falloon	8.00	5.00	2.00
□□□	91 Mike Grier	8.00	5.00	2.00
□□□	92 Bill Guerin	15.00	10.00	5.00
□□□	93 Rem Murray	8.00	5.00	2.00
□□□	94 Tom Poti	8.00	5.00	2.00
□□□	95 Tommy Salo (G)	15.00	10.00	5.00
□□□	96 Ryan Smyth	15.00	10.00	5.00

97 Doug Weight	20.00	15.00	5.00
98 Pavel Bure	30.00	20.00	10.00
99 Sean Burke (G)	20.00	15.00	5.00
100 Viktor Kozlov	10.00	5.00	2.00
101 Oleg Kvasha	8.00	5.00	2.00
102 Scott Mellanby	8.00	5.00	2.00
103 Rob Niedermayer	8.00	5.00	2.00
104 Marcus Nilson	8.00	5.00	2.00
105 Mark Parrish	15.00	10.00	5.00
106 Ray Whitney	8.00	5.00	2.00
107 Donald Audette	15.00	10.00	5.00
108 Rob Blake	20.00	15.00	5.00
109 Stéphane Fiset (G)	10.00	5.00	2.00
110 Glen Murray	15.00	10.00	5.00
111 Zigmund Palffy	20.00	15.00	5.00
112 Jamie Storr (G)	8.00	5.00	2.00
113 Jozef Stumpel	8.00	5.00	2.00
114 Benoît Brunet	8.00	5.00	2.00
115 Shayne Corson	10.00	5.00	2.00
116 Jeff Hackett (G)	10.00	5.00	2.00
117 Saku Koivu	30.00	20.00	10.00
118 Trevor Linden	15.00	10.00	5.00
119 Vladimir Malakhov	8.00	5.00	2.00
120 Martin Rucinsky	8.00	5.00	2.00
121 Igor Ulanov	8.00	5.00	2.00
122 Dainius Zubrus	8.00	5.00	2.00
123 Mike Dunham (G)	15.00	10.00	5.00
124 Tom Fitzgerald	8.00	5.00	2.00
125 Greg Johnson	8.00	5.00	2.00
126 Sergei Krivokrasov	8.00	5.00	2.00
127 David Legwand	15.00	10.00	5.00
128 Cliff Ronning	8.00	5.00	2.00
129 Scott Walker	8.00	5.00	2.00
130 Jason Arnott	15.00	10.00	5.00
131 Martin Brodeur (G)	60.00	45.00	20.00
132 Patrik Elias	30.00	20.00	10.00
133 Bobby Holik	10.00	5.00	2.00
134 John Madden RC	**20.00**	**15.00**	**5.00**
135 Randy McKay	8.00	5.00	2.00
136 Brendan Morrison	10.00	5.00	2.00
137 Scott Niedermayer	10.00	5.00	2.00
138 Brian Rolston	10.00	5.00	2.00
139 Petr* Sykora	15.00	10.00	5.00
140 Eric Brewer	15.00	10.00	5.00
141 Mariusz Czerkawski	8.00	5.00	2.00
142 Kenny Jönsson	8.00	5.00	2.00
143 Claude Lapointe	8.00	5.00	2.00
144 Mats Lindgren	8.00	5.00	2.00
145 Vladimir Orszagh RC	**10.00**	**5.00**	**2.00**
146 Félix Potvin (G)	20.00	15.00	5.00
147 Mike Watt	8.00	5.00	2.00
148 Theoren Fleury	20.00	15.00	5.00
149 Adam Graves	15.00	10.00	5.00
150 Todd Harvey	8.00	5.00	2.00
151 Valeri Kamensky	10.00	5.00	2.00
152 Brian Leetch	20.00	15.00	5.00
153 John MacLean	8.00	5.00	2.00
154 Manny Malhotra	8.00	5.00	2.00
155 Petr Nedved	10.00	5.00	2.00
156 Mike Richter (G)	15.00	10.00	5.00
157 Kevin Stevens	8.00	5.00	2.00
158 Daniel Alfredsson	20.00	15.00	5.00
159 Magnus Arvedson	8.00	5.00	2.00
160 Radek Bonk	10.00	5.00	2.00
161 Andreas Dackell	8.00	5.00	2.00
162 Marian Hossa	35.00	30.00	15.00
163 Shawn McEachern	10.00	5.00	2.00
164 Wade Redden	10.00	5.00	2.00
165 Sami Salo	8.00	5.00	2.00
166 Ron Tugnutt (G)	15.00	10.00	5.00
167 Alexei Yashin	20.00	15.00	5.00
168 Rod Brind'Amour	10.00	5.00	2.00
169 Éric Desjardins	10.00	5.00	2.00
170 Keith Jones	8.00	5.00	2.00
171 Daymond Langkow	8.00	5.00	2.00
172 John LeClair	30.00	20.00	10.00
173 Eric Lindros	35.00	30.00	15.00
174 Mark Recchi	15.00	10.00	5.00
175 Mikael Renberg	10.00	5.00	2.00
176 John Vanbiesbrouck (G)	15.00	10.00	5.00
177 Greg A. Adams	8.00	5.00	2.00
178 Dallas Drake	8.00	5.00	2.00
179 Nikolai Khabibulin (G)	15.00	10.00	5.00
180 Jyrki Lumme	8.00	5.00	2.00
181 Teppo Numminen	10.00	5.00	2.00
182 Jeremy Roenick	30.00	20.00	10.00
183 Mike Sullivan	8.00	5.00	2.00
184 Keith Tkachuk	20.00	15.00	5.00
185 Rick Tocchet	10.00	5.00	2.00
186 Matthew Barnaby	8.00	5.00	2.00
187 Tom Barrasso (G)	15.00	10.00	5.00
188 Jan Hrdina	8.00	5.00	2.00
189 Jaromir Jagr	35.00	30.00	15.00
190 Alexei Kovalev	20.00	15.00	5.00
191 Ian Moran	8.00	5.00	2.00
192 Martin Straka	10.00	5.00	2.00
193 German Titov	8.00	5.00	2.00
194 Craig Conroy	10.00	5.00	2.00
195 Pavol Demitra	15.00	10.00	5.00
196 Grant Fuhr (G)	20.00	15.00	5.00
197 Jochen Hecht RC	**15.00**	**10.00**	**5.00**
198 Al MacInnis	15.00	10.00	5.00
199 Ricard Persson	8.00	5.00	2.00
200 Chris Pronger	20.00	15.00	5.00
201 Pierre Turgeon	15.00	10.00	5.00
202 Scott A. Young	10.00	5.00	2.00
203 Vincent Damphousse	20.00	15.00	5.00
204 Jeff Friesen	10.00	5.00	2.00
205 Alexander Korolyuk	8.00	5.00	2.00
206 Patrick Marleau	15.00	10.00	5.00
207 Owen Nolan	20.00	15.00	5.00
208 Mike Ricci	10.00	5.00	2.00
209 Steve Shields (G)	8.00	5.00	2.00
210 Marco Sturm	8.00	5.00	2.00
211 Ron Sutter	8.00	5.00	2.00
212 Mike Vernon (G)	15.00	10.00	5.00
213 Karel Betik RC	**8.00**	**5.00**	**2.00**
214 Dan Cloutier (G)	15.00	10.00	5.00
215 Jassen Cullimore	8.00	5.00	2.00
216 Colin Forbes	8.00	5.00	2.00
217 Chris Gratton	8.00	5.00	2.00
218 Pavel Kubina	8.00	5.00	2.00
219 Vincent Lecavalier	35.00	30.00	15.00
220 Darcy Tucker	8.00	5.00	2.00
221 Bryan Berard	10.00	5.00	2.00
222 Sergei Berezin	8.00	5.00	2.00
223 Tie Domi	10.00	5.00	2.00
224 Mike Johnson	8.00	5.00	2.00
225 Curtis Joseph (G)	35.00	30.00	15.00
226 Derek King	8.00	5.00	2.00
227 Igor Korolev	8.00	5.00	2.00
228 Yanic Perreault	10.00	5.00	2.00
229 Steve Sullivan	10.00	5.00	2.00
230 Mats Sundin	35.00	30.00	15.00
231 Steve Thomas	8.00	5.00	2.00
232 Adrian Aucoin	8.00	5.00	2.00
233 Donald Brashear	8.00	5.00	2.00
234 Ed Jovanovski	15.00	10.00	5.00
235 Mark Messier	35.00	30.00	15.00
236 Alexander Mogilny	15.00	10.00	5.00
237 Bill Muckalt	8.00	5.00	2.00
238 Markus Näslund	35.00	30.00	15.00
239 Mattias Öhlund	10.00	5.00	2.00
240 Garth Snow (G)	10.00	5.00	2.00
241 Brian Bellows	8.00	5.00	2.00
242 Peter Bondra	20.00	15.00	5.00
243 Jan Bulis	8.00	5.00	2.00
244 Sergei Gonchar	10.00	5.00	2.00
245 Olaf Kölzig (G)	20.00	15.00	5.00
246 Steve Konowalchuk	8.00	5.00	2.00
247 Andrei Nikolishin	8.00	5.00	2.00
248 Adam Oates	15.00	10.00	5.00
249 Alexei Tezikov RC	**8.00**	**5.00**	**2.00**
250 Richard Zednik	15.00	10.00	5.00
251 Patrik Stefan RC	**20.00**	**15.00**	**5.00**

GLOVE-SIDE NET-FUSIONS

Insert Set (20 cards): 235.00

Insert (1:73 packs)	GS
1 Guy Hebert (G), Anah.	8.00
2 Byron Dafoe (G), Bost.	8.00
3 Dominik Hasek (G), Buff.	20.00
4 Arturs Irbe (G), Caro.	8.00
5 Jocelyn Thibault (G), Chic.	8.00
6 Patrick Roy (G), Colo.	60.00
7 Ed Belfour (G), Dall.	20.00
8 Chris Osgood (G), Detr.	10.00
9 Tommy Salo (G), Edmo.	8.00
10 Jeff Hackett (G), Mont.	8.00
11 Martin Brodeur (G), NJer.	30.00
12 Félix Potvin (G), Toro.	10.00
13 Mike Richter (G), NYRa.	8.00
14 Ron Tugnutt (G), Otta.	8.00
15 John Vanbiesbrouck (G), Phil.	8.00
16 Nikolai Khabibulin (G), Phoe.	8.00
17 Tom Barrasso (G), Pitt.	8.00
18 Grant Fuhr (G), SLou.	10.00
19 Curtis Joseph (G), Toro.	20.00
20 Olaf Kölzig (G), Wash.	10.00

HALL OF FAME BOUND

There are two versions: the regular insert and a Proof parallel (#/35).

Insert Set (10 cards): 1400.00 575.00

Inserts	P35	HOFB
1 Paul Kariya, Anah.	175.00	70.00
2 Raymond Bourque, Bost.	150.00	60.00
3 Dominik Hasek (G), Buff.	125.00	50.00
4 Peter Forsberg, Colo.	175.00	70.00
5 Patrick Roy (G), Colo.	375.00	150.00
6 Steve Yzerman, Detr.	300.00	120.00
7 Martin Brodeur (G), NJer.	200.00	80.00
8 Eric Lindros, Phil.	125.00	50.00
9 Jaromir Jagr, Pitt.	125.00	50.00
10 Mark Messier, Vanc.	125.00	50.00

ICE ADVANTAGE

Insert Set (20 cards): 75.00

Insert (2:25 Canadian packs)	I Adv
1 Paul Kariya, Anah. [vs. R.Courtnall]	6.00
2 Teemu Selänne, Anah.	3.00
3 Dominik Hasek (G), Buff.	4.00
4 Jarome Iginla, Calg.	3.00
5 Peter Forsberg, Colo.	6.00
6 Patrick Roy (G), Colo.	12.00
7 Joe Sakic, Colo.	7.00
8 Joe Nieuwendyk, Dall.	1.50
9 Brendan Shanahan, Detr.	4.00
10 Steve Yzerman, Detr.	10.00
11 Doug Weight, Edmo.	2.00
12 Pavel Bure, Flor.	3.00
13 Jeff Hackett (G), Mont.	1.50
14 Martin Brodeur (G), NJer.	7.00
15 Marian Hossa, Otta.	4.00
16 Eric Lindros, Phil.	4.00
17 Jaromir Jagr, Pitt.	4.00
18 Curtis Joseph (G), Toro.	4.00
19 Mats Sundin, Toro.	4.00
20 Mark Messier, Vanc.	4.00

ICE ALLIANCE

Insert Set (28 cards): 125.00

Checklist (2:37 packs)	I All
1 Paul Kariya, Anah.	8.00
2 Damian Rhodes (G), Otta. (Atla.)	2.00
3 Raymond Bourque, Bost.	7.00
4 Dominik Hasek (G), Buff.	6.00
5 Jarome Iginla, Calg.	5.00
6 Keith Primeau, Caro.	2.00
7 Tony Amonte, Chic.	3.00
8 Patrick Roy (G), Colo.	18.00
9 Mike Modano, Dall.	6.00
10 Steve Yzerman, Detr.	15.00
11 Bill Guerin, Edmo.	2.00
12 Pavel Bure, Flor.	5.00
13 Luc Robitaille, LosA.	5.00
14 Jeff Hackett (G), Mont.	2.00
15 Cliff Ronning, Nash.	2.00
16 Martin Brodeur (G), NJer.	10.00
17 Félix Potvin (G), NYIs.	3.00
18 Brian Leetch, NYRa.	3.00
19 Alexei Yashin, Otta.	3.00
20 Eric Lindros, Phil.	6.00
21 Keith Tkachuk, Phoe.	3.00
22 Jaromir Jagr, Pitt.	6.00
23 Pierre Turgeon, SLou.	2.00
24 Vincent Damphousse, SanJ.	3.00
25 Vincent Lecavalier, Tamp.	6.00
26 Curtis Joseph (G), Toro.	6.00
27 Mark Messier, Vanc.	6.00
28 Peter Bondra, Wash.	3.00

PERSONAL BEST

Insert Set (36 cards): 225.00

Insert (1:37 packs)	PB
1 Paul Kariya, Anah.	12.00
2 Teemu Selänne, Anah.	7.00
3 Raymond Bourque, Bost.	10.00
4 Sergei Samsonov, Bost.	5.00
5 Dominik Hasek (G), Buff.	8.00
6 Michael Peca, Buff.	3.00
7 Tony Amonte, Chic.	5.00
8 Chris Drury, Colo.	5.00
9 Peter Forsberg, Colo.	12.00
10 Patrick Roy (G), Colo.	25.00
11 Joe Sakic, Colo.	14.00
12 Ed Belfour (G), Dall.	8.00
13 Brett Hull, Dall.	8.00
14 Mike Modano, Dall.	8.00
15 Joe Nieuwendyk, Dall.	3.00
16 Sergei Fedorov, Detr.	8.00
17 Brendan Shanahan, Detr.	8.00
18 Steve Yzerman, Detr.	20.00
19 Pavel Bure, Flor.	7.00
20 Saku Koivu, Mont.	7.00
21 Martin Brodeur (G), NJer.	14.00
22 Theoren Fleury, Calg. (NYRa.)	5.00
23 Mike Richter (G), NYRa.	4.00
24 Alexei Yashin, Otta.	5.00
25 John LeClair, Phil.	7.00
26 Eric Lindros, Phil.	8.00
27 Mark Recchi, Phil.	3.00
28 John Vanbiesbrouck (G), Phil.	4.00
29 Jeremy Roenick, Phoe.	7.00
30 Keith Tkachuk, Phoe.	5.00
31 Jaromir Jagr, Pitt.	8.00
32 Pavol Demitra, SLou.	3.00
33 Vincent Lecavalier, Tamp.	8.00
34 Curtis Joseph (G), Toro.	8.00
35 Mats Sundin, Toro.	8.00
36 Mark Messier, Vanc.	8.00

JEWEL COLLECTION

Complete Set (251 cards): 1805.00 240.00 90.00

Player	HE	Emer.	Ruby
1 Matt Cullen, Anah.	5.00	.75	.35
2 Guy Hebert (G), Anah.	5.00	.75	.35
3 Paul Kariya, Anah.	40.00	5.00	1.50
4 Marty McInnis, Anah.	5.00	.75	.35
5 Fredrik Olausson, Anah.	5.00	.75	.35
6 Steve Rucchin, Anah.	5.00	.75	.35
7 Ruslan Salei, Anah.	5.00	.75	.35
8 Teemu Selänne, Anah.	20.00	3.00	1.00
9 Jason Botterill, Dall.	5.00	.75	.35
10 Andrew Brunette, Nash.	5.00	.75	.35
11 Kelly Buchberger, Edmo.	5.00	.75	.35
12 Matt Johnson, LosA.	5.00	.75	.35
13 Norm Maracle (G), Detr.	5.00	.75	.35
14 Damian Rhodes (G), Otta.	5.00	.75	.35
15 Steve Staios, Vanc.	5.00	.75	.35
16 Jason Allison, Bost.	15.00	2.00	.50
17 Raymond Bourque, Bost.	35.00	4.00	1.50
18 Anson Carter, Bost.	10.00	1.00	.50
19 Byron Dafoe (G), Bost.	10.00	1.00	.50
20 Jonathan Girard, Bost.	5.00	.75	.35
21 Stephen Heinze, Bost.	5.00	.75	.35
22 Dmitri Khristich, Bost.	5.00	.75	.35
23 Sergei Samsonov, Bost.	15.00	2.00	.50
24 Joe Thornton, Bost.	35.00	4.00	1.50
25 Stu Barnes, Buff.	5.00	.75	.35
26 Curtis Brown, Buff.	5.00	.75	.35
27 Michal Grosek, Buff.	5.00	.75	.35
28 Dominik Hasek (G), Buff.	30.00	3.00	1.00
29 Michael Peca, Buff.	10.00	1.00	.50
30 Geoff Sanderson, Buff.	5.00	.75	.35
31 Miroslav Satan, Buff.	5.00	1.00	.35
32 Dixon Ward, Buff.	5.00	.75	.35
33 Jason Woolley, Buff.	5.00	.75	.35
34 Alexei Zhitnik, Buff.	5.00	.75	.35
35 Valeri Bure, Calg.	5.00	1.00	.35
36 René Corbet, Calg.	5.00	.75	.35
37 Rico Fata, Calg.	5.00	.75	.35
38 J-S Giguère (G), Calg.	20.00	3.00	1.00
39 Phil Housley, Calg.	5.00	1.00	.35
40 Jarome Iginla, Calg.	20.00	3.00	1.00
41 Derek Morris, Calg.	5.00	.75	.35
42 J. Steve Smith, Calg.	5.00	.75	.35
43 Cory Stillman, Calg.	5.00	.75	.35
44 Ron Francis, Caro.	15.00	2.00	.50
45 Martin Gélinas, Caro.	5.00	.75	.35
46 Arturs Irbe (G), Caro.	10.00	1.00	.50
47 Sami Kapanen, Caro.	5.00	1.00	.35
48 Jeff O'Neill, Caro.	10.00	1.00	.50
49 Keith Primeau, Caro.	10.00	1.00	.50
50 Gary Roberts, Caro.	10.00	1.00	.50
51 Shane Willis, Caro.	5.00	.75	.35
52 Tony Amonte, Chic.	15.00	2.00	.50
53 Éric Dazé, Chic.	10.00	1.00	.50
54 Jean-Pierre Dumont, Chic.	5.00	.75	.35
55 Doug Gilmour, Chic.	15.00	2.00	.50
56 Dean McAmmond, Chic.	5.00	.75	.35
57 Boris Mironov, Chic.	5.00	.75	.35
58 Jocelyn Thibault (G), Chic.	10.00	1.00	.50
59 Alexei Zhamnov, Chic.	5.00	1.00	.35
60 Adam Deadmarsh, Colo.	5.00	1.00	.35
61 Marc Denis (G), Colo.	10.00	1.00	.50
62 Chris Drury, Colo.	15.00	2.00	.50
63 Peter Forsberg, Colo.	40.00	5.00	1.50
64 Milan Hejduk, Colo.	20.00	3.00	1.00
65 Claude Lemieux, Colo.	5.00	1.00	.35
66 Sandis Ozolinsh, Colo.	5.00	.75	.35
67 Patrick Roy (G), Colo.	90.00	11.00	3.50
68 Joe Sakic, Colo.	45.00	6.00	2.00
69 Ed Belfour (G), Dall.	30.00	3.00	1.00
70 Guy Carbonneau, Dall.	5.00	1.00	.35
71 Derian Hatcher, Dall.	5.00	1.00	.35
72 Brett Hull, Dall.	30.00	3.00	1.00
73 Jamie Langenbrunner, Dall.	5.00	.75	.35
74 Jere Lehtinen, Dall.	5.00	1.00	.35
75 Mike Modano, Dall.	30.00	3.00	1.00
76 Joe Nieuwendyk, Dall.	10.00	1.00	.50
77 Darryl Sydor, Dall.	5.00	.75	.35
78 Sergei Zubov, Dall.	5.00	.75	.35
79 Chris Chelios, Detr.	15.00	2.00	.50
80 Sergei Fedorov, Detr.	30.00	3.00	1.00
81 Vyacheslav Kozlov, Detr.	5.00	.75	.35
82 Igor Larionov, Detr.	15.00	2.00	.50

□□□	83 Nicklas Lidström, Detr.	15.00	2.00	.50
□□□	84 Darren McCarty, Detr.	5.00	1.00	.35
□□□	85 Larry Murphy, Detr.	5.00	.75	.35
□□□	86 Chris Osgood (G), Detr.	15.00	2.00	.50
□□□	87 Brendan Shanahan, Detr.	30.00	3.00	1.00
□□□	88 Steve Yzerman, Detr.	70.00	9.00	3.00
□□□	89 Josef Beranek, Edmo.	5.00	.75	.35
□□□	90 Pat Falloon, Edmo.	5.00	.75	.35
□□□	91 Mike Grier, Edmo.	5.00	.75	.35
□□□	92 Bill Guerin, Edmo.	10.00	1.00	.50
□□□	93 Rem Murray, Edmo.	5.00	.75	.35
□□□	94 Tom Poti, Edmo.	5.00	.75	.35
□□□	95 Tommy Salo (G), Edmo.	10.00	1.00	.50
□□□	96 Ryan Smyth, Edmo.	10.00	1.00	.50
□□□	97 Doug Weight, Edmo.	15.00	2.00	.50
□□□	98 Pavel Bure, Flor.	20.00	3.00	1.00
□□□	99 Sean Burke (G), Flor.	15.00	2.00	.50
□□□	100 Viktor Kozlov, Flor.	5.00	1.00	.35
□□□	101 Oleg Kvasha, Flor.	5.00	.75	.35
□□□	102 Scott Mellanby, Flor.	5.00	.75	.35
□□□	103 Rob Niedermayer, Flor.	5.00	.75	.35
□□□	104 Marcus Nilson, Flor.	5.00	.75	.35
□□□	105 Mark Parrish, Flor.	10.00	1.00	.50
□□□	106 Ray Whitney, Flor.	5.00	.75	.35
□□□	107 Donald Audette, LosA.	10.00	1.00	.50
□□□	108 Rob Blake, LosA.	15.00	2.00	.50
□□□	109 Stéphane Fiset (G), LosA.	5.00	1.00	.35
□□□	110 Glen Murray, LosA.	10.00	1.00	.50
□□□	111 Zigmund Palffy, LosA.	15.00	2.00	.50
□□□	112 Jamie Storr (G), LosA.	5.00	.75	.35
□□□	113 Jozef Stumpel, LosA.	5.00	.75	.35
□□□	114 Benoît Brunet, Mont.	5.00	.75	.35
□□□	115 Shayne Corson, Mont.	5.00	1.00	.35
□□□	116 Jeff Hackett (G), Mont.	5.00	1.00	.35
□□□	117 Saku Koivu, Mont.	20.00	3.00	1.00
□□□	118 Trevor Linden, Mont.	10.00	1.00	.50
□□□	119 Vladimir Malakhov, Mont.	5.00	.75	.35
□□□	120 Martin Rucinsky, Mont.	5.00	.75	.35
□□□	121 Igor Ulanov, Mont.	5.00	.75	.35
□□□	122 Dainius Zubrus, Mont.	5.00	.75	.35
□□□	123 Mike Dunham (G), Nash.	10.00	1.00	.50
□□□	124 Tom Fitzgerald, Nash.	5.00	.75	.35
□□□	125 Greg Johnson, Nash.	5.00	.75	.35
□□□	126 Sergei Krivokrasov, Nash.	5.00	.75	.35
□□□	127 David Legwand, Nash.	10.00	1.00	.50
□□□	128 Cliff Ronning, Nash.	5.00	.75	.35
□□□	129 Scott Walker, Nash.	5.00	.75	.35
□□□	130 Jason Arnott, NJer.	10.00	1.00	.50
□□□	131 Martin Brodeur (G), NJer.	45.00	6.00	2.00
□□□	132 Patrik Elias, NJer.	20.00	3.00	1.00
□□□	133 Bobby Holik, NJer.	5.00	1.00	.35
□□□	**134 John Madden, NJer. RC**	**10.00**	**2.00**	**2.00**
□□□	135 Randy McKay, NJer.	5.00	.75	.35
□□□	136 Brendan Morrison, NJer.	5.00	1.00	.35
□□□	137 Scott Niedermayer, NJer.	5.00	1.00	.35
□□□	138 Brian Rolston, NJer.	5.00	1.00	.35
□□□	139 Petr* Sykora, NJer.	10.00	1.00	.50
□□□	140 Eric Brewer, NYIs.	10.00	1.00	.50
□□□	141 Mariusz Czerkawski, NYIs.	5.00	.75	.35
□□□	142 Kenny Jönsson, NYIs.	5.00	.75	.35
□□□	143 Claude Lapointe, NYIs.	5.00	.75	.35
□□□	144 Mats Lindgren, NYIs.	5.00	.75	.35
□□□	**145 Vladimir Orszagh, NYIs. RC**	**5.00**	**1.00**	**1.00**
□□□	146 Félix Potvin (G), NYIs.	15.00	2.00	.50
□□□	147 Mike Watt, NYIs.	5.00	.75	.35
□□□	148 Theoren Fleury, NYRa.	15.00	2.00	.50
□□□	149 Adam Graves, NYRa.	10.00	1.00	.50
□□□	150 Todd Harvey, NYRa.	5.00	.75	.35
□□□	151 Valeri Kamensky, NYRa.	5.00	1.00	.35
□□□	152 Brian Leetch, NYRa.	15.00	2.00	.50
□□□	153 John MacLean, NYRa.	5.00	.75	.35
□□□	154 Manny Malhotra, NYRa.	5.00	.75	.35
□□□	155 Petr Nedved, NYRa.	5.00	1.00	.35
□□□	156 Mike Richter (G), NYRa.	10.00	1.00	.50
□□□	157 Kevin Stevens, NYRa.	5.00	.75	.35
□□□	158 Daniel Alfredsson, Otta.	15.00	2.00	.50
□□□	159 Magnus Arvedson, Otta.	5.00	.75	.35
□□□	160 Radek Bonk, Otta.	5.00	1.00	.35
□□□	161 Andreas Dackell, Otta.	5.00	.75	.35
□□□	162 Marian Hossa, Otta.	30.00	3.00	1.00
□□□	163 Shawn McEachern, Otta.	5.00	1.00	.35
□□□	164 Wade Redden, Otta.	5.00	1.00	.35
□□□	165 Sami Salo, Otta.	5.00	.75	.35
□□□	166 Ron Tugnutt (G), Otta.	10.00	1.00	.50
□□□	167 Alexei Yashin, Otta.	15.00	2.00	.50
□□□	168 Rod Brind'Amour, Phil.	5.00	1.00	.35
□□□	169 Éric Desjardins, Phil.	5.00	1.00	.35
□□□	170 Keith Jones, Phil.	5.00	.75	.35
□□□	171 Daymond Langkow, Phil.	5.00	.75	.35
□□□	172 John LeClair, Phil.	20.00	3.00	1.00
□□□	173 Eric Lindros, Phil.	30.00	3.00	1.00
□□□	174 Mark Recchi, Phil.	10.00	1.00	.50
□□□	175 Mikael Renberg, Phil.	5.00	1.00	.35
□□□	176 John Vanbiesbrouck (G), Phil.	10.00	1.00	.50
□□□	177 Greg A. Adams, Phoe.	5.00	.75	.35
□□□	178 Dallas Drake, Phoe.	5.00	.75	.35
□□□	179 Nikolai Khabibulin (G), Phoe.	10.00	1.00	.50
□□□	180 Jyrki Lumme, Phoe.	5.00	.75	.35
□□□	181 Teppo Numminen, Phoe.	5.00	1.00	.35
□□□	182 Jeremy Roenick, Phoe.	20.00	3.00	1.00
□□□	183 Mike Sullivan, Phoe.	5.00	.75	.35
□□□	184 Keith Tkachuk, Phoe.	15.00	2.00	.50
□□□	185 Rick Tocchet, Phoe.	5.00	1.00	.35
□□□	186 Matthew Barnaby, Pitt.	5.00	.75	.35
□□□	187 Tom Barrasso (G), Pitt.	10.00	1.00	.50
□□□	188 Jan Hrdina, Pitt.	5.00	.75	.35
□□□	189 Jaromir Jagr, Pitt.	30.00	3.00	1.00
□□□	190 Alexei Kovalev, Pitt.	15.00	2.00	.50
□□□	191 Ian Moran, Pitt.	5.00	.75	.35
□□□	192 Martin Straka, Pitt.	5.00	1.00	.35
□□□	193 German Titov, Pitt.	5.00	.75	.35
□□□	194 Craig Conroy, SLou.	5.00	1.00	.35
□□□	195 Pavol Demitra, SLou.	10.00	1.00	.50
□□□	196 Grant Fuhr (G), SLou.	15.00	2.00	.50
□□□	**197 Jochen Hecht, SLou. RC**	**10.00**	**1.00**	**1.50**
□□□	198 Al MacInnis, SLou.	10.00	1.00	.50
□□□	199 Ricard Persson, SLou.	5.00	.75	.35
□□□	200 Chris Pronger, SLou.	15.00	2.00	.50
□□□	201 Pierre Turgeon, SLou.	10.00	1.00	.50
□□□	202 Scott A. Young, SLou.	5.00	1.00	.35
□□□	203 Vincent Damphousse, SanJ.	15.00	2.00	.50
□□□	204 Jeff Friesen, SanJ.	5.00	1.00	.35
□□□	205 Alexander Korolyuk, SanJ.	5.00	.75	.35
□□□	206 Patrick Marleau, SanJ.	10.00	1.00	.50
□□□	207 Owen Nolan, SanJ.	15.00	2.00	.50
□□□	208 Mike Ricci, SanJ.	5.00	1.00	.35
□□□	209 Steve Shields (G), SanJ.	5.00	.75	.35
□□□	210 Marco Sturm, SanJ.	5.00	.75	.35
□□□	211 Ron Sutter, SanJ.	5.00	.75	.35
□□□	212 Mike Vernon (G), SanJ.	10.00	1.00	.50
□□□	**213 Karel Betik, Tamp. RC**	**5.00**	**.75**	**.50**
□□□	214 Dan Cloutier (G), Tamp.	10.00	1.00	.50
□□□	215 Jassen Cullimore, Tamp.	5.00	.75	.35
□□□	216 Colin Forbes, Tamp.	5.00	.75	.35
□□□	217 Chris Gratton, Tamp.	5.00	.75	.35
□□□	218 Pavel Kubina, Tamp.	5.00	.75	.35
□□□	219 Vincent Lecavalier, Tamp.	30.00	3.00	1.00
□□□	220 Darcy Tucker, Tamp.	5.00	.75	.35
□□□	221 Bryan Berard, Toro.	5.00	1.00	.35
□□□	222 Sergei Berezin, Toro.	5.00	.75	.35
□□□	223 Tie Domi, Toro.	5.00	1.00	.35
□□□	224 Mike Johnson, Toro.	5.00	.75	.35
□□□	225 Curtis Joseph (G), Toro.	30.00	3.00	1.00
□□□	226 Derek King, Toro.	5.00	.75	.35
□□□	227 Igor Korolev, Toro.	5.00	.75	.35
□□□	228 Yanic Perreault, Toro.	5.00	1.00	.35
□□□	229 Steve Sullivan, Toro.	5.00	1.00	.35
□□□	230 Mats Sundin, Toro.	30.00	3.00	1.00
□□□	231 Steve Thomas, Toro.	5.00	.75	.35
□□□	232 Adrian Aucoin, Vanc.	5.00	.75	.35
□□□	233 Donald Brashear, Vanc.	5.00	.75	.35
□□□	234 Ed Jovanovski, Vanc.	10.00	1.00	.50
□□□	235 Mark Messier, Vanc.	30.00	3.00	1.00
□□□	236 Alexander Mogilny, Vanc.	10.00	1.00	.50
□□□	237 Bill Muckalt, Vanc.	5.00	.75	.35
□□□	238 Markus Näslund, Vanc.	30.00	3.00	1.00
□□□	239 Mattias Öhlund, Vanc.	5.00	1.00	.35
□□□	240 Garth Snow (G), Vanc.	5.00	1.00	.35
□□□	241 Brian Bellows, Wash.	5.00	.75	.35
□□□	242 Peter Bondra, Wash.	15.00	2.00	.50
□□□	243 Jan Bulis, Wash.	5.00	.75	.35
□□□	244 Sergei Gonchar, Wash.	5.00	1.00	.35
□□□	245 Olaf Kölzig (G), Wash.	15.00	2.00	.50
□□□	246 Steve Konowalchuk, Wash.	5.00	.75	.35
□□□	247 Andrei Nikolishin, Wash.	5.00	.75	.35
□□□	248 Adam Oates, Wash.	10.00	1.00	.50
□□□	**249 Alexei Tezikov, Wash. RC**	**5.00**	**.75**	**.50**
□□□	250 Richard Zednik, Wash.	10.00	1.00	.50
□□□	**251 Patrik Stefan, Atla. RC**	**10.00**	**6.00**	**4.00**

1999 - 2000 PANINI STICKERS

These stickers were issued in Europe.

Complete Set (360 stickers): .00
Album: 4.00
Common Player: .30

	Player	Panini
□	1 NHL Logo	.30
□	2 NHLPA Logo	.30
□	3 Jaromir Jagr, Pitt. [Award Winner]	1.00
□	4 Chris Drury, Colo. [Award Winner]	.50
□	5 Al MacInnis, SLou. [Award Winner]	.30
□	6 Dominik Hasek (G), Buff. [Award Winner]	1.00
□	7 Jere Lehtinen, Dall. [Award Winner]	.30
□	8 Joe Nieuwendyk, Dall. [Award Winner]	.30
□	9 Thrashers , Atla. [Logo]	.30
□	10 Kelly Buchberger, Atla.	.30
□	11 Johan Garpenlöv, Atla.	.30
□	12 Ray Ferraro, Atla.	.30
□	13 Nelson Emerson, Atla.	.30
□	14 Kevin Dean, Atla.	.30
□	15 Patrik Stefan, Atla.	.30
□	16 Per Svartvadet, Atla.	.30
□	17 Damian Rhodes (G), Atla.	.30
□	18 Andrew Brunette, Atla.	.30
□	19 Yannick Tremblay, Atla.	.30
□	20 Bruins , Bost. [Logo]	.30
□	21 Raymond Bourque, Bost.	1.00
□	22 Anson Carter, Bost.	.30
□	23 Byron Dafoe (G), Bost.	.30
□	24 Dave Andreychuk, Bost.	.30
□	25 Sergei Samsonov, Bost.	.50
□	26 Joe Thornton, Bost.	1.00
□	27 Jason Allison, Bost.	.50
□	28 Per Axelsson, Bost.	.30
□	29 Kyle McLaren, Bost.	.30
□	30 Rob DiMaio, Bost.	.30
□	31 Sabres , Buff. [Logo]	.30
□	32 Dominik Hasek (G), Buff.	1.00
□	33 Geoff Sanderson, Buff.	.30
□	34 Richard Smehlik, Buff.	.30
□	35 Alexei Zhitnik, Buff.	.30
□	36 Jason Woolley, Buff.	.30
□	37 Michael Peca, Buff.	.30
□	38 Miroslav Satan, Buff.	.30
□	39 Michal Grosek, Buff.	.30
□	40 Stu Barnes, Buff.	.30
□	41 Vaclav Varada, Buff.	.30
□	42 Hurricanes , Caro. [Logo]	.30
□	43 Sami Kapanen, Caro.	.30
□	44 Ron Francis, Caro.	.50
□	45 Robert Kron, Caro.	.30
□	46 Andrei Kovalenko, Caro.	.30
□	47 Martin Gélinas, Caro.	.30
□	48 Glen Wesley, Caro.	.30
□	49 Kent Manderville, Caro.	.30
□	50 Gary Roberts, Caro.	.30
□	51 Tommy Westlund, Caro.	.30
□	52 Bates Battaglia, Caro.	.30
□	53 Panthers , Flor. [Logo]	.30
□	54 Sean Burke (G), Flor.	.50
□	55 Robert Svehla, Flor.	.30
□	56 Pavel Bure, Flor.	.50
□	57 Jaroslav Spacek, Flor.	.30
□	58 Radek Dvorak, Flor.	.30
□	59 Rob Niedermayer, Flor.	.30
□	60 Viktor Kozlov, Flor.	.30
□	61 Mark Parrish, Flor.	.30
□	62 Scott Mellanby, Flor.	.30
□	63 Oleg Kvasha, Flor.	.30
□	64 Canadiens , Mont. [Logo]	.30
□	65 Saku Koivu, Mont.	.50
□	66 Trevor Linden, Mont.	.30
□	67 Brian Savage, Mont.	.30
□	68 Martin Rucinsky, Mont.	.30
□	69 Scott Lachance, Mont.	.30
□	70 Scott Thornton, Mont.	.30
□	71 Mike Ribeiro, Mont.	.30
□	72 Jeff Hackett (G), Mont.	.30
□	73 Dainius Zubrus, Mont.	.30
□	74 Eric Weinrich, Mont.	.30
□	75 Devils , NewJ. [Logo]	.30
□	76 Scott Stevens, NJer.	.30
□	77 Sergei Nemchinov, NJer.	.30
□	78 Petr Sykora, NJer.	.30
□	79 Martin Brodeur (G), NJer.	1.50
□	80 Claude Lemieux, NJer.	.30
□	81 Bobby Holik, NewJ.	.30
□	82 Brian Rafalski, NJer.	.30
□	83 Scott Gomez, NJer.	.30
□	84 Jason Arnott, NJer.	.30
□	85 Ken Daneyko, NJer.	.30
□	86 Islanders , NYIs. [Logo]	.30
□	87 Jörgen Jönsson, NYIs.	.30
□	88 Olli Jokinen, NYIs.	.30
□	89 Zdeno Chara, NYIs.	.30
□	90 Mats Lindgren, NYIs.	.30
□	91 Félix Potvin (G), NYIs.	.50
□	92 Kenny Jönsson, NYIs.	.30
□	93 Tim Connolly, NYIs.	.30
□	94 Mariusz Czerkawski, NYIs.	.30
□	95 Gino Odjick, NYIs.	.30
□	96 Brad Isbister, NYIs.	.30
□	97 Rangers , NYRa. [Logo]	.30
□	98 Brian Leetch, NYRa.	.50
□	99 Theoren Fleury, NYRa.	.50
□	100 Adam Graves, NYRa.	.30
□	101 Mike Richter (G), NYRa.	.30
□	102 Kim Johnsson, NYRa.	.30
□	103 Kevin Stevens, NYRa.	.30
□	104 Mathieu Schneider, NYRa.	.30
□	105 Stéphane Quintal, NYRa.	.30
□	106 John MacLean, NYRa.	.30
□	107 Kevin Hatcher, NYRa.	.30
□	108 Senators , Otta. [Logo]	.30
□	109 Janne Laukkanen, Otta.	.30
□	110 Andreas Dackell, Otta.	.30
□	111 Rob Zamuner, Otta.	.30
□	112 Daniel Alfredsson, Otta.	.50
□	113 Shawn McEachern, Otta.	.30
□	114 Marian Hossa, Otta.	1.00
□	115 Magnus Arvedson, Otta.	.30
□	116 Radek Bonk, Otta.	.30
□	117 Ron Tugnutt (G), Otta.	.30
□	118 Igor Kravchuk, Otta.	.30
□	119 Flyers , Phil. [Logo]	.30
□	120 Ulf Samuelsson, Phil.	.30
□	121 Eric Lindros, Phil.	1.00
□	122 Mikael Renberg, Phil.	.30
□	123 Valeri Zelepukin, Phil.	.30
□	124 Rod Brind'Amour, Phil.	.30
□	125 John LeClair, Phil.	.50
□	126 Mark Recchi, Phil.	.30
□	127 Éric Desjardins, Phil.	.30
□	128 John Vanbiesbrouck (G), Phil.	.30
□	129 Simon Gagné, Phil.	.50
□	130 Penguins , Pitt. [Logo]	.30
□	131 Jaromir Jagr, Pitt.	1.00
□	132 Jiri Slégr, Pitt.	.30
□	133 Robert Lang, Pitt.	.30
□	134 Alexei Kovalev, Pitt.	.50
□	135 Darius Kasparaitis, Pitt.	.30
□	136 Aleksey Morozov, Pitt.	.30
□	137 Tom Barrasso (G), Pitt.	.30
□	138 Martin Straka, Pitt.	.30
□	139 German Titov, Pitt.	.30
□	140 Matthew Barnaby, Pitt.	.30
□	141 Lightning , Tamp. [Logo]	.30
□	142 Michael Nylander, Tamp.	.30
□	143 Chris Gratton, Tamp.	.30
□	144 Petr* Svoboda, Tamp.	.30
□	145 Stéphane Richer, Tamp.	.30
□	146 Pavel Kubina, Tamp.	.30
□	147 Fredrik Modin, Tamp.	.30
□	148 Vincent Lecavalier, Tamp.	1.00
□	149 Andrei Zyuzin, Tamp.	.30
□	150 Dan Cloutier (G), Tamp.	.30
□	151 Darcy Tucker, Tamp.	.30
□	152 Maple Leafs , Toro. [Logo]	.30
□	153 Mats Sundin, Toro.	1.00
□	154 Steve Thomas, Toro.	.30
□	155 Alexander Karpovtsev, Toro.	.30
□	156 Jonas Höglund, Toro.	.30
□	157 Curtis Joseph (G), Toro.	1.00
□	158 Yanic Perreault, Toro.	.30
□	159 Dmitri Khristich, Toro.	.30
□	160 Bryan Berard, Toro.	.30
□	161 Sergei Berezin, Toro.	.30
□	162 Tie Domi, Toro.	.30
□	163 Capitals , Wash. [Logo]	.30
□	164 Ulf Dahlén, Wash.	.30
□	165 Dmitri Mironov, Wash.	.30
□	166 Adam Oates, Wash.	.30
□	167 Peter Bondra, Wash.	.50
□	168 Joe Sacco, Wash.	.30
□	169 Sergei Gonchar, Wash.	.30
□	170 Calle Johansson, Wash.	.30
□	171 Chris Simon, Wash.	.30
□	172 Richard Zednik, Wash.	.30
□	173 Andrei Nikolishin, Wash.	.30
□	174 Mighty Ducks , Anah. [Logo]	.30
□	175 Paul Kariya, Anah.	1.00
□	176 Teemu Selänne, Anah.	.50
□	177 Matt Cullen, Anah.	.30
□	178 Ted Donato, Anah.	.30
□	179 Niclas Hävelid, Anah.	.30
□	180 Marty McInnis, Anah.	.30
□	181 Guy Hebert (G), Anah.	.30
□	182 Steve Rucchin, Anah.	.30
□	183 Oleg Tverdovsky, Anah.	.30
□	184 Pavel Trnka, Anah.	.30
□	185 Flames , Calg. [Logo]	.30
□	186 Grant Fuhr (G), Calg.	.50
□	187 Tommy Albelin, Calg.	.30
□	188 J. Steve Smith, Calg.	.30
□	189 Valeri Bure, Calg.	.30
□	190 Jarome Iginla, Calg.	.50
□	191 Cory Stillman, Calg.	.30
□	192 Derek Morris, Calg.	.30
□	193 Phil Housley, Calg.	.30
□	194 Marc* Savard, Calg.	.30
□	195 Andrei Nazarov, Calg.	.30
□	196 Blackhawks , Chic. [Logo]	.30
□	197 Bryan McCabe, Chic.	.30
□	198 Éric Dazé, Chic.	.30
□	199 Anders Eriksson, Chic.	.30
□	200 Alexei Zhamnov, Chic.	.30
□	201 Doug Gilmour, Chic.	.50
□	202 Dean McAmmond, Chic.	.30
□	203 Tony Amonte, Chic.	.50
□	204 Jean-Pierre Dumont, Chic.	.30
□	205 Wendel Clark, Chic.	.50

	Player	
☐	206 Bryan Muir, Chic.	.30
☐	207 Avalanche , Colo. [Logo]	.30
☐	208 Alexei Gusarov, Colo.	.30
☐	209 Peter Forsberg, Colo.	1.00
☐	210 Joe Sakic, Colo.	1.50
☐	211 Patrick Roy (G), Colo.	3.00
☐	212 Milan Hejduk, Colo.	.50
☐	213 Sandis Ozolinsh, Colo.	.30
☐	214 Adam Deadmarsh, Colo.	.30
☐	215 Chris Drury, Colo.	.50
☐	216 Alex Tanguay, Colo.	.50
☐	217 Adam Foote, Colo.	.30
☐	218 Stars , Dall. [Logo]	.30
☐	219 Pavel Patera, Dall.	.30
☐	220 Guy Carbonneau, Dall.	.30
☐	221 Sergei Zubov, Dall.	.30
☐	222 Joe Nieuwendyk, Dall.	.30
☐	223 Darryl Sydor, Dall.	.30
☐	224 Derian Hatcher, Dall.	.30
☐	225 Brett Hull, Dall.	1.00
☐	226 Mike Modano, Dall.	1.00
☐	227 Ed Belfour (G), Dall.	1.00
☐	228 Jamie Langenbrunner, Dall.	.30
☐	229 Red Wings , Detr. [Logo]	.30
☐	230 Igor Larionov, Detr.	.50
☐	231 Steve Yzerman, Detr.	2.00
☐	232 Sergei Fedorov, Detr.	1.00
☐	233 Nicklas Lidström, Detr.	.50
☐	234 Brendan Shanahan, Detr.	1.00
☐	235 Larry Murphy, Detr.	.30
☐	236 Vyacheslav Kozlov, Detr.	.30
☐	237 Steve Duchesne, Detr.	.30
☐	238 Chris Chelios, Detr.	.50
☐	239 Chris Osgood (G), Detr.	.50
☐	240 Oilers , Edmo. [Logo]	.30
☐	241 Tommy Salo (G), Edmo.	.30
☐	242 Tom Poti, Edmo.	.30
☐	243 Doug Weight, Edmo.	.50
☐	244 Ryan Smyth, Edmo.	.30
☐	245 Janne Niinimaa, Edmo.	.30
☐	246 Roman Hamrlik, Edmo.	.30
☐	247 Bill Guerin, Edmo.	.30
☐	248 Todd Marchant, Edmo.	.30
☐	249 Mike Grier, Edmo.	.30
☐	250 Bill Ranford (G), Edmo.	.30
☐	251 Kings , LosA. [Logo]	.30
☐	252 Rob Blake, LosA.	.50
☐	253 Mattias Norström, LosA.	.30
☐	254 Frantisek* Kaberle, LosA.	.30
☐	255 Bryan Smolinski, LosA.	.30
☐	256 Stéphane Fiset (G), LosA.	.30
☐	257 Zigmund Palffy, LosA.	.50
☐	258 Luc Robitaille, LosA.	.50
☐	259 Jozef Stumpel, LosA.	.30
☐	260 Garry Galley, LosA.	.30
☐	261 Glen Murray, LosA.	.30
☐	262 Predators , Nash. [Logo]	.30
☐	263 Ville Peltonen, Nash.	.30
☐	264 Patric Kjellberg, Nash.	.30
☐	265 Kimmo Timonen, Nash.	.30
☐	266 Scott Walker, Nash.	.30
☐	267 Dan Keczmer, Nash.	.30
☐	268 David Legwand, Nash.	.50
☐	269 Cliff Ronning, Nash.	.30
☐	270 Sergei Krivokrasov, Nash.	.30
☐	271 Tom Fitzgerald, Nash.	.30
☐	272 Vitali Yachmenev, Nash.	.30
☐	273 Coyotes , Phoe. [Logo]	.30
☐	274 Mika Alatalo, Phoe.	.30
☐	275 Juha Ylönen, Phoe.	.30
☐	276 Keith Tkachuk, Phoe.	.50
☐	277 Travis Green, Phoe.	.30
☐	278 Stanislav Neckar, Phoe.	.30
☐	279 Jyrki Lumme, Phoe.	.30
☐	280 Teppo Numminen, Phoe.	.30
☐	281 Jeremy Roenick, Phoe.	.50
☐	282 Rick Tocchet, Phoe.	.30
☐	283 Shane Doan, Phoe.	.30
☐	284 Blues , SLou. [Logo]	.30
☐	285 Roman Turek (G), SLou.	.30
☐	286 Chris Pronger, SLou.	.50
☐	287 Al MacInnis, SLou.	.30
☐	288 Scott A. Young, SLou.	.30
☐	289 Marc Bergevin, SLou.	.30
☐	290 Jochen Hecht, SLou.	.30
☐	291 Craig Conroy, SLou.	.30
☐	292 Pierre Turgeon, SLou.	.30
☐	293 Pavol Demitra, SLou.	.30
☐	294 Michal Handzus, SLou.	.30
☐	295 Sharks , SanJ. [Logo]	.30
☐	296 Jeff Friesen, SanJ.	.30
☐	297 Niklas Sundström, SanJ.	.30
☐	298 Mike Ricci, SanJ.	.30
☐	299 Gary Suter, SanJ.	.30
☐	300 Owen Nolan, SanJ.	.50
☐	301 Patrick Marleau, SanJ.	.30
☐	302 Marco Sturm, SanJ.	.30
☐	303 Vincent Damphousse, SanJ.	.50
☐	304 Brad Stuart, SanJ.	.30
☐	305 Mike Vernon (G), SanJ.	.30
☐	306 Canucks , Vanc. [Logo]	.30
☐	307 Mark Messier, Vanc.	1.00
☐	308 Mattias Öhlund, Vanc.	.30
☐	309 Alexander Mogilny, Vanc.	.30
☐	310 Markus Näslund, Vanc.	1.00
☐	311 Andrew Cassels, Vanc.	.30
☐	312 Adrian Aucoin, Vanc.	.30
☐	313 Steve Kariya, Vanc.	.30
☐	314 Peter Schaefer, Vanc.	.30
☐	315 Ed Jovanovski, Vanc.	.30
☐	316 Garth Snow (G), Vanc.	.30
☐	317 Jaromir Jagr, Pitt. [League Leader]	1.00
☐	318 Teemu Selänne, Anah. [League Leader]	.50
☐	319 Tony Amonte, Chic. [League Leader]	.50
☐	320 Peter Forsberg, Colo. [League Leader]	1.00
☐	321 Paul Kariya, Anah. [League Leader]	1.00
☐	322 Alexei Yashin, Otta. [League Leader]	.50
☐	323 Eric Lindros, Phil. [League Leader]	1.00
☐	324 Theoren Fleury, NYRa. [League Leader]	.50
☐	325 John LeClair, Phil. [League Leader]	.50
☐	326 Jason Allison, Bost. [League Leader]	.50
☐	327 Joe Sakic, Colo. [League Leader]	1.50
☐	328 Pavol Demitra, SLou. [League Leader]	.30
☐	329 Alexander Karpovtsev, Toro. [League Leader]	.30
☐	330 Dmitri Khristich, Toro. [League Leader]	.30
☐	331 Mark Messier, Vanc. [League Leader]	1.00
☐	332 Brett Hull, Dall. [League Leader]	1.00
☐	333 Scott Pellerin, SLou. [League Leader]	.30
☐	334 Brian Rolston, NJer. [League Leader]	.30
☐	335 Miroslav Satan, Buff. [League Leader]	.30
☐	336 Patrick Roy (G), Colo. [League Leader]	3.00
☐	337 John Vanbiesbrouck (G), Phil. [League Leader]	.30
☐	338 Félix Potvin (G), NYIs. [League Leader]	.50
☐	339 Mike Dunham (G), Nash. [League Leader]	.30
☐	340 Dominic Roussel (G), Anah. [League Leader]	.30
☐	341 Al MacInnis, SLou. [League Leader]	.30
☐	342 Raymond Bourque, Bost. [League Leader]	1.00
☐	343 Adrian Aucoin, Vanc. [League Leader]	.30
☐	344 Sergei Gonchar, Wash. [League Leader]	.30
☐	345 Phil Housley, Calg. [League Leader]	.30
☐	346 Nicklas Lidström, Detr. [League Leader]	.50
☐	347 Martin Brodeur (G), NJer. [League Leader]	1.50
☐	348 Ron Tugnutt (G), Otta. [League Leader]	.30
☐	349 Dominik Hasek (G), Buff. [League Leader]	1.00
☐	350 Guy Hebert (G), Anah. [League Leader]	.30
☐	351 Byron Dafoe (G), Bost. [League Leader]	.30
☐	352 Curtis Joseph (G), Toro. [League Leader]	1.00
☐	353 Peter Schaefer, Vanc. [Rookies]	.30
☐	354 Scott Gomez, NJer. [Rookies]	.30
☐	355 Alex Tanguay, Colo. [Rookies]	.50
☐	356 Steve Kariya, Vanc. [Rookies]	.30
☐	357 Frantisek* Kaberle, LosA. [Rookies]	.30
☐	358 Brian Rafalski, NJer. [Rookies]	.30
☐	359 Blue Jackets Logo	.30
☐	360 Wild Logo	.30

1999 - 2000 POST / UPPER DECK GREAT MOMENTS

Complete Set (7 cards):		25.00
	Player	Post
☐	1 Wayne Gretzky	5.00
☐	2 Wayne Gretzky	5.00
☐	3 Wayne Gretzky	5.00
☐	4 Wayne Gretzky	5.00
☐	5 Wayne Gretzky	5.00
☐	6 Wayne Gretzky	5.00
☐	7 Wayne Gretzky	5.00

1999 - 2000 POST / UPPER DECK THE GREAT ONE

Complete Set (7 cards):		25.00
	Player	Post
☐	1 Wayne Gretzky	5.00
☐	2 Wayne Gretzky	5.00
☐	3 Wayne Gretzky	5.00
☐	4 Wayne Gretzky	5.00
☐	5 Wayne Gretzky	5.00
☐	6 Wayne Gretzky	5.00
☐	7 Wayne Gretzky	5.00

1999 - 2000 PRISM

This series was released in 1999. There are six versions: the regular card, a Holographic Gold parallel (#/480), a Holographic Mirror parallel (#/160), a Holographic Puprle parallel (#/99), a Holographic Blue parallel (#/80) and a Premiere Date parallel (#/69). Premiere Date cards sell at 10-20% more than the Holographic Blue cards.

Complete Set (150 cards):		**950.00**	**295.00**	**65.00**
Common Player:		**3.00**	**1.00**	**.35**
	Player	**HM160**	**HG480**	**Prism**
☐☐☐	1 Guy Hebert (G), Anah.	3.00	1.00	.35
☐☐☐	2 Paul Kariya, Anah.	25.00	8.00	1.00
☐☐☐	3 Mike Leclerc, Anah.	3.00	1.00	.35
☐☐☐	4 Steve Rucchin, Anah.	3.00	1.00	.35
☐☐☐	5 Teemu Selänne, Anah.	15.00	4.00	.50
☐☐☐	6 Andrew Brunette, Atla.	3.00	1.00	.35
☐☐☐	7 Petr Buzek, Atla.	3.00	1.00	.35
☐☐☐	8 Damian Rhodes (G), Atla.	3.00	1.00	.35
☐☐☐	**9 Patrik Stefan, Atla. RC**	**12.00**	**5.00**	**3.00**
☐☐☐	10 Jason Allison, Bost.	10.00	3.00	.50
☐☐☐	11 Dave Andreychuk, Bost.	5.00	1.00	.35
☐☐☐	12 Raymond Bourque, Bost.	20.00	7.00	1.00
☐☐☐	13 Byron Dafoe (G), Bost.	5.00	2.00	.35
☐☐☐	14 Sergei Samsonov, Bost.	10.00	3.00	.50
☐☐☐	15 Joe Thornton, Bost.	20.00	7.00	1.00
☐☐☐	16 Maxim Afinogenov, Buff.	5.00	2.00	.50
☐☐☐	17 Martin Biron (G), Buff.	5.00	2.00	.35
☐☐☐	18 Curtis Brown, Buff.	3.00	1.00	.35
☐☐☐	19 Dominik Hasek (G), Buff.	20.00	6.00	1.00
☐☐☐	20 Michael Peca, Buff.	5.00	2.00	.35
☐☐☐	21 Miroslav Satan, Buff.	5.00	1.00	.35
☐☐☐	22 Valeri Bure, Calg.	5.00	1.00	.35
☐☐☐	23 Grant Fuhr (G), Calg.	10.00	3.00	.50
☐☐☐	24 Jarome Iginla, Calg.	15.00	4.00	.50
☐☐☐	**25 Oleg Saprykin, Calg. RC**	**9.00**	**4.00**	**2.00**
☐☐☐	26 Cory Stillman, Calg.	3.00	1.00	.35
☐☐☐	27 Bates Battaglia, Caro.	3.00	1.00	.35
☐☐☐	28 Ron Francis, Caro.	10.00	3.00	.50
☐☐☐	29 Arturs Irbe (G), Caro.	5.00	2.00	.35
☐☐☐	30 Sami Kapanen, Caro.	5.00	1.00	.35
☐☐☐	31 Keith Primeau, Caro.	5.00	2.00	.35
☐☐☐	32 Tony Amonte, Chic.	10.00	3.00	.50
☐☐☐	33 Jean-Pierre Dumont, Chic.	3.00	1.00	.35
☐☐☐	34 Doug Gilmour, Chic.	10.00	3.00	.50
☐☐☐	35 Jocelyn Thibault (G), Chic.	5.00	2.00	.35
☐☐☐	36 Alexei Zhamnov, Chic.	5.00	1.00	.35
☐☐☐	37 Chris Drury, Colo.	10.00	3.00	.50
☐☐☐	38 Peter Forsberg, Colo.	25.00	8.00	1.00
☐☐☐	39 Milan Hejduk, Colo.	15.00	4.00	.50
☐☐☐	40 Patrick Roy (G), Colo.	60.00	18.00	3.00
☐☐☐	41 Joe Sakic, Colo.	30.00	8.00	1.50
☐☐☐	42 Alex Tanguay, Colo.	10.00	3.00	1.00
☐☐☐	43 Ed Belfour (G), Dall.	20.00	6.00	1.00
☐☐☐	44 Brett Hull, Dall.	20.00	6.00	1.00
☐☐☐	45 Roman Lyashenko, Dall.	3.00	1.00	.35
☐☐☐	46 Mike Modano, Dall.	20.00	6.00	1.00
☐☐☐	47 Joe Nieuwendyk, Dall.	5.00	2.00	.35
☐☐☐	48 Brendan Shanahan, Detr.	20.00	6.00	1.00
☐☐☐	49 Chris Chelios, Chic.	10.00	3.00	.50
☐☐☐	50 Sergei Fedorov, Detr.	20.00	6.00	1.00
☐☐☐	51 Jiri Fischer, Detr.	3.00	1.00	.35
☐☐☐	52 Nicklas Lidström, Detr.	10.00	3.00	.50
☐☐☐	53 Chris Osgood (G), Detr.	10.00	3.00	.50
☐☐☐	54 Steve Yzerman, Detr.	45.00	14.00	2.00
☐☐☐	55 Bill Guerin, Edmo.	5.00	2.00	.35
☐☐☐	56 Tommy Salo (G), Edmo.	5.00	2.00	.35
☐☐☐	57 Alexander Selivanov, Edmo.	3.00	1.00	.35
☐☐☐	58 Ryan Smyth, Edmo.	5.00	2.00	.35
☐☐☐	59 Doug Weight, Edmo.	10.00	3.00	.50
☐☐☐	60 Pavel Bure, Flor.	15.00	4.00	.50
☐☐☐	61 Trevor Kidd (G), Flor.	5.00	1.00	.35
☐☐☐	62 Viktor Kozlov, Flor.	5.00	1.00	.35
☐☐☐	63 Mark Parrish, Flor.	5.00	2.00	.35
☐☐☐	64 Ray Whitney, Flor.	3.00	1.00	.35
☐☐☐	65 Rob Blake, LosA.	10.00	3.00	.50
☐☐☐	66 Stéphane Fiset (G), LosA.	5.00	1.00	.35
☐☐☐	67 Frantisek* Kaberle, LosA.	3.00	1.00	.35
☐☐☐	68 Zigmund Palffy, LosA.	10.00	3.00	.50
☐☐☐	69 Luc Robitaille, LosA.	15.00	4.00	.50
☐☐☐	**70 F. Bouillon, Mont. RC**	**4.00**	**1.00**	**1.00**
☐☐☐	71 Jeff Hackett (G), Mont.	5.00	1.00	.35
☐☐☐	72 Saku Koivu, Mont.	15.00	4.00	.50
☐☐☐	73 Trevor Linden, Mont.	5.00	2.00	.35
☐☐☐	74 Brian Savage, Mont.	5.00	1.00	.35
☐☐☐	75 Mike Dunham (G), Nash.	5.00	2.00	.35
☐☐☐	76 David Legwand, Nash.	5.00	2.00	.35
☐☐☐	77 Cliff Ronning, Nash.	3.00	1.00	.35
☐☐☐	**78 R. Valicevic, Nash. RC**	**4.00**	**1.00**	**1.00**
☐☐☐	79 Martin Brodeur (G), NJer.	30.00	8.00	1.50
☐☐☐	80 Patrik Elias, NJer.	15.00	4.00	.50
☐☐☐	81 Scott Gomez, NJer.	5.00	2.00	.50
☐☐☐	82 Bobby Holik, NJer.	5.00	1.00	.35
☐☐☐	83 Claude Lemieux, NJer.	5.00	1.00	.35
☐☐☐	84 Petr* Sykora, NJer.	5.00	2.00	.35
☐☐☐	85 Tim Connolly, NYIs.	5.00	2.00	.50
☐☐☐	86 Mariusz Czerkawski, NYIs.	3.00	1.00	.35
☐☐☐	87 Brad Isbister, NYIs.	3.00	1.00	.35
☐☐☐	88 Roberto Luongo (G), NYIs.	15.00	5.00	1.50
☐☐☐	89 Theoren Fleury, NYRa.	10.00	3.00	.50
☐☐☐	90 Jan Hlavac, NYRa.	3.00	1.00	.35
☐☐☐	91 Brian Leetch, NYRa.	10.00	3.00	.50
☐☐☐	92 Mike Richter (G), NYRa.	5.00	2.00	.35
☐☐☐	93 Mike York, NYRa.	5.00	1.00	.35
☐☐☐	94 Daniel Alfredsson, Otta.	10.00	3.00	.50
☐☐☐	95 Radek Bonk, Otta.	5.00	1.00	.35
☐☐☐	96 Marian Hossa, Otta.	20.00	6.00	1.00
☐☐☐	97 Shawn McEachern, Otta.	5.00	1.00	.35
☐☐☐	98 Ron Tugnutt (G), Otta.	5.00	2.00	.35
☐☐☐	99 Alexei Yashin, Otta.	10.00	3.00	.50
☐☐☐	100 Brian Boucher (G), Phil.	5.00	1.00	.50
☐☐☐	101 Simon Gagné, Phil.	15.00	5.00	1.50
☐☐☐	102 John LeClair, Phil.	15.00	4.00	.50
☐☐☐	103 Eric Lindros, Phil.	20.00	6.00	1.00
☐☐☐	104 Mark Recchi, Phil.	5.00	2.00	.35
☐☐☐	105 J. Vanbiesbrouck (G), Phil.	5.00	2.00	.35
☐☐☐	**106 Mika Alatalo, Phoe. RC**	**6.00**	**2.00**	**1.50**
☐☐☐	107 Travis Green, Phoe.	3.00	1.00	.35
☐☐☐	108 N. Khabibulin (G), Phoe.	5.00	2.00	.35
☐☐☐	109 Jeremy Roenick, Phoe.	15.00	4.00	.50
☐☐☐	110 Keith Tkachuk, Phoe.	10.00	3.00	.50
☐☐☐	111 Rick Tocchet, Phoe.	5.00	1.00	.35
☐☐☐	112 J-S Aubin (G), Pitt.	3.00	1.00	.35
☐☐☐	113 Andrew Ference, Pitt.	3.00	1.00	.35
☐☐☐	114 Jaromir Jagr, Pitt.	20.00	6.00	1.00
☐☐☐	115 Alexei Kovalev, Pitt.	10.00	3.00	.50
☐☐☐	116 Martin Straka, Pitt.	5.00	1.00	.35
☐☐☐	117 Pavol Demitra, SLou.	5.00	2.00	.35
☐☐☐	**118 Jochen Hecht, SLou. RC**	**9.00**	**4.00**	**2.00**
☐☐☐	119 Al MacInnis, SLou.	5.00	2.00	.35
☐☐☐	120 Chris Pronger, SLou.	10.00	3.00	.50
☐☐☐	121 Roman Turek (G), SLou.	5.00	2.00	.35
☐☐☐	122 Pierre Turgeon, SLou.	5.00	2.00	.35
☐☐☐	123 V. Damphousse, SanJ.	10.00	3.00	.50
☐☐☐	124 Jeff Friesen, SanJ.	5.00	1.00	.35
☐☐☐	125 Patrick Marleau, SanJ.	5.00	2.00	.35
☐☐☐	126 Owen Nolan, SanJ.	10.00	3.00	.50
☐☐☐	127 Steve Shields (G), SanJ.	3.00	1.00	.35
☐☐☐	128 Brad Stuart, SanJ.	5.00	2.00	.50
☐☐☐	129 Dan Cloutier (G), Tamp.	5.00	2.00	.35
☐☐☐	130 Ben Clymer, Tamp.	3.00	1.00	.35
☐☐☐	131 Chris Gratton, Tamp.	3.00	1.00	.35
☐☐☐	132 Vincent Lecavalier, Tamp.	20.00	6.00	1.00
☐☐☐	133 Darcy Tucker, Tamp.	3.00	1.00	.35
☐☐☐	**134 N. Antropov, Toro. RC**	**9.00**	**4.00**	**2.00**
☐☐☐	135 Sergei Berezin, Toro.	3.00	1.00	.35
☐☐☐	136 Tie Domi, Toro.	5.00	1.00	.35
☐☐☐	137 Curtis Joseph (G), Toro.	20.00	6.00	1.00
☐☐☐	138 Dmitri Khristich, Toro.	3.00	1.00	.35
☐☐☐	139 Mats Sundin, Toro.	20.00	6.00	1.00
☐☐☐	**140 Steve Kariya, Vanc. RC**	**9.00**	**4.00**	**2.00**
☐☐☐	141 Mark Messier, Vanc.	20.00	6.00	1.00
☐☐☐	**142 A. Michaud (G), Vanc. RC**	**6.00**	**2.00**	**1.50**
☐☐☐	143 Alexander Mogilny, Vanc.	5.00	2.00	.35
☐☐☐	**144 Jarkko Ruutu, Vanc. RC**	**6.00**	**2.00**	**1.50**
☐☐☐	145 Peter Schaefer, Vanc.	3.00	1.00	.35
☐☐☐	146 Peter Bondra, Wash.	10.00	3.00	.50
☐☐☐	147 Jan Bulis, Wash.	3.00	1.00	.35
☐☐☐	148 Olaf Kölzig (G), Wash.	10.00	3.00	.50
☐☐☐	**149 G. Metropolit, Wash. RC**	**6.00**	**2.00**	**1.50**
☐☐☐	150 Adam Oates, Wash.	5.00	2.00	.35

PARALLELS

Complete Set (150 cards):		**1900.00**	**1700.00**	**1400.00**
	Player	**PD69**	**HB80**	**HP99**
☐☐☐	1 Guy Hebert (G), Anah.	6.00	5.00	5.00
☐☐☐	2 Paul Kariya, Anah.	55.00	45.00	40.00
☐☐☐	3 Mike Leclerc, Anah.	6.00	5.00	5.00
☐☐☐	4 Steve Rucchin, Anah.	6.00	5.00	5.00
☐☐☐	5 Teemu Selänne, Anah.	30.00	25.00	20.00
☐☐☐	6 Andrew Brunette, Atla.	6.00	5.00	5.00
☐☐☐	7 Petr Buzek, Atla.	6.00	5.00	5.00
☐☐☐	8 Damian Rhodes (G), Atla.	6.00	5.00	5.00
☐☐☐	**9 Patrik Stefan, Atla. RC**	**25.00**	**20.00**	**15.00**
☐☐☐	10 Jason Allison, Bost.	20.00	20.00	15.00
☐☐☐	11 Dave Andreychuk, Bost.	10.00	10.00	5.00
☐☐☐	12 Raymond Bourque, Bost.	45.00	40.00	35.00
☐☐☐	13 Byron Dafoe (G), Bost.	15.00	10.00	10.00
☐☐☐	14 Sergei Samsonov, Bost.	20.00	20.00	15.00
☐☐☐	15 Joe Thornton, Bost.	45.00	40.00	35.00
☐☐☐	16 Maxim Afinogenov, Buff.	15.00	10.00	10.00
☐☐☐	17 Martin Biron (G), Buff.	15.00	15.00	10.00

□□□	18 Curtis Brown, Buff.	6.00	5.00	5.00
□□□	19 Dominik Hasek (G), Buff.	40.00	35.00	30.00
□□□	20 Michael Peca, Buff.	15.00	10.00	10.00
□□□	21 Miroslav Satan, Buff.	10.00	10.00	5.00
□□□	22 Valeri Bure, Calg.	10.00	10.00	5.00
□□□	23 Grant Fuhr (G), Calg.	20.00	20.00	15.00
□□□	24 Jarome Iginla, Calg.	30.00	25.00	20.00
□□□	**25 Oleg Saprykin, Calg. RC**	**10.00**	**10.00**	**10.00**
□□□	26 Cory Stillman, Calg.	6.00	5.00	5.00
□□□	27 Bates Battaglia, Caro.	6.00	5.00	5.00
□□□	28 Ron Francis, Caro.	20.00	20.00	15.00
□□□	29 Arturs Irbe (G), Caro.	15.00	10.00	10.00
□□□	30 Sami Kapanen, Caro.	10.00	10.00	5.00
□□□	31 Keith Primeau, Caro.	15.00	10.00	10.00
□□□	32 Tony Amonte, Chic.	20.00	20.00	15.00
□□□	33 Jean-Pierre Dumont, Chic.	6.00	5.00	5.00
□□□	34 Doug Gilmour, Chic.	20.00	20.00	15.00
□□□	35 Jocelyn Thibault (G), Chic.	15.00	10.00	10.00
□□□	36 Alexei Zhamnov, Chic.	10.00	10.00	5.00
□□□	37 Chris Drury, Colo.	20.00	20.00	15.00
□□□	38 Peter Forsberg, Colo.	55.00	45.00	40.00
□□□	39 Milan Hejduk, Colo.	30.00	25.00	20.00
□□□	40 Patrick Roy (G), Colo.	120.00	105.00	90.00
□□□	41 Joe Sakic, Colo.	60.00	55.00	45.00
□□□	42 Alex Tanguay, Colo.	20.00	20.00	15.00
□□□	43 Ed Belfour (G), Dall.	40.00	35.00	30.00
□□□	44 Brett Hull, Dall.	40.00	35.00	30.00
□□□	45 Roman Lyashenko, Dall.	6.00	5.00	5.00
□□□	46 Mike Modano, Dall.	40.00	35.00	30.00
□□□	47 Joe Nieuwendyk, Dall.	15.00	10.00	10.00
□□□	48 Brendan Shanahan, Detr.	40.00	35.00	30.00
□□□	49 Chris Chelios, Chic.	20.00	20.00	15.00
□□□	50 Sergei Fedorov, Detr.	40.00	35.00	30.00
□□□	51 Jiri Fischer, Detr.	6.00	5.00	5.00
□□□	52 Nicklas Lidström, Detr.	20.00	20.00	15.00
□□□	53 Chris Osgood (G), Detr.	20.00	20.00	15.00
□□□	54 Steve Yzerman, Detr.	95.00	80.00	70.00
□□□	55 Bill Guerin, Edmo.	15.00	10.00	10.00
□□□	56 Tommy Salo (G), Edmo.	15.00	10.00	10.00
□□□	57 Alexander Selivanov, Edmo.	6.00	5.00	5.00
□□□	58 Ryan Smyth, Edmo.	15.00	15.00	10.00
□□□	59 Doug Weight, Edmo.	20.00	20.00	15.00
□□□	60 Pavel Bure, Flor.	30.00	25.00	20.00
□□□	61 Trevor Kidd (G), Flor.	10.00	10.00	5.00
□□□	62 Viktor Kozlov, Flor.	10.00	10.00	5.00
□□□	63 Mark Parrish, Flor.	15.00	10.00	10.00
□□□	64 Ray Whitney, Flor.	6.00	5.00	5.00
□□□	65 Rob Blake, LosA.	20.00	20.00	15.00
□□□	66 Stéphane Fiset (G), LosA.	10.00	10.00	5.00
□□□	67 Frantisek* Kaberle, LosA.	6.00	5.00	5.00
□□□	68 Zigmund Palffy, LosA.	20.00	20.00	15.00
□□□	69 Luc Robitaille, LosA.	30.00	25.00	20.00
□□□	**70 F. Bouillon, Mont. RC**	**6.00**	**5.00**	**5.00**
□□□	71 Jeff Hackett (G), Mont.	10.00	10.00	5.00
□□□	72 Saku Koivu, Mont.	30.00	25.00	20.00
□□□	73 Trevor Linden, Mont.	15.00	10.00	10.00
□□□	74 Brian Savage, Mont.	10.00	10.00	5.00
□□□	75 Mike Dunham (G), Nash.	15.00	10.00	10.00
□□□	76 David Legwand, Nash.	15.00	10.00	10.00
□□□	77 Cliff Ronning, Nash.	6.00	5.00	5.00
□□□	**78 R. Valicevic, Nash. RC**	**6.00**	**5.00**	**5.00**
□□□	79 Martin Brodeur (G), NJer.	60.00	55.00	45.00
□□□	80 Patrik Elias, NJer.	30.00	25.00	20.00
□□□	81 Scott Gomez, NJer.	15.00	10.00	10.00
□□□	82 Bobby Holik, NJer.	10.00	10.00	5.00
□□□	83 Claude Lemieux, NJer.	10.00	10.00	5.00
□□□	84 Petr* Sykora, NJer.	15.00	10.00	10.00
□□□	85 Tim Connolly, NYIs.	15.00	10.00	10.00
□□□	86 Mariusz Czerkawski, NYIs.	6.00	5.00	5.00
□□□	87 Brad Isbister, NYIs.	6.00	5.00	5.00
□□□	88 Roberto Luongo (G), NYIs.	30.00	25.00	20.00
□□□	89 Theoren Fleury, NYRa.	20.00	20.00	15.00
□□□	90 Jan Hlavac, NYRa.	6.00	5.00	5.00
□□□	91 Brian Leetch, NYRa.	20.00	20.00	15.00
□□□	92 Mike Richter (G), NYRa.	15.00	15.00	10.00
□□□	93 Mike York, NYRa.	10.00	10.00	5.00
□□□	94 Daniel Alfredsson, Otta.	20.00	20.00	15.00
□□□	95 Radek Bonk, Otta.	10.00	10.00	5.00
□□□	96 Marian Hossa, Otta.	40.00	35.00	30.00
□□□	97 Shawn McEachern, Otta.	10.00	10.00	5.00
□□□	98 Ron Tugnutt (G), Otta.	15.00	10.00	10.00
□□□	99 Alexei Yashin, Otta.	20.00	20.00	15.00
□□□	100 Brian Boucher (G), Phil.	10.00	10.00	5.00
□□□	101 Simon Gagné, Phil.	30.00	25.00	20.00
□□□	102 John LeClair, Phil.	30.00	25.00	20.00
□□□	103 Eric Lindros, Phil.	40.00	35.00	30.00
□□□	104 Mark Recchi, Phil.	15.00	10.00	10.00
□□□	105 J. Vanbiesbrouck (G), Phil.	15.00	15.00	10.00
□□□	**106 Mika Alatalo, Phoe. RC**	**6.00**	**5.00**	**5.00**
□□□	107 Travis Green, Phoe.	6.00	5.00	5.00
□□□	108 N. Khabibulin (G), Phoe.	15.00	10.00	10.00
□□□	109 Jeremy Roenick, Phoe.	30.00	25.00	20.00
□□□	110 Keith Tkachuk, Phoe.	20.00	20.00	15.00
□□□	111 Rick Tocchet, Phoe.	10.00	10.00	5.00
□□□	112 J-S Aubin (G), Pitt.	6.00	5.00	5.00
□□□	113 Andrew Ference, Pitt.	6.00	5.00	5.00
□□□	114 Jaromir Jagr, Pitt.	40.00	35.00	30.00
□□□	115 Alexei Kovalev, Pitt.	20.00	20.00	15.00
□□□	116 Martin Straka, Pitt.	10.00	10.00	5.00
□□□	117 Pavol Demitra, SLou.	15.00	10.00	10.00
□□□	**118 J. Hecht, SLou. RC**	**10.00**	**10.00**	**10.00**
□□□	119 Al MacInnis, SLou.	15.00	10.00	10.00
□□□	120 Chris Pronger, SLou.	20.00	20.00	15.00
□□□	121 Roman Turek (G), SLou.	15.00	15.00	10.00
□□□	122 Pierre Turgeon, SLou.	15.00	10.00	10.00
□□□	123 V. Damphousse, SanJ.	20.00	20.00	15.00
□□□	124 Jeff Friesen, SanJ.	10.00	10.00	5.00
□□□	125 Patrick Marleau, SanJ.	15.00	15.00	10.00
□□□	126 Owen Nolan, SanJ.	20.00	20.00	15.00
□□□	127 Steve Shields (G), SanJ.	6.00	5.00	5.00
□□□	128 Brad Stuart, SanJ.	15.00	10.00	10.00
□□□	129 Dan Cloutier (G), Tamp.	15.00	10.00	10.00
□□□	130 Ben Clymer, Tamp.	6.00	5.00	5.00
□□□	131 Chris Gratton, Tamp.	6.00	5.00	5.00
□□□	132 Vincent Lecavalier, Tamp.	40.00	35.00	30.00
□□□	133 Darcy Tucker, Tamp.	6.00	5.00	5.00
□□□	**134 N. Antropov, Toro. RC**	**10.00**	**10.00**	**10.00**
□□□	135 Sergei Berezin, Toro.	6.00	5.00	5.00
□□□	136 Tie Domi, Toro.	10.00	10.00	5.00
□□□	137 Curtis Joseph (G), Toro.	40.00	35.00	30.00
□□□	138 Dmitri Khristich, Toro.	6.00	5.00	5.00
□□□	139 Mats Sundin, Toro.	40.00	35.00	30.00
□□□	**140 Steve Kariya, Vanc. RC**	**10.00**	**10.00**	**10.00**
□□□	141 Mark Messier, Vanc.	40.00	35.00	30.00
□□□	**142 A. Michaud (G), Vanc. RC**	**6.00**	**5.00**	**5.00**
□□□	143 Alexander Mogilny, Vanc.	15.00	15.00	10.00
□□□	**144 Jarkko Ruutu, Vanc. RC**	**6.00**	**5.00**	**5.00**
□□□	145 Peter Schaefer, Vanc.	6.00	5.00	5.00
□□□	146 Peter Bondra, Wash.	20.00	20.00	15.00
□□□	147 Jan Bulis, Wash.	6.00	5.00	5.00
□□□	148 Olaf Kölzig (G), Wash.	20.00	20.00	15.00
□□□	**149 G. Metropolit, Wash. RC**	**6.00**	**5.00**	**5.00**
□□□	150 Adam Oates, Wash.	15.00	10.00	10.00

CLEAR ADVANTAGE

Insert Set (20 cards):		**55.00**
	Insert (2:25 packs)	**CA**
□	1 Paul Kariya, Anah.	4.00
□	2 Teemu Selänne, Anah.	2.00
□	3 Dominik Hasek (G), Buff.	3.00
□	4 Peter Forsberg, Colo.	4.00
□	5 Patrick Roy (G), Colo.	9.00
□	6 Alex Tanguay, Colo.	3.00
□	7 Brett Hull, Dall.	3.00
□	8 Brendan Shanahan, Detr.	3.00
□	9 Steve Yzerman, Detr.	7.00
□	10 Pavel Bure, Flor.	2.00
□	11 Zigmund Palffy, LosA.	1.50
□	12 Martin Brodeur (G), NJer.	4.00
□	13 Theoren Fleury, NYRa.	1.50
□	14 Marian Hossa, Otta.	3.00
□	15 John LeClair, Phil.	2.00
□	16 Eric Lindros, Phil.	3.00
□	17 Mark Recchi, Phil.	1.50
□	18 Jaromir Jagr, Pitt.	3.00
□	19 Vincent Lecavalier, Tamp.	3.00
□	20 Mats Sundin, Toro.	3.00

DIAL-A-STATS

Insert Set (10 cards):		**275.00**
	Insert (1:193 packs)	**DAS**
□	1 Paul Kariya, Anah.	35.00
□	2 Teemu Selänne, Anah.	20.00
□	3 Dominik Hasek (G), Buff.	25.00
□	4 Peter Forsberg, Colo.	35.00
□	5 Patrick Roy (G), Colo.	75.00
□	6 Mike Modano, Dall.	25.00
□	7 Steve Yzerman, Detr.	60.00
□	8 Mark Messier, Vanc.	25.00
□	9 Eric Lindros, Phil.	25.00
□	10 Jaromir Jagr, Pitt.	25.00

ICE PROSPECTS

Insert Set (10 cards):		**65.00**
	Insert (1:97 Hobby packs)	**IP**
□	1 Patrik Stefan, Atla.	10.00
□	2 Martin Biron (G), Buff.	10.00
□	3 Alex Tanguay, Colo.	10.00
□	4 David Legwand, Nash.	6.00
□	5 Scott Gomez, NJer.	6.00
□	6 Simon Gagné, Phil.	15.00
□	7 Brad Stuart, SanJ.	6.00
□	8 Nikolai Antropov, Toro.	6.00
□	9 Steve Kariya, Vanc.	6.00
□	10 Peter Schaefer, Vanc.	6.00

SNO GLOBE DIE-CUTS

Insert Set (20 cards):		**120.00**
	Insert (1:25)	**SGDC**
□	1 Paul Kariya, Anah.	8.00
□	2 Teemu Selänne, Anah.	5.00
□	3 Raymond Bourque, Bost.	7.00
□	4 Dominik Hasek (G), Buff.	6.00
□	5 Peter Forsberg, Colo.	8.00
□	6 Patrick Roy (G), Colo.	18.00
□	7 Joe Sakic, Colo.	10.00
□	8 Ed Belfour (G), Dall.	6.00
□	9 Mike Modano, Dall.	6.00
□	10 Brendan Shanahan, Detr.	6.00
□	11 Steve Yzerman, Detr.	15.00
□	12 Pavel Bure, Flor.	5.00
□	13 Martin Brodeur (G), NJer.	10.00
□	14 Theoren Fleury, NYRa.	3.00
□	15 John LeClair, Phil.	5.00
□	16 Eric Lindros, Phil.	6.00
□	17 John Vanbiesbrouck (G), Phil.	3.00
□	18 Keith Tkachuk, Phoe.	3.00
□	19 Jaromir Jagr, Pitt.	6.00
□	20 Curtis Joseph (G), Toro.	6.00

1999 - 2000 REVOLUTION

This series was released in 1999. There are five versions: the regular card, a Red parallel (#/299), a Silver parallel (#/299), a Shadow Series parallel (#/99) and a Premiere Date parallel (#/42). The Red and Silver cards are priced similarly below.

Complete Set (150 cards):		**3300.00**	**1800.00**	**650.00**	**100.00**
Common Player:		**8.00**	**5.00**	**2.00**	**.50**
	Player	**PD42**	**SS99**	**R/S299**	**Reg.**
□□□□□	1 G. Hebert (G), Anah.	15.00	5.00	3.00	.50
□□□□□	2 Paul Kariya, Anah.	85.00	50.00	15.00	3.00
□□□□□	3 M. McInnis, Anah.	10.00	5.00	2.00	.50
□□□□□	4 T. Selänne, Anah.	50.00	30.00	10.00	2.00
□□□□□	5 Steve Rucchin, Anah.	15.00	5.00	3.00	.50
□□□□□	6 Buchberger, Edmo.	10.00	5.00	2.00	.50
□□□□□	7 Ray Ferraro, LosA.	10.00	5.00	2.00	.50
□□□□□	8 D. Rhodes (G), Otta.	15.00	5.00	3.00	.50
□□□□□	9 J. Garpenlöv, Flor.	8.00	5.00	2.00	.50
□□□□□	10 Jason Allison, Bost.	35.00	20.00	7.00	1.00
□□□□□	11 R. Bourque, Bost.	75.00	45.00	15.00	3.00
□□□□□	12 A. Carter, Bost.	25.00	15.00	5.00	1.00
□□□□□	13 B. Dafoe (G), Bost.	25.00	15.00	5.00	1.00
□□□□□	14 S. Samsonov, Bost.	35.00	20.00	7.00	1.00
□□□□□	15 J. Thornton, Bost.	75.00	45.00	15.00	3.00
□□□□□	16 M. Biron (G), Buff.	30.00	15.00	6.00	1.00
□□□□□	17 Curtis Brown, Buff.	10.00	5.00	2.00	.50
□□□□□	18 D. Hasek (G), Buff.	60.00	35.00	10.00	2.00
□□□□□	19 M. Peca, Buff.	25.00	15.00	5.00	1.00
□□□□□	20 M. Satan, Buff.	20.00	10.00	4.00	.50
□□□□□	21 Dixon Ward, Buff.	8.00	5.00	2.00	.50
□□□□□	22 Valeri Bure, Calg.	20.00	10.00	4.00	.50
□□□□□	23 Brathwaite (G), Calg.	20.00	10.00	4.00	.50
□□□□□	24 P. Housley, Calg.	20.00	10.00	4.00	.50
□□□□□	25 J. Iginla, Calg.	50.00	30.00	10.00	2.00
□□□□□	26 C. Stillman, Calg.	15.00	5.00	3.00	.50
□□□□□	27 R. Francis, Caro.	35.00	20.00	7.00	1.00
□□□□□	28 A. Irbe (G), Caro.	25.00	15.00	5.00	1.00
□□□□□	29 S. Kapanen, Caro.	20.00	10.00	4.00	.50
□□□□□	30 K. Primeau, Caro.	25.00	15.00	5.00	1.00
□□□□□	31 G. Roberts, Caro.	25.00	15.00	5.00	1.00
□□□□□	32 T. Amonte, Chic.	35.00	20.00	7.00	1.00
□□□□□	33 J-P Dumont, Chic.	15.00	5.00	3.00	.50
□□□□□	34 D. Gilmour, Chic.	35.00	20.00	7.00	1.00
□□□□□	35 Thibault (G), Chic.	25.00	15.00	5.00	1.00
□□□□□	36 A. Zhamnov, Chic.	20.00	10.00	4.00	.50
□□□□□	37 Deadmarsh, Colo.	20.00	10.00	4.00	.50
□□□□□	38 C. Drury, Colo.	35.00	20.00	7.00	1.00
□□□□□	39 P. Forsberg, Colo.	85.00	50.00	15.00	3.00
□□□□□	40 M. Hejduk, Colo.	50.00	30.00	10.00	2.00
□□□□□	41 C. Lemieux, Colo.	20.00	10.00	4.00	.50
□□□□□	42 P. Roy (G), Colo.	150.00	90.00	35.00	7.00
□□□□□	43 Joe Sakic, Colo.	100.00	60.00	20.00	4.00
□□□□□	44 Belfour (G), Dall.	60.00	35.00	12.00	2.00
□□□□□	45 B. Hull, Dall.	60.00	35.00	12.00	2.00
□□□□□	46 Langenbrunner, Dall.	15.00	5.00	3.00	.50
□□□□□	47 J. Lehtinen, Dall.	20.00	10.00	4.00	.50
□□□□□	48 M. Modano, Dall.	60.00	35.00	12.00	2.00
□□□□□	49 J. Nieuwendyk, Dall.	25.00	15.00	5.00	1.00
□□□□□	50 C. Chelios, Detr.	35.00	20.00	7.00	1.00
□□□□□	51 S. Fedorov, Detr.	60.00	35.00	12.00	2.00
□□□□□	52 Vy. Kozlov, Detr.	15.00	5.00	3.00	.50
□□□□□	53 N. Lidström, Detr.	35.00	20.00	7.00	1.00
□□□□□	54 Osgood (G), Detr.	35.00	20.00	7.00	1.00
□□□□□	55 B. Shanahan, Detr.	60.00	35.00	12.00	2.00
□□□□□	56 S. Yzerman, Detr.	150.00	90.00	30.00	6.00
□□□□□	57 M. Grier, Edmo.	15.00	5.00	3.00	.50
□□□□□	58 B. Guerin, Edmo.	25.00	15.00	5.00	1.00
□□□□□	59 T. Salo (G), Edmo.	25.00	15.00	5.00	1.00
□□□□□	60 R. Smyth, Edmo.	30.00	15.00	6.00	1.00
□□□□□	61 D. Weight, Edmo.	35.00	20.00	7.00	1.00
□□□□□	62 P. Bure, Flor.	50.00	30.00	10.00	2.00
□□□□□	63 S. Burke (G), Flor.	35.00	20.00	7.00	1.00
□□□□□	64 Vik. Kozlov, Flor.	20.00	10.00	4.00	.50
□□□□□	65 M. Parrish, Flor.	25.00	15.00	5.00	1.00
□□□□□	66 R. Whitney, Flor.	15.00	5.00	3.00	.50
□□□□□	67 D. Audette, LosA.	25.00	15.00	5.00	1.00
□□□□□	68 R. Blake, LosA.	35.00	20.00	7.00	1.00
□□□□□	69 S. Fiset (G), LosA.	20.00	10.00	4.00	.50
□□□□□	70 Z. Palffy, NYIs.	35.00	20.00	7.00	1.00
□□□□□	71 L. Robitaille, LosA.	50.00	30.00	10.00	2.00
□□□□□	72 J. Storr (G), LosA.	15.00	5.00	3.00	.50
□□□□□	73 S. Corson, Mont.	20.00	10.00	4.00	.50
□□□□□	74 J. Hackett (G), Phil.	20.00	10.00	4.00	.50
□□□□□	75 S. Koivu, Mont.	50.00	30.00	10.00	2.00
□□□□□	76 V. Malakhov, Mont.	10.00	5.00	2.00	.50
□□□□□	77 M. Rucinsky, Mont.	15.00	5.00	3.00	.50
□□□□□	78 Dunham (G), Nash.	25.00	15.00	5.00	1.00
□□□□□	79 G. Johnson, Nash.	10.00	5.00	2.00	.50
□□□□□	80 S. Krivokrasov, Nash.	10.00	5.00	2.00	.50
□□□□□	81 C. Ronning, Nash.	15.00	5.00	3.00	.50
□□□□□	82 S. Walker, Nash.	15.00	5.00	3.00	.50
□□□□□	83 J. Arnott, NJer.	30.00	15.00	6.00	1.00
□□□□□	84 Brodeur (G), NJer.	100.00	60.00	20.00	4.00
□□□□□	85 P. Elias, NJer.	50.00	30.00	10.00	2.00
□□□□□	86 Bobby Holik, NJer.	20.00	10.00	4.00	.50
□□□□□	87 B. Morrison, NJer.	20.00	10.00	4.00	.50
□□□□□	88 Niedermayer, NJer.	20.00	10.00	4.00	.50
□□□□□	89 P. Sykora, NJer.	25.00	15.00	5.00	1.00
□□□□□	90 Czerkawski, NYIs.	15.00	5.00	3.00	.50
□□□□□	91 K. Jönsson, NYIs.	10.00	5.00	2.00	.50
□□□□□	92 M. Lindgren, NYIs.	10.00	5.00	2.00	.50
□□□□□	93 F. Potvin (G), NYIs.	35.00	20.00	7.00	1.00
□□□□□	94 Mike Watt, NYIs.	8.00	5.00	2.00	.50
□□□□□	95 T. Fleury, Colo.	35.00	20.00	7.00	1.00
□□□□□	96 A. Graves, NYRa.	25.00	15.00	5.00	1.00
□□□□□	97 B. Leetch, NYRa.	35.00	20.00	7.00	1.00
□□□□□	98 J. MacLean, NYRa.	10.00	5.00	2.00	.50
□□□□□	99 P. Nedved, NYRa.	20.00	10.00	4.00	.50
□□□□□	100 Richter (G), NYRa.	30.00	15.00	6.00	1.00
□□□□□	101 M. Arvedson, Otta.	10.00	5.00	2.00	.50
□□□□□	102 M. Hossa, Otta.	60.00	35.00	12.00	2.00
□□□□□	103 McEachern, Otta.	20.00	10.00	4.00	.50
□□□□□	104 Tugnutt (G), Otta.	25.00	15.00	5.00	1.00
□□□□□	105 A. Yashin, Otta.	35.00	20.00	7.00	1.00
□□□□□	106 Brind'Amour, Phil.	20.00	10.00	4.00	.50
□□□□□	107 E. Lindros, Phil.	60.00	35.00	10.00	2.00
□□□□□	108 J. LeClair, Phil.	50.00	30.00	10.00	2.00
□□□□□	109 M. Recchi, Phil.	25.00	15.00	5.00	1.00
□□□□□	110 V'sbrouck (G), Phil.	30.00	15.00	6.00	1.00
□□□□□	111 Khabibulin (G), Phoe.	25.00	15.00	5.00	1.00
□□□□□	112 Numminen, Phoe.	20.00	10.00	4.00	.50
□□□□□	113 J. Roenick, Phoe.	50.00	30.00	10.00	2.00
□□□□□	114 K. Tkachuk, Phoe.	35.00	20.00	7.00	1.00
□□□□□	115 R. Tocchet, Phoe.	20.00	10.00	4.00	.50
□□□□□	116 Barrasso (G), Pitt.	25.00	15.00	5.00	1.00
□□□□□	117 Jan Hrdina, Pitt.	15.00	5.00	3.00	.50
□□□□□	118 J. Jagr, Pitt.	60.00	35.00	10.00	2.00
□□□□□	119 A. Kovalev, Pitt.	35.00	20.00	7.00	1.00
□□□□□	120 M. Straka, Pitt.	20.00	10.00	4.00	.50
□□□□□	121 P. Demitra, SLou.	25.00	15.00	5.00	1.00
□□□□□	**122 Hecht, SLou. RC**	**20.00**	**10.00**	**5.00**	**3.00**
□□□□□	123 A. MacInnis, SLou.	25.00	15.00	5.00	1.00
□□□□□	124 C. Pronger, SLou.	35.00	20.00	7.00	1.00
□□□□□	125 P. Turgeon, SLou.	25.00	15.00	5.00	1.00
□□□□□	126 Damphousse, SanJ.	35.00	20.00	7.00	1.00
□□□□□	127 J. Friesen, SanJ.	20.00	10.00	4.00	.50
□□□□□	128 P. Marleau, SanJ.	30.00	15.00	6.00	1.00
□□□□□	129 S. Shields (G), SanJ.	15.00	5.00	3.00	.50
□□□□□	130 M. Vernon (G), SanJ.	25.00	15.00	5.00	1.00
□□□□□	131 C. Gratton, Tamp.	15.00	5.00	3.00	.50
□□□□□	132 C. Forbes, Tamp.	8.00	5.00	2.00	.50
□□□□□	133 Lecavalier, Tamp.	60.00	35.00	12.00	2.00
□□□□□	134 D. Tucker, Tamp.	15.00	5.00	3.00	.50
□□□□□	135 S. Berezin, Toro.	15.00	5.00	3.00	.50
□□□□□	136 T. Domi, Toro.	20.00	10.00	4.00	.50
□□□□□	137 M. Johnson, Toro.	10.00	5.00	2.00	.50
□□□□□	138 Joseph (G), Toro.	60.00	35.00	10.00	2.00
□□□□□	139 D. King, Toro.	10.00	5.00	2.00	.50
□□□□□	140 M. Sundin, Toro.	60.00	35.00	12.00	2.00
□□□□□	141 S. Thomas, Toro.	15.00	5.00	3.00	.50
□□□□□	142 M. Messier, Vanc.	60.00	35.00	12.00	2.00

☐☐☐☐☐	143 B. Muckalt, Vanc.	10.00	5.00	2.00	.50
☐☐☐☐☐	144 M. Näslund, Vanc.	60.00	35.00	12.00	2.00
☐☐☐☐☐	145 M. Öhlund, Vanc.	20.00	10.00	4.00	.50
☐☐☐☐☐	146 G. Snow (G), Vanc.	20.00	10.00	4.00	.50
☐☐☐☐☐	147 P. Bondra, Wash.	35.00	20.00	7.00	1.00
☐☐☐☐☐	148 S. Gonchar, Wash.	20.00	10.00	4.00	.50
☐☐☐☐☐	149 O. Kölzig (G), Wash.	35.00	20.00	7.00	1.00
☐☐☐☐☐	150 A. Oates, Wash.	25.00	15.00	5.00	1.00

ICE SCULPTURES

Insert Set (10 cards): 140.00

	Insert (1:49 packs)	IS
☐	1 Paul Kariya, Anah.	15.00
☐	2 Dominik Hasek (G), Buff.	10.00
☐	3 Patrick Roy (G), Colo.	35.00
☐	4 Joe Sakic, Colo.	20.00
☐	5 Steve Yzerman, Detr.	30.00
☐	6 Pavel Bure, Vanc.	10.00
☐	7 Martin Brodeur (G), NJer.	20.00
☐	8 Theoren Fleury, NYRa.	6.00
☐	9 Eric Lindros, Phil.	10.00
☐	10 Jaromir Jagr, Pitt.	10.00

NHL ICONS

Insert Set (20 cards): 525.00

	Insert (1:121 packs)	NI
☐	1 Teemu Selänne, Anah.	25.00
☐	2 Raymond Bourque, Bost.	35.00
☐	3 Dominik Hasek (G), Buff.	30.00
☐	4 Doug Gilmour, Chic.	15.00
☐	5 Peter Forsberg, Colo.	40.00
☐	6 Patrick Roy (G), Colo.	90.00
☐	7 Joe Sakic, Colo.	50.00
☐	8 Brett Hull, Dall.	30.00
☐	9 Mike Modano, Dall.	30.00
☐	10 Brendan Shanahan, Detr.	30.00
☐	11 Steve Yzerman, Detr.	75.00
☐	12 Martin Brodeur (G), NJer.	50.00
☐	13 John LeClair, Phil.	25.00
☐	14 Eric Lindros, Phil.	30.00
☐	15 John Vanbiesbrouck (G), Phil.	15.00
☐	16 Keith Tkachuk, Phoe.	15.00
☐	17 Jaromir Jagr, Pitt.	30.00
☐	18 Curtis Joseph (G), Toro.	30.00
☐	19 Mats Sundin, Toro.	30.00
☐	20 Mark Messier, Vanc.	30.00

ORNAMENTS

Insert Set (20 cards): 175.00

	Insert (1:25)	Ornam.
☐	1 Paul Kariya, Anah. [Bell]	15.00
☐	2 Teemu Selänne, Anah. [Bell]	10.00
☐	3 Sergei Samsonov, Bost. [Stocking]	6.00
☐	4 Dominik Hasek (G), Buff. [Tree]	10.00
☐	5 Jarome Iginla, Calg. [Wreath]	10.00
☐	6 Peter Forsberg, Colo. [Ball]	15.00
☐	7 Patrick Roy (G), Colo. [Ball]	40.00
☐	8 Ed Belfour (G), Dall. [Stocking]	10.00
☐	9 Mike Modano, Dall. [Tree]	10.00
☐	10 Brendan Shanahan, Detr. [Wreath]	10.00
☐	11 Steve Yzerman, Detr. [Ball]	30.00
☐	12 Pavel Bure, Flor. [Bell]	10.00
☐	13 Martin Brodeur (G), NJer. [Stocking]	20.00
☐	14 John LeClair, Phil. [Tree]	10.00
☐	15 Eric Lindros, Phil. [Stocking]	10.00
☐	16 Jaromir Jagr, Pitt. [Ball]	10.00
☐	17 Vincent Lecavalier, Tamp. [Bell]	10.00
☐	18 Curtis Joseph (G), Toro. [Wreath]	10.00
☐	19 Mats Sundin, Toro. [Tree]	10.00
☐	20 Mark Messier, Vanc. [Wreath]	10.00

SHOWSTOPPERS

Insert Set (36 cards): 180.00

	Insert (2:25 packs)	Show.
☐	1 Paul Kariya, Anah.	10.00
☐	2 Teemu Selänne, Anah.	6.00
☐	3 Raymond Bourque, Bost.	8.00
☐	4 Byron Dafoe (G), Bost.	3.00
☐	5 Dominik Hasek (G), Buff.	6.00
☐	6 Michael Peca, Buff.	3.00
☐	7 Tony Amonte, Chic.	4.00
☐	8 Chris Drury, Colo.	4.00
☐	9 Peter Forsberg, Colo.	10.00
☐	10 Patrick Roy (G), Colo.	22.00
☐	11 Joe Sakic, Colo.	12.00
☐	12 Ed Belfour (G), Dall.	6.00
☐	13 Brett Hull, Dall.	6.00
☐	14 Mike Modano, Dall.	6.00
☐	15 Joe Nieuwendyk, Dall.	3.00
☐	16 Sergei Fedorov, Detr.	6.00
☐	17 Brendan Shanahan, Detr.	6.00
☐	18 Doug Weight, Edmo.	4.00
☐	19 Pavel Bure, Flor.	6.00
☐	20 Mark Parrish, Flor.	3.00
☐	21 Martin Brodeur (G), NJer.	12.00
☐	22 Félix Potvin (G), NYIs.	4.00
☐	23 Mike Richter (G), NYRa.	3.00
☐	24 Marian Hossa, Otta.	6.00
☐	25 Alexei Yashin, Otta.	4.00
☐	26 John LeClair, Phil.	6.00
☐	27 John Vanbiesbrouck (G), Flor.	3.00
☐	28 Jeremy Roenick, Phoe.	6.00
☐	29 Keith Tkachuk, Phoe.	4.00
☐	30 Pavol Demitra, SLou.	3.00
☐	31 Patrick Marleau, SanJ.	3.00
☐	32 Vincent Lecavalier, Tamp.	6.00
☐	33 Curtis Joseph (G), Toro.	6.00
☐	34 Mats Sundin, Toro.	6.00
☐	35 Mark Messier, Vanc.	6.00
☐	36 Peter Bondra, Wash.	4.00

TOP OF THE LINE

Insert Set (30 cards): 675.00

	Insert	TL99
☐	1 Paul Kariya, Anah.	85.00
☐	2 Sergei Samsonov, Bost.	35.00
☐	3 Brendan Shanahan, Detr.	60.00
☐	4 Pavel Bure, Flor.	50.00
☐	5 Luc Robitaille, LosA.	50.00
☐	6 Marian Hossa, Otta.	60.00
☐	7 John LeClair, Phil.	50.00
☐	8 Keith Tkachuk, Phoe.	35.00
☐	9 Pavol Demitra, SLou.	25.00
☐	10 Jeff Friesen, SanJ.	20.00
	Insert	**TL199**
☐	11 Chris Drury, Colo.	15.00
☐	12 Peter Forsberg, Colo.	40.00
☐	13 Joe Sakic, Colo.	50.00
☐	14 Steve Yzerman, Detr.	75.00
☐	15 Mike Modano, Dall.	30.00
☐	16 Joe Nieuwendyk, Dall.	10.00
☐	17 Alexei Yashin, Otta.	15.00
☐	18 Eric Lindros, Phil.	30.00
☐	19 Mats Sundin, Toro.	30.00
☐	20 Mark Messier, Vanc.	30.00
	Insert	**TL299**
☐	21 Teemu Selänne, Anah.	15.00
☐	22 Miroslav Satan, Buff.	8.00
☐	23 Jarome Iginla, Calg.	15.00
☐	24 Tony Amonte, Chic.	10.00
☐	25 Milan Hejduk, Colo.	15.00
☐	26 Brett Hull, Dall.	20.00
☐	27 Theoren Fleury, Colo. (NYRa.)	10.00
☐	28 Mark Recchi, Phil.	8.00
☐	29 Jaromir Jagr, Pitt.	20.00
☐	30 Peter Bondra, Wash.	10.00

CONTINENTAL SPORTS CARDS

There are three versions: a card limited to 25 copies, a card limited to 10 copies and a card limited to 1 copy.

Complete Set (75 cards): 1000.00 50.00

	Player	C10	C25
☐☐☐	1 Guy Hebert (G), Anah.	10.00	6.00
☐☐☐	2 Paul Kariya, Anah.	40.00	25.00
☐☐☐	4 Teemu Selänne, Anah.	20.00	15.00
☐☐☐	8 Damian Rhodes (G), Otta. (Atla.)	10.00	6.00
☐☐☐	10 Jason Allison, Bost.	15.00	10.00
☐☐☐	11 Raymond Bourque, Bost.	35.00	20.00
☐☐☐	13 Byron Dafoe (G), Bost.	10.00	6.00
☐☐☐	14 Sergei Samsonov, Bost.	15.00	10.00
☐☐☐	15 Joe Thornton, Bost.	35.00	20.00
☐☐☐	16 Martin Biron (G), Buff.	10.00	6.00
☐☐☐	18 Dominik Hasek (G), Buff.	30.00	20.00
☐☐☐	19 Michael Peca, Buff.	10.00	6.00
☐☐☐	22 Valeri Bure, Calg.	10.00	6.00
☐☐☐	25 Jarome Iginla, Calg.	20.00	15.00
☐☐☐	27 Ron Francis, Caro.	15.00	10.00
☐☐☐	28 Arturs Irbe (G), Caro.	10.00	6.00
☐☐☐	32 Tony Amonte, Chic.	15.00	10.00
☐☐☐	33 Jean-Pierre Dumont, Chic.	10.00	6.00
☐☐☐	35 Jocelyn Thibault (G), Chic.	10.00	6.00
☐☐☐	36 Alexei Zhamnov, Chic.	10.00	6.00
☐☐☐	38 Chris Drury, Colo.	15.00	10.00
☐☐☐	39 Peter Forsberg, Colo.	40.00	25.00
☐☐☐	40 Milan Hejduk, Colo.	20.00	15.00
☐☐☐	42 Patrick Roy (G), Colo.	90.00	60.00
☐☐☐	43 Joe Sakic, Colo.	45.00	30.00
☐☐☐	44 Ed Belfour (G), Dall.	30.00	20.00
☐☐☐	45 Brett Hull, Dall.	30.00	20.00
☐☐☐	48 Mike Modano, Dall.	30.00	20.00
☐☐☐	49 Joe Nieuwendyk, Dall.	10.00	6.00
☐☐☐	51 Sergei Fedorov, Detr.	30.00	20.00
☐☐☐	54 Chris Osgood (G), Detr.	15.00	10.00
☐☐☐	55 Brendan Shanahan, Detr.	30.00	20.00
☐☐☐	56 Steve Yzerman, Detr.	70.00	45.00
☐☐☐	58 Bill Guerin, Edmo.	10.00	6.00
☐☐☐	59 Tommy Salo (G), Edmo.	10.00	6.00
☐☐☐	61 Doug Weight, Edmo.	15.00	10.00
☐☐☐	62 Pavel Bure, Flor.	20.00	15.00
☐☐☐	65 Mark Parrish, Flor.	10.00	6.00
☐☐☐	70 Zigmund Palffy, NYIs. (LosA.)	15.00	10.00
☐☐☐	71 Luc Robitaille, LosA.	20.00	15.00
☐☐☐	73 Shayne Corson, Mont.	10.00	6.00
☐☐☐	75 Saku Koivu, Mont.	20.00	15.00
☐☐☐	83 Jason Arnott, NJer.	10.00	6.00
☐☐☐	84 Martin Brodeur (G), NJer.	45.00	30.00
☐☐☐	93 Félix Potvin (G), NYIs.	15.00	10.00
☐☐☐	95 Theoren Fleury, Colo. (NYRa.)	15.00	10.00
☐☐☐	97 Brian Leetch, NYRa.	15.00	10.00
☐☐☐	100 Mike Richter (G), NYRa.	10.00	6.00
☐☐☐	101 Magnus Arvedson, Otta.	10.00	6.00
☐☐☐	102 Marian Hossa, Otta.	30.00	20.00
☐☐☐	103 Shawn McEachern, Otta.	10.00	6.00
☐☐☐	104 Ron Tugnutt (G), Otta.	10.00	6.00
☐☐☐	106 Rod Brind'Amour, Phil.	10.00	6.00
☐☐☐	107 Eric Lindros, Phil.	30.00	20.00
☐☐☐	108 John LeClair, Phil.	20.00	15.00
☐☐☐	109 Mark Recchi, Phil.	10.00	6.00
☐☐☐	110 John Vanbiesbrouck (G), Phil.	10.00	6.00
☐☐☐	111 Nikolai Khabibulin (G), Phoe.	10.00	6.00
☐☐☐	113 Jeremy Roenick, Phoe.	20.00	15.00
☐☐☐	114 Keith Tkachuk, Phoe.	15.00	10.00
☐☐☐	116 Tom Barrasso (G), Pitt.	10.00	6.00
☐☐☐	118 Jaromir Jagr, Pitt.	30.00	20.00
☐☐☐	128 Patrick Marleau, SanJ.	10.00	6.00
☐☐☐	130 Mike Vernon (G), SanJ.	10.00	6.00
☐☐☐	133 Vincent Lecavalier, Tamp.	30.00	20.00
☐☐☐	135 Sergei Berezin, Toro.	10.00	6.00
☐☐☐	136 Tie Domi, Toro.	10.00	6.00
☐☐☐	137 Mike Johnson, Toro.	10.00	6.00
☐☐☐	138 Curtis Joseph (G), Toro.	30.00	20.00
☐☐☐	139 Derek King, Toro.	10.00	6.00
☐☐☐	140 Mats Sundin, Toro.	30.00	20.00
☐☐☐	141 Steve Thomas, Toro.	10.00	6.00
☐☐☐	142 Mark Messier, Vanc.	30.00	20.00
☐☐☐	147 Peter Bondra, Wash.	15.00	10.00
☐☐☐	150 Adam Oates, Wash.	10.00	6.00

1999 - 2000 SCORE

Cards of NHL stars and prospects sell at a premium (usually $1-$2).

Complete Set (165 cards): 30.00

	Player	Score
☐	1 Roman Malek, Beroun	.30
☐	2 Roman Hrubes, Beroun	.30
☐	3 Ladislav Slizek, Beroun	.30
☐	4 Jaroslav Roubik, Beroun	.30
☐	5 Jiri Kuchler, Beroun	.30
☐	6 Petr Mudroch, Beroun	.30
☐	7 Jiri Cmunt, Beroun	.30
☐	8 Lukas Palecek, Beroun	.30
☐	9 Pavel Malecek, Beroun	.30
☐	10 Vaclav Drabek, Beroun	.30
☐	11 Dalibor Sanda, Beroun	.30
☐	12 Jiri Novotny, Beroun	.30
☐	13 Dalimil Svoboda, Brno	.30
☐	14 Petr Kubena, Brno	.30
☐	15 Martin Svetlik, Brno	.30
☐	16 Jakub Ziska, Brno	.30
☐	17 Richard Kolacek, Brno	.30
☐	18 Tomas Trachta, Brno	.30
☐	19 Patrik Weber, Brno	.30
☐	20 Ales Sochorec, Brno	.30
☐	21 Alexandr Elsner, Brno	.30
☐	22 Michal Safarik, Brno	.30
☐	23 Josef Turek, Brno	.30
☐	24 Tomas Mikolasek, Brno	.30
☐	25 Pavel Malac, Choumtov	.30
☐	26 Kamil Jarina, Choumtov	.30
☐	27 Petr Martinek, Choumtov	.30
☐	28 Ladislav Bousek, Choumtov	.30
☐	29 Kamil Kolacek, Choumtov	.30
☐	30 Jiri Gombar, Choumtov	.30
☐	31 David Hajek, Choumtov	.30
☐	32 Martin Tupa, Choumtov	.30
☐	33 Stanislav Stavensky, Choumtov	.30
☐	34 Martin Stetcich, Choumtov	.30
☐	35 Radek Sip, Choumtov	.30
☐	36 Petr Altrichter, Choumtov	.30
☐	37 Lukas Stabl, Jihlva	.30
☐	38 Lukas Sablik, Jihlva	.30
☐	39 Marian Morava, Jihlva	.30
☐	40 Zdenek Fuksa, Jihlva	.30
☐	41 Petr Mokrejs, Jihlva	.30
☐	42 Miroslav Duben, Jihlva	.30
☐	43 Jiri Cihlar, Jihlva	.30
☐	44 Vaclav Adamec, Jihlva	.30
☐	45 Danie Hodek, Jihlva	.30
☐	46 Ales Polcar, Jihlva	.30
☐	47 Daniel Zapotocny, Jihlva	.30
☐	48 Richard Cachnin, Jihlva	.30
☐	49 Roman Spiler, Jindrichuv Hradec	.30
☐	50 Filip Sindelar, Jindrichuv Hradec	.30
☐	51 Petr Jaros, Jindrichuv Hradec	.30
☐	52 Marek Dvorak, Jindrichuv Hradec	.30
☐	53 Jaroslav Mares, Jindrichuv Hradec	.30
☐	54 Robert Vavroch, Jindrichuv Hradec	.30
☐	55 Vratislav Hreben, Jindrichuv Hradec	.30
☐	56 Petr Cerveny, Jindrichuv Hradec	.30
☐	57 Jaroslav Kocar, Jindrichuv Hradec	.30
☐	58 Ales Skokan, Jindrichuv Hradec	.30
☐	59 Michal Horak, Jindrichuv Hradec	.30
☐	60 Jakub Kraus, Jindrichuv Hradec	.30
☐	61 Marcel Kucera, Kadan	.30
☐	62 Miroslav Sedlacek, Kadan	.30
☐	63 Richard Richter, Kadan	.30
☐	64 Rudolf Mudra, Kadan	.30
☐	65 Jaroslav Muller, Kadan	.30
☐	66 Evzen Gal, Kadan	.30
☐	67 Petr Spojcar, Kadan	.30
☐	68 Jaroslav Kreuzmann, Kadan	.30
☐	69 Premysl Sedlak, Kadan	.30
☐	70 Martin Nosek, Kadan	.30
☐	71 Tomas Vyskocil, Kadan	.30
☐	72 Michal Lanicek, Liberec	.30
☐	73 Pavel Malac, Liberec	.30
☐	74 Ales Vala, Liberec	.30
☐	75 Martin Vyborny, Liberec	.30
☐	76 Tomas Vozka, Liberec	.30
☐	77 Petr Horcicka, Liberec	.30
☐	78 Jan Plodek, Liberec	.30
☐	79 Oldrich Nyc, Liberec	.30
☐	80 Filip Pesan, Liberec	.30
☐	81 Milan Plodek, Liberec	.30
☐	82 Jiri Matousek, Liberec	.30
☐	83 Vitezslav Jankovych, Liberec	.30
☐	84 Petr Kus, Melnik	.30
☐	85 Martin Chlad, Melnik	.30
☐	86 Hiroyuki Murakami, Melnik	.30
☐	87 Lukas Bednarik, Melnik	.30
☐	88 Michal Oliverius, Melnik	.30
☐	89 Tomas Pisa, Melnik	.30
☐	90 Jan Hranac, Melnik	.30
☐	91 Jan Bohacek, Melnik	.30
☐	92 Tomas Klimt, Melnik	.50
☐	93 Martin Zivny, Melnik	.30
☐	94 Michal Havel, Melnik	.30
☐	95 Martin Rejthar, Melnik	.30
☐	96 Karel Rakovsky, Opava	.30
☐	97 Martin Vojtek, Opava	.30
☐	98 Robert Prochazka, Opava	.30
☐	99 Daniel Vilasek, Opava	.30
☐	100 Jan Kasik, Opava	.30
☐	101 Jevgenij Alipov, Opava	.30
☐	102 Ales Kretinsky, Opava	.30
☐	103 Pavel Sebesta, Opava	.30
☐	104 David Kostelnak, Opava	.30
☐	105 Marek Harazim, Opava	.30
☐	106 Richard Brancik, Opava	.30
☐	107 Petr Rozum, Opava	.30
☐	108 Michal Pinkas, Pisek	.30
☐	109 Robert Slavik, Pisek	.30
☐	110 Josef Vachulka, Pisek	.30
☐	111 Lubos Pindiak, Pisek	.30
☐	112 Roman Zak, Pisek	.30
☐	113 David Mika, Pisek	.30
☐	114 Jiri Kudma, Pisek	.30
☐	115 Vaclav Benak, Pisek	.30
☐	116 Roman Bezpalec, Pisek	.30
☐	117 Pavel Heji, Pisek	.30
☐	118 Michal Janiga, Pisek	.30
☐	119 Vladimir Mezera, Pisek	.30
☐	120 David Pisek, Prostejov	.30
☐	121 Petr Tucek, Prostejov	.30
☐	122 Martin Palinek, Prostejov	.30
☐	123 Jiri Polak, Prostejov	.30
☐	124 Michal Cerny, Prostejov	.50
☐	125 Milan Ministr, Prostejov	.30
☐	126 Tomas Hiradecky, Prostejov	.30
☐	127 David Svec, Prostejov	.30
☐	128 Martin Jenacek, Prostejov	.30
☐	129 Jiri Hradecky, Prostejov	.30
☐	130 Radomir Brazda, Prostejov	.30
☐	131 Petr Hrachovina, Rosice	.30
☐	132 Martin Altrichter, Rosice	.30
☐	133 Jaromir Pichal, Rosice	.30
☐	134 Jiri Bures, Rosice	.30
☐	135 Jiri Mifek, Rosice	.30
☐	136 Jaroslav Smolik, Rosice	.30
☐	137 Milota Florian, Rosice	.30
☐	138 Robert Holy, Rosice	.30
☐	139 Josef Drabek, Rosice	.30
☐	140 Michal Slavik, Rosice	.30
☐	141 Tomas Kramny, Rosice	.30
☐	142 Michal Konecny, Rosice	.30
☐	143 Radek Lukes, Sumperk	.30
☐	144 Robert Hamrla, Sumperk	.30
☐	145 Petr Lustinec, Sumperk	.30
☐	146 Radek Kucera, Sumperk	.30
☐	147 Petr Sakarov, Sumperk	.30
☐	148 Pavel Kormunda, Sumperk	.30
☐	149 Petr Suchy, Sumperk	.30
☐	150 David Brezik, Sumperk	.30
☐	151 Michal Nohejl, Sumperk	.30

☐	152 Martin Jenacek, Sumperk	.30
☐	153 Dusan Barica, Sumperk	.30
☐	154 Zdenek Kucirek, Trebic	.30
☐	155 Stanislav Neruda, Trebic	.30
☐	156 Robert Pospisil, Trebic	.30
☐	157 Brendan Morrison, Trebic	1.50
☐	158 Jiri Sevcik, Trebic	.30
☐	159 Roman Hlouch, Trebic	.30
☐	160 Patrik Elias, Trebic	4.00
☐	161 Oldrich Bakus, Trebic	.30
☐	162 Jiri Oliva, Trebic	.30
☐	163 Karel Sefcik, Trebic	.30
☐	164 Marcel Hrbacek, Trebic	.30
☐	165 Rostislav Malena, Trebic	.30

DOMINATOR

Insert Set (7 cards):		10.00
	Insert	**MINT**
☐	D1 Dominik Hasek (G)	2.00
☐	D2 Dominik Hasek (G)	2.00
☐	D3 Dominik Hasek (G)	2.00
☐	D4 Dominik Hasek (G)	2.00
☐	D5 Dominik Hasek (G)	2.00
☐	D6 Dominik Hasek (G)	2.00
☐	D7 Dominik Hasek (G)	2.00

JAGR TEAM

Insert Set (28 cards):		30.00
	Insert	**MINT**
☐	JT1 Jaromir Jagr	5.00
☐	JT2 Milan Hnilicka (G)	1.00
☐	JT3 Jan Vopat	1.00
☐	JT4 Jaroslav Spacek	1.00
☐	JT5 Marek Malik	1.00
☐	JT6 Frantisek Kaberle	1.00
☐	JT7 Jiri Slegr	1.00
☐	JT8 Pavel Kubina	1.00
☐	JT9 Pavel Skrbek	1.00
☐	JT10 Pavel Patera	1.00
☐	JT11 Josef Beranek	1.00
☐	JT12 Robert Reichel	1.00
☐	JT13 Martin Rucinsky	1.00
☐	JT14 Vaclav Varada	1.00
☐	JT15 Martin Prochazka	1.00
☐	JT16 Jan Hrdina	1.00
☐	JT17 Martin Straka	1.00
☐	JT18 David Volek	1.00
☐	JT19 Vladimir Ruzicka	1.00
☐	JT20 Roman Hamrlik	1.00
☐	JT21 Radek Dvorak	1.00
☐	JT22 Milos Holan	1.00
☐	JT23 Robert Kron	1.00
☐	JT24 Leo Gudas	1.00
☐	JT25 Libor Prochazka	1.00
☐	JT26 Roman Turek (G)	2.00
☐	JT27 Jaromir Jagr	5.00
☐	JT28 Jagr Team Photo	2.00

NATIONALS

	Insert	
☐	1 Czech Republic	1.00
☐	2 Czech Republic	1.00
☐	3 Czech Republic	1.00
☐	4 Czech Republic	1.00
☐	5 Jiri Vykoukal, Czech Republic	1.00
☐	6 Czech Republic	1.00
☐	7 Czech Republic	1.00
☐	8 Czech Republic	1.00
☐	9 Martin Richter, Czech Republic	1.00
☐	10 Czech Republic	1.00
☐	11 Czech Republic	1.00
☐	12 Czech Republic	1.00
☐	13 Jan Caloun, Czech Republic	1.00
☐	14 Czech Republic	1.00
☐	15 Czech Republic	1.00
☐	16 Martin Stepanek, Czech Republic	1.00
☐	17 Czech Republic	1.00
☐	18 Czech Republic	1.00
☐	19 Czech Republic	1.00
☐	20 Czech Republic	1.00
☐	21 Czech Republic	1.00
☐	22 Czech Republic	1.00
☐	23 Czech Republic	1.00
☐	24 Czech Republic	1.00
☐	25 Czech Republic	1.00

1999 - 2000 SOBEY'S UPPER DECK

Complete Set (16 cards):		25.00
	Memorial Cup	**UD**
☐	1 Alexei Volkov (G)	3.00
☐	2 Justin Papineau	2.00
☐	3 Michael Henrich	2.00
☐	4 Kris Beech	4.00
☐	5 Mark Bell	3.00
☐	6 Andrei Shefer	1.00
☐	7 Pavel Brendl	4.00
☐	8 Blake Robson	1.00
☐	9 Ben Knopp	1.00
☐	10 Maxime Ouellet (G)	4.00
☐	11 Thatcher Bell	1.00
☐	12 Brian Finley (G)	2.00
☐	13 Jared Aulin	1.00
☐	14 Jared Newman	1.00
☐	15 Brad Boyes	2.00
☐	16 Miguel Delisle	1.00

1999 - 2000 SP AUTHENTIC

This series was released in 2000. Rookie subset cards 91-135 are limited to 1999 copies. For cards 1-90, a second variation exists without the embossing on the card front. This non-embossed variation was not seeded in packs and is tough to come by.

Shell Set (90 cards):		**35.00**
Complete Set (135 cards):		**650.00**
Common Player:		**.25**
	Player	**Reg.**
☐ ☐	1 Paul Kariya, Anah.	1.50
☐ ☐	2 Teemu Selänne, Anah.	1.00
☐ ☐	3 Guy Hebert (G), Anah.	.25
☐ ☐	4 Ray Ferraro, Atla.	.25
☐ ☐	5 Andrew Brunette, Atla.	.25
☐ ☐	6 Joe Thornton, Bost.	1.50
☐ ☐	7 Raymond Bourque, Bost.	1.50
☐ ☐	8 Sergei Samsonov, Bost.	.50
☐ ☐	9 Michael Peca, Buff.	.50
☐ ☐	10 Dominik Hasek (G), Buff.	1.00
☐ ☐	11 Miroslav Satan, Buff.	.25
☐ ☐	12 Maxim Afinogenov, Buff.	1.00
☐ ☐	13 Valeri Bure, Calg.	.25
☐ ☐	14 Marc* Savard, Calg.	.25
☐ ☐	15 Fred Brathwaite (G), Calg.	.25
☐ ☐	16 Ron Francis, Caro.	.50
☐ ☐	17 Arturs Irbe (G), Caro.	.50
☐ ☐	18 Sami Kapanen, Caro.	.25
☐ ☐	19 Tony Amonte, Chic.	.50
☐ ☐	**20 Steve Passmore (G), Chic. (RC)**	**1.00**
☐ ☐	21 Doug Gilmour, Chic.	.50
☐ ☐	22 Milan Hejduk, Colo.	1.00
☐ ☐	23 Joe Sakic, Colo.	2.00
☐ ☐	24 Patrick Roy (G), Colo.	3.50
☐ ☐	25 Chris Drury, Colo.	.50
☐ ☐	26 Peter Forsberg, Colo.	1.50
☐ ☐	27 Mike Modano, Dall.	1.00
☐ ☐	28 Brett Hull, Dall.	1.00
☐ ☐	29 Ed Belfour (G), Dall.	1.00
☐ ☐	30 Steve Yzerman, Detr.	3.00
☐ ☐	31 Chris Osgood (G), Detr.	.50
☐ ☐	32 Brendan Shanahan, Detr.	1.00
☐ ☐	33 Sergei Fedorov, Detr.	1.00
☐ ☐	34 Doug Weight, Edmo.	.50
☐ ☐	35 Bill Guerin, Edmo.	.50
☐ ☐	36 Alexander Selivanov, Edmo.	.25
☐ ☐	37 Pavel Bure, Flor.	1.00
☐ ☐	38 Trevor Kidd (G), Flor.	.25
☐ ☐	39 Viktor Kozlov, Flor.	.25
☐ ☐	40 Luc Robitaille, LosA.	1.00
☐ ☐	41 Zigmund Palffy, LosA.	.50
☐ ☐	42 Rob Blake, LosA.	.50
☐ ☐	43 Saku Koivu, Mont.	.50
☐ ☐	44 Mike Ribeiro, Mont.	.50
☐ ☐	45 José Théodore (G), Mont.	1.50
☐ ☐	46 David Legwand, Nash.	1.00
☐ ☐	47 Mike Dunham (G), Nash.	.50
☐ ☐	**48 Robert Valicevic, Nash. (RC)**	**.50**
☐ ☐	49 Martin Brodeur (G), NJer.	2.00
☐ ☐	50 Claude Lemieux, NJer.	.25
☐ ☐	51 Scott Gomez, NJer.	1.00
☐ ☐	52 Tim Connolly, NYIs.	1.00
☐ ☐	53 Roberto Luongo (G), NYIs.	2.00
☐ ☐	54 Kenny Jönsson, NYIs.	.25
☐ ☐	55 Mike Richter (G), NYRa.	.50
☐ ☐	56 Theoren Fleury, NYRa.	.50
☐ ☐	57 Mike York, NYRa.	.50
☐ ☐	58 Brian Leetch, NYRa.	.50
☐ ☐	59 Radek Bonk, Otta.	.25
☐ ☐	60 Marian Hossa, Otta.	1.00
☐ ☐	61 Patrick Lalime (G), Otta.	.50
☐ ☐	62 Keith Primeau, Phil.	.50
☐ ☐	63 Eric Lindros, Phil.	1.00
☐ ☐	64 John LeClair, Phil.	1.00
☐ ☐	65 Trevor Letowski, Phoe.	.25
☐ ☐	66 Keith Tkachuk, Phoe.	.50
☐ ☐	67 Jeremy Roenick, Phoe.	1.00
☐ ☐	68 Jaromir Jagr, Pitt.	1.00
☐ ☐	69 Alexei Kovalev, Pitt.	.50
☐ ☐	70 Martin Straka, Pitt.	.25
☐ ☐	71 Brad Stuart, SanJ.	1.00
☐ ☐	72 Steve Shields (G), SanJ.	.25
☐ ☐	73 Owen Nolan, SanJ.	.50
☐ ☐	74 Jeff Friesen, SanJ.	.25
☐ ☐	75 Pavol Demitra, SLou.	.50
☐ ☐	76 Roman Turek (G), SLou.	.50
☐ ☐	77 Pierre Turgeon, SLou.	.50
☐ ☐	78 Vincent Lecavalier, Tamp.	1.00
☐ ☐	79 Dan Cloutier (G), Tamp.	.50
☐ ☐	80 Chris Gratton, Tamp.	.25
☐ ☐	81 Mats Sundin, Toro.	1.00
☐ ☐	82 Bryan Berard, Toro.	.25
☐ ☐	83 Curtis Joseph (G), Toro.	1.00
☐ ☐	84 Jonas Höglund, Toro.	.25
☐ ☐	85 Mark Messier, Vanc.	1.00
☐ ☐	86 Peter Schaefer, Vanc.	.25
☐ ☐	87 Alexander Mogilny, Vanc.	.50
☐ ☐	88 Olaf Kölzig (G), Wash.	.50
☐ ☐	89 Adam Oates, Wash.	.50
☐ ☐	90 Peter Bondra, Wash.	.50

FUTURE WATCH

	Insert (#/2000)	**FW**
☐	**91 Patrik Stefan, Atla. RC**	**30.00**
☐	**92 Dean Sylvester, Atla. RC**	**8.00**
☐	**93 Scott Fankhouser (G), Atla. RC**	**15.00**
☐	**94 Brian Campbell, Buff. RC**	**8.00**
☐	**95 Byron Ritchie, Caro. RC**	**8.00**
☐	**96 John Grahame (G), Bost. RC**	**20.00**
☐	**97 André Savage, Bost. RC**	**8.00**
☐	**98 Oleg Saprykin, Calg. RC**	**20.00**
☐	**99 Kyle Calder, Chic. RC**	**20.00**
☐	**100 Dan Hinote, Colo. RC**	**15.00**
☐	**101 Jonathan Sim, Dall. RC**	**8.00**
☐	**102 Marc Rodgers, Detr. RC**	**8.00**
☐	**103 Paul Comrie, Edmo. RC**	**15.00**
☐	**104 Ivan Novoseltsev, Flor. RC**	**15.00**
☐	**105 Jason Blake, LosA. RC**	**20.00**
☐	**106 Brian Rafalski, NJer. RC**	**20.00**
☐	**107 John Madden, NJer. RC**	**30.00**
☐	**108 Jason Krog, NYIs. RC**	**20.00**
☐	**109 Jörgen Jönsson, NYIs. RC**	**15.00**
☐	**110 Kim Johnsson, NYRa. RC**	**15.00**
☐	**111 Mike Fisher, Otta. RC**	**20.00**
☐	**112 Michal Rozsival, Pitt. RC**	**8.00**
☐	**113 Mika Alatalo, Phoe. RC**	**15.00**
☐	**114 Tyson Nash, SLou. RC**	**15.00**
☐	**115 Ladislav Nagy, SLou. RC**	**20.00**
☐	**116 Jochen Hecht, SLou. RC**	**20.00**
☐	**117 Adam Mair, Toro. RC**	**15.00**
☐	**118 Nikolai Antropov, Toro. RC**	**25.00**
☐	**119 Steve Kariya, Vanc. RC**	**20.00**
☐	**120 Jeff Halpern, Wash. RC**	**20.00**
☐	**121 Alexandre (Jr.) Volchkov, Edmo. RC**	**8.00**
☐	**122 Pavel Brendl, Calgary Hitmen RC**	**30.00**
☐	**123 Sheldon Keefe, Barrie Colts RC**	**15.00**
☐	**124 Branislav Mezei, Belleville Bulls RC**	**15.00**
☐	**125 Milan Kraft, Prince Albert Raiders RC**	**30.00**
☐	**126 Kristian Kudroc, Québec Remparts RC**	**15.00**
☐	**127 Jaroslav Kristek, Tri-City Americans RC**	**8.00**
☐	**128 Alexander Buturlin, Sarnia Sting RC**	**8.00**
☐	**129 Andrei Shefer, Halifax Mooseheads RC**	**8.00**
☐	**130 Brad Moran, Calgary Hitmen RC**	**8.00**
☐	**131 Ryan Jardine, SSM Greyhounds RC**	**15.00**
☐	**132 Brett Lysak, Regina Pats RC**	**8.00**
☐	**133 Michal Sivek, Prince Albert Raiders RC**	**15.00**
☐	**134 Luke Sellars, Ottawa 67's RC**	**15.00**
☐	**135 Brad Ralph, Oshawa Generals RC**	**15.00**
	Sample Card	**SPA**
☐	31 Curtis Joseph (G), Toro.	1.00

HONOR ROLL

Insert Set (6 cards):		**30.00**
	Insert (1:24 packs)	**HR**
☐	HR1 Paul Kariya, Anah.	5.00
☐	HR2 Patrick Roy (G), Colo.	10.00
☐	HR3 Steve Yzerman, Detr.	8.00
☐	HR4 Martin Brodeur (G), NJer.	6.00
☐	HR5 Eric Lindros, Phil.	5.00
☐	HR6 Jaromir Jagr, Pitt.	5.00

LEGENDARY HEROES

Insert Set (5 cards):		**75.00**
	Insert (1:72 packs)	**LH**
☐	LH1 Wayne Gretzky, Edmo.	25.00
☐	LH2 Bobby Orr, Bost.	25.00
☐	LH3 Gordie Howe, Detr.	15.00
☐	LH4 Maurice Richard, Mont.	15.00
☐	LH5 Bobby Hull, Chic.	12.00

REPLICA JERSEY REDEMPTION

	Insert (1:9000 packs)	**RJR**
☐	J-BH Brett Hull, Dall.	
☐	J-CJ Curtis Joseph (G), Toro.	
☐	J-GH Gordie Howe, Detr.	
☐	J-LR Luc Robitaille, LosA.	
☐	J-PB Pavel Bure, Flor.	
☐	J-PS Patrik Stefan, Atla.	
☐	J-SF Sergei Fedorov, Detr.	
☐	J-WG Wayne Gretzky, NYRa.	

SIGN OF THE TIMES

There are two versions: the regular autograph (1:23 packs) and the Gold parallel (#/25).

Insert Set (32 cards):		**1,800.00**	**375.00**
	Inserts	**G25**	**SotT**
☐	Pavel Bure, Flor. ✍	180.00	30.00
☐	Brian Campbell, Buff. ✍	25.00	12.00
☐	Tim Connolly, NYIs. ✍	100.00	20.00
☐	Sergei Fedorov, Detr. ✍	225.00	35.00
☐	Theoren Fleury, NYRa. ✍	135.00	20.00
☐	Simon Gagné, Phil. ✍	180.00	30.00
☐	Scott Gomez, NJer. ✍	105.00	20.00
☐	Wayne Gretzky, NYRa. ✍	1100.00	275.00
☐	Jochen Hecht, SLou. ✍	60.00	12.00
☐	Marian Hossa, Otta. ✍	225.00	35.00
☐	Gordie Howe, Detr. ✍	540.00	90.00
☐	Bobby Hull, Chic. ✍	225.00	35.00
☐	Brett Hull, Dall. ✍ [Black ink]	225.00	35.00
☐	Curtis Joseph (G), Toro. ✍	225.00	35.00
☐	John LeClair, Phil. ✍	180.00	30.00
☐	David Legwand, Nash. ✍	90.00	15.00
☐	Paul Mara, Tamp. ✍	35.00	12.00
☐	Bill Muckalt, NYIs. ✍	35.00	12.00
☐	Bobby Orr, Bost. ✍	1,000.00	250.00
☐	Zigmund Palffy, LosA. ✍	135.00	20.00
☐	Mike Ribeiro, Mont. ✍	80.00	15.00
☐	Maurice Richard, Mont. ✍ •	585.00	95.00
☐	Luc Robitaille, LosA. ✍	180.00	30.00
☐	Jeremy Roenick, Phoe. ✍	180.00	30.00
☐	Sergei Samsonov, Bost. ✍	135.00	20.00
☐	Oleg Saprykin, Calg. ✍	60.00	12.00
☐	Patrik Stefan, Atla. ✍	80.00	15.00
☐	Brad Stuart, SanJ. ✍ [Black ink]	90.00	15.00
☐	Jozef Stumpel, LosA. ✍	50.00	12.00
☐	David Tanabe, Caro. ✍	40.00	12.00
☐	Alex Tanguay, Colo. ✍	160.00	30.00
☐	Steve Yzerman, Detr. ✍	550.00	90.00

SPECIAL FORCES

Insert Set (10 cards):		**30.00**
	Insert (1:12 packs)	**SF**
☐	SF1 Paul Kariya, Anah.	4.00
☐	SF2 Joe Sakic, Colo.	4.00
☐	SF3 Patrick Roy (G), Colo.	9.00
☐	SF4 Steve Yzerman, Detr.	7.00
☐	SF5 Mike Modano, Dall.	3.00
☐	SF6 Pavel Bure, Flor.	2.00
☐	SF7 Jaromir Jagr, Pitt.	3.00
☐	SF8 Eric Lindros, Phil.	3.00

☐	SF9 Curtis Joseph (G), Toro.	3.00
☐	SF10 Steve Kariya, Vanc.	2.00

SUPREME SKILL

Insert Set (11 cards):		15.00
	Insert (1:4 packs)	SS
☐	SS1 Paul Kariya, Anah.	2.00
☐	SS2 Teemu Selänne, Anah.	1.00
☐	SS3 Peter Forsberg, Colo.	2.00
☐	SS4 Brett Hull, Dall.	2.00
☐	SS5 Sergei Fedorov, Detr.	2.00
☐	SS6 Pavel Bure, Flor.	1.00
☐	SS7 Martin Brodeur (G), NJer.	3.00
☐	SS8 Theoren Fleury, NYRa.	1.00
☐	SS9 John LeClair, Phil.	1.00
☐	SS10 Keith Tkachuk, Phoe.	1.00
☐	SS11 Jaromir Jagr, Pitt.	2.00

TOMORROW'S HEADLINERS

Insert Set (10 cards):		25.00
	Insert (1:10 packs)	TH
☐	TH1 Patrik Stefan, Atla.	2.00
☐	TH2 Joe Thornton, Bost.	6.00
☐	TH3 Maxim Afinogenov, Buff.	2.00
☐	TH4 Milan Hejduk, Colo.	4.00
☐	TH5 David Legwand, Nash.	2.00
☐	TH6 Scott Gomez, NJer.	2.00
☐	TH7 Marian Hossa, Otta.	5.00
☐	TH8 Jochen Hecht, SLou.	2.00
☐	TH9 Vincent Lecavalier, Tamp.	5.00
☐	TH10 Steve Kariya, Vanc.	2.00

1999 - 2000 SP AUTHENTIC – BUYBACKS

	Buyback Autograph	**SPA**
☐	7 Raymond Bourque, Bost. ✍ {#/122}	
☐	8 Sergei Samsonov, Bost. ✍ {#/8}	
☐	11 Miroslav Satan, Buff. ✍ {#/145}	
☐	22 Milan Hejduk, Colo. ✍ {#/200}	
☐	27 Mike Modano, Dall. ✍ {#/168}	
☐	28 Brett Hull, Dall. ✍ {#/19}	
☐	30 Steve Yzerman, Detr. ✍ {#/152}	
☐	37 Pavel Bure, Flor. ✍ {#/225}	
☐	40 Luc Robitaille, LosA. ✍ {#/97}	
☐	44 Mike Ribeiro, Mont. ✍ {#/117}	
☐	46 David Legwand, Nash. ✍ {#/214}	
☐	51 Scott Gomez, NJer. ✍ {#/243}	
☐	55 Mike Richter (G), NYRa. ✍ {#/214}	
☐	57 Mike York, NYRa. ✍ {#/212}	
☐	64 John LeClair, Phil. ✍ {#/207}	
☐	67 Jeremy Roenick, Phoe. ✍ {#/98}	
☐	72 Steve Shields, SanJ. ✍ {#/195}	
☐	83 Curtis Joseph (G), Toro. ✍ {#/187}	
☐	85 Mark Messier, Vanc. ✍ {#/147}	
	Buyback Autograph • Future Watch	**SPA**
☐	**104 Ivan Novoseltsev, Flor. RC ✍ {#/1}**	
☐	**122 Pavel Brendl, Hitmen RC ✍ {#/3}**	
☐	**122 Milan Kraft, Raiders RC ✍ {#/3}**	
	Buyback Autograph • Legendary Heroes	**SPA**
☐	LH1 Wayne Gretzky, NYRa. ✍ {#/9}	
☐	LH3 Bobby Orr, Bost. ✍ {#/49}	
☐	LH5 Bobby Hull, Chic. ✍ {#/98}	
	Buyback Autograph • Special Forces	**SPA**
☐	SF4 Steve Yzerman, Detr. ✍ {#/35}	
☐	SF5 Mike Modano, Dall. ✍ {#/155}	
☐	SF6 Pavel Bure, Flor. ✍ {#/154}	
☐	SF9 Curtis Joseph (G), Toro. ✍ {#/135}	
	Buyback Autograph • Supreme Skills	**SPA**
☐	SS6 Pavel Bure, Flor. ✍ {#/69}	
☐	SS9 John LeClair, Phil. ✍ {#/116}	
	Buyback Autograph • Tomorrow's Headliners	**SPA**
☐	TH4 Milan Hejduk, Colo. ✍ {#/143}	
☐	TH5 David Legwand, Nash. ✍ {#/130}	
☐	TH6 Scott Gomez, NJer. ✍ {#/157}	

1999 - 2000 SPX

This series was released in 1999. Rookie subset cards are limited to 1999 copies. A number of the rookie subset cards are autographed (base version only, not parallels). All 180 cards have a Spectrum parallel (each #/100) and a Radiance parallel (each #/1).

Shell Set (162 cards):		-	**75.00**
Complete Set (180 cards):		**2680.00**	**325.00**
Common Player:		**5.00**	**.50**
	Player	**S100**	**Reg.**
☐☐☐	1 Damian Rhodes (G), Atla.	10.00	.50
☐☐☐	2 Nelson Emerson, Atla.	5.00	.50
☐☐☐	3 Ray Ferraro, Atla.	5.00	.50
☐☐☐	4 Paul Kariya, Anah.	60.00	1.50
☐☐☐	5 Steve Rucchin, Anah.	10.00	.50
☐☐☐	6 Guy Hebert (G), Anah.	10.00	.50
☐☐☐	7 Oleg Tverdovsky, Anah.	5.00	.50
☐☐☐	8 Ted Donato, Bost.	5.00	.50
☐☐☐	9 Raymond Bourque, Bost.	50.00	1.50
☐☐☐	10 Sergei Samsonov, Bost.	25.00	.50
☐☐☐	11 Joe Thornton, Bost.	50.00	1.50
☐☐☐	12 Jason Allison, Bost.	25.00	.50
☐☐☐	13 Byron Dafoe (G), Bost.	15.00	.50
☐☐☐	14 Jonathan Girard, Bost.	5.00	.50
☐☐☐	15 Dominik Hasek (G), Buff.	45.00	1.00
☐☐☐	16 Alexei Zhitnik, Buff.	5.00	.50
☐☐☐	17 Michael Peca, Buff.	15.00	.50
☐☐☐	18 Cory Sarich, Buff.	5.00	.50
☐☐☐	19 Martin Biron (G), Buff.	20.00	.50
☐☐☐	20 Miroslav Satan, Buff.	10.00	.50
☐☐☐	21 Valeri Bure, Calg.	10.00	.50
☐☐☐	22 Derek Morris, Calg.	10.00	.50
☐☐☐	23 Phil Housley, Calg.	10.00	.50
☐☐☐	24 Jarome Iginla, Calg.	35.00	1.00
☐☐☐	25 Rico Fata, Calg.	10.00	.50
☐☐☐	26 J-S Giguère (G), Calg.	35.00	1.00
☐☐☐	27 Marc* Savard, Calg.	10.00	.50
☐☐☐	28 Arturs Irbe (G), Caro.	15.00	.50
☐☐☐	29 Keith Primeau, Caro.	15.00	.50
☐☐☐	30 Sami Kapanen, Caro.	10.00	.50
☐☐☐	31 Ron Francis, Caro.	25.00	.50
☐☐☐	32 Wendel Clark, Chic.	35.00	1.00
☐☐☐	33 Jean-Pierre Dumont, Chic.	10.00	.50
☐☐☐	34 Ty Jones, Chic.	5.00	.50
☐☐☐	35 Tony Amonte, Chic.	25.00	.50
☐☐☐	36 Jocelyn Thibault (G), Chic.	15.00	.50
☐☐☐	37 Doug Gilmour, Chic.	25.00	.50
☐☐☐	38 Bryan McCabe, Chic.	10.00	.50
☐☐☐	39 Joe Sakic, Colo.	70.00	2.00
☐☐☐	40 Peter Forsberg, Colo.	60.00	1.50
☐☐☐	41 Alex Tanguay, Colo.	25.00	1.50
☐☐☐	42 Chris Drury, Colo.	25.00	.50
☐☐☐	43 Patrick Roy (G), Colo.	135.00	3.50
☐☐☐	44 Sandis Ozolinsh, Colo.	10.00	.50
☐☐☐	45 Adam Deadmarsh, Colo.	10.00	.50
☐☐☐	46 Milan Hejduk, Colo.	35.00	1.00
☐☐☐	47 Mike Modano, Dall.	45.00	1.00
☐☐☐	48 Brett Hull, Dall.	45.00	1.00
☐☐☐	49 Darryl Sydor, Dall.	10.00	.50
☐☐☐	50 Ed Belfour (G), Dall.	45.00	1.00
☐☐☐	51 Jere Lehtinen, Dall.	10.00	.50
☐☐☐	52 Jamie Langenbrunner, Dall.	10.00	.50
☐☐☐	53 Joe Nieuwendyk, Dall.	15.00	.50
☐☐☐	54 Sergei Fedorov, Detr.	45.00	1.00
☐☐☐	55 Steve Yzerman, Detr.	100.00	3.00
☐☐☐	56 Brendan Shanahan, Detr.	45.00	1.00
☐☐☐	57 Chris Osgood (G), Detr.	25.00	.50
☐☐☐	58 Nicklas Lidström, Detr.	25.00	.50
☐☐☐	59 Igor Larionov, Detr.	25.00	.50
☐☐☐	60 Chris Chelios, Detr.	25.00	.50
☐☐☐	61 Bill Guerin, Edmo.	15.00	.50
☐☐☐	62 Doug Weight, Edmo.	25.00	.50
☐☐☐	63 Mike Grier, Edmo.	10.00	.50
☐☐☐	64 Tommy Salo (G), Edmo.	15.00	.50
☐☐☐	65 Bill Ranford (G), Edmo.	15.00	.50
☐☐☐	66 Tom Poti, Edmo.	5.00	.50
☐☐☐	67 Daniel Cleary, Edmo.	10.00	.50
☐☐☐	68 Mark Parrish, Flor.	15.00	.50
☐☐☐	69 Pavel Bure, Flor.	35.00	1.00
☐☐☐	70 Oleg Kvasha, Flor.	5.00	.50
☐☐☐	71 Viktor Kozlov, Flor.	10.00	.50
☐☐☐	72 Trevor Kidd (G), Flor.	10.00	.50
☐☐☐	73 Rob Blake, LosA.	25.00	.50
☐☐☐	74 Pavel Rosa, LosA.	5.00	.50
☐☐☐	75 Luc Robitaille, LosA.	35.00	1.00
☐☐☐	76 Zigmund Palffy, NYIs.	25.00	.50
☐☐☐	77 Aki Berg, LosA.	5.00	.50
☐☐☐	78 Saku Koivu, Mont.	35.00	1.00
☐☐☐	79 Jeff Hackett (G), Mont.	10.00	.50
☐☐☐	80 Trevor Linden, NYIs.	15.00	.50
☐☐☐	81 Cliff Ronning, Nash.	10.00	.50
☐☐☐	82 David Legwand, Nash.	15.00	.50
☐☐☐	83 Mike Dunham (G), Nash.	15.00	.50
☐☐☐	84 Scott Stevens, NJer.	15.00	.50
☐☐☐	85 Martin Brodeur (G), NJer.	70.00	2.00
☐☐☐	86 Patrik Elias, NJer.	35.00	1.00
☐☐☐	87 Brendan Morrison, NJer.	10.00	.50
☐☐☐	88 Scott Niedermayer, NJer.	10.00	.50
☐☐☐	89 Vadim Sharifijanov, NJer.	5.00	.50
☐☐☐	90 Mike Watt, NYIs.	5.00	.50
☐☐☐	91 Félix Potvin (G), NYIs.	25.00	.50
☐☐☐	92 Eric Brewer, NYIs.	15.00	.50
☐☐☐	**93 Jörgen Jönsson, NYIs. RC**	**10.00**	**2.00**
☐☐☐	94 Kenny Jönsson, NYIs.	5.00	.50
☐☐☐	95 Olli Jokinen, LosA.	10.00	.50
☐☐☐	96 Theoren Fleury, Colo.	25.00	.50
☐☐☐	97 Brian Leetch, NYRa.	25.00	.50
☐☐☐	98 Mike Richter (G), NYRa.	20.00	.50
☐☐☐	99 Petr Nedved, NYRa.	10.00	.50
☐☐☐	100 Adam Graves, NYRa.	15.00	.50
☐☐☐	101 Manny Malhotra, NYRa.	10.00	.50
☐☐☐	102 Alexei Yashin, Otta.	25.00	.50
☐☐☐	103 Daniel Alfredsson, Otta.	25.00	.50
☐☐☐	104 Ron Tugnutt (G), Otta.	15.00	.50
☐☐☐	105 Magnus Arvedson, Otta.	5.00	.50
☐☐☐	106 Sami Salo, Otta.	5.00	.50
☐☐☐	107 Marian Hossa, Otta.	45.00	1.00
☐☐☐	108 Eric Lindros, Phil.	45.00	1.00
☐☐☐	109 John Vanbiesbrouck (G), Phil.	20.00	.50
☐☐☐	110 John LeClair, Phil.	35.00	1.00
☐☐☐	111 Rod Brind'Amour, Phil.	10.00	.50
☐☐☐	112 Mark Recchi, Phil.	15.00	.50
☐☐☐	113 Éric Desjardins, Phil.	10.00	.50
☐☐☐	114 Jeremy Roenick, Phoe.	35.00	1.00
☐☐☐	115 Keith Tkachuk, Phoe.	25.00	.50
☐☐☐	116 Rick Tocchet, Phoe.	10.00	.50
☐☐☐	**117 Robert Esche (G), Phoe. RC**	**15.00**	**2.00**
☐☐☐	118 Nikolai Khabibulin (G), Phoe.	15.00	.50
☐☐☐	119 Teppo Numminen, Phoe.	10.00	.50
☐☐☐	120 Jaromir Jagr, Pitt.	45.00	1.00
☐☐☐	121 Martin Straka, Pitt.	10.00	.50
☐☐☐	122 Jan Hrdina, Pitt.	10.00	.50
☐☐☐	123 German Titov, Pitt.	5.00	.50
☐☐☐	124 Alexei Kovalev, Pitt.	25.00	.50
☐☐☐	125 Matthew Barnaby, Pitt.	5.00	.50
☐☐☐	126 Vincent Damphousse, SanJ.	25.00	.50
☐☐☐	127 Owen Nolan, SanJ.	25.00	.50
☐☐☐	128 Jeff Friesen, SanJ.	10.00	.50
☐☐☐	129 Patrick Marleau, SanJ.	20.00	.50
☐☐☐	130 Marco Sturm, SanJ.	10.00	.50
☐☐☐	131 Mike Vernon (G), SanJ.	15.00	.50
☐☐☐	132 Pavol Demitra, SLou.	15.00	.50
☐☐☐	133 Al MacInnis, SLou.	15.00	.50
☐☐☐	134 Pierre Turgeon, SLou.	15.00	.50
☐☐☐	135 Chris Pronger, SLou.	25.00	.50
☐☐☐	**136 Jochen Hecht, SLou. RC**	**15.00**	**2.50**
☐☐☐	137 Vincent Lecavalier, Tamp.	45.00	1.00
☐☐☐	138 Paul Mara, Tamp.	5.00	.50
☐☐☐	139 Dan Cloutier (G), NYRa.	15.00	.50
☐☐☐	140 Andrei Zyuzin, SanJ.	5.00	.50
☐☐☐	141 Pavel Kubina, Tamp.	5.00	.50
☐☐☐	142 Kevin Hodson (G), Tamp.	10.00	.50
☐☐☐	143 Mats Sundin, Toro.	45.00	1.00
☐☐☐	144 Curtis Joseph (G), Toro.	45.00	1.00
☐☐☐	145 Sergei Berezin, Toro.	10.00	.50
☐☐☐	146 Bryan Berard, Toro.	10.00	.50
☐☐☐	147 Tomas Kaberle, Toro.	10.00	.50
☐☐☐	148 Danny Markov, Toro.	5.00	.50
☐☐☐	149 Mark Messier, Vanc.	45.00	1.00
☐☐☐	150 Bill Muckalt, Vanc.	5.00	.50
☐☐☐	151 Markus Näslund, Vanc.	45.00	1.00
☐☐☐	152 Mattias Öhlund, Vanc.	10.00	.50
☐☐☐	153 Ed Jovanovski, Vanc.	15.00	.50
☐☐☐	**154 Steve Kariya, Vanc. RC**	**15.00**	**2.00**
☐☐☐	155 Josh Holden, Vanc.	5.00	.50
☐☐☐	156 Richard Zednik, Wash.	15.00	.50
☐☐☐	157 Jaroslav Svejkovsky, Wash.	5.00	.50
☐☐☐	158 Adam Oates, Wash.	15.00	.50
☐☐☐	159 Peter Bondra, Wash.	25.00	.50
☐☐☐	160 Sergei Gonchar, Wash.	10.00	.50
☐☐☐	161 Olaf Kölzig (G), Wash.	25.00	.50
☐☐☐	162 Jan Bulis, Wash.	5.00	.50

ROOKIE

	Insert (#/1999)	R100	R1999
☐☐☐	**163 Patrik Stefan, Atla. RC ✍**	**70.00**	**60.00**
☐☐☐	164 Daniel Sedin, Sweden Juniors ✍	35.00	30.00
☐☐☐	165 Henrik Sedin, Sweden Juniors ✍	35.00	30.00
☐☐☐	**166 Brendl, Calgary Hitmen RC ✍**	**85.00**	**70.00**
☐☐☐	167 Brian Finley (G), Canada ✍	18.00	14.00
☐☐☐	168 Taylor Pyatt, Canada ✍	20.00	15.00
☐☐☐	169 Jamie Lundmark, Canada ✍	25.00	20.00
☐☐☐	170 Denis Shvidki, Russia Juniors	10.00	4.00
☐☐☐	171 Jani Rita, Finland Juniors	10.00	5.00
☐☐☐	**172 Oleg Saprykin, Seattle RC**	**50.00**	**25.00**
☐☐☐	173 Nick Boynton, Ottawa 67's	10.00	4.00
☐☐☐	174 Tim Connolly, U.S.A. Juniors ✍	35.00	30.00
☐☐☐	175 Kris Beech, Canada ✍	25.00	20.00
☐☐☐	176 Roberto Luongo (G), Canada	35.00	10.00
☐☐☐	177 David Legwand, Nash.	15.00	5.00
☐☐☐	178 David Tanabe, U.S.A. Juniors	8.00	4.00
☐☐☐	179 Barret Jackman, Canada	15.00	5.00
☐☐☐	180 Maxime Ouellet (G), Canada	15.00	5.00
	Sample Card		Promo
☐	SPX87 Wayne Gretzky, NYRa.		5.00

99 CHEERS

Insert Set (15 cards):		100.00
	Insert (1:17 packs)	CH
☐	CH1 Wayne Gretzky, Youth	8.00
☐	CH2 Wayne Gretzky	8.00
☐	CH3 Wayne Gretzky	8.00
☐	CH4 Wayne Gretzky, Edmo.	8.00
☐	CH5 Wayne Gretzky, Edmo.	8.00
☐	CH6 Wayne Gretzky, Edmo.	8.00
☐	CH7 Wayne Gretzky, LosA.	8.00
☐	CH8 Wayne Gretzky, LosA.	8.00
☐	CH9 Wayne Gretzky, SLou.	8.00
☐	CH10 Wayne Gretzky, NYRa.	8.00
☐	CH11 Wayne Gretzky, NHL Awards	8.00
☐	CH12 Wayne Gretzky, All-Star	8.00
☐	CH13 Wayne Gretzky, Canada	8.00
☐	CH14 Wayne Gretzky, NYRa.	8.00
☐	CH15 Wayne Gretzky, Off-Ice	8.00

HIGHLIGHT HEROES

Insert Set (10 cards):		35.00
	Insert (1:9 packs)	HH
☐	HH1 Wayne Gretzky, NYRa.	12.00
☐	HH2 Sergei Samsonov, Bost.	2.00
☐	HH3 Dominik Hasek (G), Buff.	3.00
☐	HH4 Jaromir Jagr, Pitt.	3.00
☐	HH5 Patrick Roy (G), Colo.	9.00
☐	HH6 Paul Kariya, Anah.	4.00
☐	HH7 Pavel Bure, Flor.	2.00
☐	HH8 Peter Forsberg, Colo.	4.00
☐	HH9 Eric Lindros, Phil.	3.00
☐	HH10 Teemu Selänne, Anah.	2.00

PROLIFICS

Insert Set (15 cards):		55.00
	Insert (1:17 packs)	P
☐	P1 Paul Kariya, Anah.	6.00
☐	P2 Jaromir Jagr, Pitt.	4.00
☐	P3 Brett Hull, Dall.	4.00
☐	P4 Joe Sakic, Colo.	7.00
☐	P5 Sergei Samsonov, Bost.	3.00
☐	P6 Keith Tkachuk, Phoe.	3.00
☐	P7 Brendan Shanahan, Detr.	4.00
☐	P8 Vincent Lecavalier, Tamp.	4.00
☐	P9 Steve Yzerman, Detr.	10.00
☐	P10 Jeremy Roenick, Phoe.	3.00
☐	P11 Mike Modano, Dall.	4.00
☐	P12 John LeClair, Phil.	3.00
☐	P13 Peter Forsberg, Colo.	6.00

□	P14 Raymond Bourque, Bost.	5.00
□	P15 David Legwand, Nash.	3.00

SPXCITEMENT

	Insert Set (20 cards):	**45.00**
	Insert (1:3 packs)	**X**
□	X1 Wayne Gretzky, Edmo.	10.00
□	X2 Patrick Roy (G), Colo.	7.00
□	X3 Pavel Bure, Flor.	2.00
□	X4 Steve Yzerman, Detr.	6.00
□	X5 David Legwand, Nash.	1.00
□	X6 Dominik Hasek (G), Buff.	2.00
□	X7 Sergei Samsonov, Bost.	1.00
□	X8 Patrik Stefan, Atla.	1.00
□	X9 Eric Lindros, Phil.	2.00
□	X10 Brett Hull, Dall.	2.00
□	X11 Steve Kariya, Vanc.	1.00
□	X12 Keith Tkachuk, Phoe.	1.00
□	X13 Alex Tanguay, Colo.	1.00
□	X14 Peter Forsberg, Colo.	3.00
□	X15 Jaromir Jagr, Pitt.	2.00
□	X16 Paul Kariya, Anah.	3.00
□	X17 Brendan Shanahan, Detr.	2.00
□	X18 Mike Modano, Dall.	2.00
□	X19 John LeClair, Phil.	2.00
□	X20 Teemu Selänne, Anah.	2.00

SPXTREME

	Insert Set (20 cards):	**70.00**
	Insert (1:6 packs)	**XT**
□	XT1 Al MacInnis, SLou.	2.50
□	XT2 Keith Tkachuk, Phoe.	2.50
□	XT3 Peter Forsberg, Colo.	5.00
□	XT4 Teemu Selänne, Anah.	3.00
□	XT5 Patrick Roy (G), Colo.	11.00
□	XT6 Sergei Samsonov, Bost.	2.50
□	XT7 Brendan Shanahan, Detr.	3.00
□	XT8 Mike Modano, Dall.	3.00
□	XT9 Eric Lindros, Phil.	3.00
□	XT10 Paul Kariya, Anah.	5.00
□	XT11 Jaromir Jagr, Pitt.	3.00
□	XT12 Brett Hull, Dall.	3.00
□	XT13 Mats Sundin, Toro.	3.00
□	XT14 Dominik Hasek (G), Buff.	3.00
□	XT15 Raymond Bourque, Bost.	4.00
□	XT16 Curtis Joseph (G), Toro.	3.00
□	XT17 John LeClair, Phil.	3.00
□	XT18 Ed Belfour (G), Dall.	3.00
□	XT19 David Legwand, Nash.	2.50
□	XT20 Wayne Gretzky, LosA.	15.00

STARSCAPE

	Insert Set (10 cards):	**25.00**
	Insert (1:9 packs)	**S**
□	S1 Brett Hull, Dall.	3.00
□	S2 Jaromir Jagr, Pitt.	3.00
□	S3 Pavel Bure, Flor.	2.00
□	S4 Dominik Hasek (G), Buff.	3.00
□	S5 Eric Lindros, Phil.	3.00
□	S6 Paul Kariya, Anah.	4.00
□	S7 Peter Forsberg, Colo.	4.00
□	S8 Teemu Selänne, Anah.	2.00
□	S9 Patrick Roy (G), Colo.	9.00
□	S10 Keith Tkachuk, Phoe.	2.00

WINNING MATERIALS

	Insert Set (10 cards):	**1060.00**
	Insert (1:252 packs)	**WM**
□	Raymond Bourque, Bost. ✂	75.00
□	Martin Brodeur (G), NJer. ✂	125.00
□	Wayne Gretzky, NYRa. ✂	325.00
□	Dominik Hasek (G), Buff. ✂	75.00
□	Brett Hull, All-Star '93	75.00
□	Jaromir Jagr, Pitt. ✂	75.00
□	Eric Lindros, Phil. ✂	75.00
□	Mike Modano, Dall. ✂	75.00
□	Patrick Roy (G), Colo. ✂	175.00
□	Steve Yzerman, Detr. ✂	175.00
	Autograph (#/25)	**WM**
□	Wayne Gretzky, NYRa. ✍ ✂	1700.00
□	Brett Hull, All-Star '93 ✍ ✂	400.00

1999 - 2000 STADIUM CLUB

This series was released in 1999-2000. There are three versions: the regular card, a One-of-a-Kind parallel (#/150) and a First Day Issue parallel (#/150). The One-of-a-Kind and First Day Issue cards are priced similarly below. Four differente unique Printing Plates (each #/1) were also included in packs: Black Plate, Cyan Plate, Magenta Plate and Yellow Plate.

	Complete Set (200 cards):	**1600.00**	**60.00**
	Common Player:	**3.00**	**.20**
	Player	**FD/OK**	**Reg.**
□□□	1 Jaromir Jagr, Pitt.	30.00	1.00
□□□	2 Mats Sundin, Toro.	30.00	1.00
□□□	3 Mark Messier, Vanc.	30.00	1.00
□□□	4 Paul Kariya, Anah.	40.00	1.00
□□□	5 Raymond Bourque, Bost.	35.00	1.00
□□□	6 Tony Amonte, Chic.	15.00	.50
□□□	7 Dominik Hasek (G), Buff.	30.00	1.00
□□□	8 Peter Forsberg, Colo.	40.00	1.00
□□□	9 Pavel Bure, Flor.	20.00	.50
□□□	10 Nicklas Lidström, Detr.	15.00	.50
□□□	11 Kenny Jönsson, NYIs.	5.00	.20
□□□	12 Brian Leetch, NYRa.	15.00	.50
□□□	13 Eric Lindros, Phil.	30.00	1.00
□□□	14 Al MacInnis, SLou.	10.00	.20
□□□	15 Keith Tkachuk, Phoe.	15.00	.50
□□□	16 Martin Brodeur (G), NJer.	45.00	1.50
□□□	17 Saku Koivu, Mont.	20.00	.50
□□□	18 Jeff Friesen, SanJ.	5.00	.20
□□□	19 Olaf Kölzig (G), Wash.	15.00	.50
□□□	20 Mike Modano, Dall.	30.00	1.00
□□□	21 Jarome Iginla, Calg.	20.00	.50
□□□	22 Alexei Kovalev, Pitt.	15.00	.50
□□□	23 Vincent Lecavalier, Tamp.	30.00	1.00
□□□	24 Greg Johnson, Nash.	3.00	.20
□□□	25 Ron Francis, Caro.	15.00	.50
□□□	26 Steve Konowalchuk, Wash.	5.00	.20
□□□	27 Luc Robitaille, LosA.	20.00	.50
□□□	28 Alexei Yashin, Otta.	15.00	.50
□□□	29 Mark Parrish, Flor.	10.00	.20
□□□	30 Todd Warriner, Toro.	3.00	.20
□□□	31 Brett Hull, Dall.	30.00	1.00
□□□	32 Steve Dubinsky, Calg.	3.00	.20
□□□	33 Rod Brind'Amour, Phil.	5.00	.20
□□□	34 Bill Muckalt, Vanc.	3.00	.20
□□□	35 Bryan Berard, Toro.	5.00	.20
□□□	36 Manny Malhotra, NYRa.	5.00	.20
□□□	37 Jozef Stumpel, LosA.	5.00	.20
□□□	38 Sergei Fedorov, Detr.	30.00	1.00
□□□	39 Roman Vopat, Phil.	3.00	.20
□□□	40 Teemu Selänne, Anah.	20.00	.50
□□□	41 Teppo Numminen, Phoe.	5.00	.20
□□□	42 Mats Lindgren, NYIs.	3.00	.20
□□□	43 Chris Gratton, Tamp.	5.00	.20
□□□	44 Owen Nolan, SanJ.	15.00	.50
□□□	45 Scott Niedermayer, NJer.	5.00	.20
□□□	46 Sergei Krivokrasov, Nash.	3.00	.20
□□□	47 Joe Sakic, Colo.	45.00	1.50
□□□	48 Bill Guerin, Edmo.	10.00	.20
□□□	49 Shayne Corson, Mont.	5.00	.20
□□□	50 Éric Dazé, Chic.	10.00	.20
□□□	51 Clarke Wilm, Calg.	3.00	.20
□□□	52 Magnus Arvedson, Otta.	3.00	.20
□□□	53 Sergei Berezin, Toro.	5.00	.20
□□□	54 Derian Hatcher, Dall.	5.00	.20
□□□	55 Jeremy Roenick, Phoe.	20.00	.50
□□□	56 Adam Oates, Wash.	10.00	.20
□□□	57 Dixon Ward, Buff.	3.00	.20
□□□	58 Petr Nedved, NYRa.	5.00	.20
□□□	59 Joe Reekie, Wash.	3.00	.20
□□□	60 Milan Hejduk, Colo.	20.00	.50
□□□	61 Mike Grier, Edmo.	5.00	.20
□□□	62 Martin Straka, Pitt.	5.00	.20
□□□	63 Petr* Sykora, NJer.	10.00	.20
□□□	64 Harry York, Vanc.	3.00	.20
□□□	65 John LeClair, Phil.	20.00	.50
□□□	66 Patrick Roy (G), Colo.	90.00	3.00
□□□	67 Arturs Irbe (G), Caro.	10.00	.20
□□□	68 Murray Baron, Vanc.	3.00	.20
□□□	69 Félix Potvin (G), NYIs.	15.00	.50
□□□	70 Pavol Demitra, SLou.	10.00	.20
□□□	71 Ray Whitney, Flor.	5.00	.20
□□□	72 Patrick Marleau, SanJ.	10.00	.20
□□□	73 Tom Fitzgerald, Nash.	3.00	.20
□□□	74 Jamal Mayers, SLou.	3.00	.20
□□□	75 Joe Thornton, Bost.	35.00	1.00
□□□	76 Craig Rivet, Mont.	3.00	.20
□□□	77 Ed Belfour (G), Dall.	30.00	1.00
□□□	78 Stéphane Fiset (G), LosA.	5.00	.20
□□□	79 Alexander Karpovtsev, Toro.	3.00	.20
□□□	80 Miroslav Satan, Buff.	5.00	.20
□□□	81 Doug Weight, Edmo.	15.00	.50
□□□	82 Marian Hossa, Otta.	30.00	1.00
□□□	83 Markus Näslund, Vanc.	30.00	1.00
□□□	84 Derek Morris, Calg.	5.00	.20
□□□	85 Mike Richter (G), NYRa.	10.00	.20
□□□	86 Scott A. Young, SLou.	5.00	.20
□□□	87 Darcy Tucker, Tamp.	5.00	.20
□□□	88 Jason Allison, Bost.	15.00	.50
□□□	89 Chris Osgood (G), Detr.	15.00	.50
□□□	90 Doug Gilmour, Chic.	15.00	.50
□□□	91 Ron Tugnutt (G), Otta.	10.00	.20
□□□	93 Byron Dafoe (G), Bost.	10.00	.20
□□□	94 Rick Tocchet, Phoe.	5.00	.20
□□□	95 Mike Johnson, Toro.	5.00	.20
□□□	96 Guy Hebert (G), Anah.	5.00	.20
□□□	97 Adam Deadmarsh, Colo.	5.00	.20
□□□	97 Cory Stillman, Calg.	5.00	.20
□□□	98 Daniel Alfredsson, Otta.	15.00	.50
□□□	99 Tom Barrasso (G), Pitt.	10.00	.20
□□□	100 Peter Bondra, Wash.	15.00	.50
□□□	101 Rob Blake, LosA.	15.00	.50
□□□	102 Gary Roberts, Caro.	10.00	.20
□□□	103 Cliff Ronning, Nash.	5.00	.20
□□□	104 Jason Woolley, Buff.	3.00	.20
□□□	105 Keith Primeau, Caro.	10.00	.20
□□□	106 Brendan Shanahan, Detr.	30.00	1.00
□□□	107 Alexei Zhamnov, Chic.	5.00	.20
□□□	108 Bobby Holik, Buff.	5.00	.20
□□□	109 Mark Recchi, Phil.	10.00	.20
□□□	110 Eric Brewer, NYIs.	10.00	.20
□□□	111 Mike Ricci, SanJ.	5.00	.20
□□□	112 Pierre Turgeon, SLou.	10.00	.20
□□□	113 Martin Rucinsky, Mont.	5.00	.20
□□□	**114 Chris McAllister, Toro. RC**	**6.00**	**.50**
□□□	115 Patrik Elias, NJer.	20.00	.50
□□□	116 Alexander Selivanov, Edmo.	3.00	.20
□□□	117 Fredrik Olausson, Anah.	5.00	.20
□□□	118 Curtis Joseph (G), Toro.	30.00	1.00
□□□	119 Wade Redden, Otta.	5.00	.20
□□□	120 Nikolai Khabibulin (G), Phoe.	10.00	.20
□□□	121 Chris Drury, Colo.	15.00	.50
□□□	122 Chris Chelios, Chic.	15.00	.50
□□□	123 Vincent Damphousse, SanJ.	15.00	.50
□□□	124 Mattias Öhlund, Vanc.	5.00	.20
□□□	125 Mike Dunham (G), Nash.	10.00	.20
□□□	126 John Vanbiesbrouck (G), Phil.	10.00	.20
□□□	127 John MacLean, NYRa.	3.00	.20
□□□	128 Jocelyn Thibault (G), Chic.	10.00	.20
□□□	129 Jan Hrdina, Pitt.	5.00	.20
□□□	130 Mariusz Czerkawski, NYIs.	5.00	.20
□□□	131 Pavel Kubina, Tamp.	3.00	.20
□□□	132 Scott Stevens, NJer.	10.00	.20
□□□	133 Mattias Norström, LosA.	5.00	.20
□□□	134 Sami Kapanen, Caro.	5.00	.20
□□□	135 Sergei Samsonov, Bost.	15.00	.50
□□□	136 Tom Poti, Edmo.	3.00	.20
□□□	137 Steve Shields (G), SanJ.	5.00	.20
□□□	138 Anson Carter, Bost.	10.00	.20
□□□	139 Chris McAlpine, Toro.	3.00	.20
□□□	140 Rob Niedermeyer, Flor.	5.00	.20
□□□	141 Michael Peca, Buff.	10.00	.20
□□□	142 Valeri Bure, Calg.	5.00	.20
□□□	143 Joe Nieuwendyk, Dall.	10.00	.20
□□□	144 José Théodore (G), Mont.	35.00	1.00
□□□	145 Steve Yzerman, Detr.	70.00	2.00
□□□	146 Chris Pronger, SLou.	15.00	.50
□□□	147 Marty McInnis, Anah.	3.00	.20
□□□	148 Jere Lehtinen, Dall.	5.00	.20
□□□	149 Adam Graves, NYRa.	10.00	.20
□□□	150 Deron Quint, Phoe.	3.00	.20
□□□	151 Ray Ferraro, Atla.	3.00	.20
□□□	152 Niklas Sundström, SanJ.	5.00	.20
□□□	**153 Mark Eaton, Phil. RC**	**6.00**	**.50**
□□□	154 Zigmund Palffy, LosA.	15.00	.50
□□□	155 Valeri Kamensky, NYRa.	5.00	.20
□□□	156 Oleg Tverdovsky, Anah.	3.00	.20
□□□	157 Bill Ranford (G), Edmo.	10.00	.20
□□□	158 Kelly Buchberger, Atla.	3.00	.20
□□□	159 Trevor Linden, Mont.	10.00	.20
□□□	160 Bryan McCabe, Chic.	5.00	.20
□□□	161 Dan Cloutier (G), Tamp.	10.00	.20
□□□	162 Olli Jokinen, NYIs.	5.00	.20
□□□	163 Theoren Fleury, NYRa.	15.00	.50
□□□	164 Dave Andreychuk, Bost.	5.00	.20
□□□	165 Gord Murphy, Atla.	3.00	.20
□□□	166 Steve Duchesne, Dewt.	5.00	.20
□□□	167 Marc* Savard, Calg.	5.00	.20
□□□	168 Maxim Afinogenov, Buff.	10.00	.50
□□□	169 Damian Rhodes (G), Atla.	5.00	.20
□□□	**170 Pavel Patera, Dall. RC**	**6.00**	**.50**
□□□	**171 Nikolai Antropov, Toro. RC**	**14.00**	**1.50**
□□□	**172 Ivan Novoseltsev, Flor. RC**	**12.00**	**1.50**
□□□	**173 Jochen Hecht, SLou. RC**	**14.00**	**2.00**
□□□	174 Mike Ribeiro, Mont.	5.00	.50
□□□	**175 Yuri Butsayev, Detr. RC**	**6.00**	**.50**
□□□	**176 Jörgen Jönsson, NYIs. RC**	**12.00**	**1.50**
□□□	**177 Dan Hinote, Colo. RC**	**12.00**	**1.50**
□□□	178 David Tanabe, Caro.	3.00	.20
□□□	**179 John Grahame (G), Bost. RC**	**14.00**	**1.50**
□□□	**180 Mika Alatalo, Phoe. RC**	**8.00**	**1.00**
□□□	**181 Patrik Stefan, Atla. RC**	**18.00**	**2.00**
□□□	**182 Mike Fisher, Otta. RC**	**14.00**	**1.50**
□□□	**183 Niclas Hävelid, Anah. RC**	**6.00**	**.50**
□□□	**184 Paul Comrie, Edmo. RC**	**8.00**	**1.00**
□□□	**185 Michal Rozsival, Pitt. RC**	**6.00**	**.50**
□□□	**186 Oleg Saprykin, Calg. RC**	**14.00**	**1.50**
□□□	187 Martin Skoula, Colo.	5.00	.20
□□□	188 Simon Gagné, Phil.	20.00	1.50
□□□	**189 Brian Rafalski, NJer. RC**	**14.00**	**1.50**
□□□	190 Jean-Pierre Dumont, Chic.	5.00	.20
□□□	191 Martin Biron (G), Buff.	10.00	.20
□□□	192 Rico Fata, Calg.	5.00	.20
□□□	193 Jan Hlavac, NYRa.	5.00	.20
□□□	194 Alex Tanguay, Colo.	15.00	1.00
□□□	195 Brad Stuart, SanJ.	10.00	.50
□□□	196 Brian Boucher (G), Phil.	5.00	.50
□□□	**197 Steve Kariya, Vanc. RC**	**14.00**	**1.50**
□□□	198 Scott Gomez, NJer.	10.00	.50
□□□	199 Tim Connolly, NYIs.	10.00	.50
□□□	200 David Legwand, Nash.	10.00	.20

CHROME

There are two versions: the Chrome card (1:4 packs) and the Chrome Refractor (1:8 packs).

	Insert Set (50 cards):	**165.00**	**90.00**
	Player	**Refr.**	**Reg.**
□□	1 Jaromir Jagr, Pitt.	5.00	3.00
□□	2 Mats Sundin, Toro.	5.00	3.00
□□	3 Mark Messier, Vanc.	5.00	3.00
□□	4 Paul Kariya, Anah.	7.00	4.00
□□	5 Raymond Bourque, Bost.	6.00	3.00
□□	6 Tony Amonte, Chic.	3.00	1.00
□□	7 Dominik Hasek (G), Buff.	5.00	3.00
□□	8 Peter Forsberg, Colo.	7.00	4.00
□□	9 Pavel Bure, Flor.	4.00	2.00
□□	10 Nicklas Lidström, Detr.	3.00	1.00
□□	11 Brian Leetch, NYRa.	3.00	1.00
□□	12 Eric Lindros, Phil.	5.00	3.00
□□	13 Al MacInnis, SLou.	2.00	1.00
□□	14 Keith Tkachuk, Phoe.	3.00	1.00
□□	15 Martin Brodeur (G), NJer.	8.00	4.00
□□	16 Saku Koivu, Mont.	4.00	2.00
□□	17 Jeff Friesen, SanJ.	2.00	1.00
□□	18 Mike Modano, Dall.	5.00	3.00
□□	19 Vincent Lecavalier, Tamp.	5.00	3.00
□□	20 Luc Robitaille, LosA.	4.00	2.00
□□	21 Brett Hull, Dall.	5.00	3.00
□□	22 Teemu Selänne, Anah.	4.00	2.00
□□	23 Joe Sakic, Colo.	8.00	4.00
□□	24 Jeremy Roenick, Phoe.	4.00	2.00
□□	25 John LeClair, Phil.	4.00	2.00
□□	26 Patrick Roy (G), Colo.	15.00	9.00
□□	27 Joe Thornton, Bost.	6.00	3.00
□□	28 Ed Belfour (G), Dall.	5.00	3.00
□□	29 Doug Weight, Edmo.	3.00	1.00
□□	30 Marian Hossa, Otta.	5.00	3.00
□□	31 Chris Osgood (G), Detr.	3.00	1.00
□□	32 Daniel Alfredsson, Otta.	3.00	1.00
□□	33 Peter Bondra, Wash.	3.00	1.00
□□	34 Brendan Shanahan, Detr.	5.00	3.00
□□	35 Curtis Joseph (G), Toro.	5.00	3.00
□□	36 Chris Drury, Colo.	3.00	1.00
□□	37 Sergei Samsonov, Bost.	3.00	1.00
□□	38 Anson Carter, Bost.	2.00	1.00
□□	39 Joe Nieuwendyk, Dall.	2.00	1.00
□□	40 Steve Yzerman, Detr.	12.00	7.00
□□	41 Zigmund Palffy, LosA.	3.00	1.00
□□	42 Theoren Fleury, NYRa.	3.00	1.00
□□	**43 Patrik Stefan, Atla. RC**	**6.00**	**4.00**
□□	44 Simon Gagné, Phil.	6.00	4.00
□□	45 Jean-Pierre Dumont, Chic.	2.00	1.00
□□	46 Alex Tanguay, Colo.	4.00	3.00
□□	**47 Steve Kariya, Vanc. RC**	**4.00**	**3.00**
□□	48 Scott Gomez, NJer.	3.00	2.00
□□	49 Tim Connolly, NYIs.	3.00	2.00
□□	50 David Legwand, Nash.	3.00	2.00

CHROME OVERSIZE

There are two version: the regular Oversize card (1 per Box) and the Oversize Refractor.

	Insert Set (20 cards):	**136.00**	**93.00**
	Player	**Refr.**	**Reg.**
□□	1 Jaromir Jagr, Pitt.	7.00	5.00
□□	2 Mats Sundin, Toro.	7.00	5.00
□□	3 Paul Kariya, Anah.	10.00	7.00
□□	4 Raymond Bourque, Bost.	9.00	6.00
□□	5 Dominik Hasek (G), Buff.	7.00	5.00

☐☐ 6 Peter Forsberg, Colo.	10.00	7.00
☐☐ 7 Pavel Bure, Flor.	6.00	4.00
☐☐ 8 Eric Lindros, Phil.	7.00	5.00
☐☐ 9 Martin Brodeur (G), NJer.	12.00	8.00
☐☐ 10 Mike Modano, Dall.	7.00	5.00
☐☐ 11 Teemu Selänne, Anah.	6.00	4.00
☐☐ 12 Joe Sakic, Colo.	12.00	8.00
☐☐ 13 Patrick Roy (G), Colo.	22.00	15.00
☐☐ 14 Marian Hossa, Otta.	7.00	5.00
☐☐ 15 Curtis Joseph (G), Toro.	7.00	5.00
☐☐ 16 Steve Yzerman, Detr.	18.00	12.00
☐☐ 17 Theoren Fleury, NYRa.	4.00	3.00
☐☐ 18 Patrik Stefan, Atla.	3.00	2.00
☐☐ 19 Steve Kariya, Vanc.	3.00	2.00
☐☐ 20 David Legwand, Nash.	3.00	2.00

CAPTURE THE ACTION

There are two versions: the regular insert (1:12 packs) and the Game View parallel (1:118 packs).

Insert Set (30 cards):	**1,000**	**85.00**
Inserts	**CAGV**	**CA**
☐☐ CA1 Bill Muckalt, Vanc. [Rookies]	6.00	1.00
☐☐ CA2 Chris Drury, Colo. [Rookies]	25.00	2.00
☐☐ CA3 Milan Hejduk, Colo. [Rookies]	35.00	3.00
☐☐ CA4 Mark Parrish, Flor. [Rookies]	15.00	1.00
☐☐ CA5 Marian Hossa, Otta. [Rookies]	45.00	4.00
☐☐ CA6 Manny Malhotra, NYRa. [Rookies]	10.00	1.00
☐☐ CA7 Jean-Pierre Dumont, Chic. [Rookies]	10.00	1.00
☐☐ CA8 Eric Brewer, NYIs. [Rookies]	15.00	1.00
☐☐ CA9 Vincent Lecavalier, Tamp. [Rookies]	45.00	4.00
☐☐ CA10 Jan Hrdina, Pitt. [Rookies]	10.00	1.00
☐☐ CA11 Paul Kariya, Anah. [Stars]	65.00	5.00
☐☐ CA12 Peter Forsberg, Colo. [Stars]	65.00	5.00
☐☐ CA13 Eric Lindros, Phil. [Stars]	45.00	4.00
☐☐ CA14 Martin Brodeur (G), NJer. [Stars]	75.00	6.00
☐☐ CA15 Teemu Selänne, Anah. [Stars]	35.00	3.00
☐☐ CA16 Keith Tkachuk, Phoe. [Stars]	25.00	2.00
☐☐ CA17 Mats Sundin, Toro. [Stars]	45.00	4.00
☐☐ CA18 Pavel Bure, Flor. [Stars]	35.00	3.00
☐☐ CA19 Mike Modano, Dall. [Stars]	45.00	4.00
☐☐ CA20 Nicklas Lidström, Detr. [Stars]	25.00	2.00
☐☐ CA21 Raymond Bourque, Bost. [Legends]	55.00	4.00
☐☐ CA22 Dominik Hasek (G), Buff. [Legends]	45.00	4.00
☐☐ CA23 Patrick Roy (G), Colo. [Legends]	140.00	12.00
☐☐ CA24 Mark Messier, Vanc. [Legends]	45.00	4.00
☐☐ CA25 Steve Yzerman, Detr. [Legends]	110.00	9.00
☐☐ CA26 Jaromir Jagr, Pitt. [Legends]	45.00	4.00
☐☐ CA27 Paul Coffey, Caro. [Legends]	25.00	2.00
☐☐ CA28 Brett Hull, Dall. [Legends]	45.00	4.00
☐☐ CA29 Al MacInnis, SLou. [Legends]	15.00	1.00
☐☐ CA30 Larry Murphy, Detr. [Legends]	10.00	1.00

CO-SIGNERS

These cards are signed by two players.

Insert Set (15 cards):	**680.00**
Inserts	**CS**
☐ CS1 C. Drury ✍ / B. Morrison ✍	25.00
☐ CS2 B. Morrison ✍ / M. Hossa ✍	40.00
☐ CS3 M. Hossa ✍ / C. Drury ✍	50.00
☐ CS4 M. Sundin ✍ / J. Jagr ✍	90.00
☐ CS5 J. Jagr ✍ / A. Yashin ✍	80.00
☐ CS6 J. LeClair ✍ / J. Jagr ✍	85.00
☐ CS7 A. Yashin ✍ / M. Sundin ✍	50.00
☐ CS8 J. LeClair ✍ / M. Sundin ✍	55.00
☐ CS9 A. Yashin ✍ / J. LeClair ✍	40.00
☐ CS10 E. Belfour (G) ✍ / C. Osgood ✍	50.00
☐ CS11 C. Osgood ✍ / Cu. Joseph ✍	50.00
☐ CS12 Cu. Joseph ✍ / E. Belfour (G) ✍	60.00
☐ CS13 R. Bourque ✍ / A. MacInnis ✍	55.00
☐ CS14 A. MacInnis ✍ / W. Redden ✍	25.00
☐ CS15 W. Redden ✍ / R. Bourque ✍	50.00

EYES OF THE GAME

There are two versions: the regular insert (1:15 packs) and the Refractor parallel (1:75 packs).

Insert Set (10 cards):	**65.00**	**15.00**
Inserts	**EGR**	**EG**
☐☐ EG1 Jaromir Jagr, Pitt.	8.00	2.00
☐☐ EG2 Peter Forsberg, Colo.	12.00	3.00
☐☐ EG3 Paul Kariya, Anah.	12.00	3.00
☐☐ EG4 Teemu Selänne, Anah.	7.00	2.00
☐☐ EG5 Joe Sakic, Colo.	14.00	4.00
☐☐ EG6 Eric Lindros, Phil.	8.00	2.00
☐☐ EG7 Jason Allison, Bost.	5.00	1.00
☐☐ EG8 Mats Sundin, Toro.	8.00	2.00
☐☐ EG9 Pavol Demitra, SLou.	3.00	1.00
☐☐ EG10 Rod Brind'Amour, Phil.	3.00	1.00

GOALIE CAM

Insert Set (7 cards):	**20.00**
Inserts (1:24 packs)	**GC**
☐ GC1 Dominik Hasek (G), Buff.	5.00
☐ GC2 Martin Brodeur (G), NJer.	8.00
☐ GC3 Byron Dafoe (G), Bost.	3.00
☐ GC4 Olaf Kölzig (G), Wash.	3.00
☐ GC5 Mike Richter (G), NYRa.	3.00
☐ GC6 Ron Tugnutt (G), Otta.	3.00
☐ GC7 Tom Barrasso (G), Pitt.	3.00

LONE STAR SIGNATURES

Insert Set (13 cards):	**505.00**
Autograph	**LSS**
☐ LS8 Ed Belfour (G), Dall.	55.00
☐ LS4 Raymond Bourque, Bost.	75.00
☐ LS11 Chris Drury, Colo.	25.00
☐ LS13 Marian Hossa, Otta.	45.00
☐ LS1 Jaromir Jagr, Pitt.	125.00
☐ LS9 Curtis Joseph (G), Toro.	55.00
☐ LS10 John LeClair, Phil.	40.00
☐ LS5 Al MacInnis, SLou.	20.00
☐ LS12 Brendan Morrison, NJer.	15.00
☐ LS7 Chris Osgood (G), Detr.	30.00
☐ LS6 Wade Redden, Otta.	15.00
☐ LS3 Mats Sundin, Toro.	60.00
☐ LS2 Alexei Yashin, Otta.	35.00

ONYX EXTREME

There are two versions: the regular insert (1:15 packs) and the Die-Cut parallel (1:75 packs).

Insert Set (10 cards):	**70.00**	**15.00**
Inserts	**EOEDC**	**OE**
☐☐ OE1 Jaromir Jagr, Pitt.	8.00	2.00
☐☐ OE2 Peter Forsberg, Colo.	12.00	3.00
☐☐ OE3 Dominik Hasek (G), Buff.	8.00	2.00
☐☐ OE4 Eric Lindros, Phil.	8.00	2.00
☐☐ OE5 Paul Kariya, Anah.	12.00	3.00
☐☐ OE6 Joe Sakic, Colo.	14.00	4.00
☐☐ OE7 Nicklas Lidström, Detr.	5.00	1.00
☐☐ OE8 Teemu Selänne, Anah.	7.00	2.00
☐☐ OE9 John LeClair, Phil.	7.00	2.00
☐☐ OE10 Pavel Bure, Flor.	7.00	2.00

SOUVENIRS

Insert Set (10 cards):	**120.00**
Inserts	**Souv.**
☐ Ed Belfour (G), Dall. [Stick]	31.00
☐ Marian Hossa, SLou. [Jersey]	25.00
☐ John LeClair, Toro. [Stick]	25.00
☐ Al MacInnis, SLou. [Stick]	20.00
☐ Chris Osgood (G), Detr. [Jersey]	20.00
☐ Mats Sundin, Toro. [Jersey]	25.00

PRE-PRODUCTION SAMPLE

Complete Set (6 cards):	**6.00**
Player	**PP**
☐ PP1 Chris Osgood (G), Detr.	1.50
☐ PP2 Steve Konowalchuk, Wash.	1.00
☐ PP3 Jeremy Roenick, Phoe.	2.00
☐ PP4 Rod Brind'Amour, Caro.	1.00
☐ PP5 Mattias Norström, LosA.	1.00
☐ PP6 Clarke Wilm, Calg.	1.00

1999 - 2000 STARTING LINEUP

An Upper Deck card was packaged with each figure.

Upper Deck Set (17 cards):	**25.00**
Player	**MT**
☐ 31 Paul Kariya, Anah.	2.00
☐ 39 Sergei Samsonov, Bost.	1.00
☐ 44 Dominik Hasek (G), Buff.	2.00
☐ 69 Peter Forsberg, Colo.	2.00
☐ 83 Nicklas Lidström, Detr.	1.00
☐ 85 Steve Yzerman, Detr.	4.00
☐ 135 Wayne Gretzky, NYRa.	8.00
☐ 157 Nikolai Khabibulin (G), Phoe.	1.00
☐ 161 Jaromir Jagr, Pitt.	2.00
☐ 174 Chris Pronger, SLou.	1.00
☐ 191 Curtis Joseph (G), Toro.	2.00
☐ 205 Olaf Kölzig (G), Wash.	1.00
☐ 210 Mike Dunham (G), Nash.	1.00
☐ 237 Keith Primeau, Caro.	1.00
☐ 256 Mike Modano, Dall.	2.00
☐ 333 Eric Lindros, Phil.	2.00
☐ Jeff Hackett (G), Mont.	1.00

FIGURES

Priced below are retail selling prices for packaged figures (each package includes one Upper Deck card) and loose figures.

Packaged Set (17 packages):	**225.00**	**-**
Figure Set (17 loose figures):	**-**	**55.00**
Player	**Pack**	**Loose**
☐ Mike Dunham (G), Nash.	20.00	5.00
☐ Peter Forsberg, Colo.	15.00	4.00
☐ Wayne Gretzky, NYRa.	20.00	5.00
☐ Jeff Hackett (G), Mont.	18.00	5.00
☐ Dominik Hasek (G), Buff.	20.00	5.00
☐ Jaromir Jagr, Pitt.	15.00	4.00
☐ Curtis Joseph (G), Toro.	25.00	5.00
☐ Paul Kariya, Anah.	15.00	4.00
☐ Nikolai Khabibulin (G), Phoe.	18.00	5.00
☐ Olaf Kölzig (G), Wash.	18.00	5.00
☐ Nicklas Lidström, Detr.	15.00	3.00
☐ Eric Lindros, Phil.	15.00	4.00
☐ Mike Modano, Dall.	12.00	3.00
☐ Keith Primeau, Caro.	12.00	3.00
☐ Chris Pronger, SLou.	15.00	3.00
☐ Sergei Samsonov, Bost.	15.00	4.00
☐ Steve Yzerman, Detr.	15.00	4.00

1999 - 2000 TOPPS & O-PEE-CHEE

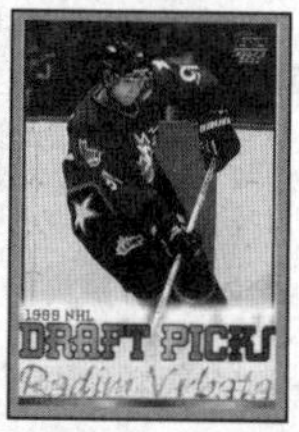

These series were released in 1999. The O-Pee-Chee and Topps cards are similar in design but have different brand logos on the card fronts. There are five versions (per brand) for each Magic Moments card.

Complete Set (336 cards):	**120.00**
Shell Set (286 cards):	**55.00**
Common Player:	**.20**
Player	**Reg.**
☐☐ 1 Joe Sakic, Colo.	1.00
☐☐ 2 Alexei Yashin, Otta.	.20
☐☐ 3 Paul Kariya, Anah.	.50
☐☐ 4 Keith Tkachuk, Phoe.	.20
☐☐ 5 Jaromir Jagr, Pitt.	.50
☐☐ 6 Mike Modano, Dall.	.50
☐☐ 7 Eric Lindros, Phil.	.50
☐☐ 8 Zigmund Palffy, LosA.	.20
☐☐ 9 Dominik Hasek (G), Buff.	.50
☐☐ 10 Pavel Bure, Flor.	.50
☐☐ 11 Raymond Bourque, Bost.	.50
☐☐ 12 Peter Forsberg, Colo.	.50
☐☐ 13 Al MacInnis, SLou.	.20
☐☐ 14 Steve Yzerman, Detr.	1.50
☐☐ 15 Mats Sundin, Toro.	.50
☐☐ 16 Patrick Roy (G), Colo.	1.50
☐☐ 17 Teemu Selänne, Anah.	.50
☐☐ 18 Keith Primeau, Caro.	.20
☐☐ 19 John LeClair, Phil.	.50
☐☐ 20 Martin Brodeur (G), NJer.	1.00
☐☐ 21 Joe Thornton, Bost.	.50
☐☐ 22 Rob Blake, LosA.	.20
☐☐ 23 Ron Francis, Caro.	.20
☐☐ 24 Grant Fuhr (G), SLou.	.20
☐☐ 25 Nicklas Lidström, Detr.	.20
☐☐ **26 Vladimir Orszagh, NYIs. (RC)**	**1.00**
☐☐ 27 Glen Wesley, Caro.	.20
☐☐ 28 Adam Deadmarsh, Colo.	.20
☐☐ 29 Zdeno Chara, NYIs.	.20
☐☐ 30 Brian Leetch, NYRa.	.20
☐☐ 31 Valeri Bure, Calg.	.20
☐☐ 32 Ryan Smyth, Edmo.	.20
☐☐ 33 Jean-Sébastien Aubin (G), Pitt.	.20
☐☐ 34 David Reid, Dall.	.20
☐☐ 35 Ed Jovanovski, Vanc.	.20
☐☐ 36 Anders Eriksson, Chic.	.20
☐☐ 37 Mike Ricci, SanJ.	.20
☐☐ 38 Todd Bertuzzi, Vanc.	.50
☐☐ 39 Shawn Bates, Bost.	.20
☐☐ 40 Kip Miller, Pitt.	.20
☐☐ 41 Jozef Stumpel, LosA.	.20
☐☐ 42 Jeremy Roenick, Phoe.	.50
☐☐ 43 Todd Marchant, Edmo.	.20
☐☐ 44 Josh Holden, Vanc.	.20
☐☐ 45 Rob Niedermayer, Flor.	.20
☐☐ 46 Cory Sarich, Buff.	.20
☐☐ 47 Nikolai Khabibulin (G), Phoe.	.20
☐☐ 48 Marty McInnis, Anah.	.20
☐☐ 49 Marty Reasoner, SLou.	.20
☐☐ 50 Gary Roberts, Caro.	.20
☐☐ 51 Manny Malhotra, NYRa.	.20
☐☐ 52 Adam Foote, Colo.	.20
☐☐ 53 Luc Robitaille, LosA.	.50
☐☐ 54 Bryan Marchment, SanJ.	.20
☐☐ 55 Mark Janssens, Chic.	.20
☐☐ 56 Stephen Heinze, Bost.	.20
☐☐ 57 Cory Stillman, Calg.	.20
☐☐ 58 Guy Hebert (G), Anah.	.20
☐☐ 59 Mike Richter (G), NYRa.	.20
☐☐ 60 Jamie Langenbrunner, Dall.	.20
☐☐ 61 Wade Redden, Otta.	.20
☐☐ 62 J. Steve Smith, Calg.	.20
☐☐ 63 Danny Markov, Toro.	.20
☐☐ 64 Erik Rasmussen, Buff.	.20
☐☐ 65 Glen Murray, LosA.	.20
☐☐ 66 Alexei Kovalev, Pitt.	.20
☐☐ 67 Peter Bondra, Wash.	.20
☐☐ 68 Dmitri Khristich, Bost.	.20
☐☐ 69 Sami Kapanen, Caro.	.20
☐☐ 70 Tom Poti, Edmo.	.20
☐☐ 71 Trevor Linden, Mont.	.20
☐☐ 72 Tomas Vokoun (G), Nash.	.20
☐☐ 73 Steve Webb, NYIs.	.20
☐☐ 74 Jarome Iginla, Calg.	.50
☐☐ 75 Scott Mellanby, Flor.	.20
☐☐ 76 Mattias Öhlund, Vanc.	.20
☐☐ 77 Steve Konowalchuk, Wash.	.20
☐☐ 78 Bryan Berard, Toro.	.20
☐☐ 79 Chris Pronger, SLou.	.20
☐☐ 80 Teppo Numminen, Phoe.	.20
☐☐ 81 John MacLean, NYRa.	.20
☐☐ 82 Jeff Hackett (G), Mont.	.20
☐☐ 83 Ray Whitney, Flor.	.20
☐☐ 84 Chris Osgood (G), Detr.	.20
☐☐ 85 Doug Zmolek, Chic.	.20
☐☐ 86 Curtis Brown, Buff.	.20
☐☐ 87 Reid Simpson, Chic.	.20
☐☐ 88 Milan Hejduk, Colo.	.50
☐☐ 89 Donald Audette, LosA.	.20
☐☐ 90 Saku Koivu, Mont.	.50
☐☐ 91 Martin Straka, Pitt.	.20
☐☐ 92 Mark Messier, Vanc.	.50
☐☐ 93 Richard Zednik, Wash.	.20
☐☐ 94 Curtis Joseph (G), Toro.	.50
☐☐ 95 Colin Forbes, Tamp.	.20
☐☐ 96 Jeff Friesen, SanJ.	.20
☐☐ 97 Eric Brewer, NYIs.	.20
☐☐ 98 Darius Kasparaitis, Pitt.	.20
☐☐ 99 Marian Hossa, Otta.	.50
☐☐ 100 Petr* Sykora, NJer.	.20
☐☐ 101 Vladimir Malakhov, Mont.	.20

☐☐ 102 Jamie Storr (G), LosA. .20
☐☐ 103 Doug Gilmour, Chic. .20
☐☐ 104 Doug Weight, Edmo. .20
☐☐ 105 Derian Hatcher, Dall. .20
☐☐ 106 Chris Drury, Colo. .20
☐☐ 107 Arturs Irbe (G), Caro. .20
☐☐ 108 Fred Brathwaite (G), Calg. .20
☐☐ 109 Jason Allison, Bost. .20
☐☐ 110 Roman Hamrlik, Edmo. .20
☐☐ 111 Rico Fata, Calg. .20
☐☐ 112 Janne Niinimaa, Edmo. .20
☐☐ 113 Kenny Jönsson, NYIs. .20
☐☐ 114 Marco Sturm, SanJ. .20
☐☐ 115 Steve Thomas, Toro. .20
☐☐ 116 Garth Snow (G), Vanc. .20
☐☐ 117 Rick Tocchet, Phoe. .20
☐☐ 118 Jean-Marc Pelletier (G), Phil. .20
☐☐ 119 Bobby Holik, NJer. .20
☐☐ 120 Sergei Fedorov, Detr. .50
☐☐ 121 Jean-Pierre Dumont, Chic. .20
☐☐ 122 Jason Woolley, Buff. .20
☐☐ 123 James Patrick, Buff. .20
☐☐ 124 Blake Sloan, Dall. .20
☐☐ 125 Marcus Nilson, Flor. .20
☐☐ 126 Shayne Corson, Mont. .20
☐☐ 127 Tom Fitzgerald, Nash. .20
☐☐ 128 Brian Rolston, NJer. .20
☐☐ 129 Ron Tugnutt (G), Otta. .20
☐☐ 130 Mark Recchi, Phil. .20
☐☐ 131 Matthew Barnaby, Pitt. .20
☐☐ 132 Olaf Kölzig (G), Wash. .20
☐☐ 133 Paul Mara, Tamp. .20
☐☐ 134 Patrick Marleau, SanJ. .20
☐☐ 135 Magnus Arvedson, Otta. .20
☐☐ 136 Félix Potvin (G), NYIs. .20
☐☐ 137 Bill Guerin, Edmo. .20
☐☐ 138 Brett Hull, Dall. .50
☐☐ 139 Vitali Yachmenev, Nash. .20
☐☐ 140 Ruslan Salei, Anah. .20
☐☐ 141 Mark Parrish, Flor. .20
☐☐ 142 Randy Cunneyworth, Buff. .20
☐☐ 143 Damian Rhodes (G), Otta. .20
☐☐ 144 Daniel Brière, Phoe. .20
☐☐ 145 Craig Conroy, SLou. .20
☐☐ 146 Sergei Gonchar, Wash. .20
☐☐ 147 Vincent Lecavalier, Tamp. .50
☐☐ 148 Adam Graves, NYRa. .20
☐☐ 149 Doug Bodger, LosA. .20
☐☐ 150 Jeff O'Neill, Caro. .20
☐☐ 151 Darby Hendrickson, Vanc. .20
☐☐ 152 Sergei Samsonov, Bost. .20
☐☐ 153 Ed Belfour (G), Dall. .50
☐☐ 154 Robert Svehla, Flor. .20
☐☐ 155 Cliff Ronning, Nash. .20
☐☐ 156 Brendan Morrison, NJer. .20
☐☐ 157 Daniel Alfredsson, Otta. .20
☐☐ 158 Éric Desjardins, Phil. .20
☐☐ 159 Mike Vernon (G), SanJ. .20
☐☐ 160 Vadim Sharifijanov, NJer. .20
☐☐ 161 Jaroslav Svejkovsky, Wash. .20
☐☐ 162 Michael Peca, Buff. .20
☐☐ 163 Shane Willis, Caro. .20
☐☐ 164 Sandis Ozolinsh, Colo. .20
☐☐ 165 Mathieu Dandenault, Detr. .20
☐☐ 166 Martin Rucinsky, Mont. .20
☐☐ 167 Scott Stevens, NJer. .20
☐☐ 168 Sami Salo, Otta. .20
☐☐ 169 Tom Barrasso (G), Pitt. .20
☐☐ 170 Chris Gratton, Tamp. .20
☐☐ 171 Markus Näslund, Vanc. .50
☐☐ 172 Mike Johnson, Toro. .20
☐☐ 173 Bob Boughner, Nash. .20
☐☐ 174 Todd Simpson, Calg. .20
☐☐ 175 Fredrik Olausson, Anah. .20
☐☐ 176 Jocelyn Thibault (G), Chic. .20
☐☐ 177 Juha Ylönen, Phoe. .20
☐☐ 178 Brad Bombardir, NJer. .20
☐☐ 179 Jan Hrdina, Pitt. .20
☐☐ 180 Adrian Aucoin, Vanc. .20
☐☐ 181 Mike Eagles, Wash. .20
☐☐ 182 Petr Nedved, NYRa. .20
☐☐ 183 Rem Murray, Edmo. .20
☐☐ 184 Mikael Renberg, Phil. .20
☐☐ 185 Mike Eastwood, SLou. .20
☐☐ 186 Byron Dafoe (G), Bost. .20
☐☐ 187 Tony Amonte, Chic. .20
☐☐ 188 Darren McCarty, Detr. .20
☐☐ 189 Sergei Krivokrasov, Nash. .20
☐☐ 190 Dave Lowry, SanJ. .20
☐☐ 191 Michal Handzus, SLou. .20
☐☐ 192 Tie Domi, Toro. .20
☐☐ 193 Brian Holzinger, Buff. .20
☐☐ 194 Jason Arnott, NJer. .20
☐☐ 195 José Théodore (G), Mont. .50
☐☐ 196 Brendan Shanahan, Detr. .50
☐☐ 197 Derek Morris, Calg. .20
☐☐ 198 Steve Rucchin, Anah. .20
☐☐ 199 Kevin Hodson (G), Tamp. .20
☐☐ 200 Oleg Kvasha, Flor. .20
☐☐ 201 John Vanbiesbrouck (G), Phil. .20
☐☐ 202 Adam Oates, Wash. .20
☐☐ 203 Anson Carter, Bost. .20
☐☐ 204 Sébastien Bordeleau, Nash. .20
☐☐ 205 Pavol Demitra, SLou. .20
☐☐ 206 Owen Nolan, SanJ. .20
☐☐ 207 Pavel Rosa, LosA. .20
☐☐ 208 Petr' Svoboda, Tamp. .20
☐☐ 209 Tomas Kaberle, Toro. .20
☐☐ 210 Claude Lapointe, NYIs. .20
☐☐ 211 Todd Harvey, NYRa. .20
☐☐ 212 Trent McCleary, Mont. .20
☐☐ 213 Vyacheslav Kozlov, Detr. .20
☐☐ 214 Marc Denis (G), Colo. .20
☐☐ 215 Joe Nieuwendyk, Dall. .20
☐☐ 216 Kelly Buchberger, Edmo. .20
☐☐ 217 Tommy Albelin, Calg. [XCX: Aalto] .20
☐☐ 218 Kyle McLaren, Bost. .20
☐☐ 219 Chris Chelios, Detr. .20
☐☐ 220 Joël Bouchard, Nash. .20
☐☐ 221 Mats Lindgren, NYIs. .20
☐☐ 222 Jyrki Lumme, Phoe. .20
☐☐ 223 Pierre Turgeon, SLou. .20
☐☐ 224 Bill Muckalt, Vanc. .20
☐☐ 225 Antti Aalto, Anah. .20
☐☐ 226 Jere Lehtinen, Dall. .20
☐☐ 227 Theoren Fleury, NYRa. .20
☐☐ 228 Dmitri Mironov, Wash. .20
☐☐ 229 Scott Niedermayer, NJer. .20
☐☐ 230 Sean Burke (G), Flor. .20
☐☐ 231 Éric Dazé, Chic. .20
☐☐ 232 Alexei Zhitnik, Buff. .20
☐☐ 233 Christian Matte, Colo. .20
☐☐ 234 Patrik Elias, NJer. .50
☐☐ 235 Alexander Korolyuk, SanJ. .20
☐☐ 236 Sergei Berezin, Toro. .20
☐☐ 237 Ray Ferraro, LosA. .20
☐☐ 238 Rod Brind'Amour, Phil. .20
☐☐ 239 Darcy Tucker, Tamp. .20
☐☐ 240 Darryl Sydor, Dall. .20
☐☐ 241 Mike Dunham (G), Nash. .20
☐☐ 242 Marc Bergevin, SLou. .20
☐☐ 243 Ray Sheppard, Caro. .20
☐☐ 244 Miroslav Satan, Buff. .20
☐☐ 245 Andreas Dackell, Otta. .20
☐☐ 246 Mike Grier, Edmo. .20
☐☐ 247 Alexei Zhamnov, Chic. .20
☐☐ 248 David Legwand, CHL All-Stars [CHL All-Stars] .20
☐☐ 249 Daniel Tkaczuk, CHL All-Stars [CHL All-Stars] .20
☐☐ 250 R. Luongo (G), CHL All-Stars [CHL All-Stars] 1.00
☐☐ 251 Simon Gagné [Draft Picks] 1.00
☐☐ 252 Jamie Lundmark [Draft Picks] .20
☐☐ **253 Alexandre Giroux [Draft Picks] (RC) .50**
☐☐ **254 Dusty Jamieson [Draft Picks] (RC) .50**
☐☐ **255 Jamie Chamberlain [Draft Picks] (RC) .50**
☐☐ **256 Radim Vrbata [Draft Picks] (RC) 6.00**
☐☐ **257 Scott Cameron [Draft Picks] (RC) .50**
☐☐ **258 Simon Lajeunesse (G) [Draft Picks] (RC) 1.00**
☐☐ 259 Tim Connolly [Draft Picks] .50
☐☐ 260 Kris Beech [Draft Picks] .20
☐☐ 261 Brian Finley (G) [Draft Picks] .20
☐☐ **262 Alex Auld (G) [Draft Picks] (RC) 1.50**
☐☐ **263 Martin Grenier [Draft Picks] (RC) .50**
☐☐ **264 Sheldon Keefe [Draft Picks] (RC) 1.00**
☐☐ **265 Justin Mapletoft [Draft Picks] (RC) 1.00**
☐☐ **266 Edward Hill [Draft Picks] (RC) .50**
☐☐ **267 Nolan Yonkman [Draft Picks] (RC) .50**
☐☐ **268 Oleg Saprykin [Draft Picks] (RC) 1.50**
☐☐ **269 Branislav Mezei [Draft Picks] (RC) 1.00**
☐☐ **270 Chris Kelly [Draft Picks] (RC) .50**
☐☐ **271 Pavel Brendl [Draft Picks] (RC) 3.50**
☐☐ **272 Brett Lysak [Draft Picks] (RC) .50**
☐☐ **273 Matt Carkner [Draft Picks] (RC) .50**
☐☐ **274 Luke Sellars [Draft Picks] (RC) 1.00**
☐☐ **275 Brad Ralph [Draft Picks] (RC) 1.00**
☐☐ 276 Raymond Bourque [1000 Points] 1.50
☐☐ 276 Raymond Bourque [16 All-Star Games] 1.50
☐☐ 276 Raymond Bourque [1980 Calder Trophy] 1.50
☐☐ 276 Raymond Bourque [1996 All-Star MVP] 1.50
☐☐ 276 Raymond Bourque [5-Time Norris] 1.50
☐☐ 277 Peter Forsberg [1994 Gold Medal Goal] 1.50
☐☐ 277 Peter Forsberg [1994 Gold Medal] 1.50
☐☐ 277 Peter Forsberg [1995 Calder Trophy] 1.50
☐☐ 277 Peter Forsberg [1996 Stanley Cup] 1.50
☐☐ 277 Peter Forsberg [3 NHL All-Star Games] 1.50
☐☐ 278 Joe Nieuwendyk [1988 Calder Trophy] .50
☐☐ 278 Joe Nieuwendyk [1989 Stanley Cup] .50
☐☐ 278 Joe Nieuwendyk [1999 Conn Smythe Trophy] .50
☐☐ 278 Joe Nieuwendyk [1999 Stanley Cup] .50
☐☐ 278 Joe Nieuwendyk [4 NHL All-Star Games] .50
☐☐ 279 Dominik Hasek (G) [1998 Gold Medal] 1.00
☐☐ 279 Dominik Hasek (G) [2-Time Hart] 1.00
☐☐ 279 Dominik Hasek (G) [2-Time Pearson] 1.00
☐☐ 279 Dominik Hasek (G) [4 NHL All-Star Games] 1.00
☐☐ 279 Dominik Hasek (G) [5-Time Vézina] 1.00
☐☐ 280 Jaromir Jagr [1998 Gold Medal] 1.00
☐☐ 280 Jaromir Jagr [1999 Hart Trophy] 1.00
☐☐ 280 Jaromir Jagr [2-Time Stanley Cup] 1.00
☐☐ 280 Jaromir Jagr [3-Time Scoring Leader] 1.00
☐☐ 280 Jaromir Jagr [8 NHL All-Star Games] 1.00
☐☐ 281 Paul Kariya [1993 NCAA Championship] 1.50
☐☐ 281 Paul Kariya [1994 Silver Medal] 1.50
☐☐ 281 Paul Kariya [2-Time Lady Byng] 1.50
☐☐ 281 Paul Kariya [3 NHL All-Star Games] 1.50
☐☐ 281 Paul Kariya [50 Goal Season] 1.50
☐☐ 282 Eric Lindros [1991 #1 Draft Pick] 1.00
☐☐ 282 Eric Lindros [1995 Hart Trophy] 1.00
☐☐ 282 Eric Lindros [1995 Pearson Award] 1.00
☐☐ 282 Eric Lindros [5 NHL All-Star Games] 1.00
☐☐ 282 Eric Lindros [Magic Moments] 1.00
☐☐ 283 Mark Messier [13 NHL All-Star Games] 1.00
☐☐ 283 Mark Messier [1984 Conn Smythe Trophy] 1.00
☐☐ 283 Mark Messier [2-Time Hart] 1.00
☐☐ 283 Mark Messier [2-Time Pearson] 1.00
☐☐ 283 Mark Messier [6-Time Stanley Cup] 1.00
☐☐ 284 Patrick Roy (G) [2-Time Conn Smythe] 3.50
☐☐ 284 Patrick Roy (G) [3-Time Stanley Cup] 3.50
☐☐ 284 Patrick Roy (G) [3-Time Vézina] 3.50
☐☐ 284 Patrick Roy (G) [8 NHL All-Star Games] 3.50
☐☐ 284 Patrick Roy (G) [All-Time Playoff Wins Leader] 3.50
☐☐ 285 Joe Sakic [1988 Cdn. Jr. POY] 2.00
☐☐ 285 Joe Sakic [1996 Conn Smythe Trophy] 2.00
☐☐ 285 Joe Sakic [1996 Stanley Cup] 2.00
☐☐ 285 Joe Sakic [50-Goal Season] 2.00
☐☐ 285 Joe Sakic [7 NHL All-Star Games] 2.00
☐☐ 286 Steve Yzerman [1989 Pearson Award] 3.00
☐☐ 286 Steve Yzerman [1998 Conn Smythe Trophy] 3.00
☐☐ 286 Steve Yzerman [2-Time Stanley Cup] 3.00
☐☐ 286 Steve Yzerman [500 NHL Goals] 3.00
☐☐ 286 Steve Yzerman [8 NHL All-Star Games] 3.00

Checklist **Reg.**
☐☐ 1 Checklist .25
☐☐ 2 Checklist .25
☐☐ 3 Checklist .25
☐☐ 4 Checklist .25
☐☐ 5 Checklist .25
☐☐ 6 Checklist .25

O-PEE-CHEE OVERSIZE

We do not have a full checklist for this series.

ALL-TOPPS

There is both an O-Pee-Chee and a Topps version.

Insert Set (15 cards): **65.00**
Insert (1:18 packs) **AT**
☐☐ AT1 Dominik Hasek (G), Buff. 5.00
☐☐ AT2 Martin Brodeur (G), NJer. 8.00
☐☐ AT3 Raymond Bourque, Bost. 6.00
☐☐ AT4 Al MacInnis, SLou. 2.00
☐☐ AT5 Nicklas Lidström, Detr. 3.00
☐☐ AT6 Brian Leetch, NYRa. 3.00
☐☐ AT7 John LeClair, Phil. 4.00
☐☐ AT8 Paul Kariya, Anah. 7.00
☐☐ AT9 Keith Tkachuk, Phoe. 3.00
☐☐ AT10 Eric Lindros, Phil. 5.00
☐☐ AT11 Peter Forsberg, Colo. 7.00
☐☐ AT12 Steve Yzerman, Detr. 12.00
☐☐ AT13 Jaromir Jagr, Pitt. 5.00
☐☐ AT14 Teemu Selänne, Anah. 4.00
☐☐ AT15 Pavel Bure, Flor. 4.00

CERTIFIED AUTOGRAPH ISSUE

Insert Set (10 cards): **250.00**
Insert (1:517 packs) **TA**
☐ Chris Drury, Colo. ✍ 20.00
☐ Dominik Hasek (G), Buff. ✍ 40.00
☐ Milan Hejduk, Colo. ✍ 25.00
☐ Marian Hossa, Otta. ✍ 30.00
☐ Curtis Joseph (G), Toro. ✍ 30.00
☐ Vincent Lecavalier, Tamp. ✍ 30.00
☐ Joe Sakic, Colo. ✍ 50.00
☐ Mats Sundin, Toro. ✍ 30.00
☐ Joe Thornton, Bost. ✍ 35.00
☐ Alexei Yashin, Otta. ✍ 20.00

ICE MASTERS

There is both an O-Pee-Chee and a Topps version.

Insert Set (20 cards): **140.00**
Insert (1:30) **IM**
☐☐ IM1 Joe Sakic, Colo. 12.00
☐☐ IM2 Dominik Hasek (G), Buff. 7.00
☐☐ IM3 Eric Lindros, Phil. 7.00
☐☐ IM4 Jaromir Jagr, Pitt. 7.00
☐☐ IM5 John LeClair, Phil. 6.00
☐☐ IM6 Mats Sundin, Toro. 7.00
☐☐ IM7 Raymond Bourque, Bost. 9.00
☐☐ IM8 Mike Modano, Dall. 7.00
☐☐ IM9 Peter Forsberg, Colo. 10.00
☐☐ IM10 Brian Leetch, NYRa. 4.00
☐☐ IM11 Martin Brodeur (G), NJer. 12.00
☐☐ IM12 Al MacInnis, SLou. 3.00
☐☐ IM13 Paul Kariya, Anah. 10.00
☐☐ IM14 Alexei Yashin, Otta. 4.00
☐☐ IM15 Steve Yzerman, Detr. 18.00
☐☐ IM16 Ed Belfour (G), Dall. 7.00
☐☐ IM17 Keith Tkachuk, Phoe. 4.00
☐☐ IM18 Patrick Roy (G), Colo. 22.00
☐☐ IM19 Nicklas Lidström, Detr. 4.00
☐☐ IM20 Teemu Selänne, Anah. 6.00

NOW STARRING

There is both an O-Pee-Chee and a Topps version.

Insert Set (15 cards): **30.00**
Insert (1:18) **NS**
☐☐ NS1 Anson Carter, Bost. 2.00
☐☐ NS2 Marian Hossa, Otta. 5.00
☐☐ NS3 Michael Peca, Buff. 2.00
☐☐ NS4 Kenny Jönsson, NYIs. 2.00
☐☐ NS5 Petr' Sykora, NJer. 2.00
☐☐ NS6 Chris Drury, Colo. 3.00
☐☐ NS7 Byron Dafoe (G), Bost. 2.00
☐☐ NS8 Wade Redden, Otta. 2.00
☐☐ NS9 Jeff Friesen, SanJ. 2.00
☐☐ NS10 Jamie Langenbrunner, Dall. 2.00
☐☐ NS11 Mike Johnson, Toro. 2.00
☐☐ NS12 Keith Primeau, Caro. 2.00
☐☐ NS13 Vincent Lecavalier, Tamp. 5.00
☐☐ NS14 Mattias Öhlund, Vanc. 2.00
☐☐ NS15 Pavol Demitra, SLou. 2.00

SEASON'S BEST

There is both an O-Pee-Chee and a Topps version.

Insert Set (30 cards): **45.00**
Insert (1:10) **SB**
☐☐ AM1 Jaromir Jagr, Pitt. 2.00
☐☐ AM2 Peter Forsberg, Colo. 3.00
☐☐ AM3 Paul Kariya, Anah. 3.00
☐☐ AM4 Teemu Selänne, Anah. 2.00
☐☐ AM5 Joe Sakic, Colo. 4.00
☐☐ AM6 Eric Lindros, Phil. 2.00
☐☐ FF1 Teemu Selänne, Anah. 2.00
☐☐ FF2 Jaromir Jagr, Pitt. 2.00
☐☐ FF3 Tony Amonte, Chic. 1.50
☐☐ FF4 Alexei Yashin, Otta. 1.50
☐☐ FF5 John LeClair, Phil. 2.00
☐☐ FF6 Joe Sakic, Colo. 4.00
☐☐ IF1 Mark Parrish, Flor. 1.50
☐☐ IF2 Chris Drury, Colo. 1.50
☐☐ IF3 Bill Muckalt, Vanc. 1.50
☐☐ IF4 Marian Hossa, Otta. 2.00
☐☐ IF5 Milan Hejduk, Colo. 2.00
☐☐ IF6 Brendan Morrison, NJer. 1.50
☐☐ PP1 Alexander Karpovtsev, Toro. 1.50
☐☐ PP2 John LeClair, Phil. 2.00
☐☐ PP3 Eric Lindros, Phil. 2.00
☐☐ PP4 Magnus Arvedson, Otta. 1.50
☐☐ PP5 Al MacInnis, SLou. 1.50
☐☐ PP6 Jere Lehtinen, Dall. 1.50
☐☐ PM1 Dominik Hasek (G), Buff. 2.00
☐☐ PM2 Byron Dafoe (G), Bost. 1.50
☐☐ PM3 Nikolai Khabibulin (G), Phoe. 1.50
☐☐ PM4 Ed Belfour (G), Dall. 2.00
☐☐ PM5 Patrick Roy (G), Colo. 7.00
☐☐ PM6 Martin Brodeur (G), NJer. 4.00

STANLEY CUP HEROES

There are up to three versions for each player: a regular insert (SC1-SC20, 1:23 packs), a Refractor parallel (SC1-SC20, 1:120 packs) and an Autographed parallel (SC1-SC6, 1:697 packs).

		Refr.	Insert
Insert Set (20 cards):		**500.00**	**130.00**
Inserts		**Refr.**	**Insert**
☐☐	SC1 Mario Lemieux, Pitt.	75.00	18.00
☐☐	SC2 Mike Bossy, NYIs.	40.00	10.00
☐☐	SC3 Guy Lafleur, Mont.	50.00	12.00
☐☐	SC4 Maurice Richard, Mont.	70.00	17.00
☐☐	SC5 Lanny McDonald, Calg.	20.00	5.00
☐☐	SC6 Frank Mahovlich, Toro.	25.00	6.00
☐☐	SC7 Steve Yzerman, Detr.	60.00	15.00
☐☐	SC8 Mark Messier, Edmo.	25.00	6.00
☐☐	SC9 Patrick Roy (G), Mont.	75.00	18.00
☐☐	SC10 Joe Sakic, Colo.	40.00	10.00
☐☐	SC11 Jaromir Jagr, Pitt.	25.00	6.00
☐☐	SC12 Peter Forsberg, Colo.	35.00	8.00
☐☐	SC13 Claude Lemieux, NJer.	12.00	4.00

☐☐ SC14 Martin Brodeur (G), NJer.	40.00	10.00
☐☐ SC15 Brian Leetch, NYRa.	15.00	4.00
☐☐ SC16 Mike Richter (G), NYRa.	12.00	4.00
☐☐ SC17 Theoren Fleury, Calg.	15.00	4.00
☐☐ SC18 Chris Osgood (G), Detr.	15.00	4.00
☐☐ SC19 Ed Belfour (G), Dall.	25.00	6.00
☐☐ SC20 Joe Nieuwendyk, Dall.	12.00	4.00

STANLEY CUP HEROES AUTOGRAPH

Autographed Set (6 cards):	400.00
Inserts	Auto.
☐ Mike Bossy, NYIs. ✍	50.00
☐ Guy Lafleur, Mont. ✍	50.00
☐ Mario Lemieux, Pitt. ✍	200.00
☐ Frank Mahovlich, Toro. ✍	35.00
☐ Lanny McDonald, Calg. ✍	35.00
☐ Maurice Richard, Mont. ✍ •	125.00

TOP OF THE WORLD

There is both an O-Pee-Chee and a Topps version.

Insert Set (30 cards):	85.00
Insert (1:30)	TW
☐☐ TW1 Teemu Selänne, Anah. [Finland]	5.00
☐☐ TW2 Saku Koivu, Mont. [Finland]	5.00
☐☐ TW3 Jere Lehtinen, Dall. [Finland]	3.00
☐☐ TW4 Peter Forsberg, Colo. [Sweden]	8.00
☐☐ TW5 Mats Sundin, Toro. [Sweden]	6.00
☐☐ TW6 Nicklas Lidström, Detr. [Sweden]	3.00
☐☐ TW7 Alexei Yashin, Otta. [Russia]	3.00
☐☐ TW8 Nikolai Khabibulin (G), Phoe. [Russia]	3.00
☐☐ TW9 Pavel Bure, Flor. [Russia]	5.00
☐☐ TW10 John LeClair, Phil. [United States]	5.00
☐☐ TW11 Keith Tkachuk, Phoe. [United States]	3.00
☐☐ TW12 Mike Modano, Dall. [United States]	6.00
☐☐ TW13 Paul Kariya, Anah. [Canada]	8.00
☐☐ TW14 Joe Sakic, Colo. [Canada]	10.00
☐☐ TW15 Martin Brodeur (G), NJer. [Canada]	10.00
☐☐ TW16 Dominik Hasek (G), Buff. [Czech Republic]	6.00
☐☐ TW17 Jaromir Jagr, Pitt. [Czech Republic]	6.00
☐☐ TW18 Peter Bondra, Wash. [Slovakia]	3.00
☐☐ TW19 Olaf Kölzig (G), Wash. [Germany]	3.00
☐☐ TW20 Marco Sturm, SanJ. [Germany]	3.00

PRE-PRODUCTION SAMPLE

Complete Set (6 cards):	5.00
Player	PP
☐ PP1 Adam Graves, NYRa.	1.00
☐ PP2 Martin Straka, Pitt.	1.00
☐ PP3 Darryl Sydor, Dall.	1.00
☐ PP4 Valeri Bure, Calg.	1.00
☐ PP5 Keith Primeau, Caro.	1.00
☐ PP6 Tom Fitzgerald, Nash.	1.00

1999 - 2000 TOPPS CHROME & O-PEE-CHEE CHROME

These series were released in 1999. The O-Pee-Chee Chrome and Topps Chrome cards are similar in design but have different brand logos on the card fronts. The O-Pee-Chee Chrome card backs also include French bios below the English bios. Both the O-Pee-Chee Chrome and Topps Chrome cards have a Refractor parallel. There are five versions (per brand and parallel) for each Magic Moments card.

Complete Set (341 cards):	**4000.00**	**350.00**
Shell Set (297 cards):	**-**	**245.00**
Common Player:	**4.00**	**.50**
Player	**Refr.**	**Chrome**
☐☐☐☐ 1 Joe Sakic, Colo.	40.00	4.00
☐☐☐☐ 2 Alexei Yashin, Otta.	15.00	1.50
☐☐☐☐ 3 Paul Kariya, Anah.	35.00	3.50
☐☐☐☐ 4 Keith Tkachuk, Phoe.	15.00	1.50
☐☐☐☐ 5 Jaromir Jagr, Pitt.	25.00	2.50
☐☐☐☐ 6 Mike Modano, Dall.	25.00	2.50
☐☐☐☐ 7 Eric Lindros, Phil.	25.00	2.50
☐☐☐☐ 8 Zigmund Palffy, LosA.	15.00	1.50
☐☐☐☐ 9 Dominik Hasek (G), Buff.	25.00	2.50
☐☐☐☐ 10 Pavel Bure, Flor.	20.00	2.00
☐☐☐☐ 11 Raymond Bourque, Bost.	30.00	3.00
☐☐☐☐ 12 Peter Forsberg, Colo.	35.00	3.50
☐☐☐☐ 13 Al MacInnis, SLou.	10.00	1.00
☐☐☐☐ 14 Steve Yzerman, Detr.	60.00	6.00
☐☐☐☐ 15 Mats Sundin, Toro.	25.00	2.50
☐☐☐☐ 16 Patrick Roy (G), Colo.	75.00	7.50
☐☐☐☐ 17 Teemu Selänne, Anah.	20.00	2.00
☐☐☐☐ 18 Keith Primeau, Caro.	10.00	1.00
☐☐☐☐ 19 John LeClair, Phil.	20.00	2.00
☐☐☐☐ 20 Martin Brodeur (G), NJer.	40.00	4.00
☐☐☐☐ 21 Joe Thornton, Bost.	30.00	3.00
☐☐☐☐ 22 Rob Blake, LosA.	15.00	1.50
☐☐☐☐ 23 Ron Francis, Caro.	15.00	1.50
☐☐☐☐ 24 Grant Fuhr (G), SLou.	15.00	1.50
☐☐☐☐ 25 Nicklas Lidström, Detr.	15.00	1.50
☐☐☐☐ **26 Vladimir Orszagh, NYIs.**	**8.00**	**3.50**
☐☐☐☐ 27 Glen Wesley, Caro.	4.00	.50
☐☐☐☐ 28 Adam Deadmarsh, Colo.	8.00	.50
☐☐☐☐ 29 Zdeno Chara, NYIs.	6.00	.50
☐☐☐☐ 30 Brian Leetch, NYRa.	15.00	1.50
☐☐☐☐ 31 Valeri Bure, Calg.	8.00	.50
☐☐☐☐ 32 Ryan Smyth, Edmo.	12.00	1.00
☐☐☐☐ 33 Jean-Sébastien Aubin (G), Pitt.	6.00	.50
☐☐☐☐ 34 David Reid, Dall.	4.00	.50
☐☐☐☐ 35 Ed Jovanovski, Vanc.	10.00	1.00
☐☐☐☐ 36 Anders Eriksson, Chic.	4.00	.50
☐☐☐☐ 37 Mike Ricci, SanJ.	8.00	.50
☐☐☐☐ 38 Todd Bertuzzi, Vanc.	30.00	3.00
☐☐☐☐ 39 Shawn Bates, Bost.	4.00	.50
☐☐☐☐ 40 Kip Miller, Pitt.	4.00	.50
☐☐☐☐ 41 Jozef Stumpel, LosA.	6.00	.50
☐☐☐☐ 42 Jeremy Roenick, Phoe.	20.00	2.00
☐☐☐☐ 43 Todd Marchant, Edmo.	6.00	.50
☐☐☐☐ 44 Josh Holden, Vanc.	4.00	.50
☐☐☐☐ 45 Rob Niedermayer, Flor.	6.00	.50
☐☐☐☐ 46 Cory Sarich, Buff.	4.00	.50
☐☐☐☐ 47 Nikolai Khabibulin (G), Phoe.	10.00	1.00
☐☐☐☐ 48 Marty McInnis, Anah.	4.00	.50
☐☐☐☐ 49 Marty Reasoner, SLou.	6.00	.50
☐☐☐☐ 50 Gary Roberts, Caro.	10.00	1.00
☐☐☐☐ 51 Manny Malhotra, NYRa.	6.00	.50
☐☐☐☐ 52 Adam Foote, Colo.	8.00	.50
☐☐☐☐ 53 Luc Robitaille, LosA.	20.00	2.00
☐☐☐☐ 54 Bryan Marchment, SanJ.	4.00	.50
☐☐☐☐ 55 Mark Janssens, Chic.	4.00	.50
☐☐☐☐ 56 Stephen Heinze, Bost.	4.00	.50
☐☐☐☐ 57 Cory Stillman, Calg.	6.00	.50
☐☐☐☐ 58 Guy Hebert (G), Anah.	6.00	.50
☐☐☐☐ 59 Mike Richter (G), NYRa.	12.00	1.00
☐☐☐☐ 60 Jamie Langenbrunner, Dall.	6.00	.50
☐☐☐☐ 61 Wade Redden, Otta.	8.00	.50
☐☐☐☐ 62 J. Steve Smith, Calg.	6.00	.50
☐☐☐☐ 63 Danny Markov, Toro.	4.00	.50
☐☐☐☐ 64 Erik Rasmussen, Buff.	6.00	.50
☐☐☐☐ 65 Glen Murray, LosA.	12.00	1.00
☐☐☐☐ 66 Alexei Kovalev, Pitt.	15.00	1.50
☐☐☐☐ 67 Peter Bondra, Wash.	15.00	1.50
☐☐☐☐ 68 Dmitri Khristich, Bost.	4.00	.50
☐☐☐☐ 69 Sami Kapanen, Caro.	8.00	.50
☐☐☐☐ 70 Tom Poti, Edmo.	4.00	.50
☐☐☐☐ 71 Trevor Linden, Mont.	10.00	1.00
☐☐☐☐ 72 Tomas Vokoun (G), Nash.	6.00	.50
☐☐☐☐ 73 Steve Webb, NYIs.	4.00	.50
☐☐☐☐ 74 Jarome Iginla, Calg.	20.00	2.00
☐☐☐☐ 75 Scott Mellanby, Flor.	6.00	.50
☐☐☐☐ 76 Mattias Öhlund, Vanc.	8.00	.50
☐☐☐☐ 77 Steve Konowalchuk, Wash.	6.00	.50
☐☐☐☐ 78 Bryan Berard, Toro.	8.00	.50
☐☐☐☐ 79 Chris Pronger, SLou.	15.00	1.50
☐☐☐☐ 80 Teppo Numminen, Phoe.	8.00	.50
☐☐☐☐ 81 John MacLean, NYRa.	4.00	.50
☐☐☐☐ 82 Jeff Hackett (G), Mont.	8.00	.50
☐☐☐☐ 83 Ray Whitney, Flor.	6.00	.50
☐☐☐☐ 84 Chris Osgood (G), Detr.	15.00	1.50
☐☐☐☐ 85 Doug Zmolek, Chic.	4.00	.50
☐☐☐☐ 86 Curtis Brown, Buff.	4.00	.50
☐☐☐☐ 87 Reid Simpson, Chic.	4.00	.50
☐☐☐☐ 88 Milan Hejduk, Colo.	20.00	2.00
☐☐☐☐ 89 Donald Audette, LosA.	10.00	1.00
☐☐☐☐ 90 Saku Koivu, Mont.	20.00	2.00
☐☐☐☐ 91 Martin Straka, Pitt.	8.00	.50
☐☐☐☐ 92 Mark Messier, Vanc.	25.00	2.50
☐☐☐☐ 93 Richard Zednik, Wash.	10.00	1.00
☐☐☐☐ 94 Curtis Joseph (G), Toro.	25.00	2.50
☐☐☐☐ 95 Colin Forbes, Tamp.	4.00	.50
☐☐☐☐ 96 Jeff Friesen, SanJ.	8.00	.50
☐☐☐☐ 97 Eric Brewer, NYIs.	10.00	1.00
☐☐☐☐ 98 Darius Kasparaitis, Pitt.	6.00	.50
☐☐☐☐ 99 Marian Hossa, Otta.	25.00	2.50
☐☐☐☐ 100 Petr* Sykora, NJer.	10.00	1.00
☐☐☐☐ 101 Vladimir Malakhov, Mont.	4.00	.50
☐☐☐☐ 102 Jamie Storr (G), LosA.	6.00	.50
☐☐☐☐ 103 Doug Gilmour, Chic.	15.00	1.50
☐☐☐☐ 104 Doug Weight, Edmo.	15.00	1.50
☐☐☐☐ 105 Derian Hatcher, Dall.	8.00	.50
☐☐☐☐ 106 Chris Drury, Colo.	15.00	1.50
☐☐☐☐ 107 Arturs Irbe (G), Caro.	10.00	1.00
☐☐☐☐ 108 Fred Brathwaite (G), Calg.	8.00	.50
☐☐☐☐ 109 Jason Allison, Bost.	15.00	1.50
☐☐☐☐ 110 Roman Hamrlik, Edmo.	6.00	.50
☐☐☐☐ 111 Rico Fata, Calg.	6.00	.50
☐☐☐☐ 112 Janne Niinimaa, Edmo.	6.00	.50
☐☐☐☐ 113 Kenny Jönsson, NYIs.	5.00	.50
☐☐☐☐ 114 Marco Sturm, SanJ.	6.00	.50
☐☐☐☐ 115 Steve Thomas, Toro.	6.00	.50
☐☐☐☐ 116 Garth Snow (G), Vanc.	8.00	.50
☐☐☐☐ 117 Rick Tocchet, Phoe.	8.00	.50
☐☐☐☐ 118 Jean-Marc Pelletier (G), Phil.	4.00	.50
☐☐☐☐ 119 Bobby Holik, NJer.	8.00	.50
☐☐☐☐ 120 Sergei Fedorov, Detr.	25.00	2.50
☐☐☐☐ 121 Jean-Pierre Dumont, Chic.	6.00	.50
☐☐☐☐ 122 Jason Woolley, Buff.	4.00	.50
☐☐☐☐ 123 James Patrick, Buff.	4.00	.50
☐☐☐☐ 124 Blake Sloan, Dall.	4.00	.50
☐☐☐☐ 125 Marcus Nilson, Flor.	4.00	.50
☐☐☐☐ 126 Shayne Corson, Mont.	8.00	.50
☐☐☐☐ 127 Tom Fitzgerald, Nash.	4.00	.50
☐☐☐☐ 128 Brian Rolston, NJer.	8.00	.50
☐☐☐☐ 129 Ron Tugnutt (G), Otta.	10.00	1.00
☐☐☐☐ 130 Mark Recchi, Phil.	10.00	1.00
☐☐☐☐ 131 Matthew Barnaby, Pitt.	4.00	.50
☐☐☐☐ 132 Olaf Kölzig (G), Wash.	15.00	1.50
☐☐☐☐ 133 Paul Mara, Tamp.	4.00	.50
☐☐☐☐ 134 Patrick Marleau, SanJ.	12.00	1.00
☐☐☐☐ 135 Magnus Arvedson, Otta.	4.00	.50
☐☐☐☐ 136 Félix Potvin (G), NYIs.	15.00	1.50
☐☐☐☐ 137 Bill Guerin, Edmo.	10.00	1.00
☐☐☐☐ 138 Brett Hull, Dall.	25.00	2.50
☐☐☐☐ 139 Vitali Yachmenev, Nash.	4.00	.50
☐☐☐☐ 140 Ruslan Salei, Anah.	4.00	.50
☐☐☐☐ 141 Mark Parrish, Flor.	10.00	1.00
☐☐☐☐ 142 Randy Cunneyworth, Buff.	4.00	.50
☐☐☐☐ 143 Damian Rhodes (G), Otta.	6.00	.50
☐☐☐☐ 144 Daniel Brière, Phoe.	12.00	1.00
☐☐☐☐ 145 Craig Conroy, SLou.	8.00	.50
☐☐☐☐ 146 Sergei Gonchar, Wash.	8.00	.50
☐☐☐☐ 147 Vincent Lecavalier, Tamp.	25.00	2.50
☐☐☐☐ 148 Adam Graves, NYRa.	10.00	1.00
☐☐☐☐ 149 Doug Bodger, LosA.	4.00	.50
☐☐☐☐ 150 Jeff O'Neill, Caro.	10.00	1.00
☐☐☐☐ 151 Darby Hendrickson, Vanc.	4.00	.50
☐☐☐☐ 152 Sergei Samsonov, Bost.	15.00	1.50
☐☐☐☐ 153 Ed Belfour (G), Dall.	25.00	2.50
☐☐☐☐ 154 Robert Svehla, Flor.	6.00	.50
☐☐☐☐ 155 Cliff Ronning, Nash.	6.00	.50
☐☐☐☐ 156 Brendan Morrison, NJer.	8.00	.50
☐☐☐☐ 157 Daniel Alfredsson, Otta.	15.00	1.50
☐☐☐☐ 158 Éric Desjardins, Phil.	8.00	.50
☐☐☐☐ 159 Mike Vernon (G), SanJ.	10.00	1.00
☐☐☐☐ 160 Vadim Sharifijanov, NJer.	4.00	.50
☐☐☐☐ 161 Jaroslav Svejkovsky, Wash.	4.00	.50
☐☐☐☐ 162 Michael Peca, Buff.	10.00	1.00
☐☐☐☐ 163 Shane Willis, Caro.	6.00	1.00
☐☐☐☐ 164 Sandis Ozolinsh, Colo.	6.00	.50
☐☐☐☐ 165 Mathieu Dandenault, Detr.	4.00	.50
☐☐☐☐ 166 Martin Rucinsky, Mont.	6.00	.50
☐☐☐☐ 167 Scott Stevens, NJer.	10.00	1.00
☐☐☐☐ 168 Sami Salo, Otta.	4.00	.50
☐☐☐☐ 169 Tom Barrasso (G), Pitt.	10.00	1.00
☐☐☐☐ 170 Chris Gratton, Tamp.	6.00	.50
☐☐☐☐ 171 Markus Näslund, Vanc.	25.00	2.50
☐☐☐☐ 172 Mike Johnson, Toro.	5.00	.50
☐☐☐☐ 173 Bob Boughner, Nash.	4.00	.50
☐☐☐☐ 174 Todd Simpson, Calg.	4.00	.50
☐☐☐☐ 175 Fredrik Olausson, Anah.	6.00	.50
☐☐☐☐ 176 Jocelyn Thibault (G), Chic.	10.00	1.00
☐☐☐☐ 177 Juha Ylönen, Phoe.	4.00	.50
☐☐☐☐ 178 Brad Bombardir, NJer.	4.00	.50
☐☐☐☐ 179 Jan Hrdina, Pitt.	6.00	.50
☐☐☐☐ 180 Adrian Aucoin, Vanc.	4.00	.50
☐☐☐☐ 181 Mike Eagles, Wash.	4.00	.50
☐☐☐☐ 182 Petr Nedved, NYRa.	8.00	.50
☐☐☐☐ 183 Rem Murray, Edmo.	4.00	.50
☐☐☐☐ 184 Mikael Renberg, Phil.	8.00	.50
☐☐☐☐ 185 Mike Eastwood, SLou.	4.00	.50
☐☐☐☐ 186 Byron Dafoe (G), Bost.	10.00	1.00
☐☐☐☐ 187 Tony Amonte, Chic.	15.00	1.50
☐☐☐☐ 188 Darren McCarty, Detr.	8.00	.50
☐☐☐☐ 189 Sergei Krivokrasov, Nash.	4.00	.50
☐☐☐☐ 190 Dave Lowry, SanJ.	6.00	.50
☐☐☐☐ 191 Michal Handzus, SLou.	6.00	.50
☐☐☐☐ 192 Tie Domi, Toro.	8.00	.50
☐☐☐☐ 193 Brian Holzinger, Buff.	4.00	.50
☐☐☐☐ 194 Jason Arnott, NJer.	12.00	1.00
☐☐☐☐ 195 José Théodore (G), Mont.	30.00	3.00
☐☐☐☐ 196 Brendan Shanahan, Detr.	25.00	2.50
☐☐☐☐ 197 Derek Morris, Calg.	6.00	.50
☐☐☐☐ 198 Steve Rucchin, Anah.	6.00	.50
☐☐☐☐ 199 Kevin Hodson (G), Tamp.	6.00	.50
☐☐☐☐ 200 Oleg Kvasha, Flor.	4.00	.50
☐☐☐☐ 201 John Vanbiesbrouck (G), Phil.	12.00	1.00
☐☐☐☐ 202 Adam Oates, Wash.	10.00	1.00
☐☐☐☐ 203 Anson Carter, Bost.	10.00	1.00
☐☐☐☐ 204 Sébastien Bordeleau, Nash.	4.00	.50
☐☐☐☐ 205 Pavol Demitra, SLou.	10.00	1.00
☐☐☐☐ 206 Owen Nolan, SanJ.	15.00	1.50
☐☐☐☐ 207 Pavel Rosa, LosA.	4.00	.50
☐☐☐☐ 208 Petr* Svoboda, Tamp.	6.00	.50
☐☐☐☐ 209 Tomas Kaberle, Toro.	8.00	.50
☐☐☐☐ 210 Claude Lapointe, NYIs.	4.00	.50
☐☐☐☐ 211 Todd Harvey, NYRa.	6.00	.50
☐☐☐☐ 212 Trent McCleary, Mont.	4.00	.50
☐☐☐☐ 213 Vyacheslav Kozlov, Detr.	6.00	.50
☐☐☐☐ 214 Marc Denis (G), Colo.	12.00	1.00
☐☐☐☐ 215 Joe Nieuwendyk, Dall.	10.00	1.00
☐☐☐☐ 216 Kelly Buchberger, Edmo.	4.00	.50
☐☐☐☐ 217 Tommy Albelin, Calg. [XCX: Aalto]	4.00	.50
☐☐☐☐ 218 Kyle McLaren, Bost.	6.00	.50
☐☐☐☐ 219 Chris Chelios, Detr.	15.00	1.50
☐☐☐☐ 220 Joël Bouchard, Nash.	4.00	.50
☐☐☐☐ 221 Mats Lindgren, NYIs.	4.00	.50
☐☐☐☐ 222 Jyrki Lumme, Phoe.	6.00	.50
☐☐☐☐ 223 Pierre Turgeon, SLou.	10.00	1.00
☐☐☐☐ 224 Bill Muckalt, Vanc.	4.00	.50
☐☐☐☐ 225 Antti Aalto, Anah.	4.00	.50
☐☐☐☐ 226 Jere Lehtinen, Dall.	8.00	.50
☐☐☐☐ 227 Theoren Fleury, NYRa.	15.00	1.50
☐☐☐☐ 228 Dmitri Mironov, Wash.	4.00	.50
☐☐☐☐ 229 Scott Niedermayer, NJer.	8.00	.50
☐☐☐☐ 230 Sean Burke (G), Flor.	15.00	1.50
☐☐☐☐ 231 Éric Dazé, Chic.	10.00	1.00
☐☐☐☐ 232 Alexei Zhitnik, Buff.	4.00	.50
☐☐☐☐ 233 Christian Matte, Colo.	4.00	.50
☐☐☐☐ 234 Patrik Elias, NJer.	20.00	2.00
☐☐☐☐ 235 Alexander Korolyuk, SanJ.	4.00	.50
☐☐☐☐ 236 Sergei Berezin, Toro.	6.00	.50
☐☐☐☐ 237 Ray Ferraro, LosA.	4.00	.50
☐☐☐☐ 238 Rod Brind'Amour, Phil.	8.00	.50
☐☐☐☐ 239 Darcy Tucker, Tamp.	6.00	.50
☐☐☐☐ 240 Darryl Sydor, Dall.	6.00	.50
☐☐☐☐ 241 Mike Dunham (G), Nash.	10.00	1.00
☐☐☐☐ 242 Marc Bergevin, SLou.	4.00	.50
☐☐☐☐ 243 Ray Sheppard, Caro.	4.00	.50
☐☐☐☐ 244 Miroslav Satan, Buff.	8.00	.50
☐☐☐☐ 245 Andreas Dackell, Otta.	4.00	.50
☐☐☐☐ 246 Mike Grier, Edmo.	6.00	.50
☐☐☐☐ 247 Alexei Zhamnov, Chic.	8.00	.50
☐☐☐☐ 248 David Legwand	10.00	1.00
☐☐☐☐ 249 Daniel Tkaczuk	6.00	.50
☐☐☐☐ 250 Roberto Luongo (G)	20.00	4.00
☐☐☐☐ 251 Simon Gagné	20.00	4.00
☐☐☐☐ 252 Jamie Lundmark	8.00	.50
☐☐☐☐ **253 Alexandre Giroux**	**5.00**	**2.00**
☐☐☐☐ **254 Dusty Jamieson**	**5.00**	**2.00**
☐☐☐☐ **255 Jamie Chamberlain**	**5.00**	**2.00**
☐☐☐☐ **256 Radim Vrbata**	**60.00**	**25.00**
☐☐☐☐ **257 Scott Cameron**	**5.00**	**2.00**
☐☐☐☐ **258 Simon Lajeunesse (G)**	**10.00**	**4.50**
☐☐☐☐ 259 Tim Connolly	10.00	1.00
☐☐☐☐ 260 Kris Beech	8.00	.50
☐☐☐☐ 261 Brian Finley (G)	5.00	.50
☐☐☐☐ **262 Alex Auld (G)**	**12.00**	**5.00**
☐☐☐☐ **263 Martin Grenier**	**5.00**	**2.00**
☐☐☐☐ **264 Sheldon Keefe**	**10.00**	**4.50**
☐☐☐☐ **265 Justin Mapletoft**	**8.00**	**3.50**
☐☐☐☐ **266 Edward Hill**	**5.00**	**2.00**
☐☐☐☐ **267 Nolan Yonkman**	**5.00**	**2.00**
☐☐☐☐ **268 Oleg Saprykin**	**12.00**	**5.00**
☐☐☐☐ **269 Branislav Mezei**	**8.00**	**3.50**
☐☐☐☐ **270 Chris Kelly**	**5.00**	**2.00**
☐☐☐☐ **271 Pavel Brendl**	**30.00**	**12.00**
☐☐☐☐ **272 Brett Lysak**	**5.00**	**2.00**
☐☐☐☐ **273 Matt Carkner**	**5.00**	**2.00**
☐☐☐☐ **274 Luke Sellars**	**8.00**	**3.50**
☐☐☐☐ **275 Brad Ralph**	**8.00**	**3.50**
☐☐☐☐ 276 Bourque [1000 Points]	45.00	4.50
☐☐☐☐ 276 Bourque [16 All-Star Games]	45.00	4.50
☐☐☐☐ 276 Bourque [1980 Calder Trophy]	45.00	4.50
☐☐☐☐ 276 Bourque [1996 All-Star MVP]	45.00	4.50
☐☐☐☐ 276 Bourque [5-Time Norris]	45.00	4.50
☐☐☐☐ 277 Forsberg [1994 Gold Medal Goal]	52.00	5.00
☐☐☐☐ 277 Forsberg [1994 Gold Medal]	52.00	5.00
☐☐☐☐ 277 Forsberg [1995 Calder Trophy]	52.00	5.00
☐☐☐☐ 277 Forsberg [1996 Stanley Cup]	52.00	5.00
☐☐☐☐ 277 Forsberg [3 NHL All-Star Games]	52.00	5.00
☐☐☐☐ 278 Nieuwendyk [1988 Calder Trophy]	15.00	1.50
☐☐☐☐ 278 Nieuwendyk [1989 Stanley Cup]	15.00	1.50
☐☐☐☐ 278 Nieuwendyk [1999 Smythe Trophy]	15.00	1.50
☐☐☐☐ 278 Nieuwendyk [1999 Stanley Cup]	15.00	1.50
☐☐☐☐ 278 Nieuwendyk [4 All-Star Games]	15.00	1.50
☐☐☐☐ 279 Hasek (G) [1998 Gold Medal]	37.00	3.50
☐☐☐☐ 279 Hasek (G) [2-Time Hart]	37.00	3.50
☐☐☐☐ 279 Hasek (G) [2-Time Pearson]	37.00	3.50
☐☐☐☐ 279 Hasek (G) [4 All-Star Games]	37.00	3.50
☐☐☐☐ 279 Hasek (G) [5-Time Vézina]	37.00	3.50
☐☐☐☐ 280 Jagr [1998 Gold Medal]	37.00	3.50
☐☐☐☐ 280 Jagr [1999 Hart Trophy]	37.00	3.50
☐☐☐☐ 280 Jagr [2-Time Stanley Cup]	37.00	3.50
☐☐☐☐ 280 Jagr [3-Time Scoring Leader]	37.00	3.50
☐☐☐☐ 280 Jagr [8 NHL All-Star Games]	37.00	3.50
☐☐☐☐ 281 Kariya [1993 NCAA Champ.]	52.00	5.00
☐☐☐☐ 281 Kariya [1994 Silver Medal]	52.00	5.00
☐☐☐☐ 281 Kariya [2-Time Lady Byng]	52.00	5.00
☐☐☐☐ 281 Kariya [3 NHL All-Star Games]	52.00	5.00
☐☐☐☐ 281 Kariya [50 Goal Season]	52.00	5.00
☐☐☐☐ 282 Lindros [1991 #1 Draft Pick]	37.00	3.50

□□□□	282 Lindros [1995 Hart Trophy]	37.00	3.50
□□□□	282 Lindros [1995 Pearson Award]	37.00	3.50
□□□□	282 Lindros [5 NHL All-Star Games]	37.00	3.50
□□□□	282 Lindros [Magic Moments]	37.00	3.50
□□□□	283 Messier [13 NHL All-Star Games]	37.00	3.50
□□□□	283 Messier [1984 Smythe Trophy]	37.00	3.50
□□□□	283 Messier [2-Time Hart]	37.00	3.50
□□□□	283 Messier [2-Time Pearson]	37.00	3.50
□□□□	283 Messier [6-Time Stanley Cup]	37.00	3.50
□□□□	284 Roy (G) [2-Time Conn Smythe]	112.00	10.00
□□□□	284 Roy (G) [3-Time Stanley Cup]	112.00	10.00
□□□□	284 Roy (G) [3-Time Vézina]	112.00	10.00
□□□□	284 Roy (G) [8 NHL All-Star Games]	112.00	10.00
□□□□	284 Roy (G) [All-Time Playoff Wins]	112.00	10.00
□□□□	285 Sakic [1988 Cdn. Jr. POY]	60.00	6.00
□□□□	285 Sakic [1996 Smythe Trophy]	60.00	6.00
□□□□	285 Sakic [1996 Stanley Cup]	60.00	6.00
□□□□	285 Sakic [50-Goal Season]	60.00	6.00
□□□□	285 Sakic [7 NHL All-Star Games]	60.00	6.00
□□□□	286 Yzerman [1989 Pearson Award]	90.00	9.00
□□□□	286 Yzerman [1998 Smythe Trophy]	90.00	9.00
□□□□	286 Yzerman [2-Time Stanley Cup]	90.00	9.00
□□□□	286 Yzerman [500 NHL Goals]	90.00	9.00
□□□□	286 Yzerman [8 NHL All-Star Games]	90.00	9.00
□□□□	287 Alex Tanguay, Colo.	15.00	3.00
□□□□	288 Brad Stuart, SanJ.	10.00	2.00
□□□□	289 Brian Boucher (G), Phil.	8.00	1.50
□□□□	**290 Steve Kariya, Vanc.**	**12.00**	**5.00**
□□□□	291 Scott Gomez, NJer.	10.00	2.00
□□□□	**292 Mikko Eloranta, Bost.**	**5.00**	**2.00**
□□□□	**293 Patrik Stefan, Atla.**	**16.00**	**5.00**
□□□□	**294 John Madden, NJer.**	**16.00**	**7.00**
□□□□	295 Per Svartvadet, Atla.	4.00	.50
□□□□	296 Jiri Fischer, Detr.	6.00	1.00
□□□□	**297 Nikolai Antropov, Toro.**	**12.00**	**5.00**

ALL-TOPPS

There are four versions: an O-Pee-Chee Chrome card (1:24 O-Pee-Chee packs), an O-Pee-Chee Chrome Refractor parallel (1:120 O-Pee-Chee packs), a Topps Chrome card (1:24 Topps packs) and a Topps Chrome Refractor parallel (1:120 Topps packs).

Insert Set (15 cards):		**135.00**	**49.00**
	Inserts	**ATR**	**AT**
□□	AT1 Dominik Hasek (G), Buff.	11.00	4.00
□□	AT2 Martin Brodeur (G), NJer.	18.00	7.00
□□	AT3 Raymond Bourque, Bost.	13.00	5.00
□□	AT4 Al MacInnis, SLou.	4.00	1.50
□□	AT5 Nicklas Lidström, Detr.	6.00	2.00
□□	AT6 Brian Leetch, NYRa.	6.00	2.00
□□	AT7 John LeClair, Phil.	9.00	3.00
□□	AT8 Paul Kariya, Anah.	15.00	6.00
□□	AT9 Keith Tkachuk, Phoe.	6.00	2.00
□□	AT10 Eric Lindros, Phil.	11.00	4.00
□□	AT11 Peter Forsberg, Colo.	15.00	6.00
□□	AT12 Steve Yzerman, Detr.	27.00	10.00
□□	AT13 Jaromir Jagr, Pitt.	11.00	4.00
□□	AT14 Teemu Selänne, Anah.	9.00	3.00
□□	AT15 Pavel Bure, Flor.	9.00	3.00

ICE MASTERS

There are four versions: an O-Pee-Chee Chrome card (1:18 O-Pee-Chee packs), an O-Pee-Chee Chrome Refractor parallel (1:90 O-Pee-Chee packs), a Topps Chrome card (1:18 Topps packs) and a Topps Chrome Refractor parallel (1:90 Topps packs).

Insert Set (20 cards):		**164.00**	**67.00**
	Inserts	**IMR**	**IM**
□□	IM1 Joe Sakic, Colo.	14.00	6.00
□□	IM2 Dominik Hasek (G), Buff.	8.00	3.00
□□	IM3 Eric Lindros, Phil.	8.00	3.00
□□	IM4 Jaromir Jagr, Pitt.	8.00	3.00
□□	IM5 John LeClair, Phil.	7.00	3.00
□□	IM6 Mats Sundin, Toro.	8.00	3.00
□□	IM7 Raymond Bourque, Bost.	10.00	4.00
□□	IM8 Mike Modano, Dall.	8.00	3.00
□□	IM9 Peter Forsberg, Colo.	12.00	5.00
□□	IM10 Brian Leetch, NYRa.	5.00	2.00
□□	IM11 Martin Brodeur (G), NJer.	14.00	6.00
□□	IM12 Al MacInnis, SLou.	3.00	1.00
□□	IM13 Paul Kariya, Anah.	12.00	5.00
□□	IM14 Alexei Yashin, Otta.	5.00	2.00
□□	IM15 Steve Yzerman, Detr.	21.00	9.00
□□	IM16 Ed Belfour (G), Dall.	8.00	3.00
□□	IM17 Keith Tkachuk, Phoe.	5.00	2.00
□□	IM18 Patrick Roy (G), Colo.	26.00	11.00
□□	IM19 Nicklas Lidström, Detr.	5.00	2.00
□□	IM20 Teemu Selänne, Anah.	7.00	3.00

SEASON'S BEST

There are four versions: an O-Pee-Chee Chrome card (1:24 O-Pee-Chee packs), an O-Pee-Chee Chrome Refractor parallel (1:120 O-Pee-Chee packs), a Topps Chrome card (1:24 Topps packs) and a Topps Chrome Refractor parallel (1:120 Topps packs).

Insert Set (30 cards):		**277.00**	**114.00**
	Inserts	**SBR**	**SB**
□□	AM1 Jaromir Jagr, Pitt.	12.00	5.00
□□	AM2 Peter Forsberg, Colo.	17.00	7.00
□□	AM3 Paul Kariya, Anah.	17.00	7.00
□□	AM4 Teemu Selänne, Anah.	10.00	4.00
□□	AM5 Joe Sakic, Colo.	20.00	8.00
□□	AM6 Eric Lindros, Phil.	12.00	5.00
□□	FF1 Teemu Selänne, Anah.	10.00	4.00
□□	FF2 Jaromir Jagr, Pitt.	12.00	5.00
□□	FF3 Tony Amonte, Chic.	7.00	3.00
□□	FF4 Alexei Yashin, Otta.	7.00	3.00
□□	FF5 John LeClair, Phil.	10.00	4.00
□□	FF6 Joe Sakic, Colo.	20.00	8.00
□□	IF1 Mark Parrish, Flor.	5.00	2.00
□□	IF2 Chris Drury, Colo.	7.00	3.00
□□	IF3 Bill Muckalt, Vanc.	4.00	2.00
□□	IF4 Marian Hossa, Otta.	12.00	5.00
□□	IF5 Milan Hejduk, Colo.	10.00	4.00
□□	IF6 Brendan Morrison, NJer.	4.00	2.00
□□	PP1 Alexander Karpovtsev, Toro.	4.00	2.00
□□	PP2 John LeClair, Phil.	10.00	4.00
□□	PP3 Eric Lindros, Phil.	12.00	5.00
□□	PP4 Magnus Arvedson, Otta.	4.00	2.00
□□	PP5 Al MacInnis, SLou.	5.00	2.00
□□	PP6 Jere Lehtinen, Dall.	4.00	2.00
□□	PM1 Dominik Hasek (G), Buff.	12.00	5.00
□□	PM2 Byron Dafoe (G), Bost.	5.00	2.00
□□	PM3 Nikolai Khabibulin (G), Phoe.	5.00	2.00
□□	PM4 Ed Belfour (G), Dall.	12.00	5.00
□□	PM5 Patrick Roy (G), Colo.	37.00	15.00
□□	PM6 Martin Brodeur (G), NJer.	20.00	8.00

1999 - 2000 TOPPS GOLD LABEL

This series was released in 2000. All 100 base cards are available as either a Class 1, a Class 2 or a Class 3 card; each Class version has a Black Label parallel and a Red Label parallel. For the Class 1 series, base cards 1-100 are seeded regularly, Black Label cards are seeded 1:18 packs and Red Label cards are limited to 100 copies. For the Class 2 series, base cards 1-100 are seeded, Black Label cards are seeded 1:32 packs and Red Label cards are limited to 50 copies. For the Class 3 series, base cards 1-100 are seeded, Black Label cards are seeded 1:72 packs and Red Label cards are limited to 25 copies. For all versions (regular, Black and Gold) for each Class (1,2,3) there is a one-of-one version (#/1).

Class 1 Set (100 cards):		**2450.00**	**445.00**	**90.00**
Common Player:		**8.00**	**2.00**	**.50**
	Player	**Red**	**Black**	**Reg.**
□□□□□□	1 Dominik Hasek (G), Buff.	60.00	10.00	2.00
□□□□□□	2 Al MacInnis, SLou.	20.00	4.00	.50
□□□□□□	3 Luc Robitaille, LosA.	45.00	8.00	1.50
□□□□□□	4 Steve Yzerman, Detr.	140.00	24.00	4.50
□□□□□□	5 Michael Peca, Buff.	20.00	4.00	.50
□□□□□□	6 Keith Tkachuk, Phoe.	35.00	6.00	1.00
□□□□□□	7 Saku Koivu, Mont.	45.00	8.00	1.50
□□□□□□	8 Tony Amonte, Chic.	35.00	6.00	1.00
□□□□□□	9 Peter Bondra, Wash.	35.00	6.00	1.00
□□□□□□	10 Pavel Bure, Flor.	45.00	8.00	1.50
□□□□□□	11 Ron Francis, Caro.	35.00	6.00	1.00
□□□□□□	12 Eric Lindros, Phil.	60.00	10.00	2.00
□□□□□□	13 Paul Kariya, Anah.	80.00	14.00	2.50
□□□□□□	14 Theoren Fleury, NYRa.	35.00	6.00	1.00
□□□□□□	15 Jaromir Jagr, Pitt.	60.00	10.00	2.00
□□□□□□	16 Patrick Roy (G), Colo.	180.00	30.00	6.00
□□□□□□	17 Zigmund Palffy, LosA.	35.00	6.00	1.00
□□□□□□	18 Ed Belfour (G), Dall.	60.00	10.00	2.00
□□□□□□	19 Sergei Samsonov, Bost.	35.00	6.00	1.00
□□□□□□	20 Nicklas Lidström, Detr.	35.00	6.00	1.00
□□□□□□	21 Pavol Demitra, SLou.	20.00	4.00	.50
□□□□□□	22 Sergei Fedorov, Detr.	60.00	10.00	2.00
□□□□□□	23 Teemu Selänne, Anah.	45.00	8.00	1.50
□□□□□□	24 Martin Brodeur (G), NJer.	95.00	16.00	3.00
□□□□□□	25 John LeClair, Phil.	45.00	8.00	1.50
□□□□□□	26 Raymond Bourque, Bost.	70.00	12.00	2.00
□□□□□□	27 Peter Forsberg, Colo.	80.00	14.00	2.50
□□□□□□	28 Doug Weight, Edmo.	35.00	6.00	1.00
□□□□□□	29 Brian Leetch, NYRa.	35.00	6.00	1.00
□□□□□□	30 Mark Recchi, Phil.	20.00	4.00	.50
□□□□□□	31 Jason Allison, Bost.	35.00	6.00	1.00
□□□□□□	32 Rob Blake, LosA.	35.00	6.00	1.00
□□□□□□	33 Scott Niedermayer, NJer.	15.00	3.00	.50
□□□□□□	34 Chris Pronger, SLou.	35.00	6.00	1.00
□□□□□□	35 Joe Sakic, Colo.	95.00	16.00	3.00
□□□□□□	36 Mark Messier, Vanc.	60.00	10.00	2.00
□□□□□□	37 Daniel Alfredsson, Otta.	35.00	6.00	1.00
□□□□□□	38 Guy Hebert (G), Anah.	10.00	2.00	.50
□□□□□□	39 Bobby Holik, NJer.	15.00	3.00	.50
□□□□□□	40 Joe Thornton, Bost.	70.00	12.00	2.00
□□□□□□	41 Ron Tugnutt (G), Otta.	20.00	4.00	.50
□□□□□□	42 Jeff Friesen, SanJ.	15.00	3.00	.50
□□□□□□	43 Jeremy Roenick, Phoe.	45.00	8.00	1.50
□□□□□□	44 Wade Redden, Otta.	15.00	3.00	.50
□□□□□□	45 Chris Osgood (G), Detr.	35.00	6.00	1.00
□□□□□□	46 Arturs Irbe (G), Caro.	20.00	4.00	.50
□□□□□□	47 Valeri Bure, Calg.	15.00	3.00	.50
□□□□□□	48 Chris Drury, Colo.	35.00	6.00	1.00
□□□□□□	49 Owen Nolan, SanJ.	35.00	6.00	1.00
□□□□□□	50 Kenny Jönsson, NYIs.	10.00	2.00	.50
□□□□□□	51 Petr* Sykora, NJer.	20.00	4.00	.50
□□□□□□	52 Byron Dafoe (G), Bost.	20.00	4.00	.50
□□□□□□	53 Brett Hull, Dall.	60.00	10.00	2.00
□□□□□□	54 Mike Richter (G), NYRa.	25.00	4.00	.50
□□□□□□	55 Brendan Shanahan, Detr.	60.00	10.00	2.00
□□□□□□	56 Mats Sundin, Toro.	60.00	10.00	2.00
□□□□□□	57 Miroslav Satan, Buff.	15.00	3.00	.50
□□□□□□	58 Markus Näslund, Vanc.	60.00	10.00	2.00
□□□□□□	59 Rod Brind'Amour, Phil.	15.00	3.00	.50
□□□□□□	60 Joe Nieuwendyk, Dall.	20.00	4.00	.50
□□□□□□	61 Petr Nedved, NYRa.	15.00	3.00	.50
□□□□□□	62 Sergei Berezin, Toro.	10.00	2.00	.50
□□□□□□	63 Trevor Linden, Mont.	20.00	4.00	.50
□□□□□□	64 Marian Hossa, Otta.	60.00	10.00	2.00
□□□□□□	65 Pierre Turgeon, SLou.	20.00	4.00	.50
□□□□□□	66 Vincent Lecavalier, Tamp.	60.00	10.00	2.00
□□□□□□	67 Sami Kapanen, Caro.	15.00	3.00	.50
□□□□□□	68 Andrew Brunette, Atla.	8.00	2.00	.50
□□□□□□	69 Brian Savage, Mont.	15.00	3.00	.50
□□□□□□	70 Derian Hatcher, Dall.	15.00	3.00	.50
□□□□□□	71 Curtis Joseph (G), Toro.	60.00	10.00	2.00
□□□□□□	72 Scott Stevens, NJer.	20.00	4.00	.50
□□□□□□	73 Radek Bonk, Otta.	15.00	3.00	.50
□□□□□□	74 Jarome Iginla, Calg.	45.00	8.00	1.50
□□□□□□	75 Adam Graves, NYRa.	20.00	4.00	.50
□□□□□□	76 A. Selivanov, Edmo.	8.00	2.00	.50
□□□□□□	77 Alexander Mogilny, Vanc.	25.00	4.00	.50
□□□□□□	78 Cliff Ronning, Nash.	10.00	2.00	.50
□□□□□□	79 V. Damphousse, SanJ.	35.00	6.00	1.00
□□□□□□	80 Alexei Kovalev, NYRa.	35.00	6.00	1.00
□□□□□□	81 Yanic Perreault, Toro.	15.00	3.00	.50
□□□□□□	82 Alexander Korolyuk, SanJ.	8.00	2.00	.50
□□□□□□	83 Jozef Stumpel, LosA.	10.00	2.00	.50
□□□□□□	84 Viktor Kozlov, Flor.	15.00	3.00	.50
□□□□□□	85 Mike Modano, Dall.	60.00	10.00	2.00
□□□□□□	86 David Legwand, Nash.	20.00	4.00	1.50
□□□□□□	87 Scott Gomez, NJer.	20.00	4.00	1.50
□□□□□□	88 Tim Connolly, NYIs.	20.00	4.00	1.50
□□□□□□	89 Brad Stuart, SanJ.	20.00	4.00	1.50
□□□□□□	90 Peter Schaefer, Vanc.	8.00	2.00	.50
□□□□□□	91 Alex Tanguay, Colo.	35.00	6.00	2.00
□□□□□□	92 Simon Gagné, Phil.	45.00	8.00	3.00
□□□□□□	93 David Tanabe, Caro.	8.00	2.00	.50
□□□□□□	94 R. Luongo (G), NYIs.	45.00	8.00	3.00
□□□□□□	95 Martin Biron (G), Buff.	25.00	4.00	1.50
□□□□□□	**96 Mike Fisher, Otta. RC**	**20.00**	**7.00**	**3.00**
□□□□□□	**97 P. Stefan, Atla. RC**	**25.00**	**9.00**	**4.00**
□□□□□□	**98 N. Antropov, Toro. RC**	**20.00**	**7.00**	**3.00**
□□□□□□	**99 J. Hecht, SLou. RC**	**20.00**	**7.00**	**3.00**
□□□□□□	**100 S. Kariya, Vanc. RC**	**20.00**	**7.00**	**3.00**

CLASS 2

Common Player:		**10.00**	**3.00**	**1.00**
Class 2 Set (100 cards):		**8,600**	**2,000**	**400**
	Player	**Red**	**Black**	**Reg.**
□□□□□□	1 Dominik Hasek (G)	70.00	15.00	3.50
□□□□□□	2 Al MacInnis	30.00	5.00	1.50
□□□□□□	3 Luc Robitaille	60.00	10.00	3.00
□□□□□□	4 Steve Yzerman	180.00	35.00	9.00
□□□□□□	5 Michael Peca	30.00	5.00	1.50
□□□□□□	6 Keith Tkachuk	45.00	5.00	2.00
□□□□□□	7 Saku Koivu	60.00	10.00	3.00
□□□□□□	8 Tony Amonte	45.00	5.00	2.00
□□□□□□	9 Peter Bondra	45.00	5.00	2.00
□□□□□□	10 Pavel Bure	60.00	10.00	3.00
□□□□□□	11 Ron Francis	45.00	5.00	2.00
□□□□□□	12 Eric Lindros	70.00	15.00	3.50
□□□□□□	13 Paul Kariya	105.00	20.00	5.00
□□□□□□	14 Theoren Fleury	45.00	5.00	2.00
□□□□□□	15 Jaromir Jagr	75.00	15.00	3.50
□□□□□□	16 Patrick Roy (G)	225.00	45.00	10.00
□□□□□□	17 Zigmund Palffy	45.00	5.00	2.00
□□□□□□	18 Ed Belfour (G)	75.00	15.00	3.50
□□□□□□	19 Sergei Samsonov	45.00	5.00	2.00
□□□□□□	20 Nicklas Lidström	45.00	5.00	2.00
□□□□□□	21 Pavol Demitra	30.00	5.00	1.50
□□□□□□	22 Sergei Fedorov	75.00	15.00	3.50
□□□□□□	23 Teemu Selänne	60.00	10.00	3.00
□□□□□□	24 Martin Brodeur (G)	120.00	20.00	6.00
□□□□□□	25 John LeClair	60.00	10.00	3.00
□□□□□□	26 Raymond Bourque	90.00	15.00	4.50
□□□□□□	27 Peter Forsberg	100.00	20.00	5.00
□□□□□□	28 Doug Weight	45.00	5.00	2.00
□□□□□□	29 Brian Leetch	45.00	5.00	2.00
□□□□□□	30 Mark Recchi	30.00	5.00	1.50
□□□□□□	31 Jason Allison	45.00	5.00	2.00
□□□□□□	32 Rob Blake	45.00	5.00	2.00
□□□□□□	33 Scott Niedermayer	20.00	3.00	1.00
□□□□□□	34 Chris Pronger	45.00	5.00	2.00
□□□□□□	35 Joe Sakic	120.00	20.00	6.00
□□□□□□	36 Mark Messier	75.00	15.00	3.50
□□□□□□	37 Daniel Alfredsson	45.00	5.00	2.00
□□□□□□	38 Guy Hebert (G)	15.00	3.00	1.00
□□□□□□	39 Bobby Holik	20.00	3.00	1.00
□□□□□□	40 Joe Thornton	90.00	15.00	4.50
□□□□□□	41 Ron Tugnutt (G)	30.00	5.00	1.50
□□□□□□	42 Jeff Friesen	20.00	3.00	1.00
□□□□□□	43 Jeremy Roenick	60.00	10.00	3.00
□□□□□□	44 Wade Redden	20.00	3.00	1.00
□□□□□□	45 Chris Osgood (G)	45.00	5.00	2.00
□□□□□□	46 Arturs Irbe (G)	30.00	5.00	1.50
□□□□□□	47 Valeri Bure	20.00	3.00	1.00
□□□□□□	48 Chris Drury	45.00	5.00	2.00
□□□□□□	49 Owen Nolan	45.00	5.00	2.00
□□□□□□	50 Kenny Jönsson	15.00	3.00	1.00
□□□□□□	51 Petr* Sykora	30.00	5.00	1.50
□□□□□□	52 Byron Dafoe (G)	30.00	5.00	1.50
□□□□□□	53 Brett Hull	75.00	15.00	3.50
□□□□□□	54 Mike Richter (G)	35.00	5.00	1.50
□□□□□□	55 Brendan Shanahan	75.00	15.00	3.50
□□□□□□	56 Mats Sundin	75.00	15.00	3.50
□□□□□□	57 Miroslav Satan	20.00	3.00	1.00
□□□□□□	58 Markus Näslund	75.00	15.00	3.50
□□□□□□	59 Rod Brind'Amour	20.00	3.00	1.00
□□□□□□	60 Joe Nieuwendyk	30.00	5.00	1.50
□□□□□□	61 Petr Nedved	20.00	3.00	1.00
□□□□□□	62 Sergei Berezin	15.00	3.00	1.00
□□□□□□	63 Trevor Linden	30.00	5.00	1.50
□□□□□□	64 Marian Hossa	75.00	15.00	3.50
□□□□□□	65 Pierre Turgeon	30.00	5.00	1.50
□□□□□□	66 Vincent Lecavalier	75.00	15.00	3.50
□□□□□□	67 Sami Kapanen	20.00	3.00	1.00
□□□□□□	68 Andrew Brunette	10.00	3.00	1.00
□□□□□□	69 Brian Savage	20.00	3.00	1.00
□□□□□□	70 Derian Hatcher	20.00	3.00	1.00
□□□□□□	71 Curtis Joseph (G)	75.00	15.00	3.50
□□□□□□	72 Scott Stevens	30.00	5.00	1.50
□□□□□□	73 Radek Bonk	20.00	3.00	1.00
□□□□□□	74 Jarome Iginla	60.00	10.00	3.00
□□□□□□	75 Adam Graves	30.00	5.00	1.50
□□□□□□	76 Alexander Selivanov	10.00	3.00	1.00
□□□□□□	77 Alexander Mogilny	35.00	5.00	1.50
□□□□□□	78 Cliff Ronning	15.00	3.00	1.00
□□□□□□	79 Vincent Damphousse	45.00	5.00	2.00
□□□□□□	80 Alexei Kovalev	45.00	5.00	2.00
□□□□□□	81 Yanic Perreault	20.00	3.00	1.00
□□□□□□	82 Alexander Korolyuk	10.00	3.00	1.00
□□□□□□	83 Jozef Stumpel	15.00	3.00	1.00
□□□□□□	84 Viktor Kozlov	20.00	3.00	1.00
□□□□□□	85 Mike Modano	75.00	15.00	3.50
□□□□□□	86 David Legwand	30.00	5.00	2.00
□□□□□□	87 Scott Gomez	30.00	5.00	2.00
□□□□□□	88 Tim Connolly	30.00	5.00	2.00
□□□□□□	89 Brad Stuart	30.00	5.00	2.00
□□□□□□	90 Peter Schaefer	10.00	3.00	1.00
□□□□□□	91 Alex Tanguay	45.00	5.00	3.00
□□□□□□	92 Simon Gagné	60.00	10.00	4.50
□□□□□□	93 David Tanabe	10.00	3.00	1.00
□□□□□□	94 Roberto Luongo (G)	60.00	10.00	4.50
□□□□□□	95 Martin Biron (G)	35.00	5.00	2.50
□□□□□□	**96 Mike Fisher RC**	**25.00**	**10.00**	**4.50**
□□□□□□	**97 Patrik Stefan RC**	**35.00**	**14.00**	**6.00**
□□□□□□	**98 Nikolai Antropov RC**	**25.00**	**10.00**	**4.50**

Player	Red	Black	Reg.
□□□□□□ **99 Jochen Hecht RC**	**25.00**	**10.00**	**5.00**
□□□□□□ **100 Steve Kariya RC**	**25.00**	**10.00**	**4.50**

CLASS 3

Class 3 Set (100 cards):	**7,500**	**2,500**	**350**
Common Player:	**20.00**	**10.00**	**3.00**
Player	**Red**	**Black**	**Reg.**
□□□□□□ 1 Dominik Hasek (G)	185.00	60.00	7.00
□□□□□□ 2 Al MacInnis	75.00	20.00	3.00
□□□□□□ 3 Luc Robitaille	150.00	45.00	6.00
□□□□□□ 4 Steve Yzerman	450.00	140.00	18.00
□□□□□□ 5 Michael Peca	75.00	20.00	3.00
□□□□□□ 6 Keith Tkachuk	110.00	35.00	4.00
□□□□□□ 7 Saku Koivu	150.00	45.00	6.00
□□□□□□ 8 Tony Amonte	110.00	35.00	4.00
□□□□□□ 9 Peter Bondra	110.00	35.00	4.00
□□□□□□ 10 Pavel Bure	150.00	45.00	6.00
□□□□□□ 11 Ron Francis	110.00	35.00	4.00
□□□□□□ 12 Eric Lindros	185.00	60.00	7.00
□□□□□□ 13 Paul Kariya	260.00	80.00	10.00
□□□□□□ 14 Theoren Fleury	110.00	35.00	4.00
□□□□□□ 15 Jaromir Jagr	185.00	60.00	7.00
□□□□□□ 16 Patrick Roy (G)	550.00	180.00	22.00
□□□□□□ 17 Zigmund Palffy	110.00	35.00	4.00
□□□□□□ 18 Ed Belfour (G)	185.00	60.00	7.00
□□□□□□ 19 Sergei Samsonov	110.00	35.00	4.00
□□□□□□ 20 Nicklas Lidström	110.00	35.00	4.00
□□□□□□ 21 Pavol Demitra	75.00	20.00	3.00
□□□□□□ 22 Sergei Fedorov	185.00	60.00	7.00
□□□□□□ 23 Teemu Selänne	150.00	45.00	6.00
□□□□□□ 24 Martin Brodeur (G)	300.00	95.00	12.00
□□□□□□ 25 John LeClair	150.00	45.00	6.00
□□□□□□ 26 Raymond Bourque	225.00	70.00	9.00
□□□□□□ 27 Peter Forsberg	260.00	80.00	10.00
□□□□□□ 28 Doug Weight	110.00	35.00	4.00
□□□□□□ 29 Brian Leetch	110.00	35.00	4.00
□□□□□□ 30 Mark Recchi	75.00	20.00	3.00
□□□□□□ 31 Jason Allison	110.00	35.00	4.00
□□□□□□ 32 Rob Blake	110.00	35.00	4.00
□□□□□□ 33 Scott Niedermayer	60.00	15.00	3.00
□□□□□□ 34 Chris Pronger	110.00	35.00	4.00
□□□□□□ 35 Joe Sakic	300.00	95.00	12.00
□□□□□□ 36 Mark Messier	185.00	60.00	7.00
□□□□□□ 37 Daniel Alfredsson	110.00	35.00	4.00
□□□□□□ 38 Guy Hebert (G)	45.00	10.00	3.00
□□□□□□ 39 Bobby Holik	60.00	15.00	3.00
□□□□□□ 40 Joe Thornton	225.00	70.00	9.00
□□□□□□ 41 Ron Tugnutt (G)	75.00	20.00	3.00
□□□□□□ 42 Jeff Friesen	60.00	15.00	3.00
□□□□□□ 43 Jeremy Roenick	150.00	45.00	6.00
□□□□□□ 44 Wade Redden	60.00	15.00	3.00
□□□□□□ 45 Chris Osgood (G)	110.00	35.00	4.00
□□□□□□ 46 Arturs Irbe (G)	75.00	20.00	3.00
□□□□□□ 47 Valeri Bure	60.00	15.00	3.00
□□□□□□ 48 Chris Drury	110.00	35.00	4.00
□□□□□□ 49 Owen Nolan	110.00	35.00	4.00
□□□□□□ 50 Kenny Jönsson	35.00	10.00	3.00
□□□□□□ 51 Petr* Sykora	75.00	20.00	3.00
□□□□□□ 52 Byron Dafoe (G)	75.00	20.00	3.00
□□□□□□ 53 Brett Hull	185.00	60.00	7.00
□□□□□□ 54 Mike Richter (G)	90.00	25.00	3.00
□□□□□□ 55 Brendan Shanahan	185.00	60.00	7.00
□□□□□□ 56 Mats Sundin	185.00	60.00	7.00
□□□□□□ 57 Miroslav Satan	60.00	15.00	3.00
□□□□□□ 58 Markus Näslund	185.00	60.00	7.00
□□□□□□ 59 Rod Brind'Amour	60.00	15.00	3.00
□□□□□□ 60 Joe Nieuwendyk	75.00	20.00	3.00
□□□□□□ 61 Petr Nedved	60.00	15.00	3.00
□□□□□□ 62 Sergei Berezin	45.00	10.00	3.00
□□□□□□ 63 Trevor Linden	75.00	20.00	3.00
□□□□□□ 64 Marian Hossa	185.00	60.00	7.00
□□□□□□ 65 Pierre Turgeon	75.00	20.00	3.00
□□□□□□ 66 Vincent Lecavalier	185.00	60.00	7.00
□□□□□□ 67 Sami Kapanen	60.00	15.00	3.00
□□□□□□ 68 Andrew Brunette	30.00	10.00	3.00
□□□□□□ 69 Brian Savage	60.00	15.00	3.00
□□□□□□ 70 Derian Hatcher	60.00	15.00	3.00
□□□□□□ 71 Curtis Joseph (G)	185.00	60.00	7.00
□□□□□□ 72 Scott Stevens	75.00	20.00	3.00
□□□□□□ 73 Radek Bonk	60.00	15.00	3.00
□□□□□□ 74 Jarome Iginla	150.00	45.00	6.00
□□□□□□ 75 Adam Graves	75.00	20.00	3.00
□□□□□□ 76 Alexander Selivanov	20.00	10.00	3.00
□□□□□□ 77 Alexander Mogilny	90.00	25.00	3.00
□□□□□□ 78 Cliff Ronning	45.00	10.00	3.00
□□□□□□ 79 Vincent Damphousse	110.00	35.00	4.00
□□□□□□ 80 Alexei Kovalev	110.00	35.00	4.00
□□□□□□ 81 Yanic Perreault	60.00	15.00	3.00
□□□□□□ 82 Alexander Korolyuk	20.00	10.00	3.00
□□□□□□ 83 Jozef Stumpel	45.00	10.00	3.00
□□□□□□ 84 Viktor Kozlov	60.00	15.00	3.00
□□□□□□ 85 Mike Modano	185.00	60.00	7.00
□□□□□□ 86 David Legwand	75.00	20.00	3.00
□□□□□□ 87 Scott Gomez	75.00	20.00	3.00
□□□□□□ 88 Tim Connolly	75.00	20.00	3.00
□□□□□□ 89 Brad Stuart	75.00	20.00	3.00
□□□□□□ 90 Peter Schaefer	30.00	10.00	3.00
□□□□□□ 91 Alex Tanguay	110.00	35.00	5.00
□□□□□□ 92 Simon Gagné	150.00	45.00	7.00
□□□□□□ 93 David Tanabe	30.00	10.00	3.00
□□□□□□ 94 Roberto Luongo (G)	150.00	45.00	7.00
□□□□□□ 95 Martin Biron (G)	90.00	25.00	4.00
□□□□□□ **96 Mike Fisher RC**	**45.00**	**25.00**	**9.00**
□□□□□□ **97 Patrik Stefan RC**	**60.00**	**35.00**	**12.00**
□□□□□□ **98 Nikolai Antropov RC**	**45.00**	**25.00**	**9.00**
□□□□□□ **99 Jochen Hecht RC**	**45.00**	**25.00**	**10.00**
□□□□□□ **100 Steve Kariya RC**	**45.00**	**25.00**	**9.00**
Checklist			**Reg.**
□ Checklist (Samsonov)			.25

FRESH GOLD

There are six versions: a Gold Label insert (1:30 packs), a Black Label (1:150 packs), a Red Label (#/25), a Gold Label One-to-One parallel (#/1), a Black Label One-to-One parallel (#/1) and a Red Label One-to-One parallel (#/1).

Insert Set (20 cards):	**1300.00**	**225.00**	**55.00**
Player	**Red**	**Black**	**Reg.**
□□□□□□ FG1 Sergei Samsonov	110.00	18.00	4.00
□□□□□□ FG2 Joe Thornton	225.00	36.00	9.00
□□□□□□ FG3 Wade Redden	60.00	10.00	3.00
□□□□□□ FG4 Chris Drury	110.00	18.00	4.00
□□□□□□ FG5 Petr* Sykora	75.00	12.00	3.00
□□□□□□ FG6 Patrik Stefan	60.00	19.00	4.00
□□□□□□ FG7 Anson Carter	75.00	12.00	3.00
□□□□□□ FG8 Martin Biron (G)	90.00	14.00	3.00
□□□□□□ FG9 Alex Tanguay	110.00	18.00	4.00
□□□□□□ FG10 Milan Hejduk	150.00	24.00	6.00
□□□□□□ FG11 Mark Parrish	75.00	12.00	3.00
□□□□□□ FG12 David Legwand	75.00	12.00	3.00
□□□□□□ FG13 Brendan Morrison	60.00	10.00	3.00
□□□□□□ FG14 Scott Gomez	75.00	12.00	3.00
□□□□□□ FG15 Tim Connolly	75.00	12.00	3.00
□□□□□□ FG16 Marian Hossa	185.00	30.00	7.00
□□□□□□ FG17 Jan Hrdina	45.00	10.00	3.00
□□□□□□ FG18 Steve Kariya	45.00	14.00	3.00
□□□□□□ FG19 Jochen Hecht	45.00	14.00	3.00
□□□□□□ FG20 Vincent Lecavalier	185.00	30.00	7.00

PRIME GOLD

There are six versions: a Gold Label insert (1:20 packs), a Black Label (1:100 packs), a Red Label (#/25), a Gold Label One-to-One parallel (#/1), a Black Label One-to-One parallel (#/1) and a Red Label One-to-One parallel (#/1).

Insert Set (20 cards):	**1900.00**	**255.00**	**60.00**
Player	**Red**	**Black**	**Reg.**
□□□□□□ PG1 Dominik Hasek (G)	185.00	25.00	6.00
□□□□□□ PG2 Paul Kariya	260.00	35.00	8.00
□□□□□□ PG3 Theoren Fleury	110.00	15.00	3.00
□□□□□□ PG4 Jaromir Jagr	185.00	25.00	6.00
□□□□□□ PG5 Zigmund Palffy	110.00	15.00	3.00
□□□□□□ PG6 Nicklas Lidström	110.00	15.00	3.00
□□□□□□ PG7 Teemu Selänne	150.00	20.00	5.00
□□□□□□ PG8 John LeClair	150.00	20.00	5.00
□□□□□□ PG9 Raymond Bourque	225.00	30.00	7.00
□□□□□□ PG10 Peter Forsberg	260.00	35.00	8.00
□□□□□□ PG11 Joe Sakic	300.00	40.00	10.00
□□□□□□ PG12 Jeremy Roenick	150.00	20.00	5.00
□□□□□□ PG13 Mike Modano	185.00	25.00	6.00
□□□□□□ PG14 Pavel Bure	150.00	20.00	5.00
□□□□□□ PG15 Curtis Joseph (G)	185.00	25.00	6.00

QUEST FOR THE CUP

There are six versions: a Gold Label insert (1:12 packs), a Black Label (1:60 packs), a Red Label (#/25), a Gold Label One-to-One parallel (#/1), a Black Label One-to-One parallel (#/1) and a Red Label One-to-One parallel (#/1).

Insert Set (20 cards):	**1600.00**	**130.00**	**25.00**
Player	**Red**	**Black**	**Reg.**
□□□□□□ QC1 Steve Yzerman	450.00	36.00	9.00
□□□□□□ QC2 Keith Tkachuk	110.00	9.00	2.00
□□□□□□ QC3 Eric Lindros	185.00	15.00	3.00
□□□□□□ QC4 Patrick Roy (G)	550.00	45.00	10.00
□□□□□□ QC5 Martin Brodeur (G)	300.00	24.00	6.00
□□□□□□ QC6 Chris Pronger	110.00	9.00	2.00
□□□□□□ QC7 Daniel Alfredsson	110.00	9.00	2.00
□□□□□□ QC8 Owen Nolan	110.00	9.00	2.00
□□□□□□ QC9 Brett Hull	185.00	15.00	3.00
□□□□□□ QC10 Mats Sundin	185.00	15.00	3.00

1999 - 2000 TOPPS PREMIER PLUS

This series was released in 2000. There are two versions: the regular card and a Foil die-cut parallel (#/250).

Complete Set (140 cards):	**1100.00**	**65.00**
Common Player:	**3.00**	**.25**
Player	**F250**	**Reg.**
□□ 1 Curtis Joseph (G), Toro.	20.00	1.00
□□ 2 Peter Bondra, Wash.	12.00	.50
□□ 3 Theoren Fleury, NYRa.	12.00	.50
□□ 4 Steve Yzerman, Detr.	48.00	2.00
□□ 5 Peter Forsberg, Colo.	28.00	1.00
□□ 6 Raymond Bourque, Bost.	24.00	1.00
□□ 7 Dominik Hasek (G), Buff.	20.00	1.00
□□ 8 Chris Drury, Colo.	12.00	.50
□□ 9 Brett Hull, Dall.	20.00	1.00
□□ 10 Chris Osgood (G), Detr.	12.00	.50
□□ 11 Luc Robitaille, LosA.	16.00	.50
□□ 12 Bobby Holik, NJer.	6.00	.25
□□ 13 John LeClair, Phil.	16.00	.50
□□ 14 Jeremy Roenick, Phoe.	16.00	.50
□□ 15 Owen Nolan, SanJ.	12.00	.50
□□ 16 Wade Redden, Otta.	6.00	.25
□□ 17 Teemu Selänne, Anah.	16.00	.50
□□ 18 Doug Weight, Edmo.	12.00	.50
□□ 19 Vincent Lecavalier, Tamp.	20.00	1.00
□□ 20 Pierre Turgeon, SLou.	8.00	.25
□□ 21 Ron Francis, Caro.	12.00	.50
□□ 22 Sergei Samsonov, Bost.	12.00	.50
□□ 23 Patrick Roy (G), Colo.	60.00	3.00
□□ 24 Mark Messier, Vanc.	20.00	1.00
□□ 25 Al MacInnis, SLou.	8.00	.25
□□ 26 Mark Parrish, Flor.	8.00	.25
□□ 27 Ron Tugnutt (G), Otta.	8.00	.25
□□ 28 Joe Nieuwendyk, Dall.	8.00	.25
□□ 29 Valeri Bure, Calg.	6.00	.25
□□ 30 Jason Allison, Bost.	12.00	.50
□□ 31 Tony Amonte, Chic.	12.00	.50
□□ 32 Scott Niedermayer, NJer.	6.00	.25
□□ 33 Kenny Jönsson, NYIs.	4.00	.25
□□ 34 Jaromir Jagr, Pitt.	20.00	1.00
□□ 35 Sergei Berezin, Toro.	4.00	.25
□□ 36 Olaf Kölzig (G), Wash.	12.00	.50
□□ 37 Byron Dafoe (G), Bost.	8.00	.25
□□ 38 Adam Deadmarsh, Colo.	6.00	.25
□□ 39 Alexei Zhitnik, Buff.	3.00	.25
□□ 40 Paul Kariya, Anah.	28.00	1.00
□□ 41 Chris Pronger, SLou.	12.00	.50
□□ 42 Markus Näslund, Vanc.	20.00	1.00
□□ 43 Damian Rhodes (G), Atla.	4.00	.25
□□ 44 Marian Hossa, Otta.	20.00	1.00
□□ 45 Adam Graves, NYRa.	8.00	.25
□□ 46 Scott Stevens, NJer. [XCX: Jagr]	8.00	.25
□□ 47 Nicklas Lidström, Detr.	12.00	.50
□□ 48 Ed Belfour (G), Dall.	20.00	1.00
□□ 49 Miroslav Satan, Buff.	6.00	.25
□□ 50 Rob Blake, LosA.	12.00	.50
□□ 51 Petr Nedved, NYRa.	6.00	.25
□□ 52 Mark Recchi, Phil.	8.00	.25
□□ 53 Jeff Friesen, SanJ.	6.00	.25
□□ 54 Mats Sundin, Toro.	20.00	1.00
□□ 55 Arturs Irbe (G), Caro.	8.00	.25
□□ 56 Derian Hatcher, Dall.	6.00	.25
□□ 57 Mike Modano, Dall.	20.00	1.00
□□ 58 Brendan Shanahan, Detr.	20.00	1.00
□□ 59 Zigmund Palffy, LosA.	12.00	.50
□□ 60 Saku Koivu, Mont.	16.00	.50
□□ 61 Brian Leetch, NYRa.	12.00	.50
□□ 62 Rod Brind'Amour, Phil.	6.00	.25
□□ 63 Keith Tkachuk, Phoe.	12.00	.50
□□ 64 Pavol Demitra, SLou.	8.00	.25
□□ 65 Magnus Arvedson, Otta.	3.00	.25
□□ 66 Martin Brodeur (G), NJer.	32.00	1.50
□□ 67 Chris Chelios, Detr.	12.00	.50
□□ 68 Joe Sakic, Colo.	32.00	1.50
□□ 69 Anson Carter, Bost.	8.00	.25
□□ 70 Sergei Fedorov, Detr.	20.00	1.00
□□ 71 Pavel Bure, Flor.	16.00	.50
□□ 72 Petr* Sykora, NJer.	8.00	.25
□□ 73 Daniel Alfredsson, Otta.	12.00	.50
□□ 74 Guy Hebert (G), Anah.	4.00	.25
□□ 75 Jere Lehtinen, Dall.	6.00	.25
□□ 76 Mike Richter (G), NYRa.	9.00	.25
□□ 77 Michael Peca, Buff.	8.00	.25
□□ 78 Sandis Ozolinsh, Colo.	4.00	.25
□□ 79 Joe Thornton, Bost.	24.00	1.00
□□ 80 Eric Lindros, Phil.	20.00	1.00
□□ 81 Milan Hejduk, Colo.	16.00	.50
□□ **82 Ladislav Nagy, SLou. RC**	**12.00**	**1.50**
□□ **83 Francis Bouillon, Mont. RC**	**5.00**	**.50**
□□ **84 Mark Eaton, Phil. RC**	**5.00**	**.50**
□□ **85 Robert Valicevic, Nash. RC**	**5.00**	**.50**
□□ **86 Sami Helenius, Colo. RC**	**5.00**	**.50**
□□ **87 Travis Brigley, Calg. RC**	**5.00**	**.50**
□□ **88 Glen Metropolit, Wash. RC**	**8.00**	**1.00**
□□ **89 Alan Letang, Dall. RC**	**5.00**	**.50**
□□ **90 Brad Chartrand, LosA. RC**	**5.00**	**.50**
□□ **91 Marc Rodgers, Detr. RC**	**5.00**	**.50**
□□ **92 Hans Jonsson, Pitt. RC**	**5.00**	**.50**
□□ **93 Kim Johnsson, NYRa. RC**	**8.00**	**1.00**
□□ **94 Richard Lintner, Nash. RC**	**5.00**	**.50**
□□ 95 Andrew Ference, Pitt.	3.00	.25
□□ **96 Jeff Halpern, Wash. RC**	**12.00**	**1.50**
□□ **97 Brad Lukowich, Dall. RC**	**8.00**	**1.00**
□□ **98 Tyson Nash, SLou. RC**	**8.00**	**1.00**
□□ **99 Oleg Saprykin, Calg. RC**	**12.00**	**1.50**
□□ **100 John Grahame (G), Bost. RC**	**12.00**	**1.50**
□□ **101 Patrik Stefan, Atla. RC**	**16.00**	**2.00**
□□ **102 Jason Blake, LosA. RC**	**12.00**	**1.50**
□□ **103 Kyle Calder, Chic. RC**	**12.00**	**1.50**
□□ **104 John Madden, NJer. RC**	**16.00**	**2.00**
□□ **105 Dan Hinote, Colo. RC**	**10.00**	**1.50**
□□ **106 Pavel Patera, Dall. RC**	**5.00**	**.50**
□□ **107 Yuri Butsayev, Detr. RC**	**5.00**	**.50**
□□ **108 Paul Comrie, Edmo. RC**	**8.00**	**1.00**
□□ **109 Ivan Novoseltsev, Flor. RC**	**10.00**	**1.50**
□□ **110 Niclas Hävelid, Anah. RC**	**5.00**	**.50**
□□ **111 Brian Rafalski, NJer. RC**	**12.00**	**1.50**
□□ **112 Jörgen Jönsson, NYIs. RC**	**10.00**	**1.50**
□□ **113 Mike Fisher, Otta. RC**	**12.00**	**1.50**
□□ **114 Mika Alatalo, Phoe. RC**	**8.00**	**1.00**
□□ **115 Michal Rozsival, Pitt. RC**	**5.00**	**.50**
□□ **116 Jochen Hecht, SLou. RC**	**12.00**	**1.50**
□□ **117 Nikolai Antropov, Toro. RC**	**12.00**	**1.50**
□□ **118 Steve Kariya, Vanc. RC**	**12.00**	**1.50**
□□ **119 Brian Campbell, Buff. RC**	**5.00**	**.50**
□□ 120 Maxim Afinogenov, Buff.	8.00	.50
□□ 121 Roberto Luongo (G), NYIs.	16.00	1.50
□□ 122 Petr Buzek, Atla.	3.00	.25
□□ 123 Per Svartvadet, Atla.	3.00	.25
□□ 124 David Tanabe, Caro.	3.00	.25
□□ 125 Brad Stuart, SanJ.	8.00	.50
□□ 126 Mike York, NYRa.	6.00	.50
□□ 127 Jiri Fischer, Detr.	4.00	.25
□□ 128 Peter Schaefer, Vanc.	3.00	.25
□□ 129 Martin Biron (G), Buff.	9.00	.50
□□ 130 Rico Fata, Calg.	4.00	.25
□□ 131 Jean-Pierre Dumont, Chic.	4.00	.25
□□ 132 Martin Skoula, Colo.	4.00	.25
□□ 133 Alex Tanguay, Colo.	12.00	1.00
□□ 134 Mike Ribeiro, Mont.	6.00	.50
□□ 135 David Legwand, Nash.	8.00	.50
□□ 136 Scott Gomez, NJer.	8.00	.50
□□ 137 Tim Connolly, NYIs.	8.00	.50
□□ 138 Jan Hlavac, NYRa.	4.00	.25
□□ 139 Simon Gagné, Phil.	16.00	1.50
□□ 140 Brian Boucher (G), Phil.	6.00	.50
Autograph		**CTW**
Checklist		**CL**
□ Curtis Joseph (G), Toro.		1.00
Autograph		**CTW**
□ CTW1 Chris Drury, Colo. ✍		25.00

CALLING ALL CALDERS

Insert Set (10 cards):	**35.00**
Insert (1:16)	**CAC**
□ CAC1 Chris Drury, Colo.	3.00
□ CAC2 Sergei Samsonov, Bost.	3.00
□ CAC3 Daniel Alfredsson, Otta.	3.00
□ CAC4 Peter Forsberg, Colo.	7.00

□	CAC5 Martin Brodeur (G), NJer.	8.00
□	CAC6 Teemu Selänne, Anah.	4.00
□	CAC7 Pavel Bure, Flor.	4.00
□	CAC8 Ed Belfour (G), Dall.	5.00
□	CAC9 Joe Nieuwendyk, Dall.	2.00
□	CAC10 Brian Leetch, NYRa.	3.00

CLUB SIGNINGS

Insert Set (9 cards):		1000.00
	Autograph	CS
□	Raymond Bourque, Bost. ✍	85.00
□	Johnny Bower, Toro. ✍	35.00
□	Jaromir Jagr, Pitt. ✍	125.00
□	Curtis Joseph (G), Toro. ✍	60.00
□	Mario Lemieux, Pitt. ✍	185.00
□	Cam Neely, Bost. ✍	60.00
□	1 R. Bourque ✍ / C. Neely ✍	175.00
□	2 J. Bower ✍ / Cu. Joseph ✍	100.00
□	3 J. Jagr ✍ / M. Lemieux ✍	375.00

CODE RED

Insert Set (8 cards):		30.00
	Insert (1:40 packs)	CR
□	CR1 Keith Tkachuk, Phoe.	3.00
□	CR2 Teemu Selänne, Anah.	4.00
□	CR3 Zigmund Palffy, LosA.	3.00
□	CR4 Steve Yzerman, Detr.	12.00
□	CR5 Theoren Fleury, NYRa.	3.00
□	CR6 Jaromir Jagr, Pitt.	5.00
□	CR7 Peter Bondra, Wash.	3.00
□	CR8 Pavel Bure, Flor.	4.00

FEATURE PRESENTATIONS

Insert Set (8 cards):		20.00
	Insert (1:10 packs)	FP
□	FP1 Joe Sakic, Colo.	4.00
□	FP2 Mark Messier, Vanc.	3.00
□	FP3 Steve Yzerman, Detr.	7.00
□	FP4 Mike Modano, Dall.	3.00
□	FP5 Paul Kariya, Anah.	4.00
□	FP6 Pavel Bure, Flor.	2.00
□	FP7 Jaromir Jagr, Pitt.	3.00
□	FP8 Raymond Bourque, Bost.	3.00

GAME PIECES

Insert Set (6 cards):		200.00
	Insert	GP
□	Chris Drury, Colo. ✂ [Stick]	60.00
□	Scott Gomez, NJer. ✂ [Jersey]	25.00
□	David Legwand, Nash. ✂ [Stick]	40.00
□	Nicklas Lidström, Detr. ✂ [Jersey]	35.00
□	Mike Richter (G), NYRa. ✂ [Stick]	45.00
□	Doug Weight, Edmo. ✂ [Jersey]	35.00

IMPERIAL GUARD

Insert Set (8 cards):		45.00
	Insert (1:40 packs)	IG
□	IG1 Ed Belfour (G), Dall.	6.00
□	IG2 Patrick Roy (G), Colo.	18.00
□	IG3 Martin Brodeur (G), NJer.	10.00
□	IG4 Dominik Hasek (G), Buff.	6.00
□	IG5 Curtis Joseph (G), Toro.	6.00
□	IG6 John Vanbiesbrouck (G), Phil.	3.00
□	IG7 Mike Richter (G), NYRa.	3.00
□	IG8 Byron Dafoe (G), Bost.	3.00

PREMIER ROOKIES

These cards have a Blue parallel.

Insert Set (10 cards):		75.00	15.00
	Inserts	PRB	PR
□ □	PR1 Alex Tanguay, Colo.	16.00	3.00
□ □	PR2 Brad Stuart, SanJ.	10.00	2.00
□ □	PR3 Peter Schaefer, Vanc.	8.00	2.00
□ □	PR4 Scott Gomez, NJer.	10.00	2.00
□ □	PR5 Patrik Stefan, Atla.	8.00	2.00
□ □	PR6 Jochen Hecht, SLou.	8.00	2.00
□ □	PR7 David Legwand, Nash.	10.00	2.00
□ □	PR8 Steve Kariya, Vanc.	8.00	2.00
□ □	PR9 Jean-Pierre Dumont, Chic.	8.00	2.00
□ □	PR10 Simon Gagné, Phil.	20.00	4.00

PREMIER TEAM

These cards have a Blue parallel.

Insert Set (10 cards):		235.00	35.00
	Insert (1:229 packs)	PTB	PT
□ □	PT1 Paul Kariya, Anah.	30.00	5.00
□ □	PT2 Jaromir Jagr, Pitt.	20.00	3.00
□ □	PT3 Eric Lindros, Phil.	20.00	3.00
□ □	PT4 Mike Modano, Dall.	20.00	3.00
□ □	PT5 Mats Sundin, Toro.	20.00	3.00
□ □	PT6 Peter Forsberg, Colo.	30.00	5.00
□ □	PT7 Steve Yzerman, Detr.	50.00	9.00
□ □	PT8 Patrick Roy (G), Colo.	65.00	10.00
□ □	PT9 Martin Brodeur (G), NJer.	35.00	6.00
□ □	PT10 Dominik Hasek (G), Buff.	20.00	3.00

SIGNING BONUS

Insert Set (5 cards):		100.00
	Insert (1:229 packs)	Auto.
□	Scott Gomez, NJer. ✍	25.00
□	David Legwand, Nash. ✍	25.00
□	Peter Schaefer, Vanc. ✍	15.00
□	Patrik Stefan, Atla. ✍	20.00
□	Alex Tanguay, Colo. ✍	35.00

THE NEXT ONES

Insert Set (10 cards):		25.00
	Insert (1:10 packs)	TNO
□	TNO1 Vincent Lecavalier, Tamp.	5.00
□	TNO2 Marian Hossa, Otta.	5.00
□	TNO3 Chris Drury, Colo.	3.00
□	TNO4 Joe Thornton, Bost.	6.00
□	TNO5 Steve Kariya, Vanc.	2.00
□	TNO6 David Legwand, Nash.	2.00
□	TNO7 Patrik Stefan, Atla.	3.00
□	TNO8 Milan Hejduk, Colo.	4.00

PRE-PRODUCTION SAMPLE

Complete Set (6 cards):		9.00
	Player	PP
□	PP1 Curtis Joseph (G), Toro.	2.50
□	PP2 Jean-Pierre Dumont, Chic.	1.00
□	PP3 Marian Hossa, Otta.	2.50
□	PP4 Saku Koivu, Mont.	2.00
□	PP5 Chris Drury, Colo.	1.50
□	PP6 Ron Francis, Caro.	1.50

1999 - 2000 ULTIMATE VICTORY

These cards were released in February 2000. There are four versions: the regular card, a Victory Collection parallel, an Ultimate Collection parallel (#/100) and a One of One parallel (#/1).

Shell Set (90 cards):		-	-	30.00
Complete Set (120 cards):		2485.00	230.00	140.00
Common Player:		5.00	.75	.25
	Player	UC100	VC	Reg.
□□□□	1 Paul Kariya	60.00	4.00	1.50
□□□□	2 Teemu Selänne	35.00	2.00	1.00
□□□□	3 Jason Marshall	5.00	.75	.25
□□□□	4 David Harlock	5.00	.75	.25
□□□□	5 Ray Ferraro	5.00	.75	.25
□□□□	6 Kelly Buchberger	5.00	.75	.25
□□□□	7 Sergei Samsonov	25.00	1.00	.50
□□□□	8 Raymond Bourque	50.00	3.00	1.50
□□□□	9 Darren Van Impe	5.00	.75	.25
□□□□	10 Dominik Hasek (G)	45.00	3.00	1.00
□□□□	11 Miroslav Satan	10.00	.75	.25
□□□□	12 Geoff Sanderson	10.00	.75	.25
□□□□	13 Valeri Bure	10.00	.75	.25
□□□□	14 Cale Hulse	5.00	.75	.25
□□□□	15 Cory Stillman	10.00	.75	.25
□□□□	16 Ron Francis	25.00	1.00	.50
□□□□	17 Andrei Kovalenko	5.00	.75	.25
□□□□	18 Sami Kapanen	10.00	.75	.25
□□□□	19 Tony Amonte	25.00	1.00	.50
□□□□	20 Steve Sullivan	10.00	.75	.25
□□□□	21 Doug Gilmour	25.00	1.00	.50
□□□□	22 Milan Hejduk	35.00	2.00	1.00
□□□□	23 Joe Sakic	70.00	4.00	2.00
□□□□	24 Patrick Roy (G)	135.00	9.00	3.50
□□□□	25 Chris Drury	25.00	1.00	.50
□□□□	26 Peter Forsberg	60.00	4.00	1.50
□□□□	27 Mike Modano	45.00	3.00	1.00
□□□□	28 Brett Hull	45.00	3.00	1.00
□□□□	29 Ed Belfour (G)	45.00	3.00	1.00
□□□□	30 Blake Sloan	5.00	.75	.25
□□□□	31 Steve Yzerman	105.00	7.00	3.00
□□□□	32 Chris Osgood (G)	25.00	1.00	.50
□□□□	33 Brendan Shanahan	45.00	3.00	1.00
□□□□	34 Larry Murphy	10.00	.75	.25
□□□□	35 Doug Weight	25.00	1.00	.50
□□□□	36 Christian Laflamme	5.00	.75	.25
□□□□	37 Alexander Selivanov	5.00	.75	.25
□□□□	38 Pavel Bure	35.00	2.00	1.00
□□□□	39 Jaroslav Spacek	5.00	.75	.25
□□□□	40 Viktor Kozlov	10.00	.75	.25
□□□□	41 Luc Robitaille	35.00	2.00	1.00
□□□□	42 Zigmund Palffy	25.00	1.00	.50
□□□□	43 Rob Blake	25.00	1.00	.50
□□□□	44 Saku Koivu	35.00	2.00	1.00
□□□□	45 Patrick Poulin	5.00	.75	.25
□□□□	46 Brian Savage	10.00	.75	.25
□□□□	47 David Legwand	15.00	1.00	.50
□□□□	48 Sergei Krivokrasov	5.00	.75	.25
□□□□	**49 Robert Valicevic RC**	**5.00**	**.75**	**.50**
□□□□	50 Martin Brodeur (G)	70.00	4.00	2.00
□□□□	51 Scott Stevens	15.00	1.00	.50
□□□□	52 Krzysztof Oliwa	10.00	.75	.25
□□□□	53 Jamie Heward	5.00	.75	.25
□□□□	54 Mariusz Czerkawski	10.00	.75	.25
□□□□	55 Kenny Jönsson	5.00	.75	.25
□□□□	56 Mike Richter (G)	20.00	1.00	.50
□□□□	57 Theoren Fleury	25.00	1.00	.50
□□□□	58 Tim Taylor	5.00	.75	.25
□□□□	59 Brian Leetch	25.00	1.00	.50
□□□□	60 Andreas Dackell	5.00	.75	.25
□□□□	61 Marian Hossa	45.00	3.00	1.00
□□□□	62 Ron Tugnutt (G)	15.00	1.00	.50
□□□□	63 Craig Berube	5.00	.75	.25
□□□□	64 Eric Lindros	45.00	3.00	1.00
□□□□	65 John LeClair	35.00	2.00	1.00
□□□□	66 Dallas Drake	5.00	.75	.25
□□□□	67 Keith Tkachuk	25.00	1.00	.50
□□□□	68 Jeremy Roenick	35.00	2.00	1.00
□□□□	69 Jaromir Jagr	45.00	3.00	1.00
□□□□	70 Martin Straka	10.00	.75	.25
□□□□	71 Rob (Jr.) Brown	5.00	.75	.25
□□□□	72 Marcus Ragnarsson	10.00	.75	.25
□□□□	73 Steve Shields (G)	10.00	.75	.25
□□□□	74 Owen Nolan	25.00	1.00	.50
□□□□	75 Jeff Friesen	10.00	.75	.25
□□□□	76 Pavol Demitra	15.00	1.00	.50
□□□□	77 Roman Turek (G)	20.00	1.00	.50
□□□□	78 Mike Eastwood	5.00	.75	.25
□□□□	79 Vincent Lecavalier	45.00	3.00	1.00
□□□□	80 Dan Cloutier (G)	15.00	1.00	.50
□□□□	81 Stan Drulia	5.00	.75	.25
□□□□	82 Mats Sundin	45.00	3.00	1.00
□□□□	83 Igor Korolev	5.00	.75	.25
□□□□	84 Curtis Joseph (G)	45.00	3.00	1.00
□□□□	85 Mark Messier	45.00	3.00	1.00
□□□□	86 Harry York	5.00	.75	.25
□□□□	87 Peter Schaefer	5.00	.75	.25
□□□□	88 Olaf Kölzig (G)	25.00	1.00	.50
□□□□	89 Steve Konowalchuk	10.00	.75	.25
□□□□	90 Peter Bondra	25.00	1.00	.50

PROSPECTS / GRETZKY

	Inserts	UC100	VC	Reg.
□□□□	**91 Patrik Stefan RC**	**40.00**	**10.00**	**8.00**
□□□□	**92 Brian Campbell RC**	**10.00**	**4.00**	**3.00**
□□□□	**93 Mikko Eloranta RC**	**10.00**	**4.00**	**3.00**
□□□□	**94 Oleg Saprykin RC**	**30.00**	**7.00**	**6.00**
□□□□	**95 Kyle Calder RC**	**35.00**	**9.00**	**6.00**
□□□□	**96 Jonathan Sim RC**	**10.00**	**4.00**	**3.00**
□□□□	**97 Marc Rodgers RC**	**10.00**	**4.00**	**3.00**
□□□□	**98 Paul Comrie RC**	**20.00**	**5.00**	**4.00**
□□□□	**99 Ivan Novoseltsev RC**	**25.00**	**6.00**	**5.00**
□□□□	**100 Jason Blake RC**	**30.00**	**7.00**	**6.00**
□□□□	**101 Brian Rafalski RC**	**30.00**	**7.00**	**6.00**
□□□□	**102 Jörgen Jönsson RC**	**25.00**	**6.00**	**5.00**
□□□□	**103 Nikolai Antropov RC**	**30.00**	**7.00**	**6.00**
□□□□	**104 Steve Kariya RC**	**30.00**	**7.00**	**6.00**
□□□□	**105 Glen Metropolit RC**	**20.00**	**5.00**	**4.00**
□□□□	**106 Jochen Hecht RC**	**35.00**	**9.00**	**6.00**
□□□□	**107 Sheldon Keefe RC**	**25.00**	**6.00**	**5.00**
□□□□	**108 Branislav Mezei RC**	**20.00**	**5.00**	**4.00**
□□□□	**109 Pavel Brendl RC**	**50.00**	**12.00**	**8.00**
□□□□	**110 Milan Kraft RC**	**50.00**	**12.00**	**8.00**
□□□□	111 Wayne Gretzky,SSM	90.00	6.00	4.00
□□□□	112 Wayne Gretzky, Edmo.	90.00	6.00	4.00
□□□□	113 Wayne Gretzky, Edmo.	90.00	6.00	4.00
□□□□	114 Wayne Gretzky, Edmo.	90.00	6.00	4.00
□□□□	115 Wayne Gretzky, Edmo.	90.00	6.00	4.00
□□□□	116 Wayne Gretzky, LosA.	90.00	6.00	4.00
□□□□	117 Wayne Gretzky, LosA.	90.00	6.00	4.00
□□□□	118 Wayne Gretzky, All-Star	90.00	6.00	4.00
□□□□	119 Wayne Gretzky, NYRa.	90.00	6.00	4.00
□□□□	120 Wayne Gretzky, Off-Ice	90.00	6.00	4.00

FROZEN FURY

Insert Set (10 cards):		40.00
	Insert (1:23 packs)	FF
□	FF-1 Eric Lindros, Phil.	4.00
□	FF-2 Paul Kariya, Anah.	6.00
□	FF-3 Pavel Bure, Flor.	3.00
□	FF-4 Steve Kariya, Vanc.	2.00
□	FF-5 Mike Modano, Dall.	4.00
□	FF-6 Patrik Stefan, Atla.	2.00
□	FF-7 Martin Brodeur (G), NJer.	7.00
□	FF-8 Jaromir Jagr, Pitt.	4.00
□	FF-9 Joe Sakic, Colo.	7.00
□	FF-10 Steve Yzerman, Detr.	10.00

LEGENDARY FABRICS

	Insert	LF
□	Bobby Orr, Bost. ✂ {#/99}	
□	Wayne Gretzky, NYRa. ✂ {#/99}	
□	Bobby Orr, Bost. ✍ ✂ {#/4}	

NET WORK

Insert Set (10 cards):		25.00
	Insert (1:11 packs)	NW
□	NW1 Dominik Hasek (G), Buff.	3.00
□	NW2 Patrick Roy (G), Colo.	10.00
□	NW3 Chris Osgood (G), Detr.	2.00
□	NW4 Ed Belfour (G), Dall.	3.00
□	NW5 Mike Richter (G), NYRa.	2.00
□	NW6 Roman Turek (G), SLou.	2.00
□	NW7 Steve Shields (G), SanJ.	2.00
□	NW8 Curtis Joseph (G), Toro.	3.00
□	NW9 Guy Hebert (G), Anah.	2.00
□	NW10 Martin Brodeur (G), NJer.	6.00

SMOKING GUNS

Insert Set (12 cards):		15.00
	Insert (1:11 packs)	SG
□	sg-1 Jaromir Jagr, Pitt.	2.00
□	sg-2 Paul Kariya, Anah.	3.00

sg-3 Sergei Fedorov, Detr.	2.00
sg-4 Steve Kariya, Vanc.	1.00
sg-5 Peter Forsberg, Colo.	3.00
sg-6 Marian Hossa, Otta.	2.00
sg-7 Theoren Fleury, NYRa.	1.00
sg-8 Patrik Stefan, Atla.	1.00
sg-9 Pavel Bure, Flor.	2.00
sg-10 Eric Lindros, Phil.	2.00
sg-11 Brett Hull, Dall.	2.00
sg-12 Teemu Selänne, Anah.	2.00

STATURE

Insert Set (10 cards):	**15.00**
Insert (1:6 packs)	**S**
S1 Paul Kariya, Anah.	2.00
S2 Joe Sakic, Colo.	3.00
S3 Peter Forsberg, Colo.	2.00
S4 Mike Modano, Dall.	2.00
S5 Brendan Shanahan, Detr.	2.00
S6 Pavel Bure, Flor.	1.00
S7 Martin Brodeur (G), NJer.	3.00
S8 Theoren Fleury, NYRa.	1.00
S9 Eric Lindros, Phil.	2.00
S10 Keith Tkachuk, Phoe.	1.00
S11 Jaromir Jagr, Pitt.	2.00
S12 Raymond Bourque, Bost.	2.00

THE VICTORS

Insert Set (8 cards):	**30.00**
Insert (1:23 packs)	**TV**
TV1 Mark Messier, Vanc.	3.00
TV2 Brett Hull, Dall.	3.00
TV3 Steve Yzerman, Detr.	8.00
TV4 Jaromir Jagr, Pitt.	3.00
TV5 Patrick Roy (G), Colo.	10.00
TV6 Martin Brodeur (G), NJer.	6.00
TV7 Peter Forsberg, Colo.	5.00
TV8 Theoren Fleury, NYRa.	2.00

ULTIMATE FABRICS

Insert	**UF**
UF Bobby Orr ✂ / Wayne Gretzky ✂ {#/99}	1500.00
UF Bobby Orr ✍ ✂ / Wayne Gretzky ✍ ✂ {#/10}	

UV EXTRA

Insert Set (8 cards):	**40.00**
Insert (1:23 packs)	**UV**
UV-1 Jaromir Jagr, Pitt.	3.00
UV-2 Patrick Roy (G), Colo.	10.00
UV-3 Pavel Bure, Flor.	3.00
UV-4 Bobby Orr, Bost.	15.00
UV-5 Paul Kariya, Anah.	5.00
UV-6 Peter Forsberg, Colo.	5.00
UV-7 Steve Yzerman, Detr.	8.00
UV-8 Eric Lindros, Phil.	3.00

1999 - 2000 ULTIMATE VICTORY – BUYBACKS

Buyback Autograph	**UV**
41 Luc Robitaille, LosA. ✍ {#/1}	

1999 - 2000 UPPER DECK

This series was distributed in two separate releases: a Series One release in October 1999 and a Series Two release in January 2000. For each series, there is a regular base card, a Bronze Exclusive parallel limited to 100 copies and a Gold Exclusive parallel limited to 1 copy each. In Series One, short-print subset cards 136-170 are seeded 1:4 packs. In Series Two, short-print subset cards 306-335 are seeded 1:4 packs.

Series One Set (170 cards):	**2900.00**	**105.00**
Series Two Set (165 cards):	**1300.00**	**80.00**
Common Player:	**5.00**	**.20**
Player	**BE100**	**Reg.**
1 Wayne Gretzky, Edmo.	140.00	3.00
2 Wayne Gretzky, Edmo.	140.00	3.00
3 Wayne Gretzky, Edmo.	140.00	3.00
4 Wayne Gretzky, Edmo.	140.00	3.00
5 Wayne Gretzky, Edmo.	140.00	3.00
6 Wayne Gretzky, Edmo.	140.00	3.00
7 Wayne Gretzky, Edmo.	140.00	3.00
8 Wayne Gretzky, Edmo.	140.00	3.00
9 Wayne Gretzky, Edmo.	140.00	3.00
10 Wayne Gretzky, LosA.	140.00	3.00
11 Paul Kariya, Anah.	60.00	1.00
12 Matt Cullen, Anah.	10.00	.20
13 Steve Rucchin, Anah.	10.00	.20
14 Fredrik Olausson, Anah.	10.00	.20
15 Damian Rhodes (G), Otta.	10.00	.20
16 Jody Hull, Phil.	5.00	.20
17 Raymond Bourque, Bost.	50.00	1.00
18 Joe Thornton, Bost.	50.00	1.00
19 Jonathan Girard, Bost.	5.00	.20
20 Shawn Bates, Bost.	5.00	.20
21 Byron Dafoe (G), Bost.	15.00	.20
22 Dominik Hasek (G), Buff.	45.00	1.00
23 Michael Peca, Buff.	15.00	.20
24 Miroslav Satan, Buff.	10.00	.20
25 Dixon Ward, Buff.	5.00	.20
26 Valeri Bure, Calg.	10.00	.20
27 Derek Morris, Calg.	10.00	.20
28 Jarome Iginla, Calg.	35.00	.50
29 Rico Fata, Calg.	10.00	.20
30 J-S Giguère (G), Calg.	35.00	.50
31 Arturs Irbe (G), Caro.	15.00	.20
32 Sami Kapanen, Caro.	10.00	.20
33 Gary Roberts, Caro.	15.00	.20
34 Bates Battaglia, Caro.	10.00	.20
35 Jean-Pierre Dumont, Chic.	10.00	.20
36 Ty Jones, Chic.	5.00	.20
37 Tony Amonte, Chic.	25.00	.50
38 Anders Eriksson, Chic.	5.00	.20
39 Peter Forsberg, Colo.	60.00	1.00
40 Adam Foote, Colo.	10.00	.20
41 Chris Drury, Colo.	25.00	.50
42 Milan Hejduk, Colo.	35.00	.50
43 Brett Hull, Dall.	45.00	1.00
44 Ed Belfour (G), Dall.	45.00	1.00
45 Jamie Langenbrunner, Dall.	10.00	.20
46 Derian Hatcher, Dall.	10.00	.20
47 Jonathan Sim, Dall. RC	**5.00**	**.50**
48 Joe Nieuwendyk, Dall.	15.00	.20
49 Steve Yzerman, Detr.	100.00	2.00
50 Brendan Shanahan, Detr.	45.00	1.00
51 Nicklas Lidström, Detr.	25.00	.50
52 Igor Larionov, Detr.	25.00	.50
53 Vyacheslav Kozlov, Detr.	10.00	.20
54 Bill Guerin, Edmo.	15.00	.20
55 Mike Grier, Edmo.	10.00	.20
56 Tommy Salo (G), Edmo.	15.00	.20
57 Tom Poti, Edmo.	5.00	.20
58 Mark Parrish, Flor.	15.00	.20
59 Pavel Bure, Flor.	35.00	.50
60 Scott Mellanby, Flor.	10.00	.20
61 Chris Allen, Flor.	5.00	.20
62 Rob Blake, LosA.	25.00	.50
63 Pavel Rosa, LosA.	5.00	.20
64 Donald Audette, LosA.	15.00	.20
65 Vladimir Tsyplakov, LosA.	5.00	.20
66 Manny Legacé (G), LosA.	10.00	.20
67 Saku Koivu, Mont.	35.00	.50
68 Eric Weinrich, Mont.	5.00	.20
69 Jeff Hackett (G), Mont.	10.00	.20
70 Arron Asham, Mont.	5.00	.20
71 Trevor Linden, NYIs.	15.00	.20
72 Cliff Ronning, Nash.	10.00	.20
73 David Legwand, Nash.	15.00	.20
74 Kimmo Timonen, Nash.	5.00	.20
75 Sergei Krivokrasov, Nash.	5.00	.20
76 Mike Dunham (G), Nash.	15.00	.20
77 Martin Brodeur (G), NJer.	70.00	1.50
78 Patrik Elias, NJer.	35.00	.50
79 Petr* Sykora, NJer.	15.00	.20
80 Vadim Sharifijanov, NJer.	5.00	.20
81 John Madden, NJer. RC	**20.00**	**2.00**
82 Eric Brewer, NYIs.	15.00	.20
83 Dimitri Nabokov, NYIs.	5.00	.20
84 Kenny Jönsson, NYIs.	5.00	.20
85 Zdeno Chara, NYIs.	10.00	.20
86 Wayne Gretzky, NYRa.	180.00	4.00
87 Mike Richter (G), NYRa.	20.00	.20
88 Adam Graves, NYRa.	15.00	.20
89 Manny Malhotra, NYRa.	10.00	.20
90 Alexei Yashin, Otta.	25.00	.50
91 Sami Salo, Otta.	5.00	.20
92 Marian Hossa, Otta.	45.00	1.00
93 Shawn McEachern, Otta.	10.00	.20
94 Eric Lindros, Phil.	45.00	1.00
95 Jean-Marc Pelletier (G), Phil.	5.00	.20
96 Rod Brind'Amour, Phil.	10.00	.20
97 Mark Recchi, Phil.	15.00	.20
98 Éric Desjardins, Phil.	10.00	.20
99 Robert Reichel, Phoe.	10.00	.20
100 Keith Tkachuk, Phoe.	25.00	.50
101 Robert Esche (G), Phoe. RC	**15.00**	**1.50**
102 Oleg Tverdovsky, Anah.	5.00	.20
103 Trevor Letowski, Phoe.	5.00	.20
104 Jaromir Jagr, Pitt.	45.00	1.00
105 Tom Barrasso (G), Pitt.	15.00	.20
106 Jan Hrdina, Pitt.	10.00	.20
107 Matthew Barnaby, Pitt.	5.00	.20
108 Vinent Damphousse, SanJ.	25.00	.20
109 Jeff Friesen, SanJ.	10.00	.20
110 Patrick Marleau, SanJ.	20.00	.20
111 Mike Ricci, SanJ.	10.00	.20
112 Scott Hannan, SanJ.	5.00	.20
113 Pavol Demitra, SLou.	15.00	.20
114 Al MacInnis, SLou.	15.00	.20
115 Lubos Bartecko, SLou.	5.00	.20
116 Jochen Hecht, SLou. RC	**15.00**	**1.50**
117 Vincent Lecavalier, Tamp.	45.00	1.00
118 Paul Mara, Tamp.	5.00	.20
119 Kevin Hodson (G), Tamp.	10.00	.20
120 Dan Cloutier (G), NYRa.	15.00	.20
121 Mats Sundin, Toro.	45.00	1.00
122 Danny Markov, Toro.	5.00	.20
123 Sergei Berezin, Toro.	10.00	.20
124 Steve Thomas, Toro.	10.00	.20
125 Tomas Kaberle, Toro.	10.00	.20
126 Mark Messier, Vanc.	45.00	1.00
127 Bill Muckalt, Vanc.	5.00	.20
128 Kevin Weekes (G), Vanc.	10.00	.20
129 Josh Holden, Vanc.	5.00	.20
130 Jaroslav Svejkovsky, Wash.	5.00	.20
131 Adam Oates, Wash.	15.00	.20
132 Peter Bondra, Wash.	25.00	.50
133 Jan Bulis, Wash.	5.00	.20
134 Wayne Gretzky, Edmo. [CL]	100.00	1.50
135 Wayne Gretzky, LosA. [CL]	100.00	1.50
136 Wayne Gretzky, NYRa.	180.00	10.00
137 Eric Lindros, Phil.	45.00	2.50
138 Jaromir Jagr, Pitt.	45.00	2.50
139 Paul Kariya, Anah.	60.00	3.50
140 Steve Yzerman, Detr.	105.00	6.00
141 Patrick Roy (G), Colo.	135.00	7.50
142 Chris Drury, Colo.	25.00	2.00
143 Sergei Samsonov, Bost.	25.00	2.00
144 Brett Hull, Dall.	45.00	2.50
145 Dominik Hasek (G), Buff.	45.00	2.50
146 Keith Tkachuk, Phoe.	25.00	2.00
147 Alexei Yashin, Otta.	25.00	2.00
148 Martin Brodeur (G), NJer.	70.00	4.00
149 Pavel Bure, Flor.	35.00	2.00
150 Paul Mara, Tamp.	5.00	2.00
151 Peter Bondra, Wash.	25.00	2.00
152 Mike Modano, Dall.	45.00	2.50
153 Teemu Selänne, Anah.	35.00	2.00
154 Peter Forsberg, Colo.	60.00	3.50
155 Brendan Shanahan, Detr.	45.00	2.50
156 Raymond Bourque, Bost.	50.00	3.00
157 Saku Koivu, Mont.	35.00	2.00
158 John LeClair, Phil.	35.00	2.00
159 Joe Sakic, Colo.	70.00	4.00
160 David Legwand, Nash.	15.00	2.00
161 Patrik Stefan, Atla. RC	**20.00**	**10.00**
162 Nick Boynton, Ottawa 67's	10.00	2.00
163 Roberto Luongo (G), CHL	35.00	4.00
164 Rico Fata, Calg.	10.00	2.00
165 Daniel Sedin, Swe.	15.00	2.00
166 Henrik Sedin, Swe.	15.00	2.00
167 Brad Stuart, CHL	15.00	2.00
168 Tony Amonte, Chic.	25.00	2.00
169 Oleg Saprykin, Seattle RC	**15.00**	**7.50**
170 Denis Shvidki, CHL	10.00	2.00
171 Guy Hebert (G), Anah.	10.00	.20
172 Niclas Hävelid, Anah. RC	**5.00**	**.50**
173 Oleg Tverdovsky, Anah.	5.00	.20
174 Teemu Selänne, Anah.	35.00	.50
175 Damian Rhodes (G), Atla.	10.00	.20
176 Nelson Emerson, Atla.	5.00	.20
177 Per Svartvadet, Atla.	5.00	.20
178 Ray Ferraro, Atla.	5.00	.20
179 Kelly Buchberger, Atla.	5.00	.20
180 Norm Maracle (G), Atla.	5.00	.20
181 Patrik Stefan, Atla.	20.00	.50
182 Dave Andreychuk, Bost.	10.00	.20
183 Sergei Samsonov, Bost.	25.00	.50
184 John Grahame (G), Bost. RC	**15.00**	**1.50**
185 Jason Allison, Bost.	25.00	.50
186 Kyle McLaren, Bost.	10.00	.20
187 Anson Carter, Bost.	15.00	.20
188 Martin Biron (G), Buff.	20.00	.20
189 Brian Campbell, Buff. RC	**5.00**	**.50**
190 Curtis Brown, Buff.	5.00	.20
191 Alexei Zhitnik, Buff.	5.00	.20
192 David Moravec, Buff. RC	**5.00**	**.50**
193 Oleg Saprykin, Calg.	15.00	.20
194 Grant Fuhr (G), Calg.	25.00	.50
195 Phil Housley, Calg.	10.00	.20
196 Marc* Savard, Calg.	10.00	.20
197 Robyn Regehr, Calg.	5.00	.20
198 Martin Gélinas, Caro.	10.00	.20
199 Ron Francis, Caro.	25.00	.50
200 Jeff O'Neill, Caro.	15.00	.20
201 Keith Primeau, Caro.	15.00	.20
202 Paul Ranheim, Caro.	5.00	.20
203 Kyle Calder, Chic. RC	**15.00**	**1.50**
204 Jocelyn Thibault (G), Chic.	15.00	.20
205 Wendel Clark, Chic.	35.00	.50
206 Doug Gilmour, Chic.	25.00	.50
207 Josef Marha, Chic.	5.00	.20
208 Alexei Zhamnov, Chic.	10.00	.20
209 Dan Hinote, Colo. RC	**10.00**	**1.00**
210 Patrick Roy (G), Colo.	135.00	3.00
211 Joe Sakic, Colo.	70.00	1.50
212 Alex Tanguay, Colo.	25.00	.50
213 Sandis Ozolinsh, Colo.	10.00	.20
214 Adam Deadmarsh, Colo.	10.00	.20
215 Jere Lehtinen, Dall.	10.00	.20
216 Mike Modano, Dall.	45.00	1.00
217 Darryl Sydor, Dall.	10.00	.20
218 Sergei Zubov, Dall.	10.00	.20
219 Pavel Patera, Dall. RC	**5.00**	**.50**
220 Jamie Pushor, Dall.	5.00	.20
221 Chris Osgood (G), Detr.	25.00	.50
222 Tomas Holmström, Detr.	10.00	.20
223 Chris Chelios, Detr.	25.00	.50
224 Sergei Fedorov, Detr.	45.00	1.00
225 Jiri Fischer, Detr.	10.00	.20
226 Paul Comrie, Edmo. RC	**10.00**	**1.00**
227 Frantisek (Frank) Musil, Edmo.	10.00	.20
228 Janne Niinimaa, Edmo.	10.00	.20
229 Doug Weight, Edmo.	25.00	.50
230 Trevor Kidd (G), Flor.	10.00	.20
231 Oleg Kvasha, Flor.	5.00	.20
232 Viktor Kozlov, Flor.	10.00	.20
233 Rob Niedermayer, Flor.	10.00	.20
234 Luc Robitaille, LosA.	35.00	.50
235 Aki Berg, LosA.	5.00	.20
236 Bryan Smolinski, LosA.	5.00	.20
237 Jozef Stumpel, LosA.	10.00	.20
238 Zigmund Palffy, LosA.	25.00	.50
239 Stéphane Fiset (G), LosA.	10.00	.20
240 Jason Blake, LosA. RC	**15.00**	**1.50**
241 Scott Lachance, Mont.	5.00	.20
242 Vladimir Malakhov, Mont.	5.00	.20
243 Mike Ribeiro, Mont.	10.00	.50
244 Brian Savage, Mont.	10.00	.20
245 Tomas Vokoun (G), Nash.	10.00	.20
246 Randy Robitaille, Nash.	5.00	.20
247 Sergei Nemchinov, NJer.	10.00	.20
248 Brendan Morrison, NJer.	10.00	.20
249 Scott Niedermayer, NJer.	10.00	.20
250 Scott Stevens, NJer.	15.00	.20
251 Scott Gomez, NJer.	15.00	.50
252 Mark Lawrence, NYIs.	5.00	.20
253 Félix Potvin (G), NYIs.	25.00	.50
254 Olli Jokinen, NYIs.	10.00	.20
255 Tim Connolly, NYIs.	15.00	.50
256 Mariusz Czerkawski, NYIs.	10.00	.20
257 Valeri Kamensky, NYRa.	10.00	.20
258 Brian Leetch, NYRa.	25.00	.50
259 Petr Nedved, NYRa.	10.00	.20
260 Theoren Fleury, NYRa.	25.00	.50
261 Kevin Hatcher, NYRa.	5.00	.20
262 Mike York, NYRa.	10.00	.20
263 Ron Tugnutt (G), Otta.	15.00	.20
264 Chris Phillips, Otta.	10.00	.20
265 Daniel Alfredsson, Otta.	25.00	.50
266 Radek Bonk, Otta.	10.00	.20
267 Wade Redden, Otta.	10.00	.20
268 John Vanbiesbrouck (G), Phil.	20.00	.20
269 John LeClair, Phil.	35.00	.50
270 Simon Gagné, Phil.	35.00	1.50
271 Nikolai Khabibulin (G), Phoe.	15.00	.20
272 Daniel Brière, Phoe.	20.00	.20
273 Jeremy Roenick, Phoe.	35.00	.50
274 Andrew Ference, Pitt.	5.00	.20
275 Alexei Kovalev, Pitt.	25.00	.50
276 Martin Straka, Pitt.	10.00	.20
277 Aleksey Morozov, Pitt.	10.00	.20
278 Steve Shields (G), SanJ.	10.00	.20
279 Marco Sturm, SanJ.	10.00	.20
280 Niklas Sundström, SanJ.	10.00	.20
281 Brad Stuart, SanJ.	15.00	.20
282 Owen Nolan, SanJ.	25.00	.50
283 Roman Turek (G), SLou.	20.00	.20
284 Chris Pronger, SLou.	25.00	.50
285 Jim Campbell, SLou.	5.00	.20
286 Michal Handzus, SLou.	10.00	.20
287 Pierre Turgeon, SLou.	15.00	.20
288 Darcy Tucker, Tamp.	10.00	.20
289 Andrei Zyuzin, Tamp.	5.00	.20
290 Stephen Guolla, Tamp.	5.00	.20
291 Curtis Joseph (G), Toro.	45.00	1.00
292 Jonas Höglund, Toro.	5.00	.20
293 Bryan Berard, Toro.	10.00	.20
294 Mike Johnson, Toro.	5.00	.20
295 Garth Snow (G), Vanc.	10.00	.20
296 Jason Strudwick, Vanc.	5.00	.20

□□□	**297 Steve Kariya, Vanc. RC**	**15.00**	**1.50**
□□□	298 Markus Näslund, Vanc.	45.00	1.00
□□□	299 Mattias Öhlund, Vanc.	10.00	.20
□□□	300 Alexander Mogilny, Vanc.	20.00	.20
□□□	301 Olaf Kölzig (G), Wash.	25.00	.50
□□□	**302 Alexei Tezikov, Wash. RC**	**5.00**	**.50**
□□□	**303 Al. (Jr.) Volchkov, Wash. RC**	**5.00**	**.50**
□□□	304 Steve Yzerman, Detr. [Checklist]	60.00	.50
□□□	305 Curtis Joseph (G), Toro. [Checklist]	25.00	.20
□□□	**306 P. Brendl, Calgary Hitmen RC**	**20.00**	**10.00**
□□□	307 Daniel Sedin, MoDo	15.00	2.00
□□□	308 Henrik Sedin, MoDo	15.00	2.00
□□□	**309 Sheldon Keefe, Barrie Colts RC**	**10.00**	**6.00**
□□□	**310 R. Jardine, Sault Ste. Marie RC**	**10.00**	**5.00**
□□□	311 Maxime Ouellet (G), Québec	10.00	2.00
□□□	312 Barret Jackman, Regina Pats	15.00	2.00
□□□	**313 Kristian Kudroc, Québec RC**	**10.00**	**5.00**
□□□	**314 B. Mezei, Belleville Bulls RC**	**10.00**	**5.00**
□□□	315 Denis Shvidki, Barrie Colts	10.00	2.00
□□□	316 Brian Finley (G), Barrie Colts	5.00	2.00
□□□	317 Jonathan Cheechoo, Belleville	10.00	2.00
□□□	318 Mark Bell, Ottawa 67s	10.00	2.00
□□□	319 Taylor Pyatt, Sudbury Wolves	10.00	2.00
□□□	320 Norm Milley, Sudbury Wolves	5.00	2.00
□□□	321 Jamie Lundmark, Moose Jaw	10.00	2.00
□□□	**322 Alexander Buturlin, Sarnia RC**	**5.00**	**3.00**
□□□	**323 Jaroslav Kristek, Tri-City RC**	**5.00**	**3.00**
□□□	324 Kris Beech, Calgary Hitmen	10.00	2.00
□□□	325 Scott Kelman, Seattle	5.00	2.00
□□□	**326 Milan Kraft, Prince Albert RC**	**20.00**	**10.00**
□□□	327 Mattias Weinhandl, MoDo	5.00	2.00
□□□	328 Alexei Volkov (G), Halifax	10.00	2.00
□□□	**329 Andrei Shefer, Halifax RC**	**5.00**	**3.00**
□□□	330 Mat. Chouinard (G), Shawinigan	5.00	2.00
□□□	331 Justin Papineau, Belleville Bulls	5.00	2.00
□□□	332 Mike Van Ryn, Sarnia Sting	10.00	2.00
□□□	333 Jeff Heerema, Sarnia Sting	5.00	2.00
□□□	334 Michael Zigomanis, Calgary	5.00	2.00
□□□	**335 Bryan Kazarian, Owen Sound RC**	**5.00**	**3.00**

ALL-STAR CLASS

There are three versions: the regular insert (1:23 packs), the Quantum Silver parallel (#/100) and the Quantum Gold parallel (#/1).

Series Two Insert Set (20 cards): 935.00 85.00

	Inserts	QS	AS
□□□	AS1 Dominik Hasek (G), Buff.	45.00	4.00
□□□	AS2 Patrick Roy (G), Colo.	135.00	13.00
□□□	AS3 Jaromir Jagr, Pitt.	45.00	4.00
□□□	AS4 Paul Kariya, Anah.	60.00	6.00
□□□	AS5 Teemu Selänne, Anah.	35.00	3.00
□□□	AS6 Keith Tkachuk, Phoe.	25.00	2.00
□□□	AS7 Pavel Bure, Flor.	35.00	3.00
□□□	AS8 John LeClair, Phil.	35.00	3.00
□□□	AS9 Mats Sundin, Toro.	45.00	4.00
□□□	AS10 Steve Yzerman, Detr.	100.00	10.00
□□□	AS11 Peter Forsberg, Colo.	60.00	6.00
□□□	AS12 Eric Lindros, Phil.	45.00	4.00
□□□	AS13 Steve Kariya, Vanc.	15.00	2.00
□□□	AS14 Ed Belfour (G), Dall.	45.00	4.00
□□□	AS15 Nicklas Lidström, Detr.	25.00	2.00
□□□	AS16 Raymond Bourque, Bost.	50.00	5.00
□□□	AS17 Sandis Ozolinsh, Colo.	10.00	1.50
□□□	AS18 Al MacInnis, SLou.	15.00	1.50
□□□	AS19 Martin Brodeur (G), NJer.	70.00	7.00
□□□	AS20 Patrik Stefan, Atla.	20.00	2.00

NEW ICE AGE

There are three versions: the regular insert (1:23 packs), the Quantum Silver parallel (#/100) and the Quantum Gold parallel (#/1).

Series One Insert Set (20 cards): 485.00 45.00

	Inserts	QS	NIA
□□□	N1 Jaromir Jagr, All-Star '99	45.00	4.00
□□□	N2 Paul Kariya, Anah.	60.00	6.00
□□□	N3 Sergei Samsonov, Bost.	25.00	2.00
□□□	N4 Vadim Sharifijanov, NJer.	5.00	1.50
□□□	N5 Ty Jones, Chic.	5.00	1.50
□□□	N6 Teemu Selänne, Anah.	35.00	3.00
□□□	N7 Martin Brodeur (G), NJer.	70.00	7.00
□□□	N8 David Legwand, Nash.	15.00	1.50
□□□	N9 Vincent Lecavalier, Tamp.	45.00	4.00
□□□	N10 Paul Mara, Tamp.	5.00	1.50
□□□	N11 Jean-Marc Pelletier (G), Phil.	5.00	1.50
□□□	N12 J-S Giguère (G), Calg.	35.00	3.00
□□□	N13 Marian Hossa, Otta.	45.00	4.00
□□□	N14 Milan Hejduk, Colo.	35.00	3.00
□□□	N15 Chris Drury, Colo.	25.00	2.00
□□□	N16 Rico Fata, Calg.	10.00	1.50
□□□	N17 Patrik Elias, NJer.	35.00	3.00
□□□	N18 Eric Brewer, NYIs.	15.00	1.50
□□□	N19 Joe Thornton, Bost.	50.00	5.00
□□□	N20 Jean-Pierre Dumont, Chic.	10.00	1.50

CRUNCH TIME

There are three versions: the regular insert (1:4 packs), the Quantum Silver parallel (#/100) and the Quantum Gold parallel (#/1).

Series One Insert Set (30 cards): 565.00 25.00

	Inserts	QS	CT
□□□	CT1 Vincent Lecavalier, Tamp.	45.00	2.00
□□□	CT2 Steve Yzerman, Detr.	100.00	6.00
□□□	CT3 Curtis Joseph (G), Toro.	45.00	2.00
□□□	CT4 Jean-Marc Pelletier (G), Phil.	5.00	1.00
□□□	CT5 Brendan Shanahan, Detr.	45.00	2.00
□□□	CT6 Joe Sakic, Colo.	70.00	4.00
□□□	CT7 J-S Giguère (G), Calg.	35.00	2.00
□□□	CT8 Brett Hull, Dall.	45.00	2.00
□□□	CT9 Jaromir Jagr, Pitt.	45.00	2.00
□□□	CT10 Eric Brewer, NYIs.	15.00	1.00
□□□	CT11 Sergei Samsonov, Bost.	25.00	1.00
□□□	CT12 Alexei Yashin, Otta.	25.00	1.00
□□□	CT13 Mats Sundin, Toro.	45.00	2.00
□□□	CT14 Mike Modano, Dall.	45.00	2.00
□□□	CT15 Al MacInnis, SLou.	15.00	1.00
□□□	CT16 Paul Mara, Tamp.	5.00	1.00
□□□	CT17 David Legwand, Nash.	15.00	1.00
□□□	CT18 Eric Lindros, Phil.	45.00	2.00
□□□	CT19 Peter Forsberg, Colo.	60.00	3.00
□□□	CT20 Raymond Bourque, Bost.	50.00	3.00
□□□	CT21 Teemu Selänne, Anah.	35.00	2.00
□□□	CT22 John LeClair, Phil.	35.00	2.00
□□□	CT23 Dominik Hasek (G), Buff.	45.00	2.00
□□□	CT24 Martin Brodeur (G), NJer.	70.00	4.00
□□□	CT25 Tony Amonte, Chic.	25.00	1.00
□□□	CT26 Keith Tkachuk, Phoe.	25.00	1.00
□□□	CT27 Patrick Roy (G), Colo.	135.00	7.00
□□□	CT28 Pavel Bure, Flor.	35.00	2.00
□□□	CT29 Paul Kariya, Anah.	60.00	3.00
□□□	CT30 Peter Bondra, Wash.	25.00	1.00

SIXTH SENSE

There are three versions: the regular insert (1:5 packs), the Quantum Silver parallel (#/100) and the Quantum Gold parallel (#/1).

Series Two Insert Set (20 cards): 790.00 35.00

	Inserts	QS	SS
□□□	SS1 Paul Kariya, Anah.	60.00	3.00
□□□	SS2 Patrick Roy (G), Colo.	135.00	7.00
□□□	SS3 Brett Hull, Dall.	45.00	2.00
□□□	SS4 Eric Lindros, Phil.	45.00	2.00
□□□	SS5 Sergei Samsonov, Bost.	25.00	1.00
□□□	SS6 Peter Forsberg, Colo.	60.00	3.00
□□□	SS7 Patrik Stefan, Atla.	20.00	1.00
□□□	SS8 Steve Yzerman, Detr.	100.00	6.00
□□□	SS9 Jaromir Jagr, Pitt.	45.00	2.00
□□□	SS10 David Legwand, Nash.	15.00	1.00
□□□	SS11 Steve Kariya, Vanc.	15.00	1.00
□□□	SS12 Tim Connolly, NYIs.	15.00	1.00
□□□	SS13 Pavel Bure, Flor.	35.00	2.00
□□□	SS14 Brendan Shanahan, Detr.	45.00	2.00
□□□	SS15 Martin Brodeur (G), NJer.	70.00	4.00
□□□	SS16 Dominik Hasek (G), Buff.	45.00	2.00
□□□	SS17 Mats Sundin, Toro.	45.00	2.00
□□□	SS18 Vincent Lecavalier, Tamp.	45.00	2.00
□□□	SS19 Keith Tkachuk, Phoe.	25.00	1.00
□□□	SS20 Mike Modano, Dall.	45.00	2.00

FANTASTIC FINISHERS

There are three versions: the regular insert (1:11 packs), the Quantum Silver parallel (#/100) and the Quantum Gold parallel (#/1).

Series One Insert Set (15 cards): 510.00 30.00

	Inserts	QS	FF
□□□	FF1 Brett Hull, Dall.	45.00	3.00
□□□	FF2 John LeClair, Phil.	35.00	2.00
□□□	FF3 Eric Lindros, Phil.	45.00	3.00
□□□	FF4 Jaromir Jagr, Pitt.	45.00	3.00
□□□	FF5 Sergei Samsonov, Bost.	25.00	1.00
□□□	FF6 Teemu Selänne, Anah.	35.00	2.00
□□□	FF7 Alexei Yashin, Otta.	25.00	1.00
□□□	FF8 Keith Tkachuk, Phoe.	25.00	1.00
□□□	FF9 Pavel Bure, Flor.	35.00	2.00
□□□	FF10 Peter Forsberg, Colo.	60.00	4.00
□□□	FF11 Brendan Shanahan, Detr.	45.00	3.00
□□□	FF12 Tony Amonte, Chic.	25.00	1.00
□□□	FF13 Paul Kariya, Anah.	60.00	4.00
□□□	FF14 Steve Yzerman, Detr.	100.00	7.00
□□□	FF15 Joe Sakic, Colo.	70.00	4.00

MARQUEE ATTRACTIONS

There are three versions: the regular insert (1:11 packs), the Quantum Silver parallel (#/100) and the Quantum Gold parallel (#/1).

Series One Insert Set (15 cards): 630.00 40.00

	Inserts	QS	MA
□□□	MA1 Raymond Bourque, Bost.	50.00	3.00
□□□	MA2 Paul Kariya, Anah.	60.00	4.00
□□□	MA3 Eric Lindros, Phil.	45.00	3.00
□□□	MA4 Jaromir Jagr, Pitt.	45.00	3.00
□□□	MA5 Dominik Hasek (G), Buff.	45.00	3.00
□□□	MA6 Patrick Roy (G), Colo.	135.00	9.00
□□□	MA7 Alexei Yashin, Otta.	25.00	1.00
□□□	MA8 Mats Sundin, Toro.	45.00	3.00
□□□	MA9 Steve Yzerman, Detr.	100.00	7.00
□□□	MA10 Pavel Bure, Flor.	35.00	2.00
□□□	MA11 Vincent Lecavalier, Tamp.	45.00	3.00
□□□	MA12 Teemu Selänne, Anah.	35.00	2.00
□□□	MA13 Mike Modano, Dall.	45.00	3.00
□□□	MA14 Keith Tkachuk, Phoe.	25.00	1.00
□□□	MA15 Peter Forsberg, Colo.	60.00	4.00

GRETZKY PROFILES

There are three versions: the regular insert (1:23 packs), the Quantum Silver parallel (#/100) and the Quantum Gold parallel (#/1).

Series One Insert Set (10 cards): 1020.00 100.00

	Inserts	QS	GP
□□□	GP1 Wayne Gretzky, Edmo.	120.00	12.00
□□□	GP2 Wayne Gretzky, Edmo.	120.00	12.00
□□□	GP3 Wayne Gretzky, Edmo.	120.00	12.00
□□□	GP4 Wayne Gretzky, All-Star	120.00	12.00
□□□	GP5 Wayne Gretzky, Cdn.	120.00	12.00
□□□	GP6 Wayne Gretzky, SLou.	120.00	12.00
□□□	GP7 Wayne Gretzky, NYRa.	120.00	12.00
□□□	GP8 Wayne Gretzky, NYRa.	120.00	12.00
□□□	GP9 Wayne Gretzky, NYRa.	120.00	12.00
□□□	GP10 Wayne Gretzky, NYRa.	120.00	12.00

HEADED FOR THE HALL

There are three versions: the regular insert (1:23 packs), the Quantum Silver parallel (#/100) and the Quantum Gold parallel (#/1). These cards have a HOF prefix.

Series Two Insert Set (10 cards): 765.00 60.00

	Inserts	QS	AS
□□□	HOF1 Wayne Gretzky, NYRa.	180.00	15.00
□□□	HOF2 Dominik Hasek (G), Buff.	45.00	3.00
□□□	HOF3 Raymond Bourque, Bost.	50.00	4.00
□□□	HOF4 Steve Yzerman, Detr.	100.00	9.00
□□□	HOF5 Jaromir Jagr, Pitt.	45.00	3.00
□□□	HOF6 Brett Hull, Dall.	45.00	3.00
□□□	HOF7 Eric Lindros, Phil.	45.00	3.00
□□□	HOF8 Adam Oates, Wash.	15.00	1.50
□□□	HOF9 Brian Leetch, NYRa.	25.00	2.00
□□□	HOF10 Patrick Roy (G), Colo.	135.00	11.00
□□□	HOF11 Mark Messier, Vanc.	45.00	3.00
□□□	HOF12 Luc Robitaille, LosA.	35.00	3.00
□□□	HOF13 Joe Sakic, Colo.	70.00	6.00
□□□	HOF14 Chris Chelios, Detr.	25.00	2.00
□□□	HOF15 Curtis Joseph (G), Toro.	45.00	3.00

ICE GALLERY

There are three versions: the regular insert (1:72 packs), the Quantum Silver parallel (#/100) and the Quantum Gold parallel (#/1).

Series Two Insert Set (10 cards): 420.00 100.00

	Inserts	QS	IG
□□□	IG1 Jaromir Jagr, Pitt.	45.00	11.00
□□□	IG2 Paul Kariya, Anah.	60.00	15.00
□□□	IG3 Peter Forsberg, Colo.	60.00	15.00
□□□	IG4 Dominik Hasek (G), Buff.	45.00	11.00
□□□	IG5 Patrick Roy (G), Colo.	135.00	30.00
□□□	IG6 Teemu Selänne, Anah.	35.00	9.00
□□□	IG7 Eric Lindros, Phil.	45.00	11.00
□□□	IG8 Patrik Stefan, Atla.	20.00	7.00
□□□	IG9 Steve Kariya, Vanc.	15.00	5.00
□□□	IG10 Pavel Bure, Flor.	35.00	9.00

NHL SCRAPBOOK

There are three versions: the regular insert (1:11 packs), the Quantum Silver parallel (#/100) and the Quantum Gold parallel (#/1).

Series Two Insert Set (15 cards): 650.00 40.00

	Inserts	QS	SB
□□□	SB-1 Patrick Roy (G), Colo.	135.00	9.00
□□□	SB-2 Raymond Bourque, Bost.	50.00	3.00
□□□	SB-3 Steve Yzerman, Detr.	100.00	7.00
□□□	SB-4 Jaromir Jagr, Pitt.	45.00	3.00
□□□	SB-5 Paul Kariya, Anah.	60.00	4.00
□□□	SB-6 Peter Forsberg, Colo.	60.00	4.00
□□□	SB-7 Pavel Bure, Flor.	35.00	2.00
□□□	SB-8 Curtis Joseph (G), Toro.	45.00	3.00
□□□	SB-9 Brett Hull, Dall.	45.00	3.00
□□□	SB-10 Eric Lindros, Phil.	45.00	3.00
□□□	SB-11 Teemu Selänne, Anah.	35.00	2.00
□□□	SB-12 Brendan Shanahan, Detr.	45.00	3.00
□□□	SB-13 John LeClair, Phil.	35.00	2.00
□□□	SB-14 Steve Kariya, Vanc.	15.00	2.00
□□□	SB-15 Patrik Stefan, Atla.	20.00	2.00

ULTIMATE DEFENSE

There are three versions: the regular insert (1:9 packs), the Quantum Silver parallel (#/100) and the Quantum Gold parallel (#/1).

	Series Two Insert Set (10 cards):	**365.00**	**15.00**
	Inserts	**QS**	**UD**
☐☐☐	UD-1 Byron Dafoe (G), Bost.	15.00	1.00
☐☐☐	UD-2 Dominik Hasek (G), Buff.	45.00	2.00
☐☐☐	UD-3 Patrick Roy (G), Colo.	135.00	7.00
☐☐☐	UD-4 Chris Osgood (G), Detr.	25.00	1.00
☐☐☐	UD-5 Ed Belfour (G), Dall.	45.00	2.00
☐☐☐	UD-6 Roman Turek (G), SLou.	20.00	1.00
☐☐☐	UD-7 Mike Richter (G), NYRa.	20.00	1.00
☐☐☐	UD-8 Nikolai Khabibulin (G), Phoe.	15.00	1.00
☐☐☐	UD-9 Martin Brodeur (G), NJer.	70.00	4.00
☐☐☐	UD-10 Curtis Joseph (G), Toro.	45.00	2.00

GAME JERSEY 1

There are up to four different versions for each card: the Game Jersey card (1:2500 packs or 1:287 Hobby packs), the Game Jersey Signed card (#/25), the Game Jersey Patch (1:7500 packs) and the Game Jersey Patch Gold (#/1). Cards in the Game Jersey Patch Gold series are marked below GJPG. The regular Dual Jersey card of Gretzky (WG-2) is limited to 99 copies.

	Game Jersey Set (18 cards):	**-**	**1700.00**
	Inserts	**GJP**	**GJ**
☐☐	Raymond Bourque, Bost. ✂	300.00	50.00
☐☐	Martin Brodeur (G), NJer. ✂	400.00	65.00
☐☐	Sergei Fedorov, Detr. ✂	250.00	40.00
☐☐☐	Peter Forsberg, Colo. ✂ [GJPG]	350.00	55.00
☐☐	WG-1 Gretzky, NYRa. ✂ [GJPG]	1000.00	175.00
☐	WG-2 Wayne Gretzky, NYRa. ✂ ✂	-	1000.00
☐☐	WG-3 Gretzky, NYRa. ✂ [GJPG]	1000.00	170.00
☐☐☐	Dominik Hasek (G), Buff. ✂ [GJPG]	250.00	40.00
☐☐	Brett Hull, Dall. ✂	250.00	40.00
☐☐☐	Jaromir Jagr, Pitt. ✂ [GJPG]	250.00	40.00
☐☐	John LeClair, All-Star '99	200.00	30.00
☐☐☐	Eric Lindros, Phil. ✂ [GJPG]	250.00	40.00
☐☐☐	Mike Modano, Dall. ✂ [GJPG]	250.00	40.00
☐☐☐	Patrick Roy (G), Colo. ✂ [GJPG]	600.00	100.00
☐☐	Joe Sakic, Colo. ✂	400.00	65.00
☐☐	Sergei Samsonov, Bost. ✂	150.00	30.00
☐☐☐	T. Selänne, All-Star '98 [GJPG]	200.00	30.00
☐☐	Steve Yzerman, Detr. ✂	600.00	100.00

GAME JERSEY 1 SIGNED

	Insert (#/25)	**GJA**
☐	Raymond Bourque, Bost. ✍ ✂	550.00
☐	Wayne Gretzky, NYRa. ✍ ✂	1700.00
☐	Brett Hull, Dall. ✍ ✂	400.00
☐	Steve Yzerman, Detr. ✍ ✂	900.00

GAME JERSEY 2

There are up to four different versions for each card: the Game Jersey card (1:2500 packs or 1:287 Hobby packs), the Game Jersey Signed card (#/25), the Game Jersey Patch (1:7500 packs) and the Game Jersey Patch Gold (#/1).

	Game Jersey Set (17 cards):	**-**	**900.00**
	Insert (1:252 packs)	**GJP**	**GJ**
☐☐☐	Ed Belfour (G), Dall. ✂ [GJPG]	250.00	40.00
☐☐	Martin Brodeur (G), NJer. ✂	400.00	65.00
☐☐	Sergei Fedorov, Detr. ✂	250.00	40.00
☐☐	Peter Forsberg, Colo. ✂	350.00	55.00
☐☐☐	Wayne Gretzky, NYRa. ✂ [GJPG]	1000.00	175.00
☐☐☐	Dominik Hasek (G), Buff. ✂ [GJPG]	250.00	40.00
☐☐☐	Jaromir Jagr, Pitt. ✂ [GJPG]	250.00	40.00
☐☐☐	Curtis Joseph (G), Toro. ✂ [GJPG]	250.00	40.00
☐☐☐	Paul Kariya, Anah. ✂ [GJPG]	350.00	55.00
☐☐☐	John LeClair, Phil. ✂ [GJPG]	200.00	30.00
☐☐	Al MacInnis, SLou. ✂	150.00	30.00
☐☐	Jeremy Roenick, Phoe. ✂	150.00	30.00
☐☐☐	Patrick Roy (G), Colo. ✂ [GJPG]	600.00	100.00
☐☐	Teemu Selänne, Anah. ✂	150.00	30.00
☐☐	Joe Thornton, Bost. ✂	300.00	50.00
☐☐☐	Steve Yzerman, Detr. ✂ [GJPG]	600.00	100.00
☐☐	SY-C Steve Yzerman, Detr. ✂	150.00	180.00

GAME JERSEY 2 SIGNED

	Insert (1:252 packs)	**GJP**
☐	Ed Belfour (G), Dall. ✍ ✂	475.00
☐	Wayne Gretzky, NYRa. ✍ ✂	1700.00
☐	Curtis Joseph (G), Toro. ✍ ✂	400.00
☐	Steve Yzerman, Detr. ✍ ✂	900.00

GAME PADS

	Game Pads (1:1500 packs)	**GP**
☐	Curtis Joseph (G), Toro. ✂	200.00

POWERDECK

	Insert Set (9 cards):	**205.00**
	Insert (1:252 packs)	**PD**
☐	PD1 Dominik Hasek (G), Buff.	6.00
☐	PD2 Paul Kariya, Anah.	8.00
☐	PD3 Jaromir Jagr, Pitt.	6.00
☐	PD4 Steve Yzerman, Detr.	15.00
☐	PD5 Patrick Roy (G), Colo.	18.00
☐	PD6 Brett Hull, Dall.	6.00
☐	PD7 Wayne Gretzky, NYRa.	25.00
☐	PD8 Wayne Gretzky, LosA.	80.00
☐	PD9 Wayne Gretzky, Edmo.	80.00

1999 - 2000 UPPER DECK – BUYBACKS

	Buyback Autograph	**UD**
☐	9 Wayne Gretzky, Edmo. ✍ {#/1}	
☐	10 Wayne Gretzky, LosA. ✍ {#/1}	
☐	49 Steve Yzerman, Detr. ✍ {#/1}	
☐	77 Martin Brodeur (G), NJer. ✍ {#/3}	
☐	87 Mike Richter (G), NYRa. ✍ {#/1}	
☐	100 Keith Tkachuk, Phoe. ✍ {#/25}	
☐	126 Mark Messier, Vanc. ✍ {#/4}	
☐	165 Daniel Sedin, Sweden ✍ {#/2}	
☐	166 Henrik Sedin, Sweden ✍ {#/3}	
☐	216 Mike Modano, Dall. ✍ {#/9}	
☐	234 Luc Robitaille, LosA. ✍ {#/3}	
☐	243 Mike Ribeiro, Mont. ✍ {#/25}	
☐	251 Scott Gomez, NJer. ✍ {#/9}	
☐	269 John LeClair, Phil. ✍ {#/2}	
☐	304 Steve Yzerman, Detr. ✍ {#/4}	
☐	306 Pavel Brendl, Calgary Hitmen ✍ {#/9}	
☐	307 Daniel Sedin, MoDo ✍ {#/10}	
☐	308 Henrik Sedin, MoDo ✍ {#/13}	
	Buyback Autograph • Game Jersey	**UD**
☐	Steve Yzerman ✂ ✍ {#/1}	
	Buyback Autograph • Game Jersey Patch	**UD**
☐	Steve Yzerman ✂ ✍ {#/1}	

1999 - 2000 UPPER DECK BLACK DIAMOND

This series was released in 1999-2000. Rookie subset cards are short printed. There are three versions for all base-numbered cards: a regular card, a Diamond Cut parallel and a Final Cut parallel (#/50).

	Shell Set (90 cards):	**-**	**-**	**45.00**
	Complete Set (120 cards):	**1800.00**	**200.00**	**115.00**
	Common Player:	**5.00**	**1.00**	**.20**
	Player	**FC50**	**DC**	**BD**
☐☐☐	1 Paul Kariya, Anah.	60.00	6.00	1.50
☐☐☐	2 Teemu Selänne, Anah.	35.00	3.00	1.00
☐☐☐	3 Guy Hebert (G), Anah.	10.00	1.00	.20
☐☐☐	4 Damian Rhodes (G), Atla.	10.00	1.00	.20
☐☐☐	**5 Patrik Stefan, Atla. RC**	**20.00**	**2.00**	**3.00**
☐☐☐	**6 Dean Sylvester, Atla. RC**	**5.00**	**1.00**	**1.00**
☐☐☐	7 Sergei Samsonov, Bost.	25.00	2.00	.50
☐☐☐	8 Byron Dafoe (G), Bost.	15.00	1.00	.50
☐☐☐	9 Raymond Bourque, Bost.	50.00	5.00	1.50
☐☐☐	10 Joe Thornton, Bost.	50.00	5.00	1.50
☐☐☐	11 Dominik Hasek (G), Buff.	45.00	4.00	1.00
☐☐☐	12 Michael Peca, Buff.	15.00	1.00	.50
☐☐☐	13 Miroslav Satan, Buff.	10.00	1.00	.20
☐☐☐	14 Martin Biron (G), Buff.	20.00	2.00	.50
☐☐☐	**15 Oleg Saprykin, Calg. RC**	**15.00**	**2.00**	**2.00**
☐☐☐	16 Valeri Bure, Calg.	10.00	1.00	.20
☐☐☐	17 Robyn Regehr, Calg.	5.00	1.00	.20
☐☐☐	18 David Tanabe, Caro.	5.00	1.00	.20
☐☐☐	19 Arturs Irbe (G), Caro.	15.00	1.00	.50
☐☐☐	20 Sami Kapanen, Caro.	10.00	1.00	.20
☐☐☐	**21 Kyle Calder, Chic. RC**	**15.00**	**2.00**	**3.00**
☐☐☐	22 Tony Amonte, Chic.	25.00	2.00	.50
☐☐☐	23 Doug Gilmour, Chic.	25.00	2.00	.50
☐☐☐	24 Patrick Roy (G), Colo.	135.00	13.00	3.50
☐☐☐	25 Joe Sakic, Colo.	70.00	7.00	2.00
☐☐☐	26 Peter Forsberg, Colo.	60.00	6.00	1.50
☐☐☐	27 Chris Drury, Colo.	25.00	2.00	.50
☐☐☐	28 Milan Hejduk, Colo.	35.00	3.00	1.00
☐☐☐	29 Mike Modano, Dall.	45.00	4.00	1.00
☐☐☐	30 Brett Hull, Dall.	45.00	4.00	1.00
☐☐☐	31 Ed Belfour (G), Dall.	45.00	4.00	1.00
☐☐☐	**32 Jonathan Sim, Dall. RC**	**5.00**	**1.00**	**1.00**
☐☐☐	33 Nicklas Lidström, Detr.	25.00	2.00	.50
☐☐☐	34 Sergei Fedorov, Detr.	45.00	4.00	1.00
☐☐☐	35 Brendan Shanahan, Detr.	45.00	4.00	1.00
☐☐☐	36 Steve Yzerman, Detr.	105.00	10.00	3.00
☐☐☐	37 Chris Osgood (G), Detr.	25.00	2.00	.50
☐☐☐	**38 Paul Comrie, Edmo. RC**	**10.00**	**1.00**	**1.50**
☐☐☐	39 Bill Guerin, Edmo.	15.00	1.00	.50
☐☐☐	40 Doug Weight, Edmo.	25.00	2.00	.50
☐☐☐	41 Pavel Bure, Flor.	35.00	3.00	1.00
☐☐☐	**42 I. Novoseltsev, Flor. RC**	**10.00**	**1.00**	**2.00**
☐☐☐	43 Trevor Kidd (G), Flor.	10.00	1.00	.20
☐☐☐	44 Zigmund Palffy, LosA.	25.00	2.00	.50
☐☐☐	45 Luc Robitaille, LosA.	35.00	3.00	1.00
☐☐☐	46 Stéphane Fiset (G), LosA.	10.00	1.00	.20
☐☐☐	47 Mike Ribeiro, Mont.	10.00	1.00	.50
☐☐☐	48 Saku Koivu, Mont.	35.00	3.00	1.00
☐☐☐	49 David Legwand, Nash.	15.00	1.00	.50
☐☐☐	**50 R. Valicevic, Nash. RC**	**5.00**	**1.00**	**1.00**
☐☐☐	51 Martin Brodeur (G), NJer.	70.00	7.00	2.00
☐☐☐	52 Scott Gomez, NJer.	15.00	1.00	1.00
☐☐☐	**53 Brian Rafalski, NJer. RC**	**15.00**	**2.00**	**2.00**
☐☐☐	54 Tim Connolly, NYIs.	15.00	1.00	1.00
☐☐☐	**55 J. Jönsson, NYIs. RC**	**10.00**	**1.00**	**2.00**
☐☐☐	56 Theoren Fleury, NYRa.	25.00	2.00	.50
☐☐☐	57 Brian Leetch, NYRa.	25.00	2.00	.50
☐☐☐	58 Mike Richter (G), NYRa.	20.00	2.00	.50
☐☐☐	59 Marian Hossa, Otta.	45.00	4.00	1.00
☐☐☐	60 Radek Bonk, Otta.	10.00	1.00	.20
☐☐☐	**61 Mike Fisher, Otta. RC**	**15.00**	**2.00**	**2.00**
☐☐☐	62 Eric Lindros, Phil.	45.00	4.00	1.00
☐☐☐	63 Keith Primeau, Phil.	15.00	1.00	.50
☐☐☐	64 John LeClair, Phil.	35.00	3.00	1.00
☐☐☐	65 Jeremy Roenick, Phoe.	35.00	3.00	1.00
☐☐☐	66 Keith Tkachuk, Phoe.	25.00	2.00	.50
☐☐☐	**67 Mika Alatalo, Phoe. RC**	**10.00**	**1.00**	**1.50**
☐☐☐	68 Jaromir Jagr, Pitt.	45.00	4.00	1.00
☐☐☐	69 Martin Straka, Pitt.	10.00	1.00	.20
☐☐☐	70 Alexei Kovalev, Pitt.	25.00	2.00	.50
☐☐☐	**71 Jochen Hecht, SLou. RC**	**15.00**	**2.00**	**3.00**
☐☐☐	72 Pavol Demitra, SLou.	15.00	1.00	.50
☐☐☐	73 Chris Pronger, SLou.	25.00	2.00	.50
☐☐☐	74 Patrick Marleau, SanJ.	20.00	2.00	.50
☐☐☐	75 Owen Nolan, SanJ.	25.00	2.00	.50
☐☐☐	76 Jeff Friesen, SanJ.	10.00	1.00	.20
☐☐☐	77 Steve Shields (G), SanJ.	10.00	1.00	.20
☐☐☐	78 Vincent Lecavalier, Tamp.	45.00	4.00	1.00
☐☐☐	79 Dan Cloutier (G), Tamp.	15.00	1.00	.50
☐☐☐	**80 Adam Mair, Toro. RC**	**10.00**	**1.00**	**1.50**
☐☐☐	81 Mike Johnson, Toro.	5.00	1.00	.20
☐☐☐	82 Mats Sundin, Toro.	45.00	4.00	1.00
☐☐☐	**83 N. Antropov, Toro. RC**	**15.00**	**2.00**	**2.00**
☐☐☐	84 Curtis Joseph (G), Toro.	45.00	4.00	1.00
☐☐☐	**85 Steve Kariya, Vanc. RC**	**15.00**	**2.00**	**2.00**
☐☐☐	86 Mark Messier, Vanc.	45.00	4.00	1.00
☐☐☐	87 Alexander Mogilny, Vanc.	20.00	2.00	.50
☐☐☐	88 Olaf Kölzig (G), Wash.	25.00	2.00	.50
☐☐☐	89 Peter Bondra, Wash.	25.00	2.00	.50
☐☐☐	**90 A. Volchkov, Wash. RC**	**5.00**	**1.00**	**1.00**

DIAMONDS IN THE ROUGH

	Inserts	**FC50**	**DC**	**BD**
☐☐☐	**91 P. Brendl, CalgaryRC**	**20.00**	**9.00**	**8.00**
☐☐☐	92 J. Lundmark, Moose Jaw	10.00	2.50	2.00
☐☐☐	93 K. Beech, Calgary	10.00	2.50	2.00
☐☐☐	94 M. Zigomanis, Kingston	5.00	1.00	1.00
☐☐☐	**95 B. Mezei, Belleville RC**	**10.00**	**3.50**	**4.00**
☐☐☐	**96 S. Keefe, Barrie RC**	**10.00**	**4.50**	**5.00**
☐☐☐	97 B. Finley (G), Barrie	5.00	1.50	1.00
☐☐☐	98 T. Pyatt, Sudbury	10.00	2.00	1.00
☐☐☐	99 D. Shvidki, Barrie	10.00	2.00	1.00
☐☐☐	100 B. Jackman, Regina	15.00	3.50	3.00
☐☐☐	101 M. Ouellet (G), Québec	15.00	3.50	3.00
☐☐☐	**102 M. Kraft, P.Albert RC**	**20.00**	**9.00**	**8.00**
☐☐☐	**103 B. Ralph, Oshawa RC**	**10.00**	**3.50**	**4.00**
☐☐☐	104 A. Volkov (G), Halifax	10.00	2.00	1.00
☐☐☐	105 Chouinard (G), Shawinigan	5.00	1.00	1.00
☐☐☐	106 M. Bell, Ottawa	10.00	2.00	1.00
☐☐☐	**107 R. Jardine, SSM RC**	**10.00**	**3.50**	**4.00**
☐☐☐	**108 K. Kudroc, Québec RC**	**10.00**	**3.50**	**4.00**
☐☐☐	109 N. Milley, Sudbury	5.00	1.00	1.00
☐☐☐	110 J. Heerema, Sarnia	5.00	1.00	1.00
☐☐☐	**111 J. Kristek, Tri-City RC**	**5.00**	**2.00**	**2.00**
☐☐☐	**112 L. Sellars, Ottawa RC**	**10.00**	**3.50**	**4.00**
☐☐☐	**113 B. Kazarian, O.Sound RC**	**5.00**	**2.00**	**2.00**
☐☐☐	**114 B. Lysak, Regina RC**	**5.00**	**2.00**	**2.00**
☐☐☐	**115 A. Shefer, Halifax RC**	**5.00**	**2.00**	**2.00**
☐☐☐	**116 M. Sivek, P.Albert RC**	**10.00**	**3.50**	**4.00**
☐☐☐	117 J. Papineau, Belleville	5.00	1.00	1.00
☐☐☐	118 M. Weinhandl, MoDo	5.00	1.00	1.00
☐☐☐	119 D. Sedin, MoDo	15.00	3.50	3.00
☐☐☐	120 H. Sedin, MoDo	15.00	3.50	3.00

DIAMONATION

	Insert Set (20 cards):	**10.00**
	Insert (1:4 packs)	**D**
☐	D1 Paul Kariya, Anah.	3.00
☐	D2 Patrik Stefan, Atla.	2.00
☐	D3 Sergei Samsonov, Bost.	1.00
☐	D4 Teemu Selänne, Anah.	2.00
☐	D5 Patrick Roy (G), Colo.	7.00
☐	D6 Mike Modano, Dall.	2.00
☐	D7 Sergei Fedorov, Detr.	2.00
☐	D8 Pavel Bure, Flor.	2.00
☐	D9 David Legwand, Nash.	1.00
☐	D10 Martin Brodeur (G), NJer.	4.00
☐	D11 Theoren Fleury, NYIs.	1.00
☐	D12 Eric Lindros, Phil.	2.00
☐	D13 Keith Tkachuk, Phoe.	1.00
☐	D14 Jaromir Jagr, Pitt.	2.00
☐	D15 Mats Sundin, Toro.	2.00
☐	D16 Steve Kariya, Vanc.	1.00
☐	D17 Peter Bondra, Wash.	1.00
☐	D18 Peter Forsberg, Colo.	3.00
☐	D19 Steve Yzerman, Detr.	6.00
☐	D20 Zigmund Palffy, LosA.	1.00

DIAMOND MIGHT

	Insert Set (10 cards):	**20.00**
	Insert (1:9 packs)	**DM**
☐	DM1 Peter Forsberg, Colo.	4.00
☐	DM2 Brendan Shanahan, Detr.	3.00
☐	DM3 Eric Lindros, Phil.	3.00
☐	DM4 John LeClair, Phil.	2.00
☐	DM5 Jaromir Jagr, Pitt.	3.00
☐	DM6 Keith Tkachuk, Phoe.	1.50
☐	DM7 Teemu Selänne, Anah.	2.00
☐	DM8 Mats Sundin, Toro.	3.00
☐	DM9 Mark Messier, Vanc.	3.00
☐	DM10 Theoren Fleury, NYRa.	1.50

DIAMOND SKILLS

	Insert Set (10 cards):	**60.00**
	Insert (1:24 packs)	**DS**
☐	DS-1 Teemu Selänne, Anah.	5.00
☐	DS-2 Paul Kariya, Anah.	8.00
☐	DS-3 Patrick Roy (G), Colo.	18.00
☐	DS-4 Pavel Bure, Flor.	5.00
☐	DS-5 Sergei Fedorov, Detr.	6.00
☐	DS-6 Eric Lindros, Phil.	6.00
☐	DS-7 Jaromir Jagr, Pitt.	6.00
☐	DS-8 Martin Brodeur (G), NJer.	10.00
☐	DS-9 Theoren Fleury, NYRa.	3.00
☐	DS-10 Curtis Joseph (G), Toro.	6.00

MYRIAD

	Insert Set (10 cards):	**55.00**
	Insert (1:24 packs)	**M**
☐	M1 Patrik Stefan, Atla.	4.00
☐	M2 Teemu Selänne, Anah.	5.00
☐	M3 Sergei Samsonov, Bost.	3.00

☐	M4 Joe Sakic, Colo.	10.00
☐	M5 Brett Hull, Dall.	6.00
☐	M6 Pavel Bure, Flor.	5.00
☐	M7 Steve Yzerman, Detr.	15.00
☐	M8 Jaromir Jagr, Pitt.	6.00
☐	M9 Eric Lindros, Phil.	6.00
☐	M10 Paul Kariya, Anah.	8.00

A PIECE OF HISTORY

There are three versions: the regular insert (1:336 packs), the Double parallel (1:1008 packs) and the Triple parallel (#/1).

Insert Set (20 cards):		1425.00	765.00
	Inserts	POHD	POH
☐☐☐	Brett Hull, Dall. ✂ [Gold]	50.00	30.00
☐☐☐	Dominik Hasek (G), Buff. ✂ [Silver]	50.00	30.00
☐☐☐	Ed Belfour (G), Dall. ✂ [Gold]	50.00	30.00
☐☐☐	Eric Lindros, Phil. ✂ [Gold]	50.00	30.00
☐☐☐	Gordie Howe, Detr. ✂ [Gold]	175.00	85.00
☐☐☐	Jaromir Jagr, Pitt. ✂ [Silver]	50.00	30.00
☐☐☐	John LeClair, Phil. ✂ [Silver]	50.00	25.00
☐☐☐	Joe Sakic, Colo. ✂ [Gold]	100.00	50.00
☐☐☐	Keith Tkachuk, Phoe. ✂ [Gold]	40.00	25.00
☐☐☐	Martin Brodeur (G), NJer. ✂ [Gold]	100.00	50.00
☐☐☐	Mike Modano, Dall. ✂ [Silver]	50.00	30.00
☐☐☐	Pavel Bure, Flor. ✂ [Gold]	50.00	25.00
☐☐☐	Peter Forsberg, Colo. ✂ [Silver]	75.00	40.00
☐☐☐	Paul Kariya, Anah. ✂ [Gold]	75.00	40.00
☐☐☐	Patrick Roy (G), Colo. ✂ [Silver]	150.00	75.00
☐☐☐	Raymond Bourque, Bost. ✂ [Silver]	75.00	35.00
☐☐☐	Steve Yzerman, Detr. ✂ [Silver]	150.00	70.00
☐☐☐	Tim Connolly, NYIs. ✂ [Gold]	40.00	25.00
☐☐☐	Teemu Selänne, Anah. ✂ [Silver]	50.00	25.00
☐☐☐	Wayne Gretzky, NYRa. ✂ [Silver]	250.00	150.00

GORDIE HOWE GALLERY

Insert Set (10 cards):		65.00
	Insert (1:12 packs)	GH
☐	GH1 Gordie Howe, Detr.	8.00
☐	GH2 Gordie Howe, Detr.	8.00
☐	GH3 Gordie Howe, Detr.	8.00
☐	GH4 Gordie Howe, Detr.	8.00
☐	GH5 Gordie Howe, Detr.	8.00
☐	GH6 Gordie Howe, Detr.	8.00
☐	GH7 Gordie Howe, Detr.	8.00
☐	GH8 Gordie Howe, Detr.	8.00
☐	GH9 Gordie Howe, Hart.	8.00
☐	GH10 Gordie Howe, Off Ice	8.00

1999 - 2000 UPPER DECK CENTURY LEGENDS

This series was released in 1999. There are two versions: the regular card and a Century Collections parallel (#/100). The Sporting News ranks the top-50 players of all time from cards 1-50. Card #23 was not released.

Complete Set (89 cards):		2300.00	55.00
Common Player:		.50	.25
	Player	CC100	Reg.
☐☐	1 Wayne Gretzky, Edmo. [TSN Top 50]	180.00	4.00
☐☐	2 Bobby Orr, Bost. [TSN Top 50]	140.00	4.00
☐☐	3 Gordie Howe, Detr. [TSN Top 50]	100.00	2.50
☐☐	4 Mario Lemieux, Pitt. [TSN Top 50]	135.00	3.00
☐☐	5 Maurice Richard, Mont. [TSN Top 50]	100.00	2.50
☐☐	6 Jean Béliveau, Mont. [TSN Top 50]	60.00	2.00
☐☐	7 Doug Harvey, Mont. [TSN Top 50]	45.00	1.00
☐☐	8 Bobby Hull, Chic. [TSN Top 50]	60.00	1.50
☐☐	9 Jacques Plante (G), Mont. [TSN Top 50]	50.00	1.50
☐☐	10 Eddie Shore, Bost. [TSN Top 50]	50.00	1.00
☐☐	11 Guy Lafleur, Mont. [TSN Top 50]	50.00	2.00
☐☐	12 Mark Messier, Edmo. [TSN Top 50]	45.00	1.00
☐☐	13 Terry Sawchuk (G), Detr. [TSN Top 50]	70.00	2.00
☐☐	14 Howie Morenz, Mont. [TSN Top 50]	60.00	1.50
☐☐	15 Denis Potvin, NYIs. [TSN Top 50]	25.00	.50
☐☐	16 Raymond Bourque, Bost. [TSN Top 50]	50.00	1.00
☐☐	17 Glenn Hall (G), SLou. [TSN Top 50]	30.00	1.00
☐☐	18 Stan Mikita, Chic. [TSN Top 50]	25.00	.50
☐☐	19 Phil Esposito, Bost. [TSN Top 50]	35.00	1.00
☐☐	20 Mike Bossy, NYIs. [TSN Top 50]	45.00	1.50
☐☐	21 Ted Lindsay, Detr. [TSN Top 50]	35.00	1.00
☐☐	22 Leonard (Red) Kelly, Detr. [TSN Top 50]	25.00	.50
☐☐	24 Bobby Clarke, Phil. [TSN Top 50]	25.00	.50
☐☐	25 Larry Robinson, All-Star [TSN Top 50]	25.00	.50
☐☐	26 Milt Schmidt, Bost. [TSN Top 50]	20.00	.50
☐☐	27 Frank Mahovlich, Toro. [TSN Top 50]	20.00	1.00
☐☐	28 Henri Richard, Mont. [TSN Top 50]	20.00	1.00
☐☐	29 Paul Coffey, Edmo. [TSN Top 50]	20.00	.50
☐☐	30 Bryan Trottier, NYIs. [TSN Top 50]	30.00	1.00
☐☐	31 Dickie Moore, Mont. [TSN Top 50]	20.00	.50
☐☐	32 Newsy Lalonde, Mont. [TSN Top 50]	30.00	.50
☐☐	33 Syl (Sr.) Apps, Toro. [TSN Top 50]	30.00	.50
☐☐	34 Bill Durnan (G), Mont. [TSN Top 50]	20.00	.50
☐☐	35 Patrick Roy (G), Mont. [TSN Top 50]	100.00	3.00
☐☐	36 Peter Stastny, SLou. [TSN Top 50]	20.00	.50
☐☐	37 Jaromir Jagr, Pitt. [TSN Top 50]	35.00	1.00
☐☐	38 Charlie Conacher, Toro. [TSN Top 50]	20.00	.50
☐☐	39 Marcel Dionne, LosA. [TSN Top 50]	30.00	1.00
☐☐	40 Tim Horton, Toro. [TSN Top 50]	30.00	1.00
☐☐	41 Joe Malone, Mont. [TSN Top 50]	20.00	.50
☐☐	42 Chris Chelios, Detr. [TSN Top 50]	20.00	.50
☐☐	43 Bernie Geoffrion, Mont. [TSN Top 50]	20.00	.50
☐☐	44 Dit Clapper, Bost. [TSN Top 50]	20.00	.50
☐☐	45 Bill Cook, NYRa. [TSN Top 50]	20.00	.50
☐☐	46 Johnny Bucyk, Bost. [TSN Top 50]	20.00	.50
☐☐	47 Serge Savard, Mont. [TSN Top 50]	15.00	.25
☐☐	48 Jari Kurri, Edmo. [TSN Top 50]	35.00	1.00
☐☐	49 Max Bentley, Toro. [TSN Top 50]	20.00	.50
☐☐	50 Gilbert Perreault, Buff. [TSN Top 50]	20.00	.50
☐☐	51 D. Hasek (G), Buff. [Contemporaries]	35.00	1.00
☐☐	52 Jaromir Jagr, Pitt. [Contemporaries]	35.00	1.00
☐☐	53 Peter Forsberg, Colo. [Contemporaries]	50.00	1.00
☐☐	54 Paul Kariya, Anah. [Contemporaries]	50.00	1.00
☐☐	55 P. Roy (G), Colo. [Contemporaries]	100.00	3.00
☐☐	56 Steve Yzerman, Detr. [Contemporaries]	90.00	2.00
☐☐	57 R. Bourque, Bost. [Contemporaries]	45.00	1.00
☐☐	58 Pavel Bure, Flor. [Contemporaries]	30.00	.50
☐☐	59 Teemu Selänne, Anah. [Contemporaries]	30.00	.50
☐☐	60 Mike Modano, Dall. [Contemporaries]	35.00	1.00
☐☐	61 Eric Lindros, Phil. [Contemporaries]	35.00	1.00
☐☐	62 Brett Hull, Dall. [Contemporaries]	35.00	1.00
☐☐	63 M. Brodeur (G), NJer. [Contemporaries]	60.00	1.50
☐☐	64 Keith Tkachuk, Phoe. [Contemporaries]	20.00	.50
☐☐	65 Joe Sakic, Colo. [Contemporaries]	60.00	1.50
☐☐	66 Mats Sundin, Toro. [Contemporaries]	35.00	1.00
☐☐	67 John LeClair, Phil. [Contemporaries]	30.00	.50
☐☐	68 Alexei Yashin, Otta. [Contemporaries]	20.00	.50
☐☐	69 Peter Bondra, Wash. [Contemporaries]	20.00	.50
☐☐	70 B. Shanahan, Detr. [Contemporaries]	35.00	1.00
☐☐	71 Sergei Samsonov, Bost. [Phenoms]	20.00	.50
☐☐	72 Vincent Lecavalier, Tamp. [Phenoms]	35.00	1.00
☐☐	73 Marian Hossa, Otta. [Phenoms]	35.00	1.00
☐☐	74 Chris Drury, Colo. [Phenoms]	20.00	.50
☐☐	75 Milan Hejduk, Colo. [Phenoms]	30.00	.50
☐☐	76 Paul Mara, Tamp. [Phenoms]	5.00	.25
☐☐	77 David Legwand, Nash. [Phenoms]	15.00	.25
☐☐	78 Joe Thornton, Bost. [Phenoms]	45.00	1.00
☐☐	79 Pavel Rosa, LosA. [Phenoms]	5.00	.25
☐☐	80 Patrik Elias, NJer. [Phenoms]	30.00	.50
☐☐	81 Wayne Gretzky, Edmo.	100.00	2.00
☐☐	82 Wayne Gretzky, Edmo.	100.00	2.00
☐☐	83 Wayne Gretzky, Edmo.	100.00	2.00
☐☐	84 Wayne Gretzky, Edmo.	100.00	2.00
☐☐	85 Wayne Gretzky, Cdn.	100.00	2.00
☐☐	86 Wayne Gretzky, LosA.	100.00	2.00
☐☐	87 Wayne Gretzky, All-Star	100.00	2.00
☐☐	88 Wayne Gretzky, SLou.	100.00	2.00
☐☐	89 Wayne Gretzky, NYRa.	100.00	2.00
☐☐	90 Wayne Gretzky, NYRa.	100.00	2.00

ALL-CENTURY TEAM

Insert Set (12 cards):		75.00
	Insert (1:11 packs)	AC
☐	AC1 Wayne Gretzky, Edmo.	14.00
☐	AC2 Gordie Howe, Detr.	10.00
☐	AC3 Bobby Hull, Chic.	6.00
☐	AC4 Bobby Orr, Bost.	14.00
☐	AC5 Doug Harvey, Mont.	4.00
☐	AC6 Jacques Plante (G), Mont.	6.00
☐	AC7 Mario Lemieux, Pitt.	10.00
☐	AC8 Maurice Richard, Mont.	10.00
☐	AC9 Ted Lindsay, Detr.	2.00
☐	AC10 Eddie Shore, Bost.	4.00
☐	AC11 Raymond Bourque, Bost.	4.00
☐	AC12 Terry Sawchuk (G), Detr.	6.00

CENTURY ARTIFACTS

	Insert (#/1)
☐	C1 W. Gretzky [Stick]
☐	C2 W. Gretzky [Jersey]
☐	C3 W. Gretzky [Jersey]
☐	C4 Autographed Collection [Card Set]
☐	C5 Autographed Collection [Puck Set]
☐	C6 Bobby Orr [Jersey]
☐	C7 Gordie Howe [Jersey]
☐	C8 W. Gretzky [Lithograph]
☐	C9 J. Plante (G) [Cut Piece]
☐	C10 T. Sawchuk (G) [Cut Piece]

EPIC SIGNATURE

There are two versions: the regular autograph (1:23 packs) and the Gold parallel (#/100). Some autographs are produced in smaller quantites than others.

Insert Set (23 cards):		3,500.00	900.00
	Autographs	ESG	ES
☐☐	Jean Béliveau, Mont. ✍	175.00	35.00
☐☐	Mike Bossy, NYIs. ✍	200.00	40.00
☐☐	Raymond Bourque, Bost. ✍	175.00	35.00
☐☐	Johnny Bucyk, Bost. ✍	75.00	15.00
☐☐	Pavel Bure, Flor. ✍	100.00	20.00
☐☐	Gerry Cheevers (G), Bost. ✍	100.00	20.00
☐☐	Bobby Clarke, Phil. ✍	75.00	15.00
☐☐	Marcel Dionne, LosA. ✍	100.00	20.00
☐☐	Phil Esposito, Bost. ✍	150.00	30.00
☐☐	Tony Esposito (G), Chic. ✍	125.00	25.00
☐☐	Wayne Gretzky, NYRa. ✍	550.00	
☐☐	Gordie Howe, Detr. ✍	300.00	150.00
☐☐	Bobby Hull, Chic. ✍	125.00	25.00
☐☐	Brett Hull, Dall. ✍	125.00	25.00
☐☐	Mario Lemieux, Pitt. ✍	375.00	185.00
☐☐	Ted Lindsay, Detr. ✍	125.00	20.00
☐☐	Frank Mahovlich, Toro. ✍	100.00	20.00
☐☐	Stan Mikita, Chic. ✍	100.00	20.00
☐☐	Bobby Orr, Bost. ✍	500.00	250.00
☐☐	Brad Park, NYRa. ✍	75.00	15.00
☐☐	Maurice Richard, Mont. ✍ •	325.00	75.00
☐☐	Larry Robinson, Mont. ✍	75.00	15.00
☐☐	Sergei Samsonov, Bost. ✍	75.00	15.00

ESSENSE OF THE GAME

Insert Set (8 cards):		40.00
	Insert (1:11 packs)	EotG
☐	E1 W. Gretzky / P. Kariya	10.00
☐	E2 B. Orr / R. Bourque	8.00
☐	E3 M. Lemieux / J. Jagr	6.00
☐	E4 G. Howe / E. Lindros	6.00
☐	E5 J. Plante / P. Roy	8.00
☐	E6 M. Richard / P. Bure	6.00
☐	E7 Bo. Hull / Br. Hull	4.00
☐	E8 T. Lindsay / K. Tkachuk	2.00

GREAT MOMENTS

Insert Set (10 cards):		100.00
	Insert (1:12 packs)	GM
☐	GM1 Wayne Gretzky, Edmo. [Feb. 24, 1982]	12.00
☐	GM2 Wayne Gretzky, Edmo. [May 19. 1984]	12.00
☐	GM3 Wayne Gretzky, Edmo. [1985-86]	12.00
☐	GM4 Wayne Gretzky, Edmo. [May 27. 1988]	12.00
☐	GM5 Wayne Gretzky, LosA. [Oct. 15, 1989]	12.00
☐	GM6 Wayne Gretzky, LosA. [Mar. 23, 1994]	12.00
☐	GM7 Wayne Gretzky, LosA. [1993 Finals]	12.00
☐	GM8 Wayne Gretzky, All-Star [Jan. 24, 1999]	12.00
☐	GM9 Wayne Gretzky, NYRa. [Mar. 29, 1999]	12.00
☐	GM10 Wayne Gretzky, NYRa. [Apr. 18, 1999]	12.00

JERSEYS OF THE CENTURY

Insert Set (6 cards):		700.00
	Inserts	JotC
☐	JC1 Bobby Clarke, Phil. ✂	75.00
☐	JC2 Mike Bossy, NYIs. ✂	75.00
☐	JC3 Larry Robinson, LosA. ✂	75.00
☐	JC4 Raymond Bourque, Bost. ✂	90.00
☐	JC5 Mario Lemieux, Pitt. ✂	225.00
☐	JC6 Wayne Gretzky, NYRa. ✂	300.00

JERSEYS OF THE CENTURY SIGNED

	Autograph (#/25)	JotC
☐	JC1 Bobby Clarke, Phil. ✂	300.00
☐	JC5 Mario Lemieux, Pitt. ✂	1800.00

1999 - 2000 UPPER DECK CENTURY LEGENDS – BUYBACKS

	Buyback Autograph	UDCL
☐	1 Wayne Gretzky, Edmo. ✍ {#/1}	
☐	2 Bobby Orr, Bost. ✍ {#/2}	
☐	3 Gordie Howe, Detr. ✍ {#/3}	

1999 - 2000 UPPER DECK ELITSERIEN

Cards of NHL stars and prospects sell at a premium (usually $1-$2).

Complete Set (210 cards):		35.00
Common Player:		.25
	Player	UD
☐	1 Mattias Pettersson, AIK	.20
☐	2 Rikard Franzén, AIK	.20
☐	3 Mathias Svedberg, AIK	.20
☐	4 Dick Tärnström, AIK	.20
☐	5 Jan Sandström, AIK	.20
☐	6 Anders Myrvold, AIK	.50
☐	7 Henrik Tallinder, AIK	.20
☐	8 Per-Anton Lundström, AIK	.20
☐	9 Kristian Gahn, AIK	.20
☐	10 Björn Ahlström, AIK	.20
☐	11 Stefan Gustavson, AIK	.20
☐	12 Jarkko Varvio, AIK	.20
☐	13 Fredrik Krekula, AIK	.20
☐	14 Erik Norbäck, AIK	.20
☐	15 Niklas Anger, AIK	.20
☐	16 Mats Lindberg, AIK	.20
☐	17 Erik Andersson, AIK	.20
☐	18 Johan Holmqvist (G), Brynäs	1.00
☐	19 Tommy Sjödin, Brynäs	.20
☐	20 Marko Tuulola, Brynäs	.20
☐	21 Henrik Petré, Brynäs	.20
☐	22 Pär Djoos, Brynäs Gavle	.20
☐	23 Niclas Wallin, Brynäs	.20
☐	24 Roger Kyrö, Brynäs	.20
☐	25 Ove Molin, Brynäs	.20
☐	26 Stefan Lundqvist, Brynäs	.20
☐	27 Göran Hermansson, Brynäs	.20
☐	28 Jan Larsson, Brynäs	.20
☐	29 Daniel Rudslätt, Brynäs	.20
☐	30 Tom Bissett, Brynäs	.20
☐	31 Kenneth Bergqvist, Brynäs	.20
☐	32 Mikko Luovi, Brynäs	.20
☐	33 Johan Lindström, Brynäs	.20
☐	34 Daniel Olsson, Brynäs	.20
☐	35 Tommy Söderström, Djurgården	.50
☐	36 Björn Nord, Djurgården	.20
☐	37 Niklas Kronwall, Djurgården	.20
☐	38 Thomas Johansson, Djurgården	.20
☐	39 Daniel Tjärnqvist, Djurgården	.20
☐	40 Mikael Magnusson, Djurgården	.20
☐	41 Mikael Johansson, Djurgården	.20
☐	42 Nichlas Falk, Djurgården	.20
☐	43 Mikael Håkansson, Djurgården	.20
☐	44 Charles Berglund, Djurgården	.20
☐	45 Lars-Göran Wiklander, Djurgården	.20
☐	46 Per Eklund, Djurgården	.20
☐	47 Kristofer Ottosson, Djurgården	.20
☐	48 Mathias Tjärnqvist, Djurgården	.20
☐	49 Espen (Shampoo) Knutsen, Djurgården	.50
☐	50 Jimmie Ölvestad, Djurgården	.20
☐	51 Mikko Konttila, Djurgården	.20
☐	52 Vesa Toskala, Färjestad	.20
☐	53 Roger Johansson, Färjestad	.20
☐	54 Sergei Fokin, Färjestad	.20
☐	55 Greger Artursson, Färjestad	.20
☐	56 Jonas Elofsson, Färjestad	.20
☐	57 Radek Hamr, Färjestad	.20
☐	58 Henrik Rehnberg, Färjestad	.20
☐	59 Peter Nordström, Färjestad	.20
☐	60 Niklas Sjökvist, Färjestad	.20
☐	61 Trond Magnussen, Färjestad	.20
☐	62 Peter Hagström, Färjestad	.20
☐	63 Pelle Prestberg, Färjestad	.20
☐	64 Mathias Johansson, Färjestad	.20
☐	65 Tore Vikingstad, Färjestad	.20
☐	66 Clas Eriksson, Färjestad	.20
☐	67 Marko Jantunen, Färjestad	.20
☐	68 Christian Berglund, Färjestad	.20
☐	69 Mario Brunetta, Frölunda	.20
☐	70 Petter Nilsson, Frölunda	.20
☐	71 Magnus Johansson, Frölunda	.20
☐	72 Ronnie Sundin, Vastra Frölunda	.20
☐	73 Stefan Larsson, Frölunda	.20
☐	74 Christian Bäckman, Frölunda	.20
☐	75 Pär Edlund, Frölunda	.20
☐	76 Reid Simonton, Frölunda	.20
☐	77 Kristian Huselius, Frölunda	3.00
☐	78 Pasi Saarela, Frölunda	.20

☐ 79 Juha Ikonen, Frölunda .20
☐ 80 Linus Fagemo, Frölunda .20
☐ 81 Patrik Carnbäck, Frölunda .20
☐ 82 Peter Berndtsson, Frölunda .20
☐ 83 Peter Ström, Frölunda .20
☐ 84 Henrik Nilsson, Frölunda .20
☐ 85 Jonas Johnsson, Vastra Frölunda .20
☐ 86 Kari Takko, HV71 .20
☐ 87 David Petrasek, HV71 .20
☐ 88 Joacim Esbjörs, HV71 .20
☐ 89 Per* Gustafsson, HV 71 Jonkoping .20
☐ 90 Jani Nikko, HV71 .20
☐ 91 Mikael Lindman, HV71 .20
☐ 92 Oleg Belov, HV71 .20
☐ 93 Jonas Esbjörs, HV71 .20
☐ 94 Johan Forsander, HV71 .20
☐ 95 Peter Ekelund, HV 71 Jonkoping .20
☐ 96 Antti Törmänen, HV71 .20
☐ 97 Anders Lönn, HV71 .20
☐ 98 Gabriel Karlsson, HV71 .20
☐ 99 Johan Hult, HV71 .20
☐ 100 Mattias Remstam, HV71 .20
☐ 101 Daniel Wallin, HV71 .20
☐ 102 Johan Lindbom, HV71 .20
☐ 103 Reinhard Divis, Leksand .50
☐ 104 Jan Huokko, Leksand .20
☐ 105 Torbjörn Johansson, Leksand .20
☐ 106 Per Lundell, Leksand .20
☐ 107 David Ytfeldt, Leksand .20
☐ 108 Stefan Bergkvist, Leksand .20
☐ 109 Patrik Allvin, Leksand .20
☐ 110 Niklas Persson, Leksand .20
☐ 111 Martin Jansson, Leksand .20
☐ 112 Anders Carlsson, Leksand .20
☐ 113 Niklas Eriksson, Leksand .20
☐ 114 Stefan Hellkvist, Leksand .20
☐ 115 Jens Nielsen, Leksand .20
☐ 116 Morten Green, Leksand .20
☐ 117 Markus Åkerblom, Leksand .20
☐ 118 Mikael Karlberg, Leksand .20
☐ 119 Mattias Elm, Linköping .20
☐ 120 Edvin Frylén, Linköping .20
☐ 121 Martin Knold, Linköping .20
☐ 122 Erkki Saramaa, Linköping .20
☐ 123 Nicklas Nordquist, Linköping .20
☐ 124 Jesper Andersson, Linköping .20
☐ 125 Henrik Andersson, Linköping .20
☐ 126 Henrik Nordfeldt, Linköping .20
☐ 127 Ulf Söderström, Linköping .20
☐ 128 Ragnar Karlsson, Linköping .20
☐ 129 Fredrik Emvall, Linköping .20
☐ 130 Peter Casparsson, Linköping .20
☐ 131 Dennis Ejdeholm, Linköping .20
☐ 132 Mattias Nilimaa, Linköping .20
☐ 133 Mike Helber, Linköping .20
☐ 134 Johan Bülow, Linköping .20
☐ 135 Jarmo Myllys (G), Luleå .50
☐ 136 Vaclav Burda, Luleå .20
☐ 137 Osmo Soutukorva, Luleå .20
☐ 138 Johan Finnström, Luleå .20
☐ 139 Roger Åkerström, Luleå .20
☐ 140 Torbjörn Lindberg, Luleå .20
☐ 141 Jonas Rönnqvist, Luleå .20
☐ 142 Jonathan Hedström, Luleå .20
☐ 143 Tomas Berglund, Luleå .20
☐ 144 Mikael Lövgren, Luleå .20
☐ 145 Anders Burström, Luleå .20
☐ 146 Jörgen Bemström, Luleå .20
☐ 147 Martin Hostak, Luleå .20
☐ 148 Hans Huczkowski, Luleå .20
☐ 149 Lars Edström, Luleå .20
☐ 150 Jiri Kucera, Luleå .20
☐ 151 Andreas Hadelöv, Malmö .20
☐ 152 Johan Tornberg, Malmö .20
☐ 153 Mats Lusth, Malmö .20
☐ 154 Andreas Lilja, Malmö .20
☐ 155 Peter Jakobsson, Malmö .20
☐ 156 Henrik Malmström, Malmö .20
☐ 157 Tomas Sandström, Malmö .50
☐ 158 Kim Staal, Malmö .20
☐ 159 Jan Hammar, Malmö .20
☐ 160 Marcus Magnertoft, Malmö .20
☐ 161 Marcus Thuresson, Malmö .20
☐ 162 Magnus Nilsson, Malmö .20
☐ 163 Mikael Lindholm, Malmö .20
☐ 164 Juha Riihijärvi, Malmö .20
☐ 165 Jesper Mattsson, Malmö .20
☐ 166 Niklas Sundblad, Malmö .20
☐ 167 Toivo Suursoo, Malmö .20
☐ 168 Tobias Lundström, MoDo .20
☐ 169 Pierre Hedin, MoDo .20
☐ 170 Per Hållberg, MoDo .20
☐ 171 Jan-Axel Alavaara, MoDo .20
☐ 172 Jesper Duus, MoDo .20
☐ 173 François Bouchard, MoDo .20
☐ 174 Andreas Pihl, MoDo .20
☐ 175 Andreas Salomonsson, MoDo .20
☐ 176 Magnus Wernblom, MoDo .20
☐ 177 Mikael Pettersson, MoDo .20
☐ 178 Mattias Weinhandl, MoDo .20
☐ 179 Daniel Sedin, MoDo 4.00
☐ 180 Henrik Sedin, MoDo 4.00
☐ 181 Tommy Pettersson, MoDo .20
☐ 182 Samuel Påhlsson, MoDo .50
☐ 183 Anders Söderberg, MoDo .20
☐ 184 Mattias Karlin, MoDo .20
☐ 185 Magnus Eriksson, Västerås .20
☐ 186 Andrei Lulin, Västerås .20
☐ 187 Denis Chervyakov, Västerås .20
☐ 188 Dimitri Chikin, Västerås .20
☐ 189 Joakim Lundberg, Västerås .20
☐ 190 Henric Björkman, Västerås .20
☐ 191 Roger Jönsson, Västerås .20
☐ 192 Peter Nylander, Västerås .20
☐ 193 Mikael Pettersson, Västerås .20
☐ 194 Patrik Zetterberg, Västerås .20
☐ 195 Daniel Rydmark, Västerås .20
☐ 196 Johan Molin, Västerås .20
☐ 197 Paul Andersson-Everberg, Västerås .20
☐ 198 Jonas Finn-Olsson, Västerås .20
☐ 199 Fredrik Öberg, Västerås .20
☐ 200 Roger Rosén, Västerås .20
☐ 201 Henrik Tallinder, AIK .20
☐ 202 Kenneth Bergqvist, Brynäs .20
☐ 203 Mathias Tjärnqvist, Djurgården .20
☐ 204 Jimmie Ölvestad, Djurgården .20
☐ 205 Jonas Elofsson, Färjestad .20
☐ 206 Christian Berglund, Färjestad .20
☐ 207 Johan Forsander, HV71 .20
☐ 208 David Ytfeldt, Leksand .20
☐ 209 Niklas Persson, Leksand .20
☐ 210 Henrik Andersson, Linköping .20
☐ 211 Jonathan Hedström, Luleå .20
☐ 212 Kim Staal, Malmö .20
☐ 213 Pierre Hedin, MoDo .20
☐ 214 Mattias Weinhandl, MoDo .20
☐ 215 Rikard Ekström, Västerås .20
☐ 216 Christian Bäckman, Frölunda .20
☐ 217 Daniel Sedin, MoDo 1.50
☐ 218 Peter Ekelund, HV 71 Jonkoping .20
☐ 219 Tommy Söderström (G), Djurgården .50
☐ 220 Henrik Sedin, MoDo 1.50

AUTHENTICS

Insert Set (20 cards): 250.00
Insert (1:35 packs) Auto.
☐ Magnus Eriksson, Västerås ✍ 8.00
☐ Rikard Franzén, AIK ✍ 8.00
☐ Per* Gustafsson, HV 71 Jonkoping ✍ 8.00
☐ Stefan Gustavson, AIK ✍ 8.00
☐ Stefan Hellkvist, Leksand ✍ 8.00
☐ Johan Holmqvist (G), Brynäs ✍ 20.00
☐ Kristian Huselius, Frolunda ✍ 40.00
☐ Marko Jantunen, Farjestad ✍ 8.00
☐ Jonas Johnsson, Frolunda ✍ 8.00
☐ Espen Knutsen, Djurgården ✍ 15.00
☐ Johan Lindbom, HV71 ✍ 8.00
☐ Jarmo Myllys (G), Lulea ✍ 8.00
☐ Peter Nordström, Farjestad ✍ 8.00
☐ Tomas Sandström, Malmö ✍ 15.00
☐ Daniel Sedin, MoDo ✍ 50.00
☐ Henrik Sedin, MoDo ✍ 50.00
☐ Tommy Sjödin, Brynäs ✍ 8.00
☐ Tommy Söderström (G), Djurgården ✍ 8.00
☐ Ulf Söderström, Linköping ✍ 8.00
☐ Johan Tornberg, Malmö ✍ 8.00

HANDS OF GOLD

Insert Set (15 cards): 25.00
Insert (1:6 packs) H
☐ H1 Mats Lindberg, AIK 1.00
☐ H2 Tom Bissett, Brynäs 1.00
☐ H3 Jan Larsson, Brynäs 1.00
☐ H4 Per Eklund, Djurgården 1.00
☐ H5 Thomas Johansson, Djurgården 1.00
☐ H6 Mathias Johansson, Färjestad 1.00
☐ H7 Peter Ekelund, HV 71 Jonkoping 1.00
☐ H8 Anders Carlsson, Leksand 1.00
☐ H9 Ulf Söderström, Linköping 1.00
☐ H10 Jonas Rönnqvist, Luleå 1.00
☐ H11 Marcus Thuresson, Malmö 1.00
☐ H12 Daniel Sedin, MoDo 8.00
☐ H13 Henrik Sedin, MoDo 8.00
☐ H14 Daniel Rydmark, Västerås 1.00
☐ H15 Kristian Huselius, Frölunda 6.00

LASTING IMPRESSIONS

Insert Set (12 cards): 30.00
Insert (1:35 packs) L
☐ L1 Ri
☐ L1 Rikard Franzén, AIK 3.00
☐ L2 Pär Djoos, Brynäs Gavle 3.00
☐ L3 Charles Berglund, Djurgården 3.00
☐ L4 Roger Johansson, Färjestad 3.00
☐ L5 Kari Takko (G), HV71 3.00
☐ L6 Anders Carlsson, Leksand 3.00
☐ L7 Mike Helber, Linköping 3.00
☐ L8 Jiri Kucera, Luleå 3.00
☐ L9 Juha Riihijärvi, Malmö 3.00
☐ L10 Samuel Påhlsson, MoDo 4.00
☐ L11 Magnus Eriksson, Västerås 3.00
☐ L12 Patrik Carnbäck, Frölunda 3.00

POWERDECK

Insert (1:35 packs) PD
☐ PD1 Elitserien 8.00
☐ PD2 Daniel & Henrik Sedin 20.00

SNAPSHOTS

Insert Set (15 cards): 25.00
Insert (1:17 packs) S
☐ S1 Anders Myrvold, AIK 2.00
☐ S2 Johan Holmqvist (G), Brynäs 2.00
☐ S3 Ove Molin, Brynäs 2.00
☐ S4 Tommy Söderström (G), Djurgården 2.00
☐ S5 Espen Knutsen, Djurgården 4.00
☐ S6 Peter Nordström, Färjestad 2.00
☐ S7 Per* Gustafsson, HV 71 Jonkoping 2.00
☐ S8 Stefan Bergkvist, Leksand 2.00
☐ S9 Mattias Elm, Linköping 2.00
☐ S10 Jarmo Myllys (G), Luleå 2.00
☐ S11 Tomas Sandström, Malmö 2.00
☐ S12 Magnus Wernblom, MoDo 2.00
☐ S13 Mattias Weinhandl, MoDo 2.00
☐ S14 Denis Chervyakov, Västerås 2.00
☐ S15 Kristian Huselius, Frölunda 6.00

1999 - 2000 UPPER DECK GOLD RESERVE

This series was distributed in two separate releases: a Series One release in 1999 and an Update release in 2000. Cards 336-350 are new additions not included in the regular Upper Deck brand Series Two release.

Series One Set (170 cards): 85.00
Series Two Set (180 cards): 160.00
Common Player: .25
Player UDGR
☐ 1 Wayne Gretzky, Edmo. 4.00
☐ 2 Wayne Gretzky, Edmo. 4.00
☐ 3 Wayne Gretzky, Edmo. 4.00
☐ 4 Wayne Gretzky, Edmo. 4.00
☐ 5 Wayne Gretzky, Edmo. 4.00
☐ 6 Wayne Gretzky, Edmo. 4.00
☐ 7 Wayne Gretzky, Edmo. 4.00
☐ 8 Wayne Gretzky, Edmo. 4.00
☐ 9 Wayne Gretzky, Edmo. 4.00
☐ 10 Wayne Gretzky, LosA. 4.00
☐ 11 Paul Kariya, Anah. 1.50
☐ 12 Matt Cullen, Anah. .25
☐ 13 Steve Rucchin, Anah. .25
☐ 14 Fredrik Olausson, Anah. .25
☐ 15 Damian Rhodes (G), Otta. .25
☐ 16 Jody Hull, Phil. .25
☐ 17 Raymond Bourque, Bost. 1.50
☐ 18 Joe Thornton, Bost. 1.50
☐ 19 Jonathan Girard, Bost. .25
☐ 20 Shawn Bates, Bost. .25
☐ 21 Byron Dafoe (G), Bost. .50
☐ 22 Dominik Hasek (G), Buff. 1.00
☐ 23 Michael Peca, Buff. .50
☐ 24 Miroslav Satan, Buff. .25
☐ 25 Dixon Ward, Buff. .25
☐ 26 Valeri Bure, Calg. .25
☐ 27 Derek Morris, Calg. .25
☐ 28 Jarome Iginla, Calg. 1.00
☐ 29 Rico Fata, Calg. .25
☐ 30 Jean-Sébastien Giguère (G), Calg. 1.00
☐ 31 Arturs Irbe (G), Caro. .50
☐ 32 Sami Kapanen, Caro. .25
☐ 33 Gary Roberts, Caro. .50
☐ 34 Bates Battaglia, Caro. .25
☐ 35 Jean-Pierre Dumont, Chic. .25
☐ 36 Ty Jones, Chic. .25
☐ 37 Tony Amonte, Chic. .50
☐ 38 Anders Eriksson, Chic. .25
☐ 39 Peter Forsberg, Colo. 1.50
☐ 40 Adam Foote, Colo. .25
☐ 41 Chris Drury, Colo. .50
☐ 42 Milan Hejduk, Colo. 1.00
☐ 43 Brett Hull, Dall. 1.00
☐ 44 Ed Belfour (G), Dall. 1.00
☐ 45 Jamie Langenbrunner, Dall. .25
☐ 46 Derian Hatcher, Dall. .25
☐ **47 Jonathan Sim, Dall. RC 1.00**
☐ 48 Joe Nieuwendyk, Dall. .50
☐ 49 Steve Yzerman, Detr. 3.00
☐ 50 Brendan Shanahan, Detr. 1.00
☐ 51 Nicklas Lidström, Detr. .50
☐ 52 Igor Larionov, Detr. .50
☐ 53 Vyacheslav Kozlov, Detr. .25
☐ 54 Bill Guerin, Edmo. .50
☐ 55 Mike Grier, Edmo. .25
☐ 56 Tommy Salo (G), Edmo. .50
☐ 57 Tom Poti, Edmo. .25
☐ 58 Mark Parrish, Flor. .50
☐ 59 Pavel Bure, Flor. 1.00
☐ 60 Scott Mellanby, Flor. .25
☐ 61 Chris Allen, Flor. .25
☐ 62 Rob Blake, LosA. .50
☐ 63 Pavel Rosa, LosA. .25
☐ 64 Donald Audette, LosA. .50
☐ 65 Vladimir Tsyplakov, LosA. .25
☐ 66 Manny Legacé (G), LosA. .25
☐ 67 Saku Koivu, Mont. 1.00
☐ 68 Eric Weinrich, Mont. .25
☐ 69 Jeff Hackett (G), Mont. .25
☐ 70 Arron Asham, Mont. .25
☐ 71 Trevor Linden, NYIs. .50
☐ 72 Cliff Ronning, Nash. .25
☐ 73 David Legwand, Nash. .50
☐ 74 Kimmo Timonen, Nash. .25
☐ 75 Sergei Krivokrasov, Nash. .25
☐ 76 Mike Dunham (G), Nash. .50
☐ 77 Martin Brodeur (G), NJer. 2.00
☐ 78 Patrik Elias, NJer. 1.00
☐ 79 Petr* Sykora, NJer. .50
☐ 80 Vadim Sharifijanov, NJer. .25
☐ **81 John Madden, NJer. RC 3.00**
☐ 82 Eric Brewer, NYIs. .50
☐ 83 Dimitri Nabokov, NYIs. .25
☐ 84 Kenny Jönsson, NYIs. .25
☐ 85 Zdeno Chara, NYIs. .25
☐ 86 Wayne Gretzky, NYRa. 5.00
☐ 87 Mike Richter (G), NYRa. .50
☐ 88 Adam Graves, NYRa. .50
☐ 89 Manny Malhotra, NYRa. .25
☐ 90 Alexei Yashin, Otta. .50
☐ 91 Sami Salo, Otta. .25
☐ 92 Marian Hossa, Otta. 1.00
☐ 93 Shawn McEachern, Otta. .25
☐ 94 Eric Lindros, Phil. 1.00
☐ 95 Jean-Marc Pelletier (G), Phil. .25
☐ 96 Rod Brind'Amour, Phil. .25
☐ 97 Mark Recchi, Phil. .50
☐ 98 Éric Desjardins, Phil. .25
☐ 99 Robert Reichel, Phoe. .25
☐ 100 Keith Tkachuk, Phoe. .50
☐ **101 Robert Esche (G), Phoe. RC 2.00**
☐ 102 Oleg Tverdovsky, Anah. .25
☐ 103 Trevor Letowski, Phoe. .25
☐ 104 Jaromir Jagr, Pitt. 1.00
☐ 105 Tom Barrasso (G), Pitt. .50
☐ 106 Jan Hrdina, Pitt. .25
☐ 107 Matthew Barnaby, Pitt. .25
☐ 108 Vincent Damphousse, SanJ. .50
☐ 109 Jeff Friesen, SanJ. .25
☐ 110 Patrick Marleau, SanJ. .50
☐ 111 Mike Ricci, SanJ. .25
☐ 112 Scott Hannan, SanJ. .25
☐ 113 Pavol Demitra, SLou. .50
☐ 114 Al MacInnis, SLou. [cameo: Pellerin] .50
☐ 115 Lubos Bartecko, SLou. .25
☐ **116 Jochen Hecht, SLou. RC 2.50**
☐ 117 Vincent Lecavalier, Tamp. 1.00
☐ 118 Paul Mara, Tamp. .25
☐ 119 Kevin Hodson (G), Tamp. .25
☐ 120 Dan Cloutier (G), NYRa. .50
☐ 121 Mats Sundin, Toro. 1.00
☐ 122 Danny Markov, Toro. .25
☐ 123 Sergei Berezin, Toro. .25
☐ 124 Steve Thomas, Toro. .25
☐ 125 Tomas Kaberle, Toro. .25
☐ 126 Mark Messier, Vanc. 1.00
☐ 127 Bill Muckalt, Vanc. .25
☐ 128 Kevin Weekes (G), Vanc. .25
☐ 129 Josh Holden, Vanc. .25
☐ 130 Jaroslav Svejkovsky, Wash. .25
☐ 131 Adam Oates, Wash. .50
☐ 132 Peter Bondra, Wash. .50
☐ 133 Jan Bulis, Wash. .25
☐ 134 Wayne Gretzky, Edmo. [Checklist] 2.00

□	135 Wayne Gretzky, LosA. [Checklist]	2.00
□	136 Wayne Gretzky, NYRa. [Star Power]	5.00
□	137 Eric Lindros, Phil. [Star Power]	1.00
□	138 Jaromir Jagr, Pitt. [Star Power]	1.00
□	139 Paul Kariya, Anah. [Star Power]	1.50
□	140 Steve Yzerman, Detr. [Star Power]	3.00
□	141 Patrick Roy (G), Colo. [Star Power]	3.50
□	142 Chris Drury, Colo. [Star Power]	.50
□	143 Sergei Samsonov, Bost. [Star Power]	.50
□	144 Brett Hull, Dall. [Star Power]	1.00
□	145 Dominik Hasek (G), Buff. [Star Power]	1.00
□	146 Keith Tkachuk, Phoe. [Star Power]	.50
□	147 Alexei Yashin, Otta. [Star Power]	.50
□	148 Martin Brodeur (G), NJer. [Star Power]	2.00
□	149 Pavel Bure, Flor. [Star Power]	1.00
□	150 Paul Mara, Tamp. [Star Power]	.25
□	151 Peter Bondra, Wash. [Star Power]	.50
□	152 Mike Modano, Dall. [Star Power]	1.00
□	153 Teemu Selänne, Anah. [Star Power]	1.00
□	154 Peter Forsberg, Colo. [Star Power]	1.50
□	155 Brendan Shanahan, Detr. [Star Power]	1.00
□	156 Raymond Bourque, Bost. [Star Power]	1.50
□	157 Saku Koivu, Mont. [Star Power]	1.00
□	158 John LeClair, Phil. [Star Power]	1.00
□	159 Joe Sakic, Colo. [Star Power]	2.00
□	160 David Legwand, Nash. [Star Power]	.50
□	**161 Patrik Stefan, Atla. [Young Guns] RC**	**3.00**
□	162 Nick Boynton, Ottawa 67's [Young Guns]	.50
□	163 Roberto Luongo (G), CHL [Young Guns]	2.00
□	164 Rico Fata, Calg. [Star Power]	.25
□	165 Daniel Sedin, Swe. [Young Guns]	.50
□	166 Henrik Sedin, Swe. [Young Guns]	1.00
□	167 Brad Stuart, CHL [Young Guns]	1.00
□	168 Tony Amonte, Chic. [Star Power]	.50
□	**169 Oleg Saprykin, Seattle [Young Guns] RC**	**2.00**
□	170 Denis Shvidki, CHL [Young Guns]	.50
□	171 Guy Hebert (G), Anah.	.25
□	**172 Niclas Hävelid, Anah. RC**	**1.00**
□	173 Oleg Tverdovsky, Anah.	.25
□	174 Teemu Selänne, Anah.	1.00
□	175 Damian Rhodes (G), Atla.	.25
□	176 Nelson Emerson, Atla.	.25
□	177 Per Svartvadet, Atla.	.25
□	178 Ray Ferraro, Atla.	.25
□	179 Kelly Buchberger, Atla.	.25
□	180 Norm Maracle (G), Atla.	.25
□	181 Patrik Stefan, Atla. RC.	.50
□	182 Dave Andreychuk, Bost.	.50
□	183 Sergei Samsonov, Bost.	.50
□	**184 John Grahame (G), Bost. RC**	**2.00**
□	185 Jason Allison, Bost.	.50
□	186 Kyle McLaren, Bost.	.25
□	187 Anson Carter, Bost.	.50
□	188 Martin Biron (G), Buff.	.50
□	**189 Brian Campbell, Buff. RC**	**1.00**
□	190 Curtis Brown, Buff.	.25
□	191 Alexei Zhitnik, Buff.	.25
□	**192 David Moravec, Buff. RC**	**1.00**
□	193 Oleg Saprykin, Calg.	.50
□	194 Grant Fuhr (G), Calg.	.50
□	195 Phil Housley, Calg.	.25
□	196 Marc* Savard, Calg.	.25
□	197 Robyn Regehr, Calg.	.25
□	198 Martin Gélinas, Caro.	.25
□	199 Ron Francis, Caro.	.50
□	200 Jeff O'Neill, Caro.	.50
□	201 Keith Primeau, Caro.	.50
□	202 Paul Ranheim, Caro.	.25
□	**203 Kyle Calder, Chic. RC**	**2.50**
□	204 Jocelyn Thibault (G), Chic.	.50
□	205 Wendel Clark, Chic.	1.00
□	206 Doug Gilmour, Chic.	.50
□	207 Josef Marha, Chic.	.25
□	208 Alexei Zhamnov, Chic.	.25
□	**209 Dan Hinote, Colo. RC**	**2.00**
□	210 Patrick Roy (G), Colo.	3.50
□	211 Joe Sakic, Colo.	2.00
□	212 Alex Tanguay, Colo.	1.50
□	213 Sandis Ozolinsh, Colo.	.25
□	214 Adam Deadmarsh, Colo.	.25
□	215 Jere Lehtinen, Dall.	.25
□	216 Mike Modano, Dall.	1.00
□	217 Darryl Sydor, Dall.	.25
□	218 Sergei Zubov, Dall.	.25
□	**219 Pavel Patera, Dall. RC**	**1.00**
□	220 Jamie Pushor, Dall.	.25
□	221 Chris Osgood (G), Detr.	.50
□	222 Tomas Holmström, Detr.	.25
□	223 Chris Chelios, Detr.	.50
□	224 Sergei Fedorov, Detr.	1.00
□	225 Jiri Fischer, Detr.	.50
□	**226 Paul Comrie, Edmo. RC**	**1.50**
□	227 Frantisek (Frank) Musil, Edmo.	.25
□	228 Janne Niinimaa, Edmo.	.25
□	229 Doug Weight, Edmo.	.50
□	230 Trevor Kidd (G), Flor.	.25
□	231 Oleg Kvasha, Flor.	.25
□	232 Viktor Kozlov, Flor.	.25
□	233 Rob Niedermayer, Flor.	.25
□	234 Luc Robitaille, LosA.	1.00
□	235 Aki Berg, LosA.	.25
□	236 Bryan Smolinski, LosA.	.25
□	237 Jozef Stumpel, LosA.	.25
□	238 Zigmund Palffy, LosA.	.50
□	239 Stéphane Fiset (G), LosA.	.25
□	**240 Jason Blake, LosA. RC**	**2.00**
□	241 Scott Lachance, Mont.	.25
□	242 Vladimir Malakhov, Mont.	.25
□	243 Mike Ribeiro, Mont.	.50
□	244 Brian Savage, Mont.	.25
□	245 Tomas Vokoun (G), Nash.	.25
□	246 Randy Robitaille, Nash.	.25
□	247 Sergei Nemchinov, NJer.	.25
□	248 Brendan Morrison, NJer.	.25
□	249 Scott Niedermayer, NJer.	.25
□	250 Scott Stevens, NJer.	.50
□	251 Scott Gomez, NJer.	1.00
□	252 Mark Lawrence, NYIs.	.25
□	253 Félix Potvin (G), NYIs.	.50
□	254 Olli Jokinen, NYIs.	.25
□	255 Tim Connolly, NYIs.	1.00
□	256 Mariusz Czerkawski, NYIs.	.25
□	257 Valeri Kamensky, NYRa.	.25
□	258 Brian Leetch, NYRa.	.50
□	259 Petr Nedved, NYRa.	.25
□	260 Theoren Fleury, NYRa.	.50
□	261 Kevin Hatcher, NYRa.	.25
□	262 Mike York, NYRa.	.50
□	263 Ron Tugnutt (G), Otta.	.50
□	264 Chris Phillips, Otta.	.25
□	265 Daniel Alfredsson, Otta.	.50
□	266 Radek Bonk, Otta.	.25
□	267 Wade Redden, Otta.	.25
□	268 J. Vanbiesbrouck (G), Phil.	.50
□	269 John LeClair, Phil.	1.00
□	270 Simon Gagné, Phil.	2.00
□	271 Nikolai Khabibulin (G), Phoe.	.50
□	272 Daniel Brière, Phoe.	.50
□	273 Jeremy Roenick, Phoe.	1.00
□	274 Andrew Ference, Pitt.	.25
□	275 Alexei Kovalev, Pitt.	.50
□	276 Martin Straka, Pitt.	.25
□	277 Aleksey Morozov, Pitt.	.25
□	278 Steve Shields (G), SanJ.	.25
□	279 Marco Sturm, SanJ.	.25
□	280 Niklas Sundström, SanJ.	.25
□	281 Brad Stuart, SanJ.	1.00
□	282 Owen Nolan, SanJ.	.50
□	283 Roman Turek (G), SLou.	.50
□	284 Chris Pronger, SLou.	.50
□	285 Jim Campbell, SLou.	.25
□	286 Michal Handzus, SLou.	.25
□	287 Pierre Turgeon, SLou.	.50
□	288 Darcy Tucker, Tamp.	.25
□	289 Andrei Zyuzin, Tamp.	.25
□	290 Stephen Guolla, Tamp.	.25
□	291 Curtis Joseph (G), Toro.	1.00
□	292 Jonas Höglund, Toro.	.25
□	293 Bryan Berard, Toro.	.25
□	294 Mike Johnson, Toro.	.25
□	295 Garth Snow (G), Vanc.	.25
□	296 Jason Strudwick, Vanc.	.25
□	**297 Steve Kariya, Vanc. RC**	**2.00**
□	298 Markus Näslund, Vanc.	1.00
□	299 Mattias Öhlund, Vanc.	.25
□	300 Alexander Mogilny, Vanc.	.50
□	301 Olaf Kölzig (G), Wash.	.50
□	**302 Alexei Tezikov, Wash. RC**	**1.00**
□	**303 Alexandre (Jr.) Volchkov, Edmo. RC**	**1.00**
□	304 Steve Yzerman, Detr. [Checklist]	1.00
□	305 Curtis Joseph (G), Toro. [Checklist]	.50

PROSPECTS

	Insert (#/2500)	UDGR
□	**306 Pavel Brendl, Calgary Hitmen RC**	**20.00**
□	307 Daniel Sedin, MoDo	8.00
□	308 Henrik Sedin, MoDo	8.00
□	**309 Sheldon Keefe, Barrie Colts RC**	**12.00**
□	**310 Ryan Jardine, Sault Ste. Marie RC**	**10.00**
□	311 Maxime Ouellet (G), Québec Remparts	6.00
□	312 Barret Jackman, Regina Pats	8.00
□	**313 Kristian Kudroc, Québec Remparts RC**	**10.00**
□	**314 Branislav Mezei, Belleville Bulls RC**	**10.00**
□	315 Denis Shvidki, Barrie Colts	4.00
□	316 Brian Finley (G), Barrie Colts	4.00
□	317 Jonathan Cheechoo, Belleville Bulls	6.00
□	318 Mark Bell, Ottawa 67s	4.00
□	319 Taylor Pyatt, Sudbury Wolves	4.00
□	320 Norm Milley, Sudbury Wolves	4.00
□	321 Jamie Lundmark, Moose Jaw Warriors	6.00
□	**322 Alexander Buturlin, Sarnia Sting RC**	**6.00**
□	**323 Jaroslav Kristek, Tri-City Americans RC**	**6.00**
□	324 Kris Beech, Calgary Hitmen	6.00
□	325 Scott Kelman, Seattle Thunderbirds	4.00
□	**326 Milan Kraft, Prince Albert Raiders RC**	**20.00**
□	327 Mattias Weinhandl, MoDo	4.00
□	328 Alexei Volkov (G), Halifax Moosehead	4.00
□	**329 Andrei Shefer, Halifax Moosehead RC**	**6.00**
□	330 Mathieu Chouinard (G), Shawinigan Cataractes	4.00
□	331 Justin Papineau, Belleville Bulls	4.00
□	332 Mike Van Ryn, Sarnia Sting	4.00
□	333 Jeff Heerema, Sarnia Sting	4.00
□	334 Michael Zigomanis, Calgary Hitmen	4.00
□	**335 Bryan Kazarian, Owen Sound Platers RC**	**6.00**

UPDATE EXCLUSIVE

	Player	UDGR
□	336 Antti Aalto, Anah.	.50
□	**337 Andreas Karlsson, Atla.RC**	**1.00**
□	**338 Joel Prpic, Bost. RC**	**1.00**
□	**339 Travis Brigley, Calg. RC**	**1.00**
□	**340 Steve Passmore (G), Chic. RC**	**1.50**
□	**341 Georges Laraque, Edmo. RC**	**1.50**
□	**342 Brad Chartrand, LosA. RC**	**1.00**
□	**343 Francis Bouillon, Mont. RC**	**1.00**
□	**344 Karlis Skrastins, Nash. RC**	**1.00**
□	**345 Karel Rachunek, Otta. RC**	**2.00**
□	**346 Andy Delmore, Phil. RC**	**2.00**
□	**347 Martin Sonnenberg, Pitt. RC**	**1.00**
□	348 Ben Clymer, Tamp.	.50
□	**349 Chris McAllister, Toro. RC**	**1.00**
□	350 Harold Druken, Vanc.	.50

GAME-USED SOUVENIR

Update Series Insert Set (7 cards):		**575.00**
	Insert (1:480 packs)	**GUS**
□	Brett Hull, Dall. ✂	50.00
□	Eric Lindros, Phil. ✂	50.00
□	Pavel Bure, Flor. ✂	30.00
□	Paul Kariya, Anah. ✂	75.00
□	Patrick Roy (G), Colo. ✂	125.00
□	Steve Yzerman, Detr. ✂	125.00
□	Wayne Gretzky, NYRa. ✂	225.00

UD AUTHENTICS

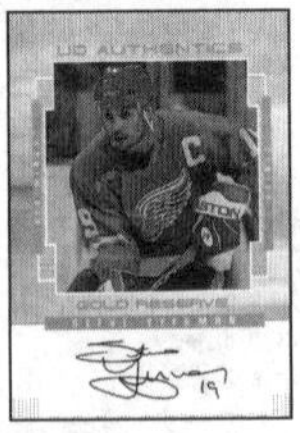

Insert Set (9 cards):		**500.00**
	Insert (1:480 packs)	**UDA1**
□	Brett Hull, Dall. ✍	60.00
□	Bill Muckalt, Vanc. ✍	15.00
□	Chris Drury, Colo. ✍	35.00
□	Curtis Joseph (G), Toro. ✍	60.00
□	David Legwand, Nash. ✍	25.00
□	Pavel Bure, Flor. ✍	50.00
	Insert (1:480 packs)	**UDA2**
□	Brett Hull, Dall. ✍	60.00
□	Brian Leetch, NYRa. ✍	35.00
□	Curtis Joseph (G), Toro. ✍	60.00
□	Patrik Stefan, Atla. ✍	20.00
□	Sergei Samsonov, Bost. ✍	35.00
□	Steve Yzerman, Detr. ✍	150.00

STAR FACTOR AND YOUNG GUNS BACKUPS

These cards were not supposed to be distributed. They did, however, make their way to the secondary market.

	Player
□	161 Marian Hossa, Otta.
□	162 Doug Weight, Edmo.
□	163 Milan Hejduk, Colo.
□	164 Pavel Brendl, NYRa.
□	165 Al MacInnis, SLou.
□	166 Jeff Friesen, SanJ.
□	167 Ed Belfour (G), Dall.
□	168 Jeff Jillson, SanJ.
□	169 J-M Pelletier (G), Phil.
□	170 Jean-Sébastien Giguère (G), Calg.

1999 - 2000 UPPER DECK GOLD RESERVE – BUYBACKS

	Buyback Autograph	UD
□	165 Daniel Sedin, Sweden ✍ {#/2}	
□	166 Henrik Sedin, Sweden ✍ {#/3}	
□	308 Henrik Sedin, MoDo ✍ {#/1}	

1999 - 2000 UPPER DECK GRETZKY EXCLUSIVE

This cross-brand series was included in 1999-2000 hobby boxes released during the 1999 calendar year. Each marked hobby box of the Upper Deck product included a pack of Gretzky Exclusive. All 99 base cards have a Gold parallel (#/99).

Complete Set (99 cards):		**5600.00**	**250.00**
Common Player:		**50.00**	**2.00**
	Player	**G99**	**Reg.**
□ □	1 Wayne Gretzky	80.00	4.00
□ □	2 Wayne Gretzky	80.00	4.00
□ □	3 Wayne Gretzky	80.00	4.00
□ □	4 Wayne Gretzky	80.00	4.00
□ □	5 Wayne Gretzky	80.00	4.00
□ □	6 Wayne Gretzky	80.00	4.00
□ □	7 Wayne Gretzky	80.00	4.00
□ □	8 Wayne Gretzky	80.00	4.00
□ □	9 Wayne Gretzky	80.00	4.00
□ □	10 Wayne Gretzky	80.00	4.00
□ □	11 Wayne Gretzky	80.00	4.00
□ □	12 Wayne Gretzky	80.00	4.00
□ □	13 Wayne Gretzky	80.00	4.00
□ □	14 Wayne Gretzky	80.00	4.00
□ □	15 Wayne Gretzky	80.00	4.00
□ □	16 Wayne Gretzky	80.00	4.00
□ □	17 Wayne Gretzky	80.00	4.00
□ □	18 Wayne Gretzky	80.00	4.00
□ □	19 Wayne Gretzky	80.00	4.00
□ □	20 Wayne Gretzky	80.00	4.00
□ □	21 Wayne Gretzky	80.00	4.00
□ □	22 Wayne Gretzky	80.00	4.00
□ □	23 Wayne Gretzky	80.00	4.00
□ □	24 Wayne Gretzky	80.00	4.00
□ □	25 Wayne Gretzky	80.00	4.00
□ □	26 Wayne Gretzky	80.00	4.00
□ □	27 Wayne Gretzky	80.00	4.00
□ □	28 Wayne Gretzky	80.00	4.00
□ □	29 Wayne Gretzky	80.00	4.00
□ □	30 Wayne Gretzky	80.00	4.00
□ □	31 Wayne Gretzky	80.00	4.00

☐☐	32 Wayne Gretzky	80.00	4.00
☐☐	33 Wayne Gretzky	80.00	4.00
☐☐	34 Wayne Gretzky	80.00	4.00
☐☐	35 Wayne Gretzky	80.00	4.00
☐☐	36 Wayne Gretzky	80.00	4.00
☐☐	37 Wayne Gretzky	80.00	4.00
☐☐	38 Wayne Gretzky	80.00	4.00
☐☐	39 Wayne Gretzky	80.00	4.00
☐☐	40 Wayne Gretzky	80.00	4.00
☐☐	41 Wayne Gretzky	80.00	4.00
☐☐	42 Wayne Gretzky	80.00	4.00
☐☐	43 Wayne Gretzky	80.00	4.00
☐☐	44 Wayne Gretzky	80.00	4.00
☐☐	45 Wayne Gretzky	80.00	4.00
☐☐	46 Wayne Gretzky	80.00	4.00
☐☐	47 Wayne Gretzky	80.00	4.00
☐☐	48 Wayne Gretzky	80.00	4.00
☐☐	49 Wayne Gretzky	80.00	4.00
☐☐	50 Wayne Gretzky	80.00	4.00
☐☐	51 Wayne Gretzky	80.00	4.00
☐☐	52 Wayne Gretzky	80.00	4.00
☐☐	53 Wayne Gretzky	80.00	4.00
☐☐	54 Wayne Gretzky	80.00	4.00
☐☐	55 Wayne Gretzky	80.00	4.00
☐☐	56 Wayne Gretzky	80.00	4.00
☐☐	57 Wayne Gretzky	80.00	4.00
☐☐	58 Mark Messier, NYRa. [w/ Gretzky]	60.00	2.50
☐☐	59 Brett Hull, SLou. [w/ Gretzky]	60.00	2.50
☐☐	60 Grant Fuhr (G), SLou. [w/ Gretzky]	50.00	2.00
☐☐	61 Marty McSorley, LosA. [w/ Gretzky]	50.00	2.00
☐☐	62 Eric Lindros, Cdn. [w/ Gretzky]	60.00	2.50
☐☐	63 Paul Coffey, Edmo. [w/ Gretzky]	50.00	2.00
☐☐	64 Luc Robitaille, LosA. [w/ Gretzky]	60.00	2.00
☐☐	65 Brian Leetch, NYRa. [w/ Gretzky]	50.00	2.00
☐☐	66 Jaromir Jagr, All-Star [w/ Gretzky]	60.00	2.50
☐☐	67 Raymond Bourque, Bost. [w/ Gretzky]	60.00	2.50
☐☐	68 Mike Richter (G), NYRa. [w/ Gretzky]	50.00	2.00
☐☐	69 Adam Graves, NYRa. [w/ Gretzky]	50.00	2.00
☐☐	70 Rob Blake, LosA. [w/ Gretzky]	50.00	2.00
☐☐	71 Steve Yzerman, Canada [w/ Gretzky]	80.00	3.00
☐☐	72 Petr Nedved, NYRa. [w/ Gretzky]	50.00	2.00
☐☐	73 Jaromir Jagr, Pitt. [w/ Gretzky]	60.00	2.50
☐☐	74 Paul Kariya, Anah. [w/ Gretzky]	60.00	2.50
☐☐	75 Eric Lindros, Phil. [w/ Gretzky]	60.00	2.50
☐☐	76 Pavel Bure, Flor. [w/ Gretzky]	60.00	2.00
☐☐	77 Teemu Selänne, Anah. [w/ Gretzky]	60.00	2.00
☐☐	78 Mats Sundin, Toro. [w/ Gretzky]	60.00	2.50
☐☐	79 Sergei Samsonov, Bost. [w/ Gretzky]	50.00	2.00
☐☐	80 Keith Tkachuk, Phoe. [w/ Gretzky]	50.00	2.00
☐☐	81 Alexei Yashin, Otta. [w/ Gretzky]	50.00	2.00
☐☐	82 Vincent Lecavalier, Tamp. [w/ Gretzky]	60.00	2.50
☐☐	83 David Legwand, Nash. [w/ Gretzky]	50.00	2.00
☐☐	84 Marian Hossa, Otta. [w/ Gretzky]	60.00	2.50
☐☐	85 Joe Thornton, Bost. [w/ Gretzky]	60.00	2.50
☐☐	86 Chris Drury, Colo. [w/ Gretzky]	50.00	2.00
☐☐	87 Milan Hejduk, Colo. [w/ Gretzky]	60.00	2.00
☐☐	88 Wayne Gretzky	80.00	4.00
☐☐	89 Glen Sather, Edmo. [w/ Gretzky]	50.00	4.00
☐☐	90 John Muckler, NYRa. [w/ Gretzky]	50.00	2.00
☐☐	91 Mark Messier [w/ Gretzky]	60.00	2.50
☐☐	92 Wayne Gretzky	80.00	4.00
☐☐	93 Ty Gretzky, [w/ Wayne Gretzky]	50.00	4.00
☐☐	94 Wayne Gretzky, Edmo. [w/ Stanley Cup]	80.00	4.00
☐☐	95 Wayne Gretzky, LosA. [Impressions]	80.00	4.00
☐☐	96 Wayne Gretzky, NYRa. [Impressions]	80.00	4.00
☐☐	97 Wayne Gretzky, NYRa. [Impressions]	80.00	4.00
☐☐	98 Wayne Gretzky, Edmo. [Checklist]	80.00	4.00
☐☐	99 Wayne Gretzky, NYRa. [Checklist]	80.00	4.00

AUTOGRAPHS

	Autograph	Auto.
☐	Wayne Gretzky, Edmo. ✍ {#/50}	1000.00
☐	Wayne Gretzky, LosA. ✍ {#/99}	500.00
☐	Wayne Gretzky, SLou. ✍ {#/99}	500.00
☐	Wayne Gretzky, NYRa. ✍ {#/25}	1500.00

1999 - 2000 UPPER DECK LIVING LEGEND

This series was released in 1999. There are four versions: the regular card, a Year of the Great One parallel (#/1999), a More Than A Number parallel (#/99) and a Only One parallel (#/1).

Complete Set (99 cards): 5525.00 200.00 25.00

	Player	M99	G1999	Reg.
☐☐☐☐	1 Wayne Gretzky	80.00	3.00	.50
☐☐☐☐	2 Wayne Gretzky	80.00	3.00	.50
☐☐☐☐	3 Wayne Gretzky	80.00	3.00	.50
☐☐☐☐	4 Wayne Gretzky	80.00	3.00	.50
☐☐☐☐	5 Wayne Gretzky	80.00	3.00	.50
☐☐☐☐	6 Wayne Gretzky	80.00	3.00	.50
☐☐☐☐	7 Wayne Gretzky	80.00	3.00	.50
☐☐☐☐	8 Wayne Gretzky	80.00	3.00	.50
☐☐☐☐	9 Wayne Gretzky	80.00	3.00	.50
☐☐☐☐	10 Wayne Gretzky	80.00	3.00	.50
☐☐☐☐	11 Wayne Gretzky	80.00	3.00	.50
☐☐☐☐	12 Wayne Gretzky	80.00	3.00	.50
☐☐☐☐	13 Wayne Gretzky	80.00	3.00	.50
☐☐☐☐	14 Wayne Gretzky	80.00	3.00	.50
☐☐☐☐	15 Wayne Gretzky	80.00	3.00	.50
☐☐☐☐	16 Wayne Gretzky	80.00	3.00	.50
☐☐☐☐	17 Wayne Gretzky	80.00	3.00	.50
☐☐☐☐	18 Wayne Gretzky	80.00	3.00	.50
☐☐☐☐	19 Wayne Gretzky	80.00	3.00	.50
☐☐☐☐	20 Wayne Gretzky	80.00	3.00	.50
☐☐☐☐	21 Wayne Gretzky	80.00	3.00	.50
☐☐☐☐	22 Wayne Gretzky	80.00	3.00	.50
☐☐☐☐	23 Wayne Gretzky	80.00	3.00	.50
☐☐☐☐	24 Wayne Gretzky	80.00	3.00	.50
☐☐☐☐	25 Wayne Gretzky	80.00	3.00	.50
☐☐☐☐	26 Wayne Gretzky	80.00	3.00	.50
☐☐☐☐	27 Wayne Gretzky	80.00	3.00	.50
☐☐☐☐	28 Wayne Gretzky	80.00	3.00	.50
☐☐☐☐	29 Wayne Gretzky	80.00	3.00	.50
☐☐☐☐	30 Wayne Gretzky	80.00	3.00	.50
☐☐☐☐	31 Wayne Gretzky	80.00	3.00	.50
☐☐☐☐	32 Wayne Gretzky	80.00	3.00	.50
☐☐☐☐	33 Wayne Gretzky	80.00	3.00	.50
☐☐☐☐	34 Wayne Gretzky	80.00	3.00	.50
☐☐☐☐	35 Wayne Gretzky	80.00	3.00	.50
☐☐☐☐	36 Wayne Gretzky	80.00	3.00	.50
☐☐☐☐	37 Wayne Gretzky	80.00	3.00	.50
☐☐☐☐	38 Wayne Gretzky	80.00	3.00	.50
☐☐☐☐	39 Wayne Gretzky	80.00	3.00	.50
☐☐☐☐	40 Wayne Gretzky	80.00	3.00	.50
☐☐☐☐	41 Wayne Gretzky	80.00	3.00	.50
☐☐☐☐	42 Wayne Gretzky	80.00	3.00	.50
☐☐☐☐	43 Wayne Gretzky	80.00	3.00	.50
☐☐☐☐	44 Wayne Gretzky	80.00	3.00	.50
☐☐☐☐	45 Wayne Gretzky	80.00	3.00	.50
☐☐☐☐	46 Wayne Gretzky	80.00	3.00	.50
☐☐☐☐	47 Wayne Gretzky	80.00	3.00	.50
☐☐☐☐	48 Wayne Gretzky	80.00	3.00	.50
☐☐☐☐	49 Wayne Gretzky	80.00	3.00	.50
☐☐☐☐	50 Wayne Gretzky	80.00	3.00	.50
☐☐☐☐	51 Wayne Gretzky	80.00	3.00	.50
☐☐☐☐	52 Wayne Gretzky	80.00	3.00	.50
☐☐☐☐	53 Wayne Gretzky	80.00	3.00	.50
☐☐☐☐	54 Wayne Gretzky	80.00	3.00	.50
☐☐☐☐	55 Wayne Gretzky	80.00	3.00	.50
☐☐☐☐	56 Wayne Gretzky	80.00	3.00	.50
☐☐☐☐	57 Wayne Gretzky	80.00	3.00	.50
☐☐☐☐	58 Wayne Gretzky	80.00	3.00	.50
☐☐☐☐	59 Wayne Gretzky	80.00	3.00	.50
☐☐☐☐	60 Wayne Gretzky	80.00	3.00	.50
☐☐☐☐	61 Wayne Gretzky	80.00	3.00	.50
☐☐☐☐	62 Wayne Gretzky	80.00	3.00	.50
☐☐☐☐	63 Wayne Gretzky	80.00	3.00	.50
☐☐☐☐	64 Wayne Gretzky	80.00	3.00	.50
☐☐☐☐	65 Wayne Gretzky	80.00	3.00	.50
☐☐☐☐	66 Wayne Gretzky	80.00	3.00	.50
☐☐☐☐	67 Wayne Gretzky	80.00	3.00	.50
☐☐☐☐	68 Wayne Gretzky	80.00	3.00	.50
☐☐☐☐	69 Wayne Gretzky	80.00	3.00	.50
☐☐☐☐	70 Wayne Gretzky	80.00	3.00	.50
☐☐☐☐	71 Wayne Gretzky	80.00	3.00	.50
☐☐☐☐	72 Wayne Gretzky	80.00	3.00	.50
☐☐☐☐	73 Wayne Gretzky	80.00	3.00	.50
☐☐☐☐	74 Wayne Gretzky	80.00	3.00	.50
☐☐☐☐	75 Wayne Gretzky	80.00	3.00	.50
☐☐☐☐	76 Wayne Gretzky	80.00	3.00	.50
☐☐☐☐	77 Wayne Gretzky	80.00	3.00	.50
☐☐☐☐	78 Wayne Gretzky	80.00	3.00	.50
☐☐☐☐	79 Wayne Gretzky	80.00	3.00	.50
☐☐☐☐	80 Wayne Gretzky	80.00	3.00	.50
☐☐☐☐	81 Wayne Gretzky	80.00	3.00	.50
☐☐☐☐	82 Wayne Gretzky	80.00	3.00	.50
☐☐☐☐	83 Wayne Gretzky	80.00	3.00	.50
☐☐☐☐	84 Wayne Gretzky	80.00	3.00	.50
☐☐☐☐	85 Wayne Gretzky	80.00	3.00	.50
☐☐☐☐	86 Wayne Gretzky	80.00	3.00	.50
☐☐☐☐	87 Wayne Gretzky	80.00	3.00	.50
☐☐☐☐	88 Wayne Gretzky	80.00	3.00	.50
☐☐☐☐	89 Wayne Gretzky	80.00	3.00	.50
☐☐☐☐	90 Wayne Gretzky	80.00	3.00	.50
☐☐☐☐	91 Wayne Gretzky	80.00	3.00	.50
☐☐☐☐	92 Wayne Gretzky	80.00	3.00	.50
☐☐☐☐	93 Wayne Gretzky	80.00	3.00	.50
☐☐☐☐	94 Wayne Gretzky	80.00	3.00	.50
☐☐☐☐	95 Wayne Gretzky	80.00	3.00	.50
☐☐☐☐	96 Wayne Gretzky	80.00	3.00	.50
☐☐☐☐	97 Wayne Gretzky	80.00	3.00	.50
☐☐☐☐	98 Wayne Gretzky	80.00	3.00	.50
☐☐☐☐	99 Wayne Gretzky	80.00	3.00	.50

AUTHENTICS

Authentic puck-piece cards were seeded once every 288 packs while authentic stick-piece cards were seeded once every 1252 packs. The jersey-piece cards are limited to 99 copies.

Insert Set (9 cards): 1725.00

	Insert	Auth.
☐	W. Gretzky All-Star Jersey (#/99)	1200.00
☐	1 Wayne Gretzky (Puck)	75.00
☐	2 Wayne Gretzky (Puck)	75.00
☐	3 Wayne Gretzky (Puck)	75.00
☐	4 Wayne Gretzky (Puck)	75.00
☐	5 Wayne Gretzky (Puck)	75.00
☐	6 Wayne Gretzky (Puck)	75.00
☐	1 Wayne Gretzky (Stick)	200.00
☐	2 Wayne Gretzky (Stick)	200.00

EXCLUSIVE

Insert Set (24 cards): 120.00

	Insert (1:23 packs)	Excl.
☐	GS1 Wayne Gretzky	6.00
☐	GS2 Wayne Gretzky	6.00
☐	GS3 Wayne Gretzky	6.00
☐	GS4 Wayne Gretzky	6.00
☐	GS5 Wayne Gretzky	6.00
☐	GS6 Wayne Gretzky	6.00
☐	L1 Wayne Gretzky	6.00
☐	L2 Wayne Gretzky	6.00
☐	L3 Wayne Gretzky	6.00
☐	L4 Wayne Gretzky	6.00
☐	L5 Wayne Gretzky	6.00
☐	L6 Wayne Gretzky	6.00
☐	MM1 Wayne Gretzky	6.00
☐	MM2 Wayne Gretzky	6.00
☐	MM3 Wayne Gretzky	6.00
☐	MM4 Wayne Gretzky	6.00
☐	MM5 Wayne Gretzky	6.00
☐	MM6 Wayne Gretzky	6.00
☐	WL1 Wayne Gretzky	6.00
☐	WL2 Wayne Gretzky	6.00
☐	WL3 Wayne Gretzky	6.00
☐	WL4 Wayne Gretzky	6.00
☐	WL5 Wayne Gretzky	6.00
☐	WL6 Wayne Gretzky	6.00

GOODWILL AMBASSADOR

Insert Set (9 cards): 30.00

	Insert (1:11 packs)	GW
☐	GW1 Wayne Gretzky	4.00
☐	GW2 Wayne Gretzky	4.00
☐	GW3 Wayne Gretzky	4.00
☐	GW4 Wayne Gretzky	4.00
☐	GW5 Wayne Gretzky	4.00
☐	GW6 Wayne Gretzky	4.00
☐	GW7 Wayne Gretzky	4.00
☐	GW8 Wayne Gretzky	4.00
☐	GW9 Wayne Gretzky	4.00

GREAT ACCOLADES

Insert Set (45 cards): 110.00

	Insert (1:6 packs)	GA
☐	GA01 Wayne Gretzky	3.00
☐	GA02 Wayne Gretzky	3.00
☐	GA03 Wayne Gretzky	3.00
☐	GA04 Wayne Gretzky	3.00
☐	GA05 Wayne Gretzky	3.00
☐	GA06 Wayne Gretzky	3.00
☐	GA07 Wayne Gretzky	3.00
☐	GA08 Wayne Gretzky	3.00
☐	GA09 Wayne Gretzky	3.00
☐	GA10 Wayne Gretzky	3.00
☐	GA11 Wayne Gretzky	3.00
☐	GA12 Wayne Gretzky	3.00
☐	GA13 Wayne Gretzky	3.00
☐	GA14 Wayne Gretzky	3.00
☐	GA15 Wayne Gretzky	3.00
☐	GA16 Wayne Gretzky	3.00
☐	GA17 Wayne Gretzky	3.00
☐	GA18 Wayne Gretzky	3.00
☐	GA19 Wayne Gretzky	3.00
☐	GA20 Wayne Gretzky	3.00
☐	GA21 Wayne Gretzky	3.00
☐	GA22 Wayne Gretzky	3.00
☐	GA23 Wayne Gretzky	3.00
☐	GA24 Wayne Gretzky	3.00
☐	GA25 Wayne Gretzky	3.00
☐	GA26 Wayne Gretzky	3.00
☐	GA27 Wayne Gretzky	3.00
☐	GA28 Wayne Gretzky	3.00
☐	GA29 Wayne Gretzky	3.00
☐	GA30 Wayne Gretzky	3.00
☐	GA31 Wayne Gretzky	3.00
☐	GA32 Wayne Gretzky	3.00
☐	GA33 Wayne Gretzky	3.00
☐	GA34 Wayne Gretzky	3.00
☐	GA35 Wayne Gretzky	3.00
☐	GA36 Wayne Gretzky	3.00
☐	GA37 Wayne Gretzky	3.00
☐	GA38 Wayne Gretzky	3.00
☐	GA39 Wayne Gretzky	3.00
☐	GA40 Wayne Gretzky	3.00
☐	GA41 Wayne Gretzky	3.00
☐	GA42 Wayne Gretzky	3.00
☐	GA43 Wayne Gretzky	3.00
☐	GA44 Wayne Gretzky	3.00
☐	GA45 Wayne Gretzky	3.00

THE GREAT ONE

Insert Set (9 cards): 15.00

	Insert (1:2 packs)	GO
☐	GO1 Wayne Gretzky	2.00
☐	GO2 Wayne Gretzky	2.00
☐	GO3 Wayne Gretzky	2.00
☐	GO4 Wayne Gretzky	2.00
☐	GO5 Wayne Gretzky	2.00
☐	GO6 Wayne Gretzky	2.00
☐	GO7 Wayne Gretzky	2.00
☐	GO8 Wayne Gretzky	2.00
☐	GO9 Wayne Gretzky	2.00

1999 - 2000 UPPER DECK MVP

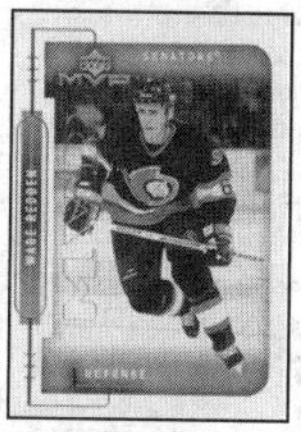

This series was released in 1999. There are four versions: the regular card, a Silver Script parallel (1:2 packs), a Gold Script parallel (#/100) and a Super Script parallel (#/25).

	Complete Set (220 cards):	-	-	100.00	30.00
	Complete Set (218 cards):	8,800	2,800	-	-
	Common Player:	15.00	5.00	.50	.20
☐☐☐☐	1 W. Gretzky, Edmo.	500.00	175.00	7.00	3.00
☐☐☐☐	2 D. Rhodes (G), Atla.	30.00	10.00	.50	.20
☐☐☐☐	3 Jody Hull, Atla.	15.00	5.00	.50	.20
☐☐☐☐	4 Paul Kariya, Anah.	175.00	60.00	2.00	1.00
☐☐☐☐	5 Teemu Selänne, Anah.	100.00	35.00	1.00	.50
☐☐☐☐	6 Guy Hebert (G), Anah.	30.00	10.00	.50	.20
☐☐☐☐	7 Matt Cullen, Anah.	30.00	10.00	.50	.20
☐☐☐☐	8 Steve Rucchin, Anah.	30.00	10.00	.50	.20
☐☐☐☐	9 Oleg Tverdovsky, Anah.	20.00	5.00	.50	.20
☐☐☐☐	10 J. Davidsson, Anah.	15.00	5.00	.50	.20
☐☐☐☐	11 R. Bourque, Bost.	150.00	50.00	2.00	.50
☐☐☐☐	12 S. Samsonov, Bost.	75.00	25.00	1.00	.20
☐☐☐☐	13 Joe Thornton, Bost.	75.00	25.00	1.00	.20
☐☐☐☐	14 Anson Carter, Bost.	50.00	15.00	.50	.20
☐☐☐☐	15 Jason Allison, Bost.	75.00	25.00	1.00	.20
☐☐☐☐	16 Kyle McLaren, Bost.	30.00	10.00	.50	.20
☐☐☐☐	17 Byron Dafoe (G), Bost.	50.00	15.00	.50	.20
☐☐☐☐	18 Shawn Bates, Bost.	20.00	5.00	.50	.20
☐☐☐☐	19 Jonathan Girard, Bost.	15.00	5.00	.50	.20
☐☐☐☐	20 Hal Gill, Bost.	15.00	5.00	.50	.20
☐☐☐☐	21 D. Hasek (G), Buff.	125.00	40.00	1.00	.50
☐☐☐☐	22 Joé Juneau, Buff.	30.00	10.00	.50	.20
☐☐☐☐	23 Michael Peca, Buff.	50.00	15.00	.50	.20
☐☐☐☐	24 Cory Sarich, Buff.	20.00	5.00	.50	.20
☐☐☐☐	25 Martin Biron (G), Buff.	60.00	20.00	.50	.20
☐☐☐☐	26 Miroslav Satan, Buff.	40.00	10.00	.50	.20
☐☐☐☐	27 Dixon Ward, Buff.	15.00	5.00	.50	.20
☐☐☐☐	28 Michal Grosek, Buff.	15.00	5.00	.50	.20
☐☐☐☐	29 Valeri Bure, Calg.	40.00	10.00	.50	.20
☐☐☐☐	30 Phil Housley, Calg.	40.00	10.00	.50	.20
☐☐☐☐	31 Derek Morris, Calg.	30.00	10.00	.50	.20
☐☐☐☐	32 Jarome Iginla, Calg.	100.00	35.00	1.00	.50
☐☐☐☐	33 Wade Belak, Calg.	15.00	5.00	.50	.20
☐☐☐☐	34 Rico Fata, Calg.	30.00	10.00	.50	.20
☐☐☐☐	35 J-S Giguère (G), Calg.	100.00	35.00	1.00	.50
☐☐☐☐	36 René Corbet, Calg.	20.00	5.00	.50	.20

37 Arturs Irbe (G), Caro.	50.00	15.00	.50	.20
38 Keith Primeau, Caro.	50.00	15.00	.50	.20
39 Sami Kapanen, Caro.	40.00	10.00	.50	.20
40 Ron Francis, Caro.	75.00	25.00	1.00	.20
41 Shane Willis, Caro.	30.00	10.00	.50	.20
42 Gary Roberts, Caro.	50.00	15.00	.50	.20
43 Bates Battaglia, Caro.	30.00	10.00	.50	.20
44 J-P Dumont, Chic.	30.00	10.00	.50	.20
45 Ty Jones, Chic.	15.00	5.00	.50	.20
46 Tony Amonte, Chic.	75.00	25.00	1.00	.20
47 J. Thibault (G), Chic.	50.00	15.00	.50	.20
48 Doug Gilmour, Chic.	75.00	25.00	1.00	.20
49 Rémi Royer, Chic.	15.00	5.00	.50	.20
50 Alexei Zhamnov, Chic.	40.00	10.00	.50	.20
51 Joe Sakic, Colo.	200.00	70.00	3.00	1.00
52 Peter Forsberg, Colo.	175.00	60.00	2.00	1.00
53 Theoren Fleury, Colo.	75.00	25.00	1.00	.20
54 Chris Drury, Colo.	75.00	25.00	1.00	.20
55 P. Roy (G), Colo.	375.00	130.00	5.00	2.00
56 S. Ozolinsh, Colo.	30.00	10.00	.50	.20
57 A. Deadmarsh, Colo.	40.00	10.00	.50	.20
58 Milan Hejduk, Colo.	100.00	35.00	1.00	.50
59 Mike Modano, Dall.	125.00	40.00	1.00	.50
60 Brett Hull, Dall.	125.00	40.00	1.00	.50
61 Darryl Sydor, Dall.	30.00	10.00	.50	.20
62 Ed Belfour (G), Dall.	125.00	40.00	1.00	.50
63 Jere Lehtinen, Dall.	40.00	10.00	.50	.20
64 Langenbrunner, Dall.	30.00	10.00	.50	.20
65 Derian Hatcher, Dall.	40.00	10.00	.50	.20
66 J. Sim, Dall. RC	**25.00**	**10.00**	**.50**	**.50**
67 Joe Nieuwendyk, Dall.	50.00	15.00	.50	.20
68 S. Fedorov, Detr.	125.00	40.00	1.00	.50
69 S. Yzerman, Detr.	300.00	105.00	4.00	1.50
70 B. Shanahan, Detr.	125.00	40.00	1.00	.50
71 C. Osgood (G), Detr.	75.00	25.00	1.00	.20
72 Nicklas Lidström, Detr.	75.00	25.00	1.00	.20
73 Chris Chelios, Detr.	75.00	25.00	1.00	.20
74 Igor Larionov, Detr.	75.00	25.00	1.00	.20
75 T. Holmström, Detr.	30.00	10.00	.50	.20
76 V. Kozlov, Detr.	30.00	10.00	.50	.20
77 Josef Beranek, Edmo.	20.00	5.00	.50	.20
78 Bill Guerin, Edmo.	50.00	15.00	.50	.20
79 Doug Weight, Edmo.	75.00	25.00	1.00	.20
80 T. Salo (G), Edmo.	50.00	15.00	.50	.20
81 Mike Grier, Edmo.	30.00	10.00	.50	.20
82 Tom Poti, Edmo.	20.00	5.00	.50	.20
83 F. Lindquist, Edmo.	20.00	5.00	.50	.20
83 Pavel Rosa, LosA.	15.00	5.00	.50	.20
84 Mark Parrish, Flor.	50.00	15.00	.50	.20
85 Pavel Bure, Flor.	100.00	35.00	1.00	.50
86 Viktor Kozlov, Flor.	40.00	10.00	.50	.20
87 Ray Whitney, Flor.	30.00	10.00	.50	.20
88 R. Niedermayer, Flor.	30.00	10.00	.50	.20
89 Oleg Kvasha, Flor.	20.00	5.00	.50	.20
90 Scott Mellanby, Flor.	30.00	10.00	.50	.20
91 Chris Allen, Flor.	15.00	5.00	.50	.20
92 Rob Blake, LosA.	75.00	25.00	1.00	.20
94 S. Fiset (G), LosA.	40.00	10.00	.50	.20
95 D. Audette, LosA.	50.00	15.00	.50	.20
96 Luc Robitaille, LosA.	100.00	35.00	1.00	.50
97 Jozef Stumpel, LosA.	30.00	10.00	.50	.20
98 V. Tsyplakov, LosA.	15.00	5.00	.50	.20
99 M. Legacé (G), LosA.	40.00	10.00	.50	.20
100 Saku Koivu, Mont.	100.00	35.00	1.00	.50
101 M. Rucinsky, Mont.	30.00	10.00	.50	.20
102 V. Malakhov, Mont.	20.00	5.00	.50	.20
103 Eric Weinrich, Mont.	15.00	5.00	.50	.20
104 J. Hackett (G), Mont.	40.00	10.00	.50	.20
105 Arron Asham, Mont.	15.00	5.00	.50	.20
106 Trevor Linden, NYIs.	50.00	15.00	.50	.20
107 Brian Savage, Mont.	40.00	10.00	.50	.20
108 Cliff Ronning, Nash.	30.00	10.00	.50	.20
109 S. Krivokrasov, Nash.	20.00	5.00	.50	.20
110 D. Legwand, Nash.	50.00	15.00	.50	.20
111 K. Timonen, Nash.	20.00	5.00	.50	.20
112 Mowers, Nash. RC	**25.00**	**10.00**	**.50**	**.50**
113 M. Dunham (G), Nash.	50.00	15.00	.50	.20
114 Scott Stevens, NJer.	50.00	15.00	.50	.20
115 Brodeur (G), NJer.	200.00	70.00	3.00	1.00
116 Patrik Elias, NJer.	100.00	35.00	1.00	.50
117 B. Morrison, NJer.	40.00	10.00	.50	.20
118 S.Niedermayer, NJer.	40.00	10.00	.50	.20
119 Petr Sykora, NJer.	50.00	15.00	.50	.20
120 Jason Arnott, NJer.	60.00	20.00	.50	.20
121 V. Sharifijanov, NJer.	15.00	5.00	.50	.20
122 J.Madden, NJer. RC	**80.00**	**30.00**	**3.00**	**1.50**
123 M. Czerkawski, NYIs.	30.00	10.00	.50	.20
124 F. Potvin (G), NYIs.	75.00	25.00	1.00	.20
125 Mike Watt, NYIs.	15.00	5.00	.50	.20
126 Eric Brewer, NYIs.	50.00	15.00	.50	.20
127 D. Nabokov, NYIs.	20.00	5.00	.50	.20
128 C. Lapointe, NYIs.	20.00	5.00	.50	.20
129 K. Jönsson, NYIs.	25.00	5.00	.50	.20
130 Zdeno Chara, NYIs.	30.00	10.00	.50	.20
131 W. Gretzky, NYRa.	500.00	175.00	7.00	3.00
132 Brian Leetch, NYRa.	75.00	25.00	1.00	.20
133 M. Richter (G), NYRa.	60.00	20.00	.50	.20
134 P. Nedved, NYRa.	40.00	10.00	.50	.20
135 A. Graves, NYRa.	50.00	15.00	.50	.20
136 M. Malhotra, NYRa.	30.00	10.00	.50	.20
137 J. MacLean, NYRa.	20.00	5.00	.50	.20
138 Alexei Yashin, Otta.	75.00	25.00	1.00	.20
139 M. Arvedson, Otta.	20.00	5.00	.50	.20
140 D. Alfredsson, Otta.	75.00	25.00	1.00	.20
141 Wade Redden, Otta.	40.00	10.00	.50	.20
142 R. Tugnutt (G), Otta.	50.00	15.00	.50	.20
143 Sami Salo, Otta.	15.00	5.00	.50	.20
144 Marian Hossa, Otta.	125.00	40.00	1.00	.50
145 S. McEachern, Otta.	40.00	10.00	.50	.20
146 Eric Lindros, Phil.	125.00	40.00	1.00	.50
147 J-M Pelletier (G), Phil.	20.00	5.00	.50	.20
148 John LeClair, Phil.	100.00	35.00	1.00	.50
149 R. Brind'Amour, Phil.	40.00	10.00	.50	.20
150 Mark Recchi, Phil.	50.00	15.00	.50	.20
151 Keith Jones, Phil.	20.00	5.00	.50	.20
152 Éric Desjardins, Phil.	40.00	10.00	.50	.20
153 R. Bast, Phil. RC	**25.00**	**10.00**	**.50**	**.50**
154 Wesenberg, Phil. RC	**25.00**	**10.00**	**.50**	**.50**
155 V'sbrouck (G), Phil.	60.00	20.00	.50	.20
156 J. Roenick, Phoe.	100.00	35.00	1.00	.50
157 R. Reichel, Phoe.	40.00	10.00	.50	.20
158 Keith Tkachuk, Phoe.	75.00	25.00	1.00	.20
159 Rick Tocchet, Phoe.	40.00	10.00	.50	.20
160 Esche (G), Phoe. RC	**60.00**	**25.00**	**2.00**	**1.00**
161 Khabibulin (G), Phoe.	50.00	15.00	.50	.20
162 Daniel Brière, Phoe.	60.00	20.00	.50	.20
163 Greg Adams, Phoe.	20.00	5.00	.50	.20
164 T. Letowski, Phoe.	20.00	5.00	.50	.20
165 Jaromir Jagr, Pitt.	125.00	40.00	1.00	.50
166 Martin Straka, Pitt.	40.00	10.00	.50	.20
167 German Titov, Pitt.	15.00	5.00	.50	.20
168 T. Barrasso (G), Pitt.	50.00	15.00	.50	.20
169 Jan Hrdina, Pitt.	30.00	10.00	.50	.20
170 Alexei Kovalev, Pitt.	75.00	25.00	1.00	.20
171 M. Barnaby, Pitt.	15.00	5.00	.50	.20
172 J-S Aubin (G), Pitt.	30.00	10.00	.50	.20
173 Damphousse, SanJ.	75.00	25.00	1.00	.20
174 Owen Nolan, SanJ.	75.00	25.00	1.00	.20
175 Jeff Friesen, SanJ.	40.00	10.00	.50	.20
176 P. Marleau, SanJ.	60.00	20.00	.50	.20
177 Marco Sturm, SanJ.	30.00	10.00	.50	.20
178 Mike Ricci, SanJ.	40.00	10.00	.50	.20
179 Gary Suter, SanJ.	30.00	10.00	.50	.20
180 Scott Hannan, SanJ.	15.00	5.00	.50	.20
181 Andy Sutton, SanJ.	15.00	5.00	.50	.20
182 P. Demitra, SLou.	50.00	15.00	.50	.20
183 Al MacInnis, SLou.	50.00	15.00	.50	.20
184 P. Turgeon, SLou.	50.00	15.00	.50	.20
185 G. Fuhr (G), SLou.	75.00	25.00	1.00	.20
186 C. Pronger, SLou.	75.00	25.00	1.00	.20
187 L. Bartecko, SLou.	20.00	5.00	.50	.20
188 J. Hecht, SLou. RC	**90.00**	**30.00**	**2.00**	**1.50**
189 M. Handzus, SLou.	30.00	10.00	.50	.20
190 V. Lecavalier, Tamp.	125.00	40.00	1.00	.50
191 Paul Mara, Tamp.	20.00	5.00	.50	.20
192 Darcy Tucker, Tamp.	30.00	10.00	.50	.20
193 Chris Gratton, Tamp.	30.00	10.00	.50	.20
194 Pavel Kubina, Tamp.	20.00	5.00	.50	.20
195 K. Hodson (G), Tamp.	30.00	10.00	.50	.20
196 Mats Sundin, Toro.	125.00	40.00	1.00	.50
197 Danny Markov, Toro.	20.00	5.00	.50	.20
198 C. Joseph (G), Toro.	125.00	40.00	1.00	.50
199 Sergei Berezin, Toro.	30.00	10.00	.50	.20
200 Steve Thomas, Toro.	30.00	10.00	.50	.20
201 Bryan Berard, Toro.	40.00	10.00	.50	.20
202 Mike Johnson, Toro.	25.00	5.00	.50	.20
203 T. Kaberle, Toro.	40.00	10.00	.50	.20
204 M. Messier, Vanc.	125.00	40.00	1.00	.50
205 Bill Muckalt, Vanc.	20.00	5.00	.50	.20
206 M. Näslund, Vanc.	125.00	40.00	1.00	.50
207 M. Öhlund, Vanc.	40.00	10.00	.50	.20
208 K. Weekes (G), Vanc.	30.00	10.00	.50	.20
209 E. Jovanovski, Vanc.	50.00	15.00	.50	.20
210 A. Mogilny, Vanc.	60.00	20.00	.50	.20
211 Josh Holden, Vanc.	20.00	5.00	.50	.20
212 R. Zednik, Wash.	50.00	15.00	.50	.20
213 J. Svejkovsky, Wash.	20.00	5.00	.50	.20
214 Adam Oates, Wash.	50.00	15.00	.50	.20
215 Peter Bondra, Wash.	75.00	25.00	1.00	.20
216 S. Gonchar, Wash.	40.00	10.00	.50	.20
217 O. Kölzig (G), Wash.	75.00	25.00	1.00	.20
218 Jan Bulis, Wash.	15.00	5.00	.50	.20
219 Gretzky, NYRa. [CL]	-	-	3.00	1.00
220 Gretzky, NYRa. [CL]	-	-	3.00	1.00

DRAW YOUR OWN TRADING CARD

Insert Set (45 cards):	150.00
Insert (1:6 packs)	**W**
W1 Joey Kocur, Detr.	.50
W2 Mike Richter (G), NYRa.	.50

W3 Wayne Gretzky, NYRa.	8.00
W4 Dominik Hasek (G), Buff.	2.00
W5 Steve Yzerman, Detr.	6.00
W6 Raymond Bourque, Bost.	2.00
W7 Arturs Irbe (G), Vanc. (Caro.)	.50
W8 Wayne Gretzky, NYRa.	8.00
W9 Martin Brodeur (G), NJer.	4.00
W10 Patrick Roy (G), Colo.	8.00
W11 Wayne Gretzky, NYRa.	8.00
W12 Paul Kariya, Anah.	4.00
W13 Wayne Gretzky, NYRa.	8.00
W14 Jaromir Jagr, Pitt.	2.00
W15 Wayne Gretzky, NYRa.	8.00
W16 Félix Potvin (G), Toro. (NYIs.)	.50
W17 Marc Denis (G), Colo.	.50
W18 Dominik Hasek (G), Buff.	2.00
W19 Patrick Roy (G), Colo.	8.00
W20 Robert Svehla, Flor.	.50
W21 Joé Juneau, Wash.	.50
W22 Mattias Öhlund, Vanc.	.50
W23 Kirk Muller, Flor.	.50
W24 Peter Forsberg, Colo.	4.00
W25 Stu Barnes, Pitt. (Buff.)	.50
W26 Nikolai Khabibulin (G), Phoe.	.50
W27 Sergei Samsonov, Bost.	.50
W28 Jeremy Roenick, Phoe.	2.00
W29 Wayne Gretzky, NYRa.	8.00
W30 Sergei Fedorov, Detr.	2.00
W31 Wayne Gretzky, NYRa.	8.00
W32 Wayne Gretzky, NYRa.	8.00
W33 Wayne Gretzky, NYRa.	8.00
W34 Wayne Gretzky, NYRa.	8.00
W35 Wayne Gretzky, NYRa.	8.00
W36 Wayne Gretzky, NYRa.	8.00
W37 Wayne Gretzky, NYRa.	8.00
W38 Wayne Gretzky, NYRa.	8.00
W39 Wayne Gretzky, NYRa.	8.00
W40 Wayne Gretzky, NYRa.	8.00
W41 Wayne Gretzky, NYRa.	8.00
W42 Wayne Gretzky, NYRa.	8.00
W43 Wayne Gretzky, NYRa.	8.00
W44 Wayne Gretzky, NYRa.	8.00
W45 Wayne Gretzky, NYRa.	8.00

21ST CENTURY NHL

Insert Set (10 cards):	15.00
Insert (1:13 packs)	**21st**
21st-1 David Legwand, Nash.	1.00
21st-2 Sergei Samsonov, Bost.	1.00
21st-3 Paul Kariya, Anah.	4.00
21st-4 Peter Forsberg, Colo.	4.00
21st-5 Vincent Lecavalier, Tamp.	3.00
21st-6 Jaromir Jagr, Pitt.	3.00
21st-7 Paul Mara, Tamp.	1.00
21st-8 Marian Hossa, Otta.	3.00
21st-9 Pavel Bure, Vanc.	2.00
21st-10 Chris Drury, Colo.	1.00

90S SNAPSHOTS

Insert Set (10 cards):	65.00
Insert (1:27 packs)	**90s**
S1 Wayne Gretzky, NYRa.	20.00
S2 Jaromir Jagr, Pitt.	5.00
S3 Patrick Roy (G), Colo.	15.00
S4 Eric Lindros, Phil.	5.00
S5 Brendan Shanahan, Detr.	5.00
S6 Peter Forsberg, Colo.	7.00
S7 Steve Yzerman, Detr.	12.00
S8 Teemu Selänne, Anah.	4.00
S9 Dominik Hasek (G), Buff.	5.00
S10 Pavel Bure, Flor.	4.00

AUTHENTIC GAME-USED SOUVENIR

These souvenir cards, either affixed with a piece of game-used puck or game-used stick, are seeded one card per 130 packs. There are two autographed parallels (Gretzky and Bure) limited to just 25 copies each.

Insert Set (28 cards):	675.00
Insert	**GU**
Pavel Bure, Flor. [Puck]	15.00
Pavel Bure, Flor. [Stick]	20.00
Peter Forsberg, Colo. [Stick]	35.00
Wayne Gretzky, NYRa. [Puck]	80.00
Wayne Gretzky, NYRa. [Stick]	100.00
Dominik Hasek (G), Buff. [Stick]	25.00
Marian Hossa, Otta. [Puck]	20.00
Brett Hull, Dall. [Puck]	20.00
Jaromir Jagr, Pitt. [Stick]	25.00
Curtis Joseph (G), Toro. [Stick]	25.00
Curtis Joseph (G), Toro. [Puck]	25.00
Paul Kariya, Anah. [Puck]	25.00
Paul Kariya, Anah. [Stick]	35.00
Eric Lindros, Phil. [Puck]	20.00
Eric Lindros, Phil. [Stick]	25.00
Jeremy Roenick, Phoe. [Stick]	20.00
Joe Sakic, Colo. [Stick]	40.00
Sergei Samsonov, Bost. [Puck]	10.00
Teemu Selänne, Anah. [Puck]	15.00
Teemu Selänne, Anah. [Stick]	20.00
Brendan Shanahan, Detr. [Puck]	20.00
Brendan Shanahan, Detr. [Stick]	25.00
Keith Tkachuk, Phoe. [Puck]	10.00
Keith Tkachuk, Phoe. [Stick]	15.00
Alexei Yashin, Otta. [Stick]	15.00
Alexei Yashin, Otta. [Puck]	15.00
Steve Yzerman, Detr. [Stick]	60.00
Steve Yzerman, Detr. [Puck]	60.00

AUTHENTIC GAME-USED SOUVENIR SIGNED

Insert	**Aut.**
GU6 Wayne Gretzky, NYRa. ✍ [Puck]	1300.00
GU18 Pavel Bure, Flor. ✍ ✂ [Stick]	300.00

DRAFT REPORT

Insert Set (10 cards):	5.00
Insert (1:6 packs)	**DR**
DR1 Damian Rhodes (G), Otta. (Atla.)	.50
DR2 Bill Muckalt, Vanc.	.50
DR3 Wayne Gretzky, NYRa.	4.00
DR4 Eric Brewer, NYIs.	.50
DR5 David Legwand, Nash.	.50
DR6 Peter Bondra, Wash.	.50
DR7 Rico Fata, Calg.	.50
DR8 Mark Parrish, Flor.	.50
DR9 Tom Poti, Edmo.	.50
DR10 Jeff Friesen, SanJ.	.50

HANDS OF GOLD

Insert Set (11 cards):	25.00
Insert (1:9 packs)	**HG**
H1 Wayne Gretzky, NYRa.	10.00
H2 Brett Hull, Dall.	2.00
H3 Pavel Bure, Flor.	2.00
H4 Teemu Selänne, Anah.	2.00
H5 Sergei Samsonov, Bost.	1.00
H6 Peter Forsberg, Colo.	3.00
H7 Eric Lindros, Phil.	2.00
H8 Paul Kariya, Anah.	3.00
H9 Jaromir Jagr, Pitt.	2.00

☐	H10 Steve Yzerman, Detr.	6.00
☐	H11 Mike Modano, Dall.	2.00

LAST LINE OF DEFENSE

	Insert Set (10 cards):	15.00
	Insert (1:9 packs)	**LL**
☐	LL1 Dominik Hasek (G), Buff.	2.00
☐	LL2 Martin Brodeur (G), NJer.	4.00
☐	LL3 Patrick Roy (G), Colo.	7.00
☐	LL4 Byron Dafoe (G), Bost.	1.00
☐	LL5 Ed Belfour (G), Dall.	2.00
☐	LL6 Curtis Joseph (G), Toro.	2.00
☐	LL7 John Vanbiesbrouck (G), Phil.	1.00
☐	LL8 Tom Barrasso (G), Pitt.	1.00
☐	LL9 Chris Osgood (G), Detr.	1.00
☐	LL10 Nikolai Khabibulin (G), Phoe.	1.00

LEGENDARY ONE

	Insert Set (10 cards):	65.00
	Insert (1:27 packs)	**LO**
☐	LO-1 Wayne Gretzky	8.00
☐	LO-2 Wayne Gretzky	8.00
☐	LO-3 Wayne Gretzky	8.00
☐	LO-4 Wayne Gretzky	8.00
☐	LO-5 Wayne Gretzky	8.00
☐	LO-6 Wayne Gretzky	8.00
☐	LO-7 Wayne Gretzky	8.00
☐	LO-8 Wayne Gretzky	8.00
☐	LO-9 Wayne Gretzky	8.00
☐	LO-10 Wayne Gretzky	8.00

MVP TALENT

	Insert Set (10 cards):	40.00
	Insert (1:13 packs)	**MVP**
☐	MVP1 Wayne Gretzky, NYRa.	12.00
☐	MVP2 Paul Kariya, Anah.	4.00
☐	MVP3 Dominik Hasek (G), Buff.	3.00
☐	MVP4 Eric Lindros, Phil.	3.00
☐	MVP5 Raymond Bourque, Bost.	3.00
☐	MVP6 Steve Yzerman, Detr.	7.00
☐	MVP7 Patrick Roy (G), Colo.	9.00
☐	MVP8 Jaromir Jagr, Pitt.	3.00
☐	MVP9 Martin Brodeur (G), NJer.	4.00
☐	MVP10 Mike Modano, Dall.	3.00

PROSIGN

	Insert Set (31 cards):	950.00
	Autograph (1:144 Retail)	**PS**
☐	Donald Audette, LosA. ✍	20.00
☐	Raymond Bourque, Bost. ✍	70.00
☐	Rod Brind'Amour, Phil. ✍	15.00
☐	Pavel Bure, Flor. ✍	40.00
☐	Wendel Clark, Detr. ✍	40.00
☐	Matt Cullen, Anah. ✍	10.00
☐	Pavol Demitra, SLou. ✍	20.00
☐	Tie Domi, Toro. ✍	15.00
☐	Chris Drury, Colo. ✍	30.00
☐	Theoren Fleury, Colo. ✍	30.00
☐	Jeff Friesen, SanJ. ✍	15.00
☐	Sergei Gonchar, Wash. ✍	15.00
☐	Wayne Gretzky, NYRa. ✍	285.00
☐	Jeff Hackett (G), Mont. ✍	15.00
☐	Jan Hrdina, Pitt. ✍	10.00
☐	Brett Hull, Dall. ✍	50.00
☐	Tomas Kaberle, Toro. ✍	15.00
☐	Sami Kapanen, Caro. ✍	15.00
☐	Igor Larionov, Detr. ✍	30.00
☐	Trevor Linden, NYIs. ✍	20.00
☐	Derek Morris, Calg. ✍	10.00
☐	Bill Muckalt, Vanc. ✍	10.00
☐	Glen Murray, LosA. ✍	20.00
☐	Michael Peca, Buff. ✍	20.00
☐	Tom Poti, Edmo. ✍	10.00
☐	Bob Probert, Chic. ✍	16.00
☐	Luc Robitaille, LosA. ✍	40.00
☐	Jeremy Roenick, Phoe. ✍	40.00
☐	Joe Thornton, Bost. ✍	60.00
☐	Ron Tugnutt (G), Otta. ✍	20.00
☐	Steve Yzerman, Detr. ✍	120.00

1999 - 2000 UPPER DECK MVP STANLEY CUP

This series was released in 2000. There are four versions: the regular card, a Silver Script parallel (1:2 packs), a Gold Script parallel (#/100) and a Super Script parallel (#/25).

	S25	G100	Silv.	Reg.
Complete Set (220 cards):	-	-	100.00	35.00
Complete Set (218 cards):	8,500	4,000	-	-
Common Player:	15.00	5.00	.50	.20
Player	**S25**	**G100**	**Silv.**	**Reg.**
☐☐☐☐ 1 Teemu Selänne	100.00	50.00	1.00	.50
☐☐☐☐ 2 Paul Kariya	175.00	85.00	2.00	1.00
☐☐☐☐ 3 Guy Hebert (G)	30.00	15.00	.50	.20
☐☐☐☐ 4 Oleg Tverdovsky	20.00	10.00	.50	.20
☐☐☐☐ 5 Tony Hrkac	20.00	10.00	.50	.20
☐☐☐☐ 6 Mike Leclerc	20.00	10.00	.50	.20
☐☐☐☐ 7 Ladislav Kohn	20.00	10.00	.50	.20
☐☐☐☐ 8 Ray Ferraro	20.00	10.00	.50	.20
☐☐☐☐ 9 Ed Ward	15.00	5.00	.50	.20
☐☐☐☐ 10 N. Maracle (G)	20.00	10.00	.50	.20
☐☐☐☐ **11 D. Sylvester RC**	**25.00**	**15.00**	**1.00**	**.50**
☐☐☐☐ 12 Y. Tremblay	15.00	5.00	.50	.20
☐☐☐☐ **13 P. Stefan RC**	**80.00**	**45.00**	**3.00**	**1.50**
☐☐☐☐ 14 Johan Garpenlöv	15.00	5.00	.50	.20
☐☐☐☐ 15 Per Axelsson	20.00	10.00	.50	.20
☐☐☐☐ 16 Joe Thornton	150.00	75.00	2.00	.50
☐☐☐☐ 17 S. Samsonov	75.00	35.00	1.00	.20
☐☐☐☐ **18 Jay Henderson RC**	**25.00**	**15.00**	**1.00**	**.50**
☐☐☐☐ 19 Byron Dafoe (G)	50.00	25.00	.50	.20
☐☐☐☐ 20 Stephen Heinze	20.00	10.00	.50	.20
☐☐☐☐ 21 Marty McSorley	30.00	15.00	.50	.20
☐☐☐☐ 22 Dominik Hasek (G)	125.00	60.00	2.00	.50
☐☐☐☐ 23 Miroslav Satan	40.00	20.00	.50	.20
☐☐☐☐ 24 Curtis Brown	20.00	10.00	.50	.20
☐☐☐☐ 25 Martin Biron (G)	60.00	30.00	.50	.20
☐☐☐☐ 26 Jason Woolley	15.00	5.00	.50	.20
☐☐☐☐ 27 Michael Peca	50.00	25.00	.50	.20
☐☐☐☐ 28 Wayne Primeau	20.00	10.00	.50	.20
☐☐☐☐ 29 Valeri Bure	40.00	20.00	.50	.20
☐☐☐☐ 30 Derek Morris	30.00	15.00	.50	.20
☐☐☐☐ 31 Cory Stillman	30.00	15.00	.50	.20
☐☐☐☐ 32 Fred Brathwaite (G)	40.00	20.00	.50	.20
☐☐☐☐ 33 Jarome Iginla	100.00	50.00	1.00	.50
☐☐☐☐ 34 Andrei Nazarov	20.00	10.00	.50	.20
☐☐☐☐ 35 Jeff Shantz	15.00	5.00	.50	.20
☐☐☐☐ 36 Ron Francis	75.00	35.00	1.00	.20
☐☐☐☐ 37 Jeff O'Neill	50.00	25.00	.50	.20
☐☐☐☐ 38 Arturs Irbe (G)	50.00	25.00	.50	.20
☐☐☐☐ 39 Sami Kapanen	40.00	20.00	.50	.20
☐☐☐☐ 40 Sean Hill	15.00	5.00	.50	.20
☐☐☐☐ **41 Byron Ritchie RC**	**25.00**	**15.00**	**1.00**	**.50**
☐☐☐☐ **42 Tommy Westlund RC**	**25.00**	**15.00**	**1.00**	**.50**
☐☐☐☐ 43 Tony Amonte	75.00	35.00	1.00	.20
☐☐☐☐ 44 Doug Gilmour	75.00	35.00	1.00	.20
☐☐☐☐ 45 Blair Atcheynum	15.00	5.00	.50	.20
☐☐☐☐ 46 Alexei Zhamnov	40.00	20.00	.50	.20
☐☐☐☐ 47 Dean McAmmond	20.00	10.00	.50	.20
☐☐☐☐ 48 Michael Nylander	30.00	15.00	.50	.20
☐☐☐☐ 49 Aaron Miller	15.00	5.00	.50	.20
☐☐☐☐ 50 Milan Hejduk	100.00	50.00	1.00	.50
☐☐☐☐ 51 Patrick Roy (G)	375.00	185.00	6.00	2.00
☐☐☐☐ 52 Joe Sakic	200.00	100.00	3.00	1.00
☐☐☐☐ 53 Chris Drury	75.00	35.00	1.00	.20
☐☐☐☐ 54 Peter Forsberg	175.00	85.00	2.00	1.00
☐☐☐☐ 55 Raymond Bourque	150.00	75.00	2.00	.50
☐☐☐☐ 56 Marc Denis (G)	60.00	30.00	.50	.20
☐☐☐☐ 57 Brett Hull	125.00	60.00	2.00	.50
☐☐☐☐ 58 Mike Modano	125.00	60.00	2.00	.50
☐☐☐☐ 59 Ed Belfour (G)	125.00	60.00	2.00	.50
☐☐☐☐ 60 Kirk Muller	40.00	20.00	.50	.20
☐☐☐☐ 61 Brenden Morrow	40.00	20.00	.50	.20
☐☐☐☐ 62 Mike Keane	20.00	10.00	.50	.20
☐☐☐☐ **63 Brad Lukowich RC**	**40.00**	**20.00**	**1.00**	**.50**
☐☐☐☐ 64 Sergei Fedorov	125.00	60.00	2.00	.50
☐☐☐☐ 65 Steve Yzerman	300.00	150.00	4.00	1.50
☐☐☐☐ 66 Chris Osgood (G)	75.00	35.00	1.00	.20
☐☐☐☐ 67 Brendan Shanahan	125.00	60.00	2.00	.50
☐☐☐☐ 68 Martin Lapointe	50.00	25.00	.50	.20
☐☐☐☐ 69 Pat Verbeek	40.00	20.00	.50	.20
☐☐☐☐ 70 Stacy Roest	20.00	10.00	.50	.20
☐☐☐☐ 71 Tommy Salo (G)	50.00	25.00	.50	.20
☐☐☐☐ 72 Doug Weight	75.00	35.00	1.00	.20
☐☐☐☐ 73 Alexander Selivanov	15.00	5.00	.50	.20
☐☐☐☐ 74 Ryan Smyth	60.00	30.00	.50	.20
☐☐☐☐ 75 Boyd Devereaux	30.00	15.00	.50	.20
☐☐☐☐ 76 Ethan Moreau	20.00	10.00	.50	.20
☐☐☐☐ 77 Pavel Bure	100.00	50.00	1.00	.50
☐☐☐☐ 78 Viktor Kozlov	40.00	20.00	.50	.20
☐☐☐☐ 79 Mike Vernon (G)	50.00	25.00	.50	.20
☐☐☐☐ **80 Ivan Novoseltsev RC**	**50.00**	**30.00**	**2.00**	**1.00**
☐☐☐☐ 81 Ray Whitney	30.00	15.00	.50	.20
☐☐☐☐ **82 Filip Kuba RC**	**40.00**	**20.00**	**1.00**	**.50**
☐☐☐☐ 83 Ray Sheppard	20.00	10.00	.50	.20
☐☐☐☐ 84 Zigmund Palffy	75.00	35.00	1.00	.20
☐☐☐☐ 85 Luc Robitaille	100.00	50.00	1.00	.50
☐☐☐☐ 86 Bryan Smolinski	20.00	10.00	.50	.20
☐☐☐☐ 87 Rob Blake	75.00	35.00	1.00	.20
☐☐☐☐ 88 Jere Karalahti	15.00	5.00	.50	.20
☐☐☐☐ 89 Marko Tuomainen	15.00	5.00	.50	.20
☐☐☐☐ 90 Garry Galley	15.00	5.00	.50	.20
☐☐☐☐ 91 Saku Koivu	100.00	50.00	1.00	.50
☐☐☐☐ 92 Dainius Zubrus	30.00	15.00	.50	.20
☐☐☐☐ 93 José Théodore (G)	150.00	75.00	2.00	1.00
☐☐☐☐ 94 Karl Dykhuis	15.00	5.00	.50	.20
☐☐☐☐ 95 Sergei Zholtok	20.00	10.00	.50	.20
☐☐☐☐ **96 Francis Bouillon RC**	**25.00**	**15.00**	**1.00**	**.50**
☐☐☐☐ 97 David Legwand	50.00	25.00	.50	.50
☐☐☐☐ 98 Mike Dunham (G)	50.00	25.00	.50	.20
☐☐☐☐ **99 Robert Valicevic RC**	**25.00**	**15.00**	**1.00**	**.50**
☐☐☐☐ 100 Cliff Ronning	30.00	15.00	.50	.20
☐☐☐☐ 101 Drake Berehowsky	20.00	10.00	.50	.20
☐☐☐☐ 102 Greg Johnson	20.00	10.00	.50	.20
☐☐☐☐ 103 Patric Kjellberg	20.00	10.00	.50	.20
☐☐☐☐ 104 Martin Brodeur (G)	200.00	100.00	3.00	1.00
☐☐☐☐ 105 Scott Stevens	50.00	25.00	.50	.20
☐☐☐☐ 106 Claude Lemieux	40.00	20.00	.50	.20
☐☐☐☐ 107 Scott Gomez	50.00	25.00	.50	.50
☐☐☐☐ 108 Patrik Elias	100.00	50.00	1.00	.50
☐☐☐☐ 109 Randy McKay	15.00	5.00	.50	.20
☐☐☐☐ 110 Sergei Brylin	20.00	10.00	.50	.20
☐☐☐☐ 111 Tim Connolly	50.00	25.00	.50	.50
☐☐☐☐ 112 Roberto Luongo (G)	100.00	50.00	1.00	1.00
☐☐☐☐ 113 Dave Scatchard	15.00	5.00	.50	.20
☐☐☐☐ 114 Kenny Jönsson	25.00	10.00	.50	.20
☐☐☐☐ **115 V. Orszagh RC**	**40.00**	**20.00**	**1.00**	**.50**
☐☐☐☐ 116 Ted Drury	15.00	5.00	.50	.20
☐☐☐☐ 117 Theoren Fleury	75.00	35.00	1.00	.20
☐☐☐☐ 118 Mike Richter (G)	60.00	30.00	.50	.20
☐☐☐☐ 119 Mike York	40.00	20.00	.50	.20
☐☐☐☐ 120 Brian Leetch	75.00	35.00	1.00	.20
☐☐☐☐ 121 Petr Nedved	40.00	20.00	.50	.20
☐☐☐☐ 122 Radek Dvorak	30.00	15.00	.50	.20
☐☐☐☐ 123 Jan Hlavac	30.00	15.00	.50	.20
☐☐☐☐ 124 Marian Hossa	125.00	60.00	2.00	.50
☐☐☐☐ 125 Radek Bonk	40.00	20.00	.50	.20
☐☐☐☐ 126 Daniel Alfredsson	75.00	35.00	1.00	.20
☐☐☐☐ 127 Ron Tugnutt (G)	50.00	25.00	.50	.20
☐☐☐☐ 128 Rob Zamuner	30.00	15.00	.50	.20
☐☐☐☐ 129 Jason York	20.00	10.00	.50	.20
☐☐☐☐ 130 Shaun Van Allen	20.00	10.00	.50	.20
☐☐☐☐ 131 Eric Lindros	125.00	60.00	2.00	.50
☐☐☐☐ 132 John LeClair	100.00	50.00	1.00	.50
☐☐☐☐ 133 Simon Gagné	100.00	50.00	1.00	1.00
☐☐☐☐ 134 Mark Recchi	50.00	25.00	.50	.20
☐☐☐☐ 135 Keith Primeau	50.00	25.00	.50	.20
☐☐☐☐ 136 Daymond Langkow	30.00	15.00	.50	.20
☐☐☐☐ 137 Brian Boucher (G)	40.00	20.00	.50	.20
☐☐☐☐ 138 Luke Richardson	20.00	10.00	.50	.20
☐☐☐☐ 139 Keith Tkachuk	75.00	35.00	1.00	.20
☐☐☐☐ 140 Jeremy Roenick	100.00	50.00	1.00	.50
☐☐☐☐ 141 Travis Green	30.00	15.00	.50	.20
☐☐☐☐ 142 Dallas Drake	20.00	10.00	.50	.20
☐☐☐☐ 143 Jyrki Lumme	30.00	15.00	.50	.20
☐☐☐☐ 144 Shane Doan	30.00	15.00	.50	.20
☐☐☐☐ 145 Sean Burke (G)	75.00	35.00	1.00	.20
☐☐☐☐ 146 Jaromir Jagr	125.00	60.00	2.00	.50
☐☐☐☐ 147 Alexei Kovalev	75.00	35.00	1.00	.20
☐☐☐☐ 148 Tom Barrasso (G)	50.00	25.00	.50	.20
☐☐☐☐ **149 M. Sonnenberg RC**	**25.00**	**15.00**	**1.00**	**.50**
☐☐☐☐ 150 Robert Lang	30.00	15.00	.50	.20
☐☐☐☐ 151 Robert Dome	20.00	10.00	.50	.20
☐☐☐☐ 152 Darius Kasparaitis	30.00	15.00	.50	.20
☐☐☐☐ 153 Owen Nolan	75.00	35.00	1.00	.20
☐☐☐☐ 154 Jeff Friesen	40.00	20.00	.50	.20
☐☐☐☐ 155 Steve Shields (G)	30.00	15.00	.50	.20
☐☐☐☐ 156 V. Damphousse	75.00	35.00	1.00	.20
☐☐☐☐ 157 Mike Rathje	20.00	10.00	.50	.20
☐☐☐☐ 158 Alexander Korolyuk	15.00	5.00	.50	.20
☐☐☐☐ 159 Todd Harvey	30.00	15.00	.50	.20
☐☐☐☐ 160 Pavol Demitra	50.00	25.00	.50	.20
☐☐☐☐ 161 Pierre Turgeon	50.00	25.00	.50	.20
☐☐☐☐ 162 Roman Turek (G)	60.00	30.00	.50	.20
☐☐☐☐ 163 Chris Pronger	75.00	35.00	1.00	.20
☐☐☐☐ **164 Jochen Hecht RC**	**90.00**	**45.00**	**3.00**	**1.00**
☐☐☐☐ **165 Todd Reirden RC**	**25.00**	**15.00**	**1.00**	**.50**
☐☐☐☐ 166 Scott A. Young	40.00	20.00	.50	.20
☐☐☐☐ 167 Vincent Lecavalier	125.00	60.00	2.00	.50
☐☐☐☐ 168 Dan Cloutier (G)	50.00	25.00	.50	.20
☐☐☐☐ 169 Chris Gratton	30.00	15.00	.50	.20
☐☐☐☐ 170 Todd Warriner	20.00	10.00	.50	.20
☐☐☐☐ 171 Mike Sillinger	20.00	10.00	.50	.20
☐☐☐☐ 172 Petr* Svoboda	30.00	15.00	.50	.20
☐☐☐☐ 173 Mats Sundin	125.00	60.00	2.00	.50
☐☐☐☐ 174 Curtis Joseph (G)	125.00	60.00	2.00	.50
☐☐☐☐ 175 Jonas Höglund	20.00	10.00	.50	.20
☐☐☐☐ 176 Sergei Berezin	30.00	15.00	.50	.20
☐☐☐☐ **177 N. Dempsey RC**	**40.00**	**20.00**	**1.00**	**.50**
☐☐☐☐ **178 N. Antropov RC**	**60.00**	**35.00**	**2.00**	**1.00**
☐☐☐☐ 179 Alyn McCauley	40.00	20.00	.50	.20
☐☐☐☐ 180 Alexander Karpovtsev	15.00	5.00	.50	.20
☐☐☐☐ **181 Steve Kariya RC**	**60.00**	**35.00**	**2.00**	**1.00**
☐☐☐☐ 182 Mark Messier	125.00	60.00	2.00	.50
☐☐☐☐ 183 Markus Näslund	125.00	60.00	2.00	.50
☐☐☐☐ 184 Adrian Aucoin	20.00	10.00	.50	.20
☐☐☐☐ 185 Andrew Cassels	30.00	15.00	.50	.20
☐☐☐☐ 186 Artem Chubarov	20.00	10.00	.50	.20
☐☐☐☐ 187 Brad May	20.00	10.00	.50	.20
☐☐☐☐ 188 Peter Bondra	75.00	35.00	1.00	.20
☐☐☐☐ 189 Olaf Kölzig (G)	75.00	35.00	1.00	.20
☐☐☐☐ 190 Dmitri Mironov	20.00	10.00	.50	.20
☐☐☐☐ **191 Jeff Halpern RC**	**60.00**	**35.00**	**2.00**	**1.00**
☐☐☐☐ 192 Andrei Nikolishin	20.00	10.00	.50	.20
☐☐☐☐ 193 Terry Yake	15.00	5.00	.50	.20
☐☐☐☐ **194 Pavel Brendl RC**	**120.00**	**60.00**	**6.00**	**2.50**
☐☐☐☐ **195 Sheldon Keefe RC**	**50.00**	**30.00**	**2.00**	**1.00**
☐☐☐☐ **196 Branislav Mezei RC**	**40.00**	**20.00**	**1.00**	**.50**
☐☐☐☐ **197 Milan Kraft RC**	**120.00**	**60.00**	**6.00**	**2.50**
☐☐☐☐ **198 Ryan Jardine RC**	**40.00**	**20.00**	**1.00**	**.50**
☐☐☐☐ **199 Kristian Kudroc RC**	**40.00**	**20.00**	**1.00**	**.50**
☐☐☐☐ **200 A. Buturlin RC**	**25.00**	**15.00**	**1.00**	**.50**
☐☐☐☐ **201 Jaroslav Kristek RC**	**25.00**	**15.00**	**1.00**	**.50**
☐☐☐☐ **202 Andrei Shefer RC**	**25.00**	**15.00**	**1.00**	**.50**
☐☐☐☐ **203 Brad Moran RC**	**25.00**	**15.00**	**1.00**	**.50**
☐☐☐☐ **204 Brett Lysak RC**	**25.00**	**15.00**	**1.00**	**.50**
☐☐☐☐ **205 Michal Sivek RC**	**40.00**	**20.00**	**1.00**	**.50**
☐☐☐☐ **206 Luke Sellars RC**	**40.00**	**20.00**	**1.00**	**.50**
☐☐☐☐ **207 Brad Ralph RC**	**40.00**	**20.00**	**1.00**	**.50**
☐☐☐☐ **208 Bryan Kazarian RC**	**25.00**	**15.00**	**1.00**	**.50**
☐☐☐☐ 209 Barrett Jackman	50.00	25.00	.50	.50
☐☐☐☐ 210 Brian Finley (G)	25.00	10.00	.50	.20
☐☐☐☐ 211 Jamie Lundmark	40.00	20.00	.50	.20
☐☐☐☐ 212 Denis Shvidki	30.00	15.00	.50	.20
☐☐☐☐ 213 Taylor Pyatt	30.00	15.00	.50	.20
☐☐☐☐ 214 Kris Beech	40.00	20.00	.50	.20
☐☐☐☐ 215 Michael Zigomanis	20.00	10.00	.50	.20
☐☐☐☐ 216 Justin Papineau	20.00	10.00	.50	.20
☐☐☐☐ 217 Daniel Sedin	50.00	25.00	.50	.50
☐☐☐☐ 218 Henrik Sedin	50.00	25.00	.50	.50
☐☐☐☐ 219 Checklist	-	-	.50	.20
☐☐☐☐ 220 Checklist	-	-	.50	.20

CUP CONTENDERS

	Insert Set (10 cards):	10.00
	Insert (1:9 packs)	**CC**
☐	CC1 Patrik Stefan, Atla.	1.00
☐	CC2 Sergei Samsonov, Bost.	1.50
☐	CC3 Milan Hejduk, Colo.	2.00
☐	CC4 Chris Drury, Colo.	1.50
☐	CC5 David Legwand, Nash.	1.00
☐	CC6 Scott Gomez, NJer.	1.00
☐	CC7 Marian Hossa, Otta.	3.00
☐	CC8 Jeff Friesen, SanJ.	.50
☐	CC9 Vincent Lecavalier, Tamp.	3.00
☐	CC10 Steve Kariya, Vanc.	.50

CLUTCH PERFORMERS

	Insert Set (10 cards):	**50.00**
	Insert (1:28 packs)	**CP**
☐	CP1 Paul Kariya, Anah.	7.00
☐	CP2 Raymond Bourque, Bost.	6.00
☐	CP3 Joe Sakic, Colo.	8.00
☐	CP4 Steve Yzerman, Detr.	12.00
☐	CP5 Luc Robitaille, LosA.	4.00
☐	CP6 Martin Brodeur (G), NJer.	8.00
☐	CP7 Theoren Fleury, NYRa.	3.00
☐	CP8 John LeClair, Phil.	4.00
☐	CP9 Jaromir Jagr, Pitt.	5.00
☐	CP10 Curtis Joseph (G), Toro.	5.00

GAME-USED SOUVENIR

	Insert Set (18 cards):	**320.00**
	Insert (1:130 packs)	**GUS**
☐	Kris Beech, Calgary Hitmen [Stick]	10.00
☐	Raymond Bourque, Bost. ✄ [Stick]	30.00
☐	Pavel Brendl, Calgary Hitmen [Stick]	10.00
☐	Pavel Bure, Flor. ✄ [Stick]	20.00
☐	Peter Forsberg, Colo. ✄ [Stick]	35.00
☐	Brett Hull, Dall. ✄ [Stick]	25.00
☐	Barret Jackman, Regina Pats [Stick]	10.00
☐	Curtis Joseph (G), Toro. ✄ [Stick]	25.00
☐	Scott Kelman, Seattle Thunderbirds [Stick]	10.00
☐	Milan Kraft, Prince Albert Raiders [Stick]	10.00
☐	John LeClair, Phil. ✄ [Stick]	20.00
☐	Eric Lindros, Phil. ✄ [Stick]	25.00
☐	Maxime Ouellet (G), Québec Remparts [Stick]	10.00
☐	Taylor Pyatt, Sudbury Wolves [Stick]	10.00
☐	Joe Sakic, Colo. ✄ [Stick]	40.00
☐	Teemu Selänne, Anah. ✄ [Stick]	20.00
☐	Denis Shvidki, Barrie Colts [Stick]	10.00
☐	Steve Yzerman, Detr. ✄ [Stick]	60.00

GOLDEN MEMORIES

	Insert Set (10 cards):	**25.00**
	Insert (1:14 packs)	**GM**
☐	GM1 Paul Kariya, Anah.	3.00
☐	GM2 Patrick Roy (G), Colo.	7.00
☐	GM3 Peter Forsberg, Colo.	3.00
☐	GM4 Mike Modano, Dall.	2.00
☐	GM5 Steve Yzerman, Detr.	6.00
☐	GM6 Martin Brodeur (G), NJer.	4.00
☐	GM7 Theoren Fleury, NYRa.	1.00
☐	GM8 Eric Lindros, Phil.	2.00
☐	GM9 Jaromir Jagr, Pitt.	2.00
☐	GM10 Curtis Joseph (G), Toro.	2.00

GREAT CONNECTIONS

There are two versions: the regular insert (1:196 Hobby packs) and the parallel version (#/25).

	Insert Set (16 cards):	**1700.00**	**600.00**
	Inserts	**GC25**	**GC**
☐☐	P. Bure / Vi. Kozlov	70.00	20.00
☐☐	W. Gretzky / B. Leetch	280.00	100.00
☐☐	W. Gretzky / M. Richter	280.00	95.00
☐☐	Br. Hull / M. Modano	120.00	40.00
☐☐	D. Hasek / M. Peca	80.00	30.00
☐☐	J. Jagr / M. Straka	80.00	25.00
☐☐	P. Kariya / T. Selänne	130.00	45.00
☐☐	J. LeClair / E. Lindros	110.00	35.00
☐☐	V. Lecavalier / P. Svoboda	70.00	25.00
☐☐	P. Roy / P. Forsberg	270.00	95.00
☐☐	B. Shanahan / S. Fedorov	120.00	40.00
☐☐	M. Sundin / Cu. Joseph (G)	120.00	40.00
☐☐	P. Stefan / D. Rhodes	50.00	12.00
☐☐	K. Tkachuk / J. Roenick	80.00	30.00
☐☐	J. Thornton / S. Samsonov	110.00	35.00
☐☐	S. Yzerman / C. Osgood	180.00	65.00

PLAYOFF HEROES

	Insert Set (10 cards):	**110.00**
	Insert (1:84 packs)	**PH**
☐	PH1 Paul Kariya, Anah.	14.00
☐	PH2 Dominik Hasek (G), Buff.	10.00
☐	PH3 Patrick Roy (G), Colo.	30.00
☐	PH4 Mike Modano, Dallas	10.00
☐	PH5 Sergei Fedorov, Detr.	10.00
☐	PH6 Pavel Bure, Flor.	8.00
☐	PH7 Martin Brodeur (G), NJer.	18.00
☐	PH8 Eric Lindros, Phil.	10.00
☐	PH9 Jaromir Jagr, Pitt.	10.00
☐	PH10 Mark Messier, Vanc.	10.00

PROSIGN

	Insert Set (24 cards):	**525.00**
	Insert (1:144 Retail packs)	**MVP**
☐	Dave Andreychuk, Bost. ✍	16.00
☐	Kris Beech, Calgary Hitmen	16.00
☐	Martin Biron (G), Buff. ✍	24.00
☐	Pavel Brendl, Calgary Hitmen	16.00
☐	Pavel Bure, Flor. ✍	40.00
☐	Brian Finley (G), Barrie Colts	10.00
☐	Simon Gagné, Phil. ✍	40.00
☐	Jochen Hecht, SLou. ✍	12.00
☐	Brett Hull, Dall. ✍	50.00
☐	Barret Jackman, Regina Pats	20.00
☐	Curtis Joseph (G), Toro. ✍	50.00
☐	Scott Kelman, Seattle Thunderbirds	10.00
☐	Milan Kraft, Prince Albert Raiders	16.00
☐	Brian Leetch, NYRa. ✍	30.00
☐	David Legwand, Nash. ✍	20.00
☐	Al MacInnis, SLou. ✍	20.00
☐	Maxime Ouellet (G), Québec Remparts	16.00
☐	Taylor Pyatt, Sudbury Wolves	12.00
☐	Sergei Samsonov, Bost. ✍	30.00
☐	Denis Shvidki, Barrie Colts	12.00
☐	Patrik Stefan, Atla. ✍	16.00
☐	Jozef Stumpel, LosA. ✍	12.00
☐	Alex Tanguay, Colo. ✍	30.00
☐	Steve Yzerman, Detr. ✍	120.00

SECOND SEASON SNIPERS

	Insert Set (12 cards):	**35.00**
	Insert (1:28 packs)	**SSS**
☐	SS1 Teemu Selänne, Anah.	3.00
☐	SS2 Joe Thornton, Bost.	5.00
☐	SS3 Peter Forsberg, Colo.	6.00
☐	SS4 Brendan Shanahan, Detr.	4.00
☐	SS5 Pavel Bure, Flor.	3.00
☐	SS6 Claude Lemieux, NJer.	2.00
☐	SS7 Eric Lindros, Phil.	4.00
☐	SS8 John LeClair, Phil.	3.00
☐	SS9 Keith Tkachuk, Phoe.	2.00
☐	SS10 Jaromir Jagr, Pitt.	4.00
☐	SS11 Mats Sundin, Toro.	4.00
☐	SS12 Mark Messier, Vanc.	4.00

STANLEY CUP TALENT

	Insert Set (20 cards):	**15.00**
	Insert (1:5 packs)	**SCT**
☐	SC1 Paul Kariya, Anah.	2.00
☐	SC2 Teemu Selänne, Anah.	1.00
☐	SC3 Raymond Bourque, Bost.	1.00
☐	SC4 Joe Sakic, Colo.	2.00
☐	SC5 Patrick Roy (G), Colo.	4.00
☐	SC6 Brett Hull, Dall.	1.00
☐	SC7 Sergei Fedorov, Detr.	1.00
☐	SC8 Pavel Bure, Flor.	1.00
☐	SC9 Zigmund Palffy, LosA.	.50
☐	SC10 Martin Brodeur (G), NJer.	2.00
☐	SC11 Theoren Fleury, NYRa.	.50
☐	SC12 Eric Lindros, Phil.	1.00
☐	SC13 John LeClair, Phil.	1.00
☐	SC14 Jaromir Jagr, Pitt.	1.00
☐	SC15 Jeremy Roenick, Phoe.	1.00
☐	SC16 Keith Tkachuk, Phoe.	.50
☐	SC17 Steve Shields (G), SanJ.	.50
☐	SC18 Mats Sundin, Toro.	1.00
☐	SC19 Mark Messier, Vanc.	1.00
☐	SC20 Peter Bondra, Wash.	.50

SUPER GAME-USED SOUVENIR

	Insert Set (4 cards):	**190.00**
	Insert (1:130 Canadian packs)	**SGUS**
☐	Kris Beech, Calgary Hitmen ✄	60.00
☐	Pavel Brendl, Calgary Hitmen ✄	60.00
☐	Milan Kraft, Prince Albert Raiders ✄	60.00
☐	Denis Shvidki, Barrie Colts ✄	45.00

1999 - 2000 UPPER DECK MVP STANLEY CUP – BUYBACKS

	Buyback Autograph	**MVP SC**
☐	17 Sergei Samsonov, Bost. ✍ {#/29}	
☐	93 José Théodore, Mont. ✍ {#/357}	
☐	107 Scott Gomez, NJer. ✍ {#/357}	
☐	194 Pavel Brendl, Calgary Hitmen RC ✍ {#/301}	
☐	217 Daniel Sedin, MoDo ✍ {#/329}	
☐	218 Henrik Sedin, MoDo ✍ {#/324}	
	Buyback Autograph • Silver Script parallel	**MVP SC**
☐	107 Scott Gomez, NJer. ✍ {#/27}	
	Buyback Autograph • Game-Used Souvenir	**MVP SC**
☐	Curtis Joseph (G), Toro. ✍ {#/30}	
☐	Teemu Selänne, Anah. ✍ {#/12}	
☐	Steve Yzerman, Detr. ✍ {#/7}	

1999 - 2000 UPPER DECK OVATION

This series was released in 2000. There are two versions: the regular card and a Standing Ovation parallel (#/50).

	Shell Set (60 cards):	**-**	**30.00**
	Complete Set (90 cards):	**3100.00**	**110.00**
	Common Player:	**10.00**	**.25**
	Player	**SO50**	**Reg.**
☐☐	1 Paul Kariya, Anah.	140.00	1.50
☐☐	2 Teemu Selänne, Anah.	80.00	1.00
☐☐	**3 Patrik Stefan, Atla. RC**	**30.00**	**3.00**
☐☐	4 Sergei Samsonov, Bost.	60.00	.50
☐☐	5 Raymond Bourque, Bost.	120.00	1.50
☐☐	6 Dominik Hasek (G), Buff.	100.00	1.00
☐☐	7 Michael Peca, Buff.	40.00	.50
☐☐	8 Miroslav Satan, Buff.	30.00	.25
☐☐	**9 Oleg Saprykin, Calg. RC**	**20.00**	**2.00**
☐☐	10 Valeri Bure, Calg.	30.00	.25
☐☐	11 Ron Francis, Caro.	60.00	.50
☐☐	12 David Tanabe, Caro.	15.00	.25
☐☐	13 Tony Amonte, Chic.	60.00	.50
☐☐	14 Jean-Pierre Dumont, Chic.	20.00	.25
☐☐	15 Patrick Roy (G), Colo.	300.00	3.50
☐☐	16 Alex Tanguay, Colo.	60.00	1.50
☐☐	17 Joe Sakic, Colo.	160.00	2.00
☐☐	18 Peter Forsberg, Colo.	140.00	1.50
☐☐	19 Mike Modano, Dall.	100.00	1.00
☐☐	20 Ed Belfour (G), Dall.	100.00	1.00
☐☐	21 Brett Hull, Dall.	100.00	1.00
☐☐	22 Sergei Fedorov, Detr.	100.00	1.00
☐☐	23 Chris Osgood (G), Detr.	60.00	.50
☐☐	24 Steve Yzerman, Detr.	240.00	3.00
☐☐	25 Doug Weight, Edmo.	60.00	.50
☐☐	26 Tom Poti, Edmo.	15.00	.25
☐☐	27 Pavel Bure, Flor.	80.00	1.00
☐☐	**28 Ivan Novoseltsev, Flor. RC**	**20.00**	**2.00**
☐☐	29 Luc Robitaille, LosA.	80.00	1.00
☐☐	30 Zigmund Palffy, LosA.	60.00	.50
☐☐	31 Mike Ribeiro, Mont.	30.00	.50
☐☐	32 David Legwand, Nash.	40.00	.50
☐☐	33 Martin Brodeur (G), NJer.	160.00	2.00
☐☐	34 Scott Gomez, NJer.	40.00	1.00
☐☐	35 Tim Connolly, NYIs.	40.00	1.00
☐☐	36 Theoren Fleury, NYRa.	60.00	.50
☐☐	37 Mike Richter (G), NYRa.	45.00	.50
☐☐	38 Brian Leetch, NYRa.	60.00	.50
☐☐	39 Marian Hossa, Otta.	100.00	1.00
☐☐	40 Daniel Alfredsson, Otta.	60.00	.50
☐☐	41 Eric Lindros, Phil.	100.00	1.00
☐☐	42 John LeClair, Phil.	80.00	1.00
☐☐	43 Simon Gagné, Phil.	80.00	2.00
☐☐	44 Keith Tkachuk, Phoe.	60.00	.50
☐☐	45 Jeremy Roenick, Phoe.	80.00	1.00
☐☐	46 Jaromir Jagr, Pitt.	100.00	1.00
☐☐	47 Alexei Kovalev, Pitt.	60.00	.50
☐☐	48 Pavol Demitra, SLou.	40.00	.50
☐☐	49 Al MacInnis, SLou.	40.00	.50
☐☐	50 Owen Nolan, SanJ.	60.00	.50
☐☐	51 Brad Stuart, SanJ.	40.00	1.00
☐☐	52 Steve Shields (G), SanJ.	20.00	.25
☐☐	53 Vincent Lecavalier, Tamp.	100.00	1.00
☐☐	54 Paul Mara, Tamp.	15.00	.25
☐☐	55 Curtis Joseph (G), Toro.	100.00	1.00
☐☐	56 Mats Sundin, Toro.	100.00	1.00
☐☐	**57 Steve Kariya, Vanc. RC**	**20.00**	**2.00**
☐☐	58 Mark Messier, Vanc.	100.00	1.00
☐☐	59 Peter Bondra, Wash.	60.00	.50
☐☐	60 Olaf Kölzig (G), Wash.	60.00	.50

SUBSET

	Insert (1:3)	**SO50**	**PP**
☐☐	**61 Pavel Brendl, Calgary Hitmen RC**	**110.00**	**8.00**
☐☐	62 Daniel Sedin, MoDo	40.00	3.00
☐☐	63 Henrik Sedin, MoDo	40.00	3.00
☐☐	**64 Sheldon Keefe, Barrie Colts RC**	**60.00**	**5.00**
☐☐	65 Jeff Heerema, Sarnia Sting	15.00	2.00
☐☐	66 Norm Milley, Sudbury Wolves	15.00	2.00
☐☐	**67 Branislav Mezei, Belleville Bulls RC**	**45.00**	**4.00**
☐☐	68 Denis Shvidki, Barrie Colts	20.00	2.00
☐☐	69 Brian Finley (G), Barrie Colts	20.00	2.00
☐☐	70 Taylor Pyatt, Sudbury Wolves	20.00	2.00
☐☐	71 Jamie Lundmark, Moose Jaw Warriors	30.00	2.00
☐☐	**72 Milan Kraft, Prince Albert RC**	**110.00**	**8.00**
☐☐	73 Kris Beech, Calgary Hitmen	30.00	2.00
☐☐	74 Alexei Volkov (G), Halifax Moosehead	20.00	2.00
☐☐	75 Mathieu Chouinard (G), Shawinigan	15.00	2.00
☐☐	76 Justin Papineau, Belleville Bulls	15.00	2.00
☐☐	**77 Brad Moran, Seattle Thunderbirds RC**	**30.00**	**2.00**
☐☐	78 Jonathan Cheechoo, Belleville Bulls	30.00	2.00
☐☐	79 Mark Bell, Ottawa 67's	20.00	2.00
☐☐	80 Mattias Weinhandl, MoDo Hockey	15.00	2.00

SUBSET

	Insert (1:6)	**SO50**	**PP**
☐☐	81 Jaromir Jagr, Pitt.	100.00	3.00
☐☐	82 Steve Kariya, Vanc.	20.00	2.00
☐☐	83 Dominik Hasek (G), Buff.	100.00	3.00
☐☐	84 Paul Kariya, Anah.	140.00	5.00
☐☐	85 Eric Lindros, Phil.	100.00	3.00
☐☐	86 Patrick Roy (G), Colo.	300.00	10.00
☐☐	87 Steve Yzerman, Detr.	240.00	9.00
☐☐	88 Pavel Bure, Flor.	80.00	3.00
☐☐	89 Theoren Fleury, NYRa.	60.00	2.00
☐☐	90 Patrik Stefan, Atla.	30.00	3.00

A PIECE OF HISTORY

	Insert Set (13 cards):	**350.00**
	Insert (1:118 packs)	**POH**
☐	Brett Hull, Dall. [Puck]	30.00
☐	Curtis Joseph (G), Toro. [Puck]	30.00
☐	Jaromir Jagr, Pitt. [Puck]	30.00
☐	Martin Brodeur (G), NJer. [Puck]	45.00
☐	Mike Ribeiro, Mont. [Puck]	12.00
☐	Pavel Bure, Flor. [Puck]	20.00
☐	Steve Kariya, Vanc. [Puck]	12.00
☐	Patrick Roy (G), Colo. [Puck]	90.00
☐	Patrik Stefan, Atla. [Puck]	12.00
☐	Steve Kariya, Vanc. [Puck]	12.00
☐	Sergei Samsonov, Bost. [Puck]	15.00
☐	Tim Connolly, NYIs. [Puck]	12.00
☐	Wayne Gretzky, NYRa. [Puck]	120.00

A PIECE OF HISTORY AUTOGRAPH

	Insert (1:118 packs)	**Aut25**
☐	Brett Hull, Dall. ✍ [Puck]	300.00
☐	Curtis Joseph (G), Toro. ✍ [Puck]	300.00
☐	Pavel Bure, Flor. ✍ [Puck]	240.00
☐	Patrik Stefan, Atla. ✍ [Puck]	115.00

CENTER STAGE

Insertion odds are as follows: cards 1-10 are seeded one card per 9 packs; cards 11-20 are seeded one card per 39 packs; cards 21-30 are seeded one per 99 packs.

Insert Set (30 cards): 550.00

Insert (1:9) CS

☐ CS1 Wayne Gretzky, Edmo. [Silver] 5.00
☐ CS2 Wayne Gretzky, Edmo. [Silver] 5.00
☐ CS3 Wayne Gretzky, LosA. [Silver] 5.00
☐ CS4 Wayne Gretzky, SLou. [Silver] 5.00
☐ CS5 Wayne Gretzky, NYRa. [Silver] 5.00
☐ CS6 Gordie Howe, Detr. [Silver] 3.00
☐ CS7 Gordie Howe, Detr. [Silver] 3.00
☐ CS8 Gordie Howe, Detr. [Silver] 3.00
☐ CS9 Gordie Howe, Detr. [Silver] 3.00
☐ CS10 Gordie Howe, Detr. [Silver] 3.00

Insert (1:39) CS

☐ CS11 Wayne Gretzky, Edmo. [Gold] 20.00
☐ CS12 Wayne Gretzky, Edmo. [Gold] 20.00
☐ CS13 Wayne Gretzky, LosA. [Gold] 20.00
☐ CS14 Wayne Gretzky, NYRa. [Gold] 20.00
☐ CS15 Wayne Gretzky, NYRa. [Gold] 20.00
☐ CS16 Gordie Howe, Detr. [Gold] 14.00
☐ CS17 Gordie Howe, Hart. [Gold] 14.00
☐ CS18 Gordie Howe, Detr. [Gold] 14.00
☐ CS19 Gordie Howe, Detr. [Gold] 14.00
☐ CS20 Gordie Howe, Edmo. [Gold] 14.00

Insert (1:99) CS

☐ CS21 W. Gretzky / G. Howe [Rainbow] 50.00
☐ CS22 Wayne Gretzky, Edmo. [Rainbow] 50.00
☐ CS23 Wayne Gretzky, All-Star [Rainbow] 50.00
☐ CS24 Wayne Gretzky, LosA. [Rainbow] 50.00
☐ CS25 Wayne Gretzky, NYRa. [Rainbow] 50.00
☐ CS26 Gordie Howe, WHA All-Star [Rainbow] 35.00
☐ CS27 Gordie Howe, Detr. [Rainbow] 35.00
☐ CS28 W. Gretzky / G. Howe [Rainbow] 40.00
☐ CS29 W. Gretzky / G. Howe [Rainbow] 40.00
☐ CS30 W. Gretzky / G. Howe [Rainbow] 40.00

LEAD PERFORMERS

Insert Set (20 cards): 40.00

Insert (1:4 packs) LP

☐ LP1 Mike Modano, Dall. 2.00
☐ LP2 Theoren Fleury, NYRa. 1.00
☐ LP3 Paul Kariya, Anah. 3.00
☐ LP4 Peter Forsberg, Colo. 3.00
☐ LP5 Pavel Bure, Flor. 2.00
☐ LP6 John LeClair, Phil. 2.00
☐ LP7 Keith Tkachuk, Phoe. 1.00
☐ LP8 Jaromir Jagr, Pitt. 2.00
☐ LP9 Patrik Stefan, Atla. 1.00
☐ LP10 Steve Kariya, Vanc. 1.00
☐ LP11 Raymond Bourque, Bost. 3.00
☐ LP12 Teemu Selänne, Anah. 2.00
☐ LP13 Zigmund Palffy, LosA. 1.00
☐ LP14 Steve Yzerman, Detr. 6.00
☐ LP15 Eric Lindros, Phil. 2.00
☐ LP16 Dominik Hasek (G), Buff. 2.00
☐ LP17 Martin Brodeur (G), NJer. 4.00
☐ LP18 Brendan Shanahan, Detr. 2.00
☐ LP19 Ed Belfour (G), Dall. 2.00
☐ LP20 Patrick Roy (G), Colo. 7.00

SUPER SIGNATURES

Insert Set (7 cards): 5700.00

Autographs SS

☐ SS-RC Wayne Gretzky ✍ / Gordie Howe ✍ {#/9} 2900.00
☐ SS1 Wayne Gretzky, NYRa. ✍ {#/99} 400.00
☐ SS2 Gordie Howe, Detr. ✍ {#/99} 275.00
☐ SS-G1 Wayne Gretzky, NYRa. ✍ {#/50} 700.00
☐ SS-G2 Gordie Howe, Detr. ✍ {#/50} 475.00
☐ SS-R1 Wayne Gretzky, NYRa. ✍ {#/25} 1200.00
☐ SS-R2 Gordie Howe, Detr. ✍ {#/25} 825.00

SUPERSTAR THEATER

Insert Set (20 cards): 20.00

Insert (1:9 packs) ST

☐ ST1 Paul Kariya, Anah. 3.00
☐ ST2 Sergei Fedorov, Detr. 2.00
☐ ST3 Brett Hull, Dall. 2.00
☐ ST4 Patrick Roy (G), Colo. 7.00
☐ ST5 Dominik Hasek (G), Buff. 2.00
☐ ST6 Eric Lindros, Phil. 2.00
☐ ST7 Jaromir Jagr, Pitt. 2.00
☐ ST8 Martin Brodeur (G), NJer. 4.00
☐ ST9 Pavel Bure, Flor. 2.00
☐ ST10 Teemu Selänne, Anah. 2.00

1999 - 2000 UPPER DECK OVATION – BUYBACKS

Buyback Autograph UDO

☐ 29 Luc Robitaille, LosA. ✍ {#/7}
☐ 31 Mike Ribeiro, Mont. ✍ {#/1}

Buyback Autograph UDO

☐ Gordie Howe, Detr. ✍ {#/29}

1999 - 2000 UPPER DECK POWERDECK

This series was released in 1999-2000. There are two versions: the PowerDeck CD-ROM card and an Auxiliary regular card.

PowerDeck Set (20 cards): - 110.00
Auxiliary Set (21 cards): 45.00 -

	Player	Aux.	CD
☐☐	1 Paul Kariya, Anah.	3.00	7.00
☐☐	2 Teemu Selänne, Anah.	2.00	4.00
☐☐	3 Patrik Stefan, Atla.	1.00	8.00
☐☐	4 Raymond Bourque, Bost.	3.00	6.00
☐☐	5 Sergei Samsonov, Bost.	1.00	3.00
☐☐	6 Dominik Hasek (G), Buff.	2.00	5.00
☐☐	7 Peter Forsberg, Colo.	3.00	7.00
☐☐	8 Patrick Roy (G), Colo.	7.00	15.00
☐☐	9 Brett Hull, Dall.	2.00	5.00
☐☐	10 Mike Modano, Dall.	2.00	5.00
☐☐	11 Steve Yzerman, Detr.	6.00	12.00
☐☐	12 Pavel Bure, Flor.	2.00	4.00
☐☐	13 David Legwand, Nash.	1.00	2.00
☐☐	14 Martin Brodeur (G), NJer.	4.00	8.00
☐☐	15 Theoren Fleury, NYRa.	1.00	3.00
☐☐	16 Eric Lindros, Phil.	2.00	5.00
☐☐	17 Jaromir Jagr, Pitt.	2.00	5.00
☐☐	18 Bobby Orr, Bost.	10.00	20.00
☐☐	19 Gordie Howe, Detr.	7.00	14.00
☐☐	20 Wayne Gretzky, NYRa.	10.00	20.00
☐	CK Steve Yzerman, Detr.	.10	-

POWERFUL MOMENT

Insert Set (4 cards): 50.00 65.00

	Inserts	Aux.	CD
☐☐	P1 Wayne Gretzky, LosA.	15.00	20.00
☐☐	P2 Wayne Gretzky, LosA.	15.00	20.00
☐☐	P3 Wayne Gretzky, Edmo.	15.00	20.00
☐☐	P4 Wayne Gretzky, NYRa.	15.00	20.00

TIME CAPSULE

Insert Set (8 cards): 65.00 100.00

	Inserts	Aux.	CD
☐☐	T1 Jaromir Jagr, Pitt.	4.00	6.00
☐☐	T2 Paul Kariya, Anah.	6.00	10.00
☐☐	T3 Patrick Roy (G), Colo.	16.00	22.00
☐☐	T4 Bobby Orr, Bost.	22.00	30.00
☐☐	T5 Dominik Hasek (G), Buff.	4.00	6.00
☐☐	T6 Gordie Howe, Detr.	14.00	20.00
☐☐	T7 Steve Yzerman, Detr.	12.00	18.00
☐☐	T8 Brett Hull, Dall.	4.00	6.00

1999 - 2000 UPPER DECK PROSPECTS

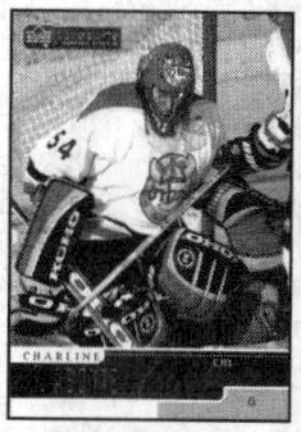

This series was released in 2000.

Complete Set (90 cards): 50.00
Common Player: .25

Player UD

☐ 1 Wayne Gretzky, Sault Ste. Marie Greyhounds 3.00
☐ 2 Jason Spezza, Mississauga IceDogs 6.00
☐ 3 Sheldon Keefe, Barrie Colts .50
☐ 4 Mark Bell, Ottawa 67s 1.00
☐ 5 Justin Papineau, Belleville Bulls .50
☐ 6 Denis Shvidki, Barrie Colts 1.00
☐ 7 Darryl Bootland, Toronto St. Mike's .25
☐ 8 Michael Zigomanis, Kingston Frontenacs .50
☐ 9 Chris Eade, North Bay Centennials .25
☐ 10 Brad Boyes, Erie Otters 1.00
☐ 11 Michael Henrich, Barrie Colts .50
☐ 12 Nikita Alexeev, Erie Otters 1.00
☐ 13 Libor Ustrnul, Plymouth Whalers .25
☐ 14 Brian Finley (G), Barrie Colts .50
☐ 15 Chris Berti, Sarnia Sting .25
☐ 16 Agris Saviels, Owen Sound Platers .25
☐ 17 Kris Newbury, Belleville Bulls .25
☐ 18 Jared Newman, Plymouth Whalers .25
☐ 19 Samu Isosalo, North Bay Centennials .25
☐ 20 Mike Van Ryn, Sarnia Sting 1.00
☐ 21 Miguel Delisle, Ottawa 67s .25
☐ 22 Rostislav Klesla, Brampton Battalion 1.00
☐ 23 Raffi Torres, Brampton Battalion 1.00
☐ 24 Kurtis Foster, Peterborough Petes .25
☐ 25 Lou Dickenson, Mississauga IceDogs .50
☐ 26 Milan Kraft, Prince Albert Raiders 1.00
☐ 27 Jamie Lundmark, Moose Jaw Warriors 1.00
☐ 28 Scott Hartnell, Prince Albert Raiders 1.00
☐ 29 Ben Knopp, Calgary Hitmen .25
☐ 30 Mike Wiril, Brandon Wheat Kings .25
☐ 31 Ryan Craig, Brandon Wheat Kings .25
☐ 32 Kris Beech, Calgary Hitmen 1.00
☐ 33 Pavel Brendl, Calgary Hitmen 1.00
☐ 34 Blake Robson, Portland Winte Hakws .25
☐ 35 Jarret Stoll, Kootenay Ice .50
☐ 36 Oleg Saprykin, Calgary Hitmen 1.00
☐ 37 Eric Johansson, Tri-City Americans .25
☐ 38 Warren Peters, Saskatoon Blades .25
☐ 39 Marcel Hossa, Portland Winte Hakws 1.50
☐ 40 Shane Endicott, Seattle Thunderbirds .25
☐ 41 Craig Olynick, Seattle Thunderbirds .25
☐ 42 Brent Krahn, Calgary Hitmen 1.00
☐ 43 Matt Pettinger, Calgary Hitmen .50
☐ 44 Jaroslav Kristek, Tri-City Americans .25
☐ 45 Milan Bartovic, Tri-City Americans .25
☐ 46 Jared Aulin, Kamloops Blazers 1.00
☐ 47 Jakub Cutta, Swift Current Broncos .50
☐ 48 Blake Ward, Tri-City Americans .25
☐ 49 Lynn Lyons, Spokane Chiefs .25
☐ 50 Jay Bouwmeester, Medicine Hat Tigers 5.00
☐ 51 Nick Schultz, Prince Albert Raiders .50
☐ 52 Filip Novak, Regina Pats .25
☐ 53 Michael Bubnick, Calgary Hitmen .25
☐ 54 Charline Labonté (G), Bathurst Titan 4.00
☐ 55 Thatcher Bell, Rimouski Océanic .50
☐ 56 Yanick Lehoux, Baie-Comeau .25
☐ 57 Antoine Vermette, Victoriaville Tigres .25
☐ 58 Alexei Volkov (G), Halifax Mooseheads 1.00
☐ 59 Michal Sivek, Prince Albert Raiders .50
☐ 60 Carl Mallette, Victoriaville Tigres .25
☐ 61 Maxime Ouellet (G), Québec Remparts 1.50
☐ 62 Simon Lagacé-Daigle, Drummondville Voltigeurs .25
☐ 63 Andrei Shefer, Halifax Mooseheads .25
☐ 64 Mathieu Chouinard (G), Shawinigan Cataractes .50
☐ 65 Philippe Sauvé (G), Drummondville Voltigeurs 1.00
☐ 66 Daniel Sedin, MoDo 1.50
☐ 67 Henrik Sedin, MoDo 1.50
☐ 68 Thatcher Bell, Canada Juniors .25
☐ 69 Brad Boyes, Canada Juniors 1.00
☐ 70 Jared Aulin, Canada Juniors 1.00
☐ 71 Dany Heatley, Canada Juniors 6.00
☐ 72 Ryan Hare, Canada Juniors .50
☐ 73 Scott Hartnell, Canada Juniors 1.00
☐ 74 Jay Bouwmeester, Canada Juniors 5.00
☐ 75 Kiel McLeod, Canada Juniors .50
☐ 76 Kris Newbury, Canada Juniors .50
☐ 77 Blake Robson, Canada Juniors .50
☐ 78 Jarret Stoll, Canada Juniors .50
☐ 79 Antoine Vermette, Canada Juniors .50
☐ 80 Mike Wiril, Canada Juniors .50
☐ 81 Jason Spezza, Canada Juniors 6.00
☐ 82 Jay Harrison, Canada Juniors .50
☐ 83 Brandon Janes, Canada Juniors .50
☐ 84 Craig Olynick, Canada Juniors .50
☐ 85 Mark Popovic, Canada Juniors .50
☐ 86 Nick Schultz, Canada Juniors .50
☐ 87 Karl St. Pierre, Canada Juniors .50
☐ 88 Pascal Leclaire (G), Canada Juniors 2.00
☐ 89 Blake Ward, Canada Juniors .50
☐ 90 Checklist .25

CHL CLASS

Insert Set (10 cards): 24.00

Insert (1:4) MT

☐ C1 Jason Spezza, Mississauga IceDogs 6.00
☐ C2 Justin Papineau, Belleville Bulls 1.00
☐ C3 Mark Bell, Ottawa 67's 2.00
☐ C4 Kris Beech, Calgary Hitmen 3.00
☐ C5 Jay Bouwmeester, Medicine Hat Tigers 7.00
☐ C6 Denis Shvidki, Barrie Colts 2.00
☐ C7 Pavel Brendl, Calgary Hitmen 3.00
☐ C8 Brian Finley (G), Barrie Colts 2.00
☐ C9 Jamie Lundmark, Moose Jaw Warriors 3.00
☐ C10 Thatcher Bell, Rimouski Océanic 1.00

DESTINATION: THE SHOW

Insert Set (10 cards): 40.00

Insert (1:17) MT

☐ DS1 Jason Spezza, Mississauga IceDogs 9.00
☐ DS2 Pavel Brendl, Calgary Hitmen 4.00
☐ DS3 Henrik Sedin, Sweden Juniors 6.00
☐ DS4 Daniel Sedin, Sweden Juniors 6.00
☐ DS5 Jamie Lundmark, Moose Jaw Warriors 4.00
☐ DS6 Taylor Pyatt, Sudbury Wolves 3.00
☐ DS7 Brian Finley (G), Barrie Colts 3.00
☐ DS8 Kris Beech, Calgary Hitmen 4.00
☐ DS9 Denis Shvidki, Barrie Colts 3.00
☐ DS10 Jay Bouwmeester, Medicine Hat Tigers 10.00

INTERNATIONAL STARS

Insert Set (10 cards): 40.00

Insert (1:9) IN

☐ IN1 Daniel Sedin, MoDo 7.00
☐ IN2 Henrik Sedin, MoDo 7.00
☐ IN3 Pavel Brendl, Calgary Hitmen 5.00
☐ IN4 Alexei Volkov (G), Halifax Mooseheads 4.00
☐ IN5 Denis Shvidki, Barrie Colts 4.00
☐ IN6 Milan Kraft, Prince Albert Raiders 5.00
☐ IN7 Nikita Alexeev, Erie Otters 4.00
☐ IN8 Oleg Saprykin, Calgary Hitmen 4.00
☐ IN9 Jaroslav Kristek, Tri-City Americans 1.50
☐ IN10 Marcel Hossa, Portland Winter Hawks 7.00

JERSEY

Insert Set (9 cards): 475.00

Player GJ

☐ Charline Labonté (G), Bathurst Titan ✂ 80.00
☐ Daniel Sedin, Sweden Juniors ✂ 70.00
☐ Henrik Sedin, Sweden Juniors ✂ 70.00
☐ Jay Bouwmeester, Medicine Hat Tigers ✂ 80.00
☐ Jason Spezza, Mississauga IceDogs ✂ 105.00
☐ Kris Beech, Calgary Hitmen ✂ 55.00

☐	Lou Dickenson, Mississauga IceDogs ✂	35.00
☐	Pavel Brendl, Calgary Hitmen ✂	55.00
☐	Thatcher Bell, Rimouski Océanic ✂	35.00

SIGNATURE

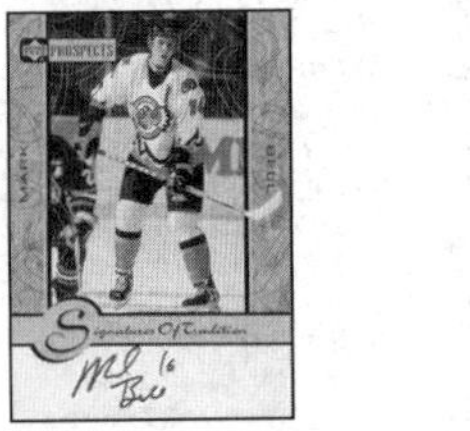

	Insert Set (18 cards):	575.00
	Player	MT
☐	Alexei Volkov (G), Halifax Mooseheads ✍	12.00
☐	Brian Finley (G), Barrie Colts ✍	12.00
☐	Branislav Mezei, Belleville Bulls ✍	12.00
☐	Charline Labonté (G), Bathurst Titan ✍	30.00
☐	Daniel Sedin, Sweden Juniors ✍	30.00
☐	Denis Shvidki, Barrie Colts ✍	12.00
☐	Henrik Sedin, Sweden Juniors ✍	30.00
☐	Jay Bouwmeester, Medicine Hat Tigers ✍	45.00
☐	Jamie Lundmark, Moose Jaw Warriors ✍	15.00
☐	Jason Spezza, Mississauga IceDogs ✍	75.00
☐	Kris Beech, Calgary Hitmen ✍	15.00
☐	Mark Bell, Ottawa 67's ✍	12.00
☐	Mathieu Chouinard (G), Shawinigan Cataractes ✍	12.00
☐	Maxime Ouellet (G), Québec Remparts ✍	15.00
☐	Mike Van Ryn, Sarnia Sting ✍	12.00
☐	Pavel Brendl, Calgary Hitmen ✍	15.00
☐	Taylor Pyatt, Sudbury Wolves ✍	12.00
☐	Wayne Gretzky, Sault Ste. Marie Greyhounds ✍	400.00

1999 - 2000 UPPER DECK RETRO

This series was released in 1999. There are three versions: the regular card, a Gold parallel (#/150) and a Platinum parallel (#/1). Card 82 does not exist.

	Complete Set (109 cards):	2500.00	60.00
	Common Player:	4.00	.25
	Player	G150	Reg.
☐☐☐	1 Paul Kariya, Anah.	55.00	1.00
☐☐☐	2 Teemu Selänne, Anah.	30.00	.50
☐☐☐	3 Jim McKenzie, Anah.	4.00	.25
☐☐☐	4 Raymond Bourque, Bost.	45.00	1.00
☐☐☐	5 Sergei Samsonov, Bost.	20.00	.50
☐☐☐	6 Joe Thornton, Bost.	45.00	1.00
☐☐☐	7 Dominik Hasek (G), Buff.	40.00	1.00
☐☐☐	8 Miroslav Satan, Buff.	10.00	.25
☐☐☐	9 Michael Peca, Buff.	15.00	.25
☐☐☐	10 Todd Simpson, Calg.	4.00	.25
☐☐☐	11 Valeri Bure, Calg.	10.00	.25
☐☐☐	12 Jarome Iginla, Calg.	30.00	.50
☐☐☐	13 Kent Manderville, Caro.	4.00	.25
☐☐☐	14 Keith Primeau, Caro.	15.00	.25
☐☐☐	15 Sami Kapanen, Caro.	10.00	.25
☐☐☐	16 Mark Janssens, Chic.	4.00	.25
☐☐☐	17 Tony Amonte, Chic.	20.00	.50
☐☐☐	18 Doug Gilmour, Chic.	20.00	.50
☐☐☐	19 Peter Forsberg, Colo.	55.00	1.00
☐☐☐	20 Patrick Roy (G), Colo.	120.00	3.00
☐☐☐	21 Joe Sakic, Colo.	60.00	1.50
☐☐☐	22 Theoren Fleury, Colo.	20.00	.50
☐☐☐	23 Chris Drury, Colo.	20.00	.50
☐☐☐	24 Mike Modano, Dall.	40.00	1.00
☐☐☐	25 Brett Hull, Dall.	40.00	1.00
☐☐☐	26 Ed Belfour (G), Dall.	40.00	1.00
☐☐☐	27 Steve Yzerman, Detr.	95.00	2.00
☐☐☐	28 Sergei Fedorov, Detr.	40.00	1.00
☐☐☐	29 Brendan Shanahan, Detr.	40.00	1.00
☐☐☐	30 Chris Chelios, Detr.	20.00	.50
☐☐☐	31 Doug Weight, Edmo.	20.00	.50
☐☐☐	32 Bill Guerin, Edmo.	15.00	.25
☐☐☐	33 Tom Poti, Edmo.	5.00	.25
☐☐☐	34 Gord Murphy, Flor.	4.00	.25
☐☐☐	35 Pavel Bure, Flor.	30.00	.50
☐☐☐	36 Mark Parrish, Flor.	15.00	.25
☐☐☐	37 Rob Blake, LosA.	20.00	.50
☐☐☐	38 Pavel Rosa, LosA.	5.00	.25
☐☐☐	39 Luc Robitaille, LosA.	30.00	.50
☐☐☐	40 Stéphane Quintal, Mont.	5.00	.25
☐☐☐	41 Saku Koivu, Mont.	30.00	.50
☐☐☐	42 Bob Boughner, Nash.	4.00	.25
☐☐☐	43 David Legwand, Nash.	15.00	.25
☐☐☐	44 Mike Dunham (G), Nash.	15.00	.25
☐☐☐	45 Martin Brodeur (G), NJer.	60.00	1.50
☐☐☐	46 Scott Stevens, NJer.	15.00	.25
☐☐☐	**47 John Madden, NJer. RC**	**20.00**	**1.50**
☐☐☐	48 Vadim Sharifijanov, NJer.	4.00	.25
☐☐☐	49 Wayne Gretzky, NYRa.	160.00	4.00
☐☐☐	50 Manny Malhotra, NYRa.	5.00	.25
☐☐☐	51 Brian Leetch, NYRa.	20.00	.50
☐☐☐	52 Mike Richter (G), NYRa.	15.00	.25
☐☐☐	53 Eric Brewer, NYIs.	15.00	.25
☐☐☐	54 Alexei Yashin, Otta.	20.00	.50
☐☐☐	55 Marian Hossa, Otta.	40.00	1.00
☐☐☐	56 Chris Phillips, Otta.	5.00	.25
☐☐☐	57 Eric Lindros, Phil.	40.00	1.00
☐☐☐	58 John LeClair, Phil.	30.00	.50
☐☐☐	59 Mark Recchi, Phil.	15.00	.25
☐☐☐	60 Jeremy Roenick, Phoe.	30.00	.50
☐☐☐	61 Keith Tkachuk, Phoe.	20.00	.50
☐☐☐	62 Nikolai Khabibulin (G), Phoe.	15.00	.25
☐☐☐	**63 Robert Esche (G), Phoe. RC**	**15.00**	**1.00**
☐☐☐	64 Jaromir Jagr, Pitt.	40.00	1.00
☐☐☐	65 Martin Straka, Pitt.	10.00	.25
☐☐☐	66 Jeff Friesen, SanJ.	10.00	.25
☐☐☐	67 Vincent Damphousse, SanJ.	20.00	.50
☐☐☐	68 Chris Pronger, SLou.	20.00	.50
☐☐☐	69 Pavol Demitra, SLou.	15.00	.25
☐☐☐	70 Al MacInnis, SLou.	15.00	.25
☐☐☐	71 Paul Mara, Tamp.	5.00	.25
☐☐☐	72 Vincent Lecavalier, Tamp.	40.00	1.00
☐☐☐	73 Sergei Berezin, Toro.	5.00	.25
☐☐☐	74 Mats Sundin, Toro.	40.00	1.00
☐☐☐	75 Curtis Joseph (G), Toro.	40.00	1.00
☐☐☐	76 Markus Näslund, Vanc.	40.00	1.00
☐☐☐	77 Mark Messier, Vanc.	40.00	1.00
☐☐☐	78 Bill Muckalt, Vanc.	5.00	.25
☐☐☐	79 Peter Bondra, Wash.	20.00	.50
☐☐☐	80 Adam Oates, Wash.	15.00	.25
☐☐☐	81 Bobby Orr, Bost.	160.00	4.00
☐☐☐	83 Mario Lemieux, Pitt.	120.00	3.00
☐☐☐	84 Maurice Richard, Mont.	110.00	2.50
☐☐☐	85 Jean Béliveau, Mont.	85.00	2.00
☐☐☐	86 Bobby Hull, Chic.	70.00	1.50
☐☐☐	87 Terry Sawchuk (G), Detr.	80.00	2.00
☐☐☐	88 Eddie Shore, Bost.	55.00	1.00
☐☐☐	89 Alex Delvecchio, Detr.	15.00	.25
☐☐☐	90 Jacques Plante (G), Mont.	60.00	1.50
☐☐☐	91 Stan Mikita, Chic.	30.00	.50
☐☐☐	92 Gerry Cheevers (G), Bost.	30.00	.50
☐☐☐	93 Glenn Hall (G), Chic.	40.00	1.00
☐☐☐	94 Phil Esposito, Bost.	45.00	1.00
☐☐☐	95 Lanny McDonald, Calg.	30.00	.50
☐☐☐	96 Mike Bossy, NYIs.	60.00	1.50
☐☐☐	97 Ted Lindsay, Detr.	40.00	1.00
☐☐☐	98 Leonard (Red) Kelly, Detr.	20.00	.50
☐☐☐	99 Bobby Clarke, Phil.	30.00	.50
☐☐☐	100 Larry Robinson, Mont.	20.00	.50
☐☐☐	101 Ken Dryden (G), Mont.	80.00	2.00
☐☐☐	**102 Vladislav Tretiak (G), USSR RC**	**45.00**	**3.00**
☐☐☐	103 Marcel Dionne, LosA.	40.00	1.00
☐☐☐	104 Bernie Geoffrion, Mont.	30.00	.50
☐☐☐	105 Johnny Bucyk, Bost.	20.00	.50
☐☐☐	106 Brad Park, NYRa.	20.00	.50
☐☐☐	107 Tony Esposito (G), Chic.	40.00	1.00
☐☐☐	108 Jari Kurri, Edmo.	40.00	1.00
☐☐☐	109 Henri Richard, Mont.	40.00	1.00
☐☐☐	110 Mike Gartner, Phoe.	30.00	.50

DISTANT REPLAY

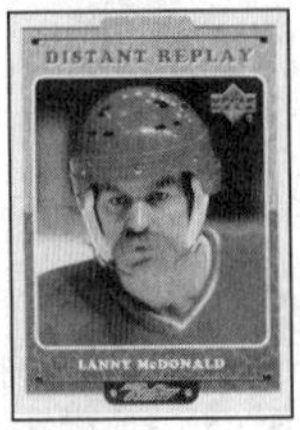

There are two versions: the regular insert (1:11 packs) and the parallel insert (#/100).

	Insert Set (15 cards):	950.00	115.00
	Inserts	DR100	DR
☐☐	DR1 Raymond Bourque, Bost.	50.00	6.00
☐☐	DR2 Martin Brodeur (G), NJer.	70.00	8.00
☐☐	DR3 Jaromir Jagr, Pitt.	45.00	5.00
☐☐	DR4 Paul Kariya, Anah.	60.00	7.00
☐☐	DR5 Steve Yzerman, Detr.	105.00	12.00
☐☐	DR6 Mark Messier, Vanc.	45.00	5.00
☐☐	DR7 Patrick Roy (G), Colo.	135.00	15.00
☐☐	DR8 Dominik Hasek (G), Buff.	45.00	5.00
☐☐	DR9 Wayne Gretzky, NYRa.	180.00	20.00
☐☐	DR10 Bobby Orr, Bost.	140.00	20.00
☐☐	DR12 Mario Lemieux, Pitt.	135.00	15.00
☐☐	DR13 Lanny McDonald, Calg.	25.00	4.00
☐☐	DR14 Maurice Richard, Mont.	100.00	14.00
☐☐	DR15 Vladislav Tretiak (G), USSR	45.00	6.00

EPIC GRETZKY

There are two versions: the regular insert (1:23 packs) and the parallel insert (#/50).

	Insert Set (10 cards):	1900.00	170.00
	Inserts	EG50	EG
☐☐	EG1 Wayne Gretzky, Edmo.	225.00	20.00
☐☐	EG2 Wayne Gretzky, Edmo.	225.00	20.00
☐☐	EG3 Wayne Gretzky, Edmo.	225.00	20.00
☐☐	EG4 Wayne Gretzky, Edmo.	225.00	20.00
☐☐	EG5 Wayne Gretzky, Edmo.	225.00	20.00
☐☐	EG6 Wayne Gretzky, Edmo.	225.00	20.00
☐☐	EG7 Wayne Gretzky, Edmo.	225.00	20.00
☐☐	EG8 Wayne Gretzky, LosA.	225.00	20.00
☐☐	EG9 Wayne Gretzky, LosA.	225.00	20.00
☐☐	EG10 Wayne Gretzky, NYRa.	225.00	20.00

GENERATIONS

There are two versions: the regular insert (1:3 packs) and the parallel insert (#/500). Card G2A does not exist.

	Insert Set (10 cards):	225.00	75.00
	Inserts	G500	G
☐☐	G1A Bobby Orr, Bost.	30.00	10.00
☐☐	G1B Brian Leetch, NYRa.	4.00	1.00
☐☐	G1C Bryan Berard, Toro.	3.00	1.00
☐☐	G2B Bobby Clarke, Phil.	6.00	2.00
☐☐	G2C Keith Tkachuk, Phoe.	4.00	1.00
☐☐	G3A Glenn Hall (G), Chic.	6.00	2.00
☐☐	G3B Patrick Roy (G), Colo.	22.00	7.00
☐☐	G3C Jean-Marc Pelletier (G), Phil.	3.00	1.00
☐☐	G4A Eddie Shore, Bost.	10.00	3.00
☐☐	G4B Bobby Orr, Bost.	30.00	10.00
☐☐	G4C Raymond Bourque, Bost.	8.00	3.00
☐☐	G5A Jean Béliveau, Mont.	16.00	5.00
☐☐	G5B Mario Lemieux, Pitt.	22.00	7.00
☐☐	G5C Vincent Lecavalier, Tamp.	6.00	2.00
☐☐	G6A Maurice Richard, Mont.	20.00	7.00
☐☐	G6B Pavel Bure, Flor.	6.00	2.00
☐☐	G6C Sergei Samsonov, Bost.	4.00	1.00
☐☐	G7A Stan Mikita, Chic.	6.00	2.00
☐☐	G7B Theoren Fleury, Colo.	4.00	1.00
☐☐	G7C Paul Kariya, Anah.	10.00	3.00
☐☐	G8A Jari Kurri, Edmo.	6.00	2.00
☐☐	G8B Teemu Selänne, Anah.	6.00	2.00
☐☐	G8C Olli Jokinen, NYIs.	3.00	1.00
☐☐	G9A Phil Esposito, Bost.	8.00	3.00
☐☐	G9B Brendan Shanahan, Detr.	6.00	2.00
☐☐	G9C Mark Parrish, Flor.	3.00	1.00
☐☐	G10A Terry Sawchuk (G), Detr.	14.00	5.00
☐☐	G10B Dominik Hasek (G), Buff.	6.00	2.00
☐☐	G10C Jean-Sébastien Giguère (G), Calg.	6.00	2.00

INKREDIBLE

There are two versions: the regular insert (1:23 packs) and the Gold parallel (#/25).

	Insert Set (29 cards):	7000.00	1100.00
	Autographs	G25	Ink
☐	Tony Amonte, Chic. ✍	135.00	20.00
☐	Jean Béliveau, Mont. ✍	315.00	50.00
☐	Mike Bossy, NYIs. ✍	360.00	60.00
☐	Raymond Bourque, Bost. ✍	315.00	50.00
☐	Johnny Bucyk, Bost. ✍	135.00	20.00
☐	Pavel Bure, Flor. ✍	180.00	30.00
☐	Gerry Cheevers (G), Bost. ✍	180.00	30.00
☐	Bobby Clarke, Phil. ✍	135.00	20.00
☐	Alex Delvecchio, Detr. ✍	108.00	15.00
☐	Marcel Dionne, LosA. ✍	225.00	35.00
☐	Tony Esposito (G), Chic. ✍	225.00	35.00
☐	Phil Esposito, Bost. ✍	270.00	45.00
☐	Bernie Geoffrion, Mont. ✍	180.00	30.00
☐	Wayne Gretzky, NYRa. ✍	990.00	165.00
☐	Bobby Hull, Chic. ✍	225.00	35.00
☐	Brett Hull, Dall. ✍	225.00	35.00
☐	Vincent Lecavalier, Tamp. ✍	225.00	35.00
☐	Mario Lemieux, Pitt. ✍	675.00	110.00
☐	Ted Lindsay, Detr. ✍	225.00	30.00
☐	Lanny McDonald, Calg. ✍	180.00	30.00
☐	Stan Mikita, Chic. ✍	180.00	30.00
☐	Bobby Orr, Bost. ✍	900.00	150.00
☐	Brad Park, NYRa. ✍	135.00	20.00
☐	Keith Primeau, Caro. ✍	90.00	15.00
☐	Maurice Richard, Mont. ✍ •	585.00	95.00
☐	Sergei Samsonov, Bost. ✍	135.00	20.00
☐	Vladislav Tretiak (G), USSR ✍	270.00	45.00
☐	Doug Weight, Edmo. ✍	135.00	20.00
☐	Steve Yzerman, Detr. ✍	540.00	90.00

RETRO MOMENTOS

	Insert Set (5 cards):	900.00
	Insert	RM
☐	Marcel Dionne, LosA. ✂	100.00
☐	Ken Dryden (G), Mont. ✂	200.00
☐	Phil Esposito, All-Star ✂	120.00
☐	Wayne Gretzky, NYRa. ✂	400.00
☐	Mario Lemieux, Pitt. ✂	300.00

TURN OF THE CENTURY

	Insert Set (15 cards):	200.00
	Insert (1:23 packs)	TotC
☐	TC1 Vincent Lecavalier, Tamp.	10.00
☐	TC2 Martin Brodeur (G), NJer.	15.00
☐	TC3 Jaromir Jagr, Pitt.	10.00
☐	TC4 Paul Kariya, Anah.	10.00
☐	TC5 Steve Yzerman, Detr.	20.00
☐	TC6 Raymond Bourque, Bost.	10.00
☐	TC7 Patrick Roy (G), Colo.	30.00
☐	TC8 Dominik Hasek (G), Buff.	10.00
☐	TC9 Wayne Gretzky, NYRa.	40.00
☐	TC10 Bobby Clarke, Phil.	5.00
☐	TC11 Larry Robinson, Mont.	5.00
☐	TC13 Mario Lemieux, Pitt.	30.00
☐	TC14 Maurice Richard, Mont.	25.00
☐	TC15 Bobby Orr, Bost.	40.00

LUNCH BOXES

	Complete Set (4 boxes):	75.00
	Insert	LB
☐	Wayne Gretzky	20.00
☐	Wayne Gretzky Tribute	35.00
☐	Wayne Gretzky	20.00
☐	Wayne Gretzky	20.00

1999 - 2000 UPPER DECK RETRO – BUYBACKS

Buyback Autograph	Retro
☐ 4 Raymond Bourque, Bost. ✍ {#/4}	
☐ 39 Luc Robitaille, LosA. ✍ {#/3}	

1999 - 2000 VICTORY

This series was released in 1999 as a retail-only product.

Complete Set (440 cards): 80.00
Common Player: .20

Player	Reg.
☐ 1 Paul Kariya, Anah. [Checklist]	.50
☐ 2 Paul Kariya, Anah.	1.00
☐ 3 Teemu Selänne, Anah.	.50
☐ 4 Matt Cullen, Anah.	.20
☐ 5 Steve Rucchin, Anah.	.20
☐ 6 Oleg Tverdovsky, Anah.	.20
☐ 7 Guy Hebert (G), Anah.	.20
☐ 8 Fredrik Olausson, Anah.	.20
☐ 9 Ted Donato, Anah.	.20
☐ 10 Marty McInnis, Anah.	.20
☐ 11 Damian Rhodes (G), Otta. [Checklist]	.20
☐ 12 Jody Hull, Phil.	.20
☐ 13 Damian Rhodes (G), Otta.	.20
☐ 14 Kelly Buchberger, Edmo.	.20
☐ **15 Scott Langkow (G), Phoe. RC**	**1.00**
☐ 16 Norm Maracle (G), Detr.	.20
☐ 17 Jason Botterill, Dall.	.20
☐ 18 Randy Robitaille, Bost.	.20
☐ 19 Ray Ferraro, Atla.	.20
☐ 20 Raymond Bourque, Bost. [Checklist]	.20
☐ 21 Raymond Bourque, Bost.	.50
☐ 22 Sergei Samsonov, Bost.	.20
☐ 23 Joe Thornton, Bost.	.50
☐ 24 Shawn Bates, Bost.	.20
☐ 25 Byron Dafoe (G), Bost.	.20
☐ 26 Jonathan Girard, Bost.	.20
☐ 27 Jason Allison, Bost.	.20
☐ 28 Anson Carter, Bost.	.20
☐ 29 Hal Gill, Bost.	.20
☐ 30 Kyle McLaren, Bost.	.20
☐ 31 Don Sweeney, Bost.	.20
☐ 32 Dominik Hasek (G), Buff. [Checklist]	.20
☐ 33 Dominik Hasek (G), Buff.	.50
☐ 34 Michael Peca, Buff.	.20
☐ 35 Miroslav Satan, Buff.	.20
☐ 36 Dixon Ward, Buff.	.20
☐ 37 Martin Biron (G), Buff.	.20
☐ 38 Joé Juneau, Buff.	.20
☐ 39 Cory Sarich, Buff.	.20
☐ 40 Brian Holzinger, Buff.	.20
☐ 41 Rhett Warrener, Buff.	.20
☐ 42 Alexei Zhitnik, Buff.	.20
☐ 43 Jean-Sébastien Giguère (G), Calg. [Checklist]	.20
☐ 44 Valeri Bure, Calg.	.20
☐ 45 Jean-Sébastien Giguère (G), Calg.	.50
☐ 46 Jarome Iginla, Calg.	.50
☐ 47 Rico Fata, Calg.	.20
☐ 48 Derek Morris, Calg.	.20
☐ 49 René Corbet, Calg.	.20
☐ 50 Phil Housley, Calg.	.20
☐ **51 Tyrone Garner (G), Calg. RC**	**1.00**
☐ 52 Marc* Savard, NYRa.	.20
☐ 53 Keith Primeau, Caro. [Checklist]	.20
☐ 54 Sami Kapanen, Caro.	.20
☐ 55 Bates Battaglia, Caro.	.20
☐ 56 Arturs Irbe (G), Caro.	.20
☐ 57 Keith Primeau, Caro.	.20
☐ 58 Gary Roberts, Caro.	.20
☐ 59 Ron Francis, Caro.	.20
☐ 60 Paul Coffey, Caro.	.20
☐ 61 Martin Gélinas, Caro.	.20
☐ 62 Jeff O'Neill, Caro.	.20
☐ 63 Glen Wesley, Caro.	.20
☐ 64 Tony Amonte, Chic. [Checklist]	.20
☐ 65 Tony Amonte, Chic.	.20
☐ 66 Jean-Pierre Dumont, Chic.	.20
☐ 67 Doug Gilmour, Chic.	.20
☐ 68 Ty Jones, Chic.	.20
☐ 69 Anders Eriksson, Chic.	.20
☐ 70 Rémi Royer, Chic.	.20
☐ 71 Jocelyn Thibault (G), Chic.	.20
☐ 72 Alexei Zhamnov, Chic.	.20
☐ 73 Éric Dazé, Chic.	.20
☐ 74 Bryan McCabe, Chic.	.20
☐ 75 Peter Forsberg, Colo. [Checklist]	.50
☐ 76 Chris Drury, Colo.	.20
☐ 77 Peter Forsberg, Colo.	1.00
☐ 78 Patrick Roy (G), Colo.	2.00
☐ 79 Joe Sakic, Colo.	1.00
☐ 80 Milan Hejduk, Colo.	.50
☐ 81 Adam Deadmarsh, Colo.	.20
☐ 82 Adam Foote, Colo.	.20
☐ 83 Sandis Ozolinsh, Colo.	.20
☐ 84 Claude Lemieux, Colo.	.20
☐ 86 Ed Belfour (G), Dall.	.50
☐ 86 Brett Hull, Dall. [Checklist]	.20
☐ 87 Brett Hull, Dall.	.50
☐ 88 Mike Modano, Dall.	.50
☐ 89 Derian Hatcher, Dall.	.20
☐ 90 Jamie Langenbrunner, Dall.	.20
☐ 91 Joe Nieuwendyk, Dall.	.20
☐ **92 Jonathan Sim, Dall. RC**	**.50**
☐ 93 Jere Lehtinen, Dall.	.20
☐ 94 Darryl Sydor, Dall.	.20
☐ 95 Sergei Zubov, Dall.	.20
☐ 96 Steve Yzerman, Detr. [Checklist]	.50
☐ 97 Brendan Shanahan, Detr.	.50
☐ 98 Steve Yzerman, Detr.	1.50
☐ 99 Chris Chelios, Detr.	.20
☐ 100 Sergei Fedorov, Detr.	.50
☐ 101 Vyacheslav Kozlov, Detr.	.20
☐ 102 Igor Larionov, Detr.	.20
☐ 103 Nicklas Lidström, Detr.	.20
☐ 104 Tomas Holmström, Detr.	.20
☐ 105 Chris Osgood (G), Detr.	.20
☐ 106 Kris Draper, Detr.	.20
☐ 107 Darren McCarty, Detr.	.20
☐ 108 Doug Weight, Edmo. [Checklist]	.20
☐ 109 Bill Guerin, Edmo.	.20
☐ 110 Tom Poti, Edmo.	.20
☐ 111 Mike Grier, Edmo.	.20
☐ 112 Tommy Salo (G), Edmo.	.20
☐ 113 Doug Weight, Edmo.	.20
☐ 114 Josef Beranek, Edmo.	.20
☐ 115 Fredrik Lindquist, Edmo.	.20
☐ 116 Roman Hamrlik, Edmo.	.20
☐ 117 Todd Marchant, Edmo.	.20
☐ 118 Janne Niinimaa, Edmo.	.20
☐ 119 Pavel Bure, Flor. [Checklist]	.20
☐ 120 Pavel Bure, Flor.	.50
☐ 121 Mark Parrish, Flor.	.20
☐ 122 Scott Mellanby, Flor.	.20
☐ 122 Pavel Rosa, LosA.	.20
☐ 123 Viktor Kozlov, Flor.	.20
☐ 124 Oleg Kvasha, Flor.	.20
☐ 125 Rob Niedermayer, Flor.	.20
☐ 126 Bret Hedican, Flor.	.20
☐ 127 Trevor Kidd (G), Caro.	.20
☐ 128 Robert Svehla, Flor.	.20
☐ 129 Peter Worrell, Flor.	.20
☐ 130 Rob Blake, LosA. [Checklist]	.20
☐ 131 Rob Blake, LosA.	.20
☐ 133 Donald Audette, LosA.	.20
☐ 134 Luc Robitaille, LosA.	.50
☐ 135 Vladimir Tsyplakov, LosA.	.20
☐ 136 Jozef Stumpel, LosA.	.20
☐ 137 Nathan Lafayette, LosA.	.20
☐ 138 Glen Murray, LosA.	.20
☐ 139 Zigmund Palffy, NYIs.	.20
☐ 140 Bryan Smolinski, NYIs.	.20
☐ 141 Jamie Storr (G), LosA.	.20
☐ 142 Saku Koivu, Mont. [Checklist]	.20
☐ 143 Saku Koivu, Mont.	.50
☐ 144 Arron Asham, Mont.	.20
☐ 145 Jeff Hackett (G), Mont.	.20
☐ 146 Trevor Linden, NYIs.	.20
☐ 147 Eric Weinrich, Mont.	.20
☐ 148 Vladimir Malakhov, Mont.	.20
☐ 149 Martin Rucinsky, Mont.	.20
☐ 150 Brian Savage, Mont.	.20
☐ 151 Shayne Corson, Mont.	.20
☐ 152 Scott Lachance, Mont.	.20
☐ 153 José Théodore (G), Mont.	1.00
☐ 154 David Legwand, Nash. [Checklist]	.20
☐ 155 Mike Dunham (G), Nash.	.20
☐ 156 David Legwand, Nash.	.20
☐ 157 Sergei Krivokrasov, Nash.	.20
☐ 158 Cliff Ronning, Nash.	.20
☐ 159 Kimmo Timonen, Nash.	.20
☐ 160 Bob Boughner, Nash.	.20
☐ **161 Mark Mowers, Nash. RC**	**.50**
☐ 162 Patrick* Côté, Nash.	.20
☐ 163 Tomas Vokoun (G), Nash.	.20
☐ 164 Jan Vopat, Nash.	.20
☐ 165 Martin Brodeur (G), NJer. [Checklist]	.50
☐ 166 Martin Brodeur (G), NJer.	1.00
☐ **167 John Madden, NJer. RC**	**2.00**
☐ 168 Vadim Sharifijanov, NJer.	.20
☐ 169 Patrik Elias, NJer.	.50
☐ 170 Scott Stevens, NJer.	.20
☐ 171 Petr* Sykora, NJer.	.20
☐ 172 Jason Arnott, NJer.	.20
☐ 173 Brendan Morrison, NJer.	.20
☐ 174 Scott Niedermayer, NJer.	.20
☐ 175 Bobby Holik, NJer.	.20
☐ 176 Eric Brewer, NYIs. [Checklist]	.20
☐ 177 Eric Brewer, NYIs.	.20
☐ 178 Zdeno Chara, NYIs.	.20
☐ 179 Kenny Jönsson, NYIs.	.20
☐ 180 Dimitri Nabokov, NYIs.	.20
☐ 181 Mariusz Czerkawski, NYIs.	.20
☐ 182 Brad Isbister, NYIs.	.20
☐ 183 Olli Jokinen, LosA.	.20
☐ 184 Félix Potvin (G), NYIs.	.20
☐ 185 Mike Watt, NYIs.	.20
☐ 186 Claude Lapointe, NYIs.	.20
☐ 187 Brian Leetch, NYRa. [Checklist]	.20
☐ 188 Manny Malhotra, NYRa.	.20
☐ 189 Mike Richter (G), NYRa.	.20
☐ 190 Theoren Fleury, Colo.	.20
☐ 191 Adam Graves, NYRa.	.20
☐ 192 Brian Leetch, NYRa.	.20
☐ 193 Petr Nedved, NYRa.	.20
☐ 194 Brent Fedyk, NYRa.	.20
☐ 195 Barry Richter, NYRa.	.20
☐ 196 Valeri Kamensky, Colo.	.20
☐ 197 Kirk McLean (G), Flor.	.20
☐ 198 Kevin Stevens, NYRa.	.20
☐ 199 Alexei Yashin, Otta. [Checklist]	.20
☐ 200 Marian Hossa, Otta.	.50
☐ 201 Alexei Yashin, Otta.	.20
☐ 202 Shawn McEachern, Otta.	.20
☐ 203 Sami Salo, Otta.	.20
☐ 204 Daniel Alfredsson, Otta.	.20
☐ 205 Magnus Arvedson, Otta.	.20
☐ 206 Wade Redden, Otta.	.20
☐ 207 Ron Tugnutt (G), Otta.	.20
☐ 208 Chris Phillips, Otta.	.20
☐ 209 Vaclav Prospal, Otta.	.20
☐ 210 Eric Lindros, Phil. [Checklist]	.20
☐ 211 John LeClair, Phil.	.50
☐ 212 Eric Lindros, Phil.	.50
☐ 213 Mark Recchi, Phil.	.20
☐ 214 Rod Brind'Amour, Phil.	.20
☐ 215 Éric Desjardins, Phil.	.20
☐ 216 Jean-Marc Pelletier (G), Phil.	.20
☐ **217 Ryan Bast, Phil. RC**	**.50**
☐ 218 Keith Jones, Phil.	.20
☐ 219 John Vanbiesbrouck (G), Phil.	.20
☐ **220 Brian Wesenberg, Phil. RC**	**.50**
☐ 221 Dan McGillis, Phil.	.20
☐ 222 Keith Tkachuk, Phoe. [Checklist]	.20
☐ **223 Robert Esche (G), Phoe. RC**	**1.50**
☐ 224 Keith Tkachuk, Phoe.	.20
☐ 225 Nikolai Khabibulin (G), Phoe.	.20
☐ 226 Trevor Letowski, Phoe.	.20
☐ 227 Robert Reichel, Phoe.	.20
☐ 228 Jeremy Roenick, Phoe.	.50
☐ 229 Greg A. Adams, Phoe.	.20
☐ 230 Daniel Brière, Phoe.	.20
☐ 231 Rick Tocchet, Phoe.	.20
☐ 232 Stanislav Neckar, Phoe.	.20
☐ 233 Teppo Numminen, Phoe.	.20
☐ 234 Jaromir Jagr, Pitt. [Checklist]	.20
☐ 235 Jaromir Jagr, Pitt.	.50
☐ 236 Matthew Barnaby, Pitt.	.20
☐ 237 Tom Barrasso (G), Pitt.	.20
☐ 238 Jan Hrdina, Pitt.	.20
☐ 239 Martin Straka, Pitt.	.20
☐ 240 Jean-Sébastien Aubin (G), Pitt.	.20
☐ 241 Alexei Kovalev, Pitt.	.20
☐ 242 German Titov, Pitt.	.20
☐ 243 Kevin Hatcher, Pitt.	.20
☐ 244 Kip Miller, Pitt.	.20
☐ 245 Aleksey Morozov, Pitt.	.20
☐ 246 Jeff Friesen, SanJ. [Checklist]	.20
☐ 247 Vincent Damphousse, SanJ.	.20
☐ 248 Jeff Friesen, SanJ.	.20
☐ 249 Scott Hannan, SanJ.	.20
☐ 250 Patrick Marleau, SanJ.	.20
☐ 251 Mike Ricci, SanJ.	.20
☐ 252 Owen Nolan, SanJ.	.20
☐ 253 Marco Sturm, SanJ.	.20
☐ 254 Gary Suter, SanJ.	.20
☐ 255 Jeff Norton, SanJ.	.20
☐ 256 Steve Shields (G), SanJ.	.20
☐ 257 Mike Vernon (G), SanJ.	.20
☐ 258 Al MacInnis, SLou. [Checklist]	.20
☐ 259 Pavol Demitra, SLou.	.20
☐ 260 Al MacInnis, SLou.	.20
☐ 261 Lubos Bartecko, SLou.	.20
☐ **262 Jochen Hecht, SLou. RC**	**2.00**
☐ 263 Chris Pronger, SLou.	.20
☐ 264 Grant Fuhr (G), SLou.	.20
☐ 265 Michal Handzus, SLou.	.20
☐ 266 Pierre Turgeon, SLou.	.20
☐ 267 Jim Campbell, SLou.	.20
☐ 268 Roman Turek (G), Dall.	.20
☐ 269 Vincent Lecavalier, Tamp. [Checklist]	.20
☐ 270 Vincent Lecavalier, Tamp.	.50
☐ 271 Paul Mara, Tamp.	.20
☐ 272 Kevin Hodson (G), Tamp.	.20
☐ 273 Dan Cloutier (G), NYRa.	.20
☐ 274 Chris Gratton, Tamp.	.20
☐ 275 Pavel Kubina, Tamp.	.20
☐ 276 Darcy Tucker, Tamp.	.20
☐ 277 Alexandre Daigle, Tamp.	.20
☐ 278 Stéphane Richer, Tamp.	.20
☐ 279 Niklas Sundström, NYRa.	.20
☐ 280 Mats Sundin, Toro. [Checklist]	.20
☐ 281 Mats Sundin, Toro.	.50
☐ 282 Bryan Berard, Toro.	.20
☐ 283 Sergei Berezin, Toro.	.20
☐ 284 Curtis Joseph (G), Toro.	.50
☐ 285 Tomas Kaberle, Toro.	.20
☐ 286 Danny Markov, Toro.	.20
☐ 287 Steve Thomas, Toro.	.20
☐ 288 Mike Johnson, Toro.	.20
☐ 289 Tie Domi, Toro.	.20
☐ 290 Yanic Perreault, Toro.	.20
☐ 291 Derek King, Toro.	.20
☐ 292 Mark Messier, Vanc. [Checklist]	.20
☐ 293 Mark Messier, Vanc.	.50
☐ 294 Bill Muckalt, Vanc.	.20
☐ 295 Josh Holden, Vanc.	.20
☐ 296 Markus Näslund, Vanc.	.50
☐ 297 Kevin Weekes (G), Vanc.	.20
☐ 298 Ed Jovanovski, Vanc.	.20
☐ 299 Alexander Mogilny, Vanc.	.20
☐ 300 Mattias Öhlund, Vanc.	.20
☐ 301 Todd Bertuzzi, Vanc.	.50
☐ 302 Peter Schaefer, Vanc.	.20
☐ 303 Peter Bondra, Wash. [Checklist]	.20
☐ 304 Peter Bondra, Wash.	.20
☐ 305 Adam Oates, Wash.	.20
☐ 306 Jan Bulis, Wash.	.20
☐ 307 Jaroslav Svejkovsky, Wash.	.20
☐ 308 Sergei Gonchar, Wash.	.20
☐ 309 Olaf Kölzig (G), Wash.	.20
☐ 310 Richard Zednik, Wash.	.20
☐ **311 Benoît Gratton, Wash. RC**	**.50**
☐ 312 Matt Herr, Wash.	.20
☐ 313 Nolan Baumgartner, Wash.	.20
☐ 314 Peter Forsberg, Colo. [All-Victory]	.50
☐ 315 Jaromir Jagr, Pitt. [All-Victory]	.20
☐ 316 Paul Kariya, Anah. [All-Victory]	.50
☐ 317 Raymond Bourque, Bost. [All-Victory]	.50
☐ 318 Al MacInnis, SLou. [All-Victory]	.20
☐ 319 Dominik Hasek (G), Buff. [All-Victory]	.20
☐ 320 Steve Yzerman, Detr. [All-Victory]	1.00
☐ 321 Teemu Selänne, Anah. [All-Victory]	.20
☐ 322 Brett Hull, Dall. [All-Victory]	.20
☐ 323 Chris Pronger, SLou. [All-Victory]	.20
☐ 324 Nicklas Lidström, Detr. [All-Victory]	.20
☐ 325 Patrick Roy (G), Colo. [All-Victory]	1.00
☐ 326 Teemu Selänne, Anah. [Season Leader]	.20
☐ 327 Tony Amonte, Chic. [Season Leader]	.20
☐ 328 Jaromir Jagr, Pitt. [Season Leader]	.20
☐ 329 Alexei Yashin, Otta. [Season Leader]	.20
☐ 330 John LeClair, Phil. [Season Leader]	.20
☐ 331 Jaromir Jagr, Pitt. [Season Leader]	.20
☐ 332 Peter Forsberg, Colo. [Season Leader]	.50
☐ 333 Paul Kariya, Anah. [Season Leader]	.50
☐ 334 Teemu Selänne, Anah. [Season Leader]	.20
☐ 335 Joe Sakic, Colo. [Season Leader]	.50
☐ 336 Jaromir Jagr, Pitt. [Season Leader]	.20
☐ 337 Teemu Selänne, Anah. [Season Leader]	.20
☐ 338 Paul Kariya, Anah. [Season Leader]	.50
☐ 339 Peter Forsberg, Colo. [Season Leader]	.50
☐ 340 Joe Sakic, Colo. [Season Leader]	.50
☐ 341 Al MacInnis, SLou. [Season Leader]	.20
☐ 342 Nicklas Lidström, Detr. [Season Leader]	.20
☐ 343 Raymond Bourque, Bost. [Season Leader]	.50
☐ 344 Fredrik Olausson, Anah. [Season Leader]	.20
☐ 345 Brian Leetch, NYRa. [Season Leader]	.20
☐ 346 Martin Brodeur (G), NJer. [Season Leader]	.50
☐ 347 Ed Belfour (G), Dall. [Season Leader]	.20
☐ 348 Curtis Joseph (G), Toro. [Season Leader]	.20
☐ 349 Chris Osgood (G), Detr. [Season Leader]	.20
☐ 350 Patrick Roy (G), Colo. [Season Leader]	1.00
☐ 351 Milan Hejduk, Colo. [Season Leader]	.20
☐ 352 Brendan Morrison, NJer. [Season Leader]	.20
☐ 353 Chris Drury, Colo. [Season Leader]	.20
☐ 354 Jan Hrdina, Pitt. [Season Leader]	.20
☐ 355 Mark Parrish, Flor. [Season Leader]	.20
☐ **356 Oleg Saprykin, Calg. RC**	**1.50**
☐ **357 Patrik Stefan, Atla. RC**	**2.00**
☐ **358 Pavel Brendl, Calgary Hitmen RC**	**4.00**
☐ 359 Roberto Luongo (G), CHL	1.00
☐ 360 Scott Gomez, NJer.	.50
☐ **361 Sheldon Keefe, CHL RC**	**1.50**
☐ 362 Simon Gagné, Phil.	1.00
☐ **363 Steve Kariya, Vanc. RC**	**1.50**
☐ 364 Alex Tanguay, Colo.	.50
☐ 365 Brad Stuart, SanJ.	.50
☐ **366 Branislav Mezei, CHL RC**	**1.00**
☐ **367 Brian Campbell, Buff. RC**	**.50**
☐ 368 Daniel Sedin, MoDo	.20
☐ 369 Henrik Sedin, MoDo	.20
☐ 370 Mike Ribeiro, Mont.	.20
☐ **371 Ivan Novoseltsev, Sarnia Sting RC**	**1.50**
☐ 372 Nick Boynton, Ottawa 67's	.20

☐	373 Nikos Tselios, Plymouth Whalers	.20
☐	374 Tim Connolly, NYIs.	.50
☐	**375 Jean-François Damphousse (G), CHL RC**	**2.00**
☐	376 Patrick Roy (G), Colo. [Stacking the Pads]	2.00
☐	377 Ed Belfour (G), Dall. [Stacking the Pads]	.50
☐	378 Chris Osgood (G), Detr. [Stacking the Pads]	.20
☐	379 Arturs Irbe (G), Caro. [Stacking the Pads]	.20
☐	380 Nikolai Khabibulin (G), Phoe. [Stacking the Pads]	.20
☐	381 Dominik Hasek (G), Buff. [Stacking the Pads]	.50
☐	382 Byron Dafoe (G), Bost. [Stacking the Pads]	.20
☐	383 J-S Giguère (G), Calg. [Stacking the Pads]	.50
☐	384 Olaf Kölzig (G), Wash. [Stacking the Pads]	.20
☐	385 J. Vanbiesbrouck (G), Phil. [Stacking the Pads]	.20
☐	386 Martin Brodeur (G), NJer. [Stacking the Pads]	1.00
☐	387 Dan Cloutier (G), NYRa. [Stacking the Pads]	.20
☐	388 Damian Rhodes (G), Otta. [Stacking the Pads]	.20
☐	389 Curtis Joseph (G), Toro. [Stacking the Pads]	.50
☐	390 Mike Richter (G), NYRa. [Stacking the Pads]	.20
☐	391 Wayne Gretzky, Hespeler	1.50
☐	392 Wayne Gretzky, Hespeler	1.50
☐	393 Wayne Gretzky, Sault Ste. Marie Greyhounds	1.50
☐	394 Wayne Gretzky, Sault Ste. Marie Greyhounds	1.50
☐	395 Wayne Gretzky, Indianapolis Racers	1.50
☐	396 Wayne Gretzky, Edmo.	1.50
☐	397 Wayne Gretzky, WHA All-Star	1.50
☐	398 Wayne Gretzky, Edmo.	1.50
☐	399 Wayne Gretzky, Edmo.	1.50
☐	400 Wayne Gretzky, Edmo.	1.50
☐	401 Wayne Gretzky, AW	1.50
☐	402 Wayne Gretzky, Edmo.	1.50
☐	403 Wayne Gretzky, All-Star	1.50
☐	404 Wayne Gretzky, Edmo.	1.50
☐	405 Wayne Gretzky, Edmo.	1.50
☐	406 Wayne Gretzky, NHL Awards	1.50
☐	407 Wayne Gretzky, Edmo.	1.50
☐	408 Wayne Gretzky, NHL Awards	1.50
☐	409 Wayne Gretzky, Edmo.	1.50
☐	410 Wayne Gretzky, Edmo.	1.50
☐	411 Wayne Gretzky, Edmo.	1.50
☐	412 Wayne Gretzky, Edmo.	1.50
☐	413 Wayne Gretzky, LosA.	1.50
☐	414 Wayne Gretzky, NHL Awards	1.50
☐	415 Wayne Gretzky, LosA. [cameo: M.Messier]	1.50
☐	416 Wayne Gretzky, LosA.	1.50
☐	417 Wayne Gretzky, LosA.	1.50
☐	418 Wayne Gretzky, LosA.	1.50
☐	419 Wayne Gretzky, AW	1.50
☐	420 Wayne Gretzky, SLou.	1.50
☐	421 Wayne Gretzky, SLou. [w/ Hull]	1.50
☐	422 Wayne Gretzky, NYRa.	1.50
☐	423 Wayne Gretzky, NYRa. [w/ Messier]	1.50
☐	424 Wayne Gretzky, NYRa.	1.50
☐	425 Wayne Gretzky, NYRa.	1.50
☐	426 Wayne Gretzky, NYRa.	1.50
☐	427 Wayne Gretzky, NYRa.	1.50
☐	428 Wayne Gretzky, All-Star	1.50
☐	429 Wayne Gretzky, Canada '98	1.50
☐	430 Wayne Gretzky, NYRa. [Scoreboard]	1.50
☐	431 Wayne Gretzky, NYRa.	1.50
☐	432 Wayne Gretzky, NYRa.	1.50
☐	433 Wayne Gretzky, NYRa.	1.50
☐	434 Wayne Gretzky, AW	1.50
☐	435 Wayne Gretzky, LosA.	1.50
☐	436 Wayne Gretzky, Edmo.	1.50
☐	437 Wayne Gretzky, Cdn. '91	1.50
☐	438 Wayne Gretzky, Edmo. [Statue]	1.50
☐	439 Wayne Gretzky, LosA.	1.50
☐	440 Wayne Gretzky, NYRa.	1.50
	Description (1:1)	**WG**
☐	victorycards.com (picture of Gretzky jersey)	.25

1999 - 2000 WAYNE GRETZKY

This series was released in 2000.

	Complete Set (180 cards):	**45.00**
	Common Player:	**.20**
	Player	**Reg.**
☐	1 Paul Kariya, Anah.	1.00
☐	2 Guy Hebert (G), Anah.	.20
☐	3 Steve Rucchin, Anah.	.20
☐	4 Teemu Selänne, Anah.	.50
☐	5 Oleg Tverdovsky, Anah.	.20
☐	6 Matt Cullen, Anah.	.20
☐	7 Jeff Nielsen, Anah.	.20
☐	**8 Patrik Stefan, Atla. RC**	**2.00**
☐	9 Kelly Buchberger, Atla.	.20
☐	10 Andrew Brunette, Atla.	.20
☐	11 Ray Ferraro, Atla.	.20
☐	12 Nelson Emerson, Atla.	.20
☐	13 Damian Rhodes (G), Atla.	.20
☐	14 Sergei Samsonov, Bost.	.50
☐	**15 John Grahame (G), Bost. RC**	**1.50**
☐	16 Joe Thornton, Bost.	1.00
☐	17 Jason Allison, Bost.	.50
☐	18 Kyle McLaren, Bost.	.20
☐	19 Rob DiMaio, Bost.	.20
☐	20 Raymond Bourque, Bost.	1.00
☐	21 Dominik Hasek (G), Buff.	1.00
☐	22 Miroslav Satan, Buff.	.20
☐	23 Alexei Zhitnik, Buff.	.20
☐	24 Stu Barnes, Buff.	.20
☐	25 Curtis Brown, Buff.	.20
☐	**26 Brian Campbell, Buff. RC**	**.50**
☐	27 Michael Peca, Buff.	.20
☐	28 Marc* Savard, Calg.	.20
☐	29 Valeri Bure, Calg.	.20
☐	30 Phil Housley, Calg.	.20
☐	31 Grant Fuhr (G), Calg.	.50
☐	32 Cory Stillman, Calg.	.20
☐	**33 Oleg Saprykin, Calg. RC**	**1.50**
☐	34 Sami Kapanen, Caro.	.20
☐	35 Bates Battaglia, Caro.	.20
☐	36 David Tanabe, Caro.	.20
☐	37 Ron Francis, Caro.	.50
☐	38 Arturs Irbe (G), Caro.	.20
☐	39 Keith Primeau, Caro.	.20
☐	40 Doug Gilmour, Chic.	.50
☐	41 Jean-Pierre Dumont, Chic.	.20
☐	42 Éric Dazé, Chic.	.20
☐	43 Tony Amonte, Chic.	.50
☐	44 Alexei Zhamnov, Chic.	.20
☐	**45 Kyle Calder, Chic. RC**	**1.50**
☐	46 Joe Sakic, Colo.	1.50
☐	47 Chris Drury, Colo.	.50
☐	48 Milan Hejduk, Colo.	.50
☐	49 Adam Deadmarsh, Colo.	.20
☐	50 Patrick Roy (G), Colo.	3.00
☐	51 Peter Forsberg, Colo.	1.00
☐	52 Alex Tanguay, Colo.	1.00
☐	53 Mike Modano, Dall.	1.00
☐	54 Brett Hull, Dall.	1.00
☐	55 Ed Belfour (G), Dall.	1.00
☐	56 Jamie Langenbrunner, Dall.	.20
☐	**57 Pavel Patera, Dall. RC**	**.50**
☐	58 Joe Nieuwendyk, Dall.	.20
☐	59 Jere Lehtinen, Dall.	.20
☐	60 Steve Yzerman, Detr.	2.00
☐	61 Jiri Fischer, Detr.	.20
☐	62 Brendan Shanahan, Detr.	1.00
☐	63 Chris Osgood (G), Detr.	.50
☐	64 Chris Chelios, Detr.	.50
☐	65 Sergei Fedorov, Detr.	1.00
☐	66 Nicklas Lidström, Detr.	.50
☐	67 Doug Weight, Edmo.	.50
☐	68 Mike Grier, Edmo.	.20
☐	69 Ryan Smyth, Edmo.	.20
☐	70 Jason Smith, Edmo.	.20
☐	71 Tom Poti, Edmo.	.20
☐	72 Pavel Bure, Flor.	.50
☐	73 Mark Parrish, Flor.	.20
☐	**74 Ivan Novoseltsev, Flor. RC**	**1.00**
☐	75 Trevor Kidd (G), Flor.	.20
☐	76 Viktor Kozlov, Flor.	.20
☐	77 Scott Mellanby, Flor.	.20
☐	78 Rob Blake, LosA.	.50
☐	79 Ian Laperrière, LosA.	.20
☐	80 Zigmund Palffy, LosA.	.50
☐	81 Luc Robitaille, LosA.	.50
☐	82 Jozef Stumpel, LosA.	.20
☐	83 Aki Berg, LosA.	.20
☐	84 Stéphane Fiset (G), LosA.	.20
☐	85 Saku Koivu, Mont.	.50
☐	86 Brian Savage, Mont.	.20
☐	87 Trevor Linden, Mont.	.20
☐	88 Jeff Hackett (G), Mont.	.20
☐	89 Eric Weinrich, Mont.	.20
☐	90 David Legwand, Nash.	.20
☐	91 Sergei Krivokrasov, Nash.	.20
☐	92 Randy Robitaille, Nash.	.20
☐	93 Kimmo Timonen, Nash.	.20
☐	94 Mike Dunham (G), Nash.	.20
☐	95 Brendan Morrison, NJer.	.20
☐	96 Scott Stevens, NJer.	.20
☐	97 Sheldon Souray, NJer.	.20
☐	98 Petr* Sykora, NJer.	.20
☐	99 Wayne Gretzky, NYRa.	4.00
☐	100 Martin Brodeur (G), NJer.	1.50
☐	101 Scott Niedermayer, NJer.	.20
☐	102 Patrik Elias, NJer.	.50
☐	103 Tim Connolly, NYIs.	.50
☐	**104 Jörgen Jönsson, NYIs. RC**	**1.00**
☐	105 Mathieu Biron, NYIs.	.20
☐	106 Claude Lapointe, NYIs.	.20
☐	107 Kenny Jönsson, NYIs.	.20
☐	108 Félix Potvin (G), NYIs.	.50
☐	109 Theoren Fleury, NYRa.	.50
☐	110 Petr Nedved, NYRa.	.20
☐	111 Valeri Kamensky, NYRa.	.20
☐	112 Adam Graves, NYRa.	.20
☐	113 Manny Malhotra, NYRa.	.20
☐	114 Brian Leetch, NYRa.	.50
☐	115 Mike Richter (G), NYRa.	.20
☐	116 Marian Hossa, Otta.	1.00
☐	117 Radek Bonk, Otta.	.20
☐	118 Joé Juneau, Otta.	.20
☐	119 Wade Redden, Otta.	.20
☐	120 Ron Tugnutt (G), Otta.	.20
☐	121 Daniel Alfredsson, Otta.	.50
☐	122 Eric Lindros, Phil.	1.00
☐	123 John LeClair, Phil.	.50
☐	124 Marc Bureau, Phil.	.20
☐	125 Simon Gagné, Phil.	1.50
☐	126 Mark Recchi, Phil.	.20
☐	127 Rod Brind'Amour, Phil.	.20
☐	128 John Vanbiesbrouck (G), Phil.	.20
☐	129 Keith Tkachuk, Phoe.	.50
☐	130 Jeremy Roenick, Phoe.	.50
☐	131 Daniel Brière, Phoe.	.20
☐	132 Bob Essensa (G), Phoe.	.20
☐	133 J.J. Daigneault, Phoe.	.20
☐	**134 Mika Alatalo, Phoe. RC**	**1.00**
☐	135 Travis Green, Phoe.	.20
☐	136 Jaromir Jagr, Pitt.	1.00
☐	137 Martin Straka, Pitt.	.20
☐	138 Aleksey Morozov, Pitt.	.20
☐	139 Jan Hrdina, Pitt.	.20
☐	140 Alexei Kovalev, Pitt.	.50
☐	141 Peter Skudra (G), Pitt.	.20
☐	142 John Slaney, Pitt.	.20
☐	143 Pierre Turgeon, SLou.	.20
☐	144 Roman Turek (G), SLou.	.20
☐	145 Pavol Demitra, SLou.	.20
☐	146 Al MacInnis, SLou.	.20
☐	147 Chris Pronger, SLou.	.50
☐	**148 Jochen Hecht, Blues RC**	**1.50**
☐	149 Jeff Friesen, SanJ.	.20
☐	150 Steve Shields (G), SanJ.	.20
☐	151 Patrick Marleau, SanJ.	.20
☐	152 Vincent Damphousse, SanJ.	.50
☐	153 Marco Sturm, SanJ.	.20
☐	154 Brad Stuart, SanJ.	.50
☐	155 Darcy Tucker, Tamp.	.20
☐	156 Vincent Lecavalier, Tamp.	1.00
☐	157 Andrei Zyuzin, Tamp.	.20
☐	158 Chris Gratton, Tamp.	.20
☐	159 Fredrik Modin, Tamp.	.20
☐	160 Mats Sundin, Toro.	1.00
☐	161 Steve Thomas, Toro.	.20
☐	162 Sergei Berezin, Toro.	.20
☐	163 Mike Johnson, Toro.	.20
☐	164 Dmitri Khristich, Toro.	.20
☐	165 Bryan Berard, Toro.	.20
☐	166 Curtis Joseph (G), Toro.	1.00
☐	167 Mark Messier, Vanc.	1.00
☐	168 Alexander Mogilny, Vanc.	.20
☐	169 Kevin Weekes (G), Vanc.	.20
☐	170 Markus Näslund, Vanc.	1.00
☐	**171 Steve Kariya, Vanc. RC**	**1.50**
☐	172 Peter Schaefer, Vanc.	.20
☐	173 Peter Bondra, Wash.	.50
☐	174 Joe Sacco, Wash.	.20
☐	175 Adam Oates, Wash.	.20
☐	176 Olaf Kölzig (G), Wash.	.50
☐	177 Jan Bulis, Wash.	.20
☐	**178 Alexandre (Jr.) Volchkov, Wash. RC**	**.50**
☐	179 Wayne Gretzky, NYRa. [Checklist]	1.50
☐	180 Curtis Joseph (G), Toro. [Checklist]	1.00
	Promo	**Sample**
☐	90 Steve Yzerman, Detr.	2.00

CHANGING THE GAME

	Insert Set (10 cards):	**30.00**
	Insert (1:27 packs)	**CG**
☐	CG1 Peter Forsberg, Colo.	5.00
☐	CG2 Eric Lindros, Phil.	3.00
☐	CG3 Paul Kariya, Anah.	5.00
☐	CG4 Jaromir Jagr, Pitt.	3.00
☐	CG5 Dominik Hasek (G), Buff.	3.00
☐	CG6 Sergei Samsonov, Bost.	2.00
☐	CG7 Theoren Fleury, Colo.	2.00
☐	CG8 Al MacInnis, SLou.	1.50
☐	CG9 Pavel Bure, Flor.	3.00
☐	CG10 Patrick Roy (G), Colo.	10.00

ELEMENTS OF THE GAME

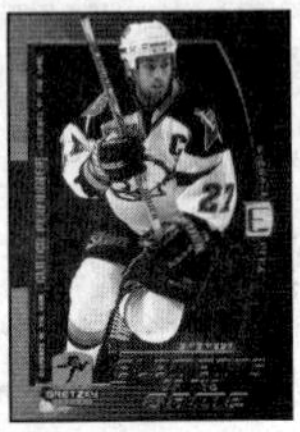

	Insert Set (15 cards):	**20.00**
	Insert (1:6 packs)	**EG**
☐	EG1 Teemu Selänne, Anah.	1.00
☐	EG2 Michael Peca, Buff.	1.00
☐	EG3 Sergei Samsonov, Bost.	1.00
☐	EG4 Sergei Fedorov, Detr.	2.00
☐	EG5 Peter Forsberg, Colo.	2.00
☐	EG6 Brett Hull, Dall.	2.00
☐	EG7 Eric Lindros, Phil.	2.00
☐	EG8 Pavel Bure, Flor.	1.00
☐	EG9 Theoren Fleury, NYRa.	1.00
☐	EG10 Martin Brodeur (G), NJer.	3.00
☐	EG11 Jaromir Jagr, Pitt.	2.00
☐	EG12 Keith Tkachuk, Phoe.	1.00
☐	EG13 Peter Bondra, Wash.	1.00
☐	EG14 Joe Sakic, Colo.	3.00
☐	EG15 Curtis Joseph (G), Toro.	2.00

GREAT HEROES

	Insert Set (10 cards):	**55.00**
	Insert (1:27 packs)	**GH**
☐	GH1 Jaromir Jagr, Pitt.	5.00
☐	GH2 Paul Kariya, Anah.	7.00
☐	GH3 Joe Sakic, Colo.	8.00
☐	GH4 Dominik Hasek (G), Buff.	5.00
☐	GH5 Patrick Roy (G), Colo.	15.00
☐	GH6 Steve Yzerman, Detr.	12.00
☐	GH7 Eric Lindros, Phil.	5.00
☐	GH8 Patrik Stefan, Atla.	2.00
☐	GH9 Teemu Selänne, Anah.	4.00
☐	GH10 Pavel Bure, Flor.	4.00

GREAT MEMORABILIA

	Insert (1:2351)	**GM**
☐	GM1 Wayne Gretzky, NYRa. [Puck]	175.00

HALL OF FAME CAREER

	Insert Set (30 cards):	**25.00**
	Insert (1:1 packs)	**HOF**
☐	HOF1 Wayne Gretzky, All-Star	1.00
☐	HOF2 Wayne Gretzky, Sault Ste. Marie Greyhounds	1.00
☐	HOF3 Wayne Gretzky, All-Star	1.00
☐	HOF4 Wayne Gretzky, Indianapolis Racers	1.00
☐	HOF5 Wayne Gretzky, Edmo.	1.00
☐	HOF6 Wayne Gretzky, Edmo.	1.00
☐	HOF7 Wayne Gretzky, Edmo.	1.00
☐	HOF8 Wayne Gretzky, Edmo.	1.00
☐	HOF9 Wayne Gretzky, Edmo.	1.00
☐	HOF10 Wayne Gretzky, Edmo.	1.00
☐	HOF11 Wayne Gretzky, Edmo.	1.00
☐	HOF12 Wayne Gretzky, LosA.	1.00
☐	HOF13 Wayne Gretzky, LosA.	1.00
☐	HOF14 Wayne Gretzky, LosA.	1.00
☐	HOF15 Wayne Gretzky, LosA.	1.00
☐	HOF16 Wayne Gretzky, LosA.	1.00
☐	HOF17 Wayne Gretzky, NHL Awards	1.00
☐	HOF18 Wayne Gretzky, All-Star	1.00
☐	HOF19 Wayne Gretzky, Edmo.	1.00
☐	HOF20 Wayne Gretzky, All-Star	1.00
☐	HOF21 Wayne Gretzky, SLou.	1.00
☐	HOF22 Wayne Gretzky, SLou.	1.00
☐	HOF23 Wayne Gretzky / Mark Messier	3.00
☐	HOF24 Wayne Gretzky, NYRa.	1.00
☐	HOF25 Wayne Gretzky, NYRa.	1.00
☐	HOF26 Wayne Gretzky, NYRa.	1.00

☐ HOF27 Wayne Gretzky, NYRa.	1.00
☐ HOF28 Wayne Gretzky, All-Star '99	1.00
☐ HOF29 Wayne Gretzky, NYRa.	1.00
☐ HOF30 Wayne Gretzky, Hall of Fame	1.00

SIGNS OF GREATNESS

Insert Set (15 cards):	700.00
Autographs (1:139 Retail packs)	SoG
☐ Arturs Irbe (G), Caro. ✍	20.00
☐ Brett Hull, Dall. ✍	75.00
☐ Chris Drury, Colo. ✍	30.00
☐ Curtis Joseph (G), Toro. ✍	75.00
☐ Chris Osgood (G), Detr. ✍	30.00
☐ David Legwand, Nash. ✍	20.00
☐ Mark Parrish, Flor. ✍	20.00
☐ Nikolai Khabibulin (G), Phoe. ✍	20.00
☐ Pavel Bure, Flor. ✍	60.00
☐ Paul Mara, Tamp. ✍	15.00
☐ Patrik Stefan, Atla. ✍	24.00
☐ Raymond Bourque, Bost. ✍	70.00
☐ Sergei Samsonov, Bost. ✍	45.00
☐ Vadim Sharifijanov, NJer. ✍	15.00
☐ Wayne Gretzky, NYRa. ✍	330.00

TOOLS OF GREATNESS

Insert Set (19 cards):	900.00
Insert (1:139 Hobby packs)	ToG
☐ Arturs Irbe (G), Caro. ✂	25.00
☐ Brett Hull, Dall. ✂	60.00
☐ Brendan Shanahan, Detr. ✂	60.00
☐ Curtis Joseph (G), Toro. ✂	60.00
☐ Doug Weight, Edmo. ✂	35.00
☐ Ed Belfour (G), Dall. ✂	60.00
☐ Eric Lindros, Phil. ✂	60.00
☐ Luc Robitaille, LosA. ✂	50.00
☐ Mike Richter (G), NYRa. ✂	30.00
☐ Mats Sundin, Toro. ✂	60.00
☐ Nikolai Khabibulin (G), Phoe. ✂	25.00
☐ Pavel Bure, Flor. ✂	50.00
☐ Peter Forsberg, Colo. ✂	85.00
☐ Paul Kariya, Anah. ✂	85.00
☐ Patrick Roy (G),	150.00
☐ Raymond Bourque, Bost. ✂	75.00
☐ Sergei Samsonov, Bost. ✂	35.00
☐ Tony Amonte, Chic. ✂	35.00
☐ Teemu Selänne, Anah. ✂	50.00

VISIONARY

Insert Set (10 cards):	325.00
Insert (1:167 packs)	V
☐ V1 Wayne Gretzky, Edmo.	40.00
☐ V2 Wayne Gretzky, Edmo.	40.00
☐ V3 Wayne Gretzky, Edmo.	40.00
☐ V4 Wayne Gretzky, LosA.	40.00
☐ V5 Wayne Gretzky, LosA.	40.00
☐ V6 Wayne Gretzky, SLou.	40.00
☐ V7 Wayne Gretzky, NYRa.	40.00
☐ V8 Wayne Gretzky, NYRa.	40.00
☐ V9 Wayne Gretzky, NYRa.	40.00
☐ V10 Wayne Gretzky, NYRa.	40.00

WILL TO WIN

Insert Set (10 cards):	30.00
Insert (1:13 packs)	WtW
☐ W1 Paul Kariya, Anah.	4.00
☐ W2 Steve Yzerman, Detr.	7.00
☐ W3 Jaromir Jagr, Pitt.	3.00
☐ W4 Dominik Hasek (G), Buff.	3.00
☐ W5 Patrick Roy (G), Colo.	9.00
☐ W6 Jeremy Roenick, Phoe.	2.00
☐ W7 Raymond Bourque, Bost.	3.00
☐ W8 John LeClair, Phil.	2.00
☐ W9 Mats Sundin, Toro.	3.00
☐ W10 Mark Messier, Vanc.	3.00

1999 - 2000 WAYNE GRETZKY HOCKEY – BUYBACKS

Buyback Autograph • Tools of the Game	WGH
☐ Curtis Joseph (G), Toro. ✂ ✍ {#/3}	

2000 CSAS SIGNATURE SERIES

These autographed cards are limited to 2000 copies.

Complete Set (6 cards):	140.00
Player	Auto.
☐ Jim Morrison, Bost. ✍	20.00
☐ Ed Litzenberger, Chic. ✍	20.00
☐ Leonard (Red) Kelly, Detr. ✍	30.00
☐ Jean Béliveau, Mont. ✍	50.00
☐ Lou Fontinato, NYRa. ✍	20.00
☐ Red Horner, Toro. ✍	30.00

2000 GATORADE STICKERS

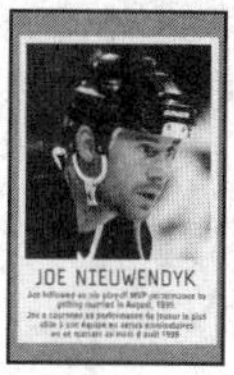

Complete Set (24 stickers):

Player

- ☐ Daniel Alfredsson, NHLPA
- ☐ Vincent Damphousse, NHLPA
- ☐ Tie Domi, NHLPA
- ☐ Grant Fuhr (G), NHLPA
- ☐ Bill Guerin, NHLPA
- ☐ Jarome Iginla, NHLPA
- ☐ Jaromir Jagr, NHLPA
- ☐ Paul Kariya, NHLPA
- ☐ Saku Koivu, NHLPA
- ☐ Eric Lindros, NHLPA
- ☐ Mark Messier, NHLPA
- ☐ Mike Modano, NHLPA
- ☐ Alexander Mogilny, NHLPA
- ☐ Joe Nieuwendyk, NHLPA
- ☐ Chris Pronger, NHLPA
- ☐ Mark Recchi, NHLPA
- ☐ Luc Robitaille, NHLPA
- ☐ Patrick Roy (G), NHLPA
- ☐ Joe Sakic, NHLPA
- ☐ Teemu Selänne, NHLPA
- ☐ Mats Sundin, NHLPA
- ☐ José Théodore (G), NHLPA
- ☐ Ron Tugnutt (G), NHLPA
- ☐ Doug Weight, NHLPA

2000 UPPER DECK A PIECE OF HISTORY 500 GOAL CLUB

This cross-brand insert series was included in 1999-2000 and 2000-01 Upper Deck series released during the 2000-calendar year.

Jersey	Jersey
☐ Brett Hull, SLou. ✂ [99-00 SP Authentic]	150.00
☐ Bryan Trottier, NYIs. ✂ [99-00 UD MVP Cup]	150.00
☐ Dino Ciccarelli, Detr. ✂ [99-00 UD PowerDeck]	50.00
☐ Dale Hawerchuk, SLou. ✂ [00-01 UD BD]	75.00
☐ Jari Kurri, Edmo. ✂ [00-01 Upper Deck-1]	150.00
☐ Joe Mullen, Pitt. ✂ [00-01 Upper Deck-1]	50.00
☐ Luc Robitaille, LosA. ✂ [99-00 UD Ovation]	100.00
☐ Marcel Dionne, LosA. ✂ [99-00 UD Ovation]	150.00
☐ Mike Gartner, Wash. ✂ [00-01 UD BD]	100.00
☐ Mario Lemieux, Pitt. ✂ [00-01 SPx]	450.00
☐ Mark Messier, Edmo. ✂ [00-01 UD Vintage]	150.00
☐ Pat Verbeek, Dall. ✂ [00-01 SPx]	50.00
☐ Steve Yzerman, Detr. ✂ [99-00 UD PowerDeck]	350.00
☐ Wayne Gretzky, Edmo. ✂ [00-01 Upper Deck-1]	600.00
Stick	Stick
☐ Bobby Hull, Chic. ✂ [99-00 SP Authentic]	175.00
☐ Frank Mahovlich, Toro. ✂ [00-01 UD MVP]	100.00
☐ Gordie Howe, Detr. ✂ [99-00 Upper Deck-2]	275.00
☐ Guy Lafleur, Mont. ✂ [99-00 Gretzky Hockey]	200.00
☐ Gilbert Perreault, Buff. ✂ [99-00 Ultimate Victory]	75.00
☐ Jean Béliveau, Mont. ✂ [99-00 Gretzky Hockey	225.00
☐ Mike Bossy, NYIs. ✂ [99-00 UD MVP Cup]	150.00
☐ Michel Goulet, Chic. ✂ [99-00 UD BD]	50.00
☐ Maurice Richard, Mont. ✂ [Stick]	275.00
☐ Phil Esposito, Bost. ✂ [00-01 UD Ice]	125.00
☐ Stan Mikita, Chic. ✂ [99-00 UD BD]	75.00

500 GOAL CLUB AUTOGRAPH

Jersey	Aut25
☐ Brett Hull, SLou. ✍ ✂ [99-00 SP Authentic]	450.00
☐ Bryan Trottier, NYIs. ✍ ✂ [99-00 UD MVP Cup]	450.00
☐ Dino Ciccarelli, Detr. ✍ ✂ [99-00 UD PowerDeck]	125.00
☐ Dale Hawerchuk, SLou. ✍ ✂ [00-01 UD BD]	250.00
☐ Jari Kurri, Edmo. ✍ ✂ [00-01 Upper Deck-1]	450.00
☐ Joe Mullen, Pitt. ✍ ✂ [00-01 Upper Deck-1]	175.00
☐ Luc Robitaille, LosA. ✍ ✂ [99-00 UD Ovation]	350.00
☐ Marcel Dionne, LosA. ✍ ✂ [99-00 UD Ovation]	350.00
☐ Mike Gartner, Wash. ✍ ✂ [00-01 UD BD]	350.00
☐ Mario Lemieux, Pitt. ✍ ✂ [00-01 SPx]	1300.00
☐ Mark Messier, Edmo. ✍ ✂ [00-01 UD Vintage]	525.00
☐ Pat Verbeek, Dall. ✍ ✂ [00-01 SPx]	125.00
☐ S. Yzerman, Detr. ✍ ✂ [99-00 UD PowerDeck]	1000.00
☐ W Gretzky, Edmo. ✍ ✂ [00-01 Upper Deck-1]	2300.00
Stick	Aut25
☐ Bobby Hull, Chic. ✍ ✂ [99-00 SP Authentic]	325.00
☐ Frank Mahovlich, Toro. ✍ ✂ [00-01 UD MVP]	250.00
☐ Gordie Howe, Detr. ✍ ✂ [99-00 Upper Deck-2]	775.00
☐ Guy Lafleur, Mont. ✍ ✂ [99-00 Gretzky Hockey]	325.00
☐ G. Perreault, Buff. ✍ ✂ [99-00 Ultimate Victory]	250.00
☐ J. Béliveau, Mont. ✍ ✂ [99-00 Gretzky Hockey	450.00
☐ Mike Bossy, NYIs. ✍ ✂ [99-00 UD MVP Cup]	375.00
☐ Michel Goulet, Chic. ✍ ✂ [99-00 UD BD]	150.00
☐ Maurice Richard, Mont. ✍ • ✂ [Stick]	825.00
☐ Phil Esposito, Bost. ✍ ✂ [00-01 UD Ice]	325.00
☐ Stan Mikita, Chic. ✍ ✂ [99-00 UD BD]	250.00

2000 WAYNE GRETZKY MASTER COLLECTION

This series was released in 2000.

Complete Set (18 cards):	
Player	MINT
☐ 1 Wayne Gretzky	
☐ 2 Wayne Gretzky	
☐ 3 Wayne Gretzky	
☐ 4 Wayne Gretzky	
☐ 5 Wayne Gretzky	
☐ 6 Wayne Gretzky	
☐ 7 Wayne Gretzky	
☐ 8 Wayne Gretzky	
☐ 9 Wayne Gretzky	
☐ 10 Wayne Gretzky	
☐ 11 Wayne Gretzky	
☐ 12 Wayne Gretzky	
☐ 13 Wayne Gretzky	
☐ 14 Wayne Gretzky	
☐ 15 Wayne Gretzky	
☐ 16 Wayne Gretzky	
☐ 17 Wayne Gretzky	
☐ 18 Wayne Gretzky	

GREAT JERSEY

Complete Set (4 cards):	6,000.00
Player	MINT
☐ GJC-1 Wayne Gretzky ✂ {#/99}	800.00
☐ GJC-A Wayne Gretzky ✍ ✂ {#/9}	2000.00
☐ GPC-1 Wayne Gretzky ✂ Patch {#/15}	1500.00
☐ GPC-A Wayne Gretzky ✍ ✂ Patch {#/9}	2500.00

JERSEY

Complete Set (12 cards):	3,500.00
Insert (#/50)	MINT
☐ AS1 Wayne Greatzky ✂	400.00
☐ AS2 Wayne Gretzky ✂	400.00
☐ AS3 Wayne Gretzky ✂	400.00
☐ ED1 Wayne Gretzky ✂	400.00
☐ ED2 Wayne Gretzky ✂	400.00
☐ ED3 Wayne Gretzky ✂	400.00
☐ LA1 Wayne Gretzky ✂	400.00
☐ LA2 Wayne Gretzky ✂	400.00
☐ LA3 Wayne Gretzky ✂	400.00
☐ NY1 Wayne Gretzky ✂	400.00
☐ NY2 Wayne Gretzky ✂	400.00
☐ NY3 Wayne Gretzky ✂	400.00

JERSEY AUTOGRAPH

Complete Set (6 cards):	3500.00
Insert (#/50)	MINT
☐ ED1 Wayne Gretzky ✂ ✍	900.00
☐ ED2 Wayne Gretzky ✂ ✍	900.00
☐ ED3 Wayne Gretzky ✂ ✍	900.00
☐ NY1 Wayne Gretzky ✂ ✍	900.00
☐ NY2 Wayne Gretzky ✂ ✍	900.00
☐ NY3 Wayne Gretzky ✂ ✍	900.00

ULTIMATE GRETZKY

Complete Set (18 cards):

Insert (#/1)

- ☐ UG1 Wayne Gretzky
- ☐ UG2 Wayne Gretzky
- ☐ UG3 Wayne Gretzky
- ☐ UG4 Wayne Gretzky
- ☐ UG5 Wayne Gretzky
- ☐ UG6 Wayne Gretzky
- ☐ UG7 Wayne Gretzky
- ☐ UG8 Wayne Gretzky
- ☐ UG9 Wayne Gretzky
- ☐ UG10 Wayne Gretzky
- ☐ UG11 Wayne Gretzky
- ☐ UG12 Wayne Gretzky
- ☐ UG13 Wayne Gretzky
- ☐ UG14 Wayne Gretzky
- ☐ UG15 Wayne Gretzky
- ☐ UG16 Wayne Gretzky
- ☐ UG17 Wayne Gretzky
- ☐ UG18 Wayne Gretzky

2000 - 01 ALFABILDER

We have no pricing information on this set.

Description	
☐ B-A Gustafsson	☐ Lennart Häggroth
☐ Anders Hedberg	☐ Göran Högosta
☐ Leif Holmqvist	☐ Sven Johansson
☐ Anders Kallur	☐ Håkan Loob
☐ Tord Lundström	☐ Eilert Määttä
☐ Peter Lindmark	☐ Mats Näslund
☐ Kent Nilsson	☐ Nisse Nilsson
☐ Stefan Persson	☐ Börje Salming
☐ Ulf Sterner	☐ Roland Stoltz

2000 - 01 AURORA

This series was issued in September 2000. All 200 base cards (regular and Striped) have a Premiere Date parallel (#/50).

Shell Set (150 cards):	-	35.00
Complete Set (200 cards):	2,200	55.00
Description	PD50	Base
☐☐ 1 Guy Hebert (G), Anah.	8.00	.25
☐☐ 2 Paul Kariya, Anah.	55.00	1.00
☐☐ 3 Steve Rucchin, Anah.	8.00	.25
☐☐ 4 Teemu Selänne, Anah.	30.00	.50
☐☐ 5 Andrew Brunette, Atla.	8.00	.25
☐☐ 6 Scott Fankhouser (G), Atla.	8.00	.25
☐☐ 7 Damian Rhodes (G), Atla.	8.00	.25
☐☐ 8 Patrik Stefan, Atla.	10.00	.25
☐☐ 9 Jason Allison, Bost.	20.00	.50
☐☐ 10 Anson Carter, Bost.	15.00	.25
☐☐ 11 Paul Coffey, Caro. (Bost.)	20.00	.50
☐☐ 12 Byron Dafoe (G), Bost.	15.00	.25
☐☐ 13 John Grahame (G), Bost. [Rookie]	8.00	.25
☐☐ 14 Sergei Samsonov, Bost.	20.00	.50
☐☐ 15 Joe Thornton, Bost.	45.00	1.00
☐☐ 16 Maxim Afinogenov, Buff.	15.00	.25
☐☐ 17 Martin Biron (G), Buff.	15.00	.25
☐☐ 18 Doug Gilmour, Buff.	20.00	.50
☐☐ 19 Dominik Hasek (G), Buff.	40.00	1.00
☐☐ 20 Michael Peca, Buff.	15.00	.25
☐☐ 21 Miroslav Satan, Buff.	10.00	.25
☐☐ 22 Fred Brathwaite (G), Calg.	10.00	.25
☐☐ 23 Valeri Bure, Calg.	10.00	.25
☐☐ 24 Jarome Iginla, Calg.	30.00	.50
☐☐ 25 Derek Morris, Calg.	8.00	.25
☐☐ 26 Marc Savard, Calg.	8.00	.25
☐☐ 27 Rod Brind'Amour, Caro.	10.00	.25
☐☐ 28 Ron Francis, Caro.	20.00	.50
☐☐ 29 Arturs Irbe (G), Caro.	15.00	.25
☐☐ 30 Sami Kapanen, Caro.	10.00	.25
☐☐ 31 Tony Amonte, Chic.	20.00	.50
☐☐ 32 Eric Dazé, Chic.	15.00	.25
☐☐ 33 Steve Sullivan, Chic.	10.00	.25
☐☐ 34 Jocelyn Thibault (G), Chic.	15.00	.25
☐☐ 35 Alexei Zhamnov, Chic.	10.00	.25
☐☐ 36 Raymond Bourque, Colo.	45.00	1.00
☐☐ 37 Chris Drury, Colo.	20.00	.50
☐☐ 38 Peter Forsberg, Colo.	55.00	1.00

□□	39 Milan Hejduk, Colo.	30.00	.50
□□	40 Patrick Roy (G), Colo.	120.00	3.00
□□	41 Joe Sakic, Colo.	60.00	1.50
□□	42 Alex Tanguay, Colo.	20.00	.50
□□	43 Ed Belfour (G), Dall.	40.00	1.00
□□	44 Brett Hull, Dall.	40.00	1.00
□□	45 Mike Modano, Dall.	40.00	1.00
□□	46 Brenden Morrow, Dall.	10.00	.25
□□	47 Joe Nieuwendyk, Dall.	15.00	.25
□□	48 Chris Chelios, Detr.	20.00	.50
□□	49 Sergei Fedorov, Detr.	40.00	1.00
□□	50 Nicklas Lidström, Detr.	20.00	.50
□□	51 Chris Osgood (G), Detr.	20.00	.50
□□	52 Brendan Shanahan, Detr.	40.00	1.00
□□	53 Pat Verbeek, Detr.	10.00	.25
□□	54 Steve Yzerman, Detr.	95.00	2.00
□□	55 Mike Grier, Edmo.	8.00	.25
□□	56 Bill Guerin, Edmo.	15.00	.25
□□	57 Tommy Salo (G), Edmo.	15.00	.25
□□	58 Ryan Smyth, Edmo.	15.00	.25
□□	59 Doug Weight, Edmo.	20.00	.50
□□	60 Pavel Bure, Flor.	30.00	.50
□□	61 Trevor Kidd (G), Flor.	10.00	.25
□□	62 Viktor Kozlov, Flor.	10.00	.25
□□	63 Roberto Luongo (G), NYIs. (Flor.) [Rookie]	30.00	.50
□□	64 Ray Whitney, Flor.	8.00	.25
□□	65 Rob Blake, LosA.	20.00	.50
□□	66 Stéphane Fiset (G), LosA.	10.00	.25
□□	67 Zigmund Palffy, LosA.	20.00	.50
□□	68 Luc Robitaille, LosA.	30.00	.50
□□	69 Jamie Storr (G), LosA.	8.00	.25
□□	70 Jozef Stumpel, LosA.	8.00	.25
□□	71 Jeff Hackett (G), Mont.	10.00	.25
□□	72 Saku Koivu, Mont.	45.00	.50
□□	73 Trevor Linden, Mont.	15.00	.25
□□	74 Martin Rucinsky, Mont.	8.00	.25
□□	75 José Théodore (G), Mont.	45.00	1.00
□□	76 Mike Dunham (G), Nash.	15.00	.25
□□	77 Patric Kjellberg, Nash.	8.00	.25
□□	78 David Legwand, Nash.	15.00	.25
□□	79 Cliff Ronning, Nash.	8.00	.25
□□	80 Jason Arnott, NJer.	15.00	.25
□□	81 Martin Brodeur (G), NJer.	60.00	1.50
□□	82 Patrik Elias, NJer.	30.00	.50
□□	83 Scott Gomez, NJer.	15.00	.25
□□	84 John Madden, NJer.	10.00	.25
□□	85 Scott Stevens, NJer.	15.00	.25
□□	86 Petr Sykora, NJer.	15.00	.25
□□	87 Tim Connolly, NYIs.	15.00	.25
□□	88 Mariusz Czerkawski, NYIs.	8.00	.25
□□	89 Brad Isbister, NYIs.	8.00	.25
□□	90 Mark Parrish, Flor. (NYIs.)	15.00	.25
□□	91 John Vanbiesbrouck (G), Phil. (NYIs.)	15.00	.25
□□	92 Theoren Fleury, NYRa.	20.00	.50
□□	93 Adam Graves, NYRa.	15.00	.25
□□	94 Jan Hlavac, NYRa.	8.00	.25
□□	95 Brian Leetch, NYRa.	20.00	.50
□□	96 Mark Messier, Vanc. (NYRa.)	40.00	1.00
□□	97 Petr Nedved, NYRa.	10.00	.25
□□	98 Mike Richter (G), NYRa.	15.00	.25
□□	99 Daniel Alfredsson, Otta.	20.00	.50
□□	100 Radek Bonk, Otta.	10.00	.25
□□	101 Marian Hossa, Otta.	40.00	1.00
□□	102 Shawn McEachern, Otta.	10.00	.25
□□	103 Vaclav Prospal, Otta.	10.00	.25
□□	104 Brian Boucher (G), Phil.	10.00	.25
□□	105 Éric Desjardins, Phil.	10.00	.25
□□	106 Simon Gagné, Phil.	30.00	.50
□□	107 John LeClair, Phil.	30.00	.50
□□	108 Eric Lindros, Phil.	40.00	1.00
□□	109 Mark Recchi, Phil.	15.00	.25
□□	110 Shane Doan, Phoe.	8.00	.25
□□	111 Joé Juneau, Otta. (Phoe.)	8.00	.25
□□	112 Jeremy Roenick, Phoe.	30.00	.50
□□	113 Keith Tkachuk, Phoe.	20.00	.50
□□	114 Jean-Sébastien Aubin (G), Pitt.	8.00	.25
□□	115 Jan Hrdina, Pitt.	8.00	.25
□□	116 Jaromir Jagr, Pitt.	40.00	1.00
□□	117 Alex Kovalev, Pitt.	20.00	.50
□□	118 Martin Straka, Pitt.	10.00	.25
□□	119 Pavol Demitra, SLou.	15.00	.25
□□	120 Dallas Drake, Phoe. (SLou.)	8.00	.25
□□	121 Michal Handzus, SLou.	8.00	.25
□□	122 Al MacInnis, SLou.	15.00	.25
□□	123 Chris Pronger, SLou.	20.00	.50
□□	124 Roman Turek (G), SLou.	15.00	.25
□□	125 Pierre Turgeon, SLou.	15.00	.25
□□	126 Vincent Damphousse, SanJ.	20.00	.50
□□	127 Jeff Friesen, SanJ.	10.00	.25
□□	128 Patrick Marleau, SanJ.	15.00	.25
□□	129 Owen Nolan, SanJ.	20.00	.50
□□	130 Steve Shields (G), SanJ.	8.00	.25
□□	131 Dan Cloutier (G), Tamp.	15.00	.25
□□	**132 Matt Elich, Tamp. [Rookie] RC**	**30.00**	**.50**
□□	133 Mike Johnson, Tamp.	8.00	.25
□□	134 Vincent Lecavalier, Tamp.	40.00	1.00
□□	135 Kevin Weekes (G), NYIs. (Tamp.)	8.00	.25
□□	136 Nikolai Antropov, Toro.	8.00	.25
□□	137 Tie Domi, Toro.	10.00	.25
□□	138 Jeff Farkas, Toro. [Rookie]	15.00	.25
□□	139 Curtis Joseph (G), Toro.	40.00	1.00
□□	140 Mats Sundin, Toro.	40.00	1.00
□□	141 Steve Thomas, Toro.	8.00	.25
□□	142 Andrew Cassels, Vanc.	8.00	.25
□□	143 Steve Kariya, Vanc.	8.00	.25
□□	144 Markus Näslund, Vanc.	40.00	1.00
□□	145 Félix Potvin (G), Vanc.	45.00	.50
□□	146 Peter Bondra, Wash.	20.00	.50
□□	147 Jeff Halpern, Wash.	8.00	.25
□□	148 Olaf Kölzig (G), Wash.	20.00	.50
□□	149 Adam Oates, Wash.	15.00	.25
□□	150 Chris Simon, Wash.	8.00	.25

PINSTRIPES

	Description	PD	Aurora
□□	2 Paul Kariya, Anah.	55.00	2.00
□□	4 Teemu Selänne, Anah.	30.00	1.00
□□	8 Patrik Stefan, Atla.	10.00	.25
□□	9 Jason Allison, Bost.	20.00	.50
□□	18 Doug Gilmour, Buff.	20.00	.50
□□	19 Dominik Hasek (G), Buff.	40.00	1.50
□□	22 Fred Brathwaite (G), Calg.	10.00	.25
□□	23 Valeri Bure, Calg.	10.00	.25
□□	25 Derek Morris, Calg.	8.00	.25
□□	31 Tony Amonte, Chic.	20.00	.50
□□	36 Raymond Bourque, Colo.	45.00	1.50
□□	37 Chris Drury, Colo.	20.00	.50
□□	38 Peter Forsberg, Colo.	55.00	2.00
□□	40 Patrick Roy (G), Colo.	120.00	4.50
□□	41 Joe Sakic, Colo.	60.00	2.00
□□	42 Alex Tanguay, Colo.	20.00	.50
□□	43 Ed Belfour (G), Dall.	40.00	1.50
□□	44 Brett Hull, Dall.	40.00	1.50
□□	45 Mike Modano, Dall.	40.00	1.50
□□	46 Brenden Morrow, Dall.	10.00	.25
□□	48 Chris Chelios, Detr.	20.00	.50
□□	49 Sergei Fedorov, Detr.	40.00	1.50
□□	52 Brendan Shanahan, Detr.	40.00	1.50
□□	54 Steve Yzerman, Detr.	95.00	3.50
□□	55 Mike Grier, Edmo. [Rookie]	8.00	.25
□□	60 Pavel Bure, Flor.	30.00	1.00
□□	63 Roberto Luongo (G), NYIs. (Flor.)	30.00	1.00
□□	68 Luc Robitaille, LosA.	30.00	1.00
□□	70 Jozef Stumpel, LosA.	8.00	.25
□□	75 José Théodore (G), Mont.	45.00	1.50
□□	78 David Legwand, Nash.	15.00	.50
□□	81 Martin Brodeur (G), NJer.	60.00	2.00
□□	83 Scott Gomez, NJer.	15.00	.50
□□	92 Theoren Fleury, NYRa.	20.00	.50
□□	96 Mark Messier, Vanc. (NYRa.)	40.00	1.50
□□	101 Marian Hossa, Otta.	40.00	1.50
□□	104 Brian Boucher (G), Phil.	10.00	.25
□□	107 John LeClair, Phil.	30.00	1.00
□□	109 Mark Recchi, Phil.	15.00	.50
□□	112 Jeremy Roenick, Phoe.	30.00	1.00
□□	113 Keith Tkachuk, Phoe.	20.00	.50
□□	114 Jean-Sébastien Aubin (G), Pitt.	8.00	.25
□□	116 Jaromir Jagr, Pitt.	40.00	1.50
□□	124 Roman Turek (G), SLou.	15.00	.50
□□	129 Owen Nolan, SanJ.	20.00	.50
□□	136 Nikolai Antropov, Toro.	8.00	.25
□□	139 Curtis Joseph (G), Toro.	40.00	1.50
□□	140 Mats Sundin, Toro.	40.00	1.50
□□	145 Félix Potvin (G), Vanc.	45.00	.50
□□	148 Olaf Kölzig (G), Wash.	20.00	.50

AUTHENTIC AUTOGRAPHS

Insert Set (10 cards):		150.00
	Insert	**Auto.**
□	23 Valeri Bure, Calg. ✍ (#/300)	15.00
□	37 Chris Drury, Colo. ✍ (#/250)	25.00
□	42 Alex Tanguay, Colo. ✍ (#/500)	20.00
□	46 Brenden Morrow, Dall. ✍ (#/500)	15.00
□	55 Mike Grier, Edmo. ✍ (#/500)	15.00
□	75 José Théodore (G), Mont. ✍ (#/500)	45.00
□	78 David Legwand, Nash. ✍ (#/500)	15.00
□	114 Jean-Sébastien Aubin (G), Pitt. ✍ (#/500)	15.00
□	136 Nikolai Antropov, Toro. ✍ (#/500)	15.00
□	148 Olaf Kölzig (G), Wash. ✍ (#/250)	25.00

CANVAS CREATIONS

Insert Set (10 cards):		500.00
	Insert (1:361)	**CC**
□	1 Paul Kariya, Anah.	60.00
□	2 Peter Forsberg, Colo.	60.00
□	3 Patrick Roy (G), Colo.	130.00
□	4 Mike Modano, Dall.	40.00
□	5 Steve Yzerman, Detr.	100.00
□	6 Pavel Bure, Flor.	30.00
□	7 Martin Brodeur (G), NJer.	70.00
□	8 John LeClair, Phil.	30.00
□	9 Jaromir Jagr, Pitt.	40.00
□	10 Curtis Joseph (G), Toro.	40.00

CHAMPIONSHIP FEVER

There are four versions: the regular insert (4:37 packs), the Silver parallel (#/221), the Platinum Blue parallel (#/92) and the Copper parallel (#/90). The Platinum Blue and Copper parallels are priced similarly below. There are also four versions of the John LeClair's autographed cards: the regular insert autographed (#/197), the Silver parallel autographed (#/1), the Platinum Blue parallel autographed (#/1) and the Copper parallel autographed (#/1).

Insert Set (20 cards):		650.00	375.00	65.00
	Description	**CF92**	**CF221**	**CF**
□□□□	1 Paul Kariya, Anah.	45.00	25.00	4.50
□□□□	2 Teemu Selänne, Anah.	25.00	15.00	2.50
□□□□	3 Dominik Hasek (G), Buff.	35.00	20.00	3.50
□□□□	4 Raymond Bourque, Colo.	40.00	25.00	4.00
□□□□	5 Peter Forsberg, Colo.	45.00	25.00	4.50
□□□□	6 Patrick Roy (G), Colo.	105.00	60.00	10.00
□□□□	7 Ed Belfour (G), Dall.	35.00	20.00	3.50
□□□□	8 Brett Hull, Dall.	35.00	20.00	3.50
□□□□	9 Mike Modano, Dall.	35.00	20.00	3.50
□□□□	10 Sergei Fedorov, Detr.	35.00	20.00	3.50
□□□□	11 Brendan Shanahan, Detr.	35.00	20.00	3.50
□□□□	12 Steve Yzerman, Detr.	80.00	50.00	8.00
□□□□	13 Pavel Bure, Flor.	25.00	15.00	2.50
□□□□	14 Martin Brodeur (G), NJer.	55.00	30.00	5.50
□□□□	15 Scott Gomez, NJer.	10.00	5.00	2.00
□□□□	16 Brian Boucher (G), Phil.	10.00	5.00	2.00
□□□□	17 John LeClair, Phil.	25.00	15.00	2.50
□□□□	18 Jaromir Jagr, Pitt.	35.00	20.00	3.50
□□□□	19 Curtis Joseph (G), Toro.	35.00	20.00	3.50
□□□□	20 Mark Messier, Vanc.	35.00	20.00	3.50
	Autograph			**Auto**
□□□□	17 John LeClair, Phil. ✍			65.00

GAME-WORN JERSEY

There are two versions for cards 1-10: the Jersey card and the Jersey Patch variation (#/10). Cards 11-14 are Dual Jersey cards (#/200).

Jersey Set (10 cards):		2,400	175.00
	Insert	**Patch**	**Jersey**
□□	10 Peter Bondra, Wash. ✂	200.00	15.00
□□	1 Paul Coffey, Caro. ✂	200.00	15.00
□□	6 Saku Koivu, Mont. ✂	400.00	20.00
□□	9 Eric Lindros, Phil. ✂	350.00	25.00
□□	5 Roberto Luongo (G), NYIs. ✂	275.00	20.00
□□	8 Mark Messier, Vanc. ✂	350.00	25.00
□□	3 Brendan Shanahan, Detr. ✂	350.00	25.00
□□	7 Petr Sykora, NJer. ✂	125.00	15.00
□□	2 John Vanbiesbrouck (G), Flor. ✂	150.00	15.00
□□	4 Steve Yzerman, Detr. ✂	825.00	65.00

GAME-WORN JERSEY

Insert Set (4 cards):		325.00
	Insert	**GWJD**
□	1 P. Sykora ✂ / S. Koivu ✂	75.00
□	2 J. Vanbiesbrouck ✂ / R. Luongo ✂	75.00
□	3 B. Shanahan ✂ / S. Yzerman ✂	140.00
□	4 J. Jagr ✂ / P. Bondra ✂	90.00

SCOUTING REPORT

Insert Set (20 cards):		115.00
	Insert (2:37 Hobby packs)	**SR**
□	1 Paul Kariya, Anah.	10.00
□	2 Teemu Selänne, Anah.	6.00
□	3 Patrik Stefan, Atla.	4.00
□	4 Joe Thornton, Bost.	9.00
□	5 Peter Forsberg, Colo.	10.00
□	6 Milan Hejduk, Colo.	6.00
□	7 Brett Hull, Dall.	7.00
□	8 Ed Belfour (G), Dall.	7.00
□	9 Sergei Fedorov, Detr.	7.00
□	10 Brendan Shanahan, Detr.	7.00
□	11 Pavel Bure, Flor.	6.00
□	12 Roberto Luongo (G), NYIs. (Flor.)	6.00
□	13 Martin Brodeur (G), NJer.	12.00
□	14 Scott Gomez, NJer.	4.00
□	15 Marian Hossa, Otta.	7.00
□	16 Brian Boucher (G), Phil.	4.00
□	17 John LeClair, Phil.	6.00
□	18 Vincent Lecavalier, Tamp.	7.00
□	19 Curtis Joseph (G), Toro.	7.00
□	20 Mats Sundin, Toro.	7.00

TEAM PLAYER STYROTECHS

The A cards were seeded in Hobby packs while the B cards were seeded in Retail packs.

Insert Set (20 cards):		175.00
	Insert (1:37 packs)	**TPS**
□	1A Paul Kariya, Anah.	15.00
□	1B Teemu Selänne, Anah.	5.00
□	2A Doug Gilmour, Buff.	5.00
□	2B Dominik Hasek (G), Buff.	10.00
□	3A Peter Forsberg, Colo.	15.00
□	3B Patrick Roy (G), Colo.	30.00
□	4A Joe Sakic, Colo.	15.00
□	4B Raymond Bourque, Colo.	10.00
□	5A Brett Hull, Detr.	10.00
□	5B Mike Modano, Dall.	10.00
□	6A Brendan Shanahan, Detr.	10.00
□	6B Steve Yzerman, Detr.	25.00
□	7A Scott Gomez, NJer.	5.00
□	7B Martin Brodeur (G), NJer.	15.00
□	8A John LeClair, Phil.	5.00
□	8B Brian Boucher (G), Phil.	5.00
□	9A Jaromir Jagr, Pitt.	10.00
□	9B Jean-Sébastien Aubin (G), Pitt.	5.00
□	10A Curtis Joseph (G), Toro.	10.00
□	10B Mats Sundin, Toro.	10.00

2000 - 01 BE A PLAYER ALL-STAR FANTASY

Complete Set (10 cards):

	Description
□	AS-1 Patrick Roy (G), Colo. ✂
□	AS-2 Joe Sakic, Colo. ✂
□	AS-3 Raymond Bourque, Colo. ✂
□	AS-4 Peter Forsberg, Colo. ✂
□	AS-5 Chris Drury, Colo. ✂
□	AS-6 Milan Hejduk, Colo. ✂
□	AS-7 Alex Tanguay, Colo. ✂
□	AS-8 Adam Foote, Colo. ✂
□	AS-9 Adam Deadmarsh, Colo. ✂
□	AS-10 Chris Dingman, Colo. ✂

2000 - 01 BE A PLAYER MEMORABILIA

This series was distributed in three parts: the original release in August 2000 (base cards 1-396), the Rookie & Traded release in January 2001 (base cards 397-497) and the Final Update release in May 2001 (base cards 498-521). Base cards 1-497 have a Ruby parallel (#/200), a Sapphire parallel (#/100) and an Emerald parallel (#/10).

Cross-brand Parkhurst insert cards are listed under their own heading (2000 - 01 Be A Player Parkhurst). Parkhurst cards P-1 to P-100 were inserted in packs of Be A Player Memorabilia while Parkhurst cards P-101 to P-150 were inserted in boxes of Be A Player Memorabilia Rookie & Traded.

A number of wrapper-redemption unsigned parallels exist. These wrapper-redemption cards were available at: the 2000 Chicago Times show (Gold, Ruby and Sapphire versions limited to 10 copies each); the 2000 Sportsfest (Bronze, Gold, Purple and Teal versions each limited to 10 copies each); the 2000 Montréal show (Copper, Gold and Ruby versions limited to 10 copies each); the 2000 Toronto Fall Expo (Copper, Gold and Ruby versions limited to 10 copies each); and the 2001 All-Star FANtasy (Black, Emerald, Ruby and Sapphire versions limited to 10 copies each). These wrapper-redemption cards sell for considerably less than the Emerald parallels (each limited to ten copies). Common Wrapper-redemption singles start at $5-10 each.

Original series (396 cards):	**80.00**
Rookie & Traded series (101 cards):	**30.00**
Final Update series (24 cards):	**25.00**
Complete Set (521 cards):	**100.00**
Common Player:	**.20**

	Description	BAPM
☐	1 Jaromir Jagr, Pitt.	1.00
☐	2 Scott Mellanby, Flor.	.20
☐	3 Mike Fisher, Otta.	.20
☐	4 Vyacheslav Kozlov, Detr.	.20
☐	**5 S. Valiquette (G), NYIs. RC**	**1.00**
☐	6 Simon Gagné, Phil.	1.00
☐	7 Aleksey Morozov, Pitt.	.20
☐	8 Alexei Zhitnik, Buff.	.20
☐	9 Jochen Hecht, SLou.	.20
☐	10 Jamie Allison, Chic.	.20
☐	11 Olli Jokinen, NYIs.	.20
☐	12 Bobby Holik, NJer.	.20
☐	13 Keith Primeau, Phil.	.50
☐	14 Bryan McCabe, Chic.	.20
☐	15 Tim Connolly, NYIs.	.50
☐	16 Marco Sturm, SanJ.	.20
☐	17 Craig Darby, Mont.	.20
☐	**18 Jeff Cowan, Calg. RC**	**.50**
☐	19 Brad Stuart, SanJ.	.50
☐	20 Sean O'Donnell, LosA. (MinW.)	.20
☐	**21 Mike Minard (G), Edmo. RC**	**1.00**
☐	22 Rob Blake, LosA.	.50
☐	23 Marek Malík, Caro.	.20
☐	24 Marek Posmyk, Tamp.	.20
☐	25 Alex Tanguay, Colo.	.50
☐	26 Steve McCarthy, Chic.	.20
☐	27 Bill Guerin, Edmo.	.50
☐	28 Ed Jovanovski, Vanc.	.50
☐	29 Martin Skoula, Colo.	.20
☐	30 Jeff Hackett (G), Mont.	.20
☐	31 Vladimir Tsyplakov, Buff.	.20
☐	32 Sergei Zubov, Dall.	.20
☐	33 Damian Rhodes (G), Atla.	.20
☐	**34 Brent Sopel, Vanc. RC**	**1.00**
☐	35 Frantisek Kaberle, Atla.	.20
☐	36 Michael Peca, Buff.	.50
☐	37 Steve Kelly, NJer.	.20
☐	38 Geoff Sanderson, Buff. (Colu.)	.20
☐	39 Petr Svoboda, Tamp.	.20
☐	40 Martin Brodeur (G), NJer.	2.00
☐	41 Markus Näslund, Vanc.	1.00
☐	42 Steve Thomas, Toro.	.20
☐	43 Anson Carter, Bost.	.50
☐	44 Theoren Fleury, NYRa.	.50
☐	45 Félix Potvin (G), Vanc.	.50
☐	46 Adam Deadmarsh, Colo.	.20
☐	47 David Tanabe, Caro.	.20
☐	48 Trevor Kidd (G), Flor.	.20
☐	49 Jeff Friesen, SanJ.	.20
☐	**50 Marc Moro, Nash. RC**	**.50**
☐	51 Luc Robitaille, LosA.	1.00
☐	52 Mike Richter (G), NYRa.	.50
☐	53 Éric Desjardins, Phil.	.20
☐	54 Jean-Sébastien Aubin (G), Pitt.	.20
☐	55 Paul Laus, Flor.	.20
☐	56 Kimmo Timonen, Nash.	.20
☐	57 Steve Sullivan, Chic.	.20
☐	58 Eric Cairns, NYIs.	.20
☐	59 Scott Stevens, NJer.	.50
☐	60 Andy Delmore, Phil.	.20
☐	61 Jeff Nielsen, Anah. (MinW.)	.20
☐	62 Mathieu Biron, NYIs.	.20
☐	63 Juha Lind, Mont.	.20
☐	64 Maxim Afinogenov, Buff.	.50
☐	65 Guy Hebert (G), Anah.	.20
☐	66 Sergei Brylin, NJer.	.20
☐	67 Mike Modano, Dall.	1.00
☐	68 Tommy Salo (G), Edmo.	.50
☐	69 Bryan Smolinski, LosA.	.20
☐	70 Sergei Varlamov, Calg.	.20
☐	71 Paul Mara, Tamp.	.20
☐	72 Peter Forsberg, Colo.	1.50
☐	73 Doug Weight, Edmo.	.50
☐	74 Peter Bondra, Wash.	.50
☐	75 Marc Denis (G), Colo. (Colu.)	.50
☐	76 Jamie Storr (G), LosA.	.20
☐	77 Alex Kovalev, Pitt.	.50
☐	78 Danius Zubrus, Mont.	.20
☐	79 Mike Grier, Edmo.	.20
☐	80 Olaf Kölzig (G), Wash.	.50
☐	**81 Bryan Adams, Atla. RC**	**.50**
☐	82 Scott Niedermayer, NJer.	.20
☐	**83 David Gosselin, Nash. RC**	**.50**
☐	84 Boris Mironov, Chic.	.20
☐	85 Kyle McLaren, Bost.	.20
☐	86 Steve Kariya, Vanc.	.20
☐	87 Dmitry Yushkevich, Toro.	.20
☐	88 Paul Kariya, Anah.	1.50
☐	89 Brian Leetch, NYRa.	.50
☐	90 Jeff Daniels, Caro.	.20
☐	91 Brendan Morrison, Vanc.	.20
☐	92 Brian Campbell, Buff.	.20
☐	93 Ray Whitney, Flor.	.20
☐	94 Marian Hossa, Otta.	1.00
☐	95 Sergei Samsonov, Bost.	.50
☐	96 Mike York, NYRa.	.20
☐	97 Mark Eaton, Phil.	.20
☐	98 Ryan VandenBussche, Chic.	.20
☐	99 Vladimir Malakhov, NJer.	.20
☐	100 Jeff Finley, SLou.	.20
☐	101 John Vanbiesbrouck (G), Phil.	.50
☐	102 Brad Isbister, NYIs.	.20
☐	103 John Madden, NJer.	.20
☐	104 Patrick Roy (G), Colo.	3.50
☐	105 Radek Bonk, Otta.	.20
☐	106 Brett Hull, Dall.	1.00
☐	107 Andreas Dackell, Otta.	.20
☐	108 Pierre Turgeon, SLou.	.50
☐	109 Jason Woolley, Buff.	.20
☐	110 Jeff O'Neill, Caro.	.50
☐	111 John LeClair, Phil.	1.00
☐	112 Darryl Sydor, Dall.	.20
☐	113 Ryan Smyth, Edmo.	.50
☐	114 Curtis Joseph (G), Toro.	1.00
☐	115 Gary Roberts, Caro.	.50
☐	116 Pavel Kubina, Tamp.	.20
☐	117 Roman Hamrlik, Edmo.	.20
☐	118 Sandis Ozolinsh, Colo.	.20
☐	119 M. Fernandez (G), Dall. (MinW.)	.50
☐	120 Adam Oates, Wash.	.50
☐	121 D. Hendrickson, Vanc. (MinW.)	.20
☐	122 Glenn Murray, LosA.	.50
☐	123 Jiri Slegr, Pitt.	.20
☐	124 Steve Yzerman, Detr.	3.00
☐	125 Mats Lindgren, NYIs.	.20
☐	126 Sergei Gonchar, Wash.	.20
☐	127 Joe Thornton, Bost.	1.50
☐	128 Petr Sykora, NJer.	.50
☐	129 Pavol Demitra, SLou.	.50
☐	130 Tyler Wright, Pitt. (Colu.)	.20
☐	131 Johan Davidsson, NYIs.	.20
☐	132 Brian Rolston, Bost.	.20
☐	133 Mark Messier, Vanc.	1.00
☐	134 Darcy Tucker, Toro.	.20
☐	135 Oleg Tverdovsky, Anah.	.20
☐	136 Petr Nedved, NYRa.	.20
☐	137 Harold Druken, Vanc.	.20
☐	138 Valeri Bure, Calg.	.20
☐	139 Mikael Andersson, NYIs.	.20
☐	140 Evgeni Nabokov (G), SanJ.	1.50
☐	141 Janne Laukkanen, Pitt.	.20
☐	142 Radek Dvorak, NYRa.	.20
☐	143 Brian Boucher (G), Phil.	.20
☐	144 Éric Dazé, Chic.	.50
☐	145 Dan Cloutier (G), Tamp.	.50
☐	146 Scott Gomez, NJer.	.50
☐	147 Dallas Drake, Phoe. (Colu.)	.20
☐	148 Shawn McEachern, Otta.	.20
☐	149 Joe Nieuwendyk, Dall.	.50
☐	150 Kenny Jönsson, NYIs.	.20
☐	151 Saku Koivu, Mont.	1.00
☐	152 Roman Turek (G), SLou.	.50
☐	153 Chris Gratton, Buff.	.20
☐	154 Steve Rucchin, Anah.	.20
☐	155 Teppo Numminen, Phoe.	.20
☐	156 Jamie Langenbrunner, Dall.	.20
☐	157 Johnathan Aitken, Bost.	.20
☐	158 Nikolai Antropov, Toro.	.20
☐	159 Stéphane Fiset (G), LosA.	.20
☐	160 Manny Malhotra, NYRa.	.20
☐	161 Pavel Bure, Flor.	1.00
☐	162 Chris Drury, Colo.	.50
☐	163 Roberto Luongo (G), NYIs.	1.00
☐	164 Norm Maracle (G), Atla.	.20
☐	165 Brendan Shanahan, Detr.	1.00
☐	166 Calle Johansson, Wash.	.20
☐	167 Cory Stillman, Calg.	.20
☐	168 Jozef Stümpel, LosA.	.20
☐	169 Ron Tugnutt (G), Pitt.	.50
☐	170 Brian Savage, Mont.	.20
☐	171 Viktor Kozlov, Flor.	.20
☐	172 Chris Simon, Wash.	.20
☐	173 Chris Joseph, Phoe.	.20
☐	**174 Willie Mitchell, NJer. RC**	**1.00**
☐	175 Randy Robitaille, Nash.	.20
☐	176 Sami Kapanen, Caro.	.20
☐	177 Jonathan Girard, Bost.	.20
☐	178 Andrew Cassels, Vanc.	.20
☐	**179 Jani Hurme (G), Otta. RC**	**1.50**
☐	180 Maxim Balmochnykh, Anah.	.20
☐	181 Adam Graves, NYRa.	.50
☐	182 Steve Shields (G), SanJ.	.20
☐	183 Marc Savard, Calg.	.20
☐	184 Zigmund Palffy, LosA.	.50
☐	185 Magnus Arvedson, Otta.	.20
☐	186 Byron Dafoe (G), Bost.	.50
☐	187 Jan Hlavac, NYRa.	.20
☐	188 Len Barrie, Flor.	.20
☐	189 Jocelyn Thibault (G), Chic.	.50
☐	190 Fred Brathwaite (G), Calg.	.20
☐	191 Fredrik Modin, Tamp.	.20
☐	192 Shane Doan, Phoe.	.20
☐	**193 Petr Mika, NYIs. RC**	**.50**
☐	194 Larry Murphy, Detr.	.20
☐	195 Daniel Alfredsson, Otta.	.50
☐	196 Brenden Morrow, Dall.	.20
☐	197 Martin Rucinsky, Mont.	.20
☐	198 Michal Handzus, SLou.	.20
☐	199 Dominik Hasek (G), Buff.	1.00
☐	200 Rod Brind'Amour, Caro.	.20
☐	201 Trevor Letowski, Phoe.	.20
☐	202 Derian Hatcher, Dall.	.20
☐	203 Phil Housley, Calg.	.20
☐	204 Martin Biron (G), Buff.	.50
☐	205 Sergei Berezin, Toro.	.20
☐	206 Ron Francis, Caro.	.50
☐	207 Cliff Ronning, Nash.	.20
☐	208 Robert Svehla, Flor.	.20
☐	209 Vincent Lecavalier, Tamp.	1.00
☐	210 Kent Manderville, Phil.	.20
☐	211 Andrew Brunette, Atla.	.20
☐	212 Chris Chelios, Detr.	.50
☐	213 Alexander Karpovtsev, Toro.	.20
☐	214 Robyn Regehr, Calg.	.20
☐	215 Mika Alatalo, Phoe.	.20
☐	216 Jan Hrdina, Pitt.	.20
☐	217 Nicklas Lidström, Detr.	.50
☐	218 Ivan Novoseltsev, Flor.	.20
☐	219 Alexander Mogilny, NJer.	.50
☐	220 Chris Pronger, SLou.	.50
☐	221 Paul Coffey, Caro.	.50
☐	222 John Grahame (G), Bost.	.20
☐	223 Jeff Farkas, Toro.	.50
☐	224 Eric Lindros, Phil.	1.00
☐	225 Jörgen Jönsson, Anah.	.20
☐	**226 J-F Labbé (G), NYRa. RC**	**1.00**
☐	227 Owen Nolan, SanJ.	.50
☐	228 Oleg Saprykin, Calg.	.20
☐	229 Patrick Marleau, SanJ.	.50
☐	**230 Aaron Downey, Bost. RC**	**1.00**
☐	231 Chris Osgood (G), Detr.	.50
☐	232 Mike Wilson, Flor.	.20
☐	233 Joe Sakic, Colo.	2.00
☐	**234 D. Kochan (G), Tamp. RC**	**1.00**
☐	235 Jeremy Roenick, Phoe.	1.00
☐	236 Alexei Zhamnov, Chic.	.20
☐	237 Sergei Fedorov, Detr.	1.00
☐	238 Petr Schastlivy, Otta.	.20
☐	239 Milan Hejduk, Colo.	1.00
☐	240 Patrice Brisebois, Mont.	.20
☐	241 Marty Reasoner, SLou.	.20
☐	242 Ed Belfour (G), Dall.	1.00
☐	243 Vitaly Vishnevski, Anah.	.20
☐	244 Keith Tkachuk, Phoe.	.50
☐	245 Petr Buzek, Atla.	.20
☐	246 Miroslav Satan, Buff.	.20
☐	247 Adam Mair, Toro.	.20
☐	248 Jere Karalahti, LosA.	.20
☐	249 Mike Dunham (G), Nash.	.50
☐	250 Mike Sillinger, Flor.	.20
☐	**251 A. Skopintsev, Tamp. RC**	**.50**
☐	**252 S. Vyshedkevich, Atla. RC**	**1.00**
☐	253 Steve Duchesne, Detr.	.20
☐	254 Tomas Kaberle, Toro.	.20
☐	255 Arturs Irbe (G), Caro.	.50
☐	256 Niklas Sundström, SanJ.	.20
☐	257 Al MacInnis, SLou.	.50
☐	258 Mike Ribeiro, Mont.	.20
☐	259 Rob Niedermayer, Flor.	.20
☐	**260 Jean-Guy Trudel, Phoe. RC**	**1.00**
☐	261 Martin Straka, Pitt.	.20
☐	262 Jason Arnott, NJer.	.50
☐	263 David Legwand, Nash.	.50
☐	264 Tony Amonte, Chic.	.50
☐	265 Jason Allison, Bost.	.50
☐	266 Patrik Elias, NJer.	1.00
☐	267 Mark Recchi, Phil.	.50
☐	268 Patrik Stefan, Atla.	.20
☐	269 Mariusz Czerkawski, NYIs.	.20
☐	270 Vincent Damphousse, SanJ.	.50
☐	271 S. Krivokrasov, Calg. (MinW.)	.20
☐	272 Teemu Selänne, Anah.	1.00
☐	273 Patrick Lalime (G), Otta.	.50
☐	274 Nick Boynton, Bost.	.50
☐	275 Darren McCarty, Detr.	.20
☐	276 Jaroslav Spacek, Flor.	.20
☐	277 Chris Dingman, Colo.	.20
☐	278 Jarome Iginla, Calg.	1.00
☐	279 Andrei Zyuzin, Tamp.	.20
☐	280 Jyrki Lumme, Phoe.	.20
☐	281 Michal Grosek, Chic.	.20
☐	282 Janne Niinimaa, Edmo.	.20
☐	283 Wade Redden, Otta.	.20
☐	284 Raymond Bourque, Colo.	1.50
☐	285 Trevor Linden, Mont.	.50
☐	286 Ladislav Nagy, SLou.	.50
☐	287 José Théodore (G), Mont.	1.50
☐	288 Bates Battaglia, Caro.	.20
☐	289 Mikeal Renberg, Phoe.	.20
☐	290 Donald Audette, Atla.	.50
☐	291 Doug Gilmour, Buff.	.50
☐	292 Yanic Perreault, Toro.	.20
☐	293 Anders Eriksson, Chic.	.20
☐	294 Gary Suter, SanJ.	.20
☐	295 Brad Ference, Flor.	.20
☐	296 Mats Sundin, Toro.	1.00
☐	297 Ray Ferraro, Atla.	.20
☐	298 Jiri Fischer, Detr.	.20
☐	299 Todd Bertuzzi, Vanc.	1.50
☐	300 Derek Morris, Calg.	.20
☐	301 Patric Kjellberg, Nash.	.20
☐	302 Pat Verbeek, Detr.	.20
☐	303 Kip Miller, Anah.	.20
☐	304 Alexei Vasiliev, NYRa.	.20
☐	305 Marcus Ragnarsson, SanJ.	.20
☐	306 Arron Asham, Mont.	.20
☐	307 Sylvain Cote, Dall.	.20
☐	308 Vaclav Prospal, Otta.	.20
☐	309 Aki Berg, LosA.	.20
☐	310 Alexander Selivanov, Edmo.	.20
☐	311 Wayne Primeau, Tamp.	.20
☐	312 Brian Rafalski, NJer.	.20
☐	313 Jonas Höglund, Toro.	.20
☐	314 Adam Foote, Colo.	.20
☐	315 Steve Konowalchuk, Wash.	.20
☐	316 Robert Dome, Pitt.	.20
☐	317 Antti Laaksonen, Bost.	.20
☐	318 Mike Ricci, SanJ.	.20
☐	319 Gino Odjick, Phil.	.20
☐	320 Eric Weinrich, Mont.	.20
☐	321 Jason Strudwick, Vanc.	.20
☐	322 Kim Johnsson, NYRa.	.20
☐	323 Dimitri Kalinin, Buff.	.20
☐	324 Daymond Langkow, Phil.	.20
☐	325 Todd Marchant, Edmo.	.20
☐	326 Richard Matvichuk, Dall.	.20
☐	327 Travis Green, Phoe.	.20
☐	328 Igor Larionov, Detr.	.50
☐	329 Mattias Öhlund, Vanc.	.20
☐	330 Igor Kravchuk, Otta.	.20
☐	331 Richard Zednik, Wash.	.50
☐	332 Curtis Brown, Buff.	.20
☐	333 Krzysztof Oliwa, NJer. (Colu.)	.20
☐	334 Darius Kasparaitis, NYIs.	.20
☐	335 Michael Nylander, Chic.	.20
☐	336 Stan Drulia, Tamp.	.20
☐	337 Nelson Emerson, LosA.	.20
☐	338 Greg Johnson, Nash.	.20
☐	339 Sean Hill, Caro.	.20
☐	340 Keith Jones, Phil.	.20
☐	341 Bill Muckalt, NYIs.	.20
☐	342 Randy McKay, NJer.	.20
☐	343 Stu Grimson, Anah.	.20
☐	344 Tyson Nash, SLou.	.20
☐	345 Dan Hinote, Colo.	.20
☐	346 Mike Rathje, SanJ.	.20
☐	347 Brian Holzinger, Tamp.	.20
☐	**348 Eric Nickulas, Bost. RC**	**.50**
☐	349 Alexandre Daigle, NYRa.	.20
☐	350 Jan Bulis, Wash.	.20
☐	351 Tom Poti, Edmo.	.20
☐	352 Kevyn Adams, Toro. (Colu.)	.20
☐	353 Scott Thornton, Dall.	.20
☐	354 Sean Burke (G), Phoe.	.50
☐	355 Peter Worrell, Flor.	.20
☐	356 Josef Beranek, Pitt.	.20
☐	357 Matt Cullen, Anah.	.20
☐	358 Sandy McCarthy, Caro.	.20
☐	359 Sergei Zholtok, Mont.	.20
☐	360 Darren Langdon, NYRa.	.20
☐	361 Martin Lapointe, Detr.	.50
☐	362 Adrian Aucoin, Vanc.	.20
☐	363 Dimitri Nabokov, NYIs.	.20
☐	364 Jason Blake, LosA.	.20
☐	365 Jeff Halpern, Wash.	.20
☐	366 Rico Fata, Calg.	.20
☐	367 Dave Reid, Colo.	.20
☐	368 Vitali Yachmenev, Nash.	.20
☐	369 Hnat Domenichelli, Atla.	.20
☐	370 Rick Tocchet, Phil.	.20
☐	371 Tommy Westlund, Caro.	.20
☐	372 Chris Phillips, Otta.	.20
☐	373 Claude Lemieux, NJer.	.20
☐	374 Greg Adams, Phoe.	.20
☐	375 Todd Simpson, Flor.	.20
☐	376 Ken Klee, Wash.	.20
☐	377 André Savage, Bost.	.20
☐	378 Bryan Marchment, SanJ.	.20
☐	379 Dean McAmmond, Chic.	.20

380 Mike Johnson, Tamp.	.20
381 Tomas Holmström, Detr.	.20
382 Robert Lang, Pitt.	.20
383 Daniel McGillis, Phil.	.20
384 Jamie Rivers, NYIs.	.20
385 Dave Andreychuk, Colo.	.20
386 Marty McInnis, Anah.	.20
387 Sami Salo, Otta.	.20
388 Dan Cleary, Edmo.	.20
389 Robert Esche (G), Phoe.	.20
390 Aaron Gavey, Dall. (MinW.)	.20
391 Andrei Nikolishin, Wash.	.20
392 Jason Krog, NYIs.	.20
393 Stu Barnes, Buff.	.20
394 Tomas Vokoun (G), Nash.	.20
395 Peter Schaefer, Vanc.	.20
396 Danny Markov, Toro.	.20
397 Daniel Sedin, Vanc.	1.00
398 Kris Beech, Wash.	.20
399 Samuel Påhlsson, Bost.	.20
400 Gary Roberts, Toro.	.50
401 Marian Gaborik, MinW. RC	**6.00**
402 Oleg Kvasha, NYIs.	.20
403 Martin Havlat, Otta. RC	**3.50**
404 Roman Simicek, Pitt. RC	**.50**
405 Dallas Drake, SLou.	.20
406 Jakub Cutta, Wash. RC	**1.00**
407 German Titov, Anah.	.20
408 Jarno Kultanen, Bost. RC	**.50**
409 Sandis Ozolinsh, Caro.	.20
410 David Vyborny, Colu.	.20
411 Olli Jokinen, Flor.	.20
412 Maxim Sushinsky, MinW.	.20
413 J. Vanbiesbrouck (G), NYIs.	.50
414 Shane Hnidy, Otta. RC	**1.00**
415 Milan Kraft, Pitt.	.20
416 A. Kharitonov, Tamp. RC	**.50**
417 Andrei Nazarov, Anah.	.20
418 Dave Andreychuk, Buff.	.20
419 Niclas Wallin, Caro. RC	**.50**
420 Rostislav Klesla, Colu. RC	**2.00**
421 Denis Shvidki, Flor.	.20
422 Mathieu Garon (G), Mont.	.50
423 Taylor Pyatt, NYIs.	.20
424 R. Cechmanek (G), Phil. RC	**2.50**
425 Mark Smith, SanJ. RC	**.50**
426 Shayne Corson, Toro.	.20
427 Jonas Rönnqvist, Anah. RC	**1.00**
428 Jean-Pierre Dumont, Buff.	.20
429 Josef Vasicek, Caro. RC	**1.50**
430 Tyler Bouck, Dall. RC	**1.00**
431 Mathieu Schneider, LosA.	.20
432 Andrei Markov, Mont.	.20
433 Vladimir Malakhov, NYRa.	.20
434 Maxime Ouellet (G), Phil.	.20
435 Matt Bradley, SanJ.	.20
436 Dave Manson, Toro.	.20
437 Brad Tapper, Atla. RC	**1.00**
438 Eric Boulton, Buff. RC	**1.00**
439 Brent Johnson (G), SLou.	.50
440 Marty Turco (G), Dall. RC	**3.50**
441 Tomas Vlasak, LosA.	.20
442 Greg Classen, Nash. RC	**1.00**
443 Mark Messier, NYRa.	1.00
444 Justin Williams, Phil. RC	**2.00**
445 Sean Hill, SLou.	.20
446 Bryan McCabe, Toro.	.20
447 Andreas Karlsson, Atla.	.20
448 Mika Noronen (G), Buff.	.50
449 Alexander Karpovtsev, Chic.	.20
450 Boyd Devereaux, Detr.	.20
451 L. Visnovsky, LosA. RC	**1.00**
452 Scott Hartnell, Nash. RC	**1.50**
453 J. LaBarbera (G), NYRa. RC	**1.00**
454 Petr Hubacek, Phil. RC	**.50**
455 A. Khavanov, SLou. RC	**1.00**
456 Petr Svoboda, Toro. RC**	**1.00**
457 Tomi Kallio, Atla.	.20
458 Mike Vernon (G), Calg.	.50
459 Reto von Arx, Chic. RC	**1.00**
460 Maxim Kuznetsov, Detr.	.20
461 S. Reinprecht, LosA. RC	**2.00**
462 Turner Stevenson, NJer.	.20
463 Roberto Luongo (G), Flor.	1.00
464 Brad Richards, Tamp.	1.00
465 Bryce Salvador, SLou. RC	**1.00**
466 Kevin Hatcher, Caro.	.20
467 Paul Coffey, Bost.	.50
468 Marty Murray, Calg.	.20
469 Todd Fedoruk, Phil. RC	**.50**
470 Brian Swanson, Edmo.	.20
471 Christian Matte, MinW.	.20
472 Sascha Goc, NJer. RC	**1.00**
473 Dale Purinton, NYRa. RC	**1.00**
474 Brad May, Phoe.	.20
475 Brad Brown, NYRa.	.20
476 Petteri Nummelin, Colu. RC	**1.00**
477 R. Fedotenko, Phil. RC	**1.00**
478 R. Petrovicky, Calg. RC	**1.00**
479 D. Aebischer (G), Colo. RC	**2.00**
480 Michel Riesen, Edmo. RC	**1.00**
481 Ladislav Benysek, Minn. RC	**.50**
482 Mark Parrish, NYIs.	.50
483 Mike Mottau, NYRa.	.20
484 Ossi Väänänen, Phoe. RC	**1.00**
485 A. Raycroft (G), Bost. RC	**1.50**
486 Sylvain Côté, Wash.	.20
487 Richard Jackman, Dall.	.20
488 Toni Lydman, Calg.	.20
489 Ron Tugnutt (G), Colu.	.50
490 Igor Larionov, Flor.	.50
491 L. Sekeras, MinW. RC	**1.00**
492 Roman Hamrlik, NYIs.	.20
493 J. Holmqvist (G), NYRa. RC	**2.00**
494 Josef Melichar, Pitt. RC	**.50**
495 Sheldon Keefe, Tamp.	.20
496 Henrik Sedin, Vanc.	1.00
497 Rick DiPietro (G), NYIs. RC	**3.00**
498 Teemu Selänne, SanJ.	1.50
499 Keith Tkachuk, SLou.	1.00
500 Rob Blake, Colo.	1.00
501 Mario Lemieux, Pitt.	6.00
502 Johan Hedberg (G), Pitt. RC	**8.00**
503 Félix Potvin (G), LosA.	1.00
504 Branislav Mezei, NYIs.	.50
505 Mike Comrie, Edmo. RC	**8.00**
506 Miikka Kiprusoff (G), SanJ.	1.00
507 Petr Tenkrat, Anah. RC	**1.50**
508 Mark Bell, Chic.	.50
509 Steve Gainey, Dall. RC	**1.50**
510 Jason Williams, Detr. RC	**2.00**
511 Shawn Horcoff, Edmo. RC	**1.50**
512 Éric Chouinard, Mont.	.50
513 Derek Gustafson, MinW. RC	**1.00**
514 Bryan Allen, Vanc.	.50
515 Kristian Kudroc, Tamp.	.50
516 G. Naumenko (G), Anah. RC	**1.50**
517 Pierre Dagenais, NJer.	.50
518 Juraj Kolnik, NYIs. RC	**1.50**
519 Tomas Kloucek, NYRa. RC	**1.00**
520 Andreas Lilja, LosA. RC	**1.00**
521 A. Ponikarovsky, Toro. RC	**1.50**

PARALLELS

	E10	S100	R200
Complete Set (497 cards):	21,000	2,300	1,400
Common Player:	**20.00**	**4.00**	**2.00**
Description	**E10**	**S100**	**R200**
1 Jaromir Jagr	175.00	15.00	10.00
2 Scott Mellanby	25.00	4.00	2.00
3 Mike Fisher	25.00	4.00	2.00
4 Vyacheslav Kozlov	25.00	4.00	2.00
5 S. Valiquette (G) RC	**35.00**	**4.00**	**4.00**
6 Simon Gagné	150.00	15.00	8.00
7 Aleksey Morozov	25.00	4.00	2.00
8 Alexei Zhitnik	25.00	4.00	2.00
9 Jochen Hecht	25.00	4.00	2.00
10 Jamie Allison	20.00	4.00	2.00
11 Olli Jokinen	50.00	5.00	3.00
12 Bobby Holik	50.00	5.00	3.00
13 Keith Primeau	75.00	5.00	4.00
14 Bryan McCabe	25.00	4.00	2.00
15 Tim Connolly	75.00	5.00	4.00
16 Marco Sturm	25.00	4.00	2.00
17 Craig Darby	25.00	4.00	2.00
18 Jeff Cowan RC	**20.00**	**4.00**	**2.50**
19 Brad Stuart	75.00	5.00	4.00
20 Sean O'Donnell (MinW.)	20.00	4.00	2.00
21 Mike Minard (G) RC	**35.00**	**4.00**	**4.00**
22 Rob Blake	100.00	10.00	6.00
23 Marek Malík	20.00	4.00	2.00
24 Marek Posmyk	20.00	4.00	2.00
25 Alex Tanguay	100.00	10.00	6.00
26 Steve McCarthy	25.00	4.00	2.00
27 Bill Guerin	75.00	5.00	4.00
28 Ed Jovanovski	75.00	5.00	4.00
29 Martin Skoula	25.00	4.00	2.00
30 Jeff Hackett (G)	50.00	5.00	3.00
31 Vladimir Tsyplakov	20.00	4.00	2.00
32 Sergei Zubov	25.00	4.00	2.00
33 Damian Rhodes (G)	25.00	4.00	2.00
34 Brent Sopel RC	**35.00**	**4.00**	**4.00**
35 Frantisek Kaberle	25.00	4.00	2.00
36 Michael Peca	75.00	5.00	4.00
37 Steve Kelly	20.00	4.00	2.00
38 Geoff Sanderson (Colu.)	25.00	4.00	2.00
39 Petr Svoboda	25.00	4.00	2.00
40 Martin Brodeur (G)	300.00	30.00	16.00
41 Markus Näslund	175.00	15.00	10.00
42 Steve Thomas	25.00	4.00	2.00
43 Anson Carter	75.00	5.00	4.00
44 Theoren Fleury	100.00	10.00	6.00
45 Félix Potvin (G)	225.00	20.00	6.00
46 Adam Deadmarsh	50.00	5.00	3.00
47 David Tanabe	25.00	4.00	2.00
48 Trevor Kidd (G)	50.00	5.00	3.00
49 Jeff Friesen	50.00	5.00	3.00
50 Marc Moro RC	**20.00**	**4.00**	**2.50**
51 Luc Robitaille	150.00	15.00	8.00
52 Mike Richter (G)	75.00	5.00	4.50
53 Éric Desjardins	50.00	5.00	3.00
54 Jean-Sébastien Aubin (G)	25.00	4.00	2.00
55 Paul Laus	20.00	4.00	2.00
56 Kimmo Timonen	25.00	4.00	2.00
57 Steve Sullivan	50.00	5.00	3.00
58 Eric Cairns	20.00	4.00	2.00
59 Scott Stevens	75.00	5.00	4.00
60 Andy Delmore	25.00	4.00	2.00
61 Jeff Nielsen (MinW.)	20.00	4.00	2.00
62 Mathieu Biron	25.00	4.00	2.00
63 Juha Lind	25.00	4.00	2.00
64 Maxim Afinogenov	75.00	5.00	4.00
65 Guy Hebert (G)	25.00	4.00	2.00
66 Sergei Brylin	25.00	4.00	2.00
67 Mike Modano	175.00	15.00	10.00
68 Tommy Salo (G)	75.00	5.00	4.00
69 Bryan Smolinski	25.00	4.00	2.00
70 Sergei Varlamov	25.00	4.00	2.00
71 Paul Mara	25.00	4.00	2.00
72 Peter Forsberg	250.00	25.00	14.00
73 Doug Weight	100.00	10.00	6.00
74 Peter Bondra	100.00	10.00	6.00
75 Marc Denis (G) (Colu.)	75.00	5.00	4.50
76 Jamie Storr (G)	25.00	4.00	2.00
77 Alex Kovalev	100.00	10.00	6.00
78 Darius Zubrus	25.00	4.00	2.00
79 Mike Grier	25.00	4.00	2.00
80 Olaf Kölzig (G)	100.00	10.00	6.00
81 Bryan Adams RC	**20.00**	**4.00**	**2.50**
82 Scott Niedermayer	50.00	5.00	3.00
83 David Gosselin RC	**20.00**	**4.00**	**2.50**
84 Boris Mironov	25.00	4.00	2.00
85 Kyle McLaren	25.00	4.00	2.00
86 Steve Kariya	25.00	4.00	2.00
87 Dmitry Yushkevich	25.00	4.00	2.00
88 Paul Kariya	250.00	25.00	14.00
89 Brian Leetch	100.00	10.00	6.00
90 Jeff Daniels	20.00	4.00	2.00
91 Brendan Morrison	50.00	5.00	3.00
92 Brian Campbell	20.00	4.00	2.00
93 Ray Whitney	25.00	4.00	2.00
94 Marian Hossa	175.00	15.00	10.00
95 Sergei Samsonov	100.00	10.00	6.00
96 Mike York	50.00	5.00	3.00
97 Mark Eaton	20.00	4.00	2.00
98 Ryan VandenBussche	20.00	4.00	2.00
99 Vladimir Malakhov	25.00	4.00	2.00
100 Jeff Finley	20.00	4.00	2.00
101 John Vanbiesbrouck (G)	75.00	5.00	4.50
102 Brad Isbister	25.00	4.00	2.00
103 John Madden	50.00	5.00	3.00
104 Patrick Roy (G)	550.00	55.00	30.00
105 Radek Bonk	50.00	5.00	3.00
106 Brett Hull	175.00	15.00	10.00
107 Andreas Dackell	25.00	4.00	2.00
108 Pierre Turgeon	75.00	5.00	4.00
109 Jason Woolley	20.00	4.00	2.00
110 Jeff O'Neill	75.00	5.00	4.00
111 John LeClair	150.00	15.00	8.00
112 Darryl Sydor	25.00	4.00	2.00
113 Ryan Smyth	75.00	5.00	4.50
114 Curtis Joseph (G)	175.00	15.00	10.00
115 Gary Roberts	75.00	5.00	4.00
116 Pavel Kubina	25.00	4.00	2.00
117 Roman Hamrlik	25.00	4.00	2.00
118 Sandis Ozolinsh	25.00	4.00	2.00
119 M. Fernandez (G) (MinW.)	75.00	5.00	4.00
120 Adam Oates	75.00	5.00	4.00
121 D. Hendrickson (MinW.)	25.00	4.00	2.00
122 Glenn Murray	75.00	5.00	4.50
123 Jiri Slegr	25.00	4.00	2.00
124 Steve Yzerman	450.00	45.00	24.00
125 Mats Lindgren	25.00	4.00	2.00
126 Sergei Gonchar	50.00	5.00	3.00
127 Joe Thornton	225.00	20.00	12.00
128 Petr Sykora	75.00	5.00	4.00
129 Pavol Demitra	75.00	5.00	4.00
130 Tyler Wright (Colu.)	20.00	4.00	2.00
131 Johan Davidsson	20.00	4.00	2.00
132 Brian Rolston	50.00	5.00	3.00
133 Mark Messier	175.00	15.00	10.00
134 Darcy Tucker	25.00	4.00	2.00
135 Oleg Tverdovsky	25.00	4.00	2.00
136 Petr Nedved	50.00	5.00	3.00
137 Harold Druken	50.00	5.00	3.00
138 Valeri Bure	50.00	5.00	3.00
139 Mikael Andersson	20.00	4.00	2.00
140 Evgeni Nabokov (G)	100.00	10.00	9.00
141 Janne Laukkanen	20.00	4.00	2.00
142 Radek Dvorak	25.00	4.00	2.00
143 Brian Boucher (G)	50.00	5.00	3.00
144 Éric Dazé	75.00	5.00	4.00
145 Dan Cloutier (G)	75.00	5.00	4.00
146 Scott Gomez	75.00	5.00	4.00
147 Dallas Drake (Colu.)	25.00	4.00	2.00
148 Shawn McEachern	50.00	5.00	3.00
149 Joe Nieuwendyk	75.00	5.00	4.00
150 Kenny Jönsson	25.00	4.00	2.00
151 Saku Koivu	225.00	20.00	8.00
152 Roman Turek (G)	75.00	5.00	4.50
153 Chris Gratton	25.00	4.00	2.00
154 Steve Rucchin	25.00	4.00	2.00
155 Teppo Numminen	50.00	5.00	3.00
156 Jamie Langenbrunner	25.00	4.00	2.00
157 Johnathan Aitken	20.00	4.00	2.00
158 Nikolai Antropov	25.00	4.00	2.00
159 Stéphane Fiset (G)	50.00	5.00	3.00
160 Manny Malhotra	25.00	4.00	2.00
161 Pavel Bure	150.00	15.00	8.00
162 Chris Drury	100.00	10.00	6.00
163 Roberto Luongo (G)	150.00	15.00	8.00
164 Norm Maracle (G)	25.00	4.00	2.00
165 Brendan Shanahan	175.00	15.00	10.00
166 Calle Johansson	25.00	4.00	2.00
167 Cory Stillman	25.00	4.00	2.00
168 Jozef Stümpel	25.00	4.00	2.00
169 Ron Tugnutt (G)	75.00	5.00	4.00
170 Brian Savage	50.00	5.00	3.00
171 Viktor Kozlov	50.00	5.00	3.00
172 Chris Simon	25.00	4.00	2.00
173 Chris Joseph	20.00	4.00	2.00
174 Willie Mitchell RC	**35.00**	**4.00**	**4.00**
175 Randy Robitaille	25.00	4.00	2.00
176 Sami Kapanen	50.00	5.00	3.00
177 Jonathan Girard	20.00	4.00	2.00
178 Andrew Cassels	25.00	4.00	2.00
179 Jani Hurme (G) RC	**50.00**	**5.00**	**6.00**
180 Maxim Balmochnykh	25.00	4.00	2.00
181 Adam Graves	75.00	5.00	4.00
182 Steve Shields (G)	25.00	4.00	2.00
183 Marc Savard	25.00	4.00	2.00
184 Zigmund Palffy	100.00	10.00	6.00
185 Magnus Arvedson	25.00	4.00	2.00
186 Byron Dafoe (G)	75.00	5.00	4.00
187 Jan Hlavac	25.00	4.00	2.00
188 Len Barrie	20.00	4.00	2.00
189 Jocelyn Thibault (G)	75.00	5.00	4.00
190 Fred Brathwaite (G)	50.00	5.00	3.00
191 Fredrik Modin	25.00	4.00	2.00
192 Shane Doan	25.00	4.00	2.00
193 Petr Mika RC	**20.00**	**4.00**	**2.50**
194 Larry Murphy	25.00	4.00	2.00
195 Daniel Alfredsson	225.00	10.00	6.00
196 Brenden Morrow	50.00	5.00	3.00
197 Martin Rucinsky	25.00	4.00	2.00
198 Michal Handzus	25.00	4.00	2.00
199 Dominik Hasek (G)	175.00	15.00	10.00
200 Rod Brind'Amour	50.00	5.00	3.00
201 Trevor Letowski	25.00	4.00	2.00
202 Derian Hatcher	50.00	5.00	3.00
203 Phil Housley	50.00	5.00	3.00
204 Martin Biron (G)	75.00	5.00	4.50
205 Sergei Berezin	75.00	5.00	2.00
206 Ron Francis	100.00	10.00	6.00
207 Cliff Ronning	25.00	4.00	2.00
208 Robert Svehla	25.00	4.00	2.00
209 Vincent Lecavalier	175.00	15.00	10.00
210 Kent Manderville	20.00	4.00	2.00
211 Andrew Brunette	25.00	4.00	2.00
212 Chris Chelios	100.00	10.00	6.00
213 Alexander Karpovtsev	20.00	4.00	2.00
214 Robyn Regehr	25.00	4.00	2.00
215 Mika Alatalo	25.00	4.00	2.00
216 Jan Hrdina	25.00	4.00	2.00
217 Nicklas Lidström	100.00	10.00	6.00
218 Ivan Novoseltsev	25.00	4.00	2.00
219 Alexander Mogilny	75.00	5.00	4.50
220 Chris Pronger	100.00	10.00	6.00
221 Paul Coffey	100.00	10.00	6.00
222 John Grahame (G)	25.00	4.00	2.00
223 Jeff Farkas	25.00	4.00	3.50
224 Eric Lindros	175.00	15.00	10.00
225 Jörgen Jönsson	25.00	4.00	2.00
226 J-F Labbé (G) RC	**35.00**	**4.00**	**4.00**
227 Owen Nolan	100.00	10.00	6.00
228 Oleg Saprykin	25.00	4.00	2.00
229 Patrick Marleau	75.00	5.00	4.50
230 Aaron Downey RC	**35.00**	**4.00**	**4.00**
231 Chris Osgood (G)	100.00	10.00	6.00
232 Mike Wilson	20.00	4.00	2.00
233 Joe Sakic	300.00	30.00	16.00
234 D. Kochan (G) RC	**35.00**	**4.00**	**4.00**
235 Jeremy Roenick	150.00	15.00	8.00
236 Alexei Zhamnov	50.00	5.00	3.00
237 Sergei Fedorov	175.00	15.00	10.00
238 Petr Schastlivy	25.00	4.00	2.00
239 Milan Hejduk	150.00	15.00	8.00
240 Patrice Brisebois	25.00	4.00	2.00
241 Marty Reasoner	25.00	4.00	2.00

□□□	242 Ed Belfour (G)	175.00	15.00	10.00
□□□	243 Vitaly Vishnevski	25.00	4.00	2.00
□□□	244 Keith Tkachuk	100.00	10.00	6.00
□□□	245 Petr Buzek	20.00	4.00	2.00
□□□	246 Miroslav Satan	50.00	5.00	3.00
□□□	247 Adam Mair	25.00	4.00	2.00
□□□	248 Jere Karalahti	20.00	4.00	2.00
□□□	249 Mike Dunham (G)	75.00	5.00	4.00
□□□	250 Mike Sillinger	25.00	4.00	2.00
□□□	**251 A. Skopintsev RC**	**20.00**	**4.00**	**2.50**
□□□	**252 S. Vyshedkevich RC**	**35.00**	**4.00**	**4.00**
□□□	253 Steve Duchesne	25.00	4.00	2.00
□□□	254 Tomas Kaberle	50.00	5.00	3.00
□□□	255 Arturs Irbe (G)	75.00	5.00	4.00
□□□	256 Niklas Sundström	25.00	4.00	2.00
□□□	257 Al MacInnis	75.00	5.00	4.00
□□□	258 Mike Ribeiro	50.00	5.00	3.00
□□□	259 Rob Niedermayer	25.00	4.00	2.00
□□□	**260 Jean-Guy Trudel RC**	**35.00**	**4.00**	**4.00**
□□□	261 Martin Straka	50.00	5.00	3.00
□□□	262 Jason Arnott	75.00	5.00	4.50
□□□	263 David Legwand	75.00	5.00	4.00
□□□	264 Tony Amonte	100.00	10.00	6.00
□□□	265 Jason Allison	100.00	10.00	6.00
□□□	266 Patrik Elias	150.00	15.00	8.00
□□□	267 Mark Recchi	75.00	5.00	4.00
□□□	268 Patrik Stefan	50.00	5.00	3.00
□□□	269 Mariusz Czerkawski	25.00	4.00	2.00
□□□	270 Vincent Damphousse	100.00	10.00	6.00
□□□	271 S. Krivokrasov (MinW.)	25.00	4.00	2.00
□□□	272 Teemu Selänne	150.00	15.00	8.00
□□□	273 Patrick Lalime (G)	100.00	10.00	6.00
□□□	274 Nick Boynton	25.00	4.00	3.50
□□□	275 Darren McCarty	50.00	5.00	3.00
□□□	276 Jaroslav Spacek	20.00	4.00	2.00
□□□	277 Chris Dingman	25.00	4.00	2.00
□□□	278 Jarome Iginla	150.00	15.00	8.00
□□□	279 Andrei Zyuzin	25.00	4.00	2.00
□□□	280 Jyrki Lumme	25.00	4.00	2.00
□□□	281 Michal Grosek	20.00	4.00	2.00
□□□	282 Janne Niinimaa	25.00	4.00	2.00
□□□	283 Wade Redden	50.00	5.00	3.00
□□□	284 Raymond Bourque	225.00	20.00	12.00
□□□	285 Trevor Linden	75.00	5.00	4.00
□□□	286 Ladislav Nagy	25.00	4.00	3.50
□□□	287 José Théodore (G)	225.00	20.00	12.00
□□□	288 Bates Battaglia	25.00	4.00	2.00
□□□	289 Mikeal Renberg	50.00	5.00	3.00
□□□	290 Donald Audette	75.00	5.00	4.00
□□□	291 Doug Gilmour	100.00	10.00	6.00
□□□	292 Yanic Perreault	50.00	5.00	3.00
□□□	293 Anders Eriksson	20.00	4.00	2.00
□□□	294 Gary Suter	25.00	4.00	2.00
□□□	295 Brad Ference	25.00	4.00	2.00
□□□	296 Mats Sundin	175.00	15.00	10.00
□□□	297 Ray Ferraro	25.00	4.00	2.00
□□□	298 Jiri Fischer	25.00	4.00	2.00
□□□	299 Todd Bertuzzi	225.00	20.00	12.00
□□□	300 Derek Morris	25.00	4.00	2.00
□□□	301 Patric Kjellberg	25.00	4.00	2.00
□□□	302 Pat Verbeek	50.00	5.00	3.00
□□□	303 Kip Miller	25.00	4.00	2.00
□□□	304 Alexei Vasiliev	20.00	4.00	2.00
□□□	305 Marcus Ragnarsson	25.00	4.00	2.00
□□□	306 Arron Asham	20.00	4.00	2.00
□□□	307 Sylvain Cote	25.00	4.00	2.00
□□□	308 Vaclav Prospal	50.00	5.00	3.00
□□□	309 Aki Berg	25.00	4.00	2.00
□□□	310 Alexander Selivanov	20.00	4.00	2.00
□□□	311 Wayne Primeau	25.00	4.00	2.00
□□□	312 Brian Rafalski	25.00	4.00	2.00
□□□	313 Jonas Höglund	25.00	4.00	2.00
□□□	314 Adam Foote	50.00	5.00	3.00
□□□	315 Steve Konowalchuk	25.00	4.00	2.00
□□□	316 Robert Dome	25.00	4.00	2.00
□□□	317 Antti Laaksonen	20.00	4.00	2.00
□□□	318 Mike Ricci	50.00	5.00	3.00
□□□	319 Gino Odjick	25.00	4.00	2.00
□□□	320 Eric Weinrich	20.00	4.00	2.00
□□□	321 Jason Strudwick	20.00	4.00	2.00
□□□	322 Kim Johnsson	25.00	4.00	2.00
□□□	323 Dimitri Kalinin	20.00	4.00	2.00
□□□	324 Daymond Langkow	25.00	4.00	2.00
□□□	325 Todd Marchant	25.00	4.00	2.00
□□□	326 Richard Matvichuk	25.00	4.00	2.00
□□□	327 Travis Green	25.00	4.00	2.00
□□□	328 Igor Larionov	100.00	10.00	6.00
□□□	329 Mattias Öhlund	50.00	5.00	3.00
□□□	330 Igor Kravchuk	25.00	4.00	2.00
□□□	331 Richard Zednik	75.00	5.00	4.00
□□□	332 Curtis Brown	25.00	4.00	2.00
□□□	333 Krzysztof Oliwa (Colu.)	25.00	4.00	2.00
□□□	334 Darius Kasparaitis	25.00	4.00	2.00
□□□	335 Michael Nylander	25.00	4.00	2.00
□□□	336 Stan Drulia	20.00	4.00	2.00
□□□	337 Nelson Emerson	25.00	4.00	2.00
□□□	338 Greg Johnson	25.00	4.00	2.00
□□□	339 Sean Hill	20.00	4.00	2.00
□□□	340 Keith Jones	25.00	4.00	2.00
□□□	341 Bill Muckalt	25.00	4.00	2.00
□□□	342 Randy McKay	20.00	4.00	2.00
□□□	343 Stu Grimson	25.00	4.00	2.00
□□□	344 Tyson Nash	25.00	4.00	2.00
□□□	345 Dan Hinote	25.00	4.00	2.00
□□□	346 Mike Rathje	25.00	4.00	2.00
□□□	347 Brian Holzinger	25.00	4.00	2.00
□□□	**348 Eric Nickulas RC**	**20.00**	**4.00**	**2.50**
□□□	349 Alexandre Daigle	25.00	4.00	2.00
□□□	350 Jan Bulis	20.00	4.00	2.00
□□□	351 Tom Poti	25.00	4.00	2.00
□□□	352 Kevyn Adams (Colu.)	25.00	4.00	2.00
□□□	353 Scott Thornton	20.00	4.00	2.00
□□□	354 Sean Burke (G)	100.00	10.00	6.00
□□□	355 Peter Worrell	25.00	4.00	2.00
□□□	356 Josef Beranek	25.00	4.00	2.00
□□□	357 Matt Cullen	25.00	4.00	2.00
□□□	358 Sandy McCarthy	25.00	4.00	2.00
□□□	359 Sergei Zholtok	25.00	4.00	2.00
□□□	360 Darren Langdon	25.00	4.00	2.00
□□□	361 Martin Lapointe	75.00	5.00	4.00
□□□	362 Adrian Aucoin	25.00	4.00	2.00
□□□	363 Dimitri Nabokov	25.00	4.00	2.00
□□□	364 Jason Blake	25.00	4.00	2.00
□□□	365 Jeff Halpern	25.00	4.00	2.00
□□□	366 Rico Fata	25.00	4.00	2.00
□□□	367 Dave Reid	25.00	4.00	2.00
□□□	368 Vitali Yachmenev	25.00	4.00	2.00
□□□	369 Hnat Domenichelli	25.00	4.00	2.00
□□□	370 Rick Tocchet	50.00	5.00	3.00
□□□	371 Tommy Westlund	20.00	4.00	2.00
□□□	372 Chris Phillips	25.00	4.00	2.00
□□□	373 Claude Lemieux	50.00	5.00	3.00
□□□	374 Greg Adams	25.00	4.00	2.00
□□□	375 Todd Simpson	20.00	4.00	2.00
□□□	376 Ken Klee	20.00	4.00	2.00
□□□	377 André Savage	20.00	4.00	2.00
□□□	378 Bryan Marchment	25.00	4.00	2.00
□□□	379 Dean McAmmond	25.00	4.00	2.00
□□□	380 Mike Johnson	25.00	4.00	2.00
□□□	381 Tomas Holmström	25.00	4.00	2.00
□□□	382 Robert Lang	25.00	4.00	2.00
□□□	383 Daniel McGillis	30.00	4.00	2.00
□□□	384 Jamie Rivers	20.00	4.00	2.00
□□□	385 Dave Andreychuk	50.00	5.00	3.00
□□□	386 Marty McInnis	25.00	4.00	2.00
□□□	387 Sami Salo	20.00	4.00	2.00
□□□	388 Dan Cleary	50.00	5.00	3.00
□□□	389 Robert Esche (G)	25.00	4.00	2.00
□□□	390 Aaron Gavey (MinW.)	25.00	4.00	2.00
□□□	391 Andrei Nikolishin	25.00	4.00	2.00
□□□	392 Jason Krog	25.00	4.00	2.00
□□□	393 Stu Barnes	20.00	4.00	2.00
□□□	394 Tomas Vokoun (G)	25.00	4.00	2.00
□□□	395 Peter Schaefer	25.00	4.00	2.00
□□□	396 Danny Markov	25.00	4.00	2.00
□□□	397 Daniel Sedin	75.00	5.00	6.00
□□□	398 Kris Beech	50.00	5.00	3.00
□□□	399 Samuel Påhlsson	25.00	4.00	2.00
□□□	400 Gary Roberts	75.00	5.00	4.00
□□□	**401 Marian Gaborik RC**	**300.00**	**45.00**	**25.00**
□□□	402 Oleg Kvasha	25.00	4.00	2.00
□□□	**403 Martin Havlat RC**	**125.00**	**20.00**	**15.00**
□□□	**404 Roman Simicek RC**	**20.00**	**4.00**	**2.50**
□□□	405 Dallas Drake	25.00	4.00	2.00
□□□	**406 Jakub Cutta RC**	**35.00**	**4.00**	**4.00**
□□□	407 German Titov	20.00	4.00	2.00
□□□	**408 Jarno Kultanen RC**	**20.00**	**4.00**	**2.50**
□□□	409 Sandis Ozolinsh	25.00	4.00	2.00
□□□	410 David Vyborny	25.00	4.00	2.00
□□□	411 Olli Jokinen	50.00	5.00	3.00
□□□	412 Maxim Sushinsky	25.00	4.00	2.00
□□□	413 J. Vanbiesbrouck (G)	75.00	5.00	4.50
□□□	**414 Shane Hnidy RC**	**35.00**	**4.00**	**4.00**
□□□	415 Milan Kraft	50.00	5.00	3.00
□□□	**416 A. Kharitonov RC**	**20.00**	**4.00**	**2.50**
□□□	417 Andrei Nazarov	25.00	4.00	2.00
□□□	418 Dave Andreychuk	50.00	5.00	3.00
□□□	**419 Niclas Wallin RC**	**20.00**	**4.00**	**2.50**
□□□	**420 Rostislav Klesla RC**	**125.00**	**15.00**	**8.00**
□□□	421 Denis Shvidki	25.00	4.00	2.00
□□□	422 Mathieu Garon (G)	75.00	10.00	4.00
□□□	423 Taylor Pyatt	25.00	4.00	2.00
□□□	**424 R. Cechmanek (G) RC**	**75.00**	**10.00**	**10.00**
□□□	**425 Mark Smith RC**	**20.00**	**4.00**	**2.50**
□□□	426 Shayne Corson	50.00	5.00	3.00
□□□	**427 Jonas Rönnqvist RC**	**35.00**	**4.00**	**4.00**
□□□	428 Jean-Pierre Dumont	25.00	4.00	2.00
□□□	**429 Josef Vasicek RC**	**50.00**	**5.00**	**6.00**
□□□	**430 Tyler Bouck RC**	**35.00**	**4.00**	**4.00**
□□□	431 Mathieu Schneider	25.00	4.00	2.00
□□□	432 Andrei Markov	25.00	4.00	2.00
□□□	433 Vladimir Malakhov	25.00	4.00	2.00
□□□	434 Maxime Ouellet (G)	75.00	5.00	4.00
□□□	435 Matt Bradley	25.00	4.00	2.00
□□□	436 Dave Manson	25.00	4.00	2.00
□□□	**437 Brad Tapper RC**	**35.00**	**4.00**	**4.00**
□□□	**438 Eric Boulton RC**	**35.00**	**4.00**	**4.00**
□□□	439 Brent Johnson (G)	75.00	5.00	4.00
□□□	**440 Marty Turco (G) RC**	**125.00**	**15.00**	**15.00**
□□□	441 Tomas Vlasak	20.00	4.00	2.00
□□□	**442 Greg Classen RC**	**35.00**	**4.00**	**4.00**
□□□	443 Mark Messier	175.00	15.00	10.00
□□□	**444 Justin Williams RC**	**50.00**	**5.00**	**8.00**
□□□	445 Sean Hill	20.00	4.00	2.00
□□□	446 Bryan McCabe	25.00	4.00	2.00
□□□	447 Andreas Karlsson	20.00	4.00	2.00
□□□	448 Mika Noronen (G)	75.00	5.00	4.00
□□□	449 Alexander Karpovtsev	20.00	4.00	2.00
□□□	450 Boyd Devereaux	25.00	4.00	2.00
□□□	**451 L. Visnovsky RC**	**35.00**	**4.00**	**4.00**
□□□	**452 Scott Hartnell RC**	**25.00**	**4.00**	**6.00**
□□□	**453 J. LaBarbera (G) RC**	**35.00**	**4.00**	**4.00**
□□□	**454 Petr Hubacek RC**	**20.00**	**4.00**	**2.50**
□□□	**455 A. Khavanov RC**	**35.00**	**4.00**	**4.00**
□□□	**456 Petr** Svoboda RC**	**35.00**	**4.00**	**4.00**
□□□	457 Tomi Kallio	25.00	4.00	2.00
□□□	458 Mike Vernon (G)	75.00	10.00	4.00
□□□	**459 Reto von Arx RC**	**30.00**	**4.00**	**4.00**
□□□	460 Maxim Kuznetsov	20.00	4.00	2.00
□□□	**461 S. Reinprecht RC**	**50.00**	**5.00**	**8.00**
□□□	462 Turner Stevenson	25.00	4.00	2.00
□□□	463 Roberto Luongo (G)	150.00	15.00	8.00
□□□	464 Brad Richards	100.00	10.00	7.00
□□□	**465 Bryce Salvador RC**	**30.00**	**4.00**	**4.00**
□□□	466 Kevin Hatcher	25.00	4.00	2.00
□□□	467 Paul Coffey	100.00	10.00	6.00
□□□	468 Marty Murray	20.00	4.00	2.00
□□□	**469 Todd Fedoruk RC**	**20.00**	**4.00**	**2.50**
□□□	470 Brian Swanson	25.00	4.00	2.00
□□□	471 Christian Matte	20.00	4.00	2.00
□□□	**472 Sascha Goc RC**	**30.00**	**4.00**	**4.00**
□□□	**473 Dale Purinton RC**	**35.00**	**4.00**	**4.00**
□□□	474 Brad May	25.00	4.00	2.00
□□□	475 Brad Brown	20.00	4.00	2.00
□□□	**476 Petteri Nummelin RC**	**35.00**	**4.00**	**4.00**
□□□	**477 R. Fedotenko RC**	**35.00**	**4.00**	**4.00**
□□□	**478 R. Petrovicky RC**	**35.00**	**4.00**	**4.00**
□□□	**479 D. Aebischer (G) RC**	**50.00**	**5.00**	**8.00**
□□□	**480 Michel Riesen RC**	**35.00**	**4.00**	**4.00**
□□□	**481 Ladislav Benysek RC**	**20.00**	**4.00**	**2.50**
□□□	482 Mark Parrish	75.00	10.00	4.00
□□□	483 Mike Mottau	25.00	4.00	2.00
□□□	**484 Ossi Väänänen RC**	**35.00**	**4.00**	**4.00**
□□□	**485 A. Raycroft (G) RC**	**50.00**	**5.00**	**6.00**
□□□	486 Sylvain Côté	25.00	4.00	2.00
□□□	487 Richard Jackman	25.00	4.00	2.00
□□□	488 Toni Lydman	25.00	4.00	2.00
□□□	489 Ron Tugnutt (G)	75.00	5.00	4.00
□□□	490 Igor Larionov	100.00	10.00	6.00
□□□	**491 L. Sekeras RC**	**35.00**	**4.00**	**4.00**
□□□	492 Roman Hamrlik	25.00	4.00	2.00
□□□	**493 J. Holmqvist (G) RC**	**50.00**	**5.00**	**8.00**
□□□	**494 Josef Melichar RC**	**20.00**	**4.00**	**2.50**
□□□	495 Sheldon Keefe	25.00	4.00	2.00
□□□	496 Henrik Sedin	75.00	5.00	6.00
□□□	**497 Rick DiPietro (G) RC**	**100.00**	**10.00**	**12.00**

ALL-STAR GAME TICKET

Insert Set (10 cards):		**625.00**
	Insert (1:864 packs)	**AST**
□	1990 All-Star Game	75.00
□	1991 All-Star Game	75.00
□	1992 All-Star Game	75.00
□	1993 All-Star Game	75.00
□	1994 All-Star Game	75.00
□	1996 All-Star Game	75.00
□	1997 All-Star Game	75.00
□	1998 All-Star Game	75.00
□	1999 All-Star Game	75.00
□	2000 All-Star Game	75.00

ALL-STAR JERSEY, ETC.

There are four versions: the Jersey card (1:360 packs, prefix J-), the Jersey & Stick card (1:999 packs, prefix JS-), the In The Numbers card (1:999 packs, prefix N-) and the Emblem card (1:999 packs, prefix E-).

Insert Set (40 cards):		**4,200**	**3,700**	**3,100**	**2,300**
	Inserts	**E**	**ITN**	**JS**	**J**
□□□□	27 D. Alfredsson, AS'97 ✂	175	150	125	100
□□□□	11 T. Amonte, AS'00 ✂	75	75	60	50
□□□□	33 E. Belfour (G), AS'96 ✂	150	125	100	75
□□□□	39 R. Blake, AS'94 ✂	75	75	60	50
□□□□	37 R. Bourque, AS'94 ✂	175	150	125	100
□□□□	4 M. Brodeur (G), AS'00 ✂	225	200	150	125
□□□□	3 P. Bure, AS'00 ✂	100	100	75	50
□□□□	28 P. Coffey, AS'97 ✂	75	75	60	50
□□□□	35 S. Fedorov, AS'94 ✂	150	125	100	75
□□□□	18 T. Fleury, AS'99 ✂	75	75	60	50
□□□□	14 P. Forsberg, AS'99 ✂	200	175	150	100
□□□□	25 W. Gretzky, AS'98 ✂	600	525	425	350
□□□□	13 D. Hasek (G), AS'99 ✂	150	125	100	75
□□□□	30 B. Hull, AS'96 ✂	150	125	100	75
□□□□	9 J. Jagr, AS'00 ✂	150	125	100	75
□□□□	40 C. Joseph (G), AS'94 ✂	150	125	100	75
□□□□	31 P. Kariya, AS'96 ✂	200	175	150	100
□□□□	21 N. Khabibulin (G), AS'98 ✂	60	60	60	40
□□□□	10 O. Kölzig (G), AS'00 ✂	75	75	60	50
□□□□	32 J. LeClair, AS'96 ✂	100	100	75	50
□□□□	38 B. Leetch, AS'94 ✂	75	75	60	50
□□□□	17 N. Lidström, AS'99 ✂	75	75	60	50
□□□□	16 E. Lindros, AS'99 ✂	150	125	100	75
□□□□	8 A. MacInnis, AS'00 ✂	60	60	60	40
□□□□	23 M. Messier, AS'98 ✂	150	125	100	75
□□□□	20 M. Modano, AS'99 ✂	150	125	100	75
□□□□	26 O. Nolan, AS'97 ✂	75	75	60	50
□□□□	22 S. Ozolinsh, AS'98 ✂	60	60	60	40
□□□□	7 C. Pronger, AS'00 ✂	75	75	60	50
□□□□	36 M. Recchi, AS'94 ✂	60	60	60	40
□□□□	5 M. Richter (G), AS'00 ✂	60	60	60	40
□□□□	1 J. Roenick, AS'00 ✂	100	100	75	50
□□□□	34 P. Roy (G), AS'94 ✂	350	300	250	200
□□□□	24 J. Sakic, AS'98 ✂	225	200	150	125
□□□□	15 T. Selänne, AS'99 ✂	100	100	75	50
□□□□	6 B. Shanahan, AS'00 ✂	150	125	100	75
□□□□	12 S. Stevens, AS'00 ✂	60	60	60	40
□□□□	2 M. Sundin, AS'00 ✂	150	125	100	75
□□□□	19 D. Sydor, AS'99 ✂	60	60	60	40
□□□□	29 S. Yzerman, AS'97 ✂	350	300	250	200

GOALIE MEMORABILIA

Insert Set (30 cards):		**7,000**
	Insert (1:999 packs)	**GM**
□	G-1 Mike Richter (G) Jersey ✂ Stick ✂	150.00
□	G-2 Patrick Roy (G) Glove ✂ Stick ✂	400.00
□	G-3 Dominik Hasek (G) Glove ✂ Stick ✂	175.00
□	G-4 Ed Belfour (G) Jersey ✂ Stick ✂	175.00
□	G-5 Curtis Joseph (G) Glove ✂ Jersey ✂	175.00
□	G-6 Terry Sawchuk (G) Glove ✂ Stick ✂	400.00
□	G-7 Vladislav Tretiak (G) Glove ✂ Jersey ✂	300.00
□	G-8 Gerry Cheevers (G) Pads ✂ Stick ✂	150.00
□	G-9 Félix Potvin (G) Glove ✂ Jersey ✂	150.00
□	G-10 Frank Brimsek (G) Glove ✂ Jersey ✂	150.00
□	G-11 Bernie Parent (G) Pads ✂ Jersey ✂	150.00
□	G-12 B. Parent Jersey ✂ / T. Esposito Stick ✂	250.00
□	G-13 J. Bower Stick ✂ / C.Joseph Stick ✂	250.00
□	G-14 F. Brimsek Glove ✂ / G. Cheevers Stick ✂	175.00
□	G-15 P. Roy Stick ✂ / J. Plante Glove ✂	525.00
□	G-16 T. Esposito Stick ✂ / V. Tretiak Jersey ✂	325.00
□	G-17 Joseph (G) Jersey ✂ / Sawchuk Stick ✂	450.00
□	G-18 T. Broda Glove ✂ / C. Joseph Jersey ✂	250.00
□	G-19 J. Bower Glove ✂ / T. Broda Glove ✂	225.00
□	G-20 C. Joseph (G) Stick ✂ / F. Potvin Glove ✂	225.00
□	G-21 P. Roy Jersey ✂ / E. Belfour Jersey ✂	500.00
□	G-22 V. Tretiak Jersey ✂ / E. Belfour Jersey ✂	475.00
□	G-23 J. Plante Glove ✂ / T. Sawchuk Stick ✂	525.00
□	G-24 J. Bower Stick ✂ / T. Sawchuk Stick ✂	400.00
□	G-25 G. Cheevers Stick ✂ / T. Esposito Stick ✂	250.00
□	G-26 F. Brimsek Glove ✂ / G. Cheevers Pads ✂	175.00
□	G-27 T. Broda Glove ✂ / C. Joseph Glove ✂	250.00
□	G-28 P. Roy Glove ✂ / T. Sawchuk Glove ✂	800.00
□	G-29 Bower Stick ✂ / Joseph Stick ✂ / Sawchuk Stick ✂	650.00
□	G-30 Cheevers Stick ✂ / Esposito Stick ✂ / Parent Stick ✂	500.00

HERITAGE MEMORABILIA

There are two versions: the regular insert (1:5 Update boxes) and the Gold parallel (#/1).

Insert Set (22 cards):		**2,000**
	Insert (1:999 packs)	**HM**
□□	H-6 Ed Belfour (G), Chic. ✂	150.00
□□	H-16 Raymond Bourque, Bost. ✂	175.00
□□	H-2 Pavel Bure, Vanc. ✂	125.00
□□	H-12 Chris Chelios, Chic. ✂	75.00
□□	H-3 Paul Coffey, Edmo. ✂	75.00
□□	H-14 Theoren Fleury, Calg. ✂	75.00
□□	H-8 Brett Hull, SLou. ✂	150.00
□□	H-5 Curtis Joseph (G), SLou. ✂	150.00
□□	H-20 Trevor Linden, Vanc. ✂	75.00
□□	H-13 Al MacInnis, Calg. ✂	75.00
□□	H-1 Mark Messier, Edmo. ✂	150.00
□□	H-7 Mike Modano, MinN. ✂	150.00
□□	H-18 Owen Nolan, Québ. ✂	75.00
□□	H-22 Adam Oates, Bost. ✂	75.00
□□	H-19 Félix Potvin (G), Toro. ✂	75.00
□□	H-15 Keith Primeau, Detr. ✂	75.00
□□	H-11 Patrick Roy (G), Mont. ✂	375.00
□□	H-9 Teemu Selänne, Winn. ✂	125.00
□□	H-17 Brendan Shanahan, Hart. ✂	150.00
□□	H-21 Scott Stevens, Wash. ✂	75.00
□□	H-4 Mats Sundin, Québ. ✂	150.00
□□	H-10 Keith Tkachuk, Winn. ✂	75.00

LEGEND SERIES

There are two versions: the regular insert (30 copies each, 1:2400 packs) and the autographed parallel (#/6).

Insert Set (10 cards):	5,700
Inserts	**LS30**
☐☐ L-1 Mario Lemieux 87-88 Jersey ✂	600.00
☐☐ L-2 Mario Lemieux 91-92 Jersey ✂	600.00
☐☐ L-3 Lemieux 87-88 Jersey ✂ 91-92 Glove ✂	800.00
☐☐ L-4 Mario Lemieux 91-92 Jersey ✂ Glove ✂	800.00
☐☐ L-5 Mario Lemieux 91-92 Emblem ✂	800.00
☐☐ L-6 Mario Lemieux 91-92 Number ✂	800.00
☐☐ L-7 Mario Lemieux 91-92 Glove ✂	600.00
☐☐ L-8 Mario Lemieux AS'96 Jersey ✂	600.00
☐☐ L-9 Lemieux 87-88 Jersey ✂ AS'96 Jersey ✂	1000.00
☐☐ L-10 Lemieux 91-92 Jersey ✂ AS'96 Jersey ✂	1000.00

LINDEN FOUNDATION

Description	
☐ Trevor Linden (Card Offer)	.25
☐ Trevor Linden ✍ (Signature Card)	30.00

PATENTED POWER

There are two versions: the regular insert (1:5 Update boxes) and the Gold parallel (#/1).

Insert Set (6 cards):	2,300
Insert (1:4800 packs)	**PP**
☐ PP-1 W. Gretzky ✂ / M. Lemieux ✂	1200.00
☐ PP-2 P. Kariya ✂ / S. Yzerman ✂	550.00
☐ PP-3 P. Bure ✂ / J. Jagr ✂	350.00
☐ PP-4 P. Forsberg ✂ / M. Sundin ✂	350.00
☐ PP-5 T. Selänne ✂ / B. Hull ✂	350.00
☐ PP-6 B. Shanahan ✂ / J. LeClair ✂	350.00

RECORD BREAKERS

There are two versions: the regular insert and the Gold parallel (#/1).

Insert Set (2 cards):	900.00
Insert (1:4800 packs)	**RB**
☐☐ BB-1 P. Bure ✂ / V. Bure ✂	350.00
☐☐ RB-1 P. Roy / T. Sawchuk ✂ (#/33)	600.00

TEAMMATES

There are two versions: the regular insert (1:5 Update boxes) and the Gold parallel (#/1).

Insert Set (40 cards):	4,500
Inserts	**TM**
☐☐ TM-1 M. Brodeur ✂ / P. Sykora ✂	200.00
☐☐ TM-2 S. Gonchar ✂ / A. Oates ✂	50.00
☐☐ TM-3 J. Jagr ✂ / M. Lemieux ✂	400.00
☐☐ TM-4 T. Amonte ✂ / B. Probert ✂	75.00
☐☐ TM-5 J. Roenick ✂ / K. Tkachuk ✂	125.00
☐☐ TM-6 D. Hasek ✂ / M. Peca ✂	125.00
☐☐ TM-7 B. Leetch ✂ / M. Messier ✂	150.00
☐☐ TM-8 P. Bure ✂ / P. Laus ✂	75.00
☐☐ TM-9 T. Domi ✂ / C. Joseph (G) ✂	125.00
☐☐ TM-10 M. Brodeur ✂ / S. Niedermayer ✂	175.00
☐☐ TM-11 B. Dafoe ✂ / K. McLaren ✂	50.00
☐☐ TM-12 C. Chelios ✂ / N. Lidström ✂	100.00
☐☐ TM-13 D. McCarty ✂ / S. Yzerman ✂	250.00
☐☐ TM-14 E. Belfour ✂ / D. Sydor ✂	100.00
☐☐ TM-15 Br. Hull ✂ / M. Modano ✂	200.00
☐☐ TM-16 S. Fedorov ✂ / B. Shanahan ✂	200.00
☐☐ TM-17 V. Kozlov ✂ / N. Lidström ✂	75.00
☐☐ TM-18 P. Forsberg ✂ / P. Roy ✂	375.00
☐☐ TM-19 T. Fleury ✂ / M. Richter ✂	100.00
☐☐ TM-20 J. Jagr ✂ / M. Straka ✂	125.00
☐☐ TM-21 J. Arnott ✂ / S. Stevens ✂	75.00
☐☐ TM-22 C. Osgood ✂ / B. Shanahan ✂	150.00
☐☐ TM-23 G. Hebert ✂ / P. Kariya ✂	150.00
☐☐ TM-24 C. Joseph ✂ / M. Sundin ✂	200.00
☐☐ TM-25 T. Amonte ✂ / É. Dazé ✂	100.00
☐☐ TM-26 P. Kariya ✂ / T. Selänne ✂	200.00
☐☐ TM-27 J. Arnott ✂ / P. Sykora ✂	75.00
☐☐ TM-28 P. Roy ✂ / J. Sakic ✂	400.00
☐☐ TM-29 S. Fedorov ✂ / S. Yzerman ✂	325.00
☐☐ TM-30 T. Numminen ✂ / K. Tkachuk ✂	75.00
☐☐ TM-31 S. Niedermayer ✂ / S. Stevens ✂	50.00
☐☐ TM-32 M. Messier ✂ / M. Richter ✂	125.00
☐☐ TM-33 N. Khabibulin ✂ / T. Numminen ✂	50.00
☐☐ TM-34 P. Forsberg ✂ / J. Sakic ✂	300.00
☐☐ TM-35 Vy. Kozlov ✂ / C. Osgood ✂	75.00
☐☐ TM-36 E. Belfour ✂ / M. Modano ✂	200.00
☐☐ TM-37 T. Domi ✂ / C. Joseph (G) ✂	125.00
☐☐ TM-38 N. Khabibulin ✂ / J. Roenick ✂	100.00
☐☐ TM-39 G. Hebert ✂ / T. Selänne ✂	100.00
☐☐ TM-40 T. Fleury ✂ / B. Leetch ✂	100.00

TOUGH MATERIAL

There are two versions: the regular insert and the Gold parallel (#/1).

Insert Set (26 cards):	1,200
Inserts	**Tough**
☐☐ T-8 Wade Belak, Calg.	50.00
☐☐ T-25 Craig Berube, Wash.	50.00
☐☐ T-21 Bob Boughner, Pitt.	50.00
☐☐ T-6 Donald Brashear, Vanc.	75.00
☐☐ T-15 Brad Brown, Chic.	50.00
☐☐ T-4 Eric Cairns, NYIs.	50.00
☐☐ T-9 Kelly Chase, SLou.	50.00
☐☐ T-19 Enrico Ciccone, Mont.	50.00
☐☐ T-18 Chris Dingman, Colo.	50.00
☐☐ T-2 Tie Domi, Toro.	100.00
☐☐ T-24 Jean-Luc Grand-Pierre, Colu.	50.00
☐☐ T-3 Stu Grimson, LosA.	75.00
☐☐ T-23 Matt Johnson, MinW.	50.00
☐☐ T-26 Ian Laperrière, LosA.	50.00
☐☐ T-5 Paul Laus, Flor.	50.00
☐☐ T-14 Sandy McCarthy, NYRa.	50.00
☐☐ T-11 Darren McCarty, Detr.	100.00
☐☐ T-17 Jeff Odgers, Atla.	50.00
☐☐ T-22 Gino Odjick, Phil.	50.00
☐☐ T-13 Krzysztof Oliwa, Colu.	75.00
☐☐ T-1 Bob Probert, Chic.	100.00
☐☐ T-7 Rob Ray, Buff.	75.00
☐☐ T-16 Luke Richardson, Phil.	50.00
☐☐ T-12 Todd Simpson, Flor.	50.00
☐☐ T-20 Ryan VandenBussche, Chic.	50.00
☐☐ T-10 Peter Worrell, Flor.	75.00

VÉZINA MEMORABILIA

These cards feature a cut-piece of a Georges Vézina game-used leg pad.

Insert Set (16 cards):	7,300
Inserts	**VM**
☐ V-1 G. Vézina ✂ / O. Kölzig (G)	500.00
☐ V-2 G. Vézina ✂ / D. Hasek (G)	600.00
☐ V-3 G. Vézina ✂ / D. Hasek (G)	600.00
☐ V-4 G. Vézina ✂ / D. Hasek (G)	600.00
☐ V-5 G. Vézina ✂ / J. Carey (G)	500.00
☐ V-6 G. Vézina ✂ / D. Hasek (G)	600.00
☐ V-7 G. Vézina ✂ / D. Hasek (G)	600.00
☐ V-8 G. Vézina ✂ / E. Belfour (G)	500.00
☐ V-9 G. Vézina ✂ / P. Roy (G)	700.00
☐ V-10 G. Vézina ✂ / E. Belfour (G)	500.00
☐ V-11 G. Vézina ✂ / P. Roy (G)	700.00
☐ V-12 G. Vézina ✂ / P. Roy (G)	700.00
☐ V-13 G. Vézina ✂ / G. Fuhr (G)	500.00
☐ V-14 G. Vézina ✂ / J. Vanbiesbrouck (G)	500.00
☐ V-15 G. Vézina ✂ / T. Barrasso (G)	500.00
☐ V-16 Georges Vézina, Mont.	1200.00

FOR PROMOTIONAL USE

Promotional Set (100 cards):	50.00
Description	**Promo**
☐ 1 Jaromir Jagr, Pitt.	2.00
☐ 5 S. Valiquette (G), NYIs. RC	1.00
☐ 6 Simon Gagné, Phil.	1.50
☐ 9 Jochen Hecht, SLou.	.35
☐ 13 Keith Primeau, Phil.	.50
☐ 15 Tim Connolly, NYIs.	.50
☐ 22 Rob Blake, LosA.	1.00
☐ 25 Alex Tanguay, Colo.	1.00
☐ 28 Ed Jovanovski, Vanc.	.50
☐ 34 Brent Sopel, Vanc. RC	1.00
☐ 37 Steve Kelly, NJer.	.35
☐ 40 Martin Brodeur (G), NJer.	3.00
☐ 42 Steve Thomas, Toro.	.35
☐ 44 Theoren Fleury, NYRa.	1.00
☐ 45 Félix Potvin (G), Vanc.	1.00
☐ 51 Luc Robitaille, LosA.	1.50
☐ 58 Eric Cairns, NYIs.	.35
☐ 59 Scott Stevens, NJer.	.50
☐ 64 Maxim Afinogenov, Buff.	.50
☐ 67 Mike Modano, Dall.	2.00
☐ 68 Tommy Salo (G), Edmo.	.50
☐ 70 Sergei Varlamov, Calg.	.35
☐ 72 Peter Forsberg, Colo.	2.50
☐ 73 Doug Weight, Edmo.	1.00
☐ 74 Peter Bondra, Wash.	1.00
☐ 77 Alex Kovalev, Pitt.	1.00
☐ 80 Olaf Kölzig (G), Wash.	1.00
☐ 85 Kyle McLaren, Bost.	.35
☐ 86 Steve Kariya, Vanc.	.35
☐ 88 Paul Kariya, Anah.	2.50
☐ 89 Brian Leetch, NYRa.	1.00
☐ 91 Brendan Morrison, Vanc.	.50
☐ 94 Marian Hossa, Otta.	2.00
☐ 103 John Madden, NJer.	.50
☐ 104 Patrick Roy (G), Colo.	6.00
☐ 105 Radek Bonk, Otta.	.50
☐ 106 Brett Hull, Dall.	2.00
☐ 108 Pierre Turgeon, SLou.	.50
☐ 111 John LeClair, Phil.	1.50
☐ 112 Darryl Sydor, Dall.	.35
☐ 114 Curtis Joseph (G), Toro.	2.00
☐ 117 Roman Hamrlik, Edmo.	.35
☐ 120 Adam Oates, Wash.	.50
☐ 124 Steve Yzerman, Detr.	4.50
☐ 128 Petr Sykora, NJer.	.50
☐ 129 Pavol Demitra, SLou.	.50
☐ 132 Brian Rolston, Bost.	.50
☐ 134 Darcy Tucker, Toro.	.35
☐ 135 Oleg Tverdovsky, Anah.	.35
☐ 138 Valeri Bure, Calg.	.50
☐ 142 Radek Dvorak, NYRa.	.35
☐ 143 Brian Boucher (G), Phil.	.50
☐ 144 Éric Dazé, Chic.	.50
☐ 145 Dan Cloutier (G), Tamp.	.50
☐ 149 Joe Nieuwendyk, Dall.	.50
☐ 151 Saku Koivu, Mont.	1.50
☐ 152 Roman Turek (G), SLou.	.50
☐ 153 Chris Gratton, Buff.	.35
☐ 154 Steve Rucchin, Anah.	.35
☐ 155 Teppo Numminen, Phoe.	.50
☐ 158 Nikolai Antropov, Toro.	.35
☐ 161 Pavel Bure, Flor.	1.50
☐ 163 Roberto Luongo (G), NYIs.	1.50
☐ 165 Brendan Shanahan, Detr.	2.00
☐ 167 Cory Stillman, Calg.	.35
☐ 171 Viktor Kozlov, Flor.	.50
☐ 179 Jani Hurme (G), Otta.	2.00
☐ 180 Maxim Balmochnykh, Anah.	.35
☐ 181 Adam Graves, NYRa.	.50
☐ 184 Zigmund Palffy, LosA.	1.00
☐ 189 Jocelyn Thibault (G), Chic.	.50
☐ 192 Shane Doan, Phoe.	.35
☐ 195 Daniel Alfredsson, Otta.	1.00
☐ 196 Brenden Morrow, Dall.	.50
☐ 197 Martin Rucinsky, Mont.	.35
☐ 200 Rod Brind'Amour, Caro.	.50
☐ 202 Derian Hatcher, Dall.	.50
☐ 205 Sergei Berezin, Toro.	.35
☐ 209 Vincent Lecavalier, Tamp.	2.00
☐ 212 Chris Chelios, Detr.	1.00
☐ 214 Robyn Regehr, Calg.	.35
☐ 217 Nicklas Lidström, Detr.	1.00
☐ 220 Chris Pronger, SLou.	1.00
☐ 223 Jeff Farkas, Toro.	.50
☐ 227 Owen Nolan, SanJ.	1.00
☐ 229 Patrick Marleau, SanJ.	.50
☐ 243 Vitaly Vishnevski, Anah.	.35
☐ 252 S. Vyshedkevich, Atla.	1.00
☐ 257 Al MacInnis, SLou.	.50
☐ 262 Jason Arnott, NJer.	.50
☐ 263 David Legwand, Nash.	.50
☐ 267 Mark Recchi, Phil.	.50
☐ 270 Vincent Damphousse, SanJ.	1.00
☐ 272 Teemu Selänne, Anah.	1.50
☐ 284 Raymond Bourque, Colo.	2.00
☐ 287 José Théodore (G), Mont.	2.00
☐ 292 Yanic Perreault, Toro.	.50
☐ 295 Brad Ference, Flor.	.35
☐ 296 Mats Sundin, Toro.	2.00
☐ 299 Todd Bertuzzi, Vanc.	2.00

2000 - 01 CARDSET

NHL stars and prospects sometimes sell at a premium (usually $1-2).

Complete Set (360 cards):	60.00
Common Player:	**.25**
Description	**Cardset**
☐ 1 Checklist	.25
☐ 2 Checklist	.25
☐ 3 Checklist	.25
☐ 4 Mika Oksa, Blues Kiekko-Espoo	.25
☐ 5 Peter Ahola, Blues Kiekko-Espoo	.50
☐ 6 Jermu Pisto, Blues Kiekko-Espoo	.25
☐ 7 Jiri Vykoukal, Blues Kiekko-Espoo	.25
☐ 8 Niclas Hedberg, Blues Kiekko-Espoo	.25
☐ 9 Teemu Siren, Blues Kiekko-Espoo	.25
☐ 10 Joonas Jääskeläinen, Blues Kiekko-Espoo	.25
☐ 11 Timo Hirvonen, Blues Kiekko-Espoo	.25
☐ 12 Mikko Kaukokari, Blues Kiekko-Espoo	.25
☐ 13 Ari Ahonen, HIFK Helsinki	3.00
☐ 14 Marek Zidlicky, HIFK Helsinki	.25
☐ 15 Jarno Kultanen, HIFK Helsinki	.50
☐ 16 Toni Sihvonen, HIFK Helsinki	.25
☐ 17 Aki Uusikartano, HIFK Helsinki	.25
☐ 18 Pasi Nielikäinen, HIFK Helsinki	.25
☐ 19 Hannes Hyvönen, HIFK Helsinki	.25
☐ 20 Mika Nieminen, HIFK Helsinki	.25
☐ 21 Mika Kortelainen, HIFK Helsinki	.25
☐ 22 Kimmo Kapanen (G), HPK Hämeenlinna	.25
☐ 23 Jonas Andersson-Junkka, HPK Hämeenlinna	.25
☐ 24 Kimmo Peltonen, HPK Hämeenlinna	.25
☐ 25 Sebastian Sulku, HPK Hämeenlinna	.25
☐ 26 Teemu Aalto, HPK Hämeenlinna	.25
☐ 27 Antti Miettinen, HPK Hämeenlinna	.25
☐ 28 Riku Hahl, HPK Hämeenlinna	2.00
☐ 29 Marko Palo, HPK Hämeenlinna	.25
☐ 30 Juha Pitkämäki, Ilves Tampere	.25
☐ 31 Arto Tukio, Ilves Tampere	.25
☐ 32 Tapio Sammalkangas, Ilves Tampere	.25
☐ 33 Tomi Pettinen, Ilves Tampere	.25
☐ 34 Jarkko Nikander, Ilves Tampere	.25
☐ 35 Raimo Helminen, Ilves Tampere	.50
☐ 36 Juha Hautamaa, Ilves Tampere	.25
☐ 37 Sami Karjalainen, Ilves Tampere	.25
☐ 38 Pasi Nurminen, Jokerit Helsinki	3.00
☐ 39 Ossi Väänänen, Jokerit Helsinki	.50
☐ 40 Marko Kauppinen, Jokerit Helsinki	.25
☐ 41 Tom Koivisto, Jokerit Helsinki	.25
☐ 42 Rami Alanko, Jokerit Helsinki	.25
☐ 43 Petri Varis, Jokerit Helsinki	.25
☐ 44 Jan Benda, Jokerit Helsinki	.25
☐ 45 Jani Rita, Jokerit Helsinki	1.50
☐ 46 Markus Kankaanperä, JyP HT Jyväskylä	.25
☐ 47 Jarkko Glad, JyP HT Jyväskylä	.25
☐ 48 Jyrki Välivaara, JyP HT Jyväskylä	.25
☐ 49 Tuomas Pihlman, JyP HT Jyväskylä	.25
☐ 50 Jussi Pesonen, JyP HT Jyväskylä	.25
☐ 51 Petr Ton, JyP HT Jyväskylä	.25
☐ 52 Markus Korhonen, Oulu Kärpät	.25
☐ 53 Harri Aho, Oulu Kärpät	.25
☐ 54 Karri Kivi, Oulu Kärpät	.25
☐ 55 Mikko Haapakoski, Oulu Kärpät	.25
☐ 56 Jaako Niskavaara, Oulu Kärpät	.25
☐ 57 Niklas Hagman, Oulu Kärpät	.50
☐ 58 Sakari Palsola, Oulu Kärpät	.25
☐ 59 Jari Laukkanen, Oulu Kärpät	.25
☐ 60 Petri Isotalus, Oulu Kärpät	.25
☐ 61 Jari Viuhkola, Oulu Kärpät	.25
☐ 62 Allan Measures, Rauman Lukko	.25
☐ 63 Mika Laaksonen, Rauman Lukko	.25
☐ 64 Marko Toivonen, Rauman Lukko	.25
☐ 65 Matti Kaipainen, Rauman Lukko	.25
☐ 66 Petri Lätti, Rauman Lukko	.25
☐ 67 Sami Torkki, Rauman Lukko	.25
☐ 68 Jokke Heinänen, Rauman Lukko	.25
☐ 69 Sami Lehtinen, Pelicans Lahti	.25
☐ 70 Veli-Pekka Laitinen, Pelicans Lahti	.25
☐ 71 Kaj Lindström, Pelicans Lahti	.25
☐ 72 Mika Niskanen, Pelicans Lahti	.25
☐ 73 Jani Keinänen, Pelicans Lahti	.25
☐ 74 Tommi Turunen, Pelicans Lahti	.25
☐ 75 Mikko Juutilainen, Pelicans Lahti	.25
☐ 76 Veli-Pekka Nutikka, Pelicans Lahti	.25
☐ 77 Mikko Jokela, SaiPa Lappeenranta	.25
☐ 78 Martin Richter, SaiPa Lappeenranta	.25
☐ 79 Pekka Tirkkonen, SaiPa Lappeenranta	.25
☐ 80 Vladimir Machulda, SaiPa Lappeenranta	.25
☐ 81 Ville Hämäläinen, SaiPa Lappeenranta	.25
☐ 82 Mika Skyttä, SaiPa Lappeenranta	.25
☐ 83 Ville Immonen, SaiPa Lappeenranta	.25
☐ 84 Sami Kaartinen, SaiPa Lappeenranta	.25
☐ 85 Tuukka Mäntylä, Tappara Tampere	.25
☐ 86 Miska Kangasniemi, Tappara Tampere	.25
☐ 87 Janne Grönvall, Tappara Tampere	.25
☐ 88 Jussi Tarvainen, Tappara Tampere	.25
☐ 89 Janne Ojanen, Tappara Tampere	.50
☐ 90 Jaakko Uhlbäck, Tappara Tampere	.25
☐ 91 Johannes Alanen, Tappara Tampere	.25
☐ 92 Jani Hassinen, Tappara Tampere	.25
☐ 93 Fredrik Norrena, TPS Turku	.25
☐ 94 Jouni Loponen, TPS Turku	.25
☐ 95 Tommi Rajamäki, TPS Turku	.25
☐ 96 Kimmo Eronen, TPS Turku	.25
☐ 97 Kimmo Rintanen, TPS Turku	.25
☐ 98 Tony Virta, TPS Turku	.50
☐ 99 Jani Kiviharju, TPS Turku	.25
☐ 100 Teemu Elomo, TPS Turku	.25

□ 101 Mikko Rautee, TPS Turku .25
□ 102 Jim Hrivnak, Porin Ässät .50
□ 103 Pasi Peltonen, Porin Ässät .25
□ 104 Timo Willman, Porin Ässät .25
□ 105 Pauli Levokari, Porin Ässät .25
□ 106 Tuomo Kyhä, Porin Ässät .25
□ 107 Janne Laitila, Porin Ässät .25
□ 108 Janne Mäkelä, Porin Ässät .25
□ 109 Samu Wesslin, Porin Ässät .25
□ 110 Hannu Tala, Porin Ässät .25
□ 111 Vesa Toskala .25
□ 112 Aki Berg .50
□ 113 Antti-Jussi Niemi .25
□ 114 Janne Niinimaa 1.00
□ 115 Ville Peltonen .25
□ 116 Olli Jokinen 1.50
□ 117 Teemu Selänne 4.00
□ 118 Marko Tuomainen .25
□ 119 Juha Lind .25
□ 120 Niko Kapanen 1.00
□ 121 Checklist .25
□ 122 Checklist .25
□ 123 Checklist .25
□ 124 Arto Laatikainen, Blues Kiekko-Espoo .25
□ 125 Tero Määttä, Blues Kiekko-Espoo .25
□ 126 Juha Gustafsson, Blues Kiekko-Espoo .25
□ 127 Toni Koivunen, Blues Kiekko-Espoo .25
□ 128 Teemu Virkkunen, Blues Kiekko-Espoo .25
□ 129 Valeri Krykov, Blues Kiekko-Espoo .25
□ 130 Frank Banham, Blues Kiekko-Espoo .50
□ 131 Semir Ben-Amor, Blues Kiekko-Espoo .25
□ 132 Jiri Burger, Blues Kiekko-Espoo .25
□ 133 Aki Tuominen, HIFK Helsinki .25
□ 134 Ray Giroux, HIFK Helsinki .50
□ 135 Mikko Kurvinen, HIFK Helsinki .25
□ 136 Patrik Hucko, HIFK Helsinki .25
□ 137 Jari Kauppila, HIFK Helsinki .25
□ 138 Tony Salmelainen, HIFK Helsinki .25
□ 139 Kimmo Kuhta, HIFK Helsinki .25
□ 140 Jaroslav Bednar, HIFK Helsinki .50
□ 141 Ari Vallin, HPK Hämeenlinna .25
□ 142 Sami Nuutinen, HPK Hämeenlinna .25
□ 143 Jani Virtanen, HPK Hämeenlinna .25
□ 144 Timo Ahmaoja, HPK Hämeenlinna .25
□ 145 Tomi Suoniemi, HPK Hämeenlinna .25
□ 146 Jari Kesti, HPK Hämeenlinna .25
□ 147 Tommi Santala, HPK Hämeenlinna .25
□ 148 Pavel Rosa, HPK Hämeenlinna .50
□ 149 Eero Somervuori, HPK Hämeenlinna .25
□ 150 Mika Pietilä, Ilves Tampere .25
□ 151 Ivan Majesky, Ilves Tampere .25
□ 152 Antti Bruun, Ilves Tampere .25
□ 153 Matt Smith, Ilves Tampere .25
□ 154 Jari-Pekka Pajula, Ilves Tampere .25
□ 155 Kimmo Vähä-Ruohola, Ilves Tampere .25
□ 156 Toni Dahlman, Ilves Tampere .50
□ 157 Antti Hilden, Ilves Tampere .25
□ 158 Timo Koskela, Ilves Tampere .25
□ 159 Vesa Viitakoski, Ilves Tampere .25
□ 160 Kari Haakana, Jokerit Helsinki .25
□ 161 Pasi Saarinen, Jokerit Helsinki .25
□ 162 Santeri Heiskanen, Jokerit Helsinki .25
□ 163 Antti Törmänen, Jokerit Helsinki .25
□ 164 Juha Virtanen, Jokerit Helsinki .25
□ 165 Tuomo Ruutu, Jokerit Helsinki 6.00
□ 166 Niko Mikkola, Jokerit Helsinki .25
□ 167 Aigars Cipruss, Jokerit Helsinki .25
□ 168 Mika Lehto, JyP HT Jyväskylä .25
□ 169 Chris MacKenzie, JyP HT Jyväskylä .25
□ 170 Pekka Poikolainen, JyP HT Jyväskylä .25
□ 171 Riku Varjamo, JyP HT Jyväskylä .25
□ 172 Markku Paukkunen, JyP HT Jyväskylä .25
□ 173 Mika Paananen, JyP HT Jyväskylä .25
□ 174 Juha-Pekka Hytönen, JyP HT Jyväskylä .25
□ 175 Janne Hauhtonen, JyP HT Jyväskylä .25
□ 176 Jouni Kulonen, JyP HT Jyväskylä .25
□ 177 Antti Virtanen, JyP HT Jyväskylä .25
□ 178 Kristian Taubert, Oulu Kärpät .25
□ 179 Mikko Lehtonen, Oulu Kärpät .25
□ 180 Lasse Kukkonen, Oulu Kärpät .25
□ 181 Kimmo Koskenkorva, Oulu Kärpät .25
□ 182 Tuomo Harjula, Oulu Kärpät .25
□ 183 Juha Joenväärä, Oulu Kärpät .25
□ 184 Brett Lievers, Oulu Kärpät .25
□ 185 Miikka Rousu, Oulu Kärpät .25
□ 186 Bruce Racine, Rauman Lukko .25
□ 187 Ismo Kuoppala, Rauman Lukko .25
□ 188 Topi Lehtonen, Rauman Lukko .25
□ 189 Toni Koivisto, Rauman Lukko .25
□ 190 Jonni Vauhkonen, Rauman Lukko .25
□ 191 Jimmy Provencher, Rauman Lukko .25
□ 192 Pasi Saarela, Rauman Lukko .25
□ 193 Pasi Kuivalainen, Pelicans Lahti .25
□ 194 Antti-Jussi Reimari, Pelicans Lahti .25
□ 195 Jan Latvala, Pelicans Lahti .25
□ 196 Roman Vopat, Pelicans Lahti .25
□ 197 Janne Sinkkonen, Pelicans Lahti .25
□ 198 Ales Kratoska, Pelicans Lahti .25
□ 199 Mikko Peltola, Pelicans Lahti .25
□ 200 Niklas Bäckström, SaiPa Lappeenranta .25
□ 201 Oleg Romanov, SaiPa Lappeenranta .25
□ 202 Riku Kallioniemi, SaiPa Lappeenranta .25
□ 203 Petri Kokko, SaiPa Lappeenranta .25
□ 204 Juha Pursiainen, SaiPa Lappeenranta .25
□ 205 Joni Yli-Torkko, SaiPa Lappeenranta .25
□ 206 Pasi Tuominen, SaiPa Lappeenranta .25
□ 207 Ludek Krayzel, SaiPa Lappeenranta .25
□ 208 Mika Kauppinen, SaiPa Lappeenranta .25
□ 209 Jussi Markkanen, Tappara Tampere .25
□ 210 Alain Côté, Tappara Tampere .25
□ 211 Pekka Saravo, Tappara Tampere .25
□ 212 Niki Siren, Tappara Tampere .25
□ 213 Timo Vertala, Tappara Tampere .25
□ 214 Tero Lehterä, Tappara Tampere .25
□ 215 Arto Kuki, Tappara Tampere .25
□ 216 Henrik Tallinder, TPS Turku .25
□ 217 Martti Järventie, TPS Turku .50
□ 218 Marco Tuokko, TPS Turku .25
□ 219 Joni Lius, TPS Turku .25
□ 220 Jarkko Varvio, TPS Turku .50
□ 221 Mikael Holmqvist, TPS Turku .25
□ 222 Mikko Koivu, TPS Turku 6.00
□ 223 Ari Vapola, Porin Ässät .25
□ 224 Curtis Sheptak, Porin Ässät .25
□ 225 Marcus Kristoffersson, Porin Ässät .25
□ 226 Jari Korpisalo, Porin Ässät .25
□ 227 Gabriel Karlsson, Porin Ässät .25
□ 228 Sami Salonen, Porin Ässät .25
□ 229 Jarkko Väänänen, Porin Ässät .25
□ 230 Niklas Hede, Porin Ässät .25
□ 231 Ari Sulander .25
□ 232 Jere Karalahti .50
□ 233 Toni Lydman .50
□ 234 Petteri Nummelin .50
□ 235 Raimo Helminen .50
□ 236 Tomi Kallio .50
□ 237 Toni Sihvonen .25
□ 238 Jukka Hentunen .25
□ 239 Tony Virta .50
□ 240 Esa Tikkanen .50
□ 241 Checklist .25
□ 242 Checklist .25
□ 243 Checklist .25
□ 244 Tom Draper, Blues Kiekko-Espoo .50
□ 245 Timo Willman, Blues Kiekko-Espoo .25
□ 246 Asko Rantanen, Blues Kiekko-Espoo .25
□ 247 Jukka Tiilikainen, Blues Kiekko-Espoo .25
□ 248 Mikael Jämsänen, Blues Kiekko-Espoo .25
□ 249 Kari Kalto, Blues Kiekko-Espoo .25
□ 250 Esa Pirnes, Blues Kiekko-Espoo .25
□ 251 Johan Davidsson, Blues Kiekko-Espoo .50
□ 252 Shayne Toporowski, Blues Kiekko-Espoo .50
□ 253 Sakari Lindfors, HIFK Helsinki .25
□ 254 Tomi Nyman, HIFK Helsinki .25
□ 255 Kari Rajala, HIFK Helsinki .25
□ 256 Martin Stepanek, HIFK Helsinki .25
□ 257 Veli-Pekka Kautonen, HIFK Helsinki .25
□ 258 Toni Mäkiaho, HIFK Helsinki .25
□ 259 Lasse Pirjetä, HIFK Helsinki .25
□ 260 Markku Hurme, HIFK Helsinki .25
□ 261 Erkki Rajamäki, HIFK Helsinki .25
□ 262 Jan Caloun, HIFK Helsinki .50
□ 263 Joonas Vihko, HIFK Helsinki .25
□ 264 Jan Lundell, HPK Hämeenlinna .25
□ 265 Dan Ratushny, HPK Hämeenlinna .50
□ 266 Darcy Werenka, HPK Hämeenlinna .50
□ 267 Timo Pärssinen, HPK Hämeenlinna .25
□ 268 Tomas Vlasak, HPK Hämeenlinna .25
□ 269 Jyrki Louhi, HPK Hämeenlinna .25
□ 270 Pasi Määttänen, HPK Hämeenlinna .25
□ 271 Petr Kuchyna, Ilves Tampere .25
□ 272 Jani Nikko, Ilves Tampere .25
□ 273 Tommi Miettinen, Ilves Tampere .25
□ 274 Jesse Welling, Ilves Tampere .25
□ 275 Oliver Setzinger, Ilves Tampere .25
□ 276 Jarno Peltonen, Ilves Tampere .25
□ 277 Tony Salmelainen, Ilves Tampere .25
□ 278 Kari Lehtonen, Jokerit Helsinki .25
□ 279 Pauli Levokari, Jokerit Helsinki .25
□ 280 Thomas Johansson, Jokerit Helsinki .25
□ 281 Lee Sorochan, Jokerit Helsinki .25
□ 282 Tomek Valtonen, Jokerit Helsinki .25
□ 283 Jukka Hentunen, Jokerit Helsinki .25
□ 284 Mikko Ruutu, Jokerit Helsinki .25
□ 285 Timo Saarikoski, Jokerit Helsinki .25
□ 286 Teemu Sainomaa, Jokerit Helsinki .25
□ 287 Ari-Pekka Siekkinen, JyP HT Jyväskylä .25
□ 288 Tomi Hirvonen, JyP HT Jyväskylä .25
□ 289 Jarno Tiilikainen, JyP HT Jyväskylä .25
□ 290 Radoslav Kropac, JyP HT Jyväskylä .25
□ 291 Zdenek Sedlak, JyP HT Jyväskylä .25
□ 292 Tuomo Jääskeläinen, JyP HT Jyväskylä .25
□ 293 Antti Kangas, Oulu Kärpät .25
□ 294 Steve Shieffers, Oulu Kärpät .25
□ 295 Pekka Kangasalusta, Oulu Kärpät .25
□ 296 Vyacheslav Fandul, Oulu Kärpät .25
□ 297 Kimmo Salminen, Oulu Kärpät .25
□ 298 Sami Alalauri, Oulu Kärpät .25
□ 299 Andrei Potaichuk, Oulu Kärpät .25
□ 300 Petri Vehanen, Rauman Lukko .25
□ 301 Erik Hämäläinen, Rauman Lukko .25
□ 302 Tuomas Grönman, Rauman Lukko .50
□ 303 Kimmo Lotvonen, Rauman Lukko .25
□ 304 Janne Siivonen, Rauman Lukko .25
□ 305 Marko Kivenmäki, Rauman Lukko .25
□ 306 Zdenek Nedved, Rauman Lukko .25
□ 307 Petri Pakaslahti, Rauman Lukko .25
□ 308 Harri Sillgren, Rauman Lukko .25
□ 309 Samu Isosalo, Rauman Lukko .25
□ 310 Henri Laurila, Pelicans Lahti .25
□ 311 Jussi Salminen, Pelicans Lahti .25
□ 312 Kalle Koskinen, Pelicans Lahti .25
□ 313 Jarkko Ollikainen, Pelicans Lahti .25
□ 314 Toni Saarinen, Pelicans Lahti .25
□ 315 Teemu Riihijärvi, Pelicans Lahti .25
□ 316 Lasse Jämsen, Pelicans Lahti .25
□ 317 Jouko Myrrä, Pelicans Lahti .25
□ 318 Pasi Häkkinen, SaiPa Lappeenranta .25
□ 319 Juha Kuokkanen, SaiPa Lappeenranta .25
□ 320 Roland Carlsson, SaiPa Lappeenranta .25
□ 321 Harri Tikkanen, SaiPa Lappeenranta .25
□ 322 Yuri Kuznetsov, SaiPa Lappeenranta .25
□ 323 Ville Kiiskinen, SaiPa Lappeenranta .25
□ 324 Olli Sipiläinen, SaiPa Lappeenranta .25
□ 325 Tuomas Reijonen, SaiPa Lappeenranta .25
□ 326 Joel Salonen, SaiPa Lappeenranta .25
□ 327 Sami Ahlberg, SaiPa Lappeenranta .25
□ 328 Sasu Hovi, Tappara Tampere .25
□ 329 Janne Vuorela, Tappara Tampere .25
□ 330 Mikko Luoma, Tappara Tampere .25
□ 331 Miro Laitinen, Tappara Tampere .25
□ 332 Sami Venäläinen, Tappara Tampere .25
□ 333 Marko Ojanen, Tappara Tampere .25
□ 334 Marko Mäkinen, Tappara Tampere .25
□ 335 Alexander Barkov, Tappara Tampere .25
□ 336 Antero Niittymäki, TPS Turku .25
□ 337 Markus Seikola, TPS Turku .25
□ 338 Ilkka Mikkola, TPS Turku .25
□ 339 Mika Lehtinen, TPS Turku .25
□ 340 Niko Kapanen, TPS Turku 1.00
□ 341 Ville Vahalahti, TPS Turku .25
□ 342 Kalle Sahlstedt, TPS Turku .25
□ 343 Kristian Antila, Porin Ässät .25
□ 344 Pasi Puistola, Porin Ässät .25
□ 345 Vesa Salo, Porin Ässät .25
□ 346 Veli-Pekka Hård, Porin Ässät .25
□ 347 Eric Perrin, Porin Ässät .25
□ 348 Tomas Kucharcík, Porin Ässät .25
□ 349 Markku Tähtinen, Porin Ässät .25
□ 350 Mikko Konttila, Porin Ässät .25
□ 351 Pasi Nurminen 3.00
□ 352 Kimmo Timonen .25
□ 353 Jyrki Lumme 1.00
□ 354 Janne Laukkanen .50
□ 355 Kimmo Rintanen .25
□ 356 Saku Koivu 4.00
□ 357 Jere Lehtinen 1.50
□ 358 Sami Kapanen 1.50
□ 359 Antti Aalto .50
□ 360 Mika Alatalo .50

Insert (#/1000) **Special**
□ Ari Ahonen (G) (Masked Marvel) 4.50
□ Saku Koivu (Millenium Thunder) 12.00
□ Pasi Nurminen (Masked Marvel) 4.50

MASKIT

Series Two Insert Set (9 cards):
Insert (1:5 packs) **Mask**
□ 1 Mika Pietilä, Ilves 1.50
□ 2 Bruce Racine, Lukko 1.50
□ 3 Sami Lehtinen, Pelicans 1.50
□ 4 Niklas Bäckström, SaiPa 1.50
□ 5 Antero Niittymäki, TPS 1.50
□ 6 Markus Korhonen, Kärpät 1.50
□ 7 Jussi Markkanen, Tappara 2.00
□ 8 Tom Draper, Blues 2.00
□ 9 Kristian Antila, Ässät 1.50

MASTER BLASTERS

Series One Insert Set (9 cards): 10.00
Insert (1:5 packs) **MB**
□ 1 Kai Nurminen, TPS 1.50
□ 2 Jan Caloun, HIFK 1.50
□ 3 Petr Tenkrat, HPK/Ilves 2.00
□ 4 Jaroslav Bednar, JYP 2.00
□ 5 Dale McTavish, Blues 1.50
□ 6 Kalle Sahlstedt, TPS 1.50
□ 7 Zdenek Nedved, Lukko 1.50
□ 8 Tomi Kallio, TPS 2.00
□ 9 Timo Pärssinen, HPK 1.50

NEXT GENERATION

Series Three Insert Set (9 cards): **25.00**
Insert (1:5 packs) **NG**
□ 1 Mikko Koivu, TPS Turku 5.00
□ 2 Tuukka Mäntylä, Tappara 2.00
□ 3 Tuomo Ruutu, Jokerit 5.00
□ 4 Jani Rita, Jokerit 7.00
□ 5 Ari Ahonen (G), HIFK 5.00
□ 6 Arto Tukio, Ilves 2.00
□ 7 Antti Miettinen, HPK 2.00
□ 8 Markus Kankaanperä, JYP 2.00
□ 9 Antero Niittymäki, TPS 2.00

2000 - 01 CROWN ROYALE

This series was issued in March 2001. Base cards 1-108 have a Red parallel, a Premiere Date parallel (#/80), an Ice Blue parallel (#/75) and a Limited Series parallel (#/25). Premiere Date and Ice Blue parallels are priced similarly below.

		LS25	PD80	Red	CR
	Shell Set (108 cards):	-	-	-	75.00
	Parallel Set (108 cards):	3,900	1,800	175.00	-
	Complete Set (144 cards):	-	-	-	600.00
	Common Player:	12.00	6.00	1.00	.75
	Description	**LS25**	**PD80**	**Red**	**CR**
□□□□□□	1 Guy Hebert (G)	15.00	6.00	1.00	.75
□□□□□□	2 Paul Kariya	100.00	50.00	7.00	3.50
□□□□□□	3 Teemu Selänne	60.00	30.00	4.00	2.00
□□□□□□	4 Donald Audette	30.00	15.00	2.00	1.00
□□□□□□	5 Andrew Brunette	12.00	6.00	1.00	.75
□□□□□□	6 Damian Rhodes (G)	15.00	6.00	1.00	.75
□□□□□□	7 Patrik Stefan	20.00	10.00	1.50	.75
□□□□□□	8 Jason Allison	45.00	20.00	3.00	1.50
□□□□□□	9 Byron Dafoe (G)	30.00	15.00	2.00	1.00
□□□□□□	10 Bill Guerin	30.00	15.00	2.00	1.00
□□□□□□	11 Sergei Samsonov	45.00	20.00	3.00	1.50
□□□□□□	12 Joe Thornton	90.00	45.00	6.00	3.00
□□□□□□	13 Doug Gilmour	45.00	20.00	3.00	1.50
□□□□□□	14 Chris Gratton	15.00	6.00	1.00	.75
□□□□□□	15 Dominik Hasek (G)	75.00	35.00	5.00	2.50
□□□□□□	16 Michael Peca	30.00	15.00	2.00	1.00
□□□□□□	17 Valeri Bure	20.00	10.00	1.50	.75
□□□□□□	18 Jarome Iginla	60.00	30.00	4.00	2.00
□□□□□□	19 Marc Savard	15.00	6.00	1.00	.75
□□□□□□	20 Ron Francis	45.00	20.00	3.00	1.50
□□□□□□	21 Arturs Irbe (G)	30.00	15.00	2.00	1.00
□□□□□□	22 Sami Kapanen	20.00	10.00	1.50	.75
□□□□□□	23 Tony Amonte	45.00	20.00	3.00	1.50
□□□□□□	24 J. Thibault (G)	30.00	15.00	2.00	1.00
□□□□□□	25 Alexei Zhamnov	20.00	10.00	1.50	.75
□□□□□□	26 Raymond Bourque	90.00	45.00	6.00	3.00
□□□□□□	27 Chris Drury	45.00	20.00	3.00	1.50
□□□□□□	28 Peter Forsberg	100.00	50.00	7.00	3.50
□□□□□□	29 Milan Hejduk	60.00	30.00	4.00	2.00
□□□□□□	30 Patrick Roy (G)	225.00	110.00	15.00	7.50
□□□□□□	31 Joe Sakic	120.00	60.00	8.00	4.00
□□□□□□	32 Geoff Sanderson	15.00	6.00	1.00	.75
□□□□□□	33 Ron Tugnutt (G)	30.00	15.00	2.00	1.00
□□□□□□	34 Ed Belfour (G)	75.00	35.00	5.00	2.50
□□□□□□	35 Brett Hull	75.00	35.00	5.00	2.50
□□□□□□	36 Mike Modano	75.00	35.00	5.00	2.50
□□□□□□	37 Joe Nieuwendyk	30.00	15.00	2.00	1.00
□□□□□□	38 Sergei Fedorov	75.00	35.00	5.00	2.50
□□□□□□	39 Chris Osgood (G)	45.00	20.00	3.00	1.50
□□□□□□	40 Brendan Shanahan	75.00	35.00	5.00	2.50
□□□□□□	41 Steve Yzerman	180.00	90.00	12.00	6.00
□□□□□□	42 Tommy Salo (G)	30.00	15.00	2.00	1.00
□□□□□□	43 Ryan Smyth	35.00	15.00	2.00	1.00
□□□□□□	44 Doug Weight	45.00	20.00	3.00	1.50
□□□□□□	45 Pavel Bure	60.00	30.00	4.00	2.00
□□□□□□	46 Rob Niedermayer	15.00	6.00	1.00	.75
□□□□□□	47 Ray Whitney	15.00	6.00	1.00	.75
□□□□□□	48 Stéphane Fiset (G)	20.00	10.00	1.50	.75
□□□□□□	49 Zigmund Palffy	45.00	20.00	3.00	1.50
□□□□□□	50 Luc Robitaille	60.00	30.00	4.00	2.00
□□□□□□	51 Jamie Storr (G)	15.00	6.00	1.00	.75

□□□□□	52 Jim Dowd	12.00	6.00	1.00	.75
□□□□□	53 J. McLennan (G)	12.00	6.00	1.00	.75
□□□□□	54 Scott Pellerin	12.00	6.00	1.00	.75
□□□□□	55 Saku Koivu	90.00	45.00	4.00	2.00
□□□□□	56 Martin Rucinsky	15.00	6.00	1.00	.75
□□□□□	57 Brian Savage	20.00	10.00	1.50	.75
□□□□□	58 José Théodore (G)	90.00	45.00	6.00	3.00
□□□□□	59 Mike Dunham (G)	30.00	15.00	2.00	1.00
□□□□□	60 David Legwand	30.00	15.00	2.00	1.00
□□□□□	61 Vitali Yachmenev	12.00	6.00	1.00	.75
□□□□□	62 M. Brodeur (G)	120.00	60.00	8.00	4.00
□□□□□	63 Patrik Elias	60.00	30.00	4.00	2.00
□□□□□	64 Scott Gomez	30.00	15.00	2.00	1.00
□□□□□	65 Alexander Mogilny	35.00	15.00	2.00	1.00
□□□□□	66 Tim Connolly	30.00	15.00	2.00	1.00
□□□□□	67 Brad Isbister	15.00	6.00	1.00	.75
□□□□□	68 Vanbiesbrouck (G)	35.00	15.00	2.00	1.00
□□□□□	69 Theoren Fleury	45.00	20.00	3.00	1.50
□□□□□	70 Brian Leetch	45.00	20.00	3.00	1.50
□□□□□	71 Mark Messier	75.00	35.00	5.00	2.50
□□□□□	72 Mike Richter (G)	35.00	15.00	2.00	1.00
□□□□□	73 Daniel Alfredsson	90.00	45.00	3.00	1.50
□□□□□	74 Radek Bonk	20.00	10.00	1.50	.75
□□□□□	75 Marian Hossa	75.00	35.00	5.00	2.50
□□□□□	76 Patrick Lalime (G)	45.00	20.00	3.00	1.50
□□□□□	77 Alexei Yashin	45.00	20.00	3.00	1.50
□□□□□	78 Brian Boucher (G)	20.00	10.00	1.50	.75
□□□□□	79 Simon Gagné	60.00	30.00	4.00	2.00
□□□□□	80 John LeClair	60.00	30.00	4.00	2.00
□□□□□	81 Eric Lindros	75.00	35.00	5.00	2.50
□□□□□	82 Sean Burke (G)	45.00	20.00	3.00	1.50
□□□□□	83 Shane Doan	15.00	6.00	1.00	.75
□□□□□	84 Jeremy Roenick	60.00	30.00	4.00	2.00
□□□□□	85 Keith Tkachuk	45.00	20.00	3.00	1.50
□□□□□	86 Jaromir Jagr	75.00	35.00	5.00	2.50
□□□□□	87 Mario Lemieux	225.00	110.00	15.00	7.50
□□□□□	88 Martin Straka	20.00	10.00	1.50	.75
□□□□□	89 Chris Pronger	45.00	20.00	3.00	1.50
□□□□□	90 Roman Turek (G)	35.00	15.00	2.00	1.00
□□□□□	91 Pierre Turgeon	30.00	15.00	2.00	1.00
□□□□□	92 Scott A. Young	20.00	10.00	1.50	.75
□□□□□	93 Patrick Marleau	35.00	15.00	2.00	1.00
□□□□□	94 Owen Nolan	45.00	20.00	3.00	1.50
□□□□□	95 Steve Shields (G)	15.00	6.00	1.00	.75
□□□□□	96 Vincent Lecavalier	75.00	35.00	5.00	2.50
□□□□□	97 Fredrik Modin	15.00	6.00	1.00	.75
□□□□□	98 Kevin Weekes (G)	15.00	6.00	1.00	.75
□□□□□	99 Sergei Berezin	35.00	15.00	2.00	.75
□□□□□	100 Curtis Joseph (G)	75.00	35.00	5.00	2.50
□□□□□	101 Gary Roberts	30.00	15.00	2.00	1.00
□□□□□	102 Mats Sundin	75.00	35.00	5.00	2.50
□□□□□	103 Andrew Cassels	15.00	6.00	1.00	.75
□□□□□	104 Markus Näslund	75.00	35.00	5.00	2.50
□□□□□	105 Félix Potvin (G)	90.00	45.00	3.00	1.50
□□□□□	106 Peter Bondra	45.00	20.00	3.00	1.50
□□□□□	107 Olaf Kölzig (G)	45.00	20.00	3.00	1.50
□□□□□	108 Adam Oates	30.00	15.00	2.00	1.00

ROOKIES

	Insert (#/400)	**R400**
□	109 Samuel Påhlsson, Bost.	6.00
□	110 Tomi Kallio, Atla.	6.00
□	**111 A. Raycroft (G), Bost. RC**	**20.00**
□	**112 Eric Boulton, Buff. RC**	**15.00**
□	113 Dimitri Kalinin, Buff.	6.00
□	114 Oleg Saprykin, Calg.	6.00
□	**115 Josef Vasicek, Caro. RC**	**20.00**
□	116 Shane Willis, Caro.	6.00
□	117 Steve McCarthy, Chic.	6.00
□	**118 D. Aebischer (G), Colo. RC**	**30.00**
□	**119 Serge Aubin, Colu. RC**	**15.00**
□	120 Marc Denis (G), Colu.	12.00
□	121 David Vyborny, Colu.	6.00
□	**122 Marty Turco (G), Dall. RC**	**55.00**
□	123 Roberto Luongo (G), Flor.	20.00
□	124 Ivan Novoseltsev, Flor.	6.00
□	125 Denis Shvidki, Flor.	6.00
□	**126 S. Reinprecht, LosA. RC**	**30.00**
□	**127 M. Gaborik, MinW. RC**	**90.00**
□	128 Filip Kuba, MinW.	6.00
□	129 Andrei Markov, Mont.	6.00
□	**130 Scott Hartnell, Nash. RC**	**20.00**
□	**131 Colin White, NJer. RC**	**15.00**
□	**132 R. DiPietro (G), NYIs. RC**	**45.00**
□	133 Taylor Pyatt, NYIs.	6.00
□	**134 Martin Havlat, Otta. RC**	**55.00**
□	**135 Jani Hurme (G), Otta. RC**	**20.00**
□	**136 Justin Williams, Phil. RC**	**30.00**
□	137 Robert Esche (G), Phoe.	6.00
□	138 Milan Kraft, Pitt.	8.00
□	139 Brent Johnson (G), SLou.	10.00
□	140 Evgeni Nabokov (G), SanJ.	15.00
□	141 Sheldon Keefe, Tamp.	6.00
□	142 Brad Richards, Tamp.	12.00
□	143 Daniel Sedin, Vanc.	10.00
□	144 Henrik Sedin, Vanc.	10.00

21ST CENTURY ROOKIES

	Insert Set (25 cards):	**50.00**
	Insert (1:1)	**21CR**
□	1 Tomi Kallio, Atla.	.50
□	2 Andrew Raycroft (G), Bost.	3.00
□	3 Eric Boulton, Buff.	2.00
□	4 Oleg Saprykin, Calg.	1.00
□	5 Shane Willis, Caro.	1.00
□	6 Steve McCarthy, Chic.	.50
□	7 David Aebischer (G), Colo.	4.00
□	8 Marc Denis (G), Colu.	2.00
□	9 Marty Turco (G), Dall.	6.00
□	10 Roberto Luongo (G), Flor.	4.00
□	11 Steven Reinprecht, LosA.	4.00
□	12 Marian Gaborik, MinW.	10.00
□	13 Andrei Markov, Mont.	.50
□	14 Colin White, NJer.	2.00
□	15 Rick DiPietro (G), NYIs.	6.00
□	16 Taylor Pyatt, NYIs.	1.00
□	17 Martin Havlat, Otta.	6.00
□	18 Jani Hurme (G), Otta.	3.00
□	19 Justin Williams, Phil.	4.00
□	20 Milan Kraft, Pitt.	1.50
□	21 Brent Johnson (G), SLou.	2.00
□	22 Evgeni Nabokov (G), SanJ.	3.00
□	23 Brad Richards, Tamp.	2.00
□	24 Daniel Sedin, Vanc.	2.00
□	25 Henrik Sedin, Vanc.	2.00

GAME-WORN JERSEY

There are two versions for each card: the Jersey card and the Jersey Patch variation. Production numbers listed to the right of each name are in same order as the pricing columns: Jersey Patch and Jersey.

	Standard-Size Jersey Set (25 cards):	**700.00**	**300.00**
	Description	**Patch**	**Jersey**
□□	7 Belfour (G) ✂ (#/145; #/608)	75.00	25.00
□□	2 V. Bure ✂ (#/145; #/599)	20.00	12.00
□□	13 Chelios ✂ (#/192; #/1157)	35.00	12.00
□□	1 Dafoe (G) ✂ (#/141; #/602)	30.00	12.00
□□	19 Desjardins ✂ (#/145; #/594)	20.00	12.00
□□	3 Fata ✂ (#/144; #/596)	20.00	12.00
□□	6 Forsberg ✂ (#/141; #/624)	100.00	35.00
□□	4 Housley ✂ (#/144; #/599)	20.00	12.00
□□	8 Hull ✂ (#/144; #/591)	75.00	25.00
□□	16 Kjellberg ✂ (#/136; #/594)	20.00	12.00
□□	9 Langenbrunner ✂ (#/143; #/599)	20.00	12.00
□□	20 LeClair ✂ (#/144; #/594)	60.00	20.00
□□	21 Lumme ✂ (#/144; #/592)	20.00	12.00
□□	10 Marshall ✂ (#/144; #/593)	20.00	12.00
□□	11 Modano ✂ (#/143; #/587)	75.00	25.00
□□	12 Nieuwendyk ✂ (#/142; #/597)	30.00	12.00
□□	14 Osgood (G) ✂ (#/143; #/592)	45.00	15.00
□□	25 Potvin (G) ✂ (#/144; #/585)	50.00	15.00
□□	17 Richter (G) ✂ (#/135; #/596)	35.00	12.00
□□	22 Rozsival ✂ (#/144; #/591)	20.00	12.00
□□	5 Savard ✂ (#/144; #/597)	20.00	12.00
□□	15 Shanahan ✂ (#/163; #/781)	75.00	20.00
□□	23 Straka ✂ (#/144; #/581)	20.00	12.00
□□	24 Sundin ✂ (#/104; #/343)	100.00	30.00
□□	18 Yashin ✂ (#/283; #/946)	30.00	12.00

GAME-WORN JERSEY PREMIUM SIZE

	Premium-Size Jersey Set (24 cards):	**475.00**
	Description	**J**
□	7 Belfour (G) ✂ (#/352)	35.00
□	2 V. Bure ✂ (#/349)	20.00
□	13 Chelios ✂ (#/94)	35.00
□	1 Dafoe (G) ✂ (#/343)	20.00
□	19 Desjardins ✂ (#/349)	20.00
□	3 Fata ✂ (#/343)	20.00
□	6 Forsberg ✂ (#/95)	75.00
□	4 Housley ✂ (#/344)	20.00
□	8 Hull ✂ (#/317)	35.00
□	16 Kjellberg ✂ (#/327)	20.00
□	9 Langenbrunner ✂ (#/338)	20.00
□	20 LeClair ✂ (#/330)	30.00
□	21 Lumme ✂ (#/336)	20.00
□	10 Marshall ✂ (#/342)	20.00
□	11 Modano ✂ (#/320)	35.00
□	12 Nieuwendyk ✂ (#/333)	20.00
□	14 Osgood (G) ✂ (#/351)	20.00
□	25 Potvin (G) ✂ (#/345)	20.00
□	17 Richter (G) ✂ (#/346)	20.00
□	22 Rozsival ✂ (#/357)	20.00
□	5 Savard ✂ (#/343)	20.00
□	15 Shanahan ✂ (#/96)	60.00
□	23 Straka ✂ (#/344)	20.00
□	18 Yashin ✂ (#/345)	20.00

JERSEY REDEMPTION

	Insert Set (11 cards):	**350.00**
	Insert	**JR**
□	7 Daniel Alfredsson, Otta. ✂ (#/475)	20.00
□	1 Stu Barnes, Buff. ✂ (#/475)	20.00
□	6 Theoren Fleury, NYRa. ✂ (#/475)	20.00
□	2 Jarome Iginla, Calg. ✂ (#/475)	30.00
□	9 Jaromir Jagr, Pitt. ✂ (#/475)	20.00
□	10 Curtis Joseph (G), Toro. ✂ (#/475)	40.00
□	4 David Legwand, Nash. ✂ (#/475)	20.00
□	11 Mario Lemieux, Pitt. ✂ (#/100)	200.00
□	5 Scott Niedermayer, NJer. ✂ (#/475)	20.00
□	8 Jeremy Roenick, Phoe. ✂ (#/475)	30.00
□	3 Joe Sakic, Colo. ✂ (#/475)	60.00

JEWEL OF THE CROWN

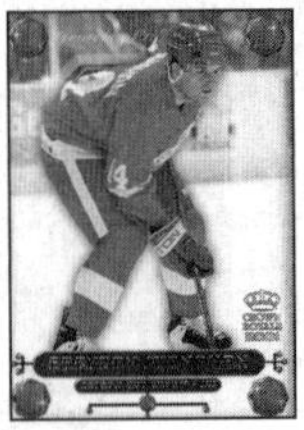

	Insert Set (25 cards):	**45.00**
	Insert (1:1)	**JotC**
□	1 Paul Kariya, Anah.	3.50
□	2 Teemu Selänne, Anah.	2.00
□	3 Patrik Stefan, Atla.	.50
□	4 Jason Allison, Bost.	1.50
□	5 Joe Thornton, Bost.	3.00
□	6 Dominik Hasek (G),	2.50
□	7 Raymond Bourque, Colo.	3.00
□	8 Peter Forsberg, Colo.	3.50
□	9 Patrick Roy (G), Colo.	7.50
□	10 Joe Sakic, Colo.	4.00
□	11 Brett Hull, Dall.	2.50
□	12 Mike Modano, Dall.	2.50
□	13 Brendan Shanahan, Detr.	2.50
□	14 Steve Yzerman, Detr.	6.00
□	15 Doug Weight, Edmo.	1.50
□	16 Pavel Bure, Flor.	2.00
□	17 Martin Brodeur (G), NJer.	4.00
□	18 Mark Messier, NYRa.	2.50
□	19 John LeClair, Phil.	2.00
□	20 Eric Lindros, Phil.	2.50
□	21 Jaromir Jagr, Pitt.	2.50
□	22 Mario Lemieux, Pitt.	7.50
□	23 Vincent Lecavalier, Tamp.	2.50
□	24 Curtis Joseph (G), Toro.	2.50
□	25 Mats Sundin, Toro.	2.50

LANDMARKS

	Insert Set (10 cards):	**375.00**
	Insert (#/99)	**LM**
□	1 Paul Kariya, Anah.	40.00
□	2 Dominik Hasek (G), Buff.	30.00
□	3 Peter Forsberg, Colo.	40.00
□	4 Patrick Roy (G), Colo.	70.00
□	5 Steve Yzerman, Detr.	70.00
□	6 Pavel Bure, Flor.	20.00
□	7 Martin Brodeur (G), NJer.	50.00
□	8 Jaromir Jagr, Pitt.	30.00
□	9 Mario Lemieux, Pitt.	90.00
□	10 Curtis Joseph (G), Toro.	30.00

NOW PLAYING

	Insert Set (20 cards):	**115.00**
	Insert (1:25 packs)	**NP**
□	1 Paul Kariya, Anah.	5.00
□	2 Teemu Selänne, Anah.	4.00
□	3 Jason Allison, Bost.	2.00
□	4 Raymond Bourque, Colo.	6.00
□	5 Peter Forsberg, Colo.	5.00
□	6 Patrick Roy (G), Colo.	15.00
□	7 Brett Hull, Dall.	6.00
□	8 Steve Yzerman, Detr.	15.00
□	9 Pavel Bure, Flor.	5.00
□	10 Marian Gaborik, MinW.	15.00
□	11 Martin Brodeur (G), NJer.	10.00
□	12 Theoren Fleury, NYRa.	2.00
□	13 John LeClair, Phil.	4.00
□	14 Jaromir Jagr, Pitt.	5.00
□	15 Mario Lemieux, Pitt.	15.00
□	16 Vincent Lecavalier, Tamp.	6.00
□	17 Curtis Joseph (G), Toro.	6.00
□	18 Mats Sundin, Toro.	6.00
□	19 Daniel Sedin, Vanc.	4.00
□	20 Henrik Sedin, Vanc.	4.00

2000 - 01 CROWN ROYALE CALDER COLLECTION

	Complete Set (8 cards):	**65.00**
	Player (#/1000)	**CC**
□	David Aebischer (G), Colo.	8.00
□	Rick DiPietro (G), NYIs.	8.00
□	Marian Gaborik, MinW.	20.00
□	Martin Havlat, Otta.	12.00
□	Evgeni Nabokov (G), SanJ.	8.00
□	Brad Richards, Tamp.	8.00
□	Daniel Sedin, Vanc.	8.00
□	Henrik Sedin, Vanc.	8.00

2000 - 01 CROWN ROYALE GOLD ROOKIES

These cards were issued as wrapper-redemption prizes at the Toronto 2001 Spring Expo.

	Complete Set (8 cards):	**80.00**
	Description (#/500)	**GR**
□	G-1 Marty Turco (G), Dall.	15.00
□	G-2 Mike Comrie, Edmo.	20.00
□	G-3 Rick DiPietro (G), NYIs.	10.00
□	G-4 Martin Havlat, Otta.	15.00
□	G-5 Roman Cechmanek (G), Phil.	10.00
□	G-6 Brent Johnson (G), SLou.	8.00
□	G-7 Evgeni Nabokov (G), SanJ.	10.00
□	G-8 Brad Richards, Tamp.	10.00

2000 - 01 DS

NHL stars and prospects sometimes sell at a premium (usually $1-2).

	Complete Set (168 cards):	**35.00**
	Common Player:	**.25**
	Description	**DS**
□	1 Petr Briza (G), Sparta Praha	.25
□	2 Petr Prikryl, Sparta Praha	.25
□	3 Libor Zabransky, Sparta Praha	.50
□	4 Vlastimil Kroupa, Sparta Praha	.50
□	5 Frantisek Ptacek, Sparta Praha	.25
□	6 Michal Dobron, Sparta Praha	.25
□	7 Vladimir Vujtek, Sparta Praha	.25
□	8 Jaroslav Hlinka, Sparta Praha	.25
□	9 Martin Chabada, Sparta Praha	.25
□	10 Ondrej Kratena, Sparta Praha	.25
□	11 Michal Bros, Sparta Praha	.25
□	12 Richard Zemlicka, Sparta Praha	.25
□	13 Jaroslav Kames, Vsetin	.25
□	14 Ivo Pesat, Vsetin	.25
□	15 Jan Srdinko, Vsetin	.25
□	16 Milan Nedoma, Vsetin	.25
□	17 Martin Strbak, Vsetin	.25
□	18 Radim Tesarik, Vsetin	.25
□	19 Jan Pardavy, Vsetin	.25
□	20 Jiri Dopita, Vsetin	.50
□	21 Jan Sochor, Vsetin	.25
□	22 Jan Lipiansky, Vsetin	.25
□	23 Jiri Hudler, Vsetin	6.00
□	24 Ondrej Vesely, Vsetin	.25
□	25 Dusan Salficky, Plzen	.25
□	26 Petr Kus, Plzen	.25
□	27 Josef Reznicek, Plzen	.25

☐	28 Martin Cech, Plzen	.25
☐	29 Ivan Vlcek, Plzen	.25
☐	30 Jiri Hanzlik, Plzen	.25
☐	31 Pavel Vostrak, Plzen	.25
☐	32 Petr Korinek, Plzen	.25
☐	33 Milan Volak, Plzen	.25
☐	34 Michal Straka, Plzen	.25
☐	35 David Pospisil, Plzen	.25
☐	36 Milan Antos, Plzen	.25
☐	37 Zdenek Orct, Litvinov	.25
☐	38 Michal Podolka, Litvinov	.25
☐	39 Angel Nikolov, Litvinov	.25
☐	40 Karel Pilar, Litvinov	2.00
☐	41 Radek Mrazek, Litvinov	.25
☐	42 Vladimir Gyna, Litvinov	.25
☐	43 Robert Reichel, Litvinov	1.50
☐	44 Petr Rosol, Litvinov	.25
☐	45 Vojtech Kubincak, Litvinov	.25
☐	46 Kamil Piros, Litvinov	2.00
☐	47 Vesa Karjalainen, Litvinov	.25
☐	48 Robert Kysela, Litvinov	.25
☐	49 Vladimir Hudacek (G), Zlin	.25
☐	50 Richard Hrazdira, Zlin	.25
☐	51 Tomas Zizka, Zlin	.25
☐	52 Jiri Marusak, Zlin	.25
☐	53 Martin Hamrlik, Zlin	.25
☐	54 Miroslav Barus, Zlin	.25
☐	55 Miroslav Okal, Zlin	.25
☐	56 Petr Cajanek, Zlin	.25
☐	57 Jaroslav Balastik, Zlin	.25
☐	58 Petr Vala, Zlin	.25
☐	59 Martin Ambruz, Zlin	.25
☐	60 Petr Leska, Zlin	.25
☐	61 Marek Novotny, Trinec	.25
☐	62 Vlastimil Lakosil, Trinec	.25
☐	63 Marek Zadina, Trinec	.25
☐	64 Mario Cartelli, Trinec	.25
☐	65 Vladimir Vlk, Trinec	.25
☐	66 Jiri Kuntos, Trinec	.25
☐	67 Richard Kral, Trinec	.25
☐	68 Viktor Ujcik, Trinec	.50
☐	69 Jozef Dano, Trinec	.25
☐	70 Petr Gregorek, Trinec	.25
☐	71 Richard Kapus, Trinec	.25
☐	72 Pavel Janku, Trinec	.25
☐	73 Michal Marik, Ceske Budejovice	.25
☐	74 Ivo Capek, Ceske Budejovice	.25
☐	75 Radek Martinek, Ceske Budejovice	.50
☐	76 Rudolf Suchanek, Ceske Budejovice	.25
☐	77 Stanislav Jasecko, Ceske Budejovice	.25
☐	78 Vaclav Kral, Ceske Budejovice	.25
☐	79 Filip Turek, Ceske Budejovice	.25
☐	80 Lubos Rob, Ceske Budejovice	.25
☐	81 Radek Belohlav, Ceske Budejovice	.25
☐	82 Jiri Simanek, Ceske Budejovice	.25
☐	83 Ales Kotalik, Ceske Budejovice	5.00
☐	84 Kamil Brabenec, Ceske Budejovice	.25
☐	85 Libor Barta, Pardubice	.25
☐	86 Adam Svoboda, Pardubice	.25
☐	87 Ales Pisa, Pardubice	1.00
☐	88 Jiri Malinsky, Pardubice	.25
☐	89 Petr Jancarik, Pardubice	.25
☐	90 Otakar Janecky, Pardubice	.25
☐	91 Ladislav Lubina, Pardubice	.25
☐	92 Tomas Blazek, Pardubice	.25
☐	93 Jaroslav Kudrna, Pardubice	.25
☐	94 Michal Mileska, Pardubice	.25
☐	95 Stanislav Prochazka, Pardubice	.25
☐	96 Michal Tvrdik, Pardubice	.25
☐	97 Oldrich Svoboda, Znojmo	.25
☐	98 Ladislav Kudma, Znojmo	.25
☐	99 Tomas Jakes, Znojmo	.25
☐	100 Jiri Hes, Znojmo	.25
☐	101 Pavel Kumstat, Znojmo	.25
☐	102 Karel Soudek, Znojmo	.25
☐	103 Peter Pucher, Znojmo	.25
☐	104 David Havir, Znojmo	.25
☐	105 Zbynek Marak, Znojmo	.25
☐	106 Milan Prochazka, Znojmo	.25
☐	107 Radek Haman, Znojmo	.25
☐	108 David Pazourek, Znojmo	.25
☐	109 Ladislav Blazek, Slavia Praha	.25
☐	110 Roman Malek, Slavia Praha	.25
☐	111 Petr Kadlec, Slavia Praha	.25
☐	112 Jan Novak, Slavia Praha	.25
☐	113 Angel Krstev, Slavia Praha	.25
☐	114 Jan Snopek, Slavia Praha	.25
☐	115 Daniel Branda, Slavia Praha	.25
☐	116 Jan Alinc, Slavia Praha	.25
☐	117 Viktor Hubl, Slavia Praha	.25
☐	118 Petr Hrbek, Slavia Praha	.25
☐	119 Jan Bohac, Slavia Praha	.25
☐	120 Zdenek Skorepa, Slavia Praha	.25
☐	121 Petr Franek, Karlovy Vary	.25
☐	122 Zdenek Smid, Karlovy Vary	.25
☐	123 Libor Prochazka, Karlovy Vary	.50
☐	124 Normunds Sejejs, Karlovy Vary	.25
☐	125 Jiri Polak, Karlovy Vary	.25
☐	126 Roman Zak, Karlovy Vary	.25
☐	127 Jaromir Kverka, Karlovy Vary	.25
☐	128 Tomas Chlubna, Karlovy Vary	.25
☐	129 Radek Prochazka, Karlovy Vary	.25
☐	130 David Hruska, Karlovy Vary	.25
☐	131 Robert Tomik, Karlovy Vary	.25
☐	132 Pavel Kasparik, Karlovy Vary	.25
☐	133 Lubos Horcicka, Kladno	.25
☐	134 Marek Pinc, Kladno	.25
☐	135 Jan Krulis, Kladno	.25
☐	136 Michal Madl, Kladno	.25
☐	137 Radek Gardon, Kladno	.25
☐	138 Jan Bohacek, Kladno	.25
☐	139 Ladislav Svoboda, Kladno	.25
☐	140 Tomas Horna, Kladno	.25
☐	141 Jiri Holsan, Kladno	.25
☐	142 Ondrej Kriz, Kladno	.25
☐	143 Ladislav Vicek, Kladno	.25
☐	144 Jozef Voskar, Kladno	.25
☐	145 Radovan Biegl, Havirov	.25
☐	146 Radek Masny, Havirov	.25
☐	147 Michael Vyhlidal, Havirov	.25
☐	148 Miroslav Javin, Havirov	.25
☐	149 Petr Pavlas, Havirov	.25
☐	150 Tomas Srsen, Havirov	.25
☐	151 Petr Folta, Havirov	.25
☐	152 Libor Pivko, Havirov	.25
☐	153 Daniel Bohac, Havirov	.25
☐	154 Roman Horak, Havirov	.25
☐	155 Jan Peterek, Havirov	.25
☐	156 Richard Pavlikovsky, Havirov	.25
☐	157 Martin Prusek, Vitkovice	2.00
☐	158 Jiri Trvaj, Vitkovice	.25
☐	159 Zdenek Pavelek, Vitkovice	.25
☐	160 Vitezslav Skuta, Vitkovice	.25
☐	161 Dmitri Jerofejev, Vitkovice	.25
☐	162 David Moravec, Vitkovice	.50
☐	163 Roman Kadera, Vitkovice	.25
☐	164 Zbynek Irgl, Vitkovice	.25
☐	165 Marek Ivan, Vitkovice	.25
☐	166 Martin Prochazka, Vitkovice	.50
☐	167 Josef Straub, Vitkovice	.25
☐	168 Ivan Padelek, Vitkovice	.25

BEST OF THE BEST

	Insert (1:10)	**BotB**
☐	BBH1 Dominik Hasek (G)	6.00
☐	BBJ1 Jaromir Jagr	6.00
	Insert (1:25)	**BotB**
☐	BBH1 Dominik Hasek (G)	14.00
☐	BBH2 Dominik Hasek (G)	14.00
☐	BBJ1 Jaromir Jagr	14.00
☐	BBJ2 Jaromir Jagr	14.00
	Autograph (#/200)	**Auto.**
☐	BBH1 Dominik Hasek (G) ✍	
☐	BBJ1 Jaromir Jagr ✍	

GOALIES

Insert Set (14 cards):		**65.00**
	Insert (1:8 packs)	**G**
☐	G1 Petr Briza (G)	6.00
☐	G2 Jaroslav Kames (G)	5.00
☐	G3 Dusan Salficky (G)	6.00
☐	G4 Zdenek Orct (G)	5.00
☐	G5 Vladimir Hudacek (G)	5.00
☐	G6 Vlastimil Lakosil (G)	5.00
☐	G7 Ivo Capek (G)	5.00
☐	G8 Adam Svoboda (G)	5.00
☐	G9 Oldrich Svoboda (G)	5.00
☐	G10 Roman Malek (G)	5.00
☐	G11 Zdenek Smid (G)	5.00
☐	G12 Marek Pinc (G)	5.00
☐	G13 Radovan Biegl (G)	5.00
☐	G14 Martin Prusek (G)	14.00

JAGR TEAM

There is a subset card (1:1.3 packs) and a parallel card (1:35 packs, #/300).

Insert Set (16 cards):		**90.00**	**35.00**
	Insert	**JT300**	**JT**
☐ ☐	JT1 Roman Turek (G)	6.00	3.50
☐ ☐	JT2 Milan Hnilicka (G)	6.00	2.00
☐ ☐	JT3 Petr Sykora	6.00	3.00
☐ ☐	JT4 Roman Hamrlik	6.00	2.00
☐ ☐	JT5 Martin Straka	6.00	2.00
☐ ☐	JT6 Pavel Kubina	6.00	2.00
☐ ☐	JT7 Petr Nedved	6.00	2.00
☐ ☐	JT8 Martin Prochazka	6.00	2.00
☐ ☐	JT9 Vaclav Prospal	6.00	2.00
☐ ☐	JT10 David Volek	6.00	2.00
☐ ☐	JT11 Milan Hejduk	12.00	6.00
☐ ☐	JT12 Jaromir Jagr	14.00	7.50
☐ ☐	JT13 Jan Hlavac	6.00	2.00
☐ ☐	JT14 Pavel Patera	6.00	2.00
☐ ☐	JT15 Tomas Vlasak	6.00	2.00
☐ ☐	JT16 Vaclav Varada	6.00	2.00

NATIONAL TEAM

Insert Set (9 cards):		**35.00**
	Insert	**NT**
☐	NT1 Dusan Salficky (G)	4.00
☐	NT2 Roman Cechmanek (G)	4.50
☐	NT3 Martin Stepanek	4.00
☐	NT4 Vladimir Vujtek	4.00
☐	NT5 Robert Reichel	4.00
☐	NT6 Jiri Dopita	4.00
☐	NT7 Martin Rucinsky	4.00
☐	NT8 Martin Havlat	9.00
☐	NT9 Tomas Vlasak	4.00

TOP STARS

Insert Set (6 cards):		**20.00**
	Insert (1:17)	**TS**
☐	TS1 Petr Briza (G)	4.00
☐	TS2 Radek Martinek	4.00
☐	TS3 Petr Cajanek	4.00
☐	TS4 Jiri Dopita	4.00
☐	TS5 Robert Reichel	7.00
☐	TS6 Martin Prochazka	4.00

VALUABLE PLAYERS

Insert Set (6 cards):		**20.00**
	Insert	**VP**
☐	VP1 Vladimir Hudacek (G)	4.00
☐	VP2 Frantisek Kucera	4.00
☐	VP3 Michal Sykora	4.00
☐	VP4 Robert Reichel	7.00
☐	VP5 Jiri Dopita	4.00
☐	VP6 Petr Cajanek	4.00

WORLD CHAMPIONS

Insert Set (11 cards):		**40.00**
	Insert (1:9)	**WCH**
☐	WCH1 Roman Cechmanek (G)	9.00
☐	WCH2 Dusan Salficky (G)	4.00
☐	WCH3 Radek Marinek	4.00
☐	WCH4 Martin Stepanek	4.00
☐	WCH5 Frantisek Kucera	4.00
☐	WCH6 Michal Sykora	4.00
☐	WCH7 Martin Havlat	13.00
☐	WCH8 Robert Reichel	7.00
☐	WCH9 Tomas Vlasak	4.00
☐	WCH10 David Vyborny	4.00
☐	WCH11 Michal Bros	4.00

2000 - 01 KRAFT

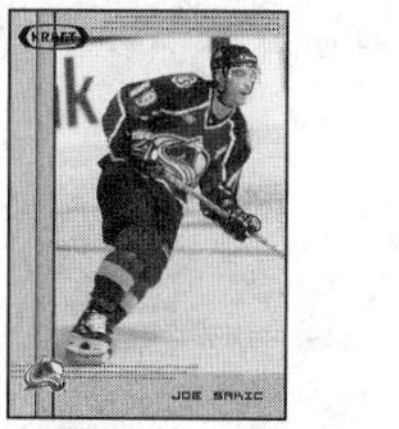

This series was produced as a premium for Kraft dealers.

Complete Set (30 cards):		**50.00**
	Description.	**Kraft**
☐	1 Jaromir Jagr, Pitt.	2.50
☐	2 Markus Näslund, Vanc.	2.50
☐	3 Luc Robitaille, LosA.	2.00
☐	4 Scott Stevens, NJer.	1.00
☐	5 Mike Modano, Dall.	2.50
☐	6 Doug Weight, Edmo.	1.50
☐	7 Peter Bondra, Wash.	1.50
☐	8 Paul Kariya, Anah.	3.50
☐	9 Radek Bonk, Otta.	1.00
☐	10 John LeClair, Phil.	2.00
☐	11 Sandis Ozolinsh, Caro.	1.00
☐	12 Steve Yzerman, Detr.	6.00
☐	13 Joe Thornton, Bost.	3.00
☐	14 Valeri Bure, Calg.	1.00
☐	15 Pavel Bure, Flor.	2.00
☐	16 Cliff Ronning, Nash.	1.00
☐	17 Dominik Hasek (G), Buff.	2.50
☐	18 Vincent Lecavalier, Tamp.	2.50
☐	19 Andrew Brunette, Atla.	1.00
☐	20 Chris Pronger, SLou.	1.50
☐	21 Owen Nolan, SanJ.	1.50
☐	22 Joe Sakic, Colo.	4.00
☐	23 Jeremy Roenick, Phoe.	2.00
☐	24 Tony Amonte, Chic.	1.50
☐	25 Mariusz Czerkawski, NYIs.	1.00
☐	26 Trevor Linden, Mont.	1.00
☐	27 Mats Sundin, Toro.	2.50
☐	28 Mark Messier, NYRa.	2.50
☐	29 Ron Tugnutt (G), Colu.	1.00
☐	30 Scott Pellerin, MinW.	1.00

2000 - 01 KUDOS

This set featured players of the British Superleague. Singles start at 20¢.

	Description		
☐	1 ISL	☐	2 Jim Lynch
☐	3 Paul Heavey	☐	4 P. DeRouville (G)
☐	5 Colin Ryder	☐	6 Trevor Doyle
☐	7 Derek Eberle	☐	8 Anders Hillstorm
☐	9 Jan Mikel	☐	10 Johan Silfwerplatz
☐	11 Scott Young	☐	12 Dainius Bauyba
☐	13 Cam Bristow	☐	14 Shawn Bryam
☐	15 Ed Courtenay	☐	16 Tony Hand
☐	17 Rhett Gordon	☐	18 Mike Harding
☐	19 Mark Montanari	☐	20 Jonathon Weaver
☐	21 Teeder Wynne	☐	22 Dave Whistle
☐	23 Mark Cavallin	☐	24 Todd Kelman
☐	25 Kevin Riehl	☐	26 Paxton Schulte
☐	27 Colin Ward	☐	28 Jeff Hoad
☐	29 Shane Johnson	☐	30 Enio Sacilotto
☐	31 Brian Greer	☐	32 Joe Watkins
☐	33 Matej Bukna	☐	34 Jimmy Drolet
☐	35 Jason Mansoff	☐	36 Mark Matier
☐	37 Steve O'Rourke	☐	38 Reid Simonton
☐	39 Brent Bobyck	☐	40 Chris Brant
☐	41 Mark Bultje	☐	42 Joe Cardarelli
☐	43 Dan Ceman	☐	44 Joe Ciccarello
☐	45 Darren Hurley	☐	46 Blaxe Knox
☐	47 Stephane Roy	☐	48 Brad Wingfield
☐	49 Doug McCarthy	☐	50 Troy Walkington
☐	51 Stevie Lyle	☐	52 Derek Herlofsky
☐	53 Frank Evans	☐	54 Kip Noble
☐	55 Clayton Norris	☐	56 Dwight Parrish
☐	57 Alan Schuler	☐	58 Rick Strachan
☐	59 Denis Chassé	☐	60 James Hanlon
☐	61 Rick Kowalsky	☐	62 Ivan Matulik
☐	63 Ian Macintyre	☐	64 Steve Moria
☐	65 John Parco	☐	66 Vezio Sacratini
☐	67 Steve Thornton	☐	68 Mike Ware
☐	69 Chris Mcsorley	☐	70 Trevor Robins
☐	71 Shawn Silver	☐	72 Rich Bronilla
☐	73 Martin Neal	☐	74 Randy Perry
☐	75 Mikael Tjallden	☐	76 Nicky Chinn
☐	77 Pat Ferschweiler	☐	78 Claude Jutras
☐	79 Mikko Koivynoro	☐	80 Mark Kolesar
☐	81 Jay Neal	☐	82 Ryan Richardson
☐	83 Paul Rushforth	☐	84 David Vallieres
☐	85 Darby Walker	☐	86 Brendan Yarema
☐	87 Terry Cristensen	☐	88 Daryl Lipsey
☐	89 Frank Pietrangelo	☐	90 Dave Trofimenkoff
☐	91 Curtis Bowen	☐	92 Matt Eldred
☐	93 Perry Johnson	☐	94 Troy Neumeier
☐	95 Rob Robinson	☐	96 Blair Scott
☐	97 Pierre Allard	☐	98 Kevin Brown
☐	99 Greg Bullock	☐	100 Doug Doull
☐	101 Marty Flichel	☐	102 Trevor Gallant
☐	103 Jason Glover	☐	104 Mike Morin
☐	105 Corey Spring	☐	106 S. Stevenson
☐	107 Rob Trumbly	☐	108 Jukka Jalonen
☐	109 Jimmy Hibbert	☐	110 Tommi Satosaari
☐	111 Craig Binns	☐	112 Santeri Immonen
☐	113 Arttu Kaykho	☐	114 Miroslav Mosnar
☐	115 D. McAusland	☐	116 Rob Wilson
☐	117 Tero Arkiomaa	☐	118 Louis Bedard
☐	119 Tomas Kupka	☐	120 Matt Oates
☐	121 Joel Poirer	☐	122 Timo Salonen
☐	123 Tommi Sova	☐	124 Alex Dampier
☐	125 Eoin McInerney	☐	126 Willis Jordan
☐	127 Greg Burke	☐	128 Ryan Gillis
☐	129 Éric Lavigne	☐	130 Daryl Lavoie
☐	131 Jim Paek	☐	132 Duncan Paterson
☐	133 Pierre Drouin	☐	134 Graham Garden
☐	135 Greg Hadden	☐	136 Jamie Leach
☐	137 Daryl Moxam	☐	138 Barry Nieckar
☐	139 David Struch	☐	140 Ashley Tait
☐	141 Randall Weber	☐	142 Mike Blaisdell
☐	143 Mike O'Neill	☐	144 Steve Carpenter
☐	145 Shayne McCosh	☐	146 Jeff Sebastian
☐	147 Kayle Short	☐	148 Adam Smith
☐	149 Dennis Vial	☐	150 Scott Allison
☐	151 Paul Beraldo	☐	152 Rick Brebant
☐	153 Dale Craigwell	☐	154 David Longstaff
☐	155 Scott Metcalfe	☐	156 Warren Norris
☐	157 Steve Roberts	☐	158 Kent Simpson
☐	159 Jason Weaver	☐	160 Brent Bobyck
☐	161 Scottish Eagles	☐	162 Belfast Giants
☐	163 Bracknell Bees	☐	164 Bt Cardiff Devils
☐	165 London Knights	☐	166 Manchester Storm
☐	167 Newcastle	☐	168 Nottingham
☐	169 Sheffield Steelers	☐	170 Lucky card

2000 - 01 McDONALD'S

This series was issued in December 2000 at McDonald's restaurants in Canada. Base cards 1-36 have a Platinum Blue parallel (1:4 packs).

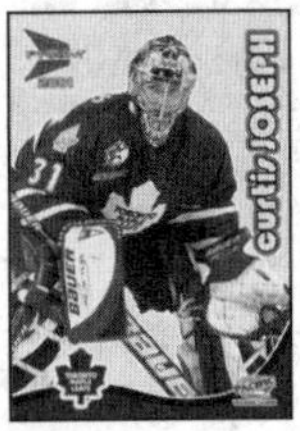

Complete Set (36 cards):	**120.00**	**25.00**
Description	**Blue**	**McD**
☐ ☐ 1 Paul Kariya	7.00	1.50
☐ ☐ 2 Teemu Selänne	4.00	1.00
☐ ☐ 3 Patrik Stefan	1.50	.35
☐ ☐ 4 Joe Thornton	6.00	1.50
☐ ☐ 5 Dominik Hasek (G)	5.00	1.00
☐ ☐ 6 Valeri Bure	1.50	.35
☐ ☐ 7 Raymond Bourque	6.00	1.50
☐ ☐ 8 Peter Forsberg	7.00	1.50
☐ ☐ 9 Patrick Roy (G)	15.00	3.50
☐ ☐ 10 Joe Sakic	8.00	2.00
☐ ☐ 11 Brett Hull	5.00	1.00
☐ ☐ 12 Mike Modano	5.00	1.00
☐ ☐ 13 Chris Osgood (G)	3.00	.50
☐ ☐ 14 Brendan Shanahan	5.00	1.00
☐ ☐ 15 Steve Yzerman	12.00	3.00
☐ ☐ 16 Doug Weight	3.00	.50
☐ ☐ 17 Pavel Bure	4.00	1.00
☐ ☐ 18 Jeff Hackett (G)	1.50	.35
☐ ☐ 19 Saku Koivu	4.00	1.00
☐ ☐ 20 Martin Brodeur (G)	8.00	2.00
☐ ☐ 21 Scott Gomez	2.00	.50
☐ ☐ 22 Scott Stevens	2.00	.50
☐ ☐ 23 Marian Hossa	5.00	1.00
☐ ☐ 24 Brian Boucher (G)	1.50	.35
☐ ☐ 25 John LeClair	4.00	1.00
☐ ☐ 26 Eric Lindros	5.00	1.00
☐ ☐ 27 Jaromir Jagr	5.00	1.00
☐ ☐ 28 Chris Pronger	3.00	.50
☐ ☐ 29 Roman Turek (G)	2.00	.50
☐ ☐ 30 Vincent Lecavalier	5.00	1.00
☐ ☐ 31 Nikolai Antropov	1.00	.35
☐ ☐ 32 Curtis Joseph (G)	5.00	1.00
☐ ☐ 33 Mats Sundin	5.00	1.00
☐ ☐ 34 Mattias Öhlund	1.50	.35
☐ ☐ 35 Félix Potvin (G)	3.00	.50
☐ ☐ 36 Olaf Kölzig (G)	3.00	.50

CHECKLIST

Insert Set (9 cards):	**4.00**
Insert	**CL**
☐ 1 Valeri Bure	.35
☐ 2 Doug Weight	.50
☐ 3 Jeff Hackett (G)	.35
☐ 4 Saku Koivu	1.00
☐ 5 Marian Hossa	1.00
☐ 6 Curtis Joseph (G)	1.00
☐ 7 Mats Sundin	1.00
☐ 8 Mattias Öhlund	.35
☐ 9 Félix Potvin (G)	.50

DIAL-A-STATS

Insert Set (6 cards):	**25.00**
Insert	**DAS**
☐ 1 Paul Kariya	7.00
☐ 2 Steve Yzerman	12.00
☐ 3 Pavel Bure	4.00
☐ 4 Eric Lindros	5.00
☐ 5 Jaromir Jagr	5.00
☐ 6 Mats Sundin	5.00

GAME-WORN JERSEY

Insert Set (10 cards):	**990.00**
Insert	**GWJ**
☐ 1 Teemu Selänne ✂	100.00
☐ 2 Peter Forsberg ✂	125.00
☐ 3 Patrick Roy (G) ✂	225.00
☐ 4 Mike Modano ✂	100.00
☐ 5 Steve Yzerman ✂	225.00
☐ 6 Pavel Bure ✂	100.00
☐ 7 Martin Brodeur (G) ✂	150.00
☐ 8 Eric Lindros ✂	100.00
☐ 9 Jaromir Jagr ✂	100.00
☐ 10 Mats Sundin ✂	100.00

GLOVE-SIDE NET-FUSIONS

Insert Set (6 cards):	**30.00**
Insert	**GSNF**
☐ 1 Dominik Hasek (G)	5.00
☐ 2 Patrick Roy (G)	12.00
☐ 3 Chris Osgood (G)	4.00
☐ 4 Martin Brodeur (G)	8.00
☐ 5 Brian Boucher (G)	4.00
☐ 6 Curtis Joseph (G)	5.00

GOLD-CROWN DIE-CUTS

Insert Set (6 cards):	**12.00**
Insert	**GCDC**
☐ 1 Patrik Stefan	2.00
☐ 2 Alex Tanguay	3.00
☐ 3 David Legwand	2.00
☐ 4 Scott Gomez	2.00
☐ 5 Tim Connolly	2.00
☐ 6 Vincent Lecavalier	5.00

2000 - 01 MIR

NHL stars and prospects sometimes sell at a premium (usually $1-2).

Complete Set (392 cards):	**75.00**
Common Player:	**.30**
Description	**Mir**
☐ 1 Oleg Filimonov, Amur	.30
☐ 2 Alexei Lazarenko, Amur	.30
☐ 3 Sergei Yasakov, Amur	.30
☐ 4 Steve Pluff, Amur	.30
☐ 5 Alexander Tychkin, Amur	.30
☐ 6 Igor Boldin, Amur	.30
☐ 7 Vitali Evdokimov, Amur	.30
☐ 8 Igor Andryushenko, Amur	.30
☐ 9 Alexander Grishin, Amur	.30
☐ 10 Andrei Kiselev, Amur	.30
☐ 11 Dmitri Tarasov, Amur	.30
☐ 12 Anatoli Ustyugov, Amur	.30
☐ 13 Ruslan Bernikov, Amur	.30
☐ 14 Oleg Naumenko, Amur	.30
☐ 15 Igor Nikolaev, Amur	.30
☐ 16 Renat Khairetdinov, Amur	.30
☐ 17 Vadim Pokotilo, Amur	.30
☐ 18 Vladimir Tyurikov, Amur	.30
☐ 19 Dmitri Uchaikin, Amur	.30
☐ 20 Konstantin Mitroshkin, Amur	.30
☐ 21 Alexei Plotnikov, Amur	.30
☐ 22 Oleg Vevcherenko, Amur	.30
☐ 23 Dmitri Shulakov, Amur	.30
☐ 24 Sergei Butko, Amur	.30
☐ 25 Dmitri Levinski, Amur	.30
☐ 26 Vladimir Gusev, Amur	.30
☐ 27 Denis Martynyuk, Amur	.30
☐ 28 Kharis Ross, Amur	.30
☐ 29 Nikolai Pronin, CSKA Moscow	.30
☐ 30 Sergei Zolotov, AkBars	.30
☐ 31 Dmitri Bykov, AkBars	3.00
☐ 32 Remir Khaidarov, AkBars	.30
☐ 33 Eduard Kudermetov, AkBars	.30
☐ 34 Dmitri Yachanov, AkBars	.30
☐ 35 Dmitri Balmin, AkBars	.30
☐ 36 Alexander Zhdan, AkBars	.30
☐ 37 Alexei Chupin, AkBars	.30
☐ 38 Almaz Garifullin, AkBars	.30
☐ 39 Alexander Zavyalov, AkBars	.30
☐ 40 Ilnur Gizatullin, AkBars	.30
☐ 41 Alexei Tertyshny, AkBars	.30
☐ 42 Evgeni Varlamov, Akbars	.30
☐ 43 Oleg Glebov, Soviet Wings	.30
☐ 44 Sergei Mylnikov, Soviet Wings	.30
☐ 45 Leonid Kanareikin, Soviet Wings	.30
☐ 46 Ildar Yubin, Soviet Wings	.30
☐ 47 Anton Volchenkov, Soviet Wings	1.50
☐ 48 Andrei Loginov, Soviet Wings	.30
☐ 49 Vitali Dryndin, Soviet Wings	.30
☐ 50 Pavel Kanarski, Soviet Wings	.30
☐ 51 Vladimir Kramskoi, Soviet Wings	.30
☐ 52 Oleg Mikulchik, Soviet Wings	.50
☐ 53 Vyacheslav Zavalnyuk, Soviet Wings	.30
☐ 54 Sergei Soin, Soviet Wings	1.00
☐ 55 Andrei Galkin, Soviet Wings	.30
☐ 56 Valeri Chernin, Soviet Wings	.30
☐ 57 Andrei Posnov, Soviet Wings	.30
☐ 58 Alexander Ardashev, Soviet Wings	.30
☐ 59 Roman Salnikov, Soviet Wings	.30
☐ 60 Eduard Gorbachev, Soviet Wings	.30
☐ 61 Sergei Martinov, Soviet Wings	.30
☐ 62 Dmitri Pirozhkov, Soviet Wings	.30
☐ 63 Alexander Frolov, Soviet Wings	2.00
☐ 64 Vladimir Zavyalov, Soviet Wings	.30
☐ 65 Lev Berdichevsky, Soviet Wings	.50
☐ 66 Andrei Maksimenko, Soviet Wings	.30
☐ 67 Dmitri Teplyakov, Soviet Wings	.30
☐ 68 Boris Kuzimin, Soviet Wings	.30
☐ 69 Nikolai Ryzheinkov, Soviet Wings	.30
☐ 70 Maxim Osipov, Soviet Wings	.30
☐ 71 Vladimir Loginov, Soviet Wings	.30
☐ 72 Andrei Kuzimin, Soviet Wings	.30
☐ 73 Ilia Dokshin, SKA	.30
☐ 74 Sergei Yakimovich, SKA	.30
☐ 75 Oleg Kyzimin, SKA	.30
☐ 76 Yuri Trubachev, SKA	.30
☐ 77 Fedor Tyutin, SKA	.30
☐ 78 Alexei Tsvetkov, SKA	.30
☐ 79 Alexander Shinkari, SKA	.30
☐ 80 Georgie Kabanov, Dizelist	.30
☐ 81 Vitali Chumichev, Spartak	.30
☐ 82 Artem Chernov, Novokuznetsk	1.00
☐ 83 Dmitri Khramchenko, Torpedo NN	.30
☐ 84 Andrei Sharapov, Torpedo NN	.30
☐ 85 Oleg Antonenko, Torpedo NN	.30
☐ 86 Oleg Namestnikov, Torpedo NN	.30
☐ 87 Andrei Poddyakon, Torpedo NN	.30
☐ 88 Vasili Smirnov, Torpedo NN	.30
☐ 89 Vitali Novopashin, Torpedo NN	.30
☐ 90 Roman Malov, Torpedo NN	.30
☐ 91 Vadim Averkin, Torpedo NN	.30
☐ 92 Nikolai Voevodin, Torpedo NN	.30
☐ 93 Vladimir Fedosov, Torpedo NN	.30
☐ 94 Vasili Chistokletov, Torpedo NN	.30
☐ 95 Anatoli Filatov, Torpedo NN	.30
☐ 96 Igor Safonov, Torpedo NN	.30
☐ 97 Mikhail Belobragin, Torpedo NN	.30
☐ 98 Maxim Ovchinnikov, Torpedo NN	.30
☐ 99 Alexei Vorobiev, Torpedo NN	.30
☐ 100 Igor Shavtsov, Torpedo NN	.30
☐ 101 Sergei Fadeev, Torpedo NN	.30
☐ 102 Dmitri Pankov, Torpedo NN	.30
☐ 103 Sergei Berdnikov, Severstal	.30
☐ 105 Sergei Voronov, Magnitogorsk	.30
☐ 106 Alexei Kalyukhny, Magnitogorsk	.30
☐ 107 Yuri Kuznetsov, Magnitogorsk	.50
☐ 108 Alexander Goltz, Magnitogorsk	.30
☐ 109 Sergei Klishin, Torpedo NN	.30
☐ 110 Igor Melyakov, Torpedo NN	.30
☐ 111 Sergei Kiselev, Torpedo NN	.30
☐ 112 Igor Karpenko, Magnitogorsk	.30
☐ 113 Igor Karpenko, Magnitogorsk	.30
☐ 114 Sergei Nikolaev, SKA	.30
☐ 115 Igor Sipchenko, SKA	.30
☐ 116 Valeri Pokrovski, SKA	.30
☐ 117 Sergei Gubernatorov, SKA	.30
☐ 118 Igor Samoilov, SKA	.30
☐ 119 Alexander Urakin, SKA	.30
☐ 120 Oleg Eremeev, SKA	.30
☐ 121 Della Paolo, Magnitogorsk	.30
☐ 122 Vyacheslav Bezukladnikov, Lada	.30
☐ 123 Alexei Troshinski, Magnitogorsk	.30
☐ 124 Vladimir Antipin, Lada	.30
☐ 125 Alexander Yudin, Neftikhimik	.50
☐ 126 Vitali Proshkin, AkBars	.30
☐ 127 Ilya Kovalchuk, Spartak	25.00
☐ 128 Dmitri Ryabikin, Avangard	.30
☐ 129 Alexander Zhurik, Avangard	.30
☐ 130 Igor Shastin, Avangard	.30
☐ 131 Mikhail Shukaev, Torpedo NN	.30
☐ 132 Anvar Gatiyatulin, Torpedo NN	.30
☐ 133 Andrei Anisimov, Torpedo NN	.30
☐ 134 Maxim Solobiev, Novokuznetsk	.30
☐ 135 Konstantin Bezborodov, Soviet Wings	.30
☐ 136 Ravil Yakubov, Avangard	.50
☐ 137 Alexander Prokopiev, Avangard	.30
☐ 138 Oleg Shargorodski, Avangard	.30
☐ 139 Ruslan Batirshin, Avangard	.30
☐ 140 Alexei Kupreenkov, Spartak	.30
☐ 141 Pavel Komarov, Salavat	.30
☐ 142 Alexei Sharnin, Salavat	.30
☐ 143 Sergei* Fedotov, Salavat	.50
☐ 144 Denis Khlistov, Salavat	.30
☐ 145 Mikhail Potapov, Salavat	.30
☐ 146 Alexander Semak, Salavat	.50
☐ 147 Andrei Vasilevski, Salavat	.30
☐ 148 Azat Sharipov, Salavat	.30
☐ 149 Andrei Sidyakin, Salavat	.30
☐ 150 Sergei Shikhanov, Magnitogorsk	.30
☐ 151 Sergei Gomalyako, Lada	.30
☐ 152 Dmitri Nabokov, Lada	.30
☐ 153 Valentin Morozov, Lada	.30
☐ 154 Denis Metlyuk, Lada	.50
☐ 155 Ilja Bryzgalov, Lada	5.00
☐ 156 Alexander Lyubimov, Lada	.30
☐ 157 Ilya Byakin, Lada	.50
☐ 158 Sergei Tertyshny, Lada	.30
☐ 159 Valeri Karpov, Lada	.50
☐ 160 Andrei Tarasenko, Lada	.30
☐ 161 Alexander Yudin, Lada	.50
☐ 162 Nikolai Zavarukhin, Lada	.50
☐ 163 Oleg Belkin, Lada	.30
☐ 164 Andrei Skabelka, Lada	.30
☐ 165 Leonid Fatikov, Lada	.30
☐ 166 Oleg Khmyl, Lada	.30
☐ 167 Denis Afinogenov, Lada	.30
☐ 168 Alexander Nesterov, Lada	.30
☐ 169 Andrei Kruchinin, Lada	.30
☐ 170 Andrei Petrunin, Lada	.50
☐ 171 Vladimir Malenkikh, Lada	.30
☐ 172 Sergei Shabanov, Novokuznetsk	.30
☐ 173 Vadim Tarasov, Novokuznetsk	.30
☐ 174 Igor Zelenchev, Novokuznetsk	.30
☐ 175 Sergei Shalamai, Novokuznetsk	.30
☐ 176 Yuri Zyev, Novokuznetsk	.30
☐ 177 Artem Argokov, Novokuznetsk	.30
☐ 178 Evgeni Pupkov, Novokuznetsk	.30
☐ 179 Sergei Moskalev, Novokuznetsk	.30
☐ 180 Alexander Filippov, Amur	.30
☐ 181 Igor Dyakiv, Novokuznetsk	.30
☐ 182 Stanislav Pinevski, Novokuznetsk	.30
☐ 183 Alexander Agnevshikov, Novokuznetsk	.30
☐ 184 Sergei Zherebtsov, Novokuznetsk	.30
☐ 185 Roman Kukhtinov, Novokuznetsk	.30
☐ 186 Evgeni Lapin, Novokuznetsk	.30
☐ 187 Nikolai Kurochkin, Novokuznetsk	.30
☐ 188 Alexei Alekseev, Novokuznetsk	.30
☐ 189 Alexei Koledaev, Novokuznetsk	.30
☐ 190 Sergei Verenikin, Novokuznetsk	.30
☐ 191 Denis Tyurin, Novokuznetsk	.30
☐ 192 Rail Rozakov, Novokuznetsk	.30
☐ 193 Vladimir Pozdnyakov, Novokuznetsk	.30
☐ 194 Pavel Desyatkov, Novokuznetsk	.50
☐ 195 Alexei Krovopuskov, Novokuznetsk	.30
☐ 196 Sergei Sevastyanov, Lada	.30
☐ 197 Mikhail Yakubov, Lada	2.00
☐ 199 Pavel Torgajev, Torpedo NN	.50
☐ 199 Vadim Glovatskin, Magnitogorsk	.30
☐ 200 Denis Tyulyapkin, Torpedo NN	.30
☐ 201 Dmitri Altarev, Torpedo NN	.30
☐ 202 Maxim Savosin, Torpedo NN	.30
☐ 203 Leonid Toropchenko, Khimik Voskresensk	.30
☐ 204 Stanislav Timakov, Khimik Voskresensk	.30
☐ 205 Valeri Emelyanov, Khimik Voskresensk	.30
☐ 206 Igor Grachev, Khimik Voskresensk	.30
☐ 207 Stanislav Udyanski, Khimik Voskresensk	.30
☐ 208 Yuris Ozols, Khimik Voskresensk	.30
☐ 209 Alexander Galkin, Khimik Voskresensk	.30
☐ 210 Sergei Makarov, Khimik Voskresensk	.30
☐ 211 Sergei Selyutin, Khimik Voskresensk	.30
☐ 212 Alexander Popov, Khimik Voskresensk	.30
☐ 213 Sergei Zadelenko, Energiya	.30
☐ 215 Dmitri Shulga, Energiya	.30
☐ 216 Denis Sokolov, Energiya	.30
☐ 217 Maxim Kraev, Energiya	.30
☐ 218 Rinat Khasanov, Lokomotive	.30
☐ 219 Boris Tortunov, Lokomotive	.30

☐ 220 Dmitri Krasotkin, Lokomotive .30
☐ 221 Maxim Velikov, CSKA Moscow .30
☐ 222 Yuri Panov, Avangard .30
☐ 223 Alexander Vyukhin, Avangard .30
☐ 224 Vadim Shakhraichuk, Avangard .30
☐ 225 Alexei Badyukov, Avangard .30
☐ 226 Alexander Korobolin, Avangard .30
☐ 227 Dmitri Zatonski, Avangard .30
☐ 228 Kirill Koltsov, Avangard 1.00
☐ 229 Alexander Svitov, Avangard 8.00
☐ 230 Ilya Gorbushin, Avangard .30
☐ 231 Andrei Samokhvalov, Avangard .30
☐ 232 Igor Nikitin, Avangard .30
☐ 233 Ramil Saifullin, Avangard .30
☐ 234 Victor Chistov, Severstal .30
☐ 235 Vladimir Vorobiev, Severstal .50
☐ 236 Igor Nikulin, Severstal .30
☐ 237 Alexander Sidorovski, Tver .30
☐ 238 Oleg Polkovnikov, Dynamo Moscow .30
☐ 239 Dmitri Dudarev, Dynamo Moscow .30
☐ 240 Andrei Sapozhnikov, Severstal .30
☐ 241 Andrei Kudinov, Magnitogorsk .30
☐ 242 Alik Gareev, Salavat .30
☐ 243 Ruslan Nurtdinov, Salavat .30
☐ 244 Alexander Ageev, Salavat .30
☐ 245 Andrei Yakhanov, Salavat .30
☐ 246 Vener Safin, Salavat .30
☐ 247 Sergei Komarov, Salavat .30
☐ 248 Nail Shayakhmetov, Salavat .30
☐ 249 Vladislav Ozolin, Salavat .30
☐ 250 Nikolai Tsulygin, Salavat .50
☐ 251 Albert Leshchev, CSKA Moscow .30
☐ 252 Stanislav Shalnov, CSKA Moscow .30
☐ 253 Maxim Orlov, CSKA Moscow .30
☐ 254 Alexei Chernikov, CSKA Moscow .30
☐ 255 Sergei Makarov, CSKA Moscow .30
☐ 256 Sergei Zimakov, CSKA Moscow .50
☐ 257 Gennadi Savilov, CSKA Moscow .30
☐ 258 Vasili Turkovski, CSKA Moscow .30
☐ 259 Igor Mikhailov, CSKA Moscow .30
☐ 260 Georgi Evtyukhin, Spartak .30
☐ 261 Alexei Tkachuk, Spartak .30
☐ 262 Mikhail Volkov, Spartak .30
☐ 263 Dmitri Gogolev, Spartak .30
☐ 264 Pavel Agarkov, Spartak .30
☐ 265 Vladimir Korsunov, Spartak .30
☐ 266 Andrei Medvedev (G), Spartak 3.00
☐ 267 Dmitri Bykov, National Team 3.00
☐ 268 Ruslan Zainullin, AkBars .30
☐ 269 Dmitri Starostenko, CSKA Moscow .30
☐ 270 Alexander Schev, Magnitogorsk .30
☐ 271 Andrei Petrakov, Magnitogorsk .30
☐ 272 Sergei Klimentiev, Magnitogorsk .30
☐ 273 Yuri Kuznetsov, Magnitogorsk .50
☐ 274 Igor Knyazev, Spartak 1.00
☐ 275 Vladimir Tikhomirov, Spartak .30
☐ 276 Vladimir Repnev, CSKA Moscow .30
☐ 277 Alexandre Boikov, CSKA Moscow .50
☐ 278 Sergei Voronov, Magnitogorsk .30
☐ 279 Rustem Kamaletdinov, CSKA Moscow .30
☐ 280 Konstantin Molodtsov, CSKA Moscow .30
☐ 281 Andrei Frolkin, CSKA Moscow .30
☐ 282 Vladimir Terekhov, CSKA Moscow .30
☐ 283 Dmitri Klevakin, Spartak .50
☐ 284 Denis Denisov, Russia .50
☐ 285 Vladimir Korneev, Russia .50
☐ 286 Evgeni Muratov, Russia .50
☐ 287 Pavel Duma, Russia 1.00
☐ 288 Egor Shastin, Russia 1.00
☐ 289 Artem Chernov, Russia 1.00
☐ 290 Rail Rozakov, Russia 1.00
☐ 291 Alexander Chagodaev, Russia 1.00
☐ 292 Alexander Buturlin, Russia 1.00
☐ 293 Mikhail Yakubov, Russia 2.00
☐ 294 Alexei Petrov, Russia 1.00
☐ 295 Pavel Vorobiev, Russia 2.00
☐ 296 Ilya Kovalchuk, Russia 25.00
☐ 297 Vladimir Tikhomirov, Spartak .50
☐ 298 Igor Bakhmutov, Dynamo Moscow .50
☐ 299 Sergei Zolotov, Russia .50
☐ 300 Vadim Tarasov (G), Russia 2.00
☐ 301 Andrei Medvedev (G), Russia 3.00
☐ 302 Anton Volchenkov, Russia 4.00
☐ 303 Denis Grabeshkov, Russia .50
☐ 304 Andrei Shefer, Russia 1.00
☐ 305 Alexander Seluyanov, Russia .50
☐ 306 Ivan Nepryaev, Russia .50
☐ 307 Stanislav Chistov, Russia 12.00
☐ 308 Alexander Barkunov, Russia .50
☐ 309 Alexander Svitov, Russia 8.00
☐ 310 Igor Boriskov, CSKA Moscow .30
☐ 311 Alexander Zhdan, Russia .30
☐ 312 Ilia Nikulin, Dynamo Moscow .30
☐ 313 Mikhail Donika, Dynamo Moscow .30
☐ 314 Andrei Kuzmin, Dynamo Moscow .30
☐ 315 Alexei Smirnov, Dynamo Moscow 1.50
☐ 316 Vadim Brezgunov, CSKA Moscow .50
☐ 317 Mikhail Shtalenkov, Dynamo Moscow .50
☐ 318 Sergei Klimovich, Dynamo Moscow .50
☐ 319 Alexander Kharlamov, Dynamo Moscow .50
☐ 320 Dmitri Subbotin, Dynamo Moscow .30
☐ 321 Alexander Karpovtsev, Dynamo Moscow .50
☐ 322 Oleg Shevtsov, Dynamo Moscow .30
☐ 323 Evgeni Gribko, Dynamo Moscow .30
☐ 324 Denis Khlopotnov (G), CSKA Moscow .50
☐ 325 Pavel Boichenko, CSKA Moscow .30
☐ 326 Alexander Stepanov, Dynamo Moscow .30
☐ 327 Nikolai Ignatov, CSKA Moscow .30
☐ 328 Alexander Skoptsov, CSKA Moscow .30
☐ 329 Maxim Mikhailovsky, CSKA Moscow .50
☐ 330 Sergei Semin, CSKA Moscow .30
☐ 331 Pavel Trakhanov, CSKA Moscow .30
☐ 332 Dmitri Ryabikin, Russia .30
☐ 333 Ravil Yakubov, Russia .50
☐ 334 Pavel Datsyuk, Russia 20.00
☐ 335 Andrei Evstafiev, Russia .30
☐ 336 Andrei Razin, Russia .30
☐ 337 Denis Afinogenov, Russia .30
☐ 338 Oleg Orekhovsky, Russia .30
☐ 339 Ilya Gorbushin, Russia .30
☐ 340 Victor Chistov, Russia .30
☐ 341 Valeri Oleinik, Lipetsk .30
☐ 342 Sergei Shumikhin, Lipetsk .30
☐ 343 Oleg Romashko, Lipetsk .30
☐ 344 Yuri Bogusevich, Lipetsk .30
☐ 345 Nikolai Koptin, Lipetsk .30
☐ 346 Vladislav Pustovalov, Lipetsk .30
☐ 347 Andrei Gavrilin, Lipetsk .30
☐ 348 Dmitri Chikin, Lipetsk .30
☐ 349 Evgeni Letov, Lipetsk .30
☐ 350 Vadim Navrotskin, Lipetsk .30
☐ 351 Vitali Chumichev, Lipetsk .30
☐ 352 Sergei Mozyakin, CSKA Moscow .30
☐ 353 Alexei Simakov, Energiya .30
☐ 354 Vadim Gusev, Energiya .30
☐ 355 Sergei Kutyavin, Energiya .30
☐ 356 Lev Trifonov, Energiya .30
☐ 357 Roman Oksiuta, Khimik Voskresensk .50
☐ 358 Alexei Chervyakov, Khimik Voskresensk .30
☐ 359 Sergei Erkovich, Lokomotive .30
☐ 360 Oleg Volkov, Lada .30
☐ 361 Sergei Gomolyako, Lada .30
☐ 362 Evgeni Bobariko, Spartak .30
☐ 363 Evgeni Bobariko, Torpedo NN .30
☐ 364 Igor Boldin, Spartak .30
☐ 365 Oleg Komissarov, Spartak .30
☐ 366 Yuri Zlov, Soviet Wings .30
☐ 367 Andrei Pchelyakov, Severstal .30
☐ 368 Oleg Boltunov, Severstal .30
☐ 369 Nikolai Babenko, Severstal .30
☐ 370 Igor Varitskin, Severstal .30
☐ 371 Andrei Rasolko, Severstal .30
☐ 372 Dmitri Denisov, Severstal .30
☐ 373 Konstantin Maslyukov, Severstal .30
☐ 374 Vadim Epantchinsev, Severstal .50
☐ 375 Alexei Krivchenkov, Severstal .30
☐ 376 Maxim Sokolov, Severstal .30
☐ 377 Alexei Koznev, Severstal .30
☐ 378 Evgeni Petrochinin, Severstal .30
☐ 379 Vladislav Luchkin, Severstal .30
☐ 380 Artur Oktyabriev, Severstal .30
☐ 381 Vladimir Kopat, Severstal .30
☐ 382 Vladimir Kochin, Severstal .30
☐ 383 Igor Emeleev, CSKA Moscow .30
☐ 384 Sergei Shitkovski, Severstal .30
☐ 385 Andrei Kozrev, Severstal .30
☐ 386 Alexander Smagin, Neftikhimik .30
☐ 387 Rafik Yakubov, Neftikhimik .30
☐ 388 Ildar Mukhometov, Neftikhimik 1.00
☐ 389 Ivan Tkachenko, Neftikhimik .30
☐ 390 Evgeni Akhmetov, Neftikhimik .30
☐ 391 Vitali Lyutkevich, Neftikhimik .30
☐ 392 Alexander Vinogradov, Vityaz .30
☐ 393 Evgeni Artyukhin, Vityaz .30
☐ 394 Andrei Trefilov (G), Neftikhimik .50

2000 - 01 MIR FETISOV FAREWELL

NHL stars and prospects sometimes sell at a premium (usually $1-2).

Complete Set (41 cards): 25.00

Description	Mir
☐ 1 Alexander Korolyuk	.50
☐ 2 Pavel Bure	2.00
☐ 3 Aleksey Morozov	.50
☐ 4 Viktor Kozlov	.50
☐ 5 Sergei Makarov	1.00
☐ 6 Valeri Kamensky	.50
☐ 7 Maxim Afinogenov	1.00
☐ 8 Viacheslav Fetisov	1.50
☐ 9 Maxim Sokolov	.50
☐ 10 Vladimir Malakhov	.50
☐ 11 Alexei Yashin	1.50
☐ 12 Sergei Vyshedkevich	.50
☐ 13 Oleg Tverdovsky	.50
☐ 14 Sergei Brylin	.50
☐ 15 Vladimir Krutov	.50
☐ 16 Gennady Tsycankov	.50
☐ 17 Igor Podomatski	.50
☐ 18 Vitaly Vishnevski	.50
☐ 19 Sergei Nemchinov	.50
☐ 20 Danny Markov	.50
☐ 21 Alexander Kharitonov	.50
☐ 22 Vyacheslav Bykov	.50
☐ 23 Bob Carpenter	.50
☐ 24 Scott Stevens	1.00
☐ 25 Ken Daneyko	.50
☐ 26 Jari Kurri	2.50
☐ 27 Vyacheslav Kozlov	.50
☐ 28 Anders Eriksson	.50
☐ 29 Darius Kasparaitis	.50
☐ 30 Doug Brown	.50
☐ 31 Ilkka Sinisalo	.50
☐ 32 Valeri Shiryev	.50
☐ 33 Martin Brodeur	4.00
☐ 34 Christian Ruuttu	.50
☐ 35 Randy McKay	.50
☐ 36 Dzhino Odzhik	.50
☐ 37 Igor Larionov	1.50
☐ 38 Martin Lapointe	1.00
☐ 39 Larry Robinson	1.50
☐ 40 Viktor Tikhonov	.50
☐ 41 Scotty Bowman	1.50

2000 - 01 NORTEL NETWORKS

These cards were issued at the 2001 All-Star FANtasy in sheets of six cards each.

Complete Set (12 cards): 25.00

Description	Nortel
☐ 1 Jaromir Jagr, Pitt.	3.00
☐ 2 Peter Forsberg, Colo.	4.00
☐ 3 Pavel Bure, Flor.	2.00
☐ 4 Nicklas Lidström, Detr.	1.50
☐ 5 Dominik Hasek (G), Buff.	3.00
☐ 6 Sandis Ozolinsh, Caro.	1.00
☐ 7 Paul Kariya, Anah.	4.00
☐ 8 Joe Sakic, Colo.	4.50
☐ 9 Theoren Fleury, NYRa.	1.50
☐ 10 Raymond Bourque, Colo.	3.50
☐ 11 Patrick Roy (G), Colo.	9.00
☐ 12 Chris Pronger, SLou.	1.50

2000 - 01 O-PEE-CHEE

Please see 2000 - 01 Topps & O-Pee-Chee.

2000 - 01 OFS

NHL stars and prospects sometimes sell at a premium (usually $1-2).

Complete Set (421 cards): 60.00
Common Player: .30

Description	OFS
☐ 1 Team Logo, Ceske Budejovice	.30
☐ 2 Jaroslav Liska, Ceske Budejovice	.30
☐ 3 Jaroslav Parizek, Ceske Budejovice	.30
☐ 4 Jan Tlacil, Ceske Budejovice	.30
☐ 5 Jaroslav Pouzar, Ceske Budejovice	.50
☐ 6 Michal Marik, Ceske Budejovice	.30
☐ 7 Ivo Capek, Ceske Budejovice	.30
☐ 8 Radek Martinek, Ceske Budejovice	.50
☐ 9 Rudolf Suchanek, Ceske Budejovice	.30
☐ 10 Stanislav Jasecko, Ceske Budejovice	.30
☐ 11 Pavel Mojzis, Ceske Budejovice	.30
☐ 12 Vaclav Benak, Ceske Budejovice	.30
☐ 13 Ladislav Cierny, Ceske Budejovice	.30
☐ 14 Josef Jindra, Ceske Budejovice	.30
☐ 15 Vaclav Kral, Ceske Budejovice	.30
☐ 16 Filip Turek, Ceske Budejovice	.30
☐ 17 Lubos Rob, Ceske Budejovice	.30
☐ 18 Radek Belohlav, Ceske Budejovice	.30
☐ 19 Ales Kotalik, Ceske Budejovice	5.00
☐ 20 Kamil Brabenec, Ceske Budejovice	.30
☐ 21 Jiri Simanek, Ceske Budejovice	.30
☐ 22 Martin Strba, Ceske Budejovice	.30
☐ 23 Petr Sailer, Ceske Budejovice	.30
☐ 24 Milan Filipi, Ceske Budejovice	.30
☐ 25 Jiri Broz, Ceske Budejovice	.30
☐ 26 Jiri Novotny, Ceske Budejovice	8.00
☐ 27 Michal Vondrka, Ceske Budejovice	.30
☐ 28 Team Logo, Pardubice	.30
☐ 29 Josef Palecek, Pardubice	.30
☐ 30 Petr Hemsky, Pardubice	.30
☐ 31 Libor Barta, Pardubice	.30
☐ 32 Adam Svoboda, Pardubice	.30
☐ 33 Martin Barek, Pardubice	.30
☐ 34 Ales Pisa, Pardubice	.50
☐ 35 Jiri Malinsky, Pardubice	.30
☐ 36 Petr Jancarik, Pardubice	.30
☐ 37 Miroslav Duben, Pardubice	.30
☐ 38 Tomas Pacal, Pardubice	.30
☐ 39 Michal Divisek, Pardubice	.30
☐ 40 Andrej Novotny, Pardubice	.30
☐ 41 Petr Mudroch, Pardubice	.30
☐ 42 Otakar Janecky, Pardubice	.30
☐ 43 Ladislav Lubina, Pardubice	.30
☐ 44 Tomas Blazek, Pardubice	.50
☐ 45 Jaroslav Kudma, Pardubice	.30
☐ 46 Michal Mikeska, Pardubice	.30
☐ 47 Stanislav Prochazka, Pardubice	.30
☐ 48 Michal Tvrdik, Pardubice	.30
☐ 49 Martin Filip, Pardubice	.30
☐ 50 Martin Koudelka, Pardubice	.30
☐ 51 Pavel Kabrt, Pardubice	.30
☐ 52 Petr Sykora, Pardubice	.30
☐ 53 Tomas Rolinek, Pardubice	.30
☐ 54 Jan Kolar, Pardubice	.30
☐ 55 Team Logo, Plzen	.30
☐ 56 Marek Sykora, Plzen	.30
☐ 57 Dusan Salficky (G), Plzen	1.00
☐ 58 Petr Kus, Plzen	.30
☐ 59 Josef Reznicek, Plzen	.30
☐ 60 Martin Cech, Plzen	.30
☐ 61 Ivan Vlcek, Plzen	.30
☐ 62 Jiri Hanzlik, Plzen	.30
☐ 63 Jaroslav Spelda, Plzen	.30
☐ 64 Zdenek Touzimsky, Plzen	.30
☐ 65 Jiri Dobrovolny, Plzen	.30
☐ 66 Jan Choteborsky, Plzen	.30
☐ 67 Pavel Vostrak, Plzen	.30
☐ 68 Petr Korinek, Plzen	.30
☐ 69 Milan Volak, Plzen	.30
☐ 70 Michal Straka, Plzen	.30
☐ 71 David Pospisil, Plzen	.30
☐ 72 Josef Straka, Plzen	.30
☐ 73 Milan Antos, Plzen	.30
☐ 74 Andrej Nedorost, Plzen	.50
☐ 75 Vaclav Eiselt, Plzen	.30
☐ 76 Jiri Jelen, Plzen	.30
☐ 77 Michal Dvorak, Plzen	.30
☐ 78 Jiri Zurek, Plzen	.30
☐ 79 Dusan Andrasovsky, Plzen	.30
☐ 80 Team Logo, Slavia Praha	.30
☐ 81 Jaromir Sindel, Slavia Praha	.30
☐ 82 Ondrej Weissmann, Slavia Praha	.30
☐ 83 Ladislav Blazek, Slavia Praha	.30
☐ 84 Roman Malek, Slavia Praha	.30
☐ 85 Petr Kadlek, Slavia Praha	.30
☐ 86 Jan Novak, Slavia Praha	.30
☐ 87 Angel Krstev, Slavia Praha	.30
☐ 88 Jan Snopek, Slavia Praha	.30
☐ 89 Jan Kloboucek, Slavia Praha	.30
☐ 90 Jan Hejda, Slavia Praha	.30
☐ 91 Petr Martinek, Slavia Praha	.30
☐ 92 Jan Slavik, Slavia Praha	.30
☐ 93 Daniel Branda, Slavia Praha	.30
☐ 94 Jan Alinc, Slavia Praha	.30
☐ 95 Viktor Hubl, Slavia Praha	.30
☐ 96 Jan Kopecky, Slavia Praha	.30
☐ 97 Jan Bohac, Slavia Praha	.30
☐ 98 Zdenek Skorepa, Slavia Praha	.30
☐ 99 Michal Sup, Slavia Praha	.30
☐ 100 Radek Matejovsky, Slavia Praha	.30
☐ 101 Robin Bacul, Slavia Praha	.30
☐ 102 Leos Cermak, Slavia Praha	.30
☐ 103 Petr Jira, Slavia Praha	.30
☐ 104 Marek Tomica, Slavia Praha	.30
☐ 105 Petr Hrbek, Slavia Praha	.30
☐ 106 Team Logo, Kladno	.30
☐ 107 Eduard Novak, Kladno	.30
☐ 108 Petr Fiala, Kladno	.30
☐ 109 Lubos Horcicka, Kladno	.30
☐ 110 Marek Pinc, Kladno	.30
☐ 111 Jan Pospisil, Kladno	.30
☐ 112 Jan Krulis, Kladno	.30
☐ 113 Michal Madl, Kladno	.30
☐ 114 Ondrej Kriz, Kladno	.30
☐ 115 Jan Bohacek, Kladno	.30
☐ 116 David Hajek, Kladno	.30
☐ 117 Jan Dlouhy, Kladno	.30
☐ 118 Martin Taborsky, Kladno	.30
☐ 119 Jiri Kames, Kladno	.30
☐ 120 Ladislav Svoboda, Kladno	.30
☐ 121 Pavel Geffert, Kladno	.30
☐ 122 Tomas Horna, Kladno	.30
☐ 123 Jiri Holsan, Kladno	.30
☐ 124 Radek Gardon, Kladno	.30
☐ 125 Ladislav Vlcek, Kladno	.30
☐ 126 Jozef Voskar, Kladno	.30
☐ 127 Tomas Klimt, Kladno	.50
☐ 128 Premysl Sedlak, Kladno	.30
☐ 129 Tomas Plekanec, Kladno	.30

130 Michal Havel, Kladno	.30
131 Vaclav Skuhravy, Kladno	.30
132 Team Logo, Litvinov	.30
133 Vaclav Sykora, Litvinov	.30
134 Otakar Vejvoda, Litvinov	.30
135 Zdenek Orct, Litvinov	.30
136 Michal Podolka, Litvinov	.30
137 Angel Nikolov, Litvinov	.30
138 Karel Pilar, Litvinov	.50
139 Radek Mrazek, Litvinov	.30
140 Marek Cernosek, Litvinov	.30
141 Vladimir Gyna, Litvinov	.30
142 Martin Tupa, Litvinov	.30
143 Jan Hranac, Litvinov	.30
144 Petr Suchy, Litvinov	.30
145 Robert Reichel, Litvinov	1.50
146 Petr Rosol, Litvinov	.30
147 Vojtech Kubincak, Litvinov	.30
148 Kamil Piros, Litvinov	.50
149 Jindrich Kotrla, Litvinov	.30
150 Vesa Karjalainen, Litvinov	.30
151 Robert Kysela, Litvinov	.30
152 Stanislav Stavensky, Litvinov	.30
153 Tomas Martinec, Litvinov	.30
154 Zdenek Zak, Litvinov	.30
155 Martin Tvrznik, Litvinov	.30
156 Lukas Bednarik, Litvinov	.30
157 Team Logo, Karlovy Vary	.30
158 Radim Rulik, Karlovy Vary	.30
159 Martin Pesout, Karlovy Vary	.30
160 Petr Franek, Karlovy Vary	.30
161 Zdenek Smid, Karlovy Vary	.30
162 Pavel Csipka, Karlovy Vary	.30
163 Libor Prochazka, Karlovy Vary	.50
164 Robert Kantor, Karlovy Vary	.30
165 Jiri Polak, Karlovy Vary	.30
166 Normunds Sejejs, Karlovy Vary	.30
167 Roman Prosek, Karlovy Vary	.30
168 Roman Zak, Karlovy Vary	.30
169 Ivan Puncochar, Karlovy Vary	.30
170 Petr Puncochar, Karlovy Vary	.30
171 Jakub Grof, Karlovy Vary	.30
172 Jaromir Kverka, Karlovy Vary	.30
173 Tomas Chlubna, Karlovy Vary	.30
174 Radek Prochazka, Karlovy Vary	.30
175 David Hruska, Karlovy Vary	.30
176 Robert Tomik, Karlovy Vary	.30
177 Pavel Kasparik, Karlovy Vary	.30
178 Martin Rousek, Karlovy Vary	.30
179 Jaroslav Kalla, Karlovy Vary	.30
180 Petr Bohunicky, Karlovy Vary	.30
181 Jan Kostal, Karlovy Vary	.30
182 Petr Domin, Karlovy Vary	.30
183 Petr Sinagl, Karlovy Vary	.30
184 Team Logo, Znojmo	.30
185 Milan Chalupa, Znojmo	.30
186 Pavel Pazourek, Znojmo	.30
187 Oldrich Svoboda, Znojmo	.30
188 Ladislav Kudrna, Znojmo	.30
189 Miloslav Bahensky, Znojmo	.30
190 Tomas Jakes, Znojmo	.30
191 Jiri Hes, Znojmo	.30
192 Pavel Kumstat, Znojmo	.30
193 Karel Soudek, Znojmo	.30
194 Pavol Valko, Znojmo	.30
195 David Havir, Znojmo	.30
196 David Petlak, Znojmo	.30
197 Vladimir Holik, Znojmo	.30
198 Peter Pucher, Znojmo	.30
199 Marek Uram, Znojmo	.30
200 Karel Plasek, Znojmo	.30
201 Zbynek Marak, Znojmo	.30
202 Milan Prochazka, Znojmo	.30
203 Patrik Fink, Znojmo	.30
204 David Pazourek, Znojmo	.30
205 Marek Vorel, Znojmo	.30
206 Radek Haman, Znojmo	.30
207 Petr Lipina, Znojmo	.30
208 Petr Kumstat, Znojmo	.30
209 Team Logo, Trinec	.30
210 Vladimir Vujtek, Trinec	.30
211 Ales Mach, Trinec	.30
212 Marek Novotny, Trinec	.30
213 Vlastimil Lakosil, Trinec	.30
214 Mario Cartelli, Trinec	.30
215 Vladimir Vlk, Trinec	.30
216 Jiri Kuntos, Trinec	.30
217 Petr Gregorek, Trinec	.30
218 Robert Prochazka, Trinec	.30
219 Ondrej Zetek, Trinec	.30
220 David Nosek, Trinec	.30
221 Tomas Houdek, Trinec	.30
222 Tomas Harant, Trinec	.30
223 Richard Kral, Trinec	.30
224 Viktor Ujcik, Trinec	.50
225 Jozef Dano, Trinec	.30
226 Richard Kapus, Trinec	.50
227 Pavel Janku, Trinec	.30
228 Marek Zadina, Trinec	.30
229 Branislav Janos, Trinec	.30
230 Tomas Nemcicky, Trinec	.30
231 Patrik Moskal, Trinec	.30
232 David Appel, Trinec	.30
233 Jan Marek, Trinec	.30
234 Jiri Hasek, Trinec	.30
235 Team Logo, Vitkovice	.30
236 Alois Hadamczik, Vitkovice	.30
237 Kamil Konecny, Vitkovice	.30
238 Mojmir Trlicik, Vitkovice	.30
239 Martin Prusek, Vitkovice	1.50
240 Jiri Trvaj, Vitkovice	.30
241 Lukas Smolka, Vitkovice	.30
242 Vitezslav Skuta, Vitkovice	.30
243 Dmitri Jerofejev, Vitkovice	.30
244 Daniel Kapotocny, Vitkovice	.30
245 Petr Jurecka, Vitkovice	.30
246 Radek Philipp, Vitkovice	.30
247 Lukas Zatopek, Vitkovice	.30
248 Daniel Seman, Vitkovice	.30
249 Jan Vytisk, Vitkovice	.30
250 David Moravec, Vitkovice	.50
251 Martin Prochazka, Vitkovice	.50
252 Ivan Padelek, Vitkovice	.30
253 Josef Straub, Vitkovice	.30
254 Roman Kadera, Vitkovice	.30
255 Marek Ivan, Vitkovice	.30
256 Zdenek Pavelek, Vitkovice	.30
257 Martin Tomasek, Vitkovice	.30
258 Pavel Selingr, Vitkovice	.30
259 Jan Pleva, Vitkovice	.30
260 Ales Padelek, Vitkovice	.30
261 Team Logo, Havirov	.30
262 Ivo Pestuka, Havirov	.30
263 Jiri Reznar, Havirov	.30
264 Radovan Biegl, Havirov	.30
265 Radek Masny, Havirov	.30
266 Michael Vyhlidal, Havirov	.30
267 Miroslav Javin, Havirov	.30
268 Richard Pavlikovsky, Havirov	.30
269 Petr Pavlas, Havirov	.30
270 Patrik Rimmel, Havirov	.30
271 Ales Tomasek, Havirov	.30
272 Petr Suchanek, Havirov	.30
273 Tomas Srsen, Havirov	.30
274 Petr Folta, Havirov	.30
275 Libor Pivko, Havirov	.30
276 Daniel Bohac, Havirov	.30
277 Roman Horak, Havirov	.30
278 Jan Peterek, Havirov	.30
279 Marek Melenovsky, Havirov	.30
280 Pavel Zdrahal, Havirov	.30
281 Roman Kontsek, Havirov	.30
282 Michal Cech, Havirov	.30
283 Tomas Sykora, Havirov	.30
284 Martin Streit, Havirov	.30
285 Milos Melicherik, Havirov	.30
286 Team Logo, Sparta Praha	.30
287 Milos Riha, Sparta Praha	.30
288 Frantisek Vyborny, Sparta Praha	.30
289 Pavel Hynek, Sparta Praha	.30
290 Petr Briza, Sparta Praha	.30
291 Petr Prikryl, Sparta Praha	.30
292 Tomas Duba, Sparta Praha	3.00
293 Libor Zabransky, Sparta Praha	.50
294 Vlastimil Kroupa, Sparta Praha	.50
295 Frantisek Ptacek, Sparta Praha	.30
296 Michal Dobron, Sparta Praha	.30
297 Pavel Srek, Sparta Praha	.30
298 Jaroslav Nedved, Sparta Praha	.30
299 Martin Holy, Sparta Praha	.30
300 Miha Rebolj, Sparta Praha	.30
301 Jan Hanzlik, Sparta Praha	.30
302 Vladimir Vujtek, Sparta Praha	.30
303 Jaroslav Hlinka, Sparta Praha	.30
304 Martin Chabada, Sparta Praha	.30
305 Ondrej Kratena, Sparta Praha	.30
306 Michal Bros, Sparta Praha	.30
307 Patrik Martinec, Sparta Praha	.30
308 Richard Zemlicka, Sparta Praha	.30
309 Jiri Zelenka, Sparta Praha	.30
310 Vaclav Novak, Sparta Praha	.30
311 Petr Havelka, Sparta Praha	.30
312 Michal Sivek, Sparta Praha	2.00
313 Petr Hrbek, Sparta Praha	.30
314 Radek Duda, Sparta Praha	.30
315 Josef Slanec, Sparta Praha	.30
316 Petr Kanko, Sparta Praha	.30
317 Team Logo, Vsetin	.30
318 Zdislav Tabara, Vsetin	.30
319 Miroslav Venkrbec, Vsetin	.30
320 Jaroslav Kames, Vsetin	.30
321 Ivo Pesat, Vsetin	.30
322 Lukas Plsek, Vsetin	.30
323 Jan Srdinko, Vsetin	.30
324 Milan Nedoma, Vsetin	.30
325 Martin Strbak, Vsetin	.30
326 Radim Tesarik, Vsetin	.30
327 Pavel Zubicek, Vsetin	.30
328 Alexei Jaskin, Vsetin	.30
329 Petr Kubos, Vsetin	.30
330 Zbynek Spitzer, Vsetin	.30
331 Michal Safarik, Vsetin	.30
332 Pavel Augusta, Vsetin	.30
333 Jan Pardavy, Vsetin	.30
334 Jiri Dopita, Vsetin	.50
335 Jan Tomajko, Vsetin	.30
336 Roman Stantien, Vsetin	.30
337 Jan Sochor, Vsetin	.30
338 Martin Paroulek, Vsetin	.30
339 Jan Lipiansky, Vsetin	.30
340 Jiri Hudler, Vsetin	4.00
341 Ondrej Vesely, Vsetin	.30
342 Jiri Jantovsky, Vsetin	.30
343 Petr Zajgla, Vsetin	.30
344 Tomas Demel, Vsetin	.30
345 Petr Vampola, Vsetin	.30
346 Team Logo, Zlin	.30
347 Antonin Stavjana, Zlin	.30
348 Zdenek Venera, Zlin	.30
349 Vladimir Hudacek (G), Zlin	.30
350 Richard Hrazdira, Zlin	.30
351 Petr Tucek, Zlin	.30
352 Tomas Zizka, Zlin	.30
353 Jiri Marusak, Zlin	.30
354 Martin Hamrlik, Zlin	.30
355 Patrik Luza, Zlin	.30
356 Rostislav Malena, Zlin	.30
357 Jan Homer, Zlin	.30
358 Lukas Zib, Zlin	.30
359 Boris Zabka, Zlin	.30
360 Miroslav Okal, Zlin	.30
361 Petr Cajanek, Zlin	.50
362 Jaroslav Belastik, Zlin	.30
363 Petr Vala, Zlin	.30
364 Martin Ambruz, Zlin	.30
365 Petr Leska, Zlin	.30
366 Miroslav Barus, Zlin	.30
367 Martin Kotasek, Zlin	.30
368 Lubomir Korhon, Zlin	.30
369 Ivan Rachunek, Zlin	.30
370 Radovan Somik, Zlin	.30
371 Filip Cech, Zlin	.30
372 Martin Jenacek, Zlin	.30
373 Pavel Mojzis, Zlin	.30
374 Milan Navratil, Zlin	.30
375 Michal Safarik, Zlin	.30
376 Miroslav Blatak, Zlin	.30
377 Team Logo, Jagr Team	.30
378 Roman Turek (G), Jagr Team	2.00
379 Milan Hnilicka (G), Jagr Team	1.00
380 Tomas Kaberle, Jagr Team	1.50
381 Frantisek Kaberle, Jagr Team	.30
382 Roman Hamrlik, Jagr Team	1.00
383 Pavel Kubina, Jagr Team	.50
384 Jaromir Jagr, Jagr Team	5.00
385 Patrik Elias, Jagr Team	4.00
386 Milan Hejduk, Jagr Team	4.00
387 Radek Dvorak, Jagr Team	1.00
388 Petr Nedved, Jagr Team	1.50
389 Vaclav Prospal, Jagr Team	1.50
390 Pavel Patera, Jagr Team	.50
391 Petr Sykora, Jagr Team	.30
392 Vaclav Varada, Jagr Team	.50
393 Martin Straka, Jagr Team	1.50
394 Jan Hrdina, Jagr Team	1.00
395 David Volek, Jagr Team	.50
396 Tomas Vlasak, Jagr Team	.50
397 Michal Rozsival, Jagr Team	.50
398 Team Logo, Ruzicka Team	.30
399 Ladislav Blazek, Ruzicka Team	.30
400 Miloslav Horava, Ruzicka Team	.30
401 Frantisek Kucera, Ruzicka Team	.30
402 Lubomir Sekeras, Ruzicka Team	.50
403 Petr Kadlec, Ruzicka Team	.30
404 Jaroslav Spacek, Ruzicka Team	.50
405 Frantisek Prochazka, Ruzicka Team	.30
406 Antonin Stavjana, Ruzicka Team	.30
407 Vladimir Ruzicka, Ruzicka Team	1.00
408 Petr Rosol, Ruzicka Team	.30
409 Robert Reichel, Ruzicka Team	1.50
410 Martin Rucinsky, Ruzicka Team	1.00
411 Josef Beranek, Ruzicka Team	.50
412 Viktor Ujcik, Ruzicka Team	.50
413 Michal Sup, Ruzicka Team	.30
414 Ivo Prorok, Ruzicka Team	.30
415 Zdeno Ciger, Ruzicka Team	.50
416 Jiri Hrdina, Ruzicka Team	.50
417 J. Jagr / V. Ruzicka	3.00
418 Checklist	.25
419 Checklist	.25
420 Checklist	.25
421 Checklist	.25

STAR

There are three versions: the Emerald card (1:2 packs), the Violet card (1:3 packs) and the Pink card (1:6 packs).

Complete Set (36 cards):	65.00	35.00	15.00
Description	Pink	Vio.	Eme.
1 Jaroslav Kames, Vsetin	2.00	1.00	.50
2 Jiri Dopita, Vsetin	2.00	1.50	1.00
3 Jan Pardavy, Vsetin	2.00	1.00	.50
4 Vladimir Hudacek (G), Zlin	2.00	1.00	.50
5 Petr Cajanek, Zlin	2.00	1.00	.50
6 Richard Hrazdira, Zlin	2.00	1.00	.50
7 Petr Briza, Sparta Praha	2.00	1.00	.50
8 Jiri Zelenka, Sparta Praha	2.00	1.00	.50
9 R. Zemlicka, Sparta Praha	2.00	1.00	.50
10 Libor Barta, Pardubice	2.00	1.00	.50
11 Adam Svoboda, Pardubice	2.00	1.00	.50
12 Otakar Janecky, Pardubice	2.00	1.00	.50
13 V. Kral, Ceske Budejovice	2.00	1.00	.50
14 Suchanek, Ceske Budejovice	2.00	1.00	.50
15 M. Marik, Ceske Budejovice	2.00	1.00	.50
16 Dusan Salficky, Plzen	2.00	1.00	.50
17 Petr Korinek, Plzen	2.00	1.00	.50
18 Ivan Vlcek, Plzen	2.00	1.00	.50
19 Zdenek Orct, Litvinov	2.00	1.00	.50
20 Robert Reichel, Litvinov	4.50	3.50	2.50
21 Petr Franek, Karlovy Vary	2.00	1.00	.50
22 L. Prochazka, Karlovy Vary	2.00	1.00	.50
23 Vlastimil Lakosil, Trinec	2.00	1.00	.50
24 Richard Kral, Trinec	2.00	1.00	.50
25 Viktor Ujcik, Trinec	2.00	1.50	1.00
26 Martin Prusek, Vitkovice	4.50	3.50	2.50
27 Martin Prochazka, Vitkovice	2.00	1.00	.50
28 Josef Straub, Vitkovice	2.00	1.00	.50
29 Radek Gardon, Kladno	2.00	1.00	.50
30 Lubos Horcicka, Kladno	2.00	1.00	.50
31 Tomas Srsen, Havirov	2.00	1.00	.50
32 Radovan Biegl, Havirov	2.00	1.00	.50
33 Oldrich Svoboda, Znojmo	2.00	1.00	.50
34 Marek Uram, Znojmo	2.00	1.00	.50
35 L. Blazek, Slavia Praha	2.00	1.00	.50
36 Roman Malek, Slavia Praha	2.00	1.00	.50

2000 - 01 PACIFIC

This series was issued in August 2000. All 450 base cards have a Copper parallel (#/40), a Premiere Date parallel (#/40), a Gold (#/50) and an Ice Blue parallel (#/45). Copper and Premiere Date parallels are all priced similarly below. Players (1-430) were sorted by teams in alphabetical order.

Complete Set (450 cards):	2,000	40.00
Common Player:	8.00	.20
Description	G50	Pacific
1 Maxim Balmochnykh	8.00	.20
2 Matt Cullen	10.00	.20
3 Ted Donato	8.00	.20
4 Guy Hebert (G)	10.00	.20
5 Paul Kariya	60.00	1.00
6 Ladislav Kohn	8.00	.20
7 Marty McInnis	8.00	.20
8 Kip Miller	8.00	.20
9 Dominic Roussel (G)	8.00	.20
10 Steve Rucchin	10.00	.20
11 Teemu Selänne	35.00	.50
12 Oleg Tverdovsky	8.00	.20
13 Vitaly Vishnevski	10.00	.20
14 Donald Audette	15.00	.20
15 Andrew Brunette	8.00	.20
16 Petr Buzek	8.00	.20
17 Hnat Domenichelli	8.00	.20
18 Ray Ferraro	8.00	.20
19 Stephen Guolla	8.00	.20
20 Denny Lambert	8.00	.20
22 Mike Stapleton	10.00	.20
21 Damian Rhodes (G)	8.00	.20
24 Per Svartvadet	10.00	.20
23 Patrik Stefan	8.00	.20
25 Dean Sylvester	8.00	.20
26 Yannick Tremblay	8.00	.20
27 B.Adams RC / Fankhouser	**15.00**	**.50**
28 Vasiljevs RC / Vyshedkevich RC	**20.00**	**1.00**
29 Jason Allison	25.00	.50
30 Per Axelsson	8.00	.20
31 Anson Carter	15.00	.20
32 Byron Dafoe (G)	15.00	.20
33 Hal Gill	8.00	.20
34 John Grahame (G)	10.00	.20

35 Stephen Heinze	8.00	.20
36 Joe Hulbig	8.00	.20
37 Mike Knuble	8.00	.20
38 Kyle McLaren	10.00	.20
39 Eric Nickulas RC	**10.00**	**.50**
40 Brian Rolston	10.00	.20
41 Sergei Samsonov	25.00	.50
42 André Savage	8.00	.20
43 Joe Thornton	50.00	1.00
44 Darren Van Impe	8.00	.20
45 J. Aitken / N. Boynton	10.00	.20
46 Maxim Afinogenov	15.00	.20
47 Stu Barnes	8.00	.20
48 Martin Biron (G)	20.00	.20
49 Curtis Brown	8.00	.20
50 Doug Gilmour	25.00	.50
51 Chris Gratton	10.00	.20
52 Dominik Hasek (G)	45.00	1.00
53 Michael Peca	15.00	.20
54 Erik Rasmussen	10.00	.20
55 Rob Ray	10.00	.20
56 Geoff Sanderson	10.00	.20
57 Miroslav Satan	10.00	.20
58 Vladimir Tsyplakov	8.00	.20
59 Vaclav Varada	8.00	.20
60 Jason Woolley	8.00	.20
61 Fred Brathwaite (G)	10.00	.20
62 Valeri Bure	10.00	.20
63 Bobby Dollas	8.00	.20
64 J-S Giguère (G)	35.00	.50
65 Phil Housley	10.00	.20
66 Jarome Iginla	35.00	.50
67 Andreas Johansson	10.00	.20
68 Sergei Krivokrasov	8.00	.20
69 Bill Lindsay	8.00	.20
70 Derek Morris	10.00	.20
72 Oleg Saprykin	8.00	.20
71 Andrei Nazarov	10.00	.20
73 Marc Savard	10.00	.20
74 Jeff Shantz	8.00	.20
75 Cory Stillman	10.00	.20
76 Jason Wiemer	8.00	.20
77 C. Clark / S. Varlamov	8.00	.20
78 Bates Battaglia	10.00	.20
79 Rod Brind'Amour	10.00	.20
80 Paul Coffey	25.00	.50
81 Ron Francis	25.00	.50
82 Sean Hill	8.00	.20
83 Arturs Irbe (G)	15.00	.20
84 Sami Kapanen	10.00	.20
85 Dave Karpa	8.00	.20
86 Andrei Kovalenko	8.00	.20
87 Robert Kron	8.00	.20
88 Jeff O'Neill	15.00	.20
89 Gary Roberts	15.00	.20
90 David Tanabe	8.00	.20
91 Tommy Westlund	8.00	.20
92 Tony Amonte	25.00	.50
93 Éric Dazé	15.00	.20
94 Kevin Dean	8.00	.20
95 Michal Grosek	8.00	.20
96 Dean McAmmond	8.00	.20
97 Bryan McCabe	10.00	.20
98 Steven McCarthy	8.00	.20
99 Boris Mironov	8.00	.20
100 Michael Nylander	10.00	.20
101 Bob Probert	10.00	.20
102 Steve Sullivan	10.00	.20
103 Jocelyn Thibault (G)	15.00	.20
104 Ryan VandenBussche	8.00	.20
105 Alexei Zhamnov	10.00	.20
106 Dave Andreychuk	10.00	.20
107 Raymond Bourque	50.00	1.00
108 Adam Deadmarsh	10.00	.20
109 Marc Denis (G)	20.00	.20
110 Greg de Vries	8.00	.20
111 Chris Drury	25.00	.50
112 Adam Foote	10.00	.20
113 Peter Forsberg	60.00	1.00
114 Alexei Gusarov	8.00	.20
115 Milan Hejduk	35.00	.50
116 Éric Messier	8.00	.20
117 Sandis Ozolinsh	10.00	.20
118 Shjon Podein	10.00	.20
119 Dave Reid	8.00	.20
120 Patrick Roy (G)	135.00	3.00
121 Joe Sakic	70.00	1.50
122 Martin Skoula	10.00	.20
123 Alex Tanguay	25.00	.50
124 Stéphane Yelle	8.00	.20
125 Aubin RC / Nieminen RC	**25.00**	**2.00**
126 Ed Belfour (G)	45.00	1.00
127 Guy Carbonneau	10.00	.20
128 Sylvain Côté	8.00	.20
129 Manny Fernandez (G)	15.00	.20
130 Derian Hatcher	10.00	.20
131 Brett Hull	45.00	1.00
132 Mike Keane	8.00	.20
133 Jamie Langenbrunner	10.00	.20
134 Jere Lehtinen	10.00	.20
135 Dave Manson	8.00	.20
137 Mike Modano	10.00	.20
136 Richard Matvichuk	45.00	1.00
138 Brenden Morrow	10.00	.20
139 Joe Nieuwendyk	15.00	.20
140 Blake Sloan	8.00	.20
141 Darryl Sydor	10.00	.20
142 Scott Thornton	8.00	.20
142 Sergei Zubov	10.00	.20
144 Doug Brown	8.00	.20
145 Chris Chelios	25.00	.50
146 Kris Draper	10.00	.20
147 Sergei Fedorov	45.00	1.00
148 Tomas Holmström	10.00	.20
149 Vyacheslav Kozlov	10.00	.20
150 Darryl Laplante	8.00	.20
151 Martin Lapointe	15.00	.20
152 Igor Larionov	25.00	.50
153 Nicklas Lidström	25.00	.50
154 Kirk Maltby	10.00	.20
155 Darren McCarty	10.00	.20
156 Larry Murphy	10.00	.20
157 Chris Osgood (G)	25.00	.50
158 Brendan Shanahan	45.00	1.00
159 Pat Verbeek	10.00	.20
160 Jesse Wallin	8.00	.20
161 Ken Wregget (G)	10.00	.20
162 Steve Yzerman	105.00	2.00
163 Boyd Devereaux	10.00	.20
164 Jim Dowd	8.00	.20
165 Mike Grier	10.00	.20
166 Bill Guerin	15.00	.20
167 Roman Hamrlik	10.00	.20
168 Georges Laraque	8.00	.20
169 Todd Marchant	10.00	.20
170 Ethan Moreau	8.00	.20
171 Tom Poti	8.00	.20
172 Tommy Salo (G)	15.00	.20
173 Alexander Selivanov	8.00	.20
174 Ryan Smyth	20.00	.20
175 German Titov	8.00	.20
176 Doug Weight	25.00	.50
177 Pavel Bure	35.00	.50
178 Trevor Kidd (G)	10.00	.20
179 Viktor Kozlov	10.00	.20
180 Oleg Kvasha	8.00	.20
181 Paul Laus	8.00	.20
182 Scott Mellanby	10.00	.20
183 Rob Niedermayer	10.00	.20
184 Ivan Novoseltsev	8.00	.20
185 Mark Parrish	15.00	.20
186 Mikhail Shtalenkov	8.00	.20
187 Robert Svehla	10.00	.20
188 Mike Vernon (G)	15.00	.20
189 Ray Whitney	10.00	.20
190 Peter Worrell	10.00	.20
191 E. Boguniecki / B. Ference	10.00	.20
192 Aki Berg	8.00	.20
193 Rob Blake	25.00	.50
194 Kelly Buchberger	8.00	.20
195 Nelson Emerson	8.00	.20
196 Stéphane Fiset (G)	10.00	.20
197 Garry Galley	8.00	.20
198 Glen Murray	20.00	.20
199 Jan Nemecek	8.00	.20
200 Zigmund Palffy	25.00	.50
201 Luc Robitaille	35.00	.50
202 Bryan Smolinski	8.00	.20
203 Jamie Storr (G)	10.00	.20
204 Jozef Stümpel	10.00	.20
205 Patrice Brisebois	8.00	.20
206 Benoît Brunet	8.00	.20
207 Shayne Corson	10.00	.20
208 Jeff Hackett (G)	10.00	.20
209 Saku Koivu	50.00	.50
210 Trevor Linden	15.00	.20
211 Oleg Petrov	10.00	.20
212 Martin Rucinsky	10.00	.20
213 Brian Savage	10.00	.20
214 Sheldon Souray	8.00	.20
215 José Théodore (G)	50.00	1.00
216 Eric Weinrich	8.00	.20
217 Sergei Zhotlok	8.00	.20
218 Dainius Zubrus	10.00	.20
219 Sébastien Bordeleau	8.00	.20
220 Mike Dunham (G)	15.00	.20
221 Tom Fitzgerald	8.00	.20
222 Greg Johnson	8.00	.20
224 Craig Millar	15.00	.20
223 David Legwand	8.00	.20
225 Cliff Ronning	10.00	.20
226 Kimmo Timonen	8.00	.20
227 Tomas Vokoun (G)	10.00	.20
228 Scott Walker	10.00	.20
229 Boikov / Moro (RCs)	**10.00**	**.50**
230 Gosselin / C.Mason (RCs)	**15.00**	**.50**
231 Jason Arnott	20.00	.20
232 Martin Brodeur (G)	70.00	1.50
233 Patrik Elias	35.00	.50
234 Scott Gomez	15.00	.20
235 Bobby Holik	10.00	.20
236 Claude Lemieux	10.00	.20
237 John Madden	10.00	.20
238 Vladimir Malakhov	8.00	.20
239 Randy McKay	8.00	.20
240 Alexander Mogilny	20.00	.20
241 Scott Niedermayer	10.00	.20
242 Brian Rafalski	10.00	.20
243 Scott Stevens	15.00	.20
244 Petr Sykora	15.00	.20
245 Chris Terreri (G)	8.00	.20
246 Mitchell RC / White RC	**20.00**	**1.00**
247 Tim Connolly	15.00	.20
248 Mariusz Czerkawski	10.00	.20
249 Josh Green	8.00	.20
250 Brad Isbister	10.00	.20
251 Jason Krog	10.00	.20
252 Claude Lapointe	8.00	.20
253 Roberto Luongo (G)	35.00	.50
254 Petr Mika RC	**10.00**	**.50**
255 Dave Scatchard	8.00	.20
256 S. Valiquette (G) RC	**20.00**	**1.00**
257 Kevin Weekes (G)	10.00	.20
258 Alexandre Daigle	8.00	.20
259 Radek Dvorak	10.00	.20
260 Theoren Fleury	25.00	.50
261 Adam Graves	15.00	.20
262 Jan Hlavac	10.00	.20
263 Kim Johnsson	8.00	.20
264 Valeri Kamensky	10.00	.20
265 Brian Leetch	25.00	.50
266 John MacLean	8.00	.20
267 Kirk McLean (G)	10.00	.20
268 Petr Nedved	10.00	.20
269 Mike Richter (G)	20.00	.20
270 Mathieu Schneider	10.00	.20
271 Johan Witehall RC	**20.00**	**1.00**
272 Mike York	10.00	.20
273 Daniel Alfredsson	50.00	.50
274 Magnus Arvedson	8.00	.20
275 Tom Barrasso (G)	15.00	.20
276 Radek Bonk	10.00	.20
277 Mike Fisher	10.00	.20
278 Marian Hossa	45.00	1.00
279 Jani Hurme (G) RC	**30.00**	**1.50**
280 Joé Juneau	10.00	.20
281 Patrick Lalime (G)	25.00	.50
282 Grant Ledyard	8.00	.20
283 Shawn McEachern	10.00	.20
284 Chris Phillips	10.00	.20
286 Wade Redden	10.00	.20
285 Vaclav Prospal	10.00	.20
287 Sami Salo	8.00	.20
288 Alexei Yashin	25.00	.50
289 Jason York	8.00	.20
290 Rob Zamuner	10.00	.20
291 Goldmann RC / Schastlivy	**20.00**	**1.00**
292 Craig Berube	8.00	.20
293 Brian Boucher (G)	10.00	.20
294 Andy Delmore	10.00	.20
295 Éric Desjardins	10.00	.20
296 Simon Gagné	35.00	.50
297 Jody Hull	8.00	.20
298 Keith Jones	8.00	.20
299 Daymond Langkow	10.00	.20
300 John LeClair	35.00	.50
301 Eric Lindros	45.00	1.00
302 Kent Manderville	8.00	.20
303 Daniel McGillis	8.00	.20
304 Gino Odjick	8.00	.20
305 Keith Primeau	15.00	.20
306 Mark Recchi	15.00	.20
307 Chris Therien	8.00	.20
308 Rick Tocchet	10.00	.20
309 John Vanbiesbrouck (G)	20.00	.20
310 Valeri Zelepukin	8.00	.20
311 Sean Burke (G)	25.00	.50
312 Keith Carney	8.00	.20
313 Louie DeBrusk	8.00	.20
314 Shane Doan	10.00	.20
315 Dallas Drake	8.00	.20
316 Travis Green	10.00	.20
318 Trevor Letowski	15.00	.20
317 Nikolai Khabibulin (G)	8.00	.20
319 Jyrki Lumme	10.00	.20
320 Mikael Renberg	10.00	.20
321 Jeremy Roenick	35.00	.50
322 Keith Tkachuk	25.00	.50
323 W. Smith / R. Esche	10.00	.20
324 J-S Aubin (G)	10.00	.20
325 Matthew Barnaby	8.00	.20
326 Pat Falloon	8.00	.20
327 Jan Hrdina	10.00	.20
328 Jaromir Jagr	45.00	1.00
329 Darius Kasparaitis	10.00	.20
330 Alex Kovalev	25.00	.50
331 Robert Lang	10.00	.20
332 Janne Laukkanen	8.00	.20
333 Stephen Leach	8.00	.20
334 Aleksey Morozov	10.00	.20
335 Michal Rozsival	8.00	.20
336 Jiri Slegr	8.00	.20
337 Martin Straka	10.00	.20
338 Ron Tugnutt (G)	15.00	.20
339 Lubos Bartecko	8.00	.20
340 Marc Bergevin	8.00	.20
341 Pavol Demitra	15.00	.20
342 Mike Eastwood	8.00	.20
343 Dave Ellett	8.00	.20
344 Michal Handzus	10.00	.20
345 Jochen Hecht	10.00	.20
346 Al MacInnis	15.00	.20
347 Jamie McLennan (G)	8.00	.20
348 Tyson Nash	8.00	.20
350 Marty Reasoner	25.00	.50
349 Chris Pronger	10.00	.20
351 Stéphane Richer	10.00	.20
352 Roman Turek (G)	20.00	.20
352 Scott Young	10.00	.20
353 Pierre Turgeon	15.00	.20
355 Bekar RC / Nagy	**20.00**	**1.00**
356 Vincent Damphousse	25.00	.50
357 Jeff Friesen	10.00	.20
358 Todd Harvey	10.00	.20
359 Alexander Korolyuk	8.00	.20
360 Patrick Marleau	20.00	.20
361 Stéphane Matteau	8.00	.20
362 Evgeni Nabokov (G)	40.00	1.00
363 Owen Nolan	25.00	.50
364 Mike Ricci	10.00	.20
365 Steve Shields (G)	10.00	.20
366 Brad Stuart	15.00	.20
367 Marco Sturm	10.00	.20
368 Gary Suter	10.00	.20
369 Dan Cloutier (G)	15.00	.20
370 Stan Drulia	8.00	.20
371 Matt Elich RC	**20.00**	**1.00**
372 Brian Holzinger	8.00	.20
373 Mike Johnson	8.00	.20
374 Ryan Johnson	8.00	.20
375 Dieter Kochan (G) RC	**20.00**	**1.00**
377 Vincent Lecavalier	8.00	.20
376 Pavel Kubina	45.00	1.00
379 Wayne Primeau	10.00	.20
378 Fredrik Modin	8.00	.20
380 Cory Sarich	8.00	.20
381 Petr Svoboda	10.00	.20
382 Astashenko / Freadrich (RCs)	**10.00**	**.50**
383 Posmyk / Dwyer RC	**10.00**	**.50**
384 Nikolai Antropov	10.00	.20
385 Sergei Berezin	20.00	.20
386 Wendel Clark	35.00	.50
387 Tie Domi	10.00	.20
388 Gerald Diduck	8.00	.20
389 Jeff Farkas	15.00	.20
390 Glenn Healy (G)	10.00	.20
391 Jonas Höglund	8.00	.20
392 Curtis Joseph (G)	45.00	1.00
393 Tomas Kaberle	10.00	.20
394 Alexander Karpovtsev	8.00	.20
395 Dmitri Khristich	8.00	.20
396 Igor Korolev	8.00	.20
397 Yanic Perreault	10.00	.20
398 D.J. Smith	8.00	.20
399 Mats Sundin	45.00	1.00
400 Steve Thomas	10.00	.20
401 Darcy Tucker	10.00	.20
402 Dmitry Yushkevich	10.00	.20
403 Adrian Aucoin	8.00	.20
404 Todd Bertuzzi	50.00	1.00
405 Donald Brashear	10.00	.20
406 Andrew Cassels	10.00	.20
407 Harold Druken	10.00	.20
408 Ed Jovanovski	15.00	.20
409 Steve Kariya	10.00	.20
410 Trent Klatt	8.00	.20
412 Markus Näslund	45.00	1.00
411 Mark Messier	45.00	1.00
413 Mattias Öhlund	10.00	.20
414 Félix Potvin (G)	50.00	.50
415 Peter Schaefer	8.00	.20
416 Garth Snow (G)	10.00	.20
417 A. Michaud / J. Ruutu	8.00	.20
418 Peter Bondra	25.00	.50
419 Martin Brochu (G) RC	**20.00**	**1.00**
420 Jan Bulis	8.00	.20
421 Sergei Gonchar	10.00	.20
422 Jeff Halpern	10.00	.20

□□□□□	423 Calle Johansson	10.00	.20
□□□□□	424 Ken Klee	8.00	.20
□□□□□	425 Olaf Kölzig (G)	25.00	.50
□□□□□	426 Steve Konowalchuk	10.00	.20
□□□□□	427 Glen Metropolit	8.00	.20
□□□□□	428 Adam Oates	15.00	.20
□□□□□	429 Chris Simon	10.00	.20
□□□□□	430 Richard Zednik	15.00	.20
□□□□□	431 Jörgen Jönsson [Sweden]	8.00	.20
□□□□□	432 Teemu Selänne [Finland]	35.00	.50
□□□□□	433 Sami Kapanen [Finland]	10.00	.20
□□□□□	434 Peter Forsberg [Sweden]	60.00	1.00
□□□□□	435 Jere Lehtinen [Finland]	10.00	.20
□□□□□	436 Nicklas Lidström [Sweden]	25.00	.50
□□□□□	437 Janne Niinimaa [Finland]	10.00	.20
□□□□□	438 Tommy Salo (G) [Sweden]	15.00	.20
□□□□□	439 Saku Koivu [Finland]	50.00	.50
□□□□□	440 Patric Kjellberg [Sweden]	8.00	.20
□□□□□	441 Olli Jokinen [Finland]	10.00	.20
□□□□□	442 Kenny Jönsson [Sweden]	8.00	.20
□□□□□	443 Daniel Alfredsson [Sweden]	50.00	.50
□□□□□	444 Andreas Dackell [Sweden]	8.00	.20
□□□□□	445 Teppo Numminen [Finland]	10.00	.20
□□□□□	446 Marcus Ragnarsson [Sweden]	10.00	.20
□□□□□	447 Niklas Sundström [Sweden]	10.00	.20
□□□□□	448 Mats Sundin [Sweden]	45.00	1.00
□□□□□	449 Markus Näslund [Sweden]	45.00	1.00
□□□□□	450 Ulf Dahlén, Wash.	8.00	.20

2001 ICE ODYSSEY

Insert Set (20 cards):		**150.00**
	Insert (1:37 packs)	**IO**
□	1 Paul Kariya, Anah.	12.00
□	2 Teemu Selänne, Anah.	6.00
□	3 Martin Biron (G), Buff.	5.00
□	4 Jarome Iginla, Calg.	6.00
□	5 Chris Drury, Colo.	5.00
□	6 Peter Forsberg, Colo.	12.00
□	7 Milan Hejduk, Colo.	6.00
□	8 Patrick Roy (G), Colo.	25.00
□	9 Steve Yzerman, Detr.	20.00
□	10 Pavel Bure, Flor.	6.00
□	11 José Théodore (G), Mont.	10.00
□	12 Martin Brodeur (G), NJer.	14.00
□	13 Patrik Elias, NJer.	6.00
□	14 Scott Gomez, NJer.	5.00
□	15 Roberto Luongo (G), NYIs.	6.00
□	16 Marian Hossa, Otta.	8.00
□	17 Brian Boucher (G), Phil.	5.00
□	18 Jaromir Jagr, Pitt.	8.00
□	19 Vincent Lecavalier, Tamp.	8.00
□	20 Mats Sundin, Toro.	8.00

AUTHENTIC AUTOGRAPH

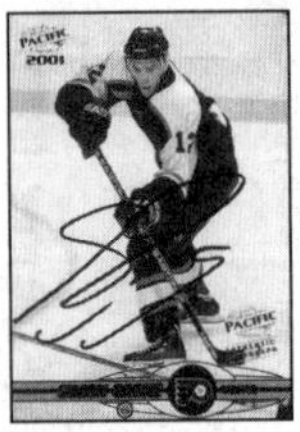

Insert Set (19 cards):		**300.00**
	Description	**Auto.**
□	384 Nikolai Antropov, Toro. ✍ (#/250)	15.00
□	126 Ed Belfour (G), Dall. ✍ (#/250)	30.00
□	233 Patrik Elias, NJer. ✍ (#/500)	20.00
□	296 Simon Gagné, Phil. ✍ (#/1000)	20.00
□	234 Scott Gomez, NJer. ✍ (#/500)	15.00
□	262 Jan Hlavac, NYRa. ✍ (#/500)	15.00
□	251 Jason Krog, NYIs. ✍ (#/500)	15.00
□	377 Vincent Lecavalier, Tamp. ✍ (#/1000)	25.00
□	300 John LeClair, Phil. ✍ (#/250)	25.00
□	223 David Legwand, Nash. ✍ (#/250)	15.00
□	169 Todd Marchant, Edmo. ✍ (#/250)	15.00
□	137 Mike Modano, Dall. ✍ (#/250)	30.00
□	138 Brenden Morrow, Dall. ✍ (#/500)	15.00
□	172 Tommy Salo (G), Edmo. ✍ (#/500)	15.00
□	57 Miroslav Satan, Buff. ✍ (#/500)	15.00
□	123 Alex Tanguay, Colo. ✍ (#/250)	15.00
□	215 José Théodore (G), Mont. ✍ (#/250)	35.00
□	352 Roman Turek (G), SLou. ✍ (#/500)	15.00
□	272 Mike York, NYIs. ✍ (#/500)	15.00

CRAMER'S CHOICE AWARDS

Insert Set (10 cards):		**600.00**
	Insert (1:721 packs)	**CCA**
□	1 Paul Kariya, Anah.	70.00
□	2 Teemu Selänne, Anah.	40.00
□	3 Peter Forsberg, Colo.	70.00
□	4 Patrick Roy (G), Colo.	150.00
□	5 Steve Yzerman, Detr.	120.00
□	6 Pavel Bure, Flor.	40.00
□	7 Martin Brodeur (G), NJer.	80.00
□	8 Scott Gomez, NJer.	40.00
□	9 Jaromir Jagr, Pitt.	50.00
□	10 Mats Sundin, Toro.	50.00

EURO STARS

Insert Set (10 cards):		**55.00**
	Insert (1:37 packs)	**ES**
□	1 Teemu Selänne, Anah.	6.00
□	2 Dominik Hasek (G), Buff.	7.00
□	3 Peter Forsberg, Colo.	10.00
□	4 Sergei Fedorov, Detr.	7.00
□	5 Pavel Bure, Flor.	6.00
□	6 Jaromir Jagr, Pitt.	7.00
□	7 Pavol Demitra, SLou.	5.00
□	8 Roman Turek (G), SLou.	5.00
□	9 Mats Sundin, Toro.	7.00
□	10 Olaf Kölzig (G), Wash.	5.00

GAME-WORN JERSEY

There are two versions: the Jersey card and the Jersey Patch variation (#/10).

Insert Set (15 cards):		**3,600**	**300.00**
	Inserts	**P10**	**J**
□□	1 Raymond Bourque, Colo. ✂	300.00	30.00
□□	9 Pavel Bure, Flor. ✂	200.00	20.00
□□	10 Éric Desjardins, Phil. ✂	200.00	15.00
□□	12 Shane Doan, Phoe. ✂	200.00	15.00
□□	13 Jaromir Jagr, Pitt. ✂	250.00	20.00
□□	15 Olaf Kölzig (G), Wash. ✂	200.00	15.00
□□	11 Daymond Langkow, Phil. ✂	200.00	15.00
□□	14 Mark Messier, Vanc. ✂	250.00	20.00
□□	2 Éric Messier, Colo. ✂	200.00	15.00
□□	5 Mike Modano, Dall. ✂	250.00	20.00
□□	3 Patrick Roy (G), Colo. ✂	600.00	60.00
□□	4 Joe Sakic, Colo. ✂	400.00	40.00
□□	7 Brendan Shanahan, Detr. ✂	250.00	20.00
□□	6 Darryl Sydor, Dall. ✂	200.00	15.00
□□	8 Steve Yzerman, Detr. ✂	600.00	60.00

GOLD-CROWN DIE-CUTS

Insert Set (36 cards):		**225.00**
	Insert (1:37 packs)	**GCDC**
□	1 Paul Kariya, Anah.	12.00
□	2 Teemu Selänne, Anah.	6.00
□	3 Joe Thornton, Bost.	10.00
□	4 Dominik Hasek (G), Buff.	8.00
□	5 Valeri Bure, Calg.	4.00
□	6 Tony Amonte, Chic.	4.00
□	7 Raymond Bourque, Colo.	10.00
□	8 Peter Forsberg, Colo.	12.00
□	9 Milan Hejduk, Colo.	6.00
□	10 Joe Sakic, Colo.	10.00
□	11 Patrick Roy (G), Colo.	25.00
□	12 Brett Hull, Dall.	8.00
□	13 Mike Modano, Dall.	8.00
□	14 Brendan Shanahan, Detr.	8.00
□	15 Steve Yzerman, Detr.	20.00
□	16 Pavel Bure, Flor.	6.00
□	17 Luc Robitaille, LosA.	6.00
□	18 Martin Brodeur (G), NJer.	10.00
□	19 Scott Gomez, NJer.	4.00
□	20 Roberto Luongo (G), NYIs.	6.00
□	21 Marian Hossa, Otta.	8.00
□	22 Brian Boucher (G), Phil.	4.00
□	23 John LeClair, Phil.	6.00
□	24 Eric Lindros, Phil.	8.00
□	25 Mark Recchi, Phil.	4.00
□	26 Keith Tkachuk, Phoe.	4.00
□	27 Jeremy Roenick, Phoe.	6.00
□	28 Jaromir Jagr, Pitt.	8.00
□	29 Chris Pronger, SLou.	4.00
□	30 Roman Turek (G), SLou.	4.00
□	31 Owen Nolan, SanJ.	4.00
□	32 Vincent Lecavalier, Tamp.	8.00
□	33 Mats Sundin, Toro.	8.00
□	34 Curtis Joseph (G), Toro.	8.00
□	35 Mark Messier, Vanc.	8.00
□	36 Olaf Kölzig (G), Wash.	4.00

IN THE CAGE

Insert Set (10 cards):		**160.00**
	Insert (1:73 packs)	**ITC**
□	1 Dominik Hasek (G), Buff.	20.00
□	2 Fred Brathwaite (G), Calg.	10.00
□	3 Patrick Roy (G), Colo.	60.00
□	4 Mike Vernon (G), Flor.	10.00
□	5 Stéphane Fiset (G), LosA.	10.00
□	6 Jeff Hackett (G), Mont.	10.00
□	7 Martin Brodeur (G), NJer.	30.00
□	8 Mike Richter (G), NYRa.	10.00
□	9 Brian Boucher (G), Phil.	10.00
□	10 Curtis Joseph (G), Toro.	20.00

NORTH AMERICAN STARS

Insert Set (10 cards):		**75.00**
	Insert (1:37 packs)	**NAAS**
□	1 Paul Kariya, Anah.	10.00
□	2 Joe Sakic, Colo.	10.00
□	3 Patrick Roy (G), Colo.	20.00
□	4 Mike Modano, Dall.	5.00
□	5 Brendan Shanahan, Detr.	5.00
□	6 Steve Yzerman, Detr.	15.00
□	7 Martin Brodeur (G), NJer.	10.00
□	8 Scott Gomez, NJer.	5.00
□	9 John LeClair, Phil.	5.00
□	10 Curtis Joseph (G), Toro.	5.00

PACIFIC REFLECTIONS

Insert Set (20 cards):		**425.00**
	Insert (1:145 packs)	**PR**
□	1 Paul Kariya, Anah.	35.00
□	2 Teemu Selänne, Anah.	20.00
□	3 Doug Gilmour, Buff.	15.00
□	4 Raymond Bourque, Colo.	30.00
□	5 Peter Forsberg, Colo.	35.00
□	6 Joe Sakic, Colo.	40.00
□	7 Brett Hull, Dall.	25.00
□	8 Mike Modano, Dall.	25.00
□	9 Brendan Shanahan, Detr.	25.00
□	10 Steve Yzerman, Detr.	60.00
□	11 Pavel Bure, Flor.	20.00
□	12 Zigmund Palffy, LosA.	15.00
□	13 Scott Gomez, NJer.	12.00
□	14 Marian Hossa, Otta.	25.00
□	15 John LeClair, Phil.	20.00
□	16 Eric Lindros, Phil.	25.00
□	17 Jaromir Jagr, Pitt.	25.00
□	18 Vincent Lecavalier, Tamp.	25.00
□	19 Mats Sundin, Toro.	25.00
□	20 Mark Messier, Vanc.	25.00

2000 - 01 PACIFIC PARAMOUNT

This series was issued in November 2000. Base cards 1-252 have a one-per-hobby-pack Copper parallel, a one-per-retail-pack Gold parallel, a hobby-pack Holo-Silver parallel (#/74), a retail-pack Holo-Gold parallel (#/74), an Ice Blue parallel (#/50) and a Premiere Date parallel (#/45). Priced similarly below are Copper and Gold parallels, Holo-Silver and Holo-Gold parallels and Ice Blue and Premiere Date parallels. Players (1-250) are sorted by team alphabetically.

Complete Set (252 cards):		**100.00**	**25.00**
Common Player:		**.50**	**.20**
	Description	**Cop.**	**Param.**
□□□	1 Antti Aalto	.50	.20
□□□	2 Maxim Balmochnykh	.50	.20
□□□	3 Matt Cullen	.50	.20
□□□	4 Guy Hebert (G)	.50	.20
□□□	5 Paul Kariya	4.00	1.00
□□□	6 Steve Rucchin	.50	.20
□□□	7 Teemu Selänne	2.00	.50
□□□	8 Oleg Tverdovsky	.50	.20
□□□	9 Donald Audette	1.00	.20
□□□	10 Andrew Brunette	.50	.20
□□□	11 Shean Donovan	.50	.20
□□□	12 Scott Fankhouser (G)	.50	.20
□□□	13 Ray Ferraro	.50	.20
□□□	14 Damian Rhodes (G)	.50	.20
□□□	15 Patrik Stefan	.50	.20
□□□	16 Jason Allison	1.50	.20
□□□	17 Anson Carter	1.00	.20
□□□	18 Byron Dafoe (G)	1.00	.20
□□□	19 John Grahame (G)	.50	.20
□□□	20 Brian Rolston	.50	.20
□□□	21 Sergei Samsonov	1.50	.20
□□□	22 Don Sweeney	.50	.20
□□□	23 Joe Thornton	3.50	.50
□□□	24 Maxim Afinogenov	1.00	.20
□□□	25 Stu Barnes	.50	.20
□□□	26 Martin Biron (G)	1.00	.20
□□□	27 Curtis Brown	.50	.20
□□□	28 Doug Gilmour	1.50	.20
□□□	29 Chris Gratton	.50	.20
□□□	30 Dominik Hasek (G)	3.00	.50
□□□	31 Michael Peca	1.00	.20
□□□	32 Miroslav Satan	.50	.20
□□□	33 Fred Brathwaite (G)	.50	.20
□□□	34 Valeri Bure	.50	.20
□□□	35 Phil Housley	.50	.20
□□□	36 Jarome Iginla	2.00	.50
□□□	37 Oleg Saprykin	.50	.20
□□□	38 Marc Savard	.50	.20
□□□	39 Cory Stillman	.50	.20
□□□	40 Clarke Wilm	.50	.20
□□□	41 Rod Brind'Amour	.50	.20
□□□	42 Ron Francis	1.50	.20
□□□	43 Arturs Irbe (G)	1.00	.20
□□□	44 Sami Kapanen	.50	.20
□□□	45 Jeff O'Neill	1.00	.20
□□□	46 David Tanabe	.50	.20
□□□	47 Glen Wesley	.50	.20
□□□	48 Tony Amonte	1.50	.20
□□□	49 Michal Grosek	.50	.20
□□□	50 Dean McAmmond	.50	.20
□□□	51 Boris Mironov	.50	.20
□□□	52 Michael Nylander	.50	.20
□□□	53 Steve Sullivan	.50	.20
□□□	54 Jocelyn Thibault (G)	1.00	.20
□□□	55 Alexei Zhamnov	.50	.20
□□□	56 Raymond Bourque	3.50	.50
□□□	57 Adam Deadmarsh	.50	.20
□□□	58 Chris Drury	1.50	.20
□□□	59 Adam Foote	.50	.20
□□□	60 Peter Forsberg	4.00	1.00
□□□	61 Milan Hejduk	2.00	.50
□□□	62 Patrick Roy (G)	9.00	2.00
□□□	63 Joe Sakic	4.50	1.00
□□□	64 Martin Skoula	.50	.20
□□□	65 Alex Tanguay	1.50	.20
□□□	66 Kevyn Adams	.50	.20
□□□	**67 Serge Aubin RC**	**2.50**	**.50**
□□□	68 Marc Denis (G)	1.00	.20
□□□	69 Ted Drury	.50	.20
□□□	70 Stephen Heinze	.50	.20
□□□	71 Lyle Odelein	.50	.20
□□□	72 Ron Tugnutt (G)	1.00	.20
□□□	73 Ed Belfour (G)	3.00	.50
□□□	74 Derian Hatcher	.50	.20
□□□	75 Brett Hull	3.00	.50
□□□	76 Jamie Langenbrunner	.50	.20
□□□	77 Jere Lehtinen	.50	.20
□□□	78 Roman Lyashenko	.50	.20
□□□	79 Mike Modano	3.00	.50
□□□	80 Brenden Morrow	.50	.20
□□□	81 Joe Nieuwendyk	1.00	.20
□□□	82 Sergei Zubov	.50	.20
□□□	83 Chris Chelios	1.50	.20
□□□	84 Mathieu Dandenault	.50	.20
□□□	85 Sergei Fedorov	3.00	.50
□□□	86 Martin Lapointe	1.00	.20
□□□	87 Nicklas Lidström	1.50	.20
□□□	88 Chris Osgood (G)	1.50	.20

☐☐☐	89 Brendan Shanahan	3.00	.50
☐☐☐	90 Pat Verbeek	.50	.20
☐☐☐	91 Jesse Wallin	.50	.20
☐☐☐	92 Ken Wregget (G)	.50	.20
☐☐☐	93 Steve Yzerman	7.00	1.50
☐☐☐	94 Mike Grier	.50	.20
☐☐☐	95 Bill Guerin	1.00	.20
☐☐☐	96 Todd Marchant	.50	.20
☐☐☐	97 Tom Poti	.50	.20
☐☐☐	98 Tommy Salo (G)	1.00	.20
☐☐☐	99 Alexander Selivanov	.50	.20
☐☐☐	100 Ryan Smyth	1.00	.20
☐☐☐	101 Doug Weight	1.50	.20
☐☐☐	102 Pavel Bure	2.00	.50
☐☐☐	103 Brad Ference	.50	.20
☐☐☐	104 Trevor Kidd (G)	.50	.20
☐☐☐	105 Viktor Kozlov	.50	.20
☐☐☐	106 Scott Mellanby	.50	.20
☐☐☐	107 Ivan Novoseltsev	.50	.20
☐☐☐	108 Robert Svehla	.50	.20
☐☐☐	109 Ray Whitney	.50	.20
☐☐☐	110 Rob Blake	1.50	.20
☐☐☐	111 Stéphane Fiset (G)	.50	.20
☐☐☐	112 Glen Murray	1.00	.20
☐☐☐	113 Zigmund Palffy	1.50	.20
☐☐☐	114 Luc Robitaille	2.00	.50
☐☐☐	115 Bryan Smolinski	.50	.20
☐☐☐	116 Jamie Storr (G)	.50	.20
☐☐☐	117 Jozef Stümpel	.50	.20
☐☐☐	118 Manny Fernandez (G)	1.00	.20
☐☐☐	119 Sergei Krivokrasov	.50	.20
☐☐☐	120 Jamie McLennan (G)	.50	.20
☐☐☐	121 Jeff Nielsen	.50	.20
☐☐☐	122 Sean O'Donnell	.50	.20
☐☐☐	123 Jeff Odgers	.50	.20
☐☐☐	124 Scott Pellerin	.50	.20
☐☐☐	125 Jeff Hackett (G)	.50	.20
☐☐☐	126 Saku Koivu	2.00	.50
☐☐☐	127 Trevor Linden	1.00	.20
☐☐☐	128 Patrick Poulin	.50	.20
☐☐☐	129 Mike Ribeiro	.50	.20
☐☐☐	130 Martin Rucinsky	.50	.20
☐☐☐	131 Brian Savage	.50	.20
☐☐☐	132 José Théodore (G)	3.50	.50
☐☐☐	133 Dainius Zubrus	.50	.20
☐☐☐	134 Mike Dunham (G)	1.00	.20
☐☐☐	135 Greg Johnson	.50	.20
☐☐☐	136 David Legwand	1.00	.20
☐☐☐	137 Cliff Ronning	.50	.20
☐☐☐	138 Robert Valicevic	.50	.20
☐☐☐	139 Tomas Vokoun (G)	.50	.20
☐☐☐	140 Vitali Yachmenev	.50	.20
☐☐☐	141 Jason Arnott	1.00	.20
☐☐☐	142 Martin Brodeur (G)	4.50	1.00
☐☐☐	143 Patrik Elias	2.00	.50
☐☐☐	144 Scott Gomez	1.00	.20
☐☐☐	145 John Madden	.50	.20
☐☐☐	146 Alexander Mogilny	1.00	.20
☐☐☐	147 Scott Niedermayer	.50	.20
☐☐☐	148 Brian Rafalski	.50	.20
☐☐☐	149 Scott Stevens	1.00	.20
☐☐☐	150 Petr* Sykora	1.00	.20
☐☐☐	**151 Colin White RC**	**2.50**	**.50**
☐☐☐	152 Tim Connolly	1.00	.20
☐☐☐	153 Mariusz Czerkawski	.50	.20
☐☐☐	154 Brad Isbister	.50	.20
☐☐☐	155 Jason Krog	.50	.20
☐☐☐	156 Claude Lapointe	.50	.20
☐☐☐	157 Bill Muckalt	.50	.20
☐☐☐	**158 S. Valiquette (G) RC**	**2.00**	**.50**
☐☐☐	159 Radek Dvorak	.50	.20
☐☐☐	160 Theoren Fleury	1.50	.20
☐☐☐	161 Adam Graves	1.00	.20
☐☐☐	162 Jan Hlavac	.50	.20
☐☐☐	163 Brian Leetch	1.50	.20
☐☐☐	164 Sylvain Lefebvre	.50	.20
☐☐☐	165 Mark Messier	3.00	.50
☐☐☐	166 Petr Nedved	.50	.20
☐☐☐	167 Mike Richter (G)	1.00	.20
☐☐☐	168 Mike York	.50	.20
☐☐☐	169 Daniel Alfredsson	1.50	.20
☐☐☐	170 Magnus Arvedson	.50	.20
☐☐☐	171 Radek Bonk	.50	.20
☐☐☐	172 Marian Hossa	3.00	.50
☐☐☐	**173 Jani Hurme (G) RC**	**2.00**	**1.00**
☐☐☐	174 Patrick Lalime (G)	1.50	.20
☐☐☐	175 Shawn McEachern	.50	.20
☐☐☐	176 Vaclav Prospal	.50	.20
☐☐☐	177 Brian Boucher (G)	.50	.20
☐☐☐	178 Andy Delmore	.50	.20
☐☐☐	179 Éric Desjardins	.50	.20
☐☐☐	180 Simon Gagné	2.00	.50
☐☐☐	181 Daymond Langkow	.50	.20
☐☐☐	182 John LeClair	2.00	.50
☐☐☐	183 Eric Lindros	3.00	.50
☐☐☐	184 Keith Primeau	1.00	.20
☐☐☐	185 Mark Recchi	1.00	.20
☐☐☐	186 Rick Tocchet	.50	.20
☐☐☐	187 Shane Doan	.50	.20
☐☐☐	188 Robert Esche (G)	.50	.20
☐☐☐	189 Travis Green	.50	.20
☐☐☐	190 Trevor Letowski	.50	.20
☐☐☐	191 Stanislav Neckar	.50	.20
☐☐☐	192 Teppo Numminen	.50	.20
☐☐☐	193 Jeremy Roenick	2.00	.50
☐☐☐	194 Keith Tkachuk	1.50	.20
☐☐☐	195 Jean-Sébastien Aubin (G)	.50	.20
☐☐☐	196 Matthew Barnaby	.50	.20
☐☐☐	197 Jan Hrdina	.50	.20
☐☐☐	198 Jaromir Jagr	3.00	.50
☐☐☐	199 Alex Kovalev	1.50	.20
☐☐☐	200 Robert Lang	.50	.20
☐☐☐	201 John Slaney	.50	.20
☐☐☐	202 Martin Straka	.50	.20
☐☐☐	203 Lubos Bartecko	.50	.20
☐☐☐	204 Pavol Demitra	1.00	.20
☐☐☐	205 Michal Handzus	.50	.20
☐☐☐	206 Al MacInnis	1.00	.20
☐☐☐	207 Jamal Mayers	.50	.20
☐☐☐	208 Chris Pronger	1.50	.20
☐☐☐	209 Roman Turek (G)	1.00	.20
☐☐☐	210 Pierre Turgeon	1.00	.20
☐☐☐	211 Scott Young	.50	.20
☐☐☐	212 Vincent Damphousse	1.50	.20
☐☐☐	213 Jeff Friesen	.50	.20
☐☐☐	214 Patrick Marleau	1.00	.20
☐☐☐	215 Owen Nolan	1.50	.20
☐☐☐	216 Mike Ricci	.50	.20
☐☐☐	217 Steve Shields (G)	.50	.20
☐☐☐	218 Brad Stuart	1.00	.20
☐☐☐	219 Dan Cloutier (G)	1.00	.20
☐☐☐	220 Brian Holzinger	.50	.20
☐☐☐	221 Mike Johnson	.50	.20
☐☐☐	222 Vincent Lecavalier	3.00	.50
☐☐☐	223 Fredrik Modin	.50	.20
☐☐☐	224 Petr* Svoboda	.50	.20
☐☐☐	225 Todd Warriner	.50	.20
☐☐☐	226 Nikolai Antropov	.50	.20
☐☐☐	227 Sergei Berezin	.50	.20
☐☐☐	228 Tie Domi	.50	.20
☐☐☐	229 Jeff Farkas	.50	.20
☐☐☐	230 Curtis Joseph (G)	3.00	.50
☐☐☐	231 Tomas Kaberle	.50	.20
☐☐☐	232 Yanic Perreault	.50	.20
☐☐☐	233 Mats Sundin	3.00	.50
☐☐☐	234 Steve Thomas	.50	.20
☐☐☐	235 Darcy Tucker	.50	.20
☐☐☐	236 Todd Bertuzzi	3.50	.50
☐☐☐	237 Andrew Cassels	.50	.20
☐☐☐	238 Ed Jovanovski	1.00	.20
☐☐☐	239 Steve Kariya	.50	.20
☐☐☐	240 Markus Näslund	3.00	.50
☐☐☐	241 Mattias Öhlund	.50	.20
☐☐☐	242 Félix Potvin (G)	1.50	.20
☐☐☐	243 Peter Bondra	1.50	.20
☐☐☐	244 Sergei Gonchar	.50	.20
☐☐☐	245 Jeff Halpern	.50	.20
☐☐☐	246 Olaf Kölzig (G)	1.50	.20
☐☐☐	247 Steve Konowalchuk	.50	.20
☐☐☐	248 Adam Oates	1.00	.20
☐☐☐	249 Chris Simon	.50	.20
☐☐☐	250 Richard Zednik	1.00	.20
☐☐☐	251 Daniel Sedin	6.00	4.00
☐☐☐	252 Henrik Sedin	6.00	4.00

SERIAL-NUMBERED PARALLELS

	Complete Set (252 cards):	**1,900**	**1,600**
	Common Player:	**8.00**	**6.00**
	Description	**IB50**	**HS74**
☐☐☐☐	1 Antti Aalto	8.00	6.00
☐☐☐☐	2 Maxim Balmochnykh	8.00	6.00
☐☐☐☐	3 Matt Cullen	10.00	6.00
☐☐☐☐	4 Guy Hebert (G)	10.00	6.00
☐☐☐☐	5 Paul Kariya	60.00	50.00
☐☐☐☐	6 Steve Rucchin	10.00	6.00
☐☐☐☐	7 Teemu Selänne	35.00	30.00
☐☐☐☐	8 Oleg Tverdovsky	8.00	6.00
☐☐☐☐	9 Donald Audette	15.00	15.00
☐☐☐☐	10 Andrew Brunette	8.00	6.00
☐☐☐☐	11 Shean Donovan	8.00	6.00
☐☐☐☐	12 Scott Fankhouser (G)	8.00	6.00
☐☐☐☐	13 Ray Ferraro	8.00	6.00
☐☐☐☐	14 Damian Rhodes (G)	10.00	6.00
☐☐☐☐	15 Patrik Stefan	10.00	10.00
☐☐☐☐	16 Jason Allison	25.00	20.00
☐☐☐☐	17 Anson Carter	15.00	15.00
☐☐☐☐	18 Byron Dafoe (G)	15.00	15.00
☐☐☐☐	19 John Grahame (G)	10.00	6.00
☐☐☐☐	20 Brian Rolston	10.00	10.00
☐☐☐☐	21 Sergei Samsonov	25.00	20.00
☐☐☐☐	22 Don Sweeney	8.00	6.00
☐☐☐☐	23 Joe Thornton	50.00	45.00
☐☐☐☐	24 Maxim Afinogenov	15.00	15.00
☐☐☐☐	25 Stu Barnes	8.00	6.00
☐☐☐☐	26 Martin Biron (G)	20.00	15.00
☐☐☐☐	27 Curtis Brown	8.00	6.00
☐☐☐☐	28 Doug Gilmour	25.00	20.00
☐☐☐☐	29 Chris Gratton	10.00	6.00
☐☐☐☐	30 Dominik Hasek (G)	45.00	35.00
☐☐☐☐	31 Michael Peca	15.00	15.00
☐☐☐☐	32 Miroslav Satan	10.00	10.00
☐☐☐☐	33 Fred Brathwaite (G)	10.00	10.00
☐☐☐☐	34 Valeri Bure	10.00	10.00
☐☐☐☐	35 Phil Housley	10.00	10.00
☐☐☐☐	36 Jarome Iginla	35.00	30.00
☐☐☐☐	37 Oleg Saprykin	10.00	6.00
☐☐☐☐	38 Marc Savard	10.00	6.00
☐☐☐☐	39 Cory Stillman	10.00	6.00
☐☐☐☐	40 Clarke Wilm	8.00	6.00
☐☐☐☐	41 Rod Brind'Amour	10.00	10.00
☐☐☐☐	42 Ron Francis	25.00	20.00
☐☐☐☐	43 Arturs Irbe (G)	15.00	15.00
☐☐☐☐	44 Sami Kapanen	10.00	10.00
☐☐☐☐	45 Jeff O'Neill	15.00	15.00
☐☐☐☐	46 David Tanabe	8.00	6.00
☐☐☐☐	47 Glen Wesley	8.00	6.00
☐☐☐☐	48 Tony Amonte	25.00	20.00
☐☐☐☐	49 Michal Grosek	8.00	6.00
☐☐☐☐	50 Dean McAmmond	8.00	6.00
☐☐☐☐	51 Boris Mironov	8.00	6.00
☐☐☐☐	52 Michael Nylander	10.00	6.00
☐☐☐☐	53 Steve Sullivan	10.00	10.00
☐☐☐☐	54 Jocelyn Thibault (G)	15.00	15.00
☐☐☐☐	55 Alexei Zhamnov	10.00	10.00
☐☐☐☐	56 Raymond Bourque	50.00	45.00
☐☐☐☐	57 Adam Deadmarsh	10.00	10.00
☐☐☐☐	58 Chris Drury	25.00	20.00
☐☐☐☐	59 Adam Foote	10.00	10.00
☐☐☐☐	60 Peter Forsberg	60.00	50.00
☐☐☐☐	61 Milan Hejduk	35.00	30.00
☐☐☐☐	62 Patrick Roy (G)	135.00	110.00
☐☐☐☐	63 Joe Sakic	70.00	60.00
☐☐☐☐	64 Martin Skoula	10.00	6.00
☐☐☐☐	65 Alex Tanguay	25.00	20.00
☐☐☐☐	66 Kevyn Adams	8.00	6.00
☐☐☐☐	**67 Serge Aubin RC**	**10.00**	**10.00**
☐☐☐☐	68 Marc Denis (G)	20.00	15.00
☐☐☐☐	69 Ted Drury	8.00	6.00
☐☐☐☐	70 Stephen Heinze	8.00	6.00
☐☐☐☐	71 Lyle Odelein	8.00	6.00
☐☐☐☐	72 Ron Tugnutt (G)	15.00	15.00
☐☐☐☐	73 Ed Belfour (G)	45.00	35.00
☐☐☐☐	74 Derian Hatcher	10.00	10.00
☐☐☐☐	75 Brett Hull	45.00	35.00
☐☐☐☐	76 Jamie Langenbrunner	10.00	6.00
☐☐☐☐	77 Jere Lehtinen	10.00	10.00
☐☐☐☐	78 Roman Lyashenko	8.00	6.00
☐☐☐☐	79 Mike Modano	45.00	35.00
☐☐☐☐	80 Brenden Morrow	10.00	10.00
☐☐☐☐	81 Joe Nieuwendyk	15.00	15.00
☐☐☐☐	82 Sergei Zubov	10.00	6.00
☐☐☐☐	83 Chris Chelios	25.00	20.00
☐☐☐☐	84 Mathieu Dandenault	8.00	6.00
☐☐☐☐	85 Sergei Fedorov	45.00	35.00
☐☐☐☐	86 Martin Lapointe	15.00	15.00
☐☐☐☐	87 Nicklas Lidström	25.00	20.00
☐☐☐☐	88 Chris Osgood (G)	25.00	20.00
☐☐☐☐	89 Brendan Shanahan	45.00	35.00
☐☐☐☐	90 Pat Verbeek	10.00	10.00
☐☐☐☐	91 Jesse Wallin	8.00	6.00
☐☐☐☐	92 Ken Wregget (G)	10.00	6.00
☐☐☐☐	93 Steve Yzerman	105.00	90.00
☐☐☐☐	94 Mike Grier	10.00	6.00
☐☐☐☐	95 Bill Guerin	15.00	15.00
☐☐☐☐	96 Todd Marchant	10.00	6.00
☐☐☐☐	97 Tom Poti	8.00	6.00
☐☐☐☐	98 Tommy Salo (G)	15.00	15.00
☐☐☐☐	99 Alexander Selivanov	8.00	6.00
☐☐☐☐	100 Ryan Smyth	20.00	15.00
☐☐☐☐	101 Doug Weight	25.00	20.00
☐☐☐☐	102 Pavel Bure	35.00	30.00
☐☐☐☐	103 Brad Ference	8.00	6.00
☐☐☐☐	104 Trevor Kidd (G)	10.00	10.00
☐☐☐☐	105 Viktor Kozlov	10.00	10.00
☐☐☐☐	106 Scott Mellanby	10.00	6.00
☐☐☐☐	107 Ivan Novoseltsev	8.00	6.00
☐☐☐☐	108 Robert Svehla	10.00	6.00
☐☐☐☐	109 Ray Whitney	10.00	6.00
☐☐☐☐	110 Rob Blake	25.00	20.00
☐☐☐☐	111 Stéphane Fiset (G)	10.00	10.00
☐☐☐☐	112 Glen Murray	20.00	15.00
☐☐☐☐	113 Zigmund Palffy	25.00	20.00
☐☐☐☐	114 Luc Robitaille	35.00	30.00
☐☐☐☐	115 Bryan Smolinski	8.00	6.00
☐☐☐☐	116 Jamie Storr (G)	10.00	6.00
☐☐☐☐	117 Jozef Stümpel	10.00	6.00
☐☐☐☐	118 Manny Fernandez (G)	15.00	15.00
☐☐☐☐	119 Sergei Krivokrasov	8.00	6.00
☐☐☐☐	120 Jamie McLennan (G)	8.00	6.00
☐☐☐☐	121 Jeff Nielsen	8.00	6.00
☐☐☐☐	122 Sean O'Donnell	8.00	6.00
☐☐☐☐	123 Jeff Odgers	8.00	6.00
☐☐☐☐	124 Scott Pellerin	8.00	6.00
☐☐☐☐	125 Jeff Hackett (G)	10.00	10.00
☐☐☐☐	126 Saku Koivu	50.00	30.00
☐☐☐☐	127 Trevor Linden	15.00	15.00
☐☐☐☐	128 Patrick Poulin	8.00	6.00
☐☐☐☐	129 Mike Ribeiro	10.00	10.00
☐☐☐☐	130 Martin Rucinsky	10.00	6.00
☐☐☐☐	131 Brian Savage	10.00	10.00
☐☐☐☐	132 José Théodore (G)	50.00	45.00
☐☐☐☐	133 Dainius Zubrus	10.00	6.00
☐☐☐☐	134 Mike Dunham (G)	15.00	15.00
☐☐☐☐	135 Greg Johnson	8.00	6.00
☐☐☐☐	136 David Legwand	15.00	15.00
☐☐☐☐	137 Cliff Ronning	10.00	6.00
☐☐☐☐	138 Robert Valicevic	8.00	6.00
☐☐☐☐	139 Tomas Vokoun (G)	10.00	6.00
☐☐☐☐	140 Vitali Yachmenev	8.00	6.00
☐☐☐☐	141 Jason Arnott	20.00	15.00
☐☐☐☐	142 Martin Brodeur (G)	70.00	60.00
☐☐☐☐	143 Patrik Elias	35.00	30.00
☐☐☐☐	144 Scott Gomez	15.00	15.00
☐☐☐☐	145 John Madden	10.00	10.00
☐☐☐☐	146 Alexander Mogilny	20.00	15.00
☐☐☐☐	147 Scott Niedermayer	10.00	10.00
☐☐☐☐	148 Brian Rafalski	10.00	6.00
☐☐☐☐	149 Scott Stevens	15.00	15.00
☐☐☐☐	150 Petr* Sykora	15.00	15.00
☐☐☐☐	**151 Colin White RC**	**10.00**	**10.00**
☐☐☐☐	152 Tim Connolly	15.00	15.00
☐☐☐☐	153 Mariusz Czerkawski	10.00	6.00
☐☐☐☐	154 Brad Isbister	10.00	6.00
☐☐☐☐	155 Jason Krog	10.00	6.00
☐☐☐☐	156 Claude Lapointe	8.00	6.00
☐☐☐☐	157 Bill Muckalt	8.00	6.00
☐☐☐☐	**158 S. Valiquette (G) RC**	**10.00**	**10.00**
☐☐☐☐	159 Radek Dvorak	10.00	6.00
☐☐☐☐	160 Theoren Fleury	25.00	20.00
☐☐☐☐	161 Adam Graves	15.00	15.00
☐☐☐☐	162 Jan Hlavac	10.00	6.00
☐☐☐☐	163 Brian Leetch	25.00	20.00
☐☐☐☐	164 Sylvain Lefebvre	8.00	6.00
☐☐☐☐	165 Mark Messier	45.00	35.00
☐☐☐☐	166 Petr Nedved	10.00	10.00
☐☐☐☐	167 Mike Richter (G)	20.00	15.00
☐☐☐☐	168 Mike York	10.00	10.00
☐☐☐☐	169 Daniel Alfredsson	50.00	20.00
☐☐☐☐	170 Magnus Arvedson	8.00	6.00
☐☐☐☐	171 Radek Bonk	10.00	10.00
☐☐☐☐	172 Marian Hossa	45.00	35.00
☐☐☐☐	**173 Jani Hurme (G) RC**	**20.00**	**15.00**
☐☐☐☐	174 Patrick Lalime (G)	25.00	20.00
☐☐☐☐	175 Shawn McEachern	10.00	10.00
☐☐☐☐	176 Vaclav Prospal	10.00	10.00
☐☐☐☐	177 Brian Boucher (G)	10.00	10.00
☐☐☐☐	178 Andy Delmore	10.00	6.00
☐☐☐☐	179 Éric Desjardins	10.00	10.00
☐☐☐☐	180 Simon Gagné	35.00	30.00
☐☐☐☐	181 Daymond Langkow	10.00	6.00
☐☐☐☐	182 John LeClair	35.00	30.00
☐☐☐☐	183 Eric Lindros	45.00	35.00
☐☐☐☐	184 Keith Primeau	15.00	15.00
☐☐☐☐	185 Mark Recchi	15.00	15.00
☐☐☐☐	186 Rick Tocchet	10.00	10.00
☐☐☐☐	187 Shane Doan	10.00	6.00
☐☐☐☐	188 Robert Esche (G)	10.00	6.00
☐☐☐☐	189 Travis Green	10.00	6.00
☐☐☐☐	190 Trevor Letowski	8.00	6.00
☐☐☐☐	191 Stanislav Neckar	8.00	6.00
☐☐☐☐	192 Teppo Numminen	10.00	10.00
☐☐☐☐	193 Jeremy Roenick	35.00	30.00
☐☐☐☐	194 Keith Tkachuk	25.00	20.00
☐☐☐☐	195 Jean-Sébastien Aubin (G)	10.00	6.00
☐☐☐☐	196 Matthew Barnaby	8.00	6.00
☐☐☐☐	197 Jan Hrdina	10.00	6.00
☐☐☐☐	198 Jaromir Jagr	45.00	35.00
☐☐☐☐	199 Alex Kovalev	25.00	20.00
☐☐☐☐	200 Robert Lang	10.00	6.00
☐☐☐☐	201 John Slaney	10.00	6.00
☐☐☐☐	202 Martin Straka	10.00	10.00
☐☐☐☐	203 Lubos Bartecko	8.00	6.00
☐☐☐☐	204 Pavol Demitra	15.00	15.00
☐☐☐☐	205 Michal Handzus	10.00	6.00
☐☐☐☐	206 Al MacInnis	15.00	15.00
☐☐☐☐	207 Jamal Mayers	8.00	6.00
☐☐☐☐	208 Chris Pronger	25.00	20.00
☐☐☐☐	209 Roman Turek (G)	20.00	15.00
☐☐☐☐	210 Pierre Turgeon	15.00	15.00
☐☐☐☐	211 Scott Young	10.00	10.00
☐☐☐☐	212 Vincent Damphousse	25.00	20.00
☐☐☐☐	213 Jeff Friesen	10.00	10.00
☐☐☐☐	214 Patrick Marleau	20.00	15.00
☐☐☐☐	215 Owen Nolan	25.00	20.00
☐☐☐☐	216 Mike Ricci	10.00	10.00
☐☐☐☐	217 Steve Shields (G)	10.00	6.00
☐☐☐☐	218 Brad Stuart	15.00	15.00
☐☐☐☐	219 Dan Cloutier (G)	15.00	15.00

□□□□ 220 Brian Holzinger	8.00	6.00
□□□□ 221 Mike Johnson	8.00	6.00
□□□□ 222 Vincent Lecavalier	45.00	35.00
□□□□ 223 Fredrik Modin	10.00	6.00
□□□□ 224 Petr* Svoboda	10.00	6.00
□□□□ 225 Todd Warriner	8.00	6.00
□□□□ 226 Nikolai Antropov	10.00	6.00
□□□□ 227 Sergei Berezin	20.00	6.00
□□□□ 228 Tie Domi	10.00	10.00
□□□□ 229 Jeff Farkas	10.00	6.00
□□□□ 230 Curtis Joseph (G)	45.00	35.00
□□□□ 231 Tomas Kaberle	10.00	10.00
□□□□ 232 Yanic Perreault	10.00	10.00
□□□□ 233 Mats Sundin	45.00	35.00
□□□□ 234 Steve Thomas	10.00	6.00
□□□□ 235 Darcy Tucker	10.00	6.00
□□□□ 236 Todd Bertuzzi	50.00	45.00
□□□□ 237 Andrew Cassels	10.00	6.00
□□□□ 238 Ed Jovanovski	15.00	15.00
□□□□ 239 Steve Kariya	10.00	6.00
□□□□ 240 Markus Näslund	45.00	35.00
□□□□ 241 Mattias Öhlund	10.00	10.00
□□□□ 242 Félix Potvin (G)	50.00	20.00
□□□□ 243 Peter Bondra	25.00	20.00
□□□□ 244 Sergei Gonchar	10.00	10.00
□□□□ 245 Jeff Halpern	10.00	6.00
□□□□ 246 Olaf Kölzig (G)	25.00	20.00
□□□□ 247 Steve Konowalchuk	10.00	6.00
□□□□ 248 Adam Oates	15.00	15.00
□□□□ 249 Chris Simon	10.00	6.00
□□□□ 250 Richard Zednik	15.00	15.00
□□□□ 251 Daniel Sedin	25.00	30.00
□□□□ 252 Henrik Sedin	25.00	30.00

GAME-WORN JERSEY & PATCH

Insert Set (10 cards):	980
Insert (#/30)	JAP30
□ 2 Tony Amonte, Chic. ✄	80.00
□ 3 Raymond Bourque, Colo. ✄	175.00
□ 8 Éric Desjardins, Phil. ✄	80.00
□ 9 Shane Doan, Phoe. ✄	80.00
□ 1 Jarome Iginla, Calg. ✄	100.00
□ 6 Saku Koivu, Mont. ✄	175.00
□ 10 Olaf Kölzig (G), Wash. ✄	80.00
□ 4 Joe Sakic, Colo. ✄	225.00
□ 5 Darryl Sydor, Dall. ✄	80.00
□ 7 John Vanbiesbrouck (G), NYIs. ✄	80.00

EPIC SCOPE

Insert Set (20 cards):	120.00
Insert (2:37 packs)	ES
□ 1 Paul Kariya, Anah.	8.00
□ 2 Teemu Selänne, Anah.	5.00
□ 3 Dominik Hasek (G), Buff.	6.00
□ 4 Raymond Bourque, Colo.	7.00
□ 5 Peter Forsberg, Colo.	8.00
□ 6 Patrick Roy (G), Colo.	18.00
□ 7 Joe Sakic, Colo.	10.00
□ 8 Brett Hull, Dall.	6.00
□ 9 Mike Modano, Dall.	6.00
□ 10 Brendan Shanahan, Detr.	6.00
□ 11 Steve Yzerman, Detr.	15.00
□ 12 Pavel Bure, Flor.	5.00
□ 13 Martin Brodeur (G), NJer.	10.00
□ 14 Scott Gomez, NJer.	4.00
□ 15 Brian Boucher (G), Phil.	4.00
□ 16 John LeClair, Phil.	5.00
□ 17 Jaromir Jagr, Pitt.	6.00
□ 18 Vincent Lecavalier, Tamp.	6.00
□ 19 Mats Sundin, Toro.	6.00
□ 20 Curtis Joseph (G), Toro.	6.00

FREEZE FRAME

Insert Set (36 cards):	200.00
Insert (1:37 packs)	FF
□ 1 Paul Kariya, Anah.	10.00
□ 2 Teemu Selänne, Anah.	5.00
□ 3 Doug Gilmour, Buff.	5.00
□ 4 Dominik Hasek (G), Buff.	5.00
□ 5 Valeri Bure, Calg.	5.00
□ 6 Tony Amonte, Chic.	5.00
□ 7 Raymond Bourque, Colo.	10.00
□ 8 Peter Forsberg, Colo.	10.00
□ 9 Joe Sakic, Colo.	10.00
□ 10 Patrick Roy (G), Colo.	25.00
□ 11 Ed Belfour (G), Dall.	5.00
□ 12 Brett Hull, Dall.	5.00
□ 13 Mike Modano, Dall.	5.00
□ 14 Sergei Fedorov, Detr.	5.00
□ 15 Brendan Shanahan, Detr.	5.00
□ 16 Steve Yzerman, Detr.	20.00
□ 17 Doug Weight, Edmo.	5.00
□ 18 Pavel Bure, Flor.	5.00
□ 19 Luc Robitaille, LosA.	5.00
□ 20 Saku Koivu, Mont.	5.00
□ 21 Martin Brodeur (G), NJer.	10.00
□ 22 Scott Gomez, NJer.	5.00
□ 23 Tim Connolly, NYIs.	5.00
□ 24 Marian Hossa, Otta.	5.00
□ 25 Brian Boucher (G), Phil.	5.00
□ 26 John LeClair, Phil.	5.00
□ 27 Mark Recchi, Phil.	5.00
□ 28 Jaromir Jagr, Pitt.	5.00
□ 29 Jeremy Roenick, Phoe.	5.00
□ 30 Chris Pronger, SLou.	5.00
□ 31 Roman Turek (G), SLou.	5.00
□ 32 Owen Nolan, SanJ.	5.00
□ 33 Vincent Lecavalier, Tamp.	5.00
□ 34 Mats Sundin, Toro.	5.00
□ 35 Curtis Joseph (G), Toro.	5.00
□ 36 Olaf Kölzig (G), Wash.	5.00

GAME-USED STICK

Insert Set (17 cards):	540.00
Description	GUS
□ 8 Ed Belfour (G), Dall. ✄ (#/205)	50.00
□ 2 Raymond Bourque, Colo. ✄ (#/190)	60.00
□ 9 Chris Chelios, Detr. ✄ (#/165)	30.00
□ 3 Adam Deadmarsh, Colo. ✄ (#/200)	20.00
□ 4 Chris Drury, Colo. ✄ (#/205)	30.00
□ 14 Theoren Fleury, NYRa. ✄ (#/190)	30.00
□ 1 Ron Francis, Caro. ✄ (#/165)	30.00
□ 17 Curtis Joseph (G), Toro. ✄ (#/150)	60.00
□ 15 Eric Lindros, Phil. ✄ (#/190)	50.00
□ 16 Al MacInnis, SLou. ✄ (#/165)	20.00
□ 13 Alexander Mogilny, NJer. ✄ (#/155)	30.00
□ 10 Chris Osgood (G), Detr. ✄ (#/205)	30.00
□ 12 Luc Robitaille, LosA. ✄ (#/185)	40.00
□ 5 Joe Sakic, Colo. ✄ (#/190)	80.00
□ 6 Martin Skoula, Colo. ✄ (#/200)	20.00
□ 7 Alex Tanguay, Colo. ✄ (#/200)	30.00
□ 11 Doug Weight, Edmo. ✄ (#/165)	30.00

GLOVE-SIDE NET FUSIONS

There are two versions: the regular insert (1:73 packs) and the Platinum parallel (#/25).

Insert Set (20 cards):	1,130	250.00
Inserts	GS25	GSNF
□□ 1 Byron Dafoe (G), Bost.	30.00	10.00
□□ 2 Martin Biron (G), Buff.	30.00	10.00
□□ 3 Dominik Hasek (G), Buff.	100.00	20.00
□□ 4 Fred Brathwaite (G), Calg.	30.00	10.00
□□ 5 Arturs Irbe (G), Caro.	30.00	10.00
□□ 6 Jocelyn Thibault (G), Chic.	30.00	10.00
□□ 7 Patrick Roy (G), Colo.	250.00	50.00
□□ 8 Ed Belfour (G), Dall.	100.00	20.00
□□ 9 Chris Osgood (G), Detr.	50.00	10.00
□□ 10 Tommy Salo (G), Edmo.	30.00	10.00
□□ 11 José Théodore (G), Mont.	100.00	20.00
□□ 12 Martin Brodeur (G), NJer.	150.00	30.00
□□ 13 Mike Richter (G), NYRa.	30.00	10.00
□□ 14 Brian Boucher (G), Phil.	30.00	10.00
□□ 15 Jean-Sébastien Aubin (G), Pitt.	30.00	10.00
□□ 16 Roman Turek (G), SLou.	30.00	10.00
□□ 17 Steve Shields (G), SanJ.	30.00	10.00
□□ 18 Curtis Joseph (G), Toro.	100.00	20.00
□□ 19 Félix Potvin (G), Vanc.	100.00	10.00
□□ 20 Olaf Kölzig (G), Wash.	50.00	10.00

HALL OF FAME BOUND

There are three versions: the regular insert (1:361 packs), the Proof parallel (#/25) and the Canvas Proof parallel (#/1).

Insert Set (10 cards):	1,100	350.00
Inserts	HOF25	HOFB
□□□ 1 Paul Kariya, Anah.	150.00	50.00
□□□ 2 Dominik Hasek (G), Buff.	100.00	25.00
□□□ 3 Raymond Bourque, Colo.	125.00	25.00
□□□ 4 Patrick Roy (G), Colo.	250.00	100.00
□□□ 5 Brett Hull, Dall.	100.00	25.00
□□□ 6 Steve Yzerman, Detr.	250.00	75.00
□□□ 7 Pavel Bure, Flor.	75.00	25.00
□□□ 8 Martin Brodeur (G), NJer.	175.00	50.00
□□□ 9 John LeClair, Phil.	75.00	25.00
□□□ 10 Jaromir Jagr, Pitt.	100.00	25.00

SUB-ZERO

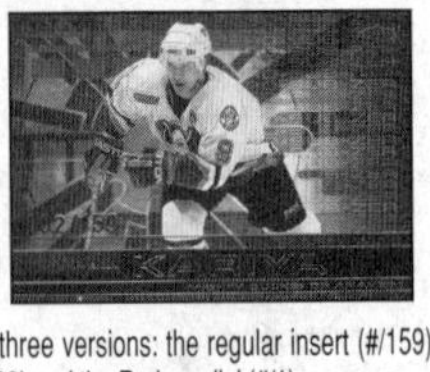

There are three versions: the regular insert (#/159), the Gold parallel (#/99) and the Red parallel (#/1).

Insert Set (10 cards):	375.00	200.00
Inserts	SZ99	SZ159
□□□ 1 Paul Kariya, Anah.	50.00	25.00
□□□ 2 Peter Forsberg, Colo.	50.00	25.00
□□□ 3 Patrick Roy (G), Colo.	75.00	55.00
□□□ 4 Brendan Shanahan, Detr.	30.00	15.00
□□□ 5 Steve Yzerman, Detr.	75.00	45.00
□□□ 6 Pavel Bure, Flor.	30.00	15.00
□□□ 7 Martin Brodeur (G), NJer.	50.00	30.00
□□□ 8 Jaromir Jagr, Pitt.	30.00	15.00
□□□ 9 Curtis Joseph (G), Toro.	30.00	15.00
□□□ 10 Mats Sundin, Toro.	30.00	15.00

WRAPPER REDEMPTION

These redemption cards were available at the Toronto 2000 Fall Expo.

Insert Set (20 cards):	425.00
Description (#/15)	Wrapper
□ 5 Paul Kariya, Anah.	35.00
□ 7 Teemu Selänne, Anah.	20.00
□ 15 Patrik Stefan, Atla.	5.00
□ 30 Dominik Hasek (G), Buff.	25.00
□ 62 Patrick Roy (G), Colo.	75.00
□ 75 Brett Hull, Dall.	25.00
□ 93 Steve Yzerman, Detr.	60.00
□ 102 Pavel Bure, Flor.	20.00
□ 114 Luc Robitaille, LosA.	20.00
□ 132 José Théodore (G), Mont.	30.00
□ 142 Martin Brodeur (G), NJer.	40.00
□ 172 Marian Hossa, Otta.	25.00
□ 177 Brian Boucher (G), Phil.	5.00
□ 182 John LeClair, Phil.	20.00
□ 198 Jaromir Jagr, Pitt.	25.00
□ 222 Vincent Lecavalier, Tamp.	25.00
□ 226 Nikolai Antropov, Toro.	5.00
□ 230 Curtis Joseph (G), Toro.	25.00
□ 233 Mats Sundin, Toro.	25.00
□ 239 Steve Kariya, Vanc.	10.00

2000 - 01 PANINI STICKER

These stickers were produced for European release only.

Complete Set (212 stickers):	50.00
Description	Sticker
□ 1 NHL	.25
□ 2 NHLPA	.25
□ 3 Thrashers Atla.	.25
□ 4 Johan Garpenlöv, Atla.	.25
□ 5 Patrik Stefan, Atla.	.25
□ 6 Andrew Brunette, Atla.	.25
□ 7 Andreas Karlsson, Atla.	.25
□ 8 Ray Ferraro, Atla.	.25
□ 9 Petr Buzek, Atla.	.25
□ 10 Bruins Bost.	.25
□ 11 Sergei Samsonov, Bost.	.50
□ 12 P.J. Axelsson, Bost.	.25
□ 13 Anson Carter, Bost.	.50
□ 14 Eric Nickulas, Bost.	.25
□ 15 Mikko Eloranta, Bost.	.25
□ 16 Joe Thornton, Bost.	1.50
□ 17 Sabres Buff.	.25
□ 18 Dominik Hasek (G), Buff.	1.00
□ 19 Curtis Brown, Buff.	.25
□ 20 Michael Peca, Buff.	.50
□ 21 Vaclav Varada, Buff.	.25
□ 22 Alexei Zhitnik, Buff.	.25
□ 23 Miroslav Satan, Buff.	.25
□ 24 Hurricanes Caro.	.25
□ 25 Sami Kapanen, Caro.	.25
□ 26 Paul Coffey, Caro. (Bost.)	.50
□ 27 Marek Malik, Caro.	.25
□ 28 Andrei Kovalenko, Caro. (Bost.)	.25
□ 29 Arturs Irbe (G), Caro.	.50
□ 30 Ron Francis, Caro.	.50
□ 31 Panthers Flor.	.25
□ 32 Scott Mellanby, Flor.	.25
□ 33 Viktor Kozlov, Flor.	.25
□ 34 Jaroslav Spacek, Flor.	.25
□ 35 Ray Whitney, Flor.	.25
□ 36 Robert Svehla, Flor.	.25
□ 37 Pavel Bure, Flor.	1.00
□ 38 Canadiens Mont.	.25
□ 39 Saku Koivu, Mont.	1.00
□ 40 Trevor Linden, Mont.	.50
□ 41 Karl Dykhuis, Mont.	.25
□ 42 Sergei Zholtok, Mont.	.25
□ 43 Martin Rucinsky, Mont.	.25
□ 44 Dainius Zubrus, Mont.	.25
□ 45 Devils NJer.	.25
□ 46 Alexander Mogilny, NJer.	.50
□ 47 Petr Sykora, NJer.	.50
□ 48 Martin Brodeur (G), NJer.	2.00
□ 49 Bobby Holik, NJer.	.25
□ 50 Scott Gomez, NJer.	.50
□ 51 Patrik Elias, NJer.	1.00
□ 52 Islanders NYIs.	.25
□ 53 Brad Isbister, NYIs.	.25
□ 54 Mariusz Czerkawski, NYIs.	.25
□ 55 Mats Lindgren, NYIs.	.25
□ 56 Tim Connolly, NYIs.	.50
□ 57 Kenny Jönsson, NYIs.	.25
□ 58 Olli Jokinen, NYIs. (Flor.)	.25
□ 59 Rangers NYRa.	.25
□ 60 Brian Leetch, NYRa.	.50
□ 61 Petr Nedved, NYRa.	.25
□ 62 Radek Dvorak, NYRa.	.25
□ 63 Valeri Kamensky, NYRa.	.25
□ 64 Theoren Fleury, NYRa.	.50
□ 65 Jan Hlavac, NYRa.	.25
□ 66 Senators Otta.	.25
□ 67 Magnus Arvedson, Otta.	.25
□ 68 Igor Kravchuk, Otta.	.25
□ 69 Vaclav Prospal, Otta.	.25
□ 70 Daniel Alfredsson, Otta.	.50
□ 71 Shawn McEachern, Otta.	.25
□ 72 Radek Bonk, Otta.	.25
□ 73 Flyers Phil.	.25
□ 74 John LeClair, Phil.	1.00
□ 75 Eric Lindros, Phil.	1.00
□ 76 Mark Recchi, Phil.	.50
□ 77 Daymond Langkow, Phil.	.25
□ 78 Ulf Samuelsson, Phil.	.25
□ 79 Valeri Zelepukin, Phil. (Chic.)	.25
□ 80 Penguins Pitt.	.25
□ 81 Jaromir Jagr, Pitt.	1.00
□ 82 Martin Straka, Pitt.	.25
□ 83 Aleksey Morozov, Pitt.	.25
□ 84 Alex Kovalev, Pitt.	.50
□ 85 Robert Lang, Pitt.	.25
□ 86 Darius Kasparaitis, Pitt.	.25
□ 87 Lightning Tamp.	.25
□ 88 Vincent Lecavalier, Tamp.	1.00
□ 89 Fredrik Modin, Tamp.	.25
□ 90 Jaroslav Svejkovsky, Tamp.	.25
□ 91 Mike Johnson, Tamp.	.25
□ 92 Pavel Kubina, Tamp.	.25
□ 93 Petr* Svoboda, Tamp.	.25
□ 94 Maple Leafs Toro.	.25
□ 95 Mats Sundin, Toro.	1.00
□ 96 Darcy Tucker, Toro.	.25
□ 97 Steve Thomas, Toro.	.25
□ 98 Jonas Höglund, Toro.	.25
□ 99 Igor Korolev, Toro.	.25
□ 100 Yanic Perreault, Toro.	.25
□ 101 Capitals Wash.	.25
□ 102 Peter Bondra, Wash.	.50
□ 103 Sergei Gonchar, Wash.	.25
□ 104 Joe Sacco, Wash.	.25
□ 105 Ulf Dahlén, Wash.	.25
□ 106 Adam Oates, Wash.	.50
□ 107 Calle Johansson, Wash.	.25
□ 108 Mighty Ducks Anah.	.25
□ 109 Paul Kariya, Anah.	1.50
□ 110 Guy Hebert (G), Anah.	.25
□ 111 Teemu Selänne, Anah.	1.00
□ 112 Ruslan Salei, Anah.	.25
□ 113 Vitaly Vishnevski, Anah.	.25
□ 114 Oleg Tverdovsky, Anah.	.25
□ 115 Flames Calg.	.25
□ 116 Valeri Bure, Calg.	.25
□ 117 Jarome Iginla, Calg.	1.00
□ 118 Marc Savard, Calg.	.25
□ 119 Andrei Nazarov, Calg.	.25
□ 120 Phil Housley, Calg.	.25
□ 121 Derek Morris, Calg.	.25
□ 122 Blackhawks Chic.	.25
□ 123 Michael Nylander, Chic.	.25
□ 124 Boris Mironov, Chic.	.25
□ 125 Alexei Zhamnov, Chic.	.25
□ 126 Tony Amonte, Chic.	.50
□ 127 Michal Grosek, Chic.	.25
□ 128 Steve Sullivan, Chic.	.25
□ 129 Avalanche Colo.	.25
□ 130 Peter Forsberg, Colo.	1.50
□ 131 Patrick Roy (G), Colo.	3.50

☐ 132 Joe Sakic, Colo. 2.00
☐ 133 Stéphane Yelle, Colo. .25
☐ 134 Sandis Ozolinsh, Colo. (Caro.) .25
☐ 135 Milan Hejduk, Colo. 1.00
☐ 136 Blue Jackets Colu. .25
☐ 137 Geoff Sanderson, Buff. (Colu.) .25
☐ 138 Ron Tugnutt (G), Pitt. (Colu.) .50
☐ 139 Radim Bicanek, Chic. (Colu.) .25
☐ 140 Mattias Timander, Bost. (Colu.) .25
☐ 141 Krzysztof Oliwa, NJer. (Colu.) .25
☐ 142 Espen Knutsen, Anah. (Colu.) .25
☐ 143 Stars Dall. .25
☐ 144 Mike Modano, Dall. 1.00
☐ 145 Joe Nieuwendyk, Dall. .50
☐ 146 Sergei Zubov, Dall. .25
☐ 147 Richard Matvichuk, Dall. .25
☐ 148 Brett Hull, Dall. 1.00
☐ 149 Jamie Langenbrunner, Dall. .25
☐ 150 Red Wings Detr. .25
☐ 151 Sergei Fedorov, Detr. 1.00
☐ 152 Brendan Shanahan, Detr. 1.00
☐ 153 Nicklas Lidström, Detr. .50
☐ 154 Vyacheslav Kozlov, Detr. .25
☐ 155 Igor Larionov, Detr. (Flor.) .50
☐ 156 Steve Yzerman, Detr. 3.00
☐ 157 Oilers Edmo. .25
☐ 158 Doug Weight, Edmo. .50
☐ 159 German Titov, Edmo. (Anah.) .25
☐ 160 Janne Niinimaa, Edmo. .25
☐ 161 Roman Hamrlik, Edmo. .25
☐ 162 Ryan Smyth, Edmo. .50
☐ 163 Alexander Selivanov, Edmo. .25
☐ 164 Kings LosA. .25
☐ 165 Rob Blake, LosA. .50
☐ 166 Luc Robitaille, LosA. 1.00
☐ 167 Zigmund Palffy, LosA. .50
☐ 168 Jozef Stümpel, LosA. .25
☐ 169 Glen Murray, LosA. .50
☐ 170 Mattias Norström, LosA. .25
☐ 171 Wild MinW. .25
☐ 172 Curtis Leschyshyn, Caro. (MinW.) .25
☐ 173 Sergei Krivokrasov, Calg. (MinW.) .25
☐ 174 Antti Laaksonen, Bost. (MinW.) .25
☐ 175 Pavel Patera, Dall. (MinW.) .25
☐ 176 Sean O'Donnell, LosA. (MinW.) .25
☐ 177 Manny Fernandez (G), Dall. (MinW.) .50
☐ 178 Predators Nash. .25
☐ 179 Vitali Yachmenev, Nash. .25
☐ 180 Patrick Kjellberg, Nash. .25
☐ 181 Ville Peltonen, Nash. .25
☐ 182 Cliff Ronning, Nash. .25
☐ 183 Greg Johnson, Nash. .25
☐ 184 Kimmo Timonen, Nash. .25
☐ 185 Coyotes Phoe. .25
☐ 186 Jeremy Roenick, Phoe. 1.00
☐ 187 Jyrki Lumme, Phoe. .25
☐ 188 Travis Green, Phoe. .25
☐ 189 Teppo Numminen, Phoe. .25
☐ 190 Keith Tkachuk, Phoe. .50
☐ 191 Radoslav Suchy, Phoe. .25
☐ 192 Blues SLou. .25
☐ 193 Chris Pronger, SLou. .50
☐ 194 Pierre Turgeon, SLou. .50
☐ 195 Pavol Demitra, SLou. .50
☐ 196 Roman Turek (G), SLou. .50
☐ 197 Michal Handzus, SLou. .25
☐ 198 Stéphane J.J. Richer, SLou. .25
☐ 199 Sharks SanJ. .25
☐ 200 Vincent Damphousse, SanJ. .50
☐ 201 Niklas Sundström, SanJ. .25
☐ 202 Stéphane Matteau, SanJ. .25
☐ 203 Marcus Ragnarsson, SanJ. .25
☐ 204 Owen Nolan, SanJ. .50
☐ 205 Alex Korolyuk, SanJ. .25
☐ 206 Canucks Vanc. .25
☐ 207 Andrew Cassels, Vanc. .25
☐ 208 Artem Chubarov, Vanc. .25
☐ 209 Mark Messier, Vanc. (NYRa.) 1.00
☐ 210 Mattias Öhlund, Vanc. .25
☐ 211 Todd Bertuzzi, Vanc. 1.50
☐ 212 Markus Näslund, Vanc. 1.00

2000 - 01 PARKHURST

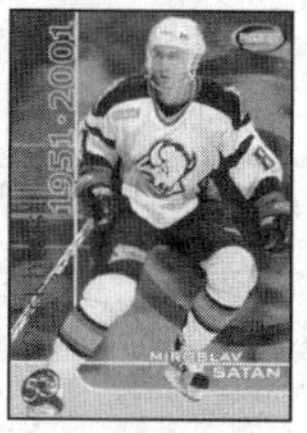

These cross-brand insert cards were distributed as follows: P-1 to P-100 in packs of Be A Player Memorabilia; P-101 to P-150 in boxes of Be A Player Memorabilia Rookie & Traded; P-151- to P-250 in packs of Signature Series.

Complete Set (250 cards): 300.00
Common Player: 1.00

Description — Parkie

☐ P-1 Pavel Bure, Flor. 2.50
☐ P-2 Tony Amonte, Chic. 2.00
☐ P-3 Chris Pronger, SLou. 2.00
☐ P-4 John Madden, NJer. 1.00
☐ P-5 Kimmo Timonen, Nash. 1.00
☐ P-6 Marc Savard, Calg. 1.00
☐ P-7 Peter Forsberg, Colo. 4.50
☐ P-8 Arturs Irbe (G), Caro. 1.00
☐ P-9 Mike York, NYRa. 1.00
☐ P-10 Brendan Shanahan, Detr. 3.50
☐ P-11 Simon Gagné, Phil. 2.50
☐ P-12 Maxim Afinogenov, Buff. 1.00
☐ P-13 Joe Sakic, Colo. 5.50
☐ P-14 Curtis Joseph (G), Toro. 3.50
☐ P-15 Jozef Stümpel, LosA. 1.00
☐ P-16 Vitaly Vishnevski, Anah. 1.00
☐ P-17 Owen Nolan, SanJ. 2.00
☐ P-18 Jan Hrdina, Pitt. 1.00
☐ P-19 Brenden Morrow, Dall. 1.00
☐ P-20 Todd Bertuzzi, Vanc. 4.00
☐ P-21 Vincent Lecavalier, Tamp. 3.50
☐ P-22 Andrew Brunette, Atla. 1.00
☐ P-23 Brendan Morrison, Vanc. 1.00
☐ P-24 Rod Brind'Amour, Caro. 1.00
☐ P-25 Patrik Elias, NJer. 2.50
☐ P-26 Joe Thornton, Bost. 4.00
☐ P-27 Roman Turek (G), SLou. 1.50
☐ P-28 Fred Brathwaite (G), Calg. 1.00
☐ P-29 Brian Leetch, NYRa. 2.00
☐ P-30 Trevor Linden, Mont. 1.00
☐ P-31 Janne Niinimaa, Edmo. 1.00
☐ P-32 Nikolai Antropov, Toro. 1.00
☐ P-33 Teemu Selänne, Anah. 2.50
☐ P-34 Calle Johansson, Wash. 1.00
☐ P-35 Boris Mironov, Chic. 1.00
☐ P-36 Éric Desjardins, Phil. 1.00
☐ P-37 Mark Parrish, Flor. 1.00
☐ P-38 Alex Tanguay, Colo. 2.00
☐ P-39 Jason Arnott, NJer. 1.50
☐ P-40 Vincent Damphousse, SanJ. 2.00
☐ P-41 Dominik Hasek (G), Buff. 3.50
☐ P-42 Teppo Numminen, Phoe. 1.00
☐ P-43 Patrick Lalime (G), Otta. 2.00
☐ P-44 Valeri Bure, Calg. 1.00
☐ P-45 Adam Oates, Wash. 1.00
☐ P-46 Sergei Zubov, Dall. 1.00
☐ P-47 Tim Connolly, NYIs. 1.00
☐ P-48 Pavel Kubina, Tamp. 1.00
☐ P-49 Nicklas Lidström, Detr. 2.00
☐ P-50 Mark Recchi, Phil. 1.00
☐ P-51 Chris Drury, Colo. 2.00
☐ P-52 Kyle McLaren, Bost. 1.00
☐ P-53 Steve Kariya, Vanc. 1.00
☐ P-54 Scott Gomez, NJer. 1.00
☐ P-55 Rob Blake, LosA. 2.00
☐ P-56 Miroslav Satan, Buff. 1.00
☐ P-57 Cliff Ronning, Nash. 1.00
☐ P-58 Radek Dvorak, NYRa. 1.00
☐ P-59 Jeff O'Neill, Caro. 1.00
☐ P-60 Dainius Zubrus, Mont. 1.00
☐ P-61 Brad Ference, Flor. 1.00
☐ P-62 Jarome Iginla, Calg. 2.50
☐ P-63 Chris Simon, Wash. 1.00
☐ P-64 Darryl Sydor, Dall. 1.00
☐ P-65 Daniel Alfredsson, Otta. 2.00
☐ P-66 Sandis Ozolinsh, Colo. 1.00
☐ P-67 Brian Rafalski, NJer. 1.00
☐ P-68 Ryan Smyth, Edmo. 1.50
☐ P-69 John LeClair, Phil. 2.50
☐ P-70 Patrik Stefan, Atla. 1.00
☐ P-71 Patrick Marleau, SanJ. 1.50
☐ P-72 Roberto Luongo (G), NYIs. 2.50
☐ P-73 Chris Osgood (G), Detr. 2.00
☐ P-74 Pierre Turgeon, SLou. 1.00
☐ P-75 Zigmund Palffy, LosA. 2.00
☐ P-76 Jeff Farkas, Toro. 1.00
☐ P-77 Milan Hejduk, Colo. 2.50
☐ P-78 Ray Whitney, Flor. 1.00
☐ P-79 Félix Potvin (G), Vanc. 2.00
☐ P-80 Chris Gratton, Buff. 1.00
☐ P-81 Brad Stuart, SanJ. 1.00
☐ P-82 Ron Francis, Caro. 2.00
☐ P-83 Oleg Tverdovsky, Anah. 1.00
☐ P-84 Alex Kovalev, Pitt. 2.00
☐ P-85 Sergei Fedorov, Detr. 3.50
☐ P-86 Nick Boynton, Bost. 1.00
☐ P-87 David Legwand, Nash. 1.00
☐ P-88 Robyn Regehr, Calg. 1.00
☐ P-89 Brian Boucher (G), Phil. 1.00
☐ P-90 Roman Hamrlik, Edmo. 1.00
☐ P-91 Jochen Hecht, SLou. 1.00
☐ P-92 Alexei Zhamnov, Chic. 1.00
☐ P-93 Olaf Kölzig (G), Wash. 2.00
☐ P-94 José Théodore (G), Mont. 4.00
☐ P-95 Jeremy Roenick, Phoe. 2.50
☐ P-96 Theoren Fleury, NYRa. 2.00
☐ P-97 Patrick Roy (G), Colo. 10.00
☐ P-98 Marian Hossa, Otta. 3.50
☐ P-99 Martin Brodeur (G), NJer. 5.50
☐ P-100 Brett Hull, Dall. 3.50
☐ P-101 Daniel Sedin, Vanc. 2.50
☐ P-102 Paul Coffey, Bost. 2.00
☐ P-103 Raymond Bourque, Colo. 4.00
☐ P-104 Glen Murray, LosA. 1.50
☐ P-105 Mariusz Czerkawski, NYIs. 1.00
☐ P-106 Jeff Friesen, SanJ. 1.00
☐ P-107 Sergei Samsonov, Bost. 2.00
☐ P-108 Tyler Wright, Colu. 1.00
☐ P-109 Manny Fernandez (G), MinW. 1.00
☐ P-110 Mike Richter (G), NYRa. 1.50
☐ P-111 Alexander Mogilny, NJer. 1.50
☐ P-112 Brian Rolston, Bost. 1.00
☐ P-113 Ron Tugnutt (G), Colu. 1.00
☐ P-114 Pavol Demitra, SLou. 1.00
☐ P-115 Radek Bonk, Otta. 1.00
☐ P-116 Al MacInnis, SLou. 1.00
☐ P-117 Jean-Pierre Dumont, Buff. 1.00
☐ P-118 Ed Belfour (G), Dall. 3.50
☐ P-119 Jeff Hackett (G), Mont. 1.00
☐ P-120 Shawn McEachern, Otta. 1.00
☐ P-121 Dan Cloutier (G), Tamp. 1.00
☐ P-122 Mika Noronen (G), Buff. 1.00
☐ P-123 Derian Hatcher, Dall. 1.00
☐ P-124 Saku Koivu, Mont. 2.50
☐ P-125 Keith Primeau, Phil. 1.00
☐ P-126 Mats Sundin, Toro. 3.50
☐ P-127 Damian Rhodes (G), Atla. 1.00
☐ P-128 Chris Chelios, Detr. 2.00
☐ P-129 Mike Dunham (G), Nash. 1.00
☐ P-130 Keith Tkachuk, Phoe. 2.00
☐ P-131 Steve Thomas, Toro. 1.00
☐ P-132 Phil Housley, Calg. 1.00
☐ P-133 Doug Weight, Edmo. 2.00
☐ P-134 Kris Beech, Wash. 1.00
☐ P-135 Jyrki Lumme, Phoe. 1.00
☐ P-136 Guy Hebert (G), Anah. 1.00
☐ P-137 Sami Kapanen, Caro. 1.00
☐ P-138 Trevor Kidd (G), Flor. 1.00
☐ **P-139 Marian Gaborik, MinW. RC 15.00**
☐ P-140 Martin Straka, Pitt. 1.00
☐ P-141 Ed Jovanovski, Vanc. 1.00
☐ P-142 Jean-Sébastien Aubin (G), Pitt. 1.00
☐ P-143 Viktor Kozlov, Flor. 1.00
☐ P-144 Scott Stevens, NJer. 1.00
☐ P-145 Jirí Slégr, Pitt. 1.00
☐ P-146 Steve Yzerman, Detr. 8.00
☐ P-147 Jocelyn Thibault (G), Chic. 1.00
☐ P-148 Stéphane Fiset (G), LosA. 1.00
☐ P-149 Kenny Jönsson, NYIs. 1.00
☐ P-150 Steve Shields (G), SanJ. 1.00
☐ P-151 Paul Kariya, Anah. 4.50
☐ P-152 Shane Willis, Caro. 1.50
☐ P-153 Martin Lapointe, Detr. 1.00
☐ P-154 Brian Savage, Mont. 1.00
☐ P-155 Alexei Yashin, Otta. 2.00
☐ P-156 Marcus Ragnarsson, SanJ. 1.00
☐ **P-157 Petr Tenkrat, Anah. RC 2.00**
☐ P-158 Sandis Ozolinsh, Caro. 1.00
☐ P-159 Anson Carter, Edmo. 1.00
☐ **P-160 Scott Hartnell, Nash. RC 3.00**
☐ P-161 Rick Tocchet, Phil. 1.00
☐ P-162 Brad Richards, Tamp. 3.00
☐ P-163 Byron Dafoe (G), Bost. 1.00
☐ P-164 Marc Denis (G), Colu. 1.50
☐ **P-165 Steven Reinprecht, LosA. RC 5.00**
☐ P-166 Mario Lemieux, Pitt. 10.00
☐ P-167 Taylor Pyatt, NYIs. 1.00
☐ P-168 Mike Vernon (G), Calg. 1.00
☐ P-169 Scott Niedermayer, NJer. 1.00
☐ P-170 Milan Kraft, Pitt. 1.00
☐ P-171 Donald Audette, Atla. 1.00
☐ P-172 Steve Sullivan, Chic. 1.00
☐ P-173 Todd Marchant, Edmo. 1.00
☐ P-174 Scott Walker, Nash. 1.00
☐ P-175 Daymond Langkow, Phil. 1.00
☐ P-176 Fredrik Modin, Tamp. 1.00
☐ P-177 Ray Ferraro, Atla. 1.00
☐ P-178 Michael Nylander, Chic. 1.00
☐ P-179 Robert Svehla, Flor. 1.00
☐ P-180 Petr* Sykora, NJer. 1.00
☐ P-181 Claude Lemieux, Phoe. 1.00
☐ P-182 Sergei Berezin, Toro. 1.00
☐ P-183 Doug Gilmour, Buff. 2.00
☐ P-184 Jere Lehtinen, Dall. 1.00
☐ P-185 Maxim Sushinsky, MinW. 1.00
☐ P-186 Jan Hlavac, NYRa. 1.00
☐ P-187 Michal Handzus, SLou. 1.00
☐ P-188 Jamie Langenbrunner, Dall. 1.00
☐ P-189 John Vanbiesbrouck (G), NYIs. 1.50
☐ P-190 Brent Johnson (G), SLou. 1.00
☐ P-191 Jason Allison, Bost. 2.00
☐ P-192 Adam Deadmarsh, Colo. 1.00
☐ P-193 Scott Mellanby, Flor. 1.00
☐ P-194 Sergei Brylin, NJer. 1.00
☐ P-195 Shane Doan, Phoe. 1.00
☐ P-196 Jonas Höglund, Toro. 1.00
☐ P-197 Bill Guerin, Bost. 1.00
☐ P-198 Espen (Shampoo) Knutsen, Colu. 1.00
☐ P-199 Bryan Smolinski, LosA. 1.00
☐ P-200 Brad Isbister, NYIs. 1.00
☐ P-201 Robert Lang, Pitt. 1.00
☐ P-202 Andrew Cassels, Vanc. 1.00
☐ P-203 Daniel Tkaczuk, Calg. 1.00
☐ P-204 Igor Larionov, Detr. 2.00
☐ P-205 Andrei Markov, Mont. 1.00
☐ P-206 Magnus Arvedson, Otta. 1.00
☐ P-207 Henrik Sedin, Vanc. 2.50
☐ P-208 Manny Legacé (G), Detr. 1.00
☐ P-209 Adam Graves, NYRa. 1.00
☐ **P-210 Marty Turco (G), Dall. RC 10.00**
☐ P-211 Stu Barnes, Buff. 1.00
☐ P-212 Geoff Sanderson, Colu. 1.00
☐ P-213 Luc Robitaille, LosA. 2.50
☐ P-214 Roman Hamrlik, NYIs. 1.00
☐ P-215 Jaromir Jagr, Pitt. 3.50
☐ P-216 Markus Näslund, Vanc. 3.50
☐ P-217 Alexei Zhitnik, Buff. 1.00
☐ P-218 Joe Nieuwendyk, Dall. 1.00
☐ **P-219 Lubomir Sekeras, MinW. RC 2.00**
☐ P-220 Petr Nedved, NYRa. 1.00
☐ P-221 Dallas Drake, SLou. 1.00
☐ P-222 Sergei Gonchar, Wash. 1.00
☐ P-223 David Tanabe, Caro. 1.00
☐ P-224 Tommy Salo (G), Edmo. 1.00
☐ **P-225 Rick DiPietro (G), NYIs. RC 8.00**
☐ **P-226 Justin Williams, Phil. RC 5.00**
☐ P-227 Dmitri Khristich, Wash. 1.00
☐ **P-228 L'ubomír Visnovsky, LosA. RC 2.00**
☐ **P-229 Jani Hurme (G), Otta. RC 3.00**
☐ **P-230 Roman Cechmanek (G), Phil. RC 7.00**
☐ P-231 Cory Stillman, Calg. 1.00
☐ P-232 Mike Modano, Dall. 3.50
☐ P-233 Scott Pellerin, MinW. 1.00
☐ P-234 Mark Messier, NYRa. 3.50
☐ P-235 Scott A. Young, SLou. 1.00
☐ P-236 Peter Bondra, Wash. 2.00
☐ P-237 Oleg Saprykin, Calg. 1.00
☐ P-238 Pat Verbeek, Detr. 1.00
☐ P-239 Martin Rucinsky, Mont. 1.00
☐ **P-240 Martin Havlat, Otta. RC 10.00**
☐ P-241 Evgeni Nabokov (G), SanJ. 4.00
☐ P-242 Tomi Kallio, Atla. 1.00
☐ P-243 Éric Dazé, Chic. 1.00
☐ P-244 Roberto Luongo (G), Flor. 2.50
☐ P-245 Bobby Holik, NJer. 1.00
☐ P-246 Sean Burke (G), Phoe. 2.00
☐ P-247 Martin Biron (G), Buff. 1.50
☐ P-248 Mathieu Garon (G), Mont. 1.00
☐ P-249 Jamie Storr (G), LosA. 1.00
☐ P-250 Maxime Ouellet (G), Phil. 1.00

2000 - 01 PREMIER PLUS

This series was released in March 2001. Cards 1-140 have a Blue Ice parallel (#/250). Veteran players have a red border on the card front design while rookie players have a blue border on the card front design.

Complete Set (140 cards): 475.00 55.00
Common Player: 6.00 .20

	Player	BI	Reg.
☐ ☐	1 Scott Gomez, NJer.	4.00	.20
☐ ☐	2 Brian Boucher (G), Phil.	3.00	.20
☐ ☐	3 Patrik Stefan, Atla.	3.00	.20
☐ ☐	4 David Legwand, Nash.	4.00	.20
☐ ☐	5 Tim Connolly, NYIs.	4.00	.20
☐ ☐	6 Jaromir Jagr, Pitt.	10.00	1.00
☐ ☐	7 Owen Nolan, SanJ.	6.00	.50
☐ ☐	8 Patrick Roy (G), Colo.	30.00	3.00
☐ ☐	9 Joe Thornton, Bost.	12.00	1.00
☐ ☐	10 Paul Kariya, Anah.	10.00	1.00
☐ ☐	11 Mark Messier, NYRa.	10.00	1.00
☐ ☐	12 Jeremy Roenick, Phoe.	8.00	.50

☐☐	13 Jeff Friesen, SanJ.	3.00	.20
☐☐	14 Al MacInnis, SLou.	4.00	.20
☐☐	15 Curtis Joseph (G), Toro.	10.00	1.00
☐☐	16 Olaf Kölzig (G), Wash.	6.00	.50
☐☐	17 Dominik Hasek (G), Buff.	10.00	1.00
☐☐	18 Arturs Irbe (G), Caro.	4.00	.20
☐☐	19 Joe Sakic, Colo.	16.00	1.50
☐☐	20 Sergei Fedorov, Detr.	10.00	1.00
☐☐	21 Zigmund Palffy, LosA.	6.00	.50
☐☐	22 Jason Arnott, NJer.	4.00	.20
☐☐	23 Marian Hossa, Otta.	10.00	1.00
☐☐	24 Pierre Turgeon, SLou.	4.00	.20
☐☐	25 Ron Tugnutt (G), Colu.	4.00	.20
☐☐	26 Valeri Bure, Calg.	3.00	.20
☐☐	27 Tony Amonte, Chic.	6.00	.50
☐☐	28 Jeff Hackett (G), Mont.	3.00	.20
☐☐	29 Mariusz Czerkawski, NYIs.	2.00	.20
☐☐	30 Wade Redden, Otta.	3.00	.20
☐☐	31 Mark Recchi, Phil.	4.00	.20
☐☐	32 Jean-Sébastien Aubin (G), Pitt.	2.00	.20
☐☐	33 Jason Allison, Bost.	6.00	.50
☐☐	34 Michael Peca, Buff.	4.00	.20
☐☐	35 Teemu Selänne, Anah.	8.00	.50
☐☐	36 Martin Brodeur (G), NJer.	16.00	1.50
☐☐	37 Simon Gagné, Phil.	8.00	.50
☐☐	38 Chris Simon, Wash.	2.00	.20
☐☐	39 Doug Weight, Edmo.	6.00	.50
☐☐	40 Jocelyn Thibault (G), Chic.	4.00	.20
☐☐	41 Ed Belfour (G), Dall.	10.00	1.00
☐☐	42 Raymond Bourque, Colo.	12.00	1.00
☐☐	43 Mike Richter (G), NYRa.	4.00	.20
☐☐	44 Curtis Leschyshyn, MinW.	1.00	.20
☐☐	45 Pavol Demitra, SLou.	4.00	.20
☐☐	46 Alex Kovalev, Pitt.	6.00	.50
☐☐	47 Brad Stuart, SanJ.	4.00	.20
☐☐	48 Jarome Iginla, Calg.	8.00	.50
☐☐	49 Ron Francis, Caro.	6.00	.50
☐☐	50 Brendan Shanahan, Detr.	10.00	1.00
☐☐	51 Rob Blake, LosA.	6.00	.50
☐☐	52 Miroslav Satan, Buff.	3.00	.20
☐☐	53 Theoren Fleury, NYRa.	6.00	.50
☐☐	54 John LeClair, Phil.	8.00	.50
☐☐	55 Roman Turek (G), SLou.	4.00	.20
☐☐	56 Brett Hull, Dall.	10.00	1.00
☐☐	57 Peter Forsberg, Colo.	14.00	1.00
☐☐	58 Steve Yzerman, Detr.	20.00	2.00
☐☐	59 Derian Hatcher, Dall.	3.00	.20
☐☐	60 Pavel Bure, Flor.	8.00	.50
☐☐	61 Patrik Elias, NJer.	8.00	.50
☐☐	62 Daniel Alfredsson, Otta.	6.00	.50
☐☐	63 Adam Oates, Wash.	4.00	.20
☐☐	64 Andrew Brunette, Atla.	1.00	.20
☐☐	65 Chris Pronger, SLou.	6.00	.50
☐☐	66 Mario Lemieux, Pitt.	30.00	3.00
☐☐	67 Keith Tkachuk, Phoe.	6.00	.50
☐☐	68 Markus Näslund, Vanc.	10.00	1.00
☐☐	69 Mike Modano, Dall.	10.00	1.00
☐☐	70 Nicklas Lidström, Detr.	6.00	.50
☐☐	71 Scott Stevens, NJer.	4.00	.20
☐☐	72 Vincent Lecavalier, Tamp.	10.00	1.00
☐☐	73 Luc Robitaille, LosA.	8.00	.50
☐☐	74 Mats Sundin, Toro.	10.00	1.00
☐☐	75 Milan Hejduk, Colo.	8.00	.50
☐☐	76 Rod Brind'Amour, Caro.	3.00	.20
☐☐	77 Tommy Salo (G), Edmo.	4.00	.20
☐☐	78 Byron Dafoe (G), Bost.	4.00	.20
☐☐	79 Doug Gilmour, Buff.	6.00	.50
☐☐	80 Guy Hebert (G), Anah.	2.00	.20
☐☐	81 Keith Primeau, Phil.	4.00	.20
☐☐	82 Chris Drury, Colo.	6.00	.50
☐☐	83 Saku Koivu, Mont.	8.00	.50
☐☐	84 Alexei Yashin, Otta.	6.00	.50
☐☐	85 Martin St-Louis, Tamp.	4.00	.20
☐☐	86 Steve McCarthy, Chic.	1.00	.20
☐☐	87 Henrik Sedin, Vanc.	6.00	.50
☐☐	88 Kris Beech, Wash.	3.00	.20
☐☐	89 Dimitri Kalinin, Buff.	1.00	.20
☐☐	90 Maxime Ouellet (G), Phil.	4.00	.50
☐☐	91 Shawn Heins, SanJ.	1.00	.20
☐☐	92 Mika Noronen (G), Buff.	4.00	.20
☐☐	93 Taylor Pyatt, NYIs.	3.00	.20
☐☐	94 Brent Johnson (G), SLou.	6.00	.50
☐☐	95 Oleg Saprykin, Calg.	2.00	.20
☐☐	96 Daniel Tkaczuk, Calg.	2.00	.20
☐☐	97 Daniel Sedin, Vanc.	6.00	.50
☐☐	98 Milan Kraft, Pitt.	4.00	.50
☐☐	99 Jeff Farkas, Toro.	2.00	.20
☐☐	100 Denis Shvidki, Flor.	2.00	.20
☐☐	101 Mathieu Garon (G), Mont.	4.00	.20
☐☐	102 Mike Mottau, NYRa.	1.00	.20
☐☐	103 Andréi Markov, Mont.	1.00	.20
☐☐	104 Brad Richards, Tamp.	7.00	.50
☐☐	105 Brian Swanson, Edmo.	3.00	.20
☐☐	**106 Josef Vasicek, Caro. RC**	**4.00**	**1.50**
☐☐	**107 Reto von Arx, Chic. RC**	**3.00**	**1.00**
☐☐	**108 Lubomir Sekeras, MinW. RC**	**3.00**	**1.00**
☐☐	**109 Ruslan Fedotenko, Phil. RC**	**3.00**	**1.00**
☐☐	**110 Roman Simicek, Pitt. RC**	**2.00**	**.50**
☐☐	**111 Michel Riesen, Edmo. RC**	**3.00**	**1.00**
☐☐	**112 Petteri Nummelin, Colu. RC**	**3.00**	**1.00**
☐☐	**113 Brad Tapper, Atla. RC**	**3.00**	**1.00**
☐☐	**114 Alexandre Kharitonov, Tamp. RC**	**2.00**	**.50**
☐☐	**115 Andrew Raycroft (G), Bost. RC**	**4.00**	**1.50**
☐☐	**116 Ossi Väänänen, Phoe. RC**	**3.00**	**1.00**
☐☐	**117 Tyler Bouck, Dall. RC**	**3.00**	**1.00**
☐☐	**118 Steven Reinprecht, LosA. RC**	**9.00**	**2.00**
☐☐	**119 Rostislav Klesla, Colu. RC**	**9.00**	**2.00**
☐☐	**120 Martin Havlat, Otta. RC**	**24.00**	**3.50**
☐☐	**121 Scott Hartnell, Nash. RC**	**4.00**	**1.50**
☐☐	**122 David Aebischer (G), Colo. RC**	**6.00**	**2.00**
☐☐	**123 Bryce Salvador, SLou. RC**	**3.00**	**1.00**
☐☐	**124 Jani Hurme (G), Otta. RC**	**4.00**	**1.50**
☐☐	**125 Éric Belanger, LosA. RC**	**3.00**	**1.00**
☐☐	**126 Marty Turco (G), Dall. RC**	**12.00**	**3.50**
☐☐	**127 Rick DiPietro (G), NYIs. RC**	**9.00**	**3.00**
☐☐	**128 Justin Williams, Phil. RC**	**6.00**	**2.00**
☐☐	**129 Dale Purinton, NYRa. RC**	**3.00**	**1.00**
☐☐	**130 Marian Gaborik, MinW. RC**	**40.00**	**6.00**
☐☐	**131 Petr Svoboda, Toro. RC**	**3.00**	**1.00**
☐☐	**132 Niclas Wallin, Caro. RC**	**2.00**	**.50**
☐☐	**133 Petr Hubacek, Phil. RC**	**2.00**	**.50**
☐☐	**134 Colin White, NJer. RC**	**3.00**	**1.00**
☐☐	**135 Greg Classen, Nash. RC**	**3.00**	**1.00**
☐☐	**136 Roman Cechmanek (G), Phil. RC**	**20.00**	**2.50**
☐☐	**137 Eric Boulton, Buff. RC**	**3.00**	**1.00**
☐☐	**138 Sascha Goc, NJer. RC**	**3.00**	**1.00**
☐☐	**139 Lubomir Visnovsky, LosA. RC**	**3.00**	**1.00**
☐☐	**140 Ronald Petrovicky, Calg. RC**	**3.00**	**1.00**
	Description		**- Gomez**
☐	CTW1 Scott Gomez Autograph		- 35.00
☐	Scott Gomez Checklist		- 2.00

CLUB SIGNINGS

Insert Set (9 cards):		**290.00**
	Autograph	**CS**
☐	CS-4 Bobby Clarke, Phil.	25.00
☐	CS-6 Marcel Dionne, LosA.	25.00
☐	CS-3 John LeClair, Phil.	25.00
☐	CS-5 Luc Robitaille, LosA.	25.00
☐	CS-1 Billy Smith, NYIs.	25.00
☐	CS-2 John Vanbiesbrouck (G), NYIs.	25.00
☐	Combo-1 Bi. Smith / J. Vanbiesbrouck	50.00
☐	Combo-2 B. Clarke / J. LeClair	75.00
☐	Combo-3 M. Dionne/ L. Robitaille	75.00

GAME PIECES

Insert Set (18 cards):		**475.00**
	Player	**GP**
☐	GP-MB Maxim Balmochnykh, Anah. ✂ Jersey	20.00
☐	GP-KB Kris Beech, Wash. ✂ Jersey	20.00
☐	GP-EB Ed Belfour (G), Dall. ✂ Stick	50.00
☐	GP-VB Valeri Bure, Calg. ✂ Stick	20.00
☐	GP-RF Rico Fata, Calg. ✂ Jersey	20.00
☐	GP-JI Jarome Iginla, Calg. ✂ Stick	25.00
☐	GP-AO Adam Oates, Wash. ✂ Stick	20.00
☐	GP-TP Taylor Pyatt, NYIs. ✂ Jersey	20.00
☐	GP-OS Oleg Saprykin, Calg. ✂ Jersey	20.00
☐	GP-TS Teemu Selänne, Anah. ✂ Stick	25.00
☐	GP-MT Marty Turco (G), Dall. ✂ Jersey	50.00
☐	GP-JV John Vanbiesbrouck (G), NYIs. ✂ Stick	20.00
☐	AO/KB K. Beech ✂ / A. Oates ✂	30.00
☐	EB/MT E. Belfour (G) ✂ / M. Turco (G) ✂	75.00
☐	JI/RF R. Fata ✂ / J. Iginla ✂	50.00
☐	JV/TP T. Pyatt ✂ / J. Vanbiesbrouck (G) ✂	30.00
☐	TS/MB M. Balmochnykh ✂ / T. Selänne ✂	50.00
☐	VB/OS V. Bure ✂ / O. Saprykin ✂	35.00

MASTERS OF THE BREAK

Insert Set (20 cards):		**80.00**
	Insert (1:24)	**MB**
☐	MB1 Jaromir Jagr, Pitt.	5.00
☐	MB2 Teemu Selänne, Anah.	4.00
☐	MB3 Pavel Bure, Flor.	4.00
☐	MB4 Tony Amonte, Chic.	3.00
☐	MB5 Milan Hejduk, Colo.	4.00
☐	MB6 Patrik Elias, NJer.	4.00
☐	MB7 Paul Kariya, Anah.	7.00
☐	MB8 Peter Forsberg, Colo.	7.00
☐	MB9 Sergei Fedorov, Detr.	5.00
☐	MB10 Mike Modano, Dall.	5.00
☐	MB11 Martin Brodeur (G), NJer.	8.00
☐	MB12 Patrick Roy (G), Colo.	15.00
☐	MB13 Ed Belfour (G), Dall.	5.00
☐	MB14 Curtis Joseph (G), Toro.	5.00
☐	MB15 Dominik Hasek (G), Buff.	5.00
☐	MB16 Olaf Kölzig (G), Wash.	3.00
☐	MB17 Roman Turek (G), SLou.	2.00
☐	MB18 Brian Boucher (G), Phil.	2.00
☐	MB19 Mike Richter (G), NYRa.	2.00
☐	MB20 Tommy Salo (G), Edmo.	2.00

PREMIER ASPIRATIONS

Insert Set (10 cards):		**20.00**
	Insert (1:16)	**PA**
☐	PA1 Scott Gomez, NJer.	2.00
☐	PA2 Vincent Lecavalier, Tamp.	5.00
☐	PA3 Maxim Afinogenov, Buff.	1.50
☐	PA4 Milan Hejduk, Colo.	3.00
☐	PA5 Joe Thornton, Bost.	6.00
☐	PA6 Marian Hossa, Otta.	5.00
☐	PA7 Oleg Saprykin, Calg.	1.50
☐	PA8 Shane Willis, Caro.	1.50
☐	PA9 David Legwand, Nash.	1.50
☐	PA10 Tim Connolly, NYIs.	1.50

PREMIER ROOKIES

These cards have a Blue Ice parallel (#/250).

Insert Set (10 cards):		**90.00**	**30.00**
	Inserts	**BI250**	**PR**
☐☐	PR1 Marian Gaborik, MinW.	30.00	15.00
☐☐	PR2 Henrik Sedin, Vanc.	12.00	2.00
☐☐	PR3 Rostislav Klesla, Colu.	9.00	4.00
☐☐	PR4 Brad Richards, Tamp.	14.00	2.00
☐☐	PR5 Justin Williams, Phil.	9.00	4.00
☐☐	PR6 Josef Vasicek, Caro.	7.00	3.00
☐☐	PR7 Daniel Sedin, Vanc.	12.00	2.00
☐☐	PR8 Maxime Ouellet (G), Phil.	9.00	1.50
☐☐	PR9 Andréi Markov, Mont.	6.00	1.50
☐☐	PR10 Oleg Saprykin, Calg.	7.00	1.50

PREMIER TEAM

These cards have a Blue Ice parallel.

Insert Set (10 cards):		**40.00**	**.00**
	Inserts	**BI**	**PT**
☐☐	PT1 Paul Kariya, Anah.	5.00	4.00
☐☐	PT2 Peter Forsberg, Colo.	8.00	4.00
☐☐	PT3 John LeClair, Phil.	5.00	2.00
☐☐	PT4 Mike Modano, Dall.	6.00	3.00
☐☐	PT5 Martin Brodeur (G), NJer.	10.00	4.00
☐☐	PT6 Pavel Bure, Flor.	5.00	2.00
☐☐	PT7 Curtis Joseph (G), Toro.	6.00	3.00
☐☐	PT8 Jaromi Jagr, Pitt.	5.00	3.00
☐☐	PT9 Chris Pronger, SLou.	3.00	1.50
☐☐	PT10 Teemu Selänne, Anah.	5.00	2.00

PRIVATE SIGNINGS

Insert Set (9 cards):		**300.00**
	Autograph	**PS**
☐	Brad Richards, Tamp. ✍	35.00
☐	Brad Stuart, SanJ. ✍	30.00
☐	Chris Pronger, SLou. ✍	30.00
☐	Evgeni Nabokov (G), SanJ. ✍	30.00
☐	Martin Brodeur (G), NJer. ✍	80.00
☐	Marian Gaborik, MinW. ✍	65.00
☐	Milan Kraft, Pitt. ✍	20.00
☐	Marty Turco (G), Dall. ✍	45.00
☐	Scott Hartnell, Nash. ✍	20.00

TROPHY TRIBUTE

Insert Set (15 cards):		**20.00**
	Insert (1:16)	**TT**
☐	TT1 Dominik Hasek (G), Buff.	3.00
☐	TT2 Jaromi Jagr, Pitt.	3.00
☐	TT3 Patrick Roy (G), Colo.	10.00
☐	TT4 Chris Pronger, SLou.	2.00
☐	TT5 Paul Kariya, Anah.	4.00
☐	TT6 Ed Belfour (G), Dall.	3.00
☐	TT7 Mark Messier, NYRa.	3.00
☐	TT8 Raymond Bourque, Colo.	4.00
☐	TT9 Steve Yzerman, Detr.	8.00
☐	TT10 Sergei Fedorov, Detr.	3.00
☐	TT11 Brett Hull, Dall.	3.00
☐	TT12 Ron Francis, Caro.	2.00
☐	TT13 Pavel Bure, Flor.	2.00
☐	TT14 Teemu Selänne, Anah.	2.00
☐	TT15 Brian Leetch, NYRa.	2.00

WORLD PREMIER

Insert Set (20 cards):		**20.00**
	Insert (1:24)	**WP**
☐	WP1 Patrick Roy (G), Colo.	15.00
☐	WP2 Martin Brodeur (G), NJer.	8.00
☐	WP3 Chris Pronger, SLou.	3.00
☐	WP4 Sergei Zubov, Dall.	2.00
☐	WP5 Scott Stevens, NJer.	2.00
☐	WP6 Raymond Bourque, Colo.	6.00
☐	WP7 Nicklas Lidström, Detr.	3.00
☐	WP8 Rob Blake, LosA.	3.00
☐	WP9 Paul Kariya, Anah.	7.00
☐	WP10 John LeClair, Phil.	4.00
☐	WP11 Keith Tkachuk, Phoe.	3.00
☐	WP12 Brendan Shanahan, Detr.	5.00
☐	WP13 Vincent Lecavalier, Tamp.	5.00
☐	WP14 Steve Yzerman, Detr.	12.00
☐	WP15 Mike Modano, Dall.	5.00
☐	WP16 Peter Forsberg, Colo.	7.00
☐	WP17 Pavel Bure, Flor.	4.00
☐	WP18 Teemu Selänne, Anah.	4.00
☐	WP19 Brett Hull, Dall.	5.00
☐	WP20 Jaromir Jagr, Pitt.	5.00

PRE-PRODUCTION SAMPLE

Complete Set (6 cards):		**8.00**
	Player	**Promo**
☐	PP1 Scott Gomez, NJer.	1.00
☐	PP2 Joe Sakic, Colo.	4.00
☐	PP3 Zigmund Palffy, LosA.	1.50
☐	PP4 Tony Amonte, Chic.	1.50
☐	PP5 David Legwand, Nash.	1.00
☐	PP6 Jeff Farkas, Toro.	1.00

2000 - 01 PRIVATE STOCK

This series was issued in January 2001. Hobby packs contained regular gold-foil base cards (1-100, 152), short-printed gold-foil rookie-subset cards (101-151, each #/155), Portraits in Gold parallel cards (1-152, each #/75) and Premiere Date parallel cards (1-152, each #/60). Retail packs contained regular silver-foil base cards (1-100, 152), short-printed silver-foil rookie-subset cards (101-151, each #/230) and Portraits in Silver parallel cards (1-152, each #/120).

Shell Set (101 cards):				**50.00**
Complete Set (152 cards):		**2,500**	**2,400**	**1,550**
Common Player:		**8.00**	**6.00**	**.35**
	Hobby	**PD60**	**FiG75**	**Hobby**
☐☐☐	1 Guy Hebert (G), Anah.	8.00	6.00	.35
☐☐☐	2 Paul Kariya, Anah.	40.00	40.00	2.50
☐☐☐	3 Teemu Selänne, Anah.	25.00	20.00	1.50
☐☐☐	4 Ray Ferraro, Atla.	8.00	6.00	.35
☐☐☐	5 Damian Rhodes (G), Atla.	8.00	6.00	.35
☐☐☐	6 Patrik Stefan, Atla.	10.00	6.00	.50
☐☐☐	7 Byron Dafoe (G), Bost.	10.00	10.00	.50
☐☐☐	8 Sergei Samsonov, Bost.	15.00	15.00	1.00
☐☐☐	9 Joe Thornton, Bost.	35.00	35.00	2.00
☐☐☐	10 Maxim Afinogenov, Buff.	10.00	10.00	.50

11 Doug Gilmour, Buff.	15.00	15.00	1.00
12 Dominik Hasek (G), Buff.	30.00	30.00	2.00
13 Miroslav Satan, Buff.	10.00	6.00	.50
14 Fred Brathwaite (G), Calg.	10.00	6.00	.50
15 Valeri Bure, Calg.	10.00	6.00	.50
16 Ron Francis, Caro.	15.00	15.00	1.00
17 Arturs Irbe (G), Caro.	10.00	10.00	.50
18 Sami Kapanen, Caro.	10.00	6.00	.50
19 Tony Amonte, Chic.	15.00	15.00	1.00
20 Jocelyn Thibault (G), Chic.	10.00	10.00	.50
21 Alexei Zhamnov, Chic.	10.00	6.00	.50
22 Raymond Bourque, Colo.	35.00	35.00	2.00
23 Peter Forsberg, Colo.	40.00	40.00	2.50
24 Milan Hejduk, Colo.	25.00	20.00	1.50
25 Patrick Roy (G), Colo.	90.00	90.00	6.00
26 Joe Sakic, Colo.	50.00	45.00	3.00
27 Marc Denis (G), Colu.	15.00	10.00	.50
28 Ted Drury, Colu.	8.00	6.00	.35
29 Geoff Sanderson, Colu.	8.00	6.00	.35
30 Ed Belfour (G), Dall.	30.00	30.00	2.00
31 Brett Hull, Dall.	30.00	30.00	2.00
32 Mike Modano, Dall.	30.00	30.00	2.00
33 Brenden Morrow, Dall.	10.00	6.00	.50
34 Joe Nieuwendyk, Dall.	10.00	10.00	.50
35 Sergei Fedorov, Detr.	30.00	30.00	2.00
36 Chris Osgood (G), Detr.	15.00	15.00	1.00
37 Brendan Shanahan, Detr.	30.00	30.00	2.00
38 Steve Yzerman, Detr.	75.00	70.00	4.50
39 Tommy Salo (G), Edmo.	10.00	10.00	.50
40 Ryan Smyth, Edmo.	15.00	10.00	.50
41 Doug Weight, Edmo.	15.00	15.00	1.00
42 Pavel Bure, Flor.	25.00	20.00	1.50
43 Trevor Kidd (G), Flor.	10.00	6.00	.50
44 Viktor Kozlov, Flor.	10.00	6.00	.50
45 Stéphane Fiset (G), LosA.	10.00	6.00	.50
46 Zigmund Palffy, LosA.	15.00	15.00	1.00
47 Luc Robitaille, LosA.	25.00	20.00	1.50
48 M. Fernandez (G), MinW.	10.00	10.00	.50
49 Sergei Krivokrasov, MinW.	8.00	6.00	.35
50 Stacy Roest, MinW.	8.00	6.00	.35
51 Saku Koivu, Mont.	35.00	35.00	1.50
52 Trevor Linden, Mont.	10.00	10.00	.50
53 José Théodore (G), Mont.	35.00	35.00	2.00
54 Mike Dunham (G), Nash.	10.00	10.00	.50
55 David Legwand, Nash.	10.00	10.00	.50
56 Jason Arnott, NJer.	15.00	10.00	.50
57 Martin Brodeur (G), NJer.	50.00	45.00	3.00
58 Patrik Elias, NJer.	25.00	20.00	1.50
59 Scott Gomez, NJer.	10.00	10.00	.50
60 Petr* Sykora, NJer.	10.00	10.00	.50
61 Tim Connolly, NYIs.	10.00	10.00	.50
62 Mariusz Czerkawski, NYIs.	8.00	6.00	.35
63 Vanbiesbrouck (G), NYIs.	15.00	10.00	.50
64 Theoren Fleury, NYRa.	15.00	15.00	1.00
65 Brian Leetch, NYRa.	15.00	15.00	1.00
66 Mark Messier, NYRa.	30.00	30.00	2.00
67 Mike Richter (G), NYRa.	15.00	10.00	.50
68 Daniel Alfredsson, Otta.	35.00	35.00	1.00
69 Radek Bonk, Otta.	10.00	6.00	.50
70 Marian Hossa, Otta.	30.00	30.00	2.00
71 Brian Boucher (G), Phil.	10.00	6.00	.50
72 Simon Gagné, Phil.	25.00	20.00	1.50
73 John LeClair, Phil.	25.00	20.00	1.50
74 Eric Lindros, Phil.	30.00	30.00	2.00
75 N. Khabibulin (G), Phoe.	10.00	10.00	.50
76 Jeremy Roenick, Phoe.	25.00	20.00	1.50
77 Keith Tkachuk, Phoe.	15.00	15.00	1.00
78 J-S Aubin (G), Pitt.	8.00	6.00	.35
79 Jan Hrdina, Pitt.	8.00	6.00	.35
80 Jaromir Jagr, Pitt.	30.00	30.00	2.00
81 Martin Straka, Pitt.	10.00	6.00	.50
82 Pavol Demitra, SLou.	10.00	10.00	.50
83 Al MacInnis, SLou.	10.00	10.00	.50
84 Chris Pronger, SLou.	15.00	15.00	1.00
85 Roman Turek (G), SLou.	15.00	10.00	.50
86 Pierre Turgeon, SLou.	10.00	10.00	.50
87 V. Damphousse, SanJ.	15.00	15.00	1.00
88 Jeff Friesen, SanJ.	10.00	6.00	.50
89 Owen Nolan, SanJ.	15.00	15.00	1.00
90 Dan Cloutier (G), Tamp.	10.00	10.00	.50
91 Vincent Lecavalier, Tamp.	30.00	30.00	2.00
92 Nikolai Antropov, Toro.	8.00	6.00	.35
93 Curtis Joseph (G), Toro.	30.00	30.00	2.00
94 Mats Sundin, Toro.	30.00	30.00	2.00
95 Steve Kariya, Vanc.	8.00	6.00	.35
96 Markus Näslund, Vanc.	30.00	30.00	2.00
97 Félix Potvin (G), Vanc.	35.00	35.00	1.00
98 Jeff Halpern, Wash.	8.00	6.00	.35
99 Olaf Kölzig (G), Wash.	15.00	15.00	1.00
100 Adam Oates, Wash.	10.00	10.00	.50
152 Mario Lemieux, Pitt.	160.00	155.00	10.00

HOBBY ROOKIES

Hobby Insert	PD60	FiG75	H155
101 J. Rönnqvist, Anah. RC	**20.00**	**20.00**	**25.00**
102 Samuel Påhlsson, Bost.	10.00	6.00	5.00
103 Raycroft (G), Bost. RC	**30.00**	**35.00**	**50.00**

104 Eric Boulton, Buff. RC	**20.00**	**20.00**	**25.00**
105 Dimitri Kalinin, Buff.	8.00	6.00	5.00
106 Mika Noronen (G), Buff.	25.00	20.00	20.00
107 Oleg Saprykin, Calg.	15.00	10.00	10.00
108 J. Vasicek, Caro. RC	**30.00**	**35.00**	**50.00**
109 Shane Willis, Caro.	15.00	10.00	10.00
110 Steve McCarthy, Chic.	10.00	6.00	5.00
111 Aebischer (G), Colo. RC	**40.00**	**45.00**	**75.00**
112 Serge Aubin, Colu. RC	**20.00**	**20.00**	**25.00**
113 R. Klesla, Colu. RC	**90.00**	**90.00**	**125.00**
114 David Vyborny, Colu.	10.00	6.00	5.00
115 Tyler Bouck, Dall. RC	**20.00**	**20.00**	**25.00**
116 Richard Jackman, Dall.	10.00	6.00	5.00
117 M. Turco (G), Dall. RC	**75.00**	**90.00**	**250.00**
118 Dan LaCouture, Edmo.	8.00	6.00	5.00
119 Brian Swanson, Edmo.	8.00	6.00	5.00
120 Denis Shvidki, Flor.	15.00	10.00	10.00
121 Éric Bélanger, LosA. RC	**20.00**	**20.00**	**25.00**
122 S. Reinprecht, LosA. RC	**75.00**	**85.00**	**75.00**
123 L. Visnovsky, LosA. RC	**20.00**	**20.00**	**25.00**
124 M. Fernandez (G), MinW.	25.00	20.00	15.00
125 M. Gaborik, MinW. RC	**260.00**	**300.00**	**450.00**
126 Filip Kuba, MinW.	10.00	6.00	5.00
127 Maxim Sushinsky, MinW.	10.00	6.00	5.00
128 Andrei Markov, Mont.	10.00	6.00	5.00
129 S. Hartnell, Nash. RC	**30.00**	**35.00**	**50.00**
130 Colin White, NJer. RC	**20.00**	**20.00**	**25.00**
131 Taylor Pyatt, NYIs.	15.00	10.00	10.00
132 M. Havlat, Otta. RC	**155.00**	**180.00**	**250.00**
133 J. Hurme (G), Otta. RC	**30.00**	**35.00**	**50.00**
134 Karel Rachunek, Otta.	10.00	6.00	5.00
135 Maxime Ouellet (G), Phil.	20.00	15.00	15.00
136 Ju. Williams, Phil. RC	**40.00**	**45.00**	**75.00**
137 Robert Esche (G), Phoe.	15.00	10.00	10.00
138 Wyatt Smith, Phoe.	8.00	6.00	5.00
139 O. Väänänen, Phoe. RC	**20.00**	**20.00**	**25.00**
140 Brent Johnson (G), SLou.	15.00	15.00	15.00
141 Ladislav Nagy, SLou.	15.00	10.00	10.00
142 Mike Van Ryn, SLou.	15.00	10.00	10.00
143 B. Salvador, SLou. RC	**20.00**	**20.00**	**25.00**
144 E. Nabokov (G), SanJ.	8.00	6.00	5.00
145 Kharitonov, Tamp. RC	**20.00**	**15.00**	**25.00**
146 Brad Richards, Tamp.	8.00	6.00	5.00
147 P. Svoboda, Toro. RC	**20.00**	**20.00**	**25.00**
148 Daniel Sedin, Vanc.	8.00	6.00	5.00
149 Henrik Sedin, Vanc.	8.00	6.00	5.00
150 Kris Beech, Wash.	20.00	15.00	15.00
151 R. DiPietro (G), NYIs. RC	**110.00**	**125.00**	**150.00**

RETAIL

Shell Set (101 cards):		**50.00**
Complete Set (152 cards):	**1,500**	**900**
Common Player:	**4.00**	**.35**
Retail	**FiS120**	**Retail**
1 Guy Hebert (G), Anah.	4.00	.35
2 Paul Kariya, Anah.	25.00	2.50
3 Teemu Selänne, Anah.	15.00	1.50
4 Ray Ferraro, Atla.	4.00	.35
5 Damian Rhodes (G), Atla.	4.00	.35
6 Patrik Stefan, Atla.	5.00	.50
7 Byron Dafoe (G), Bost.	5.00	.50
8 Sergei Samsonov, Bost.	10.00	1.00
9 Joe Thornton, Bost.	20.00	2.00
10 Maxim Afinogenov, Buff.	5.00	.50
11 Doug Gilmour, Buff.	10.00	1.00
12 Dominik Hasek (G), Buff.	20.00	2.00
13 Miroslav Satan, Buff.	5.00	.50
14 Fred Brathwaite (G), Calg.	5.00	.50
15 Valeri Bure, Calg.	5.00	.50
16 Ron Francis, Caro.	10.00	1.00
17 Arturs Irbe (G), Caro.	5.00	.50
18 Sami Kapanen, Caro.	5.00	.50
19 Tony Amonte, Chic.	10.00	1.00
20 Jocelyn Thibault (G), Chic.	5.00	.50
21 Alexei Zhamnov, Chic.	5.00	.50
22 Raymond Bourque, Colo.	20.00	2.00
23 Peter Forsberg, Colo.	25.00	2.50
24 Milan Hejduk, Colo.	15.00	1.50
25 Patrick Roy (G), Colo.	60.00	6.00
26 Joe Sakic, Colo.	30.00	3.00
27 Marc Denis (G), Colu.	5.00	.50
28 Ted Drury, Colu.	4.00	.35
29 Geoff Sanderson, Colu.	4.00	.35
30 Ed Belfour (G), Dall.	20.00	2.00
31 Brett Hull, Dall.	20.00	2.00
32 Mike Modano, Dall.	20.00	2.00
33 Brenden Morrow, Dall.	5.00	.50
34 Joe Nieuwendyk, Dall.	5.00	.50
35 Sergei Fedorov, Detr.	20.00	2.00
36 Chris Osgood (G), Detr.	10.00	1.00
37 Brendan Shanahan, Detr.	20.00	2.00
38 Steve Yzerman, Detr.	45.00	4.50
39 Tommy Salo (G), Edmo.	5.00	.50
40 Ryan Smyth, Edmo.	5.00	.50
41 Doug Weight, Edmo.	10.00	1.00
42 Pavel Bure, Flor.	15.00	1.50
43 Trevor Kidd (G), Flor.	5.00	.50
44 Viktor Kozlov, Flor.	5.00	.50
45 Stéphane Fiset (G), LosA.	5.00	.50
46 Zigmund Palffy, LosA.	10.00	1.00
47 Luc Robitaille, LosA.	15.00	1.50
48 Manny Fernandez (G), MinW.	5.00	.50
49 Sergei Krivokrasov, MinW.	4.00	.35
50 Stacy Roest, MinW.	4.00	.35
51 Saku Koivu, Mont.	20.00	1.50
52 Trevor Linden, Mont.	5.00	.50
53 José Théodore (G), Mont.	20.00	2.00
54 Mike Dunham (G), Nash.	5.00	.50
55 David Legwand, Nash.	5.00	.50
56 Jason Arnott, NJer.	5.00	.50
57 Martin Brodeur (G), NJer.	30.00	3.00
58 Patrik Elias, NJer.	15.00	1.50
59 Scott Gomez, NJer.	5.00	.50
60 Petr* Sykora, NJer.	5.00	.50
61 Tim Connolly, NYIs.	5.00	.50
62 Mariusz Czerkawski, NYIs.	4.00	.35
63 John Vanbiesbrouck (G), NYIs.	5.00	.50
64 Theoren Fleury, NYRa.	10.00	1.00
65 Brian Leetch, NYRa.	10.00	1.00
66 Mark Messier, NYRa.	20.00	2.00
67 Mike Richter (G), NYRa.	5.00	.50
68 Daniel Alfredsson, Otta.	10.00	1.00
69 Radek Bonk, Otta.	5.00	.50
70 Marian Hossa, Otta.	20.00	2.00
71 Brian Boucher (G), Phil.	5.00	.50
72 Simon Gagné, Phil.	15.00	1.50
73 John LeClair, Phil.	15.00	1.50
74 Eric Lindros, Phil.	20.00	2.00
75 Nikolai Khabibulin (G), Phoe.	5.00	.50
76 Jeremy Roenick, Phoe.	15.00	1.50
77 Keith Tkachuk, Phoe.	10.00	1.00
78 Jean-Sébastien Aubin (G), Pitt.	4.00	.35
79 Jan Hrdina, Pitt.	4.00	.35
80 Jaromir Jagr, Pitt.	20.00	2.00
81 Martin Straka, Pitt.	5.00	.50
82 Pavol Demitra, SLou.	5.00	.50
83 Al MacInnis, SLou.	5.00	.50
84 Chris Pronger, SLou.	10.00	1.00
85 Roman Turek (G), SLou.	5.00	.50
86 Pierre Turgeon, SLou.	5.00	.50
87 Vincent Damphousse, SanJ.	10.00	1.00
88 Jeff Friesen, SanJ.	5.00	.50
89 Owen Nolan, SanJ.	10.00	1.00
90 Dan Cloutier (G), Tamp.	5.00	.50
91 Vincent Lecavalier, Tamp.	20.00	2.00
92 Nikolai Antropov, Toro.	4.00	.35
93 Curtis Joseph (G), Toro.	20.00	2.00
94 Mats Sundin, Toro.	20.00	2.00
95 Steve Kariya, Vanc.	4.00	.35
96 Markus Näslund, Vanc.	20.00	2.00
97 Félix Potvin (G), Vanc.	10.00	1.00
98 Jeff Halpern, Wash.	4.00	.35
99 Olaf Kölzig (G), Wash.	10.00	1.00
100 Adam Oates, Wash.	5.00	.50
152 Mario Lemieux, Pitt.	60.00	10.00

RETAIL ROOKIE

Retail Rookie	FiS120	R230
101 J. Rönnqvist, Anah. RC	**12.00**	**25.00**
102 Samuel Påhlsson, Bost.	6.00	6.00
103 Andrew Raycroft (G), Bost. RC	**20.00**	**25.00**
104 Eric Boulton, Buff. RC	**12.00**	**25.00**
105 Dimitri Kalinin, Buff.	5.00	4.00
106 Mika Noronen (G), Buff.	16.00	15.00
107 Oleg Saprykin, Calg.	9.00	9.00
108 Josef Vasicek, Caro. RC	**20.00**	**25.00**
109 Shane Willis, Caro.	9.00	9.00
110 Steve McCarthy, Chic.	6.00	6.00
111 D. Aebischer (G), Colo. RC	**30.00**	**50.00**
112 Serge Aubin, Colu. RC	**12.00**	**25.00**
113 R. Klesla, Colu. RC	**60.00**	**75.00**
114 David Vyborny, Colu.	6.00	6.00
115 Tyler Bouck, Dall. RC	**12.00**	**25.00**
116 Richard Jackman, Dall.	6.00	6.00
117 Marty Turco (G), Dall. RC	**60.00**	**125.00**
118 Dan LaCouture, Edmo.	5.00	4.00
119 Brian Swanson, Edmo.	10.00	10.00
120 Denis Shvidki, Flor.	9.00	9.00
121 Éric Bélanger, LosA. RC	**12.00**	**25.00**
122 S. Reinprecht, LosA. RC	**50.00**	**50.00**
123 L. Visnovsky, LosA. RC	**12.00**	**25.00**
124 Manny Fernandez (G), MinW.	16.00	15.00
125 M. Gaborik, MinW. RC	**200.00**	**225.00**
126 Filip Kuba, MinW.	6.00	6.00
127 Maxim Sushinsky, MinW.	6.00	6.00
128 Andrei Markov, Mont.	6.00	6.00
129 S. Hartnell, Nash. RC	**20.00**	**25.00**
130 Colin White, NJer. RC	**12.00**	**25.00**
131 Taylor Pyatt, NYIs.	9.00	9.00
132 Martin Havlat, Otta. RC	**120.00**	**175.00**
133 J. Hurme (G), Otta. RC	**20.00**	**25.00**
134 Karel Rachunek, Otta.	6.00	6.00
135 Maxime Ouellet (G), Phil.	12.00	12.00
136 Ju. Williams, Phil. RC	**30.00**	**50.00**
137 Robert Esche (G), Phoe.	9.00	9.00
138 Wyatt Smith, Phoe.	5.00	4.00
139 O. Väänänen, Phoe. RC	**12.00**	**25.00**
140 Brent Johnson (G), SLou.	12.00	11.00
141 Ladislav Nagy, SLou.	9.00	9.00
142 Mike Van Ryn, SLou.	9.00	9.00
143 B. Salvador, SLou. RC	**12.00**	**25.00**
144 Evgeni Nabokov (G), SanJ.	20.00	20.00
145 A. Kharitonov, Tamp. RC	**12.00**	**18.00**
146 Brad Richards, Tamp.	10.00	10.00
147 P. Svoboda, Toro. RC	**12.00**	**25.00**
148 Daniel Sedin, Vanc.	10.00	10.00
149 Henrik Sedin, Vanc.	10.00	10.00
150 Kris Beech, Wash.	12.00	12.00
151 R. DiPietro (G), NYIs. RC	**80.00**	**100.00**

ARTIST'S CANVAS

There are two versions: the regular insert (seeded 1:29 Hobby packs and 1:49 Retail packs) and the Proof parallel (#/1).

Insert Set (20 cards):	**175.00**
Insert	**AC**
1 Paul Kariya, Anah.	10.00
2 Teemu Selänne, Anah.	5.00
3 Joe Thornton, Bost.	10.00
4 Maxim Afinogenov, Buff.	5.00
5 Dominik Hasek (G), Buff.	10.00
6 Peter Forsberg, Colo.	10.00
7 Patrick Roy (G), Colo.	30.00
8 Joe Sakic, Colo.	15.00
9 Brett Hull, Dall.	10.00
10 Mike Modano, Dall.	10.00
11 Brendan Shanahan, Detr.	10.00
12 Steve Yzerman, Detr.	20.00
13 Pavel Bure, Flor.	5.00
14 Martin Brodeur (G), NJer.	15.00
15 Mark Messier, NYRa.	10.00
16 John LeClair, Phil.	5.00
17 Jeremy Roenick, Phoe.	5.00
18 Jaromir Jagr, Pitt.	10.00
19 Vincent Lecavalier, Tamp.	10.00
20 Curtis Joseph (G), Toro.	10.00

EXTREME ACTION

These inserts are seeded 2:21 Hobby packs and 1:25 Retail packs.

Insert Set (20 cards):	**85.00**
Insert	**EA**
1 Paul Kariya, Anah.	6.00
2 Teemu Selänne, Anah.	4.00
3 Dominik Hasek (G), Buff.	4.00
4 Patrick Roy (G), Colo.	14.00
5 Joe Sakic, Colo.	8.00
6 Ed Belfour (G), Dall.	4.00
7 Brett Hull, Dall.	4.00
8 Mike Modano, Dall.	4.00
9 Steve Yzerman, Detr.	12.00
10 Luc Robitaille, LosA.	4.00
11 Trevor Linden, Mont.	2.00
12 Petr* Sykora, NJer.	2.00
13 Martin Brodeur (G), NJer.	8.00
14 Tim Connolly, NYIs.	2.00
15 John LeClair, Phil.	4.00
16 Eric Lindros, Phil.	4.00
17 Jeremy Roenick, Phoe.	4.00
18 Jaromir Jagr, Pitt.	4.00
19 Vincent Lecavalier, Tamp.	4.00
20 Curtis Joseph (G), Toro.	4.00

GAME-USED GEAR

Gear Set (105 cards):	**1,100**
Description	**GUG**
15 Tony Amonte Jersey ✂	15.00
4 Shawn Bates Jersey ✂	8.00
34 Ed Belfour (G) Stick ✂	30.00
100 Craig Berube Stick ✂	10.00

☐	54 Rob Blake Stick ✂	15.00
☐	101 Peter Bondra Jersey ✂	15.00
☐	18 Raymond Bourque Jersey ✂	35.00
☐	19 Raymond Bourque Stick ✂	35.00
☐	12 Rod Brind'Amour Stick ✂	10.00
☐	48 Anson Carter Jersey ✂	10.00
☐	67 Zdeno Chara Jersey ✂	8.00
☐	43 Chris Chelios Stick ✂	15.00
☐	Paul Coffey Jersey & Stick ✂	20.00
☐	5 Paul Coffey Stick ✂	15.00
☐	68 Tim Connolly Stick ✂	10.00
☐	95 Shayne Corson Jersey ✂	8.00
☐	102 Sylvain Côté Stick ✂	10.00
☐	69 Mariusz Czerkawski Jersey ✂	8.00
☐	80 Andreas Dackell Jersey ✂	8.00
☐	103 Ulf Dahlén Jersey ✂	8.00
☐	Vincent Damphousse Jersey & Stick ✂	20.00
☐	91 Vincent Damphousse Jersey ✂	15.00
☐	16 Éric Dazé Jersey ✂	10.00
☐	20 Greg de Vries Jersey ✂	8.00
☐	33 Marc Denis (G) Stick ✂	10.00
☐	81 Éric Desjardins Jersey ✂	8.00
☐	21 Chris Dingman Jersey ✂	8.00
☐	87 Shane Doan Jersey ✂	8.00
☐	90 Dallas Drake Jersey ✂	8.00
☐	22 Chris Drury Stick ✂	15.00
☐	44 Sergei Fedorov Jersey ✂	30.00
☐	23 Adam Foote Stick ✂	10.00
☐	Peter Forsberg Jersey & Stick ✂	55.00
☐	24 Peter Forsberg Stick ✂	40.00
☐	73 Adam Graves Stick ✂	10.00
☐	7 Bill Guerin Stick ✂	10.00
☐	56 Jeff Hackett (G) Jersey ✂	8.00
☐	9 Dominik Hasek (G) Stick ✂	30.00
☐	13 Kevin Hatcher Stick ✂	10.00
☐	35 Derian Hatcher Jersey ✂	8.00
☐	36 Derian Hatcher Jersey ✂	8.00
☐	1 Guy Hebert (G) Jersey ✂	8.00
☐	63 Bobby Holik Jersey ✂	8.00
☐	11 Jarome Iginla Jersey ✂	20.00
☐	89 Jaromir Jagr Jersey ✂	30.00
☐	51 Olli Jokinen Stick ✂	10.00
☐	96 Curtis Joseph (G) Stick ✂	30.00
☐	74 Valeri Kamensky Stick ✂	10.00
☐	57 Saku Koivu Jersey ✂	20.00
☐	Olaf Kölzig (G) Jersey & Stick ✂	20.00
☐	37 Jamie Langenbrunner Jersey ✂	8.00
☐	82 Daymond Langkow Jersey ✂	8.00
☐	70 Claude Lapointe Jersey ✂	8.00
☐	93 Vincent Lecavalier Stick ✂	30.00
☐	83 John LeClair Jersey ✂	20.00
☐	Brian Leetch Jersey & Stick ✂	20.00
☐	75 Brian Leetch Jersey ✂	15.00
☐	38 Jere Lehtinen Jersey ✂	8.00
☐	45 Nicklas Lidström Jersey ✂	15.00
☐	58 Trevor Linden Stick ✂	10.00
☐	71 Mats Lindgren Jersey ✂	8.00
☐	85 Eric Lindros Stick ✂	30.00
☐	84 Eric Lindros Jersey ✂	30.00
☐	52 Roberto Luongo (G) Jersey ✂	20.00
☐	2 Marty McInnis Jersey ✂	8.00
☐	10 Jay McKee Jersey ✂	8.00
☐	53 Scott Mellanby Stick ✂	10.00
☐	77 Mark Messier Jersey ✂	30.00
☐	26 Éric Messier Jersey ✂	8.00
☐	27 Aaron Miller Jersey ✂	8.00
☐	39 Mike Modano Jersey ✂	30.00
☐	64 Scott Niedermayer Jersey ✂	8.00
☐	105 Adam Oates Stick ✂	10.00
☐	46 Chris Osgood (G) Jersey ✂	15.00
☐	14 Sandis Ozolinsh Stick ✂	10.00
☐	55 Zigmund Palffy Stick ✂	15.00
☐	97 Yanic Perreault Stick ✂	10.00
☐	78 Mike Richter (G) Jersey ✂	10.00
☐	79 Mike Richter (G) Jersey ✂	10.00
☐	98 Gary Roberts Stick ✂	10.00
☐	62 Cliff Ronning Stick ✂	10.00
☐	28 Patrick Roy (G) Stick ✂	70.00
☐	Joe Sakic Jersey & Stick ✂	60.00
☐	30 Joe Sakic Jersey ✂	45.00
☐	49 Tommy Salo (G) Stick ✂	10.00
☐	8 Sergei Samsonov Jersey ✂	15.00
☐	59 Brian Savage Stick ✂	10.00
☐	3 Teemu Selänne Jersey ✂	20.00
☐	47 Brendan Shanahan Jersey ✂	30.00
☐	31 Martin Skoula Stick ✂	10.00
☐	88 Radoslav Suchy Jersey ✂	8.00
☐	99 Mats Sundin Jersey ✂	30.00
☐	94 Petr Svoboda Jersey ✂	8.00
☐	40 Darryl Sydor Jersey ✂	8.00
☐	41 Darryl Sydor Jersey ✂	8.00
☐	65 Petr* Sykora Jersey ✂	10.00
☐	32 Alex Tanguay Stick ✂	15.00
☐	66 Chris Terreri (G) Jersey ✂	8.00
☐	86 Rick Tocchet Stick ✂	10.00
☐	72 John Vanbiesbrouck (G) Jersey ✂	10.00
☐	50 Doug Weight Jersey ✂	15.00
☐	60 Eric Weinrich Stick ✂	10.00
☐	17 Alexei Zhamnov Jersey ✂	8.00
☐	42 Sergei Zubov Jersey ✂	8.00
☐	61 Dainius Zubrus Jersey ✂	8.00

GAME-USED GEAR PATCH VARIATION

	Patch Set (59 cards):	**1,500**
	Patch Variation	**GUGP**
☐	15 Tony Amonte, Chic. ✂	45.00
☐	4 Shawn Bates, Bost. ✂	15.00
☐	101 Peter Bondra, Wash. ✂	35.00
☐	18 Raymond Bourque, Colo. ✂	150.00
☐	48 Anson Carter, Bost. ✂	25.00
☐	67 Zdeno Chara, NYIs. ✂	15.00
☐	95 Shayne Corson, Toro. ✂	20.00
☐	69 Mariusz Czerkawski, NYIs. ✂	15.00
☐	80 Andreas Dackell, Otta. ✂	15.00
☐	103 Ulf Dahlén, Wash. ✂	15.00
☐	16 Éric Dazé, Chic. ✂	25.00
☐	20 Greg de Vries, Colo. ✂	15.00
☐	81 Éric Desjardins, Phil. ✂	55.00
☐	21 Chris Dingman, Colo. ✂	15.00
☐	87 Shane Doan, Phoe. ✂	20.00
☐	90 Dallas Drake	15.00
☐	44 Sergei Fedorov, Detr. ✂	65.00
☐	56 Jeff Hackett (G), Mont. ✂	20.00
☐	35 Derian Hatcher, Dall. ✂	20.00
☐	36 Derian Hatcher, Dall. ✂	20.00
☐	1 Guy Hebert (G), Anah. ✂	15.00
☐	63 Bobby Holik, NJer. ✂	20.00
☐	11 Jarome Iginla, Calg. ✂	70.00
☐	89 Jaromir Jagr, Pitt. ✂	15.00
☐	57 Saku Koivu, Mont. ✂	200.00
☐	37 Jamie Langenbrunner, Dall. ✂	15.00
☐	82 Daymond Langkow, Phil. ✂	20.00
☐	70 Claude Lapointe, NYIs. ✂	15.00
☐	83 John LeClair, Phil. ✂	60.00
☐	75 Brian Leetch, NYRa. ✂	45.00
☐	38 Jere Lehtinen, Dall. ✂	20.00
☐	45 Nicklas Lidström, Detr. ✂	35.00
☐	71 Mats Lindgren, NYIs. ✂	15.00
☐	52 Roberto Luongo (G), Flor. ✂	55.00
☐	2 Marty McInnis, Anah. ✂	15.00
☐	10 Jay McKee, Buff. ✂	15.00
☐	77 Mark Messier, NYRa. ✂	100.00
☐	26 Éric Messier, Colo. ✂	15.00
☐	27 Aaron Miller, Colo. ✂	15.00
☐	39 Mike Modano, Dall. ✂	40.00
☐	64 Scott Niedermayer, NJer. ✂	25.00
☐	46 Chris Osgood (G), Detr. ✂	45.00
☐	78 Mike Richter (G), NYRa. ✂	30.00
☐	79 Mike Richter (G), NYRa. ✂	30.00
☐	8 Sergei Samsonov, Bost. ✂	50.00
☐	3 Teemu Selänne, Anah. ✂	50.00
☐	47 Brendan Shanahan, Detr. ✂	225.00
☐	88 Radoslav Suchy, Phoe. ✂	15.00
☐	99 Mats Sundin, Toro. ✂	85.00
☐	94 Petr Svoboda, Tamp. ✂	15.00
☐	40 Darryl Sydor, Dall. ✂	25.00
☐	41 Darryl Sydor, Dall. ✂	20.00
☐	65 Petr* Sykora, NJer. ✂	20.00
☐	66 Chris Terreri (G), NJer. ✂	15.00
☐	72 John Vanbiesbrouck (G), NYIs. ✂	40.00
☐	50 Doug Weight, Edmo. ✂	45.00
☐	17 Alexei Zhamnov, Chic. ✂	20.00
☐	42 Sergei Zubov, Dall. ✂	15.00
☐	61 Dainius Zubrus, Mont. ✂	15.00

RESERVE

	Insert Set (20 cards):	**135.00**
	Insert (1:21 Hobby packs)	**Res.**
☐	1 Paul Kariya, Anah.	10.00
☐	2 Teemu Selänne, Anah.	6.00
☐	3 Patrik Stefan, Atla.	4.00
☐	4 Dominik Hasek (G), Buff.	6.00
☐	5 Peter Forsberg, Colo.	10.00
☐	6 Patrick Roy (G), Colo.	20.00
☐	7 Joe Sakic, Colo.	12.00
☐	8 Mike Modano, Dall.	6.00
☐	9 Brendan Shanahan, Detr.	6.00
☐	10 Steve Yzerman, Detr.	15.00
☐	11 Pavel Bure, Flor.	6.00
☐	12 Saku Koivu, Mont.	6.00
☐	13 Scott Gomez, NJer.	4.00
☐	14 Martin Brodeur (G), NJer.	12.00
☐	15 Mark Messier, NYRa.	6.00
☐	16 John LeClair, Phil.	6.00
☐	17 Eric Lindros, Phil.	6.00
☐	18 Jaromir Jagr, Pitt.	6.00
☐	19 Vincent Lecavalier, Tamp.	6.00
☐	20 Curtis Joseph (G), Toro.	6.00

PS-2001

	Insert Set (60 cards):	**25.00**
	Insert (2:1 packs)	**PS**
☐	1 Paul Kariya, Anah.	1.50
☐	2 Teemu Selänne, Anah.	1.00
☐	3 Sergei Samsonov, Bost.	.50
☐	4 Joe Thornton, Bost.	1.50
☐	5 Maxim Afinogenov, Buff.	.50
☐	6 Doug Gilmour, Buff.	.50
☐	7 Dominik Hasek (G), Buff.	1.00
☐	8 Raymond Bourque, Colo.	1.50
☐	9 Chris Drury, Colo.	.50
☐	10 Peter Forsberg, Colo.	1.50
☐	11 Milan Hejduk, Colo.	1.00
☐	12 Patrick Roy (G), Colo.	3.50
☐	13 Joe Sakic, Colo.	2.00
☐	14 Alex Tanguay, Colo.	.50
☐	15 Marc Denis (G), Colu.	.50
☐	16 Ed Belfour (G), Dall.	1.00
☐	17 Brett Hull, Dall.	1.00
☐	18 Mike Modano, Dall.	1.00
☐	19 Chris Chelios, Detr.	.50
☐	20 Sergei Fedorov, Detr.	1.00
☐	21 Chris Osgood (G), Detr.	.50
☐	22 Brendan Shanahan, Detr.	1.00
☐	23 Steve Yzerman, Detr.	3.00
☐	24 Doug Weight, Edmo.	.50
☐	25 Pavel Bure, Flor.	1.00
☐	26 Zigmund Palffy, LosA.	.50
☐	27 Luc Robitaille, LosA.	1.00
☐	28 Saku Koivu, Mont.	1.00
☐	29 José Théodore (G), Mont.	1.50
☐	30 David Legwand, Nash.	.50
☐	31 Martin Brodeur (G), NJer.	2.00
☐	32 Patrik Elias, NJer.	1.00
☐	33 Scott Gomez, NJer.	.50
☐	34 Petr* Sykora, NJer.	.50
☐	35 Tim Connolly, NYIs.	.50
☐	36 Theoren Fleury, NYRa.	.50
☐	37 Brian Leetch, NYRa.	.50
☐	38 Mark Messier, NYRa.	1.00
☐	39 Mike Richter (G), NYRa.	.50
☐	40 Marian Hossa, Otta.	1.00
☐	41 Brian Boucher (G), Phil.	.50
☐	42 John LeClair, Phil.	1.00
☐	43 Eric Lindros, Phil.	1.00
☐	44 Jeremy Roenick, Phoe.	1.00
☐	45 Keith Tkachuk, Phoe.	.50
☐	46 Jan Hrdina, Pitt.	.50
☐	47 Jaromir Jagr, Pitt.	1.00
☐	48 Martin Straka, Pitt.	.50
☐	49 Jeff Friesen, SanJ.	.50
☐	50 Owen Nolan, SanJ.	.50
☐	51 Pavol Demitra, SLou.	.50
☐	52 Chris Pronger, SLou.	.50
☐	53 Pierre Turgeon, SLou.	.50
☐	54 Vincent Lecavalier, Tamp.	1.00
☐	55 Curtis Joseph (G), Toro.	1.00
☐	56 Mats Sundin, Toro.	1.00
☐	57 Steve Kariya, Vanc.	.50
☐	58 Markus Näslund, Vanc.	1.00
☐	59 Peter Bondra, Wash.	.50
☐	60 Olaf Kölzig (G), Wash.	.50

PS-2001 NEW WAVE

	Insert Set (26 cards):	**125.00**
	Insert (#/70)	**NW70**
☐	1 Patrik Stefan, Atla.	8.00
☐	2 Joe Thornton, Bost.	15.00
☐	3 Maxim Afinogenov, Buff.	8.00
☐	4 Sami Kapanen, Caro.	8.00
☐	5 Valeri Bure, Calg.	8.00
☐	6 Oleg Saprykin, Calg.	8.00
☐	7 Jocelyn Thibault (G), Chic.	8.00
☐	8 Milan Hejduk, Colo.	10.00
☐	9 Marc Denis (G), Colu.	8.00
☐	10 Brenden Morrow, Dall.	8.00
☐	11 José Théodore (G), Mont.	15.00
☐	12 David Legwand, Nash.	8.00
☐	13 Patrik Elias, NJer.	10.00
☐	14 Scott Gomez, NJer.	8.00
☐	15 Tim Connolly, NYIs.	8.00
☐	16 Marian Hossa, Otta.	15.00
☐	17 Brian Boucher (G), Phil.	8.00
☐	18 Simon Gagné, Phil.	10.00
☐	19 Jean-Sébastien Aubin (G), Pitt.	8.00
☐	20 Roman Turek (G), SLou.	8.00
☐	21 Jeff Friesen, SanJ.	8.00
☐	22 Dan Cloutier (G), Tamp.	8.00
☐	23 Vincent Lecavalier, Tamp.	15.00
☐	24 Nikolai Antropov, Toro.	8.00
☐	25 Steve Kariya, Vanc.	8.00
☐	26 Rick DiPietro (G), NYIs.	35.00

PS-2001 ROOKIES

	Insert Set (26 cards):	**400.00**
	Insert (#/45)	**R45**
☐	1 Samuel Påhlsson, Bost.	10.00
☐	**2 Andrew Raycroft (G), Bost. RC**	**30.00**
☐	3 Dimitri Kalinin, Buff.	10.00
☐	4 Oleg Saprykin, Calg.	10.00
☐	**5 Josef Vasicek, Caro. RC**	**30.00**
☐	**6 David Aebischer (G), Colo. RC**	**40.00**
☐	7 David Vyborny, Colu.	10.00
☐	**8 Marty Turco (G), Dall. RC**	**75.00**
☐	**9 Éric Bélanger, LosA. RC**	**20.00**
☐	**10 Steven Reinprecht, LosA. RC**	**40.00**
☐	**11 Marian Gaborik, MinW. RC**	**125.00**
☐	12 Andrei Markov, Mont.	10.00
☐	**13 Colin White, NJer. RC**	**20.00**
☐	**14 Martin Havlat, Otta. RC**	**75.00**
☐	15 Maxime Ouellet (G), Phil.	15.00
☐	**16 Justin Williams, Phil. RC**	**40.00**
☐	17 Wyatt Smith, Phoe.	10.00
☐	**18 Ossi Väänänen, Phoe. RC**	**10.00**
☐	19 Brent Johnson (G), SLou.	15.00
☐	20 Ladislav Nagy, SLou.	10.00
☐	21 Evgeni Nabokov (G), SanJ.	30.00
☐	**22 Alexander Kharitonov, Tamp. RC**	**10.00**
☐	23 Brad Richards, Tamp.	20.00
☐	24 Daniel Sedin, Vanc.	20.00
☐	25 Henrik Sedin, Vanc.	20.00
☐	**26 Rick DiPietro (G), NYIs. RC**	**60.00**

PS-2001 STARS

	Insert Set (25 cards):	**175.00**
	Insert (#/105)	**S105**
☐	1 Paul Kariya, Anah.	15.00
☐	2 Teemu Selänne, Anah.	10.00
☐	3 Sergei Samsonov, Bost.	8.00
☐	4 Dominik Hasek (G), Buff.	10.00
☐	5 Raymond Bourque, Colo.	15.00
☐	6 Peter Forsberg, Colo.	15.00
☐	7 Patrick Roy (G), Colo.	35.00
☐	8 Joe Sakic, Colo.	20.00
☐	9 Brett Hull, Dall.	10.00
☐	10 Mike Modano, Dall.	10.00
☐	11 Sergei Fedorov, Detr.	10.00
☐	12 Brendan Shanahan, Detr.	10.00
☐	13 Steve Yzerman, Detr.	30.00
☐	14 Pavel Bure, Flor.	10.00
☐	15 Luc Robitaille, LosA.	10.00
☐	16 Saku Koivu, Mont.	10.00
☐	17 Martin Brodeur (G), NJer.	20.00
☐	18 Mark Messier, NYRa.	10.00
☐	19 John LeClair, Phil.	10.00
☐	20 Eric Lindros, Phil.	10.00
☐	21 Jeremy Roenick, Phoe.	10.00
☐	22 Jaromir Jagr, Pitt.	10.00
☐	23 Pierre Turgeon, SLou.	8.00
☐	24 Curtis Joseph (G), Toro.	10.00
☐	25 Mats Sundin, Toro.	10.00

2000 - 01 PRIVATE STOCK TITANIUM

This series was issued in April 2001. Hobby packs contained regular cards (1-100), short-printed rookies (101-150, #/99), Premiere Date parallels (1-100, #/185), Titanium Gold parallels (1-100, #/99), and Titanium Blue parallels (1-100, numbered to player's jersey number). Retail packs contained regular cards (1-100), short-printed rookies (101-150, #/199), and Titanium Red parallels (1-100, #/299).

Shell Set (100 cards): 25.00

	TG99	PD185	Hobby
Parallel Set (100 cards):	600.00	400.00	
Complete Set (150 cards):			-
Common Player:	4.00	3.00	.35
Description	**TG99**	**PD185**	**Hobby**
1 Paul Kariya, Anah.	25.00	20.00	2.00
2 Teemu Selänne, Anah.	15.00	10.00	1.00
3 Donald Audette, Atla.	5.00	5.00	.50
4 Jason Allison, Bost.	10.00	5.00	.50
5 Byron Dafoe (G), Bost.	5.00	5.00	.50
6 Bill Guerin, Bost.	5.00	5.00	.50
7 Joe Thornton, Bost.	20.00	15.00	1.50
8 Jean-Pierre Dumont, Buff.	4.00	3.00	.35
9 Doug Gilmour, Buff.	10.00	5.00	.50
10 Dominik Hasek (G), Buff.	15.00	15.00	1.50
11 Jarome Iginla, Calg.	15.00	10.00	1.00
12 Marc* Savard, Calg.	4.00	3.00	.35
13 Mike Vernon (G), Calg.	5.00	5.00	.50
14 Ron Francis, Caro.	10.00	5.00	.50
15 Arturs Irbe (G), Caro.	5.00	5.00	.50
16 Tony Amonte, Chic.	10.00	5.00	.50
17 Steve Sullivan, Chic.	5.00	3.00	.35
18 Jocelyn Thibault (G), Chic.	5.00	5.00	.50
19 Raymond Bourque, Colo.	20.00	15.00	1.50
20 Peter Forsberg, Colo.	25.00	20.00	2.00
21 Milan Hejduk, Colo.	15.00	10.00	1.00
22 Patrick Roy (G), Colo.	55.00	45.00	4.50
23 Joe Sakic, Colo.	30.00	20.00	2.00
24 A. Tanguay, Colo. [Photo: Skoula]	10.00	5.00	.50
25 Geoff Sanderson, Colu.	4.00	3.00	.35
26 Ron Tugnutt (G), Colu.	5.00	5.00	.50
27 Ed Belfour (G), Dall.	15.00	15.00	1.50
28 Brett Hull, Dall.	15.00	15.00	1.50
29 Mike Modano, Dall.	15.00	15.00	1.50
30 Joe Nieuwendyk, Dall.	5.00	5.00	.50
31 Sergei Fedorov, Detr.	15.00	15.00	1.50
32 Manny Legacé (G), Detr.	5.00	3.00	.35
33 Nicklas Lidström, Detr.	10.00	5.00	.50
34 Brendan Shanahan, Detr.	15.00	15.00	1.50
35 Steve Yzerman, Detr.	45.00	35.00	3.50
36 Tommy Salo (G), Edmo.	5.00	5.00	.50
37 Ryan Smyth, Edmo.	5.00	5.00	.50
38 Doug Weight, Edmo.	10.00	5.00	.50
39 Pavel Bure, Flor.	15.00	10.00	1.00
40 Trevor Kidd (G), Flor.	5.00	3.00	.35
41 Rob Blake, LosA.	10.00	5.00	.50
42 Zigmund Palffy, LosA.	10.00	5.00	.50
43 Luc Robitaille, LosA.	15.00	10.00	1.00
44 Jamie Storr (G), LosA.	4.00	3.00	.35
45 M. Fernandez (G), MinW.	5.00	5.00	.50
46 Scott Pellerin, MinW.	4.00	3.00	.35
47 Saku Koivu, Mont.	20.00	15.00	1.00
48 Trevor Linden, Mont.	5.00	5.00	.50
49 Martin Rucinsky, Mont.	4.00	3.00	.35
50 José Théodore (G), Mont.	20.00	15.00	1.50
51 David Legwand, Nash.	5.00	5.00	.50
52 Cliff Ronning, Nash.	4.00	3.00	.35
53 Jason Arnott, NJer.	5.00	5.00	.50
54 Martin Brodeur (G), NJer.	30.00	20.00	2.00
55 Patrik Elias, NJer.	15.00	10.00	1.00
56 Alexander Mogilny, NJer.	5.00	5.00	.50
57 Tim Connolly, NYIs.	5.00	5.00	.50
58 Mariusz Czerkawski, NYIs.	4.00	3.00	.35
59 J. Vanbiesbrouck (G), NYIs.	5.00	5.00	.50
60 Theoren Fleury, NYRa.	10.00	5.00	.50
61 Brian Leetch, NYRa.	10.00	5.00	.50
62 Mark Messier, NYRa.	15.00	15.00	1.50
63 Mike Richter (G), NYRa.	5.00	5.00	.50
64 Radek Bonk, Otta.	5.00	3.00	.35
65 Marian Hossa, Otta.	15.00	15.00	1.50
66 Patrick Lalime (G), Otta.	10.00	5.00	.50
67 Alexei Yashin, Otta.	10.00	5.00	.50
68 Brian Boucher (G), Phil.	5.00	3.00	.35
69 Simon Gagné, Phil.	15.00	10.00	1.00
70 John LeClair, Phil.	15.00	10.00	1.00
71 Eric Lindros, Phil.	15.00	15.00	1.50
72 Sean Burke (G), Phoe.	10.00	5.00	.50
73 Jeremy Roenick, Phoe.	15.00	10.00	1.00
74 Keith Tkachuk, Phoe.	10.00	5.00	.50
75 Jaromir Jagr, Pitt.	15.00	15.00	1.50
76 Alex Kovalev, Pitt.	10.00	5.00	.50
77 Mario Lemieux, Pitt.	55.00	45.00	4.00
78 Garth Snow (G), Pitt.	5.00	3.00	.35
79 Martin Straka, Pitt.	5.00	3.00	.35
80 Pavol Demitra, SLou.	5.00	5.00	.50
81 Chris Pronger, SLou.	10.00	5.00	.50
82 Roman Turek (G), SLou.	5.00	5.00	.50
83 Pierre Turgeon, SLou.	5.00	5.00	.50
84 V. Damphousse, SanJ.	10.00	5.00	.50
85 Patrick Marleau, SanJ.	5.00	5.00	.50
86 Owen Nolan, SanJ.	10.00	5.00	.50
87 Steve Shields (G), SanJ.	4.00	3.00	.35
88 Mike Johnson, Tamp.	4.00	3.00	.35
89 Vincent Lecavalier, Tamp.	15.00	15.00	1.50
90 Sergei Berezin, Toro.	4.00	3.00	.35
91 Curtis Joseph (G), Toro.	15.00	15.00	1.50
92 Gary Roberts, Toro.	5.00	5.00	.50
93 Mats Sundin, Toro.	15.00	15.00	1.50
94 Andrew Cassels, Vanc.	4.00	3.00	.35
95 Brendan Morrison, Vanc.	5.00	3.00	.35
96 Markus Näslund, Vanc.	15.00	15.00	1.50
97 Félix Potvin (G), Vanc.	20.00	15.00	.50
98 Peter Bondra, Wash.	10.00	5.00	.50
99 Olaf Kölzig (G), Wash.	10.00	5.00	.50
100 Adam Oates, Wash.	5.00	5.00	.50

HOBBY ROOKIE

Hobby Rookie (#/99)	R99
101 Samuel Påhlsson, Anah.	15.00
102 Scott Fankhouser (G), Atla.	15.00
103 Tomi Kallio, Atla.	15.00
104 Brad Tapper, Atla. RC	**50.00**
105 Andrew Raycroft (G), Bost. RC	**75.00**
106 Denis Hamel, Buff.	15.00
107 Jeff Cowan, Calg. RC	**25.00**
108 Oleg Saprykin, Calg.	15.00
109 Josef Vasicek, Caro. RC	**75.00**
110 Shane Willis, Caro.	15.00
111 David Aebischer (G), Colo. RC	**100.00**
112 Serge Aubin, Colu. RC	**50.00**
113 Marc Denis (G), Colu.	25.00
114 Chris Nielsen, Colu. RC	**50.00**
115 David Vyborny, Colu.	15.00
116 Marty Turco (G), Dall. RC	**300.00**
117 Shawn Horcoff, Edmo. RC	**50.00**
118 Mike Comrie, Edmo. RC	**400.00**
119 Domenic Pittis, Edmo.	15.00
120 Roberto Luongo (G), Flor.	45.00
121 Ivan Novoseltsev, Flor.	15.00
122 Serge Payer, Flor.	15.00
123 Denis Shvidki, Flor.	15.00
124 Steven Reinprecht, LosA. RC	**100.00**
125 L'ubomir Visnovsky, LosA. RC	**50.00**
126 Marian Gaborik, MinW. RC	**600.00**
127 Filip Kuba, MinW.	15.00
128 Mathieu Garon (G), Mont.	20.00
129 Éric Landry, Mont. RC	**25.00**
130 Andrei Markov, Mont.	15.00
131 Marian Cisar, Nash.	15.00
132 Scott Hartnell, Nash. RC	**75.00**
133 Rick DiPietro (G), NYIs. RC	**200.00**
134 Martin Havlat, Otta. RC	**350.00**
135 Jani Hurme (G), Otta. RC	**75.00**
136 Petr Schastlivy, Otta.	15.00
137 Ruslan Fedotenko, Phil. RC	**50.00**
138 Justin Williams, Phil. RC	**100.00**
139 Robert Esche (G), Phoe.	15.00
140 Milan Kraft, Pitt.	15.00
141 Brent Johnson (G), SLou.	20.00
142 Reed Low, SLou. RC	**50.00**
143 Evgeni Nabokov (G), SanJ.	35.00
144 Alexander Kharitonov, Tamp. RC	**25.00**
145 Dieter Kochan (G), Tamp. RC	**50.00**
146 Brad Richards, Tamp.	25.00
147 Adam Mair, Toro.	15.00
148 Daniel Sedin, Vanc.	20.00
149 Henrik Sedin, Vanc.	20.00
150 Trent Whitfield, Wash.	15.00

TITANIUM ICE

Complete Set (100 cards):

Description	TI
1 Paul Kariya, Anah.	
2 Teemu Selänne, Anah.	
3 Donald Audette, Atla.	
4 Jason Allison, Bost.	
5 Byron Dafoe (G), Bost.	
6 Bill Guerin, Bost.	
7 Joe Thornton, Bost.	
8 Jean-Pierre Dumont, Buff.	
9 Doug Gilmour, Buff.	
10 Dominik Hasek (G), Buff.	
11 Jarome Iginla, Calg.	
12 Marc* Savard, Calg.	
13 Mike Vernon (G), Calg.	
14 Ron Francis, Caro.	
15 Arturs Irbe (G), Caro.	
16 Tony Amonte, Chic.	
17 Steve Sullivan, Chic.	
18 Jocelyn Thibault (G), Chic.	
19 Raymond Bourque, Colo.	
20 Peter Forsberg, Colo.	
21 Milan Hejduk, Colo.	
22 Patrick Roy (G), Colo.	
23 Joe Sakic, Colo.	
24 A. Tanguay, Colo. [Photo: Skoula]	
25 Geoff Sanderson, Colu.	
26 Ron Tugnutt (G), Colu.	
27 Ed Belfour (G), Dall.	
28 Brett Hull, Dall.	
29 Mike Modano, Dall.	
30 Joe Nieuwendyk, Dall.	
31 Sergei Fedorov, Detr.	
32 Manny Legacé (G), Detr.	
33 Nicklas Lidström, Detr.	
34 Brendan Shanahan, Detr.	
35 Steve Yzerman, Detr.	
36 Tommy Salo (G), Edmo.	
37 Ryan Smyth, Edmo.	
38 Doug Weight, Edmo.	
39 Pavel Bure, Flor.	
40 Trevor Kidd (G), Flor.	
41 Rob Blake, LosA.	
42 Zigmund Palffy, LosA.	
43 Luc Robitaille, LosA.	
44 Jamie Storr (G), LosA.	
45 Manny Fernandez (G), MinW.	
46 Scott Pellerin, MinW.	
47 Saku Koivu, Mont.	
48 Trevor Linden, Mont.	
49 Martin Rucinsky, Mont.	
50 José Théodore (G), Mont.	
51 David Legwand, Nash.	
52 Cliff Ronning, Nash.	
53 Jason Arnott, NJer.	
54 Martin Brodeur (G), NJer.	
55 Patrik Elias, NJer.	
56 Alexander Mogilny, NJer.	
57 Tim Connolly, NYIs.	
58 Mariusz Czerkawski, NYIs.	
59 John Vanbiesbrouck (G), NYIs.	
60 Theoren Fleury, NYRa.	
61 Brian Leetch, NYRa.	
62 Mark Messier, NYRa.	
63 Mike Richter (G), NYRa. {#/35}	
64 Radek Bonk, Otta.	
65 Marian Hossa, Otta.	
66 Patrick Lalime (G), Otta.	
67 Alexei Yashin, Otta.	
68 Brian Boucher (G), Phil.	
69 Simon Gagné, Phil.	
70 John LeClair, Phil.	
71 Eric Lindros, Phil.	
72 Sean Burke (G), Phoe.	
73 Jeremy Roenick, Phoe.	
74 Keith Tkachuk, Phoe.	
75 Jaromir Jagr, Pitt.	
76 Alex Kovalev, Pitt.	
77 Mario Lemieux, Pitt.	
78 Garth Snow (G), Pitt.	
79 Martin Straka, Pitt.	
80 Pavol Demitra, SLou.	
81 Chris Pronger, SLou.	
82 Roman Turek (G), SLou.	
83 Pierre Turgeon, SLou.	
84 Vincent Damphousse, SanJ.	
85 Patrick Marleau, SanJ.	
86 Owen Nolan, SanJ.	
87 Steve Shields (G), SanJ.	
88 Mike Johnson, Tamp.	
89 Vincent Lecavalier, Tamp.	
90 Sergei Berezin, Toro.	
91 Curtis Joseph (G), Toro.	
92 Gary Roberts, Toro.	
93 Mats Sundin, Toro.	
94 Andrew Cassels, Vanc.	
95 Brendan Morrison, Vanc.	
96 Markus Näslund, Vanc.	
97 Félix Potvin (G), Vanc.	
98 Peter Bondra, Wash.	
99 Olaf Kölzig (G), Wash.	
100 Adam Oates, Wash.	

RETAIL

	R299	Retail
Shell Set (100 cards):		35.00
Parallel Set (100 cards):	225.00	
Complete Set (150 cards):		1,700.00
Common Player:	3.00	.35
Description	**R299**	**Retail**
1 Paul Kariya, Anah.	15.00	2.00
2 Teemu Selänne, Anah.	5.00	1.00
3 Donald Audette, Atla.	2.00	.50
4 Jason Allison, Bost.	5.00	.50
5 Byron Dafoe (G), Bost.	2.00	.50
6 Bill Guerin, Bost.	2.00	.50
7 Joe Thornton, Bost.	10.00	1.50
8 Jean-Pierre Dumont, Buff.	2.00	.35
9 Doug Gilmour, Buff.	5.00	.50
10 Dominik Hasek (G), Buff.	10.00	1.50
11 Jarome Iginla, Calg.	5.00	1.00
12 Marc* Savard, Calg.	2.00	.35
13 Mike Vernon (G), Calg.	2.00	.50
14 Ron Francis, Caro.	5.00	.50
15 Arturs Irbe (G), Caro.	2.00	.50
16 Tony Amonte, Chic.	5.00	.50
17 Steve Sullivan, Chic.	2.00	.35
18 Jocelyn Thibault (G), Chic.	2.00	.50
19 Raymond Bourque, Colo.	10.00	1.50
20 Peter Forsberg, Colo.	15.00	2.00
21 Milan Hejduk, Colo.	5.00	1.00
22 Patrick Roy (G), Colo.	30.00	4.50
23 Joe Sakic, Colo.	15.00	2.00
24 A. Tanguay, Colo. [Photo: Skoula]	5.00	.50
25 Geoff Sanderson, Colu.	2.00	.35
26 Ron Tugnutt (G), Colu.	2.00	.50
27 Ed Belfour (G), Dall.	10.00	1.50
28 Brett Hull, Dall.	10.00	1.50
29 Mike Modano, Dall.	10.00	1.50
30 Joe Nieuwendyk, Dall.	2.00	.50
31 Sergei Fedorov, Detr.	10.00	1.50
32 Manny Legacé (G), Detr.	2.00	.35
33 Nicklas Lidström, Detr.	5.00	.50
34 Brendan Shanahan, Detr.	10.00	1.50
35 Steve Yzerman, Detr.	25.00	3.50
36 Tommy Salo (G), Edmo.	2.00	.50
37 Ryan Smyth, Edmo.	5.00	.50
38 Doug Weight, Edmo.	5.00	.50
39 Pavel Bure, Flor.	5.00	1.00
40 Trevor Kidd (G), Flor.	2.00	.35
41 Rob Blake, LosA.	5.00	.50
42 Zigmund Palffy, LosA.	5.00	.50
43 Luc Robitaille, LosA.	5.00	1.00
44 Jamie Storr (G), LosA.	2.00	.35
45 Manny Fernandez (G), MinW.	2.00	.50
46 Scott Pellerin, MinW.	2.00	.35
47 Saku Koivu, Mont.	5.00	1.00
48 Trevor Linden, Mont.	2.00	.50
49 Martin Rucinsky, Mont.	2.00	.35
50 José Théodore (G), Mont.	10.00	1.50
51 David Legwand, Nash.	2.00	.50
52 Cliff Ronning, Nash.	2.00	.35
53 Jason Arnott, NJer.	5.00	.50
54 Martin Brodeur (G), NJer.	15.00	2.00
55 Patrik Elias, NJer.	5.00	1.00
56 Alexander Mogilny, NJer.	5.00	.50
57 Tim Connolly, NYIs.	2.00	.50
58 Mariusz Czerkawski, NYIs.	2.00	.35
59 John Vanbiesbrouck (G), NYIs.	5.00	.50
60 Theoren Fleury, NYRa.	5.00	.50
61 Brian Leetch, NYRa.	5.00	.50
62 Mark Messier, NYRa.	10.00	1.50
63 Mike Richter (G), NYRa.	5.00	.50
64 Radek Bonk, Otta.	2.00	.35
65 Marian Hossa, Otta.	10.00	1.50
66 Patrick Lalime (G), Otta.	5.00	.50
67 Alexei Yashin, Otta.	5.00	.50
68 Brian Boucher (G), Phil.	2.00	.35
69 Simon Gagné, Phil.	5.00	1.00
70 John LeClair, Phil.	5.00	1.00
71 Eric Lindros, Phil.	10.00	1.50
72 Sean Burke (G), Phoe.	5.00	.50
73 Jeremy Roenick, Phoe.	5.00	1.00
74 Keith Tkachuk, Phoe.	5.00	.50
75 Jaromir Jagr, Pitt.	10.00	1.50
76 Alex Kovalev, Pitt.	5.00	.50
77 Mario Lemieux, Pitt.	65.00	9.00
78 Garth Snow (G), Pitt.	2.00	.35
79 Martin Straka, Pitt.	2.00	.35
80 Pavol Demitra, SLou.	2.00	.50
81 Chris Pronger, SLou.	5.00	.50
82 Roman Turek (G), SLou.	5.00	.50
83 Pierre Turgeon, SLou.	2.00	.50
84 Vincent Damphousse, SanJ.	5.00	.50
85 Patrick Marleau, SanJ.	5.00	.50
86 Owen Nolan, SanJ.	5.00	.50
87 Steve Shields (G), SanJ.	2.00	.35
88 Mike Johnson, Tamp.	2.00	.35
89 Vincent Lecavalier, Tamp.	10.00	1.50
90 Sergei Berezin, Toro.	2.00	.35
91 Curtis Joseph (G), Toro.	10.00	1.50
92 Gary Roberts, Toro.	2.00	.50
93 Mats Sundin, Toro.	10.00	1.50
94 Andrew Cassels, Vanc.	2.00	.35
95 Brendan Morrison, Vanc.	2.00	.35
96 Markus Näslund, Vanc.	10.00	1.50
97 Félix Potvin (G), Vanc.	5.00	.50
98 Peter Bondra, Wash.	5.00	.50
99 Olaf Kölzig (G), Wash.	5.00	.50
100 Adam Oates, Wash.	2.00	.50

RETAIL ROOKIE

Retail Rookie (#/199)	R199
101 Samuel Påhlsson, Anah.	5.00
102 Scott Fankhouser (G), Atla.	5.00
103 Tomi Kallio, Atla.	5.00
104 Brad Tapper, Atla. RC	**40.00**
105 Andrew Raycroft (G), Bost. RC	**60.00**
106 Denis Hamel, Buff.	5.00
107 Jeff Cowan, Calg. RC	**25.00**
108 Oleg Saprykin, Calg.	10.00
109 Josef Vasicek, Caro. RC	**60.00**
110 Shane Willis, Caro.	10.00
111 David Aebischer (G), Colo. RC	**80.00**
112 Serge Aubin, Colu. RC	**40.00**
113 Marc Denis (G), Colu.	20.00
114 Chris Nielsen, Colu. RC	**40.00**
115 David Vyborny, Colu.	5.00
116 Marty Turco (G), Dall. RC	**175.00**

☐	**117 Shawn Horcoff, Edmo. RC**	**40.00**
☐	**118 Mike Comrie, Edmo. RC**	**225.00**
☐	119 Domenic Pittis, Edmo.	5.00
☐	120 Roberto Luongo (G), Flor.	40.00
☐	121 Ivan Novoseltsev, Flor.	10.00
☐	122 Serge Payer, Flor.	5.00
☐	123 Denis Shvidki, Flor.	10.00
☐	**124 Steven Reinprecht, LosA. RC**	**75.00**
☐	**125 L'ubomir Visnovsky, LosA. RC**	**40.00**
☐	**126 Marian Gaborik, MinW. RC**	**250.00**
☐	127 Filip Kuba, MinW.	5.00
☐	128 Mathieu Garon (G), Mont.	20.00
☐	**129 Éric Landry, Mont. RC**	**25.00**
☐	130 Andrei Markov, Mont.	5.00
☐	131 Marian Cisar, Nash.	5.00
☐	**132 Scott Hartnell, Nash. RC**	**60.00**
☐	**133 Rick DiPietro (G), NYIs. RC**	**125.00**
☐	**134 Martin Havlat, Otta. RC**	**225.00**
☐	**135 Jani Hurme (G), Otta. RC**	**60.00**
☐	136 Petr Schastlivy, Otta.	10.00
☐	**137 Ruslan Fedotenko, Phil. RC**	**40.00**
☐	**138 Justin Williams, Phil. RC**	**80.00**
☐	139 Robert Esche (G), Phoe.	10.00
☐	140 Milan Kraft, Pitt.	15.00
☐	141 Brent Johnson (G), SLou.	20.00
☐	**142 Reed Low, SLou. RC**	**40.00**
☐	143 Evgeni Nabokov (G), SanJ.	30.00
☐	**144 Alexander Kharitonov, Tamp. RC**	**25.00**
☐	**145 Dieter Kochan (G), Tamp. RC**	**40.00**
☐	146 Brad Richards, Tamp.	20.00
☐	147 Adam Mair, Toro.	5.00
☐	148 Daniel Sedin, Vanc.	20.00
☐	149 Henrik Sedin, Vanc.	20.00
☐	150 Trent Whitfield, Wash.	5.00

THREE-STAR SELECTIONS

	Insert Set (30 cards):	**125.00**
	Insert (#/1400)	**G1400**
☐	1 Dominik Hasek (G), Buff.	2.00
☐	2 Patrick Roy (G), Colo.	10.00
☐	3 Ed Belfour (G), Dall.	2.00
☐	4 Martin Brodeur (G), NJer.	6.00
☐	5 Mike Richter (G), NYRa.	2.00
☐	6 Brian Boucher (G), Phil.	2.00
☐	7 Roman Turek (G), SLou.	2.00
☐	8 Curtis Joseph (G), Toro.	2.00
☐	9 Félix Potvin (G), Vanc.	2.00
☐	10 Olaf Kölzig (G), Wash.	2.00
	Insert (#/1000)	**S1000**
☐	11 Paul Kariya, Anah.	6.00
☐	12 Joe Sakic, Colo.	8.00
☐	13 Mike Modano, Dall.	4.00
☐	14 Sergei Fedorov, Detr.	4.00
☐	15 Zigmund Palffy, LosA.	2.00
☐	16 Theoren Fleury, NYRa.	2.00
☐	17 Jaromir Jagr, Pitt.	4.00
☐	18 Mario Lemieux, Pitt.	15.00
☐	19 Vincent Lecavalier, Tamp.	4.00
☐	20 Mats Sundin, Toro.	4.00
	Insert (#/750)	**R750**
☐	21 Shane Willis, Caro.	2.00
☐	22 Steven Reinprecht, LosA.	6.00
☐	23 Marian Gaborik, MinW.	18.00
☐	24 Rick DiPietro (G), NYIs.	8.00
☐	25 Martin Havlat, Otta.	10.00
☐	26 Brent Johnson (G), SLou.	4.00
☐	27 Evgeni Nabokov (G), SanJ.	6.00
☐	28 Brad Richards, Tamp.	6.00
☐	29 Daniel Sedin, Vanc.	4.00
☐	30 Henrik Sedin, Vanc.	4.00

GAME-USED GEAR

	Gear Set (155 cards):	**500**
	Description	**GG**
☐	123 Mika Alatalo Jersey ✂	8.00
☐	41 Daniel Alfredsson Stick ✂	20.00
☐	119 Daniel Alfredsson Jersey ✂	15.00
☐	5 Tony Amonte Stick ✂	15.00
☐	130 Jean-Sébastien Aubin (G) Jersey ✂	8.00
☐	55 Per Axelsson Jersey ✂	8.00
☐	143 Matthew Barnaby Jersey ✂	8.00
☐	58 Stu Barnes Jersey ✂	8.00
☐	81 Ed Belfour (G) Jersey ✂	25.00
☐	19 Rob Blake Stick ✂	15.00
☐	20 Rob Blake Stick ✂	15.00
☐	64 Fred Brathwaite (G) Jersey ✂	8.00
☐	105 Martin Brodeur (G) Jersey ✂	40.00
☐	100 Benoît Brunet Jersey ✂	8.00
☐	65 Valeri Bure Jersey ✂	8.00
☐	124 Sean Burke (G) Jersey ✂	15.00
☐	48 Andrew Cassels Stick ✂	10.00
☐	16 Chris Chelios Stick ✂	15.00
☐	94 Chris Chelios Jersey ✂	15.00
☐	144 Dan Cloutier (G) Jersey ✂	10.00
☐	131 René Corbet Jersey ✂	8.00
☐	31 Mariusz Czerkawski Stick ✂	10.00
☐	108 Mariusz Czerkawski Jersey ✂	8.00
☐	56 Byron Dafoe (G) Jersey ✂	10.00
☐	95 Mathieu Dandenault Jersey ✂	8.00
☐	11 Marc Denis (G) Stick ✂	15.00
☐	121 Éric Desjardins Jersey ✂	8.00
☐	12 Kevin Dineen Stick ✂	10.00
☐	125 Shane Doan Jersey ✂	8.00
☐	145 Tie Domi Jersey ✂	8.00
☐	14 Ted Donato Stick ✂	10.00
☐	32 Radek Dvorak Stick ✂	10.00
☐	21 Nelson Emerson Stick ✂	10.00
☐	66 Rico Fata Jersey ✂	8.00
☐	109 Wade Flaherty (G) Jersey ✂	8.00
☐	33 Theoren Fleury Stick ✂	15.00
☐	111 Theoren Fleury Jersey ✂	15.00
☐	112 Theoren Fleury Jersey ✂	15.00
☐	7 Peter Forsberg Stick ✂	40.00
☐	74 Peter Forsberg Jersey ✂	35.00
☐	2 Martin Gélinas Stick ✂	10.00
☐	34 Adam Graves Stick ✂	10.00
☐	113 Adam Graves Jersey ✂	10.00
☐	26 Jeff Hackett (G) Stick ✂	10.00
☐	59 Dominik Hasek (G) Jersey ✂	25.00
☐	82 Derian Hatcher Jersey ✂	8.00
☐	146 Glenn Healy (G) Jersey ✂	8.00
☐	51 Guy Hebert (G) Jersey ✂	8.00
☐	52 Guy Hebert (G) Jersey ✂	8.00
☐	83 Benoît Hogue Jersey ✂	8.00
☐	1 Phil Housley Stick ✂	10.00
☐	67 Phil Housley Jersey ✂	8.00
☐	132 Jan Hrdina Jersey ✂	8.00
☐	15 Brett Hull Stick ✂	30.00
☐	84 Brett Hull Jersey ✂	25.00
☐	68 Jarome Iginla Jersey ✂	20.00
☐	133 Jaromir Jagr Jersey ✂	25.00
☐	18 Olli Jokinen Stick ✂	10.00
☐	110 Kenny Jönsson Jersey ✂	8.00
☐	147 Curtis Joseph (G) Jersey ✂	25.00
☐	35 Valeri Kamensky Stick ✂	10.00
☐	3 Sami Kapanen Stick ✂	10.00
☐	134 Darius Kasparaitis Jersey ✂	8.00
☐	85 Mike Keane Jersey ✂	8.00
☐	126 Nikolai Khabibulin (G) Jersey ✂	10.00
☐	103 Patric Kjellberg Jersey ✂	8.00
☐	75 Jon Klemm Jersey ✂	8.00
☐	150 Olaf Kölzig (G) Jersey ✂	15.00
☐	50 Steve Konowalchuk Stick ✂	10.00
☐	135 Alex Kovalev Jersey ✂	15.00
☐	136 Robert Lang Jersey ✂	8.00
☐	86 Jamie Langenbrunner Jersey ✂	8.00
☐	42 John LeClair Stick ✂	25.00
☐	122 John LeClair Jersey ✂	20.00
☐	53 Mike Leclerc Jersey ✂	8.00
☐	36 Brian Leetch Stick ✂	15.00
☐	114 Brian Leetch Jersey ✂	15.00
☐	115 Sylvain Lefebvre Jersey ✂	8.00
☐	104 David Legwand Jersey ✂	10.00
☐	87 Jere Lehtinen Jersey ✂	8.00
☐	44 Mario Lemieux Stick ✂	120.00
☐	151 Mario Lemieux Jersey ✂	75.00
☐	27 Trevor Linden Stick ✂	10.00
☐	28 Trevor Linden Stick ✂	10.00
☐	127 Jyrki Lumme Jersey ✂	8.00
☐	116 Manny Malhotra Jersey ✂	8.00
☐	88 Grant Marshall Jersey ✂	8.00
☐	37 Sandy McCarthy Stick ✂	10.00
☐	38 Kirk McLean (G) Stick ✂	10.00
☐	39 Kirk McLean (G) Stick ✂	10.00
☐	76 Aaron Miller Jersey ✂	8.00
☐	72 Boris Mironov Jersey ✂	8.00
☐	89 Mike Modano Jersey ✂	25.00
☐	30 Alexander Mogilny Stick ✂	15.00
☐	137 Aleksey Morozov Jersey ✂	8.00
☐	40 Petr Nedved Stick ✂	10.00
☐	117 Petr Nedved Jersey ✂	8.00
☐	106 Scott Niedermayer Jersey ✂	8.00
☐	90 Joe Nieuwendyk Jersey ✂	10.00
☐	43 Teppo Numminen Stick ✂	10.00
☐	128 Teppo Numminen Jersey ✂	8.00
☐	80 Lyle Odelein Jersey ✂	8.00
☐	96 Chris Osgood (G) Jersey ✂	15.00
☐	4 Sandis Ozolinsh Stick ✂	10.00
☐	22 Zigmund Palffy Stick ✂	15.00
☐	23 Zigmund Palffy Stick ✂	15.00
☐	138 Rich Parent (G) Jersey ✂	8.00
☐	46 Yanic Perreault Stick ✂	10.00
☐	49 Félix Potvin (G) Stick ✂	15.00
☐	149 Félix Potvin (G) Jersey ✂	15.00
☐	139 Wayne Primeau Jersey ✂	8.00
☐	60 Erik Rasmussen Jersey ✂	8.00
☐	61 Rob Ray Jersey ✂	8.00
☐	77 Dave Reid Jersey ✂	8.00
☐	118 Mike Richter (G) Jersey ✂	10.00
☐	47 Gary Roberts Stick ✂	10.00
☐	129 Jeremy Roenick Jersey ✂	20.00
☐	8 Patrick Roy (G) Stick ✂	75.00
☐	78 Patrick Roy (G) Jersey ✂	75.00
☐	140 Michal Rozsival Jersey ✂	8.00
☐	9 Joe Sakic Stick ✂	50.00
☐	79 Joe Sakic Jersey ✂	40.00
☐	57 André Savage Jersey ✂	8.00
☐	69 Marc" Savard Jersey ✂	8.00
☐	54 Teemu Selänne Jersey ✂	20.00
☐	97 Brendan Shanahan Jersey ✂	25.00
☐	70 Jeff Shantz Jersey ✂	8.00
☐	91 Blake Sloan Jersey ✂	8.00
☐	62 Richard Smehlik Jersey ✂	8.00
☐	24 Bryan Smolinski Stick ✂	10.00
☐	141 Kevin Stevens Jersey ✂	8.00
☐	71 Cory Stillman Jersey ✂	8.00
☐	142 Martin Straka Jersey ✂	8.00
☐	25 Jozef Stümpel Stick ✂	10.00
☐	99 Robert Svehla Jersey ✂	8.00
☐	92 Darryl Sydor Jersey ✂	8.00
☐	107 Chris Terreri (G) Jersey ✂	8.00
☐	13 Ron Tugnutt (G) Stick ✂	10.00
☐	45 Roman Turek (G) Stick ✂	15.00
☐	29 Eric Weinrich Stick ✂	10.00
☐	101 Eric Weinrich Jersey ✂	8.00
☐	120 Alexei Yashin Jersey ✂	15.00
☐	10 Stéphane Yelle Stick ✂	10.00
☐	148 Dmitry Yushkevich Jersey ✂	8.00
☐	98 Steve Yzerman Jersey ✂	50.00
☐	17 Steve Yzerman Stick ✂	75.00
☐	6 Alexei Zhamnov Stick ✂	10.00
☐	73 Alexei Zhamnov Jersey ✂	8.00
☐	63 Alexei Zhitnik Jersey ✂	8.00
☐	102 Sergei Zholtok Jersey ✂	8.00
☐	93 Sergei Zubov Jersey ✂	8.00
☐	152 Jaromir Jagr ✂ / Mario Lemieux ✂ {#/100}	250.00
☐	153 Peter Forsberg ✂ / Joe Sakic ✂ {#/100}	175.00
☐	154 Brett Hull ✂ / Mike Modano ✂ {#/100}	125.00
☐	155 Alex Kovalev ✂ / Martin Straka ✂ {#/100}	75.00

GAME-USED GEAR PATCH VARIATION

	Patch Set (101 cards):	
	Description	**GGP**
☐	123 Mika Alatalo ✂	
☐	119 Daniel Alfredsson ✂	
☐	130 Jean-Sébastien Aubin (G) ✂	
☐	55 Per Axelsson ✂	
☐	143 Matthew Barnaby ✂	
☐	58 Stu Barnes ✂	
☐	81 Ed Belfour (G) ✂	
☐	64 Fred Brathwaite (G) ✂	
☐	105 Martin Brodeur (G) ✂	
☐	100 Benoît Brunet ✂	
☐	65 Valeri Bure ✂	
☐	124 Sean Burke (G) ✂	
☐	94 Chris Chelios ✂	
☐	144 Dan Cloutier (G) ✂	
☐	131 René Corbet ✂	
☐	108 Mariusz Czerkawski ✂	
☐	56 Byron Dafoe (G) ✂	
☐	95 Mathieu Dandenault ✂	
☐	121 Éric Desjardins ✂	
☐	125 Shane Doan ✂	
☐	145 Tie Domi ✂	
☐	66 Rico Fata ✂	
☐	109 Wade Flaherty (G) ✂	
☐	111 Theoren Fleury ✂	
☐	112 Theoren Fleury ✂	
☐	74 Peter Forsberg ✂	
☐	113 Adam Graves ✂	
☐	59 Dominik Hasek (G) ✂	
☐	82 Derian Hatcher ✂	
☐	146 Glenn Healy (G) ✂	
☐	51 Guy Hebert (G) ✂	
☐	52 Guy Hebert (G) ✂	
☐	83 Benoît Hogue ✂	
☐	67 Phil Housley ✂	
☐	132 Jan Hrdina ✂	
☐	84 Brett Hull ✂	
☐	68 Jarome Iginla ✂	
☐	133 Jaromir Jagr ✂	
☐	110 Kenny Jönsson ✂	
☐	147 Curtis Joseph (G) ✂	
☐	134 Darius Kasparaitis ✂	
☐	85 Mike Keane ✂	
☐	126 Nikolai Khabibulin (G) ✂	
☐	103 Patric Kjellberg ✂	
☐	75 Jon Klemm ✂	
☐	150 Olaf Kölzig (G) ✂ {#/50}	
☐	135 Alex Kovalev ✂	
☐	136 Robert Lang ✂	
☐	86 Jamie Langenbrunner ✂	
☐	122 John LeClair ✂	
☐	53 Mike Leclerc ✂	
☐	114 Brian Leetch ✂	
☐	115 Sylvain Lefebvre ✂	
☐	104 David Legwand ✂	
☐	87 Jere Lehtinen ✂	
☐	151 Mario Lemieux ✂	
☐	127 Jyrki Lumme ✂	
☐	116 Manny Malhotra ✂	
☐	88 Grant Marshall ✂	
☐	76 Aaron Miller ✂	
☐	72 Boris Mironov ✂	
☐	89 Mike Modano ✂	
☐	137 Aleksey Morozov ✂	
☐	117 Petr Nedved ✂	
☐	106 Scott Niedermayer ✂	
☐	90 Joe Nieuwendyk ✂	
☐	128 Teppo Numminen ✂	
☐	80 Lyle Odelein ✂	
☐	96 Chris Osgood (G) ✂	
☐	138 Rich Parent (G) ✂	
☐	149 Félix Potvin (G) ✂	
☐	139 Wayne Primeau ✂	
☐	60 Erik Rasmussen ✂	
☐	61 Rob Ray ✂	
☐	77 Dave Reid ✂	
☐	118 Mike Richter (G) ✂	
☐	129 Jeremy Roenick ✂	
☐	78 Patrick Roy (G) ✂	
☐	140 Michal Rozsival ✂	
☐	79 Joe Sakic ✂	
☐	57 André Savage ✂	
☐	69 Marc" Savard ✂	
☐	54 Teemu Selänne ✂	
☐	97 Brendan Shanahan ✂	
☐	70 Jeff Shantz ✂	
☐	91 Blake Sloan ✂	
☐	62 Richard Smehlik ✂	
☐	141 Kevin Stevens ✂	
☐	71 Cory Stillman ✂	
☐	142 Martin Straka ✂	
☐	99 Robert Svehla ✂	
☐	92 Darryl Sydor ✂	
☐	107 Chris Terreri (G) ✂	
☐	101 Eric Weinrich ✂	
☐	120 Alexei Yashin ✂	
☐	148 Dmitry Yushkevich ✂	
☐	98 Steve Yzerman ✂	
☐	73 Alexei Zhamnov ✂	
☐	63 Alexei Zhitnik ✂	
☐	102 Sergei Zholtok ✂	
☐	93 Sergei Zubov ✂	

NORTH AMERICA ALL-STARS

	Insert Set (10 cards):	**75.00**
	Insert (#/1000)	**NAAS**
☐	1 Paul Kariya, NHL All-Star '00	6.00
☐	2 Bill Guerin, NHL All-Star '00	3.00
☐	3 Raymond Bourque, NHL All-Star '00	6.00
☐	4 Patrick Roy (G), NHL All-Star '00	15.00
☐	5 Joe Sakic, NHL All-Star '00	8.00
☐	6 Brett Hull, NHL All-Star '00	4.00
☐	7 Martin Brodeur (G), NHL All-Star '00	8.00
☐	8 Theoren Fleury, NHL All-Star '00	3.00
☐	9 Mario Lemieux, NHL All-Star '00	15.00
☐	10 North America All-Stars {#/100}	25.00

WORLD ALL-STARS

	Insert Set (10 cards):	**50.00**
	Insert (#/1000)	**WAS**
☐	1 Dominik Hasek (G), NHL All-Star '00	4.00
☐	2 Peter Forsberg, NHL All-Star '00	6.00
☐	3 Sergei Fedorov, NHL All-Star '00	4.00
☐	4 Nicklas Lidström, NHL All-Star '00	3.00
☐	5 Pavel Bure, NHL All-Star '00	4.00
☐	6 Zigmund Palffy, NHL All-Star '00	3.00
☐	7 Marian Hossa, NHL All-Star '00	4.00
☐	8 Evgeni Nabokov (G), NHL All-Star '00	6.00
☐	9 Mats Sundin, NHL All-Star '00	4.00
☐	10 World All-Stars {#/100}	25.00

2000 - 01 PRIVATE STOCK TITANIUM DRAFT DAY

This series was issued in June 2001. Each pack includes one memorabilia-affixed Game-Used Gear card (1-100) and one rookie-subset card (101-176). Game-Used Gear Patch cards (1-100 skip numbered) also exist. Production numbers for Jersey and Jersey patch cards are listed after each player's name. Promo versions (marked Sample on the card back) exist for Rookie subset cards 101-176.

Complete Set (176 cards):	500
Description	**Jersey**
☐ 74 Mika Alatalo ✂ {#/535}	8.00
☐ 70 Daniel Alfredsson ✂ {#/520}	15.00
☐ 16 Tony Amonte ✂ {#/1020}	10.00
☐ 80 J-S Aubin (G) ✂ {#/1015}	8.00
☐ 3 Per Axelsson ✂ {#/520}	8.00
☐ 10 Stu Barnes ✂ {#/535}	8.00
☐ 28 Ed Belfour (G) {J#/110}	60.00
☐ 98 Peter Bondra {J#/15}	150.00
☐ 13 Fred Brathwaite (G) ✂ {#/1010}	8.00
☐ 49 Benoît Brunet ✂ {#/1015}	8.00
☐ 46 Pavel Bure ✂ {#/55}	80.00
☐ 14 Valeri Bure ✂ {#/1020}	8.00
☐ 75 Sean Burke (G) ✂ {#/1010}	10.00
☐ 43 Anson Carter {J#/55}	50.00
☐ 36 Chris Chelios ✂ {#/520}	15.00
☐ 94 Shayne Corson ✂ {#/1010}	8.00
☐ 61 Mariusz Czerkawski ✂ {#/1020}	8.00
☐ 4 Byron Dafoe (G) ✂ {#/520}	10.00
☐ 99 Ulf Dahlén {J#/535}	8.00
☐ 91 Vincent Damphousse ✂ {#/1015}	10.00
☐ 37 Mathieu Dandenault ✂ {#/520}	8.00
☐ 17 Éric Dazé ✂ {#/1020}	8.00
☐ 72 Éric Desjardins {J#/520}	8.00
☐ 23 Chris Dingman ✂ {#/520}	8.00
☐ 76 Shane Doan {J#/535}	8.00
☐ 95 Tie Domi ✂ {#/535}	8.00
☐ 89 Dallas Drake ✂ {#/535}	8.00
☐ 52 Mike Dunham (G) ✂ {#/1020}	8.00
☐ 53 Tom Fitzgerald {J#/520}	8.00
☐ 65 Theoren Fleury ✂ {#/870}	10.00
☐ 24 Peter Forsberg ✂ {#/520}	30.00
☐ 1 J-S Giguère (G) ✂ {#/1010}	15.00
☐ 50 Jeff Hackett (G) {J#/520}	8.00
☐ 11 Dominik Hasek (G) {J#/535}	25.00
☐ 29 Derian Hatcher ✂ {#/990}	8.00
☐ 59 Bobby Holik ✂ {#/520}	8.00
☐ 81 Jan Hrdina ✂ {#/1020}	8.00
☐ 30 Brett Hull {J#/115}	60.00
☐ 82 Jaromir Jagr {J#/520}	20.00
☐ 62 Kenny Jönsson ✂ {#/520}	8.00
☐ 96 Curtis Joseph (G) {J#/535}	25.00
☐ 83 Darius Kasparaitis ✂ {#/1010}	8.00
☐ 54 Patric Kjellberg ✂ {#/520}	8.00
☐ 84 Alex Kovalev ✂ {#/1015}	10.00
☐ 85 Milan Kraft ✂ {#/1015}	8.00
☐ 31 Jamie Langenbrunner ✂ {#/985}	8.00
☐ 63 Claude Lapointe ✂ {#/1015}	8.00
☐ 93 Vincent Lecavalier {J#/535}	25.00
☐ 73 John LeClair ✂ {#/520}	20.00
☐ 2 Mike Leclerc ✂ {#/520}	8.00
☐ 66 Brian Leetch ✂ {#/520}	15.00
☐ 55 David Legwand ✂ {#/520}	10.00
☐ 32 Jere Lehtinen {J#/520}	8.00
☐ 86 Mario Lemieux {J#/115}	175.00
☐ 38 Nicklas Lidström {J#/110}	40.00
☐ 77 Jyrki Lumme ✂ {#/520}	8.00
☐ 39 Darren McCarty {J#/520}	8.00
☐ 5 Kyle McLaren {J#/520}	8.00
☐ 18 Boris Mironov ✂ {#/1020}	8.00
☐ 33 Mike Modano ✂ {#/1015}	20.00
☐ 67 Petr Nedved ✂ {#/1015}	8.00
☐ 60 Scott Niedermayer ✂ {#/995}	8.00
☐ 34 Joe Nieuwendyk ✂ {#/1015}	8.00
☐ 19 Michael Nylander ✂ {#/1020}	8.00
☐ 27 Lyle Odelein ✂ {#/535}	8.00
☐ 40 Chris Osgood (G) ✂ {#/1020}	10.00
☐ 48 Félix Potvin (G) {J#/100}	40.00
☐ 12 Erik Rasmussen ✂ {#/1020}	8.00
☐ 68 Mike Richter (G) ✂ {#/1010}	8.00
☐ 78 Jeremy Roenick ✂ {#/520}	20.00
☐ 56 Cliff Ronning ✂ {#/520}	8.00
☐ 25 Patrick Roy (G) {J#/68}	200.00
☐ 26 Joe Sakic {J#/535}	40.00
☐ 6 Sergei Samsonov ✂ {#/520}	15.00
☐ 15 Marc Savard ✂ {#/1020}	8.00
☐ 92 Teemu Selänne ✂ {#/1020}	15.00
☐ 41 Brendan Shanahan ✂ {#/520}	25.00
☐ 44 Ryan Smyth ✂ {#/1015}	8.00
☐ 87 Kevin Stevens ✂ {#/1020}	8.00
☐ 90 Cory Stillman ✂ {#/1010}	8.00
☐ 88 Martin Straka ✂ {#/1010}	8.00
☐ 79 Radoslav Suchy ✂ {#/1015}	8.00
☐ 20 Steve Sullivan ✂ {#/1020}	8.00
☐ 97 Mats Sundin {J#/535}	25.00
☐ 47 Robert Svehla ✂ {#/1015}	8.00
☐ 7 Don Sweeney {J#/535}	8.00
☐ 35 Darryl Sydor ✂ {#/835}	8.00
☐ 64 Chris Terreri (G) ✂ {#/1020}	8.00
☐ 21 Jocelyn Thibault (G) ✂ {#/1020}	8.00
☐ 8 Joe Thornton ✂ {#/535}	30.00
☐ 57 Kimmo Timonen {J#/520}	8.00
☐ 58 Scott Walker ✂ {#/520}	8.00
☐ 45 Doug Weight ✂ {#/520}	15.00
☐ 9 Eric Weinrich ✂ {#/1020}	8.00
☐ 71 Alexei Yashin ✂ {#/285}	20.00
☐ 69 Mike York ✂ {#/1015}	8.00
☐ 42 Steve Yzerman {J#/105}	150.00
☐ 22 Alexei Zhamnov ✂ {#/1020}	8.00
☐ 51 Sergei Zholtok ✂ {#/1010}	8.00
☐ 100 Dainius Zubrus {J#/520}	8.00

ROOKIE

Rookie (#/1000)	R1000
☐☐ 101 Samuel Påhlsson, Anah.	4.00
☐☐ 102 Scott Fankhouser (G), Atla.	4.00
☐☐ 103 Tomi Kallio, Atla.	4.00
☐☐ **104 Brad Tapper, Atla. RC**	**8.00**
☐☐ **105 Andrew Raycroft (G), Bost. RC**	**12.00**
☐☐ 106 Denis Hamel, Buff.	4.00
☐☐ **107 Jeff Cowan, Calg. RC**	**6.00**
☐☐ 108 Oleg Saprykin, Calg.	4.00
☐☐ **109 Josef Vasicek, Caro. RC**	**12.00**
☐☐ 110 Shane Willis, Caro.	4.00
☐☐ **111 David Aebischer (G), Colo. RC RC**	**15.00**
☐☐ **112 Serge Aubin, Colu. RC RC**	**8.00**
☐☐ 113 Marc Denis (G), Colu.	6.00
☐☐ **114 Chris Nielsen, Colu. RC**	**8.00**
☐☐ 115 David Vyborny, Colu.	4.00
☐☐ **116 Marty Turco (G), Dall. RC**	**30.00**
☐☐ **117 Shawn Horcoff, Edmo. RC**	**8.00**
☐☐ **118 Mike Comrie, Edmo. RC RC**	**40.00**
☐☐ 119 Domenic Pittis, Edmo.	4.00
☐☐ 120 Roberto Luongo (G), Flor.	10.00
☐☐ 121 Ivan Novoseltsev, Flor.	4.00
☐☐ 122 Serge Payer, Flor.	4.00
☐☐ 123 Denis Shvidki, Flor.	4.00
☐☐ **124 Steven Reinprecht, LosA. RC**	**15.00**
☐☐ **125 L'ubomir Visnovsky, LosA. RC**	**8.00**
☐☐ **126 Marian Gaborik, MinW. RC**	**50.00**
☐☐ 127 Filip Kuba, MinW.	4.00
☐☐ 128 Mathieu Garon (G), Mont.	4.00
☐☐ **129 Éric Landry, Mont. RC**	**6.00**
☐☐ 130 Andrei Markov, Mont.	4.00
☐☐ 131 Marian Cisar, Nash.	4.00
☐☐ **132 Scott Hartnell, Nash. RC**	**12.00**
☐☐ **133 Rick DiPietro (G), NYIs. RC**	**20.00**
☐☐ **134 Martin Havlat, Otta. RC**	**30.00**
☐☐ **135 Jani Hurme (G), Otta. RC**	**10.00**
☐☐ 136 Petr Schastlivy, Otta.	4.00
☐☐ **137 Ruslan Fedotenko, Phil. RC**	**8.00**
☐☐ **138 Justin Williams, Phil. RC**	**15.00**
☐☐ 139 Robert Esche (G), Phoe.	4.00
☐☐ 140 Milan Kraft, Pitt.	4.00
☐☐ 141 Brent Johnson (G), SLou.	4.00
☐☐ **142 Reed Low, SLou. RC**	**8.00**
☐☐ 143 Evgeni Nabokov (G), SanJ.	6.00
☐☐ **144 Alexander Kharitonov, Tamp. RC RC**	**6.00**
☐☐ **145 Dieter Kochan (G), Tamp. RC RC**	**8.00**
☐☐ 146 Brad Richards, Tamp.	6.00
☐☐ 147 Adam Mair, Toro.	4.00
☐☐ 148 Daniel Sedin, Vanc.	4.00
☐☐ 149 Henrik Sedin, Vanc.	4.00
☐☐ 150 Trent Whitfield, Wash.	4.00
☐☐ **151 Marc Chouinard, Anah. RC**	**6.00**
☐☐ **152 Jonas Rönnqvist, Anah. RC**	**8.00**
☐☐ **153 Petr Tenkrat, Anah. RC**	**8.00**
☐☐ **154 Ronald Petrovicky, Calg. RC**	**8.00**
☐☐ **155 Craig Adams, Caro. RC**	**6.00**
☐☐ **156 Niclas Wallin, Caro. RC**	**6.00**
☐☐ **157 Rostislav Klesla, Colu. RC**	**15.00**
☐☐ **158 Petteri Nummelin, Colu. RC**	**8.00**
☐☐ **159 Tyler Bouck, Dall. RC**	**8.00**
☐☐ **160 Michel Riesen, Edmo. RC**	**8.00**
☐☐ **161 Éric Bélanger, LosA. RC**	**8.00**
☐☐ **162 Roman Simicek, MinW. RC**	**6.00**
☐☐ 163 Xavier Delisle, Mont.	4.00
☐☐ **164 Greg Classen, Nash. RC**	**8.00**
☐☐ **165 Mike Commodore, NJer. RC**	**6.00**
☐☐ **166 Sascha Goc, NJer. RC**	**8.00**
☐☐ **167 Jeff Ulmer, NYRa. RC**	**6.00**
☐☐ **168 Shane Hnidy, Otta. RC**	**6.00**
☐☐ **169 Roman Cechmanek (G), Phil. RC**	**20.00**
☐☐ **170 Todd Fedoruk, Phil. RC**	**6.00**
☐☐ **171 Ossi Väänänen, Phoe. RC**	**8.00**
☐☐ **172 Bryce Salvador, SLou. RC**	**8.00**
☐☐ **173 Mark Smith, SanJ. RC**	**6.00**
☐☐ **174 Mike Brown, Vanc. RC**	**8.00**
☐☐ **175 Jakub Cutta, Wash. RC**	**8.00**
☐☐ **176 Johan Hedberg (G), Pitt. RC**	**30.00**

GAME-WORN JERSEY PATCH VARIATION

Insert Set (74 cards):	800
Insert	**Patch**
☐ 74 Mika Alatalo ✂ {#/117}	20.00
☐ 70 Daniel Alfredsson ✂ {#/56}	95.00
☐ 16 Tony Amonte ✂ {#/110}	35.00
☐ 80 J-S Aubin (G) ✂ {#/112}	20.00
☐ 3 Per Axelsson ✂ {#/114}	20.00
☐ 10 Stu Barnes ✂ {#/57}	20.00
☐ 13 Fred Brathwaite (G) ✂ {#/106}	20.00
☐ 49 Benoît Brunet ✂ {#/111}	20.00
☐ 46 Pavel Bure ✂ {#/116}	50.00
☐ 14 Valeri Bure ✂ {#/110}	20.00
☐ 75 Sean Burke (G) ✂ {#/111}	35.00
☐ 36 Chris Chelios ✂ {#/112}	35.00
☐ 94 Shayne Corson ✂ {#/38}	30.00
☐ 61 Mariusz Czerkawski ✂ {#/79}	20.00
☐ 4 Byron Dafoe (G) ✂ {#/70}	30.00
☐ 91 Vincent Damphousse ✂ {#/114}	35.00
☐ 37 Mathieu Dandenault ✂ {#/115}	20.00
☐ 17 Éric Dazé ✂ {#/114}	25.00
☐ 23 Chris Dingman ✂ {#/120}	20.00
☐ 95 Tie Domi ✂ {#/110}	20.00
☐ 89 Dallas Drake ✂ {#/36}	20.00
☐ 52 Mike Dunham (G) ✂ {#/113}	25.00
☐ 65 Theoren Fleury ✂ {#/38}	50.00
☐ 24 Peter Forsberg ✂ {#/112}	50.00
☐ 1 J-S Giguère (G) ✂ {#/115}	50.00
☐ 29 Derian Hatcher ✂ {#/114}	20.00
☐ 59 Bobby Holik ✂ {#/49}	25.00
☐ 81 Jan Hrdina ✂ {#/112}	20.00
☐ 62 Kenny Jönsson ✂ {#/92}	20.00
☐ 83 Darius Kasparaitis ✂ {#/114}	20.00
☐ 54 Patric Kjellberg ✂ {#/118}	20.00
☐ 84 Alex Kovalev ✂ {#/114}	35.00
☐ 85 Milan Kraft ✂ {#/112}	20.00
☐ 31 Jamie Langenbrunner ✂ {#/109}	20.00
☐ 63 Claude Lapointe ✂ {#/40}	20.00
☐ 73 John LeClair ✂ {#/89}	55.00
☐ 2 Mike Leclerc ✂ {#/114}	20.00
☐ 66 Brian Leetch ✂ {#/117}	35.00
☐ 55 David Legwand ✂ {#/116}	25.00
☐ 77 Jyrki Lumme ✂ {#/108}	20.00
☐ 18 Boris Mironov ✂ {#/116}	20.00
☐ 33 Mike Modano ✂ {#/112}	65.00
☐ 67 Petr Nedved ✂ {#/34}	30.00
☐ 60 Scott Niedermayer ✂ {#/102}	20.00
☐ 34 Joe Nieuwendyk ✂ {#/106}	25.00
☐ 19 Michael Nylander ✂ {#/113}	20.00
☐ 27 Lyle Odelein ✂ {#/114}	20.00
☐ 40 Chris Osgood (G) ✂ {#/106}	35.00
☐ 12 Erik Rasmussen ✂ {#/113}	20.00
☐ 68 Mike Richter (G) ✂ {#/114}	30.00
☐ 78 Jeremy Roenick ✂ {#/42}	70.00
☐ 56 Cliff Ronning ✂ {#/56}	20.00
☐ 6 Sergei Samsonov ✂ {#/43}	50.00
☐ 15 Marc Savard ✂ {#/106}	20.00
☐ 92 Teemu Selänne ✂ {#/118}	50.00
☐ 41 Brendan Shanahan ✂ {#/117}	60.00
☐ 44 Ryan Smyth ✂ {#/24}	50.00
☐ 87 Kevin Stevens ✂ {#/115}	20.00
☐ 90 Cory Stillman ✂ {#/114}	20.00
☐ 88 Martin Straka ✂ {#/108}	20.00
☐ 79 Radoslav Suchy ✂ {#/107}	20.00
☐ 20 Steve Sullivan ✂ {#/113}	20.00
☐ 47 Robert Svehla ✂ {#/105}	20.00
☐ 35 Darryl Sydor ✂ {#/107}	20.00
☐ 64 Chris Terreri (G) ✂ {#/72}	20.00
☐ 21 Jocelyn Thibault (G) ✂ {#/113}	25.00
☐ 8 Joe Thornton ✂ {#/24}	125.00
☐ 58 Scott Walker ✂ {#/94}	20.00
☐ 45 Doug Weight ✂ {#/110}	35.00
☐ 9 Eric Weinrich ✂ {#/116}	20.00
☐ 71 Alexei Yashin ✂ {#/46}	50.00
☐ 69 Mike York ✂ {#/109}	20.00
☐ 22 Alexei Zhamnov ✂ {#/116}	20.00
☐ 51 Sergei Zholtok ✂ {#/103}	20.00

2000 - 01 REVOLUTION

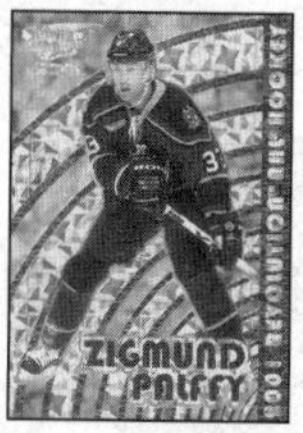

This series was issued in December 2000. Base cards 1-150 have a retail-pack Red parallel (#/99), a hobby-pack Premiere Date parallel (#/60) and a hobby-pack Ice Blue parallel (#/85).

Complete Set (150):	2000	2000	1500	75.00
Common Player:	8.00	6.00	5.00	.50
Description	**PD60**	**IB85**	**R99**	**Rev.**
☐☐☐☐ 1 Guy Hebert (G)	8.00	8.00	6.00	.50
☐☐☐☐ 2 Paul Kariya	55.00	55.00	40.00	2.50
☐☐☐☐ 3 Steve Rucchin	8.00	8.00	6.00	.50
☐☐☐☐ 4 Teemu Selänne	30.00	30.00	20.00	1.50
☐☐☐☐ 5 Andrew Brunette	8.00	6.00	5.00	.50
☐☐☐☐ 6 Ray Ferraro	8.00	6.00	5.00	.50
☐☐☐☐ 7 Damian Rhodes (G)	8.00	8.00	6.00	.50
☐☐☐☐ 8 Patrik Stefan	12.00	12.00	8.00	.50
☐☐☐☐ 9 Anson Carter	16.00	16.00	12.00	.50
☐☐☐☐ 10 Byron Dafoe (G)	16.00	16.00	12.00	.50
☐☐☐☐ 11 John Grahame (G)	8.00	8.00	6.00	.50
☐☐☐☐ 12 Sergei Samsonov	20.00	20.00	18.00	1.00
☐☐☐☐ 13 Joe Thornton	45.00	45.00	35.00	2.00
☐☐☐☐ 14 Maxim Afinogenov	16.00	16.00	12.00	.50
☐☐☐☐ 15 Martin Biron (G)	18.00	18.00	14.00	.50
☐☐☐☐ 16 Doug Gilmour	20.00	20.00	18.00	1.00
☐☐☐☐ 17 Dominik Hasek (G)	40.00	40.00	30.00	2.00
☐☐☐☐ 18 Michael Peca	16.00	16.00	12.00	.50
☐☐☐☐ 19 Miroslav Satan	12.00	12.00	8.00	.50
☐☐☐☐ 20 Fred Brathwaite (G)	12.00	12.00	8.00	.50
☐☐☐☐ 21 Valeri Bure	12.00	12.00	8.00	.50
☐☐☐☐ 22 Phil Housley	12.00	12.00	8.00	.50
☐☐☐☐ 23 Jarome Iginla	30.00	30.00	20.00	1.50
☐☐☐☐ 24 Oleg Saprykin	8.00	8.00	6.00	.50
☐☐☐☐ 25 Rod Brind'Amour	12.00	12.00	8.00	.50
☐☐☐☐ 26 Ron Francis	20.00	20.00	18.00	1.00
☐☐☐☐ 27 Arturs Irbe (G)	15.00	15.00	12.00	.50
☐☐☐☐ 28 Sami Kapanen	12.00	12.00	8.00	.50
☐☐☐☐ 29 Tony Amonte	20.00	20.00	18.00	1.00
☐☐☐☐ 30 Michal Grosek	8.00	6.00	5.00	.50
☐☐☐☐ 31 Steve Sullivan	12.00	12.00	8.00	.50
☐☐☐☐ 32 Jocelyn Thibault (G)	16.00	16.00	12.00	.50
☐☐☐☐ 33 Alexei Zhamnov	12.00	12.00	8.00	.50
☐☐☐☐ 34 R. Bourque	45.00	45.00	35.00	2.00
☐☐☐☐ 35 Chris Drury	20.00	20.00	18.00	1.00
☐☐☐☐ 36 Peter Forsberg	55.00	55.00	40.00	2.50
☐☐☐☐ 37 Milan Hejduk	30.00	30.00	24.00	1.50
☐☐☐☐ 38 Patrick Roy (G)	120.00	120.00	90.00	6.00
☐☐☐☐ 39 Joe Sakic	60.00	60.00	45.00	3.00
☐☐☐☐ 40 Alex Tanguay	20.00	20.00	18.00	1.00
☐☐☐☐ 41 Kevyn Adams	8.00	6.00	5.00	.50
☐☐☐☐ 42 Marc Denis (G)	18.00	18.00	14.00	.50
☐☐☐☐ 43 Krzystzof Oliwa	8.00	8.00	6.00	.50
☐☐☐☐ 44 Geoff Sanderson	8.00	8.00	6.00	.50
☐☐☐☐ 45 Ed Belfour (G)	40.00	40.00	30.00	2.00
☐☐☐☐ 46 Brett Hull	40.00	40.00	30.00	2.00
☐☐☐☐ 47 Mike Modano	40.00	40.00	30.00	2.00
☐☐☐☐ 48 Brenden Morrow	12.00	12.00	8.00	.50
☐☐☐☐ 49 Joe Nieuwendyk	16.00	16.00	12.00	.50
☐☐☐☐ 50 Chris Chelios	20.00	20.00	18.00	1.00
☐☐☐☐ 51 Sergei Fedorov	40.00	40.00	30.00	2.00
☐☐☐☐ 52 Nicklas Lidström	20.00	20.00	18.00	1.00
☐☐☐☐ 53 Chris Osgood (G)	20.00	20.00	18.00	1.00
☐☐☐☐ 54 B. Shanahan	40.00	40.00	30.00	2.00
☐☐☐☐ 55 Steve Yzerman	95.00	95.00	70.00	4.50
☐☐☐☐ 56 Bill Guerin	16.00	16.00	12.00	.50
☐☐☐☐ 57 Todd Marchant	8.00	8.00	6.00	.50
☐☐☐☐ 58 Tommy Salo (G)	16.00	16.00	12.00	.50
☐☐☐☐ 59 Ryan Smyth	15.00	15.00	14.00	.50

□□□□ 60 Doug Weight	20.00	20.00	18.00	1.00
□□□□ 61 Pavel Bure	30.00	30.00	20.00	1.50
□□□□ 62 Trevor Kidd (G)	12.00	12.00	8.00	.50
□□□□ 63 Viktor Kozlov	12.00	12.00	8.00	.50
□□□□ 64 Scott Mellanby	8.00	8.00	6.00	.50
□□□□ 65 Ray Whitney	8.00	8.00	6.00	.50
□□□□ 66 Rob Blake	20.00	20.00	18.00	1.00
□□□□ 67 S. Fiset (G)	12.00	12.00	8.00	.50
□□□□ 68 Zigmund Palffy	20.00	20.00	18.00	1.00
□□□□ 69 Luc Robitaille	30.00	30.00	20.00	1.50
□□□□ 70 Jamie Storr (G)	8.00	8.00	6.00	.50
□□□□ 71 M. Fernandez (G)	16.00	16.00	12.00	.50
□□□□ 72 J. McLennan (G)	8.00	6.00	5.00	.50
□□□□ 73 S. O'Donnell	8.00	6.00	5.00	.50
□□□□ 74 S. Roest	8.00	6.00	5.00	.50
□□□□ 75 Jeff Hackett (G)	12.00	12.00	8.00	.50
□□□□ 76 Saku Koivu	45.00	45.00	35.00	1.50
□□□□ 77 Trevor Linden	16.00	16.00	12.00	.50
□□□□ 78 Martin Rucinsky	8.00	8.00	6.00	.50
□□□□ 79 J. Théodore (G)	45.00	45.00	35.00	2.00
□□□□ 80 Mike Dunham (G)	16.00	16.00	12.00	.50
□□□□ **81 D. Gosselin RC**	**8.00**	**8.00**	**6.00**	**1.00**
□□□□ 82 David Legwand	16.00	16.00	12.00	.50
□□□□ 83 Cliff Ronning	8.00	8.00	6.00	.50
□□□□ 84 Jason Arnott	15.00	15.00	14.00	.50
□□□□ 85 M. Brodeur (G)	60.00	60.00	45.00	3.00
□□□□ 86 Patrik Elias	30.00	30.00	20.00	1.50
□□□□ 87 Scott Gomez	16.00	16.00	12.00	.50
□□□□ 88 Scott Stevens	16.00	16.00	12.00	.50
□□□□ 89 Petr Sykora	16.00	16.00	12.00	.50
□□□□ 90 Tim Connolly	16.00	16.00	12.00	.50
□□□□ 91 M. Czerkawski	8.00	8.00	6.00	.50
□□□□ 92 Brad Isbister	8.00	8.00	6.00	.50
□□□□ **93 S. Valiquette (G) RC**	**12.00**	**12.00**	**8.00**	**1.50**
□□□□ 94 Theoren Fleury	20.00	20.00	15.00	1.00
□□□□ 95 Adam Graves	16.00	16.00	12.00	.50
□□□□ 96 Brian Leetch	20.00	20.00	18.00	1.00
□□□□ 97 Mark Messier	40.00	40.00	30.00	2.00
□□□□ 98 Petr Nedved	12.00	12.00	8.00	.50
□□□□ 99 Mike Richter (G)	18.00	18.00	14.00	.50
□□□□ 100 Mike York	12.00	12.00	8.00	.50
□□□□ 101 D. Alfredsson	45.00	45.00	35.00	1.00
□□□□ 102 Radek Bonk	12.00	12.00	8.00	.50
□□□□ 103 Marian Hossa	40.00	40.00	30.00	2.00
□□□□ 104 P. Lalime (G)	20.00	20.00	18.00	1.00
□□□□ 105 S. McEachern	12.00	12.00	8.00	.50
□□□□ 106 B. Boucher (G)	12.00	12.00	8.00	.50
□□□□ 107 Éric Desjardins	12.00	12.00	8.00	.50
□□□□ 108 Simon Gagné	30.00	30.00	20.00	1.50
□□□□ 109 John LeClair	30.00	30.00	20.00	1.50
□□□□ 110 Eric Lindros	40.00	40.00	30.00	2.00
□□□□ 111 Mark Recchi	16.00	16.00	12.00	.50
□□□□ 112 Shane Doan	8.00	8.00	6.00	.50
□□□□ 113 N. Khabibulin (G)	16.00	16.00	12.00	.50
□□□□ 114 Jeremy Roenick	30.00	30.00	20.00	1.50
□□□□ 115 Keith Tkachuk	20.00	20.00	18.00	1.00
□□□□ 116 J-S Aubin (G)	8.00	8.00	6.00	.50
□□□□ 117 Jan Hrdina	8.00	8.00	6.00	.50
□□□□ 118 Jaromir Jagr	40.00	40.00	30.00	2.00
□□□□ 119 Alex Kovalev	20.00	20.00	18.00	1.00
□□□□ 120 Martin Straka	12.00	12.00	8.00	.50
□□□□ 121 Pavol Demitra	16.00	16.00	12.00	.50
□□□□ 122 Michal Handzus	8.00	8.00	6.00	.50
□□□□ 123 Al MacInnis	16.00	16.00	12.00	.50
□□□□ 124 Chris Pronger	20.00	20.00	18.00	1.00
□□□□ 125 Roman Turek (G)	15.00	15.00	14.00	.50
□□□□ 126 Pierre Turgeon	16.00	16.00	12.00	.50
□□□□ 127 V. Damphousse	20.00	20.00	18.00	1.00
□□□□ 128 Jeff Friesen	12.00	12.00	8.00	.50
□□□□ 129 Patrick Marleau	18.00	18.00	14.00	.50
□□□□ 130 Owen Nolan	20.00	20.00	18.00	1.00
□□□□ 131 Steve Shields (G)	8.00	8.00	6.00	.50
□□□□ 132 Dan Cloutier (G)	16.00	16.00	12.00	.50
□□□□ 133 Mike Johnson	8.00	8.00	6.00	.50
□□□□ **134 D. Kochan (G) RC**	**12.00**	**12.00**	**8.00**	**1.50**
□□□□ 135 V. Lecavalier	40.00	40.00	30.00	2.00
□□□□ 136 Nikolai Antropov	8.00	8.00	6.00	.50
□□□□ 137 Tie Domi	12.00	12.00	8.00	.50
□□□□ 138 Jeff Farkas	18.00	18.00	14.00	.50
□□□□ 139 C. Joseph (G)	40.00	40.00	30.00	2.00
□□□□ 140 Mats Sundin	40.00	40.00	30.00	2.00
□□□□ 141 Darcy Tucker	8.00	8.00	6.00	.50
□□□□ 142 Todd Bertuzzi	45.00	45.00	35.00	2.00
□□□□ 143 Steve Kariya	8.00	8.00	6.00	.50
□□□□ 144 Markus Näslund	40.00	40.00	30.00	2.00
□□□□ 145 Félix Potvin (G)	45.00	45.00	35.00	1.00
□□□□ 146 Peter Bondra	20.00	20.00	18.00	1.00
□□□□ 147 Jeff Halpern	8.00	8.00	6.00	.50
□□□□ 148 Olaf Kölzig (G)	20.00	20.00	18.00	1.00
□□□□ 149 Adam Oates	16.00	16.00	12.00	.50
□□□□ 150 Chris Simon	8.00	8.00	6.00	.50

GAME-USED GEAR

Insert Set (10 cards):	**275.00**
Insert (#/200)	**GG200**
□ 10 Peter Bondra, Wash. ✂	25.00
□ 4 Sergei Fedorov, Detr. ✂	25.00
□ 1 Peter Forsberg, Colo. ✂	50.00
□ 9 Jaromir Jagr, Pitt. ✂	25.00
□ 8 Nikolai Khabibulin (G), Phoe. ✂	25.00
□ 5 Nicklas Lidström, Detr. ✂	25.00
□ 7 Mark Messier, NYRa. ✂	25.00
□ 3 Mike Modano, Dall. ✂	25.00
□ 2 Joe Sakic, Colo. ✂	50.00
□ 6 Steve Yzerman, Detr. ✂	100.00

GAME-WORN JERSEY

There are two versions: the Jersey card (#/400) and the Patch variation (#/50).

Insert Set (10 cards):	**450.00**	**125.00**
Description	**P50**	**J400**
□□ 4 Tony Amonte, Chic. ✂	60.00	15.00
□□ 2 Anson Carter, Bost. ✂	50.00	15.00
□□ 7 Zdeno Chara, NYIs. ✂	50.00	15.00
□□ 9 Andreas Dackell, Otta. ✂	50.00	15.00
□□ 3 Jarome Iginla, Calg. ✂	80.00	25.00
□□ 6 Saku Koivu, Mont. ✂	120.00	25.00
□□ 5 Jamie Langenbrunner, Dall. ✂	50.00	15.00
□□ 8 Brian Leetch, NYRa. ✂	60.00	15.00
□□ 1 Marty McInnis, Anah. ✂	50.00	15.00
□□ 10 Petr Svoboda, Tamp. ✂	50.00	15.00

HD-NHL

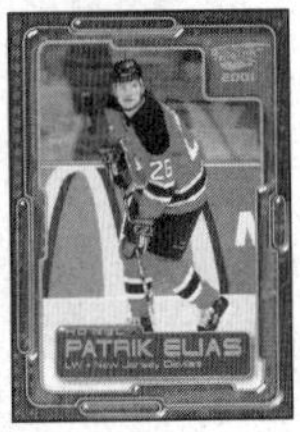

Insert Set (36 cards):	**75.00**
Insert (2:25 packs)	**HD**
□ 1 Paul Kariya, Anah.	10.00
□ 2 Teemu Selänne, Anah.	6.00
□ 3 Patrik Stefan, Atla.	4.00
□ 4 Joe Thornton, Bost.	8.00
□ 5 Dominik Hasek (G), Buff.	6.00
□ 6 Jarome Iginla, Calg.	6.00
□ 7 Tony Amonte, Chic.	4.00
□ 8 Peter Forsberg, Colo.	10.00
□ 9 Milan Hejduk, Colo.	6.00
□ 10 Joe Sakic, Colo.	12.00
□ 11 Patrick Roy (G), Colo.	20.00
□ 12 Ed Belfour (G), Dall.	6.00
□ 13 Brett Hull, Dall.	6.00
□ 14 Sergei Fedorov, Detr.	6.00
□ 15 Brendan Shanahan, Detr.	6.00
□ 16 Pavel Bure, Flor.	6.00
□ 17 Zigmund Palffy, LosA.	4.00
□ 18 Luc Robitaille, LosA.	6.00
□ 19 Saku Koivu, Mont.	6.00
□ 20 Martin Brodeur (G), NJer.	12.00
□ 21 Patrik Elias, NJer.	6.00
□ 22 Scott Gomez, NJer.	4.00
□ 23 Marian Hossa, Otta.	6.00
□ 24 Brian Boucher (G), Phil.	4.00
□ 25 John LeClair, Phil.	6.00
□ 26 Mark Recchi, Phil.	4.00
□ 27 Jeremy Roenick, Phoe.	6.00
□ 28 Keith Tkachuk, Phoe.	4.00
□ 29 Chris Pronger, SLou.	4.00
□ 30 Roman Turek (G), SLou.	4.00
□ 31 Owen Nolan, SanJ.	4.00
□ 32 Vincent Lecavalier, Tamp.	6.00
□ 33 Nikolai Antropov, Toro.	4.00
□ 34 Mats Sundin, Toro.	6.00
□ 35 Curtis Joseph (G), Toro.	6.00
□ 36 Olaf Kölzig (G), Wash.	4.00

ICE IMMORTALS

Insert Set (20 cards):	**60.00**
Insert (1:25 packs)	**II**
□ 1 Paul Kariya, Anah.	10.00
□ 2 Teemu Selänne, Anah.	5.00
□ 3 Dominik Hasek (G), Buff.	5.00
□ 4 Raymond Bourque, Colo.	5.00
□ 5 Peter Forsberg, Colo.	10.00
□ 6 Patrick Roy (G), Colo.	20.00
□ 7 Ed Belfour (G), Dall.	5.00
□ 8 Brett Hull, Dall.	5.00
□ 9 Mike Modano, Dall.	5.00
□ 10 Brendan Shanahan, Detr.	5.00
□ 11 Steve Yzerman, Detr.	15.00
□ 12 Pavel Bure, Flor.	5.00
□ 13 Martin Brodeur (G), NJer.	10.00
□ 14 Scott Gomez, NJer.	5.00
□ 15 John LeClair, Phil.	5.00
□ 16 Mark Recchi, Phil.	5.00
□ 17 Jeremy Roenick, Phoe.	5.00
□ 18 Jaromir Jagr, Pitt.	5.00
□ 19 Curtis Joseph (G), Toro.	5.00
□ 20 Olaf Kölzig (G), Wash.	5.00

NHL ICONS

Insert Set (20 cards):	**125.00**
Insert (1:121 packs)	**Icon**
□ 1 Paul Kariya, Anah.	40.00
□ 2 Teemu Selänne, Anah.	20.00
□ 3 Doug Gilmour, Buff.	20.00
□ 4 Dominik Hasek (G), Buff.	20.00
□ 5 Raymond Bourque, Colo.	35.00
□ 6 Peter Forsberg, Colo.	40.00
□ 7 Patrick Roy (G), Colo.	90.00
□ 8 Joe Sakic, Colo.	45.00
□ 9 Brett Hull, Dall.	20.00
□ 10 Mike Modano, Dall.	20.00
□ 11 Brendan Shanahan, Detr.	20.00
□ 12 Steve Yzerman, Detr.	70.00
□ 13 Pavel Bure, Flor.	20.00
□ 14 Luc Robitaille, LosA.	20.00
□ 15 Martin Brodeur (G), NJer.	45.00
□ 16 John LeClair, Phil.	20.00
□ 17 Jaromir Jagr, Pitt.	20.00
□ 18 Curtis Joseph (G), Toro.	20.00
□ 19 Mats Sundin, Toro.	20.00
□ 20 Olaf Kölzig (G), Wash.	20.00

STAT MASTERS

Insert Set (30 cards):	**40.00**
Insert (#/99)	**SM99**
□ 1 Teemu Selänne, Anah.	30.00
□ 2 Tony Amonte, Chic.	20.00
□ 3 Milan Hejduk, Colo.	30.00
□ 4 Brett Hull, Dall.	35.00
□ 5 Brendan Shanahan, Detr.	35.00
□ 6 Pavel Bure, Flor.	30.00
□ 7 Luc Robitaille, LosA.	30.00
□ 8 John LeClair, Phil.	30.00
□ 9 Jaromir Jagr, Pitt.	35.00
□ 10 Owen Nolan, SanJ.	20.00
Insert (#/199)	**SM199**
□ 11 Martin Biron (G), Buff.	8.00
□ 12 Dominik Hasek (G), Buff.	15.00
□ 13 Patrick Roy (G), Colo.	55.00
□ 14 Ed Belfour (G), Dall.	15.00
□ 15 José Théodore (G), Mont.	20.00
□ 16 Martin Brodeur (G), NJer.	30.00
□ 17 Brian Boucher (G), Phil.	8.00
□ 18 Roman Turek (G), SLou.	8.00
□ 19 Curtis Joseph (G), Toro.	15.00
□ 20 Olaf Kölzig (G), Wash.	10.00
Insert (#/299)	**SM299**
□ 21 Paul Kariya, Anah.	10.00
□ 22 Doug Gilmour, Buff.	5.00
□ 23 Raymond Bourque, Colo.	10.00
□ 24 Joe Sakic, Colo.	15.00
□ 25 Mike Modano, Dall.	10.00
□ 26 Steve Yzerman, Detr.	20.00
□ 27 Scott Gomez, NJer.	5.00
□ 28 Mark Recchi, Phil.	5.00
□ 29 Mats Sundin, Toro.	10.00
□ 30 Adam Oates, Wash.	5.00

2000 - 01 SIGNATURE SERIES

This series was issued in March 2001. Base cards 1-300 have a have a Ruby parallel (#/200), a Sapphire parallel (#/100) and an Emerald parallel (#/10). Base cards 251-275 are limited to 1,000 copies each; cards 276-300 are limited to 500 copies each.

A number of wrapper-redemption unsigned parallels exist. These wrapper-redemption cards were available at: the 2001 Toronto Spring Expo (Bronze, Emerald and Sapphire versions limited to 10 copies each); and the 2001 Cleveland National (Ruby, Emerald, Sapphire and Bronze versions limited to 10 copies each). These wrapper-redemption cards sell for considerably less than the Emerald parallels (each limited to ten copies). Common Wrapper-redemption singles start at $5-10 each.

Shell Set (250 cards):				**150.00**
Complete Set (300 cards):		**1,800**	**900**	**525.00**
Common Player:	**30.00**	**5.00**	**3.00**	**.75**
Description	**E10**	**S100**	**R200**	**BAP**
□□□□ 1 Doug Gilmour	150.00	10.00	5.00	1.50
□□□□ 2 Todd Reirden	30.00	5.00	3.00	.75
□□□□ 3 Mike Johnson	50.00	5.00	3.00	.75
□□□□ 4 Scott Walker	60.00	5.00	3.00	.75
□□□□ 5 Mike York	80.00	5.00	3.00	.75
□□□□ 6 Roman Turek (G)	120.00	10.00	5.00	1.00
□□□□ 7 Sergei Zubov	60.00	5.00	3.00	.75
□□□□ 8 Brad Stuart	100.00	5.00	3.00	1.00
□□□□ 9 Michael Peca	100.00	5.00	3.00	1.00
□□□□ 10 Jyrki Lumme	60.00	5.00	3.00	.75
□□□□ 11 Steve Yzerman	600.00	55.00	25.00	7.00
□□□□ 12 Olaf Kölzig (G)	150.00	10.00	5.00	1.50
□□□□ 13 R. Bourque	300.00	25.00	10.00	3.50
□□□□ 14 Clarke Wilm	30.00	5.00	3.00	.75
□□□□ 15 Éric Desjardins	80.00	5.00	3.00	.75
□□□□ 16 Rod Brind'Amour	80.00	5.00	3.00	.75
□□□□ 17 Marc Savard	60.00	5.00	3.00	.75
□□□□ 18 Jarome Iginla	200.00	15.00	5.00	2.00
□□□□ 19 D. Alfredsson	300.00	25.00	5.00	1.50
□□□□ 20 Alexei Yashin	150.00	10.00	5.00	1.50
□□□□ 21 Keith Tkachuk	150.00	10.00	5.00	1.50
□□□□ 22 Jaromir Jagr	250.00	20.00	10.00	3.00
□□□□ 23 Trevor Kidd (G)	80.00	5.00	3.00	.75
□□□□ 24 Alexei Kovalev	150.00	10.00	5.00	1.50
□□□□ 25 Jan Hrdina	60.00	5.00	3.00	.75
□□□□ 26 Tom Poti	40.00	5.00	3.00	.75
□□□□ 27 Jere Karalahti	30.00	5.00	3.00	.75
□□□□ 28 Janne Niinimaa	60.00	5.00	3.00	.75
□□□□ 29 Ray Whitney	60.00	5.00	3.00	.75
□□□□ 30 Nicklas Lidström	150.00	10.00	5.00	1.50
□□□□ 31 Martin Lapointe	100.00	5.00	3.00	1.00
□□□□ 32 Matt Cullen	60.00	5.00	3.00	.75
□□□□ 33 Theoren Fleury	150.00	10.00	5.00	1.50
□□□□ 34 Mats Sundin	250.00	20.00	10.00	3.00
□□□□ 35 Kimmo Timonen	40.00	5.00	3.00	.75
□□□□ 36 Joe Thornton	300.00	25.00	10.00	3.50
□□□□ 37 Adam Graves	100.00	5.00	3.00	1.00
□□□□ 38 Andrei Zyuzin	40.00	5.00	3.00	.75
□□□□ 39 Michal Handzus	60.00	5.00	3.00	.75
□□□□ 40 Jamie Storr (G)	60.00	5.00	3.00	.75
□□□□ 41 Teemu Selänne	200.00	15.00	5.00	2.00
□□□□ 42 Brian Rafalski	60.00	5.00	3.00	.75
□□□□ 43 Aaron Gavey	30.00	5.00	3.00	.75
□□□□ 44 J. Théodore (G)	300.00	25.00	10.00	3.50
□□□□ 45 Tyler Wright	30.00	5.00	3.00	.75
□□□□ 46 A. Mogilny	120.00	10.00	5.00	1.00
□□□□ 47 Brad Isbister	60.00	5.00	3.00	.75
□□□□ 48 Guy Hebert (G)	60.00	5.00	3.00	.75
□□□□ 49 Chris Simon	60.00	5.00	3.00	.75
□□□□ 50 D. Hasek (G)	250.00	20.00	10.00	3.00
□□□□ 51 Dan Cloutier (G)	100.00	5.00	3.00	1.00
□□□□ 52 Brian Holzinger	40.00	5.00	3.00	.75
□□□□ 53 Dmitri Khristich	40.00	5.00	3.00	.75
□□□□ 54 Tyson Nash	40.00	5.00	3.00	.75
□□□□ 55 Patrick Marleau	120.00	10.00	5.00	1.00
□□□□ 56 Marty Reasoner	60.00	5.00	3.00	.75
□□□□ 57 Fernandez (G)	100.00	5.00	3.00	1.00
□□□□ 58 Brenden Morrow	80.00	5.00	3.00	.75
□□□□ 59 Darren McCarty	80.00	5.00	3.00	.75
□□□□ 60 Milan Hejduk	200.00	15.00	5.00	2.00
□□□□ 61 D. Kasparaitis	60.00	5.00	3.00	.75
□□□□ 62 Jere Lehtinen	80.00	5.00	3.00	.75
□□□□ 63 Andrew Brunette	40.00	5.00	3.00	.75
□□□□ 64 W. Gretzky	1000.00	95.00	45.00	12.00
□□□□ 65 Robyn Regehr	40.00	5.00	3.00	.75
□□□□ 66 Travis Green	60.00	5.00	3.00	.75
□□□□ 67 J. Grahame (G)	60.00	5.00	3.00	.75
□□□□ 68 Mike Fisher	60.00	5.00	3.00	.75
□□□□ 69 Josef Marha	30.00	5.00	3.00	.75
□□□□ 70 Randy McKay	30.00	5.00	3.00	.75
□□□□ 71 Brett Hull	250.00	20.00	10.00	3.00
□□□□ 72 Anson Carter	100.00	5.00	3.00	1.00
□□□□ 73 Owen Nolan	150.00	10.00	5.00	1.50

74 Sean Burke (G)	150.00	10.00	5.00	1.50
75 Mario Lemieux	750.00	70.00	35.00	9.00
76 Brian Savage	80.00	5.00	3.00	.75
77 Jason Ward	100.00	5.00	3.00	1.00
78 P. Lalime (G)	150.00	10.00	5.00	1.50
79 Glen Murray	120.00	10.00	5.00	1.00
80 Mathieu Biron	40.00	5.00	3.00	.75
81 Todd Bertuzzi	300.00	25.00	10.00	3.50
82 Chris Drury	150.00	10.00	5.00	1.50
83 M. Afinogenov	100.00	5.00	3.00	1.00
84 Michal Rozsival	30.00	5.00	3.00	.75
85 Glen Metropolit	40.00	5.00	3.00	.75
86 M. Czerkawski	60.00	5.00	3.00	.75
87 Byron Dafoe (G)	100.00	5.00	3.00	1.00
88 Mark Recchi	100.00	5.00	3.00	1.00
89 Mike Modano	250.00	20.00	10.00	3.00
90 Félix Potvin (G)	300.00	25.00	5.00	1.50
91 Saku Koivu	300.00	25.00	5.00	2.00
92 Jay Pandolfo	40.00	5.00	3.00	.75
93 Todd Simpson	30.00	5.00	3.00	.75
94 Calle Johansson	60.00	5.00	3.00	.75
95 Bill Guerin	100.00	5.00	3.00	1.00
96 Oleg Tverdovsky	40.00	5.00	3.00	.75
97 Kyle McLaren	60.00	5.00	3.00	.75
98 Mark Messier	250.00	20.00	10.00	3.00
99 Chris Gratton	60.00	5.00	3.00	.75
100 Sergei Brylin	40.00	5.00	3.00	.75
101 David Legwand	100.00	5.00	3.00	1.00
102 Jason Allison	150.00	10.00	5.00	1.50
103 Daniel Cleary	80.00	5.00	3.00	.75
104 C. Joseph (G)	250.00	20.00	10.00	3.00
105 S. Fedorov	250.00	20.00	10.00	3.00
106 J. Roenick	200.00	15.00	5.00	2.00
107 F. Kaberle	40.00	5.00	3.00	.75
108 Chris Pronger	150.00	10.00	5.00	1.50
109 Martin Skoula	60.00	5.00	3.00	.75
110 Jirí Slégr	40.00	5.00	3.00	.75
111 Trevor Letowski	40.00	5.00	3.00	.75
112 Colin Forbes	30.00	5.00	3.00	.75
113 Sergei Zholtok	40.00	5.00	3.00	.75
114 David Harlock	30.00	5.00	3.00	.75
115 Scott Stevens	100.00	5.00	3.00	1.00
116 David Tanabe	40.00	5.00	3.00	.75
117 M. Timander	30.00	5.00	3.00	.75
118 Stu Barnes	30.00	5.00	3.00	.75
119 Simon Gagné	200.00	15.00	5.00	2.00
120 Paul Coffey	150.00	10.00	5.00	1.50
121 Peter Bondra	150.00	10.00	5.00	1.50
122 Ed Jovanovski	100.00	5.00	3.00	1.00
123 J-P Dumont	60.00	5.00	3.00	.75
124 Pavol Demitra	100.00	5.00	3.00	1.00
125 Mike Vernon (G)	100.00	5.00	3.00	1.00
126 B. Morrison	80.00	5.00	3.00	.75
127 Dainius Zubrus	60.00	5.00	3.00	.75
128 Al MacInnis	100.00	5.00	3.00	1.00
129 Kevyn Adams	40.00	5.00	3.00	.75
130 Petr Buzek	30.00	5.00	3.00	.75
131 Steve Kariya	60.00	5.00	3.00	.75
132 Keith Primeau	100.00	5.00	3.00	1.00
133 Kenny Jönsson	50.00	5.00	3.00	.75
134 Lance Pitlick	30.00	5.00	3.00	.75
135 Randy Robitaille	40.00	5.00	3.00	.75
136 Brian Rolston	80.00	5.00	3.00	.75
137 Alex Tanguay	150.00	10.00	5.00	1.50
138 Alexei Zhamnov	80.00	5.00	3.00	.75
139 Peter Forsberg	350.00	30.00	15.00	4.00
140 Cam Stewart	30.00	5.00	3.00	.75
141 V. Vishnevsky	60.00	5.00	3.00	.75
142 Tim Connolly	100.00	5.00	3.00	1.00
143 Tie Domi	80.00	5.00	3.00	.75
144 Jaroslav Modry	30.00	5.00	3.00	.75
145 J. Kultanen RC	**35.00**	**5.00**	**3.00**	**1.50**
146 Igor Larionov	150.00	10.00	5.00	1.50
147 Derian Hatcher	80.00	5.00	3.00	.75
148 S. Niedermayer	80.00	5.00	3.00	.75
149 S. McEachern	80.00	5.00	3.00	.75
150 Sergei Berezin	120.00	10.00	3.00	.75
151 Rob Blake	150.00	10.00	5.00	1.50
152 Steve Thomas	60.00	5.00	3.00	.75
153 Ryan Smyth	120.00	10.00	5.00	1.00
154 Petr Nedved	80.00	5.00	3.00	.75
155 Jochen Hecht	60.00	5.00	3.00	.75
156 R. Zedník	100.00	5.00	3.00	1.00
157 T. Salo (G)	100.00	5.00	3.00	1.00
158 Ed Belfour (G)	250.00	20.00	10.00	3.00
159 Lyle Odelein	40.00	5.00	3.00	.75
160 Steve Sullivan	80.00	5.00	3.00	.75
161 V. Damphousse	150.00	10.00	5.00	1.50
162 Andy Delmore	60.00	5.00	3.00	.75
163 Harold Druken	80.00	5.00	3.00	.75
164 M. Brodeur (G)	400.00	35.00	15.00	4.50
165 M. Richter (G)	120.00	10.00	5.00	1.00
166 Radek Bonk	80.00	5.00	3.00	.75
167 Joe Sakic	400.00	35.00	15.00	4.50
168 V'sbrouck (G)	120.00	10.00	5.00	1.00
169 Jeff Shantz	30.00	5.00	3.00	.75
170 J-S Aubin (G)	60.00	5.00	3.00	.75
171 Shayne Corson	80.00	5.00	3.00	.75
172 Jeff Friesen	80.00	5.00	3.00	.75
173 Jeff Hackett (G)	80.00	5.00	3.00	.75
174 Jozef Stümpel	60.00	5.00	3.00	.75
175 D. Langkow	60.00	5.00	3.00	.75
176 N. Antropov	60.00	5.00	3.00	.75
177 R. Tugnutt (G)	100.00	5.00	3.00	1.00
178 Viktor Kozlov	80.00	5.00	3.00	.75
179 Adam Oates	100.00	5.00	3.00	1.00
180 Steve Webb	30.00	5.00	3.00	.75
181 Pierre Turgeon	100.00	5.00	3.00	1.00
182 Brathwaite (G)	80.00	5.00	3.00	.75
183 M. Biron (G)	120.00	10.00	5.00	1.00
184 John LeClair	200.00	15.00	5.00	2.00
185 Steve Rucchin	60.00	5.00	3.00	.75
186 Patrik Elias	200.00	15.00	5.00	2.00
187 Boris Mironov	40.00	5.00	3.00	.75
188 Mika Alatalo	40.00	5.00	3.00	.75
189 J. Thibault (G)	100.00	5.00	3.00	1.00
190 Jason York	40.00	5.00	3.00	.75
191 Zigmund Palffy	150.00	10.00	5.00	1.50
192 Paul Kariya	350.00	30.00	15.00	4.00
193 Stu Grimson	60.00	5.00	3.00	.75
194 Jeff Halpern	60.00	5.00	3.00	.75
195 Scott Gomez	100.00	5.00	3.00	1.00
196 Tomas Vlasak	30.00	5.00	3.00	.75
197 Roman Hamrlik	60.00	5.00	3.00	.75
198 Radek Dvorak	60.00	5.00	3.00	.75
199 Martin Straka	80.00	5.00	3.00	.75
200 Martin Rucinsky	60.00	5.00	3.00	.75
201 Valeri Bure	80.00	5.00	3.00	.75
202 Scott Mellanby	60.00	5.00	3.00	.75
203 Steve McKenna	30.00	5.00	3.00	.75
204 Luc Robitaille	200.00	15.00	5.00	2.00
205 J. Nieuwendyk	100.00	5.00	3.00	1.00
206 B. Shanahan	250.00	20.00	10.00	3.00
207 Robert Lang	60.00	5.00	3.00	.75
208 Todd Marchant	60.00	5.00	3.00	.75
209 Doug Weight	150.00	10.00	5.00	1.50
210 André Roy	40.00	5.00	3.00	.75
211 Patrick Roy (G)	750.00	70.00	35.00	9.00
212 V. Lecavalier	250.00	20.00	10.00	3.00
213 Trevor Linden	100.00	5.00	3.00	1.00
214 Patrik Stefan	80.00	5.00	3.00	.75
215 Jan Hlavac	60.00	5.00	3.00	.75
216 Ron Francis	150.00	10.00	5.00	1.50
217 B. Boucher (G)	80.00	5.00	3.00	.75
218 Tony Hrkac	40.00	5.00	3.00	.75
219 Brian Leetch	150.00	10.00	5.00	1.50
220 Tony Amonte	150.00	10.00	5.00	1.50
221 Khabibulin (G)	100.00	5.00	3.00	1.00
222 Sandis Ozolinsh	60.00	5.00	3.00	.75
223 Darryl Sydor	60.00	5.00	3.00	.75
224 Bobby Holik	80.00	5.00	3.00	.75
225 Sami Kapanen	80.00	5.00	3.00	.75
226 Pavel Bure	200.00	15.00	5.00	2.00
227 S. Konowalchuk	60.00	5.00	3.00	.75
228 Brent Gilchrist	30.00	5.00	3.00	.75
229 Jeff O'Neill	100.00	5.00	3.00	1.00
230 André Savage	30.00	5.00	3.00	.75
231 Pavel Kubina	40.00	5.00	3.00	.75
232 Jason Arnott	120.00	10.00	5.00	1.00
233 Petr* Sykora	100.00	5.00	3.00	1.00
234 Miroslav Satan	80.00	5.00	3.00	.75
235 C. Osgood (G)	150.00	10.00	5.00	1.50
236 S. Samsonov	150.00	10.00	5.00	1.50
237 Marian Hossa	250.00	20.00	10.00	3.00
238 Arturs Irbe (G)	100.00	5.00	3.00	1.00
239 Josh Holden	40.00	5.00	3.00	.75
240 Phil Housley	80.00	5.00	3.00	.75
241 D. Yushkevich	60.00	5.00	3.00	.75
242 Cliff Ronning	60.00	5.00	3.00	.75
243 John Madden	80.00	5.00	3.00	.75
244 Jaroslav Spacek	30.00	5.00	3.00	.75
245 Craig Darby	40.00	5.00	3.00	.75
246 Eric Lindros	250.00	20.00	10.00	3.00
247 M. Näslund	250.00	20.00	10.00	3.00
248 Sergei Gonchar	80.00	5.00	3.00	.75
249 Gary Roberts	100.00	5.00	3.00	1.00
250 S. Shields (G)	60.00	5.00	3.00	.75

ROOKIE

Rookie (#/1000)	E10	S100	R200	R1000
251 P. Nummelin RC	**80.00**	**15.00**	**8.00**	**6.00**
252 Mika Noronen (G)	100.00	14.00	8.00	4.00
253 Raycroft (G) RC	**120.00**	**20.00**	**14.00**	**9.00**
254 Taylor Pyatt	60.00	8.00	5.00	3.00
255 Toni Lydman	40.00	5.00	5.00	3.00
256 Matt Bradley	40.00	5.00	5.00	3.00
257 Petr Hubacek RC	**50.00**	**5.00**	**8.00**	**6.00**
258 Ossi Väänänen RC	**80.00**	**15.00**	**8.00**	**6.00**
259 Dimitri Kalinin	30.00	5.00	5.00	3.00
260 Ju. Williams RC	**160.00**	**30.00**	**18.00**	**10.00**
261 Jeff Farkas	60.00	8.00	5.00	3.00
262 Brent Sopel RC	**80.00**	**15.00**	**8.00**	**6.00**
263 Samuel Påhlsson	40.00	5.00	5.00	3.00
264 Josef Vasicek RC	**120.00**	**20.00**	**14.00**	**9.00**
265 Shane Willis	60.00	8.00	5.00	3.00
266 Petr Svoboda RC	**80.00**	**15.00**	**8.00**	**6.00**
267 Petr Schastlivy	60.00	8.00	5.00	3.00
268 R. Simicek RC	**50.00**	**5.00**	**8.00**	**6.00**
269 Reto von Arx RC	**80.00**	**15.00**	**8.00**	**6.00**
270 Colin White RC	**80.00**	**15.00**	**8.00**	**6.00**
271 L. Sekeras RC	**80.00**	**15.00**	**8.00**	**6.00**
272 A. Kharitonov RC	**50.00**	**5.00**	**8.00**	**6.00**
273 M. Sushinsky	40.00	5.00	5.00	3.00
274 Vyshedkevich RC	**80.00**	**15.00**	**8.00**	**6.00**
275 Brad Ference RC	**40.00**	**5.00**	**5.00**	**3.00**

Rookie (#/500)	E10	S100	R200	R500
276 M. Havlat RC	**450.00**	**70.00**	**50.00**	**30.00**
277 Maxime Ouellet (G)	80.00	11.00	7.00	4.00
278 R. Luongo (G)	200.00	28.00	19.00	10.00
279 M. Gaborik RC	**750.00**	**120.00**	**80.00**	**50.00**
280 Daniel Sedin	100.00	14.00	9.00	5.00
281 Henrik Sedin	100.00	14.00	9.00	5.00
282 Milan Kraft	80.00	11.00	7.00	4.00
283 Denis Shvidki	60.00	8.00	5.00	4.00
284 Kris Beech	80.00	11.00	7.00	4.00
285 R. Klesla RC	**375.00**	**60.00**	**20.00**	**15.00**
286 J. Hurme (G) RC	**120.00**	**20.00**	**18.00**	**10.00**
287 Oleg Saprykin	60.00	8.00	5.00	4.00
288 M. Turco (G) RC	**300.00**	**55.00**	**35.00**	**30.00**
289 Brad Richards	120.00	17.00	11.00	6.00
290 Steve McCarthy	40.00	5.00	5.00	4.00
291 Tomi Kallio	40.00	5.00	5.00	4.00
292 E. Nabokov (G)	150.00	21.00	14.00	7.00
293 S. Reinprecht RC	**200.00**	**30.00**	**20.00**	**15.00**
294 Andrei Markov	40.00	5.00	5.00	4.00
295 Brent Johnson (G)	100.00	14.00	9.00	5.00
296 DiPietro (G) RC	**300.00**	**50.00**	**35.00**	**20.00**
297 Cechmanek (G) RC	**200.00**	**35.00**	**20.00**	**20.00**
298 Daniel Tkaczuk	60.00	8.00	5.00	4.00
299 Mathieu Garon (G)	100.00	14.00	9.00	5.00
300 S. Hartnell RC	**120.00**	**20.00**	**18.00**	**10.00**

AUTOGRAPHS

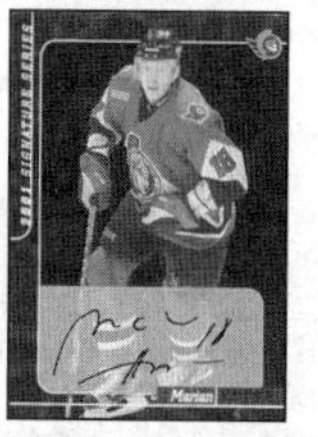

There are two versions: the Silver Autograph (silver-foil board, roughly 1500 copies) and the Gold Autograph (gold-foil board, roughly 500 copies). Most short-print autographs are limited to 450 Silver copies and 50 Gold copies. The Tie Domi is one exception. The Wayne Gretzky short-print autographs are the most limited cards. Limited cards (LTD) and First Signature Cards [FSC] are marked below.

Complete Set (250 cards):	7,600	3,500
Description	Gold	Silv.
1 Pavel Bure, Flor. ✍ (LTD)	100.00	50.00
2 Valeri Bure, Calg. ✍ (LTD)	45.00	20.00
3 Nikolai Antropov, Toro. ✍	10.00	6.00
4 Rob Blake, LosA. ✍	20.00	15.00
5 Brendan Morrison, Vanc. ✍	10.00	8.00
6 David Legwand, Nash. ✍	15.00	10.00
7 Dimitri Kalinin, Buff. ✍ [FSC]	10.00	6.00
8 Jeff Farkas, Toro. ✍ [FSC]	10.00	6.00
9 Brian Savage, Mont. ✍	10.00	8.00
10 Dan Cloutier (G), Tamp. ✍	15.00	10.00
11 Tom Poti, Edmo. ✍	10.00	6.00
12 Doug Gilmour, Buff. ✍ (LTD)	90.00	35.00
13 Steve Konowalchuk, Wash. ✍	10.00	6.00
14 Scott Mellanby, Flor. ✍	10.00	6.00
15 Brent Sopel, Vanc. ✍ [FSC]	10.00	6.00
16 Ron Tugnutt (G), Colu. ✍ (LTD)	60.00	24.00
17 Steve Thomas, Toro. ✍	10.00	6.00
18 Dainius Zubrus, Mont. ✍	10.00	6.00
19 Jason Allison, Bost. ✍ (LTD)	90.00	30.00
20 Jason Ward, Mont. ✍ [FSC]	10.00	6.00
21 Brian Holzinger, Tamp. ✍	10.00	6.00
22 Jere Karalahti, LosA. ✍ [FSC]	10.00	6.00
23 Todd Reirden, SLou. ✍ [FSC]	10.00	6.00
24 Brent Gilchrist, Detr. ✍	10.00	6.00
25 Steve McKenna, MinW. ✍	10.00	6.00
26 Viktor Kozlov, Flor. ✍	10.00	8.00
27 Ryan Smyth, Edmo. ✍	15.00	10.00
28 Al MacInnis, SLou. ✍ (LTD)	60.00	25.00
29 Daniel Cleary, Edmo. ✍	10.00	8.00
30 Patrick Lalime (G), Otta. ✍	20.00	15.00
31 Dmitri Khristich, Toro. ✍	10.00	6.00
32 Janne Niinimaa, Edmo. ✍	10.00	6.00
33 Mike Johnson, Tamp. ✍	10.00	6.00
34 Jeff O'Neill, Caro. ✍ (LTD)	60.00	25.00
35 Luc Robitaille, LosA. ✍ (LTD)	100.00	50.00
36 Adam Oates, Wash. ✍ (LTD)	60.00	25.00
37 Petr Nedved, NYRa. ✍	10.00	8.00
38 Kevyn Adams, Colu. ✍ [FSC]	10.00	6.00
39 Curtis Joseph (G), Toro. ✍ (LTD)	150.00	50.00
40 Glen Murray, LosA. ✍	15.00	10.00
41 Tyson Nash, SLou. ✍ [FSC]	10.00	6.00
42 Ray Whitney, Flor. ✍	10.00	6.00
43 Scott Walker, Nash. ✍	10.00	6.00
44 André Savage, Bost. ✍ [FSC]	10.00	6.00
45 Joe Nieuwendyk, Dall. ✍ (LTD)	60.00	25.00
46 Steve Webb, NYIs. ✍ [FSC]	10.00	6.00
47 Jochen Hecht, SLou. ✍ [FSC]	10.00	10.00
48 Petr Buzek, Atla. ✍ [FSC]	10.00	6.00
49 Sergei Fedorov, Detr. ✍ (LTD)	150.00	60.00
50 Mathieu Biron, NYIs. ✍ [FSC]	10.00	6.00
51 Patrick Marleau, SanJ. ✍	15.00	10.00
52 Nicklas Lidström, Detr. ✍ (LTD)	90.00	35.00
53 Mike York, NYRa. ✍	10.00	8.00
54 Pavel Kubina, Tamp. ✍	10.00	6.00
55 Brendan Shanahan, Detr. ✍ (LTD)	150.00	60.00
56 Pierre Turgeon, SLou. ✍ (LTD)	60.00	25.00
57 Richard Zedník, Wash. ✍ [FSC]	15.00	10.00
58 Steve Kariya, Vanc. ✍	10.00	6.00
59 Jeremy Roenick, Phoe. ✍ (LTD)	100.00	50.00
60 Todd Bertuzzi, Vanc. ✍	45.00	30.00
61 Marty Reasoner, SLou. ✍ [FSC]	10.00	6.00
62 Martin Lapointe, Detr. ✍	15.00	10.00
63 Roman Turek (G), SLou. ✍	15.00	10.00
64 Jason Arnott, NJer. ✍ (LTD)	70.00	30.00
65 Robert Lang, Pitt. ✍	10.00	6.00
66 Fred Brathwaite (G), Calg. ✍ [FSC]	10.00	10.00
67 Tommy Salo (G), Edmo. ✍	15.00	10.00
68 Keith Primeau, Phil. ✍ (LTD)	60.00	25.00
69 Frantisek Kaberle, Atla. ✍ [FSC]	10.00	6.00
70 Chris Drury, Colo. ✍	20.00	15.00
71 Manny Fernandez (G), MinW. ✍ [FSC]	15.00	10.00
72 Shane Willis, Caro. ✍ [FSC]	15.00	6.00
73 Matt Cullen, Anah. ✍	10.00	6.00
74 Sergei Zubov, Dall. ✍	10.00	6.00
75 Petr* Sykora, NJer. ✍	15.00	10.00
76 Todd Marchant, Edmo. ✍	10.00	6.00
77 Martin Biron (G), Buff. ✍	15.00	10.00
78 Ed Belfour (G), Dall. ✍ (LTD)	150.00	60.00
79 Kenny Jönsson, NYIs. ✍ (LTD)	30.00	12.00
80 Chris Pronger, SLou. ✍ (LTD)	90.00	35.00
81 Maxim Afinogenov, Buff. ✍ [FSC]	15.00	10.00
82 Brenden Morrow, Dall. ✍ [FSC]	10.00	10.00
83 Theoren Fleury, NYRa. ✍ (LTD)	75.00	30.00
84 Brad Stuart, SanJ. ✍	15.00	10.00
85 Miroslav Satan, Buff. ✍	10.00	8.00
86 Doug Weight, Edmo. ✍ (LTD)	90.00	30.00
87 John LeClair, Phil. ✍ (LTD)	100.00	50.00
88 Lyle Odelein, Colu. ✍	10.00	6.00
89 Lance Pitlick, Flor. ✍	10.00	6.00
90 Martin Skoula, Colo. ✍ [FSC]	10.00	6.00
91 Michal Rozsival, Pitt. ✍ [FSC]	10.00	6.00
92 Darren McCarty, Detr. ✍	10.00	8.00
93 Mats Sundin, Toro. ✍ (LTD)	150.00	60.00
94 Michael Peca, Buff. ✍	15.00	10.00
95 Chris Osgood (G), Detr. ✍ (LTD)	75.00	30.00
96 André Roy, Otta. ✍ [FSC]	10.00	6.00
97 Steve Rucchin, Anah. ✍	10.00	6.00
98 Steve Sullivan, Chic. ✍	10.00	8.00
99 Randy Robitaille, Nash. ✍ [FSC]	10.00	6.00
100 Jiri Slégr, Pitt. ✍	10.00	6.00
101 Glen Metropolit, Wash. ✍ [FSC]	10.00	6.00
102 Milan Hejduk, Colo. ✍	30.00	20.00
103 Kimmo Timonen, Nash. ✍ [FSC]	10.00	6.00
104 Jyrki Lumme, Phoe. ✍	10.00	6.00
105 Sergei Samsonov, Bost. ✍ (LTD)	90.00	35.00
106 Patrick Roy (G), Colo. ✍ (LTD)	450.00	175.00
107 Patrik Elias, NJer. ✍ (LTD)	100.00	50.00
108 Vincent Damphousse, SanJ. ✍	20.00	15.00
109 Brian Rolston, Bost. ✍	10.00	8.00
110 Peter Forsberg, Colo. ✍ (LTD)	200.00	75.00
111 Mariusz Czerkawski, NYIs. ✍	10.00	6.00
112 Darius Kasparaitis, Pitt. ✍	10.00	6.00
113 Joe Thornton, Bost. ✍	45.00	30.00
114 Steve Yzerman, Detr. ✍ (LTD)	350.00	150.00
115 Marian Hossa, Otta. ✍	35.00	25.00
116 Vincent Lecavalier, Tamp. ✍	35.00	25.00
117 Colin White, NJer. ✍ [FSC]	10.00	8.00
118 Boris Mironov, Chic. ✍	10.00	6.00
119 Andy Delmore, Phil. ✍ [FSC]	10.00	6.00
120 Alex Tanguay, Colo. ✍	20.00	15.00
121 Colin Forbes, Otta. ✍ [FSC]	10.00	6.00
122 Byron Dafoe (G), Bost. ✍	15.00	10.00
123 Jere Lehtinen, Dall. ✍	10.00	8.00
124 Adam Graves, NYRa. ✍	15.00	10.00
125 Olaf Kölzig (G), Wash. ✍ (LTD)	90.00	35.00
126 Arturs Irbe (G), Caro. ✍	15.00	10.00
127 Trevor Linden, Mont. ✍	15.00	10.00
128 Mika Alatalo, Phoe. ✍ [FSC]	10.00	6.00
129 Harold Druken, Vanc. ✍ [FSC]	10.00	10.00
130 Alexei Zhamnov, Chic. ✍	10.00	8.00
131 Sergei Zholtok, Mont. ✍	10.00	6.00
132 Mark Recchi, Phil. ✍ (LTD)	60.00	25.00
133 Andrew Brunette, Atla. ✍	10.00	6.00

☐ ☐	134 Andrei Zyuzin, Tamp. ✍	10.00	6.00
☐ ☐	135 Raymond Bourque, Colo. ✍ (LTD)	175.00	70.00
☐ ☐	136 Josh Holden, Vanc. ✍ [FSC]	10.00	6.00
☐ ☐	137 Patrik Stefan, Atla. ✍	10.00	8.00
☐ ☐	138 Jocelyn Thibault (G), Chic. ✍	15.00	10.00
☐ ☐	139 Martin Brodeur (G), NJer. ✍ (LTD)	225.00	100.00
☐ ☐	140 Trevor Letowski, Phoe. ✍	10.00	6.00
☐ ☐	141 David Harlock, Atla. ✍ [FSC]	10.00	6.00
☐ ☐	142 Mike Modano, Dall. ✍ (LTD)	150.00	60.00
☐ ☐	143 Wayne Gretzky, NYRa. ✍ (X-LTD)	2200.00	825.00
☐ ☐	144 Michal Handzus, SLou. ✍ [FSC]	10.00	6.00
☐ ☐	145 Clarke Wilm, Calg. ✍ [FSC]	10.00	6.00
☐ ☐	146 Phil Housley, Calg. ✍	10.00	8.00
☐ ☐	147 Jan Hlavac, NYRa. ✍	10.00	6.00
☐ ☐	148 Jason York, Otta. ✍	10.00	6.00
☐ ☐	149 Mike Richter (G), NYRa. ✍ (LTD)	70.00	30.00
☐ ☐	150 Sergei Vyshedkevich, Atla. ✍ [FSC]	10.00	6.00
☐ ☐	151 Cam Stewart, MinW. ✍ [FSC]	10.00	6.00
☐ ☐	152 Scott Stevens, NJer. ✍ (LTD)	60.00	25.00
☐ ☐	153 Félix Potvin (G), Vanc. ✍	20.00	15.00
☐ ☐	154 Robyn Regehr, Calg. ✍ [FSC]	10.00	6.00
☐ ☐	155 Jamie Storr (G), LosA. ✍	10.00	6.00
☐ ☐	156 Éric Desjardins, Phil. ✍	10.00	8.00
☐ ☐	157 Dmitry Yushkevich, Toro. ✍	10.00	6.00
☐ ☐	158 Ron Francis, Caro. ✍ (LTD)	90.00	35.00
☐ ☐	159 Zigmund Palffy, LosA. ✍ (LTD)	90.00	35.00
☐ ☐	160 Radek Bonk, Otta. ✍	10.00	8.00
☐ ☐	161 Vitali Vishnevsky, Anah. ✍ [FSC]	10.00	6.00
☐ ☐	162 David Tanabe, Caro. ✍ [FSC]	10.00	6.00
☐ ☐	163 Saku Koivu, Mont. ✍	30.00	20.00
☐ ☐	164 Travis Green, Phoe. ✍	10.00	6.00
☐ ☐	165 Teemu Selänne, Anah. ✍ (LTD)	100.00	50.00
☐ ☐	166 Rod Brind'Amour, Caro. ✍	10.00	8.00
☐ ☐	167 Cliff Ronning, Nash. ✍	10.00	6.00
☐ ☐	168 Brian Boucher (G), Phil. ✍ [FSC]	10.00	10.00
☐ ☐	169 Paul Kariya, Anah. ✍ (LTD)	200.00	75.00
☐ ☐	170 Joe Sakic, Colo. ✍ (LTD)	225.00	100.00
☐ ☐	171 Tim Connolly, NYIs. ✍	15.00	10.00
☐ ☐	172 Mattias Timander, Colu. ✍	10.00	6.00
☐ ☐	173 Jay Pandolfo, NJer. ✍ [FSC]	10.00	6.00
☐ ☐	174 John Grahame (G), Bost. ✍ [FSC]	10.00	6.00
☐ ☐	175 Brian Rafalski, NJer. ✍	10.00	6.00
☐ ☐	176 Marc Savard, Calg. ✍ [FSC]	10.00	6.00
☐ ☐	177 John Madden, NJer. ✍ [FSC]	10.00	10.00
☐ ☐	178 Tony Hrkac, Anah. ✍ [FSC]	10.00	6.00
☐ ☐	179 Stu Grimson, LosA. ✍	10.00	6.00
☐ ☐	180 John Vanbiesbrouck (G), NYIs. ✍ (LTD)	70.00	30.00
☐ ☐	181 Tie Domi, Toro. ✍	20.00	20.00
☐ ☐	182 Stu Barnes, Buff. ✍	10.00	6.00
☐ ☐	183 Todd Simpson, Flor. ✍	10.00	6.00
☐ ☐	184 Mike Fisher, Otta. ✍ [FSC]	10.00	6.00
☐ ☐	185 Aaron Gavey, MinW. ✍	10.00	6.00
☐ ☐	186 Jarome Iginla, Calg. ✍	30.00	20.00
☐ ☐	187 Jaroslav Spacek, Chic. ✍ [FSC]	10.00	6.00
☐ ☐	188 Brian Leetch, NYRa. ✍ (LTD)	90.00	35.00
☐ ☐	189 Jeff Halpern, Wash. ✍ [FSC]	10.00	6.00
☐ ☐	190 Jeff Shantz, Calg. ✍	10.00	6.00
☐ ☐	191 Jaroslav Modry, LosA. ✍ [FSC]	10.00	6.00
☐ ☐	192 Simon Gagné, Phil. ✍	30.00	20.00
☐ ☐	193 Calle Johansson, Wash. ✍	10.00	6.00
☐ ☐	194 Josef Marha, Chic. ✍ [FSC]	10.00	6.00
☐ ☐	195 José Théodore (G), Mont. ✍	45.00	30.00
☐ ☐	196 Daniel Alfredsson, Otta. ✍	20.00	15.00
☐ ☐	197 Craig Darby, Mont. ✍ [FSC]	10.00	6.00
☐ ☐	198 Tony Amonte, Chic. ✍ (LTD)	90.00	35.00
☐ ☐	199 Scott Gomez, NJer. ✍ [FSC]	15.00	10.00
☐ ☐	200 Jean-Sébastien Aubin (G), Pitt. ✍ [FSC]	10.00	6.00
☐ ☐	201 Jarno Kultanen, Bost. ✍ [FSC]	10.00	6.00
☐ ☐	202 Paul Coffey, Bost. ✍ (LTD)	90.00	35.00
☐ ☐	203 Bill Guerin, Bost. ✍ (LTD)	60.00	25.00
☐ ☐	204 Roberto Luongo (G), Flor. ✍ [FSC]	30.00	25.00
☐ ☐	205 Randy McKay, NJer. ✍	10.00	6.00
☐ ☐	206 Tyler Wright, Colu. ✍	10.00	6.00
☐ ☐	207 Alexei Yashin, Otta. ✍	20.00	15.00
☐ ☐	208 Eric Lindros, Phil. ✍ (LTD)	150.00	50.00
☐ ☐	209 Nikolai Khabibulin (G), Phoe. ✍	15.00	10.00
☐ ☐	210 Tomas Vlasak, LosA. ✍ [FSC]	10.00	6.00
☐ ☐	211 Shayne Corson, Toro. ✍	10.00	8.00
☐ ☐	212 Igor Larionov, Flor. ✍ (LTD)	90.00	35.00
☐ ☐	213 Peter Bondra, Wash. ✍ (LTD)	90.00	35.00
☐ ☐	214 Mika Noronen (G), Buff. ✍ [FSC]	20.00	10.00
☐ ☐	215 Andrew Raycroft (G), Bost. ✍ [FSC]	15.00	10.00
☐ ☐	216 Taylor Pyatt, NYIs. ✍ [FSC]	10.00	6.00
☐ ☐	217 Toni Lydman, Calg. ✍ [FSC]	10.00	6.00
☐ ☐	218 Matt Bradley, SanJ. ✍ [FSC]	10.00	6.00
☐ ☐	219 Brad Richards, Tamp. ✍ [FSC]	35.00	15.00
☐ ☐	220 Steve McCarthy, Chic. ✍ [FSC]	10.00	6.00
☐ ☐	221 Tomi Kallio, Atla. ✍ [FSC]	10.00	6.00
☐ ☐	222 Justin Williams, Phil. ✍ [FSC]	20.00	10.00
☐ ☐	223 Brad Ference, Flor. ✍ [FSC]	10.00	6.00
☐ ☐	224 Steve Reinprecht, LosA. ✍ [FSC]	20.00	10.00
☐ ☐	225 Samuel Pahlsson, Anah. ✍ [FSC]	10.00	6.00
☐ ☐	226 Josef Vasicek, Caro. ✍ [FSC]	15.00	10.00
☐ ☐	227 Jani Hurme (G), Otta. ✍ [FSC]	15.00	10.00
☐ ☐	228 Petr** Svoboda, Toro. ✍ [FSC]	10.00	8.00
☐ ☐	229 Petr Schastlivy, Otta. ✍	10.00	6.00
☐ ☐	230 Roman Simicek, Pitt. ✍ [FSC]	10.00	6.00
☐ ☐	231 Reto von Arx, Chic. ✍ [FSC]	10.00	8.00
☐ ☐	232 Oleg Saprykin, Calg. ✍	10.00	6.00
☐ ☐	233 Lubomir Sekeras, MinW. ✍ [FSC]	10.00	8.00
☐ ☐	234 Alexander Kharitonov, Tamp. ✍ [FSC]	10.00	6.00
☐ ☐	235 Maxim Sushinsky, MinW. ✍ [FSC]	10.00	6.00
☐ ☐	236 Andrei Markov, Mont. ✍ [FSC]	10.00	6.00
☐ ☐	237 Scott Hartnell, Nash. ✍ [FSC]	15.00	10.00
☐ ☐	238 Martin Havlat, Otta. ✍ [FSC]	45.00	20.00
☐ ☐	239 Maxime Ouellet (G), Phil. ✍ [FSC]	15.00	10.00
☐ ☐	240 Petteri Nummelin, Colu. ✍ [FSC]	10.00	8.00
☐ ☐	241 Marian Gaborik, MinW. ✍ [FSC]	75.00	40.00
☐ ☐	242 Daniel Sedin, Vanc. ✍ [FSC]	30.00	15.00
☐ ☐	243 Henrik Sedin, Vanc. ✍ [FSC]	30.00	15.00
☐ ☐	244 Milan Kraft, Pitt. ✍ [FSC]	15.00	10.00
☐ ☐	245 Denis Shvidki, Flor. ✍ [FSC]	10.00	6.00
☐ ☐	246 Kris Beech, Wash. ✍ [FSC]	15.00	10.00
☐ ☐	247 Rostislav Klesla, Colu. ✍ [FSC]	20.00	10.00
☐ ☐	248 Petr Hubacek, Phil. ✍ [FSC]	10.00	6.00
☐ ☐	249 Ossi Väänänen, Phoe. ✍ [FSC]	10.00	8.00
☐ ☐	250 Marty Turco (G), Dall. ✍ [FSC]	45.00	20.00

DEPARTMENT OF DEFENCE

Multi-colour swatches usually sell at a premium above the below-listed prices.

Insert Set (20 cards):		**800**
	Insert (#/100)	**DD**
☐	DD-1 Brian Leetch, NYRa. ✂	75.00
☐	DD-2 Raymond Bourque, Colo. ✂	150.00
☐	DD-3 Chris Chelios, Detr. ✂	75.00
☐	DD-4 Nicklas Lidström, Detr. ✂	75.00
☐	DD-5 Sandis Ozolinsh, Caro. ✂	35.00
☐	DD-6 Scott Stevens, NJer. ✂	50.00
☐	DD-7 Al MacInnis, SLou. ✂	50.00
☐	DD-8 Kyle McLaren, Bost. ✂	35.00
☐	DD-9 Kenny Jönsson, NYIs. ✂	35.00
☐	DD-10 Teppo Numminen, Phoe. ✂	35.00
☐	DD-11 Sergei Zubov, Dall. ✂	35.00
☐	DD-12 Scott Niedermayer, NJer. ✂	35.00
☐	DD-13 Paul Coffey, Bost. ✂	75.00
☐	DD-14 Adam Foote, Colo. ✂	35.00
☐	DD-15 Sergei Gonchar, Wash. ✂	35.00
☐	DD-16 Phil Housley, Calg. ✂	35.00
☐	DD-17 Eric Desjardins, Phil. ✂	35.00
☐	DD-18 Dmitry Yushkevich, Toro. ✂	35.00
☐	DD-19 Chris Pronger, SLou. ✂	75.00
☐	DD-20 Rob Blake, LosA. ✂	75.00

FRANCHISE

Insert Set (30 cards):		**1,500**
	Insert (#/30)	**F**
☐	F-1 Paul Kariya, Anah.	100.00
☐	F-2 Patrik Stefan, Atla.	50.00
☐	F-3 Joe Thornton, Bost.	75.00
☐	F-4 Dominik Hasek (G), Buff.	75.00
☐	F-5 Jarome Iginla, Calg.	50.00
☐	F-6 Jeff O'Neill, Caro.	50.00
☐	F-7 Tony Amonte, Chic.	50.00
☐	F-8 Peter Forsberg, Colo.	100.00
☐	F-9 Ron Tugnutt (G), Colu.	50.00
☐	F-10 Mike Modano, Dall.	75.00
☐	F-11 Steve Yzerman, Detr.	175.00
☐	F-12 Doug Weight, Edmo.	50.00
☐	F-13 Pavel Bure, Flor.	50.00
☐	F-14 Rob Blake, LosA.	50.00
☐	F-15 Marian Gaborik, MinW.	100.00
☐	F-16 Saku Koivu, Mont.	75.00
☐	F-17 David Legwand, Nash.	50.00
☐	F-18 Martin Brodeur (G), NJer.	100.00
☐	F-19 Mariusz Czerkawski, NYIs.	50.00
☐	F-20 Brian Leetch, NYRa.	50.00
☐	F-21 Marian Hossa, Otta.	75.00
☐	F-22 John LeClair, Phil.	50.00
☐	F-23 Keith Tkachuk, Phoe.	50.00
☐	F-24 Jaromir Jagr, Pitt.	75.00
☐	F-25 Chris Pronger, SLou.	50.00
☐	F-26 Owen Nolan, SanJ.	50.00
☐	F-27 Vincent Lecavalier, Tamp.	75.00
☐	F-28 Curtis Joseph (G), Toro.	75.00
☐	F-29 Daniel Sedin, Vanc.	50.00
☐	F-30 Olaf Kölzig (G), Wash.	50.00

JERSEY

Jersey Set (40 cards):		**2,000**
	Inserts	**J**
☐	J-1 Theoren Fleury, NYRa. ✂	50.00
☐	J-2 Brendan Shanahan, Detr. ✂	75.00
☐	J-3 Curtis Joseph (G), Toro. ✂	75.00
☐	J-4 Saku Koivu, Mont. ✂	100.00
☐	J-5 Dominik Hasek (G), Buff. ✂	75.00
☐	J-6 Al MacInnis, SLou. ✂	40.00
☐	J-7 John LeClair, Phil. ✂	50.00
☐	J-8 Teemu Selänne, Anah. ✂	50.00
☐	J-9 Scott Niedermayer, NJer. ✂	40.00
☐	J-10 Pavel Bure, Flor. ✂	50.00
☐	J-11 Mark Messier, NYRa. ✂	75.00
☐	J-12 Jaromir Jagr, Pitt. ✂	75.00
☐	J-13 Chris Pronger, SLou. ✂	50.00
☐	J-14 Chris Osgood (G), Detr. ✂	50.00
☐	J-15 Mats Sundin, Toro. ✂	75.00
☐	J-16 Paul Kariya, Anah. ✂	100.00
☐	J-17 Scott Stevens, NJer. ✂	40.00
☐	J-18 Kenny Jönsson, NYIs. ✂	40.00
☐	J-19 Sergei Fedorov, Detr. ✂	75.00
☐	J-20 Peter Forsberg, Colo. ✂	100.00
☐	J-21 Brett Hull, Dall. ✂	75.00
☐	J-22 Tony Amonte, Chic. ✂	50.00
☐	J-23 Patrick Roy (G), Colo. ✂	200.00
☐	J-24 Ed Belfour (G), Dall. ✂	75.00
☐	J-25 Martin Brodeur (G), NJer. ✂	125.00
☐	J-26 Brian Leetch, NYRa. ✂	50.00
☐	J-27 Mike Modano, Dall. ✂	75.00
☐	J-28 Jeff Friesen, SanJ. ✂	40.00
☐	J-29 Jeremy Roenick, Phoe. ✂	50.00
☐	J-30 Steve Yzerman, Detr. ✂	200.00
☐	J-31 Joe Sakic, Colo. ✂	125.00
☐	J-32 Michael Peca, Buff. ✂	40.00
☐	J-33 Luc Robitaille, LosA. ✂	50.00
☐	J-34 Adam Oates, Wash. ✂	40.00
☐	J-35 Valeri Bure, Calg. ✂	40.00
☐	J-36 Kyle McLaren, Bost. ✂	40.00
☐	J-37 Nicklas Lidström, Detr. ✂	50.00
☐	J-38 Jason Arnott, NJer. ✂	40.00
☐	J-39 Mike Richter (G), NYRa. ✂	40.00
☐	J-40 Keith Tkachuk, Phoe. ✂	50.00

JERSEY AUTOGRAPH

There are no Jeff Friesen Jerey autographed cards.

Autograph Set (39 cards):		**15,000**
	Inserts	**JA10**
☐	J-1 Theoren Fleury, NYRa. ✍ ✂	300.00
☐	J-2 Brendan Shanahan, Detr. ✍ ✂	600.00
☐	J-3 Curtis Joseph (G), Toro. ✍ ✂	600.00
☐	J-4 Saku Koivu, Mont. ✍ ✂	700.00
☐	J-5 Dominik Hasek (G), Buff. ✍ ✂	600.00
☐	J-6 Al MacInnis, SLou. ✍ ✂	300.00
☐	J-7 John LeClair, Phil. ✍ ✂	500.00
☐	J-8 Teemu Selänne, Anah. ✍ ✂	500.00
☐	J-9 Scott Niedermayer, NJer. ✍ ✂	300.00
☐	J-10 Pavel Bure, Flor. ✍ ✂	500.00
☐	J-11 Mark Messier, NYRa. ✍ ✂	600.00
☐	J-12 Jaromir Jagr, Pitt. ✍ ✂	600.00
☐	J-13 Chris Pronger, SLou. ✍ ✂	300.00
☐	J-14 Chris Osgood (G), Detr. ✍ ✂	300.00
☐	J-15 Mats Sundin, Toro. ✍ ✂	600.00
☐	J-16 Paul Kariya, Anah. ✍ ✂	800.00
☐	J-17 Scott Stevens, NJer. ✍ ✂	300.00
☐	J-18 Kenny Jönsson, NYIs. ✍ ✂	300.00
☐	J-19 Sergei Fedorov, Detr. ✍ ✂	600.00
☐	J-20 Peter Forsberg, Colo. ✍ ✂	800.00
☐	J-21 Brett Hull, Dall. ✍ ✂	600.00
☐	J-22 Tony Amonte, Chic. ✍ ✂	300.00
☐	J-23 Patrick Roy (G), Colo. ✍ ✂	1800.00
☐	J-24 Ed Belfour (G), Dall. ✍ ✂	600.00
☐	J-25 Martin Brodeur (G), NJer. ✍ ✂	1000.00
☐	J-26 Brian Leetch, NYRa. ✍ ✂	300.00
☐	J-27 Mike Modano, Dall. ✍ ✂	600.00
☐	J-29 Jeremy Roenick, Phoe. ✍ ✂	500.00
☐	J-30 Steve Yzerman, Detr. ✍ ✂	1500.00
☐	J-31 Joe Sakic, Colo. ✍ ✂	1000.00
☐	J-32 Michael Peca, Buff. ✍ ✂	300.00
☐	J-33 Luc Robitaille, LosA. ✍ ✂	500.00
☐	J-34 Adam Oates, Wash. ✍ ✂	300.00
☐	J-35 Valeri Bure, Calg. ✍ ✂	300.00
☐	J-36 Kyle McLaren, Bost. ✍ ✂	300.00
☐	J-37 Nicklas Lidström, Detr. ✍ ✂	300.00
☐	J-38 Jason Arnott, NJer. ✍ ✂	300.00
☐	J-39 Mike Richter (G), NYRa. ✍ ✂	300.00
☐	J-40 Keith Tkachuk, Phoe. ✍ ✂	300.00

GAME MEMORABILIA, ETC.

The three versions listed below are: Stick & Jersey (#/100, prefix JS-), In The Numbers (#/10, prefix N-) and Emblem (#/10, prefix E-).

Insert Set (40 cards):		**9,000**	**9,000**	**2,700**
	Inserts	**E10**	**ITN10**	**JS100**
☐ ☐ ☐	1 Theoren Fleury, NYRa. ✂	200.00	200.00	60.00
☐ ☐ ☐	2 B. Shanahan, Detr. ✂	250.00	250.00	100.00
☐ ☐ ☐	3 C. Joseph (G), Toro. ✂	250.00	250.00	100.00
☐ ☐ ☐	4 Saku Koivu, Mont. ✂	300.00	300.00	125.00
☐ ☐ ☐	5 D. Hasek (G), Buff. ✂	250.00	250.00	100.00
☐ ☐ ☐	6 Al MacInnis, SLou. ✂	200.00	200.00	60.00
☐ ☐ ☐	7 John LeClair, Phil. ✂	200.00	200.00	75.00
☐ ☐ ☐	8 Teemu Selänne, Anah. ✂	200.00	200.00	75.00
☐ ☐ ☐	9 S. Niedermayer, NJer. ✂	200.00	200.00	60.00
☐ ☐ ☐	10 Pavel Bure, Flor. ✂	200.00	200.00	75.00
☐ ☐ ☐	11 Mark Messier, NYRa. ✂	250.00	250.00	100.00
☐ ☐ ☐	12 Jaromir Jagr, Pitt. ✂	250.00	250.00	100.00
☐ ☐ ☐	13 Chris Pronger, SLou. ✂	200.00	200.00	60.00
☐ ☐ ☐	14 C. Osgood (G), Detr. ✂	200.00	200.00	60.00
☐ ☐ ☐	15 Mats Sundin, Toro. ✂	250.00	250.00	100.00
☐ ☐ ☐	16 Paul Kariya, Anah. ✂	350.00	350.00	125.00
☐ ☐ ☐	17 Scott Stevens, NJer. ✂	200.00	200.00	60.00
☐ ☐ ☐	18 Kenny Jönsson, NYIs. ✂	200.00	200.00	60.00
☐ ☐ ☐	19 Sergei Fedorov, Detr. ✂	250.00	250.00	100.00
☐ ☐ ☐	20 Peter Forsberg, Colo. ✂	350.00	350.00	125.00
☐ ☐ ☐	21 Brett Hull, Dall. ✂	250.00	250.00	100.00
☐ ☐ ☐	22 Tony Amonte, Chic. ✂	200.00	200.00	60.00
☐ ☐ ☐	23 Patrick Roy (G), Colo. ✂	500.00	500.00	250.00
☐ ☐ ☐	24 Ed Belfour (G), Dall. ✂	250.00	250.00	100.00
☐ ☐ ☐	25 M. Brodeur (G), NJer. ✂	400.00	400.00	150.00
☐ ☐ ☐	26 Brian Leetch, NYRa. ✂	200.00	200.00	60.00
☐ ☐ ☐	27 Mike Modano, Dall. ✂	250.00	250.00	100.00
☐ ☐ ☐	28 Jeff Friesen, SanJ. ✂	200.00	200.00	60.00
☐ ☐ ☐	29 J. Roenick, Phoe. ✂	200.00	200.00	75.00
☐ ☐ ☐	30 S. Yzerman, Detr. ✂	600.00	600.00	250.00
☐ ☐ ☐	31 Joe Sakic, Colo. ✂	400.00	400.00	150.00
☐ ☐ ☐	32 Michael Peca, Buff. ✂	200.00	200.00	60.00
☐ ☐ ☐	33 Luc Robitaille, LosA. ✂	200.00	200.00	75.00
☐ ☐ ☐	34 Adam Oates, Wash. ✂	200.00	200.00	60.00
☐ ☐ ☐	35 Valeri Bure, Calg. ✂	200.00	200.00	60.00
☐ ☐ ☐	36 Kyle McLaren, Bost. ✂	200.00	200.00	60.00
☐ ☐ ☐	37 Nicklas Lidström, Detr. ✂	200.00	200.00	60.00
☐ ☐ ☐	38 Jason Arnott, NJer. ✂	200.00	200.00	60.00
☐ ☐ ☐	39 M. Richter (G), NYRa. ✂	200.00	200.00	60.00
☐ ☐ ☐	40 Keith Tkachuk, Phoe. ✂	200.00	200.00	60.00

HE SHOOTS HE SCORES REDEMPTION

These point-based cards were redeemable for Jersey cards (listed after this 20-card set).

Insert Set (20 cards):		
	Insert	**HSHS**
☐	Mario Lemieux, Pitt. [Three Points]	2.00
☐	Patrick Roy (G), Colo. [Two Points]	2.00
☐	Steve Yzerman, Detr. [Three Points]	1.50
☐	Martin Brodeur (G), NJer. [One Point]	1.00
☐	Pavel Bure, Flor. [Three Points]	.50
☐	Theoren Fleury, NYRa. [Three Points]	.25
☐	Peter Forsberg, Colo. [One Point]	1.00
☐	Peter Forsberg, Colo. [Three Points]	1.00
☐	Dominik Hasek (G), Buff. [Two Points]	.50
☐	Brett Hull, Dall. [Two Points]	.50
☐	Jaromir Jagr, Pitt. [Three Points]	.50
☐	Curtis Joseph (G), Toro. [One Point]	.50
☐	Paul Kariya, Anah. [Two Points]	1.00
☐	Mark Messier, NYRa. [Two Points]	.50
☐	Mike Modano, Dall. [Two Points]	.50
☐	Zigmund Palffy, LosA. [One Point]	.25
☐	Luc Robitaille, LosA. [Two Points]	.50
☐	Joe Sakic, Colo. [Two Points]	1.00
☐	Brendan Shanahan, Detr. [One Point]	.50
☐	Mats Sundin, Toro. [One Point]	.50

HE SHOOTS HE SCORES JERSEY

There has been too little distribution of these cards for them to be priced.

Insert Set (40 cards):		**7,000**
	Redeemed (#/20)	**HSHS**
☐	1 Pavel Bure, Flor. ✂	150.00
☐	2 Milan Hejduk, Colo. ✂	150.00
☐	3 Patrick Roy (G), Colo. ✂	475.00
☐	4 Roberto Luongo (G), Flor. ✂	150.00
☐	5 Alexei Yashin, Otta. ✂	100.00
☐	6 Peter Bondra, Wash. ✂	100.00
☐	7 Martin Brodeur (G), NJer. ✂	300.00
☐	8 Steve Yzerman, Detr. ✂	475.00
☐	9 Vincent Lecavalier, Tamp. ✂	200.00
☐	10 Mike Modano, Dall. ✂	200.00
☐	11 Wayne Gretzky, NYRa. ✂	800.00
☐	12 Peter Forsberg, Colo. ✂	275.00
☐	13 Mark Recchi, Phil. ✂	100.00
☐	14 Olaf Kölzig (G), Wash. ✂	100.00
☐	15 Arturs Irbe (G), Caro. ✂	100.00
☐	16 Patrik Stefan, Atla. ✂	100.00
☐	17 Al MacInnis, SLou. ✂	100.00
☐	18 Luc Robitaille, LosA. ✂	150.00
☐	19 Dominik Hasek (G), Buff. ✂	200.00

☐ 20 Curtis Joseph (G), Toro. ✂ 200.00
☐ 21 Paul Kariya, Anah. ✂ 275.00
☐ 22 Joe Sakic, Colo. ✂ 300.00
☐ 23 Sergei Fedorov, Detr. ✂ 200.00
☐ 24 Ed Belfour (G), Dall. ✂ 200.00
☐ 25 Keith Tkachuk, Phoe. ✂ 100.00
☐ 26 Chris Pronger, SLou. ✂ 100.00
☐ 27 Nicklas Lidström, Detr. ✂ 100.00
☐ 28 Brendan Shanahan, Detr. ✂ 200.00
☐ 29 Brett Hull, Dall. ✂ 200.00
☐ 30 Brian Leetch, NYRa. ✂ 100.00
☐ 31 Mark Messier, NYRa. ✂ 200.00
☐ 32 Jeremy Roenick, Phoe. ✂ 150.00
☐ 33 Keith Primeau, Phil. ✂ 100.00
☐ 34 Tony Amonte, Chic. ✂ 100.00
☐ 35 Scott Gomez, NJer. ✂ 100.00
☐ 36 Jason Arnott, NJer. ✂ 100.00
☐ 37 Mats Sundin, Toro. ✂ 200.00
☐ 38 Chris Osgood (G), Detr. ✂ 100.00
☐ 39 Mario Lemieux, Pitt. ✂ 600.00
☐ 40 Jaromir Jagr, Pitt. ✂ 200.00

LEGEND - GOALIE SIGNATURES

Insert Set (5 cards): 1,000
Insert (#/150) LG
☐ GLS-1 Johnny Bower (G), Toro. ✂ ✍ 200.00
☐ GLS-2 Gerry Cheevers (G), Bost. ✂ ✍ 200.00
☐ GLS-3 Tony Esposito (G), Chic. ✂ ✍ 300.00
☐ GLS-4 Vladislav Tretiak (G) ✂ ✍ 400.00
☐ GLS-5 Bernie Parent (G), Phil. ✂ ✍ 200.00

LEGEND - LEMIEUX

Insert Set (5 cards): 4,700
Insert (#/30) LL30
☐ ML-1 Mario Lemieux Number ✂ Emblem ✂ 1200.00
☐ ML-2 Mario Lemieux Jersey ✂ Glove ✂ 925.00
☐ ML-3 Mario Lemieux Jersey ✂ Glove ✂ 925.00
☐ ML-4 Mario Lemieux Jersey ✂ Jersey ✂ 1400.00
☐ ML-5 Mario Lemieux Jersey ✂ ✂ ✂ 1500.00

LEGEND - LEMIEUX (SIGNED)

Insert Set (5 cards):
Insert (#/6) LL6
☐ ML-1 Mario Lemieux ✍ Number ✂ Emblem ✂
☐ ML-2 Mario Lemieux ✍ Jersey ✂ Glove ✂
☐ ML-3 Mario Lemieux ✍ Jersey ✂ Glove ✂
☐ ML-4 Mario Lemieux ✍ Jersey ✂ Jersey ✂
☐ ML-5 Mario Lemieux ✍ Jersey ✂ ✂ ✂

RETROSPECTIVE

Insert Set (20 cards):
Insert ML
☐ R-1 Mario Lemieux [282 Points in Junior] 6.00
☐ R-2 Mario Lemieux [1984 Amateur Draft] 6.00
☐ R-3 Mario Lemieux [First NHL Game] 6.00
☐ R-4 Mario Lemieux [First NHL Season] 6.00
☐ R-5 Mario Lemieux [Wins Pearson Award] 6.00
☐ R-6 Mario Lemieux [First 50-Goal Season] 6.00
☐ R-7 Mario Lemieux [Canada Cup Winning Goal] 6.00
☐ R-8 Mario Lemieux [First Art Ross and Hart Trophies] 6.00
☐ R-9 Mario Lemieux [Five Goal Game] 6.00
☐ R-10 Mario Lemieux [1991 Stanley Cup] 6.00
☐ R-11 Mario Lemieux [Another Championship Season] 6.00
☐ R-12 Mario Lemieux [160 Points in 60 Games] 6.00
☐ R-13 Mario Lemieux [Dedication to Hockey] 6.00
☐ R-14 Mario Lemieux [500th NHL Goal] 6.00
☐ R-15 Mario Lemieux [NHL All-Star Game Heroics] 6.00
☐ R-16 Mario Lemieux [Mario Bids Farewell] 6.00
☐ R-17 Mario Lemieux [Penguins Retire #66] 6.00
☐ R-18 Mario Lemieux [Hall of Fame Induction] 6.00
☐ R-19 Mario Lemieux [Mario Returns to the NHL] 6.00
☐ R-20 Mario Lemieux [1,500th NHL Point] 6.00

2000 - 01 SP AUTHENTIC

This series was released in April 2001. Rookie-subset cards 91-165 are limited to 900 copies.

Shell Set (90 cards): 35.00
Complete Set (165 cards): 1,400.00
Common Player: .25
Player SPA
☐ 1 Paul Kariya, Anah. 2.00
☐ 2 Jean-Sébastien Giguère (G), Anah. 1.00

☐ 3 Oleg Tverdovsky, Anah. .25
☐ 4 Patrik Stefan, Atla. .25
☐ 5 Donald Audette, Atla. .50
☐ 6 Damian Rhodes (G), Atla. .25
☐ 7 Joe Thornton, Bost. 1.50
☐ 8 Jason Allison, Bost. .50
☐ 9 Bill Guerin, Bost. .50
☐ 10 Dominik Hasek (G), Buff. 1.50
☐ 11 Maxim Afinogenov, Buff. .50
☐ 12 Doug Gilmour, Buff. .50
☐ 13 Valeri Bure, Calg. .25
☐ 14 Marc Savard, Calg. .25
☐ 15 Jarome Iginla, Calg. 1.00
☐ 16 Ron Francis, Caro. .50
☐ 17 Jeff O'Neill, Caro. .50
☐ 18 Sandis Ozolinsh, Caro. .25
☐ 19 Steve Sullivan, Chic. .25
☐ 20 Tony Amonte, Chic. .50
☐ 21 Rob Blake, Colo. .50
☐ 22 Raymond Bourque, Colo. 1.50
☐ 23 Patrick Roy (G), Colo. 4.50
☐ 24 Peter Forsberg, Colo. 2.00
☐ 25 Joe Sakic, Colo. 2.00
☐ 26 Ron Tugnutt (G), Colu. .50
☐ 27 Geoff Sanderson, Colu. .25
☐ 28 Ed Belfour (G), Dall. 1.50
☐ 29 Mike Modano, Dall. 1.50
☐ 30 Brett Hull, Dall. 1.50
☐ 31 Steve Yzerman, Detr. 3.50
☐ 32 Brendan Shanahan, Detr. 1.50
☐ 33 Nicklas Lidström, Detr. .50
☐ 34 Sergei Fedorov, Detr. 1.50
☐ 35 Doug Weight, Edmo. .50
☐ 36 Ryan Smyth, Edmo. .50
☐ 37 Tommy Salo (G), Edmo. .50
☐ 38 Pavel Bure, Flor. 1.00
☐ 39 Ray Whitney, Flor. .25
☐ 40 Ivan Novoseltsev, Flor. .25
☐ 41 Adam Deadmarsh, LosA. .25
☐ 42 Zigmund Palffy, LosA. .50
☐ 43 Luc Robitaille, LosA. 1.00
☐ 44 Darby Hendrickson, MinW. .25
☐ 45 Manny Fernandez (G), MinW. .50
☐ 46 José Théodore (G), Mont. 1.50
☐ 47 Andréi Markov, Mont. .25
☐ 48 Trevor Linden, Mont. .50
☐ 49 David Legwand, Nash. .50
☐ 50 Mike Dunham (G), Nash. .50
☐ 51 Cliff Ronning, Nash. .25
☐ 52 Scott Gomez, NJer. .50
☐ 53 Martin Brodeur (G), NJer. 2.00
☐ 54 Jason Arnott, NJer. .50
☐ 55 Mark Messier, NYRa. 1.50
☐ 56 Theoren Fleury, NYRa. .50
☐ 57 Brian Leetch, NYRa. .50
☐ 58 Tim Connolly, NYIs. .50
☐ 59 Brad Isbister, NYIs. .25
☐ 60 Taylor Pyatt, NYIs. .50
☐ 61 Alexei Yashin, Otta. .50
☐ 62 Marian Hossa, Otta. 1.50
☐ 63 Patrick Lalime (G), Otta. .50
☐ 64 John LeClair, Phil. 1.00
☐ 65 Simon Gagné, Phil. 1.00
☐ 66 Mark Recchi, Phil. .50
☐ 67 Jeremy Roenick, Phoe. 1.00
☐ 68 Keith Tkachuk, Phoe. .50
☐ 69 Shane Doan, Phoe. .25
☐ 70 Jaromir Jagr, Pitt. 1.50
☐ 71 Alexei Kovalev, Pitt. .50
☐ 72 Mario Lemieux, Pitt. 4.50
☐ 73 Owen Nolan, SanJ. .50
☐ 74 Patrick Marleau, SanJ. .50
☐ 75 Evgeni Nabokov, SanJ. .50
☐ 76 Pierre Turgeon, SLou. .50
☐ 77 Chris Pronger, SLou. .50
☐ 78 Roman Turek (G), SLou. .50
☐ 79 Brad Richards, Tamp. 1.00
☐ 80 Vincent Lecavalier, Tamp. 1.50
☐ 81 Fredrik Modin, Tamp. .25
☐ 82 Mats Sundin, Toro. 1.50
☐ 83 Curtis Joseph (G), Toro. 1.50
☐ 84 Gary Roberts, Toro. .50
☐ 85 Daniel Sedin, Vanc. 1.00
☐ 86 Henrik Sedin, Vanc. 1.00
☐ 87 Markus Näslund, Vanc. 1.50
☐ 88 Peter Bondra, Wash. .50
☐ 89 Olaf Kölzig (G), Wash. .50
☐ 90 Adam Oates, Wash. .50

FUTURE WATCH

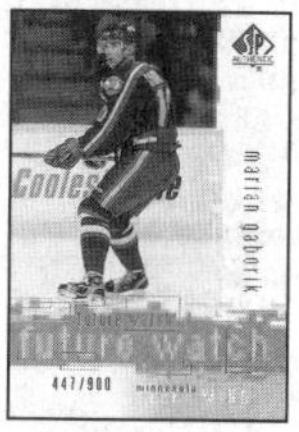

Insert (#/900) SPA
☐ 91 Petr Tenkrat, Anah. RC 15.00
☐ 92 Andy McDonald, Anah. RC 15.00
☐ 93 Brad Tapper, Atla. RC 15.00
☐ 94 Andrew Raycroft (G), Bost. RC 20.00
☐ 95 Lee Goren, Bost. RC 15.00
☐ 96 Josef Vasicek, Caro. RC 20.00
☐ 97 Reto von Arx, Chic. RC 15.00
☐ 98 David Aebischer (G), Colo. RC 30.00
☐ 99 Ville Nieminen, Colo. RC 45.00
☐ 100 Serge Aubin, Colu. RC 15.00
☐ 101 Rostislav Klesla, Colu. RC 60.00
☐ 102 Marty Turco (G), Dall. RC 125.00
☐ 103 Tyler Bouck, Dall. RC 15.00
☐ 104 Jason Williams, Detr. RC 20.00
☐ 105 Shawn Horcoff, Edmo. RC 15.00
☐ 106 Mike Comrie, Edmo. RC 150.00
☐ 107 Éric Bélanger, LosA. RC 15.00
☐ 108 Steven Reinprecht, Colo. RC 35.00
☐ 109 Lubomir Visnovsky, LosA. RC 15.00
☐ 110 Marian Gaborik, MinW. RC 300.00
☐ 111 Peter Bartos, MinW. RC 15.00
☐ 112 Scott Hartnell, Nash. RC 20.00
☐ 113 Chris Mason (G), Nash. RC 15.00
☐ 114 Rick DiPietro (G), NYIs. RC 55.00
☐ 115 Martin Havlat, Otta. RC 100.00
☐ 116 Jani Hurme (G), Otta. RC 20.00
☐ 117 Petr Hubacek, Phil. RC 10.00
☐ 118 Justin Williams, Phil. RC 30.00
☐ 119 Roman Cechmanek (G), Phil. RC 40.00
☐ 120 Ruslan Fedotenko, Phil. RC 15.00
☐ 121 Roman Simicek, Pitt. RC 10.00
☐ 122 Mark Smith, SanJ. RC 10.00
☐ 123 Alexander Kharitonov, Tamp. RC 10.00
☐ 124 Alexei Ponikarovsky, Toro. RC 15.00
☐ 125 Matt Pettinger, Wash. RC 15.00
☐ 126 Zdenek Blatny RC 15.00
☐ 127 Damian Surma RC 15.00
☐ 128 Marc-André Thinel RC 15.00
☐ 129 Fedor Fedorov RC 15.00
☐ 130 Jason Jaspers RC 15.00
☐ 131 Jordan Krestanovich RC 15.00
☐ 132 Jeff Bateman RC 15.00
☐ 133 Marc Chouinard, Anah. RC 10.00
☐ 134 Darcy Hordichuk, Atla. RC 10.00
☐ 135 Bryan Adams, Atla. RC 10.00
☐ 136 Jarno Kultanen, Bost. RC 10.00
☐ 137 Eric Boulton, Buff. RC 15.00
☐ 138 Ronald Petrovicky, Calg. RC 15.00
☐ 139 Martin Brochu (G), Calg. RC 15.00
☐ 140 Craig Adams, Caro. RC 10.00
☐ 141 Chris Nielsen, Colu. RC 15.00
☐ 142 Petteri Nummelin, Colu. RC 15.00
☐ 143 Brian Swanson, Edmo. 8.00
☐ 144 Michel Riesen, Edmo. RC 15.00
☐ 145 Lance Ward, Flor. 8.00
☐ 146 Travis Scott, LosA. RC 15.00
☐ 147 Lubomir Sekeras, MinW. RC 15.00
☐ 148 Éric Landry, Mont. RC 10.00
☐ 149 Greg Classen, Nash. RC 15.00
☐ 150 Sascha Goc, NJer. RC 15.00
☐ 151 Mike Commodore, NJer. RC 10.00
☐ 152 Johan Holmqvist (G), NYRa. RC 30.00
☐ 153 Vitali Yeremeyev (G), NYRa. RC 10.00
☐ 154 Tomas Kloucek, NYRa. RC 10.00
☐ 155 Dale Purinton, NYRa. RC 15.00
☐ 156 Shane Hnidy, Otta. RC 15.00
☐ 157 Todd Fedoruk, Phil. RC 10.00
☐ 158 Jean-Guy Trudel, Phoe. RC 15.00
☐ 159 Ossi Väänänen, Phoe. RC 15.00
☐ 160 Greg Andrusak, SanJ. RC 10.00
☐ 161 Alexander Khavanov, SLou. RC 15.00
☐ 162 Bryce Salvador, SLou. RC 15.00
☐ 163 Reed Low, SLou. RC 15.00
☐ 164 Petr Svoboda, Toro. RC 15.00
☐ 165 Brent Sopel, Vanc. RC 15.00
Sample SPA
☐ 11 Mark Messier, NYRa. 2.00

NHLPA PARENTS' SCRAPBOOK

Insert Set (7 cards): 14.00
Insert (1:24) PS
☐ PS1 Paul Kariya, Anah. 3.00
☐ PS2 Joe Thornton, Bost. 3.00
☐ PS3 Mike Modano, Dall. 2.00
☐ PS4 Scott Gomez, NJer. 1.50
☐ PS5 Martin Brodeur (G), NJer. 4.00
☐ PS6 John LeClair, Phil. 2.00
☐ PS7 Vincent Lecavalier, Tamp. 2.00

POWER SKATERS

Insert Set (7 cards): 50.00
Insert (1:24) P
☐ P1 Bobby Orr, Bost. 10.00
☐ P2 Bobby Hull, Chic. 4.00
☐ P3 Gordie Howe, Detr. 7.00
☐ P4 Wayne Gretzky, Edmo. 10.00
☐ P5 Wayne Gretzky, LosA. 10.00
☐ P6 Wayne Gretzky, SLou. 10.00
☐ P7 Wayne Gretzky, NYRa. 10.00

SIGNIFICANT STARS

Insert Set (7 cards): 20.00
Insert (1:24) ST
☐ ST1 Peter Forsberg, Colo. 3.00
☐ ST2 Brett Hull, Dall. 2.00
☐ ST3 Steve Yzerman, Detr. 6.00
☐ ST4 Pavel Bure, Flor. 2.00
☐ ST5 Mark Messier, NYRa. 2.00
☐ ST6 Jaromir Jagr, Pitt. 2.00
☐ ST7 Mario Lemieux, Pitt. 7.00

SP HONOR

Insert Set (7 cards): 20.00
Insert (1:24) SP
☐ SP1 Paul Kariya, Anah. 3.00
☐ SP2 Patrick Roy (G), Colo. 7.00
☐ SP3 Pavel Bure, Flor. 2.00
☐ SP4 Martin Brodeur (G), NJer. 4.00
☐ SP5 Mark Messier, NYRa. 2.00
☐ SP6 Mario Lemieux, Pitt. 7.00
☐ SP7 Jaromir Jagr, Pitt. 2.00

SPECIAL FORCES

Insert Set (7 cards): 10.00
Insert (1:24) SF
☐ SF1 Teemu Selänne, Anah. 2.00
☐ SF2 Mike Modano, Dall. 2.00

☐	SF3 Brendan Shanahan, Detr.	2.00
☐	SF4 Pavel Bure, Flor.	2.00
☐	SF5 John LeClair, Phil.	2.00
☐	SF6 Keith Tkachuk, Phoe.	1.50
☐	SF7 Jaromir Jagr, Pitt.	2.00

SUPER STOPPERS

	Insert Set (7 cards):	15.00
	Insert (1:24)	**SS**
☐	SS1 Dominik Hasek (G), Buff.	2.00
☐	SS2 Patrick Roy (G), Colo.	7.00
☐	SS3 Ed Belfour (G), Dall.	2.00
☐	SS4 Martin Brodeur (G), NJer.	4.00
☐	SS5 Roman Turek (G), SLou.	1.50
☐	SS6 Curtis Joseph (G), Toro.	2.00
☐	SS7 Olaf Kölzig (G), Wash.	1.50

REPLICA JERSEY REDEMPTION

These cards can be redeemed for a Replic Jersey.

	Player
☐	Martin Brodeur (G), NJer.
☐	Scott Gomez, NJer.
☐	John LeClair, Phil.
☐	Mike Modano, Dall.
☐	Daniel Sedin, Vanc.
☐	Henrik Sedin, Vanc.

SIGN OF THE TIMES

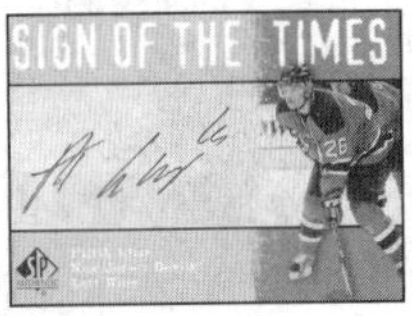

	Insert Set (53 cards):	2,200
	Autograph	**SotT**
☐	Anson Carter, Edmo. ✍	15.00
☐	Anders Eriksson, Flor. ✍	10.00
☐	Serge Aubin, Colu. ✍	10.00
☐	Byron Dafoe (G), Bost. ✍	15.00
☐	Bobby Hull, Chic. ✍	45.00
☐	Martin Biron (G), Buff. ✍	20.00
☐	Bobby Orr, Bost. (#/44) ✍	300.00
☐	Pavel Brendl, Hitmen ✍	10.00
☐	Curtis Joseph (G), Toro. ✍	45.00
☐	David Gosselin, Nash. ✍	10.00
☐	David Legwand, Nash. ✍	15.00
☐	Daniel Sedin, Vanc. ✍	20.00
☐	Félix Potvin (G), Vanc. ✍	25.00
☐	Gordie Howe, Detr. ✍	200.00
☐	Martin Havlat, Otta. ✍	40.00
☐	Henrik Sedin, Vanc. ✍	20.00
☐	Ivan Novoseltsev, Flor. ✍	10.00
☐	Jean-Sébastien Aubin (G), Pitt. ✍	10.00
☐	Jani Hurme (G), Otta. ✍	15.00
☐	John LeClair, Phil. ✍	35.00
☐	José Théodore (G), Mont. ✍	50.00
☐	Lubos Bartecko, SLou. ✍	10.00
☐	Luc Robitaille, LosA. ✍	35.00
☐	Martin Brodeur (G), NJer. ✍	70.00
☐	Marc Denis (G), Colu. ✍	20.00
☐	Marian Gaborik, MinW. ✍	55.00
☐	Milan Hejduk, Colo. (#/49) ✍	120.00
☐	Milan Kraft, Pitt. ✍	15.00
☐	Mario Lemieux, Pitt. (#/49) ✍	225.00
☐	Mark Messier, NYRa. (#/47) ✍	90.00
☐	Mike Modano, Dall. ✍	45.00
☐	Mike Richter (G), NYRa. ✍	20.00
☐	Miroslav Satan, Buff. ✍	10.00
☐	Marty Turco (G), Dall. ✍	40.00
☐	Mike York, NYRa. ✍	10.00
☐	Nicklas Lidström, Detr. ✍	25.00
☐	Pavel Bure, Flor. ✍	35.00
☐	Patrik Elias, NJer. ✍	35.00
☐	Petr* Sykora, NJer. ✍	15.00
☐	Raymond Bourque, Colo. (#/19) ✍	300.00
☐	Rick DiPietro (G), NYIs. ✍	30.00
☐	Mike Ribeiro, Mont. ✍	10.00
☐	Michel Riesen, Edmo. ✍	10.00
☐	Rostislav Klesla, Colu. ✍	10.00
☐	Ron Tugnutt (G), Colu. ✍	15.00
☐	Sergei Samsonov, Bost. ✍	25.00
☐	Scott Gomez, NJer. ✍	15.00
☐	Scott Hartnell, Nash. ✍	10.00
☐	Steven Reinprecht, LosA. ✍	20.00
☐	Steve Shields (G), SanJ. ✍	10.00
☐	Steve Yzerman, Detr. ✍	100.00
☐	Tommy Salo (G), Edmo. ✍	15.00
☐	Wayne Gretzky, Edmo. (#/24) ✍	650.00

SIGN OF THE TIMES DOUBLE

	Insert Set (11 cards):	2,200
	Autographs	**SotT**
☐	P. Bure ✍ / I. Novoseltsev ✍	50.00
☐	M. Brodeur ✍ / P. Sykora ✍	125.00
☐	P. Brendl ✍ / M. York ✍	30.00
☐	P. Elias ✍ / S. Gomez ✍	75.00
☐	G. Howe ✍ / W. Gretzky ✍	650.00
☐	Br. Hull ✍ / Bo. Hull ✍	125.00
☐	M. Lemieux ✍ / M. Kraft ✍	225.00
☐	M. Messier ✍ / W. Gretzky ✍	600.00
☐	B. Orr ✍ / R. Bourque ✍	500.00
☐	D. Sedin ✍ / H. Sedin ✍	50.00
☐	S. Yzerman ✍ / N. Lidström ✍	200.00

SIGN OF THE TIMES TRIPLE

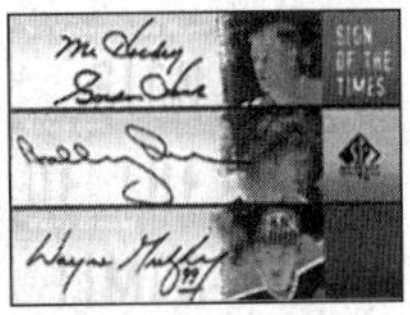

	Insert Set (5 cards):	4,200
	Autographs	**MT**
☐	BGE M. Brodeur / S. Gomez / P. Elias	200.00
☐	GMF W. Gretzky / M. Messier / G. Fuhr	1500.00
☐	HLY Bo. Hull / M. Lemieux / S. Yzerman	600.00
☐	HOG G. Howe / B. Orr / W. Gretzky	2500.00
☐	LMB J. LeClair / M. Modano / P. Bure	200.00

2000 - 01 SP AUTHENTIC – BUYBACKS

	Buyback Autograph • Future Watch	**SPA**
☐	106 Mike Comrie, Edmo. ✍ {#/1}	

2000 - 01 SP GAME-USED EDITION

This series was released in March 2001. Rookie-subset cards 61-90 are limited to 900 copies. Each pack of SP Game-Used Edition included one memorabilia-affixed Tools of the Game insert card.

	Shell Set (60 cards):	**150.00**
	Complete Set (90 cards):	**875.00**
	Common Player:	**1.50**
	Player	**Reg.**
☐	1 Paul Kariya, Anah.	8.00
☐	2 Teemu Selänne, Anah.	5.00
☐	3 Patrik Stefan, Atla.	2.00
☐	4 Byron Dafoe (G), Bost.	2.00
☐	5 Joe Thornton, Bost.	7.00
☐	6 Dominik Hasek (G), Buff.	6.00
☐	7 Maxim Afinogenov, Buff.	2.00
☐	8 Valeri Bure, Calg.	2.00
☐	9 Ron Francis, Caro.	3.00
☐	10 Arturs Irbe (G), Caro.	2.00
☐	11 Tony Amonte, Chic.	3.00
☐	12 Steve Sullivan, Chic.	2.00
☐	13 Patrick Roy (G), Colo.	18.00
☐	14 Joe Sakic, Colo.	10.00
☐	15 Peter Forsberg, Colo.	8.00
☐	16 Raymond Bourque, Colo.	7.00
☐	17 Ron Tugnutt (G), Colu.	2.00
☐	18 Mike Modano, Dall.	6.00
☐	19 Brett Hull, Dall.	6.00
☐	20 Ed Belfour (G), Dall.	6.00
☐	21 Steve Yzerman, Detr.	15.00
☐	22 Brendan Shanahan, Detr.	6.00
☐	23 Sergei Fedorov, Detr.	6.00
☐	24 Nicklas Lidström, Detr.	3.00
☐	25 Doug Weight, Edmo.	3.00
☐	26 Tommy Salo (G), Edmo.	2.00
☐	27 Pavel Bure, Flor.	5.00
☐	28 Trevor Kidd (G), Flor.	2.00
☐	29 Luc Robitaille, LosA.	5.00
☐	30 Zigmund Palffy, LosA.	3.00
☐	31 Manny Fernandez (G), MinW.	2.00
☐	32 José Théodore (G), Mont.	7.00
☐	33 Trevor Linden, Mont.	2.00
☐	34 Mike Dunham (G), Nash.	2.00
☐	35 David Legwand, Nash.	2.00
☐	36 Martin Brodeur (G), NJer.	10.00
☐	37 Scott Gomez, NJer.	2.00
☐	38 Tim Connolly, NYIs.	2.00
☐	39 John Vanbiesbrouck (G), NYIs.	3.00
☐	40 Mike Richter (G), NYRa.	3.00
☐	41 Mark Messier, NYRa.	6.00
☐	42 Marian Hossa, Otta.	6.00
☐	43 Alexei Yashin, Otta.	3.00
☐	44 Brian Boucher (G), Phil.	2.00
☐	45 John LeClair, Phil.	5.00
☐	46 Jeremy Roenick, Phoe.	5.00
☐	47 Keith Tkachuk, Phoe.	3.00
☐	48 Jaromir Jagr, Pitt.	6.00
☐	49 Mario Lemieux, Pitt.	18.00
☐	50 Steve Shields (G), SanJ.	1.50
☐	51 Owen Nolan, SanJ.	3.00
☐	52 Roman Turek (G), SLou.	3.00
☐	53 Pavol Demitra, SLou.	2.00
☐	54 Vincent Lecavalier, Tamp.	6.00
☐	55 Curtis Joseph (G), Toro.	6.00
☐	56 Mats Sundin, Toro.	6.00
☐	57 Daniel Sedin, Vanc.	5.00
☐	58 Henrik Sedin, Vanc.	5.00
☐	59 Olaf Kölzig (G), Wash.	3.00
☐	60 Chris Simon, Wash.	1.50

NEW STYLE

	Insert (#/900)	**NS900**
☐	**61 Jonas Rönnqvist, Anah. RC**	**15.00**
☐	**62 Andy McDonald, Anah. RC**	**15.00**
☐	**63 Andrew Raycroft (G), Bost. RC**	**25.00**
☐	**64 Josef Vasicek, Caro. RC**	**25.00**
☐	**65 David Aebischer (G), Colo. RC**	**35.00**
☐	**66 Rostislav Klesla, Colu. RC**	**35.00**
☐	**67 Marty Turco (G), Dall. RC**	**125.00**
☐	**68 Tyler Bouck, Dall. RC**	**15.00**
☐	**69 Steven Reinprecht, LosA. RC**	**35.00**
☐	**70 Marian Gaborik, MinW. RC**	**200.00**
☐	**71 Scott Hartnell, Nash. RC**	**25.00**
☐	**72 Greg Classen, Nash. RC**	**15.00**
☐	**73 Rick DiPietro (G), NYIs. RC**	**50.00**
☐	**74 Jason LaBarbera (G), NYRa. RC**	**15.00**
☐	**75 Martin Havlat, Otta. RC**	**90.00**
☐	**76 Jani Hurme (G), Otta. RC**	**25.00**
☐	**77 Roman Cechmanek (G), Phil. RC**	**45.00**
☐	**78 Ruslan Fedotenko, Phil. RC**	**15.00**
☐	**79 Justin Williams, Phil. RC**	**35.00**
☐	**80 Roman Simicek, Pitt. RC**	**10.00**
☐	**81 Mark Smith, SanJ. RC**	**10.00**
☐	**82 Matt Elich, Tamp. RC**	**15.00**
☐	**83 Alexander Kharitonov, Tamp. RC**	**10.00**
☐	**84 Fedor Fedorov, Sudbury Wolves RC**	**15.00**
☐	**85 Marc-André Thinel, Victoriaville Tigres RC**	**15.00**
☐	**86 Zdenek Blatny, Kootenay Ice RC**	**15.00**
☐	**87 Jeff Bateman, Brampton Batallion RC**	**15.00**
☐	**88 Jason Jaspers, Sudbury Wolves RC**	**15.00**
☐	**89 Jordan Krestanovich, Calgary Hitmen RC**	**15.00**
☐	**90 Damian Surma, Plymouth Whalers RC**	**15.00**

TOOLS OF THE GAME

There are two versions: the regular insert (1:1) and the Exclusive parallel (#/350).

	Insert Set (38 cards):	1,400	900
	Inserts	**E350**	**TotG**
☐☐	Al MacInnis, SLou. ✂	20.00	15.00
☐☐	Brian Boucher (G), Phil. ✂ Black	20.00	15.00
☐☐	Byron Dafoe (G), Bost. ✂	20.00	15.00
☐☐	Brett Hull, Dall. ✂	40.00	30.00
☐☐	Brian Leetch, NYRa. ✂	25.00	15.00
☐☐	Chris Osgood (G), Detr. ✂	25.00	15.00
☐☐	David Legwand, Nash. ✂	20.00	15.00
☐☐	Eric Lindros, Phil. ✂	40.00	30.00
☐☐	Gordie Howe, WHA All-Star	120.00	80.00
☐☐	Jaromir Jagr, Pitt. ✂	40.00	30.00
☐☐	John LeClair, Phil. ✂	35.00	25.00
☐☐	Joe Nieuwendyk, Dall. ✂	20.00	15.00
☐☐	Jeremy Roenick, Phoe. ✂	35.00	25.00
☐☐	Joe Sakic, Colo. ✂	70.00	50.00
☐☐	Keith Tkachuk, Phoe. ✂	25.00	15.00
☐☐	Martin Brodeur (G), NJer. ✂	70.00	50.00
☐☐	Michal Handzus, SLou. ✂	20.00	15.00
☐☐	Mario Lemieux, Pitt. ✂	130.00	90.00
☐☐	Mark Messier, NYRa. ✂	40.00	30.00
☐☐	Mike Modano, Dall. ✂	40.00	30.00
☐☐	Michael Peca, Buff. ✂	20.00	15.00
☐☐	Mike Richter (G), NYRa. ✂	20.00	15.00
☐☐	Mats Sundin, Toro. ✂	40.00	30.00
☐☐	Nicklas Lidström, Detr. ✂	25.00	15.00
☐☐	Pavel Bure, Flor. ✂	35.00	25.00
☐☐	Pavol Demitra, SLou. ✂	20.00	15.00
☐☐	Peter Forsberg, Colo. ✂	60.00	40.00
☐☐	Paul Kariya, Anah. ✂	60.00	40.00
☐☐	Patrick Marleau, SanJ. ✂	20.00	15.00
☐☐	Patrick Roy (G), Colo. ✂	105.00	75.00
☐☐	Raymond Bourque, Colo. ✂	50.00	35.00
☐☐	Sergei Fedorov, Detr. ✂	40.00	30.00
☐☐	Sandis Ozolinsh, Caro. ✂	20.00	15.00
☐☐	Sergei Samsonov, Bost. ✂	25.00	15.00
☐☐	Steve Yzerman, Detr. ✂	105.00	75.00
☐☐	Tony Amonte, Chic. ✂	25.00	15.00
☐☐	Teemu Selänne, Anah. ✂	35.00	25.00
☐☐	Wayne Gretzky, NYRa. ✂	175.00	125.00

TOOLS OF THE GAME COMBO

	Insert Set (18 cards):	2,700
	Insert (#/100)	**C100**
☐	Pavel Bure ✂ / Sergei Fedorov ✂	100.00
☐	Martin Brodeur ✂ / Mike Richter ✂	100.00
☐	Doug Gilmour ✂ / Mats Sundin ✂	75.00
☐	Brett Hull ✂ / Ed Belfour (G) ✂	100.00
☐	Gordie Howe ✂ / Wayne Gretzky ✂	500.00
☐	Dominik Hasek ✂ / Michael Peca ✂	75.00
☐	Paul Kariya ✂ / Teemu Selänne ✂	125.00
☐	Brian Boucher (G) ✂ / John LeClair ✂	60.00
☐	Mario Lemieux ✂ / Wayne Gretzky ✂	400.00
☐	Mario Lemieux ✂ / Jaromir Jagr ✂	225.00
☐	Mark Messier ✂ / Wayne Gretzky ✂	400.00
☐	Mike Modano ✂ / Joe Nieuwendyk ✂	75.00
☐	Chris Osgood ✂ / Nicklas Lidström ✂	60.00
☐	Patrick Roy ✂ / Peter Forsberg ✂	225.00
☐	Jeremy Roenick ✂ / Keith Tkachuk ✂	75.00
☐	Brendan Shanahan ✂ / Gordie Howe ✂	200.00
☐	Joe Sakic ✂ ✂	150.00
☐	Steve Yzerman ✂ / Gordie Howe ✂	275.00

TOOLS OF THE GAME PATCH

	Insert Set (28 cards):	6,200
	Insert (#/50)	**P50**
☐	Mario Lemieux ✂ / Jaromir Jagr ✂	475.00
☐	Wayne Gretzky ✂ / Jaromir Jagr ✂	525.00
☐	Wayne Gretzky ✂ / Mark Messier ✂	600.00
☐	Patrick Roy ✂ / Peter Forsberg ✂	375.00
☐	Brian Boucher (G), Phil. ✂	90.00
☐	Brett Hull, Dall. ✂	150.00
☐	Bobby Orr, Bost. ✂	600.00
☐	Gordie Howe ✂	400.00
☐	Jaromir Jagr, Pitt. ✂	150.00
☐	John LeClair, Phil. ✂	100.00

□ Jeremy Roenick, Phoe. ✂ 100.00
□ Joe Sakic, Colo. ✂ 225.00
□ Keith Tkachuk, Phoe. ✂ 90.00
□ Martin Brodeur (G), Njer. ✂ 225.00
□ Mario Lemieux, Pitt. ✂ 450.00
□ Mark Messier, NYRa. ✂ 150.00
□ Mike Modano, Dall. ✂ 150.00
□ Mats Sundin, Toro. ✂ 150.00
□ Pavel Bure, Flor. ✂ 100.00
□ Peter Forsberg, Colo. ✂ 200.00
□ Paul Kariya, Anah. ✂ 200.00
□ Patrick Roy (G), Colo. ✂ 350.00
□ Raymond Bourque, Colo. ✂ 175.00
□ Sergei Fedorov, Detr. ✂ 150.00
□ Steve Yzerman, Detr. ✂ 350.00
□ Tony Amonte, Chic. ✂ 90.00
□ Teemu Selänne, Anah. ✂ 100.00
□ Wayne Gretzky, NYRa. ✂ 600.00

TOOLS OF THE GAME SIGNED

There are three versions: the Bronze card (#/300), the Silver card (#/100) and the Bronze card (#/25).

Insert Set (6 cards):	3,100	1,300	850.00
Inserts	G25	S100	B300
□□□ Brett Hull, Dall. ✍✂	350.00	150.00	100.00
□□□ John LeClair, Phil. ✍✂	275.00	125.00	75.00
□□□ Pavel Bure, Flor. ✍✂	275.00	125.00	75.00
□□□ R. Bourque, Colo. ✍✂	475.00	200.00	125.00
□□□ Steve Yzerman, Detr. ✍✂	825.00	350.00	250.00
□□□ Wayne Gretzky, NYRa. ✍✂	1525.00	650.00	450.00

2000 - 01 SP GAME USED EDITION – BUYBACKS

Buyback Autograph • Future Watch — SPA
□ 9 Arturs Irbe (G), Caro. ✍ {#/9}

2000 - 01 SP^X

This series was distributed in two releases: the original release in 2000 and the Update released as part of the 2000 - 01 Upper Deck Rookie Update product in April 2001. In the original 130-card release, there are rookie-subset cards 91-120 limited to 1,500 copies and CHL game-used jersey subset cards 121-130. In the Update release, there are rookie-subset cards limited to 1,500 copies. Base cards (1-90) have a Spectrum parallel (#/50).

Shell Set (90 cards):	-	40.00
Complete Set (187 cards):	-	475.00
Parallel Set (90 cards):	3,100	-
Common Player:	-	.35
Player	Spec.	Reg.
□□ 1 Paul Kariya, Anah.	85.00	1.50
□□ 2 Teemu Selänne, Anah.	50.00	1.00
□□ 3 Patrik Stefan, Atla.	20.00	.35
□□ 4 Jason Allison, Bost.	35.00	.50
□□ 5 Sergei Samsonov, Bost.	35.00	.50
□□ 6 Dominik Hasek (G), Buff.	60.00	1.00
□□ 7 Miroslav Satan, Buff.	20.00	.35
□□ 8 Fred Brathwaite (G), Calg.	20.00	.35
□□ 9 Valeri Bure, Calg.	20.00	.35
□□ 10 Ron Francis, Caro.	35.00	.50
□□ 11 Arturs Irbe (G), Caro.	25.00	.50
□□ 12 Tony Amonte, Chic.	35.00	.50
□□ 13 Joe Sakic, Colo.	100.00	2.00
□□ 14 Milan Hejduk, Colo.	50.00	1.00
□□ 15 Patrick Roy (G), Colo.	185.00	3.50
□□ 16 Peter Forsberg, Colo.	85.00	1.50
□□ 17 Raymond Bourque, Colo.	75.00	1.50
□□ 18 Ron Tugnutt (G), Colu.	25.00	.50
□□ 19 Brett Hull, Dall.	60.00	1.00
□□ 20 Ed Belfour (G), Dall.	60.00	1.00
□□ 21 Mike Modano, Dall.	60.00	1.00
□□ 22 Sergei Fedorov, Detr.	60.00	1.00
□□ 23 Brendan Shanahan, Detr.	60.00	1.00
□□ 24 Chris Osgood (G), Detr.	35.00	.50
□□ 25 Steve Yzerman, Detr.	150.00	3.00
□□ 26 Doug Weight, Edmo.	35.00	.50
□□ 27 Tommy Salo (G), Edmo.	25.00	.50
□□ 28 Pavel Bure, Flor.	50.00	1.00
□□ 29 Trevor Kidd (G), Flor.	20.00	.35
□□ 30 Viktor Kozlov, Flor.	20.00	.35
□□ 31 Rob Blake, LosA.	35.00	.50
□□ 32 Zigmund Palffy, LosA.	35.00	.50
□□ 33 Luc Robitaille, LosA.	50.00	1.00
□□ 34 M. Fernandez (G), MinW. [Photo McLennan]	25.00	.50
□□ 35 Saku Koivu, Mont.	75.00	1.00
□□ 36 David Legwand, Nash.	25.00	.50
□□ 37 Martin Brodeur (G), NJer.	100.00	2.00
□□ 38 Patrik Elias, NJer.	50.00	1.00
□□ 39 Scott Gomez, NJer.	25.00	.50
□□ 40 Scott Stevens, NJer.	25.00	.50
□□ 41 Mariusz Czerkawski, NYIs.	15.00	.35
□□ 42 Tim Connolly, NYIs.	25.00	.50
□□ 43 Mark Messier, NYRa.	60.00	1.00
□□ 44 Mike York, NYRa.	20.00	.35
□□ 45 Theoren Fleury, NYRa.	35.00	.50
□□ 46 Marian Hossa, Otta.	60.00	1.00
□□ 47 Radek Bonk, Otta.	20.00	.35
□□ 48 Simon Gagné, Phil.	50.00	1.00
□□ 49 Brian Boucher (G), Phil.	20.00	.35
□□ 50 Rick Tocchet, Phil.	20.00	.35
□□ 51 John LeClair, Phil.	50.00	1.00
□□ 52 Jeremy Roenick, Phoe.	50.00	1.00
□□ 53 Keith Tkachuk, Phoe.	35.00	.50
□□ 54 Jaromir Jagr, Pitt.	60.00	1.00
□□ 55 Jean-Sébastien Aubin (G), Pitt.	15.00	.35
□□ 56 Jeff Friesen, SanJ.	20.00	.35
□□ 57 Steve Shields (G), SanJ.	15.00	.35
□□ 58 Brad Stuart, SanJ.	25.00	.50
□□ 59 Chris Pronger, SLou.	35.00	.50
□□ 60 Pavol Demitra, SLou.	25.00	.50
□□ 61 Roman Turek (G), SLou.	30.00	.50
□□ 62 Dan Cloutier (G), Tamp.	25.00	.50
□□ 63 Vincent Lecavalier, Tamp.	60.00	1.00
□□ 64 Nikolai Antropov, Toro.	15.00	.35
□□ 65 Curtis Joseph (G), Toro.	60.00	1.00
□□ 66 Mats Sundin, Toro.	60.00	1.00
□□ 67 Félix Potvin (G), Vanc.	75.00	.50
□□ 68 Markus Näslund, Vanc.	60.00	1.00
□□ 69 Adam Oates, Wash.	25.00	.50
□□ 70 Olaf Kölzig (G), Wash.	35.00	.50
□□ 71 Peter Forsberg, Colo. [Xtra Effort]	85.00	1.50
□□ 72 Brendan Shanahan, Detr. [Xtra Effort]	60.00	1.00
□□ 73 Scott Stevens, NJer. [Xtra Effort]	25.00	.50
□□ 74 Mark Messier, NYRa. [Xtra Effort]	60.00	1.00
□□ 75 John LeClair, Phil. [Xtra Effort]	50.00	1.00
□□ 76 Keith Primeau, Phil. [Xtra Effort]	25.00	.50
□□ 77 Keith Tkachuk, Phoe. [Xtra Effort]	35.00	.50
□□ 78 Jeremy Roenick, Phoe. [Xtra Effort]	50.00	1.00
□□ 79 Owen Nolan, SanJ. [Xtra Effort]	35.00	.50
□□ 80 Chris Pronger, SLou. [Xtra Effort]	35.00	.50
□□ 81 Paul Kariya, Anah. [Prominence]	85.00	1.50
□□ 82 Dominik Hasek (G), Buff. [Prominence]	60.00	1.00
□□ 83 Patrick Roy (G), Colo. [Prominence]	185.00	3.50
□□ 84 Raymond Bourque, Colo. [Prominence]	75.00	1.50
□□ 85 Mike Modano, Dall. [Prominence]	60.00	1.00
□□ 86 Steve Yzerman, Detr. [Prominence]	150.00	3.00
□□ 87 Pavel Bure, Flor. [Prominence]	50.00	1.00
□□ 88 Martin Brodeur (G), NJer. [Prominence]	100.00	2.00
□□ 89 John LeClair, Phil. [Prominence]	50.00	1.00
□□ 90 Jaromir Jagr, Pitt. [Prominence]	60.00	1.00

ROOKIE

Insert (#/1500)	R1500
□ **91 Herbert Vasiljevs, Atla. RC**	8.00
□ **92 Eric Nickulas, Bost. RC**	6.00
□ **93 Brandon Smith, Bost. RC**	6.00
□ **94 Jeff Cowan, Calg. RC**	6.00
□ **95 Serge Aubin, Colu. RC**	8.00
□ **96 Mike Minard (G), Oilers RC**	8.00
□ **97 Steven Reinprecht, LosA. RC**	15.00
□ **98 David Gosselin, Nash. RC**	6.00
□ **99 Colin White, NJer. RC**	8.00
□ **100 Willie Mitchell, NJer. RC**	8.00
□ **101 Steve Brûlé, NJer. RC**	6.00
□ **102 Stephen Valiquette (G), NYIs. RC**	8.00
□ **103 Petr Mika, NYIs. RC**	6.00
□ **104 Chris Kenady, NYRa. RC**	6.00
□ **105 Johan Witehall, NYRa. RC**	8.00
□ **106 Jani Hurme (G), Otta. RC**	10.00
□ **107 Jean-Guy Trudel, Phoe. RC**	8.00
□ **108 Dale Rominski, Tamp. RC**	6.00
□ **109 Greg Andrusak, SanJ. RC**	6.00
□ **110 Martin Havlat, Otta. RC**	30.00
□ **111 Jeremy Stevenson, Anah. RC**	6.00
□ **112 Sergei Vyshedkevich, Atla. RC**	8.00
□ 113 Johnathan Aitken, Bost.	4.00
□ **114 Keith Aldridge, Dall. RC**	6.00
□ **115 Rich Parent (G), Tamp. RC**	8.00
□ **116 Kaspars Astashenko, Tamp. RC**	6.00
□ **117 Matt Elich, Tamp. RC**	8.00
□ **118 Dieter Kochan (G), Tamp. RC**	8.00
□ **119 Kyle Freadrich, Tamp. RC**	6.00
□ **120 Justin Williams, Phil. RC**	15.00

ROOKIE JERSEY

Insert (1:13)	Rookie
□ **121 Andrew Raycroft (G), Kingston RC**	15.00
□ **122 Zdenek Blatny, Kootenay Ice RC**	12.00
□ 123 Pavel Brendl, Calgary Hitmen	12.00
□ **124 Jason Jaspers, Sudbury Wolves RC**	12.00
□ **125 Fedor Fedorov, Windsor Spitfires RC**	12.00
□ **126 Jordan Krestanovich, Calgary Hitmen RC**	12.00
□ **127 Marc-André Thinel, Victoriaville Tigres RC**	12.00
□ **128 Damian Surma, Plymouth Whalers RC**	12.00
□ **129 Jeff Bateman, Brampton Batallion RC**	12.00
□ 130 Sheldon Keefe, Barrie Colts	12.00

UPDATE

Common Player:	.35
Player	Update
□ 131 Ray Ferraro, Atla.	.35
□ 132 Bill Guerin, Bost.	.50
□ **133 Ronald Petrovicky, Calg. RC**	1.00
□ 134 Shane Willis, Caro.	.50
□ **135 Chris Nielsen, Colu. RC**	1.00
□ **136 Petteri Nummelin, Colu. RC**	1.00
□ 137 Igor Larionov, Detr.	.50
□ **138 Shawn Horcoff, Edmo. RC**	1.00
□ 139 Lance Ward, Flor.	.50
□ 140 Manny Fernandez (G), MinW.	.50
□ 141 Scott Niedermayer, NJer.	.35
□ 142 Alexei Yashin, Otta.	.50
□ 143 Claude Lemieux, Phoe.	.35
□ 144 Mario Lemieux, Pitt.	3.50
□ 145 Milan Kraft, Pitt.	.50
□ 146 Evgeni Nabokov, SanJ.	.50
□ 147 Keith Tkachuk, SLou.	.50
□ 148 Gary Roberts, Toro.	.50
□ 149 Daniel Sedin, Vanc.	1.00
□ 150 Henrik Sedin, Vanc.	1.00
□ 151 Kris Beech, Wash.	.50

UPDATE ROOKIE

Insert (#/1500)	Update
□ **152 Lee Goren, Bost. RC**	8.00
□ **153 Pavel Kolarik, Bost. RC**	6.00
□ **154 Greg Kuznik, Caro. RC**	6.00
□ **155 Josef Vasicek, Caro. RC**	10.00
□ **156 Rick Berry, Colo. RC**	6.00
□ **157 David Aebischer (G), Colo. RC**	15.00
□ **158 Rostislav Klesla, Colu. RC**	15.00
□ **159 Marty Turco (G), Dall. RC**	30.00
□ **160 Tyler Bouck, Dall. RC**	8.00
□ **161 Mike Comrie, Edmo. RC**	40.00
□ **162 Éric Bélanger, LosA. RC**	8.00
□ **163 Marian Gaborik, MinW. RC**	60.00
□ **164 Scott Hartnell, Nash. RC**	10.00
□ **165 Jason LaBarbera (G), NYRa. RC**	8.00
□ **166 Rick DiPietro (G), NYIs. RC**	20.00
□ **167 Ruslan Fedotenko, Phil. RC**	8.00
□ **168 Petr Hubacek, Phil. RC**	6.00
□ **169 Roman Cechmanek (G), Phil. RC**	20.00
□ **170 Roman Simicek, MinW. RC**	6.00
□ **171 Mark Smith, SanJ. RC**	6.00
□ **172 Jakub Cutta, Wash. RC**	8.00
□ **173 Marc Chouinard, Anah. RC**	6.00
□ **174 Darcy Hordichuk, Atla. RC**	6.00
□ **175 Bryan Adams, Atla. RC**	6.00
□ **176 Jarno Kultanen, Bost. RC**	6.00
□ **177 Eric Boulton, Buff. RC**	8.00
□ 178 Brian Swanson, Edmo.	4.00
□ **179 Lubomir Sekeras, MinW. RC**	8.00
□ **180 Éric Landry, Mont. RC**	6.00
□ **181 Mike Commodore, NJer. RC**	6.00
□ **182 Johan Holmqvist (G), New York RC**	15.00
□ **183 Jeff Ulmer, New York RC**	6.00
□ **184 Ossi Väänänen, Phoe. RC**	8.00
□ **185 Alexander Khavanov, SLou. RC**	8.00
□ **186 Bryce Salvador, SLou. RC**	8.00
□ **187 Reed Low, SLou. RC**	8.00

HIGHLIGHT HEROES

Insert Set (14 cards):	20.00
Insert (1:7)	HH
□ HH1 Paul Kariya, Anah.	3.00
□ HH2 Patrik Stefan, Atla.	1.50
□ HH3 Joe Thornton, Bost.	3.00
□ HH4 Valeri Bure, Calg.	1.50
□ HH5 Milan Hejduk, Colo.	2.00
□ HH6 Brett Hull, Dall.	2.00
□ HH7 Brendan Shanahan, Detr.	2.00
□ HH8 Pavel Bure, Flor.	2.00
□ HH9 Marian Hossa, Otta.	2.00
□ HH10 Brian Boucher (G), Phil.	1.50
□ HH11 Jeremy Roenick, Phoe.	2.00
□ HH12 Jaromir Jagr, Pitt.	2.00
□ HH13 Chris Pronger, SLou.	1.50
□ HH14 Curtis Joseph (G), Toro.	2.00

PROLIFICS

Insert Set (7 cards):	15.00
Insert (1:14)	P
□ P1 Dominik Hasek (G), Buff.	2.00
□ P2 Raymond Bourque, Colo.	3.00
□ P3 Brett Hull, Dall.	2.00
□ P4 Steve Yzerman, Detr.	6.00
□ P5 Mark Messier, NYRa.	2.00
□ P6 John LeClair, Phil.	2.00
□ P7 Jaromir Jagr, Pitt.	2.00

SPXCITEMENT

Insert Set (14 cards):	25.00
Insert (1:7)	X
□ X1 Teemu Selänne, Anah.	2.00
□ X2 Sergei Samsonov, Bost.	1.50
□ X3 Tony Amonte, Chic.	1.50
□ X4 Joe Sakic, Colo.	4.00
□ X5 Mike Modano, Dall.	2.00
□ X6 Sergei Fedorov, Detr.	2.00
□ X7 Pavel Bure, Flor.	2.00
□ X8 Martin Brodeur (G), NJer.	4.00
□ X9 Simon Gagné, Phil.	2.00
□ X10 Jaromir Jagr, Pitt.	2.00
□ X11 Jeff Friesen, SanJ.	1.50
□ X12 Roman Turek (G), SLou.	1.50
□ X13 Vincent Lecavalier, Tamp.	2.00
□ X14 Mats Sundin, Toro.	2.00

SPXTREME

Insert Set (7 cards):	15.00
Insert (1:14)	S
□ S1 Paul Kariya, Anah.	3.00
□ S2 Peter Forsberg, Colo.	3.00
□ S3 Mike Modano, Dall.	2.00
□ S4 Martin Brodeur (G), NJer.	4.00
□ S5 Mark Messier, NYRa.	2.00
□ S6 John LeClair, Phil.	2.00
□ S7 Jaromir Jagr, Pitt.	2.00

ROOKIE REDEMPTION

These cards could be redeemed for a 2001 - 02 SPx Rookie card.

WINNING MATERIALS

Insert Set (48 cards):	1,700
Player	WM
□ Anson Carter, Bost. ✂ [*]	80.00
□ Brett Hull, Dall. ✂ [*]	70.00
□ Brendan Shanahan, Detr. ✂	35.00
□ Curtis Joseph (G), Toro. ✂	30.00
□ Chris Osgood (G), Detr. ✂	20.00
□ Dominik Hasek (G), Buff. ✂	30.00
□ Félix Potvin (G), NYIs. ✂	20.00

	Player	Price
☐	Jaromir Jagr, Pitt. ✂	30.00
☐	John LeClair, Phil. ✂	30.00
☐	Jeremy Roenick, Phoe. ✂	30.00
☐	Joe Sakic, Colo. ✂	60.00
☐	Kenny Jönsson, NYIs. ✂	20.00
☐	Keith Tkachuk, Phoe. ✂	20.00
☐	Martin Brodeur (G), NJer. ✂ [*]	100.00
☐	Mario Lemieux, Pitt. ✂	100.00
☐	Mike Modano, Dall. ✂ [*]	70.00
☐	Nicklas Lidström, Detr. ✂	20.00
☐	Peter Bondra, NHL All-Star [*]	40.00
☐	Pavol Demitra, SLou. ✂ [*]	40.00
☐	Peter Forsberg, Colo. ✂	50.00
☐	Paul Kariya, Anah. ✂ [*]	125.00
☐	Patrick Roy (G), Colo. ✂	100.00
☐	Raymond Bourque, Bost. ✂	40.00
☐	Sergei Fedorov, Detr. ✂	35.00
☐	Steve Yzerman, Detr. ✂	90.00
☐	Tony Amonte, Chic. ✂	20.00
☐	Teemu Selänne, Anah. ✂	30.00
☐	Wayne Gretzky, NYRa. ✂	150.00
☐	Brian Boucher (G), Phil. ✂	20.00
☐	Ed Belfour (G), Dall. ✂	35.00
☐	Martin Biron (G), Buff. ✂	20.00
☐	Raymond Bourque, Colo. ✂	45.00
☐	Valeri Bure, Calg. ✂	20.00
☐	Sergei Fedorov, Detr. ✂	35.00
☐	Wayne Gretzky, LosA. ✂	150.00
☐	Jaromir Jagr, Pitt. ✂	35.00
☐	Paul Kariya, Anah. ✂	50.00
☐	John LeClair, Phil. ✂	30.00
☐	Roberto Luongo (G), NYIs. ✂	30.00
☐	Jeremy Roenick, Phoe. ✂	30.00
☐	Patrick Roy (G), Colo. ✂	110.00
☐	Miroslav Satan, Buff. ✂	20.00
☐	Teemu Selänne, Anah. ✂	30.00
☐	Mats Sundin, Toro. ✂	35.00
☐	Jocelyn Thibault (G), Chic. ✂	20.00
☐	Joe Thornton, Bost. ✂	40.00
☐	Keith Tkachuk, Phoe. ✂	20.00
☐	Steve Yzerman, Detr. ✂	90.00

WINNING MATERIALS SIGNED

Insert Set (10 cards):		4,900
	Insert (#/25)	**WMS25**
☐	Brett Hull, Dall. ✍ ✂	325.00
☐	Curtis Joseph (G), Toro. ✍ ✂	325.00
☐	Félix Potvin (G), NYIs. ✍ ✂	400.00
☐	John LeClair, Phil. ✍ ✂	275.00
☐	Keith Tkachuk, Phoe. ✍ ✂	200.00
☐	Martin Brodeur (G), NJer. ✍ ✂	550.00
☐	Mario Lemieux, Pitt. ✍ ✂	1000.00
☐	Raymond Bourque, Bost. ✍ ✂	475.00
☐	Steve Yzerman, Detr. ✍ ✂	825.00
☐	Wayne Gretzky, NYRa. ✍ ✂	1500.00

2000 - 01 STADION

These unlicensed cards feature athletes from several sports. Because the cards are unlicensed, some dealers will not stock these cards.

	Description	
☐	5 Dominik Hasek (G)	1.00
☐	13 Roman Turek (G)	.50
☐	57 Jaromir Jagr	1.00
☐	61 Mike Ricci, SanJ.	.25
☐	64 Marty McSorley	.25
☐	65 Martin Brodeur (G)	2.00
☐	66 Olaf Kölzig (G)	.50
☐	67 Mark Messier	1.00
☐	68 Eric Lindros, Phil.	1.00
☐	69 Robert Lang	.25
☐	71 Milan Hejduk, Colo.	1.00
☐	72 Alexei Yashin	.50
☐	74 Owen Nolan	.50
☐	75 Patrick Roy (G), Colo.	3.50
☐	76 Petr' Svoboda	.25
☐	77 Martin Straka	.25
☐	79 Mario Lemieux, NHL Awards	3.50
☐	80 Petr Nedved	.25
☐	81 Mats Sundin	1.00
☐	82 Wayne Gretzky	5.00
☐	83 Jaromir Jagr, Pitt.	1.00
☐	84 Saku Koivu	1.00
☐	85 Steve Yzerman	3.00
☐	87 Mike Modano	1.00
☐	90 Brian Leetch	.50
☐	91 Patrik Stefan	.25
☐	92 Ed Belfour (G)	1.00
☐	93 Curtis Joseph (G)	1.00
☐	94 Brett Hull	1.00
☐	95 Scott Stevens	.50
☐	96 Patrik Elias	1.00
☐	99 Pavel Bure, NHL All-Star '00	1.00
☐	109 Roman Turek, SLou.	.50
☐	110 Arturs Irbe, Caro.	.50
☐	111 Radek Dvorak, NYRa.	.50
☐	112 Valeri Kamensky, NYRa.	.50
☐	113 Jiri Slegr, Pitt.	.50
☐	114 Alexander Mogilnyj, NJer.	.50
☐	115 Peter Forsberg, Colo.	1.50
☐	116 Martin Havlat, Otta.	.50
☐	117 Daniel Alfredsson, Otta.	.50
☐	118 Theoren Fleury, NYRa.	.50
☐	119 Sergei Brylin, NJer.	.50
☐	120 Patrick Roy, Colo.	3.50
☐	121 Patrick Lalime, Otta.	.50
☐	122 Tomas Vokoun, Nash.	.50
☐	123 Marian Hossa, Otta.	1.00
☐	124 Zigmund Palffy, LosA.	.50
☐	125 Evgeni Nabokov, SanJ.	.50
☐	126 Jaroslav Modry, LosA.	.50
☐	145 Rob Blake, LosA.	.50
☐	146 Jaromir Jagr, Pitt.	1.00
☐	147 Mario Lemieux, Pitt.	3.50
☐	148 Mario Lemieux, Pitt.	3.50
☐	149 Al MacInnis, SLou.	.50
☐	150 Mark Messier, NYRa.	1.00
☐	151 Chris Pronger, SLou.	.50
☐	152 Mike Richter, NYRa.	.50
☐	153 Brian Savage, Mont.	.50
☐	154 Maxim Afinogenov, Buff.	.50
☐	155 Martin Biron, Buff.	.50
☐	156 Martin Brodeur, NJer.	2.00
☐	157 Paul Coffey, Bost.	.50
☐	158 Mariusz Czerkawski, NYIs.	.50
☐	159 Wayne Gretzky, NYRa.	5.00
☐	160 Michal Grosek, NYRa.	.50
☐	161 Adam Graves, NYRa.	.50
☐	162 Mario Lemieux / Jaromir Jagr	2.50
☐	190 Dominik Hasek, Buff.	1.00
☐	191 Milan Hnilicka, Atla.	.50
☐	192 Joe Sakic, Colo.	2.00
☐	193 Jocelyn Thibault, Chic.	.50
☐	194 Vladimir Chebaturkin, SLou.	.50
☐	195 Bill Guerin, Bost.	.50
☐	196 Krzysztof Oliwa, NJer.	.50
☐	197 Rob Probert, Chic.	.50
☐	198 Rick Tocchet, Phoe.	.50

2000 - 01 STADIUM CLUB

This series was released in February 2001. Rookie cards were short printed and seeded 1:3 packs.

Complete Set (260 cards):		100.00
Common Player:		.20
	Player	**Reg.**
☐	1 Pavel Bure, Flor.	1.00
☐	2 Brendan Shanahan, Detr.	1.00
☐	3 Chris Pronger, SLou.	.50
☐	4 Doug Weight, Edmo.	.50
☐	5 Peter Forsberg, Colo.	1.50
☐	6 Jaromir Jagr, Pitt.	1.00
☐	7 Ed Belfour (G), Dall.	1.00
☐	8 Rod Brind'Amour, Caro.	.20
☐	9 Mike Richter (G), NYRa.	.50
☐	10 Mike Ricci, SanJ.	.20
☐	11 Dmitry Yushkevich, Toro.	.20
☐	12 Dominik Hasek (G), Buff.	1.00
☐	13 Teemu Selänne, Anah.	1.00
☐	14 Ed Jovanovski, Vanc.	.50
☐	15 Damian Rhodes (G), Atla.	.20
☐	16 Martin Brodeur (G), NJer.	2.00
☐	17 Keith Primeau, Phil.	.50
☐	18 Byron Dafoe (G), Bost.	.50
☐	19 Jeff Hackett (G), Mont.	.20
☐	20 Brad Isbister, NYIs.	.20
☐	21 Jeremy Roenick, Phoe.	1.00
☐	22 Jocelyn Thibault (G), Chic.	.50
☐	23 Raymond Bourque, Colo.	1.50
☐	24 Steve Yzerman, Detr.	3.00
☐	25 Mike Dunham (G), Nash.	.50
☐	26 Bill Guerin, Edmo.	.50
☐	27 Dan Cloutier (G), Tamp.	.50
☐	28 Pavol Demitra, SLou.	.50
☐	29 Richard Smehlik, Buff.	.20
☐	30 Ron Francis, Caro.	.50
☐	31 Zigmund Palffy, LosA.	.50
☐	32 David Legwand, Nash.	.50
☐	33 Scott Stevens, NJer.	.50
☐	34 Daniel Alfredsson, Otta.	.50
☐	35 Michal Rozsíval, Pitt.	.20
☐	36 John LeClair, Phil.	1.00
☐	37 Vincent Lecavalier, Tamp.	1.00
☐	38 Jason Allison, Bost.	.50
☐	39 Kenny Jönsson, NYIs.	.20
☐	40 Patrick Roy (G), Colo.	3.50
☐	41 Derian Hatcher, Dall.	.20
☐	42 Chris Osgood (G), Detr.	.50
☐	43 Owen Nolan, SanJ.	.50
☐	44 Mike York, NYRa.	.20
☐	45 Ryan Smyth, Edmo.	.50
☐	46 Alexei Kovalev, Pitt.	.50
☐	47 Roman Turek (G), SLou.	.50
☐	48 Mark Recchi, Phil.	.50
☐	49 Ray Ferraro, Atla.	.20
☐	50 Sergei Samsonov, Bost.	.50
☐	51 Paul Kariya, Anah.	1.50
☐	52 Jarome Iginla, Calg.	1.00
☐	53 Martin Biron (G), Buff.	.50
☐	54 Tom Poti, Edmo.	.20
☐	55 Trevor Linden, Mont.	.50
☐	56 Pierre Turgeon, SLou.	.50
☐	57 Scott Gomez, NJer.	.50
☐	58 Mattias Öhlund, Vanc.	.20
☐	59 Tony Amonte, Chic.	.50
☐	60 Yannick Tremblay, Atla.	.20
☐	61 Cliff Ronning, Nash.	.20
☐	62 Marc Savard, Calg.	.20
☐	63 Viktor Kozlov, Flor.	.20
☐	64 Pavel Kubina, Tamp.	.20
☐	65 Arturs Irbe (G), Caro.	.50
☐	66 Stéphane Fiset (G), LosA.	.20
☐	67 John Madden, NJer.	.20
☐	68 Steve Shields (G), SanJ.	.20
☐	69 Theoren Fleury, NYRa.	.50
☐	70 Chris Simon, Wash.	.20
☐	71 Andy Delmore, Phil.	.20
☐	72 Radek Bonk, Otta.	.20
☐	73 Michal Handzus, SLou.	.20
☐	74 Tommy Salo (G), Edmo.	.50
☐	75 Félix Potvin (G), Vanc.	.50
☐	76 Teppo Numminen, Phoe.	.20
☐	77 Bobby Holik, NJer.	.20
☐	78 Phil Housley, Calg.	.20
☐	79 Sergei Gonchar, Wash.	.20
☐	80 Shawn McEachern, Otta.	.20
☐	81 Simon Gagné, Phil.	1.00
☐	82 Mike Sillinger, Flor.	.20
☐	83 Tim Connolly, NYIs.	.50
☐	84 Eric Dazé, Chic.	.50
☐	85 Andrew Brunette, Atla.	.20
☐	86 Mike Modano, Dall.	1.00
☐	87 Chris Drury, Colo.	.50
☐	88 Nicklas Lidström, Detr.	.50
☐	89 Joe Thornton, Bost.	1.50
☐	90 Michael Peca, Buff.	.50
☐	91 Matt Cullen, Anah.	.20
☐	92 Robyn Regehr, Calg.	.20
☐	93 Todd Marchant, Edmo.	.20
☐	94 Brett Hull, Dall.	1.00
☐	95 Rob Blake, LosA.	.50
☐	96 Sergei Zholtok, Mont.	.20
☐	97 Eric Lindros, Phil.	1.00
☐	98 Jean-Sébastien Aubin (G), Pitt.	.20
☐	99 Jason Arnott, NJer.	.50
☐	100 Keith Tkachuk, Phoe.	.50
☐	101 Wade Redden, Otta.	.20
☐	102 Sean Burke (G), Phoe.	.50
☐	103 Marian Hossa, Otta.	1.00
☐	104 Robert Lang, Pitt.	.20
☐	105 Curtis Joseph (G), Toro.	1.00
☐	106 Jeff Friesen, SanJ.	.20
☐	107 Dennis Bonvie, Pitt.	.20
☐	108 Alexander Korolyuk, SanJ.	.20
☐	109 Éric Lacroix, NYRa.	.20
☐	110 Todd Bertuzzi, Vanc.	1.50
☐	111 Bates Battaglia, Caro.	.20
☐	112 Jozef Stümpel, LosA.	.20
☐	113 Alexei Zhamnov, Chic.	.20
☐	114 Milan Hejduk, Colo.	1.00
☐	115 Chris Chelios, Detr.	.50
☐	116 Adam Graves, NYRa.	.50
☐	117 Patrik Stefan, Atla.	.20
☐	118 Guy Hebert (G), Anah.	.20
☐	119 Anson Carter, Bost.	.50
☐	120 Fred Brathwaite (G), Calg.	.20
☐	121 Maxim Afinogenov, Buff.	.50
☐	122 Éric Messier, Colo.	.20
☐	123 Ray Whitney, Flor.	.20
☐	124 Bob Bassen, SLou.	.20
☐	125 Patrick Lalime (G), Otta.	.50
☐	126 Jonas Höglund, Toro.	.20
☐	127 Mike Johnson, Tamp.	.20
☐	128 Peter Schaefer, Vanc.	.20
☐	129 Olaf Kölzig (G), Wash.	.50
☐	130 Jamie Langenbrunner, Dall.	.20
☐	131 Scott Niedermayer, NJer.	.20
☐	132 Mariusz Czerkawski, NYIs.	.20
☐	133 Petr Buzek, Atla.	.20
☐	134 Michal Grosek, Chic.	.20
☐	135 Valeri Bure, Calg.	.20
☐	136 Igor Korolev, Toro.	.20
☐	137 Oleg Tverdovsky, Anah.	.20
☐	138 Fredrik Modin, Tamp.	.20
☐	139 Kyle McLaren, Bost.	.20
☐	140 Todd Gill, Detr.	.20
☐	141 Miroslav Satan, Buff.	.20
☐	142 Jeff O'Neill, Caro.	.50
☐	143 Steve Sullivan, Chic.	.20
☐	144 Jon Klemm, Colo.	.20
☐	145 Joe Nieuwendyk, Dall.	.50
☐	146 Luc Robitaille, LosA.	1.00
☐	147 Patrice Brisebois, Mont.	.20
☐	148 Travis Green, Phoe.	.20
☐	149 Patric Kjellberg, Nash.	.20
☐	150 Mats Sundin, Toro.	1.00
☐	151 Brian Rolston, Bost.	.20
☐	152 Patrik Elias, NJer.	1.00
☐	153 Markus Näslund, Vanc.	1.00
☐	154 Trevor Letowski, Phoe.	.20
☐	155 Brad Stuart, SanJ.	.50
☐	156 Doug Gilmour, Buff.	.50
☐	157 Alexander Mogilny, NJer.	.50
☐	158 Glen Wesley, Caro.	.20
☐	159 Petr Nedved, NYRa.	.20
☐	160 Peter Bondra, Wash.	.50
☐	161 Alex Tanguay, Colo.	.50
☐	162 Steve Rucchin, Anah.	.20
☐	163 Nikolai Antropov, Toro.	.20
☐	164 Anders Eriksson, Chic.	.20
☐	165 Martin Rucinsky, Mont.	.20
☐	166 Trevor Kidd (G), Flor.	.20
☐	167 Zdeno Chara, NYIs.	.20
☐	168 Adam Oates, Wash.	.50
☐	169 Éric Desjardins, Phil.	.20
☐	170 Petr Sykora, NJer.	.50
☐	171 Brenden Morrow, Dall.	.20
☐	172 Al MacInnis, SLou.	.50
☐	173 Ethan Moreau, Edmo.	.20
☐	174 Chris Tamer, Atla.	.20
☐	175 Jaroslav Spacek, Flor.	.20
☐	176 Paul Mara, Tamp.	.20
☐	177 Bryan Smolinski, LosA.	.20
☐	178 Yanic Perreault, Toro.	.20
☐	179 Vaclav Prospal, Otta.	.20
☐	180 Vitali Yachmenev, Nash.	.20
☐	181 Pavel Trnka, Anah.	.20
☐	182 Joe Sakic, Colo.	2.00
☐	183 Vincent Damphousse, SanJ.	.50
☐	184 Sergei Fedorov, Detr.	1.00
☐	185 Brian Rafalski, NJer.	.20
☐	186 Jochen Hecht, SLou.	.20
☐	187 Shane Doan, Phoe.	.20
☐	188 Saku Koivu, Mont.	1.00
☐	189 Richard Zednik, Wash.	.50
☐	190 Brian Boucher (G), Phil.	.20
☐	191 Jeff Halpern, Wash.	.20
☐	192 Matt Cooke, Vanc.	.20
☐	193 Darcy Tucker, Toro.	.20
☐	194 Brian Leetch, NYRa.	.50
☐	195 Glen Murray, LosA.	.50
☐	196 Robert Svehla, Flor.	.20
☐	197 Kimmo Timonen, Nash.	.20
☐	198 Claude Lapointe, NYIs.	.20
☐	199 Brian Savage, Mont.	.20
☐	200 Sami Kapanen, Caro.	.20
☐	201 Scott Pellerin, MinW.	.20
☐	202 Cam Stewart, MinW.	.20
☐	203 Sergei Krivokrasov, MinW.	.20
☐	204 Manny Fernandez (G), MinW.	.50
☐	205 Darby Hendrickson, MinW.	.20
☐	206 Jamie McLennan (G), MinW.	.20
☐	207 Kevyn Adams, Colu.	.20
☐	208 Lyle Odelein, Colu.	.20
☐	209 Marc Denis (G), Colu.	.50
☐	210 Ron Tugnutt (G), Colu.	.50
☐	211 Tyler Wright, Colu.	.20
☐	212 Geoff Sanderson, Colu.	.20
☐	213 Mark Messier, NYRa.	1.00
☐	214 Mike Vernon (G), Calg.	.50
☐	215 Dave Andréychuk, Buff.	.20
☐	216 Chris Murray, SLou.	.20
☐	217 Joé Juneau, Phoe.	.20
☐	218 Vladimir Malakhov, NYRa.	.20
☐	219 Paul Coffey, Bost.	.50
☐	220 Roberto Luongo (G), Flor.	1.00
☐	221 Roman Hamrlik, NYIs.	.20
☐	222 Sandis Ozolinsh, Caro.	.20
☐	223 Gary Roberts, Toro.	.50
☐	224 Boyd Devereaux, Detr.	.20
☐	225 Scott Thornton, SanJ.	.20
☐	226 Igor Larionov, Flor.	.50
☐	227 John Vanbiesbrouck (G), NYIs.	.50

ROOKIE

	Insert (1:3)	Rookie
☐	228 Milan Kraft, Pitt.	1.50
☐	229 Steve McCarthy, Chic.	1.00
☐	230 Kris Beech, Wash.	1.50
☐	231 Henrik Sedin, Vanc.	2.00
☐	232 Daniel Sedin, Vanc.	2.00
☐	233 Oleg Saprykin, Calg.	1.00
☐	234 Maxime Ouellet (G), Phil.	1.50
☐	235 Taylor Pyatt, NYIs.	1.00
☐	236 Brent Johnson (G), SLou.	2.00
☐	237 Shawn Heins, SanJ.	1.00
☐	238 Mika Noronen (G), Buff.	1.00
☐	239 Samuel Påhlsson, Bost.	1.00
☐	240 Dimitri Kalinin, Buff.	1.00
☐	**241 Marian Gaborik, MinW. RC**	**12.00**
☐	**242 Petr Svoboda, Toro. RC**	**2.00**
☐	**243 Niclas Wallin, Caro. RC**	**1.50**
☐	**244 Dale Purinton, NYRa. RC**	**2.00**
☐	**245 Justin Williams, Phil. RC**	**4.00**
☐	**246 Roman Simicek, Pitt. RC**	**1.50**
☐	**247 Brad Tapper, Atla. RC**	**2.00**
☐	**248 Rostislav Klesla, Colu. RC**	**4.00**
☐	**249 Martin Havlat, Otta. RC**	**7.00**
☐	**250 Scott Hartnell, Nash. RC**	**3.00**
☐	**251 Andrew Raycroft (G), Bost. RC**	**3.00**
☐	**252 Ossi Väänänen, Phoe. RC**	**2.00**
☐	**253 S. Reinprecht, LosA. RC**	**4.00**
☐	**254 Josef Vasicek, Caro. RC**	**3.00**
☐	**255 Petr Hubacek, Phil. RC**	**1.50**
☐	**256 L. Sekeras, MinW. RC**	**2.00**
☐	**257 D. Aebischer (G), Colo. RC**	**4.00**
☐	**258 Jani Hurme (G), Otta. RC**	**3.00**
☐	**259 Marty Turco (G), Dall. RC**	**7.00**
☐	**260 Jarno Kultanen, Bost. RC**	**1.50**
	Checklist	
☐	Pavel Bure, Flor.	1.50

11X14 AUTOGRAPHED PRINT

	Autograph
☐	Daniel Alfredsson, Otta. ✍
☐	Nikolai Antropov, Toro. ✍
☐	Martin Brodeur (G), NJer. ✍
☐	Pavel Bure, Flor. ✍
☐	Anson Carter, Bost. ✍
☐	Pavol Demitra, SLou. ✍
☐	Scott Gomez, NJer. ✍
☐	Mike York, NYRa. ✍
☐	José Théodore (G), Mont. ✍
☐	Mike York, NYRa. ✍

BEAM TEAM

	Insert Set (30 cards):	300.00
	Insert (#/500)	BT500
☐	BT1 Paul Kariya, Anah.	15.00
☐	BT2 Peter Forsberg, Colo.	15.00
☐	BT3 Mike Modano, Dall.	10.00
☐	BT4 Steve Yzerman, Detr.	30.00
☐	BT5 Pavel Bure, Flor.	10.00
☐	BT6 Jaromir Jagr, Pitt.	10.00
☐	BT7 Brett Hull, Dall.	10.00
☐	BT8 Joe Sakic, Colo.	20.00
☐	BT9 Scott Gomez, NJer.	8.00
☐	BT10 Teemu Selänne, Anah.	10.00
☐	BT11 Vincent Lecavalier, Tamp.	10.00
☐	BT12 Patrick Roy (G), Colo.	35.00
☐	BT13 Martin Brodeur (G), NJer.	20.00
☐	BT14 Dominik Hasek (G), Buff.	10.00
☐	BT15 Joe Thornton, Bost.	15.00
☐	BT16 Valeri Bure, Calg.	8.00
☐	BT17 Ed Belfour (G), Dall.	10.00
☐	BT18 Ray Bourque, Colo.	15.00
☐	BT19 Mark Messier, NYRa.	10.00
☐	BT20 Curtis Joseph (G), Toro.	10.00
☐	BT21 Jason Arnott, NJer.	8.00
☐	BT22 Brian Boucher (G), Phil.	8.00
☐	BT23 Tony Amonte, Chic.	8.00
☐	BT24 Milan Hejduk, Colo.	10.00
☐	BT25 Mark Recchi, Phil.	8.00
☐	BT26 Patrik Elias, NJer.	10.00
☐	BT27 Zigmund Palffy, LosA.	8.00
☐	BT28 Jeremy Roenick, Phoe.	10.00
☐	BT29 Eric Lindros, Phil.	10.00
☐	BT30 Chris Pronger, SLou.	8.00

CAPTURE THE ACTION GAME VIEW

	Insert Set (15 cards):	525.00
	Insert (#/100)	CAGV
☐	CA1 Jaromir Jagr, Pitt.	50.00
☐	CA2 Martin Brodeur (G), NJer.	80.00
☐	CA3 Scott Gomez, NJer.	20.00
☐	CA4 Ed Belfour (G), Dall.	50.00
☐	CA5 Dominik Hasek (G), Buff.	50.00
☐	CA6 Olaf Kölzig (G), Wash.	30.00
☐	CA7 Pavel Bure, Flor.	40.00
☐	CA8 John LeClair, Phil.	40.00
☐	CA9 Curtis Joseph (G), Toro.	50.00
☐	CA10 Chris Pronger, SLou.	30.00
☐	CA11 Peter Forsberg, Colo.	70.00
☐	CA12 Teemu Selänne, Anah.	40.00
☐	CA13 Patrik Stefan, Atla.	16.00
☐	CA14 Vincent Lecavalier, Tamp.	50.00
☐	CA15 Tim Connolly, NYIs.	20.00

CAPTURE THE ACTION

	Insert Set (15 cards):	25.00
	Player	CA
☐	CA1 Jaromir Jagr vs. Flyers	2.50
☐	CA2 Martin Brodeur (G) vs. Eric Lindros	3.50
☐	CA3 Scott Gomez, NJer.	1.50
☐	CA4 Ed Belfour (G) vs. John LeClair	2.00
☐	CA5 Dominik Hasek (G), Buff.	2.50
☐	CA6 Olaf Kölzig (G) vs. John Madden	1.50
☐	CA7 Pavel Bure vs. Jeff Hackett (G)	1.50
☐	CA8 John LeClair, Phil.	2.00
☐	CA9 Curtis Joseph (G) vs. Mariusz Czerkawski	1.50
☐	CA10 Chris Pronger, SLou.	1.50
☐	CA11 Peter Forsberg, Colo.	3.50
☐	CA12 Teemu Selänne, Anah.	2.00
☐	CA13 Patrik Stefan, Atla.	1.50
☐	CA14 V. Lecavalier vs. K. Weekes & K. Jönsson	1.50
☐	CA15 T. Connolly vs. M. Schneider & M. Richter	1.50

CO-SIGNERS

	Insert Set (4 cards):	250.00
	Player	CS
☐	P. Bure ✍ / P. Demitra ✍	65.00
☐	M. Brodeur ✍ / S. Gomez ✍	150.00
☐	D. Alfredsson ✍ / N. Antropov ✍	50.00
☐	A. Carter ✍ / M. York ✍	50.00

GLOVE SAVE

	Insert Set (10 cards):	60.00
	Insert (1:10)	GS
☐	GS1 Martin Brodeur (G), NJer.	10.00
☐	GS2 Ed Belfour (G), Dall.	5.00
☐	GS3 Patrick Roy (G), Colo.	25.00
☐	GS4 Curtis Joseph (G), Toro.	5.00
☐	GS5 Brian Boucher (G), Phil.	5.00
☐	GS6 Roman Turek (G), SLou.	5.00
☐	GS7 Olaf Kölzig (G), Wash.	5.00
☐	GS8 Dominik Hasek (G), Buff.	5.00
☐	GS9 Chris Osgood (G), Detr.	5.00
☐	GS10 Fred Brathwaite (G), Calg.	5.00

LONE STAR SIGNATURES

	Insert Set (10 cards):	275.00
	Autograph	LSS
☐	Pavel Bure, Flor. ✍	45.00
☐	Martin Brodeur (G), NJer. ✍	90.00
☐	Scott Gomez, NJer. ✍	20.00
☐	Daniel Alfredsson, Otta. ✍	30.00
☐	Nikolai Antropov, Toro. ✍	20.00
☐	José Théodore (G), Mont. ✍	65.00
☐	Anson Carter, Bost. ✍	20.00
☐	Pavol Demitra, SLou. ✍	20.00
☐	Michael York, NYRa. ✍	20.00
☐	Brad Stuart, SanJ. ✍	20.00

SPECIAL FORCES

	Insert Set (20 cards):	30.00
	Insert (1:18)	SF
☐	SF1 Scott Stevens, NJer.	1.00
☐	SF2 Chris Pronger, SLou.	1.00
☐	SF3 Paul Kariya, Anah.	3.00
☐	SF4 Peter Forsberg, Colo.	3.00
☐	SF5 Mike Modano, Dall.	2.00
☐	SF6 Steve Yzerman, Detr.	6.00
☐	SF7 Pavel Bure, Flor.	2.00
☐	SF8 Jaromir Jagr, Pitt.	2.00
☐	SF9 John LeClair, Phil.	2.00
☐	SF10 Mats Sundin, Toro.	2.00
☐	SF11 Owen Nolan, SanJ.	1.00
☐	SF12 Brendan Shanahan, Detr.	2.00
☐	SF13 Pavol Demitra, SLou.	1.00
☐	SF14 Nicklas Lidström, Detr.	1.00
☐	SF15 Ron Francis, Caro.	1.00
☐	SF16 Patrick Roy (G), Colo.	7.00
☐	SF17 Martin Brodeur (G), NJer.	4.00
☐	SF18 Dominik Hasek (G), Buff.	2.00
☐	SF19 Keith Tkachuk, Phoe.	1.00
☐	SF20 Curtis Joseph (G), Toro.	2.00

STADIUM CLUB SOUVENIRS

	Insert Set (8 cards):	120.00
	Insert (1:88)	SCS
☐	SCS-1 Wade Redden, Otta. ✂	15.00
☐	SCS-2 Joe Sakic, Colo. ✂	40.00
☐	SCS-3 Derian Hatcher, Dall. ✂	15.00
☐	SCS-4 Jeff Hackett (G), Mont. ✂ Red	15.00
☐	SCS-5 Kenny Jönsson, NYIs. ✂	15.00
☐	SCS-6 Sergei Samsonov, Bost. ✂	15.00
☐	SCS-7 Darren McCarty, Detr. ✂	15.00
☐	SCS-8 Tie Domi, Toro. ✂	15.00

PRE-PRODUCTION SAMPLE

	Complete Set (6 cards):	5.00
	Player	Promo
☐	PP1 Bill Guerin, Edmo.	1.00
☐	PP2 Alexei Kovalev, Pitt.	1.50
☐	PP3 Keith Primeau, Phil.	1.00
☐	PP4 Jocelyn Thibault (G), Chic.	1.00
☐	PP5 Brad Isbister, Phoe.	1.00
☐	PP6 Adam Graves, NYRa.	1.00

2000 - 01 STARTING LINEUP

A card produced by Pacific was packaged with each figure.

	Complete Set (22 cards):	25.00
	Description	SLU
☐	1 Adam Deadmarsh, Colo.	1.00
☐	2 Joe Sakic, Colo.	3.00
☐	3 Anson Carter, Bost.	1.00
☐	4 Raymond Bourque, Bost.	2.00
☐	5 Saku Koivu, Mont.	1.50
☐	6 Adam Oates, Wash.	1.00
☐	7 Guy Hebert (G), Anah.	1.00
☐	8 John Vanbiesbrouck (G), Phil.	1.00
☐	9 Keith Primeau, Phil.	1.00
☐	10 Rod Brind'Amour, Caro.	1.00
☐	11 Arturs Irbe (G), Caro.	1.00
☐	12 Stéphane Fiset (G), LosA.	1.00
☐	13 Vincent Lecavalier, Tamp.	2.00
☐	14 Curtis Joseph (G), Toro.	2.00
☐	15 Mike Grier, Edmo.	1.00
☐	16 Jaromir Jagr, Pitt.	2.00
☐	17 Steve Yzerman, Detr.	4.50
☐	18 Ron Tugnutt (G), Otta.	1.00
☐	19 Niklas Sundström, SanJ.	1.00
☐	20 Ed Belfour (G), Dall.	2.00
☐	21 Derian Hatcher, Dall.	1.00
☐	22 Damian Rhodes (G), Atla.	1.00

FIGURES

Figures were available in American (English text) and Canadian (bilingual text) packaging. The figures and cards in each type of package are the same. Priced below are retail selling prices for packaged figures (each package includes one card) and loose figures.

	Packaged Set (24 packages):	315.00	
	Figure Set (24 figures):		90.00
	Player	Pack.	Loose
☐	Ed Belfour (G), Dall.	18.00	5.00
☐	Raymond Bourque, Colo.	15.00	4.00
☐	Raymond Bourque, Bost.	20.00	5.00
☐	Rod Brind'Amour, Caro.	12.00	4.00
☐	Anson Carter, Bost.	12.00	4.00
☐	Adam Deadmarsh, Colo.	15.00	4.00
☐	Stéphane Fiset (G), LosA.	18.00	5.00
☐	Mike Grier, Edmo.	15.00	4.00
☐	Derian Hatcher, Dall.	15.00	4.00
☐	Guy Hebert (G), Anah.	15.00	5.00
☐	Arturs Irbe (G), Caro.	15.00	5.00
☐	Jaromir Jagr, Pitt.	12.00	4.00
☐	Curtis Joseph (G), Toro.	15.00	5.00
☐	Saku Koivu, Mont.	18.00	4.00
☐	Vincent Lecavalier, Tamp.	20.00	5.00
☐	Adam Oates, Wash.	12.00	4.00
☐	Keith Primeau, Phil.	12.00	4.00
☐	Damian Rhodes (G), Atla.	15.00	5.00
☐	Joe Sakic, Colo.	15.00	4.00
☐	Niklas Sundström, SanJ.	15.00	4.00
☐	Ron Tugnutt (G), Pitt.	15.00	4.00
☐	Ron Tugnutt (G), Colu.	30.00	6.00
☐	John Vanbiesbrouck (G), Phil.	12.00	4.00
☐	Steve Yzerman, Detr.	15.00	5.00

2000 - 01 STARTING LINEUP CLASSIC DOUBLES

Two cards produced by Pacific were packaged with each pair of figures.

	Complete Set (8 cards):	15.00
	Description	SLU
☐	1 Olaf Kölzig (G), Wash.	1.00
☐	2 Patrick Roy (G), Colo.	6.00
☐	3 Paul Kariya, Anah.	2.50
☐	4 Miroslav Satan, Buff.	1.00
☐	5 Jaromir Jagr, Pitt.	2.00
☐	6 Pavel Bure, Flor.	1.50
☐	7 Peter Forsberg, Colo.	2.50
☐	8 Sergei Fedorov, Detr.	2.00

FIGURES

Each pair of figures were packaged with two cards.

	Packaged Set (4 packages):	70.00
	Players	Pack.
☐	Peter Forsberg / Sergei Fedorov	20.00
☐	Jaromir Jagr / Pavel Bure	20.00
☐	Paul Kariya / Miroslav Satan	20.00
☐	Olaf Kölzig (G) / Patrick Roy (G)	25.00

2000 - 01 TOPPS & O-PEE-CHEE

These series were issued in August 2000. The O-Pee-Chee and Topps cards are similar in design but have different brand logos on the card fronts. The O-Pee-Chee card backs also include French bios below the English bios. Cards 1-250 and 271-330 feature the same players in both the O-Pee-Chee and Topps series; cards 251-270 feature different players in each series. Topps packs have an O-Pee-Chee foil parallel (#/100) while O-Pee-Chee packs have a Topps foil parallel (#/100).

	Topps Set (330 cards):	2,800	35.00
	O-Pee-Chee Set (330 cards):	2,800	35.00
	Common Player:	4.00	.20
	Player	F100	Reg.
☐☐☐☐	1 Jaromir Jagr [PIT-1]	35.00	.50
☐☐☐☐	2 Patrick Roy (G) [COL-1]	110.00	2.00
☐☐☐☐	3 Paul Kariya [ANA-1]	50.00	1.00
☐☐☐☐	4 Mats Sundin [TOR-1]	35.00	.50
☐☐☐☐	5 Ron Francis [CAR-1]	20.00	.20
☐☐☐☐	6 Pavel Bure [FLA-1]	30.00	.50
☐☐☐☐	7 John LeClair [PHI-1]	30.00	.50
☐☐☐☐	8 Olaf Kölzig (G) [WAS-1]	20.00	.20
☐☐☐☐	9 Chris Pronger [STL-1]	20.00	.20
☐☐☐☐	10 Jeremy Roenick [PHO-1]	30.00	.50
☐☐☐☐	11 Owen Nolan [SJ-1]	20.00	.20
☐☐☐☐	12 Theoren Fleury [NYR-1]	20.00	.20
☐☐☐☐	13 Zigmund Palffy [LA-1]	20.00	.20
☐☐☐☐	14 Patrik Stefan [ATL-1]	10.00	.20
☐☐☐☐	15 Jarome Iginla [CAL-1]	30.00	.50
☐☐☐☐	16 Joe Thornton [BOS-1]	45.00	.50
☐☐☐☐	17 Tony Amonte [CHI-1]	20.00	.20
☐☐☐☐	18 Mike Modano [DAL-1]	35.00	.50
☐☐☐☐	19 Alexander Mogilny [NJ-1]	15.00	.20

□□□□ 20 Mark Messier [VAN-1] 35.00 .50
□□□□ 21 Dominik Hasek (G) [BUF-1] 35.00 .50
□□□□ 22 Steve Yzerman [DET-1] 90.00 1.50
□□□□ 23 Marian Hossa [OTT-1] 35.00 .50
□□□□ 24 David Legwand [NAS-1] 15.00 .20
□□□□ 25 José Théodore (G) [MON-1] 45.00 .50
□□□□ 26 Vincent Lecavalier [TB-1] 35.00 .50
□□□□ 27 Mike Ricci [SJ-2] 10.00 .20
□□□□ 28 Scott Stevens [NJ-2] 15.00 .20
□□□□ 29 K. Weekes [NYI-1] 5.00 .20
□□□□ 30 Sean Burke (G) [PHO-2] 20.00 .20
□□□□ 31 Alexei Kovalev [PIT-2] 20.00 .20
□□□□ 32 Trevor Linden [MON-2] 15.00 .20
□□□□ 33 Joé Juneau [OTT-2] 5.00 .20
□□□□ 34 Niklas Sundstrom [SJ-3] 5.00 .20
□□□□ 35 Dan Cloutier (G) [TB-2] 15.00 .20
□□□□ 36 Drake Berehowsky [NAS-2] 5.00 .20
□□□□ 37 Jonas Höglund [TOR-2] 5.00 .20
□□□□ 38 Sami Kapanen [CAR-9] 10.00 .20
□□□□ 39 Matthew Barnaby [PIT-3] 4.00 .20
□□□□ 40 Anson Carter [BOS-2] 15.00 .20
□□□□ 41 Miroslav Satan [BUF-2] 10.00 .20
□□□□ 42 Mark Recchi [PHI-2] 15.00 .20
□□□□ 43 Pavol Demitra [STL-2] 15.00 .20
□□□□ 44 Peter Bondra [WAS-2] 20.00 .20
□□□□ 45 Mike Richter (G) [NYR-2] 15.00 .20
□□□□ 46 Guy Hebert (G) [ANA-2] 5.00 .20
□□□□ 47 Robert Svehla [FLA-2] 5.00 .20
□□□□ 48 Martin Skoula [COL-2] 5.00 .20
□□□□ 49 Ed Belfour (G) [DAL-2] 35.00 .50
□□□□ 50 Alexei Zhamnov [CHI-2] 10.00 .20
□□□□ 51 Fred Brathwaite (G) [CAL-2] 10.00 .20
□□□□ 52 Andrew Brunette [ATL-2] 5.00 .20
□□□□ 53 Byron Dafoe (G) [BOS-3] 15.00 .20
□□□□ 54 Claude Lemieux [NJ-3] 10.00 .20
□□□□ 55 Sergei Berezin [TOR-3] 15.00 .20
□□□□ 56 Félix Potvin (G) [VAN-2] 45.00 .20
□□□□ 57 Rod Brind'Amour [CAR-2] 10.00 .20
□□□□ 58 Doug Gilmour [BUF-3] 20.00 .20
□□□□ 59 Brett Hull [DAL-3] 35.00 .50
□□□□ 60 Nicklas Lidström [DET-2] 20.00 .20
□□□□ 61 Mike York [NYR-3] 10.00 .20
□□□□ 62 Al MacInnis [STL-3] 15.00 .20
□□□□ 63 Brian Boucher (G) [PHI-3] 10.00 .20
□□□□ 64 Teemu Selänne [ANA-3] 30.00 .50
□□□□ 65 Mike Vernon [FLA-3] 15.00 .20
□□□□ 66 Bill Guerin [EDM-1] 15.00 .20
□□□□ 67 Raymond Bourque [COL-3] 45.00 .50
□□□□ 68 Bryan McCabe [CHI-3] 5.00 .20
□□□□ 69 Ray Ferraro [ATL-3] 5.00 .20
□□□□ 70 Stéphane Fiset (G) [LA-2] 10.00 .20
□□□□ 71 Sergei Gonchar [WAS-3] 10.00 .20
□□□□ 72 Mattias Öhlund [VAN-3] 10.00 .20
□□□□ 73 Todd Marchant [EDM-2] 5.00 .20
□□□□ 74 Derek Morris [CAL-3] 5.00 .20
□□□□ 75 Brian Rolston [BOS-4] 10.00 .20
□□□□ 76 Damian Rhodes (G) [ATL-4] 5.00 .20
□□□□ 77 Chris Drury [COL-4] 20.00 .20
□□□□ 78 Curtis Joseph (G) [TOR-4] 35.00 .50
□□□□ 79 Teppo Numminen [PHO-3] 10.00 .20
□□□□ 80 Petr Nedved [NYR-4] 10.00 .20
□□□□ 81 Doug Weight [EDM-3] 20.00 .20
□□□□ 82 Arturs Irbe (G) [CAR-3] 15.00 .20
□□□□ 83 Chris Osgood (G) [DET-3] 20.00 .20
□□□□ 84 Chris Gratton [BUF-4] 5.00 .20
□□□□ 85 Jocelyn Thibault (G) [CHI-4] 15.00 .20
□□□□ 86 Oleg Tverdovsky [ANA-4] 5.00 .20
□□□□ 87 Derian Hatcher [DAL-4] 10.00 .20
□□□□ 88 Ray Whitney [FLA-4] 5.00 .20
□□□□ 89 Saku Koivu [MON-3] 45.00 .50
□□□□ 90 Cliff Ronning [NAS-3] 5.00 .20
□□□□ 91 Claude Lapointe [NYI-2] 5.00 .20
□□□□ 92 Fredrik Modin [TB-3] 5.00 .20
□□□□ 93 Chris Simon [WAS-4] 5.00 .20
□□□□ 94 Todd Harvey [SJ-4] 5.00 .20
□□□□ 95 Martin Rucinsky [MON-4] 5.00 .20
□□□□ 96 Valeri Bure [CAL-4] 10.00 .20
□□□□ 97 Brad Isbister [NYI-3] 5.00 .20
□□□□ 98 Daymond Langkow [PHI-4] 5.00 .20
□□□□ 99 Todd Bertuzzi [VAN-4] 45.00 .50
□□□□ 100 Roman Turek (G) [STL-4] 15.00 .20
□□□□ 101 Kenny Jönsson [NYI-4] 5.00 .20
□□□□ 102 Mike Dunham (G) [NAS-4] 15.00 .20
□□□□ 103 Rob Blake [LA-3] 20.00 .20
□□□□ 104 Darius Kasparaitis [PIT-4] 5.00 .20
□□□□ 105 Daniel Alfredsson [OTT-3] 45.00 .20
□□□□ 106 Bobby Holik [NJ-4] 10.00 .20
□□□□ 107 Tommy Salo (G) [EDM-10] 15.00 .20
□□□□ 108 Sergei Samsonov [BOS-5] 20.00 .20
□□□□ 109 Joe Sakic [COL-5] 60.00 1.00
□□□□ 110 Bryan Smolinski [LA-4] 5.00 .20
□□□□ 111 Luc Robitaille [LA-5] 30.00 .50
□□□□ 112 Ryan Smyth [EDM-4] 15.00 .20
□□□□ 113 Éric Dazé [CHI-5] 15.00 .20
□□□□ 114 Mariusz Czerkawski [NYI-5] 5.00 .20
□□□□ 115 Brendan Shanahan [DET-4] 35.00 .50
□□□□ 116 Brian Rafalski [NJ-5] 5.00 .20
□□□□ 117 Mark Parrish [FLA-05] 15.00 .20
□□□□ 118 Jamie Langenbrunner [DAL-5] 5.00 .20
□□□□ 119 Peter Forsberg [COL-6] 50.00 1.00
□□□□ 120 Phil Housley [CAL-5] 10.00 .20
□□□□ 121 Jeff O'Neill [CAR-4] 15.00 .20
□□□□ 122 Stu Barnes [BUF-5] 4.00 .20
□□□□ 123 Glen Murray [LA-6] 15.00 .20
□□□□ 124 Jeff Hackett (G) [MON-5] 10.00 .20
□□□□ 125 Sergei Fedorov [DET-5] 35.00 .50
□□□□ 126 Kyle McLaren [BOS-6] 5.00 .20
□□□□ 127 Michael Nylander [CHI-6] 5.00 .20
□□□□ 128 Sergei Zubov [DAL-6] 5.00 .20
□□□□ 129 Steve Rucchin [ANA-5] 5.00 .20
□□□□ 130 Nelson Emerson [LA-7] 5.00 .20
□□□□ 131 Martin Brodeur (G) [NJ-6] 60.00 1.00
□□□□ 132 Mike Grier [EDM-5] 5.00 .20
□□□□ 133 Paul Coffey [CAR-5] 20.00 .20
□□□□ 134 Radek Bonk [OTT-4] 10.00 .20
□□□□ 135 Marc Savard [CAL-6] 5.00 .20
□□□□ 136 Milan Hejduk [COL-7] 30.00 .50
□□□□ 137 Curtis Brown [BUF-6] 5.00 .20
□□□□ 138 Viktor Kozlov [FLA-6] 10.00 .20
□□□□ 139 Jason Woolley [BUF-7] 4.00 .20
□□□□ 140 Adam Foote [COL-8] 10.00 .20
□□□□ 141 Radek Dvorak [NYR-5] 5.00 .20
□□□□ 142 Jason Arnott [NJ-7] 15.00 .20
□□□□ 143 German Titov [EDM-6] 4.00 .20
□□□□ 144 Scott Thornton [DAL-7] 4.00 .20
□□□□ 145 Brendan Morrison [VAN-5] 10.00 .20
□□□□ 146 Keith Tkachuk [PHO-4] 20.00 .20
□□□□ 147 Patrik Elias [NJ-8] 30.00 .50
□□□□ 148 Donald Audette [ATL-5] 15.00 .20
□□□□ 149 Jochen Hecht [STL-5] 5.00 .20
□□□□ 150 Dave Scatchard [NYI-6] 4.00 .20
□□□□ 151 Tom Barrasso (G) [OTT-5] 15.00 .20
□□□□ 152 Adam Deadmarsh [COL-9] 10.00 .20
□□□□ 153 Brian Leetch [NYR-6] 20.00 .20
□□□□ 154 Sergei Krivokrasov [CAL-7] 5.00 .20
□□□□ 155 Randy Robitaille [NAS-5] 5.00 .20
□□□□ 156 Petr Sykora [NJ-9] 15.00 .20
□□□□ 157 Dave Andréychuk [COL-10] 10.00 .20
□□□□ 158 Mathieu Biron [NYI-7] 5.00 .20
□□□□ 159 Sergei Zholtok [MON-6] 5.00 .20
□□□□ 160 Shawn McEachern [OTT-6] 10.00 .20
□□□□ 161 Steve Shields (G) [SJ-5] 5.00 .20
□□□□ 162 Petr Svoboda [TB-4] 5.00 .20
□□□□ 163 Nikolai Antropov [TOR-5] 5.00 .20
□□□□ 164 Michal Handzus [STL-6] 5.00 .20
□□□□ 165 Martin Straka [PIT-5] 10.00 .20
□□□□ 166 Shane Doan [PHO-5] 5.00 .20
□□□□ 167 Éric Desjardins [PHI-5] 10.00 .20
□□□□ 168 Peter Schaefer [VAN-6] 5.00 .20
□□□□ 169 Adam Oates [WAS-5] 15.00 .20
□□□□ 170 Scott Niedermayer [NJ-10] 10.00 .20
□□□□ 171 Dallas Drake [PHO-6] 5.00 .20
□□□□ 172 Josh Green [NYI-8] 5.00 .20
□□□□ 173 Mike Sillinger [FLA-7] 5.00 .20
□□□□ 174 Adam Graves [NYR-7] 15.00 .20
□□□□ 175 Lubos Bartecko [STL-7] 5.00 .20
□□□□ 176 Steve Konowalchuk [WAS-6] 5.00 .20
□□□□ 177 Jozef Stümpel [LA-8] 5.00 .20
□□□□ 178 Vincent Damphousse [SJ-6] 20.00 .20
□□□□ 179 Tomas Kaberle [TOR-6] 10.00 .20
□□□□ 180 Maxim Afinogenov [BUF-8] 15.00 .20
□□□□ 181 Marty McInnis [ANA-6] 5.00 .20
□□□□ 182 Chris Chelios [DET-6] 20.00 .20
□□□□ 183 Joe Nieuwendyk [DAL-8] 15.00 .20
□□□□ 184 Petr Buzek [ATL-6] 4.00 .20
□□□□ 185 Calle Johansson [WAS-7] 5.00 .20
□□□□ 186 Jeff Friesen [SJ-7] 10.00 .20
□□□□ 187 Paul Mara [TB-5] 5.00 .20
□□□□ 188 Markus Näslund [VAN-7] 35.00 .50
□□□□ 189 Scott Young [STL-8] 10.00 .20
□□□□ 190 Trevor Letowski [PHO-7] 5.00 .20
□□□□ 191 Steve Thomas [TOR-7] 5.00 .20
□□□□ 192 Martin Biron (G) [BUF-9] 15.00 .20
□□□□ 193 Jason Allison [BOS-7] 20.00 .20
□□□□ 194 Bob Probert [CHI-7] 10.00 .20
□□□□ 195 Jere Lehtinen [DAL-9] 10.00 .20
□□□□ 196 Tom Poti [EDM-7] 10.00 .20
□□□□ 197 Eric Lindros [PHI-6] 35.00 .50
□□□□ 198 Rob Niedermayer [FLA-8] 5.00 .20
□□□□ 199 Gary Roberts [CAR-6] 15.00 .20
□□□□ 200 Richard Zednik [WAS-8] 15.00 .20
□□□□ 201 Dainius Zubrus [MON-7] 5.00 .20
□□□□ 202 Tom Fitzgerald [NAS-6] 4.00 .20
□□□□ 203 Scott Gomez [NJ-11] 15.00 .20
□□□□ 204 Travis Green [PHO-8] 5.00 .20
□□□□ 205 Pierre Turgeon [STL-9] 15.00 .20
□□□□ 206 Ed Jovanovski [VAN-8] 15.00 .20
□□□□ 207 Trevor Kidd (G) [FLA-9] 10.00 .20
□□□□ 208 Jan Hrdina [PIT-6] 5.00 .20
□□□□ 209 Valeri Zelepukin [PHI-7] 4.00 .20
□□□□ 210 Vaclav Prospal [OTT-7] 10.00 .20
□□□□ 211 Matt Cullen [ANA-7] 5.00 .20
□□□□ 212 Karlis Skrastins [NAS-7] 4.00 .20
□□□□ 213 Robyn Regehr [CAL-8] 5.00 .20
□□□□ 214 Darren McCarty [DET-7] 10.00 .20
□□□□ 215 John Madden [NJ-12] 10.00 .20
□□□□ 216 Scott Mellanby [FLA-10] 5.00 .20
□□□□ 217 Tim Connolly [NYI-9] 15.00 .20
□□□□ 218 Pat Verbeek [DET-8] 10.00 .20
□□□□ 219 Richard Matvichuk [DAL-10] 5.00 .20
□□□□ 220 Rick Tocchet [PHI-8] 10.00 .20
□□□□ 221 Jan Hlavac [NYR-8] 5.00 .20
□□□□ 222 Jeff Halpern [WAS-9] 5.00 .20
□□□□ 223 Patrick Marleau [SJ-8] 15.00 .20
□□□□ 224 Robert Lang [PIT-7] 5.00 .20
□□□□ 225 Wade Redden [OTT-8] 10.00 .20
□□□□ 226 Stéphane Richer [STL-10] 5.00 .20
□□□□ 227 Kim Johnsson [NYR-9] 5.00 .20
□□□□ 228 Greg Adams [PHO-9] 5.00 .20
□□□□ 229 Alex Tanguay [COL-11] 20.00 .20
□□□□ 230 André Savage [BOS-8] 4.00 .20
□□□□ 231 Vyacheslav Kozlov [DET-9] 5.00 .20
□□□□ 232 Steve Sullivan [CHI-8] 10.00 .20
□□□□ 233 Alexander Selivanov [EDM-8] 4.00 .20
□□□□ 234 Tommy Westlund [CAR-7] 4.00 .20
□□□□ 235 Darcy Tucker [TOR-8] 5.00 .20
□□□□ 236 Simon Gagné [PHI-9] 30.00 .50
□□□□ 237 Brad Stuart [SJ-9] 15.00 .20
□□□□ 238 Jean-Sébastien Aubin (G) [PIT-8] 5.00 .20
□□□□ 239 Mike Johnson [TB-6] 5.00 .20
□□□□ 240 Shayne Corson [MON-8] 10.00 .20
□□□□ 241 Michael Peca [BUF-10] 15.00 .20
□□□□ 242 Keith Primeau [PHI-10] 15.00 .20
□□□□ 243 Martin Lapointe [DET-10] 15.00 .20
□□□□ 244 Tie Domi [TOR-9] 10.00 .20
□□□□ 245 Janne Niinimaa [EDM-9] 5.00 .20
□□□□ 246 Brenden Morrow [DAL-11] 10.00 .20
□□□□ 247 Sandis Ozolinsh [COL-12] 5.00 .20
□□□□ 248 Ron Tugnutt [PIT-9] 15.00 .20
□□□□ 249 Andréi Nazarov [CAL-9] 5.00 .20
□□□□ 250 Bates Battaglia [CAR-8] 5.00 .20
□□ 251 Dean Sylvester [ATL-8] (Topps) 4.00 .30
□□ 252 Hal Gill [BOS-11] (Topps) 4.00 .30
□□ 253 V. Tsyplakov [BUF-13] (Topps) 4.00 .30
□□ 254 Sean Hill [CAR-12] (Topps) 4.00 .30
□□ 255 Michal Grosek [CHI-11] (Topps) 4.00 .30
□□ 256 Darryl Sydor [DAL-15] (Topps) 5.00 .30
□□ 257 I. Larionov [DET-13] (Topps) 20.00 .30
□□ 258 Jaroslav Spacek [FLA-13] (Topps) 4.00 .30
□□ 259 Mattias Norström [LA-9] (Topps) 5.00 .30
□□ 260 Ladislav Kohn [ANA-10] (Topps) 5.00 .30
□□ 261 Patric Kjellberg [NAS-9] (Topps) 5.00 .30
□□ 262 Marty Reasoner [STL-12] (Topps) 5.00 .30
□□ 263 Zdeno Chara [NYI-15] (Topps) 5.00 .30
□□ 264 M. Schneider [NYR-10] (Topps) 5.00 .30
□□ 265 V'sbrouck (G) [PHI-13] (Topps) 15.00 .30
□□ 266 Jyrki Lumme [PHO-12] (Topps) 5.00 .30
□□ 267 Janne Laukkanen [PIT-10] (Topps) 4.00 .30
□□ 268 Alexander Korolyuk [SJ-12] (Topps) 4.00 .30
□□ 269 Pavel Kubina [TB-9] (Topps) 5.00 .30
□□ 270 Ulf Dahlén [WAS-12] (Topps) 5.00 .30
□□□□ 271 Roberto Luongo [NYI-10] 30.00 .50
□□□□ 272 Harold Druken [VAN-9] 10.00 .20
□□□□ 273 Marc Denis [COL-13] 15.00 .20
□□□□ 274 Oleg Saprykin [CAL-10] 5.00 .20
□□□□ 275 Glen Metropolit [WAS-10] 5.00 .20
□□□□ 276 Mark Eaton [PHI-11] 4.00 .20
□□□□ 277 Dmitri Yakushin [TOR-10] 4.00 .20
□□□□ 278 Scott Hannan [SJ-10] 4.00 .20
□□□□ 279 David Tanabe [CAR-10] 5.00 .20
□□□□ 280 Jiri Fischer [DET-11] 5.00 .20
□□□□ 281 Dimitri Nabokov [NYI-11] 5.00 .20
□□□□ 282 Ivan Novoseltsev [FLA-11] 5.00 .20
□□□□ 283 M. Fernandez [DAL-12] 15.00 .20
□□□□ 284 Maxim Balmochnykh [ANA-8] 5.00 .20
□□□□ 285 Brian Campbell [BUF-11] 4.00 .20
□□□□ 286 Sergei Varlamov [CAL-11] 5.00 .20
□□□□ **287 Ville Nieminen [COL-14] RC 15.00 1.00**
□□□□ **288 Colin White [NJ-13] RC 10.00 .50**
□□□□ 289 Mike Fisher [OTT-9] 5.00 .20
□□□□ **290 Matt Elich [TB-7] RC 10.00 .50**
□□□□ 291 Zenith Komarniski [VAN-10] 4.00 .20
□□□□ **292 Eric Nickulas [BOS-9] RC 5.00 .50**
□□□□ 293 Steve McCarthy [CHI-9] 5.00 .20
□□□□ 294 Jason Krog [NYI-12] 5.00 .20
□□□□ 295 Robert Esche (G) [PHO-10] 5.00 .20
□□□□ 296 Adam Mair [TOR-11] 5.00 .20
□□□□ 297 Ladislav Nagy [STL-11] 5.00 .20
□□□□ **298 S. Vyshedkevich [ATL-7] RC 10.00 .50**
□□□□ 299 Steve Bégin [CAL-12] 5.00 .20
□□□□ 300 Brad Ference [FLA-12] 5.00 .20
□□□□ 301 Andy Delmore [PHI-12] 5.00 .20
□□□□ **302 Brent Sopel [VAN-11] RC 10.00 .50**
□□□□ 303 Evgeni Nabokov (G) [SJ-11] 20.00 .20
□□□□ **304 David Gosselin [NAS-8] RC 5.00 .50**
□□□□ 305 Tavis Hansen [PHO-11] 4.00 .20
□□□□ 306 Raymond Giroux [NYI-13] 4.00 .20
□□□□ **307 S. Aubin (Colu.) [COL-15] RC 10.00 .50**
□□□□ 308 Shane Willis [CAR-11] 5.00 .20
□□□□ 309 Vitaly Vishnevski [ANA-9] 5.00 .20
□□□□ 310 Richard Jackman [DAL-13] 5.00 .20
□□□□ 311 Petr Schastlivy [OTT-10] 5.00 .20
□□□□ 312 Ryan Bonni [VAN-12] 4.00 .20
□□□□ 313 Alexei Tezikov [WAS-11] 4.00 .20
□□□□ 314 Zac Bierk [TB-8] 5.00 .20
□□□□ 315 Mike Ribeiro [MON-9] 10.00 .20
□□□□ 316 Darryl Laplante [DET-12] 4.00 .20
□□□□ 317 Kyle Calder [CHI-10] 5.00 .20
□□□□ 318 Dimitri Kalinin [BUF-12] 4.00 .20
□□□□ 319 J-S Giguère (G) [CAL-13] 30.00 .50
□□□□ **320 Willie Mitchell [NJ-14] RC 10.00 .50**
□□□□ **321 S. Valiquette (G) [NYI-14] RC 10.00 .50**
□□□□ 322 Brian Willsie [COL-16] 4.00 .20
□□□□ 323 Jarkko Ruutu [VAN-13] 5.00 .20
□□□□ 324 Jonathan Sim [DAL-14] 4.00 .20
□□□□ 325 Jonathan Girard [BOS-10] 4.00 .20
□□□□ 326 Martin Brodeur (G) 45.00 .50
□□□□ 327 Raymond Bourque 35.00 .50
□□□□ 328 V. Bure / P. Bure 20.00 .20
□□□□ 329 Steve Yzerman 70.00 1.00
□□□□ 330 Brett Hull 30.00 .50

O-Pee-Chee Exclusive F100 OPC

□□ 251 Yannick Tremblay [ATLA-8] (OPC) 4.00 .30
□□ 252 Grant Fuhr (G) [CAL-14] (OPC) 22.00 .30
□□ 253 Cory Stillman [CAL-15] (OPC) 9.00 .30
□□ 254 Jason Wiemer [CAL-16] (OPC) 4.00 .30
□□ 255 Martin Gélinas [CAR-12] (OPC) 9.00 .30
□□ 256 Mike Keane [DAL-15] (OPC) 6.00 .30
□□ 257 Ethan Moreau [EDM-11] (OPC) 6.00 .30
□□ 258 Jason Smith [EDM-12] (OPC) 6.00 .30
□□ 259 Kelly Buchberger [LA-9] (OPC) 6.00 .30
□□ 260 Benoît Brunet [MON-10] (OPC) 4.00 .30
□□ 261 Brian Savage [MON-11] (OPC) 12.00 .30
□□ 262 Sheldon Souray [MON-12] (OPC) 4.00 .30
□□ 263 Greg Johnson [NAS-9] (OPC) 6.00 .30
□□ 264 M. Arvedson [OTT-11] (OPC) 6.00 .30
□□ 265 P. Lalime (G) [OTT-12] (OPC) 22.00 .30
□□ 266 Wayne Primeau [TB-9] (OPC) 6.00 .30
□□ 267 Igor Korolev [TOR-12] (OPC) 6.00 .30
□□ 268 Yanic Perreault [TOR-13] (OPC) 12.00 .30
□□ 269 Adrian Aucoin [VAN-14] (OPC) 6.00 .30
□□ 270 Andrew Cassels [VAN-15] (OPC) 9.00 .30

1000-POINT CLUB

There is a Topps insert and an O-Pee-Chee insert. These cards have a 1000PC- prefix.

Insert Set (16 cards): 60.00

Insert (1:27) PC

□□ 1 Mark Messier, Vanc. 6.00
□□ 2 Steve Yzerman, Detr. 15.00
□□ 3 Ron Francis, Caro. 3.00
□□ 4 Paul Coffey, Caro. 3.00
□□ 5 Raymond Bourque, Colo. 7.00
□□ 6 Doug Gilmour, Buff. 3.00
□□ 7 Adam Oates, Wash. 3.00
□□ 8 Larry Murphy, Detr. 3.00
□□ 9 Dave Andréychuk, Colo. 3.00
□□ 10 Luc Robitaille, LosA. 5.00
□□ 11 Phil Housley, Calg. 3.00
□□ 12 Brett Hull, Dall. 6.00
□□ 13 Al MacInnis, SLou. 3.00
□□ 14 Pierre Turgeon, SLou. 3.00
□□ 15 Joe Sakic, Colo. 10.00
□□ 16 Pat Verbeek, Detr. 3.00

CERTIFIED AUTOGRAPH ISSUE

Insert Set (11 cards): 300.00

Autograph CAI

□ Chris Pronger, SLou. ✍ 30.00
□ Fred Brathwaite (G), Calg. ✍ 15.00
□ John LeClair, Phil. ✍ 40.00
□ José Théodore (G), Mont. ✍ 60.00
□ Mike Modano, Dall. ✍ 50.00
□ Mark Recchi, Phil. ✍ 20.00
□ Raymond Bourque, Colo. ✍ 70.00
□ Roman Turek (G), SLou. ✍ 20.00
□ Scott Gomez, NJer. ✍ 20.00
□ Tony Amonte, Chic. ✍ 30.00
□ Valeri Bure, Calg. ✍ 15.00

COMBOS

There is a Topps insert and an O-Pee-Chee insert as well as a Topps oversize card and an O-Pee-Chee oversize card.

Insert Set (10 cards): 80.00 50.00

Inserts Big Reg.

□□□□ TC1 V. Bure / P. Bure 8.00 6.00
□□□□ TC2 P. Kariya / T. Selänne 8.00 6.00
□□□□ TC3 T. Amonte / J. LeClair 8.00 6.00

☐☐☐☐	TC4 D. Hasek / C. Joseph	8.00	6.00
☐☐☐☐	TC5 P. Forsberg / M. Modano	8.00	6.00
☐☐☐☐	TC6 R. Bourque / C. Pronger	8.00	6.00
☐☐☐☐	TC7 J. Thornton / V. Lecavalier	8.00	6.00
☐☐☐☐	TC8 P. Roy / M. Brodeur	16.00	14.00
☐☐☐☐	TC9 B. Hull / S. Yzerman	12.00	10.00
☐☐☐☐	TC10 J. Jagr / M. Lemieux	14.00	12.00

COMMEMORATIVE SERIES

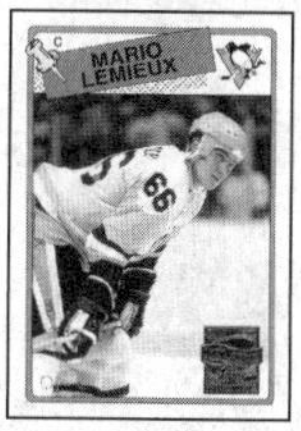

	Insert Set (23 cards):	100.00
	Insert	CS
☐	1 Mario Lemieux [85-86 Topps]	10.00
☐	2 Mario Lemieux [85-86 OPC]	10.00
☐	3 Mario Lemieux [86-87 Topps]	6.00
☐	4 Mario Lemieux [86-87 OPC]	6.00
☐	5 Mario Lemieux [87-88 Topps]	6.00
☐	6 Mario Lemieux [87-88 OPC]	6.00
☐	7 Mario Lemieux [88-89 Topps]	6.00
☐	8 Mario Lemieux [88-89 OPC]	6.00
☐	9 Mario Lemieux [89-90 Topps]	6.00
☐	10 Mario Lemieux [89-90 OPC]	6.00
☐	11 Mario Lemieux [90-91 Topps]	6.00
☐	12 Mario Lemieux [90-91 OPC]	6.00
☐	13 Mario Lemieux [90-91 OPC Premier]	6.00
☐	14 Mario Lemieux [91-92 Topps]	6.00
☐	15 Mario Lemieux [91-92 OPC]	6.00
☐	16 Mario Lemieux [92-93 Topps]	6.00
☐	17 Mario Lemieux [92-93 OPC]	6.00
☐	18 Mario Lemieux [93-94 Topps Premier]	6.00
☐	19 Mario Lemieux [93-94 OPC Premier]	6.00
☐	20 Mario Lemieux [94-95 Topps Premier]	6.00
☐	21 Mario Lemieux [94-95 OPC Premier]	6.00
☐	22 Mario Lemieux [95-96 Topps]	6.00
☐	23 Mario Lemieux [96-97 Topps]	6.00

COMMEMORATIVE SERIES AUTOGRAPH

	Insert Set (23 cards):	5,000
	Insert	Auto
☐	1 Mario Lemieux ✍ [85-86 Topps]	400.00
☐	2 Mario Lemieux ✍ [85-86 OPC]	400.00
☐	3 Mario Lemieux ✍ [86-87 Topps]	250.00
☐	4 Mario Lemieux ✍ [86-87 OPC]	250.00
☐	5 Mario Lemieux ✍ [87-88 Topps]	250.00
☐	6 Mario Lemieux ✍ [87-88 OPC]	250.00
☐	7 Mario Lemieux ✍ [88-89 Topps]	250.00
☐	8 Mario Lemieux ✍ [88-89 OPC]	250.00
☐	9 Mario Lemieux ✍ [89-90 Topps]	250.00
☐	10 Mario Lemieux ✍ [89-90 OPC]	250.00
☐	11 Mario Lemieux ✍ [90-91 Topps]	250.00
☐	12 Mario Lemieux ✍ [90-91 OPC]	250.00
☐	13 Mario Lemieux ✍ [90-91 OPC Premier]	250.00
☐	14 Mario Lemieux ✍ [91-92 Topps]	250.00
☐	15 Mario Lemieux ✍ [91-92 OPC]	250.00
☐	16 Mario Lemieux ✍ [92-93 Topps]	250.00
☐	17 Mario Lemieux ✍ [92-93 OPC]	250.00
☐	18 Mario Lemieux ✍ [93-94 Topps Premier]	250.00
☐	19 Mario Lemieux ✍ [93-94 OPC Premier]	250.00
☐	20 Mario Lemieux ✍ [94-95 Topps Premier]	250.00
☐	21 Mario Lemieux ✍ [94-95 OPC Premier]	250.00
☐	22 Mario Lemieux ✍ [95-96 Topps]	250.00
☐	23 Mario Lemieux ✍ [96-97 Topps]	250.00

GAME-WORN SWEATER

	Insert Set (6 cards):	200.00
	Insert	GWS
☐	Adam Graves, NYRa. ✂	35.00
☐	Bobby Holik, NJer. ✂	70.00
☐	David Legwand, Nash. ✂	35.00
☐	Darren McCarty, Detr. ✂	35.00
☐	Jaromir Jagr, Pitt. ✂	50.00
☐	Tie Domi, Toro. ✂	35.00

HOBBY MASTERS

There is a Topps insert and an O-Pee-Chee insert.

	Insert Set (10 cards):	45.00
	Insert (1:18)	HM
☐☐	HM1 Martin Brodeur (G), NJer.	6.00
☐☐	HM2 Pavel Bure, Flor.	3.00
☐☐	HM3 Peter Forsberg, Colo.	5.00
☐☐	HM4 Dominik Hasek (G), Buff.	4.00
☐☐	HM5 Jaromir Jagr, Pitt.	4.00
☐☐	HM6 Curtis Joseph (G), Toro.	4.00
☐☐	HM7 Paul Kariya, Anah.	5.00
☐☐	HM8 Mike Modano, Dall.	4.00
☐☐	HM9 Patrick Roy (G), Colo.	12.00
☐☐	HM10 Steve Yzerman, Detr.	9.00

NHL DRAFT

There is a Topps insert and an O-Pee-Chee insert. These cards have an NHLD- prefix.

	Insert Set (14 cards):	60.00
	Insert (1:31)	NHLD
☐☐	1 Vincent Lecavalier, Tamp. [1 Selection]	6.00
☐☐	2 Eric Lindros, Phil. [1 Selection]	6.00
☐☐	3 Mike Modano, Dall. [1 Selection]	6.00
☐☐	4 Owen Nolan, SanJ. [1 Selection]	4.00
☐☐	5 Patrik Stefan, Atla. [1 Selection]	4.00
☐☐	6 Mats Sundin, Toro. [1 Selection]	6.00
☐☐	7 Joe Thornton, Bost. [1 Selection]	7.00
☐☐	8 Pavel Bure, Flor. [Hidden Gems]	5.00
☐☐	9 Anson Carter, Bost. [Hidden Gems]	4.00
☐☐	10 Pavol Demitra, SLou. [Hidden Gems]	4.00
☐☐	11 Doug Gilmour, Buff. [Hidden Gems]	4.00
☐☐	12 Dominik Hasek (G), Buff. [Hidden Gems]	6.00
☐☐	13 Brett Hull, Dall. [Hidden Gems]	6.00
☐☐	14 Luc Robitaille, LosA. [Hidden Gems]	5.00

OWN THE GAME

There is a Topps insert and an O-Pee-Chee insert.

	Insert Set (30 cards):	100.00
	Insert (1:7)	OTG
☐☐	OTG1 Jaromir Jagr, Pitt. [Points]	5.00
☐☐	OTG2 Pavel Bure, Flor. [Points]	4.00
☐☐	OTG3 Mark Recchi, Phil. [Points]	2.00
☐☐	OTG4 Paul Kariya, Anah. [Points]	7.00
☐☐	OTG5 Teemu Selänne, Anah. [Points]	4.00
☐☐	OTG6 Owen Nolan, SanJ. [Points]	3.00
☐☐	OTG7 Tony Amonte, Chic. [Points]	3.00
☐☐	OTG8 Mike Modano, Dall. [Points]	5.00
☐☐	OTG9 Joe Sakic, Colo. [Points]	8.00
☐☐	OTG10 Steve Yzerman, Detr. [Points]	12.00
☐☐	OTG11 Martin Brodeur (G), NJer. [Victories]	8.00
☐☐	OTG12 Roman Turek (G), SLou. [Victories]	2.00
☐☐	OTG13 Olaf Kölzig (G), Wash. [Victories]	3.00
☐☐	OTG14 Curtis Joseph (G), Toro. [Victories]	5.00
☐☐	OTG15 Arturs Irbe (G), Caro. [Victories]	2.00
☐☐	OTG16 Patrick Roy (G), Colo. [Victories]	15.00
☐☐	OTG17 Ed Belfour (G), Dall. [Victories]	5.00
☐☐	OTG18 Chris Osgood (G), Detr. [Victories]	3.00
☐☐	OTG19 Guy Hebert (G), Anah. [Victories]	2.00
☐☐	OTG20 Steve Shields (G), SanJ. [Victories]	2.00
☐☐	OTG21 Scott Gomez, NJer. [Rookie Points]	2.00
☐☐	OTG22 Alex Tanguay, Colo. [Rookie Points]	3.00
☐☐	OTG24 Simon Gagné, Phil. [Rookie Points]	2.00
☐☐	OTG23 Mike York, NYRa. [Rookie Points]	4.00
☐☐	OTG26 Trevor Letowski, Phoe. [Rookie Points]	2.00
☐☐	OTG25 Jan Hlavac, NYRa. [Rookie Points]	2.00
☐☐	OTG28 Maxim Afinogenov, Buff. [Rookie Points]	2.00
☐☐	OTG27 Brad Stuart, SanJ. [Rookie Points]	2.00
☐☐	OTG29 Tim Connolly, NYIs. [Rookie Points]	2.00
☐☐	OTG30 Jochen Hecht, SLou. [Rookie Points]	2.00

STANLEY CUP HEROES

	Insert Set (5 cards):	40.00
	Insert (1:55)	SCH
☐	Bob Gainey, Mont.	10.00
☐	Bernie Parent (G), Phil.	10.00
☐	Bryan Trottier, NYIs.	12.00
☐	Larry Robinson, Mont.	10.00
☐	Ted Lindsay, Detr.	12.00

STANLEY CUP HEROES AUTOGRAPH

	Insert Set (5 cards):	250.00
	Insert (1:1104)	Aut
☐	Bob Gainey, Mont. ✍	50.00
☐	Bernie Parent (G), Phil. ✍	60.00
☐	Bryan Trottier, NYIs. ✍	75.00
☐	Larry Robinson, Mont. ✍	50.00
☐	Ted Lindsay, Detr. ✍	75.00

PRE-PRODUCTION SAMPLE

There is a Topps promo and an O-Pee-Chee promo.

	Complete Set (6 cards):	5.00
	Player	Promo
☐☐	PP1 Mariusz Czerkawski, NYIs.	1.00
☐☐	PP2 Sami Kapanen, Caro.	1.00
☐☐	PP3 Tommy Salo (G), Edmo.	1.00
☐☐	PP4 Radek Bonk, Otta.	1.00
☐☐	PP5 Pat Verbeek, Detr.	1.00
☐☐	PP6 Luc Robitaille, LosA.	2.00

2000 - 01 TOPPS CHROME

This series was released in January 2001. Topps Chrome cards 1-240 have a Topps Chrome Refractor parallel and an O-Pee-Chee Chrome Refractor parallel. Topps Chrome rookie cards 241-251 have a Blue border and a Red border parallel with each of the three base versions sequentially numbered to 1250 copies. All three base versions of the rookie cards have an O-Pee-Chee Chrome Refractor parallel (each #/35) and a Topps Chrome Refractor parallel (each #/25).

	Shell Set (240 cards):	-	-	200.00
	Regular Set (251 cards):	2,100	1,500	300.00
	Complete Set (273 cards):	4,200	3,100	500.00
	Common Player:	3.00	2.00	.50
	Player	TR	OR	TC
☐☐☐	1 Jaromir Jagr, Pitt.	12.00	10.00	2.50
☐☐☐	2 Patrick Roy (G), Colo.	35.00	30.00	7.50
☐☐☐	3 Paul Kariya, Anah.	17.00	14.00	3.50
☐☐☐	4 Mats Sundin, Toro.	12.00	10.00	2.50
☐☐☐	5 Ron Francis, Caro.	7.00	6.00	1.50
☐☐☐	6 Pavel Bure, Flor.	10.00	8.00	2.00
☐☐☐	7 John LeClair, Phil.	10.00	8.00	2.00
☐☐☐	8 Olaf Kölzig (G), Wash.	7.00	6.00	1.50
☐☐☐	9 Chris Pronger, SLou.	7.00	6.00	1.50
☐☐☐	10 Jeremy Roenick, Phoe.	10.00	8.00	2.00
☐☐☐	11 Owen Nolan, SanJ.	7.00	6.00	1.50
☐☐☐	12 Theoren Fleury, NYRa.	7.00	6.00	1.50
☐☐☐	13 Zigmund Palffy, LosA.	7.00	6.00	1.50
☐☐☐	14 Patrik Stefan, Atla.	4.00	3.00	.50
☐☐☐	15 Jarome Iginla, Calg.	10.00	8.00	2.00
☐☐☐	16 Joe Thornton, Bost.	15.00	12.00	3.00
☐☐☐	17 Tony Amonte, Chic.	7.00	6.00	1.50
☐☐☐	18 Mike Modano, Dall.	12.00	10.00	2.50
☐☐☐	19 Mark Messier, NYRa.	12.00	10.00	2.50
☐☐☐	20 Dominik Hasek (G), Buff.	12.00	10.00	2.50
☐☐☐	21 Steve Yzerman, Detr.	30.00	20.00	6.00
☐☐☐	22 Marian Hossa, Otta.	12.00	10.00	2.50
☐☐☐	23 David Legwand, Nash.	5.00	4.00	1.00
☐☐☐	24 José Théodore (G), Mont.	15.00	12.00	3.00
☐☐☐	25 Vincent Lecavalier, Tamp.	12.00	10.00	2.50
☐☐☐	26 Scott Stevens, NJer.	5.00	4.00	1.00
☐☐☐	27 Mark Parrish, NYIs.	5.00	4.00	1.00
☐☐☐	28 Sean Burke (G), Phoe.	7.00	6.00	1.50
☐☐☐	29 Alexei Kovalev, Pitt.	7.00	6.00	1.50
☐☐☐	30 Dan Cloutier (G), Tamp.	5.00	4.00	1.00
☐☐☐	31 Sami Kapanen, Caro.	4.00	3.00	.50
☐☐☐	32 Anson Carter, Bost.	5.00	4.00	1.00
☐☐☐	33 Miroslav Satan, Buff.	4.00	3.00	.50
☐☐☐	34 Mark Recchi, Phil.	5.00	4.00	1.00
☐☐☐	35 Pavol Demitra, SLou.	5.00	4.00	1.00
☐☐☐	36 Peter Bondra, Wash.	7.00	6.00	1.50
☐☐☐	37 Mike Richter (G), NYRa.	6.00	4.00	1.00
☐☐☐	38 Guy Hebert (G), Anah.	3.00	2.00	.50
☐☐☐	39 Martin Skoula, Colo.	3.00	2.00	.50
☐☐☐	40 Ed Belfour (G), Dall.	12.00	10.00	2.50
☐☐☐	41 Fred Brathwaite (G), Calg.	4.00	3.00	.50
☐☐☐	42 Andrew Brunette, Atla.	3.00	2.00	.50
☐☐☐	43 Byron Dafoe (G), Bost.	5.00	4.00	1.00
☐☐☐	44 Félix Potvin (G), Vanc.	7.00	6.00	1.50
☐☐☐	45 Rod Brind'Amour, Caro.	4.00	3.00	.50
☐☐☐	46 Doug Gilmour, Buff.	7.00	6.00	1.50
☐☐☐	47 Brett Hull, Dall.	12.00	10.00	2.50
☐☐☐	48 Nicklas Lidström, Detr.	7.00	6.00	1.50
☐☐☐	49 Mike York, NYRa.	4.00	3.00	.50
☐☐☐	50 Al MacInnis, SLou.	5.00	4.00	1.00
☐☐☐	51 Brian Boucher (G), Phil.	4.00	3.00	.50
☐☐☐	52 Teemu Selänne, Anah.	10.00	8.00	2.00
☐☐☐	53 Bill Guerin, Edmo.	5.00	4.00	1.00
☐☐☐	54 Raymond Bourque, Colo.	15.00	12.00	3.00
☐☐☐	55 Ray Ferraro, Atla.	3.00	2.00	.50
☐☐☐	56 Sergei Gonchar, Wash.	4.00	3.00	.50
☐☐☐	57 Mattias Öhlund, Vanc.	4.00	3.00	.50
☐☐☐	58 Todd Marchant, Edmo.	3.00	2.00	.50
☐☐☐	59 Damian Rhodes (G), Atla.	3.00	2.00	.50
☐☐☐	60 Chris Drury, Colo.	7.00	6.00	1.50
☐☐☐	61 Curtis Joseph (G), Toro.	12.00	10.00	2.50
☐☐☐	62 Teppo Numminen, Phoe.	4.00	3.00	.50
☐☐☐	63 Petr Nedved, NYRa.	4.00	3.00	.50
☐☐☐	64 Doug Weight, Edmo.	7.00	6.00	1.50
☐☐☐	65 Arturs Irbe (G), Caro.	5.00	4.00	1.00
☐☐☐	66 Chris Osgood (G), Detr.	7.00	6.00	1.50
☐☐☐	67 Jocelyn Thibault (G), Chic.	5.00	4.00	1.00
☐☐☐	68 Oleg Tverdovsky, Anah.	3.00	2.00	.50
☐☐☐	69 Derian Hatcher, Dall.	4.00	3.00	.50
☐☐☐	70 Ray Whitney, Flor.	3.00	2.00	.50
☐☐☐	71 Saku Koivu, Mont.	10.00	8.00	2.00
☐☐☐	72 Cliff Ronning, Nash.	3.00	2.00	.50
☐☐☐	73 Claude Lapointe, NYIs.	3.00	2.00	.50
☐☐☐	74 Chris Simon, Wash.	3.00	2.00	.50
☐☐☐	75 Martin Rucinsky, Mont.	3.00	2.00	.50
☐☐☐	76 Valeri Bure, Calg.	4.00	3.00	.50
☐☐☐	77 Brad Isbister, NYIs.	3.00	2.00	.50
☐☐☐	78 Roman Turek (G), SLou.	6.00	4.00	1.00
☐☐☐	79 Kenny Jönsson, NYIs.	3.00	2.00	.50
☐☐☐	80 Mike Dunham (G), Nash.	5.00	4.00	1.00
☐☐☐	81 Rob Blake, LosA.	7.00	6.00	1.50
☐☐☐	82 Daniel Alfredsson, Otta.	7.00	6.00	1.50
☐☐☐	83 Tommy Salo (G), Edmo.	5.00	4.00	1.00
☐☐☐	84 Sergei Samsonov, Bost.	7.00	6.00	1.50
☐☐☐	85 Joe Sakic, Colo.	20.00	16.00	4.00
☐☐☐	86 Bryan Smolinski, LosA.	3.00	2.00	.50
☐☐☐	87 Luc Robitaille, LosA.	10.00	8.00	2.00
☐☐☐	88 Mariusz Czerkawski, NYIs.	3.00	2.00	.50
☐☐☐	89 Brendan Shanahan, Detr.	12.00	10.00	2.50
☐☐☐	90 Brian Rafalski, NJer.	3.00	2.00	.50
☐☐☐	91 Jamie Langenbrunner, Dall.	3.00	2.00	.50
☐☐☐	92 Peter Forsberg, Colo.	17.00	14.00	3.50
☐☐☐	93 Phil Housley, Calg.	4.00	3.00	.50
☐☐☐	94 Glen Murray, LosA.	6.00	4.00	1.00
☐☐☐	95 Jeff Hackett (G), Mont.	4.00	3.00	.50
☐☐☐	96 Sergei Fedorov, Detr.	12.00	10.00	2.50
☐☐☐	97 Sergei Zubov, Dall.	3.00	2.00	.50
☐☐☐	98 Martin Brodeur (G), NJer.	20.00	16.00	4.00
☐☐☐	99 Mike Grier, Edmo.	3.00	2.00	.50
☐☐☐	100 Paul Coffey, Bost.	7.00	6.00	1.50
☐☐☐	101 Radek Bonk, Otta.	4.00	3.00	.50
☐☐☐	102 Milan Hejduk, Colo.	10.00	8.00	2.00
☐☐☐	103 Viktor Kozlov, Flor.	4.00	3.00	.50
☐☐☐	104 Jason Arnott, NJer.	6.00	4.00	1.00
☐☐☐	105 Brendan Morrison, Vanc.	4.00	3.00	.50
☐☐☐	106 Keith Tkachuk, Phoe.	7.00	6.00	1.50
☐☐☐	107 Patrik Elias, NJer.	10.00	8.00	2.00
☐☐☐	108 Jochen Hecht, SLou.	3.00	2.00	.50
☐☐☐	109 Brian Leetch, NYRa.	7.00	6.00	1.50
☐☐☐	110 Petr Sykora, NJer.	5.00	4.00	1.00
☐☐☐	111 Dave Andreychuk, Buff.	4.00	3.00	.50
☐☐☐	112 Steve Shields (G), SanJ.	3.00	2.00	.50
☐☐☐	113 Nikolai Antropov, Toro.	3.00	2.00	.50
☐☐☐	114 Martin Straka, Pitt.	4.00	3.00	.50
☐☐☐	115 Éric Desjardins, Phil.	4.00	3.00	.50
☐☐☐	116 Adam Oates, Wash.	5.00	4.00	1.00
☐☐☐	117 Adam Graves, NYRa.	5.00	4.00	1.00
☐☐☐	118 Jozef Stumpel, LosA.	3.00	2.00	.50
☐☐☐	119 V. Damphousse, SanJ.	7.00	6.00	1.50
☐☐☐	120 Maxim Afinogenov, Buff.	5.00	4.00	1.00
☐☐☐	121 Chris Chelios, Detr.	7.00	6.00	1.50
☐☐☐	122 Joe Nieuwendyk, Dall.	5.00	4.00	1.00
☐☐☐	123 Petr Buzek, Atla.	3.00	2.00	.50
☐☐☐	124 Jeff Friesen, SanJ.	4.00	3.00	.50
☐☐☐	125 Markus Näslund, Vanc.	12.00	10.00	2.50
☐☐☐	126 Trevor Letowski, Phoe.	3.00	2.00	.50
☐☐☐	127 Steve Thomas, Toro.	3.00	2.00	.50
☐☐☐	128 Jason Allison, Bost.	7.00	6.00	1.50
☐☐☐	129 Jere Lehtinen, Dall.	4.00	3.00	.50
☐☐☐	130 Tom Poti, Edmo.	3.00	2.00	.50
☐☐☐	131 Eric Lindros, Phil.	12.00	10.00	2.50
☐☐☐	132 Rob Niedermayer, Flor.	3.00	2.00	.50
☐☐☐	133 Gary Roberts, Toro.	5.00	4.00	1.00
☐☐☐	134 Scott Gomez, NJer.	5.00	4.00	1.00
☐☐☐	135 Pierre Turgeon, SLou.	5.00	4.00	1.00
☐☐☐	136 Trevor Kidd (G), Flor.	4.00	3.00	.50
☐☐☐	137 Jan Hrdina, Pitt.	3.00	2.00	.50
☐☐☐	138 John Madden, NJer.	4.00	3.00	.50
☐☐☐	139 Tim Connolly, NYIs.	5.00	4.00	1.00
☐☐☐	140 Pat Verbeek, Detr.	4.00	3.00	.50
☐☐☐	141 Jeff Halpern, Wash.	3.00	2.00	.50
☐☐☐	142 Patrick Marleau, SanJ.	6.00	4.00	1.00
☐☐☐	143 Wade Redden, Otta.	4.00	3.00	.50
☐☐☐	144 Alex Tanguay, Colo.	7.00	6.00	1.50
☐☐☐	145 Darcy Tucker, Toro.	3.00	2.00	.50
☐☐☐	146 Simon Gagné, Phil.	10.00	8.00	2.00
☐☐☐	147 Brad Stuart, SanJ.	5.00	4.00	1.00
☐☐☐	148 J-S Aubin (G), Pitt.	3.00	2.00	.50
☐☐☐	149 Mike Johnson, Tamp.	3.00	2.00	.50
☐☐☐	150 Shayne Corson, Toro.	4.00	3.00	.50

151 Michael Peca, Buff.	5.00	4.00	1.00
152 Keith Primeau, Phil.	5.00	4.00	1.00
153 Tie Domi, Toro.	4.00	3.00	.50
154 Brenden Morrow, Dall.	4.00	3.00	.50
155 Sandis Ozolinsh, Caro.	3.00	2.00	.50
156 Mike Keane, Dall.	3.00	2.00	.50
157 Patric Kjellberg, Nash.	3.00	2.00	.50
158 Patrick Lalime (G), Otta.	7.00	6.00	1.50
159 Vanbiesbrouck (G), NYIs.	6.00	4.00	1.00
160 Andrew Cassels, Vanc.	3.00	2.00	.50
161 Scott Stevens, NJer.	5.00	4.00	1.00
162 Ed Belfour (G), Dall.	12.00	10.00	2.50
163 Martin Brodeur (G), NJer.	20.00	16.00	4.00
164 Mike Modano, Dall.	12.00	10.00	2.50
165 Jason Arnott, NJer.	6.00	4.00	1.00
166 Roberto Luongo (G), Flor.	10.00	8.00	2.00
167 Harold Druken, Vanc.	4.00	3.00	.50
168 Marc Denis (G), Colu.	6.00	4.00	1.00
169 Oleg Saprykin, Calg.	3.00	2.00	.50
170 Glen Metropolit, Wash.	3.00	2.00	.50
171 Daniel Sedin, Vanc.	5.00	4.00	2.00
172 Dmitry Yakushin, Toro.	3.00	2.00	.50
173 Scott Hannan, SanJ.	3.00	2.00	.50
174 David Tanabe, Caro.	3.00	2.00	.50
175 Jiri Fischer, Detr.	3.00	2.00	.50
176 Dimitri Nabokov, NYIs.	3.00	2.00	.50
177 Ivan Novoseltsev, Flor.	3.00	2.00	.50
178 M. Fernandez (G), MinW.	5.00	4.00	1.00
179 M. Balmochnykh, Anah.	3.00	2.00	.50
180 Brian Campbell, Buff.	3.00	2.00	.50
181 Sergei Varlamov, Calg.	3.00	2.00	.50
182 V. Nieminen, Colo. RC	**30.00**	**20.00**	**12.00**
183 Colin White, NJer. RC	**10.00**	**8.00**	**5.00**
184 Mike Fisher, Otta.	3.00	2.00	.50
185 Matt Elich, Tamp. RC	**10.00**	**8.00**	**5.00**
186 Zenith Komarniski, Vanc.	3.00	2.00	.50
187 Eric Nickulas, Bost. RC	**6.00**	**5.00**	**3.00**
188 Steve McCarthy, Chic.	3.00	2.00	.50
189 Jason Krog, NYIs.	3.00	2.00	.50
190 Robert Esche (G), Phoe.	3.00	2.00	.50
191 Adam Mair, Toro.	3.00	2.00	.50
192 Ladislav Nagy, SLou.	3.00	2.00	1.00
193 Vyshedkevich, Atla. RC	**10.00**	**8.00**	**5.00**
194 Steve Bégin, Calg.	3.00	2.00	1.00
195 Brad Ference, Flor.	3.00	2.00	.50
196 Andy Delmore, Phil.	3.00	2.00	.50
197 Brent Sopel, Vanc. RC	**10.00**	**8.00**	**5.00**
198 E. Nabokov (G), SanJ.	7.00	6.00	1.50
199 D. Gosselin, Nash. RC	**6.00**	**5.00**	**3.00**
200 Tavis Hansen, Phoe.	3.00	2.00	.50
201 Ray Giroux, NYIs.	3.00	2.00	.50
202 Serge Aubin, Colu. RC	**10.00**	**8.00**	**5.00**
203 Shane Willis, Caro.	3.00	2.00	1.00
204 Vitaly Vishnevski, Anah.	3.00	2.00	.50
205 Richard Jackman, Dall.	3.00	2.00	.50
206 Petr Schastlivy, Otta.	3.00	2.00	.50
207 Ryan Bonni, Vanc.	3.00	2.00	.50
208 Alexei Tezikov, Wash.	3.00	2.00	.50
209 Henrik Sedin, Vanc.	5.00	4.00	2.00
210 Mike Ribeiro, Mont.	4.00	3.00	.50
211 Darryl Laplante, MinW.	3.00	2.00	.50
212 Kyle Calder, Chic.	3.00	2.00	.50
213 Dimitri Kalinin, Buff.	3.00	2.00	.50
214 J-S Giguère (G), Anah.	10.00	8.00	2.00
215 W. Mitchell, NJer. RC	**10.00**	**8.00**	**5.00**
216 Valiquette (G), NYIs. RC	**10.00**	**8.00**	**5.00**
217 Brian Willsie, Colo.	3.00	2.00	.50
218 Jarkko Ruutu, Vanc.	3.00	2.00	.50
219 Jonathan Sim, Dall.	3.00	2.00	.50
220 Jonathan Girard, Bost.	3.00	2.00	.50
221 Ron Tugnutt (G), Colu.	5.00	4.00	1.00
222 Lyle Odelein, Colu.	3.00	2.00	.50
223 J-L Grand-Pierre, Colu.	3.00	2.00	.50
224 Geoff Sanderson, Colu.	3.00	2.00	.50
225 Robert Kron, Colu.	3.00	2.00	.50
226 Kevin Dineen, Colu.	3.00	2.00	.50
227 Kevyn Adams, Colu.	3.00	2.00	.50
228 Tyler Wright, Colu.	3.00	2.00	.50
229 Jamie Pushor, Colu.	3.00	2.00	.50
230 David Vyborny, Colu.	3.00	2.00	.50
231 J. McLennan (G), MinW.	3.00	2.00	.50
232 Jeff Nielsen, MinW.	3.00	2.00	.50
233 Scott Pellerin, MinW.	3.00	2.00	.50
234 Darby Hendrickson, MinW.	3.00	2.00	.50
235 Jim Dowd, MinW.	3.00	2.00	.50
236 Filip Kuba, MinW.	3.00	2.00	.50
237 Stacy Roest, MinW.	3.00	2.00	.50
238 Sean O'Donnell, MinW.	3.00	2.00	.50
239 Aaron Gavey, MinW.	3.00	2.00	.50
240 Sergei Krivokrasov, MinW.	3.00	2.00	.50

ROOKIES

Rookie	TR25	OR35	T1250
241 Justin Williams RC	**100.00**	**65.00**	**10.00**
242 Marian Gaborik RC	**375.00**	**270.00**	**30.00**
243 Marty Turco (G) RC	**180.00**	**125.00**	**15.00**
244 D. Aebischer (G) RC	**100.00**	**65.00**	**10.00**
245 Rostislav Klesla. RC	**175.00**	**150.00**	**10.00**
246 Petr Hubacek RC	**30.00**	**21.00**	**6.00**
247 Scott Hartnell RC	**70.00**	**50.00**	**6.00**
248 Martin Havlat RC	**240.00**	**160.00**	**15.00**
249 Steven Reinprech. RC	**100.00**	**80.00**	**10.00**
250 A. Raycroft (G) RC	**70.00**	**50.00**	**6.00**
251 Rick DiPietro (G) RC	**150.00**	**120.00**	**15.00**
Rookie • Blue	**TR25**	**OR35**	**T1250**
241 Justin Williams RC	**100.00**	**65.00**	**10.00**
242 Marian Gaborik RC	**375.00**	**270.00**	**30.00**
243 Marty Turco (G) RC	**180.00**	**125.00**	**15.00**
244 D. Aebischer (G) RC	**100.00**	**65.00**	**10.00**
245 Rostislav Klesla. RC	**175.00**	**150.00**	**10.00**
246 Petr Hubacek RC	**30.00**	**20.00**	**6.00**
247 Scott Hartnell RC	**70.00**	**50.00**	**6.00**
248 Martin Havlat RC	**240.00**	**160.00**	**15.00**
249 Steven Reinprech. RC	**100.00**	**80.00**	**10.00**
250 A. Raycroft (G) RC	**70.00**	**50.00**	**6.00**
251 Rick DiPietro (G) RC	**150.00**	**120.00**	**15.00**
Rookie • Red	**TR25**	**OR35**	**T1250**
241 Justin Williams RC	**100.00**	**65.00**	**10.00**
242 Marian Gaborik RC	**375.00**	**270.00**	**30.00**
243 Marty Turco (G) RC	**180.00**	**125.00**	**15.00**
244 D. Aebischer (G) RC	**100.00**	**65.00**	**10.00**
245 Rostislav Klesla. RC	**175.00**	**150.00**	**10.00**
246 Petr Hubacek RC	**30.00**	**20.00**	**6.00**
247 Scott Hartnell RC	**70.00**	**50.00**	**6.00**
248 Martin Havlat RC	**240.00**	**160.00**	**15.00**
249 Steven Reinprech. RC	**100.00**	**80.00**	**10.00**
250 A. Raycroft (G) RC	**70.00**	**50.00**	**6.00**
251 Rick DiPietro (G) RC	**150.00**	**120.00**	**15.00**

1000-POINT CLUB REFRACTOR

Insert Set (16 cards):	200.00
Insert (1:250 Retail)	MT
1 Mark Messier, Vanc.	18.00
2 Steve Yzerman, Detr.	45.00
3 Ron Francis, Caro.	11.00
4 Paul Coffey, Caro.	11.00
5 Raymond Bourque, Colo.	22.00
6 Doug Gilmour, Buff.	11.00
7 Adam Oates, Wash.	8.00
8 Larry Murphy, Detr.	8.00
9 Dave Andréychuk, Colo.	8.00
10 Luc Robitaille, LosA.	15.00
11 Phil Housley, Calg.	8.00
12 Brett Hull, Dall.	18.00
13 Al MacInnis, SLou.	8.00
14 Pierre Turgeon, SLou.	8.00
15 Joe Sakic, Colo.	30.00
16 Pat Verbeek, Detr.	8.00

COMBOS

There are two versions: the regular insert (1:20 packs) and the Refractor parallel (1:200 packs).

Insert Set (10 cards):	120.00	50.00
Inserts	TCR	TC
TC1 V. Bure / P. Bure	6.00	3.00
TC2 P. Kariya / T. Selänne	12.00	6.00
TC3 T. Amonte / J. LeClair	8.00	4.00
TC4 D. Hasek / C. Joseph	12.00	6.00
TC5 P. Forsberg / M. Modano	14.00	6.00
TC6 R. Bourque / C. Pronger	10.00	4.00
TC7 J. Thornton / V. Lecavalier	12.00	6.00
TC8 P. Roy / M. Brodeur	28.00	14.00
TC9 B. Hull / S. Yzerman	20.00	10.00
TC10 J. Jagr / M. Lemieux	24.00	12.00

COMMEMORATIVE SERIES

There are two versions: the regular insert (1:18 packs) and the Refractor parallel (1:180 packs).

Insert Set (23 cards):	400.00	175.00
Player	CSR	CS
1 Mario Lemieux [85-86 Topps]	30.00	12.00
2 Mario Lemieux [85-86 OPC]	30.00	12.00
3 Mario Lemieux [86-87 Topps]	20.00	10.00
4 Mario Lemieux [86-87 OPC]	20.00	10.00
5 Mario Lemieux [87-88 Topps]	20.00	10.00
6 Mario Lemieux [87-88 OPC]	20.00	10.00
7 Mario Lemieux [88-89 Topps]	20.00	10.00
8 Mario Lemieux [88-89 OPC]	20.00	10.00
9 Mario Lemieux [89-90 Topps]	20.00	10.00
10 Mario Lemieux [89-90 OPC]	20.00	10.00
11 Mario Lemieux [90-91 Topps]	20.00	10.00
12 Mario Lemieux [90-91 OPC]	20.00	10.00
13 Mario Lemieux [90-91 OPC Premier]	20.00	10.00
14 Mario Lemieux [91-92 Topps]	20.00	10.00
15 Mario Lemieux [91-92 OPC]	20.00	10.00
16 Mario Lemieux [92-93 Topps]	20.00	10.00
17 Mario Lemieux [92-93 OPC]	20.00	10.00
18 Mario Lemieux [93-94 Topps Premier]	20.00	10.00
19 Mario Lemieux [93-94 OPC Premier]	20.00	10.00
20 Mario Lemieux [94-95 Topps Premier]	20.00	10.00
21 Mario Lemieux [94-95 OPC Premier]	20.00	10.00
22 Mario Lemieux [95-96 Topps]	20.00	10.00
23 Mario Lemieux [96-97 Topps]	20.00	10.00

HOBBY MASTER REFRACTOR

Insert Set (10 cards):	230.00
Insert (1:400 Hobby)	HMR
HM1 Martin Brodeur (G), NJer.	30.00
HM2 Pavel Bure, Flor.	15.00
HM3 Peter Forsberg, Colo.	25.00
HM4 Dominik Hasek (G), Buff.	20.00
HM5 Jaromir Jagr, Pitt.	20.00
HM6 Curtis Joseph (G), Toro.	20.00
HM7 Paul Kariya, Anah.	25.00
HM8 Mike Modano, Dall.	20.00
HM9 Patrick Roy (G), Colo.	60.00
HM10 Steve Yzerman, Detr.	45.00

ROCKET'S FLARE

There are two versions: the regular insert (1:14 packs) and the Refractor parallel (1:140 packs).

Insert Set (10 cards):	50.00	25.00
Inserts	RFR	RF
RF1 Pavel Bure, Flor.	6.00	3.00
RF2 Paul Kariya, Anah.	10.00	5.00
RF3 John LeClair, Phil.	6.00	3.00
RF4 Jaromir Jagr, Pitt.	7.00	3.00
RF5 Luc Robitaille, LosA.	6.00	3.00
RF6 Milan Hejduk, Colo.	6.00	3.00
RF7 Tony Amonte, Chic.	6.00	3.00
RF8 Patrik Elias, NJer.	6.00	3.00
RF9 Miroslav Satan, Buff.	6.00	3.00
RF10 Teemu Selänne, Anah.	6.00	3.00

2000 - 01 TOPPS GOLD LABEL

This series was released in April 2001. All 115 base cards are available as either a Class 1, a Class 2 or a Class 3 card; each Class version has a gold parallel. For the Class 1 series, base cards 1-100 are seeded regularly while Gold cards 1-100 are each limited to 399 copies; Class 1 rookie cards 101-115 are each limited to 999 copies while Gold rookie cards 101-115 are each limited to 99 copies. For the Class 2 series, base cards 101-100 are each seeded 1:4 packs while Gold cards 1-100 are each limited to 299 copies; Class 2 rookie cards 101-115 are each limited to 666 copies while Gold rookie cards 101-115 are each limited to 66 copies. For the Class 3 series, base cards 101-100 are each seeded 1:8 packs while Gold cards 1-100 are each limited to 199 copies; Class 3 rookie cards 101-115 are each limited to 333 copies while Gold rookie cards 101-115 are each limited to 33 copies.

Class 1 Shell Set (100 cards):	-	75.00
Class 1 Set (115 cards):	700.00	175.00
Common Player:	1.00	.35
Player	G399	Reg.
1 Raymond Bourque, Colo.	7.00	2.00
2 Brendan Shanahan, Detr.	6.00	2.00
3 Mark Recchi, Phil.	2.00	.50
4 Olaf Kölzig (G), Wash.	3.00	1.00
5 Brett Hull, Dall.	6.00	2.00
6 Valeri Bure, Calg.	2.00	.50
7 Joe Thornton, Bost.	7.00	2.00
8 Pavel Bure, Flor.	5.00	1.50
9 Jeff Hackett (G), Mont.	2.00	.50
10 Patrik Elias, NJer.	5.00	1.50
11 Marian Hossa, Otta.	6.00	2.00
12 Patrick Marleau, SanJ.	3.00	.50
13 Markus Näslund, Vanc.	6.00	2.00
14 Jaromir Jagr, Pitt.	6.00	2.00
15 Tim Connolly, NYIs.	2.00	.50
16 Zigmund Palffy, LosA.	3.00	1.00
17 Peter Forsberg, Colo.	8.00	2.50
18 Byron Dafoe (G), Bost.	2.00	.50
19 Patrik Stefan, Atla.	2.00	.50
20 Arturs Irbe (G), Caro.	2.00	.50
21 Jocelyn Thibault (G), Chic.	2.00	.50
22 Bill Guerin, Bost.	2.00	.50
23 Keith Primeau, Phil.	2.00	.50
24 Mats Sundin, Toro.	6.00	2.00
25 Adam Oates, Wash.	2.00	.50
26 Owen Nolan, SanJ.	3.00	1.00
27 Mike Richter (G), NYRa.	3.00	.50
28 Luc Robitaille, LosA.	5.00	1.50
29 Chris Drury, Colo.	3.00	1.00
30 Maxim Afinogenov, Buff.	2.00	.50
31 Jarome Iginla, Calg.	5.00	1.50
32 Joe Nieuwendyk, Dall.	2.00	.50
33 Maxim Sushinsky, MinW.	1.00	.50
34 Daniel Alfredsson, Otta.	3.00	1.00
35 Pierre Turgeon, SLou.	2.00	.50
36 Jason Allison, Bost.	3.00	1.00
37 Mario Lemieux, Pitt.	18.00	6.00
38 Sergei Fedorov, Detr.	6.00	2.00
39 Paul Kariya, Anah.	8.00	2.50
40 Scott Stevens, NJer.	2.00	.50
41 Keith Tkachuk, Phoe.	3.00	1.00
42 Curtis Joseph (G), Toro.	6.00	2.00
43 Peter Bondra, Wash.	3.00	1.00
44 Roman Turek (G), SLou.	3.00	.50
45 Alexei Kovalev, Pitt.	3.00	1.00
46 Brian Boucher (G), Phil.	2.00	.50
47 Mark Messier, NYRa.	6.00	2.00
48 Saku Koivu, Mont.	5.00	1.50
49 Tommy Salo (G), Edmo.	2.00	.50
50 Ron Tugnutt (G), Colu.	2.00	.50
51 Patrick Roy (G), Colo.	18.00	6.00
52 Fred Brathwaite (G), Calg.	2.00	.50
53 Donald Audette, Atla.	2.00	.50
54 Doug Gilmour, Buff.	3.00	1.00
55 Alexander Mogilny, NJer.	3.00	.50
56 John LeClair, Phil.	5.00	1.50
57 Scott A. Young, SLou.	2.00	.50
58 Jeff Friesen, SanJ.	2.00	.50
59 Simon Gagné, Phil.	5.00	1.50
60 Theoren Fleury, NYRa.	3.00	1.00
61 Scott Gomez, NJer.	2.00	.50
62 Guy Hebert (G), Anah.	1.00	.35
63 Roberto Luongo (G), Flor.	5.00	1.50
64 Mike Modano, Dall.	6.00	2.00
65 Joe Sakic, Colo.	10.00	3.00
66 Dominik Hasek (G), Buff.	6.00	2.00
67 Pavol Demitra, SLou.	2.00	.50
68 Daniel Sedin, Vanc.	2.00	1.50
69 Vincent Lecavalier, Tamp.	6.00	2.00
70 Jeremy Roenick, Phoe.	5.00	1.50
71 Martin Brodeur (G), NJer.	10.00	3.00
72 Rob Blake, LosA.	3.00	1.00
73 Ed Belfour (G), Dall.	6.00	2.00
74 Tony Amonte, Chic.	3.00	1.00
75 Miroslav Satan, Buff.	2.00	.50
76 Alexei Yashin, Otta.	3.00	1.00
77 Henrik Sedin, Vanc.	2.00	1.50
78 David Legwand, Nash.	2.00	.50
79 Steve Yzerman, Detr.	15.00	4.50
80 Ron Francis, Caro.	3.00	1.00
81 Milan Hejduk, Colo.	5.00	1.50
82 Teemu Selänne, Anah.	5.00	1.50
83 Brad Isbister, NYIs.	1.00	.35
84 Jean-Sébastien Aubin (G), Pitt.	1.00	.35
85 Chris Pronger, SLou.	3.00	1.00
86 Nicklas Lidström, Detr.	3.00	1.00
87 Brad Richards, Tamp.	3.00	1.50
88 Brent Johnson (G), SLou.	2.00	1.50
89 Oleg Saprykin, Calg.	1.00	.35
90 Anson Carter, Edmo.	2.00	.50
91 Brian Leetch, NYRa.	3.00	1.00

☐☐ 92 Evgeni Nabokov, SanJ.	3.00	1.00
☐☐ 93 Ian Laperrière, LosA.	1.00	.35
☐☐ 94 Peter White, Phil.	1.00	.35
☐☐ 95 Wes Walz, MinW.	1.00	.35
☐☐ 96 Jason Arnott, NJer.	3.00	.50
☐☐ 97 Tommy Albelin, Calg.	1.00	.35
☐☐ 98 Jeff Toms, NYIs.	1.00	.35
☐☐ 99 Brad Brown, NYRa.	1.00	.35
☐☐ 100 Garry Valk, Toro.	1.00	.35

CLASS 1 ROOKIE

Rookie	G99	R999
☐☐ **101 Andrew Raycroft (G), Bost. RC**	**24.00**	**6.00**
☐☐ **102 Marian Gaborik, MinW. RC**	**140.00**	**30.00**
☐☐ **103 David Aebischer (G), Colo. RC**	**30.00**	**10.00**
☐☐ **104 Scott Hartnell, Nash. RC**	**24.00**	**6.00**
☐☐ **105 Marty Turco (G), Dall. RC**	**60.00**	**15.00**
☐☐ **106 Justin Williams, Phil. RC**	**30.00**	**10.00**
☐☐ **107 Steven Reinprecht, LosA. RC**	**40.00**	**10.00**
☐☐ **108 Josef Vasicek, Caro. RC**	**24.00**	**6.00**
☐☐ **109 Martin Havlat, Otta. RC**	**80.00**	**15.00**
☐☐ **110 Rostislav Klesla, Colu. RC**	**75.00**	**10.00**
☐☐ **111 Jani Hurme (G), Otta. RC**	**20.00**	**6.00**
☐☐ **112 Rick DiPietro (G), NYIs. RC**	**60.00**	**15.00**
☐☐ **113 Alexandre Kharitonov, Tamp. RC**	**10.00**	**6.00**
☐☐ **114 Tyler Bouck, Dall. RC**	**16.00**	**6.00**
☐☐ **115 Roman Cechmanek (G), Phil. RC**	**40.00**	**10.00**

CLASS 2

Class 2 Set (115 cards):	**1,200**	**500.00**
Common Player:	**2.00**	**1.00**
Player	**G299**	**Reg.**
☐☐ 1 Raymond Bourque, Colo.	18.00	6.00
☐☐ 2 Brendan Shanahan, Detr.	14.00	5.00
☐☐ 3 Mark Recchi, Phil.	6.00	2.00
☐☐ 4 Olaf Kölzig (G), Wash.	9.00	3.00
☐☐ 5 Brett Hull, Dall.	14.00	5.00
☐☐ 6 Valeri Bure, Calg.	4.00	1.00
☐☐ 7 Joe Thornton, Bost.	18.00	6.00
☐☐ 8 Pavel Bure, Flor.	12.00	4.00
☐☐ 9 Jeff Hackett (G), Mont.	4.00	1.00
☐☐ 10 Patrik Elias, NJer.	12.00	4.00
☐☐ 11 Marian Hossa, Otta.	15.00	5.00
☐☐ 12 Patrick Marleau, SanJ.	7.00	2.00
☐☐ 13 Markus Näslund, Vanc.	15.00	5.00
☐☐ 14 Jaromir Jagr, Pitt.	14.00	5.00
☐☐ 15 Tim Connolly, NYIs.	6.00	2.00
☐☐ 16 Zigmund Palffy, LosA.	9.00	3.00
☐☐ 17 Peter Forsberg, Colo.	20.00	7.00
☐☐ 18 Byron Dafoe (G), Bost.	6.00	2.00
☐☐ 19 Patrik Stefan, Atla.	4.00	1.00
☐☐ 20 Arturs Irbe (G), Caro.	6.00	2.00
☐☐ 21 Jocelyn Thibault (G), Chic.	6.00	2.00
☐☐ 22 Bill Guerin, Bost.	6.00	2.00
☐☐ 23 Keith Primeau, Phil.	6.00	2.00
☐☐ 24 Mats Sundin, Toro.	14.00	5.00
☐☐ 25 Adam Oates, Wash.	6.00	2.00
☐☐ 26 Owen Nolan, SanJ.	9.00	3.00
☐☐ 27 Mike Richter (G), NYRa.	7.00	2.00
☐☐ 28 Luc Robitaille, LosA.	12.00	4.00
☐☐ 29 Chris Drury, Colo.	9.00	3.00
☐☐ 30 Maxim Afinogenov, Buff.	6.00	2.00
☐☐ 31 Jarome Iginla, Calg.	12.00	4.00
☐☐ 32 Joe Nieuwendyk, Dall.	6.00	2.00
☐☐ 33 Maxim Sushinsky, MinW.	2.00	1.00
☐☐ 34 Daniel Alfredsson, Otta.	9.00	3.00
☐☐ 35 Pierre Turgeon, SLou.	6.00	2.00
☐☐ 36 Jason Allison, Bost.	9.00	3.00
☐☐ 37 Mario Lemieux, Pitt.	45.00	15.00
☐☐ 38 Sergei Fedorov, Detr.	15.00	5.00
☐☐ 39 Paul Kariya, Anah.	21.00	7.00
☐☐ 40 Scott Stevens, NJer.	6.00	2.00
☐☐ 41 Keith Tkachuk, Phoe.	9.00	3.00
☐☐ 42 Curtis Joseph (G), Toro.	14.00	5.00
☐☐ 43 Peter Bondra, Wash.	9.00	3.00
☐☐ 44 Roman Turek (G), SLou.	7.00	2.00
☐☐ 45 Alexei Kovalev, Pitt.	9.00	3.00
☐☐ 46 Brian Boucher (G), Phil.	4.00	1.00
☐☐ 47 Mark Messier, NYRa.	14.00	5.00
☐☐ 48 Saku Koivu, Mont.	12.00	4.00
☐☐ 49 Tommy Salo (G), Edmo.	6.00	2.00
☐☐ 50 Ron Tugnutt (G), Colu.	6.00	2.00
☐☐ 51 Patrick Roy (G), Colo.	45.00	15.00
☐☐ 52 Fred Brathwaite (G), Calg.	4.00	1.00
☐☐ 53 Donald Audette, Atla.	6.00	2.00
☐☐ 54 Doug Gilmour, Buff.	9.00	3.00
☐☐ 55 Alexander Mogilny, NJer.	7.00	2.00
☐☐ 56 John LeClair, Phil.	12.00	4.00
☐☐ 57 Scott A. Young, SLou.	4.00	1.00
☐☐ 58 Jeff Friesen, SanJ.	4.00	1.00
☐☐ 59 Simon Gagné, Phil.	12.00	4.00
☐☐ 60 Theoren Fleury, NYRa.	9.00	3.00
☐☐ 61 Scott Gomez, NJer.	6.00	2.00
☐☐ 62 Guy Hebert (G), Anah.	3.00	1.00
☐☐ 63 Roberto Luongo (G), Flor.	12.00	4.00
☐☐ 64 Mike Modano, Dall.	15.00	5.00
☐☐ 65 Joe Sakic, Colo.	24.00	8.00
☐☐ 66 Dominik Hasek (G), Buff.	14.00	5.00
☐☐ 67 Pavol Demitra, SLou.	6.00	2.00
☐☐ 68 Daniel Sedin, Vanc.	6.00	2.00
☐☐ 69 Vincent Lecavalier, Tamp.	14.00	5.00
☐☐ 70 Jeremy Roenick, Phoe.	12.00	4.00
☐☐ 71 Martin Brodeur (G), NJer.	24.00	8.00
☐☐ 72 Rob Blake, LosA.	9.00	3.00
☐☐ 73 Ed Belfour (G), Dall.	15.00	5.00
☐☐ 74 Tony Amonte, Chic.	9.00	3.00
☐☐ 75 Miroslav Satan, Buff.	4.00	1.00
☐☐ 76 Alexei Yashin, Otta.	9.00	3.00
☐☐ 77 Henrik Sedin, Vanc.	6.00	2.00
☐☐ 78 David Legwand, Nash.	6.00	2.00
☐☐ 79 Steve Yzerman, Detr.	36.00	12.00
☐☐ 80 Ron Francis, Caro.	9.00	3.00
☐☐ 81 Milan Hejduk, Colo.	12.00	4.00
☐☐ 82 Teemu Selänne, Anah.	12.00	4.00
☐☐ 83 Brad Isbister, NYIs.	3.00	1.00
☐☐ 84 Jean-Sébastien Aubin (G), Pitt.	3.00	1.00
☐☐ 85 Chris Pronger, SLou.	9.00	3.00
☐☐ 86 Nicklas Lidström, Detr.	9.00	3.00
☐☐ 87 Brad Richards, Tamp.	7.00	2.00
☐☐ 88 Brent Johnson (G), SLou.	6.00	3.00
☐☐ 89 Oleg Saprykin, Calg.	3.00	1.00
☐☐ 90 Anson Carter, Edmo.	6.00	2.00
☐☐ 91 Brian Leetch, NYRa.	9.00	3.00
☐☐ 92 Evgeni Nabokov, SanJ.	9.00	3.00
☐☐ 93 Ian Laperrière, LosA.	2.00	1.00
☐☐ 94 Peter White, Phil.	2.00	1.00
☐☐ 95 Wes Walz, MinW.	3.00	1.00
☐☐ 96 Jason Arnott, NJer.	7.00	2.00
☐☐ 97 Tommy Albelin, Calg.	2.00	1.00
☐☐ 98 Jeff Toms, NYIs.	2.00	1.00
☐☐ 99 Brad Brown, NYRa.	2.00	1.00
☐☐ 100 Garry Valk, Toro.	2.00	1.00

CLASS 2 ROOKIE

Rookie	G66	R666
☐☐ **101 Andrew Raycroft (G), Bost. RC**	**35.00**	**15.00**
☐☐ **102 Marian Gaborik, MinW. RC**	**150.00**	**75.00**
☐☐ **103 David Aebischer (G), Colo. RC**	**45.00**	**20.00**
☐☐ **104 Scott Hartnell, Nash. RC**	**35.00**	**15.00**
☐☐ **105 Marty Turco (G), Dall. RC**	**90.00**	**45.00**
☐☐ **106 Justin Williams, Phil. RC**	**45.00**	**20.00**
☐☐ **107 Steven Reinprecht, LosA. RC**	**45.00**	**30.00**
☐☐ **108 Josef Vasicek, Caro. RC**	**35.00**	**15.00**
☐☐ **109 Martin Havlat, Otta. RC**	**90.00**	**60.00**
☐☐ **110 Rostislav Klesla, Colu. RC**	**90.00**	**30.00**
☐☐ **111 Jani Hurme (G), Otta. RC**	**35.00**	**15.00**
☐☐ **112 Rick DiPietro (G), NYIs. RC**	**70.00**	**45.00**
☐☐ **113 Alexandre Kharitonov, Tamp. RC**	**15.00**	**8.00**
☐☐ **114 Tyler Bouck, Dall. RC**	**20.00**	**10.00**
☐☐ **115 Roman Cechmanek (G), Phil. RC**	**60.00**	**30.00**

CLASS 3

Class 3 Set (115 cards):	**2,000**	**900.00**
Common Player:	**6.00**	**4.00**
Player	**G199**	**Reg.**
☐☐ 1 Raymond Bourque, Colo.	36.00	12.00
☐☐ 2 Brendan Shanahan, Detr.	30.00	10.00
☐☐ 3 Mark Recchi, Phil.	12.00	4.00
☐☐ 4 Olaf Kölzig (G), Wash.	18.00	6.00
☐☐ 5 Brett Hull, Dall.	30.00	10.00
☐☐ 6 Valeri Bure, Calg.	9.00	4.00
☐☐ 7 Joe Thornton, Bost.	36.00	12.00
☐☐ 8 Pavel Bure, Flor.	24.00	8.00
☐☐ 9 Jeff Hackett (G), Mont.	9.00	4.00
☐☐ 10 Patrik Elias, NJer.	24.00	8.00
☐☐ 11 Marian Hossa, Otta.	30.00	10.00
☐☐ 12 Patrick Marleau, SanJ.	14.00	4.00
☐☐ 13 Markus Näslund, Vanc.	30.00	10.00
☐☐ 14 Jaromir Jagr, Pitt.	30.00	10.00
☐☐ 15 Tim Connolly, NYIs.	12.00	4.00
☐☐ 16 Zigmund Palffy, LosA.	18.00	6.00
☐☐ 17 Peter Forsberg, Colo.	42.00	14.00
☐☐ 18 Byron Dafoe (G), Bost.	12.00	4.00
☐☐ 19 Patrik Stefan, Atla.	9.00	4.00
☐☐ 20 Arturs Irbe (G), Caro.	12.00	4.00
☐☐ 21 Jocelyn Thibault (G), Chic.	12.00	4.00
☐☐ 22 Bill Guerin, Bost.	12.00	4.00
☐☐ 23 Keith Primeau, Phil.	12.00	4.00
☐☐ 24 Mats Sundin, Toro.	30.00	10.00
☐☐ 25 Adam Oates, Wash.	12.00	4.00
☐☐ 26 Owen Nolan, SanJ.	18.00	6.00
☐☐ 27 Mike Richter (G), NYRa.	14.00	4.00
☐☐ 28 Luc Robitaille, LosA.	24.00	8.00
☐☐ 29 Chris Drury, Colo.	18.00	6.00
☐☐ 30 Maxim Afinogenov, Buff.	12.00	4.00
☐☐ 31 Jarome Iginla, Calg.	24.00	8.00
☐☐ 32 Joe Nieuwendyk, Dall.	12.00	4.00
☐☐ 33 Maxim Sushinsky, MinW.	6.00	4.00
☐☐ 34 Daniel Alfredsson, Otta.	18.00	6.00
☐☐ 35 Pierre Turgeon, SLou.	12.00	4.00
☐☐ 36 Jason Allison, Bost.	18.00	6.00
☐☐ 37 Mario Lemieux, Pitt.	9.00	30.00
☐☐ 38 Sergei Fedorov, Detr.	30.00	10.00
☐☐ 39 Paul Kariya, Anah.	40.00	14.00
☐☐ 40 Scott Stevens, NJer.	12.00	4.00
☐☐ 41 Keith Tkachuk, Phoe.	18.00	6.00
☐☐ 42 Curtis Joseph (G), Toro.	30.00	10.00
☐☐ 43 Peter Bondra, Wash.	18.00	6.00
☐☐ 44 Roman Turek (G), SLou.	14.00	4.00
☐☐ 45 Alexei Kovalev, Pitt.	18.00	6.00
☐☐ 46 Brian Boucher (G), Phil.	9.00	4.00
☐☐ 47 Mark Messier, NYRa.	30.00	10.00
☐☐ 48 Saku Koivu, Mont.	24.00	8.00
☐☐ 49 Tommy Salo (G), Edmo.	12.00	4.00
☐☐ 50 Ron Tugnutt (G), Colu.	12.00	4.00
☐☐ 51 Patrick Roy (G), Colo.	90.00	30.00
☐☐ 52 Fred Brathwaite (G), Calg.	9.00	4.00
☐☐ 53 Donald Audette, Atla.	12.00	4.00
☐☐ 54 Doug Gilmour, Buff.	18.00	6.00
☐☐ 55 Alexander Mogilny, NJer.	14.00	4.00
☐☐ 56 John LeClair, Phil.	24.00	8.00
☐☐ 57 Scott A. Young, SLou.	9.00	4.00
☐☐ 58 Jeff Friesen, SanJ.	9.00	4.00
☐☐ 59 Simon Gagné, Phil.	24.00	8.00
☐☐ 60 Theoren Fleury, NYRa.	18.00	6.00
☐☐ 61 Scott Gomez, NJer.	12.00	4.00
☐☐ 62 Guy Hebert (G), Anah.	7.00	4.00
☐☐ 63 Roberto Luongo (G), Flor.	24.00	8.00
☐☐ 64 Mike Modano, Dall.	30.00	10.00
☐☐ 65 Joe Sakic, Colo.	48.00	16.00
☐☐ 66 Dominik Hasek (G), Buff.	30.00	10.00
☐☐ 67 Pavol Demitra, SLou.	12.00	4.00
☐☐ 68 Daniel Sedin, Vanc.	12.00	4.00
☐☐ 69 Vincent Lecavalier, Tamp.	30.00	10.00
☐☐ 70 Jeremy Roenick, Phoe.	24.00	8.00
☐☐ 71 Martin Brodeur (G), NJer.	48.00	16.00
☐☐ 72 Rob Blake, LosA.	18.00	6.00
☐☐ 73 Ed Belfour (G), Dall.	30.00	10.00
☐☐ 74 Tony Amonte, Chic.	18.00	6.00
☐☐ 75 Miroslav Satan, Buff.	9.00	4.00
☐☐ 76 Alexei Yashin, Otta.	18.00	6.00
☐☐ 77 Henrik Sedin, Vanc.	12.00	4.00
☐☐ 78 David Legwand, Nash.	12.00	4.00
☐☐ 79 Steve Yzerman, Detr.	70.00	24.00
☐☐ 80 Ron Francis, Caro.	18.00	6.00
☐☐ 81 Milan Hejduk, Colo.	24.00	8.00
☐☐ 82 Teemu Selänne, Anah.	24.00	8.00
☐☐ 83 Brad Isbister, NYIs.	7.00	4.00
☐☐ 84 Jean-Sébastien Aubin (G), Pitt.	7.00	4.00
☐☐ 85 Chris Pronger, SLou.	18.00	6.00
☐☐ 86 Nicklas Lidström, Detr.	18.00	6.00
☐☐ 87 Brad Richards, Tamp.	14.00	4.00
☐☐ 88 Brent Johnson (G), SLou.	12.00	8.00
☐☐ 89 Oleg Saprykin, Calg.	7.00	4.00
☐☐ 90 Anson Carter, Edmo.	12.00	4.00
☐☐ 91 Brian Leetch, NYRa.	18.00	6.00
☐☐ 92 Evgeni Nabokov, SanJ.	18.00	6.00
☐☐ 93 Ian Laperrière, LosA.	6.00	4.00
☐☐ 94 Peter White, Phil.	6.00	4.00
☐☐ 95 Wes Walz, MinW.	7.00	4.00
☐☐ 96 Jason Arnott, NJer.	14.00	4.00
☐☐ 97 Tommy Albelin, Calg.	6.00	4.00
☐☐ 98 Jeff Toms, NYIs.	6.00	4.00
☐☐ 99 Brad Brown, NYRa.	6.00	4.00
☐☐ 100 Garry Valk, Toro.	6.00	4.00

CLASS 3 ROOKIE

Rookie	G33	R333
☐☐ **101 Andrew Raycroft (G), Bost. RC**	**45.00**	**25.00**
☐☐ **102 Marian Gaborik, MinW. RC**	**200.00**	**110.00**
☐☐ **103 David Aebischer (G), Colo. RC**	**65.00**	**35.00**
☐☐ **104 Scott Hartnell, Nash. RC**	**45.00**	**25.00**
☐☐ **105 Marty Turco (G), Dall. RC**	**120.00**	**65.00**
☐☐ **106 Justin Williams, Phil. RC**	**65.00**	**35.00**
☐☐ **107 Steven Reinprecht, LosA. RC**	**65.00**	**40.00**
☐☐ **108 Josef Vasicek, Caro. RC**	**45.00**	**25.00**
☐☐ **109 Martin Havlat, Otta. RC**	**120.00**	**100.00**
☐☐ **110 Rostislav Klesla, Colu. RC**	**120.00**	**40.00**
☐☐ **111 Jani Hurme (G), Otta. RC**	**45.00**	**25.00**
☐☐ **112 Rick DiPietro (G), NYIs. RC**	**95.00**	**60.00**
☐☐ **113 Alexandre Kharitonov, Tamp. RC**	**20.00**	**12.00**
☐☐ **114 Tyler Bouck, Dall. RC**	**30.00**	**15.00**
☐☐ **115 Roman Cechmanek (G), Phil. RC**	**80.00**	**45.00**

CERTIFIED AUTOGRAPH ISSUE

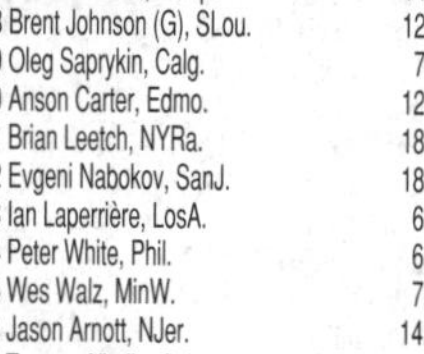

Insert Set (10 cards):	**250.00**
Autograph (1:57)	**GLA**
☐ Brian Boucher (G), Phil. ✍	20.00
☐ Brad Richards, Tamp. ✍	25.00
☐ Justin Williams, Phil. ✍	20.00
☐ Marian Gaborik, MinW. ✍	55.00
☐ Milan Kraft, Pitt. ✍	20.00
☐ Marty Turco (G), Dall. ✍	30.00
☐ Michael York, NYRa. ✍	20.00
☐ Raymond Bourque, Colo. ✍	75.00
☐ Scott Gomez, NJer. ✍	20.00
☐ Scott Hartnell, Nash. ✍	20.00

BEHIND THE MASK

There are two versions: the regular insert (1:7 packs) and a One to One parallel (#/1).

Insert Set (10 cards):	**40.00**
Inserts	**BTM**
☐☐ BTM1 Curtis Joseph (G), Toro.	5.00
☐☐ BTM2 Ed Belfour (G), Dall.	5.00
☐☐ BTM3 Dominik Hasek (G), Buff.	5.00
☐☐ BTM4 Martin Brodeur (G), NJer.	8.00
☐☐ BTM5 Brian Boucher (G), Phil.	2.00
☐☐ BTM6 Roman Turek (G), SLou.	2.00
☐☐ BTM7 Olaf Kölzig (G), Wash.	3.00
☐☐ BTM8 Patrick Roy (G), Colo.	15.00
☐☐ BTM9 Arturs Irbe (G), Caro.	2.00
☐☐ BTM10 Mike Richter (G), NYRa.	2.00

BULLION

Insert Set (10 cards):	**70.00**
Insert (1:21)	**B**
☐ B1 J. Arnott / M. Brodeur / S. Gomez	8.00
☐ B2 E. Belfour (G) / Br. Hull / M. Modano	10.00
☐ B3 S. Fedorov / B. Shanahan / S. Yzerman	14.00
☐ B4 R. Bourque / P. Forsberg / P. Roy	18.00
☐ B5 P. Demitra / C. Pronger / R. Turek	6.00
☐ B6 T. Domi / Cu. Joseph / M. Sundin	8.00
☐ B7 T. Numminen / J. Roenick / K. Tkachuk	6.00
☐ B8 J. Friesen / P. Marleau / O. Nolan	6.00
☐ B9 B. Leetch / M. Messier / M. Richter	6.00
☐ B10 M. Näslund / D. Sedin / H. Sedin	6.00

GAME JERSEY

Insert Set (6 cards):	**150.00**
Insert	**GLJ**
☐ GLJ-JL John LeClair, Phil. ✂	25.00
☐ GLJ-KT Keith Tkachuk, Phoe. ✂	25.00
☐ GLJ-MB Martin Brodeur (G), NJer. ✂	45.00
☐ GLJ-PF Peter Forsberg, Colo. ✂	40.00
☐ GLJ-PM Patrick Marleau, SanJ. ✂	25.00
☐ GLJ-SF Sergei Fedorov, Detr. ✂	30.00

GOLDEN GREATS

There are two versions: the regular insert (1:5 packs) and the One to One parallel (#/1).

Insert Set (15 cards):	**60.00**
Inserts	**GG**
☐☐ GG1 Pavel Bure, Flor.	4.00
☐☐ GG2 Paul Kariya, Anah.	7.00
☐☐ GG3 Jaromir Jagr, Pitt.	5.00
☐☐ GG4 John LeClair, Phil.	4.00
☐☐ GG5 Steve Yzerman, Detr.	12.00
☐☐ GG6 Brett Hull, Dall.	5.00
☐☐ GG7 Alexander Mogilny, NJer.	2.00
☐☐ GG8 Joe Sakic, Colo.	8.00
☐☐ GG9 Keith Tkachuk, Phoe.	3.00
☐☐ GG10 Teemu Selänne, Anah.	4.00
☐☐ GG11 Sergei Fedorov, Detr.	5.00
☐☐ GG12 Luc Robitaille, LosA.	4.00

☐☐ GG13 Mike Modano, Dall.	5.00
☐☐ GG14 Brendan Shanahan, Detr.	5.00
☐☐ GG15 Jeremy Roenick, Phoe.	4.00

NEW GENERATION

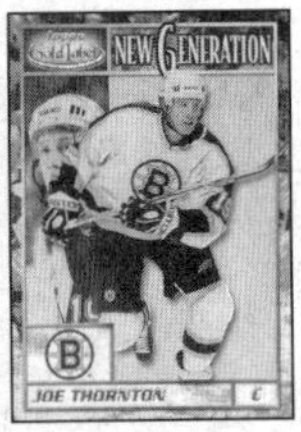

There are two versions: the regular insert (1:4 packs) and the One to One parallel (#/1).

Insert Set (15 cards):	50.00
Player	NG
☐☐ NG1 Scott Gomez, NJer.	3.00
☐☐ NG2 Vincent Lecavalier, Tamp.	6.00
☐☐ NG3 Joe Thornton, Bost.	6.00
☐☐ NG4 Alex Tanguay, Colo.	3.00
☐☐ NG5 Marian Hossa, Otta.	6.00
☐☐ NG6 Brad Stuart, SanJ.	3.00
☐☐ NG7 Henrik Sedin, Vanc.	3.00
☐☐ NG8 Marian Gaborik, MinW.	18.00
☐☐ NG9 Roberto Luongo (G), Flor.	4.00
☐☐ NG10 David Legwand, Nash.	3.00
☐☐ NG11 Daniel Sedin, Vanc.	3.00
☐☐ NG12 Patrik Stefan, Atla.	3.00
☐☐ NG13 Brian Boucher (G), Phil.	3.00
☐☐ NG14 Chris Drury, Colo.	3.00
☐☐ NG15 Tim Connolly, NYIs.	3.00

2000 - 01 TOPPS HERITAGE

This series was released in April 2001. The card design mimicks the original 1954-55 Topps hockey card design. Rookie cards 74-100 are limited to 1955 copies; cards 1-100 have a Chrome parallel limited to 555 copies.

Shell Set (220 cards):	-	60.00
Chrome Set (110 cards):	590.00	-
Complete Set (247 cards):	-	75.00
Common Player:	2.00	.30
Player	TC555	Reg.
☐☐ 1 Raymond Bourque, Colo.	10.00	1.50
☐☐ 2 Martin Brodeur (G), NJer.	14.00	2.00
☐☐ 3 Jaromir Jagr, Pitt.	8.00	1.50
☐☐ 4 Vincent Lecavalier, Tamp.	8.00	1.50
☐☐ 5 Olaf Kölzig (G), Wash.	5.00	.50
☐☐ 6 Alexei Yashin, Otta.	5.00	.50
☐☐ 7 Mark Messier, NYRa.	8.00	1.50
☐☐ 8 Paul Kariya, Anah.	12.00	2.00
☐☐ 9 Pavel Bure, Flor.	7.00	1.00
☐☐ 10 Steve Yzerman, Detr.	20.00	3.50
☐☐ 11 Patrik Stefan, Atla.	2.00	.30
☐☐ 12 Joe Thornton, Bost.	10.00	1.50
☐☐ 13 Mats Sundin, Toro.	8.00	1.50
☐☐ 14 Brett Hull, Dall.	8.00	1.50
☐☐ 15 Zigmund Palffy, LosA.	5.00	.50
☐☐ 16 Peter Bondra, Wash.	5.00	.50
☐☐ 17 Owen Nolan, SanJ.	5.00	.50
☐☐ 18 Tony Amonte, Chic.	5.00	.50
☐☐ 19 Henrik Sedin, Vanc.	3.00	1.00
☐☐ 20 Keith Tkachuk, Phoe.	5.00	.50
☐☐ 21 Tim Connolly, NYIs.	3.00	.50
☐☐ 22 Doug Weight, Edmo.	5.00	.50
☐☐ 23 Ed Belfour (G), Dall.	8.00	1.50
☐☐ 24 Patrick Roy (G), Colo.	25.00	4.50
☐☐ 25 Brad Richards, Tamp.	4.00	1.00
☐☐ 26 Dominik Hasek (G), Buff.	8.00	1.50
☐☐ 27 Brendan Shanahan, Detr.	8.00	1.50
☐☐ 28 Teemu Selänne, Anah.	7.00	1.00
☐☐ 29 Scott Gomez, NJer.	3.00	.50
☐☐ 30 John LeClair, Phil.	7.00	1.00
☐☐ 31 Chris Pronger, SLou.	5.00	.50
☐☐ 32 Ron Francis, Caro.	5.00	.50
☐☐ 33 Daniel Sedin, Vanc.	3.00	1.00
☐☐ 34 Curtis Joseph (G), Toro.	8.00	1.50
☐☐ 35 Roman Turek (G), SLou.	4.00	.50
☐☐ 36 Jeremy Roenick, Phoe.	7.00	1.00
☐☐ 37 Mark Recchi, Phil.	3.00	.50
☐☐ 38 Patrik Elias, NJer.	7.00	1.00
☐☐ 39 Saku Koivu, Mont.	7.00	1.00
☐☐ 40 Luc Robitaille, LosA.	7.00	1.00
☐☐ 41 Sergei Fedorov, Detr.	8.00	1.50
☐☐ 42 Peter Forsberg, Colo.	12.00	2.00
☐☐ 43 Milan Kraft, Pitt.	2.00	.50
☐☐ 44 Jason Allison, Bost.	5.00	.50
☐☐ 45 Mike Modano, Dall.	8.00	1.50
☐☐ 46 Roberto Luongo (G), Flor.	7.00	1.00
☐☐ 47 David Legwand, Nash.	3.00	.50
☐☐ 48 Pierre Turgeon, SLou.	3.00	.50
☐☐ 49 Maxime Ouellet (G), Phil.	2.00	.50
☐☐ 50 Oleg Saprykin, Calg.	2.00	.30
☐☐ 51 Pavol Demitra, SLou.	3.00	.50
☐☐ 52 Adam Oates, Wash.	3.00	.50
☐☐ 53 Doug Gilmour, Buff.	5.00	.50
☐☐ 54 Joe Sakic, Colo.	14.00	2.00
☐☐ 55 Daniel Alfredsson, Otta.	5.00	.50
☐☐ 56 Brian Leetch, NYRa.	5.00	.50
☐☐ 57 Bill Guerin, Bost.	3.00	.50
☐☐ 58 Brent Johnson (G), SLou.	3.00	1.00
☐☐ 59 Scott Stevens, NJer.	3.00	.50
☐☐ 60 Rob Blake, LosA.	5.00	.50
☐☐ 61 Nicklas Lidström, Detr.	5.00	.50
☐☐ 62 Milan Hejduk, Colo.	7.00	1.00
☐☐ 63 Arturs Irbe (G), Caro.	3.00	.50
☐☐ 64 Maxim Afinogenov, Buff.	3.00	.50
☐☐ 65 Taylor Pyatt, NYIs.	2.00	.50
☐☐ 66 Tommy Salo (G), Edmo.	3.00	.50
☐☐ 67 Theoren Fleury, NYRa.	5.00	.50
☐☐ 68 Marian Hossa, Otta.	8.00	1.50
☐☐ 69 Simon Gagné, Phil.	7.00	1.00
☐☐ 70 Jarome Iginla, Calg.	7.00	1.00
☐☐ 71 Alexander Mogilny, NJer.	4.00	.50
☐☐ 72 Chris Drury, Colo.	5.00	.50
☐☐ 73 Mario Lemieux, Pitt.	25.00	4.50
☐☐ **74 Petr Hubacek, Phil. RC**	**10.00**	**8.00**
☐☐ **75 Marty Turco (G), Dall. RC**	**48.00**	**40.00**
☐☐ **76 Rostislav Klesla, Colu. RC**	**18.00**	**15.00**
☐☐ **77 Martin Havlat, Otta. RC**	**.00**	**30.00**
☐☐ **78 David Aebischer (G), Colo. RC**	**18.00**	**15.00**
☐☐ **79 Reto von Arx, Chic. RC**	**10.00**	**8.00**
☐☐ **80 Mike Comrie, Edmo. RC**	**60.00**	**50.00**
☐☐ **81 Tomas Kloucek, NYRa. RC**	**10.00**	**8.00**
☐☐ **82 Steven Reinprecht, LosA. RC**	**18.00**	**15.00**
☐☐ **83 Brad Tapper, Atla. RC**	**10.00**	**8.00**
☐☐ **84 Petr Svoboda, Toro. RC**	**10.00**	**8.00**
☐☐ **85 Marian Gaborik, MinW. RC**	**.00**	**65.00**
☐☐ **86 Josef Vasicek, Caro. RC**	**12.00**	**10.00**
☐☐ **87 Lubomir Visnovsky, LosA. RC**	**10.00**	**8.00**
☐☐ **88 Roman Cechmanek (G), Phil. RC**	**24.00**	**20.00**
☐☐ **89 Reed Low, SLou. RC**	**10.00**	**8.00**
☐☐ **90 Jani Hurme (G), Otta. RC**	**12.00**	**10.00**
☐☐ **91 Petteri Nummelin, Colu. RC**	**10.00**	**8.00**
☐☐ **92 Colin White, NJer. RC**	**10.00**	**8.00**
☐☐ **93 Andrew Raycroft (G), Bost. RC**	**12.00**	**10.00**
☐☐ **94 Greg Classen, Nash. RC**	**10.00**	**8.00**
☐☐ **95 Alexandre Kharitonov, Tamp. RC**	**10.00**	**8.00**
☐☐ **96 Rick DiPietro (G), NYIs. RC**	**30.00**	**25.00**
☐☐ **97 Justin Williams, Phil. RC**	**18.00**	**15.00**
☐☐ **98 Éric Belanger, LosA. RC**	**10.00**	**8.00**
☐☐ **99 Scott Hartnell, Nash. RC**	**12.00**	**10.00**
☐☐ **100 Michel Riesen, Edmo. RC**	**10.00**	**8.00**
☐☐ 101 Brian Boucher (G), Phil.	2.50	.30
☐☐ 102 Mike Richter (G), NYRa.	4.00	.50
☐☐ 103 John Vanbiesbrouck (G), NYIs.	4.00	.50
☐☐ 104 Jamie McLennan (G), MinW.	2.00	.30
☐☐ 105 Andréi Markov, Mont.	2.00	.30
☐☐ 106 Ron Tugnutt (G), Colu.	3.50	.50
☐☐ 107 Jean-Sebastien Aubin (G), Pitt.	2.00	.30
☐☐ 108 Brad Stuart, SanJ.	3.50	.50
☐☐ 109 Gary Roberts, Toro.	3.50	.50
☐☐ 110 Rod Brind'Amour, Caro.	2.50	.30
☐ 111 Keith Primeau, Phil.	-	.50
☐ 112 Jeff Halpern, Wash.	-	.30
☐ 113 Jochen Hecht, SLou.	-	.30
☐ 114 Valeri Bure, Calg.	-	.30
☐ 115 Donald Audette, Atla.	-	.50
☐ 116 Brenden Morrow, Dall.	-	.30
☐ 117 Mike Mottau, NYRa.	-	.30
☐ 118 Kevin Weekes (G), Tamp.	-	.30
☐ 119 Jamie Storr (G), LosA.	-	.30
☐ 120 Shane Willis, Caro.	-	.50
☐ 121 Matt Cooke, Vanc.	-	.30
☐ 122 Martin Lapointe, Detr.	-	.50
☐ 123 Alexei Kovalev, Pitt.	-	.50
☐ 124 Félix Potvin (G), Vanc.	-	.50
☐ 125 Sean Burke (G), Phoe.	-	.50
☐ 126 Jeff Hackett (G), Mont.	-	.30
☐ 127 Brad Isbister, NYIs.	-	.30
☐ 128 Derian Hatcher, Dall.	-	.30
☐ 129 Marc Savard, Calg.	-	.30
☐ 130 Sergei Samsonov, Bost.	-	.50
☐ 131 Maxim Sushinsky, MinW.	-	.30
☐ 132 Radek Bonk, Otta.	-	.30
☐ 133 Mika Noronen (G), Buff.	-	.50
☐ 134 Adam Graves, NYRa.	-	.50
☐ 135 Sheldon Keefe, Tamp.	-	.50
☐ 136 Markus Näslund, Vanc.	-	1.50
☐ 137 Trevor Letowski, Phoe.	-	.30
☐ 138 Jeff Friesen, SanJ.	-	.30
☐ 139 Alex Tanguay, Colo.	-	.50
☐ 140 Byron Dafoe (G), Bost.	-	.50
☐ 141 Chris Osgood (G), Detr.	-	.50
☐ 142 Michael York, NYRa.	-	.30
☐ 143 Scott Young, SLou.	-	.30
☐ 144 Sami Kapanen, Caro.	-	.30
☐ 145 Evgeni Nabokov (G), SanJ.	-	.50
☐ 146 Brendan Morrison, Vanc.	-	.30
☐ 147 Joe Nieuwendyk, Dall.	-	.50
☐ 148 Tomi Kallio, Atla.	-	.30
☐ 149 Guy Hebert (G), Anah.	-	.30
☐ 150 Randy McKay, NJer.	-	.30
☐ 151 Mike Johnson, Tamp.	-	.30
☐ 152 Miroslav Satan, Buff.	-	.30
☐ 153 Patrick Marleau, SanJ.	-	.50
☐ 154 Jocelyn Thibault (G), Chic.	-	.50
☐ 155 Martin Straka, Pitt.	-	.30
☐ 156 Fred Brathwaite (G), Calg.	-	.30
☐ 157 Cliff Ronning, Nash.	-	.30
☐ 158 Denis Shvidki, Flor.	-	.30
☐ 159 Espen Knutsen, Colu.	-	.30
☐ 160 Alexei Zhamnov, Chic.	-	.30
☐ 161 Georges Laraque, Edmo.	-	.30
☐ 162 José Théodore (G), Mont.	-	1.50
☐ 163 Rick Tocchet, Phil.	-	.30
☐ 164 Donald Brashear, Vanc.	-	.30
☐ 165 Darren Langdon, Caro.	-	.30
☐ 166 Rob Ray, Buff.	-	.30
☐ 167 Matthew Barnaby, Pitt.	-	.30
☐ 168 Chris Simon, Wash.	-	.30
☐ 169 Ken Belanger, Bost.	-	.30
☐ 170 Tie Domi, Toro.	-	.30
☐ 171 Roman Hamrlik, NYIs.	-	.30
☐ 172 Olli Jokinen, Flor.	-	.30
☐ 173 Steve Rucchin, Anah.	-	.30
☐ 174 Jim Cummins, Anah.	-	.30
☐ 175 Tyson Nash, SLou.	-	.30
☐ 176 Scott Parker, Colo.	-	.30
☐ 177 Matt Johnson, MinW.	-	.30
☐ 178 Sandy McCarthy, NYRa.	-	.30
☐ 179 Daniel Cleary, Edmo.	-	.30
☐ 180 Michal Handzus, SLou.	-	.30
☐ 181 Nikolai Antropov, Toro.	-	.30
☐ 182 Scott Thornton, SanJ.	-	.30
☐ 183 Shane Doan, Phoe.	-	.30
☐ 184 Wade Redden, Otta.	-	.30
☐ 185 Ray Whitney, Flor.	-	.30
☐ 186 Teppo Numminen, Phoe.	-	.30
☐ 187 Pat Verbeek, Detr.	-	.30
☐ 188 Bobby Holik, NJer.	-	.30
☐ 189 Mike Dunham (G), Nash.	-	.50
☐ 190 Rob Niedermayer, Flor.	-	.30
☐ 191 Ray Ferraro, Atla.	-	.30
☐ 192 Steve Sullivan, Chic.	-	.30
☐ 193 Sergei Zubov, Dall.	-	.30
☐ 194 Scott Walker, Nash.	-	.30
☐ 195 Geoff Sanderson, Colu.	-	.30
☐ 196 Bob Probert, Chic.	-	.30
☐ 197 Andrew Brunette, Atla.	-	.30
☐ 198 Marty Murray, Calg.	-	.30
☐ 199 Steve Staios, Atla.	-	.30
☐ 200 Kay Whitmore (G), Bost.	-	.30
☐ 201 Jonas Hoglund, Toro.	-	.30
☐ 202 Niklas Andersson, Calg.	-	.30
☐ 203 Joaquin Gage (G), Edmo.	-	.30
☐ 204 Mike Ricci, SanJ.	-	.30
☐ 205 Bryan Helmer, Vanc.	-	.30
☐ 206 Patrick Traverse, Bost.	-	.30
☐ 207 Mike Rucinski, Caro.	-	.30
☐ 208 Brantt Myhres, Nash.	-	.30
☐ 209 Claude Lapointe, NYIs.	-	.30
☐ 210 Frank Musil, Edmo.	-	.30
☐ 211 Sandis Ozolinsh, Caro.	-	.30
☐ 212 Tomas Vokoun (G), Nash.	-	.30
☐ 213 Jarrod Skalde, Atla.	-	.30
☐ 214 Sergei Gonchar, Wash.	-	.30
☐ 215 Anson Carter, Edmo.	-	.50
☐ 216 Steve Yzerman, Detr. [All-Star]	-	2.00
☐ 217 Mike Modano, Dall. [All-Star]	-	1.00
☐ 218 Paul Kariya, Anah. [All-Star]	-	1.00
☐ 219 Brendan Shanahan, Detr. [All-Star]	-	1.00
☐ 220 Pavel Bure, Flor. [All-Star]	-	.50
☐ 221 Jaromir Jagr, Pitt. [All-Star]	-	1.00
☐ 222 Chris Pronger, SLou. [All-Star]	-	.50
☐ 223 Nicklas Lidström, Detr. [All-Star]	-	.50
☐ 224 Rob Blake, LosA. [All-Star]	-	.50
☐ 225 Éric Desjardins, Phil. [All-Star]	-	.30
☐ 226 Olaf Kölzig (G), Wash. [All-Star]	-	.50
☐ 227 Roman Turek (G), SLou. [All-Star]	-	.30
☐ 228 S. Stevens / C. Pronger	-	.50
☐ 229 S. Gomez / A. Tanguay [Photo: M.Skoula]	-	.50
☐ 230 P. Bure / O. Nolan	-	.50
☐ 231 M. Brodeur / R. Turek	-	1.00
☐ 232 M. Czerkawski / O. Nolan	-	.30
☐ 233 J. Théodore / E. Belfour (G)	-	1.00
☐ 234 J. Madden / T. Amonte	-	.30
☐ 235 J. Jagr / P. Kariya	-	1.00
☐ 236 É. Desjardins / N. Lidström	-	.30
☐ 237 B. Boucher (G) / R. Turek	-	.30
☐ 238 Steve Yzerman, Detr. [Award Winner]	-	2.00
☐ 239 Scott Stevens, NJer. [Award Winner]	-	.30
☐ 240 Scott Gomez, NJer. [Award Winner]	-	.30
☐ 241 Roman Turek (G), SLou. [Award Winner]	-	.30
☐ 242 Pavol Demitra, SLou. [Award Winner]	-	.30
☐ 243 Pavel Bure, Flor. [Award Winner]	-	.50
☐ 244 Olaf Kölzig (G), Wash. [Award Winner]	-	.50
☐ 245 Jaromir Jagr, Pitt. [Award Winner]	-	1.00
☐ 246 Chris Pronger, SLou. [Award Winner]	-	.50
☐ 247 Stanley Cup finals	-	.30

CERTIFIED AUTOGRAPH ISSUE

Insert Set (12 cards):	470.00
Autograph	HA
☐ Andy Bathgate, NYRa. ✍	25.00
☐ Alex Delvecchio, Detr. ✍	25.00
☐ Adam Graves, NYRa. ✍	25.00
☐ Curtis Joseph (G), Toro. ✍	45.00
☐ Gordie Howe, Detr. ✍	200.00
☐ Jeff Hackett (G), Mont. ✍	25.00
☐ Joe Thornton, Bost. ✍	50.00
☐ Lorne Worsley, NYRa. ✍	35.00
☐ Red Kelly, Detr. ✍	25.00
☐ Sergei Fedorov, Detr. ✍	45.00
☐ Tony Amonte, Chic. ✍	25.00
☐ Ted Lindsay, Detr. ✍	35.00

HERITAGE HEROES

Insert Set (20 cards):	70.00
Insert (1:14)	HH
☐ HH1 Raymond Bourque, Colo.	4.00
☐ HH2 Jaromir Jagr, Pitt.	4.00
☐ HH3 Steve Yzerman, Detr.	10.00
☐ HH4 Mike Modano, Dall.	4.00
☐ HH5 Patrick Roy (G), Colo.	12.00
☐ HH6 Martin Brodeur (G), NJer.	6.00
☐ HH7 Mark Messier, NYRa.	4.00
☐ HH8 Peter Forsberg, Colo.	6.00
☐ HH9 Scott Stevens, NJer.	2.00
☐ HH10 Teemu Selänne, Anah.	2.00
☐ HH11 Pavel Bure, Flor.	2.00
☐ HH12 Curtis Joseph (G), Toro.	4.00
☐ HH13 John LeClair, Phil.	2.00
☐ HH14 Brett Hull, Dall.	4.00
☐ HH15 Keith Tkachuk, Phoe.	2.00
☐ HH16 Tony Amonte, Chic.	2.00
☐ HH17 Ed Belfour (G), Dall.	4.00
☐ HH18 Brendan Shanahan, Detr.	4.00
☐ HH19 Dominik Hasek (G), Buff.	4.00
☐ HH20 Paul Kariya, Anah.	6.00

NEW TRADITION

Insert Set (10 cards):	30.00
Insert (1:8)	NT
☐ NT1 Marian Hossa, Otta.	5.00
☐ NT2 Daniel Sedin, Vanc.	2.00
☐ NT3 Milan Hejduk, Colo.	4.00
☐ NT4 Vincent Lecavalier, Tamp.	5.00
☐ NT5 Joe Thornton, Bost.	6.00
☐ NT6 Scott Gomez, NJer.	2.00
☐ NT7 Chris Drury, Colo.	3.00
☐ NT8 Brian Boucher (G), Phil.	1.50
☐ NT9 Henrik Sedin, Vanc.	2.00
☐ NT10 Marian Gaborik, MinW.	10.00

ORIGINAL SIX ARENA RELICS

Insert Set (13 cards):	875.00
Player	OSA
☐ OSA Six teams {#/55}	600.00
☐ Bill Gadsby, Chic.	20.00
☐ Gordie Howe, Detr.	70.00
☐ Joe Thornton, Bost.	35.00
☐ Lorne Worsley, NYRa.	25.00
☐ Mark Messier, NYRa.	30.00
☐ Maurice Richard, Mont.	70.00
☐ Milt Schmidt, Bost.	30.00

□	Mats Sundin, Toro.	20.00
□	Saku Koivu, Mont.	25.00
□	Steve Yzerman, Detr.	75.00
□	Tony Amonte, Chic.	20.00
□	Ted Kennedy, Toro.	20.00

ORIGINAL SIX ARENA RELICS AUTOGRAPHS

	Insert (#/25)	Auto25
□	Gordie Howe, Detr. ✍	600.00
□	Gump Worlsey, Toro. ✍	200.00

THE ORIGINAL SIX

The cards in this series feature an affixed swatch from either a player-worn jersey (not game-worn) and a game-used stick.

Insert Set (13 cards): 525.00

	Insert	TOS
□	OSJ Six teams {#/55}	350.00
□	Alexei Zhamnov, Chic. White	15.00
□	Chris Osgood (G), Detr. White	15.00
□	Joe Thornton, Bost. Black	30.00
□	Joe Thornton, Bost. Yellow	30.00
□	Joe Thornton, Bost. White	30.00
□	Saku Koivu, Mont. Red	20.00
□	Saku Koivu, Mont. White/Blue	30.00
□	Tie Domi, Toro. White	15.00
□	Theoren Fleury, NYRa. White	15.00
□	Bob Probert, Chic. ✂ Stick	15.00
□	Jason Allison, Bost. ✂ Stick	15.00
□	Jeff Hackett (G), Mont. ✂ Stick	15.00
□	Mark Messier, NYRa. ✂ Stick	20.00
□	Mats Sundin, Toro. ✂ Stick	20.00
□	Steve Yzerman, Detr. ✂ Stick	50.00

THE ORIGINAL SIX AUTOGRAPH

As Tony Amonte did not sign his card, the OSJA-TA redemption cards were redeemed with alternate prize cards.

Insert Set (2 cards): 325.00

	Autograph	Auto25
□	Jeff Hackett (G), Mont. ✍	80.00
□	Joe Thornton, Bost. ✍	300.00

2000 - 01 TOPPS HERITAGE ALL-STAR FANTASY

These cards were distributed at the All-Star FANtasy.

Insert Set (6 cards):

	Avalanche
□	1 Raymond Bourque, Colo.
□	2 Patrick Roy (G), Colo.
□	3 Peter Forsberg, Colo.
□	4 Joe Sakic, Colo.
□	5 Milan Hejduk, Colo.
□	6 Chris Drury, Colo.

2000 - 01 TOPPS HERITAGE SPORTSCARD EXPO

These cards were distributed at the Spring 2001 Toronto Sportscard Expo. We do not have the full checklist.

Insert Set (6 cards):

	Expo
□	1 Curtis Joseph, Toro.
□	2
□	3
□	4
□	5
□	6

2000 - 01 TOPPS STARS

This series was released in March 2001. All 150 base cards have a Blue parallel; while Blue cards 1-100 are limited to 299 copies, Blue cards 101-150 are limited to 99 copies.

	Complete Set (150 cards):	**1,200**	**80.00**
	Common Player:	**1.00**	**.20**
	Player	**Blue**	**Reg.**
□ □	1 Vincent Lecavalier, Tamp.	10.00	1.00
□ □	2 Patrick Roy (G), Colo.	30.00	3.50
□ □	3 Scott Gomez, NJer.	4.00	.50
□ □	4 Steve Yzerman, Detr.	24.00	3.00
□ □	5 Paul Kariya, Anah.	14.00	1.50
□ □	6 Dominik Hasek (G), Buff.	10.00	1.00
□ □	7 Mike Modano, Dall.	10.00	1.00
□ □	8 Zigmund Palffy, LosA.	6.00	.50
□ □	9 John LeClair, Phil.	8.00	1.00
□ □	10 Mats Sundin, Toro.	10.00	1.00
□ □	11 Owen Nolan, SanJ.	6.00	.50
□ □	12 Tony Amonte, Chic.	6.00	.50
□ □	13 Patrik Stefan, Atla.	3.00	.20
□ □	14 Brett Hull, Dall.	10.00	1.00
□ □	15 Chris Pronger, SLou.	6.00	.50
□ □	16 Jeremy Roenick, Phoe.	8.00	1.00
□ □	17 Martin Brodeur (G), NJer.	16.00	2.00
□ □	18 Doug Weight, Edmo.	6.00	.50
□ □	19 Raymond Bourque, Colo.	12.00	1.50
□ □	20 Olaf Kölzig (G), Wash.	6.00	.50
□ □	21 Jaromir Jagr, Pitt.	10.00	1.00
□ □	22 Daniel Alfredsson, Otta.	6.00	.50
□ □	23 Jeff Hackett (G), Mont.	3.00	.20
□ □	24 Jason Allison, Bost.	6.00	.50
□ □	25 Joe Sakic, Colo.	16.00	2.00
□ □	26 Brendan Shanahan, Detr.	10.00	1.00
□ □	27 David Legwand, Nash.	4.00	.50
□ □	28 Tim Connolly, NYIs.	4.00	.50
□ □	29 Mark Recchi, Phil.	4.00	.50
□ □	30 Brad Stuart, SanJ.	4.00	.50
□ □	31 Pierre Turgeon, SLou.	4.00	.50
□ □	32 Ed Belfour (G), Dall.	10.00	1.00
□ □	33 Valeri Bure, Calg.	3.00	.20
□ □	34 Pavel Bure, Flor.	8.00	1.00
□ □	35 Teemu Selänne, Anah.	8.00	1.00
□ □	36 Patrik Elias, NJer.	8.00	1.00
□ □	37 Mattias Öhlund, Vanc.	3.00	.20
□ □	38 Rod Brind'Amour, Caro.	3.00	.20
□ □	39 Derian Hatcher, Dall.	3.00	.20
□ □	40 Peter Forsberg, Colo.	14.00	1.50
□ □	41 Eric Lindros, Phil.	10.00	1.00
□ □	42 Curtis Joseph (G), Toro.	10.00	1.00
□ □	43 Keith Tkachuk, Phoe.	6.00	.50
□ □	44 Mike Ricci, SanJ.	3.00	.20
□ □	45 Al MacInnis, SLou.	4.00	.50
□ □	46 Nicklas Lidström, Detr.	6.00	.50
□ □	47 Rob Blake, LosA.	6.00	.50
□ □	48 Scott Stevens, NJer.	4.00	.50
□ □	49 Milan Hejduk, Colo.	8.00	1.00
□ □	50 Theoren Fleury, NYRa.	6.00	.50
□ □	51 Joe Thornton, Bost.	12.00	1.50
□ □	52 Tommy Salo (G), Edmo.	4.00	.50
□ □	53 Éric Desjardins, Phil.	3.00	.20
□ □	54 Pavol Demitra, SLou.	4.00	.50
□ □	55 Adam Oates, Wash.	4.00	.50
□ □	56 Jeff Friesen, SanJ.	3.00	.20
□ □	57 Mariusz Czerkawski, NYIs.	2.00	.20
□ □	58 Luc Robitaille, LosA.	8.00	1.00
□ □	59 Jeff O'Neill, Caro.	4.00	.50
□ □	60 Andrew Brunette, Atla.	1.00	.20
□ □	61 Fred Brathwaite (G), Calg.	3.00	.20
□ □	62 Robert Svehla, Flor.	2.00	.20
□ □	63 Kimmo Timonen, Nash.	1.00	.20
□ □	64 Teppo Numminen, Phoe.	3.00	.20
□ □	65 Nikolai Antropov, Toro.	2.00	.20
□ □	66 Marian Hossa, Otta.	10.00	1.00
□ □	67 Joe Nieuwendyk, Dall.	4.00	.50
□ □	68 Michael Peca, Buff.	4.00	.50
□ □	69 Saku Koivu, Mont.	8.00	1.00
□ □	70 Alexei Kovalev, Pitt.	6.00	.50
□ □	71 Sergei Gonchar, Wash.	3.00	.20
□ □	72 Brian Leetch, NYRa.	6.00	.50
□ □	73 Ryan Smyth, Edmo.	4.00	.50
□ □	74 Jarome Iginla, Calg.	8.00	1.00
□ □	75 Byron Dafoe (G), Bost.	4.00	.50
□ □	76 Ray Whitney, Flor.	2.00	.20
□ □	77 Wade Redden, Otta.	3.00	.20
□ □	78 Pavel Kubina, Tamp.	1.00	.20
□ □	79 Markus Näslund, Vanc.	10.00	1.00
□ □	80 Brian Boucher (G), Phil.	3.00	.20
□ □	81 Martin Rucinsky, Mont.	2.00	.20
□ □	82 Roman Turek (G), SLou.	4.00	.50
□ □	83 Jocelyn Thibault (G), Chic.	4.00	.50
□ □	84 Miroslav Satan, Buff.	3.00	.20
□ □	85 Cliff Ronning, Nash.	2.00	.20
□ □	86 Mike Richter (G), NYRa.	4.00	.50
□ □	87 Chris Chelios, Detr.	6.00	.50
□ □	88 Arturs Irbe (G), Caro.	4.00	.50
□ □	89 Steve Thomas, Toro.	2.00	.20
□ □	90 Félix Potvin (G), Vanc.	6.00	.50
□ □	91 Jason Arnott, NJer.	4.00	.50
□ □	92 Mark Messier, NYRa.	10.00	1.00
□ □	93 Scott Pellerin, MinW.	1.00	.20
□ □	94 John Vanbiesbrouck (G), NYIs.	4.00	.50
□ □	95 Dave Andréychuk, Buff.	3.00	.20
□ □	96 Paul Coffey, Bost.	6.00	.50
□ □	97 Ron Tugnutt (G), Caro.	4.00	.50
□ □	98 Larry Robinson, Mont. [Hall of Fame]	6.00	.50
□ □	99 Billy Smith, NYIs. [Hall of Fame]	8.00	1.00
□ □	100 Mario Lemieux, Pitt. [Hall of Fame]	30.00	3.50
□ □	**101 Martin Havlat, Otta. [Rookie] RC**	**45.00**	**3.50**
□ □	**102 Petr Hubacek, Phil. [Rookie] RC**	**5.00**	**.50**
□ □	**103 Niclas Wallin, Caro. [Rookie] RC**	**5.00**	**.50**
□ □	**104 A. Khavanov, SLou. [Rookie] RC**	**6.00**	**1.00**
□ □	**105 R. Cechmanek (G), Phil. [Rookie] RC**	**32.00**	**2.50**
□ □	**106 Bryce Salvador, SLou. [Rookie] RC**	**6.00**	**1.00**
□ □	**107 Jonas Rönnqvist, Anah. [Rookie] RC**	**6.00**	**1.00**
□ □	**108 Rostislav Klesla, Colu. [Rookie] RC**	**24.00**	**2.00**
□ □	**109 Justin Williams, Phil. [Rookie] RC**	**12.00**	**2.00**
□ □	**110 Sascha Goc, NJer. [Rookie] RC**	**6.00**	**1.00**
□ □	**111 A. Raycroft (G), Bost. [Rookie] RC**	**9.00**	**1.50**
□ □	**112 Marty Turco (G), Dall. [Rookie] RC**	**20.00**	**5.00**
□ □	**113 Marian Gaborik, MinW. [Rookie] RC**	**80.00**	**8.00**
□ □	**114 Josef Vasicek, Caro. [Rookie] RC**	**9.00**	**1.50**
□ □	**115 S. Reinprecht, LosA. [Rookie] RC**	**12.00**	**2.00**
□ □	**116 Jani Hurme (G), Otta. [Rookie] RC**	**9.00**	**1.50**
□ □	**117 D. Aebischer (G), Colo. [Rookie] RC**	**12.00**	**2.00**
□ □	**118 Dale Purinton, NYRa. [Rookie] RC**	**6.00**	**1.00**
□ □	**119 Jarno Kultanen, Bost. [Rookie] RC**	**5.00**	**.50**
□ □	**120 Petr Svoboda, Toro. [Rookie] RC**	**6.00**	**1.00**
□ □	**121 Éric Bélanger, LosA. [Rookie] RC**	**6.00**	**1.00**
□ □	**122 Petteri Nummelin, Colu. [Rookie] RC**	**6.00**	**1.00**
□ □	**123 Michel Riesen, Edmo. [Rookie] RC**	**6.00**	**1.00**
□ □	**124 J. LaBarbera (G), NYRa. [Rookie] RC**	**6.00**	**1.00**
□ □	**125 Tyler Bouck, Dall. [Rookie] RC**	**6.00**	**1.00**
□ □	126 Martin Brodeur (G), NJer. [Spotlights]	60.00	2.00
□ □	127 Pavel Bure, Flor. [Spotlights]	30.00	1.00
□ □	128 Peter Forsberg, Colo. [Spotlights]	55.00	1.50
□ □	129 Scott Gomez, NJer. [Spotlights]	16.00	.50
□ □	130 Dominik Hasek (G), Buff. [Spotlights]	40.00	1.00
□ □	131 Brett Hull, Dall. [Spotlights]	40.00	1.00
□ □	132 Jaromir Jagr, Pitt. [Spotlights]	40.00	1.00
□ □	133 Curtis Joseph (G), Toro. [Spotlights]	40.00	1.00
□ □	134 Paul Kariya, Anah. [Spotlights]	55.00	1.50
□ □	135 Chris Pronger, SLou. [Spotlights]	24.00	.50
□ □	136 Patrick Roy (G), Colo. [Spotlights]	120.00	3.50
□ □	137 Joe Sakic, Colo. [Spotlights]	60.00	2.00
□ □	138 Teemu Selänne, Anah. [Spotlights]	30.00	1.00
□ □	139 Steve Yzerman, Detr. [Spotlights]	95.00	3.00
□ □	140 Vincent Lecavalier, Tamp. [Spotlights]	40.00	1.00
□ □	141 Samuel Påhlsson, Bost. [Spotlights]	6.00	.20
□ □	142 Maxime Ouellet (G), Phil. [Spotlights]	12.00	.50
□ □	143 Kris Beech, Wash. [Spotlights]	12.00	.50
□ □	144 Henrik Sedin, Vanc. [Spotlights]	16.00	1.00
□ □	145 Daniel Sedin, Vanc. [Spotlights]	16.00	1.00
□ □	146 Milan Kraft, Pitt. [Spotlights]	12.00	.50
□ □	147 Marty Turco (G), Dall. [Spotlights]	25.00	1.50
□ □	148 Oleg Saprykin, Calg. [Spotlights]	9.00	.50
□ □	149 Brent Johnson (G), SLou. [Spotlights]	16.00	1.00
□ □	150 Marian Gaborik, MinW. [Spotlights]	40.00	3.50

ALL-STAR AUTHORITY

Insert Set (11 cards): 25.00

	Insert (1:9)	ASA
□	AS1 Raymond Bourque, Colo.	3.00
□	AS2 Brett Hull, Dall.	2.00
□	AS3 Mark Messier, NYRa.	2.00
□	AS4 Patrick Roy (G), Colo.	7.00
□	AS5 Jaromir Jagr, Pitt.	2.00
□	AS6 Dominik Hasek (G), Buff.	2.00
□	AS7 Teemu Selänne, Anah.	2.00
□	AS8 Steve Yzerman, Detr.	6.00
□	AS9 Joe Sakic, Colo.	4.00
□	AS10 Pavel Bure, Flor.	2.00
□	AS11 John LeClair, Phil.	2.00

PROGRESSION

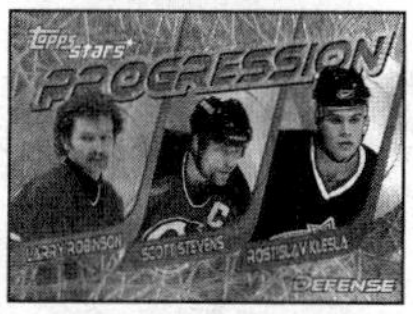

Insert Set (9 cards): 30.00

	Insert (1:11)	P
□	P1 V. Lecavalier / M. Modano / M. Lemieux	7.00
□	P2 P. Stefan / P. Forsberg / M. Lemieux	6.00
□	P3 S. Gomez / S. Yzerman / M. Lemieux	8.00
□	P4 R. Luongo / P. Roy / Bi. Smith	6.00
□	P5 M. Turco / M. Brodeur / Bi. Smith	4.00
□	P6 B. Boucher / E. Belfour (G) / Bi. Smith	2.00
□	P7 R. Klesla / S. Stevens / L. Robinson	1.50
□	P8 B. Stuart / R. Bourque / L. Robinson	3.00
□	P9 M. Skoula / C. Pronger / L. Robinson	2.00

WALL OF FAME

Insert Set (10 cards): 25.00

	Insert (1:10)	WoF
□	WF1 Pavel Bure, Flor.	2.00
□	WF2 Paul Kariya, Anah.	3.00
□	WF3 Jaromir Jagr, Pitt.	2.00
□	WF4 Peter Forsberg, Colo.	3.00
□	WF5 Mike Modano, Dall.	2.00
□	WF6 Patrick Roy (G), Colo.	7.00
□	WF7 Steve Yzerman, Detr.	6.00
□	WF8 Dominik Hasek (G), Buff.	2.00
□	WF9 John LeClair, Phil.	2.00
□	WF10 Martin Brodeur (G), NJer.	4.00

CERTIFIED AUTOGRAPH

Insert Set (9 cards): 375.00

	Autograph	CA
□	Brian Boucher (G), Phil.	20.00
□	Billy Smith, NYIs.	35.00
□	Brad Stuart, SanJ.	20.00
□	Chris Pronger, SLou.	25.00
□	Larry Robinson, Mont.	25.00
□	Mario Lemieux, Pitt.	225.00
□	Mike Modano, Dall.	45.00
□	Mike York, NYRa.	20.00
□	Vincent Lecavalier, Tamp.	45.00

GAME GEAR

Insert Set (19 cards): 300.00

	Player	GG
□	Adam Graves, NYRa. ✂ Jersey	15.00
□	Chris Pronger, SLou. ✂ Jersey	15.00
□	Don Cherry Suit	35.00
□	David Legwand, Nash. ✂ Jersey	15.00
□	Darren McCarty, Detr. ✂ Jersey	15.00
□	Jason Allison, Bost. ✂ Jersey	15.00
□	Keith Tkachuk, Phoe. ✂ Stick	15.00
□	Mariusz Czerkawski, NYIs. ✂ Jersey	15.00
□	Martin Lapointe, Detr. ✂ Jersey	15.00
□	Mike Modano, Dall. ✂ Stick	30.00
□	Mark Recchi, Phil. ✂ Stick	15.00
□	Mike Richter (G), NYRa. ✂ Jersey	15.00
□	Phil Housley, Calg. ✂ Jersey	15.00
□	Patrick Roy (G), Colo. ✂ Jersey	60.00
□	Ron Tugnutt (G), Colu. ✂ Stick	15.00
□	Sergei Zubov, Dall. ✂ Jersey	15.00
□	Tony Amonte, Chic. ✂ Jersey	15.00
□	Teemu Selänne, Anah. ✂ Jersey	20.00
□	Zigmund Palffy, LosA. ✂ Stick	15.00

GAME GEAR AUTOGRAPH

	Player	Auto.
☐	Chris Pronger, SLou. ✍ ✂ Jersey	225.00
☐	Don Cherry ✍ Suit	125.00
☐	Mike Modano, Dall. ✍ ✂ Stick	300.00

PRE-PRODUCTION SAMPLE

Complete Set (6 cards): 8.00

	Player	Promo
☐	PP1 Jason Arnott, NJer.	1.00
☐	PP2 Peter Forsberg, Colo.	3.50
☐	PP3 David Legwand, Nash.	1.00
☐	PP4 Steve Thomas, Toro.	1.00
☐	PP5 Félix Potvin (G), Vanc.	1.50
☐	PP6 Vincent Lecavalier, Tamp.	2.50

2000 - 01 UD HEROES

This series was released in 2001.

Complete Set (180 cards): 60.00
Common Player: .20

	Player	Reg.
☐	1 Steve Rucchin, Anah.	.20
☐	2 Marty McInnis, Anah.	.20
☐	3 Oleg Tverdovsky, Anah.	.20
☐	4 Guy Hebert (G), Anah.	.20
☐	5 Patrik Stefan, Atla.	.20
☐	6 Donald Audette, Atla.	.20
☐	7 Andrew Brunette, Atla.	.20
☐	8 Jason Allison, Bost.	.50
☐	9 Sergei Samsonov, Bost.	.50
☐	10 Joe Thornton, Bost.	1.00
☐	11 Byron Dafoe (G), Bost.	.20
☐	12 Dominik Hasek (G), Buff.	1.00
☐	13 Miroslav Satan, Buff.	.20
☐	14 Doug Gilmour, Buff.	.50
☐	15 J-P Dumont, Buff.	.20
☐	16 Fred Brathwaite (G), Calg.	.20
☐	17 Valeri Bure, Calg.	.20
☐	18 Marc Savard, Calg.	.20
☐	19 Cory Stillman, Calg.	.20
☐	20 Ron Francis, Caro.	.50
☐	21 Arturs Irbe (G), Caro.	.20
☐	22 Jeff O'Neill, Caro.	.20
☐	23 Sandis Ozolinsh, Caro.	.20
☐	24 Tony Amonte, Chic.	.50
☐	25 Jocelyn Thibault (G), Chic.	.20
☐	26 Alexei Zhamnov, Chic.	.20
☐	27 Steve Sullivan, Chic.	.20
☐	28 Chris Drury, Colo.	.50
☐	29 Milan Hejduk, Colo.	.50
☐	30 Alex Tanguay, Colo.	.50
☐	31 Peter Forsberg, Colo.	1.00
☐	32 Adam Deadmarsh, Colo.	.20
☐	33 Marc Denis (G), Colu.	.20
☐	34 Ron Tugnutt (G), Colu.	.20
☐	35 Tyler Wright, Colu.	.20
☐	36 David Vyborny, Colu.	.20
☐	37 Brett Hull, Dall.	1.00
☐	38 Ed Belfour (G), Dall.	1.00
☐	39 Joe Nieuwendyk, Dall.	.20
☐	40 Sergei Zubov, Dall.	.20
☐	41 Jere Lehtinen, Dall.	.20
☐	42 Sergei Fedorov, Detr.	1.00
☐	43 Martin Lapointe, Detr.	.20
☐	44 Chris Osgood (G), Detr.	.50
☐	45 Pat Verbeek, Detr.	.20
☐	46 Nicklas Lidström, Detr.	.50
☐	47 Doug Weight, Edmo.	.50
☐	48 Tommy Salo (G), Edmo.	.20
☐	49 Ryan Smyth, Edmo.	.20
☐	50 Sean Brown, Edmo.	.20
☐	51 Ray Whitney, Flor.	.20
☐	52 Trevor Kidd (G), Flor.	.20
☐	53 Viktor Kozlov, Flor.	.20
☐	54 Denis Shvidki, Flor.	.20
☐	55 Rob Blake, LosA.	.50
☐	56 Zigmund Palffy, LosA.	.50
☐	57 Luc Robitaille, LosA.	.50
☐	58 Glen Murray, LosA.	.20
☐	59 Manny Fernandez (G), MinW.	.20
☐	60 Scott Pellerin, MinW.	.20
☐	61 Maxim Sushinsky, MinW.	.20
☐	62 Saku Koivu, Mont.	.50
☐	63 José Théodore (G), Mont.	1.00
☐	64 Martin Rucinsky, Mont.	.20
☐	65 Darryl Shannon, Mont.	.20
☐	66 Cliff Ronning, Nash.	.20
☐	67 Randy Robitaille, Nash.	.20
☐	68 David Legwand, Nash.	.20
☐	69 Mike Dunham (G), Nash.	.20
☐	70 Alexander Mogilny, NJer.	.20
☐	71 Patrik Elias, NJer.	.50
☐	72 Bobby Holik, NJer.	.20
☐	73 Scott Stevens, NJer.	.20
☐	74 Mariusz Czerkawski, NYIs.	.20
☐	75 Tim Connolly, NYIs.	.20
☐	76 Aris Brimanis, NYIs.	.20
☐	77 John Vanbiesbrouck (G), NYIs.	.20
☐	78 Brian Leetch, NYRa.	.50
☐	79 Mike York, NYRa.	.20
☐	80 Theoren Fleury, NYRa.	.50
☐	81 Mike Richter (G), NYRa.	.20
☐	82 Alexei Yashin, Otta.	.50
☐	83 Ricard Persson, Otta.	.20
☐	84 Radek Bonk, Otta.	.20
☐	85 Patrick Lalime (G), Otta.	.50
☐	86 Simon Gagné, Phil.	.50
☐	87 Brian Boucher (G), Phil.	.20
☐	88 Keith Primeau, Phil.	.20
☐	89 Mark Grieg, Phil.	.20
☐	90 Teppo Numminen, Phoe.	.20
☐	91 Shane Doan, Phoe.	.20
☐	92 Keith Tkachuk, Phoe.	.50
☐	93 Sean Burke (G), Phoe.	.50
☐	94 Milan Kraft, Pitt.	.50
☐	95 Alexei Kovalev, Pitt.	.50
☐	96 Jean-Sébastien Aubin (G), Pitt.	.20
☐	97 Martin Straka, Pitt.	.20
☐	98 Vincent Damphousse, SanJ.	.50
☐	99 Steve Shields (G), SanJ.	.20
☐	100 Brad Stuart, SanJ.	.20
☐	101 Owen Nolan, SanJ.	.50
☐	102 Chris Pronger, SLou.	.50
☐	103 Pavol Demitra, SLou.	.20
☐	104 Roman Turek (G), SLou.	.20
☐	105 Pierre Turgeon, SLou.	.20
☐	106 Dan Cloutier (G), Tamp.	.20
☐	107 Brad Richards, Tamp.	.50
☐	108 Paul Mara, Tamp.	.20
☐	109 Gary Roberts, Toro.	.20
☐	110 Sergei Berezin, Toro.	.20
☐	111 Mats Sundin, Toro.	1.00
☐	112 Bryan McCabe, Toro.	.20
☐	113 Henrik Sedin, Vanc.	.50
☐	114 Daniel Sedin, Vanc.	.50
☐	115 Greg Hawgood, Vanc.	.20
☐	116 Adam Oates, Wash.	.20
☐	117 Olaf Kölzig (G), Wash.	.50
☐	118 Sergei Gonchar, Wash.	.20
☐	119 Bobby Orr, Bost. [Hockey Immortals]	4.00
☐	120 Cam Neely, Bost. [Hockey Immortals]	1.00
☐	121 Gilbert Perreault, Buff. [Hockey Immortals]	.50
☐	122 Bobby Hull, Chic. [Hockey Immortals]	1.50
☐	123 Stan Mikita, Chic. [Hockey Immortals]	.50
☐	124 Tony Esposito (G), Chic. [Hockey Immortals]	1.00
☐	125 Gordie Howe, Detr. [Hockey Immortals]	2.50
☐	126 Wayne Gretzky, Edmo. [Hockey Immortals]	4.00
☐	127 Marcel Dionne, LosA. [Hockey Immortals]	1.00
☐	128 Maurice Richard, Mont. [Hockey Immortals]	2.50
☐	129 Guy Lafleur, Mont. [Hockey Immortals]	2.00
☐	130 Jean Béliveau, Mont. [Hockey Immortals]	2.00
☐	131 Bryan Trottier, NYIs. [Hockey Immortals]	1.00
☐	132 Denis Potvin, NYIs. [Hockey Immortals]	.50
☐	133 Mike Bossy, NYIs. [Hockey Immortals]	1.50
☐	134 Bobby Clarke, Phil. [Hockey Immortals]	.50
☐	135 Bernie Parent (G), Phil. [Hockey Immortals]	.50
☐	136 Mario Lemieux, Pitt. [Hockey Immortals]	3.00
☐	137 Michel Goulet, Québ. [Hockey Immortals]	.20
☐	138 Frank Mahovlich, Toro. [Hockey Immortals]	1.00
☐	139 Paul Kariya, Anah. [Portrayals]	1.00
☐	140 Teemu Selänne, Anah. [Portrayals]	.50
☐	141 Patrick Roy (G), Colo. [Portrayals]	3.00
☐	142 Joe Sakic, Colo. [Portrayals]	1.50
☐	143 Peter Forsberg, Colo. [Portrayals]	1.00
☐	144 Raymond Bourque, Colo. [Portrayals]	1.00
☐	145 Mike Modano, Dall. [Portrayals]	1.00
☐	146 Steve Yzerman, Detr. [Portrayals]	2.00
☐	147 Brendan Shanahan, Detr. [Portrayals]	1.00
☐	148 Pavel Bure, Flor. [Portrayals]	.50
☐	149 Martin Brodeur (G), NJer. [Portrayals]	1.50
☐	150 Scott Gomez, NJer. [Portrayals]	.20
☐	151 Mark Messier, NYRa. [Portrayals]	1.00
☐	152 Marian Hossa, Otta. [Portrayals]	1.00
☐	153 John LeClair, Phil. [Portrayals]	.50
☐	154 Jeremy Roenick, Phoe. [Portrayals]	.50
☐	155 Jaromir Jagr, Pitt. [Portrayals]	1.00
☐	156 Jeff Friesen, SanJ. [Portrayals]	.20
☐	157 Vincent Lecavalier, Tamp. [Portrayals]	1.00
☐	158 Curtis Joseph (G), Toro. [Portrayals]	1.00
☐	**159 Jonas Ronnqvist, Anah. [Future Heroes] RC**	**1.00**
☐	**160 Jeff Cowan, Calg. [Future Heroes] RC**	**.50**
☐	**161 D. Aebischer (G), Colo. [Future Heroes] RC**	**2.00**
☐	**162 Rostislav Klesla, Colu. [Future Heroes] RC**	**2.00**
☐	**163 Tyler Bouck, Dall. [Future Heroes] RC**	**1.00**
☐	**164 Michel Riesen, Edmo. [Future Heroes] RC**	**1.00**
☐	**165 S. Reinprecht, LosA. [Future Heroes] RC**	**2.00**
☐	**166 Marian Gaborik, MinW. [Future Heroes] RC**	**7.50**
☐	**167 David Gosselin, Nash. [Future Heroes] RC**	**.50**
☐	**168 Scott Hartnell, Nash. [Future Heroes] RC**	**1.50**
☐	**169 Colin White, NJer. [Future Heroes] RC**	**1.00**
☐	**170 Rick DiPietro (G), NYIs. [Future Heroes] RC**	**3.50**
☐	**171 J. Holmqvist (G), NYRa. [Future Heroes] RC**	**2.00**
☐	**172 Jani Hurme (G), Otta. [Future Heroes] RC**	**1.50**
☐	**173 Martin Havlat, Otta. [Future Heroes] RC**	**4.50**
☐	**174 Justin Williams, Phil. [Future Heroes] RC**	**2.00**
☐	**175 R. Cechmanek (G), Phil. [Future Heroes] RC**	**3.00**
☐	**176 Roman Simicek, Pitt. [Future Heroes] RC**	**.50**
☐	**177 Zdenek Blatny [Future Heroes] RC**	**1.00**
☐	**178 Jordan Krestanovich [Future Heroes] RC**	**1.00**
☐	179 Mark Messier, NYRa. [Checklist]	.50
☐	180 Wayne Gretzky, NYRa. [Checklist]	2.00

NHL LEADERS

Insert Set (10 cards): 20.00

	Insert (1:13)	L
☐	L1 Paul Kariya, Anah.	3.00
☐	L2 Ray Bourque, Colo.	3.00
☐	L3 Joe Sakic, Colo.	4.00
☐	L4 Steve Yzerman, Detr.	6.00
☐	L5 Mark Messier, NYRa.	2.00
☐	L6 Alexei Yashin, Otta.	1.50
☐	L7 John LeClair, Phil.	2.00
☐	L8 Keith Tkachuk, Phoe.	1.50
☐	L9 Jaromir Jagr, Pitt.	2.00
☐	L10 Al MacInnis, SLou.	1.50

PLAYER IDOLS

Insert Set (6 cards): 10.00

	Insert (1:23)	PI
☐	PI1 B. Shanahan / M. Messier	2.00
☐	PI2 M. Brodeur / P. Roy	5.00
☐	PI3 M. Afinogenov / P. Bure	1.50
☐	PI4 P. Kariya / W. Gretzky	6.00
☐	PI5 V. Lecavalier / M. Lemieux	5.00
☐	PI6 R. Turek / D. Hasek	1.50

SECOND SEASON HEROES

Insert Set (10 cards): 30.00

	Insert (1:13)	SS
☐	SS1 Patrick Roy (G), Colo.	7.00
☐	SS2 Peter Forsberg, Colo.	3.00
☐	SS3 Mike Modano, Dall.	2.00
☐	SS4 Ed Belfour (G), Dall.	2.00
☐	SS5 Steve Yzerman, Detr.	6.00
☐	SS6 Wayne Gretzky, Edmo.	10.00
☐	SS7 Martin Brodeur (G), NJer.	4.00
☐	SS8 Mark Messier, NYRa.	2.00
☐	SS9 John LeClair, Phil.	2.00
☐	SS10 Jaromir Jagr, Pitt.	2.00

TIMELESS MOMENTS

Insert Set (10 cards): 20.00

	Insert (1:13)	TM
☐	TM1 Teemu Selänne, Anah.	2.00
☐	TM2 Dominik Hasek (G), Buff.	2.00
☐	TM3 Patrick Roy (G), Colo.	7.00
☐	TM4 Brett Hull, Dall.	2.00
☐	TM5 Pavel Bure, Flor.	2.00
☐	TM6 Martin Brodeur (G), NJer.	4.00
☐	TM7 Mike York, NYRa.	1.50
☐	TM8 Brian Boucher (G), Phil.	1.50
☐	TM9 Jaromir Jagr, Pitt.	2.00
☐	TM10 Curtis Joseph (G), Toro.	2.00

TODAY'S SNIPERS

Insert Set (6 cards): 10.00

	Insert (1:23)	TS
☐	TS1 Paul Kariya, Anah.	3.00
☐	TS2 Brendan Shanahan, Detr.	2.00
☐	TS3 Pavel Bure, Flor.	2.00
☐	TS4 John LeClair, Phil.	2.00
☐	TS5 Jaromir Jagr, Pitt.	2.00
☐	TS6 Mats Sundin, Toro.	2.00

GAME-USED TWIGS

Insert Set (20 cards): 1000.00

	Insert (1:83 Hobby)	GUT
☐	Bobby Hull, Chic. ✂	50.00
☐	Bobby Orr, Bost. ✂	250.00
☐	Martin Brodeur (G), NJer. ✂	55.00
☐	Steve Yzerman, Detr. ✂	80.00
☐	Mats Sundin, Toro. ✂	35.00
☐	Mike Bossy, NYIs. ✂	55.00
☐	Curtis Joseph (G), Toro. ✂	35.00
☐	Dominik Hasek (G), Buff. ✂	35.00
☐	Gordie Howe, Detr. ✂	75.00
☐	Gilbert Perreault, Buff. ✂	25.00
☐	Jaromir Jagr, Pitt. ✂	35.00
☐	John LeClair, Phil. ✂	25.00
☐	Mario Lemieux, Pitt. ✂	100.00
☐	Mark Messier, NYRa. ✂	35.00
☐	Paul Kariya, Anah. ✂	45.00
☐	Patrick Roy (G), Colo. ✂	80.00
☐	Raymond Bourque, Colo. ✂	40.00
☐	Theoren Fleury, NYRa. ✂	20.00
☐	Teemu Selänne, Anah. ✂	25.00
☐	Wayne Gretzky, NYRa. ✂	125.00

GAME-USED TWIGS GOLD

Insert Set (10 cards): 2,200

	Insert (#/50)	GUT
☐	R. Bourque ✂ / B. Orr ✂	450.00
☐	P. Roy ✂ / M. Brodeur ✂	325.00
☐	C. Joseph (G) ✂ / M. Sundin ✂	150.00
☐	T. Fleury ✂ / J. LeClair ✂	100.00
☐	W. Gretzky ✂ / M. Messier ✂	375.00
☐	Bo. Hull ✂ / M. Bossy ✂	175.00
☐	D. Hasek ✂ / G. Perreault ✂	100.00
☐	G. Howe ✂ / S. Yzerman ✂	500.00
☐	P. Kariya ✂ / T. Selänne ✂	150.00
☐	M. Lemieux ✂ / J. Jagr ✂	300.00

SIGNS OF GREATNESS

Insert Set (33 cards): 1,900

	Insert (1:71)	SoG
☐	Bobby Clarke, Phil. ✍	15.00
☐	Bobby Hull, Chic. ✍ (#/50)	100.00
☐	Bobby Orr, Bost. ✍ (#/75)	350.00
☐	Bernie Parent (G), Phil. ✍	25.00
☐	Bryan Trottier, NYIs. ✍	30.00
☐	Cam Neely, Bost. ✍	30.00
☐	Denis Potvin, NYIs. ✍	25.00
☐	Frank Mahovlich, Toro. ✍	25.00
☐	Félix Potvin (G), Vanc. ✍	15.00
☐	Gordie Howe, Detr. ✍ (#/50)	225.00
☐	Guy Lafleur, Mont. ✍	30.00
☐	Gilbert Perreault, Buff. ✍	25.00
☐	Jean Béliveau, Mont. ✍	40.00
☐	John LeClair, Phil. ✍	25.00
☐	Jeremy Roenick, Phoe. ✍ (#/100)	60.00
☐	Kenny Jönsson, NYIs. ✍	12.00
☐	Marc Denis (G), Colu. ✍	15.00
☐	Marcel Dionne, LosA. ✍	25.00
☐	Michel Goulet, Québ. ✍	15.00
☐	Mario Lemieux, Pitt. ✍ (#/25)	450.00
☐	Mark Messier, NYRa. ✍ (#/50)	100.00
☐	Miroslav Satan, Buff. ✍	12.00
☐	Mike York, NYRa. ✍	12.00
☐	Pavel Brendl, Calgary Hitmen	12.00
☐	Peter Bondra, Wash. ✍	15.00
☐	Pavel Bure, Vanc. ✍ (#/100)	50.00
☐	Roberto Luongo (G), Flor. ✍	25.00
☐	Roman Turek (G), SLou. ✍	15.00
☐	Scott Gomez, NJer. ✍	12.00
☐	Stan Mikita, Chic. ✍	25.00
☐	Steve Yzerman, Detr. ✍	75.00
☐	Tommy Salo (G), Edmo. ✍	12.00
☐	Wayne Gretzky, Edmo. ✍ (#/50)	450.00

2000 - 01 UD RESERVE

This series was released in 2001. Rookie-subset cards are seeded 1:2 packs.

Complete Set (120 cards): 100.00
Common Player: .25

	Player	Reg.
☐	1 Paul Kariya, Anah.	1.50
☐	2 Steve Rucchin, Anah.	.25
☐	3 Teemu Selänne, Anah.	1.00
☐	4 Damian Rhodes (G), Atla.	.25
☐	5 Patrik Stefan, Atla.	.25
☐	6 Byron Dafoe (G), Bost.	.50
☐	7 Jason Allison, Bost.	.50
☐	8 Joe Thornton, Bost.	1.50
☐	9 Doug Gilmour, Buff.	.50
☐	10 Dominik Hasek (G), Buff.	1.00
☐	11 Miroslav Satan, Buff.	.25
☐	12 Jarome Iginla, Calg.	1.00
☐	13 Oleg Saprykin, Calg.	.25
☐	14 Valeri Bure, Calg.	.25
☐	15 Sandis Ozolinsh, Caro.	.25
☐	16 Ron Francis, Caro.	.50
☐	17 Sami Kapanen, Caro.	.25
☐	18 Steve Sullivan, Chic.	.25
☐	19 Alexei Zhamnov, Chic.	.25
☐	20 Tony Amonte, Chic.	.50
☐	21 Raymond Bourque, Colo.	1.50
☐	22 Patrick Roy (G), Colo.	3.50
☐	23 Peter Forsberg, Colo.	1.50
☐	24 Joe Sakic, Colo.	2.00
☐	25 Ron Tugnutt (G), Colu.	.50
☐	26 Stephen Heinze, Colu.	.25
☐	27 Mike Modano, Dall.	1.00
☐	28 Brett Hull, Dall.	1.00
☐	29 Ed Belfour (G), Dall.	1.00
☐	30 Brenden Shanahan, Detr.	1.00
☐	31 Sergei Fedorov, Detr.	1.00
☐	32 Steve Yzerman, Detr.	3.00
☐	33 Ryan Smyth, Edmo.	.50
☐	34 Tommy Salo (G), Edmo.	.50
☐	35 Doug Weight, Edmo.	.50
☐	36 Pavel Bure, Flor.	1.00
☐	37 Ray Whitney, Flor.	.25
☐	38 Roberto Luongo (G), Flor.	1.00
☐	39 Luc Robitaille, LosA.	1.00
☐	40 Zigmund Palffy, LosA.	.50
☐	41 Jamie Storr (G), LosA.	.25
☐	42 Jamie McLennan (G), MinW.	.25
☐	43 Jim Dowd, MinW.	.25
☐	44 Brian Savage, Mont.	.25
☐	45 José Théodore (G), Mont.	1.50
☐	46 Saku Koivu, Mont.	1.00
☐	47 David Legwand, Nash.	.50
☐	48 Cliff Ronning, Nash.	.25
☐	49 Tomas Vokoun (G), Nash.	.25
☐	50 Scott Gomez, NJer.	.50
☐	51 Patrik Elias, NJer.	1.00
☐	52 Martin Brodeur (G), NJer.	2.00
☐	53 Tim Connolly, NYIs.	.50
☐	54 Roman Hamrlik, NYIs.	.25
☐	55 John Vanbiesbrouck (G), NYIs.	.50
☐	56 Theoren Fleury, NYRa.	.50
☐	57 Mark Messier, NYRa.	1.00
☐	58 Brian Leetch, NYRa.	.50
☐	59 Marian Hossa, Otta.	1.00
☐	60 Patrick Lalime (G), Otta.	.50
☐	61 Alexei Yashin, Otta.	.50
☐	62 John LeClair, Phil.	1.00
☐	63 Mark Recchi, Phil.	.50
☐	64 Keith Primeau, Phil.	.50
☐	65 Jeremy Roenick, Phoe.	1.00
☐	66 Sean Burke (G), Phoe.	.50
☐	67 Keith Tkachuk, Phoe.	.50
☐	68 Jaromir Jagr, Pitt.	1.00
☐	69 Milan Kraft, Pitt.	.50
☐	70 Mario Lemieux, Pitt.	3.50
☐	71 Owen Nolan, SanJ.	.50
☐	72 Jeff Friesen, SanJ.	.25
☐	73 Evgeni Nabokov, SanJ.	.50
☐	74 Chris Pronger, SLou.	.50
☐	75 Scott A. Young, SLou.	.25
☐	76 Roman Turek (G), SLou.	.50
☐	77 Vincent Lecavalier, Tamp.	1.00
☐	78 Brad Richards, Tamp.	1.00
☐	79 Mike Johnson, Tamp.	.25
☐	80 Curtis Joseph (G), Toro.	1.00
☐	81 Mats Sundin, Toro.	1.00
☐	82 Sergei Berezin, Toro.	.25
☐	83 Markus Näslund, Vanc.	1.00
☐	84 Daniel Sedin, Vanc.	1.00
☐	85 Henrik Sedin, Vanc.	1.00
☐	86 Chris Simon, Wash.	.25
☐	87 Peter Bondra, Wash.	.50
☐	88 Olaf Kölzig (G), Wash.	.50

RESERVE ROOKIES

	Insert (1:2)	RR
☐	**89 Andrew Raycroft (G), Bost. RC**	**3.00**
☐	**90 Josef Vasicek, Caro. RC**	**3.00**
☐	**91 David Aebischer (G), Colo. RC**	**4.00**
☐	**92 Rostislav Klesla, Colu. RC**	**4.00**
☐	**93 Marty Turco (G), Dall. RC**	**9.00**
☐	**94 Tyler Bouck, Dall. RC**	**2.00**
☐	**95 Shawn Horcoff, Edmo. RC**	**2.00**
☐	**96 Éric Belanger, LosA. RC**	**2.00**
☐	**97 Steven Reinprecht, LosA. RC**	**4.00**
☐	**98 Marian Gaborik, MinW. RC**	**15.00**
☐	**99 Peter Bartos, MinW. RC**	**2.00**
☐	**100 Scott Hartnell, Nash. RC**	**3.00**
☐	**101 Greg Classen, Nash. RC**	**2.00**
☐	**102 Chris Mason (G), Nash. RC**	**2.00**
☐	**103 Willie Mitchell, NJer. RC**	**2.00**
☐	**104 Rick DiPietro (G), NYIs. RC**	**7.00**
☐	**105 Jason LaBarbera (G), NYRa. RC**	**2.00**
☐	**106 Jani Hurme (G), Otta. RC**	**3.00**
☐	**107 Martin Havlat, Otta. RC**	**9.00**
☐	**108 Ruslan Fedotenko, Phil. RC**	**2.00**
☐	**109 Justin Williams, Phil. RC**	**4.00**
☐	**110 Petr Hubacek, Phil. RC**	**1.50**
☐	**111 Roman Cechmanek (G), Phil. RC**	**6.00**
☐	**112 Mark Smith, SanJ. RC**	**1.50**
☐	**113 Alexander Khavanov, SLou. RC**	**2.00**
☐	**114 Alexander Kharitonov, Tamp. RC**	**1.50**
☐	**115 Marc-André Thinel, Victoriaville Tigres RC**	**2.00**
☐	**116 Zdenek Blatney, Kootenay Ice RC**	**2.00**
☐	**117 Jordan Krestanovich, Calgary Hitmen RC**	**2.00**
☐	**118 Jeff Bateman, Brampton Batallion RC**	**2.00**

CHECKLIST

	Player	CL
☐	119 Mark Messier, NYRa. [Checklist]	.25
☐	120 Curtis Joseph (G), Toro. [Checklist]	.25

GOLD STRIKE

	Insert Set (10 cards):	25.00
	Insert (1:14)	GS
☐	GS1 Teemu Selänne, Anah.	2.00
☐	GS2 Joe Sakic, Colo.	4.00
☐	GS3 Mike Modano, Dall.	3.00
☐	GS4 Sergei Fedorov, Detr.	3.00
☐	GS5 Pavel Bure, Flor.	2.00
☐	GS6 Scott Gomez, NJer.	2.00
☐	GS7 Theoren Fleury, NYRa.	2.00
☐	GS8 Mario Lemieux, Pitt.	9.00
☐	GS9 Mats Sundin, Toro.	3.00
☐	GS10 Olaf Kölzig (G), Wash.	2.00

GOLDEN GOALIES

	Insert Set (10 cards):	25.00
	Insert (1:14)	GG
☐	GG1 Guy Hebert (G), Anah.	2.00
☐	GG2 Dominik Hasek (G), Buff.	3.00
☐	GG3 Patrick Roy (G), Colo.	9.00
☐	GG4 Tommy Salo (G), Edmo.	2.00
☐	GG5 José Théodore (G), Mont.	3.00
☐	GG6 Mike Dunham (G), Nash.	2.00
☐	GG7 Martin Brodeur (G), NJer.	4.00
☐	GG8 John Vanbiesbrouck (G), NYIs.	2.00
☐	GG9 Roman Turek (G), SLou.	2.00
☐	GG10 Curtis Joseph (G), Toro.	3.00

ON-ICE SUCCESS

	Insert Set (6 cards):	10.00
	Insert (1:23)	OS
☐	OS1 Paul Kariya, Anah.	4.00
☐	OS2 Tony Amonte, Chic.	2.00
☐	OS3 Joe Sakic, Colo.	4.00
☐	OS4 Pavel Bure, Flor.	2.00
☐	OS5 Luc Robitaille, Kings	2.00
☐	OS6 Mark Messier, NYRa.	3.00

POWER PORTFOLIOS

	Insert Set (6 cards):	20.00
	Insert (1:23)	PP
☐	PP1 Patrick Roy (G), Colo.	9.00
☐	PP2 Brett Hull, Dall.	3.00
☐	PP3 Steve Yzerman, Detr.	7.00
☐	PP4 Martin Brodeur (G), NJer.	4.00
☐	PP5 Mark Messier, NYRa.	3.00
☐	PP6 Jaromir Jagr, Pitt.	3.00

THE BIG TICKET

	Insert Set (10 cards):	30.00
	Insert (1:14)	TBT
☐	BT1 Paul Kariya, Anah.	4.00
☐	BT2 Dominik Hasek (G), Buff.	3.00
☐	BT3 Raymond Bourque, Colo.	3.00
☐	BT4 Steve Yzerman, Detr.	7.00
☐	BT5 Pavel Bure, Flor.	2.00
☐	BT6 Marian Gaborik, MinW.	9.00
☐	BT7 Martin Brodeur (G), NJer.	4.00
☐	BT8 John LeClair, Phil.	2.00
☐	BT9 Jaromir Jagr, Pitt.	3.00
☐	BT10 Vincent Lecavalier, Tamp.	3.00

PRACTICE SESSION JERSEY

	Jersey Set (10 cards):	250.00
	Insert (1:239)	PJ
☐	Chris Osgood (G), Detr.	20.00
☐	Jaromir Jagr, NHL All-Star	35.00
☐	John LeClair, NHL All-Star	30.00
☐	Joe Thornton, Bost.	45.00
☐	Mark Messier, NHL All-Star	35.00
☐	Mike Modano, NHL All-Star	35.00
☐	Mark Recchi, Phil.	20.00
☐	Peter Forsberg, Québ.	50.00
☐	Theoren Fleury, Calg.	20.00
☐	Teemu Seänne, NHL All-Star	30.00

PRACTICE SESSION JERSEY SIGNED

	Autograph Set (6 cards):	275.00
	Insert (1:479)	Aut
☐	Chris Osgood (G), Detr. ✍	35.00
☐	John LeClair, NHL All-Star ✍	50.00
☐	Joe Thornton, Bost. ✍	75.00
☐	Mark Messier, NHL All-Star ✍	75.00
☐	Mike Modano, NHL All-Star ✍	75.00
☐	Mark Recchi, Phil. ✍	35.00

2000 - 01 ULTIMATE MEMORABILIA

This series was issued in May 2001. Every card in this series (including every insert card) is encased and sequentially numbered. Base cards 1-50 (all autographed, limited to 90 copies each) have a Gold parallel (also all autographed, limited to 10 copies each).

	Autographed Set (50 cards):	18,400	5,000
	Description	U10	U90
☐☐	Theoren Fleury, NYRa. ✍	250.00	75.00
☐☐	Brendan Shanahan, Detr. ✍	450.00	125.00
☐☐	Curtis Joseph (G), Toro. ✍	450.00	125.00
☐☐	Saku Koivu, Mont. ✍	550.00	150.00
☐☐	Olaf Kölzig (G), Wash. ✍	250.00	75.00
☐☐	Al MacInnis, SLou. ✍	200.00	50.00
☐☐	John LeClair, Phil. ✍	350.00	100.00
☐☐	Teemu Selänne, Anah. ✍	350.00	100.00
☐☐	Wayne Gretzky, NYRa. ✍	2000.00	550.00
☐☐	Pavel Bure, Flor. ✍	350.00	100.00
☐☐	Mario Lemieux, Pitt. ✍	1350.00	375.00
☐☐	Milan Hejduk, Colo. ✍	350.00	100.00
☐☐	Raymond Bourque, Colo. ✍	550.00	150.00
☐☐	Daniel Alfredsson, Otta. ✍	825.00	150.00
☐☐	Mats Sundin, Toro. ✍	450.00	125.00
☐☐	Paul Kariya, Anah. ✍	600.00	175.00
☐☐	Scott Gomez, NJer. ✍	200.00	50.00
☐☐	Eric Lindros, NHL All-Star	450.00	125.00
☐☐	Sergei Fedorov, Detr. ✍	450.00	125.00
☐☐	Peter Forsberg, Colo. ✍	600.00	175.00
☐☐	Vincent Lecavalier, Tamp. ✍	450.00	125.00
☐☐	Tony Amonte, Chic. ✍	250.00	75.00
☐☐	Patrick Roy (G), Colo. ✍	1100.00	300.00
☐☐	Ed Belfour (G), Dall. ✍	450.00	125.00
☐☐	Martin Brodeur (G), NJer. ✍	700.00	200.00
☐☐	Brian Leetch, NYRa. ✍	250.00	75.00
☐☐	Mike Modano, Dall. ✍	450.00	125.00
☐☐	Joe Sakic, Colo. ✍	700.00	200.00
☐☐	Jeremy Roenick, Phoe. ✍	350.00	100.00
☐☐	Steve Yzerman, Detr. ✍	1100.00	300.00
☐☐	Nikolai Khabibulin (G), Phoe. ✍	200.00	50.00
☐☐	Roman Turek (G), SLou. ✍	200.00	50.00
☐☐	Keith Primeau, Phil. ✍	200.00	50.00
☐☐	Mike Richter (G), NYRa. ✍	200.00	50.00
☐☐	Patrik Stefan, Atla. ✍	200.00	40.00
☐☐	Scott Stevens, NJer. ✍	200.00	50.00
☐☐	Valeri Bure, Calg. ✍	200.00	40.00
☐☐	Doug Weight, Edmo. ✍	250.00	75.00
☐☐	Nicklas Lidström, Detr. ✍	250.00	75.00
☐☐	Chris Drury, Colo. ✍	250.00	75.00
☐☐	Michael Peca, Buff. ✍	200.00	50.00
☐☐	Chris Pronger, SLou. ✍	250.00	75.00
☐☐	Rob Blake, LosA. ✍	250.00	75.00
☐☐	Luc Robitaille, LosA. ✍	350.00	100.00
☐☐	Joe Thornton, Bost. ✍	550.00	150.00
☐☐	Jason Arnott, NJer. ✍	200.00	50.00
☐☐	Daniel Sedin, Vanc. ✍	350.00	75.00
☐☐	Pierre Turgeon, SLou. ✍	200.00	50.00
☐☐	Brad Stuart, SanJ. ✍	200.00	50.00
☐☐	Adam Oates, Wash. ✍	200.00	50.00

ACTIVE-8

	Insert Set (8 cards):	2,800
	Insert (#/30)	AE30
☐	AE-1 Messier ✂ / Yzerman ✂ / Lemieux ✂	650.00
☐	AE-2 Messier ✂ / Yzerman ✂ / Francis ✂	400.00
☐	AE-3 Lemieux ✂ / Hull ✂ / Bure ✂	500.00
☐	AE-4 Lemieux ✂ / Lindros ✂ / Jagr ✂	500.00
☐	AE-5 Roy ✂ / Vernon ✂ / Vanbiesbrouck ✂	400.00
☐	AE-6 Belfour (G) ✂ / Roy ✂ / Hasek ✂	500.00
☐	AE-7 Brodeur ✂ / Hasek ✂ / Osgood ✂	300.00
☐	AE-8 Hasek ✂ / Brodeur ✂ / Hebert ✂	250.00

DYNASTY

There are two versions: the Jersey card (#/50, prefix D-) and the Jersey Emblem card (#/10, prefix DE-).

	Insert Set (20 cards):	5,800	1,700
	Inserts	DE10	DJ50
☐☐	1 Wayne Gretzky, Edmo. ✂	1400.00	450.00
☐☐	2 Mark Messier, Edmo. ✂	350.00	110.00
☐☐	3 Grant Fuhr (G), Edmo. ✂	210.00	60.00
☐☐	4 Paul Coffey, Edmo. ✂	210.00	60.00
☐☐	5 Bill Ranford (G), Edmo. ✂	200.00	50.00
☐☐	6 Mario Lemieux, Pitt. ✂	1050.00	330.00
☐☐	7 Paul Coffey, Pitt. ✂	210.00	60.00
☐☐	8 Jaromir Jagr, Pitt. ✂	350.00	110.00
☐☐	9 Tom Barrasso (G), Pitt. ✂	200.00	50.00
☐☐	10 Ron Francis, Pitt. ✂	210.00	60.00
☐☐	11 Larry Murphy, Pitt. ✂	200.00	50.00
☐☐	12 Ulf Samuelsson, Pitt. ✂	200.00	50.00
☐☐	13 Steve Yzerman, Detr. ✂	840.00	270.00
☐☐	14 Chris Osgood (G), Detr. ✂	210.00	60.00
☐☐	15 Nicklas Lidström, Detr. ✂	210.00	60.00
☐☐	16 Sergei Fedorov, Detr. ✂	350.00	110.00
☐☐	17 Brendan Shanahan, Detr. ✂	350.00	110.00
☐☐	18 Darren McCarty, Detr. ✂	200.00	50.00
☐☐	19 Vyacheslav Kozlov, Detr. ✂	200.00	50.00
☐☐	20 Mike Vernon (G), Detr. ✂	200.00	50.00

GOALIE LEGENDS

	Insert Set (5 cards):	1,000
	Autograph (#/50)	GL50
☐	UG-1 Gerry Cheevers (G), Bost. ✍ ✂	225.00
☐	UG-2 Vladislav Tretiak (G), CSKA Moscow ✍ ✂	400.00
☐	UG-3 Tony Esposito (G), Chic. ✍ ✂	275.00
☐	UG-4 Johnny Bower (G), Toro. ✍ ✂	225.00
☐	UG-5 Bernie Parent (G), Phil. ✍ ✂	225.00

GOALIE STICK MEMORABILIA

	Insert Set (30 cards):	1,500
	Insert (#/50)	GS50
☐	G-1 Guy Hebert (G), Anah. ✂	40.00
☐	G-2 Damian Rhodes (G), Atla. ✂	40.00
☐	G-3 Byron Dafoe (G), Bost. ✂	40.00
☐	G-4 Dominik Hasek (G), Buff. ✂	100.00
☐	G-5 Mike Vernon (G), Calg. ✂	40.00
☐	G-6 Arturs Irbe (G), Caro. ✂	40.00
☐	G-7 Jocelyn Thibault (G), Chic. ✂	40.00
☐	G-8 Patrick Roy (G), Colo. ✂	300.00
☐	G-9 Marc Denis (G), Colu. ✂	40.00
☐	G-10 Ed Belfour (G), Dall. ✂	100.00
☐	G-11 Chris Osgood (G), Detr. ✂	60.00
☐	G-12 Tommy Salo (G), Edmo. ✂	40.00
☐	G-13 Roberto Luongo (G), Flor. ✂	80.00
☐	G-14 Jamie Storr (G), LosA. ✂	40.00
☐	G-15 Manny Fernandez (G), MinW. ✂	40.00
☐	G-16 Jeff Hackett (G), Mont. ✂	40.00

	Card	Price
□	G-17 Mike Dunham (G), Nash. ✂	40.00
□	G-18 Martin Brodeur (G), NJer. ✂	160.00
□	G-19 John Vanbiesbrouck (G), NYIs. ✂	40.00
□	G-20 Mike Richter (G), NYRa. ✂	40.00
□	G-21 Patrick Lalime (G), Otta. ✂	60.00
□	G-22 Brian Boucher (G), Phil. ✂	40.00
□	G-23 Nikolai Khabibulin (G), Phoe. ✂	40.00
□	G-24 Jean-Sébastien Aubin (G), Pitt. ✂	40.00
□	G-25 Roman Turek (G), SLou. ✂	40.00
□	G-26 Steve Shields (G), SanJ. ✂	40.00
□	G-27 Dan Cloutier (G), Tamp. ✂	40.00
□	G-28 Curtis Joseph (G), Toro. ✂	100.00
□	G-29 Félix Potvin (G), Vanc. ✂	120.00
□	G-30 Olaf Kölzig (G), Wash. ✂	60.00

GORDIE HOWE 9

	Insert Set (3 cards):	600.00
	Insert (*50)	J50
□	#9-1 Gordie Howe, Detr. ✂	250.00
□	#9-2 Gordie Howe, New England Whalers ✂	250.00
□	#9-3 Gordie Howe, Houston Aeros ✂	250.00

GORDIE HOWE 9 AUTOGRAPH

	Insert Set (3 cards):	1,600
	Insert (*20)	Aut20
□	#9-1 Gordie Howe, Detr. ✍ ✂	700.00
□	#9-2 Gordie Howe, New England Whalers ✍ ✂	700.00
□	#9-3 Gordie Howe, Houston Aeros ✍ ✂	700.00

HART MEMORABILIA

	Insert Set (20 cards):	500
	Insert (#/30)	J30
□	H-1 Chris Pronger, SLou.	100.00
□	H-2 Jaromir Jagr, Pitt.	100.00
□	H-3 Dominik Hasek (G), Buff.	100.00
□	H-4 Dominik Hasek (G), Buff.	100.00
□	H-5 Mario Lemieux, Pitt.	325.00
□	H-6 Eric Lindros, Phil.	100.00
□	H-7 Sergei Fedorov, Detr.	100.00
□	H-8 Mario Lemieux, Pitt.	325.00
□	H-9 Mark Messier, NYRa.	100.00
□	H-10 Brett Hull, SLou.	100.00
□	H-11 Mark Messier, Edmo.	100.00
□	H-12 Wayne Gretzky, LosA.	400.00
□	H-13 Mario Lemieux, Pitt.	325.00
□	H-14 Wayne Gretzky, Edmo.	400.00
□	H-15 Wayne Gretzky, Edmo.	400.00
□	H-16 Wayne Gretzky, Edmo.	400.00
□	H-17 Wayne Gretzky, Edmo.	400.00
□	H-18 Wayne Gretzky, Edmo.	400.00
□	H-19 Wayne Gretzky, Edmo.	400.00
□	H-20 Wayne Gretzky, Edmo.	400.00

JACQUES PLANTE MEMORABILIA

There are two versions: the Plante Jersey card (#/30, prefix PJ-) and the Plante Skates card (#/20, prefix PS-).

	Insert Set (15 cards):	1,900	1,400
	Description	Sk20	J30
□□	1 Jacques Plante ✂ [w/ Roy]	300.00	250.00
□□	2 Jacques Plante ✂ [w/ Belfour (G)]	175.00	125.00
□□	3 Jacques Plante ✂ [w/ Brodeur]	200.00	175.00
□□	4 Jacques Plante ✂ [w/ Hasek]	175.00	125.00
□□	5 Jacques Plante ✂ [w/ Osgood]	150.00	100.00
□□	6 Jacques Plante ✂ [w/ Joseph (G)]	175.00	125.00
□□	7 Jacques Plante ✂ [w/ Hackett]	125.00	100.00
□□	8 Jacques Plante ✂ [w/ Richter]	125.00	100.00
□□	9 Jacques Plante ✂ [w/ Hebert (G)]	125.00	100.00
□□	10 Jacques Plante ✂ [w/ Luongo]	150.00	125.00
□□	11 Jacques Plante ✂ [w/ Turek]	125.00	100.00
□□	12 Jacques Plante ✂ [w/ Kölzig]	150.00	100.00
□□	13 Jacques Plante ✂ [w/ Thibault]	125.00	100.00
□□	14 Jacques Plante ✂ [w/ Potvin]	150.00	100.00
□□	15 Jacques Plante ✂ [w/ Boucher (G)]	125.00	100.00

JERSEY

	Insert Set (50 cards):	3,300
	Insert (#/60)	J60
□	J-1 Theoren Fleury, NYRa. ✂	50.00
□	J-2 Brendan Shanahan, Detr. ✂	100.00
□	J-3 Curtis Joseph (G), Toro. ✂	100.00
□	J-4 Roman Turek (G), SLou. ✂	30.00
□	J-5 Dominik Hasek (G), Buff. ✂	100.00
□	J-6 Al MacInnis, SLou. ✂	30.00
□	J-7 John LeClair, Phil. ✂	75.00
□	J-8 Teemu Selänne, Anah. ✂	75.00
□	J-9 Wayne Gretzky, NYRa. ✂	400.00
□	J-10 Pavel Bure, Flor. ✂	75.00
□	J-11 Mark Messier, NYRa. ✂	100.00
□	J-12 Jaromir Jagr, Pitt. ✂	100.00
□	J-13 Arturs Irbe (G), Caro. ✂	30.00
□	J-14 Vincent Lecavalier, Tamp. ✂	100.00
□	J-15 Mats Sundin, Toro. ✂	100.00
□	J-16 Paul Kariya, Anah. ✂	125.00
□	J-17 Marian Hossa, Otta. ✂	100.00
□	J-18 Owen Nolan, SanJ. ✂	50.00
□	J-19 Sergei Fedorov, Detr. ✂	100.00
□	J-20 Peter Forsberg, Colo. ✂	125.00
□	J-21 Brett Hull, Dall. ✂	100.00
□	J-22 Tony Amonte, Chic. ✂	50.00
□	J-23 Patrick Roy (G), Colo. ✂	225.00
□	J-24 Ed Belfour (G), Dall. ✂	100.00
□	J-25 Martin Brodeur (G), NJer. ✂	150.00
□	J-26 Brian Leetch, NYRa. ✂	50.00
□	J-27 Mike Modano, Dall. ✂	100.00
□	J-28 Joe Sakic, Colo. ✂	150.00
□	J-29 Jeremy Roenick, Phoe. ✂	75.00
□	J-30 Steve Yzerman, Detr. ✂	225.00
□	J-31 Jason Allison, Bost. ✂	50.00
□	J-32 Milan Hejduk, Colo. ✂	75.00
□	J-33 Mike Richter (G), NYRa. ✂	30.00
□	J-34 Patrik Stefan, Atla. ✂	30.00
□	J-35 Kyle McLaren, Bost. ✂	30.00
□	J-36 Valeri Bure, Calg. ✂	30.00
□	J-37 Félix Potvin (G), Vanc. ✂	100.00
□	J-38 Chris Pronger, SLou. ✂	50.00
□	J-39 Scott Stevens, NJer. ✂	30.00
□	J-40 Luc Robitaille, LosA. ✂	75.00
□	J-41 Roberto Luongo (G), Flor. ✂	75.00
□	J-42 Chris Osgood (G), Detr. ✂	50.00
□	J-43 Olaf Kölzig (G), Wash. ✂	50.00
□	J-44 Scott Gomez, NJer. ✂	30.00
□	J-45 Jason Arnott, NJer. ✂	30.00
□	J-46 Rob Blake, LosA. ✂	50.00
□	J-47 Keith Tkachuk, Phoe. ✂	50.00
□	J-48 Saku Koivu, Mont. ✂	100.00
□	J-49 Alexei Yashin, Otta. ✂	50.00
□	J-50 Nicklas Lidström, Detr. ✂	50.00

JERSEY IN THE NUMBERS, JERSEY EMBLEM

There are two versions: the In The Numbers card (#/10, prefix N-) and the Emblem card (#/10, prefix E-).

	Insert Set (40 cards):	12,000	10,300
	Description	JE10	JN10
□□	1 Brendan Shanahan, Detr. ✂	350.00	300.00
□□	2 Curtis Joseph (G), Toro. ✂	350.00	300.00
□□	3 Roman Turek (G), SLou. ✂	200.00	175.00
□□	4 Dominik Hasek (G), Buff. ✂	350.00	300.00
□□	5 John LeClair, Phil. ✂	275.00	225.00
□□	6 Teemu Selänne, Anah. ✂	275.00	225.00
□□	7 Wayne Gretzky, NYRa. ✂	1400.00	1200.00
□□	8 Pavel Bure, Flor. ✂	275.00	225.00
□□	9 Mark Messier, NYRa. ✂	350.00	300.00
□□	10 Jaromir Jagr, Pitt. ✂	350.00	300.00
□□	11 Arturs Irbe (G), Caro. ✂	200.00	175.00
□□	12 Vincent Lecavalier, Tamp. ✂	350.00	300.00
□□	13 Mats Sundin, Toro. ✂	350.00	300.00
□□	14 Paul Kariya, Anah. ✂	475.00	400.00
□□	15 Marian Hossa, Otta. ✂	350.00	300.00
□□	16 Owen Nolan, SanJ. ✂	200.00	175.00
□□	17 Sergei Fedorov, Detr. ✂	350.00	300.00
□□	18 Peter Forsberg, Colo. ✂	475.00	400.00
□□	19 Brett Hull, Dall. ✂	350.00	300.00
□□	20 Tony Amonte, Chic. ✂	200.00	175.00
□□	21 Patrick Roy (G), Colo. ✂	1050.00	900.00
□□	22 Ed Belfour (G), Dall. ✂	350.00	300.00
□□	23 Martin Brodeur (G), NJer. ✂	550.00	475.00
□□	24 Mike Modano, Dall. ✂	350.00	300.00
□□	25 Joe Sakic, Colo. ✂	550.00	475.00
□□	26 Steve Yzerman, Detr. ✂	825.00	700.00
□□	27 Jason Allison, Bost. ✂	200.00	175.00
□□	28 Milan Hejduk, Colo. ✂	275.00	225.00
□□	29 Mike Richter (G), NYRa. ✂	200.00	175.00
□□	30 Patrik Stefan, Atla. ✂	200.00	175.00
□□	31 Chris Pronger, SLou. ✂	200.00	175.00
□□	32 Luc Robitaille, LosA. ✂	275.00	225.00
□□	33 Roberto Luongo (G), Flor. ✂	275.00	225.00
□□	34 Chris Osgood (G), Detr. ✂	200.00	175.00
□□	35 Olaf Kölzig (G), Wash. ✂	200.00	175.00
□□	36 Scott Gomez, NJer. ✂	200.00	175.00
□□	37 Jason Arnott, NJer. ✂	200.00	175.00
□□	38 Rob Blake, LosA. ✂	200.00	175.00
□□	39 Keith Tkachuk, Phoe. ✂	200.00	175.00
□□	40 Alexei Yashin, Otta. ✂	200.00	175.00

JOURNEY

There are three versions: the Jersey card (#/50, prefix JJ-), the Jersey Numbers card (#/10, prefix JN-) and the Jersey Stick card (#/10, prefix JE-).

	Insert Set (20 cards):	6,000	5,100	1,700
	Description	JE10	JN10	JJ50
□□□	1 Wayne Gretzky, NYRa. ✂	1400.00	1200.00	450.00
□□□	2 Mark Messier, NYRa. ✂	350.00	300.00	100.00
□□□	3 Pavel Bure, Flor. ✂	275.00	225.00	75.00
□□□	4 Jeff Hackett (G), Mont. ✂	200.00	175.00	50.00
□□□	5 Mats Sundin, Toro. ✂	350.00	300.00	100.00
□□□	6 Curtis Joseph (G), Toro. ✂	350.00	300.00	100.00
□□□	7 Ed Belfour (G), Dall. ✂	350.00	300.00	100.00
□□□	8 Mike Modano, Dall. ✂	350.00	300.00	100.00
□□□	9 Brett Hull, Dall. ✂	350.00	300.00	100.00
□□□	10 Teemu Selänne, Anah. ✂	275.00	225.00	75.00
□□□	11 Keith Tkachuk, Phoe. ✂	200.00	175.00	50.00
□□□	12 Patrick Roy (G), Colo. ✂	1050.00	900.00	325.00
□□□	13 Chris Chelios, Detr. ✂	200.00	175.00	50.00
□□□	14 Al MacInnis, SLou. ✂	200.00	175.00	50.00
□□□	15 Theoren Fleury, NYRa. ✂	200.00	175.00	50.00
□□□	16 Jason Allison, Bost. ✂	200.00	175.00	50.00
□□□	17 Jeremy Roenick, Phoe. ✂	275.00	225.00	75.00
□□□	18 B. Shanahan, Detr. ✂	350.00	300.00	100.00
□□□	19 Owen Nolan, SanJ. ✂	200.00	175.00	50.00
□□□	20 Félix Potvin (G), Vanc. ✂	400.00	350.00	125.00

MAGNIFICENT ONES

	Insert Set (10 cards):	2,500
	Insert (#/40)	MO40
□	ML-1 Mario Lemieux ✂ [w/ Yzerman]	375.00
□	ML-2 Mario Lemieux ✂ [w/ Jagr]	275.00
□	ML-3 Mario Lemieux ✂ [w/ Brodeur]	300.00
□	ML-4 Mario Lemieux ✂ [w/ Messier]	275.00
□	ML-5 Mario Lemieux ✂ [w/ Roy]	400.00
□	ML-6 Mario Lemieux ✂ [w/ Bourque]	275.00
□	ML-7 Mario Lemieux ✂ [w/ Francis]	250.00
□	ML-8 Mario Lemieux ✂ [w/ Hasek]	275.00
□	ML-9 Mario Lemieux ✂ [w/ Gretzky]	475.00
□	ML-10 Mario Lemieux ✂ [w/ Coffey]	250.00

MAGNIFICENT ONES AUTOGRAPHED

	Insert Set (10 cards):	3,000
	Insert (#/6)	Auto.
□	ML-1 Mario Lemieux ✂ [w/ Yzerman]	450.00
□	ML-2 Mario Lemieux ✂ [w/ Jagr]	350.00
□	ML-3 Mario Lemieux ✂ [w/ Brodeur]	400.00
□	ML-4 Mario Lemieux ✂ [w/ Messier]	350.00
□	ML-5 Mario Lemieux ✂ [w/ Roy]	525.00
□	ML-6 Mario Lemieux ✂ [w/ Bourque]	350.00
□	ML-7 Mario Lemieux ✂ [w/ Francis]	300.00
□	ML-8 Mario Lemieux ✂ [w/ Hasek]	350.00
□	ML-9 Mario Lemieux ✂ [w/ Gretzky]	600.00
□	ML-10 Mario Lemieux ✂ [w/ Coffey]	300.00

NHL RECORDS

	Insert Set (10 cards):	2,000
	Insert (#/30)	R30
□	RE-1 Terry Sawchuk (G), Toro. ✂	275.00
□	RE-2 Patrick Roy (G), Colo. ✂	400.00
□	RE-3 Tony Esposito (G), Chic. ✂	100.00
□	RE-4 Jacques Plante, Mont. ✂	200.00
□	RE-5 Bill Mosienko, Chic. ✂	100.00
□	RE-6 Teemu Selänne, Winn. ✂	100.00
□	RE-7 Mario Lemieux, Pitt. ✂	400.00
□	RE-8 Raymond Bourque	150.00
□	RE-9 Gordie Howe, Detr. ✂	325.00
□	RE-10 Wayne Gretzky, NYRa. ✂	550.00

NORRIS TROPHY

	Insert Set (10 cards):	500.00
	Insert (#/50)	N50
□	N-1 Chris Pronger, SLou. ✂	60.00
□	N-2 Al MacInnis, SLou. ✂	60.00
□	N-3 Rob Blake, LosA. ✂	60.00
□	N-4 Brian Leetch, NYRa. ✂	60.00
□	N-5 Chris Chelios, Chic. ✂	60.00
□	N-6 Paul Coffey, Detr. ✂	60.00
□	N-7 Raymond Bourque, Bost. ✂	125.00
□	N-8 Chris Chelios, Chic. ✂	60.00
□	N-9 Brian Leetch, NYRa. ✂	60.00
□	N-10 Raymond Bourque, Bost. ✂	125.00

RETRO ACTIVE

	Insert Set (10 cards):	2,200
	Insert (#/30)	RA30
□	RA-1 G. Howe ✂ / C. Pronger ✂	225.00
□	RA-2 T. Sawchuk ✂ / P. Roy ✂	350.00
□	RA-3 T. Esposito ✂ / M. Lemieux ✂	300.00
□	RA-4 T. Esposito ✂ / E. Belfour (G) ✂	125.00
□	RA-5 B. Parent ✂ / S. Yzerman ✂	225.00
□	RA-6 G. Howe ✂ / M. Lemieux ✂	425.00
□	RA-7 B. Mosienko ✂ / P. Kariya ✂	125.00
□	RA-8 J. Plante ✂ / P. Roy ✂	325.00
□	RA-9 G. Howe ✂ / J. Jagr ✂	275.00
□	RA-10 W. Gretzky ✂ / M. Messier ✂	400.00

RETROSPECTIVE

	Insert Set (7 cards):	1,800
	Insert (#/50)	R50
□	1 Gordie Howe, Detr. ✂	250.00
□	2 Gordie Howe, New England Whalers ✂	250.00
□	3 Gordie Howe, Houston Aeros ✂	250.00
□	4 Gordie Howe, Detr. ✂ New England ✂	350.00
□	5 Gordie Howe, Detr. ✂ Houston ✂	350.00
□	6 Gordie Howe, Houston ✂ New England ✂	350.00
□	7 Howe, Detr. ✂ New England ✂ Houston ✂	525.00

RETROSPECTIVE AUTOGRAPH

	Insert Set (7 cards):	3,900
	Insert (#/50)	R50
□	1 Gordie Howe ✍ Detr. ✂	550.00
□	2 Gordie Howe ✍ New England Whalers ✂	550.00
□	3 Gordie Howe ✍ Houston Aeros ✂	550.00
□	4 Gordie Howe ✍ Detr. ✂ New England ✂	550.00
□	5 Gordie Howe ✍ Detr. ✂ Houston ✂	550.00
□	6 Gordie Howe ✍ Houston ✂ New England ✂	550.00
□	7 Howe ✍ Detr. ✂ New England ✂ Houston ✂	1600.00

RICHARD AUTOGRAPH

These cards featured an affixed cut autograph.

	Insert Set (5 cards):	2,800
	Insert (#/10)	MRA10
□	RR-1 Maurice Richard, Mont. ✍ •	700.00
□	RR-2 Maurice Richard, Mont. ✍ •	700.00
□	RR-3 Maurice Richard, Mont. ✍ •	700.00
□	RR-4 Maurice Richard, Mont. ✍ •	700.00
□	RR-5 Maurice Richard, Mont. ✍ •	700.00

STICK

	Insert Set (50 cards):	2,600
	Insert (#/90)	S90
□	S-1 Theoren Fleury, NYRa. ✂	35.00
□	S-2 Brendan Shanahan, Detr. ✂	75.00
□	S-3 Curtis Joseph (G), Toro. ✂	75.00
□	S-4 Roman Turek (G), SLou. ✂	35.00
□	S-5 Dominik Hasek (G), Buff. ✂	75.00
□	S-6 Al MacInnis, SLou. ✂	35.00
□	S-7 John LeClair, Phil. ✂	50.00
□	S-8 Teemu Selänne, Anah. ✂	50.00
□	S-9 Wayne Gretzky, NYRa. ✂	300.00
□	S-10 Pavel Bure, Flor. ✂	50.00
□	S-11 Mark Messier, NYRa. ✂	75.00
□	S-12 Jaromir Jagr, Pitt. ✂	75.00
□	S-13 Arturs Irbe (G), Caro. ✂	35.00
□	S-14 Vincent Lecavalier, Tamp. ✂	75.00
□	S-15 Mats Sundin, Toro. ✂	75.00
□	S-16 Paul Kariya, Anah. ✂	100.00
□	S-17 Marian Hossa, Otta. ✂	75.00
□	S-18 Owen Nolan, SanJ. ✂	35.00
□	S-19 Sergei Fedorov, Detr. ✂	75.00
□	S-20 Peter Forsberg, Colo. ✂	100.00
□	S-21 Brett Hull, Dall. ✂	75.00
□	S-22 Tony Amonte, Chic. ✂	35.00
□	S-23 Patrick Roy (G), Colo. ✂	225.00
□	S-24 Ed Belfour (G), Dall. ✂	75.00
□	S-25 Martin Brodeur (G), NJer. ✂	100.00
□	S-26 Brian Leetch, NYRa. ✂	35.00
□	S-27 Mike Modano, Dall. ✂	75.00
□	S-28 Joe Sakic, Colo. ✂	100.00
□	S-29 Jeremy Roenick, Phoe. ✂	50.00
□	S-30 Steve Yzerman, Detr. ✂	175.00
□	S-31 Jason Allison, Bost. ✂	35.00
□	S-32 Milan Hejduk, Colo. ✂	50.00
□	S-33 Mike Richter (G), NYRa. ✂	35.00
□	S-34 Patrik Stefan, Atla. ✂	35.00
□	S-35 Kyle McLaren, Bost. ✂	35.00
□	S-36 Valeri Bure, Calg. ✂	35.00
□	S-37 Félix Potvin (G), LosA. ✂	75.00
□	S-38 Chris Pronger, SLou. ✂	35.00
□	S-39 Scott Stevens, NJer. ✂	35.00
□	S-40 Luc Robitaille, LosA. ✂	50.00
□	S-41 Roberto Luongo (G), Flor. ✂	50.00
□	S-42 Chris Osgood (G), Detr. ✂	35.00
□	S-43 Olaf Kölzig (G), Wash. ✂	35.00
□	S-44 Scott Gomez, NJer. ✂	35.00
□	S-45 Jason Arnott, NJer. ✂	35.00
□	S-46 Rob Blake, LosA. ✂	35.00
□	S-47 Keith Tkachuk, Phoe. ✂	35.00
□	S-48 Saku Koivu, Mont. ✂	75.00
□	S-49 Alexei Yashin, Otta. ✂	35.00
□	S-50 Nicklas Lidström, Detr. ✂	35.00

TEAMMATES

	Insert Set (40 cards):	1,700
	Insert (#/70)	T70
□	T-1 S. Yzerman ✂ / S. Fedorov ✂	150.00
□	T-2 B. Shanahan ✂ / Vy. Kozlov ✂	50.00
□	T-3 S. Yzerman ✂ / C. Chelios ✂	150.00
□	T-4 S. Yzerman ✂ / B. Shanahan ✂	150.00
□	T-5 J. Roenick ✂ / K. Tkachuk ✂	50.00
□	T-6 N. Lidström ✂ / S. Fedorov ✂	75.00
□	T-7 N. Lidström ✂ / C. Osgood ✂	50.00
□	T-8 N. Lidström ✂ / B. Shanahan ✂	75.00
□	T-9 C. Osgood ✂ / S. Fedorov ✂	75.00
□	T-10 N. Khabibulin ✂ / J. Roenick ✂	50.00
□	T-11 S. Gonchar ✂ / A. Oates ✂	35.00
□	T-12 Cu. Joseph (G) ✂ / M. Sundin ✂	100.00
□	T-13 Cu. Joseph ✂ / T. Domi ✂	50.00
□	T-14 M. Sundin ✂ / T. Domi ✂	50.00
□	T-15 P. Forsberg ✂ / P. Roy ✂	200.00
□	T-16 P. Forsberg ✂ / J. Sakic ✂	150.00
□	T-17 J. Sakic ✂ / P. Roy ✂	225.00
□	T-18 B. Mironov ✂ / T. Amonte ✂	35.00
□	T-19 P. Bure ✂ / P. Laus ✂	35.00
□	T-20 M. Peca ✂ / D. Hasek ✂	50.00
□	T-21 P. Kariya ✂ / T. Selänne ✂	100.00
□	T-22 G. Hebert (G) ✂ / T. Selänne ✂	50.00
□	T-23 P. Kariya ✂ / G. Hebert (G) ✂	75.00

☐	T-24 Br. Hull ✂ / M. Modano ✂	100.00
☐	T-25 Br. Hull ✂ / E. Belfour (G) ✂	100.00
☐	T-26 E. Belfour (G) ✂ / M. Modano ✂	100.00
☐	T-27 S. Zubov ✂ / E. Belfour (G) ✂	50.00
☐	T-28 Br. Hull ✂ / D. Sydor ✂	50.00
☐	T-29 É. Desjardins ✂ / J. LeClair ✂	50.00
☐	T-30 J. Arnott ✂ / M. Brodeur ✂	100.00
☐	T-31 S. Yzerman ✂ / M. Vernon ✂	125.00
☐	T-32 Br. Hull ✂ / Cu. Joseph ✂	100.00
☐	T-33 K. Tkachuk ✂ / T. Selänne ✂	50.00
☐	T-34 M. Sundin ✂ / O. Nolan ✂	75.00
☐	T-35 C. Chelios ✂ / E. Belfour (G) ✂	75.00
☐	T-36 M. Messier ✂ / W. Gretzky ✂	250.00
☐	T-37 T. Fleury ✂ / A. MacInnis ✂	50.00
☐	T-38 F. Potvin ✂ / M. Sundin ✂	100.00
☐	T-39 M. Lemieux ✂ / J. Jagr ✂	200.00
☐	T-40 R. Bourque ✂ / A. Oates ✂	75.00

ULTIMATE CAPTAINS

Insert Set (10 cards):		**2,500**
	Insert (#/5)	**UC5**
☐	UC-1 Steve Yzerman, Detr. ✂	1300.00
☐	UC-2 Keith Tkachuk, Phoe. ✂	300.00
☐	UC-3 Mats Sundin, Toro. ✂	500.00
☐	UC-4 Saku Koivu, Mont. ✂	600.00
☐	UC-5 Jaromir Jagr, Pitt. ✂	500.00
☐	UC-6 Paul Kariya, Anah. ✂	700.00
☐	UC-7 Mark Messier, NYRa. ✂	500.00
☐	UC-8 Joe Sakic, Colo. ✂	800.00
☐	UC-9 Wayne Gretzky, Edmo. ✂	2200.00
☐	UC-10 Mario Lemieux, Pitt. ✂	1600.00

ULTIMATE GOALIE COLLECTION

Insert Set (20 cards):		**3,200**
	Insert (#/30)	**GM30**
☐	GM-1 J. Plante / P. Roy	350.00
☐	GM-2 T. Sawchuk / P. Roy	400.00
☐	GM-3 M. Vernon / C. Osgood	100.00
☐	GM-4 Cu. Joseph (G) / F. Potvin	100.00
☐	GM-5 T. Esposito / E. Belfour (G)	150.00
☐	GM-6 T. Broda / J. Bower	100.00
☐	GM-7 B. Parent / B. Boucher (G)	100.00
☐	GM-8 T. Esposito / G. Cheevers	100.00
☐	GM-9 B. Parent / G. Cheevers	100.00
☐	GM-10 Jacques Plante, Mont.	150.00
☐	GM-11 P. Roy / E. Belfour (G)	350.00
☐	GM-12 Cu. Joseph / D. Hasek	150.00
☐	GM-13 R. Turek / E. Belfour (G)	100.00
☐	GM-14 M. Brodeur / J. Plante	200.00
☐	GM-15 M. Richter / J. Vanbiesbrouck	100.00
☐	GM-16 Jacques Plante, Mont.	150.00
☐	GM-17 T. Esposito / B. Parent / V. Tretiak	200.00
☐	GM-18 F. Brimsek / B. Dafoe / G. Cheevers	200.00
☐	GM-19 J. Bower / T. Broda / T. Sawchuk	250.00
☐	GM-20 P. Roy / G. Vézina / T. Sawchuk	650.00

2000 - 01 UPPER DECK

This series was distributed in two separate releases: a Series One release in October 2000 and a Series Two release in January 2001. For each series, there is a regular base card, a UD Exclusives silver-foil parallel limited to 100 copies and a UD Exclusives gold-foil parallel limited to 25 copies. In Series One, Young Guns subset cards 181-230 are seeded 1:4 packs with the last 20 cards (211-230) being more limited than the first 30 cards (181-210). In Series Two, Young Guns subet cards 411-440 are seeded 1:4 packs. Also in Series Two, Upper Deck reprinted Young Guns subset cards 211-230 so that production numbers for these cards would match those of other Young Guns subset cards. These reprint cards, however, have a 2001-copyright date as opposed to the 2000-copyright date that appears on the originals. Young Guns reprints 211-230 are listed below as an insert set after the regular set.

Series One Set (230 cards):		**5,700**	**2,300**	**275.00**
Series Two Set (210 cards):		**4,400**	**1,700**	**100.00**
Common Player:		**12.00**	**5.00**	**.20**
	Player	**E25**	**E100**	**Reg.**
☐☐☐	1 Paul Kariya, Anah.	175.00	70.00	1.00
☐☐☐	2 Steve Rucchin, Anah.	30.00	12.00	.20
☐☐☐	3 Oleg Tverdovsky, Anah.	20.00	8.00	.20
☐☐☐	4 Mike Leclerc, Anah.	20.00	8.00	.20
☐☐☐	5 Ladislav Kohn, Anah.	20.00	8.00	.20
☐☐☐	6 Guy Hebert (G), Anah.	30.00	12.00	.20
☐☐☐	7 Dean Sylvester, Atla.	12.00	5.00	.20
☐☐☐	8 Andrew Brunette, Atla.	20.00	8.00	.20
☐☐☐	9 Ray Ferraro, Atla.	20.00	8.00	.20
☐☐☐	10 Donald Audette, Atla.	50.00	20.00	.20
☐☐☐	11 Damian Rhodes (G), Atla.	30.00	12.00	.20
☐☐☐	12 Patrik Stefan, Atla.	40.00	16.00	.20
☐☐☐	13 Joe Thornton, Bost.	150.00	60.00	1.00
☐☐☐	14 Brian Rolston, Bost.	40.00	16.00	.20
☐☐☐	15 John Grahame (G), Bost.	30.00	12.00	.20
☐☐☐	16 Jason Allison, Bost.	75.00	30.00	.50
☐☐☐	17 Kyle McLaren, Bost.	30.00	12.00	.20
☐☐☐	18 André Savage, Bost.	12.00	5.00	.20
☐☐☐	19 Martin Biron (G), Buff.	60.00	24.00	.20
☐☐☐	20 Doug Gilmour, Buff.	75.00	30.00	.50
☐☐☐	21 Chris Gratton, Buff.	30.00	12.00	.20
☐☐☐	22 Miroslav Satan, Buff.	40.00	16.00	.20
☐☐☐	23 Maxim Afinogenov, Buff.	50.00	20.00	.20
☐☐☐	24 Dimitri Kalinin, Buff.	12.00	5.00	.20
☐☐☐	25 Oleg Saprykin, Calg.	30.00	12.00	.20
☐☐☐	26 Valeri Bure, Calg.	40.00	16.00	.20
☐☐☐	27 Derek Morris, Calg.	30.00	12.00	.20
☐☐☐	28 Marc Savard, Calg.	30.00	12.00	.20
☐☐☐	29 Clarke Wilm, Calg.	12.00	5.00	.20
☐☐☐	30 Fred Brathwaite (G), Calg.	40.00	16.00	.20
☐☐☐	31 Ron Francis, Caro.	75.00	30.00	.50
☐☐☐	32 Sami Kapanen, Caro.	40.00	16.00	.20
☐☐☐	33 Bates Battaglia, Caro.	30.00	12.00	.20
☐☐☐	34 Arturs Irbe (G), Caro.	50.00	20.00	.20
☐☐☐	35 David Tanabe, Caro.	20.00	8.00	.20
☐☐☐	36 Rod Brind'Amour, Caro.	40.00	16.00	.20
☐☐☐	37 Michal Grosek, Chic.	12.00	5.00	.20
☐☐☐	38 Steve Sullivan, Chic.	40.00	16.00	.20
☐☐☐	39 Éric Dazé, Chic.	50.00	20.00	.20
☐☐☐	40 Bryan McCabe, Chic.	30.00	12.00	.20
☐☐☐	41 Michael Nylander, Chic.	30.00	12.00	.20
☐☐☐	42 Alexei Zhamnov, Chic.	40.00	16.00	.20
☐☐☐	43 Milan Hejduk, Colo.	100.00	40.00	.50
☐☐☐	44 Raymond Bourque, Colo.	150.00	60.00	1.00
☐☐☐	45 Patrick Roy (G), Colo.	375.00	150.00	3.00
☐☐☐	46 Peter Forsberg, Colo.	175.00	70.00	1.00
☐☐☐	47 Martin Skoula, Colo.	30.00	12.00	.20
☐☐☐	48 Shjon Podein, Colo.	30.00	12.00	.20
☐☐☐	49 Aaron Miller, Colo.	12.00	5.00	.20
☐☐☐	50 E. Knutsen, Anah. (Colu.)	30.00	12.00	.20
☐☐☐	51 Jamie Pushor, Colu.	12.00	5.00	.20
☐☐☐	52 Kevyn Adams, Colu.	20.00	8.00	.20
☐☐☐	53 Marc Denis (G), Colu.	60.00	24.00	.20
☐☐☐	54 R. Tugnutt (G), Pitt. (Colu.)	50.00	20.00	.20
☐☐☐	55 Mike Modano, Dall.	125.00	50.00	1.00
☐☐☐	56 Joe Nieuwendyk, Dall.	50.00	20.00	.20
☐☐☐	57 Mike Keane, Dall.	20.00	8.00	.20
☐☐☐	58 Darryl Sydor, Dall.	30.00	12.00	.20
☐☐☐	59 Brenden Morrow, Dall.	40.00	16.00	.20
☐☐☐	60 Jere Lehtinen, Dall.	40.00	16.00	.20
☐☐☐	61 Derian Hatcher, Dall.	40.00	16.00	.20
☐☐☐	62 Brendan Shanahan, Detr.	125.00	50.00	1.00
☐☐☐	63 Sergei Fedorov, Detr.	125.00	50.00	1.00
☐☐☐	64 Darren McCarty, Detr.	40.00	16.00	.20
☐☐☐	65 Tomas Holmström, Detr.	30.00	12.00	.20
☐☐☐	66 Chris Osgood (G), Detr.	75.00	30.00	.50
☐☐☐	67 Nicklas Lidström, Detr.	75.00	30.00	.50
☐☐☐	68 Ryan Smyth, Edmo.	60.00	24.00	.20
☐☐☐	69 Igor Ulanov, Edmo.	20.00	8.00	.20
☐☐☐	70 Tommy Salo (G), Edmo.	50.00	20.00	.20
☐☐☐	71 Ethan Moreau, Edmo.	20.00	8.00	.20
☐☐☐	72 Daniel Cleary, Edmo.	40.00	16.00	.20
☐☐☐	73 Bill Guerin, Edmo.	50.00	20.00	.20
☐☐☐	74 Pavel Bure, Flor.	100.00	40.00	.50
☐☐☐	75 Ray Whitney, Flor.	30.00	12.00	.20
☐☐☐	76 Lance Pitlick, Flor.	12.00	5.00	.20
☐☐☐	77 Trevor Kidd (G), Flor.	40.00	16.00	.20
☐☐☐	78 Mike Wilson, Flor.	12.00	5.00	.20
☐☐☐	79 Ivan Novoseltsev, Flor.	25.00	10.00	.20
☐☐☐	80 Luc Robitaille, LosA.	100.00	40.00	.50
☐☐☐	81 Stéphane Fiset (G), LosA.	40.00	16.00	.20
☐☐☐	82 Rob Blake, LosA.	75.00	30.00	.50
☐☐☐	83 Jozef Stumpel, LosA.	30.00	12.00	.20
☐☐☐	84 Craig Johnson, LosA.	12.00	5.00	.20
☐☐☐	85 Glen Murray, LosA.	60.00	24.00	.20
☐☐☐	86 Kelly Buchberger, LosA.	20.00	8.00	.20
☐☐☐	87 Fernanadez, Dall. (MinW.)	50.00	20.00	.20
☐☐☐	88 S. Roest [Photo A. Jacques]	20.00	8.00	.20
☐☐☐	89 A. Sutton, SanJ. (MinW.)	12.00	5.00	.20
☐☐☐	90 S. Pellerin, SLou. (MinW.)	20.00	8.00	.20
☐☐☐	91 Jim Dowd, Edmo. (MinW.)	12.00	5.00	.20
☐☐☐	92 Dainius Zubrus, Mont.	30.00	12.00	.20
☐☐☐	93 Brian Savage, Mont.	40.00	16.00	.20
☐☐☐	94 Martin Rucinsky, Mont.	30.00	12.00	.20
☐☐☐	95 Craig Darby, Mont.	20.00	8.00	.20
☐☐☐	96 José Théodore (G), Mont.	150.00	60.00	1.00
☐☐☐	97 David Legwand, Nash.	50.00	20.00	.20
☐☐☐	98 Rob Valicevic, Nash.	12.00	5.00	.20
☐☐☐	99 Randy Robitaille, Nash.	20.00	8.00	.20
☐☐☐	100 Mike Dunham (G), Nash.	50.00	20.00	.20
☐☐☐	101 Kimmo Timonen, Nash.	20.00	8.00	.20
☐☐☐	102 Scott Gomez, NJer.	50.00	20.00	.20
☐☐☐	103 Petr* Sykora, NJer.	50.00	20.00	.20
☐☐☐	104 Alexander Mogilny, NJer.	60.00	24.00	.20
☐☐☐	105 John Madden, NJer.	40.00	16.00	.20
☐☐☐	106 Jason Arnott, NJer.	60.00	24.00	.20
☐☐☐	107 Sergei Brylin, NJer.	20.00	8.00	.20
☐☐☐	108 Scott Stevens, NJer.	50.00	20.00	.20
☐☐☐	109 Tim Connolly, NYIs.	50.00	20.00	.20
☐☐☐	110 Mariusz Czerkawski, NYIs.	30.00	12.00	.20
☐☐☐	111 Zdeno Chara, NYIs.	30.00	12.00	.20
☐☐☐	112 Kenny Jönsson, NYIs.	25.00	10.00	.20
☐☐☐	113 Claude Lapointe, NYIs.	20.00	8.00	.20
☐☐☐	114 Theoren Fleury, NYRa.	75.00	30.00	.50
☐☐☐	115 Mike Richter (G), NYRa.	60.00	24.00	.20
☐☐☐	116 Mike York, NYRa.	40.00	16.00	.20
☐☐☐	117 Jan Hlavac, NYRa.	30.00	12.00	.20
☐☐☐	118 Adam Graves, NYRa.	50.00	20.00	.20
☐☐☐	119 Mark Messier, NYRa.	125.00	50.00	1.00
☐☐☐	120 Marian Hossa, Otta.	125.00	50.00	1.00
☐☐☐	121 Daniel Alfredsson, Otta.	150.00	60.00	.50
☐☐☐	122 Mike Fisher, Otta.	30.00	12.00	.20
☐☐☐	123 Patrick Lalime (G), Otta.	75.00	30.00	.50
☐☐☐	124 Wade Redden, Otta.	40.00	16.00	.20
☐☐☐	125 Shawn McEachern, Otta.	40.00	16.00	.20
☐☐☐	126 John LeClair, Phil.	100.00	40.00	.50
☐☐☐	127 Mark Recchi, Phil.	50.00	20.00	.20
☐☐☐	128 Brian Boucher (G), Phil.	40.00	16.00	.20
☐☐☐	129 Simon Gagné, Phil.	100.00	40.00	.50
☐☐☐	130 Éric Desjardins, Phil.	40.00	16.00	.20
☐☐☐	131 Rick Tocchet, Phil.	40.00	16.00	.20
☐☐☐	132 Jeremy Roenick, Phoe.	100.00	40.00	.50
☐☐☐	133 Travis Green, Phoe.	30.00	12.00	.20
☐☐☐	134 Trevor Letowski, Phoe.	20.00	8.00	.20
☐☐☐	135 Teppo Numminen, Phoe.	40.00	16.00	.20
☐☐☐	136 Shane Doan, Phoe.	30.00	12.00	.20
☐☐☐	137 Mike Sullivan, Phoe.	12.00	5.00	.20
☐☐☐	138 Jaromir Jagr, Pitt.	125.00	50.00	1.00
☐☐☐	139 Robert Lang, Pitt.	30.00	12.00	.20
☐☐☐	140 Jan Hrdina, Pitt.	30.00	12.00	.20
☐☐☐	141 Matthew Barnaby, Pitt.	12.00	5.00	.20
☐☐☐	142 J-S Aubin (G), Pitt.	30.00	12.00	.20
☐☐☐	143 Jirí Slégr, Pitt.	20.00	8.00	.20
☐☐☐	144 Owen Nolan, SanJ.	75.00	30.00	.50
☐☐☐	145 Jeff Friesen, SanJ.	40.00	16.00	.20
☐☐☐	146 Patrick Marleau, SanJ.	60.00	24.00	.20
☐☐☐	147 Brad Stuart, SanJ.	50.00	20.00	.20
☐☐☐	148 Steve Shields (G), SanJ.	30.00	12.00	.20
☐☐☐	149 Todd Harvey, SanJ.	30.00	12.00	.20
☐☐☐	150 Pavol Demitra, SLou.	50.00	20.00	.20
☐☐☐	151 Chris Pronger, SLou.	75.00	30.00	.50
☐☐☐	152 Scott Young, SLou.	40.00	16.00	.20
☐☐☐	153 Todd Reirden, SLou.	12.00	5.00	.20
☐☐☐	154 Roman Turek (G), SLou.	60.00	24.00	.20
☐☐☐	155 Marty Reasoner, SLou.	30.00	12.00	.20
☐☐☐	156 Mike Johnson, Tamp.	25.00	10.00	.20
☐☐☐	157 Todd Warriner, Tamp.	20.00	8.00	.20
☐☐☐	158 Paul Mara, Tamp.	20.00	8.00	.20
☐☐☐	159 Dan Cloutier (G), Tamp.	50.00	20.00	.20
☐☐☐	160 Fredrik Modin, Tamp.	30.00	12.00	.20
☐☐☐	161 Curtis Joseph (G), Toro.	125.00	50.00	1.00
☐☐☐	162 Steve Thomas, Toro.	30.00	12.00	.20
☐☐☐	163 Darcy Tucker, Toro.	30.00	12.00	.20
☐☐☐	164 Yanic Perreault, Toro.	40.00	16.00	.20
☐☐☐	165 Sergei Berezin, Toro.	60.00	24.00	.20
☐☐☐	166 Dmitry Yushkevich, Toro.	30.00	12.00	.20
☐☐☐	167 Markus Näslund, Vanc.	125.00	50.00	1.00
☐☐☐	168 Andrew Cassels, Vanc.	30.00	12.00	.20
☐☐☐	169 Todd Bertuzzi, Vanc.	150.00	60.00	1.00
☐☐☐	170 Félix Potvin (G), Vanc.	150.00	60.00	.50
☐☐☐	171 Ed Jovanovski, Vanc.	50.00	20.00	.20
☐☐☐	172 Trent Klatt, Vanc.	20.00	8.00	.20
☐☐☐	173 Adam Oates, Wash.	50.00	20.00	.20
☐☐☐	174 Chris Simon, Wash.	30.00	12.00	.20
☐☐☐	175 Richard Zednik, Wash.	50.00	20.00	.20
☐☐☐	176 Calle Johansson, Wash.	30.00	12.00	.20
☐☐☐	177 Andréi Nikolishin, Wash.	20.00	8.00	.20
☐☐☐	178 Jeff Halpern, Wash.	30.00	12.00	.20
☐☐☐	179 S. Yzerman, Detr. [CL]	300.00	120.00	1.00
☐☐☐	180 C. Joseph (G), Toro. [CL]	125.00	50.00	.50
☐☐☐	**181 Eric Nickulas, Bost. RC**	**12.00**	**5.00**	**2.50**
☐☐☐	**182 Aubin, Colo.(Colu.) RC**	**20.00**	**8.00**	**4.00**
☐☐☐	**183 Keith Aldridge, Dall. RC**	**12.00**	**5.00**	**2.50**
☐☐☐	**184 Minard (G), Edmo. RC**	**20.00**	**8.00**	**4.00**
☐☐☐	**185 Reinprecht, LosA. RC**	**40.00**	**16.00**	**10.00**
☐☐☐	**186 Gosselin, Nash. RC**	**12.00**	**5.00**	**2.50**
☐☐☐	187 Andy Berenzweig, Nash.	12.00	5.00	2.00
☐☐☐	**188 W. Mitchell, NJer. RC**	**20.00**	**8.00**	**4.00**
☐☐☐	**189 Colin White, NJer. RC**	**20.00**	**8.00**	**4.00**
☐☐☐	**190 Peter Mika, NYIs. RC**	**12.00**	**5.00**	**2.50**
☐☐☐	**191 Valiquette (G), NYIs. RC**	**20.00**	**8.00**	**4.00**
☐☐☐	**192 Freadrich, Tamp. RC**	**12.00**	**5.00**	**2.50**
☐☐☐	**193 Rich Parent (G), Tamp. (Otta.) RC**	**20.00**	**8.00**	**4.00**
☐☐☐	**194 G. Andrusak, Toro. RC**	**12.00**	**5.00**	**2.50**
☐☐☐	**195 Brent Sopel, Vanc. RC**	**20.00**	**8.00**	**4.00**
☐☐☐	**196 Matt Pettinger RC**	**20.00**	**8.00**	**4.00**
☐☐☐	**197 Chris Nielsen RC**	**20.00**	**8.00**	**4.00**
☐☐☐	**198 Dany Heatley RC**	**125.00**	**50.00**	**55.00**
☐☐☐	**199 Matt Zultek RC**	**12.00**	**5.00**	**2.50**
☐☐☐	**200 D. Afanasenkov RC**	**20.00**	**8.00**	**4.00**
☐☐☐	**201 Tyler Bouck RC**	**20.00**	**8.00**	**4.00**
☐☐☐	**202 Jonas Andersson RC**	**12.00**	**5.00**	**2.50**
☐☐☐	**203 Marc-André Thinel RC**	**20.00**	**8.00**	**4.00**
☐☐☐	**204 Jaroslav Svoboda RC**	**30.00**	**12.00**	**6.00**
☐☐☐	**205 Josef Vasicek RC**	**30.00**	**12.00**	**6.00**
☐☐☐	**206 A. Raycroft (G) RC**	**30.00**	**12.00**	**6.00**
☐☐☐	**207 Juraj Kolnik RC**	**20.00**	**8.00**	**4.00**
☐☐☐	**208 Zdenek Blatny RC**	**20.00**	**8.00**	**4.00**
☐☐☐	**209 S. Caron (G) RC**	**30.00**	**12.00**	**6.00**
☐☐☐	**210 Michael Ryder RC**	**20.00**	**8.00**	**4.00**
☐☐☐	**211 Jason Jaspers RC ©'00**	**20.00**	**8.00**	**10.00**
☐☐☐	212 P. Brendl, Calgary ©'00	40.00	16.00	4.50
☐☐☐	213 Kraft, Prince Albert ©'00	40.00	16.00	4.50
☐☐☐	**214 . Williams, Phil. RC ©'00**	**40.00**	**16.00**	**20.00**
☐☐☐	**215 Karlsson, Atla. RC ©'00**	**12.00**	**5.00**	**6.00**
☐☐☐	**216 Vasiljevs, Atla. RC ©'00**	**20.00**	**8.00**	**10.00**
☐☐☐	**217 Vyshedkevich RC ©'00**	**20.00**	**8.00**	**10.00**
☐☐☐	218 J. Aitken, Bost. ©'00	12.00	5.00	3.00
☐☐☐	**219 B. Smith, Bost. RC ©'00**	**12.00**	**5.00**	**6.00**
☐☐☐	**220 J. Cowan, Calg. RC ©'00**	**12.00**	**5.00**	**6.00**
☐☐☐	**221 S. Brûlé, NJer. RC ©'00**	**12.00**	**5.00**	**6.00**
☐☐☐	**222 Witehall, NYRa. RC ©'00**	**20.00**	**8.00**	**10.00**
☐☐☐	**223 Hurme (G),Otta. RC ©'00**	**30.00**	**12.00**	**15.00**
☐☐☐	**224 Trudel, Phoe. RC ©'00**	**20.00**	**8.00**	**10.00**
☐☐☐	**225 Astashenko RC ©'00**	**12.00**	**5.00**	**6.00**
☐☐☐	**226 Hartnell, Nash. RC ©'00**	**30.00**	**12.00**	**15.00**
☐☐☐	**227 Kochan (G) RC ©'00**	**20.00**	**8.00**	**10.00**
☐☐☐	**228 R. Klesla, Colu. RC ©'00**	**75.00**	**30.00**	**25.00**
☐☐☐	**229 Gaborik RC ©'00**	**125.00**	**50.00**	**75.00**
☐☐☐	230 Michaud (G), Vanc. ©'00	20.00	8.00	3.00
☐☐☐	231 Teemu Selänne, Anah.	100.00	40.00	.50
☐☐☐	232 Matt Cullen, Anah.	30.00	12.00	.20
☐☐☐	233 German Titov, Anah.	12.00	5.00	.20
☐☐☐	234 Vitaly Vishnevski, Anah.	30.00	12.00	.20
☐☐☐	235 Pavel Trnka, Anah.	12.00	5.00	.20
☐☐☐	236 Marty McInnis, Anah.	20.00	8.00	.20
☐☐☐	237 Hnat Domenichelli, Atla.	20.00	8.00	.20
☐☐☐	238 Per Svartvadet, Atla.	12.00	5.00	.20
☐☐☐	239 Stephen Guolla, Atla.	12.00	5.00	.20
☐☐☐	240 Frantisek Kaberle, Atla.	20.00	8.00	.20
☐☐☐	241 Steve Staios, Atla.	12.00	5.00	.20
☐☐☐	242 Byron Dafoe (G), Bost.	50.00	20.00	.20
☐☐☐	243 Peter Popovic, Bost.	12.00	5.00	.20
☐☐☐	244 Paul Coffey, Bost.	75.00	30.00	.50
☐☐☐	245 Sergei Samsonov, Bost.	75.00	30.00	.50
☐☐☐	246 Andréi Kovalenko, Bost.	20.00	8.00	.20
☐☐☐	247 Shawn Bates, Bost.	20.00	8.00	.20
☐☐☐	248 Dominik Hasek (G), Buff.	125.00	50.00	1.00
☐☐☐	249 Stu Barnes, Buff.	12.00	5.00	.20
☐☐☐	250 Curtis Brown, Buff.	20.00	8.00	.20
☐☐☐	251 Alexei Zhitnik, Buff.	20.00	8.00	.20
☐☐☐	252 Jay McKee, Buff.	12.00	5.00	.20
☐☐☐	253 Vaclav Varada, Buff.	20.00	8.00	.20
☐☐☐	254 Jarome Iginla, Calg.	100.00	40.00	.50
☐☐☐	255 Phil Housley, Calg.	40.00	16.00	.20
☐☐☐	256 Cory Stillman, Calg.	30.00	12.00	.20
☐☐☐	257 Mike Vernon (G), Calg.	50.00	20.00	.20
☐☐☐	258 Jeff Shantz, Calg.	12.00	5.00	.20
☐☐☐	259 Brad Werenka, Calg.	12.00	5.00	.20
☐☐☐	260 Jeff O'Neill, Caro.	50.00	20.00	.20
☐☐☐	261 Martin Gélinas, Caro.	30.00	12.00	.20
☐☐☐	262 Tommy Westlund, Caro.	12.00	5.00	.20
☐☐☐	263 Stevenn Halko, Caro.	12.00	5.00	.20
☐☐☐	264 Sandis Ozolinsh, Caro.	30.00	12.00	.20
☐☐☐	265 Rob DiMaio, Caro.	20.00	8.00	.20
☐☐☐	266 Tony Amonte, Chic.	75.00	30.00	.50
☐☐☐	267 J. Thibault (G), Chic.	50.00	20.00	.20
☐☐☐	268 Boris Mironov, Chic.	20.00	8.00	.20
☐☐☐	269 Dean McAmmond, Chic.	20.00	8.00	.20
☐☐☐	270 Jean-Yves Leroux, Chic.	12.00	5.00	.20
☐☐☐	271 Valeri Zelepukin, Chic.	12.00	5.00	.20
☐☐☐	272 Nolan Pratt, Colo.	12.00	5.00	.20
☐☐☐	273 Joe Sakic, Colo.	200.00	80.00	1.50
☐☐☐	274 Chris Drury, Colo.	75.00	30.00	.50
☐☐☐	275 Alex Tanguay, Colo.	75.00	30.00	.50
☐☐☐	276 Adam Deadmarsh, Colo.	40.00	16.00	.20
☐☐☐	277 Stéphane Yelle, Colo.	20.00	8.00	.20
☐☐☐	278 Ron Tugnutt (G), Colu.	50.00	20.00	.20
☐☐☐	279 Geoff Sanderson, Colu.	30.00	12.00	.20
☐☐☐	280 Stephen Heinze, Colu.	20.00	8.00	.20
☐☐☐	281 J-L Grand-Pierre, Colu.	12.00	5.00	.20
☐☐☐	282 Robert Kron, Colu.	20.00	8.00	.20
☐☐☐	283 Kevin Dineen, Colu.	20.00	8.00	.20
☐☐☐	284 Brett Hull, Dall.	125.00	50.00	1.00
☐☐☐	285 Sergei Zubov, Dall.	30.00	12.00	.20
☐☐☐	286 J. Langenbrunner, Dall.	30.00	12.00	.20
☐☐☐	287 Ed Belfour (G), Dall.	125.00	50.00	1.00
☐☐☐	288 Roman Lyashenko, Dall.	12.00	5.00	.20
☐☐☐	289 Ted Donato, Dall.	12.00	5.00	.20
☐☐☐	290 Martin Lapointe, Detr.	50.00	20.00	.20
☐☐☐	291 Chris Chelios, Detr.	75.00	30.00	.50
☐☐☐	292 Vyacheslav Kozlov, Detr.	30.00	12.00	.20
☐☐☐	293 Steve Yzerman, Detr.	300.00	120.00	2.00
☐☐☐	294 Larry Murphy, Detr.	30.00	12.00	.20
☐☐☐	295 Brent Gilchrist, Detr.	12.00	5.00	.20

□□□ 296 Doug Weight, Edmo. 75.00 30.00 .50
□□□ 297 Eric Brewer, Edmo. 50.00 20.00 .20
□□□ 298 Todd Marchant, Edmo. 30.00 12.00 .20
□□□ 299 Tom Poti, Edmo. 20.00 8.00 .20
□□□ 300 Mike Grier, Edmo. 30.00 12.00 .20
□□□ 301 Georges Laraque, Edmo. 20.00 8.00 .20
□□□ 302 Igor Larionov, Flor. 75.00 30.00 .50
□□□ 303 R. Luongo (G), Flor. 100.00 40.00 .50
□□□ 304 Olli Jokinen, Flor. 40.00 16.00 .20
□□□ 305 Viktor Kozlov, Flor. 40.00 16.00 .20
□□□ 306 Robert Svehla, Flor. 30.00 12.00 .20
□□□ 307 Mike Sillinger, Flor. 20.00 8.00 .20
□□□ 308 Jere Karalahti, LosA. 12.00 5.00 .20
□□□ 309 Zigmund Palffy, LosA. 75.00 30.00 .50
□□□ 310 Mattias Norström, LosA. 30.00 12.00 .20
□□□ 311 Bryan Smolinski, LosA. 20.00 8.00 .20
□□□ 312 Jamie Storr (G), LosA. 30.00 12.00 .20
□□□ 313 Ian Laperrière, LosA. 20.00 8.00 .20
□□□ 314 M. Fernandez (G), MinW. 50.00 20.00 .20
□□□ 315 Sergei Krivokrasov, MinW. 20.00 8.00 .20
□□□ 316 Darryl Laplante, MinW. 12.00 5.00 .20
□□□ 317 Sean O'Donnell, MinW. 12.00 5.00 .20
□□□ 318 Scott Pellerin, MinW. 20.00 8.00 .20
□□□ 319 Saku Koivu, Mont. 150.00 60.00 .50
□□□ 320 Sergei Zholtok, Mont. 20.00 8.00 .20
□□□ 321 Jeff Hackett (G), Mont. 40.00 16.00 .20
□□□ 322 Eric Weinrich, Mont. 12.00 5.00 .20
□□□ 323 Karl Dykhuis, Mont. 12.00 5.00 .20
□□□ 324 Benoît Brunet, Mont. 12.00 5.00 .20
□□□ 325 Cliff Ronning, Nash. 30.00 12.00 .20
□□□ 326 Patric Kjellberg, Nash. 20.00 8.00 .20
□□□ 327 Drake Berehowsky, Nash. 20.00 8.00 .20
□□□ 328 Vitali Yachmenev, Nash. 20.00 8.00 .20
□□□ 329 Tomas Vokoun (G), Nash. 30.00 12.00 .20
□□□ 330 Greg Johnson, Nash. 20.00 8.00 .20
□□□ 331 Patrik Elias, NJer. 100.00 40.00 .50
□□□ 332 Bobby Holik, NJer. 40.00 16.00 .20
□□□ 333 Randy McKay, NJer. 12.00 5.00 .20
□□□ 334 Brian Rafalski, NJer. 30.00 12.00 .20
□□□ 335 M. Brodeur (G), NJer. 200.00 80.00 1.50
□□□ 336 Sergei Brylin, NJer. 20.00 8.00 .20
□□□ 337 Brad Isbister, NYIs. 30.00 12.00 .20
□□□ 338 Roman Hamrlik, NYIs. 30.00 12.00 .20
□□□ 339 Vanbiesbrouck (G), NYIs. 60.00 24.00 .20
□□□ 340 Dave Scatchard, NYIs. 12.00 5.00 .20
□□□ 341 Oleg Kvasha, NYIs. 20.00 8.00 .20
□□□ 342 Mark Parrish, NYIs. 50.00 20.00 .20
□□□ 343 Petr Nedved, NYRa. 40.00 16.00 .20
□□□ 344 Brian Leetch, NYRa. 75.00 30.00 .50
□□□ 345 Radek Dvorak, NYRa. 30.00 12.00 .20
□□□ 346 Vladimir Malakhov, NYRa. 20.00 8.00 .20
□□□ 347 Valeri Kamensky, NYRa. 40.00 16.00 .20
□□□ 348 Rich Pilon, NYRa. 12.00 5.00 .20
□□□ 349 Radek Bonk, Otta. 40.00 16.00 .20
□□□ 350 Vaclav Prospal, Otta. 40.00 16.00 .20
□□□ 351 Jason York, Otta. 20.00 8.00 .20
□□□ 352 Andreas Dackell, Otta. 20.00 8.00 .20
□□□ 353 Magnus Arvedson, Otta. 20.00 8.00 .20
□□□ 354 Rob Zamuner, Otta. 30.00 12.00 .20
□□□ 355 Daymond Langkow, Phil. 30.00 12.00 .20
□□□ 356 Keith Primeau, Phil. 50.00 20.00 .20
□□□ 357 Daniel McGillis, Phil. 20.00 8.00 .20
□□□ 358 Andy Delmore, Phil. 30.00 12.00 .20
□□□ 359 Jody Hull, Phil. 12.00 5.00 .20
□□□ 360 Luke Richardson, Phil. 20.00 8.00 .20
□□□ 361 Joé Juneau, Phoe. 30.00 12.00 .20
□□□ 362 Mika Alatalo, Phoe. 20.00 8.00 .20
□□□ 363 Keith Tkachuk, Phoe. 75.00 30.00 .50
□□□ 364 Radoslav Suchy, Phoe. 12.00 5.00 .20
□□□ 365 Louie DeBrusk, Phoe. 12.00 5.00 .20
□□□ 366 Sean Burke (G), Phoe. 75.00 30.00 .50
□□□ 367 Martin Straka, Pitt. 40.00 16.00 .20
□□□ 368 Alexei Kovalev, Pitt. 75.00 30.00 .50
□□□ 369 Aleksey Morozov, Pitt. 30.00 12.00 .20
□□□ 370 Josef Beranek, Pitt. 20.00 8.00 .20
□□□ 371 Milan Kraft, Pitt. 40.00 16.00 .50
□□□ 372 Darius Kasparaitis, Pitt. 30.00 12.00 .20
□□□ 373 V. Damphousse, SanJ. 75.00 30.00 .50
□□□ 374 Mike Ricci, SanJ. 40.00 16.00 .20
□□□ 375 Scott Thornton, SanJ. 12.00 5.00 .20
□□□ 376 Niklas Sundström, SanJ. 30.00 12.00 .20
□□□ 377 Marco Sturm, SanJ. 30.00 12.00 .20
□□□ 378 Jeff Norton, SanJ. 12.00 5.00 .20
□□□ 379 Pierre Turgeon, SLou. 50.00 20.00 .20
□□□ 380 Al MacInnis, SLou. 50.00 20.00 .20
□□□ 381 Jochen Hecht, SLou. 30.00 12.00 .20
□□□ 382 Sean Hill, SLou. 12.00 5.00 .20
□□□ 383 Pavol Demitra, SLou. 50.00 20.00 .20
□□□ 384 Michal Handzus, SLou. 30.00 12.00 .20
□□□ 385 Mike Eastwood, SLou. 12.00 5.00 .20
□□□ 386 V. Lecavalier, Tamp. 125.00 50.00 1.00
□□□ 387 Brian Holzinger, Tamp. 20.00 8.00 .20
□□□ 388 Pavel Kubina, Tamp. 20.00 8.00 .20
□□□ 389 Andréi Zyzuin, Tamp. 20.00 8.00 .20
□□□ 390 Wayne Primeau, Tamp. 20.00 8.00 .20
□□□ 391 Mats Sundin, Toro. 125.00 50.00 1.00
□□□ 392 Gary Roberts, Toro. 50.00 20.00 .20
□□□ 393 Igor Korolev, Toro. 20.00 8.00 .20
□□□ 394 Shayne Corson, Toro. 40.00 16.00 .20
□□□ 395 Tomas Kaberle, Toro. 40.00 16.00 .20
□□□ 396 Cory Cross, Toro. 12.00 5.00 .20
□□□ 397 Peter Schaefer, Vanc. 20.00 8.00 .20
□□□ 398 Adrian Aucoin, Vanc. 20.00 8.00 .20
□□□ 399 Brendan Morrison, Vanc. 40.00 16.00 .20
□□□ 400 Daniel Sedin, Vanc. 50.00 20.00 .50
□□□ 401 Donald Brashear, Vanc. 30.00 12.00 .20
□□□ 402 Henrik Sedin, Vanc. 50.00 20.00 .50
□□□ 403 Joe Murphy, Wash. 20.00 8.00 .20
□□□ 404 S. Konowalchuk, Wash. 30.00 12.00 .20
□□□ 405 Joe Reekie, Wash. 12.00 5.00 .20
□□□ 406 Sergei Gonchar, Wash. 40.00 16.00 .20
□□□ 407 Peter Bondra, Wash. 75.00 30.00 .50
□□□ 408 Olaf Kölzig (G), Wash. 75.00 30.00 .50
□□□ 409 S. Yzerman, Detr. [CL] 300.00 120.00 1.00
□□□ 410 M. Messier, NYRa. [CL] 125.00 50.00 .50
□□□ **411 DiPietro (G), NYIs. RC 60.00 24.00 12.00**
□□□ **412 M. Riesen, Edmo. RC 20.00 8.00 4.00**
□□□ **413 Reto von Arx, Chic. RC 20.00 8.00 4.00**
□□□ **414 Martin Havlat, Otta. RC 75.00 30.00 15.00**
□□□ **415 Matt Elich, Tamp. RC 20.00 8.00 4.00**
□□□ **416 J. Rönnqvist, Anah. RC 20.00 8.00 4.00**
□□□ **417 LaBarbera (G), NYRa. RC 20.00 8.00 4.00**
□□□ **418 Marc Moro, Nash. RC 12.00 5.00 2.50**
□□□ **419 Mark Smith, SanJ. RC 12.00 5.00 2.50**
□□□ **420 Petr Hubacek, Phil. RC 12.00 5.00 2.50**
□□□ **421 Niclas Wallin, Caro. RC 12.00 5.00 2.50**
□□□ 422 Brian Swanson, Edmo. 20.00 8.00 2.00
□□□ **423 P. Nummelin, Colu. RC 20.00 8.00 4.00**
□□□ **424 A. Boikov, Nash. RC 12.00 5.00 2.50**
□□□ **425 O. Väänänen, Phoe. RC 20.00 8.00 4.00**
□□□ **426 R. Simicek, Pitt. RC 12.00 5.00 2.50**
□□□ **427 G. Classen, Nash. RC 20.00 8.00 4.00**
□□□ **428 M. Turco (G), Dall. RC 75.00 30.00 15.00**
□□□ **429 S. Hnidy, Otta. RC 20.00 8.00 4.00**
□□□ **430 L. Visnovsky, LosA. RC 20.00 8.00 4.00**
□□□ **431 B. Salvador, SLou. RC 20.00 8.00 4.00**
□□□ **432 L. Sekeras, MinW. 20.00 8.00 4.00**
□□□ **433 Aebischer (G), Colo. RC 40.00 16.00 8.00**
□□□ **434 P. Ratchuk, Flor. RC 12.00 5.00 2.50**
□□□ **435 Cechmanek (G), Phil. RC 50.00 20.00 10.00**
□□□ **436 É. Bélanger, LosA. RC 20.00 8.00 4.00**
□□□ **437 A. Kharitonov, Tamp. RC12.00 5.00 2.50**
□□□ **438 Bateman, Brampton RC 20.00 8.00 4.00**
□□□ **439 Surma, Plymouth RC 20.00 8.00 4.00**
□□□ **440 Krestanovich, Calgary RC 20.00 8.00 4.00**

YOUNG GUNS INSERTS

These series-two inserts have a ©2001 mark on the card back.

Series Two Insert Set (20 cards): 90.00
Insert (©2001) YG

□ **211 Jason Jaspers RC 4.00**
□ 212 Pavel Brendl, Calgary Hitmen 3.00
□ 213 Milan Kraft, Prince Albert Raiders 3.00
□ **214 Justin Williams, Phil. RC 8.00**
□ **215 Andreas Karlsson, Atla. 2.00**
□ **216 Herbert Vasiljevs, Atla. RC 4.00**
□ **217 Sergei Vyshedkevich, Atla. RC 4.00**
□ 218 Johnathan Aitken, Bost. 2.00
□ **219 Brandon Smith, Bost. RC 2.00**
□ **220 Jeff Cowan, Calg. RC 2.00**
□ **221 Steve Brûlé, NJer. RC 2.00**
□ **222 Johan Witehall, NYRa. RC 4.00**
□ **223 Jani Hurme (G), Otta. RC 6.00**
□ **224 Jean-Guy Trudel, Phoe. RC 4.00**
□ **225 Kaspars Astashenko, Tamp. RC 2.00**
□ **226 Scott Hartnell, Nash. RC 6.00**
□ **227 Dieter Kochan (G), Tamp. RC 4.00**
□ **228 Rostislav Klesla, Colu. RC 10.00**
□ **229 Marian Gaborik, MinW. RC 35.00**
□ 230 Alfie Michaud (G), Vanc. 2.00

GATE ATTRACTIONS

Series One Insert Set (11 cards): 35.00
Insert (1:11) GA

□ GA1 Paul Kariya, Anah. 4.00
□ GA2 Dominik Hasek (G), Buff. 3.00
□ GA3 Raymond Bourque, Colo. 3.00
□ GA4 Patrick Roy (G), Colo. 9.00
□ GA5 Mike Modano, Dall. 3.00
□ GA6 Steve Yzerman, Detr. 7.00
□ GA7 Pavel Bure, Flor. 2.00
□ GA8 Martin Brodeur (G), NJer. 4.00

□ GA9 John LeClair, Phil. 2.00
□ GA10 Jaromir Jagr, Pitt. 3.00
□ GA11 Curtis Joseph (G), Toro. 3.00

NUMBER CRUNCHERS

Series One Insert Set (10 cards): 20.00
Insert (1:9) NC

□ NC1 Peter Forsberg, Colo. 4.00
□ NC2 Brendan Shanahan, Detr. 3.00
□ NC3 John LeClair, Phil. 2.00
□ NC4 Eric Lindros, Phil. 3.00
□ NC5 Keith Tkachuk, Phoe. 2.00
□ NC6 Jeremy Roenick, Phoe. 2.00
□ NC7 Jaromir Jagr, Pitt. 3.00
□ NC8 Owen Nolan, SanJ. 2.00
□ NC9 Chris Pronger, SLou. 2.00
□ NC10 Mark Messier, Vanc. 3.00

PROSPECTS: IN DEPTH

Series One Insert Set (10 cards): 15.00
Insert (1:11) PID

□ P1 Patrik Stefan, Atla. 2.00
□ P2 Maxim Afinogenov, Buff. 2.00
□ P3 Alex Tanguay, Colo. 2.00
□ P4 Brenden Morrow, Dall. 2.00
□ P5 Scott Gomez, NJer. 2.00
□ P6 Tim Connolly, NYIs. 2.00
□ P7 Mike York, NYRa. 2.00
□ P8 Simon Gagné, Phil. 3.00
□ P9 Brian Boucher (G), Phil. 2.00
□ P10 Jochen Hecht, SLou. 2.00

SKILLED STARS

Series One Insert Set (20 cards): 50.00
Insert (1:5) SS

□ SS1 Paul Kariya, Anah. 4.00
□ SS2 Teemu Selänne, Anah. 2.00
□ SS3 Dominik Hasek (G), Buff. 3.00
□ SS4 Valeri Bure, Calg. 2.00
□ SS5 Patrick Roy (G), Colo. 9.00
□ SS6 Peter Forsberg, Colo. 4.00
□ SS7 Ed Belfour (G), Dall. 3.00
□ SS8 Mike Modano, Dall. 3.00
□ SS9 Sergei Fedorov, Detr. 3.00
□ SS10 Brendan Shanahan, Detr. 3.00
□ SS11 Pavel Bure, Flor. 2.00
□ SS12 Zigmund Palffy, LosA. 2.00
□ SS13 Martin Brodeur (G), NJer. 4.00
□ SS14 Tim Connolly, NYIs. 2.00
□ SS15 John LeClair, Phil. 2.00
□ SS16 Jeremy Roenick, Phoe. 2.00
□ SS17 Jaromir Jagr, Pitt. 3.00
□ SS18 Vincent Lecavalier, Tamp. 3.00
□ SS19 Mats Sundin, Toro. 3.00
□ SS20 Olaf Kölzig (G), Wash. 2.00

FROZEN IN TIME

Insert Set (8 cards): 20.00
Insert (1:12) FT

□ FT1 Doug Gilmour, Buff. 2.00
□ FT2 Raymond Bourque, Colo. 3.00

□ FT3 Brett Hull, Dall. 3.00
□ FT4 Steve Yzerman, Detr. 7.00
□ FT5 Mark Messier, NYRa. 3.00
□ FT6 Jeremy Roenick, Phoe. 2.00
□ FT7 Jaromir Jagr, Pitt. 3.00
□ FT8 Curtis Joseph (G), Toro. 3.00

FUN-DAMENTALS

Series Two Insert Set (9 cards): 20.00
Insert (1:10) F

□ F1 Paul Kariya, Anah. 4.00
□ F2 Dominik Hasek (G), Buff. 3.00
□ F3 Peter Forsberg, Colo. 4.00
□ F4 Mike Modano, Dall. 3.00
□ F5 Sergei Fedorov, Detr. 3.00
□ F6 Pavel Bure, Flor. 2.00
□ F7 Marian Hossa, Otta. 3.00
□ F8 Jaromir Jagr, Pitt. 3.00
□ F9 Curtis Joseph (G), Toro. 3.00

LORD STANLEY'S HEROES

Series Two Insert Set (9 cards): 30.00
Insert (1:10) LSH

□ L1 Patrick Roy (G), Colo. 9.00
□ L2 Joe Sakic, Colo. 4.00
□ L3 Brett Hull, Dall. 3.00
□ L4 Steve Yzerman, Detr. 7.00
□ L5 Brendan Shanahan, Detr. 3.00
□ L6 Martin Brodeur (G), NJer. 4.00
□ L7 Scott Gomez, NJer. 2.00
□ L8 Mark Messier, NYRa. 3.00
□ L9 Jaromir Jagr, Pitt. 3.00

RISE TO PROMINENCE

Series Two Insert Set (8 cards): 15.00
Insert (1:12) RTP

□ RP1 Paul Kariya, Anah. 4.00
□ RP2 Pavel Bure, Flor. 2.00
□ RP3 José Théodore (G), Mont. 3.00
□ RP4 Scott Gomez, NJer. 2.00
□ RP5 Marian Hossa, Otta. 3.00
□ RP6 Brian Boucher (G), Phil. 2.00
□ RP7 Roman Turek (G), SLou. 2.00
□ RP8 Vincent Lecavalier, Tamp. 3.00

UD FLASHBACK

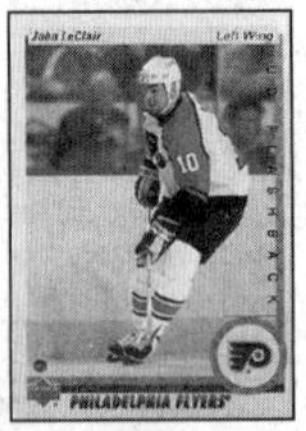

Series Two Insert Set (8 cards): 10.00
Insert (1:12) UDF

□ UD1 Teemu Selänne, Anah. 2.00
□ UD2 Tony Amonte, Chic. 2.00
□ UD3 Milan Hejduk, Colo. 2.00
□ UD4 Scott Gomez, NJer. 2.00

□ UD5 Tim Connolly, NYIs. 2.00
□ UD6 John LeClair, Phil. 2.00
□ UD7 Keith Tkachuk, Phoe. 2.00
□ UD8 Olaf Kölzig (G), Wash. 2.00

ALL-STAR CLASS

Series Two Insert Set (10 cards): 30.00
Insert (1:23) ASC

□ A1 Teemu Selänne, Anah. 4.00
□ A2 Valeri Bure, Calg. 3.00
□ A3 Milan Hejduk, Colo. 4.00
□ A4 Mike Modano, Dall. 5.00
□ A5 Pavel Bure, Flor. 4.00
□ A6 Marian Hossa, Otta. 5.00
□ A7 Brian Boucher (G), Phil. 3.00
□ A8 Keith Tkachuk, Phoe. 3.00
□ A9 Jaromir Jagr, Pitt. 5.00
□ A10 Curtis Joseph (G), Toro. 5.00

DIGNITARIES

Series One Insert Set (10 cards): 55.00
Insert (1:23) D

□ D1 Paul Kariya, Anah. 7.00
□ D2 Raymond Bourque, Colo. 6.00
□ D3 Patrick Roy (G), Colo. 15.00
□ D4 Brett Hull, Dall. 5.00
□ D5 Steve Yzerman, Detr. 12.00
□ D6 Pavel Bure, Flor. 4.00
□ D7 Luc Robitaille, LosA. 4.00
□ D8 Brian Leetch, NYRa. 3.00
□ D9 Jaromir Jagr, Pitt. 5.00
□ D10 Mark Messier, NYRa. 5.00

FANTASTIC FINISHERS

Series One Insert Set (10 cards): 50.00
Insert (1:23) FF

□ FF1 Paul Kariya, Anah. 7.00
□ FF2 Teemu Selänne, Anah. 4.00
□ FF3 Peter Forsberg, Colo. 7.00
□ FF4 Brett Hull, Dall. 5.00
□ FF5 Steve Yzerman, Detr. 12.00
□ FF6 Pavel Bure, Flor. 4.00
□ FF7 John LeClair, Phil. 4.00
□ FF8 Keith Tkachuk, Phoe. 3.00
□ FF9 Jaromir Jagr, Pitt. 5.00
□ FF10 Owen Nolan, SanJ. 3.00
□ FF11 Mats Sundin, Toro. 5.00

PROFILES

Series Two Insert Set (10 cards): 40.00
Insert (1:23) GG

□ P1 Dominik Hasek (G), Buff. 5.00
□ P2 Joe Sakic, Colo. 8.00
□ P3 Mike Modano, Dall. 5.00
□ P4 Brendan Shanahan, Detr. 5.00
□ P5 Pavel Bure, Flor. 4.00
□ P6 Martin Brodeur (G), NJer. 8.00
□ P7 John LeClair, Phil. 4.00
□ P8 Jaromir Jagr, Pitt. 5.00
□ P9 Mats Sundin, Toro. 5.00
□ P10 Olaf Kölzig (G), Wash. 3.00

E-CARD

Complete Set (12 cards): 20.00
Player eC

□ EC1 Sergei Samsonov, Bost. 1.00
□ EC2 Brett Hull, Dall. 3.00
□ EC3 Steve Yzerman, Detr. 7.00
□ EC4 Pavel Bure, Flor. 2.00
□ EC5 John LeClair, Phil. 2.00
□ EC6 Curtis Joseph (G), Toro. 3.00
□ EC7 Martin Brodeur (G), NJer. 4.00
□ EC8 Mark Messier, NYRa. 3.00
□ EC9 Chris Osgood (G), Detr. 1.00
□ EC10 Mike Richter (G), NYRa. 1.00
□ EC11 Raymond Bourque, Bost. 3.00
□ EC12 Jeremy Roenick, Phoe. 2.00

E-VOLVE JERSEY

Complete Set (12 cards): 600.00
Player J300

□ Sergei Samsonov, Bost. ✂ 40.00
□ Brett Hull, Dall. ✂ 50.00
□ Steve Yzerman, Detr. ✂ 150.00
□ Pavel Bure, Flor. ✂ 50.00
□ John LPhil. ✂ 50.00
□ Curtis Joseph (G), Toro. ✂ 50.00
□ Martin Brodeur (G), NJer. ✂ 100.00
□ Mark Messier, NYRa. ✂ 50.00
□ Chris Osgood (G), Detr. ✂ 40.00
□ Mike Richter (G), NYRa. ✂ 40.00
□ Raymond Bourque, Bost. ✂ 75.00
□ Jeremy Roenick, Phoe. ✂ 50.00

E-VOLVE JERSEY SIGNED

Complete Set (12 cards): 1,400
Player JA50

□ Sergei Samsonov, Bost. ✍ ✂ 75.00
□ Brett Hull, Dall. ✍ ✂ 150.00
□ Steve Yzerman, Detr. ✍ ✂ 350.00
□ Pavel Bure, Flor. ✍ ✂ 100.00
□ John LPhil. ✍ ✂ 100.00
□ Curtis Joseph (G), Toro. ✍ ✂ 150.00
□ Martin Brodeur (G), NJer. ✍ ✂ 225.00
□ Mark Messier, NYRa. ✍ ✂ 175.00
□ Chris Osgood (G), Detr. ✍ ✂ 75.00
□ Mike Richter (G), NYRa. ✍ ✂ 60.00
□ Raymond Bourque, Bost. ✍ ✂ 200.00
□ Jeremy Roenick, Phoe. ✍ ✂ 100.00

E-VOLVE SIGNED

Complete Set (12 cards): 700.00
Player A200

□ Sergei Samsonov, Bost. ✍ 40.00
□ Brett Hull, Dall. ✍ 60.00
□ Steve Yzerman, Detr. ✍ 160.00
□ Pavel Bure, Flor. ✍ 50.00
□ John LPhil. ✍ 50.00
□ Curtis Joseph (G), Toro. ✍ 60.00
□ Martin Brodeur (G), NJer. ✍ 110.00
□ Mark Messier, NYRa. ✍ 80.00
□ Chris Osgood (G), Detr. ✍ 40.00
□ Mike Richter (G), NYRa. ✍ 40.00
□ Raymond Bourque, Bost. ✍ 90.00
□ Jeremy Roenick, Phoe. ✍ 50.00

TRIPLE THREAT

Series Two Insert Set (10 cards): 120.00
Insert (1:72) TT

□ TT1 P. Kariya / S. Gomez / M. Hejduk 13.00
□ TT2 P. Roy / M. Brodeur / E. Belfour (G) 28.00
□ TT3 P. Forsberg / M. Sundin / Sedin 14.00
□ TT4 Br. Hull / J. Roenick / J. LeClair 13.00
□ TT5 S. Yzerman / J. Sakic / M. Modano 26.00
□ TT6 B. Shanahan / K. Tkachuk / M. Messier 13.00
□ TT7 P. Bure / S. Samsonov / S. Fedorov 12.00
□ TT8 R. Bourque / C. Pronger / R. Blake 12.00
□ TT9 J. Jagr / T. Selänne / M. Kraft 11.00
□ TT10 R. Turek / D. Hasek / O. Kölzig 10.00

COMBO GAME JERSEY

Series Two Insert Set (10 cards): 1,500
Insert (#/100) CGJ

□ Brett Hull, SLou. ✂ / Dall. ✂ 150.00
□ Brendan Shanahan, Hart. ✂ / Detr. ✂ 150.00
□ Dominik Hasek (G), Chic. ✂ / Buff. ✂ 150.00
□ Félix Potvin (G), Toro. ✂ / NYIs. ✂ 175.00
□ Jaromir Jagr, Pitt. ✂ / All-Star '96 ✂ 150.00
□ Joe Nieuwendyk, Dall. ✂ / Calg. ✂ 75.00
□ Joe Sakic, Québ. ✂ / Colo. ✂ 225.00
□ Pavel Bure, Flor. ✂ / Vanc. ✂ 100.00
□ Teemu Selänne, Anah. ✂ / All-Star '98 ✂ 100.00
□ Wayne Gretzky, NYRa. ✂ / All-Star '99 ✂ 600.00

GAME JERSEY SERIES 1

Insert Set (15 cards): 1,000
Player GJ

□ Brendan Shanahan, Detr. ✂ 75.00
□ Chris Pronger, SLou. ✂ 35.00
□ Jaromir Jagr, Pitt. ✂ 75.00
□ John LeClair, Phil. ✂ 50.00
□ Joe Nieuwendyk, Dall. ✂ 35.00
□ Joe Sakic, Colo. ✂ 100.00
□ Joe Thornton, Bost. ✂ 75.00
□ Keith Tkachuk, Phoe. ✂ 35.00
□ Martin Brodeur, NJer. ✂ 100.00
□ Mats Sundin, Toro. ✂ 75.00
□ Peter Bondra, Wash. ✂ 35.00
□ Paul Kariya, Anah. ✂ 100.00
□ Sergei Fedorov, Detr. ✂ 75.00
□ Teemu Selänne, Anah. ✂ 50.00
□ Wayne Gretzky, NYRa. ✂ 300.00

GAME JERSEY PATCH SERIES 1

There are two versions: the Patch card (1:2500 packs) and the Patch Exclusive parallel (#/1).

Insert Set (25 cards): 7,400
Inserts GJP

□ □ Brett Hull, Dall. ✂ 300.00
□ □ Brendan Shanahan, Detr. ✂ 300.00
□ □ Curtis Joseph (G), Toro. ✂ 300.00
□ □ Dominik Hasek, Buff. ✂ 300.00
□ □ Eric Lindros, Phil. ✂ 300.00
□ □ Jochen Hecht, SLou. ✂ 150.00
□ □ Jaromir Jagr, Pitt. ✂ 300.00
□ □ John LeClair, Phil. ✂ 225.00
□ □ Joe Sakic, Colo. ✂ 475.00
□ □ Joe Thornton, Bost. ✂ 350.00
□ □ Keith Tkachuk, Phoe. ✂ 175.00
□ □ Martin Brodeur, NJer. ✂ 475.00
□ □ Mark Messier, Vanc. ✂ 300.00
□ □ Mike York, NYRa. ✂ 150.00
□ □ Pavel Bure, Flor. ✂ 225.00
□ □ Peter Forsberg, Colo. ✂ 400.00
□ □ Paul Kariya, Anah. ✂ 400.00
□ □ Patrick Roy, Colo. ✂ 700.00
□ □ Sergei Fedorov, Detr. ✂ 300.00
□ □ Scott Gomez, NJer. ✂ 150.00
□ □ Sergei Samsonov, Bost. ✂ 175.00
□ □ Steve Yzerman, Detr. ✂ 700.00
□ □ Tim Connolly, NYIs. ✂ 150.00
□ □ Teemu Selänne, Anah. ✂ 225.00
□ □ Wayne Gretzky, NYRa. ✂ 1200.00

GAME JERSEY SIGNED SERIES 1

Insert Set (10 cards): 1,100
Insert (1:287 Hobby) GJA

□ Brett Hull, Dall. ✍ ✂ 200.00
□ Jochen Hecht, SLou. ✍ ✂ 75.00
□ Martin Biron (G), Buff. ✍ ✂ 75.00
□ Mike York, NYRa. ✍ ✂ 75.00
□ Nicklas Lidström, Detr. ✍ ✂ 100.00
□ Pavel Bure, Flor. ✍ ✂ 150.00
□ Scott Gomez, NJer. ✍ ✂ 75.00
□ Sergei Samsonov, Bost. ✍ ✂ 100.00
□ Steve Yzerman, Detr. ✍ ✂ 475.00
□ Tim Connolly, NYIs. ✍ ✂ 75.00

GAME JERSEY EXCLUSIVE SIGNED SERIES 1

Insert Set (22 cards): 8,000
Autograph (#/25) GJA

□ Brett Hull, Dall. ✍ ✂ 375.00
□ Brendan Shanahan, Detr. ✍ ✂ 375.00
□ Chris Pronger, SLou. ✍ ✂ 225.00
□ Jaromir Jagr, Pitt. ✍ ✂ 750.00
□ John LeClair, Phil. ✍ ✂ 300.00
□ Joe Nieuwendyk, Dall. ✍ ✂ 200.00
□ Joe Sakic, Colo. ✍ ✂ 600.00
□ Joe Thornton, Bost. ✍ ✂ 450.00
□ Keith Tkachuk, Phoe. ✍ ✂ 225.00
□ Martin Biron (G), Buff. ✍ ✂ 200.00
□ Martin Brodeur, NJer. ✍ ✂ 600.00
□ Mats Sundin, Toro. ✍ ✂ 375.00
□ Mike York, NYRa. ✍ ✂ 200.00
□ Nicklas Lidström, Detr. ✍ ✂ 225.00
□ Peter Bondra, Wash. ✍ ✂ 225.00
□ Pavel Bure, Flor. ✍ ✂ 300.00
□ Paul Kariya, Anah. ✍ ✂ 525.00
□ Sergei Fedorov, Detr. ✍ ✂ 375.00
□ Steve Yzerman, Detr. ✍ ✂ 900.00
□ Tim Connolly, NYIs. ✍ ✂ 200.00
□ Teemu Selänne, Anah. ✍ ✂ 300.00
□ Wayne Gretzky, NYRa. ✍ ✂ 1500.00

GAME JERSEY SERIES 2

Insert Set (10 cards): 850.00
Player GJ

□ Brendan Shanahan, Detr. ✂ 75.00
□ Jaromir Jagr, Pitt. ✂ 75.00
□ Joe Sakic, Colo. ✂ 100.00
□ Mats Sundin, Toro. ✂ 75.00
□ Pavel Bure, Flor. ✂ 50.00
□ Peter Forsberg, Colo. ✂ 100.00
□ Paul Kariya, Anah. ✂ 100.00
□ Sergei Fedorov, Detr. ✂ 75.00
□ Teemu Selänne, Anah. ✂ 50.00
□ Wayne Gretzky, NHL All-Star 300.00

GAME JERSEY PATCH SERIES 2

There are two versions: the Patch card (1:5000 packs) and the Patch Exclusive parallel (#/25).

Insert Set (11 cards): 4,700 3,700

Inserts	GJP25	GJP
□ □ Brendan Shanahan, Detr. ✂	375.00	300.00
□ □ Chris Osgood, Detr. ✂	225.00	175.00
□ □ Jaromir Jagr, Pitt. ✂	375.00	300.00
□ □ John LeClair, Phil. ✂	300.00	225.00
□ □ Keith Tkachuk, Phoe. ✂	225.00	175.00
□ □ Peter Forsberg, Colo. ✂	525.00	400.00
□ □ Paul Kariya, Anah. ✂	525.00	400.00
□ □ Sergei Fedorov, Detr. ✂	375.00	300.00
□ □ Steve Yzerman, Detr. ✂	900.00	700.00
□ □ Teemu Selänne, Anah. ✂	300.00	225.00
□ □ Wayne Gretzky, NHL All-Star	1500.00	1200.00

GAME JERSEY SIGNED SERIES 2

Insert Set (8 cards): 1,100
Insert (1:287 Hobby) GJA

□ Chris Osgood, Detr. ✍ ✂ 100.00
□ John LeClair, Phil. ✍ ✂ 150.00
□ Jeremy Roenick, Phoe. ✍ ✂ 150.00
□ Joe Thornton, Bost. ✍ ✂ 225.00
□ Keith Tkachuk, Phoe. ✍ ✂ 100.00
□ Mike Richter, NYRa. ✍ ✂ 75.00
□ Sergei Samsonov, Bost. ✍ ✂ 100.00
□ Steve Yzerman, Detr. ✍ ✂ 475.00

GAME JERSEY EXCLUSIVE SIGNED SERIES 2

Insert Set (12 cards): 4,500
Autograph (#/25) GJA

□ Chris Osgood, Detr. ✍ ✂ 225.00
□ John LeClair, Phil. ✍ ✂ 300.00
□ Joe Nieuwendyk, Dall. ✍ ✂ 200.00
□ Jeremy Roenick, Phoe. ✍ ✂ 300.00
□ Joe Thornton, Bost. ✍ ✂ 450.00
□ Keith Tkachuk, Phoe. ✍ ✂ 225.00
□ Mike Richter, NYRa. ✍ ✂ 200.00
□ Pavel Bure, Flor. ✍ ✂ 300.00
□ Sergei Fedorov, Detr. ✍ ✂ 375.00
□ Sergei Samsonov, Bost. ✍ ✂ 225.00
□ Steve Yzerman, Detr. ✍ ✂ 900.00
□ Wayne Gretzky, All-Star '93 ✍ ✂ 1600.00

GAME JERSEY CANADIAN HERO

Insert Set (4 cards): 300.00
Autograph CJ

□ José Théodore (G), Mont. ✍ ✂ 90.00
□ Mark Messier, NYRa. ✍ ✂ 90.00
□ Curtis Joseph (G), Toro. ✍ ✂ 90.00
□ Roberto Luongo (G), NYIs. ✍ ✂ 90.00

GAME JERSEY DUAL

Insert Set (15 cards): 5,400
Insert (#/50) JD

□ R. Bourque ✂ / P. Forsberg ✂ 375.00
□ E. Belfour (G) ✂ / D. Hasek ✂ 300.00
□ T. Connolly ✂ / R. Luongo ✂ 175.00
□ S. Fedorov ✂ / P. Bure ✂ 250.00
□ S. Gomez ✂ / M. Brodeur ✂ 300.00
□ W. Gretzky ✂ / Bre. Hull ✂ 750.00
□ W. Gretzky ✂ / M. Lemieux ✂ 1200.00
□ W. Gretzky ✂ / M. Messier ✂ 750.00
□ J. Jagr ✂ / M. Lemieux ✂ 600.00
□ J. LeClair ✂ / B. Clarke ✂ 200.00
□ M. Sundin ✂ / Cu. Joseph (G) ✂ 300.00
□ T. Selänne ✂ / P. Kariya ✂ 325.00
□ J. Thornton ✂ / S. Samsonov ✂ 250.00
□ M. York ✂ / B. Leetch ✂ 150.00
□ S. Yzerman ✂ / B. Shanahan ✂ 500.00

GAME JERSEY PATCH EXCLUSIVE SIGNED

Insert Set (3 cards): 2,600
Insert JES

□ John LeClair, Phil. ✍ ✂ (#/10) 400.00
□ Steve Yzerman, Detr. ✍ ✂ (#/19) 1500.00
□ Wayne Gretzky, All-Star ✍ ✂ (#/99) 1200.00

SIGNS OF GREATNESS

Series Two Insert Set (9 cards): 725.00
Autograph (#/250) SoG

□ Bobby Orr, Bost. ✍ 275.00
□ Curtis Joseph (G), Toro. ✍ 60.00
□ Keith Tkachuk, Phoe. ✍ 35.00
□ Martin Brodeur (G), NJer. ✍ 100.00
□ Mike York, NYRa. ✍ 30.00
□ Pavel Brendl, Calgary Hitmen 30.00
□ Sergei Samsonov, Bost. ✍ 35.00
□ Tony Amonte, Chic. ✍ 35.00
□ Wayne Gretzky, NYRa. ✍ 275.00

2000 - 01 UPPER DECK ALL-STAR FANTASY

Complete Set (15 cards):	
Player	
CA1 Raymond Bourque, Colo.	
CA2 Adam Foote, Colo.	
CA3 Adam Deadmarsh, Colo.	
CA4 Alex Tanguay, Colo.	
CA5 Aaron Miller, Colo.	
CA6 Stéphane Yelle, Colo.	
PP1 Patrick Roy (G), Colo.	
PP2 Joe Sakic, Colo.	
PP3 Peter Forsberg, Colo.	
PP4 Chris Drury, Colo.	
PP5 Milan Hejduk, Colo.	
PP6 David Aebischer (G), Colo.	
HH1 David Aebischer (G) / Patrick Roy (G)	
HH2 Milan Hejduk / Peter Forsberg	
HH3 Joe Sakic / Raymond Bourque	

2000 - 01 UPPER DECK – BUYBACKS

It is not known whether Gaborik, Hartnell, and Klesla signed the Series One cards (© 2000) or Series Two inserts (©2001).

Buyback Autograph	UD
198 Dany Heatley, Canada RC ✍ {#/50}	
226 Scott Hartnell, Nash. RC ✍ {#/82}	
228 Rostislav Klesla, Colu RC. ✍ {#/44}	
229 Marian Gaborik, MinW. RC ✍ {#/31}	
411 Rick DiPietro (G), NYIs. RC ✍ {#/31}	
414 Martin Havlat, Otta. RC ✍ {#/35}	
428 Marty Turco, Dall. RC ✍ {#/35}	
Buyback Autograph • Game Jersey	**UD**
Wayne Gretzky ✍ ✂ {#/3}	
John LeClair ✍ ✂ {#/5}	
Teemu Selänne ✍ ✂ {#/8}	

2000 - 01 UPPER DECK BLACK DIAMOND

This series was distributed in two releases: the original release in December 2000 and the Update releasd as part of the 2000 - 01 Upper Deck Rookie Update product in April 2001. In the original release (1-90), rookie CHL subset cards 61-75 are limited to 1999 copies, rookie NHL subset cards 76-84 are limited to 1250 copies and star subset cards 85-90 are limited to 500 copies. In the Update release, rookie-subset cards are limited to 1999 copies. For all base cards in each series, there is a Gold parallel limited to 100 copies.

Shell Set (60 cards):	-	25.00
Complete Set (132 cards):	-	525.00
Common Player:	6.00	.20
Player	Gold	Reg.
1 Paul Kariya, Anah.	70.00	1.50
2 Teemu Selänne, Anah.	40.00	1.00
3 Patrik Stefan, Atla.	16.00	.25
4 Joe Thornton, Bost.	60.00	1.50
5 Sergei Samsonov, Bost.	30.00	.50
6 Dominik Hasek (G), Buff.	50.00	1.00
7 Maxim Afinogenov, Buff.	20.00	.50
8 Valeri Bure, Calg.	16.00	.25
9 Marc Savard, Calg.	12.00	.25
10 Ron Francis, Caro.	30.00	.50
11 Jeff O'Neill, Caro.	20.00	.50
12 Tony Amonte, Chic.	30.00	.50
13 Michal Grosek, Chic.	6.00	.25
14 Patrick Roy (G), Colo.	150.00	3.50
15 Raymond Bourque, Colo.	60.00	1.50
16 Milan Hejduk, Colo.	40.00	1.00
17 Peter Forsberg, Colo.	70.00	1.50
18 Brett Hull, Dall.	50.00	1.00
19 Ed Belfour (G), Dall.	50.00	1.00
20 Mike Modano, Dall.	50.00	1.00
21 Brendan Shanahan, Detr.	50.00	1.00
22 Chris Osgood (G), Detr.	30.00	.50
23 Steve Yzerman, Detr.	120.00	3.00
24 Doug Weight, Edmo.	30.00	.50
25 Tommy Salo (G), Edmo.	20.00	.50
26 Pavel Bure, Flor.	40.00	1.00
27 Trevor Kidd (G), Flor.	16.00	.25
28 Rob Blake, LosA.	30.00	.50
29 Luc Robitaille, LosA.	40.00	1.00
30 José Théodore (G), Mont.	60.00	1.50
31 Saku Koivu, Mont.	60.00	1.00
32 David Legwand, Nash.	20.00	.50
33 Martin Brodeur (G), NJer.	80.00	2.00
34 Scott Gomez, NJer.	20.00	.50
35 Scott Stevens, NJer.	20.00	.50
36 Tim Connolly, NYIs.	20.00	.50
37 Mariusz Czerkawski, NYIs.	12.00	.25
38 Mark Messier, NYRa.	50.00	1.00
39 Theoren Fleury, NYRa.	30.00	.50
40 Marian Hossa, Otta.	50.00	1.00
41 Radek Bonk, Otta.	16.00	.25
42 Brian Boucher (G), Phil.	16.00	.25
43 John LeClair, Phil.	40.00	1.00
44 Simon Gagné, Phil.	40.00	1.00
45 Jeremy Roenick, Phoe.	40.00	1.00
46 Keith Tkachuk, Phoe.	30.00	.50
47 Jaromir Jagr, Pitt.	50.00	1.00
48 Martin Straka, Pitt.	16.00	.25
49 Steve Shields (G), SanJ.	12.00	.25
50 Jeff Friesen, SanJ.	16.00	.25
51 Chris Pronger, SLou.	30.00	.50
52 Roman Turek (G), SLou.	24.00	.50
53 Vincent Lecavalier, Tamp.	50.00	1.00
54 Dan Cloutier (G), Tamp.	20.00	.50
55 Curtis Joseph (G), Toro.	50.00	1.00
56 Mats Sundin, Toro.	50.00	1.00
57 Markus Näslund, Vanc.	50.00	1.00
58 Félix Potvin (G), Vanc.	60.00	.50
59 Olaf Kölzig (G), Wash.	30.00	.50
60 Jeff Halpern, Wash.	12.00	.25

PRECIOUS GEMS

Insert (#/1999)	PG
61 Matt Pettinger RC (#/1999)	**10.00**
62 Chris Nielsen RC (#/1999)	**10.00**
63 Dany Heatley RC (#/1999)	**150.00**
64 Matt Zultek RC (#/1999)	**6.00**
65 Dmitry Afanasenkov RC (#/1999)	**10.00**
66 Tyler Bouck RC (#/1999)	**10.00**
67 Jonas Andersson RC (#/1999)	**6.00**
68 Marc-André Thinel RC (#/1999)	**10.00**
69 Jaroslav Svoboda RC (#/1999)	**15.00**
70 Josef Vasicek RC (#/1999)	**15.00**
71 Andrew Raycroft (G) RC (#/1999)	**15.00**
72 Juraj Kolnik RC (#/1999)	**10.00**
73 Zdenek Blatny RC (#/1999)	**10.00**
74 Sébastien Caron (G) RC (#/1999)	**15.00**
75 Michael Ryder RC (#/1999)	**10.00**

PRECIOUS GEMS

Insert (#/1250)	PG
76 Eric Nickulas, Bost. RC (#/1250)	**8.00**
77 Jeff Cowan, Calg. RC (#/1250)	**8.00**
78 Steven Reinprecht, LosA. RC (#/1250)	**20.00**
79 David Gosselin, Nash. RC (#/1250)	**8.00**
80 Colin White, NJer. RC (#/1250)	**10.00**
81 Stephen Valiquette (G), NYIs. RC (#/1250)	**10.00**
82 Jani Hurme (G), Otta. RC (#/1250)	**15.00**
83 Jean-Guy Trudel, Phoe. RC (#/1250)	**10.00**
84 Dieter Kochan (G), Tamp. RC (#/1250)	**10.00**

PRECIOUS GEMS

Insert (#/500)	PG
85 Paul Kariya, Anah. (#/500)	25.00
86 Patrick Roy (G), Colo. (#/500)	60.00
87 Steve Yzerman, Detr. (#/500)	45.00
88 Pavel Bure, Flor. (#/500)	15.00
89 Martin Brodeur (G), NJer. (#/500)	30.00
90 Jaromir Jagr, Pitt. (#/500)	20.00

UPDATE

Player	Update
91 Samuel Påhlsson, Anah.	.25
92 Eric Boulton, Buff. RC	**1.50**
93 Daniel Tkaczuk, Calg.	.50
94 Rob Shearer, Colo. RC	**1.00**
95 David Vyborny, Colu.	.25
96 Tyler Bouck, Dall.	1.00
97 Mike Comrie, Edmo. RC	**10.00**
98 Anson Carter, Edmo.	.50
99 Roman Simicek, MinW. RC	**1.00**
100 Andréi Markov, Mont.	.25
101 Jason Arnott, NJer.	.50
102 Mike Mottau, NYRa.	.25
103 Taylor Pyatt, NYIs.	.50
104 Alexei Yashin, Otta.	.50
105 Todd Fedoruk, Phil. RC	**1.00**
106 Milan Kraft, Pitt.	.50
107 Mario Lemieux, Pitt.	3.50
108 Evgeni Nabokov, SanJ.	.50
109 Brad Richards, Tamp.	1.00
110 Daniel Sedin, Vanc.	1.00
111 Henrik Sedin, Vanc.	1.00

PRECIOUS GEMS

Insert (#/1999)	PG
112 Petr Tenkrat, Anah. RC	**8.00**
113 Lee Goren, Bost. RC	**8.00**
114 David Aebischer (G), Colo. RC	**15.00**
115 Yuri Babenko, Colo. RC	**6.00**
116 Rostislav Klesla, Colu. RC	**15.00**
117 Marty Turco (G), Dall. RC	**30.00**
118 Jason Williams, Detr. RC	**10.00**
119 Michel Riesen, Edmo. RC	**8.00**
120 Lubomir Visnovski, LosA. RC	**8.00**
121 Travis Scott, LosA. RC	**8.00**
122 Peter Bartos, MinW. RC	**8.00**
123 Marian Gaborik, MinW. RC	**50.00**
124 Scott Hartnell, Nash. RC	**10.00**
125 Rick DiPietro (G), NYIs. RC	**20.00**
126 Vitali Yeremeyev (G), NYRa. RC	**6.00**
127 Martin Havlat, Otta. RC	**30.00**
128 Roman Cechmanek (G), Phil. RC	**20.00**
129 Justin Williams, Phil. RC	**15.00**
130 Ruslan Fedotenko, Phil. RC	**8.00**
131 Alexandre Kharitonov, Tamp. RC	**6.00**
132 Alexei Ponikarovsky, Toro. RC	**8.00**

DIAMONATION

Insert Set (9 cards):	45.00
Insert (1:12)	IG
IG1 Paul Kariya, Anah.	7.00
IG2 Patrick Roy (G), Colo.	15.00
IG3 Sergei Fedorov, Detr.	5.00
IG4 Pavel Bure, Flor.	4.00
IG5 Scott Gomez, NJer.	3.00
IG6 John LeClair, Phil.	4.00
IG7 Jaromir Jagr, Pitt.	5.00
IG8 Vincent Lecavalier, Tamp.	5.00
IG9 Curtis Joseph (G), Toro.	5.00

DIAMOND MIGHT

Insert Set (9 cards):	40.00
Insert (1:12)	FP
FP1 Teemu Selänne, Anah.	4.00
FP2 Peter Forsberg, Colo.	7.00
FP3 Raymond Bourque, Colo.	6.00
FP4 Mike Modano, Dall.	5.00
FP5 Brendan Shanahan, Detr.	5.00
FP6 Pavel Bure, Flor.	4.00
FP7 Martin Brodeur (G), NJer.	8.00
FP8 John LeClair, Phil.	4.00
FP9 Jaromir Jagr, Pitt.	5.00

DIAMOND SKILLS

Insert Set (6 cards):	40.00
Insert (1:17)	IC
IC1 Patrick Roy (G), Colo.	15.00
IC2 Mike Modano, Dall.	5.00
IC3 Steve Yzerman, Detr.	12.00
IC4 Martin Brodeur (G), NJer.	8.00
IC5 John LeClair, Phil.	4.00
IC6 Jaromir Jagr, Pitt.	5.00

MYRIAD

Insert Set (6 cards):	25.00
Insert (1:17)	M
CC1 Paul Kariya, Anah.	7.00
CC2 Peter Forsberg, Colo.	7.00
CC3 Pavel Bure, Flor.	4.00
CC4 Scott Gomez, NJer.	3.00
CC5 Jaromir Jagr, Pitt.	5.00
CC6 Curtis Joseph (G), Toro.	5.00

GAME GEAR

These cards were inserted 1:23 original series packs and 1:30 Rookie Update packs.

Insert Set (31 cards):	1,000
Insert (1:12)	GG
John Vanbiesbrouck (G), Phil. ✂ Blocker	25.00
Sean Burke (G), Caro. ✂ Blocker	25.00
Tom Barasso, Pitt. ✂ Blocker	25.00
Tommy Salo (G), Edmo. ✂ Blocker	25.00
John Vanbiesbrouck (G), Phil. ✂ Catcher	25.00
Kirk McLean (G), NYRa. ✂ Catcher	25.00
Sean Burke (G), Caro. ✂ Catcher	25.00
Tom Barasso, Pitt. ✂ Catcher	25.00
Tommy Salo (G), Edmo. ✂ Catcher	25.00
Eric Lindros, Phil. ✂ Glove	40.00
Teemu Selänne, Anah. ✂ Glove	35.00
Wayne Gretzky, LosA. ✂ Glove	180.00
Byron Dafoe (G), Bost. ✂ Leg Pad	25.00
Curtis Joseph (G), Toro. ✂ Leg Pad	45.00
Dominik Hasek (G), Buff. ✂ Leg Pad	45.00
John Vanbiesbrouck (G), Phil. ✂ Leg Pad	25.00
Martin Biron (G), Buff. ✂ Leg Pad	25.00
Olaf Kölzig (G), Wash. ✂ Leg Pad	25.00
Roberto Luongo (G), NYIs. ✂ Leg Pad	35.00
Steve Shields (G), SanJ. ✂ Leg Pad	25.00
Mark Messier, Vanc. ✂ Skates	125.00
Chris Drury, Colo. ✂ Glove	25.00
Sergei Fedorov, Detr. ✂ Glove	45.00
Joe Sakic, Colo. ✂ Glove	70.00
Joe Thornton, Bost. ✂ Glove	50.00
Alexei Yashin, Otta. ✂ Glove	25.00
Jean-Sébastien Aubin (G), Pitt. ✂ Leg Pad	25.00
Marc Denis (G), Colo. ✂ Leg Pad	25.00
Chris Osgood (G), Detr. ✂ Leg Pad	25.00
Roman Turek (G), SLou. ✂ Leg Pad	25.00
Jaromir Jagr, Pitt. ✂ Skate	45.00

2000 - 01 UPPER DECK BLACK DIAMOND – BUYBACKS

Buyback Autograph • Game Gear	UD
Martin Biron (G), Buff. ✍ ✂ Leg Pad {#/41}	
Curtis Joseph (G), Toro. ✍ ✂ Leg Pad {#/4}	
Olaf Kölzig (G), Wash. ✍ ✂ Leg Pad {#/18}	
Tommy Salo (G), Edmo. ✍ ✂ Blocker {#/8}	
Tommy Salo (G), Edmo. ✍ ✂ Catcher {#/5}	
Teemu Selänne, Anah. ✍ ✂ Glove {#/3}	

2000 - 01 UPPER DECK DEL

Complete Set (240 cards):	40.00
Common Player:	.25
Player	DEL
1 Gordon Hynes, Adler Mannheim	.25
2 Dave Tomlinson, Adler Mannheim	.25
3 Stéphane J.G. Richer, Adler Mannheim	.25
4 Steve Junker, Adler Mannheim	.25
5 Wayne Hynes, Adler Mannheim	.25
6 Bradley Bergen, Adler Mannheim	.25
7 Devin Edgerton, Adler Mannheim	.25
8 Ron Pasco, Adler Mannheim	.25
9 François Groleau, Adler Mannheim	.25
10 Todd Hlushko, Adler Mannheim	.25

☐ 11 Mike Rosati, Adler Mannheim .25
☐ 12 Chris Straube, Adler Mannheim .25
☐ 13 Jean-François Jomphe, Adler Mannheim .25
☐ 14 Jan Alston, Adler Mannheim .25
☐ 15 Sven Rampf, Augsburg Panther .25
☐ 16 Sergei Vostrikov, Augsburg Panther .25
☐ 17 Igor Maslennikov, Augsburg Panther .25
☐ 18 Reemt Pyka, Augsburg Panther .25
☐ 19 Dave Chyzowski, Augsburg Panther .25
☐ 20 Arnaud Briand, Augsburg Panther .25
☐ 21 Sergei Stas, Augsburg Panther .25
☐ 22 Sébastien Klenner, Augsburg Panther .25
☐ 23 Vasily Pankov, Augsburg Panther .25
☐ 24 Duanne Moeser, Augsburg Panther .25
☐ 25 Jason Muzzatti, Augsburg Panther .25
☐ 26 Herbert Hohenberger, Augsburg Panther .25
☐ 27 Ryan Savoia, Augsburg Panther .25
☐ 28 Jim Camazzola, Augsburg Panther .25
☐ 29 Tommy Jakobsen, Augsburg Panther .25
☐ 30 Andrei Mezin, Berlin Capitals .25
☐ 31 Markus Pottinger, Berlin Capitals .25
☐ 32 Thomas Sjögren, Berlin Capitals .25
☐ 33 Jim Hiller, Berlin Capitals .25
☐ 34 Pavel Gross, Berlin Capitals .25
☐ 35 Robert Guillet, Berlin Capitals .25
☐ 36 Udo Dohler, Berlin Capitals .25
☐ 37 Anders Huusko, Berlin Capitals .25
☐ 38 Heinz Ehlers, Berlin Capitals .25
☐ 39 Greg Johnston, Berlin Capitals .25
☐ 40 Petri Liimatainen, Berlin Capitals .25
☐ 41 Johan Norgren, Berlin Capitals .25
☐ 42 Martin Ulrich, Berlin Capitals .25
☐ 43 Iain Fraser, Berlin Capitals .25
☐ 44 Gary Shuchuk, Dusseldorfer EG .25
☐ 45 Torsten Kienass, Dusseldorfer EG .25
☐ 46 Niki Mondt, Dusseldorfer EG .25
☐ 47 Bernd Kuhnhauser, Dusseldorfer EG .25
☐ 48 Craig Reichert, Dusseldorfer EG .25
☐ 49 Niklas Sundblad, Dusseldorfer EG .25
☐ 50 Sergei Sorokin, Dusseldorfer EG .25
☐ 51 Peter Franke, Dusseldorfer EG .25
☐ 52 Ivan Droppa, Dusseldorfer EG .25
☐ 53 Christopher Bartolone, Dusseldorfer EG .25
☐ 54 Leo Stefan, Dusseldorfer EG .25
☐ 55 Viktor Gordiouk, Dusseldorfer EG .25
☐ 56 Lorenz Funk, Dusseldorfer EG .25
☐ 57 Boris Lingemann, Dusseldorfer EG .25
☐ 58 Andrei Trefilov, Dusseldorfer EG .25
☐ 59 Nico Pyka, Eisbaren Berlin .25
☐ 60 Alexander Jung, Eisbaren Berlin .25
☐ 61 Alexander Godynyuk, Eisbaren Berlin .25
☐ 62 Derek Mayer, Eisbaren Berlin .25
☐ 63 Sven Felski, Eisbaren Berlin .25
☐ 64 Marc Fortier, Eisbaren Berlin .25
☐ 65 John Chabot, Eisbaren Berlin .25
☐ 66 Derek Cormier, Eisbaren Berlin .25
☐ 67 Steve Walker, Eisbaren Berlin .25
☐ 68 Lubomir Vaic, Eisbaren Berlin .25
☐ 69 Klaus Merk, Eisbaren Berlin .25
☐ 70 Daniel Laperrière, Eisbaren Berlin .25
☐ 71 Rob Cowie, Eisbaren Berlin .25
☐ 72 Martin Lindman, Eisbaren Berlin .25
☐ 73 Chris Govedaris, Eisbaren Berlin .25
☐ 74 Michael Bresagk, Frankfurt Lions .25
☐ 75 Leonardo Conti, Frankfurt Lions .25
☐ 76 Robin Doyle, Frankfurt Lions .25
☐ 77 Toni Porkka, Frankfurt Lions .25
☐ 78 Johnny Walker, Frankfurt Lions .25
☐ 79 Jean-Marc Richard, Frankfurt Lions .25
☐ 80 Jason Ruff, Frankfurt Lions .25
☐ 81 Jason Cirone, Frankfurt Lions .25
☐ 82 José Charbonneau, Frankfurt Lions .25
☐ 83 Victor Gervais, Frankfurt Lions .25
☐ 84 Patrice Lefebvre, Frankfurt Lions .25
☐ 85 Martin Gendron, Frankfurt Lions .25
☐ 86 Ken Quinney, Frankfurt Lions .25
☐ 87 Keith Aldridge, Frankfurt Lions .25
☐ 88 Eldon (Pokey) Reddick, Frankfurt Lions .25
☐ 89 Oscar Ackerström, Hannover Scorpions .25
☐ 90 Mattias Lööf, Hannover Scorpions .25
☐ 91 Igor Bashkatov, Hannover Scorpions .25
☐ 92 Mark Kosturik, Hannover Scorpions .25
☐ 93 Wallace Schreiber, Hannover Scorpions .25
☐ 94 Dominic Lavoie, Hannover Scorpions .25
☐ 95 Rob Murphy, Hannover Scorpions .25
☐ 96 Pavel Cagas, Hannover Scorpions .25
☐ 97 Igor Chibirev, Hannover Scorpions .25
☐ 98 Kevin Grant, Hannover Scorpions .25
☐ 99 Jan Munster, Hannover Scorpions .25
☐ 100 Chris Snell, Hannover Scorpions .25
☐ 101 Patrik Zetterberg, Hannover Scorpions .25
☐ 102 Colin Beardsmore, Iserlohn Roosters .25
☐ 103 Calle Carlsson, Iserlohn Roosters .25
☐ 104 Tomas Martinec, Iserlohn Roosters .25
☐ 105 Teal Fowler, Iserlohn Roosters .25
☐ 106 Alexander Kuzminsky, Iserlohn Roosters .25
☐ 107 Terence Campbell, Iserlohn Roosters .25
☐ 108 Duane Derksen, Iserlohn Roosters .25
☐ 109 Peter Roed, Iserlohn Roosters .25
☐ 110 Torsten Fendt, Iserlohn Roosters .25
☐ 111 Shawn Anderson, Iserlohn Roosters .25
☐ 112 Manuel Kofler, Iserlohn Roosters .25
☐ 113 Radek Toth, Iserlohn Roosters .25
☐ 114 Steve Potvin, Iserlohn Roosters .25
☐ 115 Brent Tulley, Kassel Huskies .25
☐ 116 Ted Crowley, Kassel Huskies .25
☐ 117 Pat Mikesch, Kassel Huskies .25
☐ 118 Stéphane Robitaille, Kassel Huskies .25
☐ 119 Francois Guay, Kassel Huskies .25
☐ 120 Andreas Loth, Kassel Huskies .25
☐ 121 Patrice Tardif, Kassel Huskies .25
☐ 122 Scott Levins, Kassel Huskies .25
☐ 123 Joachim Appel, Kassel Huskies .25
☐ 124 Chris Rogles, Kassel Huskies .25
☐ 125 Thomas Daffner, Kassel Huskies .25
☐ 126 Klaus Kathan, Kassel Huskies .25
☐ 127 Sylvain Turgeon, Kassel Huskies .25
☐ 128 Andrew Verner, Kolner Haie .25
☐ 129 Bruno Zarrillo, Kolner Haie .25
☐ 130 Dwayne Norris, Kolner Haie .25
☐ 131 Christoph Paepke, Kolner Haie .25
☐ 132 Mirko Ludemann, Kolner Haie .25
☐ 133 Andreas Lupzig, Kolner Haie .25
☐ 134 Jason Young, Kolner Haie .25
☐ 135 Josef Heiss, Kolner Haie .25
☐ 136 Tomas Forslund, Kolner Haie .25
☐ 137 André Faust, Kolner Haie .25
☐ 138 Tino Boos, Kolner Haie .25
☐ 139 John Miner, Kolner Haie .25
☐ 140 Dave McLlwain, Kolner Haie .25
☐ 141 Dieter Kalt, Kolner Haie .25
☐ 142 Corey Millen, Kolner Haie .25
☐ 143 Marc Hussey, Krefeld Pinguine .25
☐ 144 Brent Severyn, Krefeld Pinguine .25
☐ 145 Christian Ehrhoff, Krefeld Pinguine .25
☐ 146 Neil Eisenhut, Krefeld Pinguine .25
☐ 147 Ilja Vorobiev, Krefeld Pinguine .25
☐ 148 Shayne Wright, Krefeld Pinguine .25
☐ 149 Dan Lambert, Krefeld Pinguine .25
☐ 150 Brad Purdie, Krefeld Pinguine .25
☐ 151 Christoph Brandner, Krefeld Pinguine .25
☐ 152 Roger Nordström, Krefeld Pinguine .25
☐ 153 Jeff Christian, Krefeld Pinguine .25
☐ 154 Karel Lang, Krefeld Pinguine .25
☐ 155 Thomas Brandl, Krefeld Pinguine .25
☐ 156 Martin Sychra, Moskitos Essen .25
☐ 157 Jason McBain, Moskitos Essen .25
☐ 158 Ralph Intranuovo, Moskitos Essen .25
☐ 159 Jarkko Savijoki, Moskitos Essen .25
☐ 160 Marc** Savard, Moskitos Essen .25
☐ 161 Roman Meluzin, Moskitos Essen .25
☐ 162 Todd Simon, Moskitos Essen .25
☐ 163 Jean-François Quintin, Moskitos Essen .25
☐ 164 Scott Pearson, Moskitos Essen .25
☐ 165 Kevin Wortman, Moskitos Essen .25
☐ 166 Geoff Sarjeant, Moskitos Essen .25
☐ 167 Leonard Wild, Moskitos Essen .25
☐ 168 Erich Goldmann, Moskitos Essen .25
☐ 169 Marc Laniel, Moskitos Essen .25
☐ 170 Esa Tikkanen, Moskitos Essen .25
☐ 171 Hans Lodin, Munchen Barons .25
☐ 172 Rick Girard, Munchen Barons .25
☐ 173 Christian Kunast, Munchen Barons .25
☐ 174 Simon Wheeldon, Munchen Barons .25
☐ 175 Shane Peacock, Munchen Barons .25
☐ 176 Christoph Schubert, Munchen Barons .25
☐ 177 Peter Douris, Munchen Barons .25
☐ 178 Alexander Serikow, Munchen Barons .25
☐ 179 Peter Larsson, Munchen Barons .25
☐ 180 Thomas Dolak, Munchen Barons .25
☐ 181 Jörg Handrick, Munchen Barons .25
☐ 182 Jason Herter, Munchen Barons .25
☐ 183 Andrew Schneider, Munchen Barons .25
☐ 184 Parris Duffus, Nurnberg Ice Tigers .25
☐ 185 Luciano Borsato, Nurnberg Ice Tigers .25
☐ 186 Jürgen Rumrich, Nurnberg Ice Tigers .25
☐ 187 Dimitri Dudik, Nurnberg Ice Tigers .25
☐ 188 Alexander Cherbayev, Nurnberg Ice Tigers .25
☐ 189 Martin Jiranek, Nurnberg Ice Tigers .25
☐ 190 Martin Reichel, Nurnberg Ice Tigers .25
☐ 191 Mario Chitarroni, Nurnberg Ice Tigers .25
☐ 192 Jason Miller, Nurnberg Ice Tigers .25
☐ 193 Bjorn Nord, Nurnberg Ice Tigers .25
☐ 194 Kevin Miehm, Nurnberg Ice Tigers .25
☐ 195 Marc Seliger, Nurnberg Ice Tigers .25
☐ 196 Daniel Kunce, Nurnberg Ice Tigers .25
☐ 197 Paul Stanton, Nurnberg Ice Tigers .25
☐ 198 Peter Gulda, Revier Lowen Oberhausen .25
☐ 199 Christian Kohmann, Revier Lowen Oberhausen .25
☐ 200 Mika Arvaja, Revier Lowen Oberhausen .25
☐ 201 Carsten Gosdeck, Revier Lowen Oberhausen .25
☐ 202 Aleksandrs Kercs, Revier Lowen Oberhausen .25
☐ 203 Alexander Andrijevski, Revier Lowen Oberhausen .25
☐ 204 Robert Hock, Revier Lowen Oberhausen .25
☐ 205 Josef Zajic, Revier Lowen Oberhausen .25
☐ 206 Marek Stebnicki, Revier Lowen Oberhausen .25
☐ 207 Andrei Kovalev, Revier Lowen Oberhausen .25
☐ 208 Ladislav Karabin, Revier Lowen Oberhausen .25
☐ 209 Peter Draisaitl, Revier Lowen Oberhausen .25
☐ 210 Sinuhe Wallinheimo, Revier Lowen Oberhausen .25
☐ 211 Jergus Baca, Revier Lowen Oberhausen .25
☐ 212 Peter Allen, Schwenninger Wild Wings .25
☐ 213 Alexander Duck, Schwenninger Wild Wings .25
☐ 214 Marcel Goc, Schwenninger Wild Wings 3.00
☐ 215 Jens Stramkowski, Schwenninger Wild Wings .25
☐ 216 Mark MacKay, Schwenninger Wild Wings .25
☐ 217 Vadim Slivchenko, Schwenninger Wild Wings .25
☐ 218 Jacek Plachta, Schwenninger Wild Wings .25
☐ 219 Alexei Yegorov, Schwenninger Wild Wings .25
☐ 220 Patrik Augusta, Schwenninger Wild Wings .25
☐ 221 Brad Schlegel, Schwenninger Wild Wings .25
☐ 222 Andreas Renz, Schwenninger Wild Wings .25
☐ 223 Thomas Greilinger, Schwenninger Wild Wings .25
☐ 224 Ian Gordon, Schwenninger Wild Wings .25
☐ 225 Mike Bullard, Schwenninger Wild Wings .25
☐ 226 Robert Muller, Adler Mannheim .25
☐ 227 Mike Pellegrims, Berlin Capitals .25
☐ 228 Mike Casselman, Hannover Scorpions .25
☐ 229 Leonardo Soccio, Hannover Scorpions .25
☐ 230 Andreas Pokorny, Iserlohn Roosters .25
☐ 231 Tim Schnelle, Iserlohn Roosters .25
☐ 232 Daniel Kreutzer, Kassel Huskies .25
☐ 233 Tobias Abstreiter, Kassel Huskies .25
☐ 234 Tomas Hartogs, Krefeld Pinguine .25
☐ 235 Stéphane Barin, Krefeld Pinguine .25
☐ 236 Boris Rousson, Munchen Barons .25
☐ 237 Mike Kennedy, Munchen Barons .25
☐ 238 John Craighead, Nurnberg Ice Tigres .25
☐ 239 Marc Pethke, Revier Lowen Oberhausen .25
☐ 240 Markus Janka, Schwenninger Wild Wings .25

ALL-STAR CLASS

Insert Set (10 cards): 24.00
Insert (1:17) ASC

☐ A1 Martin Jiranek, Nurnberg Ice Tigres 3.00
☐ A2 Patrice Lefebvre, Frankfurt Lions 3.00
☐ A3 Peter Douris, Munchen Barons 3.00
☐ A4 Sergei Vostrikov, Augsburg Panther 3.00
☐ A5 Greg Johnston, Berlin Capitals 3.00
☐ A6 Chris Govedaris, Eisbaren Berlin 3.00
☐ A7 Mike Casselman, Hannover Scorpions 3.00
☐ A8 Corey Millen, Kolner Haie 3.00
☐ A9 Shawn Anderson, Iserlohn Roosters 3.00
☐ A10 Sylvain Turgeon, Kassel Huskies 3.00

GAME JERSEY

Insert Set (16 cards): 400.00
Insert (1:144) GJ

☐ Bruno Zarrillo, Kolner Haie ✂ 30.00
☐ Duane Moeser, Augsburg Panther ✂ 30.00
☐ Jergus Baca, Oberhausen ✂ 30.00
☐ Jürgen Rumrich, Nurnberg Ice Tigers ✂ 30.00
☐ Leonardo Soccio, Hannover Scorpions ✂ 30.00
☐ Leo Stefan, Dusseldorfer EG ✂ 30.00
☐ Marc Fortier, Eisbaren Berlin ✂ 30.00
☐ Mark MacKay, Schwenninger Wild Wings ✂ 30.00
☐ Marc** Savard, Moskitos Essen ✂ 30.00
☐ Pavel Gross, Berlin Capitals ✂ 30.00
☐ Stéphane J.G. Richer, Adler Mannheim ✂ 30.00
☐ Simon Wheeldon, Munchen Barons ✂ 30.00
☐ Tobias Abstreiter, Kassel Huskies ✂ 30.00
☐ Teal Fowler, Iserlohn Roosters ✂ 30.00
☐ Tomas Hartogs, Krefeld Pinguine ✂ 30.00
☐ Toni Porkka, Frankfurt Lions ✂ 30.00

PROFILES

Insert Set (11 cards): 28.00
Insert (1:8) PF

☐ P1 Jan Alston, Adler Mannheim 3.00
☐ P2 Andréi Mezin, Berlin Capitals 3.00
☐ P3 John Chabot, Eisbaren Berlin 3.00
☐ P4 Wally Schreiber, Hannover Scorpions 3.00
☐ P5 Shane Peacock, Munchen Barons 3.00
☐ P6 Mike Bullard, Schwenninger Wild Wings 3.00
☐ P7 Mirko Ludemann, Kolner Haie 3.00
☐ P8 Boris Rousson (G), Munchen Barons 3.00
☐ P9 Andrei Kovalev, Revier Lowen Oberhausen 3.00
☐ P10 Mike Pellegrims, Berlin Capitals 3.00
☐ P11 Andrei Trefilov, Dusseldorfer EG 3.00

STAR ATTRACTIONS

Insert Set (10 cards): 25.00
Insert (1:17) SA

☐ S1 Ivan Droppa, Dusseldorfer EG 3.00
☐ S2 Gord Hynes, Adler Mannheim 3.00
☐ S3 Marek Stebnicki, Revier Lowen Oberhausen 3.00
☐ S4 Daniel Kreutzer, Kassel Huskies 3.00
☐ S5 Thomas Brandl, Krefeld Pinguine 3.00
☐ S6 Esa Tikkanen, Moskitos Essen 3.00
☐ S7 Bob Sweeney, Munchen Barons 3.00
☐ S8 Paul Stanton, Nurnberg Ice Tigers 3.00
☐ S9 Dave Tomlinson, Adler Mannheim 3.00
☐ S10 Brent Severyn, Krefeld Pinguine 3.00

2000 - 01 UPPER DECK E-CARD

Player MINT

☐ Wayne Gretzky, NYRa. 3.00

2000 - 01 UPPER DECK ELITSERIEN

Complete Set (220 cards): 35.00
Common Player: .25
Player UD

☐ 1 Tim Thomas (G), AIK .25
☐ 2 Per-Anton Lundstrom, AIK .25
☐ 3 Dick Tarnström, AIK .50
☐ 4 Rikard Franzén, AIK .25
☐ 5 Rikard Ekström, AIK .25
☐ 6 Jan Sandström, AIK .25
☐ 7 Stefan Gustavson, AIK .25
☐ 8 Anders Gozzi, AIK .25
☐ 9 Stefan Hellkvist, AIK .25
☐ 10 Mats Lindberg, AIK .25
☐ 11 Bjorn Danielsson, AIK .25
☐ 12 Erik Andersson, AIK .25
☐ 13 Björn Ahlström, AIK .25
☐ 14 Kristian Gahn, AIK .25
☐ 15 Petter Sandström, Bjorkloven .25
☐ 16 Mattias Hedlund, Bjorkloven .25
☐ 17 Tomi Hamal, Bjorkloven .25
☐ 18 Jörgen Hermansson, Bjorkloven .25
☐ 19 Jesper Jager, Bjorkloven .25
☐ 20 Christian Lechtaler, Bjorkloven .25
☐ 21 Alexander Beliavski, Bjorkloven .25
☐ 22 Johan Ramstedt, Bjorkloven .25
☐ 23 Lars Brieel, Bjorkloven .25
☐ 24 Johan Boman, Bjorkloven .25
☐ 25 Aleksanders Semjonovs, Bjorkloven .25
☐ 26 Mathias Bosson, Bjorkloven .25
☐ 27 Niko Halttunen, Bjorkloven .25
☐ 28 Fredrik Nasvall, Bjorkloven .25
☐ 29 Johan Asplund, Brynas .25
☐ 30 Henrik Petré, Brynas .25
☐ 31 Par Djoos, Brynas .25
☐ 32 Tommy Sjödin, Brynas .25
☐ 33 Christer Olsson, Brynas .25
☐ 34 Marko Tuulola, Brynas .25
☐ 35 Johan Molin, Brynas .25
☐ 36 Tony Martensson, Brynas .25
☐ 37 Tom Bissett, Brynas .25
☐ 38 Roger Kyro, Brynas .25
☐ 39 Ove Molin, Brynas .25
☐ 40 Mikko Luovi, Brynas .25
☐ 41 Daniel Rudslätt, Brynas .25
☐ 42 Kenneth Bergqvist, Brynas .25
☐ 43 Jan Larsson, Brynas .25
☐ 44 Mikael Tellqvist, Djurgarden 1.00
☐ 45 Niklas Kronwall, Djurgarden .25
☐ 46 François Bouchard, Djurgarden .25
☐ 47 Edvin Frylén, Djurgarden .25
☐ 48 Mikael Magnusson, Djurgarden .25
☐ 49 Daniel Tjärnqvist, Djurgarden .25
☐ 50 Charles Berglund, Djurgarden .25
☐ 51 Kristofer Ottosson, Djurgarden .25
☐ 52 Kyosti Karjalainen, Djurgarden .25
☐ 53 Nichlas Falk, Djurgarden .25
☐ 54 Mathias Tjärnqvist, Djurgarden .25
☐ 55 Jimmie Ölvestad, Djurgarden .25
☐ 56 Johan Garpenlöv, Djurgarden .25
☐ 57 Andreas Salomonsson, Djurgarden .25
☐ 58 Mikael Johansson, Djurgarden .25
☐ 59 Vladimir Orszagh, Djurgarden .25
☐ 60 Henrik Lundqvist, Frolunda .25
☐ 61 Magnus Johansson, Frolunda .25
☐ 62 Christian Bäckman, Frolunda .25
☐ 63 Nicklas Rahm, Frolunda .25
☐ 64 Ronnie Sundin, Frolunda .25
☐ 65 Par Erlund, Frolunda .25
☐ 66 Magnus Kahnberg, Frolunda .25
☐ 67 Pelle Prestberg, Frolunda .25
☐ 68 Patrik Carnbäck, Frolunda .25

☐ 69 Juha Ikonen, Frolunda	.25
☐ 70 Jari Tolsa, Frolunda	.25
☐ 71 Kristian Huselius, Frolunda	2.00
☐ 72 Peter Strom, Frolunda	.25
☐ 73 Henrik Nilsson, Frolunda	.25
☐ 74 Jonas Johnsson, Frolunda	.25
☐ 75 Mikael Andersson, Frolunda	.25
☐ 76 Magnus Eriksson, Färjestad	.25
☐ 77 Sergej Fokin, Färjestad	.25
☐ 78 Jonas Frogren, Färjestad	.25
☐ 79 Thomas Rhodin, Färjestad	.25
☐ 80 Greger Artursson, Färjestad	.25
☐ 81 Radek Hamr, Färjestad	.25
☐ 82 Roger Johansson, Färjestad	.25
☐ 83 Marko Jantunen, Färjestad	.25
☐ 84 Ulf Söderström, Färjestad	.25
☐ 85 Christian Berglund, Färjestad	.25
☐ 86 Mathias Johansson, Färjestad	.25
☐ 87 Trond Magnussen, Färjestad	.25
☐ 88 Peter Nordström, Färjestad	.25
☐ 89 Clas Eriksson, Färjestad	.25
☐ 90 Jörgen Jönsson, Färjestad	.50
☐ 91 Marcel Jenni, Färjestad	.25
☐ 92 Stefan Liv, HV 71	.25
☐ 93 Joacim Esbjörs, HV 71	.25
☐ 94 Per* Gustafsson, HV 71	.25
☐ 95 Fredrik Stillman, HV 71	.25
☐ 96 Mikael Lindman, HV 71	.25
☐ 97 Peter Ottosson, HV 71	.25
☐ 98 Oleg Belov, HV 71	.25
☐ 99 Peter Ekelund, HV 71	.25
☐ 100 Johan Hult, HV 71	.25
☐ 101 Johan Lindbom, HV 71	.25
☐ 102 Jonas Esbjörs, HV 71	.25
☐ 103 Johan Forsander, HV 71	.25
☐ 104 Mattias Remstam, HV 71	.25
☐ 105 Fredrik Oberg, HV 71	.25
☐ 106 Reinhard Divis, Leksand	1.00
☐ 107 Magnus Svensson, Leksand	.25
☐ 108 Jan Huokko, Leksand	.25
☐ 109 Stefan Bergkvist, Leksand	.25
☐ 110 Lars Jonsson, Leksand	.25
☐ 111 Per Lofstrom, Leksand	.25
☐ 112 Jens Nielsen, Leksand	.25
☐ 113 Niklas Eriksson, Leksand	.25
☐ 114 Daniel Widing, Leksand	.25
☐ 115 Niklas Persson, Leksand	.25
☐ 116 Henrik Nordfeldt, Leksand	.25
☐ 117 Tore Vikingstad, Leksand	.25
☐ 118 Mikael Karlberg, Leksand	.25
☐ 119 Robert Burakovsky, Leksand	.25
☐ 120 Jarmo Myllys, Luleå	.25
☐ 121 Torbjörn Lindberg, Luleå	.25
☐ 122 Petter Nilsson, Luleå	.25
☐ 123 Osmo Soutukorva, Luleå	.25
☐ 124 Roger Åkerström, Luleå	.25
☐ 125 Johan Finnström, Luleå	.25
☐ 126 Jiri Kucera, Luleå	.25
☐ 127 Jonathan Hedström, Luleå	.25
☐ 128 Tomas Berglund, Luleå	.25
☐ 129 Mikael Renberg, Luleå	.50
☐ 130 Anders Burström, Luleå	.25
☐ 131 Hans Huczkowski, Luleå	.25
☐ 132 Martin Hostak, Luleå	.25
☐ 133 Lars Edström, Luleå	.25
☐ 134 Sami Mettovaara, Luleå	.25
☐ 135 Andreas Hadelöv, Malmo	.25
☐ 136 David Petrasek, Malmo	.25
☐ 137 Peter Jakobsson, Malmo	.25
☐ 138 Joakim Lundberg, Malmo	.25
☐ 139 Christian Due-Boje, Malmo	.25
☐ 140 Johan Tornberg, Malmo	.25
☐ 141 Henrik Malmström, Malmo	.25
☐ 142 Marcus Thuresson, Malmo	.25
☐ 143 Daniel Rydmark, Malmo	.25
☐ 144 Juha Riihijarvi, Malmo	.25
☐ 145 Jesper Mattsson, Malmo	.25
☐ 146 Fredrik Lindquist, Malmo	.25
☐ 147 Tomas Sandström, Malmo	.25
☐ 148 Kim Staal, Malmo	.25
☐ 149 Jan Hammar, Malmo	.25
☐ 150 Tobias Lundstrom, MoDo	.25
☐ 151 Andreas Pihl, MoDo	.25
☐ 152 Pierre Hedin, MoDo	.25
☐ 153 Jan-Axel Alavaara, MoDo	.25
☐ 154 Lars Jansson, MoDo	.25
☐ 155 Per Hållberg, MoDo	.25
☐ 156 Jesper Duus, MoDo	.25
☐ 157 Magnus Wernblom, MoDo	.25
☐ 158 Anders Soderberg, MoDo	.25
☐ 159 Tommy Pettersson, MoDo	.25
☐ 160 Mattias Weinhandl, MoDo	.25
☐ 161 Peter Hogardh, MoDo	.25
☐ 162 Patrik Wallenberg, MoDo	.25
☐ 163 Jörgen Bernström, MoDo	.25
☐ 164 Stefan Öhman, MoDo	.25
☐ 165 Boo Ahl (G), Timra	.25
☐ 166 Pasi Petrilainen, Timra	.25
☐ 167 Stefan Klockare, Timra	.25
☐ 168 Daniel Casselstahl, Timra	.25
☐ 169 Marcus Karlsson, Timra	.25
☐ 170 Robert Carlsson, Timra	.25
☐ 171 Per Hallin, Timra	.25
☐ 172 Nik Zupancic, Timra	.25
☐ 173 Timo Peltomaa, Timra	.25
☐ 174 Linus Fagemo, Timra	.25
☐ 175 Henrik Zetterberg, Timrå	15.00
☐ 176 Mikael Lind, Timra	.25
☐ 177 Anders Huss, Timra	.25
☐ 178 Markus Matthiasson, Timra	.25
☐ 179 Stefan Hellkvist, AIK	.25
☐ 180 Kristian Gahn, AIK	.25
☐ 181 Björn Ahlström, AIK	.25
☐ 182 Alexander Beliavski, Bjorkloven	.25
☐ 183 Tom Bissett, Brynas	.25
☐ 184 Tommy Sjödin, Brynas	.25
☐ 185 Ove Molin, Brynas	.25
☐ 186 Mikael Tellqvist, Djurgarden	.25
☐ 187 Mikael Johansson, Djurgarden	.25
☐ 188 Vladimir Orszagh, Djurgarden	.25
☐ 189 Johan Garpenlöv, Djurgarden	.25
☐ 190 Christian Berglund, Färjestad	.25
☐ 191 Jörgen Jönsson, Färjestad	.50
☐ 192 Radek Hamr, Färjestad	.25
☐ 193 Kristian Huselius, Frolunda	2.00
☐ 194 Mikael Andersson, Frolunda	.25
☐ 195 Patrik Carnbäck, Frolunda	.25
☐ 196 Per* Gustafsson, HV 71	.25
☐ 197 Johan Lindbom, HV 71	.25
☐ 198 Oleg Belov, HV 71	.25
☐ 199 Robert Burakovsky, Leksand	.25
☐ 200 Mikael Renberg, Luleå	.50
☐ 201 Petter Nilsson, Luleå	.25
☐ 202 Jarmo Myllys, Luleå	.25
☐ 203 Tomas Sandström, Malmo	.25
☐ 204 Marcus Thuresson, Malmo	.25
☐ 205 Fredrik Lindquist, Malmo	.25
☐ 206 Magnus Wernblom, MoDo	.25
☐ 207 Mattias Weinhandl, MoDo	.25
☐ 208 Henrik Zetterberg, Timrå	10.00
☐ 209 Mats Lindberg, AIK	.25
☐ 210 Jörgen Hermansson, Bjorkloven	.25
☐ 211 Pår Djoos, Brynas	.25
☐ 212 Jimmie Ölvestad, Djurgarden	.25
☐ 213 Christian Bäckman, Frolunda	.25
☐ 214 Radek Hamr, Färjestad	.25
☐ 215 Peter Ekelund, HV 71	.25
☐ 216 Lars Jonsson, Leksand	1.00
☐ 217 Mikael Renberg, Luleå	.25
☐ 218 Fredrik Lindquist, Malmo	.25
☐ 219 Mattias Weinhandl, MoDo	.25
☐ 220 Marcus Karlsson, Timra	.25

JERSEY

Insert	GJ
☐ DS Daniel Sedin ✂	60.00
☐ HS Henrik Sedin ✂	60.00

MASKED MEN

Insert Set (7 cards): 14.00

Insert	MM
☐ M1 Tim Thomas (G), AIK	2.00
☐ M2 Mikael Tellqvist (G), Djurgarden	5.00
☐ M3 Magnus Eriksson (G), Färjestad	2.00
☐ M4 Reinhard Divis (G), Leksand	2.00
☐ M5 Jarmo Myllys (G), Luleå	2.00
☐ M6 Andreas Hadelöv (G), Malmo	2.00
☐ M7 Boo Ahl (G), Timra	2.00

SHL EXCELLENCE

Insert Set (5 cards): 4.00

Insert	SHL
☐ S1 Johan Garpenlöv / Vladimir Orszagh	1.00
☐ S2 Christian Berglund / Jörgen Jönsson	1.00
☐ S3 Patrick Cárnback / Kristian Huselius	1.00
☐ S4 Jarmo Myllys / Mikael Renberg	2.00
☐ S5 Mattias Weinhandl / Magnus Wernblom	1.00

SHL SIGNATURES

Insert Set (37 cards): 525.00

Insert	Auto.
☐ Alexander Beliavski, Bjorkloven ✍	12.00
☐ Anders Gozzi, AIK ✍	12.00
☐ Andreas Hadelöv, Malmo ✍	12.00
☐ Boo Ahl (G), Timra ✍	12.00
☐ Christian Bäckman, Frolunda ✍	12.00
☐ Daniel Rydmark, Malmo ✍	12.00
☐ Fredrik Lindquist, Malmo ✍	12.00
☐ Greger Artursson, Färjestad ✍	12.00
☐ Henrik Zetterberg, Timrå ✍	125.00
☐ Jonas Esbjörs, HV 71 ✍	12.00
☐ Johan Garpenlöv, Djurgarden ✍	12.00
☐ Jörgen Hermansson, Bjorkloven ✍	12.00
☐ Jan Larsson, Brynas ✍	15.00
☐ Jens Nielsen, Leksand ✍	12.00
☐ Jonathan Hedström, Luleå ✍	12.00
☐ Kristian Gahn, AIK ✍	12.00
☐ Kristian Huselius, Frolunda ✍	45.00
☐ Mikael Andersson, Frolunda ✍	12.00
☐ Mikael Tellqvist, Djurgarden ✍	25.00
☐ Martin Hostak, Luleå ✍	12.00
☐ Mattias Weinhandl, MoDo ✍	12.00
☐ Mikael Johansson, Djurgarden ✍	12.00
☐ Mats Lindberg, AIK ✍	12.00
☐ Mikael Renberg, Luleå ✍	20.00
☐ Mattias Remstam, HV 71 ✍	12.00
☐ Magnus Svensson, Leksand ✍	12.00
☐ Marcus Thuresson, Malmo ✍	12.00
☐ Magnus Wernblom, MoDo ✍	12.00
☐ Niklas Kronwall, Djurgarden ✍	12.00
☐ Oleg Belov, HV 71 ✍	12.00
☐ Ove Molin, Brynas ✍	12.00
☐ Patrik Carnbäck, Frolunda ✍	12.00
☐ Per Djoos, Brynas ✍	12.00
☐ Petter Nilsson, Luleå ✍	12.00
☐ Reinhard Divis, Leksand ✍	15.00
☐ Tom Bissett, Brynas ✍	12.00
☐ Tobias Lundstrom, MoDo ✍	12.00

TOP DRAWS

Insert Set (11 cards): 20.00

Insert	TD
☐ T1 Björn Ahlström, AIK	2.00
☐ T2 Ove Molin, Brynas	2.00
☐ T3 Mikael Tellqvist, Djurgarden	5.00
☐ T4 Patrik Carnbäck, Frolunda	2.00
☐ T5 Roger Johansson, Färjestad	2.00
☐ T6 Oleg Belov, HV 71	2.00
☐ T7 Jens Nielsen, Leksand	2.00
☐ T8 Jonathan Hedström, Luleå	2.00
☐ T9 Fredrik Lindquist, Malmo	2.00
☐ T10 Mattias Weinhandl, MoDo	2.00
☐ T11 Anders Huss, Timra	2.00

TOP PLAYMAKERS

Insert Set (8 cards): 7.00

Insert	TP
☐ P1 Mats Lindberg, AIK	1.00
☐ P2 Jan Larsson, Brynas	2.00
☐ P3 Mikael Johansson, Djurgarden	1.00
☐ P4 Jonas Johnsson, Frolunda	1.00
☐ P5 Jörgen Jönsson, Färjestad	1.00
☐ P6 Martin Hostak, Luleå	1.00
☐ P7 Juha Riihijarvi, Malmo	1.00
☐ P8 Mattias Weinhandl, MoDo	1.00

2000 - 01 UPPER DECK GREAT FUTURES

This card was given out at the Toronto Sport Card & Memorabilia Expo.

Autograph	
☐ Jason Spezza ✍	

2000 - 01 UPPER DECK ICE

This series was distributed in two releases: the original release in 2000 and the Update releasd as part of the 2000 - 01 Rookie Update product in April 2001. In the original release (1-60), rookie-subset cards 41-60 are limited to 1500 copies. In the Update release, rookie-subset cards are limited to 1500 copies. For all base cards in each series, there is an Ice Stars parallel limited to 500 copies, an Ice Legends parallel limited to 150 copies and an Ice Immortals parallel limited to 25 copies.

Shell Set (40 cards):	-	-	-	30.00
Parallel Set (60 cards):	3,400	775.00	300.00	-
Complete Set (123 cards):	-	-	-	500.00
Common Player:	15.00	4.00	2.00	.50
Player	I25	L150	S500	Reg.
☐☐☐☐ 1 Paul Kariya	210.00	40.00	10.00	2.50
☐☐☐☐ 2 Teemu Selänne	120.00	24.00	6.00	1.50
☐☐☐☐ 3 Patrik Stefan	45.00	9.00	2.00	.50
☐☐☐☐ 4 Joe Thornton	180.00	36.00	9.00	2.00
☐☐☐☐ 5 D. Hasek (G)	150.00	30.00	7.00	2.00
☐☐☐☐ 6 Michael Peca	60.00	12.00	3.00	.50
☐☐☐☐ 7 Valeri Bure	45.00	9.00	2.00	.50
☐☐☐☐ 8 Ron Francis	90.00	18.00	4.00	1.00
☐☐☐☐ 9 Tony Amonte	90.00	18.00	4.00	1.00
☐☐☐☐ 10 Patrick Roy (G)	450.00	90.00	22.00	6.00
☐☐☐☐ 11 R. Bourque	180.00	36.00	9.00	2.00
☐☐☐☐ 12 Milan Hejduk	120.00	24.00	6.00	1.50
☐☐☐☐ 13 Peter Forsberg	210.00	40.00	10.00	2.50
☐☐☐☐ 14 Brett Hull	150.00	29.00	7.00	2.00
☐☐☐☐ 15 Mike Modano	150.00	29.00	7.00	2.00
☐☐☐☐ 16 B. Shanahan	150.00	29.00	7.00	2.00
☐☐☐☐ 17 Chris Osgood (G)	90.00	18.00	4.00	1.00
☐☐☐☐ 18 Steve Yzerman	360.00	70.00	18.00	4.50
☐☐☐☐ 19 Doug Weight	90.00	18.00	4.00	1.00
☐☐☐☐ 20 Pavel Bure	120.00	24.00	6.00	1.50
☐☐☐☐ 21 Luc Robitaille	120.00	24.00	6.00	1.50
☐☐☐☐ 22 J. Théodore (G)	180.00	36.00	9.00	2.00
☐☐☐☐ 23 David Legwand	60.00	12.00	3.00	.50
☐☐☐☐ 24 M. Brodeur (G)	240.00	48.00	12.00	3.00
☐☐☐☐ 25 Scott Gomez	60.00	12.00	3.00	.50
☐☐☐☐ 26 Tim Connolly	60.00	12.00	3.00	.50
☐☐☐☐ 27 Mike York	45.00	9.00	2.00	.50
☐☐☐☐ 28 Marian Hossa	150.00	30.00	7.00	2.00
☐☐☐☐ 29 Brian Boucher (G)	45.00	9.00	2.00	.50
☐☐☐☐ 30 John LeClair	120.00	23.00	6.00	1.50
☐☐☐☐ 31 Jeremy Roenick	120.00	24.00	6.00	1.50
☐☐☐☐ 32 Jaromir Jagr	150.00	30.00	7.00	2.00
☐☐☐☐ 33 Steve Shields (G)	35.00	7.00	2.00	.50
☐☐☐☐ 34 Chris Pronger	90.00	18.00	4.00	1.00
☐☐☐☐ 35 Roman Turek (G)	70.00	14.00	3.00	.50
☐☐☐☐ 36 V. Lecavalier	150.00	29.00	7.00	2.00
☐☐☐☐ 37 Curtis Joseph (G)	150.00	30.00	7.00	2.00
☐☐☐☐ 38 Mats Sundin	150.00	29.00	7.00	2.00
☐☐☐☐ 39 Mark Messier	150.00	29.00	7.00	2.00
☐☐☐☐ 40 Olaf Kölzig (G)	90.00	18.00	4.00	1.00

PRIME PERFORMERS

Inserts				
☐☐☐☐ **41 M. Pettinger RC**	**35.00**	**12.00**	**10.00**	**8.00**
☐☐☐☐ **42 Chris Nielsen RC**	**35.00**	**12.00**	**10.00**	**8.00**
☐☐☐☐ **43 D. Heatley RC**	**225.00**	**150.00**	**93.00**	**200.00**
☐☐☐☐ **44 Matt Zultek RC**	**25.00**	**12.00**	**10.00**	**6.00**
☐☐☐☐ **45 Afanasenkov RC**	**35.00**	**12.00**	**10.00**	**8.00**
☐☐☐☐ **46 Tyler Bouck RC**	**35.00**	**12.00**	**10.00**	**8.00**
☐☐☐☐ **47 J. Andersson RC**	**25.00**	**12.00**	**10.00**	**6.00**
☐☐☐☐ **48 M-A Thinel RC**	**35.00**	**12.00**	**10.00**	**8.00**
☐☐☐☐ **49 J. Svoboda RC**	**50.00**	**14.00**	**12.00**	**12.00**
☐☐☐☐ **50 J. Vasicek RC**	**50.00**	**14.00**	**12.00**	**12.00**
☐☐☐☐ **51 Raycroft (G) RC**	**50.00**	**14.00**	**12.00**	**12.00**
☐☐☐☐ **52 Juraj Kolnik RC**	**35.00**	**12.00**	**10.00**	**8.00**
☐☐☐☐ **53 Z. Blatny RC**	**35.00**	**12.00**	**10.00**	**8.00**
☐☐☐☐ **54 S. Caron (G) RC**	**50.00**	**12.00**	**10.00**	**12.00**
☐☐☐☐ **55 E. Nickulas RC**	**25.00**	**12.00**	**10.00**	**6.00**
☐☐☐☐ **56 S. Aubin RC**	**35.00**	**12.00**	**10.00**	**8.00**
☐☐☐☐ **57 S. Reinprecht RC**	**70.00**	**20.00**	**16.00**	**16.00**
☐☐☐☐ **58 D. Gosselin RC**	**25.00**	**12.00**	**10.00**	**6.00**
☐☐☐☐ **59 C. White RC**	**35.00**	**12.00**	**10.00**	**8.00**
☐☐☐☐ **60 Valiquette (G) RC**	**35.00**	**12.00**	**10.00**	**8.00**

UPDATE

Insert	Ice
☐ 61 Jeff Friesen, Anah.	.50
☐ 62 Bill Guerin, Bost.	.50
☐ 63 Jean-Pierre Dumont, Buff.	.50
☐ 64 Oleg Saprykin, Calg.	.50
☐ 65 Shane Willis, Caro.	.50
☐ 66 Josef Vasicek, Caro.	.50
☐ 67 Steve Reinprecht, Colo.	1.00
☐ 68 Marc Denis (G), Colu.	.50
☐ **69 Marty Turco (G), Dall. RC**	**6.00**
☐ 70 Sergei Fedorov, Detr.	2.00
☐ 71 Adam Deadmarsh, LosA.	.50

□	72 Keith Tkachuk, SLou.	1.00
□	73 Mark Messier, NYRa.	2.00
□	74 Alexei Yashin, Otta.	1.00
□	75 Mario Lemieux, Pitt.	6.00
□	76 Evgeni Nabokov, SanJ.	1.00
□	77 Brad Richards, Tamp.	1.50
□	78 Henrik Sedin, Vanc.	1.50
□	79 Daniel Sedin, Vanc.	1.50
□	80 Matt Pettinger, Wash.	.50
□	102 Rob Blake, Colo.	1.00

PRIME PERFORMERS

	Insert (#/1500)	**PP**
□	**81 Marc Chouinard, Anah. RC**	**6.00**
□	**82 Bryan Adams, Atla. RC**	**6.00**
□	**83 Martin Brochu (G), Calg. RC**	**8.00**
□	**84 Craig Adams, Caro. RC**	**6.00**
□	**85 David Aebischer (G), Colo. RC**	**16.00**
□	**86 Rostislav Klesla, Colu. RC**	**16.00**
□	**87 Shawn Horcoff, Edmo. RC**	**8.00**
□	**88 Mike Comrie, Edmo. RC**	**40.00**
□	**89 Éric Bélanger, LosA. RC**	**8.00**
□	**90 Marian Gaborik, MinW. RC**	**50.00**
□	**91 Éric Landry, Mont. RC**	**6.00**
□	**92 Scott Hartnell, Nash. RC**	**12.00**
□	**93 Chris Mason (G), Nash. RC**	**8.00**
□	**94 Rick DiPietro (G), NYIs. RC**	**20.00**
□	**95 Martin Havlat, Otta. RC**	**30.00**
□	**96 Roman Cechmanek (G), Phil. RC**	**20.00**
□	**97 Justin Williams, Phil. RC**	**16.00**
□	**98 Ruslan Fedotenko, Phil. RC**	**8.00**
□	**99 Jean-Guy Trudel, Phoe. RC**	**8.00**
□	**100 Reed Low, SLou. RC**	**8.00**
□	**101 Alexei Ponikarovsky, Toro. RC**	**8.00**
□	**103 Andy McDonald, Anah. RC**	**8.00**
□	**104 Petr Tenkrat, Anah. RC**	**8.00**
□	**105 Brad Tapper, Atla. RC**	**8.00**
□	**106 Darcy Hordichuk, Atla. RC**	**6.00**
□	**107 J-P Vigier, Atla. RC**	**6.00**
□	**108 Pavel Kolarik, Bost. RC**	**6.00**
□	**109 Jarno Kultanen, Bost. RC**	**6.00**
□	**110 Eric Manlow, Bost. RC**	**6.00**
□	**111 Eric Boulton, Buff. RC**	**8.00**
□	112 Brian Swanson, Edmo.	4.00
□	**113 Lubomir Sekeras, MinW. RC**	**8.00**
□	**114 Greg Classen, Nash. RC**	**8.00**
□	**115 Jiri Bicek, NJer. RC**	**8.00**
□	**116 Jeff Ulmer, NYRa. RC**	**6.00**
□	**117 Johan Holmqvist (G), NYRa. RC**	**15.00**
□	**118 Shane Hnidy, Otta. RC**	**8.00**
□	**119 Ossi Väänänen, Phoe. RC**	**8.00**
□	**120 Johan Hedberg (G), Pitt. RC**	**20.00**
□	**121 Mark Smith, SanJ. RC**	**6.00**
□	**122 Alexander Khavanov, SLou. RC**	**8.00**
□	**123 Bryce Salvador, SLou. RC**	**8.00**

CLEAR CUT AUTOGRAPHS

	Insert Set (10 cards):	**350.00**
	Autograph (1:108)	**CCA**
□	Brett Hull, Dall. ✍	55.00
□	Brian Leetch, NYRa. ✍ (Redemption)	30.00
□	Curtis Joseph (G), Toro. ✍	55.00
□	Mike York, NYRa. ✍ (Redemption)	20.00
□	Pavel Bure, Flor. ✍	45.00
□	Patrik Stefan, Atla. ✍	20.00
□	Roman Turek (G), SLou. ✍	25.00
□	Scott Gomez, NJer. ✍	20.00
□	Steve Yzerman, Detr. ✍	125.00
□	Tim Connolly, NYIs. ✍ (Redemption)	20.00

COOL COMPETITORS

	Insert Set (6 cards):	**60.00**
	Insert (1:53)	**CC**
□	CC1 Paul Kariya, Anah.	18.00
□	CC2 Peter Forsberg, Colo.	18.00
□	CC3 Pavel Bure, Flor.	10.00
□	CC4 Scott Gomez, NJer.	10.00
□	CC5 Jaromir Jagr, Pitt.	12.00
□	CC6 Curtis Joseph (G), Toro.	12.00

ICE CHAMPIONS

	Insert Set (6 cards):	**40.00**
	Insert (1:18)	**IC**
□	IC1 Patrick Roy (G), Colo.	15.00
□	IC2 Mike Modano, Dall.	5.00
□	IC3 Steve Yzerman, Detr.	12.00
□	IC4 Martin Brodeur (G), NJer.	8.00
□	IC5 John LeClair, Phil.	4.00
□	IC6 Jaromir Jagr, Pitt.	5.00

ICE GALLERY

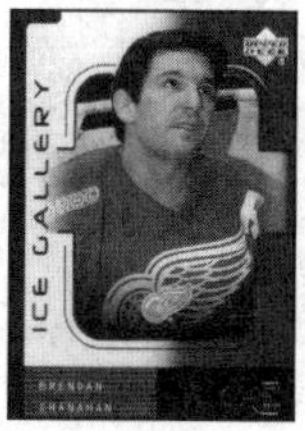

	Insert Set (9 cards):	**20.00**
	Insert (1:6)	**IG**
□	IG1 Teemu Selänne, Anah.	2.00
□	IG2 Patrick Roy (G), Colo.	9.00
□	IG3 Brendan Shanahan, Detr.	3.00
□	IG4 Pavel Bure, Flor.	2.00
□	IG5 Scott Gomez, NJer.	2.00
□	IG6 John LeClair, Phil.	2.00
□	IG7 Jaromir Jagr, Pitt.	3.00
□	IG8 Vincent Lecavalier, Tamp.	3.00
□	IG9 Curtis Joseph (G), Toro.	3.00

ICE GAME JERSEY CARD

These cards were inserted 1:46 original series packs and 1:60 Rookie Update packs.

	Insert Set (29 cards):	**675.00**
	Insert	**IJ**
□	Anson Carter, Bost. ✂	12.00
□	Brett Hull, Dall. ✂	30.00
□	Brendan Shanahan, Detr. ✂	30.00
□	Chris Osgood (G), Detr. ✂	20.00
□	David Legwand, Nash. ✂	12.00
□	Jaromir Jagr, Pitt. ✂	30.00
□	John LeClair, Phil. ✂	25.00
□	Joe Nieuwendyk, Dall. ✂	12.00
□	Martin Brodeur (G), NJer. ✂	50.00
□	Michal Handzus, SLou. ✂	12.00
□	Mike Modano, Dall. ✂	30.00
□	Miroslav Satan, Buff. ✂	12.00
□	Pavel Bure, Flor. ✂	25.00
□	Pavol Demitra, SLou. ✂	12.00
□	Paul Kariya, Anah. ✂	45.00
□	Raymond Bourque, Colo. ✂	40.00
□	Sergei Fedorov, Detr. ✂	30.00
□	Sergei Samsonov, Bost. ✂	20.00
□	Tim Connolly, NYIs. ✂	12.00
□	Teemu Selänne, Anah. ✂	25.00
□	Peter Forsberg, All-Star ✂	45.00
□	Joe Thornton, Bost. ✂ White	40.00
□	John LeClair, Phil. ✂	25.00
□	Mike Modano, Dall. ✂	30.00
□	Patrick Roy (G), Colo. ✂	80.00
□	Joe Sakic, All-Star ✂	50.00
□	Brenden Shanahan, SLou. ✂	30.00
□	Jocelyn Thibault (G), Chic. ✂ Red	12.00
□	Keith Tkachuk, Phoe. ✂	20.00

ICE RINK FAVORITES

	Insert Set (9 cards):	**40.00**
	Insert (1:9)	**IRF**
□	FP1 Paul Kariya, Anah.	6.00
□	FP2 Peter Forsberg, Colo.	6.00
□	FP3 Raymond Bourque, Colo.	5.00
□	FP4 Mike Modano, Dall.	4.00
□	FP5 Steve Yzerman, Detr.	10.00
□	FP6 Pavel Bure, Flor.	3.00
□	FP7 Martin Brodeur (G), NJer.	7.00
□	FP8 John LeClair, Phil.	3.00
□	FP9 Jaromir Jagr, Pitt.	4.00

2000 - 01 UPPER DECK LEGENDS

This series was released in 2000. There are four versions: the base card, the Legends Collection gold parallel (#/375), the Legends Collection silver parallel (#/100) and the Legends Collection bronze parallel (#/25).

		L25	L100	L375	Reg.
	Complete Set (135 cards):	**14,000**	**4,500**	**850.00**	**50.00**
	Common Player:	**15.00**	**6.00**	**3.00**	**.25**
	Player	**L25**	**L100**	**L375**	**Reg.**
□□□□	1 Paul Kariya	200.00	70.00	14.00	1.50
□□□□	2 Teemu Selänne	100.00	40.00	8.00	1.00
□□□□	3 Kariya / Selänne	150.00	55.00	11.00	1.00
□□□□	4 Patrik Stefan	25.00	16.00	3.00	.25
□□□□	5 Rhodes / Stefan	25.00	14.00	3.00	.25
□□□□	6 Bobby Orr	600.00	200.00	40.00	5.00
□□□□	7 Phil Esposito	175.00	60.00	12.00	1.50
□□□□	8 Johnny Bucyk	75.00	30.00	6.00	.50
□□□□	9 Cam Neely	150.00	50.00	10.00	1.00
□□□□	10 Eddie Shore	200.00	70.00	14.00	1.50
□□□□	11 Joe Thornton	175.00	60.00	12.00	1.50
□□□□	12 Sergei Samsonov	75.00	30.00	6.00	.50
□□□□	13 Neely / Thornton	150.00	55.00	11.00	1.00
□□□□	14 Gilbert Perreault	100.00	40.00	8.00	1.00
□□□□	15 Pat LaFontaine	75.00	30.00	6.00	.50
□□□□	16 Dominik Hasek (G)	150.00	50.00	10.00	1.00
□□□□	17 Doug Gilmour	75.00	30.00	6.00	.50
□□□□	18 Hasek / Perreault	125.00	45.00	9.00	1.00
□□□□	19 Lanny McDonald	100.00	40.00	8.00	1.00
□□□□	20 Valeri Bure	25.00	16.00	3.00	.25
□□□□	21 Bure / Fleury	50.00	23.00	4.00	.50
□□□□	22 Ron Francis	75.00	30.00	6.00	.50
□□□□	23 Arturs Irbe (G)	50.00	20.00	4.00	.50
□□□□	24 Francis / Irbe	75.00	25.00	5.00	.50
□□□□	25 Bobby Hull	250.00	90.00	18.00	2.00
□□□□	26 Stan Mikita	100.00	40.00	8.00	1.00
□□□□	27 Tony Esposito (G)	150.00	50.00	10.00	1.00
□□□□	28 Glenn Hall (G)	150.00	50.00	10.00	1.00
□□□□	29 Tony Amonte	75.00	30.00	6.00	.50
□□□□	30 Amonte / Bo. Hull	175.00	60.00	12.00	1.50
□□□□	31 Patrick Roy (G)	350.00	120.00	30.00	3.50
□□□□	32 Raymond Bourque	175.00	60.00	12.00	1.50
□□□□	33 Chris Drury	75.00	30.00	6.00	.50
□□□□	34 Peter Forsberg	200.00	70.00	14.00	1.50
□□□□	35 Milan Hejduk	100.00	40.00	8.00	1.00
□□□□	36 Forsberg / Roy	275.00	95.00	22.00	2.50
□□□□	37 Brett Hull	150.00	50.00	10.00	1.00
□□□□	38 Ed Belfour (G)	150.00	50.00	10.00	1.00
□□□□	39 Mike Modano	150.00	50.00	10.00	1.00
□□□□	40 Belfour (G) / Modano	150.00	50.00	10.00	1.00
□□□□	41 Gordie Howe	400.00	140.00	28.00	3.50
□□□□	42 Ted Lindsay	150.00	50.00	10.00	1.00
□□□□	43 Terry Sawchuk (G)	300.00	100.00	20.00	2.50
□□□□	44 Brendan Shanahan	150.00	50.00	10.00	1.00
□□□□	45 Chris Osgood (G)	75.00	30.00	6.00	.50
□□□□	46 Steve Yzerman	350.00	120.00	24.00	3.00
□□□□	47 Howe / Yzerman	375.00	130.00	26.00	3.00
□□□□	48 Grant Fuhr (G)	75.00	30.00	6.00	.50
□□□□	49 Wayne Gretzky	600.00	200.00	40.00	5.00
□□□□	50 Jarri Kurri	150.00	50.00	10.00	1.00
□□□□	51 Mark Messier	150.00	50.00	10.00	1.00
□□□□	52 Paul Coffey	75.00	30.00	6.00	.50
□□□□	53 Doug Weight	75.00	30.00	6.00	.50
□□□□	54 Gretzky / Weight	325.00	115.00	23.00	2.50
□□□□	55 Pavel Bure	100.00	40.00	8.00	1.00
□□□□	56 Viktor Kozlov	25.00	16.00	3.00	.25
□□□□	57 Bure / Vanbiesbrouck	75.00	30.00	6.00	.50
□□□□	58 Marcel Dionne	150.00	50.00	10.00	1.00
□□□□	59 Zigmund Palffy	75.00	30.00	6.00	.50
□□□□	60 Luc Robitaille	100.00	40.00	8.00	1.00
□□□□	61 Gretzky / Robitaille	350.00	120.00	24.00	3.00
□□□□	62 Dino Ciccarelli	25.00	16.00	3.00	.25
□□□□	63 Saku Koivu	175.00	40.00	8.00	1.00
□□□□	64 Jean Béliveau	325.00	110.00	22.00	2.50
□□□□	65 Doug Harvey	175.00	60.00	12.00	1.50
□□□□	66 Jacques Plante	225.00	80.00	16.00	2.00
□□□□	67 Guy Lafleur	175.00	60.00	20.00	2.50
□□□□	68 Serge Savard	50.00	24.00	4.00	.50
□□□□	69 Larry Robinson	75.00	30.00	6.00	.50
□□□□	70 Eric Weinrich	15.00	6.00	3.00	.25
□□□□	71 Bernie Geoffrion	100.00	40.00	8.00	1.00
□□□□	72 José Théodore (G)	175.00	60.00	12.00	1.50
□□□□	73 G. Lafleur / P. Roy	250.00	90.00	25.00	3.00
□□□□	74 David Legwand	50.00	20.00	4.00	.50
□□□□	75 Dunham / Legwand	50.00	20.00	4.00	.50
□□□□	76 Martin Brodeur (G)	225.00	80.00	16.00	2.00
□□□□	77 Scott Gomez	50.00	20.00	4.00	.50
□□□□	78 Scott Stevens	50.00	20.00	4.00	.50
□□□□	79 Brodeur / Stevens	150.00	50.00	10.00	1.00
□□□□	80 Denis Potvin	100.00	40.00	8.00	1.00
□□□□	81 Mike Bossy	225.00	80.00	16.00	2.00
□□□□	82 Bryan Trottier	150.00	50.00	10.00	1.00
□□□□	83 Butch Goring	25.00	16.00	3.00	.25
□□□□	84 Bob Nystrom	25.00	12.00	3.00	.25
□□□□	85 Chico Resch	25.00	16.00	3.00	.25
□□□□	86 Clark Gillies	25.00	16.00	3.00	.25
□□□□	87 Tim Connolly	50.00	20.00	4.00	.50
□□□□	88 Connolly / Trottier	100.00	35.00	7.00	.50
□□□□	89 Ed Giacomin	100.00	40.00	8.00	1.00
□□□□	90 Rod Gilbert	50.00	20.00	4.00	.50
□□□□	91 Theoren Fleury	75.00	30.00	6.00	.50
□□□□	92 Leetch / Messier	100.00	40.00	8.00	1.00
□□□□	93 Marian Hossa	150.00	50.00	10.00	1.00
□□□□	94 Radek Bonk	25.00	16.00	3.00	.25
□□□□	95 Bonk / Hossa	75.00	33.00	6.00	.50
□□□□	96 Bobby Clarke	100.00	40.00	8.00	1.00
□□□□	97 Bernie Parent (G)	100.00	40.00	8.00	1.00
□□□□	98 Eric Lindros	150.00	50.00	10.00	1.00
□□□□	99 Brian Boucher (G)	25.00	16.00	3.00	.25
□□□□	100 John LeClair	100.00	40.00	8.00	1.00
□□□□	101 Clarke / LeClair	100.00	40.00	8.00	1.00
□□□□	102 Jeremy Roenick	100.00	40.00	8.00	1.00
□□□□	103 Keith Tkachuk	75.00	30.00	6.00	.50
□□□□	104 Roenick / Tkachuk	100.00	35.00	7.00	.50
□□□□	105 Mario Lemieux	450.00	150.00	30.00	3.50
□□□□	106 Joe Mullen	50.00	20.00	4.00	.50
□□□□	107 Jaromir Jagr	150.00	50.00	10.00	1.00
□□□□	108 Jagr / Lemieux	300.00	100.00	20.00	2.50
□□□□	109 Peter Stastny	75.00	30.00	6.00	.50
□□□□	110 Michel Goulet	50.00	24.00	4.00	.50
□□□□	111 Steve Shields (G)	25.00	12.00	3.00	.25
□□□□	112 Jeff Friesen	25.00	16.00	3.00	.25
□□□□	113 Friesen / Nolan	50.00	23.00	4.00	.50
□□□□	114 Bernie Federko	25.00	16.00	3.00	.25
□□□□	115 Chris Pronger	75.00	30.00	6.00	.50
□□□□	116 Roman Turek (G)	50.00	24.00	4.00	.50
□□□□	117 Demitra / Br. Hull	100.00	35.00	7.00	.50
□□□□	118 Vincent Lecavalier	150.00	50.00	10.00	1.00
□□□□	119 Lecavalier / Mara	75.00	29.00	5.00	.50
□□□□	120 Frank Mahovlich	150.00	50.00	10.00	1.00
□□□□	121 Syl Apps	100.00	40.00	8.00	1.00
□□□□	122 Tim Horton	175.00	60.00	12.00	1.50
□□□□	123 Eddie Shack	50.00	20.00	4.00	.50
□□□□	124 Curtis Joseph (G)	150.00	50.00	10.00	1.00
□□□□	125 Mats Sundin	150.00	50.00	10.00	1.00
□□□□	126 Joseph (G) / Mahovlich	150.00	50.00	10.00	1.00
□□□□	127 Richard Brodeur	25.00	12.00	3.00	.25
□□□□	128 Brodeur / Näslund	75.00	31.00	6.00	.50
□□□□	129 Mike Gartner	100.00	40.00	8.00	1.00
□□□□	130 Adam Oates	50.00	20.00	4.00	.50
□□□□	131 Olaf Kölzig (G)	75.00	30.00	6.00	.50
□□□□	132 Gartner / Kölzig	100.00	35.00	7.00	.50
□□□□	133 Dale Hawerchuk	75.00	30.00	6.00	.50
□□□□	134 Wayne Gretzky [SL]	300.00	100.00	20.00	2.00
□□□□	135 Steve Yzerman [CL]	175.00	60.00	12.00	1.00

ENSHRINED STARS

	Insert Set (15 cards):	**100.00**
	Insert (1:12)	**ES**
□	ES1 Wayne Gretzky, Edmo.	20.00
□	ES2 Gordie Howe, Detr.	14.00
□	ES3 Mario Lemieux, Pitt.	15.00
□	ES4 Bobby Hull, Chic.	9.00
□	ES5 Marcel Dionne, LosA.	5.00
□	ES6 Denis Potvin, NYIs.	4.00
□	ES7 Guy Lafleur, Mont.	10.00
□	ES8 Mike Bossy, NYIs.	8.00
□	ES9 Bobby Clarke, Phil.	4.00
□	ES10 Frank Mahovlich, Toro.	5.00
□	ES11 Gilbert Perreault, Buff.	4.00
□	ES12 Phil Esposito, Bost.	6.00
□	ES13 Tony Esposito (G), Chic.	5.00
□	ES14 Stan Mikita, Chic.	4.00
□	ES15 Ted Lindsay, Detr.	5.00

ESSENCE OF THE GAME

	Insert Set (8 cards):	**70.00**
	Insert (1:23)	**EotG**
□	EG1 P. Kariya / G. Lafleur	8.00
□	EG2 W. Gretzky / J. Jagr	16.00
□	EG3 M. Bossy / P. Bure	6.00
□	EG4 P. Roy / T. Sawchuk	16.00
□	EG5 M. Brodeur / B. Parent	6.00
□	EG6 C. Neely / B. Shanahan	5.00
□	EG7 R. Bourque / B. Orr	13.00
□	EG8 G. Howe / S. Yzerman	16.00

LEGENDS OF THE CAGE

	Insert Set (10 cards):	**50.00**
	Insert (1:18)	**LotC**
□	LC1 Patrick Roy (G), Colo.	15.00
□	LC2 Martin Brodeur (G), NJer.	8.00
□	LC3 Dominick Hasek, Buff.	5.00
□	LC4 Curtis Joseph (G), Toro.	5.00
□	LC5 Ed Belfour (G), Dall.	5.00
□	LC6 Grant Fuhr (G), Edmo.	3.00
□	LC7 Mike Richter (G), NYRa.	3.00
□	LC8 Jacques Plante, Mont.	8.00
□	LC9 Terry Sawchuk (G), Detr.	10.00
□	LC10 Tony Esposito (G), Chic.	5.00

PLAYOFF HEROES

	Card	Price
	Insert Set (12 cards):	**90.00**
	Insert (1:15)	**PH**
□	PH1 Patrick Roy (G), Colo.	15.00
□	PH2 Steve Yzerman, Detr.	12.00
□	PH3 Jaromir Jagr, Pitt.	5.00
□	PH4 Mike Modano, Dall.	5.00
□	PH5 Peter Forsberg, Colo.	7.00
□	PH6 Mark Messier, NYRa.	5.00
□	PH7 Wayne Gretzky, Edmo.	20.00
□	PH8 Brett Hull, Dall.	5.00
□	PH9 Gordie Howe, Detr.	14.00
□	PH10 Bobby Hull, Chic.	9.00
□	PH11 Bryan Trottier, NYIs.	5.00
□	PH12 Phil Esposito, Bost.	6.00

SUPREME MILESTONES

	Card	Price
	Insert Set (15 cards):	**45.00**
	Insert (1:4)	**SM**
□	SM1 Wayne Gretzky, LosA.	8.00
□	SM2 Gordie Howe, Detr.	5.00
□	SM3 Bobby Hull, Chic.	3.00
□	SM4 Wayne Gretzky, NYRa.	8.00
□	SM5 Steve Yzerman, Detr.	4.00
□	SM6 Brett Hull, Dall.	2.00
□	SM7 Joe Sakic, Colo.	3.00
□	SM8 Mark Messier, NYRa.	2.00
□	SM9 Patrick Roy (G), Colo.	6.00
□	SM10 Luc Robitaille, LosA.	1.50
□	SM11 Mario Lemieux, Pitt.	6.00
□	SM12 Mike Bossy, NYIs.	3.00
□	SM13 Phil Esposito, Bost.	2.00
□	SM14 Tony Esposito (G), Chic.	2.00
□	SM15 Raymond Bourque, Colo.	2.00

EPIC SIGNATURES

	Card	Price
	Insert Set (44 cards):	**1,700**
	Autograph (1:23)	**Epic**
□	Bobby Clarke, Phil. ✍	25.00
□	Bernie Geoffrion, Mont. ✍	35.00
□	Brett Hull, Dall. ✍	45.00
□	Bobby Hull, Chic. ✍	45.00
□	Bobby Orr, Bost. ✍	250.00
□	Bryan Trottier, NYIs. ✍	45.00
□	Curtis Joseph (G), Toro. ✍	45.00
□	Cam Neely, Bost. ✍	45.00
□	Dale Hawerchuk, Winn. ✍	25.00
□	Denis Potvin, NYIs. ✍	35.00
□	Frank Mahovlich, Toro. ✍	45.00
□	Gordie Howe, Detr. ✍	105.00
□	Guy Lafleur, Mont. ✍	45.00
□	Gilbert Perreault, Buff. ✍	35.00
□	John Bucyk, Bost. ✍	25.00
□	Jean Béliveau, Mont. ✍	60.00
□	Jari Kurri, Edmo. ✍	45.00
□	John LeClair, Phil. ✍	35.00
□	Joe Mullen, Pitt. ✍	15.00
□	Joe Nieuwendyk, Dall. ✍	15.00
□	Joe Thornton, Bost. ✍	50.00
□	Keith Tkachuk, Phoe. ✍	25.00
□	Lanny McDonald, Calg. ✍	35.00
□	Larry Robinson, Mont. ✍	25.00
□	Mike Bossy, NYIs. ✍	50.00
□	Martin Brodeur (G), NJer. ✍	70.00
□	Marcel Dionne, LosA. ✍	35.00
□	Mike Gartner, Wash. ✍	35.00
□	Michel Goulet, Québ. ✍	20.00
□	Mario Lemieux, Pitt. ✍	125.00
□	Mark Messier, Edmo. ✍	45.00
□	Pavel Bure, Flor. ✍	35.00
□	Peter Bondra, Wash. ✍	25.00
□	Phil Esposito, Bost. ✍	45.00
□	Pat LaFontaine, Buff. ✍	25.00
□	Patrik Stefan, Atla. ✍	15.00
□	Pat Verbeek, Hart. ✍	15.00
□	Sergei Fedorov, Detr. ✍	45.00
□	Stan Mikita, Chic. ✍	35.00
□	Sergei Samsonov, Bost. ✍	25.00
□	Steve Yzerman, Detr. ✍	100.00
□	Tony Esposito (G), Chic. ✍	45.00
□	Ted Lindsay, Detr. ✍	45.00
□	Wayne Gretzky, Edmo. ✍	250.00

LEGENDARY GAME JERSEY

	Card	Price
	Insert Set (36 cards):	**1,800**
	Insert (1:23)	**LGJ**
□	Al MacInnis, SLou. ✂	15.00
□	Butch Goring, NYIs. ✂	15.00
□	Brett Hull, Dall. ✂	45.00
□	Bob Nystrom, NYIs. ✂	15.00
□	Bobby Orr, Bost. (*) ✂	300.00
□	Bryan Trottier, NYIs. ✂ White	45.00
□	Clark Gillies, NYIs. ✂	15.00
□	Chico Resch, NYIs. ✂	15.00
□	Doug Gilmour, Toro. ✂	25.00
□	Dominik Hasek (G), Buff. ✂	45.00
□	Denis Potvin, NYIs. ✂	35.00
□	Grant Fuhr (G), SLou. (*) ✂	45.00
□	Gordie Howe, WHA	125.00
□	Jaromir Jagr, Pitt. ✂	45.00
□	Jari Kurri, LosA. (*) ✂	75.00
□	John LeClair, Phil. ✂	35.00
□	Joe Sakic, Colo. ✂	70.00
□	Keith Tkachuk, Phoe. ✂	25.00
□	Larry Robinson, LosA. ✂	25.00
□	Mike Bossy, NYIs. ✂	70.00
□	Martin Brodeur (G), NJer. ✂	70.00
□	Marcel Dionne, LosA. (*) ✂	75.00
□	Mike Gartner, Wash. ✂	35.00
□	Mario Lemieux, Pitt. ✂	135.00
□	Mike Modano, Dall. ✂	45.00
□	Mats Sundin, Toro. ✂	45.00
□	Pavel Bure, Flor. ✂	35.00
□	Peter Forsberg, Colo. ✂	60.00
□	Paul Kariya, Anah. ✂	60.00
□	Pat LaFontaine, NYIs. ✂	25.00
□	Patrick Roy (G), Colo. ✂	105.00
□	Raymond Bourque, Bost. ✂	50.00
□	Sergei Fedorov, Detr. ✂	45.00
□	Steve Yzerman, Detr. ✂	105.00
□	Teemu Selänne, Anah. ✂	35.00
□	Wayne Gretzky, LosA. ✂	175.00

2000 - 01 UPPER DECK LEGENDS – BUYBACKS

	Buyback Autograph • Legendary Game Jersey	UD
□	Raymond Bourque, Bost. ✍ ✂ {#/7}	
□	Gordie Howe, Detr. ✍ ✂ {#/9}	
□	John LeClair, Phil. ✍ ✂ {#/10}	
□	Mike Modano, Dall. ✍ ✂ {#/9}	

2000 - 01 UPPER DECK MVP

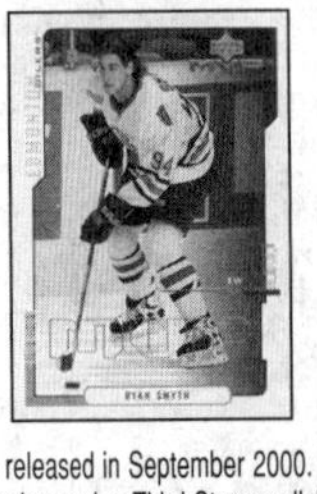

This series was released in September 2000. There are four versions: the regular card, a Third Star parallel (1:2 packs), a Second Star parallel (#/100) and a First Star parallel (#/25).

	Player	1S	2S	3S	Reg.
	Complete Set (220 cards):	**6,200**	**2,300**	**100.00**	**25.00**
	Common Player:	**12.00**	**4.00**	**.50**	**.20**
□□□□	1 Antti Aalto	12.00	4.00	.50	.20
□□□□	2 Matt Cullen	20.00	9.00	.50	.20
□□□□	3 Oleg Tverdovsky	15.00	6.00	.50	.20
□□□□	4 Paul Kariya	140.00	50.00	2.00	1.00
□□□□	5 Steve Rucchin	20.00	9.00	.50	.20
□□□□	6 Teemu Selänne	80.00	30.00	1.00	.50
□□□□	7 Maxim Balmochnykh	15.00	6.00	.50	.20
□□□□	8 Andrew Brunette	15.00	6.00	.50	.20
□□□□	9 Damian Rhodes (G)	20.00	9.00	.50	.20
□□□□	10 Dean Sylvester	12.00	4.00	.50	.20
□□□□	11 Donald Audette	40.00	15.00	.50	.20
□□□□	12 Patrik Stefan	30.00	12.00	.50	.20
□□□□	13 Ray Ferraro	15.00	6.00	.50	.20
□□□□	14 Brian Rolston	30.00	12.00	.50	.20
□□□□	15 Sergei Samsonov	60.00	22.00	1.00	.20
□□□□	16 Jason Allison	60.00	22.00	1.00	.20
□□□□	17 Joe Thornton	120.00	45.00	2.00	.50
□□□□	18 Kyle McLaren	20.00	9.00	.50	.20
□□□□	19 Byron Dafoe (G)	40.00	15.00	.50	.20
□□□□	20 Hal Gill	12.00	4.00	.50	.20
□□□□	21 Curtis Brown	15.00	6.00	.50	.20
□□□□	22 Stu Barnes	12.00	4.00	.50	.20
□□□□	23 Dominik Hasek (G)	100.00	35.00	2.00	.50
□□□□	24 Doug Gilmour	60.00	22.00	1.00	.20
□□□□	25 Maxim Afinogenov	40.00	15.00	.50	.20
□□□□	26 Michael Peca	40.00	15.00	.50	.20
□□□□	27 Miroslav Satan	30.00	12.00	.50	.20
□□□□	28 Chris Gratton	20.00	9.00	.50	.20
□□□□	29 Derek Morris	20.00	9.00	.50	.20
□□□□	30 Fred Brathwaite (G)	30.00	12.00	.50	.20
□□□□	31 Jarome Iginla	80.00	30.00	1.00	.50
□□□□	32 Marc Savard	20.00	9.00	.50	.20
□□□□	33 Phil Housley	30.00	12.00	.50	.20
□□□□	34 Valeri Bure	30.00	12.00	.50	.20
□□□□	35 Arturs Irbe (G)	40.00	15.00	.50	.20
□□□□	36 David Tanabe	15.00	6.00	.50	.20
□□□□	37 Jeff O'Neill	40.00	15.00	.50	.20
□□□□	38 Rod Brind'Amour	30.00	12.00	.50	.20
□□□□	39 Ron Francis	60.00	22.00	1.00	.20
□□□□	40 Sami Kapanen	30.00	12.00	.50	.20
□□□□	41 Alexei Zhamnov	30.00	12.00	.50	.20
□□□□	42 Éric Dazé	40.00	15.00	.50	.20
□□□□	43 Jocelyn Thibault (G)	40.00	15.00	.50	.20
□□□□	44 Michael Nylander	20.00	9.00	.50	.20
□□□□	45 Steve Sullivan	30.00	12.00	.50	.20
□□□□	46 Tony Amonte	60.00	22.00	1.00	.20
□□□□	47 Chris Drury	60.00	22.00	1.00	.20
□□□□	48 Joe Sakic	160.00	60.00	3.00	1.00
□□□□	49 Milan Hejduk	80.00	30.00	1.00	.50
□□□□	50 Patrick Roy (G)	300.00	110.00	6.00	2.00
□□□□	51 Peter Forsberg	140.00	50.00	2.00	1.00
□□□□	52 Raymond Bourque	120.00	45.00	2.00	.50
□□□□	53 Adam Deadmarsh	30.00	12.00	.50	.20
□□□□	54 Alex Tanguay	60.00	22.00	1.00	.20
□□□□	55 Marc Denis (G)	45.00	18.00	.50	.20
□□□□	56 Brenden Morrow	30.00	12.00	.50	.20
□□□□	57 Brett Hull	100.00	35.00	2.00	.50
□□□□	58 Derian Hatcher	30.00	12.00	.50	.20
□□□□	59 Ed Belfour (G)	100.00	35.00	2.00	.50
□□□□	60 Jamie Langenbrunner	20.00	9.00	.50	.20
□□□□	61 Mike Modano	100.00	35.00	2.00	.50
□□□□	62 Sergei Zubov	20.00	9.00	.50	.20
□□□□	63 Joe Nieuwendyk	40.00	15.00	.50	.20
□□□□	64 Brendan Shanahan	100.00	35.00	2.00	.50
□□□□	65 Chris Chelios	60.00	22.00	1.00	.20
□□□□	66 Chris Osgood (G)	60.00	22.00	1.00	.20
□□□□	67 Nicklas Lidström	60.00	22.00	1.00	.20
□□□□	68 Pat Verbeek	30.00	12.00	.50	.20
□□□□	69 Sergei Fedorov	100.00	35.00	2.00	.50
□□□□	70 Steve Yzerman	240.00	90.00	4.00	1.50
□□□□	71 Darren McCarty	30.00	12.00	.50	.20
□□□□	72 Tom Poti	15.00	6.00	.50	.20
□□□□	73 Bill Guerin	40.00	15.00	.50	.20
□□□□	74 Doug Weight	60.00	22.00	1.00	.20
□□□□	75 Mike Grier	20.00	9.00	.50	.20
□□□□	76 Ryan Smyth	45.00	18.00	.50	.20
□□□□	77 Tommy Salo (G)	40.00	15.00	.50	.20
□□□□	78 Bret Hedican	12.00	4.00	.50	.20
□□□□	79 Pavel Bure	80.00	30.00	1.00	.50
□□□□	80 Ray Whitney	20.00	9.00	.50	.20
□□□□	81 Scott Mellanby	20.00	9.00	.50	.20
□□□□	82 Trevor Kidd (G)	30.00	12.00	.50	.20
□□□□	83 Viktor Kozlov	30.00	12.00	.50	.20
□□□□	84 Bryan Smolinski	15.00	6.00	.50	.20
□□□□	85 Stéphane Fiset (G)	30.00	12.00	.50	.20
□□□□	86 Jozef Stumpel	20.00	9.00	.50	.20
□□□□	87 Luc Robitaille	80.00	30.00	1.00	.50
□□□□	88 Rob Blake	60.00	22.00	1.00	.20
□□□□	89 Zigmund Palffy	60.00	22.00	1.00	.20
□□□□	90 Brian Savage	30.00	12.00	.50	.20
□□□□	91 Dainius Zubrus	20.00	9.00	.50	.20
□□□□	92 José Théodore (G)	120.00	45.00	2.00	.50
□□□□	93 Martin Rucinsky	20.00	9.00	.50	.20
□□□□	94 Saku Koivu	120.00	30.00	1.00	.50
□□□□	95 Sergei Zholtok	15.00	6.00	.50	.20
□□□□	96 Manny Fernandez (G)	40.00	15.00	.50	.20
□□□□	97 Cliff Ronning	20.00	9.00	.50	.20
□□□□	98 David Legwand	40.00	15.00	.50	.20
□□□□	99 Drake Berehowsky	15.00	6.00	.50	.20
□□□□	100 Vitali Yachmenev	15.00	6.00	.50	.20
□□□□	101 Mike Dunham (G)	40.00	15.00	.50	.20
□□□□	102 Patric Kjellberg	15.00	6.00	.50	.20
□□□□	103 Alexander Mogilny	45.00	18.00	.50	.20
□□□□	104 Claude Lemieux	30.00	12.00	.50	.20
□□□□	105 John Madden	30.00	12.00	.50	.20
□□□□	106 Martin Brodeur (G)	160.00	60.00	3.00	1.00
□□□□	107 Patrik Elias	80.00	30.00	1.00	.50
□□□□	108 Scott Gomez	40.00	15.00	.50	.20
□□□□	109 Scott Stevens	40.00	15.00	.50	.20
□□□□	110 Dave Scatchard	12.00	4.00	.50	.20
□□□□	111 Kenny Jönsson	20.00	7.00	.50	.20
□□□□	112 Mariusz Czerkawski	20.00	9.00	.50	.20
□□□□	113 Mathieu Biron	15.00	6.00	.50	.20
□□□□	114 Tim Connolly	40.00	15.00	.50	.20
□□□□	115 Claude Lapointe	15.00	6.00	.50	.20
□□□□	116 Adam Graves	40.00	15.00	.50	.20
□□□□	117 Brian Leetch	60.00	22.00	1.00	.20
□□□□	118 Mike York	30.00	12.00	.50	.20
□□□□	119 Mike Richter (G)	45.00	18.00	.50	.20
□□□□	120 Petr Nedved	30.00	12.00	.50	.20
□□□□	121 Theoren Fleury	60.00	20.00	1.00	.20
□□□□	122 Daniel Alfredsson	120.00	22.00	1.00	.20
□□□□	123 Patrick Lalime (G)	60.00	22.00	1.00	.20
□□□□	124 John LeClair	80.00	30.00	1.00	.50
□□□□	125 Marian Hossa	100.00	37.00	2.00	.50
□□□□	126 Keith Primeau	40.00	15.00	.50	.20
□□□□	127 Radek Bonk	30.00	12.00	.50	.20
□□□□	128 Shawn McEachern	30.00	12.00	.50	.20
□□□□	129 Andreas Dackell	15.00	6.00	.50	.20
□□□□	130 Brian Boucher (G)	30.00	12.00	.50	.20
□□□□	131 Mark Recchi	40.00	15.00	.50	.20
□□□□	132 Simon Gagné	80.00	30.00	1.00	.50
□□□□	133 Éric Desjardins	30.00	12.00	.50	.20
□□□□	134 Jeremy Roenick	80.00	30.00	1.00	.50
□□□□	135 Keith Tkachuk	60.00	22.00	1.00	.20
□□□□	136 Teppo Numminen	30.00	12.00	.50	.20
□□□□	137 Eric Lindros	100.00	35.00	2.00	.50
□□□□	138 Shane Doan	20.00	9.00	.50	.20
□□□□	139 Travis Green	20.00	9.00	.50	.20
□□□□	140 Trevor Letowski	15.00	6.00	.50	.20
□□□□	141 Alexei Kovalev	60.00	22.00	1.00	.20
□□□□	142 Jan Hrdina	20.00	9.00	.50	.20
□□□□	143 Jaromir Jagr	100.00	35.00	2.00	.50
□□□□	144 Jéean-Sebastien Aubin (G)	20.00	9.00	.50	.20
□□□□	145 Martin Straka	30.00	12.00	.50	.20
□□□□	146 Matthew Barnaby	12.00	4.00	.50	.20
□□□□	147 Brad Stuart	40.00	15.00	.50	.20
□□□□	148 Jeff Friesen	30.00	12.00	.50	.20
□□□□	149 Mike Ricci	30.00	12.00	.50	.20
□□□□	150 Owen Nolan	60.00	22.00	1.00	.20
□□□□	151 Steve Shields (G)	20.00	9.00	.50	.20
□□□□	152 Vincent Damphousse	60.00	22.00	1.00	.20
□□□□	153 Al MacInnis	40.00	15.00	.50	.20
□□□□	154 Chris Pronger	60.00	22.00	1.00	.20
□□□□	155 Jochen Hecht	20.00	9.00	.50	.20
□□□□	156 Pavol Demitra	40.00	15.00	.50	.20
□□□□	157 Pierre Turgeon	40.00	15.00	.50	.20
□□□□	158 Roman Turek (G)	45.00	18.00	.50	.20
□□□□	159 Dan Cloutier (G)	40.00	15.00	.50	.20
□□□□	160 Fredrik Modin	20.00	9.00	.50	.20
□□□□	161 Mike Johnson	20.00	7.00	.50	.20
□□□□	162 Paul Mara	15.00	6.00	.50	.20
□□□□	163 Vincent Lecavalier	100.00	35.00	2.00	.50
□□□□	164 Petr Svoboda	20.00	9.00	.50	.20
□□□□	165 Curtis Joseph (G)	100.00	35.00	2.00	.50
□□□□	166 Darcy Tucker	20.00	9.00	.50	.20
□□□□	167 Mats Sundin	100.00	35.00	2.00	.50
□□□□	168 Nikolai Antropov	20.00	9.00	.50	.20
□□□□	169 Sergei Berezin	35.00	9.00	.50	.20
□□□□	170 Steve Thomas	20.00	9.00	.50	.20
□□□□	171 Dmitry Yushkevich	20.00	9.00	.50	.20
□□□□	172 Brendan Morrison	30.00	12.00	.50	.20
□□□□	173 Ed Jovanovski	40.00	15.00	.50	.20
□□□□	174 Félix Potvin (G)	120.00	22.00	1.00	.20
□□□□	175 Harold Druken	30.00	12.00	.50	.20
□□□□	176 Todd Bertuzzi	120.00	45.00	2.00	.50
□□□□	177 Markus Naslund	100.00	37.00	2.00	.50
□□□□	178 Adam Oates	40.00	15.00	.50	.20
□□□□	179 Chris Simon	20.00	9.00	.50	.20
□□□□	180 Jeff Halpern	20.00	9.00	.50	.20
□□□□	181 Olaf Kölzig (G)	60.00	22.00	1.00	.20
□□□□	182 Peter Bondra	60.00	22.00	1.00	.20
□□□□	183 Sergei Gonchar	30.00	12.00	.50	.20
□□□□	184 Vitaly Vishnevski	20.00	9.00	.50	.20
□□□□	185 Andreas Karlsson	12.00	4.00	.50	.20
□□□□	**186 Eric Nicklaus RC**	**12.00**	**4.00**	**1.00**	**.50**
□□□□	**187 Brandon Smith RC**	**12.00**	**4.00**	**1.00**	**.50**
□□□□	188 Dimitri Kalinin	12.00	4.00	.50	.20
□□□□	189 Chris Herperger	12.00	4.00	.50	.20
□□□□	**190 Serge Aubin RC**	**15.00**	**6.00**	**1.00**	**1.00**
□□□□	191 Alan Letang	12.00	4.00	.50	.20
□□□□	**192 Keith Aldridge RC**	**12.00**	**4.00**	**1.00**	**.50**
□□□□	**193 S. Reinprecht RC**	**30.00**	**12.00**	**3.00**	**2.50**
□□□□	194 Brad Chartrand	12.00	4.00	.50	.20
□□□□	**195 David Gosselin RC**	**12.00**	**4.00**	**1.00**	**.50**
□□□□	**196 Colin White RC**	**15.00**	**6.00**	**1.00**	**1.00**

□□□□ **197 Willie Mitchell RC**	**15.00**	**6.00**	**1.00**	**1.00**
□□□□ 198 Jason Krog	20.00	9.00	.50	.20
□□□□ **199 S. Valiquette (G) RC**	**15.00**	**6.00**	**1.00**	**1.00**
□□□□ 200 Petr Schastlivy	20.00	9.00	.50	.20
□□□□ 201 Andy Delmore	20.00	9.00	.50	.20
□□□□ 202 Mark Eaton	12.00	4.00	.50	.20
□□□□ 203 Evgeni Nabokov (G)	60.00	22.00	1.00	.20
□□□□ 204 Ladislav Nagy	20.00	9.00	.50	.20
□□□□ **205 Kyle Freadrich RC**	**12.00**	**4.00**	**1.00**	**.50**
□□□□ **206 Greg Andrusak**	**12.00**	**4.00**	**1.00**	**.50**
□□□□ 207 Alfie Michaud (G)	15.00	6.00	.50	.20
□□□□ **208 Brent Sopel RC**	**15.00**	**6.00**	**1.00**	**1.00**
□□□□ **209 Matt Pettinger RC**	**15.00**	**6.00**	**1.00**	**1.00**
□□□□ **210 Chris Nielsen RC**	**15.00**	**6.00**	**1.00**	**1.00**
□□□□ **211 Dany Heatley RC**	**100.00**	**37.00**	**13.00**	**10.00**
□□□□ **212 Josef Vasicek RC**	**20.00**	**9.00**	**2.00**	**1.50**
□□□□ **213 Matt Zultek RC**	**12.00**	**4.00**	**1.00**	**.50**
□□□□ **214 D. Afanasenkov RC**	**15.00**	**6.00**	**1.00**	**1.00**
□□□□ **215 Tyler Bouck RC**	**15.00**	**6.00**	**1.00**	**1.00**
□□□□ **216 J. Andersson RC**	**12.00**	**4.00**	**1.00**	**.50**
□□□□ **217 Juraj Kolnik RC**	**15.00**	**6.00**	**1.00**	**1.00**
□□□□ **218 A. Raycroft (G) RC**	**20.00**	**9.00**	**2.00**	**1.50**
□□□□ 219 Pavel Bure	80.00	30.00	1.00	.20
□□□□ 220 Steve Yzerman	240.00	90.00	4.00	.50

MVP TALENT

Insert Set (15 cards):	**20.00**
Insert (1:6)	**MVPT**
□ M1 Paul Kariya, Anah.	2.00
□ M2 Teemu Selänne, Anah.	1.00
□ M3 Raymond Bourque, Colo.	2.00
□ M4 Joe Sakic, Colo.	3.00
□ M5 Patrick Roy (G), Colo.	6.00
□ M6 Brett Hull, Dall.	2.00
□ M7 Sergei Fedorov, Detr.	2.00
□ M8 Pavel Bure, Flor.	1.00
□ M9 Zigmund Palffy, LosA.	1.00
□ M10 Martin Brodeur (G), NJer.	3.00
□ M11 Theoren Fleury, NYRa.	1.00
□ M12 Eric Lindros, Phil.	2.00
□ M13 John LeClair, Phil.	1.00
□ M14 Jaromir Jagr, Pitt.	2.00
□ M15 Jeremy Roenick, Phoe.	1.00

TOP DRAWS

Insert Set (10 cards):	**10.00**
Insert (1:9)	**TD**
□ TD1 Teemu Selänne, Anah.	1.00
□ TD2 Dominik Hasek (G), Buff.	2.00
□ TD3 Peter Forsberg, Colo.	2.00
□ TD4 Brenden Shanahan, Detr.	2.00
□ TD5 Pavel Bure, Flor.	1.00
□ TD6 Scott Gomez, NJer.	1.00
□ TD7 Eric Lindros, Phil.	2.00
□ TD8 John LeClair, Phil.	1.00
□ TD9 Keith Tkachuk, Phoe.	1.00
□ TD10 Jaromir Jagr, Pitt.	2.00

MASKED MEN

Insert Set (10 cards):	**30.00**
Insert (1:18)	**MM**
□ MM1 Dominik Hasek (G), Buff.	3.00
□ MM2 Patrick Roy (G), Colo.	11.00
□ MM3 Ed Belfour (G), Dall.	3.00
□ MM4 Chris Osgood (G), Detr.	2.00
□ MM5 Martin Brodeur (G), NJer.	6.00
□ MM6 Brian Boucher (G), Phil.	2.00
□ MM7 Steve Shields (G), SanJ.	2.00
□ MM8 Roman Turek (G), SLou.	2.00
□ MM9 Curtis Joseph (G), Toro.	3.00
□ MM10 Olaf Kölzig (G), Wash.	2.00

MVP EXCELLENCE

Insert Set (10 cards):	**.00**
Inserts	**MVPE**
□ ME1 R. Luongo / C. Joseph (G)	3.00
□ ME2 P. Brendl / P. Bure	2.00
□ ME3 S. Samsonov / O. Saprykin	2.00
□ ME4 M. Hejduk / I. Novoseltsev	2.00
□ ME5 P. Verbeek / S. Yzerman	6.00
□ ME6 M. Biron (G) / R. Turek	2.00
□ ME7 D. Sedin / H. Sedin	2.00
□ ME8 P. Stefan / L. Nagy	2.00
□ ME9 M. Malhotra / M. York	2.00
□ ME10 R. Bourque / W. Gretzky	12.00

TOP PLAYMAKERS

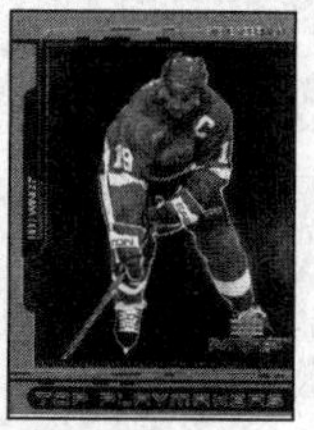

Insert Set (10 cards):	**30.00**
Insert (1:18)	**TP**
□ TP1 Paul Kariya, Anah.	5.00
□ TP2 Dominik Hasek (G), Buff.	3.00
□ TP3 Peter Forsberg, Colo.	5.00
□ TP4 Mike Modano, Dall.	3.00
□ TP5 Steve Yzerman, Detr.	9.00
□ TP6 Pavel Bure, Flor.	3.00
□ TP7 Scott Gomez, NJer.	2.00
□ TP8 Eric Lindros, Phil.	3.00
□ TP9 Jaromir Jagr, Pitt.	3.00
□ TP10 Jeremy Roenick, Phoe.	3.00

VALUABLE COMMODITIES

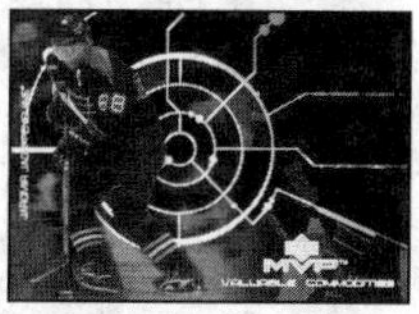

Insert Set (10 cards):	**40.00**
Insert (1:18)	**VC**
□ VC1 Paul Kariya, Anah.	5.00
□ VC2 Patrick Roy (G), Colo.	11.00
□ VC3 Peter Forsberg, Colo.	5.00
□ VC4 Mike Modano, Dall.	3.00
□ VC5 Steve Yzerman, Detr.	9.00
□ VC6 Martin Brodeur (G), NJer.	6.00
□ VC7 Theoren Fleury, NYRa.	2.00
□ VC8 Eric Lindros, Phil.	3.00
□ VC9 Jaromir Jagr, Pitt.	3.00
□ VC10 Curtis Joseph (G), Toro.	3.00

GAME-USED SOUVENIR

There are two versions: the regular insert (1:83 packs) and the Super parallel (#/50).

Insert Set (22 cards):	**1,900**	**1,000**
Insert (1:83)	**S50**	**GUS**
□□ Arturs Irbe (G), Caro. ✂	25.00	20.00
□□ Brendan Shanahan, Detr. ✂	100.00	50.00
□□ Chris Chelios, Detr. ✂	50.00	30.00
□□ Dominik Hasek (G), Buff. ✂	100.00	50.00
□□ Eric Lindros, Phil. ✂	100.00	50.00
□□ Jason Allison, Bost. ✂	50.00	30.00
□□ Jaromir Jagr, Pitt. ✂	100.00	50.00
□□ John LeClair, Phil. ✂	75.00	40.00
□□ Keith Tkachuk, Phoe. ✂	50.00	30.00
□□ Mark Messier, Vanc. ✂	100.00	50.00
□□ Mike Richter (G), NYRa. ✂	25.00	20.00
□□ Pavel Bure, Flor. ✂	75.00	40.00
□□ Peter Forsberg, Colo. ✂	125.00	70.00
□□ Paul Kariya, Anah. ✂	125.00	70.00
□□ Patrick Roy (G), Colo. ✂	225.00	120.00
□□ Raymond Bourque, Colo. ✂	100.00	60.00
□□ Roberto Luongo (G), NYIs. ✂	75.00	40.00
□□ Sergei Fedorov, Detr. ✂	100.00	50.00
□□ Steve Yzerman, Detr. ✂	225.00	120.00
□□ Teemu Selänne, Anah. ✂	75.00	40.00
□□ Wayne Gretzky, NYRa. ✂	400.00	200.00
□□ Zigmund Palffy, LosA. ✂	50.00	30.00

GAME-USED SOUVENIR CANADA

There are two versions: the regular insert (1:83 packs) and the Super parallel (#/50).

Insert Set (7 cards):	**880.00**	**400.00**
Insert (1:83)	**S50**	**GUS**
□□ Curtis Joseph (G), Toro. ✂	100.00	50.00
□□ Chris Osgood (G), Detr. ✂	60.00	30.00
□□ Ed Belfour (G), Dall. ✂	100.00	50.00
□□ Félix Potvin (G), Vanc. ✂	120.00	30.00
□□ Martin Brodeur (G), NJer. ✂	160.00	80.00
□□ Mats Sundin, Toro. ✂	100.00	50.00
□□ Wayne Gretzky, NYRa. ✂	400.00	200.00

MARK OF EXCELLENCE

Autograph Set (9 cards):	**950.00**
Inserts	**MoE50**
□ R. Luongo ✍ / C. Joseph (G) ✍	175.00
□ P. Brendl ✍ / P. Bure ✍	100.00
□ S. Samsonov ✍ / O. Saprykin ✍	75.00
□ M. Hejduk ✍ / I. Novoseltsev ✍	100.00
□ P. Verbeek ✍ / S. Yzerman ✍	250.00
□ M. Biron (G) ✍ / R. Turek ✍	75.00
□ D. Sedin ✍ / H. Sedin ✍	200.00
□ P. Stefan ✍ / L. Nagy ✍	75.00
□ M. Malhotra ✍ / M. York ✍	75.00

PROSIGN

Insert Set (18 cards):	**300.00**
Autograph (1:143 Retail)	**PS**
□ Al MacInnis, SLou. ✍	15.00
□ Brian Boucher (G), Phil. ✍	15.00
□ Brenden Morrow, Dall. ✍	15.00
□ Curtis Brown, Buff. ✍	15.00
□ Curtis Joseph (G), Toro. ✍	45.00
□ David Legwand, Nash. ✍	15.00
□ Ladislav Nagy, SLou. ✍	20.00
□ Mike Johnson, Tamp. ✍	15.00
□ Manny Malhotra, NYRa. ✍	15.00
□ Mike Ribeiro, Mont. ✍	15.00
□ Mike York, NYRa. ✍	15.00
□ Oleg Saprykin, Calg. ✍	15.00
□ Pavel Bure, Flor. ✍	35.00
□ Patrik Stefan, Atla. ✍	15.00
□ Roberto Luongo (G), NYIs. ✍	35.00
□ Roman Turek (G), SLou. ✍	20.00
□ Steve McCarthy, Chic. ✍	15.00
□ Sergei Samsonov, Bost. ✍	25.00

2000 - 01 UPPER DECK PEARSON AWARD CEREMONY

While these cards are not rare, they are tough to come by on the secondary market.

Player	**UD**
□ Joe Sakic, Colo. [Winner]	
□ Jaromir Jagr, Pitt. [Finalist]	
□ Mario Lemieux, Pitt. [Finalist]	

2000 - 01 UPPER DECK PROS & PROSPECTS

This series was released in 2001. Rookie-subset cards 91-132 are short-printed. A rookie-subset card graded by SGC was included as a topper in each box. Rookie-subset cards are available as either an SGC-92, an SGC-96, an SGC-98 or an SGC-100.

Shell Set (90 cards):	**35.00**
Complete Set (132 cards):	**370.00**
Common Player:	**.30**
Player	**Reg.**
□ 1 Paul Kariya, Anah.	1.50
□ 2 Teemu Selänne, Anah.	1.00
□ 3 Guy Hebert (G), Anah.	.30
□ 4 Donald Audette, Atla.	.50
□ 5 Adam Burt, Atla.	.30
□ 6 Patrik Stefan, Atla.	.30
□ 7 Joe Thornton, Bost.	1.50
□ 8 Jason Allison, Bost.	.50
□ 9 Sergei Samsonov, Bost.	.50
□ 10 Dominik Hasek (G), Buff.	1.00
□ 11 Doug Gilmour, Buff.	.50
□ 12 Maxim Afinogenov, Buff.	.50
□ 13 Oleg Saprykin, Calg.	.30
□ 14 Valeri Bure, Calg.	.30
□ 15 Mike Vernon (G), Calg.	.50
□ 16 Ron Francis, Caro.	.50
□ 17 Jeff O'Neill, Caro.	.50
□ 18 Arturs Irbe (G), Caro.	.50
□ 19 Steve Sullivan, Chic.	.30
□ 20 Alexei Zhamnov, Chic.	.30
□ 21 Tony Amonte, Chic.	.50
□ 22 Raymond Bourque, Colo.	1.50
□ 23 Patrick Roy (G), Colo.	3.50
□ 24 Peter Forsberg, Colo.	1.50
□ 25 Marc Denis (G), Colu.	.50
□ 26 Tyler Wright, Colu.	.30
□ 27 Mike Modano, Dall.	1.00
□ 28 Brett Hull, Dall.	1.00
□ 29 Ed Belfour (G), Dall.	1.00
□ 30 Brendan Shanahan, Detr.	1.00
□ 31 Sergei Fedorov, Detr.	1.00
□ 32 Steve Yzerman, Detr.	3.00
□ 33 Ryan Smyth, Edmo.	.50
□ 34 Tommy Salo (G), Edmo.	.50
□ 35 Doug Weight, Edmo.	.50
□ 36 Pavel Bure, Flor.	1.00
□ 37 Ray Whitney, Flor.	.30
□ 38 Viktor Kozlov, Flor.	.30
□ 39 Luc Robitaille, LosA.	1.00
□ 40 Rob Blake, LosA.	.50
□ 41 Zigmund Palffy, LosA.	.50
□ 42 Manny Fernandez (G), MinW.	.50
□ 43 Scott Pellerin, MinW.	.30
□ 44 José Théodore (G), Mont.	1.50
□ 45 Brian Savage, Mont.	.30
□ 46 Martin Rucinsky, Mont.	.30
□ 47 David Legwand, Nash.	.50
□ 48 Mike Dunham (G), Nash.	.50
□ 49 Cliff Ronning, Nash.	.30
□ 50 Scott Gomez, NJer.	.50
□ 51 Scott Stevens, NJer.	.50
□ 52 Martin Brodeur (G), NJer.	2.00
□ 53 Tim Connolly, NYIs.	.50
□ 54 Brad Isbister, NYIs.	.30
□ 55 Roman Hamrlik, NYIs.	.30
□ 56 Theoren Fleury, NYRa.	.50
□ 57 Mike Richter (G), NYRa.	.50
□ 58 Mark Messier, NYRa.	1.00
□ 59 Marian Hossa, Otta.	1.00
□ 60 Alexei Yashin, Otta.	.50
□ 61 Radek Bonk, Otta.	.30
□ 62 John LeClair, Phil.	1.00
□ 63 Mark Recchi, Phil.	.50
□ 64 Simon Gagné, Phil.	1.00
□ 65 Jeremy Roenick, Phoe.	1.00
□ 66 Shane Doan, Phoe.	.30
□ 67 Keith Tkachuk, Phoe.	.50
□ 68 Jaromir Jagr, Pitt.	1.00
□ 69 Mario Lemieux, Pitt.	3.50
□ 70 Alexei Kovalev, Pitt.	.50
□ 71 Owen Nolan, SanJ.	.50
□ 72 Jeff Friesen, SanJ.	.30
□ 73 Patrick Marleau, SanJ.	.50
□ 74 Chris Pronger, SLou.	.50
□ 75 Roman Turek (G), SLou.	.50
□ 76 Pierre Turgeon, SLou.	.50
□ 77 Kevin Weekes (G), Tamp.	.30
□ 78 Fredrik Modin, Tamp.	.30
□ 79 Vincent Lecavalier, Tamp.	1.00
□ 80 Curtis Joseph (G), Toro.	1.00
□ 81 Mats Sundin, Toro.	1.00
□ 82 Gary Roberts, Toro.	.50
□ 83 Markus Näslund, Vanc.	1.00
□ 84 Daniel Sedin, Vanc.	1.00
□ 85 Henrik Sedin, Vanc.	1.00
□ 86 Adam Oates, Wash.	.50
□ 87 Peter Bondra, Wash.	.50
□ 88 Olaf Kölzig (G), Wash.	.50
□ 89 Mark Messier, NYRa. [Checklist]	.50
□ 90 Steve Yzerman, Detr. [Checklist]	1.00

FABULOUS FIRSTS

Insert	**FF**
□ **91 Jonas Rönnqvist, Anah. RC**	**10.00**
□ **92 Andy McDonald, Anah. RC**	**10.00**
□ **93 Eric Nickulas, Bost. RC**	**6.00**
□ **94 Andrew Raycroft (G), Bost. RC**	**15.00**
□ **95 Jarno Kultanen, Bost. RC**	**6.00**
□ **96 Jeff Cowan, Calg. RC**	**6.00**
□ **97 Josef Vasicek, Caro. RC**	**15.00**
□ **98 Reto von Arx, Chic. RC**	**10.00**
□ **99 David Aebischer (G), Colo. RC**	**20.00**
□ **100 Serge Aubin, Colu. RC**	**10.00**
□ **101 Rostislav Klesla, Colu. RC**	**25.00**
□ **102 Marty Turco (G), Dall. RC**	**35.00**
□ **103 Tyler Bouck, Dall. RC**	**10.00**

104 Brian Swanson, Edmo.	4.00
105 Michel Riesen, Edmo. RC	10.00
106 Éric Bélanger, LosA. RC	10.00
107 Steven Reinprecht, LosA. RC	25.00
108 Marian Gaborik, MinW. RC	60.00
109 Scott Hartnell, Nash. RC	15.00
110 Greg Classen, Nash. RC	10.00
111 Willie Mitchell, NJer. RC	10.00
112 Colin White, NJer. RC	10.00
113 Petr Mika, NYIs. RC	6.00
114 Rick DiPietro (G), NYIs. RC	35.00
115 Jason LaBarbera (G), NYRa. RC	10.00
116 Martin Havlat, Otta. RC	50.00
117 Jani Hurme (G), Otta. RC	15.00
118 Petr Hubacek, Phil. RC	6.00
119 Justin Williams, Phil. RC	20.00
120 Roman Cechmanek (G), Phil. RC	25.00
121 Roman Simicek, Pitt. RC	6.00
122 Mark Smith, SanJ. RC	6.00
123 Alexander Kharitonov, Tamp. RC	6.00
124 Matt Elich, Tamp. RC	10.00
125 Jakub Cutta, Wash. RC	10.00
126 Fedor Fedorov, Sudbury Wolves RC	10.00
127 Marc-André Thinel, Victoriaville Tigres RC	10.00
128 Zdenek Blatny, Kootenay Ice RC	10.00
129 Jeff Bateman, Brampton Batallion RC	10.00
130 Jason Jaspers, Sudbury Wolves RC	10.00
131 Jordan Krestanovich, Calgary Hitmen RC	10.00
132 Damian Surma, Plymouth Whalers RC	10.00

CHAMPIONSHIP RINGS

Insert Set (8 cards):	35.00
Insert (1:12)	CR
CR1 Patrick Roy (G), Colo.	9.00
CR2 Brenden Shanahan, Detr.	3.00
CR3 Steve Yzerman, Detr.	7.00
CR4 Wayne Gretzky, Edmo.	12.00
CR5 Scott Stevens, NJer.	2.00
CR6 Martin Brodeur (G), NJer.	4.00
CR7 Mark Messier, NYRa.	3.00
CR8 Jaromir Jagr, Pitt.	3.00

GREAT SKATES

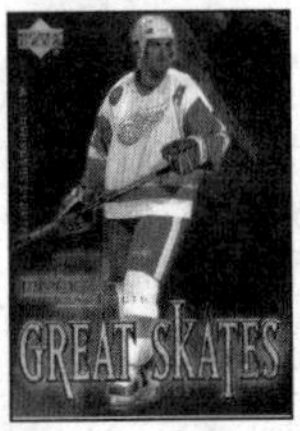

Insert Set (8 cards):	25.00
Insert (1:12)	GS
GS1 Paul Kariya, Anah.	4.00
GS2 Mario Lemieux, Pitt.	9.00
GS3 Patrick Roy (G), Colo.	9.00
GS4 Brenden Shanahan, Detr.	3.00
GS5 Pavel Bure, Flor.	2.00
GS6 Alexei Yashin, Otta.	2.00
GS7 John LeClair, Phil.	2.00
GS8 Jaromir Jagr, Pitt.	3.00

NOW APPEARING

Insert Set (8 cards):	20.00
Insert (1:12)	NA
NA1 Maxim Afinogenov, Buff.	2.00
NA2 Marian Gaborik, MinW.	9.00
NA3 Scott Hartnell, Nash.	2.00
NA4 Scott Gomez, NJer.	2.00
NA5 Rick DiPietro (G), NYIs.	4.00
NA6 Justin Williams, Phil.	2.00
NA7 Daniel Sedin, Vanc.	2.00
NA8 Henrik Sedin, Vanc.	2.00

NHL PASSION

Insert Set (9 cards):	25.00
Insert (1:10)	NP
NP1 Raymond Bourque, Colo.	3.00
NP2 Brett Hull, Dall.	3.00
NP3 Steve Yzerman, Detr.	7.00
NP4 Mark Messier, NYRa.	3.00
NP5 John LeClair, Phil.	2.00
NP6 Jeremy Roenick, Phoe.	2.00
NP7 Jaromir Jagr, Pitt.	3.00
NP8 Mario Lemieux, Pitt.	9.00
NP9 Curtis Joseph (G), Toro.	3.00

PROMOTION

Insert Set (9 cards):	20.00
Insert (1:10)	PM
PM1 Teemu Selänne, Anah.	2.00
PM2 Dominik Hasek (G), Buff.	3.00
PM3 Peter Forsberg, Colo.	4.00
PM4 Sergei Fedorov, Detr.	3.00
PM5 Mike Modano, Dall.	3.00
PM6 Pavel Bure, Flor.	2.00
PM7 Martin Brodeur (G), NJer.	4.00
PM8 John LeClair, Phil.	2.00
PM9 Jaromir Jagr, Pitt.	3.00

GAME JERSEY

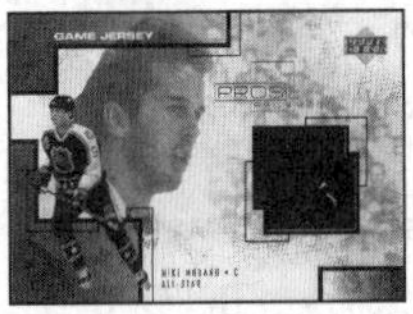

There are two versions: the Jersey card (1:30 packs) and the Exclusive parallel (#/50).

Insert Set (10 cards):	800.00	300.00
Inserts	E50	J
☐☐ Brendan Shanahan, Detr. ✂	75.00	30.00
☐☐ Chris Pronger, SLou. ✂	60.00	15.00
☐☐ Jaromir Jagr, Pitt. ✂	75.00	30.00
☐☐ Mike Modano, AS'93 ✂ Black	75.00	30.00
☐☐ Peter Forsberg, Colo. ✂	100.00	40.00
☐☐ Paul Kariya, Anah. ✂	100.00	40.00
☐☐ Patrick Roy (G), Colo. ✂	250.00	90.00
☐☐ Raymond Bourque, Bost. ✂	100.00	35.00
☐☐ Sergei Fedorov, Detr. ✂	75.00	30.00
☐☐ Teemu Selänne, Anah. ✂	60.00	25.00

SIGNED GAME JERSEY

There are two versions: the Jersey card (1:96 packs) and the Exclusive parallel (#/50).

Insert Set (10 cards):	1,400	750.00
Inserts	E50	J
☐☐ John LeClair, Phil. ✍✂	100.00	60.00
☐☐ Jeremy Roenick Phoe. ✍✂	100.00	60.00
☐☐ Keith Tkachuk, Phoe. ✍✂	75.00	45.00
☐☐ Lubos Bartecko, SLou. ✍✂	75.00	30.00
☐☐ Mark Messier, NYRa. ✍✂	150.00	90.00
☐☐ Pavel Bure, Flor. ✍✂	100.00	60.00
☐☐ Scott Gomez, NJer. ✍✂	75.00	30.00
☐☐ Sergei Samsonov, Bost. ✍✂	75.00	45.00
☐☐ Steve Yzerman, Detr. ✍✂	350.00	180.00
☐☐ Wayne Gretzky, NYRa. ✍✂	600.00	300.00

SGC GRADED CARDS

	Player	SGC100	SGC98	SGC96	SGC92
☐☐☐	91 Jonas Ronnqvist RC	-	30.00	15.00	10.00
☐☐☐	92 Andy McDonald RC	-	30.00	15.00	10.00
☐☐☐☐	93 Eric Nickulas RC (SGC)		20.00	12.00	10.00
☐☐☐	94 A. Raycroft (G) RC	-	45.00	20.00	15.00
☐☐☐	95 Jarno Kultanen RC	-	20.00	12.00	10.00
☐☐☐	96 Jeff Cowan RC	-	20.00	12.00	10.00
☐☐☐☐	97 Josef Vasicek RC(SGC)		45.00	20.00	15.00
☐☐☐	98 Reto von Arx RC	-	30.00	15.00	10.00
☐☐☐	99 D. Aebischer (G) RC	-	60.00	30.00	20.00
☐☐☐☐	100 Serge Aubin RC(SGC)		30.00	15.00	10.00
☐☐☐	101 R. Klesla RC	-	80.00	35.00	25.00
☐☐☐	102 M. Turco (G) RC	-	110.00	60.00	35.00
☐☐☐☐	103 Tyler Bouck RC (SGC)		30.00	15.00	10.00
☐☐☐	104 Brian Swanson RC	-	30.00	15.00	10.00
☐☐☐	105 Michel Riesen RC	-	30.00	15.00	10.00
☐☐☐	106 Eric Belanger RC	-	30.00	15.00	10.00
☐☐☐☐	107 S. Reinprecht RC(SGC)		80.00	35.00	20.00
☐☐☐	108 Marian Gaborik RC	-	300.00	140.00	90.00
☐☐☐	109 Scott Hartnell RC	-	45.00	20.00	15.00
☐☐☐	110 Greg Classen RC	-	30.00	15.00	10.00
☐☐☐	111 Willie Mitchell RC	-	30.00	15.00	10.00
☐☐☐☐	112 Colin White RC (SGC)		30.00	15.00	10.00
☐☐☐	113 Petr Mika RC	-	20.00	12.00	10.00
☐☐☐	114 R/ DiPietro (G) RC	-	120.00	55.00	35.00
☐☐☐	115 J. LaBarbera (G) RC	-	30.00	15.00	10.00
☐☐☐☐	116 M. Havlat RC (SGC)		180.00	85.00	50.00
☐☐☐	117 Jani Hurme (G) RC	-	45.00	20.00	15.00
☐☐☐	118 Petr Hubacek RC	-	20.00	12.00	10.00
☐☐☐	119 Justin Williams RC	-	60.00	30.00	20.00
☐☐☐	120 R. Cechmanek (G) RC	-	75.00	40.00	25.00
☐☐☐☐	121 R. Simicek RC (SGC)		20.00	12.00	10.00
☐☐☐☐	122 Mark Smith RC (SGC)		20.00	12.00	10.00
☐☐☐☐	123 A. Kharitonov RC(SGC)		20.00	12.00	10.00
☐☐☐	124 Matt Elich RC	-	30.00	15.00	10.00
☐☐☐	125 Jakub Cutta RC	-	30.00	15.00	10.00
☐☐☐	126 Fedor Fedorov RC	-	30.00	15.00	10.00
☐☐☐	127 M-A Thinel RC	-	30.00	15.00	10.00
☐☐☐	128 Zdenek Blatny RC	-	30.00	15.00	10.00
☐☐☐	129 Jeff Bateman RC	-	30.00	15.00	10.00
☐☐☐	130 Jason Jaspers RC	-	30.00	15.00	10.00
☐☐☐	131 J. Krestanovich RC	-	30.00	15.00	10.00
☐☐☐	132 Damian Surma RC	-	30.00	15.00	10.00

2000 - 01 UPPER DECK PROSPECTS

This series was released in 2000 - 01.

Complete Set (100 cards):	50.00
Common Player:	.25
Player	MT
1 Jay Harrison, Battallion	.75
2 Jay McClement, Battallion	.75
3 Adam Henrich, Battallion	.25
4 Carlo Colaiacovo, Otters	.50
5 Nikita Alexeev, Otters	1.00
6 Brad Boyes, Erie Otters	1.00
7 Peter Hamrlik, Frontenacs	.25
8 Cory Stillman, Kingston Frontenacs	.25
9 Derek Roy, Kitchener NYRa.	3.00
10 Michael Zigomanis, Frontenacs	.50
11 Jason Spezza, Windsor Spitfires	3.50
12 Chad Wiseman, Ice Dogs	.25
13 Patrick Jarrett, Ice Dogs	1.00
14 Chris Thornburn, Centenials	.25
15 John Kozoriz, Generals	.25
16 Brandon Cullen, Generals	.25
17 Jonathon Zion, 67's	.25
18 Miguel Delisle, 67's	.50
19 Ryan Ramsay, Petes	.25
20 Marcel Rodman, Petes	.25
21 Stephen Weiss, Whalers	2.00
22 Libor Ustrnul, Plymouth Whalers	.25
23 Rob Zepp (G), Plymouth Whalers	.25
24 Kris Vernarsky, Whalers	.25
25 Jason Penner, Sting	.25
26 Trevor Daley, Greyhounds	.75
27 Alexei Semenov, Wolves	.50
28 Mark Popovic, St. Mikes	.75
29 Tim Gleason, Spitfires	.75
30 Craig Kennedy, Spitfires	.50
31 Steve Ott, Spitfires	.50
32 Brian Finley (G), Barrie Colts	.50
33 Kyle Wellwood, Bulls	.75
34 Raffi Torres, Battalion	1.00
35 Chris Kelly, London Knights	.25
36 Scott Cameron, Centenialls	.25
37 Cole Jarrett, Whalers	.25
38 Maxim Rybin, Sting	.25
39 Derek MacKenzie, Wolves	.25
40 Ryan Held, Greyhounds	.25
41 Colt King, Storm	.25
42 Rick Nash, Knights	8.00
43 Greg Jacina, Attack	.25
44 Branko Radivojevic, Bulls	.50
45 Jordin Tootoo, Wheat Kings	4.00
46 Pavel Brendl, Calgary Hitmen	1.50
47 Ryan Craig, Wheat Kings	.25
48 Owen Fussey, Hitmen	.25
49 Brent Krahn (G), Calgary Hitmen	.50
50 Erik Christensen, Blazers	.75
51 Jared Aulin, Blazers	.50
52 Kiel McLeod, Rockets	.25
53 Dan Blackburn (G), Kootenay Ice	2.00
54 Jeff Woywitka, Rebels	.75
55 Ryan Hollweg, Tigers	.25
56 Jay Bouwmeester, Medicine Hat Tigers	2.50
57 Ben Knoop, Warriors	.25
58 Marcel Hossa, Winter Hawks	2.00
59 Greg Watson, Raiders	.75
60 Justin Mapletoft, Rebels	.50
61 Matt Hubbauer, Pats	.25
62 Garth Murray, Regina Pats	.25
63 Matthew Spiller, Thunderbirds	.25
64 Barrett Heisten, Thunderbirds	.50
65 Gerard Dicaire, Thunderbirds	.50
66 Jamie Lundmark, Thunderbirds	1.50
67 Duncan Milroy, Broncos	1.00
68 Nathan Smith, Broncos	.25
69 Konstantin Panov, Blazers	.25
70 Mike Comrie, Kootenay Ice	3.00
71 Tomas Kopecky, Hurricanes	.25
72 Josef Balej, Winter Hawks	.50
73 Shane Bendera, Rebels	.25
74 Blake Evans, Tri-City Americans	.25
75 Igor Pohanka, Raiders	.25
76 Robin LeBlanc, Drakkar	.25
77 Yanick Lehoux, Drakkar	.50
78 Jean-Francois Racine, Voltigeurs	.25
79 Pascal Leclaire (G), Mooseheads	1.50
80 Chris Montgomery, Rockets	1.00
81 Brent MacLellan, Rimouski Océanic	.25
82 Thatcher Bell, Oceanic	.25
83 Antoine Vermette, Tigres	.75
84 Carl Mallette, Tigres	.25
85 Nicolas Poirier, Oceanic	.25
86 Radim Vrbata, Cataracts	1.50
87 Maxime Ouellet (G), Huskies	2.00
88 Brandon Reid, Foreurs	1.00
89 Jason Spezza, Windsor Spitfires	3.50
90 Pascal Leclaire (G), Mooseheads	1.50
91 Dan Blackburn (G), Kootenay Ice	2.00
92 Stephen Weiss, Whalers	2.00
93 Tim Gleason, Spitfires	.75
94 Duncan Milroy, Broncos	1.00
95 Kiel McLeod, Rockets	.25
96 Jay McClement, Battallion	.75
97 Jay Harrison, Battallion	.75
98 Greg Watson, Raiders	.75
99 Jason Spezza, Windsor Spitfires	1.00
100 Jay Bouwmeester, Medicine Hat Tigers	1.00

CHL CLASS

Insert Set (10 cards):	30.00

s

	Insert (1:17)	CC
☐	CC1 Brian Finley (G), Barrie Colts	1.50
☐	CC2 Michael Zigomanis, Frontenacs	1.50
☐	CC3 Jason Spezza, Windsor Spitfires	7.00
☐	CC4 Jay Bouwmeester, Medicine Hat Tigers	5.00
☐	CC5 Rob Zepp (G), Plymouth Whalers	1.50
☐	CC6 Pavel Brendl, Calgary Hitmen	2.00
☐	CC7 Dan Blackburn (G), Kootenay Ice	4.00
☐	CC8 Mike Comrie, Kootenay Ice	9.00
☐	CC9 Pascal Leclaire (G), Mooseheads	3.00
☐	CC10 Maxime Ouellet (G), Huskies	3.00

CHL SUPREMACY

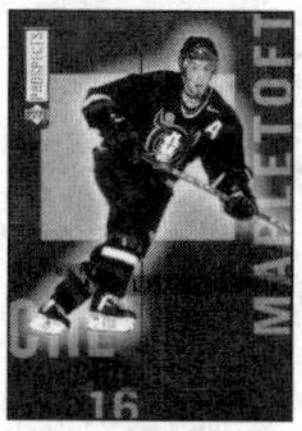

	Insert Set (10 cards):	20.00
	Insert (1:17)	CS
☐	CS1 Jason Spezza, Windsor Spitfires	7.00
☐	CS2 Brian Finley (G), Barrie Colts	1.50
☐	CS3 Raffi Torres, Battalion	1.50
☐	CS4 Rob Zepp (G), Plymouth Whalers	1.50
☐	CS5 Pavel Brendl, Calgary Hitmen	2.00
☐	CS6 Justin Mapletoft, Rebels	1.50
☐	CS7 Barrett Heisten, Thunderbirds	1.50
☐	CS8 Mike Comrie, Kootenay Ice	9.00
☐	CS9 Jay Bouwmeester, Medicine Hat Tigers	5.00
☐	CS10 Pascal Leclaire (G), Mooseheads	3.00

FUTURE LEADERS

	Insert Set (10 cards):	20.00
	Insert (1:17)	FL
☐	FL1 Jason Spezza, Windsor Spitfires	7.00
☐	FL2 Raffi Torres, Battalion	1.50
☐	FL3 Brad Boyes, Erie Otters	1.50
☐	FL4 Stephen Weiss, Whalers	1.50
☐	FL5 Michael Zigomanis, Frontenacs	1.50
☐	FL6 Jamie Lundmark, Thunderbirds	2.00
☐	FL7 Mike Comrie, Kootenay Ice	9.00
☐	FL8 Nathan Smith, Broncos	1.50
☐	FL9 Radim Vrbata, Cataracts	3.00
☐	FL10 Brandon Reid, Foreurs	1.50

DESTINATION: THE SHOW

	Insert Set (6 cards):	20.00
	Insert (1:33)	DS
☐	D1 Jason Spezza, Windsor Spitfires	9.00
☐	D2 Dan Blackburn (G), Kootenay Ice	6.00
☐	D3 Pavel Brendl, Calgary Hitmen	3.00
☐	D4 Jay Bouwmeester, Medicine Hat Tigers	7.00
☐	D5 Zdenek Blatny, Ice	2.00
☐	D6 Pascal Leclaire (G), Mooseheads	4.00

GREAT DESIRE

	Insert Set (6 cards):	20.00
	Insert (1:33)	GD
☐	GD1 Jason Spezza, Windsor Spitfires	7.00
☐	GD2 Jay Bouwmeester, Medicine Hat Tigers	5.00
☐	GD3 Mike Comrie, Kootenay Ice	9.00
☐	GD4 Raffi Torres, Battalion	2.00
☐	GD5 Brandon Reid, Foreurs	2.00
☐	GD6 Pascal Leclaire (G), Mooseheads	3.00

GAME JERSEY

	Insert Set (10 cards):	350.00
	Insert (1:18)	GJ
☐	Brent Krahn (G), Hitmen ✂	30.00
☐	Dan Blackburn (G), Ice ✂ White	50.00
☐	Jason Spezza, Spitfires ✂	60.00
☐	Jay Bouwmeester, Tigers ✂	60.00
☐	Jamie Lundmark, Warriors ✂	40.00
☐	Jason Spezza, IceDogs ✂ White	60.00
☐	Nikita Alexeev, Otters ✂	30.00
☐	Pavel Brendl, Hitmen ✂	40.00
☐	Raffi Torres, Battalion ✂	30.00
☐	Rob Zepp (G), Whalers ✂	20.00

GAME JERSEY SIGNED

	Insert Set (8 cards):	750.00
	Insert (#/100)	GJS
☐	Brent Krahn (G), Hitmen ✍ ✂	75.00
☐	Dan Blackburn (G), Ice ✍ ✂	125.00
☐	Jason Spezza, Spitfires ✍ ✂	150.00
☐	Jay Bouwmeester, Tigers ✍ ✂	150.00
☐	Jason Spezza, IceDogs ✍ ✂	150.00
☐	Pavel Brendl, Hitmen ✍ ✂	100.00
☐	Raffi Torres, Battalion ✍ ✂	75.00
☐	Rob Zepp (G), Whalers ✍ ✂	75.00

GAME JERSEY COMBO

	Insert Set (10 cards):	500.00
	Insert (#/250)	GJC
☐	Dan Blackburn (G) ✂ / Brent Krahn (G) ✂	45.00
☐	Dan Blackburn (G) ✂ / Rob Zepp (G) ✂	40.00
☐	Dan Blackburn (G) ✂ / Jamie Lundmark ✂	50.00
☐	Brent Krahn (G) ✂ / Jamie Lundmark ✂	40.00
☐	Jason Spezza ✂ / Jay Bouwmeester ✂	80.00
☐	Jason Spezza ✂ / Jamie Lundmark ✂	65.00
☐	Jason Spezza ✂ ✂	120.00
☐	Jason Spezza ✂ / Raffi Torres ✂	60.00
☐	Jason Spezza ✂ / Rob Zepp (G) ✂	50.00
☐	Raffi Torres ✂ / Rob Zepp (G) ✂	40.00

SIGNATURE

	Insert Set (9 cards):	420.00
	Autograph (1:107)	S
☐	Brent Krahn (G), Hitmen ✍	20.00
☐	Bobby Orr, Generals ✍	250.00
☐	Dan Blackburn (G), Ice ✍	35.00
☐	Jay Bouwmeester, Tigers ✍	45.00
☐	Jason Spezza, IceDogs ✍	55.00
☐	Pavel Brendl, Hitmen ✍	30.00
☐	Pascal Leclaire (G), Mooseheads ✍	30.00
☐	Raffi Torres, Battalion ✍	20.00
☐	Rob Zepp (G), Whalers ✍	20.00

2000 - 01 UPPER DECK RETURN TO EXCELLENCE

These cards were inserted into packs of Upper Deck Pros & Prospects (ML1-ML3), SP Authentic (ML4-ML6) and Upper Deck Rookie Update (ML7-ML9).

	Insert Set (9 cards):	4,900
	Jersey (#/66)	ML66
☐	ML1 Mario Lemieux, Pitt. ✂	650.00
☐	ML2 Mario Lemieux, Pitt. ✂	650.00
☐	ML3 Mario Lemieux, Pitt. ✂	650.00
☐	ML4 Mario Lemieux, Pitt. ✂	650.00
☐	ML5 Mario Lemieux, Pitt. ✂	650.00
☐	ML6 Mario Lemieux, Pitt. ✂	650.00
☐	ML7 Mario Lemieux, Pitt. ✂	650.00
☐	ML8 Mario Lemieux, Pitt. ✂	650.00
☐	ML9 Mario Lemieux, Pitt. ✂	650.00

2000 - 01 UPPER DECK ROOKIE UPDATE

This series is listed under the following three Upper Deck Company brands: SPx, Upper Deck Black Diamond and Upper Deck Ice.

2000 - 01 UPPER DECK VINTAGE

This series was released in 2001. This series has a design similar to the 1954-55 Topps hockey design.

	Complete Set (400 cards):	30.00
	Common Player:	.20
	Player	Reg.
☐	1 German Titov, Anah.	.20
☐	2 Teemu Selänne, Anah.	1.00
☐	3 Matt Cullen, Anah.	.20
☐	4 Oleg Tverdovsky, Anah.	.20
☐	5 Jean-Sébastien Giguère (G), Anah.	1.00
☐	6 Guy Hebert (G), Anah.	.20

☐	7 Mike Leclerc, Anah.	.20
☐	8 Jason Marshall, Anah.	.20
☐	9 Paul Kariya, Anah.	1.50
☐	10 Steve Rucchin, Anah.	.20
☐	11 Mighty Ducks Checklist	.50
☐	12 Mighty Ducks Team Stats	.50
☐	13 Patrik Stefan, Atla.	.20
☐	14 Damian Rhodes (G), Atla.	.20
☐	15 Donald Audette, Atla.	.50
☐	16 Yannick Tremblay, Atla.	.20
☐	17 Hnat Domenichelli, Atla.	.20
☐	18 Dean Sylvester, Atla.	.20
☐	19 Stephen Guolla, Atla.	.20
☐	20 Petr Buzek, Atla.	.20
☐	21 Andrew Brunette, Atla.	.20
☐	22 Ray Ferraro, Atla.	.20
☐	23 Thrashers Checklist	.20
☐	24 Thrashers Team Stats	.20
☐	25 Joe Thornton, Bost.	1.50
☐	26 Brian Rolston, Bost.	.20
☐	27 Kyle McLaren, Bost.	.20
☐	28 Sergei Samsonov, Bost.	.50
☐	29 Paul Coffey, Bost.	.50
☐	30 Andréi Kovalenko, Bost.	.20
☐	31 Jason Allison, Bost.	.50
☐	32 Bill Guerin, Bost.	.50
☐	33 Byron Dafoe (G), Bost.	.50
☐	34 Mikko Eloranta, Bost.	.20
☐	35 Don Sweeney, Bost.	.20
☐	36 Bruins Checklist	.50
☐	37 Bruins Team Stats	.50
☐	38 Miroslav Satan, Buff.	.20
☐	39 Dominik Hasek (G), Buff.	1.00
☐	40 Stu Barnes, Buff.	.20
☐	41 Chris Gratton, Buff.	.20
☐	42 Doug Gilmour, Buff.	.50
☐	43 Curtis Brown, Buff.	.20
☐	44 James Patrick, Buff.	.20
☐	45 Alexei Zhitnik, Buff.	.20
☐	46 Rhett Warrener, Buff.	.20
☐	47 Dave Andréychuk, Buff.	.20
☐	48 Maxim Afinogenov, Buff.	.50
☐	49 Sabres Checklist	.50
☐	50 Sabres Team Stats	.50
☐	51 Valeri Bure, Calg.	.20
☐	52 Mike Vernon (G), Calg.	.50
☐	53 Marc Savard, Calg.	.20
☐	54 Clarke Wilm, Calg.	.20
☐	55 Phil Housley, Calg.	.20
☐	56 Fred Brathwaite (G), Calg.	.20
☐	57 Cory Stillman, Calg.	.20
☐	58 Derek Morris, Calg.	.20
☐	59 Robyn Regehr, Calg.	.20
☐	60 Jarome Iginla, Calg.	1.00
☐	61 Flames Checklist	.20
☐	62 Flames Team Stats	.20
☐	63 Bates Battaglia, Caro.	.20
☐	64 Sandis Ozolinsh, Caro.	.20
☐	65 Jeff O'Neill, Caro.	.50
☐	66 Ron Francis, Caro.	.50
☐	67 Sami Kapanen, Caro.	.20
☐	68 Martin Gélinas, Caro.	.20
☐	69 Arturs Irbe (G), Caro.	.50
☐	70 David Tanabe, Caro.	.20
☐	71 Rod Brind'Amour, Caro.	.20
☐	72 Glen Wesley, Caro.	.20
☐	73 Hurricanes Checklist	.20
☐	74 Hurricanes Team Stats	.20
☐	75 Tony Amonte, Chic.	.50
☐	76 Steve Sullivan, Chic.	.20
☐	77 Éric Dazé, Chic.	.50
☐	78 Boris Mironov, Chic.	.20
☐	79 Jocelyn Thibault (G), Chic.	.50
☐	80 Jean-Yves Leroux, Chic.	.20
☐	81 Valeri Zelepukin, Chic.	.20
☐	82 Alexei Zhamnov, Chic.	.20
☐	83 Josef Marha, Chic.	.20
☐	84 Michael Nylander, Chic.	.20
☐	85 Blackhawks Checklist	.20
☐	86 Blackhawks Team Stats	.20
☐	87 Patrick Roy (G), Colo.	3.50
☐	88 Joe Sakic, Colo.	2.00
☐	89 Jon Klemm, Colo.	.20
☐	90 Adam Deadmarsh, Colo.	.20
☐	91 Raymond Bourque, Colo.	1.50
☐	92 Peter Forsberg, Colo.	1.50
☐	93 Milan Hejduk, Colo.	1.00
☐	94 Chris Drury, Colo.	.50
☐	95 Alex Tanguay, Colo.	.50
☐	96 Adam Foote, Colo.	.20
☐	97 Dave Reid, Colo.	.20
☐	98 Avalanche Checklist	1.50
☐	99 Avalanche Team Stats	2.00
☐	100 Marc Denis (G), Colu.	.50
☐	101 Geoff Sanderson, Colu.	.20
☐	102 Ron Tugnutt (G), Colu.	.50
☐	103 Lyle Odelein, Colu.	.20
☐	104 Krzysztof Oliwa, Colu.	.20
☐	105 Kevyn Adams, Colu.	.20
☐	106 Stephen Heinze, Colu.	.20
☐	107 Jamie Pushor, Colu.	.20
☐	108 Bruce Gardiner, Colu.	.20
☐	109 Jan Caloun, Colu.	.20
☐	110 Blue Jackets Checklist	.20
☐	111 Blue Jackets Team Stats	.20
☐	112 Mike Modano, Dall.	1.00
☐	113 Jere Lehtinen, Dall.	.20
☐	114 Brett Hull, Dall.	1.00
☐	115 Sergei Zubov, Dall.	.20
☐	116 Jamie Langenbrunner, Dall.	.20
☐	117 Shaun Van Allen, Dall.	.20
☐	118 Ed Belfour (G), Dall.	1.00
☐	119 Brenden Morrow, Dall.	.20
☐	120 Darryl Sydor, Dall.	.20
☐	121 Joe Nieuwendyk, Dall.	.50
☐	122 Derian Hatcher, Dall.	.20
☐	123 Stars Checklist	.50
☐	124 Stars Team Stats	.50
☐	125 Steve Yzerman, Detr.	3.00
☐	126 Nicklas Lidström, Detr.	.50
☐	127 Sergei Fedorov, Detr.	1.00
☐	128 Chris Osgood (G), Detr.	.50
☐	129 Brendan Shanahan, Detr.	1.00
☐	130 Larry Murphy, Detr.	.20
☐	131 Darren McCarty, Detr.	.20
☐	132 Chris Chelios, Detr.	.50
☐	133 Kris Draper, Detr.	.20
☐	134 Tomas Holmström, Detr.	.20
☐	135 Vyacheslav Kozlov, Detr.	.20
☐	136 Red Wings Checklist	1.00
☐	137 Red Wings Team Stats	1.00
☐	138 Doug Weight, Edmo.	.50
☐	139 Todd Marchant, Edmo.	.20
☐	140 Eric Brewer, Edmo.	.50
☐	141 Mike Grier, Edmo.	.20
☐	142 Tom Poti, Edmo.	.20
☐	143 Ryan Smyth, Edmo.	.50
☐	144 Tommy Salo (G), Edmo.	.50
☐	145 Janne Niinimaa, Edmo.	.20
☐	146 Dan Cleary, Edmo.	.20
☐	147 Bill Guerin, Edmo.	.50
☐	148 Oilers Checklist	.20
☐	149 Oilers Team Stats	.20
☐	150 Pavel Bure, Flor.	1.00
☐	151 Ray Whitney, Flor.	.20
☐	152 Viktor Kozlov, Flor.	.20
☐	153 Igor Larionov, Flor.	.50
☐	154 Scott Mellanby, Flor.	.20
☐	155 Trevor Kidd (G), Flor.	.20
☐	156 Rob Niedermayer, Flor.	.20
☐	157 Robert Svehla, Flor.	.20
☐	158 Roberto Luongo (G), Flor.	1.00
☐	159 Mike Sillinger, Flor.	.20
☐	160 Panthers Checklist	.50
☐	161 Panthers Team Stats	.50
☐	162 Zigmund Palffy, LosA.	.50
☐	163 Luc Robitaille, LosA.	1.00
☐	164 Stéphane Fiset (G), LosA.	.20
☐	165 Rob Blake, LosA.	.50
☐	166 Bryan Smolinski, LosA.	.20
☐	167 Glen Murray, Kings	.50
☐	168 Mattias Norström, LosA.	.20
☐	169 Jamie Storr (G), LosA.	.20
☐	170 Craig Johnson, LosA.	.20
☐	171 Nelson Emerson, LosA.	.20
☐	172 Kings Checklist	.20
☐	173 Kings Team Stats	.50
☐	174 Stacy Roest, MinW.	.20
☐	175 Manny Fernandez (G), MinW.	.50
☐	176 Jim Dowd, MinW.	.20
☐	177 Curtis Leschyshyn, MinW.	.20
☐	178 Jeff Nielsen, MinW.	.20
☐	179 Aaron Gavey, MinW.	.20
☐	180 Sergei Krivokrasov, MinW.	.20
☐	181 Brad Bombardir, MinW.	.20
☐	182 Cam Stewart, MinW.	.20
☐	183 Scott Pellerin, MinW.	.20
☐	184 Wild Checklist	.50
☐	185 Wild Team Stats	.20
☐	186 Saku Koivu, Mont.	1.00
☐	187 Eric Weinrich, Mont.	.20
☐	188 Sergei Zholtok, Mont.	.20

Card	Price
189 Dainius Zubrus, Mont.	.20
190 Brian Savage, Mont.	.20
191 Jeff Hackett (G), Mont.	.20
192 Patrick Poulin, Mont.	.20
193 José Théodore (G), Mont.	1.50
194 Christian Laflamme, Mont.	.20
195 Martin Rucinsky, Mont.	.20
196 Canadiens Checklist	.50
197 Canadiens Team Stats	.50
198 Greg Johnson, Nash.	.20
199 Cliff Ronning, Nash.	.20
200 Drake Berehowsky, Nash.	.20
201 Mike Dunham (G), Nash.	.50
202 David Legwand, Nash.	.50
203 Tom Fitzgerald, Nash.	.20
204 Patric Kjellberg, Nash.	.20
205 Scott Walker, Nash.	.20
206 Kimmo Timonen, Nash.	.20
207 Bill Houlder, Nash.	.20
208 Predators Checklist	.20
209 Predators Team Stats	.20
210 Scott Stevens, NJer.	.50
211 Martin Brodeur (G), NJer.	2.00
212 Jason Arnott, NJer.	.50
213 Patrik Elias, NJer.	1.00
214 Alexander Mogilny, NJer.	.50
215 Scott Gomez, NJer.	.50
216 John Madden, NJer.	.20
217 Bobby Holik, NJer.	.20
218 Petr* Sykora, NJer.	.50
219 Ken Sutton, NJer.	.20
220 Randy McKay, NJer.	.20
221 Devils Checklist	.50
222 Devils Team Stats	.50
223 Tim Connolly, NYIs.	.50
224 Kevin Haller, NYIs.	.20
225 Brad Isbister, NYIs.	.20
226 Mariusz Czerkawski, NYIs.	.20
227 Roman Hamrlik, NYIs.	.20
228 Claude Lapointe, NYIs.	.20
229 Bill Muckalt, NYIs.	.20
230 John Vanbiesbrouck (G), NYIs.	.50
231 Kenny Jönsson, NYIs.	.20
232 Mark Parrish, NYIs.	.50
233 Islanders Checklist	.20
234 Islanders Team Stats	.20
235 Theoren Fleury, NYRa.	.50
236 Brian Leetch, NYRa.	.50
237 Mark Messier, NYRa.	1.00
238 Adam Graves, NYRa.	.50
239 Mike Richter (G), NYRa.	.50
240 Vladimir Malakhov, NYRa.	.20
241 Mike York, NYRa.	.20
242 Radek Dvorak, NYRa.	.20
243 Petr Nedved, NYRa.	.20
244 Jan Hlavac, NYRa.	.20
245 Tim Taylor, NYRa.	.20
246 Rangers Checklist	.50
247 Rangers Team Stats	.50
248 Radek Bonk, Otta.	.20
249 Marian Hossa, Otta.	1.00
250 Jason York, Otta.	.20
251 Wade Redden, Otta.	.20
252 Patrick Lalime (G), Otta.	.50
253 Daniel Alfredsson, Otta.	.50
254 Shawn McEachern, Otta.	.20
255 Sami Salo, Otta.	.20
256 Petr Schastlivy, Otta.	.20
257 Vaclav Prospal, Otta.	.20
258 Senators Checklist	.50
259 Senators Team Stats	.50
260 John LeClair, Phil.	1.00
261 Rick Tocchet, Phil.	.20
262 Daymond Langkow, Phil.	.20
263 Simon Gagné, Phil.	1.00
264 Keith Primeau, Phil.	.50
265 Éric Desjardins, Phil.	.20
266 Brian Boucher (G), Phil.	.20
267 Andy Delmore, Phil.	.20
268 Mark Recchi, Phil.	.50
269 Keith Jones, Phil.	.20
270 Chris Therien, Phil.	.20
271 Flyers Checklist	.20
272 Flyers Team Stats	.50
273 Jeremy Roenick, Phoe.	1.00
274 Teppo Numminen, Phoe.	.20
275 Brad May, Phoe.	.20
276 Keith Tkachuk, Phoe.	.50
277 Trevor Letowski, Phoe.	.20
278 Shane Doan, Phoe.	.20
279 Jyrki Lumme, Phoe.	.20
280 Joé Juneau, Phoe.	.20
281 Sean Burke (G), Phoe.	.50
282 Travis Green, Phoe.	.20
283 Coyotes Checklist	.50
284 Coyotes Team Stats	.50
285 Jean-Sébastien Aubin (G), Pitt.	.20
286 Jaromir Jagr, Pitt.	1.00
287 Aleksey Morozov, Pitt.	.20
288 Josef Beranek, Pitt.	.20
289 Jan Hrdina, Pitt.	.20
290 Milan Kraft, Pitt.	.50
291 Alexei Kovalev, Pitt.	.50
292 Robert Lang, Pitt.	.20
293 Janne Laukkanen, Pitt. [Photo: Roman Simicek]	.20
294 Martin Straka, Pitt.	.20
295 Penguins Checklist	.20
296 Penguins Team Stats	.50
297 Niklas Sundström, SanJ.	.20
298 Owen Nolan, SanJ.	.50
299 Jeff Friesen, SanJ.	.20
300 Vincent Damphousse, SanJ.	.50
301 Brad Stuart, SanJ.	.50
302 Marco Sturm, SanJ.	.20
303 Alexander Korolyuk, SanJ.	.20
304 Mike Ricci, SanJ.	.20
305 Patrick Marleau, SanJ.	.50
306 Steve Shields (G), SanJ.	.20
307 Sharks Checklist	.20
308 Sharks Team Stats	.20
309 Chris Pronger, SLou.	.50
310 Pavol Demitra, SLou.	.50
311 Marty Reasoner, SLou.	.20
312 Jochen Hecht, SLou.	.20
313 Michal Handzus, SLou.	.20
314 Al MacInnis, SLou.	.50
315 Roman Turek (G), SLou.	.50
316 Lubos Bartecko, Blues	.20
317 Jamal Mayers, Blues	.20
318 Dallas Drake, Blues	.20
319 Pierre Turgeon, SLou.	.50
320 Blues Checklist	.20
321 Blues Team Stats	.50
322 Vincent Lecavalier, Tamp.	1.00
323 Mike Johnson, Tamp.	.20
324 Brad Richards, Tamp.	1.00
325 Dan Cloutier (G), Tamp.	.50
326 Paul Mara, Tamp.	.20
327 Fredrik Modin, Tamp.	.20
328 Bryan Muir, Tamp.	.20
329 Jassen Cullimore, Tamp.	.20
330 Todd Warriner, Tamp.	.20
331 Petr Svoboda, Tamp.	.20
332 Lightning Checklist	.50
333 Lightning Team Stats	.50
334 Mats Sundin, Toro.	1.00
335 Sergei Berezin, Toro.	.20
336 Nikolai Antropov, Toro.	.20
337 Steve Thomas, Toro.	.20
338 Curtis Joseph (G), Toro.	1.00
339 Jonas Höglund, Toro.	.20
340 Dmitry Yushkevich, Toro.	.20
341 Darcy Tucker, Toro.	.20
342 Gary Roberts, Toro.	.50
343 Jeff Farkas, Toro.	.20
344 Tie Domi, Toro.	.20
345 Maple Leafs Checklist	.50
346 Maple Leafs Team Stats	.50
347 Markus Näslund, Vanc.	1.00
348 Brendan Morrison, Vanc.	.20
349 Todd Bertuzzi, Vanc.	1.50
350 Adrian Aucoin, Vanc.	.20
351 Donald Brashear, Vanc.	.20
352 Murray Baron, Vanc.	.20
353 Daniel Sedin, Vanc.	1.00
354 Andrew Cassels, Vanc.	.20
355 Henrik Sedin, Vanc.	1.00
356 Mattias Öhlund, Vanc.	.20
357 Canucks Checklist	.50
358 Canucks Team Stats	.50
359 Chris Simon, Wash.	.20
360 Olaf Kölzig (G), Wash.	.50
361 Jeff Halpern, Wash.	.20
362 Andréi Nikolishin, Wash.	.20
363 Steve Konowalchuk, Wash.	.20
364 Peter Bondra, Wash.	.50
365 Adam Oates, Wash.	.50
366 Richard Zednik, Wash.	.50
367 Sergei Gonchar, Wash.	.20
368 Brendan Witt, Wash.	.20
369 Capitals Checklist	.20
370 Capitals Team Stats	.20
371 R. Klesla, Colu. [Vintage Rookies] RC	**3.00**
372 J. Rönnqvist, Anah. [Vintage Rookies] RC	**1.50**
373 Eric Nickulas, Bost. [Vintage Rookies] RC	**1.00**
374 A. Raycroft (G), Bost. [Vintage Rookies] RC	**2.00**
375 Jeff Cowan, Calg. [Vintage Rookies] RC	**1.00**
376 Reto von Arx, Chic. [Vintage Rookies] RC	**1.50**
377 Serge Aubin, Colu. [Vintage Rookies] RC	**1.50**
378 Tyler Bouck, Dall. [Vintage Rookies] RC	**1.50**
379 Michel Riesen, Edmo. [Vintage Rookies] RC	**1.50**
380 Éric Bélanger, LosA. [Vintage Rookies] RC	**1.50**
381 M. Gaborik, MinW. [Vintage Rookies] RC	**10.00**
382 Scott Hartnell, Nash. [Vintage Rookies] RC	**2.00**
383 Greg Classen, Nash. [Vintage Rookies] RC	**1.50**
384 Willie Mitchell, NJer. [Vintage Rookies] RC	**1.50**
385 Colin White, NJer. [Vintage Rookies] RC	**1.50**
386 S. Valiquette (G), NYIs. [Vintage Rookies] RC	**1.50**
387 Jani Hurme (G), Otta. [Vintage Rookies] RC	**2.00**
388 Martin Havlat, Otta. [Vintage Rookies] RC	**6.00**
389 Justin Williams, Phil. [Vintage Rookies] RC	**3.00**
390 Petr Hubacek, Phil. [Vintage Rookies] RC	**1.00**
391 Roman Simicek, Pitt. [Vintage Rookies] RC	**1.00**
392 Matt Elich, Tamp. [Vintage Rookies] RC	**1.50**
393 Brent Sopel, Vanc. [Vintage Rookies] RC	**1.50**
394 Marc-André Thinel [Vintage Rookies] RC	**1.50**
395 Zdenek Blatny [Vintage Rookies] RC	**1.50**
396 Michael Ryder [Vintage Rookies] RC	**1.50**
397 Jason Jaspers [Vintage Rookies] RC	**1.50**
398 Jordan Krestanovich [Vintage Rookies] RC	**1.50**
399 Fedor Fedorov [Vintage Rookies] RC	**1.50**
400 Jeff Bateman [Vintage Rookies] RC	**1.50**
Sample	**MT**
31 Curtis Joseph (G), Toro.	2.00

ALL-UD TEAM

Insert Set (10 cards):	**20.00**
Insert (1:23)	**UD**
UD1 Patrick Roy (G), Colo.	6.00
UD2 Martin Brodeur (G), NJer.	3.00
UD3 Chris Pronger, SLou.	1.00
UD4 Raymond Bourque, Colo.	2.00
UD5 Paul Kariya, Anah.	2.00
UD6 John LeClair, Phil.	1.00
UD7 Steve Yzerman, Detr.	4.00
UD8 Peter Forsberg, Colo.	2.00
UD9 Jaromir Jagr, Pitt.	2.00
UD10 Pavel Bure, Flor.	1.00

HEROES OF HOCKEY

Insert Set (10 cards):	**20.00**
Insert (1:23)	**HH**
HH37 Mark Messier, Edmo.	3.00
HH38 Messier & Gretzky	5.00
HH39 Mark Messier, Edmo.	3.00
HH40 Mark Messier, Edmo.	3.00
HH41 Mark Messier, NYRa.	3.00
HH42 Mark Messier, NYRa.	3.00
HH43 Mark Messier, Vanc.	3.00
HH44 Mark Messier, NHL All-Star Game	3.00
HH45 Mark Messier, NYRa.	3.00
HH46 Mark Messier, NYRa.	3.00

STAR TANDEMS

Insert Set (10 cards):	**10.00**
Insert (1:23)	**ST**
S1A Paul Kariya, Anah.	2.00
S1B Teemu Selänne, Anah.	1.00
S2A Joe Sakic, Colo.	3.00
S2B Patrick Roy (G), Colo.	6.00
S3A Steve Yzerman, Detr.	4.00
S3B Brendan Shanahan, Detr.	2.00
S4A Scott Gomez, NJer.	.75
S4B Martin Brodeur (G), NJer.	3.00
S5A John LeClair, Phil.	1.00
S5B Brian Boucher (G), Phil.	.75

DYNASTY: A PIECE OF HISTORY

There are two versions: the Jersey card (1:72 packs) and the Level 2 parallel (#/50).

Insert Set (11 cards):	**1,400**	**900**
Inserts	**D50**	**D**
B. Bourne / C. Gillies ✂	50.00	30.00
M. Bossy / A. Kallur ✂	75.00	85.00
B. Goring / B. Carroll ✂	50.00	30.00
C. Gillies / M. Hallin ✂	50.00	30.00
W. Gretzky / M. Messier ✂	525.00	400.00
M. Lemieux / J. Jagr ✂	400.00	200.00
P. LaFontaine / D. Langevin ✂	50.00	40.00
B. Nystrom / Bre. Sutter ✂	50.00	30.00
D. Potvin / C. Resch ✂	50.00	55.00
B. Trottier / S. Persson ✂	50.00	55.00
S. Yzerman / C. Osgood ✂	300.00	150.00

GREAT GLOVES

Insert Set (20 cards):	**20.00**
Insert (1:12)	**GG**
GG1 Guy Hebert (G), Anah.	1.50
GG2 Byron Dafoe (G), Bost.	1.50
GG3 Dominik Hasek (G), Buff.	2.00
GG4 Fred Brathwaite (G), Calg.	1.50
GG5 Arturs Irbe (G), Caro.	1.50
GG6 Patrick Roy (G), Colo.	6.00
GG7 Ed Belfour (G), Dall.	2.00
GG8 Chris Osgood (G), Detr.	1.50
GG9 Tommy Salo (G), Edmo.	1.50
GG10 Trevor Kidd (G), Flor.	1.50
GG11 José Théodore (G), Mont.	2.00
GG12 Mike Richter (G), NYRa.	1.50
GG13 Brian Boucher (G), Phil.	1.50
GG14 Jean-Sébastien Aubin (G), Pitt.	1.50
GG15 Steve Shields (G), SanJ.	1.50
GG16 Roman Turek (G), SLou.	1.50
GG17 Dan Cloutier (G), Tamp.	1.50
GG18 Curtis Joseph (G), Toro.	2.00
GG19 Félix Potvin (G), Vanc.	1.50
GG20 Olaf Kölzig (G), Wash.	1.50

NATIONAL HEROES

Insert Set (20 cards):	**20.00**
Insert (1:4)	**NH**
NH1 Paul Kariya, Anah.	2.00
NH2 Teemu Selänne, Anah.	1.00
NH3 Patrik Stefan, Atla.	.50
NH4 Sergei Samsonov, Bost.	1.00
NH5 Dominik Hasek (G), Buff.	2.00
NH6 Valeri Bure, Calg.	.50
NH7 Tony Amonte, Chic.	1.00
NH8 Patrick Roy (G), Colo.	6.00
NH9 Peter Forsberg, Colo.	2.00
NH10 Mike Modano, Dall.	2.00
NH11 Steve Yzerman, Detr.	4.00
NH12 Pavel Bure, Flor.	1.00
NH13 Saku Koivu, Mont.	1.00
NH14 Martin Brodeur (G), NJer.	3.00
NH15 Scott Gomez, NJer.	.50
NH16 Mark Messier, NYRa.	2.00
NH17 John LeClair, Phil.	1.00
NH18 Jeremy Roenick, Phoe.	1.00
NH19 Jaromir Jagr, Pitt.	2.00
NH20 Mats Sundin, Toro.	2.00

ORIGINAL SIX: A PIECE OF HISTORY

Each card features a swatch from a player-worn jersey. There are two versions: the Jersey card (1:72 packs) and the Level 2 parallel (#/67).

Insert Set (6 cards):	**675.00**	**200.00**
Inserts	**O67**	**O6**
O-CJ Curtis Joseph (G), Toro.	125.00	35.00
O-JT José Théodore (G), Mont.	150.00	45.00
O-MY Mike York, NYRa.	40.00	20.00
O-SS Sergei Samsonov, Bost.	75.00	20.00
O-SY Steve Yzerman, Detr.	300.00	90.00
O-TE Tony Esposito (G), Chic.	125.00	35.00

2000 - 01 VANGUARD

This series was issued in February 2001. Base cards (1-100, 151) have a hobby-pack Holographic Purple parallel (#/105), a Premiere Date parallel (#/100), a retail-pack Holographic Gold parallel (#/60) and a one-of-one Proof parallel (#/1). Holographic Purple and Premiere Date parallel cards are priced similarly below; the Proof cards are too scarce to price. Short-printed rookie-subset cards are limited to 390 copies each.

Shell Set (101 cards):			**60.00**
Parallel Set (101 cards):	**150.00**	**75.00**	
Complete Set (151 cards):			**.00**
Common Player:	**8.00**	**4.00**	**.65**

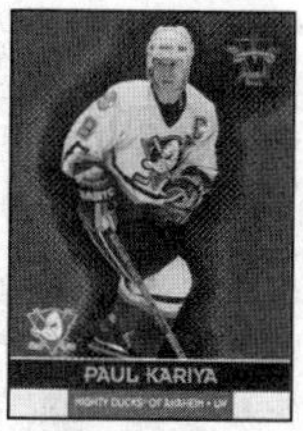

	Description	HG60	HP105	Vang.
☐☐☐☐☐	1 Guy Hebert (G)	8.00	4.00	.65
☐☐☐☐☐	2 Paul Kariya	8.00	4.00	4.00
☐☐☐☐☐	3 Teemu Selänne	8.00	4.00	2.00
☐☐☐☐☐	4 Ray Ferraro	8.00	4.00	.65
☐☐☐☐☐	5 Damian Rhodes (G)	8.00	4.00	.65
☐☐☐☐☐	6 Patrik Stefan	8.00	4.00	.65
☐☐☐☐☐	7 Jason Allison	8.00	4.00	1.50
☐☐☐☐☐	8 Bill Guerin	8.00	4.00	1.00
☐☐☐☐☐	9 Sergei Samsonov	8.00	4.00	1.50
☐☐☐☐☐	10 Joe Thornton	8.00	4.00	3.50
☐☐☐☐☐	11 Maxim Afinogenov	8.00	4.00	1.00
☐☐☐☐☐	12 Doug Gilmour	8.00	4.00	1.50
☐☐☐☐☐	13 Dominik Hasek (G)	8.00	4.00	3.00
☐☐☐☐☐	14 Miroslav Satan	8.00	4.00	.65
☐☐☐☐☐	15 Valeri Bure	8.00	4.00	.65
☐☐☐☐☐	16 Jarome Iginla	8.00	4.00	2.00
☐☐☐☐☐	17 Marc Savard	8.00	4.00	.65
☐☐☐☐☐	18 Rod Brind'Amour	8.00	4.00	.65
☐☐☐☐☐	19 Ron Francis	8.00	4.00	1.50
☐☐☐☐☐	20 Arturs Irbe (G)	8.00	4.00	1.00
☐☐☐☐☐	21 Sami Kapanen	8.00	4.00	.65
☐☐☐☐☐	22 Tony Amonte	8.00	4.00	1.50
☐☐☐☐☐	23 Jocelyn Thibault (G)	8.00	4.00	1.00
☐☐☐☐☐	24 Alexei Zhamnov	8.00	4.00	.65
☐☐☐☐☐	25 Raymond Bourque	8.00	4.00	3.50
☐☐☐☐☐	26 Chris Drury	8.00	4.00	1.50
☐☐☐☐☐	27 Peter Forsberg	8.00	4.00	4.00
☐☐☐☐☐	28 Milan Hejduk	8.00	4.00	2.00
☐☐☐☐☐	29 Patrick Roy (G)	8.00	4.00	8.00
☐☐☐☐☐	30 Joe Sakic	8.00	4.00	4.50
☐☐☐☐☐	31 Geoff Sanderson	8.00	4.00	.65
☐☐☐☐☐	32 Ron Tugnutt (G)	8.00	4.00	1.00
☐☐☐☐☐	33 Ed Belfour (G)	8.00	4.00	3.00
☐☐☐☐☐	34 Brett Hull	8.00	4.00	3.00
☐☐☐☐☐	35 Mike Modano	8.00	4.00	3.00
☐☐☐☐☐	36 Joe Nieuwendyk	8.00	4.00	1.00
☐☐☐☐☐	37 Sergei Fedorov	8.00	4.00	3.00
☐☐☐☐☐	38 Nicklas Lidström	8.00	4.00	1.50
☐☐☐☐☐	39 Chris Osgood (G)	8.00	4.00	1.50
☐☐☐☐☐	40 Brendan Shanahan	8.00	4.00	3.00
☐☐☐☐☐	41 Steve Yzerman	8.00	4.00	6.00
☐☐☐☐☐	42 Anson Carter	8.00	4.00	1.00
☐☐☐☐☐	43 Tommy Salo (G)	8.00	4.00	1.00
☐☐☐☐☐	44 Doug Weight	8.00	4.00	1.50
☐☐☐☐☐	45 Pavel Bure	8.00	4.00	2.00
☐☐☐☐☐	46 Viktor Kozlov	8.00	4.00	.65
☐☐☐☐☐	47 Ray Whitney	8.00	4.00	.65
☐☐☐☐☐	48 Zigmund Palffy	8.00	4.00	1.50
☐☐☐☐☐	49 Luc Robitaille	8.00	4.00	2.00
☐☐☐☐☐	50 Sergei Krivokrasov	8.00	4.00	.65
☐☐☐☐☐	51 Saku Koivu	8.00	4.00	2.00
☐☐☐☐☐	52 Trevor Linden	8.00	4.00	1.00
☐☐☐☐☐	53 José Théodore (G)	8.00	4.00	3.50
☐☐☐☐☐	54 David Legwand	8.00	4.00	1.00
☐☐☐☐☐	55 Randy Robitaille	8.00	4.00	.65
☐☐☐☐☐	56 Jason Arnott	8.00	4.00	1.00
☐☐☐☐☐	57 Martin Brodeur (G)	8.00	4.00	4.50
☐☐☐☐☐	58 Patrik Elias	8.00	4.00	2.00
☐☐☐☐☐	59 Scott Gomez	8.00	4.00	1.00
☐☐☐☐☐	60 Alexander Mogilny	8.00	4.00	1.00
☐☐☐☐☐	61 Tim Connolly	8.00	4.00	1.00
☐☐☐☐☐	62 Mariusz Czerkawski	8.00	4.00	.65
☐☐☐☐☐	63 John Vanbiesbrouck (G)	8.00	4.00	1.00
☐☐☐☐☐	64 Theoren Fleury	8.00	4.00	1.50
☐☐☐☐☐	65 Brian Leetch	8.00	4.00	1.50
☐☐☐☐☐	66 Mark Messier	8.00	4.00	3.00
☐☐☐☐☐	67 Mike Richter (G)	8.00	4.00	1.00
☐☐☐☐☐	68 Daniel Alfredsson	8.00	4.00	1.50
☐☐☐☐☐	69 Marian Hossa	8.00	4.00	3.00
☐☐☐☐☐	70 Alexei Yashin	8.00	4.00	1.50
☐☐☐☐☐	71 Brian Boucher (G)	8.00	4.00	.65
☐☐☐☐☐	72 Simon Gagné	8.00	4.00	2.00
☐☐☐☐☐	73 John LeClair	8.00	4.00	2.00
☐☐☐☐☐	74 Eric Lindros	8.00	4.00	3.00
☐☐☐☐☐	75 Shane Doan	8.00	4.00	.65
☐☐☐☐☐	76 Jeremy Roenick	8.00	4.00	2.00
☐☐☐☐☐	77 Keith Tkachuk	8.00	4.00	1.50
☐☐☐☐☐	78 J-S Aubin (G)	8.00	4.00	.65
☐☐☐☐☐	79 Jan Hrdina	8.00	4.00	.65
☐☐☐☐☐	80 Jaromir Jagr	8.00	4.00	3.00
☐☐☐☐☐	81 Martin Straka	8.00	4.00	.65
☐☐☐☐☐	82 Al MacInnis	8.00	4.00	1.00
☐☐☐☐☐	83 Chris Pronger	8.00	4.00	1.50
☐☐☐☐☐	84 Roman Turek (G)	8.00	4.00	1.00
☐☐☐☐☐	85 Pierre Turgeon	8.00	4.00	1.00
☐☐☐☐☐	86 Vincent Damphousse	8.00	4.00	1.50
☐☐☐☐☐	87 Jeff Friesen	8.00	4.00	.65
☐☐☐☐☐	88 Owen Nolan	8.00	4.00	1.50
☐☐☐☐☐	89 Mike Johnson	8.00	4.00	.65
☐☐☐☐☐	90 Vincent Lecavalier	8.00	4.00	3.00
☐☐☐☐☐	91 Nikolai Antropov	8.00	4.00	.65
☐☐☐☐☐	92 Tie Domi	8.00	4.00	.65
☐☐☐☐☐	93 Curtis Joseph (G)	8.00	4.00	3.00
☐☐☐☐☐	94 Mats Sundin	8.00	4.00	3.00
☐☐☐☐☐	95 Andrew Cassels	8.00	4.00	.65
☐☐☐☐☐	96 Markus Näslund	8.00	4.00	3.00
☐☐☐☐☐	97 Félix Potvin (G)	8.00	4.00	1.50
☐☐☐☐☐	98 Peter Bondra	8.00	4.00	1.50
☐☐☐☐☐	99 Olaf Kölzig (G)	8.00	4.00	1.50
☐☐☐☐☐	100 Adam Oates	8.00	4.00	1.00
☐☐☐☐☐	151 Mario Lemieux	8.00	4.00	8.00

ROOKIE

	Rookie (#/390)	R390
☐	101 Samuel Påhlsson, Bost.	4.00
☐	**102 J. Rönnqvist, Anah. RC**	**15.00**
☐	103 Milan Hnilicka (G), Atla.	4.00
☐	**104 A. Raycroft (G), Bost. RC**	**20.00**
☐	105 Dimitri Kalinin, Buff.	4.00
☐	106 Mika Noronen (G), Buff.	8.00
☐	107 Oleg Saprykin, Calg.	4.00
☐	**108 Josef Vasicek, Caro. RC**	**20.00**
☐	109 Shane Willis, Caro.	4.00
☐	110 Steve McCarthy, Chic.	4.00
☐	**111 D. Aebischer (G), Colo. RC**	**30.00**
☐	**112 Serge Aubin, Colu. RC**	**15.00**
☐	113 Marc Denis (G), Colu.	4.00
☐	**114 R. Klesla, Colu. RC**	**30.00**
☐	115 David Vyborny, Colu.	4.00
☐	**116 Tyler Bouck, Dall. RC**	**15.00**
☐	**117 Marty Turco (G), Dall. RC**	**60.00**
☐	118 Joaquin Gage (G), Edmo.	4.00
☐	**119 Michel Riesen, Edmo. RC**	**15.00**
☐	120 Brian Swanson, Edmo.	8.00
☐	121 Roberto Luongo (G), Flor.	8.00
☐	122 Ivan Novoseltsev, Flor.	4.00
☐	**123 Eric Bélanger, LosA. RC**	**15.00**
☐	**124 S. Reinprecht, LosA. RC**	**30.00**
☐	**125 L. Visnovsky, LosA. RC**	**15.00**
☐	126 Manny Fernandez (G), MinW.	8.00
☐	**127 M. Gaborik, MinW. RC**	**100.00**
☐	128 Filip Kuba, MinW.	4.00
☐	129 Mathieu Garon (G), Mont.	8.00
☐	130 Andrei Markov, Mont.	4.00
☐	**131 S. Hartnell, Nash. RC**	**20.00**
☐	**132 Colin White, NJer. RC**	**15.00**
☐	**133 R. DiPietro (G), NYIs. RC**	**45.00**
☐	134 Taylor Pyatt, NYIs.	4.00
☐	**135 Martin Havlat, Otta. RC**	**60.00**
☐	**136 J. Hurme (G), Otta. RC**	**20.00**
☐	**137 R. Cechmanek (G), Phil. RC**	**40.00**
☐	**138 Justin Williams, Phil. RC**	**30.00**
☐	139 Robert Esche (G), Phoe.	4.00
☐	140 Wyatt Smith, Phoe.	4.00
☐	**141 O. Väänänen, Phoe. RC**	**15.00**
☐	142 Milan Kraft, Pitt.	6.00
☐	143 Brent Johnson (G), SLou.	8.00
☐	144 Ladislav Nagy, SLou.	4.00
☐	145 Evgeni Nabokov (G), SanJ.	12.00
☐	146 Sheldon Keefe, Tamp.	4.00
☐	147 Brad Richards, Tamp.	9.00
☐	**148 Petr Svoboda, Toro. RC**	**15.00**
☐	149 Daniel Sedin, Vanc.	8.00
☐	150 Henrik Sedin, Vanc.	8.00

COSMIC FORCE

Insert Set (10 cards): **175.00**

	Insert (1:73 packs)	CF
☐	1 Paul Kariya, Anah.	20.00
☐	2 Dominik Hasek (G), Buff.	15.00
☐	3 Peter Forsberg, Colo.	20.00
☐	4 Patrick Roy (G), Colo.	45.00
☐	5 Steve Yzerman, Detr.	35.00
☐	6 Pavel Bure, Flor.	10.00
☐	7 Martin Brodeur (G), NJer.	25.00
☐	8 Eric Lindros, Phil.	15.00
☐	9 Jaromir Jagr, Pitt.	15.00
☐	10 Curtis Joseph (G), Toro.	15.00

DUAL GAME-WORN JERSEY

Insert Set (20 cards): **225.00**

	Description	DJ
☐	1 J. Thornton ✄ / S. Samsonov ✄	25.00
☐	2 P. Forsberg ✄ / M. Sundin ✄	100.00
☐	3 J. Sakic ✄ / E. Lindros ✄	50.00
☐	4 D. Hatcher ✄ / M. Modano ✄	20.00
☐	5 B. Shanahan ✄ / C. Chelios ✄	30.00
☐	6 S. Fedorov ✄ / C. Osgood ✄	30.00
☐	7 D. Weight ✄ / R. Smyth ✄	15.00
☐	8 B. Holik ✄ / M. Czerkawski ✄	12.00
☐	9 J. Vanbiesbrouck ✄ / M. Richter ✄	35.00
☐	10 A. Zhamnov ✄ / C. Stillman ✄	12.00
☐	11 C. Ronning ✄ / V. Yachmenev ✄	12.00
☐	12 T. Fitzgerald ✄ / K. Timonen ✄	12.00
☐	13 B. Dafoe ✄ / D. McCarty ✄	12.00
☐	14 K. McLaren ✄ / B. Dafoe ✄	12.00
☐	15 J. Lehtinen ✄ / J. Langenbrunner ✄	12.00
☐	16 É. Dazé ✄ / M. McInnis ✄	12.00
☐	17 A. Dackell ✄ / U. Dahlén ✄	12.00
☐	18 S. Corson ✄ / J. Hackett ✄	12.00
☐	19 C. Terreri ✄ / B. Dafoe ✄	12.00
☐	20 S. Niedermayer ✄ / C. Lapointe ✄	15.00

DUAL GAME-WORN JERSEY PATCH

Insert Set (19 cards):

	Description	DJP
☐	1 J. Thornton ✄ / S. Samsonov ✄	55.00
☐	2 P. Forsberg ✄ / M. Sundin ✄	150.00
☐	3 J. Sakic ✄ / E. Lindros ✄	150.00
☐	4 D. Hatcher ✄ / M. Modano ✄	40.00
☐	5 B. Shanahan ✄ / C. Chelios ✄	85.00
☐	6 S. Fedorov ✄ / C. Osgood ✄	
☐	7 D. Weight ✄ / R. Smyth ✄	30.00
☐	8 B. Holik ✄ / M. Czerkawski ✄	20.00
☐	10 A. Zhamnov ✄ / C. Stillman ✄	
☐	11 C. Ronning ✄ / V. Yachmenev ✄	
☐	12 T. Fitzgerald ✄ / K. Timonen ✄	
☐	13 B. Dafoe ✄ / D. McCarty ✄	20.00
☐	14 K. McLaren ✄ / B. Dafoe ✄	
☐	15 J. Lehtinen ✄ / J. Langenbrunner ✄	35.00
☐	16 É. Dazé ✄ / M. McInnis ✄	
☐	17 A. Dackell ✄ / U. Dahlén ✄	20.00
☐	18 S. Corson ✄ / J. Hackett ✄	45.00
☐	19 C. Terreri ✄ / B. Dafoe ✄	30.00
☐	20 S. Niedermayer ✄ / C. Lapointe ✄	

HIGH VOLTAGE

There are five versions: the regular insert (1:1 packs), the Red parallel (#/299), the Gold parallel (#/199), the Green parallel (#/99) and the Silver parallel (#/10).

Insert Set (36 cards): **15.00**

	Inserts	HV
☐	1 Paul Kariya, Anah.	2.50
☐	2 Teemu Selänne, Anah.	1.50
☐	3 Jason Allison, Bost.	1.00
☐	4 Joe Thornton, Bost.	2.00
☐	5 Dominik Hasek (G), Buff.	2.00
☐	6 Raymond Bourque, Colo.	2.00
☐	7 Peter Forsberg, Colo.	2.50
☐	8 Patrick Roy (G), Colo.	6.00
☐	9 Joe Sakic, Colo.	3.00
☐	10 Ed Belfour (G), Dall.	2.00
☐	11 Brett Hull, Dall.	2.00
☐	12 Mike Modano, Dall.	2.00
☐	13 Brendan Shanahan, Detr.	2.00
☐	14 Steve Yzerman, Detr.	4.50
☐	15 Doug Weight, Edmo.	1.00
☐	16 Pavel Bure, Flor.	1.50
☐	17 Zigmund Palffy, LosA.	1.00
☐	18 Marian Gaborik, MinW.	8.00
☐	19 Martin Brodeur (G), NJer.	3.00
☐	20 Scott Gomez, NJer.	.75
☐	21 Rick DiPietro (G), NYIs.	3.50
☐	22 Theoren Fleury, NYRa.	1.00
☐	23 Mark Messier, NYRa.	2.00
☐	24 Marian Hossa, Otta.	2.00
☐	25 John LeClair, Phil.	1.50
☐	26 Eric Lindros, Phil.	2.00
☐	27 Jeremy Roenick, Phoe.	1.50
☐	28 Keith Tkachuk, Phoe.	1.00
☐	29 Jaromir Jagr, Pitt.	2.00
☐	30 Pierre Turgeon, SLou.	.75
☐	31 Vincent Lecavalier, Tamp.	2.00
☐	32 Curtis Joseph (G), Toro.	2.00
☐	33 Mats Sundin, Toro.	2.00
☐	34 Daniel Sedin, Vanc.	1.50
☐	35 Henrik Sedin, Vanc.	1.50
☐	36 Peter Bondra, Wash.	1.00

HIGH VOLTAGE

	Insert Set (36 cards):	2,100	400	200.00	75.00
	Inserts	**S10**	**G99**	**G199**	**R299**
☐☐☐☐	1 Paul Kariya	275.00	55.00	25.00	10.00
☐☐☐☐	2 Teemu Selänne	150.00	30.00	15.00	5.00
☐☐☐☐	3 Jason Allison	100.00	20.00	10.00	5.00
☐☐☐☐	4 Joe Thornton	225.00	45.00	20.00	10.00
☐☐☐☐	5 Dominik Hasek (G)	200.00	40.00	20.00	10.00
☐☐☐☐	6 R. Bourque	225.00	45.00	20.00	10.00
☐☐☐☐	7 Peter Forsberg	275.00	55.00	25.00	10.00
☐☐☐☐	8 Patrick Roy (G)	600.00	120.00	60.00	30.00
☐☐☐☐	9 Joe Sakic	300.00	60.00	30.00	15.00
☐☐☐☐	10 Ed Belfour (G)	200.00	40.00	20.00	10.00
☐☐☐☐	11 Brett Hull	200.00	40.00	20.00	10.00
☐☐☐☐	12 Mike Modano	200.00	40.00	20.00	10.00
☐☐☐☐	13 B. Shanahan	200.00	40.00	20.00	10.00
☐☐☐☐	14 Steve Yzerman	475.00	95.00	45.00	20.00
☐☐☐☐	15 Doug Weight	100.00	20.00	10.00	5.00
☐☐☐☐	16 Pavel Bure	150.00	30.00	15.00	5.00
☐☐☐☐	17 Zigmund Palffy	100.00	20.00	10.00	5.00
☐☐☐☐	18 Marian Gaborik	400.00	80.00	40.00	20.00
☐☐☐☐	19 M. Brodeur (G)	300.00	60.00	30.00	15.00
☐☐☐☐	20 Scott Gomez	75.00	15.00	5.00	3.00
☐☐☐☐	21 Rick DiPietro (G)	175.00	35.00	15.00	5.00
☐☐☐☐	22 Theoren Fleury	100.00	20.00	10.00	5.00
☐☐☐☐	23 Mark Messier	200.00	40.00	20.00	10.00
☐☐☐☐	24 Marian Hossa	200.00	40.00	20.00	10.00
☐☐☐☐	25 John LeClair	150.00	30.00	15.00	5.00
☐☐☐☐	26 Eric Lindros	200.00	40.00	20.00	10.00
☐☐☐☐	27 Jeremy Roenick	150.00	30.00	15.00	5.00
☐☐☐☐	28 Keith Tkachuk	100.00	20.00	10.00	5.00
☐☐☐☐	29 Jaromir Jagr	200.00	40.00	20.00	10.00
☐☐☐☐	30 Pierre Turgeon	75.00	15.00	5.00	3.00
☐☐☐☐	31 Vincent Lecavalier	200.00	40.00	20.00	10.00
☐☐☐☐	32 Curtis Joseph (G)	200.00	40.00	20.00	10.00
☐☐☐☐	33 Mats Sundin	200.00	40.00	20.00	10.00
☐☐☐☐	34 Daniel Sedin	100.00	20.00	10.00	5.00
☐☐☐☐	35 Henrik Sedin	100.00	20.00	10.00	5.00
☐☐☐☐	36 Peter Bondra	100.00	20.00	10.00	5.00

IN FOCUS

Insert Set (20 cards): **20.00**

	Insert (1:25 packs)	IF
☐	1 Paul Kariya, Anah.	4.00
☐	2 Teemu Selänne, Anah.	2.00
☐	3 Jason Allison, Bost.	2.00
☐	4 Raymond Bourque, Colo.	3.00
☐	5 Peter Forsberg, Colo.	4.00
☐	6 Patrick Roy (G), Colo.	9.00
☐	7 Brett Hull, Dall.	3.00
☐	8 Sergei Fedorov, Detr.	3.00
☐	9 Steve Yzerman, Detr.	7.00
☐	10 Pavel Bure, Flor.	2.00
☐	11 Marian Gaborik, MinW.	9.00
☐	12 Martin Brodeur (G), NJer.	4.00
☐	13 Theoren Fleury, NYRa.	2.00
☐	14 John LeClair, Phil.	2.00
☐	15 Jaromir Jagr, Pitt.	3.00
☐	16 Vincent Lecavalier, Tamp.	3.00
☐	17 Curtis Joseph (G), Toro.	3.00
☐	18 Mats Sundin, Toro.	3.00
☐	19 Daniel Sedin, Vanc.	2.00
☐	20 Henrik Sedin, Vanc.	2.00

VANGUARD PRESS

Cards 1-10 were seeded in Hobby packs while cards 11-20 were seeded in Retail packs.

Insert Set (20 cards): **50.00**

	Hobby Insert (2:25)	Hobby
☐	1 Paul Kariya, Anah.	4.00
☐	2 Teemu Selänne, Anah.	2.00
☐	3 Peter Forsberg, Colo.	4.00
☐	4 Patrick Roy (G), Colo.	9.00
☐	5 Brett Hull, Dall.	3.00
☐	6 Sergei Fedorov, Detr.	3.00
☐	7 Steve Yzerman, Detr.	7.00
☐	8 Zigmund Palffy, LosA.	2.00
☐	9 Jeremy Roenick, Phoe.	2.00
☐	10 Pierre Turgeon, SLou.	2.00
	Retail Insert (2:25)	**Retail**
☐	11 Joe Thornton, Bost.	5.00
☐	12 Dominik Hasek (G), Buff.	4.00
☐	13 Pavel Bure, Flor.	3.00
☐	14 Martin Brodeur (G), NJer.	7.00
☐	15 Mark Messier, NYRa.	4.00
☐	16 Alexei Yashin, Otta.	3.00
☐	17 Eric Lindros, Phil.	4.00
☐	18 Jaromir Jagr, Pitt.	4.00
☐	19 Vincent Lecavalier, Tamp.	4.00
☐	20 Curtis Joseph (G), Toro.	4.00

2000 - 01 VICTORY

This series was released in August 2000.

Complete Set (330 cards): **30.00**

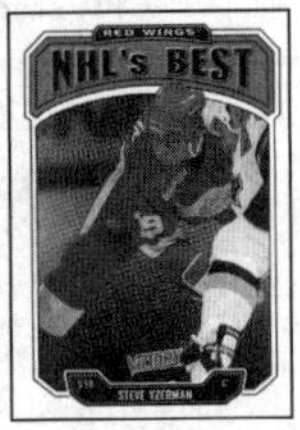

Common Player: .20

Player	Reg.
1 Paul Kariya, Anah. [CL]	.50
2 Ladislav Kohn, Anah.	.20
3 Vitaly Vishnevski, Anah.	.20
4 Steve Rucchin, Anah.	.20
5 Oleg Tverdovsky, Anah.	.20
6 Guy Hebert (G), Anah.	.20
7 Teemu Selänne, Anah.	.50
8 Paul Kariya, Anah.	.50
9 Patrik Stefan, Atla. [CL]	.20
10 Andrew Brunette, Atla.	.20
11 Patrik Stefan, Atla.	.20
12 Donald Audette, Atla.	.20
13 Damian Rhodes (G), Atla.	.20
14 Maxim Galanov, Atla.	.20
15 Dean Sylvester, Atla.	.20
16 Ray Ferraro, Atla.	.20
17 Joe Thornton, Bost. [CL]	.20
18 Brian Rolston, Bost.	.20
19 Sergei Samsonov, Bost.	.20
20 Joe Thornton, Bost.	.50
21 Byron Dafoe (G), Bost.	.20
22 Jason Allison, Bost.	.20
23 Anson Carter, Bost.	.20
24 Hal Gill, Bost.	.20
25 Dominik Hasek (G), Buff. [CL]	.20
26 Dominik Hasek (G), Buff.	.50
27 Michael Peca, Buff.	.20
28 Miroslav Satan, Buff.	.20
29 Doug Gilmour, Buff.	.20
30 Chris Gratton, Buff.	.20
31 Curtis Brown, Buff.	.20
32 Maxim Afinogenov, Buff.	.20
33 Jay McKee, Buff.	.20
34 Valeri Bure, Calg. [CL]	.20
35 Valeri Bure, Calg.	.20
36 Fred Brathwaite (G), Calg.	.20
37 Jarome Iginla, Calg.	.50
38 Phil Housley, Calg.	.20
39 Derek Morris, Calg.	.20
40 Cory Stillman, Calg.	.20
41 Marc Savard, Calg.	.20
42 Ron Francis, Caro. [CL]	.20
43 Sami Kapanen, Caro.	.20
44 Arturs Irbe (G), Caro.	.20
45 Rod Brind'Amour, Caro.	.20
46 Gary Roberts, Caro.	.20
47 Ron Francis, Caro.	.20
48 Paul Coffey, Caro.	.20
49 Jeff O'Neill, Caro.	.20
50 Tony Amonte, Chic. [CL]	.20
51 Tony Amonte, Chic.	.20
52 Steve Sullivan, Chic.	.20
53 Michal Grosek, Chic.	.20
54 Boris Mironov, Chic.	.20
55 Jocelyn Thibault (G), Chic.	.20
56 Alexei Zhamnov, Chic.	.20
57 Éric Dazé, Chic.	.20
58 Peter Forsberg, Colo. [CL]	.50
59 Chris Drury, Colo.	.20
60 Peter Forsberg, Colo.	.50
61 Patrick Roy (G), Colo.	1.50
62 Joe Sakic, Colo.	1.00
63 Raymond Bourque, Colo.	.50
64 Adam Deadmarsh, Colo.	.20
65 Milan Hejduk, Colo.	.50
66 Sandis Ozolinsh, Colo.	.20
67 Alex Tanguay, Colo.	.20
68 Adam Foote, Colo.	.20
69 Columbus Blue Jackets [CL]	.20
70 Mike Modano, Dall. [CL]	.20
71 Ed Belfour (G), Dall.	.50
72 Brett Hull, Dall.	.50
73 Sergei Zubov, Dall.	.20
74 Brenden Morrow, Dall.	.20
75 Jamie Langenbrunner, Dall.	.20
76 Joe Nieuwendyk, Dall.	.20
77 Mike Modano, Dall.	.50
78 Derian Hatcher, Dall.	.20
79 Jere Lehtinen, Dall.	.20
80 Roman Lyashenko, Dall.	.20
81 Steve Yzerman, Detr. [CL]	.50
82 Brendan Shanahan, Detr.	.50
83 Steve Yzerman, Detr.	1.50
84 Chris Chelios, Detr.	.20
85 Sergei Fedorov, Detr.	.50
86 Vyacheslav Kozlov, Detr.	.20
87 Pat Verbeek, Detr.	.20
88 Nicklas Lidström, Detr.	.20
89 Tomas Holmström, Detr.	.20
90 Chris Osgood (G), Detr.	.20
91 Martin Lapointe, Detr.	.20
92 Doug Weight, Edmo. [CL]	.20
93 Bill Guerin, Edmo.	.20
94 Tom Poti, Edmo.	.20
95 Mike Grier, Edmo.	.20
96 Tommy Salo (G), Edmo.	.20
97 Doug Weight, Edmo.	.20
98 Ryan Smyth, Edmo.	.20
99 Alexander Selivanov, Edmo.	.20
100 Pavel Bure, Flor. [CL]	.20
101 Pavel Bure, Flor.	.50
102 Mark Parrish, Flor.	.20
103 Scott Mellanby, Flor.	.20
104 Viktor Kozlov, Flor.	.20
105 Oleg Kvasha, Flor.	.20
106 Ray Whitney, Flor.	.20
107 Trevor Kidd (G), Flor.	.20
108 Rob Blake, LosA. [CL]	.20
109 Rob Blake, LosA.	.20
110 Jere Karalahti, LosA.	.20
111 Luc Robitaille, LosA.	.50
112 Jozef Stumpel, LosA.	.20
113 Glen Murray, LosA.	.20
114 Zigmund Palffy, LosA.	.20
115 Bryan Smolinski, LosA.	.20
116 Minnesota Wild [CL]	.20
117 Saku Koivu, Mont. [CL]	.20
118 Saku Koivu, Mont.	.50
119 Sergei Zholtok, Mont.	.20
120 Eric Weinrich, Mont.	.20
121 José Théodore (G), Mont.	.50
122 Martin Rucinsky, Mont.	.20
123 Brian Savage, Mont.	.20
124 Shayne Corson, Mont.	.20
125 Dainius Zubrus, Mont.	.20
126 David Legwand, Nash. [CL]	.20
127 Mike Dunham (G), Nash.	.20
128 David Legwand, Nash.	.20
129 Greg Johnson, Nash.	.20
130 Cliff Ronning, Nash.	.20
131 Kimmo Timonen, Nash.	.20
132 Patric Kjellberg, Nash.	.20
133 Drake Berehowsky, Nash.	.20
134 Martin Brodeur (G), NJer. [CL]	.50
135 Martin Brodeur (G), NJer.	1.00
136 John Madden, NJer.	.20
137 Scott Gomez, NJer.	.20
138 Patrik Elias, NJer.	.50
139 Scott Stevens, NJer.	.20
140 Jason Arnott, NJer.	.20
141 Alexander Mogilny, NJer.	.20
142 Tim Connolly, NYIs. [CL]	.20
143 Dave Scatchard, NYIs.	.20
144 Tim Connolly, NYIs.	.20
145 Kenny Jönsson, NYIs.	.20
146 Claude Lapointe, NYIs.	.20
147 Mariusz Czerkawski, NYIs.	.20
148 Brad Isbister, NYIs.	.20
149 Olli Jokinen, NYIs.	.20
150 Theoren Fleury, NYRa. [CL]	.20
151 Mike Richter (G), NYRa.	.20
152 Theoren Fleury, NYRa.	.20
153 Adam Graves, NYRa.	.20
154 Brian Leetch, NYRa.	.20
155 Petr Nedved, NYRa.	.20
156 Radek Dvorak, NYRa.	.20
157 Mike York, NYRa.	.20
158 Marian Hossa, Otta. [CL]	.20
159 Marian Hossa, Otta.	.50
160 Radek Bonk, Otta.	.20
161 Shawn McEachern, Otta.	.20
162 Vaclav Prospal, Otta.	.20
163 Daniel Alfredsson, Otta.	.20
164 Magnus Arvedson, Otta.	.20
165 Wade Redden, Otta.	.20
166 John LeClair, Phil. [CL]	.20
167 John LeClair, Phil.	.50
168 Eric Lindros, Phil.	.50
169 Mark Recchi, Phil.	.20
170 Keith Primeau, Phil.	.20
171 Éric Desjardins, Phil.	.20
172 Brian Boucher (G), Phil.	.20
173 Daymond Langkow, Phil.	.20
174 Simon Gagné, Phil.	.50
175 Jeremy Roenick, Phoe. [CL]	.20
176 Mikael Renberg, Phoe.	.20
177 Keith Tkachuk, Phoe.	.20
178 Sean Burke (G), Phoe.	.20
179 Trevor Letowski, Phoe.	.20
180 Shane Doan, Phoe.	.20
181 Jeremy Roenick, Phoe.	.50
182 Travis Green, Phoe.	.20
183 Jaromir Jagr, Pitt. [CL]	.20
184 Jaromir Jagr, Pitt.	.50
185 Matthew Barnaby, Pitt.	.20
186 Robert Lang, Pitt.	.20
187 Jan Hrdina, Pitt.	.20
188 Martin Straka, Pitt.	.20
189 Ron Tugnutt (G), Pitt.	.20
190 Alexei Kovalev, Pitt.	.20
191 Jeff Friesen, SanJ. [CL]	.20
192 Vincent Damphousse, SanJ.	.20
193 Jeff Friesen, SanJ.	.20
194 Brad Stuart, SanJ.	.20
195 Patrick Marleau, SanJ.	.20
196 Mike Ricci, SanJ.	.20
197 Owen Nolan, SanJ.	.20
198 Steve Shields (G), SanJ.	.20
199 Chris Pronger, SLou. [CL]	.20
200 Pavol Demitra, SLou.	.20
201 Al MacInnis, SLou.	.20
202 Lubos Bartecko, SLou.	.20
203 Jochen Hecht, SLou.	.20
204 Chris Pronger, SLou.	.20
205 Roman Turek (G), SLou.	.20
206 Michal Handzus, SLou.	.20
207 Pierre Turgeon, SLou.	.20
208 Vincent Lecavalier, Tamp. [CL]	.20
209 Vincent Lecavalier, Tamp.	.50
210 Paul Mara, Tamp.	.20
211 Mike Johnson, Tamp.	.20
212 Dan Cloutier (G), Tamp.	.20
213 Wayne Primeau, Tamp.	.20
214 Pavel Kubina, Tamp.	.20
215 Fredrik Modin, Tamp.	.20
216 Mats Sundin, Toro. [CL]	.20
217 Mats Sundin, Toro.	.50
218 Darcy Tucker, Toro.	.20
219 Sergei Berezin, Toro.	.20
220 Curtis Joseph (G), Toro.	.50
221 Jonas Höglund, Toro.	.20
222 Nikolai Antropov, Toro.	.20
223 Steve Thomas, Toro.	.20
224 Tie Domi, Toro.	.20
225 Mark Messier, Vanc. [CL]	.20
226 Mark Messier, Vanc.	.50
227 Andrew Cassels, Vanc.	.20
228 Brendan Morrison, Vanc.	.20
229 Markus Näslund, Vanc.	.50
230 Félix Potvin (G), Vanc.	.20
231 Ed Jovanovski, Vanc.	.20
232 Harold Druken, Vanc.	.20
233 Olaf Kölzig (G), Wash. [CL]	.20
234 Peter Bondra, Wash.	.20
235 Adam Oates, Wash.	.20
236 Jan Bulis, Wash.	.20
237 Jeff Halpern, Wash.	.20
238 Sergei Gonchar, Wash.	.20
239 Olaf Kölzig (G), Wash.	.20
240 Chris Simon, Wash.	.20
241 P. Bure / V.Bure [Season Highlights]	.20
242 P. Kariya / S. Kariya [Season Highlights]	.50
243 Dominik Hasek (G), Buff. [Season Highlights]	.50
244 Patrick Roy (G), Colo. [Season Highlights]	1.50
245 Joe Sakic, Colo. [Season Highlights]	1.00
246 Raymond Bourque, Colo. [Season Highlights]	.50
247 Brett Hull, Dall. [Season Highlights]	.50
248 Brendan Shanahan, Detr. [Season Highlights]	.50
249 Steve Yzerman, Detr. [Season Highlights]	1.50
250 Pat Verbeek, Detr. [Season Highlights]	.20
251 Pavel Bure, Flor. [Season Highlights]	.50
252 Scott Gomez, NJer. [Season Highlights]	.20
253 John LeClair, Phil. [Season Highlights]	.50
254 Brian Boucher (G), Phil. [Season Highlights]	.20
255 Jeremy Roenick, Phoe. [Season Highlights]	.50
256 Jaromir Jagr, Pitt. [Season Highlights]	.50
257 Chris Pronger, SLou. [Season Highlights]	.20
258 Roman Turek (G), SLou. [Season Highlights]	.20
259 Curtis Joseph (G), Toro. [Season Highlights]	.50
260 Wayne Gretzky [Season Highlights]	2.50
261 S. Aubin / D. Hinote RC [Prospects]	**.50**
262 A. Savage / B. Smith RC [Prospects]	**.50**
263 K. Aldridge RC / R. Christie [Prospects]	**.50**
264 B. Chartrand / S. Reinprecht RC [Prospects]	**1.00**
265 J. Krog / P. Mika RC [Prospects]	**.50**
266 V. Orszagh / S. Valiquette RC [Prospects]	**.50**
267 K. Freadrich RC / C. Sarich [Prospects]	**.50**
268 E. Nickulas RC / J. Prpic [Prospects]	**.50**
269 D. Gosselin RC / R. Lintner [Prospects]	**.50**
270 G. Andrusak RC / N. Dempsey [Prospects]	**.50**
271 A. Michaud / B. Sopel RC [Prospects]	**.50**
272 M.BalmochnykhRC /J. StevensonRC[Prospects]	**.50**
273 S. Fankhouser / A. Karlsson [Prospects]	.20
274 B. Ritchie / D. Tanabe [Prospects]	.20
275 K. Calder / S. McCarthy [Prospects]	.20
276 M. Fisher / P. Schastlivy [Prospects]	.20
277 A. Delmore / M. Eaton [Prospects]	.20
278 S. Hannan / E. Nabokov [Prospects]	.20
279 D. Heatley RC / J. Svoboda RC [Prospects]	**4.50**
280 C. Nielsen RC / M. Pettinger RC [Prospects]	**.50**
281 Teemu Selänne, Anah. [NHL's Best]	.50
282 Paul Kariya, Anah. [NHL's Best]	1.00
283 Patrik Stefan, Atla. [NHL's Best]	.30
284 Sergei Samsonov, Bost. [NHL's Best]	.30
285 Joe Thornton, Bost. [NHL's Best]	.50
286 Dominik Hasek (G), Buff. [NHL's Best]	.50
287 Doug Gilmour, Buff. [NHL's Best]	.30
288 Valeri Bure, Calg. [NHL's Best]	.30
289 Ron Francis, Caro. [NHL's Best]	.30
290 Tony Amonte, Chic. [NHL's Best]	.30
291 Peter Forsberg, Colo. [NHL's Best]	1.00
292 Patrick Roy (G), Colo. [NHL's Best]	2.00
293 Joe Sakic, Colo. [NHL's Best]	1.00
294 Raymond Bourque, Colo. [NHL's Best]	.50
295 Milan Hejduk, Colo. [NHL's Best]	.50
296 Ed Belfour (G), Dall. [NHL's Best]	.50
297 Brett Hull, Dall. [NHL's Best]	.50
298 Mike Modano, Dall. [NHL's Best]	.50
299 Brendan Shanahan, Detr. [NHL's Best]	.50
300 Steve Yzerman, Detr. [NHL's Best]	1.50
301 Sergei Fedorov, Detr. [NHL's Best]	.50
302 Chris Osgood (G), Detr. [NHL's Best]	.30
303 Doug Weight, Edmo. [NHL's Best]	.30
304 Pavel Bure, Flor. [NHL's Best]	.50
305 Zigmund Palffy, LosA. [NHL's Best]	.30
306 Rob Blake, LosA. [NHL's Best]	.30
307 Saku Koivu, Mont. [NHL's Best]	.50
308 David Legwand, Nash. [NHL's Best]	.30
309 Martin Brodeur (G), NJer. [NHL's Best]	1.00
310 Scott Gomez, NJer. [NHL's Best]	.30
311 Tim Connolly, NYIs. [NHL's Best]	.30
312 Theoren Fleury, NYRa. [NHL's Best]	.30
313 Marian Hossa, Otta. [NHL's Best]	.50
314 John LeClair, Phil. [NHL's Best]	.50
315 Eric Lindros, Phil. [NHL's Best]	.50
316 Keith Tkachuk, Phoe. [NHL's Best]	.30
317 Jeremy Roenick, Phoe. [NHL's Best]	.50
318 Jaromir Jagr, Pitt. [NHL's Best]	.50
319 Jeff Friesen, SanJ. [NHL's Best]	.30
320 Owen Nolan, SanJ. [NHL's Best]	.30
321 Al MacInnis, SLou. [NHL's Best]	.30
322 Pavol Demitra, SLou. [NHL's Best]	.30
323 Chris Pronger, SLou. [NHL's Best]	.30
324 Roman Turek (G), SLou. [NHL's Best]	.30
325 Vincent Lecavalier, Tamp. [NHL's Best]	.50
326 Mats Sundin, Toro. [NHL's Best]	.50
327 Curtis Joseph (G), Toro. [NHL's Best]	.50
328 Mark Messier, Vanc. [NHL's Best]	.50
329 Peter Bondra, Wash. [NHL's Best]	.30
330 Olaf Kölzig (G), Wash. [NHL's Best]	.30

Player	MT
www.victorycards.com (Pavel Bure)	.10

2001 UPPER DECK PROSPECTS GAME USED EDITION

Produced by The Upper Deck Company, this series was released in 2001.

Complete Set (45 cards): 50.00
Common Player: 1.00

Description	Base
1 Jason Spezza, CHL Prospect	6.00
2 Dan Blackburn (G), CHL Prospect	4.00
3 Daniel Boisclair, CHL Prospect	1.00
4 Jeff Woytwitka, CHL Prospect	1.50
5 Matthew Spiller, CHL Prospect	1.00
6 Nathan Paetsch, CHL Prospect	1.00
7 Mark Popovic, CHL Prospect	1.00
8 Jay McClement, CHL Prospect	1.00
9 Garth Murray, CHL Prospect	1.00
10 Aaron Lobb, CHL Prospect	1.00
11 Derek Roy, CHL Prospect	4.00
12 Jean-François Soucy, CHL Prospect	1.00
13 Nicolas Corbeil, CHL Prospect	1.00
14 Colt King, CHL Prospect	1.00
15 Robin Leblanc, CHL Prospect	1.00
16 Jay Harrison, CHL Prospect	1.00
17 Jiri Jakes, CHL Prospect	1.00
18 Lukas Krajicek, CHL Prospect	2.00
19 Jason Pominville, CHL Prospect	1.00
20 Shawn Collymore, CHL Prospect	1.00

□	21 Michael Garnett (G), CHL Prospect	1.50
□	22 Adam Munro, CHL Prospect	1.00
□	23 Dan Hamhuis, CHL Prospect	2.00
□	24 Doug Lynch, CHL Prospect	1.00
□	25 Shaone Morrisonn, CHL Prospect	2.00
□	26 Carlo Colaicovo, CHL Prospect	1.00
□	27 Stephen Weiss, CHL Prospect	4.00
□	28 Joel Stepp, CHL Prospect	1.00
□	29 Jeff Lucky, CHL Prospect	1.00
□	30 Cory Stillman, CHL Prospect	1.00
□	31 Chris Thorburn, CHL Prospect	1.00
□	32 Colby Armstrong, CHL Prospect	1.00
□	33 Brent MacLellan, CHL Prospect	1.00
□	34 Jordin Tootoo, CHL Prospect	8.00
□	35 Greg Watson, CHL Prospect	1.00
□	36 Martin Podlesak, CHL Prospect	1.00
□	37 Duncan Milroy, CHL Prospect	2.00
□	38 Frantisek Bakrlik, CHL Prospect	1.00
□	39 Brandon Bell, CHL Prospect	1.00
□	40 Kiel McLeod, CHL Prospect	1.00
□	41 Jason Spezza, Mississauga	4.00
□	42 Jason Spezza, Mississauga	4.00
□	43 Jason Spezza, Mississauga	4.00
□	44 Jason Spezza	4.00

SIGNATURES OF TRADITION

Insert Set (23 cards):		**675.00**
	Insert (1:6)	**SoT**
□	Dan Blackburn (G), ✍	40.00
□	Jay Bouwmeester, Tigers ✍	45.00
□	Michael Garnett, Team Orr ✍	15.00
□	Wayne Gretzky, Greyhounds ✍	200.00
□	Dan Hamhuis, Team Orr ✍	15.00
□	Jay Harrison, Team Cherry ✍	15.00
□	Colt King, Team Cherry ✍	15.00
□	Rostislav Klesla, Batallion ✍	30.00
□	Brent Krahn, Hitmen ✍	20.00
□	Pascal Leclaire, Mooseheads ✍	30.00
□	Jamie Lundmark, Thunderbirds ✍	30.00
□	Jay McClement, Team Cherry ✍	15.00
□	Kiel McLeod, Team Orr ✍	15.00
□	Duncan Milroy, Team Orr ✍	15.00
□	Adam Munro, Team Orr ✍	15.00
□	Bobby Orr, Generals ✍	200.00
□	Mark Popovic, Team Cherry ✍	15.00
□	Jason Spezza, Team Cherry ✍	60.00
□	Cory Stillman, Team Orr ✍	20.00
□	Chris Thorburn, Team Orr ✍	15.00
□	Raffi Torres, Batallion ✍	20.00
□	Greg Watson, Team Orr ✍	15.00
□	Stephen Weiss, Team Orr ✍	40.00

TPO PROSPECTS JERSEY

Insert Set (41 cards):		**550.00**
	Insert (1:1)	**J**
□	Colby Armstrong, Team Orr ✂	12.00
□	Frantisek Bakrlik, Team Orr ✂	12.00
□	Brandon Bell, Team Orr ✂ White	12.00
□	Dan Blackburn (G), Team Orr ✂	40.00
□	Daniel Boisclair, Team Cherry ✂	12.00
□	Shawn Collymore, Team Cherry ✂	12.00
□	Nicolas Corbeil, Team Cherry ✂	12.00
□	Michael Garnett, Team Orr ✂	15.00
□	Dan Hamhuis, Team Orr ✂	12.00
□	Jay Harrison, Team Cherry ✂	12.00
□	Jiri Jakes, Team Cherry ✂	12.00
□	Colt King, Team Cherry ✂	12.00
□	Lukas Krajicek, Team Cherry ✂	20.00
□	Robin Leblanc, Team Cherry ✂	12.00
□	Aaron Lobb, Team Cherry ✂	12.00
□	Jeff Lucky, Team Orr ✂	12.00
□	Doug Lynch, Team Orr ✂	12.00
□	Brent Maclellan, Team Orr ✂	12.00
□	Jay McClement, Team Cherry ✂	12.00
□	Kiel McLeod, Team Orr ✂	12.00
□	Duncan Milroy, Team Orr ✂	12.00
□	Shaone Morrisonn, Team Orr ✂	20.00
□	Adam Munro, Team Orr ✂	12.00
□	Garth Murray, Team Cherry ✂	12.00
□	Nathan Paetsch, Team Cherry ✂	12.00
□	Martin Podlesak, Team Orr ✂	12.00
□	Jason Pominville, Team Cherry ✂	12.00
□	Mark Popovic, Team Cherry ✂	12.00
□	Derek Roy, Team Cherry ✂	25.00
□	Jean-Francois Soucy, Team Cherry ✂	12.00
□	Jason Spezza, Team Cherry ✂ Purple	60.00
□	Jason Spezza, Spitfires ✂ White	60.00
□	Jason Spezza, Spitfires ✂ Blue	60.00
□	Matthew Spiller, Team Cherry ✂	12.00
□	Joel Stepp, Team Orr ✂	12.00
□	Cory Stillman, Team Orr ✂	12.00
□	Chris Thorburn, Team Orr ✂	12.00
□	Jordin Tootoo, Team Orr ✂	60.00
□	Greg Watson, Team Orr ✂	12.00
□	Stephen Weiss, Team Orr ✂	40.00
□	Jeff Woywitka, Team Cherry ✂	12.00

JERSEY SIGNED

Insert Set (17 cards):		**700.00**
	Insert (#/30)	**JS**
□	Dan Blackburn (G), Team Orr ✍ ✂	50.00
□	Michael Garnett, Team Orr ✍ ✂	50.00
□	Dan Hamhuis, Team Orr ✍ ✂	50.00
□	Jay Harrison, Team Cherry ✍ ✂	50.00
□	Colt King, Team Cherry ✍ ✂	50.00
□	Jay McClement, Team Cherry ✍ ✂	50.00
□	Kiel McLeod, Team Orr ✍ ✂	50.00
□	Duncan Milroy, Team Orr ✍ ✂	50.00
□	Adam Munro, Team Orr ✍ ✂	50.00
□	Mark Popovic, Team Cherry ✍ ✂	50.00
□	Jason Spezza, Team Cherry ✍ ✂	100.00
□	Jason Spezza, Spitfires ✍ ✂ White	100.00
□	Jason Spezza, Spitfires ✍ ✂ Blue	100.00
□	Cory Stillman, Team Orr ✍ ✂	50.00
□	Chris Thorburn, Team Orr ✍ ✂	50.00
□	Greg Watson, Team Orr ✍ ✂	50.00
□	Stephen Weiss, Team Orr ✍ ✂	50.00

JERSEY COMBO

Insert Set (21 cards):		**300.00**
	Insert (#/125)	**JC**
□	D. Blackburn ✂ / D. Milroy ✂	30.00
□	D. Boisclair ✂ / M. Garnett ✂	30.00
□	D. Blackburn ✂ / A. Munro ✂	30.00
□	D. Blackburn ✂ / J. Spezza ✂	85.00
□	D. Blackburn ✂ / S. Weiss ✂	70.00
□	J. Harrison ✂ / K. McLeod ✂	30.00
□	D. Hamhuis ✂ / S. Weiss ✂	30.00
□	L. Krajicek ✂ / M. Podlesak ✂	30.00
□	C. King ✂ / G. Watson ✂	30.00
□	J. McClement ✂ / C. Stillman ✂	30.00
□	G. Murray ✂ / C. Thorburn ✂	30.00
□	M. Popovic ✂ / D. Milroy ✂	30.00
□	D. Roy ✂ / J. Tootoo ✂	40.00
□	J. Spezza ✂ / J. Spezza ✂	100.00
□	J. Spezza ✂ / J. Spezza ✂	100.00
□	J. Spezza ✂ / D. Hamhuis ✂	30.00
□	J. Spezza ✂ / D. Milroy ✂	30.00
□	J. Spezza ✂ / J. Spezza ✂	105.00
□	J. Spezza ✂ / S. Weiss ✂	85.00
□	J. Woywitka ✂ / C. Armstrong ✂	30.00
□	S. Weiss ✂ / D. Milroy ✂	30.00

2001 - 02 ADRENALINE

Produced by Pacific Trading Cards, this series was released in December 2001. There are five versions for each card 1-200: a hobby gold-foil base card, a hobby blue-foil parallel (#/62), a hobby Premiere Date parallel (#/62), a retail silver-foil base card, and a retail red-foil parallel (#/54). Hobby gold-foil base cards have the same value as retail silver-foil base cards. Red-foil parallel cards are slightly more expensive (about 5-10%) than blue-foil and Premiere Date parallel cards.

Shell Set (200 cards):		-	**70.00**
Complete Set (225 cards):		**1,800**	**275.00**
Common Player:		**6.00**	**.25**
	Description	**PD62**	**Base**
□□□□□	1 J. Friesen	10.00	.50
□□□□□	2 J-S Giguère (G)	30.00	1.50
□□□□□	3 P. Kariya	55.00	2.50
□□□□□	4 M. McInnis	6.00	.25
□□□□□	5 S. Shields (G)	6.00	.25
□□□□□	6 O. Tverdovsky	6.00	.25
□□□□□	7 R. Ferraro	6.00	.25
□□□□□	8 M. Hnilicka (G)	6.00	.25
□□□□□	9 T. Kallio	6.00	.25
□□□□□	10 D. Rhodes (G)	6.00	.25
□□□□□	11 P. Stefan	10.00	.50
□□□□□	12 B. Dafoe (G)	15.00	.50
□□□□□	13 B. Guerin	15.00	.50
□□□□□	14 M. Lapointe	15.00	.50
□□□□□	15 S. Samsonov	20.00	1.00
□□□□□	16 J. Stümpel	6.00	.25
□□□□□	17 J. Thornton	45.00	2.00
□□□□□	18 S. Barnes	6.00	.25
□□□□□	19 M. Biron (G)	15.00	.50
□□□□□	20 T. Connolly	15.00	.50
□□□□□	21 J. Dumont	6.00	.25
□□□□□	22 C. Gratton	6.00	.25
□□□□□	23 S. Kozlov	6.00	.25
□□□□□	24 M. Satan	10.00	.50
□□□□□	25 J. Iginla	30.00	1.50
□□□□□	26 D. Morris	6.00	.25
□□□□□	27 R. Niedermayer	6.00	.25
□□□□□	28 M. Savard	6.00	.25
□□□□□	29 R. Turek (G)	15.00	.50
□□□□□	30 M. Vernon (G)	15.00	.50
□□□□□	31 R. Brind'Amour	10.00	.50
□□□□□	32 R. Francis	20.00	1.00
□□□□□	33 M. Gélinas	6.00	.25
□□□□□	34 A. Irbe (G)	15.00	.50
□□□□□	35 S. Kapanen	10.00	.50
□□□□□	36 J. O'Neill	15.00	.50
□□□□□	37 S. Willis	6.00	.25
□□□□□	38 T. Amonte	20.00	1.00
□□□□□	39 É. Dazé	15.00	.50
□□□□□	40 M. Nylander	6.00	.25
□□□□□	41 S. Sullivan	10.00	.50
□□□□□	42 J. Thibault (G)	15.00	.50
□□□□□	43 A. Zhamnov	10.00	.50
□□□□□	44 D. Aebischer (G)	10.00	.50
□□□□□	45 R. Blake	20.00	1.00
□□□□□	46 C. Drury	20.00	1.00
□□□□□	47 P. Forsberg	55.00	2.50
□□□□□	48 M. Hejduk	30.00	1.50
□□□□□	49 P. Roy (G)	120.00	6.00
□□□□□	50 J. Sakic	60.00	3.00
□□□□□	51 A. Tanguay	20.00	1.00
□□□□□	52 M. Denis (G)	15.00	.50
□□□□□	53 R. Klesla	20.00	.50
□□□□□	54 E. Knutsen	6.00	.25
□□□□□	55 G. Sanderson	6.00	.25
□□□□□	56 R. Tugnutt (G)	15.00	.50
□□□□□	57 D. Audette	15.00	.50
□□□□□	58 E. Belfour (G)	40.00	2.00
□□□□□	59 M. Modano	40.00	2.00
□□□□□	60 J. Nieuwendyk	15.00	.50
□□□□□	61 M. Turco (G)	20.00	1.00
□□□□□	62 P. Turgeon	15.00	.50
□□□□□	63 C. Chelios	20.00	1.00
□□□□□	64 S. Fedorov	40.00	2.00
□□□□□	65 D. Hasek (G)	40.00	2.00
□□□□□	66 B. Hull	40.00	2.00
□□□□□	67 N. Lidström	20.00	1.00
□□□□□	68 L. Robitaille	30.00	1.50
□□□□□	69 B. Shanahan	40.00	2.00
□□□□□	70 S. Yzerman	95.00	4.50
□□□□□	71 E. Brewer	15.00	.50
□□□□□	72 A. Carter	15.00	.50
□□□□□	73 D. Cleary	10.00	.50
□□□□□	74 M. Comrie	30.00	1.50
□□□□□	75 M. Grier	6.00	.25
□□□□□	76 J. Hecht	6.00	.25
□□□□□	77 T. Salo (G)	15.00	.50
□□□□□	78 R. Smyth	15.00	.50
□□□□□	79 P. Bure	30.00	1.50
□□□□□	80 V. Bure	10.00	.50
□□□□□	81 T. Kidd (G)	10.00	.50
□□□□□	82 V. Kozlov	10.00	.50
□□□□□	83 R. Luongo (G)	30.00	1.50
□□□□□	84 M. Nilson	6.00	.25
□□□□□	85 J. Allison	20.00	1.00
□□□□□	86 A. Deadmarsh	10.00	.50
□□□□□	87 Z. Palffy	20.00	1.00
□□□□□	88 F. Potvin (G)	45.00	1.00
□□□□□	89 M. Schneider	6.00	.25
□□□□□	90 B. Smolinski	6.00	.25
□□□□□	91 M. Fernandez (G)	15.00	.50
□□□□□	92 M. Gaborik	40.00	2.00
□□□□□	93 D. Hendrickson	6.00	.25
□□□□□	94 L. Sekeras	6.00	.25
□□□□□	95 W. Walz	6.00	.25
□□□□□	96 J. Juneau	6.00	.25
□□□□□	97 Y. Perreault	10.00	.50
□□□□□	98 O. Petrov	10.00	.50
□□□□□	99 M. Rucinsky	6.00	.25
□□□□□	100 B. Savage	10.00	.50
□□□□□	101 J. Théodore (G)	45.00	2.00
□□□□□	102 R. Zednik	15.00	.50
□□□□□	103 M. Dunham (G)	15.00	.50
□□□□□	104 S. Hartnell	6.00	.25
□□□□□	105 P. Kjellberg	6.00	.25
□□□□□	106 D. Legwand	15.00	.50
□□□□□	107 C. Ronning	6.00	.25
□□□□□	108 T. Vokoun (G)	6.00	.25
□□□□□	109 S. Walker	6.00	.25
□□□□□	110 J. Arnott	15.00	.50
□□□□□	111 M. Brodeur (G)	60.00	3.00
□□□□□	112 S. Brylin	6.00	.25
□□□□□	113 P. Elias	30.00	1.50
□□□□□	114 S. Gomez	15.00	.50
□□□□□	115 J. Madden	10.00	.50
□□□□□	116 R. McKay	6.00	.25
□□□□□	117 S. Stevens	15.00	.50
□□□□□	118 M. Czerkawski	6.00	.25
□□□□□	119 R. DiPietro	15.00	.50
□□□□□	120 B. Isbister	6.00	.25
□□□□□	121 C. Osgood (G)	20.00	1.00
□□□□□	122 M. Peca	15.00	.50
□□□□□	123 A. Yashin	20.00	1.00
□□□□□	124 R. Dvorak	6.00	.25
□□□□□	125 T. Fleury	20.00	1.00
□□□□□	126 B. Leetch	20.00	1.00
□□□□□	127 E. Lindros	40.00	2.00
□□□□□	128 M. Messier	40.00	2.00
□□□□□	129 P. Nedved	10.00	.50
□□□□□	130 M. Richter (G)	15.00	.50
□□□□□	131 D. Alfredsson	45.00	1.00
□□□□□	132 R. Bonk	10.00	.50
□□□□□	133 M. Havlat	20.00	1.00
□□□□□	134 M. Hossa	40.00	2.00
□□□□□	135 P. Lalime (G)	20.00	1.00
□□□□□	136 S. McEachern	10.00	.50
□□□□□	137 W. Redden	10.00	.50
□□□□□	138 R. Cechmanek (G)	15.00	.50
□□□□□	139 S. Gagné	30.00	1.50
□□□□□	140 J. LeClair	30.00	1.50
□□□□□	141 K. Primeau	15.00	.50
□□□□□	142 M. Recchi	15.00	.50
□□□□□	143 J. Roenick	30.00	1.50
□□□□□	144 J. Williams	10.00	.50
□□□□□	145 S. Berezin	6.00	.25
□□□□□	146 S. Burke (G)	20.00	1.00
□□□□□	147 S. Doan	6.00	.25
□□□□□	148 M. Handzus	6.00	.25
□□□□□	149 D. Langkow	6.00	.25
□□□□□	150 C. Lemieux	10.00	.50
□□□□□	151 J. Hedberg (G)	15.00	.50
□□□□□	152 J. Hrdina	6.00	.25
□□□□□	153 A. Kovalev	20.00	1.00
□□□□□	154 R. Lang	6.00	.25
□□□□□	155 M. Lemieux	120.00	6.00
□□□□□	156 M. Straka	10.00	.50
□□□□□	157 F. Brathwaite (G)	10.00	.50
□□□□□	158 P. Demitra	15.00	.50
□□□□□	159 B. Johnson (G)	15.00	.50
□□□□□	160 A. MacInnis	15.00	.50
□□□□□	161 C. Pronger	20.00	1.00
□□□□□	162 C. Stillman	6.00	.25
□□□□□	163 K. Tkachuk	20.00	1.00
□□□□□	164 D. Weight	20.00	1.00
□□□□□	165 M. Kiprusoff (G)	10.00	.50
□□□□□	166 P. Marleau	15.00	.50
□□□□□	167 E. Nabokov (G)	20.00	1.00
□□□□□	168 O. Nolan	20.00	1.00
□□□□□	169 M. Ricci	10.00	.50
□□□□□	170 T. Selänne	30.00	1.50
□□□□□	171 M. Sturm	6.00	.25
□□□□□	172 B. Holzinger	6.00	.25
□□□□□	173 N. Khabibulin (G)	15.00	.50
□□□□□	174 V. Lecavalier	40.00	2.00
□□□□□	175 F. Modin	6.00	.25
□□□□□	176 B. Richards	15.00	.50
□□□□□	177 M. St-Louis	15.00	.50
□□□□□	178 K. Weekes (G)	6.00	.25
□□□□□	179 T. Domi	10.00	.50
□□□□□	180 J. Höglund	6.00	.25
□□□□□	181 C. Joseph (G)	40.00	2.00
□□□□□	182 T. Kaberle	10.00	.50
□□□□□	183 A. Mogilny	15.00	.50
□□□□□	184 G. Roberts	15.00	.50
□□□□□	185 M. Sundin	40.00	2.00
□□□□□	186 D. Tucker	6.00	.25
□□□□□	187 T. Bertuzzi	45.00	2.00
□□□□□	188 A. Cassels	6.00	.25
□□□□□	189 D. Cloutier (G)	15.00	.50
□□□□□	190 B. Morrison	10.00	.50
□□□□□	191 M. Näslund	40.00	2.00
□□□□□	192 D. Sedin	15.00	.50
□□□□□	193 H. Sedin	15.00	.50
□□□□□	194 P. Bondra	20.00	1.00
□□□□□	195 S. Gonchar	10.00	.50
□□□□□	196 J. Halpern	6.00	.25
□□□□□	197 J. Jagr	40.00	2.00
□□□□□	198 O. Kölzig (G)	20.00	1.00
□□□□□	199 S. Konowalchuk	6.00	.25
□□□□□	200 A. Oates	15.00	.50

ROOKIES

There are five versions for each Rookie subset card 201-225: a hobby gold-foil base card (#/984), a hobby blue-foil parallel (#/62), a hobby Premiere Date parallel (#/62), a retail silver-foil base subset card (short-print, no serial numbering), and a retail red-foil parallel (#/54). Kovalchuk's hobby gold-foil base card is autographed and serial numbered to 500 copies (not 984).

	Description	Retail	PD62	Hobby
□□□□□	201 I. Bryzgalov (G) RC	6.00	15.00	10.00
□□□□□	202 T. Pärssinen RC	3.00	9.00	8.00
□	203 Kovalchuk RC ✍ *500	-	-	165.00
□□□□	203 I. Kovalchuk RC	35.00	80.00	-
□□□□□	204 K. Piros RC	6.00	10.00	10.00
□□□□□	205 E. Cole RC	8.00	15.00	15.00
□□□□□	206 V. Nedorost RC	8.00	15.00	15.00
□□□□□	207 P. Datsyuk RC	30.00	60.00	55.00
□□□□□	208 T. Conklin RC	8.00	15.00	15.00
□□□□□	209 N. Hagman RC	6.00	10.00	10.00
□□□□□	210 K. Huselius RC	12.00	25.00	20.00
□□□□□	211 J. Bednar RC	6.00	10.00	10.00
□□□□□	212 N. Schultz RC	6.00	10.00	10.00
□□□□□	213 M. Erat RC	6.00	10.00	10.00
□□□□□	214 Clemmensen (G) RC	6.00	10.00	10.00
□□□□□	215 Salomonsson RC	3.00	9.00	8.00
□□□□□	216 R. Martinek RC	3.00	9.00	8.00
□□□□□	217 D. Blackburn (G) RC	14.00	30.00	25.00
□□□□□	218 C. Neil RC	3.00	9.00	8.00
□□□□□	219 P. Brendl	4.00	25.00	6.00
□□□□□	220 J. Dopita RC	6.00	10.00	10.00
□□□□□	221 K. Kolanos RC	8.00	15.00	15.00
□□□□□	222 M. Rycroft RC	3.00	9.00	8.00
□□□□□	223 J. Jillson RC	6.00	10.00	10.00
□□□□□	224 N. Alexeev RC	8.00	15.00	15.00
□□□□□	225 B. Sutherby RC	6.00	10.00	10.00

AUTHENTIC GAME-WORN JERSEY

Insert Set (50 cards):		550.00
	Description	GWJ
□	Tony Amonte ✂	10.00
□	Ed Belfour (G) ✂	20.00
□	Fred Brathwaite (G) ✂	10.00
□	Martin Brodeur (G) ✂	30.00
□	Valeri Bure ✂	10.00
□	Andrew Cassels ✂ Blue	10.00
□	Zdeno Chara ✂	10.00
□	Shayne Corson ✂	10.00
□	Shane Doan ✂	10.00
□	Jean-Pierre Dumont ✂	10.00
□	Derian Hatcher ✂	10.00
□	Jochen Hecht ✂	10.00
□	Brett Hull ✂	20.00
□	Jarome Iginla ✂	15.00
□	Jaromir Jagr ✂	20.00
□	Nikolai Khabibulin (G) ✂	10.00
□	Patric Kjellberg ✂ White	10.00
□	Saku Koivu ✂	15.00
□	Alexei Kovalev ✂	10.00
□	Milan Kraft ✂	10.00
□	Robert Lang ✂ Black	10.00
□	Daymond Langkow ✂	10.00
□	Vincent Lecavalier ✂	20.00
□	John LeClair ✂	15.00
□	Mario Lemieux ✂	60.00
□	Eric Lindros ✂ White	20.00
□	Jay McKee ✂ Grey	10.00
□	Jamie McLennan (G) ✂	10.00
□	Petr Nedved ✂	10.00
□	Joe Nieuwendyk ✂	10.00
□	Chris Osgood (G) ✂	10.00
□	Félix Potvin (G) ✂	10.00
□	Mike Richter (G) ✂	10.00
□	Patrick Roy (G) ✂	60.00
□	Joe Sakic ✂	30.00
□	Sergei Samsonov ✂	10.00
□	Teemu Selänne ✂	15.00
□	Cory Stillman ✂	10.00
□	Mats Sundin ✂	20.00
□	Robert Svehla ✂	10.00
□	Petr Sykora ✂	10.00
□	Kimmo Timonen ✂	10.00
□	Roman Turek (G) ✂	10.00
□	Pierre Turgeon ✂	10.00
□	Oleg Tverdovsky ✂	10.00
□	Doug Weight ✂	10.00
□	Scott Young ✂	10.00
□	Dmitry Yushkevich ✂	10.00
□	Steve Yzerman ✂	45.00
□	Alexei Zhamnov ✂	10.00

BLADERUNNERS

Insert Set (10 cards):		400.00
	Insert (#/63)	B63
□	1 Paul Kariya, Anah.	45.00
□	2 Patrick Roy (G), Colo.	100.00
□	3 Joe Sakic, Colo.	50.00
□	4 Dominik Hasek (G), Detr.	30.00
□	5 Steve Yzerman, Detr.	80.00
□	6 Pavel Bure, Flor.	25.00
□	7 Martin Brodeur (G), NJer.	50.00
□	8 Eric Lindros, NYRa.	30.00
□	9 Mario Lemieux, Pitt.	100.00
□	10 Jaromir Jagr, Wash.	30.00

CREASED LIGHTNING

Insert Set (20 cards):		50.00
	Insert	CL
□	1 Martin Biron (G), Buff.	3.00
□	2 Arturs Irbe (G), Caro.	3.00
□	3 Jocelyn Thibault (G), Chic.	3.00
□	4 Patrick Roy (G), Colo.	12.00
□	5 Ed Belfour (G), Dall.	4.00
□	6 Dominik Hasek (G), Detr.	4.00
□	7 Tommy Salo (G), Edmo.	3.00
□	8 Roberto Luongo (G), Flor.	3.00
□	9 Félix Potvin (G), LosA.	3.00
□	10 José Théodore (G), Mont.	4.00
□	11 Martin Brodeur (G), NJer.	6.00
□	12 Rick DiPietro (G), NYIs.	3.00
□	13 Mike Richter (G), NYRa.	3.00
□	14 Patrick Lalime (G), Otta.	3.00
□	15 Roman Cechmanek (G), Phil.	3.00
□	16 Sean Burke (G), Phoe.	3.00
□	17 Johan Hedberg (G), Pitt.	3.00
□	18 Brent Johnson (G), Slou.	3.00
□	19 Evgeni Nabokov (G), SanJ.	3.00
□	20 Curtis Joseph (G), Toro.	4.00

PLAYMAKERS

Insert Set (10 cards):		40.00
	Insert (1:49)	PM
□	1 Joe Thornton, Bost.	8.00
□	2 Milan Hejduk, Colo.	6.00
□	3 Mike Modano, Dall.	6.00
□	4 Brett Hull, Detr.	6.00
□	5 Mike Comrie, Edmo.	6.00
□	6 Marian Gaborik, MinW.	6.00
□	7 Martin Havlat, Otta.	4.00
□	8 Teemu Selänne, SanJ.	6.00
□	9 Daniel Sedin, Vanc.	3.00
□	10 Henrik Sedin, Vanc.	3.00

POWERPLAY

Insert Set (36 cards):		25.00
	Insert	PP
□	1 J-S Giguère (G), Anah.	1.50
□	2 Steve Shields (G), Anah.	.25
□	3 Milan Hnilicka (G), Atla.	.25
□	4 Byron Dafoe (G), Bost.	.50
□	5 Martin Biron (G), Buff.	.50
□	6 Roman Turek (G), Calg.	.50
□	7 Arturs Irbe (G), Caro.	.50
□	8 Jocelyn Thibault (G), Chic.	.50
□	9 Patrick Roy (G), Colo.	6.00
□	10 Marc Denis (G), Colu.	.50
□	11 Ron Tugnutt (G), Colu.	.50
□	12 Ed Belfour (G), Dall.	2.00
□	13 Marty Turco (G), Dall.	1.00
□	14 Dominik Hasek (G), Detr.	2.00
□	15 Tommy Salo (G), Edmo.	.50
□	16 Trevor Kidd (G), Flor.	.50
□	17 Roberto Luongo (G), Flor.	1.50
□	18 Félix Potvin (G), LosA.	1.00
□	19 Manny Fernandez (G), MinW.	.50
□	20 José Théodore (G), Mont.	2.00
□	21 Mike Dunham (G), Nash.	.50
□	22 Martin Brodeur (G), NJer.	3.00
□	23 Rick DiPietro (G), NYIs.	.50
□	24 Mike Richter (G), NYRa.	.50
□	25 Patrick Lalime (G), Otta.	1.00
□	26 Roman Cechmanek (G), Phil.	.50
□	27 Sean Burke (G), Phoe.	1.00
□	28 Johan Hedberg (G), Pitt.	.50
□	29 Fred Brathwaite (G), Slou.	.50
□	30 Brent Johnson (G), Slou.	.50
□	31 Miikka Kiprusoff (G), SanJ.	.50
□	32 Evgeni Nabokov (G), SanJ.	1.00
□	33 Nikolai Khabibulin (G), Tamp.	.50
□	34 Curtis Joseph (G), Toro.	2.00
□	35 Dan Cloutier (G), Vanc.	.50
□	36 Olaf Kölzig (G), Wash.	1.00

ROOKIE REPORT

Insert Set (20 cards):		75.00
	Insert	RR
□	1 Ilja Bryzgalov (G), Anah.	4.00
□	2 Dany Heatley, Atla.	12.00
□	3 Ilya Kovalchuk, Atla.	12.00
□	4 Erik Cole, Caro.	4.00
□	5 Mark Bell, Chic.	4.00
□	6 Vaclav Nedorost, Colo.	4.00
□	7 Rostislav Klesla, Colu.	4.00
□	8 Pavel Datsyuk, Detr.	10.00
□	9 Kristian Huselius, Flor.	4.00
□	10 Jaroslav Bednar, LosA.	4.00
□	11 Rick DiPietro (G), NYIs.	6.00
□	12 Dan Blackburn (G), NYRa.	4.00
□	13 Pavel Brendl, Phil.	4.00
□	14 Krys Kolanos, Phoe.	4.00
□	15 Kris Beech, Pitt.	4.00
□	16 Johan Hedberg (G), Pitt.	4.00
□	17 Jeff Jillson, SanJ.	4.00
□	18 Miikka Kiprusoff (G), SanJ.	4.00
□	19 Nikita Alexeev, Tamp.	4.00
□	20 Brian Sutherby, Wash.	4.00

WORLD BEATERS

Insert Set (20 cards):		40.00
	Insert	WB
□	1 Paul Kariya, Anah.	4.00
□	2 Chris Drury, Colo.	2.00
□	3 Joe Sakic, Colo.	4.00
□	4 Mike Modano, Dall.	2.00
□	5 Brett Hull, Detr.	2.00
□	6 Steve Yzerman, Detr.	6.00
□	7 Pavel Bure, Flor.	2.00
□	8 Zigmund Palffy, LosA.	2.00
□	9 Marian Gaborik, MinW.	2.00
□	10 Patrik Elias, NJer.	2.00
□	11 Alexei Yashin, NYIs.	2.00
□	12 Eric Lindros, NYRa.	2.00
□	13 Martin Havlat, Otta.	2.00
□	14 John LeClair, Phil.	2.00
□	15 Alexei Kovalev, Pitt.	2.00
□	16 Mario Lemieux, Pitt.	8.00
□	17 Keith Tkachuk, Slou.	2.00
□	18 Teemu Selänne, SanJ.	2.00
□	19 Mats Sundin, Toro.	2.00
□	20 Jaromir Jagr, Wash.	2.00

2001 - 02 ALL-STAR GAME HISTORY

Produced by In The Game, this series was released in February 2002 at the All-Star Fantasy in Los Angeles, CA. Each card is sequentially numbered to 10 copies. Realised pricing on these scarce cards may vary considerably from the below listed pricing.

Complete Set (52 cards):		
	Redemption (#/10)	ASG
□	Ted Kennedy, Toro.	10.00
□	Guy Lafleur, Mont.	25.00
□	Brian Leetch, NYRa.	10.00
□	Mario Lemieux, Pitt.	100.00
□	Eric Lindros, Phil.	25.00
□	Ted Lindsay, Detr.	25.00
□	Frank Mahovlich, Mont.	10.00
□	Lanny McDonald, Toro.	10.00
□	Mark Messier, Edmo.	25.00
□	Stan Mikita, Chic.	10.00
□	Mike Modano, Dall.	25.00
□	Bill Mosienko, Chic.	10.00
□	Bernie Parent (G), Phil.	10.00
□	Gilbert Perreault, Buff.	25.00
□	Jacques Plante (G), Mont.	25.00
□	Denis Potvin, NYIs.	10.00
□	Chuck Rayner (G), Bost.	10.00
□	Henri Richard, Mont.	10.00
□	Maurice Richard, Mont.	75.00
□	Luc Robitaille, LosA.	25.00
□	Jeremy Roenick, Chic.	25.00
□	Patrick Roy (G), Mont.	75.00
□	Joe Sakic, Québ.	50.00
□	Terry Sawchuk (G), Detr.	50.00
□	Mats Sundin, Toro.	25.00
□	Bryan Trottier, NYIs.	25.00
□	Steve Yzerman, Detr.	75.00
□	Jean Béliveau, Mont.	50.00
□	Mike Bossy, NYIs.	25.00
□	Johnny Bower (G), Toro.	10.00
□	Frank Brimsek (G), Bost.	10.00
□	Turk Broda (G), Toro.	10.00
□	Johnny Bucyk, Bost.	10.00
□	Pavel Bure, Flor.	25.00
□	Bobby Clarke, Phil.	10.00
□	Paul Coffey, Edmo.	10.00
□	Marcel Dionne, LosA.	25.00
□	Tony Esposito (G), Chic.	25.00
□	Peter Forsberg, Colo.	50.00
□	Grant Fuhr (G), Edmo.	10.00
□	Bill Gadsby, Detr.	10.00
□	Ed Giacomin (G), NYRa.	10.00
□	Wayne Gretzky, Edmo.	200.00
□	Glenn Hall (G), Chic.	25.00
□	Doug Harvey, Mont.	25.00
□	Milan Hejduk, Colo.	25.00
□	Tim Horton, Toro.	25.00
□	Gordie Howe, Detr.	75.00
□	Bobby Hull, Chic.	50.00
□	Brett Hull, SLou.	25.00
□	Jaromir Jagr, Pitt.	25.00
□	Paul Kariya, Anah.	50.00

2001 - 02 AGF

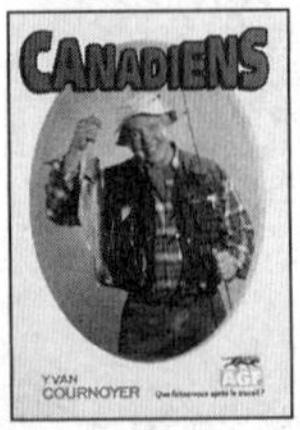

Description AGF

□	Yvan Cournoyer	□	Réjean Houle
□	Henri Richard	□	Steve Shutt

2001 - 02 ATOMIC

Produced by Pacific Trading Cards, this series was released in December 2001. There are five versions for each card 1-100: a silver-bar base card, a blue-bar parallel card (serial numbered to the player's jersey number), a hobby gold-bar parallel card (#/200), a hobby Premiere Date parallel card (#/90), and a retail red-bar parallel card (#/290). The gold-bar cards are valued 10% more than the red-bar cards.

Shell Set (100 cards):	-	-	-	**80.00**
Complete Set (125 cards):	-	-	**1,000**	**400.00**
Parallel Set (100 cards):	**375.00**	**325.00**	-	-
Common Player:	**3.00**	**2.50**	**5.00**	**.75**
Description	**G200**	**R290**	**PD90**	**Base**
☐☐☐☐ 1 P. Kariya	20.00	15.00	40.00	4.00
☐☐☐☐ 2 S. Shields (G)	4.00	3.00	5.00	.75
☐☐☐☐ 3 M. Hnilicka (G)	4.00	3.00	5.00	.75
☐☐☐☐ 4 P. Stefan	4.00	3.00	5.00	.75
☐☐☐☐ 5 J. Allison	5.00	5.00	15.00	1.50
☐☐☐☐ 6 B. Dafoe (G)	5.00	5.00	10.00	1.00
☐☐☐☐ 7 B. Guerin	5.00	5.00	10.00	1.00
☐☐☐☐ 8 S. Samsonov	5.00	5.00	15.00	1.50
☐☐☐☐ 9 J. Thornton	15.00	15.00	35.00	3.50
☐☐☐☐ 10 M. Biron (G)	5.00	5.00	10.00	1.00
☐☐☐☐ 11 T. Connolly	5.00	5.00	10.00	1.00
☐☐☐☐ 12 J. Dumont	4.00	3.00	5.00	.75
☐☐☐☐ 13 J. Iginla	10.00	10.00	20.00	2.00
☐☐☐☐ 14 M. Savard	4.00	3.00	5.00	.75
☐☐☐☐ 15 R. Turek (G)	5.00	5.00	10.00	1.00
☐☐☐☐ 16 R. Francis	5.00	5.00	15.00	1.50
☐☐☐☐ 17 A. Irbe (G)	5.00	5.00	10.00	1.00
☐☐☐☐ 18 J. O'Neill	5.00	5.00	10.00	1.00
☐☐☐☐ 19 T. Amonte	5.00	5.00	15.00	1.50
☐☐☐☐ 20 S. Sullivan	4.00	3.00	5.00	.75
☐☐☐☐ 21 J. Thibault (G)	5.00	5.00	10.00	1.00
☐☐☐☐ 22 R. Blake	5.00	5.00	15.00	1.50
☐☐☐☐ 23 C. Drury	5.00	5.00	15.00	1.50
☐☐☐☐ 24 P. Forsberg	20.00	15.00	40.00	4.00
☐☐☐☐ 25 M. Hejduk	10.00	10.00	20.00	2.00
☐☐☐☐ 26 P. Roy (G)	45.00	35.00	90.00	8.00
☐☐☐☐ 27 J. Sakic	20.00	20.00	45.00	4.50
☐☐☐☐ 28 A. Tanguay	5.00	5.00	15.00	1.50
☐☐☐☐ 29 M. Denis (G)	5.00	5.00	10.00	1.00
☐☐☐☐ 30 G. Sanderson	4.00	3.00	5.00	.75
☐☐☐☐ 31 E. Belfour (G)	15.00	10.00	30.00	3.00
☐☐☐☐ 32 M. Modano	15.00	10.00	30.00	3.00
☐☐☐☐ 33 J. Nieuwendyk	5.00	5.00	10.00	1.00
☐☐☐☐ 34 P. Turgeon	5.00	5.00	10.00	1.00
☐☐☐☐ 35 S. Fedorov	15.00	10.00	30.00	3.00
☐☐☐☐ 36 D. Hasek (G)	15.00	10.00	30.00	3.00
☐☐☐☐ 37 B. Hull	15.00	10.00	30.00	3.00
☐☐☐☐ 38 L. Robitaille	10.00	10.00	20.00	2.00
☐☐☐☐ 39 B. Shanahan	15.00	10.00	30.00	3.00
☐☐☐☐ 40 S. Yzerman	35.00	30.00	70.00	7.00
☐☐☐☐ 41 M. Comrie	10.00	10.00	20.00	2.00
☐☐☐☐ 42 T. Salo (G)	5.00	5.00	10.00	1.00
☐☐☐☐ 43 R. Smyth	5.00	5.00	10.00	1.00
☐☐☐☐ 44 P. Bure	10.00	10.00	20.00	2.00
☐☐☐☐ 45 V. Bure	4.00	3.00	5.00	.75
☐☐☐☐ 46 R. Luongo (G)	10.00	10.00	20.00	2.00
☐☐☐☐ 47 Z. Palffy	5.00	5.00	15.00	1.50
☐☐☐☐ 48 F. Potvin (G)	5.00	5.00	35.00	1.50
☐☐☐☐ 49 Fernandez (G)	5.00	5.00	10.00	1.00
☐☐☐☐ 50 M. Gaborik	15.00	10.00	30.00	3.00
☐☐☐☐ 51 S. Koivu	10.00	10.00	35.00	2.00
☐☐☐☐ 52 Y. Perreault	4.00	3.00	5.00	.75
☐☐☐☐ 53 Théodore (G)	15.00	15.00	35.00	3.50
☐☐☐☐ 54 M. Dunham (G)	5.00	5.00	10.00	1.00
☐☐☐☐ 55 D. Legwand	5.00	5.00	10.00	1.00
☐☐☐☐ 56 J. Arnott	5.00	5.00	10.00	1.00
☐☐☐☐ 57 M. Brodeur (G)	20.00	20.00	45.00	4.50
☐☐☐☐ 58 P. Elias	10.00	10.00	20.00	2.00
☐☐☐☐ 59 M. Czerkawski	4.00	3.00	5.00	.75
☐☐☐☐ 60 R. DiPietro (G)	5.00	5.00	10.00	1.00
☐☐☐☐ 61 M. Peca	5.00	5.00	10.00	1.00
☐☐☐☐ 62 A. Yashin	5.00	5.00	15.00	1.50
☐☐☐☐ 63 T. Fleury	5.00	5.00	15.00	1.50
☐☐☐☐ 64 B. Leetch	5.00	5.00	15.00	1.50
☐☐☐☐ 65 E. Lindros	15.00	10.00	30.00	3.00
☐☐☐☐ 66 M. Messier	15.00	10.00	30.00	3.00
☐☐☐☐ 67 D. Alfredsson	5.00	5.00	35.00	1.50
☐☐☐☐ 68 M. Havlat	5.00	5.00	15.00	1.50
☐☐☐☐ 69 M. Hossa	15.00	10.00	30.00	3.00
☐☐☐☐ 70 P. Lalime (G)	5.00	5.00	15.00	1.50
☐☐☐☐ 71 Cechmanek (G)	5.00	5.00	10.00	1.00
☐☐☐☐ 72 J. LeClair	10.00	10.00	20.00	2.00
☐☐☐☐ 73 M. Recchi	5.00	5.00	10.00	1.00
☐☐☐☐ 74 J. Roenick	10.00	10.00	20.00	2.00
☐☐☐☐ 75 S. Burke (G)	5.00	5.00	15.00	1.50
☐☐☐☐ 76 D. Langkow	4.00	3.00	5.00	.75
☐☐☐☐ 77 J. Hedberg (G)	5.00	5.00	10.00	1.00
☐☐☐☐ 78 A. Kovalev	5.00	5.00	15.00	1.50
☐☐☐☐ 79 M. Lemieux	45.00	35.00	90.00	8.00
☐☐☐☐ 80 M. Straka	4.00	3.00	5.00	.75
☐☐☐☐ 81 B. Johnson (G)	5.00	5.00	10.00	1.00
☐☐☐☐ 82 C. Pronger	5.00	5.00	15.00	1.50
☐☐☐☐ 83 K. Tkachuk	5.00	5.00	15.00	1.50
☐☐☐☐ 84 D. Weight	5.00	5.00	15.00	1.50
☐☐☐☐ 85 E. Nabokov (G)	5.00	5.00	15.00	1.50
☐☐☐☐ 86 O. Nolan	5.00	5.00	15.00	1.50
☐☐☐☐ 87 T. Selänne	10.00	10.00	20.00	2.00
☐☐☐☐ 88 Khabibulin (G)	5.00	5.00	10.00	1.00
☐☐☐☐ 89 V. Lecavalier	15.00	10.00	30.00	3.00
☐☐☐☐ 90 B. Richards	5.00	5.00	10.00	1.00
☐☐☐☐ 91 C. Joseph (G)	15.00	10.00	30.00	3.00
☐☐☐☐ 92 A. Mogilny	5.00	5.00	10.00	1.00
☐☐☐☐ 93 M. Sundin	15.00	10.00	30.00	3.00
☐☐☐☐ 94 M. Näslund	15.00	10.00	30.00	3.00
☐☐☐☐ 95 D. Sedin	5.00	5.00	10.00	1.00
☐☐☐☐ 96 H. Sedin	5.00	5.00	10.00	1.00
☐☐☐☐ 97 P. Bondra	5.00	5.00	15.00	1.50
☐☐☐☐ 98 J. Jagr	15.00	10.00	30.00	3.00
☐☐☐☐ 99 O. Kölzig (G)	5.00	5.00	15.00	1.50
☐☐☐☐ 100 A. Oates	5.00	5.00	10.00	1.00

ROOKIES

There are four versions for each Rookie subset card 101-125: a silver-bar base card (#/500) and a Premiere Date parallel (#/90), a Toronto Expo promo (#/500), and a Toronto Expo Premiere Date sample (no serial number).

Complete Set (25 cards):	**160.00**	**100.00**	-	-
Description	**ExpoPD**	**Expo**	**PD90**	**Base**
☐☐☐☐ **101 Bryzgalov (G) RC**	**5.00**	**5.00**	**10.00**	**25.00**
☐☐☐☐ **102 T. Pärssinen RC**	**3.00**	**2.00**	**8.00**	**12.00**
☐☐☐☐ 103 D. Heatley	35.00	30.00	60.00	35.00
☐☐☐☐ **104 I. Kovalchuk RC**	**35.00**	**30.00**	**90.00**	**125.00**
☐☐☐☐ **105 K. Piros RC**	**5.00**	**2.00**	**8.00**	**20.00**
☐☐☐☐ **106 E. Cole RC**	**5.00**	**5.00**	**10.00**	**30.00**
☐☐☐☐ **107 V. Nedorost RC**	**5.00**	**5.00**	**10.00**	**30.00**
☐☐☐☐ **108 P. Datsyuk RC**	**30.00**	**20.00**	**70.00**	**100.00**
☐☐☐☐ **109 N. Hagman RC**	**5.00**	**2.00**	**8.00**	**20.00**
☐☐☐☐ **110 K. Huselius RC**	**10.00**	**5.00**	**15.00**	**40.00**
☐☐☐☐ **111 J. Bednar RC**	**5.00**	**2.00**	**8.00**	**20.00**
☐☐☐☐ **112 P. Dupuis RC**	**5.00**	**5.00**	**10.00**	**30.00**
☐☐☐☐ **113 M. Erat RC**	**5.00**	**2.00**	**8.00**	**20.00**
☐☐☐☐ **114 Clemmensen (G) RC**	**5.00**	**2.00**	**8.00**	**20.00**
☐☐☐☐ **115 R. Martinek RC**	**3.00**	**2.00**	**8.00**	**12.00**
☐☐☐☐ **116 I. Ciernik RC**	**5.00**	**2.00**	**8.00**	**20.00**
☐☐☐☐ **117 C. Neil RC**	**3.00**	**2.00**	**8.00**	**12.00**
☐☐☐☐ 118 P. Brendl	10.00	5.00	15.00	15.00
☐☐☐☐ **119 J. Dopita RC**	**5.00**	**2.00**	**8.00**	**20.00**
☐☐☐☐ **120 K. Kolanos RC**	**5.00**	**5.00**	**10.00**	**30.00**
☐☐☐☐ 121 K. Beech	10.00	5.00	15.00	12.00
☐☐☐☐ **122 M. Rycroft RC**	**3.00**	**2.00**	**8.00**	**12.00**
☐☐☐☐ **123 J. Jillson RC**	**5.00**	**2.00**	**8.00**	**20.00**
☐☐☐☐ **124 N. Alexeev RC**	**5.00**	**5.00**	**10.00**	**30.00**
☐☐☐☐ **125 B. Sutherby RC**	**5.00**	**2.00**	**8.00**	**20.00**

BLUE

Realised pricing on scarce cards may vary considerably from below pricing.

Parallel Set (100 cards):	**3,900**
Description	**Blue**
☐ 1 Paul Kariya, Anah. {#/9}	200.00
☐ 2 Steve Shields (G), Anah. {#/31}	5.00
☐ 3 Milan Hnilicka (G), Atla. {#/33}	5.00
☐ 4 Patrik Stefan, Atla. {#/13}	25.00
☐ 5 Jason Allison, Bost. {#/41}	5.00
☐ 6 Byron Dafoe (G), Bost. {#/34}	5.00
☐ 7 Bill Guerin, Bost. {#/13}	25.00
☐ 8 Sergei Samsonov, Bost. {#/14}	50.00
☐ 9 Joe Thornton, Bost. {#/19}	75.00
☐ 10 Martin Biron (G), Bost. {#/43}	5.00
☐ 11 Tim Connolly, Buff. {#/18}	25.00
☐ 12 Jean-Pierre Dumont, Buff. {#/17}	5.00
☐ 13 Jarome Iginla, Calg. {#/12}	75.00
☐ 14 Marc Savard, Calg. {#/27}	5.00
☐ 15 Roman Turek (G), Calg. {#/1}	100.00
☐ 16 Ron Francis, Caro. {#/10}	75.00
☐ 17 Arturs Irbe (G), Caro. {#/32}	5.00
☐ 18 Jeff O'Neill (G), Caro. {#/92}	5.00
☐ 19 Tony Amonte, Chic. {#/10}	75.00
☐ 20 Steve Sullivan, Chic. {#/26}	5.00
☐ 21 Jocelyn Thibault (G), Chic. {#/41}	5.00
☐ 22 Rob Blake, Colo. {#/4}	125.00
☐ 23 Chris Drury, Colo. {#/18}	25.00
☐ 24 Peter Forsberg, Colo. {#/21}	75.00
☐ 25 Milan Hejduk, Colo. {#/23}	25.00
☐ 26 Patrick Roy (G), Colo. {#/33}	125.00
☐ 27 Joe Sakic, Colo. {#/19}	100.00
☐ 28 Alex Tanguay, Colo. {#/40}	5.00
☐ 29 Marc Denis (G), Colu. {#/30}	25.00
☐ 30 Geoff Sanderson, Colu. {#/8}	25.00
☐ 31 Ed Belfour (G), Dall. {#/20}	50.00
☐ 32 Mike Modano, Dall. {#/9}	150.00
☐ 33 Joe Nieuwendyk, Dall. {#/25}	5.00
☐ 34 Pierre Turgeon, Dall. {#/77}	5.00
☐ 35 Sergei Fedorov, Detr. {#/91}	25.00
☐ 36 Dominik Hasek (G), Detr. {#/39}	25.00
☐ 37 Brett Hull, Detr. {#/17}	75.00
☐ 38 Luc Robitaille, Detr. {#/20}	50.00
☐ 39 Brendan Shanahan, Detr. {#/14}	100.00
☐ 40 Steve Yzerman, Detr. {#/19}	150.00
☐ 41 Mike Comrie, Edmo. {#/89}	5.00
☐ 42 Tommy Salo (G), Edmo. {#/35}	5.00
☐ 43 Ryan Smyth, Edmo. {#/94}	5.00
☐ 44 Pavel Bure, Flor. {#/10}	100.00
☐ 45 Valeri Bure, Flor. {#/20}	5.00
☐ 46 Roberto Luongo (G), Flor. {#/1}	175.00
☐ 47 Zigmund Palffy, LosA. {#/33}	25.00
☐ 48 Félix Potvin (G), LosA. {#/39}	25.00
☐ 49 Manny Fernandez (G), MinW. {#/35}	5.00
☐ 50 Marian Gaborik, MinW. {#/10}	125.00
☐ 51 Saku Koivu, Mont. {#/11}	300.00
☐ 52 Yanic Perreault, Toro. (Mont.) {#/44}	5.00
☐ 53 José Théodore (G), Mont. {#/60}	25.00
☐ 54 Mike Dunham (G), Nash. {#/1}	75.00
☐ 55 David Legwand, Nash. {#/11}	50.00
☐ 56 Jason Arnott, NJer. {#/25}	25.00
☐ 57 Martin Brodeur (G), NJer. {#/30}	75.00
☐ 58 Patrik Elias, NJer. {#/26}	25.00
☐ 59 Mariusz Czerkawski, NYIs. {#/21}	5.00
☐ 60 Rick DiPietro (G), NYIs. {#/1}	100.00
☐ 61 Michael Peca, NYIs. {#/27}	5.00
☐ 62 Alexei Yashin, NYIs. {#/79}	5.00
☐ 63 Theoren Fleury, NYRa. {#/14}	50.00
☐ 64 Brian Leetch, NYRa. {#/2}	125.00
☐ 65 Eric Lindros, NYRa. {#/88}	25.00
☐ 66 Mark Messier, NYRa. {#/11}	125.00
☐ 67 Daniel Alfredsson, Otta. {#/11}	300.00
☐ 68 Martin Havlat, Otta. {#/9}	75.00
☐ 69 Marian Hossa, Otta. {#/18}	75.00
☐ 70 Patrick Lalime (G), Otta. {#/40}	5.00
☐ 71 Roman Cechmanek (G), Phil. {#/32}	5.00
☐ 72 John LeClair, Phil. {#/10}	100.00
☐ 73 Mark Recchi, Phil. {#/8}	50.00
☐ 74 Jeremy Roenick, Phil. {#/97}	5.00
☐ 75 Sean Burke (G), Phoe. {#/1}	125.00
☐ 76 Daymond Langkow, Phoe. {#/11}	25.00
☐ 77 Johan Hedberg (G), Pitt. {#/1}	75.00
☐ 78 Alexei Kovalev, Pitt. {#/27}	25.00
☐ 79 Mario Lemieux, Pitt. {#/66}	75.00
☐ 80 Martin Straka, Pitt. {#/82}	5.00
☐ 81 Brent Johnson (G), SLou. {#/35}	5.00
☐ 82 Chris Pronger, SLou. {#/44}	5.00
☐ 83 Keith Tkachuk, SLou. {#/7}	100.00
☐ 84 Doug Weight, SLou. {#/39}	5.00
☐ 85 Evgeni Nabokov (G), SanJ. {#/35}	25.00
☐ 86 Owen Nolan, SanJ. {#/11}	75.00
☐ 87 Teemu Selänne, SanJ. {#/8}	125.00
☐ 88 Nikolai Khabibulin (G), Tamp. {#/35}	5.00
☐ 89 Vincent Lecavalier, Tamp. {#/4}	200.00
☐ 90 Brad Richards, Tamp. {#/19}	25.00
☐ 91 Curtis Joseph (G), Toro. {#/31}	50.00
☐ 92 Alexander Mogilny, Toro. {#/89}	5.00
☐ 93 Mats Sundin, Toro. {#/13}	100.00
☐ 94 Markus Näslund, Vanc. {#/19}	50.00
☐ 95 Daniel Sedin, Vanc. {#/22}	5.00
☐ 96 Henrik Sedin, Vanc. {#/33}	5.00
☐ 97 Peter Bondra, Wash. {#/12}	50.00
☐ 98 Jaromir Jagr, Wash. {#/68}	25.00
☐ 99 Olaf Kölzig (G), Wash. {#/37}	25.00
☐ 100 Adam Oates, Wash. {#/77}	5.00

ATOMIC BLAST

Insert Set (10 cards):	**300.00**
Insert (1:641)	**AB**
☐ 1 Paul Kariya, Anah.	40.00
☐ 2 Peter Forsberg, Colo.	40.00
☐ 3 Joe Sakic, Colo.	45.00
☐ 4 Steve Yzerman, Detr.	70.00
☐ 5 Mike Comrie, Edmo.	20.00
☐ 6 Pavel Bure, Flor.	20.00
☐ 7 Alexei Yashin, NYIs.	20.00
☐ 8 Eric Lindros, Phil.	30.00
☐ 9 Mario Lemieux, Pitt.	90.00
☐ 10 Jaromir Jagr, Pitt.	30.00

AUTHENTIC GAME-WORN JERSEY

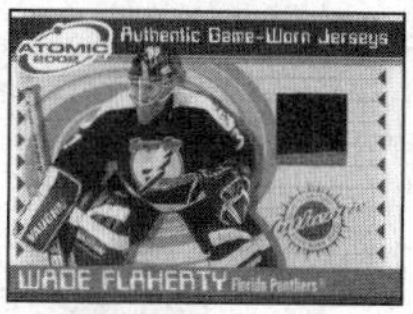

Insert Set (50 cards):	**650.00**
Description	**GWJ**
☐ Mike Alatalo ✂	10.00
☐ Tony Amonte ✂	15.00
☐ Ed Belfour (G) ✂	25.00
☐ Benoît Brunet ✂	10.00
☐ Valeri Bure ✂	10.00
☐ René Corbet ✂ Yellow	10.00
☐ Mariusz Czerkawski ✂	10.00
☐ Byron Dafoe (G) ✂	10.00
☐ Mathieu Dandenault ✂ Red	10.00
☐ Éric Dazé ✂ White	10.00
☐ Mike Dunham (G) ✂ Blue	10.00
☐ Tom Fitzgerald ✂	10.00
☐ Wade Flaherty (G) ✂ Blue	10.00
☐ Wade Flaherty (G) ✂ Blue/Orange	15.00
☐ Peter Forsberg ✂	35.00
☐ Jean-Sébastien Giguère (G) ✂	20.00
☐ Jeff Hackett (G) ✂	10.00
☐ Dominik Hasek (G) ✂	25.00
☐ Guy Hebert (G) ✂	10.00
☐ Benoît Hogue ✂	10.00
☐ Phil Housley ✂	10.00
☐ Jan Hrdina ✂	10.00
☐ Jaromir Jagr ✂	25.00
☐ Saku Koivu ✂ Red	20.00
☐ Mario Lemieux ✂	75.00
☐ Jyrki Lumme ✂ White	10.00
☐ Darren McCarty ✂ White	10.00
☐ Mike Modano ✂	25.00
☐ Scott Niedermayer ✂	10.00
☐ Lyle Odelein ✂	10.00
☐ Chris Osgood (G) ✂ Red	15.00
☐ Félix Potvin (G) ✂	15.00
☐ Erik Rasmussen ✂ Red	10.00
☐ Dave Reid ✂	10.00
☐ Patrick Roy (G) ✂	75.00
☐ Steve Rucchin ✂	10.00
☐ Joe Sakic ✂	40.00
☐ Marc Savard ✂	10.00
☐ Teemu Selänne ✂ Red	20.00
☐ Brendan Shanahan ✂	25.00
☐ Jeff Shantz ✂	10.00
☐ Kevin Stevens ✂	10.00
☐ Mats Sundin ✂ White	25.00
☐ Chris Terreri (G) ✂	10.00
☐ Jocelyn Thibault (G) ✂	10.00
☐ Scott Walker ✂	10.00
☐ Mike York ✂	10.00
☐ Dmitry Yushkevich ✂	10.00
☐ Steve Yzerman ✂	60.00
☐ Sergei Zholtok ✂	10.00
☐ Sergei Zubov ✂	10.00

AUTHENTIC GAME-WORN JERSEY PATCH VARIATION

Insert Set (50 cards):	
Description	**GWJ**
☐ Mika Alatalo ✂ {#/228}	20.00
☐ Tony Amonte ✂ {#/403}	25.00
☐ Ed Belfour (G) ✂	
☐ Benoît Brunet ✂	
☐ Valeri Bure ✂ {#/428}	20.00
☐ René Corbet ✂	
☐ Mariusz Czerkawski ✂ {#/503}	20.00
☐ Byron Dafoe (G) ✂ {#/128}	25.00
☐ Mathieu Dandenault ✂ {#/178}	20.00
☐ Éric Dazé ✂ {#/328}	20.00
☐ Mike Dunham (G) ✂	
☐ Tom Fitzgerald ✂ {#/378}	20.00
☐ Wade Flaherty (G) ✂ {#/302}	20.00
☐ Peter Forsberg ✂	
☐ Jean-Sébastien Giguère (G) ✂ {#/403}	30.00
☐ Jeff Hackett (G) ✂	
☐ Dominik Hasek (G) ✂ {#/283}	50.00
☐ Guy Hebert (G) ✂	
☐ Benoît Hogue ✂ {#/123}	20.00
☐ Phil Housley ✂ {#/106}	20.00
☐ Jan Hrdina ✂ {#/353}	20.00
☐ Jaromir Jagr ✂	
☐ Saku Koivu ✂ {#/53}	120.00
☐ Mario Lemieux ✂	
☐ Jyrki Lumme ✂ {#/303}	20.00
☐ Darren McCarty ✂	
☐ Mike Modano ✂	
☐ Scott Niedermayer ✂ {#/478}	20.00
☐ Lyle Odelein ✂ {#/153}	20.00

□	Chris Osgood (G) ✂	
□	Félix Potvin (G) ✂	
□	Erik Rasmussen ✂	
□	Dave Reid ✂	
□	Patrick Roy (G) ✂	
□	Steve Rucchin ✂ {#/303}	20.00
□	Joe Sakic ✂	
□	Marc Savard ✂ {#/402}	20.00
□	Teemu Selänne ✂ {#/153}	50.00
□	Brendan Shanahan ✂	
□	Jeff Shantz ✂	
□	Kevin Stevens ✂ {#/353}	20.00
□	Mats Sundin ✂ {#/203}	60.00
□	Chris Terreri (G) ✂ {#/153}	20.00
□	Jocelyn Thibault (G) ✂ {#/328}	20.00
□	Scott Walker ✂ {#/428}	20.00
□	Mike York ✂ {#/403}	20.00
□	Dmitry Yushkevich ✂ {#/128}	20.00
□	Steve Yzerman ✂	
□	Sergei Zholtok ✂ {#/138}	20.00
□	Sergei Zubov ✂	

CORE PLAYERS

Insert Set (20 cards):		100.00
	Insert [1:21]	CP
□	1 Paul Kariya, Anah.	10.00
□	2 Joe Thornton, Bost.	6.00
□	3 Patrick Roy (G), Colo.	6.00
□	4 Mike Modano, Dall.	6.00
□	5 Steve Yzerman, Detr.	15.00
□	6 Pavel Bure, Flor.	6.00
□	7 Zigmund Palffy, LosA.	6.00
□	8 Marian Gaborik, MinW.	6.00
□	9 Saku Koivu, Mont.	6.00
□	10 Martin Brodeur (G), NJer.	10.00
□	11 Alexei Yashin, NYIs.	6.00
□	12 Mark Messier, NYRa.	6.00
□	13 Marian Hossa, Otta.	6.00
□	14 John LeClair, Phil.	6.00
□	15 Mario Lemieux, Pitt.	20.00
□	16 Chris Pronger, SLou.	6.00
□	17 Teemu Selänne, SanJ.	6.00
□	18 Vincent Lecavalier, Tamp.	6.00
□	19 Curtis Joseph (G), Toro.	6.00
□	20 Jaromir Jagr, Wash.	6.00

POWERPLAY

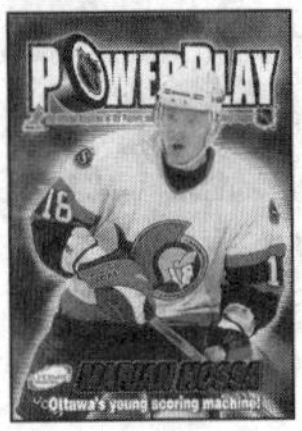

Insert Set (36 cards):		25.00
	Insert [1:1]	PP
□	1 Paul Kariya, Anah.	1.50
□	2 Patrik Stefan, Atla.	.50
□	3 Sergei Samsonov, Bost.	.50
□	4 Joe Thornton, Bost.	1.50
□	5 Jarome Iginla, Calg.	1.00
□	6 Jeff O'Neill, Caro.	.50
□	7 Tony Amonte, Chic.	.50
□	8 Peter Forsberg, Colo.	1.50
□	9 Milan Hejduk, Colo.	1.00
□	10 Joe Sakic, Colo.	2.00
□	11 Mike Modano, Dall.	1.00
□	12 Sergei Fedorov, Detr.	1.00
□	13 Brendan Shanahan, Detr.	1.00
□	14 Steve Yzerman, Detr.	3.00
□	15 Mike Comrie, Edmo.	1.00
□	16 Pavel Bure, Flor.	1.00
□	17 Zigmund Palffy, LosA.	.50
□	18 Marian Gaborik, MinW.	1.00
□	19 Saku Koivu, Mont.	1.00
□	20 Jason Arnott, NJer.	.50
□	21 Alexei Yashin, NYIs.	.50
□	22 Theoren Fleury, NYRa.	.50
□	23 Eric Lindros, NYRa.	1.00
□	24 Mark Messier, NYRa.	1.00
□	25 Marian Hossa, Otta.	1.00
□	26 John LeClair, Phil.	1.00
□	27 Mario Lemieux, Pitt.	3.50
□	28 Chris Pronger, Slou.	.50
□	29 Keith Tkachuk, Slou.	.50
□	30 Teemu Selänne, SanJ.	1.00
□	31 Vincent Lecavalier, Tamp.	1.00
□	32 Mats Sundin, Toro.	1.00
□	33 Daniel Sedin, Vanc.	.50
□	34 Henrik Sedin, Vanc.	.50
□	35 Peter Bondra, Wash.	.50
□	36 Jaromir Jagr, Wash.	1.00

ROOKIE REACTION

Insert Set (10 cards):		50.00
	Insert	RR
□	1 Dany Heatley, Atla.	15.00
□	2 Ilya Kovalchuk, Atla.	15.00
□	3 Vaclav Nedorost, Colo.	4.00
□	4 Rostislav Klesla, Colu.	4.00
□	5 Rick DiPietro (G), NYIs.	7.00
□	6 Pavel Brendl, Phil.	4.00
□	7 Jiri Dopita, Phil.	4.00
□	8 Kris Beech, Pitt.	4.00
□	9 Johan Hedberg (G), Pitt.	6.00
□	10 Nikita Alexeev, Tamp.	4.00

STATOSPHERE

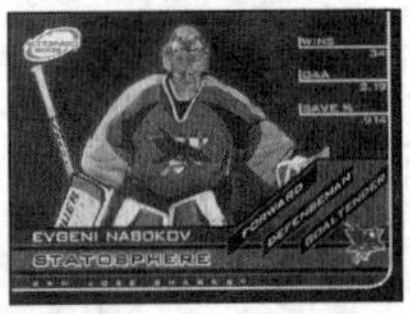

Insert Set (20 cards):		90.00
	Insert	Stat.
□	1 Patrick Roy (G), Colo.	15.00
□	2 Ed Belfour (G), Dall.	6.00
□	3 Dominik Hasek (G), Detr.	6.00
□	4 Martin Brodeur (G), NJer.	10.00
□	5 Rick DiPietro (G), NYIs.	3.00
□	6 Mike Richter (G), NYRa.	3.00
□	7 Roman Cechmanek (G), Phil.	3.00
□	8 Johan Hedberg (G), Pitt.	3.00
□	9 Evgeni Nabokov (G), SanJ.	3.00
□	10 Curtis Joseph (G), Toro.	6.00
□	11 Peter Forsberg, Colo.	8.00
□	12 Joe Sakic, Colo.	10.00
□	13 Brett Hull, Dall.	6.00
□	14 Pavel Bure, Flor.	5.00
□	15 Zigmund Palffy, LosA.	3.00
□	16 Alexei Yashin, NYIs.	3.00
□	17 Alexei Kovalev, Pitt.	3.00
□	18 Mario Lemieux, Pitt.	15.00
□	19 Martin Straka, Pitt.	3.00
□	20 Jaromir Jagr, Pitt.	6.00

TEAM NUCLEUS

Insert Set (15 cards):		65.00
	Insert	TN
□	1 Guerin / Samsonov /Thornton	5.00
□	2 Iginla / Savard / Turek (G)	5.00
□	3 Francis / Irbe (G) / O'Neill	5.00
□	4 Forsberg / Roy (G) / Sakic	12.00
□	5 Belfour (G) / Modano / Nieuwendyk	5.00
□	6 Hasek (G) / Shanahan / Yzerman	8.00
□	7 Comrie / Salo (G) / Smyth	5.00
□	8 Arnott / Brodeur (G) / Elias	5.00
□	9 DiPietro (G) / Peca / Yashin	5.00
□	10 Fleury / Lindros / Messier	5.00
□	11 Hedberg (G) / Kovalev / Lemieux	8.00
□	12 Nabokov (G) / Nolan / Selänne	5.00
□	13 Joseph (G) / Mogilny / Sundin	5.00
□	14 Näslund / D.Sedin / H.Sedin	5.00
□	15 Bondra / Jagr / Oates	5.00

SAMPLE

	Sample	Sample
□	Martin Brodeur (G), NJer.	8.00
□	Johan Hedberg (G), Pitt.	3.00
□	Patrick Roy (G), Colo.	15.00
□	Brendan Shanahan, Detr.	5.00
□	Mats Sundin, Toro.	5.00
□	Keith Tkachuk, SLou.	3.00

2001 - 02 BE A PLAYER DRAFT FLORIDA 2001

These cards were redeemed via the Draft Day redemption cards found in packs of 2001 - 02 Be A Player Memorabilia. Cards were redeemable after the player made his NHL debut. These four five cards were redeemed during the 2001-02 season. An additional six cards were redeemable during the 2002-03 season (see 2002 - 03 Be A Player Draft Florida 2001).

	Redeemed card	Draft
□	1 Ilya Kovalchuk, Atla. {*74}	400.00
□	4 Stephen Weiss, Flor. {*55}	200.00
□	10 Dan Blackburn (G), NYRa. {*67}	175.00
□	24 Lukas Krajicek, Flor. {*31}	125.00

2001 - 02 BE A PLAYER MEMORABILIA

Produced by In The Game, the original series was released in August 2001. An update (both base cards and inserts) was issued in June 2002 as part of the Be A Player Update release. There are four versions for each card 1-500: a base card, a Ruby parallel (#/200), a Sapphire parallel (#/100) and an Emerald parallel (#/10). The Emerald cards are not priced below.

The following wrapper redemption promotional versions were created: All-Star Fantasy '02 (#/10), All-Star Fantasy '02 Ruby (#/1), All-Star Fantasy '02 Sapphire (#/10), All-Star Fantasy '02 Emerald (#/1), Spring Expo '02 Ruby (#/10), Spring Expo '02 Emerald (#/1).

Complete Set (300 cards):		1,300	700	80.00
Update Set (200 cards):		700	400.00	115.00
Common Player:		6.00	3.00	.25
	Description	S100	R200	Base
□□□□	1 Rick DiPietro	6.00	6.00	.50
□□□□	2 Radek Dvorak	6.00	3.00	.25
□□□□	3 Radek Bonk	6.00	4.00	.50
□□□□	4 Evgeni Nabokov (G)	10.00	6.00	1.00
□□□□	5 Roman Turek (G)	6.00	6.00	.50
□□□□	6 Daniel Sedin	6.00	4.00	.50
□□□□	7 Jeff Halpern	6.00	3.00	.25
□□□□	8 Joe Thornton	20.00	14.00	2.00
□□□□	9 Maxim Afinogenov	6.00	4.00	.50
□□□□	10 Oleg Saprykin	6.00	3.00	.25
□□□□	11 Shane Willis	6.00	3.00	.25
□□□□	12 Jocelyn Thibault (G)	6.00	4.00	.50
□□□□	13 Alex Tanguay	10.00	6.00	1.00
□□□□	14 Brenden Morrow	6.00	4.00	.50
□□□□	15 Steve Yzerman	45.00	30.00	4.00
□□□□	16 Anson Carter	6.00	4.00	.50
□□□□	17 Brad Richards	6.00	6.00	.50
□□□□	18 Mike York	6.00	4.00	.50
□□□□	19 Brian Rafalski	6.00	3.00	.25
□□□□	20 Maxime* Ouellet (G)	6.00	4.00	.50
□□□□	21 Ruslan Fedotenko	6.00	3.00	.25
□□□□	22 Brad Stuart	6.00	4.00	.50
□□□□	23 Daniel Corso	6.00	3.00	.25
□□□□	24 Mika Noronen (G)	6.00	4.00	.50
□□□□	25 Jason Williams	6.00	3.00	.25
□□□□	26 Scott Stevens	6.00	4.00	.50
□□□□	27 Patrick Lalime (G)	10.00	6.00	1.00
□□□□	28 Johan Hedberg (G)	6.00	4.00	.50
□□□□	29 V. Damphousse	10.00	6.00	1.00
□□□□	30 Jochen Hecht	6.00	3.00	.25
□□□□	31 Ed Jovanovski	6.00	4.00	.50
□□□□	32 J-S Giguère (G)	15.00	10.00	1.00
□□□□	33 Fred Brathwaite (G)	6.00	4.00	.50
□□□□	34 Arturs Irbe (G)	6.00	4.00	.50
□□□□	35 Ron Tugnutt (G)	6.00	4.00	.50
□□□□	36 Ed Belfour (G)	20.00	12.00	1.50
□□□□	37 Chris Osgood (G)	10.00	6.00	1.00
□□□□	38 Mike Comrie	15.00	10.00	1.00
□□□□	39 Aaron Miller	6.00	3.00	.25
□□□□	40 Martin Brodeur (G)	30.00	20.00	2.50
□□□□	41 Martin Havlat	10.00	6.00	1.00
□□□□	42 R. Cechmanek (G)	6.00	4.00	.50
□□□□	43 Teppo Numminen	6.00	4.00	.50
□□□□	44 Milan Kraft	6.00	4.00	.50
□□□□	45 Pavol Demitra	6.00	4.00	.50
□□□□	46 Henrik Sedin	6.00	4.00	.50
□□□□	47 Byron Dafoe (G)	6.00	4.00	.50
□□□□	48 David Tanabe	6.00	3.00	.25
□□□□	49 Chris Drury	10.00	6.00	1.00
□□□□	50 Tommy Salo (G)	6.00	4.00	.50
□□□□	51 Lubomir Visnovsky	6.00	3.00	.25
□□□□	52 Andrei Markov	6.00	3.00	.25
□□□□	53 Jason Arnott	6.00	6.00	.50
□□□□	54 Adam Foote	6.00	4.00	.50
□□□□	55 Vitaly Vishnevski	6.00	3.00	.25
□□□□	56 Ville Nieminen	6.00	3.00	.25
□□□□	57 Mike Mottau	6.00	3.00	.25
□□□□	58 Brendan Morrison	6.00	4.00	.50
□□□□	59 Lee Goren	6.00	3.00	.25
□□□□	60 Scott Gomez	6.00	4.00	.50
□□□□	61 Tim Connolly	6.00	4.00	.50
□□□□	62 Daniel Alfredsson	20.00	6.00	1.00
□□□□	63 Owen Nolan	10.00	6.00	1.00
□□□□	64 Chris Pronger	10.00	6.00	1.00
□□□□	65 Fredrik Modin	6.00	3.00	.25
□□□□	66 Mario Lemieux	60.00	36.00	5.00
□□□□	67 Olaf Kölzig (G)	10.00	6.00	1.00
□□□□	68 Jeff Friesen	6.00	4.00	.50
□□□□	69 Patrik Stefan	6.00	4.00	.50
□□□□	70 Sergei Samsonov	10.00	6.00	1.00
□□□□	71 Jean-Pierre Dumont	6.00	3.00	.25
□□□□	72 Sandis Ozolinsh	6.00	3.00	.25
□□□□	73 Milan Hejduk	15.00	10.00	1.00
□□□□	74 Sergei Zubov	6.00	3.00	.25
□□□□	75 Sergei Fedorov	20.00	12.00	1.50
□□□□	76 Janne Niinimaa	6.00	3.00	.25
□□□□	77 Roberto Luongo (G)	15.00	10.00	1.00
□□□□	78 Félix Potvin (G)	10.00	6.00	1.00
□□□□	79 Petr* Sykora	6.00	4.00	.50
□□□□	80 Petr Nedved	6.00	4.00	.50
□□□□	81 Shawn McEachern	6.00	4.00	.50
□□□□	82 Simon Gagné	15.00	10.00	1.00
□□□□	83 Sean Burke (G)	10.00	6.00	1.00
□□□□	84 Al MacInnis	6.00	4.00	.50
□□□□	85 Vincent Lecavalier	20.00	12.00	1.50
□□□□	86 Sergei Gonchar	6.00	4.00	.50
□□□□	87 Oleg Tverdovsky	6.00	3.00	.25
□□□□	88 Bill Guerin	6.00	4.00	.50
□□□□	89 Miroslav Satan	6.00	4.00	.50
□□□□	90 Marc Savard	6.00	3.00	.25
□□□□	91 Peter Forsberg	25.00	16.00	2.00
□□□□	92 Brett Hull	20.00	12.00	1.50
□□□□	93 Nicklas Lidström	10.00	6.00	1.00
□□□□	94 Ryan Smyth	6.00	6.00	.50
□□□□	95 Luc Robitaille	15.00	10.00	1.00
□□□□	96 Alexander Mogilny	6.00	6.00	.50
□□□□	97 Mark Messier	20.00	12.00	1.50
□□□□	98 Marian Hossa	20.00	12.00	1.50
□□□□	99 Keith Primeau	6.00	4.00	.50
□□□□	100 Todd Bertuzzi	20.00	14.00	2.00
□□□□	101 Justin Williams	6.00	4.00	.50
□□□□	102 Ossi Väänänen	6.00	3.00	.25
□□□□	103 Robert Lang	6.00	3.00	.25
□□□□	104 Pavel Bure	15.00	10.00	1.00
□□□□	105 Tomas Kaberle	6.00	4.00	.50
□□□□	106 Nikolai Antropov	6.00	3.00	.25
□□□□	107 Tomi Kallio	6.00	3.00	.25
□□□□	108 David Vyborny	6.00	3.00	.25
□□□□	109 Denis Shvidki	6.00	3.00	.25
□□□□	110 Jozef Stümpel	6.00	3.00	.25
□□□□	111 Dimitri Kalinin	6.00	3.00	.25
□□□□	112 Stéphane Robidas	6.00	3.00	.25
□□□□	113 Scott Walker	6.00	3.00	.25
□□□□	114 J. Langenbrunner	6.00	3.00	.25
□□□□	115 Maxim Kuznetsov	6.00	3.00	.25
□□□□	116 Mike Grier	6.00	3.00	.25
□□□□	117 Michael Nylander	6.00	3.00	.25
□□□□	118 Derian Hatcher	6.00	4.00	.50
□□□□	119 Scott Niedermayer	6.00	4.00	.50
□□□□	120 Petr Schastlivy	6.00	3.00	.25
□□□□	**121 Tomas Divisek RC**	**6.00**	**3.00**	**.50**
□□□□	122 Toby Petersen	6.00	3.00	.25
□□□□	123 Jarkko Ruutu	6.00	3.00	.25
□□□□	124 Chris Chelios	10.00	6.00	1.00
□□□□	125 A. Raycroft (G)	6.00	3.00	.25
□□□□	126 Jason Woolley	6.00	3.00	.25
□□□□	127 Derek Morris	6.00	3.00	.25
□□□□	128 David Legwand	6.00	4.00	.50
□□□□	129 Jaromir Jagr	20.00	12.00	1.50
□□□□	130 Serge Aubin	6.00	3.00	.25
□□□□	131 Jere Lehtinen	6.00	4.00	.50
□□□□	132 Manny Legacé (G)	6.00	4.00	.50
□□□□	133 Patrick Roy (G)	60.00	36.00	5.00

134 Glen Murray	6.00	6.00	.50
135 Jan Bulis	6.00	3.00	.25
136 Mike Dunham (G)	6.00	4.00	.50
137 Jan Hlavac	6.00	3.00	.25
138 Wade Redden	6.00	4.00	.50
139 Jan Hrdina	6.00	3.00	.25
140 Keith Tkachuk	10.00	6.00	1.00
141 Yanic Perreault	6.00	4.00	.50
142 Jonas Rönnqvist	6.00	3.00	.25
143 John Madden	6.00	4.00	.50
144 Jani Hurme (G)	6.00	3.00	.25
145 Chris Gratton	6.00	3.00	.25
146 Toni Lydman	6.00	3.00	.25
147 Mike Modano	20.00	12.00	1.50
148 Boris Mironov	6.00	3.00	.25
149 Joe Sakic	30.00	20.00	2.50
150 Chris Nielsen	6.00	3.00	.25
151 Marty Turco (G)	10.00	6.00	1.00
152 Bryan Smolinski	6.00	3.00	.25
153 Daniel Cleary	6.00	4.00	.50
154 Anders Eriksson	6.00	3.00	.25
155 Pierre Dagenais	6.00	3.00	.25
156 Wes Walz	6.00	3.00	.25
157 Brian Savage	6.00	4.00	.50
158 Stu Barnes	6.00	3.00	.25
159 Éric Desjardins	6.00	4.00	.50
160 Juraj Kolnik	6.00	3.00	.25
161 Brendan Shanahan	20.00	12.00	1.50
162 Karel Rachunek	6.00	3.00	.25
163 Marc Denis (G)	6.00	6.00	.50
164 Martin Straka	6.00	4.00	.50
165 A. Kharitonov	6.00	3.00	.25
166 Sergei Brylin	6.00	3.00	.25
167 Éric Dazé	6.00	4.00	.50
168 Alexei Kovalev	10.00	6.00	1.00
169 Jiri Slegr	6.00	3.00	.25
170 Brian Rolston	6.00	4.00	.50
171 Phil Housley	6.00	4.00	.50
172 Josef Vasicek	6.00	3.00	.25
173 Patrick Marleau	6.00	6.00	.50
174 Steven Reinprecht	6.00	4.00	.50
175 Gary Roberts	6.00	4.00	.50
176 Darryl Sydor	6.00	3.00	.25
177 Michel Riesen	6.00	3.00	.25
178 Kevyn Adams	6.00	3.00	.25
179 Andreas Lilja	6.00	3.00	.25
180 Roman Hamrlik	6.00	3.00	.25
181 Mathieu Garon (G)	6.00	4.00	.50
182 Scott Hartnell	6.00	3.00	.25
183 Kenny Jönsson	6.00	3.00	.25
184 Jeff Ulmer	6.00	3.00	.25
185 Petr Hubacek	6.00	3.00	.25
186 Jeremy Roenick	15.00	10.00	1.00
187 Scott Young	6.00	4.00	.50
188 Sergei Berezin	6.00	3.00	.25
189 S. Konowalchuk	6.00	3.00	.25
190 Curtis Joseph (G)	20.00	12.00	1.50
191 Jonathan Girard	6.00	3.00	.25
192 Brian Campbell	6.00	3.00	.25
193 Markus Näslund	20.00	12.00	1.50
194 D. Aebischer (G)	6.00	4.00	.50
195 Peter Bondra	10.00	6.00	1.00
196 Paul Kariya	25.00	16.00	2.00
197 Jason Allison	10.00	6.00	1.00
198 Dominik Hasek (G)	20.00	12.00	1.50
199 Branislav Mezei	6.00	3.00	.25
200 Peter Smrek RC	6.00	3.00	.50
201 Miikka Kiprusoff (G)	6.00	4.00	.50
202 Kristian Kudroc	6.00	3.00	.25
203 Kyle McLaren	6.00	3.00	.25
204 C. Johansson	6.00	3.00	.25
205 G. Naumenko (G)	6.00	3.00	.25
206 Damian Rhodes (G)	6.00	3.00	.25
207 Willie Mitchell	6.00	3.00	.25
208 Daniel Tkaczuk	6.00	3.00	.25
209 Mike Ribeiro	6.00	4.00	.50
210 Rostislav Klesla	10.00	4.00	.50
211 Denis Arkhipov	6.00	3.00	.25
212 Andy McDonald	6.00	3.00	.25
213 Ivan Novoseltsev	6.00	3.00	.25
214 M. Fernandez (G)	6.00	4.00	.50
215 Reto von Arx	6.00	3.00	.25
216 Raymond Bourque	20.00	14.00	2.00
217 M. Danton RC	6.00	4.00	1.00
218 J. Chimera RC	6.00	4.00	1.00
219 Mattias Öhlund	6.00	4.00	.50
220 Rico Fata	6.00	3.00	.25
221 Brad Tapper	6.00	3.00	.25
222 Mike Richter (G)	6.00	6.00	.50
223 Nick Boynton	6.00	3.00	.25
224 Harold Druken	6.00	4.00	.50
225 Chris Clark	6.00	3.00	.25
226 Colin White	6.00	3.00	.25
227 Tyler Bouck	6.00	3.00	.25
228 Jesse Wallin	6.00	3.00	.25
229 Jeff Hackett (G)	6.00	4.00	.50
230 Greg Classen	6.00	3.00	.25
231 Adam Mair	6.00	3.00	.25
232 Ivan Ciernik RC	6.00	4.00	1.00
233 Marc Chouinard	6.00	3.00	.25
234 Chris Mason (G)	6.00	3.00	.25
235 Ronald Petrovicky	6.00	3.00	.25
236 Kyle Calder	6.00	3.00	.25
237 Rick Berry	6.00	3.00	.25
238 M. Darche RC	6.00	4.00	1.00
239 Theoren Fleury	10.00	6.00	1.00
240 Mike Commodore	6.00	3.00	.25
241 Michal Handzus	6.00	3.00	.25
242 Billy Tibbetts RC	6.00	3.00	1.00
243 Cory Stillman	6.00	3.00	.25
244 Valeri Bure	6.00	4.00	.50
245 Matt Pettinger	6.00	3.00	.25
246 Rod Brind'Amour	6.00	4.00	.50
247 P. Dupuis RC	6.00	6.00	2.00
248 Martin Rucinsky	6.00	3.00	.25
249 Cliff Ronning	6.00	3.00	.25
250 Brad Isbister	6.00	3.00	.25
251 Antti-Jussi Niemi	6.00	3.00	.25
252 Mark Bell	6.00	3.00	.25
253 Martin Spanhel	6.00	3.00	.50
254 Andrew Cassels	6.00	3.00	.25
255 Andrew Brunette	6.00	3.00	.25
256 Ron Francis	10.00	6.00	1.00
257 Tony Amonte	10.00	6.00	1.00
258 Espen Knutsen	6.00	3.00	.25
259 Viktor Kozlov	6.00	4.00	.50
260 S. Krivokrasov	6.00	3.00	.25
261 Richard Zednik	6.00	4.00	.50
262 A. Berenzweig	6.00	3.00	.25
263 Pavel Patera	6.00	3.00	.25
264 Mike Johnson	6.00	3.00	.25
265 Teemu Selänne	15.00	10.00	1.00
266 John LeClair	15.00	10.00	1.00
267 Adam Deadmarsh	6.00	4.00	.50
268 Herbert Vasiljevs	6.00	3.00	.25
269 Steve McCarthy	6.00	3.00	.25
270 Mathieu Schneider	6.00	3.00	.25
271 Peter Bartos	6.00	3.00	.25
272 Ray Ferraro	6.00	3.00	.25
273 Éric Chouinard	6.00	3.00	.25
274 Marian Cisar	6.00	3.00	.25
275 Jarome Iginla	15.00	10.00	1.00
276 Jeff O'Neill	6.00	4.00	.50
277 Steve Sullivan	6.00	4.00	.50
278 Rob Blake	10.00	6.00	1.00
279 Geoff Sanderson	6.00	3.00	.25
280 Niclas Wallin	6.00	3.00	.25
281 Vitali Yeremeyev (G)	6.00	3.00	.25
282 Doug Weight	10.00	6.00	1.00
283 Martin Skoula	6.00	3.00	.25
284 Zigmund Palffy	10.00	6.00	1.00
285 Marian Gaborik	20.00	12.00	1.50
286 Saku Koivu	20.00	10.00	1.00
287 Joe Nieuwendyk	6.00	4.00	.50
288 Patrik Elias	15.00	10.00	1.00
289 M. Czerkawski	6.00	3.00	.25
290 Brian Leetch	10.00	6.00	1.00
291 Alexei Yashin	10.00	6.00	1.00
292 Mark Recchi	6.00	4.00	.50
293 Shane Doan	6.00	3.00	.25
294 Brian Holzinger	6.00	3.00	.25
295 M. Samuelsson RC	6.00	3.00	.50
296 Pierre Turgeon	6.00	4.00	.50
297 Sheldon Keefe	6.00	3.00	.25
298 Mats Sundin	20.00	12.00	1.50
299 Bryan Allen	6.00	3.00	.25
300 Adam Oates	6.00	4.00	.50

UPDATE

Update	S100	R200	Base
301 Ilja Bryzgalov (G) RC	6.00	4.00	2.00
302 Erik Cole RC	6.00	6.00	2.00
303 Pavel Datsyuk RC	30.00	20.00	8.00
304 Nikolai Khabibulin (G)	6.00	5.00	.50
305 Dan Blackburn (G) RC	15.00	10.00	4.00
306 Jeff Jillson RC	6.00	4.00	1.50
307 Brian Sutherby RC	6.00	4.00	1.50
308 Vaclav Nedorost RC	6.00	6.00	2.00
309 Byron Ritchie	6.00	3.00	.25
310 Martin Erat RC	6.00	4.00	1.50
311 Vaclav Pletka RC	6.00	3.00	1.00
312 Karel Pilar RC	6.00	4.00	1.50
313 Jaroslav Obsut RC	6.00	3.00	1.00
314 Jason Allison	10.00	7.50	1.00
315 Eric Lindros	20.00	12.50	1.50
316 Mike Farrell RC	6.00	3.00	1.00
317 Doug Gilmour	10.00	7.50	1.00
318 Bruno St-Jacques RC	6.00	3.00	1.00
319 Martin Lapointe	6.00	5.00	.50
320 Dan Focht	6.00	3.00	.25
321 Ben Simon RC	6.00	3.00	1.00
322 Mike Peluso RC	6.00	4.00	1.50
323 Martin Cibak RC	6.00	3.00	1.00
324 Marcel Hossa RC	15.00	10.00	4.00
325 Chris Neil RC	6.00	3.00	1.00
326 Mark Rycroft RC	6.00	3.00	1.00
327 Timo Pärssinen RC	6.00	3.00	1.00
328 S. Charpentier (G) RC	6.00	4.00	1.50
329 Kip Brennan RC	6.00	3.00	1.00
330 Christian Berglund RC	6.00	4.00	1.50
331 Tom Kostopoulos RC	6.00	3.00	1.00
332 Pat Kavanagh RC	6.00	3.00	1.00
333 S. Centomo (G) RC	6.00	6.00	2.00
334 Andrew Brunette	6.00	3.00	.25
335 Toni Dahlman RC	6.00	3.00	1.00
336 Kamil Piros RC	6.00	4.00	1.50
337 Robert Schnabel RC	6.00	3.00	1.00
338 Radim Vrbata	10.00	8.00	.50
339 Chris Osgood (G)	10.00	7.50	1.00
340 Steve Montador RC	6.00	3.00	1.00
341 R. Divis (G) RC	6.00	4.00	1.50
342 Steve Moore RC	6.00	3.00	1.00
343 Branko Radivojevic RC	6.00	6.00	2.00
344 Zdenek Kutlak RC	6.00	3.00	1.00
345 Jiri Dopita RC	6.00	4.00	1.50
346 Josef Boumedienne RC	6.00	3.00	1.00
347 Phil Housley	6.00	4.00	.50
348 Niko Kapanen RC	6.00	6.00	2.00
349 Travis Roche RC	6.00	3.00	1.00
350 Raffi Torres RC	6.00	6.00	2.00
351 Randy Robitaille	6.00	3.00	.25
352 Chris Corrinet RC	6.00	3.00	1.00
353 Pierre Turgeon	6.00	5.00	.50
354 Pavel Skrbek RC	6.00	3.00	1.00
355 Jeremy Roenick	15.00	10.00	1.00
356 Riku Hahl RC	6.00	4.00	1.50
357 Stanislav Gron RC	6.00	3.00	1.00
358 P. Nurminen (G) RC	6.00	6.00	2.00
359 Nick Smith RC	6.00	3.00	1.00
360 Shane Endicott RC	6.00	3.00	1.00
361 Ales Kotalik RC	15.00	10.00	4.00
362 Blake Bellefeuille RC	6.00	3.00	1.00
363 Jaroslav Bednar RC	6.00	4.00	1.50
364 Andreas Salomonsson RC	6.00	3.00	1.00
365 Krys Kolanos RC	6.00	6.00	2.00
366 Tim Connolly	6.00	5.00	.50
367 Ivan Huml RC	6.00	6.00	2.00
368 Sean Avery RC	6.00	4.00	1.50
369 Trent Hunter RC	6.00	4.00	1.50
370 Richard Scott RC	6.00	3.00	1.00
371 Doug Weight	10.00	7.50	1.00
372 Ilya Kovalchuk RC	40.00	24.00	10.00
373 Dominik Hasek (G)	20.00	12.50	1.50
374 Scott Clemmensen (G) RC	6.00	4.00	1.50
375 Nikita Alexeev RC	6.00	6.00	2.00
376 Luc Robitaille	15.00	10.00	1.00
377 Mike Peca	6.00	5.00	.50
378 Brett Hull	20.00	12.50	1.50
379 Valeri Bure	6.00	4.00	.50
380 Pavel Brendl	10.00	8.00	.50
381 Jukka Hentunen RC	6.00	3.00	1.00
382 John Erskine RC	6.00	3.00	1.00
383 Nick Schultz RC	6.00	4.00	1.50
384 Radek Martinek RC	6.00	3.00	1.00
385 Dany Heatley	30.00	18.00	2.50
386 Alex Auld (G)	6.00	3.00	.50
387 Tyler Arnason RC	15.00	10.00	4.00
388 Ty Conklin (G) RC	6.00	6.00	2.00
389 Olivier Michaud (G) RC	6.00	6.00	2.00
390 Sandis Ozolinsh	6.00	3.00	.25
391 E. Konstantinov (G) RC	6.00	4.00	1.50
392 Roman Turek (G)	6.00	6.00	.50
393 Kristian Huselius RC	10.00	8.00	3.00
394 Alexei Yashin	10.00	7.50	1.00
395 Alexander Mogilny	6.00	6.00	.50
396 Éric Meloche RC	6.00	3.00	1.00
397 Andy McDonald	6.00	3.00	.25
398 Niklas Hagman RC	6.00	4.00	1.50
399 Ryan Flinn RC	6.00	3.00	1.00
400 Mike Weaver RC	6.00	3.00	1.00
401 Nolan Yonkman	6.00	3.00	.25
402 Ryan Jardine	6.00	3.00	.25
403 Andrej Nedorost RC	6.00	3.00	1.00
404 Andrei Podkonicky RC	6.00	4.00	1.50
405 Hnat Domenichelli	6.00	3.00	.25
406 Bob Wren RC	6.00	3.00	1.00
407 Brad Norton RC	6.00	3.00	1.00
408 Brian Pothier RC	6.00	3.00	1.00
409 Trevor Letowski	6.00	3.00	.25
410 Chris Bala RC	6.00	3.00	1.00
411 Tom Fitzgerald	6.00	3.00	.25
412 Petr Tenkrat	6.00	3.00	.25
413 Dan Snyder RC	6.00	3.00	1.00
414 David Cullen RC	6.00	3.00	1.00
415 David Ling RC	6.00	3.00	1.00
416 Dean Melanson RC	6.00	3.00	1.00
417 Duvie Westcott RC	6.00	3.00	1.00
418 Éric Beaudoin RC	6.00	3.00	1.00
419 Marty McInnis	6.00	3.00	.25
420 Francis Lessard RC	6.00	3.00	1.00
421 F. Cassivi (G) RC	6.00	4.00	1.50
422 Bill Lindsay	6.00	3.00	.25
423 Kim Johnsson	6.00	3.00	.25
424 Danny Markov	6.00	3.00	.25
425 Guillaume Lefebvre RC	6.00	3.00	1.00
426 Hannes Hyvonen RC	6.00	3.00	1.00
427 Jeff Daw RC	6.00	3.00	1.00
428 Jody Shelley RC	6.00	4.00	1.50
429 Joel Kwiatkowski RC	6.00	3.00	1.00
430 Josh Langfeld RC	6.00	3.00	1.00
431 Kelly Fairchild RC	6.00	3.00	1.00
432 Kevin Sawyer RC	6.00	3.00	1.00
433 Kirby Law RC	6.00	3.00	1.00
434 Kyle Rossiter RC	6.00	3.00	1.00
435 Lukas Krajicek RC	6.00	6.00	2.00
436 Mark Hartigan RC	6.00	3.00	1.00
437 Martin Prusek (G) RC	10.00	8.00	3.00
438 Matt Davidson RC	6.00	3.00	1.00
439 André Roy	6.00	3.00	.25
440 Chris Kelleher RC	6.00	3.00	1.00
441 Mike Matteucci RC	6.00	3.00	1.00
442 Nathan Perrott RC	6.00	3.00	1.00
443 Neil Little (G) RC	6.00	4.00	1.50
444 R. Thompson RC	6.00	3.00	1.00
445 Ryan Tobler RC	6.00	3.00	1.00
446 Scott Nichol RC	6.00	3.00	1.00
447 Jiri Slegr	6.00	3.00	.25
448 Stephen Weiss RC	20.00	12.00	8.00
449 Jeff Cowan	6.00	3.00	.25
450 Thomas Ziegler RC	6.00	4.00	1.50
451 Todd Rohloff RC	6.00	3.00	1.00
452 Blake Sloan	6.00	3.00	.25
453 Tony Tuzzolino RC	6.00	3.00	1.00
454 Tony Virta RC	6.00	3.00	1.00
455 Adam Oates	6.00	5.00	.50
456 Benoît Brunet	6.00	3.00	.25
457 Benoît Hogue	6.00	3.00	.25
458 Brian Savage	6.00	4.00	.50
459 Cliff Ronning	6.00	3.00	.25
460 Darius Kasparaitis	6.00	3.00	.25
461 Dean McAmmond	6.00	3.00	.25
462 Donald Brashear	6.00	3.00	.25
463 Glen Murray	6.00	6.00	.50
464 Jamie Allison	6.00	3.00	.25
465 J. Langenbrunner	6.00	3.00	.25
466 Jan Hlavac	6.00	3.00	.25
467 Jason Arnott	6.00	6.00	.50
468 Joe Nieuwendyk	6.00	5.00	.50
469 Jozef Stümpel	6.00	3.00	.25
470 Juha Ylönen	6.00	3.00	.25
471 Kevin Weekes (G)	6.00	3.00	.25
472 Kirill Safronov RC	6.00	4.00	1.50
473 Manny Malhotra	6.00	3.00	.25
474 Martin Rucinsky	6.00	3.00	.25
475 Matthew Barnaby	6.00	3.00	.25
476 Mike Keane	6.00	3.00	.25
477 Mike York	6.00	4.00	.50
478 Mikko Eloranta	6.00	3.00	.25
479 Pascal Rhéaume	6.00	3.00	.25
480 Pavel Bure	15.00	10.00	1.00
481 Pierre Dagenais	6.00	3.00	.25
482 Randy McKay	6.00	3.00	.25
483 Ray Ferraro	6.00	3.00	.25
484 Rem Murray	6.00	3.00	.25
485 Rick Berry	6.00	3.00	.25
486 Sean Brown	6.00	3.00	.25
487 Sean Hill	6.00	3.00	.25
488 Sergei Berezin	6.00	3.00	.25
489 Shane Willis	6.00	3.00	.25
490 Stéphane Fiset (G)	6.00	4.00	.50
491 Stéphane Richer	6.00	3.00	.25
492 Steve Thomas	6.00	3.00	.25
493 Tom Barrasso (G)	6.00	5.00	.50
494 Tom Poti	6.00	3.00	.25
495 Trevor Linden	6.00	5.00	.50
496 Valeri Kamensky	6.00	4.00	.50
497 Ville Nieminen	6.00	3.00	.25
498 Zdeno Chara	6.00	3.00	.25
499 Shjon Podein	6.00	3.00	.25
500 Shaun Van Allen	6.00	3.00	.25

HE SHOOTS HE SCORES REDEMPTION

Each redemption card was worth one, two, or three points. Collectors who accumulated 400 points could trade their redemption cards in for a special random jersey card. This redemption program ended on January 31, 2002.

Insert Set (20 cards):	10.00
Description	HSHS
Saku Koivu, Mont. [1 Point]	.50
Vincent Lecavalier, Tamp. [2 Points]	.50
Mark Messier, NYRa. [1 Point]	.50
Mike Modano, Dall. [1 Point]	.50
Evgeni Nabokov (G), SanJ. [1 Point]	.50
Chris Pronger, SLou. [1 Point]	.50
Teemu Selänne, SanJ. [3 Points]	.50
Mats Sundin, Toro. [1 Point]	.50
Roman Cechmanek (G), Phil. [1 Point]	.50
Martin Havlat, Otta. [1 Point]	.50
Milan Hejduk, Colo. [1 Point]	.50
Curtis Joseph (G), Toro. [1 Point]	.50
Joe Sakic, Colo. [2 Points]	1.00
Martin Brodeur (G), NJer. [2 Points]	1.00
Pavel Bure, Flor. [3 Points]	.50
Peter Forsberg, Colo. [2 Points]	1.00
Paul Kariya, Anah. [3 Points]	1.00
Steve Yzerman, Detr. [2 Points]	2.00
Patrick Roy (G), Colo. [2 Points]	2.50
Mario Lemieux, Pitt. [3 Points]	3.00

500 GOAL SCORERS

Insert Set (28 cards):	4,100
Description	500G
Dave Andreychuk, Bost. ✂ {*99}	60.00
Jean Béliveau, Mont. ✂ {*20}	300.00
Mike Bossy, NYIs. ✂ {*50}	125.00
John Bucyk, Bost. ✂ {*99}	60.00
Dino Ciccarelli, Detr. ✂ {*99}	60.00
Marcel Dionne, LosA. ✂ {*50}	100.00
Phil Esposito, NYRa. ✂ {*40}	125.00
Ron Francis, Caro. ✂ {*25}	125.00
Mike Gartner, Toro. ✂ {*99}	75.00
Michel Goulet, Chic. ✂ {*99}	60.00
Wayne Gretzky, Edmo. ✂ {*20}	900.00
Dale Hawerchuk, Phil. ✂ {*99}	60.00
Gordie Howe, Detr. ✂ {*20}	525.00
Bobby Hull, Chic. ✂ {*40}	175.00
Brett Hull, SLou. ✂ {*99}	100.00
Jari Kurri, LosA. ✂ {*99}	125.00
Guy Lafleur, Mont. ✂ {*50}	150.00
Mario Lemieux, Pitt. ✂ {*20}	675.00
Frank Mahovlich, Mont. ✂ {*40}	125.00
Lanny McDonald, Toro. ✂ {*99}	75.00
Mark Messier, NYRa. ✂ {*99}	100.00
Stan Mikita, Chic. ✂ {*40}	125.00
Joe Mullen, Calg. ✂ {*99}	60.00
Gilbert Perreault, Buff. ✂ {*99}	60.00
Maurice Richard, Mont. ✂ {*20}	525.00
Luc Robitaille, LosA. ✂ {*99}	75.00
Brendan Shanahan, Detr. ✂ {*25}	200.00
Bryan Trottier, NYIs. ✂ {*99}	75.00
Pat Verbeek, NJer. ✂ {*99}	60.00
Steve Yzerman, Detr. ✂ {*99}	250.00

ALL-STAR JERSEY

There are three versions for each card: the Jersey card (#/98), the Emblem card (#/10) and the In The Numbers card (#/10). Pricing on the scarce Emblem and In The Numbers cards vary considerably.

Insert Set (50 cards):	14,800	2,600
Insert	AS10	ASJ98
Daniel Alfredsson, AS '98 ✂	575.00	100.00
Tony Amonte, AS '01 ✂	240.00	50.00
Rob Blake, AS '01 ✂	240.00	50.00
Peter Bondra, AS '99 ✂	240.00	50.00
Radek Bonk, AS '01 ✂	200.00	50.00
Raymond Bourque, AS '01 ✂	480.00	100.00
Martin Brodeur (G), AS '01 ✂	640.00	125.00
Pavel Bure, AS '01 ✂	320.00	50.00
Pavel Bure, AS '00 ✂	320.00	50.00
Valeri Bure, AS '00 ✂	200.00	50.00
Roman Cechmanek (G), AS '01 ✂	200.00	50.00
Pavol Demitra, AS '00 ✂	200.00	50.00
Theoren Fleury, AS '01 ✂	240.00	50.00
Peter Forsberg, AS '01 ✂	560.00	100.00
Simon Gagné, AS '01 ✂	320.00	50.00
Scott Gomez, AS '00 ✂	200.00	50.00
Bill Guerin, AS '01 ✂	200.00	50.00
Dominik Hasek (G), AS '01 ✂	400.00	75.00
Milan Hejduk, AS '01 ✂	320.00	50.00
Brett Hull, AS '96 ✂	400.00	75.00
Arturs Irbe (G), AS '99 ✂	200.00	50.00
Jaromir Jagr, AS '00 ✂	400.00	75.00
Curtis Joseph (G), AS '00 ✂	400.00	75.00
Paul Kariya, AS '01 ✂	560.00	100.00
Nikolai Khabibulin (G), AS '99 ✂	200.00	50.00
Alexei Kovalev, AS '01 ✂	240.00	50.00
Viktor Kozlov, AS '00 ✂	200.00	50.00
Brian Leetch, AS '01 ✂	240.00	50.00
Mario Lemieux, AS '01 ✂	1200.00	250.00
Nicklas Lidström, AS '01 ✂	240.00	50.00
Eric Lindros, AS '99 ✂	400.00	75.00
Al MacInnis, AS '99 ✂	200.00	50.00
Mark Messier, AS '00 ✂	400.00	75.00
Mike Modano, AS '00 ✂	400.00	75.00
Evgeni Nabokov (G), AS '01 ✂	240.00	50.00
Markus Näslund, AS '99 ✂	400.00	75.00
Owen Nolan, AS '00 ✂	240.00	50.00
Teppo Numminen, AS '01 ✂	200.00	50.00
Sandis Ozolinsh, AS '01 ✂	200.00	50.00
Zigmund Palffy, AS '01 ✂	240.00	50.00
Chris Pronger, AS '99 ✂	240.00	50.00
Patrick Roy (G), AS '01 ✂	950.00	200.00
Joe Sakic, AS '01 ✂	640.00	125.00
Tommy Salo (G), AS '00 ✂	200.00	50.00
Teemu Selänne, AS '99 ✂	320.00	50.00
Keith Tkachuk, AS '99 ✂	240.00	50.00
Roman Turek (G), AS '00 ✂	200.00	50.00
Doug Weight, AS '01 ✂	240.00	50.00
Alexei Yashin, AS '99 ✂	240.00	50.00
Steve Yzerman, AS '00 ✂	960.00	200.00

DOUBLE ALL-STAR JERSEY

Insert Set (30 cards):	3,375
Insert (#/60)	DASJ
Tony Amonte, AS '01 ✂ AS '99 ✂	80.00
Rob Blake, AS '01 ✂ AS '94 ✂	80.00
Raymond Bourque, AS '01 ✂ AS '94 ✂	150.00
Martin Brodeur (G), AS '01 ✂ AS '97 ✂	200.00
Pavel Bure, AS '01 ✂ AS '97 ✂	100.00
Theoren Fleury, AS '01 ✂ AS '99 ✂	80.00
Peter Forsberg, AS '01 ✂ AS '98 ✂	175.00
Wayne Gretzky, AS '98 ✂ AS '94 ✂	525.00
Dominik Hasek (G), AS '01 ✂ AS '98 ✂	125.00
Jaromir Jagr, AS '00 ✂ AS '98 ✂	125.00
Curtis Joseph (G), AS '00 ✂ AS '94 ✂	125.00
Paul Kariya, AS '01 ✂ AS '96 ✂	175.00
John LeClair, AS '97 ✂ AS '96 ✂	100.00
Brian Leetch, AS '01 ✂ AS '94 ✂	80.00
Mario Lemieux, AS '01 ✂ AS '96 ✂	375.00
Nicklas Lidström, AS '01 ✂ AS '99 ✂	80.00
Eric Lindros, AS '99 ✂ AS '96 ✂	125.00
Al MacInnis, AS '00 ✂ AS '99 ✂	80.00
Mark Messier, AS '00 ✂ AS '94 ✂	125.00
Mike Modano, AS '00 ✂ AS '98 ✂	125.00
Owen Nolan, AS '00 ✂ AS '97 ✂	80.00
Chris Pronger, AS '00 ✂ AS '99 ✂	80.00
Jeremy Roenick, AS '00 ✂ AS '94 ✂	100.00
Patrick Roy (G), AS '01 ✂ AS '94 ✂	300.00
Joe Sakic, AS '01 ✂ AS '98 ✂	200.00
Teemu Selänne, AS '99 ✂ AS '94 ✂	100.00
Brendan Shanahan, AS '00 ✂ AS '96 ✂	125.00
Mats Sundin, AS '00/AS '97 ✂	125.00
Alexei Yashin, AS '99 ✂ AS '94 ✂	80.00
Steve Yzerman, AS '00 ✂ AS '97 ✂	300.00

ALL-STAR STARTERS

Insert Set (12 cards):	5,000
Insert (#/70)	S
Rob Blake, AS '01 ✂	50.00
Raymond Bourque, AS '01 ✂	125.00
Pavel Bure, AS '01 ✂	75.00
Theoren Fleury, AS '01 ✂	50.00
Peter Forsberg, AS '01 ✂	150.00
Dominik Hasek (G), AS '01 ✂	100.00
Milan Hejduk, AS '01 ✂	75.00
Paul Kariya, AS '01 ✂	150.00
Nicklas Lidström, AS '01 ✂	50.00
Sandis Ozolinsh, AS '01 ✂	50.00
Patrick Roy (G), AS '01 ✂	275.00
Joe Sakic, AS '01 ✂	175.00

ALL-STAR TEAMMATES

Insert Set (50 cards):	2,600
Insert (#/80)	AST
1 Hejduk ✂ / Nabokov (G) ✂ / Palffy ✂	100.00
2 Gagné ✂ / Kariya ✂ / Lemieux ✂	250.00
3 Blake ✂ / Roy (G) ✂ / Sakic ✂	225.00
4 Brodeur (G) ✂ / Leetch ✂ / Weight ✂	125.00
5 Bure ✂ Cechmanek (G) ✂ / Forsberg ✂	125.00
6 Hasek (G) ✂ / Kovalev ✂ / Lidström ✂	100.00
7 Bourque ✂ / Fleury ✂ / Leetch ✂	100.00
8 Amonte ✂ / Guerin ✂ / Weight ✂	50.00
9 Cechma. (G) ✂ / Hasek (G) ✂ / Nabokov (G) ✂	100.00
10 Fleury ✂ / Kariya ✂ / Sakic ✂	150.00
11 Forsberg ✂ / Hejduk ✂	125.00
12 Lemieux ✂ / Roy (G) ✂	325.00
13 Blake ✂ / Bourque ✂	100.00
14 P.Bure ✂ / V.Bure ✂ / Kozlov ✂	50.00
15 Brodeur (G) ✂ / Gomez ✂ / Stevens ✂	100.00
16 MacInnis ✂ / Pronger ✂	50.00
17 Amonte ✂ / Modano ✂ / Roenick ✂	100.00
18 Kölzig (G) ✂ / Salo (G) ✂ / Turek (G) ✂	50.00
19 Shanahan ✂ / Yzerman ✂	200.00
20 Salo (G) ✂ / Sundin ✂	75.00
21 Bure ✂ / Jagr ✂	100.00
22 Joseph (G) ✂ / Modano ✂ / Yzerman ✂	200.00
23 P.Bure ✂ / V.Bure ✂	50.00
24 Gomez ✂ / Messier ✂ / Yzerman ✂	150.00
25 Lindros ✂ / Modano ✂	125.00
26 Forsberg ✂ / Selänne ✂	125.00
27 Bondra ✂ / Näslund ✂ / Yashin ✂	100.00
28 Hasek (G) ✂ / Irbe (G) ✂ / Khabibulin (G) ✂	75.00
29 Lidström ✂ / Näslund ✂ / Sundin ✂	125.00
30 MacInnis ✂ / Pronger ✂	50.00
31 Amonte ✂ / Kariya ✂	125.00
32 Forsberg ✂ / Jagr ✂	150.00
33 LeClair ✂ / Modano ✂	100.00
34 Gretzky ✂ / Lindros ✂ / Modano ✂	350.00
35 Roy (G) ✂ / Sakic ✂	250.00
36 Bure ✂ / Forsberg ✂ / Jagr ✂	150.00
37 Gretzky ✂ / Roy (G) ✂	400.00
38 Bourque ✂ / Chelios ✂ / Leetch ✂	100.00
39 Lindros ✂ / Messier ✂	125.00
40 Hasek (G) ✂ / Khabibulin (G) ✂	75.00
41 Modano ✂ / Sakic ✂	150.00
42 Bourque ✂ / Hasek (G) ✂	125.00
43 Sundin ✂ / Yzerman ✂	200.00
44 Bure ✂ / Kariya ✂	125.00
45 Selänne ✂ / Sundin ✂	100.00
46 Belfour (G) ✂ / Hull ✂	125.00
47 Jagr ✂ / Lindros ✂	125.00
48 Forsberg ✂ / Kariya ✂	175.00
49 Gretzky ✂ / Joseph (G) ✂	300.00
50 Bourque ✂ / Roy (G) ✂	225.00

COUNTRY OF ORIGIN

Actual realized pricing on these scarce cards may vary considerably from listed pricing.

Insert Set (60 cards):	13,100
Insert (#/12)	OP
Daniel Alfredsson ✂	575.00
Tony Amonte ✂	200.00
Rob Blake ✂	200.00
Peter Bondra ✂	200.00
Radek Bonk ✂	200.00
Raymond Bourque ✂	350.00
Martin Brodeur (G) ✂	475.00
Pavel Bure ✂	225.00
Valeri Bure ✂	200.00
Roman Cechmanek (G) ✂	200.00
Pavol Demitra ✂	200.00
Theoren Fleury ✂	200.00
Peter Forsberg ✂	400.00
Bill Guerin ✂	200.00
Dominik Hasek (G) ✂	300.00
Milan Hejduk ✂	225.00
Jaromir Jagr ✂	300.00
Curtis Joseph (G) ✂	300.00
Paul Kariya ✂	400.00
Alexei Kovalev ✂	200.00
Brian Leetch ✂	200.00
Mario Lemieux ✂	900.00
Nicklas Lidström ✂	200.00
Eric Lindros ✂	300.00
Al MacInnis ✂	200.00
Mike Modano ✂	300.00
Markus Näslund ✂	300.00
Scott Niedermayer ✂	200.00
Teppo Numminen ✂	200.00
Sandis Ozolinsh ✂	200.00
Zigmund Palffy ✂	200.00
Jeremy Roenick ✂	225.00
Patrick Roy (G) ✂	700.00
Joe Sakic ✂	475.00
Tommy Salo (G) ✂	200.00
Teemu Selänne ✂	225.00
Keith Tkachuk ✂	200.00
Doug Weight ✂	200.00
Alexei Yashin ✂	200.00
Steve Yzerman ✂	700.00
Insert (#/10)	OP
Sean Burke (G) ✂	200.00
Vincent Damphousse ✂	200.00
Éric Dazé ✂	200.00
Patrik Elias ✂	250.00
Sergei Fedorov ✂	325.00
Jarome Iginla ✂	250.00
Ed Jovanovski ✂	200.00
Tomas Kaberle ✂	200.00
Sami Kapanen ✂	200.00
Nikolai Khabibulin (G) ✂	200.00
John LeClair ✂	250.00
Mario Lemieux ✂	975.00
Owen Nolan ✂	200.00
Chris Pronger ✂	200.00
Mark Recchi ✂	200.00
Luc Robitaille ✂	250.00
Brendan Shanahan ✂	325.00
Mats Sundin ✂	325.00
José Théodore (G) ✂	375.00
Joe Thornton ✂	375.00

DRAFT DAY REDEMPTION

These cards could be redeemed only after the player made his NHL debut. Four of these cards were redeemable during the 2001-02 season (see 2001 - 02 Be A Player Draft Florida 2001) while six of these cards were redeemable during the 2002-03 season (see 2002 - 03 Be A Player Draft Florida 2001).

Insert Set (30 cards):	
Redemption Card (#/100)	Draft
1 Expired (see 2001 - 02 Be A Player Draft Florida 2001)	
2 Expired (see 2002 - 03 Be A Player Draft Florida 2001)	
3 Expired (see 2002 - 03 Be A Player Draft Florida 2001)	
4 Expired (see 2001 - 02 Be A Player Draft Florida 2001)	
5 Expired (see 2002 - 03 Be A Player Draft Florida 2001)	
6 Draft redemption	
7 Draft redemption	
8 Expired (see 2002 - 03 Be A Player Draft Florida 2001)	
9 Draft redemption	
10 Expired (see 2001 - 02 Be A Player Draft Florida 2001)	
11 Draft redemption	
12 Draft redemption	
13 Expired (see 2002 - 03 Be A Player Draft Florida 2001)	
14 Expired (see 2002 - 03 Be A Player Draft Florida 2001)	
15 Draft redemption	
16 Draft redemption	
17 Draft redemption	
18 Draft redemption	
19 Draft redemption	
20 Draft redemption	
21 Draft redemption	
22 Draft redemption	
23 Draft redemption	
24 Expired (see 2001 - 02 Be A Player Draft Florida 2001)	
25 Draft redemption	
26 Draft redemption	
27 Draft redemption	
28 Draft redemption	
29 Draft redemption	
30 Draft redemption	

GOALIE JERSEY

Insert Set (20 cards):	1,075
Insert (#/80)	GWJ
GJ-1 Byron Dafoe (G), Bost. ✂	50.00
GJ-2 Dominik Hasek (G), Buff. ✂	75.00
GJ-3 Mike Vernon (G), Calg. ✂	50.00
GJ-4 Arturs Irbe (G), Caro. ✂	50.00
GJ-5 Jocelyn Thibault (G), Chic. ✂	50.00
GJ-6 Patrick Roy (G), Colo. ✂	200.00
GJ-7 Ed Belfour (G), Dall. ✂	75.00
GJ-8 Chris Osgood (G), Detr. ✂	50.00
GJ-9 Johan Hedberg (G), Pitt. ✂	50.00
GJ-10 T. Kidd (G) ✂ / R. Luongo (G) ✂	50.00
GJ-11 J. Hackett (G) ✂ / J. Théodore (G) ✂	75.00
GJ-12 Mike Dunham (G), Nash. ✂	50.00
GJ-13 Martin Brodeur (G), NJer. ✂	125.00
GJ-14 Mike Richter (G), NYRa. ✂	50.00
GJ-15 Brian Boucher (G), Phil. ✂	75.00
GJ-15 R. Cechmanek (G) ✂ / B. Boucher (G) ✂	50.00
GJ-16 Jean-Sébastien Aubin (G), Pitt. ✂	50.00
GJ-17 Roman Turek (G), SLou. ✂	50.00
GJ-18 Curtis Joseph (G), Toro. ✂	75.00
GJ-19 Olaf Kölzig (G), Wash. ✂	50.00
GJ-20 Félix Potvin (G), LosA. ✂	100.00

GOALIE TRADITIONS

Insert Set (42 cards):	3,800
Description	GT
1 Curtis Joseph (G), Toro. ✂ {*60}	100.00
2 Johnny Bower (G), Toro. ✂ {*60}	75.00
3 Turk Broda (G), Toro. ✂ {*60}	65.00
4 Patrick Roy (G), Mont. ✂ {*60}	250.00
5 Jacques Plante (G), Mont. ✂ {*60}	175.00
6 José Théodore (G), Mont. ✂ {*60}	125.00
7 Glenn Hall (G), Chic. ✂ {*60}	75.00
8 Tony Esposito (G), Chic. ✂ {*60}	75.00
9 Jocelyn Thibault (G), Chic. ✂ {*60}	65.00
10 Chuck Rayner (G), NYRa. ✂ {*60}	65.00
11 Ed Giacomin (G), NYRa. ✂ {*60}	75.00
12 Mike Richter (G), NYRa. ✂ {*60}	65.00
13 Frank Brimsek (G), Bost. ✂ {*60}	65.00
14 Gerry Cheevers (G), Bost. ✂ {*60}	65.00
15 Byron Dafoe (G), Bost. ✂ {*60}	65.00
16 Terry Sawchuk (G), Detr. ✂ {*60}	250.00
17 Roger Crozier (G), Detr. ✂ {*60}	65.00
18 Chris Osgood (G), Detr. ✂ {*60}	65.00
19 T. Broda (G) ✂ / C. Joseph (G) ✂ {*50}	100.00
20 J. Bower (G) ✂ / C. Joseph (G) ✂ {*50}	100.00
21 J. Bower (G) ✂ / T. Broda (G) ✂ {*50}	80.00
22 R. Crozier (G) ✂ / T. Sawchuk (G) ✂ {*50}	100.00

☐ 23 R. Crozier (G) ✂ / C. Osgood (G) ✂ {*50} 80.00
☐ 24 C. Osgood (G) ✂ / T. Sawchuk (G) ✂ {*50} 150.00
☐ 25 G. Hall (G) ✂ / J. Thibault (G) ✂ {*50} 80.00
☐ 26 T. Esposito (G) ✂ / G. Hall (G) ✂ {*50} 80.00
☐ 27 T. Esposito (G) ✂ / J. Thibault (G) ✂ {*50} 80.00
☐ 28 J. Plante (G) ✂ / P. Roy (G) ✂ {*50} 300.00
☐ 29 J. Plante (G) ✂ / J. Théodore (G) ✂ {*50} 175.00
☐ 30 P. Roy (G) ✂ / J. Théodore (G) ✂ {*50} 225.00
☐ 31 F. Brimsek (G) ✂ / B. Dafoe (G) ✂ {*50} 80.00
☐ 32 F. Brimsek (G) ✂ / G. Cheevers (G) ✂ {*50} 80.00
☐ 33 G. Cheevers (G) ✂ / B. Dafoe (G) ✂ {*50} 80.00
☐ 34 E. Giacomin (G) ✂ / C. Rayner (G) ✂ {*50} 80.00
☐ 35 C. Rayner (G) ✂ / M. Richter (G) ✂ {*50} 80.00
☐ 36 E. Giacomin (G) ✂ / M. Richter (G) ✂ {*50} 80.00

Triple (limited to 20) **GT**
☐ 37 Bower (G) ✂ / Broda (G) ✂ / Joseph (G) ✂ 200.00
☐ 38 Crozier (G) ✂ / Osgood (G) ✂ / Sawchuk (G) ✂ 200.00
☐ 39 Esposito (G) ✂ / Hall (G) ✂ / Thibault (G) ✂ 200.00
☐ 40 Plante (G) ✂ / Roy (G) ✂ / Théodore (G) ✂ 450.00
☐ 41 Brimsek (G) ✂ / Cheevers (G) ✂ / Dafoe (G) ✂ 200.00
☐ 42 Giacomin (G) ✂ / Rayner (G) ✂ / Richter (G) ✂ 200.00

PATENTED POWER

Insert Set (6 cards): **1,500**
Insert (#/20) **PP**
☐ PP-1 J. Jagr ✂ / M. Sundin ✂ 200.00
☐ PP-2 W. Gretzky ✂ / M. Lemieux ✂ 800.00
☐ PP-3 P. Bure ✂ / M. Hejduk ✂ 200.00
☐ PP-4 M. Modano ✂ / C. Pronger ✂ 200.00
☐ PP-5 P. Kariya ✂ / J. Sakic ✂ 300.00
☐ PP-6 P. Forsberg ✂ / S. Yzerman ✂ 400.00

ROCKET'S MATES

Insert Set (10 cards): **1,500**
Insert (#/50) **RM**
☐ RM-1 M. Richard ✂ / J. Plante (G) 200.00
☐ RM-2 M. Richard ✂ / D. Harvey 200.00
☐ RM-3 M. Richard ✂ / J. Béliveau 200.00
☐ RM-4 M. Richard ✂ / H. Richard 200.00
☐ RM-5 M. Richard ✂ / B. Geoffrion 200.00
☐ RM-6 M. Richard ✂ / D. St-Laurent 200.00
☐ RM-7 M. Richard ✂ / E. Lach 200.00
☐ RM-8 M. Richard ✂ / D. Moore 200.00
☐ RM-9 M. Richard ✂ / E. Bouchard 200.00
☐ RM-10 M. Richard ✂ / J. Talbot 200.00

STANLEY CUP CHAMPIONS

Insert Set (14 cards): **1,750**
Insert (#/40) **CA**
☐ 1 Patrick Roy (G), Colo. ✂ 550.00
☐ 2 Adam Foote, Colo. ✂ 80.00
☐ 3 Raymond Bourque, Colo. ✂ 350.00
☐ 4 Martin Skoula, Colo. ✂ 80.00
☐ 5 Shjon Podein, Colo. ✂ 80.00
☐ 6 Alex Tanguay, Colo. ✂ 100.00
☐ 7 Chris Dingman, Colo. ✂ 80.00
☐ 8 Milan Hejduk, Colo. ✂ 150.00
☐ 9 Peter Forsberg, Colo. ✂ 250.00
☐ 10 Joe Sakic, Colo. ✂ 300.00
☐ 11 Éric Messier, Colo. ✂ 80.00
☐ 12 Jon Klemm, Colo. ✂ 80.00
☐ 13 Dave Reid, Colo. ✂ 80.00
☐ 14 Chris Drury, Colo. ✂ 100.00

STANLEY CUP PLAYOFFS

Insert Set (32 cards): **2,800**
Description **SC**
☐ SC-1 Mats Sundin, Toro. ✂ {*95} 75.00
☐ SC-2 Daniel Alfredsson, Otta. ✂ {*95} 100.00
☐ SC-3 Scott Stevens, NJer. ✂ {*95} 40.00
☐ SC-4 Arturs Irbe (G), Caro. ✂ {*95} 40.00
☐ SC-5 Martin Straka, Pitt. ✂ {*95} 40.00
☐ SC-6 Olaf Kölzig (G), Wash. ✂ {*95} 50.00
☐ SC-7 Doug Gilmour, Buff. ✂ {*95} 50.00
☐ SC-8 Roman Cechmanek (G), Phil. ✂ {*95} 40.00
☐ SC-9 Joe Sakic, Colo. ✂ {*95} 125.00
☐ SC-10 Daniel Sedin, Vanc. ✂ {*95} 40.00
☐ SC-11 Zigmund Palffy, LosA. ✂ {*95} 50.00
☐ SC-12 Sergei Fedorov, Detr. ✂ {*95} 75.00
☐ SC-13 Ed Belfour (G), Dall. ✂ {*95} 75.00
☐ SC-14 Tommy Salo (G), Edmo. ✂ {*95} 40.00
☐ SC-15 Roman Turek (G), SLou. ✂ {*95} 40.00
☐ SC-16 Owen Nolan, SanJ. ✂ {*95} 50.00

Description **SC**
☐ SC-17 Patrick Roy (G), Colo. ✂ {*80} 225.00
☐ SC-18 Luc Robitaille, LosA. ✂ {*80} 75.00
☐ SC-19 Chris Pronger, SLou. ✂ {*80} 50.00
☐ SC-20 Mike Modano, Dall. ✂ {*80} 100.00
☐ SC-21 Martin Brodeur (G), NJer. ✂ {*80} 150.00
☐ SC-22 Curtis Joseph (G), Toro. ✂ {*80} 100.00
☐ SC-23 Dominik Hasek (G), Buff. ✂ {*80} 100.00
☐ SC-24 Mario Lemieux, Pitt. ✂ {*80} 300.00
☐ SC-25 Jason Arnott, NJer. ✂ {*60} 75.00

Description **SC**
☐ SC-26 Johan Hedberg (G), Pitt. ✂ {*60} 75.00
☐ SC-27 Raymond Bourque, Colo. ✂ {*60} 150.00
☐ SC-28 Al MacInnis, SLou. ✂ {*60} 75.00
☐ SC-29 Scott Gomez, NJer. ✂ {*40} 75.00
☐ SC-30 Chris Drury, Colo. ✂ {*40} 100.00
☐ SC-32 Patrick Roy (G), Colo. ✂ {*10} 950.00

2001 - 02 BE A PLAYER UPDATE

Please see Be A Player Memorabilia, Between the Pipes, and Parkhurst.

HE SHOOTS HE SCORES

☐ Todd Bertuzzi, Vanc. [1 Point]
☐ Theoren Fleury, NYRa. [1 Point]
☐ Marian Gaborik, MinW. [1 Point]
☐ Bill Guerin, Bost. [1 Point]
☐ Martin Havlat, Otta. [1 Point]
☐ Marian Hossa, Otta. [1 Point]
☐ Nicklas Lidström, Detr. [1 Point]
☐ Zigmund Palffy, LosA. [1 Point]
☐ Joe Thornton, Bost. [1 Point]
☐ Alexei Yashin, NYIs. [1 Point]
☐ Ed Belfour (G), Dall. [2 Points]
☐ Martin Brodeur (G), NJer. [2 Points]
☐ Pavel Bure, NYRa. [2 Points]
☐ Ron Francis, Caro. [2 Points]
☐ Luc Robitaille, Detr. [2 Points]
☐ José Théodore (G), Mont. [2 Points]
☐ Peter Forsberg, Colo. [3 Points]
☐ Dominik Hasek (G), Detr. [3 Points]
☐ Curtis Joseph (G), Toro. [3 Points]
☐ Patrick Roy (G), Colo. [3 Points]

HE SHOOTS HE SCORE JERSEYS

These cards were distributed to those collectors who redeemed 400 He Shoots He Scores points.

Jersey (#/20)
☐ Ed Belfour (G), Dall. ✂ [Signature Series]
☐ Todd Bertuzzi, Vanc. ✂ [Signature Series]
☐ Peter Bondra, Wash. ✂ [Parkhurst]
☐ Martin Brodeur, NJer. ✂ [Signature Series]
☐ Pavel Bure, NYRa. ✂ [BAP Memorabilia]
☐ Pavel Bure, NYRa. ✂ [Signature Series]
☐ Patrik Elias, NJer. ✂ [BAP Memorabilia]
☐ Theoren Fleury, NYRa. ✂ [Signature Series]
☐ Peter Forsberg, Colo. ✂ [Parkhurst]
☐ Ron Francis, Caro. ✂ [Parkhurst]
☐ Marian Gaborik, MinW. ✂ [Signature Series]
☐ Bill Guerin, Bost. ✂ [Parkhurst]
☐ Dominik Hasek (G), Detr. ✂ [BAP Memorabilia]
☐ Dominik Hasek (G), Detr. ✂ [Signature Series]
☐ Martin Havlat, Otta. ✂ [Signature Series]
☐ Marian Hossa, Otta. ✂ [Parkhurst]
☐ Jarome Iginla, Calg. ✂ [BAP Memorabilia]
☐ Curtis Joseph (G), Toro. ✂ [Signature Series]
☐ Sami Kapanen, Caro. ✂ [Parkhurst]
☐ Paul Kariya, Anah. ✂ [BAP Memorabilia]
☐ Ilya Kovalchuk, Atla. ✂ [BAP Memorabilia]
☐ Patrick Lalime, Otta. ✂ [BAP Memorabilia]
☐ Vincent Lecavalier, Tamp. ✂ [Parkhurst]
☐ Nicklas Lidstrom, Detr. ✂ [Parkhurst]
☐ Eric Lindros, NYRa. ✂ [BAP Memorabilia]
☐ Roberto Luongo, Flor. ✂ [Signature Series]
☐ Alexander Mogilny, Toro. ✂ [BAP Memorabilia]
☐ Evgeni Nabokov, SanJ. ✂ [BAP Memorabilia]
☐ Markus Naslund, Vanc. ✂ [BAP Memorabilia]
☐ Zigmund Palffy, LosA. ✂ [Parkhurst]
☐ Luc Robitaille, Detr. ✂ [BAP Memorabilia]
☐ Luc Robitaille, Detr. ✂ [Parkhurst]
☐ Jeremy Roenick, Phil. ✂ [BAP Memorabilia]
☐ Patrick Roy, Colo. ✂ [Signature Series]
☐ Alex Tanguay, Colo. ✂ [Signature Series]
☐ José Théodore, Mont. ✂ [BAP Memorabilia]
☐ José Théodore, Mont. ✂ [Signature Series]
☐ Joe Thornton, Bost. ✂ [Parkhurst]
☐ Marty Turco, Dall. ✂ [Parkhurst]
☐ Alexei Yashin, NYIs. ✂ [Parkhurst]

HERITAGE

Complete Set (6 cards): **800**
Insert (*90) **H**
☐ Jason Allison, Wash. ✂ 35.00
☐ Ed Belfour (G), Chic. ✂ 60.00
☐ Rob Blake, LosA. ✂ 35.00
☐ Pavel Bure, Vanc. ✂ 50.00
☐ Theoren Fleury, Calg. ✂ 35.00
☐ Doug Gilmour, Toro. ✂ 35.00
☐ Wayne Gretzky, LosA. ✂ 250.00
☐ Bill Guerin, Njer. ✂ 30.00
☐ Jeff Hackett, Chic. ✂ 30.00
☐ Brett Hull, Slou. ✂ 60.00
☐ Curtis Joseph (G), Slou. ✂ 60.00
☐ Ed Jovanovski, Flor. ✂ 30.00
☐ Al MacInnis, Slou. ✂ 30.00
☐ Mark Messier, Edmo. ✂ 60.00
☐ Mike Modano, Minn. ✂ 60.00
☐ Alexander Mogilny, Vanc. ✂ 30.00
☐ Owen Nolan, Québ. ✂ 35.00
☐ Adam Oates, Bost. ✂ 30.00
☐ Félix Potvin, Toro. ✂ 75.00
☐ Keith Primeau, Detr. ✂ 30.00
☐ Mark Recchi, Mont. ✂ 30.00
☐ Gary Roberts, Calg. ✂ 30.00
☐ Luc Robitaille, NYRa. ✂ 50.00
☐ Jeremy Roenick, Chic. ✂ 50.00
☐ Patrick Roy, Mont. ✂ 150.00
☐ Teemu Selänne, Winn. ✂ 50.00
☐ Brendan Shanahan, Hart. ✂ 60.00
☐ Mats Sundin, Québ. ✂ 60.00
☐ Keith Tkachuk, Phoe. ✂ 35.00
☐ Roman Turek, Dall. ✂ 30.00

PASSING THE TORCH

Complete Set (6 cards): **425.00**
Insert (*25) **PTT**
☐ J. Bucyk ✂ / C. Neely ✂ / J. Thornton ✂ 100.00
☐ Bob Hull ✂ / M. Goulet ✂ / T. Amonte ✂ 100.00
☐ S. Abel ✂ / G. Howe ✂ / S. Yzerman ✂ 225.00
☐ M. Richard ✂ / G. Lafleur ✂ / S. Koivu ✂ 225.00
☐ E. Giacomin ✂ / R. Gilbert ✂ / B. Leetch ✂ 50.00
☐ K. Clancy ✂ / T. Horton ✂ / M. Sundin ✂ 100.00

ROCKET'S RIVALS

Complete Set (10 cards):
Insert **RR**
☐ RR-3 Johnny Bower ✂ {#/30} 100.00
☐ RR-5 Frank Brimsek ✂ {#/40} 100.00
☐ RR-6 Turk Broda ✂ {#/30} 100.00
☐ RR-7 Bill Gadsby ✂ {#/30} 100.00
☐ RR-9 Glenn Hall ✂ {#/30} 100.00
☐ RR-1 Gordie Howe, Detr. ✂
☐ RR-2 Ted Lindsay ✂ {#/30} 100.00
☐ RR-10 Bill Mosienko, Chic. ✂ {#/40} 100.00
☐ RR-8 Chuck Rayner (G) ✂
☐ RR-4 Terry Sawchuk ✂ {#/30} 225.00

TOUGH CUSTOMERS

Complete Set (40 cards): **1055.00**
Insert (*90) **TC**
☐ Dave Schultz ✂ / Tiger Williams ✂ 40.00
☐ Joey Tetarenko ✂ / Darren Langdon ✂ 40.00
☐ Tie Domi ✂ / Rob Ray ✂ 40.00
☐ Krzysztof Oliwa ✂ / Peter Worrell ✂ 40.00
☐ Luke Richardson ✂ / Jeff Odgers ✂ 40.00
☐ P.J. Stock ✂ / Matthew Barnaby ✂ 40.00
☐ Wade Belak ✂ / Sandy McCarthy ✂ 40.00
☐ Donald Brashear ✂ / Georges Laraque ✂ 40.00
☐ André Roy ✂ / Jeff Odgers ✂ 40.00
☐ André Roy ✂ / Tie Domi ✂ 40.00
☐ Donald Brashear ✂ / Bob Probert ✂ 40.00
☐ Bob Probert ✂ / Tie Domi ✂ 40.00
☐ Darren Langdon ✂ / Rocky Thompson ✂ 40.00
☐ Ryan VandenBussche ✂ / Chris Simon ✂ 40.00
☐ Matt Johnson ✂ / Craig Berube ✂ 40.00
☐ Denny Lambert ✂ / Scott Parker ✂ 40.00
☐ Georges Laraque ✂ / Jeff Odgers ✂ 40.00
☐ Luke Richardson ✂ / Wade Belak ✂ 40.00
☐ Chris Dingman ✂ / Paul Laus ✂ 40.00
☐ Gino Odjick ✂ / Chris Simon ✂ 40.00
☐ Ian Laperrière ✂ / Andrei Nazarov ✂ 40.00
☐ Georges Laraque ✂ / Paul Laus ✂ 40.00
☐ Ian Laperrière ✂ / Stu Grimson ✂ 40.00
☐ Krzysztof Oliwa ✂ / Eric Cairns ✂ 40.00
☐ Maurice Richard ✂ / Ted Lindsay ✂ 200.00
☐ Gordie Howe ✂ / Stan Mikita ✂ 200.00
☐ Denny Lambert ✂ / André Roy ✂ 40.00
☐ Wendel Clark ✂ / Bob Probert ✂ 45.00
☐ Ryan VandenBussche ✂ / Jamal Mayers ✂ 40.00
☐ Rocky Thompson ✂ / P.J. Stock ✂ 40.00
☐ Scott Parker ✂ / Ken Belanger ✂ 40.00
☐ Chris Neil, Otta. ✂ / Matthew Barnaby ✂ 40.00
☐ Chris Dingman ✂ / Sandy McCarthy ✂ 40.00
☐ Peter Worrell ✂ / Craig Berube ✂ 40.00
☐ Gino Odjick ✂ / Eric Cairns ✂ 40.00
☐ Jamal Mayers ✂ / Ken Belanger ✂ 40.00
☐ Stu Grimson ✂ / Bob Probert ✂ 40.00
☐ Paul Laus ✂ / Matt Johnson ✂ 40.00
☐ Rob Ray ✂ / Chris Neil ✂ 40.00
☐ Andrei Nazarov ✂ / Brad Brown ✂ 40.00

TRAVEL PLANS

Complete Set (16 cards): **520.00**
Insert (*50) **TP**
☐ Dave Andreychuk ✂ ✂ 40.00
☐ Rob Blake ✂ ✂ 50.00
☐ Dan Cloutier / ✂ 40.00
☐ Dominik Hasek ✂ ✂ 75.00
☐ Jaromir Jagr ✂ ✂ 75.00
☐ Nikolai Khabibulin ✂ ✂ 40.00
☐ Eric Lindros ✂ ✂ 75.00
☐ Alexander Mogilny ✂ ✂ 40.00
☐ Félix Potvin ✂ ✂ 100.00
☐ Luc Robitaille ✂ ✂ 75.00
☐ Jeremy Roenick ✂ ✂ 75.00
☐ Teemu Selänne ✂ Burgandy ✂ White 75.00
☐ Keith Tkachuk ✂ ✂ 50.00
☐ Roman Turek ✂ ✂ 40.00
☐ Doug Weight ✂ Blue ✂ White 50.00
☐ Alexei Yashin ✂ ✂ 50.00

2001 - 02 BETWEEN THE PIPES

Produced by In The Game, the original series was released in March 2002. An update series (both base and insert cards) was issued in June 2002 in the Be A Player Update release.

The following wrapper redemption promotional versions were created: All-Star Fantasy (#/10), Spring Expo '02 (#/10).

Complete Set (150 cards): **90.00**
Description **Base**
☐ 1 Patrick Roy (G), Colo. 5.00
☐ 2 Jean-Sébastien Giguère (G), Anah. 1.00
☐ 3 Ron Tugnutt (G), Colu. .50
☐ 4 Rick DiPietro (G), NYIs. .50
☐ 5 Milan Hnilicka (G), Atla. .50
☐ 6 Jean-Sébastien Aubin (G), Pitt. .50
☐ 7 Craig Billington (G), Wash. .50
☐ 8 Byron Dafoe (G), Bost. .50
☐ 9 Maxime Ouellet (G), Phil. .50
☐ 10 Ed Belfour (G), Dall. 1.50
☐ 11 John Grahame (G), Bost. .50
☐ 12 Mathieu Garon (G), Mont. .50
☐ 13 Martin Biron (G), Buff. .50
☐ 14 Dan Cloutier (G), Vanc. .50
☐ 15 Tomas Vokoun (G), Nash. .50
☐ 16 Arturs Irbe (G), Caro. .50
☐ 17 Curtis Joseph (G), Toro. 1.50
☐ 18 Jocelyn Thibault (G), Chic. .50
☐ 19 Roman Cechmanek (G), Phil. .50
☐ 20 Miikka Kiprusoff (G), SanJ. .50
☐ 21 Olaf Kölzig (G), Wash. 1.00
☐ 22 Jani Hurme (G), Otta. .50
☐ 23 David Aebischer (G), Colo. .50
☐ 24 Damian Rhodes (G), Atla. .50
☐ 25 Marc Denis (G), Colu. .50
☐ 26 Marty Turco (G), Dall. 1.00
☐ 27 Evgeni Nabokov (G), SanJ. 1.00
☐ 28 Manny Legacé (G), Detr. .50
☐ 29 Mike Dunham (G), Nash. .50
☐ 30 Tommy Salo (G), Edmo. .50
☐ 31 Sean Burke (G), Phoe. 1.00
☐ 32 Andrew Raycroft (G), Bost. .50
☐ 33 Roberto Luongo (G), Flor. 1.00
☐ 34 Johan Holmqvist (G), NYRa. .50
☐ 35 Félix Potvin (G), LosA. 1.00
☐ 36 Martin Brodeur (G), NJer. 2.50
☐ 37 Gregg Naumenko (G), Anah. .50
☐ 38 Travis Scott (G), LosA. .50
☐ 39 Manny Fernandez (G), MinW. .50
☐ 40 Kevin Weekes (G), Tamp. .50
☐ 41 Steve Passmore (G), Chic. .50
☐ 42 Johan Hedberg (G), Pitt. .50
☐ 43 Patrick Lalime (G), Otta. 1.00
☐ 44 José Théodore (G), Mont. 2.00
☐ 45 Mika Noronen (G), Buff. .50

☐	46 Brent Johnson (G), SLou.	.50
☐	47 Chris Mason (G), Nash.	.50
☐	48 Mike Fountain (G), Otta.	.50
☐	49 Jamie McLennan (G), MinW.	.50
☐	50 Mike Richter (G), NYRa.	.50
☐	51 Éric Fichaud (G), Mont.	.50
☐	52 Steve Shields (G), Anah.	.50
☐	53 Rich Parent (G), Pitt.	.50
☐	54 Mike Vernon (G), Calg.	.50
☐	55 Jason LaBarbera (G), NYRa.	.50
☐	56 Dominik Hasek (G), Detr.	1.50
☐	**57 Dan Blackburn (G), NYRa. RC**	**10.00**
☐	58 Robert Esche (G), Phoe.	.50
☐	59 Joaquin Gage (G), Edmo.	.50
☐	60 Jamie Storr (G), LosA.	.50
☐	61 Brian Boucher (G), Phil.	.50
☐	62 Trevor Kidd (G), Flor.	.50
☐	63 Nikolai Khabibulin (G), Tamp.	.50
☐	64 Norm Maracle (G), Atla.	.50
☐	65 Roman Turek (G), Calg.	.50
☐	66 Tyler Moss (G), Caro.	.50
☐	67 Fred Brathwaite (G), SLou.	.50
☐	68 Garth Snow (G), NYIs.	.50
☐	69 Dieter Kochan (G), Tamp.	.50
☐	70 Bob Essensa (G), Buff.	.50
☐	71 Kirk McLean (G), NYRa.	.50
☐	72 Chris Osgood (G), NYIs.	1.00
☐	73 Jeff Hackett (G), Mont.	.50
☐	74 Stéphane Fiset (G), LosA.	.50
☐	75 Dominic Roussel (G), Edmo.	.50
☐	76 Corey Hirsch (G), Wash.	.50
☐	77 Vitali Yeremeyev (G), NYRa.	.50
☐	78 Tom Barrasso (G), Caro.	.50
☐	**79 Scott Clemmensen (G), NJer. RC**	**4.00**
☐	80 Martin Brochu (G), Vanc.	.50
☐	81 Corey Schwab (G), Toro.	.50
☐	**82 Ty Conklin (G), Edmo. RC**	**6.00**
☐	83 Dwayne Roloson (G), MinW.	.50
☐	**84 Ilja Bryzgalov (G), Anah. RC**	**5.00**
☐	**85 Olivier Michaud (G), Mont. RC**	**10.00**
☐	86 Vesa Toskala (G), SanJ.	.50
☐	87 Jussi Markkanen (G), Edmo.	.50
☐	88 Patrick Desrochers (G), Phoe.	.50
☐	89 Peter Skudra (G), Vanc.	.50
☐	90 Jean-François Damphousse (G), NJer.	.50
☐	91 Mike Dunham (G), Nash.	.50
☐	92 Mike Richter (G), NYRa.	.50
☐	93 Brian Boucher (G), Phil.	.50
☐	94 Patrick Roy (G), Colo.	4.50
☐	95 Martin Biron (G), Buff.	.50
☐	96 Jean-Sébastien Aubin (G), Pitt.	.50
☐	97 Curtis Joseph (G), Toro.	1.50
☐	98 Martin Brodeur (G), NJer.	2.00
☐	99 Arturs Irbe (G), Caro.	.50
☐	100 Jeff Hackett (G), Mont.	.50
☐	101 Ed Belfour (G), Dall.	1.50
☐	102 Jocelyn Thibault (G), Chic.	.50
☐	103 Roman Cechmanek (G), Phil.	.50
☐	104 Patrick Lalime (G), Otta.	.50
☐	105 Olaf Kölzig (G), Wash.	.50
☐	106 Byron Dafoe (G), Bost.	.50
☐	107 Johan Hedberg (G), Pitt.	.50
☐	108 Dan Cloutier (G), Vanc.	.50
☐	109 Dominik Hasek (G), Buff.	1.50
☐	110 Olaf Kölzig (G), Wash.	.50
☐	111 Patrick Roy (G), Mont.	4.50
☐	112 Ed Belfour (G), Chic.	1.50
☐	113 Grant Fuhr (G), Edmo.	.50
☐	114 Ron Hextall (G), Phil.	.50
☐	115 Pelle Lindbergh (G), Phil.	.50
☐	116 Tom Barrasso (G), Buff.	.50
☐	117 Billy Smith (G), NYIs.	1.00
☐	118 Bernie Parent (G), Phil.	1.00
☐	119 Tony Esposito (G), Chic.	1.50
☐	120 Gump Worsley (G), Mont.	1.00
☐	121 Glenn Hall (G), Chic.	1.50
☐	122 Jacques Plante (G), Mont.	2.00
☐	123 Johnny Bower (G), Toro.	1.00
☐	124 Terry Sawchuk (G), Detr.	3.00
☐	125 Harry Lumley (G), Toro.	.50
☐	126 Bill Durnan (G), Mont.	1.00
☐	127 Turk Broda (G), Toro.	1.00
☐	128 Frank Brimsek (G), Bost.	.50
☐	129 Tiny Thompson (G), Bost.	.50
☐	130 George Hainsworth (G), Mont.	.50
☐	131 Gump Worsley (G), Minn.	1.00
☐	132 Georges Vézina (G), Mont.	3.50
☐	133 Vladislav Tretiak (G), USSR	2.00
☐	134 Tiny Thompson (G), Detr.	.50
☐	135 Terry Sawchuk (G), Detr.	3.50
☐	136 Jacques Plante (G), Mont.	2.50
☐	137 Chuck Rayner (G), NYRa.	.50
☐	138 Bernie Parent (G), Phil.	1.00
☐	139 Harry Lumley (G), Toro.	.50
☐	140 Glenn Hall (G), Detr.	1.50
☐	141 George Hainsworth (G), Toro.	1.00
☐	142 Ed Giacomin (G), NYRa.	1.00
☐	143 Chuck Gardiner (G), Chic.	.50
☐	144 Tony Esposito (G), Chic.	1.50
☐	145 Bill Durnan (G), Mont.	1.00
☐	146 Gerry Cheevers (G), Bost.	1.00
☐	147 Turk Broda (G), Toro.	1.00
☐	148 Frank Brimsek (G), Bost.	.50
☐	149 Johnny Bower (G), Toro.	1.00
☐	150 Roy Worters (G), NYAm.	.50

UPDATE

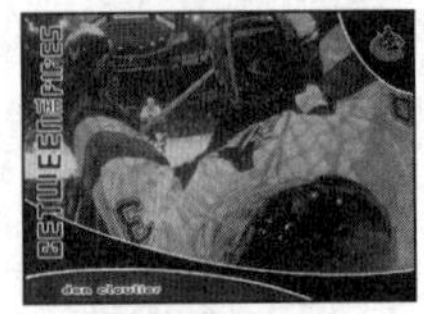

	Update	Update
☐	**151 Pasi Nurminen (G), Atla. RC**	**6.00**
☐	152 Alex Auld (G), Vanc.	.50
☐	153 John Vanbiesbrouck (G), NJer.	.50
☐	154 Wade Flaherty (G), Flor.	.50
☐	155 Kevin Weekes (G), Caro.	.50
☐	156 Tom Barrasso (G), Toro.	.50
☐	157 Stéphane Fiset (G), Mont.	.50
☐	**158 Sébastien Centomo (G), Toro. RC**	**6.00**
☐	159 Jean-François Labbé, Colu.	.50
☐	160 Simon Lajeunesse, Otta.	.50
☐	**161 Frédéric Cassivi (G), Atla. RC**	**4.00**
☐	**162 Martin Prusek (G), Otta. RC**	**8.00**
☐	163 Dominik Hasek (G), Detr.	1.50
☐	164 David Aebischer (G), Colo.	.50
☐	165 Dan Cloutier (G), Vanc.	.50
☐	166 Byron Dafoe (G), Bost.	.50
☐	167 Curtis Joseph (G), Toro.	1.50
☐	168 Ed Belfour (G), Dall.	1.50
☐	169 Tommy Salo (G), World All-Star	.50
☐	170 José Théodore (G), North American All-Star	2.00

HE SHOOTS HE SAVES REDEMPTION

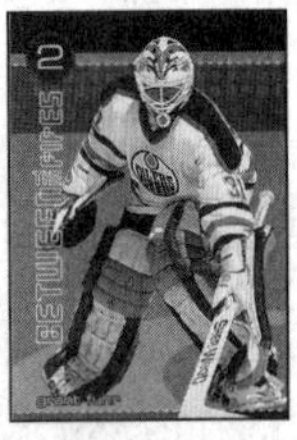

Each redemption card was worth one, two, or three points. Collectors who accumulated 400 points could trade their redemption cards in for a special random jersey card. This redemption program ends on December 31, 2002.

	Insert Set Redemption	HSHS
☐	Ed Belfour (G), Dall. [2 Points]	
☐	Brian Boucher (G), Phil. [1 Point]	
☐	Martin Brodeur (G), NJer. [2 Points]	
☐	Sean Burke (G), Phoe. [1 Point]	
☐	Byron Dafoe (G), Bost. [1 Point]	
☐	Grant Fuhr (G), Edmo. [2 Points]	
☐	Glenn Hall (G), Chic. [2 Points]	
☐	Dominik Hasek (G), Detr. [3 Points]	
☐	Curtis Joseph (G), Toro. [3 Points]	
☐	Nikolai Khabibulin (G), Tamp. [1 Point]	
☐	Olaf Kölzig (G), Wash. [1 Point]	
☐	Roberto Luongo (G), Flor. [1 Point]	
☐	Evgeni Nabokov (G), SanJ. [1 Point]	
☐	Jacques Plante (G), Mont. [2 Points]	
☐	Patrick Roy (G), Colo. [3 Points]	
☐	Tommy Salo (G), Edmo. [2 Points]	
☐	Terry Sawchuk (G), Detr. [3 Points]	
☐	José Théodore (G), Mont. [1 Point]	
☐	Jocelyn Thibault (G), Chic. [1 Point]	
☐	Roman Turek (G), Calg. [1 Point]	

ALL-STAR JERSEY

	Insert Set (32 cards): Insert (#/60)	1,000 ASJ
☐	Ed Belfour (G), AS '96 ✂	100.00
☐	Martin Brodeur (G), AS '00 ✂	150.00
☐	Roman Cechmanek (G), AS '01 ✂	50.00
☐	Dominik Hasek (G), AS '98 ✂	75.00
☐	Dominik Hasek (G), AS '97 ✂	75.00
☐	Arturs Irbe (G), AS '99 ✂	50.00
☐	Curtis Joseph (G), AS '00 ✂	75.00
☐	Curtis Joseph (G), AS '94 ✂	75.00
☐	Nikolai Khabibulin (G), AS '98 ✂	50.00
☐	Olaf Kölzig (G), AS '00 ✂	50.00
☐	Evgeni Nabokov (G), AS '01 ✂	50.00
☐	Mike Richter (G), AS '00 ✂	50.00
☐	Patrick Roy (G), AS '94 ✂	200.00
☐	Patrick Roy (G), AS '01 ✂	200.00
☐	Tommy Salo (G), AS '00 ✂	50.00
☐	Roman Turek (G), AS '00 ✂	50.00

DOUBLE MEMORABILIA

	Insert Set (30 cards): Insert (#/50)	2,200 DM
☐	18 M. Biron (G) Jersey ✂ Glove ✂	75.00
☐	20 B. Boucher (G) Jersey ✂ Pad ✂	75.00
☐	6 M. Brodeur (G) Jersey ✂ Pad ✂	200.00
☐	17 S. Burke (G) Jersey ✂ Pad ✂	75.00
☐	23 G. Cheevers (G) Stick ✂ Pad ✂	75.00
☐	7 M. Dunham (G) Jersey ✂ Pad ✂	75.00
☐	15 R. Esche (G) Jersey ✂ Pad ✂	75.00
☐	29 T. Esposito (G) Jersey ✂ Glove ✂	150.00
☐	25 G. Fuhr (G) Jersey ✂ Pad ✂	75.00
☐	30 E. Giacomin (G) Stick ✂ Glove ✂	75.00
☐	10 J. Grahame (G) Jersey ✂ Blocker ✂	75.00
☐	5 J. Hackett (G) Jersey ✂ Pad ✂	75.00
☐	3 J. Hedberg (G) Jersey ✂ Blocker ✂	75.00
☐	27 R. Hextall (G) Jersey ✂ Pad ✂	125.00
☐	21 C. Joseph (G) Jersey ✂ Pad ✂	125.00
☐	8 T. Kidd (G) Jersey ✂ Blocker ✂	75.00
☐	4 O. Kölzig (G) Jersey ✂ Blocker ✂	75.00
☐	12 M. Legacé (G) Jersey ✂ Blocker ✂	75.00
☐	11 R. Luongo (G) Jersey ✂ Blocker ✂	100.00
☐	13 E. Nabokov (G) Jersey ✂ Glove ✂	75.00
☐	16 C. Osgood (G) Jersey ✂ Pad ✂	75.00
☐	26 B. Parent (G) Jersey ✂ Pad ✂	75.00
☐	1 F. Potvin (G) Jersey ✂ Blocker ✂	150.00
☐	9 D. Rhodes (G) Jersey ✂ Blocker ✂	75.00
☐	24 T. Sawchuk (G) Jersey ✂ Pad ✂	300.00
☐	14 J. Théodore (G) Jersey ✂ Pad ✂	150.00
☐	19 J. Thibault (G) Jersey ✂ Pad ✂	75.00
☐	22 R. Turek (G) Jersey ✂ Pad ✂	75.00
☐	2 M. Vernon (G) Jersey ✂ Pad ✂	75.00
☐	28 G. Worsley (G) Stick ✂ Glove ✂	125.00

FUTURE WAVE

	Insert Set (10 cards): Insert (#/22)	1,200 FW
☐	Martin Biron (G), Buff. ✂	150.00
☐	Dan Blackburn (G), NYRa. ✂	200.00
☐	Brian Boucher (G), Phil. ✂	150.00
☐	Dan Cloutier (G), Vanc. ✂	150.00
☐	Rick DiPietro (G), NYIs. ✂	150.00
☐	Mathieu Garon (G), Mont. ✂	150.00
☐	Johan Hedberg (G), Pitt. ✂	150.00
☐	Patrick Lalime (G), Otta. ✂	150.00
☐	Roberto Luongo (G), Flor. ✂	200.00
☐	Evgeni Nabokov (G), SanJ. ✂	150.00

GAME-USED JERSEY

	Insert Set (42 cards): Insert (#/90)	1,600 GJ
☐	David Aebischer (G), Colo. ✂	40.00
☐	Jean-Sébastien Aubin (G), Pitt. ✂	40.00
☐	Ed Belfour (G), Dall. ✂	75.00
☐	Martin Biron (G), Buff. ✂	40.00
☐	Brian Boucher (G), Phil. ✂	40.00
☐	Martin Brodeur (G), NJer. ✂	125.00
☐	Sean Burke (G), Phoe. ✂	50.00
☐	Roman Cechmanek (G), Phil. ✂	40.00
☐	Dan Cloutier (G), Vanc. ✂	40.00
☐	Byron Dafoe (G), Bost. ✂	40.00
☐	Marc Denis (G), Colu. ✂	40.00
☐	Mike Dunham (G), Nash. ✂	40.00
☐	Manny Fernandez (G), MinW. ✂	40.00
☐	Mathieu Garon (G), Mont. ✂	40.00
☐	John Grahame (G), Bost. ✂	40.00
☐	Jeff Hackett (G), Mont. ✂	40.00
☐	Dominik Hasek (G), Detr. ✂	75.00
☐	Johan Hedberg (G), Pitt. ✂	40.00
☐	Johan Holmqvist (G), NYRa. ✂	40.00
☐	Arturs Irbe (G), Caro. ✂	40.00
☐	Curtis Joseph (G), Toro. ✂	75.00
☐	Nikolai Khabibulin (G), Tamp. ✂	40.00
☐	Trevor Kidd (G), Flor. ✂	40.00
☐	Miikka Kiprusoff (G), SanJ. ✂	40.00
☐	Olaf Kölzig (G), Wash. ✂	50.00
☐	Manny Legacé (G), Detr. ✂	40.00
☐	Roberto Luongo (G), Flor. ✂	50.00
☐	Evgeni Nabokov (G), SanJ. ✂	50.00
☐	Gregg Naumenko (G), Anah. ✂	40.00
☐	Chris Osgood (G), NYIs. ✂	50.00
☐	Félix Potvin (G), Toro. ✂	100.00
☐	Damian Rhodes (G), Atla. ✂	40.00
☐	Mike Richter (G), NYRa. ✂	40.00
☐	Patrick Roy (G), Colo. ✂	175.00
☐	Tommy Salo (G), Edmo. ✂	40.00
☐	Steve Shields (G), Anah. ✂	40.00
☐	José Théodore (G), Mont. ✂	100.00
☐	Jocelyn Thibault (G), Chic. ✂	40.00
☐	Ron Tugnutt (G), Colu. ✂	40.00
☐	Marty Turco (G), Dall. ✂	50.00
☐	Roman Turek (G), Calg. ✂	40.00
☐	Mike Vernon (G), Calg. ✂	40.00

GAME-USED JERSEY EMBLEM

	Insert Set (10 cards): Insert (#/20)	1,600 GUE
☐	Brian Boucher (G), Phil. ✂	150.00
☐	Dominik Hasek (G), Detr. ✂	250.00
☐	Johan Hedberg (G), Pitt. ✂	150.00
☐	Curtis Joseph (G), Toro. ✂	250.00
☐	Olaf Kölzig (G), Wash. ✂	150.00
☐	Evgeni Nabokov (G), SanJ. ✂	150.00
☐	Patrick Roy (G), Colo. ✂	600.00
☐	Tommy Salo (G), Edmo. ✂	150.00
☐	Jocelyn Thibault (G), Chic. ✂	150.00
☐	Roman Turek (G), Calg. ✂	150.00

GAME-USED STICK & JERSEY

	Insert Set (42 cards): Description	1,900 GSJ
☐	David Aebischer (G), Colo. ✂	40.00
☐	Jean-Sébastien Aubin (G), Pitt. ✂	40.00
☐	Ed Belfour (G), Dall. ✂	75.00
☐	Martin Biron (G), Buff. ✂	40.00
☐	Brian Boucher (G), Phil. ✂	40.00
☐	Martin Brodeur (G), NJer. ✂	125.00
☐	Sean Burke (G), Phoe. ✂	50.00
☐	Roman Cechmanek (G), Phil. ✂	40.00
☐	Dan Cloutier (G), Vanc. ✂	40.00
☐	Byron Dafoe (G), Bost. ✂	40.00
☐	Mike Dunham (G), Nash. ✂	40.00
☐	Tony Esposito (G), Chic. ✂	100.00
☐	Manny Fernandez (G), MinW. ✂	40.00
☐	Grant Fuhr (G), Edmo. ✂	50.00
☐	Jeff Hackett (G), Chic. ✂	40.00
☐	Glenn Hall (G), Chic. ✂	100.00
☐	Dominik Hasek (G), Detr. ✂	75.00
☐	Johan Hedberg (G), Pitt. ✂	40.00
☐	Arturs Irbe (G), Caro. ✂	40.00
☐	Curtis Joseph (G), Toro. ✂	75.00
☐	Nikolai Khabibulin (G), Tamp. ✂	40.00
☐	Trevor Kidd (G), Flor. ✂	40.00
☐	Olaf Kölzig (G), Wash. ✂	50.00
☐	Patrick Lalime (G), Otta. ✂	50.00
☐	Manny Legacé (G), Detr. ✂	40.00
☐	Roberto Luongo (G), Flor. ✂	50.00
☐	Evgeni Nabokov (G), SanJ. ✂	50.00
☐	Bernie Parent (G), Phil. ✂	50.00
☐	Jacques Plante (G), Mont. ✂	125.00
☐	Félix Potvin (G), LosA. ✂	100.00
☐	Damian Rhodes (G), Atla. ✂	40.00
☐	Mike Richter (G), NYRa. ✂	40.00
☐	Patrick Roy (G), Colo. ✂	200.00
☐	Tommy Salo (G), Edmo. ✂	40.00
☐	Terry Sawchuk (G), Detr. ✂	175.00
☐	Steve Shields (G), Anah. ✂	40.00
☐	José Théodore (G), Mont. ✂	100.00
☐	Jocelyn Thibault (G), Chic. ✂	40.00
☐	Ron Tugnutt (G), Colu. ✂	40.00
☐	Roman Turek (G), Calg. ✂	40.00
☐	Mike Vernon (G), Calg. ✂	40.00
☐	Tomas Vokoun (G), Nash. ✂	40.00

GOALIE GEAR

	Insert Set (32 cards): Description	1,100 GG
☐	Jean-Sébastien Aubin (G), Pitt. ✂	50.00
☐	Martin Biron (G), Buff. ✂	50.00
☐	Brian Boucher (G), Phil. ✂	50.00
☐	Martin Brodeur (G), NJer. ✂	50.00
☐	Sean Burke (G), Phoe. ✂	50.00
☐	Dan Cloutier (G), Vanc. ✂	50.00
☐	Rick DiPietro (G), NYIs. ✂	50.00
☐	Mike Dunham (G), Nash. ✂	50.00
☐	Robert Esche (G), Phoe. ✂	50.00
☐	Jeff Hackett (G), Mont. ✂	50.00
☐	Dominik Hasek (G), Detr. ✂	50.00
☐	Johan Hedberg (G), Pitt. ✂	50.00
☐	Arturs Irbe (G), Caro. ✂	50.00
☐	Brent Johnson (G), SLou. ✂	50.00
☐	Curtis Joseph (G), Toro. ✂	50.00
☐	Trevor Kidd (G), Flor. ✂	50.00
☐	Olaf Kölzig (G), Wash. ✂	50.00
☐	Patrick Lalime (G), Otta. ✂	50.00
☐	Manny Legacé (G), Detr. ✂	50.00
☐	Roberto Luongo (G), Flor. ✂	50.00
☐	Evgeni Nabokov (G), SanJ. ✂	50.00
☐	Chris Osgood (G), NYIs. ✂	50.00
☐	Félix Potvin (G), LosA. ✂	50.00
☐	Damian Rhodes (G), Atla. ✂	50.00
☐	Patrick Roy (G), Colo. ✂	50.00
☐	José Théodore (G), Mont. ✂	50.00
☐	Jocelyn Thibault (G), Chic. ✂	50.00
☐	Marty Turco (G), Dall. ✂	50.00
☐	Roman Turek (G), Calg. ✂	50.00
☐	Mike Vernon (G), Calg. ✂	50.00

GOALIE RECORDS

Insert Set (20 cards): 2,400

	Description	GR
☐	Ed Belfour (G), Dall. ✂	100.00
☐	Ed Belfour (G)* (G), Dall. ✂	100.00
☐	Martin Brodeur (G), NJer. ✂	150.00
☐	Martin Brodeur (G), NJer. ✂	150.00
☐	Gerry Cheevers (G), Bost. ✂	100.00
☐	Tony Esposito (G), Chic. ✂	100.00
☐	Tony Esposito (G), Chic. ✂	100.00
☐	Grant Fuhr (G), Edmo. ✂	80.00
☐	Glenn Hall (G), Chic. ✂	125.00
☐	Chris Osgood (G), NYIs. ✂	80.00
☐	Bernie Parent (G), Phil. ✂	100.00
☐	Jacques Plante (G), Mont. ✂	150.00
☐	Jacques Plante (G) ✂	150.00
☐	Jacques Plante (G), Mont. ✂	150.00
☐	Patrick Roy (G), Colo. ✂	200.00
☐	Patrick Roy (G), Colo. ✂	200.00
☐	Patrick Roy (G), Colo. ✂	200.00
☐	Patrick Roy (G), Colo. ✂	200.00
☐	Patrick Roy (G), Colo. ✂	200.00
☐	Terry Sawchuk (G), Detr. ✂	200.00
☐	Terry Sawchuk (G), Detr. ✂	200.00
☐	Terry Sawchuk (G), Detr. ✂	200.00

GOALIE TANDEMS

Insert Set (13 cards): 900

	Insert (#/50)	GT
☐	1 M. Kiprusoff (G) ✂ / E. Nabokov (G) ✂	80.00
☐	2 B. Boucher (G) ✂ / R. Cechmanek (G) ✂	80.00
☐	3 J. Hackett (G) ✂ / J. Théodore (G) ✂	125.00
☐	4 T. Kidd (G) ✂ / R. Luongo (G) ✂	80.00
☐	5 D. Aebischer (G) ✂ / P. Roy (G) ✂	200.00
☐	6 J-S Giguère (G) ✂ / S. Shields (G) ✂	80.00
☐	7 E. Belfour (G) ✂ / M. Turco (G) ✂	100.00
☐	8 R. Turek (G) ✂ / M. Vernon (G) ✂	80.00
☐	9 D. Hasek (G) ✂ / M. Legacé (G) ✂	80.00
☐	10 B. Dafoe (G) ✂ / J. Grahame (G) ✂	80.00
☐	11 S. Burke (G) ✂ / R. Esche (G) ✂	80.00
☐	12 J. Thibault (G) ✂ / S. Passmore (G) ✂	80.00
☐	13 J-S Aubin (G) ✂ / J. Hedberg (G) ✂	80.00

HE SHOOTS HE SAVES JERSEYS

These cards were distributed to those collectors who redeemed 400 He Shoots He Saves points.

	Jersey (#/20)
☐	Jean-Sébastien Aubin (G) ✂
☐	Ed Belfour (G) ✂
☐	Martin Biron (G) ✂
☐	Brian Boucher (G) ✂
☐	Martin Brodeur (G) ✂
☐	Sean Burke (G) ✂
☐	Roman Cechmanek (G) ✂
☐	Dan Cloutier (G) ✂
☐	Byron Dafoe (G) ✂
☐	Mike Dunham (G) ✂
☐	Manny Fernandez (G) ✂
☐	Grant Fuhr (G) ✂
☐	Jeff Hackett (G) ✂
☐	Glenn Hall (G) ✂
☐	Dominik Hasek (G) ✂
☐	Johan Hedberg (G) ✂
☐	Ron Hextall (G) ✂
☐	Jani Hurme (G) ✂
☐	Arturs Irbe (G) ✂
☐	Curtis Joseph (G) ✂
☐	Nikolai Khabibulin (G) ✂
☐	Mikka Kiprusoff (G) ✂
☐	Olaf Kölzig (G) ✂
☐	Patrick Lalime (G) ✂
☐	Manny Legace (G) ✂
☐	Roberto Luongo (G) ✂
☐	Evgeni Nabokov (G) ✂
☐	Bernie Parent (G) ✂
☐	Félix Potvin (G) ✂
☐	Damian Rhodes (G) ✂
☐	Mike Richter (G) ✂
☐	Patrick Roy (G) ✂
☐	Tommy Salo (G) ✂
☐	Steve Shields (G) ✂
☐	Billy Smith (G) ✂
☐	Jose Theodore (G) ✂
☐	Joceyln Thibault (G) ✂
☐	Ron Tugnutt (G) ✂
☐	Marty Turco (G) ✂
☐	Roman Turek (G) ✂

GAME-USED JERSEY IN THE NUMBERS

Insert Set (10 cards): 1,800

	Insert (#/20)	ITN
☐	Brian Boucher (G), Phil. ✂	200.00
☐	Dominik Hasek (G), Detr. ✂	250.00
☐	Johan Hedberg (G), Pitt. ✂	200.00
☐	Curtis Joseph (G), Toro. ✂	250.00
☐	Olaf Kölzig (G), Wash. ✂	200.00

☐	Evgeni Nabokov (G), SanJ. ✂	200.00
☐	Patrick Roy (G), Colo. ✂	600.00
☐	Tommy Salo (G), Edmo. ✂	200.00
☐	Jocelyn Thibault (G), Chic. ✂	200.00
☐	Roman Turek (G), Calg. ✂	200.00

THE MASK

There are three versions to each card: the regular insert, a silver parallel (#/300) and a gold parallel (#/30).

Insert Set (30 cards): 1,575 600.00 300.00

	Description	M30	M300	Mask
☐☐☐	Murray Bannerman (G), Chic.	50.00	20.00	10.00
☐☐☐	Ed Belfour (G), Dall.	50.00	20.00	10.00
☐☐☐	Martin Biron (G), Buff.	50.00	20.00	10.00
☐☐☐	Sean Burke (G), Phoe.	50.00	20.00	10.00
☐☐☐	Roman Cechmanek (G), Phil.	50.00	20.00	10.00
☐☐☐	Gerry Cheevers (G), Bost.	50.00	20.00	10.00
☐☐☐	Byron Dafoe (G), Bost.	50.00	20.00	10.00
☐☐☐	Mike Dunham (G), Nash.	50.00	20.00	10.00
☐☐☐	Manny Fernandez (G), MinW.	50.00	20.00	10.00
☐☐☐	Ed Giacomin (G), NYRa.	50.00	20.00	10.00
☐☐☐	Gilles Gratton (G), NYRa.	50.00	20.00	10.00
☐☐☐	Johan Hedberg (G), Pitt.	50.00	20.00	10.00
☐☐☐	Brent Johnson (G), SLou.	50.00	20.00	10.00
☐☐☐	Curtis Joseph (G), SLou.	50.00	20.00	10.00
☐☐☐	Curtis Joseph (G), Toro.	50.00	20.00	10.00
☐☐☐	Olaf Kölzig (G), Wash.	50.00	20.00	10.00
☐☐☐	Patrick Lalime (G), Otta.	50.00	20.00	10.00
☐☐☐	Manny Legacé (G), Detr.	50.00	20.00	10.00
☐☐☐	Roberto Luongo (G), Flor.	50.00	20.00	10.00
☐☐☐	Evgeni Nabokov (G), SanJ.	50.00	20.00	10.00
☐☐☐	Jacques Plante (G), Mont.	60.00	25.00	18.00
☐☐☐	Félix Potvin (G), LosA.	60.00	20.00	10.00
☐☐☐	Damian Rhodes (G), Atla.	50.00	20.00	10.00
☐☐☐	Mike Richter (G), NYRa.	50.00	20.00	10.00
☐☐☐	Patrick Roy (G), Chic.	150.00	45.00	20.00
☐☐☐	Tommy Salo (G), Edmo.	50.00	20.00	10.00
☐☐☐	Steve Shields (G), Anah.	50.00	20.00	10.00
☐☐☐	José Théodore (G), Mont.	60.00	20.00	10.00
☐☐☐	Roman Turek (G), Calg.	50.00	20.00	10.00
☐☐☐	John Vanbiesbrouck (G), Flor.	50.00	20.00	10.00
☐☐☐	Nikolai Khabibulin (G)	50.00	20.00	10.00
☐☐☐	Miikka Kiprusoff (G), SanJ.	50.00	20.00	10.00
☐☐☐	Jocelyn Thibault (G), Chic.	50.00	20.00	10.00
☐☐☐	Ron Tugnutt (G), Colu.	50.00	20.00	10.00
☐☐☐	Ed Belfour (G)	50.00	20.00	10.00
☐☐☐	Rick DiPietro (G), NYIs.	50.00	20.00	10.00
☐☐☐	Grant Fuhr (G)	50.00	20.00	10.00
☐☐☐	Jeff Hackett (G), Mont.	50.00	20.00	10.00
☐☐☐	Brian Hayward (G), SanJ.	50.00	20.00	10.00
☐☐☐	Milan Hnilicka (G), Atla.	50.00	20.00	10.00

TROPHY WINNERS

Insert Set (24 cards): 1,900

	Insert (#/40)	TW
☐	Ed Belfour (G), Chic. ✂	100.00
☐	Frank Brimsek (G), Bost. ✂	75.00
☐	Turk Broda (G), Toro. ✂	100.00
☐	Martin Brodeur (G), NJer. ✂	150.00
☐	Bill Durnan (G), Mont. ✂	100.00
☐	Tony Esposito (G), Chic. ✂	100.00
☐	TW-7 Glenn Hall (G), Chic. ✂	100.00
☐	TW-13 Glenn Hall (G), Chic. ✂	100.00
☐	TW-16 Glenn Hall (G), Detr. ✂	100.00
☐	TW-2 Dominik Hasek (G), Buff. ✂	75.00
☐	TW-19 Dominik Hasek (G), Buff. ✂	75.00
☐	TW-24 Dominik Hasek (G), Buff. ✂	75.00
☐	Ron Hextall (G), Phil. ✂	100.00
☐	Olaf Kölzig (G), Wash. ✂	75.00
☐	Evgeni Nabokov (G), SanJ. ✂	75.00
☐	Bernie Parent (G), Phil. ✂	100.00
☐	TW-4 Jacques Plante (G), Mont. ✂	125.00
☐	TW-18 Jacques Plante (G), Mont. ✂	125.00
☐	Patrick Roy (G), Colo. ✂	200.00
☐	TW-6 Terry Sawchuk (G), Detr. ✂	200.00
☐	TW-14 Terry Sawchuk (G), Detr. ✂	200.00
☐	TW-8 Billy Smith (G), NYIs. ✂	75.00
☐	TW-20 Billy Smith (G), NYIs. ✂	75.00
☐	Tiny Thompson (G), Bost. ✂	125.00

VINTAGE MEMORABILIA

Insert Set (20 cards): 2,600

	Insert (#/40)	VM
☐	12 Johnny Bower (G) Pad ✂	100.00
☐	7 Frank Brimsek (G) Jersey ✂ Glove ✂	75.00
☐	2 Turk Broda (G) Glove ✂	100.00
☐	3 Gerry Cheevers (G) Pad ✂	100.00
☐	17 Bill Durnan (G) Glove ✂	125.00
☐	17 Bill Durnan (G) Glove ✂	125.00
☐	9 Tony Esposito (G) Jersey ✂	125.00
☐	1 Grant Fuhr (G) Jersey ✂ Pad ✂	75.00
☐	20 Charlie Gardiner (G) Jersey ✂ Pad ✂	150.00
☐	15 Ed Giacomin (G) Stick ✂ Glove ✂	125.00
☐	8 Glenn Hall (G) Jersey ✂	125.00
☐	14 Ron Hextall (G) Jersey ✂ Pad ✂	125.00
☐	4 Bernie Parent (G) Jersey ✂ Pad ✂	125.00
☐	5 Jacques Plante (G) Jersey ✂ Pad ✂	200.00
☐	6 Terry Sawchuk (G) Jersey ✂	225.00
☐	11 Billy Smith (G) Jersey ✂	100.00
☐	19 Tiny Thompson (G) Glove ✂	150.00
☐	10 Vladislav Tretiak (G) Jersey ✂	175.00
☐	18 Rogatien Vachon (G) Glove ✂	75.00
☐	13 Georges Vézina (G) Pad ✂	1000.00
☐	16 Gump Worsley (G) Stick ✂	100.00

2001 - 02 BLIZZAK

	Description	Blizzak
☐	Kim St-Pierre (G)	

2001 - 02 BOWMAN

Produced by the Topps Company, this series was released in May 2002. There are three versions for each card 1-165: a base card, a Gold parallel and an Ice3 parallel.

Complete Set (165 cards): 100.00 400.00 80.00

Common Player: .50 2.00 .25

	Description	Ice3	Gold	Base
☐☐☐	1 Patrick Roy, Colo.	4.50	18.00	3.50
☐☐☐	2 Brett Hull, Detr.	1.50	6.00	1.00
☐☐☐	3 Mario Lemieux, Pitt.	4.50	18.00	3.50
☐☐☐	4 Jaromir Jagr, Wash.	1.50	6.00	1.00
☐☐☐	5 Mats Sundin, Toro.	1.50	6.00	1.00
☐☐☐	6 Mike Modano, Dall.	1.50	6.00	1.00
☐☐☐	7 Jarome Iginla, Calg.	1.00	5.00	1.00
☐☐☐	8 Jason Allison, LosA.	.50	3.00	.50
☐☐☐	9 Mike Richter, NYRa.	.50	3.00	.50
☐☐☐	10 Chris Pronger, SLou.	.50	3.00	.50
☐☐☐	11 Patrik Elias, NJer.	1.00	5.00	1.00
☐☐☐	12 Tommy Salo, Edmo.	.50	2.00	.50
☐☐☐	13 Tony Amonte, Chic.	.50	3.00	.50
☐☐☐	14 Joe Thornton, Bost.	1.50	7.00	1.50
☐☐☐	15 Joe Sakic, Colo.	2.00	10.00	2.00
☐☐☐	16 Pavel Bure, NYRa.	1.00	5.00	1.00
☐☐☐	17 Teemu Selänne, SanJ.	1.00	5.00	1.00
☐☐☐	18 Markus Näslund, Vanc.	1.50	6.00	1.00
☐☐☐	19 N. Khabibulin (G), Tamp.	.50	2.00	.50
☐☐☐	20 Paul Kariya, Anah.	2.00	8.00	1.50
☐☐☐	21 Dominik Hasek, Detr.	1.50	6.00	1.00
☐☐☐	22 Ron Francis, Caro.	.50	3.00	.50
☐☐☐	23 Ray Ferraro, SLou.	.50	2.00	.25
☐☐☐	24 Miroslav Satan, Buff.	.50	2.00	.25
☐☐☐	25 Milan Hejduk, Colo.	1.00	5.00	1.00
☐☐☐	26 José Théodore, Mont.	1.50	7.00	1.50
☐☐☐	27 Daniel Alfredsson, Otta.	.50	3.00	.50
☐☐☐	28 Michael Peca, NYIs.	.50	2.00	.50
☐☐☐	29 Keith Primeau, Phil.	.50	2.00	.50
☐☐☐	30 Doug Weight, SLou.	.50	3.00	.50
☐☐☐	31 Sean Burke, Phoe.	.50	3.00	.50
☐☐☐	32 Adam Oates, Phil.	.50	2.00	.50
☐☐☐	33 Brian Rolston, Bost.	.50	2.00	.25
☐☐☐	34 Rob Blake, Colo.	.50	3.00	.50
☐☐☐	35 Steve Yzerman, Detr.	3.50	15.00	3.00
☐☐☐	36 Eric Lindros, NYRa.	1.50	6.00	1.00
☐☐☐	37 Keith Tkachuk, SLou.	.50	3.00	.50
☐☐☐	38 Dan Cloutier, Vanc.	.50	2.00	.50
☐☐☐	39 Chris Osgood, Detr.	.50	3.00	.50
☐☐☐	40 Zigmund Palffy, LosA.	.50	3.00	.50
☐☐☐	41 Jocelyn Thibault, Chic.	.50	2.00	.50
☐☐☐	42 Roman Turek (G), Calg.	.50	3.00	.50
☐☐☐	43 Ed Belfour (G), Dall.	1.50	6.00	1.00
☐☐☐	44 Adam Deadmarsh, LosA.	.50	2.00	.25
☐☐☐	45 Marian Hossa, Otta.	1.50	6.00	1.00
☐☐☐	46 Owen Nolan, SanJ.	.50	3.00	.50
☐☐☐	47 Curtis Joseph (G), Toro.	1.50	6.00	1.00
☐☐☐	48 Peter Bondra, Wash.	.50	3.00	.50
☐☐☐	49 Jeremy Roenick, Phoe.	1.00	5.00	1.00
☐☐☐	50 Brendan Shanahan, Detr.	1.50	6.00	1.00
☐☐☐	51 Éric Dazé, Chic.	.50	2.00	.50
☐☐☐	52 Jean-Pierre Dumont, Buff.	.50	2.00	.25
☐☐☐	53 Bill Guerin, Bost.	.50	2.00	.50
☐☐☐	**54 J. Hentunen, Calg. RC**	**1.00**	**2.00**	**1.50**
☐☐☐	55 Brian Leetch, NYRa.	.50	3.00	.50
☐☐☐	56 Alexei Kovalev, Pitt.	.50	3.00	.50
☐☐☐	57 Olaf Kölzig, Wash.	.50	3.00	.50
☐☐☐	58 Mike York, Edmo.	.50	2.00	.25
☐☐☐	59 Félix Potvin, LosA.	.50	3.00	.50
☐☐☐	60 Pierre Turgeon, Dall.	.50	2.00	.50
☐☐☐	61 Luc Robitaille, Detr.	1.00	5.00	1.00
☐☐☐	62 Sami Kapanen, Caro.	.50	2.00	.25
☐☐☐	63 Byron Dafoe, Bost.	.50	2.00	.50
☐☐☐	64 Ryan Smyth, Edmo.	.50	3.00	.50
☐☐☐	65 John LeClair, Phil.	1.00	5.00	1.00
☐☐☐	66 Pavol Demitra, SLou.	.50	2.00	.50
☐☐☐	67 Alexei Yashin, NYIs.	.50	3.00	.50
☐☐☐	68 Vincent Lecavalier, Tamp.	1.50	6.00	1.00
☐☐☐	69 Chris Drury, Colo.	.50	3.00	.50
☐☐☐	70 Mike Dunham, Nash.	.50	2.00	.50
☐☐☐	71 Patrick Lalime, Otta.	.50	3.00	.50
☐☐☐	72 Derek Morris, Calg.	.50	2.00	.25
☐☐☐	73 Peter Forsberg, Colo.	2.00	8.00	1.50
☐☐☐	74 Sergei Fedorov, Detr.	1.50	6.00	1.00
☐☐☐	75 Mark Parrish, NYIs.	.50	2.00	.50
☐☐☐	76 Simon Gagné, Phil.	1.00	5.00	1.00
☐☐☐	77 Jeff O'Neill, Caro.	.50	2.00	.50
☐☐☐	78 Alexander Mogilny, Toro.	.50	3.00	.50
☐☐☐	79 Johan Hedberg (G), Pitt.	.50	2.00	.50
☐☐☐	80 Martin Brodeur, NJer.	2.00	10.00	2.00
☐☐☐	81 Claude Lemieux, Phoe.	.50	2.00	.25
☐☐☐	82 Mark Messier, NYRa.	1.50	6.00	1.00
☐☐☐	83 Nicklas Lidström, Detr.	.50	3.00	.50
☐☐☐	84 Stu Barnes, Buff.	.50	2.00	.25
☐☐☐	85 Steve Sullivan, Chic.	.50	2.00	.25
☐☐☐	86 Jeff Friesen, Anah.	.50	2.00	.25
☐☐☐	87 Brent Johnson, SLou.	.50	2.00	.50
☐☐☐	88 Marc Denis, Colu.	.50	3.00	.50
☐☐☐	89 Jason Arnott, Dall.	.50	3.00	.50
☐☐☐	90 Brendan Morrison, Vanc.	.50	2.00	.25
☐☐☐	91 Jere Lehtinen, Dall.	.50	2.00	.25
☐☐☐	92 Craig Conroy, Calg.	.50	2.00	.25
☐☐☐	93 Petr* Sykora, NJer.	.50	2.00	.50
☐☐☐	94 Gary Roberts, Toro.	.50	2.00	.50
☐☐☐	95 Saku Koivu, Mont.	1.00	5.00	1.00
☐☐☐	96 Scott Stevens, NJer.	.50	2.00	.50
☐☐☐	97 Radek Bonk, Otta.	.50	2.00	.25
☐☐☐	98 Roman Cechmanek, Phil.	.50	2.00	.50
☐☐☐	99 Robert Lang, Pitt.	.50	2.00	.25
☐☐☐	100 Tom Barrasso (G), Toro.	.50	2.00	.50
☐☐☐	101 Yanic Perreault, Mont.	.50	2.00	.25
☐☐☐	102 Joe Nieuwendyk, NJer.	.50	2.00	.50
☐☐☐	103 Al MacInnis, SLou.	.50	2.00	.50
☐☐☐	104 Vincent Damphousse, SanJ.	.50	3.00	.50
☐☐☐	105 Anson Carter, Edmo.	.50	2.00	.50
☐☐☐	106 Sergei Samsonov, Bost.	.50	3.00	.50
☐☐☐	107 Theoren Fleury, NYRa.	.50	3.00	.50
☐☐☐	108 Mark Recchi, Phil.	.50	2.00	.50
☐☐☐	109 Marco Sturm, SanJ.	.50	2.00	.25
☐☐☐	**110 Jiri Dopita, Phil. RC**	**1.00**	**3.00**	**1.50**
☐☐☐	111 Tim Connolly, Buff.	.50	2.00	.50
☐☐☐	112 Mike Fisher, Otta.	.50	2.00	.25
☐☐☐	113 Alex Tanguay, Colo.	.50	3.00	.50
☐☐☐	**114 C. Berglund, NJer. RC**	**1.00**	**3.00**	**1.50**
☐☐☐	**115 O. Michaud, Mont. RC**	**1.50**	**4.00**	**2.00**
☐☐☐	**116 John Erskine, Dall. RC**	**1.00**	**2.00**	**1.50**
☐☐☐	**117 M. Samuelsson, NYRa. RC**	**1.00**	**2.00**	**1.50**
☐☐☐	**118 R. Martinek, NYIs. RC**	**1.00**	**2.00**	**1.50**
☐☐☐	**119 Mark Rycroft, SLou. RC**	**1.00**	**2.00**	**1.50**
☐☐☐	120 Mike Ribeiro, Mont.	.50	2.00	.25
☐☐☐	**121 Vaclav Pletka, Phil. RC**	**1.00**	**2.00**	**1.50**
☐☐☐	122 Toni Lydman, Calg.	.50	2.00	.25
☐☐☐	**123 B. Sutherby, Wash. RC**	**1.00**	**3.00**	**1.50**
☐☐☐	124 Karel Rachunek, Otta.	.50	2.00	.25
☐☐☐	125 Robyn Regehr, Calg.	.50	2.00	.25
☐☐☐	**126 Martin Erat, Nash. RC**	**1.00**	**3.00**	**1.50**
☐☐☐	127 Nick Boynton, Bost.	.50	2.00	.25
☐☐☐	**128 Nick Schultz, MinW. RC**	**1.00**	**3.00**	**1.50**
☐☐☐	**129 T. Pärssinen, Anah. RC**	**1.00**	**2.00**	**1.50**
☐☐☐	**130 J. Bednar, LosA. RC**	**1.00**	**3.00**	**1.50**
☐☐☐	131 Roberto Luongo, Flor.	1.00	5.00	1.00
☐☐☐	**132 P. Dupuis, MinW. RC**	**1.50**	**4.00**	**2.00**
☐☐☐	133 David Tanabe, Caro.	.50	2.00	.25
☐☐☐	134 Dany Heatley, Atla.	2.00	9.00	1.50
☐☐☐	**135 Jeff Jillson, SanJ. RC**	**1.00**	**3.00**	**1.50**
☐☐☐	136 Marian Gaborik, MinW.	1.50	6.00	1.00
☐☐☐	137 Radim Vrbata, Colo.	.50	3.00	.50

☐☐☐	138 Andrew Ference, Pitt.	.50	2.00	.25
☐☐☐	139 Rostislav Klesla, Colu.	.50	2.00	.25
☐☐☐	**140 D. Blackburn (G), NYRa. RC**	**4.00**	**7.00**	**4.00**
☐☐☐	141 Andy Hilbert, Bost.	.50	2.00	.50
☐☐☐	142 Martin Havlat, Otta.	.50	3.00	.50
☐☐☐	**143 Niko Kapanen, Dall. RC**	**1.50**	**4.00**	**2.00**
☐☐☐	144 Brenden Morrow, Dall.	.50	2.00	.25
☐☐☐	145 Scott Hartnell, Nash.	.50	2.00	.25
☐☐☐	**146 Raffi Torres, NYIs. RC**	**1.50**	**4.00**	**2.00**
☐☐☐	**147 V. Nedorost, Colo. RC**	**1.50**	**4.00**	**2.00**
☐☐☐	**148 Krys Kolanos, Phoe. RC**	**1.50**	**4.00**	**2.00**
☐☐☐	149 Kyle Calder, Chic.	.50	2.00	.25
☐☐☐	**150 Niklas Hagman, Flor. RC**	**1.00**	**3.00**	**1.50**
☐☐☐	151 Brian Gionta, NJer.	.50	2.00	.50
☐☐☐	**152 K. Huselius, Flor. RC**	**2.50**	**6.00**	**3.00**
☐☐☐	153 Mike Comrie, Edmo.	1.00	5.00	1.00
☐☐☐	**154 Ty Conklin, Edmo. RC**	**1.50**	**4.00**	**2.00**
☐☐☐	155 Justin Williams, Phil.	.50	2.00	.25
☐☐☐	**156 Erik Cole, Caro. RC**	**1.50**	**4.00**	**2.00**
☐☐☐	**157 N. Alexeev, Tamp. RC**	**1.50**	**4.00**	**2.00**
☐☐☐	158 Paul Mara, Phoe.	.50	2.00	.25
☐☐☐	**159 I. Kovalchuk, Atla. RC**	**10.00**	**25.00**	**10.00**
☐☐☐	160 David Legwand, Nash.	.50	2.00	.50
☐☐☐	**161 Ilja Bryzgalov, Anah. RC**	**1.50**	**3.00**	**2.00**
☐☐☐	162 Brad Richards, Tamp.	.50	3.00	.50
☐☐☐	163 Evgeni Nabokov, SanJ.	.50	3.00	.50
☐☐☐	164 Kris Beech, Pitt.	.50	2.00	.25
☐☐☐	**165 Pavel Datsyuk, Detr. RC**	**8.00**	**15.00**	**8.00**

SIGNED PUCK

Complete Set (40 pucks):

	Insert	Puck
☐	Jason Arnott, NJer. ✍	
☐	Peter Bondra, Wash. ✍	
☐	Pavel Brendl, Phil. ✍	
☐	Roman Cechmanek, Phil. ✍	
☐	Mike Comrie, Edmo. ✍	
☐	Marian Gaborik, MinW. ✍	
☐	Martin Havlat, Otta. ✍	
☐	Johan Hedberg (G), Pitt. ✍	
☐	Milan Hejduk, Colo. ✍	
☐	Brent Johnson, Slou. ✍	
☐	Ilya Kovalchuk, Atla. ✍	
☐	Michael Peca, NYIs. ✍	
☐	Chris Pronger, Slou. ✍	
☐	Miroslav Satan, Buff. ✍	
☐	Petr Sykora, Njer. ✍	
☐	Alex Tanguay, Colo. ✍	
☐	Justin Williams, Phil. ✍	
☐	Dan Blackburn (G), YoungStars ✍	
☐	Nick Boynton, YoungStars ✍	
☐	Kyle Calder, YoungStars ✍	
☐	Mike Comrie, YoungStars ✍	
☐	Tim Connolly, YoungStars ✍	
☐	Pavel Datsyuk, YoungStars ✍	
☐	Andrew Ference, YoungStars ✍	
☐	Mike Fisher, YoungStars ✍	
☐	Marian Gaborik, YoungStars ✍	
☐	Scott Hartnell, YoungStars ✍	
☐	Dany Heatley, YoungStars ✍	
☐	Kristian Huselius, YoungStars ✍	
☐	Ilya Kovalchuk, YoungStars ✍	
☐	David Legwand, YoungStars ✍	
☐	Roberto Luongo, YoungStars ✍	
☐	Paul Mara, YoungStars ✍	
☐	Brenden Morrow, YoungStars ✍	
☐	Karel Rachunek, YoungStars ✍	
☐	Robyn Regehr, YoungStars ✍	
☐	Mike Ribeiro, YoungStars ✍	
☐	Brad Richards, YoungStars ✍	
☐	David Tanabe, YoungStars ✍	
☐	Justin Williams, YoungStars ✍	

CERTIFIED AUTOGRAPH ISSUE

	Insert Set (23 cards):	800.00
	Insert (#/50)	**YSA**
☐	Dan Blackburn (G), NYRa. ✍	35.00
☐	Nick Boynton, Bost. ✍	30.00
☐	Kyle Calder, Chic. ✍	30.00
☐	Mike Comrie, Edmo. ✍	70.00
☐	Tim Connolly, Buff. ✍	35.00
☐	Pavel Datsyuk, Detr. ✍	175.00
☐	Andrew Ference, Pitt. ✍	30.00
☐	Mike Fisher, Otta. ✍	30.00
☐	Marian Gaborik, MinW. ✍	85.00
☐	Scott Hartnell, Nash. ✍	30.00
☐	Dany Heatley, Atla. ✍	125.00
☐	Kristian Huselius, Flor. ✍	30.00
☐	Ilya Kovalchuk, Atla. ✍	125.00
☐	David Legwand, Nash. ✍	35.00
☐	Roberto Luongo (G), Flor. ✍	70.00
☐	Paul Mara, Phoe. ✍	30.00
☐	Brenden Morrow, Dall. ✍	30.00
☐	Karel Rachunek, Otta. ✍	30.00
☐	Robyn Regehr, Calg. ✍	30.00
☐	Mike Ribeiro, Mont. ✍	30.00
☐	Brad Richards, Tamp. ✍	40.00
☐	David Tanabe, Caro. ✍	30.00
☐	Justin Williams, Phil. ✍	30.00

FABRIC OF THE FUTURE JERSEY

	Insert Set (23 cards):	200.00
	Insert	**Jersey**
☐	Dan Blackburn (G), NYRa. ✂	10.00
☐	Nick Boynton, Bost. ✂	10.00
☐	Kyle Calder, Chic. ✂	10.00
☐	Mike Comrie, Edmo. ✂ White	20.00
☐	Tim Connolly, Buff. ✂	10.00
☐	Pavel Datsyuk, Detr. ✂ Red	35.00
☐	Andrew Ference, Pitt. ✂	10.00
☐	Mike Fisher, Otta. ✂	10.00
☐	Marian Gaborik, MinW. ✂	30.00
☐	Scott Hartnell, Nash. ✂	10.00
☐	Dany Heatley, Atla. ✂	30.00
☐	Kristian Huselius, Flor. ✂	10.00
☐	Ilya Kovalchuk, Atla. ✂	30.00
☐	David Legwand, Nash. ✂	10.00
☐	Roberto Luongo (G), Flor. ✂	20.00
☐	Paul Mara, Phoe. ✂	10.00
☐	Brenden Morrow, Dall. ✂	10.00
☐	Karel Rachunek, Otta. ✂	10.00
☐	Robyn Regehr, Calg. ✂	10.00
☐	Mike Ribeiro, Mont. ✂	10.00
☐	Brad Richards, Tamp. ✂	10.00
☐	David Tanabe, Caro. ✂	10.00
☐	Justin Williams, Phil. ✂	10.00

FABRIC OF THE FUTURE STICK

	Insert Set (20 cards):	200.00
	Insert	**Stick**
☐	Dan Blackburn (G), NYRa. ✂	15.00
☐	Nick Boynton, Bost. ✂	15.00
☐	Kyle Calder, Chic. ✂	15.00
☐	Mike Comrie, Edmo. ✂	15.00
☐	Tim Connolly, Buff. ✂	15.00
☐	Pavel Datsyuk, Detr. ✂	15.00
☐	Andrew Ference, Pitt. ✂	15.00
☐	Mike Fisher, Otta. ✂	15.00
☐	Marian Gaborik, MinW. ✂	18.00
☐	Scott Hartnell, Nash. ✂	15.00
☐	Dany Heatley, Atla. ✂	18.00
☐	Kristian Huselius, Flor. ✂	15.00
☐	Ilya Kovalchuk, Atla. ✂	18.00
☐	David Legwand, Nash. ✂	15.00
☐	Roberto Luongo (G), Flor. ✂	15.00
☐	Paul Mara, Phoe. ✂	15.00
☐	Brenden Morrow, Dall. ✂	15.00
☐	Karel Rachunek, Otta. ✂	15.00
☐	Robyn Regehr, Calg. ✂	15.00
☐	Mike Ribeiro, Mont. ✂	15.00
☐	Brad Richards, Tamp. ✂	15.00
☐	David Tanabe, Caro. ✂	15.00
☐	Justin Williams, Phil. ✂	15.00

FABRIC OF THE FUTURE DOUBLE STUFF

	Insert Set (23 cards):	1,700
	Insert (#/25)	**DS**
☐	Dan Blackburn (G), NYRa. ✂ ✂	75.00
☐	Nick Boynton, Bost. ✂ ✂	75.00
☐	Kyle Calder, Chic. ✂ ✂	75.00
☐	Mike Comrie, Edmo. ✂ ✂	150.00
☐	Tim Connolly, Buff. ✂ ✂	75.00
☐	Pavel Datsyuk, Detr. ✂ ✂	200.00
☐	Andrew Ference, Pitt. ✂ ✂	75.00
☐	Mike Fisher, Otta. ✂ ✂	75.00
☐	Marian Gaborik, MinW. ✂ ✂	200.00
☐	Scott Hartnell, Nash. ✂ ✂	75.00
☐	Dany Heatley, Atla. ✂ ✂	200.00
☐	Kristian Huselius, Flor. ✂ ✂	75.00
☐	Ilya Kovalchuk, Atla. ✂ ✂	200.00
☐	David Legwand, Nash. ✂ ✂	75.00
☐	Roberto Luongo (G), Flor. ✂ ✂	150.00
☐	Paul Mara, Phoe. ✂ ✂	75.00
☐	Brenden Morrow, Dall. ✂ ✂	75.00
☐	Karel Rachunek, Otta. ✂ ✂	75.00
☐	Robyn Regehr, Calg. ✂ ✂	75.00
☐	Mike Ribeiro, Mont. ✂ ✂	75.00
☐	Brad Richards, Tamp. ✂ ✂	75.00
☐	David Tanabe, Caro. ✂ ✂	75.00
☐	Justin Williams, Phil. ✂ ✂	75.00

FABRIC OF THE FUTURE RIVALS

	Insert Set (11 cards):	200.00
	Insert	**FFR**
☐	1 R. Luongo (G) ✂ / D. Blackburn (G) ✂	35.00
☐	2 B. Richards ✂ / K. Rachunek ✂	25.00
☐	3 D. Tanabe ✂ / A. Ference ✂	25.00
☐	4 R. Regehr ✂ / N. Boynton ✂	25.00
☐	5 I. Kovalchuk ✂ / M. Gaborik ✂	60.00
☐	6 D. Heatley ✂ / M. Comrie ✂	50.00
☐	7 Ju. Williams ✂ / M. Ribeiro ✂	25.00
☐	8 D. Legwand ✂ / T. Connolly ✂	25.00
☐	9 M. Fisher ✂ / P. Datsyuk ✂	30.00
☐	10 S. Hartnell ✂ / B. Morrow ✂	25.00
☐	11 K. Huselius ✂ / K. Calder ✂	25.00

SPRING EXPO

These cards were available via a wrapper redemption program at the Spring Sport Card & Memorabilia Expo in Toronto (May 2002).

	Complete Set (10 cards):	
	Insert	**Expo**
☐	1 Ilya Kovalchuk, Atla.	
☐	2 Curtis Joseph (G), Toro.	
☐	3 Pavel Datsyuk, Detr.	
☐	4 José Théodore (G), Mont.	
☐	5 Jarome Iginla, Calg.	
☐	6 Martin Brodeur (G), Njer.	
☐	7 Patrick Roy (G), Colo.	
☐	8 Dany Heatley, Atla.	
☐	9 Dan Blackburn (G), NYRa.	
☐	10 Mats Sundin, Toro.	
☐	1 Ilya Kovalchuk, Atla. ✍	100.00

2001 - 02 CROWN ROYALE

Produced by Pacific Trading Cards, this series was released in March 2002. There are five versions for each card 1-144: a hobby gold-foil base card, a hobby burgandy-foil parallel (#/35), a hobby Premiere Date parallel (#/60), a retail green-foil base card, and a retail light blue-foil parallel (#/89). Hobby gold-foil base cards have the same value as retail green-foil base cards. Retail light blue-foil parallel cards are valued at 75-90% of Premiere Date parallel cards.

Shell Set (144 cards):		-	-	**125.00**
Complete Set (180 cards):		-	-	**1,200**
Parallel Set (144 cards):		**1,000**	**3,200**	-
Common Player:		**10.00**	**6.00**	**.50**
	Description	**Bu35**	**PD60**	**Base**
☐☐☐☐☐	1 M. Cullen	10.00	12.00	.50
☐☐☐☐☐	2 J. Friesen	10.00	16.00	.50
☐☐☐☐☐	3 J-S Giguère (G)	10.00	40.00	2.00
☐☐☐☐☐	4 P. Kariya	10.00	70.00	3.50
☐☐☐☐☐	5 R. Ferraro	10.00	8.00	.50
☐☐☐☐☐	6 D. Heatley	10.00	50.00	5.00
☐☐☐☐☐	7 M. Hnilicka (G)	10.00	12.00	.50
☐☐☐☐☐	8 P. Stefan	10.00	16.00	.50
☐☐☐☐☐	9 B. Dafoe (G)	10.00	20.00	1.00
☐☐☐☐☐	10 G. Murray	10.00	24.00	1.00
☐☐☐☐☐	11 B. Rolston	10.00	16.00	.50
☐☐☐☐☐	12 S. Samsonov	10.00	30.00	1.50
☐☐☐☐☐	13 J. Thornton	10.00	60.00	3.00
☐☐☐☐☐	14 S. Barnes	10.00	6.00	.50
☐☐☐☐☐	15 M. Biron (G)	10.00	24.00	1.00
☐☐☐☐☐	16 T. Connolly	10.00	20.00	1.00
☐☐☐☐☐	17 J. Dumont	10.00	12.00	.50
☐☐☐☐☐	18 M. Satan	10.00	16.00	.50
☐☐☐☐☐	19 C. Conroy	10.00	16.00	.50
☐☐☐☐☐	20 J. Iginla	10.00	40.00	2.00
☐☐☐☐☐	21 D. McAmmond	10.00	8.00	.50
☐☐☐☐☐	22 D. Morris	10.00	12.00	.50
☐☐☐☐☐	23 M. Savard	10.00	12.00	.50
☐☐☐☐☐	24 R. Turek (G)	10.00	24.00	1.00
☐☐☐☐☐	25 R. Francis	10.00	30.00	1.50
☐☐☐☐☐	26 A. Irbe (G)	10.00	20.00	1.00
☐☐☐☐☐	27 S. Kapanen	10.00	16.00	.50
☐☐☐☐☐	28 J. O'Neill	10.00	20.00	1.00
☐☐☐☐☐	29 T. Amonte	10.00	30.00	1.50
☐☐☐☐☐	30 M. Bell	10.00	12.00	.50
☐☐☐☐☐	31 K. Calder	10.00	12.00	.50
☐☐☐☐☐	32 E. Dazé	10.00	20.00	1.00
☐☐☐☐☐	33 S. Sullivan	10.00	16.00	.50
☐☐☐☐☐	34 J. Thibault (G)	10.00	20.00	1.00
☐☐☐☐☐	35 R. Blake	10.00	30.00	1.50
☐☐☐☐☐	36 C. Drury	10.00	30.00	1.50
☐☐☐☐☐	37 P. Forsberg	10.00	70.00	3.50
☐☐☐☐☐	38 M. Hejduk	10.00	40.00	2.00
☐☐☐☐☐	39 P. Roy (G)	10.00	150.00	7.50
☐☐☐☐☐	40 J. Sakic	10.00	80.00	4.00
☐☐☐☐☐	41 A. Tanguay	10.00	30.00	1.50
☐☐☐☐☐	42 M. Denis (G)	10.00	24.00	1.00
☐☐☐☐☐	43 R. Klesla	10.00	30.00	.50
☐☐☐☐☐	44 G. Sanderson	10.00	12.00	.50
☐☐☐☐☐	45 R. Tugnutt (G)	10.00	20.00	1.00
☐☐☐☐☐	46 E. Belfour (G)	10.00	50.00	2.50
☐☐☐☐☐	47 J. Lehtinen	10.00	16.00	.50
☐☐☐☐☐	48 M. Modano	10.00	50.00	2.50
☐☐☐☐☐	49 J. Nieuwendyk	10.00	20.00	1.00
☐☐☐☐☐	50 P. Turgeon	10.00	20.00	1.00
☐☐☐☐☐	51 S. Fedorov	10.00	50.00	2.50
☐☐☐☐☐	52 D. Hasek (G)	10.00	50.00	2.50
☐☐☐☐☐	53 B. Hull	10.00	50.00	2.50
☐☐☐☐☐	54 N. Lidström	10.00	30.00	1.50
☐☐☐☐☐	55 L. Robitaille	10.00	40.00	2.00
☐☐☐☐☐	56 B. Shanahan	10.00	50.00	2.50
☐☐☐☐☐	57 S. Yzerman	10.00	120.00	6.00
☐☐☐☐☐	58 A. Carter	10.00	20.00	1.00
☐☐☐☐☐	59 D. Cleary	10.00	16.00	.50
☐☐☐☐☐	60 M. Comrie	10.00	40.00	2.00
☐☐☐☐☐	61 T. Salo (G)	10.00	20.00	1.00
☐☐☐☐☐	62 R. Smyth	10.00	24.00	1.00
☐☐☐☐☐	63 P. Bure	10.00	40.00	2.00
☐☐☐☐☐	64 V. Kozlov	10.00	16.00	.50
☐☐☐☐☐	65 R. Luongo (G)	10.00	40.00	2.00
☐☐☐☐☐	66 J. Allison	10.00	30.00	1.50
☐☐☐☐☐	67 A. Deadmarsh	10.00	16.00	.50
☐☐☐☐☐	68 S. Heinze	10.00	8.00	.50
☐☐☐☐☐	69 Z. Palffy	10.00	30.00	1.50
☐☐☐☐☐	70 F. Potvin (G)	10.00	60.00	1.50
☐☐☐☐☐	71 A. Brunette	10.00	8.00	.50
☐☐☐☐☐	72 J. Dowd	10.00	6.00	.50
☐☐☐☐☐	73 M. Fernandez (G)	10.00	20.00	1.00
☐☐☐☐☐	74 M. Gaborik	10.00	50.00	2.50
☐☐☐☐☐	75 D. Gilmour	10.00	30.00	1.50
☐☐☐☐☐	76 J. Hackett (G)	10.00	16.00	.50
☐☐☐☐☐	77 Y. Perreault	10.00	16.00	.50
☐☐☐☐☐	78 B. Savage	10.00	16.00	.50
☐☐☐☐☐	79 J. Théodore (G)	10.00	60.00	3.00
☐☐☐☐☐	80 M. Dunham (G)	10.00	20.00	1.00
☐☐☐☐☐	81 D. Legwand	10.00	20.00	1.00
☐☐☐☐☐	82 C. Ronning	10.00	12.00	.50
☐☐☐☐☐	83 S. Walker	10.00	12.00	.50
☐☐☐☐☐	84 J. Arnott	10.00	24.00	1.00
☐☐☐☐☐	85 M. Brodeur (G)	10.00	80.00	4.00
☐☐☐☐☐	86 P. Elias	10.00	40.00	2.00
☐☐☐☐☐	87 S. Stevens	10.00	20.00	1.00
☐☐☐☐☐	88 P. Sykora	10.00	20.00	1.00
☐☐☐☐☐	89 R. DiPietro	10.00	24.00	1.00
☐☐☐☐☐	90 C. Osgood (G)	10.00	30.00	1.50
☐☐☐☐☐	91 M. Parrish	10.00	20.00	1.00
☐☐☐☐☐	92 M. Peca	10.00	20.00	1.00
☐☐☐☐☐	93 A. Yashin	10.00	30.00	1.50
☐☐☐☐☐	94 T. Fleury	10.00	30.00	1.50
☐☐☐☐☐	95 B. Leetch	10.00	30.00	1.50
☐☐☐☐☐	96 E. Lindros	10.00	50.00	2.50
☐☐☐☐☐	97 M. Messier	10.00	50.00	2.50
☐☐☐☐☐	98 M. Richter (G)	10.00	24.00	1.00
☐☐☐☐☐	99 D. Alfredsson	10.00	60.00	1.50
☐☐☐☐☐	100 M. Havlat	10.00	30.00	1.50
☐☐☐☐☐	101 M. Hossa	10.00	50.00	2.50
☐☐☐☐☐	102 P. Lalime (G)	10.00	30.00	1.50
☐☐☐☐☐	103 T. White	10.00	6.00	.50
☐☐☐☐☐	104 B. Boucher (G)	10.00	16.00	.50
☐☐☐☐☐	105 R. Cechmanek (G)	10.00	20.00	1.00
☐☐☐☐☐	106 S. Gagné	10.00	40.00	2.00
☐☐☐☐☐	107 J. LeClair	10.00	40.00	2.00
☐☐☐☐☐	108 M. Recchi	10.00	20.00	1.00
☐☐☐☐☐	109 J. Roenick	10.00	40.00	2.00

□□□□□	110 D. Brière	10.00	24.00	1.00
□□□□□	111 S. Burke (G)	10.00	30.00	1.50
□□□□□	112 S. Doan	10.00	12.00	.50
□□□□□	113 C. Lemieux	10.00	16.00	.50
□□□□□	114 J. Hedberg (G)	10.00	20.00	1.00
□□□□□	115 A. Kovalev	10.00	30.00	1.50
□□□□□	116 R. Lang	10.00	12.00	.50
□□□□□	117 M. Lemieux	10.00	150.00	7.50
□□□□□	118 P. Demitra	10.00	20.00	1.00
□□□□□	119 B. Johnson (G)	10.00	20.00	1.00
□□□□□	120 C. Pronger	10.00	30.00	1.50
□□□□□	121 K. Tkachuk	10.00	30.00	1.50
□□□□□	122 D. Weight	10.00	30.00	1.50
□□□□□	123 V. Damphousse	10.00	30.00	1.50
□□□□□	124 E. Nabokov (G)	10.00	30.00	1.50
□□□□□	125 O. Nolan	10.00	30.00	1.50
□□□□□	126 T. Selänne	10.00	40.00	2.00
□□□□□	127 N. Khabibulin (G)	10.00	20.00	1.00
□□□□□	128 V. Lecavalier	10.00	50.00	2.50
□□□□□	129 B. Richards	10.00	24.00	1.00
□□□□□	130 M. St-Louis	10.00	24.00	1.00
□□□□□	131 C. Joseph (G)	10.00	50.00	2.50
□□□□□	132 A. Mogilny	10.00	24.00	1.00
□□□□□	133 G. Roberts	10.00	20.00	1.00
□□□□□	134 M. Sundin	10.00	50.00	2.50
□□□□□	135 D. Tucker	10.00	12.00	.50
□□□□□	136 D. Cloutier (G)	10.00	20.00	1.00
□□□□□	137 B. Morrison	10.00	16.00	.50
□□□□□	138 M. Näslund	10.00	50.00	2.50
□□□□□	139 D. Sedin	10.00	20.00	1.00
□□□□□	140 H. Sedin	10.00	20.00	1.00
□□□□□	141 P. Bondra	10.00	30.00	1.50
□□□□□	142 J. Jagr	10.00	50.00	2.50
□□□□□	143 O. Kölzig (G)	10.00	30.00	1.50
□□□□□	144 A. Oates	10.00	20.00	1.00

ROOKIES

	Rookie (#/267)	R267
□	**145 Ilja Bryzgalov (G), Anah. RC**	35.00
□	**146 Timo Pärssinen, Anah. RC**	20.00
□	**147 Ilya Kovalchuk, Atla. RC**	175.00
□	**148 Brian Pothier, Atla. RC**	20.00
□	**149 Jukka Hentunen, Calg. RC**	20.00
□	**150 Erik Cole, Caro. RC**	45.00
□	**151 Vaclav Nedorost, Colo. RC**	45.00
□	152 Brian Gionta, NJer.	15.00
□	**153 Mathieu Darche, Colu. RC**	30.00
□	**154 Jody Shelley, Colu. RC**	30.00
□	**155 Martin Spanhel, Colu. RC**	20.00
□	**156 Niko Kapanen, Dall. RC**	45.00
□	**157 Pavel Datsyuk, Detr. RC**	150.00
□	**158 Jason Chimera, Edmo. RC**	30.00
□	**159 Ty Conklin (G), Edmo. RC**	45.00
□	160 Jussi Markkanen, Edmo.	10.00
□	**161 Niklas Hagman, Flor. RC**	30.00
□	**162 Kristian Huselius, Flor. RC**	60.00
□	**163 Jaroslav Bednar, LosA. RC**	30.00
□	**164 David Cullen, MinW. RC**	20.00
□	**165 Pascal Dupuis, MinW. RC**	45.00
□	**166 Nick Schultz, MinW. RC**	30.00
□	**167 Martin Erat, Nash. RC**	30.00
□	**168 Andreas Salomonsson, NJer. RC**	20.00
□	**169 Radek Martinek, NYIs. RC**	20.00
□	**170 Raffi Torres, NYIs. RC**	45.00
□	**171 Dan Blackburn (G), NYRa. RC**	75.00
□	**172 Chris Neil, Otta. RC**	20.00
□	**173 Jiri Dopita, Phil. RC**	30.00
□	**174 Krys Kolanos, Phoe. RC**	45.00
□	**175 Billy Tibbetts, Pitt. RC**	30.00
□	**176 Mark Rycroft, SLou. RC**	20.00
□	**177 Jeff Jillson, SanJ. RC**	30.00
□	**178 Nikita Alexeev, Tamp. RC**	45.00
□	**179 Chris Corrinet, Wash. RC**	20.00
□	**180 Brian Sutherby, Wash. RC**	30.00

ALL-STAR HONORS

	Insert Set (20 cards):	175.00
	Insert (1:49)	ASH
□	1 Paul Kariya, Anah.	10.00
□	2 Roman Turek (G), Calg.	6.00
□	3 Rob Blake, Colo.	6.00
□	4 Patrick Roy (G), Colo.	30.00
□	5 Joe Sakic, Colo.	15.00
□	6 Mike Modano, Dall.	10.00
□	7 Dominik Hasek (G), Detr.	10.00
□	8 Brett Hull, Detr.	10.00
□	9 Brendan Shanahan, Detr.	10.00
□	10 Steve Yzerman, Detr.	20.00
□	11 Pavel Bure, Flor.	6.00
□	12 Martin Brodeur (G), NJer.	15.00
□	13 Patrik Elias, NJer.	6.00
□	14 Alexei Yashin, NYIs.	6.00
□	15 Eric Lindros, NYRa.	10.00
□	16 Mark Messier, NYRa.	10.00
□	17 Mario Lemieux, Pitt.	30.00
□	18 Doug Weight, SLou.	6.00
□	19 Curtis Joseph (G), Toro.	10.00
□	20 Mats Sundin, Toro.	10.00

CROWNING ACHIEVEMENTS

	Insert Set (20 cards):	95.00
	Insert (1:25)	CA
□	1 Dany Heatley, Atla.	10.00
□	2 Ilya Kovalchuk, Atla.	10.00
□	3 Mark Bell, Chic.	3.00
□	4 Rostislav Klesla, Colu.	3.00
□	5 Kristian Huselius, Flor.	3.00
□	6 Martin Erat, Nash.	3.00
□	7 Rick DiPietro, NYIs.	4.00
□	8 Dan Blackburn (G), NYRa.	4.00
□	9 Krys Kolanos, Phoe.	3.00
□	10 Johan Hedberg (G), Pitt.	4.00
□	11 Jarome Iginla, Calg.	4.00
□	12 Patrick Roy (G), Colo.	15.00
□	13 Joe Sakic, Colo.	8.00
□	14 Dominik Hasek (G), Detr.	5.00
□	15 Steve Yzerman, Detr.	12.00
□	16 Pavel Bure, Flor.	4.00
□	17 Martin Brodeur (G), NJer.	8.00
□	18 Eric Lindros, NYRa.	5.00
□	19 Mario Lemieux, Pitt.	15.00
□	20 Jaromir Jagr, Wash.	5.00

JEWELS OF THE CROWN

	Insert Set (30 cards):	150.00
	Insert (1:25)	JotC
□	1 Paul Kariya, Anah.	8.00
□	2 Joe Thornton, Bost.	7.00
□	3 Jarome Iginla, Calg.	5.00
□	4 Roman Turek (G), Calg.	3.00
□	5 Jeff O'Neill, Caro.	3.00
□	6 Peter Forsberg, Colo.	8.00
□	7 Patrick Roy (G), Colo.	18.00
□	8 Joe Sakic, Colo.	10.00
□	9 Mike Modano, Dall.	6.00
□	10 Dominik Hasek (G), Detr.	6.00
□	11 Brendan Shanahan, Detr.	6.00
□	12 Steve Yzerman, Detr.	15.00
□	13 Ryan Smyth, Edmo.	3.00
□	14 Pavel Bure, Flor.	5.00
□	15 Jason Allison, LosA.	3.00
□	16 Marian Gaborik, MinW.	6.00
□	17 Saku Koivu, Mont.	5.00
□	18 Martin Brodeur (G), NJer.	10.00
□	19 Patrik Elias, NJer.	5.00
□	20 Alexei Yashin, NYIs.	3.00
□	21 Eric Lindros, NYRa.	6.00
□	22 Mark Messier, NYRa.	6.00
□	23 Marian Hossa, Otta.	6.00
□	24 Jeremy Roenick, Phil.	5.00
□	25 Mario Lemieux, Pitt.	18.00
□	26 Keith Tkachuk, Slou.	3.00
□	27 Teemu Selänne, SanJ.	5.00
□	28 Curtis Joseph (G), Toro.	6.00
□	29 Mats Sundin, Toro.	6.00
□	30 Jaromir Jagr, Wash.	6.00

LEGENDARY HEROES

	Insert Set (10 cards):	600.00
	Insert (1:1152)	LH
□	1 Paul Kariya, Anah.	70.00
□	2 Patrick Roy (G), Colo.	150.00
□	3 Dominik Hasek (G), Detr.	50.00
□	4 Steve Yzerman, Detr.	120.00
□	5 Martin Brodeur (G), NJer.	80.00
□	6 Eric Lindros, NYRa.	50.00
□	7 Mark Messier, NYRa.	50.00
□	8 Mario Lemieux, Pitt.	150.00
□	9 Curtis Joseph (G), Toro.	50.00
□	10 Jaromir Jagr, Wash.	50.00

ROOKIE ROYALTY

	Insert Set (20 cards):	90.00
	Insert (1:49)	RR
□	1 Dany Heatley, Atla.	15.00
□	2 Ilya Kovalchuk, Atla.	15.00
□	3 Erik Cole, Caro.	5.00
□	4 Mark Bell, Chic.	5.00
□	5 Vaclav Nedorost, Colo.	5.00
□	6 Brian Willsie, Colo.	5.00
□	7 Rostislav Klesla, Colu.	5.00
□	8 Pavel Datsyuk, Detr.	10.00
□	9 Ty Conklin (G), Edmo.	5.00
□	10 Kristian Huselius, Flor.	5.00
□	11 Jaroslav Bednar, LosA.	5.00
□	12 Martin Erat, Nash.	5.00
□	13 Rick DiPietro, NYIs.	5.00
□	14 Dan Blackburn (G), NYRa.	5.00
□	15 Krys Kolanos, Phoe.	5.00
□	16 Kris Beech, Pitt.	5.00
□	17 Johan Hedberg (G), Pitt.	5.00
□	18 Toby Petersen, Pitt.	5.00
□	19 Jeff Jillson, SanJ.	5.00
□	20 Nikita Alexeev, Tamp.	5.00

TRIPLE THREADS

	Insert Set (20 cards):	275.00
	Insert	TT
□	1 Kariya ✂ / Rucchin ✂ / Tverdovsky ✂ {*1400}	15.00
□	2 Conroy ✂ / Savard ✂ / Turek (G) ✂ {*1400}	10.00
□	3 Samsonov ✂ / Bure ✂ / Zubov ✂ {*550}	10.00
□	4 Giguère (G) ✂ / Théodore (G) ✂ / Roy (G) ✂ {*650}	55.00
□	5 Dumont ✂ / Smehlik ✂ / Zhitnik ✂ {*350}	10.00
□	6 Calder ✂ / Dandenault ✂ / Dazé ✂ {*700}	10.00
□	7 Sakic ✂ / Roy (G) ✂ / de Vries ✂ {*800}	45.00
□	8 Modano ✂ / Turgeon ✂ / Hatcher ✂ {*850}	15.00
□	9 Iginla ✂ / Hecht ✂ / Cassels ✂ {*760}	10.00
□	10 Fitzgerald ✂ / Ronning ✂ / Yachmenev ✂ {*450}	10.00
□	11 Yzerman ✂ / Sakic ✂ / Lindros ✂ {*500}	60.00
□	12 Koivu ✂ / Sundin ✂ / Turek (G) ✂ {*1400}	20.00
□	13 Niedermayer ✂ / Terreri (G) ✂ / Malhotra ✂ {*500}	10.00
□	14 Czerkawski ✂ / Lindgren ✂ / Alatalo ✂ {*975}	10.00
□	15 Nedved ✂ White / Richter (G) ✂ White / Fleury ✂ White {*1025}	10.00
□	16 Dunham (G) ✂ / Walker ✂ / Fitzgerald ✂ {*600}	10.00
□	17 Lemieux ✂ / Straka ✂ / Kovalev ✂ {*500}	45.00
□	18 Young ✂ White / McLennan (G) ✂ Blue / Eastwood ✂ Blue {*1400}	10.00
□	19 Stillman ✂ White / Hecht ✂ Blue / Turgeon ✂ Blue {*1325}	10.00
□	20 Bondra ✂ / Jagr ✂ / Straka ✂ {*750}	15.00

2001 - 02 DS

Complete Set (61 cards):

DS

□ 1 Dominik Hasek (G), Czech Republic
□ 2 Vladimir Hudacek (G), Czech Republic
□ 3 Roman Malek (G), Czech Republic
□ 4 Mario Cartelli, Czech Republic
□ 5 Tomas Kaberle, Czech Republic
□ 6 Petr Kadlec, Czech Republic
□ 7 Angel Nikolov, Czech Republic
□ 8 Radek Phillip, Czech Republic
□ 9 Libor Prochazka, Czech Republic
□ 10 Michal Sykora, Czech Republic
□ 11 Libor Zabransky, Czech Republic
□ 12 Kamil Brabenec, Czech Republic
□ 13 Michal Bros, Czech Republic
□ 14 Jiri Burger, Czech Republic
□ 15 Petr Cajanek, Czech Republic
□ 16 Jaroslav Hlinka, Czech Republic
□ 17 Viktor Hubl, Czech Republic
□ 18 David Moravec, Czech Republic
□ 19 Martin Prochazka, Czech Republic
□ 20 Petr Sykora, Czech Republic
□ 21 Jan Tomajko, Czech Republic
□ 22 Viktor Ujcik, Czech Republic
□ 23 Pavel Vostrak, Czech Republic
□ 24 Jaroslav Bednar, Czech Republic
□ 25 Martin Rucinsky, Czech Republic
□ 26 Toman Vokoun (G), Jagr Team
□ 27 Milan Hnilicka (G), Jagr Team
□ 28 Josef Melichar, Jagr Team
□ 29 Michal Rozsival, Jagr Team
□ 30 Karel Pilar, Jagr Team
□ 31 Jan Horacek, Jagr Team
□ 32 Robert Schnabel, Jagr Team
□ 33 Pavel Kolarik, Jagr Team
□ 34 Petr Mika, Jagr Team
□ 35 Petr Tenkrat, Jagr Team
□ 36 Jaromir Jagr, Jagr Team
□ 37 Pavel Patera, Jagr Team
□ 38 Josef Beranek, Jagr Team
□ 39 Martin Straka, Jagr Team
□ 40 Petr Nedved, Jagr Team
□ 41 Martin Rucinsky, Jagr Team
□ 42 Robert Reichel, Jagr Team
□ 43 David Vyborny, Jagr Team
□ 44 Roman Hamrlik, Jagr Team
□ 45 Milan Hejduk, Jagr Team
□ 46 Patrik Elias, Jagr Team
□ 47 Vaclav Prospal, Jagr Team
□ 48 Vaclav Varada, Jagr Team
□ 49 Petr Sykora, Jagr Team
□ 50 Dusan Salficky (G)
□ 51 Petr Briza (G)
□ 52 Martin Prusek (G)
□ 53 Radek Martinek
□ 54 Karel Pilar
□ 55 Viktor Ujcik
□ 56 Vaclav Nedorost
□ 57 Ales Kotalik
□ 58 Jiri Dopita
□ 59 Robert Reichel
□ 60 Petr Cajanek
□ 61 David Moravec

BEST OF THE BEST

Best

□ BB1 Dominik Hasek (G)
□ BB2 Tomas Kaberle
□ BB3 Michal Sykora
□ BB4 Petr Cajanek
□ BB5 David Moravec
□ BB6 Martin Prochazka
□ BB7 Martin Rucinsky
□ BB8 Robert Reichel
□ BB9 Jiri Dopita

GOALIES

Goalies

□ G1 Dominik Hasek (G)
□ G2 Milan Hnilicka (G)
□ G3 Petr Briza (G)
□ G4 Roman Cechmanek (G)
□ G5 Roman Malek (G)

ICE HEROES

Ice Heroes

☐ IH1 Tomas Vokoun (G)
☐ IH10 Petr Tenkrat
☐ IH2 Jaromir Jagr
☐ IH3 Pavel Patera
☐ IH4 Josef Beranek
☐ IH5 Martin Straka
☐ IH6 Petr Nedved
☐ IH7 Martin Rucinsky
☐ IH8 Robert Reichel
☐ IH9 David Vyborny

LEGENDS

Legends

☐ L1 Jiri Holecek
☐ L10 Jaroslav Holik
☐ L11 Milan Novy
☐ L12 Jiri Lala
☐ L2 Jiri Kralik
☐ L3 Vlastimil Bubnik
☐ L4 Vaclav Rozinak
☐ L5 Vladimir Zabrodsky
☐ L6 Vladimir Martinec
☐ L7 Ivan Hlinka
☐ L8 Jan Havel
☐ L9 Frantisek Pospisil

TOP GALLERY

Top Gallery

☐ Jaromir Jagr
☐ Jaromir Jagr

2001 - 02 EA SPORTS / UPPER DECK

Produced by The Upper Deck Company, these cards were issued by EA Sports.

Complete Set (9 cards):

Description

☐ Peter Forsberg, Colo.
☐ Jere Lehtinen, Dall.
☐ Mario Lemieux, Pitt.
☐ Mario Lemieux, Pitt.
☐ Markus Näslund, Vanc.
☐ Owen Nolan, SanJ.
☐ Chris Pronger, Slou.
☐ Martin Rucinsky, Mont.
☐ Steve Yzerman, Detr.

2001 - 02 eTOPPS

Produced by the Topps Company, this series was released in January 2002 via eTopps.com. Listed below is the Initial Price Offering (IPO) in approximate Canadian dollars.

	Description	IPO-Cdn. eTopps
☐	1 Joe Sakic, Colo. (*782)	[15.00]
☐	2 Paul Kariya, Anah. (*1032)	[10.25]
☐	3 Curtis Joseph (G), Toro. (*714)	[10.25]
☐	4 Brendan Shanahan, Detr. (*2000)	[5.50]
☐	5 Patrik Elias, NJer. (*859)	[5.50]
☐	6 Evgeni Nabokov (G), SanJ. (*549)	[10.25]
☐	7 Johan Hedberg (G), Pitt. (*547)	[10.25]
☐	8 Patrick Roy (G), Colo. (*938)	[15.00]
☐	9 John LeClair, Phil. (*494)	[10.25]
☐	10 Martin Brodeur (G), NJer. (*663)	[10.25]
☐	11 Teemu Selänne, SanJ. (*784)	[5.50]
☐	12 Mike Modano, Dall. (*559)	[10.25]
☐	13 Martin Havlat, Otta. (*510)	[10.25]
☐	14 Roberto Luongo (G), Flor. (*747)	[5.50]
☐	15 Peter Forsberg, Colo. (*598)	[10.25]
☐	16 Steve Yzerman, Detr. (*796)	[15.00]
☐	17 Pavel Bure, Flor. (*896)	[5.50]
☐	18 Mark Messier, NYRa. (*618)	[10.25]
☐	19 Mike Comrie, Edmo. (*809)	[5.50]
☐	20 Mats Sundin, Toro. (*717)	[5.50]
☐	21 Owen Nolan, SanJ. (*457)	[10.25]
☐	22 Ed Belfour (G), Dall. (*730)	[5.50]
☐	23 Mario Lemieux, Pitt. (*1116)	[15.00]
☐	24 Keith Tkachuk, SLou. (*751)	[5.50]
☐	25 Milan Hejduk, Colo. (*532)	[10.25]
☐	26 Rick DiPietro (G), NYIs. (*579)	[15.00]
☐	27 Roman Cechmanek (G), Phil. (*511)	[10.25]
☐	28 Sergei Fedorov, Detr. (*710)	[10.25]
☐	29 Vincent Lecavalier, Tamp. (*550)	[10.25]
☐	30 Eric Lindros, NYRa. (*634)	[10.25]
☐	**31 Ilya Kovalchuk, Atla. RC (*2513)**	**[15.00]**
☐	32 Zigmund Palffy, LosA. (*550)	[5.50]
☐	33 Dominik Hasek (G), Detr. (*753)	[10.25]
☐	34 Jaromir Jagr, Wash. (*569)	[15.00]
☐	35 Doug Weight, SLou. (*521)	[5.50]

2001 - 02 FLEER ALL-STAR FANTASY

Produced by Fleer Trading Cards, this card was issued in February 2002 at the All-Star Fantasy in Los Angeles, CA.

	Description	ASG
☐	Mario Lemieux, Pitt.	

2001 - 02 FLEER GREATS OF THE GAME

Produced by Fleer Trading Cards, this series was released in October 2001.

	Complete Set (90 cards):	40.00
	Description	Base
☐	1 Gordie Howe, Detr.	4.00
☐	2 Glenn Hall (G), Chic.	1.50
☐	3 Jean Béliveau, Mont.	3.00
☐	4 Bob Nystrom, NYIs.	.50
☐	5 Phil Esposito, Bost.	1.50
☐	6 Dennis Maruk, Wash.	.50
☐	7 Bobby Hull, Chic.	2.50
☐	8 Guy Lafleur, Mont.	3.00
☐	9 Gilbert Perreault, Buff.	1.00
☐	10 John Davidson (G), NYRa.	.50
☐	11 Peter Stastny, NJer.	.50
☐	12 Steve Shutt, Mont.	.50
☐	13 Henri Richard, Mont.	1.50
☐	14 Johnny Bower (G), Toro.	1.00
☐	15 Barry Beck, Colo.	.50
☐	16 Marcel Dionne, NYRa.	1.50
☐	17 Billy Smith (G), NYIs.	1.00
☐	18 Dale Hunter, Wash.	.50
☐	19 Tony Esposito (G), Chic.	1.50
☐	20 Guy Lapointe, Mont.	.50
☐	21 Ed Giacomin (G), NYRa.	1.00
☐	22 Denis Savard, Chic.	.50
☐	23 Rod Gilbert, NYRa.	.50
☐	24 Steve Larmer, Chic.	.50
☐	25 Yvan Cournoyer, Mont.	.50
☐	26 Ulf Nilsson, NYRa.	.50
☐	27 Jean Ratelle, NYRa.	.50
☐	28 Dino Ciccarelli, Wash.	.50
☐	29 Bryan Trottier, NYIs.	1.50
☐	30 Tim Horton, Toro.	1.50
☐	31 Stan Mikita, Chic.	1.00
☐	32 Glenn Anderson, Edmo.	.50
☐	33 Bobby Clarke, Phil.	1.00
☐	34 Wendel Clark, Toro.	1.00
☐	35 Reggie Leach, Phil.	.50
☐	36 Terry Sawchuk (G), Detr.	3.00
☐	37 Bernie Geoffrion, Mont.	1.00
☐	38 Bill Barber, Phil.	.50
☐	39 Tiger Williams, Vanc.	.50
☐	40 Alex Delvecchio, Detr.	.50
☐	41 Bernie Parent (G), Phil.	1.00
☐	42 Paul Henderson, Toro.	.50
☐	43 Norm Ullman, Toro.	.50
☐	44 Larry Robinson, Mont.	.50
☐	45 Dave Schultz, Phil.	.50
☐	46 John Ogrodnick, Detr.	.50
☐	47 Rick MacLeish, Phil.	.50
☐	48 Richard Brodeur (G), Vanc.	.50
☐	49 Rick Martin, Buff.	.50
☐	50 Bobby Smith, Mont.	.50
☐	51 Denis Potvin, NYIs.	1.00
☐	52 Darryl Sittler, Toro.	1.00
☐	53 Lanny McDonald, Calg.	1.00
☐	54 Brian Bellows, Mont.	.50
☐	55 Frank Mahovlich, Toro.	1.50
☐	56 Cam Neely, Bost.	1.50
☐	57 Grant Fuhr (G), Edmo.	.50
☐	58 Harry Howell, NYRa.	.50
☐	59 Michel Goulet, Chic.	.50
☐	60 Gerry Cheevers (G), Bost.	1.00
☐	61 Dave Taylor, LosA.	.50
☐	62 Clark Gillies, NYIs.	.50
☐	63 Bernie Federko, SLou.	.50
☐	64 Chico Resch (G), Colo.	.50
☐	65 Andy Bathgate, NYRa.	.50
☐	66 Jacques Lemaire, Mont.	.50
☐	67 Ken Hodge, Bost.	.50
☐	68 Rogatien Vachon (G), Mont.	.50
☐	69 Brian Sutter, SLou.	.50
☐	70 Rick Middleton, Bost.	.50
☐	71 Neal Broten, Minn.	.50
☐	72 Mike Bossy, NYIs.	2.00
☐	73 Börje Salming, Toro.	1.00
☐	74 Ted Lindsay, Detr.	1.50
☐	75 Mike Gartner, Wash.	1.00
☐	76 Johnny Bucyk, Bost.	.50
☐	77 Brad Park, NYRa.	.50
☐	78 Red Kelly, Detr.	.50
☐	79 Joe Mullen, Pitt.	.50
☐	80 Terry O'Reilly, Bost.	.50
☐	81 Mario Lemieux, Pitt.	4.50
☐	82 Butch Goring, NYIs.	.50
☐	83 Mike Liut (G), SLou.	.50
☐	84 Marcel Pronovost, Detr.	.50
☐	85 Serge Savard, Mont.	.50
☐	86 Jari Kurri, Edmo.	1.50
☐	87 Rick Kehoe, Pitt.	.50
☐	88 Gump Worsley (G), Mont.	1.00
☐	89 Kent Nilsson, Calg.	.50

AUTOGRAPH

	Insert Set (85 cards):	2,000
	Insert	Auto
☐	Glenn Anderson, Edmo. ✍	20.00
☐	Bill Barber, Phil. ✍	20.00
☐	Andy Bathgate, NYRa. ✍	20.00
☐	Barry Beck, Colo. ✍	20.00
☐	Jean Béliveau, Mont. * ✍	90.00
☐	Brian Bellows, Mont. ✍	20.00
☐	Mike Bossy, NYIs. * ✍	80.00
☐	Johnny Bower (G), Toro. ✍	30.00
☐	Richard Brodeur (G), Vanc. ✍	20.00
☐	Neal Broten, Minn. ✍	20.00
☐	Johnny Bucyk, Bost. ✍	30.00
☐	Gerry Cheevers (G), Bost. ✍	40.00
☐	Dino Ciccarelli, Wash. ✍	20.00
☐	Wendel Clark, Toro. * ✍	50.00
☐	Yvan Cournoyer, Mont. ✍	30.00
☐	John Davidson (G), NYRa. ✍	20.00
☐	Alex Delvecchio, Detr. * ✍	30.00
☐	Marcel Dionne, NYRa. * ✍	50.00
☐	Phil Esposito, Bost. * ✍	60.00
☐	Tony Esposito (G), Chic. ✍	50.00
☐	Bernie Federko, SLou. ✍	20.00
☐	Grant Fuhr (G), Edmo. ✍	30.00
☐	Mike Gartner, Wash. * ✍	50.00
☐	Bernie Geoffrion, Mont. ✍	40.00
☐	Ed Giacomin (G), NYRa. ✍	40.00
☐	Rod Gilbert, NYRa. ✍	20.00
☐	Clark Gillies, NYIs. ✍	20.00
☐	Butch Goring, NYIs. ✍	20.00
☐	Michel Goulet, Chic. ✍	20.00
☐	Glenn Hall (G), Chic. * ✍	90.00
☐	Paul Henderson, Toro. * ✍	30.00
☐	Ken Hodge, Bost. ✍	20.00
☐	Gordie Howe, Detr. * ✍	225.00
☐	Harry Howell, NYRa. ✍	20.00
☐	Bobby Hull, Chic. * ✍	80.00
☐	Dale Hunter, Wash. ✍	20.00
☐	Rick Kehoe, Pitt. ✍	20.00
☐	Red Kelly, Detr. ✍	30.00
☐	Jari Kurri, Edmo. ✍	50.00
☐	Guy Lafleur, Mont. * ✍	60.00
☐	Guy Lapointe, Mont. ✍	20.00
☐	Steve Larmer, Chic. ✍	20.00
☐	Reggie Leach, Phil. ✍	20.00
☐	Jacques Lemaire, Mont. ✍	20.00
☐	Mario Lemieux, Pitt. ✍	150.00
☐	Ted Lindsay, Detr. * ✍	50.00
☐	Mike Liut (G), SLou. ✍	20.00
☐	Rick MacLeish, Phil. ✍	20.00
☐	Frank Mahovlich, Toro. ✍	40.00
☐	Rick Martin, Buff. ✍	20.00
☐	Dennis Maruk, Wash. ✍	20.00
☐	Lanny McDonald, Calg. ✍	40.00
☐	Rick Middleton, Bost. ✍	20.00
☐	Stan Mikita, Chic. * ✍	40.00
☐	Joe Mullen, Pitt. ✍	20.00
☐	Cam Neely, Bost. * ✍	50.00
☐	Kent Nilsson, Calg. ✍	20.00
☐	Ulf Nilsson, NYRa. ✍	20.00
☐	Bob Nystrom, NYIs. ✍	20.00
☐	John Ogrodnick, Detr. ✍	20.00
☐	Bernie Parent (G), Phil. ✍	40.00
☐	Brad Park, NYRa. ✍	30.00
☐	Gilbert Perreault, Buff. ✍	40.00
☐	Denis Potvin, NYIs. ✍	40.00
☐	Marcel Pronovost, Detr. ✍	20.00
☐	Jean Ratelle, NYRa. ✍	20.00
☐	Chico Resch (G), Colo. ✍	20.00
☐	Henri Richard, Mont. * ✍	50.00
☐	Larry Robinson, Mont. ✍	30.00
☐	Börje Salming, Toro. ✍	40.00
☐	Denis Savard, Chic. ✍	20.00
☐	Serge Savard, Mont. ✍	20.00
☐	Dave Schultz, Phil. ✍	20.00
☐	Steve Shutt, Mont. ✍	20.00
☐	Darryl Sittler, Toro. ✍	40.00
☐	Billy Smith (G), NYIs. ✍	40.00
☐	Bobby Smith, Mont. ✍	20.00
☐	Peter Stastny, NJer. * ✍	40.00
☐	Brian Sutter, SLou. ✍	20.00
☐	Dave Taylor, LosA. ✍	20.00
☐	Bryan Trottier, NYIs. * ✍	50.00
☐	Norm Ullman, Toro. ✍	20.00
☐	Rogatien Vachon (G), Mont. ✍	20.00
☐	Tiger Williams, Vanc. ✍	20.00
☐	Gump Worsley (G), Mont. ✍	40.00

BOARD CERTIFIED

	Insert Set (5 cards):	60.00
	Insert (1:24)	BC
☐	4 Mike Bossy, NYIs.	15.00
☐	1 Guy Lafleur, Mont.	20.00
☐	5 Mario Lemieux, Pitt.	30.00
☐	3 Cam Neely, Bost.	10.00
☐	2 Peter Stastny, Québ.	10.00

ORIGINAL SIX STICK

	Insert Set (10 cards):	240.00
	Insert (1:84)	OSS
☐	Marcel Dionne, NYRa. ✂	20.00
☐	Phil Esposito, Bost. ✂	35.00
☐	Tony Esposito (G), Chic. ✂	30.00
☐	Bobby Hull, Chic. ✂	50.00
☐	Cam Neely, Bost. ✂	30.00
☐	Willie O'Ree, Bost. ✂	20.00
☐	Brad Park, NYRa. ✂	20.00
☐	Henri Richard, Mont. ✂	30.00
☐	Terry Sawchuk (G), Detr. ✂	75.00
☐	Darryl Sittler, Toro. ✂	20.00

ORIGINAL SIX SWEATER

	Insert Set (8 cards):	500.00	130.00
	Insert (1:30)	Patch	Jersey
☐☐	Guy Lafleur, Mont. ✂	200.00	45.00
☐☐	Tony Esposito (G), Chic. ✂	100.00	20.00
☐☐	Larry Robinson, Mont. ✂	60.00	20.00
☐☐	Börje Salming, Detr. ✂	80.00	20.00
☐☐	Glen Sather, NYRa. ✂	60.00	20.00
☐☐	Denis Savard, Chic. ✂	60.00	20.00
☐☐	Dino Ciccarelli, Detr. ✂	60.00	20.00
☐☐	Michel Goulet, Chic. ✂	60.00	20.00

RETROSPECTION

	Insert Set (13 cards):	30.00
	Insert (1:6)	R
☐	1 Gordie Howe, Detr.	6.00
☐	2 Jean Béliveau, Mont.	4.00
☐	3 Phil Esposito, Bost.	2.00
☐	4 Bobby Hull, Chic.	4.00
☐	5 Guy Lafleur, Mont.	4.00
☐	6 Peter Stastny, NJer.	2.00
☐	7 Henri Richard, Mont.	2.00
☐	8 Marcel Dionne, NYRa.	2.00
☐	9 Bryan Trottier, NYIs.	2.00
☐	10 Bobby Clarke, Phil.	2.00
☐	11 Terry Sawchuk (G), Detr.	4.00
☐	12 Mario Lemieux, Pitt.	6.00
☐	13 Tony Esposito (G), Chic.	2.00

2001 - 02 FLEER LEGACY

Produced by Fleer Trading Cards, this series was released in March 2002. There are two versions for each card 1-8: a base card (#/2002) and a gold-border Ultimate parallel (#/202).

Complete Set (64 cards): 525.00 60.00
Shell Set (56 cards): - 30.00

FLEER ULTRA

	Description	U202	U2002
☐☐	1 Mario Lemieux, Pitt.	45.00	10.00
☐☐	2 Bobby Hull, Chic.	27.00	5.00
☐☐	3 Guy Lafleur, Mont.	30.00	5.00
☐☐	4 Phil Esposito, Bost.	18.00	3.00
☐☐	5 Cam Neely, Bost.	15.00	3.00
☐☐	6 Jean Béliveau, Mont.	33.00	5.00
☐☐	7 Bryan Trottier, NYIs.	15.00	3.00
☐☐	8 Jari Kurri, Edmo.	15.00	3.00

FLEER LEGACY

There are two versions for each card 9-64: a base card and a gold-border Ultimate parallel (#/202).

	Insert	U202	Base
☐☐	9 Jean Béliveau, Mont.	30.00	3.00
☐☐	10 Bob Nystrom, NYIs.	4.00	.35
☐☐	11 Phil Esposito, Bost.	15.00	1.50
☐☐	12 Bobby Hull, Chic.	25.00	2.50
☐☐	13 Guy Lafleur, Mont.	30.00	3.00
☐☐	14 Gilbert Perreault, Buff.	10.00	1.00
☐☐	15 Henri Richard, Mont.	15.00	1.50
☐☐	16 Marcel Dionne, NYRa.	15.00	1.50
☐☐	17 Tony Esposito (G), Chic.	15.00	1.50
☐☐	18 Clark Gillies, NYIs.	4.00	.35
☐☐	19 Grant Fuhr (G), Edmo.	5.00	.50
☐☐	20 Brad Park, NYRa.	5.00	.50
☐☐	21 Frank Mahovlich, Toro.	15.00	1.50
☐☐	22 Johnny Bucyk, Bost.	5.00	.50
☐☐	23 Billy Smith (G), NYIs.	10.00	1.00
☐☐	24 Ulf Samuelsson, NYRa.	4.00	.35
☐☐	25 Mario Lemieux, Pitt.	45.00	4.50
☐☐	26 Rod Gilbert, NYRa.	5.00	.50
☐☐	27 Basil McRae, Dall.	4.00	.35
☐☐	28 Dave Semenko, Edmo.	4.00	.35
☐☐	29 Neal Broten, Dall.	4.00	.35
☐☐	30 Terry Sawchuk (G), Detr.	30.00	3.00
☐☐	31 Dino Ciccarelli, Wash.	4.00	.35
☐☐	32 Mike Bossy, NYIs.	20.00	2.00
☐☐	33 Börje Salming, Toro.	10.00	1.00
☐☐	34 Stan Mikita, Chic.	10.00	1.00
☐☐	35 Ted Lindsay, Detr.	15.00	1.50
☐☐	36 Gerry Cheevers (G), Bost.	10.00	1.00
☐☐	37 Michel Goulet, Chic.	5.00	.50
☐☐	38 Red Kelly, Detr.	5.00	.50
☐☐	39 Bobby Clarke, Phil.	10.00	1.00
☐☐	40 Todd Ewen, Anah.	4.00	.35
☐☐	41 Denis Potvin, NYIs.	10.00	1.00
☐☐	42 Paul Henderson, Toro.	5.00	.50
☐☐	43 Butch Goring, NYIs.	4.00	.35
☐☐	44 Nick Fotiu, NYRa.	4.00	.35
☐☐	45 Denis Savard, Chic.	5.00	.50
☐☐	46 Larry Robinson, Mont.	5.00	.50
☐☐	47 Joey Kocur, Detr.	4.00	.35
☐☐	48 Bernie Parent (G), Phil.	10.00	1.00
☐☐	49 Mike Liut (G), SLou.	4.00	.35
☐☐	50 Bernie Geoffrion, Mont.	10.00	1.00
☐☐	51 Tony Twist, SLou.	4.00	.35
☐☐	52 Bryan Trottier, NYIs.	15.00	1.50
☐☐	53 Cam Neely, Bost.	15.00	1.50
☐☐	54 Brent Sutter, NYIs.	4.00	.35
☐☐	55 Dave Schultz, Phil.	4.00	.35
☐☐	56 Terry O'Reilly, Bost.	4.00	.35
☐☐	57 Jari Kurri, Edmo.	15.00	1.50
☐☐	58 Lanny McDonald, Calg.	10.00	1.00
☐☐	59 Mike Gartner, Wash.	10.00	1.00
☐☐	60 Alex Delvecchio, Detr.	5.00	.50
☐☐	61 Ron Hextall (G), Phil.	5.00	.50
☐☐	62 Darryl Sittler, Toro.	10.00	1.00
☐☐	63 Dale Hunter, Wash.	4.00	.35
☐☐	64 John Vanbiesbrouck (G), Flor.	5.00	.50

HOCKEY KINGS

	Insert Set (17 cards):	2,300
	Insert	HK
☐	Jean Béliveau, Mont. ✂	40.00
☐	Marcel Dionne, NYRa. ✂	20.00
☐	Phil Esposito, Bost. ✂	20.00
☐	Tony Esposito (G), Chic. ✂	20.00
☐	Mike Gartner, Wash. ✂	15.00
☐	Bobby Hull, Chic. ✂	35.00
☐	Guy Lafleur, Mont. ✂	40.00
☐	Mario Lemieux, Pitt. ✂	60.00
☐	Stan Mikita, Chic. ✂	15.00
☐	Cam Neely, Bost. ✂	20.00
☐	Brad Park, NYRa. ✂	15.00
☐	Gilbert Perreault, Buff. ✂	15.00
☐	Henri Richard, Mont. ✂	20.00
☐	Terry Sawchuk (G), Detr. ✂	40.00
☐	Darryl Sittler, Toro. ✂	15.00
☐	Bryan Trottier, NYIs. ✂	20.00
☐	John Vanbiesbrouck (G), Flor. ✂	15.00

HOCKEY KINGS AUTOGRAPHS

	Insert Set (8 cards):	2,200
	Insert	HKA
☐	Jean Béliveau, Mont. ✍✂ {*100}	75.00
☐	Phil Esposito, Bost. ✍✂ {*100}	40.00
☐	Bobby Hull, Chic. ✍✂ {*100}	50.00
☐	Guy Lafleur, Mont. ✍✂ {*100}	50.00
☐	Mario Lemieux, Pitt. ✍✂ {*100}	150.00
☐	Stan Mikita, Chic. ✍✂ {*100}	40.00
☐	Darryl Sittler, Toro. ✍✂ {*100}	40.00
☐	Bryan Trottier, NYIs. ✍✂ {*100}	40.00

IN THE CORNERS

	Insert Set (12 cards):	1,400
	Insert	ITC
☐	Dino Ciccarelli, Detr.	8.00
☐	Jari Kurri, Edmo.	10.00
☐	Guy Lafleur, Mont.	20.00
☐	Mario Lemieux, Pitt.	30.00
☐	Lanny McDonald, Calg.	8.00
☐	Cam Neely, Bost.	10.00
☐	Denis Potvin, NYIs.	8.00
☐	Larry Robinson, Mont.	8.00
☐	Börje Salming, Toro.	8.00
☐	Darryl Sittler, Toro.	8.00
☐	Billy Smith (G), NYIs.	8.00
☐	Tony Twist, SLou.	8.00

TAILOR MADE

	Insert Set (8 cards):	800.00
	Insert	TM
☐	Dino Ciccarelli, Detr. ✂ White	15.00
☐	Tony Esposito (G), Chic. ✂	20.00
☐	Michel Goulet, Chic. ✂	15.00
☐	Guy Lafleur, Mont. ✂	40.00
☐	Mario Lemieux, Pitt. ✂	60.00
☐	Larry Robinson, Mont. ✂	15.00
☐	Börje Salming, Detr. ✂	15.00
☐	Denis Savard, Chic. ✂	15.00

PUCK

	Insert Set (22 pucks):	500.00
	Insert	Puck
☐	Jean Béliveau, Mont.	40.00
☐	Mike Bossy, NYIs.	50.00
☐	Bobby Clarke, Phil.	25.00
☐	Bobby Hull, Chic.	30.00
☐	Joey Kocur, Detr.	25.00
☐	Jari Kurri, Edmo.	30.00
☐	Guy Lafleur, Mont.	30.00
☐	Mario Lemieux, Pitt.	90.00
☐	Ted Lindsay, Detr.	30.00
☐	Stan Mikita, Chic.	25.00
☐	Cam Neely, Bost.	30.00
☐	Terry O'Reilly, Bost.	25.00
☐	Bernie Parent (G), Phil.	25.00
☐	Gilbert Perreault, Buff.	25.00
☐	Denis Potvin, NYIs.	25.00
☐	Henri Richard, Mont.	30.00
☐	Larry Robinson, Mont.	25.00
☐	Denis Savard, Chic.	25.00
☐	Dave Schultz, Phil.	25.00
☐	Billy Smith (G), NYIs.	25.00
☐	Bryan Trottier, NYIs.	30.00
☐	Tony Twist, SLou.	25.00

2001 - 02 FLEER ULTRA

Please see 2001 - 02 Fleer Legacy cards 1-8.

2001 - 02 HEADS UP

Produced by Pacific Trading Cards, this series was released in October 2001. There are five versions for each card 1-100: a base card, a Red parallel card (#/165), a Blue parallel card (#/55), a Premiere Date parallel card (#/105) and a Holographic Silver parallel card (#/27). The Red cards are valued 50% of the Blue cards while the Premiere Date cards are valued 50% of the Holographic Silver cards.

		HS27	B55	Base
	Shell Set (100 cards):	-	-	55.00
	Complete Set (120 cards):	-	-	350.00
	Parallel Set (100 cards):	3,500	1,500	-
	Common Player:	12.00	6.00	.35
	Description	HS27	B55	Base
☐☐☐☐☐	1 P. Kariya	105.00	55.00	2.50
☐☐☐☐☐	2 S. Shields (G)	15.00	6.00	.35
☐☐☐☐☐	3 R. Ferraro	12.00	6.00	.35
☐☐☐☐☐	4 M. Hnilicka (G)	15.00	6.00	.35
☐☐☐☐☐	5 P. Stefan	20.00	10.00	.50
☐☐☐☐☐	6 J. Allison	45.00	20.00	1.00
☐☐☐☐☐	7 B. Dafoe (G)	30.00	15.00	.50
☐☐☐☐☐	8 B. Guerin	30.00	15.00	.50
☐☐☐☐☐	9 S. Samsonov	45.00	20.00	1.00
☐☐☐☐☐	10 J. Thornton	90.00	45.00	2.00
☐☐☐☐☐	11 J. Dumont	15.00	6.00	.35
☐☐☐☐☐	12 J. Iginla	60.00	30.00	1.50
☐☐☐☐☐	13 M. Savard	15.00	6.00	.35
☐☐☐☐☐	14 R. Turek (G)	35.00	15.00	.50
☐☐☐☐☐	15 R. Francis	45.00	20.00	1.00
☐☐☐☐☐	16 A. Irbe (G)	30.00	15.00	.50
☐☐☐☐☐	17 J. O'Neill	30.00	15.00	.50
☐☐☐☐☐	18 T. Amonte	45.00	20.00	1.00
☐☐☐☐☐	19 S. Sullivan	20.00	10.00	.50
☐☐☐☐☐	20 J. Thibault (G)	30.00	15.00	.50
☐☐☐☐☐	21 R. Blake	45.00	20.00	1.00
☐☐☐☐☐	22 C. Drury	45.00	20.00	1.00
☐☐☐☐☐	23 P. Forsberg	105.00	55.00	2.50
☐☐☐☐☐	24 M. Hejduk	60.00	30.00	1.50
☐☐☐☐☐	25 P. Roy (G)	225.00	120.00	6.00
☐☐☐☐☐	26 J. Sakic	120.00	60.00	3.00
☐☐☐☐☐	27 M. Denis (G)	35.00	15.00	.50
☐☐☐☐☐	28 G. Sanderson	15.00	6.00	.35
☐☐☐☐☐	29 E. Belfour (G)	75.00	40.00	2.00
☐☐☐☐☐	30 B. Hull	75.00	40.00	2.00
☐☐☐☐☐	31 M. Modano	75.00	40.00	2.00
☐☐☐☐☐	32 J. Nieuwendyk	30.00	15.00	.50
☐☐☐☐☐	33 P. Turgeon	30.00	15.00	.50
☐☐☐☐☐	34 S. Fodorov	75.00	40.00	2.00
☐☐☐☐☐	35 D. Hasek (G)	75.00	40.00	2.00
☐☐☐☐☐	36 C. Osgood (G)	45.00	20.00	1.00
☐☐☐☐☐	37 L. Robitaille	60.00	30.00	1.50
☐☐☐☐☐	38 B. Shanahan	75.00	40.00	2.00
☐☐☐☐☐	39 S. Yzerman	180.00	95.00	4.50
☐☐☐☐☐	40 M. Comrie	60.00	30.00	1.50
☐☐☐☐☐	41 T. Salo (G)	30.00	15.00	.50
☐☐☐☐☐	42 R. Smyth	35.00	15.00	.50
☐☐☐☐☐	43 P. Bure	60.00	30.00	1.50
☐☐☐☐☐	44 R. Luongo (G)	60.00	30.00	1.50
☐☐☐☐☐	45 S. Heinze	12.00	6.00	.35
☐☐☐☐☐	46 Z. Palffy	45.00	20.00	1.00
☐☐☐☐☐	47 F. Potvin (G)	90.00	45.00	1.00
☐☐☐☐☐	48 M. Fernandez (G)	30.00	15.00	.50
☐☐☐☐☐	49 M. Gaborik	75.00	40.00	2.00
☐☐☐☐☐	50 S. Koivu	75.00	45.00	1.50
☐☐☐☐☐	51 B. Savage	20.00	10.00	.50
☐☐☐☐☐	52 J. Théodore (G)	90.00	45.00	2.00
☐☐☐☐☐	53 M. Dunham (G)	30.00	15.00	.50
☐☐☐☐☐	54 D. Legwand	30.00	15.00	.50
☐☐☐☐☐	55 J. Arnott	35.00	15.00	.50
☐☐☐☐☐	56 M. Brodeur (G)	120.00	60.00	3.00
☐☐☐☐☐	57 P. Elias	60.00	30.00	1.50
☐☐☐☐☐	58 S. Stevens	30.00	15.00	.50
☐☐☐☐☐	59 M. Czerkawski	15.00	6.00	.35
☐☐☐☐☐	60 R. DiPietro	35.00	15.00	.50
☐☐☐☐☐	61 M. Peca	30.00	15.00	.50
☐☐☐☐☐	62 A. Yashin	45.00	20.00	1.00
☐☐☐☐☐	63 T. Fleury	45.00	20.00	1.00
☐☐☐☐☐	64 B. Leetch	45.00	20.00	1.00
☐☐☐☐☐	65 M. Messier	75.00	40.00	2.00
☐☐☐☐☐	66 M. Richter (G)	35.00	15.00	.50
☐☐☐☐☐	67 D. Alfredsson	90.00	45.00	1.00
☐☐☐☐☐	68 M. Havlat	45.00	20.00	1.00
☐☐☐☐☐	69 M. Hossa	75.00	40.00	2.00
☐☐☐☐☐	70 P. Lalime (G)	45.00	20.00	1.00
☐☐☐☐☐	71 R. Cechmanek (G)	30.00	15.00	.50
☐☐☐☐☐	72 J. LeClair	60.00	30.00	1.50
☐☐☐☐☐	73 M. Recchi	30.00	15.00	.50
☐☐☐☐☐	74 J. Roenick	60.00	30.00	1.50
☐☐☐☐☐	75 S. Burke (G)	45.00	20.00	1.00
☐☐☐☐☐	76 J. Hedberg (G)	30.00	15.00	.50
☐☐☐☐☐	77 A. Kovalev	45.00	20.00	1.00
☐☐☐☐☐	78 M. Lemieux	225.00	120.00	6.00
☐☐☐☐☐	79 F. Brathwaite (G)	20.00	10.00	.50
☐☐☐☐☐	80 C. Pronger	45.00	20.00	1.00
☐☐☐☐☐	81 K. Tkachuk	45.00	20.00	1.00
☐☐☐☐☐	82 D. Weight	45.00	20.00	1.00
☐☐☐☐☐	83 P. Marleau	35.00	15.00	.50
☐☐☐☐☐	84 E. Nabokov (G)	45.00	20.00	1.00
☐☐☐☐☐	85 T. Selänne	60.00	30.00	1.50
☐☐☐☐☐	86 N. Khabibulin (G)	30.00	15.00	.50
☐☐☐☐☐	87 V. Lecavalier	75.00	40.00	2.00
☐☐☐☐☐	88 B. Richards	35.00	15.00	.50
☐☐☐☐☐	89 C. Joseph (G)	75.00	40.00	2.00
☐☐☐☐☐	90 A. Mogilny	35.00	15.00	.50
☐☐☐☐☐	91 G. Roberts	30.00	15.00	.50
☐☐☐☐☐	92 M. Sundin	75.00	40.00	2.00
☐☐☐☐☐	93 D. Cloutier (G)	30.00	15.00	.50
☐☐☐☐☐	94 M. Näslund	75.00	40.00	2.00
☐☐☐☐☐	95 D. Sedin	30.00	15.00	.50
☐☐☐☐☐	96 H. Sedin	30.00	15.00	.50
☐☐☐☐☐	97 P. Bondra	45.00	20.00	1.00
☐☐☐☐☐	98 J. Jagr	75.00	40.00	2.00
☐☐☐☐☐	99 O. Kölzig (G)	45.00	20.00	1.00
☐☐☐☐☐	100 A. Oates	30.00	15.00	.50

ROOKIES

	Rookie (#/999)	R999
☐	**101 Ilja Bryzgalov (G), Anah. RC**	**15.00**
☐	**102 Timo Pärssinen, Anah. RC**	**10.00**
☐	**103 Ilya Kovalchuk, Atla. RC**	**75.00**
☐	**104 Erik Cole, Caro. RC**	**15.00**
☐	**105 Vaclav Nedorost, Colo. RC**	**15.00**
☐	**106 Pavel Datsyuk, Detr. RC**	**60.00**
☐	**107 Kristian Huselius, Flor. RC**	**20.00**
☐	**108 Jaroslav Bednar, LosA. RC**	**10.00**
☐	**109 Pascal Dupuis, MinW. RC**	**15.00**
☐	**110 Martin Erat, Nash. RC**	**10.00**
☐	**111 Scott Clemmensen (G), NJer. RC**	**10.00**

□ **112 Dan Blackburn (G), NYRa. RC**	**30.00**
□ **113 Chris Neil, Otta. RC**	**10.00**
□ 114 Pavel Brendl, Phil.	5.00
□ **115 Jiri Dopita, Phil. RC**	**10.00**
□ **116 Krys Kolanos, Phoe. RC**	**15.00**
□ **117 Mark Rycroft, SLou. RC**	**10.00**
□ **118 Jeff Jillson, SanJ. RC**	**10.00**
□ **119 Nikita Alexeev, Tamp. RC**	**15.00**
□ **120 Brian Sutherby, Wash. RC**	**10.00**

ALL-STAR GAME-USED NET

Insert Set (6 cards):	425.00
Insert	ASGN
□ 1 Cechmanek (G) / Nabokov (G)	75.00
□ 2 Blake / Brodeur (G)	125.00
□ 3 Guerin / Weight	75.00
□ 4 Bure / Palffy	75.00
□ 5 Kariya / Sundin	100.00
□ 6 Lidström / Pronger	75.00

AUTHENTIC GAME-WORN JERSEY QUADS

Insert Set (29 cards):	800
Insert	AGWJQ
□ 1 Giguère (G) ✂ / Leclerc ✂ / Selänne ✂ / Hebert (G) ✂	25.00
□ 2 Dafoe (G) ✂ / Thornton ✂ / Samsonov ✂ / McLaren ✂	50.00
□ 3 Axelsson ✂ / Sweeney ✂ / Niedermayer ✂ / Holik ✂	15.00
□ 4 Barnes ✂ / Hasek (G) ✂ / Czerkawski ✂ / Jönsson ✂	25.00
□ 5 Iginla ✂ / V.Bure ✂ / Savard ✂ / Fata ✂	25.00
□ 6 Amonte ✂ / Dazé ✂ / Calder ✂ / Thibault ✂	25.00
□ 7 Sullivan ✂ / Nylander ✂ / Mironov ✂ / Zhamnov ✂	15.00
□ 8 A.Miller ✂ / Forsberg ✂ / Sakic ✂ / Reid ✂	50.00
□ 9 Roy (G) ✂ / Dingman ✂ / de Vries ✂ / Klemm ✂	75.00
□ 10 D.Hatcher ✂ / Modano ✂ / Nieuwendyk ✂ / Sydor ✂	25.00
□ 11 Shanahan ✂ / Chelios ✂ / Dandenault ✂ / Osgood (G) ✂	50.00
□ 12 Brunet ✂ / Zholtok ✂ / Zubrus ✂ / Dahlén ✂	15.00
□ 13 Legwand ✂ / Dunham (G) ✂ / Fitzgerald ✂ / Walker ✂	15.00
□ 14 Leetch ✂ / Fleury ✂ / Richter (G) ✂ / Nedved ✂	25.00
□ 15 Desjardins ✂ / LeClair ✂ / K.Stevens ✂ / Ki.Miller ✂	25.00
□ 16 Roenick ✂ / Alatalo ✂ / Burke (G) ✂ / Doan ✂	25.00
□ 17 Lemieux ✂ / Hrdina ✂ / Jagr ✂ / Kasparaitis ✂	75.00
□ 18 Aubin (G) ✂ / Straka ✂ / Kovalev ✂ / Parent (G) ✂	25.00
□ 19 Alfredsson ✂ / Cloutier (G) ✂ / Domi ✂ / Healy (G) ✂	25.00
□ 20 Roy (G) ✂ / Joseph (G) ✂ / Hasek (G) ✂ / Richter (G) ✂	100.00
□ 21 Lemieux ✂ / Sakic ✂ / P.Bure ✂ / Modano ✂	175.00
□ 22 Weight ✂ / Chelios ✂ / D.Hatcher ✂ / Leetch ✂	25.00
□ 23 Zhitnik ✂ / Ray ✂ / Rasmussen ✂ / Smehlik ✂	15.00
□ 24 Lehtinen ✂ / Keane ✂ / Hogue ✂ / Sloan ✂	15.00
□ 25 Graves ✂ / York ✂ / Lefebvre ✂ / Malhotra ✂	15.00
□ 26 Burke (G) ✂ / Numminen ✂ / Suchy ✂ / Lumme ✂	25.00
□ 27 Lecavalier ✂ / W.Primeau ✂ / Barnaby ✂ / Kraft ✂	25.00
□ 28 Straka ✂ / Beranek ✂ / Morozov ✂ / Boughner ✂	15.00
□ 29 Kovalev ✂ / Rozsival ✂ / Parent ✂ / Kasparaitis ✂	15.00

BREAKING THE ICE

Insert Set (20 cards):	55.00
Insert	BTI
□ 1 Milan Hnilicka (G), Atla.	3.00
□ 2 Patrik Stefan, Atla.	3.00
□ 3 Jean-Pierre Dumont, Buff.	3.00
□ 4 Shane Willis, Caro.	3.00
□ 5 David Aebischer (G), Colo.	3.00
□ 6 Chris Drury, Colo.	4.00
□ 7 Alex Tanguay, Colo.	4.00
□ 8 Marc Denis (G), Colu.	3.00
□ 9 Marty Turco (G), Dall.	4.00
□ 10 Mike Comrie, Edmo.	6.00
□ 11 Roberto Luongo (G), Flor.	6.00
□ 12 Marian Gaborik, MinW.	6.00
□ 13 David Legwand, Nash.	3.00
□ 14 Rick DiPietro (G), NYIs.	3.00
□ 15 Martin Havlat, Otta.	4.00
□ 16 Johan Hedberg (G), Pitt.	3.00
□ 17 Evgeni Nabokov (G), SanJ.	4.00
□ 18 Brad Richards, Tamp.	3.00
□ 19 Daniel Sedin, Vanc.	3.00
□ 20 Henrik Sedin, Vanc.	3.00

HD NHL

Cards 1-10 are seeded in hobby packs while cards 11-20 are seeded in retail packs.

Insert Set (20 cards):	65.00
Insert	HD
□ 1 Paul Kariya, Anah.	5.00
□ 2 Peter Forsberg, Colo.	5.00
□ 3 Joe Sakic, Colo.	5.00
□ 4 Mike Modano, Dall.	5.00
□ 5 Steve Yzerman, Detr.	10.00
□ 6 Pavel Bure, Flor.	2.00
□ 7 Mario Lemieux, Pitt.	15.00
□ 8 Teemu Selänne, SanJ.	2.00
□ 9 Mats Sundin, Toro.	5.00
□ 10 Jaromir Jagr, Pitt.	5.00
□ 11 Roman Turek (G), Slou.	2.00
□ 12 Ed Belfour (G), Dall.	5.00
□ 13 Chris Osgood (G), Detr.	2.00
□ 14 Tommy Salo (G), Edmo.	2.00
□ 15 Félix Potvin (G), LosA.	2.00
□ 16 José Théodore (G), Mont.	5.00
□ 17 Martin Brodeur (G), NJer.	5.00
□ 18 Mike Richter (G), NYRa.	2.00
□ 19 Roman Cechmanek (G), Phil.	2.00
□ 20 Curtis Joseph (G), Toro.	5.00

PRIME PICKS

Insert Set (10 cards):	45.00
Insert	PP
□ 1 Mike Comrie, Edmo.	10.00
□ 2 Roberto Luongo (G), Flor.	10.00
□ 3 Marian Gaborik, MinW.	10.00
□ 4 Rick DiPietro (G), NYIs.	5.00
□ 5 Martin Havlat, Otta.	5.00
□ 6 Johan Hedberg (G), Pitt.	5.00
□ 7 Evgeni Nabokov (G), SanJ.	5.00
□ 8 Brad Richards, Tamp.	5.00
□ 9 Daniel Sedin, Vanc.	5.00
□ 10 Henrik Sedin, Vanc.	5.00

RINK IMMORTALS

Insert Set (10 cards):	275.00
Insert (#/99)	RI
□ 1 Paul Kariya, Anah.	25.00
□ 2 Patrick Roy (G), Colo.	75.00
□ 3 Joe Sakic, Colo.	25.00
□ 4 Dominik Hasek (G), Buff.	25.00
□ 5 Brett Hull, Dall.	25.00
□ 6 Steve Yzerman, Detr.	50.00
□ 7 Pavel Bure, Flor.	25.00
□ 8 Martin Brodeur (G), NJer.	25.00
□ 9 Mario Lemieux, Pitt.	75.00
□ 10 Jaromir Jagr, Pitt.	25.00

SHOWSTOPPERS

Insert Set (20 cards):	50.00
Insert	SS
□ 1 Steve Shields (G), SanJ.	3.00
□ 2 Byron Dafoe (G), Bost.	3.00
□ 3 Roman Turek (G), Slou.	3.00
□ 4 Patrick Roy (G), Colo.	10.00
□ 5 Ed Belfour (G), Dall.	3.50
□ 6 Dominik Hasek (G), Buff.	3.50
□ 7 Chris Osgood (G), Detr.	3.00
□ 8 Tommy Salo (G), Edmo.	3.00
□ 9 Roberto Luongo (G), Flor.	3.00
□ 10 Félix Potvin (G), LosA.	3.00
□ 11 José Théodore (G), Mont.	4.50
□ 12 Martin Brodeur (G), NJer.	6.00
□ 13 Rick DiPietro (G), NYIs.	3.00
□ 14 Mike Richter (G), NYRa.	3.00
□ 15 Patrick Lalime (G), Otta.	3.00
□ 16 Roman Cechmanek (G), Phil.	3.00
□ 17 Johan Hedberg (G), Pitt.	3.00
□ 18 Evgeni Nabokov (G), SanJ.	3.00
□ 19 Curtis Joseph (G), Toro.	3.50
□ 20 Olaf Kölzig (G), Wash.	3.00

STAT MASTERS

Insert Set (20 cards):	45.00
Insert	SM
□ 1 Paul Kariya, Anah.	4.00
□ 2 Joe Thornton, Bost.	4.00
□ 3 Peter Forsberg, Colo.	4.00
□ 4 Joe Sakic, Colo.	6.00
□ 5 Brett Hull, Dall.	2.00
□ 6 Mike Modano, Dall.	2.00
□ 7 Steve Yzerman, Detr.	8.00
□ 8 Pavel Bure, Flor.	2.00
□ 9 Zigmund Palffy, LosA.	2.00
□ 10 Jason Arnott, NJer.	1.00
□ 11 Theoren Fleury, NYRa.	2.00
□ 12 Marian Hossa, Otta.	2.00
□ 13 Jeremy Roenick, Phil.	2.00
□ 14 Mario Lemieux, Pitt.	10.00
□ 15 Keith Tkachuk, Phoe.	2.00
□ 16 Teemu Selänne, SanJ.	2.00
□ 17 Vincent Lecavalier, Tamp.	2.00
□ 18 Brad Richards, Tamp.	1.00
□ 19 Mats Sundin, Toro.	2.00
□ 20 Jaromir Jagr, Pitt.	2.00

BOBBLE DOBBLES

Produced by Alexander Global Promotions, these dolls were seeded one per Heads Up hobby box.

Player Set (11 dolls): 900.00

Insert (#/1000)	BD
□ Martin Brodeur (G), NJer.	125.00
□ Dominik Hasek (G), Detr.	90.00
□ Johan Hedberg (G), Pitt.	80.00
□ Jaromir Jagr, Wash.	100.00
□ Curtis Joseph (G), Toro.	125.00
□ Paul Kariya, Anah.	125.00
□ Mario Lemieux, Pitt.	150.00
□ Mark Messier, NYRa.	80.00
□ Patrick Roy (G), Colo.	125.00
□ Joe Sakic, Colo.	80.00
□ Steve Yzerman, Detr.	125.00

2001 - 02 McDONALD'S

Produced by Pacific Trading Cards, this series was released in November 2001.

Complete Set (42 cards):	30.00
Description	McD
□ 1 Paul Kariya, Anah.	1.00
□ 2 Joe Thornton, Bost.	1.00
□ 3 Jarome Iginla, Calg.	.50
□ 4 Raymond Bourque, Colo. [w/ Cup]	2.00
□ 5 Peter Forsberg, Colo.	1.00
□ 6 Patrick Roy (G), Colo. (*)	4.50
□ 7 Joe Sakic, Colo.	1.50
□ 8 Ed Belfour (G), Dall. (*)	1.50
□ 9 Brett Hull, Dall.	1.00
□ 10 Mike Modano, Dall.	1.00
□ 11 Sergei Fedorov, Detr.	1.00
□ 12 Dominik Hasek (G), All-Star (*)	1.50
□ 13 Chris Osgood (G), Detr. (*)	.50
□ 14 Brendan Shanahan, Detr.	1.00
□ 15 Steve Yzerman, Detr.	2.00
□ 16 Tommy Salo (G), Edmo. (*)	.50
□ 17 Ryan Smyth, Edmo.	.35
□ 18 Pavel Bure, Flor.	.50
□ 19 Félix Potvin (G), LosA. (*)	.50
□ 20 Marian Gaborik, MinW.	1.00
□ 21 Saku Koivu, Mont.	.50
□ 22 José Théodore (G), Mont. (*)	1.50
□ 23 Jason Arnott, NJer.	.35
□ 24 Martin Brodeur (G), NJer. (*)	2.00
□ 25 Rick DiPietro (G), NYIs. (*)	.50
□ 26 Marian Hossa, Otta.	1.00
□ 27 Patrick Lalime (G), Otta. (*)	.50
□ 28 Roman Cechmanek (G), Phil. (*)	.50
□ 29 John LeClair, Phil.	.50
□ 30 Johan Hedberg (G), Pitt. (*)	.50
□ 31 Mario Lemieux, Pitt. (*)	4.50
□ 32 Fred Brathwaite, Calg. (SLou.) (*)	.35
□ 33 Chris Pronger, SLou.	.50
□ 34 Doug Weight, All-Star (SLou.)	.50
□ 35 Evgeni Nabokov (G), SanJ. (*)	.50
□ 36 Teemu Selänne, SanJ.	.50
□ 37 Vincent Lecavalier, Tamp.	1.00
□ 38 Curtis Joseph (G), Toro. (*)	1.50
□ 39 Mats Sundin, Toro.	1.00
□ 40 Dan Cloutier, Vanc. (*)	.50
□ 41 Markus Näslund, Vanc.	1.00
□ 42 Jaromir Jagr, All-Star (*)	1.50

AUTHENTIC GAME-WORN JERSEY PATCH

Insert Set (20 cards): 10,600

Prize	JPS
1 Jarome Iginla ✂ {#/238}	135.00
2 Peter Forsberg ✂ {#/229}	200.00
3 Patrick Roy (G) ✂ {#/217}	350.00
4 Joe Sakic ✂ {#/231}	225.00
5 Ed Belfour (G) ✂ {#/230}	135.00
6 Brett Hull ✂ {#/234}	135.00
7 Mike Modano ✂ {#/241}	135.00
8 Joe Nieuwendyk ✂ {#/225}	135.00
9 Dominik Hasek (G) ✂ {#/211}	150.00
10 Brendan Shanahan ✂ {#/236}	135.00
11 Steve Yzerman ✂ {#/231}	350.00
12 Saku Koivu ✂ {#/239}	135.00
13 Theoren Fleury ✂ {#/236}	135.00
14 Daniel Alfredsson ✂ {#/239}	135.00
15 Mario Lemieux ✂ {#/184}	475.00
16 Teemu Selänne ✂ {#/242}	135.00
17 Vincent Lecavalier ✂ {#/246}	135.00
18 Curtis Joseph (G) ✂ {#/219}	135.00
19 Mats Sundin ✂ {#/237}	135.00
20 Jaromir Jagr ✂ {#/182}	150.00

AUTHENTIC GAME-WORN JERSEY PATCH GOLD

Insert Set (20 cards): 6,400

Prize	JPG
1 Jarome Iginla ✂ {#/12}	300.00
2 Peter Forsberg ✂ {#/21}	350.00
3 Patrick Roy (G) ✂ {#/33}	550.00
4 Joe Sakic ✂ {#/19}	400.00
5 Ed Belfour (G) ✂ {#/20}	300.00
6 Brett Hull ✂ {#/16}	300.00
7 Mike Modano ✂ {#/9}	325.00
8 Joe Nieuwendyk ✂ {#/25}	300.00
9 Dominik Hasek (G) ✂ {#/39}	300.00
10 Brendan Shanahan ✂ {#/14}	300.00
11 Steve Yzerman ✂ {#/19}	600.00
12 Saku Koivu ✂ {#/11}	500.00
13 Theoren Fleury ✂ {#/14}	300.00
14 Daniel Alfredsson ✂ {#/11}	425.00
15 Mario Lemieux ✂ {#/66}	600.00
16 Teemu Selänne ✂ {#/8}	300.00
17 Vincent Lecavalier ✂ {#/4}	500.00
18 Curtis Joseph (G) ✂ {#/31}	300.00
19 Mats Sundin ✂ {#/13}	300.00
20 Jaromir Jagr ✂ {#/68}	300.00

COSMIC FORCE

Insert Set (6 cards): 20.00

Insert (1:16)	CF
1 Doug Weight, Edmo.	2.00
2 Pavel Bure, Flor.	3.00
3 Jaromir Jagr, Pitt.	4.00
4 Mario Lemieux, Pitt.	12.00
5 Teemu Selänne, SanJ.	3.00
6 Mats Sundin, Toro.	4.00

FUTURE LEGENDS

Insert Set (6 cards): 15.00

Insert (1:16)	FL
1 Mike Comrie, Edmo.	5.00
2 Rick DiPietro (G), NYIs.	3.00
3 Martin Havlat, Otta.	4.00
4 Evgeni Nabokov (G), SanJ.	4.00
5 Daniel Sedin, Vanc.	2.50
6 Henrik Sedin, Vanc.	2.50

GLOVE-SIDE NET FUSIONS

Insert Set (6 cards): 25.00

Insert (1:16)	GSNF
1 Patrick Roy (G), Colo.	12.00
2 Tommy Salo (G), Edmo.	2.00
3 José Théodore (G), Mont.	5.00
4 Martin Brodeur (G), NJer.	7.00
5 Johan Hedberg (G), Pitt.	2.00
6 Curtis Joseph (G), Toro.	4.00

HOCKEY GREATS

Insert Set (6 cards): 25.00

Insert (1:16)	HG
1 Raymond Bourque, Colo.	5.00
2 Joe Sakic, Colo.	7.00
3 Brett Hull, Dall.	4.00
4 Dominik Hasek (G), Detr.	4.00
5 Steve Yzerman, Detr.	10.00
6 Mark Messier, NYRa.	4.00

HOMETOWN PRIDE

Insert Set (10 cards): 10.00

Checklist (1:1)	HP
1 Jeff Friesen / Wade Redden	0.50
2 Paul Kariya / Brendan Morrison	2.00
3 Scott Pellerin / Don Sweeney	0.35
4 Mike Comrie / Jarome Iginla	2.00
5 Brad Richards / Geoff Sanderson	0.50
6 Ed Belfour (G) / Theoren Fleury	2.00
7 Luc Robitaille / Vincent Lecavalier	2.00
8 Daniel Cleary / Harold Druken	1.50
9 Al MacInnis / Colin White	0.50
10 Gary Roberts / Steve Thomas	0.50

2001 - 02 NEXTEL ALL-STARS

These cards were issued at the 2002 All-Star Fantasy in Los Angeles.

Complete Set (5 cards in seal): 30.00

Complete Set (4 cards) .00

Description	Nextel
Nolan / Damphousse / Shanahan	
Pronger / Roy (G) / Blake	
Selänne / Fedorov / Jagr	
Lidström / Hasek (G) / Ozolinsh	

2001 - 02 O-PEE-CHEE

Produced by The Topps Company, this series was released in August 2001. Please see 2001 - 02 Topps for pricing.

2001 - 02 OFS

Cards of NHL stars and prospects sell at a premium (usually $1-$2).

Complete Set (284 cards): 45.00

Common Player: .25

Description	OFS
1 Lukas Hronek (G)	.50
2 Petr Martinek	.25
3 Petr Kadlec	.25
4 Roman Malek (G)	.50
5 Jan Alinc	.25
6 Josef Beranek	.50
7 Viktor Hübl	.25
8 Martin Rousek	.25
9 Radek Matejovsky	.25
10 Jan Kloboucek	.25
11 Daniel Branda	.25
12 Viktor Ujcik	.50
13 Milan Antos	.25
14 Radek Belohlav	.25
15 Michal Bros	.50
16 Petr Briza (G)	.50
17 Radek Hamr	.50
18 Jaroslav Hlinka	.25
19 Martin Chabada	.25
20 Pavel Kasparik	.25
21 Marek Ivan	.25
22 Lukas Gavlas	.25
23 Radek Simicek	.25
24 Robert Tomanek	.25
25 Jan Tomajko	.50
26 Ivan Padelek	.25
27 Zdenek Pavelek	.25
28 Radek Philipp	.25
29 Pavel srek	.25
30 David Moravec	.50
31 Jan Srdinko	.25
32 Marek Malenovsky	.25
33 Frantisek Ptacek	.25
34 Vaclav Novak	.25
35 Jaroslav Nedved	.25
36 Ludek Krayzel	.25
37 Roman Kadera	.50
38 Petr Jurecka	.25
39 Lukas Smolka (G)	.50
40 Vitezslav skuta	.25
41 Josef straub	.25
42 Jiri Trvaj (G)	.50
43 Jan Vytisk	.25
44 Daniel Zapotocny	.25
45 Pavel Selingr	.25
46 Martin Prochazka	.50
47 Vlastimil Lakosil	.25
48 Petr Gregorek	.25
49 Mario Cartelli	.25
50 Miroslav Guren	.25
51 Petr Jancarik	.25
52 Libor Prochazka	.50
53 Jan Slavik	.25
54 Pavel Janku	.25
55 Branislav Janos	.25
56 Marek Zadina	.25
57 Jiri Polak	.25
58 Ondrej Nemec	.25
59 Petr Kubos	.25
60 Slavomir Hrina	.25
61 Ivo Pesat (G)	.50
62 Radovan Biegl (G)	.50
63 Zdenek Skorepa	.25
64 Roman Meluzin	.25
65 Jan Marek	.25
66 Richard Kral	.25
67 Rostislav Vlach	.25
68 Ondrej Vetchy	.25
69 Petr Vampola	.25
70 Lukas Valko	.25
71 Michal safarcik	.25
72 Martin Streit	.25
73 Radim Kucharczyk	.25
74 Jiri Hudler	4.00
75 Jiri Burger	.25
76 Martin strbak	.25
77 Martin Ambruz	.25
78 Jakub Blazek	.25
79 Pavel Mojzis	.25
80 Jiri Marusak	.25
81 Rostisalv Malena	.25
82 Jan Homer	.25
83 Martin Hamrlik	.25
84 Petr Tucek (G)	.50
85 Vladimir Hudacek (G)	.50
86 Ales Zacha	.25
87 Radovan Somik	.25
88 Ivan Rachunek	.25
89 Libor Pivko	.25
90 Milan Ministr	.25
91 Petr Leska	.25
92 Martin Jenacek	.25
93 Petr Cajanek	.50
94 Karol Bartanus	.50
95 Jaroslav Balastik	.25
96 Petr Havelka	.25
97 Jan Hanzlik	.25
98 Petr Prikryl (G)	.50
99 Libor Zabransky	.50
100 David Hnat	.25
101 David Pazourek	.25
102 Zbynek Pazourek	.25
103 Radek Haman	.25
104 Karel Soudek	.25
105 Pavel Kumstat	.25
106 Tomas Jakes	.25
107 Vladimir Holik	.25
108 Jiri Hes	.25
109 David Havir	.25
110 Oldrich Svoboda (G)	.50
111 Ladislav Kudrna (G)	.50
112 Vlademar Jirus	.25
113 Miroslav Okal	.25
114 Petr Bohunicky	.25
115 Patrik Hucko	.25
116 Miroslav Blatak	.25
117 Tomas Netik	.25
118 Richard zemlicka	.25
119 Marek Uram	.25
120 Peter Pucher	.25
121 Lukas Krajicek	3.00
122 Michal Klimes	.25
123 Josef Jindra	.25
124 Ladislav Cierny	.25
125 Michal Marik (G)	.50
126 Josef Kucera	.25
127 Michal Kolarik	.25
128 Jiri Hasek	.25
129 David Nosek	.25
130 Martin Vojtek (G)	.50
131 Milan Nedoma	.25
132 Rudolf Suchanek	.25
133 Filip Vanecek	.25
134 Pavel Zubicek	.25
135 Kamil Brabenec	.25
136 Jiri Broz	.25
137 Dan Hlavka	.25
138 stepan Hrebejk	.25
139 Roamn Horak	.25
140 Milan Michalek	.25
141 Peter Bartos	.50
142 Michal Vondrka	.25
143 Jiri simanek	.25
144 Petr Sailer	.25
145 Lubos Rob	.25
146 Jan Rehor	.25
147 Martin Strba	.25
148 Marek Pinc (G)	.50
149 Vladimir Gyna	.25
150 Jan Hranac	.25
151 Martin Nosek	.25
152 Lukas Pozivil	.25
153 Vojtech Kubincak	.25
154 Anton Lezo	.25
155 Martin tupa	.25
156 Vlastimil Kroupa	.50
157 Jindrich Kotrla	.25
158 David Hruska	.25
159 Petr Jira	.25
160 Michal Oliverius	.25
161 Lukas Havel	.25
162 Jaroslav Buchal	.25
163 Jan sulc	.25
164 Pavol Rieciciar	.25
165 Petr Klima	.50
166 Jiri Gombar	.25
167 Tomas Kaberle	1.50
168 Ladislav Svoboda	.25
169 Pavel Geffert	.25
170 Tomas Horna	.25
171 Zdenek Orct	.25
172 Robert Kysela	.25
173 Radek Gardon	.25
174 Ondrej Kriz	.25
175 Tomas Klimt	.50
176 Jan Bohacek	.25
177 Michal Havel	.25
178 David Hajek	.25
179 Vaclav Skuhravy	.25
180 Radim Skuhrovec	.25
181 Tomas Plekanec	.25
182 Jan Dlouhy	.25
183 David Patera	.25
184 Jan Krulis	.25
185 Jan Pospisil	.25
186 David Appel	.25
187 Jakub Kraus	.25
188 Petr Macholda	.25
189 Petr Franek (G)	.50
190 Jaromir Kverka	.25
191 Michal Madl	.25
192 Marcel Kucera (G)	.50
193 Jakub Grof	.25
194 Michal Dobron	.25
195 Jan Kopecky	.25
196 Dmitrij Rodine	.25
197 David Balazs	.25
198 Roman Prosek	.25
199 Jan Kostal	.25
200 Petr Domin	.25
201 Jan Choteborsky	.25
202 Vaclavc Benak	.25
203 Miroslav simonovic (G)	.50
204 Jiri Hanzlik	.25
205 Josef reznicek	.25
206 Ivan Vlcek	.25
207 Libor Barta (G)	.50
208 Ondrej Steiner	.50
209 Dusan Andrasovsky	.25
210 Martin Vyborny	.25
211 Juraj stefanka	.25
212 Radek Duda	.25
213 Josef Slanec	.25
214 Michal Dvorak	.25
215 Libor Pavlis	.25
216 Vaclav Eiselt	.25
217 Tomas Nemcicky	.50
218 Petr Korinek	.25
219 Patrik Moskal	.25
220 Zdenek Sedlak	.25
221 Pavel Vostrak	.25

□	222 Milanb Volak	.25
□	223 Petr Mudroch	.25
□	224 Jiri Malinsky	.25
□	225 Jan Svik	.25
□	226 Petr Caslava	.25
□	227 Michal Straka	.25
□	228 Adam Svoboda (G)	.50
□	229 Josef Straka	.25
□	230 Patrik Rimmel	.25
□	231 Petr Pavlas	.25
□	232 Michael Prochazka	.25
□	233 Miroslav Javim	.25
□	234 Robin Bacul	.25
□	235 Marek cernosek	.25
□	236 Petr Folta	.25
□	237 Pavel Malac (G)	.50
□	238 Radek Krestan	.25
□	239 Lubomir Korhon	.25
□	240 Pavel Cagas (G)	.50
□	241 Radoslav Kropac	.25
□	242 Dusan Pohorelec	.25
□	243 Petr Vala	.25
□	244 Pavel Zdrahal	.25
□	245 Otakar Janecky	.25
□	246 Tomas Blazek	.50
□	247 Michael Vyhlidal	.25
□	248 Michal Sykora	.50
□	249 Tomas Pacal	.25
□	250 Andrej Novotny	.25
□	251 Tomas Rolinek	.25
□	252 Stanislav Prochazka	.25
□	253 David Pospisil	.25
□	254 Michal Mikeska	.25
□	255 Ladislav Lubina	.25
□	256 Jaroslav Kudrna	.25
□	257 Tomas Vak	.25
□	258 Michal Tvrdik	.25
□	259 Petr** Sykora	.50
□	260 Jan Bohac	.25
□	261 Milan Prochazka	.25
□	262 Patrik Fink	.25
□	263 Richard Kucirek	.25
□	264 Marek Vorel	.25
□	265 Tomas Klimes	.25
□	266 Premysl Sedlak	.25
□	267 David Hajek	.25
□	268 Ladislav Vlcek	.25
□	269 Jiri Kames	.25
□	270 Radek Krestan	.25
□	271 Jan Hejda	.25
□	272 Borek Slama	.25
□	273 Leos Cermak	.25
□	274 Jan Novak	.25
□	275 Zbynek Tuma	.25
□	276 Daniel Bohac	.25
□	277 Michal Sup	.25
□	278 Jan Snopek	.25
□	279 Adam saffer	.25
□	280 David Pojkar	.25
□	281 Marek Tomica	.25
□	282 Petr Jurecka	.25
□	283 Lukas Krenzelok	.25
□	284 Michael Prochazka	.25

CHECKLIST

Insert

□	1 Petr Franek (G)
□	2 Zdenek Orct (G)
□	3 Pavel Cagas (G)
□	4 Michal Marik (G)
□	5 Miroslav simonovic (G)
□	6 Vladimir Hudacek (G)
□	7 Radovan Biegl (G)
□	8 Lukas Smolka (G)
□	9 Martin Vojtek (G)
□	10 Roman Malek (G)
□	11 Petr Briza (G)

INSERT

Insert

□	G1 Roman Malek (G)
□	G2 Petr Franek (G)
□	G3 Petr Prikryl (G)
□	G4 Vlastimil Lakosil (G)
□	G5 Radov Biegl (G)
□	G6 Vladimir Hudacek (G)
□	G7 Oldrich Svoboda (G)
□	G8 Josef Kucera (G)
□	G9 Michal Marik (G)
□	G10 Miroslav simonovic (G)
□	G11 Pavel Malac (G)
□	H1 Lukas Hronek (G)
□	H2 Marcel Kucera (G)
□	H3 Zdenek Orct (G)
□	H4 Martin Vojtek (G)
□	H5 Jan Pospisil (G)
□	H6 Lukas Smolka (G)
□	H7 Jiri Trvaj (G)
□	H8 Ivo Pesat (G)
□	H9 Petr Tucek (G)
□	H10 Ladislav Kudrna (G)
□	H11 Marek Pinc (G)
□	H12 Pavel Cagas (G)
□	H13 Adam Svoboda (G)
□	H14 Libor Barta (G)
□	H15 Petr Briza (G)

RED

Insert

□	RE1D Viktor Ujcik
□	RE2D Josef Beranek
□	RE3D Tomas Plekanec
□	RE4D Tomas Kaberle
□	RE5D Jiri Zelenka
□	RE6D Martin Prochazka
□	RE7D David Moravec
□	RE8D Petr Klima
□	RE9D Rudolf Suchanek
□	RE10D Frantisek Kucera
□	RE11D Michal Sykora
□	RE12D Otakar Janecky
□	RE13D Pavel Zdrahal
□	RE14D Radoslav Kropac
□	RE15D Rostislav Vlach
□	RE16D Marek Uram
□	RE17D Petr Leska
□	RE18D Petr Cajanek
□	RE19D Ondrej Kratena
□	RE20D Petr Korinek
□	RE21D Jiri Hudler
□	RE22D Pavel Janku
□	RE23D Richard Kral
□	RE24D Miroslav Guren

UTKANI HVEZD I.

Insert

□	1 Martin Hamrlik
□	2 Petr Gregorek
□	3 Oldrich Svoboda (G)
□	4 Radim Tesrik
□	5 Jiri Dopita
□	6 Petr cajanek
□	7 Marek Uram
□	8 Michael Vyhlidal
□	9 Mario Cartelli
□	10 Pavel Zdrahal
□	11 Libor Prochazka
□	12 Ales Pisa
□	13 Robert Reichel
□	14 Josef reznicek
□	15 Karel Pilar
□	16 Dusan Salficky (G)
□	17 Patrik Martinec
□	18 Rudolf Suchanek
□	19 Jaromir Kverka
□	20 Ladislav Svoboda
□	21 Daniel Branda
□	22 Jan Pardavy
□	23 David Moravec
□	24 Zbynek Marak
□	25 Petr Leska
□	26 Jiri Marusak
□	27 Roman Stantien
□	28 Jan Srdinko
□	29 Martin Prusek
□	30 Libor Pivko
□	31 Zdenek Pavelek
□	32 Jaroslav Hlinka
□	33 Otakar Janecky
□	34 Petr Kadlec
□	35 Ales Kotalik
□	36 Jan Krulis
□	37 Róbert Tomik
□	38 Petr Sykora
□	39 Ivan Vlcek
□	40 Pavel Vostrak
□	41 Vladimir Vujtek

2001 - 02 PACIFIC

Produced by Pacific Trading Cards, this series was released in July 2001. There are five versions for each card 1-400: a base card, a Hobby Ltd. parallel card (#/99), a Retail Ltd. parallel card (#/149), an Extreme Ltd. parallel card (#/49), and a Premiere Date parallel card (#/45). Retail Ltd. parallel cards are valued at 75% of the Hobby Ltd. parallel cards. The Extreme Ltd. parallel cards and the Premiere Date parallel cards have the same value.

Shell Set (400 cards):	-	-	**55.00**
Complete Set (462 cards):	-	-	**250.00**
Parallel Set (400 cards):	**1,300**	**700**	**-**
Common Player:	**6.00**	**4.00**	**.20**

	Description	EL49	HL99	Base
□□□□□	1 M. Cullen	6.00	4.00	.20
□□□□□	2 J. Cummins	6.00	4.00	.20
□□□□□	3 J. Friesen	10.00	5.00	.20
□□□□□	4 J-S Giguère (G)	25.00	15.00	.50
□□□□□	5 T. Hrkac	6.00	4.00	.20
□□□□□	6 P. Kariya	45.00	25.00	1.00
□□□□□	7 M. Leclerc	6.00	4.00	.20
□□□□□	8 M. McInnis	6.00	4.00	.20
□□□□□	9 S. Rucchin	6.00	4.00	.20
□□□□□	10 R. Salei	6.00	4.00	.20
□□□□□	11 S. Shields (G)	6.00	4.00	.20
□□□□□	12 O. Tverdovsky	6.00	4.00	.20
□□□□□	**13 B. Wren RC**	**6.00**	**4.00**	**.50**
□□□□□	14 A. Brunette	6.00	4.00	.20
□□□□□	15 H. Domenichelli	6.00	4.00	.20
□□□□□	16 R. Ferraro	6.00	4.00	.20
□□□□□	17 S. Guolla	6.00	4.00	.20
□□□□□	18 M. Hnilicka (G)	6.00	4.00	.20
□□□□□	19 T. Kallio	6.00	4.00	.20
□□□□□	20 N. Maracle (G)	6.00	4.00	.20
□□□□□	21 R. Ndur	6.00	4.00	.20
□□□□□	22 J. Odgers	6.00	4.00	.20
□□□□□	23 D. Rhodes (G)	6.00	4.00	.20
□□□□□	24 J. Slegr	6.00	4.00	.20
□□□□□	25 P. Stefan	10.00	5.00	.20
□□□□□	26 J. Vigier	6.00	4.00	.20
□□□□□	27 J. Allison	20.00	10.00	.50
□□□□□	28 P. Axelsson	6.00	4.00	.20
□□□□□	29 B. Dafoe (G)	10.00	5.00	.20
□□□□□	30 J. Grahame (G)	6.00	4.00	.20
□□□□□	31 B. Guerin	10.00	5.00	.20
□□□□□	32 M. Knuble	6.00	4.00	.20
□□□□□	33 A. Kovalenko	6.00	4.00	.20
□□□□□	34 E. Manlow	6.00	4.00	.20
□□□□□	35 A. Nazarov	6.00	4.00	.20
□□□□□	36 B. Rolston	10.00	5.00	.20
□□□□□	37 S. Samsonov	20.00	10.00	.50
□□□□□	38 P. Skudra (G)	6.00	4.00	.20
□□□□□	39 D. Sweeney	6.00	4.00	.20
□□□□□	40 J. Thornton	40.00	20.00	1.00
□□□□□	41 E. Weinrich	6.00	4.00	.20
□□□□□	42 M. Afinogenov	10.00	5.00	.20
□□□□□	43 D. Andreychuk	10.00	5.00	.20
□□□□□	44 D. Audette	10.00	5.00	.20
□□□□□	45 S. Barnes	6.00	4.00	.20
□□□□□	46 M. Biron (G)	15.00	5.00	.20
□□□□□	47 J. Dumont	6.00	4.00	.20
□□□□□	48 D. Gilmour	20.00	10.00	.50
□□□□□	49 C. Gratton	6.00	4.00	.20
□□□□□	50 D. Hasek (G)	35.00	20.00	1.00
□□□□□	51 S. Heinze	6.00	4.00	.20
□□□□□	52 E. Rasmussen	6.00	4.00	.20
□□□□□	53 R. Ray	6.00	4.00	.20
□□□□□	54 M. Satan	10.00	5.00	.20
□□□□□	55 A. Zhitnik	6.00	4.00	.20
□□□□□	56 T. Albelin	6.00	4.00	.20
□□□□□	57 F. Brathwaite (G)	10.00	5.00	.20
□□□□□	58 V. Bure	10.00	5.00	.20
□□□□□	59 C. Conroy	10.00	5.00	.20
□□□□□	60 P. Housley	10.00	5.00	.20
□□□□□	61 J. Iginla	25.00	15.00	.50
□□□□□	62 D. Lowry	6.00	4.00	.20
□□□□□	63 D. Morris	6.00	4.00	.20
□□□□□	64 O. Saprykin	6.00	4.00	.20
□□□□□	65 M. Savard	6.00	4.00	.20
□□□□□	66 D. Tkaczuk	6.00	4.00	.20
□□□□□	67 M. Vernon (G)	10.00	5.00	.20
□□□□□	68 J. Wiemer	6.00	4.00	.20
□□□□□	69 B. Battaglia	6.00	4.00	.20
□□□□□	70 R. Brind'Amour	10.00	5.00	.20
□□□□□	71 R. Francis	20.00	10.00	.50
□□□□□	72 M. Gélinas	6.00	4.00	.20
□□□□□	73 K. Hatcher	6.00	4.00	.20
□□□□□	74 A. Irbe (G)	10.00	5.00	.20
□□□□□	75 S. Kapanen	10.00	5.00	.20
□□□□□	76 D. Karpa	6.00	4.00	.20
□□□□□	77 T. Moss (G)	6.00	4.00	.20
□□□□□	78 J. O'Neill	10.00	5.00	.20
□□□□□	79 S. Ozolinsh	6.00	4.00	.20
□□□□□	80 S. Pellerin	6.00	4.00	.20
□□□□□	81 S. Willis	6.00	4.00	.20
□□□□□	82 T. Amonte	20.00	10.00	.50
□□□□□	83 M. Bell	6.00	4.00	.20
□□□□□	84 É. Dazé	10.00	5.00	.20
□□□□□	85 S. Dubinsky	6.00	4.00	.20
□□□□□	86 C. Herperger	6.00	4.00	.20
□□□□□	**87 M. Larocque RC**	**15.00**	**10.00**	**.50**
□□□□□	88 M. Nylander	6.00	4.00	.20
□□□□□	89 S. Passmore (G)	6.00	4.00	.20
□□□□□	90 B. Probert	10.00	5.00	.20
□□□□□	91 S. Quintal	6.00	4.00	.20
□□□□□	92 S. Sullivan	10.00	5.00	.20
□□□□□	93 J. Thibault (G)	10.00	5.00	.20
□□□□□	94 A. Zhamnov	10.00	5.00	.20
□□□□□	95 D. Aebischer (G)	10.00	5.00	.20
□□□□□	96 R. Berry	6.00	4.00	.20
□□□□□	97 R. Blake	20.00	10.00	.50
□□□□□	98 R. Bourque	40.00	20.00	1.00
□□□□□	99 C. Drury	20.00	10.00	.50
□□□□□	100 A. Foote	10.00	5.00	.20
□□□□□	101 P. Forsberg	45.00	25.00	1.00
□□□□□	102 M. Hejduk	25.00	15.00	.50
□□□□□	103 V. Nieminen	6.00	4.00	.20
□□□□□	104 S. Podein	6.00	4.00	.20
□□□□□	105 S. Reinprecht	10.00	5.00	.20
□□□□□	106 P. Roy (G)	105.00	60.00	3.00
□□□□□	107 J. Sakic	55.00	30.00	1.50
□□□□□	108 A. Tanguay	20.00	10.00	.50
□□□□□	109 S. Aubin	6.00	4.00	.20
□□□□□	**110 M. Darche RC**	**6.00**	**4.00**	**.50**
□□□□□	**111 M. Davidson RC**	**6.00**	**4.00**	**.50**
□□□□□	112 M. Denis (G)	15.00	5.00	.20
□□□□□	113 R. Klesla	20.00	10.00	.20
□□□□□	114 E. Knutsen	6.00	4.00	.20
□□□□□	115 C. Nielsen	6.00	4.00	.20
□□□□□	116 G. Sanderson	6.00	4.00	.20
□□□□□	**117 M. Spanhel RC**	**6.00**	**4.00**	**.50**
□□□□□	118 R. Tugnutt (G)	10.00	5.00	.20
□□□□□	119 D. Vyborny	6.00	4.00	.20
□□□□□	120 R. Whitney	6.00	4.00	.20
□□□□□	121 T. Wright	6.00	4.00	.20
□□□□□	122 E. Belfour (G)	35.00	20.00	1.00
□□□□□	123 S. Gainey	6.00	4.00	.20
□□□□□	124 D. Hatcher	10.00	5.00	.20
□□□□□	125 S. Helenius	6.00	4.00	.20
□□□□□	126 Br. Hull	35.00	20.00	1.00
□□□□□	127 J. Langenbrunner	6.00	4.00	.20
□□□□□	128 J. Lehtinen	10.00	5.00	.20
□□□□□	129 B. Lukowich	6.00	4.00	.20
□□□□□	130 G. Marshall	6.00	4.00	.20
□□□□□	131 M. Modano	35.00	20.00	1.00
□□□□□	132 B. Morrow	10.00	5.00	.20
□□□□□	133 K. Muller	10.00	5.00	.20
□□□□□	134 J. Nieuwendyk	10.00	5.00	.20
□□□□□	135 D. Sydor	6.00	4.00	.20
□□□□□	136 M. Turco (G)	20.00	10.00	.50
□□□□□	137 S. Zubov	6.00	4.00	.20
□□□□□	138 C. Chelios	20.00	10.00	.50
□□□□□	139 S. Fedorov	35.00	20.00	1.00
□□□□□	140 T. Gill	6.00	4.00	.20
□□□□□	141 T. Holmström	6.00	4.00	.20
□□□□□	142 V. Kozlov	6.00	4.00	.20
□□□□□	143 M. Lapointe	10.00	5.00	.20
□□□□□	144 I. Larionov	20.00	10.00	.50
□□□□□	145 M. Legacé (G)	10.00	5.00	.20
□□□□□	146 N. Lidström	20.00	10.00	.50
□□□□□	147 D. McCarty	10.00	5.00	.20
□□□□□	148 C. Osgood (G)	20.00	10.00	.50
□□□□□	149 B. Shanahan	35.00	20.00	1.00
□□□□□	150 P. Verbeek	10.00	5.00	.20
□□□□□	151 A. Ward	6.00	4.00	.20
□□□□□	152 S. Yzerman	80.00	45.00	2.00
□□□□□	153 A. Carter	10.00	5.00	.20
□□□□□	**154 J. Chimera RC**	**6.00**	**4.00**	**.50**
□□□□□	155 D. Cleary	10.00	5.00	.20
□□□□□	156 M. Comrie	25.00	15.00	.50
□□□□□	157 M. Grier	6.00	4.00	.20
□□□□□	158 S. Horcoff	6.00	4.00	.20
□□□□□	159 G. Laraque	6.00	4.00	.20
□□□□□	160 T. Marchant	6.00	4.00	.20
□□□□□	161 R. Murray	6.00	4.00	.20
□□□□□	162 J. Niinimaa	6.00	4.00	.20
□□□□□	163 D. Roussel (G)	6.00	4.00	.20
□□□□□	164 T. Salo (G)	10.00	5.00	.20
□□□□□	165 J. Smith	6.00	4.00	.20
□□□□□	166 R. Smyth	15.00	5.00	.20
□□□□□	167 D. Weight	20.00	10.00	.50
□□□□□	168 K. Adams	6.00	4.00	.20
□□□□□	169 P. Bure	25.00	15.00	.50
□□□□□	170 A. Eriksson	6.00	4.00	.20
□□□□□	171 T. Kidd (G)	10.00	5.00	.20
□□□□□	172 V. Kozlov	10.00	5.00	.20
□□□□□	173 R. Luongo (G)	25.00	15.00	.50
□□□□□	174 R. Niedermayer	6.00	4.00	.20
□□□□□	175 M. Nilson	6.00	4.00	.20
□□□□□	**176 A. Podkonicky RC**	**6.00**	**4.00**	**.50**
□□□□□	177 R. Svehla	6.00	4.00	.20
□□□□□	178 P. Worrell	6.00	4.00	.20
□□□□□	179 É. Bélanger	6.00	4.00	.20
□□□□□	180 A. Deadmarsh	10.00	5.00	.20

□□□□□	181 S. Grimson	6.00	4.00	.20
□□□□□	182 A. Lilja	6.00	4.00	.20
□□□□□	183 G. Murray	15.00	5.00	.20
□□□□□	184 Z. Palffy	20.00	10.00	.50
□□□□□	185 F. Potvin (G)	40.00	20.00	.50
□□□□□	186 L. Robitaille	25.00	15.00	.50
□□□□□	187 M. Schneider	6.00	4.00	.20
□□□□□	188 B. Smolinski	6.00	4.00	.20
□□□□□	189 J. Storr (G)	6.00	4.00	.20
□□□□□	190 J. Stümpel	6.00	4.00	.20
□□□□□	191 L. Visnovsky	6.00	4.00	.20
□□□□□	192 J. Dowd	6.00	4.00	.20
□□□□□	193 M. Fernandez (G)	10.00	5.00	.20
□□□□□	194 M. Gaborik	35.00	20.00	1.00
□□□□□	195 D. Gustafson (G)	6.00	4.00	.20
□□□□□	196 M. Johnson	6.00	4.00	.20
□□□□□	197 F. Kuba	6.00	4.00	.20
□□□□□	198 A. Laaksonen	6.00	4.00	.20
□□□□□	199 J. McLennan (G)	6.00	4.00	.20
□□□□□	200 L. Sekeras	6.00	4.00	.20
□□□□□	201 W. Walz	6.00	4.00	.20
□□□□□	**202 F. Bélanger RC**	**6.00**	**4.00**	**.50**
□□□□□	203 P. Brisebois	6.00	4.00	.20
□□□□□	204 J. Bulis	6.00	4.00	.20
□□□□□	205 K. Dykhuis	6.00	4.00	.20
□□□□□	206 M. Garon (G)	10.00	5.00	.20
□□□□□	207 J. Hackett (G)	10.00	5.00	.20
□□□□□	208 C. Kilger	6.00	4.00	.20
□□□□□	209 S. Koivu	40.00	20.00	.50
□□□□□	210 O. Petrov	10.00	5.00	.20
□□□□□	211 M. Rucinsky	6.00	4.00	.20
□□□□□	212 B. Savage	10.00	5.00	.20
□□□□□	213 J. Théodore (G)	40.00	20.00	1.00
□□□□□	214 R. Zednik	10.00	5.00	.20
□□□□□	215 M. Cisar	6.00	4.00	.20
□□□□□	216 M. Dunham (G)	10.00	5.00	.20
□□□□□	217 S. Hartnell	6.00	4.00	.20
□□□□□	218 G. Johnson	6.00	4.00	.20
□□□□□	219 P. Kjellberg	6.00	4.00	.20
□□□□□	220 D. Legwand	10.00	5.00	.20
□□□□□	221 C. Ronning	6.00	4.00	.20
□□□□□	222 T. Vokoun (G)	6.00	4.00	.20
□□□□□	223 S. Walker	6.00	4.00	.20
□□□□□	224 V. Yachmenev	6.00	4.00	.20
□□□□□	225 J. Arnott	15.00	5.00	.20
□□□□□	226 J. Bicek	25.00	15.00	.50
□□□□□	227 M. Brodeur (G)	55.00	30.00	1.50
□□□□□	228 S. Brylin	6.00	4.00	.20
□□□□□	229 P. Elias	25.00	15.00	.50
□□□□□	230 S. Gomez	10.00	5.00	.20
□□□□□	231 B. Holik	10.00	5.00	.20
□□□□□	232 J. Madden	10.00	5.00	.20
□□□□□	233 R. McKay	6.00	4.00	.20
□□□□□	234 J. McKenzie	6.00	4.00	.20
□□□□□	235 A. Mogilny	15.00	5.00	.20
□□□□□	236 S. Nemchinov	6.00	4.00	.20
□□□□□	237 S. Niedermayer	10.00	5.00	.20
□□□□□	238 S. Stevens	10.00	5.00	.20
□□□□□	239 P. Sykora	10.00	5.00	.20
□□□□□	240 J. Vanbiesbrouck (G)	15.00	5.00	.20
□□□□□	241 E. Ward	6.00	4.00	.20
□□□□□	242 Z. Chara	6.00	4.00	.20
□□□□□	243 T. Connolly	10.00	5.00	.20
□□□□□	244 M. Czerkawski	6.00	4.00	.20
□□□□□	245 R. DiPietro	15.00	5.00	.20
□□□□□	246 G. Galley	6.00	4.00	.20
□□□□□	247 K. Haller	6.00	4.00	.20
□□□□□	248 R. Hamrlik	6.00	4.00	.20
□□□□□	249 B. Isbister	6.00	4.00	.20
□□□□□	250 K. Jönsson	6.00	4.00	.20
□□□□□	251 C. Lapointe	6.00	4.00	.20
□□□□□	252 M. Parrish	10.00	5.00	.20
□□□□□	253 D. Scatchard	6.00	4.00	.20
□□□□□	254 C. Terreri (G)	6.00	4.00	.20
□□□□□	255 R. Dvorak	6.00	4.00	.20
□□□□□	256 T. Fleury	20.00	10.00	.50
□□□□□	257 A. Graves	10.00	5.00	.20
□□□□□	258 G. Hebert (G)	6.00	4.00	.20
□□□□□	259 J. Hlavac	6.00	4.00	.20
□□□□□	260 V. Kamensky	10.00	5.00	.20
□□□□□	261 B. Leetch	20.00	10.00	.50
□□□□□	262 S. Lefebvre	6.00	4.00	.20
□□□□□	263 S. McCarthy	6.00	4.00	.20
□□□□□	264 M. Messier	35.00	20.00	1.00
□□□□□	265 P. Nedved	10.00	5.00	.20
□□□□□	266 R. Pilon	6.00	4.00	.20
□□□□□	267 M. Richter (G)	15.00	5.00	.20
□□□□□	268 M. York	10.00	5.00	.20
□□□□□	269 D. Alfredsson	40.00	20.00	.50
□□□□□	270 M. Arvedson	6.00	4.00	.20
□□□□□	271 R. Bonk	10.00	5.00	.20
□□□□□	272 M. Havlat	20.00	10.00	.50
□□□□□	273 M. Hossa	35.00	20.00	1.00
□□□□□	274 J. Hurme (G)	6.00	4.00	.20
□□□□□	275 P. Lalime (G)	20.00	10.00	.50
□□□□□	276 S. McEachern	10.00	5.00	.20
□□□□□	277 C. Phillips	6.00	4.00	.20
□□□□□	278 W. Redden	10.00	5.00	.20
□□□□□	279 A. Roy (G)	6.00	4.00	.20
□□□□□	280 M. Sillinger	6.00	4.00	.20
□□□□□	281 A. Yashin	20.00	10.00	.50
□□□□□	282 R. Zamuner	6.00	4.00	.20
□□□□□	283 B. Boucher (G)	10.00	5.00	.20
□□□□□	284 R. Cechmanek (G)	10.00	5.00	.20
□□□□□	285 É. Desjardins	10.00	5.00	.20
□□□□□	286 R. Fedotenko	6.00	4.00	.20
□□□□□	287 S. Gagné	25.00	15.00	.50
□□□□□	288 D. Langkow	6.00	4.00	.20
□□□□□	289 J. LeClair	25.00	15.00	.50
□□□□□	290 E. Lindros	35.00	20.00	1.00
□□□□□	291 D. McGillis	6.00	4.00	.20
□□□□□	292 K. Primeau	10.00	5.00	.20
□□□□□	293 P. Ranheim	6.00	4.00	.20
□□□□□	294 M. Recchi	10.00	5.00	.20
□□□□□	295 R. Tocchet	10.00	5.00	.20
□□□□□	296 J. Williams	10.00	5.00	.20
□□□□□	297 J. Bouchard	6.00	4.00	.20
□□□□□	298 D. Brière	15.00	5.00	.20
□□□□□	299 S. Burke (G)	20.00	10.00	.50
□□□□□	300 K. Carney	6.00	4.00	.20
□□□□□	301 S. Doan	6.00	4.00	.20
□□□□□	302 R. Esche (G)	6.00	4.00	.20
□□□□□	303 M. Handzus	6.00	4.00	.20
□□□□□	304 M. Johnson	6.00	4.00	.20
□□□□□	305 J. Juneau	6.00	4.00	.20
□□□□□	306 C. Lemieux	10.00	5.00	.20
□□□□□	307 T. Numminen	10.00	5.00	.20
□□□□□	308 J. Roenick	25.00	15.00	.50
□□□□□	309 L. Wilson	6.00	4.00	.20
□□□□□	310 J. Aubin (G)	6.00	4.00	.20
□□□□□	311 J. Hrdina	6.00	4.00	.20
□□□□□	312 J. Jagr	35.00	20.00	1.00
□□□□□	313 D. Kasparaitis	6.00	4.00	.20
□□□□□	314 A. Kovalev	20.00	10.00	.50
□□□□□	315 R. Lang	6.00	4.00	.20
□□□□□	316 M. Lemieux	105.00	60.00	3.00
□□□□□	317 G. Snow	10.00	5.00	.20
□□□□□	318 K. Stevens	6.00	4.00	.20
□□□□□	319 M. Straka	10.00	5.00	.20
□□□□□	320 S. Bordeleau	6.00	4.00	.20
□□□□□	321 P. Demitra	10.00	5.00	.20
□□□□□	322 D. Drake	6.00	4.00	.20
□□□□□	323 J. Hecht	6.00	4.00	.20
□□□□□	324 B. Johnson (G)	10.00	5.00	.20
□□□□□	325 R. Low	6.00	4.00	.20
□□□□□	326 A. MacInnis	10.00	5.00	.20
□□□□□	327 S. Mellanby	6.00	4.00	.20
□□□□□	**328 J. Obsut RC**	**6.00**	**4.00**	**.50**
□□□□□	329 C. Pronger	20.00	10.00	.50
□□□□□	330 D. Rumble	6.00	4.00	.20
□□□□□	331 C. Stillman	6.00	4.00	.20
□□□□□	332 K. Tkachuk	20.00	10.00	.50
□□□□□	333 R. Turek (G)	15.00	5.00	.20
□□□□□	334 P. Turgeon	10.00	5.00	.20
□□□□□	335 S. Young	10.00	5.00	.20
□□□□□	336 V. Damphousse	20.00	10.00	.50
□□□□□	337 Mi. Kiprusoff (G)	10.00	5.00	.20
□□□□□	338 B. Marchment	6.00	4.00	.20
□□□□□	339 P. Marleau	15.00	5.00	.20
□□□□□	340 E. Nabokov (G)	20.00	10.00	.50
□□□□□	341 O. Nolan	20.00	10.00	.50
□□□□□	342 J. Norton	6.00	4.00	.20
□□□□□	343 M. Ricci	10.00	5.00	.20
□□□□□	344 T. Selänne	25.00	15.00	.50
□□□□□	345 B. Stuart	10.00	5.00	.20
□□□□□	346 M. Sturm	6.00	4.00	.20
□□□□□	347 N. Sundström	6.00	4.00	.20
□□□□□	348 S. Thornton	6.00	4.00	.20
□□□□□	349 M. Barnaby	6.00	4.00	.20
□□□□□	350 B. Holzinger	6.00	4.00	.20
□□□□□	351 N. Khabibulin (G)	10.00	5.00	.20
□□□□□	352 A. Kharitonov	6.00	4.00	.20
□□□□□	353 P. Kubina	6.00	4.00	.20
□□□□□	354 K. Kudroc	6.00	4.00	.20
□□□□□	355 V. Lecavalier	35.00	20.00	1.00
□□□□□	356 F. Modin	6.00	4.00	.20
□□□□□	357 B. Richards	15.00	5.00	.20
□□□□□	358 M. St-Louis	15.00	5.00	.20
□□□□□	359 K. Weekes (G)	6.00	4.00	.20
□□□□□	**360 T. Ziegler RC**	**25.00**	**15.00**	**.50**
□□□□□	361 S. Berezin	15.00	5.00	.20
□□□□□	362 S. Corson	10.00	5.00	.20
□□□□□	363 C. Cross	6.00	4.00	.20
□□□□□	364 T. Domi	10.00	5.00	.20
□□□□□	365 G. Healy (G)	6.00	4.00	.20
□□□□□	366 J. Höglund	6.00	4.00	.20
□□□□□	367 Cu. Joseph (G)	35.00	20.00	1.00
□□□□□	368 D. MacLean	6.00	4.00	.20
□□□□□	369 D. Manson	6.00	4.00	.20
□□□□□	370 Y. Perreault	10.00	5.00	.20
□□□□□	371 A. Ponikarovsky	6.00	4.00	.20
□□□□□	372 G. Roberts	10.00	5.00	.20
□□□□□	373 M. Sundin	35.00	20.00	1.00
□□□□□	374 S. Thomas	6.00	4.00	.20
□□□□□	375 D. Tucker	6.00	4.00	.20
□□□□□	376 M. Baron	6.00	4.00	.20
□□□□□	377 T. Bertuzzi	40.00	20.00	1.00
□□□□□	378 D. Brashear	6.00	4.00	.20
□□□□□	379 A. Cassels	6.00	4.00	.20
□□□□□	380 D. Cloutier (G)	10.00	5.00	.20
□□□□□	381 B. Essensa (G)	6.00	4.00	.20
□□□□□	382 E. Jovanovski	10.00	5.00	.20
□□□□□	383 B. Morrison	10.00	5.00	.20
□□□□□	384 M. Näslund	35.00	20.00	1.00
□□□□□	385 M. Öhlund	10.00	5.00	.20
□□□□□	386 P. Schaefer	6.00	4.00	.20
□□□□□	387 D. Sedin	10.00	5.00	.20
□□□□□	388 H. Sedin	10.00	5.00	.20
□□□□□	389 C. Billington (G)	6.00	4.00	.20
□□□□□	390 P. Bondra	20.00	10.00	.50
□□□□□	391 U. Dahlén	6.00	4.00	.20
□□□□□	392 S. Gonchar	10.00	5.00	.20
□□□□□	393 J. Halpern	6.00	4.00	.20
□□□□□	394 D. Khristich	6.00	4.00	.20
□□□□□	395 O. Kölzig (G)	20.00	10.00	.50
□□□□□	396 S. Konowalchuk	6.00	4.00	.20
□□□□□	397 T. Linden	10.00	5.00	.20
□□□□□	398 A. Oates	10.00	5.00	.20
□□□□□	399 C. Simon	6.00	4.00	.20
□□□□□	400 D. Zubrus	6.00	4.00	.20

SUBSETS

There are two versions for each subset card 401-443: a silver-foil base card and a gold-foil parallel (#/100). Base cards 444-451 are autographed and limited to 500 copies. Base card 452 (Hedberg) is short-printed.

Gold Set (43 cards):		**200.00**	**-**
	Description	**G100**	**Base**
□□	401 P. Kariya / J. Cummins	15.00	.50
□□	402 R. Ferraro / J. Odgers	4.00	.20
□□	403 J. Allison / K. Belanger	5.00	.20
□□	404 Jean-Pierre Dumont / R. Ray	4.00	.20
□□	405 J. Iginla / J. Wiemer	5.00	.20
□□	406 R. Francis / D. Langdon	5.00	.20
□□	407 S. Sullivan / B. Probert	5.00	.20
□□	408 J. Sakic / S. Parker	15.00	.50
□□	409 M. Modano / G. Marshall	10.00	.50
□□	410 S. Yzerman / D. McCarty	25.00	1.00
□□	411 R. Smyth / G. Laraque	5.00	.20
□□	412 P. Bure / P. Worrell	10.00	.50
□□	413 S. Grimson / Z. Palffy	5.00	.20
□□	414 P. Elias / C. White	5.00	.20
□□	415 M. Czerkawski / Z. Chara	4.00	.20
□□	416 T. Fleury / S. McCarthy	5.00	.20
□□	417 M. Hossa / A. Roy	10.00	.50
□□	418 J. Roenick / L. DeBrusk	5.00	.20
□□	419 M. Lemieux / K. Oliwa	30.00	1.50
□□	420 P. Turgeon / R. Low	5.00	.20
□□	421 T. Selänne / B. Marchment	5.00	.20
□□	422 V. Lecavalier / M. Barnaby	10.00	.50
□□	423 M. Sundin / T. Domi	10.00	.50
□□	424 M. Näslund / D. Brashear	10.00	.50
□□	425 P. Bondra / C. Simon	5.00	.20
□□	426 J. Allison / J. Thornton	15.00	.50
□□	427 P. Roy (G) / J. Sakic	45.00	2.00
□□	428 Br. Hull / M. Modano	20.00	1.00
□□	429 S. Fedorov / N. Lidström	15.00	.50
□□	430 R. Smyth / D. Weight	10.00	.50
□□	431 P. Bure / R. Luongo (G)	15.00	.50
□□	432 Z. Palffy / L. Robitaille	10.00	.50
□□	433 P. Elias / A. Mogilny	10.00	.50
□□	434 M. Czerkawski / R. DiPietro	5.00	.20
□□	435 T. Fleury / B. Leetch	10.00	.50
□□	436 A. Yashin / M. Hossa	15.00	.50
□□	437 R. Cechmanek (G) / K. Primeau	5.00	.20
□□	438 J. Roenick / S. Burke (G)	10.00	.50
□□	439 J. Jagr / M. Lemieux	40.00	2.00
□□	440 P. Turgeon / B. Johnson (G)	5.00	.20
□□	441 E. Nabokov (G) / T. Selänne	10.00	.50
□□	442 C. Joseph (G) / M. Sundin	20.00	1.00
□□	443 P. Bondra / A. Oates	10.00	.50
□	444 David Aebischer (G), Colo. ✍ {*500}		20.00
□	445 Steven Reinprecht, Colo. ✍ {*500}		20.00
□	446 Marty Turco (G), Dall. ✍ {*500}		35.00
□	447 Marian Gaborik, MinW. ✍ {*500}		60.00
□	448 Martin Havlat, Otta. ✍ {*500}		35.00
□	449 Brent Johnson (G), SLou. ✍ {*500}		25.00
□	450 Evgeni Nabokov (G), SanJ. ✍ {*500}		35.00
□	451 Brad Richards, Tamp. ✍ {*500}		30.00
□	452 Johan Hedberg (G), Pitt. *		20.00

REDEMPTIONS

	Redemption (#/1000)	**R1000**
□	**453 Timo Pärssinen, Anah. RC**	**6.00**
□	**454 Ilya Kovalchuk, Atla. RC**	**50.00**
□	**455 Vaclav Nedorost, Colo. RC**	**10.00**
□	**456 Kristian Huselius, Flor. RC**	**15.00**
□	**457 Jaroslav Bednar, LosA. RC**	**6.00**
□	**458 Dan Blackburn (G), NYRa. RC**	**20.00**
□	**459 Jiri Dopita, Phil. RC**	**6.00**
□	**460 Krys Kolanos, Phoe. RC**	**10.00**
□	**461 Jeff Jillson, SanJ. RC**	**6.00**
□	**462 Nikita Alexeev, Tamp. RC**	**10.00**

1997-98 PACIFIC CROWN COLLECTION

These cards have two versions: the silver-foil base card and the gold-foil parallel card (#/100).

Insert Set (7 cards):		**100.00**	**14.00**
	Insert	**G100**	**PCC**
□□	66 Mario Lemieux, Pitt.	60.00	4.50
□□	352 Mike Leclerc, Anah.	5.00	2.00
□□	353 Sergei Samsonov, Bost.	10.00	2.00
□□	354 Joe Thornton, Bost.	20.00	3.50
□□	355 Patrik Elias, NJer.	15.00	2.00
□□	356 Marian Hossa, Otta.	20.00	3.00
□□	357 Steve Shields (G), SanJ.	5.00	2.00

CRAMER'S CHOICE AWARD

Insert Set (10 cards):		**800**
	Insert	**CCA**
□	1 Paul Kariya, Anah.	80.00
□	2 Raymond Bourque, Colo.	70.00
□	3 Patrick Roy (G), Colo.	180.00
□	4 Joe Sakic, Colo.	100.00
□	5 Steve Yzerman, Detr.	150.00
□	6 Pavel Bure, Flor.	50.00
□	7 Martin Brodeur (G), NJer.	100.00
□	8 Jaromir Jagr, Pitt.	60.00
□	9 Mario Lemieux, Pitt.	180.00
□	10 Curtis Joseph (G), Toro.	60.00

AUTHENTIC GAME-WORN JERSEYS

Insert Set (36 cards):		**500.00**
	Insert	**GWJ**
□	M. Alatalo ✂ {*510}	10.00
□	T. Amonte ✂ {*1135}	15.00
□	F. Brathwaite (G) ✂ {*1135}	10.00
□	M. Czerkawski ✂ {*510}	10.00
□	V. Damphousse ✂ {*1010}	15.00
□	M. Dandenault ✂ {*1135}	10.00
□	C. Dingman ✂ {*510}	10.00
□	S. Doan ✂ {*310}	10.00
□	D. Hatcher ✂ {*1135} White	10.00
□	G. Hebert (G) ✂ {*760}	10.00
□	B. Holik ✂ {*760} White	10.00
□	J. Hrdina ✂ {*510}	10.00
□	J. Jagr ✂ {*210}	50.00
□	J. Langenbrunner ✂ {*1135} Black	10.00
□	M. Lemieux ✂ {*110}	225.00
□	J. Lumme ✂ {*1135} Black	10.00
□	J. McKee ✂ {*1135}	10.00
□	A. Miller ✂ {*510}	10.00
□	K. Miller ✂ {*1135}	10.00
□	I. Moran ✂ {*1135}	10.00
□	C. Osgood (G) ✂ {*760}	15.00
□	M. Richter (G) ✂ {*760}	15.00
□	C. Ronning ✂ {*510}	10.00
□	J. Sakic ✂ {*510}	50.00
□	A. Savage ✂ {*510}	10.00
□	M. Savard ✂ {*760}	10.00
□	T. Selänne ✂ {*1135} Red	20.00
□	C. Stillman ✂ {*1135} White	10.00
□	M. Straka ✂ {*110}	20.00
□	M. Sundin ✂ {*760}	30.00
□	C. Terreri (G) ✂ {*1135} Red	10.00
□	D. Weight ✂ {*260}	25.00
□	E. Weinrich ✂ {*510}	10.00
□	A. Zhamnov ✂ {*1135} Black	10.00
□	S. Zubov ✂ {*760}	10.00
□	D. Zubrus ✂ {*760} Red	10.00

GOLD CROWN DIE-CUT

Insert Set (20 cards):		**225.00**
	Insert	**GCDC**
□	1 Paul Kariya, Anah.	15.00
□	2 Joe Thornton, Bost.	15.00
□	3 Dominik Hasek (G), Buff.	10.00
□	4 Raymond Bourque, Colo.	15.00
□	5 Peter Forsberg, Colo.	15.00
□	6 Patrick Roy (G), Colo.	35.00
□	7 Joe Sakic, Colo.	20.00
□	8 Mike Modano, Dall.	10.00
□	9 Sergei Fedorov, Detr.	10.00
□	10 Steve Yzerman, Detr.	30.00
□	11 Pavel Bure, Flor.	10.00
□	12 Martin Brodeur (G), NJer.	20.00
□	13 Rick DiPietro (G), NYIs.	8.00
□	14 Mark Messier, NYRa.	10.00
□	15 Marian Hossa, Otta.	10.00
□	16 Jaromir Jagr, Pitt.	10.00
□	17 Mario Lemieux, Pitt.	35.00
□	18 Keith Tkachuk, SLou.	8.00
□	19 Evgeni Nabokov (G), SanJ.	8.00
□	20 Curtis Joseph (G), Toro.	10.00

IMPACT ZONE

	Insert Set (20 cards):	75.00
	Insert [1:37]	IZ
□	1 Paul Kariya, Anah.	10.00
□	2 Byron Dafoe (G), Bost.	4.00
□	3 Doug Gilmour, Buff.	4.00
□	4 Dominik Hasek (G), Buff.	6.00
□	5 Ron Francis, Caro.	4.00
□	6 Raymond Bourque, Colo.	8.00
□	7 Patrick Roy (G), Colo.	20.00
□	8 Ed Belfour (G), Dall.	6.00
□	9 Derian Hatcher, Dall.	4.00
□	10 Mike Modano, Dall.	6.00
□	11 Chris Osgood (G), Detr.	4.00
□	12 Martin Brodeur (G), NJer.	12.00
□	13 Marian Hossa, Otta.	6.00
□	14 Patrick Lalime (G), Otta.	4.00
□	15 Roman Cechmanek (G), Phil.	4.00
□	16 Chris Pronger, SLou.	4.00
□	17 Tie Domi, Toro.	4.00
□	18 Curtis Joseph (G), Toro.	6.00
□	19 Mats Sundin, Toro.	6.00
□	20 Andrew Cassels, Vanc.	4.00

NORTH AMERICA ALL-STARS

	Insert Set (10 cards):	50.00
	Insert	NAAS
□	1 Paul Kariya, NHL All-Star	10.00
□	2 Bill Guerin, NHL All-Star	5.00
□	3 Raymond Bourque, NHL All-Star	5.00
□	4 Patrick Roy (G), NHL All-Star	20.00
□	5 Joe Sakic, NHL All-Star	10.00
□	6 Brett Hull, NHL All-Star	5.00
□	7 Doug Weight, NHL All-Star	5.00
□	8 Luc Robitaille, NHL All-Star	5.00
□	9 Martin Brodeur (G), NHL All-Star	10.00
□	10 Mario Lemieux, NHL All-Star	20.00

STEEL CURTAIN

	Insert Set (20 cards):	75.00
	Insert	SC
□	1 Steve Shields (G), SanJ.	4.00
□	2 Byron Dafoe (G), Bost.	4.00
□	3 Dominik Hasek (G), Buff.	6.00
□	4 Jocelyn Thibault (G), Chic.	4.00
□	5 Patrick Roy (G), Colo.	18.00
□	6 Ed Belfour (G), Dall.	6.00
□	7 Manny Legacé (G), Detr.	4.00
□	8 Tommy Salo (G), Edmo.	4.00
□	9 Roberto Luongo (G), Flor.	4.00
□	10 José Théodore (G), Mont.	6.00
□	11 Martin Brodeur (G), NJer.	10.00
□	12 Rick DiPietro (G), NYIs.	4.00
□	13 Mike Richter (G), NYRa.	4.00
□	14 Patrick Lalime (G), Otta.	4.00
□	15 Roman Cechmanek (G), Phil.	4.00
□	16 Sean Burke (G), Phoe.	4.00
□	17 Roman Turek (G), SLou.	4.00
□	18 Evgeni Nabokov (G), SanJ.	4.00
□	19 Curtis Joseph (G), Toro.	6.00
□	20 Olaf Kölzig (G), Wash.	4.00

TOP DRAFT PICKS

There are two versions for each card: the gold-text insert (1:37 packs) and the silver-text wrapper redemption card (#/499).

	Insert Set (10 cards):	60.00	45.00
	Card	T499	TDP
□□	1 Rick DiPietro (G), NYIs.	6.00	4.00
□□	2 Patrik Stefan, Atla.	6.00	4.00
□□	3 Vincent Lecavalier, Tamp.	6.00	6.00
□□	4 Joe Thornton, Bost.	10.00	7.00
□□	5 Eric Lindros, Phil.	6.00	6.00
□□	6 Owen Nolan, SanJ.	6.00	4.00
□□	7 Mats Sundin, Toro.	6.00	6.00
□□	8 Mike Modano, Dall.	6.00	6.00
□□	9 Pierre Turgeon, SLou.	6.00	4.00
□□	10 Mario Lemieux, Pitt.	25.00	18.00

WORLD ALL-STARS

	Insert Set (10 cards):	25.00
	Insert	WAS
□	1 Dominik Hasek (G), NHL All-Star	6.00
□	2 Peter Forsberg, NHL All-Star	10.00
□	3 Sergei Fedorov, NHL All-Star	6.00
□	4 Pavel Bure, NHL All-Star	6.00
□	5 Zigmund Palffy, NHL All-Star	4.00
□	6 Marian Hossa, NHL All-Star	6.00
□	7 Roman Cechmanek (G), NHL All-Star	4.00
□	8 Alexei Kovalev, NHL All-Star	4.00
□	9 Evgeni Nabokov (G), NHL All-Star	4.00
□	10 Mats Sundin, NHL All-Star	6.00

ARENA COLLECTION

These cards were intended for sale at each of the 30 local arenas.

	Arena Set (400 cards):	1,100
	Description	Arena
□	1 Matt Cullen, Anah.	8.00
□	2 Jim Cummins, Anah.	8.00
□	3 Jeff Friesen, Anah.	8.00
□	4 Jean-Sébastien Giguère (G), Anah.	8.00
□	5 Tony Hrkac, Anah.	8.00
□	6 Paul Kariya, Anah.	8.00
□	7 Mike Leclerc, Anah.	8.00
□	8 Marty McInnis, Anah.	8.00
□	9 Steve Rucchin, Anah.	8.00
□	10 Ruslan Salei, Anah.	8.00
□	11 Steve Shields (G), Anah.	8.00
□	12 Oleg Tverdovsky, Anah.	8.00
□	13 Bob Wren, Anah.	8.00
□	14 Andrew Brunette, Atla.	8.00
□	15 Hnat Domenichelli, Atla.	8.00
□	16 Ray Ferraro, Atla.	8.00
□	17 Steve Guolla, Atla.	8.00
□	18 Milan Hnilicka (G), Atla.	8.00
□	19 Tomi Kallio, Atla.	8.00
□	20 Norm Maracle (G), Atla.	8.00
□	21 Rumun Ndur, Atla.	8.00
□	22 Jeff Odgers, Atla.	8.00
□	23 Damian Rhodes (G), Atla.	8.00
□	24 Jiri Slegr, Atla.	8.00
□	25 Patrik Stefan, Atla.	8.00
□	26 Jean-Pierre Vigier, Atla.	8.00
□	27 Jason Allison, Bost.	8.00
□	28 Per Axelsson, Bost.	8.00
□	29 Byron Dafoe (G), Bost.	8.00
□	30 John Grahame (G), Bost.	8.00
□	31 Bill Guerin, Bost.	8.00
□	32 Mike Knuble, Bost.	8.00
□	33 Andrei Kovalenko, Bost.	8.00
□	34 Eric Manlow, Bost.	8.00
□	35 Andrei Nazarov, Bost.	8.00
□	36 Brian Rolston, Bost.	8.00
□	37 Sergei Samsonov, Bost.	8.00
□	38 Peter Skudra (G), Bost.	8.00
□	39 Don Sweeney, Bost.	8.00
□	40 Joe Thornton, Bost.	8.00
□	41 Eric Weinrich, Bost.	8.00
□	42 Maxim Afinogenov, Buff.	8.00
□	43 Dave Andreychuk, Buff.	8.00
□	44 Donald Audette, Buff.	8.00
□	45 Stu Barnes, Buff.	8.00
□	46 Martin Biron (G), Buff.	8.00
□	47 Jean-Pierre Dumont, Buff.	8.00
□	48 Doug Gilmour, Buff.	8.00
□	49 Chris Gratton, Buff.	8.00
□	50 Dominik Hasek (G), Buff.	8.00
□	51 Steve Heinze, Buff.	8.00
□	52 Erik Rasmussen, Buff.	8.00
□	53 Rob Ray, Buff.	8.00
□	54 Miroslav Satan, Buff.	8.00
□	55 Alexei Zhitnik, Buff.	8.00
□	56 Tommy Albelin, Calg.	8.00
□	57 Fred Brathwaite (G), Calg.	8.00
□	58 Valeri Bure, Calg.	8.00
□	59 Craig Conroy, Calg.	8.00
□	60 Phil Housley, Calg.	8.00
□	61 Jarome Iginla, Calg.	8.00
□	62 Dave Lowry, Calg.	8.00
□	63 Derek Morris, Calg.	8.00
□	64 Oleg Saprykin, Calg.	8.00
□	65 Marc* Savard, Calg.	8.00
□	66 Daniel Tkaczuk, Calg.	8.00
□	67 Mike Vernon (G), Calg.	8.00
□	68 Jason Wiemer, Calg.	8.00
□	69 Bates Battaglia, Caro.	8.00
□	70 Rod Brind'Amour, Caro.	8.00
□	71 Ron Francis, Caro.	8.00
□	72 Martin Gélinas, Caro.	8.00
□	73 Kevin Hatcher, Caro.	8.00
□	74 Arturs Irbe (G), Caro.	8.00
□	75 Sami Kapanen, Caro.	8.00
□	76 Dave Karpa, Caro.	8.00
□	77 Tyler Moss (G), Caro.	8.00
□	78 Jeff O'Neill, Caro.	8.00
□	79 Sandis Ozolinsh, Caro.	8.00
□	80 Scott Pellerin, Caro.	8.00
□	81 Shane Willis, Caro.	8.00
□	82 Tony Amonte, Chic.	8.00
□	83 Mark Bell, Chic.	8.00
□	84 Éric Dazé, Chic.	8.00
□	85 Steve Dubinsky, Chic.	8.00
□	86 Chris Herperger, Chic.	8.00
□	87 Michel Larocque, Chic.	8.00
□	88 Michael Nylander, Chic.	8.00
□	89 Steve Passmore (G), Chic.	8.00
□	90 Bob Probert, Chic.	8.00
□	91 Stéphane Quintal, Chic.	8.00
□	92 Steve Sullivan, Chic.	8.00
□	93 Jocelyn Thibault (G), Chic.	8.00
□	94 Alexei Zhamnov, Chic.	8.00
□	95 David Aebischer (G), Colo.	8.00
□	96 Rick Berry, Colo.	8.00
□	97 Rob Blake, Colo.	8.00
□	98 Raymond Bourque, Colo.	8.00
□	99 Chris Drury, Colo.	8.00
□	100 Adam Foote, Colo.	8.00
□	101 Peter Forsberg, Colo.	8.00
□	102 Milan Hejduk, Colo.	8.00
□	103 Ville Nieminen, Colo.	8.00
□	104 Shjon Podein, Colo.	8.00
□	105 Steven Reinprecht, Colo.	8.00
□	106 Patrick Roy (G), Colo.	8.00
□	107 Joe Sakic, Colo.	8.00
□	108 Alex Tanguay, Colo.	8.00
□	109 Serge Aubin, Colu.	8.00
□	110 Mathieu Darche, Colu.	8.00
□	111 Matt Davidson, Colu.	8.00
□	112 Marc Denis (G), Colu.	8.00
□	113 Rostislav Klesla, Colu.	8.00
□	114 Espen Knutsen, Colu.	8.00
□	115 Chris Nielsen, Colu.	8.00
□	116 Geoff Sanderson, Colu.	8.00
□	117 Martin Spanhel, Colu.	8.00
□	118 Ron Tugnutt (G), Colu.	8.00
□	119 David Vyborny, Colu.	8.00
□	120 Ray Whitney, Colu.	8.00
□	121 Tyler Wright, Colu.	8.00
□	122 Ed Belfour (G), Dall.	8.00
□	123 Steve Gainey, Dall.	8.00
□	124 Derian Hatcher, Dall.	8.00
□	125 Sami Helenius, Dall.	8.00
□	126 Brett Hull, Dall.	8.00
□	127 Jamie Langenbrunner, Dall.	8.00
□	128 Jere Lehtinen, Dall.	8.00
□	129 Brad Lukowich, Dall.	8.00
□	130 Grant Marshall, Dall.	8.00
□	131 Mike Modano, Dall.	8.00
□	132 Brenden Morrow, Dall.	8.00
□	133 Kirk Muller, Dall.	8.00
□	134 Joe Nieuwendyk, Dall.	8.00
□	135 Darryl Sydor, Dall.	8.00
□	136 Marty Turco (G), Dall.	8.00
□	137 Sergei Zubov, Dall.	8.00
□	138 Chris Chelios, Detr.	8.00
□	139 Sergei Fedorov, Detr.	8.00
□	140 Todd Gill, Detr.	8.00
□	141 Tomas Holmström, Detr.	8.00
□	142 Vyacheslav Kozlov, Detr.	8.00
□	143 Martin Lapointe, Detr.	8.00
□	144 Igor Larionov, Detr.	8.00
□	145 Manny Legacé (G), Detr.	8.00
□	146 Nicklas Lidström, Detr.	8.00
□	147 Darren McCarty, Detr.	8.00
□	148 Chris Osgood (G), Detr.	8.00
□	149 Brendan Shanahan, Detr.	8.00
□	150 Pat Verbeek, Detr.	8.00
□	151 Aaron Ward, Detr.	8.00
□	152 Steve Yzerman, Detr.	8.00
□	153 Anson Carter, Edmo.	8.00
□	154 Jason Chimera, Edmo.	8.00
□	155 Daniel Cleary, Edmo.	8.00
□	156 Mike Comrie, Edmo.	8.00
□	157 Mike Grier, Edmo.	8.00
□	158 Shawn Horcoff, Edmo.	8.00
□	159 Georges Laraque, Edmo.	8.00
□	160 Todd Marchant, Edmo.	8.00
□	161 Rem Murray, Edmo.	8.00
□	162 Janne Niinimaa, Edmo.	8.00
□	163 Dominic Roussel (G), Edmo.	8.00
□	164 Tommy Salo (G), Edmo.	8.00
□	165 Jason Smith, Edmo.	8.00
□	166 Ryan Smyth, Edmo.	8.00
□	167 Doug Weight, Edmo.	8.00
□	168 Kevyn Adams, Flor.	8.00
□	169 Pavel Bure, Flor.	8.00
□	170 Anders Eriksson, Flor.	8.00
□	171 Trevor Kidd (G), Flor.	8.00
□	172 Viktor Kozlov, Flor.	8.00
□	173 Roberto Luongo (G), Flor.	8.00
□	174 Rob Niedermayer, Flor.	8.00
□	175 Marcus Nilson, Flor.	8.00
□	176 Andrei Podkonicky, Flor.	8.00
□	177 Robert Svehla, Flor.	8.00
□	178 Peter Worrell, Flor.	8.00
□	179 Éric Belanger, LosA.	8.00
□	180 Adam Deadmarsh, LosA.	8.00
□	181 Stu Grimson, LosA.	8.00
□	182 Andreas Lilja, LosA.	8.00
□	183 Glen Murray, LosA.	8.00
□	184 Zigmund Palffy, LosA.	8.00
□	185 Félix Potvin (G), LosA.	8.00
□	186 Luc Robitaille, LosA.	8.00
□	187 Mathieu Schneider, LosA.	8.00
□	188 Bryan Smolinski, LosA.	8.00
□	189 Jamie Storr (G), LosA.	8.00
□	190 Jozef Stümpel, LosA.	8.00
□	191 Lubomir Visnovsky, LosA.	8.00
□	192 Jim Dowd, MinW.	8.00
□	193 Manny Fernandez (G), MinW.	8.00
□	194 Marian Gaborik, MinW.	8.00
□	195 Derek Gustafson (G), MinW.	8.00
□	196 Matt Johnson, MinW.	8.00
□	197 Filip Kuba, MinW.	8.00
□	198 Antti Laaksonen, MinW.	8.00
□	199 Jamie McLennan (G), MinW.	8.00
□	200 Lubomir Sekeras, MinW.	8.00
□	201 Wes Walz, MinW.	8.00
□	202 Francis Bélanger, Mont.	8.00
□	203 Patrice Brisebois, Mont.	8.00
□	204 Jan Bulis, Mont.	8.00
□	205 Karl Dykhuis, Mont.	8.00
□	206 Mathieu Garon (G), Mont.	8.00
□	207 Jeff Hackett (G), Mont.	8.00
□	208 Chad Kilger, Mont.	8.00
□	209 Saku Koivu, Mont.	8.00
□	210 Oleg Petrov, Mont.	8.00
□	211 Martin Rucinsk_, Mont.	8.00
□	212 Brian Savage, Mont.	8.00
□	213 José Théodore (G), Mont.	8.00
□	214 Richard Zednik, Mont.	8.00
□	215 Marian Cisar, Nash.	8.00
□	216 Mike Dunham (G), Nash.	8.00
□	217 Scott Hartnell, Nash.	8.00
□	218 Greg Johnson, Nash.	8.00
□	219 Patric Kjellberg, Nash.	8.00
□	220 David Legwand, Nash.	8.00
□	221 Cliff Ronning, Nash.	8.00
□	222 Tomas Vokoun (G), Nash.	8.00
□	223 Scott Walker, Nash.	8.00
□	224 Vitali Yachmenev, Nash.	8.00
□	225 Jason Arnott, NJer.	8.00
□	226 Jiri Bicek, NJer.	8.00
□	227 Martin Brodeur (G), NJer.	8.00
□	228 Sergei Brylin, NJer.	8.00
□	229 Patrik Elias, NJer.	8.00
□	230 Scott Gomez, NJer.	8.00
□	231 Bobby Holik, NJer.	8.00
□	232 John Madden, NJer.	8.00
□	233 Randy McKay, NJer.	8.00
□	234 Jim McKenzie, NJer.	8.00
□	235 Alexander Mogilny, NJer.	8.00
□	236 Sergei Nemchinov, NJer.	8.00
□	237 Scott Niedermayer, NJer.	8.00
□	238 Scott Stevens, NJer.	8.00
□	239 Petr* Sykora, NJer.	8.00
□	240 John Vanbiesbrouck (G), NJer.	8.00
□	241 Ed Ward, NJer.	8.00
□	242 Zdeno Chara, NYIs.	8.00
□	243 Tim Connolly, NYIs.	8.00
□	244 Mariusz Czerkawski, NYIs.	8.00
□	245 Rick DiPietro, NYIs.	8.00
□	246 Garry Galley, NYIs.	8.00
□	247 Kevin Haller, NYIs.	8.00
□	248 Roman Hamrlik, NYIs.	8.00
□	249 Brad Isbister, NYIs.	8.00
□	250 Kenny Jönsson, NYIs.	8.00
□	251 Claude Lapointe, NYIs.	8.00
□	252 Mark Parrish, NYIs.	8.00
□	253 Dave Scatchard, NYIs.	8.00
□	254 Chris Terreri (G), NYIs.	8.00
□	255 Radek Dvorak, NYRa.	8.00
□	256 Theoren Fleury, NYRa.	8.00
□	257 Adam Graves, NYRa.	8.00
□	258 Guy Hebert (G), NYRa.	8.00
□	259 Jan Hlavac, NYRa.	8.00
□	260 Valeri Kamensky, NYRa.	8.00
□	261 Brian Leetch, NYRa.	8.00
□	262 Sylvain Lefebvre, NYRa.	8.00
□	263 Sandy McCarthy, NYRa.	8.00
□	264 Mark Messier, NYRa.	8.00
□	265 Petr Nedved, NYRa.	8.00

266 Richard Pilon, NYRa.	8.00
267 Mike Richter (G), NYRa.	8.00
268 Mike York, NYRa.	8.00
269 Daniel Alfredsson, Otta.	8.00
270 Magnus Arvedson, Otta.	8.00
271 Radek Bonk, Otta.	8.00
272 Martin Havlat, Otta.	8.00
273 Marian Hossa, Otta.	8.00
274 Jani Hurme (G), Otta.	8.00
275 Patrick Lalime (G), Otta.	8.00
276 Shawn McEachern, Otta.	8.00
277 Chris Phillips, Otta.	8.00
278 Wade Redden, Otta.	8.00
279 André Roy (G), Otta.	8.00
280 Mike Sillinger, Otta.	8.00
281 Alexei Yashin, Otta.	8.00
282 Rob Zamuner, Otta.	8.00
283 Brian Boucher (G), Phil.	8.00
284 Roman Cechmanek (G), Phil.	8.00
285 Éric Desjardins, Phil.	8.00
286 Ruslan Fedotenko, Phil.	8.00
287 Simon Gagné, Phil.	8.00
288 Daymond Langkow, Phil.	8.00
289 John LeClair, Phil.	8.00
290 Eric Lindros, Phil.	8.00
291 Dan McGillis, Phil.	8.00
292 Keith Primeau, Phil.	8.00
293 Paul Ranheim, Phil.	8.00
294 Mark Recchi, Phil.	8.00
295 Rick Tocchet, Phil.	8.00
296 Justin Williams, Phil.	8.00
297 Joël Bouchard, Phoe.	8.00
298 Daniel Brière, Phoe.	8.00
299 Sean Burke (G), Phoe.	8.00
300 Keith Carney, Phoe.	8.00
301 Shane Doan, Phoe.	8.00
302 Robert Esche, Phoe.	8.00
303 Michal Handzus, Phoe.	8.00
304 Mike Johnson, Phoe.	8.00
305 Joé Juneau, Phoe.	8.00
306 Claude Lemieux, Phoe.	8.00
307 Teppo Numminen, Phoe.	8.00
308 Jeremy Roenick, Phoe.	8.00
309 Landon Wilson, Phoe.	8.00
310 Jean-Sébastien Aubin (G), Pitt.	8.00
311 Jan Hrdina, Pitt.	8.00
312 Jaromir Jagr, Pitt.	8.00
313 Darius Kasparaitis, Pitt.	8.00
314 Alexei Kovalev, Pitt.	8.00
315 Robert Lang, Pitt.	8.00
316 Mario Lemieux, Pitt.	8.00
317 Garth Snow, Pitt.	8.00
318 Kevin Stevens, Pitt.	8.00
319 Martin Straka, Pitt.	8.00
320 Sébastien Bordeleau, Nash. (SLou.)	8.00
321 Pavol Demitra, SLou.	8.00
322 Dallas Drake, SLou.	8.00
323 Jochen Hecht, SLou.	8.00
324 Brent Johnson (G), SLou.	8.00
325 Reed Low, SLou.	8.00
326 Al MacInnis, SLou.	8.00
327 Scott Mellanby, SLou.	8.00
328 Jaroslav Obsut, SLou.	8.00
329 Chris Pronger, SLou.	8.00
330 Darren Rumble, SLou.	8.00
331 Cory Stillman, SLou.	8.00
332 Keith Tkachuk, SLou.	8.00
333 Roman Turek (G), SLou.	8.00
334 Pierre Turgeon, SLou.	8.00
335 Scott Young, SLou.	8.00
336 Vincent Damphousse, SanJ.	8.00
337 Miikka Kiprusoff (G), SanJ.	8.00
338 Bryan Marchment, SanJ.	8.00
339 Patrick Marleau, SanJ.	8.00
340 Evgeni Nabokov (G), SanJ.	8.00
341 Owen Nolan, SanJ.	8.00
342 Jeff Norton, SanJ.	8.00
343 Mike Ricci, SanJ.	8.00
344 Teemu Selänne, SanJ.	8.00
345 Brad Stuart, SanJ.	8.00
346 Marco Sturm, SanJ.	8.00
347 Niklas Sundström, SanJ.	8.00
348 Scott Thornton, SanJ.	8.00
349 Matthew Barnaby, Tamp.	8.00
350 Brian Holzinger, Tamp.	8.00
351 Nikolai Khabibulin (G), Tamp.	8.00
352 Alexander Kharitonov, Tamp.	8.00
353 Pavel Kubina, Tamp.	8.00
354 Kristian Kudroc, Tamp.	8.00
355 Vincent Lecavalier, Tamp.	8.00
356 Fredrik Modin, Tamp.	8.00
357 Brad Richards, Tamp.	8.00
358 Martin St-Louis, Tamp.	8.00
359 Kevin Weekes (G), Tamp.	8.00
360 Thomas Ziegler, Tamp.	8.00
361 Sergei Berezin, Toro.	8.00
362 Shayne Corson, Toro.	8.00
363 Cory Cross, Toro.	8.00
364 Tie Domi, Toro.	8.00
365 Glenn Healy (G), Toro.	8.00
366 Jonas Höglund, Toro.	8.00
367 Curtis Joseph (G), Toro.	8.00
368 Donald MacLean, Toro.	8.00
369 Dave Manson, Toro.	8.00
370 Yanic Perreault, Toro.	8.00
371 Alexei Ponikarovsky, Toro.	8.00
372 Gary Roberts, Toro.	8.00
373 Mats Sundin, Toro.	8.00
374 Steve Thomas, Toro.	8.00
375 Darcy Tucker, Toro.	8.00
376 Murray Baron, Vanc.	8.00
377 Todd Bertuzzi, Vanc.	8.00
378 Donald Brashear, Vanc.	8.00
379 Andrew Cassels, Vanc.	8.00
380 Dan Cloutier (G), Vanc.	8.00
381 Bob Essensa (G), Vanc.	8.00
382 Ed Jovanovski, Vanc.	8.00
383 Brendan Morrison, Vanc.	8.00
384 Markus Näslund, Vanc.	8.00
385 Mattias Öhlund, Vanc.	8.00
386 Peter Schaefer, Vanc.	8.00
387 Daniel Sedin, Vanc.	8.00
388 Henrik Sedin, Vanc.	8.00
389 Craig Billington (G), Wash.	8.00
390 Peter Bondra, Wash.	8.00
391 Ulf Dahlén, Wash.	8.00
392 Sergei Gonchar, Wash.	8.00
393 Jeff Halpern, Wash.	8.00
394 Dmitri Khristich, Wash.	8.00
395 Olaf Kölzig (G), Wash.	8.00
396 Steve Konowalchuk, Wash.	8.00
397 Trevor Linden, Wash.	8.00
398 Adam Oates, Wash.	8.00
399 Chris Simon, Wash.	8.00
400 Dainius Zubrus, Wash.	8.00

SAMPLE

Promotional Set (9 cards):	15.00
Insert	**Sample**
Jason Allison, Bost.	2.00
Raymond Bourque, Colo.	3.00
Martin Brodeur (G), NJer.	4.00
Marian Hossa, Otta.	2.00
Jaromir Jagr, Pitt.	2.00
Curtis Joseph (G), Toro.	2.00
Mario Lemieux, Pitt.	7.00
Mike Modano, Dall.	2.00
Evgeni Nabokov (G), SanJ.	2.00

2001 - 02 PACIFIC TRADING CARDS / CALDER COLLECTION

Produced by Pacific Trading Cards, this series was released in early 2002. The series was available via a redemption offer.

Complete Set (10 cards):	85.00
Description	**Calder**
1 Dany Heatley, Atla.	30.00
2 Ilya Kovalchuk, Atla.	30.00
3 Erik Cole, Caro.	7.00
4 Vaclav Nedorost, Colo.	7.00
5 Kristian Huselius, Flor.	9.00
6 Jaroslav Bednar, LosA.	5.00
7 Martin Erat, Nash.	5.00
8 Dan Blackburn (G), NYRa.	12.00
9 Krys Kolanos, Phoe.	7.00
10 Jeff Jillson, SanJ.	5.00

2001 - 02 PACIFIC TRADING CARDS / ENTRY DRAFT

Produced by Pacific Trading Cards, this series was released in June 2002. The series was available via a wrapper redemption program at the NHL Entry Draft.

Complete Set (10 cards):	50.00
Redemption (#/500)	**Draft**
1 Ilya Kovalchuk, Atla.	20.00
2 Erik Cole, Caro.	5.00
3 Mark Bell, Chic.	5.00
4 Marcel Hossa, Mont.	8.00
5 Mike Ribeiro, Mont.	6.00
6 Rick DiPietro, NYIs.	9.00
7 Raffi Torres, NYIs.	5.00
8 Dan Blackburn (G), NYRa.	8.00
9 Krys Kolanos, Phoe.	5.00
10 Jeff Jillson, SanJ.	5.00

2001 - 02 PACIFIC TRADING CARDS / HIGH VOLTAGE

Produced by Pacific Trading Cards, this series was released in 2002. The series was available via a wrapper redemption program. A "Big One" parallel version was available in October 2002 at the Big One in Vancouver.

Complete Set (8 cards):		100.00
Redemption	**HV10**	**HV**
1 Dany Heatley, Atla.		30.00
2 Ilya Kovalchuk, Atla.		30.00
3 Erik Cole, Caro.		8.00
4 Vaclav Nedorost, Colo.		8.00
5 Kristian Huselius, Flor.		10.00
6 Martin Erat, Nash.		8.00
7 Dan Blackburn (G), NYRa.		15.00
8 Krys Kolanos, Phoe.		8.00

2001 - 02 PACIFIC TRADING CARDS / COLLECTORS' INTERNATIONAL

Produced by Pacific Trading Cards, this series was released in October 2002. The series was available via a wrapper redemption offer at the Montréal Collectors' International.

Complete Set (9 cards):	95.00
Card (#/499)	**M499**
1 Raymond Bourque, Colo.	12.00
2 Patrick Roy (G), Colo.	30.00
3 Roberto Luongo (G), Flor.	8.00
4 Félix Potvin (G), LosA.	6.00
5 José Théodore (G), Mont.	12.00
6 Martin Brodeur (G), NJer.	16.00
7 Patrick Lalime (G), Otta.	6.00
8 Mario Lemieux, Pitt.	30.00
9 Vincent Lecavalier, Tamp.	10.00

2001 - 02 PACIFIC TRADING CARDS / MONTRÉAL SPORT COLLECTIBLES

Produced by Pacific Trading Cards, this series was released in March 2002. The series was available via a wrapper redemption offer at the Montréal Sport Collectibles show.

Complete Set (9 cards):	90.00
Card (#/250)	**R250**
1 Dany Heatley, Atla.	30.00
2 Ilya Kovalchuk, Atla.	30.00
3 Mark Bell, Chic.	7.00
4 Radim Vrbata, Colo.	9.00
5 Kristian Huselius, Flor.	9.00
6 Mike Ribeiro, Mont.	9.00
7 Raffi Torres, NYIs.	7.00
8 Dan Blackburn (G), NYRa.	12.00
9 Krys Kolanos, Phoe.	7.00

2001 - 02 PACIFIC TRADING CARDS / NATIONAL

Produced by Pacific Trading Cards, this series was released in Summer 2002. The series was available via a wrapper redemption program at the National Sports Collectors Convention. Each card features a hockey player and a football player.

Complete Set (8 cards):	
Redemption	**National**
1 Ilya Kovalchuk, Atla. / M. Vick	
2 Joe Thornton, Bost. / T. Brady	
3 Éric Dazé, Chic. / A. Thomas	
4 Peter Forsberg, Colo. / B. Griese	
5 Mike Modano, Dall. / E. Smith	
6 Steve Yzerman, Detr. / J. Harrington	
7 Eric Lindros, NYRa. / R. Dayne	
8 Chris Pronger, SLou. / K. Warner	

2001 - 02 PACIFIC TRADING CARDS / ROOKIE COLLECTION

Produced by Pacific Trading Cards, this series was released in May 2002. The series was available via a wrapper redemption program at the Spring Sport Card & Memorabilia Expo in Toronto.

Complete Set (10 cards):	70.00
Rookie (#/500)	**R500**
Dan Heatley, Atla.	20.00
Ilya Kovalchuk, Atla.	20.00
Mark Bell, Chic.	5.00
Radim Vrbata, Colo.	6.00
Rostislav Klesla, Colu.	6.00
Pavel Datsyuk, Detr.	16.00
Kristian Huselius, Flor.	6.00
Dan Blackburn (G), NYRa.	8.00
Raffi Torres, NYIs.	5.00
Krys Kolanos, Phoe.	5.00

2001 - 02 PARKHURST

Produced by In The Game, the original series was released in November 2001. There are three versions for each card 1-100: a base card, a silver parallel (#/500) and a gold parallel (#/50). An update series (both base and insert cards) was issued in June 2002 in the Be A Player Update release.

The following wrapper redemption promotional versions were created for cards 1-300: All-Star Fantasy '02 (#/10), Spring Expo '02 (#/10). The following wrapper redemption promotional versions were created for cards 1-100 only: All-Star Fantasy '02 Silver (#/1), All-Star Fantasy '02 Gold (#/1), Spring Expo '02 Silver (#/1), Spring Expo '02 Gold (#/1).

Shell Set (250 cards):	-	-	80.00
Update Set (100 cards):	-	-	65.00
Complete Set (400 cards):	-	-	700
Parallel Set (100 cards):	1,400	100.00	-
Description	**G50**	**S500**	**Base**
1 Paul Kariya, Anah.	60.00	5.00	2.00
2 Patrik Stefan, Atla.	6.00	2.00	.25
3 Jeremy Roenick, Phil.	35.00	2.00	1.00
4 Patrick Roy (G), Colo.	135.00	10.00	4.50
5 Jarome Iginla, Calg.	35.00	2.00	1.00
6 Jeff O'Neill, Caro.	15.00	2.00	.50
7 Sergei Samsonov, Bost.	25.00	2.00	.50
8 Peter Forsberg, Colo.	60.00	5.00	2.00
9 Scott Gomez, NJer.	15.00	2.00	.50
10 Mike Modano, Dall.	45.00	2.00	1.50
11 Brendan Shanahan, Detr.	45.00	2.00	1.50
12 J-S Giguère (G), Anah.	35.00	2.00	1.00
13 Pavel Bure, Flor.	35.00	2.00	1.00
14 Zigmund Palffy, LosA.	25.00	2.00	.50
15 Marian Gaborik, MinW.	45.00	2.00	1.50
16 Pavol Demitra, SLou.	15.00	2.00	.50
17 Alexei Kovalev, Pitt.	25.00	2.00	.50
18 Patrik Elias, NJer.	35.00	2.00	1.00

☐☐☐	19 Keith Tkachuk, SLou.	25.00	2.00	.50
☐☐☐	20 Mats Sundin, Toro.	45.00	2.00	1.50
☐☐☐	21 Marian Hossa, Otta.	45.00	2.00	1.50
☐☐☐	22 Mark Recchi, Phil.	15.00	2.00	.50
☐☐☐	23 John Madden, NJer.	6.00	2.00	.25
☐☐☐	24 Mario Lemieux, Pitt.	135.00	10.00	4.50
☐☐☐	25 Teemu Selänne, SanJ.	35.00	2.00	1.00
☐☐☐	26 Joe Sakic, Colo.	70.00	5.00	2.00
☐☐☐	27 Brad Richards, Tamp.	20.00	2.00	.50
☐☐☐	28 Brian Leetch, NYRa.	25.00	2.00	.50
☐☐☐	29 Markus Näslund, Vanc.	45.00	2.00	1.50
☐☐☐	30 Peter Bondra, Wash.	25.00	2.00	.50
☐☐☐	31 Steve Yzerman, Detr.	105.00	10.00	3.50
☐☐☐	32 Michael Peca, NYIs.	15.00	2.00	.50
☐☐☐	33 Bill Guerin, Bost.	15.00	2.00	.50
☐☐☐	34 Jaromir Jagr, Wash.	45.00	2.00	1.50
☐☐☐	35 Alexei Yashin, NYIs.	25.00	2.00	.50
☐☐☐	36 Theoren Fleury, NYRa.	25.00	2.00	.50
☐☐☐	37 Al MacInnis, SLou.	15.00	2.00	.50
☐☐☐	38 Milan Hejduk, Colo.	35.00	2.00	1.00
☐☐☐	39 Martin Biron (G), Buff.	20.00	2.00	.50
☐☐☐	40 Brad Isbister, NYIs.	6.00	2.00	.25
☐☐☐	41 Nicklas Lidström, Detr.	25.00	2.00	.50
☐☐☐	42 Rick DiPietro, NYIs.	20.00	2.00	.50
☐☐☐	43 Roberto Luongo (G), Flor.	35.00	2.00	1.00
☐☐☐	44 Tim Connolly, Buff.	15.00	2.00	.50
☐☐☐	45 M. Fernandez (G), MinW.	15.00	2.00	.50
☐☐☐	46 Scott Niedermayer, NJer.	6.00	2.00	.25
☐☐☐	47 David Legwand, Nash.	15.00	2.00	.50
☐☐☐	48 Petr Sykora, NJer.	15.00	2.00	.50
☐☐☐	49 Ryan Smyth, Edmo.	20.00	2.00	.50
☐☐☐	50 Mark Messier, NYRa.	45.00	2.00	1.50
☐☐☐	51 David Tanabe, Caro.	6.00	2.00	.25
☐☐☐	52 Keith Primeau, Phil.	15.00	2.00	.50
☐☐☐	53 Teppo Numminen, Phoe.	6.00	2.00	.25
☐☐☐	54 Milan Kraft, Pitt.	6.00	2.00	.25
☐☐☐	55 Owen Nolan, SanJ.	25.00	2.00	.50
☐☐☐	56 Alexander Mogilny, Toro.	20.00	2.00	.50
☐☐☐	57 Brent Johnson (G), SLou.	15.00	2.00	.50
☐☐☐	58 Curtis Joseph (G), Toro.	45.00	2.00	1.50
☐☐☐	59 Félix Potvin (G), LosA.	50.00	2.00	.50
☐☐☐	60 Olaf Kölzig (G), Wash.	25.00	2.00	.50
☐☐☐	61 Eric Lindros, NYRa.	45.00	2.00	1.50
☐☐☐	62 Pierre Turgeon, Dall.	15.00	2.00	.50
☐☐☐	63 Martin Straka, Pitt.	6.00	2.00	.25
☐☐☐	64 Maxim Afinogenov, Buff.	15.00	2.00	.50
☐☐☐	65 Oleg Saprykin, Calg.	6.00	2.00	.25
☐☐☐	66 Shane Willis, Caro.	6.00	2.00	.25
☐☐☐	67 Brett Hull, Detr.	45.00	2.00	1.50
☐☐☐	68 Alex Tanguay, Colo.	25.00	2.00	.50
☐☐☐	69 Marc Denis (G), Colu.	20.00	2.00	.50
☐☐☐	70 Ed Belfour (G), Dall.	45.00	2.00	1.50
☐☐☐	71 R. Cechmanek (G), Phil.	15.00	2.00	.50
☐☐☐	72 Tommy Salo (G), Edmo.	15.00	2.00	.50
☐☐☐	73 Rob Blake, Colo.	25.00	2.00	.50
☐☐☐	74 José Théodore (G), Mont.	50.00	5.00	1.50
☐☐☐	75 Henrik Sedin, Vanc.	15.00	2.00	.50
☐☐☐	76 Tony Amonte, Chic.	25.00	2.00	.50
☐☐☐	77 Scott Hartnell, Nash.	6.00	2.00	.25
☐☐☐	78 Brian Rafalski, NJer.	6.00	2.00	.25
☐☐☐	79 Joe Thornton, Bost.	50.00	5.00	1.50
☐☐☐	80 Patrick Marleau, SanJ.	20.00	2.00	.50
☐☐☐	81 Daniel Alfredsson, Otta.	50.00	2.00	1.50
☐☐☐	82 Simon Gagné, Phil.	35.00	2.00	1.00
☐☐☐	83 Patrick Lalime (G), Otta.	25.00	2.00	.50
☐☐☐	84 Johan Hedberg (G), Pitt.	15.00	2.00	.50
☐☐☐	85 Adam Oates, Wash.	15.00	2.00	.50
☐☐☐	86 Chris Pronger, SLou.	25.00	2.00	.50
☐☐☐	87 Vincent Lecavalier, Tamp.	45.00	2.00	1.50
☐☐☐	88 Tomas Kaberle, Toro.	6.00	2.00	.25
☐☐☐	89 Daniel Sedin, Vanc.	15.00	2.00	.50
☐☐☐	90 Martin Lapointe, Bost.	15.00	2.00	.50
☐☐☐	91 Chris Drury, Colo.	25.00	2.00	.50
☐☐☐	92 Dominik Hasek (G), Detr.	45.00	2.00	1.50
☐☐☐	93 E. Nabokov (G), SanJ.	25.00	2.00	.50
☐☐☐	94 Ed Jovanovski, Vanc.	15.00	2.00	.50
☐☐☐	95 John LeClair, Phil.	35.00	2.00	1.00
☐☐☐	96 Sergei Fedorov, Detr.	45.00	2.00	1.50
☐☐☐	97 Martin Havlat, Otta.	25.00	2.00	.50
☐☐☐	98 Martin Brodeur (G), NJer.	70.00	5.00	2.00
☐☐☐	99 Jason Arnott, NJer.	20.00	2.00	.50
☐☐☐	100 Mike Comrie, Edmo.	35.00	2.00	1.00

☐	101 Petr Nedved, NYRa.	.25
☐	102 Ray Ferraro, Atla.	.25
☐	103 Miroslav Satan, Buff.	.25
☐	104 Rod Brind'Amour, Caro.	.25
☐	105 Ron Tugnutt (G), Colu.	.50
☐	106 Oleg Tverdovsky, Anah.	.25
☐	107 Anson Carter, Edmo.	.50
☐	108 Wes Walz, MinW.	.25
☐	109 Andrei Markov, Mont.	.25
☐	110 Mike Dunham (G), Nash.	.50
☐	111 Éric Desjardins, Phil.	.25
☐	112 Radek Dvorak, NYRa.	.25
☐	113 Pavel Kubina, Tamp.	.25
☐	114 Gary Roberts, Toro.	.50
☐	115 Andrew Cassels, Vanc.	.25
☐	116 Vitaly Vishnevski, Anah.	.25
☐	117 Byron Dafoe (G), Bost.	.50
☐	118 Chris Gratton, Buff.	.25
☐	119 Marc Savard, Calg.	.25
☐	120 Shawn McEachern, Otta.	.25
☐	121 Jocelyn Thibault (G), Chic.	.50
☐	122 Joe Nieuwendyk, Dall.	.50
☐	123 Janne Niinimaa, Edmo.	.25
☐	124 Shane Doan, Phoe.	.25
☐	125 Willie Mitchell, MinW.	.25
☐	126 Glen Murray, LosA.	.50
☐	127 Scott Walker, Nash.	.25
☐	128 Geoff Sanderson, Colu.	.25
☐	129 Kenny Jönsson, NYIs.	.25
☐	130 Radek Bonk, Otta.	.25
☐	131 Brad Stuart, SanJ.	.50
☐	132 Scott Young, SLou.	.25
☐	133 Brendan Morrison, Vanc.	.25
☐	134 Sergei Gonchar, Wash.	.25
☐	135 Jonathan Girard, Bost.	.25
☐	136 Arturs Irbe (G), Caro.	.50
☐	137 Chris Herperger, Otta.	.25
☐	138 Brenden Morrow, Dall.	.25
☐	139 Sergei Zubov, Dall.	.25
☐	140 Lubomir Visnovsky, LosA.	.25
☐	141 Aaron Miller, LosA.	.25
☐	142 Ossi Väänänen, Phoe.	.25
☐	143 Saku Koivu, Mont.	1.00
☐	144 Sean Burke (G), Phoe.	.50
☐	145 Darryl Sydor, Dall.	.25
☐	146 Chris Chelios, Detr.	.50
☐	147 Brian Savage, Mont.	.25
☐	148 Wade Redden, Otta.	.25
☐	149 Derian Hatcher, Dall.	.25
☐	150 Igor Larionov, Detr.	.50
☐	151 Steve Sullivan, Chic.	.25
☐	152 Michal Handzus, Phoe.	.25
☐	153 Ron Francis, Caro.	.50
☐	154 David Vyborny, Colu.	.25
☐	155 Manny Legacé (G), Detr.	.25
☐	156 Jeff Friesen, Anah.	.25
☐	157 Jeff Hackett (G), Mont.	.25
☐	158 Marian Cisar, Nash.	.25
☐	159 Mike York, NYRa.	.25
☐	160 Nikolai Antropov, Toro.	.25
☐	161 Trevor Linden, Wash.	.50
☐	162 Bryan Smolinski, LosA.	.25
☐	163 Janne Laukkanen, Pitt.	.25
☐	164 Dan Cloutier (G), Vanc.	.50
☐	165 Scott Stevens, NJer.	.50
☐	166 Jani Hurme (G), Otta.	.25
☐	167 Fredrik Modin, Tamp.	.25
☐	168 Steven Reinprecht, Colo.	.25
☐	169 Kevyn Adams, Flor.	.25
☐	170 Richard Zednik, Mont.	.50
☐	171 Viktor Kozlov, Flor.	.25
☐	172 Cliff Ronning, Nash.	.25
☐	173 Mariusz Czerkawski, NYIs.	.25
☐	174 Todd Bertuzzi, Vanc.	1.50
☐	175 Vincent Damphousse, SanJ.	.50
☐	176 Roman Hamrlik, NYIs.	.25
☐	177 Sandis Ozolinsh, Caro.	.25
☐	178 Mike Richter (G), NYRa.	.50
☐	179 Stu Barnes, Buff.	.25
☐	180 Patric Kjellberg, Nash.	.25
☐	181 Tomas Holmström, Detr.	.25
☐	182 Sergei Brylin, NJer.	.25
☐	183 Magnus Arvedson, Otta.	.25
☐	184 Sami Kapanen, Caro.	.25
☐	185 Niklas Sundström, SanJ.	.25
☐	186 Todd Marchant, Edmo.	.25
☐	187 Mark Parrish, NYIs.	.50
☐	188 Adam Foote, Colo.	.25
☐	189 Peter Schaefer, Vanc.	.25
☐	190 Mike Ricci, SanJ.	.25
☐	191 Alexei Zhamnov, Chic.	.25
☐	192 Dainius Zubrus, Wash.	.25
☐	193 Espen Knutsen, Colu.	.25
☐	194 Shean Donovan, Atla.	.25
☐	195 Bobby Holik, NJer.	.25
☐	196 Tom Poti, Edmo.	.25
☐	197 Marcus Ragnarsson, SanJ.	.25
☐	198 Jozef Stümpel, LosA.	.25
☐	199 Martin Rucinsky, Mont.	.25
☐	200 Matt Davidson, Colu.	.50
☐	201 Jan Bulis, Mont.	.25
☐	202 Matt Pettinger, Wash.	.25
☐	203 Rob Zamuner, Bost.	.25
☐	204 Chris Osgood (G), NYIs.	.50
☐	205 Dan Hinote, Colo.	.25
☐	206 Travis Green, Toro.	.25
☐	207 Joé Juneau, Mont.	.25
☐	208 Mikael Renberg, Toro.	.25
☐	209 Zdeno Ciger, NYRa.	.25
☐	210 Jochen Hecht, Edmo.	.25
☐	211 Jan Hlavac, Phil.	.25
☐	212 Jeff Halpern, Wash.	.25
☐	213 Tom Barrasso (G), Caro.	.50
☐	214 Bill Muckalt, Otta.	.25
☐	215 Luc Robitaille, Detr.	1.00
☐	216 Jason Wiemer, Flor.	.25
☐	217 Deron Quint, Colu.	.25
☐	218 Jyrki Lumme, Dall.	.25
☐	219 Andreas Dackell, Mont.	.25
☐	220 Tomi Kallio, Atla.	.25
☐	221 Roman Turek (G), Calg.	.50
☐	222 Taylor Pyatt, Buff.	.25
☐	223 Richard Jackman, Bost.	.25
☐	224 Michael Nylander, Chic.	.25
☐	225 Brian Pothier, Atla.	.25
☐	226 Vyacheslav Kozlov, Buff.	.25
☐	227 Kim Johnsson, Phil.	.25
☐	228 Jean-Pierre Dumont, Buff.	.25
☐	229 Marty Reasoner, Edmo.	.25
☐	230 Dimitri Kalinin, Buff.	.25
☐	231 Damian Rhodes (G), Atla.	.25
☐	232 Jason Allison, Bost.	.50
☐	233 Doug Weight, SLou.	.50
☐	234 Yanic Perreault, Mont.	.25
☐	235 Éric Dazé, Chic.	.50
☐	236 Brian Campbell, Buff.	.25
☐	237 Valeri Bure, Flor.	.25
☐	238 Adam Deadmarsh, LosA.	.25
☐	239 Robert Reichel, Toro.	.25
☐	240 Anders Eriksson, Toro.	.25
☐	241 Nikolai Khabibulin (G), Tamp.	.50
☐	242 Sean O'Donnell, Bost.	.25
☐	243 Bob Essensa (G), Buff.	.25
☐	244 Josef Vasicek, Caro.	.25
☐	245 Donald Audette, Dall.	.50
☐	246 Stephen Heinze, LosA.	.25
☐	247 Bryan Berard, NYRa.	.25
☐	248 Ville Nieminen, Colo.	.25
☐	249 Eric Weinrich, Phil.	.25
☐	250 Adam Graves, SanJ.	.50

ROOKIES

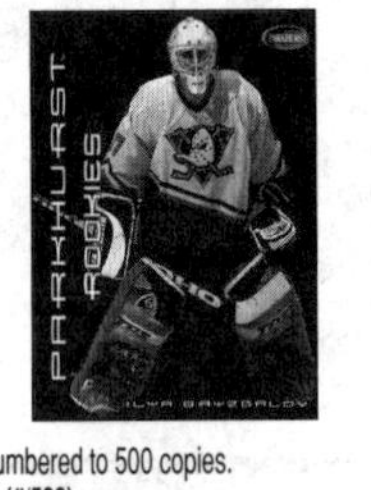

Rookies are numbered to 500 copies.

	Rookie (#/500)	R500
☐	251 Jesse Boulerice, Phil.	5.00
☐	252 Marko Kiprusoff, NYIs.	5.00
☐	**253 Ivan Ciernik, Otta. RC**	**20.00**
☐	**254 Pavel Datsyuk, Detr. RC**	**120.00**
☐	**255 Jaroslav Bednar, LosA. RC**	**20.00**
☐	**256 Andreas Salomonsson, NJer. RC**	**10.00**
☐	257 Mike Ribeiro, Mont.	5.00
☐	258 Darcy Hordichuk, Atla.	5.00
☐	**259 Chris Neil, Otta. RC**	**10.00**
☐	260 Rostislav Klesla, Colu.	5.00
☐	**261 Kristian Huselius, Flor. RC**	**45.00**
☐	**262 Brian Sutherby, Wash. RC**	**20.00**
☐	**263 Jiri Dopita, Phil. RC**	**20.00**
☐	**264 Radek Martinek, NYIs. RC**	**10.00**
☐	265 Barrett Heisten, NYRa.	5.00
☐	**266 Krys Kolanos, Phoe. RC**	**30.00**
☐	**267 Pascal Dupuis, MinW. RC**	**30.00**
☐	268 Andreas Lilja, LosA.	5.00
☐	269 Chris Mason (G), Nash.	5.00
☐	270 Mathieu Garon (G), Mont.	10.00
☐	271 Andrew Raycroft (G), Bost.	5.00
☐	**272 Jeff Jillson, SanJ. RC**	**20.00**
☐	273 Jiri Bicek, NJer.	5.00
☐	**274 Niklas Hagman, Flor. RC**	**20.00**
☐	275 Pavel Brendl, Phil.	5.00
☐	276 Stephen Peat, Wash.	5.00
☐	277 Sascha Goc, NJer.	5.00
☐	278 Nick Boynton, Bost.	5.00
☐	**279 Timo Pärssinen, Anah. RC**	**10.00**
☐	280 Mika Noronen (G), Buff.	10.00
☐	**281 Scott Clemmensen (G), NJer. RC**	**20.00**
☐	**282 Dan Blackburn (G), NYRa. RC**	**60.00**
☐	**283 Nikita Alexeev, Tamp. RC**	**30.00**
☐	**284 Vaclav Nedorost, Colo. RC**	**30.00**
☐	**285 Ilja Bryzgalov (G), Anah. RC**	**25.00**
☐	286 Dany Heatley, Atla.	25.00
☐	**287 Niko Kapanen, Dall. RC**	**30.00**
☐	288 Rick Berry, Colo.	5.00
☐	289 Mark Bell, Chic.	5.00
☐	290 Kamil Piros, Atla.	5.00
☐	291 Maxime* Ouellet (G), Phil.	5.00
☐	292 Kris Beech, Pitt.	5.00
☐	293 Miikka Kiprusoff (G), SanJ.	5.00
☐	294 Martti Järventie, Mont.	5.00
☐	**295 Ilya Kovalchuk, Atla. RC**	**150.00**
☐	**296 Nick Schultz, MinW. RC**	**20.00**
☐	297 Bryan Allen, Vanc.	5.00
☐	**298 Josef Boumedienne, NJer. RC**	**10.00**
☐	299 Jason Williams, Detr.	5.00
☐	300 Daniel Tjärnqvist, Atla.	5.00

UPDATE

	Update	Update
☐	**301 Frédéric Cassivi (G), Atla. RC**	**1.50**
☐	**302 Mark Hartigan, Atla. RC**	**1.50**
☐	**303 Pasi Nurminen (G), Atla. RC**	**2.00**
☐	**304 Ivan Huml, Bost. RC**	**2.00**
☐	**305 Zdenek Kutlak, Bost. RC**	**1.50**
☐	**306 Ales Kotalik, Buff. RC**	**4.00**
☐	**307 Jukka Hentunen, Nash. RC**	**1.50**
☐	**308 Erik Cole, Caro. RC**	**2.00**
☐	**309 Tyler Arnason, Chic. RC**	**8.00**
☐	**310 Jaroslav Obsut, Colo. RC**	**1.50**
☐	**311 Riku Hahl, Colo. RC**	**1.50**
☐	**312 Martin Spanhel, Colu. RC**	**1.50**
☐	**313 Andrej Nedorost, Colu. RC**	**1.50**
☐	**314 Ty Conklin (G), Edmo. RC**	**2.00**
☐	**315 Jason Chimera, Edmo. RC**	**1.50**
☐	**316 Kyle Rossiter, Flor. RC**	**1.50**
☐	**317 Lukas Krajicek, Flor. RC**	**2.00**
☐	**318 Stephen Weiss, Flor. RC**	**15.00**
☐	**319 Tony Virta, MinW. RC**	**1.50**
☐	**320 Marcel Hossa, Mont. RC**	**8.00**
☐	**321 Olivier Michaud (G), Mont. RC**	**2.00**
☐	**322 Henrik Tallinder, Buff. RC**	**1.50**
☐	**323 Martin Erat, Nash. RC**	**1.50**
☐	**324 Nathan Perrott, Nash. RC**	**1.50**
☐	**325 Pavel Skrbek, Nash. RC**	**1.50**
☐	**326 Robert Schnabel, Nash. RC**	**1.50**
☐	**327 Christian Berglund, NJer. RC**	**1.50**
☐	**328 Stanislav Gron, NJer. RC**	**1.50**
☐	**329 Raffi Torres, NYIs. RC**	**2.00**
☐	**330 Mikael Samuelsson, NYRa. RC**	**1.50**
☐	**331 Chris Bala, Otta. RC**	**1.50**
☐	**332 Josh Langfeld, Otta. RC**	**1.50**
☐	**333 Martin Prusek (G), Otta. RC**	**3.00**
☐	**334 Sean Avery, Detr. RC**	**1.50**
☐	**335 Neil Little (G), Phil. RC**	**1.50**
☐	**336 Tomas Divisek, Phil. RC**	**1.50**
☐	**337 Vaclav Pletka, Phil. RC**	**1.50**
☐	**338 Guillaume Lefebvre, Phil. RC**	**1.50**
☐	**339 Branko Radivojevic, Phoe. RC**	**2.00**
☐	**340 Trent Hunter, NYIs. RC**	**1.50**
☐	**341 Jan Lasak (G), Nash. RC**	**2.00**
☐	**342 Tom Kostopoulos, Pitt. RC**	**1.50**
☐	**343 Hannes Hyvonen, SanJ. RC**	**1.50**
☐	**344 Shane Endicott, Pitt. RC**	**1.50**
☐	**345 Evgeny Konstantinov (G), Tamp. RC**	**1.50**
☐	**346 Martin Cibak, Tamp. RC**	**1.50**
☐	**347 Karel Pilar, Toro. RC**	**1.50**
☐	**348 Sébastien Centomo (G), Toro. RC**	**2.00**
☐	**349 Mike Farrell, Wash. RC**	**1.50**
☐	**350 Sébastien Charpentier (G), Wash. RC**	**1.50**

UPDATE

	Update	Update
☐	351 Radim Vrbata, Colo.	.50
☐	352 Andy McDonald, Anah.	.25
☐	353 Jean-Pierre Vigier, Atla.	.25
☐	354 Donald Brashear, Phil.	.25
☐	355 Adrian Aucoin, NYIs.	.25
☐	356 Stéphane Richer, NJer.	.25
☐	357 Byron Ritchie, Flor.	.25
☐	358 Sergei Berezin, Mont.	.25
☐	359 Cliff Ronning, LosA.	.25
☐	360 Tony Hrkac, Atla.	.25
☐	361 André Roy, Tamp.	.25
☐	362 Shjon Podein, SLou.	.25
☐	363 Andrei Nazarov, Phoe.	.25
☐	364 Marty McInnis, Bost.	.25
☐	365 Petr Tenkrat, Nash.	.25
☐	366 Trevor Letowski, Vanc.	.25
☐	367 Randy Robitaille, Pitt.	.25
☐	368 Kim Johnsson, Phil.	.25
☐	369 Jozef Stümpel, Bost.	.25
☐	370 P.J. Stock, Bost.	.25
☐	371 Dean McAmmond, Calg.	.25
☐	372 Steve Thomas, Chic.	.25
☐	373 Darius Kasparaitis, Colo.	.25
☐	374 Mike Sillinger, Colu.	.25
☐	375 Jason Arnott, Dall.	.50
☐	376 Alex Auld (G), Vanc.	.25
☐	377 Mike York, Edmo.	.25
☐	378 Pierre Dagenais, Flor.	.25
☐	379 Andrew Brunette, MinW.	.25
☐	380 Sergei Zholtok, MinW.	.25
☐	381 Donald Audette, Mont.	.50
☐	382 Doug Gilmour, Mont.	.50
☐	383 Andy Delmore, Nash.	.25
☐	384 Martin Rucinsky, NYRa.	.25

☐ 385 Jamie Langenbrunner, NJer.	.25
☐ 386 Joe Nieuwendyk, NJer.	.50
☐ 387 John Vanbiesbrouck (G), NJer.	.50
☐ 388 Shawn Bates, NYIs.	.25
☐ 389 Matthew Barnaby, NYRa.	.25
☐ 390 Pavel Bure, NYRa.	1.00
☐ 391 Tom Poti, NYRa.	.25
☐ 392 Zdeno Chara, Otta.	.25
☐ 393 Adam Oates, Phil.	.50
☐ 394 Marty Murray, Phil.	.25
☐ 395 Brian Savage, Phoe.	.25
☐ 396 Danny Markov, Phoe.	.25
☐ 397 Tom Barrasso (G), Toro.	.50
☐ 398 Jan Hlavac, Vanc.	.25
☐ 399 Trevor Linden, Vanc.	.50
☐ 400 Ivan Ciernik, Wash.	.25

HE SHOOTS HE SCORES REDEMPTION

Each redemption card was worth one, two, or three points. Collectors who accumulated 400 points could trade their redemption cards in for a special random jersey card. This redemption program ends on November 30, 2002.

Insert Set (20 cards):

Insert	HSHS
☐ Mario Lemieux, Pitt. [3 Points]	
☐ Ted Lindsay, Detr. [1 Point]	
☐ Stan Mikita, Chic. [1 Point]	
☐ Jacques Plante (G), Mont. [1 Point]	
☐ Chris Pronger, Slou. [1 Point]	
☐ Maurice Richard, Mont. [3 Points]	
☐ Patrick Roy (G), Colo. [2 Points]	
☐ Joe Sakic, Colo. [2 Points]	
☐ Terry Sawchuk (G), Detr. [1 Point]	
☐ Mats Sundin, Toro. [1 Point]	
☐ Steve Yzerman, Detr. [2 Points]	
☐ Jean Béliveau, Mont. [1 Point]	
☐ Martin Brodeur (G), NJer. [2 Points]	
☐ Pavel Bure, Flor. [3 Points]	
☐ Peter Forsberg, Colo. [2 Points]	
☐ Doug Harvey, Mont. [1 Point]	
☐ Tim Horton, Toro. [1 Point]	
☐ Gordie Howe, Detr. [3 Points]	
☐ Bobby Hull, Chic. [1 Point]	
☐ Paul Kariya, Anah. [2 Points]	

500 GOAL SCORERS

Insert Set (27 cards):	2,700
Insert	PGS
☐ Dave Andreychuk, Bost. ✂ {*80}	60.00
☐ Jean Béliveau, Mont. ✂ {*80}	125.00
☐ Mike Bossy, NYIs. ✂ {*30}	150.00
☐ John Bucyk, Bost. ✂ {*80}	60.00
☐ Dino Ciccarelli, Detr. ✂ {*80}	60.00
☐ Marcel Dionne, LosA. ✂ {*30}	125.00
☐ Phil Esposito, NYRa. ✂ {*30}	125.00
☐ Mike Gartner, Toro. ✂ {*80}	75.00
☐ Michel Goulet, Chic. ✂ {*80}	60.00
☐ Dale Hawerchuk, Phil. ✂ {*80}	60.00
☐ Gordie Howe, Detr. ✂ {*30}	350.00
☐ Bobby Hull, Chic. ✂ {*30}	200.00
☐ Brett Hull, SLou. ✂ {*30}	150.00
☐ Jari Kurri, LosA. ✂ {*80}	100.00
☐ Guy Lafleur, Mont. ✂ {*30}	175.00
☐ Mario Lemieux, Pitt. ✂ {*30}	450.00
☐ Frank Mahovlich, Mont. ✂ {*80}	60.00
☐ Lanny McDonald, Toro. ✂ {*80}	75.00
☐ Mark Messier, Edmo. ✂ {*30}	150.00
☐ Stan Mikita, Chic. ✂ {*80}	60.00
☐ Joe Mullen, Calg. ✂ {*80}	60.00
☐ Gilbert Perreault, Buff. ✂ {*80}	60.00
☐ Maurice Richard, Mont. ✂ {*80}	225.00
☐ Luc Robitaille, LosA. ✂ {*30}	125.00
☐ Bryan Trottier, NYIs. ✂ {*80}	75.00
☐ Pat Verbeek, NJer. ✂ {*80}	60.00
☐ Steve Yzerman, Detr. ✂ {*30}	350.00
☐ Ron Francis, Caro. ✂ {*25}	125.00
☐ Brendan Shanahan, Detr. ✂ {*25}	150.00

GAME-USED JERSEY

Insert Set (60 cards):	1,650
Insert (#/90)	PJ
☐ Daniel Alfredsson, Otta. ✂	50.00
☐ Tony Amonte, Chic. ✂	25.00
☐ Ed Belfour (G), Dall. ✂	50.00
☐ Peter Bondra, Wash. ✂	25.00
☐ Radek Bonk, Otta. ✂	25.00
☐ Martin Brodeur (G), NJer. ✂	75.00
☐ Pavel Bure, Flor. ✂	25.00
☐ Roman Cechmanek (G), Phil. ✂	25.00
☐ Chris Chelios, Detr. ✂	25.00
☐ Byron Dafoe (G), Bost. ✂	25.00
☐ Éric Dazé, Chic. ✂	25.00
☐ Chris Drury, Colo. ✂	25.00
☐ Patrik Elias, NJer. ✂	25.00
☐ Sergei Fedorov, Detr. ✂	50.00
☐ Theoren Fleury, NYRa. ✂	25.00
☐ Adam Foote, Colo. ✂	25.00
☐ Peter Forsberg, Colo. ✂	50.00
☐ Ron Francis, Caro. ✂	25.00
☐ Jeff Friesen, Anah. ✂	25.00
☐ Scott Gomez, NJer. ✂	25.00
☐ Sergei Gonchar, Wash. ✂	25.00
☐ Milan Hejduk, Colo. ✂	25.00
☐ Marian Hossa, Otta. ✂	50.00
☐ Arturs Irbe (G), Caro. ✂	25.00
☐ Curtis Joseph (G), Toro. ✂	50.00
☐ Paul Kariya, Anah. ✂	50.00
☐ Saku Koivu, Mont. ✂	50.00
☐ Olaf Kölzig (G), Wash. ✂	25.00
☐ Viktor Kozlov, Flor. ✂	25.00
☐ Milan Kraft, Pitt. ✂	25.00
☐ Vincent Lecavalier, Tamp. ✂	50.00
☐ John LeClair, Phil. ✂	25.00
☐ Brian Leetch, NYRa. ✂	25.00
☐ Mario Lemieux, Pitt. ✂	150.00
☐ Nicklas Lidström, Detr. ✂	25.00
☐ Roberto Luongo (G), Flor. ✂	25.00
☐ Al MacInnis, SLou. ✂	25.00
☐ Darren McCarty, Detr. ✂	25.00
☐ Mark Messier, NYRa. ✂	50.00
☐ Mike Modano, Dall. ✂	50.00
☐ Fredrik Modin, Tamp. ✂	25.00
☐ Joe Nieuwendyk, Dall. ✂	25.00
☐ Owen Nolan, SanJ. ✂	25.00
☐ Zigmund Palffy, LosA. ✂	25.00
☐ Keith Primeau, Phil. ✂	25.00
☐ Chris Pronger, SLou. ✂	25.00
☐ Mark Recchi, Phil. ✂	25.00
☐ Mike Richter (G), NYRa. ✂	25.00
☐ Patrick Roy (G), Colo. ✂	100.00
☐ Joe Sakic, Colo. ✂	75.00
☐ Daniel Sedin, Vanc. ✂	25.00
☐ Brendan Shanahan, Detr. ✂	50.00
☐ Patrik Stefan, Atla. ✂	25.00
☐ Scott Stevens, NJer. ✂	25.00
☐ Martin Straka, Pitt. ✂	25.00
☐ Mats Sundin, Toro. ✂	50.00
☐ Alex Tanguay, Colo. ✂	25.00
☐ Joe Thornton, Bost. ✂	50.00
☐ Steve Yzerman, Detr. ✂	100.00
☐ Alexei Zhamnov, Chic. ✂	25.00

GAME-USED STICK

Insert Set (70 cards):	2,400
Insert	GWJ
☐ Daniel Alfredsson, Otta. ✂	50.00
☐ Tony Amonte, Chic. ✂	40.00
☐ Jason Arnott, NJer. ✂	40.00
☐ Rob Blake, Colo. ✂	40.00
☐ Peter Bondra, Wash. ✂	40.00
☐ Martin Brodeur (G), NJer. ✂	75.00
☐ Pavel Bure, Flor. ✂	40.00
☐ Chris Chelios, Detr. ✂	40.00
☐ Pavol Demitra, SLou. ✂	40.00
☐ Rick DiPietro, NYIs. ✂	40.00
☐ Chris Drury, Colo. ✂	40.00
☐ Sergei Fedorov, Detr. ✂	50.00
☐ Adam Foote, Colo. ✂	40.00
☐ Peter Forsberg, Colo. ✂	50.00
☐ Ron Francis, Caro. ✂	40.00
☐ Jeff Friesen, Anah. ✂	40.00
☐ Scott Gomez, NJer. ✂	40.00
☐ Sergei Gonchar, Wash. ✂	40.00
☐ Dominik Hasek (G), Detr. ✂	50.00
☐ Milan Hejduk, Colo. ✂	40.00
☐ Marian Hossa, Otta. ✂	50.00
☐ Brett Hull, Detr. ✂	50.00
☐ Jaromir Jagr, Wash. ✂	50.00
☐ Kenny Jönsson, NYIs. ✂	40.00
☐ Paul Kariya, Anah. ✂	50.00
☐ Olaf Kölzig (G), Wash. ✂	40.00
☐ Jari Kurri, LosA. ✂	50.00
☐ Guy Lafleur, Mont. ✂	50.00
☐ Vincent Lecavalier, Tamp. ✂	50.00
☐ John LeClair, Phil. ✂	40.00
☐ Brian Leetch, NYRa. ✂	40.00
☐ Mario Lemieux, Pitt. ✂	150.00
☐ Nicklas Lidström, Detr. ✂	40.00
☐ Eric Lindros, NYRa. ✂	50.00
☐ Al MacInnis, SLou. ✂	40.00
☐ Darren McCarty, Detr. ✂	40.00
☐ Lanny McDonald, Calg. ✂	40.00
☐ Mark Messier, NYRa. ✂	50.00
☐ Stan Mikita, Chic. ✂	40.00
☐ Mike Modano, Dall. ✂	50.00
☐ Alexander Mogilny, Toro. ✂	40.00
☐ Markus Näslund, Vanc. ✂	50.00
☐ Joe Nieuwendyk, Dall. ✂	40.00
☐ Owen Nolan, SanJ. ✂	40.00
☐ Adam Oates, Wash. ✂	40.00
☐ Sandis Ozolinsh, Caro. ✂	40.00
☐ Zigmund Palffy, LosA. ✂	40.00
☐ Keith Primeau, Phil. ✂	40.00
☐ Chris Pronger, SLou. ✂	40.00
☐ Mark Recchi, Phil. ✂	40.00
☐ Brad Richards, Tamp. ✂	40.00
☐ Gary Roberts, Toro. ✂	40.00
☐ Luc Robitaille, Detr. ✂	40.00
☐ Jeremy Roenick, Phil. ✂	40.00
☐ Patrick Roy (G), Colo. ✂	100.00
☐ Joe Sakic, Colo. ✂	75.00
☐ Sergei Samsonov, Bost. ✂	40.00
☐ Daniel Sedin, Vanc. ✂	40.00
☐ Teemu Selänne, SanJ. ✂	40.00
☐ Brendan Shanahan, Detr. ✂	50.00
☐ Patrik Stefan, Atla. ✂	40.00
☐ Scott Stevens, NJer. ✂	40.00
☐ Mats Sundin, Toro. ✂	50.00
☐ Alex Tanguay, Colo. ✂	40.00
☐ Joe Thornton, Bost. ✂	50.00
☐ Keith Tkachuk, SLou. ✂	40.00
☐ Roman Turek (G), Calg. ✂	40.00
☐ Pierre Turgeon, Dall. ✂	40.00
☐ Doug Weight, SLou. ✂	40.00
☐ Steve Yzerman, Detr. ✂	100.00

STICK & JERSEY

Insert Set (20 cards):	1,200
Insert (#/70)	PSJ
☐ Ed Belfour (G), Dall. ✂	75.00
☐ Martin Brodeur (G), NJer. ✂	100.00
☐ Pavel Bure, Flor. ✂	50.00
☐ Roman Cechmanek (G), Phil. ✂	50.00
☐ Byron Dafoe (G), Bost. ✂	50.00
☐ Sergei Fedorov, Detr. ✂	75.00
☐ Peter Forsberg, Colo. ✂	100.00
☐ Marian Hossa, Otta. ✂	75.00
☐ Paul Kariya, Anah. ✂	100.00
☐ Olaf Kölzig (G), Wash. ✂	50.00
☐ Vincent Lecavalier, Tamp. ✂	75.00
☐ John LeClair, Phil. ✂	50.00
☐ Al MacInnis, SLou. ✂	50.00
☐ Chris Pronger, SLou. ✂	50.00
☐ Mark Recchi, Phil. ✂	50.00
☐ Patrick Roy (G), Colo. ✂	175.00
☐ Joe Sakic, Colo. ✂	100.00
☐ Mats Sundin, Toro. ✂	75.00
☐ Joe Thornton, Bost. ✂	75.00
☐ Steve Yzerman, Detr. ✂	175.00

HE SHOOTS HE SCORE JERSEYS

These cards were distributed to those collectors who redeemed 400 He Shoots He Scores points.

Jersey (#/20)

- ☐ Tony Amonte, Chic. ✂
- ☐ Ed Belfour (G), Dall. ✂
- ☐ Jean Béliveau, Mont. ✂
- ☐ Rob Blake, Colo. ✂
- ☐ Martin Brodeur, NJer. ✂
- ☐ Pavel Bure, Flor. ✂
- ☐ Bobby Clarke, Phil. ✂
- ☐ Chris Drury, Colo. ✂
- ☐ Sergei Fedorov, Detr. ✂
- ☐ Dominik Hasek (G), Detr. ✂
- ☐ Milan Hejduk, Colo. ✂
- ☐ Gordie Howe, Detr. ✂
- ☐ Bobby Hull, Chic. ✂
- ☐ Jarome Iginla, Calg. ✂
- ☐ Jaromir Jagr, Wash. ✂
- ☐ Curtis Joseph (G), Toro. ✂
- ☐ Paul Kariya, Anah. ✂
- ☐ Saku Koivu, Mont. ✂
- ☐ Ilya Kovalchuk, Atla. ✂
- ☐ John LeClair, Phil. ✂
- ☐ Mario Lemieux, Pitt. ✂
- ☐ Eric Lindros, NYRa. ✂
- ☐ Ted Lindsay, Detr. ✂
- ☐ Mark Messier, NYRa. ✂
- ☐ Mike Modano, Dall. ✂
- ☐ Alexander Mogilny, Toro. ✂
- ☐ Markus Naslund, Vanc. ✂
- ☐ Jacques Plante, Mont. ✂
- ☐ Denis Potvin, NYIs. ✂
- ☐ Jeremy Roenick, Phil. ✂
- ☐ Patrick Roy, Colo. ✂
- ☐ Joe Sakic, Colo. ✂
- ☐ Tommy Salo, Edmo. ✂
- ☐ Terry Sawchuk, Detr. ✂
- ☐ Teemu Selanne, SanJ. ✂
- ☐ Brendan Shanahan, Detr. ✂
- ☐ Mats Sundin, Toro. ✂
- ☐ Alex Tanguay, Colo. ✂
- ☐ Doug Weight, SLou. ✂
- ☐ Steve Yzerman, Detr. ✂

MILESTONES

Insert Set (22 cards):	2,900
Insert (#/50)	M
☐ M-5 Ed Belfour (G), ✂	75.00
☐ M-19 Raymond Bourque ✂	75.00
☐ M-21 Raymond Bourque ✂	75.00
☐ M-2 Martin Brodeur (G), ✂	125.00
☐ M-16 Martin Brodeur (G), ✂	125.00
☐ M-15 Doug Gilmour ✂	50.00
☐ M-11 Dominik Hasek (G) ✂	75.00
☐ M-3 Jaromir Jagr ✂	50.00
☐ M-4 Jaromir Jagr ✂	50.00
☐ M-8 Jaromir Jagr ✂	50.00
☐ M-10 Curtis Joseph (G) ✂	75.00
☐ M-6 Brian Leetch, ✂	50.00
☐ M-20 Mario Lemieux ✂	250.00
☐ M-12 Mark Messier ✂	75.00
☐ M-1 Chris Osgood (G), Detr. ✂	50.00
☐ M-9 Mark Recchi ✂	50.00
☐ M-7 Luc Robitaille ✂	50.00
☐ M-22 Jeremy Roenick ✂	50.00
☐ M-18 Patrick Roy (G) ✂	200.00
☐ M-13 Scott Stevens ✂	50.00
☐ M-14 Steve Yzerman ✂	175.00
☐ M-17 Steve Yzerman ✂	175.00
Insert (#/90)	M
☐ M-44 Ed Belfour (G) ✂	50.00
☐ M-32 Peter Bondra ✂	40.00
☐ M-47 Martin Brodeur ✂	75.00
☐ M-30 Pavel Bure ✂	40.00
☐ M-54 Theoren Fleury ✂	40.00
☐ M-28 Ron Francis ✂	40.00
☐ M-48 Ron Francis ✂	40.00
☐ M-42 Dominik Hasek ✂	50.00
☐ M-24 Brett Hull ✂	40.00
☐ M-50 Brett Hull ✂	40.00
☐ M-53 Jaromir Jagr ✂	50.00
☐ M-45 Curtis Joseph (G) ✂	50.00
☐ M-25 Mario Lemieux ✂	125.00
☐ M-40 Mario Lemieux ✂	125.00
☐ M-52 Al MacInnis ✂	40.00
☐ M-39 Mark Messier ✂	50.00
☐ M-35 Mike Modano ✂	50.00
☐ M-31 Alexander Mogilny ✂	40.00
☐ M-27 Joe Nieuwendyk ✂	40.00
☐ M-38 Adam Oates ✂	40.00
☐ M-49 Adam Oates ✂	40.00
☐ M-34 Mark Recchi ✂	40.00
☐ M-46 Mike Richter ✂	40.00
☐ M-23 Luc Robitaille ✂	40.00
☐ M-56 Jeremy Roenick ✂	40.00
☐ M-41 Patrick Roy ✂	100.00
☐ M-43 Patrick Roy ✂	100.00
☐ M-51 Joe Sakic ✂	75.00
☐ M-36 Teemu Selanne ✂	40.00
☐ M-29 Brendan Shanahan ✂	40.00
☐ M-55 Brendan Shanahan ✂	40.00
☐ M-33 Mats Sundin ✂	50.00
☐ M-26 Steve Yzerman ✂	100.00
☐ M-37 Steve Yzerman ✂	100.00

NHL HEROES

Insert Set (16 cards):	2,300
Insert (#/40)	H
☐ H-1 J. Béliveau ✂ / V. Lecavalier ✂	200.00
☐ H-2 G. Howe ✂ / S. Yzerman ✂	400.00
☐ H-3 T. Sawchuk (G) ✂ / P. Roy (G) ✂	350.00
☐ H-4 M. Richard ✂ / P. Bure ✂	250.00
☐ H-5 P. Esposito ✂ / J. Thornton ✂	150.00
☐ H-6 G. Lafleur ✂ / P. Kariya ✂	200.00
☐ H-7 D. Harvey ✂ / B. Leetch ✂	125.00
☐ H-8 S. Mikita ✂ / J. Sakic ✂	175.00
☐ H-9 J. Plante (G) ✂ / M. Brodeur (G) ✂	225.00
☐ H-10 T. Lindsay ✂ / O. Nolan ✂	100.00
☐ H-11 V. Tretiak (G) ✂ / E. Belfour (G) ✂	150.00
☐ H-12 T. Horton ✂ / S. Stevens ✂	125.00
☐ H-13 Bo. Hull ✂ / Br. Hull ✂	200.00
☐ H-14 G. Perreault ✂ / M. Lemieux ✂	300.00

☐	H-15 H. Richard ✂ / S. Gomez ✂	75.00
☐	H-16 B. Gadsby ✂ / C. Pronger ✂	75.00

TEAMMATES

	Insert Set (28 cards):	**3,400**
	Insert (#/30)	**T**
☐	T-1 Lidström ✂ / Shanahan ✂ / Yzerman ✂	350.00
☐	T-2 Aubin (G) ✂ / Kraft ✂ / Lemieux ✂	300.00
☐	T-3 Fleury ✂ / Leetch ✂ / Messier ✂	175.00
☐	T-4 Allison ✂ / Dafoe (G) ✂ / Thornton ✂	175.00
☐	T-5 Drury ✂ / Foote ✂ / Sakic ✂	200.00
☐	T-6 Bondra ✂ / Gonchar ✂ / Kölzig (G) ✂	125.00
☐	T-7 Joseph (G) ✂ / Kaberle ✂ / Sundin ✂	200.00
☐	T-8 Forsberg ✂ / Hejduk ✂ / Roy (G) ✂	300.00
☐	T-9 Amonte ✂ / Dazé ✂ / Thibault (G) ✂	100.00
☐	T-10 Bure ✂ / Kozlov ✂ / Luongo (G) ✂	150.00
☐	T-11 Biron (G) ✂ / Satan ✂ / Zhitnik ✂	100.00
☐	T-12 Belfour (G) ✂ / Modano ✂ / Sydor ✂	175.00
☐	T-13 Cechmanek (G) ✂ / LeClair ✂ / Recchi ✂	125.00
☐	T-14 Brodeur (G) ✂ / Elias ✂ / Stevens ✂	225.00
☐	T-15 Arnott ✂ / Gomez ✂ / Holik ✂	100.00
☐	T-16 Alfredsson ✂ / Bonk ✂ / Hossa ✂	200.00
☐	T-17 Bertuzzi ✂ / Näslund ✂ / D.Sedin ✂	225.00
☐	T-18 Francis ✂ / Irbe (G) ✂ / Ozolinsh ✂	100.00
	Insert (#/80)	**T**
☐	S. Samsonov ✂ / J. Thornton ✂ / B. Guerin ✂	75.00
☐	S. Ozolinsh ✂ / P. Bure ✂ / R. Luongo ✂	75.00
☐	M. Turco ✂ / M. Modano ✂ / E. Belfour ✂	100.00
☐	J. Sakic ✂ / P. Roy (G) ✂ / C. Drury ✂	200.00
☐	S. Yzerman ✂ / B. Shanahan ✂ / D. Hasek (G) ✂	175.00
☐	E. Lindros ✂ / B. Leetch ✂ / M. Messier ✂	100.00
☐	T. Selänne ✂ / J. Hurme (G) ✂ / S. Kapanen ✂	60.00
☐	M. Sundin ✂ / T. Salo ✂ / M. Näslund ✂	75.00
☐	J. Jagr ✂ / D. Hasek ✂ / T. Kaberle ✂	100.00
☐	S. Yzerman ✂ / M. Lemieux ✂ / M. Brodeur (G) ✂	300.00

VINTAGE AUTOGRAPH

	Insert Set (40 cards):	**18,500**
	Insert	**PA**
☐	PA-3 Jean Béliveau, Mont. ✍ {*60}	125.00
☐	PA-6 Jean Béliveau, Mont. ✍ {*60}	125.00
☐	PA-27 Jean Béliveau, ✍ {*60}	125.00
☐	PA-29 Mike Bossy, ✍ {*80}	75.00
☐	PA-25 Butch Bouchard, ✍ {*90}	40.00
☐	PA-24 Johnny Bower (G), ✍ {*90}	40.00
☐	PA-21 Johnny Bucyk, ✍ {*90}	40.00
☐	PA-33 Gerry Cheevers (G), ✍ {*90}	40.00
☐	PA-34 Dino Ciccarelli, ✍ {*90}	40.00
☐	PA-31 Marcel Dionne, ✍ {*60}	100.00
☐	PA-9 Woody Dumart, ✍ {*20}	150.00
☐	PA-13 Phil Esposito, ✍ {*60}	100.00
☐	PA-37 Tony Esposito (G), ✍ {*60}	75.00
☐	PA-18 Bill Gadsby, ✍ {*90}	40.00
☐	PA-23 Mike Gartner, ✍ {*80}	50.00
☐	PA-14 Bernie Geoffrion, ✍ {*60}	75.00
☐	PA-2 Glenn Hall (G), ✍ {*90}	40.00
☐	PA-22 Dale Hawerchuk, ✍ {*80}	40.00
☐	PA-12 Gordie Howe, ✍ {*20}	400.00
☐	PA-26 Gordie Howe, ✍ {*20}	400.00
☐	PA-36 Gordie Howe, ✍ {*20}	400.00
☐	PA-40 Red Kelly, ✍ {*90}	40.00
☐	PA-32 Jari Kurri, ✍ {*80}	75.00
☐	PA-8 Elmer Lach, ✍ {*90}	40.00
☐	PA-28 Guy Lafleur, ✍ {*60}	150.00
☐	PA-39 Ted Lindsay, ✍ {*90}	50.00
☐	PA-1 Frank Mahovlich, ✍ {*20}	100.00
☐	PA-4 Frank Mahovlich, ✍ {*20}	100.00
☐	PA-19 Lanny McDonald, ✍ {*80}	50.00
☐	PA-35 Stan Mikita, ✍ {*60}	75.00
☐	PA-16 Dickie Moore, ✍ {*90}	40.00
☐	PA-20 Gilbert Perreault, ✍ {*60}	75.00
☐	PA-10 Chuck Rayner (G), ✍ {*90}	40.00
☐	PA-5 Henri Richard, ✍ {*90}	40.00
☐	PA-11 Henri Richard, ✍ {*90}	50.00
☐	PA-7 Milt Schmidt, ✍ {*90}	40.00
☐	PA-15 Dollard St-Laurent, ✍ {*90}	40.00
☐	PA-17 Jean-Guy Talbot, ✍ {*90}	40.00
☐	PA-30 Bryan Trottier, ✍ {*90}	50.00
☐	PA-38 Gump Worsley (G), ✍ {*90}	40.00
☐	53 Bill Barber, Phil. {*90} ✍	40.00
☐	42 Bobby Clarke, Phil. {*90} ✍	40.00
☐	52 Yvon Cournoyer, Mont. {*90} ✍	40.00
☐	50 Ron Hextall (G), Phil. {*90} ✍	65.00
☐	55 Dennis Hull, Chic. {*90} ✍	40.00
☐	46 Jacques Laperrière, Mont. {*90} ✍	40.00
☐	58 Guy Lapointe, Mont. {*90} ✍	40.00
☐	54 Reggie Leach, Phil. {*90} ✍	40.00
☐	47 Peter Mahovlich, Mont. {*90} ✍	40.00
☐	49 Cam Neely, Bost. {*90} ✍	65.00
☐	57 Bob Nystrom, NYIs. {*90} ✍	40.00
☐	56 Bernie Parent, Phil. {*90} ✍	55.00
☐	48 Denis Potvin, NYIs. {*90} ✍	55.00
☐	59 Larry Robinson, Mont. {*90} ✍	40.00
☐	45 Serge Savard, Mont. {*90} ✍	40.00
☐	43 Dave Schultz, Phil. {*90} ✍	40.00
☐	51 Steve Shutt, Mont. {*90} ✍	40.00
☐	41 Joe Watson, Phil. {*90} ✍	40.00
☐	44 Tiger Williams, Toro. {*90} ✍	40.00

VINTAGE MEMORABILIA

	Insert Set (30 cards):	**9,400**
	Insert	**PV**
☐	1 M. Richard [1955-56] Jersey ✂ {*90}	200.00
☐	2 M. Richard [1953-54] Number ✂ {*5}	1400.00
☐	3 M. Richard [1959-60] Emblem ✂ {*5}	1400.00
☐	4 J. Plante (G) [1955-56] Jersey ✂ {*90}	100.00
☐	5 J. Plante (G) [1960-61] Glove ✂ {*90}	125.00
☐	6 J. Plante (G) [1961-62] Emblem ✂ {*5}	800.00
☐	7 J. Plante (G) [1957-58] Number ✂ {*5}	800.00
☐	8 J. Plante (G) [1962-63] Stick ✂ {*90}	125.00
☐	9 B. Gadsby (G) [1953-54] Glove ✂ {*90}	50.00
☐	10 D. Harvey [1957-58] Jersey ✂ {*90}	100.00
☐	11 D. Harvey [1954-55] Emblem ✂ {*5}	700.00
☐	12 D. Harvey [1951-52] Number ✂ {*5}	700.00
☐	13 G. Howe [1963-64] Jersey ✂ {*40}	300.00
☐	14 G. Howe [1953-54] Emblem ✂ {*5}	1200.00
☐	15 G. Howe [1951-52] Number ✂ {*5}	1200.00
☐	16 B. Mosienko [1953-54] Pants ✂ {*90}	50.00
☐	17 J. Béliveau [1953-54] Jersey ✂ {*90}	100.00
☐	18 J. Béliveau [1963-64] Number ✂ {*5}	800.00
☐	19 J. Béliveau [1959-60] Emblem ✂ {*5}	800.00
☐	20 T. Broda (G) [1951-52] Glove ✂ {*90}	75.00
☐	21 T. Horton [1955-56] Pants ✂ {*90}	125.00
☐	22 H. Richard [1963-64] Jersey ✂ {*90}	50.00
☐	23 H. Richard [1957-58] Emblem ✂ {*5}	300.00
☐	24 C. Rayner (G) [1953-54] Glove ✂ {*90}	50.00
☐	25 T. Sawchuk (G) [1961-62] Glove ✂ {*90}	175.00
☐	26 T. Sawchuk (G) [1954-55] Pads ✂ {*90}	200.00
☐	27 T. Sawchuk (G) [1951-52] Jersey ✂ {*90}	150.00
☐	28 T. Lindsay [1954-55] Jersey ✂ {*90}	50.00
☐	29 T. Lindsay [1951-52] Emblem ✂ {*5}	400.00
☐	30 J. Bower (G) [1959-60] Pads ✂ {*90}	100.00

PARKHURST REPRINT

	Insert Set (150 cards):	**400.00**
	Insert	**Reprint**
☐	PR-1 G. Howe [1951-52 PH #66]	6.00
☐	PR-2 M. Richard [1957-58 PH #5]	6.00
☐	PR-3 B. Geoffrion [1962-63 PH #53]	4.00
☐	PR-4 B. Mosienko [1953-54 PH #80]	4.00
☐	PR-5 T. Sawchuk (G) [1952-53 PH #86]	4.00
☐	PR-6 W. Dumart [1953-54 PH #96]	4.00
☐	PR-7 D. Harvey [1955-56 PH #45]	4.00
☐	PR-8 F. Mahovlich [1963-64 PH #17]	4.00
☐	PR-9 J. Béliveau [1955-56 PH #74]	4.00
☐	PR-10 J. Plante (G) [1960-61 PH #53]	4.00
☐	PR-11 J. Talbot [1957-58 PH #9]	4.00
☐	PR-12 G. Howe [1962-63 PH #31]	6.00
☐	PR-13 T. Sawchuk (G) [1954-55 PH #33]	4.00
☐	PR-14 M. Richard [1952-53 PH #1]	6.00
☐	PR-15 H. Lumley (G) [1953-54 PH #1]	4.00
☐	PR-16 J. Béliveau [1955-56 PH #44]	4.00
☐	PR-17 R. Kelly [1963-64 PH #63]	4.00
☐	PR-18 B. Geoffrion [1951-52 PH #14]	4.00
☐	PR-19 D. Moore [1961-62 PH #36]	4.00
☐	PR-20 D. St-Laurent [1957-58 PH #10]	4.00
☐	PR-21 T. Sawchuk (G) [1963-64 PH #53]	4.00
☐	PR-22 H. Lumley (G) [1954-55 PH #16]	4.00
☐	PR-23 W. Dumart [1952-53 PH #72]	4.00
☐	PR-24 T. Horton [1953-54 PH #13]	4.00
☐	PR-25 G. Hainsworth (G) [1955-56 PH #59]	4.00
☐	PR-26 J. Bower (G) [1963-64 PH #5]	4.00
☐	PR-27 D. Harvey [1951-52 PH #10]	4.00
☐	PR-28 B. Gadsby [1961-62 PH #27]	4.00
☐	PR-29 D. Moore [1957-58 PH #14]	4.00
☐	PR-30 G. Howe [1962-63 PH #30]	6.00
☐	PR-31 R. Kelly [1954-55 PH #42]	4.00
☐	PR-32 B. Geoffrion [1952-53 PH #3]	4.00
☐	PR-33 J. Béliveau [1953-54 PH #27]	4.00
☐	PR-34 J. Plante (G) [1961-62 PH #49]	4.00
☐	PR-35 H. Richard [1963-64 PH #23]	4.00
☐	PR-36 C. Rayner (G) [1951-52 PH #104]	4.00
☐	PR-37 H. Richard [1961-62 PH #43]	4.00
☐	PR-38 F. Mahovlich [1957-58 PH #17]	4.00
☐	PR-39 B. Gadsby [1962-63 PH #25]	4.00
☐	PR-40 B. Geoffrion [1954-55 PH #8]	4.00
☐	PR-41 D. Harvey [1952-53 PH #14]	4.00
☐	PR-42 M. Richard [1953-54 PH #24]	6.00
☐	PR-43 G. Vézina (G) [1955-56 PH #56]	4.00
☐	PR-44 J. Talbot [1963-64 PH #22]	4.00
☐	PR-45 T. Sawchuk (G) [1951-52 PH #61]	4.00
☐	PR-46 T. Sawchuk (G) [1961-62 PH #31]	4.00
☐	PR-47 J. Plante (G) [1957-58 PH #15]	4.00
☐	PR-48 F. Mahovlich [1962-63 PH #18]	4.00
☐	PR-49 B. Gadsby [1954-55 PH #87]	4.00
☐	PR-50 E. Bouchard [1952-53 PH #13]	4.00
☐	PR-51 B. Geoffrion [1953-54 PH #29]	4.00
☐	PR-52 D. St-Laurent [1955-56 PH #48]	4.00
☐	PR-53 R. Kelly [1963-64 PH #3]	4.00
☐	PR-54 R. Kelly [1951-52 PH #55]	4.00
☐	PR-55 J. Bower (G) [1960-61 PH #3]	4.00
☐	PR-56 H. Richard [1957-58 PH #4]	4.00
☐	PR-57 B. Geoffrion [1962-63 PH #48]	4.00
☐	PR-58 Howe / Lumley [1954-55 PH #92]	4.00
☐	PR-59 C. Rayner (G) [1952-53 PH #22]	4.00
☐	PR-60 R. Kelly [1953-54 PH #40]	4.00
☐	PR-61 D. Moore [1955-56 PH #38]	4.00
☐	PR-62 B. Geoffrion [1963-64 PH #88]	4.00
☐	PR-63 E. Bouchard [1951-52 PH #3]	4.00
☐	PR-64 F. Mahovlich [1961-62 PH #2]	4.00
☐	PR-65 D. Harvey [1957-58 PH #1]	4.00
☐	PR-66 J. Plante (G) [1962-63 PH #49]	4.00
☐	PR-67 T. Horton [1961-62 PH #1]	4.00
☐	PR-68 D. St-Laurent [1952-53 PH #52]	4.00
☐	PR-69 B. Geoffrion [1960-61 PH #46]	4.00
☐	PR-70 E. Bouchard [1955-56 PH #46][	4.00
☐	PR-71 G. Howe	6.00
☐	PR-72 M. Schmidt [1951-52 PH #29]	4.00
☐	PR-73 E. Bouchard [1954-55 PH #6]	4.00
☐	PR-74 H. Richard [1958-59 PH #2]	4.00
☐	PR-75 T. Horton [1960-61 PH #1]	4.00
☐	PR-76 G. Howe [1963-64 PH #55]	6.00
☐	PR-77 D. Moore [1952-53 PH #10]	4.00
☐	PR-78 E. Lach [1953-54 PH #31]	4.00
☐	PR-79 B. Geoffrion [1955-56 PH #43]	4.00
☐	PR-80 J. Béliveau [1963-64 PH #89]	4.00
☐	PR-81 B. Gadsby [1951-52 PH #37]	4.00
☐	PR-82 J. Béliveau [1958-59 PH #34]	4.00
☐	PR-83 B. Gadsby [1963-64 PH #59]	4.00
☐	PR-84 H. Richard [1963-64 PH #82]	4.00
☐	PR-85 Sloan / Plante (G) [1954-55 PH #98]	4.00
☐	PR-86 F. Mahovlich [1960-61 PH #2]	4.00
☐	PR-87 T. Sawchuk (G) [1953-54 PH #46]	4.00
☐	PR-88 M. Richard [1955-56 PH #37]	6.00
☐	PR-89 T. Horton [1963-64 PH #16]	4.00
☐	PR-90 T. Lindsay [1951-52 PH #56]	4.00
☐	PR-91 J. Bower (G) [1958-59 PH #46]	4.00
☐	PR-92 M. Richard [1958-59 PH #38]	6.00
☐	PR-93 R. Kelly	4.00
☐	PR-94 D. Moore [1954-55 PH #2]	4.00
☐	PR-95 B. Gadsby [1952-53 PH #56]	4.00
☐	PR-96 T. Lindsay [1953-54 PH #52]	4.00
☐	PR-97 T. Horton [1955-56 PH #3]	4.00
☐	PR-98 B. Geoffrion [1963-64 PH #29]	4.00
☐	PR-99 W. Dumart [1951-52 PH #28]	4.00
☐	PR-100 D. Harvey [1958-59 PH #49]	4.00
☐	PR-101 F. Mahovlich [1958-59 PH #33]	4.00
☐	PR-102 D. Moore [1960-61 PH #38]	4.00
☐	PR-103 T. Horton [1954-55 PH #31]	4.00
☐	PR-104 H. Lumley (G) [1952-53 PH #59]	4.00
☐	PR-105 E. Bouchard [1953-54 PH #32]	4.00
☐	PR-106 T. Broda (G) [1955-56 PH #23]	4.00
☐	PR-107 J. Béliveau [1963-64 PH #30]	4.00
☐	PR-108 M. Richard [1951-52 PH #4]	6.00
☐	PR-109 R. Kelly [1962-63 PH #5]	4.00
☐	PR-110 J. Béliveau [1962-63 PH #39]	4.00
☐	PR-111 J. Talbot [1960-61 PH #52]	4.00
☐	PR-112 Geoffrion / Sawchuk (G) [1954-55 PH #100]	4.00
☐	PR-113 T. Horton [1952-53 PH #58]	4.00
☐	PR-114 D. St-Laurent [1953-54 PH #23]	4.00
☐	PR-115 D. Harvey [1958-59 PH #8]	4.00
☐	PR-116 G. Worsley (G) [1963-64 PH #98]	4.00
☐	PR-117 M. Schmidt [1952-53 PH #70]	4.00
☐	PR-118 J. Béliveau [1958-59 PH #6]	4.00
☐	PR-119 T. Horton [1962-63 PH #7]	4.00
☐	PR-120 D. Moore [1953-54 PH #28]	4.00
☐	PR-121 D. Harvey [1954-55 PH #14]	4.00
☐	PR-122 H. Richard [1959-60 PH #39]	4.00
☐	PR-123 M. Schmidt [1953-54 PH #92]	4.00
☐	PR-124 F. Mahovlich [1959-60 PH #24]	4.00
☐	PR-125 J. Bower (G) [1963-64 PH #65]	4.00
☐	PR-126 T. Lindsay [1952-53 PH #87]	4.00
☐	PR-127 T. Horton [1958-59 PH #42]	4.00
☐	PR-128 J. Plante (G) [1958-59 PH #22]	4.00
☐	PR-129 J. Talbot [1959-60 PH #49]	4.00
☐	PR-130 J. Béliveau [1961-62 PH #45]	4.00
☐	PR-131 D. Harvey [1960-61 PH #48]	4.00
☐	PR-132 G. Worsley (G) [1953-54 PH #53]	4.00
☐	PR-133 T. Sawchuk (G) [1960-61 PH #31]	4.00
☐	PR-134 F. Mahovlich [1963-64 PH #77]	4.00
☐	PR-135 B. Mosienko [1952-53 PH #27]	4.00
☐	PR-136 J. Béliveau [1954-55 PH #3]	4.00
☐	PR-137 T. Horton [1963-64 PH #76]	4.00
☐	PR-138 J. Plante (G) [1959-60 PH #41]	4.00
☐	PR-139 J. Bower (G) [1962-63 PH #16]	4.00
☐	PR-140 G. Howe	6.00
☐	PR-141 C. Rayner (G) [1953-54 PH #59]	4.00
☐	PR-142 H. Richard [1960-61 PH #47]	4.00
☐	PR-143 G. Worsley (G) [1963-64 PH #39]	4.00
☐	PR-144 R. Kelly [1952-53 PH #67]	4.00
☐	PR-145 D. Moore [1959-60 PH #14]	4.00
☐	PR-146 F. Mahovlich [1962-63 PH #4]	4.00
☐	PR-147 H. Richard [1962-63 PH #38]	4.00
☐	PR-148 J. Bower (G) [1959-60 PH #32]	4.00
☐	PR-149 R. Kelly	4.00
☐	PR-150 B. Gadsby [1953-54 PH #76]	4.00

WORLD CLASS

There are three versions to each card: the Jersey card (limited to 80), the Emblem card (limited to 20) and the In The Numbers card (limited to 20). Emblem and In The Numbers cards usually sell for the same price.

	Insert Set (8 cards):	**900**	**400.00**
	Insert	**WC20**	**WC80**
☐☐☐	Steve Yzerman, Detr. ✂	480.00	225.00
☐☐☐	Teemu Selänne, SanJ. ✂	160.00	75.00
☐☐☐	Olaf Kölzig (G), Wash. ✂	120.00	50.00
☐☐☐	Zigmund Palffy, LosA. ✂	120.00	50.00
☐☐☐	Peter Forsberg, Colo. ✂	280.00	125.00
☐☐☐	Mike Modano, Dall. ✂	200.00	100.00
☐☐☐	Jaromir Jagr, Wash. ✂	200.00	100.00
☐☐☐	Alexei Yashin, NYIs. ✂	120.00	50.00

2001 - 02 PRIVATE STOCK

Produced by Pacific Trading Cards, this series was released in January 2002. There are five versions for each card 1-100: a hobby red-foil base card, a hobby gold-foil parallel (#/106), a hobby Premiere Date parallel (#/100), a retail blue-foil base card, and a retail silver-foil parallel (#/108). Hobby red-foil base cards have the same value as retail blue-foil base cards. Premiere Date parallel cards are slightly more expensive (1-5%) than gold-foil and silver-foil parallel cards.

	Shell Set (100 cards):	**-**	**40.00**
	Complete Set (140 cards):	**900**	**500.00**
	Common Player:	**6.00**	**.25**
	Description	**PD100**	**Base**
☐☐☐☐☐	1 J. Friesen	6.00	.25
☐☐☐☐☐	2 P. Kariya	25.00	2.00
☐☐☐☐☐	3 M. Hnilicka (G)	6.00	.25
☐☐☐☐☐	4 P. Stefan	6.00	.25
☐☐☐☐☐	5 B. Guerin	6.00	.50
☐☐☐☐☐	6 S. Samsonov	10.00	.50
☐☐☐☐☐	7 J. Thornton	20.00	1.50
☐☐☐☐☐	8 M. Biron (G)	6.00	.50
☐☐☐☐☐	9 T. Connolly	6.00	.50
☐☐☐☐☐	10 J. Dumont	6.00	.25
☐☐☐☐☐	11 J. Iginla	15.00	1.00
☐☐☐☐☐	12 M. Savard	6.00	.25
☐☐☐☐☐	13 R. Turek (G)	6.00	.50
☐☐☐☐☐	14 R. Francis	10.00	.50
☐☐☐☐☐	15 A. Irbe (G)	6.00	.50
☐☐☐☐☐	16 J. O'Neill	6.00	.50
☐☐☐☐☐	17 T. Amonte	10.00	.50
☐☐☐☐☐	18 S. Sullivan	6.00	.25
☐☐☐☐☐	19 J. Thibault (G)	6.00	.50
☐☐☐☐☐	20 R. Blake	10.00	.50
☐☐☐☐☐	21 C. Drury	10.00	.50
☐☐☐☐☐	22 M. Hejduk	15.00	1.00
☐☐☐☐☐	23 P. Roy (G)	60.00	4.50
☐☐☐☐☐	24 J. Sakic	30.00	2.00
☐☐☐☐☐	25 A. Tanguay	10.00	.50
☐☐☐☐☐	26 E. Knutsen	6.00	.25
☐☐☐☐☐	27 R. Tugnutt (G)	6.00	.50
☐☐☐☐☐	28 E. Belfour (G)	20.00	1.50
☐☐☐☐☐	29 M. Modano	20.00	1.50
☐☐☐☐☐	30 J. Nieuwendyk	6.00	.50
☐☐☐☐☐	31 P. Turgeon	6.00	.50
☐☐☐☐☐	32 S. Fedorov	20.00	1.50
☐☐☐☐☐	33 D. Hasek (G)	20.00	1.50
☐☐☐☐☐	34 B. Hull	20.00	1.50
☐☐☐☐☐	35 N. Lidström	10.00	.50
☐☐☐☐☐	36 L. Robitaille	15.00	1.00

□□□□□	37 B. Shanahan	20.00	1.50
□□□□□	38 S. Yzerman	45.00	3.50
□□□□□	39 M. Comrie	15.00	1.00
□□□□□	40 T. Salo (G)	6.00	.50
□□□□□	41 R. Smyth	6.00	.50
□□□□□	42 P. Bure	15.00	1.00
□□□□□	43 R. Luongo (G)	15.00	1.00
□□□□□	44 J. Allison	10.00	.50
□□□□□	45 Z. Palffy	10.00	.50
□□□□□	46 F. Potvin (G)	20.00	.50
□□□□□	47 M. Fernandez (G)	6.00	.50
□□□□□	48 M. Gaborik	20.00	1.50
□□□□□	49 Y. Perreault	6.00	.25
□□□□□	50 B. Savage	6.00	.25
□□□□□	51 J. Théodore (G)	20.00	1.50
□□□□□	52 M. Dunham (G)	6.00	.50
□□□□□	53 D. Legwand	6.00	.50
□□□□□	54 J. Arnott	6.00	.50
□□□□□	55 M. Brodeur (G)	30.00	2.00
□□□□□	56 P. Elias	15.00	1.00
□□□□□	57 S. Gomez	6.00	.50
□□□□□	58 C. Osgood (G)	10.00	.50
□□□□□	59 M. Peca	6.00	.50
□□□□□	60 A. Yashin	10.00	.50
□□□□□	61 T. Fleury	10.00	.50
□□□□□	62 B. Leetch	10.00	.50
□□□□□	63 E. Lindros	20.00	1.50
□□□□□	64 M. Messier	20.00	1.50
□□□□□	65 M. Richter (G)	6.00	.50
□□□□□	66 D. Alfredsson	20.00	.50
□□□□□	67 M. Havlat	10.00	.50
□□□□□	68 M. Hossa	20.00	1.50
□□□□□	69 P. Lalime (G)	10.00	.50
□□□□□	70 R. Cechmanek (G)	6.00	.50
□□□□□	71 S. Gagné	15.00	1.00
□□□□□	72 J. LeClair	15.00	1.00
□□□□□	73 M. Recchi	6.00	.50
□□□□□	74 J. Roenick	15.00	1.00
□□□□□	75 S. Burke (G)	10.00	.50
□□□□□	76 D. Langkow	6.00	.25
□□□□□	77 A. Kovalev	10.00	.50
□□□□□	78 M. Lemieux	60.00	4.50
□□□□□	79 M. Straka	6.00	.25
□□□□□	80 B. Johnson (G)	6.00	.50
□□□□□	81 C. Pronger	10.00	.50
□□□□□	82 K. Tkachuk	10.00	.50
□□□□□	83 D. Weight	10.00	.50
□□□□□	84 P. Marleau	6.00	.50
□□□□□	85 E. Nabokov (G)	10.00	.50
□□□□□	86 O. Nolan	10.00	.50
□□□□□	87 T. Selänne	15.00	1.00
□□□□□	88 V. Lecavalier	20.00	1.50
□□□□□	89 B. Richards	6.00	.50
□□□□□	90 C. Joseph (G)	20.00	1.50
□□□□□	91 A. Mogilny	6.00	.50
□□□□□	92 M. Sundin	20.00	1.50
□□□□□	93 D. Cloutier (G)	6.00	.50
□□□□□	94 M. Näslund	20.00	1.50
□□□□□	95 D. Sedin	6.00	.50
□□□□□	96 H. Sedin	6.00	.50
□□□□□	97 P. Bondra	10.00	.50
□□□□□	98 J. Jagr	20.00	1.50
□□□□□	99 O. Kölzig (G)	10.00	.50
□□□□□	100 A. Oates	6.00	.50

ROOKIES

There are five versions for each Rookie subset card 101-140: a hobby red-foil base card, a hobby gold-foil parallel (#/106), a hobby Premiere Date parallel (#/100), a retail blue-foil base card, and a retail silver-foil parallel (#/108). Premiere Date parallel cards are slightly more expensive (1-5%) than gold-foil and silver-foil parallel cards. Base cards 111-140 are serial-numbered: hobby red-foil cards to 414 and retail blue-foil cards to 450.

	Description	Blue	PD100	Red
□□□□□	101 D. Heatley	25.00	20.00	25.00
□□□□□	102 M. Bell	6.00	5.00	6.00
□□□□□	103 R. Klesla	15.00	12.00	8.00
□□□□□	104 J. Williams	6.00	5.00	6.00
□□□□□	105 R. DiPietro (G)	12.00	9.00	12.00
□□□□□	106 P. Brendl	8.00	6.00	8.00
□□□□□	107 K. Beech	8.00	6.00	8.00
□□□□□	108 J. Hedberg (G)	10.00	8.00	10.00
□□□□□	109 Mi. Kiprusoff (G)	8.00	6.00	8.00
□□□□□	110 B. Allen	4.00	5.00	4.00
□□□□□	**111 I. Bryzgalov (G) RC**	**20.00**	**10.00**	**25.00**
□□□□□	**112 T. Pärssinen RC**	**10.00**	**10.00**	**15.00**
□□□□□	**113 I. Kovalchuk RC**	**135.00**	**100.00**	**125.00**
□□□□□	**114 K. Piros RC**	**15.00**	**10.00**	**20.00**
□□□□□	**115 B. Pothier RC**	**10.00**	**10.00**	**15.00**
□□□□□	**116 J. Hentunen RC**	**10.00**	**10.00**	**15.00**
□□□□□	**117 E. Cole RC**	**25.00**	**10.00**	**30.00**
□□□□□	**118 V. Nedorost RC**	**25.00**	**10.00**	**30.00**
□□□□□	**119 N. Kapanen RC**	**25.00**	**10.00**	**30.00**
□□□□□	**120 P. Datsyuk RC**	**90.00**	**60.00**	**100.00**
□□□□□	**121 J. Chimera RC**	**15.00**	**10.00**	**20.00**
□□□□□	**122 N. Hagman RC**	**15.00**	**10.00**	**20.00**
□□□□□	**123 K. Huselius RC**	**35.00**	**15.00**	**40.00**
□□□□□	**124 J. Bednar RC**	**15.00**	**10.00**	**20.00**
□□□□□	**125 P. Dupuis RC**	**25.00**	**10.00**	**30.00**
□□□□□	**126 N. Schultz RC**	**15.00**	**10.00**	**20.00**
□□□□□	**127 F. Bélanger RC**	**10.00**	**10.00**	**15.00**
□□□□□	**128 M. Erat RC**	**15.00**	**10.00**	**20.00**
□□□□□	**129 Clemmensen (G) RC**	**15.00**	**10.00**	**20.00**
□□□□□	**130 R. Martinek RC**	**10.00**	**10.00**	**15.00**
□□□□□	**131 D. Blackburn (G) RC**	**45.00**	**20.00**	**50.00**
□□□□□	**132 P. Smrek RC**	**10.00**	**10.00**	**15.00**
□□□□□	**133 C. Neil RC**	**10.00**	**10.00**	**15.00**
□□□□□	**134 J. Dopita RC**	**15.00**	**10.00**	**20.00**
□□□□□	**135 D. Cullen RC**	**10.00**	**10.00**	**15.00**
□□□□□	**136 K. Kolanos RC**	**25.00**	**10.00**	**30.00**
□□□□□	**137 J. Jillson RC**	**15.00**	**10.00**	**20.00**
□□□□□	**138 M. Rycroft RC**	**10.00**	**10.00**	**15.00**
□□□□□	**139 N. Alexeev RC**	**25.00**	**10.00**	**30.00**
□□□□□	**140 B. Sutherby RC**	**15.00**	**10.00**	**20.00**

AUTHENTIC GAME USED GEAR

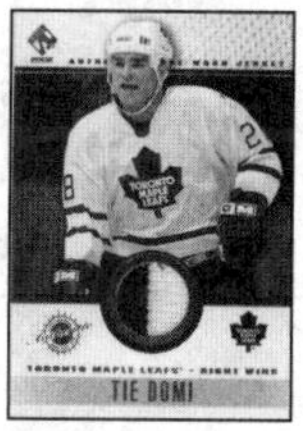

These cards feature either a swatch of a game-worn jersey or a game-used stick.

	Insert Set (98 cards):	**1,400**
	Insert	**GWJ**
□	Tony Amonte ✄ Red	15.00
□	Jean-Sébastien Aubin (G) ✄	10.00
□	Per Axelsson ✄ White	10.00
□	Stu Barnes ✄	10.00
□	Shawn Bates ✄ White	10.00
□	Shawn Bates ✄ Blue	10.00
□	Ed Belfour (G) ✄ Black	25.00
□	Peter Bondra ✄ Black	15.00
□	Fred Brathwaite (G) ✄ Red	10.00
□	Pavel Brendl ✄	10.00
□	Rod Brind'Amour ✄ Stick {*200}	20.00
□	Valeri Bure ✄ {*275}	25.00
□	Sean Burke (G) ✄	15.00
□	Kyle Calder ✄	10.00
□	Anson Carter ✄ {*130}	25.00
□	Andrew Cassels ✄	10.00
□	Craig Conroy ✄ Blue	10.00
□	Mariusz Czerkawski ✄ Blue	10.00
□	Byron Dafoe (G) ✄ Black	10.00
□	Vincent Damphousse ✄ {*400}	15.00
□	Éric Dazé ✄ {*660}	10.00
□	Shane Doan ✄ Black	10.00
□	Tie Domi ✄	10.00
□	Tie Domi ✄ Blue/White	12.00
□	Chris Drury ✄ Stick {*200}	35.00
□	Jean-Pierre Dumont ✄	10.00
□	Mike Dunham (G) ✄	10.00
□	Mike Eastwood ✄ Blue	10.00
□	Rico Fata ✄	10.00
□	Tom Fitzgerald ✄ Blue	10.00
□	Peter Forsberg ✄ {*250}	50.00
□	Jean-Sébastien Giguère (G) ✄	20.00
□	Dominik Hasek (G) ✄ {*650}	20.00
□	Derian Hatcher ✄ Black	10.00
□	Jochen Hecht ✄ Blue	10.00
□	Bobby Holik ✄ White	10.00
□	Bobby Holik ✄ Red	10.00
□	Jan Hrdina ✄ Black	10.00
□	Brett Hull ✄ {*330}	30.00
□	Jarome Iginla ✄	20.00
□	Jaromir Jagr ✄	25.00
□	Kenny Jönsson ✄	10.00
□	Curtis Joseph (G) ✄ {*400}	25.00
□	Paul Kariya ✄ Teal	35.00
□	Paul Kariya ✄ White/Teal	50.00
□	Paul Kariya ✄ White	35.00
□	Saku Koivu ✄ {<750} Blue	15.00
□	Saku Koivu ✄ {<750} Red	15.00
□	Ilya Kovalchuk ✄ Stick {*200}	90.00
□	Alexei Kovalev ✄	15.00
□	Milan Kraft ✄	15.00
□	Jamie Langenbrunner ✄ Green	10.00
□	Vincent Lecavalier ✄ {*500}	25.00
□	John LeClair ✄ {*225}	30.00
□	Mike Leclerc ✄	10.00
□	Mario Lemieux ✄ {*500} Yellow	75.00
□	Eric Lindros ✄ {*500}	25.00
□	Grant Marshall ✄	10.00
□	Jay McKee ✄ {*60}	30.00
□	Jamie McLennan (G) ✄ Blue	10.00
□	Aaron Miller ✄ White	10.00
□	Boris Mironov ✄ White	10.00
□	Mike Modano ✄ White	25.00
□	Ian Moran ✄	10.00
□	Aleksey Morozov ✄	10.00
□	Petr Nedved ✄ Blue	10.00
□	Joe Nieuwendyk ✄ White	10.00
□	Michael Nylander ✄	10.00
□	Jeff O'Neill ✄ Stick {*200}	25.00
□	Chris Osgood (G) ✄ White	15.00
□	Félix Potvin (G) ✄ {*460}	15.00
□	Wayne Primeau ✄	10.00
□	Rob Ray ✄	10.00
□	Robert Reichel ✄ Stick {*200}	20.00
□	Mike Richter (G) ✄ White	10.00
□	Cliff Ronning ✄ White	10.00
□	Cliff Ronning ✄ Blue	10.00
□	Patrick Roy (G) ✄ {*500} Burgandy	75.00
□	Michal Rozsival ✄ White	10.00
□	Steve Rucchin ✄ Teal	10.00
□	Joe Sakic ✄	40.00
□	Marc Savard ✄	10.00
□	Teemu Selänne ✄ White	20.00
□	Brendan Shanahan ✄ White	25.00
□	Blake Sloan ✄	10.00
□	Richard Smehlik ✄ {*49}	10.00
□	Ryan Smyth ✄ {*650}	10.00
□	Kevin Stevens ✄ White	10.00
□	Kevin Stevens ✄ Yellow	10.00
□	Cory Stillman ✄ Red	10.00
□	M. Straka ✄ Yellow	10.00
□	Steve Sullivan ✄ White	10.00
□	Mats Sundin ✄ Blue	10.00
□	Robert Svehla ✄	10.00
□	Darryl Sydor ✄	10.00
□	José Théodore (G) ✄ Blue	30.00
□	Jocelyn Thibault (G) ✄	10.00
□	Roman Turek (G) ✄	10.00
□	Pierre Turgeon ✄ Blue	10.00
□	Oleg Tverdovsky ✄ Teal	10.00
□	Doug Weight ✄ {*640}	10.00
□	Scott Young ✄	10.00
□	Steve Yzerman ✄ White	60.00
□	Steve Yzerman ✄ Red	60.00
□	Alexei Zhamnov ✄	10.00
□	Sergei Zubov ✄	10.00

AUTHENTIC GAME USED GEAR PATCH VARIATION

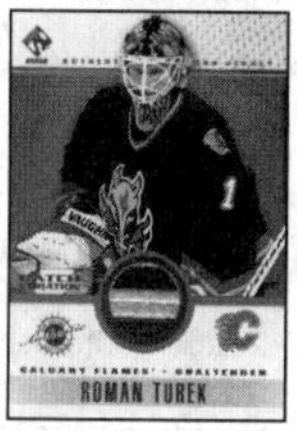

	Insert Set (93 cards):	**2,600**
	Insert	**Patch**
□	Tony Amonte ✄ {*400}	25.00
□	Jean-Sébastien Aubin (G) ✄ {*430}	20.00
□	Per Axelsson ✄ {*131}	20.00
□	Stu Barnes ✄ {*466}	20.00
□	Shawn Bates ✄ {*225}	20.00
□	Ed Belfour (G)	
□	Peter Bondra ✄ {*375}	25.00
□	Fred Brathwaite (G) ✄ {*525}	20.00
□	Pavel Brendl ✄ {*275}	20.00
□	Valeri Bure ✄ {*136}	55.00
□	Sean Burke (G) ✄ {*225}	35.00
□	Kyle Calder ✄ {*400}	20.00
□	Anson Carter ✄ {*8}	200.00
□	Andrew Cassels ✄ {*400}	20.00
□	Craig Conroy ✄ {*425}	20.00
□	Mariusz Czerkawski ✄ {*500}	20.00
□	Byron Dafoe (G) ✄ {*163}	25.00
□	Vincent Damphousse ✄ {*305}	30.00
□	Éric Dazé ✄ {*125}	25.00
□	Shane Doan ✄ {*110}	20.00
□	Tie Domi ✄ {*318}	20.00
□	Jean-Pierre Dumont ✄ {*400}	20.00
□	Mike Dunham (G) ✄ {*95}	30.00
□	Mike Eastwood ✄ {*425}	20.00
□	Rico Fata ✄ {*400}	20.00
□	Tom Fitzgerald ✄ {*135}	20.00
□	Dominik Hasek (G)	
□	Derian Hatcher ✄ {*100}	25.00
□	Jochen Hecht ✄ {*400}	20.00
□	Bobby Holik ✄ {*215}	20.00
□	Jan Hrdina ✄ {*480}	20.00
□	Brett Hull	
□	Jarome Iginla ✄ {*226}	50.00
□	Jaromir Jagr ✄ {*300}	55.00
□	Kenny Jönsson ✄ {*415}	20.00
□	Curtis Joseph (G)	
□	Paul Kariya ✄ {*375}	65.00
□	Saku Koivu ✄ {*85}	100.00
□	Alexei Kovalev ✄ {*525}	20.00
□	Milan Kraft ✄ {*330}	30.00
□	Jamie Langenbrunner ✄ {*500}	20.00
□	Vincent Lecavalier ✄ {*169}	65.00
□	John LeClair ✄ {*185}	50.00
□	Mike Leclerc ✄ {*210}	20.00
□	David Legwand ✄ {*365}	20.00
□	Mario Lemieux ✄ {*20}	375.00
□	Eric Lindros ✄ {*250}	60.00
□	Grant Marshall ✄ {*196}	20.00
□	Jay McKee ✄ {*315}	20.00
□	Jamie McLennan (G) ✄ {*400}	20.00
□	Aaron Miller ✄ {*235}	20.00
□	Boris Mironov ✄ {*258}	20.00
□	Mike Modano ✄ {*129}	70.00
□	Ian Moran ✄ {*525}	20.00
□	Aleksey Morozov ✄ {*465}	20.00
□	Petr Nedved ✄ {*400}	20.00
□	Joe Nieuwendyk ✄ {*230}	25.00
□	Michael Nylander ✄ {*500}	20.00
□	Chris Osgood (G) ✄ {*56}	60.00
□	Félix Potvin (G) ✄ {*87}	105.00
□	Wayne Primeau ✄ {*300}	20.00
□	Rob Ray ✄ {*281}	20.00
□	Mike Richter (G) ✄ {*400}	20.00
□	Jeremy Roenick ✄ {*290}	40.00
□	Cliff Ronning ✄ {*400}	20.00
□	Patrick Roy (G) ✄ {*75}	210.00
□	Michal Rozsival ✄ {*525}	20.00
□	Steve Rucchin ✄ {*45}	20.00
□	Joe Sakic ✄ {*500}	65.00
□	Marc Savard ✄ {*425}	20.00
□	Teemu Selänne ✄ {*39}	90.00
□	Brendan Shanahan	
□	Blake Sloan ✄ {*215}	20.00
□	Richard Smehlik ✄ {*250}	20.00
□	Ryan Smyth ✄ {*35}	60.00
□	Kevin Stevens	
□	Cory Stillman ✄ {*500}	20.00
□	Martin Straka ✄ {*525}	20.00
□	Steve Sullivan ✄ {*500}	20.00
□	Mats Sundin ✄ {*400}	20.00
□	Robert Svehla ✄ {*475}	20.00
□	Darryl Sydor ✄ {*440}	20.00
□	José Théodore (G) ✄ {*425}	55.00
□	Jocelyn Thibault (G) ✄ {*80}	35.00
□	Roman Turek (G) ✄ {*283}	25.00
□	Pierre Turgeon ✄ {*400}	20.00
□	Oleg Tverdovsky ✄ {*400}	20.00
□	Doug Weight ✄ {*90}	45.00
□	Alexei Yashin ✄ {*140}	40.00
□	Scott Young ✄ {*400}	20.00
□	Steve Yzerman ✄ {*115}	170.00
□	Alexei Zhamnov ✄ {*424}	20.00
□	Sergei Zubov ✄ {*120}	20.00

GOALIE RESERVE

	Insert Set (10 cards):	**70.00**
	Insert	**GR**
□	1 Martin Biron (G), Buff.	5.00
□	2 Patrick Roy (G), Colo.	30.00
□	3 Ed Belfour (G), Dall.	10.00
□	4 Dominik Hasek (G), Detr.	10.00
□	5 Tommy Salo (G), Edmo.	5.00
□	6 Roberto Luongo (G), Flor.	8.00
□	7 Martin Brodeur (G), NJer.	16.00
□	8 Roman Cechmanek (G), Phil.	5.00
□	9 Evgeni Nabokov (G), SanJ.	6.00
□	10 Curtis Joseph (G), Toro.	10.00

MOMENTS IN TIME

	Insert Set (10 cards):	275.00
	Insert (#/85)	**MIT**
☐	1 Dany Heatley, Atla.	85.00
☐	2 Ilya Kovalchuk, Atla.	85.00
☐	3 Vaclav Nedorost, Colo.	20.00
☐	4 Rostislav Klesla, Colu.	25.00
☐	5 Jaroslav Bednar, LosA.	12.00
☐	6 Rick DiPietro (G), NYIs.	40.00
☐	7 Dan Blackburn (G), NYRa.	35.00
☐	8 Pavel Brendl, Phil.	25.00
☐	9 Krys Kolanos, Phoe.	20.00
☐	10 Johan Hedberg (G), Pitt.	25.00

PRIVATE STOCK RESERVE

	Insert Set (20 cards):	140.00
	Insert	**PSR**
☐	1 Paul Kariya, Anah.	10.00
☐	2 Joe Thornton, Bost.	10.00
☐	3 Joe Sakic, Colo.	15.00
☐	4 Brendan Shanahan, Detr.	10.00
☐	5 Steve Yzerman, Detr.	20.00
☐	6 Mike Comrie, Edmo.	5.00
☐	7 Pavel Bure, Flor.	5.00
☐	8 Zigmund Palffy, LosA.	5.00
☐	9 Marian Gaborik, MinW.	10.00
☐	10 Alexei Yashin, NYIs.	5.00
☐	11 Eric Lindros, NYRa.	10.00
☐	12 Martin Havlat, Otta.	5.00
☐	13 John LeClair, Phil.	5.00
☐	14 Jeremy Roenick, Phil.	5.00
☐	15 Mario Lemieux, Pitt.	30.00
☐	16 Keith Tkachuk, Slou.	5.00
☐	17 Teemu Selänne, SanJ.	5.00
☐	18 Vincent Lecavalier, Tamp.	10.00
☐	19 Mats Sundin, Toro.	10.00
☐	20 Jaromir Jagr, Wash.	10.00

ROOKIE RESERVE

	Insert Set (10 cards):	80.00
	Insert	**RR**
☐	1 Dany Heatley, Atla.	25.00
☐	2 Ilya Kovalchuk, Atla.	25.00
☐	3 Vaclav Nedorost, Colo.	6.00
☐	4 Pavel Datsyuk, Detr.	20.00
☐	5 Jaroslav Bednar, LosA.	5.00
☐	6 Dan Blackburn (G), NYRa.	10.00
☐	7 Pavel Brendl, Phil.	8.00
☐	8 Krys Kolanos, Phoe.	6.00
☐	9 Kris Beech, Pitt.	8.00
☐	10 Nikita Alexeev, Tamp.	6.00

PS-2002

Size: 3.8 x 6.7 cm.

	Shell Set (75 cards):	25.00
	Complete Set (102 cards):	355.00
	Insert (2:1)	**PS2002**
☐	1 Paul Kariya, Anah.	1.50
☐	2 Steve Shields (G), Anah.	.30
☐	3 Ray Ferraro, Atla.	.30
☐	4 Byron Dafoe (G), Bost.	.50
☐	5 Joe Thornton, Bost.	1.50
☐	6 Stu Barnes, Buff.	.30
☐	7 Martin Biron (G), Buff.	.50
☐	8 Miroslav Satan, Buff.	.30
☐	9 Jarome Iginla, Calg.	1.00
☐	10 Derek Morris, Calg.	.30
☐	11 Sami Kapanen, Caro.	.30
☐	12 Jeff O'Neill, Caro.	.50
☐	13 Éric Dazé, Chic.	.50
☐	14 Jocelyn Thibault (G), Chic.	.50
☐	15 David Aebischer (G), Colo.	.30
☐	16 Chris Drury, Colo.	.50
☐	17 Peter Forsberg, Colo.	1.50
☐	18 Patrick Roy (G), Colo.	3.50
☐	19 Joe Sakic, Colo.	2.00
☐	20 Marc Denis (G), Colu.	.50
☐	21 Geoff Sanderson, Colu.	.30
☐	22 Ed Belfour (G), Dall.	1.00
☐	23 Mike Modano, Dall.	1.00
☐	24 Marty Turco (G), Dall.	.50
☐	25 Pat Verbeek, Dall.	.30
☐	26 Dominik Hasek (G), Detr.	1.00
☐	27 Brett Hull, Detr.	1.00
☐	28 Brendan Shanahan, Detr.	1.00
☐	29 Steve Yzerman, Detr.	3.00
☐	30 Mike Comrie, Edmo.	1.00
☐	31 Tommy Salo (G), Edmo.	.50
☐	32 Ryan Smyth, Edmo.	.50
☐	33 Pavel Bure, Flor.	1.00
☐	34 Roberto Luongo (G), Flor.	1.00
☐	35 Jason Allison, LosA.	.50
☐	36 Zigmund Palffy, LosA.	.50
☐	37 Félix Potvin (G), LosA.	.50
☐	38 Marian Gaborik, MinW.	1.00
☐	39 Doug Gilmour, Mont.	.50
☐	40 Jeff Hackett (G), Mont.	.30
☐	41 Joé Juneau, Mont.	.30
☐	42 Cliff Ronning, Nash.	.30
☐	43 Jason Arnott, NJer.	.50
☐	44 Martin Brodeur (G), NJer.	2.00
☐	45 Michael Peca, NYIs.	.50
☐	46 Alexei Yashin, NYIs.	.50
☐	47 Zdeno Ciger, NYRa.	.30
☐	48 Eric Lindros, NYRa.	1.00
☐	49 Mark Messier, NYRa.	1.00
☐	50 Petr Nedved, NYRa.	.30
☐	51 Radek Bonk, Otta.	.30
☐	52 Martin Havlat, Otta.	.50
☐	53 Roman Cechmanek (G), Phil.	.50
☐	54 John LeClair, Phil.	1.00
☐	55 Jeremy Roenick, Phil.	1.00
☐	56 Sean Burke (G), Phoe.	.50
☐	57 Shane Doan, Phoe.	.30
☐	58 Robert Lang, Pitt.	.30
☐	59 Mario Lemieux, Pitt.	3.50
☐	60 Fred Brathwaite (G), Slou.	.30
☐	61 Chris Pronger, Slou.	.50
☐	62 Keith Tkachuk, Slou.	.50
☐	63 Doug Weight, Slou.	.50
☐	64 Evgeni Nabokov (G), SanJ.	.50
☐	65 Owen Nolan, SanJ.	.50
☐	66 Teemu Selänne, SanJ.	1.00
☐	67 Nikolai Khabibulin (G), Tamp.	.50
☐	68 Vincent Lecavalier, Tamp.	1.00
☐	69 Brad Richards, Tamp.	.50
☐	70 Curtis Joseph (G), Toro.	1.00
☐	71 Mats Sundin, Toro.	1.00
☐	72 Andrew Cassels, Vanc.	.30
☐	73 Brendan Morrison, Vanc.	.30
☐	74 Peter Bondra, Wash.	.50
☐	75 Jaromir Jagr, Wash.	1.00

PS-2002 ROOKIES

Size: 3.8 x 6.7 cm.

Rookies 76-92 are short-printed (in comparison to cards 1-75).

Rookies 93-102 are short-printed and serial-numberd (#/50).

	Description	**Rookie**
☐	76 Ilja Bryzgalov (G), Anah.	3.00
☐	77 Timo Pärssinen, Anah.	1.00
☐	78 Erik Cole, Caro.	3.00
☐	79 Mark Bell, Chic.	2.00
☐	80 Pavel Datsyuk, Detr.	12.00
☐	81 Jason Williams, Detr.	2.00
☐	82 Jaroslav Bednar, LosA.	2.00
☐	83 Scott Clemmensen (G), NJer.	2.00
☐	84 Pavel Brendl, Phil.	3.00
☐	85 Jiri Dopita, Phil.	2.00
☐	86 Kris Beech, Pitt.	3.00
☐	87 Mark Rycroft, Slou.	1.00
☐	88 Jeff Jillson, SanJ.	2.00
☐	89 Miikka Kiprusoff (G), SanJ.	3.00
☐	90 Nikita Alexeev, Tamp.	3.00
☐	91 Bryan Allen, Vanc.	1.00
☐	92 Brian Sutherby, Wash.	2.00
	Description	**Rookie**
☐	93 Dany Heatley, Atla.	55.00
☐	94 Ilya Kovalchuk, Atla.	110.00
☐	95 Vaclav Nedorost, Colo.	40.00
☐	96 Rostislav Klesla, Colu.	45.00
☐	97 Kristian Huselius, Flor.	40.00
☐	98 Martin Erat, Nash.	40.00
☐	99 Rick DiPietro, NYIs.	40.00
☐	100 Dan Blackburn (G), NYRa.	40.00
☐	101 Krys Kolanos, Phoe.	40.00
☐	102 Johan Hedberg (G), Pitt.	40.00

2001 - 02 PRIVATE STOCK TITANIUM

Produced by Pacific Trading Cards, this series was released in April 2002. There are four versions for each card 1-144: the regular card, the Red hobby parallel (#/94), the Premiere Date parallel (#/94), and the retail parallel (#/131).

	Shell Set (144 cards):	600	400.00	60.00
	Common Player:	4.00	3.00	.50
	Description	**PD94**	**P131**	**Base**
☐☐☐☐	1 Jeff Friesen, Anah.	5.00	5.00	.50
☐☐☐☐	2 J-S Giguère (G), Anah.	20.00	10.00	1.00
☐☐☐☐	3 Paul Kariya, Anah.	35.00	20.00	2.00
☐☐☐☐	4 Dany Heatley, Atla.	50.00	35.00	3.50
☐☐☐☐	5 Milan Hnilicka (G), Atla.	5.00	3.00	.50
☐☐☐☐	6 Patrik Stefan, Atla.	5.00	5.00	.50
☐☐☐☐	7 Byron Dafoe (G), Bost.	10.00	5.00	.50
☐☐☐☐	8 Bill Guerin, Bost.	10.00	5.00	.50
☐☐☐☐	9 Brian Rolston, Bost.	5.00	5.00	.50
☐☐☐☐	10 Sergei Samsonov, Bost.	15.00	10.00	1.00
☐☐☐☐	11 Joe Thornton, Bost.	30.00	20.00	2.00
☐☐☐☐	12 Stu Barnes, Buff.	4.00	3.00	.50
☐☐☐☐	13 Martin Biron (G), Buff. (G)	10.00	5.00	.50
☐☐☐☐	14 Tim Connolly, Buff.	10.00	5.00	.50
☐☐☐☐	15 Jean-Pierre Dumont, Buff.	5.00	3.00	.50
☐☐☐☐	16 Miroslav Satan, Buff.	5.00	5.00	.50
☐☐☐☐	17 Craig Conroy, Calg.	5.00	5.00	.50
☐☐☐☐	18 Jarome Iginla, Calg.	20.00	10.00	1.00
☐☐☐☐	19 Dean McAmmond, Calg.	4.00	3.00	.50
☐☐☐☐	20 Derek Morris, Calg.	5.00	3.00	.50
☐☐☐☐	21 Marc Savard, Calg.	5.00	3.00	.50
☐☐☐☐	22 Roman Turek (G), Calg.	10.00	5.00	.50
☐☐☐☐	23 Tom Barrasso (G), Caro.	10.00	5.00	.50
☐☐☐☐	24 Ron Francis, Caro.	15.00	10.00	1.00
☐☐☐☐	25 Arturs Irbe (G), Caro.	10.00	5.00	.50
☐☐☐☐	26 Sami Kapanen, Caro.	5.00	5.00	.50
☐☐☐☐	27 Jeff O'Neill, Caro.	10.00	5.00	.50
☐☐☐☐	28 Tony Amonte, Chic.	15.00	10.00	1.00
☐☐☐☐	29 Mark Bell, Chic.	5.00	3.00	.50
☐☐☐☐	30 Kyle Calder, Chic.	5.00	3.00	.50
☐☐☐☐	31 Éric Dazé, Chic.	10.00	5.00	.50
☐☐☐☐	32 Jocelyn Thibault (G), Chic.	10.00	5.00	.50
☐☐☐☐	33 Alexei Zhamnov, Chic.	5.00	5.00	.50
☐☐☐☐	34 Rob Blake, Colo.	15.00	10.00	1.00
☐☐☐☐	35 Milan Hejduk, Colo.	20.00	10.00	1.00
☐☐☐☐	36 Patrick Roy (G), Colo.	75.00	50.00	5.00
☐☐☐☐	37 Joe Sakic, Colo.	40.00	25.00	2.50
☐☐☐☐	38 Radim Vrbata, Colo.	5.00	5.00	.50
☐☐☐☐	39 Marc Denis (G), Colu.	10.00	5.00	.50
☐☐☐☐	40 Rostislav Klesla, Colu.	15.00	10.00	.50
☐☐☐☐	41 Ron Tugnutt (G), Colu.	10.00	5.00	.50
☐☐☐☐	42 Ray Whitney, Colu.	5.00	3.00	.50
☐☐☐☐	43 Ed Belfour (G), Dall.	25.00	15.00	1.50
☐☐☐☐	44 Jere Lehtinen, Dall.	5.00	5.00	.50
☐☐☐☐	45 Mike Modano, Dall.	25.00	15.00	1.50
☐☐☐☐	46 Joe Nieuwendyk, Dall.	10.00	5.00	.50
☐☐☐☐	47 Pierre Turgeon, Dall.	10.00	5.00	.50
☐☐☐☐	48 Sergei Fedorov, Detr.	25.00	15.00	1.50
☐☐☐☐	49 Dominik Hasek (G), Detr.	25.00	15.00	1.50
☐☐☐☐	50 Brett Hull, Detr.	25.00	15.00	1.50
☐☐☐☐	51 Nicklas Lidström, Detr.	15.00	10.00	1.00
☐☐☐☐	52 Luc Robitaille, Detr.	20.00	10.00	1.00
☐☐☐☐	53 Brendan Shanahan, Detr.	25.00	15.00	1.50
☐☐☐☐	54 Steve Yzerman, Detr.	60.00	40.00	4.00
☐☐☐☐	55 Anson Carter, Edmo.	10.00	5.00	.50
☐☐☐☐	56 Mike Comrie, Edmo.	20.00	10.00	1.00
☐☐☐☐	57 Tommy Salo (G), Edmo.	10.00	5.00	.50
☐☐☐☐	58 Ryan Smyth, Edmo.	10.00	5.00	.50
☐☐☐☐	59 Pavel Bure, Flor.	20.00	10.00	1.00
☐☐☐☐	60 Viktor Kozlov, Flor.	5.00	5.00	.50
☐☐☐☐	61 Roberto Luongo (G), Flor.	20.00	10.00	1.00
☐☐☐☐	62 Marcus Nilson, Flor.	4.00	3.00	.50
☐☐☐☐	63 Jason Allison, LosA.	15.00	10.00	1.00
☐☐☐☐	64 Adam Deadmarsh, LosA.	5.00	5.00	.50
☐☐☐☐	65 Stephen Heinze, LosA.	4.00	3.00	.50
☐☐☐☐	66 Zigmund Palffy, LosA.	15.00	10.00	1.00
☐☐☐☐	67 Félix Potvin (G), LosA.	30.00	20.00	1.00
☐☐☐☐	68 Andrew Brunette, MinW.	4.00	3.00	.50
☐☐☐☐	69 Jim Dowd, MinW.	4.00	3.00	.50
☐☐☐☐	70 Marian Gaborik, MinW.	25.00	15.00	1.50
☐☐☐☐	71 Dwayne Roloson, MinW.	4.00	3.00	.50
☐☐☐☐	72 Doug Gilmour, Mont.	15.00	10.00	1.00
☐☐☐☐	73 Yanic Perreault, Mont.	5.00	5.00	.50
☐☐☐☐	74 Mike Ribeiro, Mont.	5.00	5.00	.50
☐☐☐☐	75 Brian Savage, Mont.	5.00	5.00	.50
☐☐☐☐	76 José Théodore (G), Mont.	30.00	20.00	2.00
☐☐☐☐	77 Mike Dunham (G), Nash.	10.00	5.00	.50
☐☐☐☐	78 Scott Hartnell, Nash.	5.00	3.00	.50
☐☐☐☐	79 David Legwand, Nash.	10.00	5.00	.50
☐☐☐☐	80 Cliff Ronning, Nash.	5.00	3.00	.50
☐☐☐☐	81 Jason Arnott, NJer.	10.00	5.00	.50
☐☐☐☐	82 Martin Brodeur (G), NJer.	40.00	25.00	2.50
☐☐☐☐	83 J-F Damphousse (G), NJer.	4.00	3.00	.50
☐☐☐☐	84 Patrik Elias, NJer.	20.00	10.00	1.00
☐☐☐☐	85 Scott Stevens, NJer.	10.00	5.00	.50
☐☐☐☐	86 Mariusz Czerkawski, NYIs.	5.00	3.00	.50
☐☐☐☐	87 Rick DiPietro, NYIs.	10.00	5.00	.50
☐☐☐☐	88 Chris Osgood (G), NYIs.	15.00	10.00	1.00
☐☐☐☐	89 Mark Parrish, NYIs.	10.00	5.00	.50
☐☐☐☐	90 Michael Peca, NYIs.	10.00	5.00	.50
☐☐☐☐	91 Alexei Yashin, NYIs.	15.00	10.00	1.00
☐☐☐☐	92 Theoren Fleury, NYRa.	15.00	10.00	1.00
☐☐☐☐	93 Brian Leetch, NYRa.	15.00	10.00	1.00
☐☐☐☐	94 Eric Lindros, NYRa.	25.00	15.00	1.50
☐☐☐☐	95 Mark Messier, NYRa.	25.00	15.00	1.50
☐☐☐☐	96 Mike Richter (G), NYRa.	10.00	5.00	.50
☐☐☐☐	97 Mike York, NYRa.	5.00	5.00	.50
☐☐☐☐	98 Daniel Alfredsson, Otta.	30.00	10.00	1.00
☐☐☐☐	99 Martin Havlat, Otta.	15.00	10.00	1.00
☐☐☐☐	100 Marian Hossa, Otta.	25.00	15.00	1.50
☐☐☐☐	101 Patrick Lalime (G), Otta.	15.00	10.00	1.00
☐☐☐☐	102 Todd White, Otta.	4.00	3.00	.50
☐☐☐☐	103 R. Cechmanek (G), Phil.	10.00	5.00	.50
☐☐☐☐	104 Simon Gagné, Phil.	20.00	10.00	1.00
☐☐☐☐	105 John LeClair, Phil.	20.00	10.00	1.00
☐☐☐☐	106 Mark Recchi, Phil.	10.00	5.00	.50
☐☐☐☐	107 Jeremy Roenick, Phil.	20.00	10.00	1.00
☐☐☐☐	108 Sean Burke (G), Phoe.	15.00	10.00	1.00
☐☐☐☐	109 Daymond Langkow, Phoe.	5.00	3.00	.50
☐☐☐☐	110 Claude Lemieux, Phoe.	5.00	5.00	.50
☐☐☐☐	111 Johan Hedberg (G), Pitt.	10.00	5.00	.50
☐☐☐☐	112 Alexei Kovalev, Pitt.	15.00	10.00	1.00
☐☐☐☐	113 Robert Lang, Pitt.	5.00	3.00	.50
☐☐☐☐	114 Mario Lemieux, Pitt.	75.00	50.00	5.00
☐☐☐☐	115 Pavol Demitra, SLou.	10.00	5.00	.50
☐☐☐☐	116 Brent Johnson (G), SLou.	10.00	5.00	.50
☐☐☐☐	117 Al MacInnis, SLou.	10.00	5.00	.50
☐☐☐☐	118 Chris Pronger, SLou.	15.00	10.00	1.00
☐☐☐☐	119 Keith Tkachuk, SLou.	15.00	10.00	1.00
☐☐☐☐	120 Doug Weight, SLou.	15.00	10.00	1.00
☐☐☐☐	121 V. Damphousse, SanJ.	15.00	10.00	1.00
☐☐☐☐	122 E. Nabokov (G), SanJ.	15.00	10.00	1.00
☐☐☐☐	123 Owen Nolan, SanJ.	15.00	10.00	1.00
☐☐☐☐	124 Teemu Selänne, SanJ.	20.00	10.00	1.00
☐☐☐☐	125 N. Khabibulin (G), Tamp.	10.00	5.00	.50
☐☐☐☐	126 V. Lecavalier, Tamp.	25.00	15.00	1.50
☐☐☐☐	127 Brad Richards, Tamp.	10.00	5.00	.50
☐☐☐☐	128 Martin St. Louis, Tamp.	10.00	5.00	.50
☐☐☐☐	129 Curtis Joseph (G), Toro.	25.00	15.00	1.50
☐☐☐☐	130 Alexander Mogilny, Toro.	10.00	5.00	.50
☐☐☐☐	131 Gary Roberts, Toro.	10.00	5.00	.50
☐☐☐☐	132 Mats Sundin, Toro.	25.00	15.00	1.50
☐☐☐☐	133 Darcy Tucker, Toro.	5.00	3.00	.50
☐☐☐☐	134 Todd Bertuzzi, Vanc.	30.00	20.00	2.00
☐☐☐☐	135 Dan Cloutier (G), Vanc.	10.00	5.00	.50
☐☐☐☐	136 Brendan Morrison, Vanc.	5.00	5.00	.50
☐☐☐☐	137 Markus Näslund, Vanc.	25.00	15.00	1.50
☐☐☐☐	138 Daniel Sedin, Vanc.	10.00	5.00	.50
☐☐☐☐	139 Henrik Sedin, Vanc.	10.00	5.00	.50
☐☐☐☐	140 Peter Bondra, Wash.	15.00	10.00	1.00
☐☐☐☐	141 Sergei Gonchar, Wash.	5.00	5.00	.50
☐☐☐☐	142 Jaromir Jagr, Wash.	25.00	15.00	1.50
☐☐☐☐	143 Olaf Kölzig (G), Wash.	15.00	10.00	1.00
☐☐☐☐	144 Adam Oates, Wash.	10.00	5.00	.50

ROOKIES

Realised pricing for scarce cards may vary considerably from pricing listed below.

	Rookie	**Hobby**
☐	**145 Ilja Bryzgalov (G), Anah. RC (#/30)**	**175.00**
☐	**146 Timo Pärssinen, Anah. RC (#/29)**	**85.00**
☐	**147 Ilya Kovalchuk, Atla. RC (#/17)**	**1500.00**

☐	148 Kamil Piros, Atla. RC {#/25}	150.00
☐	149 Brian Pothier, Atla. RC {#/3}	210.00
☐	150 Andy Hilbert, Bost. {#/29}	80.00
☐	151 Jukka Hentunen, Calg. RC {#/24}	90.00
☐	152 Erik Cole, Caro. RC {#/26}	225.00
☐	153 Vaclav Nedorost, Colo. RC {#/22}	240.00
☐	154 John Erskine, Dall. RC {#/3}	210.00
☐	155 Niko Kapanen, Dall. RC {#/39}	180.00
☐	156 Pavel Datsyuk, Detr. RC {#/13}	1100.00
☐	157 Jason Chimera, Edmo. RC {#/28}	140.00
☐	158 Ty Conklin (G), Edmo. RC {#/1}	600.00
☐	159 Jussi Markkanen, Edmo. {#/30}	80.00
☐	160 Niklas Hagman, Flor. RC {#/14}	210.00
☐	161 Kristian Huselius, Flor. RC {#/22}	320.00
☐	162 Jaroslav Bednar, LosA. RC {#/7}	280.00
☐	163 David Cullen, MinW. RC {#/24}	90.00
☐	164 Pascal Dupuis, MinW. RC {#/11}	360.00
☐	165 Nick Schultz, MinW. RC {#/55}	90.00
☐	166 Martin Erat, Nash. RC {#/19}	160.00
☐	167 Brian Gionta, NJer. {#/14}	125.00
☐	168 Andreas Salomonsson, NJer. RC {#/15}	125.00
☐	169 Radek Martinek, NYIs. RC {#/24}	90.00
☐	170 Raffi Torres, NYIs. RC {#/16}	285.00
☐	171 Dan Blackburn (G), NYRa. RC {#/31}	350.00
☐	172 Mikael Samuelsson, NYRa. RC {#/37}	80.00
☐	173 Chris Neil, Otta. RC {#/25}	90.00
☐	174 Jiri Dopita, Phil. RC {#/20}	160.00
☐	175 Bruno St-Jacques, Phil. RC {#/42}	80.00
☐	176 Krys Kolanos, Phoe. RC {#/36}	175.00
☐	177 Josef Melichar, Pitt. {#/2}	90.00
☐	178 Billy Tibbetts, Pitt. RC {#/12}	230.00
☐	179 Mark Rycroft, SLou. RC {#/42}	80.00
☐	180 Jeff Jillson, SanJ. RC {#/5}	320.00
☐	181 Nikita Alexeev, Tamp. RC {#/15}	300.00
☐	182 Brad Leeb, Vanc. RC {#/38}	80.00
☐	183 Chris Corrinet, Wash. RC {#/48}	80.00
☐	184 Brian Sutherby, Wash. RC {#/41}	120.00

RETAIL ROOKIES

These Rookie subset cards were included in the retail packaging.

	Rookie (#/534)	Retail
☐	145 Ilja Bryzgalov (G), Anah. RC	20.00
☐	146 Timo Pärssinen, Anah. RC	10.00
☐	147 Ilya Kovalchuk, Atla. RC	100.00
☐	148 Kamil Piros, Atla. RC	15.00
☐	149 Brian Pothier, Atla. RC	10.00
☐	150 Andy Hilbert, Bost.	5.00
☐	151 Jukka Hentunen, Calg. RC	10.00
☐	152 Erik Cole, Caro. RC	20.00
☐	153 Vaclav Nedorost, Colo. RC	20.00
☐	154 John Erskine, Dall. RC	10.00
☐	155 Niko Kapanen, Dall. RC	20.00
☐	156 Pavel Datsyuk, Detr. RC	80.00
☐	157 Jason Chimera, Edmo. RC	15.00
☐	158 Ty Conklin (G), Edmo. RC	20.00
☐	159 Jussi Markkanen, Edmo.	5.00
☐	160 Niklas Hagman, Flor. RC	15.00
☐	161 Kristian Huselius, Flor. RC	30.00
☐	162 Jaroslav Bednar, LosA. RC	15.00
☐	163 David Cullen, MinW. RC	10.00
☐	164 Pascal Dupuis, MinW. RC	20.00
☐	165 Nick Schultz, MinW. RC	15.00
☐	166 Martin Erat, Nash. RC	15.00
☐	167 Brian Gionta, NJer.	5.00
☐	168 Andreas Salomonsson, NJer. RC	10.00
☐	169 Radek Martinek, NYIs. RC	10.00
☐	170 Raffi Torres, NYIs. RC	20.00
☐	171 Dan Blackburn (G), NYRa. RC	40.00
☐	172 Mikael Samuelsson, NYRa. RC	10.00
☐	173 Chris Neil, Otta. RC	10.00
☐	174 Jiri Dopita, Phil. RC	15.00
☐	175 Bruno St-Jacques, Phil. RC	10.00
☐	176 Krys Kolanos, Phoe. RC	20.00
☐	177 Josef Melichar, Pitt.	5.00
☐	178 Billy Tibbetts, Pitt. RC	15.00
☐	179 Mark Rycroft, SLou. RC	10.00
☐	180 Jeff Jillson, SanJ. RC	15.00
☐	181 Nikita Alexeev, Tamp. RC	20.00
☐	182 Brad Leeb, Vanc.	5.00
☐	183 Chris Corrinet, Wash. RC	10.00
☐	184 Brian Sutherby, Wash. RC	15.00

DOUBLE-SIDED GAME-WORN JERSEYS

Insert Set (77 cards): 650

	Insert	DSGWJ
☐	1 S. Rucchin ✂ / P. Kariya ✂ {*325}	25.00
☐	2 J. Friesen ✂ Teal / O. Tverdovsky ✂ Burgandy	12.00
☐	2 J. Friesen ✂ Red / O. Tverdovsky ✂ Burgandy	12.00
☐	2 Friesen ✂ Grey/Burgandy / Tverdovsky ✂ Burgandy	12.00
☐	3 S. Samsonov ✂ / B. Guerin ✂	12.00
☐	4 J. Dumont ✂ / A. Zhitnik ✂ {*299}	12.00
☐	5 M. Savard ✂ / R. Turek (G) ✂	12.00
☐	6 R. Turek (G) ✂ / B. Boughner ✂	12.00
☐	7 J. Iginla ✂ / M. Savard ✂ {*261}	20.00
☐	8 T. Amonte ✂ / B. Mironov ✂ {*383}	12.00
☐	9 K. Calder ✂ / M. Nylander ✂ {*340}	12.00
☐	10 A. Zhamnov ✂ Red / S. Sullivan ✂ White {*560}	12.00
☐	11 M. Hejduk ✂ / C. Drury ✂	15.00
☐	12 J. Sakic ✂ Blue / A. Tanguay ✂ White	25.00
☐	13 P. Roy (G) ✂ / R. Blake ✂ {*312}	65.00
☐	14 A. Tanguay ✂ / V. Nedorost ✂	12.00
☐	15 L. Odelein ✂ / J. McLennan (G) ✂	12.00
☐	16 M. Modano ✂ / J. Langenbrunner ✂ {*386}	20.00
☐	17 Z. Palffy ✂ / F. Potvin (G) ✂	15.00
☐	18 A. Deadmarsh ✂ / B. Smolinski ✂	12.00
☐	19 R. Blake ✂ / A. Miller ✂ {*562}	12.00
☐	20 F. Potvin (G) ✂ / J. Théodore (G) ✂ {*511}	30.00
☐	21 J. Dumont ✂ / S. Stevens ✂	12.00
☐	22 C. Ronning ✂ / T. Fitzgerald ✂ {*511}	12.00
☐	23 I. Kovalchuk ✂ / D. Heatley ✂ {*527}	55.00
☐	24 M. Bell ✂ / É. Dazé ✂	12.00
☐	25 E. Lindros ✂ / T. Fleury ✂ {*720}	20.00
☐	26 B. Leetch ✂ / R. Fata ✂	12.00
☐	27 E. Lindros ✂ / M. Messier ✂ {*509}	25.00
☐	28 M. York ✂ Light Blue ✂ / T. Fleury ✂ Dark Blue {*361}	15.00
☐	29 M. Richter (G) ✂ White / B. Leetch ✂ Red {*482}	15.00
☐	30 D. Alfredsson ✂ / M. Sundin ✂ {*161}	45.00
☐	31 P. Brendl ✂ / J. Hrdina ✂	12.00
☐	32 M. Lemieux ✂ / A. Morozov ✂ {*492}	45.00
☐	33 P. Brendl ✂ Blue / J. Beranek ✂ Black	12.00
☐	34 M. Straka ✂ / M. Rozsival ✂	12.00
☐	35 J. Hrdina ✂ Black / I. Moran ✂ Black	12.00
☐	36 A. Kovalev ✂ / R. Parent (G) ✂ {*510}	12.00
☐	37 M. Eastwood ✂ / F. Brathwaite (G) ✂ {*431}	12.00
☐	38 J. Hecht ✂ / S. Young ✂ {*301}	12.00
☐	40 V. Lecavalier ✂ / P. Svoboda ✂ {*231}	30.00
☐	41 C. Joseph (G) ✂ / G. Healy (G) ✂ {*207}	30.00
☐	42 M. Sundin ✂ White / J. Sakic ✂ Blue	30.00
☐	43 J. Jagr ✂ / D. Zubrus ✂ {*304}	20.00
☐	44 T. Barrasso (G) ✂ Red / A. Irbe (G) ✂ Red	12.00
☐	44 T. Barrasso (G) ✂ Black/Red / A. Irbe (G) ✂ Black/Red	15.00
☐	45 R. Francis ✂ / J. O'Neill ✂	12.00
☐	46 R. Brind'Amour ✂ / E. Cole ✂	12.00
☐	47 M. Havlat ✂ Black / M. Hossa ✂ Black	20.00
☐	48 D. Alfredsson ✂ / P. Lalime (G) ✂	15.00
☐	49 J. Dopita ✂ / R. Cechmanek (G) ✂	12.00
☐	50 J. Roenick ✂ / J. LeClair ✂	20.00
☐	51 S. Gagné ✂ / J. LeClair ✂	20.00
☐	52 M. Modano ✂ / P. Turgeon ✂	15.00
☐	53 M. Turco (G) ✂ / E. Belfour (G) ✂	20.00
☐	54 H. Sedin ✂ / D. Sedin ✂	12.00
☐	55 T. Bertuzzi ✂ Black / B. Morrison ✂ Silver	15.00
☐	56 D. Cloutier (G) ✂ / M. Näslund ✂	15.00
☐	57 B. Morrison ✂ / M. Turco (G) ✂	12.00
☐	58 M. Näslund ✂ Blue / D. Alfredsson ✂ Black	20.00
☐	59 J. Roenick ✂ / T. Barrasso (G) ✂	15.00
☐	60 M. Havlat ✂ / R. Cechmanek (G) ✂	12.00
☐	61 R. Francis ✂ / A. Irbe (G) ✂	12.00
☐	62 J. O'Neill ✂ / E. Cole ✂	12.00
☐	63 M. Hossa ✂ / J. Dopita ✂	12.00
☐	64 P. Lalime (G) ✂ Black / S. Gagné ✂ Black	15.00
☐	65 E. Belfour (G) ✂ / P. Turgeon ✂	15.00
☐	66 M. Biron (G) ✂ Black / M. Satan ✂ Grey	12.00
☐	67 M. Gaborik ✂ / M. Fernandez (G) ✂	15.00
☐	68 M. Brodeur (G) ✂ / J. Arnott ✂	25.00
☐	69 P. Elias ✂ / S. Gomez ✂	15.00
☐	70 J. McLennan (G) ✂ / F. Kuba ✂	12.00
☐	72 K. Kolanos ✂ / D. Langkow ✂	12.00
☐	72 M. Handzus ✂ Burgandy / S. Berezin ✂ Burgandy	12.00
☐	71 M. Handzus ✂ Burgandy / S. Berezin ✂ Green/Grey	12.00
☐	73 S. Sullivan ✂ / M. Bell ✂	12.00
☐	74 J. Thornton ✂ / B. Guerin ✂	20.00
☐	75 J. Allison ✂ / Z. Palffy ✂	15.00

DOUBLE-SIDED GAME-WORN JERSEYS PATCH

Insert Set (58 cards): 1,400

	Insert	DSGWJP
☐	1 S. Rucchin ✂ / P. Kariya ✂ {*56}	75.00
☐	2 J. Friesen ✂ / O. Tverdovsky ✂ {*213}	20.00
☐	3 S. Samsonov ✂ / B. Guerin ✂ {*215}	25.00
☐	4 J. Dumont ✂ / A. Zhitnik ✂ {*181}	20.00
☐	9 K. Calder ✂ / M. Nylander ✂ {*46}	25.00
☐	11 M. Hejduk ✂ / C. Drury ✂ {*219}	25.00
☐	12 J. Sakic ✂ / A. Tanguay ✂ {*259}	50.00
☐	13 P. Roy (G) ✂ / R. Blake ✂ {*39}	200.00
☐	14 A. Tanguay ✂ / V. Nedorost ✂ {*117}	25.00
☐	16 M. Modano ✂ / J. Langenbrunner ✂ {*19}	100.00
☐	17 Z. Palffy ✂ / F. Potvin (G) ✂ {*174}	25.00
☐	18 A. Deadmarsh ✂ / B. Smolinski ✂ {*163}	20.00
☐	20 F. Potvin (G) ✂ / J. Théodore (G) ✂ {*94}	125.00
☐	21 J. Dumont ✂ / S. Stevens ✂ {*255}	20.00
☐	24 M. Bell ✂ / É. Dazé ✂ {*116}	25.00
☐	25 E. Lindros ✂ / T. Fleury ✂ {*288}	25.00
☐	26 B. Leetch ✂ / R. Fata ✂ {*198}	25.00
☐	27 E. Lindros ✂ / M. Messier ✂ {*166}	50.00
☐	28 M. Richter (G) ✂ / B. Leetch ✂ {*104}	25.00
☐	30 D. Alfredsson ✂ / M. Sundin ✂ {*63}	125.00
☐	33 P. Brendl ✂ / J. Beranek ✂ {*39}	25.00
☐	34 M. Straka ✂ / M. Rozsival ✂ {*302}	20.00
☐	35 J. Hrdina ✂ / I. Moran ✂ {*88}	20.00
☐	38 J. Hecht ✂ / S. Young ✂ {*62}	25.00
☐	40 V. Lecavalier ✂ / P. Svoboda ✂ {*45}	75.00
☐	41 C. Joseph (G) ✂ / G. Healy (G) ✂ {*140}	25.00
☐	42 M. Sundin ✂ / J. Sakic ✂ {*53}	150.00
☐	43 J. Jagr ✂ / D. Zubrus ✂ {*56}	50.00
☐	44 T. Barrasso (G) ✂ / A. Irbe (G) ✂ {*199}	25.00
☐	45 R. Francis ✂ / J. O'Neill ✂ {*194}	25.00
☐	46 R. Brind'Amour ✂ / E. Cole ✂ {*215}	20.00
☐	47 M. Havlat ✂ / M. Hossa ✂ {*118}	50.00
☐	48 D. Alfredsson ✂ / P. Lalime (G) ✂ {*114}	50.00
☐	49 J. Dopita ✂ / R. Cechmanek (G) ✂ {*202}	20.00
☐	50 J. Roenick ✂ / J. LeClair ✂ {*216}	50.00
☐	51 S. Gagné ✂ / J. LeClair ✂ {*169}	50.00
☐	52 M. Modano ✂ / P. Turgeon ✂ {*216}	25.00
☐	53 M. Turco (G) ✂ / E. Belfour (G) ✂ {*212}	50.00
☐	54 H. Sedin ✂ / D. Sedin ✂ {*218}	25.00
☐	55 T. Bertuzzi ✂ / B. Morrison ✂ {*215}	25.00
☐	56 D. Cloutier (G) ✂ / M. Näslund ✂ {*164}	50.00
☐	57 B. Morrison ✂ / M. Turco (G) ✂ {*119}	25.00
☐	58 D. Alfredsson ✂ / M. Näslund ✂ {*164}	50.00
☐	59 J. Roenick ✂ / T. Barrasso ✂ {*113}	50.00
☐	60 M. Havlat ✂ / R. Cechmanek (G) ✂ {*109}	25.00
☐	61 R. Francis ✂ / A. Irbe (G) ✂ {*154}	25.00
☐	62 J. O'Neill ✂ / E. Cole ✂ {*163}	20.00
☐	63 M. Hossa ✂ / J. Dopita ✂ {*166}	25.00
☐	64 P. Lalime (G) ✂ / S. Gagné ✂ {*163}	50.00
☐	65 E. Belfour (G) ✂ / P. Turgeon ✂ {*165}	50.00
☐	66 M. Biron (G) ✂ / M. Satan ✂ {*256}	20.00
☐	67 M. Gaborik ✂ / M. Fernandez (G) ✂ {*104}	50.00
☐	69 P. Elias ✂ / S. Gomez ✂ {*250}	25.00
☐	70 J. McLennan (G) ✂ / F. Kuba ✂ {*569}	20.00
☐	71 K. Kolanos ✂ / D. Langkow ✂ {*116}	20.00
☐	72 M. Handzus ✂ / S. Berezin ✂ {*260}	20.00
☐	73 S. Sullivan ✂ / M. Bell ✂ / {*264}	20.00
☐	75 J. Allison ✂ / Z. Palffy ✂ {*106}	50.00

DOUBLE MEMORABILIA

☐	39 T. Selänne ✂ / I. Kovalchuk ✂ Stick {*212}	90.00

SATURDAY KNIGHTS

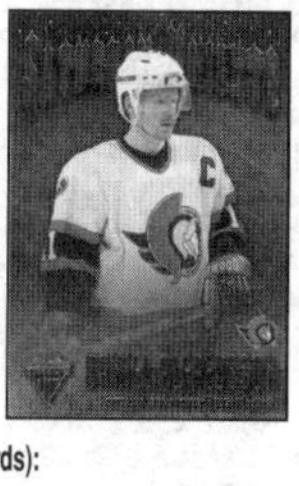

Insert Set (20 cards): 75.00

	Insert	SK
☐	1 Paul Kariya, Anah.	6.00
☐	2 Joe Thornton, Bost.	6.00
☐	3 Jarome Iginla, Calg.	4.00
☐	4 Ed Belfour (G), Dall.	4.00
☐	5 Dominik Hasek (G), Detr.	4.00
☐	6 Brendan Shanahan, Detr.	4.00
☐	7 Steve Yzerman, Detr.	12.00
☐	8 Mike Comrie, Edmo.	4.00
☐	9 Pavel Bure, Flor.	4.00
☐	10 Marian Gaborik, MinW.	4.00
☐	11 José Théodore (G), Mont.	6.00
☐	12 Martin Brodeur (G), NJer.	8.00
☐	13 Michael Peca, NYIs.	3.00
☐	14 Eric Lindros, NYRa.	4.00
☐	15 Daniel Alfredsson, Otta.	3.00
☐	16 Martin Havlat, Otta.	3.00
☐	17 Jeremy Roenick, Phil.	4.00
☐	18 Mario Lemieux, Pitt.	15.00
☐	19 Curtis Joseph (G), Toro.	4.00
☐	20 Mats Sundin, Toro.	4.00

THREE-STAR SELECTS

Insert Set (30 cards): 110.00

	Insert	TSS
☐	1 Roman Turek (G), Calg.	2.00
☐	2 Tom Barrasso (G), Caro.	2.00
☐	3 Patrick Roy (G), Colo.	9.00
☐	4 Dominik Hasek (G), Detr.	2.00
☐	5 Martin Brodeur (G), NJer.	4.00
☐	6 Chris Osgood (G), NYIs.	2.00
☐	7 Mike Richter (G), NYRa.	2.00
☐	8 Evgeni Nabokov (G), SanJ.	2.00
☐	9 Nikolai Khabibulin (G), Tamp.	2.00
☐	10 Curtis Joseph (G), Toro.	2.00
☐	11 Paul Kariya, Anah.	6.00
☐	12 Jarome Iginla, Calg.	2.00
☐	13 Joe Sakic, Colo.	6.00
☐	14 Brendan Shanahan, Detr.	4.00
☐	15 Steve Yzerman, Detr.	10.00
☐	16 Eric Lindros, NYRa.	4.00
☐	17 Mike York, NYRa.	2.00
☐	18 Mario Lemieux, Pitt.	12.00
☐	19 Mats Sundin, Toro.	4.00
☐	20 Jaromir Jagr, Pitt.	4.00
☐	21 Dany Heatley, Atla.	14.00
☐	22 Ilya Kovalchuk, Atla.	25.00
☐	23 Erik Cole, Caro.	3.00
☐	24 Mark Bell, Chic.	3.00
☐	25 Radim Vrbata, Colo.	4.00
☐	26 Kristian Huselius, Flor.	4.00
☐	27 Mike Ribeiro, Mont.	4.00
☐	28 Rick DiPietro, NYIs.	6.00
☐	29 Raffi Torres, NYIs.	3.00
☐	30 Krys Kolanos, Phoe.	3.00

TITANIUM ALL-STARS

Insert Set (20 cards): 35.00

	Insert	TAS
☐	1 Joe Thornton, All-Star '02	4.00
☐	2 Jarome Iginla, All-Star '02	2.00
☐	3 Sami Kapanen, All-Star '02	2.00
☐	4 Éric Dazé, All-Star '02	2.00
☐	5 Rob Blake, All-Star '02	2.00
☐	6 Patrick Roy (G), All-Star '02	10.00
☐	7 Dominik Hasek (G), All-Star '02	2.00
☐	8 Sergei Fedorov, All-Star '02	2.00
☐	9 Nicklas Lidström, All-Star '02	2.00
☐	10 Brendan Shanahan, All-Star '02	2.00
☐	11 Zigmund Palffy, All-Star '02	2.00
☐	12 José Théodore (G), All-Star '02	4.00
☐	13 Patrik Elias, All-Star '02	2.00
☐	14 Alexei Yashin, All-Star '02	2.00
☐	15 Chris Pronger, All-Star '02	2.00
☐	16 Owen Nolan, All-Star '02	2.00
☐	17 Teemu Selänne, All-Star '02	2.00
☐	18 Nikolai Khabibulin (G), All-Star '02	2.00
☐	19 Mats Sundin, All-Star '02	2.00
☐	20 Jaromir Jagr, All-Star '02	2.00

TITANIUM ROOKIE TEAM

Insert Set (10 cards): 315.00

	Insert (#/70)	TAS
☐	1 Dany Heatley, Atla.	85.00
☐	2 Ilya Kovalchuk, Atla.	85.00
☐	3 Erik Cole, Caro.	30.00
☐	4 Mark Bell, Chic.	30.00
☐	5 Radim Vrbata, Colo.	30.00
☐	6 Kristian Huselius, Flor.	30.00

☐ 7 Mike Ribeiro, Mont. 30.00
☐ 8 Rick DiPietro, NYIs. 40.00
☐ 9 Raffi Torres, NYIs. 30.00
☐ 10 Krys Kolanos, Phoe. 30.00

2001 - 02 PRIVATE STOCK TITANIUM DRAFT DAY

Produced by Pacific Trading Cards, this series was released in May 2002.

Complete Set (172 cards): 440.00

	Description	**Base**
☐	1 Jeff Friesen, Anah. ✂ {*1250}	8.00
☐	2 Paul Kariya, Anah. ✂ {*250}	40.00
☐	3 Oleg Tverdovsky, Anah. ✂ {*1250}	8.00
☐	4 Dany Heatley, Atla. ✂ {*500}	30.00
☐	5 Milan Hnilicka (G), Atla. ✂ {*1250}	8.00
☐	6 Tomi Kallio, Atla. ✂ {*1250}	8.00
☐	7 Ilya Kovalchuk, Atla. ✂ {*500}	30.00
☐	8 Patrik Stefan, Atla. ✂ {*1250}	8.00
☐	9 Bill Guerin, Bost. ✂ {*750}	8.00
☐	10 Kyle McLaren, Bost. ✂ {*190}	8.00
☐	11 Joe Thornton, Bost. ✂ {*500}	25.00
☐	12 Martin Biron (G), Buff. (G) ✂ {*750}	8.00
☐	13 J-P Dumont, Buff. ✂ {*580}	8.00
☐	14 Erik Rasmussen, Buff. ✂ {*120}	10.00
☐	15 Jarome Iginla, Calg. ✂ {*125}	40.00
☐	16 Marcel Savard, Calg. ✂ {*440}	8.00
☐	17 Roman Turek (G), Calg. ✂ {*1250}	8.00
☐	18 Erik Cole, Caro. ✂ {*750}	8.00
☐	19 Jeff O'Neill, Caro. ✂ {*500}	8.00
☐	20 Tony Amonte, Chic. ✂ {*180}	20.00
☐	21 Kyle Calder, Chic. ✂ {*300}	8.00
☐	22 Tom Fitzgerald, Chic. ✂ {*330}	8.00
☐	23 Phil Housley, Chic. ✂ {*125}	15.00
☐	24 Steve Sullivan, Chic. ✂ {*750}	8.00
☐	25 Rob Blake, Colo. ✂ {*500}	10.00
☐	26 Vaclav Nedorost, Colo. ✂ {*1250}	8.00
☐	27 Joe Sakic, Colo. ✂ {*175}	60.00
☐	28 Alex Tanguay, Colo. ✂ {*750}	10.00
☐	29 Marc Denis (G), Colu. ✂ {*1250}	8.00
☐	30 Rostislav Klesla, Colu. ✂ {*1250}	8.00
☐	31 Ron Tugnutt (G), Colu. ✂ {*1250}	8.00
☐	32 Jason Arnott, Dall. ✂ {*1000}	8.00
☐	33 Derian Hatcher, Dall. ✂ {*270}	8.00
☐	34 Mike Modano, Dall. ✂ {*330}	25.00
☐	35 Pierre Turgeon, Dall. ✂ {*136}	20.00
☐	36 Sergei Zubov, Dall. ✂ {*105}	10.00
☐	37 Dominik Hasek (G), Detr. ✂ {*170}	40.00
☐	38 Brett Hull, Detr. ✂	
☐	40 Jochen Hecht, Edmo. ✂ {*255}	8.00
☐	41 Jason Allison, LosA. ✂ {*1252}	10.00
☐	42 Adam Deadmarsh, LosA. ✂ {*752}	8.00
☐	43 Félix Potvin (G), LosA. ✂ {*520}	10.00
☐	44 Manny Fernandez (G), MinW. ✂ {*1000}	8.00
☐	45 Marian Gaborik, MinW. ✂ {*520}	20.00
☐	46 Filip Kuba, MinW. ✂ {*1000}	8.00
☐	47 Jamie McLennan (G), MinW. ✂ {*1252}	8.00
☐	48 Sergei Berezin, Mont. ✂ {*1000}	8.00
☐	49 Jeff Hackett (G), Mont. ✂ {*185}	10.00
☐	50 Jukka Hentunen, Nashville ✂ {*1252}	8.00
☐	51 Martin Brodeur (G), New ✂ ✂ {*520}	35.00
☐	52 Scott Gomez, New ✂ ✂ {*752}	8.00
☐	53 Bobby Holik, New ✂ ✂ {*200}	10.00
☐	54 Jamie Langenbrunner, New ✂ ✂ {*430}	8.00
☐	55 Scott Stevens, New ✂ ✂ {*752}	8.00
☐	56 Mats Lindgren, NYIs. ✂ {*480}	8.00
☐	57 Kip Miller, NY Islanders ✂ {*400}	8.00
☐	58 Chris Osgood (G), NYIs. ✂ {*290}	15.00
☐	59 Theoren Fleury, NYRa. ✂ {*1000}	10.00
☐	60 Brian Leetch, NYRa. ✂ {*750}	10.00
☐	61 Eric Lindros, NYRa. ✂ {*1000}	15.00
☐	62 Mark Messier, NYRa. ✂ {*1000}	15.00
☐	63 Mike Richter (G), NYRa. ✂ {*220}	15.00
☐	64 Daniel Alfredsson, Otta. ✂ {*750}	10.00
☐	65 Martin Havlat, Otta. ✂ {*750}	10.00
☐	66 Marian Hossa, Otta. ✂ {*750}	15.00
☐	67 Patrick Lalime (G), Otta. ✂ {*750}	10.00
☐	68 Roman Cechmanek (G), Phil. ✂ {*1000}	8.00
☐	69 Jiri Dopita, Phil. ✂ {*1000}	8.00
☐	70 Simon Gagné, Philadephia ✂ {*1000}	10.00
☐	39 Mike Comrie, Edmo. ✂	
☐	71 John LeClair, Phil. ✂ {*1000}	10.00
☐	72 Jeremy Roenick, Phil. ✂ {*1000}	10.00
☐	73 Michal Handzus, Phoe. ✂ {*1000}	8.00
☐	74 Krys Kolanos, Phoe. ✂ {*500}	8.00
☐	75 Daymond Langkow, Phoe. ✂ {*1000}	8.00
☐	76 Teppo Numminen, Phoe. ✂ {*590}	8.00
☐	77 Kris Beech, Pitt. ✂ {*1250}	8.00
☐	78 Johan Hedberg (G), Pitt. ✂ {*1000}	8.00
☐	79 Robert Lang, Pitt. ✂ {*1000}	8.00
☐	80 Mario Lemieux, Pitt. ✂ {*650}	60.00
☐	81 Rich Parent (G), Pitt. ✂ {*1000}	8.00
☐	82 Toby Petersen, Pitt. ✂ {*1250}	8.00
☐	83 Mike Eastwood, SLou. ✂ {*230}	8.00
☐	84 Ray Ferraro, SLou. ✂ {*1250}	8.00
☐	85 Patrick Marleau, SanJ. ✂ {*1000}	8.00
☐	86 Evgeni Nabokov (G), SanJ. ✂ {*1000}	10.00
☐	87 Owen Nolan, SanJ. ✂ {*1000}	10.00
☐	88 Vincent Lecavalier, Tamp. ✂ {*280}	30.00
☐	89 Tom Barrasso (G), Toro. ✂ {*1250}	8.00
☐	90 Mats Sundin, Toro. ✂ {*150}	45.00
☐	91 Dmitry Yushkevich, Toro. ✂ {*320}	8.00
☐	92 Todd Bertuzzi, Vanc. ✂ {*1000}	20.00
☐	93 Andrew Cassels, Vanc. ✂ {*150}	10.00
☐	94 Dan Cloutier (G), Vanc. ✂ {*440}	8.00
☐	95 Brendan Morrison, Vanc. ✂ {*1000}	8.00
☐	96 Markus Näslund, Vanc. ✂ {*500}	20.00
☐	97 Daniel Sedin, Vanc. ✂ {*1000}	8.00
☐	98 Henrik Sedin, Vanc. ✂ {*1000}	8.00
☐	99 Peter Bondra, Wash. ✂ {*750}	10.00
☐	100 Jaromir Jagr, Wash. ✂ {*250}	30.00

ROOKIES

	Description	**Base**
☐	**101 Ilja Bryzgalov (G), Anah. RC**	**15.00**
☐	102 Andy McDonald, Anah.	4.00
☐	**103 Timo Pärssinen, Anah. RC**	**8.00**
☐	104 Dany Heatley, Atla.	15.00
☐	**105 Ilya Kovalchuk, Atla. RC**	**70.00**
☐	**106 Pasi Nurminen (G), Atla. RC**	**15.00**
☐	**107 Kamil Piros, Atla. RC**	**10.00**
☐	**108 Brian Pothier, Atla. RC**	**8.00**
☐	109 Daniel Tjärnqvist, Atla.	4.00
☐	110 Andy Hilbert, Bost.	4.00
☐	**111 Ales Kotalik, Bost. RC**	**30.00**
☐	112 Mika Noronen (G), Buff.	5.00
☐	**113 Erik Cole, Caro. RC**	**15.00**
☐	**114 Tyler Arnason, Chic. RC**	**30.00**
☐	115 Mark Bell, Chic.	4.00
☐	**116 Vaclav Nedorost, Colo. RC**	**15.00**
☐	117 Radim Vrbata, Colo.	4.00
☐	118 Brian Willsie, Colo.	4.00
☐	**119 Mathieu Darche, Colu. RC**	**10.00**
☐	120 Rostislav Klesla, Colu.	4.00
☐	**121 Jody Shelley, Colu. RC**	**10.00**
☐	**122 Martin Spanhel, Colu. RC**	**8.00**
☐	**123 John Erskine, Dall. RC**	**8.00**
☐	**124 Niko Kapanen, Dall. RC**	**15.00**
☐	**125 Sean Avery, Detr. RC**	**10.00**
☐	**126 Pavel Datsyuk, Detr. RC**	**60.00**
☐	127 Maxim Kuznetsov, Detr.	4.00
☐	**128 Jason Chimera, Edmo. RC**	**10.00**
☐	**129 Ty Conklin (G), Edmo. RC**	**15.00**
☐	130 Jussi Markkanen, Edmo.	4.00
☐	**131 Niklas Hagman, Flor. RC**	**10.00**
☐	**132 Kristian Huselius, Flor. RC**	**20.00**
☐	**133 Stephen Weiss, Flor. RC**	**60.00**
☐	**134 Jaroslav Bednar, LosA. RC**	**10.00**
☐	**135 David Cullen, MinW. RC**	**8.00**
☐	**136 Pascal Dupuis, MinW. RC**	**15.00**
☐	**137 Nick Schultz, MinW. RC**	**10.00**
☐	138 Mathieu Garon (G), Mont.	5.00
☐	**139 Marcel Hossa, Mont. RC**	**30.00**
☐	140 Mike Ribeiro, Mont.	4.00
☐	141 Bubba Berenzweig, Nash.	4.00
☐	**142 Martin Erat, Nash. RC**	**10.00**
☐	**143 Jukka Hentunen, Nash. RC**	**8.00**
☐	**144 Nathan Perrott, Nash. RC**	**8.00**
☐	**145 Christian Berglund, NJer. RC**	**10.00**
☐	**146 Scott Clemmensen (G), NJer. RC**	**10.00**
☐	147 Jean-François Damphousse (G), NJer.	4.00
☐	148 Brian Gionta, NJer.	4.00
☐	**149 Andreas Salomonsson, NJer. RC**	**8.00**
☐	**150 Radek Martinek, NYIs. RC**	**8.00**
☐	**151 Raffi Torres, NYIs. RC**	**15.00**
☐	**152 Dan Blackburn (G), NYRa. RC**	**30.00**
☐	**153 Mikael Samuelsson, NYRa. RC**	**8.00**
☐	**154 Chris Neil, Otta. RC**	**8.00**
☐	155 Pavel Brendl, Phil.	4.00
☐	**156 Jiri Dopita, Phil. RC**	**10.00**
☐	**157 Bruno St-Jacques, Phil. RC**	**8.00**
☐	**158 Billy Tibbetts, Phil.**	**10.00**
☐	158 Darcy Hordichuk, Atla.	5.00
☐	**160 Krys Kolanos, Phoe. RC**	**15.00**
☐	161 Josef Melichar, Pitt.	4.00
☐	**162 Mark Rycroft, SLou. RC**	**8.00**
☐	163 Sergei Varlamov, SLou.	4.00
☐	164 Matt Bradley, SanJ.	4.00
☐	**165 Jeff Jillson, SanJ. RC**	**10.00**
☐	166 Vesa Toskala, SanJ.	4.00
☐	**167 Nikita Alexeev, Tamp. RC**	**15.00**
☐	168 Alexei Ponikarovsky, Toro.	4.00
☐	**169 Chris Corrinet, Wash. RC**	**8.00**
☐	170 Stephen Peat, Wash.	4.00
☐	171 Matt Pettinger, Wash.	4.00
☐	**172 Brian Sutherby, Wash. RC**	**10.00**

2001 - 02 SIGNATURE SERIES

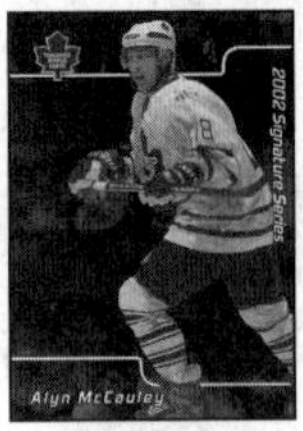

Produced by In The Game, the original series was released in April 2002. An update series (base and insert cards) was issued in June 2002 in the Be A Player Update release.

The following wrapper redemption promotional versions were created: Spring Expo '02 (#/10).

First Set (250 cards): 150.00
Update Set (25 cards): 50.00

	Description	**Base**
☐	1 Rick DiPietro, NYIs.	1.00
☐	2 Patrik Stefan,Atla.	.75
☐	3 Hal Gill, Bost.	.75
☐	4 Jean-Pierre Dumont, Buff.	.75
☐	5 Jarome Iginla, Calg.	2.00
☐	6 Shane Willis, Caro.	.75
☐	7 Chris Phillips, Otta.	.75
☐	8 Rostislav Klesla, Colu.	.75
☐	9 Brenden Morrow, Dall.	.75
☐	10 Manny Legacé (G), Detr.	.75
☐	11 Anson Carter, Edmo.	1.00
☐	12 Roberto Luongo (G), Flor.	2.00
☐	13 Aaron Miller, LosA.	.75
☐	14 Wayne Primeau, Pitt.	.75
☐	15 Brian Savage, Mont.	.75
☐	16 John Jakopin, Flor.	.75
☐	17 Greg Johnson, Nash.	.75
☐	18 Marc Chouinard, Anah.	.75
☐	19 Steve Martins, NYIs.	.75
☐	20 Marian Hossa, Otta.	2.50
☐	21 Brent Johnson (G), SLou.	1.00
☐	22 Sean Burke (G), Phoe.	1.50
☐	23 Jan Hrdina, Pitt.	.75
☐	24 Evgeni Nabokov (G), SanJ.	1.50
☐	25 Adam Deadmarsh, LosA.	.75
☐	26 Brad Richards, Tamp.	1.00
☐	27 Wade Redden, Otta.	.75
☐	28 David Legwand, Nash.	1.00
☐	29 Jean-Sébastien Giguère (G), Anah.	2.00
☐	30 Ray Ferraro,Atla.	.75
☐	31 Denis Hamel, Buff.	.75
☐	32 Marc Savard, Calg.	.75
☐	33 Craig Adams, Caro.	.75
☐	34 Landon Wilson, Phoe.	.75
☐	35 Marc Denis (G), Colu.	1.00
☐	36 Roman Lyashenko, Dall.	.75
☐	37 Tomas Holmström, Detr.	.75
☐	38 Mike Comrie, Edmo.	2.00
☐	39 Scott Hartnell, Nash.	.75
☐	40 Sergei Krivokrasov, MinW.	.75
☐	41 Mathieu Garon (G), Mont.	1.00
☐	42 Denis Arkhipov, Nash.	.75
☐	43 Roman Hamrlik, NYIs.	.75
☐	44 Mike Mottau, NYRa.	.75
☐	45 Shawn McEachern, Otta.	.75
☐	46 Peter White, Phil.	.75
☐	47 Shane Doan, Phoe.	.75
☐	48 Janne Laukkanen, Pitt.	.75
☐	49 Martin Louis, Tamp.	1.00
☐	50 Tomas Kaberle, Toro.	.75
☐	51 Daniel Sedin, Vanc.	1.00
☐	52 Jonas Rönnqvist, Anah.	.75
☐	53 Damian Rhodes (G),Atla.	.75
☐	54 Vaclav Varada, Buff.	.75
☐	55 Ronald Petrovicky, Calg.	.75
☐	56 Tommy Westlund, Caro.	.75
☐	57 Michael Nylander, Chic.	.75
☐	58 Serge Aubin, Colu.	.75
☐	59 Jiri Fischer, Detr.	.75
☐	60 Shawn Horcoff, Edmo.	.75
☐	61 Peter Worrell, Flor.	.75
☐	62 Willie Mitchell, MinW.	.75
☐	63 Oleg Petrov, Mont.	.75
☐	64 Scott Walker, Nash.	.75
☐	65 Tomi Kallio,Atla.	.75
☐	66 Jason Strudwick, Vanc.	.75
☐	67 Magnus Arvedson, Otta.	.75
☐	68 Éric Dazé, Chic.	1.00
☐	69 Johan Hedberg (G), Pitt.	1.00
☐	70 Fredrik Modin, Tamp.	.75
☐	71 Nathan Dempsey, Toro.	.75
☐	72 Henrik Sedin, Vanc.	1.00
☐	73 Mike LeClerc, Anah.	.75
☐	74 Hnat Domenichelli,Atla.	.75
☐	75 Jeff Cowan, Calg.	.75
☐	76 Brad Stuart, SanJ.	1.00
☐	77 Bryan Allen, Vanc.	.75
☐	78 Wes Walz, MinW.	.75
☐	79 Patrick Traverse, Mont.	.75
☐	80 Markus Näslund, Vanc.	2.50
☐	81 Brad Isbister, NYIs.	.75
☐	82 Jan Hlavac, NYRa.	.75
☐	83 Steve Sullivan, Chic.	.75
☐	84 Marian Gaborik, MinW.	2.50
☐	85 Kristian Kudroc, Tamp.	.75
☐	86 Peter Schaefer, Vanc.	.75
☐	87 Pascal Trépanier, Anah.	.75
☐	88 Milan Hnilicka (G),Atla.	.75
☐	89 Dave Lowry, Calg.	.75
☐	90 Jamie Allison, Chic.	.75
☐	91 Jeff Nielsen, MinW.	.75
☐	92 Sheldon Souray, Mont.	.75
☐	93 Mike Dunham (G), Nash.	1.00
☐	94 Branislav Mezei, NYIs.	.75
☐	95 Dale Purinton, NYRa.	.75
☐	96 Cory Sarich, Tamp.	.75
☐	97 Jarkko Ruutu, Vanc.	.75
☐	98 Kyle Calder, Chic.	.75
☐	99 Frantisek Musil, Edmo.	.75
☐	100 Tomas Kloucek, NYRa.	.75
☐	101 Karel Rachunek, Otta.	.75
☐	102 Darcy Tucker, Toro.	.75
☐	103 Alex Tanguay, Colo.	1.50
☐	104 Patrick Lalime (G), Otta.	1.50
☐	105 Ossi Väänänen, Phoe.	.75
☐	106 Martin Skoula, Colo.	.75
☐	107 Lubomir Visnovsky, LosA.	.75
☐	108 Richard Zednik, Mont.	1.00
☐	109 Jani Hurme (G), Otta.	.75
☐	110 Teppo Numminen, Phoe.	.75
☐	111 Scott Young, SLou.	.75
☐	112 Robert Reichel, Toro.	.75
☐	113 David Tanabe, Caro.	.75
☐	114 Steven Reinprecht, Colo.	.75
☐	115 Ryan Smyth, Edmo.	1.00
☐	116 Jozef Stümpel, Bost.	.75
☐	117 Martin Rucinsky, Mont.	.75
☐	118 Radek Dvorak, NYRa.	.75
☐	119 Chris Herperger, Otta.	.75
☐	120 Eric Weinrich, Phil.	.75
☐	121 Claude Lemieux, Phoe.	.75
☐	122 Mike Ricci, SanJ.	.75
☐	123 Cory Stillman, SLou.	.75
☐	124 Alyn McCauley, Toro.	.75
☐	125 Trevor Linden, Wash.	1.00
☐	126 Vitaly Vishnevski, Anah.	.75
☐	127 Tim Connolly, Buff.	1.00
☐	128 Oleg Saprykin, Calg.	.75
☐	129 Arturs Irbe (G), Caro.	1.00
☐	130 Ville Nieminen, Colo.	.75
☐	131 David Vyborny, Colu.	.75
☐	132 Janne Niinimaa, Edmo.	.75
☐	133 Joey Tetarenko, Flor.	.75
☐	134 Bryan Smolinski, LosA.	.75
☐	135 Stacy Roest, MinW.	.75
☐	136 Mikael Renberg, Toro.	.75
☐	137 Gino Odjick, Mont.	.75
☐	138 Petr Sykora, NJer.	1.00
☐	139 Alexei Yashin, NYIs.	1.50
☐	140 Martin Havlat, Otta.	1.50
☐	141 Rick Tocchet, Phil.	.75
☐	142 Daymond Langkow, Phoe.	.75
☐	143 Kevin Stevens, Pitt.	.75
☐	144 Patrick Marleau, SanJ.	1.00
☐	145 Reed Low, SLou.	.75
☐	146 Bryan McCabe, Toro.	.75
☐	147 Dmitri Khristich, Wash.	.75
☐	148 Oleg Tverdovsky, Anah.	.75
☐	149 Yannick Tremblay,Atla.	.75
☐	150 Martin Biron (G), Buff. (G)	1.00
☐	151 Rob Niedermayer, Calg.	.75
☐	152 Rod Brind'Amour, Caro.	.75
☐	153 Adam Foote, Colo.	.75
☐	154 Geoff Sanderson, Colu.	.75
☐	155 Pat Verbeek, Dall.	.75
☐	156 Nicklas Lidström, Detr.	1.50
☐	157 Jochen Hecht, Edmo.	.75
☐	158 Robert Svehla, Flor.	.75
☐	159 Mathieu Schneider, LosA.	.75
☐	160 Antti Laaksonen, MinW.	.75
☐	161 Jeff Hackett (G), Mont.	.75
☐	162 Scott Niedermayer, NJer.	.75
☐	163 Sandis Ozolinsh, Caro.	.75
☐	164 Radek Bonk, Otta.	.75
☐	165 Roman Cechmanek (G), Phil.	1.00
☐	166 Mike Johnson, Phoe.	.75
☐	167 Milan Kraft, Pitt.	.75
☐	168 Adam Graves, SanJ.	1.00
☐	169 Pavol Demitra, SLou.	1.00
☐	170 Kevin Weekes (G), Tamp.	.75
☐	171 Travis Green, Toro.	.75
☐	172 Jeff Halpern, Wash.	.75

☐	173 Steve Shields (G), Anah.	.75
☐	174 Lubos Bartecko,Atla.	.75
☐	175 P.J. Stock, Bost.	.75
☐	176 Maxim Afinogenov, Buff.	1.00
☐	177 Derek Morris, Calg.	.75
☐	178 Bates Battaglia, Caro.	.75
☐	179 Boris Mironov, Chic.	.75
☐	180 David Aebischer (G), Colo.	.75
☐	181 Espen Knutsen, Colu.	.75
☐	182 Darryl Sydor, Dall.	.75
☐	183 Igor Larionov, Detr.	1.50
☐	184 Eric Brewer, Edmo.	1.00
☐	185 Trevor Kidd (G), Flor.	.75
☐	186 Eric Bélanger, LosA.	.75
☐	187 Manny Fernandez (G), MinW.	1.00
☐	188 Francis Bouillon, Mont.	.75
☐	189 Patrik Elias, NJer.	2.00
☐	190 Mariusz Czerkawski, NYIs.	.75
☐	191 Daniel Alfredsson, Otta.	1.50
☐	192 Brian Boucher (G), Phil.	.75
☐	193 Sergei Berezin, Phoe.	.75
☐	194 Kris Beech, Pitt.	.75
☐	195 Vincent Damphousse, SanJ.	1.50
☐	196 Fred Brathwaite (G), SLou.	.75
☐	197 Ben Clymer, Tamp.	.75
☐	198 Wade Belak, Toro.	.75
☐	199 Ed Jovanovski, Vanc.	1.00
☐	200 Sergei Gonchar, Wash.	.75
☐	**201 Dan Blackburn (G), NYRa. RC**	**7.00**
☐	202 Daniel Tjärnqvist,Atla.	.75
☐	**203 Andreas Salomonsson, NJer. RC**	**1.00**
☐	**204 Vaclav Nedorost, Colo. RC**	**4.00**
☐	205 Justin Kurtz, Vanc.	.75
☐	**206 Jiri Dopita, Phil. RC**	**3.00**
☐	**207 Ilya Kovalchuk,Atla. RC**	**15.00**
☐	208 Richard Jackman, Bost.	.75
☐	**209 Scott Nichol, Calg. RC**	**1.00**
☐	210 Brad Larsen, Colo.	.75
☐	211 Jason Williams, Detr.	1.00
☐	**212 Kristian Huselius, Flor. RC**	**6.00**
☐	213 Andreas Lilja, LosA.	.75
☐	**214 Nick Schultz, MinW. RC**	**3.00**
☐	215 Marc Moro, Nash.	.75
☐	**216 Scott Clemmensen (G), NJer. RC**	**3.00**
☐	217 Brad Tapper,Atla.	.75
☐	218 Barrett Heisten, NYRa.	1.00
☐	**219 Chris Neil, Otta. RC**	**1.00**
☐	220 Pavel Brendl, Phil.	1.50
☐	221 Miikka Kiprusoff (G), SanJ.	1.50
☐	222 Jimmie Ölvestad, Tamp.	.75
☐	**223 Brian Sutherby, Wash. RC**	**3.00**
☐	**224 Timo Pärssinen, Anah. RC**	**1.00**
☐	225 Sascha Goc, NJer.	.75

UPDATE

	Description	Base
☐	226 Dany Heatley,Atla.	5.00
☐	227 Nick Boynton, Bost.	1.00
☐	228 Steve Bégin, Calg.	1.00
☐	**229 Erik Cole, Caro. RC**	**4.00**
☐	230 Mark Bell, Chic.	1.00
☐	231 Rick Berry, Colo.	.75
☐	**232 Niko Kapanen, Dall. RC**	**4.00**
☐	**233 Pavel Datsyuk, Detr. RC**	**15.00**
☐	**234 Niklas Hagman, Flor. RC**	**3.00**
☐	**235 Jaroslav Bednar, LosA. RC**	**3.00**
☐	**236 Pascal Dupuis, MinW. RC**	**4.00**
☐	237 Mike Ribeiro, Mont.	1.50
☐	**238 Martin Erat, Nash. RC**	**3.00**
☐	239 Jiri Bicek, NJer.	.75
☐	**240 Radek Martinek, NYIs. RC**	**1.00**
☐	**241 Ivan Ciernik, Otta. RC**	**3.00**
☐	242 Jesse Boulerice, Phil.	.75
☐	**243 Krys Kolanos, Phoe. RC**	**4.00**
☐	244 Toby Petersen, Pitt.	.75
☐	**245 Jeff Jillson, SanJ. RC**	**3.00**
☐	**246 Mark Rycroft, SLou. RC**	**1.00**
☐	**247 Kamil Piros,Atla. RC**	**3.00**
☐	**248 Nikita Alexeev, Tamp. RC**	**4.00**
☐	249 Stephen Peat, Wash.	.75
☐	250 Pierre Dagenais, NJer.	.75

HE SHOOTS HE SCORES REDEMPTION

Insert Set (20 cards):

	Insert	HSHS
☐	Eric Lindros, NYRa. [1 Point]	
☐	Mats Sundin, Toro. [1 Point]	
☐	Teemu Selänne, SanJ. [1 Point]	
☐	Mike Modano, Dall. [1 Point]	
☐	John LeClair, Phil. [1 Point]	
☐	Tony Amonte, Chic. [1 Point]	
☐	Luc Robitaille, Detr. [1 Point]	
☐	Sergei Fedorov, Detr. [1 Point]	
☐	Bill Guerin, Bost. [1 Point]	
☐	Jeremy Roenick, Phil. [1 Point]	
☐	Mark Messier, NYRa. [1 Point]	
☐	Pavel Bure, Flor. [2 Points]	
☐	Ilya Kovalchuk, Atla. [2 Points]	
☐	Brendan Shanahan, Detr. [2 Points]	
☐	Paul Kariya, Anah. [2 Points]	
☐	Jaromir Jagr, Wash. [2 Points]	
☐	Jarome Iginla, Calg. [2 Points]	
☐	Steve Yzerman, Detr. [3 Points]	
☐	Joe Sakic, Colo. [3 Points]	
☐	Mario Lemieux, Pitt. [3 Points]	

500 GOAL SCORERS

Insert Set (29 cards): 4,460

	Insert	500S
☐	Dave Andreychuk ✂ {*90}	40.00
☐	Jean Béliveau ✂ {*20}	350.00
☐	Mike Bossy ✂ {*50}	125.00
☐	Johnny Bucyk ✂ {*30}	100.00
☐	Dino Ciccarelli ✂ {*90}	40.00
☐	Marcel Dionne ✂ {*30}	125.00
☐	Phil Esposito ✂ {*30}	125.00
☐	Ron Francis ✂ {*10}	200.00
☐	Mike Gartner ✂ {*90}	75.00
☐	Michel Goulet ✂ {*90}	40.00
☐	Dale Hawerchuk ✂ {*90}	50.00
☐	Gordie Howe ✂ {*10}	800.00
☐	Brett Hull ✂ {*30}	175.00
☐	Bobby Hull ✂ {*20}	350.00
☐	Jari Kurri ✂ {*90}	100.00
☐	Guy Lafleur ✂ {*30}	200.00
☐	Mario Lemieux ✂ {*20}	750.00
☐	Frank Mahovlich ✂ {*30}	100.00
☐	Lanny McDonald ✂ {*90}	75.00
☐	Mark Messier ✂ {*30}	175.00
☐	Stan Mikita ✂ {*30}	100.00
☐	Joe Mullen ✂ {*90}	40.00
☐	Gilbert Perreault ✂ {*90}	50.00
☐	Maurice Richard ✂ {*10}	800.00
☐	Luc Robitaille ✂ {*30}	125.00
☐	Brendan Shanahan ✂ {*10}	300.00
☐	Bryan Trottier ✂ {*50}	100.00
☐	Pat Verbeek ✂ {*90}	40.00
☐	Steve Yzerman ✂ {*30}	400.00
☐	Mario Lemieux, Pitt. ✍ ✂ {*10}	1500.00
☐	Mark Messier, ✍ ✂ {*10}	500.00
☐	Steve Yzerman, Detr. ✍ ✂ {*10}	1200.00

AUTOGRAPH

Insert Set (225 cards):

	Insert	Gold	Silver
		-	-
☐ ☐	1 Rick DiPietro, NYIs. ✍ [FSC]	20.00	18.00
☐ ☐	2 Patrik Stefan,Atla. ✍	10.00	8.00
☐ ☐	3 Hal Gill, Bost. ✍ [FSC]	10.00	5.00
☐ ☐	4 Jean-Pierre Dumont, Buff. ✍	10.00	6.00
☐ ☐	5 Jarome Iginla, Calg. ✍	30.00	20.00
☐ ☐	6 Shane Willis, Caro. ✍	10.00	6.00
☐ ☐	7 Chris Phillips, Otta. ✍	10.00	6.00
☐ ☐	8 Rostislav Klesla, Colu. ✍	10.00	8.00
☐ ☐	9 Brenden Morrow, Dall. ✍	10.00	8.00
☐ ☐	10 Manny Legacé (G), Detr. ✍ [FSC]	15.00	12.00
☐ ☐	11 Anson Carter, Edmo. ✍	15.00	10.00
☐ ☐	12 Roberto Luongo (G), Flor. ✍	30.00	20.00
☐ ☐	13 Aaron Miller, LosA. ✍	10.00	5.00
☐ ☐	14 Wayne Primeau, Pitt. ✍	10.00	5.00
☐ ☐	15 Brian Savage, Mont. ✍	10.00	8.00
☐ ☐	16 John Jakopin, Flor. ✍ [FSC]	10.00	5.00
☐ ☐	17 Greg Johnson, Nash. ✍	10.00	5.00
☐ ☐	18 Marc Chouinard, Anah. ✍	10.00	5.00
☐ ☐	19 Steve Martins, NYIs. ✍ [FSC]	10.00	5.00
☐ ☐	20 Marian Hossa, Otta. ✍	35.00	25.00
☐ ☐	21 Brent Johnson (G), SLou. ✍ [FSC]	15.00	10.00
☐ ☐	22 Sean Burke (G), Phoe. ✍	20.00	15.00
☐ ☐	23 Jan Hrdina, Pitt. ✍	10.00	6.00
☐ ☐	24 Evgeni Nabokov (G), SanJ. ✍ [FSC]	20.00	15.00
☐ ☐	25 Adam Deadmarsh, LosA. ✍	10.00	8.00
☐ ☐	26 Brad Richards, Tamp. ✍	15.00	12.00
☐ ☐	27 Wade Redden, Otta. ✍	10.00	8.00
☐ ☐	28 David Legwand, Nash. ✍	15.00	10.00
☐ ☐	29 J-S Giguère (G), Anah. ✍ [FSC]	30.00	25.00
☐ ☐	30 Ray Ferraro,Atla. ✍	10.00	5.00
☐ ☐	31 Denis Hamel, Buff. ✍ [FSC]	10.00	5.00
☐ ☐	32 Marc Savard, Calg. ✍	10.00	6.00
☐ ☐	33 Craig Adams, Caro. ✍ [FSC]	10.00	5.00
☐ ☐	34 Landon Wilson, Phoe. ✍	10.00	5.00
☐ ☐	35 Marc Denis (G), Colu. ✍	15.00	12.00
☐ ☐	36 Roman Lyashenko, Dall. ✍	10.00	5.00
☐ ☐	37 Tomas Holmström, Detr. ✍	10.00	6.00
☐ ☐	38 Mike Comrie, Edmo. ✍ [FSC]	30.00	20.00
☐ ☐	39 Scott Hartnell, Nash. ✍	10.00	6.00
☐ ☐	40 Sergei Krivokrasov, MinW. ✍	10.00	5.00
☐ ☐	41 Mathieu Garon (G), Mont. ✍ [FSC]	15.00	10.00
☐ ☐	42 Denis Arkhipov, Nash. ✍ [FSC]	10.00	6.00
☐ ☐	43 Roman Hamrlik, NYIs. ✍	10.00	6.00
☐ ☐	44 Mike Mottau, NYRa. ✍ [FSC]	10.00	5.00
☐ ☐	45 Shawn McEachern, Otta. ✍	10.00	8.00
☐ ☐	46 Peter White, Phil. ✍	10.00	5.00
☐ ☐	47 Shane Doan, Phoe. ✍	10.00	6.00
☐ ☐	48 Janne Laukkanen, Pitt. ✍	10.00	5.00
☐ ☐	49 Martin St-Louis, Tamp. ✍ [FSC]	20.00	18.00
☐ ☐	50 Tomas Kaberle, Toro. ✍	10.00	8.00
☐ ☐	51 Daniel Sedin, Vanc. ✍	15.00	10.00
☐ ☐	52 Jonas Rönnqvist, Anah. ✍ FSC	10.00	5.00
☐ ☐	53 Damian Rhodes (G),Atla. ✍	10.00	6.00
☐ ☐	54 Vaclav Varada, Buff. ✍	10.00	5.00
☐ ☐	55 Ronald Petrovicky, Calg. ✍	10.00	5.00
☐ ☐	56 Tommy Westlund, Caro. ✍	10.00	5.00
☐ ☐	57 Michael Nylander, Chic. ✍	10.00	6.00
☐ ☐	58 Serge Aubin, Colu. ✍ [FSC]	10.00	5.00
☐ ☐	59 Jiri Fischer, Detr. ✍	10.00	6.00
☐ ☐	60 Shawn Horcoff, Edmo. ✍	10.00	5.00
☐ ☐	61 Peter Worrell, Flor. ✍	10.00	6.00
☐ ☐	62 Willie Mitchell, MinW. ✍ FSC	10.00	5.00
☐ ☐	63 Oleg Petrov, Mont. ✍ [FSC]	10.00	8.00
☐ ☐	64 Scott Walker, Nash. ✍	10.00	6.00
☐ ☐	65 Tomi Kallio,Atla. ✍	10.00	5.00
☐ ☐	66 Jason Strudwick, Vanc. ✍ [FSC]	10.00	5.00
☐ ☐	67 Magnus Arvedson, Otta. ✍	10.00	5.00
☐ ☐	68 Éric Dazé, Chic. ✍	15.00	10.00
☐ ☐	69 Johan Hedberg (G), Pitt. ✍ [FSC]	25.00	20.00
☐ ☐	70 Fredrik Modin, Tamp. ✍	10.00	6.00
☐ ☐	71 Nathan Dempsey, Toro. ✍ [FSC]	10.00	5.00
☐ ☐	72 Henrik Sedin, Vanc. ✍	15.00	10.00
☐ ☐	73 Mike Leclerc, Anah. ✍	10.00	5.00
☐ ☐	74 Hnat Domenichelli,Atla. ✍ [FSC]	10.00	5.00
☐ ☐	75 Jeff Cowan, Calg. ✍	10.00	5.00
☐ ☐	76 Brad Stuart, SanJ. ✍	15.00	10.00
☐ ☐	77 Bryan Allen, Vanc. ✍ [FSC]	10.00	5.00
☐ ☐	78 Wes Walz, MinW. ✍ [FSC]	10.00	6.00
☐ ☐	79 Patrick Traverse, Mont. ✍ [FSC]	10.00	5.00
☐ ☐	80 Markus Näslund, Vanc. ✍	35.00	25.00
☐ ☐	81 Brad Isbister, NYIs. ✍	10.00	6.00
☐ ☐	82 Jan Hlavac, NYRa. ✍	10.00	6.00
☐ ☐	83 Steve Sullivan, Chic. ✍	10.00	8.00
☐ ☐	84 Marian Gaborik, MinW. ✍	35.00	25.00
☐ ☐	85 Kristian Kudroc, Tamp. ✍	10.00	5.00
☐ ☐	86 Peter Schaefer, Vanc. ✍	10.00	5.00
☐ ☐	87 Pascal Trépanier, Anah. ✍ [FSC]	10.00	5.00
☐ ☐	88 Milan Hnilicka (G),Atla. ✍ [FSC]	10.00	6.00
☐ ☐	89 Dave Lowry, Calg. ✍	10.00	6.00
☐ ☐	90 Jamie Allison, Chic. ✍ [FSC]	10.00	5.00
☐ ☐	91 Jeff Nielsen, MinW. ✍	10.00	5.00
☐ ☐	92 Sheldon Souray, Mont. ✍	10.00	5.00
☐ ☐	93 Mike Dunham (G), Nash. ✍	15.00	10.00
☐ ☐	94 Branislav Mezei, NYIs. ✍	10.00	5.00
☐ ☐	95 Dale Purinton, NYRa. ✍ [FSC]	10.00	8.00
☐ ☐	96 Cory Sarich, Tamp. ✍	10.00	5.00
☐ ☐	97 Jarkko Ruutu, Vanc. ✍	10.00	5.00
☐ ☐	98 Kyle Calder, Chic. ✍ [FSC]	10.00	6.00
☐ ☐	99 Frantisek Musil, Edmo. ✍ [FSC]	10.00	6.00
☐ ☐	100 Tomas Kloucek, NYRa. ✍ [FSC]	10.00	5.00
☐ ☐	101 Karel Rachunek, Otta. ✍ [FSC]	10.00	8.00
☐ ☐	102 Darcy Tucker, Toro. ✍	10.00	6.00
☐ ☐	103 Alex Tanguay, Colo. ✍	20.00	15.00
☐ ☐	104 Patrick Lalime (G), Otta. ✍	20.00	15.00
☐ ☐	105 Ossi Väänänen, Phoe. ✍	10.00	5.00
☐ ☐	106 Martin Skoula, Colo. ✍	10.00	6.00
☐ ☐	107 Lubomir Visnovsky, LosA. ✍ [FSC]	10.00	8.00
☐ ☐	108 Richard Zednik, Mont. ✍	15.00	10.00
☐ ☐	109 Jani Hurme (G), Otta. ✍	10.00	6.00
☐ ☐	110 Teppo Numminen, Phoe. ✍	10.00	8.00
☐ ☐	111 Scott Young, SLou. ✍	10.00	8.00
☐ ☐	112 Robert Reichel, Toro. ✍	10.00	8.00
☐ ☐	113 David Tanabe, Caro. ✍	10.00	5.00
☐ ☐	114 Steven Reinprecht, Colo. ✍	10.00	8.00
☐ ☐	115 Ryan Smyth, Edmo. ✍	15.00	12.00
☐ ☐	116 Jozef Stümpel, Bost. ✍	10.00	6.00
☐ ☐	117 Martin Rucinsky, Mont. ✍	10.00	6.00
☐ ☐	118 Radek Dvorak, NYRa. ✍	10.00	6.00
☐ ☐	119 Chris Herperger, Otta. ✍ [FSC]	10.00	5.00
☐ ☐	120 Eric Weinrich, Phil. ✍	10.00	5.00
☐ ☐	121 Claude Lemieux, Phoe. ✍	10.00	8.00
☐ ☐	122 Mike Ricci, SanJ. ✍	10.00	8.00
☐ ☐	123 Cory Stillman, SLou. ✍	10.00	6.00
☐ ☐	124 Alyn McCauley, Toro. ✍	10.00	8.00
☐ ☐	125 Trevor Linden, Wash. ✍	15.00	10.00
☐ ☐	126 Vitaly Vishnevski, Anah. ✍	10.00	6.00
☐ ☐	127 Tim Connolly, Buff. ✍	15.00	10.00
☐ ☐	128 Oleg Saprykin, Calg. ✍	10.00	6.00
☐ ☐	129 Arturs Irbe (G), Caro. ✍	15.00	10.00
☐ ☐	130 Ville Nieminen, Colo. ✍ [FSC]	15.00	12.00
☐ ☐	131 David Vyborny, Colu. ✍ [FSC]	10.00	8.00
☐ ☐	132 Janne Niinimaa, Edmo. ✍	10.00	6.00
☐ ☐	133 Joey Tetarenko, Flor. ✍ [FSC]	10.00	5.00
☐ ☐	134 Bryan Smolinski, LosA. ✍	10.00	5.00
☐ ☐	135 Stacy Roest, MinW. ✍ [FSC]	10.00	8.00
☐ ☐	136 Mikael Renberg, Toro. ✍	10.00	8.00
☐ ☐	137 Gino Odjick, Mont. ✍	10.00	5.00
☐ ☐	138 Petr Sykora, NJer. ✍	15.00	10.00
☐ ☐	139 Alexei Yashin, NYIs. ✍	20.00	15.00
☐ ☐	140 Martin Havlat, Otta. ✍	20.00	15.00
☐ ☐	141 Rick Tocchet, Phil. ✍	10.00	8.00
☐ ☐	142 Daymond Langkow, Phoe. ✍	10.00	6.00
☐ ☐	143 Kevin Stevens, Pitt. ✍	10.00	6.00
☐ ☐	144 Patrick Marleau, SanJ. ✍	15.00	12.00
☐ ☐	145 Reed Low, SLou. ✍ [FSC]	10.00	8.00
☐ ☐	146 Bryan McCabe, Toro. ✍	10.00	6.00
☐ ☐	147 Dmitri Khristich, Wash. ✍	10.00	5.00
☐ ☐	148 Oleg Tverdovsky, Anah. ✍	10.00	5.00
☐ ☐	149 Yannick Tremblay,Atla. ✍ [FSC]	10.00	5.00
☐ ☐	150 Martin Biron (G), Buff. (G) ✍	15.00	12.00
☐ ☐	151 Rob Niedermayer, Calg. ✍	10.00	6.00
☐ ☐	152 Rod Brind'Amour, Caro. ✍	10.00	8.00
☐ ☐	153 Adam Foote, Colo. ✍	10.00	8.00
☐ ☐	154 Geoff Sanderson, Colu. ✍	10.00	6.00
☐ ☐	155 Pat Verbeek, Dall. ✍	10.00	8.00
☐ ☐	156 Nicklas Lidström, Detr. ✍	20.00	15.00
☐ ☐	157 Jochen Hecht, Edmo. ✍	10.00	6.00
☐ ☐	158 Robert Svehla, Flor. ✍	10.00	6.00
☐ ☐	159 Mathieu Schneider, LosA. ✍	10.00	6.00
☐ ☐	160 Antti Laaksonen, MinW. ✍ [FSC]	10.00	5.00
☐ ☐	161 Jeff Hackett (G), Mont. ✍	10.00	8.00
☐ ☐	162 Scott Niedermayer, NJer. ✍	10.00	8.00
☐ ☐	163 Sandis Ozolinsh, Caro. ✍ [FSC]	10.00	6.00
☐ ☐	164 Radek Bonk, Otta. ✍	10.00	8.00
☐ ☐	165 Roman Cechmanek (G), Phil. ✍ [FSC]	20.00	15.00
☐ ☐	166 Mike Johnson, Phoe. ✍	10.00	5.00
☐ ☐	167 Milan Kraft, Pitt. ✍	10.00	8.00
☐ ☐	168 Adam Graves, SanJ. ✍	15.00	10.00
☐ ☐	169 Pavol Demitra, SLou. ✍	15.00	10.00
☐ ☐	170 Kevin Weekes (G), Tamp. ✍ [FSC]	10.00	8.00
☐ ☐	171 Travis Green, Toro. ✍	10.00	6.00
☐ ☐	172 Jeff Halpern, Wash. ✍	10.00	6.00
☐ ☐	173 Steve Shields (G), Anah. ✍	10.00	6.00
☐ ☐	174 Lubos Bartecko,Atla. ✍ [FSC]	10.00	8.00
☐ ☐	175 P.J. Stock, Bost. ✍ [FSC]	19.00	16.00
☐ ☐	176 Maxim Afinogenov, Buff. ✍	15.00	10.00
☐ ☐	177 Derek Morris, Calg. ✍	10.00	6.00
☐ ☐	178 Bates Battaglia, Caro. ✍ [FSC]	10.00	8.00
☐ ☐	179 Boris Mironov, Chic. ✍	10.00	5.00
☐ ☐	180 David Aebischer (G), Colo. ✍ [FSC]	15.00	12.00
☐ ☐	181 Espen Knutsen, Colu. ✍ [FSC]	10.00	8.00
☐ ☐	182 Darryl Sydor, Dall. ✍	10.00	6.00
☐ ☐	183 Igor Larionov, Detr. ✍	20.00	15.00
☐ ☐	184 Eric Brewer, Edmo. ✍	15.00	10.00
☐ ☐	185 Trevor Kidd (G), Flor. ✍	10.00	8.00
☐ ☐	186 Éric Bélanger, LosA. ✍ [FSC]	10.00	8.00
☐ ☐	187 Manny Fernandez (G), MinW. ✍	15.00	10.00
☐ ☐	188 Francis Bouillon, Mont. ✍ [FSC]	10.00	5.00
☐ ☐	189 Patrik Elias, NJer. ✍	30.00	20.00
☐ ☐	190 Mariusz Czerkawski, NYIs. ✍	10.00	6.00
☐ ☐	191 Daniel Alfredsson, Otta. ✍	20.00	15.00
☐ ☐	192 Brian Boucher (G), Phil. ✍	10.00	8.00
☐ ☐	193 Sergei Berezin, Phoe. ✍	10.00	6.00
☐ ☐	194 Kris Beech, Pitt. ✍	10.00	8.00
☐ ☐	195 Vincent Damphousse, SanJ. ✍	20.00	15.00
☐ ☐	196 Fred Brathwaite (G), SLou. ✍	10.00	8.00
☐ ☐	197 Ben Clymer, Tamp. ✍ [FSC]	10.00	5.00
☐ ☐	198 Wade Belak, Toro. ✍ [FSC]	10.00	5.00
☐ ☐	199 Ed Jovanovski, Vanc. ✍	15.00	10.00
☐ ☐	200 Sergei Gonchar, Wash. ✍	10.00	8.00
☐ ☐	201 Dan Blackburn (G), NYRa. ✍ [FSC]	20.00	15.00
☐ ☐	202 Daniel Tjärnqvist,Atla. ✍ [FSC]	10.00	5.00
☐ ☐	203 A. Salomonsson, NJer. ✍ [FSC]	10.00	5.00
☐ ☐	204 Vaclav Nedorost, Colo. ✍ [FSC]	10.00	8.00
☐ ☐	205 Justin Kurtz, Vanc. ✍ [FSC]	10.00	5.00
☐ ☐	206 Jiri Dopita, Phil. ✍ [FSC]	10.00	8.00
☐ ☐	207 Ilya Kovalchuk,Atla. ✍ [FSC]	50.00	40.00
☐ ☐	208 Richard Jackman, Bost. ✍ [FSC]	10.00	8.00
☐ ☐	209 Scott Nichol, Calg. ✍ [FSC]	10.00	5.00

□□	210 Brad Larsen, Colo. ✍ [FSC]	10.00	5.00
□□	211 Jason Williams, Detr. ✍ [FSC]	10.00	8.00
□□	212 Kristian Huselius, Flor. ✍ [FSC]	18.00	15.00
□□	213 Andreas Lilja, LosA. ✍ [FSC]	10.00	5.00
□□	214 Nick Schultz, MinW. ✍ [FSC]	10.00	8.00
□□	215 Marc Moro, Nash. ✍ [FSC]	10.00	5.00
□□	216 S. Clemmensen (G), NJer. ✍ [FSC]	10.00	8.00
□□	217 Brad Tapper, Atla. ✍ [FSC]	10.00	8.00
□□	218 Barrett Heisten, NYRa. ✍ [FSC]	10.00	8.00
□□	219 Chris Neil, Otta. ✍ [FSC]	10.00	5.00
□□	220 Pavel Brendl, Phil. ✍ [FSC]	15.00	10.00
□□	221 Miikka Kiprusoff (G), SanJ. ✍ [FSC]	15.00	12.00
□□	222 Jimmie Ölvestad, Tamp. ✍ [FSC]	10.00	5.00
□□	223 Brian Sutherby, Wash. ✍ [FSC]	10.00	8.00
□□	224 Timo Pärssinen, Anah. ✍ [FSC]	10.00	5.00
□□	225 Sascha Goc, NJer. ✍ [FSC]	10.00	8.00
□□	226 Dany Heatley, Atla. ✍ [FSC]	50.00	40.00
□□	227 Nick Boynton, Bost. ✍ [FSC]	10.00	8.00
□□	228 Steve Bégin, Calg. ✍ [FSC]	10.00	8.00
□□	229 Erik Cole, Caro. ✍ [FSC]	14.00	12.00
□□	230 Mark Bell, Chic. ✍ [FSC]	10.00	8.00
□□	231 Rick Berry, Colo. ✍ [FSC]	10.00	5.00
□□	232 Niko Kapanen, Dall. ✍ [FSC]	10.00	8.00
□□	233 Pavel Datsyuk, Detr. ✍ [FSC]	45.00	40.00
□□	234 Niklas Hagman, Flor. ✍ [FSC]	10.00	8.00
□□	235 Jaroslav Bednar, LosA. ✍ [FSC]	10.00	8.00
□□	236 Pascal Dupuis, MinW. ✍ [FSC]	15.00	12.00
□□	237 Mike Ribeiro, Mont. ✍ [FSC]	15.00	10.00
□□	238 Martin Erat, Nash. ✍ [FSC]	10.00	8.00
□□	239 Jiri Bicek, NJer. ✍ [FSC]	10.00	8.00
□□	240 Radek Martinek, NYIs. ✍ [FSC]	10.00	5.00
□□	241 Ivan Ciernik, Otta. ✍ [FSC]	10.00	8.00
□□	242 Jesse Boulerice, Phil. ✍ [FSC]	10.00	5.00
□□	243 Krys Kolanos, Phoe. ✍ [FSC]	10.00	8.00
□□	244 Toby Petersen, Pitt. ✍ [FSC]	10.00	8.00
□□	245 Jeff Jillson, SanJ. ✍ [FSC]	10.00	8.00
□□	246 Mark Rycroft, SLou. ✍ [FSC]	10.00	5.00
□□	247 Kamil Piros, Atla. ✍ [FSC]	10.00	8.00
□□	248 Nikita Alexeev, Tamp. ✍ [FSC]	14.00	12.00
□□	249 Stephen Peat, Wash. ✍ [FSC]	10.00	5.00
□□	250 Pierre Dagenais, NJer. ✍ [FSC]	10.00	8.00

LIMITED AUTOGRAPHS

Insert Set (34 cards):		1,500	700
	Insert	Gold	Silver
□□	LJAL Jason Allison, LosA. ✍	75.00	35.00
□□	LDA Donald Audette, Dall. ✍	50.00	25.00
□□	LRB Rob Blake, Colo. ✍	75.00	35.00
□□	LPBO Peter Bondra, Wash. ✍	75.00	35.00
□□	LPBU Pavel Bure, Flor. ✍	100.00	50.00
□□	LBD Byron Dafoe (G), Bost. ✍	50.00	25.00
□□	LCD Chris Drury, Colo. ✍	75.00	35.00
□□	LRF Ron Francis, Caro. ✍	75.00	35.00
□□	LCG Chris Gratton, Buff. ✍	30.00	20.00
□□	LBG Bill Guerin, Bost. ✍	50.00	25.00
□□	LMH Milan Hejduk, Colo. ✍	100.00	50.00
□□	LSK Sami Kapanen, Caro. ✍	40.00	20.00
□□	LPK Paul Kariya, Anah. ✍	175.00	85.00
□□	LOK Olaf Kölzig (G), Wash. ✍	75.00	35.00
□□	LML Martin Lapointe, Bost. ✍	50.00	25.00
□□	LVL Vincent Lecavalier, Tamp. ✍	125.00	60.00
□□	LJL John LeClair, Phil. ✍	100.00	50.00
□□	LBL Brian Leetch, NYRa. ✍	75.00	35.00
□□	LAM Al MacInnis, SLou. ✍	50.00	25.00
□□	LKM Kyle McLaren, Bost. ✍	30.00	20.00
□□	LJO Jeff O'Neill, Caro. ✍	50.00	25.00
□□	LZP Zigmund Palffy, LosA. ✍	75.00	35.00
□□	LCP Chris Pronger, SLou. ✍	75.00	35.00
□□	LMR Mark Recchi, Phil. ✍	50.00	25.00
□□	LLR Luc Robitaille, Detr. ✍	100.00	50.00
□□	LJS Joe Sakic, Colo. ✍	200.00	100.00
□□	LTS Tommy Salo (G), Edmo. ✍ ,, ✍/	50.00	25.00
□□	LSSA Sergei Samsonov, Bost. ✍	75.00	35.00
□□	LBS Brendan Shanahan, Detr. ✍	125.00	60.00
□□	LSST Scott Stevens, NJer. ✍	50.00	25.00
□□	LJT Joe Thornton, Bost. ✍	150.00	75.00
□□	LRT Roman Turek (G), Calg. ✍ ,, ✍/	60.00	30.00
□□	LPT Pierre Turgeon, Dall. ✍	50.00	25.00
□□	LDW Doug Weight, SLou. ✍	75.00	35.00

CERTIFIED

There are three versions for each card 1-60: a pink card (#/100), a purple card (#/50), and a green card (#/1).

Insert Set (60 cards):		1,100	500.00
	Insert	P50	P100
□□□	C-1 Al MacInnis, SLou.	18.00	8.00
□□□	C-2 Adam Oates, Wash.	18.00	8.00
□□□	C-3 Byron Dafoe (G), Bost.	18.00	8.00
□□□	C-4 Bill Guerin, Bost.	18.00	8.00
□□□	C-5 Brian Leetch, NYRa.	18.00	8.00
□□□	C-6 Brendan Shanahan, Detr.	25.00	10.00
□□□	C-7 Chris Drury, Colo.	18.00	8.00
□□□	C-8 Chris Gratton, Buff.	18.00	8.00
□□□	C-9 Curtis Joseph (G), Toro.	25.00	10.00
□□□	C-10 Chris Pronger, SLou.	18.00	8.00
□□□	C-11 Donald Audette, Dall.	18.00	8.00
□□□	C-12 Doug Weight, SLou.	18.00	8.00
□□□	C-13 Ed Belfour (G), Dall.	25.00	10.00
□□□	C-14 Eric Lindros, NYRa.	25.00	10.00
□□□	C-15 Jason Allison, LosA.	18.00	8.00
□□□	C-16 Jason Arnott, NJer.	18.00	8.00
□□□	C-17 John LeClair, Phil.	20.00	10.00
□□□	C-18 Jeff O'Neill, Caro.	18.00	8.00
□□□	C-19 Jeremy Roenick, Phil.	20.00	10.00
□□□	C-20 Joe Sakic, Colo.	40.00	20.00
□□□	C-21 Joe Thornton, Bost.	30.00	15.00
□□□	C-22 Kyle McLaren, Bost.	18.00	8.00
□□□	C-23 Luc Robitaille, Detr.	20.00	10.00
□□□	C-24 Martin Brodeur (G), NJer.	40.00	20.00
□□□	C-25 Milan Hejduk, Colo.	20.00	10.00
□□□	C-26 Martin Lapointe, Bost.	18.00	8.00
□□□	C-27 Mike Modano, Dall.	25.00	10.00
□□□	C-28 Mark Recchi, Phil.	18.00	8.00
□□□	C-29 Mats Sundin, Toro.	25.00	10.00
□□□	C-30 Olaf Kölzig (G), Wash.	18.00	8.00
□□□	C-31 Peter Bondra, Wash.	18.00	8.00
□□□	C-32 Pavel Bure, Flor.	20.00	10.00
□□□	C-33 Paul Kariya, Anah.	35.00	15.00
□□□	C-34 Pierre Turgeon, Dall.	18.00	8.00
□□□	C-35 Rob Blake, Colo.	18.00	8.00
□□□	C-36 Ron Francis, Caro.	18.00	8.00
□□□	C-37 Roman Turek (G), Calg.	18.00	8.00
□□□	C-38 Sergei Fedorov, Detr.	25.00	10.00
□□□	C-39 Scott Gomez, NJer.	18.00	8.00
□□□	C-40 Sami Kapanen, Caro.	18.00	8.00
□□□	C-41 Saku Koivu, Mont.	30.00	15.00
□□□	C-42 Sergei Samsonov, Bost.	18.00	8.00
□□□	C-43 Scott Stevens, NJer.	18.00	8.00
□□□	C-44 Steve Yzerman, Detr.	60.00	30.00
□□□	C-45 Tony Amonte, Chic.	18.00	8.00
□□□	C-46 Theoren Fleury, NYRa.	18.00	8.00
□□□	C-47 Teemu Selänne, SanJ.	20.00	10.00
□□□	C-48 Tommy Salo (G), Edmo.	18.00	8.00
□□□	C-49 Vincent Lecavalier, Tamp.	25.00	10.00
□□□	C-50 Zigmund Palffy, LosA.	18.00	8.00
□□□	C-51 Brett Hull, Detr.	25.00	10.00
□□□	C-52 Dominik Hasek (G), Detr.	25.00	10.00
□□□	C-53 Jaromir Jagr, Wash.	25.00	10.00
□□□	C-54 Mario Lemieux, Pitt.	75.00	35.00
□□□	C-55 Mark Messier, NYRa.	25.00	10.00
□□□	C-56 Mike Vernon (G), Calg.	18.00	8.00
□□□	C-57 Owen Nolan, SanJ.	18.00	8.00
□□□	C-58 Peter Forsberg, Colo.	35.00	15.00
□□□	C-59 Patrick Roy (G), Colo.	75.00	35.00
□□□	C-60 Wayne Gretzky, NYRa.	100.00	50.00

DEPARTMENT OF DEFENSE

Insert Set (12 cards):		2,800
	Insert (*40)	DD
□	Rob Blake, Colo. ✂	70.00
□	Sergei Gonchar, Wash. ✂	40.00
□	Tomas Kaberle, Toro. ✂	40.00
□	Darius Kasparaitis, Pitt. ✂	40.00
□	Rostislav Klesla, Colu. ✂	70.00
□	Brian Leetch, NYRa. ✂	70.00
□	Nicklas Lidström, Detr. ✂	70.00
□	Al MacInnis, SLou. ✂	45.00
□	Kyle McLaren, Bost. ✂	40.00
□	Sandis Ozolinsh, Flor. ✂	40.00
□	Chris Pronger, SLou. ✂	70.00
□	Oleg Tverdovsky, Anah. ✂	40.00

FRANCHISE PLAYERS

Insert Set (30 cards):		3,000
	Insert (*28)	FP
□	Daniel Alfredsson, Otta. ✂	150.00
□	Tony Amonte, Chic. ✂	75.00
□	Martin Brodeur (G), NJer. ✂	200.00
□	Pavel Bure, Flor. ✂	100.00
□	Sean Burke (G), Phoe. ✂	75.00
□	Marian Gaborik, MinW. ✂	125.00
□	Jarome Iginla, Calg. ✂	100.00
□	Jaromir Jagr, Wash. ✂	125.00
□	Sami Kapanen, Caro. ✂	75.00
□	Paul Kariya, Anah. ✂	175.00
□	Rostislav Klesla, Colu. ✂	75.00
□	Ilya Kovalchuk, Atla. ✂	125.00
□	Vincent Lecavalier, Tamp. ✂	125.00
□	John LeClair, Phil. ✂	100.00
□	David Legwand, Nash. ✂	75.00
□	Mario Lemieux, Pitt. ✂	350.00
□	Eric Lindros, NYRa. ✂	125.00
□	Mike Modano, Dall. ✂	125.00
□	Markus Näslund, Vanc. ✂	125.00
□	Owen Nolan, SanJ. ✂	75.00
□	Zigmund Palffy, LosA. ✂	75.00
□	Joe Sakic, Colo. ✂	200.00
□	Tommy Salo (G), Edmo. ✂	75.00
□	Miroslav Satan, Buff. ✂	75.00
□	Mats Sundin, Toro. ✂	125.00
□	José Théodore (G), Mont. ✂	150.00
□	Joe Thornton, Bost. ✂	150.00
□	Doug Weight, SLou. ✂	75.00
□	Alexei Yashin, NYIs. ✂	75.00
□	Steve Yzerman, Detr. ✂	275.00

GAME-USED EMBLEM

Actual realized pricing on these scarce cards may vary considerably from below listed pricing.

Insert Set (50 cards):		14,500
	Insert (*10)	GUE
□	Daniel Alfredsson, Otta. ✂	550.00
□	Tony Amonte, Chic. ✂	225.00
□	Jason Arnott, NJer. ✂	200.00
□	Peter Bondra, Wash. ✂	225.00
□	Brian Boucher (G), Phil. ✂	200.00
□	Martin Brodeur (G), NJer. ✂	600.00
□	Pavel Bure, Flor. ✂	300.00
□	Roman Cechmanek (G), Phil. ✂	200.00
□	Byron Dafoe (G), Bost. ✂	200.00
□	Chris Drury, Colo. ✂	225.00
□	Sergei Fedorov, Detr. ✂	375.00
□	Peter Forsberg, Colo. ✂	525.00
□	Ron Francis, Caro. ✂	225.00
□	Bill Guerin, Bost. ✂	200.00
□	Dominik Hasek (G), Detr. ✂	375.00
□	Marian Hossa, Otta. ✂	375.00
□	Jarome Iginla, Calg. ✂	300.00
□	Jaromir Jagr, Wash. ✂	375.00
□	Curtis Joseph (G), Toro. ✂	375.00
□	Paul Kariya, Anah. ✂	525.00
□	Olaf Kölzig (G), Wash. ✂	225.00
□	Ilya Kovalchuk, Atla. ✂	375.00
□	Vincent Lecavalier, Tamp. ✂	375.00
□	John LeClair, Phil. ✂	300.00
□	Brian Leetch, NYRa. ✂	225.00
□	Mario Lemieux, Pitt. ✂	1,100.00
□	Nicklas Lidström, Detr. ✂	225.00
□	Eric Lindros, NYRa. ✂	375.00
□	Roberto Luongo (G), Flor. ✂	300.00
□	Al MacInnis, SLou. ✂	200.00
□	Mark Messier, NYRa. ✂	375.00
□	Mike Modano, Dall. ✂	375.00
□	Owen Nolan, SanJ. ✂	225.00
□	Adam Oates, Wash. ✂	200.00
□	Chris Pronger, SLou. ✂	225.00
□	Mark Recchi, Phil. ✂	200.00
□	Mike Richter (G), NYRa. ✂	200.00
□	Luc Robitaille, Detr. ✂	300.00
□	Jeremy Roenick, Phil. ✂	300.00
□	Patrick Roy (G), Colo. ✂	900.00
□	Joe Sakic, Colo. ✂	600.00
□	Miroslav Satan, Buff. ✂	200.00
□	Teemu Selänne, SanJ. ✂	300.00
□	Brendan Shanahan, Detr. ✂	375.00
□	Mats Sundin, Toro. ✂	375.00
□	Joe Thornton, Bost. ✂	450.00
□	Mike Vernon (G), Calg. ✂	200.00
□	Doug Weight, SLou. ✂	225.00
□	Alexei Yashin, NYIs. ✂	225.00
□	Steve Yzerman, Detr. ✂	900.00

GAME-USED JERSEY

Insert Set (98 cards):		3,100
	Insert (*60)	GJ
□	Tony Amonte, Chic. ✂	30.00
□	Jason Arnott, NJer. ✂	30.00
□	Todd Bertuzzi, Vanc. ✂	75.00
□	Rob Blake, Colo. ✂	30.00
□	Peter Bondra, Wash. ✂	30.00
□	Radek Bonk, Otta. ✂	30.00
□	Brian Boucher (G), Phil. ✂	30.00
□	Martin Brodeur (G), NJer. ✂	100.00
□	Pavel Bure, Flor. ✂	50.00
□	Roman Cechmanek (G), Phil. ✂	30.00
□	Byron Dafoe (G), Bost. ✂	30.00
□	Chris Drury, Colo. ✂	30.00
□	Sergei Fedorov, Detr. ✂	50.00
□	Theoren Fleury, NYRa. ✂	30.00
□	Ron Francis, Caro. ✂	30.00
□	Marian Gaborik, MinW. ✂	50.00
□	Scott Gomez, NJer. ✂	30.00
□	Sergei Gonchar, Wash. ✂	30.00
□	Dominik Hasek (G), Detr. ✂	50.00
□	Martin Havlat, Otta. ✂	30.00
□	Milan Hejduk, Colo. ✂	50.00
□	Marian Hossa, Otta. ✂	50.00
□	Jarome Iginla, Calg. ✂	50.00
□	Jaromir Jagr, Wash. ✂	50.00
□	Kenny Jönsson, NYIs. ✂	30.00
□	Curtis Joseph (G), Toro. ✂	50.00
□	Paul Kariya, Anah. ✂	75.00
□	Rostislav Klesla, Colu. ✂	30.00
□	Saku Koivu, Mont. ✂	75.00
□	Olaf Kölzig (G), Wash. ✂	30.00
□	Ilya Kovalchuk, Atla. ✂	50.00
□	Vincent Lecavalier, Tamp. ✂	50.00
□	John LeClair, Phil. ✂	50.00
□	Brian Leetch, NYRa. ✂	30.00
□	Mario Lemieux, Pitt. ✂	175.00
□	Nicklas Lidström, Detr. ✂	30.00
□	Eric Lindros, NYRa. ✂	50.00
□	Roberto Luongo (G), Flor. ✂	50.00
□	Al MacInnis, SLou. ✂	30.00
□	Mark Messier, NYRa. ✂	50.00
□	Mike Modano, Dall. ✂	50.00
□	Markus Näslund, Vanc. ✂	50.00
□	Scott Niedermayer, NJer. ✂	30.00
□	Owen Nolan, SanJ. ✂	30.00
□	Jeff O'Neill, Caro. ✂	30.00
□	Adam Oates, Wash. ✂	30.00
□	Zigmund Palffy, LosA. ✂	30.00
□	Keith Primeau, Phil. ✂	30.00
□	Chris Pronger, SLou. ✂	30.00
□	Mark Recchi, Phil. ✂	30.00
□	Brad Richards, Tamp. ✂	30.00
□	Mike Richter (G), NYRa. ✂	30.00
□	Luc Robitaille, Detr. ✂	50.00
□	Jeremy Roenick, Phil. ✂	50.00
□	Patrick Roy (G), Colo. ✂	150.00
□	Joe Sakic, Colo. ✂	100.00
□	Miroslav Satan, Buff. ✂	30.00
□	Brian Savage, Mont. ✂	30.00
□	Henrik Sedin, Vanc. ✂	30.00
□	Daniel Sedin, Vanc. ✂	30.00
□	Teemu Selänne, SanJ. ✂	50.00
□	Brendan Shanahan, Detr. ✂	50.00
□	Scott Stevens, NJer. ✂	30.00
□	Mats Sundin, Toro. ✂	50.00
□	Alex Tanguay, Colo. ✂	30.00
□	Joe Thornton, Bost. ✂	75.00
□	Pierre Turgeon, Dall. ✂	30.00
□	Doug Weight, SLou. ✂	30.00
□	Alexei Yashin, NYIs. ✂	30.00
□	Steve Yzerman, Detr. ✂	150.00
	Insert (*90)	GJ
□	Daniel Alfredsson, Otta. ✂	60.00
□	Ed Belfour (G), Dall. ✂	50.00
□	Pavel Bure, Flor. ✂	40.00
□	Sean Burke, Phoe. ✂	30.00
□	Chris Chelios, Detr. ✂	30.00
□	Dan Cloutier, Vanc. ✂	25.00
□	Éric Dazé, Chic. ✂	25.00
□	Patrik Elias, Njer. ✂	40.00
□	Adam Foote, Colo. ✂	25.00
□	Peter Forsberg, Colo. ✂	70.00
□	Bill Guerin, Bost. ✂	25.00
□	Kristian Huselius, Flor. ✂	30.00
□	Arturs Irbe (G), Caro. ✂	25.00
□	Sami Kapanen, Caro. ✂	25.00
□	Nikolai Khabibulin, Tamp. ✂	25.00
□	Patrick Lalime, Otta. ✂	30.00
□	Alexander Mogilny, Toro. ✂	25.00
□	Evgeni Nabokov, SanJ. ✂	30.00
□	Sandis Ozolinsh, Flor. ✂	25.00
□	Félix Potvin, LosA. ✂	60.00
□	Tommy Salo, Edmo. ✂	25.00
□	Sergei Samsonov, Bost. ✂	30.00
□	Martin Straka, Pitt. ✂	25.00
□	Petr* Sykora, Njer. ✂	25.00
□	José Théodore, Mont. ✂	60.00
□	Jocelyn Thibault, Chic. ✂	25.00
□	Keith Tkachuk, Slou. ✂	30.00
□	Roman Turek, Calg. ✂	25.00

GAME-USED JERSEY AUTOGRAPH

Actual realized pricing on these scarce cards may vary considerably from below listed pricing.

Insert Set (58 cards):		17,400
	Insert (#/10)	GJA
□	Tony Amonte, Chic. ✍ ✂	300.00
□	Todd Bertuzzi, Vanc. ✍ ✂	600.00
□	Rob Blake, Colo. ✍ ✂	300.00
□	Peter Bondra, Wash. ✍ ✂	300.00
□	Radek Bonk, Otta. ✍ ✂	200.00
□	Brian Boucher (G), Phil. ✍ ✂	200.00
□	Pavel Bure, Flor. ✍ ✂	400.00
□	Roman Cechmanek (G), Phil. ✍ ✂	200.00
□	Byron Dafoe (G), Bost. ✍ ✂	200.00
□	Chris Drury, Colo. ✍ ✂	300.00
□	Sergei Fedorov, Detr. ✍ ✂	500.00
□	Ron Francis, Caro. ✍ ✂	300.00
□	Marian Gaborik, MinW. ✍ ✂	500.00
□	Sergei Gonchar, Wash. ✍ ✂	200.00
□	Dominik Hasek (G), Detr. ✍ ✂	500.00
□	Martin Havlat, Otta. ✍ ✂	300.00
□	Milan Hejduk, Colo. ✍ ✂	400.00
□	Marian Hossa, Otta. ✍ ✂	500.00
□	Jarome Iginla, Calg. ✍ ✂	400.00
□	Kenny Jönsson, NYIs. ✍ ✂	200.00
□	Paul Kariya, Anah. ✍ ✂	700.00
□	Rostislav Klesla, Colu. ✍ ✂	450.00
□	Olaf Kölzig (G), Wash. ✍ ✂	300.00
□	Ilya Kovalchuk, Atla. ✍ ✂	500.00
□	Vincent Lecavalier, Tamp. ✍ ✂	500.00
□	John LeClair, Phil. ✍ ✂	400.00

☐	Brian Leetch, NYRa. ✍ ✂	300.00
☐	Mario Lemieux, Pitt. ✍ ✂	1500.00
☐	Mario Lemieux, Pitt. ✍ ✂	1500.00
☐	Nicklas Lidström, Detr. ✍ ✂	300.00
☐	Roberto Luongo (G), Flor. ✍ ✂	400.00
☐	Al MacInnis, SLou. ✍ ✂	200.00
☐	Mark Messier, NYRa. ✍ ✂	500.00
☐	Markus Näslund, Vanc. ✍ ✂	500.00
☐	Scott Niedermayer, NJer. ✍ ✂	200.00
☐	Owen Nolan, SanJ. ✍ ✂	300.00
☐	Jeff O'Neill, Caro. ✍ ✂	200.00
☐	Zigmund Palffy, LosA. ✍ ✂	300.00
☐	Keith Primeau, Phil. ✍ ✂	200.00
☐	Chris Pronger, SLou. ✍ ✂	300.00
☐	Brad Richards, Tamp. ✍ ✂	225.00
☐	Mike Richter, NYRa. ✍ ✂	225.00
☐	Luc Robitaille, Detr. ✍ ✂	400.00
☐	Jeremy Roenick, Phoe. ✍ ✂	400.00
☐	Joe Sakic, Colo. ✍ ✂	800.00
☐	Miroslav Satan, Buff. ✍ ✂	200.00
☐	Brian Savage, Mont. ✍ ✂	200.00
☐	Henrik Sedin, Vanc. ✍ ✂	200.00
☐	Daniel Sedin, Vanc. ✍ ✂	200.00
☐	Teemu Selänne, SanJ. ✍ ✂	400.00
☐	Brendan Shanahan, Detr. ✍ ✂	500.00
☐	Scott Stevens, NJer. ✍ ✂	200.00
☐	Alex Tanguay, Colo. ✍ ✂	300.00
☐	Joe Thornton, Bost. ✍ ✂	600.00
☐	Pierre Turgeon, Dall. ✍ ✂	200.00
☐	Doug Weight, SLou. ✍ ✂	300.00
☐	Alexei Yashin,NYIs. ✍ ✂	300.00
☐	Steve Yzerman, Detr. ✍ ✂	1200.00

GAME-USED STICK & JERSEY

	Insert Set (20 cards):	775.00
	Insert (*60)	GSJ
☐	Tony Amonte, Chic. ✂	35.00
☐	Jason Arnott, NJer. ✂	35.00
☐	Todd Bertuzzi, Vanc. ✂	75.00
☐	Rob Blake, Colo. ✂	35.00
☐	Peter Bondra, Wash. ✂	35.00
☐	Radek Bonk, Otta. ✂	35.00
☐	Brian Boucher (G), Phil. ✂	35.00
☐	Martin Brodeur (G), NJer. ✂	100.00
☐	Pavel Bure, Flor. ✂	50.00
☐	Roman Cechmanek (G), Phil. ✂	35.00
☐	Byron Dafoe (G), Bost. ✂	35.00
☐	Chris Drury, Colo. ✂	35.00
☐	Sergei Fedorov, Detr. ✂	50.00
☐	Theoren Fleury, NYRa. ✂	35.00
☐	Ron Francis, Caro. ✂	35.00
☐	Marian Gaborik, MinW. ✂	50.00
☐	Scott Gomez, NJer. ✂	35.00
☐	Sergei Gonchar, Wash. ✂	35.00
☐	Dominik Hasek (G), Detr. ✂	50.00
☐	Martin Havlat, Otta. ✂	35.00
☐	Milan Hejduk, Colo. ✂	50.00
☐	Marian Hossa, Otta. ✂	50.00
☐	Jarome Iginla, Calg. ✂	50.00
☐	Jaromir Jagr, Wash. ✂	50.00
☐	Kenny Jönsson,NYIs. ✂	35.00
☐	Curtis Joseph (G), Toro. ✂	50.00
☐	Paul Kariya, Anah. ✂	75.00
☐	Rostislav Klesla, Colu. ✂	35.00
☐	Saku Koivu, Mont. ✂	75.00
☐	Olaf Kölzig (G), Wash. ✂	35.00
☐	Ilya Kovalchuk,Atla. ✂	50.00
☐	Vincent Lecavalier, Tamp. ✂	50.00
☐	John LeClair, Phil. ✂	50.00
☐	Brian Leetch, NYRa. ✂	35.00
☐	Mario Lemieux, Pitt. ✂	175.00
☐	Nicklas Lidström, Detr. ✂	35.00
☐	Eric Lindros, NYRa. ✂	50.00
☐	Roberto Luongo (G), Flor. ✂	50.00
☐	Al MacInnis, SLou. ✂	35.00
☐	Mark Messier, NYRa. ✂	50.00
☐	Mike Modano, Dall. ✂	50.00
☐	Markus Näslund, Vanc. ✂	50.00
☐	Scott Niedermayer, NJer. ✂	35.00
☐	Owen Nolan, SanJ. ✂	35.00
☐	Jeff O'Neill, Caro. ✂	35.00
☐	Adam Oates, Wash. ✂	35.00
☐	Zigmund Palffy, LosA. ✂	35.00
☐	Keith Primeau, Phil. ✂	35.00
☐	Chris Pronger, SLou. ✂	35.00
☐	Mark Recchi, Phil. ✂	35.00
☐	Brad Richards, Tamp. ✂	35.00
☐	Mike Richter (G), NYRa. ✂	35.00
☐	Luc Robitaille, Detr. ✂	50.00
☐	Jeremy Roenick, Phil. ✂	50.00
☐	Patrick Roy (G), Colo. ✂	150.00
☐	Joe Sakic, Colo. ✂	100.00
☐	Miroslav Satan, Buff. ✂	35.00
☐	Brian Savage, Mont. ✂	35.00
☐	Henrik Sedin, Vanc. ✂	35.00
☐	Daniel Sedin, Vanc. ✂	35.00
☐	Teemu Selänne, SanJ. ✂	50.00
☐	Brendan Shanahan, Detr. ✂	50.00
☐	Scott Stevens, NJer. ✂	35.00
☐	Mats Sundin, Toro. ✂	50.00
☐	Alex Tanguay, Colo. ✂	35.00
☐	Joe Thornton, Bost. ✂	75.00
☐	Pierre Turgeon, Dall. ✂	35.00
☐	Doug Weight, SLou. ✂	35.00
☐	Alexei Yashin,NYIs. ✂	35.00
☐	Steve Yzerman, Detr. ✂	150.00

HE SHOOTS HE SCORES JERSEY

	Redemption Set (40 cards):	
	Redemption (*20)	HSHS
☐	Daniel Alfredsson, Otta. ✂	
☐	Tony Amonte, Chic. ✂	
☐	Rob Blake, Colo. ✂	
☐	Peter Bondra, Wash. ✂	
☐	Éric Dazé, Chic. ✂	
☐	Chris Drury, Colo. ✂	
☐	Sergei Fedorov, Detr. ✂	
☐	Peter Forsberg, Colo. ✂	
☐	Ron Francis, Caro. ✂	
☐	Bill Guerin, Bost. ✂	
☐	Milan Hejduk, Colo. ✂	
☐	Kristian Huselius, Flor. ✂	
☐	Jarome Iginla, Calg. ✂	
☐	Jaromir Jagr, Wash. ✂	
☐	Sami Kapanen, Caro. ✂	
☐	Paul Kariya, Anah. ✂	
☐	Saku Koivu, Mont. ✂	
☐	Ilya Kovalchuk, Atla. ✂	
☐	John LeClair, Phil. ✂	
☐	Mario Lemieux, Pitt. ✂	
☐	Eric Lindros, NYRa. ✂	
☐	Mark Messier, NYRa. ✂	
☐	Mike Modano, Dall. ✂	
☐	Alexander Mogilny, Toro. ✂	
☐	Markus Naslund, Vanc. ✂	
☐	Owen Nolan, SanJ. ✂	
☐	Zigmund Palffy, LosA. ✂	
☐	Mark Recchi, Phil. ✂	
☐	Luc Robitaille, Detr. ✂	
☐	Jeremy Roenick, Phil. ✂	
☐	Joe Sakic, Colo. ✂	
☐	Sergei Samsonov, Bost. ✂	
☐	Teemu Selanne, SanJ. ✂	
☐	Brendan Shanahan, Detr. ✂	
☐	Mats Sundin, Toro. ✂	
☐	Joe Thornton, Bost. ✂	
☐	Keith Tkachuk, SLou. ✂	
☐	Doug Weight, SLou. ✂	
☐	Alexei Yashin, NYIs. ✂	
☐	Steve Yzerman, Detr. ✂	

IN THE NUMBERS

Actual realized pricing on these scarce cards may vary considerably from below listed pricing.

	Insert Set (50 cards):	13,000
	Insert (*10)	ITN
☐	Daniel Alfredsson, Otta. ✂	550.00
☐	Tony Amonte, Chic. ✂	225.00
☐	Jason Arnott, NJer. ✂	200.00
☐	Peter Bondra, Wash. ✂	225.00
☐	Brian Boucher (G), Phil. ✂	200.00
☐	Martin Brodeur (G), NJer. ✂	600.00
☐	Pavel Bure, Flor. ✂	300.00
☐	Roman Cechmanek (G), Phil. ✂	200.00
☐	Byron Dafoe (G), Bost. ✂	200.00
☐	Chris Drury, Colo. ✂	225.00
☐	Sergei Fedorov, Detr. ✂	375.00
☐	Peter Forsberg, Colo. ✂	525.00
☐	Ron Francis, Caro. ✂	225.00
☐	Bill Guerin, Bost. ✂	200.00
☐	Dominik Hasek (G), Detr. ✂	375.00
☐	Marian Hossa, Otta. ✂	375.00
☐	Jarome Iginla, Calg. ✂	300.00
☐	Jaromir Jagr, Wash. ✂	375.00
☐	Curtis Joseph (G), Toro. ✂	375.00
☐	Paul Kariya, Anah. ✂	525.00
☐	Olaf Kölzig (G), Wash. ✂	225.00
☐	Ilya Kovalchuk,Atla. ✂	375.00
☐	Vincent Lecavalier, Tamp. ✂	375.00
☐	John LeClair, Phil. ✂	300.00
☐	Brian Leetch, NYRa. ✂	225.00
☐	Mario Lemieux, Pitt. ✂	1125.00
☐	Nicklas Lidström, Detr. ✂	225.00
☐	Eric Lindros, NYRa. ✂	375.00
☐	Roberto Luongo (G), Flor. ✂	300.00
☐	Al MacInnis, SLou. ✂	200.00
☐	Mark Messier, NYRa. ✂	375.00
☐	Mike Modano, Dall. ✂	375.00
☐	Owen Nolan, SanJ. ✂	225.00
☐	Adam Oates, Wash. ✂	200.00
☐	Chris Pronger, SLou. ✂	225.00
☐	Mark Recchi, Phil. ✂	200.00
☐	Mike Richter (G), NYRa. ✂	200.00
☐	Luc Robitaille, Detr. ✂	300.00
☐	Jeremy Roenick, Phil. ✂	300.00
☐	Patrick Roy (G), Colo. ✂	900.00
☐	Joe Sakic, Colo. ✂	600.00
☐	Miroslav Satan, Buff. ✂	200.00
☐	Teemu Selänne, SanJ. ✂	300.00
☐	Brendan Shanahan, Detr. ✂	375.00
☐	Mats Sundin, Toro. ✂	375.00
☐	Joe Thornton, Bost. ✂	450.00
☐	Mike Vernon (G), Calg. ✂	200.00
☐	Doug Weight, SLou. ✂	225.00
☐	Alexei Yashin,NYIs. ✂	225.00
☐	Steve Yzerman, Detr. ✂	900.00

INTERNATIONAL

	Insert Set (24 cards):	2,100
	Insert (*30)	I30
☐	Maxim Afinogenov, Buff. ✂	75.00
☐	Tony Amonte, Chic. ✂	75.00
☐	Rob Blake, Colo. ✂	75.00
☐	Martin Brodeur (G), Njer. ✂	200.00
☐	Valeri Bure, Flor. ✂	75.00
☐	Pavel Bure, Flor. ✂	100.00
☐	Chris Chelios, Detr. ✂	75.00
☐	Chris Drury, Colo. ✂	75.00
☐	Mike Dunham, Nash. ✂	75.00
☐	Sergei Fedorov, Detr. ✂	125.00
☐	Theoren Fleury, NYRa. ✂	75.00
☐	Sergei Gonchar, Wash. ✂	75.00
☐	Bill Guerin, Bost. ✂	75.00
☐	Brett Hull, Detr. ✂	125.00
☐	Jarome Iginla, Calg. ✂	100.00
☐	Curtis Joseph (G), Toro. ✂	125.00
☐	Paul Kariya, Anah. ✂	175.00
☐	Darius Kasparaitis, Pitt. ✂	75.00
☐	Nikolai Khabibulin (G), Tamp. ✂	75.00
☐	Ilya Kovalchuk, Atla. ✂	125.00
☐	Alexei Kovalev, Pitt. ✂	75.00
☐	Igor Larionov, Detr. ✂	75.00
☐	John LeClair, Phil. ✂	100.00
☐	Brian Leetch, NYRa. ✂	75.00
☐	Mario Lemieux, Pitt. ✂	350.00
☐	Eric Lindros, NYRa. ✂	125.00
☐	Al MacInnis, Slou. ✂	75.00
☐	Vladimir Malakhov, NYRa. ✂	75.00
☐	Mike Modano, Dall. ✂	125.00
☐	Owen Nolan, SanJ. ✂	75.00
☐	Chris Pronger, Slou. ✂	75.00
☐	Mike Richter (G), NYRa. ✂	75.00
☐	Jeremy Roenick, Phil. ✂	100.00
☐	Brian Rolston, Bost. ✂	75.00
☐	Joe Sakic, Colo. ✂	200.00
☐	Sergei Samsonov, Bost. ✂	75.00
☐	Brendan Shanahan, Detr. ✂	125.00
☐	Keith Tkachuk, Slou. ✂	75.00
☐	Oleg Tverdovsky, Anah. ✂	75.00
☐	Doug Weight, Slou. ✂	75.00
☐	Alexei Yashin, NYIs. ✂ White	75.00
☐	Steve Yzerman, Detr. ✂	275.00

TEAMMATES

	Insert Set (30 cards):	1,900
	Insert (*40)	TM
☐	1 J. Friesen ✂ / P. Kariya ✂	100.00
☐	2 I. Kovalchuk ✂ / P. Stefan ✂	100.00
☐	3 B. Dafoe (G) ✂ / B. Guerin ✂	60.00
☐	4 M. Biron (G) ✂ / M. Satan (G) ✂	60.00
☐	5 J. Iginla ✂ / R. Turek (G) ✂	75.00
☐	6 R. Francis ✂ / S. Kapanen ✂	60.00
☐	7 T. Amonte ✂ / É. Dazé ✂	60.00
☐	8 P. Roy (G) ✂ / J. Sakic ✂	200.00
☐	9 C. Drury ✂ / M. Hejduk ✂	75.00
☐	10 E. Belfour (G) ✂ / M. Modano ✂	100.00
☐	11 B. Shanahan ✂ / S. Yzerman ✂	200.00
☐	12 D. Hasek (G) ✂ / L. Robitaille ✂	100.00
☐	13 P. Bure ✂ / R. Luongo (G) ✂	75.00
☐	14 Z. Palffy ✂ / F. Potvin (G) ✂	60.00
☐	15 M. Fernandez (G) ✂ / M. Gaborik ✂	75.00
☐	16 B. Savage ✂ / J. Théodore (G) ✂	75.00
☐	17 M. Brodeur (G) ✂ White / J. Arnott ✂ Red	100.00
☐	18 S. Niedermayer ✂ / S. Stevens ✂	60.00
☐	19 E. Lindros ✂ / M. Messier ✂	100.00
☐	20 K. Jönsson ✂ / A. Yashin ✂	60.00
☐	21 D. Alfredsson ✂ / P. Lalime (G) ✂	60.00
☐	22 J. Roenick ✂ Black / M. Recchi ✂ White	60.00
☐	23 B. Boucher (G) ✂ / J. LeClair ✂	60.00
☐	24 M. Kraft ✂ White / M. Lemieux ✂ Yellow	200.00
☐	25 O. Nolan ✂ / T. Selänne ✂	75.00
☐	26 K. Tkachuk ✂ / D. Weight ✂	60.00
☐	27 N. Khabibulin (G) ✂ / V. Lecavalier ✂	75.00
☐	28 Cu. Joseph (G) ✂ / M. Sundin ✂	100.00
☐	29 M. Näslund ✂ / D. Sedin ✂	75.00
☐	30 P. Bondra ✂ / J. Jagr ✂	75.00

VINTAGE AUTOGRAPH

	Insert Set (40 cards):	3,300
	Insert	VA
☐	VA-1 Tony Esposito (G), Chic. ✍ {*60}	75.00
☐	VA-2 Phil Esposito, ✍ {*40}	150.00
☐	VA-03 Gordie Howe, ✍ {*20}	375.00
☐	VA-04 Gordie Howe, ✍ {*20}	375.00
☐	VA-05 Jean Béliveau, Mont. ✍ {*40}	175.00
☐	VA-06 Jean Béliveau, Mont. ✍ {*40}	175.00
☐	VA-07 Bobby Hull, Winn. ✍ {*40}	125.00
☐	VA-08 Bobby Hull, Chic. ✍ {*40}	125.00
☐	VA-9 Ted Lindsay, ✍ {*40}	150.00
☐	VA-10 Johnny Bower (G), Toro. ✍ {*60}	75.00
☐	VA-11 Milt Schmidt, Bost. ✍ {*80}	50.00
☐	VA-12 Red Kelly, ✍ {*80}	50.00
☐	VA-13 Glenn Hall (G), ✍ {*40}	150.00
☐	VA-14 Chuck Rayner (G), NYRa. ✍ {*40}	50.00
☐	VA-15 Elmer Lach, ✍ {*80}	50.00
☐	VA-17 Gerry Cheevers (G), Bost. ✍ {*40}	100.00
☐	VA-18 Gump Worsley (G), Minn. ✍ {*40}	100.00
☐	VA-19 Butch Bouchard, Mont. ✍ {*80}	50.00
☐	VA-20 Henri Richard, Mont. ✍ {*80}	100.00
☐	VA-21 Henri Richard, Mont. ✍ {*80}	100.00
☐	VA-22 Bernie Geoffrion, Mont. ✍ {*80}	75.00
☐	VA-23 Dollard St-Laurent, Mont. ✍ {*80}	50.00
☐	VA-24 Dickie Moore, Mont. ✍ {*70}	75.00
☐	VA-25 Jean-Guy Talbot, Mont. ✍ {*80}	50.00
☐	VA-26 Bill Gadsby, Detr. ✍ {*80}	50.00
☐	VA-27 Frank Mahovlich, ✍ {*40}	150.00
☐	VA-28 Dino Ciccarelli, ✍ {*70}	50.00
☐	VA-29 Jari Kurri, ✍ {*70}	150.00
☐	VA-30 Mike Bossy, NYIs. ✍ {*70}	150.00
☐	VA-31 Johnny Bucyk, Bost. ✍ {*90}	50.00
☐	VA-32 Michel Goulet, ✍ {*90}	50.00
☐	VA-33 Stan Mikita, Chic. ✍ {*40}	100.00
☐	VA-34 Bryan Trottier, NYIs. ✍ {*70}	125.00
☐	VA-35 Dale Hawerchuk, ✍ {*70}	75.00
☐	VA-36 Gilbert Perreault, Buff. ✍ {*40}	100.00
☐	VA-37 Marcel Dionne, ✍ {*40}	150.00
☐	VA-38 Mike Gartner, ✍ {*70}	100.00
☐	VA-39 Lanny McDonald, ✍ {*70}	100.00
☐	VA-40 Guy Lafleur, Mont. ✍ {*40}	150.00

2001 - 02 SP AUTHENTIC

Produced by The Upper Deck Company, this series was released in March 2002. There are three versions for each card 1-90: a base card, a bronze-foil SP Limited parallel (#/150), and a gold-foil SP Limited parallel (#/25).

	Shell Set (90 cards):	-	-	35.00
	Complete Set (180 cards):	5,750	2,100	1200.00
	Description	G25	B150	Base
☐☐☐	1 Jeff Friesen, Anah.	15.00	3.00	.25
☐☐☐	2 Paul Kariya, Anah.	70.00	20.00	1.50
☐☐☐	3 Dany Heatley, Atla.	50.00	15.00	2.50
☐☐☐	4 Milan Hnilicka (G), Atla.	10.00	3.00	.25
☐☐☐	5 Bill Guerin, Bost.	20.00	5.00	.50
☐☐☐	6 Joe Thornton, Bost.	60.00	15.00	1.50
☐☐☐	7 Sergei Samsonov, Bost.	30.00	5.00	.50
☐☐☐	8 Miroslav Satan, Buff.	15.00	3.00	.25
☐☐☐	9 Martin Biron (G), Buff.	20.00	5.00	.50
☐☐☐	10 Jean-Pierre Dumont, Buff.	10.00	3.00	.25
☐☐☐	11 Jarome Iginla, Calg.	40.00	10.00	1.00
☐☐☐	12 Roman Turek, Calg.	20.00	5.00	.50
☐☐☐	13 Craig Conroy, Calg.	15.00	3.00	.25
☐☐☐	14 Tony Amonte, Chic.	30.00	5.00	.50
☐☐☐	15 Steve Sullivan, Chic.	15.00	3.00	.25
☐☐☐	16 Joe Sakic, Colo.	80.00	20.00	2.00
☐☐☐	17 Milan Hejduk, Colo.	40.00	10.00	1.00
☐☐☐	18 Patrick Roy, Colo.	150.00	45.00	3.50
☐☐☐	19 Rob Blake, Colo.	30.00	5.00	.50
☐☐☐	20 Chris Drury, Colo.	30.00	5.00	.50
☐☐☐	21 Ron Tugnutt, Colu.	20.00	5.00	.50
☐☐☐	22 Geoff Sanderson, Colu.	10.00	3.00	.25
☐☐☐	23 Mike Modano, Dall.	50.00	15.00	1.00
☐☐☐	24 Ed Belfour (G), Dall.	50.00	15.00	1.00
☐☐☐	25 Pierre Turgeon, Dall.	20.00	5.00	.50
☐☐☐	26 Brett Hull, Detr.	50.00	15.00	1.00
☐☐☐	27 Dominik Hasek (G), Detr.	50.00	15.00	1.00
☐☐☐	28 Steve Yzerman, Detr.	120.00	35.00	3.00
☐☐☐	29 Sergei Fedorov, Detr.	50.00	15.00	1.00
☐☐☐	30 Luc Robitaille, Detr.	40.00	10.00	1.00
☐☐☐	31 Brendan Shanahan, Detr.	50.00	15.00	1.00
☐☐☐	32 Tommy Salo, Edmo.	20.00	5.00	.50
☐☐☐	33 Ryan Smyth, Edmo.	20.00	5.00	.50

□□□	34 Mike Comrie, Edmo.	40.00	10.00	1.00
□□□	35 Pavel Bure, Flor.	40.00	10.00	1.00
□□□	36 Valeri Bure, Flor.	15.00	3.00	.25
□□□	37 Roberto Luongo, Flor.	40.00	10.00	1.00
□□□	38 Jason Allison, LosA.	30.00	5.00	.50
□□□	39 Zigmund Palffy, LosA.	30.00	5.00	.50
□□□	40 Félix Potvin, LosA.	60.00	5.00	.50
□□□	41 Manny Fernandez, MinW.	20.00	5.00	.50
□□□	42 Marian Gaborik, MinW.	50.00	15.00	1.00
□□□	43 José Théodore (G), Mont.	60.00	15.00	1.50
□□□	44 Brian Savage, Mont.	15.00	3.00	.25
□□□	45 David Legwand, Nash.	20.00	5.00	.50
□□□	46 Mike Dunham, Nash.	20.00	5.00	.50
□□□	47 Patrik Elias, NJer.	40.00	10.00	1.00
□□□	48 Martin Brodeur, NJer.	80.00	20.00	2.00
□□□	49 Jason Arnott, NJer.	20.00	5.00	.50
□□□	50 Scott Stevens, NJer.	20.00	5.00	.50
□□□	51 Chris Osgood, NYIs.	30.00	5.00	.50
□□□	52 Alexei Yashin, NYIs.	30.00	5.00	.50
□□□	53 Mark Parrish, NYIs.	20.00	5.00	.50
□□□	54 Mark Messier, NYRa.	50.00	15.00	1.00
□□□	55 Eric Lindros, NYRa.	50.00	15.00	1.00
□□□	56 Petr Nedved, NYRa.	15.00	3.00	.25
□□□	57 Marian Hossa, Otta.	50.00	15.00	1.00
□□□	58 Radek Bonk, Otta.	15.00	3.00	.25
□□□	59 Daniel Alfredsson, Otta.	60.00	5.00	.50
□□□	60 Jeremy Roenick, Phil.	40.00	10.00	1.00
□□□	61 John LeClair, Phil.	40.00	10.00	1.00
□□□	62 Keith Primeau, Phil.	20.00	5.00	.50
□□□	63 Mark Recchi, Phil.	20.00	5.00	.50
□□□	64 Roman Cechmanek, Phil.	20.00	5.00	.50
□□□	65 Sean Burke, Phoe.	30.00	5.00	.50
□□□	66 Michal Handzus, Phoe.	10.00	3.00	.25
□□□	67 Shane Doan, Phoe.	10.00	3.00	.25
□□□	68 Mario Lemieux, Pitt.	150.00	45.00	3.50
□□□	69 Alexei Kovalev, Pitt.	30.00	5.00	.50
□□□	70 Johan Hedberg (G), Pitt.	20.00	5.00	.50
□□□	71 Teemu Selänne, SanJ.	40.00	10.00	1.00
□□□	72 Owen Nolan, SanJ.	30.00	5.00	.50
□□□	73 Evgeni Nabokov, SanJ.	30.00	5.00	.50
□□□	74 V. Damphousse, SanJ.	30.00	5.00	.50
□□□	75 Pavol Demitra, SLou.	20.00	5.00	.50
□□□	76 Doug Weight, SLou.	30.00	5.00	.50
□□□	77 Keith Tkachuk, SLou.	30.00	5.00	.50
□□□	78 Chris Pronger, SLou.	30.00	5.00	.50
□□□	79 Brad Richards, Tamp.	20.00	5.00	.50
□□□	80 Vincent Lecavalier, Tamp.	50.00	15.00	1.00
□□□	81 Nikolai Khabibulin, Tamp.	20.00	5.00	.50
□□□	82 Curtis Joseph (G), Toro.	50.00	15.00	1.00
□□□	83 Mats Sundin, Toro.	50.00	15.00	1.00
□□□	84 Alexander Mogilny, Toro.	20.00	5.00	.50
□□□	85 Markus Näslund, Vanc.	50.00	15.00	1.00
□□□	86 Daniel Sedin, Vanc.	20.00	5.00	.50
□□□	87 Henrik Sedin, Vanc.	20.00	5.00	.50
□□□	88 Peter Bondra, Wash.	30.00	5.00	.50
□□□	89 Olaf Kölzig, Wash.	30.00	5.00	.50
□□□	90 Jaromir Jagr, Wash.	50.00	15.00	1.00

ALL-TIME GREATS

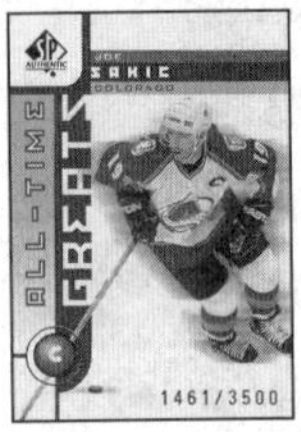

There are three versions for each card 91-110: a base card (#/3500), a bronze-foil SP Limited parallel (#/150), and a gold-foil SP Limited parallel (#/25).

	All-Time Great (#/3500)	G25	B150	Base
□□□	91 Paul Kariya, Anah.	70.00	21.00	7.00
□□□	92 Raymond Bourque, Bost.	60.00	18.00	6.00
□□□	93 Patrick Roy, Colo.	120.00	45.00	15.00
□□□	94 Joe Sakic, Colo.	80.00	24.00	8.00
□□□	95 Mike Modano, Dall.	50.00	15.00	5.00
□□□	96 Ed Belfour (G), Dall.	50.00	15.00	5.00
□□□	97 Steve Yzerman, Detr.	120.00	36.00	12.00
□□□	98 Dominik Hasek (G), Detr.	50.00	15.00	5.00
□□□	99 Gordie Howe, Detr.	140.00	42.00	14.00
□□□	100 Brett Hull, Detr.	50.00	15.00	5.00
□□□	101 Wayne Gretzky, Edmo.	200.00	60.00	20.00
□□□	102 Martin Brodeur, NJer.	80.00	24.00	8.00
□□□	103 Mark Messier, NYRa.	50.00	15.00	5.00
□□□	104 John LeClair, Phil.	40.00	12.00	4.00
□□□	105 Jeremy Roenick, Phil.	40.00	12.00	4.00
□□□	106 Mario Lemieux, Pitt.	150.00	45.00	15.00
□□□	107 Teemu Selänne, SanJ.	40.00	12.00	4.00
□□□	108 Al MacInnis, SLou.	20.00	6.00	2.00
□□□	109 Curtis Joseph (G), Toro.	50.00	15.00	5.00
□□□	110 Jaromir Jagr, Wash.	50.00	15.00	5.00

FUTURE GREATS

There are three versions for each card 111-130: a base card (#/3500), a bronze-foil SP Limited parallel (#/150), and a gold-foil SP Limited parallel (#/25).

	Future Greats (#/3500)	G25	B150	Base
□□□	111 Dany Heatley, Atla.	50.00	15.00	5.00
□□□	112 Mike Comrie, Edmo.	40.00	12.00	4.00
□□□	113 David Legwand, Nash.	20.00	6.00	2.00
□□□	114 Justin Williams, Phil.	16.00	4.00	1.00
□□□	115 Mike Van Ryn, SLou.	12.00	3.00	1.00
□□□	116 Alex Tanguay, Colo.	30.00	9.00	3.00
□□□	117 Manny Fernandez, MinW.	20.00	6.00	2.00
□□□	118 Martin Havlat, Otta.	30.00	9.00	3.00
□□□	119 Kris Beech, Pitt.	16.00	4.00	1.00
□□□	120 Nikolai Antropov, Toro.	12.00	3.00	1.00
□□□	121 Patrik Stefan, Atla.	16.00	4.00	1.00
□□□	122 Steven Reinprecht, Colo.	16.00	4.00	1.00
□□□	123 Marian Gaborik, MinW.	50.00	15.00	5.00
□□□	124 Pavel Brendl, Phil.	16.00	4.00	1.00
□□□	125 Brad Stuart, SanJ.	20.00	6.00	2.00
□□□	126 Martin Biron (G), Buff.	24.00	7.00	2.00
□□□	127 Éric Bélanger, LosA.	10.00	3.00	1.00
□□□	128 Ladislav Nagy, NYIs.	12.00	3.00	1.00
□□□	129 Rick DiPietro, Phoe.	24.00	7.00	2.00
□□□	130 Brad Richards, Tamp.	24.00	7.00	2.00

FUTURE WATCH

There are three versions for each card 131-180: a base card (#/900), a bronze-foil SP Limited parallel (#/150), and a gold-foil SP Limited parallel (#/25).

	Rookie (#/900)	G25	B150	Base
□□□	**131 Ilja Bryzgalov RC**	**40.00**	**15.00**	**20.00**
□□□	**132 Timo Pärssinen RC**	**20.00**	**10.00**	**10.00**
□□□	**133 Kevin Sawyer RC**	**20.00**	**10.00**	**10.00**
□□□	**134 Brian Pothier RC**	**20.00**	**10.00**	**10.00**
□□□	**135 Kamil Piros RC**	**30.00**	**10.00**	**15.00**
□□□	**136 Ivan Huml RC**	**45.00**	**15.00**	**25.00**
□□□	**137 Scott Nichol RC**	**20.00**	**10.00**	**10.00**
□□□	**138 Jukka Hentunen RC**	**20.00**	**10.00**	**10.00**
□□□	**139 Erik Cole RC**	**45.00**	**15.00**	**25.00**
□□□	140 Casey Hankinson, Chic.	20.00	10.00	5.00
□□□	**141 Jaroslav Obsut RC**	**20.00**	**10.00**	**10.00**
□□□	**142 Jody Shelley RC**	**30.00**	**10.00**	**15.00**
□□□	**143 Matt Davidson RC**	**20.00**	**10.00**	**10.00**
□□□	**144 Niko Kapanen RC**	**45.00**	**15.00**	**25.00**
□□□	**145 Pavel Datsyuk RC**	**160.00**	**125.00**	**125.00**
□□□	**146 Ty Conklin RC**	**45.00**	**15.00**	**25.00**
□□□	**147 Selmser, Colu. (Edmo.) RC**	**20.00**	**10.00**	**10.00**
□□□	**148 Jason Chimera RC**	**30.00**	**10.00**	**15.00**
□□□	**149 Andrei Podkonicky RC**	**30.00**	**10.00**	**15.00**
□□□	**150 Niklas Hagman RC**	**30.00**	**10.00**	**15.00**
□□□	**151 Jaroslav Bednar RC**	**30.00**	**10.00**	**15.00**
□□□	**152 Mike Matteucci RC**	**20.00**	**10.00**	**10.00**
□□□	**153 Pascal Dupuis RC**	**45.00**	**15.00**	**25.00**
□□□	**154 Francis Bélanger RC**	**20.00**	**10.00**	**10.00**
□□□	155 Martti Järventie, Mont.	20.00	10.00	5.00
□□□	**156 Pavel Skrbek RC**	**20.00**	**10.00**	**10.00**
□□□	**157 Martin Erat RC**	**30.00**	**10.00**	**15.00**
□□□	**158 A. Salomonsson RC**	**20.00**	**10.00**	**10.00**
□□□	**159 Scott Clemmensen RC**	**30.00**	**10.00**	**15.00**
□□□	**160 Josef Boumedienne RC**	**20.00**	**10.00**	**10.00**
□□□	**161 Peter Smrek RC**	**20.00**	**10.00**	**10.00**
□□□	**162 Mikael Samuelsson RC**	**20.00**	**10.00**	**10.00**
□□□	**163 Radek Martinek RC**	**20.00**	**10.00**	**10.00**
□□□	**164 Joel Kwiatkowski RC**	**20.00**	**10.00**	**10.00**
□□□	**165 Ivan Ciernik RC**	**30.00**	**10.00**	**15.00**
□□□	**166 Chris Neil RC**	**20.00**	**10.00**	**10.00**
□□□	**167 Jiri Dopita RC**	**30.00**	**10.00**	**15.00**
□□□	**168 Vaclav Pletka RC**	**20.00**	**10.00**	**10.00**
□□□	**169 David Cullen RC**	**20.00**	**10.00**	**10.00**
□□□	**170 Jeff Jillson RC**	**30.00**	**10.00**	**15.00**
□□□	**171 Mark Rycroft RC**	**20.00**	**10.00**	**10.00**
□□□	**172 Nikita Alexeev RC**	**45.00**	**15.00**	**25.00**
□□□	**173 Ryan Tobler RC**	**20.00**	**10.00**	**10.00**
□□□	**174 Bob Wren RC**	**20.00**	**10.00**	**10.00**
□□□	**175 Ilya Kovalchuk RC ✍**	**800.00**	**500.00**	**425.00**
□□□	**176 V. Nedorost RC ✍**	**175.00**	**100.00**	**50.00**
□□□	**177 K. Huselius RC ✍**	**225.00**	**150.00**	**75.00**
□□□	**178 Blackburn (G) RC ✍**	**300.00**	**200.00**	**125.00**
□□□	**179 Krys Kolanos RC ✍**	**175.00**	**100.00**	**50.00**
□□□	**180 Raffi Torres RC ✍**	**175.00**	**100.00**	**50.00**

NOTABLE NUMBERS

	Insert Set (20 cards):	475.00
	Insert	NN
□	Bob Probert, Chic. {*<1034} ✂- Red	10.00
□	Brendan Shanahan, Detr. {*<955} ✂- ✂- Red	20.00
□	Brendan Shanahan, Detr. {*<955} ✂- ✂- White	20.00
□	Chris Chelios, Detr. {*<1181} ✂- White	10.00
□	Eric Lindros, NYRa. {*<659} ✂- Blue	25.00
□	Jari Kurri, LosA. {*<601} ✂- Black	25.00
□	John LeClair, Phil. {*<627} ✂- White	20.00
□	John LeClair, Phil. {*<627} ✂- Orange	20.00
□	Joe Sakic, Colo. {*<1178} ✂- Burgandy	30.00
□	Keith Primeau, Phil. {*<496} ✂-	10.00
□	Sandy McCarthy, NYRa. {*<1206} ✂- White	10.00
□	Sandy McCarthy, NYRa. {*<1206} ✂- Red/White	10.00
□	Mike Gartner, Wash. {*<102} ✂- White	50.00
□	Mario Lemieux, Pitt. {*<648} ✂- White	75.00
□	Mark Messier, NYRa. {*<651} ✂- Blue	25.00
□	Mark Messier, NYRa. {*<651} ✂- White	25.00
□	Mike Modano, Dall. {*<900} ✂- White	20.00
□	Mark Recchi, Phil. {*<1010} ✂- White	10.00
□	Paul Kariya, Anah. {*<531} ✂- Teal	40.00
□	Raymond Bourque, Bost. {*<1169} ✂- Black	25.00
□	Rick Tocchet, Phil. {*<950} ✂- White	10.00
□	Scott Stevens, NJer. {*<1434} ✂- Red	10.00
□	Scott Stevens, NJer. {*<1434} ✂- Red/White	10.00
□	Steve Yzerman, Detr. {*<1614} ✂- Red	45.00
□	Steve Yzerman, Detr. {*<1614} ✂- Red/White	70.00
□	Tie Domi, Toro. {*<1620} ✂- Blue	10.00

PERSONAL PROLIFICS

	Insert Set (10 cards):	800
	Insert	PP
□	Brett Hull, SLou. ✂- (*<86) Blue	55.00
□	Brett Hull, SLou. ✂- (*<86) Red	55.00
□	Jaromir Jagr, Pitt. ✂- (*<87)	55.00
□	Joe Sakic, Colo. ✂- (*<54)	100.00
□	Luc Robitaille, LosA. ✂- (*<63)	50.00
□	Martin Brodeur (G), NJer. (*<43) ✂-	125.00
□	Mario Lemieux, Pitt. ✂- (*<38)	250.00
□	Patrick Roy (G), Colo. (*<52) ✂- Blue	175.00
□	Raymond Bourque, Bost. ✂- (*<77)	75.00
□	Teemu Selänne, Winn. ✂- (*<76) White	50.00
□	Wayne Gretzky, Edmo. ✂- (*<92)	200.00

SIGN OF THE TIMES

	Insert Set (54 cards):	1,900
	Insert	SotT
□	Jason Allison, LosA. ✍	20.00
□	Tony Amonte, Chic. ✍	20.00
□	Ed Belfour (G), Dall. ✍	35.00
□	Martin Biron (G), Buff. ✍	15.00
□	Rob Blake, Colo. ✍	20.00
□	Rod Brind'Amour, Caro. ✍	15.00
□	Martin Brodeur, NJer. ✍	60.00
□	Pavel Bure, Flor. ✍	30.00
□	Mike Comrie, Edmo. ✍	30.00
□	Rick DiPietro, NYIs. ✍	15.00
□	Manny Fernandez, MinW. ✍	15.00
□	Marian Gaborik, MinW. ✍	35.00
□	Simon Gagné, Phil. ✍	30.00
□	Wayne Gretzky, LosA. ✍	250.00
□	Bill Guerin, Bost. ✍	15.00
□	Scott Hartnell, Nash. ✍	15.00
□	Martin Havlat, Otta. ✍	20.00
□	Dany Heatley, Atla. ✍	50.00
□	Jochen Hecht, Edmo. ✍	15.00
□	Johan Hedberg (G), Pitt. ✍	15.00
□	Milan Hejduk, Colo. ✍	30.00
□	Marian Hossa, Otta. ✍	35.00
□	Gordie Howe, Detr. ✍	300.00
□	Jarome Iginla, Calg. ✍	30.00
□	Arturs Irbe (G), Caro. ✍	15.00
□	Curtis Joseph (G), Toro. ✍	35.00
□	Rostislav Klesla, Colu. ✍	15.00
□	Olaf Kölzig, Wash. ✍	20.00
□	Ilya Kovalchuk, Atla. ✍	50.00
□	Alexei Kovalev, Pitt. ✍	20.00
□	Milan Kraft, Pitt. ✍	15.00
□	Vincent Lecavalier, Tamp. ✍	35.00
□	John LeClair, Phil. ✍	30.00
□	Trevor Letowski, Phoe. ✍	15.00
□	Roberto Luongo, Flor. ✍	60.00
□	Al MacInnis, SLou. ✍	15.00
□	Mike Modano, Dall. ✍	35.00
□	Markus Näslund, Vanc. ✍	35.00
□	Jeff O'Neill, Caro. ✍	15.00
□	Bobby Orr, Bost. ✍	250.00
□	Zigmund Palffy, LosA. ✍	20.00
□	Félix Potvin, LosA. ✍	20.00
□	Keith Primeau, Phil. ✍	15.00
□	Mike Ribeiro, Mont. ✍	15.00
□	Patrick Roy, Colo. ✍ {*33}	500.00
□	Tommy Salo, Edmo. ✍	15.00
□	Daniel Sedin, Vanc. ✍	15.00
□	Henrik Sedin, Vanc. ✍	15.00
□	Teemu Selänne, SanJ. ✍	30.00
□	Brent Sopel, Vanc. ✍	15.00
□	Patrik Stefan, Atla. ✍	15.00
□	Joe Thornton, Bost. ✍	45.00
□	Doug Weight, SLou. ✍	20.00
□	Steve Yzerman, Detr. ✍	150.00

SIGN OF THE TIMES DOUBLE

	Insert Set (18 cards):	1,500
	Insert (#/150)	SotTD
□	BB E. Belfour (G) ✍ / M. Brodeur ✍	100.00
□	BL R. Luongo ✍ / P. Bure ✍	50.00
□	CH M. Comrie ✍ / J. Hecht ✍	35.00
□	DL R. DiPietro ✍ / R. Luongo ✍	50.00
□	ET P. Esposito ✍ / J. Thornton ✍	75.00
□	FG M. Fernandez ✍ / M. Gaborik ✍	50.00
□	GO G. Howe ✍ / B. Orr ✍	500.00
□	HH M. Havlat ✍ / M. Hossa ✍	75.00
□	HS J. Hedberg ✍ / T. Salo ✍	35.00
□	HT M. Hossa ✍ / J. Thornton ✍	75.00
□	HY G. Howe ✍ / S. Yzerman ✍	300.00
□	IH M. Hejduk ✍ / J. Iginla ✍	50.00
□	LR J. LeClair ✍ / M. Recchi ✍	50.00
□	PP Z. Palffy ✍ / F. Potvin ✍	50.00
□	SS D. Sedin ✍ / H. Sedin ✍	35.00
□	TL V. Lecavalier ✍ / J. Thornton ✍	75.00
□	WM A. MacInnis ✍ / D. Weight ✍	35.00
□	YA J. Allison ✍ / S. Yzerman ✍	125.00

SIGN OF THE TIMES TRIPLE

	Insert Set (10 cards):	3,000
	Insert (#/25)	SotTT
□	Bure ✍ / Kovalchuk ✍ / Kovalev ✍	275.00
□	Blake ✍ / Bourque ✍ / Orr ✍	650.00
□	Amonte ✍ / Guerin ✍ / Weight ✍	175.00
□	Blake ✍ / Bourque ✍ / Hejduk ✍	350.00
□	Gretzky ✍ / Howe ✍ / Yzerman ✍	1500.00
□	Havlat ✍ / Hejduk ✍ / Sykora ✍	200.00
□	Belfour (G) ✍ / Brodeur (G) ✍ / Joseph (G) ✍	400.00
□	Gaborik ✍ / Hossa ✍ / Palffy ✍	200.00
□	DiPietro (G) ✍ / Potvin (G) ✍ / Salo (G) ✍	150.00
□	Sedin ✍ / Sedin ✍ / Näslund ✍	200.00

2001 - 02 SP GAME USED EDITION

Produced by The Upper Deck Company, this series was released in January 2002.

	Shell Set (60 cards):	175.00
	Complete Set (100 cards):	1200.00
	Description	Base
□	1 Paul Kariya, Anah.	8.00
□	2 Dany Heatley, Atla.	8.00
□	3 Joe Thornton, Bost.	6.00
□	4 Bill Guerin, Bost.	2.50
□	5 Miroslav Satan, Buff.	2.00
□	6 Roman Turek, Calg.	3.00
□	7 Jeff O'Neill, Caro.	2.50

☐ 8 Tony Amonte, Chic. 3.50
☐ 9 Rob Blake, Colo. 3.50
☐ 10 Joe Sakic, Colo. 10.00
☐ 11 Chris Drury, Colo. 3.50
☐ 12 Patrick Roy, Colo. 18.00
☐ 13 Ron Tugnutt, Colu. 2.50
☐ 14 Mike Modano, Dall. 6.00
☐ 15 Ed Belfour (G), Dall. 6.00
☐ 16 Pierre Turgeon, Dall. 2.50
☐ 17 Brendan Shanahan, Detr. 6.00
☐ 18 Steve Yzerman, Detr. 15.00
☐ 19 Brett Hull, Detr. 6.00
☐ 20 Dominik Hasek (G), Detr. 6.00
☐ 21 Luc Robitaille, Detr. 5.00
☐ 22 Mike Comrie, Edmo. 4.00
☐ 23 Pavel Bure, Flor. 4.00
☐ 24 Valeri Bure, Flor. 2.00
☐ 25 Adam Deadmarsh, LosA. 2.00
☐ 26 Zigmund Palffy, LosA. 3.50
☐ 27 Marian Gaborik, MinW. 6.00
☐ 28 José Théodore (G), Mont. 6.00
☐ 29 Mike Dunham, Nash. 2.50
☐ 30 Patrik Elias, NJer. 4.00
☐ 31 Martin Brodeur, NJer. 10.00
☐ 32 Rick DiPietro, NYIs. 3.00
☐ 33 Alexei Yashin, NYIs. 3.50
☐ 34 Eric Lindros, NYRa. 6.00
☐ 35 Mark Messier, NYRa. 6.00
☐ 36 Marian Hossa, Otta. 6.00
☐ 37 Radek Bonk, Otta. 2.00
☐ 38 John LeClair, Phil. 5.00
☐ 39 Jeremy Roenick, Phil. 5.00
☐ 40 Pavel Brendl, Phil. 2.00
☐ 41 Roman Cechmanek, Phil. 2.50
☐ 42 Sean Burke, Phoe. 3.50
☐ 43 Mario Lemieux, Pitt. 18.00
☐ 44 Johan Hedberg (G), Pitt. 2.50
☐ 45 Alexei Kovalev, Pitt. 3.50
☐ 46 Teemu Selänne, SanJ. 5.00
☐ 47 Evgeni Nabokov, SanJ. 3.50
☐ 48 Keith Tkachuk, SLou. 3.50
☐ 49 Chris Pronger, SLou. 3.50
☐ 50 Pavol Demitra, SLou. 2.50
☐ 51 Doug Weight, SLou. 3.50
☐ 52 Vincent Lecavalier, Tamp. 6.00
☐ 53 Curtis Joseph (G), Toro. 6.00
☐ 54 Alexander Mogilny, Toro. 3.00
☐ 55 Mats Sundin, Toro. 6.00
☐ 56 Markus Näslund, Vanc. 6.00
☐ 57 Daniel Sedin, Vanc. 2.50
☐ 58 Jaromir Jagr, Wash. 6.00
☐ 59 Olaf Kölzig, Wash. 3.50
☐ 60 Peter Bondra, Wash. 3.50

NEW GROOVES

Rookie (#/499) R499
☐ 61 Ilja Bryzgalov, Anah. RC {*499} 30.00
☐ 62 Timo Pärssinen, Anah. RC {*499} 20.00
☐ 63 Kevin Sawyer, Anah. RC {*499} 20.00
☐ 64 Brian Pothier, Atla. RC {*499} 20.00
☐ 65 Kamil Piros, Atla. RC {*499} 25.00
☐ 66 Ilya Kovalchuk, Atla. RC {*499} 200.00
☐ 67 Zdenek Kutlak, Bost. RC {*499} 20.00
☐ 68 Scott Nichol, Calg. RC {*499} 20.00
☐ 69 Erik Cole, Caro. RC {*499} 35.00
☐ 70 Jaroslav Obsut, Colo. RC {*499} 20.00
☐ 71 Vaclav Nedorost, Colo. RC {*499} 35.00
☐ 72 Mathieu Darche, Colu. RC {*499} 25.00
☐ 73 Matt Davidson, Colu. RC {*499} 20.00
☐ 74 Niko Kapanen, Dall. RC {*499} 35.00
☐ 75 Pavel Datsyuk, Detr. RC {*499} 125.00
☐ 76 Ty Conklin, Edmo. RC {*499} 35.00
☐ 77 Jason Chimera, Edmo. RC {*499} 25.00
☐ 78 Niklas Hagman, Flor. RC {*499} 25.00
☐ 79 Kristian Huselius, Flor. RC {*499} 50.00
☐ 80 Jaroslav Bednar, LosA. RC {*499} 25.00
☐ 81 Nick Schultz, MinW. RC {*499} 25.00
☐ 82 Travis Roche, MinW. RC {*499} 20.00
☐ 83 Martin Erat, Nash. RC {*499} 25.00
☐ 84 Scott Clemmensen, NJer. RC {*499} 25.00
☐ 85 Josef Boumedienne, Tamp. RC {*499} 20.00
☐ 86 Raffi Torres, NYIs. RC {*499} 35.00
☐ 87 Radek Martinek, NYIs. RC {*499} 20.00
☐ 88 Dan Blackburn (G), NYRa. RC {*499} 60.00
☐ 89 Peter Smrek, NYRa. RC {*499} 20.00
☐ 90 Ivan Ciernik, Otta. RC {*499} 25.00
☐ 91 Chris Neil, Otta. RC {*499} 20.00
☐ 92 Vaclav Pletka, Phil. RC {*499} 20.00
☐ 93 Jiri Dopita, Phil. RC {*499} 25.00
☐ 94 Krys Kolanos, Phoe. RC {*499} 35.00
☐ 95 Jeff Jillson, SanJ. RC {*499} 25.00
☐ 96 Mark Rycroft, SLou. RC {*499} 20.00
☐ 97 Ryan Tobler, Tamp. RC {*499} 20.00
☐ 98 Nikita Alexeev, Tamp. RC {*499} 35.00
☐ 99 Chris Corrinet, Wash. RC {*499} 20.00
☐ 100 Brian Sutherby, Wash. RC {*499} 25.00

AUTHENTIC FABRIC

The complete set price includes only one swatch variation per player.

Insert Set (49 cards):
Insert AF
☐ Maxim Afinogenov ✂ Black 10.00
☐ Jaroslav Bednar ✂ White 10.00
☐ Ed Belfour (G) ✂ Black 25.00
☐ Peter Bondra ✂ 15.00
☐ Radek Bonk ✂ Red 10.00
☐ Radek Bonk ✂ Black 10.00
☐ Brian Boucher (G) ✂ White 10.00
☐ Raymond Bourque ✂ Black 30.00
☐ Raymond Bourque ✂ Yellow 30.00
☐ Martin Brodeur ✂ Black 40.00
☐ Martin Brodeur ✂ Red 40.00
☐ Pavol Demitra ✂ White 10.00
☐ Jean-Pierre Dumont ✂ 10.00
☐ Radek Dvorak ✂ Blue 10.00
☐ Radek Dvorak ✂ Red 10.00
☐ Rico Fata ✂ Red 10.00
☐ Rico Fata ✂ Red/Yellow 10.00
☐ Sergei Fedorov ✂ White 25.00
☐ Sergei Fedorov ✂ Red 25.00
☐ Ruslan Fedotenko ✂ Black 10.00
☐ Ruslan Fedotenko ✂ White 10.00
☐ Theoren Fleury ✂ Blue 15.00
☐ Theoren Fleury ✂ Blue/White 20.00
☐ Peter Forsberg ✂ White 35.00
☐ Bill Guerin ✂ 10.00
☐ Bill Guerin ✂ Black/White 15.00
☐ Dominik Hasek (G) ✂ 25.00
☐ Jan Hlavac ✂ White 10.00
☐ Jan Hlavac ✂ Red/White/Blue 12.00
☐ Gordie Howe ✂ Turquoise 100.00
☐ Jarome Iginla ✂ Red 20.00
☐ Brent Johnson ✂ Blue 10.00
☐ Paul Kariya ✂ Burgandy 35.00
☐ Saku Koivu ✂ White 20.00
☐ Saku Koivu ✂ Blue 20.00
☐ Alexei Kovalev ✂ Black 15.00
☐ Robert Lang ✂ Black 10.00
☐ John LeClair ✂ White 20.00
☐ John LeClair ✂ Black 20.00
☐ Mario Lemieux ✂ Yellow 75.00
☐ Mario Lemieux ✂ White 75.00
☐ Patrick Marleau ✂ Black 10.00
☐ Patrick Marleau ✂ Teal 10.00
☐ Mike Modano ✂ Black 25.00
☐ Markus Näslund ✂ Black 25.00
☐ Joe Nieuwendyk ✂ Green 10.00
☐ Owen Nolan ✂ 15.00
☐ Owen Nolan ✂ Black/White 15.00
☐ Mika Noronen ✂ Black 10.00
☐ Chris Osgood ✂ White 15.00
☐ Chris Osgood ✂ Red 15.00
☐ Zigmund Palffy ✂ White 15.00
☐ Félix Potvin ✂ White 15.00
☐ Keith Primeau ✂ Black 10.00
☐ Keith Primeau ✂ Orange 10.00
☐ Mark Recchi ✂ Orange 10.00
☐ Luc Robitaille ✂ Black 20.00
☐ Patrick Roy ✂ White 75.00
☐ Patrick Roy ✂ Burgandy 75.00
☐ Joe Sakic ✂ Burgandy 40.00
☐ Joe Sakic ✂ Blue 40.00
☐ Miroslav Satan ✂ Black 10.00
☐ Marc Savard ✂ White 10.00
☐ Marc Savard ✂ Red 10.00
☐ Brendan Shanahan ✂ Red 25.00
☐ Brendan Shanahan ✂ Red/White 35.00
☐ José Théodore (G) ✂ Blue 30.00
☐ José Théodore (G) ✂ Red 30.00
☐ José Théodore (G) ✂ Blue/Red 45.00
☐ Joe Thornton ✂ White 30.00
☐ Mike York ✂ White 10.00
☐ Mike York ✂ Blue 10.00
☐ Mike York ✂ White/Red 10.00
☐ Steve Yzerman ✂ Red 60.00

AUTHENTIC FABRIC GOLD

The complete set price includes only one swatch variation per player.

Insert Set (49 cards): 1,200
Insert (#/300) AFG300
☐ Maxim Afinogenov ✂ 15.00
☐ Jaroslav Bednar ✂ 15.00
☐ Ed Belfour (G) ✂ 35.00
☐ Peter Bondra ✂ Black 20.00
☐ Peter Bondra ✂ Blue 20.00
☐ Radek Bonk ✂ 15.00
☐ Brian Boucher (G) ✂ 15.00
☐ Raymond Bourque ✂ Black 45.00
☐ Martin Brodeur ✂ Red 60.00
☐ Pavol Demitra ✂ White 15.00
☐ Jean-Pierre Dumont ✂ 15.00
☐ Radek Dvorak ✂ 15.00
☐ Rico Fata ✂ Red 15.00
☐ Sergei Fedorov ✂ White 35.00
☐ Ruslan Fedotenko ✂ White 15.00
☐ Theoren Fleury ✂ 20.00
☐ Peter Forsberg ✂ Burgandy 50.00
☐ Bill Guerin ✂ 15.00
☐ Dominik Hasek (G) ✂ Black 35.00
☐ Jan Hlavac ✂ White 15.00
☐ Gordie Howe ✂ 150.00
☐ Jarome Iginla ✂ 30.00
☐ Brent Johnson ✂ Blue 15.00
☐ Paul Kariya ✂ 50.00
☐ Saku Koivu ✂ White 30.00
☐ Alexei Kovalev ✂ 20.00
☐ Robert Lang ✂ 15.00
☐ John LeClair ✂ White 30.00
☐ Mario Lemieux ✂ 110.00
☐ Patrick Marleau ✂ Black 15.00
☐ Mike Modano ✂ 35.00
☐ Markus Näslund ✂ 35.00
☐ Joe Nieuwendyk ✂ 15.00
☐ Owen Nolan ✂ 20.00
☐ Mika Noronen ✂ 15.00
☐ Chris Osgood (G) ✂ 20.00
☐ Zigmund Palffy ✂ 20.00
☐ Félix Potvin ✂ White 20.00
☐ Keith Primeau ✂ 15.00
☐ Mark Recchi ✂ 15.00
☐ Luc Robitaille ✂ Black 30.00
☐ Patrick Roy ✂ White 110.00
☐ Joe Sakic ✂ 60.00
☐ Miroslav Satan ✂ Black 15.00
☐ Marc Savard ✂ Red 15.00
☐ Brendan Shanahan ✂ 35.00
☐ José Théodore (G) ✂ Red 45.00
☐ Joe Thornton ✂ 45.00
☐ Mike York ✂ Blue 15.00
☐ Steve Yzerman ✂ Red 90.00

AUTHENTIC FABRIC ALL-STAR

The complete set price includes only one swatch variation per player card.

Insert Set (10 cards): 500.00
Insert AF
☐ Pavel Bure, AS '93 ✂ Black 25.00
☐ Wayne Gretzky, AS '96 ✂ 120.00
☐ Wayne Gretzky, AS '99 ✂ Red 120.00
☐ Wayne Gretzky, AS '91 ✂ 120.00
☐ Jaromir Jagr, AS '99 ✂ Black 30.00
☐ Jaromir Jagr, AS '99 ✂ Grey/Black/White 60.00
☐ Paul Kariya, AS '00 ✂ Black 40.00
☐ Mike Modano, AS '93 ✂ Black 30.00
☐ Joe Sakic, AS '00 ✂ Orange 50.00
☐ Teemu Selänne, AS '99 ✂ White 25.00
☐ Teemu Selänne, AS '99 ✂ Blue 25.00
☐ Scott Stevens, AS '99 ✂ Red 25.00

AUTHENTIC FABRIC GOLD

The complete set price includes only one swatch variation per player card.

Insert Set (10 cards): 1,600
Insert (#/50) AF50
☐ Pavel Bure, AS '93 ✂ 50.00
☐ Wayne Gretzky, AS '96 ✂ Purple/Grey/White 700.00
☐ Wayne Gretzky, AS '96 ✂ 350.00
☐ Wayne Gretzky, AS '99 ✂ Black 350.00
☐ Jaromir Jagr, AS '99 ✂ 75.00
☐ Paul Kariya, AS '00 ✂ 100.00
☐ Mike Modano, AS '93 ✂ 75.00
☐ Joe Sakic, AS '00 ✂ 125.00
☐ Scott Stevens, AS '99 ✂ 25.00
☐ Teemu Selänne, AS '99 ✂ Blue 50.00
☐ Wayne Gretzky, AS '91 ✂ 350.00

AUTHENTIC FABRIC DOUBLE

Insert Set (19 cards): 1,000
Insert (#/100) AFD
☐ Maxim Afinogenov ✂ / Martin Biron (G) ✂ 40.00
☐ M. Brodeur (G) ✂ Red / P. Roy (G) ✂ White 150.00
☐ J-P Dumont ✂ / Miroslav Satan ✂ 40.00
☐ T. Fleury ✂ Blue / R. Dvorak ✂ White 40.00
☐ Peter Forsberg ✂ / Joe Sakic ✂ 100.00
☐ S. Fedorov ✂ Red / B. Shanahan ✂ Red 75.00
☐ M. Savard ✂ Red / J. Iginla ✂ White 40.00
☐ John LeClair ✂ / Brian Boucher (G) ✂ 40.00
☐ M. Lemieux ✂ Yellow / W. Gretzky ✂ White 250.00
☐ M. Lemieux ✂ White / A. Kovalev ✂ White 125.00
☐ Mike Modano ✂ / Ed Belfour (G) ✂ 75.00
☐ Markus Näslund ✂ / Peter Bondra ✂ 50.00
☐ Paul Kariya ✂ ✂ 75.00
☐ Keith Primeau ✂ / John LeClair ✂ 40.00
☐ Z. Palffy ✂ Purple / F. Potvin (G) ✂ 40.00
☐ Félix Potvin (G) ✂ / José Théodore (G) ✂ 75.00
☐ M. Recchi ✂ White / R. Fedotenko ✂ Orange 40.00
☐ Joe Thornton ✂ / Bill Guerin ✂ 50.00
☐ S. Yzerman ✂ Red / C. Osgood (G) ✂ White 100.00

AUTHENTIC FABRIC TRIPLE

Insert Set (5 cards): 800
Insert (#/25) AFT
☐ Forsberg ✂ / Sakic ✂ / Roy (G) ✂ 300.00
☐ Lemieux ✂ / Kovalev ✂ / Lang ✂ 350.00
☐ LeClair ✂ / Recchi ✂ / Primeau ✂ 125.00
☐ Modano ✂ / Nieuwendyk ✂ / Belfour (G) ✂ 125.00
☐ Yzerman ✂ / Shanahan ✂ / Fedorov ✂ 250.00

AUTHENTIC FABRIC QUAD

Insert Set (4 cards): 2,500
Insert (#/10) AFQ
☐ Forsberg ✂ / Sakic ✂ / Roy (G) ✂ / Bourque ✂ 500.00
☐ Gretzky ✂ / Lemieux ✂ / Sakic ✂ / Yzerman ✂ 1200.00
☐ Howe ✂ / Gretzky ✂ / Bourque ✂ / Lemieux ✂ 1200.00
☐ Yzerman ✂ / Shanahan ✂ / Fedorov ✂ / Osgood (G) ✂ 500.00

INKED SWEATERS

Insert Set (16 cards): 900
Insert (#/100) IS
☐ Martin Biron (G), Buff. ✍ ✂ 50.00
☐ Raymond Bourque, Colo. ✍ ✂ Blue 100.00
☐ Martin Brodeur, NJer. ✍ ✂ Red 125.00
☐ Simon Gagné, Phil. ✍ ✂ 50.00
☐ Marian Hossa, Otta. ✍ ✂ 75.00
☐ Jarome Iginla, Calg. ✍ ✂ 50.00
☐ Curtis Joseph (G), Toro. ✍ ✂ 75.00
☐ Olaf Kölzig, Wash. ✍ ✂ 50.00
☐ Alexei Kovalev, Pitt. ✍ ✂ 50.00
☐ Vincent Lecavalier, Tamp. ✍ ✂ 75.00
☐ John LeClair, Phil. ✍ ✂ 50.00
☐ Mike Modano, Dall. ✍ ✂ 75.00
☐ Zigmund Palffy, LosA. ✍ ✂ 50.00
☐ Henrik Sedin, Vanc. ✍ ✂ 50.00
☐ Joe Thornton, Bost. ✍ ✂ 100.00
☐ Steve Yzerman, Detr. ✍ ✂ 200.00

INKED SWEATERS 2

Insert Set (9 cards): 1,000
Insert (#/50) IS50
☐ Curtis Joseph (G), Toro. ✍ ✂ 75.00
☐ Ed Belfour (G), Dall. ✍ ✂ 75.00
☐ Simon Gagné, Phil. ✍ ✂ 75.00
☐ Gordie Howe, Houston Aeros ✍ ✂ 225.00
☐ John LeClair, Phil. ✍ ✂ 75.00
☐ Martin Brodeur, NJer. ✍ ✂ 150.00
☐ Raymond Bourque, Colo. ✍ ✂ Blue 100.00
☐ Steve Yzerman, Detr. ✍ ✂ 225.00
☐ Wayne Gretzky, 1999 All-Star ✍ ✂ 400.00

DUAL INKED SWEATERS

Insert Set (15 cards): 5,100
Insert (#/10) DS
☐ R. Bourque ✍ ✂ / M. Hejduk ✍ ✂ 375.00
☐ Biron (G) ✍ ✂ White / Ouellet (G) ✍ ✂ White 300.00
☐ S. Gagné ✍ ✂ / M. Ouellet (G) ✍ ✂ 300.00
☐ W. Gretzky ✍ ✂ Black / Z. Palffy ✍ ✂ White 925.00
☐ G. Howe ✍ ✂ / W. Gretzky ✍ ✂ 1275.00
☐ J. Iginla ✍ ✂ / S. Gagné ✍ ✂ 300.00
☐ C. Joseph (G) ✍ ✂ / J. Théodore (G) ✍ ✂ 400.00
☐ O. Kölzig (G) ✍ ✂ / P. Bondra ✍ ✂ 300.00
☐ J. LeClair ✍ ✂ Black / S. Gagné ✍ ✂ Orange 300.00
☐ J. LeClair ✍ ✂ / A. Kovalev ✍ ✂ 300.00
☐ M. Modano ✍ ✂ / T. Amonte ✍ ✂ 300.00
☐ Z. Palffy ✍ ✂ / P. Bondra ✍ ✂ 300.00
☐ S. Samsonov ✍ ✂ / J. Thornton ✍ ✂ 325.00
☐ D. Weight ✍ ✂ A. MacInnis ✍ ✂ 300.00
☐ G. Howe ✍ ✂ / S. Yzerman ✍ ✂ 900.00

PATCH

Insert Set (30 cards):	**2,200**
Insert (#/50)	**P50**
☐ P-TA Tony Amonte, Chic. ✂	50.00
☐ P-EB Ed Belfour (G), Dall. ✂	75.00
☐ P-BI Martin Biron (G), Buff. ✂	50.00
☐ P-BO Peter Bondra, Wash. ✂	50.00
☐ P-MB Martin Brodeur, NJer. ✂	100.00
☐ P-PB Pavel Bure, Flor. ✂	50.00
☐ P-SF Sergei Fedorov, Detr. ✂	75.00
☐ P-PF Peter Forsberg, Colo. ✂	100.00
☐ P-SG Simon Gagné, Phil. ✂	50.00
☐ P-WG Wayne Gretzky, AS '99 ✂	300.00
☐ P-MH Marian Hossa, Otta. ✂	75.00
☐ P-JH Jani Hurme (G), Otta. ✂	50.00
☐ P-JI Jarome Iginla, Calg. ✂	50.00
☐ P-JJ Jaromir Jagr, Wash. ✂	75.00
☐ P-CJ Curtis Joseph (G), Toro. ✂	75.00
☐ P-PK Paul Kariya, Anah. ✂	100.00
☐ P-OK Olaf Kölzig, Wash. ✂	50.00
☐ P-JL John LeClair, Phil. ✂	50.00
☐ P-ML Mario Lemieux, Pitt. ✂	225.00
☐ P-MM Mike Modano, Dall. ✂	75.00
☐ P-KP Keith Primeau, Phil. ✂	50.00
☐ P-PR Patrick Roy, Colo. ✂	175.00
☐ P-JS Joe Sakic, Colo. ✂	100.00
☐ P-SS Sergei Samsonov, Bost. ✂	50.00
☐ P-SA Miroslav Satan, Buff. ✂	50.00
☐ P-BS Brendan Shanahan, Detr. ✂	75.00
☐ P-PS Patrik Stefan, Atla. ✂	50.00
☐ P-MS Mats Sundin, Toro. ✂	75.00
☐ P-JT Joe Thornton, Bost. ✂	75.00
☐ P-SY Steve Yzerman, Detr. ✂	175.00

SIGNED PATCH

Insert Set (20 cards):	**2,300**
Insert (#/50)	**SP50**
☐ SP-TA Tony Amonte, Chic. ✍ ✂	80.00
☐ SP-EB Ed Belfour (G), Dall. ✍ ✂	150.00
☐ SP-MB Martin Biron (G), Buff. ✍ ✂	80.00
☐ SP-PB Peter Bondra, Wash. ✍ ✂	80.00
☐ SP-MB Martin Brodeur, NJer. ✍ ✂	225.00
☐ SP-PB Pavel Bure, Flor. ✍ ✂	100.00
☐ SP-SG Simon Gagné, Phil. ✍ ✂	100.00
☐ SP-WG Wayne Gretzky, AS '99 ✍ ✂	650.00
☐ SP-MH Marian Hossa, Otta. ✍ ✂	150.00
☐ SP-JI Jarome Iginla, Calg. ✍ ✂	100.00
☐ SP-CJ Curtis Joseph (G), Toro. ✍ ✂	150.00
☐ SP-OK Olaf Kölzig, Wash. ✍ ✂	80.00
☐ SP-JL John LeClair, Phil. ✍ ✂	100.00
☐ SP-KP Keith Primeau, Phil. ✍ ✂	80.00
☐ SP-SS Sergei Samsonov, Bost. ✍ ✂	80.00
☐ SP-TS Teemu Selänne, Anah. ✍ ✂	100.00
☐ SP-PS Patrik Stefan, Atla. ✍ ✂	80.00
☐ SP-TH José Théodore (G), Mont. ✍ ✂	175.00
☐ SP-JT Joe Thornton, Bost. ✍ ✂	175.00
☐ SP-SY Steve Yzerman, Detr. ✍ ✂	350.00

PATCH COMBO

Insert Set (20 cards):	**2,100**
Insert (#/25)	**CP25**
☐ Tony Amonte ✂ / Jarome Iginla ✂	100.00
☐ Peter Bondra ✂ / Tony Amonte ✂	100.00
☐ Martin Brodeur ✂ / Curtis Joseph ✂	150.00
☐ Simon Gagné ✂ / Paul Kariya ✂	125.00
☐ Jani Hurme (G) ✂ / Martin Brodeur ✂	100.00
☐ Jani Hurme (G) ✂ / Marian Hossa ✂	100.00
☐ Marian Hossa ✂ / John LeClair ✂	100.00
☐ Jaromir Jagr ✂ / Peter Bondra ✂	100.00
☐ Olaf Kölzig ✂ / Peter Bondra ✂	100.00
☐ Olaf Kölzig ✂ / Patrick Roy ✂	175.00
☐ Paul Kariya ✂ / Sergei Samsonov ✂	125.00
☐ Mario Lemieux ✂ / Jaromir Jagr ✂	375.00
☐ John LeClair ✂ / Keith Primeau ✂	100.00
☐ Keith Primeau ✂ / Simon Gagné ✂	100.00
☐ Brendan Shanahan ✂ / Pavel Bure ✂	100.00
☐ Mats Sundin ✂ / Curtis Joseph ✂	125.00
☐ Miroslav Satan ✂ / Paul Kariya ✂	100.00
☐ Joe Sakic ✂ / Patrick Roy ✂	350.00
☐ Brendan Shanahan ✂ / Steve Yzerman ✂	200.00
☐ Steve Yzerman ✂ / Sergei Fedorov ✂	200.00

PATCH COMBO SIGNED

Insert Set (10 cards):	**2,400**
Insert (#/10)	**DSP10**
☐ Tony Amonte ✍ ✂ / Peter Bondra ✍ ✂	200.00
☐ Martin Brodeur (G) ✍ ✂ / Curtis Joseph (G) ✍ ✂	450.00
☐ Peter Bondra ✍ ✂ / Olaf Kölzig (G) ✍ ✂	200.00
☐ Pavel Bure ✍ ✂ / John LeClair ✍ ✂	250.00
☐ Wayne Gretzky ✍ ✂ / Pavel Bure ✍ ✂	1000.00
☐ Simon Gagné ✍ ✂ / Keith Primeau ✍ ✂	200.00
☐ Marian Hossa ✍ ✂ / Jarome Iginla ✍ ✂	300.00
☐ Olaf Kölzig (G) ✍ ✂ / Ed Belfour (G) ✍ ✂	250.00
☐ Olaf Kölzig (G) ✍ ✂ / Martin Biron (G) ✍ ✂	150.00
☐ Joe Thornton ✍ ✂ / Martin Biron (G) ✍ ✂	250.00

PATCH TRIPLE

Insert Set (5 cards):	**1,900**
Insert (#/10)	**TP10**
☐ Joseph (G) ✂ / Brodeur (G) ✂ / Belfour (G) ✂	400.00
☐ Kariya ✂ / Yzerman ✂ / Bure ✂	550.00
☐ Lemieux ✂ / Gretzky ✂ / Yzerman ✂	1200.00
☐ Samsonov ✂ / LeClair ✂ / Shanahan ✂	250.00
☐ Stefan ✂ / Sakic ✂ / Primeau ✂	250.00

SIGNS OF TRADITION

Insert (#/2)	**SoT**
☐ LC-SA Sid Abel, Detr. ✍	
☐ LC-CC Clarence Campbell, NHL President ✍	
☐ LC-DH Doug Harvey, Candiens ✍	
☐ LC-TH Tim Horton, Toro. ✍	
☐ LC-LS Lord Stanley, ✍	

TOOLS OF THE GAME

Insert Set (27 cards):	**1,100**
Insert	**T**
☐ T-BB Brian Boucher (G), Phil. ✂ {*100}	25.00
☐ T-AC Anson Carter, Edmo. ✂ {*100}	25.00
☐ T-RC Roman Cechmanek, Phil. ✂ {*100}	25.00
☐ T-BD Byron Dafoe, Bost. ✂ {*100}	25.00
☐ T-DA Byron Dafoe, Bost. ✂ {*100}	25.00
☐ T-DF Byron Dafoe, Bost. ✂ {*100}	25.00
☐ T-RD Rick DiPietro, NYIs. ✂ {*100}	
☐ T-TE Tony Esposito, Chic. ✂ {*100}	50.00
☐ T-SF Sergei Fedorov, Detr. ✂ {*100}	50.00
☐ T-JF Jeff Friesen, Anah. ✂ {*100}	25.00
☐ T-GF Grant Fuhr, SLou. ✂ {*100}	25.00
☐ T-WG Wayne Gretzky, LosA. ✂ {*71}	275.00
☐ T-JH Johan Hedberg (G), Pitt. ✂ {*100}	25.00
☐ T-JA Jaromir Jagr, Wash. ✂ {*100}	50.00
☐ T-JJ Jaromir Jagr, Wash. ✂ {*100}	50.00
☐ T-OK Olaf Kölzig, Wash. ✂ {*100}	25.00
☐ T-LE John LeClair, Phil. ✂ {*100}	25.00
☐ T-MM Mark Messier, NYRa. ✂ {*100}	50.00
☐ T-CO Chris Osgood, NYIs. ✂ {*100}	25.00
☐ T-GP Gilbert Perreault, Buff. ✂ {*92}	50.00
☐ T-RA Bill Ranford, Edmo. ✂ {*100}	25.00
☐ T-PR Patrick Roy, Colo. ✂ {*100}	125.00
☐ T-SA Sergei Samsonov, Bost. ✂ {*83}	25.00
☐ T-SS Sergei Samsonov, Bost. ✂ {*100}	25.00
☐ T-TH José Théodore (G), Mont. ✂ {*100}	50.00
☐ T-JT Joe Thornton, Bost. ✂ {*36}	125.00
☐ T-SY Steve Yzerman, Detr. ✂ {*30}	300.00

TOOLS OF THE GAME SIGNED

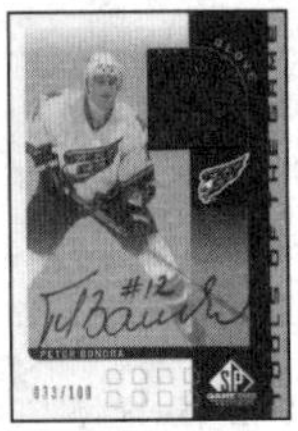

Insert Set (16 cards):	**900**
Insert (#/100)	**ST100**
☐ ST-PB Peter Bondra, Wash. ✍ ✂	50.00
☐ ST-RB Raymond Bourque, Bost. ✍ ✂	100.00
☐ ST-GF Grant Fuhr, SLou. ✍ ✂	50.00
☐ ST-JH Johan Hedberg (G), Pitt. ✍ ✂	50.00
☐ ST-JL John LeClair, Phil. ✍ ✂	75.00
☐ ST-LE John LeClair, Phil. ✍ ✂	75.00
☐ ST-GP Gilbert Perreault, Buff. ✍ ✂	75.00
☐ ST-KP Keith Primeau, Phil. ✍ ✂	50.00
☐ ST-BR Bill Ranford, Edmo. ✍ ✂	50.00
☐ ST-SA Sergei Samsonov, Bost. ✍ ✂	50.00
☐ ST-SM Sergei Samsonov, Bost. ✍ ✂	50.00
☐ ST-TS Teemu Selänne, Anah. ✍ ✂	75.00
☐ ST-JT José Théodore (G), Mont. ✍ ✂	100.00
☐ ST-JT Joe Thornton, Bost. ✍ ✂	100.00
☐ ST-TH Joe Thornton, Bost. ✍ ✂	100.00
☐ ST-SY Steve Yzerman, Detr. ✍ ✂	225.00

TOOLS OF THE GAME COMBO

Insert Set (18 cards):	**900**
Insert (#/50)	**CT50**
☐ Roman Cechmanek ✍ ✂ / Brian Boucher (G) ✍ ✂	50.00
☐ R. Cechmanek ✍ ✂ / Johan Hedberg (G) ✍ ✂	50.00
☐ Anson Carter ✍ ✂ / Sergei Samsonov ✍ ✂	50.00
☐ Byron Dafoe ✍ ✂ / Brian Boucher (G) ✍ ✂	50.00
☐ Byron Dafoe ✍ ✂ / Gerry Cheevers ✍ ✂	50.00
☐ Tony Esposito ✍ ✂ / Gerry Cheevers ✍ ✂	75.00
☐ Grant Fuhr ✍ ✂ / Roman Cechmanek ✍ ✂	50.00
☐ Sergei Fedorov ✍ ✂ / Jeff Friesen ✍ ✂	50.00
☐ Sergei Fedorov ✍ ✂ / Patrick Roy ✍ ✂	150.00
☐ Johan Hedberg ✍ ✂ / Byron Dafoe ✍ ✂	50.00
☐ Olaf Kölzig ✍ ✂ / Brian Boucher (G) ✍ ✂	50.00
☐ Olaf Kölzig ✍ ✂ / José Théodore (G) ✍ ✂	75.00
☐ John LeClair ✍ ✂ / Jaromir Jagr ✍ ✂	75.00
☐ Patrick Roy ✍ ✂ / Roman Cechmanek ✍ ✂	125.00
☐ Patrick Roy ✍ ✂ / Grant Fuhr ✍ ✂	150.00
☐ Bill Ranford ✍ ✂ / Grant Fuhr ✍ ✂	50.00
☐ Sergei Samsonov ✍ ✂ / Sergei Fedorov ✍ ✂	75.00
☐ José Théodore (G) ✍ ✂ / Byron Dafoe ✍ ✂	75.00

TOOLS OF THE GAME COMBO SIGNED

Insert Set (7 cards):	**900.00**
Insert (#/35)	**SC35**
☐ Raymond Bourque ✍ ✂ / Sergei Samsonov ✍ ✂	175.00
☐ John LeClair ✍ ✂ / Joe Thornton ✍ ✂	200.00
☐ Keith Primeau ✍ ✂ / Sergei Samsonov ✍ ✂	100.00
☐ Keith Primeau ✍ ✂ / Steve Yzerman ✍ ✂	275.00
☐ Bill Ranford (G) ✍ ✂ / Grant Fuhr (G) ✍ ✂	100.00
☐ Bill Ranford (G) ✍ ✂ / Johan Hedberg (G) ✍ ✂	100.00
☐ Joe Thornton ✍ ✂ / Steve Yzerman ✍ ✂	350.00

TOOLS OF THE GAME TRIPLE

Insert Set (7 cards):	**600.00**
Insert (#/35)	**TT35**
☐ Dafoe (G) ✂ / Esposito (G) ✂ / Roy (G) ✂	175.00
☐ Friesen ✂ / Carter ✂ / Fedorov ✂	80.00
☐ Fedorov ✂ / Samsonov ✂ / LeClair ✂	125.00
☐ Hedberg (G) ✂ / Cheevers (G) ✂ / Roy (G) ✂	175.00
☐ Kölzig (G) ✂ / Cechmanek (G) ✂ / Hedberg (G) ✂	80.00
☐ Roy (G) ✂ / Boucher (G) ✂ / Kölzig (G) ✂	150.00
☐ Ranford (G) ✂ / Fuhr (G) ✂ / Esposito (G) ✂	100.00

2001 - 02 SP^X

Produced by The Upper Deck Company, this series was released in January 2002.

Shell Set (90 cards):	**50.00**
Complete Set (170 cards):	**575.00**
Description	**Base**
☐ 1 Paul Kariya, Anah.	1.50
☐ 2 Patrik Stefan, Atla.	.35
☐ 3 Sergei Samsonov, Bost.	.50
☐ 4 Joe Thornton, Bost.	1.50
☐ 5 Bill Guerin, Bost.	.50
☐ 6 Martin Biron (G), Buff.	.50
☐ 7 Miroslav Satan, Buff.	.35
☐ 8 Jarome Iginla, Calg.	1.00
☐ 9 Marc Savard, Calg.	.35
☐ 10 Arturs Irbe (G), Caro.	.50
☐ 11 Tony Amonte, Chic.	.50
☐ 12 Steve Sullivan, Chic.	.35
☐ 13 Joe Sakic, Colo.	2.00
☐ 14 Peter Forsberg, Colo.	1.50
☐ 15 Raymond Bourque, Colo.	1.50
☐ 16 Milan Hejduk, Colo.	1.00
☐ 17 Patrick Roy, Colo.	3.50
☐ 18 Ron Tugnutt, Colu.	.50
☐ 19 Mike Modano, Dall.	1.00
☐ 20 Ed Belfour (G), Dall.	1.00
☐ 21 Pierre Turgeon, Dall.	.50
☐ 22 Steve Yzerman, Detr.	3.00
☐ 23 Brendan Shanahan, Detr.	1.00
☐ 24 Sergei Fedorov, Detr.	1.00
☐ 25 Luc Robitaille, Detr.	1.00
☐ 26 Dominik Hasek (G), Detr.	1.00
☐ 27 Tommy Salo, Edmo.	.50
☐ 28 Mike Comrie, Edmo.	1.00
☐ 29 Pavel Bure, Flor.	1.00
☐ 30 Zigmund Palffy, LosA.	.50
☐ 31 Félix Potvin, LosA.	.50
☐ 32 Adam Deadmarsh, LosA.	.35
☐ 33 Marian Gaborik, MinW.	1.00
☐ 34 Saku Koivu, Mont.	1.00
☐ 35 David Legwand, Nash.	.50
☐ 36 Mike Dunham, Nash.	.50
☐ 37 Martin Brodeur, NJer.	2.00
☐ 38 Patrik Elias, NJer.	1.00
☐ 39 Jason Arnott, NJer.	.50
☐ 40 Michael Peca, NYIs.	.50
☐ 41 Rick DiPietro, NYIs.	.50
☐ 42 Mark Messier, NYRa.	1.00
☐ 43 Theoren Fleury, NYRa.	.50
☐ 44 Marian Hossa, Otta.	1.00
☐ 45 Radek Bonk, Otta.	.35
☐ 46 Jeremy Roenick, Phil.	1.00
☐ 47 Roman Cechmanek, Phil.	.50
☐ 48 Keith Primeau, Phil.	.50
☐ 49 John LeClair, Phil.	1.00
☐ 50 Sean Burke, Phoe.	.50
☐ 51 Alexei Kovalev, Pitt.	.50
☐ 52 Mario Lemieux, Pitt.	3.50
☐ 53 Johan Hedberg (G), Pitt.	.50
☐ 54 Robert Lang, Pitt.	.35
☐ 55 Evgeni Nabokov, SanJ.	.50
☐ 56 Teemu Selänne, SanJ.	1.00
☐ 57 Owen Nolan, SanJ.	.50
☐ 58 Chris Pronger, SLou.	.50
☐ 59 Keith Tkachuk, SLou.	.50
☐ 60 Doug Weight, SLou.	.50
☐ 61 Pavol Demitra, SLou.	.50
☐ 62 Brad Richards, Tamp.	.50
☐ 63 Vincent Lecavalier, Tamp.	1.00
☐ 64 Curtis Joseph (G), Toro.	1.00
☐ 65 Mats Sundin, Toro.	1.00
☐ 66 Markus Näslund, Vanc.	1.00
☐ 67 Daniel Sedin, Vanc.	.50
☐ 68 Jaromir Jagr, Wash.	1.00
☐ 69 Peter Bondra, Wash.	.50
☐ 70 Olaf Kölzig, Wash.	.50
☐ 71 Paul Kariya, Anah.	1.50
☐ 72 Peter Forsberg, Colo.	1.50
☐ 73 Mike Modano, Dall.	1.00
☐ 74 Sergei Fedorov, Detr.	1.00
☐ 75 Steve Yzerman, Detr.	3.00
☐ 76 Pavel Bure, Flor.	1.00
☐ 77 Zigmund Palffy, LosA.	.50
☐ 78 Mario Lemieux, Pitt.	3.50
☐ 79 Vincent Lecavalier, Tamp.	1.00
☐ 80 Markus Näslund, Vanc.	1.00
☐ 81 Joe Sakic, Colo.	2.00
☐ 82 Chris Drury, Colo.	.50
☐ 83 Patrick Roy, Colo.	3.50
☐ 84 Mike Modano, Dall.	1.00
☐ 85 Steve Yzerman, Detr.	3.00
☐ 86 Pavel Bure, Flor.	1.00
☐ 87 Martin Brodeur, NJer.	2.00
☐ 88 John LeClair, Phil.	1.00
☐ 89 Mario Lemieux, Pitt.	3.50
☐ 90 Chris Pronger, SLou.	.50

ROOKIE

Rookie (#/999)	**R999**
☐ **91 Timo Pärssinen, Anah. RC**	10.00
☐ **92 Ilja Bryzgalov, Anah. RC**	20.00
☐ **93 Kevin Sawyer, Anah. RC**	10.00
☐ 94 Dany Heatley, Atla.	40.00
☐ **95 Zdenek Kutlak, Bost. RC**	10.00
☐ **96 Greg Crozier, Bost. RC**	10.00
☐ 97 Mika Noronen, Buff.	15.00
☐ **98 Scott Nichol, Calg. RC**	10.00
☐ **99 Erik Cole, Caro. RC**	20.00
☐ **100 Casey Hankinson, Chic. RC**	10.00
☐ **101 Vaclav Nedorost, Colo. RC**	20.00
☐ **102 Jaroslav Obsut, Colo. RC**	10.00
☐ **103 Niko Kapanen, Dall. RC**	20.00
☐ **104 Pavel Datsyuk, Detr. RC**	80.00
☐ **105 Niklas Hagman, Flor. RC**	15.00
☐ **106 Kristian Huselius, Flor. RC**	30.00
☐ **107 Andrei Podkonicky, Flor. RC**	15.00
☐ **108 Francis Bélanger, Mont. RC**	10.00
☐ **109 Martin Erat, Nash. RC**	15.00
☐ **110 Bill Bowler, Nash. RC**	10.00
☐ **111 Scott Clemmensen, NJer. RC**	15.00
☐ **112 Josef Boumedienne, NJer. RC**	10.00
☐ **113 Andreas Salomonsson, NJer. RC**	10.00
☐ **114 Mike Danton, NJer. RC**	15.00
☐ **115 Stanislav Gron, NJer. RC**	10.00
☐ **116 Radek Martinek, NYIs. RC**	10.00
☐ **117 Dan Blackburn (G), NYRa. RC**	40.00
☐ **118 Chris Neil, Otta. RC**	10.00
☐ **119 Ivan Ciernik, Otta. RC**	15.00
☐ 120 Pavel Brendl, Phil.	10.00
☐ **121 David Cullen, Phoe. RC**	10.00
☐ **122 Billy Tibbetts, Pitt. RC**	15.00
☐ 123 Miikka Kiprusoff, SanJ.	10.00
☐ **124 Jeff Jillson, SanJ. RC**	15.00
☐ **125 Michel Larocque, SanJ. RC**	10.00
☐ **126 Mark Rycroft, SLou. RC**	10.00
☐ **127 Thomas Ziegler, Tamp. RC**	15.00
☐ **128 Nikita Alexeev, Tamp. RC**	20.00
☐ **129 Bob Wren, Toro. RC**	10.00
☐ 130 Mike Brown, Vanc.	6.00

☐	131 Pat Kavanagh, Vanc. RC	10.00
☐	132 Brian Sutherby, Wash. RC	15.00

ROOKIE THREADS

Each card features a swatch from a player-worn jersey.

	Rookie	RT
☐	133 Brian Pothier, Atla. RC {#/800}	8.00
☐	133 Brian Pothier, Atla. RC {#/800}	8.00
☐	134 Dan Snyder, Atla. RC {#/1500}	8.00
☐	134 Dan Snyder, Atla. RC {#/1500}	8.00
☐	135 Jody Shelley, Colu. RC {#/1500}	10.00
☐	135 Jody Shelley, Colu. RC {#/1500}	10.00
☐	136 Martin Spanhel, Colu. RC {#/1500}	8.00
☐	136 Martin Spanhel, Colu. RC {#/1500}	8.00
☐	137 Mathieu Darche, Colu. RC {#/1500}	10.00
☐	137 Mathieu Darche, Colu. RC {#/1500}	10.00
☐	138 Matt Davidson, Colu. RC {#/1500}	8.00
☐	138 Matt Davidson, Colu. RC {#/1500}	8.00
☐	139 Sean Selmser, Colu. RC {#/1500}	8.00
☐	139 Sean Selmser, Colu. RC {#/1500}	8.00
☐	140 Jason Chimera, Edmo. RC {#/800}	15.00
☐	140 Jason Chimera, Edmo. RC {#/800}	15.00
☐	141 Mike Matteucci, MinW. RC {#/1500}	8.00
☐	141 Mike Matteucci, MinW. RC {#/1500}	8.00
☐	142 Pascal Dupuis, MinW. RC {#/800}	20.00
☐	142 Pascal Dupuis, MinW. RC {#/800}	20.00
☐	143 Peter Smrek, NYRa. RC {#/800}	8.00
☐	143 Peter Smrek, NYRa. RC {#/800}	8.00
☐	144 Mikael Samuelsson, NYRa. RC {#/1500}	8.00
☐	144 Mikael Samuelsson, NYRa. RC {#/1500}	8.00
☐	145 Joel Kwiatkowski, Otta. RC {#/1500}	8.00
☐	145 Joel Kwiatkowski, Otta. RC {#/1500}	8.00
☐	146 Kirby Law, Phil. RC {#/1500}	8.00
☐	146 Kirby Law, Phil. RC {#/1500}	8.00
☐	147 Tomas Divisek, Phil. RC {#/1500}	8.00
☐	147 Tomas Divisek, Phil. RC {#/1500}	8.00
☐	148 Ilya Kovalchuk, Atla. RC {#/800}	90.00
☐	148 Ilya Kovalchuk, Atla. RC {#/800}	90.00
☐	149 Jaroslav Bednar, LosA. RC {#/800}	15.00
☐	149 Jaroslav Bednar, LosA. RC {#/800}	15.00
☐	150 Jiri Dopita, Phil. RC {#/800}	15.00
☐	150 Jiri Dopita, Phil. RC {#/800}	15.00
☐	151 Krys Kolanos, Phoe. RC {#/800}	20.00
☐	151 Krys Kolanos, Phoe. RC {#/800}	20.00

UPDATE

	Update	Update
☐	152 Jeff Friesen, Anah.	.35
☐	153 Jean-Sébastien Giguère (G), Anah.	1.00
☐	154 Dany Heatley, Atla.	1.50
☐	155 Pascal Rhéaume, Atla.	.35
☐	156 Andy Hilbert, Bost.	.35
☐	157 Jozef Stümpel, Bost.	.35
☐	158 Glen Murray, Bost.	.50
☐	159 Maxim Afinogenov, Buff.	.50
☐	160 Roman Turek (G), Calg.	.50
☐	161 Craig Conroy, Calg.	.35
☐	162 Jeff O'Neill, Caro.	.50
☐	163 Sami Kapanen, Caro.	.35
☐	164 Jocelyn Thibault, Chic.	.50
☐	165 Mark Bell, Chic.	.35
☐	166 Kyle Calder, Chic.	.35
☐	167 Alex Tanguay, Colo.	.50
☐	168 Darius Kasparaitis, Colo.	.35
☐	169 Chris Drury, Colo.	.50
☐	170 Radim Vrbata, Colo.	.50
☐	171 Rostislav Klesla, Colu.	.35
☐	172 Brett Hull, Detr.	1.00
☐	173 Jani Rita, Edmo.	.35
☐	174 Mike York, Edmo.	.35
☐	175 Roberto Luongo, Flor.	1.00
☐	176 Jason Allison, LosA.	.50
☐	177 Andrew Brunette, MinW.	.35
☐	178 Sergei Berezin, Mont.	.35
☐	179 Donald Audette, Mont.	.50
☐	180 Brian Gionta, NJer.	.35
☐	181 Alexei Yashin, NYIs.	.50
☐	182 Chris Osgood, NYIs.	.50
☐	183 Pavel Bure, NYRa.	1.00
☐	184 Tom Poti, NYRa.	.35
☐	185 Eric Lindros, NYRa.	1.00
☐	186 Patrick Lalime, Otta.	.50
☐	187 Martin Havlat, Otta.	.50
☐	188 Brian Boucher (G), Phil.	.35
☐	189 Simon Gagné, Phil.	1.00
☐	190 Brian Savage, Phoe.	.35
☐	191 Brent Johnson, SLou.	.50
☐	192 Gordie Dwyer, Tamp.	.35
☐	193 Nikolai Khabibulin (G), Tamp.	.50
☐	194 Alexander Mogilny, Toro.	.50
☐	195 Brendan Morrison, Vanc.	.35
☐	196 Trevor Linden, Vanc.	.50

ROOKIE UPDATE

	Rookie (#/999)	Rookie
☐	197 Pasi Nurminen, Atla. RC {#/999}	20.00
☐	198 Ivan Huml, Bost. RC {#/999}	20.00
☐	199 Ales Kotalik, Buff. RC {#/999}	40.00
☐	200 Mike** Peluso, Chic. RC {#/999}	15.00
☐	201 Riku Hahl, Colo. RC {#/999}	15.00
☐	202 Kelly Fairchild, Colo. RC {#/999}	10.00
☐	203 Blake Bellefeuille, Colu. RC {#/999}	10.00
☐	204 Sean Avery, Detr. RC {#/999}	15.00
☐	205 Brad Norton, Flor. RC {#/999}	10.00
☐	206 Marcel Hossa, Mont. RC {#/999}	40.00
☐	207 Olivier Michaud, Mont. RC {#/999}	20.00
☐	208 Robert Schnabel, Nash. RC {#/999}	10.00
☐	209 Christian Berglund, NJer. RC {#/999}	15.00
☐	210 Raffi Torres, NYIs. RC {#/999}	20.00
☐	211 Toni Dahlman, Otta. RC {#/999}	10.00
☐	212 Branko Radivojevic, Phoe. RC {#/999}	20.00
☐	213 Shane Endicott, Pitt. RC {#/999}	10.00
☐	214 Tom Kostopoulos, Pitt. RC {#/999}	10.00
☐	215 Sébastien Centomo, Toro. RC {#/999}	20.00
☐	216 Karel Pilar, Toro. RC {#/999}	15.00

DUAL HIDDEN TREASURES

Insert Set (14 cards): 180.00

	Insert	HT
☐	M. Afinogenov ✂ / Jean-Pierre Dumont ✂	10.00
☐	P. Bondra ✂ Black / J. Jagr ✂ Black	25.00
☐	R. Blake ✂ / V. Nieminen ✂	10.00
☐	R. Fedotenko ✂ / T. Connolly ✂	10.00
☐	S. Gagné ✂ / Ju. Williams ✂	15.00
☐	M. Hejduk ✂ / R. Blake ✂	20.00
☐	Ja. Allison ✂ / A. Deadmarsh ✂	15.00
☐	Z. Palffy ✂ Purple / M. Satan ✂ Black	15.00
☐	M. Sundin ✂ / P. Forsberg ✂	40.00
☐	S. Sullivan ✂ / S. Gagné ✂	15.00
☐	T. Amonte ✂ / C. Drury ✂	20.00
☐	J. Thibault ✂ / F. Potvin ✂	15.00
☐	J. Thibault ✂ / J. Théodore (G) ✂	35.00
☐	M. York ✂ / B. Leetch ✂	15.00

TRIPLE HIDDEN TREASURES

Insert Set (8 cards): 375.00

	Insert	HTT
☐	Bondra ✂ / Selänne ✂ / Sundin ✂	50.00
☐	Brodeur ✂ / Thibault ✂ / Théodore (G) ✂	100.00
☐	Dumont ✂ / Biron ✂ / Afinogenov ✂	30.00
☐	Dazé ✂ / Sullivan ✂ / Amonte ✂	30.00
☐	Forsberg ✂ / Shanahan ✂ / Deadmarsh ✂	50.00
☐	Klesla ✂ Blue / Blake ✂ White / Lidström ✂ White	30.00
☐	Tanguay ✂ / Hinote ✂ / Nieminen ✂	30.00
☐	Yzerman ✂ / Lemieux ✂ / Sakic ✂	200.00

HOCKEY'S TREASURES

Insert Set (19 cards): 400.00

	Insert	HT
☐	Martin Brodeur, NJer. ✂	25.00
☐	Roman Cechmanek, Phil. White ✂ Stick ✂	15.00
☐	Sergei Fedorov, Detr. Red ✂ White ✂	25.00
☐	Dominik Hasek (G) Grey ✂ Stick ✂	25.00
☐	Dominik Hasek (G) Black ✂ Stick ✂	25.00
☐	Brett Hull, Dall. ✂ ✂	25.00
☐	Brett Hull, Dall. ✂ ✂	25.00
☐	Jarome Iginla, Calg. ✂ ✂	15.00
☐	Curtis Joseph (G) White ✂ Stick ✂	25.00
☐	John LeClair, Phil. ✂ ✂	15.00
☐	John LeClair, Phil. ✂ ✂	15.00
☐	Mario Lemieux Black ✂ Stick ✂	75.00
☐	Mike Modano, Dall. ✂ ✂	25.00
☐	Mike Modano, Dall. ✂ ✂	25.00
☐	Joe Nieuwendyk, Dall. ✂ ✂	15.00
☐	Keith Primeau, Phil. White ✂ Stick ✂	15.00
☐	Patrick Roy (G) Burgandy ✂ Stick ✂	75.00
☐	Sergei Samsonov, Bost. ✂ ✂	15.00
☐	Teemu Selänne, Anah. ✂ ✂	15.00
☐	Steve Yzerman, Detr. ✂ ✂	50.00

HOCKEY'S TREASURES SIGNED

Insert Set (10 cards): 1,700

	Insert (#/50)	HTS
☐	Raymond Bourque, Colo. ✍ ✂	150.00
☐	Raymond Bourque, Colo. ✍ ✂	150.00
☐	Jarome Iginla, Calg. ✍ ✂	100.00
☐	Curtis Joseph (G), Toro. ✍ ✂	125.00
☐	John LeClair, Phil. ✍ ✂	100.00
☐	John LeClair, Phil. ✍ ✂	100.00
☐	Keith Primeau, Phil. ✍ ✂	60.00
☐	Keith Primeau, Phil. ✍ ✂	60.00
☐	Marty Turco, Dall. ✍ ✂	75.00
☐	Steve Yzerman, Detr. ✍ ✂	300.00

ROOKIE REDEMPTION

See 2002 - 03 SPx Rookie for redeemed cards.

ROOKIE TREASURES

Insert Set (20 cards): 185.00

	Insert	RT
☐	Jaroslav Bednar, LosA.	10.00
☐	Jason Chimera, Edmo.	10.00
☐	Mathieu Darche, Colu.	10.00
☐	Matt Davidson, Colu.	10.00
☐	Tomas Divisek, Phil.	10.00
☐	Jiri Dopita, Phil.	10.00
☐	Pascal Dupuis, MinW.	10.00
☐	Krys Kolanos, Phoe.	10.00
☐	Ilya Kovalchuk, Atla.	60.00
☐	Joel Kwiatkowski, Otta.	10.00
☐	Kirby Law, Phil.	10.00
☐	Mike Matteucci, MinW.	10.00
☐	Brian Pothier, Atla.	10.00
☐	Mikael Samuelsson, NYRa.	10.00
☐	Sean Selmser, Edmo.	10.00
☐	Jody Shelley, Colu.	10.00
☐	Peter Smrek, NYRa.	10.00
☐	Dan Snyder, Atla.	10.00
☐	Martin Spanhel, Colu.	10.00
☐	Raffi Torres, NYIs.	10.00

SIGNS OF XCELLENCE

Insert Set (9 cards): 700.00

	Insert	SoX
☐	Mike Comrie, Edmo. ✍	50.00
☐	Simon Gagné, Phil. ✍	50.00
☐	Wayne Gretzky, NYRa. ✍	300.00
☐	Gordie Howe, Detr. ✍	150.00
☐	John LeClair, Phil. ✍	50.00
☐	Trevor Letowski, Phoe. ✍	30.00
☐	Mark Messier, NYRa. ✍	75.00
☐	Bobby Orr, Bost. ✍	275.00
☐	Doug Weight, Edmo. ✍	30.00

TRIBUTE

Insert Set (26 cards): 6200.00

	Insert	SY
☐	SY1 Steve Yzerman ✍ {#/19}	400.00
☐	SY2 Steve Yzerman ✍ {#/19}	400.00
☐	SY3 Steve Yzerman ✍ {#/19}	400.00
☐	SY4 Steve Yzerman ✍ {#/19}	400.00
☐	SY5 Steve Yzerman ✍ {#/19}	400.00
☐	SY6 Steve Yzerman ✍ {#/19}	400.00
☐	SY7 Steve Yzerman ✍ {#/19}	400.00
☐	SY8 Steve Yzerman ✍ {#/19}	400.00
☐	SY9 Steve Yzerman ✍ {#/19}	400.00
☐	SY10 Steve Yzerman ✍ {#/19}	400.00
☐	SY11 Steve Yzerman ✍ {#/19}	400.00
☐	SY12 Steve Yzerman ✍ {#/19}	400.00
☐	SY13 Steve Yzerman ✍ {#/19}	400.00
☐	SY14 Steve Yzerman ✍ {#/19}	400.00
☐	SY15 Steve Yzerman ✍ {#/19}	400.00
☐	SY16 Steve Yzerman ✍ {#/19}	400.00
☐	SY17 Steve Yzerman ✍ {#/19}	400.00
☐	SY18 Steve Yzerman ✍ {#/19}	400.00
☐	SY19 Steve Yzerman ✍ {#/19}	400.00
☐	SY20 Steve Yzerman White ✂ Stick ✂	100.00
☐	SY21 Steve Yzerman	100.00
☐	SY22 Steve Yzerman Red ✂ White ✂	100.00
☐	SY23 Steve Yzerman	100.00
☐	SY24 Steve Yzerman	100.00
☐	SY25 Steve Yzerman White ✂	60.00
☐	SY25 Steve Yzerman Red ✂	60.00
☐	SY25 Steve Yzerman White/Red ✂	75.00
☐	SY26 Steve Yzerman Red ✂	60.00

SAMPLE

☐	Steve Yzerman, Detr.	1.00

2001 - 02 SP^{X} ROOKIE

Produced by The Upper Deck Company, this series was released after October 2001. The redemption cards were seeded in packs of 2000 - 01 Upper Deck Rookie Update.

Complete Set (30 cards): 325.00

	Rookie	RR
☐	RR1 Ilja Bryzgalov, Anah. RC	15.00
☐	RR2 Ilya Kovalchuk, Atla. RC	75.00
☐	RR3 Ivan Huml, Bost. RC	15.00
☐	RR4 Ales Kotalik, Buff. RC	30.00
☐	RR5 Scott Nichol, Calg. RC	8.00
☐	RR6 Erik Cole, Caro. RC	15.00
☐	RR7 Casey Hankinson, Chic.	8.00
☐	RR8 Vaclav Nedorost, Colo. RC	15.00
☐	RR9 Martin Spanhel, Colu. RC	8.00
☐	RR10 Niko Kapanen, Dall. RC	15.00
☐	RR11 Pavel Datsyuk, Detr. RC	60.00
☐	RR12 Ty Conklin, Edmo. RC	15.00
☐	RR13 Kristian Huselius, Flor. RC	20.00
☐	RR14 Jaroslav Bednar, LosA. RC	12.00
☐	RR15 Nick Schultz, MinW. RC	12.00
☐	RR16 Martti Järventie, Mont.	8.00
☐	RR17 Martin Erat, Nash. RC	12.00
☐	RR18 Andreas Salomonsson, NJer. RC	8.00
☐	RR19 Raffi Torres, NYIs. RC	15.00
☐	RR20 Dan Blackburn (G), NYRa. RC	30.00
☐	RR21 Ivan Ciernik, Otta. RC	12.00
☐	RR22 Jiri Dopita, Phil. RC	12.00
☐	RR23 Krys Kolanos, Phoe. RC	15.00
☐	RR24 Billy Tibbetts, Pitt. RC	12.00
☐	RR25 Jeff Jillson, SanJ. RC	12.00
☐	RR26 Mark Rycroft, SLou. RC	8.00
☐	RR27 Nikita Alexeev, Tamp. RC	15.00
☐	RR28 Bob Wren, Toro. RC	8.00
☐	RR29 Pat Kavanagh, Vanc. RC	8.00
☐	RR30 Brian Sutherby, Wash. RC	12.00

2001 - 02 STADIUM CLUB

Produced by The Topps Company, this series was released in November 2001. There are three versions for each card: the base card, a Master Photo parallel (#/100) and an Award Winner parallel (#/100).

		AW100	MP100	Base
	Shell Set (120 cards):	-	-	60.00
	Complete Set (140 cards):	1,200	1,300	145.00
	Description	AW100	MP100	Base
☐☐☐	1 Martin Brodeur, NJer.	40.00	40.00	2.00
☐☐☐	2 Peter Forsberg, Colo.	35.00	35.00	1.50
☐☐☐	3 Chris Pronger, SLou.	15.00	15.00	.50
☐☐☐	4 Paul Kariya, Anah.	35.00	35.00	1.50
☐☐☐	5 Mike Modano, Dall.	25.00	25.00	1.00
☐☐☐	6 Curtis Joseph (G), Toro.	25.00	25.00	1.00
☐☐☐	7 Jason Allison, Bost.	15.00	15.00	.50
☐☐☐	8 Brendan Shanahan, Detr.	25.00	25.00	1.00
☐☐☐	9 Peter Bondra, Wash.	15.00	15.00	.50
☐☐☐	10 Mark Messier, NYRa.	25.00	25.00	1.00
☐☐☐	11 Owen Nolan, SanJ.	15.00	15.00	.50
☐☐☐	12 Saku Koivu, Mont.	30.00	30.00	1.00
☐☐☐	13 Tony Amonte, Chic.	15.00	15.00	.50
☐☐☐	14 Vincent Lecavalier, Tamp.	25.00	25.00	1.00
☐☐☐	15 Marian Hossa, Otta.	25.00	25.00	1.00
☐☐☐	16 Pavel Bure, Flor.	20.00	20.00	1.00
☐☐☐	17 Daniel Sedin, Vanc.	10.00	10.00	.50
☐☐☐	18 Mario Lemieux, Pitt.	75.00	75.00	3.50
☐☐☐	19 Rick DiPietro, NYIs.	10.00	10.00	.50
☐☐☐	20 Zigmund Palffy, LosA.	15.00	15.00	.50
☐☐☐	21 Ron Tugnutt, Colu.	10.00	10.00	.50
☐☐☐	22 Ron Francis, Caro.	15.00	15.00	.50
☐☐☐	23 Maxim Afinogenov, Buff.	10.00	10.00	.50
☐☐☐	24 Steve Yzerman, Detr.	60.00	60.00	3.00
☐☐☐	25 Ray Ferraro, Atla.	3.00	3.00	.20
☐☐☐	26 Tommy Salo, Edmo.	10.00	10.00	.50
☐☐☐	27 Marian Gaborik, MinW.	25.00	25.00	1.00
☐☐☐	28 Claude Lemieux, Phoe.	5.00	5.00	.20
☐☐☐	29 David Legwand, Nash.	10.00	10.00	.50

		Award	MP	Base
☐☐☐	30 Roman Cechmanek, Phil.	10.00	10.00	.50
☐☐☐	31 Jarome Iginla, Calg.	Win	20.00	1.00
☐☐☐	32 Sergei Fedorov, Detr.	25.00	25.00	1.00
☐☐☐	33 Bill Guerin, Bost.	10.00	10.00	.50
☐☐☐	34 Brian Leetch, NYRa.	15.00	15.00	.50
☐☐☐	35 Alexei Kovalev, Pitt.	15.00	15.00	.50
☐☐☐	36 Pavol Demitra, SLou.	10.00	10.00	.50
☐☐☐	37 Olaf Kölzig, Wash.	15.00	15.00	.50
☐☐☐	38 José Théodore, Mont.	Win	30.00	1.50
☐☐☐	39 Johan Hedberg (G), Pitt.	10.00	10.00	.50
☐☐☐	40 Teemu Selänne, SanJ.	20.00	20.00	1.00
☐☐☐	41 Adam Deadmarsh, LosA.	5.00	5.00	.20
☐☐☐	42 Miroslav Satan, Buff.	5.00	5.00	.20
☐☐☐	43 Henrik Sedin, Vanc.	10.00	10.00	.50
☐☐☐	44 Ed Belfour (G), Dall.	25.00	25.00	1.00
☐☐☐	45 Sean Burke, Phoe.	15.00	15.00	.50
☐☐☐	46 Patrik Elias, NJer.	20.00	20.00	1.00
☐☐☐	47 Daniel Alfredsson, Otta.	30.00	30.00	.50
☐☐☐	48 Evgeni Nabokov, SanJ.	15.00	15.00	.50
☐☐☐	49 Markus Näslund, Vanc.	25.00	25.00	1.00
☐☐☐	50 Mats Sundin, Toro.	25.00	25.00	1.00
☐☐☐	51 Milan Hejduk, Colo.	20.00	20.00	1.00
☐☐☐	52 Éric Bélanger, LosA.	3.00	3.00	.20
☐☐☐	53 Darren McCarty, Detr.	5.00	5.00	.20
☐☐☐	54 Keith Tkachuk, SLou.	15.00	15.00	.50
☐☐☐	55 Steve Sullivan, Chic.	5.00	5.00	.20
☐☐☐	56 Mark Recchi, Phil.	10.00	10.00	.50
☐☐☐	57 Rob Blake, Colo.	15.00	15.00	.50
☐☐☐	58 Manny Fernandez, MinW.	10.00	10.00	.50
☐☐☐	59 Patrick Lalime, Otta.	15.00	15.00	.50
☐☐☐	60 Adam Oates, Wash.	10.00	10.00	.50
☐☐☐	61 Joe Sakic, Colo.	40.00	40.00	2.00
☐☐☐	62 Lubomir Visnovsky, LosA.	3.00	3.00	.20
☐☐☐	63 Jeff Halpern, Wash.	5.00	5.00	.20
☐☐☐	64 Shane Willis, Caro.	5.00	5.00	.20
☐☐☐	65 Todd Bertuzzi, Vanc.	30.00	30.00	1.50
☐☐☐	66 Jeff Friesen, Anah.	5.00	5.00	.20
☐☐☐	67 Mike Dunham, Nash.	10.00	10.00	.50
☐☐☐	68 Alex Tanguay, Colo.	15.00	15.00	.50
☐☐☐	69 Jean-Pierre Dumont, Buff.	5.00	5.00	.20
☐☐☐	70 Patrick Marleau, SanJ.	10.00	10.00	.50
☐☐☐	71 Martin Straka, Pitt.	5.00	5.00	.20
☐☐☐	72 Petr* Sykora, NJer.	10.00	10.00	.50
☐☐☐	73 Arturs Irbe (G), Caro.	10.00	10.00	.50
☐☐☐	74 Jaromir Jagr, Pitt.	25.00	25.00	1.00
☐☐☐	75 Brad Richards, Tamp.	10.00	10.00	.50
☐☐☐	76 Mike Comrie, Edmo.	20.00	20.00	1.00
☐☐☐	77 Jason Arnott, NJer.	10.00	10.00	.50
☐☐☐	78 Tie Domi, Toro.	5.00	5.00	.20
☐☐☐	79 Martin Havlat, Otta.	15.00	15.00	.50
☐☐☐	80 Roberto Luongo, Flor.	20.00	20.00	1.00
☐☐☐	81 Nicklas Lidström, Detr.	Win	15.00	.50
☐☐☐	82 Simon Gagné, Phil.	20.00	20.00	1.00
☐☐☐	83 Marc* Savard, Calg.	5.00	5.00	.20
☐☐☐	84 John LeClair, Phil.	20.00	20.00	1.00
☐☐☐	85 Gary Roberts, Toro.	10.00	10.00	.50
☐☐☐	86 Ryan Smyth, Edmo.	10.00	10.00	.50
☐☐☐	87 Patrick Roy, Colo.	75.00	75.00	3.50
☐☐☐	88 Petr Nedved, NYRa.	5.00	5.00	.20
☐☐☐	89 Brent Johnson, SLou.	10.00	10.00	.50
☐☐☐	90 Scott Gomez, NJer.	10.00	10.00	.50
☐☐☐	91 Joe Thornton, Bost.	30.00	30.00	1.50
☐☐☐	92 Félix Potvin, LosA.	30.00	30.00	.50
☐☐☐	93 Chris Drury, Colo.	15.00	15.00	.50
☐☐☐	94 Keith Primeau, Phil.	10.00	10.00	.50
☐☐☐	95 Rod Brind'Amour, Caro.	5.00	5.00	.20
☐☐☐	96 Joe Nieuwendyk, Dall.	10.00	10.00	.50
☐☐☐	97 Espen Knutsen, Colu.	5.00	5.00	.20
☐☐☐	98 Adam Foote, Colo.	5.00	5.00	.20
☐☐☐	99 Brad Isbister, NYIs.	5.00	5.00	.20
☐☐☐	100 Marc Denis, Colu.	10.00	10.00	.50
☐☐☐	101 Eric Lindros, NYRa.	25.00	25.00	1.00
☐☐☐	102 Alexei Yashin, NYIs.	15.00	15.00	.50
☐☐☐	103 Dominik Hasek, Detr.	25.00	25.00	1.00
☐☐☐	104 Michael Peca, NYIs.	10.00	10.00	.50
☐☐☐	105 Brett Hull, Detr.	25.00	25.00	1.00
☐☐☐	106 Pierre Turgeon, Dall.	10.00	10.00	.50
☐☐☐	107 Doug Weight, SLou.	15.00	15.00	.50
☐☐☐	108 Alexander Mogilny, Toro.	10.00	10.00	.50
☐☐☐	109 Jaromir Jagr, Wash.	25.00	25.00	1.00
☐☐☐	110 Jeremy Roenick, Phil.	20.00	20.00	1.00
☐☐☐	111 Dany Heatley, Atla.	Win	25.00	7.50
☐☐☐	112 Rostislav Klesla, Colu.	15.00	15.00	3.00
☐☐☐	113 Pavel Brendl, Phil.	5.00	5.00	3.00
☐☐☐	114 Barrett Heisten, NYRa.	5.00	5.00	3.00
☐☐☐	115 Miikka Kiprusoff, SanJ.	5.00	5.00	3.00
☐☐☐	116 Kris Beech, Pitt.	5.00	5.00	3.00
☐☐☐	117 Pierre Dagenais, NJer.	3.00	3.00	3.00
☐☐☐	118 Bryan Allen, Vanc.	3.00	3.00	3.00
☐☐☐	119 Jason Williams, Detr.	5.00	5.00	3.00
☐☐☐	120 Milan Kraft, Pitt.	5.00	5.00	3.00

ROOKIE CARD

	Rookie	Award	MP	Base
☐☐☐	**121 Ilya Kovalchuk RC**	**50.00**	**50.00**	**25.00**
☐☐☐	**122 Peter Smrek RC**	**5.00**	**5.00**	**3.00**
☐☐☐	**123 Jiri Dopita RC**	**8.00**	**8.00**	**4.00**

☐☐☐	**124 Jeff Jillson RC**	**8.00**	**8.00**	**4.00**
☐☐☐	**125 Jukka Hentunen RC**	**5.00**	**5.00**	**3.00**
☐☐☐	**126 Vaclav Nedorost RC**	**12.00**	**12.00**	**6.00**
☐☐☐	**127 Timo Pärssinen RC**	**5.00**	**5.00**	**3.00**
☐☐☐	**128 Niklas Hagman RC**	**8.00**	**8.00**	**4.00**
☐☐☐	**129 A. Salomonsson RC**	**5.00**	**5.00**	**3.00**
☐☐☐	**130 Scott Nichol RC**	**5.00**	**5.00**	**3.00**
☐☐☐	**131 Dan Blackburn (G) RC**	**20.00**	**20.00**	**10.00**
☐☐☐	**132 Kristian Huselius RC**	**16.00**	**16.00**	**8.00**
☐☐☐	**133 Ivan Ciernik RC**	**8.00**	**8.00**	**4.00**
☐☐☐	**134 Scott Clemmensen RC**	**8.00**	**8.00**	**4.00**
☐☐☐	**135 Pascal Dupuis RC**	**12.00**	**12.00**	**6.00**
☐☐☐	**136 Jason Chimera RC**	**8.00**	**8.00**	**4.00**
☐☐☐	**137 Erik Cole RC**	**12.00**	**12.00**	**6.00**
☐☐☐	**138 Brian Sutherby RC**	**8.00**	**8.00**	**4.00**
☐☐☐	**139 Pavel Datsyuk RC**	**40.00**	**40.00**	**20.00**
☐☐☐	**140 Niko Kapanen RC**	**12.00**	**12.00**	**6.00**

GALLERY

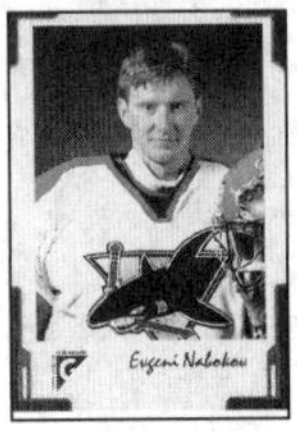

There are two versions for each card: Gallery and Gallery Gold (#/50).

	Insert Set (40 cards):	975.00	90.00
	Insert	G50	Gall
☐☐	G1 Curtis Joseph (G), Toro.	35.00	3.00
☐☐	G2 Brendan Shanahan, Detr.	35.00	3.00
☐☐	G3 Mats Sundin, Toro.	35.00	3.00
☐☐	G4 Patrik Elias, NJer.	25.00	2.00
☐☐	G5 Martin Havlat, Otta.	20.00	2.00
☐☐	G6 Joe Sakic, Colo.	55.00	5.00
☐☐	G7 Mike Modano, Dall.	35.00	3.00
☐☐	G8 Chris Drury, Colo.	20.00	2.00
☐☐	G9 Scott Stevens, NJer.	15.00	2.00
☐☐	G10 Olaf Kölzig, Wash.	20.00	2.00
☐☐	G11 Roberto Luongo, Flor.	25.00	2.00
☐☐	G12 Roman Cechmanek, Phil.	15.00	2.00
☐☐	G13 Ed Belfour (G), Dall.	35.00	3.00
☐☐	G14 Teemu Selänne, SanJ.	25.00	2.00
☐☐	G15 Henrik Sedin, Vanc.	15.00	2.00
☐☐	G16 Jaromir Jagr, Wash.	35.00	3.00
☐☐	G17 Marian Gaborik, MinW.	35.00	3.00
☐☐	G18 John LeClair, Phil.	25.00	2.00
☐☐	G19 Keith Tkachuk, SLou.	20.00	2.00
☐☐	G20 Paul Kariya, Anah.	45.00	4.00
☐☐	G21 Mario Lemieux, Pitt.	100.00	10.00
☐☐	G22 Sergei Fedorov, Detr.	35.00	3.00
☐☐	G23 Martin Brodeur, NJer.	55.00	5.00
☐☐	G24 Pavel Bure, Flor.	25.00	2.00
☐☐	G25 Mike Comrie, Edmo.	25.00	2.00
☐☐	G26 Zigmund Palffy, LosA.	20.00	2.00
☐☐	G27 Milan Hejduk, Colo.	25.00	2.00
☐☐	G28 Nicklas Lidström, Detr.	20.00	2.00
☐☐	G29 Patrick Roy, Colo.	100.00	10.00
☐☐	G30 Bill Guerin, Bost.	15.00	2.00
☐☐	G31 Evgeni Nabokov, SanJ.	20.00	2.00
☐☐	G32 Tony Amonte, Chic.	20.00	2.00
☐☐	G33 Peter Forsberg, Colo.	45.00	4.00
☐☐	G34 Rick DiPietro, NYIs.	15.00	2.00
☐☐	G35 Saku Koivu, Mont.	40.00	2.00
☐☐	G36 Chris Pronger, SLou.	20.00	2.00
☐☐	G37 Steve Yzerman, Detr.	80.00	8.00
☐☐	G38 Daniel Sedin, Vanc.	15.00	2.00
☐☐	G39 Vincent Lecavalier, Tamp.	35.00	3.00
☐☐	G40 Mark Messier, NYRa.	35.00	3.00

HEART AND SOUL

	Insert Set (10 cards):	30.00
	Insert (1:10)	HS
☐	HS1 Mark Messier, NYRa.	3.00
☐	HS2 Patrick Roy, Colo.	10.00
☐	HS3 Steve Yzerman, Detr.	8.00
☐	HS4 Mario Lemieux, Pitt.	10.00
☐	HS5 Chris Pronger, SLou.	2.00
☐	HS6 Scott Stevens, NJer.	2.00
☐	HS7 Peter Forsberg, Colo.	4.00
☐	HS8 Curtis Joseph (G), Toro.	3.00
☐	HS9 Mike Modano, Dall.	3.00
☐	HS10 Brendan Shanahan, Detr.	3.00

LONE STAR SIGNATURES

	Insert Set (7 cards):	200.00
	Insert	LSS
☐	LS5 Patrik Elias, NJer. ✍	40.00
☐	LS3 Marian Gaborik, MinW. ✍	50.00
☐	LS4 Martin Havlat, Otta. ✍	30.00
☐	LS1 Milan Hejduk, Colo. ✍	40.00
☐	LS2 Olaf Kölzig, Wash. ✍	30.00
☐	LS7 Ilya Kovalchuk, Atla. ✍	60.00
☐	LS6 Adam Oates, Wash. ✍	25.00

NEW REGIME

	Insert Set (11 cards):	20.00
	Insert (1:9)	NR
☐	NR1 Marty Turco (G), Dall.	4.00
☐	NR2 David Aebischer (G), Colo.	2.00
☐	NR3 Brent Johnson (G), SLou.	2.00
☐	NR4 Evgeni Nabokov (G), SanJ.	4.00
☐	NR5 Marc Denis (G), Colo.	3.00
☐	NR6 Roberto Luongo (G), Flor.	5.00
☐	NR7 Manny Fernandez (G), MinW.	2.00
☐	NR8 Roman Cechmanek (G), Phil.	2.00
☐	NR9 Jani Hurme (G), Otta.	2.00
☐	NR10 Johan Hedberg (G), Pitt.	2.00
☐	NR11 Rick DiPietro (G), NYIs.	3.00

NEW REGIME AUTOGRAPH

	Insert Set (9 cards):	
	Insert	NRA
☐	David Aebischer (G), Colo. ✍	30.00
☐	Roman Cechmanek, Phil. ✍	25.00
☐	Marc Denis, Colu. ✍	
☐	Manny Fernandez, MinW. ✍	
☐	Johan Hedberg (G), Pitt. ✍	30.00
☐	Brent Johnson, SLou. ✍	25.00
☐	Roberto Luongo, Flor. ✍	40.00
☐	Evgeni Nabokov, SanJ. ✍	30.00
☐	Marty Turco, Dall. ✍	30.00

NHL PASSPORT

	Insert Set (20 cards):	45.00
	Insert (1:10)	NHLP
☐	NHLP1 Peter Forsberg, Colo.	4.00
☐	NHLP2 Nicklas Lidström, Detr.	2.00
☐	NHLP3 Mats Sundin, Toro.	3.00
☐	NHLP4 Pavel Bure, Flor.	2.00
☐	NHLP5 Sergei Fedorov, Detr.	3.00
☐	NHLP6 Alexei Kovalev, Pitt.	2.00
☐	NHLP7 Saku Koivu, Mont.	2.00
☐	NHLP8 Teemu Selänne, SanJ.	2.00
☐	NHLP9 Roman Cechmanek, Phil.	2.00
☐	NHLP10 Patrik Elias, NJer.	2.00
☐	NHLP11 Milan Hejduk, Colo.	2.00
☐	NHLP12 Petr Sykora, NJer.	2.00
☐	NHLP13 Chris Drury, Colo.	2.00
☐	NHLP14 Bill Guerin, Bost.	2.00
☐	NHLP15 John LeClair, Phil.	2.00
☐	NHLP16 Mike Modano, Dall.	3.00
☐	NHLP17 Paul Kariya, Anah.	4.00
☐	NHLP18 Mario Lemieux, Pitt.	10.00
☐	NHLP19 Joe Sakic, Colo.	5.00
☐	NHLP20 Steve Yzerman, Detr.	8.00

PERENNIALS

	Insert Set (15 cards):	45.00
	Insert (1:7)	P
☐	P1 Pavel Bure, Flor.	2.00
☐	P2 Joe Sakic, Colo.	5.00
☐	P3 Martin Brodeur, NJer.	5.00
☐	P4 Peter Forsberg, Colo.	4.00
☐	P5 Patrick Roy, Colo.	10.00
☐	P6 John LeClair, Phil.	2.00
☐	P7 Paul Kariya, Anah.	4.00
☐	P8 Steve Yzerman, Detr.	8.00
☐	P9 Mario Lemieux, Pitt.	10.00
☐	P10 Ed Belfour (G), Dall.	3.00
☐	P11 Keith Tkachuk, SLou.	2.00
☐	P12 Sergei Fedorov, Detr.	3.00
☐	P13 Curtis Joseph (G), Toro.	3.00
☐	P14 Zigmund Palffy, LosA.	2.00
☐	P15 Tony Amonte, Chic.	2.00

SOUVENIR RELICS DOUBLE

	Insert Set (11 cards):	625.00
	Insert (#/25)	SRD
☐	Ed Belfour (G) ✂ / Martin Brodeur (G) ✂	75.00
☐	Jeff Hackett (G) ✂ / Saku Koivu ✂	60.00
☐	Chris Drury ✂ / Joe Sakic ✂	75.00
☐	Ed Belfour (G) ✂ / Marty Turco (G) ✂	60.00
☐	Chris Drury ✂ / Peter Forsberg ✂	75.00
☐	Peter Forsberg ✂ / Joe Sakic ✂	100.00
☐	Martin Brodeur (G) ✂ / Patrick Roy (G) ✂	150.00
☐	Pavel Bure ✂ / Sergei Fedorov ✂	60.00
☐	Pavel Bure ✂ / Sergei Samsonov ✂	60.00
☐	Tie Domi ✂ / Darren McCarty ✂	60.00
☐	Tomas Kloucek ✂ / Mike Mottau ✂	60.00

SOUVENIR RELICS TRIPLE

	Insert Set (3 cards):	625.00
	Insert (1:3616)	SRT
☐	Belfour (G) ✂ / Brodeur (G) ✂ / Roy (G) ✂	400.00
☐	Drury ✂ / Forsberg ✂ / Sakic ✂	300.00
☐	Allison ✂ / Samsonov ✂ / Thornton ✂	150.00

SOUVENIRS

	Insert Set (21 cards):	275.00
	Insert (1:16)	SRD
☐	Martin Brodeur, NJer. ✂	40.00
☐	Pavel Bure, Flor. ✂	20.00
☐	Sean Burke, Phoe. ✂ White	15.00
☐	Tie Domi, Toro. ✂	10.00
☐	Sergei Fedorov, Detr. ✂	25.00
☐	Peter Forsberg, Colo. ✂	35.00
☐	Jeff Hackett, Mont. ✂	10.00
☐	Jan Hlavac, NYRa. ✂ Blue	10.00
☐	Jarome Iginla, Calg. ✂	20.00
☐	Paul Kariya, Anah. ✂	35.00
☐	Tomas Kloucek, NYRa. ✂	10.00
☐	Saku Koivu, Mont. ✂	20.00
☐	Patrick Marleau, SanJ. ✂	10.00
☐	Chris Osgood, Detr. ✂	15.00
☐	Matt Pettinger, Wash. ✂	10.00
☐	Mark Recchi, Phil. ✂	10.00
☐	Miroslav Satan, Buff. ✂	10.00
☐	Marc Savard, Calg. ✂	10.00
☐	Joe Thornton, Bost. ✂	30.00
☐	Marty Turco, Dall. ✂	15.00
☐	Alexei Zhamnov, Chic. ✂	10.00

PRE-PRODUCTION SAMPLE

	Promotional Set (6 cards):	10.00
	Promo	PP
☐	PP1 Marian Hossa, Otta.	2.00
☐	PP2 Peter Forsberg, Colo.	3.00

☐ PP3 Daniel Alfredsson, Otta.	2.00
☐ PP4 Nicklas Lidström, Detr.	2.00
☐ PP5 Brendan Shanahan, Detr.	2.00
☐ PP6 Pavel Bure, Flor.	2.00

AWARD WINNERS

Redemption Prize	AW
☐ Ron Francis	
☐ Dany Heatley	
☐ Jarome Iginla	
☐ Nicklas Lidström	
☐ Michael Peca	
☐ José Théodore (G)	

2001 - 02 TOPPS / OPC

Produced by The Topps Company, this series was released in August 2001. There are four versions for each card 1-330: a base gold-foil Topps card, a silver-foil O-Pee-Chee parallel, a base gold-foil O-Pee-Chee card, and a silver-foil O-Pee-Chee Premier parallel.

Shell Set (330 cards):	-	-	50.00
Complete Set (360 cards):	-	-	120.00
Parallel Set (330 cards):	155.00	155.00	
Common Player:	.50	.50	.20

Description	OPP	Sil.O	Gold
☐☐☐☐ 1 Mario Lemieux, Pitt.	9.00	9.00	2.25
☐☐☐☐ 2 Steve Yzerman, Detr.	7.00	7.00	1.75
☐☐☐☐ 3 Martin Brodeur, NJer.	4.50	4.50	1.00
☐☐☐☐ 4 Brian Leetch, NYRa.	1.50	1.50	.25
☐☐☐☐ 5 Tony Amonte, Chic.	1.50	1.50	.25
☐☐☐☐ 6 Bill Guerin, Bost.	1.00	1.00	.25
☐☐☐☐ 7 Olaf Kölzig, Wash.	1.50	1.50	.25
☐☐☐☐ 8 Pavel Bure, Flor.	2.00	2.00	.50
☐☐☐☐ 9 Patrick Marleau, SanJ.	1.00	1.00	.25
☐☐☐☐ 10 Mariusz Czerkawski, NYIs.	.50	.50	.20
☐☐☐☐ 11 Teemu Selänne, SanJ.	2.00	2.00	.50
☐☐☐☐ 12 Alex Tanguay, Colo.	1.50	1.50	.25
☐☐☐☐ 13 Keith Primeau, Phil.	1.00	1.00	.25
☐☐☐☐ 14 Alexei Yashin, Otta.	1.50	1.50	.25
☐☐☐☐ 15 Markus Näslund, Vanc.	3.00	3.00	.75
☐☐☐☐ 16 Chris Pronger, SLou.	1.50	1.50	.25
☐☐☐☐ 17 Sergei Zubov, Dall.	.50	.50	.20
☐☐☐☐ 18 Marian Gaborik, MinW.	3.00	3.00	.75
☐☐☐☐ 19 Mats Sundin, Toro.	3.00	3.00	.75
☐☐☐☐ 20 Kevin Weekes, Tamp.	.50	.50	.20
☐☐☐☐ 21 Jean-Pierre Dumont, Buff.	.50	.50	.20
☐☐☐☐ 22 Nicklas Lidström, Detr.	1.50	1.50	.25
☐☐☐☐ 23 Ron Francis, Caro.	1.50	1.50	.25
☐☐☐☐ 24 Doug Weight, Edmo.	1.50	1.50	.25
☐☐☐☐ 25 Zigmund Palffy, LosA.	1.50	1.50	.25
☐☐☐☐ 26 Jason Allison, Bost.	1.50	1.50	.25
☐☐☐☐ 27 Joe Sakic, Colo.	4.50	4.50	1.00
☐☐☐☐ 28 Paul Kariya, Anah.	4.00	4.00	1.00
☐☐☐☐ 29 Marian Hossa, Otta.	3.00	3.00	.75
☐☐☐☐ 30 Owen Nolan, SanJ.	1.50	1.50	.25
☐☐☐☐ 31 Jason Arnott, NJer.	1.00	1.00	.25
☐☐☐☐ 32 Jaromir Jagr, Pitt.	3.00	3.00	.75
☐☐☐☐ 33 Justin Williams, Phil.	.50	.50	.20
☐☐☐☐ 34 Peter Bondra, Wash.	1.50	1.50	.25
☐☐☐☐ 35 Chris Drury, Colo.	1.50	1.50	.25
☐☐☐☐ 36 Radek Bonk, Otta.	.50	.50	.20
☐☐☐☐ 37 Theoren Fleury, NYRa.	1.50	1.50	.25
☐☐☐☐ 38 Keith Tkachuk, SLou.	1.50	1.50	.25
☐☐☐☐ 39 Rick DiPietro, NYIs.	1.00	1.00	.25
☐☐☐☐ 40 Ed Jovanovski, Vanc.	1.00	1.00	.25
☐☐☐☐ 41 Scott Stevens, NJer.	1.00	1.00	.25
☐☐☐☐ 42 John LeClair, Phil.	2.00	2.00	.50
☐☐☐☐ 43 Jochen Hecht, SLou.	.50	.50	.20
☐☐☐☐ 44 Vincent Lecavalier, Tamp.	3.00	3.00	.75
☐☐☐☐ 45 Henrik Sedin, Vanc.	1.00	1.00	.25
☐☐☐☐ 46 David Aebischer (G), Colo.	.50	.50	.20
☐☐☐☐ 47 Patrick Roy, Colo.	9.00	9.00	2.25
☐☐☐☐ 48 Valeri Bure, Calg.	.50	.50	.20
☐☐☐☐ 49 Dominik Hasek, Buff.	3.00	3.00	.75
☐☐☐☐ 50 Ray Ferraro, Atla.	.50	.50	.20
☐☐☐☐ 51 Milan Hejduk, Colo.	2.00	2.00	.50
☐☐☐☐ 52 Mike Modano, Dall.	3.00	3.00	.75
☐☐☐☐ 53 Sergei Fedorov, Detr.	3.00	3.00	.75
☐☐☐☐ 54 Luc Robitaille, LosA.	2.00	2.00	.50
☐☐☐☐ 55 Mark Messier, NYRa.	3.00	3.00	.75
☐☐☐☐ 56 Sean Burke, Phoe.	1.50	1.50	.25
☐☐☐☐ 57 Jeff Friesen, Anah.	.50	.50	.20
☐☐☐☐ 58 Alexander Mogilny, NJer.	1.00	1.00	.25
☐☐☐☐ 59 Roman Cechmanek, Phil.	1.00	1.00	.25
☐☐☐☐ 60 Martin Straka, Pitt.	.50	.50	.20
☐☐☐☐ 61 Pavol Demitra, SLou.	1.00	1.00	.25
☐☐☐☐ 62 Curtis Joseph (G), Toro.	3.00	3.00	.75
☐☐☐☐ 63 Daniel Sedin, Vanc.	1.00	1.00	.25
☐☐☐☐ 64 Brad Richards, Tamp.	1.00	1.00	.25
☐☐☐☐ 65 Simon Gagné, Phil.	2.00	2.00	.50
☐☐☐☐ 66 Saku Koivu, Mont.	2.00	2.00	.50
☐☐☐☐ 67 Jamie McLennan, MinW.	.50	.50	.20
☐☐☐☐ 68 Roberto Luongo, Flor.	2.00	2.00	.50
☐☐☐☐ 69 Brendan Shanahan, Detr.	3.00	3.00	.75
☐☐☐☐ 70 Espen Knutsen, Colu.	.50	.50	.20
☐☐☐☐ 71 Rob Blake, Colo.	1.50	1.50	.25
☐☐☐☐ 72 Steve Sullivan, Chic.	.50	.50	.20
☐☐☐☐ 73 Arturs Irbe (G), Caro.	1.00	1.00	.25
☐☐☐☐ 74 Maxim Afinogenov, Buff.	1.00	1.00	.25
☐☐☐☐ 75 Patrik Stefan, Atla.	.50	.50	.20
☐☐☐☐ 76 Scott Gomez, NJer.	1.00	1.00	.25
☐☐☐☐ 77 Brad Isbister, NYIs.	.50	.50	.20
☐☐☐☐ 78 Robert Lang, Pitt.	.50	.50	.20
☐☐☐☐ 79 Pierre Turgeon, SLou.	1.00	1.00	.25
☐☐☐☐ 80 Gary Roberts, Toro.	1.00	1.00	.25
☐☐☐☐ 81 Adam Oates, Wash.	1.00	1.00	.25
☐☐☐☐ 82 Evgeni Nabokov, SanJ.	1.50	1.50	.25
☐☐☐☐ 83 Petr Nedved, NYRa.	.50	.50	.20
☐☐☐☐ 84 Mike Dunham, Nash.	1.00	1.00	.25
☐☐☐☐ 85 Chris Osgood, Detr.	1.50	1.50	.25
☐☐☐☐ 86 Brett Hull, Dall.	3.00	3.00	.75
☐☐☐☐ 87 Peter Forsberg, Colo.	4.00	4.00	1.00
☐☐☐☐ 88 Joe Thornton, Bost.	3.50	3.50	.75
☐☐☐☐ 89 Raymond Bourque, Colo.	3.50	3.50	.75
☐☐☐☐ 90 Ed Belfour (G), Dall.	3.00	3.00	.75
☐☐☐☐ 91 Patrik Elias, NJer.	2.00	2.00	.50
☐☐☐☐ 92 Mike York, NYRa.	.50	.50	.20
☐☐☐☐ 93 Martin Havlat, Otta.	1.50	1.50	.25
☐☐☐☐ 94 Jeremy Roenick, Phoe.	2.00	2.00	.50
☐☐☐☐ 95 Alex Kovalev, Pitt.	1.50	1.50	.25
☐☐☐☐ 96 Al MacInnis, SLou.	1.00	1.00	.25
☐☐☐☐ 97 Marco Sturm, SanJ.	.50	.50	.20
☐☐☐☐ 98 José Théodore, Mont.	3.50	3.50	.75
☐☐☐☐ 99 Joe Nieuwendyk, Dall.	1.00	1.00	.25
☐☐☐☐ 100 Darren McCarty, Detr.	.50	.50	.20
☐☐☐☐ 101 Mark Recchi, Phil.	1.00	1.00	.25
☐☐☐☐ 102 Daniel Alfredsson, Otta.	1.50	1.50	.25
☐☐☐☐ 103 Miroslav Satan, Buff.	.50	.50	.20
☐☐☐☐ 104 Sergei Samsonov, Bost.	1.50	1.50	.25
☐☐☐☐ 105 Roman Turek, SLou.	1.00	1.00	.25
☐☐☐☐ 106 Jarome Iginla, Calg.	2.00	2.00	.50
☐☐☐☐ 107 Jeff O'Neill, Caro.	1.00	1.00	.25
☐☐☐☐ 108 Tommy Salo, Edmo.	1.00	1.00	.25
☐☐☐☐ 109 Petr Sykora, NJer.	1.00	1.00	.25
☐☐☐☐ 110 Adam Deadmarsh, LosA.	.50	.50	.20
☐☐☐☐ 111 Oleg Tverdovsky, Anah.	.50	.50	.20
☐☐☐☐ 112 Damian Rhodes, Atla.	.50	.50	.20
☐☐☐☐ 113 Bob Probert, Chic.	.50	.50	.20
☐☐☐☐ 114 Jere Lehtinen, Dall.	.50	.50	.20
☐☐☐☐ 115 Cale Hulse, Nash.	.50	.50	.20
☐☐☐☐ 116 Andy Sutton, MinW.	.50	.50	.20
☐☐☐☐ 117 Wade Redden, Otta.	.50	.50	.20
☐☐☐☐ 118 Brad Stuart, SanJ.	1.00	1.00	.25
☐☐☐☐ 119 Tomas Kaberle, Toro.	.50	.50	.20
☐☐☐☐ 120 Sergei Gonchar, Wash.	.50	.50	.20
☐☐☐☐ 121 J-S Aubin (G), Pitt.	.50	.50	.20
☐☐☐☐ 122 Adam Graves, NYRa.	1.00	1.00	.25
☐☐☐☐ 123 Teppo Numminen, Phoe.	.50	.50	.20
☐☐☐☐ 124 Martin Rucinsky, Mont.	.50	.50	.20
☐☐☐☐ 125 Scott Young, SLou.	.50	.50	.20
☐☐☐☐ 126 Pat Verbeek, Detr.	.50	.50	.20
☐☐☐☐ 127 Michael Nylander, Chic.	.50	.50	.20
☐☐☐☐ 128 Marc Savard, Calg.	.50	.50	.20
☐☐☐☐ 129 Brian Rolston, Bost.	.50	.50	.20
☐☐☐☐ 130 Sandis Ozolinsh, Caro.	.50	.50	.20
☐☐☐☐ 131 Mike Grier, Edmo.	.50	.50	.20
☐☐☐☐ 132 Éric Bélanger, LosA.	.50	.50	.20
☐☐☐☐ 133 Patrick Lalime, Otta.	1.50	1.50	.25
☐☐☐☐ 134 Steve Thomas, Toro.	.50	.50	.20
☐☐☐☐ 135 Viktor Kozlov, Flor.	.50	.50	.20
☐☐☐☐ 136 Manny Legacé, Detr.	.50	.50	.20
☐☐☐☐ 137 Oleg Saprykin, Calg.	.50	.50	.20
☐☐☐☐ 138 Sami Kapanen, Caro.	.50	.50	.20
☐☐☐☐ 139 Janne Niinimaa, Edmo.	.50	.50	.20
☐☐☐☐ 140 Scott Hartnell, Nash.	.50	.50	.20
☐☐☐☐ 141 Tim Connolly, NYIs.	1.00	1.00	.25
☐☐☐☐ 142 Travis Green, Phoe.	.50	.50	.20
☐☐☐☐ 143 Matthew Barnaby, Tamp.	.50	.50	.20
☐☐☐☐ 144 Brendan Morrison, Vanc.	.50	.50	.20
☐☐☐☐ 145 Darcy Tucker, Toro.	.50	.50	.20
☐☐☐☐ 146 Gary Suter, SanJ.	.50	.50	.20
☐☐☐☐ 147 Mattias Öhlund, Vanc.	.50	.50	.20
☐☐☐☐ 148 Patric Kjellberg, Nash.	.50	.50	.20
☐☐☐☐ 149 Lubomir Visnovsky, LosA.	.50	.50	.20
☐☐☐☐ 150 Claude Lapointe, NYIs.	.50	.50	.20
☐☐☐☐ 151 Martin Skoula, Colo.	.50	.50	.20
☐☐☐☐ 152 Mike Vernon, Calg.	1.00	1.00	.25
☐☐☐☐ 153 Stu Barnes, Buff.	.50	.50	.20
☐☐☐☐ 154 Brenden Morrow, Dall.	.50	.50	.20
☐☐☐☐ 155 Jim Dowd, MinW.	.50	.50	.20
☐☐☐☐ 156 Shane Doan, Phoe.	.50	.50	.20
☐☐☐☐ 157 Peter Schaefer, Vanc.	.50	.50	.20
☐☐☐☐ 158 Jeff Halpern, Wash.	.50	.50	.20
☐☐☐☐ 159 Sergei Berezin, Toro.	.50	.50	.20
☐☐☐☐ 160 Mike Ricci, SanJ.	.50	.50	.20
☐☐☐☐ 161 Radek Dvorak, NYRa.	.50	.50	.20
☐☐☐☐ 162 Brian Savage, Mont.	.50	.50	.20
☐☐☐☐ 163 Bryan Smolinski, LosA.	.50	.50	.20
☐☐☐☐ 164 Derian Hatcher, Dall.	.50	.50	.20
☐☐☐☐ 165 Shane Willis, Caro.	.50	.50	.20
☐☐☐☐ 166 Ron Tugnutt, Colu.	1.00	1.00	.25
☐☐☐☐ 167 Peter Worrell, Flor.	.50	.50	.20
☐☐☐☐ 168 Richard Zednik, Mont.	1.00	1.00	.25
☐☐☐☐ 169 Todd Marchant, Edmo.	.50	.50	.20
☐☐☐☐ 170 Andrew Brunette, Atla.	.50	.50	.20
☐☐☐☐ 171 Derek Morris, Calg.	.50	.50	.20
☐☐☐☐ 172 Kyle Calder, Chic.	.50	.50	.20
☐☐☐☐ 173 Félix Potvin, LosA.	1.50	1.50	.25
☐☐☐☐ 174 Bobby Holik, NJer.	.50	.50	.20
☐☐☐☐ 175 Manny Fernandez, MinW.	1.00	1.00	.25
☐☐☐☐ 176 Rick Tocchet, Phil.	.50	.50	.20
☐☐☐☐ 177 Jonas Höglund, Toro.	.50	.50	.20
☐☐☐☐ 178 Todd Bertuzzi, Vanc.	3.50	3.50	.75
☐☐☐☐ 179 Garth Snow, Pitt.	.50	.50	.20
☐☐☐☐ 180 Cliff Ronning, Nash.	.50	.50	.20
☐☐☐☐ 181 Martin Lapointe, Detr.	1.00	1.00	.25
☐☐☐☐ 182 Jason Smith, Edmo.	.50	.50	.20
☐☐☐☐ 183 Byron Dafoe, Bost.	1.00	1.00	.25
☐☐☐☐ 184 Rob Niedermayer, Flor.	.50	.50	.20
☐☐☐☐ 185 Steve Rucchin, Anah.	.50	.50	.20
☐☐☐☐ 186 Alexei Zhamnov, Chic.	.50	.50	.20
☐☐☐☐ 187 Mike Richter, NYRa.	1.00	1.00	.25
☐☐☐☐ 188 Michal Handzus, Phoe.	.50	.50	.20
☐☐☐☐ 189 Pavel Kubina, Tamp.	.50	.50	.20
☐☐☐☐ 190 Donald Brashear, Vanc.	.50	.50	.20
☐☐☐☐ 191 Trevor Letowski, Phoe.	.50	.50	.20
☐☐☐☐ 192 Randy McKay, NJer.	.50	.50	.20
☐☐☐☐ 193 Trevor Linden, Wash.	1.00	1.00	.25
☐☐☐☐ 194 Mike Sillinger, Otta.	.50	.50	.20
☐☐☐☐ 195 David Vyborny, Colu.	.50	.50	.20
☐☐☐☐ 196 David Tanabe, Caro.	.50	.50	.20
☐☐☐☐ 197 Scott Niedermayer, NJer.	.50	.50	.20
☐☐☐☐ 198 Anson Carter, Edmo.	1.00	1.00	.25
☐☐☐☐ 199 Mike Leclerc, Anah.	.50	.50	.20
☐☐☐☐ 200 Dave Scatchard, NYIs.	.50	.50	.20
☐☐☐☐ 201 Jan Hrdina, Pitt.	.50	.50	.20
☐☐☐☐ 202 Brian Holzinger, Tamp.	.50	.50	.20
☐☐☐☐ 203 Steve Konowalchuk, Wash.	.50	.50	.20
☐☐☐☐ 204 Tie Domi, Toro.	.50	.50	.20
☐☐☐☐ 205 Brent Johnson, SLou.	1.00	1.00	.25
☐☐☐☐ 206 Shawn McEachern, Otta.	.50	.50	.20
☐☐☐☐ 207 Jozef Stümpel, LosA.	.50	.50	.20
☐☐☐☐ 208 Jamie Langenbrunner, Dall.	.50	.50	.20
☐☐☐☐ 209 Jocelyn Thibault, Chic.	1.00	1.00	.25
☐☐☐☐ 210 Donald Audette, Buff.	1.00	1.00	.25
☐☐☐☐ 211 Serge Aubin, Colu.	.50	.50	.20
☐☐☐☐ 212 Andrew Cassels, Vanc.	.50	.50	.20
☐☐☐☐ 213 Tyson Nash, SLou.	.50	.50	.20
☐☐☐☐ 214 Colin White, NJer.	.50	.50	.20
☐☐☐☐ 215 Tom Poti, Edmo.	.50	.50	.20
☐☐☐☐ 216 Rod Brind'Amour, Caro.	.50	.50	.20
☐☐☐☐ 217 Fred Brathwaite (G), Calg.	.50	.50	.20
☐☐☐☐ 218 Marc Denis, Colu.	1.00	1.00	.25
☐☐☐☐ 219 Roman Simicek, MinW.	.50	.50	.20
☐☐☐☐ 220 Jan Hlavac, NYRa.	.50	.50	.20
☐☐☐☐ 221 Darius Kasparaitis, Pitt.	.50	.50	.20
☐☐☐☐ 222 Vincent Damphousse, SanJ.	1.50	1.50	.25
☐☐☐☐ 223 Bob Boughner, Pitt.	.50	.50	.20
☐☐☐☐ 224 Yanic Perreault, Toro.	.50	.50	.20
☐☐☐☐ 225 Chris Simon, Wash.	.50	.50	.20
☐☐☐☐ 226 Chris Gratton, Buff.	.50	.50	.20
☐☐☐☐ 227 Josef Vasicek, Caro.	.50	.50	.20
☐☐☐☐ 228 Vyacheslav Kozlov, Detr.	.50	.50	.20
☐☐☐☐ 229 Kelly Buchberger, LosA.	.50	.50	.20
☐☐☐☐ 230 Jeff Hackett, Mont.	.50	.50	.20
☐☐☐☐ 231 Taylor Pyatt, NYIs.	.50	.50	.20
☐☐☐☐ 232 Niklas Sundström, SanJ.	.50	.50	.20
☐☐☐☐ 233 Dan Cloutier, Vanc.	1.00	1.00	.25
☐☐☐☐ 234 Éric Dazé, Chic.	1.00	1.00	.25
☐☐☐☐ 235 Ryan Smyth, Edmo.	1.00	1.00	.25
☐☐☐☐ 236 Marty McInnis, Anah.	.50	.50	.20
☐☐☐☐ 237 John Madden, NJer.	.50	.50	.20
☐☐☐☐ 238 Claude Lemieux, Phoe.	.50	.50	.20
☐☐☐☐ 239 Stephen Heinze, Buff.	.50	.50	.20
☐☐☐☐ 240 Nikolai Antropov, Toro.	.50	.50	.20
☐☐☐☐ 241 Cory Stillman, SLou.	.50	.50	.20
☐☐☐☐ 242 Geoff Sanderson, Colu.	.50	.50	.20
☐☐☐☐ 243 Trevor Kidd, Flor.	.50	.50	.20
☐☐☐☐ 244 David Legwand, Nash.	1.00	1.00	.25
☐☐☐☐ 245 Éric Desjardins, Phil.	.50	.50	.20
☐☐☐☐ 246 Fredrik Modin, Tamp.	.50	.50	.20
☐☐☐☐ 247 Brett Clark, Atla.	.50	.50	.20
☐☐☐☐ 248 Bryan Muir, Colo.	.50	.50	.20
☐☐☐☐ 249 Ron Sutter, Calg.	.50	.50	.20
☐☐☐☐ 250 Ken Klee, Wash.	.50	.50	.20
☐☐☐☐ 251 Steve Halko, Caro.	.50	.50	.20
☐☐☐☐ 252 Steve McKenna, Pitt.	.50	.50	.20
☐☐☐☐ 253 Marc Bergevin, Pitt.	.50	.50	.20
☐☐☐☐ 254 Scott Lachance, Vanc.	.50	.50	.20
☐☐☐☐ 255 Jamie Rivers, Otta.	.50	.50	.20
☐☐☐☐ 256 Dixon Ward, Bost.	.50	.50	.20
☐☐☐☐ 257 Gord Murphy, Atla.	.50	.50	.20
☐☐☐☐ 258 Bret Hedican, Flor.	.50	.50	.20
☐☐☐☐ 259 Bob Corkum, NJer.	.50	.50	.20
☐☐☐☐ 260 Brent Sopel, Vanc.	.50	.50	.20
☐☐☐☐ 261 Todd Simpson, Phoe.	.50	.50	.20
☐☐☐☐ 262 Reid Simpson, SLou.	.50	.50	.20
☐☐☐☐ 263 Chris McAlpine, Chic.	.50	.50	.20
☐☐☐☐ 264 Deron Quint, Colu.	.50	.50	.20
☐☐☐☐ 265 Josh Holden, Vanc.	.50	.50	.20
☐☐☐☐ 266 Mike Mottau, NYRa.	.50	.50	.20
☐☐☐☐ 267 Jakub Cutta, Wash.	.50	.50	.20
☐☐☐☐ 268 Maxime* Ouellet, Phil.	.50	.50	.20
☐☐☐☐ **269 Peter Smrek, NYRa. RC**	**1.50**	**1.50**	**.25**
☐☐☐☐ 270 Daniel Corso, SLou.	.50	.50	.20
☐☐☐☐ 271 Rostislav Klesla, Colu.	.50	.50	.20
☐☐☐☐ 272 Mika Noronen, Buff.	1.00	1.00	.25
☐☐☐☐ 273 Kris Beech, Wash.	.50	.50	.20
☐☐☐☐ 274 Sheldon Keefe, Tamp.	.50	.50	.20
☐☐☐☐ 275 Miikka Kiprusoff, SanJ.	.50	.50	.20
☐☐☐☐ 276 Mathieu Garon, Mont.	1.00	1.00	.25
☐☐☐☐ **277 J. Chimera, Edmo. RC**	**2.00**	**2.00**	**.50**
☐☐☐☐ 278 Mark Bell, Chic.	.50	.50	.20
☐☐☐☐ 279 Chris Nielsen, Colu.	.50	.50	.20
☐☐☐☐ 280 Éric Chouinard, Mont.	.50	.50	.20
☐☐☐☐ 281 Pierre Dagenais, NJer.	.50	.50	.20
☐☐☐☐ 282 Branislav Mezei, NYIs.	.50	.50	.20
☐☐☐☐ 283 Milan Kraft, Pitt.	.50	.50	.20
☐☐☐☐ 284 Tomas Kloucek, NYRa.	.50	.50	.20
☐☐☐☐ 285 Petr Schastlivy, Otta.	.50	.50	.20
☐☐☐☐ 286 Lee Goren, Bost.	.50	.50	.20
☐☐☐☐ 287 Daniel Tkaczuk, Calg.	.50	.50	.20
☐☐☐☐ 288 Andreas Lilja, LosA.	.50	.50	.20
☐☐☐☐ **289 Tomas Divisek, Phil. RC**	**1.50**	**1.50**	**.25**
☐☐☐☐ 290 Alexei Ponikarovsky, Toro.	.50	.50	.20
☐☐☐☐ **291 M. Samuelsson, SanJ. RC**	**1.50**	**1.50**	**.25**
☐☐☐☐ 292 Petr2 Svoboda, Toro.	.50	.50	.20
☐☐☐☐ 293 Mike Comrie, Edmo.	2.00	2.00	.50
☐☐☐☐ 294 Johan Hedberg (G), Pitt.	1.00	1.00	.25
☐☐☐☐ 295 Tyler Moss, Caro.	.50	.50	.20
☐☐☐☐ **296 Martin Spanhel, Colu. RC**	**1.50**	**1.50**	**.25**
☐☐☐☐ 297 Mike Brown, Vanc.	.50	.50	.20
☐☐☐☐ 298 Derek Gustafson, MinW.	.50	.50	.20
☐☐☐☐ 299 Matt Pettinger, Wash.	.50	.50	.20
☐☐☐☐ 300 Mike Commodore, NJer.	.50	.50	.20
☐☐☐☐ 301 Antti-Jussi Niemi, Anah.	.50	.50	.20
☐☐☐☐ 302 Brad Tapper, Atla.	.50	.50	.20
☐☐☐☐ 303 Rick Berry, Colo.	.50	.50	.20
☐☐☐☐ 304 Andrew Raycroft, Bost.	.50	.50	.20
☐☐☐☐ 305 Bryan Allen, Vanc.	.50	.50	.20
☐☐☐☐ 306 Ivan Novoseltsev, Flor.	.50	.50	.20
☐☐☐☐ 307 Jason Williams, Detr.	.50	.50	.20
☐☐☐☐ 308 Gregg Naumenko, Anah.	.50	.50	.20
☐☐☐☐ 309 Jiri Bicek, NJer.	.50	.50	.20
☐☐☐☐ **310 Mat. Darche, Colu. RC**	**2.00**	**2.00**	**.50**
☐☐☐☐ 311 Brian Campbell, Buff.	.50	.50	.20
☐☐☐☐ 312 Jeff Farkas, Toro.	.50	.50	.20
☐☐☐☐ 313 Rico Fata, Calg.	.50	.50	.20
☐☐☐☐ 314 Kristian Kudroc, Tamp.	.50	.50	.20
☐☐☐☐ 315 R. Cechmanek [All-Star]	1.00	1.00	.25
☐☐☐☐ 316 N. Lidström [All-Star]	1.50	1.50	.25
☐☐☐☐ 317 R. Bourque [All-Star]	3.50	3.50	.75
☐☐☐☐ 318 J. Sakic [All-Star]	4.50	4.50	1.00
☐☐☐☐ 319 P. Elias [All-Star]	2.00	2.00	.50
☐☐☐☐ 320 J. Jagr [All-Star]	3.00	3.00	.75
☐☐☐☐ 321 J. Madden / R. McKay [HL]	.50	.50	.20
☐☐☐☐ 322 Mark Recchi, Phil. [HL]	1.00	1.00	.25
☐☐☐☐ 323 V. Damphousse, SanJ. [HL]	1.50	1.50	.25
☐☐☐☐ 324 Patrick Roy, Colo. [HL]	9.00	9.00	1.25
☐☐☐☐ 325 Jaromir Jagr, Pitt. [HL]	3.00	3.00	.75
☐☐☐☐ 326 Mario Lemieux [Returns]	5.00	5.00	1.25
☐☐☐☐ 327 Mario Lemieux [Returns]	5.00	5.00	1.25
☐☐☐☐ 328 Mario Lemieux [Returns]	5.00	5.00	1.25
☐☐☐☐ 329 Mario Lemieux [Returns]	5.00	5.00	1.25
☐☐☐☐ 330 Mario Lemieux [Returns]	5.00	5.00	1.25

ROOKIES

O-Pee-Chee redeemed cards are valued at 60-70% of Topps redeemed cards.

Rookie	OPC	Topps
☐☐ **331 Ilya Kovalchuk, Atla. RC**	**12.00**	**15.00**
☐☐ **332 Dan Blackburn (G), NYRa. RC**	**4.00**	**5.00**

□□ 333 Vaclav Nedorost, Colo. RC	2.00	4.00
□□ 334 Krys Kolanos, Phoe. RC	2.00	4.00
□□ 335 Kristian Huselius, Flor. RC	4.00	6.00
□□ 336 Martin Erat, Nash. RC	2.00	4.00
□□ 337 Timo Pärssinen, Anah. RC	2.00	4.00
□□ 338 Scott Nichol, Calg. RC	2.00	4.00
□□ 339 Nick Schultz, MinW. RC	2.00	4.00
□□ 340 Jukka Hentunen, Calg. RC	2.00	4.00
□□ 341 Pascal Dupuis, MinW. RC	2.00	4.00
□□ 342 Radek Martinek, NYIs. RC	2.00	4.00
□□ 343 Scott Clemmensen (G), Njer. RC	2.00	4.00
□□ 344 Jeff Jillson, SanJ. RC	2.00	4.00
□□ 345 Brian Sutherby, Wash. RC	2.00	4.00
□□ 346 Nikita Alexeev, Tamp. RC	2.00	4.00
□□ 347 Niklas Hagman, Flor. RC	2.00	4.00
□□ 348 Erik Cole, Caro. RC	2.00	4.00
□□ 349 Pavel Datsyuk, Detr. RC	10.00	15.00
□□ 350 Ilja Bryzgalov (G), Anah. RC	2.00	4.00
□□ 351 Chris Neil, Otta. RC	2.00	4.00
□□ 352 Mark Rycroft, Slou. RC	2.00	4.00
□□ 353 Kamil Piros, Atla. RC	2.00	4.00
□□ 354 Niko Kapanen, Dall. RC	2.00	4.00
□□ 355 Jiri Dopita, Phil. RC	2.00	4.00
□□ 356 Andreas Salomonsson, Njer. RC	2.00	4.00
□□ 357 Ivan Ciernik, Otta. RC	2.00	4.00
□□ 358 Jaroslav Bednar, LosA. RC	2.00	4.00
□□ 359 Ty Conklin (G), Edmo. RC	2.00	4.00
□□ 360 Raffi Torres, NYRa. RC	2.00	4.00

HERITAGE

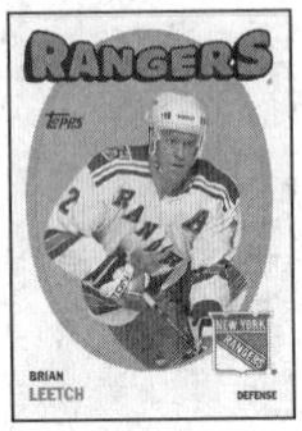

These cards feature the same back design and front photo as base cards 1-110, but they feature a front design similar to the 1971 - 72 O-Pee-Chee & Topps design. There are four versions for each card 1-110: a Topps card, an O-Pee-Chee parallel, a Topps Limited Edition parallel (#/50), and an O-Pee-Chee Limited Edition parallel (#/50).

Insert Set (110 cards):	**1,500**	**50.00**
Common Player:	**8.00**	**.35**
Insert (1:1)	**LE50**	**Heri.**
□□□□ 1 Mario Lemieux, Pitt.	110.00	4.50
□□□□ 2 Steve Yzerman, Detr.	50.00	3.50
□□□□ 3 Martin Brodeur, NJer.	60.00	2.00
□□□□ 4 Brian Leetch, NYRa.	20.00	.50
□□□□ 5 Tony Amonte, Chic.	20.00	.50
□□□□ 6 Bill Guerin, Bost.	14.00	.50
□□□□ 7 Olaf Kölzig, Wash.	20.00	.50
□□□□ 8 Pavel Bure, Flor.	30.00	1.00
□□□□ 9 Patrick Marleau, SanJ.	18.00	.50
□□□□ 10 Mariusz Czerkawski, NYIs.	8.00	.35
□□□□ 11 Teemu Selänne, SanJ.	30.00	1.00
□□□□ 12 Alex Tanguay, Colo.	20.00	.50
□□□□ 13 Keith Primeau, Phil.	14.00	.50
□□□□ 14 Alexei Yashin, Otta.	20.00	.50
□□□□ 15 Markus Näslund, Vanc.	35.00	1.50
□□□□ 16 Chris Pronger, SLou.	20.00	.50
□□□□ 17 Sergei Zubov, Dall.	8.00	.35
□□□□ 18 Marian Gaborik, MinW.	36.00	1.50
□□□□ 19 Mats Sundin, Toro.	35.00	1.50
□□□□ 20 Kevin Weekes, Tamp.	8.00	.35
□□□□ 21 Jean-Pierre Dumont, Buff.	8.00	.35
□□□□ 22 Nicklas Lidström, Detr.	20.00	.50
□□□□ 23 Ron Francis, Caro.	22.00	.50
□□□□ 24 Doug Weight, Edmo.	20.00	.50
□□□□ 25 Zigmund Palffy, LosA.	20.00	.50
□□□□ 26 Jason Allison, Bost.	20.00	.50
□□□□ 27 Joe Sakic, Colo.	60.00	2.00
□□□□ 28 Paul Kariya, Anah.	50.00	2.00
□□□□ 29 Marian Hossa, Otta.	35.00	1.50
□□□□ 30 Owen Nolan, SanJ.	20.00	.50
□□□□ 31 Jason Arnott, NJer.	15.00	.50
□□□□ 32 Jaromir Jagr, Pitt.	35.00	1.50
□□□□ 33 Justin Williams, Phil.	12.00	.35
□□□□ 34 Peter Bondra, Wash.	20.00	.50
□□□□ 35 Chris Drury, Colo.	20.00	.50
□□□□ 36 Radek Bonk, Otta.	12.00	.35
□□□□ 37 Theoren Fleury, NYRa.	20.00	.50
□□□□ 38 Keith Tkachuk, SLou.	20.00	.50
□□□□ 39 Rick DiPietro, NYIs.	18.00	.50
□□□□ 40 Ed Jovanovski, Vanc.	14.00	.50
□□□□ 41 Scott Stevens, NJer.	14.00	.50
□□□□ 42 John LeClair, Phil.	30.00	1.00
□□□□ 43 Jochen Hecht, SLou.	8.00	.35
□□□□ 44 Vincent Lecavalier, Tamp.	35.00	1.50
□□□□ 45 Henrik Sedin, Vanc.	14.00	.50
□□□□ 46 David Aebischer (G), Colo.	12.00	.35
□□□□ 47 Patrick Roy, Colo.	110.00	4.50
□□□□ 48 Valeri Bure, Calg.	12.00	.35
□□□□ 49 Dominik Hasek, Buff.	35.00	1.50
□□□□ 50 Ray Ferraro, Atla.	8.00	.35
□□□□ 51 Milan Hejduk, Colo.	30.00	1.00
□□□□ 52 Mike Modano, Dall.	35.00	1.50
□□□□ 53 Sergei Fedorov, Detr.	35.00	1.50
□□□□ 54 Luc Robitaille, LosA.	30.00	1.00
□□□□ 55 Mark Messier, NYRa.	35.00	1.50
□□□□ 56 Sean Burke, Phoe.	22.00	.50
□□□□ 57 Jeff Friesen, Anah.	12.00	.35
□□□□ 58 Alexander Mogilny, NJer.	18.00	.50
□□□□ 59 Roman Cechmanek, Phil.	14.00	.50
□□□□ 60 Martin Straka, Pitt.	12.00	.35
□□□□ 61 Pavol Demitra, SLou.	14.00	.50
□□□□ 62 Curtis Joseph (G), Toro.	35.00	1.50
□□□□ 63 Daniel Sedin, Vanc.	14.00	.50
□□□□ 64 Brad Richards, Tamp.	18.00	.50
□□□□ 65 Simon Gagné, Phil.	30.00	1.00
□□□□ 66 Saku Koivu, Mont.	30.00	1.00
□□□□ 67 Jamie McLennan, MinW.	8.00	.35
□□□□ 68 Roberto Luongo, Flor.	30.00	1.00
□□□□ 69 Brendan Shanahan, Detr.	35.00	1.50
□□□□ 70 Espen Knutsen, Colu.	8.00	.35
□□□□ 71 Rob Blake, Colo.	20.00	.50
□□□□ 72 Steve Sullivan, Chic.	12.00	.35
□□□□ 73 Arturs Irbe (G), Caro.	14.00	.50
□□□□ 74 Maxim Afinogenov, Buff.	14.00	.50
□□□□ 75 Patrik Stefan, Atla.	12.00	.35
□□□□ 76 Scott Gomez, NJer.	15.00	.50
□□□□ 77 Brad Isbister, NYIs.	8.00	.35
□□□□ 78 Robert Lang, Pitt.	8.00	.35
□□□□ 79 Pierre Turgeon, SLou.	14.00	.50
□□□□ 80 Gary Roberts, Toro.	14.00	.50
□□□□ 81 Adam Oates, Wash.	14.00	.50
□□□□ 82 Evgeni Nabokov, SanJ.	20.00	.50
□□□□ 83 Petr Nedved, NYRa.	12.00	.35
□□□□ 84 Mike Dunham, Nash.	15.00	.50
□□□□ 85 Chris Osgood, Detr.	20.00	.50
□□□□ 86 Brett Hull, Dall.	35.00	1.50
□□□□ 87 Peter Forsberg, Colo.	50.00	2.00
□□□□ 88 Joe Thornton, Bost.	45.00	1.50
□□□□ 89 Raymond Bourque, Colo.	45.00	1.50
□□□□ 90 Ed Belfour (G), Dall.	35.00	1.50
□□□□ 91 Patrik Elias, NJer.	30.00	1.00
□□□□ 92 Mike York, NYRa.	12.00	.35
□□□□ 93 Martin Havlat, Otta.	22.00	.50
□□□□ 94 Jeremy Roenick, Phoe.	30.00	1.00
□□□□ 95 Alex Kovalev, Pitt.	20.00	.50
□□□□ 96 Al MacInnis, SLou.	14.00	.50
□□□□ 97 Marco Sturm, SanJ.	8.00	.35
□□□□ 98 José Théodore, Mont.	45.00	1.50
□□□□ 99 Joe Nieuwendyk, Dall.	14.00	.50
□□□□ 100 Darren McCarty, Detr.	12.00	.35
□□□□ 101 Mark Recchi, Phil.	14.00	.50
□□□□ 102 Daniel Alfredsson, Otta.	20.00	.50
□□□□ 103 Miroslav Satan, Buff.	12.00	.35
□□□□ 104 Sergei Samsonov, Bost.	20.00	.50
□□□□ 105 Roman Turek, SLou.	18.00	.50
□□□□ 106 Jarome Iginla, Calg.	30.00	1.00
□□□□ 107 Jeff O'Neill, Caro.	14.00	.50
□□□□ 108 Tommy Salo, Edmo.	14.00	.50
□□□□ 109 Petr Sykora, NJer.	14.00	.50
□□□□ 110 Adam Deadmarsh, LosA.	12.00	.35

CAPTAIN'S CLOTH

Insert Set (3 cards):	**500.00**
Insert (1:5950)	**CC**
□ Jagr ✂ / Kariya ✂ / Lecavalier ✂ / Sakic ✂	275.00
□ Amonte ✂ / Jagr ✂ / Koivu ✂ / Pronger ✂	250.00
□ Allison ✂ / Francis ✂ / Kariya ✂ / Lecavalier ✂	250.00

CERTIFIED AUTOGRAPH ISSUE

Insert Set (10 cards):	**255.00**
Insert (1:507)	**CAI**
□ Jason Arnott, Njer. ✍	25.00
□ Chris Drury, Colo. ✍	30.00
□ Ron Francis, Caro. ✍	30.00
□ Simon Gagné, Phil. ✍	45.00
□ Martin Havlat, Otta. ✍	30.00
□ Milan Hejduk, Colo. ✍	45.00
□ Vincent Lecavalier, Tamp. ✍	55.00
□ Evgeni Nabokov (G), SanJ. ✍	30.00
□ Gary Roberts, Toro. ✍	25.00
□ Mike York, NYRa. ✍	25.00

COMMEMORATIVE SERIES

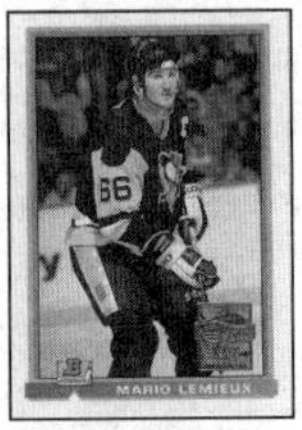

Insert Set (10 cards):	**45.00**
Insert (1:12)	**CS**
□ 1 Mario Lemieux [1989-90 OPC #319]	6.00
□ 2 Mario Lemieux [1989-90 OPC #327]	6.00
□ 3 Mario Lemieux [90-91 Bowman #204]	6.00
□ 4 Mario Lemieux [91-92 Topps #523]	6.00
□ 5 Mario Lemieux [92-93 Bowman #189]	6.00
□ 6 Mario Lemieux [92-93 OPC #240]	6.00
□ 7 Mario Lemieux [92-93 Topps #265]	6.00
□ 8 Mario Lemieux [92-93 Topps #504]	6.00
□ 9 Mario Lemieux [93-94 Premier #91]	6.00
□ 10 Mario Lemieux [91-92 Bowman #87]	6.00

AUTHENTIC GAME-WORN JERSEY

Insert Set (10 cards):	**255.00**
Insert (1:123)	**JR**
□ Jason Arnott, Njer. ✂	25.00
□ Ed Belfour (G), Dall. ✂	40.00
□ Brian Boucher (G), Phil. ✂	25.00
□ Chris Drury, Colo. ✂	25.00
□ Ron Francis, Caro. ✂	25.00
□ Simon Gagné, Phil. ✂	35.00
□ Brett Hull, Dall. ✂	40.00
□ Paul Kariya, Anah. ✂	60.00
□ Vincent Lecavalier, Tamp. ✂	40.00
□ Mike York, NYRa. ✂ White	25.00

AUTHENTIC GAME-WORN JERSEY AUTOGRAPH

Insert Set (6 cards):	**700.00**
Oversize	**JRA**
□ Jason Arnott, Njer. ✍ ✂	120.00
□ Chris Drury, Colo. ✍ ✂	150.00
□ Ron Francis, Caro. ✍ ✂	150.00
□ Simon Gagné, Phil. ✍ ✂	200.00
□ Vincent Lecavalier, Tamp. ✍ ✂	250.00
□ Mike York, NYRa. ✍ ✂	80.00

MARIO RETURNS AUTOGRAPH

Insert Set (5 cards):	**1,100**
Insert (#/66)	**MRA**
□ MR1 Mario Lemieux, Pitt. ✍	300.00
□ MR2 Mario Lemieux, Pitt. ✍	300.00
□ MR3 Mario Lemieux, Pitt. ✍	300.00
□ MR4 Mario Lemieux, Pitt. ✍	300.00
□ MR5 Mario Lemieux, All-Star ✍	300.00

OWN THE GAME

Insert Set (30 cards):	**55.00**
Insert (1:6)	**OTG**
□ OTG1 Jaromir Jagr, Pitt. [Points]	3.00
□ OTG2 Joe Sakic, Colo. [Points]	5.00
□ OTG3 Patrik Elias, NJer. [Points]	2.00
□ OTG4 Jason Allison, Bost. [Points]	2.00
□ OTG5 Alex Kovalev, Pitt. [Points]	2.00
□ OTG6 Martin Straka, Pitt. [Points]	1.50
□ OTG7 Pavel Bure, Flor. [Points]	2.00
□ OTG8 Doug Weight, Edmo. [Points]	2.00
□ OTG9 Peter Forsberg, Colo. [Points]	4.00
□ OTG10 Zigmund Palffy, LosA. [Points]	2.00
□ OTG11 Brad Richards, Tamp. [Rookie Points]	1.50
□ OTG12 Shane Willis, Caro. [Rookie Points]	1.50
□ OTG13 Martin Havlat, Otta. [Rookie Points]	2.00
□ OTG14 Lubomir Visnovsky, LosA. [Rookie Points]	1.50
□ OTG15 Marian Gaborik, MinW. [Rookie Points]	3.00
□ OTG16 Ruslan Fedotenko, Phil. [Rookie Points]	1.50
□ OTG17 Steven Reinprecht, LosA. [Rookie Points]	1.50
□ OTG18 Daniel Sedin, Vanc. [Rookie Points]	1.50
□ OTG19 Karel Rachunek, Otta. [Rookie Points]	1.50
□ OTG20 David Vyborny, Colu. [Rookie Points]	1.50
□ OTG21 Martin Brodeur, NJer. [Wins]	5.00
□ OTG22 Patrick Roy, Colo. [Wins]	10.00
□ OTG23 Dominik Hasek, Buff. [Wins]	3.00
□ OTG24 Olaf Kölzig, Wash. [Wins]	2.00
□ OTG25 Arturs Irbe (G), Caro. [Wins]	1.50
□ OTG26 Patrick Lalime, Otta. [Wins]	2.00
□ OTG27 Tommy Salo, Edmo. [Wins]	1.50
□ OTG28 Roman Cechmanek, Phil. [Wins]	1.50
□ OTG29 Ed Belfour (G), Dall. [Wins]	3.00
□ OTG30 Curtis Joseph (G), Toro. [Wins]	3.00

SHOT MASTERS

Insert Set (18 cards):	**80.00**
Insert (1:13)	**SM**
□ SM1 Mario Lemieux, Pitt.	18.00
□ SM2 Pavel Bure, Flor.	5.00
□ SM3 Brett Hull, Dall.	6.00
□ SM4 Joe Sakic, Colo.	10.00
□ SM5 Jaromir Jagr, Pitt.	6.00
□ SM6 Steve Yzerman, Detr.	15.00
□ SM7 Milan Hejduk, Colo.	5.00
□ SM8 Tony Amonte, Chic.	3.00
□ SM9 Zigmund Palffy, LosA.	3.00
□ SM10 Paul Kariya, Anah.	8.00
□ SM11 Bill Guerin, Bost.	3.00
□ SM12 Peter Bondra, Wash.	3.00
□ SM13 Patrik Elias, NJer.	5.00
□ SM14 Alex Kovalev, Pitt.	3.00
□ SM15 John LeClair, Phil.	5.00
□ SM16 Alexei Yashin, Otta.	3.00
□ SM17 Teemu Selänne, SanJ.	5.00
□ SM18 Alexander Mogilny, NJer.	3.00

STANLEY CUP HEROES

Insert Set (4 cards):	**30.00**
Insert (1:66)	**SCH**
□ Gerry Cheevers (G), Bost.	10.00
□ Yvan Cournoyer, Mont.	10.00
□ Phil Esposito, Bost.	14.00
□ Denis Potvin, NYIs.	10.00

STANLEY CUP HEROES AUTOGRAPH

Insert Set (4 cards):	**165.00**
Insert (1:1584)	**SCHA**
□ Gerry Cheevers (G), Bost. ✍	50.00
□ Yvan Cournoyer, Mont. ✍	50.00
□ Phil Esposito, Bost. ✍	75.00
□ Denis Potvin, NYIs. ✍	50.00

STARS OF THE GAME

Insert Set (10 cards):	**25.00**
Insert (1:12)	**SotG**
□ SG1 Mario Lemieux, Pitt.	10.00
□ SG2 Sean Burke, Phoe.	2.00
□ SG3 Pavel Bure, Flor.	3.00
□ SG4 Joe Sakic, Colo.	6.00
□ SG5 Patrik Elias, NJer.	3.00
□ SG6 Mike Modano, Dall.	3.00
□ SG7 Curtis Joseph (G), Toro.	3.00
□ SG8 Alex Kovalev, Pitt.	2.00
□ SG9 Sergei Fedorov, Detr.	3.00
□ SG10 Tommy Salo, Edmo.	1.50

REPRINT

Insert Set (4 cards):	**15.00**
Insert (1:22)	**Reprint**
□ Gerry Cheevers (G), Bost. [65-66 Topps]	6.00
□ Yvan Cournoyer, Mont. [65-66 Topps]	6.00
□ Phil Esposito, Chic. [65-66 Topps]	6.00
□ Denis Potvin, NYIs. [74-75 Topps]	6.00

REPRINT AUTOGRAPH

Insert Set (4 cards):	165.00
Insert (1:1584)	Reprint
☐ Gerry Cheevers (G), Bost. [65-66 Topps] ✍	50.00
☐ Yvan Cournoyer, Mont. [65-66 Topps] ✍	50.00
☐ Phil Esposito, Chic. [65-66 Topps] ✍	75.00
☐ Denis Potvin, NYIs. [74-75 Topps] ✍	50.00

PRE-PRODUCTION SAMPLE

There are two versions for each card: an O-Pee-Chee promo and a Topps promo.

Promo Set (6 cards):	5.00
Promo	PP
☐☐ PP1 Zigmund Palffy, LosA.	1.00
☐☐ PP2 Randy McKay, NJer.	1.00
☐☐ PP3 Gary Roberts, Toro.	1.00
☐☐ PP4 Manny Fernandez, MinW.	1.00
☐☐ PP5 Steve Sullivan, Chic.	1.00
☐☐ PP6 Adam Oates, Wash.	1.00

UPDATE

These cards are inserted in packs of 2001 - 02 Topps Chrome. There are two versions for each card: an O-Pee-Chee card and a Topps card.

Insert Set (10 cards):	10.00
Insert	Update
☐☐ 14 Alexei Yashin, NYIs.	1.00
☐☐ 24 Doug Weight, Slou.	1.00
☐☐ 32 Jaromir Jagr, Wash.	2.00
☐☐ 49 Dominik Hasek (G), Detr.	2.00
☐☐ 58 Alexander Mogilny, Toro.	1.00
☐☐ 79 Pierre Turgeon, Dall.	1.00
☐☐ 85 Chris Osgood (G), NYIs.	1.00
☐☐ 86 Brett Hull, Detr.	2.00
☐☐ 94 Jeremy Roenick, Phil.	2.00
☐☐ 105 Roman Turek (G), Calg.	1.00

2001 - 02 TOPPS ALL-STAR GAME

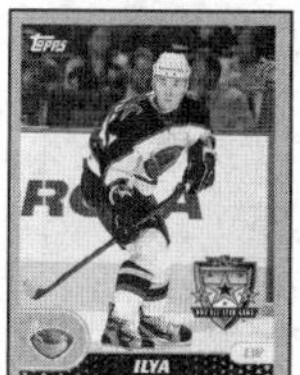

Produced by The Topps Company, this series was released at the 2002 All-Star Fantasy in February 2002.

Complete Set (6 cards):	2.00
Description	ASG
☐ 1 Paul Kariya, Anah.	1.00
☐ 2 Zigmund Palffy, LosA.	1.00
☐ 3 Joe Sakic, Colo.	1.00
☐ 4 Jaromir Jagr, Wash.	1.00
☐ 5 Dominik Hasek (G), Detr.	1.00
☐ 6 Ilya Kovalchuk, Atla.	1.00

2001 - 02 TOPPS CHROME

Produced by The Topps Company, this series was released in March 2002. Cards 1-148 have three versions: the base card, the Refractor parallel (1:6 packs) and the Black Border parallel (#/50).

Shell Set (148 cards):	-	-	100.00
Complete Set (182 cards):	2,400	500.00	325.00
Common Player:	6.00	2.00	.50
Description	BB50	Refr.	Base
☐☐☐ 1 Mario Lemieux, Pitt.	150.00	35.00	7.50
☐☐☐ 2 Steve Yzerman, Detr.	120.00	30.00	6.00
☐☐☐ 3 Martin Brodeur, NJer.	80.00	20.00	4.00
☐☐☐ 4 Brian Leetch, NYRa.	30.00	5.00	1.50
☐☐☐ 5 Tony Amonte, Chic.	30.00	5.00	1.50
☐☐☐ 6 Bill Guerin, Bost.	20.00	5.00	1.00
☐☐☐ 7 Olaf Kölzig, Wash.	30.00	5.00	1.50
☐☐☐ 8 Pavel Bure, Flor.	40.00	10.00	2.00
☐☐☐ 9 Patrick Marleau, SanJ.	20.00	5.00	1.00
☐☐☐ 10 Mariusz Czerkawski, NYIs.	10.00	2.00	.50
☐☐☐ 11 Teemu Selänne, SanJ.	40.00	10.00	2.00
☐☐☐ 12 Alex Tanguay, Colo.	30.00	5.00	1.50
☐☐☐ 13 Keith Primeau, Phil.	20.00	5.00	1.00
☐☐☐ 14 Alexei Yashin, NYIs.	30.00	5.00	1.50
☐☐☐ 15 Markus Näslund, Vanc.	50.00	10.00	2.50
☐☐☐ 16 Chris Pronger, SLou.	30.00	5.00	1.50
☐☐☐ 17 Sergei Zubov, Dall.	10.00	2.00	.50
☐☐☐ 18 Marian Gaborik, MinW.	50.00	10.00	2.50
☐☐☐ 19 Mats Sundin, Toro.	50.00	10.00	2.50
☐☐☐ 20 David Legwand, Nash.	20.00	5.00	1.00
☐☐☐ 21 Jean-Pierre Dumont, Buff.	10.00	2.00	.50
☐☐☐ 22 Nicklas Lidström, Detr.	30.00	5.00	1.50
☐☐☐ 23 Ron Francis, Caro.	30.00	5.00	1.50
☐☐☐ 24 Doug Weight, SLou.	30.00	5.00	1.50
☐☐☐ 25 Zigmund Palffy, LosA.	30.00	5.00	1.50
☐☐☐ 26 Jason Allison, LosA.	30.00	5.00	1.50
☐☐☐ 27 Joe Sakic, Colo.	80.00	20.00	4.00
☐☐☐ 28 Paul Kariya, Anah.	70.00	15.00	3.50
☐☐☐ 29 Marian Hossa, Otta.	50.00	10.00	2.50
☐☐☐ 30 Owen Nolan, SanJ.	30.00	5.00	1.50
☐☐☐ 31 Jason Arnott, NJer.	20.00	5.00	1.00
☐☐☐ 32 Jaromir Jagr, Wash.	50.00	10.00	2.50
☐☐☐ 33 Claude Lemieux, Phoe.	15.00	2.00	.50
☐☐☐ 34 Peter Bondra, Wash.	30.00	5.00	1.50
☐☐☐ 35 Chris Drury, Colo.	30.00	5.00	1.50
☐☐☐ 36 Radek Bonk, Otta.	15.00	2.00	.50
☐☐☐ 37 Theoren Fleury, NYRa.	30.00	5.00	1.50
☐☐☐ 38 Keith Tkachuk, SLou.	30.00	5.00	1.50
☐☐☐ 39 Rick DiPietro, NYIs.	20.00	5.00	1.00
☐☐☐ 40 Ed Jovanovski, Vanc.	20.00	5.00	1.00
☐☐☐ 41 Scott Stevens, NJer.	20.00	5.00	1.00
☐☐☐ 42 John LeClair, Phil.	40.00	10.00	2.00
☐☐☐ 43 Ryan Smyth, Edmo.	20.00	5.00	1.00
☐☐☐ 44 Vincent Lecavalier, Tamp.	50.00	10.00	2.50
☐☐☐ 45 Henrik Sedin, Vanc.	20.00	5.00	1.00
☐☐☐ 46 David Aebischer (G), Colo.	15.00	2.00	.50
☐☐☐ 47 Patrick Roy, Colo.	150.00	35.00	7.50
☐☐☐ 48 Valeri Bure, Flor.	15.00	2.00	.50
☐☐☐ 49 Dominik Hasek, Detr.	50.00	10.00	2.50
☐☐☐ 50 Ray Ferraro, Atla.	6.00	2.00	.50
☐☐☐ 51 Milan Hejduk, Colo.	40.00	10.00	2.00
☐☐☐ 52 Mike Modano, Dall.	50.00	10.00	2.50
☐☐☐ 53 Sergei Fedorov, Detr.	50.00	10.00	2.50
☐☐☐ 54 Luc Robitaille, Detr.	40.00	10.00	2.00
☐☐☐ 55 Mark Messier, NYRa.	50.00	10.00	2.50
☐☐☐ 56 Sean Burke, Phoe.	30.00	5.00	1.50
☐☐☐ 57 Jeff Friesen, Anah.	15.00	2.00	.50
☐☐☐ 58 Alexander Mogilny, Toro.	20.00	5.00	1.00
☐☐☐ 59 Roman Cechmanek, Phil.	20.00	5.00	1.00
☐☐☐ 60 Martin Straka, Pitt.	15.00	2.00	.50
☐☐☐ 61 Pavol Demitra, SLou.	20.00	5.00	1.00
☐☐☐ 62 Curtis Joseph (G), Toro.	50.00	10.00	2.50
☐☐☐ 63 Daniel Sedin, Vanc.	20.00	5.00	1.00
☐☐☐ 64 Brad Richards, Tamp.	20.00	5.00	1.00
☐☐☐ 65 Simon Gagné, Phil.	40.00	10.00	2.00
☐☐☐ 66 Saku Koivu, Mont.	40.00	10.00	2.00
☐☐☐ 67 Éric Dazé, Chic.	20.00	5.00	1.00
☐☐☐ 68 Roberto Luongo, Flor.	40.00	10.00	2.00
☐☐☐ 69 Brendan Shanahan, Detr.	50.00	10.00	2.50
☐☐☐ 70 Espen Knutsen, Colu.	10.00	2.00	.50
☐☐☐ 71 Rob Blake, Colo.	30.00	5.00	1.50
☐☐☐ 72 Steve Sullivan, Chic.	15.00	2.00	.50
☐☐☐ 73 Arturs Irbe (G), Caro.	20.00	5.00	1.00
☐☐☐ 74 Maxim Afinogenov, Buff.	20.00	5.00	1.00
☐☐☐ 75 Dan Cloutier, Vanc.	20.00	5.00	1.00
☐☐☐ 76 Josef Vasicek, Caro.	10.00	2.00	.50
☐☐☐ 77 V. Damphousse, SanJ.	30.00	5.00	1.50
☐☐☐ 78 Robert Lang, Pitt.	10.00	2.00	.50
☐☐☐ 79 Pierre Turgeon, Dall.	20.00	5.00	1.00
☐☐☐ 80 Gary Roberts, Toro.	20.00	5.00	1.00
☐☐☐ 81 Adam Oates, Wash.	20.00	5.00	1.00
☐☐☐ 82 Evgeni Nabokov, SanJ.	30.00	5.00	1.50
☐☐☐ 83 Petr Nedved, NYRa.	15.00	2.00	.50
☐☐☐ 84 Mike Dunham, Nash.	20.00	5.00	1.00
☐☐☐ 85 Chris Osgood, NYIs.	30.00	5.00	1.50
☐☐☐ 86 Brett Hull, Detr.	50.00	10.00	2.50
☐☐☐ 87 Peter Forsberg, Colo.	70.00	15.00	3.50
☐☐☐ 88 Joe Thornton, Bost.	60.00	15.00	3.00
☐☐☐ 89 Marc Denis, Colu.	20.00	5.00	1.00
☐☐☐ 90 Ed Belfour (G), Dall.	50.00	10.00	2.50
☐☐☐ 91 Patrik Elias, NJer.	40.00	10.00	2.00
☐☐☐ 92 Mike York, NYRa.	15.00	2.00	.50
☐☐☐ 93 Martin Havlat, Otta.	30.00	5.00	1.50
☐☐☐ 94 Jeremy Roenick, Phil.	40.00	10.00	2.00
☐☐☐ 95 Alex Kovalev, Pitt.	30.00	5.00	1.50
☐☐☐ 96 Al MacInnis, SLou.	20.00	5.00	1.00
☐☐☐ 97 Marco Sturm, SanJ.	10.00	2.00	.50
☐☐☐ 98 José Théodore, Mont.	60.00	15.00	3.00
☐☐☐ 99 Joe Nieuwendyk, Dall.	20.00	5.00	1.00
☐☐☐ 100 Darren McCarty, Detr.	15.00	2.00	.50
☐☐☐ 101 Mark Recchi, Phil.	20.00	5.00	1.00
☐☐☐ 102 Daniel Alfredsson, Otta.	30.00	5.00	1.50
☐☐☐ 103 Miroslav Satan, Buff.	15.00	2.00	.50
☐☐☐ 104 Sergei Samsonov, Bost.	30.00	5.00	1.50
☐☐☐ 105 Roman Turek, Calg.	20.00	5.00	1.00
☐☐☐ 106 Jarome Iginla, Calg.	40.00	10.00	2.00
☐☐☐ 107 Jeff O'Neill, Caro.	20.00	5.00	1.00
☐☐☐ 108 Tommy Salo, Edmo.	20.00	5.00	1.00
☐☐☐ 109 Petr* Sykora, NJer.	20.00	5.00	1.00
☐☐☐ 110 Adam Deadmarsh, LosA.	15.00	2.00	.50
☐☐☐ 111 Oleg Tverdovsky, Anah.	6.00	2.00	.50
☐☐☐ 112 Sami Kapanen, Caro.	15.00	2.00	.50
☐☐☐ 113 Scott Hartnell, Nash.	10.00	2.00	.50
☐☐☐ 114 Jere Lehtinen, Dall.	15.00	2.00	.50
☐☐☐ 115 Darcy Tucker, Toro.	10.00	2.00	.50
☐☐☐ 116 Stu Barnes, Buff.	6.00	2.00	.50
☐☐☐ 117 Jim Dowd, MinW.	6.00	2.00	.50
☐☐☐ 118 Derek Morris, Calg.	10.00	2.00	.50
☐☐☐ 119 Félix Potvin, LosA.	30.00	5.00	1.50
☐☐☐ 120 Manny Fernandez, MinW.	20.00	5.00	1.00
☐☐☐ 121 Jason Smith, Edmo.	6.00	2.00	.50
☐☐☐ 122 Byron Dafoe, Bost.	20.00	5.00	1.00
☐☐☐ 123 Teppo Numminen, Phoe.	15.00	2.00	.50
☐☐☐ 124 Mike Richter, NYRa.	20.00	5.00	1.00
☐☐☐ 125 Anson Carter, Edmo.	20.00	5.00	1.00
☐☐☐ 126 Jocelyn Thibault, Chic.	20.00	5.00	1.00
☐☐☐ 127 Dany Heatley, Atla.	50.00	10.00	5.00
☐☐☐ 128 Marc Savard, Calg.	10.00	2.00	.50
☐☐☐ 129 Brian Rolston, Bost.	15.00	2.00	.50
☐☐☐ 130 Martin Biron (G), Buff.	20.00	5.00	1.00
☐☐☐ 131 Mark Parrish, NYIs.	20.00	5.00	1.00
☐☐☐ 132 Michael Peca, NYIs.	20.00	5.00	1.00
☐☐☐ 133 Patrick Lalime, Otta.	30.00	5.00	1.50
☐☐☐ 134 Eric Lindros, NYRa.	50.00	10.00	2.50
☐☐☐ 135 Brian Boucher (G), Phil.	15.00	2.00	.50
☐☐☐ 136 Nikolai Khabibulin, Tamp.	20.00	5.00	1.00
☐☐☐ 137 John Madden, NJer.	15.00	2.00	.50
☐☐☐ 138 Rostislav Klesla, Colu.	15.00	2.00	.50
☐☐☐ 139 Mika Noronen, Buff.	20.00	5.00	1.00
☐☐☐ 140 Kris Beech, Pitt.	15.00	2.00	.50
☐☐☐ 141 Miikka Kiprusoff, SanJ.	15.00	2.00	.50
☐☐☐ 142 Mathieu Garon, Mont.	20.00	5.00	1.00
☐☐☐ 143 Mark Bell, Chic.	10.00	2.00	.50
☐☐☐ 144 Jussi Markkanen, Edmo.	6.00	2.00	.50
☐☐☐ 145 Mike Comrie, Edmo.	40.00	10.00	2.00
☐☐☐ 146 Johan Hedberg (G), Pitt.	20.00	5.00	1.00
☐☐☐ 147 Andrew Raycroft, Bost.	10.00	2.00	.50
☐☐☐ 148 Daniel Corso, SLou.	6.00	2.00	.50

ROOKIES

Cards 149-182 have three versions: the base card (1:3 packs), the Refractor parallel (1:6 packs) and the Black Border parallel (#/50).

Insert	BB50	Refr.	Base
☐☐☐ **149 I. Kovalchuk, Atla. RC**	**100.00**	**50.00**	**25.00**
☐☐☐ **150 Blackburn (G), NYRa. RC**	**25.00**	**20.00**	**10.00**
☐☐☐ **151 V. Nedorost, Colo. RC**	**15.00**	**10.00**	**6.00**
☐☐☐ **152 K. Kolanos, Phoe. RC**	**15.00**	**10.00**	**6.00**
☐☐☐ **153 K. Huselius, Flor. RC**	**25.00**	**15.00**	**6.00**
☐☐☐ **154 M. Erat, Nash. RC**	**15.00**	**10.00**	**6.00**
☐☐☐ **155 T. Pärssinen, Anah. RC**	**15.00**	**10.00**	**6.00**
☐☐☐ **156 S. Nichol, Calg. RC**	**15.00**	**10.00**	**6.00**
☐☐☐ **157 N. Schultz, MinW. RC**	**15.00**	**10.00**	**6.00**
☐☐☐ **158 J. Hentunen, Calg. RC**	**15.00**	**10.00**	**6.00**
☐☐☐ **159 P. Dupuis, MinW. RC**	**15.00**	**10.00**	**6.00**
☐☐☐ **160 R. Martinek, NYIs. RC**	**15.00**	**10.00**	**6.00**
☐☐☐ **161 Clemmensen, NJer. RC**	**15.00**	**10.00**	**6.00**
☐☐☐ **162 J. Jillson, SanJ. RC**	**15.00**	**10.00**	**6.00**
☐☐☐ **163 B. Sutherby, Wash. RC**	**15.00**	**10.00**	**6.00**
☐☐☐ **164 N. Alexeev, Tamp. RC**	**15.00**	**10.00**	**6.00**
☐☐☐ **165 N. Hagman, Flor. RC**	**15.00**	**10.00**	**6.00**
☐☐☐ **166 E. Cole, Caro. RC**	**15.00**	**10.00**	**6.00**
☐☐☐ **167 P. Datsyuk, Detr. RC**	**75.00**	**40.00**	**20.00**
☐☐☐ **168 I. Bryzgalov, Anah. RC**	**15.00**	**10.00**	**6.00**
☐☐☐ **169 C. Neil, Otta. RC**	**15.00**	**10.00**	**6.00**
☐☐☐ **170 M. Rycroft, SLou. RC**	**15.00**	**10.00**	**6.00**
☐☐☐ **171 K. Piros, Atla. RC**	**15.00**	**10.00**	**6.00**
☐☐☐ **172 N. Kapanen, Dall. RC**	**15.00**	**10.00**	**6.00**
☐☐☐ **173 J. Dopita, Phil. RC**	**15.00**	**10.00**	**6.00**
☐☐☐ **174 Salomonsson, NJer. RC**	**15.00**	**10.00**	**6.00**
☐☐☐ **175 I. Ciernik, Otta. RC**	**15.00**	**10.00**	**6.00**
☐☐☐ **176 J. Bednar, LosA. RC**	**15.00**	**10.00**	**6.00**
☐☐☐ **177 T. Conklin, Edmo. RC**	**15.00**	**10.00**	**6.00**
☐☐☐ **178 R. Scott, NYRa. RC**	**15.00**	**10.00**	**6.00**
☐☐☐ **179 R. Torres, NYIs. RC**	**15.00**	**10.00**	**6.00**
☐☐☐ **180 V. Pletka, Phil. RC**	**15.00**	**10.00**	**6.00**
☐☐☐ **181 Samuelsson, NYRa. RC**	**15.00**	**10.00**	**6.00**
☐☐☐ **182 M. Farrell, Wash. RC**	**15.00**	**10.00**	**6.00**

CHROME ARCHIVES

There are two versions of each card: the chrome insert and the Refractor parallel.

Insert Set (10 cards):	95.00	45.00
Inserts	CAR	CA
☐☐ CA1 Bi. Smith (G) [73-74 Topps]	16.00	8.00
☐☐ CA2 W. Cashman [70-71 Topps]	12.00	6.00
☐☐ CA3 B. Melrose [79-80 Topps]	12.00	6.00
☐☐ CA4 B. Federko [78-79 Topps]	12.00	6.00
☐☐ CA5 N. Broten [82-83 OPC]	12.00	6.00
☐☐ CA6 B. Clement [73-74 Topps]	12.00	6.00
☐☐ CA7 G. Lapointe [70-71 Topps]	12.00	6.00
☐☐ CA8 B. Parent [73-74 Topps]	16.00	8.00
☐☐ CA9 L. Robinson [73-74 Topps]	12.00	6.00
☐☐ CA10 K. Hodge [65-66 Topps]	12.00	6.00

CHROME ARCHIVES AUTOGRAPH

Insert Set (10 cards):	255.00
Inserts	ACA
☐ CA1 Bi. Smith (G) [73-74 Topps] ✍	45.00
☐ CA10 K. Hodge [65-66 Topps] ✍	30.00

☐ CA2 W. Cashman [70-71 Topps] ✍	30.00
☐ CA3 B. Melrose [79-80 Topps] ✍	30.00
☐ CA4 B. Federko [78-79 Topps] ✍	30.00
☐ CA5 N. Broten [82-83 OPC] ✍	30.00
☐ CA6 B. Clement [73-74 Topps] ✍	30.00
☐ CA7 G. Lapointe [70-71 Topps] ✍	30.00
☐ CA8 B. Parent [73-74 Topps] ✍	45.00
☐ CA9 L. Robinson [73-74 Topps] ✍	45.00

COMMEMORATIVE SERIES

There are two versions of each card: the chrome insert and the Refractor parallel.

Insert Set (10 cards):	150.00	75.00
Inserts	CSR	CS
☐☐ 1 Mario Lemieux, Pitt.	20.00	10.00
☐☐ 2 Mario Lemieux, Pitt.	20.00	10.00
☐☐ 3 Mario Lemieux, Pitt.	20.00	10.00
☐☐ 4 Mario Lemieux, Pitt.	20.00	10.00
☐☐ 5 Mario Lemieux, Pitt.	20.00	10.00
☐☐ 6 Mario Lemieux, Pitt.	20.00	10.00
☐☐ 7 Mario Lemieux, Pitt.	20.00	10.00
☐☐ 8 Mario Lemieux, Pitt.	20.00	10.00
☐☐ 9 Mario Lemieux, Pitt.	20.00	10.00
☐☐ 10 Mario Lemieux, Pitt.	20.00	10.00

MARIO RETURNS

There are two versions of each card: the chrome insert and the Refractor parallel.

Insert Set (5 cards):	80.00	35.00
Inserts	MRR	MR
☐☐ MR-1 Mario Lemieux, Pitt.	22.00	10.00
☐☐ MR-2 Mario Lemieux, Pitt.	22.00	10.00
☐☐ MR-3 Mario Lemieux, Pitt.	22.00	10.00
☐☐ MR-4 Mario Lemieux, Pitt.	22.00	10.00
☐☐ MR-5 Mario Lemieux, Pitt.	22.00	10.00

2001 - 02 TOPPS HERITAGE

Produced by The Topps Company, this series was released in January 2002. There are two versions for cards 1-110: the base card and a Retro Fractor parallel (#/558).

Shell Set (137 cards):	-	45.00
Complete Set (187 cards):	-	150.00
Retro Fractor Set (110 cards):	375.00	-
Common Player:	1.00	.25
Description	RF558	Base
☐☐ 1 Mario Lemieux, Pitt.	30.00	4.50
☐☐ 2 Evgeni Nabokov, SanJ.	6.00	.50
☐☐ 3 Nicklas Lidström, Detr.	6.00	.50
☐☐ 4 Patrik Elias, NJer.	8.00	1.00
☐☐ 5 Olaf Kölzig, Wash.	6.00	.50
☐☐ 6 Mats Sundin, Toro.	10.00	1.50
☐☐ 7 Jason Allison, Bost.	6.00	.50
☐☐ 8 Mike Modano, Dall.	10.00	1.50
☐☐ 9 Keith Tkachuk, SLou.	6.00	.50
☐☐ 10 John LeClair, Phil.	8.00	1.00
☐☐ 11 Pavel Bure, Flor.	8.00	1.00
☐☐ 12 Tony Amonte, Chic.	6.00	.50
☐☐ 13 Zigmund Palffy, LosA.	6.00	.50
☐☐ 14 Mark Messier, NYRa.	10.00	1.50
☐☐ 15 Sean Burke, Phoe.	6.00	.50
☐☐ 16 Markus Näslund, Vanc.	10.00	1.50
☐☐ 17 Milan Hejduk, Colo.	8.00	1.00
☐☐ 18 Teemu Selänne, SanJ.	8.00	1.00
☐☐ 19 Espen Knutsen, Colu.	2.00	.25
☐☐ 20 David Legwand, Nash.	4.00	.50
☐☐ 21 Saku Koivu, Mont.	8.00	1.00
☐☐ 22 Ron Francis, Caro.	6.00	.50
☐☐ 23 Ray Ferraro, Atla.	1.00	.25

☐ ☐	24 Brendan Shanahan, Detr.	10.00	1.50
☐ ☐	25 Rick DiPietro, NYIs.	4.00	.50
☐ ☐	26 Brad Richards, Tamp.	4.00	.50
☐ ☐	27 Henrik Sedin, Vanc.	4.00	.50
☐ ☐	28 Marian Hossa, Otta.	10.00	1.50
☐ ☐	29 Marian Gaborik, MinW.	10.00	1.50
☐ ☐	30 Ed Belfour (G), Dall.	10.00	1.50
☐ ☐	31 Miroslav Satan, Buff.	3.00	.25
☐ ☐	32 Roberto Luongo, Flor.	8.00	1.00
☐ ☐	33 Brian Leetch, NYRa.	6.00	.50
☐ ☐	34 Chris Pronger, SLou.	6.00	.50
☐ ☐	35 Peter Bondra, Wash.	6.00	.50
☐ ☐	36 Keith Primeau, Phil.	4.00	.50
☐ ☐	37 Johan Hedberg (G), Pitt.	4.00	.50
☐ ☐	38 Steve Yzerman, Detr.	24.00	3.50
☐ ☐	39 Peter Forsberg, Colo.	14.00	2.00
☐ ☐	40 Jarome Iginla, Calg.	8.00	1.00
☐ ☐	41 José Théodore, Mont.	12.00	1.50
☐ ☐	42 Curtis Joseph (G), Toro.	10.00	1.50
☐ ☐	43 Martin Havlat, Otta.	6.00	.50
☐ ☐	44 Sergei Fedorov, Detr.	10.00	1.50
☐ ☐	45 Arturs Irbe (G), Caro.	4.00	.50
☐ ☐	46 Martin Brodeur, NJer.	16.00	2.00
☐ ☐	47 Owen Nolan, SanJ.	6.00	.50
☐ ☐	48 Daniel Sedin, Vanc.	4.00	.50
☐ ☐	49 Mark Recchi, Phil.	4.00	.50
☐ ☐	50 Adam Deadmarsh, LosA.	3.00	.25
☐ ☐	51 Tommy Salo, Edmo.	4.00	.50
☐ ☐	52 Alex Kovalev, Pitt.	6.00	.50
☐ ☐	53 Steve Sullivan, Chic.	3.00	.25
☐ ☐	54 Paul Kariya, Anah.	14.00	2.00
☐ ☐	55 Vincent Lecavalier, Tamp.	10.00	1.50
☐ ☐	56 Alex Tanguay, Colo.	6.00	.50
☐ ☐	57 Joe Thornton, Bost.	12.00	1.50
☐ ☐	58 Brent Johnson, SLou.	4.00	.50
☐ ☐	59 Roman Cechmanek, Phil.	4.00	.50
☐ ☐	60 Petr Sykora, NJer.	4.00	.50
☐ ☐	61 Jean-Pierre Dumont, Buff.	2.00	.25
☐ ☐	62 Mike Comrie, Edmo.	8.00	1.00
☐ ☐	63 Daniel Alfredsson, Otta.	6.00	.50
☐ ☐	64 Éric Dazé, Chic.	4.00	.50
☐ ☐	65 Félix Potvin, LosA.	6.00	.50
☐ ☐	66 Chris Drury, Colo.	6.00	.50
☐ ☐	67 Manny Fernandez, MinW.	4.00	.50
☐ ☐	68 Claude Lemieux, Phoe.	3.00	.25
☐ ☐	69 Rob Blake, Colo.	6.00	.50
☐ ☐	70 Bill Guerin, Bost.	4.00	.50
☐ ☐	71 Mike Dunham, Nash.	4.00	.50
☐ ☐	72 Simon Gagné, Phil.	8.00	1.00
☐ ☐	73 Jeff Friesen, Anah.	3.00	.25
☐ ☐	74 Joe Sakic, Colo.	16.00	2.00
☐ ☐	75 Jason Arnott, NJer.	4.00	.50
☐ ☐	76 Patrick Roy, Colo.	30.00	4.50
☐ ☐	77 Josef Vasicek, Caro.	2.00	.25
☐ ☐	78 Marty Turco, Dall.	6.00	.50
☐ ☐	79 Al MacInnis, SLou.	4.00	.50
☐ ☐	80 Anson Carter, Edmo.	4.00	.50
☐ ☐	81 Tomi Kallio, Atla.	1.00	.25
☐ ☐	82 Éric Bélanger, LosA.	1.00	.25
☐ ☐	83 Patrick Lalime, Otta.	6.00	.50
☐ ☐	84 Scott A. Young, SLou.	3.00	.25
☐ ☐	85 Scott Gomez, NJer.	4.00	.50
☐ ☐	86 Marc Denis, Colu.	4.00	.50
☐ ☐	87 Jeff O'Neill, Caro.	4.00	.50
☐ ☐	88 Sergei Samsonov, Bost.	6.00	.50
☐ ☐	89 Robert Lang, Pitt.	2.00	.25
☐ ☐	90 Byron Dafoe, Bost.	4.00	.50
☐ ☐	91 Scott Stevens, NJer.	4.00	.50
☐ ☐	92 Adam Oates, Wash.	4.00	.50
☐ ☐	93 Patrick Marleau, SanJ.	4.00	.50
☐ ☐	94 Petr Nedved, NYRa.	3.00	.25
☐ ☐	95 Ryan Smyth, Edmo.	4.00	.50
☐ ☐	96 Adam Foote, Colo.	3.00	.25
☐ ☐	97 Marc Savard, Calg.	2.00	.25
☐ ☐	98 Brad Isbister, NYIs.	2.00	.25
☐ ☐	99 Martin Straka, Pitt.	3.00	.25
☐ ☐	100 Joe Nieuwendyk, Dall.	4.00	.50
☐ ☐	101 Shane Willis, Caro.	2.00	.25
☐ ☐	102 Pavol Demitra, SLou.	4.00	.50
☐ ☐	103 Jeff Halpern, Wash.	2.00	.25
☐ ☐	104 Sergei Zubov, Dall.	2.00	.25
☐ ☐	105 David Vyborny, Colu.	1.00	.25
☐ ☐	106 Gary Roberts, Edmo.	4.00	.50
☐ ☐	107 Martin Biron (G), Buff.	4.00	.50
☐ ☐	108 Lubomir Visnovsky, LosA.	1.00	.25
☐ ☐	109 Fredrik Modin, Tamp.	2.00	.25
☐ ☐	110 Brenden Morrow, Dall.	3.00	.25
☐	112 Nicklas Lidström, Detr.		.25
☐	113 Jaromir Jagr, Pitt.		.50
☐	114 Patrik Elias, NJer.		.50
☐	115 Joe Sakic, Colo.		1.00
☐	116 Dominik Hasek, Buff.		.50
☐	117 Rob Blake, Colo.		.25
☐	118 Scott Stevens, NJer.		.25
☐	119 Roman Cechmanek, Phil.		.25
☐	120 Mario Lemieux, Pitt.		2.00
☐	121 Pavel Bure, Flor.		.50
☐	122 Luc Robitaille, LosA.		.50
☐	123 J. Jagr / J. Sakic		.50
☐	124 P. Bure / J. Sakic		.50
☐	125 P. Elias / J. Sakic		.50
☐	126 B. Leetch / N. Lidström		.20
☐	127 A. Irbe (G) / T. Salo (G)		.20
☐	128 M. Brodeur (G) / P. Roy (G)		1.50
☐	129 R. Cechmanek (G) / M. Turco (G)		.20
☐	130 Joe Sakic, Colo.		1.00
☐	131 Patrick Roy, Colo.		2.00
☐	132 Pavel Bure, Flor.		.50
☐	133 Evgeni Nabokov, SanJ.		.20
☐	134 Nicklas Lidström, Detr.		.20
☐	135 Dominik Hasek, Buff.		.50
☐	136 John Madden, NJer.		.20
☐	137 Jaromir Jagr, Pitt.		.50

HIGH NUMBERS

	Rookie	Base
☐	**138 Ilya Kovalchuk, Atla. RC**	**18.00**
☐	**139 Niko Kapanen, Dall. RC**	**4.00**
☐	**140 Brian Sutherby, Wash. RC**	**3.00**
☐	**141 Jeff Jillson, SanJ. RC**	**3.00**
☐	**142 Jiri Dopita, Phil. RC**	**3.00**
☐	**143 Andreas Salomonsson, NJer. RC**	**2.00**
☐	**144 Timo Pärssinen, Anah. RC**	**2.00**
☐	**145 Vaclav Nedorost, Colo. RC**	**4.00**
☐	**146 Kristian Huselius, Flor. RC**	**6.00**
☐	**147 Dan Blackburn (G), NYRa. RC**	**7.00**
☐	**148 Nikita Alexeev, Tamp. RC**	**4.00**
☐	**149 Peter Smrek, NYRa. RC**	**2.00**
☐	**150 Krys Kolanos, Phoe. RC**	**4.00**
☐	**151 Pavel Datsyuk, Detr. RC**	**15.00**
☐	**152 Jaroslav Bednar, LosA. RC**	**3.00**
☐	**153 Chris Neil, Otta. RC**	**2.00**
☐	**154 Erik Cole, Caro. RC**	**4.00**
☐	**155 Niklas Hagman, Flor. RC**	**3.00**
☐	**156 Jason Chimera, Edmo. RC**	**3.00**
☐	**157 Scott Clemmensen, NJer. RC**	**3.00**
☐	158 Andrew Brunette, MinW.	2.00
☐	159 Dominik Hasek, Detr.	3.00
☐	160 Jaromir Jagr, Wash.	3.00
☐	161 Doug Weight, SLou.	2.00
☐	162 Brett Hull, Detr.	3.00
☐	163 Pierre Turgeon, Dall.	2.00
☐	164 Jeremy Roenick, Phil.	2.00
☐	165 Alexander Mogilny, Toro.	2.00
☐	166 Luc Robitaille, Detr.	2.00
☐	167 Michael Peca, NYIs.	2.00
☐	168 Roman Turek, Calg.	2.00
☐	169 Martin Lapointe, Bost.	2.00
☐	170 Alexei Yashin, NYIs.	2.00
☐	171 Adam Graves, SanJ.	2.00
☐	172 Valeri Bure, Flor.	2.00
☐	173 Tim Connolly, Buff.	2.00
☐	174 Kris Beech, Pitt.	2.00
☐	175 Donald Audette, Dall.	2.00
☐	176 Jochen Hecht, Edmo.	2.00
☐	177 Fred Brathwaite (G), SLou.	2.00
☐	178 Rob Niedermayer, Calg.	2.00
☐	179 Eric Lindros, NYRa.	3.00
☐	180 Bill Muckalt, Otta.	2.00
☐	181 Eric Weinrich, Phil.	2.00
☐	182 Taylor Pyatt, Buff.	2.00
☐	183 Daymond Langkow, Phoe.	2.00
☐	184 Dave Andreychuk, Tamp.	2.00
☐	185 Sergei Berezin, Phoe.	2.00
☐	186 Ken Sutton, NYIs.	2.00
☐	187 Vyacheslav Kozlov, Buff.	2.00

ARENA SEAT RELIC

Insert Set (4 cards): 65.00

	Insert	R
☐	R-JBE Jean Béliveau, Mont.	30.00
☐	R-JBU Johnny Bucyk, Bost.	20.00
☐	R-BG Bernie Geoffrion, Mont.	20.00
☐	R-HR Henri Richard, Mont.	20.00

ARENA SEAT RELIC

Insert Set (4 cards): 245.00

	Insert	AR
☐	AR-JBE Jean Béliveau, Mont. ✍	125.00
☐	AR-JBU Johnny Bucyk, Bost. ✍	65.00
☐	AR-BG Bernie Geoffrion, Mont. ✍	65.00
☐	AR-HR Henri Richard, Mont. ✍	75.00

ARENA SEAT RELIC DUO

Insert Set (3 cards): 90.00

	Insert	R
☐	J. Bucyk / B. Geoffrion	40.00
☐	J. Bucyk / H. Richard	40.00
☐	J. Bucyk / J. Béliveau	40.00

ARENA SEAT RELIC DUO AUTOGRAPH

Insert Set (3 cards): 300.00

	Insert (#/25)	AR
☐	J. Bucyk ✍ / B. Geoffrion ✍	100.00
☐	J. Bucyk ✍ / H. Richard ✍	100.00
☐	J. Bucyk ✍ / J. Béliveau ✍	200.00

GAME-WORN JERSEY

Insert Set (10 cards): 150.00

	Insert	J
☐	Martin Brodeur, NJer. ✂	40.00
☐	Sergei Fedorov, Detr. ✂	25.00
☐	Peter Forsberg, Colo. ✂	35.00
☐	Jarome Iginla, Calg. ✂ White	20.00
☐	Robert Lang, Pitt. ✂	15.00
☐	John LeClair, Phil. ✂	20.00
☐	Brian Leetch, NYRa. ✂	15.00
☐	Patrick Marleau, SanJ. ✂	15.00
☐	Martin Straka, Pitt. ✂ Black	15.00
☐	Joe Thornton, Bost. ✂ Black	30.00

GAME-WORN JERSEY CAPTAIN'S CLOTH

Insert Set (6 cards): 80.00

	Insert	CC
☐	Éric Desjardins, Phil. ✂	10.00
☐	Derian Hatcher, Dall. ✂	10.00
☐	Paul Kariya, Anah. ✂	35.00
☐	Saku Koivu, Mont. ✂	20.00
☐	Vincent Lecavalier, Tamp. ✂ White	25.00
☐	Adam Oates, Wash. ✂	10.00

CERTIFIED AUTOGRAPH ISSUE

Insert Set (16 cards): 400.00

	Insert	A
☐	Al Arbour, Detr. ✍	25.00
☐	Jean Béliveau, Mont. ✍	60.00
☐	Johnny Bucyk, Bost. ✍	25.00
☐	Marian Gaborik, MinW. ✍	45.00
☐	Bernie Geoffrion, Mont. ✍	25.00
☐	Glenn Hall, Chic. ✍	30.00
☐	Johan Hedberg (G), Pitt. ✍	25.00
☐	Harry Howell, NYRa. ✍	25.00
☐	Olaf Kölzig, Wash. ✍	25.00
☐	Ilya Kovalchuk, Atla. ✍	80.00
☐	Vincent Lecavalier, Tamp. ✍	45.00
☐	Pierre Pilote, Chic. ✍	25.00
☐	Henri Richard, Mont. ✍	35.00
☐	Miroslav Satan, Buff. ✍	25.00
☐	Norm Ullman, Detr. ✍	25.00
☐	Justin Williams, Phil. ✍	25.00

SALUTE

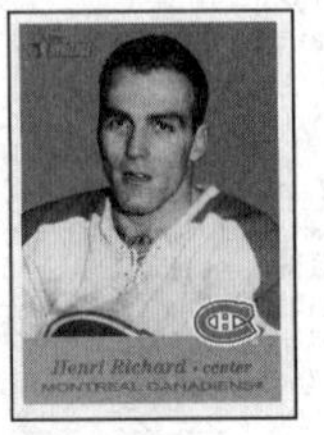

Insert Set (9 cards): 25.00

	UD1 Insert (1:144)	S
☐	S1 Johnny Bucyk, Bost.	4.00
☐	S2 Al Arbour, Detr.	4.00
☐	S3 Glenn Hall (G), Chic.	4.00
☐	S4 Harry Howell, NYRa.	4.00
☐	S5 Pierre Pilote, Chic.	4.00
☐	S6 Norm Ullman, Detr.	4.00
☐	S7 Jean Béliveau, Mont.	6.00
☐	S8 Henri Richard, Mont.	4.00
☐	S9 Bernie Geoffrion, Mont.	4.00

2001 - 02 TOPPS RESERVE

Produced by The Topps Company, this series was released in January 2002.

Shell Set (100 cards): 70.00
Complete Set (121 cards): 300.00
Common Player: .50

	Description	Base
☐	1 Joe Sakic, Colo.	3.00
☐	2 Patrik Elias, NJer.	1.50
☐	3 Mario Lemieux, Pitt.	6.00
☐	4 Chris Pronger, SLou.	1.00
☐	5 Simon Gagné, Phil.	1.50
☐	6 Steve Yzerman, Detr.	4.50
☐	7 Bill Guerin, Bost.	.50
☐	8 Pavel Bure, Flor.	1.50
☐	9 Mark Messier, NYRa.	2.00
☐	10 Evgeni Nabokov, SanJ.	1.00
☐	11 Peter Bondra, Wash.	1.00
☐	12 Martin Havlat, Otta.	1.00
☐	13 Mike Dunham, Nash.	.50
☐	14 Mike Comrie, Edmo.	1.50
☐	15 Ed Belfour (G), Dall.	2.00
☐	16 Tony Amonte, Chic.	1.00
☐	17 Patrik Stefan, Atla.	.50
☐	18 Paul Kariya, Anah.	2.50
☐	19 Patrick Roy, Colo.	6.00
☐	20 Sean Burke, Phoe.	1.00
☐	21 Vincent Lecavalier, Tamp.	2.00
☐	22 Henrik Sedin, Vanc.	.50
☐	23 Petr Sykora, NJer.	.50
☐	24 Marian Gaborik, MinW.	2.00
☐	25 Rod Brind'Amour, Caro.	.50
☐	26 Miroslav Satan, Buff.	.50
☐	27 Zigmund Palffy, LosA.	1.00
☐	28 Sergei Fedorov, Detr.	2.00
☐	29 Ron Tugnutt, Colu.	.50
☐	30 Jason Allison, LosA.	1.00
☐	31 Marian Hossa, Otta.	2.00
☐	32 John LeClair, Phil.	1.50
☐	33 Keith Tkachuk, SLou.	1.00
☐	34 Adam Oates, Wash.	.50
☐	35 Johan Hedberg (G), Pitt.	.50
☐	36 Saku Koivu, Mont.	1.50
☐	37 Peter Forsberg, Colo.	2.50
☐	38 Jarome Iginla, Calg.	1.50
☐	39 Nicklas Lidström, Detr.	1.00
☐	40 Martin Brodeur, NJer.	3.00
☐	41 Daniel Alfredsson, Otta.	1.00
☐	42 Alex Kovalev, Pitt.	1.00
☐	43 Mats Sundin, Toro.	2.00
☐	44 Brian Leetch, NYRa.	1.00
☐	45 Owen Nolan, SanJ.	1.00
☐	46 Cliff Ronning, Nash.	.50
☐	47 Mike Modano, Dall.	2.00
☐	48 Milan Hejduk, Colo.	1.50
☐	49 Joe Thornton, Bost.	2.00
☐	50 Ray Ferraro, Atla.	.50
☐	51 Geoff Sanderson, Colu.	.50
☐	52 Roberto Luongo, Flor.	1.50
☐	53 Manny Fernandez, MinW.	.50
☐	54 Mark Recchi, Phil.	.50
☐	55 Curtis Joseph (G), Toro.	2.00
☐	56 Philippe Boucher, LosA.	.50
☐	57 Patrick Lalime, Otta.	1.00
☐	58 Rick DiPietro, NYIs.	.50
☐	59 Adam Deadmarsh, LosA.	.50
☐	60 Pierre Turgeon, Dall.	.50
☐	61 Roman Turek, Calg.	.50
☐	62 Jeff Friesen, Anah.	.50
☐	63 Eric Lindros, NYRa.	2.00
☐	64 Martin Straka, Pitt.	.50
☐	65 Markus Näslund, Vanc.	2.00
☐	66 Jean-Pierre Dumont, Buff.	.50
☐	67 Daniel Sedin, Vanc.	.50
☐	68 Alexei Yashin, Otta.	1.00
☐	69 Félix Potvin, LosA.	1.00
☐	70 Chris Drury, Colo.	1.00

☐	71 Martin Biron (G), Buff.	.50
☐	72 Tommy Salo, Edmo.	.50
☐	73 Stanislav Neckar, Tamp.	.50
☐	74 Jaromir Jagr, Wash.	2.00
☐	75 Brendan Shanahan, Buff.	2.00
☐	76 José Théodore, Mont.	2.00
☐	77 Teemu Selänne, SanJ.	1.50
☐	78 Alexander Mogilny, Toro.	.50
☐	79 Niclas Hävelid, Anah.	.50
☐	80 Colin Forbes, NYRa.	.50
☐	81 Michael Peca, NYIs.	.50
☐	82 Jason Arnott, NJer.	.50
☐	83 Arturs Irbe (G), Caro.	.50
☐	84 Garry Valk, Toro.	.50
☐	85 Roman Cechmanek, Phil.	.50
☐	86 Scott Gomez, NJer.	.50
☐	87 Chris McAllister, Phil.	.50
☐	88 Shane Doan, Phoe.	.50
☐	89 David Harlock, Atla.	.50
☐	90 Jeff O'Neill, Caro.	.50
☐	91 Rob Blake, Colo.	1.00
☐	92 Dominik Hasek, Detr.	2.00
☐	93 Olaf Kölzig, Wash.	1.00
☐	94 Brent Johnson, SLou.	.50
☐	95 Jeremy Roenick, Phil.	1.50
☐	96 Brad Richards, Tamp.	.50
☐	97 Steve Sullivan, Chic.	.50
☐	98 Alex Tanguay, Colo.	1.00
☐	99 Brett Hull, Detr.	2.00
☐	100 Doug Weight, Edmo.	1.00

ROOKIES

	Rookie	Rookie
☐	**101 Niklas Hagman, Flor. {#/1099} RC**	**10.00**
☐	**102 Scott Clemmensen, NJer. {#/1099} RC**	**10.00**
☐	**103 Brian Sutherby, Wash. {#/1099} RC**	**10.00**
☐	**104 Erik Cole, Caro. {#/1599} RC**	**10.00**
☐	**105 Vaclav Nedorost, Colo. {#/1599} RC**	**10.00**
☐	**106 Jaroslav Bednar, LosA. {#/1099} RC**	**10.00**
☐	**107 Nick Schultz, MinW. {#/699} RC**	**12.00**
☐	**108 Jiri Dopita, Phil. {#/699} RC**	**12.00**
☐	**109 Krys Kolanos, Phoe. {#/1599} RC**	**10.00**
☐	**110 Jukka Hentunen, Calg. {#/1099} RC**	**10.00**
☐	**111 Niko Kapanen, Dall. {#/699} RC**	**15.00**
☐	**112 Timo Pärssinen, Anah. {#/1099} RC**	**10.00**
☐	**113 Kristian Huselius, Flor. {#/1599} RC**	**10.00**
☐	**114 Andreas Salomonsson, NJer. {#/699} RC**	**12.00**
☐	**115 Ilya Kovalchuk, Atla. {#/1599} RC**	**40.00**
☐	**116 Dan Blackburn (G), NYRa. {#/1599} RC**	**15.00**
☐	**117 Pavel Datsyuk, Detr. {#/699} RC**	**60.00**
☐	**118 Peter Smrek, NYRa. {#/699} RC**	**12.00**
☐	**119 Jeff Jillson, SanJ. {#/1099} RC**	**10.00**
☐	**120 Nikita Alexeev, Tamp. {#/1599} RC**	**10.00**
☐	**121 Scott Nichol, Calg. {#/699} RC**	**12.00**

JERSEY RELIC

There are five versions for each card: the Jersey Relic, the Logo Relic, the Name Relic, the Number Relic, and the Patch Relic.

Insert Set (56 cards): **350.00**

	Insert	JR
☐	Jason Allison, Bost. ✂ White	10.00
☐	Tony Amonte, Chic. ✂	10.00
☐	Jason Arnott, NJer. ✂	8.00
☐	Ed Belfour (G), Dall. ✂	20.00
☐	Brian Boucher (G), Phil. ✂	8.00
☐	Donald Brashear, Vanc. ✂	8.00
☐	Daniel Brière, Phoe. ✂	8.00
☐	Martin Brodeur, NJer. ✂	30.00
☐	Pavel Bure, Flor. ✂	15.00
☐	Sean Burke, Phoe. ✂	10.00
☐	Mariusz Czerkawski, NYIs. ✂	8.00
☐	Éric Desjardins, Phil. ✂	8.00
☐	Tie Domi, Toro. ✂	8.00
☐	Chris Drury, Colo. ✂	10.00
☐	Sergei Fedorov, De ✂	20.00
☐	Theoren Fleury, NYRa. ✂	10.00
☐	Peter Forsberg, Colo. ✂	25.00
☐	Ron Francis, Caro. ✂	10.00
☐	Simon Gagné, Phil. ✂ Black	15.00
☐	Jeff Hackett, Mont. ✂	8.00
☐	Derian Hatcher, Dall. ✂	8.00
☐	Jarome Iginla, Calg. ✂	15.00
☐	Kenny Jönsson, NYIs. ✂	8.00
☐	Paul Kariya, Anah. ✂	25.00
☐	Tomas Kloucek, NYRa. ✂	8.00
☐	Saku Koivu, Mont. ✂	15.00
☐	Alex Kovalev, Pitt. ✂	10.00
☐	Robert Lang, Pitt. ✂	8.00
☐	Vincent Lecavalier, Tamp. ✂ Black	20.00
☐	John LeClair, Phil. ✂	15.00
☐	Brian Leetch, NYRa. ✂	10.00
☐	Mario Lemieux, Pitt. ✂	60.00
☐	Letowski, Phoe. ✂	8.00
☐	PaMarleau, SanJ. ✂	8.00
☐	Darren McCarty, De ✂	8.00
☐	Shawn McEachern, Otta. ✂	8.00
☐	Mike Mottau, NYRa. ✂	8.00
☐	Adam Oates, Wash. ✂	8.00
☐	Krzysztof Oliwa, Pitt. ✂	8.00
☐	Matt Pettinger, Wash. ✂ White	8.00
☐	Mark Recchi, Phil. ✂	8.00
☐	Wade Redden, Otta. ✂	8.00
☐	Patrick Roy, Colo. ✂	60.00
☐	Joe Sakic, Colo. ✂	30.00
☐	Sergei Samsonov, Bost. ✂	10.00
☐	Oleg Saprykin, Calg. ✂	8.00
☐	Miroslav Satan, Buff. ✂	8.00
☐	Marc Savard, Calg. ✂ Red	8.00
☐	Martin Straka, Pitt. ✂	8.00
☐	Joe Thornton, Bost. ✂	20.00
☐	Marty Turco, Dall. ✂ White	10.00
☐	Tomas Vokoun, Nash. ✂	8.00
☐	Mike York, NYRa. ✂	8.00
☐	DmiYushkevich, Toro. ✂	8.00
☐	Alexei Zhamnov, Chic. ✂	8.00
☐	Sergei Zubov, Dall. ✂	8.00

LOGO, NAME, NUMBER AND PATCH RELICS

Logo, Name and Number relics have similar pricing.

Insert Set (56 cards): **1,600** **800**

	Insert	PR	R
☐☐☐☐	Jason Allison, Bost. ✂	60.00	30.00
☐☐☐☐	Tony Amonte, Chic. ✂	60.00	30.00
☐☐☐☐	Jason Arnott, NJer. ✂	45.00	20.00
☐☐☐☐	Ed Belfour (G), Dall. ✂	100.00	50.00
☐☐☐☐	Brian Boucher (G), Phil. ✂	30.00	15.00
☐☐☐☐	Donald Brashear, Vanc. ✂	20.00	10.00
☐☐☐☐	Daniel Brière, Phoe. ✂	45.00	20.00
☐☐☐☐	Martin Brodeur, NJer. ✂	160.00	80.00
☐☐☐☐	Pavel Bure, Flor. ✂	80.00	40.00
☐☐☐☐	Sean Burke, Phoe. ✂	60.00	30.00
☐☐☐☐	Mariusz Czerkawski, NYIs. ✂	20.00	10.00
☐☐☐☐	Éric Desjardins, Phil. ✂	30.00	15.00
☐☐☐☐	Tie Domi, Toro. ✂	30.00	15.00
☐☐☐☐	Chris Drury, Colo. ✂	60.00	30.00
☐☐☐☐	Sergei Fedorov, De ✂	100.00	50.00
☐☐☐☐	Theoren Fleury, NYRa. ✂	60.00	30.00
☐☐☐☐	Peter Forsberg, Colo. ✂	140.00	70.00
☐☐☐☐	Ron Francis, Caro. ✂	60.00	30.00
☐☐☐☐	Simon Gagné, Phil. ✂	80.00	40.00
☐☐☐☐	Jeff Hackett, Mont. ✂	30.00	15.00
☐☐☐☐	Derian Hatcher, Dall. ✂	30.00	15.00
☐☐☐☐	Jarome Iginla, Calg. ✂	80.00	40.00
☐☐☐☐	Kenny Jönsson, NYIs. ✂	20.00	10.00
☐☐☐☐	Paul Kariya, Anah. ✂	140.00	70.00
☐☐☐☐	Tomas Kloucek, NYRa. ✂	10.00	8.00
☐☐☐☐	Saku Koivu, Mont. ✂	80.00	40.00
☐☐☐☐	Alex Kovalev, Pitt. ✂	60.00	30.00
☐☐☐☐	Robert Lang, Pitt. ✂	20.00	10.00
☐☐☐☐	Vincent Lecavalier, Tamp. ✂	100.00	50.00
☐☐☐☐	John LeClair, Phil. ✂	80.00	40.00
☐☐☐☐	Brian Leetch, NYRa. ✂	60.00	30.00
☐☐☐☐	Mario Lemieux, Pitt. ✂	300.00	150.00
☐☐☐☐	Letowski, Phoe. ✂	15.00	8.00
☐☐☐☐	PaMarleau, SanJ. ✂	45.00	20.00
☐☐☐☐	Darren McCarty, De ✂	30.00	15.00
☐☐☐☐	Shawn McEachern, Otta. ✂	30.00	15.00
☐☐☐☐	Mike Mottau, NYRa. ✂	15.00	8.00
☐☐☐☐	Adam Oates, Wash. ✂	40.00	20.00
☐☐☐☐	Krzysztof Oliwa, Pitt. ✂	20.00	10.00
☐☐☐☐	Matt Pettinger, Wash. ✂	15.00	8.00
☐☐☐☐	Mark Recchi, Phil. ✂	40.00	20.00
☐☐☐☐	Wade Redden, Otta. ✂	30.00	15.00
☐☐☐☐	Patrick Roy, Colo. ✂	300.00	150.00
☐☐☐☐	Joe Sakic, Colo. ✂	160.00	80.00
☐☐☐☐	Sergei Samsonov, Bost. ✂	60.00	30.00
☐☐☐☐	Oleg Saprykin, Calg. ✂	20.00	10.00
☐☐☐☐	Miroslav Satan, Buff. ✂	30.00	15.00
☐☐☐☐	Marc Savard, Calg. ✂	20.00	10.00
☐☐☐☐	Martin Straka, Pitt. ✂	30.00	15.00
☐☐☐☐	Joe Thornton, Bost. ✂	120.00	60.00
☐☐☐☐	Marty Turco, Dall. ✂	60.00	30.00
☐☐☐☐	Tomas Vokoun, Nash. ✂	20.00	10.00
☐☐☐☐	Mike York, NYRa. ✂	30.00	15.00
☐☐☐☐	DmiYushkevich, Toro. ✂	20.00	10.00
☐☐☐☐	Alexei Zhamnov, Chic. ✂	30.00	15.00
☐☐☐☐	Sergei Zubov, Dall. ✂	20.00	10.00

SIGNED PUCK

There is one signed puck in each box of Topps Reserve. There are two versions of each puck: a silver-signed puck and a gold-signed puck (each limited to 50 copies).

Complete Set (25 pucks):

	Puck	G50	Silv.
☐☐	Ilya Kovalchuk, Atla. ✍		
☐☐	Evgeni Nabokov, SanJ. ✍		
☐☐	Adam Oates, Wash. ✍		
☐☐	Michael Peca, NYIs. ✍		
☐☐	Chris Pronger, SLou. ✍		
☐☐	Miroslav Satan, Buff. ✍		
☐☐	Ryan Smyth, Edmo. ✍		
☐☐	Petr Sykora, NJer. ✍		
☐☐	Alex Tanguay, Colo. ✍		
☐☐	José Théodore, Mont. ✍		
☐☐	Justin Williams, Phil. ✍		
☐☐	Jason Arnott, Njer. ✍		
☐☐	Todd Bertuzzi, Vanc. ✍		
☐☐	Pavel Brendl, Phil. ✍		
☐☐	Roman Cechmanek, Phil. ✍		
☐☐	Mike Comrie, Edmo. ✍		
☐☐	Marian Gaborik, MinW. ✍		
☐☐	Dominik Hasek, Buff. ✍		
☐☐	Martin Havlat, Otta. ✍		
☐☐	Johan Hedberg (G), Pitt. ✍		
☐☐	Milan Hejduk, Colo. ✍		
☐☐	Marian Hossa, Otta. ✍		
☐☐	Jarome Iginla, Calg. ✍		
☐☐	Brent Johnson, SLou. ✍		
☐☐	Curtis Joseph (G), Toro. ✍		

PSA-GRADED ROOKIES

	Rookie	PSA9
☐	**101 Niklas Hagman, Flor. {#/1099} RC**	**10.00**
☐	**102 Scott Clemmensen, NJer. {#/1099} RC**	**10.00**
☐	**103 Brian Sutherby, Wash. {#/1099} RC**	**10.00**
☐	**104 Erik Cole, Caro. {#/1599} RC**	**15.00**
☐	**105 Vaclav Nedorost, Colo. {#/1599} RC**	**15.00**
☐	**106 Jaroslav Bednar, LosA. {#/1099} RC**	**10.00**
☐	**107 Nick Schultz, MinW. {#/699} RC**	**15.00**
☐	**108 Jiri Dopita, Phil. {#/699} RC**	**15.00**
☐	**109 Krys Kolanos, Phoe. {#/1599} RC**	**15.00**
☐	**110 Jukka Hentunen, Calg. {#/1099} RC**	**10.00**
☐	**111 Niko Kapanen, Dall. {#/699} RC**	**12.00**
☐	**112 Timo Pärssinen, Anah. {#/1099} RC**	**10.00**
☐	**113 Kristian Huselius, Flor. {#/1599} RC**	**20.00**
☐	**114 Andreas Salomonsson, NJer. {#/699} RC**	**12.00**
☐	**115 Ilya Kovalchuk, Atla. {#/1599} RC**	**40.00**
☐	**116 Dan Blackburn, NYRa. {#/1599} RC**	**25.00**
☐	**117 Pavel Datsyuk, Detr. {#/699} RC**	**60.00**
☐	**118 Peter Smrek, NYRa. {#/699} RC**	**12.00**
☐	**119 Jeff Jillson, SanJ. {#/1099} RC**	**10.00**
☐	**120 Nikita Alexeev, Tamp. {#/1599} RC**	**10.00**
☐	**121 Scott Nichol, Calg. {#/699} RC**	**12.00**

2001 - 02 TOPPS / O-PEE-CHEE ARCHIVES

Produced by The Topps Company, this series was released in February 2002.

Complete Set (81 cards): **45.00**

Common Player: **.50**

	Description	Base
☐	1 A. Bathgate	.50
☐	2 B. Gadsby	.50
☐	3 T. Esposito, Chic.	2.00
☐	4 H. Howell	.50
☐	5 L. Robinson, Mont.	1.00
☐	6 J. Plante	3.00
☐	7 P. Pilote	.50
☐	8 G. Hall (G)	2.00
☐	9 D. Hunter, Québ.	.50
☐	10 G. Lapointe, Mont.	.50
☐	11 N. Ullman	.50
☐	12 B. Trottier, NYIs.	2.00
☐	13 A. Delvecchio, Detr.	.50
☐	14 S. Mikita, Chic.	1.50
☐	15 N. Broten, Minn.	.25
☐	16 B. Parent (G)	1.50
☐	17 J. Bucyk	1.00
☐	18 R. Middleton	.25
☐	19 B. Clarke, Phil.	1.50
☐	20 Billy Smith (G)	1.50
☐	21 P. Stastny, Québ.	1.00
☐	22 T. Kerr, Phil.	.25
☐	23 G. Cheevers (G)	1.50
☐	24 A. Moog (G), Edmo.	.50
☐	25 D. Hull	.50
☐	26 N. Fotiu	.25
☐	27 M. Dionne, Detr.	2.00
☐	28 G. Lafleur, Mont.	4.00
☐	29 Y. Cournoyer	1.00
☐	30 B. Mullen	.25
☐	31 W. Cashman	.25
☐	32 S. Shutt, Mont.	.50
☐	33 G. Fuhr (G), Edmo.	1.00
☐	34 E. Johnston	.25
☐	35 C. Gillies	.50
☐	36 R. MacLeish	.25
☐	37 D. Potvin, NYIs.	1.50
☐	38 B. Clement	.25
☐	39 D. Sittler, Toro.	1.50
☐	40 P. Larouche	.25
☐	41 V. Hadfield	.25
☐	42 D. Sanderson	.50
☐	43 R. Leach	.25
☐	44 B. Propp	.25
☐	45 B. Melrose	.25
☐	46 D. Gare	.25
☐	47 D. Pang (G), Chic.	.25
☐	48 D. Duff	.25
☐	49 J. Quenneville	.25
☐	50 J. Ferguson	.50
☐	51 E. Westfall	.25
☐	52 J. Bower (G)	1.50
☐	53 S. Savard, Mont.	.50
☐	54 K. Magnuson	.25
☐	55 K. Hodge	.25
☐	56 G. Unger	.25
☐	57 L. Ruff	.25
☐	58 G. Resch (G)	.50
☐	59 L. Worsley (G)	1.50
☐	60 B. Federko, SLou.	.50
☐	61 M. Foligno	.25
☐	62 M. Schmidt	1.00
☐	63 M. Bossy, NYIs.	3.00
☐	64 R. Low (G)	.25
☐	65 J. Lemaire	.50
☐	66 D. Schultz	.50
☐	67 G. Sather	.50
☐	68 D. Wilson, Chic.	.50
☐	69 T. Sawchuk (G)	4.00
☐	70 M. Milbury	.25
☐	71 T. O'Reilly	.25
☐	72 R. Kelly	1.00
☐	73 P. McNab	.25
☐	74 P. Holmgren	.25
☐	75 K. Linseman	.25
☐	76 T. Horton	2.00
☐	77 Bobby Smith, Minn.	.50
☐	78 B. Hull	3.50
☐	79 P. LaFontaine, NYIs.	1.00
☐	80 P. Mahovlich	.50
☐	81 M. Gartner, Wash.	1.50

AUTHENTIC GAME-USED STICK

Insert Set (3 cards):	80.00
Insert	S
☐ Bobby Clarke, Phil. ✄	35.00
☐ Tony Esposito (G), Chic. ✄	45.00
☐ Dale Hawerchuk, Winn. ✄	30.00

AUTHENTIC GAME-WORN JERSEY

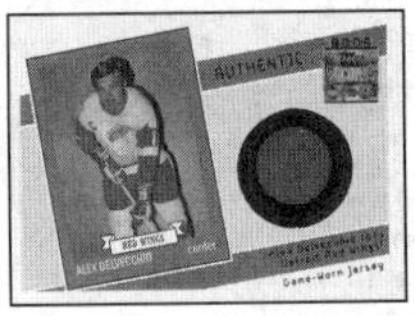

The complete set price includes only one swatch variation per player.

Insert Set (12 cards):	65.00
Insert	J
☐ Bobby Clarke, Phil. ✄ Red	25.00
☐ Bobby Clarke, Phil. ✄ Black	25.00
☐ Alex Delvecchio, Detr. ✄ White	15.00
☐ Alex Delvecchio, Detr. ✄ Red	15.00
☐ Grant Fuhr (G), Buff. ✄ Blue	15.00
☐ Grant Fuhr (G), Buff. ✄ Blue/Yellow	25.00
☐ Mike Gartner, Toro. ✄ Blue	25.00
☐ Pete Mahovlich, Mont. ✄ White	10.00
☐ Pete Mahovlich, Mont. ✄ Red	10.00
☐ Stan Mikita, Chic. ✄ White	25.00
☐ Andy Moog, Dall. ✄ Black	10.00
☐ Brian Mullen, Slou. ✄ Blue	10.00
☐ Brian Mullen, Slou. ✄ White	10.00
☐ Larry Robinson, Mont. ✄ Red	15.00
☐ Larry Robinson, Mont. ✄ Red/White	25.00
☐ Billy Smith, NYIs. ✄ White	25.00
☐ Billy Smith, NYIs. ✄ Red	25.00
☐ Bobby Smith, Dall. ✄ White	10.00
☐ Bobby Smith, Dall. ✄ Black	10.00
☐ Ed Westfall, NYIs. ✄ Blue	10.00

AUTHENTIC SEAT

Insert Set (28 cards):	.00
Insert	Seat
☐ Neal Broten, Minn. [Met Center]	6.00
☐ John Bucyk, Bost. [Boston Garden]	6.00
☐ Wayne Cashman, Bost. [Boston Garden]	6.00
☐ Gerry Cheevers (G), Bost. [Boston Garden]	10.00
☐ Yvan Cournoyer, Mont. [Montréal Forum]	6.00
☐ Alex Delvecchio, Detr. [Detroit Olympia]	6.00
☐ Marcel Dionne, Detr. [Detroit Olympia]	10.00
☐ Tony Esposito (G), Chic. [Chicago Stadium]	10.00
☐ Bernie Federko, Slou. [St. Louis Arena]	6.00
☐ Glenn Hall (G), Chic. [Chicago Stadium]	10.00
☐ Ken Hodge, Chic. [Chicago Stadium]	6.00
☐ Dennis Hull, Chic. [Chicago Stadium]	6.00
☐ Guy Lafleur, Mont. [Montréal Forum]	15.00
☐ Guy Lapointe, Mont. [Montréal Forum]	6.00
☐ Pierre Larouche, Pitt. [Pittsburgh Civic Arena]	6.00
☐ Jacques Lemaire, Mont. [Montréal Forum]	6.00
☐ Stan Mikita, Chic. [Chicago Stadium]	10.00
☐ Terry O'Reilly, Bost. [Boston Garden]	6.00
☐ Pierre Pilote, Chic. [Chicago Stadium]	6.00
☐ Larry Robinson, Mont. [Montréal Forum]	6.00
☐ Derek Sanderson, Bost. [Boston Garden]	6.00
☐ Serge Savard, Mont. [Montréal Forum]	6.00
☐ Steve Shutt, Mont. [Montréal Forum]	6.00
☐ Darryl Sittler, Toro. [Maple Leaf Gardens]	10.00
☐ Bobby Smith, Minn. [Met Center]	6.00
☐ Bryan Trottier, Pitt. [Pittsburgh Civic Arena]	10.00
☐ Norm Ullman, Detr. [Detroit Olympia]	6.00
☐ Doug Wilson, Chic. [Chicago Stadium]	6.00

CERTIFIED AUTOGRAPH ISSUE

Insert Set (29 cards):	.00
Insert	CAI
☐ John Bucyk, Bost. ✍	20.00
☐ Clark Gillies, NYIs. ✍	20.00
☐ Norm Ullman, Detr. ✍	20.00
☐ Gerry Cheevers (G), Bost. ✍	20.00
☐ Bobby Clarke, Phil. ✍	20.00
☐ Yvan Cournoyer, Mont. ✍	20.00
☐ Alex Delvecchio, Detr. ✍	20.00
☐ Peter Stastny, Québ. ✍	20.00
☐ Marcel Dionne, Detr. ✍	20.00
☐ Ed Westfall, NYIs. ✍	20.00
☐ Tony Esposito (G), Chic. ✍	30.00
☐ Grant Fuhr (G), Edmo. ✍	20.00
☐ Glenn Hall (G), Chic. ✍	25.00
☐ Bobby Hull, Chic. ✍	60.00
☐ Dennis Hull, Chic. ✍	20.00
☐ Jacques Lemaire, Mont. ✍	20.00
☐ Darryl Sittler, Toro. ✍	20.00
☐ Ken Linseman, Phil. ✍	20.00
☐ Peter McNab, Bost. ✍	20.00
☐ Guy Lafleur, Mont. ✍	25.00
☐ Stan Mikita, Chic. ✍	20.00
☐ Serge Savard, Mont. ✍	20.00
☐ Rick Middleton, NYRa. ✍	20.00
☐ Terry O'Reilly, Bost. ✍	20.00
☐ Vic Hadfield, NYRa. ✍	20.00
☐ Pierre Pilote, Chic. ✍	20.00
☐ Denis Potvin, NYIs. ✍	20.00
☐ Dave Schultz, Phil. ✍	20.00
☐ Bryan Trottier, NYIs. ✍	25.00

2001 - 02 UD PLAYMAKERS LIMITED

Produced by The Upper Deck Company, this series was released in April 2002.

Shell Set (100 cards):	25.00
Complete Set (145 cards):	170.00
Common Player:	.25
Player	Base
☐ 1 Steve Shields, Anah.	.25
☐ 2 Jeff Friesen, Anah.	.25
☐ 3 Paul Kariya, Anah.	1.00
☐ 4 Ray Ferraro, Atla.	.25
☐ 5 Milan Hnilicka (G), Atla.	.25
☐ 6 Dany Heatley, Atla.	2.00
☐ 7 Sergei Samsonov, Bost.	.50
☐ 8 Joe Thornton, Bost.	1.00
☐ 9 Byron Dafoe, Bost.	.25
☐ 10 Hal Gill, Bost.	.25
☐ 11 Miroslav Satan, Buff.	.25
☐ 12 Stu Barnes, Buff.	.25
☐ 13 Martin Biron (G), Buff.	.25
☐ 14 Marc Savard, Calg.	.25
☐ 15 Roman Turek (G), Calg.	.25
☐ 16 Jarome Iginla, Calg.	.50
☐ 17 Jeff O'Neill, Caro.	.25
☐ 18 Sami Kapanen, Caro.	.25
☐ 19 Arturs Irbe (G), Caro.	.25
☐ 20 Steve Sullivan, Chic.	.25
☐ 21 Jocelyn Thibault, Chic.	.25
☐ 22 Tony Amonte, Chic.	.50
☐ 23 Joe Sakic, Colo.	1.50
☐ 24 Milan Hejduk, Colo.	.50
☐ 25 Chris Drury, Colo.	.50
☐ 26 Patrick Roy, Colo.	3.00
☐ 27 Rob Blake, Colo.	.50
☐ 28 Marc Denis, Colu.	.25
☐ 29 Ray Whitney, Colu.	.25
☐ 30 Rostislav Klesla, Colu.	.25
☐ 31 Ed Belfour (G), Dall.	1.00
☐ 32 Pierre Turgeon, Dall.	.25
☐ 33 Mike Modano, Dall.	1.00
☐ 34 Brett Hull, Detr.	1.00
☐ 35 Dominik Hasek (G), Detr.	1.00
☐ 36 Brendan Shanahan, Detr.	1.00
☐ 37 Luc Robitaille, Detr.	.50
☐ 38 Steve Yzerman, Detr.	2.00
☐ 39 Mike Comrie, Edmo.	.50
☐ 40 Tommy Salo, Edmo.	.25
☐ 41 Ryan Smyth, Edmo.	.25
☐ 42 Anson Carter, Edmo.	.25
☐ 43 Valeri Bure, Flor.	.25
☐ 44 Roberto Luongo, Flor.	.50
☐ 45 Pavel Bure, Flor.	.50
☐ 46 Félix Potvin, LosA.	.50
☐ 47 Jason Allison, LosA.	.50
☐ 48 Zigmund Palffy, LosA.	.50
☐ 49 Manny Fernandez, MinW.	.25
☐ 50 Marian Gaborik, MinW.	1.00
☐ 51 Andrew Brunette, MinW.	.25
☐ 52 Yanic Perreault, Mont.	.25
☐ 53 José Théodore (G), Mont.	1.00
☐ 54 Brian Savage, Phoe.	.25
☐ 55 David Legwand, Nash.	.25
☐ 56 Mike Dunham, Nash.	.25
☐ 57 Cliff Ronning, Nash.	.25
☐ 58 Martin Brodeur, NJer.	1.50
☐ 59 Patrik Elias, NJer.	.50
☐ 60 Jason Arnott, NJer.	.25
☐ 61 Alexei Yashin, NYIs.	.50
☐ 62 Chris Osgood, NYIs.	.50
☐ 63 Mark Parrish, NYIs.	.25
☐ 64 Theoren Fleury, NYRa.	.50
☐ 65 Brian Leetch, NYRa.	.50
☐ 66 Mark Messier, NYRa.	1.00
☐ 67 Eric Lindros, NYRa.	1.00
☐ 68 Radek Bonk, Otta.	.25
☐ 69 Marian Hossa, Otta.	1.00
☐ 70 Martin Havlat, Otta.	.50
☐ 71 John LeClair, Phil.	.50
☐ 72 Mark Recchi, Phil.	.25
☐ 73 Roman Cechmanek, Phil.	.25
☐ 74 Jeremy Roenick, Phil.	.50
☐ 75 Michal Handzus, Phoe.	.25
☐ 76 Shane Doan, Phoe.	.25
☐ 77 Sean Burke, Phoe.	.50
☐ 78 Alex Kovalev, Pitt.	.50
☐ 79 Mario Lemieux, Pitt.	3.00
☐ 80 Johan Hedberg (G), Pitt.	.25
☐ 81 Owen Nolan, SanJ.	.50
☐ 82 Teemu Selänne, SanJ.	.50
☐ 83 Evgeni Nabokov, SanJ.	.50
☐ 84 Chris Pronger, SLou.	.50
☐ 85 Pavol Demitra, SLou.	.25
☐ 86 Keith Tkachuk, SLou.	.50
☐ 87 Doug Weight, SLou.	.50
☐ 88 Vincent Lecavalier, Tamp.	1.00
☐ 89 Brad Richards, Tamp.	.25
☐ 90 Nikolai Khabibulin (G), Tamp.	.25
☐ 91 Wade Belak, Toro.	.25
☐ 92 Alexander Mogilny, Toro.	.25
☐ 93 Mats Sundin, Toro.	1.00
☐ 94 Curtis Joseph (G), Toro.	1.00
☐ 95 Brendan Morrison, Vanc.	.25
☐ 96 Trevor Linden, Vanc.	.25
☐ 97 Markus Näslund, Vanc.	1.00
☐ 98 Peter Bondra, Wash.	.50
☐ 99 Olaf Kölzig, Wash.	.50
☐ 100 Jaromir Jagr, Wash.	1.00

ROOKIE

Insert (#/1250)	R
☐ 101 Timo Pärssinen, Anah. RC	6.00
☐ 102 Ilja Bryzgalov, Anah. RC	6.00
☐ 103 Mike Weaver, Atla. RC	6.00
☐ 104 Ilya Kovalchuk, Atla. RC	30.00
☐ 105 Ivan Huml, Bost. RC	6.00
☐ 106 Tony Tuzzolino, Bost. RC	6.00
☐ 107 Jukka Hentunen, Calg. RC	6.00
☐ 108 Scott Nichol, Calg. RC	6.00
☐ 109 Erik Cole, Caro. RC	6.00
☐ 110 Mike* Peluso, Chic. RC	6.00
☐ 111 Riku Hahl, Colo. RC	6.00
☐ 112 Vaclav Nedorost, Colo. RC	6.00
☐ 113 Blake Bellefeuille, Colu. RC	6.00
☐ 114 Niko Kapanen, Dall. RC	6.00
☐ 115 John Erskine, Dall. RC	6.00
☐ 116 Pavel Datsyuk, Detr. RC	25.00
☐ 117 Ty Conklin, Edmo. RC	6.00
☐ 118 Jason Chimera, Edmo. RC	6.00
☐ 119 Niklas Hagman, Flor. RC	6.00
☐ 120 Kristian Huselius, Flor. RC	10.00
☐ 121 Kip Brennan, LosA. RC	6.00
☐ 122 Pascal Dupuis, MinW. RC	6.00
☐ 123 Marcel Hossa, Mont. RC	10.00
☐ 124 Olivier Michaud, Mont. RC	6.00
☐ 125 Martin Erat, Nash. RC	6.00
☐ 126 Christian Berglund, NJer. RC	6.00
☐ 127 Andreas Salomonsson, NJer. RC	6.00
☐ 128 Raffi Torres, NYIs. RC	6.00
☐ 129 Radek Martinek, NYIs. RC	6.00
☐ 130 Mikael Samuelsson, NYRa. RC	6.00
☐ 131 Dan Blackburn (G), NYRa. RC	10.00
☐ 132 Toni Dahlman, Otta. RC	6.00
☐ 133 Bruno St-Jacques, Phil. RC	6.00
☐ 134 Tomas Divisek, Phil. RC	6.00
☐ 135 Jiri Dopita, Phil. RC	6.00
☐ 136 Krys Kolanos, Phoe. RC	6.00
☐ 137 Éric Meloche, Pitt. RC	6.00
☐ 138 Tom Kostopoulos, Pitt. RC	6.00
☐ 139 Jeff Jillson, SanJ. RC	6.00
☐ 140 Mark Rycroft, SLou. RC	6.00
☐ 141 Josef Boumedienne, Tamp. RC	6.00
☐ 142 Nikita Alexeev, Tamp. RC	6.00
☐ 143 Mike Farrell, Wash. RC	6.00
☐ 144 Todd Rohloff, Wash. RC	6.00
☐ 145 Brian Sutherby, Wash. RC	6.00

PLAYER'S CLUB COMBO JERSEYS

Insert Set (10 cards):	350.00	150.00
Insert	G50	C100
☐☐ Maxim Afinogenov, Buff. ✄ ✄	30.00	20.00
☐☐ Rob Blake, Colo. ✄ ✄	30.00	20.00
☐☐ Mike Dunham, Nash. ✄ ✄	30.00	20.00
☐☐ Simon Gagné, Phil. ✄ ✄	40.00	20.00
☐☐ Milan Hejduk, Colo. ✄ ✄	40.00	20.00
☐☐ Jarome Iginla, Calg. ✄ ✄	40.00	20.00
☐☐ Paul Kariya, Anah. ✄ ✄	70.00	35.00
☐☐ John LeClair, Phil. ✄ ✄	40.00	20.00
☐☐ Mark Recchi, Phil. ✄ ✄	30.00	20.00
☐☐ Patrick Roy, Colo. ✄ ✄	150.00	60.00

PLAYER'S CLUB JERSEY

Insert Set (10 cards):	300.00	150.00
Insert	PCJG	PCJ
☐ Maxim Afinogenov, Buff. ✄	25.00	15.00
☐ Martin Brodeur, NJer. ✄	60.00	30.00
☐ Peter Forsberg, Colo. ✄	50.00	25.00
☐ Simon Gagné, Phil. ✄	30.00	15.00
☐ Jarome Iginla, Calg. ✄	30.00	15.00
☐ Mario Lemieux, Pitt. ✄	110.00	45.00
☐ Zigmund Palffy, LosA. ✄	25.00	15.00
☐ Mark Recchi, Phil. ✄	25.00	15.00
☐ Teemu Selänne, SanJ. ✄	30.00	15.00
☐ Ron Tugnutt, Colu. ✄	25.00	15.00

PLAYER'S CLUB PRACTICE JERSEY

Photo Photo-need

Insert Set (10 cards):	150.00	70.00
Player	PCPJG	PCPJ
☐ Ed Belfour (G), Dall.	20.00	15.00
☐ Tyler Bouck, Phoe.	20.00	10.00
☐ Rod Brind'Amour, Caro.	20.00	10.00
☐ Rico Fata, NYRa.	20.00	10.00
☐ Simon Gagné, Phil.	20.00	10.00
☐ Milan Hejduk, Colo.	20.00	10.00
☐ Jarome Iginla, Calg.	20.00	10.00
☐ John LeClair, Phil.	20.00	10.00
☐ Maxime Ouellet, Phil.	20.00	10.00
☐ Miroslav Satan, Buff.	20.00	10.00

PLAYMAKERS

☐ Martin Brodeur, NJer. Red
☐ Martin Brodeur, NJer. White
☐ Pavel Bure, Flor. Red
☐ Pavel Bure, Flor. White
☐ Dominik Hasek (G), Detr. Red
☐ Dominik Hasek (G), Detr. White
☐ Jaromir Jagr, Wash. Black
☐ Jaromir Jagr, Wash. White
☐ Curtis Joseph (G), Toro. Blue
☐ Curtis Joseph (G), Toro. White
☐ Ilya Kovalchuk, Atla. Blue
☐ Ilya Kovalchuk, Atla. White
☐ Eric Lindros, NYRa. Blue
☐ Eric Lindros, NYRa. White
☐ Mike Modano, Dall. Green

- ☐ Mike Modano, Dall. White
- ☐ Patrick Roy, Colo. Burgandy
- ☐ Patrick Roy, Colo. White
- ☐ Joe Sakic, Colo. Burgandy
- ☐ Joe Sakic, Colo. White
- ☐ Doug Weight, SLou. Blue
- ☐ Doug Weight, SLou. White
- ☐ Steve Yzerman, Detr. Red
- ☐ Steve Yzerman, Detr. White

PLAYMAKERS SIGNED

- ☐ Martin Brodeur, NJer. Red ✍
- ☐ Martin Brodeur, NJer. White ✍
- ☐ Pavel Bure, Flor. Red ✍
- ☐ Pavel Bure, Flor. White ✍
- ☐ Curtis Joseph (G), Toro. Blue ✍
- ☐ Curtis Joseph (G), Toro. White ✍
- ☐ Ilya Kovalchuk, Atla. Blue ✍
- ☐ Ilya Kovalchuk, Atla. White ✍
- ☐ Doug Weight, SLou. Blue ✍
- ☐ Doug Weight, SLou. White ✍
- ☐ Steve Yzerman, Detr. Red ✍
- ☐ Steve Yzerman, Detr. White ✍

2001 - 02 ULTIMATE MEMORABILIA

Produced by In The Game, this series was released in May 2002.

Actual realized pricing on these rare cards may vary considerably from pricing listed below. Mint+ examples (BGS-9.5) exist for Leetch (one copy only), LeClair (one copy only), and Robitaille (two copies). Near Mint examples (BGS-7) exist for Lindsay (13 copies) and Mahovlich (eight copies).

AUTOGRAPHS

	Insert	7.5	8	8.5	9
☐	D. Alfredsson ✍ (#/40) [0,0,17,23]	-	-	75	100
☐	Tony Amonte ✍ (#/30) [1,9,19,1]	40	50	75	125
☐	Jean Béliveau ✍ (#/40) [0,3,31,6]	-	75	100	150
☐	Rob Blake ✍ (#/40) [0,2,11,27]	-	50	75	100
☐	Peter Bondra ✍ (#/40) [0,2,24,14]	-	50	75	100
☐	Pavel Bure ✍ (#/40) [0,8,24,8]	-	50	75	100
☐	Marcel Dionne ✍ (#/40) [0,7,23,10]	-	50	75	100
☐	Phil Esposito ✍ (#/40) [0,3,22,15]	-	50	75	100
☐	Sergei Fedorov ✍ (#/40) [0,2,18,20]	-	50	75	100
☐	W. Gretzky ✍ (#/30) [14,14,2,0]	450	575	800	-
☐	Milan Hejduk ✍ (#/40) [0,0,9,31]	-	-	75	100
☐	Gordie Howe ✍ (#/40) [0,7,33,0]	-	150	175	-
☐	Bobby Hull ✍ (#/40) [0,2,32,6]	-	50	75	100
☐	Jarome Iginla ✍ (#/40) [0,7,24,9]	-	50	75	100
☐	Paul Kariya ✍ (#/40) [0,14,21,5]	-	75	100	175
☐	Guy Lafleur ✍ (#/40) [0,10,27,3]	-	50	75	125
☐	John LeClair ✍ (#/40) [0,3,6,30]	-	50	75	100
☐	Brian Leetch ✍ (#/40) [0,1,6,32]	-	50	75	100
☐	M. Lemieux ✍ (#/30) [10,19,1,0]	200	250	450	-
☐	Ted Lindsay ✍ (#/20) [1,0,6,0]	50	-	75	-
☐	Al Macinnis ✍ (#/30) [0,16,14,0]	-	50	75	-
☐	Frank Mahovlich ✍ (#/30) [0,16,6,0]	-	50	75	-
☐	Mark Messier ✍ (#/40) [0,9,24,7]	-	75	75	125
☐	Stan Mikita ✍ (#/40) [0,0,28,12]	-	-	75	100
☐	Owen Nolan ✍ (#/40) [0,19,21,0]	-	50	75	-
☐	Gilbert Perreault ✍ (#/40) [0,4,17,19]	-	50	75	100
☐	Mark Recchi ✍ (#/40) [0,0,26,14]	-	-	75	100
☐	Luc Robitaille ✍ (#/40) [0,1,7,30]	-	50	75	100
☐	Jeremy Roenick ✍ (#/30) [0,0,23,7]	-	-	75	100
☐	Joe Sakic ✍ (#/40) [0,3,24,13]	-	100	100	175
☐	B. Shanahan ✍ (#/40) [0,1,14,25]	-	50	75	100
☐	Scott Stevens ✍ (#/40) [0,3,26,11]	-	50	75	100
☐	Keith Tkachuk ✍ (#/40) [0,7,28,5]	-	50	75	100
☐	Alexei Yashin ✍ (#/40) [0,18,19,3]	-	50	75	100
☐	Steve Yzerman ✍ (#/40) [0,3,25,12]	-	150	175	250

AUTOGRAPH (GOLD)

Actual realized pricing on these scarce cards may vary considerably from pricing listed below.

	Insert (#/10)	7.5	8	8.5	9
☐	Daniel Alfredsson ✍ [0,0,6,4]	-	85	225	150
☐	Tony Amonte ✍ [0,0,10,0]	-	-	100	-
☐	Jean Béliveau ✍ [0,0,5,5]	-	-	225	350
☐	Rob Blake ✍ [0,2,7,1]	-	85	100	150
☐	Peter Bondra ✍ [0,1,8,1]	-	85	100	150
☐	Pavel Bure/5 ✍ [0,0,1,4]	-	-	125	200
☐	Marcel Dionne ✍ [0,1,9,0]	-	125	150	-
☐	Phil Esposito ✍ [0,0,4,6]	-	-	125	200
☐	Sergei Fedorov ✍ [0,0,10,0]	-	-	150	-
☐	W. Gretzky ✍ [4,6,0,0]	825	1,200	-	-
☐	Milan Hejduk ✍ [0,0,10,0]	-	-	125	-
☐	Gordie Howe ✍ [0,0,6,4]	-	-	375	600
☐	Bobby Hull ✍ [0,0,9,1]	-	-	150	250
☐	Jarome Iginla ✍ [0,0,6,4]	-	-	125	200
☐	Paul Kariya ✍ [0,1,5,4]	-	175	225	350
☐	Guy Lafleur ✍ [0,0,9,1]	-	-	150	250
☐	John LeClair ✍ [0,3,6,1]	-	100	125	200
☐	Brian Leetch ✍ [0,2,5,3]	-	85	100	150
☐	Mario Lemieux ✍ [8,2,0,0]	375	400	-	-
☐	Ted Lindsay ✍ [0,2,7,1]	-	100	125	200
☐	Al Macinnis ✍ [0,3,7,0]	-	85	100	-
☐	Frank Mahovlich ✍ [0,1,6,3]	-	125	150	250
☐	Mark Messier ✍ [0,0,9,1]	-	125	150	250
☐	Stan Mikita ✍ [0,0,7,3]	-	-	100	150
☐	Owen Nolan ✍ [0,1,8,1]	-	85	100	150
☐	Gilbert Perreault ✍ [0,0,7,3]	-	-	125	200
☐	Mark Recchi ✍ [0,2,6,2]	-	-	100	125
☐	Luc Robitaille ✍ [0,0,6,4]	-	-	125	200
☐	Jeremy Roenick ✍ [0,0,3,7]	-	-	125	200
☐	Joe Sakic ✍ [0,6,3,1]	-	200	250	400
☐	Brendan Shanahan/5 ✍ [0,2,3,0]	-	125	150	-
☐	Scott Stevens ✍ [0,1,4,5]	-	85	100	125
☐	Keith Tkachuk ✍ [0,4,6,0]	-	85	100	-
☐	Alexei Yashin ✍ [0,10,0,0]	-	85	-	-
☐	Steve Yzerman ✍ [0,0,6,4]	-	-	375	600

500 GOAL SCORERS

Actual realized pricing on these rare cards may vary considerably from pricing listed below.

	Insert	8	8.5	9	9.5
☐	D. Andreychuk ✂ (#/30) [11,19,0,0]	50	75	-	-
☐	Jean Béliveau ✂ (#/10) [3,5,2,0]	175	225	350	-
☐	Mike Gartner ✂ (#/30) [2,18,10,0]	75	75	100	-
☐	John Bucyk ✂ (#/30) [2,26,2,0]	50	75	100	-
☐	Dino Ciccarelli ✂ (#/30) [2,13,15,0]	50	75	100	-
☐	Marcel Dionne ✂ (#/30) [4,16,8,2]	50	75	100	150
☐	Phil Esposito ✂ (#/30) [4,17,9,0]	50	75	100	-
☐	Ron Francis ✂ (#/30) [0,4,26,0]	-	75	100	-
☐	Mike Bossy ✂ (#/30) [3,22,5,0]	50	75	100	-
☐	Michel Goulet ✂ (#/30) [9,12,9,0]	50	75	100	-
☐	Wayne Gretzky ✂ (#/10) [3,7,0,0]	550	650	-	-
☐	Dale Hawerchuk ✂ (#/30) [6,17,7,0]	50	75	100	-
☐	Gordie Howe ✂ (#/10) [3,4,3,0]	325	375	600	-
☐	Bobby Hull ✂ (#/10) [2,6,2,0]	175	225	350	-
☐	Brett Hull ✂ (#/30) [3,22,5,0]	75	75	100	-
☐	Jari Kurri ✂ (#/30) [2,16,11,1]	75	75	125	150
☐	Guy Lafleur ✂ (#/30) [4,21,5,0]	75	100	125	-
☐	Mario Lemieux ✂ (#/10) [9,1,0,0]	400	475	-	-
☐	Frank Mahovlich ✂ (#/10) [2,5,3,0]	75	75	150	-
☐	L. McDonald ✂ (#/30) [3,10,16,1]	50	75	100	150
☐	Mark Messier ✂ (#/30) [6,18,6,0]	75	75	100	-
☐	Stan Mikita ✂ (#/30) [3,20,7,0]	50	75	100	-
☐	Joe Mullen ✂ (#/30) [3,16,11,0]	50	75	100	-
☐	Gilbert Perreault ✂ (#/30) [9,15,6,0]	50	75	100	-
☐	Maurice Richard ✂ (#/10) [4,4,2,0]	325	375	600	-
☐	Luc Robitaille ✂ (#/30) [16,13,1,0]	50	75	100	-
☐	B. Shanahan ✂ (#/30) [0,10,20,0]	-	75	100	-
☐	Bryan Trottier ✂ (#/30) [1,16,13,0]	50	75	100	-
☐	Pat Verbeek ✂ (#/30) [9,18,3,0]	50	75	100	-
☐	Steve Yzerman ✂ (#/30) [3,18,9,0]	175	200	250	-

500 GOAL SCORERS AUTOGRAPHS

Actual realized pricing on these rare cards may vary considerably from pricing listed below. Mint examples (-9) exist for Bossy (one copy only), Bucyk (one copy only), and Richard (two copies).

	Insert	7	7.5	8	8.5
☐	D. Andreychuk ✍ ✂ (#/30) [7,19,4,0]	60	75	85	-
☐	J. Béliveau ✍ ✂ (#/15) [13,2,0,0]	125	175	-	-
☐	Pat Verbeek ✍ ✂ (#/10) [4,6,0,0]	100	125	175	150
☐	John Bucyk ✍ ✂ (#/25) [0,4,12,8]	-	75	85	-
☐	D. Ciccarelli ✍ ✂ (#/10) [10,0,0,0]	60	-	-	-
☐	M. Dionne ✍ ✂ (#/25) [7,16,2,0]	60	75	100	-
☐	M. Richard ✍ • ✂ (#/10) [0,0,0,8]	100	125	-	-
☐	Mike Gartner ✍ ✂ (#/30) [0,19,9,2]	-	75	100	100
☐	Mike Bossy ✍ ✂ (#/25) [2,4,3,15]	60	75	85	100
☐	Dale Hawerchuk ✍ ✂ (#/25) [2,14,7,2]	60	75	85	100
☐	Gordie Howe ✍ ✂ (#/20) [6,10,3,1]	175	225	375	250
☐	Bobby Hull ✍ ✂ (#/25) [9,13,3,0]	60	75	150	-
☐	Jari Kurri ✍ ✂ (#/20) [8,10,2,0]	75	75	175	-
☐	Guy Lafleur ✍ ✂ (#/20) [8,9,2,1]	75	75	150	100
☐	M. Lemieux ✍ ✂ (#/10) [5,4,1,0]	325	400	600	-
☐	F. Mahovlich ✍ ✂ (#/25) [6,18,1,0]	60	75	100	-
☐	L. McDonald ✍ ✂ (#/20) [6,8,4,2]	60	75	125	100
☐	Stan Mikita ✍ ✂ (#/25) [12,12,1,0]	60	75	100	-
☐	Joe Mullen ✍ ✂ (#/20) [0,16,4,0]	-	75	85	-
☐	G. Perreault ✍ ✂ (#/15) [9,6,0,0]	75	100	-	-
☐	Michel Goulet ✍ ✂ (#/30) [1,14,12,3]	-	-	-	400
☐	Luc Robitaille ✍ ✂ (#/15) [0,11,4,0]	-	100	150	-
☐	B. Trottier ✍ ✂ (#/15) [14,1,0,0]	100	250	-	-
☐	Phil Esposito ✍ ✂ (#/15) [8,7,0,0]	60	75	-	-
☐	S. Yzerman ✍ ✂ (#/15) [8,7,0,0]	225	300	-	-

500 GOAL SCORERS EMBLEM

Actual realized pricing on these rare cards may vary considerably from pricing listed below.

	Insert (#/10)	8	8.5	9	9.5
☐	D. Andreychuk ✂ [2,3,5,0]	50	75	100	-
☐	Jean Béliveau ✂ [0,5,5,0]	-	250	400	-
☐	Mike Gartner ✂ [0,1,9,0]	-	175	300	-
☐	John Bucyk ✂ [0,7,3,0]	-	100	175	-
☐	Dino Ciccarelli ✂ [1,3,6,0]	50	75	100	-
☐	Marcel Dionne ✂ [6,4,0,0]	125	150	-	-
☐	Phil Esposito ✂ [2,8,0,0]	125	150	-	-
☐	Ron Francis ✂ [0,5,5,0]	-	100	175	-
☐	Mike Bossy ✂ [2,5,3,0]	125	150	225	-
☐	Michel Goulet ✂ [1,6,3,0]	75	75	125	-
☐	Wayne Gretzky ✂ [1,8,1,0]	650	775	1,200	-
☐	D. Hawerchuk ✂ [0,2,5,3]	-	100	175	200
☐	Gordie Howe ✂ [0,9,1,0]	-	450	700	-
☐	Bobby Hull ✂ [0,8,2,0]	-	250	400	-
☐	Brett Hull ✂ [0,7,2,1]	-	175	300	350
☐	Jari Kurri ✂ [0,4,6,0]	-	175	350	-
☐	Guy Lafleur ✂ [4,5,1,0]	175	225	350	-
☐	Mario Lemieux ✂ [0,4,6,0]	-	575	900	-
☐	Frank Mahovlich ✂ [6,4,0,0]	75	100	-	-
☐	L. McDonald ✂ [0,7,3,0]	-	100	175	-
☐	Mark Messier ✂ [0,2,8,0]	-	175	300	-
☐	Stan Mikita ✂ [0,7,3,0]	-	100	175	-
☐	Joe Mullen ✂ [0,3,7,0]	-	75	100	-
☐	G. Perreault ✂ [1,4,4,1]	75	100	175	200
☐	Maurice Richard ✂ [0,3,5,2]	-	450	700	825
☐	Luc Robitaille ✂ [0,0,9,1]	-	-	225	275
☐	B. Shanahan ✂ [1,5,4,0]	150	175	300	-
☐	Bryan Trottier ✂ [0,4,6,0]	-	150	225	-
☐	Pat Verbeek ✂ [0,5,5,0]	-	75	100	-
☐	Steve Yzerman ✂ [3,7,0,0]	375	450	-	-

500 GOAL SCORERS STICK & JERSEY

Actual realized pricing on these rare cards may vary considerably from pricing listed below.

	Insert	8	8.5	9	9.5
☐	D. Andreychuk ✂ (#/40) [0,25,15,0]	-	75	100	-
☐	Jean Béliveau ✂ (#/40) [25,15,0,0]	100	150	-	-
☐	Mike Gartner ✂ (#/40) [20,20,0,0]	75	100	-	-
☐	John Bucyk ✂ (#/40) [24,16,0,0]	50	75	-	-
☐	Dino Ciccarelli ✂ (#/40) [12,24,4,0]	50	75		-
☐	Marcel Dionne ✂ (#/40) [18,19,3,0]	50	75	100	-
☐	Phil Esposito ✂ (#/40) [16,16,8,0]	50	75	100	-
☐	Ron Francis ✂ (#/40) [8,20,11,1]	50	75	100	150
☐	Mike Bossy ✂ (#/40) [35,5,0,0]	50	75	-	-
☐	Michel Goulet ✂ (#/40) [26,12,2,0]	50	75	100	-
☐	Wayne Gretzky ✂ (#/20) [0,17,3,0]	-	425	650	-
☐	D. Hawerchuk ✂ (#/40) [27,12,1,0]	50	75	100	-
☐	Gordie Howe ✂ (#/20) [6,14,0,0]	250	275	-	-
☐	Bobby Hull ✂ (#/40) [37,3,0,0]	100	100	-	-
☐	Brett Hull ✂ (#/40) [37,3,0,0]	50	75	-	-
☐	Jari Kurri ✂ (#/40) [28,12,0,0]	50	75	-	-
☐	Guy Lafleur ✂ (#/40) [28,12,0,0]	100	125	-	-
☐	Mario Lemieux ✂ (#/20) [9,10,1,0]	275	300	475	-
☐	F. Mahovlich ✂ (#/40) [32,8,0,0]	50	75	-	-
☐	L. McDonald ✂ (#/40) [14,25,1,0]	50	75	100	-
☐	Mark Messier ✂ (#/40) [40,0,0,0]	50	-	100	-
☐	Stan Mikita ✂ (#/40) [26,13,1,0]	50	75	100	-
☐	Joe Mullen ✂ (#/40) [0,13,25,2]	-	75	100	150
☐	G. Perreault ✂ (#/40) [26,14,0,0]	50	75	-	-
☐	M. Richard ✂ (#/20) [1,10,9,0]	250	275	450	-
☐	Luc Robitaille ✂ (#/40) [20,18,2,0]	50	75	100	-
☐	B. Shanahan ✂ (#/40) [9,30,1,0]	50	75	100	-
☐	Bryan Trottier ✂ (#/40) [0,30,10,0]	-	75	100	-
☐	Pat Verbeek ✂ (#/40) [14,23,3,0]	50	75	100	-
☐	Steve Yzerman ✂ (#/40) [39,1,0,0]	125	150	-	-

ACTIVE 8

Actual realized pricing on these rare cards may vary considerably from pricing listed below.

	Insert	8	8.5	9	9.5
☐	Francis ✂ Red / Messier ✂ White / Yzerman ✂ Red [0,13,17,0]	-	150	200	-
☐	Kariya ✂ White/Grey / Lemieux ✂ White / Sakic ✂ White [0,9,19,2]	-	225	300	425
☐	Lemieux ✂ / Sundin ✂ / Yzerman ✂ [4,10,15,1]	200	250	325	475
☐	Messier ✂ / Hull ✂ / Lemieux ✂ [2,18,10,0]	100	200	250	-
☐	Roy (G) ✂ / Vernon (G) ✂ / Barrasso (G) ✂ [0,8,20,2]	-	125	150	225
☐	Selänne ✂ / Nieuwendyk ✂ / Robitaille ✂ [0,18,11,1]	-	75	100	150
☐	Messier ✂ / Francis ✂ / S.Stevens ✂ [1,12,17,0]	150	75	100	-
☐	Lemieux ✂ / Robitaille ✂ / Jagr ✂ [1,11,18,0]	50	175	250	-

ALL-STAR GAME HISTORY

Actual realized pricing on these rare cards may vary considerably from pricing listed below.

	Insert	8	8.5	9	9.5
☐	Jean Béliveau ✂ [0,1,38,1]	-	150	175	225
☐	Mike Modano ✂ [1,21,17,1]	-	-	125	175
☐	Johnny Bower (G) ✂ [0,17,23,0]	-	75	100	-
☐	Frank Brimsek (G) ✂ [0,0,40,0]	-	-	100	-
☐	Turk Broda (G) ✂ [0,32,8,0]	-	75	100	-
☐	Johnny Bucyk ✂ [0,3,35,2]	-	75	100	150
☐	Pavel Bure ✂ [0,31,9,0]	-	75	100	-
☐	Bobby Clarke ✂ [0,8,32,0]	-	75	100	-
☐	Paul Coffey ✂ [1,25,14,0]	50	75	100	-
☐	Marcel Dionne ✂ [0,8,28,4]	-	75	100	150
☐	Tony Esposito (G) ✂ [0,3,35,2]	-	75	100	150
☐	Peter Forsberg ✂ [3,26,11,0]	50	75	100	-
☐	Grant Fuhr (G) ✂ [0,34,6,0]	-	75	100	-
☐	Bill Gadsby ✂ Glove [0,28,12,0]	-	75	100	-
☐	Ed Giacomin (G) ✂ [0,12,28,0]	-	75	100	-
☐	Wayne Gretzky ✂ [0,6,34,0]	-	275	350	-
☐	Glenn Hall (G) ✂ [0,0,35,5]	-	-	100	150
☐	Doug Harvey ✂ [0,0,40,0]	-	-	100	-
☐	Milan Hejduk ✂ White/Burgandy	50	75	100	150
☐	Milan Hejduk ✂ Blue	50	75	100	150
☐	Tim Horton ✂ [0,14,26,0]	-	75	100	-
☐	Gordie Howe ✂ [0,15,24,1]	-	175	225	300
☐	Bobby Hull ✂ [0,0,35,5]	-	-	150	200
☐	Brett Hull ✂ [0,0,35,5]	-	-	100	150
☐	Jaromir Jagr ✂ [0,0,37,3]	-	-	100	150
☐	Paul Kariya ✂ [0,4,32,4]	-	75	100	150
☐	Ted Kennedy ✂ [9,20,11,0]	100	75	100	-
☐	Guy Lafleur ✂ [0,0,33,7]	-	-	175	225
☐	Brian Leetch ✂ [0,0,32,8]	-	-	100	150
☐	Mario Lemieux ✂ [0,24,16,0]	-	200	250	-
☐	Eric Lindros ✂ [0,16,22,2]	-	75	100	150
☐	Ted Lindsay ✂ [0,12,26,2]	-	75	100	150
☐	Frank Mahovlich ✂ [0,1,39,0]	-	75	100	-
☐	Lanny McDonald ✂ [0,16,24,0]	-	75	100	-
☐	Mark Messier ✂ [0,4,35,1]	-	75	100	150
☐	Stan Mikita, Chic. ✂				
☐	Mike Bossy ✂ [0,0,32,8]	50	75	100	150
☐	Bill Mosienko ✂ [0,12,28,0]	-	75	100	-
☐	Bernie Parent (G) ✂ [0,13,27,0]	-	75	100	-
☐	Gilbert Perreault ✂ [0,12,28,0]	-	75	100	-
☐	Jacques Plante (G) ✂ Blue	-	100	125	175
☐	Jacques Plante (G) ✂ White/Red	-	100	125	175
☐	Denis Potvin ✂ [0,3,36,1]	-	75	100	150
☐	Chuck Rayner (G) ✂ [0,0,0,1]				
☐	Henri Richard ✂ [0,16,24,0]	-	75	100	-
☐	Maurice Richard ✂ [0,5,35,0]	-	175	225	-
☐	Luc Robitaille ✂ [0,13,27,0]	-	75	100	-
☐	Jeremy Roenick ✂ [0,0,30,10]	-	-	100	150

		8	8.5	9	9.5
☐	Patrick Roy ✂ [0,26,14,0]	-	200	250	-
☐	Joe Sakic ✂ [0,13,27,0]	-	100	125	-
☐	Terry Sawchuk (G) ✂ [1,1,31,7]	50	125	175	225
☐	Mats Sundin ✂ [0,5,33,2]	-	75	100	150
☐	Bryan Trottier ✂ [0,14,26,0]	-	75	100	-
☐	Steve Yzerman ✂ [0,22,18,0]	-	150	200	-

BE A PLAYER LEGEND

Actual realized pricing on these rare cards may vary considerably from pricing listed below.

	Insert (#/20)	8	8.5	9	9.5
☐	Belfour (G) ✂ / Sawchuk (G) ✂ [0,5,15,0]	-	150	225	-
☐	Brodeur (G) ✂ / Sawchuk (G) ✂ [0,0,17,3]	-	-	300	400
☐	Dafoe (G) ✂ / Sawchuk (G) ✂	-	75	-	-
☐	Hasek (G) ✂ / Sawchuk (G) ✂	-	75	-	-
☐	Hedberg (G) ✂ / Sawchuk (G) ✂ [0,6,12,2]	-	125	175	250
☐	Joseph (G) ✂ / Sawchuk (G) ✂ [2,10,8]	100	150	225	-
☐	Khabibulin (G) ✂ / Sawchuk (G) ✂ [2,8,9,1]	100	125	175	250
☐	Kölzig (G) ✂ / Sawchuk (G) ✂	-	-	200	-
☐	Luongo (G) ✂ / Sawchuk (G) ✂ [0,0,18,2]	-	-	225	300
☐	Nabokov (G) ✂ / Sawchuk (G) ✂ [0,0,19,1]	-	-	200	275
☐	Potvin (G) ✂ / Sawchuk (G) ✂ [0,1,18,1]	-	125	250	275
☐	Richter (G) ✂ / Sawchuk (G) ✂ [0,1,19,0]	-	125	175	-
☐	Roy (G) ✂ / Sawchuk (G) ✂ [0,0,17,3]	-	-	375	500
☐	Salo (G) ✂ / Sawchuk (G) ✂ [0,13,7,0]	-	125	175	-
☐	Théodore (G) ✂ / Sawchuk (G) ✂ [0,0,18,2]	-	-	250	350
☐	Thibault (G) ✂ / Sawchuk (G) ✂ [0,0,17,3]	-	-	175	250

BLOODLINES

Actual realized pricing on these rare cards may vary considerably from pricing listed below.

	Insert (#/20)	8.5	9	9.5
☐	Abel ✂ Red / Br. Johnson (G) ✂ Glove [0,19,1]	-	100	150
☐	P. Bure ✂ Red / V. Bure ✂ Red [5,15,0]	75	100	-
☐	P. Esposito ✂ / T. Esposito ✂ [3,16,1]	75	125	175
☐	Br. Hull ✂ White / Bo. Hull ✂ Red [0,16,4]	-	250	325
☐	P. Kariya ✂ / S. Kariya ✂ [0,15,5]	-	150	200
☐	F. Mahovlich ✂ Red / P.Mahovlich ✂ Blue/White/Red [4,16,0]	75	100	-
☐	R. Niedermayer ✂ / S. Niedermayer ✂ [7,13,0]	75	100	-
☐	H. Richard ✂ / M. Richard ✂ [9,11,0]	175	275	-

CALDER TROPHY

Actual realized pricing on these rare cards may vary considerably from pricing listed below.

	Insert (#/30)	8.5	9	9.5
☐	Daniel Alfredsson ✂ [5,25,0]	100	125	-
☐	Tom Barrasso (G) ✂ [0,25,5]	-	100	150
☐	Ed Belfour (G) ✂ [0,25,5]	-	100	150
☐	Bryan Berard ✂ [6,24,0]	75	100	-
☐	Mike Bossy ✂ [4,26,0]	125	175	-
☐	Frank Brimsek (G) ✂ [7,23,0]	75	100	-
☐	Martin Brodeur (G) ✂ [0,27,3]	-	175	225
☐	Pavel Bure ✂ [0,18,12]	-	100	150
☐	Chris Drury ✂ [5,25,0]	75	100	-
☐	Tony Esposito (G) ✂ [0,20,10]	-	100	150
☐	Peter Forsberg ✂ [0,28,2]	-	150	200
☐	Scott Gomez ✂ [10,20,0]	75	100	-
☐	Glenn Hall (G) ✂ [0,20,10]	-	100	150
☐	Dale Hawerchuk ✂ [3,27,0]	75	100	-
☐	Brian Leetch ✂ [0,26,4]	-	100	150
☐	Mario Lemieux ✂ [0,30,0]	-	325	-
☐	Evgeni Nabokov (G) ✂ [3,27,0]	75	100	-
☐	Joe Nieuwendyk ✂ [0,21,9]	-	100	150
☐	Gilbert Perreault ✂ [4,24,2]	75	100	150
☐	Denis Potvin ✂ [5,25,0]	75	100	-
☐	Luc Robitaille ✂ [0,26,4]	-	100	150
☐	Sergei Samsonov ✂ [5,25,0]	75	100	-
☐	Terry Sawchuk (G) ✂ [0,26,4]	-	225	300
☐	Teemu Selänne ✂ [0,29,1]	-	100	150
☐	Bryan Trottier ✂ [4,26,0]	75	100	-

COMPLETE PACKAGE

Actual realized pricing on these scarce cards may vary considerably from pricing listed below.

	Insert (#/10)	8	8.5	9	9.5
☐	W. Gretzky ✂ ✂ ✂ ✂ [2,7,1]	-	800	1,200	1800
☐	T. Horton ✂ ✂ ✂ ✂ [0,10,0]	-	-	350	-
☐	J. Plante (G) ✂ ✂ ✂ ✂ [1,8,1]	-	150	225	-
☐	Eric Lindros ✂ ✂ ✂ ✂ [0,6,4]	-	400	600	-
☐	Curtis Joseph (G) ✂ ✂ ✂ ✂ [7,3,0]	-	-	300	450
☐	Guy Lafleur ✂ ✂ ✂ ✂ [5,5,0]	-	300	475	700
☐	Patrick Roy (G) ✂ ✂ ✂ ✂ [3,7,0]	-	475	700	-
☐	T. Sawchuk (G) ✂ ✂ ✂ ✂ [7,3,0]	-	400	600	-
☐	Mats Sundin ✂ ✂ ✂ ✂ [2,3,5,0]	150	200	300	-
☐	Jarome Iginla ✂ ✂ ✂ ✂ [2,8,0]	-	75	100	-

CORNERSTONES

Actual realized pricing on these rare cards may vary considerably from pricing listed below.

	Insert (#/30)	8.5	9	9.5
☐	Brimsek (G) ✂ Blue / Bucyk ✂ Yellow / Neely ✂ White / Thornton ✂ Yellow [0,20,0]	-	175	-
☐	Hull ✂ / Hall (G) ✂ / Mikita ✂ / Amonte ✂ [0,14,6]	-	225	300
☐	Lindsay ✂ / Howe ✂ / Sawchuk (G) ✂ / Yzerman ✂ [0,17,3]	-	450	600
☐	M.Richard ✂ / Béliveau ✂ / Lafleur ✂ / Roy (G) ✂ [1,18,1]	375	550	750
☐	Giacomin (G) ✂ / Rayner (G) ✂ Pad / Esposito ✂ / Leetch ✂ [0,18,2]	-	150	225
☐	Bailey ✂ / Bower (G) ✂ / McDonald ✂ / Sundin ✂ [0,18,2]	-	150	225

DECADES

Actual realized pricing on these scarce and rare cards may vary considerably from pricing listed below.

	Insert	8	8.5	9	9.5
☐	Mike Bossy ✂ [0,27,23,0]	-	75	100	-
☐	Johnny Bower (G) ✂ [1,9,36,4]	40	65	80	125
☐	Frank Brimsek (G) ✂ [2,8,0,0]	50	75	-	-
☐	Gerry Cheevers (G) ✂ [1,44,5,0]	40	65	80	-
☐	Bobby Clarke ✂ [1,35,14,0]	40	65	80	-
☐	Tony Esposito (G) ✂ [2,28,20,0]	40	65	80	-
☐	Grant Fuhr (G) ✂ [4,26,19,1]	40	65	80	125
☐	Bill Gadsby ✂ [0,0,6,4]	-	-	100	150
☐	Glenn Hall (G) ✂ [0,0,47,3]	-	-	80	125
☐	Doug Harvey ✂ [0,0,9,1]	-	-	250	300
☐	Gordie Howe ✂ [0,0,7,3]	-	-	600	700
☐	Bobby Hull ✂ [0,2,35,13]	-	75	125	175
☐	Guy Lafleur ✂ [0,30,20,0]	-	100	150	-
☐	Ted Lindsay ✂ [0,0,6,4]	-	-	200	225
☐	Al MacInnis ✂ [0,34,16,0]	-	65	80	-
☐	Stan Mikita ✂ [0,0,43,7]	-	-	80	125
☐	Cam Neely ✂ [0,33,17,0]	-	65	80	-
☐	Jacques Plante (G) ✂ [0,9,1,0]	-	175	300	-
☐	Denis Potvin ✂ [1,34,15,0]	40	65	80	-
☐	Chuck Rayner (G) ✂ [0,7,3,0]	-	75	100	-
☐	Larry Robinson ✂ [1,29,19,1]	40	65	80	125
☐	Patrick Roy (G) ✂ [0,19,30,1]	-	100	175	225
☐	Serge Savard ✂ [0,50,0,0]	-	65	-	-
☐	Terry Sawchuk (G) ✂ [0,0,4,6]	-	-	400	475

DYNAMIC DUOS

Actual realized pricing on these rare cards may vary considerably from pricing listed below.

	Insert (#/30)	8.5	9	9.5
☐	Bondra ✂ / Fleury ✂ [1,29,0]	75	100	-
☐	P. Bure ✂ / Yashin ✂ [2,28,0]	75	100	-
☐	Damphousse ✂ / Fedorov ✂ [0,26,4]	-	100	150
☐	Gretzky ✂ / Modano ✂ [17,13,0]	250	325	-
☐	Br. Hull ✂ / Hejduk ✂ [0,29,1]	-	100	150
☐	Jagr ✂ / LeClair ✂ [3,27,0]	75	100	-
☐	Kariya ✂ / Forsberg ✂ [7,23,0]	125	175	-
☐	Lindros ✂ / Kovalchuk ✂ [14,16,0]	100	125	-
☐	Messier ✂ / Iginla ✂ [0,30,0]	-	100	-
☐	Messier ✂ / Iginla ✂	-	100	-
☐	Mogilny ✂ / Recchi ✂ [3,27,0]	75	100	-

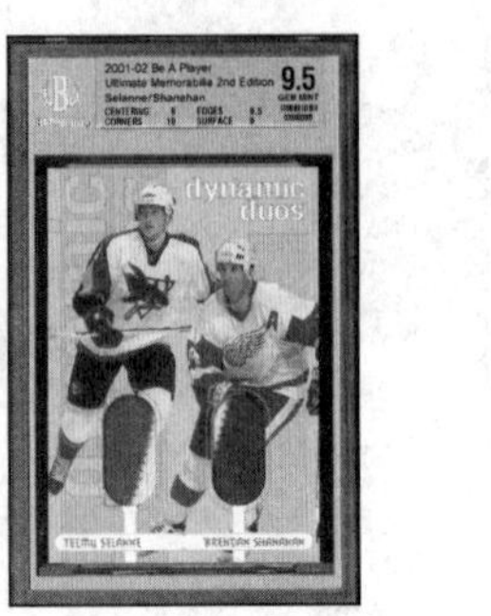

		8.5	9	9.5
☐	Robitaille ✂ / Sakic ✂ [4,26,0]	125	150	-
☐	Roenick ✂ / Lemieux ✂ [16,14,0]	200	250	-
☐	Selänne ✂ / Shanahan ✂ [5,25,0]	75	100	-
☐	Sundin ✂ / Yzerman ✂ [0,29,1]	-	225	300
☐	Tkachuk ✂ / Amonte ✂ [4,26,0]	75	100	-
☐	Weight ✂ / Alfredsson ✂ [13,17,0]	75	100	-

EMBLEM ATTIC

Photo Photo-need

Actual realized pricing on these scarce cards may vary considerably from pricing listed below.

	Insert (#/5)	9	9.5
☐	Jean Béliveau ✂ [5,0]	525	-
☐	Bobby Clarke ✂ [5,0]	225	-
☐	Phil Esposito ✂ [4,1]	300	500
☐	Wayne Gretzky ✂ [2,3]	1,500	2,500
☐	Glenn Hall (G) ✂ [4,1]	250	450
☐	Doug Harvey ✂ [0,5]	-	250
☐	Gordie Howe ✂ [1,4]	900	1,500
☐	Bobby Hull ✂ [4,1]	525	875
☐	Guy Lafleur ✂ [0,5]	-	250
☐	Ted Lindsay ✂ [2,3]	300	500
☐	Frank Mahovlich ✂ [2,3]	225	375
☐	Mark Messier ✂ [5,0]	375	-
☐	Stan Mikita ✂ [0,5]	-	250
☐	Jacques Plante (G) ✂ [0,5]	-	250
☐	Denis Potvin ✂ [3,2]	225	375
☐	Henri Richard ✂ [2,3]	225	375
☐	Maurice Richard ✂ [0,5]	-	250
☐	Larry Robinson ✂ [0,5]	-	250
☐	Terry Sawchuk (G) ✂ [0,5]	-	250
☐	Bryan Trottier ✂ [4,1]	375	625

GAME-USED EMBLEM

Actual realized pricing on these scarce cards may vary considerably from pricing listed below.

	Insert (#/10)	8	8.5	9	9.5
☐	Rob Blake ✂ [0,8,2,0]	-	100	175	-
☐	Martin Brodeur (G) ✂ [0,0,10,0]	-	-	475	-
☐	Pavel Bure ✂ [3,6,1,0]	125	150	225	-
☐	Sergei Fedorov ✂ [3,4,3,0]	150	175	300	-
☐	Bill Guerin ✂ [3,6,1,0]	50	75	100	-
☐	Dominik Hasek (G) ✂ [0,8,2,0]	-	175	300	-
☐	Jaromir Jagr ✂ [5,3,1,1]	150	175	300	350
☐	Curtis Joseph (G) ✂ [3,7,0,0]	150	175	-	-
☐	Paul Kariya ✂ [2,6,2,0]	225	250	400	-
☐	Ilya Kovalchuk ✂ [1,6,2,1]	150	175	300	350
☐	John LeClair ✂ [3,3,4,0]	125	150	225	-
☐	Brian Leetch ✂ [1,5,4,0]	75	100	175	-
☐	Mario Lemieux ✂ [0,0,10,0]	-	-	900	-
☐	Nicklas Lidström ✂ [2,6,2,0]	75	100	175	-
☐	Eric Lindros ✂ [2,8,0,0]	150	175	-	-
☐	Mark Messier ✂ [1,7,2,0]	150	175	300	-
☐	Mike Modano ✂ [1,7,2,0]	150	175	300	-
☐	Owen Nolan ✂ [2,6,2,0]	75	100	175	-
☐	Chris Pronger ✂ [2,6,2,0]	75	100	175	-
☐	Luc Robitaille ✂ [0,0,10,0]	-	-	225	-
☐	Jeremy Roenick ✂ [1,5,4,0]	125	150	225	-
☐	Patrick Roy (G) ✂ [2,6,2,0]	375	450	700	-
☐	Joe Sakic ✂ [4,6,0,0]	250	300	-	-
☐	Teemu Selänne ✂ [0,4,6,0]	-	150	225	-
☐	Brendan Shanahan ✂ [2,8,0,0]	150	175	-	-
☐	Mats Sundin ✂ [3,7,0,0]	150	175	-	-
☐	Keith Tkachuk ✂ [0,0,10,0]	-	-	175	-
☐	Doug Weight ✂ [0,0,10,0]	-	-	175	-
☐	Alexei Yashin ✂ [1,8,1,0]	75	100	175	-
☐	Steve Yzerman ✂ [0,9,1,0]	-	450	700	-

JERSEY

Actual realized pricing on these rare cards may vary considerably from pricing listed below.

	Insert (#/50)	8	8.5	9	9.5
☐	Rob Blake ✂ [11,32,7,0]	40	65	80	-
☐	Martin Brodeur (G) ✂ [9,15,25,1]	50	75	100	150
☐	Pavel Bure ✂ [19,21,10,0]	40	65	80	-
☐	Sergei Fedorov ✂ [9,32,8,1]	40	65	80	125
☐	Bill Guerin ✂ [15,26,8,1]	40	65	80	125
☐	Dominik Hasek (G) ✂ [6,27,17,0]	40	65	80	-
☐	Jaromir Jagr ✂ [7,20,21,2]	40	65	80	125
☐	Curtis Joseph (G) ✂ [18,29,2,1]	40	65	80	125
☐	Paul Kariya ✂ [20,23,7,0]	50	65	100	-
☐	Ilya Kovalchuk ✂ [0,30,20,0]	-	65	80	-
☐	John LeClair ✂ [40,9,1,0]	40	65	80	-
☐	Brian Leetch ✂ [7,25,18,0]	40	65	80	-
☐	Mario Lemieux ✂ [2,44,4,0]	100	150	225	-
☐	Nicklas Lidström ✂ [14,22,14,0]	40	65	80	-
☐	Eric Lindros ✂ [5,38,7,0]	40	65	80	-
☐	Mark Messier ✂ [8,29,11,2]	40	65	80	125
☐	Mike Modano ✂ [0,30,18,2]	-	65	80	125
☐	Owen Nolan ✂ [10,19,18,3]	40	65	80	125
☐	Chris Pronger ✂ [12,24,14,0]	40	65	80	-
☐	Luc Robitaille ✂ [8,28,11,3]	40	65	80	125
☐	Jeremy Roenick ✂ [7,21,22,0]	40	65	80	-
☐	Patrick Roy (G) ✂ [1,37,12,0]	75	100	175	-
☐	Joe Sakic ✂ [17,18,11,4]	50	75	100	150
☐	Teemu Selänne ✂ [26,21,3,0]	40	65	80	-
☐	Brendan Shanahan ✂ [4,33,12,1]	40	65	80	125
☐	Mats Sundin ✂ [9,30,11,0]	40	65	80	-
☐	Keith Tkachuk ✂ [0,0,49,1]	-	-	80	125
☐	Doug Weight ✂ [8,31,10,1]	40	65	80	125
☐	Alexei Yashin ✂ [0,0,46,4]	-	-	80	125
☐	Steve Yzerman ✂ [2,24,24,0]	75	100	175	-

GAME STICK & JERSEY

Actual realized pricing on these rare cards may vary considerably from pricing listed below.

	Insert (#/50)	8	8.5	9	9.5
☐	Rob Blake ✂ ✂ [0,3,35,12]	-	65	80	125
☐	Martin Brodeur (G) ✂ ✂ [8,35,7,0]	50	75	100	-
☐	Pavel Bure ✂ ✂ [0,24,24,2]	-	65	80	125
☐	Sergei Fedorov ✂ ✂ [3,46,1,0]	40	65	80	-
☐	Bill Guerin ✂ ✂ [0,29,20,1]	-	65	80	125
☐	Dominik Hasek (G) ✂ ✂ [2,38,10,0]	40	65	80	-
☐	Jaromir Jagr ✂ ✂ [5,23,22,0]	40	65	80	-
☐	Curtis Joseph (G) ✂ ✂ [14,33,3,0]	40	65	80	-
☐	Paul Kariya ✂ ✂ [0,21,26,3]	-	65	100	125
☐	Ilya Kovalchuk ✂ ✂ [2,41,7,0]	40	65	80	-
☐	John LeClair ✂ ✂ [0,24,21,5]	-	65	80	125
☐	Brian Leetch ✂ ✂ [1,16,33,0]	40	65	80	-
☐	Mario Lemieux ✂ ✂ [0,21,28,1]	-	150	225	300
☐	Nicklas Lidström ✂ ✂ [6,23,21,0]	40	65	80	-
☐	Eric Lindros ✂ ✂ [2,27,20,1]	40	65	80	125
☐	Mark Messier ✂ ✂ [0,13,33,4]	-	65	80	125
☐	Mike Modano ✂ ✂ [0,7,36,7]	-	65	80	125
☐	Owen Nolan ✂ ✂ [3,38,9,0]	40	65	80	-
☐	Chris Pronger ✂ ✂ [17,26,7,0]	40	65	80	-
☐	Luc Robitaille ✂ ✂ [9,39,2,0]	40	65	80	-
☐	Jeremy Roenick ✂ ✂ [4,28,18,0]	40	65	80	-
☐	Patrick Roy (G) ✂ ✂ [38,12,0,0]	75	100	-	-
☐	Joe Sakic ✂ ✂ [0,13,33,4]	-	75	100	150
☐	Teemu Selänne ✂ ✂ [3,31,16,0]	40	65	80	-
☐	B. Shanahan ✂ ✂ [3,23,21,3]	40	65	80	125
☐	Mats Sundin ✂ ✂ [0,17,32,1]	-	65	80	125
☐	Keith Tkachuk ✂ ✂ [0,27,23,0]	-	65	80	-
☐	Doug Weight ✂ ✂ [2,24,21,3]	40	65	80	125
☐	Alexei Yashin ✂ ✂ [23,24,3,0]	40	65	80	-
☐	Steve Yzerman ✂ ✂ [0,18,28,4]	-	100	175	225

GLOVES ARE OFF

Actual realized pricing on these scarce cards may vary considerably from pricing listed below.

	Insert (#/30)	8	8.5	9	9.5
☐	Ace Bailey ✂ [0,12,18,0]	-	75	100	-
☐	Chris Chelios ✂ [1,15,14,0]	50	75	100	-
☐	King Clancy ✂ [1,15,13,1]	50	75	100	150
☐	Sergei Fedorov ✂ [0,14,16,0]	-	75	100	-
☐	Bill Gadsby ✂ [2,21,7,0]	50	75	100	-
☐	Simon Gagné ✂ [0,18,11,1]	-	75	100	150
☐	Wayne Gretzky ✂ [8,18,4,0]	300	350	450	-
☐	Doug Harvey ✂ [16,12,2,0]	75	100	125	-
☐	Gordie Howe ✂ [23,7,0,0]	200	225	-	-
☐	Jarome Iginla ✂ [0,18,12,0]	-	75	100	-
☐	Ted Kennedy ✂ [2,20,8,0]	50	75	100	-
☐	Guy Lafleur ✂ [5,22,3,0]	150	175	225	-
☐	John LeClair ✂ [0,13,17,0]	-	75	100	-
☐	Mario Lemieux ✂ [1,16,12,1]	225	250	325	450
☐	Eric Lindros ✂ [0,20,10,0]	-	75	100	-

		8	8.5	9	9.5
□	Al MacInnis ✂ [1,17,11,1]	50	75	100	150
□	Dickie Moore ✂ [8,12,10,0]	50	75	100	-
□	Scott Niedermayer ✂ [0,18,12,0]	-	75	100	-
□	Maurice Richard ✂ [7,15,8,0]	200	225	300	-
□	Joe Sakic ✂ [2,18,10,0]	100	125	175	-
□	Sergei Samsonov ✂ [1,19,10,0]	50	75	100	-
□	Mats Sundin ✂ [0,4,25,1]	-	75	100	150
□	Doug Weight ✂ [1,10,19,0]	50	75	100	-
□	Alexei Yashin ✂ [3,16,11,0]	50	75	100	-

GOAL LEADERS

Actual realized pricing on these scarce cards may vary considerably from pricing listed below.

	Insert (#/40)	8	8.5	9	9.5
□	Wayne Gretzky 1982 ✂ [12,22,6,0]	225	275	350	-
□	Wayne Gretzky 1983 ✂ [8,19,12,1]	225	275	350	450
□	Wayne Gretzky 1984 ✂ [0,4,35,1]	-	275	350	450
□	Wayne Gretzky 1985 ✂ [11,18,11,0]	225	275	350	-
□	Jari Kurri 1986 ✂ [0,14,26,0]	-	65	100	-
□	Wayne Gretzky 1987 ✂ [7,17,16,0]	225	275	350	-
□	Mario Lemieux 1988 ✂ [2,21,17,0]	150	200	250	-
□	Mario Lemieux 1989 ✂ [0,6,32,2]	-	200	250	325
□	Brett Hull 1990 ✂ [5,20,14,1]	50	65	80	125
□	Brett Hull 1991 ✂ [6,8,24,2]	50	65	80	125
□	Brett Hull 1992 ✂ [2,26,12,0]	50	65	80	-
□	Mogilny ✂ / Selänne ✂ 1993 [0,1,39,0]	-	65	80	-
□	Pavel Bure 1994 ✂ [0,1,38,1]	-	65	80	125
□	Peter Bondra 1995 ✂ [2,18,20,0]	40	65	80	-
□	Mario Lemieux 1996 ✂ [8,21,10,1]	150	200	250	325
□	Keith Tkachuk 1997 ✂ [6,18,15,1]	40	65	80	125
□	Bondra ✂ / Selänne ✂ 1998 [0,0,36,4]	-	-	80	125
□	Teemu Selänne 1999 ✂ [5,19,14,2]	40	65	80	125
□	Pavel Bure 2000 ✂ [0,3,37,0]	-	65	80	-
□	Pavel Bure 2001 ✂				

IN THE NUMBERS

Actual realized pricing on these rare cards may vary considerably from pricing listed below.

	Insert (#/20)	8	8.5	9	9.5
□	Rob Blake ✂ [0,7,13,0]	-	75	100	-
□	Martin Brodeur (G) ✂ [0,7,13,0]	-	200	300	-
□	Pavel Bure ✂ [0,6,13,1]	-	100	150	200
□	Sergei Fedorov ✂ [0,6,13,1]	-	125	175	250
□	Bill Guerin ✂ [0,1,17,2]	-	75	100	150
□	Dominik Hasek (G) ✂ [0,5,15,0]	-	125	175	-
□	Jaromir Jagr ✂ [0,4,16,0]	-	125	175	-
□	Curtis Joseph (G) ✂ [0,4,15,1]	-	125	175	250
□	Paul Kariya ✂ [0,1,17,2]	-	175	250	350
□	Ilya Kovalchuk ✂ [0,0,18,2]	-	-	175	250
□	John LeClair ✂ [0,0,19,1]	-	-	150	200
□	Brian Leetch ✂ [0,2,17,1]	-	75	100	150
□	Mario Lemieux ✂ [0,10,10,0]	-	375	550	-
□	Nicklas Lidström ✂ [0,0,19,1]	-	-	100	150
□	Eric Lindros ✂ [0,6,14,0]	-	125	175	-
□	Mark Messier ✂ [0,3,17,0]	-	125	175	-
□	Mike Modano ✂ [0,9,11,0]	-	125	175	-
□	Owen Nolan ✂ [1,7,11,1]	50	75	100	150
□	Chris Pronger ✂ [0,11,9,0]	-	75	100	-
□	Luc Robitaille ✂ [0,3,17,0]	-	100	150	-
□	Jeremy Roenick ✂ [0,5,14,1]	-	100	150	200
□	Patrick Roy (G) ✂ [1,6,13,0]	250	300	450	-
□	Joe Sakic ✂ [0,7,13,0]	-	200	300	-
□	Teemu Selänne ✂ [0,1,17,2]	-	100	150	200
□	Brendan Shanahan ✂ [0,7,13,0]	-	125	175	-
□	Mats Sundin ✂ [0,0,20,0]	-	-	175	-
□	Keith Tkachuk ✂ [0,7,12,1]	-	75	100	150
□	Doug Weight ✂ [0,2,15,3]	-	75	100	150
□	Alexei Yashin ✂ [0,5,12,3]	-	75	100	150
□	Steve Yzerman ✂ [0,1,19,0]	-	300	450	-

JOURNEY EMBLEM

Actual realized pricing on these scarce cards may vary considerably from pricing listed below.

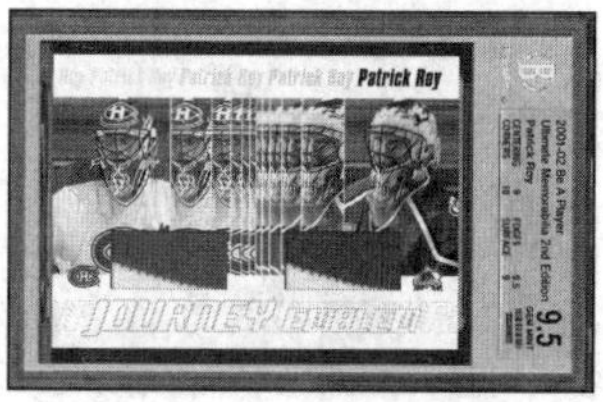

	Insert (#/10)	8	8.5	9	9.5
□	Ed Belfour (G) ✂ ✂ [0,7,2,1]	-	225	350	400
□	Rob Blake ✂ ✂ [5,5,0,0]	100	125	-	-
□	Pavel Bure ✂ ✂ [2,7,1,0]	150	175	275	-
□	Wayne Gretzky ✂ ✂ [0,2,8,0]	-	900	1,400	-
□	Dominik Hasek (G) ✂ ✂ [0,4,6,0]	-	225	350	-
□	Gordie Howe ✂ ✂ ✂	-	700	1,100	-
□	Br. Hull Calg. ✂ Slou. ✂ Dall. ✂ [0,5,5,0]	-	250	400	-
□	Jaromir Jagr ✂ ✂ [0,1,9,0]	-	225	350	-
□	Curtis Joseph (G) ✂ ✂ [0,1,9,0]	-	225	350	-
□	Mark Messier ✂ ✂ [2,4,4,0]	175	225	350	-
□	Mike Modano ✂ ✂ [0,4,6,0]	-	225	350	-
□	Alexander Mogilny ✂ ✂ [0,1,9,0]	-	100	150	-
□	Félix Potvin (G) ✂ ✂ [8,2,0,0]	100	125	-	-
□	Keith Primeau ✂ ✂ [4,6,0,0]	75	75	-	-
□	L. Robitaille NYRa. ✂ LosA. ✂ Detr. ✂ [0,1,9,0]	-	200	300	-
□	Jeremy Roenick ✂ ✂ [0,0,10,0]	-	-	275	-
□	Patrick Roy (G) ✂ ✂ [0,0,10,0]	-	-	825	-
□	Teemu Selänne ✂ ✂ [0,2,8,0]	-	175	275	-
□	Brendan Shanahan ✂ ✂ [0,5,5,0]	-	225	350	-
□	Mats Sundin ✂ ✂ [2,4,4,0]	175	225	350	-
□	Keith Tkachuk ✂ ✂ [0,1,9,0]	-	125	200	-
□	R. Turek (G) Dall. ✂ SLou. ✂ Calg. ✂ [0,2,8,0]	-	100	175	-
□	Alexei Yashin ✂ ✂ [6,4,0,0]	100	125	-	-

JOURNEY JERSEY

Actual realized pricing on these rare cards may vary considerably from pricing listed below.

	Insert (#/50)	8	8.5	9	9.5
□	Ed Belfour (G) ✂ ✂ [0,13,31,6]	-	65	80	125
□	Rob Blake ✂ ✂ [3,11,31,5]	40	65	80	125
□	Pavel Bure ✂ ✂ [0,24,26,0]	-	65	80	-
□	Wayne Gretzky ✂ ✂ [1,15,32,2]	175	250	350	475
□	Dominik Hasek (G) ✂ ✂ [1,8,35,6]	40	65	80	125
□	Gordie Howe ✂ ✂ ✂ [0,8,32,10]	-	200	275	400
□	B. Hull Calg. ✂ Slou. ✂ Dall. ✂ [0,12,37,1]	-	75	100	125
□	Jaromir Jagr ✂ ✂ [0,4,43,4]	-	65	80	125
□	Curtis Joseph (G) ✂ ✂ [1,14,32,3]	40	65	80	125
□	Mark Messier ✂ ✂ [0,5,41,4]	-	65	80	125
□	Mike Modano ✂ ✂ [0,4,27,19]	-	65	80	125
□	Alexander Mogilny ✂ ✂ [0,21,28,1]	-	65	80	125
□	Félix Potvin (G) ✂ ✂ [0,10,38,2]	-	65	100	125
□	Keith Primeau ✂ ✂	-	65	80	125
□	Luc Robitaille NYRa. ✂ LosA. ✂ Detr. ✂ [0,12,38,0]	-	65	80	-
□	Jeremy Roenick ✂ ✂ [0,10,40,0]	-	65	80	-
□	Patrick Roy (G) ✂ ✂ [3,8,27,17]	100	150	200	275
□	Teemu Selänne ✂ ✂ [0,15,35,0]	-	65	80	-
□	Brendan Shanahan ✂ ✂ [2,8,31,9]	40	65	80	125
□	Mats Sundin ✂ ✂ [1,17,31,1]	40	65	80	125
□	Keith Tkachuk ✂ ✂ [0,11,38,1]	-	65	80	125
□	Roman Turek (G) Dall. ✂ SLou. ✂ Calg. ✂ [1,6,40,3]	40	65	80	125
□	Alexei Yashin ✂ ✂ [2,11,30,7]	40	65	80	125

LES CANADIENS

Actual realized pricing on these rare cards may vary considerably from pricing listed below.

	Insert (#/40)	8	8.5	9	9.5
□	Jean Béliveau ✂ [0,16,21,3]	-	150	175	225
□	Yvan Cournoyer ✂ [14,18,7,1]	40	65	80	125
□	Bob Gainey ✂ [13,21,6,0]	40	65	80	-
□	Doug Harvey ✂ [0,16,20,4]	-	75	100	125
□	Saku Koivu ✂ [5,22,13,0]	40	65	100	-
□	Guy Lafleur ✂ [2,16,22,0]	100	125	175	-
□	Guy Lapointe ✂ [0,21,19,0]	-	65	80	-
□	Frank Mahovlich ✂ [0,0,38,2]	-	-	80	125
□	Peter Mahovlich ✂ [1,16,22,1]	40	65	80	125
□	Jacques Plante (G) ✂ [0,22,17,1]	-	100	125	175
□	Mark Recchi ✂ [10,25,4,1]	40	65	80	125
□	Maurice Richard ✂ White	150	175	225	-
□	Maurice Richard ✂ Red	150	175	225	-
□	Henri Richard ✂ [8,28,4,0]	50	65	80	-
□	Larry Robinson ✂ [20,18,2,0]	40	65	80	-
□	Patrick Roy (G) ✂ [0,14,23,3]	-	150	200	250
□	Serge Savard ✂ [0,10,28,2]	-	65	80	125
□	Steve Shutt ✂ [12,22,6,0]	40	65	80	-
□	José Théodore (G) ✂ [5,34,1,0]	50	75	100	-

NAMEPLATES

Actual realized pricing on these rare cards may vary considerably from pricing listed below.

	Insert	8	8.5	9	9.5
□	Jason Arnott ✂ (#/50) [2,19,29,0]	40	65	80	-
□	Rob Blake ✂ (#/40) [8,19,13,0]	40	65	80	-
□	Martin Brodeur (G) ✂ (#/50) [0,12,37,1]	-	75	100	150
□	Pavel Bure ✂ (#/40) [17,19,3,1]	40	65	80	125
□	Cechmanek (G) ✂ (#/50) [0,17,33,0]	-	65	80	-
□	Marcel Dionne ✂ (#/40) [18,14,8,0]	50	65	80	-
□	Phil Esposito ✂ (#/50) [3,31,16,0]	40	65	80	-
□	Sergei Fedorov ✂ (#/50) [9,23,18,0]	40	65	80	-
□	W. Gretzky LA ✂ (#/40) [0,11,29,0]	-	275	350	-
□	W. Gretzky NYR ✂ (#/50) [0,27,23,0]	-	200	300	-
□	Bill Guerin ✂ (#/50) [12,24,14,0]	40	65	80	-
□	D. Hasek (G) ✂ (#/40) [6,25,9,0]	50	65	80	-
□	Gordie Howe, Houston ✂ (#/50)				
□	Gordie Howe, New England ✂ (#/50)				
□	Jarome Iginla ✂ (#/50) [13,30,7,0]	40	65	80	-
□	Jaromir Jagr ✂ (#/50) [1,19,30,0]	40	65	80	-
□	C. Joseph (G) ✂ (#/50) [6,23,21,0]	40	65	80	-
□	P. Kariya, Anah. ✂ Burgandy (<40)	-	75	100	-
□	P. Kariya, Anah. ✂ White/Burgandy (<40)	-	75	100	-
□	Nikolai Khabibulin ✂ (#/50) [0,3,45,2]	-	65	80	125
□	Ilya Kovalchuk ✂ (#/50) [5,25,20,0]	40	65	80	-
□	John LeClair ✂ (#/50) [5,35,10,0]	40	65	80	-
□	Brian Leetch ✂ (#/50) [11,21,18,0]	40	65	80	-
□	Mario Lemieux ✂ (#/50) [0,0,1,0]				
□	N. Lidström ✂ (#/50) [2,28,20,0]	40	65	80	-
□	Eric Lindros ✂ (#/50) [18,28,4,0]	40	65	80	-
□	Mark Messier ✂ (#/50) [11,31,8,0]	40	65	80	-
□	Mike Modano ✂ (#/50) [0,7,41,2]	-	65	80	125
□	Owen Nolan ✂ (#/50) [3,23,23,1]	40	65	80	125
□	Chris Pronger ✂ (#/50) [5,39,6,0]	40	65	80	-
□	Mark Recchi ✂ (#/40) [1,16,23,0]	40	65	80	-
□	Luc Robitaille ✂ (#/50) [8,22,20,0]	40	65	80	-
□	Jeremy Roenick ✂ (#/50) [0,22,28,0]	-	65	80	-
□	Patrick Roy (G) ✂ (#/40) [0,19,21,0]	-	150	200	-
□	Joe Sakic ✂ (#/50) [8,24,18,0]	50	75	100	-
□	Teemu Selänne ✂ (#/50) [5,33,11,1]	40	65	80	125
□	Mats Sundin ✂ (#/40) [12,19,9,0]	50	65	80	-
□	Joe Thornton ✂ (#/50) [0,0,45,5]	-	-	80	125
□	Keith Tkachuk ✂ (#/50) [1,17,32,0]	40	65	80	-
□	Doug Weight ✂ (#/40) [3,22,15,0]	40	65	80	-
□	Steve Yzerman ✂ (#/50) [0,26,24,0]	-	100	175	-

PRODUCTION LINE

Actual realized pricing on these rare cards may vary considerably from pricing listed below.

	Insert (#/20)	8.5	9
□	Sid Abel ✂ [11,9]	75	100
□	Gordie Howe ✂ [10,10]	275	450
□	Ted Lindsay ✂ [8,12]	100	150
□	Abel ✂ / Howe ✂ / Lindsay ✂ [7,13]	375	500
□	Abel ✂ / Howe ✂ / Lindsay ✂ [7,13]	375	500

PROTOTYPICAL PLAYERS

Actual realized pricing on these rare cards may vary considerably from pricing listed below.

	Insert (#/40)	8	8.5	9	9.5
□	Béliveau ✂ / Lemieux ✂ [6,25,9,0]	175	200	275	-
□	Béliveau ✂ / Sakic ✂ [0,10,30,0]	-	150	200	-
□	Béliveau ✂ / Yzerman ✂ [1,19,20,0]	150	175	225	-
□	Harvey ✂ / Blake ✂ [0,18,22,0]	-	65	80	-
□	Harvey ✂ / Lidström ✂ [6,21,9,4]	50	65	80	125
□	Harvey ✂ / Pronger ✂ [0,10,30,0]	-	65	80	-
□	Howe ✂ / Bure ✂ [0,0,28,12]	-	-	175	225
□	Howe ✂ / Br. Hull ✂ [18,20,2,0]	125	150	200	-
□	Howe ✂ / Jagr ✂ [0,0,25,15]	-	-	200	250

		8	8.5	9	9.5
□	Bo. Hull ✂ / Kariya ✂ [1,10,29,0]	100	125	150	-
□	Bo. Hull ✂ Red / Robitaille ✂ White/Red	-	100	125	175
□	Bo. Hull ✂ Red / L. Robitaille ✂ Red	-	100	125	175
□	Bo. Hull ✂ / Shanahan ✂ [1,15,21,3]	75	100	125	175
□	Plante (G) ✂ / Brodeur (G) ✂				
□	Plante (G) ✂ / Hasek (G) ✂ [27,13,0,0]	75	100	-	-
□	Plante (G) ✂ White/Red / Roy (G) ✂ Burgandy	125	150	200	275
□	Plante (G) ✂ Red / Roy (G) ✂ Burgandy	125	150	200	275

RETIRED NUMBERS

Actual realized pricing on these rare cards may vary considerably from pricing listed below. We do not have grading information on the Kurri and McDonald cards.

	Insert (#/5)	8.5	9	9.5
□	Sid Abel ✂ [0,5,0]	-	175	-
□	Bill Barber ✂ [1,3,1]	125	175	250
□	Jean Béliveau ✂ [0,4,1]	-	400	700
□	Mike Bossy ✂ [1,4,0]	200	300	-
□	Johnny Bucyk ✂ [2,3,0]	125	175	-
□	Bobby Clarke ✂ [0,4,1]	-	175	300
□	Marcel Dionne ✂ [0,2,3]	-	225	400
□	Tony Esposito (G) ✂ [1,4,0]	150	200	-
□	Wayne Gretzky ✂ [0,3,2]	-	1,200	2,000
□	Glenn Hall (G) ✂ [0,4,1]	-	200	350
□	Doug Harvey ✂ [0,1,4]	-	300	500
□	Gordie Howe ✂ [0,5,0]	-	700	-
□	Bobby Hull ✂ [0,4,1]	-	400	700
□	Jari Kurri ✂			
□	Guy Lafleur ✂ [0,5,0]	-	350	-
□	Ted Lindsay ✂ [0,4,1]	-	225	400
□	Lanny McDonald ✂			
□	Stan Mikita ✂ [0,2,3]	-	175	300
□	Bernie Parent (G) ✂ [0,5,0]	-	175	-
□	Gilbert Perreault ✂ [0,2,3]	-	175	300
□	Jacques Plante (G) ✂ [0,3,2]	-	350	600
□	Denis Potvin ✂ [1,4,0]	125	175	-
□	Henri Richard ✂ [0,5,0]	-	175	-
□	Maurice Richard ✂ [0,5,0]	-	700	-
□	Terry Sawchuk (G) ✂ [0,5,0]	-	475	-
□	Billy Smith (G) ✂ [1,4,0]	125	175	-

STANLEY CUP PLAYOFF RECORDS

Actual realized pricing on these rare cards may vary considerably from pricing listed below.

	Insert (#/30)	8	8.5	9	9.5
□	Hull ✂ / Hall ✂ / Mikita ✂ [0,0,22,8]	-	-	175	250
□	Howe ✂ / Lindsay ✂ / Sawchuk (G) ✂ [0,6,21,3]	-	225	300	425
□	Gretzky ✂ / Messier ✂ / Coffey ✂ (#/10) [0,6,4]	-	550	350	-
□	Gretzky ✂ / Kurri ✂ / Robitaille ✂ [2,17,10,1]	200	225	300	425
□	M.Richard ✂ / Plante (G) ✂ / Harvey ✂ {#/10}	-	75	-	-
□	Lapointe ✂ / Savard ✂ / F.Mahovlich ✂ [0,0,22,8]	-	-	100	150
□	Cournoyer ✂ / Béliveau ✂ / Lafleur ✂ [1,10,19,0]	150	175	250	-
□	H.Richard ✂ / Béliveau ✂ / M.Richard ✂ {#/10} [0,5,5,0]	-	575	375	-
□	H.Richard ✂ / Harvey ✂ / M.Richard ✂ {#/10} [0,4,6,0]	-	475	300	-
□	Bossy ✂ / Trottier ✂ / Potvin ✂ [0,0,29,1]	-	-	175	250
□	Messier ✂ / Leetch ✂ / Gretzky ✂ [0,4,26,0]	-	225	300	-
□	Barber ✂ / Schultz ✂ / Clarke ✂ [1,10,16,3]	50	75	100	150
□	Lemieux ✂ / Coffey ✂ / Jagr ✂ [0,13,7,0]	-	175	225	-
□	Horton ✂ / Bower (G) ✂ / Sawchuk (G) ✂	-	-	200	-

RETRO-ACTIVE

Actual realized pricing on these rare cards may vary considerably from pricing listed below.

	Insert (#/25)	8	8.5	9	9.5
☐	Bossy ✂ / Sakic ✂ [3,16,6,0]	150	175	250	-
☐	Clarke ✂ / Lemieux ✂ [9,15,1,0]	175	200	300	-
☐	Clarke ✂ / Yzerman ✂ [12,12,1,0]	150	175	250	-
☐	Esposito (G) ✂ / Brodeur (G) ✂ [10,15,0,0]	125	125	-	-
☐	Gretzky ✂ / Jagr ✂ [11,11,3,0]	250	275	400	-
☐	Gretzky ✂ / Lemieux ✂ [2,23,24,1]				
☐	Gretzky ✂ / Lemieux ✂ [1,8,16,0]				
☐	Gretzky ✂ / Lemieux ✂				
☐	Gretzky ✂ / Sakic ✂ [0,19,4,2]	-	300	450	625
☐	Hall (G) ✂ / Roy (G) ✂				
☐	Hall (G) ✂ / Roy (G) ✂				
☐	Harvey ✂ / Lidström ✂ [0,16,9,0]	-	100	125	-
☐	Howe ✂ / Jagr ✂ [0,5,19,1]	-	200	300	425
☐	Kurri ✂ / Kariya ✂ [5,10,10,0]	100	125	175	-
☐	Lafleur ✂ / Lemieux ✂ [0,3,19,3]	-	275	400	550
☐	Lafleur ✂ / Sakic ✂ [0,1,23,1]	-	200	275	400
☐	McDonald ✂ / Joseph (G) ✂ [0,3,18,4]	-	100	125	200
☐	Parent (G) ✂ / Roy (G) ✂ [9,16,0,0]	150	175	-	-
☐	Sawchuk (G) ✂ / Hasek (G) ✂ [0,9,15,1]	-	150	225	325
☐	Sawchuk (G) ✂ / Nabokov (G) ✂ [2,19,4,0]	125	125	200	-

STANLEY CUP DYNASTY EMBLEM

Actual realized pricing on these scarce cards may vary considerably from pricing listed below.

	Insert (#/10)	8	8.5	9	9.5
☐	Bill Barber ✂ [0,1,5,4]	-	75	100	150
☐	Mike Bossy ✂ [0,2,5,3]	-	300	475	550
☐	Bobby Clarke ✂ [0,0,5,5]	-	-	225	275
☐	Yvan Cournoyer ✂ [1,2,6,1]	75	100	175	200
☐	Bob Gainey ✂ [0,5,5,0]	-	100	175	-
☐	Guy Lafleur ✂ [0,0,6,4]	-	-	600	700
☐	Guy Lapointe ✂ [0,4,3,3]	-	75	100	150
☐	Reggie Leach ✂ [0,3,4,3]	-	75	100	150
☐	Bob Nystrom ✂ [0,0,10,0]	-	-	100	-
☐	Bernie Parent (G) ✂ [1,3,5,1]	125	150	225	275
☐	Denis Potvin ✂ [1,2,7,0]	125	150	225	-
☐	Larry Robinson ✂ [0,1,6,3]	-	100	175	200
☐	Serge Savard ✂ [0,0,9,1]	-	-	125	150
☐	Dave Schultz ✂ [0,2,8,0]	-	75	100	-
☐	Steve Shutt ✂ [1,1,5,3]	50	75	100	150
☐	Billy Smith (G) ✂ [0,5,5,0]	-	150	225	-
☐	Bryan Trottier ✂ [0,1,9,0]	-	175	300	-
☐	Joe Watson ✂ [1,2,6,1]	50	75	100	150

STANLEY CUP DYNASTY JERSEY

Actual realized pricing on these rare cards may vary considerably from pricing listed below.

	Insert (#/50)	8	8.5	9	9.5
☐	Bill Barber ✂ [0,2,42,6]	-	65	80	125
☐	Mike Bossy ✂ [2,10,35,3]	50	75	100	150
☐	Bobby Clarke ✂ [4,22,21,3]	40	65	80	125
☐	Yvan Cournoyer ✂ [0,7,43,0]	-	65	80	-
☐	Bob Gainey ✂ [1,16,33,0]	40	65	80	-
☐	Guy Lafleur ✂ [2,23,23,2]	75	100	150	200
☐	Guy Lapointe ✂ [0,1,45,4]	-	65	80	125
☐	Reggie Leach ✂ [0,2,47,1]	-	65	80	125
☐	Bob Nystrom ✂ [5,37,8,0]	40	65	80	-
☐	Bernie Parent (G) ✂ [0,11,38,1]	-	65	80	125
☐	Denis Potvin ✂ [5,42,3,0]	40	65	80	-
☐	Larry Robinson ✂ [2,23,24,1]	40	65	80	125
☐	Serge Savard ✂ [4,14,28,4]	40	65	80	125
☐	Dave Schultz ✂ [0,1,47,2]	-	65	80	125
☐	Steve Shutt ✂ [2,14,34,0]	40	65	80	-
☐	Billy Smith (G) ✂ [15,28,6,1]	40	65	80	125
☐	Bryan Trottier ✂ [2,40,8,0]	40	65	80	-
☐	Joe Watson ✂ [6,32,12,0]	40	65	80	-

STANLEY CUP DYNASTY IN THE NUMBERS

Actual realized pricing on these scarce cards may vary considerably from pricing listed below.

	Insert (#/10)	8.5	9	9.5
☐	Bill Barber ✂ [0,4,6]	-	100	150
☐	Mike Bossy ✂ [1,4,5]	300	475	550
☐	Bobby Clarke ✂ [2,5,3]	150	225	275
☐	Yvan Cournoyer ✂ [1,7,2]	100	175	200
☐	Bob Gainey ✂ [4,3,3]	100	175	200
☐	Guy Lafleur ✂ [0,4,6]	-	600	700
☐	Guy Lapointe ✂ [1,4,5]	75	100	150
☐	Reggie Leach ✂ [0,5,5]	-	100	150
☐	Bob Nystrom ✂ [2,6,2]	75	100	150
☐	Bernie Parent (G) ✂ [0,8,2]	-	225	275
☐	Denis Potvin ✂ [3,5,2]	150	225	275
☐	Larry Robinson ✂ [2,5,3]	100	175	200
☐	Serge Savard ✂ [1,6,3]	75	125	150
☐	Dave Schultz ✂ [0,5,5]	-	100	150
☐	Steve Shutt ✂ [1,6,3]	75	100	150
☐	Billy Smith (G) ✂ [0,6,4]	-	225	275
☐	Bryan Trottier ✂ [0,7,3]	-	300	350
☐	Joe Watson ✂ [1,9,0]	75	100	-

STANLEY CUP PLAYOFF RECORDS

Actual realized pricing on these rare cards may vary considerably from pricing listed below.

	Insert	8	8.5	9	9.5
☐	M. Bossy, NYIs. ✂ (#/50) [0,0,47,3]	-	-	100	150
☐	47G W. Gretzky, Edmo. ✂ (#/10)	-	650	1,000	-
☐	382P W. Gretzky, LosA. ✂ (#/50)	150	200	300	-
☐	Wayne Gretzky ✂ (#/50)	150	200	300	-
☐	Wayne Gretzky ✂ (#/50)	150	200	300	-
☐	Wayne Gretzky ✂ (#/10)	-	650	1,000	-
☐	Wayne Gretzky ✂ (#/10)	-	650	1,000	-
☐	Wayne Gretzky ✂ (#/10)	-	650	1,000	-
☐	Wayne Gretzky ✂ (#/10)	-	650	1000	1200
☐	Jari Kurri ✂ (#/50) [0,0,49,1]	-	-	80	125
☐	Jari Kurri ✂ (#/50) [0,41,9,0]	-	65	80	-
☐	Reggie Leach ✂ (#/50) [0,0,50,0]	-	-	80	-
☐	Mario Lemieux ✂ (#/50) [0,0,33,17]	-	-	225	300
☐	14G M. Messier, Edmo. ✂ Blue (#/50)	40	65	80	-
☐	14G M. Messier, Edmo. ✂ White (#/50)	40	65	80	-
☐	Mark Messier ✂ (#/50)	40	65	80	-
☐	Maurice Richard ✂ (#/10) [0,1,9,0]	-	375	600	-
☐	Larry Robinson ✂ (#/50) [2,46,2,0]	40	65	80	-
☐	P. Roy (G) ✂ (#/50) [15,30,5,0]	100	150	225	-
☐	P. Roy (G) ✂ (#/50) [7,40,3,0]	100	150	225	-
☐	Joe Sakic ✂ (#/50) [3,16,31,0]	50	75	100	-

STANLEY CUP WINNERS

Actual realized pricing on these rare cards may vary considerably from pricing listed below.

	Insert (#/30)	8	8.5	9	9.5
☐	Jean Béliveau ✂ [0,41,9,0]	-	100	75	-
☐	Johnny Bower (G) ✂ [9,36,5,0]	50	75	100	-
☐	Turk Broda (G) ✂ (#/10) [0,10,0,0]	75	-		
☐	Yvan Cournoyer ✂ [0,0,50,0]	-	-	100	-
☐	Grant Fuhr (G) ✂ [3,42,5,0]	50	75	100	-
☐	Bob Gainey ✂ [0,6,44,0]	-	75	100	-
☐	Wayne Gretzky ✂ [2,39,9,0]	150	200	300	-
☐	Doug Harvey ✂ [1,41,8,0]	50	75	100	-
☐	Gordie Howe/10 ✂ (#/10) [1,8,1,0]	375	450	700	-
☐	Red Kelly ✂ [2,41,7,0]	50	75	100	-
☐	Ted Kennedy ✂ [6,42,2,0]	50	75	100	-
☐	Jari Kurri ✂ [0,2,48,0]	-	75	75	-
☐	Guy Lafleur ✂ [1,21,28,0]	75	100	150	-
☐	Jacques Laperrière ✂ [1,41,8,0]	50	75	100	-
☐	Guy Lapointe ✂ [1,34,15,0]	50	75	100	-
☐	Ted Lindsay ✂ [0,0,49,1]	-	-	100	150
☐	Frank Mahovlich ✂ [2,35,13,0]	50	75	100	-
☐	Mark Messier ✂ [3,43,4,0]	50	75	100	-
☐	J. Plante (G) ✂ (#/10) [0,10,0,0]	-	250	-	-
☐	Denis Potvin ✂ [2,40,8,0]	50	75	100	-
☐	Henri Richard ✂ [1,35,14,0]	50	75	100	-
☐	Maurice Richard ✂ [0,1,49,0]	-	125	200	-
☐	Larry Robinson ✂ [4,40,6,0]	50	75	100	-
☐	Serge Savard ✂ [5,20,25,0]	50	75	100	-
☐	Terry Sawchuk (G) ✂ [0,0,49,1]	-	-	150	200
☐	Steve Shutt ✂ [4,44,2,0]	50	75	100	-
☐	Billy Smith (G) ✂ [4,29,17,0]	50	75	100	-
☐	Bryan Trottier ✂ [0,0,50,0]	-	-	100	-

ULTIMATE CAPTAINS

Actual realized pricing on these scarce cards may vary considerably from pricing listed below.

	Insert (#/5)	8	8.5	9	9.5
☐	Daniel Alfredsson ✂ [1,2,2,0]	225	250	350	-
☐	Jean Béliveau ✂ [0,1,4,0]	-	275	400	-
☐	Johnny Bucyk ✂ [0,4,0,1]	-	125	-	300
☐	Ron Francis ✂ [0,2,3,0]	-	125	175	-
☐	Wayne Gretzky ✂ [0,0,5,0]	-	-	1,200	-
☐	Jaromir Jagr ✂ [0,4,1,0]	-	200	300	-
☐	Paul Kariya ✂ [0,0,1,4]	-	-	400	700
☐	Brian Leetch ✂ [0,1,4,0]	-	125	175	-
☐	Mario Lemieux ✂ [0,0,5,0]	-	-	900	-
☐	Gilbert Perreault ✂ [0,3,2,0]	-	125	175	-
☐	Denis Potvin ✂ [0,3,2,0]	-	125	175	-
☐	Chris Pronger ✂ [0,0,0,5]	-	-	-	250
☐	Henri Richard ✂ [0,3,2,0]	-	125	175	-
☐	Mats Sundin ✂ [0,0,4,1]	-	-	300	500
☐	Steve Yzerman ✂ [0,2,3,0]	-	500	700	-

WAVING THE FLAG

Actual realized pricing on these rare cards may vary considerably from pricing listed below.

	Insert (#/30)	8	8.5	9	9.5
☐	Tony Amonte ✂ [0,25,5,0]	-	75	100	150
☐	Martin Brodeur (G) ✂ [0,0,29,1]	-	-	175	225
☐	Pavel Bure ✂ [0,20,10,0]	-	75	100	-
☐	Dominik Hasek (G) ✂ [0,5,23,2]	-	75	100	150
☐	Martin Havlat ✂ [0,5,24,1]	-	75	100	150
☐	Milan Hejduk ✂ [0,4,22,4]	-	75	100	150
☐	Brett Hull ✂ [0,0,23,7]	-	-	100	150
☐	Jani Hurme (G) ✂ [0,6,24,0]	-	75	100	-
☐	Mario Lemieux ✂ [0,13,17,0]	-	75	100	150
☐	Jaromir Jagr ✂ [0,0,29,1]	-	-	100	150
☐	Curtis Joseph (G) ✂ [0,0,29,1]	-	-	100	150
☐	Sami Kapanen ✂ [0,0,28,2]	-	-	100	150
☐	Paul Kariya ✂ [0,16,14,0]	-	100	150	-
☐	Darius Kasparaitis ✂ [2,19,9,0]	50	75	100	-
☐	Nikolai Khabibulin (G) ✂ [0,3,27,0]	-	75	100	-
☐	Miikka Kiprusoff ✂ [0,5,23,2]	-	75	100	150
☐	John LeClair ✂ [1,24,5,0]	50	75	100	-
☐	Brian Leetch ✂ [0,22,8,0]	-	75	100	-
☐	Markus Näslund ✂ [0,5,21,4]	-	250	325	-
☐	Nicklas Lidström ✂ [0,0,28,2]	-	-	100	150
☐	Eric Lindros ✂ [0,0,30,0]	-	-	100	-
☐	Mike Modano ✂ [0,15,14,1]	-	75	100	150
☐	Chris Pronger ✂ [0,4,21,5]	-	75	100	150
☐	Jeremy Roenick ✂ [0,0,28,2]	-	-	100	150
☐	Joe Sakic ✂ [0,8,19,3]	-	125	175	225
☐	Tommy Salo (G) ✂ [0,0,29,1]	-	-	100	150
☐	Teemu Selänne ✂ [0,2,24,4]	-	75	100	150
☐	Mats Sundin ✂ [0,3,21,6]	-	75	100	150
☐	Keith Tkachuk ✂ [0,6,24,0]	-	75	100	-
☐	Doug Weight ✂ [0,0,30,0]	-	-	100	-
☐	Alexei Yashin ✂ [0,1,29,0]	-	75	100	-
☐	Steve Yzerman ✂ [0,4,25,1]	-	200	250	350

AWARD WINNERS

These cards are scarce. We do not have full grading information on these cards.

	Insert (#/10)	8	8.5	9	9.5
☐	Dany Heatley, Atla. Calder ✂				
☐	José Théodore, Mont. Hart ✂				
☐	José Théodore, Mont. Vézina ✂				

MADE TO ORDER

	Insert (#/1)
☐	Wayne Gretzky, Edmo. ✂
☐	Wayne Gretzky, NYRa. ✂
☐	Mario Lemieux, Pitt. Away ✂
☐	Mario Lemieux, Pitt. Home 1 ✂
☐	Mario Lemieux, Pitt. Home 2 ✂
☐	Redemption (to be determined)
☐	Redemption (to be determined)
☐	Redemption (to be determined)
☐	Redemption (to be determined)
☐	Redemption (to be determined)

2001 - 02 UPPER DECK

This brand is produced by The Upper Deck Company. Series One was released in November 2001 while Series Two was released in February 2002. There are two versions for each card 1-441: a base card and an Exclusive parallel. There is a third version (retail pack, different photo) for cards 412-441. Exclusives 1-180 and 232-411 are numbered to 100 copies each; Exclusives 181-231 and 412-441 are numbered to 50 copies each.

Shell Set 1 (180 cards):		**-**	**35.00**
Shell Set 2 (180 cards):		**-**	**35.00**
Complete Set (441 cards):		**4,500**	**500.00**

	Description	Exclusive	Base
☐ ☐	1 Paul Kariya, Anah.	40.00	1.00
☐ ☐	2 Jeff Friesen, Anah.	5.00	.20
☐ ☐	3 Mike Leclerc, Anah.	4.00	.20
☐ ☐	4 Andy McDonald, Anah.	4.00	.20
☐ ☐	5 Jean-Sébastien Giguère (G), Anah.	20.00	.50
☐ ☐	6 Steve Rucchin, Anah.	5.00	.20
☐ ☐	7 Ray Ferraro, Atla.	4.00	.20
☐ ☐	8 Milan Hnilicka (G), Atla.	5.00	.20
☐ ☐	9 Patrik Stefan, Atla.	5.00	.20
☐ ☐	10 Jiri Slegr, Atla.	4.00	.20
☐ ☐	11 Jeff Odgers, Atla.	4.00	.20
☐ ☐	12 Stephen Guolla, Atla.	4.00	.20
☐ ☐	13 Joe Thornton, Bost.	35.00	1.00
☐ ☐	14 Sergei Samsonov, Bost.	15.00	.50
☐ ☐	15 Kyle McLaren, Bost.	5.00	.20
☐ ☐	16 Jonathan Girard, Bost.	4.00	.20
☐ ☐	17 Brian Rolston, Bost.	5.00	.20
☐ ☐	18 Byron Dafoe, Bost.	10.00	.20
☐ ☐	19 Miroslav Satan, Buff.	5.00	.20
☐ ☐	20 Curtis Brown, Buff.	4.00	.20
☐ ☐	21 Stu Barnes, Buff.	4.00	.20
☐ ☐	22 Maxim Afinogenov, Buff.	10.00	.20
☐ ☐	23 Vaclav Varada, Buff.	4.00	.20
☐ ☐	24 Chris Gratton, Buff.	5.00	.20
☐ ☐	25 Jarome Iginla, Calg.	20.00	.50
☐ ☐	26 Dave Lowry, Calg.	5.00	.20
☐ ☐	27 Derek Morris, Calg.	5.00	.20
☐ ☐	28 Marc Savard, Calg.	5.00	.20
☐ ☐	29 Oleg Saprykin, Calg.	5.00	.20
☐ ☐	30 Craig Conroy, Calg.	5.00	.20
☐ ☐	31 Jeff O'Neill, Caro.	10.00	.20
☐ ☐	32 Arturs Irbe (G), Caro.	10.00	.20
☐ ☐	33 Shane Willis, Caro.	5.00	.20
☐ ☐	34 David Tanabe, Caro.	4.00	.20
☐ ☐	35 Josef Vasicek, Caro.	5.00	.20
☐ ☐	36 Sami Kapanen, Caro.	5.00	.20
☐ ☐	37 Steve Sullivan, Chic.	5.00	.20
☐ ☐	38 Tony Amonte, Chic.	15.00	.50
☐ ☐	39 Michael Nylander, Chic.	5.00	.20
☐ ☐	40 Éric Dazé, Chic.	10.00	.20
☐ ☐	41 Jocelyn Thibault, Chic.	10.00	.20
☐ ☐	42 Boris Mironov, Chic.	4.00	.20
☐ ☐	43 Ville Nieminen, Colo.	5.00	.20
☐ ☐	44 Alex Tanguay, Colo.	15.00	.50
☐ ☐	45 Milan Hejduk, Colo.	20.00	.50
☐ ☐	46 Chris Drury, Colo.	15.00	.50
☐ ☐	47 Peter Forsberg, Colo.	40.00	1.00
☐ ☐	48 Steven Reinprecht, Colo.	5.00	.20
☐ ☐	49 Ron Tugnutt, Colu.	10.00	.20
☐ ☐	50 Ray Whitney, Colu.	5.00	.20
☐ ☐	51 Geoff Sanderson, Colu.	5.00	.20
☐ ☐	52 Serge Aubin, Colu.	4.00	.20
☐ ☐	53 Espen Knutsen, Colu.	5.00	.20
☐ ☐	54 Rostislav Klesla, Colu.	5.00	.20
☐ ☐	55 Mike Modano, Dall.	30.00	1.00
☐ ☐	56 Ed Belfour (G), Dall.	30.00	1.00
☐ ☐	57 Pierre Turgeon, Dall.	10.00	.20
☐ ☐	58 Jamie Langenbrunner, Dall.	5.00	.20
☐ ☐	59 Brenden Morrow, Dall.	5.00	.20
☐ ☐	60 Donald Audette, Dall.	10.00	.20
☐ ☐	61 Steve Yzerman, Detr.	70.00	2.00
☐ ☐	62 Brett Hull, Detr.	30.00	1.00
☐ ☐	63 Nicklas Lidström, Detr.	15.00	.50
☐ ☐	64 Darren McCarty, Detr.	5.00	.20
☐ ☐	65 Luc Robitaille, Detr.	20.00	.50
☐ ☐	66 Dominik Hasek (G), Detr.	30.00	1.00
☐ ☐	67 Mike Comrie, Edmo.	20.00	.50
☐ ☐	68 Tommy Salo, Edmo.	10.00	.20
☐ ☐	69 Todd Marchant, Edmo.	5.00	.20
☐ ☐	70 Mike Grier, Edmo.	5.00	.20
☐ ☐	71 Ryan Smyth, Edmo.	10.00	.20

□□	72 Tom Poti, Edmo.	4.00	.20
□□	73 Pavel Bure, Flor.	20.00	.50
□□	74 Marcus Nilson, Flor.	4.00	.20
□□	75 Roberto Luongo, Flor.	20.00	.50
□□	76 Kevyn Adams, Flor.	4.00	.20
□□	77 Dan Boyle, Flor.	5.00	.20
□□	78 Robert Svehla, Flor.	5.00	.20
□□	79 Zigmund Palffy, LosA.	15.00	.50
□□	80 Éric Bélanger, LosA.	4.00	.20
□□	81 Ian Laperrière, LosA.	4.00	.20
□□	82 Bryan Smolinski, LosA.	4.00	.20
□□	83 Jozef Stümpel, LosA.	5.00	.20
□□	84 Adam Deadmarsh, LosA.	5.00	.20
□□	85 Marian Gaborik, MinW.	30.00	1.00
□□	86 Lubomir Sekeras, MinW.	4.00	.20
□□	87 Manny Fernandez, MinW.	10.00	.20
□□	88 Darby Hendrickson, MinW.	4.00	.20
□□	89 Roman Simicek, MinW.	4.00	.20
□□	90 Saku Koivu, Mont.	20.00	.50
□□	91 Richard Zednik, Mont.	10.00	.20
□□	92 Oleg Petrov, Mont.	5.00	.20
□□	93 Patrice Brisebois, Mont.	4.00	.20
□□	94 Brian Savage, Mont.	5.00	.20
□□	95 Jan Bulis, Mont.	4.00	.20
□□	96 David Legwand, Nash.	10.00	.20
□□	97 Cliff Ronning, Nash.	5.00	.20
□□	98 Mike Dunham, Nash.	10.00	.20
□□	99 Greg Johnson, Nash.	4.00	.20
□□	100 Kimmo Timonen, Nash.	4.00	.20
□□	101 Denis Arkhipov, Nash.	5.00	.20
□□	102 Patrik Elias, NJer.	20.00	.50
□□	103 Jason Arnott, NJer.	10.00	.20
□□	104 Scott Niedermayer, NJer.	5.00	.20
□□	105 Scott Gomez, NJer.	10.00	.20
□□	106 Scott Stevens, NJer.	10.00	.20
□□	107 John Madden, NJer.	5.00	.20
□□	108 Rick DiPietro, NYIs.	10.00	.20
□□	109 Mark Parrish, NYIs.	10.00	.20
□□	110 Brad Isbister, NYIs.	5.00	.20
□□	111 Michael Peca, NYIs.	10.00	.20
□□	112 Kenny Jönsson, NYIs.	5.00	.20
□□	113 Mariusz Czerkawski, NYIs.	5.00	.20
□□	114 Mark Messier, NYRa.	30.00	1.00
□□	115 Theoren Fleury, NYRa.	15.00	.50
□□	116 Radek Dvorak, NYRa.	5.00	.20
□□	117 Brian Leetch, NYRa.	15.00	.50
□□	118 Eric Lindros, NYRa.	30.00	1.00
□□	119 Mike Mottau, NYRa.	4.00	.20
□□	120 Radek Bonk, Otta.	5.00	.20
□□	121 Daniel Alfredsson, Otta.	15.00	.50
□□	122 Marian Hossa, Otta.	30.00	1.00
□□	123 Magnus Arvedson, Otta.	4.00	.20
□□	124 Patrick Lalime, Otta.	15.00	.50
□□	125 Martin Havlat, Otta.	15.00	.50
□□	126 Éric Desjardins, Phil.	5.00	.20
□□	127 Keith Primeau, Phil.	10.00	.20
□□	128 Mark Recchi, Phil.	10.00	.20
□□	129 Justin Williams, Phil.	5.00	.20
□□	130 Roman Cechmanek, Phil.	10.00	.20
□□	131 Jeremy Roenick, Phil.	20.00	.50
□□	132 Sean Burke, Phoe.	15.00	.50
□□	133 Shane Doan, Phoe.	5.00	.20
□□	134 Paul Mara, Phoe.	4.00	.20
□□	135 Michal Handzus, Phoe.	5.00	.20
□□	136 Ladislav Nagy, Phoe.	5.00	.20
□□	137 Mike Johnson, Phoe.	5.00	.20
□□	138 Mario Lemieux, Pitt.	90.00	3.00
□□	139 Alex Kovalev, Pitt.	15.00	.50
□□	140 Robert Lang, Pitt.	5.00	.20
□□	141 Kevin Stevens, Pitt.	5.00	.20
□□	142 Andrew Ference, Pitt.	4.00	.20
□□	143 Johan Hedberg (G), Pitt.	10.00	.20
□□	144 Owen Nolan, SanJ.	15.00	.50
□□	145 Teemu Selänne, SanJ.	20.00	.50
□□	146 Scott Thornton, SanJ.	4.00	.20
□□	147 Patrick Marleau, SanJ.	10.00	.20
□□	148 Alexander Korolyuk, SanJ.	4.00	.20
□□	149 Todd Harvey, SanJ.	5.00	.20
□□	150 Keith Tkachuk, SLou.	15.00	.50
□□	151 Pavol Demitra, SLou.	10.00	.20
□□	152 Al MacInnis, SLou.	10.00	.20
□□	153 Scott Young, SLou.	5.00	.20
□□	154 Cory Stillman, SLou.	5.00	.20
□□	155 Doug Weight, SLou.	15.00	.50
□□	156 Brad Richards, Tamp.	10.00	.20
□□	157 Nikolai Khabibulin, Tamp.	10.00	.20
□□	158 Martin St-Louis, Tamp.	10.00	.20
□□	159 Fredrik Modin, Tamp.	5.00	.20
□□	160 Matthew Barnaby, Tamp.	4.00	.20
□□	161 Gary Roberts, Toro.	10.00	.20
□□	162 Jonas Höglund, Toro.	4.00	.20
□□	163 Curtis Joseph (G), Toro.	30.00	1.00
□□	164 Mats Sundin, Toro.	30.00	1.00
□□	165 Darcy Tucker, Toro.	5.00	.20
□□	166 Shayne Corson, Toro.	5.00	.20
□□	167 Markus Näslund, Vanc.	30.00	1.00
□□	168 Daniel Sedin, Vanc.	10.00	.20
□□	169 Henrik Sedin, Vanc.	10.00	.20
□□	170 Brendan Morrison, Vanc.	5.00	.20
□□	171 Peter Schaefer, Vanc.	4.00	.20
□□	172 Harold Druken, Vanc.	5.00	.20
□□	173 Peter Bondra, Wash.	15.00	.50
□□	174 Olaf Kölzig, Wash.	15.00	.50
□□	175 Sergei Gonchar, Wash.	5.00	.20
□□	176 Jeff Halpern, Wash.	5.00	.20
□□	177 Andrei Nikolishin, Wash.	4.00	.20
□□	178 Jaromir Jagr, Wash.	30.00	1.00
□□	179 Steve Yzerman, Detr.	70.00	1.00
□□	180 Pavel Bure, Flor.	20.00	.20
□□	**181 Dan Snyder, Atla. RC**	**10.00**	**5.00**
□□	**182 Zdenek Kutlak, Bost. RC**	**10.00**	**5.00**
□□	**183 Michel Larocque, Chic. RC**	**10.00**	**5.00**
□□	184 Casey Hankinson, Chic.	10.00	2.00
□□	**185 Jody Shelley, Colu. RC**	**20.00**	**8.00**
□□	**186 Martin Spanhel, Colu. RC**	**10.00**	**5.00**
□□	**187 Mathieu Darche, Colu. RC**	**20.00**	**8.00**
□□	**188 Matt Davidson, Colu. RC**	**10.00**	**5.00**
□□	**189 Sean Selmser, Colu. RC**	**10.00**	**5.00**
□□	**190 Jason Chimera, Edmo. RC**	**20.00**	**8.00**
□□	**191 Andrei Podkonicky, Flor. RC**	**20.00**	**8.00**
□□	**192 Mike Matteucci, MinW. RC**	**10.00**	**5.00**
□□	**193 Pascal Dupuis, MinW. RC**	**30.00**	**12.00**
□□	**194 Francis Bélanger, Mont. RC**	**10.00**	**5.00**
□□	**195 Bill Bowler, Nash. RC**	**10.00**	**5.00**
□□	**196 Mike Danton, NJer. RC**	**20.00**	**8.00**
□□	**197 Stanislav Gron, NJer. RC**	**10.00**	**5.00**
□□	**198 Mikael Samuelsson, NYRa. RC**	**10.00**	**5.00**
□□	**199 Peter Smrek, NYRa. RC**	**10.00**	**5.00**
□□	**200 Joel Kwiatkowski, Otta. RC**	**10.00**	**5.00**
□□	**201 Tomas Divisek, Phil. RC**	**10.00**	**5.00**
□□	**202 Kirby Law, Phil. RC**	**10.00**	**5.00**
□□	**203 David Cullen, Phoe. RC**	**10.00**	**5.00**
□□	**204 Greg Crozier, Pitt. RC**	**10.00**	**5.00**
□□	**205 Billy Tibbetts, Pitt. RC**	**20.00**	**8.00**
□□	**206 Dale Clarke, SLou. RC**	**10.00**	**5.00**
□□	**207 Jaroslav Obsut, SLou. RC**	**10.00**	**5.00**
□□	**208 Thomas Ziegler, Tamp. RC**	**20.00**	**8.00**
□□	**209 Pat Kavanagh, Vanc. RC**	**10.00**	**5.00**
□□	**210 Mike Brown, Vanc. RC**	**20.00**	**3.00**
□□	**211 Ilya Kovalchuk, Atla. RC**	**300.00**	**60.00**
□□	212 Raymond Bourque, Bost.	50.00	5.00
□□	213 Brett Hull, Calg.	45.00	4.00
□□	214 Dominik Hasek (G), Chic.	45.00	4.00
□□	**215 Vaclav Nedorost, Colo. RC**	**30.00**	**12.00**
□□	216 Steve Yzerman, Detr.	100.00	10.00
□□	217 Mark Messier, Edmo.	45.00	4.00
□□	218 Mike Modano, Minn.	45.00	4.00
□□	219 Patrick Roy, Mont.	100.00	12.00
□□	220 John LeClair, Mont.	35.00	3.00
□□	221 Martin Brodeur, NJer.	70.00	7.00
□□	222 Tony Amonte, NYRa.	25.00	2.00
□□	223 Zigmund Palffy, NYIs.	25.00	2.00
□□	224 Roman Cechmanek, Phil.	15.00	1.00
□□	**225 Jeff Jillson, SanJ. RC**	**20.00**	**8.00**
□□	226 Jaromir Jagr, Pitt.	45.00	4.00
□□	**227 Nikita Alexeev, Tamp. RC**	**30.00**	**12.00**
□□	**228 Krys Kolanos, Phoe. RC**	**30.00**	**12.00**
□□	229 Peter Forsberg, Québ.	60.00	6.00
□□	230 Pavel Bure, Vanc.	35.00	3.00
□□	**231 Brian Sutherby, Wash. RC**	**20.00**	**8.00**
□□	232 Oleg Tverdovsky, Anah.	4.00	.20
□□	233 Steve Shields, Anah.	5.00	.20
□□	234 Matt Cullen, Anah.	5.00	.20
□□	235 Jason York, Anah.	4.00	.20
□□	236 Vitaly Vishnevski, Anah.	5.00	.20
□□	237 Marty McInnis, Anah.	4.00	.20
□□	238 Yannick Tremblay, Atla.	4.00	.20
□□	239 Dany Heatley, Atla.	75.00	2.00
□□	240 Lubos Bartecko, Atla.	4.00	.20
□□	241 Damian Rhodes, Atla.	5.00	.20
□□	242 Ilya Kovalchuk, Atla.	75.00	8.00
□□	243 Hnat Domenichelli, Atla.	4.00	.20
□□	244 Bill Guerin, Bost.	10.00	.20
□□	245 Martin Lapointe, Bost.	10.00	.20
□□	246 Scott Pellerin, Bost.	4.00	.20
□□	247 Rob Zamuner, Bost.	5.00	.20
□□	248 Jozef Stümpel, Bost.	5.00	.20
□□	249 Glen Murray, Bost.	10.00	.20
□□	250 Martin Biron (G), Buff.	10.00	.20
□□	251 Tim Connolly, Buff.	10.00	.20
□□	252 Vyacheslav Kozlov, Buff.	5.00	.20
□□	253 Jay McKee, Buff.	4.00	.20
□□	254 Jean-Pierre Dumont, Buff.	5.00	.20
□□	255 Alexei Zhitnik, Buff.	4.00	.20
□□	256 Roman Turek, Calg.	10.00	.20
□□	257 Igor Kravchuk, Calg.	4.00	.20
□□	258 Clarke Wilm, Calg.	4.00	.20
□□	259 Robyn Regehr, Calg.	4.00	.20
□□	260 Rob Niedermayer, Calg.	5.00	.20
□□	261 Dean McAmmond, Calg.	4.00	.20
□□	262 Ron Francis, Caro.	15.00	.50
□□	263 Martin Gélinas, Caro.	5.00	.20
□□	264 Rod Brind'Amour, Caro.	5.00	.20
□□	265 Sandis Ozolinsh, Caro.	5.00	.20
□□	266 Bates Battaglia, Caro.	5.00	.20
□□	267 Chris Dingman, Caro.	4.00	.20
□□	268 Igor Korolev, Chic.	4.00	.20
□□	269 Jaroslav Spacek, Chic.	4.00	.20
□□	270 Alexei Zhamnov, Chic.	5.00	.20
□□	271 Steve Thomas, Chic.	5.00	.20
□□	272 Jon Klemm, Chic.	4.00	.20
□□	273 Adam Foote, Colo.	5.00	.20
□□	274 Joe Sakic, Colo.	45.00	1.50
□□	275 Rob Blake, Colo.	15.00	.50
□□	276 Patrick Roy, Colo.	70.00	3.00
□□	277 Greg de Vries, Colo.	4.00	.20
□□	278 Dan Hinote, Colo.	5.00	.20
□□	279 Marc Denis, Colu.	10.00	.20
□□	280 David Vyborny, Colu.	4.00	.20
□□	281 Tyler Wright, Colu.	4.00	.20
□□	282 Mike Sillinger, Colu.	4.00	.20
□□	283 Bruce Gardiner, Colu.	4.00	.20
□□	284 Sergei Zubov, Dall.	5.00	.20
□□	285 Jere Lehtinen, Dall.	5.00	.20
□□	286 Joe Nieuwendyk, Dall.	10.00	.20
□□	287 Darryl Sydor, Dall.	5.00	.20
□□	288 Rob DiMaio, Dall.	4.00	.20
□□	289 Valeri Kamensky, Dall.	5.00	.20
□□	290 Brendan Shanahan, Detr.	30.00	1.00
□□	291 Igor Larionov, Detr.	15.00	.50
□□	292 Tomas Holmström, Detr.	5.00	.20
□□	293 Mathieu Dandenault, Detr.	4.00	.20
□□	294 Sergei Fedorov, Detr.	30.00	1.00
□□	295 Fredrik Olausson, Detr.	5.00	.20
□□	296 Anson Carter, Edmo.	10.00	.20
□□	297 Jochen Hecht, Edmo.	5.00	.20
□□	298 Dan Cleary, Edmo.	5.00	.20
□□	299 Janne Niinimaa, Edmo.	5.00	.20
□□	300 Rem Murray, Edmo.	4.00	.20
□□	301 Eric Brewer, Edmo.	10.00	.20
□□	302 Valeri Bure, Flor.	5.00	.20
□□	303 Viktor Kozlov, Flor.	5.00	.20
□□	304 Denis Shvidki, Flor.	5.00	.20
□□	305 Olli Jokinen, Flor.	5.00	.20
□□	306 Jason Wiemer, Flor.	4.00	.20
□□	307 Ryan Johnson, Flor.	4.00	.20
□□	308 Félix Potvin, LosA.	15.00	.50
□□	309 Jason Allison, LosA.	15.00	.50
□□	310 Mathieu Schneider, LosA.	5.00	.20
□□	311 Lubomir Visnovsky, LosA.	4.00	.20
□□	312 Mattias Norström, LosA.	5.00	.20
□□	313 Stephen Heinze, LosA.	4.00	.20
□□	314 Jim Dowd, MinW.	4.00	.20
□□	315 Wes Walz, MinW.	5.00	.20
□□	316 Filip Kuba, MinW.	4.00	.20
□□	317 Andrew Brunette, MinW.	4.00	.20
□□	318 Sergei Zholtok, MinW.	4.00	.20
□□	319 Stacy Roest, MinW.	4.00	.20
□□	320 José Théodore (G), Mont.	35.00	1.00
□□	321 Yanic Perreault, Mont.	5.00	.20
□□	322 Doug Gilmour, Mont.	15.00	.50
□□	323 Andreas Dackell, Mont.	4.00	.20
□□	324 Martin Rucinsky, Mont.	5.00	.20
□□	325 Chad Kilger, Mont.	5.00	.20
□□	326 Scott Walker, Nash.	5.00	.20
□□	327 Andy Delmore, Nash.	5.00	.20
□□	328 Patric Kjellberg, Nash.	4.00	.20
□□	329 Tomas Vokoun (G), Nash.	5.00	.20
□□	330 Vitali Yachmenev, Nash.	4.00	.20
□□	331 Bill Houlder, Nash.	4.00	.20
□□	332 Martin Brodeur, NJer.	45.00	1.50
□□	333 Bobby Holik, NJer.	5.00	.20
□□	334 Petr Sykora, NJer.	10.00	.20
□□	335 Brian Rafalski, NJer.	5.00	.20
□□	336 Sergei Brylin, NJer.	4.00	.20
□□	337 Randy McKay, NJer.	4.00	.20
□□	338 Alexei Yashin, NYIs.	15.00	.50
□□	339 Roman Hamrlik, NYIs.	5.00	.20
□□	340 Michael Peca, NYIs.	10.00	.20
□□	341 Dave Scatchard, NYIs.	4.00	.20
□□	342 Claude Lapointe, NYIs.	4.00	.20
□□	343 Chris Osgood, NYIs.	15.00	.50
□□	344 Mike Richter, NYRa.	10.00	.20
□□	345 Mike York, NYRa.	5.00	.20
□□	346 Eric Lindros, NYRa.	30.00	1.00
□□	347 Petr Nedved, NYRa.	5.00	.20
□□	348 Barrett Heisten, NYRa.	5.00	.20
□□	349 Zdeno Ciger, NYRa.	4.00	.20
□□	350 Shawn McEachern, Otta.	5.00	.20
□□	351 Wade Redden, Otta.	5.00	.20
□□	352 Bill Muckalt, Otta.	4.00	.20
□□	353 André Roy, Otta.	4.00	.20
□□	354 Sami Salo, Otta.	4.00	.20
□□	355 Todd White, Otta.	4.00	.20
□□	356 John LeClair, Phil.	20.00	.50
□□	357 Brian Boucher (G), Phil.	5.00	.20
□□	358 Pavel Brendl, Phil.	5.00	.20
□□	359 Jan Hlavac, Phil.	5.00	.20
□□	360 Daniel McGillis, Phil.	4.00	.20
□□	361 Simon Gagné, Phil.	20.00	.50
□□	362 Daymond Langkow, Phoe.	5.00	.20
□□	363 Sergei Berezin, Phoe.	5.00	.20
□□	364 Danny Markov, Phoe.	4.00	.20
□□	365 Tyler Bouck, Phoe.	4.00	.20
□□	366 Teppo Numminen, Phoe.	5.00	.20
□□	367 Trevor Letowski, Phoe.	4.00	.20
□□	368 Martin Straka, Pitt.	5.00	.20
□□	369 Jan Hrdina, Pitt.	5.00	.20
□□	370 Aleksey Morozov, Pitt.	5.00	.20
□□	371 Darius Kasparaitis, Pitt.	5.00	.20
□□	372 Toby Petersen, Pitt.	4.00	.20
□□	373 Kris Beech, Pitt.	5.00	.20
□□	374 Evgeni Nabokov, SanJ.	15.00	.50
□□	375 Mike Ricci, SanJ.	5.00	.20
□□	376 Brad Stuart, SanJ.	10.00	.20
□□	377 Adam Graves, SanJ.	10.00	.20
□□	378 Vincent Damphousse, SanJ.	15.00	.50
□□	379 Stéphane Matteau, SanJ.	4.00	.20
□□	380 Chris Pronger, SLou.	15.00	.50
□□	381 Brent Johnson, SLou.	10.00	.20
□□	382 Fred Brathwaite (G), SLou.	5.00	.20
□□	383 Dallas Drake, SLou.	4.00	.20
□□	384 Mike Eastwood, SLou.	4.00	.20
□□	385 Daniel Corso, SLou.	4.00	.20
□□	386 Brian Holzinger, Tamp.	4.00	.20
□□	387 Vincent Lecavalier, Tamp.	30.00	1.00
□□	388 Jassen Cullimore, Tamp.	4.00	.20
□□	389 Vaclav Prospal, Tamp.	5.00	.20
□□	390 Dave Andreychuk, Tamp.	5.00	.20
□□	391 Jimmie Ölvestad, Tamp.	4.00	.20
□□	392 Alexander Mogilny, Toro.	10.00	.20
□□	393 Tomas Kaberle, Toro.	5.00	.20
□□	394 Mikael Renberg, Toro.	5.00	.20
□□	395 Travis Green, Toro.	5.00	.20
□□	396 Robert Reichel, Toro.	5.00	.20
□□	397 Nikolai Antropov, Toro.	5.00	.20
□□	398 Andrew Cassels, Vanc.	5.00	.20
□□	399 Dan Cloutier, Vanc.	10.00	.20
□□	400 Ed Jovanovski, Vanc.	10.00	.20
□□	401 Todd Bertuzzi, Vanc.	35.00	1.00
□□	402 Trent Klatt, Vanc.	4.00	.20
□□	403 Donald Brashear, Vanc.	5.00	.20
□□	404 Jaromir Jagr, Wash.	30.00	1.00
□□	405 Joe Sacco, Wash.	4.00	.20
□□	406 Steve Konowalchuk, Wash.	5.00	.20
□□	407 Adam Oates, Wash.	10.00	.20
□□	408 Dmitri Khristich, Wash.	4.00	.20
□□	409 Dainius Zubrus, Wash.	5.00	.20
□□	410 John LeClair, Phil.	20.00	.20
□□	411 Martin Brodeur, NJer.	45.00	.50
□□	**412 Timo Pärssinen RC [Puck at skate]**	**10.00**	**5.00**
□□	**413 Ilja Bryzgalov RC**	**25.00**	**10.00**
□□	**414 Kevin Sawyer RC [On right skate]**	**10.00**	**5.00**
□□	**415 Kamil Piros RC [Facing forward]**	**20.00**	**8.00**
□□	**416 Ivan Huml RC**	**30.00**	**12.00**
□□	**417 Scott Nichol RC**	**10.00**	**5.00**
□□	**418 Jukka Hentunen RC [Black jersey]**	**10.00**	**5.00**
□□	**419 Erik Cole RC [On right skate]**	**30.00**	**12.00**
□□	**420 Ben Simon RC**	**10.00**	**5.00**
□□	**421 Niko Kapanen RC [Puck by stick]**	**30.00**	**12.00**
□□	**422 Pavel Datsyuk RC**	**180.00**	**40.00**
□□	**423 Ty Conklin RC**	**30**	**12.00**
□□	424 Wayne Gretzky	180.00	20.00
□□	**425 Niklas Hagman RC [Puck by stick]**	**20.00**	**8.00**
□□	**426 Kristian Huselius RC [Blue jersey]**	**40.00**	**16.00**
□□	**427 Jaroslav Bednar RC**	**20.00**	**8.00**
□□	**428 Nick Schultz RC [Green jersey]**	**20.00**	**8.00**
□□	**429 Travis Roche RC**	**10.00**	**5.00**
□□	**430 Martin Erat RC**	**20.00**	**8.00**
□□	**431 Andreas Salomonsson RC**	**10.00**	**5.00**
□□	**432 Josef Boumedienne RC**	**10.00**	**5.00**
□□	**433 Scott Clemmensen RC [Looking over shoulder]**	**20.00**	**8.00**
□□	**434 Dan Blackburn (G) RC**	**50.00**	**20.00**
□□	**435 Radek Martinek RC [Puck visible]**	**10.00**	**5.00**
□□	**436 Raffi Torres RC**	**30.00**	**12.00**
□□	**437 Ivan Ciernik RC**	**20.00**	**8.00**
□□	**438 Jiri Dopita RC**	**20.00**	**8.00**
□□	**439 Mark Rycroft RC**	**10.00**	**5.00**
□□	**440 Ryan Tobler RC [From shins up]**	**10.00**	**5.00**
□□	**441 Chris Corrinet RC**	**10.00**	**5.00**
□	**412 Timo Pärssinen RC [One hand on stick]**		**5.00**
□	**413 Ilja Bryzgalov RC**		**10.00**
□	**414 Kevin Sawyer RC [From ankles up]**		**5.00**
□	**415 Kamil Piros RC [Over the shoulder]**		**8.00**
□	**416 Ivan Huml RC**		**12.00**
□	**417 Scott Nichol RC**		**5.00**
□	**418 Jukka Hentunen RC [White jersey]**		**5.00**
□	**419 Erik Cole RC [From knees up]**		**12.00**
□	**420 Ben Simon RC**		**5.00**
□	**421 Niko Kapanen RC [Right skate crossing over]**		**12.00**
□	**422 Pavel Datsyuk RC**		**40.00**
□	**423 Ty Conklin RC**		**12.00**
□	424 Wayne Gretzky		18.00
□	**425 Niklas Hagman RC [From knees up]**		**8.00**
□	**426 Kristian Huselius RC [White jersey]**		**16.00**
□	**427 Jaroslav Bednar RC**		**8.00**
□	**428 Nick Schultz RC [White jersey]**		**8.00**

☐ 429 Travis Roche RC	5.00
☐ 430 Martin Erat RC	8.00
☐ 431 Andreas Salomonsson RC	5.00
☐ 432 Josef Boumedienne RC	5.00
☐ 433 Scott Clemmensen RC [Mask off]	8.00
☐ 434 Dan Blackburn (G) RC	20.00
☐ 435 Radek Martinek RC [Puck not visible]	5.00
☐ 436 Raffi Torres RC	12.00
☐ 437 Ivan Ciernik RC	8.00
☐ 438 Jiri Dopita RC	8.00
☐ 439 Mark Rycroft RC	5.00
☐ 440 Ryan Tobler RC [On right skate]	5.00
☐ 441 Chris Corrinet RC	5.00

CRUNCH TIMERS

Insert Set (15 cards):	30.00
UD2 Insert (1:24)	CT
☐ CT1 Joe Sakic, Colo.	5.00
☐ CT2 Milan Hejduk, Colo.	2.00
☐ CT3 Chris Drury, Colo.	2.00
☐ CT4 Mike Modano, Dall.	3.00
☐ CT5 Brett Hull, Detr.	3.00
☐ CT6 Steve Yzerman, Detr.	8.00
☐ CT7 Zigmund Palffy, LosA.	2.00
☐ CT8 Alexei Yashin, NYIs.	2.00
☐ CT9 Jeremy Roenick, Phil.	2.00
☐ CT10 Mark Recchi, Phil.	2.00
☐ CT11 Teemu Selänne, SanJ.	2.00
☐ CT12 Keith Tkachuk, SLou.	2.00
☐ CT13 Markus Näslund, Vanc.	3.00
☐ CT14 Jaromir Jagr, Wash.	3.00
☐ CT15 Peter Bondra, Wash.	2.00

FANTASTIC FINISHERS

Insert Set (10 cards):	20.00
UD1 Insert (1:36)	FF
☐ FF1 Pavel Bure, Flor.	2.00
☐ FF2 Pavol Demitra, SLou.	2.00
☐ FF3 Markus Näslund, Vanc.	3.00
☐ FF4 Mario Lemieux, Pitt.	10.00
☐ FF5 John LeClair, Phil.	2.00
☐ FF6 Keith Tkachuk, SLou.	2.00
☐ FF7 Marian Hossa, Otta.	3.00
☐ FF8 Teemu Selänne, SanJ.	2.00
☐ FF9 Joe Sakic, Colo.	5.00
☐ FF10 Zigmund Palffy, LosA.	2.00

FRANCHISE CORNERSTONES

Insert Set (15 cards):	45.00
UD1 Insert (1:24)	FC
☐ FC1 Paul Kariya, Anah.	4.00
☐ FC2 Pavel Bure, Flor.	2.00
☐ FC3 Mario Lemieux, Pitt.	10.00
☐ FC4 Peter Forsberg, Colo.	4.00
☐ FC5 Vincent Lecavalier, Tamp.	3.00
☐ FC6 Joe Sakic, Colo.	5.00
☐ FC7 Zigmund Palffy, LosA.	2.00
☐ FC8 Martin Brodeur, NJer.	5.00
☐ FC9 Patrick Roy, Colo.	10.00
☐ FC10 Steve Yzerman, Detr.	8.00
☐ FC11 Mike Modano, Dall.	3.00
☐ FC12 Tony Amonte, Chic.	2.00
☐ FC13 Teemu Selänne, SanJ.	2.00
☐ FC14 John LeClair, Phil.	2.00
☐ FC15 Mats Sundin, Toro.	3.00

GATE ATTRACTIONS

Insert Set (15 cards):	40.00
UD1 Insert (1:24)	GA
☐ GA1 Mark Messier, NYRa.	3.00
☐ GA2 Theoren Fleury, NYRa.	2.00
☐ GA3 Keith Tkachuk, SLou.	2.00
☐ GA4 John LeClair, Phil.	2.00
☐ GA5 Mario Lemieux, Pitt.	10.00
☐ GA6 Alex Kovalev, Pitt.	2.00
☐ GA7 Chris Drury, Colo.	2.00
☐ GA8 Joe Sakic, Colo.	5.00
☐ GA9 Peter Forsberg, Colo.	4.00
☐ GA10 Paul Kariya, Anah.	4.00
☐ GA11 Teemu Selänne, SanJ.	2.00
☐ GA12 Steve Yzerman, Detr.	8.00
☐ GA13 Brendan Shanahan, Detr.	3.00
☐ GA14 Mike Modano, Dall.	3.00
☐ GA15 Chris Pronger, SLou.	2.00

GOALIES IN ACTION

Insert Set (10 cards):	20.00
UD1 Insert (1:36)	GIA
☐ GL1 Curtis Joseph (G), Toro.	3.00
☐ GL2 Ed Belfour (G), Dall.	3.00
☐ GL3 Martin Brodeur, NJer.	5.00
☐ GL4 Evgeni Nabokov, SanJ.	2.00
☐ GL5 Johan Hedberg (G), Pitt.	2.00
☐ GL6 Patrick Roy, Colo.	10.00
☐ GL7 Tommy Salo, Edmo.	2.00
☐ GL8 Patrick Lalime, Otta.	2.00
☐ GL9 Olaf Kölzig, Wash.	2.00
☐ GL10 Roberto Luongo, Flor.	2.00

LAST LINE OF DEFENSE

Insert Set (10 cards):	25.00
UD2 Insert (1:36)	LL
☐ LL1 Patrick Roy, Colo.	10.00
☐ LL2 Ed Belfour (G), Dall.	3.00
☐ LL3 Dominik Hasek (G), Detr.	3.00
☐ LL4 Félix Potvin, LosA.	2.00
☐ LL5 Martin Brodeur, NJer.	5.00
☐ LL6 Roman Cechmanek, Phil.	2.00
☐ LL7 Johan Hedberg (G), Pitt.	2.00
☐ LL8 Evgeni Nabokov, SanJ.	2.00
☐ LL9 Curtis Joseph (G), Toro.	3.00
☐ LL10 Olaf Kölzig, Wash.	2.00

LEADERS OF THE PACK

Insert Set (15 cards):	35.00
UD2 Insert (1:24)	LP
☐ LP1 Paul Kariya, Anah.	4.00
☐ LP2 Tony Amonte, Chic.	2.00
☐ LP3 Joe Sakic, Colo.	5.00
☐ LP4 Mike Modano, Dall.	3.00
☐ LP5 Steve Yzerman, Detr.	8.00
☐ LP6 Pavel Bure, Flor.	2.00
☐ LP7 Scott Stevens, NJer.	2.00
☐ LP8 Mark Messier, NYRa.	3.00
☐ LP9 Michael Peca, NYIs.	2.00
☐ LP10 Daniel Alfredsson, Otta.	2.00
☐ LP11 Mario Lemieux, Pitt.	10.00
☐ LP12 Owen Nolan, SanJ.	2.00
☐ LP13 Doug Weight, SLou.	2.00
☐ LP14 Chris Pronger, SLou.	2.00
☐ LP15 Mats Sundin, Toro.	3.00

SHOOTING STARS

Insert Set (20 cards):	30.00
UD2 Insert (1:9)	SS
☐ SS1 Paul Kariya, Anah.	3.00
☐ SS2 Bill Guerin, Bost.	1.00
☐ SS3 Joe Sakic, Colo.	4.00
☐ SS4 Milan Hejduk, Colo.	2.00
☐ SS5 Brett Hull, Detr.	2.00
☐ SS6 Brendan Shanahan, Detr.	2.00
☐ SS7 Luc Robitaille, Detr.	2.00
☐ SS8 Pavel Bure, Flor.	2.00
☐ SS9 Zigmund Palffy, LosA.	1.00
☐ SS10 Patrik Elias, NJer.	2.00
☐ SS11 Alexei Yashin, NYIs.	1.00
☐ SS12 John LeClair, Phil.	2.00
☐ SS13 Alex Kovalev, Pitt.	1.00
☐ SS14 Mario Lemieux, Pitt.	7.00
☐ SS15 Owen Nolan, SanJ.	1.00
☐ SS16 Teemu Selänne, SanJ.	2.00
☐ SS17 Alexander Mogilny, Toro.	1.00
☐ SS18 Markus Näslund, Vanc.	2.00
☐ SS19 Jaromir Jagr, Wash.	2.00
☐ SS20 Peter Bondra, Wash.	1.00

SKILLED STARS

Insert Set (20 cards):	40.00
UD1 Insert (1:9)	SS
☐ SS1 Paul Kariya, Anah.	3.00
☐ SS2 Mario Lemieux, Pitt.	7.00
☐ SS3 Chris Pronger, SLou.	1.00
☐ SS4 Teemu Selänne, SanJ.	2.00
☐ SS5 Owen Nolan, SanJ.	1.00
☐ SS6 Pavel Bure, Flor.	2.00
☐ SS7 Keith Tkachuk, SLou.	1.00
☐ SS8 Mike Modano, Dall.	2.00
☐ SS9 Peter Forsberg, Colo.	3.00
☐ SS10 Zigmund Palffy, LosA.	1.00
☐ SS11 Martin Brodeur, NJer.	4.00
☐ SS12 Patrick Roy, Colo.	7.00
☐ SS13 Joe Sakic, Colo.	4.00
☐ SS14 Raymond Bourque, Colo.	3.00
☐ SS15 Steve Yzerman, Detr.	6.00
☐ SS16 Roman Cechmanek, Phil.	1.00
☐ SS17 Mark Messier, NYRa.	2.00
☐ SS18 Vincent Lecavalier, Tamp.	2.00
☐ SS19 John LeClair, Phil.	2.00
☐ SS20 Tony Amonte, Chic.	1.00

ALL-STAR JERSEY

The complete set price includes only one swatch variation per player.

Insert Set (9 cards):	150.00
UD1 Insert (1:144)	ASJ
☐ Chris Chelios, AS '93 ✂	20.00
☐ Theoren Fleury, AS ✂	20.00
☐ Jaromir Jagr, AS '99 ✂ Purple	25.00
☐ Guy Lafleur, AS '91 ✂ Black	35.00
☐ Guy Lafleur, AS '91 ✂ White	35.00
☐ Guy Lafleur, AS '91 ✂ Orange	35.00
☐ Al MacInnis, AS '99 ✂ Burgandy	20.00
☐ Al MacInnis, AS '99 ✂ White	20.00
☐ Mike Modano, AS '00 ✂ Blue	25.00
☐ Joe Sakic, AS '94 ✂	40.00
☐ Teemu Selänne, AS '99 ✂	20.00
☐ Mats Sundin, AS ✂ Red	25.00

COMBO JERSEY

Insert Set (9 cards):	525.00
UD1 Insert	Combo
☐ P. Forsberg ✂ / P. Roy ✂	100.00
☐ P. Kariya ✂ / T. Selänne ✂	50.00
☐ J. Jagr ✂ / M. Lemieux ✂	75.00
☐ M. Modano ✂ / J. Nieuwendyk ✂	25.00
☐ R. Cechmanek ✂ / K. Primeau ✂	25.00
☐ D. Sedin ✂ / H. Sedin ✂	25.00
☐ Forsberg ✂ / Roy ✂ / Sakic ✂	175.00
☐ Belfour (G) ✂ / Modano ✂ Nieuwendyk ✂	100.00
☐ Fedorov ✂ / Shanahan ✂ / Yzerman ✂	125.00

GENERATION NEXT JERSEY

Insert Set (10 cards):	100.00
UD2 Insert	GN
☐ Serge Aubin, Colu. ✂	12.00
☐ Martin Biron (G), Buff. ✂ Black	15.00
☐ Radek Bonk, Otta. ✂	12.00
☐ Rico Fata, NYRa. ✂	12.00
☐ Simon Gagné, Phil. ✂	25.00
☐ Manny Malhotra, NYRa. ✂ Blue	12.00
☐ Patrick Marleau, SanJ. ✂ Teal	15.00
☐ Maxime* Ouellet (G), Phil. ✂ [Orange]	12.00
☐ Justin Williams, Phil. ✂ White	12.00
☐ Mike York, NYRa. ✂ White	12.00
☐ Mike York, NYRa. ✂ Blue	12.00

GOALTENDERS JERSEY

Insert Set (7 cards):	150.00
UD1 Insert (1:288)	GJ
☐ Brian Boucher (G), Phil. ✂	25.00
☐ Dominik Hasek (G), Buff. ✂	30.00
☐ Jani Hurme (G), Otta. ✂	25.00
☐ Curtis Joseph (G), Toro. ✂	30.00
☐ Maxime Ouellet (G), Phil. ✂	25.00
☐ Patrick Roy (G), Colo. ✂	70.00
☐ Marty Turco (G), Dall. ✂	25.00

JERSEY PATCH

Insert Set (9 cards):	1,400
UD1 Insert	JP
☐ Raymond Bourque, Colo. ✂	175.00
☐ Sergei Fedorov, Detr. ✂	150.00
☐ Peter Forsberg, Colo. ✂	200.00
☐ Paul Kariya, Anah. ✂	200.00
☐ John LeClair, Phil. ✂	100.00
☐ Mario Lemieux, Pitt. ✂	450.00
☐ Brendan Shanahan, Detr. ✂	150.00
☐ Doug Weight, Edmo. ✂	100.00
☐ Steve Yzerman, Detr. ✂	350.00

LEGENDARY CUT SIGNATURES

Insert	Cut
☐ Clarence Campbell, NHL President ✍	
☐ Doug Harvey, Mont. ✍	
☐ Eddie Shore, Bost. ✍	
☐ Jacques Plante, Mont. ✍	
☐ King Clancy, Toro. ✍	
☐ Lord Stanley, Hockey Icon ✍	
☐ Sid Abel, Detr. ✍	
☐ Terry Sawchuk, Detr. ✍	

NEXT GENERATION JERSEY

The complete set price includes only one swatch variation per player.

Insert Set (13 cards):	200.00
UD1 Insert	NG
☐ Curtis Brown, Buff. ✂	20.00
☐ Éric Dazé, Chic. ✂ Red	20.00
☐ Shane Doan, Phoe. ✂	20.00
☐ Ruslan Fedotenko, Phil. ✂ Orange	20.00
☐ Marian Hossa, Otta. ✂	30.00
☐ Jani Hurme (G), Otta. ✂	20.00
☐ Jarome Iginla, Calg. ✂ White	25.00
☐ Jarome Iginla, Calg. ✂ Red	25.00
☐ Vincent Lecavalier, Tamp. ✂	30.00
☐ Daniel Sedin, Vanc. ✂	20.00
☐ Henrik Sedin, Vanc. ✂	20.00
☐ Patrik Stefan, Atla. ✂ Blue	20.00
☐ Marty Turco, Dall. ✂	20.00
☐ Justin Williams, Phil. ✂	20.00
☐ Mike York, NYRa. ✂	20.00

PATCH LOGOS

Insert Set (9 cards):	1,600
UD2 Insert	PL
☐ Martin Brodeur, NJer. ✂	225.00
☐ Sergei Fedorov, Detr. ✂	150.00
☐ Peter Forsberg, Colo. ✂	200.00
☐ Jaromir Jagr, Wash. ✂	150.00
☐ Paul Kariya, Anah. ✂	200.00
☐ Mario Lemieux, Pitt. ✂	450.00
☐ Mike Modano, Dall. ✂	150.00
☐ Patrick Roy, Colo. ✂	350.00
☐ Steve Yzerman, Detr. ✂	350.00

PATCH NAMES

Insert Set (7 cards):	2,000
UD2 Insert	NA
☐ Peter Forsberg, Colo. ✂	300.00
☐ John LeClair, Phil. ✂	175.00

☐	Mario Lemieux, Pitt. ✄	675.00
☐	Patrick Roy, Colo. ✄	525.00
☐	Joe Sakic, Colo. ✄	350.00
☐	Brendan Shanahan, Detr. ✄	225.00
☐	Steve Yzerman, Detr. ✄	525.00

PATCH NUMBERS

Insert Set (8 cards):		1,400
	UD2 Insert	PN
☐	Paul Kariya, Anah. ✄	200.00
☐	John LeClair, Phil. ✄	100.00
☐	Mario Lemieux, Pitt. ✄	450.00
☐	Mike Modano, Dall. ✄	150.00
☐	Patrick Roy, Colo. ✄	350.00
☐	Joe Sakic, Colo. ✄	225.00
☐	Brendan Shanahan, Detr. ✄	150.00
☐	Steve Yzerman, Detr. ✄ White	350.00

PHENOMENAL FINISHERS

The complete set price includes only one swatch variation per player.

Insert Set (10 cards):		100.00
	UD2 Insert	PF
☐	Jaromir Jagr, Wash. ✄ Black	20.00
☐	Paul Kariya, Anah. ✄	30.00
☐	Alex Kovalev, Pitt. ✄ Black	15.00
☐	Alex Kovalev, Pitt. ✄ Black/White	15.00
☐	John LeClair, Phil. ✄ Black	20.00
☐	Mario Lemieux, Pitt. ✄	65.00
☐	Markus Näslund, Vanc. ✄ White	25.00
☐	Zigmund Palffy, LosA. ✄	15.00
☐	Keith Primeau, Phil. ✄	12.00
☐	Joe Sakic, Colo. ✄	30.00
☐	Brendan Shanahan, Detr. ✄ Red	20.00

PRIDE OF A NATION

The complete set price includes only one swatch variation per player.

Insert Set (15 cards):		400.00
	UD2 Insert	PN
☐	Tony Amonte, Chic. ✄ Red	25.00
☐	Martin Brodeur (G), NJer. ✄ Red	50.00
☐	Sergei Fedorov, Detr. ✄ Red	25.00
☐	Peter Forsberg, Colo. ✄ Blue	50.00
☐	Bill Guerin, Bost. ✄ White	25.00
☐	Dominik Hasek (G), Detr. ✄ White	25.00
☐	Jaromir Jagr, Wash. ✄	25.00
☐	Saku Koivu, Mont. ✄ White	25.00
☐	Viktor Kozlov, Flor. ✄ Red	25.00
☐	Mario Lemieux, Pitt. ✄	100.00
☐	Patrick Roy (G), Colo. ✄ White	75.00
☐	Joe Sakic, Colo. ✄ White	50.00
☐	Teemu Selänne, SanJ. ✄ Blue	25.00
☐	Doug Weight, SLou. ✄ Blue	25.00
☐	Steve Yzerman, Detr. ✄	75.00

PRIDE OF A NATION DOUBLE

Insert Set (10 cards):		600.00
	UD2 Insert	PND
☐	T. Amonte ✄ Red / B. Guerin ✄ Red	50.00
☐	S. Fedorov ✄ V. Kozlov ✄	50.00
☐	P. Forsberg ✄ Blue / M. Sundin ✄ Blue	75.00
☐	D. Hasek (G) ✄ White / J. Jagr ✄ White	75.00
☐	M. Lemieux ✄ White / P. Kariya ✄ White	175.00
☐	J. LeClair ✄ White / M. Modano ✄ White	50.00
☐	P. Roy (G) ✄ White / J. Sakic ✄ White	150.00
☐	S. Stevens ✄ Red / M. Brodeur (G) ✄ White	75.00
☐	T. Selänne ✄ White / S. Koivu ✄ White	50.00
☐	S. Yzerman ✄ Red / B. Shanahan ✄ White	125.00

PRIDE OF A NATION TRIPLE

Insert Set (5 cards):		900
	UD2 Insert (#/20)	PNT
☐	Yzerman ✄ / Roy (G) ✄ / Lemieux ✄	450.00
☐	Hasek (G) ✄ White / Jagr ✄ White / Lang ✄ White	200.00
☐	Fedorov ✄ / Kovalev ✄ / Kozlov ✄	200.00
☐	Forsberg ✄ Blue / Sundin ✄ Blue / Lidström ✄ White	200.00
☐	Amonte ✄ / Weight ✄ / Leetch ✄	200.00

PRIDE OF THE LEAFS

Insert Set (9 cards):		575.00
	UD2 Insert (75 copies per player)	ML
☐	Nikolai Antropov, Toro. ✄ White/Blue	60.00
☐	Nikolai Antropov, Toro. ✄ White	60.00
☐	Sergei Berezin, Toro. ✄ White	60.00
☐	Wendel Clark, Toro. ✄ White	100.00
☐	Tie Domi, Toro. ✄ Blue	60.00
☐	Doug Gilmour, Toro. ✄ Blue	60.00
☐	Curtis Joseph (G), Toro. ✄ White	100.00
☐	Félix Potvin (G), Toro. ✄ White	100.00
☐	Börje Salming, Toro. ✄ White	100.00
☐	Mats Sundin, Toro. ✄ Blue	100.00
☐	Mats Sundin, Toro. ✄ Blue/White	150.00

STANLEY CUP FINALS SINGLE JERSEY

The complete set price includes only one swatch variation per player.

Insert Set (17 cards):		350.00
	UD2 Insert (1:144)	FJ
☐	Ed Belfour (G), Dall. ✄ White	30.00
☐	Martin Brodeur, NJer. ✄ White	40.00
☐	Chris Drury, Colo. ✄ Blue	15.00
☐	Sergei Fedorov, Detr. ✄	25.00
☐	Peter Forsberg, Colo. ✄ White	35.00
☐	Milan Hejduk, Colo. ✄ White	25.00
☐	John LeClair, Phil. ✄ Orange	25.00
☐	Claude Lemieux, NJer. ✄ White	15.00
☐	Claude Lemieux, NJer. ✄ Black/Red	15.00
☐	Mike Modano, Dall. ✄	25.00
☐	Joe Nieuwendyk, Dall. ✄	15.00
☐	Chris Osgood, Detr. ✄	15.00
☐	Patrick Roy, Colo. ✄ Burgandy	60.00
☐	Joe Sakic, Colo. ✄ White	40.00
☐	Joe Sakic, Colo. ✄ Burgandy	40.00
☐	Miroslav Satan, Buff. ✄ White	15.00
☐	Brendan Shanahan, Detr. ✄	25.00
☐	Scott Stevens, NJer. ✄ Red	15.00
☐	Scott Stevens, NJer. ✄ Red/White	15.00
☐	Steve Yzerman, Detr. ✄ Red	60.00

STANLEY CUP FINALS DOUBLE JERSEY

Insert Set (8 cards):		300.00
	UD2 Insert (1:288)	SCFSJ
☐	R. Bourque ✄ / P. Roy (G) ✄	75.00
☐	S. Fedorov ✄ Red / B. Shanahan ✄ Red	50.00
☐	M. Modano ✄ White / J. Nieuwendyk ✄ White	30.00
☐	S. Stevens ✄ Black / M. Brodeur (G) ✄ Red	50.00
☐	J. Sakic ✄ / P. Forsberg ✄	75.00
☐	M. Satan ✄ / D. Hasek (G) ✄	30.00
☐	A. Tanguay ✄ / C. Drury ✄	30.00
☐	S. Yzerman ✄ / N. Lidström ✄	75.00

STANLEY CUP FINALS TRIPLE JERSEY

Insert Set (3 cards):		500.00
	UD2 Insert	SCFTJ
☐	Nieuwendyk ✄ / Belfour (G) ✄ / Modano ✄	125.00
☐	Roy (G) ✄ / Sakic ✄ / Hejduk ✄	300.00
☐	Yzerman ✄ / Fedorov ✄ / Shanahan ✄	250.00

SUPERSTAR SWEATERS

The complete set price includes only one swatch variation per player.

Insert Set (10 cards):		325.00
	UD2 Insert (1:144)	SS
☐	Ray Bourque, Bost. ✄ White	35.00
☐	Martin Brodeur, NJer. ✄	40.00
☐	Chris Drury, Colo. ✄ Burgandy	15.00
☐	Chris Drury, Colo. ✄ Blue	15.00
☐	Peter Forsberg, Colo. ✄ White	35.00
☐	Wayne Gretzky, 1999 All-Star	125.00
☐	Paul Kariya, Anah. ✄ Purple	35.00
☐	Paul Kariya, Anah. ✄ Teal	40.00
☐	Al MacInnis, SLou. ✄ Blue	15.00
☐	Mike Modano, Dall. ✄	25.00
☐	Patrick Roy, Colo. ✄ Burgandy	60.00
☐	Steve Yzerman, Detr. ✄ Red	60.00

TANTALIZING TANDEMS

Insert Set (10 cards):		35.00
	UD2 Insert (1:36)	TT
☐	T1 Sergei Samsonov / Joe Thornton	6.00
☐	T2 Joe Sakic / Milan Hejduk	8.00
☐	T3 Brendan Shanahan / Steve Yzerman	10.00
☐	T4 Valeri Bure / Pavel Bure	3.00
☐	T5 Patrik Elias / Jason Arnott	4.00
☐	T6 Marian Hossa / Radek Bonk	4.00
☐	T7 John LeClair / Jeremy Roenick	5.00
☐	T8 Teemu Selänne / Owen Nolan	4.00
☐	T9 Keith Tkachuk / Pavol Demitra	3.00
☐	T10 Brad Richards / Vincent Lecavalier	5.00

TENDER'S THREADS

The complete set price includes only one swatch variation per player.

Insert Set (10 cards):		250.00
	UD2 Insert (1:240)	TT
☐	Brian Boucher (G), Phil. ✄ Black	25.00
☐	Brian Boucher (G), Phil. ✄ Orange	25.00
☐	Martin Brodeur (G), NJer. ✄ White	50.00
☐	Roman Cechmanek (G), Phil. ✄ Black	25.00
☐	Roman Cechmanek (G), Phil. ✄ Orange	25.00
☐	Mike Dunham (G), Nash. ✄ White	25.00
☐	Curtis Joseph (G), Toro. ✄ Blue	25.00
☐	Chris Osgood (G), NYIs. ✄	25.00
☐	Chris Osgood (G), NYIs. ✄ White/Red	25.00
☐	Mike Richter (G), NYRa. ✄ White	25.00
☐	Patrick Roy (G), Colo. ✄ Burgandy	75.00
☐	Patrick Roy (G), Colo. ✄ Grey/Blue/White	150.00
☐	José Théodore (G), Mont. ✄ White	50.00
☐	Jocelyn Thibault (G), Chic. ✄	25.00

UD JERSEY SIGNED

Insert Set (7 cards):		475.00
	UD1 Insert	JS
☐	Raymond Bourque, Colo. ✍ ✄ Blue	100.00
☐	John LeClair, Phil. ✍ ✄ White	75.00
☐	Mike Modano, Dall. ✍ ✄	75.00
☐	Daniel Sedin, Vanc. ✍ ✄	60.00
☐	Henrik Sedin, Vanc. ✍ ✄	60.00
☐	Doug Weight, SLou. ✍ ✄ Blue	60.00
☐	Steve Yzerman, Detr. ✍ ✄	225.00

UD SIGNED JERSEY

Insert Set (9 cards):		725.00
	UD2 Insert (#/150)	SJ
☐	SJ-EB Ed Belfour (G), Dall. ✍ ✄	100.00
☐	SJ-BO Raymond Bourque, Colo. ✍ ✄ White	100.00
☐	SJ-RB Raymond Bourque, Bost. ✍ ✄	100.00
☐	SJ-MB Martin Brodeur, NJer. ✍ ✄	150.00
☐	SJ-SG Simon Gagné, Phil. ✍ ✄	75.00
☐	SJ-CJ Curtis Joseph (G), Toro. ✍ ✄	100.00
☐	SJ-JL John LeClair, Phil. ✍ ✄	75.00
☐	SJ-MO Maxime* Ouellet, Phil. ✍ ✄	60.00
☐	SJ-SY Steve Yzerman, Detr. ✍ ✄	225.00

2001 - 02 UPPER DECK ALL-STAR FANTASY

Produced by The Upper Deck Company, this series was released in February 2002 at the All-Star Fantasy in Los Angeles, CA.

	Description	ASG
☐	Wayne Gretzky, All-Star	10.00
☐	Wayne Gretzky, LosA. [1989]	10.00
☐	Wayne Gretzky, LosA. [1994]	10.00

2001 - 02 UPPER DECK CHALLENGE FOR THE CUP

Produced by The Upper Deck Company, this series was released in March 2002.

Shell Set (90 cards):		30.00
Complete Set (135 cards):		200.00
	Description	Base
☐	1 Paul Kariya, Anah.	2.00
☐	2 Jeff Friesen, Anah.	.25
☐	3 Dany Heatley, Atla.	2.00
☐	4 Milan Hnilicka (G), Atla.	.25
☐	5 Joe Thornton, Bost.	1.50
☐	6 Bill Guerin, Bost.	.50
☐	7 Miroslav Satan, Buff.	.25
☐	8 Martin Biron (G), Buff.	.50
☐	9 Jarome Iginla, Calg.	1.00
☐	10 Roman Turek, Calg.	.50
☐	11 Craig Conroy, Calg.	.25
☐	12 Jeff O'Neill, Caro.	.50
☐	13 Arturs Irbe (G), Caro.	.50
☐	14 Tony Amonte, Chic.	.50
☐	15 Steve Sullivan, Chic.	.25
☐	16 Rob Blake, Colo.	.50
☐	17 Joe Sakic, Colo.	2.00
☐	18 Milan Hejduk, Colo.	1.00
☐	19 Chris Drury, Colo.	.50
☐	20 Patrick Roy, Colo.	4.50
☐	21 Espen Knutsen, Colu.	.25
☐	22 Ray Whitney, Colu.	.25
☐	23 Pierre Turgeon, Dall.	.50
☐	24 Ed Belfour (G), Dall.	1.50
☐	25 Mike Modano, Dall.	1.50
☐	26 Sergei Zubov, Dall.	.25
☐	27 Dominik Hasek (G), Detr.	1.50
☐	28 Steve Yzerman, Detr.	3.50
☐	29 Brendan Shanahan, Detr.	1.50
☐	30 Nicklas Lidström, Detr.	.50
☐	31 Luc Robitaille, Detr.	1.00
☐	32 Mike Comrie, Edmo.	1.00
☐	33 Ryan Smyth, Edmo.	.50
☐	34 Tommy Salo, Edmo.	.50
☐	35 Roberto Luongo, Flor.	1.00
☐	36 Valeri Bure, Flor.	.25
☐	37 Pavel Bure, Flor.	1.00
☐	38 Félix Potvin, LosA.	.50
☐	39 Jason Allison, LosA.	.50
☐	40 Zigmund Palffy, LosA.	.50
☐	41 Manny Fernandez, MinW.	.50
☐	42 Marian Gaborik, MinW.	1.50
☐	43 Andrew Brunette, MinW.	.25
☐	44 Brian Savage, Mont.	.25
☐	45 Jeff Hackett, Mont.	.25
☐	46 Oleg Petrov, Mont.	.25
☐	47 Cliff Ronning, Nash.	.25
☐	48 Mike Dunham, Nash.	.50
☐	49 Scott Walker, Nash.	.25
☐	50 Martin Brodeur, NJer.	2.00
☐	51 Scott Niedermayer, NJer.	.25
☐	52 Scott Gomez, NJer.	.50
☐	53 Patrik Elias, NJer.	1.00
☐	54 Alexei Yashin, NYIs.	.50
☐	55 Chris Osgood, NYIs.	.50
☐	56 Michael Peca, NYIs.	.50
☐	57 Mark Messier, NYRa.	1.50
☐	58 Theoren Fleury, NYRa.	.50
☐	59 Eric Lindros, NYRa.	1.50
☐	60 Brian Boucher (G), Phil.	.25
☐	61 John LeClair, Phil.	1.00
☐	62 Jeremy Roenick, Phil.	1.00
☐	63 Keith Primeau, Phil.	.50
☐	64 Michal Handzus, Phoe.	.25
☐	65 Claude Lemieux, Phoe.	.25
☐	66 Sean Burke, Phoe.	.50
☐	67 Alex Kovalev, Pitt.	.50
☐	68 Mario Lemieux, Pitt.	4.50
☐	69 Johan Hedberg (G), Pitt.	.50
☐	70 Martin Straka, Pitt.	.25
☐	71 Owen Nolan, SanJ.	.50
☐	72 Evgeni Nabokov, SanJ.	.50
☐	73 Teemu Selänne, SanJ.	1.00
☐	74 Doug Weight, SLou.	.50
☐	75 Brent Johnson, SLou.	.50
☐	76 Pavol Demitra, SLou.	.50
☐	77 Chris Pronger, SLou.	.50
☐	78 Keith Tkachuk, SLou.	.50
☐	79 Vincent Lecavalier, Tamp.	1.50
☐	80 Brad Richards, Tamp.	.50
☐	81 Nikolai Khabibulin, Tamp.	.50
☐	82 Curtis Joseph (G), Toro.	1.50
☐	83 Alexander Mogilny, Toro.	.50
☐	84 Mats Sundin, Toro.	1.50
☐	85 Trevor Linden, Vanc.	.50
☐	86 Markus Näslund, Vanc.	1.50
☐	87 Brendan Morrison, Vanc.	.25
☐	88 Jaromir Jagr, Wash.	1.50
☐	89 Olaf Kölzig, Wash.	.50
☐	90 Peter Bondra, Wash.	.50

UP & COMERS

	Insert (#/1000)	UC
☐	91 Ilja Bryzgalov, Anah. RC	10.00
☐	92 Timo Pärssinen, Anah. RC	5.00
☐	93 Kevin Sawyer, Anah. RC	5.00
☐	94 Brian Pothier, Atla. RC	5.00
☐	95 Ilya Kovalchuk, Atla. RC	60.00
☐	96 Kamil Piros, Atla. RC	10.00
☐	97 Ivan Huml, Bost. RC	15.00
☐	98 Jukka Hentunen, Calg. RC	5.00
☐	99 Scott Nichol, Calg. RC	5.00
☐	100 Erik Cole, Caro. RC	15.00
☐	101 Jaroslav Obsut, Colo. RC	5.00
☐	102 Vaclav Nedorost, Colo. RC	15.00
☐	103 Martin Spanhel, Colu. RC	5.00
☐	104 Niko Kapanen, Dall. RC	15.00
☐	105 Pavel Datsyuk, Detr. RC	50.00
☐	106 Ty Conklin, Edmo. RC	10.00
☐	107 Niklas Hagman, Flor. RC	10.00
☐	108 Kristian Huselius, Flor. RC	20.00
☐	109 Jaroslav Bednar, LosA. RC	10.00
☐	110 Pascal Dupuis, MinW. RC	15.00
☐	111 Mike Matteucci, MinW. RC	5.00
☐	112 Nick Schultz, MinW. RC	10.00
☐	113 Travis Roche, MinW. RC	5.00
☐	114 Martti Järventie, Mont.	4.00
☐	115 Martin Erat, Nash. RC	10.00
☐	116 Pavel Skrbek, Nash. RC	5.00
☐	117 Josef Boumedienne, NJer. RC	5.00
☐	118 Andreas Salomonsson, NJer. RC	5.00
☐	119 Scott Clemmensen, NJer. RC	10.00
☐	120 Mikael Samuelsson, NYRa. RC	5.00
☐	121 Dan Blackburn (G), NYRa. RC	25.00
☐	122 Richard Scott, NYRa. RC	5.00
☐	123 Radek Martinek, NYIs. RC	5.00
☐	124 Raffi Torres, NYIs. RC	15.00
☐	125 Ivan Ciernik, Otta. RC	10.00
☐	126 Jiri Dopita, Phil. RC	10.00
☐	127 Vaclav Pletka, Phil. RC	5.00
☐	128 Krys Kolanos, Phoe. RC	15.00
☐	129 David Cullen, Phoe. RC	5.00
☐	130 Jeff Jillson, SanJ. RC	10.00
☐	131 Mark Rycroft, SLou. RC	5.00
☐	132 Ryan Tobler, Tamp. RC	5.00
☐	133 Nikita Alexeev, Tamp. RC	15.00
☐	134 Brian Sutherby, Wash. RC	10.00
☐	135 Chris Corrinet, Wash. RC	5.00

ALL-TIME LINEUP

Insert Set (6 cards): 3035.00

	Insert (#/6)	ATL
☐	AT1 Bobby Hull, Chic.	450.00
☐	AT2 Wayne Gretzky, Edmo.	1000.00
☐	AT3 Gordie Howe, Detr.	700.00
☐	AT4 Bobby Orr, Bost.	1000.00
☐	AT5 Raymond Bourque, Bost.	300.00
☐	AT6 Patrick Roy, Colo.	600.00

BRILLIANT BACKSTOPS

Insert Set (10 cards): 240.00

	Insert (#/35)	BB
☐	BB1 Roman Turek (G), Calg.	25.00
☐	BB2 Arturs Irbe (G), Caro.	25.00
☐	BB3 Patrick Roy (G), Colo.	75.00
☐	BB4 Dominik Hasek (G), Detr.	25.00
☐	BB5 Tommy Salo (G), Edmo.	25.00
☐	BB6 Martin Brodeur (G), NJer.	50.00
☐	BB7 Roman Cechmanek (G), Phil.	25.00
☐	BB8 Evgeni Nabokov (G), SanJ.	25.00
☐	BB9 Curtis Joseph (G), Toro.	25.00
☐	BB10 Olaf Kölzig (G), Wash.	25.00

CENTURY MEN

Insert Set (10 cards): 150.00

	Insert (#/100)	CM
☐	CM1 Jeremy Roenick, Chic.	10.00
☐	CM2 Joe Sakic, Colo.	25.00
☐	CM3 Steve Yzerman, Detr.	40.00
☐	CM4 Sergei Fedorov, Detr.	15.00
☐	CM5 Luc Robitaille, LosA.	10.00
☐	CM6 Mark Messier, Edmo.	15.00
☐	CM7 Jaromir Jagr, Pitt.	15.00
☐	CM8 Mario Lemieux, Pitt.	50.00
☐	CM9 Brett Hull, SLou.	15.00
☐	CM10 Pavel Bure, Vanc.	10.00

CORNERSTONES

Insert Set (10 cards): 65.00

	Insert (#/250)	CR
☐	CR1 Paul Kariya, Anah.	5.00
☐	CR2 Ilya Kovalchuk, Atla.	15.00
☐	CR3 Joe Sakic, Colo.	10.00
☐	CR4 Mike Modano, Dall.	5.00
☐	CR5 Steve Yzerman, Detr.	15.00
☐	CR6 Pavel Bure, Flor.	5.00
☐	CR7 Mario Lemieux, Pitt.	18.00
☐	CR8 Chris Pronger, SLou.	5.00
☐	CR9 Mats Sundin, Toro.	5.00
☐	CR10 Jaromir Jagr, Wash.	5.00

FRANCHISE PLAYERS

Insert Set (10 cards): 190.00

	Insert	FP
☐	Jason Allison, LosA. ✂	12.00
☐	Tony Amonte, Chic. ✂	12.00
☐	Raymond Bourque, Colo. ✂	20.00
☐	Peter Forsberg, Colo. ✂	25.00
☐	John LeClair, Phil. ✂ White	15.00
☐	Mario Lemieux, Pitt. ✂ White	60.00
☐	Nicklas Lidström, Detr. ✂	12.00
☐	Eric Lindros, NYRa. ✂ {*SP}	30.00
☐	Doug Weight, SLou. ✂	12.00
☐	Doug Weight, SLou. ✂ White/Blue	15.00
☐	Steve Yzerman, Detr. ✂	45.00

FRANCHISE PLAYERS SIGNED

Insert Set (6 cards): 360.00

	Insert (#/75)	FPA
☐	Jason Allison, LosA. ✍ ✂	45.00
☐	Raymond Bourque, Colo. ✍ ✂	90.00
☐	Pavel Bure, Flor. ✍ ✂	60.00
☐	Jarome Iginla, Calg. ✍ ✂	60.00
☐	Doug Weight, SLou. ✍ ✂	45.00
☐	Steve Yzerman, Detr. ✍ ✂	180.00

FUTURE FAMERS

Insert Set (6 cards): 335.00

	Insert (#/25)	FF
☐	FF1 Joe Sakic, Colo.	75.00
☐	FF2 Patrick Roy, Colo.	150.00
☐	FF3 Brett Hull, Detr.	50.00
☐	FF4 Luc Robitaille, Detr.	25.00
☐	FF5 Steve Yzerman, Detr.	100.00
☐	FF6 Mark Messier, NYRa.	50.00

TERRIFIC 200

Insert Set (10 cards): 170.00

	Insert	T2
☐	Tom Barrasso (G), Caro. ✂	15.00
☐	Ed Belfour (G), Dall. ✂ Black	20.00
☐	Martin Brodeur (G), NJer. ✂ White	30.00
☐	Sean Burke (G), Phoe. ✂	15.00
☐	Dominik Hasek (G), Detr. ✂	20.00
☐	Curtis Joseph (G), Toro. ✂	20.00
☐	Chris Osgood (G), NYIs. ✂	15.00
☐	Félix Potvin (G), LosA. ✂	15.00
☐	Mike Richter (G), NYRa. ✂	15.00
☐	Patrick Roy (G), Colo. ✂ {*}	65.00

TERRIFIC 200 SIGNED

Insert Set (6 cards): 405.00

	Insert (#/75)	T2S
☐	Ed Belfour (G), Dall. ✍ ✂	75.00
☐	Martin Brodeur (G), NJer. ✍ ✂	100.00
☐	Curtis Joseph (G), Toro. ✍ ✂	75.00
☐	Félix Potvin (G), LosA. ✍ ✂	75.00
☐	Mike Richter (G), NYRa. ✍ ✂	40.00
☐	Patrick Roy (G), Colo. ✍ ✂	175.00

THEN & NOW

Insert Set (7 cards): 175.00

	Insert	TN
☐	R. Bourque, Bost. ✂ White / Colo. ✂ Blue	30.00
☐	Curtis Joseph (G), SLou. ✂ Toro. ✂	25.00
☐	Al MacInnis, Calg. ✂ SLou. ✂	20.00
☐	Keith Primeau, Detr. ✂ Phil. ✂	20.00
☐	Patrick Roy (G), Mont. ✂ Colo. ✂	75.00
☐	J. Sakic, Québ. ✂ White / Colo. ✂ Burgandy	40.00
☐	Brendan Shanahan, Hart. ✂ Detr. ✂	25.00

THEN & NOW SIGNED

Insert Set (5 cards): 600

	Insert (#/25)	TNA
☐	Ed Belfour (G), Chic. ✍ ✂ ✂	200.00
☐	Raymond Bourque, Bost. ✍ ✂ ✂	225.00
☐	Curtis Joseph (G), SLou. ✍ ✂ ✂	200.00
☐	Al MacInnis, Calg. ✍ ✂ ✂	100.00
☐	Keith Primeau, Detr. ✍ ✂ ✂	100.00

UNSTOPPABLE COMBOS

Insert Set (7 cards): 190.00

	Insert	UC
☐	J. LeClair ✂ Black / B. Boucher (G) ✂ Orange	20.00
☐	E. Lindros ✂ White / B. Leetch ✂ Blue	20.00
☐	E. Lindros ✂ Blue / B. Leetch ✂ Blue	20.00
☐	M. Modano ✂ / E. Belfour (G) ✂	25.00
☐	Z. Palffy ✂ / A. Deadmarsh ✂	20.00
☐	J. Sakic ✂ / M. Hejduk ✂ {*}	35.00
☐	M. Sundin ✂ Blue / Cu. Joseph (G) ✂ Blue	25.00
☐	B. Shanahan ✂ Red / S. Yzerman ✂ Red	40.00
☐	B. Shanahan ✂ Red / S. Yzerman ✂ White/Red	50.00

UNSTOPPABLE COMBOS SIGNED

Insert Set (4 cards): 450.00

	Insert	UCA
☐	J. Allison ✍ ✂ / Z. Palffy ✍ ✂	100.00
☐	R. Bourque ✍ ✂ / R. Blake ✍ ✂	175.00
☐	J. LeClair ✍ ✂ / S. Gagné ✍ ✂	150.00
☐	S. Samsonov ✍ ✂ / J. Thornton ✍ ✂	175.00

UP & COMERS GRADED

	Insert (#/1000)	BGS-9
☐	91 Ilja Bryzgalov, Anah. RC	12.00
☐	92 Timo Pärssinen, Anah. RC	10.00
☐	93 Kevin Sawyer, Anah. RC	10.00
☐	94 Brian Pothier, Atla. RC	10.00
☐	95 Ilya Kovalchuk, Atla. RC	70.00
☐	96 Kamil Piros, Atla. RC	12.00
☐	97 Ivan Huml, Bost. RC	20.00
☐	98 Jukka Hentunen, Calg. RC	10.00
☐	99 Scott Nichol, Calg. RC	10.00
☐	100 Erik Cole, Caro. RC	20.00
☐	101 Jaroslav Obsut, Colo. RC	10.00
☐	102 Vaclav Nedorost, Colo. RC	20.00
☐	103 Martin Spanhel, Colu. RC	10.00
☐	104 Niko Kapanen, Dall. RC	20.00
☐	105 Pavel Datsyuk, Detr. RC	60.00
☐	106 Ty Conklin, Edmo. RC	12.00
☐	107 Niklas Hagman, Flor. RC	12.00
☐	108 Kristian Huselius, Flor. RC	30.00
☐	109 Jaroslav Bednar, LosA. RC	12.00
☐	110 Pascal Dupuis, MinW. RC	20.00
☐	111 Mike Matteucci, MinW. RC	10.00
☐	112 Nick Schultz, MinW. RC	12.00
☐	113 Travis Roche, MinW. RC	10.00
☐	114 Martti Järventie, Mont.	10.00
☐	115 Martin Erat, Nash. RC	12.00
☐	116 Pavel Skrbek, Nash. RC	10.00
☐	117 Josef Boumedienne, NJer. RC	10.00
☐	118 Andreas Salomonsson, NJer. RC	10.00
☐	119 Scott Clemmensen, NJer. RC	12.00
☐	120 Mikael Samuelsson, NYRa. RC	10.00
☐	121 Dan Blackburn (G), NYRa. RC	35.00
☐	122 Richard Scott, NYRa. RC	10.00
☐	123 Radek Martinek, NYIs. RC	10.00
☐	124 Raffi Torres, NYIs. RC	20.00
☐	125 Ivan Ciernik, Otta. RC	10.00
☐	126 Jiri Dopita, Phil. RC	10.00
☐	127 Vaclav Pletka, Phil. RC	10.00
☐	128 Krys Kolanos, Phoe. RC	20.00
☐	129 David Cullen, Phoe. RC	10.00
☐	130 Jeff Jillson, SanJ. RC	12.00
☐	131 Mark Rycroft, SLou. RC	10.00
☐	132 Ryan Tobler, Tamp. RC	10.00
☐	133 Nikita Alexeev, Tamp. RC	20.00
☐	134 Brian Sutherby, Wash. RC	12.00
☐	135 Chris Corrinet, Wash. RC	10.00

2001 - 02 UPPER DECK COLLECTOR'S CLUB

Complete Set (20 cards): 25.00

	Upper Deck	UDCC
☐	1 Wayne Gretzky	6.00
☐	2 Gordie Howe	4.00
☐	3 Bobby Orr	6.00
☐	4 Raymond Bourque	1.50
☐	5 Mario Lemieux	4.50
☐	6 Patrick Roy (G)	4.50
☐	7 Steve Yzerman	3.50
☐	8 Jaromir Jagr	1.50
☐	9 Dominik Hasek (G)	1.50
☐	10 Martin Brodeur (G)	2.00
☐	11 Joe Sakic	2.00
☐	12 Paul Kariya	2.00
☐	13 Teemu Selänne	1.00
☐	14 Chris Pronger	.75
☐	15 Pavel Bure	1.00
☐	16 Peter Forsberg	2.00
☐	17 Nicklas Lidström	.75
☐	18 Ilya Kovalchuk	4.50
☐	19 Kristian Huselius	1.00
☐	20 Dan Blackburn (G)	1.50

MEMORABILIA

	Upper Deck
☐	Raymond Bourque Practice
☐	Steve Yzerman ✂

2001 - 02 UPPER DECK DEL

Produced by The Upper Deck Company, this series was released in 2001.

Complete Set (270 cards): 50.00
Common Player: .25

	Description	Base
☐	1 Igor Alexandrov, Augsburger Panther	.25
☐	2 Marc Beaucage, Augsburger Panther	.25
☐	3 Eric Dylla, Augsburger Panther	.25
☐	4 Mickey Elick, Augsburger Panther	.25
☐	5 Magnus Eriksson, Augsburger Panther	.25
☐	6 Jakub Ficenec, Augsburger Panther	.25
☐	7 Robert Guillet, Augsburger Panther	.25
☐	8 Tommy Jakobsen, Augsburger Panther	.25
☐	9 Christian Lukes, Augsburger Panther	.25
☐	10 Igor Maslennikov, Augsburger Panther	.25
☐	11 Duanne Moeser, Augsburger Panther	.25
☐	12 Vasily Pankov, Augsburger Panther	.25
☐	13 Reemt Pyka, Augsburger Panther	.25
☐	14 Reid Simonton, Augsburger Panther	.25
☐	15 Sergei Vostrikov, Augsburger Panther	.25
☐	16 Alexander Cherbayev, Berlin Capitals	.25
☐	17 Heinz Ehlers, Berlin Capitals	.25
☐	18 Ronny Arendt, Berlin Capitals	.25
☐	19 Andrei Vasiliev, Berlin Capitals	.25
☐	20 Francois Leroux, Berlin Capitals	.25
☐	21 Andrei Mezin, Berlin Capitals	.25
☐	22 Jan Münster, Berlin Capitals	.25
☐	23 Markus Pöttinger, Berlin Capitals	.25
☐	24 Patrick Senger, Berlin Capitals	.25
☐	25 Aleksandrs Kercs, Berlin Capitals	.25
☐	26 Gord Hynes, Berlin Capitals	.50
☐	27 Greg Andrusak, Berlin Capitals	.50
☐	28 Vyatcheslav Fandul, Berlin Capitals	.25
☐	29 Yvon Corriveau, Berlin Capitals	.50
☐	30 Frederik Öberg, Berlin Capitals	.25
☐	31 Keith Aldridge, Eisbären Berlin	.50
☐	32 David Cooper, Eisbären Berlin	.50
☐	33 Sven Felski, Eisbären Berlin	.25
☐	34 Marc Fortier, Eisbären Berlin	.50
☐	35 Daniel Laperrière, Eisbären Berlin	.25
☐	36 Steve Larouche, Eisbären Berlin	.50
☐	37 Scott Levins, Eisbären Berlin	.50
☐	38 Chris Marinucci, Eisbären Berlin	.50
☐	39 Klaus Merk, Eisbären Berlin	.25
☐	40 Nico Pyka, Eisbären Berlin	.25
☐	41 David Roberts, Eisbären Berlin	.50
☐	42 Jan Schertz, Eisbären Berlin	.25
☐	43 Richard Shulmistra, Eisbären Berlin	.25
☐	44 Lee Sorochan, Eisbären Berlin	.50
☐	45 Steve Walker, Eisbären Berlin	.25

☐ 46 Chris Bartolone, Düsseldorfer EG .25
☐ 47 .00
☐ 48 Ivan Droppa, Düsseldorfer EG .50
☐ 49 Neil Eisenhut, Düsseldorfer EG .50
☐ 50 Tore Vikingstad, Düsseldorfer EG .25
☐ 51 Torsten Kienass, Düsseldorfer EG .25
☐ 52 Bernd Kühnhauser, Düsseldorfer EG .25
☐ 53 Trond Magnussen, Düsseldorfer EG .25
☐ 54 Mike Pellegrims, Düsseldorfer EG .25
☐ 55 Jean-Francois Quintin, Düsseldorfer EG .25
☐ 56 Ralf Reisinger, Düsseldorfer EG .25
☐ 57 Leo Stefan, Düsseldorfer EG .25
☐ 58 Andrei Trefilov, Düsseldorfer EG .50
☐ 59 Martin Ulrich, Düsseldorfer EG .25
☐ 60 Rainer Zerwesz, Düsseldorfer EG .25
☐ 61 Frank Appel, Moskitos Essen .25
☐ 62 Lars Brüggemann, Moskitos Essen .25
☐ 63 Mike Casselman, Moskitos Essen .25
☐ 64 Ted Crowley, Moskitos Essen .50
☐ 65 Liam Garvey, Moskitos Essen .25
☐ 66 Erich Goldmann, Moskitos Essen .50
☐ 67 Todd Hawkins, Moskitos Essen .25
☐ 68 Ralph Intranuovo, Moskitos Essen .50
☐ 69 Martin Sychra, Moskitos Essen .25
☐ 70 Riku-Petteri Lehtonen, Moskitos Essen .25
☐ 71 Doug Donald, Moskitos Essen .25
☐ 72 Marc Savard, Moskitos Essen .25
☐ 73 Todd Simon, Moskitos Essen .50
☐ 74 Jimmy Waite (G), Moskitos Essen .50
☐ 75 Craig Woodcroft, Moskitos Essen .50
☐ 76 Michael Bresagk, Frankfurt Lions .25
☐ 77 Brent Cullaton, Frankfurt Lions .25
☐ 78 Rob Doyle, Frankfurt Lions .25
☐ 79 Greg Evtushevski, Frankfurt Lions .25
☐ 80 Victor Gervais, Frankfurt Lions .25
☐ 81 Rick Girard, Frankfurt Lions .50
☐ 82 Stewart Malgunas, Frankfurt Lions .50
☐ 83 Rob Pearson, Frankfurt Lions .50
☐ 84 Eldon Reddick, Frankfurt Lions .50
☐ 85 Iain Fraser, Frankfurt Lions .25
☐ 86 Alexander Selivanov, Frankfurt Lions .50
☐ 87 Vadim Slivchenko, Frankfurt Lions .25
☐ 88 Chris Snell, Frankfurt Lions .50
☐ 89 Brent Tully, Frankfurt Lions .50
☐ 90 John Walker, Frankfurt Lions .25
☐ 91 Oscar Ackeström, Hannover Scorpions .25
☐ 92 Igor Bashkatov, Hannover Scorpions .25
☐ 93 Igor Chibirev, Hannover Scorpions .50
☐ 94 Kevin Grant, Hannover Scorpions .25
☐ 95 David Haas, Hannover Scorpions .25
☐ 96 Peter Jakobsson, Hannover Scorpions .25
☐ 97 Dominic Lavoie, Hannover Scorpions .50
☐ 98 Mattias Lööf, Hannover Scorpions .25
☐ 99 Rob Murphy, Hannover Scorpions .50
☐ 100 Mark Pederson, Hannover Scorpions .50
☐ 101 Wally Schreiber, Hannover Scorpions .25
☐ 102 Len Soccio, Hannover Scorpions .25
☐ 103 Andrew Verner (G), Hannover Scorpions .50
☐ 104 Steve Wilson, Hannover Scorpions .25
☐ 105 Patrik Zetterberg, Hannover Scorpions .25
☐ 106 Doug Ast, Iserlohn Roosters .25
☐ 107 Colin Beardsmore, Iserlohn Roosters .25
☐ 108 Guy Dupuis, Iserlohn Roosters .25
☐ 109 Torsten Fendt, Iserlohn Roosters .25
☐ 110 Rusty Fitzgerald, Iserlohn Roosters .50
☐ 111 Terry Hollinger, Iserlohn Roosters .50
☐ 112 Kimmo Kapanen (G), Iserlohn Roosters .25
☐ 113 Dmitri Kotschnew, Iserlohn Roosters .25
☐ 114 Cory Laylin, Iserlohn Roosters .25
☐ 115 Paul Dyck, Iserlohn Roosters .25
☐ 116 Tomas Martinec, Iserlohn Roosters .25
☐ 117 Colin Danielsmeier, Iserlohn Roosters .25
☐ 118 David Musial, Iserlohn Roosters .25
☐ 119 Andreas Pokorny, Iserlohn Roosters .25
☐ 120 Sean Tallaire, Iserlohn Roosters .25
☐ 121 Tobias Abstreiter, Kassel Huskies .25
☐ 122 Thomas Daffner, Kassel Huskies .25
☐ 123 Doug Derraugh, Kassel Huskies .25
☐ 124 Leonid Fatikov, Kassel Huskies .25
☐ 125 Tommie Hartogs, Kassel Huskies .25
☐ 126 Klaus Kathan, Kassel Huskies .25
☐ 127 Ilpo Kauhanen, Kassel Huskies .25
☐ 128 Örjan Lindmark, Kassel Huskies .25
☐ 129 Andreas Loth, Kassel Huskies .25
☐ 130 Jeff MacLeod, Kassel Huskies .25
☐ 131 Pat Mikesch, Kassel Huskies .25
☐ 132 Jochen Molling, Kassel Huskies .25
☐ 133 Brent Peterson, Kassel Huskies .25
☐ 134 Shayne Wright, Kassel Huskies .25
☐ 135 Jeff Tory, Kassel Huskies .25
☐ 136 Tino Boos, Kölner Haie .25
☐ 137 André Faust, Kölner Haie .50
☐ 138 Alex Hicks, Kölner Haie .50
☐ 139 Petri Liimatainen, Kölner Haie .25
☐ 140 Mirko Lüdemann, Kölner Haie .25
☐ 141 Jörg Mayr, Kölner Haie .25
☐ 142 Dave McLlwain, Kölner Haie .50
☐ 143 Corey Millen, Kölner Haie .50
☐ 144 John Miner, Kölner Haie .25
☐ 145 Dwayne Norris, Kölner Haie .50
☐ 146 Toni Porkka, Kölner Haie .25
☐ 147 Andreas Renz, Kölner Haie .25
☐ 148 Chris Rogles, Kölner Haie .25
☐ 149 Niklas Sundblad, Kölner Haie .50
☐ 150 Jason Young, Kölner Haie .25
☐ 151 Patrik Augusta, Krefeld Pinguine .25
☐ 152 Stéphane Barin, Krefeld Pinguine .25
☐ 153 Thomas Brandl, Krefeld Pinguine .25
☐ 154 Steffen Ziesche, Krefeld Pinguine .25
☐ 155 .00
☐ 156 Jeff Christian, Krefeld Pinguine .25
☐ 157 Gilbert Dionne, Krefeld Pinguine .50
☐ 158 Mario Doyon, Krefeld Pinguine .50
☐ 159 Daniel Kunce, Krefeld Pinguine .25
☐ 160 Dan Lambert, Krefeld Pinguine .50
☐ 161 Roger Nordström, Krefeld Pinguine .25
☐ 162 Brad Purdie, Krefeld Pinguine .25
☐ 163 Gary Shuchuk, Krefeld Pinguine .50
☐ 164 Sergej Stas, Krefeld Pinguine .25
☐ 165 Phil Stefenelli, Krefeld Pinguine .25
☐ 166 Brad Bergen, Adler Mannheim .25
☐ 167 Fabian Brännström, Adler Mannheim .25
☐ 168 Devin Edgerton, Adler Mannheim .25
☐ 169 Todd Hlushko, Adler Mannheim .50
☐ 170 Wayne Hynes, Adler Mannheim .25
☐ 171 François Groleau, Adler Mannheim .50
☐ 172 Michel Picard, Adler Mannheim .50
☐ 173 Yves Racine, Adler Mannheim .50
☐ 174 Stéphane Richer, Adler Mannheim .25
☐ 175 Andy Roach, Adler Mannheim .25
☐ 176 Mike Rosati, Adler Mannheim .50
☐ 177 Mike Stevens, Adler Mannheim .25
☐ 178 Dave Tomlinson, Adler Mannheim .50
☐ 179 Steve Junker, Adler Mannheim .50
☐ 180 Stefan Ustorf, Adler Mannheim .50
☐ 181 Kent Fearns, München Barons .25
☐ 182 Jason Herter, München Barons .50
☐ 183 Mike Kennedy, München Barons .50
☐ 184 Derek King, München Barons .50
☐ 185 Christian Künast, München Barons .25
☐ 186 Hans Lodin, München Barons .25
☐ 187 David Oliver, München Barons .50
☐ 188 Shane Peacock, München Barons .25
☐ 189 Derek Planté, München Barons .25
☐ 190 Johan Rosén, München Barons .25
☐ 191 Boris Rousson (G), München Barons .50
☐ 192 Andy Schneider, München Barons .50
☐ 193 Peter Douris, München Barons .50
☐ 194 Heiko Smazal, München Barons .25
☐ 195 Simon Wheeldon, München Barons .25
☐ 196 Shawn Anderson, Nürnberg Ice Tigers .50
☐ 197 Luciano Borsato, Nürnberg Ice Tigers .50
☐ 198 Frédéric Chabot, Nürnberg Ice Tigers .50
☐ 199 Mario Chitarroni, Nürnberg Ice Tigers .25
☐ 200 Kevin Dahl, Nürnberg Ice Tigers .25
☐ 201 David Emma, Nürnberg Ice Tigers .50
☐ 202 Martin Jiranek, Nürnberg Ice Tigers .25
☐ 203 Chris Luongo, Nürnberg Ice Tigers .50
☐ 204 Guy Lehoux, Nürnberg Ice Tigers .25
☐ 205 Jacek Plachta, Nürnberg Ice Tigers .25
☐ 206 Martin Reichel, Nürnberg Ice Tigers .25
☐ 207 Jürgen Rumrich, Nürnberg Ice Tigers .25
☐ 208 Christian Schönmoser, Nürnberg Ice Tigers .25
☐ 209 Jan Nemecek, Nürnberg Ice Tigers .50
☐ 210 Bruno Zarrillo, Nürnberg Ice Tigers .25
☐ 211 Andreas Lupzig, Revier Löwen Oberhausen .25
☐ 212 Jergus Baca, Revier Löwen Oberhausen .50
☐ 213 Derek Cormier, Revier Löwen Oberhausen .25
☐ 214 John Craighead, Revier Löwen Oberhausen .25
☐ 215 Jesper Damgaard, Revier Löwen Oberhausen .25
☐ 216 Peter Gulda, Revier Löwen Oberhausen .25
☐ 217 Robert Hock, Revier Löwen Oberhausen .25
☐ 218 Martin Hohenberger, Revier Löwen Oberhausen .25
☐ 219 Ladislav Karabin, Revier Löwen Oberhausen .50
☐ 220 Christian Kohmann, Revier Löwen Oberhausen .25
☐ 221 Andrei Kovalev, Revier Löwen Oberhausen .25
☐ 222 Jason McBain, Revier Löwen Oberhausen .50
☐ 223 Andrei Teljukin, Revier Löwen Oberhausen .25
☐ 224 Sinuhe Wallinheimo, Revier Löwen Oberhausen .25
☐ 225 Josef Zajic, Revier Löwen Oberhausen .25
☐ 226 Micah Aivazoff, Schwenninger Wild Wings .50
☐ 227 Peter Allen, Schwenninger Wild Wings .25
☐ 228 Mike Bullard, Schwenninger Wild Wings 1.00
☐ 229 Dave Chyzowski, Schwenninger Wild Wings .50
☐ 230 Eric Dubois, Schwenninger Wild Wings .25
☐ 231 Ian Gordon, Schwenninger Wild Wings .25
☐ 232 Markus Janka, Schwenninger Wild Wings .25
☐ 233 Mark MacKay, Schwenninger Wild Wings .25
☐ 234 Neal Martin, Schwenninger Wild Wings .25
☐ 235 Jeff Nelson, Schwenninger Wild Wings .50
☐ 236 Jackson Penney, Schwenninger Wild Wings .25
☐ 237 Kent Simpson, Schwenninger Wild Wings .25
☐ 238 Jason Deleurme, Schwenninger Wild Wings .25
☐ 239 Gerhard Unterluggauer, Schwenninger Wild Wings .25
☐ 240 Darcy Werenka, Schwenninger Wild Wings .25
☐ 241 Andreas Morczinietz, Augsburger Panther .25
☐ 242 Christian Rohde, Augsburger Panther .25
☐ 243 Jonas Lanier, Berlin Capitals .25
☐ 244 Boris Blank, Eisbären Berlin .25
☐ 245 Eduard Lewandowski, Eisbären Berlin .25
☐ 246 Niki Mondt, Düsseldorfer EG .25
☐ 247 Leonard MinW., Moskitos Essen .25
☐ 248 Leonardo Conti, Frankfurt Lions .25
☐ 249 Philip Schuhmacher, Frankfurt Lions .25
☐ 250 Björn Leonhardt, Hannover Scorpions .25
☐ 251 Christian Franz, Iserlohn Roosters .25
☐ 252 Manuel Kofler, Iserlohn Roosters .25
☐ 253 Daniel Kreutzer, Kassel Huskies .25
☐ 254 Markus Guggemos, Kassel Huskies .25
☐ 255 Dimitri Pätzold, Kölner Haie .25
☐ 256 Benjamin Hinterstocker, Kölner Haie .25
☐ 257 Christian Ehrhoff, Krefeld Pinguine .25
☐ 258 Adrian Grygiel, Krefeld Pinguine .25
☐ 259 Benjamin Voigt, Krefeld Pinguine .25
☐ 260 Robert Müller, Adler Mannheim .25
☐ 261 Dennis Seidenberg, Adler Mannheim .25
☐ 262 Peter Abstreiter, München Barons .25
☐ 263 Christoph Schubert, München Barons .25
☐ 264 Andrej Strakhov, München Barons .25
☐ 265 Benjamin Hecker, Kassel Huskies .25
☐ 266 Vitalij Aab, Nürnberg Ice Tigers .25
☐ 267 Carsten Gosdeck, Revier Löwen Oberhausen .25
☐ 268 Lasse Kopitz, Revier Löwen Oberhausen .25
☐ 269 Marcel Goc, Schwenninger Wild Wings .25
☐ 270 Alexander Dück, Schwenninger Wild Wings .25

GATE ATTRACTIONS

Insert Set (9 cards):

Insert **GA**

☐ GA1 Sergej Vostrikov, Augsburger Panther
☐ GA2 Aleksandrs Kercs, Berlin Capitals
☐ GA3 Sven Felski, Eisbaren Berlin
☐ GA4 Mark MacKay, Schwenninger Wild Wings
☐ GA5 Alexander Selivanov, Frankfurt Lions
☐ GA6 Len Soccio, Hannover Scorpions
☐ GA7 Ivan Droppa, Düsseldorfer EG
☐ GA8 Gilbert Dionne, Krefeld Pinguine
☐ GA9 Stefan Ustorf, Adler Mannheim
☐ GA10 Jason Miller, Nürnberg Ice Tigers

GOALIES IN ACTION

Insert Set (10 cards):

Insert **GIA**

☐ G1 Andrei Mezin (G), Berlin Capitals
☐ G2 Klaus Merk (G), Eisbaren Berlin
☐ G3 Andrej Trefilov (G), Düsseldorfer EG
☐ G4 Andrew Verner (G), Hannover Scorpions
☐ G5 Chris Rogles (G), Kölner Haie
☐ G6 Roger Nordström (G), Krefeld Pinguine
☐ G7 Mike Rosati (G), Adler Mannheim
☐ G8 Christian Künast (G), München Barons
☐ G9 Marc Seliger (G), Nürnberg Ice Tigers
☐ G10 Sinuhe Wallinheimo (G), Revier Löwen Oberhausen

JERSEY

Insert Set (16 cards):

Insert **J**

☐ Frédéric Chabot, Nürnberg Ice Tigers ✂
☐ Magnus Eriksson, Augsburger Panther ✂
☐ LF-K Leonid Fatikov, Kassel Huskies ✂
☐ Ian Gordon, Schwenninger Wild Wings ✂
☐ Kimmo Kapanen (G), Iserlohn Roosters ✂
☐ Christian Künast, München Barons ✂
☐ Andrei Mezin (G), Berlin Capitals ✂
☐ Roger Nordström, Krefeld Pinguine ✂
☐ Eldon Reddick, Frankfurt Lions ✂
☐ Chris Rogles, Kölner Haie ✂
☐ Mike Rosati, Adler Mannheim ✂
☐ Richard Shulmistra, Eisbaren Berlin ✂
☐ Andrej Trefilov, Düsseldorfer EG ✂
☐ Andrew Verner, Hannover Scorpions ✂
☐ Jimmy Waite, Moskitos Essen ✂
☐ Sinuhe Wallinheimo, Revier Löwen Oberhausen ✂

SKILLED STARS

Insert Set (11 cards):

Insert **SS**

☐ SS1 Robert Hock, Revier Löwen Oberhausen
☐ SS2 David Cooper, Eisbären Berlin
☐ SS3 Brad Purdie, Krefeld Pinguine
☐ SS4 Todd Simon, Moskitos Essen
☐ SS5 Oscar Ackeström, Hannover Scorpions
☐ SS6 Tomas Martinec, Iserlohn Roosters
☐ SS7 Pat Mikesch, Kassel Huskies
☐ SS8 Mirko Lüdemann, Kölner Haie
☐ SS9 Stéphane Richer, Adler Mannheim
☐ SS10 Shane Peacock, München Barons
☐ SS11 Paul Stanton, Nürnberg Ice Tigers

2001 - 02 UPPER DECK HONOR ROLL

Produced by The Upper Deck Company, this series was released in March 2002.

Shell Set (60 cards): **30.00**
Complete Set (100 cards): **475.00**

Description **Base**

☐ 1 Bobby Hull, Chic. 1.00
☐ 2 Wayne Gretzky, Edmo. 3.00
☐ 3 Gordie Howe, Detr. 2.00
☐ 4 Bobby Orr, Bost. 3.00
☐ 5 Raymond Bourque, Bost. .50
☐ 6 Patrick Roy, Colo. 2.00
☐ 7 Luc Robitaille, Detr. .50
☐ 8 Mario Lemieux, Pitt. 2.00
☐ 9 Jaromir Jagr, Wash. .50
☐ 10 Chris Pronger, SLou. .20
☐ 11 Rob Blake, Colo. .20
☐ 12 Martin Brodeur, NJer. 1.00
☐ 13 Paul Kariya, Anah. 1.00
☐ 14 Joe Sakic, Colo. 1.00
☐ 15 Pavel Bure, Flor. .50
☐ 16 Nicklas Lidström, Detr. .20
☐ 17 Brian Leetch, NYRa. .20
☐ 18 Dominik Hasek (G), Detr. .50
☐ 19 Brendan Shanahan, Detr. .50
☐ 20 Steve Yzerman, Detr. 1.50
☐ 21 Teemu Selänne, SanJ. .50
☐ 22 Al MacInnis, SLou. .20
☐ 23 Scott Stevens, NJer. .20
☐ 24 Curtis Joseph (G), Toro. .50
☐ 25 Dany Heatley, Atla. 1.00
☐ 26 Joe Thornton, Bost. .50
☐ 27 Mark Parrish, NYIs. .20
☐ 28 Rostislav Klesla, Colu. .20
☐ 29 Brad Stuart, SanJ. .20
☐ 30 Rick DiPietro, NYIs. .20
☐ 31 Bobby Hull, Chic. 1.00
☐ 32 Wayne Gretzky, Edmo. 3.00
☐ 33 Gordie Howe, Detr. 2.00
☐ 34 Bobby Orr, Bost. 3.00
☐ 35 Raymond Bourque, Bost. .50
☐ 36 Patrick Roy, Colo. 2.00
☐ 37 Luc Robitaille, Detr. .50
☐ 38 Mario Lemieux, Pitt. 2.00
☐ 39 Jaromir Jagr, Wash. .50
☐ 40 Chris Pronger, SLou. .20
☐ 41 Rob Blake, Colo. .20
☐ 42 Martin Brodeur, NJer. 1.00
☐ 43 Paul Kariya, Anah. 1.00
☐ 44 Joe Sakic, Colo. 1.00
☐ 45 Pavel Bure, Flor. .50
☐ 46 Nicklas Lidström, Detr. .20
☐ 47 Brian Leetch, NYRa. .20
☐ 48 Dominik Hasek (G), Detr. .50
☐ 49 Brendan Shanahan, Detr. .50
☐ 50 Steve Yzerman, Detr. 1.50
☐ 51 Teemu Selänne, SanJ. .50

☐	52 Al MacInnis, SLou.	.20
☐	53 Scott Stevens, NJer.	.20
☐	54 Curtis Joseph (G), Toro.	.50
☐	55 Dany Heatley, Atla.	.50
☐	56 Joe Thornton, Bost.	.50
☐	57 Mark Parrish, NYIs.	.20
☐	58 Rostislav Klesla, Colu.	.20
☐	59 Brad Stuart, SanJ.	.20
☐	60 Rick DiPietro, NYIs.	.20

FRESHMAN CLASS

	Rookie	FF1500
☐	61 Ilja Bryzgalov, Anah. RC	10.00
☐	62 Mike Weaver, Atla. RC	6.00
☐	63 Kamil Piros, Atla. RC	10.00
☐	64 Ben Simon, Atla. RC	6.00
☐	65 Ivan Huml, Bost. RC	15.00
☐	66 Ales Kotalik, Buff. RC	25.00
☐	67 Scott Nichol, Calg. RC	6.00
☐	68 Kelly Fairchild, Colo. RC	6.00
☐	69 Vaclav Nedorost, Colo. RC	15.00
☐	70 Niko Kapanen, Stars	15.00
☐	71 Pavel Datsyuk, Detr. RC	50.00
☐	72 Sean Avery, Detr. RC	10.00
☐	73 Kristian Huselius, Flor. RC	20.00
☐	74 Nick Smith, Flor. RC	6.00
☐	75 Nick Schultz, MinW. RC	10.00
☐	76 Marcel Hossa, Mont. RC	25.00
☐	77 Olivier Michaud, Mont. RC	15.00
☐	78 Martin Erat, Nash. RC	10.00
☐	79 Christian Berglund, NJer. RC	10.00
☐	80 Andreas Salomonsson, NJer. RC	6.00
☐	81 Radek Martinek, NYIs. RC	6.00
☐	82 Richard Scott, NYRa. RC	6.00
☐	83 Ivan Ciernik, Otta. RC	10.00
☐	84 Bruno St-Jacques, Phil. RC	6.00
☐	85 Dan Focht, Phoe.	3.00
☐	86 Jeff Jillson, SanJ. RC	10.00
☐	87 Mark Rycroft, SLou. RC	6.00
☐	88 Nikita Alexeev, Tamp. RC	15.00
☐	89 Justin Kurtz, Vanc.	3.00
☐	90 Chris Corrinet, Wash. RC	6.00

DEAN'S LIST

	Rookie	DL1000
☐	91 Martin Spanhel RC ✂ / Tony Amonte ✂	20.00
☐	92 Matt Davidson RC ✂ / Chris Drury ✂	20.00
☐	94 J. Bednar RC ✂ Black / Z. Palffy ✂ Black	20.00
☐	94 Raffi Torres RC ✂ / Brendan Shanahan ✂	25.00
☐	95 Samuelsson ✂ White / S. Fedorov ✂ White	20.00
☐	96 D. Blackburn (G) RC ✂ White/Red / M. Richter (G) ✂ Red	25.00
☐	97 T. Divisek RC ✂ Black / J. LeClair ✂ Orange	20.00
☐	98 J. Dopita RC ✂ / P. Demitra ✂	20.00
☐	99 K. Kolanos RC ✂ / Mike Modano ✂	25.00
☐	100 I. Kovalchuk RC ✂ / J. Jagr ✂	60.00

DEFENCE FIRST

	Insert Set (6 cards):	15.00
	Insert (1:40)	DF
☐	DF1 Mike Modano, Stars	3.00
☐	DF2 Jere Lehtinen, Stars	3.00
☐	DF3 Steve Yzerman, Detr.	9.00
☐	DF4 Sergei Fedorov, Detr.	3.00
☐	DF5 John Madden, NJer.	3.00
☐	DF6 Michael Peca, NYIs.	3.00

DISTINCTIVE PUCKS

	Insert Set (12 cards):	235.00
	Insert (#/225)	DP
☐	Peter Bondra, Wash.	20.00
☐	Pavel Bure, Flor.	25.00
☐	Patrik Elias, NJer.	25.00
☐	Marian Hossa, Otta.	35.00
☐	Jarome Iginla, Calg.	25.00
☐	Saku Koivu, Mont.	25.00
☐	Alex Kovalev, Pitt.	20.00
☐	Vincent Lecavalier, Tamp.	35.00
☐	Brian Leetch, NYRa.	20.00
☐	Mark Messier, NYRa.	35.00
☐	Scott Stevens, NJer.	15.00
☐	Mats Sundin, Toro.	35.00

GRADE A JERSEYS

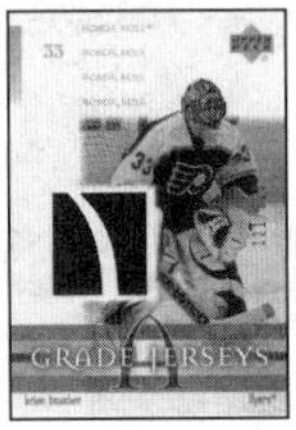

	Insert Set (32 cards):	500.00
	Insert (#/225)	GAJ
☐	Ed Belfour (G), Dall.	25.00
☐	Peter Bondra, Wash. ✂ White	15.00
☐	Brian Boucher (G), Phil. ✂ Black	15.00
☐	Raymond Bourque, Bost. ✂	30.00
☐	Martin Brodeur, NJer. ✂	40.00
☐	Tim Connolly, Buff. ✂	15.00
☐	Pavol Demitra, SLou. ✂	15.00
☐	Chris Drury, Colo. ✂	15.00
☐	Sergei Fedorov, Detr. ✂	25.00
☐	Jochen Hecht, Edmo. ✂	15.00
☐	Brett Hull, Detr. ✂	25.00
☐	Paul Kariya, Anah. ✂	35.00
☐	John LeClair, Phil. ✂ White	20.00
☐	Brian Leetch, AS White	15.00
☐	David Legwand, Nash. ✂	15.00
☐	Mario Lemieux, Pitt. ✂	75.00
☐	Nicklas Lidström, Detr. ✂ Red	15.00
☐	EL Eric Lindros, NYRa. ✂	25.00
☐	LI Eric Lindros, NYRa. ✂	25.00
☐	Roberto Luongo, Flor. ✂	20.00
☐	Mike Modano, Stars	25.00
☐	Markus Näslund, Vanc. ✂	25.00
☐	Joe Nieuwendyk, Stars	15.00
☐	Maxime Ouellet, Phil. ✂	15.00
☐	Luc Robitaille, Detr. ✂	20.00
☐	Joe Sakic, All-Star	40.00
☐	Sergei Samsonov, Bost. ✂	15.00
☐	Miroslav Satan, Buff. ✂	15.00
☐	Brendan Shanahan, Detr. ✂ White	25.00
☐	Mats Sundin, Toro. ✂	25.00
☐	Joe Thornton, Bost. ✂	30.00
☐	Doug Weight, SLou. ✂	15.00

GRADE A JERSEYS GOLD

	Insert Set (32 cards):	2000.00
	Insert (#/50)	GAJG
☐	Ed Belfour (G), Dall. ✂	100.00
☐	Peter Bondra, Wash. ✂	60.00
☐	Brian Boucher (G), Phil. ✂	32.00
☐	Raymond Bourque, Bost. ✂	120.00
☐	Martin Brodeur, NJer. ✂	160.00
☐	Tim Connolly, Buff. ✂	40.00
☐	Pavol Demitra, SLou. ✂	40.00
☐	Chris Drury, Colo. ✂	60.00
☐	Sergei Fedorov, Detr. ✂	100.00
☐	Jochen Hecht, Edmo. ✂	24.00
☐	Brett Hull, Detr. ✂	100.00
☐	Paul Kariya, Anah. ✂	140.00
☐	John LeClair, Phil. ✂	80.00
☐	Brian Leetch, All-Star	60.00
☐	David Legwand, Nash. ✂	40.00
☐	Mario Lemieux, Pitt. ✂	300.00
☐	Nicklas Lidström, Detr. ✂	60.00
☐	EL Eric Lindros, NYRa. ✂	100.00
☐	LI Eric Lindros, NYRa. ✂	100.00
☐	Roberto Luongo, Flor. ✂	80.00
☐	Mike Modano, Stars	100.00
☐	Markus Näslund, Vanc. ✂	100.00
☐	Joe Nieuwendyk, Dall. ✂	40.00
☐	Maxime Ouellet, Phil. ✂	30.00
☐	Luc Robitaille, Detr. ✂	80.00
☐	Joe Sakic, All-Star	160.00
☐	Sergei Samsonov, Bost. ✂	60.00
☐	Miroslav Satan, Buff. ✂	30.00
☐	Brendan Shanahan, Detr. ✂	100.00
☐	Mats Sundin, Toro. ✂	100.00
☐	Joe Thornton, Bost. ✂ Black	120.00
☐	Doug Weight, SLou. ✂	60.00

ORIGINAL SIX

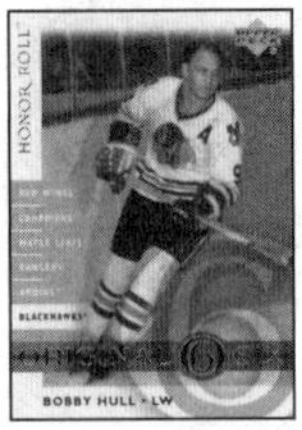

	Insert Set (6 cards):	40.00
	Insert (1:40)	OS
☐	OS1 Bobby Orr, Bost.	15.00
☐	OS2 Bobby Hull, Chic.	6.00
☐	OS3 Gordie Howe, Detr.	10.00
☐	OS4 Patrick Roy, Mont.	10.00
☐	OS5 Wayne Gretzky, NYRa.	15.00
☐	OS6 Curtis Joseph (G), Toro.	3.00

SHARP SKATERS

	Insert Set (6 cards):	15.00
	Insert (1:40)	SS
☐	SS1 Paul Kariya, Anah.	5.00
☐	SS2 Mike Modano, Stars	3.00
☐	SS3 Sergei Fedorov, Detr.	3.00
☐	SS4 Pavel Bure, Flor.	3.00
☐	SS5 Marian Hossa, Otta.	3.00
☐	SS6 Simon Gagné, Phil.	3.00

STUDENTS OF THE GAME

	Insert Set (6 cards):	20.00
	Insert (1:40)	SG
☐	SG1 Paul Kariya, Anah.	5.00
☐	SG2 Joe Sakic, Colo.	6.00
☐	SG3 Mike Modano, Stars	3.00
☐	SG4 Steve Yzerman, Detr.	9.00
☐	SG5 Patrik Elias, NJer.	3.00
☐	SG6 Mats Sundin, Toro.	3.00

TOUGH CUSTOMERS

	Insert Set (6 cards):	
	Insert (1:40)	TC
☐	TC1 Martin Lapointe, Bost.	
☐	TC2 Rob Blake, Colo.	
☐	TC3 Scott Stevens, NJer.	
☐	TC4 Jeremy Roenick, Phil.	
☐	TC5 Owen Nolan, SanJ.	
☐	TC6 Chris Pronger, SLou.	

HONOR SOCIETY

	Insert Set (4 cards):	165.00
	Insert (#/100)	HS
☐	Pavel Bure ✂ / Valeri Bure ✂	40.00
☐	Roman Cechmanek (G) ✂ / Dominik Hasek (G) ✂	40.00
☐	P. Kariya ✂ Teal / M. Hejduk ✂ Blue	40.00
☐	P. Roy (G) ✂ Burgandy / M. Brodeur (G) ✂ Black	100.00

HONOR SOCIETY GOLD

	Insert Set (4 cards):	410.00
	Insert (#/25)	HS25
☐	Pavel Bure ✂ / Valeri Bure ✂	
☐	Cechmanek (G) ✂ Black / Hasek (G) ✂ White	200.00
☐	Milan Hejduk ✂ / Paul Kariya ✂	
☐	P. Roy (G) ✂ Burgandy / M. Brodeur (G) ✂ Black	350.00

PREMIER PLAYOFF MATCHUPS

	Insert Set (6 cards):	175.00
	Insert (#/200)	PPM
☐	Brett Hull ✂ / Keith Tkachuk ✂	30.00
☐	Mario Lemieux ✂ / Dominik Hasek (G) ✂	75.00
☐	Patrick Roy (G) ✂ / Martin Brodeur (G) ✂	75.00
☐	Joe Sakic ✂ / Luc Robitaille ✂	25.00
☐	Mats Sundin ✂ / Scott Stevens ✂	25.00
☐	Alex Tanguay ✂ / Al MacInnis ✂	25.00

PREMIER PLAYOFF MATCHUPS GOLD

	Insert Set (6 cards):	800.00
	Insert (#/25)	PPM
☐	Brett Hull ✂ / Keith Tkachuk ✂	120.00
☐	Mario Lemieux ✂ / Dominik Hasek (G) ✂	300.00
☐	Patrick Roy (G) ✂ / Martin Brodeur (G) ✂	300.00
☐	Joe Sakic ✂ / Luc Robitaille ✂	175.00
☐	Mats Sundin ✂ / Scott Stevens ✂	100.00
☐	Alex Tanguay ✂ / Al MacInnis ✂	75.00

2001 - 02 UPPER DECK ICE

Produced by The Upper Deck Company, this series was released in September 2001.

	Shell Set (42 cards):	40.00
	Complete Set (84 cards):	350.00
	Description	Base
☐	1 Paul Kariya, Anah.	2.50
☐	2 Joe Thornton, Bost.	2.00
☐	3 Sergei Samsonov, Bost.	1.00
☐	4 Martin Biron (G), Buff.	.50
☐	5 Jarome Iginla, Calg.	1.50
☐	6 Arturs Irbe (G), Caro.	.50
☐	7 Tony Amonte, Chic.	1.00
☐	8 Patrick Roy, Colo.	6.00
☐	9 Peter Forsberg, Colo.	2.50
☐	10 Raymond Bourque, Colo.	2.00
☐	11 Ron Tugnutt, Colu.	.50
☐	12 Mike Modano, Dall.	2.00
☐	13 Ed Belfour (G), Dall.	2.00
☐	14 Brett Hull, Dall.	2.00
☐	15 Steve Yzerman, Detr.	4.50
☐	16 Dominik Hasek (G), Detr.	2.00
☐	17 Sergei Fedorov, Detr.	2.00
☐	18 Tommy Salo, Edmo.	.50
☐	19 Mike Comrie, Edmo.	1.50
☐	20 Pavel Bure, Flor.	1.50
☐	21 Adam Deadmarsh, LosA.	.50
☐	22 Zigmund Palffy, LosA.	1.00
☐	23 Marian Gaborik, MinW.	2.00

□	24 Manny Fernandez, MinW.	.50
□	25 José Théodore (G), Mont.	2.00
□	26 Mike Dunham, Nash.	.50
□	27 Martin Brodeur, NJer.	3.00
□	28 Patrik Elias, NJer.	1.50
□	29 Rick DiPietro, NYIs.	.50
□	30 Mark Messier, NYRa.	2.00
□	31 Martin Havlat, Otta.	1.00
□	32 Marian Hossa, Otta.	2.00
□	33 Jeremy Roenick, Phil.	1.50
□	34 Sean Burke, Phoe.	1.00
□	35 Johan Hedberg (G), Pitt.	.50
□	36 Mario Lemieux, Pitt.	6.00
□	37 Evgeni Nabokov, SanJ.	1.00
□	38 Keith Tkachuk, SLou.	1.00
□	39 Vincent Lecavalier, Tamp.	2.00
□	40 Curtis Joseph (G), Toro.	2.00
□	41 Markus Näslund, Vanc.	2.00
□	42 Jaromir Jagr, Wash.	2.00

FRESH FACES

	Rookie (#/1500)	FF1500
□	**43 Ilja Bryzgalov (G), Anah. RC**	**10.00**
□	**44 Ilya Kovalchuk, Atla. RC**	**60.00**
□	**45 Zdenek Kutlak, Bost. RC**	**8.00**
□	**46 Ales Kotalik, Buff. RC**	**25.00**
□	**47 Scott Nichol, Calg. RC**	**8.00**
□	**48 Erik Cole, Caro. RC**	**15.00**
□	49 Casey Hankinson, Chic.	5.00
□	**50 Vaclav Nedorost, Colo. RC**	**15.00**
□	**51 Martin Spanhel, Colu. RC**	**8.00**
□	**52 Niko Kapanen, Dall. RC**	**15.00**
□	**53 Pavel Datsyuk, Detr. RC**	**50.00**
□	**54 Ty Conklin, Edmo. RC**	**10.00**
□	**55 Kristian Huselius, Flor. RC**	**20.00**
□	**56 Jaroslav Bednar, LosA. RC**	**10.00**
□	**57 Nick Schultz, MinW. RC**	**10.00**
□	58 Martti Järventie, Mont.	5.00
□	**59 Martin Erat, Nash. RC**	**10.00**
□	**60 Andreas Salomonsson, NJer. RC**	**8.00**
□	**61 Raffi Torres, NYIs. RC**	**15.00**
□	**62 Dan Blackburn (G), NYRa. RC**	**25.00**
□	**63 Ivan Ciernik, Otta. RC**	**10.00**
□	**64 Jiri Dopita, Phil. RC**	**10.00**
□	**65 Krys Kolanos, Phoe. RC**	**15.00**
□	**66 Billy Tibbetts, Pitt. RC**	**10.00**
□	**67 Jeff Jillson, SanJ. RC**	**10.00**
□	**68 Mark Rycroft, SLou. RC**	**8.00**
□	**69 Nikita Alexeev, Tamp. RC**	**15.00**
□	**70 Bob Wren, Toro. RC**	**8.00**
□	**71 Pat Kavanagh, Vanc. RC**	**8.00**
□	**72 Brian Sutherby, Wash. RC**	**10.00**
□	**73 Timo Pärssinen, Anah. RC**	**8.00**
□	**74 Kamil Piros, Atla. RC**	**10.00**
□	**75 Jukka Hentunen, Calg. RC**	**8.00**
□	**76 Niklas Hagman, Flor. RC**	**10.00**
□	**77 Travis Roche, MinW. RC**	**8.00**
□	**78 Pavel Skrbek, Nash. RC**	**8.00**
□	**79 Scott Clemmensen, NJer. RC**	**10.00**
□	**80 Chris Neil, Otta. RC**	**8.00**
□	**81 Vaclav Pletka, Phil. RC**	**8.00**
□	**82 Josef Boumedienne, Tamp. RC**	**8.00**
□	**83 Ryan Tobler, Tamp. RC**	**8.00**
□	**84 Chris Corrinet, Wash. RC**	**8.00**

UPDATE

	Update	Update
□	85 Dany Heatley, Atla.	3.00
□	86 Glen Murray, Bost.	.50
□	87 Jozef Stümpel, Bost.	.50
□	88 Tim Connolly, Buff.	.50
□	89 Roman Turek (G), Calg.	.50
□	90 Joe Sakic, Colo.	3.00
□	91 Radim Vrbata, Colo.	1.00
□	92 Milan Hejduk, Colo.	1.50
□	93 Brenden Morrow, Dall.	.50
□	94 Pierre Turgeon, Dall.	.50
□	95 Brett Hull, Detr.	2.00
□	96 Luc Robitaille, Detr.	1.50
□	97 Brendan Shanahan, Detr.	2.00
□	98 Nicklas Lidström, Detr.	1.00
□	99 Sandis Ozolinsh, Flor.	.50
□	100 Jason Allison, LosA.	1.00
□	101 Félix Potvin, LosA.	1.00
□	102 Donald Audette, Mont.	.50
□	103 Chris Osgood, NYIs.	1.00
□	104 Alexei Yashin, NYIs.	1.00
□	105 Mark Parrish, NYIs.	.50
□	106 Eric Lindros, NYRa.	2.00
□	107 Theoren Fleury, NYRa.	1.00
□	108 Barrett Heisten, NYRa. (Dall.)	.50
□	109 Daniel Alfredsson, Otta.	1.00
□	110 Donald Brashear, Phil.	.50
□	111 Luke Richardson, Phil.	.50
□	112 John LeClair, Phil.	1.50
□	113 Brian Boucher (G), Phil.	.50
□	114 Alex Kovalev, Pitt.	1.00
□	115 Teemu Selänne, SanJ.	1.50
□	116 Owen Nolan, SanJ.	1.00
□	117 Pavol Demitra, SLou.	.50
□	118 Chris Pronger, SLou.	1.00
□	119 Doug Weight, SLou.	1.00
□	120 Sheldon Keefe, Tamp.	.50
□	121 Nikolai Khabibulin (G), Tamp.	.50
□	122 Mats Sundin, Toro.	2.00
□	123 Jan Hlavac, Vanc.	.50
□	124 Trevor Linden, Vanc.	.50
□	125 Peter Bondra, Wash.	1.00
□	126 Olaf Kölzig, Wash.	1.00

ROOKIE UPDATE

	Rookie (#/1000)	Update
□	**127 Pasi Nurminen, Atla. RC**	**15.00**
□	**128 Ivan Huml, Bost. RC**	**15.00**
□	**129 Tony Tuzzolino, Bost. RC**	**10.00**
□	**130 Steve Montador, Calg. RC**	**10.00**
□	**131 Mike** Peluso, Chic. RC**	**10.00**
□	**132 Steve Poapst, Chic. RC**	**10.00**
□	**133 Riku Hahl, Colo. RC**	**10.00**
□	**134 Blake Bellefeuille, Colu. RC**	**10.00**
□	**135 David Ling, Colu. RC**	**10.00**
□	**136 John Erskine, Dall. RC**	**10.00**
□	**137 Brad Norton, Flor. RC**	**10.00**
□	**138 Nick Smith, Flor. RC**	**10.00**
□	**139 Ryan Flinn, LosA. RC**	**10.00**
□	**140 Pascal Dupuis, MinW. RC**	**15.00**
□	**141 Olivier Michaud, Mont. RC**	**15.00**
□	**142 Marcel Hossa, Mont. RC**	**30.00**
□	**143 Raffi Torres, NYIs. RC**	**15.00**
□	**144 Mikael Samuelsson, NYRa. RC**	**10.00**
□	**145 Christian Berglund, NJer. RC**	**10.00**
□	**146 Shane Endicott, Pitt. RC**	**10.00**
□	**147 Éric Meloche, Pitt. RC**	**10.00**
□	**148 Steve Bancroft, SanJ. RC**	**10.00**
□	**149 Martin Cibak, Tamp. RC**	**10.00**
□	**150 Dean Melanson, Wash. RC**	**10.00**
□	**151 Mike Farrell, Wash. RC**	**10.00**

CLEAR CUT AUTOGRAPHS

Insert Set (10 cards): 325.00
Update Insert Set (12 cards): 325.00

	Insert	CCA
□	Martin Brodeur, NJer. ✍	75.00
□	Mike Comrie, Edmo. ✍	30.00
□	Wayne Gretzky, NYRa. ✍	350.00
□	Milan Kraft, Pitt. ✍	30.00
□	Roberto Luongo, Flor. ✍	30.00
□	Mike Modano, Dall. ✍	50.00
□	Daniel Sedin, Vanc. ✍	30.00
□	Henrik Sedin, Vanc. ✍	30.00
□	Petr Sykora, NJer. ✍	30.00
□	Steve Yzerman, Detr. ✍	100.00
□	Peter Bondra, Wash. ✍	30.00
□	Mike Comrie, Edmo. ✍	30.00
□	Marian Gaborik, MinW. ✍	50.00
□	Dany Heatley, Atla. ✍	50.00
□	Milan Hejduk, Colo. ✍	30.00
□	Kristian Huselius, Flor. ✍	30.00
□	Jarome Iginla, Calg. ✍	30.00
□	Arturs Irbe (G), Caro. ✍	30.00
□	Curtis Joseph (G), Toro. ✍ {#/31}	75.00
□	Rostislav Klesla, Colu. ✍	30.00
□	Krys Kolanos, Phoe. ✍	30.00
□	Ilya Kovalchuk, Atla. ✍	50.00

COMBO CARD

There are two versions for each card: the Combo jersey card and the Combo Gold jersey card (#/25).

Insert Set (10 cards): 2,100 425.00

	Inserts	G25	C
□ □	Sergei Fedorov, Detr. ✂ ✂	175.00	30.00
□ □	Jaromir Jagr, Pitt. ✂ ✂	175.00	30.00
□ □	Paul Kariya, Anah. ✂ ✂	245.00	50.00
□ □	John LeClair, Phil. ✂ ✂	140.00	30.00
□ □	Mario Lemieux, Pitt. ✂ ✂	525.00	125.00
□ □	Mike Modano, Dall. ✂ ✂	175.00	30.00
□ □	Jeremy Roenick, Phoe. ✂ ✂	140.00	30.00
□ □	Patrick Roy, Colo. ✂ ✂	525.00	100.00
□ □	Joe Sakic, Colo. ✂ ✂	280.00	50.00
□ □	Steve Yzerman, Detr. ✂ ✂	420.00	100.00

FIRST ROUNDERS

Insert Set (7 cards): 200.00

	Insert (1:36)	F
□	Jaromir Jagr, Pitt. ✂	30.00
□	Jeremy Roenick, Phoe. ✂ White	25.00
□	Joe Sakic, Colo. ✂ Burgandy	50.00
□	Mike Modano, Dall. ✂	30.00
□	Paul Kariya, Anah. ✂	40.00
□	Patrik Stefan, Atla. ✂ Blue	25.00
□	Steve Yzerman, Detr. ✂	70.00

JERSEY CARD

Insert Set (8 cards): 180.00

	Insert (1:32)	J
□	Brett Hull, Dall. ✂	30.00
□	Doug Weight, Edmo. ✂	25.00
□	Éric Dazé, Chic. ✂	25.00
□	John LeClair, Phil. ✂	25.00
□	Marc Savard, Calg. ✂	25.00
□	Patrick Roy, Colo. ✂	60.00
□	Serge Aubin, Colu. ✂	25.00
□	Sergei Fedorov, Detr. ✂	30.00

2001 - 02 UPPER DECK LEGENDS

Produced by The Upper Deck Company, this series was released in 2001.

Complete Set (100 cards): 40.00

	Description	Base
□	1 Bobby Orr, Bost.	3.00
□	2 Eddie Shore, Bost.	1.00
□	3 Phil Esposito, Bost.	.50
□	4 Johnny Bucyk, Bost.	.25
□	5 Cam Neely, Bost.	.50
□	6 Gerry Cheevers, Bost.	.50
□	7 Gilbert Perreault, Buff.	.50
□	8 René Robert, Buff.	.25
□	9 Lanny McDonald, Calg.	.50
□	10 Al Secord, Chic.	.25
□	11 Bobby Hull, Chic.	1.00
□	12 Glenn Hall, Chic.	.50
□	13 Stan Mikita, Chic.	.50
□	14 Tony Esposito, Chic.	.50
□	15 Gordie Howe, Detr.	2.00
□	16 Terry Sawchuk, Detr.	1.50
□	17 Ted Lindsay, Detr.	.50
□	18 Sid Abel, Detr.	.25
□	19 Red Kelly, Detr.	.25
□	20 Alex Delvecchio, Detr.	.25
□	21 Glenn Anderson, Edmo.	.25
□	22 Wayne Gretzky, Edmo.	3.00
□	23 Jari Kurri, Edmo.	.50
□	24 Grant Fuhr, Edmo.	.25
□	25 Bill Ranford, Edmo.	.25
□	26 Gordie Howe, Hart.	2.00
□	27 Marcel Dionne, LosA.	.50
□	28 Butch Goring, LosA.	.25
□	29 Rogatien Vachon, LosA.	.25
□	30 Maurice Richard, Mont.	2.00
□	31 Jean Béliveau, Mont.	1.50
□	32 Serge Savard, Mont.	.25
□	33 Jacques Plante, Mont.	1.00
□	34 Guy Lafleur, Mont.	1.50
□	35 Yvan Cournoyer, Mont.	.25
□	36 Steve Shutt, Mont.	.25
□	37 Rick Green, Mont.	.25
□	38 Henri Richard, Mont.	.50
□	39 Bernie Geoffrion, Mont.	.50
□	40 Guy Lapointe, Mont.	.25
□	41 Denis Potvin, NYIs.	.50
□	42 Mike Bossy, NYIs.	1.00
□	43 Bryan Trottier, NYIs.	.50
□	44 Clark Gillies, NYIs.	.25
□	45 Billy Smith, NYIs.	.50
□	46 Ed Giacomin, NYRa.	.50
□	47 Jean Ratelle, NYRa.	.25
□	48 Lester Patrick, NYRa.	.50
□	49 William Jennings, NYRa.	.25
□	50 Raymond Bourque, Bost.	.50
□	51 Frank Calder, NHL	.25
□	52 Andy van Hellemond, NHL	.25
□	53 Bobby Clarke, Phil.	.50
□	54 Bernie Parent, Phil.	.50
□	55 Bill Barber, Phil.	.25
□	56 Syl (Jr.) Apps, Pitt.	.25
□	57 Bernie Federko, SLou.	.25
□	58 Frank Mahovlich, Toro.	.50
□	59 Darryl Sittler, Toro.	.50
□	60 Tim Horton, Toro.	.50
□	61 Rick Vaive, Toro.	.25
□	62 Frank Selke, Toro.	.25
□	63 Conn Smythe, Toro.	.25
□	64 King Clancy, Toro.	.50
□	65 Tony Tanti, Vanc.	.25
□	66 Mike Ridley, Wash.	.25
□	67 Rod Langway, Wash.	.25
□	68 Mike Gartner, Wash.	.50
□	69 Kent Nilsson, Atla. [Frozen in Time]	.25
□	70 Reggie Leach, Cali. [Frozen in Time]	.25
□	71 Dennis Maruk, Clev. [Frozen in Time]	.25
□	72 Wilf Paiement, Colo. [Frozen in Time]	.25
□	73 Barry Beck, Colo. [Frozen in Time]	.25
□	74 Simon Nolet, Kans. [Frozen in Time]	.25
□	75 Don Beaupré (G), Minn. [Frozen in Time]	.25
□	76 Peter Stastny, Québ. [Frozen in Time]	.25
□	77 Michel Goulet, Québ. [Frozen in Time]	.25
□	78 Dale Hawerchuk, Winn. [Frozen in Time]	.25
□	79 Gerry Cheevers (G), Bost. [Gloves of Steel]	.50
□	80 Glenn Hall (G), Chic. [Gloves of Steel]	.50
□	81 Terry Sawchuk (G), Detr. [Gloves of Steel]	1.00
□	82 Grant Fuhr (G), Edmo. [Gloves of Steel]	.25
□	83 Bernie Parent (G), Phil. [Gloves of Steel]	.50
□	84 Jacques Plante (G), Mont. [Gloves of Steel]	1.00
□	85 Ed Giacomin (G), NYRa. [Gloves of Steel]	.50
□	86 Bill Ranford (G), Edmo. [Gloves of Steel]	.25
□	87 Billy Smith (G), NYIs. [Gloves of Steel]	.50
□	88 Tony Esposito (G), Chic. [Gloves of Steel]	.50
□	89 Bobby Orr, Bost. [Legendary Lamplighter]	2.50
□	90 Bobby Hull, Chic. [Legendary Lamplighter]	1.00
□	91 Gordie Howe, Detr. [Legendary Lamplighter]	1.50
□	92 Wayne Gretzky, Edmo. [Legendary Lamplighter]	2.50
□	93 Marcel Dionne, LosA. [Legendary Lamplighter]	.50
□	94 Maurice Richard, Mont. [Legendary Lamplighter]	1.50
□	95 Guy Lafleur, Mont. [Legendary Lamplighter]	1.00
□	96 Mike Bossy, NYIs. [Legendary Lamplighter]	1.00
□	97 Jari Kurri, Edmo. [Legendary Lamplighter]	.50
□	98 Mike Gartner, Wash. [Legendary Lamplighter]	.50
□	99 Gordie Howe, Detr. [Checklist]	1.00
□	100 Wayne Gretzky, Edmo. [Checklist]	1.50

EPIC SIGNATURES

Insert Set (18 cards): 825.00

	Insert (1:54)	ES
□	Jean Béliveau, Mont. ✍	60.00
□	Mike Bossy, NYIs. ✍	50.00
□	Bobby Clarke, Phil. ✍	25.00
□	Alex Delvecchio, Detr. ✍	25.00
□	Marcel Dionne, LosA. ✍	35.00
□	Phil Esposito, Bost. ✍	45.00
□	Tony Esposito, Chic. ✍	30.00
□	Wayne Gretzky, Edmo. ✍	200.00
□	Gordie Howe, Detr. ✍	150.00
□	Bobby Hull, Chic. ✍	45.00
□	Guy Lafleur, Mont. ✍	45.00
□	Ted Lindsay, Detr. ✍	35.00
□	Frank Mahovlich, Toro. ✍	35.00
□	Stan Mikita, Chic. ✍	25.00
□	Cam Neely, Bost. ✍	35.00
□	Bobby Orr, Bost. ✍	200.00
□	Gilbert Perreault, Buff. ✍	25.00
□	Bryan Trottier, NYIs. ✍	35.00

MILESTONES

Insert Set (16 cards): 345.00

	Insert (1:18)	M
□	Bill Barber, Phil. ✂	15.00
□	Mike Bossy, NYIs. ✂ Blue	40.00

☐	Neal Broten, Minn. ✂	15.00
☐	Bobby Clarke, Phil. ✂	20.00
☐	Marcel Dionne, LosA. ✂	25.00
☐	Mike Gartner, Wash. ✂	20.00
☐	Wayne Gretzky, LosA. ✂	100.00
☐	Guy Lafleur, Mont. ✂	30.00
☐	Lanny McDonald, Calg. ✂	20.00
☐	Cam Neely, Bost. ✂	25.00
☐	Gilbert Perreault, Buff. ✂	20.00
☐	Denis Potvin, NYIs. ✂	20.00
☐	Steve Shutt, Mont. ✂	15.00
☐	Brent Sutter, NYIs. ✂	15.00
☐	Bryan Trottier, NYIs. ✂ Blue	25.00
☐	Steve Yzerman, Detr. ✂	60.00

PIECES OF HISTORY

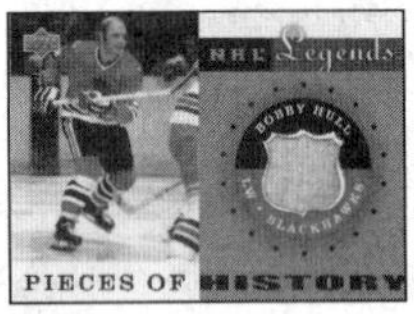

Insert Set (29 cards):		**1,000**
	Insert (1:18)	**PH**
☐	Jean Béliveau, Mont. ✂	65.00
☐	Mike Bossy, NYIs. ✂	50.00
☐	Raymond Bourque, Colo. ✂	35.00
☐	Raymond Bourque, Bost. ✂	35.00
☐	Gerry Cheevers, Bost. ✂	25.00
☐	Bobby Clarke, Phil. ✂	25.00
☐	Marcel Dionne, LosA. ✂	30.00
☐	Phil Esposito, NYRa. ✂	35.00
☐	Phil Esposito, Bost. ✂	35.00
☐	Tony Esposito, Chic. ✂	30.00
☐	Mike Gartner, Minn. ✂	25.00
☐	Wayne Gretzky, LosA. ✂	125.00
☐	Wayne Gretzky, Edmo. ✂	125.00
☐	Gordie Howe, Detr. ✂	80.00
☐	Gordie Howe, Hartnell ✂	85.00
☐	Bobby Hull, Chic. ✂	55.00
☐	Bobby Hull, Winn. ✂	55.00
☐	Jari Kurri, Edmo. ✂	30.00
☐	Guy Lafleur, Mont. ✂	35.00
☐	Frank Mahovlich, Toro. ✂	30.00
☐	Stan Mikita, Chic. ✂	25.00
☐	Bobby Orr, Bost. ✂	125.00
☐	Jacques Plante, Mont. ✂	50.00
☐	Denis Potvin, NYIs. ✂	25.00
☐	Jean Ratelle, NYRa. ✂	12.00
☐	Maurice Richard, Mont. ✂	80.00
☐	Darryl Sittler, Toro. ✂	25.00
☐	Billy Smith, NYIs. ✂	25.00
☐	Bryan Trottier, NYIs. ✂	30.00

THE FIORENTINO COLLECTION

Insert Set (15 cards):		**75.00**
	Insert (1:18)	**FC**
☐	Bobby Clarke, Phil.	3.00
☐	Bobby Hull, Chic.	6.00
☐	Bobby Orr, Bost.	15.00
☐	Bryan Trottier, NYIs.	3.00
☐	Gordie Howe, Detr.	10.00
☐	Guy Lafleur, Mont.	7.00
☐	Jacques Plante, Mont.	6.00
☐	Mike Bossy, NYIs.	6.00
☐	Marcel Dionne, LosA.	3.00
☐	Maurice Richard, Mont.	10.00
☐	Phil Esposito, Bost.	4.00
☐	Stan Mikita, Chic.	3.00
☐	Tony Esposito, Chic.	3.00
☐	Terry Sawchuk, Detr.	7.00
☐	Wayne Gretzky, Edmo.	15.00

TIMELESS TRIBUTES

Insert Set (22 cards):		**480.00**
	Insert (1:18)	**TT**
☐	Bill Barber, Phil. ✂	15.00
☐	Gerry Cheevers, Bost. ✂	20.00
☐	Phil Esposito, NYRa. ✂	30.00
☐	Mike Gartner, NYRa. ✂	20.00
☐	Mike Gartner, Minn. ✂	20.00
☐	Clark Gillies, NYIs. ✂	15.00
☐	Wayne Gretzky, Edmo. ✂	100.00
☐	Gordie Howe, Houston ✂	70.00
☐	Bobby Hull, NHL Heroes '92 ✂	45.00
☐	Guy Lafleur, Québ. ✂	30.00
☐	Guy Lafleur, NHL All-Star '91 ✂	30.00
☐	Guy Lafleur, Mont. ✂	30.00
☐	Guy Lafleur, NYRa. ✂	30.00
☐	Stan Mikita, Chic. ✂	20.00
☐	Cam Neely, Bost. ✂	25.00
☐	Gilbert Perreault, Buff. ✂	20.00
☐	Denis Potvin, NYIs. ✂	20.00
☐	Bill Ranford (G), Edmo. ✂ [Blue]	15.00
☐	Steve Shutt, Mont. ✂	15.00
☐	Billy Smith, NYIs. ✂	20.00
☐	Bryan Trottier, NYIs. ✂	25.00
☐	Andy van Hellemond, NHL Referee ✂	30.00

TIMELESS TRIBUTES COMBO

Insert Set (5 cards):		**150.00**
	Insert	**TTC**
☐	Guy Lafleur, Mont. ✂ Québ. ✂	50.00
☐	Guy Lafleur, AS '91 ✂ NYRa. ✂	50.00
☐	Bobby Hull ✂ / Stan Mikita ✂	55.00
☐	Steve Shutt ✂ / Guy Lafleur ✂	35.00
☐	Billy Smith (G) ✂ / Bryan Trottier ✂	40.00

2001 - 02 UPPER DECK MASK COLLECTION

Produced by The Upper Deck Company, this series was released in June 2002. Each box included a replica goalie mask.

Shell Set (100 cards):	**900**	**35.00**
Complete Set (190 cards):	**1,900**	**275.00**
Common Player:	**8.00**	**.20**
Description	**Gold**	**Base**
☐☐ 1 Paul Kariya, Anah.	35.00	2.00
☐☐ 2 Jeff Friesen, Anah.	8.00	.50
☐☐ 3 Matt Cullen, Anah.	8.00	.20
☐☐ 4 Dany Heatley, Atla.	25.00	2.50
☐☐ 5 Lubos Bartecko, Atla.	8.00	.20
☐☐ 6 Tony Hrkac, Atla.	8.00	.20
☐☐ 7 Sergei Samsonov, Bost.	15.00	1.00
☐☐ 8 Joe Thornton, Bost.	30.00	2.00
☐☐ 9 Bill Guerin, Bost.	10.00	.50
☐☐ 10 P.J. Stock, Bost.	8.00	.50
☐☐ 11 Stu Barnes, Buff.	8.00	.20
☐☐ 12 Tim Connolly, Buff.	10.00	.50
☐☐ 13 Jarome Iginla, Calg.	20.00	1.00
☐☐ 14 Craig Conroy, Calg.	8.00	.50
☐☐ 15 Sami Kapanen, Caro.	8.00	.50
☐☐ 16 Ron Francis, Caro.	15.00	1.00
☐☐ 17 Tony Amonte, Chic.	15.00	1.00
☐☐ 18 Mark Bell, Chic.	8.00	.20
☐☐ 19 Steve Sullivan, Chic.	8.00	.50
☐☐ 20 Chris Drury, Colo.	15.00	1.00
☐☐ 21 Milan Hejduk, Colo.	20.00	1.00
☐☐ 22 Joe Sakic, Colo.	40.00	2.50
☐☐ 23 Rob Blake, Colo.	15.00	1.00
☐☐ 24 Alex Tanguay, Colo.	15.00	1.00
☐☐ 25 Mike Sillinger, Colu.	8.00	.20
☐☐ 26 Ray Whitney, Colu.	8.00	.20
☐☐ 27 Rostislav Klesla, Colu.	8.00	.50
☐☐ 28 Pierre Turgeon, Dall.	10.00	.50
☐☐ 29 Jere Lehtinen, Dall.	8.00	.50
☐☐ 30 Mike Modano, Dall.	25.00	1.50
☐☐ 31 Sergei Zubov, Dall.	8.00	.20
☐☐ 32 Brendan Shanahan, Detr.	25.00	1.50
☐☐ 33 Steve Yzerman, Detr.	60.00	4.00
☐☐ 34 Brett Hull, Detr.	25.00	1.50
☐☐ 35 Sergei Fedorov, Detr.	25.00	1.50
☐☐ 36 Mike Comrie, Edmo.	20.00	1.00
☐☐ 37 Ryan Smyth, Edmo.	10.00	.50
☐☐ 38 Anson Carter, Edmo.	10.00	.50
☐☐ 39 Viktor Kozlov, Flor.	8.00	.50
☐☐ 40 Marcus Nilson, Flor.	8.00	.20
☐☐ 41 Sandis Ozolinsh, Flor.	8.00	.20
☐☐ 42 Adam Deadmarsh, LosA.	8.00	.50
☐☐ 43 Jason Allison, LosA.	15.00	1.00
☐☐ 44 Zigmund Palffy, LosA.	15.00	1.00
☐☐ 45 Andrew Brunette, MinW.	8.00	.20
☐☐ 46 Marian Gaborik, MinW.	25.00	1.50
☐☐ 47 Jim Dowd, MinW.	8.00	.20
☐☐ 48 Yanic Perreault, Mont.	8.00	.50
☐☐ 49 Sergei Berezin, Mont.	8.00	.20
☐☐ 50 Donald Audette, Mont.	10.00	.50
☐☐ 51 Francis Bouillon, Mont.	8.00	.20
☐☐ 52 Karlis Skrastins, Nash.	8.00	.20
☐☐ 53 David Legwand, Nash.	10.00	.50
☐☐ 54 Scott Hartnell, Nash.	8.00	.20
☐☐ 55 Bobby Holik, NJer.	8.00	.50
☐☐ 56 Joe Nieuwendyk, NJer.	10.00	.50
☐☐ 57 Patrik Elias, NJer.	20.00	1.00
☐☐ 58 Brian Rafalski, NJer.	8.00	.20
☐☐ 59 Mark Parrish, New York	10.00	.50
☐☐ 60 Michael Peca, New York	10.00	.50
☐☐ 61 Alexei Yashin, New York	15.00	1.00
☐☐ 62 Petr Nedved, New York	8.00	.50
☐☐ 63 Theoren Fleury, New York	15.00	1.00
☐☐ 64 Pavel Bure, New York	20.00	1.00
☐☐ 65 Eric Lindros, New York	25.00	1.50
☐☐ 66 Martin Havlat, Otta.	15.00	1.00
☐☐ 67 Daniel Alfredsson, Otta.	15.00	1.00
☐☐ 68 Marian Hossa, Otta.	25.00	1.50
☐☐ 69 Radek Bonk, Otta.	8.00	.50
☐☐ 70 Simon Gagné, Phil.	20.00	1.00
☐☐ 71 John LeClair, Phil.	20.00	1.00
☐☐ 72 Jeremy Roenick, Phil.	20.00	1.00
☐☐ 73 Mark Recchi, Phil.	10.00	.50
☐☐ 74 Michal Handzus, Phoe.	8.00	.20
☐☐ 75 Claude Lemieux, Phoe.	8.00	.50
☐☐ 76 Shane Doan, Phoe.	8.00	.20
☐☐ 77 Jamie Pushor, Pitt.	8.00	.20
☐☐ 78 Alex Kovalev, Pitt.	15.00	1.00
☐☐ 79 Mario Lemieux, Pitt.	75.00	5.00
☐☐ 80 Vincent Damphousse, SanJ.	15.00	1.00
☐☐ 81 Owen Nolan, SanJ.	15.00	1.00
☐☐ 82 Teemu Selänne, SanJ.	20.00	1.00
☐☐ 83 Keith Tkachuk, SLou.	15.00	1.00
☐☐ 84 Chris Pronger, SLou.	15.00	1.00
☐☐ 85 Doug Weight, SLou.	15.00	1.00
☐☐ 86 Pavol Demitra, SLou.	10.00	.50
☐☐ 87 Fredrik Modin, Tamp.	8.00	.20
☐☐ 88 Brad Richards, Tamp.	10.00	.50
☐☐ 89 Vincent Lecavalier, Tamp.	25.00	1.50
☐☐ 90 Darcy Tucker, Toro.	8.00	.20
☐☐ 91 Alexander Mogilny, Toro.	10.00	.50
☐☐ 92 Mats Sundin, Toro.	25.00	1.50
☐☐ 93 Brendan Morrison, Vanc.	8.00	.50
☐☐ 94 Todd Bertuzzi, Vanc.	30.00	2.00
☐☐ 95 Markus Näslund, Vanc.	25.00	1.50
☐☐ 96 Ed Jovanovski, Vanc.	10.00	.50
☐☐ 97 Drake Berehowsky, Phoe.	8.00	.20
☐☐ 98 Ulf Dahlén, Wash.	8.00	.20
☐☐ 99 Peter Bondra, Wash.	15.00	1.00
☐☐ 100 Jaromir Jagr, Wash.	25.00	1.50

MANNING THE NETS

Goalie	**Gold**	**MTN**
☐☐ 101 Jean-Sébastien Giguère (G), Anah.	20.00	2.00
☐☐ 102 Milan Hnilicka (G), Atla.	8.00	2.00
☐☐ 103 Byron Dafoe (G), Bost.	10.00	2.00
☐☐ 104 Martin Biron (G), Buff.	10.00	2.00
☐☐ 105 Roman Turek (G), Calg.	10.00	2.00
☐☐ 106 Arturs Irbe (G), Caro.	10.00	2.00
☐☐ 107 Jocelyn Thibault (G), Chic.	10.00	2.00
☐☐ 108 Patrick Roy (G), Colo.	75.00	10.00
☐☐ 109 Ron Tugnutt (G), Colu.	10.00	2.00
☐☐ 110 Ed Belfour (G), Dall.	25.00	2.00
☐☐ 111 Dominik Hasek (G), Detr.	25.00	2.00
☐☐ 112 Tommy Salo (G), Edmo.	10.00	2.00
☐☐ 113 Roberto Luongo (G), Flor.	20.00	2.00
☐☐ 114 Félix Potvin (G), LosA.	15.00	2.00
☐☐ 115 Manny Fernandez (G), MinW.	10.00	2.00
☐☐ 116 José Théodore (G), Mont.	30.00	4.00
☐☐ 117 Mike Dunham (G), Nash.	10.00	2.00
☐☐ 118 Martin Brodeur (G), NJer.	40.00	6.00
☐☐ 119 Chris Osgood (G), NYIs.	15.00	2.00
☐☐ 120 Mike Richter (G), NYRa.	10.00	2.00
☐☐ 121 Patrick Lalime (G), Otta.	15.00	2.00
☐☐ 122 Roman Cechmanek (G), Phil.	10.00	2.00
☐☐ 123 Sean Burke (G), Phoe.	15.00	2.00
☐☐ 124 Johan Hedberg (G), Pitt.	10.00	2.00
☐☐ 125 Evgeni Nabokov (G), SanJ.	15.00	2.00
☐☐ 126 Brent Johnson (G), SLou.	10.00	2.00
☐☐ 127 Nikolai Khabibulin (G), Tamp.	10.00	2.00
☐☐ 128 Curtis Joseph (G), Toro.	25.00	2.00
☐☐ 129 Dan Cloutier (G), Vanc.	10.00	2.00
☐☐ 130 Olaf Kölzig (G), Wash.	15.00	2.00

POTENTIAL GEMS

Rookie	**Gold**	**PG**
☐☐ **131 Frédéric Cassivi, Atla. RC**	**10.00**	**6.00**
☐☐ **132 Ilya Kovalchuk, Atla. RC**	**100.00**	**35.00**
☐☐ **133 Pasi Nurminen, Atla. RC**	**15.00**	**6.00**
☐☐ **134 Mark Hartigan, Atla. RC**	**10.00**	**6.00**
☐☐ **135 Francis Lessard, Atla. RC**	**10.00**	**6.00**
☐☐ **136 Ivan Huml, Bost. RC**	**15.00**	**6.00**
☐☐ **137 Chris Kelleher, Bost. RC**	**10.00**	**6.00**
☐☐ **138 Erik Cole, Caro. RC**	**15.00**	**6.00**
☐☐ **139 Mike** Peluso, Chic. RC**	**10.00**	**6.00**
☐☐ **140 Vaclav Nedorost, Colo. RC**	**15.00**	**6.00**
☐☐ **141 Jeff Daw, Colo. RC**	**10.00**	**6.00**
☐☐ **142 Andrej Nedorost, Colu. RC**	**10.00**	**6.00**
☐☐ **143 Sean Avery, Detr. RC**	**10.00**	**6.00**
☐☐ **144 Pavel Datsyuk, Detr. RC**	**80.00**	**30.00**
☐☐ **145 Stephen Weiss, Flor. RC**	**30.00**	**20.00**
☐☐ **146 Niklas Hagman, Flor. RC**	**10.00**	**6.00**
☐☐ **147 Kristian Huselius, Flor. RC**	**20.00**	**10.00**
☐☐ **148 Lukas Krajicek, Flor. RC**	**15.00**	**6.00**
☐☐ **149 Tony Virta, MinW. RC**	**10.00**	**6.00**
☐☐ **150 Olivier Michaud, Mont. RC**	**15.00**	**6.00**
☐☐ **151 Marcel Hossa, Mont. RC**	**30.00**	**15.00**
☐☐ **152 Martin Erat, Nash. RC**	**10.00**	**6.00**
☐☐ **153 Christian Berglund, NJer. RC**	**10.00**	**6.00**
☐☐ **154 Raffi Torres, New York RC**	**15.00**	**6.00**
☐☐ **155 Dan Blackburn (G), New York RC**	**30.00**	**15.00**
☐☐ **156 Martin Prusek, Otta. RC**	**20.00**	**10.00**
☐☐ **157 Chris Bala, Otta. RC**	**10.00**	**6.00**
☐☐ **158 Josh Langfeld, Otta. RC**	**10.00**	**6.00**
☐☐ **159 Jiri Dopita, Phil. RC**	**10.00**	**6.00**
☐☐ **160 Neil Little, Phil. RC**	**10.00**	**6.00**
☐☐ **161 Guillaume Lefebvre, Phil. RC**	**10.00**	**6.00**
☐☐ **162 Krys Kolanos, Phoe. RC**	**15.00**	**6.00**
☐☐ **163 Branko Radivojevic, Phoe. RC**	**15.00**	**6.00**
☐☐ **164 Shane Endicott, Pitt. RC**	**10.00**	**6.00**
☐☐ **165 Hannes Hyvonen, SanJ. RC**	**10.00**	**6.00**
☐☐ **166 Jeff Jillson, SanJ. RC**	**10.00**	**6.00**
☐☐ **167 Nikita Alexeev, Tamp. RC**	**15.00**	**6.00**
☐☐ **168 Gaétan Royer, Tamp. RC**	**10.00**	**6.00**
☐☐ **169 Karel Pilar, Toro. RC**	**10.00**	**6.00**
☐☐ **170 Brian Sutherby, Wash. RC**	**10.00**	**6.00**

UNMASKED WARRIORS

Goalie	**Gold**	**UW**
☐☐ 171 Byron Dafoe (G), Bost.	10.00	6.00
☐☐ 172 Martin Biron (G), Buff.	10.00	6.00
☐☐ 173 Roman Turek (G), Calg.	10.00	6.00
☐☐ 174 Arturs Irbe (G), Caro.	10.00	6.00
☐☐ 175 Patrick Roy (G), Colo.	75.00	20.00
☐☐ 176 Ed Belfour (G), Dall.	25.00	6.00
☐☐ 177 Dominik Hasek (G), Detr.	25.00	6.00
☐☐ 178 Tommy Salo (G), Edmo.	10.00	6.00
☐☐ 179 Félix Potvin (G), LosA.	15.00	6.00
☐☐ 180 Mike Dunham (G), Nash.	10.00	6.00
☐☐ 181 Martin Brodeur (G), NJer.	40.00	10.00
☐☐ 182 Chris Osgood (G), NYIs.	15.00	6.00

☐ ☐	183 Mike Richter (G), NYRa.	10.00	6.00
☐ ☐	184 Roman Cechmanek (G), Phil.	10.00	6.00
☐ ☐	185 Sean Burke (G), Phoe.	15.00	6.00
☐ ☐	186 Johan Hedberg (G), Pitt.	10.00	6.00
☐ ☐	187 Evgeni Nabokov (G), SanJ.	15.00	6.00
☐ ☐	188 Nikolai Khabibulin (G), Tamp.	10.00	6.00
☐ ☐	189 Curtis Joseph (G), Toro.	25.00	6.00
☐ ☐	190 Olaf Kölzig (G), Wash.	15.00	6.00

CAGED GREATS

Insert Set (7 cards):		155.00
	Insert (1:288)	CG
☐	Martin Brodeur (G), NJer. ✂	35.00
☐	Sean Burke (G), Phoe. ✂	25.00
☐	Dominik Hasek (G), Detr. ✂	25.00
☐	Curtis Joseph (G), Toro. ✂	25.00
☐	Chris Osgood (G), New York	25.00
☐	Mike Richter (G), NYRa. ✂	25.00
☐	Patrick Roy (G), Colo. ✂	50.00

GOALIE PADS

Insert Set (9 cards):		100.00
	Insert (1:288)	GP
☐	Martin Biron (G), Buff. ✂	15.00
☐	Byron Dafoe, Bost. ✂	15.00
☐	Marc Denis, Colu. ✂	15.00
☐	Dominik Hasek (G), Detr. ✂	20.00
☐	Johan Hedberg (G), Pitt. ✂	15.00
☐	Olaf Kölzig, Wash. ✂	15.00
☐	Patrick Roy, Colo. ✂	45.00
☐	José Théodore (G), Mont. ✂	25.00

GREAT GLOVES

Insert Set (13 cards):		200.00
	Insert (1:144)	GG
☐	Ed Belfour (G), Dall. ✂	20.00
☐	Raymond Bourque, Bost. ✂	20.00
☐	Byron Dafoe, Bost. ✂	20.00
☐	Rick DiPietro, New York ✂	20.00
☐	Chris Drury, Colo. ✂	20.00
☐	Sergei Fedorov, Detr. ✂	20.00
☐	Brett Hull, Detr. ✂	20.00
☐	Sami Kapanen, Caro. ✂	20.00
☐	Mark Messier, New York ✂	20.00
☐	Alexander Mogilny, Toro. ✂	20.00
☐	Jeremy Roenick, Phil. ✂	20.00
☐	Brendan Shanahan, Detr. ✂	20.00
☐	Keith Tkachuk, SLou. ✂	20.00

JERSEY

Insert Set (60 cards):		900.00
	Insert (#/150)	Jers
☐	David Aebischer (G), Colo. ✂	15.00
☐	Maxim Afinogenov, Buff. ✂	15.00
☐	Jason Allison, LosA. ✂	15.00
☐	Tony Amonte, Chic. ✂	15.00
☐	Ed Belfour (G), Dall. ✂	20.00
☐	Mark Bell, Chic. ✂	15.00
☐	Martin Biron (G), Buff. ✂	15.00
☐	Rob Blake, Colo. ✂	15.00
☐	Brian Boucher (G), Phil. ✂	15.00
☐	Raymond Bourque, Bost. ✂	25.00
☐	Daniel Brière, Phoe. ✂	15.00
☐	Tim Connolly, Buff. ✂	15.00
☐	Adam Deadmarsh, LosA. ✂	15.00
☐	Pavol Demitra, SLou. ✂	15.00
☐	Marc Denis, Colu. ✂	15.00
☐	Shane Doan, Phoe. ✂	15.00
☐	Chris Drury, Colo. ✂	15.00
☐	Dumont, Buff. ✂	15.00
☐	Sergei Fedorov, Detr. ✂	20.00
☐	Ruslan Fedotenko, Phil. ✂	15.00
☐	Peter Forsberg, Colo. ✂	30.00
☐	Jeff Friesen, Anah. ✂	15.00
☐	Simon Gagné, Phil. ✂	15.00
☐	Jean-Sébastien Giguère (G), Anah. ✂	15.00
☐	Milan Hejduk, Colo. ✂	15.00
☐	Jarome Iginla, Calg. ✂	15.00
☐	Jaromir Jagr, Wash. ✂	20.00
☐	Brent Johnson, SLou. ✂	15.00
☐	Paul Kariya, Anah. ✂	30.00
☐	Rostislav Klesla, Colu. ✂	15.00
☐	Espen Knutsen, Colu. ✂	15.00
☐	Saku Koivu, Mont. ✂	15.00
☐	Vyacheslav Kozlov, Buff. ✂	15.00
☐	Mario Lemieux, Pitt. ✂	65.00
☐	Nicklas Lidström, Detr. ✂	15.00
☐	Trevor Linden, Vanc. ✂	15.00
☐	Mike Modano, Dall. ✂	20.00
☐	Ville Nieminen, Pitt. ✂	15.00
☐	Joe Nieuwendyk, NJer. ✂	15.00
☐	Zigmund Palffy, LosA. ✂	15.00
☐	Félix Potvin, LosA. ✂	15.00
☐	Keith Primeau, Phil. ✂	15.00
☐	Mike Richter, New York ✂	15.00
☐	Patrick Roy, Colo. ✂	50.00
☐	Geoff Sanderson, Colu. ✂	15.00
☐	Miroslav Satan, Buff. ✂	15.00
☐	Marc Savard, Calg. ✂	15.00
☐	Teemu Selänne, SanJ. ✂	15.00
☐	Brendan Shanahan, Detr. ✂	20.00
☐	Steve Sullivan, Chic. ✂	15.00
☐	Mats Sundin, Toro. ✂	20.00
☐	Alex Tanguay, Colo. ✂	15.00
☐	José Théodore (G), Mont. ✂	25.00
☐	Jocelyn Thibault, Chic. ✂	15.00
☐	Ron Tugnutt, Colu. ✂	15.00
☐	Marty Turco, Dall. ✂	15.00
☐	Ray Whitney, Colu. ✂	15.00
☐	Justin Williams, Phil. ✂	15.00
☐	Mike York, Edmo. ✂	15.00
☐	Steve Yzerman, Detr. ✂	50.00

JERSEY PATCH

Insert Set (60 cards):		1500.00
	Insert (#/100)	JP
☐	David Aebischer (G), Colo. ✂	25.00
☐	Maxim Afinogenov, Buff. ✂	25.00
☐	Jason Allison, LosA. ✂	25.00
☐	Tony Amonte, Chic. ✂	25.00
☐	Ed Belfour (G), Dall. ✂	25.00
☐	Mark Bell, Chic. ✂	25.00
☐	Martin Biron (G), Buff. ✂	25.00
☐	Rob Blake, Colo. ✂	25.00
☐	Brian Boucher (G), Phil. ✂	25.00
☐	Raymond Bourque, Bost. ✂	50.00
☐	Daniel Brière, Phoe. ✂	25.00
☐	Tim Connolly, Buff. ✂	25.00
☐	Adam Deadmarsh, LosA. ✂	25.00
☐	Pavol Demitra, SLou. ✂	25.00
☐	Marc Denis, Colu. ✂	25.00
☐	Shane Doan, Phoe. ✂	25.00
☐	Chris Drury, Colo. ✂	25.00
☐	Jean-Pierre Dumont, Buff. ✂	25.00
☐	Sergei Fedorov, Detr. ✂	25.00
☐	Ruslan Fedotenko, Phil. ✂	25.00
☐	Peter Forsberg, Colo. ✂	50.00
☐	Jeff Friesen, Anah. ✂	25.00
☐	Simon Gagné, Phil. ✂	25.00
☐	Jean-Sébastien Giguère (G), Anah. ✂	25.00
☐	Milan Hejduk, Colo. ✂	25.00
☐	Jarome Iginla, Calg. ✂	25.00
☐	Jaromir Jagr, Wash. ✂	25.00
☐	Brent Johnson, SLou. ✂	25.00
☐	Paul Kariya, Anah. ✂	50.00
☐	Rostislav Klesla, Colu. ✂	25.00
☐	Espen Knutsen, Colu. ✂	25.00
☐	Saku Koivu, Mont. ✂	25.00
☐	Vyacheslav Kozlov, Buff. ✂	25.00
☐	Mario Lemieux, Pitt. ✂	125.00
☐	Nicklas Lidström, Detr. ✂	25.00
☐	Trevor Linden, Vanc. ✂	25.00
☐	Mike Modano, Dall. ✂	25.00
☐	Ville Nieminen, Pitt. ✂	25.00
☐	Joe Nieuwendyk, NJer. ✂	25.00
☐	Zigmund Palffy, LosA. ✂	25.00
☐	Félix Potvin, LosA. ✂	25.00
☐	Keith Primeau, Phil. ✂	25.00
☐	Mike Richter, New York ✂	25.00
☐	Patrick Roy, Colo. ✂	100.00
☐	Geoff Sanderson, Colu. ✂	25.00
☐	Miroslav Satan, Buff. ✂	25.00
☐	Marc Savard, Calg. ✂	25.00
☐	Teemu Selänne, SanJ. ✂	25.00
☐	Brendan Shanahan, Detr. ✂	25.00
☐	Steve Sullivan, Chic. ✂	25.00
☐	Mats Sundin, Toro. ✂	25.00
☐	Alex Tanguay, Colo. ✂	25.00
☐	José Théodore (G), Mont. ✂	50.00
☐	Jocelyn Thibault, Chic. ✂	25.00
☐	Ron Tugnutt, Colu. ✂	25.00
☐	Marty Turco, Dall. ✂	25.00
☐	Ray Whitney, Colu. ✂	25.00
☐	Justin Williams, Phil. ✂	25.00
☐	Mike York, Edmo. ✂	25.00
☐	Steve Yzerman, Detr. ✂	100.00

DOUBLE PATCH

Insert Set (60 cards):		2700.00
	Insert (#/50)	DP
☐	David Aebischer (G), Colo. ✂	40.00
☐	Maxim Afinogenov, Buff. ✂	40.00
☐	Jason Allison, LosA. ✂	40.00
☐	Tony Amonte, Chic. ✂	40.00
☐	Ed Belfour (G), Dall. ✂	65.00
☐	Mark Bell, Chic. ✂	40.00
☐	Martin Biron (G), Buff. ✂	40.00
☐	Rob Blake, Colo. ✂	40.00
☐	Brian Boucher (G), Phil. ✂	40.00
☐	Raymond Bourque, Bost. ✂	80.00
☐	Daniel Brière, Phoe. ✂	40.00
☐	Tim Connolly, Buff. ✂	40.00
☐	Adam Deadmarsh, LosA. ✂	40.00
☐	Pavol Demitra, SLou. ✂	40.00
☐	Marc Denis, Colu. ✂	40.00
☐	Shane Doan, Phoe. ✂	40.00
☐	Chris Drury, Colo. ✂	40.00
☐	Jean-Pierre Dumont, Buff. ✂	40.00
☐	Sergei Fedorov, Detr. ✂	65.00
☐	Ruslan Fedotenko, Phil. ✂	40.00
☐	Peter Forsberg, Colo. ✂	90.00
☐	Jeff Friesen, Anah. ✂	40.00
☐	Simon Gagné, Phil. ✂	50.00
☐	Jean-Sébastien Giguère (G), Anah. ✂	50.00
☐	Milan Hejduk, Colo. ✂	50.00
☐	Jarome Iginla, Calg. ✂	50.00
☐	Jaromir Jagr, Wash. ✂	65.00
☐	Brent Johnson, SLou. ✂	40.00
☐	Paul Kariya, Anah. ✂	90.00
☐	Rostislav Klesla, Colu. ✂	40.00
☐	Espen Knutsen, Colu. ✂	40.00
☐	Saku Koivu, Mont. ✂	50.00
☐	Vyacheslav Kozlov, Buff. ✂	40.00
☐	Mario Lemieux, Pitt. ✂	200.00
☐	Nicklas Lidström, Detr. ✂	40.00
☐	Trevor Linden, Vanc. ✂	40.00
☐	Mike Modano, Dall. ✂	65.00
☐	Ville Nieminen, Pitt. ✂	40.00
☐	Joe Nieuwendyk, NJer. ✂	40.00
☐	Zigmund Palffy, LosA. ✂	40.00
☐	Félix Potvin, LosA. ✂	40.00
☐	Keith Primeau, Phil. ✂	40.00
☐	Mike Richter, New York ✂	40.00
☐	Patrick Roy, Colo. ✂	160.00
☐	Geoff Sanderson, Colu. ✂	40.00
☐	Miroslav Satan, Buff. ✂	40.00
☐	Marc Savard, Calg. ✂	40.00
☐	Teemu Selänne, SanJ. ✂	50.00
☐	Brendan Shanahan, Detr. ✂	65.00
☐	Steve Sullivan, Chic. ✂	40.00
☐	Mats Sundin, Toro. ✂	65.00
☐	Alex Tanguay, Colo. ✂	40.00
☐	José Théodore (G), Mont. ✂	80.00
☐	Jocelyn Thibault, Chic. ✂	40.00
☐	Ron Tugnutt, Colu. ✂	40.00
☐	Marty Turco, Dall. ✂	40.00
☐	Ray Whitney, Colu. ✂	40.00
☐	Justin Williams, Phil. ✂	40.00
☐	Mike York, Edmo. ✂	40.00
☐	Steve Yzerman, Detr. ✂	160.00

PATCH SIGNED

Insert Set (8 cards):		1175.00
	Insert (#/25)	SP
☐	Ed Belfour (G), Dall. ✍ ✂	150.00
☐	Martin Biron (G), Buff. ✍ ✂	100.00
☐	Martin Brodeur (G), NJer. ✍ ✂	250.00
☐	Curtis Joseph (G), Toro. ✍ ✂	150.00
☐	Félix Potvin (G), LosA. ✍ ✂	100.00
☐	Mike Richter (G), New York ✍ ✂	100.00
☐	Patrick Roy (G), Colo. ✍ ✂	375.00
☐	José Théodore (G), Mont. ✍ ✂	175.00

MASKED MARVELS

Insert Set (8 cards):		100.00
	Insert (1:288)	MM
☐	David Aebischer (G), Colo. ✂	15.00
☐	Brian Boucher (G), Phil. ✂	15.00
☐	Sean Burke (G), Phoe. ✂	15.00
☐	Byron Dafoe (G), Bost. ✂	15.00
☐	Mike Dunham (G), Nash. ✂	15.00
☐	Jocelyn Thibault (G), Chic. ✂	15.00
☐	Ron Tugnutt (G), Colu. ✂	15.00
☐	Marty Turco (G), Dall. ✂	15.00

MEN BEHIND THE MASK

Insert Set (11 cards):		150.00
	Insert (1:288)	MB
☐	B. Boucher (G) ✂ / R. Cechmanek (G) ✂	25.00
☐	M. Brodeur (G) ✂ / J. Théodore (G) ✂	30.00
☐	Curtis Joseph (G), Toro. ✂ ✂	25.00
☐	Félix Potvin (G), LosA. ✂ ✂	25.00
☐	Patrick Roy (G), Colo. ✂ ✂	50.00
☐	M. Dunham (G) ✂ / M. Richter (G) ✂	25.00
☐	E. Belfour (G) ✂ / J. Thibault (G) ✂	25.00

PREMIER MATCHUP

Insert Set (7 cards):		175.00
	Insert (1:288)	PM
☐	T. Amonte ✂ / M. Dunham (G) ✂	25.00
☐	J. Arnott ✂ / Cu. Joseph (G) ✂	25.00
☐	S. Fedorov ✂ / J. Thibault (G) ✂	25.00
☐	S. Gagné ✂ / M. Biron (G) ✂	25.00
☐	M. Modano ✂ / Br. Johnson (G) ✂	25.00
☐	J. Sakic ✂ / M. Brodeur (G) ✂	35.00
☐	S. Yzerman ✂ / P. Roy (G) ✂	50.00

STELLAR STICKHANDLERS

Insert Set (7 cards):		100.00
	Insert (1:288)	SS
☐	Brian Boucher (G), Phil. ✂	15.00
☐	Martin Brodeur (G), NJer. ✂	35.00
☐	Dominik Hasek (G), Detr. ✂	20.00
☐	Olaf Kölzig (G), Wash. ✂	15.00
☐	Félix Potvin (G), LosA. ✂	15.00
☐	Tommy Salo (G), Edmo. ✂	15.00
☐	José Théodore (G), Mont. ✂	25.00

STYLING TENDERS

Insert Set (8 cards):		150.00
	Insert (1:288)	SY
☐	David Aebischer (G), Colo. ✂	20.00
☐	Ed Belfour (G), Dall. ✂	20.00
☐	Brian Boucher (G), Phil. ✂	20.00
☐	Roman Cechmanek (G), Phil. ✂	20.00
☐	Mike Dunham (G), Nash. ✂	20.00
☐	Jean-Sébastien Giguère (G), Anah. ✂	20.00
☐	Mika Noronen (G), Buff. ✂	20.00
☐	Patrick Roy (G), Colo. ✂	45.00

SUPER STOPPERS

Insert Set (8 cards):		125.00
	Insert (1:288)	SS
☐	Martin Biron (G), Buff. ✂	20.00
☐	Byron Dafoe (G), Bost. ✂	20.00
☐	Brent Johnson (G), SLou. ✂	20.00
☐	Roberto Luongo (G), Flor. ✂	20.00
☐	Félix Potvin (G), LosA. ✂	20.00
☐	José Théodore (G), Mont. ✂	35.00
☐	Jocelyn Thibault (G), Chic. ✂	20.00
☐	Ron Tugnutt (G), Colu. ✂	20.00

VIEW FROM THE CAGE

Insert Set (8 cards):		150.00
	Insert (1:288)	VC
☐	Ed Belfour (G), Dall. ✂	20.00
☐	Martin Brodeur (G), NJer. ✂	30.00
☐	Sean Burke (G), Phoe. ✂	20.00
☐	Roman Cechmanek (G), Phil. ✂	20.00
☐	Mike Dunham (G), Nash. ✂	20.00
☐	Félix Potvin (G), LosA. ✂	20.00
☐	Patrick Roy (G), Colo. ✂	45.00
☐	Marty Turco (G), Dall. ✂	20.00

MASK

Insert Set (9 masks):			
	Insert (1:box)	Chrome	Mask
☐ ☐	Ed Belfour (G), Dall.		
☐ ☐	Ed Belfour (G), Dall.		
☐ ☐	Martin Brodeur, NJer.		
☐ ☐	Johan Hedberg (G), Pitt.		
☐ ☐	Curtis Joseph (G), Toro.		
☐ ☐	Evgeni Nabokov, SanJ.		
☐ ☐	Patrick Roy, Colo.		
☐ ☐	Patrick Roy, Mont.		
☐ ☐	José Théodore (G), Mont.		

2001 - 02 UPPER DECK MVP

Produced by The Upper Deck Company, this series was released in 2001.

Complete Set (220 cards):		35.00
	Description	Base
☐	1 Jean-Sébastien Giguère (G), Anah.	.50
☐	2 Paul Kariya, Anah.	1.00

☐ 3 Jeff Friesen, Anah.	.20
☐ 4 Oleg Tverdovsky, Anah.	.20
☐ 5 Mike Leclerc, Anah.	.20
☐ 6 Milan Hnilicka (G), Atla.	.20
☐ 7 Patrik Stefan, Atla.	.20
☐ 8 Ray Ferraro, Atla.	.20
☐ 9 Jiri Slegr, Atla.	.20
☐ 10 Hnat Domenichelli, Atla.	.20
☐ 11 Jason Allison, Bost.	.25
☐ 12 Joe Thornton, Bost.	.75
☐ 13 Bill Guerin, Bost.	.25
☐ 14 Sergei Samsonov, Bost.	.25
☐ 15 Kyle McLaren, Bost.	.20
☐ 16 Jonathan Girard, Bost.	.20
☐ 17 Maxim Afinogenov, Buff.	.25
☐ 18 Stu Barnes, Buff.	.20
☐ 19 Doug Gilmour, Buff.	.25
☐ 20 Chris Gratton, Buff.	.20
☐ 21 Martin Biron (G), Buff.	.25
☐ 22 Jean-Pierre Dumont, Buff.	.20
☐ 23 Miroslav Satan, Buff.	.20
☐ 24 Craig Conroy, Calg.	.20
☐ 25 Jarome Iginla, Calg.	.50
☐ 26 Rico Fata, Calg.	.20
☐ 27 Derek Morris, Calg.	.20
☐ 28 Marc Savard, Calg.	.20
☐ 29 Oleg Saprykin, Calg.	.20
☐ 30 Arturs Irbe (G), Caro.	.25
☐ 31 Shane Willis, Caro.	.20
☐ 32 Rod Brind'Amour, Caro.	.20
☐ 33 Jeff O'Neill, Caro.	.25
☐ 34 Sami Kapanen, Caro.	.20
☐ 35 Ron Francis, Caro.	.25
☐ 36 David Tanabe, Caro.	.20
☐ 37 Steve Sullivan, Chic.	.20
☐ 38 Tony Amonte, Chic.	.25
☐ 39 Jaroslav Spacek, Chic.	.20
☐ 40 Eric Dazé, Chic.	.25
☐ 41 Michael Nylander, Chic.	.20
☐ 42 Alexei Zhamnov, Chic.	.20
☐ 43 Joe Sakic, Colo.	1.00
☐ 44 Peter Forsberg, Colo.	1.00
☐ 45 Milan Hejduk, Colo.	.50
☐ 46 Chris Drury, Colo.	.25
☐ 47 Rob Blake, Colo.	.25
☐ 48 Raymond Bourque, Colo.	.75
☐ 49 Patrick Roy, Colo.	2.25
☐ 50 Alex Tanguay, Colo.	.25
☐ 51 Geoff Sanderson, Colu.	.20
☐ 52 Espen Knutsen, Colu.	.20
☐ 53 Ray Whitney, Colu.	.20
☐ 54 Rostislav Klesla, Colu.	.20
☐ 55 Ron Tugnutt, Colu.	.25
☐ 56 Tyler Wright, Colu.	.20
☐ 57 Mike Modano, Dall.	.75
☐ 58 Jere Lehtinen, Dall.	.20
☐ 59 Sergei Zubov, Dall.	.20
☐ 60 Brenden Morrow, Dall.	.20
☐ 61 Ed Belfour (G), Dall.	.75
☐ 62 Joe Nieuwendyk, Dall.	.25
☐ 63 Pierre Turgeon, Dall.	.25
☐ 64 Steve Yzerman, Detr.	1.75
☐ 65 Brendan Shanahan, Detr.	.75
☐ 66 Brett Hull, Detr.	.75
☐ 67 Luc Robitaille, Detr.	.50
☐ 68 Sergei Fedorov, Detr.	.75
☐ 69 Dominik Hasek (G), Detr.	.75
☐ 70 Darren McCarty, Detr.	.20
☐ 71 Mike Grier, Edmo.	.20
☐ 72 Ryan Smyth, Edmo.	.25
☐ 73 Anson Carter, Edmo.	.25
☐ 74 Tom Poti, Edmo.	.20
☐ 75 Tommy Salo, Edmo.	.25
☐ 76 Mike Comrie, Edmo.	.50
☐ 77 Todd Marchant, Edmo.	.20
☐ 78 Pavel Bure, Flor.	.50
☐ 79 Viktor Kozlov, Flor.	.20
☐ 80 Marcus Nilson, Flor.	.20
☐ 81 Kevyn Adams, Flor.	.20
☐ 82 Roberto Luongo, Flor.	.50
☐ 83 Denis Shvidki, Flor.	.20
☐ 84 Zigmund Palffy, LosA.	.25
☐ 85 Jozef Stümpel, LosA.	.20
☐ 86 Adam Deadmarsh, LosA.	.20
☐ 87 Mathieu Schneider, LosA.	.20
☐ 88 Bryan Smolinski, LosA.	.20
☐ 89 Éric Bélanger, LosA.	.20
☐ 90 Lubomir Visnovsky, LosA.	.20
☐ 91 Marian Gaborik, MinW.	.75
☐ 92 Lubomir Sekeras, MinW.	.20
☐ 93 Wes Walz, MinW.	.20
☐ 94 Manny Fernandez, MinW.	.25
☐ 95 Roman Simicek, MinW.	.20
☐ 96 Stacy Roest, MinW.	.20
☐ 97 Saku Koivu, Mont.	.50
☐ 98 Oleg Petrov, Mont.	.20
☐ 99 Patrice Brisebois, Mont.	.20
☐ 100 José Théodore (G), Mont.	.75
☐ 101 Richard Zednik, Mont.	.25
☐ 102 Martin Rucinsky, Mont.	.20
☐ 103 Andrei Markov, Mont.	.20
☐ 104 David Legwand, Nash.	.25
☐ 105 Cliff Ronning, Nash.	.20
☐ 106 Mike Dunham, Nash.	.25
☐ 107 Kimmo Timonen, Nash.	.20
☐ 108 Scott Walker, Nash.	.20
☐ 109 Patric Kjellberg, Nash.	.20
☐ 110 Martin Brodeur, NJer.	1.00
☐ 111 Scott Stevens, NJer.	.25
☐ 112 Patrik Elias, NJer.	.50
☐ 113 Scott Niedermayer, NJer.	.20
☐ 114 Petr Sykora, NJer.	.25
☐ 115 Jason Arnott, NJer.	.25
☐ 116 Scott Gomez, NJer.	.25
☐ 117 Rick DiPietro, NYIs.	.25
☐ 118 Mark Parrish, NYIs.	.25
☐ 119 Roman Hamrlik, NYIs.	.20
☐ 120 Mariusz Czerkawski, NYIs.	.20
☐ 121 Kenny Jönsson, NYIs.	.20
☐ 122 Dave Scatchard, NYIs.	.20
☐ 123 Mark Messier, NYRa.	.75
☐ 124 Brian Leetch, NYRa.	.25
☐ 125 Jan Hlavac, NYRa.	.20
☐ 126 Theoren Fleury, NYRa.	.25
☐ 127 Eric Lindros, NYRa.	.75
☐ 128 Petr Nedved, NYRa.	.20
☐ 129 Daniel Alfredsson, Otta.	.25
☐ 130 Radek Bonk, Otta.	.20
☐ 131 Marian Hossa, Otta.	.75
☐ 132 Shawn McEachern, Otta.	.20
☐ 133 Patrick Lalime, Otta.	.25
☐ 134 Wade Redden, Otta.	.20
☐ 135 Magnus Arvedson, Otta.	.20
☐ 136 Martin Havlat, Otta.	.25
☐ 137 Simon Gagné, Phil.	.50
☐ 138 Roman Cechmanek, Phil.	.25
☐ 139 Justin Williams, Phil.	.20
☐ 140 John LeClair, Phil.	.50
☐ 141 Mark Recchi, Phil.	.25
☐ 142 Éric Desjardins, Phil.	.20
☐ 143 Jeremy Roenick, Phil.	.50
☐ 144 Paul Mara, Phoe.	.20
☐ 145 Shane Doan, Phoe.	.20
☐ 146 Landon Wilson, Phoe.	.20
☐ 147 Sean Burke, Phoe.	.25
☐ 148 Michal Handzus, Phoe.	.20
☐ 149 Ladislav Nagy, Phoe.	.20
☐ 150 Mario Lemieux, Pitt.	2.25
☐ 151 Jan Hrdina, Pitt.	.20
☐ 152 Johan Hedberg (G), Pitt.	.25
☐ 153 Robert Lang, Pitt.	.20
☐ 154 Alex Kovalev, Pitt.	.25
☐ 155 Martin Straka, Pitt.	.20
☐ 156 Owen Nolan, SanJ.	.25
☐ 157 Vincent Damphousse, SanJ.	.25
☐ 158 Brad Stuart, SanJ.	.25
☐ 159 Teemu Selänne, SanJ.	.50
☐ 160 Evgeni Nabokov, SanJ.	.25
☐ 161 Mike Ricci, SanJ.	.20
☐ 162 Chris Pronger, SLou.	.25
☐ 163 Keith Tkachuk, SLou.	.25
☐ 164 Scott Young, SLou.	.20
☐ 165 Pavol Demitra, SLou.	.25
☐ 166 Doug Weight, SLou.	.25
☐ 167 Al MacInnis, SLou.	.25
☐ 168 Cory Stillman, SLou.	.20
☐ 169 Vincent Lecavalier, Tamp.	.75
☐ 170 Brad Richards, Tamp.	.25
☐ 171 Nikolai Khabibulin, Tamp.	.25
☐ 172 Fredrik Modin, Tamp.	.20
☐ 173 Mats Sundin, Toro.	.75
☐ 174 Gary Roberts, Toro.	.25
☐ 175 Curtis Joseph (G), Toro.	.75
☐ 176 Nikolai Antropov, Toro.	.20
☐ 177 Darcy Tucker, Toro.	.20
☐ 178 Jonas Höglund, Toro.	.20
☐ 179 Markus Näslund, Vanc.	.75
☐ 180 Brendan Morrison, Vanc.	.20
☐ 181 Todd Bertuzzi, Vanc.	.75
☐ 182 Daniel Sedin, Vanc.	.25
☐ 183 Ed Jovanovski, Vanc.	.25
☐ 184 Peter Bondra, Wash.	.25
☐ 185 Sergei Gonchar, Wash.	.20
☐ 186 Jeff Halpern, Wash.	.20
☐ 187 Olaf Kölzig, Wash.	.25
☐ 188 Jaromir Jagr, Wash.	.75
☐ 189 Gregg Naumenko (G), Anah.	.20
☐ **190 Dan Snyder, Atla. RC**	**.25**
☐ **191 Zdenek Kutlak, Bost. RC**	**.25**
☐ 192 Niclas Wallin, Caro.	.20
☐ **193 Michel Larocque, Chic. RC**	**.25**
☐ 194 Casey Hankinson, Chic.	.20
☐ 195 Chris Nielsen, Colu.	.20
☐ **196 Martin Spanhel, Colu. RC**	**.25**
☐ **197 Mathieu Darche, Colu. RC**	**.50**
☐ 198 Matt Davidson, Colu.	.20
☐ 199 Brad Larsen, Colo.	.20
☐ **200 Steve Gainey, Dall.**	**.50**
☐ **201 Jason Chimera, Edmo. RC**	**.50**
☐ **202 Andrei Podkonicky, Flor. RC**	**.50**
☐ **203 Mike Matteucci, MinW. RC**	**.25**
☐ **204 Pascal Dupuis, MinW. RC**	**.75**
☐ **205 Francis Bélanger, Mont. RC**	**.25**
☐ **206 Mike Danton, NJer. RC**	**.50**
☐ **207 Stanislav Gron, NJer. RC**	**.25**
☐ **208 Peter Smrek, NYRa. RC**	**.25**
☐ **209 Joel Kwiatkowski, Otta. RC**	**.25**
☐ **210 Kirby Law, Phil. RC**	**.25**
☐ **211 Tomas Divisek, Phil. RC**	**.25**
☐ **212 David Cullen, Phoe. RC**	**.25**
☐ **213 Billy Tibbetts, Pitt. RC**	**.50**
☐ 214 Dan LaCouture, Pitt.	.20
☐ **215 Jaroslav Obsut, SLou. RC**	**.25**
☐ **216 Dale Clarke, SLou. RC**	**.25**
☐ **217 Thomas Ziegler, Tamp. RC**	**.50**
☐ 218 Mike Brown, Vanc.	.20
☐ 219 Steve Yzerman, Detr.	.75
☐ 220 Curtis Joseph (G), Toro.	.75

ROOKIE UPDATE

Rookie	Rookie
☐ **221 Ilya Kovalchuk, Atla. RC**	**18.00**
☐ **222 Erik Cole, Caro. RC**	**4.00**
☐ **223 Pavel Datsyuk, Detr. RC**	**15.00**
☐ **224 Kristian Huselius, Flor. RC**	**5.00**
☐ **225 Marcel Hossa, Mont. RC**	**5.00**
☐ **226 Martin Erat, Nash. RC**	**4.00**
☐ **227 Christian Berglund, NJer. RC**	**4.00**
☐ **228 Raffi Torres, NYIs. RC**	**4.00**
☐ **229 Dan Blackburn (G), NYRa. RC**	**5.00**
☐ **230 Jiri Dopita, Phil. RC**	**4.00**
☐ **231 Krys Kolanos, Phoe. RC**	**4.00**
☐ **232 Brian Sutherby, Wash. RC**	**4.00**
☐ **233 Olivier Michaud, Mont. RC**	**4.00**

AUTHENTIC GOALIES

Insert Set (15 cards):	**425.00**
Insert (1:288)	**GS**
☐ Ed Belfour (G), Dall. ✂	35.00
☐ Martin Brodeur (G), NJer. ✂	60.00
☐ Roman Cechmanek (G), Phil. ✂	30.00
☐ Byron Dafoe (G), Bost. ✂	30.00
☐ Rick DiPietro (G), NYIs. ✂	30.00
☐ Dominik Hasek (G), Buff. ✂	35.00
☐ Arturs Irbe (G), Caro. ✂	30.00
☐ Curtis Joseph (G), Toro. ✂	35.00
☐ Nikolai Khabibulin (G), Tamp. ✂	30.00
☐ Olaf Kölzig (G), Wash. ✂	30.00
☐ Chris Osgood (G), Detr. ✂	30.00
☐ Mike Richter (G), NYRa. ✂	30.00
☐ Patrick Roy (G), Colo. ✂	90.00
☐ Tommy Salo (G), Edmo. ✂	30.00
☐ José Théodore (G), Mont. ✂	45.00

MASKED MEN

Insert Set (14 cards):	**30.00**
Insert (1:12)	**MM**
☐ MM1 Martin Brodeur, NJer.	5.00
☐ MM2 Ed Belfour (G), Dall.	3.00
☐ MM3 Patrick Roy, Colo.	10.00
☐ MM4 Jocelyn Thibault, Chic.	2.00
☐ MM5 Tommy Salo, Edmo.	2.00
☐ MM6 Olaf Kölzig, Wash.	2.00
☐ MM7 Johan Hedberg (G), Pitt.	2.00
☐ MM8 Evgeni Nabokov, SanJ.	2.00
☐ MM9 Patrick Lalime, Otta.	2.00
☐ MM10 Sean Burke, Phoe.	2.00
☐ MM11 Curtis Joseph (G), Toro.	3.00
☐ MM12 Arturs Irbe (G), Caro.	2.00
☐ MM13 Roman Cechmanek, Phil.	2.00
☐ MM14 Félix Potvin, LosA.	2.00

MORNING SKATE

Insert Set (15 cards):	**245.00**
Insert (1:96)	**MS**
☐ Brian Boucher (G), Phil.	15.00
☐ Rod Brind'Amour, Phil.	15.00
☐ Peter Forsberg, Québ.	35.00
☐ Simon Gagné, Phil.	20.00
☐ Milan Hejduk, AS '00	20.00
☐ Jarome Iginla, Calg.	20.00
☐ Jarome Iginla, Calg.	20.00
☐ Jaromir Jagr, Pitt.	25.00
☐ John LeClair, Phil.	20.00
☐ John LeClair, Phil.	20.00
☐ Eric Lindros, Phil.	25.00
☐ Mike Modano, Minn.	25.00
☐ Keith Primeau, Phil.	15.00
☐ Mark Recchi, Phil.	15.00
☐ Joe Sakic, Québ.	40.00

MORNING SKATE SIGNED

Insert Set (10 cards):	**305.00**
Insert (#/100)	**MSS**
☐ Brian Boucher (G), Phil. ✍	25.00
☐ Rod Brind'Amour, Phil. ✍	25.00
☐ Simon Gagné, Phil. ✍	50.00
☐ Milan Hejduk, AS '00 ✍	50.00
☐ Jarome Iginla, Calg. ✍	50.00
☐ Jarome Iginla, Calg. ✍	50.00
☐ John LeClair, Phil. ✍	50.00
☐ Mike Modano, Minn. ✍	60.00
☐ Keith Primeau, Phil. ✍	25.00
☐ Mark Recchi, Phil. ✍	25.00

MVP SOUVENIRS

Insert Set (20 cards):	**575.00**
Insert (1:96)	**S**
☐ Jason Allison, Bost.	20.00
☐ Tony Amonte, Chic.	20.00
☐ Peter Bondra, Wash.	20.00
☐ Raymond Bourque, Colo.	45.00
☐ Peter Forsberg, Colo.	50.00
☐ Scott Hartnell, Nash.	15.00
☐ Brett Hull, Dall.	35.00
☐ Jaromir Jagr, Pitt.	35.00
☐ John LeClair, Phil.	30.00
☐ Mario Lemieux, Pitt.	100.00
☐ Mark Messier, NYRa.	35.00
☐ Alexander Mogilny, NJer.	15.00
☐ Mark Recchi, Phil.	15.00
☐ Luc Robitaille, LosA.	30.00
☐ Teemu Selänne, Anah.	30.00
☐ Brendan Shanahan, Detr.	35.00
☐ Patrik Stefan, Atla.	15.00
☐ Mats Sundin, Toro.	35.00
☐ Keith Tkachuk, SLou.	20.00
☐ Steve Yzerman, Detr.	90.00

SOUVENIR COMBO

Insert Set (10 cards):	**425.00**
Insert	**SC**
☐ Daniel Alfredsson, Otta. ✂	35.00
☐ Pavel Bure, Flor. ✂	40.00
☐ Wayne Gretzky, NYRa. ✂	200.00
☐ Vincent Lecavalier, Tamp. ✂	50.00
☐ Al MacInnis, SLou. ✂	20.00
☐ Mike Modano, Dall. ✂	50.00
☐ Zigmund Palffy, LosA. ✂	30.00
☐ Jeremy Roenick, Phoe. ✂	40.00
☐ Joe Sakic, Colo. ✂	80.00
☐ Sergei Samsonov, Bost. ✂	30.00

TALENT

Insert Set (14 cards):	**40.00**
Insert (1:12)	**MT**
☐ MT1 Peter Forsberg, Colo.	4.00
☐ MT2 Joe Sakic, Colo.	5.00

☐	MT3 Mike Modano, Dall.	3.00
☐	MT4 Mario Lemieux, Pitt.	10.00
☐	MT5 Sergei Fedorov, Detr.	3.00
☐	MT6 Steve Yzerman, Detr.	8.00
☐	MT7 Pavel Bure, Flor.	2.00
☐	MT8 Paul Kariya, Anah.	4.00
☐	MT9 Teemu Selänne, SanJ.	2.00
☐	MT10 Patrik Elias, NJer.	2.00
☐	MT11 Zigmund Palffy, LosA.	2.00
☐	MT12 John LeClair, Phil.	2.00
☐	MT13 Chris Pronger, SLou.	2.00
☐	MT14 Martin Brodeur, NJer.	5.00

VALUABLE COMMODITIES

	Insert Set (7 cards):	**25.00**
	Insert (1:24)	**VC**
☐	VC1 Steve Yzerman, Detr.	8.00
☐	VC2 Pavel Bure, Flor.	2.00
☐	VC3 Joe Sakic, Colo.	5.00
☐	VC4 Martin Brodeur, NJer.	5.00
☐	VC5 Mario Lemieux, Pitt.	10.00
☐	VC6 Peter Forsberg, Colo.	4.00
☐	VC7 Mike Modano, Dall.	3.00

WATCH

	Insert Set (7 cards):	**20.00**
	Insert (1:24)	**MW**
☐	MW1 Mario Lemieux, Pitt.	10.00
☐	MW2 Joe Sakic, Colo.	5.00
☐	MW3 Jaromir Jagr, Pitt.	3.00
☐	MW4 Brett Hull, Dall.	3.00
☐	MW5 Sergei Fedorov, Detr.	3.00
☐	MW6 Mark Messier, NYRa.	3.00
☐	MW7 Chris Pronger, SLou.	2.00

2001 - 02 UPPER DECK / 23RD NATIONAL

This 15-card set was issued at the 23rd National Sports Collectors Convention from August 5-11 in Chicago.

	Upper Deck
☐	Bobby Orr
☐	Wayne Gretzky
☐	Gordie Howe

2001 - 02 UPPER DECK PEARSON AWARD CEREMONY

While these cards are not rare, they are tough to come by on the secondary market.

	Player	**UD**
☐	Jarome Iginla, Calg. [Winner]	
☐	Sean Burke (G), Phoe. [Finalist]	
☐	Patrick Roy (G), Colo. [Finalist]	

2001 - 02 UPPER DECK PREMIER COLLECTION

Produced by The Upper Deck Company, this series was released in June 2002.

	Shell Set (50 cards):	**300.00**
	Complete Set (114 cards):	**2,500**
	Common Player:	**5.00**
	Description	**UD PC**
☐	1 Paul Kariya, Anah.	10.00
☐	2 Dany Heatley, Atla.	15.00
☐	3 Joe Thornton, Bost.	10.00
☐	4 Raymond Bourque, Bost.	10.00
☐	5 Bobby Orr, Bost.	40.00
☐	6 Sergei Samsonov, Bost.	5.00
☐	7 Tim Connolly, Buff.	5.00
☐	8 Jarome Iginla, Calg.	5.00
☐	9 Arturs Irbe (G), Caro.	5.00
☐	10 Jocelyn Thibault, Chic.	5.00
☐	11 Joe Sakic, Colo.	15.00
☐	12 Patrick Roy, Colo.	30.00
☐	13 Peter Forsberg, Colo.	10.00
☐	14 Chris Drury, Colo.	5.00
☐	15 Milan Hejduk, Colo.	5.00
☐	16 Rostislav Klesla, Colu.	5.00
☐	17 Mike Modano, Dall.	10.00
☐	18 Ed Belfour (G), Dall.	10.00
☐	19 Gordie Howe, Detr.	25.00
☐	20 Brendan Shanahan, Detr.	10.00
☐	21 Steve Yzerman, Detr.	20.00
☐	22 Brett Hull, Detr.	10.00
☐	23 Dominik Hasek (G), Detr.	10.00
☐	24 Sergei Fedorov, Detr.	10.00
☐	25 Wayne Gretzky, Edmo.	40.00
☐	26 Tommy Salo, Edmo.	5.00
☐	27 Roberto Luongo, Flor.	5.00
☐	28 Félix Potvin, LosA.	5.00
☐	29 Marian Gaborik, MinW.	10.00
☐	30 José Théodore (G), Mont.	10.00
☐	31 Mike Dunham, Nash.	5.00
☐	32 Martin Brodeur, NJer.	15.00
☐	33 Alexei Yashin, New York	5.00
☐	34 Eric Lindros, New York	10.00
☐	35 Pavel Bure, New York	5.00
☐	36 Marian Hossa, Otta.	10.00
☐	37 Jeremy Roenick, Phil.	5.00
☐	38 John LeClair, Phil.	5.00
☐	39 Simon Gagné, Phil.	5.00
☐	40 Sean Burke, Phoe.	5.00
☐	41 Mario Lemieux, Pitt.	30.00
☐	42 Evgeni Nabokov, SanJ.	5.00
☐	43 Teemu Selänne, SanJ.	5.00
☐	44 Keith Tkachuk, SLou.	5.00
☐	45 Chris Pronger, SLou.	5.00
☐	46 Brad Richards, Tamp.	5.00
☐	47 Curtis Joseph (G), Toro.	10.00
☐	48 Mats Sundin, Toro.	10.00
☐	49 Markus Näslund, Vanc.	10.00
☐	50 Jaromir Jagr, Wash.	10.00

SUPER ROOKIE

	Rookie (#/399)	**R399**
☐	**51 Timo Pärssinen, Anah. RC**	**15.00**
☐	**52 Ben Simon, Atla. RC**	**15.00**
☐	**53 Frédéric Cassivi, Atla. RC**	**20.00**
☐	**54 Ales Kotalik, Buff. RC**	**60.00**
☐	**55 Mike** Peluso, Chic. RC**	**20.00**
☐	**56 Steve Moore, Colo. RC**	**15.00**
☐	**57 Martin Spanhel, Colu. RC**	**15.00**
☐	**58 Matt Davidson, Colu. RC**	**15.00**
☐	**59 Mathieu Darche, Colu. RC**	**20.00**
☐	**60 Duvie Westcott, Colu. RC**	**15.00**
☐	**61 Blake Bellefeuille, Colu. RC**	**15.00**
☐	**62 Ty Conklin, Edmo. RC**	**20.00**
☐	**63 Stephen Weiss, Flor. RC**	**200.00**
☐	**64 Jaroslav Bednar, LosA. RC**	**20.00**
☐	**65 Pascal Dupuis, MinW. RC**	**35.00**
☐	**66 Nick Schultz, MinW. RC**	**20.00**
☐	**67 Travis Roche, MinW. RC**	**15.00**
☐	**68 Nathan Perrott, Nash. RC**	**15.00**
☐	**69 Scott Clemmensen, NJer. RC**	**20.00**
☐	**70 Andreas Salomonsson, NJer. RC**	**15.00**
☐	**71 Stanislav Gron, NJer. RC**	**15.00**
☐	**72 Radek Martinek, NYIs. RC**	**15.00**
☐	**73 Mikael Samuelsson, NYRa. RC**	**15.00**
☐	**74 Toni Dahlman, Otta. RC**	**15.00**
☐	**75 Bruno St-Jacques, Phil. RC**	**15.00**
☐	**76 Tomas Divisek, Phil. RC**	**15.00**
☐	**77 Vaclav Pletka, Phil. RC**	**15.00**
☐	**78 Éric Meloche, Pitt. RC**	**15.00**
☐	**79 Tom Kostopoulos, Pitt. RC**	**15.00**
☐	**80 Mark Rycroft, SLou. RC**	**15.00**
☐	**81 Martin Cibak, Tamp. RC**	**15.00**
☐	**82 Josef Boumedienne, Tamp. RC**	**15.00**
☐	**83 Karel Pilar, Toro. RC**	**20.00**
☐	**84 Sébastien Centomo, Toro. RC**	**35.00**
☐	85 Justin Kurtz, Vanc.	8.00
☐	**86 Ivan Ciernik, Wash. RC**	**20.00**
☐	**87 Chris Corrinet, Wash. RC**	**15.00**

SUPER ROOKIE

	Rookie (#/250)	**R250**
☐	**88 Ilja Bryzgalov, Anah. RC**	**50.00**
☐	**89 Pasi Nurminen, Atla. RC**	**60.00**
☐	**90 Ivan Huml, Bost. RC**	**60.00**
☐	**91 Erik Cole, Caro. RC**	**80.00**
☐	**92 Tyler Arnason, Chic. RC**	**125.00**
☐	**93 Riku Hahl, Colo. RC**	**40.00**
☐	**94 Niko Kapanen, Dall. RC**	**60.00**
☐	**95 Pavel Datsyuk, Detr. RC**	**275.00**
☐	**96 Sean Avery, Detr. RC**	**40.00**
☐	**97 Niklas Hagman, Flor. RC**	**40.00**
☐	**98 Olivier Michaud, Mont. RC**	**60.00**
☐	**99 Marcel Hossa, Mont. RC**	**100.00**
☐	**100 Martin Erat, Nash. RC**	**40.00**
☐	**101 Christian Berglund, NJer. RC**	**40.00**
☐	**102 Lukas Krajicek, Flor. RC**	**60.00**
☐	**103 Jiri Dopita, Phil. RC**	**40.00**
☐	**104 Branko Radivojevic, Phoe. RC**	**60.00**
☐	**105 Shane Endicott, Pitt. RC**	**30.00**
☐	**106 Jeff Jillson, SanJ. RC**	**40.00**
☐	**107 Nikita Alexeev, Tamp. RC**	**60.00**
☐	**108 Brian Sutherby, Wash. RC**	**40.00**

SUPER ROOKIE

	Rookie (#/199)	**R199**
☐	**109 Ilya Kovalchuk, Atla. RC ✍**	**550.00**
☐	**110 Vaclav Nedorost, Colo. RC ✍**	**100.00**
☐	**111 Kristian Huselius, Flor. RC ✍**	**150.00**
☐	**112 Raffi Torres, New York RC ✍**	**100.00**
☐	**113 Dan Blackburn (G), NYRa. RC ✍**	**200.00**
☐	**114 Krys Kolanos, Phoe. RC ✍**	**100.00**

JERSEY BRONZE

	Insert Set (30 cards):	**600.00**
	Insert (#/300)	**Jers**
☐	Tony Amonte, Chic. ✄	15.00
☐	Ed Belfour (G), Dall. ✄	25.00
☐	Peter Bondra, Wash. ✄	15.00
☐	Ray Bourque, Colo. ✄	30.00
☐	Pavel Bure, New York ✄	20.00
☐	Chris Drury, Colo. ✄	15.00
☐	Sergei Fedorov, Detr. ✄	25.00
☐	Theoren Fleury, NYRa. ✄	15.00
☐	Peter Forsberg, Colo. ✄	35.00
☐	Simon Gagné, Phil. ✄	20.00
☐	Wayne Gretzky, 1996 All-Star ✄	100.00
☐	Milan Hejduk, Colo. ✄	20.00
☐	Jarome Iginla, Calg. ✄	20.00
☐	Jaromir Jagr, 1996 All-Star ✄	20.00
☐	Jaromir Jagr, Wash. ✄	20.00
☐	Paul Kariya, 2001 All-Star ✄	35.00
☐	Saku Koivu, Mont. ✄	20.00
☐	Olaf Kölzig, Wash. ✄	15.00
☐	Ilya Kovalchuk, Atla. ✄	25.00
☐	John LeClair, Phil. ✄	20.00
☐	Eric Lindros, New York ✄	25.00
☐	Zigmund Palffy, LosA. ✄	15.00
☐	Mike Richter, New York ✄	15.00
☐	Patrick Roy, Mont. ✄	60.00
☐	Joe Sakic, 2000 All-Star ✄	40.00
☐	Sergei Samsonov, Bost. ✄	15.00
☐	Teemu Selänne, SanJ. ✄	20.00
☐	Brendan Shanahan, Detr. ✄	25.00
☐	Mats Sundin, Toro. ✄	25.00
☐	José Théodore (G), Mont. ✄	30.00

JERSEY SILVER

	Insert Set (7 cards):	**200.00**
	Insert (#/150)	**Jers**
☐	Martin Brodeur, NJer. ✄	45.00
☐	Dominik Hasek (G), Detr. ✄	30.00
☐	Curtis Joseph (G), Toro. ✄	30.00
☐	Paul Kariya, Anah. ✄	40.00
☐	Mike Modano, Dall. ✄	30.00
☐	Joe Sakic, Colo. ✄	45.00
☐	Joe Thornton, Bost. ✄	35.00

JERSEY GOLD

	Insert Set (7 cards):	**700.00**
	Insert (#/50)	**Jers**
☐	Raymond Bourque, Bost. ✄	60.00
☐	Wayne Gretzky, LosA. ✄	200.00
☐	Gordie Howe, Houston ✄	200.00
☐	Bobby Hull, 92 Heroes of Hockey	60.00
☐	Mario Lemieux, Pitt. ✄	150.00
☐	Patrick Roy, Colo. ✄	150.00
☐	Steve Yzerman, Detr. ✄	120.00

JERSEY DUAL

	Insert Set (35 cards):	**2200.00**	**1500.00**
	Insert (#/100)	**J50**	**J100**
☐☐	T. Amonte ✄ / J. Thibault (G) ✄	40.00	30.00
☐☐	P. Bure ✄ / M. Afinogenov ✄	40.00	30.00
☐☐	R. Bourque ✄ / R. Blake ✄	50.00	30.00
☐☐	R. Blake ✄ / C. Pronger ✄	40.00	30.00
☐☐	M. Brodeur (G) ✄ / J. Théodore (G) ✄	75.00	50.00
☐☐	J. Thornton ✄ / R. Bourque ✄	50.00	50.00
☐☐	R. Cechmanek (G) ✄ / B. Boucher (G) ✄	40.00	30.00
☐☐	C. Drury ✄ / M. Modano ✄	40.00	30.00
☐☐	A. Deadmarsh ✄ / F. Potvin (G) ✄	40.00	30.00
☐☐	S. Fedorov ✄ / P. Bure ✄	50.00	30.00
☐☐	P. Forsberg ✄ / C. Drury ✄	50.00	30.00
☐☐	W. Gretzky ✄ / Br. Hull ✄	150.00	100.00
☐☐	W. Gretzky ✄ / P. Kariya ✄	150.00	100.00
☐☐	W. Gretzky ✄ / M. Lemieux ✄	275.00	200.00
☐☐	W. Gretzky ✄ / M. Messier ✄	150.00	100.00
☐☐	D. Hasek (G) ✄ / R. Cechmanek (G) ✄	40.00	30.00
☐☐	W. Gretzky ✄ / G. Howe ✄	275.00	200.00
☐☐	M. Hejduk ✄ / J. Jagr ✄	50.00	30.00
☐☐	J. Jagr ✄ / P. Bondra ✄	40.00	30.00
☐☐	C. Joseph (G) ✄ / F. Potvin (G) ✄	40.00	30.00
☐☐	P. Kairya ✄ / J. Iginla ✄	50.00	30.00
☐☐	P. Kariya ✄ / J. Sakic ✄	75.00	50.00
☐☐	N. Lidström ✄ / D. Hasek (G) ✄	40.00	30.00
☐☐	M. Lemieux ✄ / P. Kariya ✄	125.00	75.00
☐☐	B. Leetch ✄ / M. Richter (G) ✄	40.00	30.00
☐☐	E. Belfour (G) ✄ / M. Modano ✄	50.00	30.00
☐☐	P. Roy (G) ✄ / M. Brodeur (G) ✄	100.00	75.00
☐☐	C. Joseph (G) ✄ / M. Richter (G) ✄	40.00	30.00
☐☐	T. Selänne ✄ / V. Nieminen ✄	40.00	30.00
☐☐	T. Selänne ✄ / Z. Palffy ✄	40.00	30.00
☐☐	J. Sakic ✄ / P. Roy (G) ✄	100.00	75.00
☐☐	J. Thornton ✄ / S. Samsonov ✄	50.00	30.00
☐☐	B. Shanahan ✄ / S. Yzerman ✄	100.00	75.00
☐☐	J. Thibault (G) ✄ / S. Burke (G) ✄	40.00	30.00
☐☐	J. Nieuwendyk ✄ / J. Thornton ✄	40.00	30.00

PREMIER SIGNATURES BRONZE

There are two versions: the regular insert and the Black parallel (#/100).

	Insert Set (14 cards):	**275.00**	**200.00**
	Bronze	**PSB100**	**PSB**
☐☐	Tony Amonte, Chic. ✍	20.00	15.00
☐☐	Martin Biron (G), Buff. ✍	20.00	12.00
☐☐	Mike Comrie, Edmo. ✍	20.00	20.00
☐☐	Marian Gaborik, MinW. ✍	30.00	30.00
☐☐	Martin Havlat, Otta. ✍	20.00	15.00
☐☐	Johan Hedberg (G), Pitt. ✍	20.00	12.00
☐☐	Marian Hossa, Otta. ✍	30.00	30.00
☐☐	Arturs Irbe (G), Caro. ✍	20.00	12.00
☐☐	Rostislav Klesla, Colu. ✍	20.00	12.00
☐☐	Alex Kovalev, Pitt. ✍	20.00	15.00
☐☐	Markus Näslund, Vanc. ✍	30.00	30.00
☐☐	Tommy Salo, Edmo. ✍	20.00	12.00
☐☐	José Théodore (G), Mont. ✍	35.00	35.00
☐☐	Raffi Torres, New York ✍	20.00	12.00

PREMIER SIGNATURES SILVER

There are two versions: the regular insert and the Black parallel (#/50).

	Insert Set (14 cards):	**825.00**	**325.00**
	Silver	**PSS50**	**PSS**
☐☐	Rob Blake, Colo. ✍	60.00	25.00
☐☐	Peter Bondra, Wash. ✍	60.00	25.00
☐☐	Mike Bossy, New York ✍	120.00	45.00
☐☐	Simon Gagné, Phil. ✍	80.00	30.00
☐☐	Bill Guerin, Bost. ✍	40.00	25.00
☐☐	Dany Heatley, Atla. ✍	100.00	50.00
☐☐	Milan Hejduk, Colo. ✍	80.00	30.00
☐☐	Jarome Iginla, Calg. ✍	80.00	30.00
☐☐	Olaf Kölzig, Wash. ✍	60.00	25.00
☐☐	John LeClair, Phil. ✍	80.00	30.00
☐☐	Cam Neely, Bost. ✍	100.00	40.00
☐☐	Zigmund Palffy, LosA. ✍	60.00	25.00
☐☐	Félix Potvin, LosA. ✍	60.00	25.00
☐☐	Doug Weight, SLou. ✍	60.00	25.00

PREMIER SIGNATURES GOLD

There are two versions: the regular insert and the Black parallel (#/5).

	Insert Set (14 cards):	**11475.00**	**1425.00**
	Silver	**PSG5**	**PSG**
☐☐	Raymond Bourque, Bost. ✍	700.00	85.00
☐☐	Wayne Gretzky, NYRa. ✍	1900.00	250.00
☐☐	Wayne Gretzky, Edmo. ✍	1900.00	250.00
☐☐	Gordie Howe, Detr. ✍	1400.00	175.00
☐☐	Bobby Hull, Chic. ✍	500.00	60.00
☐☐	Curtis Joseph (G), Toro. ✍	500.00	60.00
☐☐	Ilya Kovalchuk, Atla. ✍	500.00	80.00
☐☐	Bobby Orr, Bost. ✍	2000.00	250.00
☐☐	Patrick Roy, Colo. ✍	1500.00	150.00
☐☐	Teemu Selänne, SanJ. ✍	400.00	50.00
☐☐	Steve Yzerman, Detr. ✍	1200.00	150.00
☐☐	M. Richter (G) ✍ / D. Blackburn (G) ✍	200.00	40.00
☐☐	S. Samsonov ✍ / J. Thornton ✍	500.00	65.00
☐☐	P. Bure ✍ / K. Huselius ✍	300.00	40.00

2001 - 02 UPPER DECK STANLEY CUP CHAMPS

Produced by The Upper Deck Company, this series was released as a cross-brand insert in 2001.

	Complete Set (86 cards):	**100.00**
	Description	**Base**
☐	1 Phil Esposito, Bost.	3.00
☐	2 Bobby Orr, Bost.	10.00
☐	3 Glenn Hall, Chic.	2.50
☐	4 Bobby Hull, Chic.	4.00
☐	5 Raymond Bourque, Bost.	3.00
☐	6 Gordie Howe, Detr.	7.00

☐	7 Ted Lindsay, Detr.	2.50
☐	8 Terry Sawchuk, Detr.	5.00
☐	9 Grant Fuhr, Edmo.	1.50
☐	10 Wayne Gretzky, Edmo.	10.00
☐	11 Jari Kurri, Edmo.	2.50
☐	12 Bill Ranford, Edmo.	1.00
☐	13 Jean Béliveau, Mont.	5.00
☐	14 Yvan Cournoyer, Mont.	1.50
☐	15 Guy Lafleur, Mont.	5.00
☐	16 Jacques Plante, Mont.	4.00
☐	17 Maurice Richard, Mont.	7.00
☐	18 Henri Richard, Mont.	2.50
☐	19 Mike Bossy, NYIs.	4.00
☐	20 Bob Nystrom, NYIs.	.75
☐	21 Ken Morrow, NYIs.	.75
☐	22 Bryan Trottier, NYIs.	2.50
☐	23 Bobby Clarke, Phil.	2.00
☐	24 Bernie Parent, Phil.	2.00
☐	25 Tim Horton, Toro.	3.00
☐	26 Frank Mahovlich, Toro.	2.50
☐	27 Mike Vernon, Calg.	1.00
☐	28 Theoren Fleury, Calg.	1.50
☐	29 Al MacInnis, Calg.	1.00
☐	30 Peter Forsberg, Colo.	3.50
☐	31 Dan Hinote, Colo.	.75
☐	32 Milan Hejduk, Colo.	2.00
☐	33 Alex Tanguay, Colo.	1.50
☐	34 David Aebischer (G), Colo.	.75
☐	35 Chris Drury, Colo.	1.50
☐	36 Rob Blake, Colo.	1.50
☐	37 Joe Sakic, Colo.	4.00
☐	38 Patrick Roy, Colo.	7.00
☐	39 Ville Nieminen, Colo.	.75
☐	40 Steven Reinprecht, Colo.	.75
☐	41 Adam Foote, Colo.	.75
☐	42 Adam Deadmarsh, Colo.	.75
☐	43 Jon Klemm, Colo.	.75
☐	44 Sandis Ozolinsh, Colo.	.75
☐	45 Mike Keane, Colo.	.75
☐	46 Mike Modano, Dall.	2.50
☐	47 Brett Hull, Dall.	2.50
☐	48 Joe Nieuwendyk, Dall.	1.00
☐	49 Sergei Zubov, Dall.	.75
☐	50 Ed Belfour (G), Dall.	2.50
☐	51 Derian Hatcher, Dall.	.75
☐	52 Jamie Langenbrunner, Dall.	.75
☐	53 Grant Marshall, Dall.	.75
☐	54 Jere Lehtinen, Dall.	.75
☐	55 Darryl Sydor, Dall.	.75
☐	56 Sergei Fedorov, Detr.	2.50
☐	57 Steve Yzerman, Detr.	6.00
☐	58 Nicklas Lidström, Detr.	1.50
☐	59 Mathieu Dandenault, Detr.	.75
☐	60 Vyacheslav Kozlov, Detr.	.75
☐	61 Chris Osgood, Detr.	1.50
☐	62 Darren McCarty, Detr.	.75
☐	63 Kirk Maltby, Detr.	.75
☐	64 Brendan Shanahan, Detr.	2.50
☐	65 Tomas Holmström, Detr.	.75
☐	66 John LeClair, Mont.	2.00
☐	67 Patrick Roy, Mont.	7.00
☐	68 Éric Desjardins, Mont.	.75
☐	69 Scott Stevens, NJer.	1.00
☐	70 Patrik Elias, NJer.	2.00
☐	71 Randy McKay, NJer.	.75
☐	72 Jason Arnott, NJer.	1.00
☐	73 Alexander Mogilny, NJer.	1.00
☐	74 Petr* Sykora, NJer.	1.00
☐	75 Scott Gomez, NJer.	1.00
☐	76 Sergei Brylin, NJer.	.75
☐	77 Bobby Holik, NJer.	.75
☐	78 Martin Brodeur, NJer.	4.00
☐	79 John Madden, NJer.	.75
☐	80 Scott Niedermayer, NJer.	.75
☐	81 Claude Lemieux, NJer.	.75
☐	82 Brian Leetch, NYRa.	1.50
☐	83 Mike Richter, NYRa.	1.00
☐	84 Mark Messier, NYRa.	2.50
☐	85 Jaromir Jagr, Pitt.	2.50
☐	86 Mario Lemieux, Pitt.	7.00

CHAMPIONSHIP STICKS

Insert Set		1400.00
	Insert (#/150)	**S150**
☐	Mike Bossy, NYIs. ✂	80.00
☐	Raymond Bourque, Colo. ✂	60.00
☐	Martin Brodeur (G), NJer. ✂	80.00
☐	Sergei Fedorov, Detr. ✂	50.00
☐	Peter Forsberg, Colo. ✂	70.00
☐	Wayne Gretzky, Edmo. ✂	200.00
☐	Gordie Howe, Detr. ✂	200.00
☐	Brett Hull, Dall. ✂	50.00
☐	Jaromir Jagr, Pitt. ✂	50.00
☐	Guy Lafleur, Mont. ✂	60.00
☐	Mario Lemieux, Pitt. ✂	150.00
☐	Al MacInnis, Calg. ✂	25.00
☐	Mike Modano, Dall. ✂	50.00
☐	Joe Nieuwendyk, Calg. ✂	25.00
☐	Patrick Roy, Colo. ✂	100.00
☐	Patrick Roy, Mont. ✂	100.00
☐	Joe Sakic, Colo. ✂	80.00
☐	Brendan Shanahan, Detr. ✂	50.00
☐	Bryan Trottier, NYIs. ✂	50.00
☐	Steve Yzerman, Detr. ✂	120.00

PIECES OF GLORY

Insert Set		**2,175**
	Insert (#/50)	**PoG**
☐	Mike Bossy, NYIs. ✂	125.00
☐	Sergei Fedorov, Detr. ✂	75.00
☐	Theoren Fleury, Calg. ✂	50.00
☐	Martin Brodeur (G), NJer. ✂	125.00
☐	Mike Richter (G), NYRa. ✂	40.00
☐	Peter Forsberg, Colo. ✂	100.00
☐	Raymond Bourque, Colo. ✂	100.00
☐	Ed Belfour (G), Dall. ✂	75.00
☐	Brett Hull, Dall. ✂	75.00
☐	Jaromir Jagr, Pitt. ✂	50.00
☐	Guy Lafleur, Mont. ✂	100.00
☐	Mario Lemieux, Pitt. ✂	250.00
☐	Al MacInnis, Calg. ✂	40.00
☐	Mike Modano, Dall. ✂	75.00
☐	Joe Nieuwendyk, Calg. ✂	40.00
☐	Mark Messier ✂	75.00
☐	Steve Yzerman, Detr. ✂	200.00
☐	Wayne Gretzky, Edmo. ✂	350.00
☐	Patrick Roy, Mont. ✂	175.00
☐	Joe Sakic, Colo. ✂	125.00
☐	Brendan Shanahan, Detr. ✂	75.00
☐	Bryan Trottier, NYIs. ✂	75.00
☐	Patrick Roy (G), Colo.	175.00

TREASURED SWEATERS

Insert Set		**575.00**
	Insert (#/200)	**TS**
☐	Mario Lemieux, Pitt. ✂	125.00
☐	Patrick Roy, Colo. ✂	75.00
☐	Steve Yzerman, Detr. ✂	100.00
☐	Joe Sakic, Colo. ✂	50.00
☐	Mike Bossy, NYIs. ✂	50.00
☐	Peter Forsberg, Colo. ✂	50.00
☐	Brendan Shanahan, Detr. ✂	25.00
☐	Guy Lafleur, Mont. ✂	50.00
☐	Jaromir Jagr, Pitt. ✂	25.00
☐	Raymond Bourque, Colo. ✂	50.00
☐	Sergei Fedorov, Detr. ✂	25.00
☐	Patrick Roy, Mont. ✂	75.00

2001 - 02 UPPER DECK TOP SHELF

Produced by The Upper Deck Company, this series was released in 2001.

Shell Set (45 cards):		**50.00**
Complete Set (105 cards):		**775.00**
	Description	**Base**
☐	1 Paul Kariya, Anah.	2.50
☐	2 Patrik Stefan, Atla.	.50
☐	3 Joe Thornton, Bost.	2.00
☐	4 Miroslav Satan, Buff.	.50
☐	5 Jarome Iginla, Calg.	1.50
☐	6 Jeff O'Neill, Caro.	.50
☐	7 Tony Amonte, Chic.	1.00
☐	8 Joe Sakic, Colo.	3.00
☐	9 Peter Forsberg, Colo.	2.50
☐	10 Raymond Bourque, Colo.	2.00
☐	11 Milan Hejduk, Colo.	1.50
☐	12 Patrick Roy, Colo.	6.00
☐	13 Rostislav Klesla, Colu.	.50
☐	14 Mike Modano, Dall.	2.00
☐	15 Steve Yzerman, Detr.	4.50
☐	16 Luc Robitaille, Detr.	1.50
☐	17 Dominik Hasek (G), Detr.	2.00
☐	18 Tommy Salo, Edmo.	.50
☐	19 Pavel Bure, Flor.	1.50
☐	20 Zigmund Palffy, LosA.	1.00
☐	21 Brett Hull, Detr.	2.00
☐	22 Marian Gaborik, MinW.	2.00
☐	23 Saku Koivu, Mont.	1.50
☐	24 David Legwand, Nash.	.50
☐	25 Martin Brodeur, NJer.	3.00
☐	26 Patrik Elias, NJer.	1.50
☐	27 Rick DiPietro, NYIs.	.50
☐	28 Eric Lindros, NYRa.	2.00
☐	29 Marian Hossa, Otta.	2.00
☐	30 Jeremy Roenick, Phil.	1.50
☐	31 Roman Cechmanek, Phil.	.50
☐	32 Sean Burke, Phoe.	1.00
☐	33 Alex Kovalev, Pitt.	1.00
☐	34 Mario Lemieux, Pitt.	6.00
☐	35 Johan Hedberg (G), Pitt.	.50
☐	36 Evgeni Nabokov, SanJ.	1.00
☐	37 Teemu Selänne, SanJ.	1.50
☐	38 Chris Pronger, SLou.	1.00
☐	39 Keith Tkachuk, SLou.	1.00
☐	40 Vincent Lecavalier, Tamp.	2.00
☐	41 Curtis Joseph (G), Toro.	2.00
☐	42 Mats Sundin, Toro.	2.00
☐	43 Markus Näslund, Vanc.	2.00
☐	44 Daniel Sedin, Vanc.	.50
☐	45 Jaromir Jagr, Wash.	2.00

ROOKIE ACTION

	Rookie	**FF1500**
☐	**46 Mikael Samuelsson, SanJ. RC**	**6.00**
☐	**46 Mikael Samuelsson, SanJ. RC**	**6.00**
☐	**47 Dan Snyder, Atla. RC**	**6.00**
☐	**47 Dan Snyder, Atla. RC**	**6.00**
☐	**48 Zdenek Kutlak, Bost. RC**	**6.00**
☐	**48 Zdenek Kutlak, Bost. RC**	**6.00**
☐	**49 Michel Larocque, Chic. RC**	**6.00**
☐	**49 Michel Larocque, Chic. RC**	**6.00**
☐	50 Casey Hankinson, Chic.	6.00
☐	50 Casey Hankinson, Chic.	6.00
☐	**51 Bill Bowler, Colu. RC**	**6.00**
☐	**51 Bill Bowler, Colu. RC**	**6.00**
☐	**52 Martin Spanhel, Colu. RC**	**6.00**
☐	**52 Martin Spanhel, Colu. RC**	**6.00**
☐	**53 Mathieu Darche, Colu. RC**	**6.00**
☐	**53 Mathieu Darche, Colu. RC**	**6.00**
☐	**54 Jason Chimera, Edmo. RC**	**6.00**
☐	**54 Jason Chimera, Edmo. RC**	**6.00**
☐	**55 Andrei Podkonicky, Flor. RC**	**6.00**
☐	**55 Andrei Podkonicky, Flor. RC**	**6.00**
☐	**56 Pascal Dupuis, MinW. RC**	**6.00**
☐	**56 Pascal Dupuis, MinW. RC**	**6.00**
☐	**57 Francis Bélanger, Mont. RC**	**6.00**
☐	**57 Francis Bélanger, Mont. RC**	**6.00**
☐	**58 Mike Danton, NJer. RC**	**6.00**
☐	**58 Mike Danton, NJer. RC**	**6.00**
☐	**59 Stanislav Gron, NJer. RC**	**6.00**
☐	**59 Stanislav Gron, NJer. RC**	**6.00**
☐	**60 Joel Kwiatkowski, Otta. RC**	**6.00**
☐	**60 Joel Kwiatkowski, Otta. RC**	**6.00**
☐	**61 Kirby Law, Phil. RC**	**6.00**
☐	**61 Kirby Law, Phil. RC**	**6.00**
☐	**62 Tomas Divisek, Phil. RC**	**6.00**
☐	**62 Tomas Divisek, Phil. RC**	**6.00**
☐	**63 Billy Tibbetts, Pitt. RC**	**6.00**
☐	**63 Billy Tibbetts, Pitt. RC**	**6.00**
☐	**64 Thomas Ziegler, Tamp. RC**	**6.00**
☐	**64 Thomas Ziegler, Tamp. RC**	**6.00**
☐	65 Mike Brown, Vanc.	6.00
☐	65 Mike Brown, Vanc.	6.00
☐	**66 Pat Kavanagh, Vanc. RC**	**6.00**
☐	**66 Pat Kavanagh, Vanc. RC**	**6.00**

ROOKIE ACTION

	Rookie (#/500)	**FF1500**
☐	**67 Ilja Bryzgalov, Anah. RC**	**30.00**
☐	**68 Ilya Kovalchuk, Atla. RC**	**150.00**
☐	**69 Vaclav Nedorost, Colo. RC**	**35.00**
☐	**70 Niko Kapanen, Dall. RC**	**35.00**
☐	**71 Kristian Huselius, Flor. RC**	**45.00**
☐	**72 Dan Blackburn (G), NYRa. RC**	**60.00**
☐	**73 Krys Kolanos, Phoe. RC**	**35.00**
☐	**74 Jiri Dopita, Phil. RC**	**20.00**
☐	**75 Nikita Alexeev, Tamp. RC**	**35.00**
☐	**76 Brian Sutherby, Wash. RC**	**20.00**

UPDATE

	Description	**Base**
☐	77 Dany Heatley, Atla.	3.00
☐	78 Sergei Samsonov, Bost.	1.00
☐	79 Bill Guerin, Bost.	.50
☐	80 Byron Dafoe, Bost.	.50
☐	81 Martin Biron (G), Buff.	.50
☐	82 Roman Turek (G), Calg.	.50
☐	83 Arturs Irbe (G), Caro.	.50
☐	84 Steve Sullivan, Chic.	.50
☐	85 Mark Bell, Chic.	.50
☐	86 Rob Blake, Colo.	1.00
☐	87 Alex Tanguay, Colo.	1.00
☐	88 Chris Drury, Colo.	1.00
☐	89 Espen Knutsen, Colu.	.50
☐	90 Jason Arnott, Dall.	.50
☐	91 Brendan Shanahan, Detr.	2.00
☐	92 Nicklas Lidström, Detr.	1.00
☐	93 Sergei Fedorov, Detr.	2.00
☐	94 Mike Comrie, Edmo.	1.00
☐	95 Roberto Luongo, Flor.	1.00
☐	96 Félix Potvin, LosA.	1.00
☐	97 Jason Allison, LosA.	1.00
☐	98 José Théodore (G), Mont.	2.00
☐	99 Joe Nieuwendyk, NJer.	.50
☐	100 Brian Gionta, NJer.	.50
☐	101 Alexei Yashin, NYIs.	1.00
☐	102 Michael Peca, NYIs.	.50
☐	103 Chris Osgood, NYIs.	1.00
☐	104 Mark Parrish, NYIs.	.50
☐	105 Juraj Kolnik, NYIs.	.50
☐	106 Theoren Fleury, NYRa.	1.00
☐	107 Mike Richter, NYRa.	.50
☐	108 Brian Leetch, NYRa.	1.00
☐	109 Pavel Bure, NYRa.	1.00
☐	110 Martin Havlat, Otta.	1.00
☐	111 Adam Oates, Phil.	.50
☐	112 John LeClair, Phil.	1.00
☐	113 Keith Primeau, Phil.	.50
☐	114 Owen Nolan, SanJ.	1.00
☐	115 Pavol Demitra, SLou.	.50
☐	116 Brent Johnson, SLou.	.50
☐	117 Doug Weight, SLou.	1.00
☐	118 Nikolai Khabibulin (G), Tamp.	.50
☐	119 Brad Richards, Tamp.	.50
☐	120 Peter Bondra, Wash.	1.00
☐	121 Olaf Kölzig, Wash.	1.00

ROOKIE UPDATE

	Insert (#/900)	**RA**
☐	**122 Pasi Nurminen, Atla. RC**	**15.00**
☐	**123 Ivan Huml, Bost. RC**	**15.00**
☐	**124 Erik Cole, Caro. RC**	**15.00**
☐	**125 Mike Peluso, Chic. RC**	**10.00**
☐	**126 Riku Hahl, Colo. RC**	**10.00**
☐	**127 Pavel Datsyuk, Detr. RC**	**50.00**
☐	**128 Niklas Hagman, Flor. RC**	**10.00**
☐	**129 Olivier Michaud, Mont. RC**	**15.00**
☐	**130 Marcel Hossa, Mont. RC**	**25.00**
☐	**131 Martin Erat, Nash. RC**	**10.00**
☐	**132 Christian Berglund, NJer. RC**	**10.00**
☐	**133 Raffi Torres, NYIs. RC**	**15.00**
☐	**134 Branko Radivojevic, Phoe. RC**	**15.00**
☐	**135 Jeff Jillson, SanJ. RC**	**10.00**

ALL-STAR GAME NET

Insert Set (6 cards):		**300.00**
	Insert (1:287)	**ASGN**
☐	Martin Brodeur, AS '01	90.00
☐	Sean Burke, AS '01	40.00
☐	Roman Cechmanek, AS '01	40.00
☐	Dominik Hasek (G), AS '01	55.00
☐	Evgeni Nabokov, AS '01	40.00
☐	Patrick Roy, AS '01	135.00

GAME-USED PATCH

Insert Set (6 cards):		**575.00**
	Insert	**GP**
☐	Martin Brodeur, NJer. ✂	125.00
☐	Peter Forsberg, Colo. ✂	100.00
☐	Jaromir Jagr, Pitt. ✂	75.00
☐	Mike Modano, Dall. ✂	75.00
☐	Patrick Roy, Colo. ✂	200.00
☐	Steve Yzerman, Detr. ✂	200.00

GOALIE GEAR

	Insert Set (14 cards):	300.00
	Insert	**GG**
☐	Martin Biron (G), Buff. Pad ✂	25.00
☐	Brian Boucher (G), Phil. Pad ✂	25.00
☐	Roman Cechmanek, Phil. Pad ✂	25.00
☐	Gerry Cheevers, Bost. Pad ✂	35.00
☐	Byron Dafoe, Bost. Pad ✂	25.00
☐	Dominik Hasek (G), Buff. Pad ✂	45.00
☐	Johan Hedberg (G), Pitt. Blocker ✂	25.00
☐	Johan Hedberg (G), Pitt. Glove ✂	25.00
☐	Johan Hedberg (G), Pitt. Pad ✂	25.00
☐	Roberto Luongo, NYIs. Pad ✂	35.00
☐	Chris Osgood, Detr. Skate ✂	25.00
☐	Steve Shields, SanJ. Pad ✂	25.00
☐	José Théodore (G), Mont. Pad ✂	50.00
☐	John Vanbiesbrouck, Phil. Pad ✂	25.00

JERSEY

The complete set price includes only one swatch variation per player.

	Insert Set (16 cards):	225.00
	Update Insert Set (16 cards):	**150.00**
	Insert	**J**
☐	Jason Allison, Bost. ✂ Black	15.00
☐	Jason Allison, Bost. ✂ White	15.00
☐	Jason Allison, Bost. ✂ Yellow	15.00
☐	Peter Bondra, Wash. ✂ Black	15.00
☐	Valeri Bure, Calg. ✂ Red	15.00
☐	Marian Hossa, Otta. ✂ Red	30.00
☐	Marian Hossa, Otta. ✂ White	30.00
☐	Jarome Iginla, Calg. ✂ Red	25.00
☐	Jarome Iginla, Calg. ✂ White	25.00
☐	Paul Kariya, Anah. ✂ Teal	40.00
☐	Paul Kariya, Anah. ✂ White	40.00
☐	Vincent Lecavalier, Tamp. ✂ Black	30.00
☐	Daniel Sedin, Vanc. ✂ White	15.00
☐	Henrik Sedin, Vanc. ✂ White	15.00
☐	Teemu Selänne, Winn. ✂ White	25.00
☐	Teemu Selänne, Winn. ✂ Red/White	35.00
☐	Patrik Stefan, Atla. ✂ White	15.00
☐	José Théodore (G), Mont. ✂ Red	35.00
☐	José Théodore (G), Mont. ✂ Blue/White	55.00
☐	José Théodore (G), Mont. ✂ Red/Blue	55.00
☐	Joe Thornton, Bost. ✂ White	35.00
☐	Marty Turco, Dall. ✂ Green	15.00
☐	Marty Turco, Dall. ✂ White	15.00
☐	Doug Weight, Edmo. ✂ Blue	15.00
☐	Doug Weight, Edmo. ✂ Orange	15.00
☐	Doug Weight, Edmo. ✂ White	15.00
☐	Alexei Yashin, Otta. ✂ Black	15.00
☐	Alexei Yashin, Otta. ✂ White	15.00
☐	Pavol Demitra, SLou. ✂	15.00
☐	Chris Drury, Colo. ✂	15.00
☐	Milan Hejduk, AS'01 ✂ Red	25.00
☐	Jarome Iginla, Calg. ✂	25.00
☐	Paul Kariya, AS'01 ✂ Blue	40.00
☐	Markus Näslund, Vanc. ✂ White	30.00
☐	Zigmund Palffy, LosA. ✂ Purple	15.00
☐	Miroslav Satan, Buff. ✂ White	15.00
☐	Brendan Shanahan, Detr. ✂	30.00
☐	Justin Williams, Phil. ✂	15.00

SIGNED JERSEY

The complete set price includes only one swatch variation per player.

	Insert Set (12 cards):	475.00
	Insert (#/100)	**SJ**
☐	Jason Allison, Bost. ✍ ✂	40.00
☐	Marian Hossa, Otta. ✍ ✂	65.00
☐	Jarome Iginla, Calg. ✍ ✂	55.00
☐	Vincent Lecavalier, Tamp. ✍ ✂	65.00
☐	Daniel Sedin, Vanc. ✍ ✂	40.00
☐	Henrik Sedin, Vanc. ✍ ✂	40.00
☐	Teemu Selänne, Winn. ✍ ✂	55.00
☐	Patrik Stefan, Atla. ✍ ✂	40.00
☐	José Théodore (G), Mont. ✍ ✂	80.00
☐	Joe Thornton, Bost. ✍ ✂	80.00
☐	Marty Turco, Dall. ✍ ✂	40.00
☐	Doug Weight, Edmo. ✍ ✂	40.00

JERSEY STANLEY CUP CHAMPION

The complete set price includes only one swatch variation per player.

	Insert Set (14 cards):	475.00
	Insert	**J**
☐	Ed Belfour (G), Dall. ✂ Black/Gold	45.00
☐	Raymond Bourque, Colo. ✂	35.00
☐	Sergei Fedorov, Detr. ✂ Red	30.00
☐	Peter Forsberg, Colo. ✂ White	40.00
☐	Brett Hull, Dall. ✂ Black	30.00
☐	Jaromir Jagr, Pitt. ✂ Black	30.00
☐	John LeClair, Phil. ✂ Black	25.00
☐	John LeClair, Phil. ✂ White	25.00
☐	Mario Lemieux, Pitt. ✂	90.00
☐	Mike Modano, Dall. ✂ Orange	30.00
☐	Mike Richter, NYRa. ✂ White	15.00
☐	Mike Richter, NYRa. ✂ Blue	15.00
☐	Patrick Roy, Colo. ✂ Burgandy	75.00
☐	Joe Sakic, Colo. ✂	50.00
☐	Brendan Shanahan, Detr. ✂ Red	30.00
☐	Steve Yzerman, Detr. ✂ White	75.00

SIGNED JERSEY STANLEY CUP CHAMPION

The complete set price includes only one swatch variation per player.

	Insert Set (6 cards):	300.00
	Insert (#/100)	**SJ**
☐	Ed Belfour (G), Dall. ✍ ✂	50.00
☐	Raymond Bourque, Colo. ✍ ✂	75.00
☐	Sergei Fedorov, Detr. ✍ ✂	50.00
☐	John LeClair, Phil. ✍ ✂	50.00
☐	Mike Modano, Dall. ✍ ✂	50.00
☐	Steve Yzerman, Detr. ✍ ✂	150.00

STICK

There are two versions for each card: the stick insert and the Gold parallel (#/50).

	Insert Set (24 cards):	1375.00	650.00
	Insert (1:12)	**G50**	**Stick**
☐ ☐	Peter Bondra, Wash. ✂	40.00	15.00
☐ ☐	Raymond Bourque, Colo. ✂	75.00	35.00
☐ ☐	Martin Brodeur, NJer. ✂	100.00	45.00
☐ ☐	Pavel Bure, Flor. ✂	50.00	20.00
☐ ☐	Sergei Fedorov, Detr. ✂	50.00	30.00
☐ ☐	Theoren Fleury, NYRa. ✂	40.00	15.00
☐ ☐	Peter Forsberg, Colo. ✂	75.00	40.00
☐ ☐	Wayne Gretzky, NYRa. ✂	250.00	120.00
☐ ☐	Dominik Hasek (G), Buff. ✂	50.00	30.00
☐ ☐	Brett Hull, Dall. ✂	50.00	30.00
☐ ☐	Paul Kariya, Anah. ✂	75.00	40.00
☐ ☐	John LeClair, Phil. ✂	50.00	20.00
☐ ☐	Mario Lemieux, Pitt. ✂	175.00	90.00
☐ ☐	Nicklas Lidström, Detr. ✂	40.00	15.00
☐ ☐	Mark Messier, NYRa. ✂	50.00	30.00
☐ ☐	Sandis Ozolinsh, Caro. ✂	40.00	15.00
☐ ☐	Zigmund Palffy, LosA. ✂	40.00	15.00
☐ ☐	Chris Pronger, SLou. ✂	40.00	15.00
☐ ☐	Jeremy Roenick, Phoe. ✂	50.00	20.00
☐ ☐	Patrick Roy, Colo. ✂	175.00	70.00
☐ ☐	Joe Sakic, Colo. ✂	100.00	45.00
☐ ☐	Brendan Shanahan, Detr. ✂	50.00	30.00
☐ ☐	Keith Tkachuk, Phoe. ✂	40.00	15.00
☐ ☐	Steve Yzerman, Detr. ✂	150.00	70.00

STICK TRIPLE

Photo Photo-need

There are two versions for each card: the stick insert and the Gold parallel (#/50).

	Insert Set (5 cards):	325.00	225.00
	Insert	**G50**	**Stick**
☐	Bure ✂ / Forsberg ✂ / Jagr ✂	-	50.00
☐	Bourque ✂ / Pronger ✂ / Roy (G) ✂	125.00	70.00
☐	Fleury ✂ / Kariya ✂ / Sakic ✂	100.00	55.00
☐	Hasek (G) ✂ / Lidström ✂ / Ozolinsh ✂	50.00	50.00
☐	Forsberg ✂ / Roy (G) ✂ / Sakic ✂	175.00	100.00

2001 - 02 UPPER DECK VINTAGE

Produced by The Upper Deck Company, this series was released in January 2002.

	Complete Set (300 cards):	75.00
	Common Player:	**.20**
	Description	**Base**
☐	1 Jean-Sébastien Giguère (G), Anah.	.50
☐	2 Jeff Friesen, Anah.	.20
☐	3 Paul Kariya, Anah.	1.00
☐	4 Oleg Tverdovsky, Anah.	.20
☐	5 Steve Rucchin, Anah.	.20
☐	6 Mike Leclerc, Anah.	.20
☐	7 Dan Bylsma, Anah.	.20
☐	8 Paul Kariya, Anah.	.50
☐	9 Checklist	.20
☐	10 Patrik Stefan, Atla.	.20
☐	11 Tomi Kallio, Atla.	.20
☐	12 Chris Tamer, Atla.	.20
☐	13 Milan Hnilicka (G), Atla.	.20
☐	14 Ray Ferraro, Atla.	.20
☐	15 Stephen Guolla, Atla.	.20
☐	16 Ray Ferraro, Atla.	.20
☐	17 Checklist	.20
☐	18 Kyle McLaren, Bost.	.20
☐	19 Brian Rolston, Bost.	.20
☐	20 Byron Dafoe, Bost.	.20
☐	21 Mikko Eloranta, Bost.	.20
☐	22 Sergei Samsonov, Bost.	.50
☐	23 Joe Thornton, Bost.	1.00
☐	24 Bill Guerin, Bost.	.20
☐	25 Joe Thornton, Bost.	.50
☐	26 Checklist	.20
☐	27 Martin Biron (G), Buff.	.20
☐	28 Maxim Afinogenov, Buff.	.20
☐	29 Jean-Pierre Dumont, Buff.	.20
☐	30 Chris Gratton, Buff.	.20
☐	31 Rhett Warrener, Buff.	.20
☐	32 Miroslav Satan, Buff.	.20
☐	33 Curtis Brown, Buff.	.20
☐	34 Miroslav Satan, Buff.	.20
☐	35 Checklist	.20
☐	36 Marc Savard, Calg.	.20
☐	37 Jarome Iginla, Calg.	.50
☐	38 Derek Morris, Calg.	.20
☐	39 Oleg Saprykin, Calg.	.20
☐	40 Jeff Shantz, Calg.	.20
☐	41 Craig Conroy, Calg.	.20
☐	42 Jarome Iginla, Calg.	.50
☐	43 Checklist	.20
☐	44 Jeff O'Neill, Caro.	.20
☐	45 Arturs Irbe (G), Caro.	.20
☐	46 Shane Willis, Caro.	.20
☐	47 David Tanabe, Caro.	.20
☐	48 Rod Brind'Amour, Caro.	.20
☐	49 Sami Kapanen, Caro.	.20
☐	50 Ron Francis, Caro.	.50
☐	51 Jeff O'Neill, Caro.	.20
☐	52 Checklist	.20
☐	53 Éric Dazé, Chic.	.20
☐	54 Alexei Zhamnov, Chic.	.20
☐	55 Jaroslav Spacek, Chic.	.20
☐	56 Michael Nylander, Chic.	.20
☐	57 Tony Amonte, Chic.	.50
☐	58 Steve Sullivan, Chic.	.20
☐	59 Kevin Dean, Chic.	.20
☐	60 Steve Sullivan, Chic.	.20
☐	61 Checklist	.20
☐	62 Chris Drury, Colo.	.50
☐	63 Rob Blake, Colo.	.50
☐	64 Joe Sakic, Colo.	1.50
☐	65 Peter Forsberg, Colo.	1.00
☐	66 Raymond Bourque, Colo.	1.00
☐	67 Milan Hejduk, Colo.	.50
☐	68 Patrick Roy, Colo.	3.00
☐	69 Joe Sakic, Colo.	1.00
☐	70 Checklist	1.00
☐	71 Ron Tugnutt, Colu.	.20
☐	72 Geoff Sanderson, Colu.	.20
☐	73 Espen Knutsen, Colu.	.20
☐	74 Tyler Wright, Colu.	.20
☐	75 Rostislav Klesla, Colu.	.20
☐	76 Jamie Heward, Colu.	.20
☐	77 Geoff Sanderson, Colu.	.20
☐	78 Checklist	.20
☐	79 Mike Modano, Dall.	1.00
☐	80 Ed Belfour (G), Dall.	1.00
☐	81 Pierre Turgeon, Dall.	.20
☐	82 Joe Nieuwendyk, Dall.	.20
☐	83 Sergei Zubov, Dall.	.20
☐	84 Jere Lehtinen, Dall.	.20
☐	85 Donald Audette, Dall.	.20
☐	86 Mike Modano, Dall.	.50
☐	87 Checklist	.20
☐	88 Steve Yzerman, Detr.	2.00
☐	89 Brendan Shanahan, Detr.	1.00
☐	90 Sergei Fedorov, Detr.	1.00
☐	91 Luc Robitaille, Detr.	.50
☐	92 Dominik Hasek (G), Detr.	1.00
☐	93 Nicklas Lidström, Detr.	.50
☐	94 Darren McCarty, Detr.	.20
☐	95 Brendan Shanahan, Detr.	.50
☐	96 Checklist	.50
☐	97 Tommy Salo, Edmo.	.20
☐	98 Mike Comrie, Edmo.	.50
☐	99 Tom Poti, Edmo.	.20
☐	100 Mike Grier, Edmo.	.20
☐	101 Janne Niinimaa, Edmo.	.20
☐	102 Ryan Smyth, Edmo.	.20
☐	103 Anson Carter, Edmo.	.20
☐	104 Ryan Smyth, Edmo.	.20
☐	105 Checklist	.20
☐	106 Pavel Bure, Flor.	.50
☐	107 Viktor Kozlov, Flor.	.20
☐	108 Marcus Nilson, Flor.	.20
☐	109 Denis Shvidki, Flor.	.20
☐	110 Bret Hedican, Flor.	.20
☐	111 Roberto Luongo, Flor.	.50
☐	112 Pavel Bure, Flor.	.50
☐	113 Checklist	.20
☐	114 Zigmund Palffy, LosA.	.50
☐	115 Félix Potvin, LosA.	.50
☐	116 Adam Deadmarsh, LosA.	.20
☐	117 Glen Murray, Bost.	.20
☐	118 Éric Bélanger, LosA.	.20
☐	119 Jason Holland, LosA.	.20
☐	120 Jozef Stümpel, Bost.	.20
☐	121 Zigmund Palffy, LosA.	.20
☐	122 Checklist	.20
☐	123 Marian Gaborik, MinW.	1.00
☐	124 Manny Fernandez, MinW.	.20
☐	125 Brad Bombardir, MinW.	.20
☐	126 Lubomir Sekeras, MinW.	.20
☐	127 Wes Walz, MinW.	.20
☐	128 Antti Laaksonen, MinW.	.20
☐	129 Marian Gaborik, MinW.	.50
☐	130 Checklist	.20
☐	131 Saku Koivu, Mont.	.50
☐	132 Oleg Petrov, Mont.	.20
☐	133 Martin Rucinsky, Mont.	.20
☐	134 José Théodore (G), Mont.	1.00
☐	135 Brian Savage, Mont.	.20
☐	136 Andrei Markov, Mont.	.20
☐	137 Richard Zednik, Mont.	.20
☐	138 Saku Koivu, Mont.	.50
☐	139 Checklist	.20
☐	140 David Legwand, Nash.	.20
☐	141 Mike Dunham, Nash.	.20
☐	142 Scott Walker, Nash.	.20
☐	143 Cliff Ronning, Nash.	.20
☐	144 Patric Kjellberg, Nash.	.20
☐	145 Greg Johnson, Nash.	.20
☐	146 Vitali Yachmenev, Nash.	.20
☐	147 Cliff Ronning, Nash.	.20
☐	148 Checklist	.20
☐	149 Martin Brodeur, NJer.	1.50
☐	150 Patrik Elias, NJer.	.50
☐	151 Jason Arnott, NJer.	.20
☐	152 Scott Niedermayer, NJer.	.20
☐	153 Petr Sykora, NJer.	.20
☐	154 Scott Gomez, NJer.	.20
☐	155 Scott Stevens, NJer.	.20
☐	156 Patrik Elias, NJer.	.50
☐	157 Jason Arnott, NJer.	.20
☐	158 Michael Peca, NYIs.	.20
☐	159 Rick DiPietro, NYIs.	.20
☐	160 Mariusz Czerkawski, NYIs.	.20
☐	161 Roman Hamrlik, NYIs.	.20
☐	162 Dave Scatchard, NYIs.	.20
☐	163 Brad Isbister, NYIs.	.20
☐	164 Mark Parrish, NYIs.	.20
☐	165 Checklist	.20
☐	166 Mark Messier, NYRa.	1.00
☐	167 Theoren Fleury, NYRa.	.50
☐	168 Mike Richter, NYRa.	.20
☐	169 Brian Leetch, NYRa.	.50
☐	170 Kim Johnsson, Phil.	.20
☐	171 Radek Dvorak, NYRa.	.20
☐	172 Theoren Fleury, NYRa.	.20
☐	173 Checklist	.20
☐	174 Marian Hossa, Otta.	1.00
☐	175 Radek Bonk, Otta.	.20
☐	176 Martin Havlat, Otta.	.50
☐	177 Daniel Alfredsson, Otta.	.50
☐	178 Magnus Arvedson, Otta.	.20
☐	179 Patrick Lalime, Otta.	.50
☐	180 Shawn McEachern, Otta.	.20
☐	181 Radek Bonk, Otta.	.20
☐	182 Daniel Alfredsson, Otta.	.20
☐	183 Jeremy Roenick, Phil.	.50
☐	184 Roman Cechmanek, Phil.	.20
☐	185 Keith Primeau, Phil.	.20
☐	186 John LeClair, Phil.	.50
☐	187 Kent Manderville, Phil.	.20
☐	188 Mark Recchi, Phil.	.20
☐	189 Éric Desjardins, Phil.	.20
☐	190 Mark Recchi, Phil.	.20
☐	191 Checklist	.20
☐	192 Sean Burke, Phoe.	.50
☐	193 Shane Doan, Phoe.	.20
☐	194 Michal Handzus, Phoe.	.20
☐	195 Teppo Numminen, Phoe.	.20
☐	196 Ladislav Nagy, Phoe.	.20
☐	197 Landon Wilson, Phoe.	.20
☐	198 Sean Burke, Phoe.	.20
☐	199 Checklist	.20
☐	200 Alex Kovalev, Pitt.	.50
☐	201 Mario Lemieux, Pitt.	3.00

□	202 Johan Hedberg (G), Pitt.	.20
□	203 Robert Lang, Pitt.	.20
□	204 Martin Straka, Pitt.	.20
□	205 Andrew Ference, Pitt.	.20
□	206 Kevin Stevens, Pitt.	.20
□	207 Alex Kovalev, Pitt.	.20
□	208 Checklist	.50
□	209 Evgeni Nabokov, SanJ.	.50
□	210 Teemu Selänne, SanJ.	.50
□	211 Owen Nolan, SanJ.	.50
□	212 Mike Ricci, SanJ.	.20
□	213 Scott Thornton, SanJ.	.20
□	214 Vincent Damphousse, SanJ.	.50
□	215 Brad Stuart, SanJ.	.20
□	216 Evgeni Nabokov, SanJ.	.20
□	217 Checklist	.20
□	218 Chris Pronger, SLou.	.50
□	219 Keith Tkachuk, SLou.	.50
□	220 Doug Weight, SLou.	.50
□	221 Pavol Demitra, SLou.	.20
□	222 Cory Stillman, SLou.	.20
□	223 Al MacInnis, SLou.	.20
□	224 Bryce Salvador, SLou.	.20
□	225 Scott Young, SLou.	.20
□	226 Checklist	.20
□	227 Brad Richards, Tamp.	.20
□	228 Vincent Lecavalier, Tamp.	1.00
□	229 Nikolai Khabibulin, Tamp.	.20
□	230 Fredrik Modin, Tamp.	.20
□	231 Martin St-Louis, Tamp.	.20
□	232 Pavel Kubina, Tamp.	.20
□	233 Brad Richards, Tamp.	.20
□	234 Checklist	.20
□	235 Curtis Joseph (G), Toro.	1.00
□	236 Mats Sundin, Toro.	1.00
□	237 Shayne Corson, Toro.	.20
□	238 Darcy Tucker, Toro.	.20
□	239 Nikolai Antropov, Toro.	.20
□	240 Gary Roberts, Toro.	.20
□	241 Bryan McCabe, Toro.	.20
□	242 Mats Sundin, Toro.	.50
□	243 Checklist	.20
□	244 Markus Näslund, Vanc.	1.00
□	245 Daniel Sedin, Vanc.	.20
□	246 Peter Schaefer, Vanc.	.20
□	247 Andrew Cassels, Vanc.	.20
□	248 Brendan Morrison, Vanc.	.20
□	249 Todd Bertuzzi, Vanc.	1.00
□	250 Markus Näslund, Vanc.	.50
□	251 Todd Bertuzzi, Vanc.	.20
□	252 Steve Konowalchuk, Wash.	.20
□	253 Sergei Gonchar, Wash.	.20
□	254 Calle Johansson, Wash.	.20
□	255 Peter Bondra, Wash.	.50
□	256 Jaromir Jagr, Wash.	1.00
□	257 Olaf Kölzig, Wash.	.50
□	258 Andrei Nikolishin, Wash.	.20
□	259 Olaf Kölzig, Wash.	.20
□	260 Checklist	.20
□	261 League leaders	.50
□	262 League leaders	.20
□	263 League leaders	.50
□	264 League leaders	.50
□	265 League leaders	.50
□	266 League leaders	.20
□	267 League leaders	1.00
□	268 League leaders	.20
□	269 League leaders	.20
□	270 League leaders	.50
□	271 Timo Pärssinen, Anah.	1.00
□	272 Ilja Bryzgalov, Anah.	1.50
□	273 Kevin Sawyer, Anah.	1.00
□	274 Kamil Piros, Atla.	1.00
□	275 Ilya Kovalchuk, Atla.	8.00
□	276 Brian Pothier, Atla.	1.00
□	277 Zdenek Kutlak, Bost.	1.00
□	278 Vaclav Nedorost, Colo.	1.50
□	279 Jaroslav Obsut, Colo.	1.00
□	280 Niko Kapanen, Dall.	1.50
□	281 Kristian Huselius, Flor.	2.00
□	282 Jaroslav Bednar, LosA.	1.00
□	283 Martin Erat, Nash.	1.00
□	284 Josef Boumedienne, NJer.	1.00
□	285 Scott Clemmensen, NJer.	1.00
□	286 Andreas Salomonsson, NJer.	1.00
□	287 Radek Martinek, NYIs.	1.00
□	288 Mikael Samuelsson, NYRa.	1.00
□	289 Peter Smrek, NYRa.	1.00
□	290 Ivan Ciernik, Otta.	1.00
□	291 Chris Neil, Otta.	1.00
□	292 Jiri Dopita, Phil.	1.00
□	293 David Cullen, Phoe.	1.00
□	294 Krys Kolanos, Phoe.	1.50
□	295 Jeff Jillson, SanJ.	1.00
□	296 Mark Rycroft, SLou.	1.00
□	297 Nikita Alexeev, Tamp.	1.50
□	298 Thomas Ziegler, Tamp.	1.00
□	299 Bob Wren, Toro.	1.00
□	300 Brian Sutherby, Wash.	1.00

GOLDEN GOALIES

Insert Set (5 cards):		**60.00**
	Insert (1:96)	**GG**
□	Andy Moog (G), Bost. ✂	15.00
□	Billy Smith (G), NYIs. ✂	20.00
□	Gerry Cheevers (G), Bost. ✂	20.00
□	Grant Fuhr (G), Edmo. ✂	15.00
□	Rogatien Vachon (G), LosA. ✂ Purple	15.00

NEXT IN LINE

Insert Set (6 cards):		**560.00**
	Insert (#/50)	**NL**
□	Raymond Bourque ✂ / Nicklas Lidström ✂	75.00
□	Gerry Cheevers ✂ / Maxime Ouellet ✂	50.00
□	Wayne Gretzky ✂ / Joe Sakic ✂	225.00
□	Gordie Howe ✂ / Steve Yzerman ✂	250.00
□	Paul Kariya ✂ / Guy Lafleur ✂	100.00
□	Roman Cechmanek ✂ / Billy Smith ✂	50.00

STANLEY CUP SUPERSTARS

Insert Set (5 cards):		**140.00**
	Insert (1:144)	**SC**
□	Billy Smith (G), NYIs. ✂ Blue	15.00
□	Bryan Trottier, NYIs. ✂ White	20.00
□	Mike Bossy, NYIs. ✂ Blue	30.00
□	Steve Yzerman, Detr. ✂ White	45.00
□	Wayne Gretzky, Edmo. ✂	80.00

STARS OF THE DECADE

Insert Set (6 cards):		**115.00**
	Insert (1:144)	**SD**
□	Bobby Clarke, Phil. ✂	15.00
□	Gordie Howe, Houston Aeros	55.00
□	Guy Lafleur, Mont. ✂ Red	20.00
□	Gilbert Perreault, Buff. ✂	15.00
□	Mike Bossy, NYIs. ✂	30.00
□	Phil Esposito, NYRa. ✂	20.00

SWEATERS OF HONOR

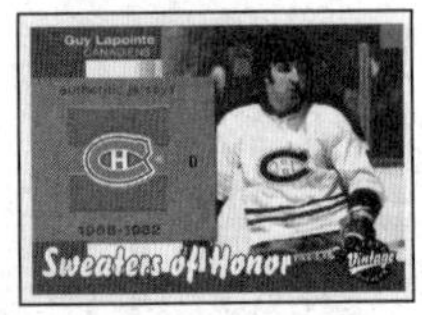

Insert Set (4 cards):		**45.00**
	Insert (1:96)	**SH**
□	Guy Lafleur, Mont. ✂	20.00
□	Guy Lapointe, Mont. ✂ Red	15.00
□	Michel Larocque, Mont. ✂ Red	15.00
□	Steve Shutt, Mont. ✂	15.00

2001 - 02 VANGUARD

Produced by Pacific Trading Cards, this series was released in February 2002. There are five versions for each card 1-130: a base card, a blue parallel (#/89), a red parallel (#/38), a Premiere Date parallel (#/83), and a vinyl One of One parallel (#/1). Blue and Premiere Date parallel cards have the same value. The Vinyl one-of-one parallel cards are not priced.

Shell Set (100 cards):		**-**	**-**	**75.00**
Complete Set (130 cards):		**700**	**400**	**400.00**
Common Player:		**15.00**	**5.00**	**.50**
	Description	**R38**	**B89**	**Base**
□□□□□	1 J. Friesen	10.00	5.00	.50
□□□□□	2 P. Kariya	60.00	35.00	4.00
□□□□□	3 D. Heatley	45.00	25.00	4.50
□□□□□	4 M. Hnilicka (G)	10.00	5.00	.50
□□□□□	5 B. Dafoe (G)	15.00	10.00	1.00
□□□□□	6 G. Murray	20.00	10.00	1.00
□□□□□	7 S. Samsonov	25.00	15.00	1.50
□□□□□	8 J. Thornton	50.00	30.00	3.50
□□□□□	9 M. Biron (G)	20.00	10.00	1.00
□□□□□	10 T. Connolly	15.00	10.00	1.00
□□□□□	11 J. Dumont	10.00	5.00	.50
□□□□□	12 J. Iginla	35.00	20.00	2.00
□□□□□	13 M. Savard	10.00	5.00	.50
□□□□□	14 R. Turek (G)	20.00	10.00	1.00
□□□□□	15 R. Francis	25.00	15.00	1.50
□□□□□	16 A. Irbe (G)	15.00	10.00	1.00
□□□□□	17 J. O'Neill	15.00	10.00	1.00
□□□□□	18 T. Amonte	25.00	15.00	1.50
□□□□□	19 M. Bell	10.00	5.00	.50
□□□□□	20 K. Calder	10.00	5.00	.50
□□□□□	21 É. Dazé	15.00	10.00	1.00
□□□□□	22 J. Thibault (G)	15.00	10.00	1.00
□□□□□	23 R. Blake	25.00	15.00	1.50
□□□□□	24 C. Drury	25.00	15.00	1.50
□□□□□	25 M. Hejduk	35.00	20.00	2.00
□□□□□	26 P. Roy (G)	105.00	60.00	9.00
□□□□□	27 J. Sakic	70.00	40.00	4.50
□□□□□	28 A. Tanguay	25.00	15.00	1.50
□□□□□	29 R. Klesla	10.00	5.00	.50
□□□□□	30 R. Tugnutt (G)	15.00	10.00	1.00
□□□□□	31 E. Belfour (G)	45.00	25.00	3.00
□□□□□	32 M. Modano	45.00	25.00	3.00
□□□□□	33 P. Turgeon	15.00	10.00	1.00
□□□□□	34 S. Fedorov	45.00	25.00	3.00
□□□□□	35 D. Hasek (G)	45.00	25.00	3.00
□□□□□	36 B. Hull	45.00	25.00	3.00
□□□□□	37 B. Shanahan	45.00	25.00	3.00
□□□□□	38 S. Yzerman	105.00	60.00	7.00
□□□□□	39 M. Comrie	35.00	20.00	2.00
□□□□□	40 T. Salo (G)	15.00	10.00	1.00
□□□□□	41 R. Smyth	20.00	10.00	1.00
□□□□□	42 P. Bure	35.00	20.00	2.00
□□□□□	43 R. Luongo (G)	35.00	20.00	2.00
□□□□□	44 J. Allison	25.00	15.00	1.50
□□□□□	45 Z. Palffy	25.00	15.00	1.50
□□□□□	46 F. Potvin (G)	25.00	15.00	1.50
□□□□□	47 M. Fernandez (G)	15.00	10.00	1.00
□□□□□	48 M. Gaborik	45.00	25.00	3.00
□□□□□	49 D. Gilmour	25.00	15.00	1.50
□□□□□	50 Y. Perreault	10.00	5.00	.50
□□□□□	51 B. Savage	10.00	5.00	.50
□□□□□	52 J. Théodore (G)	50.00	30.00	3.50
□□□□□	53 M. Dunham (G)	15.00	10.00	1.00
□□□□□	54 D. Legwand	15.00	10.00	1.00
□□□□□	55 J. Arnott	20.00	10.00	1.00
□□□□□	56 M. Brodeur (G)	70.00	40.00	4.50
□□□□□	57 P. Elias	35.00	20.00	2.00
□□□□□	58 R. DiPietro	20.00	10.00	1.00
□□□□□	59 C. Osgood (G)	25.00	15.00	1.50
□□□□□	60 M. Parrish	15.00	10.00	1.00
□□□□□	61 M. Peca	15.00	10.00	1.00
□□□□□	62 A. Yashin	25.00	15.00	1.50
□□□□□	63 B. Leetch	25.00	15.00	1.50
□□□□□	64 E. Lindros	45.00	25.00	3.00
□□□□□	65 M. Messier	45.00	25.00	3.00
□□□□□	66 M. Richter (G)	20.00	10.00	1.00
□□□□□	67 D. Alfredsson	25.00	15.00	1.50
□□□□□	68 M. Havlat	25.00	15.00	1.50
□□□□□	69 M. Hossa	45.00	25.00	3.00
□□□□□	70 P. Lalime (G)	25.00	15.00	1.50
□□□□□	71 P. Brendl	10.00	5.00	.50
□□□□□	72 R. Cechmanek (G)	15.00	10.00	1.00
□□□□□	73 J. LeClair	35.00	20.00	2.00
□□□□□	74 J. Roenick	35.00	20.00	2.00
□□□□□	75 S. Burke (G)	25.00	15.00	1.50
□□□□□	76 S. Doan	10.00	5.00	.50
□□□□□	77 D. Langkow	10.00	5.00	.50
□□□□□	78 K. Beech	10.00	5.00	.50
□□□□□	79 J. Hedberg (G)	15.00	10.00	1.00
□□□□□	80 M. Lemieux	135.00	75.00	9.00
□□□□□	81 B. Johnson (G)	15.00	10.00	1.00
□□□□□	82 C. Pronger	25.00	15.00	1.50
□□□□□	83 K. Tkachuk	25.00	15.00	1.50
□□□□□	84 D. Weight	25.00	15.00	1.50
□□□□□	85 P. Marleau	20.00	10.00	1.00
□□□□□	86 E. Nabokov (G)	25.00	15.00	1.50
□□□□□	87 O. Nolan	25.00	15.00	1.50
□□□□□	88 T. Selänne	35.00	20.00	2.00
□□□□□	89 V. Lecavalier	45.00	25.00	3.00
□□□□□	90 B. Richards	20.00	10.00	1.00
□□□□□	91 M. St-Louis	20.00	10.00	1.00
□□□□□	92 C. Joseph (G)	45.00	25.00	3.00
□□□□□	93 A. Mogilny	20.00	10.00	1.00
□□□□□	94 M. Sundin	45.00	25.00	3.00
□□□□□	95 D. Cloutier (G)	15.00	10.00	1.00
□□□□□	96 B. Morrison	10.00	5.00	.50
□□□□□	97 M. Näslund	45.00	25.00	3.00
□□□□□	98 P. Bondra	25.00	15.00	1.50
□□□□□	99 J. Jagr	45.00	25.00	3.00
□□□□□	100 O. Kölzig (G)	25.00	15.00	1.50

ROOKIES

There are five versions for each card 1-130: a base card (#/404), a blue parallel (#/89), a red parallel (#/38), a Premiere Date parallel (#/83), and a vinyl One of One parallel (#/1). Blue and Premiere Date parallel cards have the same value. The Vinyl one-of-one parallel cards are not priced.

	Description	**R38**	**B89**	**Ro404**
□□□□□	**101 Bryzgalov (G) RC**	**25.00**	**15.00**	**20.00**
□□□□□	**102 T. Pärssinen RC**	**20.00**	**15.00**	**12.00**
□□□□□	**103 I. Kovalchuk RC**	**150.00**	**75.00**	**100.00**
□□□□□	**104 B. Pothier RC**	**20.00**	**15.00**	**12.00**
□□□□□	**105 J. Hentunen RC**	**20.00**	**15.00**	**12.00**
□□□□□	**106 E. Cole RC**	**30.00**	**15.00**	**20.00**
□□□□□	**107 V. Nedorost RC**	**30.00**	**15.00**	**20.00**
□□□□□	**108 N. Kapanen RC**	**30.00**	**15.00**	**20.00**
□□□□□	**109 P. Datsyuk RC**	**125.00**	**60.00**	**80.00**
□□□□□	**110 J. Chimera RC**	**20.00**	**15.00**	**15.00**
□□□□□	**111 Conklin (G) RC**	**30.00**	**15.00**	**20.00**
□□□□□	112 J. Markkanen (G)	12.00	10.00	8.00
□□□□□	**113 N. Hagman RC**	**20.00**	**15.00**	**15.00**
□□□□□	**114 K. Huselius RC**	**40.00**	**20.00**	**30.00**
□□□□□	**115 J. Bednar RC**	**20.00**	**15.00**	**15.00**
□□□□□	**116 P. Dupuis RC**	**30.00**	**15.00**	**20.00**
□□□□□	**117 N. Schultz RC**	**20.00**	**15.00**	**15.00**
□□□□□	**118 M. Erat RC**	**20.00**	**15.00**	**15.00**
□□□□□	**119 Salomonsson RC**	**20.00**	**15.00**	**12.00**
□□□□□	**120 R. Martinek RC**	**20.00**	**15.00**	**12.00**
□□□□□	**121 R. Torres RC**	**30.00**	**15.00**	**20.00**
□□□□□	**122 Blackburn (G) RC**	**50.00**	**30.00**	**40.00**
□□□□□	**123 C. Neil RC**	**20.00**	**15.00**	**12.00**
□□□□□	**124 J. Dopita RC**	**20.00**	**15.00**	**15.00**
□□□□□	**125 D. Cullen RC**	**20.00**	**15.00**	**12.00**
□□□□□	**126 K. Kolanos RC**	**30.00**	**15.00**	**20.00**
□□□□□	**127 M. Rycroft RC**	**20.00**	**15.00**	**12.00**
□□□□□	**128 J. Jillson RC**	**20.00**	**15.00**	**15.00**
□□□□□	**129 N. Alexeev RC**	**30.00**	**15.00**	**20.00**
□□□□□	**130 B. Sutherby RC**	**20.00**	**15.00**	**15.00**

DUAL GAME-USED MEMORABILIA

Most Dual Game-Used Memorabilia cards feature a jersey swatch on both the card front and the card back. Card 42 features a Jagr jersey and a Kovalchuk stick. Cards 45-50 feature All-Star Game Net pieces on both the card front and the card back.

Insert Set (50 cards):		**200**
	Description	**DGUM**
□	1 P. Kariya ✂ / O. Tverdovsky ✂ {*515}	25.00
□	2 P. Kariya ✂ / G. Hebert (G) ✂ {*600}	20.00
□	3 S. Samsonov ✂ / D. Sweeney ✂ {*390}	10.00
□	4 J. Iginla ✂ / M. Savard ✂ {*590}	15.00
□	5 F. Brathwaite (G) ✂ / R. Turek (G) ✂ {*2000}	10.00
□	6 C. Stillman ✂ / C. Conroy ✂ {*1800}	10.00
□	7 B. Mironov ✂ / M. Nylander ✂ {*500}	10.00
□	8 T. Amonte ✂ / S. Sullivan ✂ {*150}	20.00
□	9 J. Sakic ✂ / P. Forsberg ✂ {*635}	40.00
□	10 P. Roy (G) ✂ / J. Sakic ✂ {*500}	65.00
□	11 M. Modano ✂ / D. Hatcher ✂ {*1125}	10.00
□	12 J. Langenbrunner ✂ / D. Sydor ✂ {*1375}	10.00
□	13 S. Yzerman ✂ / C. Chelios ✂ {*440}	50.00
□	14 N. Lidström ✂ / S. Fedorov ✂ {*135}	45.00
□	15 S. Koivu ✂ / T. Selänne ✂ {*600}	20.00
□	16 C. Ronning ✂ / V. Yachmenev ✂ {*700}	10.00
□	17 B. Holik ✂ / S. Niedermayer ✂ {*150}	15.00
□	18 M. Czerkawski ✂ / S. Bates ✂ {*1450}	10.00
□	19 E. Lindros ✂ / P. Brendl ✂ {*1500}	10.00
□	20 M. Richter (G) ✂ / M. York ✂ {*250}	15.00
□	21 J. Roenick ✂ / E. Weinrich ✂ {*245}	15.00
□	22 J. Lehtinen ✂ / J. Lumme ✂ {*285}	10.00
□	23 M. Straka ✂ / J. Beranek ✂ {*790}	10.00
□	24 J. Hrdina ✂ / B. Boughner ✂ {*790}	10.00
□	25 A. Kovalev ✂ / D. Kasparaitis ✂ {*1840}	10.00
□	26 M. Lemieux ✂ / R. Lang ✂ {*480}	50.00
□	27 M. Straka ✂ / R. Parent (G) ✂ {*1775}	10.00
□	28 D. Drake ✂ / M. Eastwood ✂ {*1235}	10.00
□	29 J. Hecht ✂ / J. McLennan (G) ✂ {*290}	10.00
□	30 P. Turgeon ✂ / V. Lecavalier ✂ {*785}	15.00
□	31 J. Dumont ✂ / S. Young ✂ {*490}	10.00
□	32 Cu. Joseph ✂ / J. Théodore (G) ✂ {*1000}	25.00
□	33 J. Jagr ✂ / P. Bondra ✂ {*800}	20.00
□	34 M. Sundin ✂ / A. Cassels ✂ {*745}	15.00
□	35 O. Kölzig (G) ✂ / D. Cloutier (G) ✂ {*160}	25.00
□	36 C. Lapointe ✂ / M. Lindgren ✂ {*230}	10.00
□	37 G. de Vries ✂ / É. Messier ✂ {*135}	10.00
□	38 M. Messier ✂ / E. Lindros ✂ {*100}	50.00
□	39 A. Kovalev ✂ / K. Miller ✂ {*1925}	10.00
□	40 L. Odelein ✂ / A. Savage ✂ {*1075}	10.00
□	41 M. Savard ✂ / R. Turek (G) ✂ {*1000}	10.00

☐	42 J. Jagr ✂ / I. Kovalchuk ✂ {*200}	55.00
☐	43 P. Roy (G) ✂ / J. Théodore (G) ✂ {*550}	55.00
☐	44 M. Lemieux ✂ / M. Sundin ✂ {*500}	65.00
☐	45 T. Fleury ✂ / M. Hossa ✂ {*200}	35.00
☐	46 Br. Hull ✂ / P. Bure ✂ {*200}	35.00
☐	47 D. Weight ✂ / P. Forsberg ✂ {*200}	40.00
☐	48 J. Allison ✂ / Z. Palffy ✂ {*200}	25.00
☐	49 R. Blake ✂ / M. Hejduk✂ {*200}	30.00
☐	50 M. Brodeur (G) ✂ / D. Hasek (G) ✂ {*200}	55.00

DUAL GAME-USED MEMORABILIA PATCH

Insert Set (16 cards):		**600**
	Insert	**DGUM**
☐	3 S. Samsonov ✂ / D. Sweeney ✂ {*30}	50.00
☐	5 F. Brathwaite (G) ✂ / R. Turek (G) ✂ {*180}	35.00
☐	6 C. Stillman ✂ / C. Conroy ✂ {*160}	35.00
☐	10 P. Roy (G) ✂ / J. Sakic ✂ {*50}	350.00
☐	12 J. Langenbrunner ✂ / D. Sydor ✂ {*80}	35.00
☐	21 J. Roenick ✂ / E. Weinrich ✂ {*80}	50.00
☐	22 J. Lehtinen ✂ / J. Lumme ✂ {*85}	35.00
☐	23 M. Straka ✂ / J. Beranek ✂ {*275}	35.00
☐	25 A. Kovalev ✂ / D. Kasparaitis ✂ {*275}	35.00
☐	27 M. Straka ✂ / R. Parent (G) ✂ {*160}	35.00
☐	28 D. Drake ✂ / M. Eastwood ✂ {*125}	35.00
☐	33 J. Jagr ✂ / P. Bondra ✂ {*70}	100.00
☐	37 G. de Vries ✂ / É. Messier ✂ {*50}	35.00
☐	38 M. Messier ✂ / E. Lindros ✂ {*25}	150.00
☐	39 A. Kovalev ✂ / K. Miller ✂ {*275}	35.00
☐	41 M. Savard ✂ / R. Turek (G) ✂ {*270}	35.00

EAST MEETS WEST

Insert Set (10 cards):		**100.00**
	Insert (1:97)	**EMW**
☐	1 M. Lemieux / J. Jagr	25.00
☐	2 P. Roy (G) / D. Hasek (G)	25.00
☐	3 J. Sakic / P. Forsberg	15.00
☐	4 M. Brodeur (G) / J. Hedberg	10.00
☐	5 E. Lindros / A. Yashin	10.00
☐	6 P. Kariya / T. Selänne	10.00
☐	7 S. Yzerman / S. Fedorov	20.00
☐	8 B. Shanahan / P. Bure	10.00
☐	9 J. Iginla / M. Sundin	10.00
☐	10 C. Pronger / N. Lidström	8.00

IN FOCUS

Insert Set (10 cards):		**225.00**
	Insert (#/55)	**IF**
☐	1 Patrick Roy (G), Colo.	50.00
☐	2 Joe Sakic, Colo.	35.00
☐	3 Dominik Hasek (G), Detr.	20.00
☐	4 Brendan Shanahan, Detr.	20.00
☐	5 Steve Yzerman, Detr.	50.00
☐	6 Pavel Bure, Flor.	15.00
☐	7 Martin Brodeur (G), NJer.	35.00
☐	8 Mario Lemieux, Pitt.	65.00
☐	9 Mats Sundin, Toro.	20.00
☐	10 Jaromir Jagr, Wash.	20.00

PRIME PROSPECTS

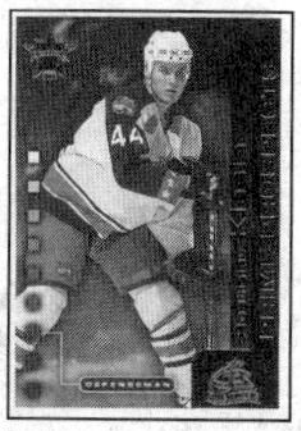

Insert Set (20 cards):		**120.00**
	Insert (1:25)	**PP**
☐	1 Dany Heatley, Atla.	12.00
☐	2 Ilya Kovalchuk, Atla.	25.00
☐	3 Vaclav Nedorost, Colo.	4.00
☐	4 Rostislav Klesla, Colu.	4.00
☐	5 Pavel Datsyuk, Detr.	20.00
☐	6 Mike Comrie, Edmo.	10.00
☐	7 Kristian Huselius, Flor.	4.00
☐	8 Jaroslav Bednar, LosA.	4.00
☐	9 Marian Gaborik, MinW.	12.00
☐	10 Martin Erat, Nash.	4.00
☐	11 Rick DiPietro (G), NYIs.	6.00
☐	12 Dan Blackburn (G), NYRa.	5.00
☐	13 Martin Havlat, Otta.	7.00
☐	14 Pavel Brendl, Phil.	4.00
☐	15 Krys Kolanos, Phoe.	4.00
☐	16 Brent Johnson (G), SLou.	5.00
☐	17 Jeff Jillson, SanJ.	4.00
☐	18 Nikita Alexeev, Tamp.	4.00
☐	19 Daniel Sedin, Vanc.	5.00
☐	20 Henrik Sedin, Vanc.	5.00

QUÉBEC TOURNAMENT HEROES

Cards 1-10 were inserted in packs of Vanguard. Cards 11-20 were polybagged with copies of Canadian Sports Collector.

Insert Set (10 cards):		**30.00**
Promotional Set (10 cards):		**35.00**
	Insert	**QTH**
☐	1 Brett Hull, Detr.	3.00
☐	2 Mario Lemieux, Pitt.	10.00
☐	3 Patrick Roy (G), Colo.	10.00
☐	4 Steve Yzerman, Detr.	8.00
☐	5 Mike Modano, Dall.	3.00
☐	6 Jeremy Roenick, Phil.	2.00
☐	7 Brendan Shanahan, Detr.	3.00
☐	8 Félix Potvin (G), LosA.	2.00
☐	9 Doug Weight, SLou.	2.00
☐	10 Eric Lindros, NYRa.	3.00
☐	11 Jocelyn Thibault (G), Chic.	4.00
☐	12 Jason Allison, LosA.	4.00
☐	13 Chris Drury, Colo.	4.00
☐	14 Jeff O'Neill, Caro.	4.00
☐	15 Sergei Samsonov, Bost.	4.00
☐	16 Alex Tanguay, Colo.	4.00
☐	17 Marian Hossa, Otta.	7.00
☐	18 Simon Gagné, Phil.	6.00
☐	19 Vincent Lecavalier, Tamp.	7.00
☐	20 Rick DiPietro, NYIs.	4.00

STONEWALLERS

Insert Set (20 cards):		**75.00**
	Insert	**SW**
☐	1 Milan Hnilicka (G), Atla.	3.00
☐	2 Byron Dafoe (G), Bost.	3.00
☐	3 Martin Biron (G), Buff.	3.00
☐	4 Roman Turek (G), Calg.	3.00
☐	5 Patrick Roy (G), Colo.	15.00
☐	6 Ed Belfour (G), Dall.	6.00
☐	7 Dominik Hasek (G), Detr.	6.00
☐	8 Tommy Salo (G), Edmo.	3.00
☐	9 Roberto Luongo (G), Flor.	5.00
☐	10 José Théodore (G), Mont.	7.00
☐	11 Martin Brodeur (G), NJer.	10.00
☐	12 Chris Osgood (G), NYIs.	3.00
☐	13 Mike Richter (G), NYRa.	3.00
☐	14 Patrick Lalime (G), Otta.	3.00
☐	15 Roman Cechmanek (G), Phil.	3.00
☐	16 Johan Hedberg (G), Pitt.	3.00
☐	17 Evgeni Nabokov (G), SanJ.	3.00
☐	18 Nikolai Khabibulin (G), Tamp.	3.00
☐	19 Curtis Joseph (G), Toro.	6.00
☐	20 Olaf Kölzig (G), Wash.	3.00

V-TEAM

Insert Set (20 cards):		**90.00**
	Insert	**VT**
☐	1 Roman Turek (G), Calg.	3.00
☐	2 Patrick Roy (G), Colo.	15.00
☐	3 Ed Belfour (G), Dall.	5.00
☐	4 Dominik Hasek (G), Detr.	5.00
☐	5 Martin Brodeur (G), NJer.	8.00
☐	6 Chris Osgood (G), NYIs.	3.00
☐	7 Roman Cechmanek (G), Phil.	3.00
☐	8 Johan Hedberg (G), Pitt.	3.00
☐	9 Evgeni Nabokov (G), SanJ.	3.00
☐	10 Curtis Joseph (G), Toro.	5.00
☐	11 Jarome Iginla, Calg.	4.00
☐	12 Joe Sakic, Colo.	8.00
☐	13 Brendan Shanahan, Detr.	5.00
☐	14 Steve Yzerman, Detr.	12.00
☐	15 Pavel Bure, Flor.	4.00
☐	16 Eric Lindros, NYRa.	5.00
☐	17 Mario Lemieux, Pitt.	15.00
☐	18 Teemu Selänne, SanJ.	4.00
☐	19 Mats Sundin, Toro.	5.00
☐	20 Jaromir Jagr, Wash.	5.00

2001 - 02 VICTORY

Produced by The Upper Deck Company, this series was released in August 2001.

Complete Set (440 cards):		**155.00**	**65.00**
Common Player:		**.35**	**.20**
	Description	**Gold**	**Base**
☐ ☐	1 J-S Giguère (G), Anah. [Checklist]	1.00	.25
☐ ☐	2 Steve Rucchin, Anah.	.35	.20
☐ ☐	3 Oleg Tverdovsky, Anah.	.35	.20
☐ ☐	4 Matt Cullen, Anah.	.35	.20
☐ ☐	5 Vitaly Vishnevski, Anah.	.35	.20
☐ ☐	6 Jean-Sébastien Giguère (G), Anah.	1.00	.50
☐ ☐	7 Mike Leclerc, Anah.	.35	.20
☐ ☐	8 Petr Tenkrat, Anah.	.35	.20
☐ ☐	9 Paul Kariya, Anah.	2.00	1.00
☐ ☐	10 Samuel Påhlsson, Anah.	.35	.20
☐ ☐	11 Jeff Friesen, Anah.	.35	.20
☐ ☐	12 Milan Hnilicka (G), Atla. [Checklist]	.35	.20
☐ ☐	13 Patrik Stefan, Atla.	.35	.20
☐ ☐	14 Andrew Brunette, Atla. (MinW.)	.35	.20
☐ ☐	15 Hnat Domenichelli, Atla.	.35	.20
☐ ☐	16 Jiri Slegr, Atla.	.35	.20
☐ ☐	17 Tomi Kallio, Atla.	.35	.20
☐ ☐	18 Steve Staios, Atla.	.35	.20
☐ ☐	19 Steve Guolla, Atla.	.35	.20
☐ ☐	20 Milan Hnilicka (G), Atla.	.35	.20
☐ ☐	21 Ray Ferraro, Atla.	.35	.20
☐ ☐	22 Frantisek Kaberle, Atla.	.35	.20
☐ ☐	23 Ladislav Kohn, Atla.	.35	.20
☐ ☐	24 Byron Dafoe, Bost. [Checklist]	.50	.20
☐ ☐	25 Sergei Samsonov, Bost.	.75	.25
☐ ☐	26 Joe Thornton, Bost.	1.75	.75
☐ ☐	27 Cameron Mann, Bost.	.35	.20
☐ ☐	28 Brian Rolston, Bost.	.35	.20
☐ ☐	29 Mikko Eloranta, Bost.	.35	.20
☐ ☐	30 Jason Allison, Bost.	.75	.25
☐ ☐	31 Mike Knuble, Bost.	.35	.20
☐ ☐	32 Eric Weinrich, Bost.	.35	.20
☐ ☐	33 Byron Dafoe, Bost.	.50	.25
☐ ☐	34 Bill Guerin, Bost.	.50	.25
☐ ☐	35 Kyle McLaren, Bost.	.35	.20
☐ ☐	36 Dominik Hasek (G), Buff. [Checklist]	1.50	.25
☐ ☐	37 Curtis Brown, Buff.	.35	.20
☐ ☐	38 Miroslav Satan, Buff.	.35	.20
☐ ☐	39 Dominik Hasek (G), Buff.	1.50	.75
☐ ☐	40 Maxim Afinogenov, Buff.	.50	.25
☐ ☐	41 Stu Barnes, Buff.	.35	.20
☐ ☐	42 Jean-Pierre Dumont, Buff.	.35	.20
☐ ☐	43 Martin Biron (G), Buff.	.50	.25
☐ ☐	44 Alexei Zhitnik, Buff.	.35	.20
☐ ☐	45 Dmitri Kalinin, Buff.	.35	.20
☐ ☐	46 Chris Gratton, Buff.	.35	.20
☐ ☐	47 Denis Hamel, Buff.	.35	.20
☐ ☐	48 Fred Brathwaite (G), Calg. [Checklist]	.35	.20
☐ ☐	49 Jarome Iginla, Calg.	1.00	.50
☐ ☐	50 Marc* Savard, Calg.	.35	.20
☐ ☐	51 Fred Brathwaite (G), Calg.	.35	.20
☐ ☐	52 Derek Morris, Calg.	.35	.20
☐ ☐	53 Dave Lowry, Calg.	.35	.20
☐ ☐	54 Craig Conroy, Calg.	.35	.20
☐ ☐	55 Valeri Bure, Calg.	.35	.20
☐ ☐	56 Oleg Saprykin, Calg.	.35	.20
☐ ☐	57 Clarke Wilm, Calg.	.35	.20
☐ ☐	58 Toni Lydman, Calg.	.35	.20
☐ ☐	59 Arturs Irbe (G), Caro. [Checklist]	.50	.20
☐ ☐	60 Rod Brind'Amour, Caro.	.35	.20
☐ ☐	61 Ron Francis, Caro.	.75	.25
☐ ☐	62 Sami Kapanen, Caro.	.35	.20
☐ ☐	63 Jeff O'Neill, Caro.	.50	.25
☐ ☐	64 Sandis Ozolinsh, Caro.	.35	.20
☐ ☐	65 Arturs Irbe (G), Caro.	.50	.25
☐ ☐	66 David Tanabe, Caro.	.35	.20
☐ ☐	67 Shane Willis, Caro.	.35	.20
☐ ☐	68 Josef Vasicek, Caro.	.35	.20
☐ ☐	69 Tommy Westlund, Caro.	.35	.20
☐ ☐	70 Bates Battaglia, Caro.	.35	.20
☐ ☐	71 Jocelyn Thibault, Chic. [Checklist]	.50	.20
☐ ☐	72 Steve Sullivan, Chic.	.35	.20
☐ ☐	73 Tony Amonte, Chic.	.75	.25
☐ ☐	74 Éric Dazé, Chic.	.50	.25
☐ ☐	75 Steve McCarthy, Chic.	.35	.20
☐ ☐	76 Alexei Zhamnov, Chic.	.35	.20
☐ ☐	77 Jaroslav Spacek, Chic.	.35	.20
☐ ☐	78 Jocelyn Thibault, Chic.	.50	.25
☐ ☐	79 Michael Nylander, Chic.	.35	.20
☐ ☐	80 Kyle Calder, Chic.	.35	.20
☐ ☐	81 Chris Herperger, Chic.	.35	.20
☐ ☐	82 Ryan Vandenbussche, Chic.	.35	.20
☐ ☐	83 Patrick Roy, Colo. [Checklist]	4.50	1.00
☐ ☐	84 Peter Forsberg, Colo.	2.00	1.00
☐ ☐	85 Raymond Bourque, Colo.	1.75	.75
☐ ☐	86 Milan Hejduk, Colo.	1.00	.50
☐ ☐	87 Alex Tanguay, Colo.	.75	.25
☐ ☐	88 David Aebischer (G), Colo.	.35	.20
☐ ☐	89 Chris Drury, Colo.	.75	.25
☐ ☐	90 Rob Blake, Colo.	.75	.25
☐ ☐	91 Joe Sakic, Colo.	2.25	1.00
☐ ☐	92 Patrick Roy, Colo.	4.50	2.00
☐ ☐	93 Ville Nieminen, Colo.	.35	.20
☐ ☐	94 Steven Reinprecht, Colo.	.35	.20
☐ ☐	95 Adam Foote, Colo.	.35	.20
☐ ☐	96 Ron Tugnutt, Colu. [Checklist]	.50	.20
☐ ☐	97 Geoff Sanderson, Colu.	.35	.20
☐ ☐	98 Serge Aubin, Colu.	.35	.20
☐ ☐	99 David Vyborny, Colu.	.35	.20
☐ ☐	100 Ron Tugnutt, Colu.	.50	.25
☐ ☐	101 Espen Knutsen, Colu.	.35	.20
☐ ☐	102 Tyler Wright, Colu.	.35	.20
☐ ☐	103 Lyle Odelein, Colu.	.35	.20
☐ ☐	104 Marc Denis, Colu.	.50	.25
☐ ☐	105 Blake Sloan, Colu.	.35	.20
☐ ☐	106 Jean-Luc Grand-Pierre, Colu.	.35	.20
☐ ☐	107 Mike Maneluk, Colu.	.35	.20
☐ ☐	108 Ed Belfour (G), Dall. [Checklist]	1.50	.25
☐ ☐	109 Mike Modano, Dall.	1.50	.75
☐ ☐	110 Brett Hull, Dall.	1.50	.75
☐ ☐	111 Brenden Morrow, Dall.	.35	.20
☐ ☐	112 Joe Nieuwendyk, Dall.	.50	.25
☐ ☐	113 Sergei Zubov, Dall.	.35	.20
☐ ☐	114 Ed Belfour (G), Dall.	1.50	.75
☐ ☐	115 Derian Hatcher, Dall.	.35	.20
☐ ☐	116 Jamie Langenbrunner, Dall.	.35	.20
☐ ☐	117 Grant Marshall, Dall.	.35	.20
☐ ☐	118 Marty Turco, Dall.	.75	.25
☐ ☐	119 Jere Lehtinen, Dall.	.35	.20
☐ ☐	120 Darryl Sydor, Dall.	.35	.20
☐ ☐	121 Chris Osgood, Detr. [Checklist]	.75	.25
☐ ☐	122 Sergei Fedorov, Detr.	1.50	.75
☐ ☐	123 Steve Yzerman, Detr.	3.50	1.50
☐ ☐	124 Nicklas Lidström, Detr.	.75	.25
☐ ☐	125 Mathieu Dandenault, Detr.	.35	.20
☐ ☐	126 Vyacheslav Kozlov, Detr.	.35	.20
☐ ☐	127 Chris Osgood, Detr.	.75	.25
☐ ☐	128 Darren McCarty, Detr.	.35	.20
☐ ☐	129 Kirk Maltby, Detr.	.35	.20
☐ ☐	130 Boyd Devereaux, Detr.	.35	.20
☐ ☐	131 Manny Legacé, Detr.	.35	.20
☐ ☐	132 Brendan Shanahan, Detr.	1.50	.75
☐ ☐	133 Tomas Holmström, Detr.	.35	.20
☐ ☐	134 Tommy Salo, Edmo. [Checklist]	.50	.20
☐ ☐	135 Anson Carter, Edmo.	.50	.25
☐ ☐	136 Todd Marchant, Edmo.	.35	.20
☐ ☐	137 Ryan Smyth, Edmo.	.50	.25
☐ ☐	138 Tommy Salo, Edmo.	.50	.25
☐ ☐	139 Doug Weight, Edmo.	.75	.25
☐ ☐	140 Janne Niinimaa, Edmo.	.35	.20
☐ ☐	141 Rem Murray, Edmo.	.35	.20
☐ ☐	142 Daniel Cleary, Edmo.	.35	.20
☐ ☐	143 Tom Poti, Edmo.	.35	.20
☐ ☐	144 Georges Laraque, Edmo.	.35	.20
☐ ☐	145 Mike Grier, Edmo.	.35	.20
☐ ☐	146 Roberto Luongo, Flor. [Checklist]	1.00	.25
☐ ☐	147 Kevyn Adams, Flor.	.35	.20
☐ ☐	148 Viktor Kozlov, Flor.	.35	.20
☐ ☐	149 Marcus Nilson, Flor.	.35	.20
☐ ☐	150 Robert Svehla, Flor.	.35	.20
☐ ☐	151 Pavel Bure, Flor.	1.00	.50
☐ ☐	152 Anders Eriksson, Flor.	.35	.20
☐ ☐	153 Vaclav Prospal, Flor.	.35	.20
☐ ☐	154 Roberto Luongo, Flor.	1.00	.50
☐ ☐	155 Denis Shvidki, Flor.	.35	.20

□□ 156 Peter Worrell, Flor.	.35	.20
□□ 157 Rob Niedermayer, Flor.	.35	.20
□□ 158 Félix Potvin, LosA. [Checklist]	.75	.25
□□ 159 Luc Robitaille, LosA.	1.00	.50
□□ 160 Zigmund Palffy, LosA.	.75	.25
□□ 161 Jozef Stümpel, LosA.	.35	.20
□□ 162 Bryan Smolinski, LosA.	.35	.20
□□ 163 Glen Murray, LosA.	.50	.25
□□ 164 Aaron Miller, LosA.	.35	.20
□□ 165 Adam Deadmarsh, LosA.	.35	.20
□□ 166 Jaroslav Modry, LosA.	.35	.20
□□ 167 Félix Potvin, LosA.	.75	.25
□□ 168 Éric Bélanger, LosA.	.35	.20
□□ 169 Ian Laperrière, LosA.	.35	.20
□□ 170 Manny Fernandez, MinW. [Checklist]	.50	.20
□□ 171 Marian Gaborik, MinW.	1.50	.75
□□ 172 Stacy Roest, MinW.	.35	.20
□□ 173 Wes Walz, MinW.	.35	.20
□□ 174 Lubomir Sekeras, MinW.	.35	.20
□□ 175 Manny Fernandez, MinW.	.50	.25
□□ 176 Darby Hendrickson, MinW.	.35	.20
□□ 177 Aaron Gavey, MinW.	.35	.20
□□ 178 Roman Simicek, MinW.	.35	.20
□□ 179 Jamie McLennan, MinW.	.35	.20
□□ 180 Antti Laaksonen, MinW.	.35	.20
□□ 181 Andy Sutton, MinW.	.35	.20
□□ 182 José Théodore (G), Mont. [Checklist]	1.75	.25
□□ 183 Richard Zednik, Mont.	.50	.25
□□ 184 Martin Rucinsky, Mont.	.35	.20
□□ 185 Saku Koivu, Mont.	1.00	.50
□□ 186 José Théodore (G), Mont.	1.75	.75
□□ 187 Brian Savage, Mont.	.35	.20
□□ 188 Oleg Petrov, Mont.	.35	.20
□□ 189 Patrice Brisebois, Mont.	.35	.20
□□ 190 Chad Kilger, Mont.	.35	.20
□□ 191 Craig Darby, Mont.	.35	.20
□□ 192 Andrei Markov, Mont.	.35	.20
□□ 193 Mike Dunham, Nash. [Checklist]	.50	.20
□□ 194 Cliff Ronning, Nash.	.35	.20
□□ 195 Vitali Yachmenev, Nash.	.35	.20
□□ 196 Scott Walker, Nash.	.35	.20
□□ 197 Kimmo Timonen, Nash.	.35	.20
□□ 198 Patric Kjellberg, Nash.	.35	.20
□□ 199 Mike Dunham, Nash.	.50	.25
□□ 200 Greg Johnson, Nash.	.35	.20
□□ 201 David Legwand, Nash.	.50	.25
□□ 202 Scott Hartnell, Nash.	.35	.20
□□ 203 Tom Fitzgerald, Nash.	.35	.20
□□ 204 Tomas Vokoun (G), Nash.	.35	.20
□□ 205 Martin Brodeur, NJer. [Checklist]	2.25	.50
□□ 206 Scott Stevens, NJer.	.50	.25
□□ 207 Patrik Elias, NJer.	1.00	.50
□□ 208 Randy McKay, NJer.	.35	.20
□□ 209 Jason Arnott, NJer.	.50	.25
□□ 210 Alexander Mogilny, NJer.	.50	.25
□□ 211 Petr Sykora, NJer.	.50	.25
□□ 212 Scott Gomez, NJer.	.50	.25
□□ 213 Sergei Brylin, NJer.	.35	.20
□□ 214 Bobby Holik, NJer.	.35	.20
□□ 215 Martin Brodeur, NJer.	2.25	1.00
□□ 216 John Madden, NJer.	.35	.20
□□ 217 Scott Niedermayer, NJer.	.35	.20
□□ 218 Rick DiPietro, NYIs. [Checklist]	.50	.20
□□ 219 Mariusz Czerkawski, NYIs.	.35	.20
□□ 220 Taylor Pyatt, NYIs.	.35	.20
□□ 221 Roman Hamrlik, NYIs.	.35	.20
□□ 222 Tim Connolly, NYIs.	.50	.25
□□ 223 Rick DiPietro, NYIs.	.50	.25
□□ 224 Dave Scatchard, NYIs.	.35	.20
□□ 225 Brad Isbister, NYIs.	.35	.20
□□ 226 Mark Parrish, NYIs.	.50	.25
□□ 227 Kenny Jönsson, NYIs.	.35	.20
□□ 228 Oleg Kvasha, NYIs.	.35	.20
□□ 229 Mike Richter, NYRa. [Checklist]	.50	.20
□□ 230 Mark Messier, NYRa.	1.50	.75
□□ 231 Mike York, NYRa.	.35	.20
□□ 232 Theoren Fleury, NYRa.	.75	.25
□□ 233 Brian Leetch, NYRa.	.75	.25
□□ 234 Petr Nedved, NYRa.	.35	.20
□□ 235 Radek Dvorak, NYRa.	.35	.20
□□ 236 Jan Hlavac, NYRa.	.35	.20
□□ 237 Mike Richter, NYRa.	.50	.25
□□ 238 Manny Malhotra, NYRa.	.35	.20
□□ 239 Tomas Kloucek, NYRa.	.35	.20
□□ 240 Guy Hebert (G), NYRa.	.35	.20
□□ 241 Patrick Lalime, Otta. [Checklist]	.75	.25
□□ 242 Marian Hossa, Otta.	1.50	.75
□□ 243 Shawn McEachern, Otta.	.35	.20
□□ 244 Wade Redden, Otta.	.35	.20
□□ 245 Daniel Alfredsson, Otta.	.75	.25
□□ 246 Radek Bonk, Otta.	.35	.20
□□ 247 Martin Havlat, Otta.	.75	.25
□□ 248 Patrick Lalime, Otta.	.75	.25
□□ 249 Magnus Arvedson, Otta.	.35	.20
□□ 250 Karel Rachunek, Otta.	.35	.20
□□ 251 Andreas Dackell, Otta.	.35	.20
□□ 252 Jani Hurme (G), Otta.	.35	.20
□□ 253 Roman Cechmanek, Phil. [Checklist]	.50	.20
□□ 254 John LeClair, Phil.	1.00	.50
□□ 255 Daymond Langkow, Phil.	.35	.20
□□ 256 Keith Primeau, Phil.	.50	.25
□□ 257 Justin Williams, Phil.	.35	.20
□□ 258 Simon Gagné, Phil.	1.00	.50
□□ 259 Roman Cechmanek, Phil.	.50	.25
□□ 260 Mark Recchi, Phil.	.50	.25
□□ 261 Ruslan Fedotenko, Phil.	.35	.20
□□ 262 Dan McGillis, Phil.	.35	.20
□□ 263 Éric Desjardins, Phil.	.35	.20
□□ 264 Brian Boucher (G), Phil.	.35	.20
□□ 265 Sean Burke, Phoe. [Checklist]	.75	.25
□□ 266 Shane Doan, Phoe.	.35	.20
□□ 267 Mike Johnson, Phoe.	.35	.20
□□ 268 Michal Handzus, Phoe.	.35	.20
□□ 269 Landon Wilson, Phoe.	.35	.20
□□ 270 Jeremy Roenick, Phoe.	1.00	.50
□□ 271 Travis Green, Phoe.	.35	.20
□□ 272 Sean Burke, Phoe.	.75	.25
□□ 273 Daniel Brière, Phoe.	.50	.25
□□ 274 Trevor Letowski, Phoe.	.35	.20
□□ 275 Teppo Numminen, Phoe.	.35	.20
□□ 276 Ladislav Nagy, Phoe.	.35	.20
□□ 277 Johan Hedberg (G), Pitt. [Checklist]	.50	.20
□□ 278 Jaromir Jagr, Pitt.	1.50	.75
□□ 279 Jan Hrdina, Pitt.	.35	.20
□□ 280 Mario Lemieux, Pitt.	4.50	2.00
□□ 281 Alex Kovalev, Pitt.	.75	.25
□□ 282 Robert Lang, Pitt.	.35	.20
□□ 283 Martin Straka, Pitt.	.35	.20
□□ 284 Aleksey Morozov, Pitt.	.35	.20
□□ 285 Janne Laukkanen, Pitt.	.35	.20
□□ 286 René Corbet, Pitt.	.35	.20
□□ 287 Jean-Sébastien Aubin (G), Pitt.	.35	.20
□□ 288 Darius Kasparaitis, Pitt.	.35	.20
□□ 289 Evgeni Nabokov, SanJ. [Checklist]	.75	.25
□□ 290 Teemu Selänne, SanJ.	1.00	.50
□□ 291 Patrick Marleau, SanJ.	.50	.25
□□ 292 Owen Nolan, SanJ.	.75	.25
□□ 293 Marcus Ragnarsson, SanJ.	.35	.20
□□ 294 Brad Stuart, SanJ.	.50	.25
□□ 295 Mike Ricci, SanJ.	.35	.20
□□ 296 Vincent Damphousse, SanJ.	.75	.25
□□ 297 Scott Thornton, SanJ.	.35	.20
□□ 298 Mike Rathje, SanJ.	.35	.20
□□ 299 Marco Sturm, SanJ.	.35	.20
□□ 300 Evgeni Nabokov, SanJ.	.75	.25
□□ 301 Alexander Korolyuk, SanJ.	.35	.20
□□ 302 Roman Turek, SLou. [Checklist]	.50	.20
□□ 303 Keith Tkachuk, SLou.	.75	.25
□□ 304 Cory Stillman, SLou.	.35	.20
□□ 305 Chris Pronger, SLou.	.75	.25
□□ 306 Scott A. Young, SLou.	.35	.20
□□ 307 Pavol Demitra, SLou.	.50	.25
□□ 308 Al MacInnis, SLou.	.50	.25
□□ 309 Jochen Hecht, SLou.	.35	.20
□□ 310 Pierre Turgeon, SLou.	.50	.25
□□ 311 Tyson Nash, SLou.	.35	.20
□□ 312 Lubos Bartecko, SLou.	.35	.20
□□ 313 Roman Turek, SLou.	.50	.25
□□ 314 Kevin Weekes, Tamp. [Checklist]	.35	.20
□□ 315 Vincent Lecavalier, Tamp.	1.50	.75
□□ 316 Brad Richards, Tamp.	.50	.25
□□ 317 Brian Holzinger, Tamp.	.35	.20
□□ 318 Fredrik Modin, Tamp.	.35	.20
□□ 319 Kevin Weekes, Tamp.	.35	.20
□□ 320 Pavel Kubina, Tamp.	.35	.20
□□ 321 Todd Warriner, Tamp.	.35	.20
□□ 322 Martin St-Louis, Tamp.	.50	.25
□□ 323 Matthew Barnaby, Tamp.	.35	.20
□□ 324 Nikolai Khabibulin, Tamp.	.50	.25
□□ 325 Curtis Joseph (G), Toro. [Checklist]	1.50	.25
□□ 326 Mats Sundin, Toro.	1.50	.75
□□ 327 Gary Roberts, Toro.	.50	.25
□□ 328 Bryan McCabe, Toro.	.35	.20
□□ 329 Curtis Joseph (G), Toro.	1.50	.75
□□ 330 Tomas Kaberle, Toro.	.35	.20
□□ 331 Jonas Höglund, Toro.	.35	.20
□□ 332 Darcy Tucker, Toro.	.35	.20
□□ 333 Nikolai Antropov, Toro.	.35	.20
□□ 334 Tie Domi, Toro.	.35	.20
□□ 335 Aki Berg, Toro.	.35	.20
□□ 336 Dmitry Yushkevich, Toro.	.35	.20
□□ 337 Dan Cloutier, Vanc. [Checklist]	.50	.20
□□ 338 Markus Näslund, Vanc.	1.50	.75
□□ 339 Donald Brashear, Vanc.	.35	.20
□□ 340 Andrew Cassels, Vanc.	.35	.20
□□ 341 Todd Bertuzzi, Vanc.	1.75	.75
□□ 342 Ed Jovanovski, Vanc.	.50	.25
□□ 343 Brendan Morrison, Vanc.	.35	.20
□□ 344 Daniel Sedin, Vanc.	.50	.25
□□ 345 Henrik Sedin, Vanc.	.50	.25
□□ 346 Dan Cloutier, Vanc.	.50	.25
□□ 347 Peter Schaefer, Vanc.	.35	.20
□□ 348 Harold Druken, Vanc.	.35	.20
□□ 349 Olaf Kölzig, Wash. [Checklist]	.75	.25
□□ 350 Peter Bondra, Wash.	.75	.25
□□ 351 Sergei Gonchar, Wash.	.35	.20
□□ 352 Steve Konowalchuk, Wash.	.35	.20
□□ 353 Chris Simon, Wash.	.35	.20
□□ 354 Adam Oates, Wash.	.50	.25
□□ 355 Olaf Kölzig, Wash.	.75	.25
□□ 356 Jeff Halpern, Wash.	.35	.20
□□ 357 Trevor Linden, Wash.	.50	.25
□□ 358 Calle Johansson, Wash.	.35	.20
□□ 359 Dainius Zubrus, Wash.	.35	.20
□□ 360 Andrei Nikolishin, Wash.	.35	.20
□□ 361 Gregg Naumenko, Anah.	.35	.20
□□ **362 B. Pothier RC / D. Snyder RC / JP. Vigier**	**.35**	**.25**
□□ **363 Z. Kutlak RC / L. Goren / P. Kolarik**	**.35**	**.25**
□□ 364 Mika Noronen, Buff.	.50	.50
□□ 365 R. Fata / M. Murray / R. Petrovicky	.35	.25
□□ 366 M. Larocque RC / M. Bell / C. Hankinson	.35	.50
□□ 367 Y. Babenko / R. Shearer	.35	.20
□□ 368 Steve Gainey, Dall.	.35	.20
□□ 369 M. Kuznetsov / Ja. Williams	.35	.25
□□ **370 J. Chimera RC / M. Comrie / C. Hajt**	**.50**	**1.00**
□□ **371 Bowler RC / Spanhel RC / Klesla**	**.35**	**.50**
□□ **372 M. Darche RC / M. Davidson RC**	**.35**	**.25**
□□ **373 A. Podkonicky RC / R. Thompson RC**	**.35**	**.25**
□□ 374 A. Lilja / T. Scott	.35	.20
□□ **375 Pascal Dupuis, MinW. RC**	**.35**	**.75**
□□ **376 M. Matteucci RC / D. Gustafson**	**.35**	**.25**
□□ **377 Francis Bélanger, Mont. RC**	**.35**	**.25**
□□ **378 P. Skrbek / C. Mason RC**	**.35**	**.25**
□□ 379 M. Danton RC / P. Dagenais	.35	.50
□□ 380 Juraj Kolnik, NYIs.	.35	.20
□□ 381 P. Smrek RC / J. Ulmer / V. Yeremeyev	.35	.25
□□ 382 Joel Kwiatkowski, Otta. RC	.35	.25
□□ 383 Maxime Ouellet, Phil.	.35	.25
□□ 384 David Cullen, Phoe. RC	.35	.25
□□ 385 Crozier RC / Tibbetts RC / Hedberg	.35	.75
□□ 386 M. Samuelsson RC / M. Kiprusoff	.35	.75
□□ 387 J. Obsut RC / M. Van Ryn	.35	.50
□□ 388 D. Afanasenkov / T. Ziegler	.35	.20
□□ 389 J. Farkas / A. Ponikarovsky	.35	.25
□□ 390 M. Pettinger / K. Beech	.35	.25
□□ 391 Mario Lemieux [Mr. Hockey's Greats]	4.25	1.00
□□ 392 Jaromir Jagr [Mr. Hockey's Greats]	2.75	.75
□□ 393 Chris Pronger [Mr. Hockey's Greats]	2.50	.75
□□ 394 Peter Forsberg [Mr. Hockey's Greats]	3.00	1.00
□□ 395 Pavel Bure [Mr. Hockey's Greats]	2.50	.75
□□ 396 Patrick Roy [Mr. Hockey's Greats]	4.25	1.00
□□ 397 Joe Sakic [Mr. Hockey's Greats]	3.25	1.00
□□ 398 Dominik Hasek (G) [Mr. Hockey's Greats]	2.75	.75
□□ 399 John LeClair [Mr. Hockey's Greats]	2.50	.75
□□ 400 Sergei Fedorov [Mr. Hockey's Greats]	2.75	.75
□□ 401 Nicklas Lidström [Mr. Hockey's Greats]	2.50	.75
□□ 402 Martin Brodeur [Mr. Hockey's Greats]	3.25	1.00
□□ 403 Ed Belfour (G) [Mr. Hockey's Greats]	2.75	.75
□□ 404 Steve Yzerman [Mr. Hockey's Greats]	3.75	1.25
□□ 405 Owen Nolan [Mr. Hockey's Greats]	2.50	.75
□□ 406 Keith Tkachuk [Mr. Hockey's Greats]	2.50	.75
□□ 407 Olaf Kölzig [Mr. Hockey's Greats]	2.50	.75
□□ 408 Rob Blake [Mr. Hockey's Greats]	2.50	.75
□□ 409 Brett Hull [Mr. Hockey's Greats]	2.75	.75
□□ 410 Brian Leetch [Mr. Hockey's Greats]	2.50	.75
□□ 411 Raymond Bourque [Mr. Hockey's Greats]	3.00	1.00
□□ 412 Pierre Turgeon [Mr. Hockey's Greats]	2.25	.75
□□ 413 Alexei Yashin [Mr. Hockey's Greats]	2.50	.75
□□ 414 Mike Modano [Mr. Hockey's Greats]	2.75	.75
□□ 415 Curtis Joseph (G) [Mr. Hockey's Greats]	2.75	.75
□□ 416 Alex Kovalev [Mr. Hockey's Greats]	2.50	.75
□□ 417 Marian Hossa [Mr. Hockey's Greats]	2.75	.75
□□ 418 Milan Hejduk [Mr. Hockey's Greats]	2.50	.75
□□ 419 Markus Näslund [Mr. Hockey's Greats]	2.75	.75
□□ 420 Theoren Fleury [Mr. Hockey's Greats]	2.50	.75
□□ 421 Bill Guerin [Mr. Hockey's Greats]	2.25	.75
□□ 422 Doug Weight [Mr. Hockey's Greats]	2.50	.75
□□ 423 Luc Robitaille [Mr. Hockey's Greats]	2.50	.75
□□ 424 Zigmund Palffy [Mr. Hockey's Greats]	2.50	.75
□□ 425 Jeremy Roenick [Mr. Hockey's Greats]	2.50	.75
□□ 426 Mats Sundin [Mr. Hockey's Greats]	2.75	.75
□□ 427 Alexander Mogilny [Mr. Hockey's Greats]	2.25	.75
□□ 428 Ed Jovanovski [Mr. Hockey's Greats]	2.25	.75
□□ 429 Adam Foote [Mr. Hockey's Greats]	2.25	.75
□□ 430 Peter Bondra [Mr. Hockey's Greats]	2.50	.75
□□ 431 Mark Recchi [Mr. Hockey's Greats]	2.25	.75
□□ 432 Radek Bonk [Mr. Hockey's Greats]	2.25	.75
□□ 433 Simon Gagné [Mr. Hockey's Greats]	2.50	.75
□□ 434 Scott Stevens [Mr. Hockey's Greats]	2.25	.75
□□ 435 Steve Sullivan [Mr. Hockey's Greats]	2.25	.75
□□ 436 Martin Straka [Mr. Hockey's Greats]	2.25	.75
□□ 437 Evgeni Nabokov [Mr. Hockey's Greats]	2.50	.75
□□ 438 Keith Primeau [Mr. Hockey's Greats]	2.25	.75
□□ 439 Brendan Shanahan [Mr. Hockey's Greats]	2.75	.75
□□ 440 Vincent Lecavalier [Mr. Hockey's Greats]	2.75	.75

ROOKIE UPDATE

Rookie	Rookie
□ **441 Ilya Kovalchuk, Atla. RC**	**20.00**
□ **442 Erik Cole, Caro. RC**	**5.00**
□ **443 Pavel Datsyuk, Detr. RC**	**18.00**

□ **444 Kristian Huselius, Flor. RC**	**6.00**
□ **445 Marcel Hossa, Mont. RC**	**8.00**
□ **446 Martin Erat, Nash. RC**	**5.00**
□ **447 Christian Berglund, NJer. RC**	**5.00**
□ **448 Raffi Torres, NYIs. RC**	**5.00**
□ **449 Dan Blackburn (G), NYRa. RC**	**8.00**
□ **450 Jiri Dopita, Phil. RC**	**5.00**
□ **451 Krys Kolanos, Phoe. RC**	**5.00**
□ **452 Brian Sutherby, Wash. RC**	**5.00**
□ **453 Olivier Michaud, Mont. RC**	**5.00**

2001 - 02 WAVING THE FLAG

Produced by In The Game, this series was released in February 2002. The series was available via a redemption offer.

The following wrapper redemption promotional versions exist for cards 1-32: Spring Expo '02 (#/10), Spring Expo '02 (#/1).

Complete Set (33 cards): 75.00

Description	WTF
□ 1 Mario Lemieux, Pitt.	15.00
□ 2 Joe Sakic, Colo.	8.00
□ 3 Steve Yzerman, Detr.	12.00
□ 4 Paul Kariya, Anah.	7.00
□ 5 Curtis Joseph (G), Toro.	5.00
□ 6 Martin Brodeur (G), NJer.	8.00
□ 7 Eric Lindros, NYRa.	5.00
□ 8 Chris Pronger, Slou.	3.00
□ 9 Jaromir Jagr, Wash.	5.00
□ 10 Milan Hejduk, Colo.	4.00
□ 11 Dominik Hasek (G), Detr.	5.00
□ 12 Martin Havlat, Otta.	3.00
□ 13 Teemu Selänne, SanJ.	4.00
□ 14 Jani Hurme (G), Otta.	2.00
□ 15 Miikka Kiprusoff (G), SanJ.	2.00
□ 16 Sami Kapanen, Caro.	2.00
□ 17 Mats Sundin, Toro.	5.00
□ 18 Nicklas Lidström, Detr.	3.00
□ 19 Tommy Salo (G), Edmo.	2.00
□ 20 Kristian Huselius, Flor.	2.00
□ 21 Jeremy Roenick, Phil.	4.00
□ 22 Doug Weight, Slou.	3.00
□ 23 Tony Amonte, Chic.	3.00
□ 24 Brian Leetch, NYRa.	3.00
□ 25 Mike Modano, Dall.	5.00
□ 26 Brett Hull, Detr.	5.00
□ 27 John LeClair, Phil.	4.00
□ 28 Keith Tkachuk, Slou.	3.00
□ 29 Alexei Yashin, NYIs.	3.00
□ 30 Pavel Bure, Flor.	4.00
□ 31 Nikolai Khabibulin (G), Tamp.	2.00
□ 32 Darius Kasparaitis, Pitt.	2.00

2002 - 03 AGF

We do not have a checklist for this series. This series is similar to the 2001 - 02 AGF series, but features new players.

2002 - 03 ATOMIC

Produced by Pacific Trading Cards, this series was released in November 2002. There are five versions for each card 1-100: the regular silver-bar card, the silver-bar Hobby Uncut parallel (#/775), the blue-bar U.S.-pack parallel (#/175), the red-bar Canada-pack parallel (#/125), and the gold-bar Hobby parallel (#/99).

Shell Set (100 cards):	-	-	85.00
Complete Set (125 cards):	1100.00	1200.00	425.00
Common Player:	5.00	2.00	.75
Description	**G99**	**775**	**Base**
□□□ 1 J-S Giguère (G), Anah.	10.00	5.00	2.00
□□□ 2 Paul Kariya, Anah.	25.00	8.00	4.00
□□□ 3 Adam Oates, Anah.	5.00	2.00	1.00

☐☐☐ 4 Dany Heatley, Atla.	15.00	6.00	3.00
☐☐☐ 5 Ilya Kovalchuk, Atla.	15.00	6.00	3.00
☐☐☐ 6 Glen Murray, Bost.	5.00	3.00	1.00
☐☐☐ 7 Sergei Samsonov, Bost.	10.00	3.00	1.00
☐☐☐ 8 Joe Thornton, Bost.	20.00	7.00	3.00
☐☐☐ 9 Martin Biron (G), Buff.	5.00	3.00	1.00
☐☐☐ 10 Jean-Pierre Dumont, Buff.	5.00	2.00	.75
☐☐☐ 11 Miroslav Satan, Buff.	5.00	2.00	.75
☐☐☐ 12 Craig Conroy, Calg.	5.00	2.00	.75
☐☐☐ 13 Jarome Iginla, Calg.	10.00	5.00	2.00
☐☐☐ 14 Roman Turek (G), Calg.	5.00	3.00	1.00
☐☐☐ 15 Erik Cole, Caro.	5.00	2.00	.75
☐☐☐ 16 Ron Francis, Caro.	10.00	3.00	1.00
☐☐☐ 17 Arturs Irbe (G), Caro.	5.00	2.00	1.00
☐☐☐ 18 Jeff O'Neill, Caro.	5.00	2.00	1.00
☐☐☐ 19 Mark Bell, Chic.	5.00	2.00	.75
☐☐☐ 20 Éric Dazé, Chic.	5.00	2.00	1.00
☐☐☐ 21 Jocelyn Thibault (G), Chic.	5.00	2.00	1.00
☐☐☐ 22 Rob Blake, Colo.	10.00	3.00	1.00
☐☐☐ 23 Chris Drury, Colo.	10.00	3.00	1.00
☐☐☐ 24 Peter Forsberg, Colo.	25.00	8.00	4.00
☐☐☐ 25 Steven Reinprecht, Colo.	5.00	2.00	.75
☐☐☐ 26 Patrick Roy (G), Colo.	50.00	18.00	9.00
☐☐☐ 27 Joe Sakic, Colo.	25.00	10.00	4.00
☐☐☐ 28 Marc Denis (G), Colu.	5.00	3.00	1.00
☐☐☐ 29 Espen Knutsen, Colu.	5.00	2.00	.75
☐☐☐ 30 Ray Whitney, Colu.	5.00	2.00	.75
☐☐☐ 31 Jason Arnott, Dall.	5.00	3.00	1.00
☐☐☐ 32 Bill Guerin, Dall.	5.00	2.00	1.00
☐☐☐ 33 Mike Modano, Dall.	15.00	6.00	3.00
☐☐☐ 34 Marty Turco (G), Dall.	10.00	3.00	1.00
☐☐☐ 35 Pavel Datsyuk, Detr.	10.00	5.00	2.00
☐☐☐ 36 Sergei Fedorov, Detr.	15.00	6.00	3.00
☐☐☐ 37 Brett Hull, Detr.	15.00	6.00	3.00
☐☐☐ 38 Curtis Joseph (G), Detr.	15.00	6.00	3.00
☐☐☐ 39 Nicklas Lidström, Detr.	10.00	3.00	1.00
☐☐☐ 40 Brendan Shanahan, Detr.	15.00	6.00	3.00
☐☐☐ 41 Steve Yzerman, Detr.	40.00	15.00	7.00
☐☐☐ 42 Mike Comrie, Edmo.	10.00	5.00	2.00
☐☐☐ 43 Tommy Salo (G), Edmo.	5.00	2.00	1.00
☐☐☐ 44 Ryan Smyth, Edmo.	5.00	3.00	1.00
☐☐☐ 45 Kristian Huselius, Flor.	5.00	2.00	.75
☐☐☐ 46 Roberto Luongo (G), Flor.	10.00	5.00	2.00
☐☐☐ 47 Stephen Weiss, Flor.	5.00	2.00	1.00
☐☐☐ 48 Jason Allison, LosA.	10.00	3.00	1.00
☐☐☐ 49 Zigmund Palffy, LosA.	10.00	3.00	1.00
☐☐☐ 50 Félix Potvin (G), LosA.	20.00	3.00	1.00
☐☐☐ 51 Andrew Brunette, MinW.	5.00	2.00	.75
☐☐☐ 52 M. Fernandez (G), MinW.	5.00	2.00	1.00
☐☐☐ 53 Marian Gaborik, MinW.	15.00	6.00	3.00
☐☐☐ 54 Doug Gilmour, Mont.	10.00	3.00	1.00
☐☐☐ 55 Saku Koivu, Mont.	20.00	5.00	2.00
☐☐☐ 56 Yanic Perreault, Mont.	5.00	2.00	.75
☐☐☐ 57 José Théodore (G), Mont.	20.00	7.00	3.00
☐☐☐ 58 Denis Arkhipov, Nash.	5.00	2.00	.75
☐☐☐ 59 Mike Dunham (G), Nash.	5.00	2.00	1.00
☐☐☐ 60 Martin Brodeur (G), NJer.	25.00	10.00	4.00
☐☐☐ 61 Patrik Elias, NJer.	10.00	5.00	2.00
☐☐☐ 62 Joe Nieuwendyk, NJer.	5.00	2.00	1.00
☐☐☐ 63 Chris Osgood (G), NYIs.	10.00	3.00	1.00
☐☐☐ 64 Michael Peca, NYIs.	5.00	2.00	1.00
☐☐☐ 65 Alexei Yashin, NYIs.	10.00	3.00	1.00
☐☐☐ 66 Dan Blackburn (G), NYRa.	5.00	2.00	1.00
☐☐☐ 67 Pavel Bure, NYRa.	10.00	5.00	2.00
☐☐☐ 68 Eric Lindros, NYRa.	15.00	6.00	3.00
☐☐☐ 69 Mike Richter (G), NYRa.	5.00	3.00	1.00
☐☐☐ 70 Daniel Alfredsson, Otta.	20.00	3.00	1.00
☐☐☐ 71 Marian Hossa, Otta.	15.00	6.00	3.00
☐☐☐ 72 Patrick Lalime (G), Otta.	10.00	3.00	1.00
☐☐☐ 73 R. Cechmanek (G), Phil.	5.00	2.00	1.00
☐☐☐ 74 Simon Gagné, Phil.	10.00	5.00	2.00
☐☐☐ 75 Jeremy Roenick, Phil.	10.00	5.00	2.00
☐☐☐ 76 Tony Amonte, Phoe.	10.00	3.00	1.00
☐☐☐ 77 Daniel Brière, Phoe.	5.00	3.00	1.00
☐☐☐ 78 Sean Burke (G), Phoe.	10.00	3.00	1.00
☐☐☐ 79 Johan Hedberg (G), Pitt.	5.00	2.00	1.00
☐☐☐ 80 Mario Lemieux, Pitt.	50.00	18.00	9.00
☐☐☐ 81 Aleksey Morozov, Pitt.	5.00	2.00	.75
☐☐☐ 82 Brent Johnson (G), SLou.	5.00	2.00	1.00
☐☐☐ 83 Chris Pronger, SLou.	10.00	3.00	1.00
☐☐☐ 84 Keith Tkachuk, SLou.	10.00	3.00	1.00
☐☐☐ 85 Patrick Marleau, SanJ.	5.00	3.00	1.00
☐☐☐ 86 Evgeni Nabokov (G), SanJ.	10.00	3.00	1.00
☐☐☐ 87 Owen Nolan, SanJ.	10.00	3.00	1.00
☐☐☐ 88 Teemu Selänne, SanJ.	10.00	5.00	2.00
☐☐☐ 89 N. Khabibulin (G), Tamp.	5.00	2.00	1.00
☐☐☐ 90 Vincent Lecavalier, Tamp.	15.00	6.00	3.00
☐☐☐ 91 Ed Belfour (G), Toro.	15.00	6.00	3.00
☐☐☐ 92 Alexander Mogilny, Toro.	5.00	3.00	1.00
☐☐☐ 93 Gary Roberts, Toro.	5.00	2.00	1.00
☐☐☐ 94 Mats Sundin, Toro.	15.00	6.00	3.00
☐☐☐ 95 Todd Bertuzzi, Vanc.	20.00	7.00	3.00
☐☐☐ 96 Dan Cloutier (G), Vanc.	5.00	2.00	1.00
☐☐☐ 97 Markus Näslund, Vanc.	15.00	6.00	3.00
☐☐☐ 98 Peter Bondra, Wash.	10.00	3.00	1.00
☐☐☐ 99 Jaromir Jagr, Wash.	15.00	6.00	3.00
☐☐☐ 100 Olaf Kölzig (G), Wash.	10.00	3.00	1.00

ROOKIE

There are five versions for each card 101-125: the regular silver-bar card (#/1300), the silver-bar Hobby Uncut parallel (#/775), the blue-bar U.S.-pack parallel (#/175), the red-bar Canada-pack parallel (#/125), and the gold-bar Hobby parallel (#/99).

Insert	G99	775	R1300
☐☐☐ **101 S. Chistov, Anah. RC**	**35**	**25**	**25**
☐☐☐ **102 M. Gerber (G), Anah. RC**	**10**	**10**	**10**
☐☐☐ **103 A. Smirnov, Anah. RC**	**10**	**10**	**10**
☐☐☐ **104 C. Kobasew, Calg. RC**	**14**	**10**	**10**
☐☐☐ **105 Rick Nash, Colu. RC**	**60**	**45**	**45**
☐☐☐ **106 Dmitri Bykov, Detr. RC**	**14**	**10**	**10**
☐☐☐ **107 H. Zetterberg, Detr. RC**	**60**	**45**	**45**
☐☐☐ **108 K. Haakana, Edmo. RC**	**14**	**10**	**10**
☐☐☐ **109 A. Hemsky, Edmo. RC**	**35**	**25**	**25**
☐☐☐ **110 Alex Henry, Edmo. RC**	**14**	**10**	**10**
☐☐☐ **111 J. Bouwmeester, Flor. RC**	**35**	**25**	**25**
☐☐☐ **112 A. Frolov, LosA. RC**	**25**	**20**	**20**
☐☐☐ **113 P-M Bouchard, MinW. RC**	**35**	**25**	**25**
☐☐☐ **114 S. Blouin, MinW. RC**	**14**	**10**	**10**
☐☐☐ **115 Ron Hainsey, Mont. RC**	**14**	**10**	**10**
☐☐☐ **116 Adam Hall, Nash. RC**	**14**	**10**	**10**
☐☐☐ **117 S. Upshall, Nash. RC**	**20**	**15**	**15**
☐☐☐ 118 Mike Danton, NJer.	8	5	6
☐☐☐ **119 Ray Schultz, NYIs. RC**	**14**	**10**	**10**
☐☐☐ **120 A. Volchenkov, Otta. RC**	**14**	**10**	**10**
☐☐☐ **121 D. Seidenberg, Phil. RC**	**14**	**10**	**10**
☐☐☐ **122 Patrick Sharp, Phil. RC**	**14**	**10**	**10**
☐☐☐ 123 Dick Tarnstrom, Pitt.	8	10	6
☐☐☐ **124 A. Svitov, Tamp. RC**	**20**	**15**	**15**
☐☐☐ **125 Steve Eminger, Wash. RC**	**14**	**10**	**10**

ROOKIE

Insert Set (6 cards):	65.00
Insert	R
☐ **126 Jordan Leopold, Calg. RC**	**12.00**
☐ **127 Stéphane Veilleux, MinW. RC**	**8.00**
☐ **128 Jason Spezza, Otta. RC**	**30.00**
☐ **129 Radovan Somik, Phil. RC**	**8.00**
☐ **130 Jeff Taffe, Phoe. RC**	**12.00**
☐ **131 Tom Koivisto, SLou. RC**	**8.00**

CHANNEL SPECIFIC PARALLELS

Channel specific parallels are Blue (U.S. packs, #/175) and Red (Canada packs, #/125).

Complete Set (125 cards):	1,000	800
Common Player:	4.00	3.50
Description	R125	B175
☐☐ 1 Jean-Sébastien Giguère (G), Anah.	12.00	10.00
☐☐ 2 Paul Kariya, Anah.	20.00	15.00
☐☐ 3 Adam Oates, Anah.	6.00	5.00
☐☐ 4 Dany Heatley, Atla.	15.00	10.00
☐☐ 5 Ilya Kovalchuk, Atla.	15.00	10.00
☐☐ 6 Glen Murray, Bost.	6.00	5.00
☐☐ 7 Sergei Samsonov, Bost.	6.00	5.00
☐☐ 8 Joe Thornton, Bost.	18.00	15.00
☐☐ 9 Martin Biron (G), Buff.	6.00	5.00
☐☐ 10 Jean-Pierre Dumont, Buff.	4.00	3.50
☐☐ 11 Miroslav Satan, Buff.	4.00	3.50
☐☐ 12 Craig Conroy, Calg.	4.00	3.50
☐☐ 13 Jarome Iginla, Calg.	12.00	10.00
☐☐ 14 Roman Turek (G), Calg.	6.00	5.00
☐☐ 15 Erik Cole, Caro.	4.00	3.50
☐☐ 16 Ron Francis, Caro.	6.00	5.00
☐☐ 17 Arturs Irbe (G), Caro.	6.00	5.00
☐☐ 18 Jeff O'Neill, Caro.	6.00	5.00
☐☐ 19 Mark Bell, Chic.	4.00	3.50
☐☐ 20 Éric Dazé, Chic.	6.00	5.00
☐☐ 21 Jocelyn Thibault (G), Chic.	6.00	5.00
☐☐ 22 Rob Blake, Colo.	6.00	5.00
☐☐ 23 Chris Drury, Colo.	6.00	5.00
☐☐ 24 Peter Forsberg, Colo.	20.00	15.00
☐☐ 25 Steven Reinprecht, Colo.	4.00	3.50
☐☐ 26 Patrick Roy (G), Colo.	45.00	35.00
☐☐ 27 Joe Sakic, Colo.	24.00	20.00
☐☐ 28 Marc Denis (G), Colu.	6.00	5.00
☐☐ 29 Espen Knutsen, Colu.	4.00	3.50
☐☐ 30 Ray Whitney, Colu.	4.00	3.50
☐☐ 31 Jason Arnott, Dall.	6.00	5.00
☐☐ 32 Bill Guerin, Dall.	6.00	5.00
☐☐ 33 Mike Modano, Dall.	15.00	10.00
☐☐ 34 Marty Turco (G), Dall.	6.00	5.00
☐☐ 35 Pavel Datsyuk, Detr.	12.00	10.00
☐☐ 36 Sergei Fedorov, Detr.	15.00	10.00
☐☐ 37 Brett Hull, Detr.	15.00	10.00
☐☐ 38 Curtis Joseph (G), Detr.	15.00	10.00
☐☐ 39 Nicklas Lidström, Detr.	6.00	5.00
☐☐ 40 Brendan Shanahan, Detr.	15.00	10.00
☐☐ 41 Steve Yzerman, Detr.	35.00	30.00
☐☐ 42 Mike Comrie, Edmo.	12.00	10.00
☐☐ 43 Tommy Salo, Edmo.	6.00	5.00
☐☐ 44 Ryan Smyth, Edmo.	6.00	5.00
☐☐ 45 Kristian Huselius, Flor.	4.00	3.50
☐☐ 46 Roberto Luongo (G), Flor.	12.00	10.00
☐☐ 47 Stephen Weiss, Flor.	6.00	5.00
☐☐ 48 Jason Allison, LosA.	6.00	5.00
☐☐ 49 Zigmund Palffy, LosA.	6.00	5.00
☐☐ 50 Félix Potvin (G), LosA.	6.00	5.00
☐☐ 51 Andrew Brunette, MinW.	4.00	3.50
☐☐ 52 Manny Fernandez (G), MinW.	6.00	5.00
☐☐ 53 Marian Gaborik, MinW.	15.00	10.00
☐☐ 54 Doug Gilmour, Mont.	6.00	5.00
☐☐ 55 Saku Koivu, Mont.	12.00	10.00
☐☐ 56 Yanic Perreault, Mont.	4.00	3.50
☐☐ 57 José Théodore (G), Mont.	18.00	15.00
☐☐ 58 Denis Arkhipov, Nash.	4.00	3.50
☐☐ 59 Mike Dunham (G), Nash.	6.00	5.00
☐☐ 60 Martin Brodeur (G), NJer.	24.00	20.00
☐☐ 61 Patrik Elias, NJer.	12.00	10.00
☐☐ 62 Joe Nieuwendyk, NJer.	6.00	5.00
☐☐ 63 Chris Osgood (G), NYIs.	6.00	5.00
☐☐ 64 Michael Peca, NYIs.	6.00	5.00
☐☐ 65 Alexei Yashin, NYIs.	6.00	5.00
☐☐ 66 Dan Blackburn (G), NYRa.	6.00	5.00
☐☐ 67 Pavel Bure, NYRa.	12.00	10.00
☐☐ 68 Eric Lindros, NYRa.	15.00	10.00
☐☐ 69 Mike Richter (G), NYRa.	6.00	5.00
☐☐ 70 Daniel Alfredsson, Otta.	6.00	5.00
☐☐ 71 Marian Hossa, Otta.	15.00	10.00
☐☐ 72 Patrick Lalime (G), Otta.	6.00	5.00
☐☐ 73 Roman Cechmanek (G), Phil.	6.00	5.00
☐☐ 74 Simon Gagné, Phil.	12.00	10.00
☐☐ 75 Jeremy Roenick, Phil.	12.00	10.00
☐☐ 76 Tony Amonte, Phoe.	6.00	5.00
☐☐ 77 Daniel Brière, Phoe.	6.00	5.00
☐☐ 78 Sean Burke (G), Phoe.	6.00	5.00
☐☐ 79 Johan Hedberg (G), Pitt.	6.00	5.00
☐☐ 80 Mario Lemieux, Pitt.	45.00	35.00
☐☐ 81 Aleksey Morozov, Pitt.	4.00	3.50
☐☐ 82 Brent Johnson (G), SLou.	6.00	5.00
☐☐ 83 Chris Pronger, SLou.	6.00	5.00
☐☐ 84 Keith Tkachuk, SLou.	6.00	5.00
☐☐ 85 Patrick Marleau, SanJ.	6.00	5.00
☐☐ 86 Evgeni Nabokov (G), SanJ.	6.00	5.00
☐☐ 87 Owen Nolan, SanJ.	6.00	5.00
☐☐ 88 Teemu Selänne, SanJ.	12.00	10.00
☐☐ 89 Nikolai Khabibulin (G), Tamp.	6.00	5.00
☐☐ 90 Vincent Lecavalier, Tamp.	15.00	10.00
☐☐ 91 Ed Belfour (G), Toro.	15.00	10.00
☐☐ 92 Alexander Mogilny, Toro.	6.00	5.00
☐☐ 93 Gary Roberts, Toro.	6.00	5.00
☐☐ 94 Mats Sundin, Toro.	15.00	10.00
☐☐ 95 Todd Bertuzzi, Vanc.	18.00	15.00
☐☐ 96 Dan Cloutier (G), Vanc.	6.00	5.00
☐☐ 97 Markus Näslund, Vanc.	15.00	10.00
☐☐ 98 Peter Bondra, Wash.	6.00	5.00
☐☐ 99 Jaromir Jagr, Wash.	15.00	10.00
☐☐ 100 Olaf Kölzig (G), Wash.	6.00	5.00
☐☐ **101 Stanislav Chistov, Anah. RC**	**24.00**	**20.00**
☐☐ **102 Martin Gerber (G), Anah. RC**	**6.00**	**5.00**
☐☐ **103 Alexei Smirnov, Anah. RC**	**12.00**	**10.00**
☐☐ **104 Chuck Kobasew, Calg. RC**	**12.00**	**10.00**
☐☐ **105 Rick Nash, Colu. RC**	**60.00**	**50.00**
☐☐ **106 Dmitri Bykov, Detr. RC**	**6.00**	**5.00**
☐☐ **107 Henrik Zetterberg, Detr. RC**	**60.00**	**50.00**
☐☐ **108 Kari Haakana, Edmo. RC**	**4.00**	**5.00**
☐☐ **109 Ales Hemsky, Edmo. RC**	**24.00**	**20.00**
☐☐ **110 Alex Henry, Edmo. RC**	**4.00**	**5.00**
☐☐ **111 Jay Bouwmeester, Flor. RC**	**24.00**	**20.00**
☐☐ **112 Alexander Frolov, LosA. RC**	**24.00**	**20.00**
☐☐ **113 Pierre-Marc Bouchard, MinW. RC**	**24.00**	**20.00**
☐☐ **114 Sylvain Blouin, MinW. RC**	**4.00**	**5.00**
☐☐ **115 Ron Hainsey, Mont. RC**	**12.00**	**10.00**
☐☐ **116 Adam Hall, Nash. RC**	**12.00**	**10.00**
☐☐ **117 Scottie Upshall, Nash. RC**	**18.00**	**15.00**
☐☐ 118 Mike Danton, NJer.	6.00	5.00
☐☐ **119 Ray Schultz, NYIs. RC**	**4.00**	**5.00**
☐☐ **120 Anton Volchenkov, Otta. RC**	**6.00**	**5.00**
☐☐ **121 Dennis Seidenberg, Phil. RC**	**6.00**	**5.00**
☐☐ **122 Patrick Sharp, Phil. RC**	**4.00**	**5.00**
☐☐ 123 Dick Tarnstrom, Pitt.	12.00	10.00
☐☐ **124 Alexander Svitov, Tamp. RC**	**18.00**	**15.00**
☐☐ **125 Steve Eminger, Wash. RC**	**6.00**	**5.00**

AUTHENTIC GAME-WORN JERSEY

Insert Set (25 cards):	325.00
Insert (4:21)	GWJ
☐ 1 Adam Oates, Anah. ✂	10.00
☐ 2 Roman Turek (G), Calg. ✂ Blue	10.00
☐ 3 Jason Arnott, Dall. ✂	10.00
☐ 4 Bill Guerin, Bost. ✂	10.00
☐ 4 Bill Guerin, Bost. ✂ Black/White/Yellow	15.00
☐ 5 Scott Young, SLou. ✂	10.00
☐ 6 Dominik Hasek (G), Detr. ✂	20.00
☐ 7 Brett Hull, Detr. ✂	20.00
☐ 8 Curtis Joseph (G), Detr. ✂	20.00
☐ 9 Luc Robitaille, Detr. ✂	15.00
☐ 10 Ryan Smyth, Edmo. ✂	10.00
☐ 11 José Théodore (G), Mont. ✂ Blue	30.00
☐ 12 Jeff Friesen, Anah. ✂ Burgandy	10.00
☐ 13 Oleg Tverdovsky, NJer. ✂	10.00
☐ 14 Alexei Yashin, NYIs. ✂	10.00
☐ 15 Pavel Bure, NYIs. ✂	15.00
☐ 16 Mark Messier, NYRa. ✂	20.00
☐ 17 John LeClair, Phil. ✂	15.00
☐ 18 Daymond Langkow, Phoe. ✂	10.00
☐ 19 Mario Lemieux, Pitt. ✂	75.00
☐ 20 Pavol Demitra, SLou. ✂	10.00
☐ 21 Ray Ferraro, SLou. ✂	10.00
☐ 22 Tom Barrasso (G), Toro. ✂	10.00
☐ 23 Darcy Tucker, Toro. ✂	10.00
☐ 24 Jaromir Jagr, Wash. ✂	20.00
☐ 25 Robert Lang, Pitt. ✂ White	10.00

AUTHENTIC GAME-WORN JERSEY GOLD

Insert Set (25 cards):	1000.00
Insert (4:21)	G25
☐ 1 Adam Oates, Anah. ✂	30.00
☐ 2 Roman Turek (G), Calg. ✂	35.00
☐ 3 Jason Arnott, Dall. ✂	35.00
☐ 4 Bill Guerin, Dall. ✂	30.00
☐ 5 Scott Young, Dall. ✂	25.00
☐ 6 Dominik Hasek (G), Detr. ✂	75.00
☐ 7 Brett Hull, Detr. ✂	75.00
☐ 8 Curtis Joseph (G), Detr. ✂	75.00
☐ 9 Luc Robitaille, Detr. ✂	60.00
☐ 10 Ryan Smyth, Edmo. ✂	35.00
☐ 11 José Théodore (G), Mont. ✂	90.00
☐ 12 Jeff Friesen, NJer. ✂	25.00
☐ 13 Oleg Tverdovsky, NJer. ✂	25.00
☐ 14 Alexei Yashin, NYIs. ✂	45.00
☐ 15 Pavel Bure, NYIs. ✂	60.00
☐ 16 Mark Messier, NYRa. ✂	75.00
☐ 17 John LeClair, Phil. ✂	60.00
☐ 18 Daymond Langkow, Phoe. ✂	25.00
☐ 19 Mario Lemieux, Pitt. ✂	225.00
☐ 20 Pavol Demitra, SLou. ✂	30.00
☐ 21 Ray Ferraro, SLou. ✂	25.00
☐ 22 Tom Barrasso (G), Toro. ✂	30.00
☐ 23 Darcy Tucker, Toro. ✂	25.00
☐ 24 Jaromir Jagr, Wash. ✂	75.00
☐ 25 Robert Lang, Wash. ✂	25.00

AUTHENTIC GAME-WORN JERSEY PATCH

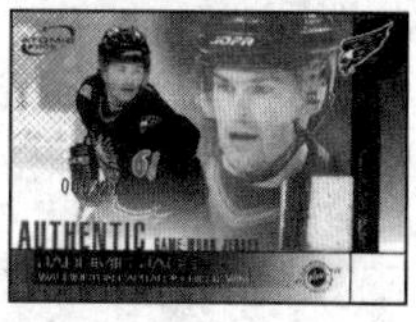

Insert Set (25 cards):	900.00
Insert	Patch
☐ 1 Adam Oates, Anah. ✂ {#/200}	25.00
☐ 2 Roman Turek (G), Calg. ✂ {#/61}	40.00
☐ 3 Jason Arnott, Dall. ✂ {#/339}	25.00
☐ 4 Bill Guerin, Dall. ✂ {#/209}	25.00
☐ 5 Scott Young, Dall. ✂ {#/70}	25.00
☐ 6 Dominik Hasek (G), Detr. ✂ {#/225}	65.00
☐ 7 Brett Hull, Detr. ✂ {#/265}	60.00
☐ 8 Curtis Joseph (G), Detr. ✂ {#/237}	60.00
☐ 9 Luc Robitaille, Detr. ✂ {#/293}	45.00
☐ 10 Ryan Smyth, Edmo. ✂ {#/295}	25.00
☐ 11 José Théodore (G), Mont. ✂ {#/66}	100.00
☐ 12 Jeff Friesen, NJer. ✂ {#/205}	20.00
☐ 13 Oleg Tverdovsky, NJer. ✂ {#/322}	20.00
☐ 14 Alexei Yashin, NYIs. ✂ {#/285}	35.00
☐ 15 Pavel Bure, NYIs. ✂ {#/281}	45.00
☐ 16 Mark Messier, NYRa. ✂ {#/312}	55.00
☐ 17 John LeClair, Phil. ✂ {#/164}	55.00

☐	18 Daymond Langkow, Phoe. ✄ {#/203}	20.00
☐	19 Mario Lemieux, Pitt. ✄ {#/70}	250.00
☐	20 Pavol Demitra, SLou. ✄ {#/322}	20.00
☐	21 Ray Ferraro, SLou. ✄ {#/322}	20.00
☐	22 Tom Barrasso (G), Toro. ✄ {#/335}	20.00
☐	23 Darcy Tucker, Toro. ✄ {#/320}	20.00
☐	24 Jaromir Jagr, Wash. ✄ {#/211}	65.00
☐	25 Robert Lang, Wash. ✄ {#/250}	20.00

COLD FUSION

Insert Set (24 cards):		**60.00**
	Insert (1:11)	**CF**
☐	1 Paul Kariya, Anah.	4.00
☐	2 Dany Heatley, Atla.	3.00
☐	3 Ilya Kovalchuk, Atla.	3.00
☐	4 Joe Thornton, Bost.	4.00
☐	5 Jarome Iginla, Calg.	2.00
☐	6 Jeff O'Neill, Caro.	2.00
☐	7 Éric Dazé, Chic.	2.00
☐	8 Peter Forsberg, Colo.	4.00
☐	9 Joe Sakic, Colo.	5.00
☐	10 Pavel Datsyuk, Detr.	2.00
☐	11 Brendan Shanahan, Detr.	3.00
☐	12 Steve Yzerman, Detr.	8.00
☐	13 Mike Comrie, Edmo.	2.00
☐	14 Kristian Huselius, Flor.	2.00
☐	15 Saku Koivu, Mont.	2.00
☐	16 Pavel Bure, NYRa.	2.00
☐	17 Eric Lindros, NYRa.	3.00
☐	18 Daniel Alfredsson, Otta.	2.00
☐	19 Simon Gagné, Phil.	2.00
☐	20 Mario Lemieux, Pitt.	10.00
☐	21 Teemu Selänne, SanJ.	2.00
☐	22 Mats Sundin, Toro.	3.00
☐	23 Markus Näslund, Vanc.	3.00
☐	24 Jaromir Jagr, Wash.	3.00

DENIED

Insert Set (20 cards):		**100.00**
	Insert (1:41)	**D**
☐	1 Jean-Sébastien Giguère (G), Anah.	5.00
☐	2 Roman Turek (G), Calg.	5.00
☐	3 Arturs Irbe (G), Caro.	5.00
☐	4 Jocelyn Thibault (G), Chic.	5.00
☐	5 Patrick Roy (G), Colo.	15.00
☐	6 Marty Turco (G), Dall.	5.00
☐	7 Curtis Joseph (G), Detr.	6.00
☐	8 Roberto Luongo (G), Flor.	5.00
☐	9 Félix Potvin (G), LosA.	5.00
☐	10 José Théodore (G), Mont.	7.00
☐	11 Martin Brodeur (G), NJer.	10.00
☐	12 Chris Osgood (G), NYIs.	5.00
☐	13 Mike Richter (G), NYRa.	5.00
☐	14 Patrick Lalime (G), Otta.	5.00
☐	15 Roman Cechmanek (G), Phil.	5.00
☐	16 Sean Burke (G), Phoe.	5.00
☐	17 Brent Johnson (G), SLou.	5.00
☐	18 Evgeni Nabokov (G), SanJ.	5.00
☐	19 Nikolai Khabibulin (G), Tamp.	5.00
☐	20 Ed Belfour (G), Dall. (Toro.)	6.00

NATIONAL PRIDE U.S.A.

Insert Set (10 cards):		**30.00**
	Insert (1:21)	**NP**
☐	1 Bill Guerin, Dall.	3.00
☐	2 Mike Modano, Dall.	6.00
☐	3 Chris Chelios, Detr.	3.00
☐	4 Brett Hull, Detr.	6.00
☐	5 Brian Leetch, NYRa.	3.00
☐	6 Mike Richter (G), NYRA.	3.00
☐	7 Jeremy Roenick, Phil.	5.00
☐	8 Tony Amonte, Phoe.	3.00
☐	9 Keith Tkachuk, SLou.	3.00
☐	10 Tom Barrasso (G), Toro.	3.00

NATIONAL PRIDE CANADA

Insert Set (10 cards):		**65.00**
	Insert (1:21)	**NP**
☐	1 Paul Kariya, Anah.	8.00
☐	2 Jarome Iginla, Calg.	4.00
☐	3 Rob Blake, Colo.	3.00
☐	4 Joe Sakic, Colo.	10.00
☐	5 Curtis Joseph (G), Detr.	6.00
☐	6 Brendan Shanahan, Detr.	6.00
☐	7 Steve Yzerman, Detr.	15.00
☐	8 Martin Brodeur (G), NJer.	10.00
☐	9 Mario Lemieux, Pitt.	18.00
☐	10 Chris Pronger, SLou.	3.00

POWER CONVERTERS

Insert Set (20 cards):		**55.00**
	Insert (1:21)	**PC**
☐	1 Dany Heatley, Atla.	5.00
☐	2 Ilya Kovalchuk, Atla.	5.00
☐	3 Miroslav Satan, Buff.	3.00
☐	4 Jarome Iginla, Calg.	4.00
☐	5 Ron Francis, Caro.	3.00
☐	6 Sami Kapanen, Caro.	3.00
☐	7 Nicklas Lidström, Detr.	3.00
☐	8 Luc Robitaille, Detr.	4.00
☐	9 Jason Allison, LosA.	3.00
☐	10 Zigmund Palffy, LosA.	3.00
☐	11 Andrew Brunette, MinW.	3.00
☐	12 Alexei Yashin, NYIs.	3.00
☐	13 Pavel Bure, NYRa.	4.00
☐	14 Eric Lindros, NYRa.	5.00
☐	15 Daniel Brière, Phoe.	3.00
☐	16 Pavol Demitra, SLou.	3.00
☐	17 Keith Tkachuk, SLou.	3.00
☐	18 Todd Bertuzzi, Vanc.	6.00
☐	19 Markus Näslund, Vanc.	5.00
☐	20 Peter Bondra, Wash.	3.00

SUPER COLLIDERS

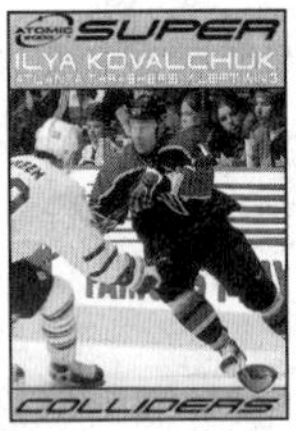

Insert Set (16 cards):		**50.00**
	Insert (1:21)	**SC**
☐	1 Ilya Kovalchuk, Atla.	6.00
☐	2 Joe Thornton, Bost.	7.00
☐	3 Jarome Iginla, Calg.	5.00
☐	4 Erik Cole, Caro.	2.00
☐	5 Jason Arnott, Dall.	3.00
☐	6 Brendan Shanahan, Detr.	6.00
☐	7 Ryan Smyth, Edmo.	3.00
☐	8 Jason Allison, LosA.	3.00
☐	9 Michael Peca, NYIs.	2.00
☐	10 Eric Lindros, NYRa.	6.00
☐	11 Jeremy Roenick, Phil.	5.00
☐	12 Chris Pronger, SLou.	3.00
☐	13 Keith Tkachuk, SLou.	3.00
☐	14 Owen Nolan, SanJ.	3.00
☐	15 Gary Roberts, Toro.	2.00
☐	16 Todd Bertuzzi, Vanc.	7.00

2002 - 03 BAP ALL-STAR EDITION

Produced by In The Game, this series was released in January 2003.

Shell Set (100 cards):	**75.00**
Complete Set (150 cards):	**2,300**
Common Player:	**.50**

	Description	**Base**
☐	1 Daniel Alfredsson, AS'97 (Otta.)	1.00
☐	2 Tony Amonte, AS'01 (Chic.)	1.00
☐	3 Ed Belfour (G), AS'96 (Chic.)	2.00
☐	4 Rob Blake, AS'02 (Colo.)	1.00
☐	5 Peter Bondra, AS'99 (Wash.)	1.00
☐	6 Radek Bonk, AS'00 (Otta.)	.50
☐	7 Martin Brodeur (G), AS'96 (NJer.)	2.50
☐	8 Martin Brodeur (G), AS'97 (NJer.)	2.50
☐	9 Martin Brodeur (G), AS'00 (NJer.)	2.50
☐	10 Valeri Bure, AS'00 (Flor.)	.50
☐	11 Pavel Bure, AS'97 (Vanc.)	1.00
☐	12 Pavel Bure, AS'00 (Flor.)	1.00
☐	13 Sean Burke, AS'02 (Phoe.)	1.00
☐	14 Roman Cechmanek (G), AS'01 (Phil.)	.50
☐	15 Chris Chelios, AS'02 (Detr.)	1.00
☐	16 Vincent Damphousse, AS'02 (SanJ.)	1.00
☐	17 Éric Dazé, AS'02 (Chic.)	.50
☐	18 Pavol Demitra, AS'00 (SLou.)	.50
☐	19 Patrik Elias, AS'02 (NJer.)	1.50
☐	20 Sergei Fedorov, AS'02 (Detr.)	1.50
☐	21 Sergei Fedorov, AS'96 (Detr.)	1.50
☐	22 Theoren Fleury, AS'97 (Calg.)	1.00
☐	23 Peter Forsberg, AS'01 (Colo.)	2.50
☐	24 Peter Forsberg, AS'96 (Colo.)	2.50
☐	25 Peter Forsberg, AS'98 (Colo.)	2.50
☐	26 Simon Gagné, AS'01 (Phil.)	1.50
☐	27 Scott Gomez, AS'00 (NJer.)	.50
☐	28 Bill Guerin, AS'01 (Bost.)	.50
☐	29 Milan Hejduk, AS'01 (Colo.)	1.50
☐	30 Phil Housley, AS'00 (Calg.)	.50
☐	31 Brett Hull, AS'94 (SLou.)	2.00
☐	32 Jarome Iginla, AS'02 (Calg.)	1.50
☐	33 Arturs Irbe (G), AS'99 (Caro.)	.50
☐	34 Jaromir Jagr, AS'00 (Pitt.)	1.50
☐	35 Jaromir Jagr, AS'98 (Pitt.)	1.50
☐	36 Jaromir Jagr, AS'96 (Pitt.)	1.50
☐	37 Curtis Joseph (G), AS'00 (Toro.)	2.00
☐	38 Ed Jovanovski, AS'02 (Vanc.)	.50
☐	39 Tomas Kaberle, AS'02 (Toro.)	.50
☐	40 Sami Kapanen, AS'02 (Caro.)	.50
☐	41 Paul Kariya, AS'97 (Anah.)	2.50
☐	42 Paul Kariya, AS'01 (Anah.)	2.50
☐	43 Paul Kariya, AS'96 (Anah.)	2.50
☐	44 Nikolai Khabibulin (G), AS'02 (Tamp.)	.50
☐	45 Saku Koivu, AS'98 (Mont.)	1.50
☐	46 Olaf Kölzig (G), AS'00 (Wash.)	1.00
☐	47 Alex Kovalev, AS'01 (Pitt.)	1.00
☐	48 John LeClair, AS'97 (Phil.)	1.50
☐	49 Brian Leetch, AS'01 (NYRa.)	1.00
☐	50 Brian Leetch, AS'94 (NYRa.)	1.00
☐	51 Mario Lemieux, AS'02 (Pitt.)	5.00
☐	52 Mario Lemieux, AS'96 (Pitt.)	5.00
☐	53 Mario Lemieux, AS'01 (Pitt.)	5.00
☐	54 Nicklas Lidström, AS'99 (Detr.)	1.00
☐	55 Nicklas Lidström, AS'01 (Detr.)	1.00
☐	56 Eric Lindros, AS'00 (Phil.)	2.00
☐	57 Al MacInnis, AS'00 (SLou.)	.50
☐	58 Mark Messier, AS'94 (NYRa.)	1.50
☐	59 Mark Messier, AS'96 (NYRa.)	1.50
☐	60 Mike Modano, AS'99 (Dall.)	1.50
☐	61 Mike Modano, AS'00 (Dall.)	1.50
☐	62 Alexander Mogilny, AS'96 (Vanc.)	.50
☐	63 Evgeni Nabokov (G), AS'01 (SanJ.)	1.00
☐	64 Markus Näslund, AS'01 (Vanc.)	2.00
☐	65 Scott Niedermayer, AS'98 (NJer.)	.50
☐	66 Owen Nolan, AS'02 (SanJ.)	1.00
☐	67 Teppo Numminen, AS'01 (Phoe.)	.50
☐	68 Chris Osgood (G), AS'96 (Detr.)	1.00
☐	69 Sandis Ozolinsh, AS'02 (Flor.)	.50
☐	70 Zigmund Palffy, AS'01 (LosA.)	1.00
☐	71 Félix Potvin (G), AS'96 (Toro.)	1.00
☐	72 Chris Pronger, AS'00 (SLou.)	1.00
☐	73 Mark Recchi, AS'00 (Phil.)	.50
☐	74 Mike Richter (G), AS'00 (NYRa.)	.50
☐	75 Luc Robitaille, AS'99 (LosA.)	1.50
☐	76 Jeremy Roenick, AS'00 (Phoe.)	1.50
☐	77 Patrick Roy (G), AS'02 (Colo.)	5.00
☐	78 Patrick Roy (G), AS'01 (Colo.)	5.00
☐	79 Patrick Roy (G), AS'94 (Mont.)	5.00
☐	80 Joe Sakic, AS'98 (Colo.)	2.50
☐	81 Joe Sakic, AS'01 (Colo.)	2.50
☐	82 Tommy Salo (G), AS'00 (Edmo.)	.50
☐	83 Teemu Selänne, AS'02 (SanJ.)	1.50
☐	84 Brendan Shanahan, AS'02 (Detr.)	1.50
☐	85 Brendan Shanahan, AS'00 (Detr.)	1.50
☐	86 Brendan Shanahan, AS'96 (Hart.)	1.50
☐	87 Scott Stevens, AS'00 (NJer.)	.50
☐	88 Mats Sundin, AS'00 (Toro.)	1.50
☐	89 Mats Sundin, AS'97 (Toro.)	1.50
☐	90 Darryl Sydor, AS'99 (Dall.)	.50
☐	91 José Théodore (G), AS'02 (Mont.)	2.00
☐	92 Joe Thornton, AS'02 (Bost.)	2.00
☐	93 Keith Tkachuk, AS'99 (Phoe.)	1.00
☐	94 Ron Tugnutt (G), AS'99 (Otta.)	.50
☐	95 Roman Turek (G), AS'00 (SLou.)	.50
☐	96 Doug Weight, AS'01 (Edmo.)	1.00
☐	97 Alexei Yashin, AS'94 (Otta.)	1.00
☐	98 Steve Yzerman, AS'97 (Detr.)	4.00
☐	99 Steve Yzerman, AS'00 (Detr.)	4.00
☐	100 Alexei Zhamnov, AS'02 (Chic.)	.50

FUTURE ALL-STAR

Cards 101-150 have three versions: the regular dufex card (#/100), the Silver dufex card (#/20), and the Gold dufex card (#/1).

	Insert	**R20**	**R100**
☐☐☐	101 Dany Heatley, Atla.	150	35
☐☐☐	102 Ilya Kovalchuk, Atla.	150	35
☐☐☐	103 Marian Gaborik, MinW.	150	35
☐☐☐	104 Marty Turco (G), Dall.	75	20
☐☐☐	105 Mike Comrie, Edmo.	125	30
☐☐☐	**106 Cody Rudkowsky, SLou. RC**	**75**	**40**
☐☐☐	**107 Levente Szuper (G), Calg. RC**	**75**	**40**
☐☐☐	**108 Alex Henry, Wash. RC**	**50**	**25**
☐☐☐	**109 Lynn Loyns, SanJ. RC**	**50**	**25**
☐☐☐	**110 Tomi Pettinen, NYIs. RC**	**50**	**25**
☐☐☐	**111 Micki Dupont, Calg. RC**	**75**	**40**
☐☐☐	**112 Shaone Morrisonn, Bost. RC**	**75**	**40**
☐☐☐	**113 Ryan Miller (G), Buff. RC**	**200**	**100**
☐☐☐	**114 Mikael Tellqvist (G), Toro. RC**	**75**	**40**
☐☐☐	**115 Dany Sabourin, Calg. RC**	**50**	**25**
☐☐☐	**116 Tim Thomas (G), Bost. RC**	**75**	**40**
☐☐☐	**117 Kurt Sauer, Anah. RC**	**50**	**25**
☐☐☐	**118 Kari Haakana, Edmo. RC**	**50**	**25**
☐☐☐	**119 Lasse Pirjetä, Colu. RC**	**50**	**25**
☐☐☐	**120 Shawn Thornton, Chic. RC**	**75**	**40**
☐☐☐	**121 Curtis Sanford (G), SLou. RC**	**75**	**40**
☐☐☐	122 Dick Tarnström, Pitt.	40	20
☐☐☐	**123 Radovan Somik, Phil. RC**	**50**	**25**
☐☐☐	**124 Martin Gerber (G), Anah. RC**	**75**	**40**
☐☐☐	**125 Dennis Seidenberg, Phil. RC**	**75**	**40**
☐☐☐	**126 P-M Bouchard, MinW. RC**	**225**	**120**
☐☐☐	**127 Alexei Smirnov, Anah. RC**	**100**	**60**
☐☐☐	**128 Ales Hemsky, Edmo. RC**	**225**	**120**
☐☐☐	**129 Stéphane Veilleux, MinW. RC**	**50**	**25**
☐☐☐	**130 Tom Koivisto, SLou. RC**	**50**	**25**
☐☐☐	**131 Jeff Taffe, Phoe. RC**	**100**	**60**
☐☐☐	**132 Jordan Leopold, Calg. RC**	**100**	**60**
☐☐☐	**133 Stanislav Chistov, Anah. RC**	**225**	**120**
☐☐☐	**134 Rick Nash, Colu. RC**	**400**	**250**

◆ The Rick Nash one-of-one gold dufex parallel #134 closed at $990 U.S. (approx. $1,535 Cdn.) in a March Internet auction at eBay.ca.

☐☐☐	**135 Chuck Kobasew, Calg. RC**	**100**	**60**
☐☐☐	**136 Alexander Svitov, Tamp. RC**	**150**	**80**
☐☐☐	**137 Carlo Colaiacovo, Toro. RC**	**100**	**60**
☐☐☐	**138 Jason Spezza, Otta. RC**	**300**	**150**

◆ The Jason Spezza one-of-one gold dufex parallel #138 was purchased for $849.99 U.S. (approx. $1,275 Cdn.) at eBay.ca on May 11, 2003.

☐☐☐	**139 Henrik Zetterberg, Detr. RC**	**400**	**275**
☐☐☐	**140 Anton Volchenkov, Otta. RC**	**75**	**40**
☐☐☐	**141 Ron Hainsey, Mont. RC**	**100**	**60**
☐☐☐	**142 Jay Bouwmeester, Flor. RC**	**225**	**120**
☐☐☐	**143 Adam Hall, Nash. RC**	**100**	**60**
☐☐☐	**144 Steve Eminger, Wash. RC**	**75**	**40**
☐☐☐	**145 Mike Cammalleri, LosA. RC**	**150**	**80**
☐☐☐	**146 Dmitri Bykov, Detr. RC**	**75**	**40**
☐☐☐	**147 Ivan Majesky, Flor. RC**	**50**	**25**
☐☐☐	**148 Alexander Frolov, LosA. RC**	**200**	**100**
☐☐☐	**149 Scottie Upshall, Nash. RC**	**150**	**80**
☐☐☐	**150 Patrick Sharp, Phil. RC**	**50**	**25**

HE SHOOTS HE SCORES

Each redemption card was worth one, two, or three points. Collectors could trade 400 points for a special random jersey card. This redemption program ends on December 31, 2003.

Insert Set (20 cards):		
	Insert	**HSHS**
☐	Brian Leetch, AS'94 (NYRa.) [1 Point]	
☐	Eric Lindros, AS'98 (Phil.) [1 Point]	

☐ Mark Messier, AS'96 (NYRa.) [1 Point]
☐ Owen Nolan, AS'97 (SanJ.) [1 Point]
☐ Teemu Selänne, AS'94 (Winn.) [1 Point]
☐ Brendan Shanahan, AS'96 (Hart.) [1 Point]
☐ Mats Sundin [1 Point]
☐ Alexei Yashin, AS'94 (Otta.) [1 Point]
☐ Martin Brodeur (G) [2 Points]
☐ Pavel Bure, AS'00 (Flor.) [2 Points]
☐ Sergei Fedorov, AS'94 (Detr.) [2 Points]
☐ Jaromir Jagr, AS'00 (Pitt.) [2 Points]
☐ Curtis Joseph (G), AS'00 [2 Points]
☐ Nicklas Lidström, AS'01 (Detr.) [2 Points]
☐ Mike Modano, AS'00 (Dall.) [2 Points]
☐ Patrick Roy (G), AS'01 (Colo.) [2 Points]
☐ Joe Sakic, AS'98 (Colo.) [2 Points]
☐ Peter Forsberg, AS'98 (Colo.) [3 Points]
☐ Mario Lemieux [3 Points]
☐ Steve Yzerman, AS'00 (Detr.) [3 Points]

JERSEY

These cards have three versions: the Jersey card (100 copies each), the silver Jersey card (30 copies each), and the gold Jersey card (10 copies each).

Insert Set (100 cards):	20,500	5,000	2,500
Insert	J10	J30	J100
☐☐☐ 1 Daniel Alfredsson ✂	175	45	45
☐☐☐ 2 Tony Amonte ✂	175	45	25
☐☐☐ 3 Ed Belfour (G) ✂	300	75	35
☐☐☐ 4 Rob Blake ✂	175	45	25
☐☐☐ 5 Peter Bondra ✂	175	45	25
☐☐☐ 6 Radek Bonk ✂	100	40	25
☐☐☐ 7 Martin Brodeur (G) ✂	450	100	50
☐☐☐ 8 Martin Brodeur (G) ✂	450	100	50
☐☐☐ 9 Martin Brodeur (G) ✂	450	100	50
☐☐☐ 10 Valeri Bure ✂	75	40	25
☐☐☐ 11 Pavel Bure ✂	225	50	25
☐☐☐ 12 Pavel Bure ✂	225	50	25
☐☐☐ 13 Sean Burke ✂	175	45	25
☐☐☐ 14 Roman Cechmanek (G) ✂	125	40	25
☐☐☐ 15 Chris Chelios ✂	175	45	25
☐☐☐ 16 Vincent Damphousse ✂	175	45	25
☐☐☐ 17 Éric Dazé ✂	125	40	25
☐☐☐ 18 Pavol Demitra ✂	125	40	25
☐☐☐ 19 Patrik Elias Burgandy ✂	250	60	30
☐☐☐ 20 Sergei Fedorov ✂	275	65	30
☐☐☐ 21 Sergei Fedorov ✂	275	65	30
☐☐☐ 22 Theoren Fleury ✂	175	45	25
☐☐☐ 23 Peter Forsberg ✂	375	90	45
☐☐☐ 24 Peter Forsberg ✂	375	90	45
☐☐☐ 25 Peter Forsberg ✂	375	90	45
☐☐☐ 26 Simon Gagné ✂	250	60	30
☐☐☐ 27 Scott Gomez ✂	125	40	25
☐☐☐ 28 Bill Guerin ✂	125	40	25
☐☐☐ 29 Milan Hejduk ✂	250	60	30
☐☐☐ 30 Phil Housley ✂	100	40	25
☐☐☐ 31 Brett Hull ✂	300	75	35
☐☐☐ 32 Jarome Iginla ✂	250	60	30
☐☐☐ 33 Arturs Irbe (G) ✂	125	40	25
☐☐☐ 34 Jaromir Jagr ✂	275	65	30
☐☐☐ 35 Jaromir Jagr ✂	275	65	30
☐☐☐ 36 Jaromir Jagr ✂	275	65	30
☐☐☐ 37 Curtis Joseph (G) ✂	300	75	35
☐☐☐ 38 Ed Jovanovski ✂	125	40	25
☐☐☐ 39 Tomas Kaberle ✂	100	40	25
☐☐☐ 40 Sami Kapanen ✂	100	40	25
☐☐☐ 41 Paul Kariya ✂	375	90	45
☐☐☐ 42 Paul Kariya ✂	375	90	45
☐☐☐ 43 Paul Kariya ✂	375	90	45
☐☐☐ 44 Nikolai Khabibulin (G) ✂	125	40	25
☐☐☐ 45 Saku Koivu ✂	250	60	45
☐☐☐ 46 Olaf Kölzig (G) ✂	175	45	25
☐☐☐ 47 Alex Kovalev ✂	175	45	25
☐☐☐ 48 John LeClair ✂	250	60	30
☐☐☐ 49 Brian Leetch ✂	150	40	25
☐☐☐ 50 Brian Leetch ✂	150	40	25
☐☐☐ 51 Mario Lemieux ✂	825	200	100
☐☐☐ 52 Mario Lemieux ✂	825	200	100
☐☐☐ 53 Mario Lemieux ✂	825	200	100
☐☐☐ 54 Nicklas Lidström ✂	150	40	25
☐☐☐ 55 Nicklas Lidström ✂	150	40	25
☐☐☐ 56 Eric Lindros ✂	300	75	35
☐☐☐ 57 Al MacInnis ✂	125	40	25
☐☐☐ 58 Mark Messier ✂	275	65	30
☐☐☐ 59 Mark Messier ✂	275	65	30
☐☐☐ 60 Mike Modano ✂	275	65	30
☐☐☐ 61 Mike Modano ✂	275	65	30
☐☐☐ 62 Alexander Mogilny ✂	150	40	25
☐☐☐ 63 Evgeni Nabokov (G) ✂	175	45	25
☐☐☐ 64 Markus Näslund ✂	300	75	35
☐☐☐ 65 Scott Niedermayer ✂	100	40	25
☐☐☐ 66 Owen Nolan ✂	175	45	25
☐☐☐ 67 Teppo Numminen ✂	100	40	25
☐☐☐ 68 Chris Osgood (G) ✂	175	45	25
☐☐☐ 69 Sandis Ozolinsh ✂	75	40	25
☐☐☐ 70 Zigmund Palffy ✂	175	45	25
☐☐☐ 71 Félix Potvin (G) ✂	175	45	45
☐☐☐ 72 Chris Pronger ✂	175	45	25
☐☐☐ 73 Mark Recchi ✂	125	40	25
☐☐☐ 74 Mike Richter (G) ✂	150	40	25
☐☐☐ 75 Luc Robitaille ✂	250	60	30
☐☐☐ 76 Jeremy Roenick ✂	250	60	30
☐☐☐ 77 Patrick Roy (G) ✂	675	150	80
☐☐☐ 78 Patrick Roy (G) ✂	675	150	80
☐☐☐ 79 Patrick Roy (G) ✂	675	150	80
☐☐☐ 80 Joe Sakic ✂	450	100	50
☐☐☐ 81 Joe Sakic ✂	450	100	50
☐☐☐ 82 Tommy Salo (G) ✂	125	40	25
☐☐☐ 83 Teemu Selänne ✂	250	60	30
☐☐☐ 84 Brendan Shanahan ✂	275	65	30
☐☐☐ 85 Brendan Shanahan ✂	275	65	30
☐☐☐ 86 Brendan Shanahan ✂	275	65	30
☐☐☐ 87 Scott Stevens ✂	125	40	25
☐☐☐ 88 Mats Sundin ✂	275	65	30
☐☐☐ 89 Mats Sundin ✂	275	65	30
☐☐☐ 90 Darryl Sydor ✂	75	40	25
☐☐☐ 91 José Théodore (G) ✂	375	90	45
☐☐☐ 92 Joe Thornton ✂	375	90	45
☐☐☐ 93 Keith Tkachuk ✂	175	45	25
☐☐☐ 94 Ron Tugnutt (G) ✂	125	40	25
☐☐☐ 95 Roman Turek (G) ✂	150	40	25
☐☐☐ 96 Doug Weight ✂	175	45	25
☐☐☐ 97 Alexei Yashin ✂	175	45	25
☐☐☐ 98 Steve Yzerman ✂	675	150	80
☐☐☐ 99 Steve Yzerman ✂	675	150	80
☐☐☐ 100 Alexei Zhamnov ✂	100	40	25

FOREVER COLLECTIBLES

Insert Set (10 dolls):	275.00
One-per-box insert	BAPAS
☐ Martin Brodeur Brodeur, AS'99 {*1530}	30.00
☐ Pavel Bure Bure, AS'01 {*2010}	25.00
☐ Peter Forsberg Forsberg, AS'98 {*2031}	25.00
☐ Jaromir Jagr Jagr, AS'96 {*2068}	25.00
☐ Curtis Joseph Joseph, AS'00 {*1031}	25.00
☐ Mario Lemieux Lemieux, AS'02 {*1066}	60.00
☐ Patrick Roy Roy, AS'93 {*1033}	60.00
☐ Joe Sakic Sakic, AS'94 {*1519}	30.00
☐ José Théodore, AS'02 {*1560}	25.00
☐ Steve Yzerman Yzerman, AS'97 {*2019}	40.00

2002 - 03 BE A PLAYER DRAFT FLORIDA 2001

These cards were redeemed via the Draft Day redemption cards found in packs of 2001 - 02 Be A Player Memorabilia. They were redeemable after the player made his NHL debut. The first four cards were redeemed during the 2001 - 02 season (see 2001 - 02 Be A Player Draft Florida 2001).

Description	Draft
☐ 2 Jason Spezza, Otta.	
☐ 3 Alexander Svitov, Tamp.	
☐ 5 Stanislav Chistov, Anah.	
☐ 8 Pascal Leclaire (G), Colu.	
☐ 13 Ales Hemsky, Edmo.	
☐ 14 Chuck Kobasew, Calg.	

2002 - 03 BE A PLAYER DRAFT TORONTO 2002

These cards were redeemed via the Draft Day redemption cards found in packs of 2002 - 03 Be A Player Memorabilia. They were redeemable after the player made his NHL debut.

Description	Draft
☐ **1 Rick Nash, Colu. RC**	
☐ **3 Jay Bouwmeester, Flor. RC**	
☐ **6 Scottie Upshall, Nash. RC**	
☐ **8 Pierre-Marc Bouchard, MinW. RC**	
☐ **12 Steve Eminger, Wash. RC**	

2002 - 03 BE A PLAYER MEMORABILIA

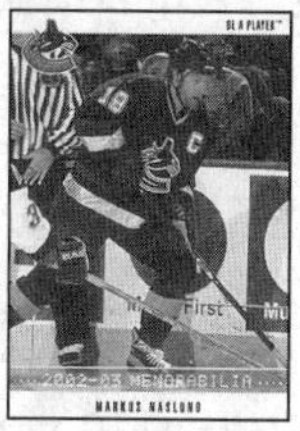

Produced by In The Game, this series was released in November 2002. There are four versions for each card 1-300: the base card, the Ruby parallel (#/200), the Sapphire parallel (#/100), and the Emerald parallel (#/10). Please see the appendix for pricing on scarce cards.

Shell Set (200 cards):	-	-	75.00
Complete Set (300 cards):	2,500	1,100	300.00
Common Player:	6.00	3.00	.25
Description	S100	R200	Base
☐☐☐☐ 1 Steve Yzerman, Detr.	45	20	4.50
☐☐☐☐ 2 Steven Reinprecht, Colo.	6	2	.50
☐☐☐☐ 3 J-S Giguère (G), Anah.	20	10	2.00
☐☐☐☐ 4 Chris Simon, Wash.	6	2	.25
☐☐☐☐ 5 Dany Heatley, Atla.	20	10	2.00
☐☐☐☐ 6 Brendan Morrison, Vanc.	6	2	.50
☐☐☐☐ 7 Bill Guerin, Dall.	6	2	.50
☐☐☐☐ 8 Alexander Mogilny, Toro.	6	2	.50
☐☐☐☐ 9 Martin Biron (G), Buff.	6	2	.50
☐☐☐☐ 10 Brad Richards, Tamp.	6	2	.50
☐☐☐☐ 11 Craig Conroy, Calg.	6	2	.50
☐☐☐☐ 12 Al MacInnis, SLou.	6	2	.50
☐☐☐☐ 13 Arturs Irbe (G), Caro.	6	2	.50
☐☐☐☐ 14 Evgeni Nabokov (G), SanJ.	10	5	1.00
☐☐☐☐ 15 Alexei Zhamnov, Chic.	6	2	.50
☐☐☐☐ 16 Daniel Brière, Phoe.	6	2	.50
☐☐☐☐ 17 Alex Tanguay, Colo.	10	5	1.00
☐☐☐☐ 18 Milan Kraft, Pitt.	6	2	.50
☐☐☐☐ 19 Marc Denis (G), Colu.	6	2	.50
☐☐☐☐ 20 Adam Oates, Anah.	6	2	.50
☐☐☐☐ 21 Darryl Sydor, Dall.	6	2	.25
☐☐☐☐ 22 Daniel Alfredsson, Otta.	20	5	1.00
☐☐☐☐ 23 Brendan Shanahan, Detr.	20	10	2.00
☐☐☐☐ 24 Brian Leetch, NYRa.	10	5	1.00
☐☐☐☐ 25 Anson Carter, Edmo.	6	2	.50
☐☐☐☐ 26 Adrian Aucoin, NYIs.	6	2	.25
☐☐☐☐ 27 Kristian Huselius, Flor.	6	2	.50
☐☐☐☐ 28 Jamie Langenbrunner, NJer.	6	2	.25
☐☐☐☐ 29 Adam Deadmarsh, LosA.	6	2	.50
☐☐☐☐ 30 Denis Arkhipov, Nash.	6	2	.25
☐☐☐☐ 31 Andrew Brunette, MinW.	6	2	.25
☐☐☐☐ 32 Donald Audette, Mont.	6	2	.50
☐☐☐☐ 33 Rob Blake, Colo.	10	5	1.00
☐☐☐☐ 34 Jaromir Jagr, Wash.	20	10	2.00
☐☐☐☐ 35 Félix Potvin (G), LosA.	20	5	1.00
☐☐☐☐ 36 Dan Cloutier (G), Vanc.	6	2	.50
☐☐☐☐ 37 Niklas Hagman, Flor.	6	2	.25
☐☐☐☐ 38 Alyn McCauley, Toro.	6	2	.50
☐☐☐☐ 39 Eric Brewer, Edmo.	6	2	.50
☐☐☐☐ 40 Nikolai Khabibulin (G), Tamp.	6	2	.50
☐☐☐☐ 41 Brett Hull, Detr.	20	10	2.00
☐☐☐☐ 42 Brent Johnson (G), SLou.	6	2	.50
☐☐☐☐ 43 Brenden Morrow, Dall.	6	2	.50
☐☐☐☐ 44 Mike Ricci, SanJ.	6	2	.50
☐☐☐☐ 45 Ray Whitney, Colu.	6	2	.25
☐☐☐☐ 46 Alexei Kovalev, Pitt.	10	5	1.00
☐☐☐☐ 47 Chris Drury, Colo.	10	5	1.00
☐☐☐☐ 48 Daymond Langkow, Phoe.	6	2	.25
☐☐☐☐ 49 Éric Dazé, Chic.	6	2	.50
☐☐☐☐ 50 Pavel Brendl, Phil.	6	2	.50
☐☐☐☐ 51 Bates Battaglia, Caro.	6	2	.25
☐☐☐☐ 52 Jani Hurme (G), Otta.	6	2	.25
☐☐☐☐ 53 Dean McAmmond, Calg.	6	2	.25
☐☐☐☐ 54 Dan Blackburn (G), NYRa.	6	2	.50
☐☐☐☐ 55 Maxim Afinogenov, Buff.	6	2	.50
☐☐☐☐ 56 Alexei Yashin, NYIs.	10	5	1.00
☐☐☐☐ 57 Steve Shields (G), Bost.	6	2	.25
☐☐☐☐ 58 Joe Nieuwendyk, NJer.	6	2	.50
☐☐☐☐ 59 Frantisek Kaberle, Atla.	6	2	.25
☐☐☐☐ 60 Jan Lasak (G), Nash.	6	2	.25
☐☐☐☐ 61 Ron Francis, Caro.	10	5	1.00
☐☐☐☐ 62 Jeff Friesen, NJer.	6	2	.50
☐☐☐☐ 63 Doug Gilmour, Mont.	10	5	1.00
☐☐☐☐ 64 Jeff Halpern, Wash.	6	2	.25
☐☐☐☐ 65 Ilya Kovalchuk, Atla.	20	10	2.00
☐☐☐☐ 66 Daniel Sedin, Vanc.	6	2	.50
☐☐☐☐ 67 Glen Murray, Bost.	6	2	.50
☐☐☐☐ 68 Bryan McCabe, Toro.	6	2	.25
☐☐☐☐ 69 Miroslav Satan, Buff.	6	2	.50
☐☐☐☐ 70 Pavel Kubina, Tamp.	6	2	.25
☐☐☐☐ 71 Derek Morris, Calg.	6	2	.25
☐☐☐☐ 72 Chris Pronger, SLou.	10	5	1.00
☐☐☐☐ 73 Erik Cole, Caro.	6	2	.25
☐☐☐☐ 74 Owen Nolan, SanJ.	10	5	1.00
☐☐☐☐ 75 Jocelyn Thibault (G), Chic.	6	2	.50
☐☐☐☐ 76 Jan Hrdina, Pitt.	6	2	.25
☐☐☐☐ 77 Greg Vries, Colo.	6	2	.25
☐☐☐☐ 78 Krys Kolanos, Phoe.	6	2	.25
☐☐☐☐ 79 David Vyborny, Colu.	6	2	.25
☐☐☐☐ 80 Jeremy Roenick, Phil.	15	5	1.50
☐☐☐☐ 81 Jason Arnott, Dall.	6	2	.50
☐☐☐☐ 82 Mike Leclerc, Anah.	6	2	.25
☐☐☐☐ 83 Marian Hossa, Otta.	20	10	2.00
☐☐☐☐ 84 Chris Chelios, Detr.	10	5	1.00
☐☐☐☐ 85 Eric Lindros, NYRa.	20	10	2.00
☐☐☐☐ 86 Jochen Hecht, Buff.	6	2	.25
☐☐☐☐ 87 Chris Osgood (G), NYIs.	10	5	1.00
☐☐☐☐ 88 Roberto Luongo (G), Flor.	15	5	1.50
☐☐☐☐ 89 Martin Brodeur (G), NJer.	30	15	3.00
☐☐☐☐ 90 Jaroslav Modry, LosA.	6	2	.25
☐☐☐☐ 91 Martin Erat, Nash.	6	2	.25
☐☐☐☐ 92 Manny Fernandez (G), MinW.	6	2	.50
☐☐☐☐ 93 José Théodore (G), Mont.	20	10	2.00
☐☐☐☐ 94 Olaf Kölzig (G), Wash.	10	5	1.00
☐☐☐☐ 95 Ed Jovanovski, Vanc.	6	2	.50
☐☐☐☐ 96 Sandis Ozolinsh, Flor.	6	2	.25
☐☐☐☐ 97 Corey Schwab, NJer.	6	2	.25
☐☐☐☐ 98 Sami Kapanen, Caro.	6	2	.50
☐☐☐☐ 99 Mike Comrie, Edmo.	15	5	1.50
☐☐☐☐ 100 Shane Willis, Tamp.	6	2	.25
☐☐☐☐ 101 Dominik Hasek, Detr.	20	10	2.00
☐☐☐☐ 102 Jason Allison, LosA.	10	5	1.00
☐☐☐☐ 103 Doug Weight, SLou.	10	5	1.00
☐☐☐☐ 104 Marty Turco (G), Dall.	10	5	1.00
☐☐☐☐ 105 Patrick Marleau, SanJ.	6	2	.50
☐☐☐☐ 106 Rostislav Klesla, Colu.	6	2	.50
☐☐☐☐ 107 Johan Hedberg (G), Pitt.	6	2	.50
☐☐☐☐ 108 Joe Sakic, Colo.	30	15	3.00
☐☐☐☐ 109 Marian Gaborik, MinW.	20	10	2.00
☐☐☐☐ 110 Sean Burke (G), Phoe.	10	5	1.00
☐☐☐☐ 111 Mark Bell, Chic.	6	2	.25
☐☐☐☐ 112 John LeClair, Phil.	15	5	1.50
☐☐☐☐ 113 Jaroslav Svoboda, Caro.	6	2	.25
☐☐☐☐ 114 Todd Bertuzzi, Vanc.	20	10	2.00
☐☐☐☐ 115 Martin Havlat, Otta.	10	5	1.00
☐☐☐☐ 116 Pavel Datsyuk, Detr.	15	5	1.50
☐☐☐☐ 117 Jarome Iginla, Calg.	15	5	1.50
☐☐☐☐ 118 Mark Messier, NYRa.	20	10	2.00
☐☐☐☐ 119 Stu Barnes, Buff.	6	2	.25
☐☐☐☐ 120 Shayne Corson, Toro.	6	2	.50
☐☐☐☐ 121 Mark Parrish, NYIs.	6	2	.50
☐☐☐☐ 122 Joe Thornton, Bost.	20	10	2.00
☐☐☐☐ 123 Patrik Elias, NJer.	15	5	1.50
☐☐☐☐ 124 Milan Hnilicka (G), Atla.	6	2	.25
☐☐☐☐ 125 Mike Dunham (G), Nash.	6	2	.50
☐☐☐☐ 126 Oleg Tverdovsky, NJer.	6	2	.25
☐☐☐☐ 127 Richard Zednik, Mont.	6	2	.50
☐☐☐☐ 128 Peter Forsberg, Colo.	25	10	2.50
☐☐☐☐ 129 Mikko Eloranta, LosA.	6	2	.25
☐☐☐☐ 130 Zdeno Chara, Otta.	6	2	.25
☐☐☐☐ 131 Curtis Joseph (G), Detr.	20	10	2.00
☐☐☐☐ 132 Steve Rucchin, Anah.	6	2	.25
☐☐☐☐ 133 Sergei Fedorov, Detr.	20	10	2.00
☐☐☐☐ 134 Josef Vasicek, Caro.	6	2	.25
☐☐☐☐ 135 Ryan Smyth, Edmo.	6	2	.50
☐☐☐☐ 136 Scott Niedermayer, NJer.	6	2	.50
☐☐☐☐ 137 Shane Doan, Phoe.	6	2	.25
☐☐☐☐ 138 Steve Sullivan, Chic.	6	2	.50
☐☐☐☐ 139 Stephen Weiss, Flor.	6	2	.50
☐☐☐☐ 140 Alexandre Daigle, Pitt.	6	2	.25
☐☐☐☐ 141 Fred Brathwaite (G), SLou.	6	2	.50
☐☐☐☐ 142 Peter Bondra, Wash.	10	5	1.00
☐☐☐☐ 143 Patrik Stefan, Atla.	6	2	.50
☐☐☐☐ 144 Tony Amonte, Phoe.	10	5	1.00
☐☐☐☐ 145 Valeri Bure, Flor.	6	2	.50
☐☐☐☐ 146 Rick DiPietro (G), NYIs.	6	2	.50
☐☐☐☐ 147 Martin Straka, Pitt.	6	2	.50
☐☐☐☐ 148 Jeff O'Neill, Caro.	6	2	.50
☐☐☐☐ 149 Milan Hejduk, Colo.	15	5	1.50
☐☐☐☐ 150 Kirk Maltby, Detr.	6	2	.25
☐☐☐☐ 151 Mike York, Edmo.	6	2	.50
☐☐☐☐ 152 Scott Gomez, NJer.	6	2	.50
☐☐☐☐ 153 Michael Peca, NYIs.	6	2	.50
☐☐☐☐ 154 Mike Richter (G), NYRa.	6	2	.50
☐☐☐☐ 155 Patrick Lalime (G), Otta.	10	5	1.00
☐☐☐☐ 156 Justin Williams, Phil.	6	2	.50
☐☐☐☐ 157 Mario Lemieux, Pitt.	60	30	6.00
☐☐☐☐ 158 Kevin Weekes (G), Caro.	6	2	.25
☐☐☐☐ 159 Scott Young, Dall.	6	2	.50

□□□□	160 Tommy Salo (G), Edmo.	6	2	.50
□□□□	161 Steve Webb, NYIs.	6	2	.25
□□□□	162 Teemu Selänne, SanJ.	15	5	1.50
□□□□	163 Jozef Stümpel, Bost.	6	2	.25
□□□□	164 Patrick Roy (G), Colo.	45	30	6.00
□□□□	165 Zigmund Palffy, LosA.	10	5	1.00
□□□□	166 Pavel Bure, NYRa.	15	5	1.50
□□□□	167 V. Damphousse, SanJ.	10	5	1.00
□□□□	168 Sergei Gonchar, Wash.	6	2	.50
□□□□	169 Sergei Samsonov, Bost.	10	5	1.00
□□□□	170 Luc Robitaille, Detr.	15	5	1.50
□□□□	171 Scott Stevens, NJer.	6	2	.50
□□□□	172 Robert Lang, Wash.	6	2	.25
□□□□	173 Henrik Sedin, Vanc.	6	2	.50
□□□□	174 Tim Connolly, Buff.	6	2	.50
□□□□	175 Pierre Turgeon, Dall.	6	2	.50
□□□□	176 Yanic Perreault, Mont.	6	2	.50
□□□□	177 Radek Bonk, Otta.	6	2	.50
□□□□	178 Keith Tkachuk, SLou.	10	5	1.00
□□□□	179 Paul Kariya, Anah.	25	10	2.50
□□□□	180 Mike Modano, Dall.	20	10	2.00
□□□□	181 Saku Koivu, Mont.	20	5	1.50
□□□□	182 Mark Recchi, Phil.	6	2	.50
□□□□	183 Roman Turek (G), Calg.	6	2	.50
□□□□	184 Kris Draper, Detr.	6	2	.25
□□□□	185 Scott Hartnell, Nash.	6	2	.25
□□□□	186 Keith Primeau, Phil.	6	2	.50
□□□□	187 Vincent Lecavalier, Tamp.	20	10	2.00
□□□□	188 Darcy Tucker, Toro.	6	2	.25
□□□□	189 Markus Näslund, Vanc.	20	10	2.00
□□□□	190 Pavol Demitra, SLou.	6	2	.50
□□□□	191 Gary Roberts, Toro.	6	2	.50
□□□□	192 Rod Brind'Amour, Caro.	6	2	.50
□□□□	193 Radim Vrbata, Colo.	6	2	.50
□□□□	194 Nicklas Lidström, Detr.	10	5	1.00
□□□□	195 Tom Poti, NYRa.	6	2	.25
□□□□	196 Roman Cechmanek (G), Phil.	6	2	.50
□□□□	197 Scott Mellanby, SLou.	6	2	.25
□□□□	198 Mats Sundin, Toro.	20	10	2.00
□□□□	199 Filip Kuba, MinW.	6	2	.25
□□□□	200 Simon Gagné, Phil.	15	5	1.50
□□□□	201 Paul Kariya, Anah.	25	10	4.00
□□□□	202 Ilya Kovalchuk, Atla.	20	10	3.00
□□□□	203 Joe Thornton, Bost.	20	10	3.50
□□□□	204 Miroslav Satan, Buff.	6	2	.75
□□□□	205 Jarome Iginla, Calg.	15	5	2.00
□□□□	206 Ron Francis, Caro.	10	5	1.50
□□□□	207 Éric Dazé, Chic.	6	2	1.00
□□□□	208 Patrick Roy (G), Colo.	45	30	9.00
□□□□	209 Rostislav Klesla, Colu.	6	2	.75
□□□□	210 Mike Modano, Dall.	20	10	3.00
□□□□	211 Steve Yzerman, Detr.	45	20	7.00
□□□□	212 Mike Comrie, Edmo.	15	5	2.00
□□□□	213 Roberto Luongo (G), Flor.	15	5	2.00
□□□□	214 Zigmund Palffy, LosA.	10	5	1.50
□□□□	215 Marian Gaborik, MinW.	20	10	3.00
□□□□	216 José Théodore (G), Mont.	20	10	3.50
□□□□	217 Scott Hartnell, Nash.	6	2	.75
□□□□	218 Martin Brodeur (G), NJer.	30	15	4.50
□□□□	219 Alexei Yashin, NYIs.	10	5	1.50
□□□□	220 Pavel Bure, NYRa.	15	5	2.00
□□□□	221 Marian Hossa, Otta.	20	10	3.00
□□□□	222 Simon Gagné, Phil.	15	5	2.00
□□□□	223 Daniel Brière, Phoe.	6	2	1.00
□□□□	224 Mario Lemieux, Pitt.	60	30	9.00
□□□□	225 Chris Pronger, SLou.	10	5	1.50
□□□□	226 Owen Nolan, SanJ.	10	5	1.50
□□□□	227 Nikolai Khabibulin (G), Tamp.	6	2	1.00
□□□□	228 Mats Sundin, Toro.	20	10	3.00
□□□□	229 Markus Näslund, Vanc.	20	10	3.00
□□□□	230 Jaromir Jagr, Wash.	20	10	3.00
□□□□	231 P. Forsberg / E. Lindros	20	10	3.50
□□□□	232 P. Roy (G) / J. Thibault (G)	25	15	5.00
□□□□	233 J. Buyck / T. Sawchuk (G)	25	10	3.50
□□□□	234 J. Plante (G) / Worlsey (G)	20	10	3.50
□□□□	235 C. Pronger / B. Shanahan	15	5	2.00
□□□□	236 P. Brendl / E. Lindros	10	5	1.50
□□□□	237 K. Beech / J. Jagr	10	5	1.50
□□□□	238 P. Bure / E. Jovanovski	10	5	1.50
□□□□	239 J. Iginla / J. Nieuwendyk	10	5	1.50
□□□□	240 É. Dazé / D. Hasek	10	5	2.00
□□□□	241 C. Chelios / D. Savard	10	5	1.50
□□□□	242 J. Allison / A. Oates	10	5	1.50
□□□□	243 D. Hasek / Vy. Kozlov	10	5	1.50
□□□□	244 R. Svehla / D. Yushkevich	6	2	.75
□□□□	245 T. Bertuzzi / T. Linden	15	5	2.00
□□□□	246 G. Lafleur / S. Zubov	20	10	3.00
□□□□	247 J. Arnott / B. Guerin	6	2	1.00
□□□□	248 A. Mogilny / M. Peca	6	2	1.00
□□□□	249 K. Primeau / B. Shanahan	10	5	2.00
□□□□	250 J. LeClair / M. Recchi	10	5	1.50
□□□□	251 R. Blake / A. Deadmarsh	6	2	1.00
□□□□	252 J. Roenick / A. Zhamnov	10	5	1.50
□□□□	253 T. Connolly / M. Peca	6	2	1.00
□□□□	254 O. Nolan / S. Ozolinsh	6	2	1.00
□□□□	255 C. Drury / M. Fernandez (G)	10	5	1.50
□□□□	256 Brathwaite (G) / Turek (G)	6	2	1.00
□□□□	257 J. Arnott / J. Nieuwendyk	6	2	1.00
□□□□	258 D. Andreychuk / B. Rolston	6	2	.75
□□□□	259 B. Berard / F. Potvin (G)	6	2	1.00
□□□□	260 V. Bure / R. Niedermayer	6	2	.75
□□□□	261 B. Boucher / M. Handzus	6	2	.75
□□□□	262 Adam Oates, Anah.	6	2	1.00
□□□□	263 Bobby Holik, NYRa.	6	2	.75
□□□□	264 Robert Lang, Wash.	6	2	.75
□□□□	265 Curtis Joseph (G), Detr.	20	10	3.00
□□□□	266 Ed Belfour (G), Toro.	20	10	3.00
□□□□	267 Darius Kasparaitis, NYRa.	6	2	.75
□□□□	268 Bill Guerin, Dall.	6	2	1.00
□□□□	269 P. Sykora / O. Tverdovsky	6	2	.75
□□□□	270 Tony Amonte, Phoe.	10	5	1.50

ROOKIE

	Insert	S100	R200	Base
□□□□	271 P-M Bouchard, MinW. RC	15	5	12.00
□□□□	272 Rick Nash, Colu. RC	55	25	20.00
□□□□	273 D. Seidenberg, Phil. RC	12	8	4.00
□□□□	274 J. Bouwmeester, Flor. RC	15	8	12.00
□□□□	275 S. Chistov, Anah. RC	15	8	12.00
□□□□	276 Kurt Sauer, Anah. RC	12	8	4.00
□□□□	277 Ivan Majesky, Flor. RC	12	8	4.00
□□□□	278 C. Kobasew, Calg. RC	12	8	8.00
□□□□	279 Jeff Taffe, Phoe. RC	12	8	6.00
□□□□	280 M. Tellqvist (G), Toro. RC	12	8	4.00
□□□□	281 Ales Hemsky, Edmo. RC	15	8	12.00
□□□□	282 Patrick Sharp, Phil. RC	12	8	4.00
□□□□	283 Jordan Leopold, Calg. RC	12	8	6.00
□□□□	284 Dmitri Bykov, Detr. RC	12	8	4.00
□□□□	285 Alex Henry, Edmo. RC	12	8	4.00
□□□□	286 H. Zetterberg, Detr. RC	55	25	20.00
□□□□	287 A. Frolov, LosA. RC	15	8	10.00
□□□□	288 Steve Eminger, Wash. RC	12	8	4.00
□□□□	289 C. Colaiacovo, Toro. RC	12	8	6.00
□□□□	290 Tom Koivisto, SLou. RC	12	8	4.00
□□□□	291 Shawn Thornton, Chic. RC	12	8	4.00
□□□□	292 Ron Hainsey, Mont. RC	12	8	6.00
□□□□	293 M. Gerber (G), Anah. RC	12	8	4.00
□□□□	294 Adam Hall (G), Nash. RC	12	8	6.00
□□□□	295 Jason Spezza, Otta. RC	40	20	15.00
□□□□	296 A. Volchenkov, Otta. RC	12	8	4.00
□□□□	297 Jeff Paul, Colo. RC	12	8	4.00
□□□□	298 Scottie Upshall, Nash. RC	12	8	8.00
□□□□	299 A. Svitov, Tamp. RC	12	8	8.00
□□□□	300 A. Smirnov, Anah. RC	12	8	6.00

UPDATE

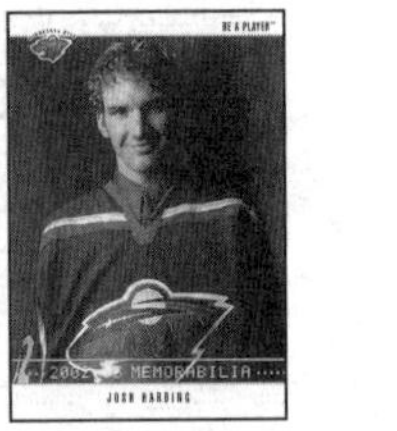

	Insert	Base
□	301 Ed Belfour (G), Toro.	2.00
□	302 Ryan Bayda, Caro. RC	.50
□	303 Jerred Smithson, LosA. RC	.50
□	304 Mike Komisarek, Mont. RC	1.50
□	305 Jarret Stoll, Edmo. RC	1.50
□	306 Radovan Somik, Phil. RC	.50
□	307 Rob Davison, SanJ. RC	.50
□	308 Jason King, Vanc. RC	.50
□	309 Tony Amonte, Phil.	1.00
□	310 Cam Severson, Anah. RC	.50
□	311 Matt Walker, SLou. RC	.50
□	312 Jesse Fibiger, SanJ. RC	.50
□	313 Ray Emery, Otta. RC	1.00
□	314 Vernon Fiddler, Nash. RC	.50
□	315 Alex Kovalev, NYRa.	1.00
□	316 Marc-Andre Bergeron, Edmo. RC	.50
□	317 Jason Elliott (G), Detr. RC	1.00
□	318 Craig Andersson (G), Chic. RC	1.50
□	319 Sandis Ozolinsh, Anah.	.50
□	320 Ryan Miller, Buff. RC	5.00
□	321 Chris Osgood (G), SLou.	1.00
□	322 Michael Garnett (G), Atla. RC	1.00
□	323 Bobby Allen, Edmo. RC	.50
□	324 Cristobal Huet, LosA. RC	1.00
□	325 Curtis Murphy, MinW. RC	.50
□	326 Darren Haydar, Nash. RC	.50
□	327 Mathieu Schneider, Detr.	.50
□	328 Ray Schultz, NYIs. RC	.50
□	329 Jim Vandermeer, Phil. RC	1.00
□	330 Miroslav Zalesak, SanJ. RC	.50
□	331 Christian Backman, SLou. RC	.50
□	332 John Craighead, Vanc. RC	.50
□	333 Doug Gilmour, Toro.	1.00
□	334 Dick Tarnstrom, Pitt.	.50
□	335 Chad Wiseman, SanJ. RC	.50
□	336 John Tripp, NYRa. RC	.50
□	337 Ari Ahonen, NJer. RC	1.50
□	338 Rickard Wallin, MinW. RC	.50
□	339 Jonathan Hedstrom, Anah. RC	.50
□	340 Daniel Briere, Buff.	.50
□	341 Paul Manning, Colu. RC	.50
□	342 Igor Radulov, Chic. RC	4.00
□	343 Tomas Malec, Caro. RC	.50
□	344 Sean McMorrow, Buff. RC	.50
□	345 Dany Sabourin (G), Calg. RC	.50
□	346 Steve Thomas, Anah.	.50
□	347 Shaone Morrisonn, Bost. RC	1.00
□	348 Brad Defauw, Caro. RC	.50
□	349 Michael Leighton, Chic. RC	1.00
□	350 Pascal Leclaire (G), Colu. RC	5.00
□	351 Chris Schmidt, LosA. RC	.50
□	352 Stéphane Veilleux, MinW. RC	.50
□	353 Jim Fahey, SanJ. RC	.50
□	354 Konstantin Koltsov, Pitt. RC	.50
□	355 Cody Rudkowsky (G), SLou. RC	1.00
□	356 Anson Carter, NYRa.	.50
□	357 Francois Beauchemin, Mont. RC	.50
□	358 Patrick Boileau, Detr. RC	.50
□	359 Sylvain Blouin, Mont. RC	.50
□	360 Eric Bertrand, Colo. RC	.50
□	361 Jamie Hodson (G), Toro. RC	.50
□	362 Curtis Sanford (G), SLou. RC	1.00
□	363 Ryan Kraft, SanJ. RC	.50
□	364 Owen Nolan, Toro.	1.00
□	365 Niko Dimitrakos, SanJ. RC	.50
□	366 Simon Gamache, Atla. RC	.50
□	367 Doug Janik, Buff. RC	.50
□	368 Tomas Kurka, Caro. RC	.50
□	369 Josh Harding, MinW. RC	8.00
□	370 Radoslav Hecl, Buff. RC	.50
□	371 Kris Vernarsky, Bost. RC	.50
□	372 Steve Ott, Dall. RC	1.50
□	373 Frédéric Cloutier (G), MinW. RC	.50
□	374 Eric Godard, NYIs. RC	.50
□	375 Kari Haakana, Edmo. RC	.50
□	376 Tomi Pettinen, NYIs. RC	.50
□	377 Brooks Orpik, Pitt. RC	1.50
□	378 Lynn Loyns, SanJ. RC	.50
□	379 Radim Vrbata, Caro.	.50
□	380 Fernando Pisani, Edmo. RC	.50
□	381 Alexei Semenov, Edmo. RC	1.00
□	382 Burke (G) Henry, Chic. RC	.50
□	383 Tim Thomas (G), Bost. RC	1.00
□	384 Mike Siklenka, Phil. RC	.50
□	385 Lasse Pirjetä, Colu. RC	.50
□	386 Tomas Zizka, LosA. RC	.50
□	387 Tomas Surovy, Pitt. RC	1.00
□	388 Paul Gaustad, Buff. RC	.50
□	389 Martin Samuelsson, Bost. RC	.50
□	390 Matt Henderson, Chic. RC	.50
□	391 Mike Dunham (G), NYRa.	.50
□	392 Levente Szuper (G), Calg. RC	1.00
□	393 Jared Aulin, LosA. RC	1.50
□	394 Brandon Reid, Vanc. RC	4.00
□	395 Mike Cammalleri, LosA. RC	4.00
□	396 Ian MacNeil, Phil. RC	.50
□	397 Brad Isbister, Edmo.	.50
□	398 Garnet Exelby, Atla. RC	.50
□	399 Jason Bacashihua, Dall. RC	1.00
□	400 Sami Kapanen, Phil.	.50

HE SHOOTS HE SCORES

Each redemption card was worth one, two, or three points. Collectors could trade 400 points for a special random jersey card.

Insert Set (20 cards):		-
	Insert	HSHS
□	Ron Francis, Caro. [1 Point]	
□	Dany Heatley, Atla. [1 Point]	
□	Mike Modano, Dall. [1 Point]	
□	Owen Nolan, SanJ. [1 Point]	
□	Chris Pronger, SLou. [1 Point]	
□	Jeremy Roenick, Phil. [1 Point]	
□	Brendan Shanahan, Detr. [1 Point]	
□	José Théodore (G), Mont. [1 Point]	
□	Martin Brodeur (G), NJer. [2 Point]	
□	Pavel Bure, NYRa. [2 Point]	
□	Peter Forsberg, Colo. [2 Point]	
□	Dominik Hasek, Detr. [2 Point]	
□	Jaromir Jagr, Wash. [2 Point]	
□	Paul Kariya, Anah. [2 Point]	
□	Ilya Kovalchuk, Atla. [2 Point]	
□	Eric Lindros, NYRa. [2 Point]	
□	Joe Sakic, Colo. [2 Point]	
□	Mario Lemieux, Pitt. [3 Point]	
□	Patrick Roy (G), Colo. [3 Point]	
□	Steve Yzerman, Detr. [3 Point]	

ALL-STAR JERSEY

Insert Set (60 cards):		1,800
	Insert (*90)	ASJ90
□	ASJ-1 Daniel Alfredsson, AS'98 ✂	50.00
□	ASJ-2 Tony Amonte, AS'00 ✂	25.00
□	ASJ-3 Ed Belfour (G), AS'98 ✂	50.00
□	ASJ-4 Rob Blake, AS'94 ✂	25.00
□	ASJ-5 Peter Bondra, AS'99 ✂	25.00
□	ASJ-6 Martin Brodeur (G), AS'97 ✂	75.00
□	ASJ-7 Pavel Bure, AS'98 ✂	25.00
□	ASJ-8 Chris Chelios, AS'96 ✂	25.00
□	ASJ-9 Éric Dazé, AS'02 ✂	25.00
□	ASJ-10 Pavol Demitra, AS'00 ✂	25.00
□	ASJ-11 Patrik Elias, AS'02 ✂	25.00
□	ASJ-12 Sergei Fedorov, AS'02 ✂	50.00
□	ASJ-13 Theoren Fleury, AS'99 ✂	25.00
□	ASJ-14 Peter Forsberg, AS'01 ✂	50.00
□	ASJ-15 Simon Gagné, AS'01 ✂	25.00
□	ASJ-16 Bill Guerin, AS'01 ✂	25.00
□	ASJ-17 Dominik Hasek, AS'01 ✂	50.00
□	ASJ-18 Milan Hejduk, AS'01 ✂	25.00
□	ASJ-19 Brett Hull, AS'96 ✂	50.00
□	ASJ-20 Jarome Iginla, AS'02 ✂	25.00
□	ASJ-21 Arturs Irbe (G), AS'99 ✂	25.00
□	ASJ-22 Jaromir Jagr, AS'98 ✂	50.00
□	ASJ-23 Curtis Joseph (G), AS'00 ✂	50.00
□	ASJ-24 Ed Jovanovski, AS'02 ✂	25.00
□	ASJ-25 Paul Kariya, AS'01 ✂	50.00
□	ASJ-26 Nikolai Khabibulin (G), AS'98 ✂	25.00
□	ASJ-27 Saku Koivu, AS'98 ✂	50.00
□	ASJ-28 Alexei Kovalev, AS'01 ✂	25.00
□	ASJ-29 John LeClair, AS'97 ✂	25.00
□	ASJ-30 Brian Leetch, AS'94 ✂	25.00
□	ASJ-31 Mario Lemieux, AS'02 ✂	150.00
□	ASJ-32 Nicklas Lidström, AS'99 ✂	25.00
□	ASJ-33 Eric Lindros, AS'00 ✂	50.00
□	ASJ-34 Al MacInnis, AS'00 ✂	25.00
□	ASJ-35 Mark Messier, AS'98 ✂	50.00
□	ASJ-36 Mike Modano, AS'98 ✂	50.00
□	ASJ-37 Alexander Mogilny, AS'96 ✂	25.00
□	ASJ-38 Evgeni Nabokov (G), AS'01 ✂	25.00
□	ASJ-39 Markus Näslund, AS'01 ✂	50.00
□	ASJ-40 Scott Niedermayer, AS'98 ✂	25.00
□	ASJ-41 Owen Nolan, AS'02 ✂	25.00
□	ASJ-43 Sandis Ozolinsh, AS'01 ✂	25.00
□	ASJ-44 Zigmund Palffy, AS'01 ✂	25.00
□	ASJ-42 Félix Potvin (G), AS'96 ✂	50.00
□	ASJ-45 Chris Pronger, AS'00 ✂	25.00
□	ASJ-46 Mark Recchi, AS'00 ✂	25.00
□	ASJ-47 Mike Richter (G), AS'00 ✂	25.00
□	ASJ-48 Luc Robitaille, AS'99 ✂	25.00
□	ASJ-49 Jeremy Roenick, AS'94 ✂	25.00
□	ASJ-50 Patrick Roy (G), AS'01 ✂	100.00
□	ASJ-51 Joe Sakic, AS'98 ✂	75.00
□	ASJ-52 Teemu Selänne, AS'02 ✂	25.00
□	ASJ-53 Brendan Shanahan, AS'96 ✂	50.00
□	ASJ-54 Mats Sundin, AS'97 ✂	50.00
□	ASJ-55 José Théodore (G), AS'02 ✂	50.00
□	ASJ-56 Joe Thornton, AS'02 ✂	50.00
□	ASJ-57 Keith Tkachuk, AS'99 ✂	25.00
□	ASJ-58 Doug Weight, AS'01 ✂	25.00
□	ASJ-59 Alexei Yashin, AS'99 ✂	25.00
□	ASJ-60 Steve Yzerman, AS'00 ✂	100.00

ALL-STAR JERSEY EMBLEM & ALL-STAR IN THE NUMBERS

Both the All-Star Jersey Emblem (prefix ASE-) and All-Star In The Numbers (prefix ASN-) are limited to 10 copies per card. Realised pricing on scarce cards may vary considerably from below pricing.

Insert Set (25 cards):		6,800
	Insert (*10)	E/N10
□□	Martin Brodeur (G), AS'97 ✂	400.00
□□	Pavel Bure, AS'98 ✂	200.00
□□	Sergei Fedorov, AS'02 ✂	300.00
□□	Peter Forsberg, AS'01 ✂	400.00
□□	Dominik Hasek, AS'01 ✂	300.00
□□	Brett Hull, AS'96 ✂	300.00
□□	Jarome Iginla, AS'02 ✂	200.00
□□	Jaromir Jagr, AS'98 ✂	300.00
□□	Curtis Joseph (G), AS'00 ✂	300.00
□□	Paul Kariya, AS'01 ✂	400.00
□□	Brian Leetch, AS'94 ✂	200.00
□□	Mario Lemieux, AS'02 ✂	900.00
□□	Nicklas Lidström, AS'99 ✂	200.00
□□	Eric Lindros, AS'00 ✂	300.00

☐☐	Mark Messier, AS'98 ✂	300.00
☐☐	Mike Modano, AS'98 ✂	300.00
☐☐	Owen Nolan, AS'02 ✂	200.00
☐☐	Luc Robitaille, AS'99 ✂	200.00
☐☐	Patrick Roy (G), AS'01 ✂	700.00
☐☐	Joe Sakic, AS'98 ✂	400.00
☐☐	Teemu Selänne, AS'02 ✂	200.00
☐☐	Brendan Shanahan, AS'96 ✂	300.00
☐☐	Mats Sundin, AS'97 ✂	300.00
☐☐	José Théodore (G), AS'02 ✂	300.00
☐☐	Steve Yzerman, AS'00 ✂	700.00

ALL-STAR JERSEY TRIPLE

Insert Set (20 cards):		1,600
	Insert (*50)	AST50
☐	Rob Blake, AS'94 ✂ AS'01 ✂ AS'02 ✂	50.00
☐	Martin Brodeur (G), AS'97 ✂ AS'00 ✂ AS'01 ✂	150.00
☐	Pavel Bure, AS'98 ✂ AS'00 ✂ AS'01 ✂	75.00
☐	Peter Forsberg, AS'98 ✂ AS'99 ✂ AS'01 ✂	125.00
☐	Dominik Hasek, AS'98 ✂ AS'99 ✂ AS'01 ✂	100.00
☐	Jaromir Jagr, AS'98 ✂ AS'00 ✂ AS'02 ✂	100.00
☐	Paul Kariya, AS'96 ✂ AS'97 ✂ AS'01 ✂	125.00
☐	John LeClair, AS'96 ✂ AS'97 ✂ AS'98 ✂	75.00
☐	Brian Leetch, AS'94 ✂ AS'98 ✂ AS'01 ✂	50.00
☐	Mario Lemieux, AS'96 ✂ AS'01 ✂ AS'02 ✂	300.00
☐	Nicklas Lidström, AS'99 ✂ AS'01 ✂ AS'02 ✂	50.00
☐	Eric Lindros, AS'98 ✂ AS'99 ✂ AS'00 ✂	100.00
☐	Al MacInnis, AS'94 ✂ AS'99 ✂ AS'00 ✂	50.00
☐	Mark Messier, AS'94 ✂ AS'96 ✂ AS'00 ✂	100.00
☐	Mike Modano, AS'98 ✂ AS'99 ✂ AS'00 ✂	100.00
☐	Owen Nolan, AS'97 ✂ AS'00 ✂ AS'02 ✂	50.00
☐	Patrick Roy (G), AS'94 ✂ AS'01 ✂ AS'02 ✂	225.00
☐	Teemu Selänne, AS'94 ✂ AS'99 ✂ AS'02 ✂	75.00
☐	Brendan Shanahan, AS'96 ✂ AS'99 ✂ AS'02 ✂	100.00
☐	Mats Sundin, AS'97 ✂ AS'99 ✂ AS'00 ✂	100.00

ALL-STAR STARTING LINEUP

Insert Set (12 cards):		600
	Insert (*40)	ASSL40
☐	Rob Blake, AS'02 ✂	50.00
☐	Vincent Damphousse, AS'02 ✂	50.00
☐	Sergei Fedorov, AS'02 ✂	75.00
☐	Dominik Hasek, AS'02 ✂	75.00
☐	Jaromir Jagr, AS'02 ✂	75.00
☐	Nicklas Lidström, AS'02 ✂	50.00
☐	Owen Nolan, AS'02 ✂	50.00
☐	Sandis Ozolinsh, AS'02 ✂	50.00
☐	Chris Pronger, AS'02 ✂	50.00
☐	Patrick Roy (G), AS'02 ✂	175.00
☐	Teemu Selänne, AS'02 ✂	50.00
☐	Brendan Shanahan, AS'02 ✂	75.00

ALL-STAR TEAMMATES

Insert Set (30 cards):		1,500
	Insert (*75)	AST75
☐	1 S. Fedorov AS'94 ✂ / T. Selänne AS'94 ✂	50.00
☐	2 Cu. Joseph (G) AS'94 ✂ / J. Roenick AS'94 ✂	50.00
☐	3 M. Messier AS'94 ✂ / P. Roy (G) AS'94 ✂	100.00
☐	4 M. Messier AS'96 ✂ / M. Lemieux AS'96 ✂	125.00
☐	5 J. Jagr AS'96 ✂ / B. Shanahan AS'96 ✂	50.00
☐	6 P. Kariya AS'96 ✂ / A. Mogilny AS'96 ✂	50.00
☐	7 O. Nolan AS'97 ✂ / S. Yzerman AS'97 ✂	75.00
☐	8 S. Yzerman AS'97 ✂ / M. Sundin AS'97 ✂	50.00
☐	9 Brodeur (G) AS'97 ✂ / Hasek (G) AS'97 ✂	75.00
☐	10 P. Bure AS'98 ✂ / P. Forsberg AS'98 ✂	50.00
☐	11 D. Hasek (G) AS'98 ✂ / J. Jagr AS'98 ✂	50.00
☐	12 E. Lindros AS'98 ✂ / M. Modano AS'98 ✂	50.00
☐	13 E. Lindros AS'99 ✂ / K. Tkachuk AS'99 ✂	50.00
☐	15 P. Forsberg AS'99 ✂ / D. Hasek (G) AS'99 ✂	75.00
☐	15 T. Selänne AS'99 ✂ / A. Yashin AS'99 ✂	35.00
☐	16 J. Jagr AS'00 ✂ / M. Sundin AS'00 ✂	50.00
☐	17 J. Roenick AS'00 ✂ / S. Yzerman AS'00 ✂	100.00
☐	18 Brodeur (G) AS'00 ✂ / Joseph (G) AS'00 ✂	75.00
☐	19 T. Amonte AS'00 ✂ / C. Pronger AS'00 ✂	35.00
☐	20 E. Lindros AS'00 ✂ / M. Messier AS'00 ✂	50.00
☐	21 B. Guerin AS'01 ✂ / J. Sakic AS'01 ✂	50.00
☐	22 M. Lemieux AS'01 ✂ / P. Roy (G) AS'01 ✂	150.00
☐	23 Hasek (G) AS'01 ✂ / Nabokov (G) AS'01 ✂	50.00
☐	24 P. Bure AS'01 ✂ / P. Forsberg AS'01 ✂	50.00
☐	25 M. Brodeur (G) AS'01 ✂ / P. Kariya AS'01 ✂	75.00
☐	26 Roy (G) AS'02 ✂ / Théodore (G) AS'02 ✂	100.00
☐	27 O. Nolan AS'02 ✂ / B. Shanahan AS'02 ✂	50.00
☐	28 J. Iginla AS'02 ✂ / M. Lemieux AS'02 ✂	100.00
☐	29 J. Jagr AS'02 ✂ / N. Lidström AS'02 ✂	50.00
☐	30 S. Fedorov AS'02 ✂ / T. Selänne AS'02 ✂	50.00

DRAFT REDEMPTION

These cards could be redeemed only after the player made his NHL debut. Five of these cards were redeemable during the 2002-03 season (see 2002 - 03 Be A Player Draft Toronto 2002).

Insert Set (30 cards):		
	Insert (*100)	Draft
☐	1 Expired (see 2002 - 03 Be A Player Draft Toronto 2002)	
☐	2 Draft redemption	
☐	3 Expired (see 2002 - 03 Be A Player Draft Toronto 2002)	
☐	4 Draft redemption	
☐	5 Draft redemption	
☐	6 Expired (see 2002 - 03 Be A Player Draft Toronto 2002)	
☐	7 Draft redemption	
☐	8 Expired (see 2002 - 03 Be A Player Draft Toronto 2002)	
☐	9 Draft redemption	
☐	10 Draft redemption	
☐	11 Draft redemption	
☐	12 Expired (see 2002 - 03 Be A Player Draft Toronto 2002)	
☐	13 Draft redemption	
☐	14 Draft redemption	
☐	15 Draft redemption	
☐	16 Draft redemption	
☐	17 Draft redemption	
☐	18 Draft redemption	
☐	19 Draft redemption	
☐	20 Draft redemption	
☐	21 Draft redemption	
☐	22 Draft redemption	
☐	23 Draft redemption	
☐	24 Draft redemption	
☐	25 Draft redemption	
☐	26 Draft redemption	
☐	27 Draft redemption	
☐	28 Draft redemption	
☐	29 Draft redemption	
☐	30 Draft redemption	

FRANCHISE

Insert Set (30 cards):		1,700
	Insert (*40)	FP40
☐	Daniel Brière, Phoe. ✂	40.00
☐	Martin Brodeur (G), NJer. ✂	100.00
☐	Pavel Bure, NYRa. ✂	50.00
☐	Mike Comrie, Edmo. ✂	50.00
☐	Éric Dazé, Chic. ✂	40.00
☐	Ron Francis, Caro. ✂	40.00
☐	Marian Gaborik, MinW. ✂	75.00
☐	Simon Gagné, Phil. ✂	50.00
☐	Scott Hartnell, Nash. ✂	40.00
☐	Marian Hossa, Otta. ✂	75.00
☐	Jarome Iginla, Calg. ✂	50.00
☐	Jaromir Jagr, Wash. ✂	75.00
☐	Paul Kariya, Anah. ✂	100.00
☐	Nikolai Khabibulin (G), Tamp. ✂	40.00
☐	Rostislav Klesla, Colu. ✂	40.00
☐	Ilya Kovalchuk, Atla. ✂	75.00
☐	Mario Lemieux, Pitt. ✂	225.00
☐	Roberto Luongo (G), Flor. ✂	50.00
☐	Mike Modano, Dall. ✂	75.00
☐	Markus Näslund, Vanc. ✂	75.00
☐	Owen Nolan, SanJ. ✂	40.00
☐	Zigmund Palffy, LosA. ✂	40.00
☐	Chris Pronger, SLou. ✂	40.00
☐	Patrick Roy (G), Colo. ✂	175.00
☐	Miroslav Satan, Buff. ✂	40.00
☐	Mats Sundin, Toro. ✂	75.00
☐	José Théodore (G), Mont. ✂	75.00
☐	Joe Thornton, Bost. ✂	75.00
☐	Alexei Yashin, NYIs. ✂	40.00
☐	Steve Yzerman, Detr. ✂	175.00

FUTURE OF THE GAME

Insert Set (20 cards):		900
	Insert (*30)	FG20
☐	Dan Blackburn (G), NYRa. ✂	50.00
☐	Kyle Calder, Chic. ✂	50.00
☐	Mike Comrie, Edmo. ✂	50.00
☐	Pavel Datsyuk, Detr. ✂	50.00
☐	Rick DiPietro (G), NYIs. ✂	50.00
☐	Marian Gaborik, MinW. ✂	75.00
☐	Simon Gagné, Phil. ✂	50.00
☐	Scott Hartnell, Nash. ✂	50.00
☐	Martin Havlat, Otta. ✂	50.00
☐	Dany Heatley, Atla. ✂	75.00
☐	Trent Hunter, NYIs. ✂	50.00
☐	Kristian Huselius, Flor. ✂	50.00
☐	Rostislav Klesla, Colu. ✂	50.00
☐	Ilya Kovalchuk, Atla. ✂	75.00
☐	Roberto Luongo (G), Flor. ✂	50.00
☐	Brad Richards, Tamp. ✂	50.00
☐	Alex Tanguay, Colo. ✂	50.00
☐	José Théodore (G), Mont. ✂	100.00
☐	Joe Thornton, Bost. ✂	100.00
☐	Justin Williams, Phil. ✂	50.00

HE SHOOTS HE SCORES JERSEY

Redemption Set (30 cards):		-
	Redemption (*20)	J20
☐	Todd Bertuzzi, Vanc. ✂	
☐	Martin Brodeur (G), NJer. ✂	
☐	Pavel Bure, NYRa. ✂	
☐	Pavel Datsyuk, Detr. ✂	
☐	Sergei Fedorov, Detr. ✂	
☐	Peter Forsberg, Colo. ✂	
☐	Ron Francis, Caro. ✂	
☐	Marian Gaborik, MinW. ✂	
☐	Dominik Hasek, Detr. ✂	
☐	Dany Heatley, Atla. ✂	
☐	Jarome Iginla, Calg. ✂	
☐	Jaromir Jagr, Wash. ✂	
☐	Paul Kariya, Anah. ✂	
☐	Ilya Kovalchuk, Atla. ✂	
☐	Mario Lemieux, Pitt. ✂	
☐	Nicklas Lidström, Detr. ✂	
☐	Eric Lindros, NYRa. ✂	
☐	Roberto Luongo (G), Flor. ✂	
☐	Mark Messier, NYRa. ✂	
☐	Mike Modano, Dall. ✂	
☐	Owen Nolan, SanJ. ✂	
☐	Chris Pronger, SLou. ✂	
☐	Jeremy Roenick, Phil. ✂	
☐	Patrick Roy (G), Colo. ✂	
☐	Joe Sakic, Colo. ✂	
☐	Teemu Selänne, SanJ. ✂	
☐	Brendan Shanahan, Detr. ✂	
☐	Mats Sundin, Toro. ✂	
☐	José Théodore (G), Mont. ✂	
☐	Steve Yzerman, Detr. ✂	

MAGNIFICENT

Insert Set (10 cards):		5,000
	Insert	Mario
☐	MI-1 Mario Lemieux ✂ {#/40}	225.00
☐	MI-2 Mario Lemieux ✂ {#/40}	225.00
☐	MI-3 Mario Lemieux ✂ {#/40}	225.00
☐	MI-4 Mario Lemieux ✂ {#/40}	225.00
☐	MI-5 Mario Lemieux ✂✂ {#/40}	250.00
☐	MI-6 Mario Lemieux ✂ {#/10}	900.00
☐	MI-7 Mario Lemieux ✂ {#/10}	900.00
☐	MI-8 Mario Lemieux ✂ ✂ ✂ {#/10}	
☐	MI-9 Mario Lemieux ✂ ✂ ✂ ✂ {#/10}	
☐	MI-10 Mario Lemieux ✂ ✂ ✂ ✂ {#/10}	

MAGNIFICENT AUTOGRAPH

Insert Set (10 cards):		11,000
	Autograph	Mario
☐	MI-1 Mario Lemieux ✂ ✍ {#/15}	1000.00
☐	MI-2 Mario Lemieux ✂ ✍ {#/15}	1000.00
☐	MI-3 Mario Lemieux ✂ ✍ {#/15}	1000.00
☐	MI-4 Mario Lemieux ✂ ✍ {#/15}	1000.00
☐	MI-5 Mario Lemieux ✂✂ ✍ {#/15}	1200.00
☐	MI-6 Mario Lemieux ✂ ✍ {#/5}	1500.00
☐	MI-7 Mario Lemieux ✂ ✍ {#/5}	1500.00
☐	MI-8 Mario Lemieux ✂ ✂✂ ✍ {#/5}	
☐	MI-9 Mario Lemieux ✂ ✂✂ ✍ {#/5}	
☐	MI-10 Mario Lemieux ✂ ✂ ✂✂ ✍ {#/5}	

STANLEY CUP CHAMPIONS

Insert Set (15 cards):		1,100
	Insert (*40)	SCC40
☐	Chris Chelios, Detr. ✂	75.00
☐	Mathieu Dandenault, Detr. ✂	40.00
☐	Pavel Datsyuk, Detr. ✂	100.00
☐	Sergei Fedorov, Detr. ✂	125.00
☐	Jiri Fischer, Detr. ✂	40.00
☐	Dominik Hasek, Detr. ✂	125.00
☐	Tomas Holmström, Detr. ✂	40.00
☐	Brett Hull, Detr. ✂ Glove	125.00
☐	Manny Legacé (G), Detr. ✂	40.00
☐	Nicklas Lidström, Detr. ✂	75.00
☐	Darren McCarty, Detr. ✂	40.00
☐	Luc Robitaille, Detr. ✂	100.00
☐	Brendan Shanahan, Detr. ✂	125.00
☐	Jason Williams, Detr. ✂	40.00
☐	Steve Yzerman, Detr. ✂	300.00

STANLEY CUP PLAYOFFS

Cards 1-16 (first round) are limited to 90 copies; cards 17-24 (second round) are limited to 60 copies; cards 25-28 (third round) are limited to 40 copies; cards 29-30 (final) are limited to 30 copies; and cards 31-32 (winners) are limited to 10 copies.

Insert Set (32 cards):		1,900
	Insert	SCP
☐	SC-1 Roman Cechmanek (G), Phil. ✂	25.00
☐	SC-2 Patrick Lalime (G), Otta. ✂	25.00
☐	SC-3 Gary Roberts, Toro. ✂	25.00
☐	SC-4 Alexei Yashin, NYIs. ✂	25.00
☐	SC-5 Joe Thornton, Bost. ✂	50.00
☐	SC-6 José Théodore (G), Mont. ✂	50.00
☐	SC-7 Ron Francis, Caro. ✂	25.00
☐	SC-8 Martin Brodeur (G), NJer. ✂	50.00
☐	SC-9 Owen Nolan, SanJ. ✂	25.00
☐	SC-10 Sean Burke (G), Phoe. ✂	25.00
☐	SC-11 Félix Potvin (G), LosA. ✂	50.00
☐	SC-12 Peter Forsberg, Colo. ✂	50.00
☐	SC-13 Todd Bertuzzi, Vanc. ✂	50.00
☐	SC-14 Steve Yzerman, Detr. ✂	100.00
☐	SC-15 Éric Dazé, Chic. ✂	25.00
☐	SC-16 Brent Johnson (G), SLou. ✂	25.00
☐	SC-17 Teemu Selänne, SanJ. ✂	50.00
☐	SC-18 Chris Drury, Colo. ✂	35.00
☐	SC-19 Alexander Mogilny, Toro. ✂	35.00
☐	SC-20 Daniel Alfredsson, Otta. ✂	75.00
☐	SC-21 Sergei Fedorov, Detr. ✂	50.00
☐	SC-22 Keith Tkachuk, SLou. ✂	35.00
☐	SC-23 Saku Koivu, Mont. ✂	75.00
☐	SC-24 Jeff O'Neill, Caro. ✂	35.00
☐	SC-25 Curtis Joseph (G), Toro. ✂	75.00
☐	SC-26 Arturs Irbe (G), Caro. ✂	50.00
☐	SC-27 Dominik Hasek, Detr. ✂	75.00
☐	SC-28 Patrick Roy (G), Colo. ✂	175.00
☐	SC-29 Ron Francis, Caro. ✂	100.00
☐	SC-30 Dominik Hasek, Detr. ✂	75.00
☐	SC-31 Steve Yzerman, Detr. ✂	700.00
☐	SC-32 Nicklas Lidström, Detr. ✂	175.00

TEAMMATES

Insert Set (20 cards):		800
	Insert (*70)	TM70
☐	1 D. Hasek (G) AS'01 ✂ / S. Yzerman AS'00 ✂	100.00
☐	2 S. Fedorov AS'02 ✂ /B. Shanahan AS'02 ✂	50.00
☐	3 Br. Hull AS'96 ✂ / Robitaille AS'99 ✂	50.00
☐	4 P. Forsberg AS'01 ✂ / J. Sakic AS'01 ✂	75.00
☐	5 R. Blake AS'02 ✂ / P. Roy (G) AS'02 ✂	75.00
☐	6 E. Lindros AS'00 ✂ / P. Bure AS'00 ✂	50.00
☐	7 B. Leetch AS'01 ✂ / M. Messier AS'00 ✂	50.00
☐	8 Cu. Joseph (G) AS'00 ✂ / M. Sundin AS'00 ✂	50.00
☐	9 Cechmanek (G) AS'01 ✂ / Roenick AS'00 ✂	35.00
☐	10 S. Gagné AS'01 ✂ / M. Recchi AS'00 ✂	35.00
☐	11 P. Bondra AS'99 ✂ / J. Jagr AS'02 ✂	50.00
☐	12 S. Koivu AS'98 ✂ / J. Théodore (G) AS'02 ✂	75.00
☐	13 Z. Palffy AS'01 ✂ / F. Potvin (G) AS'96 ✂	35.00
☐	14 M. Brodeur (G) AS'01 ✂ / P. Elias AS'02 ✂	75.00
☐	15 A. Kovalev AS'01 ✂ / M. Lemieux AS'02 ✂	100.00
☐	16 A. MacInnis AS'00 ✂ / C. Pronger AS'00 ✂	35.00
☐	17 K. Tkachuk AS'99 ✂ / D. Weight AS'01 ✂	35.00
☐	18 O. Nolan AS'02 ✂ / T. Selänne AS'02 ✂	35.00
☐	19 E. Jovanovski AS'02 ✂ / M. Näslund AS'01 ✂	35.00
☐	20 R. Turek (G) AS'00 ✂ / J. Iginla AS'02 ✂	35.00

STANLEY CUP

Complete Set (40 Stanley Cups):		900.00
	Stanley Cup	Cup
☐	Johnny Bower (G), Toro.	20.00
☐	Tim Horton, Toro.	30.00
☐	Jean Béliveau, Mont.	55.00
☐	Gump Worlsey (G), Mont.	20.00
☐	Terry Sawchuk (G), Toro.	50.00
☐	Serge Savard, Mont.	20.00
☐	Henri Richard, Mont.	25.00
☐	Phil Esposito, Bost.	30.00
☐	Frank Mahovlich, Mont.	25.00
☐	Gerry Cheevers (G), Bost.	20.00
☐	Yvan Cournoyer, Mont.	20.00
☐	Bobby Clarke, Phil.	20.00
☐	Bernie Parent (G), Phil.	20.00
☐	Steve Shutt, Mont.	20.00
☐	Larry Robinson, Mont.	20.00
☐	Guy Lafleur, Mont.	50.00
☐	Guy Lapointe, Mont.	20.00
☐	Bryan Trottier, NYIs.	25.00
☐	Mike Bossy, NYIs.	40.00
☐	Denis Potvin, NYIs.	20.00
☐	Bob Nystrom, NYIs.	20.00
☐	Mark Messier, Edmo.	25.00
☐	Andy Moog, Edmo.	20.00
☐	Patrick Roy (G), Mont.	75.00

☐	Jari Kurri, Edmo.	25.00
☐	Grant Fuhr (G), Edmo.	20.00
☐	Doug Gilmour, Calg.	20.00
☐	Adam Graves, Edmo.	20.00
☐	Mario Lemieux, Pitt.	75.00
☐	Jaromir Jagr, Pitt.	25.00
☐	John LeClair, Mont.	20.00
☐	Brian Leetch, NYRa.	20.00
☐	Martin Brodeur (G), NJer.	40.00
☐	Peter Forsberg, Colo.	35.00
☐	Steve Yzerman, Detr.	60.00
☐	Nicklas Lidström, Detr.	20.00
☐	Mike Modano, Dall.	25.00
☐	Scott Stevens, NJer.	20.00
☐	Joe Sakic, Colo.	40.00
☐	Dominik Hasek, Detr.	25.00

2002 - 03 BETWEEN THE PIPES

Produced by the In The Game, this series was released in February 2003. There are three versions for each card 1-150: the regular card, the silver parallel (#/100), and the gold parallel (#/10). Please see the appendix for pricing on scarce cards.

Complete Set (150 cards): 600.00 110.00
Common Player: 4.00 .50

	Description	S100	Base
☐☐☐	1 Patrick Roy (G), Colo.	45.00	6.50
☐☐☐	2 José Théodore (G), Mont.	15.00	2.50
☐☐☐	3 Olaf Kölzig (G), Wash.	5.00	1.00
☐☐☐	4 Roberto Luongo (G), Flor.	10.00	1.50
☐☐☐	5 Tommy Salo (G), Edmo.	5.00	.50
☐☐☐	6 Dan Blackburn (G), NYRa.	5.00	.50
☐☐☐	7 Patrick Lalime (G), Otta.	5.00	1.00
☐☐☐	8 Martin Brodeur (G), NJer.	20.00	3.50
☐☐☐	9 Evgeni Nabokov (G), SanJ.	5.00	1.00
☐☐☐	10 Jani Hurme (G), Flor.	4.00	.50
☐☐☐	11 Dan Cloutier (G), Vanc.	5.00	.50
☐☐☐	12 Mike Dunham (G), NYRa.	5.00	.50
☐☐☐	13 Miikka Kiprusoff (G), SanJ.	4.00	.50
☐☐☐	14 Rick DiPietro (G), NYIs.	5.00	1.00
☐☐☐	15 Martin Biron (G), Buff.	5.00	1.00
☐☐☐	16 Steve Passmore (G), Chic.	4.00	.50
☐☐☐	17 Curtis Joseph (G), Detr.	15.00	2.00
☐☐☐	18 Manny Fernandez (G), MinW.	5.00	.50
☐☐☐	19 Kevin Weekes (G), Caro.	4.00	.50
☐☐☐	20 Stéphane Fiset (G), Mont.	4.00	.50
☐☐☐	21 Jocelyn Thibault (G), Chic.	5.00	.50
☐☐☐	22 David Aebischer (G), Colo.	4.00	.50
☐☐☐	23 Marty Turco (G), Dall.	5.00	1.00
☐☐☐	24 Jamie Storr (G), LosA.	4.00	.50
☐☐☐	25 Marc Denis (G), Colu.	5.00	1.00
☐☐☐	26 Arturs Irbe (G), Caro.	5.00	.50
☐☐☐	27 Félix Potvin (G), LosA.	5.00	1.00
☐☐☐	28 Manny Legacé (G), Detr.	4.00	.50
☐☐☐	29 Mike Richter (G), NYRa.	5.00	1.00
☐☐☐	30 Jean-Sébastien Aubin (G), Pitt.	4.00	.50
☐☐☐	31 Sean Burke (G), Phoe.	5.00	1.00
☐☐☐	32 Milan Hnilicka (G), Atla.	4.00	.50
☐☐☐	33 Ed Belfour (G), Toro.	15.00	2.00
☐☐☐	34 Roman Turek (G), Calg.	5.00	1.00
☐☐☐	35 Frédéric Cassivi (G), Atla.	4.00	.50
☐☐☐	36 Tomas Vokoun (G), Nash.	4.00	.50
☐☐☐	37 Travis Scott (G), LosA.	4.00	.50
☐☐☐	38 Dwayne Roloson (G), MinW.	4.00	.50
☐☐☐	39 Roman Cechmanek (G), Phil.	5.00	.50
☐☐☐	40 Johan Hedberg (G), Pitt.	5.00	.50
☐☐☐	41 Neil Little (G), Phil.	4.00	.50
☐☐☐	42 Jeff Hackett (G), Mont.	4.00	.50
☐☐☐	43 John Grahame (G), Bost.	4.00	.50
☐☐☐	44 Norm Maracle (G), Atla.	4.00	.50
☐☐☐	45 Ty Conklin (G), Edmo.	4.00	.50
☐☐☐	46 Trevor Kidd (G), Toro.	4.00	.50
☐☐☐	47 Nikolai Khabibulin (G), Tamp.	5.00	.50
☐☐☐	48 Dieter Kochan (G), MinW.	4.00	.50
☐☐☐	49 Robert Esche (G), Phil.	4.00	.50
☐☐☐	50 Chris Osgood (G), NYIs.	5.00	1.00
☐☐☐	51 Jean-Sébastien Giguère (G), Anah.	15.00	2.00
☐☐☐	52 Steve Shields (G), Bost.	4.00	.50
☐☐☐	53 Wade Flaherty (G), Flor.	4.00	.50
☐☐☐	54 Peter Skudra (G), Anah.	4.00	.50
☐☐☐	55 Brent Johnson (G), SLou.	5.00	.50
☐☐☐	56 Brian Boucher, Phoe.	4.00	.50
☐☐☐	57 Garth Snow (G), NYIs.	4.00	.50
☐☐☐	58 Fred Brathwaite (G), SLou.	4.00	.50
☐☐☐	59 Ron Tugnutt (G), Dall.	5.00	.50
☐☐☐	60 Craig Billington (G), Wash.	4.00	.50
☐☐☐	61 Martin Brochu (G), Vanc.	4.00	.50
☐☐☐	62 Corey Schwab, NJer.	4.00	.50
☐☐☐	**63 Tim Thomas (G), Bost. RC**	**4.00**	**1.50**
☐☐☐	64 J-F Labbé (G), Colu.	4.00	.50
☐☐☐	65 Damian Rhodes (G), Atla.	4.00	.50
☐☐☐	66 Kevin Hodson (G), Tamp.	4.00	.50
☐☐☐	67 Jamie McLennan (G), Calg.	4.00	.50
☐☐☐	68 Tyler Moss, Anah.	4.00	.50
☐☐☐	69 Tom Barrasso (G), SLou.	5.00	.50
☐☐☐	70 Corey Hirsch (G), Dall.	4.00	.50
☐☐☐	71 Éric Fichaud (G), Mont.	4.00	.50
☐☐☐	72 Byron Dafoe (G), Atla.	5.00	.50
☐☐☐	73 Mika Noronen (G), Buff.	5.00	.50
☐☐☐	74 Alex Auld (G), Vanc.	4.00	.50
☐☐☐	**75 Curtis Sanford (G), SLou. RC**	**4.00**	**4.00**
☐☐☐	**76 Martin Gerber (G), Anah. RC**	**4.00**	**4.00**
☐☐☐	**77 Mikael Tellqvist (G), Toro. RC**	**4.00**	**4.00**
☐☐☐	78 J-M Pelletier (G), Caro.	4.00	.50
☐☐☐	79 J-F Damphousse (G), Anah.	4.00	.50
☐☐☐	80 Johan Holmqvist (G), NYRa.	4.00	.50
☐☐☐	81 Mathieu Garon (G), Mont.	5.00	.50
☐☐☐	82 Martin Prusek (G), Otta.	4.00	.50
☐☐☐	83 Ilja Bryzgalov (G), Anah.	4.00	.50
☐☐☐	84 Andrew Raycroft (G), Bost.	4.00	.50
☐☐☐	85 Derek Gustafson (G), MinW.	4.00	.50
☐☐☐	86 Jason LaBarbera (G), NYRa.	4.00	.50
☐☐☐	87 Marc Lamothe (G), Detr.	4.00	.50
☐☐☐	88 Scott Clemmensen (G), NJer.	4.00	.50
☐☐☐	**89 Cody Rudkowsky (G), SLou. RC**	**4.00**	**4.00**
☐☐☐	**90 Craig Andersson (G), Chic. RC**	**4.00**	**6.00**
☐☐☐	91 Maxime Ouellet (G), Wash.	5.00	.50
☐☐☐	92 Jan Lasak (G), Nash.	4.00	.50
☐☐☐	93 Patrick DesRochers (G), Phoe.	4.00	.50
☐☐☐	94 Pasi Nurminen (G), Atla.	4.00	.50
☐☐☐	95 Sébastien Centomo (G), Toro.	4.00	.50
☐☐☐	96 Jussi Markkanen (G), Edmo.	4.00	.50
☐☐☐	97 Sébastien Charpentier (G), Wash.	4.00	.50
☐☐☐	98 Reinhard Divis (G), SLou.	4.00	.50
☐☐☐	99 Simon Lajeunesse (G), Otta.	4.00	.50
☐☐☐	100 Vesa Toskala (G), SanJ.	4.00	.50
☐☐☐	101 Olivier Michaud (G), Mont.	4.00	.50
☐☐☐	**102 Levente Szuper (G), Calg. RC**	**4.00**	**4.00**
☐☐☐	103 Philippe Sauvé (G), Colo.	4.00	.50
☐☐☐	**104 Dany Sabourin (G), Calg. RC**	**4.00**	**2.00**
☐☐☐	**105 Ryan Miller, Buff. RC**	**5.00**	**10.00**
☐☐☐	106 Chris Mason (G), Flor.	4.00	.50
☐☐☐	107 Stephen Valiquette (G), NYIs.	4.00	.50
☐☐☐	**108 Pascal Leclaire (G), Colu. RC**	**5.00**	**10.00**
☐☐☐	**109 Jason Elliott (G), Detr. RC**	**4.00**	**4.00**
☐☐☐	**110 Michael Garnett (G), Atla. RC**	**4.00**	**2.00**
☐☐☐	111 Tiny Thompson (G), Detr.	5.00	.50
☐☐☐	112 Frank Brimsek (G), Bost.	5.00	1.00
☐☐☐	113 Jacques Plante (G), Mont.	20.00	3.50
☐☐☐	114 Terry Sawchuk (G), Toro.	30.00	4.50
☐☐☐	115 Georges Vézina (G), Mont.	30.00	4.50
☐☐☐	116 Chuck Rayner (G), NYRa.	5.00	.50
☐☐☐	117 Glenn Hall (G), Chic.	15.00	2.00
☐☐☐	118 Turk Broda (G), Toro.	10.00	1.50
☐☐☐	119 George Hainsworth (G), Toro.	5.00	1.00
☐☐☐	120 Roy Worters (G), NYAm.	5.00	.50
☐☐☐	121 J-S Giguère (G), Anah.	15.00	2.00
☐☐☐	122 Milan Hnilicka (G), Atla.	4.00	.50
☐☐☐	123 Steve Shields (G), Bost.	4.00	.50
☐☐☐	124 Martin Biron (G), Buff.	5.00	.50
☐☐☐	125 Roman Turek (G), Calg.	5.00	.50
☐☐☐	126 Arturs Irbe (G), Caro.	5.00	.50
☐☐☐	127 Jocelyn Thibault (G), Chic.	5.00	.50
☐☐☐	128 Patrick Roy (G), Colo.	45.00	6.00
☐☐☐	129 Marc Denis (G), Colu.	5.00	.50
☐☐☐	130 Marty Turco (G), Dall.	5.00	1.00
☐☐☐	131 Curtis Joseph (G), Detr.	15.00	2.00
☐☐☐	132 Tommy Salo (G), Edmo.	5.00	.50
☐☐☐	133 Roberto Luongo (G), Flor.	10.00	1.50
☐☐☐	134 Félix Potvin (G), LosA.	5.00	1.00
☐☐☐	135 Manny Fernandez (G), MinW.	5.00	.50
☐☐☐	136 José Théodore (G), Mont.	15.00	2.00
☐☐☐	137 Tomas Vokoun (G), Nash.	4.00	.50
☐☐☐	138 Martin Brodeur (G), NJer.	20.00	3.00
☐☐☐	139 Chris Osgood (G), NYIs.	5.00	1.00
☐☐☐	140 Mike Richter (G), NYRa.	5.00	.50
☐☐☐	141 Patrick Lalime (G), Otta.	5.00	1.00
☐☐☐	142 Roman Cechmanek (G), Phil.	5.00	.50
☐☐☐	143 Sean Burke (G), Phoe.	5.00	1.00
☐☐☐	144 Johan Hedberg (G), Pitt.	5.00	.50
☐☐☐	145 Brent Johnson (G), SLou.	5.00	.50
☐☐☐	146 Evgeni Nabokov (G), SanJ.	5.00	1.00
☐☐☐	147 Nikolai Khabibulin (G), Tamp.	5.00	.50
☐☐☐	148 Ed Belfour (G), Toro.	15.00	2.00
☐☐☐	149 Dan Cloutier (G), Vanc.	5.00	.50
☐☐☐	150 Olaf Kölzig (G), Wash.	5.00	1.00

HE SHOOTS HE SCORES

Each redemption card was worth one, two, or three points. Collectors could trade 400 points for a special random jersey card. This redemption program ends on December 31, 2003.

Insert Set (20 cards):

	Insert	HSHS
☐	Sean Burke (G), Phoe. [1 Point]	
☐	Roman Cechmanek (G), Phil. [1 Point]	
☐	Dan Cloutier (G), Vanc. [1 Point]	
☐	Johan Hedberg (G), Pitt. [1 Point]	
☐	Arturs Irbe (G), Caro. [1 Point]	
☐	Patrick Lalime (G), Otta. [1 Point]	
☐	Evgeni Nabokov (G), SanJ. [1 Point]	
☐	Félix Potvin (G), LosA. [1 Point]	
☐	Mike Richter (G), NYRa. [1 Point]	
☐	Marty Turco (G), Dall. [1 Point]	
☐	Roman Turek (G), Calg. [1 Point]	
☐	Dan Blackburn (G), NYRa. [2 Points]	
☐	Nikolai Khabibulin (G), Tamp. [2 Points]	
☐	Olaf Kölzig (G), Wash. [2 Points]	
☐	Roberto Luongo (G), Flor. [2 Points]	
☐	Tommy Salo (G), Edmo. [2 Points]	
☐	Jocelyn Thibault (G), Chic. [2 Points]	
☐	Martin Brodeur (G), NJer. [3 Points]	
☐	Patrick Roy (G), Colo. [3 Points]	
☐	José Théodore (G), Mont. [3 Points]	

ALL-STAR STICK & JERSEY

Insert Set (16 cards): 970.00

	Insert (*40)	ASSJ
☐	Ed Belfour (G), AS'96 ✂ ✂	100.00
☐	Martin Brodeur (G), AS'00 ✂ ✂	150.00
☐	Sean Burke (G), AS'02 ✂ ✂	50.00
☐	Roman Cechmanek (G), AS'01 ✂ ✂	40.00
☐	Arturs Irbe (G), AS'99 ✂ ✂	40.00
☐	Curtis Joseph (G), AS'00 ✂ ✂	100.00
☐	Nikolai Khabibulin (G), AS'02 ✂ ✂	40.00
☐	Olaf Kölzig (G), AS'00 ✂ ✂	50.00
☐	Evgeni Nabokov (G), AS'01 ✂ ✂	50.00
☐	Chris Osgood (G), AS'96 ✂ ✂	50.00
☐	Félix Potvin (G), AS'96 ✂ ✂	100.00
☐	Mike Richter (G), AS'00 ✂ ✂	40.00
☐	Patrick Roy (G), AS'94 ✂ ✂	225.00
☐	Tommy Salo (G), AS'00 ✂ ✂	40.00
☐	José Théodore (G), AS'02 ✂ ✂	100.00
☐	Roman Turek (G), AS'00 ✂ ✂	40.00

BEHIND THE MASK

Insert Set (20 cards): 1000.00

	Insert (*30)	BTM
☐	Ed Belfour (G), Toro. ✂	75.00
☐	Martin Brodeur (G), NJer. ✂	125.00
☐	Sean Burke (G), Phoe. ✂	50.00
☐	Dan Cloutier (G), Vanc. ✂	40.00
☐	Marc Denis (G), Colu. ✂	40.00
☐	Rick DiPietro (G), NYIs. ✂	40.00
☐	Mike Dunham (G), Nash. ✂	40.00
☐	Johan Hedberg (G), Pitt. ✂	40.00
☐	Arturs Irbe (G), Caro. ✂	40.00
☐	Nikolai Khabibulin (G), Tamp. ✂	40.00
☐	Olaf Kölzig (G), Wash. ✂	50.00
☐	Patrick Lalime (G), Otta. ✂	50.00
☐	Roberto Luongo (G), Flor. ✂	50.00
☐	Félix Potvin (G), LosA. ✂	100.00
☐	Patrick Roy (G), Colo. ✂	200.00
☐	Tommy Salo (G), Edmo. ✂	40.00
☐	Steve Shields (G), Bost. ✂	40.00
☐	José Théodore (G), Mont. ✂	100.00
☐	Jocelyn Thibault (G), Chic. ✂	40.00
☐	Marty Turco (G), Dall. ✂	50.00

COMPLETE PACKAGE

Insert Set (12 cards): 2800.00

	Insert (*10)	CP
☐	Sean Burke (G), Phoe. ✂ ✂ ✂ ✂	175.00
☐	Roman Cechmanek (G), Phil. ✂ ✂ ✂ ✂	150.00
☐	Grant Fuhr (G), Edmo. ✂ ✂ ✂ ✂	175.00
☐	Johan Hedberg (G), Pitt. ✂ ✂ ✂ ✂	150.00
☐	Curtis Joseph (G), Toro. ✂ ✂ ✂ ✂	300.00
☐	Nikolai Khabibulin (G), Tamp. ✂ ✂ ✂ ✂	150.00
☐	Bernie Parent (G), Phil. ✂ ✂ ✂ ✂	300.00
☐	Jacques Plante (G), Mont. ✂ ✂ ✂ ✂	475.00
☐	Patrick Roy (G), Mont. ✂ ✂ ✂ ✂	700.00
☐	Terry Sawchuk (G), Detr. ✂ ✂ ✂ ✂	600.00
☐	Jocelyn Thibault (G), Chic. ✂ ✂ ✂ ✂	150.00
☐	Marty Turco (G), Dall. ✂ ✂ ✂ ✂	175.00

DOUBLE MEMORABILIA

Insert Set (20 cards): 1280.00

	Insert (*40)	DM
☐	Jean-Sébastien Aubin (G), Pitt. ✂ ✂	40.00
☐	Martin Brodeur (G), NJer. ✂ ✂	175.00
☐	Sean Burke (G), Phoe. ✂ ✂	50.00
☐	Dan Cloutier (G), Vanc. ✂ ✂	40.00
☐	Roger Crozier (G), Detr. ✂ ✂	40.00
☐	Mike Dunham (G), Nash. ✂ ✂	40.00
☐	Johan Hedberg (G), Pitt. ✂ ✂	40.00
☐	Nikolai Khabibulin (G), Tamp. ✂ ✂	40.00
☐	Trevor Kidd (G), Toro. ✂ ✂	40.00
☐	Olaf Kölzig (G), Wash. ✂ ✂	50.00
☐	Manny Legacé (G), Detr. ✂ ✂	40.00
☐	Chris Osgood (G), NYIs. ✂ ✂	50.00
☐	Jacques Plante (G), Mont. ✂ ✂	175.00
☐	Patrick Roy (G), Colo. ✂ ✂	250.00
☐	Tommy Salo (G), Edmo. ✂ ✂	40.00
☐	Terry Sawchuk (G), Detr. ✂ ✂	225.00
☐	José Théodore (G), Mont. ✂ ✂	125.00
☐	Jocelyn Thibault (G), Chic. ✂ ✂	40.00
☐	Marty Turco (G), Dall. ✂ ✂	50.00
☐	Roman Turek (G), Calg. ✂ ✂	50.00

EMBLEMS & IN THE NUMBERS

Both the Jersey Emblem (prefix GUE-) and In The Numbers (prefix ITN-) are limited to 10 copies per card. Realised pricing on scarce cards may vary considerably from below pricing.

Insert Set (30 cards): 4500.00

	Insert (*10)	GUE
☐☐	David Aebischer (G), Colo. ✂	150.00
☐☐	Jean-Sébastien Aubin (G), Pitt. ✂	150.00
☐☐	Martin Biron (G), Buff. ✂	150.00
☐☐	Dan Blackburn (G), NYRa. ✂	150.00
☐☐	Martin Brodeur (G), NJer. ✂	400.00
☐☐	Sean Burke (G), Phoe. ✂	150.00
☐☐	Roman Cechmanek (G), Phil. ✂	150.00
☐☐	Dan Cloutier (G), Vanc. ✂	150.00
☐☐	Rick DiPietro (G), NYIs. ✂	150.00
☐☐	Mike Dunham (G), Nash. ✂	150.00
☐☐	Manny Fernandez (G), MinW. ✂	150.00
☐☐	Jean-Sébastien Giguère (G), Anah. ✂	250.00
☐☐	Johan Hedberg (G), Pitt. ✂	150.00
☐☐	Jani Hurme (G), Otta. ✂	150.00
☐☐	Arturs Irbe (G), Caro. ✂	150.00
☐☐	Nikolai Khabibulin (G), Tamp. ✂	150.00
☐☐	Miikka Kiprusoff (G), SanJ. ✂	150.00
☐☐	Olaf Kölzig (G), Wash. ✂	150.00
☐☐	Patrick Lalime (G), Otta. ✂	150.00
☐☐	Roberto Luongo (G), Flor. ✂	200.00
☐☐	Evgeni Nabokov (G), SanJ. ✂	150.00
☐☐	Mika Noronen (G), Buff. ✂	150.00
☐☐	Félix Potvin (G), LosA. ✂	300.00
☐☐	Mike Richter (G), NYRa. ✂	150.00
☐☐	Patrick Roy (G), Colo. ✂	600.00

☐☐ Tommy Salo (G), Edmo. ✂ 150.00
☐☐ José Théodore (G), Mont. ✂ 300.00
☐☐ Jocelyn Thibault (G), Chic. ✂ 150.00
☐☐ Marty Turco (G), Dall. ✂ 150.00
☐☐ Roman Turek (G), Calg. ✂ 150.00

FUTURE WAVE

Insert Set (12 cards): 500.00
Insert (*60) FW
☐ Alex Auld (G), Vanc. ✂ 50.00
☐ Martin Biron (G), Buff. ✂ 50.00
☐ Dan Blackburn (G), NYRa. ✂ 50.00
☐ Dan Cloutier (G), Vanc. ✂ 50.00
☐ Rick DiPietro (G), NYIs. ✂ 50.00
☐ Mathieu Garon (G), Mont. ✂ 50.00
☐ Johan Hedberg (G), Pitt. ✂ 50.00
☐ Brent Johnson (G), SLou. ✂ 50.00
☐ Miikka Kiprusoff (G), SanJ. ✂ 50.00
☐ Roberto Luongo (G), Flor. ✂ 50.00
☐ José Théodore (G), Mont. ✂ 75.00
☐ Marty Turco (G), Dall. ✂ 50.00

GAME-USED BLOCKER

Insert Set (18 cards): 780.00
Insert (*60) GUB
☐ Sean Burke (G), Phoe. ✂ 50.00
☐ Roman Cechmanek (G), Phil. ✂ 50.00
☐ Mike Dunham (G), Nash. ✂ 50.00
☐ Jean-Sébastien Giguère (G), Anah. ✂ 75.00
☐ Johan Hedberg (G), Pitt. ✂ 50.00
☐ Jani Hurme (G), Otta. ✂ 50.00
☐ Curtis Joseph (G), Detr. ✂ 75.00
☐ Nikolai Khabibulin (G), Tamp. ✂ 50.00
☐ Trevor Kidd (G), Toro. ✂ 50.00
☐ Olaf Kölzig (G), Wash. ✂ 50.00
☐ Patrick Lalime (G), Otta. ✂ 50.00
☐ Roberto Luongo (G), Flor. ✂ 50.00
☐ Evgeni Nabokov (G), SanJ. ✂ 50.00
☐ Félix Potvin (G), LosA. ✂ 75.00
☐ Tommy Salo (G), Edmo. ✂ 50.00
☐ Jocelyn Thibault (G), Chic. ✂ 50.00
☐ Marty Turco (G), Dall. ✂ 50.00
☐ Roman Turek (G), Calg. ✂ 50.00

GAME-USED JERSEYS

Insert Set (50 cards): 1120.00
Insert (*90) GUJ
☐ David Aebischer (G), Colo. ✂ 25.00
☐ Jean-Sébastien Aubin (G), Pitt. ✂ 25.00
☐ Ed Belfour (G), Toro. ✂ 25.00
☐ Martin Biron (G), Buff. ✂ 25.00
☐ Dan Blackburn (G), NYRa. ✂ 25.00
☐ Fred Brathwaite (G), SLou. ✂ 25.00
☐ Martin Brodeur (G), NJer. ✂ 50.00
☐ Sean Burke (G), Phoe. ✂ 25.00
☐ Roman Cechmanek (G), Phil. ✂ 25.00
☐ Sébastien Centomo (G), Toro. ✂ 25.00
☐ Sébastien Charpentier (G), Wash. ✂ 25.00
☐ Dan Cloutier (G), Vanc. ✂ 25.00
☐ Rick DiPietro (G), NYIs. ✂ 25.00
☐ Reinhard Divis (G), SLou. ✂ 25.00
☐ Mike Dunham (G), Nash. ✂ 25.00
☐ Robert Esche (G), Phil. ✂ 25.00
☐ Manny Fernandez (G), MinW. ✂ 25.00
☐ Martin Gerber (G), Anah. ✂ 25.00
☐ Jean-Sébastien Giguère (G), Anah. ✂ 25.00
☐ John Grahame (G), Bost. ✂ 25.00
☐ Jeff Hackett (G), Mont. ✂ 25.00
☐ Johan Hedberg (G), Pitt. ✂ 25.00
☐ Milan Hnilicka (G), Atla. ✂ 25.00
☐ Jani Hurme (G), Otta. ✂ 25.00
☐ Arturs Irbe (G), Caro. ✂ 25.00
☐ Nikolai Khabibulin (G), Tamp. ✂ 25.00
☐ Trevor Kidd (G), Toro. ✂ 25.00
☐ Miikka Kiprusoff (G), SanJ. ✂ 25.00
☐ Olaf Kölzig (G), Wash. ✂ 25.00
☐ Simon Lajeunesse (G), Otta. ✂ 25.00
☐ Patrick Lalime (G), Otta. ✂ 25.00
☐ Roberto Luongo (G), Flor. ✂ 25.00
☐ Jussi Markkanen (G), Edmo. ✂ 25.00
☐ Evgeni Nabokov (G), SanJ. ✂ 25.00
☐ Mika Noronen (G), Buff. ✂ 25.00
☐ Maxime Ouellet (G), Wash. ✂ 25.00
☐ Félix Potvin (G), LosA. ✂ 50.00
☐ Martin Prusek (G), Otta. ✂ 25.00
☐ Mike Richter (G), NYRa. ✂ 25.00
☐ Patrick Roy (G), Colo. ✂ 100.00
☐ Tommy Salo (G), Edmo. ✂ 25.00
☐ Curtis Sanford (G), SLou. ✂ 25.00
☐ Steve Shields (G), Bost. ✂ 25.00
☐ Jamie Storr (G), LosA. ✂ 25.00
☐ José Théodore (G), Mont. ✂ 50.00
☐ Jocelyn Thibault (G), Chic. ✂ 25.00
☐ Tim Thomas (G), Bost. ✂ 25.00
☐ Ron Tugnutt (G), Dall. ✂ 25.00
☐ Marty Turco (G), Dall. ✂ 25.00
☐ Roman Turek (G), Calg. ✂ 25.00

GAME-USED PADS

Insert Set (14 cards): 760.00
Insert (*50) GUP
☐ Jean-Sébastien Aubin (G), Pitt. ✂ 50.00
☐ Ed Belfour (G), Toro. ✂ 75.00
☐ Martin Brodeur (G), NJer. ✂ 100.00
☐ Sean Burke (G), Phoe. ✂ 50.00
☐ Dan Cloutier (G), Vanc. ✂ 50.00
☐ Mike Dunham (G), Nash. ✂ 50.00
☐ Curtis Joseph (G), Detr. ✂ 75.00
☐ Nikolai Khabibulin (G), Tamp. ✂ 50.00
☐ Chris Osgood (G), NYIs. ✂ 50.00
☐ Patrick Roy (G), Colo. ✂ 175.00
☐ Steve Shields (G), Bost. ✂ 50.00
☐ José Théodore (G), Mont. ✂ 75.00
☐ Jocelyn Thibault (G), Chic. ✂ 50.00
☐ Marty Turco (G), Dall. ✂ 50.00

GAME-USED STICK & JERSEY

Insert Set (30 cards): 760.00
Insert (*90) GUSJ
☐ David Aebischer (G), Colo. ✂ ✂ 25.00
☐ Jean-Sébastien Aubin (G), Pitt. ✂ ✂ 25.00
☐ Martin Biron (G), Buff. ✂ ✂ 25.00
☐ Dan Blackburn (G), NYRa. ✂ ✂ 25.00
☐ Martin Brodeur (G), NJer. ✂ ✂ 75.00
☐ Sean Burke (G), Phoe. ✂ ✂ 25.00
☐ Roman Cechmanek (G), Phil. ✂ ✂ 25.00
☐ Dan Cloutier (G), Vanc. ✂ ✂ 25.00
☐ Rick DiPietro (G), NYIs. ✂ ✂ 25.00
☐ Mike Dunham (G), Nash. ✂ ✂ 25.00
☐ Manny Fernandez (G), MinW. ✂ ✂ 25.00
☐ Jean-Sébastien Giguère (G), Anah. ✂ ✂ 50.00
☐ Johan Hedberg (G), Pitt. ✂ ✂ 25.00
☐ Jani Hurme (G), Otta. ✂ ✂ 25.00
☐ Arturs Irbe (G), Caro. ✂ ✂ 25.00
☐ Nikolai Khabibulin (G), Tamp. ✂ ✂ 25.00
☐ Miikka Kiprusoff (G), SanJ. ✂ ✂ 25.00
☐ Olaf Kölzig (G), Wash. ✂ ✂ 25.00
☐ Patrick Lalime (G), Otta. ✂ ✂ 25.00
☐ Roberto Luongo (G), Flor. ✂ ✂ 25.00
☐ Evgeni Nabokov (G), SanJ. ✂ ✂ 25.00
☐ Mika Noronen (G), Buff. ✂ ✂ 25.00
☐ Félix Potvin (G), LosA. ✂ ✂ 50.00
☐ Mike Richter (G), NYRa. ✂ ✂ 25.00
☐ Patrick Roy (G), Colo. ✂ ✂ 100.00
☐ Tommy Salo (G), Edmo. ✂ ✂ 25.00
☐ José Théodore (G), Mont. ✂ ✂ 50.00
☐ Jocelyn Thibault (G), Chic. ✂ ✂ 25.00
☐ Marty Turco (G), Dall. ✂ ✂ 25.00
☐ Roman Turek (G), Calg. ✂ ✂ 25.00

GAME-USED TRAPPERS

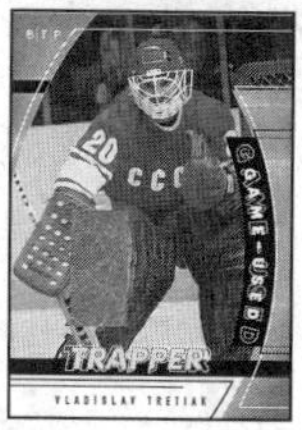

Insert Set (18 cards): 825.00
Insert (*60) GUT
☐ Sean Burke (G), Phoe. ✂ 30.00
☐ Dan Cloutier (G), Vanc. ✂ 30.00
☐ Roger Crozier (G), Detr. ✂ 30.00
☐ Byron Dafoe (G), Bost. ✂ 30.00
☐ Bill Durnan (G), Mont. ✂ 75.00
☐ Grant Fuhr (G), Edmo. ✂ 30.00
☐ Johan Hedberg (G), Pitt. ✂ 30.00
☐ Charlie Hodge (G), Mont. ✂ 30.00
☐ Nikolai Khabibulin (G), Tamp. ✂ 30.00
☐ Olaf Kölzig (G), Wash. ✂ 30.00
☐ Harry Lumley (G), Chic. ✂ 30.00
☐ Bernie Parent (G), Phil. ✂ 75.00
☐ Jacques Plante (G), Mont. ✂ 100.00
☐ Patrick Roy (G), Mont. ✂ 175.00
☐ Terry Sawchuk (G), Detr. ✂ 150.00
☐ Jocelyn Thibault (G), Chic. ✂ 30.00
☐ Vladislav Tretiak (G), CSKA ✂ 100.00
☐ Marty Turco (G), Dall. ✂ 30.00

GOALIE AUTOGRAPH

Insert Set (25 cards): 1440.00
Insert (*50) GA
☐ Martin Biron (G), Buff. ✍ 50.00
☐ Dan Blackburn (G), NYRa. ✍ 50.00
☐ Sean Burke (G), Phoe. ✍ 75.00
☐ Marc Denis (G), Colu. ✍ 50.00
☐ Jean-Sébastien Giguère (G), Anah. ✍ 125.00
☐ Johan Hedberg (G), Pitt. ✍ 50.00
☐ Milan Hnilicka (G), Atla. ✍ 50.00
☐ Arturs Irbe (G), Caro. ✍ 50.00
☐ Brent Johnson (G), SLou. ✍ 50.00
☐ Curtis Joseph (G), Detr. ✍ 125.00
☐ Nikolai Khabibulin (G), Tamp. ✍ 50.00
☐ Olaf Kölzig (G), Wash. ✍ 75.00
☐ Patrick Lalime (G), Otta. ✍ 75.00
☐ Roberto Luongo (G), Flor. ✍ 100.00
☐ Evgeni Nabokov (G), SanJ. ✍ 75.00
☐ Chris Osgood (G), NYIs. ✍ 75.00
☐ Félix Potvin (G), LosA. ✍ 150.00
☐ Dwayne Roloson (G), MinW. ✍ 50.00
☐ Tommy Salo (G), Edmo. ✍ 50.00
☐ Steve Shields (G), Bost. ✍ 50.00
☐ José Théodore (G), Mont. ✍ 150.00
☐ Jocelyn Thibault (G), Chic. ✍ 50.00
☐ Marty Turco (G), Dall. ✍ 75.00
☐ Roman Turek (G), Calg. ✍ 50.00
☐ Dan Cloutier (G), Vanc. ✍ 50.00

GOALIE NIGHTMARES

Insert Set (10 cards): 605.00
Insert (*60) GN
☐ GN-1 Blackburn (G) ✂ / Kovalchuk ✂ 50.00
☐ GN-2 Richter (G) ✂ / Lemieux ✂ 150.00
☐ GN-3 T.Salo (G) ✂ / Jagr ✂ 50.00
☐ GN-4 Potvin ✂ / Yzerman ✂ 150.00
☐ GN-4 Fiset (G) ✂ / P.Bure ✂ 35.00
☐ GN-6 Richter (G) ✂ / Iginla ✂ 50.00
☐ GN-7 T.Salo (G) ✂ / Forsberg ✂ 75.00
☐ GN-8 C.Joseph (G) ✂ / Sakic ✂ 100.00
☐ GN-9 Kölzig (G) ✂ / Lindros ✂ 50.00
☐ GN-10 Barrasso (G) ✂ / Sundin ✂ 50.00

HE SHOOTS HE SAVES JERSEY

Redemption Set (30 cards):
Redemption (*20) J20
☐ Dan Blackburn (G), NYRa. ✂
☐ Martin Brodeur (G), NJer. ✂
☐ Sean Burke (G), Phoe. ✂
☐ Roman Cechmanek (G), Phil. ✂
☐ Gerry Cheevers (G), Bost. ✂
☐ Dan Cloutier (G), Vanc. ✂
☐ Roger Crozier (G), Detr. ✂
☐ Tony Esposito (G), Chic. ✂
☐ Ed Giacomin (G), NYRa. ✂
☐ George Hainsworth (G), Mont. ✂
☐ Glenn Hall (G), Chic. ✂
☐ Johan Hedberg (G), Pitt. ✂
☐ Arturs Irbe (G), Caro. ✂
☐ Nikolai Khabibulin (G), Tamp. ✂
☐ Olaf Kölzig (G), Wash. ✂
☐ Patrick Lalime (G), Otta. ✂
☐ Harry Lumley (G), Chic. ✂
☐ Roberto Luongo (G), Flor. ✂
☐ Evgeni Nabokov (G), SanJ. ✂
☐ Bernie Parent (G), Phil. ✂
☐ Félix Potvin (G), LosA. ✂
☐ Mike Richter (G), NYRa. ✂
☐ Patrick Roy (G), Colo. ✂
☐ Tommy Salo (G), Edmo. ✂
☐ Terry Sawchuk (G), Detr. ✂
☐ José Théodore (G), Mont. ✂
☐ Jocelyn Thibault (G), Chic. ✂
☐ Marty Turco (G), Dall. ✂
☐ Roman Turek (G), Calg. ✂
☐ Roy Worters (G), NYAm. ✂

INSPIRATION

Insert Set (10 cards): 830.00
Insert (*40) Insp
☐ I-1 Roy ✂ / Plante (G) ✂ 175.00
☐ I-2 Sawchuk (G) ✂ / Hainsworth (G) ✂ 125.00
☐ I-3 Théodore (G) ✂ / Roy ✂ 150.00
☐ I-4 Luongo (G) ✂ / Roy ✂ 125.00
☐ I-5 Burke (G) ✂ / Parent ✂ 50.00
☐ I-6 Belfour (G) ✂ / Tretiak (G) ✂ 100.00
☐ I-7 Blackburn (G) ✂ / Joseph (G) ✂ 50.00
☐ I-8 Brodeur (G) ✂ / Roy ✂ 175.00
☐ I-9 Richter (G) ✂ / Cheevers (G) ✂ 50.00
☐ I-10 DiPietro (G) ✂ / Hextall ✂ 40.00

RECORD BREAKERS

Insert Set (16 cards): 1500.00
Insert (*40) RB
☐ Terry Sawchuk (G), Detr. ✂ 150.00
☐ Bernie Parent (G), Phil. ✂ 75.00
☐ Terry Sawchuk (G), Detr. ✂ 150.00
☐ Patrick Roy (G), Mont. ✂ 175.00
☐ Johnny Bower (G), Toro. ✂ 75.00
☐ Ed Belfour (G), Chic. ✂ 75.00
☐ Patrick Roy (G), Colo. ✂ 175.00
☐ Terry Sawchuk (G), Detr. ✂ 150.00
☐ Patrick Roy (G), Mont. ✂ 175.00
☐ George Hainsworth (G), Mont. ✂ 75.00
☐ Jacques Plante (G), Mont. ✂ 100.00
☐ Patrick Roy (G), Colo. ✂ 175.00
☐ Glenn Hall (G), Chic. ✂ 75.00
☐ Tony Esposito (G), Chic. ✂ 75.00
☐ Gerry Cheevers (G), Bost. ✂ 75.00
☐ Martin Brodeur (G), NJer. ✂ 100.00

TANDEMS

Insert Set (36 cards):	800.00
Insert (*30)	T
1 Richter (G) ✂ / Blackburn (G) ✂	50.00
2 Roy ✂ / Aebischer (G) ✂	100.00
3 Thibault (G) ✂ / Passmore (G) ✂	50.00
4 Nabokov (G) ✂ / Kiprusoff (G) ✂	50.00
5 Lalime (G) ✂ / Prusek (G) ✂	50.00
6 Biron (G) ✂ / Noronen (G) ✂	50.00
7 Hedberg (G) ✂ / Aubin (G) ✂	50.00
8 Cechmanek (G) ✂ / Esche (G) ✂	50.00
9 Théodore (G) ✂ / Hackett (G) ✂	75.00
10 Potvin ✂ / Storr (G) ✂	50.00
11 Dunham (G) ✂ / Vokoun (G) ✂	50.00
12 Cloutier (G) ✂ / Auld (G) ✂	50.00
13 Giguère (G) ✂ / Gerber (G) ✂	50.00
14 Belfour (G) ✂ / Kidd (G) ✂	50.00
15 Johnson ✂ / Brathwaite (G) ✂	50.00
16 Osgood (G) ✂ / DiPietro (G) ✂	50.00
17 Shields (G) ✂ / Grahame (G) ✂	50.00
18 Salo ✂ / Markkanen (G) ✂	50.00
19 Turco (G) ✂ / Tugnutt (G) ✂	50.00
20 Kölzig (G) ✂ / Ouellet (G) ✂	50.00

THE MASK II

Insert Set (30 cards):	1280.00	500.00	245.00
Insert	G30	S300	Mask
M-1 J-S Giguère (G), Anah.	50.00	20.00	10.00
M-2 Milan Hnilicka (G), Atla.	50.00	20.00	10.00
M-3 Steve Shields (G), Bost.	50.00	20.00	10.00
M-4 Martin Biron (G), Buff.	50.00	20.00	10.00
M-5 Roman Turek (G), Calg.	50.00	20.00	10.00
M-6 Kevin Weekes (G), Caro.	50.00	20.00	10.00
M-7 J. Thibault (G), Chic.	50.00	20.00	10.00
M-8 Patrick Roy (G), Colo.	150.00	45.00	20.00
M-9 Marc Denis (G), Colu.	50.00	20.00	10.00
M-10 Marty Turco (G), Dall.	50.00	20.00	10.00
M-11 Curtis Joseph (G), Detr.	50.00	20.00	10.00
M-12 Tommy Salo (G), Edmo.	50.00	20.00	10.00
M-13 Luongo (G), Flor.	50.00	20.00	10.00
M-14 Félix Potvin (G), LosA.	50.00	20.00	10.00
M-15 Fernandez (G), MinW.	50.00	20.00	10.00
M-16 Théodore (G), Mont.	50.00	20.00	10.00
M-17 Mike Dunham (G), Nash.	50.00	20.00	10.00
M-18 Mike Richter (G), NYRa.	50.00	20.00	10.00
M-19 Rick DiPietro (G), NYIs.	50.00	20.00	10.00
M-20 Patrick Lalime (G), Otta.	50.00	20.00	10.00
M-21 Cechmanek (G), Phil.	50.00	20.00	10.00
M-22 Sean Burke (G), Phoe.	50.00	20.00	10.00
M-23 Johan Hedberg (G), Pitt.	50.00	20.00	10.00
M-24 Nabokov (G), SanJ.	50.00	20.00	10.00
M-25 Kiprusoff (G), SanJ.	50.00	20.00	10.00
M-26 Johnson (G), SLou.	50.00	20.00	10.00
M-27 Khabibulin (G), Tamp.	50.00	20.00	10.00
M-28 Ed Belfour (G), Toro.	50.00	20.00	10.00
M-29 Jeff Hackett (G), Mont.	50.00	20.00	10.00
M-30 Olaf Kölzig (G), Wash.	50.00	20.00	10.00

VINTAGE GOALIE AUTOGRAPHS

Insert Set (11 cards):	655.00
Insert (*90)	VA
Johnny Bower (G), Toro. ✍	50.00
Gerry Cheevers (G), Bost. ✍	75.00
John Davidson, NYRa. ✍	40.00
Tony Esposito (G), Chic. ✍	100.00
Ed Giacomin (G), NYRa. ✍	75.00
Glenn Hall (G), Chic. ✍	100.00
Charlie Hodge (G), Mont. ✍	40.00
Bernie Parent (G), Phil. ✍	75.00
Vladislav Tretiak (G), CSKA ✍	125.00
Rogatien Vachon (G), Mont. ✍	40.00
Gump Worsley (G), Mont. ✍ {*40}	100.00

VINTAGE MEMORABILIA

Insert Set (20 cards):	3400.00
Insert (*20)	VM
Johnny Bower (G), Toro. ✂	200.00
Frank Brimsek (G), Bost. ✂	150.00
Gerry Cheevers (G), Bost. ✂	200.00
Roger Crozier (G), Detr. ✂	100.00
Bill Durnan (G), Mont. ✂	225.00
Tony Esposito (G), Chic. ✂	225.00
Charlie Gardiner (G), Chic. ✂	225.00
Ed Giacomin (G), NYRa. ✂	200.00
Ed Giacomin (G), NYRa. ✂	200.00
George Hainsworth (G), Mont. ✂	225.00
Glenn Hall (G), Chic. ✂	225.00
Charlie Hodge (G), Mont. ✂	100.00
Harry Lumley (G), Chic. ✂	150.00
Bernie Parent (G), Phil. ✂	200.00
Bernie Parent (G), Phil. ✂	200.00
Jacques Plante (G), Mont. ✂	300.00
Terry Sawchuk (G), Detr. ✂	400.00
Tiny Thompson (G), Bost. ✂	225.00
Vladislav Tretiak (G), CSKA ✂	300.00
Roy Worters (G), NYAm. ✂	200.00

2002 - 03 BOWMAN

Produced by the Upper Deck Company, this series was released in April 2003.

Complete Set (165 cards):	120.00	475.00	90.00
Common Player:	.25	1.00	.20
Description	I3	G250	B
1 Nicklas Lidström, Detr.	1.00	4.00	.50
2 Martin Brodeur (G), NJer.	3.00	12.00	2.00
3 Tony Amonte, Phoe.	1.00	4.00	.50
4 Todd Bertuzzi, Vanc.	2.00	9.00	1.50
5 Joe Thornton, Bost.	2.00	9.00	1.50
6 Ron Francis, Caro.	1.00	4.00	.50
7 Paul Kariya, Anah.	2.00	10.00	2.00
8 Eric Lindros, NYRa.	2.00	7.00	1.50
9 John LeClair, Phil.	1.00	6.00	1.00
10 Doug Weight, SLou.	1.00	4.00	.50
11 Jaromir Jagr, Wash.	2.00	7.00	1.50
12 Mats Sundin, Toro.	2.00	7.00	1.50
13 Saku Koivu, Mont.	1.00	6.00	1.00
14 Peter Forsberg, Colo.	2.00	10.00	2.00
15 Alexei Yashin, NYIs.	1.00	4.00	.50
16 Mike Modano, Dall.	2.00	7.00	1.50
17 Chris Drury, Calg.	1.00	4.00	.50
18 Ryan Smyth, Edmo.	.50	3.00	.50
19 Tomas Vokoun (G), Nash.	.25	1.00	.25
20 Marian Hossa, Otta.	2.00	7.00	1.50
21 Owen Nolan, SanJ.	1.00	4.00	.50
22 Vincent Lecavalier, Tamp.	2.00	7.00	1.50
23 Jocelyn Thibault (G), Chic.	.50	3.00	.50
24 Marc Denis (G), Colu.	.50	3.00	.50
25 Roberto Luongo (G), Flor.	1.00	6.00	1.00
26 Mario Lemieux, Pitt.	6.00	22.00	4.50
27 Keith Tkachuk, SLou.	1.00	4.00	.50
28 Radek Bonk, Otta.	.50	2.00	.25
29 Bill Guerin, Dall.	.50	3.00	.50
30 Jason Allison, LosA.	1.00	4.00	.50
31 Jeff O'Neill, Caro.	.50	3.00	.50
32 Alexei Zhamnov, Chic.	.25	2.00	.25
33 Scott Stevens, NJer.	.50	3.00	.50
34 Mark Recchi, Phil.	.50	3.00	.50
35 Alexander Mogilny, Toro.	.50	3.00	.50
36 Olaf Kölzig (G), Wash.	1.00	4.00	.50
37 Sean Burke (G), Phoe.	1.00	4.00	.50
38 Brett Hull, Detr.	2.00	7.00	1.50
39 Andrew Cassels, Colu.	.25	1.00	.25
40 Jarome Iginla, Calg.	1.00	6.00	1.00
41 Joe Sakic, Colo.	3.00	12.00	2.00
42 Brian Leetch, NYRa.	1.00	4.00	.50
43 Simon Gagné, Phil.	1.00	6.00	1.00
44 Dan Cloutier (G), Vanc.	.50	3.00	.50
45 Brian Rolston, Bost.	.25	2.00	.25
46 Milan Hejduk, Colo.	1.00	6.00	1.00
47 Steve Yzerman, Detr.	3.00	18.00	3.50
48 Martin Havlat, Otta.	1.00	4.00	.50
49 Alex Kovalev, NYRa.	1.00	4.00	.50
50 Pavol Demitra, SLou.	.50	3.00	.50
51 Mark Parrish, NYIs.	.50	3.00	.50
52 Félix Potvin (G), LosA.	1.00	4.00	.50
53 Brenden Morrow, Dall.	.25	2.00	.25
54 Steve Sullivan, Chic.	.25	2.00	.25
55 Patrick Roy (G), Colo.	6.00	22.00	4.50
56 M. Fernandez (G), MinW.	.50	3.00	.50
57 V. Damphousse, SanJ.	1.00	4.00	.50
58 Michael Peca, NYIs.	.50	3.00	.50
59 Anson Carter, Edmo.	.50	3.00	.50
60 Kevin Weekes (G), Caro.	.25	1.00	.25
61 Peter Bondra, Wash.	1.00	4.00	.50
62 Brad Richards, Tamp.	.50	3.00	.50
63 Johan Hedberg (G), Pitt.	.50	3.00	.50
64 Olli Jokinen, Flor.	.25	2.00	.25
65 Miroslav Satan, Buff.	.25	2.00	.25
66 Petr Sykora, Anah.	.50	3.00	.50
67 Al MacInnis, SLou.	.50	3.00	.50
68 Markus Näslund, Vanc.	2.00	7.00	1.50
69 Mark Messier, NYRa.	2.00	7.00	1.50
70 Rob Blake, Colo.	1.00	4.00	.50
71 Sergei Samsonov, Bost.	1.00	4.00	.50
72 José Théodore (G), Mont.	2.00	9.00	1.50
73 Eric Boguniecki, SLou.	.25	2.00	.25
74 Nikolai Khabibulin (G), Tamp.	.50	3.00	.50
75 Marco Sturm, SanJ.	.25	1.00	.25
76 Patrick Lalime (G), Otta.	1.00	4.00	.50
77 Jeremy Roenick, Phil.	1.00	6.00	1.00
78 John Madden, NJer.	.25	2.00	.25
79 Steve Rucchin, Anah.	.25	1.00	.25
80 Jere Lehtinen, Dall.	.25	2.00	.25
81 Stu Barnes, Buff.	.25	1.00	.25
82 Roman Turek (G), Calg.	.50	3.00	.50
83 Curtis Joseph (G), Detr.	2.00	7.00	1.50
84 Evgeni Nabokov (G), SanJ.	1.00	4.00	.50
85 Daniel Alfredsson, Otta.	1.00	4.00	.50
86 Brendan Morrison, Vanc.	.25	2.00	.25
87 Roman Cechmanek (G), Phil.	.50	3.00	.50
88 Chris Osgood (G), NYIs.	1.00	4.00	.50
89 Tommy Salo (G), Edmo.	.50	3.00	.50
90 Craig Conroy, Calg.	.25	2.00	.25
91 Zigmund Palffy, LosA.	1.00	4.00	.50
92 Pavel Bure, NYRa.	1.00	6.00	1.00
93 Brent Johnson (G), SLou.	.50	3.00	.50
94 Ed Belfour (G), Toro.	2.00	7.00	1.50
95 Shane Doan, Phoe.	.25	1.00	.25
96 David Legwand, Nash.	.50	3.00	.50
97 Sergei Fedorov, Detr.	2.00	7.00	1.50
98 Jason Arnott, Dall.	.50	3.00	.50
99 Keith Primeau, Phil.	.50	3.00	.50
100 Martin St_Louis, Tamp.	.50	3.00	.50
101 Teemu Selänne, SanJ.	1.00	6.00	1.00
102 Patrik Elias, NJer.	1.00	6.00	1.00
103 Ray Whitney, Colu.	.25	1.00	.25
104 Brendan Shanahan, Detr.	2.00	7.00	1.50
105 Taylor Pyatt, Buff.	.25	1.00	.25
106 Niklas Hagman, Flor.	.25	1.00	.25
107 Henrik Tallinder, Buff.	.25	1.00	.25
108 Rostislav Klesla, Colu.	.25	2.00	.25
109 David Aebischer (G), Colo.	.25	2.00	.25
110 Marcel Hossa, Mont.	.50	3.00	.50
111 Pavel Brendl, Phil.	.25	2.00	.25
112 Ossi Väänänen, Phoe.	.25	1.00	.25
113 Erik Cole, Caro.	.25	1.00	.25
114 Marian Gaborik, MinW.	2.00	7.00	1.50
115 A. Svitov, Tamp. RC	**4.00**	**6.00**	**4.00**
116 S. Chistov, Anah. RC	**6.00**	**9.00**	**6.00**
117 J. Leopold, Calg. RC	**3.00**	**4.00**	**3.00**
118 R. Miller (G), Buff. RC	**5.00**	**8.00**	**5.00**
119 Kurt Sauer, Anah. RC	**1.00**	**2.00**	**1.00**
120 Jonathan Cheechoo, SanJ.	.25	2.00	.25
121 R. Somik, Phil. RC	**1.00**	**2.00**	**1.00**
122 A. Volchenkov, Otta. RC	**2.00**	**3.00**	**2.00**
123 Pavel Datsyuk, Detr.	1.00	6.00	1.00
124 A. Frolov, LosA. RC	**5.00**	**8.00**	**5.00**
125 Steve Ott, Dall. RC	**3.00**	**4.00**	**3.00**
126 Jason Spezza, Otta. RC	**7.50**	**12.00**	**7.50**
127 Barret Jackman, SLou.	.50	3.00	.50
128 Steve Eminger, Wash.	.25	1.00	.25
129 Pascal Dupuis, MinW.	.25	1.00	.25
130 Brian Sutherby, Wash.	.25	1.00	.25
131 Dan Blackburn, NYRa.	.50	3.00	.50
132 Ron Hainsey, Mont. RC	**3.00**	**4.00**	**3.00**
133 Bouwmeester, Flor. RC	**3.50**	**7.00**	**3.50**
134 Adam Hall, Nash. RC	**1.50**	**3.00**	**1.50**
135 Mike Comrie, Edmo.	1.00	6.00	1.00
136 Nick Schultz, MinW.	.25	1.00	.25
137 H. Zetterberg, Detr. RC	**10.00**	**16.00**	**10.00**
138 Radim Vrbata, Colo.	.25	2.00	.25
139 Jaroslav Svoboda, Caro.	.25	1.00	.25
140 Tyler Arnason, Chic.	.50	3.00	.50
141 Dany Heatley, Atla.	2.00	7.00	1.50
142 Ivan Huml, Bost.	.25	1.00	.25
143 Kristian Huselius, Flor.	.25	2.00	.25
144 M. Gerber (G), Anah. RC	**2.00**	**3.00**	**2.00**
145 Tom Koivisto, SLou. RC	**1.00**	**2.00**	**1.00**
146 M. Tellqvist, Toro. RC	**2.00**	**3.00**	**2.00**
147 D. Seidenberg, Phil. RC	**2.00**	**3.00**	**2.00**
148 M. Cammalleri, LosA. RC	**6.00**	**6.00**	**4.00**
149 Niko Kapanen, Dall.	.25	1.00	.25
150 S. Thornton, Chic. RC	**3.00**	**3.00**	**2.00**
151 A. Smirnov, Anah. RC	**3.00**	**4.00**	**3.00**
152 Jamie Lundmark, NYRa.	.25	2.00	.25
153 Shawn Horcoff, Edmo.	.25	1.00	.25
154 Branko Radivojevic, Phoe.	.25	1.00	.25
155 Rick Nash, Colu. RC	**10.00**	**16.00**	**10.00**
156 Mattias Weinhandl, NYIs.	.25	1.00	.25
157 Stephen Weiss, Flor.	.50	3.00	.50
158 Dmitri Bykov, Detr. RC	**2.00**	**3.00**	**2.00**
159 Ales Hemsky, Edmo. RC	**6.00**	**9.00**	**6.00**
160 C. Kobasew, Calg. RC	**4.00**	**6.00**	**4.00**
161 Bouchard, MinW. RC	**6.00**	**9.00**	**6.00**
162 S. Upshall, Nash. RC	**4.00**	**6.00**	**4.00**
163 Patrick Sharp, Phil. RC	**1.00**	**2.00**	**1.00**
164 Derrick Walser, Colu.	.25	1.00	.25
165 Ilya Kovalchuk, Atla.	2.00	7.00	1.50

FABRIC OF THE FUTURE DOUBLE STUFF

Insert Set (27 cards):	1215.00
Insert (*25)	FFDS
David Aebischer (G), Colo. ✂	50.00
Tyler Arnason, Chic. ✂	60.00
Jay Bouwmeester, Flor. ✂	70.00
Pavel Brendl, Phil. ✂	50.00
Stanislav Chistov, Anah. ✂	70.00
Alexander Frolov, LosA. ✂	60.00
Niklas Hagman, Flor. ✂	50.00
Adam Hall, Nash. ✂	50.00
Shawn Horcoff, Edmo. ✂	50.00
Marcel Hossa, Mont. ✂	60.00
Barret Jackman, SLou. ✂	60.00
Niko Kapanen, Dall. ✂	50.00
Rostislav Klesla, Colu. ✂	50.00
Jordan Leopold, Calg. ✂	50.00
Ryan Miller (G), Buff. ✂	60.00
Rick Nash, Colu. ✂	120.00
Taylor Pyatt, Buff. ✂	50.00
Branko Radivojevic, Phoe. ✂	50.00
Nick Schultz, MinW. ✂	50.00
Dennis Seidenberg, Phil. ✂	50.00
Brian Sutherby, Wash. ✂	50.00
Alexander Svitov, Tamp. ✂	50.00
Henrik Tallinder, Buff. ✂	50.00
Ossi Väänänen, Phoe. ✂	50.00
Anton Volchenkov, Otta. ✂	50.00
Mattias Weinhandl, NYIs. ✂	50.00
Stephen Weiss, Flor. ✂	60.00

FABRIC OF THE FUTURE JERSEY

Insert Set (27 cards):	235.00
Insert	FFJ
David Aebischer (G), Colo. ✂	10.00
Tyler Arnason, Chic. ✂	10.00
Jay Bouwmeester, Flor. ✂ Red	15.00
Pavel Brendl, Phil. ✂	10.00
Stanislav Chistov, Anah. ✂	15.00
Alexander Frolov, LosA. ✂	10.00
Niklas Hagman, Flor. ✂	10.00
Adam Hall, Nash. ✂ Silver	10.00
Shawn Horcoff, Edmo. ✂	10.00
Marcel Hossa, Mont. ✂ Red	10.00
Barret Jackman, SLou. ✂	10.00
Niko Kapanen, Dall. ✂	10.00
Rostislav Klesla, Colu. ✂	10.00
Jordan Leopold, Calg. ✂	10.00
Ryan Miller (G), Buff. ✂	10.00
Rick Nash, Colu. ✂	25.00
Taylor Pyatt, Buff. ✂	10.00
Branko Radivojevic, Phoe. ✂	10.00
Nick Schultz, MinW. ✂ Green	10.00
Dennis Seidenberg, Phil. ✂ White	10.00
Brian Sutherby, Wash. ✂	10.00
Alexander Svitov, Tamp. ✂	10.00
Henrik Tallinder, Buff. ✂	10.00
Ossi Väänänen, Phoe. ✂	10.00
Anton Volchenkov, Otta. ✂	10.00
Mattias Weinhandl, NYIs. ✂ Orange	10.00
Stephen Weiss, Flor. ✂	10.00

FABRIC OF THE FUTURE PATCH

Insert Set (27 cards):	775.00

	Insert (*50)	FFP
☐	David Aebischer (G), Colo. ✂	35.00
☐	Tyler Arnason, Chic. ✂	45.00
☐	Jay Bouwmeester, Flor. ✂	55.00
☐	Pavel Brendl, Phil. ✂	35.00
☐	Stanislav Chistov, Anah. ✂	55.00
☐	Alexander Frolov, LosA. ✂	45.00
☐	Niklas Hagman, Flor. ✂	25.00
☐	Adam Hall, Nash. ✂	25.00
☐	Shawn Horcoff, Edmo. ✂	25.00
☐	Marcel Hossa, Mont. ✂	45.00
☐	Barret Jackman, SLou. ✂	45.00
☐	Niko Kapanen, Dall. ✂	25.00
☐	Rostislav Klesla, Colu. ✂	35.00
☐	Jordan Leopold, Calg. ✂	25.00
☐	Ryan Miller (G), Buff. ✂	45.00
☐	Rick Nash, Colu. ✂	100.00
☐	Taylor Pyatt, Buff. ✂	25.00
☐	Branko Radivojevic, Phoe. ✂	25.00
☐	Nick Schultz, MinW. ✂	25.00
☐	Dennis Seidenberg, Phil. ✂	25.00
☐	Brian Sutherby, Wash. ✂	25.00
☐	Alexander Svitov, Tamp. ✂	35.00
☐	Henrik Tallinder, Buff. ✂	25.00
☐	Ossi Väänänen, Phoe. ✂	25.00
☐	Anton Volchenkov, Otta. ✂	25.00
☐	Mattias Weinhandl, NYIs. ✂	25.00
☐	Stephen Weiss, Flor. ✂	45.00

FABRIC OF THE FUTURE RIVALS

	Insert Set (13 cards):	180.00
	Insert (*250)	FFR
☐	A. Frolov ✂ / A. Svitov ✂	20.00
☐	A. Hall ✂ / M. Weinhandl ✂	15.00
☐	B. Jackman ✂ / D. Seidenberg ✂	15.00
☐	B. Radivojevic ✂ / P. Brendl ✂	15.00
☐	D. Aebischer (G) ✂ / R. Miller ✂	15.00
☐	J. Leopold ✂ / T. Pyatt ✂	15.00
☐	N. Kapanen ✂ White / Marcel Hossa ✂ White	15.00
☐	N. Schultz ✂ / N. Hagman ✂	15.00
☐	O. Väänänen ✂ / H. Tallinder ✂	15.00
☐	R. Klesla ✂ / A. Volchenkov ✂	15.00
☐	R. Nash ✂ / J. Bouwmeester ✂	35.00
☐	S. Chistov ✂ / S. Weiss ✂	25.00
☐	T. Arnson ✂ / B. Sutherby ✂	15.00

FABRIC OF THE FUTURE RIVALS PATCH

	Insert Set (13 cards):	1500.00
	Insert (*10)	FFRP
☐	A. Frolov ✂ / A. Svitov ✂	175.00
☐	B. Radivojevic ✂ / P. Brendl ✂	100.00
☐	T. Arnson ✂ / B. Sutherby ✂	125.00
☐	D. Aebischer (G) ✂ / R. Miller ✂	125.00
☐	B. Jackman ✂ / D. Seidenberg ✂	100.00
☐	A. Hall ✂ / M. Weinhandl ✂	100.00
☐	N. Schultz ✂ / N. Hagman ✂	150.00
☐	N. Kapanen ✂ / Marcel Hossa ✂	100.00
☐	O. Väänänen ✂ / H. Tallinder ✂	100.00
☐	R. Klesla ✂ / A. Volchenkov ✂	175.00
☐	R. Nash ✂ / J. Bouwmeester ✂	300.00
☐	S. Chistov ✂ / S. Weiss ✂	200.00
☐	J. Leopold ✂ / T. Pyatt ✂	125.00

FABRIC OF THE FUTURE STICK

	Insert Set (27 cards):	345.00
	Insert	FFS
☐	David Aebischer (G), Colo. ✂	15.00
☐	Tyler Arnason, Chic. ✂	15.00
☐	Jay Bouwmeester, Flor. ✂	15.00
☐	Pavel Brendl, Phil. ✂	15.00
☐	Stanislav Chistov, Anah. ✂	15.00
☐	Alexander Frolov, LosA. ✂	15.00
☐	Niklas Hagman, Flor. ✂	15.00
☐	Adam Hall, Nash. ✂	15.00
☐	Shawn Horcoff, Edmo. ✂	15.00
☐	Marcel Hossa, Mont. ✂	15.00
☐	Barret Jackman, SLou. ✂	15.00
☐	Niko Kapanen, Dall. ✂	15.00
☐	Rostislav Klesla, Colu. ✂	15.00
☐	Jordan Leopold, Calg. ✂	15.00
☐	Ryan Miller (G), Buff. ✂	15.00
☐	Rick Nash, Colu. ✂	45.00
☐	Taylor Pyatt, Buff. ✂	15.00
☐	Branko Radivojevic, Phoe. ✂	15.00
☐	Nick Schultz, MinW. ✂	15.00
☐	Dennis Seidenberg, Phil. ✂	15.00
☐	Brian Sutherby, Wash. ✂	15.00
☐	Alexander Svitov, Tamp. ✂	15.00
☐	Henrik Tallinder, Buff. ✂	15.00
☐	Ossi Väänänen, Phoe. ✂	15.00
☐	Anton Volchenkov, Otta. ✂	15.00
☐	Mattias Weinhandl, NYIs. ✂	15.00
☐	Stephen Weiss, Flor. ✂	15.00

FABRIC OF THE FUTURE TRIPLE STUFF

	Insert Set (27 cards):	3360.00
	Insert (*10)	FFTS
☐	David Aebischer (G), Colo. ✂ ✂ ✂	150.00
☐	Tyler Arnason, Chic. ✂ ✂ ✂	200.00
☐	Jay Bouwmeester, Flor. ✂ ✂ ✂	225.00
☐	Pavel Brendl, Phil. ✂ ✂ ✂	150.00
☐	Stanislav Chistov, Anah. ✂ ✂ ✂	225.00
☐	Alexander Frolov, LosA. ✂ ✂ ✂	200.00
☐	Niklas Hagman, Flor. ✂ ✂ ✂	80.00
☐	Adam Hall, Nash. ✂ ✂ ✂	100.00
☐	Shawn Horcoff, Edmo. ✂ ✂ ✂	80.00
☐	Marcel Hossa, Mont. ✂ ✂ ✂	200.00
☐	Barret Jackman, SLou. ✂ ✂ ✂	200.00
☐	Niko Kapanen, Dall. ✂ ✂ ✂	100.00
☐	Rostislav Klesla, Colu. ✂ ✂ ✂	300.00
☐	Jordan Leopold, Calg. ✂ ✂ ✂	100.00
☐	Ryan Miller (G), Buff. ✂ ✂ ✂	200.00
☐	Rick Nash, Colu. ✂ ✂ ✂	400.00
☐	Taylor Pyatt, Buff. ✂ ✂ ✂	100.00
☐	Branko Radivojevic, Phoe. ✂ ✂ ✂	100.00
☐	Nick Schultz, MinW. ✂ ✂ ✂	80.00
☐	Dennis Seidenberg, Phil. ✂ ✂ ✂	80.00
☐	Brian Sutherby, Wash. ✂ ✂ ✂	80.00
☐	Alexander Svitov, Tamp. ✂ ✂ ✂	150.00
☐	Henrik Tallinder, Buff. ✂ ✂ ✂	80.00
☐	Ossi Väänänen, Phoe. ✂ ✂ ✂	80.00
☐	Anton Volchenkov, Otta. ✂ ✂ ✂	80.00
☐	Mattias Weinhandl, NYIs. ✂ ✂ ✂	80.00
☐	Stephen Weiss, Flor. ✂ ✂ ✂	200.00

YOUNGSTARS AUTOGRAPH

	Insert Set (27 cards):	1325.00
	Insert (*50)	YS
☐	David Aebischer (G), Colo. ✍	65.00
☐	Tyler Arnason, Chic. ✍	85.00
☐	Jay Bouwmeester, Flor. ✍	100.00
☐	Pavel Brendl, Phil. ✍	65.00
☐	Stanislav Chistov, Anah. ✍	100.00
☐	Alexander Frolov, LosA. ✍	85.00
☐	Niklas Hagman, Flor. ✍	30.00
☐	Adam Hall, Nash. ✍	50.00
☐	Shawn Horcoff, Edmo. ✍	30.00
☐	Marcel Hossa, Mont. ✍	85.00
☐	Barret Jackman, SLou. ✍	85.00
☐	Niko Kapanen, Dall. ✍	50.00
☐	Rostislav Klesla, Colu. ✍	65.00
☐	Jordan Leopold, Calg. ✍	50.00
☐	Ryan Miller (G), Buff. ✍	85.00
☐	Rick Nash, Colu. ✍	170.00
☐	Taylor Pyatt, Buff. ✍	50.00
☐	Branko Radivojevic, Phoe. ✍	50.00
☐	Nick Schultz, MinW. ✍	30.00
☐	Dennis Seidenberg, Phil. ✍	30.00
☐	Brian Sutherby, Wash. ✍	30.00
☐	Alexander Svitov, Tamp. ✍	65.00
☐	Henrik Tallinder, Buff. ✍	30.00
☐	Ossi Väänänen, Phoe. ✍	30.00
☐	Anton Volchenkov, Otta. ✍	30.00
☐	Mattias Weinhandl, NYIs. ✍	30.00
☐	Stephen Weiss, Flor. ✍	85.00

YOUNGSTARS MVP PUCK RELIC

	Insert	MVP
☐	YSMVP-BS Brian Sutherby, Wash.	

PUCK SIGNED

	Insert Set (27 pucks):	
	Insert	Puck
☐	David Aebischer (G) ✍	
☐	Tyler Arnason ✍	
☐	Jay Bouwmeester ✍	
☐	Pavel Brendl ✍	
☐	Stanislav Chistov ✍	
☐	Alexander Frolov ✍	
☐	Niklas Hagman ✍	
☐	Adam Hall ✍	
☐	Shawn Horcoff ✍	
☐	Marcel Hossa ✍	
☐	Barret Jackman ✍	
☐	Niko Kapanen ✍	
☐	Rostislav Klesla ✍	
☐	Jordan Leopold ✍	
☐	Ryan Miller (G) ✍	
☐	Rick Nash ✍	
☐	Taylor Pyatt ✍	
☐	Branko Radivojevic ✍	
☐	Nick Schultz ✍	
☐	Dennis Seidenberg ✍	
☐	Brian Sutherby ✍	
☐	Alexander Svitov ✍	
☐	Henrik Tallinder ✍	
☐	Ossi Väänänen ✍	
☐	Anton Volchenkov ✍	
☐	Mattias Weinhandl ✍	
☐	Stephen Weiss ✍	

2002 - 03 CALDER

Produced by Pacific Trading Cards, this series was released in June 2003.

	Shell Set (100 cards):	**50.00**
	Complete Set (150 cards):	**425.00**
	Common Player:	**.50**
	Description	**Base**
☐	1 Dany Heatley, Atla.	2.00
☐	2 Ilya Kovalchuk, Atla.	2.00
☐	3 Evgeni Nabokov (G), SanJ.	1.00
☐	4 Brad Richards, Tamp.	.50
☐	5 Scott Gomez, NJer.	.50
☐	6 Brad Stuart, SanJ.	.50
☐	7 Chris Drury, Calg.	1.00
☐	8 Marian Hossa, Otta.	2.00
☐	9 Sergei Samsonov, Bost.	1.00
☐	10 Mattias Öhlund, Vanc.	.50
☐	11 Bryan Berard, Bost.	.50
☐	12 Jarome Iginla, Calg.	1.50
☐	13 Daniel Alfredsson, Otta.	1.00
☐	14 Éric Dazé, Chic.	.50
☐	15 Peter Forsberg, Colo.	2.50
☐	16 Martin Brodeur (G), NJer.	3.00
☐	17 Jason Arnott, Dall.	.50
☐	18 Teemu Selänne, SanJ.	1.50
☐	19 Pavel Bure, NYRa.	1.50
☐	20 Nicklas Lidström, Detr.	1.00
☐	21 Ed Belfour (G), Toro.	2.00
☐	22 Sergei Fedorov, Detr.	2.00
☐	23 Mike Modano, Dall.	2.00
☐	24 Brian Leetch, NYRa.	1.00
☐	25 Joe Nieuwendyk, NJer.	.50
☐	26 Luc Robitaille, Detr.	1.50
☐	27 Mario Lemieux, Pitt.	6.00
☐	28 Chris Chelios, Detr.	1.00
☐	29 Steve Yzerman, Detr.	4.50
☐	30 Paul Kariya, Anah.	2.50
☐	31 Joe Thornton, Bost.	2.00
☐	32 Theoren Fleury, Chic.	1.00
☐	33 Milan Hejduk, Colo.	1.50
☐	34 Patrick Roy (G), Colo.	6.00
☐	35 Joe Sakic, Colo.	3.00
☐	36 Marty Turco (G), Dall.	1.00
☐	37 Brett Hull, Detr.	2.00
☐	38 Curtis Joseph (G), Detr.	2.00
☐	39 Brendan Shanahan, Detr.	2.00
☐	40 Mike Comrie, Edmo.	1.50
☐	41 Marian Gaborik, MinW.	2.00
☐	42 Saku Koivu, Mont.	1.50
☐	43 José Théodore (G), Mont.	2.00
☐	44 Alexei Yashin, NYIs.	1.00
☐	45 Alex Kovalev, NYRa.	1.00
☐	46 Eric Lindros, NYRa.	2.00
☐	47 Mark Messier, NYRa.	2.00
☐	48 Tony Amonte, Phil.	1.00
☐	49 Vincent Lecavalier, Tamp.	2.00
☐	50 Mats Sundin, Toro.	2.00
☐	51 Markus Näslund, Vanc.	2.00
☐	52 Jaromir Jagr, Wash.	2.00
☐	53 Dan Snyder, Atla.	.50
☐	54 Lee Goren, Bost.	.50
☐	55 Ivan Huml, Bost.	.50
☐	56 Andrew Raycroft (G), Bost.	.50
☐	57 Ales Kotalik, Buff.	.50
☐	58 Mika Noronen (G), Buff.	.50
☐	59 Henrik Tallinder, Buff.	.50
☐	60 Pavel Brendl, Phil. (Caro.)	.50
☐	61 Jeff Heerema, Caro.	.50
☐	62 Jaroslav Svoboda, Caro.	.50
☐	63 Tyler Arnason, Chic.	.50
☐	64 Riku Hahl, Colo.	.50
☐	65 Vaclav Nedorost, Colo.	.50
☐	66 Niko Kapanen, Dall.	.50
☐	67 Jesse Wallin, Detr.	.50
☐	68 Jason Chimera, Edmo.	.50
☐	69 Jani Rita, Edmo.	.50
☐	70 Raffi Torres, NYIs. (Edmo.)	.50
☐	71 Jaroslav Bednar, Flor.	.50
☐	72 Stephen Weiss, Flor.	.50
☐	73 Joe Corvo, LosA.	.50
☐	74 Kyle Wanvig, MinW.	.50
☐	75 Mathieu Garon (G), Mont.	.50
☐	76 Marcel Hossa, Mont.	.50
☐	77 Jan Lasak (G), Nash.	.50
☐	78 Christian Berglund, NJer.	.50
☐	79 Jiri Bicek, NJer.	.50
☐	80 Michael Rupp, NYIs. (NJer.)	.50
☐	81 Rick DiPietro (G), NYIs.	.50
☐	82 Justin Mapletoft, NYIs.	.50
☐	83 Mattias Weinhandl, NYIs.	.50
☐	84 Jamie Lundmark, NYRa.	.50
☐	85 Ales Pisa, Edmo. (NYRa.)	.50
☐	86 Toni Dahlman, Otta.	.50
☐	87 Éric Chouinard, Phil.	.50
☐	88 Ramzi Abid, Phoe. (Pitt.)	.50
☐	89 Sébastien Caron (G), Pitt.	.50
☐	90 Dan Focht, Phoe. (Pitt.)	.50
☐	91 Barret Jackman, SLou.	.50
☐	92 Justin Papineau, SLou.	.50
☐	93 Jonathan Cheechoo, SanJ.	.50
☐	94 Miikka Kiprusoff (G), SanJ.	.50
☐	95 Vesa Toskala (G), SanJ.	.50
☐	96 Karel Pilar, Toro.	.50
☐	97 Fedor Fedorov, Vanc.	.50
☐	98 Sébastien Charpentier (G), Wash.	.50
☐	99 Joel Kwiatkowski, Wash.	.50
☐	100 Brian Sutherby, Wash.	.50

ROOKIE

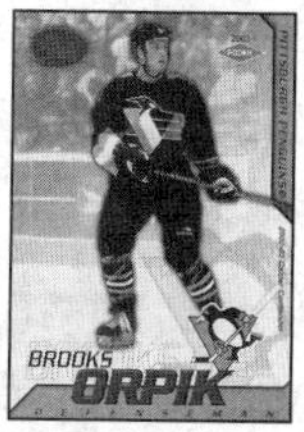

There are two versions for each card 101-150: a gold foil Rookie base insert (#/825) and a silver foil Rookie base parallel (#/299).

	Rookie	S299	G825
☐ ☐	**101 Stanislav Chistov, Anah. RC**	**15.00**	**15.00**
☐ ☐	**102 Kurt Sauer, Anah. RC**	**6.00**	**6.00**
☐ ☐	**103 Alexei Smirnov, Anah. RC**	**6.00**	**6.00**
☐ ☐	**104 Shaone Morrisonn, Bost. RC**	**6.00**	**6.00**
☐ ☐	**105 Kris Vernarsky, Bost. RC**	**6.00**	**6.00**
☐ ☐	**106 Ryan Miller (G), Buff. RC**	**15.00**	**15.00**
☐ ☐	**107 Chuck Kobasew, Calg. RC**	**10.00**	**10.00**
☐ ☐	**108 Jordan Leopold, Calg. RC**	**6.00**	**6.00**
☐ ☐	**109 Ryan Bayda, Caro. RC**	**6.00**	**6.00**
☐ ☐	**110 Igor Radulov, Chic. RC**	**10.00**	**10.00**
☐ ☐	**111 Pascal Leclaire (G), Colu. RC**	**15.00**	**15.00**
☐ ☐	**112 Rick Nash, Colu. RC**	**30.00**	**30.00**
☐ ☐	**113 Jason Bacashihua (G), Dall. RC**	**6.00**	**6.00**
☐ ☐	**114 Steve Ott, Dall. RC**	**6.00**	**6.00**
☐ ☐	**115 Dmitri Bykov, Detr. RC**	**6.00**	**6.00**
☐ ☐	**116 Henrik Zetterberg, Detr. RC**	**30.00**	**30.00**
☐ ☐	**117 Ales Hemsky, Edmo. RC**	**15.00**	**15.00**
☐ ☐	**118 Fernando Pisani, Edmo. RC**	**6.00**	**6.00**
☐ ☐	**119 Jay Bouwmeester, Flor. RC**	**15.00**	**15.00**
☐ ☐	**120 Jared Aulin, LosA. RC**	**6.00**	**6.00**
☐ ☐	**121 Mike Cammalleri, LosA. RC**	**10.00**	**10.00**
☐ ☐	**122 Alexander Frolov, LosA. RC**	**15.00**	**15.00**
☐ ☐	**123 Cristobal Huet (G), LosA. RC**	**6.00**	**6.00**
☐ ☐	**124 Pierre-Marc Bouchard, MinW. RC**	**15.00**	**15.00**
☐ ☐	**125 Stéphane Veilleux, MinW. RC**	**6.00**	**6.00**
☐ ☐	**126 Ron Hainsey, Mont. RC**	**6.00**	**6.00**
☐ ☐	**127 Mike Komisarek, Mont. RC**	**6.00**	**6.00**
☐ ☐	**128 Vernon Fiddler, Nash. RC**	**6.00**	**6.00**
☐ ☐	**129 Adam Hall, Nash. RC**	**6.00**	**6.00**
☐ ☐	**130 Scottie Upshall, Nash. RC**	**10.00**	**10.00**
☐ ☐	**131 Eric Godard, NYIs. RC**	**6.00**	**6.00**
☐ ☐	**132 Ray Emery (G), Otta. RC**	**6.00**	**6.00**
☐ ☐	**133 Jason Spezza, Otta. RC**	**20.00**	**20.00**
☐ ☐	**134 Anton Volchenkov, Otta. RC**	**6.00**	**6.00**
☐ ☐	**135 Dennis Seidenberg, Phil. RC**	**6.00**	**6.00**
☐ ☐	**136 Radovan Somik, Phil. RC**	**6.00**	**6.00**
☐ ☐	**137 Jim Vandermeer, Phil. RC**	**6.00**	**6.00**
☐ ☐	**138 Jeff Taffe, Phoe. RC**	**6.00**	**6.00**
☐ ☐	**139 Brooks Orpik, Pitt. RC**	**6.00**	**6.00**
☐ ☐	**140 Tomas Surovy, Pitt. RC**	**6.00**	**6.00**
☐ ☐	**141 Curtis Sanford (G), SLou. RC**	**6.00**	**6.00**
☐ ☐	**142 Matt Walker, SLou. RC**	**6.00**	**6.00**
☐ ☐	**143 Niko Dimitrakos, SanJ. RC**	**6.00**	**6.00**
☐ ☐	**144 Jim Fahey, SanJ. RC**	**6.00**	**6.00**
☐ ☐	**145 Lynn Loyns, SanJ. RC**	**6.00**	**6.00**
☐ ☐	**146 Alexander Svitov, Tamp. RC**	**10.00**	**10.00**
☐ ☐	**147 Carlo Colaiacovo, Toro. RC**	**6.00**	**6.00**
☐ ☐	**148 Mikael Tellqvist (G), Toro. RC**	**6.00**	**6.00**
☐ ☐	**149 Steve Eminger, Wash. RC**	**6.00**	**6.00**
☐ ☐	**150 Alex Henry, Wash. RC**	**6.00**	**6.00**

CALDER REFLECTIONS

	Insert Set (20 cards):	70.00
	Insert (1:5)	MO
☐	1 Stanislav Chistov, Anah.	5.00
☐	2 Ivan Huml, Bost.	2.00
☐	3 Ales Kotalik, Buff.	4.00

☐	4 Ryan Miller (G), Buff.	4.00
☐	5 Jordan Leopold, Calg.	2.00
☐	6 Tyler Arnason, Chic.	4.00
☐	7 Pascal Leclaire (G), Colu.	4.00
☐	8 Rick Nash, Colu.	8.00
☐	9 Henrik Zetterberg, Detr.	8.00
☐	10 Ales Hemsky, Edmo.	5.00
☐	11 Jay Bouwmeester, Flor.	5.00
☐	12 Stephen Weiss, Flor.	4.00
☐	13 Mike Cammalleri, LosA.	3.00
☐	14 Alexander Frolov, LosA.	4.00
☐	15 Pierre-Marc Bouchard, MinW.	5.00
☐	16 Marcel Hossa, Mont.	4.00
☐	17 Rick DiPietro (G), NYIs.	5.00
☐	18 Jason Spezza, Otta.	6.00
☐	19 Barret Jackman, SLou.	4.00
☐	20 Jonathan Cheechoo, SanJ.	3.00

CHASING GLORY

	Insert Set (10 cards):	45.00
	Insert (1:13)	CG
☐	1 Joe Thornton, Bost.	4.00
☐	2 Peter Forsberg, Colo.	5.00
☐	3 Patrick Roy (G), Colo.	12.00
☐	4 Mike Modano, Dall.	4.00
☐	5 Marty Turco (G), Dall.	2.00
☐	6 Martin Brodeur (G), NJer.	6.00
☐	7 Marian Hossa, Otta.	4.00
☐	8 Mario Lemieux, Pitt.	12.00
☐	9 Ed Belfour (G), Toro.	4.00
☐	10 Markus Näslund, Vanc.	4.00

GAME-WORN JERSEYS

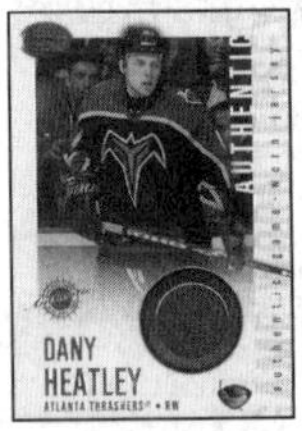

	Insert Set (20 cards):	100.00
	Insert (1:6)	Jers
☐	1 Dany Heatley, Atla. ✂ {*475}	30.00
☐	2 Patrik Stefan, Atla. ✂ {*1000}	10.00
☐	3 Glen Murray, Bost. ✂ {*1000}	10.00
☐	4 Joe Thornton, Bost. ✂ {*1000}	20.00
☐	5 Miroslav Satan, Buff. ✂ {*1000}	10.00
☐	6 Alexei Zhamnov, Chic. ✂ {*475}	10.00
☐	7 Peter Forsberg, Colo. ✂ {*750}	35.00
☐	8 Patrick Roy (G), Colo. ✂ {*750}	75.00
☐	9 Marty Turco (G), Dall. ✂ {*900}	10.00
☐	10 Luc Robitaille, Detr. ✂ {*850}	15.00
☐	11 Olli Jokinen, Flor. ✂ {*1000}	10.00
☐	12 Yanic Perreault, Mont. ✂ {*1000}	10.00
☐	13 Tomas Vokoun (G), Nash. ✂ {*1000}	10.00
☐	14 Rick DiPietro (G), NYIs. ✂ {*1000}	10.00
☐	15 Daniel Alfredsson, Otta. ✂ {*750}	15.00
☐	16 Jason Spezza, Otta. ✂ {*900}	10.00
☐	17 Roman Cechmanek (G), Phil. ✂ {*1000}	10.00
☐	18 Mario Lemieux, Pitt. ✂ {*500}	90.00
☐	19 Valeri Bure, SLou. ✂ {*1000}	10.00
☐	20 Doug Weight, SLou. ✂ {*1000}	10.00
☐	21 Ed Belfour (G), Toro. ✂ {*750}	25.00
☐	22 Mats Sundin, Toro. ✂ {*1000}	20.00
☐	23 Brendan Morrison, Vanc. ✂ {*1000}	10.00
☐	24 Markus Näslund, Vanc. ✂ {*900}	20.00
☐	25 Jaromir Jagr, Wash. ✂ {*1000}	20.00

HARDWARE HEROES

	Insert Set (12 cards):	45.00
	Insert (1:9)	HH
☐	1 Dany Heatley, Atla.	3.00
☐	2 Patrick Roy (G), Colo.	10.00
☐	3 Joe Sakic, Colo.	5.00
☐	4 Brett Hull, Detr.	3.00
☐	5 Nicklas Lidström, Detr.	2.00
☐	6 Steve Yzerman, Detr.	8.00
☐	7 José Théodore (G), Mont.	4.00
☐	8 Eric Lindros, NYRa.	3.00
☐	9 Mark Messier, NYRa.	3.00
☐	10 Mario Lemieux, Pitt.	10.00
☐	11 Ed Belfour (G), Toro.	3.00
☐	12 Jaromir Jagr, Wash.	3.00

HART STOPPERS

	Insert Set (8 cards):	25.00
	Insert (1:13)	HS
☐	1 Joe Thornton, Bost.	4.00
☐	2 Peter Forsberg, Colo.	4.00
☐	3 Patrick Roy (G), Colo.	10.00
☐	4 Mike Modano, Dall.	3.00
☐	5 Marty Turco (G), Dall.	2.00
☐	6 Martin Brodeur (G), NJer.	5.00
☐	7 Marian Hossa, Otta.	3.00
☐	8 Markus Näslund, Vanc.	3.00

2002 - 03 CANADA POST

Produced by Canada Post and printed by Pacific Trading Cards, this series was released in January 2003.

	Complete Set (24 cards):	60.00
	Description	Card
☐	Syl Apps, Toro.	1.50
☐	Jean Béliveau, Mont.	4.00
☐	Mike Bossy, NYIs.	3.00
☐	Raymond Bourque, Bost.	2.00
☐	Bill Durnan, Mont.	1.50
☐	Phil Esposito, Bost.	2.00
☐	Wayne Gretzky, Edmo.	8.00
☐	Glenn Hall, Chic.	2.00
☐	Doug Harvey, Mont.	2.00
☐	Tim Horton, Toro.	2.00
☐	Gordie Howe, Detr.	5.00
☐	Bobby Hull, Chic.	3.00
☐	Red Kelly, Toro.	1.50
☐	Guy Lafleur, Mont.	4.00
☐	Frank Mahovlich, Toro.	2.00
☐	Stan Mikita, Chic.	1.50
☐	Howie Morenz, Mont.	3.00
☐	Bobby Orr, Bost.	8.00
☐	Jacques Plante, Mont.	3.00
☐	Denis Potvin, NYIs.	1.50
☐	Maurice Richard, Mont.	5.00
☐	Serge Savard, Mont.	1.50
☐	Terry Sawchuk, Detr.	4.00
☐	Eddie Shore, Bost.	2.00

AUTOGRAPH

	Insert	Aut.
☐	Jean Béliveau, Mont. ✍	350.00
☐	Glenn Hall, Chic. ✍	200.00
☐	Bobby Hull, Chic. ✍	250.00
☐	Guy Lafleur, Mont. ✍	250.00

2002 - 03 CANADIAN MUSEUM OF CIVILIZATION

When closed, this card measures 12.7 cm x 17.7 cm (5" x 7"). The card reads "Season's greetings and best wishes for a healthy and happy 2003".

	Description	Card
☐	Maurice Richard's 1959-60 jersey	

2002 - 03 CARDSET

Distributed in Finland, this series features past and present players from the Finnish sm-Liiga.

	Series One Set (150 cards):	35.00
	Series Two Set (150 cards):	35.00
	Common Player:	.25
	Description	smL
☐	1 Peter Ahola	.25
☐	2 Mika Alatalo	.50
☐	3 Kristian Antila	.25
☐	4 Frank Banham	.25
☐	5 Jaroslav Bednar	.50
☐	6 Jan Benda	.25
☐	7 Frantisek Bombic	.25
☐	8 Jan Caloun	.25
☐	9 Martin Cech	.25
☐	10 Tomas Chlubna	.25
☐	11 Toni Dahlman	.25
☐	12 Johan Davidsson	.25
☐	13 Tom Draper (G)	.50
☐	14 Tomas Duba	1.00
☐	15 Miika Elomo	.25
☐	16 Mikko Eloranta	.25
☐	17 Vjatsheslav Fandul	.25
☐	18 Theoren Fleury	2.00
☐	19 Janne Grönvall	.25
☐	20 Kari Haakana	.25
☐	21 Niklas Hagman	.50
☐	22 Riku Hahl	.50
☐	23 Jaakko Harikkala	.25
☐	24 Jani Hassinen	.25
☐	25 Timo Hirvonen	.25
☐	26 Sasu Hovi	.25
☐	27 Markku Hurme	.25
☐	28 Ville Immonen	.25
☐	29 Otakar Janecky	.25
☐	30 Olli Jokinen	1.00
☐	31 Martti Järventie	.25
☐	32 Erik Kakko	.25
☐	33 Tomi Kallio	.50
☐	34 Kimmo Kapanen (G)	.25
☐	35 Niko Kapanen	.50
☐	36 Sami Kapanen	1.00
☐	37 Jari Kauppila	.25
☐	38 Markus Ketterer	.50
☐	39 Marko Kiprusoff	.25
☐	40 Miikka Kiprusoff (G)	1.00
☐	41 Tom Koivisto	.25
☐	42 Markus Korhonen	.25
☐	43 Jari Korpisalo	.25
☐	44 Mika Kortelainen	.25
☐	45 Kimmo Koskenkorva	.25
☐	46 Valeri Krykov	.25
☐	47 Kimmo Kuhta	.25
☐	48 Pasi Kuivalainen	.25
☐	49 Jarno Kultanen	.25
☐	50 Mikko Kuparinen	.25
☐	51 Jari Kurri	4.00
☐	52 Jarmo Kuusisto	.25
☐	53 Yuri Kuznetsov	.25
☐	54 Arto Laatikainen	.25
☐	55 Veli-Pekka Laitinen	.25
☐	56 Peter Larsson	.25
☐	57 Mikko Lehtonen	.25
☐	58 Pertti Lehtonen	.25
☐	59 Jari Levonen	.25
☐	60 Brett Lievers	.25
☐	61 Juha Lind	.50
☐	62 Sakari Lindfors	.25
☐	63 Kimmo Lotvonen	.25
☐	64 Jyrki Lumme	.50
☐	65 Petri Lätti	.25
☐	66 Vladimir Machulda	.25
☐	67 Ivan Majesky	.25
☐	68 Olli Malmivaara	.25
☐	69 Jussi Markkanen (G)	.50
☐	70 Kari Martikainen	.25
☐	71 Dale McTavish	.25
☐	72 Sami Mettovaara	.25
☐	73 Antti Miettinen	1.00
☐	74 Niko Mikkola	.25
☐	75 Cory Murphy	.25
☐	76 Jason Muzzatti	.50
☐	77 Tuukka Mäkelä	.25
☐	78 Marko Mäkinen	.25
☐	79 David Nemirovsky	.25
☐	80 Ville Nieminen	.50
☐	81 Antero Niittymäki	4.00
☐	82 Angel Nikolov	.25
☐	83 Janne Niskala	.25
☐	84 Fredrik Norrena	1.00
☐	85 Petteri Nummelin	.50
☐	86 Kai Nurminen	.25
☐	87 Janne Ojanen	.25
☐	88 Mika Oksa	.25
☐	89 Petri Pakaslahti	.25
☐	90 Mikko Peltola	.25
☐	91 Kimmo Peltonen	.25
☐	92 Pasi Peltonen	.25
☐	93 Tomi Pettinen	.25
☐	94 Tuomas Pihlman	1.00
☐	95 Ilkka Pikkarainen	.25
☐	96 Lasse Pirjetä	.25
☐	97 Esa Pirnes	.25
☐	98 Andrei Potaitshuk	.25
☐	99 Pasi Puistola	.25
☐	100 Joni Puurula	.25
☐	101 Timo Pärssinen	.25
☐	102 Bruce Racine	.50
☐	103 Brian Rafalski	.50
☐	104 Jamie Ram (G)	.50
☐	105 Martin Richter	.25
☐	106 Juha Riihijärvi	.25
☐	107 Teemu Riihijärvi	.25
☐	108 Kimmo Rintanen	.25
☐	109 Pavel Rosa	.50
☐	110 Boris Rousson (G)	.50
☐	111 Christian Ruuttu	.50
☐	112 Pasi Saarela	.25
☐	113 Peter Schaefer	.50
☐	114 Markus Seikola	.25
☐	115 Teemu Selänne	3.00
☐	116 Oliver Setzinger	.25
☐	117 Vladimir Sicak	.25
☐	118 Ari-Pekka Siekkinen	.25
☐	119 Toni Sihvonen	.25
☐	120 Mike Stapleton	.25
☐	121 Ari Sulander	1.00
☐	122 Sebastian Sulku	.25
☐	123 Kari Takko (G)	.25
☐	124 Jussi Tarvainen	.25
☐	125 Esa Tikkanen	.50
☐	126 Harri Tikkanen	.25
☐	127 Petr Ton	.25
☐	128 Vesa Toskala (G)	.25
☐	129 Arto Tukio	.25
☐	130 Tommi Turunen	.25
☐	131 Marko Tuulola	.25
☐	132 Markku Tähtinen	.25
☐	133 Antti Törmänen	.25
☐	134 Ville Vahalahti	.25
☐	135 Ari Vallin	.25
☐	136 Petri Varis	.25
☐	137 Timo Vertala	.25
☐	138 Joonas Vihko	.25
☐	139 Mika Viinanen	.25
☐	140 Vesa Viitakoski	.25
☐	141 Tony Virta	.25
☐	142 Tomas Vlasak	.25
☐	143 Pavel Vostrak	.25
☐	144 Vladimir Vujtek	.25
☐	145 Jiri Vykoukal	.25
☐	146 Marek Zidlicky	.25
☐	147 Kari Lehtonen (G)	.25
☐	148 Niklas Bäckström	.25
☐	149 Petri Vehanen	.25
☐	150 Tomas Duba	.25
☐	151 Antti Aalto, Jokerit	.25
☐	152 Teemu Aalto, HPK	.25
☐	153 Ari Ahonen (G), HIFK	.50
☐	154 Rami Alanko, Blues	.25
☐	155 Drew Bannister, Kärpät	.25
☐	156 Aleksander Barkov, Tappara	.25
☐	157 Aki Berg, Suomi	.50
☐	158 Sean Bergenheim, Jokerit	1.00
☐	159 Tom Bissett, Tappara	.25
☐	160 Niklas Bäckström, Kärpät	.25
☐	161 Aigars Cipruss, SaiPa	.25
☐	162 Parris Duffus (G), HIFK	.50
☐	163 Jason Elliott, TPS	.50
☐	164 Teemu Elomo, Blues	.25
☐	165 Jarkko Glad, Ässät	.25
☐	166 Carlo Grünn, HIFK	.25
☐	167 Tuomas Grönman, TPS	.25

168 Juha Gustafsson, Blues	.25
169 Timo Hakanen, Ässät	.25
170 Quinn Hancock, Lukko	.25
171 Markus Helanen, Jokerit	.25
172 Raimo Helminen, Ilves	.50
173 Jukka Hentunen, Jokerit	.25
174 Michael Holmkvist, TPS	.25
175 Antti Hulkkonen, SaiPa	.25
176 Jani Hurme (G), TPS	.50
177 Hannes Hyvönen, HIFK	.25
178 Erik Hämäläinen, Lukko	.25
179 Toni Häppölä, HIFK	.25
180 Juha Ikonen, Blues	.25
181 Jarkko Immonen, JYP	.25
182 Mikko Jokela, SaiPa	.50
183 Jussi Jokinen, Kärpät	.25
184 Timo Jutila, Tappara	.50
185 Lasse Jämsen, Pelicans	.25
186 Joonas Jääskeläinen, Pelicans	.25
187 Matti Kaipainen, Lukko	.25
188 Robert Kantor, HIFK	.25
189 Jere Karalahti, HIFK	.25
190 Marko Kauppinen, TPS	.25
191 Mika Kauppinen, SaiPa	.25
192 Jani Keinänen, Pelicans	.25
193 Max Kenig, HPK	.25
194 Esa Keskinen, TPS	.25
195 Jani Kiviharju, TPS	.25
196 Toni Koivisto, Lukko	.25
197 Mikko Koivu, TPS	.50
198 Saku Koivu, Suomi	3.00
199 Toni Koivunen, Pelicans	.25
200 Tomas Kucharcik, HPK	.25
201 Arto Kuki, Tappara	.25
202 Lasse Kukkonen, Kärpät	.25
203 Juha Kuokkanen, SaiPa	.25
204 Janne Laakkonen, HPK	.25
205 Antti Laaksonen, Suomi	.25
206 Jukka-Pekka Laamanen, Ilves	.25
207 Scott Langkow (G), Ässät	.50
208 Jan Latvala, Pelicans	.25
209 Janne Laukkanen, Suomi	.25
210 Jari Laukkanen, Kärpät	.25
211 Tero Lehterä, HPK	.25
212 Jere Lehtinen, TPS	1.00
213 Mika Lehto, Tappara	.25
214 Kari Lehtonen (G), Suomi	5.00
215 Tero Leinonen, JYP	.25
216 Pauli Levokari, HIFK	.25
217 Joni Lius, TPS	.25
218 Jouni Loponen, TPS	.25
219 Mikko Luoma, Tappara	.25
220 Toni Lydman, HIFK	.50
221 Jyri Marttinen, JYP	.25
222 Ilkka Mikkola, Jokerit	.25
223 Mikko Myllykoski, Kärpät	.25
224 Jere Myllyniemi, Blues	.25
225 Jarmo Myllys (G), Blues	.50
226 Toni Mäkiaho, Tappara	.25
227 Tuukka Mäntylä, Tappara	1.00
228 Tero Määttä, Blues	.25
229 Antti-Jussi Niemi, Jokerit	.25
230 Mika Nieminen, Ilves	.25
231 Janne Niinimaa, Suomi	.50
232 Jesse Niinimäki, Ilves	.25
233 Tuomas Nissinen, Ilves	.25
234 Mika Noronen (G), Tappara	1.50
235 Teppo Numminen, Suomi	1.00
236 Pasi Nurminen (G), Jokerit	.50
237 Michael Nylander, JYP	.50
238 Matti Näätänen, Blues	.25
239 Marko Ojanen, Tappara	.25
240 Marko Palo, HPK	.25
241 Sakari Palsola, Kärpät	.25
242 Jan Pardavy, HPK	.25
243 Timo Peltomaa, Ilves	.25
244 Ville Peltonen, Jokerit	.25
245 Eric Perrin, JYP	.25
246 Jussi Pesonen, Jokerit	.25
247 Pasi Petriläinen, TPS	.25
248 Juha Pitkämäki, JYP	.25
249 Joni Pitkänen, Kärpät	2.00
250 Toni Porkka, Lukko	.25
251 Mika Pyörälä, Kärpät	.25
252 Erkki Rajamäki, HPK	.25
253 Jani Rita, Jokerit	1.00
254 Jarkko Ruutu, Suomi	.50
255 Mikko Ruutu, Jokerit	.25
256 Tuomo Ruutu, HIFK	1.50
257 Mikko Rämö, Pelicans	.25
258 Timo Saarikoski, SaiPa	.25
259 Pasi Saarinen, HIFK	.25
260 Kalle Sahlstedt, TPS	.25
261 Teemu Sainomaa, Pelicans	.25
262 Tony Salmelainen, Ilves	.25
263 Sami Salo, Suomi	.25
264 Timo Salonen, Ässät	.25
265 Tommi Santala, HPK	.25
266 Peter Sarno, Blues	.25
267 Tommi Satosaari, Ilves	.25
268 Steve Shirreffs, Ässät	.25
269 Harri Sillgren, JYP	.25
270 Roman Simicek, HIFK	.25
271 Eero Somervuori, HPK	.25
272 Dave Stathos, HIFK	.25
273 Mika Strömberg, Jokerit	.25
274 Raimo Summanen, TPS	.25
275 Henrik Tallinder, TPS	.25
276 Petr Tenkrat, Kärpät	.50
277 Tim Thomas (G), Kärpät	.50
278 Kimmo Timonen, Suomi	.50
279 Pekka Tirkkonen, SaiPa	.25
280 Hannu Toivonen, HPK	.25
281 Sami Torkki, Lukko	.25
282 Marco Tuokko, TPS	.25
283 Marko Tuomainen, Blues	.25
284 Aki Uusikartano, SaiPa	.25
285 Lubomir Vaic, SaiPa	.25
286 Tomek Valtonen, Jokerit	.25
287 Petri Vehanen, Lukko	.25
288 Samu Wesslin, Ässät	.25
289 Hannu Virta, TPS	.25
290 Antti Virtanen, JYP	.25
291 Jari Viuhkola, Kärpät	.25
292 Roman Vopat, HIFK	.25
293 Jukka Voutilainen, Jokerit	1.00
294 Jyrki Välivaara, Tappara	.25
295 Ossi Väänänen, Jokerit	.50
296 Juha Ylönen, Blues	.50
297 Dave Stathos,	.25
298 Scott Langkow (G)	.50
299 Tero Leinonen,	.25
300 Mika Lehto,	.25

BOUND FOR GLORY

Insert Set (10 cards):

Insert	BG
1 Sean Bergenheim	
2 Jussi Jokinen	
3 Mikko Koivu	
4 Kari Lehtonen (G)	
5 Jesse Niinimäki	
6 Joni Pitkänen	
7 Tuomo Ruutu	
8 Oliver Setzinger	
9 Jussi Timonen	
10 Hannu Toivonen	

BOUND FOR GLORY AUTOGRAPH

Insert Set (10 cards):

Insert	BGAut
1 Sean Bergenheim ✍	
2 Jussi Jokinen ✍	
3 Mikko Koivu ✍	
4 Kari Lehtonen (G) ✍	
5 Jesse Niinimäki ✍	
6 Joni Pitkänen ✍	
7 Tuomo Ruutu ✍	
8 Oliver Setzinger ✍	
9 Jussi Timonen ✍	
10 Hannu Toivonen ✍	

DYNAMIC DUO

Insert Set (10 cards):

Insert	DD
1 M. Koivu / S. Koivu	
2 K. Lehtonen (G) / P. Nurminen (G)	
3 T. Ruutu / S. Kapanen	
4 J. Pitkänen / J. Niinimaa	
5 J. Voutilainen / O. Jokinen	
6 T. Mäntylä / V. Nieminen	
7 T. Pihlman / T. Kallio	
8 T. Duba / J. Hurme (G)	
9 A. Miettinen / N. Kapanen	
10 S. Bergenheim / T. Selänne	

LEHTONEN

Insert Set (3 cards):

Insert	KL
1 Kari Lehtonen (G)	
1 Kari Lehtonen (G)	
1 Kari Lehtonen (G)	

NIMIKIRJOITUSKORTIT

Insert Set (8 cards):

Insert	N
Tomas Duba, SaiPa	
Teemu Elomo, Blues	
Lasse Kukkonen, Kärpät	
Antti Miettinen, HPK	
Janne Niskala, Lukko	
Tuomas Pihlman, JYP	
Joonas Vihko, HIFK	
Jukka Voutilainen, Jokerit	

SOLID GOLD SIX PACK

Insert Set (6 cards):

Insert	SGSP
1 Pasi Nurminen	
2 Janne Niinimaa	
3 Sami Salo	
4 Sami Kapanen	
5 Saku Koivu	
6 Teemu Selänne	

SOLID GOLD SIX PACK

Insert Set (6 cards):

Insert	SGSP
1 Jussi Markkanen	
2 Toni Lydman	
3 Ossi Väänänen	
4 Niklas Hagman	
5 Olli Jokinen	
6 Niko Kapanen	

TROPHY SET

Insert Set (3 cards):

Insert	TS1000
1 Kari Lehtonen (G)	
2 Kari Lehtonen (G)	
3 Kari Lehtonen (G)	

2002 - 03 CHOICE TOP PROSPECTS

Produced by Choice Marketing, this series was released in February 2003.

Complete Set (45 cards): 30.00

Description	Card
Ramzi Abid, Springfield Falcons	2.00
Alex Auld (G), Manitoba Moose	2.00
Jared Aulin, Manchester Monarchs	2.00
Jason Bacashihua, Utah Grizzlies	1.00
Kris Beech, Wilkes-Barre/Scranton Penguins	3.50
Brad Boyes, St. John's Maple Leafs	2.00
Scott Clemmensen, Albany River Rats	1.00
Ty Conklin, Hamilton Bulldogs	2.00
Niko Dimitrakos, Cleveland Barons	.50
Rick DiPietro (G), Bridgeport Sound Tigers	5.50
Micki Dupont, Saint John Flames	1.00
Ray Emery (G), Binghampton Senators	1.00
Shane Endicott, Wilkes-Barre/Scranton Penguins	.50
Garnet Exelby, Chicago Wolves	.50
Jim Fahey, Cleveland Barons	.50
Ron Hainsey, Hamilton Bulldogs	2.00
Darren Haydar, Milwaukee Admirals	.50
Jonathan Hedstrom, Cincinnati Mighty Ducks	.50
Jeff Heerema, Lowell Lock Monsters	1.00
Andy Hilbert, Providence Bruins	2.00
Trent Hunter, Bridgeport Sound Tigers	1.00
Mike Komisarek, Hamilton Bulldogs	2.00
Tomas Kopecky, Grand Rapids Griffins	.50
Pascal Leclaire, Syracuse Crunch	4.50
Guillaume Lefebvre, Philadelphia Phantoms	.50
Michael Leighton (G), Norfolk Admirals	1.00
Roman Lyashenko, Hartford Wolf Pack	.50
Tomas Malec, Lowell Lock Monsters	.50
Ryan Miller (G), Rochester Americans	4.50
Shaone Morrisonn, Providence Bruins	1.00
Filip Novak, San Antonio Rampage	.50
Steve Ott, Utah Grizzlies	2.00
Maxime Ouellet (G), Portland Pirates	4.50
Justin Papineau, Worcester IceCats	1.00
John Pohl, Worcester IceCats	.50
Brandon Reid, Manitoba Moose	2.50
Jani Rita, Hamilton Bulldogs	3.50
Philippe Sauvé, Hershey Bears	2.00
Jason Spezza, Binghampton Senators	7.00
Charlie Stephens, Hershey Bears	.50
Jeff Taffe, Springfield Falcons	2.50
JP Vigier, Chicago Wolves	.50
Kyle Wanvig, Houston Aeros	1.00
Duvie Westcott, Syracuse Crunch	.50
Tomas Zizka, Manchester Monarchs	.50

2002 - 03 CROWN ROYALE

Produced by Pacific Trading Cards, this series was released in February 2003. Cards 1-100 have three versions: the gold hobby base card, the red hobby parallel card, and the silver retail card. Gold hobby and silver retail cards sell for the same price.

Shell Set (100 cards):		100.00
Complete Set (140 cards):	500.00	300.00
Common Player:	1.00	.50
Description	Red	H/R
1 J-S Giguère (G), Anah.	3.00	2.50
2 Paul Kariya, Anah.	5.00	3.50
3 Adam Oates, Anah.	1.00	1.00
4 Dany Heatley, Atla.	3.00	2.50
5 Ilya Kovalchuk, Atla.	3.00	2.50
6 Glen Murray, Bost.	1.00	1.00
7 Sergei Samsonov, Bost.	2.00	1.50
8 Steve Shields (G), Bost.	1.00	.50
9 Joe Thornton, Bost.	4.00	3.00
10 Martin Biron (G), Buff.	1.00	1.00
11 Chris Gratton, Buff.	1.00	.50
12 Miroslav Satan, Buff.	1.00	.50
13 Chris Drury, Calg.	2.00	1.50
14 Jarome Iginla, Calg.	3.00	2.00
15 Roman Turek (G), Calg.	1.00	1.00
16 Rod Brind'Amour, Caro.	1.00	.50
17 Ron Francis, Caro.	2.00	1.50
18 Arturs Irbe (G), Caro.	1.00	1.00
19 Jeff O'Neill, Caro.	1.00	1.00
20 Éric Dazé, Chic.	1.00	1.00
21 Jocelyn Thibault (G), Chic.	1.00	1.00
22 Alexei Zhamnov, Chic.	1.00	.50
23 Peter Forsberg, Colo.	5.00	3.50
24 Milan Hejduk, Colo.	3.00	2.00
25 Patrick Roy (G), Colo.	11.00	7.50
26 Joe Sakic, Colo.	6.00	4.00
27 Andrew Cassels, Colu.	1.00	.50
28 Marc Denis (G), Colu.	1.00	1.00
29 Bill Guerin, Dall.	1.00	1.00
30 Mike Modano, Dall.	3.00	2.50
31 Marty Turco (G), Dall.	2.00	1.50
32 Sergei Fedorov, Detr.	3.00	2.50
33 Brett Hull, Detr.	3.00	2.50
34 Curtis Joseph (G), Detr.	3.00	2.50
35 Nicklas Lidström, Detr.	2.00	1.50
36 Brendan Shanahan, Detr.	3.00	2.50
37 Steve Yzerman, Detr.	9.00	6.00
38 Anson Carter, Edmo.	1.00	1.00
39 Mike Comrie, Edmo.	3.00	2.00
40 Tommy Salo (G), Edmo.	1.00	1.00
41 Ryan Smyth, Edmo.	1.00	1.00
42 Kristian Huselius, Flor.	1.00	.50
43 Roberto Luongo (G), Flor.	3.00	2.00
44 Jason Allison, LosA.	2.00	1.50
45 Zigmund Palffy, LosA.	2.00	1.50
46 Félix Potvin (G), LosA.	2.00	1.50
47 Manny Fernandez (G), MinW.	1.00	1.00
48 Marian Gaborik, MinW.	3.00	2.50
49 Bill Muckalt, MinW.	1.00	.50
50 Jeff Hackett (G), Mont.	1.00	.50
51 Saku Koivu, Mont.	3.00	2.00
52 José Théodore (G), Mont.	4.00	3.00
53 Richard Zednik, Mont.	1.00	1.00
54 Mike Dunham (G), Nash.	1.00	1.00
55 David Legwand, Nash.	1.00	1.00
56 Martin Brodeur (G), NJer.	6.00	4.00
57 Patrik Elias, NJer.	3.00	2.00
58 Scott Gomez, NJer.	1.00	1.00
59 Joe Nieuwendyk, NJer.	1.00	1.00
60 Chris Osgood (G), NYIs.	2.00	1.50
61 Michael Peca, NYIs.	1.00	1.00
62 Alexei Yashin, NYIs.	2.00	1.50
63 Pavel Bure, NYRa.	3.00	2.00
64 Eric Lindros, NYRa.	3.00	2.50
65 Mike Richter (G), NYRa.	1.00	1.00
66 Daniel Alfredsson, Otta.	2.00	1.50
67 Marian Hossa, Otta.	3.00	2.50
68 Patrick Lalime (G), Otta.	2.00	1.50
69 Roman Cechmanek (G), Phil.	1.00	1.00
70 Simon Gagné, Phil.	3.00	2.00
71 John LeClair, Phil.	3.00	2.00
72 Jeremy Roenick, Phil.	3.00	2.00
73 Tony Amonte, Phoe.	2.00	1.50
74 Daniel Brière, Phoe.	1.00	1.00
75 Sean Burke (G), Phoe.	2.00	1.50
76 Johan Hedberg (G), Pitt.	1.00	1.00
77 Alex Kovalev, Pitt.	2.00	1.50
78 Mario Lemieux, Pitt.	11.00	7.50
79 Aleksey Morozov, Pitt.	1.00	.50
80 Pavol Demitra, SLou.	1.00	1.00

☐☐☐	81 Brent Johnson (G), SLou.	1.00	1.00
☐☐☐	82 Keith Tkachuk, SLou.	2.00	1.50
☐☐☐	83 Doug Weight, SLou.	2.00	1.50
☐☐☐	84 Vincent Damphousse, SanJ.	2.00	1.50
☐☐☐	85 Evgeni Nabokov (G), SanJ.	2.00	1.50
☐☐☐	86 Teemu Selänne, SanJ.	3.00	2.00
☐☐☐	87 Nikolai Khabibulin (G), Tamp.	1.00	1.00
☐☐☐	88 Vincent Lecavalier, Tamp.	3.00	2.50
☐☐☐	89 Martin St-Louis, Tamp.	1.00	1.00
☐☐☐	90 Ed Belfour (G), Toro.	3.00	2.50
☐☐☐	91 Trevor Kidd (G), Toro.	1.00	.50
☐☐☐	92 Alexander Mogilny, Toro.	1.00	1.00
☐☐☐	93 Mats Sundin, Toro.	3.00	2.50
☐☐☐	94 Todd Bertuzzi, Vanc.	4.00	3.00
☐☐☐	95 Dan Cloutier (G), Vanc.	1.00	1.00
☐☐☐	96 Brendan Morrison, Vanc.	1.00	.50
☐☐☐	97 Markus Näslund, Vanc.	3.00	2.50
☐☐☐	98 Peter Bondra, Wash.	2.00	1.50
☐☐☐	99 Jaromir Jagr, Wash.	3.00	2.50
☐☐☐	100 Olaf Kölzig (G), Wash.	2.00	1.50

HOBBY ROOKIES

In hobby packs, cards 101-140 are availble in four versions: the gold base insert (#/2299), the red parallel (#/350), the purple parallel (#/799), and the silver retail base insert (1:7 packs). Hobby gold and retail silver cards have similar pricing.

Purple Set (40 cards): 300.00

	Insert	P799	R350	G2299
☐☐☐☐	**101 S. Chistov, Anah. RC**	12	15	10
☐☐☐☐	**102 Martin Gerber (G), Anah. RC**	8	8	4
☐☐☐☐	**103 Alexei Smirnov, Anah. RC**	8	8	5
☐☐☐☐	**104 Tim Thomas (G), Bost. RC**	8	8	4
☐☐☐☐	**105 Ryan Miller (G), Bost. RC**	12	15	10
☐☐☐☐	**106 C. Kobasew, Calg. RC**	8	10	5
☐☐☐☐	**107 Jordan Leopold, Calg. RC**	8	8	5
☐☐☐☐	**108 Rick Nash, Colu. RC**	24	30	20
☐☐☐☐	**109 Lasse Pirjetä, Colu. RC**	8	8	2
☐☐☐☐	**110 Dmitri Bykov, Detr. RC**	8	8	4
☐☐☐☐	**111 H. Zetterberg, Detr. RC**	24	30	20
☐☐☐☐	**112 Kari Haakana, Edmo. RC**	8	8	2
☐☐☐☐	**113 Ales Hemsky, Edmo. RC**	12	15	10
☐☐☐☐	**114 J. Bouwmeester, Flor. RC**	12	15	10
☐☐☐☐	**115 Ivan Majesky, Flor. RC**	8	8	2
☐☐☐☐	**116 M. Cammalleri, LosA. RC**	8	10	5
☐☐☐☐	**117 A. Frolov, LosA. RC**	12	15	10
☐☐☐☐	**118 P-M Bouchard, MinW. RC**	12	15	10
☐☐☐☐	**119 S. Veilleux, MinW. RC**	8	8	2
☐☐☐☐	120 Kyle Wanvig, MinW.	8	8	2
☐☐☐☐	**121 Sylvain Blouin, MinW. RC**	8	8	2
☐☐☐☐	**122 Ron Hainsey, Mont. RC**	8	8	6
☐☐☐☐	**123 Adam Hall, Nash. RC**	8	8	6
☐☐☐☐	**124 Scottie Upshall, Nash. RC**	8	10	5
☐☐☐☐	**125 Ray Schultz, NYIs. RC**	8	8	2
☐☐☐☐	126 Mattias Weinhandl, NYIs.	8	8	2
☐☐☐☐	**127 Jason Spezza, Otta. RC**	18	20	15
☐☐☐☐	**128 A. Volchenkov, Otta. RC**	8	8	4
☐☐☐☐	**129 D. Seidenberg, Phil. RC**	8	8	4
☐☐☐☐	**130 Patrick Sharp, Phil. RC**	8	8	2
☐☐☐☐	**131 Radovan Somik, Phil. RC**	8	8	2
☐☐☐☐	**132 Jeff Taffe, Phoe. RC**	8	8	5
☐☐☐☐	133 Dick Tarnstrom, Pitt.	8	8	2
☐☐☐☐	**134 Tom Koivisto, SLou. RC**	8	8	2
☐☐☐☐	**135 C. Sanford (G), SLou. RC**	8	8	4
☐☐☐☐	**136 Lynn Loyns, SanJ. RC**	8	8	2
☐☐☐☐	**137 A. Svitov, Tamp. RC**	8	10	5
☐☐☐☐	**138 C. Colaiacovo, Toro. RC**	8	8	6
☐☐☐☐	**139 Steve Eminger, Wash. RC**	8	8	4
☐☐☐☐	**140 Alex Henry, Wash. RC**	8	8	2

GAME-WORN DUAL PATCHES

Insert Set (23 cards): 675.00

	Insert	Patch
☐	D. Heatley ✂ / I. Kovalchuk ✂	90.00
☐	M. Biron (G) ✂ / JP. Dumont ✂	20.00
☐	R. Brind'Amour ✂ / E. Cole ✂	20.00
☐	S. Sullivan ✂ / A. Zhamnov ✂	20.00
☐	P. Forsberg ✂ / P. Roy (G) ✂	110.00
☐	M. Hejduk ✂ / J. Sakic ✂	60.00
☐	M. Denis ✂ / R. Klesla ✂	20.00
☐	M. Modano ✂ / P. Turgeon ✂	40.00
☐	L. Robitaille ✂ / S. Fedorov ✂	55.00
☐	T. Salo (G) ✂ / R. Smyth ✂	20.00
☐	V. Bure ✂ / K. Huselius ✂	20.00
☐	B. Smolinski ✂ / A. Deadmarsh ✂	20.00
☐	M. Fernandez (G) ✂ / M. Gaborik ✂	35.00
☐	M. Brodeur (G) ✂ / P. Elias ✂	60.00
☐	M. Peca ✂ / A. Yashin ✂	25.00
☐	M. Richter (G) ✂ / M. Messier ✂	35.00
☐	A. Morozov ✂ / M. Lemieux ✂	80.00
☐	P. Demitra ✂ / K. Tkachuk ✂	25.00
☐	E. Nabokov (G) ✂ / P.Marleau ✂	25.00
☐	N. Khabibulin (G) ✂ / B. Richards ✂	20.00
☐	D. Tucker ✂ / A. Mogilny ✂	20.00
☐	H. Sedin ✂ / D. Sedin ✂	20.00
☐	P. Bondra ✂ / O. Kölzig (G) ✂	30.00

GAME-WORN JERSEYS

Insert Set (25 cards): 325.00

	Insert	Jers
☐	Dany Heatley, Atla. ✂	20.00
☐	Ilya Kovalchuk, Atla. ✂	20.00
☐	Joe Sakic, Colo. ✂	30.00
☐	Geoff Sanderson, Colu. ✂	12.00
☐	Marty Turco (G), Dall. ✂	12.00
☐	Mike Comrie, Edmo. ✂	15.00
☐	Valeri Bure, Flor. ✂	12.00
☐	Zigmund Palffy, LosA. ✂	12.00
☐	José Théodore (G), Mont. ✂	20.00
☐	Martin Brodeur (G), NJer. ✂	30.00
☐	Patrik Elias, NJer. ✂	15.00
☐	Michael Peca, NYIs. ✂	12.00
☐	Brian Leetch, NYRa. ✂	12.00
☐	Martin Havlat, Otta. ✂	12.00
☐	Jeremy Roenick, Phil. ✂	15.00
☐	Mario Lemieux, Pitt. ✂	60.00
☐	Aleksey Morozov, Pitt. ✂	12.00
☐	Chris Pronger, SLou. ✂	12.00
☐	Sergei Varlamov, SLou. ✂	12.00
☐	Owen Nolan, SanJ. ✂	12.00
☐	Fredrik Modin, Tamp. ✂	12.00
☐	Alexander Mogilny, Toro. ✂	12.00
☐	Markus Näslund, Vanc. ✂	20.00
☐	Peter Bondra, Wash. ✂	12.00
☐	Jaromir Jagr, Wash. ✂	20.00

GAME-WORN JERSEYS GOLD

Insert Set (25 cards): 1200.00

	Insert (#/25)	JG25
☐	Peter Bondra, Wash. ✂	45.00
☐	Martin Brodeur (G), NJer. ✂	120.00
☐	Valeri Bure, Flor. ✂	35.00
☐	Mike Comrie, Edmo. ✂	60.00
☐	Patrik Elias, NJer. ✂	60.00
☐	Martin Havlat, Otta. ✂	45.00
☐	Dany Heatley, Atla. ✂	75.00
☐	Jaromir Jagr, Wash. ✂	75.00
☐	Ilya Kovalchuk, Atla. ✂	75.00
☐	Brian Leetch, NYRa. ✂	45.00
☐	Mario Lemieux, Pitt. ✂	225.00
☐	Fredrik Modin, Tamp. ✂	35.00
☐	Alexander Mogilny, Toro. ✂	35.00
☐	Aleksey Morozov, Pitt. ✂	35.00
☐	Markus Näslund, Vanc. ✂	75.00
☐	Owen Nolan, SanJ. ✂	45.00
☐	Zigmund Palffy, LosA. ✂	45.00
☐	Michael Peca, NYIs. ✂	35.00
☐	Chris Pronger, SLou. ✂	45.00
☐	Jeremy Roenick, Phil. ✂	60.00
☐	Joe Sakic, Colo. ✂	120.00
☐	Geoff Sanderson, Colu. ✂	35.00
☐	José Théodore (G), Mont. ✂	90.00
☐	Marty Turco (G), Dall. ✂	45.00
☐	Sergei Varlamov, SLou. ✂	35.00

COATS OF ARMOR

Insert Set (10 cards): 35.00

	Insert (1:8)	CA
☐	1 Patrick Roy (G), Colo.	10.00
☐	2 Marty Turco (G), Dall.	4.00
☐	3 Curtis Joseph (G), Detr.	4.00
☐	4 Roberto Luongo (G), Flor.	4.00
☐	5 José Théodore (G), Mont.	4.00
☐	6 Martin Brodeur (G), NJer.	6.00
☐	7 Mike Richter (G), NYRa.	4.00
☐	8 Patrick Lalime (G), Otta.	4.00
☐	9 Nikolai Khabibulin (G), Tamp.	4.00
☐	10 Ed Belfour (G), Toro.	4.00

LORDS OF THE RINK

Insert Set (20 cards): 60.00

	Insert (1:5)	LR
☐	1 Paul Kariya, Anah.	4.00
☐	2 Dany Heatley, Atla.	3.00
☐	3 Ilya Kovalchuk, Atla.	3.00
☐	4 Joe Thornton, Bost.	4.00
☐	5 Jarome Iginla, Calg.	2.00
☐	6 Peter Forsberg, Colo.	4.00
☐	7 Joe Sakic, Colo.	5.00
☐	8 Mike Modano, Dall.	3.00
☐	9 Brendan Shanahan, Detr.	3.00
☐	10 Steve Yzerman, Detr.	8.00
☐	11 Zigmund Palffy, LosA.	2.00
☐	12 Marian Gaborik, MinW.	3.00
☐	13 Saku Koivu, Mont.	2.00
☐	14 Pavel Bure, NYRa.	2.00
☐	15 Eric Lindros, NYRa.	3.00
☐	16 Mario Lemieux, Pitt.	10.00
☐	17 Teemu Selänne, SanJ.	2.00
☐	18 Vincent Lecavalier, Tamp.	3.00
☐	19 Mats Sundin, Toro.	3.00
☐	20 Jaromir Jagr, Wash.	3.00

ROOKIE ROYALTY

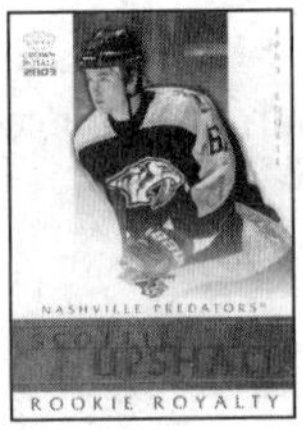

Insert Set (20 cards): 70.00

	Insert (1:5)	RR
☐	1 Stanislav Chistov, Anah.	6.00
☐	2 Martin Gerber (G), Anah.	2.00
☐	3 Alexei Smirnov, Anah.	3.00
☐	4 Ivan Huml, Bost.	2.00
☐	5 Chuck Kobasew, Calg.	4.00
☐	6 Tyler Arnason, Chic.	4.00
☐	7 Rick Nash, Colu.	10.00
☐	8 Jordan Leopold, Calg.	3.00
☐	9 Henrik Zetterberg, Detr.	10.00
☐	10 Ales Hemsky, Edmo.	6.00
☐	11 Jay Bouwmeester, Flor.	6.00
☐	12 Stephen Weiss, Flor.	5.00
☐	13 Alexander Frolov, LosA.	4.00
☐	14 Scottie Upshall, Nash.	4.00
☐	15 Justin Mapletoft, NYIs.	2.00
☐	16 Jamie Lundmark, NYRa.	3.00
☐	17 Jason Spezza, Otta.	8.00
☐	18 Petr Cajanek, SLou.	2.00
☐	19 Jonathan Cheechoo, SanJ.	3.00
☐	20 Alexander Svitov, Tamp.	4.00

ROYAL PORTRAITS

Insert Set (10 cards): 175.00

	Insert (1:45)	RP
☐	1 Paul Kariya, Anah.	15.00
☐	2 Ilya Kovalchuk, Atla.	10.00
☐	3 Patrick Roy (G), Colo.	35.00
☐	4 Joe Sakic, Colo.	20.00
☐	5 Rick Nash, Colu.	40.00
☐	6 Steve Yzerman, Detr.	30.00
☐	7 Martin Brodeur (G), NJer.	20.00
☐	8 Jason Spezza, Otta.	30.00
☐	9 Mario Lemieux, Pitt.	35.00
☐	10 Jaromir Jagr, Wash.	10.00

2002 - 03 ETOPPS

Produced by the Topps Company, this series was released via the Internet site www.eTopps.com.

Complete Set (48 cards):

	Description	eT
☐	1 Jarome Iginla, Calg. {*1668}	
☐	2 Pavel Bure, NYRa. {*1475}	
☐	3 Patrick Roy (G), Colo. {*1500}	
☐	4 Mats Sundin, Toro. {*1320}	
☐	5 Jaromir Jagr, Wash. {*1500}	
☐	6 Martin Brodeur (G), Njer. {*1459}	
☐	7 José Théodore (G), Mont. {*1181}	
☐	8 Nicklas Lidström, Detr. {*1551}	
☐	9 Joe Sakic, Colo. {*1162}	
☐	10 Ilya Kovalchuk, Atla. {*1500}	
☐	11 Mike Modano, Dall. {*922}	
☐	12 Sergei Fedorov, Detr. {*1583}	
☐	13 Pavel Datsyuk, Detr. {*1500}	
☐	14 Saku Koivu, Mont. {*1276}	
☐	15 Peter Forsberg, Colo. {*1240}	
☐	16 Dany Heatley, Atla. {*2580}	
☐	17 Erik Cole, Caro. {*1952}	
☐	18 Mario Lemieux, Pitt. {*2000}	
☐	19 Eric Lindros, NYRa. {*1243}	
☐	20 Patrik Elias, NJer. {*1500}	
☐	21 Steve Yzerman, Detr. {*1000}	
☐	22 Michael Peca, NYIs. {*837}	
☐	23 Todd Bertuzzi, Vanc. {*2000}	
☐	24 Evgeni Nabokov (G), SanJ. {*925}	
☐	25 Paul Kariya, Anah. {*971}	
☐	26 Peter Bondra, Wash. {*1102}	
☐	27 Chris Pronger, SLou. {*1147}	
☐	28 Alexei Yashin, NYIs. {*1133}	
☐	29 Daniel Alfredsson, Otta. {*840}	
☐	30 Teemu Selänne, SanJ. {*949}	
☐	31 Brendan Shanahan, Detr. {*1078}	
☐	32 Brett Hull, Detr. {*1739}	
☐	33 Ron Francis, Caro. {*1063}	
☐	34 Simon Gagné, Phil. {*1500}	
☐	35 Marty Turco (G), Dall. {*1500}	
☐	36 Roberto Luongo (G), Flor. {*918}	
☐	37 Joe Thornton, Bost. {*1500}	
☐	38 Mike Comrie, Edmo. {*1196}	
☐	**39 Rick Nash, Colu. RC {*3000}**	
☐	**40 Stanislav Chistov, Anah. RC {*2000}**	
☐	**41 Henrik Zetterberg, Detr. RC {*3000}**	
☐	**42 Ales Hemsky, Edmo. RC {*2000}**	
☐	**43 Jay Bouwmeester, Flor. RC {*3000}**	
☐	**44 Alexei Smirnov, Anah. RC {*2000}**	
☐	**45 Chuck Kobasew, Calg. RC {*2000}**	
☐	**46 Pierre-Marc Bouchard, MinW. RC {*2000}**	
☐	**47 Jason Spezza, Otta. RC {*2000}**	
☐	**48 Alexander Svitov, Tamp. RC {*2000}**	
☐	49 Marian Gaborik, MinW. {*2000}	
☐	50 Jeremy Roenick, Phil. {*1260}	
☐	51 Olli Jokinen, Flor. {*1260}	
☐	52 Marian Hossa, Otta. {*2000}	
☐	53 Markus Näslund, Vanc. {*2000}	
☐	**54 Ryan Miller (G), Buff. RC {*2000}**	
☐	55 Martin St-Louis, Tamp. {*1489}	
☐	56 Jocelyn Thibault (G), Chic. {*930}	

INTRODUCING

These cards were inserted as decoy cards into Topps Company 2002 - 03 hockey packs.

Insert Set (4 cards):

	Insert	Update
☐	Martin Brodeur (G), NJer.	.20
☐	Pavel Bure, NYRa.	.20
☐	Jarome Iginla, Calg.	.20
☐	Mats Sundin, Toro.	.20

2002 - 03 EXCLUSIVE

Produced by Pacific Trading Cards, this series was released in December 2002. There are two versions for each card 1-175: a regular base card and a Gold parallel. There are three versions for each card 176-192: a regular base card, a Gold parallel, and a hobby-exclusive Blue parallel (listed separately). At last, there are four versions for each card 193-200: a regular retail-exclusive base card, a Gold parallel, a hobby-exclusive Blue parallel (listed separately), and a numbered Autograph hobby-exclusive card (listed separately).

Shell Set (175 cards):			**100.00**
Complete Set (201 cards):		**575.00**	**375.00**
Common Player:		**1.00**	**.50**
	Description	**G**	**Base**
☐☐	1 Jean-Sébastien Giguère (G), Anah.	5.00	2.50
☐☐	2 Paul Kariya, Anah.	7.00	3.50
☐☐	3 Adam Oates, Anah.	2.00	1.00
☐☐	4 Petr Sykora, Anah.	2.00	1.00
☐☐	5 Dany Heatley, Atla.	5.00	2.50
☐☐	6 Milan Hnilicka (G), Atla.	1.00	.50
☐☐	7 Tomi Kallio, Atla.	1.00	.50
☐☐	8 Ilya Kovalchuk, Atla.	5.00	2.50
☐☐	9 Patrik Stefan, Atla.	1.00	.50
☐☐	10 Nick Boynton, Bost.	1.00	.50
☐☐	11 Glen Murray, Bost.	2.00	1.00
☐☐	12 Brian Rolston, Bost.	1.00	.50
☐☐	13 Sergei Samsonov, Bost.	3.00	1.50
☐☐	14 Steve Shields (G), Bost.	1.00	.50
☐☐	15 Joe Thornton, Bost.	6.00	3.00
☐☐	16 Martin Biron (G), Buff.	2.00	1.00
☐☐	17 Tim Connolly, Buff.	2.00	1.00
☐☐	18 Jean-Pierre Dumont, Buff.	1.00	.50
☐☐	19 Mika Noronen (G), Buff.	2.00	1.00
☐☐	20 Miroslav Satan, Buff.	1.00	.50
☐☐	21 Craig Conroy, Calg.	1.00	.50
☐☐	22 Chris Drury, Calg.	3.00	1.50
☐☐	23 Jarome Iginla, Calg.	4.00	2.00
☐☐	24 Roman Turek (G), Calg.	2.00	1.00
☐☐	25 Bates Battaglia, Caro.	1.00	.50
☐☐	26 Rod Brind'Amour, Caro.	1.00	.50
☐☐	27 Erik Cole, Caro.	1.00	.50
☐☐	28 Ron Francis, Caro.	3.00	1.50
☐☐	29 Arturs Irbe (G), Caro.	2.00	1.00
☐☐	30 Sami Kapanen, Caro.	1.00	.50
☐☐	31 Jeff O'Neill, Caro.	2.00	1.00
☐☐	32 Jaroslav Svoboda, Caro.	1.00	.50
☐☐	33 Josef Vasicek, Caro.	1.00	.50
☐☐	34 Mark Bell, Chic.	1.00	.50
☐☐	35 Éric Dazé, Chic.	2.00	1.00
☐☐	36 Theoren Fleury, Chic.	3.00	1.50
☐☐	37 Jocelyn Thibault (G), Chic.	2.00	1.00
☐☐	38 Alexei Zhamnov, Chic.	1.00	.50
☐☐	39 Rob Blake, Colo.	3.00	1.50
☐☐	40 Peter Forsberg, Colo.	7.00	3.50
☐☐	41 Milan Hejduk, Colo.	4.00	2.00
☐☐	42 Dean McAmmond, Colo.	1.00	.50
☐☐	43 Derek Morris, Colo.	1.00	.50
☐☐	44 Steven Reinprecht, Colo.	1.00	.50
☐☐	45 Patrick Roy (G), Colo.	15.00	7.50
☐☐	46 Joe Sakic, Colo.	8.00	4.00
☐☐	47 Alex Tanguay, Colo.	3.00	1.50
☐☐	48 Radim Vrbata, Colo.	1.00	.50
☐☐	49 Andrew Cassels, Colu.	1.00	.50
☐☐	50 Marc Denis (G), Colu.	2.00	1.00
☐☐	51 Rostislav Klesla, Colu.	1.00	.50
☐☐	52 Espen Knutsen, Colu.	1.00	.50
☐☐	53 Ray Whitney, Colu.	1.00	.50
☐☐	54 Jason Arnott, Dall.	2.00	1.00
☐☐	55 Bill Guerin, Dall.	2.00	1.00
☐☐	56 Jere Lehtinen, Dall.	1.00	.50
☐☐	57 Mike Modano, Dall.	5.00	2.50
☐☐	58 Marty Turco (G), Dall.	3.00	1.50
☐☐	59 Pierre Turgeon, Dall.	2.00	1.00
☐☐	60 Chris Chelios, Detr.	3.00	1.50
☐☐	61 Pavel Datsyuk, Detr.	4.00	2.00
☐☐	62 Sergei Fedorov, Detr.	5.00	2.50
☐☐	63 Brett Hull, Detr.	5.00	2.50
☐☐	64 Curtis Joseph (G), Detr.	5.00	2.50
☐☐	65 Nicklas Lidström, Detr.	3.00	1.50
☐☐	66 Luc Robitaille, Detr.	4.00	2.00
☐☐	67 Brendan Shanahan, Detr.	5.00	2.50
☐☐	68 Steve Yzerman, Detr.	12.00	6.00
☐☐	69 Anson Carter, Edmo.	2.00	1.00
☐☐	70 Mike Comrie, Edmo.	4.00	2.00
☐☐	71 Tommy Salo (G), Edmo.	2.00	1.00
☐☐	72 Jason Smith, Edmo.	1.00	.50
☐☐	73 Ryan Smyth, Edmo.	2.00	1.00
☐☐	74 Mike York, Edmo.	1.00	.50
☐☐	75 Valeri Bure, Flor.	1.00	.50
☐☐	76 Kristian Huselius, Flor.	1.00	.50
☐☐	77 Roberto Luongo (G), Flor.	4.00	2.00
☐☐	78 Stephen Weiss, Flor.	2.00	1.00
☐☐	79 Jason Allison, LosA.	3.00	1.50
☐☐	80 Adam Deadmarsh, LosA.	1.00	.50
☐☐	81 Zigmund Palffy, LosA.	3.00	1.50
☐☐	82 Félix Potvin (G), LosA.	3.00	1.50
☐☐	83 Bryan Smolinski, LosA.	1.00	.50
☐☐	84 Andrew Brunette, MinW.	1.00	.50
☐☐	85 Pascal Dupuis, MinW.	1.00	.50
☐☐	86 Manny Fernandez (G), MinW.	2.00	1.00
☐☐	87 Marian Gaborik, MinW.	5.00	2.50
☐☐	88 Cliff Ronning, MinW.	1.00	.50
☐☐	89 Mariusz Czerkawski, Mont.	1.00	.50
☐☐	90 Marcel Hossa, Mont.	2.00	1.00
☐☐	91 Saku Koivu, Mont.	4.00	2.00
☐☐	92 Yanic Perreault, Mont.	1.00	.50
☐☐	93 Oleg Petrov, Mont.	1.00	.50
☐☐	94 José Théodore (G), Mont.	6.00	3.00
☐☐	95 Richard Zednik, Mont.	2.00	1.00
☐☐	96 Denis Arkhipov, Nash.	1.00	.50
☐☐	97 Mike Dunham (G), Nash.	2.00	1.00
☐☐	98 Scott Hartnell, Nash.	1.00	.50
☐☐	99 Greg Johnson, Nash.	1.00	.50
☐☐	100 David Legwand, Nash.	2.00	1.00
☐☐	101 Christian Berglund, NJer.	1.00	.50
☐☐	102 Martin Brodeur (G), NJer.	8.00	4.00
☐☐	103 Patrik Elias, NJer.	4.00	2.00
☐☐	104 Jeff Friesen, NJer.	1.00	.50
☐☐	105 Joe Nieuwendyk, NJer.	2.00	1.00
☐☐	106 Rick DiPietro (G), NYIs.	2.00	1.00
☐☐	107 Brad Isbister, NYIs.	1.00	.50
☐☐	108 Chris Osgood (G), NYIs.	3.00	1.50
☐☐	109 Mark Parrish, NYIs.	2.00	1.00
☐☐	110 Michael Peca, NYIs.	2.00	1.00
☐☐	111 Alexei Yashin, NYIs.	3.00	1.50
☐☐	112 Dan Blackburn (G), NYRa.	2.00	1.00
☐☐	113 Pavel Bure, NYRa.	4.00	2.00
☐☐	114 Bobby Holik, NYRa.	1.00	.50
☐☐	115 Brian Leetch, NYRa.	3.00	1.50
☐☐	116 Eric Lindros, NYRa.	5.00	2.50
☐☐	117 Mark Messier, NYRa.	5.00	2.50
☐☐	118 Mike Richter (G), NYRa.	2.00	1.00
☐☐	119 Daniel Alfredsson, Otta.	3.00	1.50
☐☐	120 Radek Bonk, Otta.	1.00	.50
☐☐	121 Martin Havlat, Otta.	3.00	1.50
☐☐	122 Marian Hossa, Otta.	5.00	2.50
☐☐	123 Patrick Lalime (G), Otta.	3.00	1.50
☐☐	124 Pavel Brendl, Phil.	1.00	.50
☐☐	125 Roman Cechmanek (G), Phil.	2.00	1.00
☐☐	126 Simon Gagné, Phil.	4.00	2.00
☐☐	127 John LeClair, Phil.	4.00	2.00
☐☐	128 Mark Recchi, Phil.	2.00	1.00
☐☐	129 Jeremy Roenick, Phil.	4.00	2.00
☐☐	130 Tony Amonte, Phoe.	3.00	1.50
☐☐	131 Brian Boucher (G), Phoe.	1.00	.50
☐☐	132 Daniel Brière, Phoe.	2.00	1.00
☐☐	133 Sean Burke (G), Phoe.	3.00	1.50
☐☐	134 Krys Kolanos, Phoe.	1.00	.50
☐☐	135 Daymond Langkow, Phoe.	1.00	.50
☐☐	136 Johan Hedberg (G), Pitt.	2.00	1.00
☐☐	137 Alex Kovalev, Pitt.	3.00	1.50
☐☐	138 Mario Lemieux, Pitt.	15.00	7.50
☐☐	139 Aleksey Morozov, Pitt.	1.00	.50
☐☐	140 Martin Straka, Pitt.	1.00	.50
☐☐	141 Pavol Demitra, SLou.	2.00	1.00
☐☐	142 Barret Jackman, SLou.	2.00	1.00
☐☐	143 Brent Johnson (G), SLou.	2.00	1.00
☐☐	144 Al MacInnis, SLou.	2.00	1.00
☐☐	145 Chris Pronger, SLou.	3.00	1.50
☐☐	146 Keith Tkachuk, SLou.	3.00	1.50
☐☐	147 Doug Weight, SLou.	3.00	1.50
☐☐	148 Vincent Damphousse, SanJ.	3.00	1.50
☐☐	149 Patrick Marleau, SanJ.	2.00	1.00
☐☐	150 Evgeni Nabokov (G), SanJ.	3.00	1.50
☐☐	151 Owen Nolan, SanJ.	3.00	1.50
☐☐	152 Teemu Selänne, SanJ.	4.00	2.00
☐☐	153 Scott Thornton, SanJ.	1.00	.50
☐☐	154 Dave Andreychuk, Tamp.	1.00	.50
☐☐	155 Nikolai Khabibulin (G), Tamp.	2.00	1.00
☐☐	156 Vincent Lecavalier, Tamp.	5.00	2.50
☐☐	157 Brad Richards, Tamp.	2.00	1.00
☐☐	158 Shane Willis, Tamp.	1.00	.50
☐☐	159 Ed Belfour (G), Toro.	5.00	2.50
☐☐	160 Alyn McCauley, Toro.	1.00	.50
☐☐	161 Alexander Mogilny, Toro.	2.00	1.00
☐☐	162 Gary Roberts, Toro.	2.00	1.00
☐☐	163 Mats Sundin, Toro.	5.00	2.50
☐☐	164 Darcy Tucker, Toro.	1.00	.50
☐☐	165 Todd Bertuzzi, Vanc.	6.00	3.00
☐☐	166 Dan Cloutier (G), Vanc.	2.00	1.00
☐☐	167 Ed Jovanovski, Vanc.	2.00	1.00
☐☐	168 Brendan Morrison, Vanc.	1.00	.50
☐☐	169 Markus Näslund, Vanc.	5.00	2.50
☐☐	170 Peter Bondra, Wash.	3.00	1.50
☐☐	171 Sergei Gonchar, Wash.	1.00	.50
☐☐	172 Jaromir Jagr, Wash.	5.00	2.50
☐☐	173 Olaf Kölzig (G), Wash.	3.00	1.50
☐☐	174 Robert Lang, Wash.	1.00	.50
☐☐	175 Dainius Zubrus, Wash.	1.00	.50

ROOKIE

	Rookie	**Gold**	**R**
☐☐	**176 Martin Gerber (G), Anah. RC**	**5.00**	**4.00**
☐☐	**177 Dmitri Bykov, Detr. RC**	**5.00**	**4.00**
☐☐	**178 Ales Hemsky, Edmo. RC**	**15.00**	**12.00**
☐☐	**179 Alex Henry, Edmo. RC**	**3.00**	**3.00**
☐☐	**179 Jason Spezza, Otta. RC (*)**	**35.00**	**75.00**
☐☐	**180 Pierre-Marc Bouchard, MinW. RC**	**15.00**	**12.00**
☐☐	**181 Ron Hainsey, Mont. RC**	**5.00**	**6.00**
☐☐	**182 Adam Hall, Nash. RC**	**5.00**	**6.00**
☐☐	**183 Scottie Upshall, Nash. RC**	**10.00**	**8.00**
☐☐	184 Mike Danton, NJer.	2.00	3.00
☐☐	185 Jamie Lundmark, NYRa.	5.00	3.00
☐☐	**186 Anton Volchenkov, Otta. RC**	**5.00**	**4.00**
☐☐	**187 Dennis Seidenberg, Phil. RC**	**5.00**	**4.00**
☐☐	**188 Patrick Sharp, Phil. RC**	**3.00**	**3.00**
☐☐	189 Petr Cajanek, SLou.	2.00	3.00
☐☐	190 Jonathan Cheechoo, SanJ.	2.00	3.00
☐☐	191 Fedor Fedorov, Vanc.	2.00	3.00
☐☐	**192 Steve Eminger, Wash. RC**	**5.00**	**4.00**
☐☐	**193 Stanislav Chistov, Anah. RC**	**15.00**	**10.00**
☐☐	**194 Alexei Smirnov, Anah. RC**	**5.00**	**6.00**
☐☐	**195 Chuck Kobasew, Calg. RC**	**10.00**	**8.00**
☐☐	**196 Rick Nash, Colu. RC**	**35.00**	**20.00**
☐☐	**197 Henrik Zetterberg, Detr. RC**	**35.00**	**20.00**
☐☐	**198 Jay Bouwmeester, Flor. RC**	**15.00**	**12.00**
☐☐	**199 Alexander Frolov, LosA. RC**	**15.00**	**10.00**
☐☐	**200 Alexander Svitov, Tamp. RC**	**10.00**	**8.00**

ROOKIE AUTOGRAPH

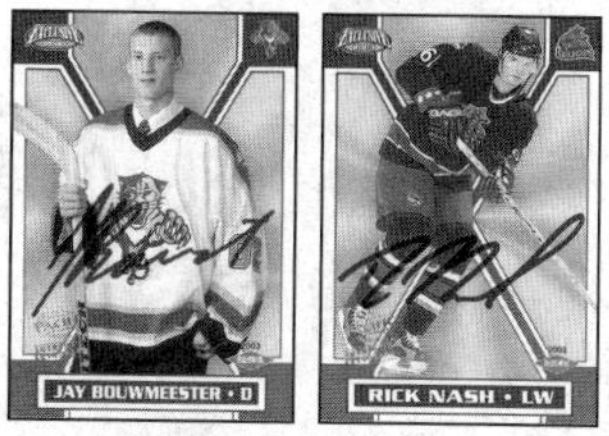

	Insert (#/1000)	**A1000**
☐	**193 Stanislav Chistov, Anah. RC** ✍	**60.00**
☐	**194 Alexei Smirnov, Anah. RC** ✍	**30.00**
☐	**195 Chuck Kobasew, Calg. RC** ✍	**40.00**
☐	**196 Rick Nash, Colu. RC** ✍	**100.00**
☐	**197 Henrik Zetterberg, Detr. RC** ✍	**120.00**
☐	**198 Jay Bouwmeester, Flor. RC** ✍	**60.00**
☐	**199 Alexander Frolov, LosA. RC** ✍	**50.00**
☐	**200 Alexander Svitov, Tamp. RC** ✍	**40.00**

BLUE

Insert Set (25 cards):		**175.00**
	Insert (#/699)	**B699**
☐	**176 Martin Gerber (G), Anah. RC**	**5.00**
☐	**177 Dmitri Bykov, Detr. RC**	**5.00**
☐	**178 Ales Hemsky, Edmo. RC**	**15.00**
☐	**179 Alex Henry, Edmo. RC**	**5.00**
☐	**180 Pierre-Marc Bouchard, MinW. RC**	**15.00**
☐	**181 Ron Hainsey, Mont. RC**	**5.00**
☐	**182 Adam Hall, Nash. RC**	**5.00**
☐	**183 Scottie Upshall, Nash. RC**	**10.00**
☐	184 Mike Danton, NJer.	5.00
☐	185 Jamie Lundmark, NYRa.	5.00
☐	**186 Anton Volchenkov, Otta. RC**	**5.00**
☐	**187 Dennis Seidenberg, Phil. RC**	**5.00**
☐	**188 Patrick Sharp, Phil. RC**	**5.00**
☐	189 Petr Cajanek, SLou.	5.00
☐	190 Jonathan Cheechoo, SanJ.	5.00
☐	191 Fedor Fedorov, Vanc.	5.00
☐	**192 Steve Eminger, Wash. RC**	**5.00**
☐	**193 Stanislav Chistov, Anah. RC**	**15.00**
☐	**194 Alexei Smirnov, Anah. RC**	**5.00**
☐	**195 Chuck Kobasew, Calg. RC**	**10.00**
☐	**196 Rick Nash, Colu. RC**	**30.00**
☐	**197 Henrik Zetterberg, Detr. RC**	**30.00**
☐	**198 Jay Bouwmeester, Flor. RC**	**15.00**
☐	**199 Alexander Frolov, LosA. RC**	**15.00**
☐	**200 Alexander Svitov, Tamp. RC**	**10.00**

AUTHENTIC GAME-WORN JERSEY

Insert Set (25 cards):		**275.00**
	Insert	**Jers**
☐	1 Tomi Kallio, Atla. ✂ {*1000}	10.00
☐	2 Joe Thornton, Bost. ✂ {*500}	30.00
☐	3 Miroslav Satan, Buff. ✂ {*1000}	10.00
☐	4 Theoren Fleury, NYRa. ✂ {*950}	10.00
☐	5 Milan Hejduk, Colo. ✂ {*500}	20.00
☐	6 Pierre Turgeon, Dall. ✂ {*500}	10.00
☐	7 Sergei Fedorov, Detr. ✂ {*500}	25.00
☐	8 Nicklas Lidström, Detr. ✂ {*1000}	10.00
☐	9 Tommy Salo (G), Edmo. ✂ {*1000}	10.00
☐	10 Kristian Huselius, Flor. ✂ {*1000}	10.00
☐	11 Roberto Luongo (G), Flor. ✂ {*500}	20.00
☐	12 Bryan Smolinski, LosA. ✂ {*1000}	10.00
☐	13 Manny Fernandez (G), MinW. ✂ {*500}	10.00
☐	14 Mariusz Czerkawski, NYIs. ✂ {*700}	10.00
☐	15 David Legwand, Nash. ✂ {*1000}	10.00
☐	16 Bobby Holik, NJer. ✂ {*175}	10.00
☐	17 Eric Lindros, NYRa. ✂ {*500}	25.00
☐	18 Marian Hossa, Otta. ✂ {*500}	25.00
☐	19 Michal Handzus, Phil. ✂ {*1000}	10.00
☐	20 Alex Kovalev, Pitt. ✂ {*150}	30.00
☐	21 Keith Tkachuk, SLou. ✂ {*1000}	10.00
☐	22 Patrick Marleau, SanJ. ✂ {*1000}	10.00
☐	23 Brad Richards, Tamp. ✂ {*1000}	10.00
☐	24 Mats Sundin, Toro. ✂ {*1000} Blue	20.00
☐	25 Olaf Kölzig (G), Wash. ✂ {*1000}	10.00

AUTHENTIC GAME-WORN JERSEY GOLD

Insert Set (25 cards):		**900.00**
	Insert (#/25)	**JG**
☐	1 Tomi Kallio, Atla. ✂	30.00
☐	2 Joe Thornton, Bost. ✂	90.00
☐	3 Miroslav Satan, Buff. ✂	30.00
☐	4 Theoren Fleury, NYRa. ✂	45.00
☐	5 Milan Hejduk, Colo. ✂	60.00
☐	6 Pierre Turgeon, Dall. ✂	30.00
☐	7 Sergei Fedorov, Detr. ✂	75.00
☐	8 Nicklas Lidström, Detr. ✂	45.00
☐	9 Tommy Salo (G), Edmo. ✂	30.00
☐	10 Kristian Huselius, Flor. ✂	30.00
☐	11 Roberto Luongo (G), Flor. ✂	60.00
☐	12 Bryan Smolinski, LosA. ✂	30.00
☐	13 Manny Fernandez (G), MinW. ✂	30.00
☐	14 Mariusz Czerkawski, NYIs. ✂	30.00
☐	15 David Legwand, Nash. ✂	30.00
☐	16 Bobby Holik, NJer. ✂	30.00
☐	17 Eric Lindros, NYRa. ✂	75.00
☐	18 Marian Hossa, Otta. ✂	75.00
☐	19 Michal Handzus, Phil. ✂	30.00
☐	20 Alex Kovalev, Pitt. ✂	45.00
☐	21 Keith Tkachuk, SLou. ✂	45.00
☐	22 Patrick Marleau, SanJ. ✂	35.00
☐	23 Brad Richards, Tamp. ✂	35.00
☐	24 Mats Sundin, Toro. ✂	75.00
☐	25 Olaf Kölzig (G), Wash. ✂	45.00

DESTINED FOR GREATNESS

Insert Set (10 cards):		**25.00**
	Insert (1:11)	**DG**
☐	1 Stanislav Chistov, Anah.	3.00
☐	2 Dany Heatley, Atla.	5.00
☐	3 Ilya Kovalchuk, Atla.	5.00
☐	4 Ivan Huml, Bost.	2.00
☐	5 Rick Nash, Colu.	9.00
☐	6 Pavel Datsyuk, Detr.	4.00
☐	7 Kristian Huselius, Flor.	2.00
☐	8 Stephen Weiss, Flor.	2.00
☐	9 Jamie Lundmark, NYRa.	2.00
☐	10 Jonathan Cheechoo, SanJ.	2.00

ETCHED IN STONE

Insert Set (10 cards):		**65.00**
	Insert (1:21)	**MD**
☐	1 Paul Kariya, Anah.	7.00
☐	2 Ron Francis, Caro.	3.00
☐	3 Patrick Roy (G), Colo.	15.00
☐	4 Joe Sakic, Colo.	8.00
☐	5 Brett Hull, Detr.	5.00
☐	6 Steve Yzerman, Detr.	12.00
☐	7 Martin Brodeur (G), NJer.	8.00
☐	8 Eric Lindros, NYRa.	5.00
☐	9 Mario Lemieux, Pitt.	15.00
☐	10 Jaromir Jagr, Wash.	5.00

EXCLUSIVE ADVANTAGE

Insert Set (15 cards):		**25.00**
	Insert (1:6)	**EA**
☐	1 Jean-Sébastien Giguère (G), Anah.	2.00
☐	2 Roman Turek (G), Calg.	2.00
☐	3 Arturs Irbe (G), Caro.	2.00
☐	4 Patrick Roy (G), Colo.	6.00
☐	5 Marc Denis (G), Colu.	2.00

☐ 6 Marty Turco (G), Dall. 2.00
☐ 7 Curtis Joseph (G), Detr. 2.00
☐ 8 Roberto Luongo (G), Flor. 2.00
☐ 9 Félix Potvin (G), LosA. 2.00
☐ 10 José Théodore (G), Mont. 2.00
☐ 11 Martin Brodeur (G), NJer. 3.00
☐ 12 Mike Richter (G), NYRa. 2.00
☐ 13 Brent Johnson (G), SLou. 2.00
☐ 14 Evgeni Nabokov (G), SanJ. 2.00
☐ 15 Ed Belfour (G), Dall. 2.00

GREAT EXPECTATIONS

Insert Set (15 cards): **25.00**
Insert (1:6) **GE**
☐ 1 Dany Heatley, Atla. 3.00
☐ 2 Ilya Kovalchuk, Atla. 3.00
☐ 3 Ivan Huml, Bost. 2.00
☐ 4 Erik Cole, Caro. 2.00
☐ 5 Radim Vrbata, Colo. 2.00
☐ 6 Pavel Datsyuk, Detr. 2.00
☐ 7 Mike Comrie, Edmo. 2.00
☐ 8 Kristian Huselius, Flor. 2.00
☐ 9 Stephen Weiss, Flor. 2.00
☐ 10 Marian Gaborik, MinW. 3.00
☐ 11 Marcel Hossa, Mont. 2.00
☐ 12 Rick DiPietro (G), NYIs. 2.00
☐ 13 Dan Blackburn (G), NYRa. 2.00
☐ 14 Krys Kolanos, Phoe. 2.00
☐ 15 Barret Jackman, SLou. 2.00

MAXIMUM OVERDRIVE

Insert Set (20 cards): **25.00**
Insert (1:6) **MO**
☐ 1 Paul Kariya, Anah. 3.00
☐ 2 Dany Heatley, Atla. 2.00
☐ 3 Ilya Kovalchuk, Atla. 2.00
☐ 4 Joe Thornton, Bost. 3.00
☐ 5 Jarome Iginla, Calg. 2.00
☐ 6 Peter Forsberg, Colo. 3.00
☐ 7 Joe Sakic, Colo. 4.00
☐ 8 Mike Modano, Dall. 2.00
☐ 9 Sergei Fedorov, Detr. 2.00
☐ 10 Steve Yzerman, Detr. 6.00
☐ 11 Saku Koivu, Mont. 2.00
☐ 12 Patrik Elias, NJer. 2.00
☐ 13 Alexei Yashin, NYIs. 1.50
☐ 14 Pavel Bure, NYRa. 2.00
☐ 15 Simon Gagné, Phil. 2.00
☐ 16 Mario Lemieux, Pitt. 7.00
☐ 17 Teemu Selänne, SanJ. 2.00
☐ 18 Mats Sundin, Toro. 2.00
☐ 19 Markus Näslund, Vanc. 2.00
☐ 20 Jaromir Jagr, Wash. 2.00

2002 - 03 FIRST EDITION

Produced by In The Game, this series was released in August 2002.

Complete Set (450 cards): **150.00**
Shell Set (400 cards): **125.00**
Common Player: **.30**
Description **FE**
☐ 1 Mario Lemieux, Pitt. 4.50
☐ 2 Sergei Gonchar, Wash. .30

☐ 3 Brian Leetch, NYRa. .50
☐ 4 Félix Potvin (G), LosA. .50
☐ 5 Sandis Ozolinsh, Flor. .30
☐ 6 Steven Reinprecht, Colo. .30
☐ 7 Byron Dafoe (G), Bost. .50
☐ 8 Mark Bell, Chic. .30
☐ 9 Jeff O'Neill, Caro. .50
☐ 10 Sean Burke (G), Phoe. .50
☐ 11 Darcy Tucker, Toro. .30
☐ 12 Scott Stevens, NJer. .50
☐ 13 David Aebischer (G), Colo. .30
☐ 14 Jocelyn Thibault (G), Chic. .50
☐ 15 Radek Bonk, Otta. .30
☐ 16 Milan Hejduk, Colo. 1.00
☐ 17 Zigmund Palffy, LosA. .50
☐ 18 Luc Robitaille, Detr. 1.00
☐ 19 Tomas Kaberle, Toro. .30
☐ 20 Rostislav Klesla, Colu. .30
☐ 21 Alexei Zhamnov, Chic. .30
☐ 22 Ron Francis, Caro. .50
☐ 23 Mike Fisher, Otta. .30
☐ 24 Dany Heatley, Atla. 1.50
☐ 25 Kyle McLaren, Bost. .30
☐ 26 Doug Weight, SLou. .50
☐ 27 Henrik Sedin, Vanc. .50
☐ 28 Roman Turek (G), Calg. .50
☐ 29 Adam Deadmarsh, LosA. .30
☐ 30 Sami Kapanen, Caro. .30
☐ 31 Sergei Samsonov, Bost. .50
☐ 32 Kristian Huselius, Flor. .30
☐ 33 Dmitry Yushkevich, Toro. .30
☐ 34 Patrik Elias, NJer. 1.00
☐ 35 Nick Boynton, Bost. .30
☐ 36 Martin Biron (G), Buff. .50
☐ 37 Brad Richards, Tamp. .50
☐ 38 Alyn McCauley, Toro. .30
☐ 39 Daniel Sedin, Vanc. .50
☐ 40 Teppo Numminen, Phoe. .30
☐ 41 Luke Richardson, Phil. .30
☐ 42 Manny Fernandez (G), MinW. .50
☐ 43 Vincent Lecavalier, Tamp. 1.50
☐ 44 Mattias Öhlund, Vanc. .30
☐ 45 Milan Kraft, Pitt. .30
☐ 46 Mike Dunham (G), Nash. .50
☐ 47 Derian Hatcher, Dall. .30
☐ 48 Oleg Tverdovsky, Anah. .30
☐ 49 Shane Doan, Phoe. .30
☐ 50 Martin Skoula, Colo. .30
☐ 51 John LeClair, Phil. 1.00
☐ 52 Tommy Salo (G), Edmo. .50
☐ 53 Miroslav Satan, Buff. .30
☐ 54 Bryan Berard, NYRa. .30
☐ 55 Roman Cechmanek (G), Phil. .50
☐ 56 Aleksey Morozov, Pitt. .30
☐ 57 Jean-Sébastien Giguère (G), Anah. 1.50
☐ 58 Pierre Turgeon, Dall. .50
☐ 59 Martin Straka, Pitt. .30
☐ 60 Stéphane Yelle, Colo. .30
☐ 61 Marc Savard, Calg. .30
☐ 62 Sergei Zubov, Dall. .30
☐ 63 Jeff Friesen, Anah. .30
☐ 64 Daniel Brière, Phoe. .50
☐ 65 Patrik Stefan, Atla. .30
☐ 66 Pavol Demitra, SLou. .50
☐ 67 Radek Dvorak, NYRa. .30
☐ 68 Marty Turco (G), Dall. .50
☐ 69 Keith Tkachuk, SLou. .50
☐ 70 Maxim Afinogenov, Buff. .50
☐ 71 Mika Noronen (G), Buff. .50
☐ 72 Evgeni Nabokov (G), SanJ. .50
☐ 73 Todd Bertuzzi, Vanc. 1.50
☐ 74 Valeri Bure, Flor. .30
☐ 75 Marian Hossa, Otta. 1.50
☐ 76 J.P. Dumont, Buff. .30
☐ 77 Niklas Sundström, SanJ. .30
☐ 78 Éric Dazé, Chic. .50
☐ 79 Brian Boucher, Phil. .30
☐ 80 Nikolai Khabibulin (G), Tamp. .50
☐ 81 Darren McCarty, Detr. .30
☐ 82 Pavel Brendl, Phil. .30
☐ 83 Mark Recchi, Phil. .50
☐ 84 Dan Cloutier (G), Vanc. .50
☐ 85 Manny Legacé (G), Detr. .30
☐ 86 Keith Primeau, Phil. .50
☐ 87 Alex Tanguay, Colo. .50
☐ 88 Ed Jovanovski, Vanc. .50
☐ 89 Roberto Luongo (G), Flor. 1.00
☐ 90 Andreas Johansson, NYRa. .30
☐ 91 Steve Shields (G), Anah. .30
☐ 92 Saku Koivu, Mont. 1.00
☐ 93 Chris Drury, Colo. .50
☐ 94 Olaf Kölzig (G), Wash. .50
☐ 95 Jan Hrdina, Pitt. .30
☐ 96 Ivan Novoseltsev, Flor. .30
☐ 97 Kenny Jönsson, NYIs. .30
☐ 98 Martin Havlat, Otta. .50
☐ 99 Scott Niedermayer, NJer. .30
☐ 100 Chris Phillips, Otta. .30
☐ 101 Tony Amonte, Chic. .50
☐ 102 Alexander Mogilny, Toro. .50
☐ 103 Chris Pronger, SLou. .50
☐ 104 Chris Gratton, Buff. .30
☐ 105 Sergei Fedorov, Detr. 1.50
☐ 106 David Legwand, Nash. .50
☐ 107 Ron Tugnutt (G), Colu. .50
☐ 108 Steve McCarthy, Chic. .30
☐ 109 Brian Rolston, Bost. .30
☐ 110 Bobby Holik, NJer. .30
☐ 111 Darryl Sydor, Dall. .30
☐ 112 Steve Sullivan, Chic. .30
☐ 113 Toby Petersen, Pitt. .30
☐ 114 Scott Gomez, NJer. .50
☐ 115 Adam Foote, Colo. .30
☐ 116 Rob Niedermayer, Calg. .30
☐ 117 Arturs Irbe (G), Caro. .50
☐ 118 Al MacInnis, SLou. .50
☐ 119 Jeff Hackett (G), Mont. .30
☐ 120 Pavel Bure, NYRa. 1.00
☐ 121 Patrick Lalime (G), Otta. .50
☐ 122 Vincent Damphousse, SanJ. .50
☐ 123 Steve Passmore (G), Chic. .30
☐ 124 Simon Gagné, Phil. 1.00
☐ 125 Shawn McEachern, Otta. .30
☐ 126 Bryan McCabe, Toro. .30
☐ 127 Jamie Storr (G), LosA. .30
☐ 128 Mike Richter (G), NYRa. .50
☐ 129 Petr Sykora, NJer. .50
☐ 130 Trevor Kidd (G), Flor. .30
☐ 131 Jaromir Jagr, Wash. 1.50
☐ 132 Bill Guerin, Bost. .50
☐ 133 Mark Messier, NYRa. 1.50
☐ 134 Ilya Kovalchuk, Atla. 1.50
☐ 135 Teemu Selänne, SanJ. 1.00
☐ 136 Dominik Hasek, Detr. 1.50
☐ 137 Mats Sundin, Toro. 1.50
☐ 138 José Théodore (G), Mont. 1.50
☐ 139 Brendan Shanahan, Detr. 1.50
☐ 140 Daniel Alfredsson, Otta. .50
☐ 141 Martin Brodeur (G), NJer. 2.00
☐ 142 Jarome Iginla, Calg. 1.00
☐ 143 Peter Bondra, Wash. .50
☐ 144 Peter Forsberg, Colo. 2.00
☐ 145 Curtis Joseph (G), Toro. 1.50
☐ 146 Alexei Yashin, NYIs. .50
☐ 147 Patrick Roy (G), Colo. 4.50
☐ 148 Markus Näslund, Vanc. 1.50
☐ 149 Jeremy Roenick, Phil. 1.00
☐ 150 Eric Lindros, NYRa. 1.50
☐ 151 Steve Yzerman, Detr. 3.50
☐ 152 Marian Gaborik, MinW. 1.50
☐ 153 Mike Modano, Dall. 1.50
☐ 154 Joe Sakic, Colo. 2.00
☐ 155 Paul Kariya, Anah. 2.00
☐ 156 Owen Nolan, SanJ. .50
☐ 157 Rob Blake, Colo. .50
☐ 158 Nicklas Lidström, Detr. .50
☐ 159 Joe Thornton, Bost. 1.50
☐ 160 Mario Lemieux, Pitt. 4.50
☐ 161 Magnus Arvedson, Otta. .30
☐ 162 Chris Clark, Calg. .30
☐ 163 Don Sweeney, Bost. .30
☐ 164 Fredrik Modin, Tamp. .30
☐ 165 Matt Cooke, Vanc. .30
☐ 166 Rhett Warrener, Buff. .30
☐ 167 Tim Taylor, Tamp. .30
☐ 168 Viktor Kozlov, Flor. .30
☐ 169 Michal Rozsival, Pitt. .30
☐ 170 Mathieu Schneider, LosA. .30
☐ 171 Matt Cullen, Anah. .30
☐ 172 Vladimir Malakhov, NYRa. .30
☐ 173 Mattias Norström, LosA. .30
☐ 174 Greg Johnson, Nash. .30
☐ 175 Éric Desjardins, Phil. .30
☐ 176 Damian Rhodes (G), Atla. .30
☐ 177 Stéphane Quintal, Mont. .30
☐ 178 Sami Salo, Otta. .30
☐ 179 Craig Rivet, Mont. .30
☐ 180 Oleg Saprykin, Calg. .30
☐ 181 Chris Therien, Phil. .30
☐ 182 Robyn Regehr, Calg. .30
☐ 183 Erik Cole, Caro. .50
☐ 184 Ed Belfour (G), Dall. 1.50
☐ 185 Chris Chelios, Detr. .50
☐ 186 Pavel Datsyuk, Detr. 1.00
☐ 187 Mike Comrie, Edmo. 1.00
☐ 188 Doug Gilmour, Mont. .50
☐ 189 Johan Hedberg (G), Pitt. .50
☐ 190 Brett Hull, Detr. 1.50
☐ 191 Theoren Fleury, NYRa. .50
☐ 192 Rick DiPietro (G), NYIs. .50
☐ 193 Marcus Ragnarsson, SanJ. .30
☐ 194 Michael Peca, NYIs. .50
☐ 195 Ryan Smyth, Edmo. .50
☐ 196 Ruslan Salei, Anah. .30
☐ 197 Anson Carter, Edmo. .50
☐ 198 Eric Brewer, Edmo. .50
☐ 199 Alexei Kovalev, Pitt. .50
☐ 200 Gary Roberts, Toro. .50
☐ **201 Micki Dupont, Calg. RC** **1.00**
☐ 202 Pat Verbeek, Dall. .30
☐ 203 Dimitri Kalinin, Buff. .30
☐ 204 Brad Stuart, SanJ. .50
☐ 205 Brent Johnson (G), SLou. .50
☐ 206 Todd White, Otta. .30
☐ 207 Andy McDonald, Anah. .30
☐ 208 Glen Murray, Bost. .50
☐ 209 Chris Osgood (G), NYIs. .50
☐ 210 Tim Connolly, Buff. .50
☐ 211 Scott Hartnell, Nash. .30
☐ 212 Radim Vrbata, Colo. .30
☐ 213 Dmitri Khristich, Wash. .30
☐ 214 Brendan Morrison, Vanc. .30
☐ **215 Matt Henderson, Chic. RC** **.50**
☐ 216 Jason Allison, LosA. .50
☐ 217 Ray Whitney, Colu. .30
☐ 218 Niklas Hagman, Flor. .30
☐ 219 Andrew Brunette, MinW. .30
☐ 220 Brian Rafalski, NJer. .30
☐ 221 Mark Parrish, NYIs. .50
☐ 222 Dave Andreychuk, Tamp. .30
☐ 223 Dainius Zubrus, Wash. .30
☐ 224 P.J. Stock, Bost. .30
☐ 225 Espen Knutsen, Colu. .30
☐ 226 Jiri Dopita, Phil. .30
☐ 227 Jeff Jillson, SanJ. .30
☐ 228 Tie Domi, Toro. .30
☐ 229 Milan Hnilicka (G), Atla. .30
☐ 230 Martin Lapointe, Bost. .50
☐ 231 Taylor Pyatt, Buff. .30
☐ 232 Kyle Calder, Chic. .30
☐ 233 Marc Denis (G), Colu. .50
☐ 234 Brenden Morrow, Dall. .30
☐ 235 Cliff Ronning, LosA. .30
☐ 236 Wade Redden, Otta. .30
☐ 237 Kris Beech, Pitt. .30
☐ 238 Patrick Marleau, SanJ. .50
☐ 239 Miikka Kiprusoff (G), SanJ. .30
☐ 240 Nikita Alexeev, Tamp. .30
☐ 241 Corey Schwab, Toro. .30
☐ 242 Jason Arnott, Dall. .50
☐ 243 Joe Nieuwendyk, NJer. .50
☐ 244 Adam Oates, Phil. .50
☐ 245 Darius Kasparaitis, Colo. .30
☐ 246 Mike York, Edmo. .30
☐ 247 Donald Brashear, Phil. .30
☐ 248 Kevin Weekes (G), Caro. .30
☐ 249 Jaroslav Spacek, Colu. .30
☐ 250 Alex Auld (G), Vanc. .30
☐ 251 Denis Arkhipov, Nash. .30
☐ 252 Cory Stillman, SLou. .30
☐ 253 Craig Conroy, Calg. .30
☐ 254 Dan Blackburn (G), NYRa. .50
☐ 255 Vaclav Nedorost, Colo. .30
☐ 256 Ladislav Nagy, Phoe. .30
☐ 257 Lukas Krajicek, Flor. .30
☐ 258 Raffi Torres, NYIs. .30
☐ 259 Richard Zednik, Mont. .50
☐ 260 Brad Bombardir, MinW. .30
☐ 261 Dwayne Roloson (G), MinW. .30
☐ 262 Frédéric Cassivi (G), Atla. .30
☐ 263 Geoff Sanderson, Colu. .30
☐ 264 Ilja Bryzgalov (G), Anah. .30
☐ 265 Jani Hurme (G), Otta. .30
☐ 266 Sébastien Centomo (G), Toro. .30
☐ 267 Jeff Halpern, Wash. .30
☐ 268 Mikael Renberg, Toro. .30
☐ 269 Vaclav Prospal, Tamp. .30
☐ **270 Sylvain Blouin, MinW. RC** **.30**
☐ 271 Olivier Michaud (G), Mont. .30
☐ 272 Pascal Dupuis, MinW. .30
☐ 273 Michael Nylander, Chic. .30
☐ 274 Daymond Langkow, Phoe. .30
☐ 275 Mike Sillinger, Colu. .30
☐ 276 Yanic Perreault, Mont. .30
☐ 277 Oleg Petrov, Mont. .30
☐ 278 Rod Brind'Amour, Caro. .30
☐ 279 Scott Clemmensen (G), NJer. .30
☐ 280 Jason Smith, Edmo. .30
☐ 281 Vladimir Orszagh, Nash. .30
☐ 282 Stephen Weiss, Flor. 1.00
☐ 283 Tony Hrkac, Atla. .30
☐ 284 Ty Conklin (G), Edmo. .30
☐ 285 Ulf Dahlén, Wash. .30
☐ 286 Karel Pilar, Toro. .30
☐ 287 Krys Kolanos, Phoe. .30
☐ 288 Marcel Hossa, Mont. .50
☐ 289 Martin Prusek (G), Otta. .30
☐ 290 Robert Svehla, Flor. .30

□	291 Radoslav Suchy, Phoe.	.30
□	292 Alexander Khavanov, SLou.	.30
□	293 Andy Delmore, Nash.	.30
□	294 Adrian Aucoin, NYIs.	.30
□	295 Bates Battaglia, Caro.	.30
□	296 Jussi Markkanen (G), Edmo.	.30
□	297 Martin Erat, Nash.	.30
□	298 Jim Dowd, MinW.	.30
□	299 Mark Hartigan, Atla.	.30
□	300 Neil Little (G), Phil.	.30

SUBSETS

	Insert	FE
□	301 Markus Näslund, Vanc. [Up Close...]	2.00
□	302 Bill Guerin, Bost. [Up Close...]	.60
□	303 Nicklas Lidström, Detr. [Up Close...]	1.00
□	304 Sergei Fedorov, Detr. [Up Close...]	2.00
□	305 Mats Sundin, Toro. [Up Close...]	2.00
□	306 Teemu Selänne, SanJ. [Up Close...]	1.50
□	307 Sergei Gonchar, Wash. [Up Close...]	.60
□	308 Brian Leetch, NYRa. [Up Close...]	1.00
□	309 Jeremy Roenick, Phil. [Up Close...]	1.50
□	310 Jaromir Jagr, Wash. [Up Close...]	2.00
□	311 Mark Recchi, Phil. [Up Close...]	.60
□	312 Sandis Ozolinsh, Flor. [Up Close...]	.60
□	313 Jarome Iginla, Calg. [Up Close...]	1.50
□	314 José Théodore (G), Mont. [Up Close...]	2.00
□	315 Steve Yzerman, Detr. [Up Close...]	4.50
□	316 Paul Kariya, Anah. [Up Close...]	2.50
□	317 Eric Dazé, Chic. [Up Close...]	.60
□	318 Ilya Kovalchuk, Atla. [Up Close...]	2.00
□	319 Brendan Shanahan, Detr. [Up Close...]	2.00
□	320 Marian Gaborik, MinW. [Up Close...]	2.00
□	321 Joe Sakic, Colo. [Up Close...]	3.00
□	322 Peter Forsberg, Colo. [Up Close...]	2.50
□	323 Mario Lemieux, Pitt. [Up Close...]	6.00
□	324 Luc Robitaille, Detr. [Up Close...]	1.50
□	325 Eric Lindros, NYRa. [Up Close...]	2.00
□	326 Mike Modano, Dall. [Up Close...]	2.00
□	327 Patrick Roy (G), Colo. [Up Close...]	6.00
□	328 Dominik Hasek, Detr. [Up Close...]	2.00
□	329 Scott Stevens, NJer. [Up Close...]	.60
□	330 Martin Brodeur (G), NJer. [Up Close...]	3.00
□	331 Keith Tkachuk, SLou. [Up Close...]	1.00
□	332 Rostislav Klesla, Colu. [Up Close...]	.60
□	333 Joe Thornton, Bost. [Up Close...]	2.00
□	334 Alexei Yashin, NYIs. [Up Close...]	1.00
□	335 Brett Hull, Detr. [Up Close...]	2.00
□	336 Olaf Kölzig (G), Wash. [Up Close...]	1.00
□	337 Roberto Luongo (G), Flor. [Up Close...]	1.50
□	338 Pavel Bure, NYRa. [Up Close...]	1.50
□	339 Chris Chelios, Detr. [Up Close...]	1.00
□	340 Owen Nolan, SanJ. [Up Close...]	1.00
□	341 Paul Kariya, Anah. [Franchise]	2.50
□	342 Ilya Kovalchuk, Atla. [Franchise]	2.00
□	343 Joe Thornton, Bost. [Franchise]	2.00
□	344 Miroslav Satan, Buff. [Franchise]	.60
□	345 Jarome Iginla, Calg. [Franchise]	1.50
□	346 Jeff O'Neill, Caro. [Franchise]	.60
□	347 Éric Dazé, Chic. [Franchise]	.60
□	348 Patrick Roy (G), Colo. [Franchise]	6.00
□	349 Rostislav Klesla, Colu. [Franchise]	.60
□	350 Mike Modano, Dall. [Franchise]	2.00
□	351 Steve Yzerman, Detr. [Franchise]	4.50
□	352 Mike Comrie, Edmo. [Franchise]	1.50
□	353 Roberto Luongo (G), Flor. [Franchise]	1.50
□	354 Zigmund Palffy, LosA. [Franchise]	1.00
□	355 Marian Gaborik, MinW. [Franchise]	2.00
□	356 José Théodore (G), Mont. [Franchise]	2.00
□	357 Scott Hartnell, Nash. [Franchise]	.60
□	358 Martin Brodeur (G), NJer. [Franchise]	3.00
□	359 Alexei Yashin, NYIs. [Franchise]	1.00
□	360 Pavel Bure, NYRa. [Franchise]	1.50
□	361 Marian Hossa, Otta. [Franchise]	2.00
□	362 Simon Gagné, Phil. [Franchise]	1.50
□	363 Daniel Brière, Phoe. [Franchise]	.60
□	364 Mario Lemieux, Pitt. [Franchise]	6.00
□	365 Chris Pronger, SLou. [Franchise]	1.00
□	366 Owen Nolan, SanJ. [Franchise]	1.00
□	367 Nikolai Khabibulin (G), Tamp. [Franchise]	.60
□	368 Mats Sundin, Toro. [Franchise]	2.00
□	369 Markus Näslund, Vanc. [Franchise]	2.00
□	370 Jaromir Jagr, Wash. [Franchise]	2.00
□	371 J. Iginla / M. Näslund / T. Bertuzzi	2.00
□	372 J. Iginla / M. Sundin / G. Murray / B. Guerin	1.00
□	373 A. Oates / J. Allison / J. Sakic	1.50
□	374 C. Chelios / J. Roenick / G. Murray / S. Gagné	1.00
□	375 P. Worrell / B. Ference / C. Neil	.60
□	376 P. Roy (G) / R. Cechmanek (G) / M. Turco (G)	2.50
□	377 Théodore (G) / Roy (G) / Cechmanek (G) / Turco (G)	2.50
□	378 P. Demitra / G. Murray / M. Sundin	1.00
□	379 B. Rolston / M. Peca / M. Satan	.60
□	380 D. Hasek / M. Brodeur (G) / E. Nabokov (G)	2.00
□	381 R. Svehla / D. Kasparaitis / D. Hatcher	.60
□	382 N. Lidström / S. Gonchar	.60
□	383 D. Heatley / I. Kovalchuk / K. Huselius	1.50
□	384 I.Kovalchuk / D. Heatley / K. Huselius	1.50
□	385 A. Aucoin / C. Pronger / N. Lidström	.60
□	386 Y. Perreault / R. Brind'Amour / R. Francis	.60
□	387 P. Bondra / J. Iginla	1.00
□	388 D. Brière / A. Deadmarsh / J. Hrdina	.60
□	389 Patrick Roy (G), North America All-Star	6.00
□	390 Chris Pronger, North America All-Star	1.00
□	391 Rob Blake, North America All-Star	1.00
□	392 Vincent Damphousse, North America All-Star	1.00
□	393 Owen Nolan, North America All-Star	1.00
□	394 Brendan Shanahan, North America All-Star	2.00
□	395 Dominik Hasek, World All-Star	2.00
□	396 Nicklas Lidström, World All-Star	1.00
□	397 Sandis Ozolinsh, World All-Star	.60
□	398 Sergei Fedorov, World All-Star	2.00
□	399 Jaromir Jagr, World All-Star	2.00
□	400 Teemu Selänne, World All-Star	1.50

FIRST ROUND DRAFT PICK / HOBBY

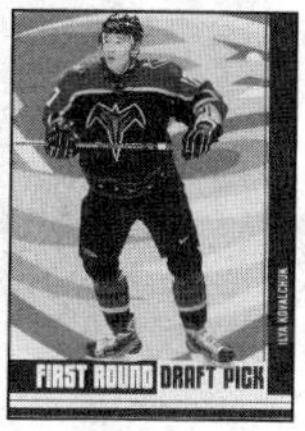

	Insert	H
□	401 Mike Modano, Minn.	2.00
□	402 Jeremy Roenick, Chic.	1.50
□	403 Bill Guerin, NJer.	.75
□	404 Owen Nolan, Québ.	1.00
□	405 Martin Brodeur (G), NJer.	3.00
□	406 Scott Niedermayer, NJer.	.75
□	407 Markus Näslund, Pitt.	2.00
□	408 Chris Pronger, Hart.	1.00
□	409 Jason Arnott, Edmo.	.75
□	410 Adam Deadmarsh, Québ.	.75
□	411 Todd Bertuzzi, NYIs.	2.00
□	412 Jeff O'Neill, Hart.	.75
□	413 Dan Cloutier (G), NYRa.	.75
□	414 J-S Giguère (G), Hart.	2.00
□	415 Petr Sykora, NJer.	.75
□	416 Marc Denis (G), Colo.	.75
□	417 Roberto Luongo (G), NYIs.	1.50
□	418 Sergei Samsonov, Bost.	1.00
□	419 Vincent Lecavalier, Tamp.	2.00
□	420 Alex Tanguay, Colo.	1.00
□	421 Martin Havlat, Otta.	1.00
□	422 Dany Heatley, Atla.	2.00
□	423 Rostislav Klesla, Colu.	.75
□	424 Ilya Kovalchuk, Atla.	2.00
□	425 Dan Blackburn (G), NYRa.	.75

FIRST ROUND DRAFT PICK / HOBBY REDEMPTION

	Redemption	H
□	426 Steve Yzerman, Detr.	
□	427 Gary Roberts, Calg.	
□	428 Brendan Shanahan, NJer.	
□	429 Joe Sakic, Québ.	
□	430 Keith Tkachuk, Winn.	
□	**431 Steve Ott, Dall. RC**	
□	**432 Pascal Leclaire (G), Colu. RC**	
□	**433 Alexei Smirnov, Anah. RC**	
□	**434 Alexander Frolov, LosA.**	
□	**435 Jeff Taffe, Phoe. RC**	
□	**436 Alexander Svitov, Tamp. RC**	
□	**437 Chuck Kobasew, Calg. RC**	
□	**438 Carlo Colaiacovo, Toro. RC**	
□	**439 Rick Nash, Colu. RC**	
□	**440 Pierre-Marc Bouchard, MinW. RC**	

FIRST ROUND DRAFT PICK / RETAIL

	Insert	R
□	401 Trevor Linden, Vanc.	.75
□	402 Mats Sundin, Québ.	2.00
□	403 Olaf Kölzig (G), Wash.	1.00
□	404 Jaromir Jagr, Pitt.	2.00
□	405 Eric Lindros, Phil.	2.00
□	406 Peter Forsberg, Québ.	2.50
□	407 Alexei Yashin, Otta.	1.00
□	408 Paul Kariya, Anah.	2.50
□	409 Jocelyn Thibault (G), Québ.	.75
□	410 Jason Allison, Wash.	1.00
□	411 Ed Jovanovski, Flor.	.75
□	412 Ryan Smyth, Edmo.	.75
□	413 Jarome Iginla, Calg.	1.50
□	414 Martin Biron (G), Buff.	.75
□	415 Brian Boucher, Phil.	.75
□	416 Joe Thornton, Bost.	2.00
□	417 Eric Brewer, NYIs.	.75
□	418 Marian Hossa, Otta.	2.00
□	419 Mark Bell, Chic.	.75
□	420 Simon Gagné, Phil.	1.50
□	421 Rick DiPietro (G), NYIs.	.75
□	422 Marian Gaborik, MinW.	2.00
□	423 Scott Hartnell, Nash.	.75
□	424 Stephen Weiss, Flor.	1.00
□	425 Lukas Krajicek, Flor.	.75

FIRST ROUND DRAFT PICK / REDEMPTION

	Insert	R
□	426 Mario Lemieux, Pitt.	6.00
□	427 Brian Leetch, NYRa.	1.00
□	428 Pierre Turgeon, Buff.	.75
□	429 Teemu Selänne, Winn.	1.50
□	430 Daniel & Henrik Sedin, Vanc.	.75
□	**431 Brooks Orpik, Pitt.**	**2.00**
□	**432 Shaone Morrisonn, Bost. RC**	**1.50**
□	**433 Ron Hainsey, Mont. RC**	**2.00**
□	**434 Anton Volchenkov, Otta. RC**	**1.50**
□	**435 Jason Spezza, Otta. RC**	**6.00**
□	**436 Stanislav Chistov, Anah. RC**	**4.50**
□	**437 Ales Hemsky, Edmo. RC**	**4.50**
□	**438 Jay Bouwmeester, Flor. RC**	**4.50**
□	**439 Scottie Upshall, Nash. RC**	**3.00**
□	**440 Steve Eminger, Wash. RC**	**1.50**

HE SHOOTS HE SCORES

Each redemption card was worth one, two, or three points. Collectors could trade 400 points for a special random jersey card. This redemption program expired on July 31, 2003.

Insert Set (20 cards):

	Insert
□	Sergei Fedorov, Detr. [1 Point]
□	Ron Francis, Caro. [1 Point]
□	Dany Heatley, Atla. [1 Point]
□	Milan Hejduk, Colo. [1 Point]
□	Saku Koivu, Mont. [1 Point]
□	Ilya Kovalchuk, Atla. [1 Point]
□	Eric Lindros, NYRa. [1 Point]
□	Mark Messier, NYRa. [1 Point]
□	Owen Nolan, SanJ. [1 Point]
□	Teemu Selänne, SanJ. [1 Point]
□	Joe Thornton, Bost. [1 Point]
□	Pavel Bure, NYRa. [2 Points]
□	Jarome Iginla, Calg. [2 Points]
□	Paul Kariya, Anah. [2 Points]
□	Mike Modano, Dall. [2 Points]
□	Joe Sakic, Colo. [2 Points]
□	Steve Yzerman, Detr. [2 Points]
□	Peter Forsberg, Colo. [3 Points]
□	Mario Lemieux, Pitt. [3 Points]
□	Mats Sundin, Toro. [3 Points]

GAME JERSEY

	Insert Set (160 cards):	**10,000**
	Insert (*100)	**GJ100**
□	David Aebischer (G), Colo. ✂	15.00
□	Maxim Afinogenov, Buff. ✂	20.00
□	Daniel Alfredsson, Otta. ✂	65.00
□	Tony Amonte, Chic. ✂	30.00
□	Mark Bell, Chic. ✂	15.00
□	Bryan Berard, NYRa. ✂	15.00
□	Todd Bertuzzi, Vanc. ✂	50.00
□	Martin Biron (G), Buff. ✂	25.00
□	Rob Blake, Colo. ✂	30.00
□	Peter Bondra, Wash. ✂	30.00
□	Radek Bonk, Otta. ✂	15.00
□	Brian Boucher, Phil. ✂	15.00
□	Nick Boynton, Bost. ✂	15.00
□	Pavel Brendl, Phil. ✂	15.00
□	Daniel Brière, Phoe. ✂	25.00
□	Martin Brodeur (G), NJer. ✂	75.00
□	Pavel Bure, NYRa. ✂	40.00
□	Valeri Bure, Flor. ✂	15.00
□	Sean Burke (G), Phoe. ✂	30.00
□	Roman Cechmanek (G), Phil. ✂	20.00
□	Dan Cloutier (G), Vanc. ✂	20.00
□	Byron Dafoe (G), Bost. ✂	20.00
□	Vincent Damphousse, SanJ. ✂	30.00
□	Éric Dazé, Chic. ✂	20.00
□	Adam Deadmarsh, LosA. ✂	15.00
□	Pavol Demitra, SLou. ✂	20.00
□	Shane Doan, Phoe. ✂	15.00
□	Chris Drury, Colo. ✂	30.00
□	Jean-Pierre Dumont, Buff. ✂	15.00
□	Mike Dunham (G), Nash. ✂	20.00
□	Radek Dvorak, NYRa. ✂	15.00
□	Patrik Elias, NJer. ✂	25.00
□	Sergei Fedorov, Detr. ✂	50.00
□	Manny Fernandez (G), MinW. ✂	20.00
□	Mike Fisher, Otta. ✂	15.00
□	Adam Foote, Colo. ✂	15.00
□	Peter Forsberg, Colo. ✂	70.00
□	Ron Francis, Caro. ✂	30.00
□	Jeff Friesen, Anah. ✂	15.00
□	Marian Gaborik, MinW. ✂	50.00
□	Simon Gagné, Phil. ✂	25.00
□	J-S Giguère (G), Anah. ✂	55.00
□	Scott Gomez, NJer. ✂	20.00
□	Sergei Gonchar, Wash. ✂	15.00
□	Chris Gratton, Buff. ✂	15.00
□	Bill Guerin, Bost. ✂	20.00
□	Jeff Hackett (G), Mont. ✂	15.00
□	Dominik Hasek, Detr. ✂	50.00
□	Derian Hatcher, Dall. ✂	15.00
□	Martin Havlat, Otta. ✂	30.00
□	Dany Heatley, Atla. ✂	50.00
□	Milan Hejduk, Colo. ✂	45.00
□	Bobby Holik, NJer. ✂	15.00
□	Marian Hossa, Otta. ✂	50.00
□	Jan Hrdina, Pitt. ✂	15.00
□	Kristian Huselius, Flor. ✂	15.00
□	Jarome Iginla, Calg. ✂	25.00
□	Arturs Irbe (G), Caro. ✂	20.00
□	Jaromir Jagr, Wash. ✂	50.00
□	Andreas Johansson, NYRa. ✂	15.00
□	Kenny Jönsson, NYIs. ✂	15.00
□	Curtis Joseph (G), Toro. ✂	50.00
□	Ed Jovanovski, Vanc. ✂	20.00
□	Tomas Kaberle, Toro. ✂	15.00
□	Sami Kapanen, Caro. ✂	15.00
□	Paul Kariya, Anah. ✂	75.00
□	Nikolai Khabibulin (G), Tamp. ✂	20.00
□	Trevor Kidd (G), Flor. ✂	15.00
□	Rostislav Klesla, Colu. ✂	30.00
□	Saku Koivu, Mont. ✂	50.00
□	Olaf Kölzig (G), Wash. ✂	30.00
□	Ilya Kovalchuk, Atla. ✂	50.00
□	Milan Kraft, Pitt. ✂	15.00
□	Patrick Lalime (G), Otta. ✂	30.00
□	Vincent Lecavalier, Tamp. ✂	50.00
□	John LeClair, Phil. ✂	25.00
□	Brian Leetch, NYRa. ✂	30.00
□	Manny Legacé (G), Detr. ✂	15.00
□	David Legwand, Nash. ✂	20.00
□	Mario Lemieux, Pitt. ✂	150.00
□	Mario Lemieux, Pitt. ✂	165.00
□	Nicklas Lidström, Detr. ✂	30.00
□	Eric Lindros, NYRa. ✂	50.00
□	Roberto Luongo (G), Flor. ✂	25.00
□	Al MacInnis, SLou. ✂	20.00
□	Bryan McCabe, Toro. ✂	15.00
□	Steve McCarthy, Chic. ✂	15.00
□	Darren McCarty, Detr. ✂	15.00
□	Alyn McCauley, Toro. ✂	15.00
□	Shawn McEachern, Otta. ✂	15.00
□	Kyle McLaren, Bost. ✂	15.00
□	Mark Messier, NYRa. ✂	50.00
□	Mike Modano, Dall. ✂	50.00
□	Alexander Mogilny, Toro. ✂	25.00
□	Aleksey Morozov, Pitt. ✂	15.00
□	Evgeni Nabokov (G), SanJ. ✂	30.00
□	Markus Näslund, Vanc. ✂	50.00
□	Rob Niedermayer, Calg. ✂	15.00

☐	Scott Niedermayer, NJer. ✂	15.00
☐	Owen Nolan, SanJ. ✂	30.00
☐	Mika Noronen (G), Buff. ✂	20.00
☐	Ivan Novoseltsev, Flor. ✂	15.00
☐	Teppo Numminen, Phoe. ✂	15.00
☐	Jeff O'Neill, Caro. ✂	20.00
☐	Mattias Öhlund, Vanc. ✂	15.00
☐	Sandis Ozolinsh, Flor. ✂	15.00
☐	Zigmund Palffy, LosA. ✂	30.00
☐	Steve Passmore (G), Chic. ✂	15.00
☐	Toby Petersen, Pitt. ✂	15.00
☐	Chris Phillips, Otta. ✂	15.00
☐	Félix Potvin (G), LosA. ✂	65.00
☐	Keith Primeau, Phil. ✂	20.00
☐	Chris Pronger, SLou. ✂	30.00
☐	Mark Recchi, Phil. ✂	20.00
☐	Steven Reinprecht, Colo. ✂	15.00
☐	Brad Richards, Tamp. ✂	25.00
☐	Luke Richardson, Phil. ✂	15.00
☐	Mike Richter (G), NYRa. ✂	25.00
☐	Luc Robitaille, Detr. ✂	25.00
☐	Jeremy Roenick, Phil. ✂	25.00
☐	Brian Rolston, Bost. ✂	15.00
☐	Patrick Roy (G), Colo. ✂	125.00
☐	Joe Sakic, Colo. ✂	75.00
☐	Tommy Salo (G), Edmo. ✂	20.00
☐	Sergei Samsonov, Bost. ✂	30.00
☐	Miroslav Satan, Buff. ✂	15.00
☐	Marc Savard, Calg. ✂	15.00
☐	Daniel Sedin, Vanc. ✂	20.00
☐	Henrik Sedin, Vanc. ✂	20.00
☐	Teemu Selänne, SanJ. ✂	25.00
☐	Brendan Shanahan, Detr. ✂	50.00
☐	Steve Shields (G), Anah. ✂	15.00
☐	Martin Skoula, Colo. ✂	15.00
☐	Patrik Stefan, Atla. ✂	15.00
☐	Scott Stevens, NJer. ✂	20.00
☐	Jamie Storr (G), LosA. ✂	15.00
☐	Martin Straka, Pitt. ✂	15.00
☐	Steve Sullivan, Chic. ✂	15.00
☐	Mats Sundin, Toro. ✂	50.00
☐	Niklas Sundström, SanJ. ✂	15.00
☐	Darryl Sydor, Dall. ✂	15.00
☐	Petr Sykora, NJer. ✂	20.00
☐	Alex Tanguay, Colo. ✂	30.00
☐	José Théodore (G), Mont. ✂	50.00
☐	Jocelyn Thibault (G), Chic. ✂	20.00
☐	Joe Thornton, Bost. ✂	50.00
☐	Keith Tkachuk, SLou. ✂	30.00
☐	Darcy Tucker, Toro. ✂	15.00
☐	Ron Tugnutt (G), Colu. ✂	20.00
☐	Marty Turco (G), Dall. ✂	30.00
☐	Roman Turek (G), Calg. ✂	25.00
☐	Pierre Turgeon, Dall. ✂	20.00
☐	Oleg Tverdovsky, Anah. ✂	15.00
☐	Doug Weight, SLou. ✂	30.00
☐	Alexei Yashin, NYIs. ✂	30.00
☐	Stéphane Yelle, Colo. ✂	15.00
☐	Dmitry Yushkevich, Toro. ✂	15.00
☐	Steve Yzerman, Detr. ✂	125.00
☐	Alexei Zhamnov, Chic. ✂	15.00
☐	Sergei Zubov, Dall. ✂	15.00

DEBUT GAME JERSEY

Insert Set (20 cards):		1,400
	Insert (*50)	**DGJ50**
☐	Ed Belfour (G), Chic. ✂	75.00
☐	Martin Brodeur (G), NJer. ✂	125.00
☐	Pavel Bure, Vanc. ✂	50.00
☐	Marian Gaborik, MinW. ✂	75.00
☐	Jarome Iginla, Calg. ✂	50.00
☐	Jaromir Jagr, Pitt. ✂	75.00
☐	Curtis Joseph (G), SLou. ✂	75.00
☐	Paul Kariya, Anah. ✂	100.00
☐	Ilya Kovalchuk, Atla. ✂	100.00
☐	Nicklas Lidström, Detr. ✂	50.00
☐	Eric Lindros, Phil. ✂	85.00
☐	Mark Messier, Edmo. ✂	85.00
☐	Owen Nolan, Québ. ✂	50.00
☐	Patrick Roy (G), Mont. ✂	200.00
☐	Joe Sakic, Québ. ✂	125.00
☐	Teemu Selänne, Winn. ✂	70.00
☐	Mats Sundin, Québ. ✂	75.00
☐	Joe Thornton, Bost. ✂	100.00
☐	Keith Tkachuk, Winn. ✂	50.00
☐	Steve Yzerman, Detr. ✂	200.00

HE SHOOTS HE SCORES JERSEY

Redemption Set (30 cards):		
	Insert (*100)	**Jers20**
☐	Martin Brodeur (G), NJer. ✂	
☐	Pavel Bure, NYRa. ✂	
☐	Sergei Fedorov, Detr. ✂	
☐	Peter Forsberg, Colo. ✂	
☐	Ron Francis, Caro. ✂	
☐	Marian Gaborik, MinW. ✂	
☐	Dany Heatley, Atla. ✂	
☐	Milan Hejduk, Colo. ✂	
☐	Jarome Iginla, Calg. ✂	
☐	Jarome Iginla, Calg. ✂	
☐	Jaromir Jagr, Wash. ✂	
☐	Paul Kariya, Anah. ✂	
☐	Saku Koivu, Mont. ✂	
☐	Ilya Kovalchuk, Atla. ✂	
☐	Mario Lemieux, Pitt. ✂	
☐	Eric Lindros, NYRa. ✂	
☐	Mark Messier, NYRa. ✂	
☐	Mike Modano, Dall. ✂	
☐	Markus Näslund, Vanc. ✂	
☐	Owen Nolan, SanJ. ✂	
☐	Jeremy Roenick, Phil. ✂	
☐	Patrick Roy (G), Colo. ✂	
☐	Joe Sakic, Colo. ✂	
☐	Teemu Selänne, SanJ. ✂	
☐	Brendan Shanahan, Detr. ✂	
☐	Mats Sundin, Toro. ✂	
☐	José Théodore (G), Mont. ✂	
☐	Joe Thornton, Bost. ✂	
☐	Keith Tkachuk, SLou. ✂	
☐	Steve Yzerman, Detr. ✂	

MAGNIFICENT

Insert Set (20 cards):		4,800
	Insert	**Mag**
☐	1 Mario Lemieux, Pitt. ✂ {#/40}	300.00
☐	2 Mario Lemieux, Pitt. ✂ {#/40}	300.00
☐	3 Mario Lemieux, Pitt. ✂ {#/40}	300.00
☐	4 Mario Lemieux, Pitt. ✂ {#/40}	300.00
☐	5 Mario Lemieux, Pitt. ✂ ✂ {#/40}	350.00
☐	6 Mario Lemieux, Pitt. ✂ {#/10}	900.00
☐	7 Mario Lemieux, Pitt. ✂ {#/10}	900.00
☐	8 Mario Lemieux, Pitt. ✂ ✂ ✂ {#/10}	
☐	9 Mario Lemieux, Pitt. ✂ ✂ ✂ ✂ {#/10}	
☐	10 Mario Lemieux, Pitt. ✂ ✂ ✂ ✂ {#/10}	

TEAM SCORING LEADERS

Insert Set (20 cards):		1,025
	Insert (*50)	**TSL50**
☐	Daniel Alfredsson, Otta. ✂	100.00
☐	Éric Dazé, Chic. ✂	25.00
☐	Patrik Elias, NJer. ✂	50.00
☐	Ron Francis, Caro. ✂	50.00
☐	Dany Heatley, Atla. ✂	75.00
☐	Jarome Iginla, Calg. ✂	50.00
☐	Jaromir Jagr, Wash. ✂	75.00
☐	Paul Kariya, Anah. ✂	100.00
☐	Alexei Kovalev, Pitt. ✂	50.00
☐	Eric Lindros, NYRa. ✂	75.00
☐	Mike Modano, Dall. ✂	75.00
☐	Markus Näslund, Vanc. ✂	75.00
☐	Owen Nolan, SanJ. ✂	50.00
☐	Brad Richards, Tamp. ✂	25.00
☐	Jeremy Roenick, Phil. ✂	50.00
☐	Joe Sakic, Colo. ✂	125.00
☐	Sergei Samsonov, Bost. ✂	50.00
☐	Brendan Shanahan, Detr. ✂	75.00
☐	Mats Sundin, Toro. ✂	75.00
☐	Alexei Yashin, NYIs. ✂	50.00

2002 - 03 FLEER THROWBACKS

Produced by Fleer Trading Cards, this series was released in January 2003. Each card 1-91 has two versions: the regular card, the one-per-pack Gold parallel and the Platinum parallel (#/50). Card 92 was available via a wrapper redemption program at the 2003 NHL All-Star Block Party.

		P50	Gold	Base
Shell Set (91 cards):		580.00	80.00	45.00
Complete Set (92 cards):				45.00
Common Player:		5.00	1.00	.50
	Description	**P50**	**Gold**	**Base**
☐☐☐	1 Terry O'Reilly, Bost.	5.00	1.00	.50
☐☐☐	2 Barry Beck, NYRa.	5.00	1.00	.50
☐☐☐	3 Bobby Clarke, Phil.	30.00	3.00	1.50
☐☐☐	4 Mike Foligno, Buff.	5.00	1.00	.50
☐☐☐	5 Danny Gare, Buff.	5.00	1.00	.50
☐☐☐	6 Clark Gillies, NYIs.	10.00	1.00	.50
☐☐☐	7 Bernie Federko, SLou.	10.00	1.00	.50
☐☐☐	8 Dale Hunter, Québ.	10.00	1.00	.50
☐☐☐	9 Kris King, Winn.	5.00	1.00	.50
☐☐☐	10 Ted Lindsay, Detr.	40.00	4.00	2.00
☐☐☐	11 Tie Domi, Toro.	10.00	1.00	.50
☐☐☐	12 Rob Ramage, SLou.	5.00	1.00	.50
☐☐☐	13 Jim Schoenfeld, Buff.	5.00	1.00	.50
☐☐☐	14 Steve Smith, Calg.	5.00	1.00	.50
☐☐☐	15 Harold Snepsts, Vanc.	5.00	1.00	.50
☐☐☐	16 Rod Langway, Wash.	15.00	1.00	.50
☐☐☐	17 Denis Potvin, NYIs.	30.00	3.00	1.50
☐☐☐	18 Johnny Bucyk, Bost.	20.00	2.00	1.00
☐☐☐	19 Dirk Graham, Chic.	5.00	1.00	.50
☐☐☐	20 Lanny McDonald, Calg.	30.00	3.00	1.50
☐☐☐	21 Stan Smyl, Vanc.	5.00	1.00	.50
☐☐☐	22 André Dupont, Phil.	5.00	1.00	.50
☐☐☐	23 Todd Ewen, SanJ.	5.00	1.00	.50
☐☐☐	24 George McPhee, NYRa.	5.00	1.00	.50
☐☐☐	25 Paul Baxter, Pitt.	5.00	1.00	.50
☐☐☐	26 Keith Magnuson, Chic.	5.00	1.00	.50
☐☐☐	27 Kevin Kaminski, Wash.	5.00	1.00	.50
☐☐☐	28 Mike Peluso, NJer.	5.00	1.00	.50
☐☐☐	29 Dave Semenko, Edmo.	5.00	1.00	.50
☐☐☐	30 David Maley, NJer.	5.00	1.00	.50
☐☐☐	31 Jeff Beukeboom, NYRa.	5.00	1.00	.50
☐☐☐	32 Dave Brown, Phil.	5.00	1.00	.50
☐☐☐	33 Troy Crowder, NJer.	5.00	1.00	.50
☐☐☐	34 Bobby Hull, Chic.	70.00	7.00	3.50
☐☐☐	35 Dan Maloney, LosA.	5.00	1.00	.50
☐☐☐	36 Jimmy Mann, Québ.	5.00	1.00	.50
☐☐☐	37 Rudy Poeschek, Tamp.	5.00	1.00	.50
☐☐☐	38 John Wensink, Bost.	5.00	1.00	.50
☐☐☐	39 Kim Clackson, Québ.	5.00	1.00	.50
☐☐☐	40 Jay Wells, LosA.	5.00	1.00	.50
☐☐☐	41 Glen Cochrane, Phil.	5.00	1.00	1.00
☐☐☐	42 Alan May, Wash.	5.00	1.00	.50
☐☐☐	43 Willi Plett, Minn.	5.00	1.00	.50
☐☐☐	44 Kevin McClelland, Edmo.	5.00	1.00	.50
☐☐☐	45 Jim Cummins, Chic.	5.00	1.00	.50
☐☐☐	46 Basil McRae, Minn.	5.00	1.00	.50
☐☐☐	47 Ron Delorme, ColR.	5.00	1.00	.50
☐☐☐	48 John Ferguson, Mont.	10.00	1.00	.50
☐☐☐	49 Gord Donnelly, Québ.	5.00	1.00	.50
☐☐☐	50 Nick Kypreos, NYRa.	5.00	1.00	.50
☐☐☐	51 Larry Playfair, LosA.	5.00	1.00	.50
☐☐☐	52 Marty McSorley, LosA.	5.00	1.00	.50
☐☐☐	53 Tim Hunter, Calg.	5.00	1.00	.50
☐☐☐	54 Billy Smith, NYIs.	30.00	3.00	1.50
☐☐☐	55 Laurie Boschman, Winn.	5.00	1.00	.50
☐☐☐	56 Wayne Cashman, Bost.	5.00	1.00	.50
☐☐☐	57 Link Gaetz, SanJ.	5.00	1.00	.50
☐☐☐	58 Darin Kimble, Québ.	5.00	1.00	.50
☐☐☐	59 Bob Nystrom, NYIs.	5.00	1.00	.50
☐☐☐	60 Ronnie Stern, Calg.	5.00	1.00	.50
☐☐☐	61 Ken Baumgartner, NYIs.	5.00	1.00	.50
☐☐☐	62 Ken Linseman, Phil.	5.00	1.00	.50
☐☐☐	63 Kelly Chase, SLou.	5.00	1.00	.50
☐☐☐	64 Bob Gassoff, SLou.	5.00	1.00	.50
☐☐☐	65 Joey Kocur, Detr.	5.00	1.00	.50
☐☐☐	66 Chris Nilan, Mont.	5.00	1.00	.50
☐☐☐	67 Dave Schultz, Phil.	10.00	1.00	.50
☐☐☐	68 Tony Twist, SLou.	5.00	1.00	.50
☐☐☐	69 Enrico Ciccone, Tamp.	5.00	1.00	.50
☐☐☐	70 Jay Miller, Bost.	5.00	1.00	.50
☐☐☐	71 Phil Russell, Chic.	5.00	1.00	.50
☐☐☐	72 Bryan Watson, Pitt.	5.00	1.00	.50
☐☐☐	73 Paul Holmgren, Phil.	5.00	1.00	.50
☐☐☐	74 Garth Butcher, Vanc.	5.00	1.00	.50
☐☐☐	75 Al Iafrate, Wash.	5.00	1.00	.50
☐☐☐	76 Barclay Plager, SLou.	5.00	1.00	.50
☐☐☐	77 Brent Severyn, Flor.	5.00	1.00	.50
☐☐☐	78 Ron Hextall, Phil.	20.00	2.00	1.00
☐☐☐	79 Shane Churla, Minn.	5.00	1.00	.50
☐☐☐	80 Dino Ciccarelli, Wash.	10.00	1.00	.50
☐☐☐	81 Cam Neely, Bost.	40.00	4.00	2.00
☐☐☐	82 Ulf Samuelsson, Hart.	5.00	1.00	.50
☐☐☐	83 Mick Vukota, NYIs.	5.00	1.00	.50
☐☐☐	84 Garry Howatt, NYIs.	5.00	1.00	.50
☐☐☐	85 Gary Rissling, Pitt.	5.00	1.00	1.00
☐☐☐	86 Behn Wilson, Phil.	5.00	1.00	.50
☐☐☐	87 Jack Carlson, Minn.	15.00	1.00	4.00
☐☐☐	88 Bob Bassen, SLou.	5.00	1.00	.50
☐☐☐	89 Curt Brackenbury, Edmo.	5.00	1.00	.50
☐☐☐	90 Mario Roberge, Mont.	5.00	1.00	.50
☐☐☐	91 Serge Roberge, Québ.	5.00	1.00	.50
☐	92 Bob Probert, Detr.	3.00		

AUTOGRAPH

Insert Set (23 cards):		425.00
	Insert	**Auto**
☐	Ken Baumgartner, NYIs. ✍	15.00
☐	Dave Brown, Phil. ✍	15.00
☐	Kelly Chase, SLou. ✍	15.00
☐	Bobby Clarke, Phil. ✍	40.00
☐	Tie Domi, Toro. ✍	16.00
☐	Todd Ewen, Anah. ✍	15.00
☐	Clark Gillies, NYIs. ✍	16.00
☐	Bobby Hull, Chic. ✍	90.00
☐	Dale Hunter, Wash. ✍	16.00
☐	Kevin Kaminski, Wash. ✍	15.00
☐	Joey Kocur, Detr. ✍	15.00
☐	Ted Lindsay, Detr. ✍	50.00
☐	Basil McRae, Dall. ✍	15.00
☐	Marty McSorley, LosA. ✍	15.00
☐	Bob Nystrom, NYIs. ✍	15.00
☐	Terry O'Reilly, Bost. ✍	15.00
☐	Larry Playfair, LosA. ✍	15.00
☐	Denis Potvin, NYIs. ✍	40.00
☐	Bob Probert, Detr. ✍	16.00
☐	Jim Schoenfeld, Buff. ✍	15.00
☐	Dave Schultz, Phil. ✍	16.00
☐	Billy Smith, NYIs. ✍	40.00
☐	Tony Twist, SLou. ✍	15.00

DROP THE GLOVES

Insert Set (5 cards):		120.00
	Insert	**DTG**
☐	Jim Cummins, Anah. ✂	20.00
☐	Ron Hextall, Phil. ✂	60.00
☐	Marty McSorley, LosA. ✂	20.00
☐	Bob Probert, Detr. ✂	30.00
☐	Tony Twist, SLou. ✂	20.00

SCRAPS

Insert Set (8 cards):		70.00
	Insert	**Scrap**
☐	1SC Basil McRae, SLou. ✂	10.00
☐	2SC Enrico Ciccone, Tamp. ✂	10.00
☐	3SC Bob Bassen, Dall. ✂	10.00
☐	4SC Joey Kocur, Detr. ✂	10.00
☐	5SC Clark Gillies, NYIs. ✂	15.00
☐	6SC Marty McSorley, LosA. ✂	10.00
☐	7SC Tony Twist, SLou. ✂	10.00
☐	8SC Dale Hunter, Wash. ✂	15.00

SCRAPS TIE DOWN

Insert Set (8 cards):		250.00
	Insert	**STD**
☐	Bob Bassen, Dall. ✂	30.00
☐	Enrico Ciccone, Tamp. ✂	30.00
☐	Clark Gillies, NYIs. ✂	60.00
☐	Dale Hunter, Wash. ✂	60.00
☐	Joey Kocur, Detr. ✂	30.00
☐	Basil McRae, SLou. ✂	30.00
☐	Marty McSorley, LosA. ✂	45.00
☐	Tony Twist, SLou. ✂	30.00

SQUARING OFF

Insert Set (9 cards):		25.00
	Insert	**SO**
☐	1SO Bob Probert, Chic. / Joey Kocur, Detr.	2.00
☐	2SO Dave Schultz, Phil. / Clark Gillies, NYIs.	3.00
☐	3SO Cam Neely, Bost. / Ulf Samuelsson, Hart.	5.00
☐	4SO Terry O'Reilly, Bost. / Jim Schoenfeld, Buff.	2.00
☐	5SO Barry Beck, NYRa. / Denis Potvin, NYIs.	4.00
☐	6SO Bobby Clarke, Phil. / Dale Hunter, Wash.	5.00
☐	7SO Tony Twist, SLou. / Marty McSorley, LosA.	2.00
☐	8SO Dave Brown, Phil. / Dave Schultz, Phil.	2.00
☐	9SO Ron Hextall, Phil. / Billy Smith, NYIs.	7.00

SQUARING OFF MEMORABILIA

Insert Set (9 cards):		160.00
	Insert	**SOM**
☐	1SO B. Probert, Chic. ✂ / Joey Kocur, Detr. ✂	15.00
☐	2SO Dave Schultz, Phil. ✂ / C. Gillies, NYIs. ✂	15.00
☐	3SO C. Neely, Bost. ✂ / U. Samuelsson, Hart. ✂	30.00
☐	4SO T. O'Reilly, Bost. ✂ / J. Schoenfeld, Buff. ✂	15.00
☐	5SO Barry Beck, NYRa. ✂ / D. Potvin, NYIs. ✂	25.00
☐	6SO B. Clarke, Phil. ✂ / D. Hunter, Wash. ✂	30.00
☐	7SO T. Twist, SLou. ✂ / M. McSorley, LosA. ✂	15.00
☐	8SO Dave Brown, Phil. ✂ / D. Schultz, Phil. ✂	15.00
☐	9SO R. Hextall, Phil. ✂ / Billy Smith, NYIs. ✂	40.00

STICKWORK

Insert Set (13 cards): 135.00

	Insert	Stick
☐	Curt Brackenbury, Edmo. ✂	10.00
☐	Kelly Chase, SLou. ✂	10.00
☐	Enrico Ciccone, Tamp. ✂	10.00
☐	Bobby Clarke, Phil. ✂	15.00
☐	Jim Cummins, Chic. ✂	10.00
☐	Todd Ewen, Anah. ✂	10.00
☐	Bobby Hull, Chic. ✂	35.00
☐	Dale Hunter, Wash. ✂	10.00
☐	Marty McSorley, LosA. ✂	10.00
☐	Cam Neely, Bost. ✂	20.00
☐	Rudy Poeschek, Tamp. ✂	10.00
☐	Bob Probert, Chic. ✂	10.00
☐	Jay Wells, LosA. ✂	10.00

2002 - 03 HEADS UP

Produced by Pacific Trading Cards, this series was released in September 2002. There are four versions for each card 1-125: the base card, the Blue parallel (#/240), the Red parallel (#/80), and the Purple parallel (#/30).

	Description	P30	R80	B240	Base
	Complete Set (125 cards):	2,400	1,000	375.00	90.00
	Common Player:	10	5	2.00	.35
☐☐☐☐	1 J-S Giguère (G), Anah.	75	30	10.00	2.50
☐☐☐☐	2 Paul Kariya, Anah.	100	40	10.00	3.50
☐☐☐☐	3 Adam Oates, Phil.	25	10	4.00	1.00
☐☐☐☐	4 Dany Heatley, Atla.	75	30	12.00	3.50
☐☐☐☐	5 Milan Hnilicka (G), Atla.	10	5	2.00	.50
☐☐☐☐	6 Ilya Kovalchuk, Atla.	75	30	12.00	3.50
☐☐☐☐	7 Byron Dafoe (G), Bost.	25	10	4.00	1.00
☐☐☐☐	8 Glen Murray, Bost.	25	10	4.00	1.00
☐☐☐☐	9 Brian Rolston, Bost.	10	5	2.00	.50
☐☐☐☐	10 S. Samsonov, Bost.	25	15	6.00	1.50
☐☐☐☐	11 Joe Thornton, Bost.	75	35	12.00	3.00
☐☐☐☐	12 Martin Biron (G), Buff.	25	10	4.00	1.00
☐☐☐☐	13 J-P Dumont, Buff.	10	5	2.00	.50
☐☐☐☐	14 Miroslav Satan, Buff.	10	5	2.00	.50
☐☐☐☐	15 Craig Conroy, Calg.	10	5	2.00	.50
☐☐☐☐	16 Jarome Iginla, Calg.	50	20	8.00	2.00
☐☐☐☐	17 D. McAmmond, Calg.	10	5	2.00	.35
☐☐☐☐	18 R. Turek (G), Calg.	25	10	4.00	1.00
☐☐☐☐	19 Erik Cole, Caro.	10	5	2.00	.50
☐☐☐☐	20 Ron Francis, Caro.	25	15	6.00	1.50
☐☐☐☐	21 Arturs Irbe (G), Caro.	25	10	4.00	1.00
☐☐☐☐	22 Sami Kapanen, Caro.	10	5	2.00	.50
☐☐☐☐	23 Jeff O'Neill, Caro.	25	10	4.00	1.00
☐☐☐☐	24 Tony Amonte, Chic.	25	15	6.00	1.50
☐☐☐☐	25 Éric Dazé, Chic.	25	10	4.00	1.00
☐☐☐☐	26 J. Thibault (G), Chic.	25	10	4.00	1.00
☐☐☐☐	27 A. Zhamnov, Chic.	10	5	2.00	.50
☐☐☐☐	28 Rob Blake, Colo.	25	15	6.00	1.50
☐☐☐☐	29 Chris Drury, Colo.	25	15	6.00	1.50
☐☐☐☐	30 P. Forsberg, Colo.	100	40	14.00	3.50
☐☐☐☐	31 Milan Hejduk, Colo.	50	20	8.00	2.00
☐☐☐☐	32 P. Roy (G), Colo.	225	90	30.00	7.50
☐☐☐☐	33 Joe Sakic, Colo.	100	45	15.00	4.00
☐☐☐☐	34 Marc Denis (G), Colu.	25	10	4.00	1.00
☐☐☐☐	35 R. Klesla, Colu.	10	5	2.00	.50
☐☐☐☐	36 Ray Whitney, Colu.	10	5	2.00	.50
☐☐☐☐	37 Jason Arnott, Dall.	25	10	4.00	1.00
☐☐☐☐	38 Bill Guerin, Bost.	25	10	4.00	1.00
☐☐☐☐	39 Mike Modano, Dall.	75	30	10.00	2.50
☐☐☐☐	40 Marty Turco (G), Dall.	25	15	6.00	1.50
☐☐☐☐	41 Sergei Fedorov, Detr.	75	30	10.00	2.50
☐☐☐☐	42 Dominik Hasek, Detr.	75	30	10.00	2.50
☐☐☐☐	43 Brett Hull, Detr.	75	30	10.00	2.50
☐☐☐☐	44 C. Joseph (G), Toro.	75	30	10.00	2.50
☐☐☐☐	45 N. Lidström, Detr.	25	15	6.00	1.50
☐☐☐☐	46 Luc Robitaille, Detr.	50	20	8.00	2.00
☐☐☐☐	47 B. Shanahan, Detr.	75	30	10.00	2.50
☐☐☐☐	48 S. Yzerman, Detr.	175	70	20.00	6.00
☐☐☐☐	49 Mike Comrie, Edmo.	50	20	8.00	2.00
☐☐☐☐	50 T. Salo (G), Edmo.	25	10	4.00	1.00
☐☐☐☐	51 Ryan Smyth, Edmo.	25	10	4.00	1.00
☐☐☐☐	52 K. Huselius, Flor.	10	5	2.00	.50
☐☐☐☐	53 R. Luongo (G), Flor.	50	20	8.00	2.00
☐☐☐☐	54 S. Weiss, Flor.	25	10	8.00	2.00
☐☐☐☐	55 Jason Allison, LosA.	25	15	6.00	1.50
☐☐☐☐	56 A. Deadmarsh, LosA.	10	5	2.00	.50
☐☐☐☐	57 Z. Palffy, LosA.	25	15	6.00	1.50
☐☐☐☐	58 Félix Potvin (G), LosA.	75	35	6.00	1.50
☐☐☐☐	59 A. Brunette, MinW.	10	5	2.00	.35
☐☐☐☐	60 Fernandez (G), MinW.	25	10	4.00	1.00
☐☐☐☐	61 M. Gaborik, MinW.	75	30	10.00	2.50
☐☐☐☐	62 D. Audette, Mont.	25	10	4.00	1.00
☐☐☐☐	63 Doug Gilmour, Mont.	25	15	6.00	1.50
☐☐☐☐	64 Saku Koivu, Mont.	75	35	8.00	2.00
☐☐☐☐	65 Y. Perreault, Mont.	10	5	2.00	.50
☐☐☐☐	66 J. Théodore (G), Mont.	75	35	12.00	3.00
☐☐☐☐	67 D. Arkhipov, Nash.	10	5	2.00	.50
☐☐☐☐	68 Scott Hartnell, Nash.	10	5	2.00	.50
☐☐☐☐	69 D. Legwand, Nash.	25	10	4.00	1.00
☐☐☐☐	70 M. Brodeur (G), NJer.	100	45	15.00	4.00
☐☐☐☐	71 Patrik Elias, NJer.	50	20	8.00	2.00
☐☐☐☐	72 J. Nieuwendyk, NJer.	25	10	4.00	1.00
☐☐☐☐	73 Chris Osgood (G), NYIs.	25	15	6.00	1.50
☐☐☐☐	74 Mark Parrish, NYIs.	25	10	4.00	1.00
☐☐☐☐	75 Michael Peca, NYIs.	25	10	4.00	1.00
☐☐☐☐	76 Alexei Yashin, NYIs.	25	15	6.00	1.50
☐☐☐☐	77 D. Blackburn (G), NYRa.	25	10	4.00	1.00
☐☐☐☐	78 Pavel Bure, NYRa.	50	20	8.00	2.00
☐☐☐☐	79 T. Fleury, NYRa.	25	15	6.00	1.50
☐☐☐☐	80 Bobby Holik, NJer.	10	5	2.00	.50
☐☐☐☐	81 Brian Leetch, NYRa.	25	15	6.00	1.50
☐☐☐☐	82 Eric Lindros, NYRa.	75	30	10.00	2.50
☐☐☐☐	83 Mike Richter (G), NYRa.	25	10	4.00	1.00
☐☐☐☐	84 D. Alfredsson, Otta.	25	15	6.00	1.50
☐☐☐☐	85 Radek Bonk, Otta.	10	5	2.00	.50
☐☐☐☐	86 Martin Havlat, Otta.	25	15	6.00	1.50
☐☐☐☐	87 Marian Hossa, Otta.	75	30	10.00	2.50
☐☐☐☐	88 Patrick Lalime (G), Otta.	25	15	6.00	1.50
☐☐☐☐	89 R. Cechmanek (G), Phil.	25	10	4.00	1.00
☐☐☐☐	90 Simon Gagné, Phil.	50	20	8.00	2.00
☐☐☐☐	91 John LeClair, Phil.	50	20	8.00	2.00
☐☐☐☐	92 Mark Recchi, Phil.	25	10	4.00	1.00
☐☐☐☐	93 J. Roenick, Phil.	50	20	8.00	2.00
☐☐☐☐	94 Daniel Brière, Phoe.	25	10	4.00	1.00
☐☐☐☐	95 Sean Burke (G), Phoe.	25	15	6.00	1.50
☐☐☐☐	96 Krys Kolanos, Phoe.	10	5	2.00	.50
☐☐☐☐	97 D. Langkow, Phoe.	10	5	2.00	.50
☐☐☐☐	98 Johan Hedberg (G), Pitt.	25	10	4.00	1.00
☐☐☐☐	99 Alex Kovalev, Pitt.	25	15	6.00	1.50
☐☐☐☐	100 M. Lemieux, Pitt.	225	90	30.00	7.50
☐☐☐☐	101 A. Morozov, Pitt.	10	5	2.00	.50
☐☐☐☐	102 P. Demitra, SLou.	25	10	4.00	1.00
☐☐☐☐	103 B. Johnson (G), SLou.	25	10	4.00	1.00
☐☐☐☐	104 C. Pronger, SLou.	25	15	6.00	1.50
☐☐☐☐	105 K. Tkachuk, SLou.	25	15	6.00	1.50
☐☐☐☐	106 D. Weight, SLou.	25	15	6.00	1.50
☐☐☐☐	107 P. Marleau, SanJ.	25	10	4.00	1.00
☐☐☐☐	108 E. Nabokov (G), SanJ.	25	15	6.00	1.50
☐☐☐☐	109 Owen Nolan, SanJ.	25	15	6.00	1.50
☐☐☐☐	110 T. Selänne, SanJ.	50	20	8.00	2.00
☐☐☐☐	111 N. Khabibulin (G), Tamp.	25	10	4.00	1.00
☐☐☐☐	112 V. Lecavalier, Tamp.	75	30	10.00	2.50
☐☐☐☐	113 B. Richards, Tamp.	25	10	4.00	1.00
☐☐☐☐	114 Ed Belfour (G), Dall.	75	30	10.00	2.50
☐☐☐☐	115 A. McCauley, Toro.	10	5	2.00	.50
☐☐☐☐	116 A. Mogilny, Toro.	25	10	4.00	1.00
☐☐☐☐	117 Gary Roberts, Toro.	25	10	4.00	1.00
☐☐☐☐	118 Mats Sundin, Toro.	75	30	10.00	2.50
☐☐☐☐	119 Todd Bertuzzi, Vanc.	75	35	12.00	3.00
☐☐☐☐	120 Dan Cloutier (G), Vanc.	25	10	4.00	1.00
☐☐☐☐	121 B. Morrison, Vanc.	10	5	2.00	.50
☐☐☐☐	122 M. Näslund, Vanc.	75	30	10.00	2.50
☐☐☐☐	123 P. Bondra, Wash.	25	15	6.00	1.50
☐☐☐☐	124 J. Jagr, Wash.	75	30	10.00	2.50
☐☐☐☐	125 O. Kölzig (G), Wash.	25	15	6.00	1.50

ROOKIE

	Insert (#/1000)	R
☐	**126 Stanislav Chistov, Anah. RC**	15.00
☐	**127 Martin Gerber (G), Anah. RC**	6.00
☐	**128 Alexei Smirnov, Anah. RC**	7.00
☐	**129 Chuck Kobasew, Calg. RC**	10.00
☐	**130 Rick Nash, Colu. RC**	25.00
☐	**131 Dmitri Bykov, Detr. RC**	6.00
☐	**132 Henrik Zetterberg, Detr. RC**	25.00
☐	**133 Ales Hemsky, Edmo. RC**	15.00
☐	**134 Jay Bouwmeester, Flor. RC**	15.00
☐	**135 Alexander Frolov, LosA. RC**	12.00
☐	**136 Sylvain Blouin, MinW. RC**	6.00
☐	**137 Pierre-Marc Bouchard, MinW. RC**	15.00
☐	**138 Ron Hainsey, Mont. RC**	7.00
☐	**139 Scottie Upshall, Nash. RC**	10.00
☐	140 Mike Danton,NJer.	6.00
☐	**141 Ray Schultz, NYIs. RC**	6.00
☐	**142 Anton Volchenkov, Otta.**	6.00
☐	**143 Dennis Seidenberg, Phil. RC**	6.00
☐	**144 Alexander Svitov, Tamp. RC**	10.00
☐	**145 Steve Eminger, Wash. RC**	6.00

AUTHENTIC GAME-WORN JERSEY QUADS

Photo Photo-hk023_HeadsUp_4Jers

	Insert	Q304	GWJQ
	Insert Set (36 cards):	2,250	800
☐☐	1 Friesen ✂ / Tverdovsky ✂ / Allison ✂ / Deadmarsh ✂	50.00	15.00
☐☐	2 Kovalchuk ✂ / Stefan ✂ / Hnilicka (G) ✂ / Kallio ✂	50.00	20.00
☐☐	3 Samsonov ✂ / Thornton ✂ / McLaren ✂ / Sweeney ✂	75.00	30.00
☐☐	4 Dumont ✂ / Biron (G) ✂ / McKee ✂ / Satan ✂	40.00	15.00
☐☐	5 Turek (G) ✂ / Savard ✂ / Comrie ✂ / Smyth ✂	75.00	25.00
☐☐	6 Francis ✂ / Irbe (G) ✂ / Brind'Amour ✂ / O'Neill ✂	50.00	20.00
☐☐	7 Amonte ✂ / Dazé ✂ / Bell ✂ / Sullivan ✂	50.00	20.00
☐☐	8 Drury ✂ / Hejduk ✂ / Tanguay ✂ / Nedorost ✂	75.00	30.00
☐☐	9 Blake ✂ / Sakic ✂ / Robitaille ✂ / Fedorov ✂	150.00	55.00
☐☐	10 Denis ✂ / Tugnutt (G) ✂ / Klesla ✂ / Sanderson ✂	50.00	20.00
☐☐	11 Belfour (G) ✂ / Turco (G) ✂ / Turgeon ✂ / Modano ✂	100.00	40.00
☐☐	12 Hasek ✂ / Hull ✂ / Lidström ✂ / Williams ✂	100.00	35.00
☐☐	13 Allison ✂ / Palffy ✂ / Potvin (G) ✂ / Smolinski ✂	100.00	25.00
☐☐	14 Gaborik ✂ / Kuba ✂ / McLennan (G) ✂ / Fernandez (G) ✂	50.00	20.00
☐☐	15 Théodore (G) ✂ / Perreault ✂ / Berezin ✂ / Koivu ✂	125.00	35.00
☐☐	16 Erat ✂ / Legwand ✂ / Walker ✂ / Hentunen ✂	40.00	15.00
☐☐	17 Brodeur (G) ✂ / Elias ✂ / Gomez ✂ / Stevens ✂	125.00	45.00
☐☐	18 Peca ✂ / Yashin ✂ / Lindros ✂ / Fleury ✂	100.00	35.00
☐☐	19 Alfredsson ✂ / Lalime (G) ✂ / Havlat ✂ / Hossa ✂	125.00	35.00
☐☐	20 Oates ✂ / Roenick ✂ / Cechmanek (G) ✂ / Dopita ✂	50.00	20.00
☐☐	21 Kolanos ✂ / Handzus ✂ / Langkow ✂ / Doan ✂	40.00	15.00
☐☐	22 Hedberg (G) ✂ / Lang ✂ / Petersen ✂ / Beech ✂	40.00	15.00
☐☐	23 Pronger ✂ / Tkachuk ✂ / Demitra ✂ / Varlamov ✂	50.00	20.00
☐☐	24 Nabokov (G) ✂ / Nolan ✂ / Kiprusoff (G) ✂ / Marleau ✂	75.00	25.00
☐☐	25 Khabibulin (G) ✂ / Richards ✂ / Bure ✂ / Luongo (G) ✂	75.00	25.00
☐☐	26 Joseph (G) ✂ / Roberts ✂ / Mogilny ✂ / Tucker ✂	75.00	25.00
☐☐	27 Cloutier (G) ✂ / Bertuzzi ✂ / Sedin ✂ / Sedin ✂	75.00	30.00
☐☐	28 Lemieux ✂ / Pronger ✂ / Brodeur (G) ✂ / Joseph (G) ✂	250.00	85.00
☐☐	29 Guerin ✂ / Modano ✂ / Hull ✂ / Leetch ✂	100.00	40.00
☐☐	30 Bure ✂ / Khabibulin (G) ✂ / Fedorov ✂ / Yashin ✂	100.00	35.00
☐☐	31 Sundin ✂ / Alfredsson ✂ / Salo (G) ✂ / Hedberg (G) ✂	100.00	30.00
☐☐	32 Jagr ✂ / Hasek (G) ✂ / Hejduk ✂ / Elias ✂	125.00	50.00
☐☐	33 Selänne ✂ / Lehtinen ✂ / Lumme ✂ / Kallio ✂	50.00	20.00
☐☐	34 Bondra ✂ / Gaborik ✂ / Demitra ✂ / Palffy ✂	100.00	35.00
☐☐	35 Kovalchuk ✂ / Heatley ✂ / Kolanos ✂ / Cole ✂	100.00	30.00
☐☐	36 Huselius ✂ / Dopita ✂ / Erat ✂ / Hentunen ✂	40.00	15.00

ETCHED IN TIME

	Insert (1:289)	EiT
	Insert Set (15 cards):	450.00
☐	1 Paul Kariya, Anah.	35.00
☐	2 Ilya Kovalchuk, Atla.	35.00
☐	3 Joe Thornton, Bost.	30.00
☐	4 Jarome Iginla, Calg.	20.00
☐	5 Ron Francis, Caro.	20.00
☐	6 Peter Forsberg, Colo.	35.00
☐	7 Patrick Roy (G), Colo.	75.00
☐	8 Joe Sakic, Colo.	40.00
☐	9 Dominik Hasek, Detr.	25.00
☐	10 Steve Yzerman, Detr.	60.00
☐	11 Martin Brodeur (G), NJer.	40.00
☐	12 Eric Lindros, NYRa.	25.00
☐	13 Mario Lemieux, Pitt.	75.00
☐	14 Mats Sundin, Toro.	25.00
☐	15 Jaromir Jagr, Wash.	25.00

HEAD FIRST

Insert Set (16 cards): 55.00

	Insert (1:19)	HF
☐	1 Dany Heatley, Atla.	6.00
☐	2 Ilya Kovalchuk, Atla.	6.00
☐	3 Sergei Samsonov, Bost.	4.00
☐	4 Joe Thornton, Bost.	8.00
☐	5 Stephen Weiss, Flor.	3.00
☐	6 Marian Gaborik, MinW.	6.00
☐	7 Scott Hartnell, Nash.	3.00
☐	8 Rick DiPietro (G), NYIs.	3.00
☐	9 Raffi Torres, NYIs.	3.00
☐	10 Dan Blackburn (G), NYRa.	3.00
☐	11 Martin Havlat, Otta.	4.00
☐	12 Simon Gagné, Phil.	6.00
☐	13 Krys Kolanos, Phoe.	3.00
☐	14 Vincent Lecavalier, Tamp.	6.00
☐	15 Daniel Sedin, Vanc.	3.00
☐	16 Henrik Sedin, Vanc.	3.00

INSIDE THE NUMBERS

	Insert (1:10)	ITN
	Insert Set (24 cards):	65.00
☐	1 Adam Oates, Phil.	2.00
☐	2 Dany Heatley, Atla.	4.00
☐	3 Ilya Kovalchuk, Atla.	4.00
☐	4 Joe Thornton, Bost.	4.00
☐	5 Jarome Iginla, Calg.	2.00
☐	6 Ron Francis, Caro.	2.00
☐	7 Patrick Roy (G), Colo.	10.00
☐	8 Joe Sakic, Colo.	6.00
☐	9 Mike Modano, Dall.	2.00
☐	10 Dominik Hasek, Detr.	2.00
☐	11 Brendan Shanahan, Detr.	2.00
☐	12 José Théodore (G), Mont.	4.00
☐	13 Martin Brodeur (G), NJer.	6.00
☐	14 Alexei Yashin, NYIs.	2.00
☐	15 Eric Lindros, NYRa.	2.00
☐	16 Daniel Alfredsson, Otta.	2.00
☐	17 Mario Lemieux, Pitt.	10.00
☐	18 Pavol Demitra, SLou.	2.00
☐	19 Evgeni Nabokov (G), SanJ.	2.00
☐	20 Nikolai Khabibulin (G), Tamp.	2.00
☐	21 Mats Sundin, Toro.	2.00
☐	22 Todd Bertuzzi, Vanc.	4.00
☐	23 Markus Näslund, Vanc.	2.00
☐	24 Jaromir Jagr, Wash.	2.00

POSTSEASON PICKS

	Insert (1:37)	PSP
	Insert Set (10 cards):	70.00
☐	1 Erik Cole, Caro.	4.00
☐	2 Ron Francis, Caro.	4.00
☐	3 Peter Forsberg, Colo.	10.00
☐	4 Patrick Roy (G), Colo.	20.00
☐	5 Joe Sakic, Colo.	12.00
☐	6 Dominik Hasek, Detr.	6.00
☐	7 Brendan Shanahan, Detr.	6.00
☐	8 Steve Yzerman, Detr.	15.00
☐	9 José Théodore (G), Mont.	8.00
☐	10 Mats Sundin, Toro.	6.00

SHOWSTOPPERS

	Insert (1:10)	SS
	Insert Set (20 cards):	40.00
☐	1 Jean-Sébastien Giguère (G), Anah.	2.00
☐	2 Byron Dafoe (G), Bost.	2.00
☐	3 Roman Turek (G), Calg.	2.00
☐	4 Arturs Irbe (G), Caro.	2.00

□	5 Jocelyn Thibault (G), Chic.	2.00
□	6 Patrick Roy (G), Colo.	10.00
□	7 Marty Turco (G), Dall.	2.00
□	8 Dominik Hasek, Detr.	2.00
□	9 Curtis Joseph (G), Toro. (Detr.)	2.00
□	10 Roberto Luongo (G), Flor.	2.00
□	11 Félix Potvin (G), LosA.	2.00
□	12 José Théodore (G), Mont.	4.00
□	13 Martin Brodeur (G), NJer.	6.00
□	14 Chris Osgood (G), NYIs.	2.00
□	15 Patrick Lalime (G), Otta.	2.00
□	16 Sean Burke (G), Phoe.	2.00
□	17 Brent Johnson (G), SLou.	2.00
□	18 Evgeni Nabokov (G), SanJ.	2.00
□	19 Nikolai Khabibulin (G), Tamp.	2.00
□	20 Dan Cloutier (G), Vanc.	2.00

STAT MASTERS

Insert Set (10 cards): 100.00

	Insert (1:73)	SM
□	1 Paul Kariya, Anah.	10.00
□	2 Ilya Kovalchuk, Atla.	6.00
□	3 Dany Heatley, Atla.	6.00
□	4 Joe Thornton, Bost.	8.00
□	5 Jarome Iginla, Calg.	6.00
□	6 Ron Francis, Caro.	5.00
□	7 Joe Sakic, Colo.	12.00
□	8 Brett Hull, Detr.	6.00
□	9 Steve Yzerman, Detr.	18.00
□	10 Pavel Bure, NYRa.	6.00
□	11 Eric Lindros, NYRa.	6.00
□	12 Mario Lemieux, Pitt.	22.00
□	13 Mats Sundin, Toro.	6.00
□	14 Todd Bertuzzi, Vanc.	8.00
□	15 Jaromir Jagr, Wash.	6.00

BOBBLE DOBBLES

Insert Set (14 Dolls): 325.00

	Insert (1:12)	Bobble
□	Jason Allison, LosA.	35.00
□	Pavel Bure, NYRa.	35.00
□	Mike Comrie, Edmo.	35.00
□	Peter Forsberg, Colo.	50.00
□	Jarome Iginla, Calg.	35.00
□	Saku Koivu, Mont.	35.00
□	Ilya Kovalchuk, Atla.	50.00
□	Eric Lindros, NYRa.	50.00
□	Evgeni Nabokov (G), SanJ.	35.00
□	Brendan Shanahan, Detr.	50.00
□	Mats Sundin, Toro.	50.00
□	José Théodore (G), Mont.	75.00
□	Joe Thornton, Bost.	50.00
□	Alexei Yashin, NYIs.	35.00

2002 - 03 IN THE GAME-USED

Produced by the In The Game, this series was released in March 2003. Dufex cards feature players in a light jersey while Shimmer cards feature players in a dark jersey. Each three-card pack included one Dufex card, one Shimmer card, and one memorabilia card.

Dufex Set (80 cards): 325.00
Shimmer Set (80 cards): 250.00
Complete Set (200 cards): 2900.00
Common Player: 5.00

	Description	Base
□	1 Adam Oates, Anah.	5.00
□	2 Paul Kariya, Anah.	12.00
□	3 Petr Sykora, Anah.	5.00
□	4 Dany Heatley, Atla.	8.00
□	5 Ilya Kovalchuk, Atla.	8.00
□	6 Jeff O'Neill, Caro.	5.00
□	7 Joe Thornton, Bost.	10.00
□	8 Sergei Samsonov, Bost.	5.00
□	9 Jarome Iginla, Calg.	6.00
□	10 Ron Francis, Caro.	5.00
□	11 Jocelyn Thibault (G), Chic.	5.00
□	12 Alex Tanguay, Colo.	5.00
□	13 Joe Sakic, Colo.	14.00
□	14 Milan Hejduk, Colo.	6.00
□	15 Patrick Roy (G), Colo.	25.00
□	16 Peter Forsberg, Colo.	12.00
□	17 Rob Blake, Colo.	5.00
□	18 Rostislav Klesla, Colu.	5.00
□	19 Brett Hull, Detr.	8.00
□	20 Marty Turco (G), Dall.	5.00
□	21 Mike Modano, Dall.	8.00
□	22 Bill Guerin, Dall.	5.00
□	23 Brendan Shanahan, Detr.	8.00
□	24 Chris Chelios, Detr.	5.00
□	25 Curtis Joseph (G), Detr.	8.00
□	26 Luc Robitaille, Detr.	6.00
□	27 Nicklas Lidström, Detr.	5.00
□	28 Pavel Datsyuk, Detr.	6.00
□	29 Sergei Fedorov, Detr.	8.00
□	30 Steve Yzerman, Detr.	20.00
□	31 Mike Comrie, Edmo.	6.00
□	32 Erik Cole, Caro.	5.00
□	33 Kristian Huselius, Flor.	5.00
□	34 Roberto Luongo (G), Flor.	6.00
□	35 Félix Potvin (G), LosA.	5.00
□	36 Jason Allison, LosA.	5.00
□	37 Zigmund Palffy, LosA.	5.00
□	38 Marian Gaborik, MinW.	8.00
□	39 José Théodore (G), Mont.	10.00
□	40 Saku Koivu, Mont.	6.00
□	41 Martin Brodeur (G), NJer.	14.00
□	42 Patrik Elias, NJer.	6.00
□	43 Scott Gomez, NJer.	5.00
□	44 Alexei Yashin, NYIs.	5.00
□	45 Chris Osgood (G), NYIs.	5.00
□	46 Rick DiPietro (G), NYIs.	5.00
□	47 Brian Leetch, NYRa.	5.00
□	48 Eric Lindros, NYRa.	8.00
□	49 Mark Messier, NYRa.	8.00
□	50 Mike Richter (G), NYRa.	5.00
□	51 Pavel Bure, NYRa.	6.00
□	52 Daniel Alfredsson, Otta.	5.00
□	53 Marian Hossa, Otta.	8.00
□	54 Martin Havlat, Otta.	5.00
□	55 Jeremy Roenick, Phil.	6.00
□	56 John LeClair, Phil.	6.00
□	57 Mark Recchi, Phil.	5.00
□	58 Simon Gagné, Phil.	6.00
□	59 Nikolai Khabibulin (G), Tamp.	5.00
□	60 Sean Burke (G), Phoe.	5.00
□	61 Johan Hedberg (G), Pitt.	5.00
□	62 Mario Lemieux, Pitt.	25.00
□	63 Evgeni Nabokov (G), SanJ.	5.00
□	64 Owen Nolan, SanJ.	5.00
□	65 Teemu Selänne, SanJ.	6.00
□	66 Al MacInnis, SLou.	5.00
□	67 Chris Pronger, SLou.	5.00
□	68 Doug Weight, SLou.	5.00
□	69 Keith Tkachuk, SLou.	5.00
□	70 Vincent Lecavalier, Tamp.	8.00
□	71 Ed Belfour (G), Toro.	8.00
□	72 Mats Sundin, Toro.	8.00
□	73 Daniel Sedin, Vanc.	5.00
□	74 Henrik Sedin, Vanc.	5.00
□	75 Markus Näslund, Vanc.	8.00
□	76 Todd Bertuzzi, Vanc.	10.00
□	77 Jaromir Jagr, Wash.	8.00
□	78 Olaf Kölzig (G), Wash.	5.00
□	79 Peter Bondra, Wash.	5.00
□	80 Tony Amonte, Phoe.	5.00

ROOKIES

	Insert (*100)	R
□	**81 Pierre-Marc Bouchard, MinW. RC**	**100.00**
□	**82 Rick Nash, Colu. RC**	**200.00**
□	**83 Jay Bouwmeester, Flor. RC**	**100.00**
□	**84 Dennis Seidenberg, Phil. RC**	**35.00**
□	**85 Stanislav Chistov, Anah. RC**	**100.00**
□	**86 Tom Koivisto, SLou. RC**	**35.00**
□	**87 Ivan Majesky, Flor. RC**	**35.00**
□	**88 ChuckKobasew, Calg. RC**	**75.00**
□	**89 Ales Hemsky, Edmo. RC**	**100.00**
□	**90 Radovan Somik, Phil. RC**	**35.00**
□	**91 Dmitri Bykov, Detr. RC**	**35.00**
□	**92 Ryan Miller, Buff. RC**	**100.00**
□	**93 Ron Hainsey, Mont. RC**	**50.00**
□	**94 Anton Volchenkov, Otta. RC**	**35.00**
□	95 Dick Tarnström, Pitt.	35.00
□	**96 Scottie Upshall, Nash. RC**	**75.00**
□	**97 Jordan Leopold, Calg. RC**	**50.00**
□	**98 Carlo Colaiacovo, Toro. RC**	**50.00**
□	**99 Levente Szuper (G), Calg. RC**	**35.00**
□	**100 Lynn Loyns, SanJ. RC**	**35.00**

SHIMMER

	Description	S
□	101 Adam Oates, Anah.	5.00
□	102 Paul Kariya, Anah.	5.00
□	103 Petr Sykora, Anah.	5.00
□	104 Dany Heatley, Atla.	5.00
□	105 Ilya Kovalchuk, Atla.	5.00
□	106 Jeff O'Neill, Caro.	5.00
□	107 Joe Thornton, Bost.	5.00
□	108 Sergei Samsonov, Bost.	5.00
□	109 Jarome Iginla, Calg.	5.00
□	110 Ron Francis, Caro.	5.00
□	111 Jocelyn Thibault (G), Chic.	5.00
□	112 Alex Tanguay, Colo.	5.00
□	113 Joe Sakic, Colo.	10.00
□	114 Milan Hejduk, Colo.	5.00
□	115 Patrick Roy (G), Colo.	15.00
□	116 Peter Forsberg, Colo.	5.00
□	117 Rob Blake, Colo.	5.00
□	118 Rostislav Klesla, Colu.	5.00
□	119 Brett Hull, Detr.	5.00
□	120 Marty Turco (G), Dall.	5.00
□	121 Mike Modano, Dall.	5.00
□	122 Bill Guerin, Dall.	5.00
□	123 Brendan Shanahan, Detr.	5.00
□	124 Chris Chelios, Detr.	5.00
□	125 Curtis Joseph (G), Detr.	5.00
□	126 Luc Robitaille, Detr.	5.00
□	127 Nicklas Lidström, Detr.	5.00
□	128 Pavel Datsyuk, Detr.	5.00
□	129 Sergei Fedorov, Detr.	5.00
□	130 Steve Yzerman, Detr.	15.00
□	131 Mike Comrie, Edmo.	5.00
□	132 Erik Cole, Caro.	5.00
□	133 Kristian Huselius, Flor.	5.00
□	134 Roberto Luongo (G), Flor.	5.00
□	135 Félix Potvin (G), LosA.	5.00
□	136 Jason Allison, LosA.	5.00
□	137 Zigmund Palffy, LosA.	5.00
□	138 Marian Gaborik, MinW.	5.00
□	139 José Théodore (G), Mont.	5.00
□	140 Saku Koivu, Mont.	5.00
□	141 Martin Brodeur (G), NJer.	10.00
□	142 Patrik Elias, NJer.	5.00
□	143 Scott Gomez, NJer.	5.00
□	144 Alexei Yashin, NYIs.	5.00
□	145 Chris Osgood (G), NYIs.	5.00
□	146 Rick DiPietro (G), NYIs.	5.00
□	147 Brian Leetch, NYRa.	5.00
□	148 Eric Lindros, NYRa.	5.00
□	149 Mark Messier, NYRa.	5.00
□	150 Mike Richter (G), NYRa.	5.00
□	151 Pavel Bure, NYRa.	5.00
□	152 Daniel Alfredsson, Otta.	5.00
□	153 Marian Hossa, Otta.	5.00
□	154 Martin Havlat, Otta.	5.00
□	155 Jeremy Roenick, Phil.	5.00
□	156 John LeClair, Phil.	5.00
□	157 Mark Recchi, Phil.	5.00
□	158 Simon Gagné, Phil.	5.00
□	159 Nikolai Khabibulin (G), Phoe.	5.00
□	160 Sean Burke (G), Phoe.	5.00
□	161 Johan Hedberg (G), Pitt.	5.00
□	162 Mario Lemieux, Pitt.	15.00
□	163 Evgeni Nabokov (G), SanJ.	5.00
□	164 Owen Nolan, SanJ.	5.00
□	165 Teemu Selänne, SanJ.	5.00
□	166 Al MacInnis, SLou.	5.00
□	167 Chris Pronger, SLou.	5.00
□	168 Doug Weight, SLou.	5.00
□	169 Keith Tkachuk, SLou.	5.00
□	170 Vincent Lecavalier, Tamp.	5.00
□	171 Ed Belfour (G), Toro.	5.00
□	172 Mats Sundin, Toro.	5.00
□	173 Daniel Sedin, Vanc.	5.00
□	174 Henrik Sedin, Vanc.	5.00
□	175 Markus Näslund, Vanc.	5.00
□	176 Todd Bertuzzi, Vanc.	5.00
□	177 Jaromir Jagr, Wash.	5.00
□	178 Olaf Kölzig (G), Wash.	5.00
□	179 Peter Bondra, Wash.	5.00
□	180 Tony Amonte, Phoe.	5.00

ROOKIES

	Insert (*100)	R
□	**181 Shaone Morrisonn, Bost. RC**	**35.00**
□	**182 Kari Haakana, Edmo. RC**	**35.00**
□	**183 Ray Emery, Otta. RC**	**35.00**
□	**184 Mike Cammalleri, LosA. RC**	**75.00**
□	**185 Ari Ahonen, NJer. RC**	**50.00**
□	**186 Martin Gerber (G), Anah. RC**	**35.00**
□	**187 Adam Hall (G), Nash. RC**	**50.00**
□	**188 Lasse Pirjetä, Colu. RC**	**35.00**
□	**189 Stéphane Veilleux, MinW. RC**	**35.00**
□	**190 Jeff Taffe, Phoe. RC**	**50.00**
□	**191 Mikael Tellqvist (G), Toro. RC**	**35.00**
□	**192 Alexander Frolov, LosA. RC**	**100.00**
□	**193 Steve Eminger, Wash. RC**	**35.00**
□	**194 Shawn Thornton, Chic. RC**	**35.00**
□	**195 Alexander Svitov, Tamp. RC**	**75.00**
□	**196 Alexei Smirnov, Anah. RC**	**50.00**
□	**197 Curtis Sanford (G), SLou. RC**	**35.00**
□	**198 Henrik Zetterberg, Detr. RC**	**225.00**
□	**199 Eric Godard, NYIs. RC**	**35.00**
□	**200 Jason Spezza, Otta. RC**	**150.00**

CALDER GAME-USED JERSEY

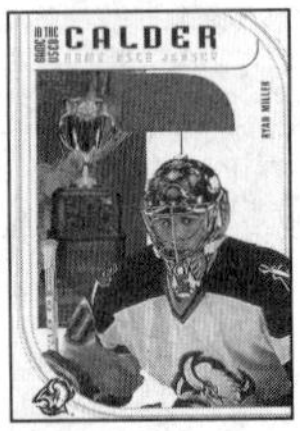

Insert Set (20 cards): 1100.00

	Insert (*50)	C50
□	Jay Bouwmeester, Flor. ✂	75.00
□	Mike Cammalleri, LosA. ✂	60.00
□	Stanislav Chistov, Anah. ✂	75.00
□	Alexander Frolov, LosA. ✂	75.00
□	Ron Hainsey, Mont. ✂	60.00
□	Adam Hall (G), Nash. ✂	60.00
□	Ales Hemsky, Edmo. ✂	75.00
□	Ivan Huml, Bost. ✂	60.00
□	Niko Kapanen, Dall. ✂	60.00
□	Chuck Kobasew, Calg. ✂	60.00
□	Jordan Leopold, Calg. ✂ Red	60.00
□	Ryan Miller, Buff. ✂	75.00

☐ Rick Nash, Colu. ✂ 150.00
☐ Dennis Seidenberg, Phil. ✂ 60.00
☐ Alexei Smirnov, Anah. ✂ 60.00
☐ Radovan Somik, Phil. ✂ 60.00
☐ Jason Spezza, Otta. ✂ 100.00
☐ Alexander Svitov, Tamp. ✂ 60.00
☐ Anton Volchenkov, Otta. ✂ 60.00
☐ Stephen Weiss, Flor. ✂ 75.00

CALDER GAME-USED JERSEY GOLD

Actual realised pricing on these scarce cards may vary considerably from listed prices.

Insert Set (20 cards): 2800.00
Insert (*10) CG
☐ Jay Bouwmeester, Flor. ✂ 200.00
☐ Mike Cammalleri, LosA. ✂ 150.00
☐ Stanislav Chistov, Anah. ✂ 200.00
☐ Alexander Frolov, LosA. ✂ 175.00
☐ Ron Hainsey, Mont. ✂ 150.00
☐ Adam Hall (G), Nash. ✂ 150.00
☐ Ales Hemsky, Edmo. ✂ 200.00
☐ Ivan Huml, Bost. ✂ 150.00
☐ Niko Kapanen, Dall. ✂ 150.00
☐ Chuck Kobasew, Calg. ✂ 150.00
☐ Jordan Leopold, Calg. ✂ 150.00
☐ Ryan Miller, Buff. ✂ 175.00
☐ Rick Nash, Colu. ✂ 350.00
☐ Dennis Seidenberg, Phil. ✂ 150.00
☐ Alexei Smirnov, Anah. ✂ 150.00
☐ Radovan Somik, Phil. ✂ 150.00
☐ Jason Spezza, Otta. ✂ 250.00
☐ Alexander Svitov, Tamp. ✂ 150.00
☐ Anton Volchenkov, Otta. ✂ 150.00
☐ Stephen Weiss, Flor. ✂ 175.00

EMBLEM

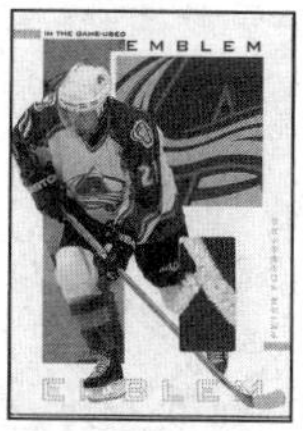

Actual realised pricing on these scarce cards may vary considerably from listed prices.

Insert Set (40 cards): 10800.00
Insert (*9) E9
☐ Daniel Alfredsson, Otta. ✂ 400.00
☐ Jay Bouwmeester, Flor. ✂ 300.00
☐ Martin Brodeur (G), NJer. ✂ 500.00
☐ Pavel Bure, NYRa. ✂ 200.00
☐ Sergei Fedorov, Detr. ✂ 300.00
☐ Peter Forsberg, Colo. ✂ 400.00
☐ Marian Gaborik, MinW. ✂ 300.00
☐ Dany Heatley, Atla. ✂ 300.00
☐ Milan Hejduk, Colo. ✂ 200.00
☐ Bobby Holik, NYRa. ✂ 200.00
☐ Brett Hull, Detr. ✂ 300.00
☐ Jarome Iginla, Calg. ✂ 200.00
☐ Jaromir Jagr, Wash. ✂ 300.00
☐ Paul Kariya, Anah. ✂ 400.00
☐ Saku Koivu, Mont. ✂ 400.00
☐ Ilya Kovalchuk, Atla. ✂ 300.00
☐ John LeClair, Phil. ✂ 200.00
☐ Brian Leetch, NYRa. ✂ 200.00
☐ Mario Lemieux, Pitt. ✂ 1000.00
☐ Nicklas Lidström, Detr. ✂ 200.00
☐ Eric Lindros, NYRa. ✂ 300.00
☐ Al MacInnis, SLou. ✂ 200.00
☐ Mark Messier, NYRa. ✂ 300.00
☐ Mike Modano, Dall. ✂ 300.00
☐ Alexander Mogilny, Toro. ✂ 200.00
☐ Rick Nash, Colu. ✂ 500.00
☐ Markus Näslund, Vanc. ✂ 300.00
☐ Owen Nolan, SanJ. ✂ 200.00
☐ Jeremy Roenick, Phil. ✂ 200.00
☐ Patrick Roy (G), Colo. ✂ 800.00
☐ Joe Sakic, Colo. ✂ 500.00
☐ Teemu Selänne, SanJ. ✂ 200.00
☐ Brendan Shanahan, Detr. ✂ 300.00
☐ Jason Spezza, Otta. ✂ 400.00
☐ Mats Sundin, Toro. ✂ 300.00
☐ José Théodore (G), Mont. ✂ 400.00
☐ Joe Thornton, Bost. ✂ 400.00
☐ Keith Tkachuk, SLou. ✂ 200.00
☐ Alexei Yashin, NYIs. ✂ 200.00
☐ Steve Yzerman, Detr. ✂ 800.00

EMBLEM GOLD

Insert Set (20 cards):
Insert (*1) EG1
☐ Daniel Alfredsson, Otta. ✂
☐ Jay Bouwmeester, Flor. ✂
☐ Martin Brodeur (G), NJer. ✂
☐ Pavel Bure, NYRa. ✂
☐ Sergei Fedorov, Detr. ✂
☐ Peter Forsberg, Colo. ✂
☐ Marian Gaborik, MinW. ✂
☐ Dany Heatley, Atla. ✂
☐ Milan Hejduk, Colo. ✂
☐ Bobby Holik, NYRa. ✂
☐ Brett Hull, Detr. ✂
☐ Jarome Iginla, Calg. ✂
☐ Jaromir Jagr, Wash. ✂
☐ Paul Kariya, Anah. ✂
☐ Saku Koivu, Mont. ✂
☐ Ilya Kovalchuk, Atla. ✂
☐ John LeClair, Phil. ✂
☐ Brian Leetch, NYRa. ✂
☐ Mario Lemieux, Pitt. ✂
☐ Nicklas Lidström, Detr. ✂
☐ Eric Lindros, NYRa. ✂
☐ Al MacInnis, SLou. ✂
☐ Mark Messier, NYRa. ✂
☐ Mike Modano, Dall. ✂
☐ Alexander Mogilny, Toro. ✂
☐ Rick Nash, Colu. ✂
☐ Markus Näslund, Vanc. ✂
☐ Owen Nolan, SanJ. ✂
☐ Jeremy Roenick, Phil. ✂
☐ Patrick Roy (G), Colo. ✂
☐ Joe Sakic, Colo. ✂
☐ Teemu Selänne, SanJ. ✂
☐ Brendan Shanahan, Detr. ✂
☐ Jason Spezza, Otta. ✂
☐ Mats Sundin, Toro. ✂
☐ José Théodore (G), Mont. ✂
☐ Joe Thornton, Bost. ✂
☐ Keith Tkachuk, SLou. ✂
☐ Alexei Yashin, NYIs. ✂
☐ Steve Yzerman, Detr. ✂

FRANCHISE JERSEY

Insert Set (30 cards): 1600.00
Insert (*65) FrJers65
☐ Daniel Brière, Phoe. ✂ 35.00
☐ Martin Brodeur (G), NJer. ✂ 100.00
☐ Pavel Bure, NYRa. ✂ 50.00
☐ Mike Comrie, Edmo. ✂ 50.00
☐ Éric Dazé, Chic. ✂ 35.00
☐ Marian Gaborik, MinW. ✂ 75.00
☐ Simon Gagné, Phil. ✂ 50.00
☐ Scott Hartnell, Nash. ✂ 35.00
☐ Marian Hossa, Otta. ✂ 75.00
☐ Jarome Iginla, Calg. ✂ 50.00
☐ Jaromir Jagr, Wash. ✂ 75.00
☐ Paul Kariya, Anah. ✂ 100.00
☐ Nikolai Khabibulin (G), Tamp. ✂ 35.00
☐ Rostislav Klesla, Colu. ✂ 35.00
☐ Ilya Kovalchuk, Atla. ✂ 75.00
☐ Mario Lemieux, Pitt. ✂ 225.00
☐ Roberto Luongo (G), Flor. ✂ 50.00
☐ Mike Modano, Dall. ✂ 75.00
☐ Markus Näslund, Vanc. ✂ 75.00
☐ Owen Nolan, SanJ. ✂ 35.00
☐ Jeff O'Neill, Caro. ✂ 35.00
☐ Zigmund Palffy, LosA. ✂ 35.00
☐ Chris Pronger, SLou. ✂ 35.00
☐ Patrick Roy (G), Colo. ✂ 175.00
☐ Miroslav Satan, Buff. ✂ 35.00
☐ Mats Sundin, Toro. ✂ 75.00
☐ José Théodore (G), Mont. ✂ 75.00
☐ Joe Thornton, Bost. ✂ 75.00
☐ Alexei Yashin, NYIs. ✂ 35.00
☐ Steve Yzerman, Detr. ✂ 175.00

FRANCHISE JERSEY GOLD

Actual realised pricing on these scarce cards may vary considerably from listed prices.

Insert Set (30 cards): 7100.00
Insert (*10) FJG
☐ Daniel Brière, Phoe. ✂ 150.00
☐ Martin Brodeur (G), NJer. ✂ 475.00
☐ Pavel Bure, NYRa. ✂ 225.00
☐ Mike Comrie, Edmo. ✂ 225.00
☐ Éric Dazé, Chic. ✂ 150.00
☐ Marian Gaborik, MinW. ✂ 300.00
☐ Simon Gagné, Phil. ✂ 225.00
☐ Scott Hartnell, Nash. ✂ 150.00
☐ Marian Hossa, Otta. ✂ 300.00
☐ Jarome Iginla, Calg. ✂ 225.00
☐ Jaromir Jagr, Wash. ✂ 300.00
☐ Paul Kariya, Anah. ✂ 400.00
☐ Nikolai Khabibulin (G), Tamp. ✂ 150.00
☐ Rostislav Klesla, Colu. ✂ 175.00
☐ Ilya Kovalchuk, Atla. ✂ 300.00
☐ Mario Lemieux, Pitt. ✂ 900.00
☐ Roberto Luongo (G), Flor. ✂ 225.00
☐ Mike Modano, Dall. ✂ 300.00
☐ Markus Näslund, Vanc. ✂ 300.00
☐ Owen Nolan, SanJ. ✂ 175.00
☐ Jeff O'Neill, Caro. ✂ 150.00
☐ Zigmund Palffy, LosA. ✂ 175.00
☐ Chris Pronger, SLou. ✂ 175.00
☐ Patrick Roy (G), Colo. ✂ 700.00
☐ Miroslav Satan, Buff. ✂ 150.00
☐ Mats Sundin, Toro. ✂ 300.00
☐ José Théodore (G), Mont. ✂ 350.00
☐ Joe Thornton, Bost. ✂ 350.00
☐ Alexei Yashin, NYIs. ✂ 175.00
☐ Steve Yzerman, Detr. ✂ 700.00

FRANCHISE JERSEY SIGNED

Actual realised pricing on these scarce cards may vary considerably from listed prices.

Insert Set (26 cards): 7300.00
Insert (*10) Aut
☐ Daniel Brière, Phoe. ✍ ✂ 200.00
☐ Pavel Bure, NYRa. ✍ ✂ 300.00
☐ Mike Comrie, Edmo. ✍ ✂ 300.00
☐ Éric Dazé, Chic. ✍ ✂ 200.00
☐ Marian Gaborik, MinW. ✍ ✂ 300.00
☐ Simon Gagné, Phil. ✍ ✂ 300.00
☐ Scott Hartnell, Nash. ✍ ✂ 200.00
☐ Marian Hossa, Otta. ✍ ✂ 300.00
☐ Jarome Iginla, Calg. ✍ ✂ 300.00
☐ Paul Kariya, Anah. ✍ ✂ 500.00
☐ Nikolai Khabibulin (G), Tamp. ✍ ✂ 200.00
☐ Rostislav Klesla, Colu. ✍ ✂ 200.00
☐ Ilya Kovalchuk, Atla. ✍ ✂ 300.00
☐ Mario Lemieux, Pitt. ✍ ✂ 1100.00
☐ Roberto Luongo (G), Flor. ✍ ✂ 300.00
☐ Markus Näslund, Vanc. ✍ ✂ 300.00
☐ Jeff O'Neill, Caro. ✍ ✂ 200.00
☐ Zigmund Palffy, LosA. ✍ ✂ 200.00
☐ Chris Pronger, SLou. ✍ ✂ 200.00
☐ Patrick Roy (G), Colo. ✍ ✂ 900.00
☐ Miroslav Satan, Buff. ✍ ✂ 200.00
☐ Mats Sundin, Toro. ✍ ✂ 300.00
☐ José Théodore (G), Mont. ✍ ✂ 400.00
☐ Joe Thornton, Bost. ✍ ✂ 400.00
☐ Alexei Yashin, NYIs. ✍ ✂ 200.00
☐ Steve Yzerman, Detr. ✍ ✂ 900.00

GOALIE PAD & JERSEY

Insert Set (20 cards): 1600.00
Insert (*50) GP
☐ Aubin (G), Pitt. ✂ ✂ 60.00
☐ Ed Belfour (G), Dall. ✂ ✂ 125.00
☐ Brian Boucher, Phil. ✂ ✂ 60.00
☐ Martin Brodeur (G), NJer. ✂ ✂ 200.00
☐ Sean Burke (G), Phoe. ✂ ✂ 75.00
☐ Roman Cechmanek (G), Phil. ✂ ✂ 60.00
☐ Gerry Cheevers (G), Bost. ✂ ✂ 125.00
☐ Dan Cloutier (G), Vanc. ✂ ✂ 60.00
☐ Mike Dunham (G), Nash. ✂ ✂ 60.00
☐ Jeff Hackett (G), Mont. ✂ ✂ 60.00
☐ Ron Hextall, Phil. ✂ ✂ 75.00
☐ Chris Osgood (G), Detr. ✂ ✂ 75.00
☐ Bernie Parent (G), Phil. ✂ ✂ 125.00
☐ Patrick Roy (G), Mont. ✂ ✂ 300.00
☐ Terry Sawchuk (G), Detr. ✂ ✂ 250.00
☐ José Théodore (G), Mont. ✂ ✂ 150.00
☐ Jocelyn Thibault (G), Chic. ✂ ✂ 60.00
☐ Marty Turco (G), Dall. ✂ ✂ 75.00
☐ Roman Turek (G), Dall. ✂ ✂ 60.00
☐ Tomas Vokoun (G), Nash. ✂ ✂ 60.00

GOALIE PAD & JERSEY GOLD

Actual realised pricing on these scarce cards may vary considerably from listed prices.

Insert Set (20 cards): 4000.00
Insert (*10) GP
☐ Aubin (G), Pitt. ✂ ✂ 150.00
☐ Ed Belfour (G), Dall. ✂ ✂ 300.00
☐ Brian Boucher, Phil. ✂ ✂ 150.00
☐ Martin Brodeur (G), NJer. ✂ ✂ 475.00
☐ Sean Burke (G), Phoe. ✂ ✂ 175.00
☐ Roman Cechmanek (G), Phil. ✂ ✂ 150.00
☐ Gerry Cheevers (G), Bost. ✂ ✂ 300.00
☐ Dan Cloutier (G), Vanc. ✂ ✂ 150.00
☐ Mike Dunham (G), Nash. ✂ ✂ 150.00
☐ Jeff Hackett (G), Mont. ✂ ✂ 150.00
☐ Ron Hextall, Phil. ✂ ✂ 175.00
☐ Chris Osgood (G), Detr. ✂ ✂ 175.00
☐ Bernie Parent (G), Phil. ✂ ✂ 300.00
☐ Patrick Roy (G), Mont. ✂ ✂ 700.00
☐ Terry Sawchuk (G), Detr. ✂ ✂ 600.00
☐ José Théodore (G), Mont. ✂ ✂ 350.00
☐ Jocelyn Thibault (G), Chic. ✂ ✂ 150.00
☐ Marty Turco (G), Dall. ✂ ✂ 175.00
☐ Roman Turek (G), Dall. ✂ ✂ 150.00
☐ Tomas Vokoun (G), Nash. ✂ ✂ 150.00

INTERNATIONAL EXPERIENCE

Insert Set (28 cards): 1300.00
Insert (*60) IE
☐ Tony Amonte, Phoe. ✂ 35.00
☐ Radek Bonk, Otta. ✂ 35.00
☐ Martin Brodeur (G), NJer. ✂ 100.00
☐ Roman Cechmanek (G), Phil. ✂ 35.00
☐ Chris Chelios, Detr. ✂ 35.00
☐ Peter Forsberg, Colo. ✂ 100.00
☐ Bill Guerin, Dall. ✂ 35.00
☐ Johan Hedberg (G), Pitt. ✂ 35.00
☐ Bobby Holik, NYRa. ✂ 35.00
☐ Jaromir Jagr, Wash. ✂ 75.00
☐ Curtis Joseph (G), Detr. ✂ 75.00
☐ Darius Kasparaitis, NYRa. ✂ 35.00
☐ Nikolai Khabibulin (G), Tamp. ✂ 35.00
☐ Saku Koivu, Mont. ✂ 75.00
☐ Olaf Kölzig (G), Wash. ✂ 35.00
☐ Brian Leetch, NYRa. ✂ 35.00
☐ Mario Lemieux, Pitt. ✂ 225.00
☐ Nicklas Lidström, Detr. ✂ 35.00
☐ Mike Modano, Dall. ✂ 75.00
☐ Alexander Mogilny, Toro. ✂ 35.00
☐ Zigmund Palffy, LosA. ✂ 35.00
☐ Joe Sakic, Colo. ✂ 100.00
☐ Tommy Salo (G), Edmo. ✂ 35.00
☐ Teemu Selänne, SanJ. ✂ 50.00
☐ Mats Sundin, Toro. ✂ 75.00
☐ Roman Turek (G), Calg. ✂ 35.00
☐ Alexei Yashin, NYIs. ✂ 35.00
☐ Steve Yzerman, Detr. ✂ 175.00

INTERNATIONAL EXPERIENCE GOLD

Actual realised pricing on these scarce cards may vary considerably from listed prices.

Insert Set (28 cards): 5900.00
Insert (*10) IEG
☐ Tony Amonte, Phoe. ✂ 175.00
☐ Radek Bonk, Otta. ✂ 150.00
☐ Martin Brodeur (G), NJer. ✂ 475.00
☐ Roman Cechmanek (G), Phil. ✂ 150.00
☐ Chris Chelios, Detr. ✂ 175.00
☐ Peter Forsberg, Colo. ✂ 400.00
☐ Bill Guerin, Dall. ✂ 150.00
☐ Johan Hedberg (G), Pitt. ✂ 150.00
☐ Bobby Holik, NYRa. ✂ 150.00
☐ Jaromir Jagr, Wash. ✂ 300.00
☐ Curtis Joseph (G), Detr. ✂ 300.00
☐ Darius Kasparaitis, NYRa. ✂ 150.00
☐ Nikolai Khabibulin (G), Tamp. ✂ 150.00
☐ Saku Koivu, Mont. ✂ 350.00
☐ Olaf Kölzig (G), Wash. ✂ 175.00
☐ Brian Leetch, NYRa. ✂ 175.00
☐ Mario Lemieux, Pitt. ✂ 900.00
☐ Nicklas Lidström, Detr. ✂ 175.00
☐ Mike Modano, Dall. ✂ 300.00
☐ Alexander Mogilny, Toro. ✂ 150.00
☐ Zigmund Palffy, LosA. ✂ 175.00
☐ Joe Sakic, Colo. ✂ 475.00

☐	Tommy Salo (G), Edmo. ✂	150.00
☐	Teemu Selänne, SanJ. ✂	225.00
☐	Mats Sundin, Toro. ✂	300.00
☐	Roman Turek (G), Calg. ✂	150.00
☐	Alexei Yashin, NYIs. ✂	175.00
☐	Steve Yzerman, Detr. ✂	700.00

JERSEY

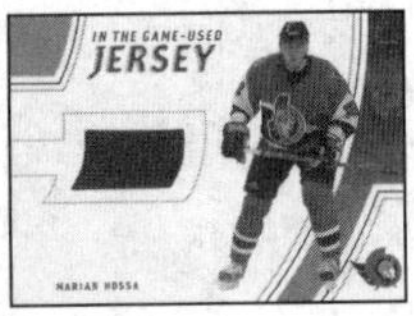

Insert Set (50 cards): 2300.00

	Insert (*75)	Jers75
☐	Daniel Alfredsson, Otta. ✂	75.00
☐	Todd Bertuzzi, Vanc. ✂	75.00
☐	Rob Blake, Colo. ✂	40.00
☐	Peter Bondra, Wash. ✂	40.00
☐	Martin Brodeur (G), NJer. ✂	100.00
☐	Pavel Bure, NYRa. ✂ Blue	50.00
☐	Chris Chelios, Detr. ✂	40.00
☐	Mike Comrie, Edmo. ✂	50.00
☐	Éric Dazé, Chic. ✂	40.00
☐	Sergei Fedorov, Detr. ✂	50.00
☐	Peter Forsberg, Colo. ✂	75.00
☐	Ron Francis, Caro. ✂	40.00
☐	Marian Gaborik, MinW. ✂	50.00
☐	Dany Heatley, Atla. ✂	50.00
☐	Milan Hejduk, Colo. ✂	50.00
☐	Marian Hossa, Otta. ✂	50.00
☐	Jarome Iginla, Calg. ✂	50.00
☐	Jaromir Jagr, Wash. ✂	50.00
☐	Paul Kariya, Anah. ✂	75.00
☐	Saku Koivu, Mont. ✂	75.00
☐	Ilya Kovalchuk, Atla. ✂	50.00
☐	John LeClair, Phil. ✂	50.00
☐	Brian Leetch, NYRa. ✂	40.00
☐	Mario Lemieux, Pitt. ✂	200.00
☐	Nicklas Lidström, Detr. ✂	40.00
☐	Eric Lindros, NYRa. ✂	50.00
☐	Al MacInnis, SLou. ✂	40.00
☐	Mark Messier, NYRa. ✂	50.00
☐	Mike Modano, Dall. ✂	50.00
☐	Alexander Mogilny, Toro. ✂	40.00
☐	Markus Näslund, Vanc. ✂	50.00
☐	Owen Nolan, SanJ. ✂	40.00
☐	Zigmund Palffy, LosA. ✂	40.00
☐	Chris Pronger, SLou. ✂	40.00
☐	Mark Recchi, Phil. ✂	40.00
☐	Luc Robitaille, Detr. ✂	50.00
☐	Jeremy Roenick, Phil. ✂	50.00
☐	Patrick Roy (G), Colo. ✂	150.00
☐	Joe Sakic, Colo. ✂	100.00
☐	Sergei Samsonov, Bost. ✂	40.00
☐	Teemu Selänne, SanJ. ✂	50.00
☐	Brendan Shanahan, Detr. ✂	50.00
☐	Mats Sundin, Toro. ✂	50.00
☐	José Théodore (G), Mont. ✂	75.00
☐	Joe Thornton, Bost. ✂	75.00
☐	Keith Tkachuk, SLou. ✂	40.00
☐	Pierre Turgeon, Dall. ✂	40.00
☐	Doug Weight, SLou. ✂	40.00
☐	Alexei Yashin, NYIs. ✂	40.00
☐	Steve Yzerman, Detr. ✂	150.00

JERSEY GOLD

Actual realised pricing on these scarce cards may vary considerably from listed prices.

Insert Set (50 cards): 11300.00

	Insert (*10)	JG
☐	Daniel Alfredsson, Otta. ✂	350.00
☐	Todd Bertuzzi, Vanc. ✂	350.00
☐	Rob Blake, Colo. ✂	175.00
☐	Peter Bondra, Wash. ✂	175.00
☐	Martin Brodeur (G), NJer. ✂	475.00
☐	Pavel Bure, NYRa. ✂	225.00
☐	Chris Chelios, Detr. ✂	175.00
☐	Mike Comrie, Edmo. ✂	225.00
☐	Éric Dazé, Chic. ✂	150.00
☐	Sergei Fedorov, Detr. ✂	300.00
☐	Peter Forsberg, Colo. ✂	400.00
☐	Ron Francis, Caro. ✂	175.00
☐	Marian Gaborik, MinW. ✂	300.00
☐	Dany Heatley, Atla. ✂	300.00
☐	Milan Hejduk, Colo. ✂	225.00
☐	Marian Hossa, Otta. ✂	300.00
☐	Jarome Iginla, Calg. ✂	225.00
☐	Jaromir Jagr, Wash. ✂	300.00
☐	Paul Kariya, Anah. ✂	400.00
☐	Saku Koivu, Mont. ✂	350.00
☐	Ilya Kovalchuk, Atla. ✂	300.00
☐	John LeClair, Phil. ✂	225.00
☐	Brian Leetch, NYRa. ✂	175.00
☐	Mario Lemieux, Pitt. ✂	900.00
☐	Nicklas Lidström, Detr. ✂	175.00
☐	Eric Lindros, NYRa. ✂	300.00
☐	Al MacInnis, SLou. ✂	150.00
☐	Mark Messier, NYRa. ✂	300.00
☐	Mike Modano, Dall. ✂	300.00
☐	Alexander Mogilny, Toro. ✂	150.00
☐	Markus Näslund, Vanc. ✂	300.00
☐	Owen Nolan, SanJ. ✂	175.00
☐	Zigmund Palffy, LosA. ✂	175.00
☐	Chris Pronger, SLou. ✂	175.00
☐	Mark Recchi, Phil. ✂	150.00
☐	Luc Robitaille, Detr. ✂	225.00
☐	Jeremy Roenick, Phil. ✂	225.00
☐	Patrick Roy (G), Colo. ✂	700.00
☐	Joe Sakic, Colo. ✂	475.00
☐	Sergei Samsonov, Bost. ✂	175.00
☐	Teemu Selänne, SanJ. ✂	225.00
☐	Brendan Shanahan, Detr. ✂	300.00
☐	Mats Sundin, Toro. ✂	300.00
☐	José Théodore (G), Mont. ✂	350.00
☐	Joe Thornton, Bost. ✂	350.00
☐	Keith Tkachuk, SLou. ✂	175.00
☐	Pierre Turgeon, Dall. ✂	150.00
☐	Doug Weight, SLou. ✂	175.00
☐	Alexei Yashin, NYIs. ✂	175.00
☐	Steve Yzerman, Detr. ✂	700.00

JERSEY SIGNED

Actual realised pricing on these scarce cards may vary considerably from listed prices.

Insert Set (42 cards): 12300.00

	Insert (*10)	Aut
☐	Daniel Alfredsson, Otta. ✍ ✂	450.00
☐	Todd Bertuzzi, Vanc. ✍ ✂	450.00
☐	Rob Blake, Colo. ✍ ✂	225.00
☐	Peter Bondra, Wash. ✍ ✂	225.00
☐	Pavel Bure, NYRa. ✍ ✂	300.00
☐	Chris Chelios, Detr. ✍ ✂	225.00
☐	Mike Comrie, Edmo. ✍ ✂	300.00
☐	Éric Dazé, Chic. ✍ ✂	200.00
☐	Sergei Fedorov, Detr. ✍ ✂	375.00
☐	Peter Forsberg, Colo. ✍ ✂	525.00
☐	Ron Francis, Caro. ✍ ✂	225.00
☐	Marian Gaborik, MinW. ✍ ✂	375.00
☐	Dany Heatley, Atla. ✍ ✂	375.00
☐	Marian Hossa, Otta. ✍ ✂	375.00
☐	Jarome Iginla, Calg. ✍ ✂	300.00
☐	Paul Kariya, Anah. ✍ ✂	525.00
☐	Saku Koivu, Mont. ✍ ✂	450.00
☐	Ilya Kovalchuk, Atla. ✍ ✂	375.00
☐	John LeClair, Phil. ✍ ✂	300.00
☐	Brian Leetch, NYRa. ✍ ✂	225.00
☐	Mario Lemieux, Pitt. ✍ ✂	1125.00
☐	Nicklas Lidström, Detr. ✍ ✂	225.00
☐	Al MacInnis, SLou. ✍ ✂	200.00
☐	Markus Näslund, Vanc. ✍ ✂	375.00
☐	Zigmund Palffy, LosA. ✍ ✂	225.00
☐	Chris Pronger, SLou. ✍ ✂	225.00
☐	Mark Recchi, Phil. ✍ ✂	200.00
☐	Luc Robitaille, Detr. ✍ ✂	300.00
☐	Jeremy Roenick, Phil. ✍ ✂	300.00
☐	Patrick Roy (G), Colo. ✍ ✂	900.00
☐	Joe Sakic, Colo. ✍ ✂	600.00
☐	Sergei Samsonov, Bost. ✍ ✂	225.00
☐	Teemu Selänne, SanJ. ✍ ✂	300.00
☐	Brendan Shanahan, Detr. ✍ ✂	375.00
☐	Mats Sundin, Toro. ✍ ✂	375.00
☐	José Théodore (G), Mont. ✍ ✂	450.00
☐	Joe Thornton, Bost. ✍ ✂	450.00
☐	Keith Tkachuk, SLou. ✍ ✂	225.00
☐	Pierre Turgeon, Dall. ✍ ✂	200.00
☐	Doug Weight, SLou. ✍ ✂	225.00
☐	Alexei Yashin, NYIs. ✍ ✂	225.00
☐	Steve Yzerman, Detr. ✍ ✂	900.00

MAGNIFICENT

Insert Set (10 cards): 4800.00

	Insert	ML
☐	MI-1 Mario Lemieux, Pitt. ✂ {#/40}	300.00
☐	MI-2 Mario Lemieux, Pitt. ✂ {#/40}	300.00
☐	MI-3 Mario Lemieux, Pitt. ✂ {#/40}	300.00
☐	MI-4 Mario Lemieux, Pitt. ✂ {#/40}	300.00
☐	MI-5 Mario Lemieux, Pitt. ✂ {#/40}	
☐	MI-6 Mario Lemieux, Pitt. ✂ {#/10}	900.00
☐	MI-7 Mario Lemieux, Pitt. ✂ {#/10}	900.00
☐	MI-8 Mario Lemieux, Pitt. ✂ ✂ ✂ {#/10}	
☐	MI-9 Mario Lemieux, Pitt. ✂ ✂ ✂ ✂ {#/10}	
☐	MI-10 Mario Lemieux, Pitt. ✂ ✂ ✂ ✂ {#/10}	

MAGNIFICENT AUTOGRAPHED

Actual realised pricing on these scarce cards may vary considerably from listed prices.

Insert Set (10 cards): 9800.00

	Insert	ML
☐	MI-1 Mario Lemieux, Pitt. ✍ ✂ {#/15}	1200.00
☐	MI-2 Mario Lemieux, Pitt. ✍ ✂ {#/15}	1200.00
☐	MI-3 Mario Lemieux, Pitt. ✍ ✂ {#/15}	1200.00
☐	MI-4 Mario Lemieux, Pitt. ✍ ✂ {#/15}	1200.00
☐	MI-5 Mario Lemieux, Pitt. ✍ ✂ ✂ {#/15}	1200.00
☐	MI-6 Mario Lemieux, Pitt. ✍ ✂ {#/5}	1500.00
☐	MI-7 Mario Lemieux, Pitt. ✍ ✂ {#/5}	1500.00
☐	MI-8 Mario Lemieux, Pitt. ✍ ✂ ✂ ✂ {#/5}	
☐	MI-9 Mario Lemieux, Pitt. ✍ ✂ ✂ ✂ ✂ {#/5}	

◆ The Mario Lemieux #MI-9, hand-numbered 5/5, sold for $2,200 U.S. (approx. $3,300 Cdn.) at eBay.ca on April 30, 2003.

☐	MI-10 Mario Lemieux, Pitt. ✍ ✂ ✂ ✂ ✂ {#/5}	

STICK & JERSEY

Insert Set (50 cards): 2600.00

	Insert (*75)	SJ75
☐	Daniel Alfredsson, Otta. ✂ ✂	75.00
☐	Todd Bertuzzi, Vanc. ✂ ✂	75.00
☐	Rob Blake, Colo. ✂ ✂	35.00
☐	Peter Bondra, Wash. ✂ ✂	35.00
☐	Martin Brodeur (G), NJer. ✂ ✂	100.00
☐	Pavel Bure, NYRa. ✂ ✂	50.00
☐	Chris Chelios, Detr. ✂ ✂	35.00
☐	Mike Comrie, Edmo. ✂ ✂	50.00
☐	Éric Dazé, Chic. ✂ ✂	35.00
☐	Sergei Fedorov, Detr. ✂ ✂	75.00
☐	Peter Forsberg, Colo. ✂ ✂	100.00
☐	Ron Francis, Caro. ✂ ✂	35.00
☐	Marian Gaborik, MinW. ✂ ✂	75.00
☐	Dany Heatley, Atla. ✂ ✂	75.00
☐	Milan Hejduk, Colo. ✂ ✂	50.00
☐	Marian Hossa, Otta. ✂ ✂	75.00
☐	Jarome Iginla, Calg. ✂ ✂	50.00
☐	Jaromir Jagr, Wash. ✂ ✂	75.00
☐	Paul Kariya, Anah. ✂ ✂	100.00
☐	Saku Koivu, Mont. ✂ ✂	75.00
☐	Ilya Kovalchuk, Atla. ✂ ✂	75.00
☐	John LeClair, Phil. ✂ ✂	50.00
☐	Brian Leetch, NYRa. ✂ ✂	35.00
☐	Mario Lemieux, Pitt. ✂ White ✂ Stick	225.00
☐	Nicklas Lidström, Detr. ✂ ✂	35.00
☐	Eric Lindros, NYRa. ✂ ✂	75.00
☐	Al MacInnis, SLou. ✂ ✂	35.00
☐	Mark Messier, NYRa. ✂ ✂	75.00
☐	Mike Modano, Dall. ✂ ✂	75.00
☐	Alexander Mogilny, Toro. ✂ ✂	35.00
☐	Markus Näslund, Vanc. ✂ ✂	75.00
☐	Owen Nolan, SanJ. ✂ ✂	35.00
☐	Zigmund Palffy, LosA. ✂ ✂	35.00
☐	Chris Pronger, SLou. ✂ ✂	35.00
☐	Mark Recchi, Phil. ✂ ✂	35.00
☐	Luc Robitaille, Detr. ✂ ✂	50.00
☐	Jeremy Roenick, Phil. ✂ ✂	50.00
☐	Patrick Roy (G), Colo. ✂ ✂	175.00
☐	Joe Sakic, Colo. ✂ ✂	100.00
☐	Sergei Samsonov, Bost. ✂ ✂	35.00
☐	Teemu Selänne, SanJ. ✂ ✂	50.00
☐	Brendan Shanahan, Detr. ✂ ✂	75.00
☐	Mats Sundin, Toro. ✂ ✂	75.00
☐	José Théodore (G), Mont. ✂ ✂	75.00
☐	Joe Thornton, Bost. ✂ ✂	75.00
☐	Keith Tkachuk, SLou. ✂ ✂	35.00
☐	Pierre Turgeon, Dall. ✂ ✂	35.00
☐	Doug Weight, SLou. ✂ ✂	35.00
☐	Alexei Yashin, NYIs. ✂ ✂	35.00
☐	Steve Yzerman, Detr. ✂ ✂	175.00

STICK & JERSEY GOLD

Actual realised pricing on these scarce cards may vary considerably from listed prices.

Insert Set (50 cards): 11300.00

	Insert (*10)	SJG
☐	Daniel Alfredsson, Otta. ✂ ✂	350.00
☐	Todd Bertuzzi, Vanc. ✂ ✂	350.00
☐	Rob Blake, Colo. ✂ ✂	175.00
☐	Peter Bondra, Wash. ✂ ✂	175.00
☐	Martin Brodeur (G), NJer. ✂ ✂	475.00
☐	Pavel Bure, NYRa. ✂ ✂	225.00
☐	Chris Chelios, Detr. ✂ ✂	175.00
☐	Mike Comrie, Edmo. ✂ ✂	225.00
☐	Éric Dazé, Chic. ✂ ✂	150.00
☐	Sergei Fedorov, Detr. ✂ ✂	300.00
☐	Peter Forsberg, Colo. ✂ ✂	400.00
☐	Ron Francis, Caro. ✂ ✂	175.00
☐	Marian Gaborik, MinW. ✂ ✂	300.00
☐	Dany Heatley, Atla. ✂ ✂	300.00
☐	Milan Hejduk, Colo. ✂ ✂	225.00
☐	Marian Hossa, Otta. ✂ ✂	300.00
☐	Jarome Iginla, Calg. ✂ ✂	225.00
☐	Jaromir Jagr, Wash. ✂ ✂	300.00
☐	Paul Kariya, Anah. ✂ ✂	400.00
☐	Saku Koivu, Mont. ✂ ✂	350.00
☐	Ilya Kovalchuk, Atla. ✂ ✂	300.00
☐	John LeClair, Phil. ✂ ✂	225.00
☐	Brian Leetch, NYRa. ✂ ✂	175.00
☐	Mario Lemieux, Pitt. ✂ ✂	900.00
☐	Nicklas Lidström, Detr. ✂ ✂	175.00
☐	Eric Lindros, NYRa. ✂ ✂	300.00
☐	Al MacInnis, SLou. ✂ ✂	150.00
☐	Mark Messier, NYRa. ✂ ✂	300.00
☐	Mike Modano, Dall. ✂ ✂	300.00
☐	Alexander Mogilny, Toro. ✂ ✂	150.00
☐	Markus Näslund, Vanc. ✂ ✂	300.00
☐	Owen Nolan, SanJ. ✂ ✂	175.00
☐	Zigmund Palffy, LosA. ✂ ✂	175.00
☐	Chris Pronger, SLou. ✂ ✂	175.00
☐	Mark Recchi, Phil. ✂ ✂	150.00
☐	Luc Robitaille, Detr. ✂ ✂	225.00
☐	Jeremy Roenick, Phil. ✂ ✂	225.00
☐	Patrick Roy (G), Colo. ✂ ✂	700.00
☐	Joe Sakic, Colo. ✂ ✂	475.00
☐	Sergei Samsonov, Bost. ✂ ✂	175.00
☐	Teemu Selänne, SanJ. ✂ ✂	225.00
☐	Brendan Shanahan, Detr. ✂ ✂	300.00
☐	Mats Sundin, Toro. ✂ ✂	300.00
☐	José Théodore (G), Mont. ✂ ✂	350.00
☐	Joe Thornton, Bost. ✂ ✂	350.00
☐	Keith Tkachuk, SLou. ✂ ✂	175.00
☐	Pierre Turgeon, Dall. ✂ ✂	150.00
☐	Doug Weight, SLou. ✂ ✂	175.00
☐	Alexei Yashin, NYIs. ✂ ✂	175.00
☐	Steve Yzerman, Detr. ✂ ✂	700.00

TEAMMATES

The complete set price includes only one swatch variation per duo.

Insert Set (20 cards): 600.00

	Insert (*70)	T70
☐	T-1 M. Lemieux ✂ / A. Kovalev ✂	125.00
☐	T-2 P. Forsberg ✂ / P. Roy (G) ✂	125.00
☐	T-3 J. Thornton ✂ / S. Samsonov ✂	50.00
☐	T-4 P.Bure ✂ / E. Lindros ✂	50.00
☐	T-5 S. Yzerman ✂ / C. Chelios ✂	100.00
☐	T-6 S. Koivu ✂ / J. Théodore (G) ✂	75.00
☐	T-7 I. Kovalchuk ✂ / D. Heatley ✂	75.00
☐	T-8 C. Pronger ✂ / K. Tkachuk ✂	40.00
☐	T-9 N. Lidstöm ✂ / B. Shanahan ✂	50.00
☐	T-10 R. Blake ✂ / J. Sakic ✂	75.00
☐	T-11 B. Leetch ✂ / M. Messier ✂	50.00
☐	T-12 M. Sundin ✂ / A. Mogilny ✂	50.00
☐	T-13 M. Modano ✂ / M. Turco (G) ✂	50.00
☐	T-14 Brodeur (G) ✂ White / Niedermayer ✂ Red	50.00
☐	T-14 Brodeur (G) ✂ Black / Niedermayer ✂ Black	150.00
☐	T-15 S. Gagné ✂ / J. LeClair ✂	50.00
☐	T-16 O. Nolan ✂ / T. Selänne ✂	50.00
☐	T-17 Z. Palffy ✂ / F. Potvin (G) ✂	50.00
☐	T-18 J.Jagr ✂ / O. Kölzig (G) ✂	50.00
☐	T-19 M. Näslund ✂ / T. Bertuzzi ✂	75.00
☐	T-20 S. Fedorov ✂ / B. Hull ✂	75.00

TEAMMATES GOLD

Actual realised pricing on these scarce cards may vary considerably from listed prices.

Insert Set (20 cards): 4600.00

	Insert (*10)	TG
☐	T-1 M. Lemieux ✂ / A. Kovalev ✂	525.00
☐	T-2 P. Forsberg ✂ / P. Roy (G) ✂	550.00
☐	T-3 J. Thornton ✂ / S. Samsonov ✂	250.00
☐	T-4 P.Bure ✂ / E. Lindros ✂	250.00
☐	T-5 S. Yzerman ✂ / C. Chelios ✂	450.00
☐	T-6 S. Koivu ✂ / J. Théodore (G) ✂	350.00
☐	T-7 I. Kovalchuk ✂ / D. Heatley ✂	300.00
☐	T-8 C. Pronger ✂ / K. Tkachuk ✂	175.00
☐	T-9 N. Lidstöm ✂ / B. Shanahan ✂	225.00
☐	T-10 R. Blake ✂ / J. Sakic ✂	325.00
☐	T-11 B. Leetch ✂ / M. Messier ✂	225.00
☐	T-12 M. Sundin ✂ / A. Mogilny ✂	200.00

☐	T-13 M. Modano ✂ / M. Turco (G) ✂	225.00
☐	T-14 M. Brodeur (G) ✂ / S. Niedermayer ✂	275.00
☐	T-15 S. Gagné ✂ / J. LeClair ✂	225.00
☐	T-16 O. Nolan ✂ / T. Selänne ✂	200.00
☐	T-17 Z. Palffy ✂ / F. Potvin (G) ✂	250.00
☐	T-18 J.Jagr ✂ / O. Kölzig (G) ✂	225.00
☐	T-19 M. Näslund ✂ / T. Bertuzzi ✂	325.00
☐	T-20 S. Fedorov ✂ / B. Hull ✂	300.00

TRIPLE MEMORABILIA

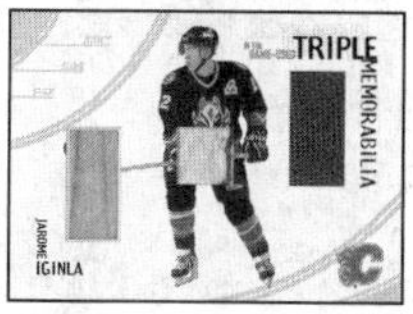

Insert Set (20 cards):		2100.00
	Insert (*35)	TM35
☐	Rob Blake, Colo. ✂ ✂ ✂	75.00
☐	Chris Chelios, Detr. ✂ ✂ ✂	75.00
☐	Adam Deadmarsh, LosA. ✂ ✂ ✂	60.00
☐	Sergei Fedorov, Detr. ✂ ✂ ✂	150.00
☐	Simon Gagné, Phil. ✂ ✂ ✂	100.00
☐	Brett Hull, Detr. ✂ ✂ ✂	150.00
☐	Jarome Iginla, Calg. ✂ ✂ ✂	100.00
☐	John LeClair, Phil. ✂ ✂ ✂	100.00
☐	Mario Lemieux, Pitt. ✂ ✂ ✂	450.00
☐	Nicklas Lidström, Detr. ✂ ✂ ✂	75.00
☐	Eric Lindros, NYRa. ✂ ✂ ✂	150.00
☐	Al MacInnis, SLou. ✂ ✂ ✂	60.00
☐	Scott Niedermayer, NJer. ✂ ✂ ✂	60.00
☐	Joe Sakic, Colo. ✂ ✂ ✂	225.00
☐	Sergei Samsonov, Bost. ✂ ✂ ✂	75.00
☐	Mats Sundin, Toro. ✂ ✂ ✂	150.00
☐	Joe Thornton, Bost. ✂ ✂ ✂	175.00
☐	Doug Weight, SLou. ✂ ✂ ✂	75.00
☐	Alexei Yashin, NYIs. ✂ ✂ ✂	75.00
☐	Steve Yzerman, Detr. ✂ ✂ ✂	350.00

TRIPLE MEMORABILIA GOLD

Actual realised pricing on these scarce cards may vary considerably from listed prices.

Insert Set (20 cards):		4100.00
	Insert (*10)	TMG
☐	Rob Blake, Colo. ✂ ✂ ✂	175.00
☐	Chris Chelios, Detr. ✂ ✂ ✂	175.00
☐	Adam Deadmarsh, LosA. ✂ ✂ ✂	175.00
☐	Sergei Fedorov, Detr. ✂ ✂ ✂	250.00
☐	Simon Gagné, Phil. ✂ ✂ ✂	200.00
☐	Brett Hull, Detr. ✂ ✂ ✂	250.00
☐	Jarome Iginla, Calg. ✂ ✂ ✂	200.00
☐	John LeClair, Phil. ✂ ✂ ✂	200.00
☐	Mario Lemieux, Pitt. ✂ ✂ ✂	750.00
☐	Nicklas Lidström, Detr. ✂ ✂ ✂	175.00
☐	Eric Lindros, NYRa. ✂ ✂ ✂	250.00
☐	Al MacInnis, SLou. ✂ ✂ ✂	175.00
☐	Scott Niedermayer, NJer. ✂ ✂ ✂	175.00
☐	Joe Sakic, Colo. ✂ ✂ ✂	400.00
☐	Sergei Samsonov, Bost. ✂ ✂ ✂	175.00
☐	Mats Sundin, Toro. ✂ ✂ ✂	250.00
☐	Joe Thornton, Bost. ✂ ✂ ✂	300.00
☐	Doug Weight, SLou. ✂ ✂ ✂	175.00
☐	Alexei Yashin, NYIs. ✂ ✂ ✂	175.00
☐	Steve Yzerman, Detr. ✂ ✂ ✂	600.00

VINTAGE MEMORABILIA

Insert Set (20 cards):		4000.00
	Insert (*38)	VM38
☐	Ace Bailey, Toro. ✂	300.00
☐	Jean Béliveau, Mont. ✂	300.00
☐	Johnny Bower (G), Toro. ✂	200.00
☐	Frank Brimsek (G), Bost. ✂	150.00
☐	King Clancy, Toro. ✂	300.00
☐	Alex Delvecchio, Detr. ✂	150.00
☐	Bill Durnan (G), Mont. ✂	225.00
☐	George Hainsworth (G), Mont. ✂	225.00
☐	Doug Harvey, Mont. ✂	275.00
☐	Tim Horton, Toro. ✂	300.00
☐	Red Kelly, Toro. ✂	150.00
☐	Newsy Lalonde, Mont. ✂	225.00
☐	Harry Lumley (G), Chic. ✂	150.00
☐	Bill Mosienko, Chic. ✂	100.00
☐	Jacques Plante (G), Mont. ✂	300.00
☐	Maurice Richard, Mont. ✂	550.00
☐	Terry Sawchuk (G), Detr. ✂	400.00
☐	Eddie Shore, Bost. ✂	300.00
☐	Tiny Thompson (G), Bost. ✂	225.00
☐	Roy Worters (G), NYAm. ✂	200.00

VINTAGE MEMORABILIA GOLD

Actual realised pricing on these scarce cards may vary considerably from listed prices.

Insert Set (20 cards):		7200.00
	Insert (*10)	VMG
☐	Ace Bailey, Toro. ✂	550.00
☐	Jean Béliveau, Mont. ✂	550.00
☐	Johnny Bower (G), Toro. ✂	350.00
☐	Frank Brimsek (G), Bost. ✂	275.00
☐	King Clancy, Toro. ✂	550.00
☐	Alex Delvecchio, Detr. ✂	275.00
☐	Bill Durnan (G), Mont. ✂	400.00
☐	George Hainsworth (G), Mont. ✂	400.00
☐	Doug Harvey, Mont. ✂	475.00
☐	Tim Horton, Toro. ✂	550.00
☐	Red Kelly, Toro. ✂	275.00
☐	Newsy Lalonde, Mont. ✂	400.00
☐	Harry Lumley (G), Chic. ✂	275.00
☐	Bill Mosienko, Chic. ✂	200.00
☐	Jacques Plante (G), Mont. ✂	550.00
☐	Maurice Richard, Mont. ✂	975.00
☐	Terry Sawchuk (G), Detr. ✂	700.00
☐	Eddie Shore, Bost. ✂	550.00
☐	Tiny Thompson (G), Bost. ✂	400.00
☐	Roy Worters (G), NYAm. ✂	350.00

2002 - 03 MCDONALD'S

Produced by Pacific Trading Cards, this series was released in early November at McDonald's restaurants in Canada.

Complete Set (42 cards):		25.00
Common Player:		.35
	Description	Prism
☐	1 Paul Kariya, Anah.	1.25
☐	2 Dany Heatley, Atla.	1.00
☐	3 Ilya Kovalchuk, Atla.	1.00
☐	4 Joe Thornton, Bost.	1.00
☐	5 Jarome Iginla, Calg.	.75
☐	6 Derek Morris, Calg.	.35
☐	7 Roman Turek (G), Calg.	.35
☐	8 Peter Forsberg, Colo.	1.25
☐	9 Patrick Roy (G), Colo.	3.00
☐	10 Joe Sakic, Colo.	1.50
☐	11 Dominik Hasek, Detr.	1.00
☐	12 Brendan Shanahan, Detr.	1.00
☐	13 Steve Yzerman, Detr.	2.25
☐	14 Anson Carter, Edmo.	.35
☐	15 Mike Comrie, Edmo.	.75
☐	16 Ryan Smyth, Edmo.	.35
☐	17 Roberto Luongo (G), Flor.	.75
☐	18 Jason Allison, LosA.	.50
☐	19 Marian Gaborik, MinW.	1.00
☐	20 Doug Gilmour, Mont.	.50
☐	21 Saku Koivu, Mont.	.75
☐	22 José Théodore (G), Mont.	1.00
☐	23 Martin Brodeur (G), NJer.	1.50
☐	24 Michael Peca, NYIs.	.35
☐	25 Alexei Yashin, NYIs.	.50
☐	26 Pavel Bure, NYRa.	.75
☐	27 Eric Lindros, NYRa.	1.00
☐	28 Daniel Alfredsson, Otta.	.50
☐	29 Marian Hossa, Otta.	1.00
☐	30 Patrick Lalime (G), Otta.	.50
☐	31 Simon Gagné, Phil.	.75
☐	32 Mario Lemieux, Pitt.	3.00
☐	33 Chris Pronger, SLou.	.50
☐	34 Evgeni Nabokov (G), SanJ.	.50
☐	35 Teemu Selänne, SanJ.	.75
☐	36 Curtis Joseph (G), Toro.	1.00
☐	37 Gary Roberts, Toro.	.35
☐	38 Mats Sundin, Toro.	1.00
☐	39 Todd Bertuzzi, Vanc.	1.00
☐	40 Brendan Morrison, Vanc.	.35
☐	41 Markus Näslund, Vanc.	1.00
☐	42 Jaromir Jagr, Wash.	1.00

ATOMIC

Insert Set (6 cards):		20.00
	Insert (1:12)	Atomic
☐	1 Paul Kariya, Anah.	6.00
☐	2 Ron Francis, Caro.	3.00
☐	3 Brett Hull, Detr.	4.00
☐	4 Steve Yzerman, Detr.	10.00
☐	5 Mats Sundin, Toro.	4.00
☐	6 Jaromir Jagr, Wash.	4.00

CLEAR ADVANTAGE

Insert Set (6 cards):		25.00
	Insert (1:12)	CA
☐	1 Dany Heatley, Atla.	6.00
☐	2 Ilya Kovalchuk, Atla.	6.00
☐	3 Jarome Iginla, Calg.	5.00
☐	4 Mike Comrie, Edmo.	5.00
☐	5 Martin Havlat, Otta.	4.00
☐	6 Todd Bertuzzi, Vanc.	8.00

CUP CONTENDERS

Insert Set (6 cards):		20.00
	Insert (1:12)	CC
☐	1 Joe Thornton, Bost.	5.00
☐	2 Patrick Roy (G), Colo.	12.00
☐	3 Sergei Fedorov, Detr.	4.00
☐	4 Saku Koivu, Mont.	3.00
☐	5 Daniel Alfredsson, Otta.	3.00
☐	6 Mats Sundin, Toro.	4.00

GLOVE-SIDE NET FUSIONS

Insert Set (6 cards):		25.00
	Insert (1:12)	GSNF
☐	1 Patrick Roy (G), Colo.	12.00
☐	2 Dominik Hasek, Detr.	4.00
☐	3 Tommy Salo (G), Edmo.	4.00
☐	4 José Théodore (G), Mont.	5.00
☐	5 Patrick Lalime (G), Otta.	4.00
☐	6 Evgeni Nabokov (G), SanJ.	4.00

JERSEY PATCH

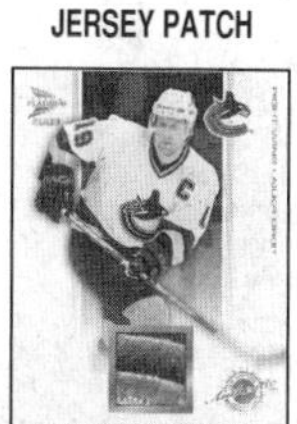

Insert Set (20 cards):		2800.00
	Insert	JP
☐	1 Dany Heatley, Atla. ✂ {#/235}	150.00
☐	2 Ilya Kovalchuk, Atla. ✂ {#/233}	150.00
☐	3 Ron Francis, Caro. ✂ {#/240}	150.00
☐	4 Joe Sakic, Colo. ✂ {#/231}	225.00
☐	5 Dominik Hasek, Detr. ✂ {#/211}	150.00
☐	6 Mike Comrie, Edmo. ✂ {#/161}	150.00
☐	7 Yanic Perreault, Mont. ✂ {#/156}	150.00
☐	8 José Théodore (G), Mont. ✂ {#/190}	175.00
☐	9 Martin Brodeur (G), NJer. ✂ {#/220}	225.00
☐	10 Pavel Bure, NYRa. ✂ {#/241}	150.00
☐	11 Eric Lindros, NYRa. ✂ {#/162}	150.00
☐	12 Daniel Alfredsson, Otta. ✂ {#/239}	150.00
☐	13 Adam Oates, Phil. ✂ {#/173}	150.00
☐	14 Mario Lemieux, Pitt. ✂ {#/184}	475.00
☐	15 Chris Pronger, SLou. ✂ {#/206}	150.00
☐	16 Curtis Joseph (G), Toro. ✂ {#/219}	150.00
☐	17 Alexander Mogilny, Toro. ✂ {#/161}	150.00
☐	18 Gary Roberts, Toro. ✂ {#/243}	150.00
☐	19 Markus Näslund, Vanc. ✂ {#/231}	150.00
☐	20 Jaromir Jagr, Wash. ✂ {#/182}	150.00

JERSEY PATCH GOLD

Insert Set (20 cards):		4200.00
	Insert	JPG
☐	1 Dany Heatley, Atla. ✂ {#/15}	275.00
☐	2 Ilya Kovalchuk, Atla. ✂ {#/17}	250.00
☐	3 Ron Francis, Caro. ✂ {#/10}	200.00
☐	4 Joe Sakic, Colo. ✂ {#/19}	400.00
☐	5 Dominik Hasek, Detr. ✂ {#/39}	225.00
☐	6 Mike Comrie, Edmo. ✂ {#/89}	200.00
☐	7 Yanic Perreault, Mont. ✂ {#/94}	200.00
☐	8 José Théodore (G), Mont. ✂ {#/60}	250.00
☐	9 Martin Brodeur (G), NJer. ✂ {#/30}	375.00
☐	10 Pavel Bure (Fla), NYRa. ✂ {#/9}	250.00
☐	11 Eric Lindros, NYRa. ✂ {#/88}	200.00
☐	12 Daniel Alfredsson, Otta. ✂ {#/11}	350.00
☐	13 Adam Oates (Wa), Phil. ✂ {#/77}	200.00
☐	14 Mario Lemieux, Pitt. ✂ {#/66}	625.00
☐	15 Chris Pronger, SLou. ✂ {#/44}	200.00
☐	16 Curtis Joseph (G), Toro. ✂ {#/31}	225.00
☐	17 Alexander Mogilny, Toro. ✂ {#/89}	200.00
☐	18 Gary Roberts, Toro. ✂ {#/7}	200.00
☐	19 Markus Näslund, Vanc. ✂ {#/19}	250.00
☐	20 Jaromir Jagr, Wash. ✂ {#/68}	200.00

SALT LAKE GOLD

Insert Set (10 cards):		5.00
	Insert (1:12)	SLG
☐	1 Belfour (G) / Brodeur (G) / Joseph (G)	1.00
☐	2 Blake / Foote / Stevens	.65
☐	3 Jovanovski / MacInnis / Pronger	.65
☐	4 Brewer / Smyth	.65
☐	5 Shanahan / Yzerman	2.00
☐	6 Fleury / Lindros	1.00
☐	7 Kariya / Nieuwendyk	1.00
☐	8 Iginla / Nolan	.65
☐	9 Peca / Sakic	1.00
☐	10 Gagné / Lemieux	2.00

2002 - 03 MIKE'S RESTAURANT TRIO THÉO

The separated cards measure 10.2 cm x 15.2 cm (4" x 6") while the intact cards measure 20.4 cm x 15.2 cm. Collectors would receive one of three José Théodore cards each time they ordered the Trio Théo special at Mike's Restaurants.

Complete Set (3 cards):		
	Description	Mike's
☐	José Théodore (G) [MONT red, standing]	3.00
☐	José Théodore (G) [MONT white]	3.00
☐	José Théodore (G) [MONT, red, on right knee]	3.00

2002 - 03 PACIFIC

Produced by Pacific Trading Cards, this series was released in July 2002. There are three versions for each card 1-400: a base card, a Red parallel, and a Blue parallel (#/45).

		Blue	Red	Base
Complete Set (400 cards):		3,900	150.00	80.00
Common Player:		6.00	.50	.25

	Description	Blue	Red	Base
☐☐☐	1 Matt Cullen, Anah.	6.00	.50	.25
☐☐☐	2 Jeff Friesen, Anah.	10.00	.50	.25
☐☐☐	3 J-S Giguère (G), Anah.	35.00	1.50	1.00
☐☐☐	4 Paul Kariya, Anah.	50.00	2.50	1.50
☐☐☐	5 Mike Leclerc, Anah.	6.00	.50	.25
☐☐☐	6 Andy McDonald, Anah.	6.00	.50	.25
☐☐☐	7 Steve Rucchin, Anah.	6.00	.50	.25
☐☐☐	8 Steve Shields (G), Anah.	6.00	.50	.25
☐☐☐	9 German Titov, Anah.	6.00	.50	.25
☐☐☐	10 Oleg Tverdovsky, Anah.	6.00	.50	.25
☐☐☐	11 Jason York, Anah.	6.00	.50	.25
☐☐☐	12 Lubos Bartecko, Atla.	6.00	.50	.25
☐☐☐	13 Dany Heatley, Atla.	35.00	1.50	1.00
☐☐☐	14 Milan Hnilicka (G), Atla.	6.00	.50	.25
☐☐☐	15 Tony Hrkac, Atla.	6.00	.50	.25
☐☐☐	16 Frantisek Kaberle, Atla.	6.00	.50	.25
☐☐☐	17 Tomi Kallio, Atla.	6.00	.50	.25
☐☐☐	18 Ilya Kovalchuk, Atla.	35.00	1.50	1.00
☐☐☐	19 Jeff Odgers, Atla.	6.00	.50	.25
☐☐☐	20 Damian Rhodes, Atla.	6.00	.50	.25
☐☐☐	21 Patrik Stefan, Atla.	10.00	.50	.25
☐☐☐	22 Daniel Tjärnqvist, Atla.	6.00	.50	.25
☐☐☐	23 Nick Boynton, Bost.	6.00	.50	.25
☐☐☐	24 Sean Brown, Bost.	6.00	.50	.25
☐☐☐	25 Byron Dafoe (G), Bost.	15.00	.50	.50
☐☐☐	26 Hal Gill, Bost.	6.00	.50	.25
☐☐☐	27 John Grahame (G), Bost.	6.00	.50	.25
☐☐☐	28 Bill Guerin, Bost.	15.00	.50	.50
☐☐☐	29 Martin Lapointe, Bost.	15.00	.50	.50
☐☐☐	30 Glen Murray, Bost.	15.00	.50	.50
☐☐☐	31 Brian Rolston, Bost.	10.00	.50	.25
☐☐☐	32 Sergei Samsonov, Bost.	20.00	1.00	.50
☐☐☐	33 P.J. Stock, Bost.	10.00	.50	.25
☐☐☐	34 Jozef Stümpel, Bost.	6.00	.50	.25
☐☐☐	35 Joe Thornton, Bost.	45.00	2.00	1.50
☐☐☐	36 Maxim Afinogenov, Buff.	15.00	.50	.50
☐☐☐	37 Stu Barnes, Buff.	6.00	.50	.25
☐☐☐	38 Martin Biron (G), Buff.	15.00	.50	.50
☐☐☐	39 Curtis Brown, Buff.	6.00	.50	.25
☐☐☐	40 Tim Connolly, Buff.	15.00	.50	.50
☐☐☐	41 Jean-Pierre Dumont, Buff.	6.00	.50	.25
☐☐☐	42 Chris Gratton, Buff.	6.00	.50	.25
☐☐☐	43 Ales Kotalik, Buff.	15.00	.50	.50
☐☐☐	44 Vyacheslav Kozlov, Buff.	6.00	.50	.25
☐☐☐	45 Jay McKee, Buff.	6.00	.50	.25
☐☐☐	46 Mika Noronen (G), Buff.	15.00	.50	.50
☐☐☐	47 Rob Ray, Buff.	6.00	.50	.25
☐☐☐	48 Miroslav Satan, Buff.	10.00	.50	.25
☐☐☐	49 Alexei Zhitnik, Buff.	6.00	.50	.25
☐☐☐	50 Bob Boughner, Calg.	6.00	.50	.25
☐☐☐	51 Chris Clark, Calg.	6.00	.50	.25
☐☐☐	52 Craig Conroy, Calg.	10.00	.50	.25
☐☐☐	53 Denis Gauthier, Calg.	6.00	.50	.25
☐☐☐	54 Jarome Iginla, Calg.	30.00	1.50	1.00
☐☐☐	55 Toni Lydman, Calg.	6.00	.50	.25
☐☐☐	56 Dean McAmmond, Calg.	6.00	.50	.25
☐☐☐	57 Derek Morris, Calg.	6.00	.50	.25
☐☐☐	58 Rob Niedermayer, Calg.	6.00	.50	.25
☐☐☐	59 Marc Savard, Calg.	6.00	.50	.25
☐☐☐	60 Roman Turek (G), Calg.	15.00	.50	.50
☐☐☐	61 Mike Vernon (G), Calg.	15.00	.50	.50
☐☐☐	62 Bates Battaglia, Caro.	6.00	.50	.25
☐☐☐	63 Rod Brind'Amour, Caro.	10.00	.50	.25
☐☐☐	64 Erik Cole, Caro.	6.00	.50	.50
☐☐☐	65 Ron Francis, Caro.	20.00	1.00	.50
☐☐☐	66 Bret Hedican, Caro.	6.00	.50	.25
☐☐☐	67 Arturs Irbe (G), Caro.	15.00	.50	.50
☐☐☐	68 Sami Kapanen, Caro.	10.00	.50	.25
☐☐☐	69 Jeff O'Neill, Caro.	15.00	.50	.50
☐☐☐	70 David Tanabe, Caro.	6.00	.50	.25
☐☐☐	71 Josef Vasicek, Caro.	6.00	.50	.25
☐☐☐	72 Kevin Weekes (G), Caro.	6.00	.50	.25
☐☐☐	73 Tony Amonte, Chic.	20.00	1.00	.50
☐☐☐	74 Mark Bell, Chic.	6.00	.50	.25
☐☐☐	75 Kyle Calder, Chic.	6.00	.50	.25
☐☐☐	76 Éric Dazé, Chic.	15.00	.50	.50
☐☐☐	77 Phil Housley, Chic.	10.00	.50	.25
☐☐☐	78 Jon Klemm, Chic.	6.00	.50	.25
☐☐☐	79 Boris Mironov, Chic.	6.00	.50	.25
☐☐☐	80 Steve Passmore (G), Chic.	6.00	.50	.25
☐☐☐	81 Bob Probert, Chic.	10.00	.50	.25
☐☐☐	82 Steve Sullivan, Chic.	10.00	.50	.25
☐☐☐	83 Jocelyn Thibault (G), Chic.	15.00	.50	.50
☐☐☐	84 Steve Thomas, Chic.	6.00	.50	.25
☐☐☐	85 Alexei Zhamnov, Chic.	10.00	.50	.25
☐☐☐	86 David Aebischer (G), Colo.	10.00	.50	.25
☐☐☐	87 Rob Blake, Colo.	20.00	1.00	.50
☐☐☐	88 Chris Drury, Colo.	20.00	1.00	.50
☐☐☐	89 Adam Foote, Colo.	10.00	.50	.25
☐☐☐	90 Peter Forsberg, Colo.	50.00	2.50	1.50
☐☐☐	91 Milan Hejduk, Colo.	30.00	1.50	1.00
☐☐☐	92 Darius Kasparaitis, Colo.	6.00	.50	.25
☐☐☐	93 Scott Parker, Colo.	6.00	.50	.25
☐☐☐	94 Steven Reinprecht, Colo.	10.00	.50	.25
☐☐☐	95 Patrick Roy (G), Colo.	110.00	5.50	3.50
☐☐☐	96 Joe Sakic, Colo.	60.00	3.00	2.00
☐☐☐	97 Alex Tanguay, Colo.	20.00	1.00	.50
☐☐☐	98 Radim Vrbata, Colo.	10.00	.50	.25
☐☐☐	99 Marc Denis (G), Colu.	15.00	.50	.50
☐☐☐	100 Rostislav Klesla, Colu.	10.00	.50	.25
☐☐☐	101 Espen Knutsen, Colu.	6.00	.50	.25
☐☐☐	102 Grant Marshall, Colu.	6.00	.50	.25
☐☐☐	103 Deron Quint, Colu.	6.00	.50	.25
☐☐☐	104 Geoff Sanderson, Colu.	6.00	.50	.25
☐☐☐	105 Jody Shelley, Colu.	6.00	.50	.25
☐☐☐	106 Mike Sillinger, Colu.	6.00	.50	.25
☐☐☐	107 Ron Tugnutt (G), Colu.	15.00	.50	.50
☐☐☐	108 David Vyborny, Colu.	6.00	.50	.25
☐☐☐	109 Ray Whitney, Colu.	6.00	.50	.25
☐☐☐	110 Jason Arnott, Dall.	15.00	.50	.50
☐☐☐	111 Ed Belfour (G), Dall.	35.00	1.50	1.00
☐☐☐	112 Derian Hatcher, Dall.	10.00	.50	.25
☐☐☐	113 Jere Lehtinen, Dall.	10.00	.50	.25
☐☐☐	114 Mike Modano, Dall.	35.00	1.50	1.00
☐☐☐	115 Brenden Morrow, Dall.	10.00	.50	.25
☐☐☐	116 Kirk Muller, Dall.	10.00	.50	.25
☐☐☐	117 Scott Pellerin, Dall.	6.00	.50	.25
☐☐☐	118 Darryl Sydor, Dall.	6.00	.50	.25
☐☐☐	119 Marty Turco (G), Dall.	20.00	1.00	.50
☐☐☐	120 Pierre Turgeon, Dall.	15.00	.50	.50
☐☐☐	121 Pat Verbeek, Dall.	10.00	.50	.25
☐☐☐	122 Sergei Zubov, Dall.	6.00	.50	.25
☐☐☐	123 Chris Chelios, Detr.	20.00	1.00	.50
☐☐☐	124 Pavel Datsyuk, Detr.	30.00	1.50	1.00
☐☐☐	125 Boyd Devereaux, Detr.	6.00	.50	.25
☐☐☐	126 Kris Draper, Detr.	6.00	.50	.25
☐☐☐	127 Sergei Fedorov, Detr.	35.00	1.50	1.00
☐☐☐	128 Dominik Hasek, Detr.	35.00	1.50	1.00
☐☐☐	129 Brett Hull, Detr.	35.00	1.50	1.00
☐☐☐	130 Igor Larionov, Detr.	20.00	1.00	.50
☐☐☐	131 Manny Legacé (G), Detr.	10.00	.50	.25
☐☐☐	132 Nicklas Lidström, Detr.	20.00	1.00	.50
☐☐☐	133 Luc Robitaille, Detr.	30.00	1.50	1.00
☐☐☐	134 Brendan Shanahan, Detr.	35.00	1.50	1.00
☐☐☐	135 Jiri Slegr, Detr.	6.00	.50	.25
☐☐☐	136 Jason Williams, Detr.	6.00	.50	.25
☐☐☐	137 Steve Yzerman, Detr.	90.00	4.50	3.00
☐☐☐	138 Eric Brewer, Edmo.	15.00	.50	.50
☐☐☐	139 Anson Carter, Edmo.	15.00	.50	.50
☐☐☐	140 Dan Cleary, Edmo.	10.00	.50	.25
☐☐☐	141 Mike Comrie, Edmo.	30.00	1.50	1.00
☐☐☐	142 Mike Grier, Edmo.	6.00	.50	.25
☐☐☐	143 Jochen Hecht, Edmo.	6.00	.50	.25
☐☐☐	144 Georges Laraque, Edmo.	6.00	.50	.25
☐☐☐	145 Todd Marchant, Edmo.	6.00	.50	.25
☐☐☐	146 J. Markkanen (G), Edmo.	6.00	.50	.25
☐☐☐	147 Janne Niinimaa, Edmo.	6.00	.50	.25
☐☐☐	148 Tommy Salo (G), Edmo.	15.00	.50	.50
☐☐☐	149 Ryan Smyth, Edmo.	15.00	.50	.50
☐☐☐	150 Mike York, Edmo.	10.00	.50	.25
☐☐☐	151 Éric Beaudoin, Flor.	6.00	.50	.25
☐☐☐	152 Valeri Bure, Flor.	10.00	.50	.25
☐☐☐	153 Niklas Hagman, Flor.	6.00	.50	.25
☐☐☐	154 Kristian Huselius, Flor.	10.00	.50	.25
☐☐☐	155 Trevor Kidd (G), Flor.	10.00	.50	.25
☐☐☐	156 Roberto Luongo (G), Flor.	30.00	1.50	1.00
☐☐☐	157 Marcus Nilson, Flor.	6.00	.50	.25
☐☐☐	158 Sandis Ozolinsh, Flor.	6.00	.50	.25
☐☐☐	159 Nick Smith, Flor.	6.00	.50	.25
☐☐☐	160 Robert Svehla, Flor.	6.00	.50	.25
☐☐☐	161 Stephen Weiss, Flor.	15.00	.50	1.00
☐☐☐	162 Jason Wiemer, Flor.	6.00	.50	.25
☐☐☐	163 Peter Worrell, Flor.	6.00	.50	.25
☐☐☐	164 Jason Allison, LosA.	20.00	1.00	.50
☐☐☐	165 Adam Deadmarsh, LosA.	10.00	.50	.25
☐☐☐	166 Stephen Heinze, LosA.	6.00	.50	.25
☐☐☐	167 Craig Johnson, LosA.	6.00	.50	.25
☐☐☐	168 Ian Laperrière, LosA.	6.00	.50	.25
☐☐☐	169 Aaron Miller, LosA.	6.00	.50	.25
☐☐☐	170 Jaroslav Modry, LosA.	6.00	.50	.25
☐☐☐	171 Zigmund Palffy, LosA.	20.00	1.00	.50
☐☐☐	172 Félix Potvin (G), LosA.	45.00	1.00	.50
☐☐☐	173 Cliff Ronning, LosA.	6.00	.50	.25
☐☐☐	174 Mathieu Schneider, LosA.	6.00	.50	.25
☐☐☐	175 Bryan Smolinski, LosA.	6.00	.50	.25
☐☐☐	176 Jamie Storr (G), LosA.	6.00	.50	.25
☐☐☐	177 Andrew Brunette, MinW.	6.00	.50	.25
☐☐☐	178 Hnat Domenichelli, MinW.	6.00	.50	.25
☐☐☐	179 Jim Dowd, MinW.	6.00	.50	.25
☐☐☐	180 Pascal Dupuis, MinW.	6.00	.50	.25
☐☐☐	181 M. Fernandez (G), MinW.	15.00	.50	.50
☐☐☐	182 Marian Gaborik, MinW.	35.00	1.50	1.00
☐☐☐	183 Darby Hendrickson, MinW.	6.00	.50	.25
☐☐☐	184 Filip Kuba, MinW.	6.00	.50	.25
☐☐☐	185 Antti Laaksonen, MinW.	6.00	.50	.25
☐☐☐	186 Stacy Roest, MinW.	6.00	.50	.25
☐☐☐	187 D. Roloson (G), MinW.	6.00	.50	.25
☐☐☐	188 Wes Walz, MinW.	6.00	.50	.25
☐☐☐	189 Sergei Zholtok, MinW.	6.00	.50	.25
☐☐☐	190 Donald Audette, Mont.	15.00	.50	.50
☐☐☐	191 Sergei Berezin, Mont.	15.00	.50	.25
☐☐☐	192 Patrice Brisebois, Mont.	6.00	.50	.25
☐☐☐	193 Andreas Dackell, Mont.	6.00	.50	.25
☐☐☐	194 S. Fiset (G), Mont.	10.00	.50	.25
☐☐☐	195 M. Garon (G), Mont.	15.00	.50	.50
☐☐☐	196 Doug Gilmour, Mont.	20.00	1.00	.50
☐☐☐	197 Joé Juneau, Mont.	6.00	.50	.25
☐☐☐	198 Saku Koivu, Mont.	30.00	1.50	1.00
☐☐☐	199 Andrei Markov, Mont.	6.00	.50	.25
☐☐☐	200 Yanic Perreault, Mont.	10.00	.50	.25
☐☐☐	201 Oleg Petrov, Mont.	10.00	.50	.25
☐☐☐	202 Mike Ribeiro, Mont.	10.00	.50	.25
☐☐☐	203 J. Théodore (G), Mont.	45.00	2.00	1.50
☐☐☐	204 Richard Zednik, Mont.	15.00	.50	.50
☐☐☐	205 Denis Arkhipov, Nash.	6.00	.50	.25
☐☐☐	206 Andy Delmore, Nash.	6.00	.50	.25
☐☐☐	207 Mike Dunham (G), Nash.	15.00	.50	.50
☐☐☐	208 Martin Erat, Nash.	6.00	.50	.25
☐☐☐	209 Stu Grimson, Nash.	6.00	.50	.25
☐☐☐	210 Scott Hartnell, Nash.	6.00	.50	.25
☐☐☐	211 Greg Johnson, Nash.	6.00	.50	.25
☐☐☐	212 David Legwand, Nash.	15.00	.50	.50
☐☐☐	213 Vladimir Orszagh, Nash.	6.00	.50	.25
☐☐☐	214 Kimmo Timonen, Nash.	6.00	.50	.25
☐☐☐	215 Tomas Vokoun (G), Nash.	6.00	.50	.25
☐☐☐	216 Scott Walker, Nash.	6.00	.50	.25
☐☐☐	217 Vitali Yachmenev, Nash.	6.00	.50	.25
☐☐☐	218 M. Brodeur (G), NJer.	60.00	3.00	2.00
☐☐☐	219 Sergei Brylin, NJer.	6.00	.50	.25
☐☐☐	220 Patrik Elias, NJer.	30.00	1.50	1.00
☐☐☐	221 Brian Gionta, NJer.	6.00	.50	.25
☐☐☐	222 Scott Gomez, NJer.	15.00	.50	.50
☐☐☐	223 Bobby Holik, NJer.	10.00	.50	.25
☐☐☐	224 J. Langenbrunner, NJer.	6.00	.50	.25
☐☐☐	225 John Madden, NJer.	10.00	.50	.25
☐☐☐	226 Scott Niedermayer, NJer.	10.00	.50	.25
☐☐☐	227 Joe Nieuwendyk, NJer.	15.00	.50	.50
☐☐☐	228 Brian Rafalski, NJer.	6.00	.50	.25
☐☐☐	229 Scott Stevens, NJer.	15.00	.50	.50
☐☐☐	230 Petr Sykora, NJer.	15.00	.50	.50
☐☐☐	231 J. Vanbiesbrouck, NJer.	15.00	.50	.50
☐☐☐	232 Adrian Aucoin, NYIs.	6.00	.50	.25
☐☐☐	233 Shawn Bates, NYIs.	6.00	.50	.25
☐☐☐	234 M. Czerkawski, NYIs.	6.00	.50	.25
☐☐☐	235 Rick DiPietro (G), NYIs.	15.00	.50	.50
☐☐☐	236 Roman Hamrlik, NYIs.	6.00	.50	.25
☐☐☐	237 Brad Isbister, NYIs.	6.00	.50	.25
☐☐☐	238 Kenny Jönsson, NYIs.	6.00	.50	.25
☐☐☐	239 Kip Miller, NYIs.	6.00	.50	.25
☐☐☐	240 Chris Osgood (G), NYIs.	20.00	1.00	.50
☐☐☐	241 Mark Parrish, NYIs.	15.00	.50	.50
☐☐☐	242 Michael Peca, NYIs.	15.00	.50	.50
☐☐☐	243 Garth Snow (G), NYIs.	10.00	.50	.25
☐☐☐	244 Raffi Torres, NYIs.	6.00	.50	.25
☐☐☐	245 Alexei Yashin, NYIs.	20.00	1.00	.50
☐☐☐	246 Matthew Barnaby, NYRa.	6.00	.50	.25
☐☐☐	247 Bryan Berard, NYRa.	10.00	.50	.25
☐☐☐	248 Dan Blackburn (G), NYRa.	15.00	.50	.50
☐☐☐	249 Pavel Bure, NYRa.	30.00	1.50	1.00
☐☐☐	250 Radek Dvorak, NYRa.	6.00	.50	.25
☐☐☐	251 Theoren Fleury, NYRa.	20.00	1.00	.50
☐☐☐	252 Brian Leetch, NYRa.	20.00	1.00	.50
☐☐☐	253 Eric Lindros, NYRa.	35.00	1.50	1.00
☐☐☐	254 Vladimir Malakhov, NYRa.	6.00	.50	.25
☐☐☐	255 Sandy McCarthy, NYRa.	6.00	.50	.25
☐☐☐	256 Mark Messier, NYRa.	35.00	1.50	1.00
☐☐☐	257 Petr Nedved, NYRa.	10.00	.50	.25
☐☐☐	258 Mike Richter (G), NYRa.	15.00	.50	.50
☐☐☐	259 Martin Rucinsky, NYRa.	6.00	.50	.25
☐☐☐	260 Daniel Alfredsson, Otta.	45.00	1.00	.50
☐☐☐	261 Magnus Arvedson, Otta.	6.00	.50	.25
☐☐☐	262 Chris Bala, Otta.	6.00	.50	.25
☐☐☐	263 Radek Bonk, Otta.	10.00	.50	.25
☐☐☐	264 Zdeno Chara, Otta.	6.00	.50	.25
☐☐☐	265 Mike Fisher, Otta.	6.00	.50	.25
☐☐☐	266 Martin Havlat, Otta.	20.00	1.00	.50
☐☐☐	267 Marian Hossa, Otta.	35.00	1.50	1.00
☐☐☐	268 Jani Hurme (G), Otta.	6.00	.50	.25
☐☐☐	269 Patrick Lalime (G), Otta.	20.00	1.00	.50
☐☐☐	270 Shawn McEachern, Otta.	10.00	.50	.25
☐☐☐	271 Chris Phillips, Otta.	6.00	.50	.25
☐☐☐	272 Wade Redden, Otta.	10.00	.50	.25
☐☐☐	273 Sami Salo, Otta.	6.00	.50	.25
☐☐☐	274 Todd White, Otta.	6.00	.50	.25
☐☐☐	275 Brian Boucher (G), Phil.	10.00	.50	.25
☐☐☐	276 Donald Brashear, Phil.	6.00	.50	.25
☐☐☐	277 R. Cechmanek (G), Phil.	15.00	.50	.50
☐☐☐	278 Éric Desjardins, Phil.	10.00	.50	.25
☐☐☐	279 Jiri Dopita, Phil.	6.00	.50	.25
☐☐☐	280 Simon Gagné, Phil.	30.00	1.50	1.00
☐☐☐	281 Kim Johnsson, Phil.	6.00	.50	.25
☐☐☐	282 John LeClair, Phil.	30.00	1.50	1.00
☐☐☐	283 Neil Little, Phil.	6.00	.50	.25
☐☐☐	284 Adam Oates, Phil.	15.00	.50	.50
☐☐☐	285 Keith Primeau, Phil.	15.00	.50	.50
☐☐☐	286 Mark Recchi, Phil.	15.00	.50	.50
☐☐☐	287 Jeremy Roenick, Phil.	30.00	1.50	1.00
☐☐☐	288 Billy Tibbetts, Phil.	6.00	.50	.25
☐☐☐	289 Eric Weinrich, Phil.	6.00	.50	.25
☐☐☐	290 Justin Williams, Phil.	10.00	.50	.25
☐☐☐	291 Daniel Brière, Phoe.	15.00	.50	.50
☐☐☐	292 Sean Burke (G), Phoe.	20.00	1.00	.50
☐☐☐	293 Shane Doan, Phoe.	6.00	.50	.25
☐☐☐	294 Robert Esche (G), Phoe.	6.00	.50	.25
☐☐☐	295 Michal Handzus, Phoe.	6.00	.50	.25
☐☐☐	296 Mike Johnson, Phoe.	6.00	.50	.25
☐☐☐	297 Krys Kolanos, Phoe.	6.00	.50	.25
☐☐☐	298 Daymond Langkow, Phoe.	6.00	.50	.25
☐☐☐	299 Claude Lemieux, Phoe.	10.00	.50	.25
☐☐☐	300 Danny Markov, Phoe.	6.00	.50	.25
☐☐☐	301 Ladislav Nagy, Phoe.	6.00	.50	.25
☐☐☐	302 Andrei Nazarov, Phoe.	6.00	.50	.25
☐☐☐	303 Teppo Numminen, Phoe.	10.00	.50	.25
☐☐☐	304 Brian Savage, Phoe.	10.00	.50	.25
☐☐☐	305 J-S Aubin (G), Pitt.	6.00	.50	.25
☐☐☐	306 Kris Beech, Pitt.	10.00	.50	.25
☐☐☐	307 Johan Hedberg (G), Pitt.	15.00	.50	.50
☐☐☐	308 Jan Hrdina, Pitt.	6.00	.50	.25
☐☐☐	309 Alex Kovalev, Pitt.	20.00	1.00	.50
☐☐☐	310 Milan Kraft, Pitt.	10.00	.50	.25
☐☐☐	311 Robert Lang, Pitt.	6.00	.50	.25
☐☐☐	312 Mario Lemieux, Pitt.	110.00	5.50	3.50
☐☐☐	313 Aleksey Morozov, Pitt.	6.00	.50	.25
☐☐☐	314 Toby Petersen, Pitt.	6.00	.50	.25
☐☐☐	315 Wayne Primeau, Pitt.	6.00	.50	.25
☐☐☐	316 Randy Robitaille, Pitt.	6.00	.50	.25
☐☐☐	317 Michal Rozsival, Pitt.	6.00	.50	.25
☐☐☐	318 Martin Straka, Pitt.	10.00	.50	.25
☐☐☐	319 Fred Brathwaite (G), SLou.	10.00	.50	.25
☐☐☐	320 Pavol Demitra, SLou.	15.00	.50	.50
☐☐☐	321 Dallas Drake, SLou.	6.00	.50	.25
☐☐☐	322 Ray Ferraro, SLou.	6.00	.50	.25
☐☐☐	323 Brent Johnson (G), SLou.	15.00	.50	.50
☐☐☐	324 Reed Low, SLou.	6.00	.50	.25
☐☐☐	325 Al MacInnis, SLou.	15.00	.50	.50
☐☐☐	326 Scott Mellanby, SLou.	6.00	.50	.25
☐☐☐	327 Chris Pronger, SLou.	20.00	1.00	.50
☐☐☐	328 Cory Stillman, SLou.	6.00	.50	.25
☐☐☐	329 Keith Tkachuk, SLou.	20.00	1.00	.50
☐☐☐	330 Doug Weight, SLou.	20.00	1.00	.50
☐☐☐	331 Scott Young, SLou.	10.00	.50	.25
☐☐☐	332 V. Damphousse, SanJ.	20.00	1.00	.50
☐☐☐	333 Adam Graves, SanJ.	15.00	.50	.50
☐☐☐	334 Jeff Jillson, SanJ.	6.00	.50	.25
☐☐☐	335 Bryan Marchment, SanJ.	6.00	.50	.25
☐☐☐	336 Patrick Marleau, SanJ.	15.00	.50	.50
☐☐☐	337 E. Nabokov (G), SanJ.	20.00	1.00	.50
☐☐☐	338 Owen Nolan, SanJ.	20.00	1.00	.50
☐☐☐	339 Mike Ricci, SanJ.	10.00	.50	.25
☐☐☐	340 Teemu Selänne, SanJ.	30.00	1.50	1.00
☐☐☐	341 Brad Stuart, SanJ.	15.00	.50	.50
☐☐☐	342 Marco Sturm, SanJ.	6.00	.50	.25
☐☐☐	343 Gary Suter, SanJ.	6.00	.50	.25
☐☐☐	344 Scott Thornton, SanJ.	6.00	.50	.25
☐☐☐	345 Nikita Alexeev, Tamp.	6.00	.50	.25
☐☐☐	346 Dave Andreychuk, Tamp.	10.00	.50	.25
☐☐☐	347 Ben Clymer, Tamp.	6.00	.50	.25
☐☐☐	348 N. Khabibulin (G), Tamp.	15.00	.50	.50
☐☐☐	349 Dieter Kochan (G), Tamp.	6.00	.50	.25
☐☐☐	350 Pavel Kubina, Tamp.	6.00	.50	.25
☐☐☐	351 V. Lecavalier, Tamp.	35.00	1.50	1.00
☐☐☐	352 Fredrik Modin, Tamp.	6.00	.50	.25
☐☐☐	353 Vaclav Prospal, Tamp.	10.00	.50	.25
☐☐☐	354 Brad Richards, Tamp.	15.00	.50	.50
☐☐☐	355 Martin St-Louis, Tamp.	15.00	.50	.50
☐☐☐	356 Shane Willis, Tamp.	6.00	.50	.25
☐☐☐	357 Tom Barrasso (G), Toro.	15.00	.50	.50
☐☐☐	358 Shayne Corson, Toro.	10.00	.50	.25
☐☐☐	359 Tie Domi, Toro.	10.00	.50	.25
☐☐☐	360 Travis Green, Toro.	6.00	.50	.25
☐☐☐	361 Curtis Joseph (G), Toro.	35.00	1.50	1.00
☐☐☐	362 Tomas Kaberle, Toro.	10.00	.50	.25
☐☐☐	363 Bryan McCabe, Toro.	6.00	.50	.25
☐☐☐	364 Alyn McCauley, Toro.	10.00	.50	.25
☐☐☐	365 Alexander Mogilny, Toro.	15.00	.50	.50
☐☐☐	366 Robert Reichel, Toro.	10.00	.50	.25
☐☐☐	367 Mikael Renberg, Toro.	10.00	.50	.25
☐☐☐	368 Gary Roberts, Toro.	15.00	.50	.50
☐☐☐	369 Corey Schwab (G), Toro.	6.00	.50	.25
☐☐☐	370 Mats Sundin, Toro.	35.00	1.50	1.00
☐☐☐	371 Darcy Tucker, Toro.	6.00	.50	.25
☐☐☐	372 Dmitry Yushkevich, Toro.	6.00	.50	.25
☐☐☐	373 Todd Bertuzzi, Vanc.	45.00	2.00	1.50
☐☐☐	374 Andrew Cassels, Vanc.	6.00	.50	.25
☐☐☐	375 Dan Cloutier (G), Vanc.	15.00	.50	.50
☐☐☐	376 Matt Cooke, Vanc.	6.00	.50	.25
☐☐☐	377 Jan Hlavac, Vanc.	6.00	.50	.25
☐☐☐	378 Ed Jovanovski, Vanc.	15.00	.50	.50
☐☐☐	379 Trevor Linden, Vanc.	15.00	.50	.50

☐☐☐ 380 Brendan Morrison, Vanc. 10.00 .50 .25
☐☐☐ 381 Markus Näslund, Vanc. 35.00 1.50 1.00
☐☐☐ 382 Mattias Öhlund, Vanc. 10.00 .50 .25
☐☐☐ 383 Daniel Sedin, Vanc. 15.00 .50 .50
☐☐☐ 384 Henrik Sedin, Vanc. 15.00 .50 .50
☐☐☐ 385 Peter Skudra (G), Vanc. 6.00 .50 .25
☐☐☐ 386 Brent Sopel, Vanc. 6.00 .50 .25
☐☐☐ 387 Craig Billington (G), Wash. 6.00 .50 .25
☐☐☐ 388 Peter Bondra, Wash. 20.00 1.00 .50
☐☐☐ 389 Ulf Dahlén, Wash. 6.00 .50 .25
☐☐☐ 390 Sergei Gonchar, Wash. 10.00 .50 .25
☐☐☐ 391 Jeff Halpern, Wash. 6.00 .50 .25
☐☐☐ 392 Jaromir Jagr, Wash. 35.00 1.50 1.00
☐☐☐ 393 Calle Johansson, Wash. 6.00 .50 .25
☐☐☐ 394 Dmitri Khristich, Wash. 6.00 .50 .25
☐☐☐ 395 Olaf Kölzig (G), Wash. 20.00 1.00 .50
☐☐☐ 396 S. Konowalchuk, Wash. 6.00 .50 .25
☐☐☐ 397 Andrei Nikolishin, Wash. 6.00 .50 .25
☐☐☐ 398 Stephen Peat, Wash. 6.00 .50 .25
☐☐☐ 399 Chris Simon, Wash. 6.00 .50 .25
☐☐☐ 400 Dainius Zubrus, Wash. 6.00 .50 .25

ROOKIE

Insert (#/999) R
☐ **401 Stanislav Chistov, Anah. RC 15.00**
☐ **402 Alexei Smirnov, Anah. RC 7.00**
☐ **403 Chuck Kobasew, Calg. RC 10.00**
☐ **404 Rick Nash, Colu. RC 25.00**
☐ **405 Henrik Zetterberg, Detr. RC 25.00**
☐ **406 Ales Hemsky, Edmo. RC 15.00**
☐ **407 Jay Bouwmeester, Flor. RC 15.00**
☐ **408 Alexander Frolov, LosA. RC 12.00**
☐ **409 Perre-Marc Bouchard, MinW. RC 15.00**
☐ **410 Alexander Svitov, Tamp. RC 10.00**

AUTHENTIC GAME-WORN JERSEY

Insert Set (50 cards): 600.00
Insert (2:37) AGWJ
☐ Jason Allison, LosA. Bost. ✂ Black {*628} 10.00
☐ Tony Amonte, Chic. ✂ {*349} 15.00
☐ Jason Arnott, Dall. NJer. ✂ Black {*625} 10.00
☐ Sergei Berezin, Mont. ✂ White {*626} 10.00
☐ Rob Blake, Colo. ✂ {*353} 15.00
☐ Pavel Bure, NYRa. Flor. ✂ Red {*629} 15.00
☐ Dan Cloutier (G), Vanc. ✂ {*354} 10.00
☐ Pavol Demitra, SLou. ✂ Blue {*628} 10.00
☐ Marc Denis (G), Colu. ✂ Blue {*628} 10.00
☐ Jiri Dopita, Phil. ✂ {*629} 10.00
☐ Chris Drury, Colo. ✂ White {*625} 10.00
☐ Martin Erat, Nash. ✂ Blue {*628} 10.00
☐ Sergei Fedorov, Detr. ✂ White {*351} 25.00
☐ Manny Fernandez (G), MinW. ✂ White {*654} 10.00
☐ Ray Ferraro, SLou. Atla. ✂ Blue {*624} 10.00
☐ Wade Flaherty (G), Flor. NYIs. ✂ Blue {*579} 10.00
☐ Theoren Fleury, NYRa. ✂ {*625} 10.00
☐ Simon Gagné, Phil. ✂ {*353} 20.00
☐ Dominik Hasek, Detr. ✂ {*353} 25.00
☐ Martin Havlat, Otta. ✂ {*<353} 15.00
☐ Martin Havlat, Otta. ✂ Gold/Black {*<353} 20.00
☐ Dany Heatley, Atla. ✂ Blue {*353} 25.00
☐ Jukka Hentunen, Nash. Calg. ✂ Red {*627} 10.00
☐ Milan Hnilicka (G), Atla. ✂ {*628} 10.00
☐ Arturs Irbe (G), Caro. ✂ {*352} 10.00
☐ Jaromir Jagr, Wash. Pitt. ✂ White {*591} 20.00
☐ Jamie Langenbrunner, NJer. Dall. ✂ {*267} 10.00
☐ Daymond Langkow, Phoe. ✂ {*628} 10.00
☐ Mario Lemieux, Pitt. ✂ {*<364} 70.00
☐ M. Lemieux, Pitt. ✂ Black/White/Yellow {*<364} 150.00
☐ Mark Messier, NYRa. ✂ Blue {*351} 25.00
☐ Aaron Miller, LosA. Colo. ✂ Burgandy {*311} 10.00
☐ Mike Modano, Dall. ✂ Black {*353} 25.00
☐ Fredrik Modin, Tamp. ✂ {*<628} 10.00
☐ Fredrik Modin, Tamp. ✂ White/Blue {*<628} 10.00
☐ Alexander Mogilny, Toro. ✂ {*353} 10.00
☐ Evgeni Nabokov (G), SanJ. ✂ Black {*354} 15.00
☐ Joe Nieuwendyk, NJer. Dall. ✂ {#/133} 20.00
☐ Adam Oates, Phil. Wash. ✂ {*628} 10.00
☐ Michael Peca, NYIs. ✂ White {*353} 10.00
☐ Yanic Perreault, Mont. ✂ Blue {*627} 10.00
☐ Cliff Ronning, LosA. Nash. ✂ {*422} 10.00
☐ Joe Sakic, Colo. ✂ {*354} 40.00
☐ Tommy Salo (G), Edmo. ✂ {*629} 10.00
☐ Miroslav Satan, Buff. ✂ {*628} 10.00
☐ Steve Sullivan, Chic. ✂ Black {*629} 10.00
☐ José Théodore (G), Mont. ✂ {*627} 25.00
☐ Joe Thornton, Bost. ✂ Black {*353} 30.00
☐ Darcy Tucker, Toro. ✂ Blue {*354} 10.00
☐ Ron Tugnutt (G), Colu. ✂ {*623} 10.00
☐ Roman Turek (G), Calg. SLou. ✂ Blue {*626} 10.00
☐ Jason Williams, Detr. ✂ White {*628} 10.00
☐ Alexei Yashin, NYIs. ✂ {*353} 15.00

AUTHENTIC GAME-WORN JERSEY SILVER

Insert Set (50 cards): 1,300
Insert (#/40) AGWJS
☐ Jason Allison, LosA. Bost. ✂ Black 30.00
☐ Tony Amonte, Chic. ✂ 30.00
☐ Jason Arnott, Dall. NJer. ✂ Black 30.00
☐ Sergei Berezin, Mont. ✂ White 20.00
☐ Rob Blake, Colo. ✂ 30.00
☐ Pavel Bure, NYRa. Flor. ✂ Red 50.00
☐ Dan Cloutier (G), Vanc. ✂ 20.00
☐ Pavol Demitra, SLou. ✂ Blue 20.00
☐ Marc Denis (G), Colu. ✂ Blue 30.00
☐ Jiri Dopita, Phil. ✂ 20.00
☐ Chris Drury, Colo. ✂ White 30.00
☐ Martin Erat, Nash. ✂ Blue 20.00
☐ Sergei Fedorov, Detr. ✂ White 60.00
☐ Manny Fernandez (G), MinW. ✂ White 20.00
☐ Ray Ferraro, SLou. Atla. ✂ Blue 20.00
☐ Wade Flaherty (G), Flor. NYIs. ✂ Blue 20.00
☐ Theoren Fleury, NYRa. ✂ 30.00
☐ Simon Gagné, Phil. ✂ 50.00
☐ Dominik Hasek, Detr. ✂ 60.00
☐ Martin Havlat, Otta. ✂ 30.00
☐ Dany Heatley, Atla. ✂ Blue 60.00
☐ Jukka Hentunen, Nash. Calg. ✂ Red 20.00
☐ Milan Hnilicka (G), Atla. ✂ 20.00
☐ Arturs Irbe (G), Caro. ✂ 20.00
☐ Jaromir Jagr, Wash. Pitt. ✂ White 60.00
☐ Jamie Langenbrunner, NJer. Dall. ✂ 20.00
☐ Daymond Langkow, Phoe. ✂ 20.00
☐ Mario Lemieux, Pitt. ✂ 175.00
☐ Mark Messier, NYRa. ✂ Blue 60.00
☐ Aaron Miller, LosA. Colo. ✂ Burgandy 20.00
☐ Mike Modano, Dall. ✂ Black 60.00
☐ Fredrik Modin, Tamp. ✂ 20.00
☐ Alexander Mogilny, Toro. ✂ 30.00
☐ Evgeni Nabokov (G), SanJ. ✂ Black 30.00
☐ Joe Nieuwendyk, NJer. Dall. ✂ 20.00
☐ Adam Oates, Phil. Wash. ✂ 20.00
☐ Michael Peca, NYIs. ✂ White 20.00
☐ Yanic Perreault, Mont. ✂ Blue 20.00
☐ Cliff Ronning, LosA. Nash. ✂ 20.00
☐ Joe Sakic, Colo. ✂ 100.00
☐ Tommy Salo (G), Edmo. ✂ 20.00
☐ Miroslav Satan, Buff. ✂ 20.00
☐ Steve Sullivan, Chic. ✂ Black 20.00
☐ José Théodore (G), Mont. ✂ 70.00
☐ Joe Thornton, Bost. ✂ Black 70.00
☐ Darcy Tucker, Toro. ✂ Blue 20.00
☐ Ron Tugnutt (G), Colu. ✂ 20.00
☐ Roman Turek (G), Calg. SLou. ✂ Blue 30.00
☐ Jason Williams, Detr. ✂ White 20.00
☐ Alexei Yashin, NYIs. ✂ 30.00

CRAMER'S CHOICE AWARD

Insert Set (10 cards): 575.00
Insert (#/95) CCA
☐ 1 Dany Heatley, Atla. 40.00
☐ 2 Ilya Kovalchuk, Atla. 60.00
☐ 3 Joe Thornton, Bost. 50.00
☐ 4 Peter Forsberg, Colo. 60.00
☐ 5 Patrick Roy (G), Colo. 100.00
☐ 6 Dominik Hasek, Detr. 40.00
☐ 7 Steve Yzerman, Detr. 100.00
☐ 8 Martin Brodeur (G), NJer. 70.00
☐ 9 Mario Lemieux, Pitt. 130.00
☐ 10 Mats Sundin, Toro. 40.00

IMPACT ZONE

Insert Set (10 cards): 25.00
Insert (1:9) IZ
☐ 1 Paul Kariya, Anah. 4.00
☐ 2 Ilya Kovalchuk, Atla. 3.00
☐ 3 Joe Thornton, Bost. 3.00
☐ 4 Jarome Iginla, Calg. 2.00
☐ 5 Joe Sakic, Colo. 4.00
☐ 6 Brendan Shanahan, Detr. 3.00
☐ 7 Saku Koivu, Mont. 2.00
☐ 8 Eric Lindros, NYRa. 3.00
☐ 9 Mario Lemieux, Pitt. 8.00
☐ 10 Teemu Selänne, SanJ. 2.00

LAMPLIGHTERS

Insert Set (14 cards): 75.00
Insert (1:20) LL
☐ 1 Dany Heatley, Atla. 5.00
☐ 2 Ilya Kovalchuk, Atla. 6.00
☐ 3 Joe Thornton, Bost. 6.00
☐ 4 Jarome Iginla, Calg. 4.00
☐ 5 Peter Forsberg, Colo. 7.00
☐ 6 Joe Sakic, Colo. 8.00
☐ 7 Steve Yzerman, Detr. 12.00
☐ 8 Alexei Yashin, NYIs. 3.00
☐ 9 Pavel Bure, NYRa. 4.00
☐ 10 Eric Lindros, NYRa. 5.00
☐ 11 Mario Lemieux, Pitt. 15.00
☐ 12 Mats Sundin, Toro. 5.00
☐ 13 Todd Bertuzzi, Vanc. 6.00
☐ 14 Jaromir Jagr, Wash. 5.00

MAIN ATTRACTIONS

Insert Set (20 cards): 65.00
Insert (1:12) MA
☐ 1 Paul Kariya, Anah. 5.00
☐ 2 Ilya Kovalchuk, Atla. 4.00
☐ 3 Joe Thornton, Bost. 4.00
☐ 4 Jarome Iginla, Calg. 3.00
☐ 5 Patrick Roy (G), Colo. 11.00
☐ 6 Mike Modano, Dall. 3.00
☐ 7 Steve Yzerman, Detr. 9.00
☐ 8 Mike Comrie, Edmo. 3.00
☐ 9 Jason Allison, LosA. 2.00
☐ 10 José Théodore (G), Mont. 4.00
☐ 11 Martin Brodeur (G), NJer. 6.00
☐ 12 Alexei Yashin, NYIs. 2.00
☐ 13 Pavel Bure, NYRa. 3.00
☐ 14 Daniel Alfredsson, Otta. 2.00
☐ 15 Jeremy Roenick, Phil. 3.00
☐ 16 Mario Lemieux, Pitt. 11.00
☐ 17 Keith Tkachuk, SLou. 2.00
☐ 18 Mats Sundin, Toro. 3.00
☐ 19 Markus Näslund, Vanc. 3.00
☐ 20 Jaromir Jagr, Wash. 3.00

MAXIMUM IMPACT

Insert Set (16 cards): 60.00
Insert (1:12) MI
☐ 1 Roman Turek (G), Calg. 2.00
☐ 2 Patrick Roy (G), Colo. 10.00
☐ 3 Dominik Hasek, Detr. 3.00
☐ 4 José Théodore (G), Mont. 4.00
☐ 5 Martin Brodeur (G), NJer. 6.00
☐ 6 Sean Burke (G), Phoe. 2.00
☐ 7 Evgeni Nabokov (G), SanJ. 2.00
☐ 8 Curtis Joseph (G), Toro. 3.00
☐ 9 Ilya Kovalchuk, Atla. 4.00
☐ 10 Joe Thornton, Bost. 4.00
☐ 11 Jarome Iginla, Calg. 3.00
☐ 12 Joe Sakic, Colo. 6.00
☐ 13 Steve Yzerman, Detr. 9.00
☐ 14 Eric Lindros, NYRa. 3.00
☐ 15 Mario Lemieux, Pitt. 10.00
☐ 16 Mats Sundin, Toro. 3.00

SHINING MOMENTS

Insert Set (10 cards): 30.00
Insert (1:20) SM
☐ 1 Dany Heatley, Atla. 7.00
☐ 2 Ilya Kovalchuk, Atla. 7.00
☐ 3 Erik Cole, Caro. 2.00

☐ 4 Radim Vrbata, Colo. 2.00
☐ 5 Pavel Datsyuk, Detr. 6.00
☐ 6 Kristian Huselius, Flor. 2.00
☐ 7 Stephen Weiss, Flor. 3.00
☐ 8 Mike Ribeiro, Mont. 2.00
☐ 9 Dan Blackburn (G), NYRa. 3.00
☐ 10 Krys Kolanos, Phoe. 2.00

STICK JERSEY AUTOGRAPH

Insert (#/500) SJ
☐ 1 Ilya Kovalchuk, Atla. ✍ ✂ 200.00

2002 - 03 PACIFIC COMPLETE

Produced by Pacific Trading Cards, this series was issued in several 2003 PTC brands. Cards 1-100 were available in Private Stock Reserve, cards 101-200 were available in Crown Royale, cards 201-300 were available in Vanguard, and cards 301-400 were available in Private Stock Titanium.

Set 1-100 (100 cards): 50.00
Set 101-200 (100 cards): 50.00
Set 201-300 (100 cards): 45.00
Set 301-400 (100 cards): 45.00
Set 401-500 (100 cards): 55.00
Set 501-600 (100 cards): 95.00
Common Player: .50
Description Base
☐ 1 Nicklas Lidström, Detr. 1.50
☐ 2 Mika Noronen (G), Buff. 1.00
☐ 3 Alex Kovalev, Pitt. 1.50
☐ 4 Jason Allison, LosA. 1.50
☐ 5 Erik Cole, Caro. .50
☐ 6 Sami Kapanen, Caro. .50
☐ 7 Marty Turco (G), Dall. 1.50
☐ 8 Brad Isbister, NYIs. .50
☐ 9 Saku Koivu, Mont. 2.00
☐ 10 Jarome Iginla, Calg. 2.00
☐ 11 Jean-Sébastien Giguère (G), Anah. 2.50
☐ 12 Roman Turek (G), Calg. 1.00
☐ 13 Joe Sakic, Colo. 4.00
☐ 14 Peter Bondra, Wash. 1.50
☐ 15 Dany Heatley, Atla. 2.50
☐ 16 Vincent Lecavalier, Tamp. 2.50
☐ 17 Manny Fernandez (G), MinW. 1.00
☐ 18 Simon Gagné, Phil. 2.00
☐ 19 Rick DiPietro (G), NYIs. 1.00
☐ 20 Mark Recchi, Phil. 1.00
☐ 21 Mike Richter (G), NYRa. 1.00
☐ 22 Daymond Langkow, Phoe. .50
☐ 23 Pavel Datsyuk, Detr. 2.00
☐ 24 Mark Messier, NYRa. 2.50
☐ 25 Ed Belfour (G), Toro. 2.50
☐ 26 Michael Peca, NYIs. 1.00
☐ 27 Krys Kolanos, Phoe. .50
☐ 28 Alexander Mogilny, Toro. 1.00
☐ 29 Martin Straka, Pitt. .50
☐ 30 Shane Willis, Tamp. .50
☐ 31 Alyn McCauley, Toro. .50
☐ 32 Ryan Smyth, Edmo. 1.00
☐ 33 Tomi Kallio, Atla. .50
☐ 34 Doug Weight, SLou. 1.50
☐ 35 Nick Boynton, Bost. .50
☐ 36 Pascal Dupuis, MinW. .50
☐ 37 Jaroslav Svoboda, Caro. .50
☐ 38 Al MacInnis, SLou. 1.00
☐ 39 Peter Forsberg, Colo. 3.50
☐ 40 Rostislav Klesla, Colu. .50

☐	41 Kimmo Timonen, Nash.	.50
☐	42 Darren McCarty, Detr.	.50
☐	43 Brian Savage, Phoe.	.50
☐	44 Ethan Moreau, Edmo.	.50
☐	45 Peter Worrell, Flor.	.50
☐	46 Doug Gilmour, Mont.	1.50
☐	47 David Aebischer (G), Colo.	.50
☐	48 Aaron Miller, LosA.	.50
☐	49 Nick Schultz, MinW.	.50
☐	50 Magnus Arvedson, Otta.	.50
☐	51 Cale Hulse, Nash.	.50
☐	52 Brian Gionta, NJer.	.50
☐	53 Trevor Linden, Vanc.	1.00
☐	54 Raffi Torres, NYIs.	.50
☐	55 Jean-Sébastien Aubin (G), Pitt.	.50
☐	56 Zdeno Chara, Otta.	.50
☐	57 Mattias Öhlund, Vanc.	.50
☐	58 Travis Green, Toro.	.50
☐	59 Michael Nylander, Wash.	.50
☐	60 Andreas Dackell, Mont.	.50
☐	61 Craig Billington (G), Wash.	.50
☐	62 Chris Therien, Phil.	.50
☐	63 Eric Brewer, Edmo.	1.00
☐	64 Shayne Corson, Toro.	.50
☐	65 Patrice Brisebois, Mont.	.50
☐	66 Sean O'Donnell, Bost.	.50
☐	67 Sergei Varlamov, SLou.	.50
☐	68 Donald Brashear, Phil.	.50
☐	69 Vaclav Prospal, Tamp.	.50
☐	70 Mike Ricci, SanJ.	.50
☐	71 Fredrik Modin, Tamp.	.50
☐	72 Stu Grimson, Nash.	.50
☐	73 Jeff Jillson, SanJ.	.50
☐	74 André Roy, Tamp.	.50
☐	75 Filip Kuba, MinW.	.50
☐	76 Martin Skoula, Colo.	.50
☐	77 Sandis Ozolinsh, Flor.	.50
☐	78 Robert Reichel, Toro.	.50
☐	79 Wes Walz, MinW.	.50
☐	80 Keith Carney, Anah.	.50
☐	81 Steve Kariya, Vanc.	.50
☐	82 David Tanabe, Caro.	.50
☐	83 Robert Svehla, Toro.	.50
☐	84 Rob Ray, Buff.	.50
☐	85 Niklas Hagman, Flor.	.50
☐	86 Stu Barnes, Buff.	.50
☐	87 Scott Gomez, NJer.	1.00
☐	88 Rob Niedermayer, Calg.	.50
☐	89 Dave Scatchard, NYIs.	.50
☐	90 Petr Nedved, NYRa.	.50
☐	91 Bob Probert, Chic.	.50
☐	92 Dallas Drake, SLou.	.50
☐	93 Mike Leclerc, Anah.	.50
☐	94 Janne Niinimaa, Edmo.	.50
☐	95 Rob Zamuner, Bost.	.50
☐	96 Jim Dowd, MinW.	.50
☐	97 Richard Matvichuk, Dall.	.50
☐	98 Boyd Devereaux, Detr.	.50
☐	99 Jamie Storr (G), LosA.	.50
☐	100 Rem Murray, NYRa.	.50
☐	101 Jaromir Jagr Wash.	2.50
☐	102 Todd Bertuzzi Vanc.	3.00
☐	103 Mike Modano Dall.	2.50
☐	104 Sergei Fedorov Detr.	2.50
☐	105 Ilya Kovalchuk Atla.	2.50
☐	106 Patrik Elias NJer.	2.00
☐	107 Marian Hossa Otta.	2.50
☐	108 Paul Kariya Anah.	3.50
☐	109 Manny Legacé (G) Detr.	.50
☐	110 Milan Hejduk Colo.	2.00
☐	111 Adam Deadmarsh LosA.	.50
☐	112 Owen Nolan SanJ.	1.50
☐	113 Patrick Marleau SanJ.	1.00
☐	114 Adam Oates Anah.	1.00
☐	115 Donald Audette Mont.	1.00
☐	116 Steven Reinprecht Colo.	.50
☐	117 Jere Lehtinen Dall.	.50
☐	118 Joe Nieuwendyk NJer.	1.00
☐	119 Roman Cechmanek (G) Phil.	1.00
☐	120 Brian Rolston Bost.	.50
☐	121 Chris Drury Calg.	1.50
☐	122 Jean_Pierre Dumont Buff.	.50
☐	123 Denis Arkhipov Nash.	.50
☐	124 Sergei Zubov Dall.	.50
☐	125 Scott Hartnell Nash.	.50
☐	126 Espen Knutsen Colo.	.50
☐	127 Vyacheslav Kozlov Atla.	.50
☐	128 Roberto Luongo (G) Flor.	2.00
☐	129 John LeClair Phil.	2.00
☐	130 Daniel Sedin Vanc.	1.00
☐	131 Justin Williams Phil.	.50
☐	132 Kyle Calder Chic.	.50
☐	133 Bryan Smolinski LosA.	.50
☐	134 Scott Mellanby SLou.	.50
☐	135 Martin Lapointe Bost.	1.00
☐	136 Dwayne Roloson (G) MinW.	.50
☐	137 Niklas Sundström SanJ.	.50
☐	138 Ladislav Nagy Phoe.	.50
☐	139 Mathieu Schneider LosA.	.50
☐	140 Scott Walker Nash.	.50
☐	141 Marcus Nilson Flor.	.50
☐	142 Steve Thomas Chic.	.50
☐	143 Kevin Weekes (G) Caro.	.50
☐	144 Vladimir Orszagh Nash.	.50
☐	145 Brad Stuart SanJ.	1.00
☐	146 Shawn Bates NYIs.	.50
☐	147 Oleg Tverdovsky NJer.	.50
☐	148 Andy Delmore Nash.	.50
☐	149 Stanislav Neckar Tamp.	.50
☐	150 Phil Housley Chic.	.50
☐	151 Matt Cooke Vanc.	.50
☐	152 Scott Niedermayer NJer.	.50
☐	153 Jeff Hackett (G) Mont.	.50
☐	154 Ruslan Fedotenko Phil.	.50
☐	155 Dan Cleary Edmo.	.50
☐	156 Martin Prusek (G) Otta.	.50
☐	157 Matt Cullen Anah.	.50
☐	158 Jason Woolley Buff. (Detr.)	.50
☐	159 Fred Brathwaite (G) SLou.	.50
☐	160 Adam Graves SanJ.	1.00
☐	161 Kenny Jönsson NYIs.	.50
☐	162 Todd Marchant Edmo.	.50
☐	163 Jason Williams Detr.	.50
☐	164 Joé Juneau Mont.	.50
☐	165 Patrick Roy (G) Colo.	7.50
☐	166 Tie Domi Toro.	.50
☐	167 Adrian Aucoin NYIs.	.50
☐	168 Dan Blackburn (G) NYRa.	1.00
☐	169 Vitali Yachmenev Nash.	.50
☐	170 Derian Hatcher Dall.	.50
☐	171 Mike Ribeiro Mont.	.50
☐	172 Mike Van Ryn SLou.	.50
☐	173 Brian Willsie Colo.	.50
☐	174 Chris Phillips Otta.	.50
☐	175 Jason York Nash.	.50
☐	176 Kris Draper Detr.	.50
☐	177 Sean Burke (G) Phoe.	1.50
☐	178 Kevin Dineen Colu.	.50
☐	179 Toni Lydman Calg.	.50
☐	180 Artem Chubarov Vanc.	.50
☐	181 Trevor Letowski Phoe.	.50
☐	182 Per Axelsson Bost.	.50
☐	183 Lubos Bartecko Atla.	.50
☐	184 Mike Knuble Bost.	.50
☐	185 Ossi Väänänen Phoe.	.50
☐	186 David Vyborny Colu.	.50
☐	187 Kevyn Adams Caro.	.50
☐	188 Johan Hedberg (G) Pitt.	1.00
☐	189 Brent Gilchrist Nash.	.50
☐	190 Eric Boguniecki SLou.	.50
☐	191 Marcus Ragnarsson SanJ. (Phil.)	.50
☐	192 Eric Weinrich Phil.	.50
☐	193 Yannick Tremblay Atla.	.50
☐	194 Mike Keane Colo.	.50
☐	195 Chad Kilger Mont.	.50
☐	196 Glen Metropolit Wash.	.50
☐	197 Stéphane Quintal Mont.	.50
☐	198 Tyler Arnason Chic.	1.00
☐	199 Jan Bulis Mont.	.50
☐	200 Patric Kjellberg Anah.	.50
☐	201 Eric Lindros, NYRa.	2.50
☐	202 Markus Näslund, Vanc.	2.50
☐	203 Zigmund Palffy, LosA.	1.50
☐	204 Brian Rafalski, NJer.	.50
☐	205 Miroslav Satan, Buff.	.50
☐	206 Marian Gaborik, MinW.	2.50
☐	207 Tony Amonte, Phoe.	1.50
☐	208 Tomas Kaberle, Toro.	.50
☐	209 Ray Whitney, Colu.	.50
☐	210 Ron Francis, Caro.	1.50
☐	211 Steve Sullivan, Chic.	.50
☐	212 Bryan Berard, Bost.	.50
☐	213 Keith Primeau, Phil.	1.00
☐	214 Vincent Damphousse, SanJ.	1.50
☐	215 Richard Zednik, Mont.	1.00
☐	216 Ed Jovanovski, Vanc.	1.00
☐	217 Valeri Bure, Flor.	.50
☐	218 Jozef Stümpel, Bost.	.50
☐	219 Alexei Zhamnov, Chic.	.50
☐	220 Mariusz Czerkawski, Mont.	.50
☐	221 John Grahame (G), Bost. (Tamp.)	.50
☐	222 Mark Parrish, NYIs.	1.00
☐	223 Mike York, Edmo.	.50
☐	224 Chris Osgood (G), NYIs.	1.50
☐	225 Scott_A Young, Dall.	.50
☐	226 Derek Morris, Colo.	.50
☐	227 Brendan Morrison, Vanc.	.50
☐	228 Mike Sillinger, Colu.	.50
☐	229 Todd White, Otta.	.50
☐	230 Tom Poti, NYRa.	.50
☐	231 Sergei Zholtok, MinW.	.50
☐	232 Kip Miller, Wash.	.50
☐	233 Pasi Nurminen (G), Atla.	.50
☐	234 Michal Handzus, Phil.	.50
☐	235 Henrik Sedin, Vanc.	1.00
☐	236 Steve McCarthy, Chic.	.50
☐	237 Jeff Halpern, Wash.	.50
☐	238 Stephen Weiss, Flor.	1.00
☐	239 Pavel Kubina, Tamp.	.50
☐	240 Luc Robitaille, Detr.	2.00
☐	241 Michal Rozsival, Pitt.	.50
☐	242 Martin Gélinas, Calg.	.50
☐	243 Curtis Brown, Buff.	.50
☐	244 Steve Passmore (G), Chic.	.50
☐	245 Tony Hrkac, Atla.	.50
☐	246 Alexei Yashin, NYIs.	1.50
☐	247 Richard Park, MinW.	.50
☐	248 Viktor Kozlov, Flor.	.50
☐	249 Andrei Markov, Mont.	.50
☐	250 Dan Boyle, Tamp.	.50
☐	251 Paul Mara, Phoe.	.50
☐	252 Jeremy Roenick, Phil.	2.00
☐	253 Randy McKay, Mont.	.50
☐	254 Tommy Salo (G), Edmo.	1.00
☐	255 Jaroslav Spacek, Colu.	.50
☐	256 Adam Foote, Colo.	.50
☐	257 Martin Erat, Nash.	.50
☐	258 Jamal Mayers, SLou.	.50
☐	259 Chris Neil, Otta.	.50
☐	260 Mark Bell, Chic.	.50
☐	261 Matt Bradley, SanJ.	.50
☐	262 Boris Mironov, Chic.	.50
☐	263 Trevor Kidd (G), Toro.	.50
☐	264 Dave Andreychuk, Tamp.	.50
☐	265 Jaroslav Modry, LosA.	.50
☐	266 Vaclav Varada, Buff.	.50
☐	267 Marty Murray, Phil.	.50
☐	268 Ben Clymer, Tamp.	.50
☐	269 Mikael Renberg, Toro.	.50
☐	270 Sean Hill, Caro.	.50
☐	271 Eric Belanger, LosA.	.50
☐	272 Andy McDonald, Anah.	.50
☐	273 Miikka Kiprusoff (G), SanJ.	.50
☐	274 Brad May, Phoe.	.50
☐	275 Dan LaCouture, Pitt.	.50
☐	276 Andy Sutton, Atla.	.50
☐	277 Kirk Maltby, Detr.	.50
☐	278 Kirk Muller, Dall.	.50
☐	279 Alex Tanguay, Colo.	1.50
☐	280 Bryan Marchment, SanJ.	.50
☐	281 Jason Smith, Edmo.	.50
☐	282 Dan Bylsma, Anah.	.50
☐	283 Jyrki Lumme, Toro.	.50
☐	284 Chris Gratton, Buff.	.50
☐	285 Chris Clark, Calg.	.50
☐	286 David Legwand, Nash.	1.00
☐	287 Alexander Khavanov, SLou.	.50
☐	288 Marc Chouinard, Anah.	.50
☐	289 Rob DiMaio, Dall.	.50
☐	290 Sean Avery, Detr.	.50
☐	291 Tommy Albelin, NJer.	.50
☐	292 Jean-François Fortin, Wash.	.50
☐	293 Matthew Barnaby, NYRa.	.50
☐	294 Jan Hrdina, Pitt.	.50
☐	295 Harold Druken, Toro.	.50
☐	296 Jody Hull, Otta.	.50
☐	297 Shjon Podein, SLou.	.50
☐	298 Jochen Hecht, Buff.	.50
☐	299 Glen Murray, Bost.	1.00
☐	300 Sergei Brylin, NJer.	.50
☐	301 Pavel Bure, NYRa.	2.00
☐	302 Mike Comrie, Edmo.	2.00
☐	303 Mario Lemieux, Pitt.	7.50
☐	304 Mats Sundin, Toro.	2.50
☐	305 Jason Blake, NYIs.	.50
☐	306 Robert Lang, Wash.	.50
☐	307 Bill Guerin, Dall.	1.00
☐	308 Brad Richards, Tamp.	1.00
☐	309 Radek Bonk, Otta.	.50
☐	310 Craig Conroy, Calg.	.50
☐	311 Brett Hull, Detr.	2.50
☐	312 Dainius Zubrus, Wash.	.50
☐	313 Petr Sykora, Anah.	1.00
☐	314 Craig Rivet, Mont.	.50
☐	315 Andrew Brunette, MinW.	.50
☐	316 Kristian Huselius, Flor.	.50
☐	317 Rod Brind'Amour, Caro.	.50
☐	318 Tim Connolly, Buff.	1.00
☐	319 Anson Carter, Edmo.	1.00
☐	320 Cory Stillman, SLou.	.50
☐	321 Teppo Numminen, Phoe.	.50
☐	322 Jason Arnott, Dall.	1.00
☐	323 Oleg Petrov, Mont.	.50
☐	324 Shawn McEachern, Atla.	.50
☐	325 Scott Thornton, SanJ.	.50
☐	326 Oleg Kvasha, NYIs.	.50
☐	327 Byron Dafoe (G), Atla.	1.00
☐	328 Glen Wesley, Caro.	.50
☐	329 Éric Messier, Colo.	.50
☐	330 Brad Lukowich, Tamp.	.50
☐	331 Jon Klemm, Chic.	.50
☐	332 Tomas Vokoun (G), Nash.	.50
☐	333 Scott Hannan, SanJ.	.50
☐	334 Mike Eastwood, Chic.	.50
☐	335 Peter Skudra (G), Vanc.	.50
☐	336 Roman Hamrlik, NYIs.	.50
☐	337 Josef Vasicek, Caro.	.50
☐	338 Bryan McCabe, Toro.	.50
☐	339 Igor Larionov, Detr.	1.50
☐	340 Darryl Sydor, Dall.	.50
☐	341 Mike Fisher, Otta.	.50
☐	342 Greg Johnson, Nash.	.50
☐	343 Danny Markov, Phoe.	.50
☐	344 Frantisek Kaberle, Atla.	.50
☐	345 Michal Grosek, Bost.	.50
☐	346 Ivan Novoseltsev, Flor.	.50
☐	347 Marty McInnis, Bost.	.50
☐	348 Éric Desjardins, Phil.	.50
☐	349 Jason Wiemer, NYIs.	.50
☐	350 Fredrik Olausson, Anah.	.50
☐	351 Bill Muckalt, MinW.	.50
☐	352 Ville Nieminen, Pitt.	.50
☐	353 Taylor Pyatt, Buff.	.50
☐	354 Mike Rathje, SanJ.	.50
☐	355 Trent Klatt, Vanc.	.50
☐	356 Bret Hedican, Caro.	.50
☐	357 Tyler Wright, Colu.	.50
☐	358 Greg de Vries, Colo.	.50
☐	359 Lubomir Sekeras, MinW.	.50
☐	360 Jonas Höglund, Toro.	.50
☐	361 Mike Grier, Wash.	.50
☐	362 Wade Redden, Otta.	.50
☐	363 Nikolai Antropov, Toro.	.50
☐	364 Philippe Boucher (G), Dall.	.50
☐	365 Clarke Wilm, Nash.	.50
☐	366 Erik Rasmussen, LosA.	.50
☐	367 Per Svartvadet, Atla.	.50
☐	368 Félix Potvin (G), LosA.	1.50
☐	369 Igor Korolev, Chic.	.50
☐	370 Vladimir Malakhov, NYRa.	.50
☐	371 Mathieu Dandenault, Detr.	.50
☐	372 Brent Johnson (G), SLou.	1.00
☐	373 Shaun Van Allen, Otta.	.50
☐	374 Scott Pellerin, Dall.	.50
☐	375 Radim Vrbata, Colo.	.50
☐	376 Mike Johnson, Phoe.	.50
☐	377 Mikael Samuelsson, NYRa.	.50
☐	378 Radek Martinek, NYIs.	.50
☐	379 Curtis Joseph (G), Detr.	2.50
☐	380 Craig Johnson, LosA.	.50
☐	381 Kelly Buchberger, Phoe.	.50
☐	382 Todd Harvey, SanJ.	.50
☐	383 Jason Chimera, Edmo.	.50
☐	384 Claude Lapointe, NYIs.	.50
☐	385 Marc Denis (G), Colu.	1.00
☐	386 Lyle Odelein, Chic.	.50
☐	387 Dimitri Kalinin, Buff.	.50
☐	388 Scott Nichol, Calg.	.50
☐	389 Tom Fitzgerald, Toro.	.50
☐	390 Darius Kasparaitis, NYRa.	.50
☐	391 Bryan Allen, Vanc.	.50
☐	392 Jamie McLennan (G), Calg.	.50
☐	393 Martin St-Louis, Tamp.	1.00
☐	394 Landon Wilson, Phoe.	.50
☐	395 Kim Johnsson, Phil.	.50
☐	396 Pavel Trnka, Anah.	.50
☐	397 P.J. Stock, Bost.	.50
☐	398 Alexandre Daigle, Pitt.	.50
☐	399 Andrew Cassels, Colu.	.50
☐	400 Wayne Primeau, Pitt.	.50
☐	401 Theoren Fleury, Chic.	1.50
☐	402 Cliff Ronning, MinW.	.50
☐	403 Sergei Samsonov, Bost.	1.50
☐	404 Jean-François Labbé (G), Colu.	.50
☐	405 Darcy Tucker, Toro.	.50
☐	406 Daniel Brière, Buff.	1.00
☐	407 Marc Savard, Atla.	.50
☐	408 Blake Sloan, Calg.	.50
☐	409 Sergei Berezin, Wash.	.50
☐	410 Ron Tugnutt (G), Dall.	1.00
☐	411 Jocelyn Thibault (G), Chic.	1.00
☐	412 José Théodore (G), Mont.	3.00
☐	413 Sheldon Keefe, Tamp.	.50
☐	414 Yanic Perreault, Mont.	.50
☐	415 Jason Krog, Anah.	.50
☐	416 John Madden, NJer.	.50
☐	417 Jonathan Girard, Bost.	.50
☐	418 Niclas Hävelid, Anah.	.50
☐	419 Daniel Alfredsson, Otta.	1.50
☐	420 Dean McAmmond, Calg.	.50
☐	421 Brenden Morrow, Dall.	.50
☐	422 Dmitry Yushkevich, Phil.	.50
☐	423 Alexei Zhitnik, Buff.	.50
☐	424 Jani Hurme (G), Flor.	.50
☐	425 Antti Laaksonen, MinW.	.50
☐	426 Corey Schwab (G), NJer.	.50
☐	427 Geoff Sanderson, Colu.	.50
☐	428 Brian Leetch, NYRa.	1.50
☐	429 Brad Tapper, Atla.	.50
☐	430 Derek Armstrong, LosA.	.50
☐	431 Evgeni Nabokov (G), SanJ.	1.50
☐	432 Jan Hlavac, Caro.	.50
☐	433 Bob Boughner, Calg.	.50
☐	434 Andreas Johansson, Nash.	.50
☐	435 Jeff Odgers, Atla.	.50
☐	436 Teemu Selänne, SanJ.	2.00
☐	437 Pavol Demitra, SLou.	1.00
☐	438 Tomas Holmström, Detr.	.50
☐	439 Jeff Friesen, NJer.	.50
☐	440 Eric Boulton, Buff.	.50

	Card	Price
☐	441 Oleg Saprykin, Calg.	.50
☐	442 Chris Chelios, Detr.	1.50
☐	443 Stéphane Yelle, Calg.	.50
☐	444 Martin Havlat, Otta.	1.50
☐	445 Jeff O'Neill, Caro.	1.00
☐	446 Dan Cloutier (G), Vanc.	1.00
☐	447 Nikolai Khabibulin (G), Tamp.	1.00
☐	448 Grant Marshall, NJer.	.50
☐	449 Pierre Turgeon, Dall.	1.00
☐	450 Jamie Langenbrunner, NJer.	.50
☐	451 Steve Staios, Edmo.	.50
☐	452 Aleksey Morozov, Pitt.	.50
☐	453 Shawn Horcoff, Edmo.	.50
☐	454 Adam Mair, Buff.	.50
☐	455 Ruslan Salei, Anah.	.50
☐	456 Robert Esche (G), Phil.	.50
☐	457 Brent Sopel, Vanc.	.50
☐	458 Aaron Ward, Caro.	.50
☐	459 Martin Biron (G), Buff.	1.00
☐	460 Brian Boucher (G), Phoe.	.50
☐	461 Richard Jackman, Toro.	.50
☐	462 Jarkko Ruutu, Vanc.	.50
☐	463 Bates Battaglia, Colo.	.50
☐	464 Sergei Gonchar, Wash.	.50
☐	465 Martin Brodeur (G), NJer.	4.00
☐	466 Patrik Stefan, Atla.	.50
☐	467 Scott Stevens, NJer.	1.00
☐	468 Gary Roberts, Toro.	1.00
☐	469 Shane Doan, Phoe.	.50
☐	470 Keith Tkachuk, SLou.	1.50
☐	471 Brendan Witt, Wash.	.50
☐	472 Todd Fedoruk, Phil.	.50
☐	473 Patrick Lalime (G), Otta.	1.50
☐	474 Mike Dunham (G), NYRa.	1.00
☐	475 Ulf Dahlén, Dall.	.50
☐	476 Olli Jokinen, Flor.	.50
☐	477 Garth Snow (G), NYIs.	.50
☐	478 Sean Pronger, Colu.	.50
☐	479 Milan Kraft, Pitt.	.50
☐	480 Aki Berg, Toro.	.50
☐	481 Steve Shields (G), Bost.	.50
☐	482 Sami Salo, Vanc.	.50
☐	483 Brendan Shanahan, Detr.	2.50
☐	484 Niclas Wallin, Caro.	.50
☐	485 Sandy McCarthy, NYRa.	.50
☐	486 Olaf Kölzig (G), Wash.	1.50
☐	487 Cory Sarich, Tamp.	.50
☐	488 Zac Bierk, Phoe.	.50
☐	489 Luke Richardson, Colu.	.50
☐	490 Colin White, NJer.	.50
☐	491 Reed Low, SLou.	.50
☐	492 Joe Thornton, Bost.	3.00
☐	493 Rob Blake, Colo.	1.50
☐	494 Bobby Holik, NYRa.	.50
☐	495 Chris Simon, Chic.	.50
☐	496 Wade Belak, Toro.	.50
☐	497 Éric Dazé, Chic.	1.00
☐	498 Hal Gill, Bost.	.50
☐	499 Chris Pronger, SLou.	1.50
☐	500 Steve Yzerman, Detr.	6.00
☐	501 Justin Papineau, NYIs.	.50
☐	502 Alex Auld (G), Vanc.	.50
☐	503 Niko Kapanen, Dall.	.50
☐	**504 Mike Cammalleri, LosA. RC**	**4.00**
☐	505 Sébastien Charpentier (G), Wash.	.50
☐	**506 Stanislav Chistov, Anah. RC**	**6.00**
☐	507 Jiri Bicek, NJer.	.50
☐	508 Ryan Flinn, LosA.	.50
☐	509 Christian Berglund, NJer.	.50
☐	**510 Vernon Fiddler, Nash. RC**	**1.00**
☐	511 Andrej Nedorost, Colu.	.50
☐	**512 Lynn Loyns, SanJ. RC**	**1.00**
☐	**513 Niko Dimitrakos, SanJ. RC**	**1.00**
☐	**514 Ryan Bayda, Caro. RC**	**1.00**
☐	**515 Curtis Sanford (G), SLou. RC**	**2.00**
☐	**516 Pierre-Marc Bouchard, MinW. RC**	**6.00**
☐	517 Sébastien Caron (G), Pitt.	.50
☐	**518 Steve Ott, Dall. RC**	**3.00**
☐	519 Dan Snyder, Atla.	.50
☐	520 Mattias Weinhandl, NYIs.	.50
☐	**521 Henrik Zetterberg, Detr. RC**	**10.00**
☐	**522 Tomas Surovy, Pitt. RC**	**2.00**
☐	**523 Ales Hemsky, Edmo. RC**	**6.00**
☐	524 Jamie Lundmark, NYRa.	.50
☐	525 Barret Jackman, SLou.	1.00
☐	526 Toni Dahlman, Otta.	.50
☐	527 Jaroslav Bednar, Flor.	.50
☐	528 Ales Pisa, NYRa.	.50
☐	529 Joel Kwiatkowski, Wash.	.50
☐	530 Jan Lasak (G), Nash.	.50
☐	**531 Jim Fahey, SanJ. RC**	**1.00**
☐	532 Pavel Brendl, Caro.	.50
☐	**533 Stéphane Veilleux, MinW. RC**	**1.00**
☐	534 Vaclav Nedorost, Colo.	.50
☐	**535 Tomas Malec, Caro. RC**	**1.00**
☐	536 Jeff Heerema, Caro.	.50
☐	**537 Dmitri Bykov, Detr. RC**	**2.00**
☐	**538 Dennis Seidenberg, Phil. RC**	**2.00**
☐	539 Jonathan Cheechoo, SanJ.	.50
☐	**540 Fernando Pisani, Edmo. RC**	**1.00**
☐	541 Riku Hahl, Colo.	.50
☐	542 Jani Rita, Edmo.	.50
☐	**543 Jim Vandermeer, Phil. RC**	**2.00**
☐	**544 Jordan Leopold, Calg. RC**	**3.00**
☐	545 Joe Corvo, LosA.	.50
☐	546 Ales Kotalik, Buff.	1.00
☐	**547 Ryan Miller (G), Buff. RC**	**5.00**
☐	**548 Tomas Kurka, Caro. RC**	**1.00**
☐	549 Arturs Irbe (G), Caro.	1.00
☐	**550 Radovan Somik, Phil. RC**	**1.00**
☐	551 Mathieu Garon (G), Mont.	1.00
☐	552 Jesse Wallin, Detr.	.50
☐	**553 Steve Eminger, Wash. RC**	**2.00**
☐	**554 Jason Bacashihua (G), Dall. RC**	**2.00**
☐	555 Ramzi Abid, Pitt.	.50
☐	556 Marcel Hossa, Mont.	1.00
☐	**557 Rick Nash, Colu. RC**	**10.00**
☐	**558 Kris Vernarsky, Bost. RC**	**1.00**
☐	559 Brian Sutherby, Wash.	.50
☐	**560 Adam Hall, Nash. RC**	**3.00**
☐	561 Éric Chouinard, Phil.	.50
☐	562 Henrik Tallinder, Buff.	.50
☐	**563 Alexander Svitov, Tamp. RC**	**4.00**
☐	**564 Kurt Sauer, Anah. RC**	**1.00**
☐	**565 Matt Walker, SLou. RC**	**1.00**
☐	**566 Ray Emery (G), Otta. RC**	**2.00**
☐	**567 Eric Godard, NYIs. RC**	**1.00**
☐	**568 Jay Bouwmeester, Flor. RC**	**6.00**
☐	569 Kip Brennan, LosA.	.50
☐	**570 Mike Komisarek, Mont. RC**	**3.00**
☐	**571 Alex Henry, Wash. RC**	**1.00**
☐	**572 Scottie Upshall, Nash. RC**	**4.00**
☐	**573 Chuck Kobasew, Calg. RC**	**4.00**
☐	**574 Anton Volchenkov, Otta. RC**	**2.00**
☐	**575 Carlo Colaiacovo, Toro. RC**	**3.00**
☐	**576 Pascal Leclaire (G), Colu. RC**	**5.00**
☐	**577 Jason Spezza, Otta. RC**	**7.50**
☐	**578 Jeff Taffe, Phoe. RC**	**3.00**
☐	**579 Alexander Frolov, LosA. RC**	**5.00**
☐	**580 Shaone Morrisonn, Bost. RC**	**2.00**
☐	**581 Ron Hainsey, Mont. RC**	**3.00**
☐	**582 Alexei Smirnov, Anah. RC**	**3.00**
☐	583 Andrew Raycroft (G), Bost.	.50
☐	**584 Brooks Orpik, Pitt. RC**	**3.00**
☐	585 Dan Focht, Pitt.	.50
☐	586 Fedor Fedorov, Vanc.	.50
☐	587 Ivan Huml, Bost.	.50
☐	**588 Jared Aulin, LosA. RC**	**3.00**
☐	589 Justin Mapletoft, NYIs.	.50
☐	590 Karel Pilar, Toro.	.50
☐	591 Kyle Wanvig, MinW.	.50
☐	592 Lee Goren, Bost.	.50
☐	**593 Cristobal Huet (G), LosA. RC**	**2.00**
☐	**594 Mikael Tellqvist (G), Toro. RC**	**2.00**
☐	**595 Igor Radulov, Chic. RC**	**4.00**
☐	596 Kirill Safronov, Atla.	.50
☐	**597 Jerred Smithson, LosA. RC**	**1.00**
☐	598 Vesa Toskala (G), SanJ.	.50
☐	599 Dick Tarnström, Pitt.	.50
☐	**600 Martin Gerber (G), Anah. RC**	**2.00**

2002 - 03 PACIFIC TRADING CARDS / ALL-STAR GAME CALDER

Produced by Pacific Trading Cards, this series was issued as part of a wrapper redemption program at the NHL All-Star Block Party.

	Complete Set (10 cards):	**55.00**
	Redemption (#/500)	**AS500**
☐	1 Stanislav Chistov, Anah.	10.00
☐	2 Chuck Kobasew, Calg.	5.00
☐	3 Jordan Leopold, Calg.	5.00
☐	4 Rick Nash, Colu.	20.00
☐	5 Henrik Zetterberg, Detr.	20.00
☐	6 Jay Bouwmeester, Flor.	10.00
☐	7 Alexander Frolov, LosA.	10.00
☐	8 Pierre-Marc Bouchard, MinW.	10.00
☐	9 Jason Spezza, Otta.	15.00
☐	10 Alexander Svitov, Tamp.	5.00

ALL-STAR GAME NETS

Produced by Pacific Trading Cards, these cards were issued at the All-Star Game Block Party.

	Redemption	**ASGN**
☐	North America All-Stars	
☐	World All-Stars	

2002 - 03 PACIFIC TRADING CARDS / LES GARDIENS

Produced by Pacific Trading Cards, this series was issued as part of a wrapper redemption program at the Montréal Collectors' International (October 18-20). Cards are hand-numbered to 199 copies.

	Complete Set (7 cards):	**40.00**
	Redemption (#/199)	**G199**
☐	1 Jean-Sébastien Giguère (G), Anah.	10.00
☐	2 Jocelyn Thibault (G), Chic.	5.00
☐	3 Patrick Roy (G), Colo.	30.00
☐	4 Roberto Luongo (G), Flor.	5.00
☐	5 José Théodore (G), Mont.	10.00
☐	6 Martin Brodeur (G), Njer.	15.00
☐	7 Patrick Lalime (G), Otta.	5.00

2002 - 03 PACIFIC TRADING CARDS / MONTRÉAL COLLECTIONS

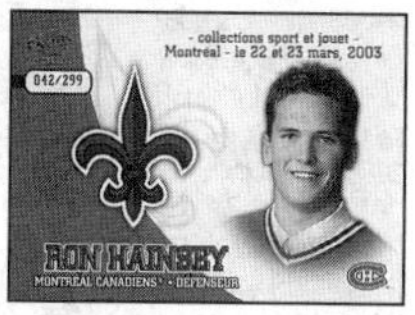

Produced by Pacific Trading Cards, this series was issued as part of a wrapper redemption program at the Montréal Collectors' International (March 22-23).

	Complete Set (8 cards):	**50.00**
	Redemption (#/299)	**M299**
☐	1 Stanislav Chistov, Anah.	10.00
☐	2 Pascal Leclaire, Colu.	10.00
☐	3 Rick Nash, Colu.	20.00
☐	4 Henrik Zetterberg, Detr.	20.00
☐	5 Jay Bouwmeester, Flor.	10.00
☐	6 Alexander Frolov, LosA.	10.00
☐	7 Ron Hainsey, Mont.	5.00
☐	8 Jason Spezza, Otta.	15.00

2002 - 03 PACIFIC TRADING CARDS / TORONTO SPRING EXPO

Produced by Pacific Trading Cards, this series was issued as part of a wrapper redemption program at the Toronto Sport Card & Memorabilia Expo (April 25-27).

	Complete Set (8 cards):	**45.00**
	Redemption (#/499)	**Expo**
☐	1 Stanislav Chistov, Anah.	10.00
☐	2 Ryan Miller (G), Buff.	10.00
☐	3 Rick Nash, Colu.	20.00
☐	4 Henrik Zetterberg, Detr.	20.00
☐	5 Jay Bouwmeester, Flor.	10.00
☐	6 Mike Cammalleri, LosA.	5.00
☐	7 Jason Spezza, Otta.	15.00
☐	8 Carlo Colaiacovo, Toro.	5.00

2002 - 03 PARKHURST

Produced by the In The Game, this series was released in February 2003. There are three versions for each card 1-150: the regular card, the bronze parallel (#/100), the silver parallel (#/50), and the gold parallel (#/10). Please see the appendix for pricing on scarce cards.

Shell Set (200 cards):	-	-	**80.00**
Complete Set (250 cards):	**2,000**	**1,200**	**650**
Common Player:	**6.00**	**4.00**	**.25**

	Description	S50	B100	Base
☐☐☐☐	1 Rod Brind'Amour, Caro.	6	4	.25
☐☐☐☐	2 Alex Kovalev, Pitt.	15	5	.50
☐☐☐☐	3 Brad Richards, Tamp.	10	5	.50
☐☐☐☐	4 Milan Hnilicka (G), Atla.	6	4	.25
☐☐☐☐	5 Arturs Irbe (G), Caro.	10	5	.50
☐☐☐☐	6 Al MacInnis, SLou.	10	5	.50
☐☐☐☐	7 Pavel Bure, NYRa.	20	10	1.00
☐☐☐☐	8 Patrick Lalime (G), Otta.	15	5	.50
☐☐☐☐	9 Vincent Damphousse, SanJ.	15	5	.50
☐☐☐☐	10 Bates Battaglia, Caro.	6	4	.25
☐☐☐☐	11 Evgeni Nabokov (G), SanJ.	15	5	.50
☐☐☐☐	12 Glen Murray, Bost.	10	5	.50
☐☐☐☐	13 Chris Osgood (G), NYIs.	15	5	.50
☐☐☐☐	14 Pierre Turgeon, Dall.	10	5	.50
☐☐☐☐	15 Scott Stevens, NJer.	10	5	.50
☐☐☐☐	16 Daniel Brière, Phoe.	10	5	.50
☐☐☐☐	17 Patrik Stefan, Atla.	6	4	.25
☐☐☐☐	18 Pavol Demitra, SLou.	10	5	.50
☐☐☐☐	19 Mark Parrish, NYIs.	10	5	.50
☐☐☐☐	20 Jason Allison, LosA.	15	5	.50
☐☐☐☐	21 Jaromir Jagr, Wash.	25	15	1.50
☐☐☐☐	22 Mike Modano, Dall.	25	15	1.50
☐☐☐☐	23 Mark Messier, NYRa.	25	15	1.50
☐☐☐☐	24 Ilya Kovalchuk, Atla.	25	15	1.50
☐☐☐☐	25 Teemu Selänne, SanJ.	20	10	1.00
☐☐☐☐	26 Marty Turco (G), Dall.	15	5	.50
☐☐☐☐	27 Keith Tkachuk, SLou.	15	5	.50
☐☐☐☐	28 Simon Gagné, Phil.	20	10	1.00
☐☐☐☐	29 Brent Johnson (G), SLou.	10	5	.50
☐☐☐☐	30 Anson Carter, Edmo.	10	5	.50
☐☐☐☐	31 Jeff Jillson, SanJ.	6	4	.25
☐☐☐☐	32 Gary Roberts, Toro.	10	5	.50
☐☐☐☐	33 Mike Richter (G), NYRa.	10	5	.50
☐☐☐☐	34 Martin Lapointe, Bost.	10	5	.50
☐☐☐☐	35 Todd Bertuzzi, Vanc.	30	15	1.50
☐☐☐☐	36 Valeri Bure, Flor.	6	4	.25
☐☐☐☐	37 Marian Hossa, Otta.	25	15	1.50
☐☐☐☐	38 Éric Dazé, Chic.	10	5	.50
☐☐☐☐	39 Nikolai Khabibulin (G), Tamp.	10	5	.50
☐☐☐☐	40 Miikka Kiprusoff (G), SanJ.	6	4	.25
☐☐☐☐	41 Kevin Weekes (G), Caro.	6	4	.25
☐☐☐☐	42 Mark Recchi, Phil.	10	5	.50
☐☐☐☐	43 Dan Cloutier (G), Vanc.	10	5	.50
☐☐☐☐	44 Keith Primeau, Phil.	10	5	.50
☐☐☐☐	45 Alex Tanguay, Colo.	15	5	.50
☐☐☐☐	46 Ed Jovanovski, Vanc.	10	5	.50
☐☐☐☐	47 Roberto Luongo (G), Flor.	20	10	1.00
☐☐☐☐	48 Saku Koivu, Mont.	30	15	1.00
☐☐☐☐	49 Chris Drury, Calg.	15	5	.50
☐☐☐☐	50 Olaf Kölzig (G), Wash.	15	5	.50
☐☐☐☐	51 Dan Blackburn (G), NYRa.	10	5	.50
☐☐☐☐	52 Erik Cole, Caro.	6	4	.25
☐☐☐☐	53 Darcy Tucker, Toro.	6	4	.25
☐☐☐☐	54 Chris Chelios, Detr.	15	5	.50
☐☐☐☐	55 Pavel Datsyuk, Detr.	20	10	1.00
☐☐☐☐	56 Mike Comrie, Edmo.	20	10	1.00
☐☐☐☐	57 Paul Kariya, Anah.	35	20	2.00
☐☐☐☐	58 Eric Lindros, NYRa.	25	15	1.50
☐☐☐☐	59 Martin Havlat, Otta.	15	5	.50
☐☐☐☐	60 Scott Niedermayer, NJer.	6	4	.25
☐☐☐☐	61 Krys Kolanos, Phoe.	6	4	.25
☐☐☐☐	62 Rostislav Klesla, Colu.	6	4	.25
☐☐☐☐	63 Jocelyn Thibault (G), Chic.	10	5	.50
☐☐☐☐	64 Mike Dunham (G), NYRa.	10	5	.50
☐☐☐☐	65 Shane Doan, Phoe.	6	4	.25
☐☐☐☐	66 John LeClair, Phil.	20	10	1.00
☐☐☐☐	67 Tommy Salo (G), Edmo.	10	5	.50
☐☐☐☐	68 Doug Gilmour, Mont.	15	5	.50
☐☐☐☐	69 Johan Hedberg (G), Pitt.	10	5	.50
☐☐☐☐	70 Brett Hull, Detr.	25	15	1.50
☐☐☐☐	71 Alexander Mogilny, Toro.	10	5	.50
☐☐☐☐	72 Chris Pronger, SLou.	15	5	.50
☐☐☐☐	73 Sergei Fedorov, Detr.	25	15	1.50
☐☐☐☐	74 David Legwand, Nash.	10	5	.50
☐☐☐☐	75 Kristian Huselius, Flor.	6	4	.25
☐☐☐☐	76 Manny Fernandez (G), MinW.	10	5	.50
☐☐☐☐	77 Vincent Lecavalier, Tamp.	25	15	1.50
☐☐☐☐	78 Rick DiPietro (G), NYIs.	10	5	.50
☐☐☐☐	79 Michael Peca, NYIs.	10	5	.50
☐☐☐☐	80 Ryan Smyth, Edmo.	10	5	.50
☐☐☐☐	81 Brian Rolston, Bost.	6	4	.25
☐☐☐☐	82 Brian Leetch, NYRa.	15	5	.50
☐☐☐☐	83 Steve Sullivan, Chic.	6	4	.25
☐☐☐☐	84 Scott Gomez, NJer.	10	5	.50
☐☐☐☐	85 Adam Foote, Colo.	6	4	.25
☐☐☐☐	86 Scott Hartnell, Nash.	6	4	.25
☐☐☐☐	87 Alexei Zhamnov, Chic.	6	4	.25

□□□□ 88 Marc Denis (G), Colu.	10	5	.50
□□□□ 89 Joe Nieuwendyk, NJer.	10	5	.50
□□□□ 90 Brad Stuart, SanJ.	10	5	.50
□□□□ 91 Patrik Elias, NJer.	20	10	1.00
□□□□ 92 Mats Sundin, Toro.	25	15	1.50
□□□□ 93 José Théodore (G), Mont.	30	15	1.50
□□□□ 94 Brendan Shanahan, Detr.	25	15	1.50
□□□□ 95 Daniel Alfredsson, Otta.	30	15	.50
□□□□ 96 Martin Brodeur (G), NJer.	40	20	2.00
□□□□ 97 Jarome Iginla, Calg.	20	10	1.00
□□□□ 98 Peter Bondra, Wash.	15	5	.50
□□□□ 99 Peter Forsberg, Colo.	35	20	2.00
□□□□ 100 Steve Yzerman, Detr.	60	35	3.50
□□□□ 101 Alexei Yashin, NYIs.	15	5	.50
□□□□ 102 Patrick Roy (G), Colo.	60	35	4.50
□□□□ 103 Markus Näslund, Vanc.	25	15	1.50
□□□□ 104 Jeremy Roenick, Phil.	20	10	1.00
□□□□ 105 Darius Kasparaitis, NYRa.	6	4	.25
□□□□ 106 Curtis Joseph (G), Detr.	25	15	1.50
□□□□ 107 Marian Gaborik, MinW.	25	15	1.50
□□□□ 108 Bill Guerin, Dall.	10	5	.50
□□□□ 109 Joe Sakic, Colo.	40	20	2.00
□□□□ 110 Adam Oates, Anah.	10	5	.50
□□□□ 111 Owen Nolan, SanJ.	15	5	.50
□□□□ 112 Rob Blake, Colo.	15	5	.50
□□□□ 113 Nicklas Lidström, Detr.	15	5	.50
□□□□ 114 Joe Thornton, Bost.	30	15	1.50
□□□□ 115 Mario Lemieux, Pitt.	75	45	4.50
□□□□ 116 Sergei Gonchar, Wash.	6	4	.25
□□□□ 117 Bobby Holik, NYRa.	6	4	.25
□□□□ 118 Sandis Ozolinsh, Flor.	6	4	.25
□□□□ 119 Steven Reinprecht, Colo.	6	4	.25
□□□□ 120 Jeff O'Neill, Caro.	10	5	.50
□□□□ 121 Radek Bonk, Otta.	6	4	.25
□□□□ 122 Milan Hejduk, Colo.	20	10	1.00
□□□□ 123 Zigmund Palffy, LosA.	15	5	.50
□□□□ 124 Luc Robitaille, Detr.	20	10	1.00
□□□□ 125 Dany Heatley, Atla.	25	15	1.50
□□□□ 126 Doug Weight, SLou.	15	5	.50
□□□□ 127 Fredrik Modin, Tamp.	6	4	.25
□□□□ 128 Ron Francis, Caro.	15	5	.50
□□□□ 129 Roman Turek (G), Calg.	10	5	.50
□□□□ 130 Adam Deadmarsh, LosA.	6	4	.25
□□□□ 131 Sami Kapanen, Caro.	6	4	.25
□□□□ 132 Sergei Samsonov, Bost.	15	5	.50
□□□□ 133 Jeff Friesen, NJer.	6	4	.25
□□□□ 134 Martin St-Louis, Tamp.	10	5	.50
□□□□ 135 Phil Housley, Bost.	6	4	.25
□□□□ 136 Mark Bell, Chic.	6	4	.25
□□□□ 137 Félix Potvin (G), LosA.	30	15	.50
□□□□ 138 Ed Belfour (G), Toro.	25	15	1.50
□□□□ 139 Martin Biron (G), Buff.	10	5	.50
□□□□ 140 Alyn McCauley, Toro.	6	4	.25
□□□□ 141 Miroslav Satan, Buff.	6	4	.25
□□□□ 142 Jan Hrdina, Pitt.	6	4	.25
□□□□ 143 Ron Tugnutt (G), Dall.	10	5	.50
□□□□ 144 Steve Shields (G), Bost.	6	4	.25
□□□□ 145 Cliff Ronning, MinW.	6	4	.25
□□□□ 146 Wade Redden, Otta.	6	4	.25
□□□□ 147 Patrick Marleau, SanJ.	10	5	.50
□□□□ 148 Tony Amonte, Phoe.	15	5	.50
□□□□ 149 Byron Dafoe (G), Atla.	10	5	.50
□□□□ 150 Roman Cechmanek (G), Phil.	10	5	.50
□□□□ 151 Martin Straka, Pitt.	6	4	.25
□□□□ 152 Sergei Zubov, Dall.	6	4	.25
□□□□ 153 Maxim Afinogenov, Buff.	10	5	.50
□□□□ 154 Brian Boucher, Phoe.	6	4	.25
□□□□ 155 Jason Arnott, Dall.	10	5	.50
□□□□ 156 Oleg Tverdovsky, NJer.	6	4	.25
□□□□ 157 Daymond Langkow, Phoe.	6	4	.25
□□□□ 158 Andrew Brunette, MinW.	6	4	.25
□□□□ 159 Brian Rafalski, NJer.	6	4	.25
□□□□ 160 Mike York, Edmo.	6	4	.25
□□□□ 161 Richard Zednik, Mont.	10	5	.50
□□□□ 162 Radim Vrbata, Colo.	6	4	.25
□□□□ 163 Tim Connolly, Buff.	10	5	.50
□□□□ 164 Jamie Storr (G), LosA.	6	4	.25
□□□□ 165 Henrik Sedin, Vanc.	10	5	.50
□□□□ 166 Sean Burke (G), Phoe.	15	5	.50
□□□□ 167 Daniel Sedin, Vanc.	10	5	.50
□□□□ 168 Jason Smith, Edmo.	6	4	.25
□□□□ 169 Stephen Weiss, Flor.	10	5	.50
□□□□ 170 Bryan McCabe, Toro.	6	4	.25
□□□□ 171 Theoren Fleury, Chic.	15	5	.50
□□□□ 172 J-S Giguère (G), Anah.	25	15	1.50
□□□□ 173 Espen Knutsen, Colu.	6	4	.25
□□□□ 174 Mika Noronen (G), Buff.	10	5	.50
□□□□ 175 Michael Nylander, Wash.	6	4	.25
□□□□ 176 Yanic Perreault, Mont.	6	4	.25
□□□□ 177 Donald Brashear, Phil.	6	4	.25
□□□□ 178 Denis Arkhipov, Nash.	6	4	.25
□□□□ 179 Adrian Aucoin, NYIs.	6	4	.25
□□□□ 180 Tie Domi, Toro.	6	4	.25
□□□□ 181 Andrew Cassels, Colu.	6	4	.25
□□□□ 182 Eric Brewer, Edmo.	10	5	.50
□□□□ 183 Trevor Linden, Vanc.	10	5	.50
□□□□ 184 Brendan Witt, Wash.	6	4	.25
□□□□ 185 Robert Lang, Wash.	6	4	.25
□□□□ 186 Brendan Morrison, Vanc.	6	4	.25
□□□□ 187 Mike Fisher, Otta.	6	4	.25
□□□□ 188 Aleksey Morozov, Pitt.	6	4	.25
□□□□ 189 Martin Erat, Nash.	6	4	.25
□□□□ 190 Jeff Hackett (G), Mont.	6	4	.25
□□□□ 191 Mariusz Czerkawski, Mont.	6	4	.25
□□□□ 192 Olli Jokinen, Flor.	6	4	.25
□□□□ 193 Brad Isbister, NYIs.	6	4	.25
□□□□ 194 Niklas Hagman, Flor.	6	4	.25
□□□□ 195 Jere Lehtinen, Dall.	6	4	.25
□□□□ 196 Igor Larionov, Detr.	15	5	.50
□□□□ 197 Curtis Brown, Buff.	6	4	.25
□□□□ 198 Ray Whitney, Colu.	6	4	.25
□□□□ 199 Grant Marshall, Colu.	6	4	.25
□□□□ 200 Craig Conroy, Calg.	6	4	.25

ROOKIES

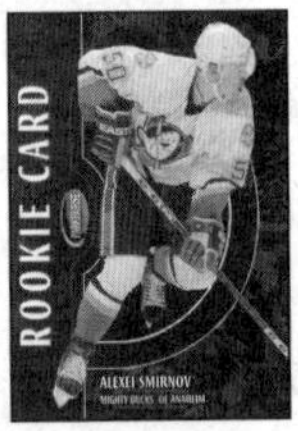

Description	S50	B100	R500
□□□□ 201 P-M Bouchard, MinW. RC	60	50	45
□□□□ 202 Rick Nash, Colu. RC	110	95	80
□□□□ 203 D. Seidenberg, Phil. RC	12	8	15
□□□□ 204 Bouwmeester, Flor. RC	60	50	45
□□□□ 205 S. Chistov, Anah. RC	60	50	45
□□□□ 206 Jared Aulin, LosA. RC	20	20	20
□□□□ 207 Ivan Majesky, Flor. RC	12	8	10
□□□□ 208 Chuck Kobasew, Calg. RC	40	35	30
□□□□ 209 Jordan Leopold, Calg. RC	20	20	20
□□□□ 210 Ryan Miller, Buff. RC	50	45	40
□□□□ 211 Ales Hemsky, Edmo. RC	60	50	45
□□□□ 212 Patrick Sharp, Phil. RC	12	8	10
□□□□ 213 Kari Haakana, Edmo. RC	12	8	10
□□□□ 214 Dmitri Bykov, Detr. RC	12	8	15
□□□□ 215 P. Leclaire (G), Colu. RC	50	45	40
□□□□ 216 H. Zetterberg, Detr. RC	110	95	80
□□□□ 217 A. Frolov, LosA. RC	50	45	40
□□□□ 218 Steve Eminger, Wash. RC	12	8	15
□□□□ 219 Scottie Upshall, Nash. RC	40	35	30
□□□□ 220 Tom Koivisto, SLou. RC	12	8	10
□□□□ 221 S. Morrisonn, Bost. RC	12	8	15
□□□□ 222 Ron Hainsey, Mont. RC	20	20	20
□□□□ 223 M. Gerber (G), Anah. RC	12	8	15
□□□□ 224 Adam Hall (G), Nash. RC	20	20	20
□□□□ 225 Lasse Pirjetä, Colu. RC	12	8	10
□□□□ 226 A. Volchenkov, Otta. RC	12	8	15
□□□□ 227 Andersson (G), Chic. RC	20	20	20
□□□□ 228 Rickard Wallin, MinW. RC	12	8	10
□□□□ 229 A. Svitov, Tamp. RC	40	35	30
□□□□ 230 Alexei Smirnov, Anah. RC	20	20	20
□□□□ 231 Jeff Taffe, Phoe. RC	20	20	20
□□□□ 232 M. Tellqvist (G), Toro. RC	12	8	15
□□□□ 233 Radovan Somik, Phil. RC	12	8	10
□□□□ 234 Dick Tarnström, Pitt.	12	8	15
□□□□ 235 Steve Ott, Dall. RC	20	20	20
□□□□ 236 Brooks Orpik, Pitt. RC	20	20	20
□□□□ 237 Éric Bertrand, Colo. RC	12	8	10
□□□□ 238 Sylvain Blouin, Mont. RC	12	8	10
□□□□ 239 Greg Koehler, Nash. RC	12	8	10
□□□□ 240 S. Veilleux, MinW. RC	12	8	10
□□□□ 241 C. Sanford (G), SLou. RC	12	8	15
□□□□ 242 C. Colaiacovo, Toro. RC	20	20	20
□□□□ 243 Patrick Boileau, Detr. RC	12	8	10
□□□□ 244 Tim Thomas (G), Bost. RC	12	8	15
□□□□ 245 M. Cammalleri, LosA. RC	40	35	30
□□□□ 246 L. Szuper (G), Calg. RC	12	8	15
□□□□ 247 Jason Spezza, Otta. RC	80	70	60
□□□□ 248 Rudkowsky (G), SLou. RC	12	8	15
□□□□ 249 Eric Godard, NYIs. RC	12	8	10
□□□□ 250 V. Kharlamov, U.S.S.R. RC	50	45	40

HE SHOOTS HE SCORES

Each redemption card was worth one, two, or three points. Collectors could trade 400 points for a special random jersey card. This redemption program ends on January 31, 2004.

Insert Set (20 cards):	
Insert	HSHS
□ Joe Thornton, Bost. [1 Point]	
□ Martin Brodeur (G), NJer. [1 Point]	
□ Peter Forsberg, Colo. [1 Point]	
□ Mark Messier, NYRa. [1 Point]	
□ Owen Nolan, SanJ. [1 Point]	
□ Jeremy Roenick, Phil. [1 Point]	
□ Patrick Roy (G), Colo. [1 Point]	
□ Joe Sakic, Colo. [1 Point]	
□ Brendan Shanahan, Detr. [1 Point]	
□ Mats Sundin, Toro. [1 Point]	
□ José Théodore (G), Mont. [1 Point]	
□ Pavel Bure, NYRa. [2 Points]	
□ Jaromir Jagr, Wash. [2 Points]	
□ Paul Kariya, Anah. [2 Points]	
□ Eric Lindros, NYRa. [2 Points]	
□ Mike Modano, Dall. [2 Points]	
□ Steve Yzerman, Detr. [2 Points]	
□ Jarome Iginla, Calg. [3 Points]	
□ Ilya Kovalchuk, Atla. [3 Points]	
□ Mario Lemieux, Pitt. [3 Points]	

COLLEGE RANKS

Insert Set (18 cards):	160.00
Insert (*100)	CR
□ 1 Chris Drury, Calg.	10.00
□ 2 Erik Cole, Caro.	8.00
□ 3 Keith Tkachuk, SLou.	10.00
□ 4 Rick DiPietro (G), NYIs.	8.00
□ 5 Rob Blake, Colo.	10.00
□ 6 Adam Oates, Anah.	8.00
□ 7 Chris Chelios, Detr.	10.00
□ 8 Brett Hull, Detr.	15.00
□ 9 Paul Kariya, Anah.	25.00
□ 10 Tony Amonte, Phoe.	10.00
□ 11 Doug Weight, SLou.	10.00
□ 12 Dany Heatley, Atla.	15.00
□ 13 Steven Reinprecht, Colo.	8.00
□ 14 Curtis Joseph (G), Detr.	15.00
□ 15 Anson Carter, Edmo.	8.00
□ 16 Mike Dunham (G), Nash.	8.00
□ 17 Mike Richter (G), NYRa.	8.00
□ 18 Ed Belfour (G), Toro.	15.00

COLLEGE RANKS MEMORABILIA

Insert Set (18 cards):	530.00
Insert (*60)	CR
□ Tony Amonte, Phoe. ✂	30.00
□ Ed Belfour (G), Toro. ✂	50.00
□ Rob Blake, Colo. ✂	30.00
□ Anson Carter, Edmo. ✂	30.00
□ Chris Chelios, Detr. ✂	30.00
□ Erik Cole, Caro. ✂	30.00
□ Rick DiPietro (G), NYIs. ✂	30.00
□ Chris Drury, Calg. ✂	30.00
□ Mike Dunham (G), Nash. ✂	30.00
□ Dany Heatley, Atla. ✂	50.00
□ Brett Hull, Detr. ✂	50.00
□ Curtis Joseph (G), Detr. ✂	50.00
□ Paul Kariya, Anah. ✂	75.00
□ Adam Oates, Anah. ✂	30.00
□ Steven Reinprecht, Colo. ✂	30.00
□ Mike Richter (G), NYRa. ✂	30.00
□ Keith Tkachuk, SLou. ✂	30.00
□ Doug Weight, SLou. ✂	30.00

FRANCHISE PLAYERS

Insert Set (30 cards):	1400.00
Insert (*50)	FP
□ Daniel Brière, Phoe. ✂	30.00
□ Martin Brodeur (G), NJer. ✂	100.00
□ Pavel Bure, NYRa. ✂	50.00
□ Mike Comrie, Edmo. ✂	50.00
□ Éric Dazé, Chic. ✂	30.00
□ Marian Gaborik, MinW. ✂	50.00
□ Simon Gagné, Phil. ✂	50.00
□ Scott Hartnell, Nash. ✂	30.00
□ Marian Hossa, Otta. ✂	50.00
□ Jarome Iginla, Calg. ✂	50.00
□ Jaromir Jagr, Wash. ✂	50.00
□ Paul Kariya, Anah. ✂	75.00
□ Nikolai Khabibulin (G), Tamp. ✂	30.00
□ Rostislav Klesla, Colu. ✂	30.00
□ Ilya Kovalchuk, Atla. ✂	50.00
□ Mario Lemieux, Pitt. ✂	200.00
□ Roberto Luongo (G), Flor. ✂	50.00
□ Mike Modano, Dall. ✂	50.00
□ Markus Näslund, Vanc. ✂	50.00
□ Owen Nolan, SanJ. ✂	30.00
□ Jeff O'Neill, Caro. ✂	30.00
□ Zigmund Palffy, LosA. ✂	30.00
□ Chris Pronger, SLou. ✂	30.00
□ Patrick Roy (G), Colo. ✂	150.00
□ Miroslav Satan, Buff. ✂	30.00
□ Mats Sundin, Toro. ✂	50.00
□ José Théodore (G), Mont. ✂	75.00
□ Joe Thornton, Bost. ✂	75.00
□ Alexei Yashin, NYIs. ✂	30.00
□ Steve Yzerman, Detr. ✂	150.00

GAME-USED JERSEY

Insert Set (58 cards):	1600.00
Insert (*90)	GJ
□ Daniel Alfredsson, Otta. ✂	50.00
□ Todd Bertuzzi, Vanc. ✂	50.00
□ Rob Blake, Colo. ✂	25.00
□ Peter Bondra, Wash. ✂	25.00
□ Jay Bouwmeester, Flor. ✂	20.00
□ Martin Brodeur (G), NJer. ✂	50.00
□ Pavel Bure, NYRa. ✂	35.00
□ Éric Dazé, Chic. ✂	20.00
□ Sergei Fedorov, Detr. ✂	40.00
□ Peter Forsberg, Colo. ✂	50.00
□ Ron Francis, Caro. ✂	25.00
□ Marian Gaborik, MinW. ✂	40.00
□ Ron Hainsey, Mont. ✂	20.00
□ Dany Heatley, Atla. ✂	40.00
□ Milan Hejduk, Colo. ✂	35.00
□ Jarome Iginla, Calg. ✂	35.00
□ Jaromir Jagr, Wash. ✂	40.00
□ Sami Kapanen, Caro. ✂	20.00
□ Paul Kariya, Anah. ✂	50.00
□ Rostislav Klesla, Colu. ✂	25.00
□ Chuck Kobasew, Calg. ✂	20.00
□ Saku Koivu, Mont. ✂	50.00
□ Ilya Kovalchuk, Atla. ✂	40.00
□ John LeClair, Phil. ✂	35.00
□ Brian Leetch, NYRa. ✂	25.00
□ Mario Lemieux, Pitt. ✂	125.00
□ Jordan Leopold, Calg. ✂	20.00
□ Nicklas Lidström, Detr. ✂	25.00
□ Eric Lindros, NYRa. ✂	40.00
□ Al MacInnis, SLou. ✂	20.00
□ Mark Messier, NYRa. ✂	40.00
□ Mike Modano, Dall. ✂	40.00
□ Alexander Mogilny, Toro. ✂	20.00
□ Rick Nash, Colu. ✂	35.00
□ Markus Näslund, Vanc. ✂	40.00
□ Owen Nolan, SanJ. ✂	25.00
□ Jeff O'Neill, Caro. ✂	20.00
□ Zigmund Palffy, LosA. ✂	25.00
□ Chris Pronger, SLou. ✂	25.00
□ Mark Recchi, Phil. ✂	20.00
□ Gary Roberts, Toro. ✂	20.00
□ Luc Robitaille, Detr. ✂	35.00
□ Jeremy Roenick, Phil. ✂	35.00
□ Patrick Roy (G), Colo. ✂	100.00
□ Joe Sakic, Colo. ✂	50.00
□ Sergei Samsonov, Bost. ✂	25.00
□ Teemu Selänne, SanJ. ✂	35.00
□ Brendan Shanahan, Detr. ✂	40.00
□ Jason Spezza, Otta. ✂	25.00
□ Mats Sundin, Toro. ✂	40.00
□ Alex Tanguay, Colo. ✂	25.00
□ José Théodore (G), Mont. ✂	50.00
□ Joe Thornton, Bost. ✂	50.00
□ Scottie Upshall, Nash. ✂	20.00
□ Doug Weight, SLou. ✂	25.00
□ Stephen Weiss, Flor. ✂	20.00
□ Alexei Yashin, NYIs. ✂	25.00
□ Steve Yzerman, Detr. ✂	100.00

GAME-USED STICK & JERSEY

Insert Set (50 cards):	1600.00
Insert (*90)	GJS
□ Daniel Alfredsson, Otta. ✂	50.00
□ Todd Bertuzzi, Vanc. ✂	50.00
□ Rob Blake, Colo. ✂	25.00
□ Peter Bondra, Wash. ✂	25.00
□ Martin Brodeur (G), NJer. ✂	75.00
□ Pavel Bure, NYRa. ✂	25.00
□ Éric Dazé, Chic. ✂	25.00
□ Sergei Fedorov, Detr. ✂	50.00
□ Peter Forsberg, Colo. ✂	50.00
□ Ron Francis, Caro. ✂	25.00
□ Marian Gaborik, MinW. ✂	50.00
□ Dany Heatley, Atla. ✂	50.00
□ Milan Hejduk, Colo. ✂	25.00
□ Jarome Iginla, Calg. ✂	25.00
□ Jaromir Jagr, Wash. ✂	50.00
□ Sami Kapanen, Caro. ✂	25.00
□ Paul Kariya, Anah. ✂	50.00
□ Rostislav Klesla, Colu. ✂	25.00
□ Saku Koivu, Mont. ✂	50.00
□ Ilya Kovalchuk, Atla. ✂	50.00
□ John LeClair, Phil. ✂	25.00
□ Brian Leetch, NYRa. ✂	25.00
□ Mario Lemieux, Pitt. ✂	150.00
□ Nicklas Lidström, Detr. ✂	25.00

☐ Eric Lindros, NYRa. ✂ 50.00
☐ Al MacInnis, SLou. ✂ 25.00
☐ Mark Messier, NYRa. ✂ 50.00
☐ Mike Modano, Dall. ✂ 50.00
☐ Alexander Mogilny, Toro. ✂ 25.00
☐ Markus Näslund, Vanc. ✂ 50.00
☐ Owen Nolan, SanJ. ✂ 25.00
☐ Jeff O'Neill, Caro. ✂ 25.00
☐ Zigmund Palffy, LosA. ✂ 25.00
☐ Chris Pronger, SLou. ✂ 25.00
☐ Mark Recchi, Phil. ✂ 25.00
☐ Gary Roberts, Toro. ✂ 25.00
☐ Luc Robitaille, Detr. ✂ 25.00
☐ Jeremy Roenick, Phil. ✂ 25.00
☐ Patrick Roy (G), Colo. ✂ 100.00
☐ Joe Sakic, Colo. ✂ 75.00
☐ Sergei Samsonov, Bost. ✂ 25.00
☐ Teemu Selänne, SanJ. ✂ 25.00
☐ Brendan Shanahan, Detr. ✂ 50.00
☐ Mats Sundin, Toro. ✂ 50.00
☐ Alex Tanguay, Colo. ✂ 25.00
☐ José Théodore (G), Mont. ✂ 50.00
☐ Joe Thornton, Bost. ✂ 50.00
☐ Doug Weight, SLou. ✂ 25.00
☐ Alexei Yashin, NYIs. ✂ 25.00
☐ Steve Yzerman, Detr. ✂ 100.00

HE SHOOTS HE SCORES JERSEY

Redemption Set (30 cards):
Redemption (*20) J20

☐ Rob Blake, Colo. ✂
☐ Martin Brodeur (G), NJer. ✂
☐ Pavel Bure, NYRa. ✂
☐ Éric Dazé, Chic. ✂
☐ Peter Forsberg, Colo. ✂
☐ Dany Heatley, Atla. ✂
☐ Milan Hejduk, Colo. ✂
☐ Jarome Iginla, Calg. ✂
☐ Jaromir Jagr, Wash. ✂
☐ Paul Kariya, Anah. ✂
☐ Ilya Kovalchuk, Atla. ✂
☐ John LeClair, Phil. ✂
☐ Brian Leetch, NYRa. ✂
☐ Mario Lemieux, Pitt. ✂
☐ Nicklas Lidström, Detr. ✂
☐ Eric Lindros, NYRa. ✂
☐ Mark Messier, NYRa. ✂
☐ Mike Modano, Dall. ✂
☐ Owen Nolan, SanJ. ✂
☐ Luc Robitaille, Detr. ✂
☐ Jeremy Roenick, Phil. ✂
☐ Patrick Roy (G), Colo. ✂
☐ Joe Sakic, Colo. ✂
☐ Teemu Selänne, SanJ. ✂
☐ Brendan Shanahan, Detr. ✂
☐ Mats Sundin, Toro. ✂
☐ José Théodore (G), Mont. ✂
☐ Joe Thornton, Bost. ✂
☐ Keith Tkachuk, SLou. ✂
☐ Steve Yzerman, Detr. ✂

HOCKEY HARDWARE CALDER

Insert Set (10 cards):
Insert HH

☐ 1 Chuck Kobasew, Calg.
☐ 2 Henrik Zetterberg, Detr.
☐ 3 Alexander Svitov, Tamp.
☐ 4 Jay Bouwmeester, Flor.
☐ 5 Jordan Leopold, Calg.
☐ 6 Ron Hainsey, Mont.
☐ 7 Rick Nash, Colu.
☐ 8 Stanislav Chistov, Anah.
☐ 9 Stephen Weiss, Flor.
☐ 10 Wildcard

HOCKEY HARDWARE HART

Insert Set (10 cards):
Insert HH

☐ 1 Eric Lindros, NYRa.
☐ 2 Jarome Iginla, Calg.
☐ 3 Jaromir Jagr, Wash.
☐ 4 Joe Sakic, Colo.
☐ 5 José Théodore (G), Mont.
☐ 6 Markus Näslund, Vanc.
☐ 7 Pavel Bure, NYRa.
☐ 8 Peter Forsberg, Colo.
☐ 9 Mario Lemieux, Pitt.
☐ 10 Wildcard

HOCKEY HARDWARE NORRIS

Insert Set (10 cards):
Insert HH

☐ 1 Nicklas Lidström, Detr.
☐ 2 Sergei Gonchar, Wash.
☐ 3 Rob Blake, Colo.
☐ 4 Ed Jovanovski, Anah.
☐ 5 Brian Rafalski, NJer.
☐ 6 Bryan McCabe, Toro.
☐ 7 Chris Chelios, Detr.
☐ 8 Adrian Aucoin, NYIs.
☐ 9 Brian Leetch, NYRa.
☐ 10 Wildcard

HOCKEY HARDWARE PEARSON

Insert Set (10 cards):
Insert HH

☐ 1 Eric Lindros, NYRa.
☐ 2 Jarome Iginla, Calg.
☐ 3 Jaromir Jagr, Wash.
☐ 4 Joe Sakic, Colo.
☐ 5 Markus Näslund, Vanc.
☐ 6 Pavel Bure, NYRa.
☐ 7 Peter Forsberg, Colo.
☐ 8 Mario Lemieux, Pitt.
☐ 9 Mats Sundin, Toro.
☐ 10 Wildcard

HOCKEY HARDWARE ROSS

Insert Set (10 cards):
Insert HH

☐ 1 Eric Lindros, NYRa.
☐ 2 Jarome Iginla, Calg.
☐ 3 Jaromir Jagr, Wash.
☐ 4 Joe Sakic, Colo.
☐ 5 Markus Näslund, Vanc.
☐ 6 Pavel Bure, NYRa.
☐ 7 Peter Forsberg, Colo.
☐ 8 Mario Lemieux, Pitt.
☐ 9 Mats Sundin, Toro.
☐ 10 Wildcard

HOCKEY HARDWARE VÉZINA

Insert Set (10 cards):
Insert HH

☐ 1 Curtis Joseph (G), Detr.
☐ 2 Evgeni Nabokov (G), SanJ.
☐ 3 José Théodore (G), Mont.
☐ 4 Martin Brodeur (G), NJer.
☐ 5 Mike Richter (G), NYRa.
☐ 6 Patrick Lalime (G), Otta.
☐ 7 Patrick Roy (G), Colo.
☐ 8 Roberto Luongo (G), Flor.
☐ 9 Olaf Kölzig (G), Wash.
☐ 10 Wildcard

MAGNIFICENT

Insert Set (10 cards): 180.00
Insert MO

☐ MI-01 Mario Lemieux, ✂ {*40} 225.00
☐ MI-02 Mario Lemieux, ✂ {*40}
☐ MI-03 Mario Lemieux, ✂ {*40}
☐ MI-04 Mario Lemieux, ✂ {*40}
☐ MI-05 Mario Lemieux, ✂ ✂ {*40}
☐ MI-06 Mario Lemieux, ✂ {*10}
☐ MI-07 Mario Lemieux, ✂ {*10}
☐ MI-08 Mario Lemieux, ✂ ✂ ✂ {*10}
☐ MI-09 Mario Lemieux, ✂ ✂ ✂ ✂ {*10}
☐ MI-10 Mario Lemieux, ✂ ✂ ✂ ✂ {*10}

MAGNIFICENT

Insert Set (10 cards):
Insert MO

☐ MI-01 Mario Lemieux, ✂ ✍ {*15}
☐ MI-02 Mario Lemieux, ✂ ✍ {*15}
☐ MI-03 Mario Lemieux, ✂ ✍ {*15}
☐ MI-04 Mario Lemieux, ✂ ✍ {*15}
☐ MI-05 Mario Lemieux, ✂ ✂ ✍ {*15}
☐ MI-06 Mario Lemieux, ✂ ✍ {*5}
☐ MI-07 Mario Lemieux, ✂ ✍ {*5}
☐ MI-08 Mario Lemieux, ✂ ✂ ✂ ✍ {*5}
☐ MI-09 Mario Lemieux, ✂ ✂ ✂ ✂ ✍ {*5}
☐ MI-10 Mario Lemieux, ✂ ✂ ✂ ✂ ✍ {*5}

MARIO'S MATES

Insert Set (10 cards):
Insert (*25) MM

☐ MM-1 Mario Lemieux ✂ / P. Roy (G)
☐ MM-2 Mario Lemieux ✂ / S. Yzerman
☐ MM-3 Mario Lemieux ✂ / J. Jagr
☐ MM-4 Mario Lemieux ✂ / M. Brodeur (G)
☐ MM-5 Mario Lemieux ✂ / E. Lindros
☐ MM-6 Mario Lemieux ✂ / R. Francis
☐ MM-7 Mario Lemieux ✂ / M. Sundin
☐ MM-8 Mario Lemieux ✂ / J. Sakic
☐ MM-9 Mario Lemieux ✂ / P. Kariya
☐ MM-10 Mario Lemieux ✂ / J. Théodore (G)

MILESTONES

Insert Set (11 cards): 500.00
Insert Mile

☐ Ed Belfour (G), Toro. ✂ {*60} 50.00
☐ Martin Brodeur (G), NJer. ✂ {*60} 100.00
☐ Pavel Bure, NYRa. ✂ {*60} 50.00
☐ Vincent Damphousse, SanJ. ✂ {*60} 30.00
☐ Peter Forsberg, Colo. ✂ {*60} 75.00
☐ Ron Francis, Caro. ✂ {*60} 30.00
☐ Jaromir Jagr, Wash. ✂ {*60} 50.00
☐ Mike Richter (G), NYRa. ✂ {*60} 30.00
☐ Jeremy Roenick, Phil. ✂ {*60} 50.00
☐ Patrick Roy (G), Colo. ✂ {*33} 225.00
☐ Mats Sundin, Toro. ✂ {*60} 50.00

NHL HEROES

Insert Set (12 cards): 1700.00
Insert (*25) NH

☐ NH-1 Kovalchuk ✂ / Kharlamov ✂ 150.00
☐ NH-2 Thornton ✂ / Yzerman ✂ 250.00
☐ NH-3 Iginla ✂ / Messier ✂ 125.00
☐ NH-4 Yzerman ✂ / Trottier ✂ 250.00
☐ NH-5 Gagné ✂ / Lemieux ✂ 275.00
☐ NH-6 Lindros ✂ / Messier ✂ 150.00
☐ NH-7 Lemieux ✂ / Lafleur ✂ 300.00
☐ NH-8 Nash ✂ / Sundin ✂ 125.00
☐ NH-9 Pronger ✂ / MacInnis ✂ 75.00
☐ NH-10 Bouwmeester ✂ / Yzerman ✂ 200.00
☐ NH-11 Heatley ✂ / Hull ✂ 150.00
☐ NH-12 Weiss ✂ / Forsberg ✂ 125.00

PATENTED POWER

Insert Set (10 cards): 1500.00
Insert (*20) GJ

☐ PP-1 Lemieux ✂ / Shanahan ✂ 325.00
☐ PP-2 Yzerman ✂ / Sundin ✂ 275.00
☐ PP-3 Jagr ✂ / Selänne ✂ 125.00
☐ PP-4 Kariya ✂ / Roenick ✂ 175.00
☐ PP-5 Sakic ✂ / Modano ✂ 200.00
☐ PP-6 Bure ✂ / Heatley ✂ 125.00
☐ PP-7 Forsberg ✂ / Fedorov ✂ 175.00
☐ PP-8 Lindros ✂ / Bertuzzi ✂ 175.00
☐ PP-9 Kovalchuk ✂ / Messier ✂ 150.00
☐ PP-10 Hull ✂ / Thornton ✂ 175.00

REPRINT

Insert Set (150 cards): 350.00
Insert Reprint

☐ 151 Floyd Curry Mont. ['51-52 Parkie] 3.00
☐ 152 Billy Reay Mont. ['51-52 Parkie] 3.00
☐ 153 Jim Henry Bost. ['51-52 Parkie] 3.00
☐ 154 Ed Sandford Bost. ['51-52 Parkie] 3.00
☐ 155 Pentti Lund Bost. ['51-52 Parkie] 3.00
☐ 156 Al Dewsbury Chic. ['51-52 Parkie] 3.00
☐ 157 Bill Barilko Toro. ['51-52 Parkie] 3.00
☐ 158 Jack Stewart Chic. ['51-52 Parkie] 3.00
☐ 159 Alex Delvecchio Detr. ['51-52 Parkie] 3.00
☐ 160 Sid Abel Detr. ['51-52 Parkie] 3.00
☐ 161 Ray Timgren Toro. ['51-52 Parkie] 3.00
☐ 162 Ed Kullman NYRa. ['51-52 Parkie] 3.00
☐ 163 Billy Reay Mont. ['52-53 Parkie] 3.00
☐ 164 Floyd Curry Mont. ['52-53 Parkie] 3.00
☐ 165 Al Dewsbury Chic. ['52-53 Parkie] 3.00
☐ 166 Allan Stanley NYRa. ['52-53 Parkie] 3.00
☐ 167 Paul Ronty NYRa. ['52-53 Parkie] 3.00
☐ 168 Gaye Stewart NYRa. ['52-53 Parkie] 3.00
☐ 169 Al Rollins Chic. ['52-53 Parkie] 3.00
☐ 170 Leo Boivin Toro. ['52-53 Parkie] 3.00
☐ 171 George Gee Chic. ['52-53 Parkie] 3.00
☐ 172 Ted Kennedy Toro. ['52-53 Parkie] 3.00
☐ 173 Alex Delvecchio Detr. ['52-53 Parkie] 3.00
☐ 174 Marcel Pronovost Detr. ['52-53 Parkie] 3.00
☐ 175 Leo Boivin Toro. ['53-54 Parkie] 3.00
☐ 176 Ted Kennedy Toro. ['53-54 Parkie] 3.00
☐ 177 Ron Stewart Toro. ['53-54 Parkie] 3.00
☐ 178 Bud MacPherson Mont. ['53-54 Parkie] 3.00
☐ 179 Marcel Pronovost Detr. ['53-54 Parkie] 3.00
☐ 180 Alex Delvecchio Detr. ['53-54 Parkie] 3.00
☐ 181 Max Bentley NYRa. ['53-54 Parkie] 3.00
☐ 182 Andy Bathgate NYRa. ['53-54 Parkie] 3.00
☐ 183 Harry Howell NYRa. ['53-54 Parkie] 3.00
☐ 184 Allan Stanley NYRa. ['53-54 Parkie] 3.00
☐ 185 Ed Sandford Bost. ['53-54 Parkie] 3.00
☐ 186 Bill Quackenbush Bost. ['53-54 Parkie] 3.00
☐ 187 Eddie Mazur Mont. ['54-55 Parkie] 3.00
☐ 188 Floyd Curry Mont. ['54-55 Parkie] 3.00
☐ 189 Eric Nesterenko Toro. ['54-55 Parkie] 3.00
☐ 190 Ron Stewart Toro. ['54-55 Parkie] 3.00
☐ 191 Leo Boivin Toro. ['54-55 Parkie] 3.00
☐ 192 Ted Kennedy Toro. ['54-55 Parkie] 3.00
☐ 193 Alex Delvecchio Detr. ['54-55 Parkie] 3.00
☐ 194 Bob Armstrong Bost. ['54-55 Parkie] 3.00
☐ 195 Paul Ronty NYRa. ['54-55 Parkie] 3.00
☐ 196 Camille Henry NYRa. ['54-55 Parkie] 3.00
☐ 197 Al Rollins Chic. ['54-55 Parkie] 3.00
☐ 198 Al Dewsbury Chic. ['54-55 Parkie] 3.00
☐ 199 Netminder's nightmare ['54-55 Parkie] 3.00
☐ 200 Ron Stewart Toro. ['55-56 Parkie] 3.00
☐ 201 Dick Duff Toro. ['55-56 Parkie] 3.00
☐ 202 Lorne Chabot Toro. ['55-56 Parkie] 3.00
☐ 203 Harvey Jackson Toro. ['55-56 Parkie] 3.00
☐ 204 Joe Primeau Toro. ['55-56 Parkie] 3.00
☐ 205 Harold Cotton Toro. ['55-56 Parkie] 3.00
☐ 206 King Clancy Toro. ['55-56 Parkie] 3.00
☐ 207 Hap Day Toro. ['55-56 Parkie] 3.00
☐ 208 Newsy Lalonde Mont. ['55-56 Parkie] 3.00
☐ 209 Albert Leduc Mont. ['55-56 Parkie] 3.00
☐ 210 Babe Siebert Mont. ['55-56 Parkie] 3.00
☐ 211 Toe Blake Mont. ['55-56 Parkie] 3.00
☐ 212 Claude Provost Mont. ['57-58 Parkie] 3.00
☐ 213 Toe Blake Mont. ['57-58 Parkie] 3.00
☐ 214 Charlie Hodge (G) Mont. ['57-58 Parkie] 3.00
☐ 215 Floyd Curry Mont. ['57-58 Parkie] 3.00
☐ 216 Len Broderick Mont. ['57-58 Parkie] 3.00
☐ 217 Bernie Geoffrion Mont. ['57-58 Parkie] 3.00
☐ 218 George Armstrong Toro. ['57-58 Parkie] 3.00
☐ 219 Dick Duff Toro. ['57-58 Parkie] 3.00
☐ 220 Ron Stewart Toro. ['57-58 Parkie] 3.00
☐ 221 Billy Harris Toro. ['57-58 Parkie] 3.00
☐ 222 Bob Baun Toro. ['57-58 Parkie] 3.00
☐ 223 Hap Day Toro. ['57-58 Parkie] 3.00
☐ 224 Billy Harris Toro. ['58-59 Parkie] 3.00
☐ 225 Toe Blake Mont. ['58-59 Parkie] 3.00
☐ 226 Bob Nevin Toro. ['58-59 Parkie] 3.00
☐ 227 Bob Baun Toro. ['58-59 Parkie] 3.00
☐ 228 Charlie Hodge (G) Mont. ['58-59 Parkie] 3.00
☐ 229 Allan Stanley Toro. ['58-59 Parkie] 3.00
☐ 230 Billy Reay Toro. ['58-59 Parkie] 3.00
☐ 231 Dick Duff Toro. ['58-59 Parkie] 3.00
☐ 232 Marcel Bonin Mont. ['58-59 Parkie] 3.00
☐ 233 Claude Provost Mont. ['58-59 Parkie] 3.00
☐ 234 Canadiens on guard Mont. ['59-60 Parkie] 3.00
☐ 235 Lach & Richard Mont. ['53-54 Parkie] 3.00
☐ 236 Billy Harris Toro. ['59-60 Parkie] 3.00
☐ 237 Punch Imlach Toro. ['59-60 Parkie] 3.00
☐ 238 Charlie Hodge (G) Mont. ['59-60 Parkie] 3.00
☐ 239 Bob Baun Toro. ['59-60 Parkie] 3.00
☐ 240 Ron Stewart Toro. ['59-60 Parkie] 3.00
☐ 241 Toe Blake Mont. ['59-60 Parkie] 3.00
☐ 242 Action around the net ['59-60 Parkie] 3.00
☐ 243 Officials intervene ['59-60 Parkie] 3.00
☐ 244 Frank Selke Mont. ['59-60 Parkie] 3.00
☐ 245 King Clancy Toro. ['59-60 Parkie] 3.00
☐ 246 Ron Stewart Toro. ['60-61 Parkie] 3.00
☐ 247 Bob Baun Toro. ['60-61 Parkie] 3.00
☐ 248 Dick Duff Toro. ['60-61 Parkie] 3.00
☐ 249 Billy Harris Toro. ['60-61 Parkie] 3.00
☐ 250 Allan Stanley Toro. ['60-61 Parkie] 3.00
☐ 251 Jacques Plante (G) Mont. ['55-56 Parkie] 3.00
☐ 252 Sid Abel Detr. ['60-61 Parkie] 3.00
☐ 253 Norm Ullman Detr. ['60-61 Parkie] 3.00
☐ 254 Marcel Pronovost Detr. ['60-61 Parkie] 3.00
☐ 255 Alex Delvecchio Detr. ['60-61 Parkie] 3.00
☐ 256 Marcel Bonin Mont. ['60-61 Parkie] 3.00
☐ 257 Claude Provost Mont. ['60-61 Parkie] 3.00
☐ 258 Ron Stewart Toro. ['61-62 Parkie] 3.00
☐ 259 Bob Nevin Toro. ['61-62 Parkie] 3.00
☐ 260 Bob Baun Toro. ['61-62 Parkie] 3.00
☐ 261 Dick Duff Toro. ['61-62 Parkie] 3.00
☐ 262 Billy Harris Toro. ['61-62 Parkie] 3.00
☐ 263 Allan Stanley Toro. ['61-62 Parkie] 3.00
☐ 264 Maurice Richard Mont. ['60-61 Parkie] 5.00
☐ 265 Alex Delvecchio Detr. ['61-62 Parkie] 3.00
☐ 266 Norm Ullman Detr. ['61-62 Parkie] 3.00
☐ 267 Ed Litzenberger Detr. ['61-62 Parkie] 3.00
☐ 268 Marcel Pronovost Detr. ['61-62 Parkie] 3.00
☐ 269 Marcel Bonin Mont. ['61-62 Parkie] 3.00
☐ 270 Billy Harris Toro. ['62-63 Parkie] 3.00
☐ 271 Dick Duff Toro. ['62-63 Parkie] 3.00
☐ 272 Bob Baun Toro. ['62-63 Parkie] 3.00
☐ 273 Maurice Richard Mont. ['59-60 Parkie] 5.00
☐ 274 Allan Stanley Toro. ['62-63 Parkie] 3.00
☐ 275 Bob Nevin Toro. ['62-63 Parkie] 3.00
☐ 276 Ed Litzenberger Toro. ['62-63 Parkie] 3.00
☐ 277 Norm Ullman Detr. ['62-63 Parkie] 3.00
☐ 278 Alex Delvecchio Detr. ['62-63 Parkie] 3.00
☐ 279 Marcel Pronovost Detr. ['62-63 Parkie] 3.00
☐ 280 Sid Abel Detr. ['62-63 Parkie] 3.00
☐ 281 Claude Provost Mont. ['62-63 Parkie] 3.00
☐ 282 Jean_Claude Tremblay Mont. ['62-63 Parkie] 3.00
☐ 283 Allan Stanley Toro. ['63-64 Parkie] 3.00
☐ 284 Ed Litzenberger Toro. ['63-64 Parkie] 3.00
☐ 285 Maurice Richard Mont. ['55-56 Parkie] 5.00
☐ 286 Bob Nevin Toro. ['63-64 Parkie] 3.00
☐ 287 Jacques Laperrière Mont. ['63-64 Parkie] 3.00
☐ 288 Jean_Claude Tremblay Mont. ['63-64 Parkie] 3.00

☐ 289 John Ferguson Mont. ['63-64 Parkie]	3.00
☐ 290 Toe Blake Mont. ['63-64 Parkie]	3.00
☐ 291 Marcel Pronovost Detr. ['63-64 Parkie]	3.00
☐ 292 Alex Delvecchio Detr. ['63-64 Parkie]	3.00
☐ 293 Allan Stanley Toro. ['63-64 Parkie]	3.00
☐ 294 Dick Duff Toro. ['63-64 Parkie]	3.00
☐ 295 Maurice Richard Mont. ['54-55 Parkie]	5.00
☐ 296 Ron Stewart Toro. ['63-64 Parkie]	3.00
☐ 297 J.C. Tremblay Mont. ['63-64 Parkie]	3.00
☐ 298 John Ferguson Mont. ['63-64 Parkie]	3.00
☐ 299 Toe Blake Mont. ['63-64 Parkie]	3.00
☐ 300 Bill Quackenbush	3.00

TRIPLE TEAMMATES

Insert Set (20 cards):	1500.00
Insert (*60)	TT
☐ TT-1 Lindros ✂ / Leetch ✂ / Bure ✂	100.00
☐ TT-2 LeClair ✂ / Recchi ✂ / Gagné ✂	75.00
☐ TT-3 Sundin ✂ / Mogilny ✂ / Roberts ✂	75.00
☐ TT-4 Yzerman ✂ / Shanahan ✂ / Fedorov ✂	175.00
☐ TT-5 Brodeur (G) ✂ / Stevens ✂ / Elias ✂	100.00
☐ TT-6 Potvin (G) ✂ / Palffy ✂ / Allison ✂	100.00
☐ TT-7 Koivu ✂ / Théodore (G) ✂ / Rivet ✂	100.00
☐ TT-8 Thornton ✂ / Samsonov ✂ / McLaren ✂	75.00
☐ TT-9 Kovalchuk ✂ / Heatley ✂ / Stefan ✂	100.00
☐ TT-10 Dunham (G) ✂ / Legwand ✂ / Hartnell ✂	40.00
☐ TT-11 Alfredsson ✂ / Havlat ✂ / Hossa ✂	100.00
☐ TT-12 Satan ✂ / Connolly ✂ / Dumont ✂	40.00
☐ TT-13 Dazé ✂ / Thibault (G) ✂ / Zhamnov ✂	40.00
☐ TT-14 Lemieux ✂ / Hedberg (G) ✂ / Kovalev ✂	275.00
☐ TT-15 Nolan ✂ / Selänne ✂ / Nabokov (G) ✂	75.00
☐ TT-16 Pronger ✂ / MacInnis ✂ / Weight ✂	50.00
☐ TT-17 Jagr ✂ / Kölzig (G) ✂ / Bondra ✂	75.00
☐ TT-18 Cloutier (G) ✂ / Bertuzzi ✂ / Näslund ✂	100.00
☐ TT-19 Forsberg ✂ / Sakic ✂ / Roy ✂	250.00
☐ TT-20 Burke (G) ✂ / Brière ✂ / Numminen ✂	50.00

VINTAGE MEMORABILIA

Insert Set (20 cards):	3500.00
Insert (*20)	VM
☐ Johnny Bucyk, Bost. ✂	125.00
☐ Frank Mahovlich, Mont. ✂	200.00
☐ Henri Richard, Mont. ✂	200.00
☐ Maurice Richard, Mont. ✂	550.00
☐ Tiny Thompson (G), Bost. ✂	125.00
☐ Bernie Parent (G), Phil. ✂	150.00
☐ Tim Horton, Toro. ✂	225.00
☐ Terry Sawchuk (G), Detr. ✂	400.00
☐ Vladislav Tretiak (G), CSKA ✂	225.00
☐ Gerry Cheevers (G), Bost. ✂	150.00
☐ Ted Kennedy, Toro. ✂	125.00
☐ Gilbert Perreault, Buff. ✂	150.00
☐ Bill Gadsby, Detr. ✂	125.00
☐ Bobby Hull, Chic. ✂	350.00
☐ Stan Mikita, Chic. ✂	150.00
☐ Marcel Dionne, LosA. ✂	200.00
☐ Jari Kurri, LosA. ✂	200.00
☐ Jean Béliveau, Mont. ✂	425.00
☐ Doug Harvey, Mont. ✂	225.00
☐ Guy Lafleur, Mont. ✂	400.00

VINTAGE TEAMMATES

Insert Set (20 cards):	1500.00
Insert (*40)	VT
☐ VT-1 Bobby Hull ✂ / Dennis Hull ✂	200.00
☐ VT-2 Giacomin (G) ✂ / P. Esposito ✂	200.00
☐ VT-3 Bucyk ✂ / Cheevers (G) ✂	125.00
☐ VT-4 S.Savard ✂ / Robinson ✂	125.00
☐ VT-5 T.Esposito ✂ / Mikita ✂	175.00
☐ VT-6 Sawchuk (G) ✂ / Abel ✂	250.00
☐ VT-7 F.Mahovlich ✂ / P. Mahovlich ✂	125.00
☐ VT-8 Béliveau ✂ / Harvey ✂	325.00
☐ VT-9 Lafleur ✂ / H.Richard ✂	300.00
☐ VT-10 Trottier ✂ / Bossy ✂	250.00
☐ VT-11 Potvin ✂ / Nystrom ✂	125.00
☐ VT-12 Clarke ✂ / Barber ✂	125.00
☐ VT-13 B.Parent ✂ / Schultz ✂	125.00
☐ VT-14 T.Horton ✂ / Kelly ✂	175.00
☐ VT-15 Kharlamov ✂ / Tretiak (G) ✂	275.00
☐ VT-16 Mosienko ✂ / H.Lumley (G) ✂	125.00
☐ VT-17 Delvecchio ✂ / Crozier (G) ✂	125.00
☐ VT-18 A.Bailey ✂ / Clancy ✂	125.00
☐ VT-19 Shore ✂ / Thompson ✂	175.00
☐ VT-20 McDonald ✂ / T.Williams ✂	125.00

2002 - 03 PARKHURST RETRO

Produced by the In The Game, this series was released in April 2003. Cards 1-200 have two versions: the standard-size card and the retro-size card (1 3/4" by 2 1/2").

Shell Set (200 cards):		70.00
Complete Set (250 cards):	1,000	1,200
Common Player:	.50	.35
Description	Mini	PR
☐☐ 1 Mario Lemieux, Pitt.	6.50	4.50
☐☐ 2 Jarome Iginla, Calg.	1.50	1.00
☐☐ 3 Jaromir Jagr, Wash.	2.00	1.50

Description	Mini	PR
☐☐ 4 Alex Kovalev, NYRa.	1.00	.50
☐☐ 5 Todd Bertuzzi, Vanc.	2.50	1.50
☐☐ 6 Joe Thornton, Bost.	2.50	1.50
☐☐ 7 Jason Allison, LosA.	1.00	.50
☐☐ 8 Markus Näslund, Vanc.	2.00	1.50
☐☐ 9 Eric Lindros, NYRa.	2.00	1.50
☐☐ 10 Keith Tkachuk, SLou.	1.00	.50
☐☐ 11 Adam Oates, Anah.	.50	.50
☐☐ 12 Mike Modano, Dall.	2.00	1.50
☐☐ 13 Pavel Bure, NYRa.	1.50	1.00
☐☐ 14 Ron Francis, Caro.	1.00	.50
☐☐ 15 Joe Sakic, Colo.	3.50	2.00
☐☐ 16 Brendan Shanahan, Detr.	2.00	1.50
☐☐ 17 Alexei Yashin, NYIs.	1.00	.50
☐☐ 18 Patrick Roy (G), Colo.	6.50	4.50
☐☐ 19 Dwayne Roloson (G), MinW.	.50	.35
☐☐ 20 Pavol Demitra, SLou.	.50	.50
☐☐ 21 Sergei Samsonov, Bost.	1.00	.50
☐☐ 22 Steve Yzerman, Detr.	5.00	3.50
☐☐ 23 Mats Sundin, Toro.	2.00	1.50
☐☐ 24 Peter Bondra, Wash.	1.00	.50
☐☐ 25 Daniel Alfredsson, Otta.	1.00	.50
☐☐ 26 Jeremy Roenick, Phil.	1.50	1.00
☐☐ 27 Zigmund Palffy, LosA.	1.00	.50
☐☐ 28 Ray Whitney, Colu.	.50	.35
☐☐ 29 Sami Kapanen, Phil.	.50	.35
☐☐ 30 Alexei Zhamnov, Chic.	.50	.35
☐☐ 31 Radek Bonk, Otta.	.50	.35
☐☐ 32 Éric Dazé, Chic.	.50	.50
☐☐ 33 Tommy Salo (G), Edmo.	.50	.50
☐☐ 34 Marian Gaborik, MinW.	2.00	1.50
☐☐ 35 Alexander Mogilny, Toro.	1.00	.50
☐☐ 36 Glen Murray, Bost.	1.00	.50
☐☐ 37 Patrik Elias, NJer.	1.50	1.00
☐☐ 38 Simon Gagné, Phil.	1.50	1.00
☐☐ 39 Ryan Smyth, Edmo.	1.00	.50
☐☐ 40 Bill Guerin, Dall.	.50	.50
☐☐ 41 Jeff O'Neill, Caro.	.50	.50
☐☐ 42 Miroslav Satan, Buff.	.50	.35
☐☐ 43 Adam Deadmarsh, LosA.	.50	.35
☐☐ 44 Sergei Fedorov, Detr.	2.00	1.50
☐☐ 45 Owen Nolan, Toro.	1.00	.50
☐☐ 46 Tony Amonte, Phoe.	1.00	.50
☐☐ 47 Doug Weight, SLou.	1.00	.50
☐☐ 48 Marian Hossa, Otta.	2.00	1.50
☐☐ 49 Mark Parrish, NYIs.	.50	.50
☐☐ 50 Theoren Fleury, Chic.	1.00	.50
☐☐ 51 Steven Reinprecht, Colo.	.50	.35
☐☐ 52 Dany Heatley, Atla.	2.00	1.50
☐☐ 53 Sergei Gonchar, Wash.	.50	.35
☐☐ 54 Ilya Kovalchuk, Atla.	2.00	1.50
☐☐ 55 Brett Hull, Detr.	2.00	1.50
☐☐ 56 Daniel Brière, Phoe.	1.00	.50
☐☐ 57 Brad Richards, Tamp.	1.00	.50
☐☐ 58 Brendan Morrison, Vanc.	.50	.35
☐☐ 59 Steve Sullivan, Chic.	.50	.35
☐☐ 60 Mike York, Edmo.	.50	.35
☐☐ 61 Nicklas Lidström, Detr.	1.00	.50
☐☐ 62 Michael Peca, NYIs.	.50	.50
☐☐ 63 Mark Recchi, Phil.	.50	.50
☐☐ 64 Daymond Langkow, Phoe.	.50	.35
☐☐ 65 Tyler Arnason, Chic.	.50	.50
☐☐ 66 Rob Blake, Colo.	1.00	.50
☐☐ 67 Mike Comrie, Edmo.	1.50	1.00
☐☐ 68 Félix Potvin (G), LosA.	1.00	.50
☐☐ 69 Brian Rolston, Bost.	.50	.35
☐☐ 70 Martin Brodeur (G), NJer.	3.50	2.00
☐☐ 71 Anson Carter, Edmo.	.50	.50
☐☐ 72 Roberto Luongo (G), Flor.	1.50	1.00
☐☐ 73 Joe Nieuwendyk, NJer.	.50	.50
☐☐ 74 Dean McAmmond, Colo.	.50	.35
☐☐ 75 Niko Kapanen, Dall.	.50	.35
☐☐ 76 Jan Hrdina, Pitt.	.50	.35
☐☐ 77 Vincent Damphousse, SanJ.	1.00	.50
☐☐ 78 Jozef Stümpel, Bost.	.50	.35
☐☐ 79 Milan Hejduk, Colo.	1.50	1.00
☐☐ 80 Stu Barnes, Buff.	.50	.35
☐☐ 81 Pierre Turgeon, Dall.	.50	.50
☐☐ 82 Marty Turco (G), Dall.	1.00	.50
☐☐ 83 Bryan McCabe, Toro.	.50	.35
☐☐ 84 Gary Roberts, Toro.	.50	.50
☐☐ 85 Martin Havlat, Otta.	1.00	.50
☐☐ 86 Kyle Calder, Chic.	.50	.35
☐☐ 87 Paul Kariya, Anah.	3.00	2.00
☐☐ 88 Martin Straka, Pitt.	.50	.35
☐☐ 89 Yanic Perreault, Mont.	.50	.35
☐☐ 90 Brian Boucher, Phoe.	.50	.35
☐☐ 91 Darcy Tucker, Toro.	.50	.35
☐☐ 92 Mike Ricci, SanJ.	.50	.35
☐☐ 93 Keith Primeau, Phil.	.50	.50
☐☐ 94 Bobby Holik, NYRa.	.50	.35
☐☐ 95 Chris Osgood (G), NYIs.	1.00	.50
☐☐ 96 Brian Leetch, NYRa.	1.00	.50
☐☐ 97 Teemu Selänne, SanJ.	1.50	1.00
☐☐ 98 Alex Tanguay, Colo.	1.00	.50
☐☐ 99 Rod Brind'Amour, Caro.	.50	.35
☐☐ 100 Petr Sykora, Anah.	.50	.50
☐☐ 101 Jere Lehtinen, Dall.	.50	.35
☐☐ 102 Kevin Weekes (G), Caro.	.50	.35
☐☐ 103 Jason Arnott, Dall.	1.00	.50
☐☐ 104 Al MacInnis, SLou.	.50	.50
☐☐ 105 Scott Gomez, NJer.	.50	.50
☐☐ 106 Byron Dafoe (G), Atla.	.50	.50
☐☐ 107 Evgeni Nabokov (G), SanJ.	1.00	.50
☐☐ 108 Sandis Ozolinsh, Anah.	.50	.35
☐☐ 109 John LeClair, Phil.	1.50	1.00
☐☐ 110 Mike Dunham (G), NYRa.	.50	.50
☐☐ 111 Manny Fernandez (G), MinW.	.50	.35
☐☐ 112 Johan Hedberg (G), Pitt.	.50	.50
☐☐ 113 Chris Pronger, SLou.	1.00	.50
☐☐ 114 Fredrik Modin, Tamp.	.50	.35
☐☐ 115 Rostislav Klesla, Colu.	.50	.35
☐☐ 116 Manny Legacé (G), Detr.	.50	.35
☐☐ 117 Teppo Numminen, Phoe.	.50	.35
☐☐ 118 Shane Doan, Phoe.	.50	.35
☐☐ 119 Martin Biron (G), Buff.	1.00	.50
☐☐ 120 Luc Robitaille, Detr.	1.50	1.00
☐☐ 121 Igor Larionov, Detr.	1.00	.50
☐☐ 122 Doug Gilmour, Mont.	1.00	.50
☐☐ 123 Roman Cechmanek (G), Phil.	.50	.50
☐☐ 124 Marc Savard, Atla.	.50	.35
☐☐ 125 Scott Stevens, NJer.	.50	.50
☐☐ 126 Steve Rucchin, Anah.	.50	.35
☐☐ 127 Olaf Kölzig (G), Wash.	1.00	.50
☐☐ 128 Ed Jovanovski, Vanc.	.50	.50
☐☐ 129 Petr Nedved, NYRa.	.50	.35
☐☐ 130 Valeri Bure, Flor.	.50	.35
☐☐ 131 Jean-Pierre Dumont, Buff.	.50	.35
☐☐ 132 Jocelyn Thibault (G), Chic.	.50	.50
☐☐ 133 Martin Lapointe, Bost.	.50	.35
☐☐ 134 Tomas Kaberle, Toro.	.50	.35
☐☐ 135 José Théodore (G), Mont.	2.50	1.50
☐☐ 136 Bates Battaglia, Caro.	.50	.35
☐☐ 137 Chris Drury, Calg.	1.00	.50
☐☐ 138 Patrick Lalime (G), Otta.	1.00	.50
☐☐ 139 Derek Morris, Colo.	.50	.35
☐☐ 140 Sean Burke (G), Phoe.	1.00	.50
☐☐ 141 Radek Dvorak, NYRa.	.50	.35
☐☐ 142 Ladislav Nagy, Phoe.	.50	.35
☐☐ 143 Oleg Petrov, Mont.	.50	.35
☐☐ 144 Kristian Huselius, Flor.	.50	.35
☐☐ 145 Mark Messier, NYRa.	2.00	1.50
☐☐ 146 Curtis Joseph (G), Detr.	2.00	1.50
☐☐ 147 Tim Connolly, Buff.	.50	.50
☐☐ 148 Arturs Irbe (G), Caro.	.50	.50
☐☐ 149 Espen Knutsen, Colu.	.50	.35
☐☐ 150 Ed Belfour (G), Toro.	2.00	1.50
☐☐ 151 Jaroslav Modry, LosA.	.50	.35
☐☐ 152 Dan Cloutier (G), Vanc.	.50	.50
☐☐ 153 Jeff Friesen, NJer.	.50	.35
☐☐ 154 Janne Niinimaa, Edmo.	.50	.35
☐☐ 155 Nikolai Khabibulin (G), Tamp.	.50	.50
☐☐ 156 Justin Williams, Phil.	.50	.35
☐☐ 157 Kyle McLaren, SanJ.	.50	.35
☐☐ 158 Sergei Zubov, Dall.	.50	.35
☐☐ 159 Brian Savage, Phoe.	.50	.35
☐☐ 160 Chris Chelios, Detr.	1.00	.50
☐☐ 161 Roman Hamrlik, NYIs.	.50	.35
☐☐ 162 Scott Niedermayer, NJer.	.50	.35
☐☐ 163 Danny Markov, Phoe.	.50	.35
☐☐ 164 Marc Denis (G), Colu.	1.00	.50
☐☐ 165 Scott Hartnell, Nash.	.50	.35
☐☐ 166 Roman Turek (G), Calg.	1.00	.50
☐☐ 167 Brenden Morrow, Dall.	.50	.35
☐☐ 168 David Legwand, Nash.	.50	.50
☐☐ 169 Henrik Sedin, Vanc.	.50	.35
☐☐ 170 Oleg Tverdovsky, NJer.	.50	.35
☐☐ 171 Peter Forsberg, Colo.	3.00	2.00
☐☐ 172 Vincent Lecavalier, Tamp.	2.00	1.50
☐☐ 173 Pavel Datsyuk, Detr.	1.50	1.00
☐☐ 174 Dan Blackburn (G), NYRa.	.50	.50
☐☐ 175 Adam Foote, Colo.	.50	.35
☐☐ 176 Joé Juneau, Mont.	.50	.35
☐☐ 177 Mike Richter (G), NYRa.	1.00	.50
☐☐ 178 Shawn Bates, NYIs.	.50	.35
☐☐ 179 Erik Cole, Caro.	.50	.35
☐☐ 180 Jean-Sébastien Giguère (G), Anah.	2.00	1.50
☐☐ 181 Saku Koivu, Mont.	1.50	1.00
☐☐ 182 Zdeno Chara, Otta.	.50	.35
☐☐ 183 Stephen Weiss, Flor.	.50	.50
☐☐ 184 Robert Svehla, Toro.	.50	.35
☐☐ 185 Patrik Stefan, Atla.	.50	.35
☐☐ 186 Robert Lang, Wash.	.50	.35
☐☐ 187 Olli Jokinen, Flor.	.50	.35
☐☐ 188 Pavel Brendl, Caro.	.50	.35
☐☐ 189 Brent Johnson (G), SLou.	.50	.50
☐☐ 190 Boris Mironov, NYRa.	.50	.35
☐☐ 191 Tomas Vokoun (G), Nash.	.50	.35
☐☐ 192 Darius Kasparaitis, NYRa.	.50	.35
☐☐ 193 Martin St-Louis, Tamp.	1.00	.50
☐☐ 194 Radim Vrbata, Colo.	.50	.35
☐☐ 195 Jeff Hackett (G), Bost.	.50	.35
☐☐ 196 Nikolai Antropov, Toro.	.50	.35
☐☐ 197 Craig Conroy, Calg.	.50	.35
☐☐ 198 Nick Boynton, Bost.	.50	.35
☐☐ 199 Richard Zednik, Mont.	.50	.50
☐☐ 200 Vaclav Prospal, Tamp.	.50	.35

ROOKIES

Cards 201-250 have two versions: the standard-size card (#/300) and the retro-size card (1 3/4" by 2 1/2").

Description	Mini	Retro
☐☐ **201 Pierre-Marc Bouchard, MinW. RC**	45.00	50.00
☐☐ **202 Rick Nash, Colu. RC**	80.00	100.00
☐☐ **203 Dennis Seidenberg, Phil. RC**	15.00	20.00
☐☐ **204 Jay Bouwmeester, SLou. RC**	45.00	50.00
☐☐ **205 Stanislav Chistov, Anah. RC**	45.00	50.00
☐☐ **206 Pascal Leclaire (G), Colu. RC**	40.00	50.00
☐☐ **207 Jared Aulin, LosA. RC**	20.00	30.00
☐☐ **208 Chuck Kobasew, Calg. RC**	30.00	40.00
☐☐ **209 Jordan Leopold, Calg. RC**	20.00	30.00
☐☐ **210 Steve Ott, Dall. RC**	20.00	30.00
☐☐ **211 Ales Hemsky, Edmo. RC**	45.00	50.00
☐☐ **212 Matt Walker, SLou. RC**	10.00	15.00
☐☐ **213 Tomas Malec, Caro. RC**	10.00	15.00
☐☐ **214 Dmitri Bykov, Detr. RC**	15.00	20.00
☐☐ **215 Michael Leighton, Chic. RC**	15.00	20.00
☐☐ **216 Henrik Zetterberg, Detr. RC**	80.00	100.00
☐☐ **217 Alexander Frolov, LosA. RC**	40.00	50.00
☐☐ **218 Steve Eminger, Wash. RC**	15.00	20.00
☐☐ **219 Scottie Upshall, Nash. RC**	30.00	40.00
☐☐ **220 Rickard Wallin, MinW. RC**	10.00	15.00
☐☐ **221 Alexei Semenov, Edmo. RC**	15.00	20.00
☐☐ **222 Ron Hainsey, Mont. RC**	20.00	30.00
☐☐ **223 Martin Gerber (G), Anah. RC**	15.00	20.00
☐☐ **224 Adam Hall (G), Nash. RC**	20.00	30.00
☐☐ **225 Ray Emery, Otta. RC**	15.00	20.00
☐☐ **226 Anton Volchenkov, Otta. RC**	15.00	20.00
☐☐ **227 Levente Szuper (G), Calg. RC**	15.00	20.00
☐☐ **228 Carlo Colaiacovo, Toro. RC**	20.00	30.00
☐☐ **229 Alexander Svitov, Tamp. RC**	30.00	40.00
☐☐ **230 Alexei Smirnov, Anah. RC**	20.00	30.00
☐☐ **231 Jeff Taffe, Phoe. RC**	20.00	30.00
☐☐ **232 Mikael Tellqvist (G), Toro. RC**	15.00	20.00
☐☐ **233 Ari Ahonen, NJer. RC**	20.00	30.00
☐☐ **234 Martin Samuelsson, Bost. RC**	10.00	15.00
☐☐ **235 Shaone Morrisonn, Bost. RC**	15.00	20.00
☐☐ **236 Craig Andersson (G), Chic. RC**	20.00	30.00
☐☐ **237 Jim Fahey, SanJ. RC**	10.00	15.00
☐☐ **238 Brooks Orpik, Pitt. RC**	20.00	30.00
☐☐ **239 Mike Komisarek, Mont. RC**	20.00	30.00
☐☐ **240 Frédéric Cloutier (G), MinW. RC**	10.00	15.00
☐☐ **241 Curtis Sanford (G), SLou. RC**	15.00	20.00
☐☐ **242 Jim Vandermeer, Phil. RC**	15.00	20.00
☐☐ **243 Paul Manning, Colu. RC**	10.00	15.00
☐☐ **244 Kris Vernarsky, Bost. RC**	10.00	15.00
☐☐ **245 Dany Sabourin (G), Calg. RC**	10.00	15.00
☐☐ **246 Mike Cammalleri, LosA. RC**	30.00	40.00
☐☐ **247 Jason Spezza, Otta. RC**	60.00	75.00
☐☐ **248 Cristobal Huet, LosA. RC**	15.00	20.00
☐☐ **249 Ryan Miller, Buff. RC**	40.00	50.00
☐☐ 250 Dick Tarnström, Pitt.	10.00	15.00

HE SHOOTS HE SCORES

Each redemption card was worth one, two, or three points. Collectors could trade 400 points for a special random jersey card.

Insert Set (20 cards):	
Insert	HSHS
☐ Marian Gaborik, MinW. [1 Point]	
☐ Dany Heatley, Atla. [1 Point]	
☐ Marian Hossa, Otta. [1 Point]	
☐ Mike Modano, Dall. [1 Point]	
☐ Rick Nash, Colu. [1 Point]	
☐ Brendan Shanahan, Detr. [1 Point]	
☐ Joe Thornton, Bost. [1 Point]	
☐ Marty Turco (G), Dall. [1 Point]	
☐ Ed Belfour (G), Toro. [2 Points]	
☐ Martin Brodeur (G), NJer. [2 Points]	
☐ Pavel Bure, NYRa. [2 Points]	
☐ Peter Forsberg, Colo. [2 Points]	
☐ Jaromir Jagr, Wash. [2 Points]	
☐ Paul Kariya, Anah. [2 Points]	
☐ Ilya Kovalchuk, Atla. [2 Points]	
☐ Eric Lindros, NYRa. [2 Points]	
☐ Joe Sakic, Colo. [2 Points]	
☐ Mario Lemieux, Pitt. [3 Points]	
☐ Patrick Roy (G), Colo. [3 Points]	
☐ Steve Yzerman, Detr. [3 Points]	

BACK IN TIME

Insert Set (15 cards):	2700.00
Insert (*30)	BIT
☐ BIT-1 Mario Lemieux, Pitt. ✂	225.00
☐ BIT-2 Mario Lemieux, Pitt. ✂	225.00
☐ BIT-3 Mario Lemieux, Pitt. ✂	225.00

☐	BIT-4 Mario Lemieux, Pitt. ✂	225.00
☐	BIT-5 Mario Lemieux, Pitt. ✂	225.00
☐	BIT-6 Mario Lemieux, Pitt. ✂	225.00
☐	BIT-7 Mario Lemieux, Pitt. ✂	225.00
☐	BIT-8 Mario Lemieux, Pitt. ✂	225.00
☐	BIT-9 Mario Lemieux, Pitt. ✂	225.00
☐	BIT-10 Mario Lemieux, Pitt. ✂	225.00
☐	BIT-11 Mario Lemieux, Pitt. ✂	225.00
☐	BIT-12 Mario Lemieux, Pitt. ✂	225.00
☐	BIT-13 Mario Lemieux, Pitt. ✂	225.00
☐	BIT-14 Mario Lemieux, Pitt. ✂	225.00
☐	BIT-15 Mario Lemieux, Pitt. ✂	225.00

CALDER HOPEFULS

Insert Set (8 cards):		**300.00**
	Insert (*30)	**CH**
☐	Tyler Arnason, Chic. ✂	50.00
☐	Jay Bouwmeester, Flor. ✂	50.00
☐	Stanislav Chistov, Anah. ✂	50.00
☐	Alexander Frolov, LosA. ✂	50.00
☐	Barret Jackman, SLou. ✂	50.00
☐	Niko Kapanen, Dall. ✂	25.00
☐	Ryan Miller, Buff. ✂	50.00
☐	Rick Nash, Colu. ✂	100.00

FRANCHISE

Insert Set (30 cards):		**1100.00**
	Insert (*60)	**RF**
☐	Jason Allison, LosA. ✂	25.00
☐	Daniel Brière, Phoe. ✂	25.00
☐	Martin Brodeur (G), NJer. ✂	75.00
☐	Pavel Bure, NYRa. ✂	25.00
☐	Mike Comrie, Edmo. ✂	50.00
☐	Ron Francis, Caro. ✂	25.00
☐	Marian Gaborik, MinW. ✂	50.00
☐	Dany Heatley, Atla. ✂	50.00
☐	Marian Hossa, Otta. ✂	50.00
☐	Jarome Iginla, Calg. ✂	50.00
☐	Jaromir Jagr, Wash. ✂	50.00
☐	Paul Kariya, Anah. ✂	50.00
☐	Vincent Lecavalier, Tamp. ✂	50.00
☐	David Legwand, Nash. ✂	25.00
☐	Mario Lemieux, Pitt. ✂	150.00
☐	Roberto Luongo (G), Flor. ✂	25.00
☐	Mike Modano, Dall. ✂	50.00
☐	Rick Nash, Colu. ✂	75.00
☐	Markus Näslund, Vanc. ✂	50.00
☐	Michael Peca, NYIs. ✂	25.00
☐	Chris Pronger, SLou. ✂	25.00
☐	Jeremy Roenick, Phil. ✂	25.00
☐	Joe Sakic, Colo. ✂	75.00
☐	Miroslav Satan, Buff. ✂	25.00
☐	Teemu Selänne, SanJ. ✂	25.00
☐	Mats Sundin, Toro. ✂	50.00
☐	José Théodore (G), Mont. ✂	50.00
☐	Jocelyn Thibault (G), Chic. ✂	25.00
☐	Joe Thornton, Bost. ✂	50.00
☐	Steve Yzerman, Detr. ✂	125.00

GAME-USED JERSEY

Insert Set (40 cards):		**3000.00**
	Insert (*90)	**RJ**
☐	Ed Belfour (G), Toro. ✂	35.00
☐	Todd Bertuzzi, Vanc. ✂	45.00
☐	Jay Bouwmeester, Flor. ✂	30.00
☐	Martin Brodeur (G), NJer. ✂	50.00
☐	Pavel Bure, NYRa. ✂	25.00
☐	Sergei Fedorov, Detr. ✂	35.00
☐	Peter Forsberg, Colo. ✂	50.00
☐	Marian Gaborik, MinW. ✂	35.00
☐	Bill Guerin, Dall. ✂	20.00
☐	Dany Heatley, Atla. ✂	35.00
☐	Marian Hossa, Otta. ✂	35.00
☐	Brett Hull, Detr. ✂	35.00
☐	Jaromir Jagr, Wash. ✂	35.00
☐	Paul Kariya, Anah. ✂	50.00
☐	Saku Koivu, Mont. ✂	50.00
☐	Ilya Kovalchuk, Atla. ✂	35.00
☐	Vincent Lecavalier, Tamp. ✂	35.00
☐	John LeClair, Phil. ✂	35.00
☐	Mario Lemieux, Pitt. ✂	100.00
☐	Nicklas Lidström, Detr. ✂	20.00
☐	Eric Lindros, NYRa. ✂	35.00
☐	Roberto Luongo (G), Flor. ✂	30.00
☐	Mark Messier, NYRa. ✂	35.00
☐	Mike Modano, Dall. ✂	35.00
☐	Rick Nash, Colu. ✂	50.00
☐	Markus Näslund, Vanc. ✂	35.00
☐	Chris Pronger, SLou. ✂	20.00
☐	Jeremy Roenick, Phil. ✂	25.00
☐	Patrick Roy (G), Colo. ✂	75.00
☐	Joe Sakic, Colo. ✂	50.00
☐	Sergei Samsonov, Bost. ✂	20.00
☐	Teemu Selänne, SanJ. ✂	25.00
☐	Brendan Shanahan, Detr. ✂	35.00
☐	Jason Spezza, Otta. ✂	35.00
☐	Mats Sundin, Toro. ✂	35.00
☐	José Théodore (G), Mont. ✂	40.00
☐	Jocelyn Thibault (G), Chic. ✂	20.00
☐	Joe Thornton, Bost. ✂	40.00
☐	Marty Turco (G), Dall. ✂	20.00
☐	Steve Yzerman, Detr. ✂	75.00

GAME-USED STICK & JERSEY

Insert Set (30 cards):		**700.00**
	Insert (*60)	**RSJ**
☐	Todd Bertuzzi, Vanc. ✂ ✂	75.00
☐	Martin Brodeur (G), NJer. ✂ ✂	100.00
☐	Pavel Bure, NYRa. ✂ ✂	50.00
☐	Sergei Fedorov, Detr. ✂ ✂	65.00
☐	Peter Forsberg, Colo. ✂ ✂	75.00
☐	Marian Gaborik, MinW. ✂ ✂	60.00
☐	Dany Heatley, Atla. ✂ ✂	60.00
☐	Marian Hossa, Otta. ✂ ✂	60.00
☐	Brett Hull, Detr. ✂ ✂	60.00
☐	Jaromir Jagr, Wash. ✂ ✂	60.00
☐	Paul Kariya, Anah. ✂ ✂	75.00
☐	Ilya Kovalchuk, Atla. ✂ ✂	60.00
☐	Mario Lemieux, Pitt. ✂ ✂	200.00
☐	Nicklas Lidström, Detr. ✂ ✂	35.00
☐	Eric Lindros, NYRa. ✂ ✂	60.00
☐	Mark Messier, NYRa. ✂ ✂	65.00
☐	Mike Modano, Dall. ✂ ✂	60.00
☐	Chris Pronger, SLou. ✂ ✂	35.00
☐	Jeremy Roenick, Phil. ✂ ✂	50.00
☐	Patrick Roy (G), Colo. ✂ ✂	150.00
☐	Joe Sakic, Colo. ✂ ✂	100.00
☐	Sergei Samsonov, Bost. ✂ ✂	40.00
☐	Brendan Shanahan, Detr. ✂ ✂	60.00
☐	Jason Spezza, Otta. ✂ ✂	65.00
☐	Mats Sundin, Toro. ✂ ✂	60.00
☐	José Théodore (G), Mont. ✂ ✂	75.00
☐	Jocelyn Thibault (G), Chic. ✂ ✂	25.00
☐	Joe Thornton, Bost. ✂ ✂	75.00
☐	Marty Turco (G), Dall. ✂ ✂	35.00
☐	Steve Yzerman, Detr. ✂ ✂	150.00

HART HOPEFULS

Insert Set (8 cards):		**400.00**
	Insert (*30)	**HH**
☐	Marian Gaborik, MinW. ✂	50.00
☐	Marian Hossa, Otta. ✂	50.00
☐	Jaromir Jagr, Wash. ✂	50.00
☐	Mario Lemieux, Pitt. ✂	225.00
☐	Nicklas Lidström, Detr. ✂	25.00
☐	Markus Näslund, Vanc. ✂	50.00
☐	Joe Thornton, Bost. ✂	75.00
☐	Marty Turco (G), Dall. ✂	25.00

HE SHOOTS HE SCORES JERSEY

Redemption Set (30 cards):		
	Redemption (*20)	**J20**
☐	Ed Belfour (G), Toro. ✂	
☐	Todd Bertuzzi, Vanc. ✂	
☐	Martin Brodeur (G), NYRa. ✂	
☐	Pavel Bure, NYRa. ✂	
☐	Sergei Fedorov, Detr. ✂	
☐	Peter Forsberg, Colo. ✂	
☐	Marian Gaborik, Minn. ✂	
☐	Dany Heatley, Atla. ✂	
☐	Milan Hejduk, Colo. ✂	
☐	Marian Hossa, Otta. ✂	
☐	Jarome Iginla, Calg. ✂	
☐	Jaromir Jagr, Wash. ✂	
☐	Paul Kariya, Anah. ✂	
☐	Ilya Kovalchuk, Atla. ✂	
☐	Mario Lemieux, Pitt. ✂	
☐	Nicklas Lidström, Detr. ✂	
☐	Eric Lindros, NYRa. ✂	
☐	Roberto Luongo (G), Flor. ✂	
☐	Mike Modano, Dall. ✂	
☐	Rick Nash, Colu. ✂	
☐	Markus Näslund, Vanc. ✂	
☐	Patrick Roy (G), Colo. ✂	
☐	Joe Sakic, Colo. ✂	
☐	Teemu Selänne, SanJ. ✂	
☐	Brendan Shanahan, Detr. ✂	
☐	Mats Sundin, Toro. ✂	
☐	José Théodore (G), Mont. ✂	
☐	Joe Thornton, Bost. ✂	
☐	Marty Turco (G), Dall. ✂	
☐	Steve Yzerman, Detr. ✂	

MAGNIFICENT

Insert Set (10 cards):		**4000.00**
	Insert	**ML**
☐	Mario Lemieux, Pitt. ✂	200.00
☐	Mario Lemieux, Pitt. ✂	200.00
☐	Mario Lemieux, Pitt. ✂	200.00
☐	Mario Lemieux, Pitt. ✂	200.00
☐	Mario Lemieux, Pitt. ✂ ✂	
☐	Mario Lemieux, Pitt. ✂	800.00
☐	Mario Lemieux, Pitt. ✂	800.00
☐	Mario Lemieux, Pitt. ✂ ✂ ✂	
☐	Mario Lemieux, Pitt. ✂ ✂ ✂ ✂	
☐	Mario Lemieux, Pitt. ✂ ✂ ✂ ✂	

MAGNIFICENT AUTOGRAPHED

Insert Set (10 cards):		
	Insert	**ML**
☐	Mario Lemieux, Pitt. ✍ ✂	
☐	Mario Lemieux, Pitt. ✍ ✂	
☐	Mario Lemieux, Pitt. ✍ ✂	
☐	Mario Lemieux, Pitt. ✍ ✂	
☐	Mario Lemieux, Pitt. ✍ ✂ ✂	
☐	Mario Lemieux, Pitt. ✍ ✂	
☐	Mario Lemieux, Pitt. ✍ ✂	
☐	Mario Lemieux, Pitt. ✍ ✂ ✂ ✂	
☐	Mario Lemieux, Pitt. ✍ ✂ ✂ ✂ ✂	
☐	Mario Lemieux, Pitt. ✍ ✂ ✂ ✂ ✂	

NICKNAMES

Insert Set (30 cards):		**2800.00**
	Insert	**NN**
☐	Ace Bailey, Toro. ✂	200.00
☐	Jean Béliveau, Mont. ✂	150.00
☐	Johnny Bower (G), Toro. ✂	100.00
☐	Frank Brimsek (G), Bost. ✂	150.00
☐	Turk Broda (G), Toro. ✂	200.00
☐	Johnny Bucyk, Bost. ✂	100.00
☐	Pavel Bure, NYRa. ✂	25.00
☐	Gerry Cheevers (G), Bost. ✂	75.00
☐	King Clancy, Toro. ✂	225.00
☐	Tony Esposito (G), Chic. ✂	150.00
☐	Bernie Geoffrion, Mont. ✂	200.00
☐	Ed Giacomin (G), NYRa. ✂	100.00
☐	Glenn Hall (G), Chic. ✂	100.00
☐	Bobby Hull, Chic. ✂	150.00
☐	Brett Hull, Detr. ✂	25.00
☐	Red Kelly, Toro. ✂	100.00
☐	Olaf Kölzig (G), Wash. ✂	25.00
☐	Mario Lemieux, Pitt. ✂	150.00
☐	Eric Lindros, NYRa. ✂	25.00
☐	F. Mahovlich ✂ / P. Mahovlich ✂	100.00
☐	Stan Mikita, Chic. ✂	75.00
☐	Jacques Plante (G), Mont. ✂	150.00
☐	Félix Potvin (G), LosA. ✂	50.00
☐	Henri Richard, Mont. ✂	100.00
☐	Maurice Richard, Mont. ✂	400.00
☐	Patrick Roy (G), Colo. ✂	100.00
☐	Teemu Selänne, SanJ. ✂	25.00
☐	Gump Worsley (G), Mont. ✂	100.00
☐	Roy Worters (G), NYAm. ✂	150.00
☐	Steve Yzerman, Detr. ✂	100.00

NORRIS HOPEFULS

Insert Set (8 cards):		**200.00**
	Insert (*30)	**NH**
☐	Rob Blake, Colo. ✂	50.00
☐	Adam Foote, Colo. ✂	35.00
☐	Derian Hatcher, Dall. ✂	35.00
☐	Ed Jovanovski, Vanc. ✂	35.00
☐	Tomas Kaberle, Toro. ✂	35.00
☐	Nicklas Lidström, Detr. ✂	35.00
☐	Al MacInnis, SLou. ✂	35.00
☐	Sergei Zubov, Dall. ✂	35.00

RETRO MEMORABILIA

Insert Set (30 cards):		**1900.00**
	Insert	**RM**
☐	Jay Bouwmeester, Flor. ✂	45.00
☐	Martin Brodeur (G), NJer. ✂	75.00
☐	Pavel Bure, NYRa. ✂	45.00
☐	Sergei Fedorov, Detr. ✂	60.00
☐	Peter Forsberg, Colo. ✂	75.00
☐	Dany Heatley, Atla. ✂	55.00
☐	Marian Hossa, Otta. ✂	55.00
☐	Brett Hull, Detr. ✂	100.00
☐	Jaromir Jagr, Wash. ✂	50.00
☐	Paul Kariya, Anah. ✂	70.00
☐	Nikolai Khabibulin (G), Tamp. ✂	100.00
☐	Saku Koivu, Mont. ✂	75.00
☐	Ilya Kovalchuk, Atla. ✂	50.00
☐	Mario Lemieux, Pitt. ✂	225.00
☐	Mario Lemieux, Pitt. ✂	175.00
☐	Mario Lemieux, Pitt. ✂	175.00
☐	Nicklas Lidström, Detr. ✂	35.00
☐	Mike Modano, Dall. ✂	50.00
☐	Rick Nash, Colu. ✂	75.00
☐	Patrick Roy (G), Colo. ✂	125.00
☐	Joe Sakic, Colo. ✂	75.00
☐	Joe Sakic, Colo. ✂	75.00
☐	Brendan Shanahan, Detr. ✂	55.00
☐	Jason Spezza, Otta. ✂	55.00
☐	Mats Sundin, Toro. ✂	55.00
☐	José Théodore (G), Mont. ✂	70.00
☐	Joe Thornton, Bost. ✂	100.00
☐	Joe Thornton, Bost. ✂	70.00
☐	Marty Turco (G), Dall. ✂	35.00
☐	Steve Yzerman, Detr. ✂	125.00

RICHARD HOPEFULS

Insert Set (8 cards):		**300.00**
	Insert (*30)	**RR**
☐	Marian Gaborik, MinW. ✂	50.00
☐	Milan Hejduk, Colo. ✂	50.00
☐	Marian Hossa, Otta. ✂	50.00
☐	Jaromir Jagr, Wash. ✂	50.00
☐	Ilya Kovalchuk, Atla. ✂	50.00
☐	Markus Näslund, Vanc. ✂	50.00
☐	Mats Sundin, Toro. ✂	50.00
☐	Joe Thornton, Bost. ✂	75.00

VÉZINA HOPEFULS

Insert Set (8 cards):		**400.00**
	Insert (*30)	**VH**
☐	Ed Belfour (G), Toro. ✂	75.00
☐	Martin Brodeur (G), NJer. ✂	100.00
☐	Giguère (G), Anah. ✂	75.00
☐	Nikolai Khabibulin (G), Tamp. ✂	25.00
☐	Patrick Lalime (G), Otta. ✂	50.00
☐	Patrick Roy (G), Colo. ✂	175.00
☐	Jocelyn Thibault (G), Chic. ✂	25.00
☐	Marty Turco (G), Dall. ✂	25.00

2002 - 03 PRIVATE STOCK RESERVE

Produced by Pacific Trading Cards, this series was released in January 2003. There are four versions for each card 1-100: the hobby base card, the Blue parallel (#/499), the Red parallel (#/50), and the silver retail base card. The hobby and retail base cards sell at the same price.

Shell Set (100 cards):	**1300.00**	**150.00**	**45.00**
Complete Set (185 cards):			
Common Player:	**6.00**	**1.00**	**.50**
Description	**R50**	**B499**	**H/R**
☐☐☐☐ 1 J-S Giguère (G), Anah.	50.00	7.00	2.00
☐☐☐☐ 2 Paul Kariya, Anah.	70.00	9.00	2.50
☐☐☐☐ 3 Petr Sykora, Anah.	20.00	2.00	.50
☐☐☐☐ 4 Milan Hnilicka (G), Atla.	10.00	1.00	.50
☐☐☐☐ 5 Patrik Stefan, Atla.	15.00	2.00	.50
☐☐☐☐ 6 Glen Murray, Bost.	20.00	3.00	.50
☐☐☐☐ 7 Brian Rolston, Bost.	15.00	2.00	.50
☐☐☐☐ 8 Sergei Samsonov, Bost.	30.00	4.00	1.00
☐☐☐☐ 9 Steve Shields, Bost.	10.00	1.00	.50
☐☐☐☐ 10 Martin Biron (G), Buff.	20.00	3.00	.50
☐☐☐☐ 11 Tim Connolly, Buff.	20.00	2.00	.50
☐☐☐☐ 12 Jean_Pierre Dumont, Buff.	10.00	1.00	.50
☐☐☐☐ 13 Craig Conroy, Calg.	15.00	2.00	.50
☐☐☐☐ 14 Chris Drury, Calg.	30.00	4.00	1.00
☐☐☐☐ 15 Rod Brind'Amour, Caro.	15.00	2.00	.50
☐☐☐☐ 16 Erik Cole, Caro.	10.00	1.00	.50
☐☐☐☐ 17 Arturs Irbe (G), Caro.	20.00	2.00	.50
☐☐☐☐ 18 Jeff O'Neill, Caro.	20.00	2.00	.50
☐☐☐☐ 19 Mark Bell, Chic.	10.00	1.00	.50
☐☐☐☐ 20 Éric Dazé, Chic.	20.00	2.00	.50
☐☐☐☐ 21 Jocelyn Thibault (G), Chic.	20.00	2.00	.50
☐☐☐☐ 22 Alexei Zhamnov, Chic.	15.00	2.00	.50
☐☐☐☐ 23 Rob Blake, Colo.	30.00	4.00	1.00
☐☐☐☐ 24 Peter Forsberg, Colo.	70.00	9.00	2.50
☐☐☐☐ 25 Milan Hejduk, Colo.	40.00	5.00	1.50
☐☐☐☐ 26 Dean McAmmond, Colo.	6.00	1.00	.50
☐☐☐☐ 27 Steven Reinprecht, Colo.	15.00	2.00	.50
☐☐☐☐ 28 Alex Tanguay, Colo.	30.00	4.00	1.00
☐☐☐☐ 29 Radim Vrbata, Colo.	15.00	2.00	.50
☐☐☐☐ 30 Andrew Cassels, Colu.	10.00	1.00	.50
☐☐☐☐ 31 Espen Knutsen, Colu.	10.00	1.00	.50
☐☐☐☐ 32 Ray Whitney, Colu.	10.00	1.00	.50
☐☐☐☐ 33 Marty Turco (G), Dall.	30.00	4.00	1.00
☐☐☐☐ 34 Pierre Turgeon, Dall.	20.00	2.00	.50
☐☐☐☐ 35 Chris Chelios, Detr.	30.00	4.00	1.00
☐☐☐☐ 36 Brett Hull, Detr.	50.00	7.00	2.00
☐☐☐☐ 37 Brendan Shanahan, Detr.	50.00	7.00	2.00
☐☐☐☐ 38 Anson Carter, Edmo.	20.00	2.00	.50
☐☐☐☐ 39 Ryan Smyth, Edmo.	20.00	3.00	.50
☐☐☐☐ 40 Mike York, Edmo.	15.00	2.00	.50
☐☐☐☐ 41 Valeri Bure, Flor.	15.00	2.00	.50
☐☐☐☐ 42 Kristian Huselius, Flor.	15.00	2.00	.50
☐☐☐☐ 43 Stephen Weiss, Flor.	20.00	2.00	.50
☐☐☐☐ 44 Jason Allison, LosA.	30.00	4.00	1.00
☐☐☐☐ 45 Adam Deadmarsh, LosA.	15.00	2.00	.50
☐☐☐☐ 46 Zigmund Palffy, LosA.	30.00	4.00	1.00
☐☐☐☐ 47 Bryan Smolinski, LosA.	6.00	1.00	.50
☐☐☐☐ 48 Andrew Brunette, MinW.	6.00	1.00	.50
☐☐☐☐ 49 M. Fernandez (G), MinW.	20.00	2.00	.50
☐☐☐☐ 50 Cliff Ronning, MinW.	10.00	1.00	.50
☐☐☐☐ 51 Mariusz Czerkawski, Mont.	10.00	1.00	.50
☐☐☐☐ 52 Marcel Hossa, Mont.	20.00	2.00	.50
☐☐☐☐ 53 Saku Koivu, Mont.	60.00	5.00	1.50
☐☐☐☐ 54 Yanic Perreault, Mont.	15.00	2.00	.50
☐☐☐☐ 55 Richard Zednik, Mont.	20.00	2.00	.50

□□□□	56 Denis Arkhipov, Nash.	10.00	1.00	.50
□□□□	57 Mike Dunham (G), Nash.	20.00	2.00	.50
□□□□	58 Scott Hartnell, Nash.	10.00	1.00	.50
□□□□	59 Greg Johnson, Nash.	6.00	1.00	.50
□□□□	60 Christian Berglund, NJer.	6.00	1.00	.50
□□□□	61 Jeff Friesen, NJer.	15.00	2.00	.50
□□□□	62 Joe Nieuwendyk, NJer.	20.00	2.00	.50
□□□□	63 Chris Osgood (G), NYIs.	30.00	4.00	1.00
□□□□	64 Mark Parrish, NYIs.	20.00	2.00	.50
□□□□	65 Dan Blackburn (G), NYRa.	20.00	2.00	.50
□□□□	66 Pavel Bure, NYRa.	40.00	5.00	1.50
□□□□	67 Bobby Holik, NYRa.	15.00	2.00	.50
□□□□	68 Brian Leetch, NYRa.	30.00	4.00	1.00
□□□□	69 Mike Richter (G), NYRa.	20.00	3.00	.50
□□□□	70 Daniel Alfredsson, Otta.	60.00	4.00	1.00
□□□□	71 Radek Bonk, Otta.	15.00	2.00	.50
□□□□	72 Martin Havlat, Otta.	30.00	4.00	1.00
□□□□	73 Patrick Lalime (G), Otta.	30.00	4.00	1.00
□□□□	74 John LeClair, Phil.	40.00	5.00	1.50
□□□□	75 Jeremy Roenick, Phil.	40.00	5.00	1.50
□□□□	76 Tony Amonte, Phoe.	30.00	4.00	1.00
□□□□	77 Daniel Brière, Phoe.	20.00	3.00	.50
□□□□	78 Sean Burke (G), Phoe.	30.00	4.00	1.00
□□□□	79 Johan Hedberg (G), Pitt.	20.00	2.00	.50
□□□□	80 Alex Kovalev, Pitt.	30.00	4.00	1.00
□□□□	81 Aleksey Morozov, Pitt.	10.00	1.00	.50
□□□□	82 Pavol Demitra, SLou.	20.00	2.00	.50
□□□□	83 Barret Jackman, SLou.	20.00	2.00	.50
□□□□	84 Brent Johnson (G), SLou.	20.00	2.00	.50
□□□□	85 Doug Weight, SLou.	30.00	4.00	1.00
□□□□	86 V. Damphousse, SanJ.	30.00	4.00	1.00
□□□□	87 Patrick Marleau, SanJ.	20.00	3.00	.50
□□□□	88 Teemu Selänne, SanJ.	40.00	5.00	1.50
□□□□	89 Scott Thornton, SanJ.	6.00	1.00	.50
□□□□	90 Dave Andreychuk, Tamp.	15.00	2.00	.50
□□□□	91 Vincent Lecavalier, Tamp.	50.00	7.00	2.00
□□□□	92 Alexander Mogilny, Toro.	20.00	3.00	.50
□□□□	93 Gary Roberts, Toro.	20.00	2.00	.50
□□□□	94 Darcy Tucker, Toro.	10.00	1.00	.50
□□□□	95 Dan Cloutier (G), Vanc.	20.00	2.00	.50
□□□□	96 Brendan Morrison, Vanc.	15.00	2.00	.50
□□□□	97 Markus Näslund, Vanc.	50.00	7.00	2.00
□□□□	98 Sergei Gonchar, Wash.	15.00	2.00	.50
□□□□	99 Olaf Kölzig (G), Wash.	30.00	4.00	1.00
□□□□	100 Dainius Zubrus, Wash.	10.00	1.00	.50

GAME GEAR

	Insert	GWJ
□	101 Adam Oates, Anah. ✂ White {<1225}	10.00
□	102 Dany Heatley, Atla. ✂ Red {<975}	25.00
□	103 Ilya Kovalchuk, Atla. ✂ White {<725}	25.00
□	104 Joe Thornton, Bost. ✂ Black {<1475}	30.00
□	105 Miroslav Satan, Buff. ✂ White {<1510}	10.00
□	106 Jarome Iginla, Calg. ✂ White {<125}	40.00
□	107 Roman Turek (G), Calg. ✂ Blue {<1475}	10.00
□	108 Ron Francis, Caro. ✂ Black {<1175}	10.00
□	109 Theoren Fleury, Chic. ✂ Black {<1300}	15.00
□	110 Patrick Roy (G), Colo. ✂ {<475}	90.00
□	111 Joe Sakic, Colo. ✂ Blue {<975}	40.00
□	112 Marc Denis (G), Colu. ✂ Blue {<1175}	10.00
□	113 Jason Arnott, Dall. ✂ Red {<1475}	10.00
□	114 Bill Guerin, Dall. ✂ Black {<875}	10.00
□	115 Mike Modano, Dall. ✂White {<975}	25.00
□	116 Sergei Fedorov, Detr. ✂ White {<1475}	25.00
□	117 Dominik Hasek (G), Detr. ✂ White {<1475}	25.00
□	118 Curtis Joseph (G), Detr. ✂ Blue {<1475}	25.00
□	119 Nicklas Lidström, Detr. ✂ Red {<1475}	15.00
□	120 Luc Robitaille, Detr. ✂ White {<1475}	20.00
□	121 Steve Yzerman, Detr. ✂ Red {<730}	65.00
□	122 Mike Comrie, Edmo. ✂ Blue {<1475}	20.00
□	123 Tommy Salo (G), Edmo. ✂ White {<1475}	10.00
□	124 Roberto Luongo (G), Flor. ✂ Blue {<1475}	20.00
□	125 Félix Potvin (G), LosA. ✂ White {<1250}	10.00
□	126 Marian Gaborik, MinW. ✂ Green {<1175}	20.00
□	127 José Théodore (G), Mont. ✂ Red {<1475}	30.00
□	128 David Legwand, Nash. ✂ Blue {<1475}	10.00
□	129 Martin Brodeur (G), NJer. ✂ Red {<975}	40.00
□	130 Patrik Elias, NJer. ✂ Red {<1475}	20.00
□	131 Michael Peca, NYIs. ✂ Blue {<1475}	10.00
□	132 Alexei Yashin, NYIs. ✂ Blue {<1475}	15.00
□	133 Eric Lindros, NYRa. ✂ Blue {<1475}	25.00
□	134 Marian Hossa, Otta. ✂ Red {<1100}	20.00
□	135 Roman Cechmanek (G), Phil. ✂ White {<1475}	10.00
□	136 Simon Gagné, Phil. ✂ Orange {<1475}	20.00
□	137 Daymond Langkow, Phoe. ✂ White {<1175}	10.00
□	137 Daymond Langkow, Phoe. ✂ Green {<1175}	10.00
□	138 Mario Lemieux, Pitt. ✂ Black {<531}	90.00
□	139 Chris Pronger, SLou. ✂ Blue {*<1475}	15.00
□	140 Keith Tkachuk, SLou. ✂ Black {<1475}	15.00
□	141 Evgeni Nabokov (G), SanJ. ✂ White {<1475}	15.00
□	142 Owen Nolan, SanJ. ✂ White {<1475}	15.00
□	142 Owen Nolan, SanJ. ✂ Teal {<1475}	15.00
□	143 Nikolai Khabibulin (G), Tamp. ✂ White {<1475}	10.00
□	144 Brad Richards, Tamp. ✂ Black {<1475}	10.00
□	145 Ed Belfour (G), Toro. ✂ Green {<865}	25.00
□	146 Mats Sundin, Toro. ✂ White {<1200}	20.00
□	147 Todd Bertuzzi, Vanc. ✂ Red {<1475}	30.00
□	147 Todd Bertuzzi, Vanc. ✂ White {<1475}	30.00
□	148 Peter Bondra, Wash. ✂ White {<1475}	15.00
□	149 Jaromir Jagr, Wash. ✂ White {<1475}	25.00
□	149 Jaromir Jagr, Wash. ✂ Blue {<1475}	25.00
□	150 Robert Lang, Wash. ✂ Black {<1475}	10.00

HOBBY ROOKIES

There are four versions for each card 151-185: the hobby base card (#/99), the Blue parallel (#/250), and the Red parallel (#/50), and the silver retail base card (#/1550). Please see the retail listings below.

	Hobby Insert	R50	B250	R99
□□□	**151 S. Chistov, Anah. RC**	150	35	150
□□□	**152 M. Gerber (G), Anah. RC**	25	25	35
□□□	**153 A. Smirnov, Anah. RC**	50	25	50
□□□	**154 Tim Thomas (G), Bost. RC**	25	25	35
□□□	**155 C. Kobasew, Calg. RC**	75	25	75
□□□	**156 J. Leopold, Calg. RC**	50	25	50
□□□	**157 Rick Nash, Colu. RC**	325	80	300
□□□	**158 Lasse Pirjetä, Colu. RC**	15	25	35
□□□	**159 Dmitri Bykov, Detr. RC**	25	25	35
□□□	**160 H. Zetterberg, Detr. RC**	375	80	350
□□□	**161 Kari Haakana, Edmo. RC**	15	25	35
□□□	**162 Ales Hemsky, Edmo. RC**	150	35	150
□□□	**163 J. Bouwmeester, Flor. RC**	150	35	150
□□□	**164 A. Frolov, LosA. RC**	125	30	125
□□□	**165 P-M Bouchard, MinW. RC**	150	35	150
□□□	**166 S. Veilleux, MinW. RC**	15	25	35
□□□	**167 Sylvain Blouin, Mont. RC**	15	25	35
□□□	**168 Ron Hainsey, Mont. RC**	50	25	50
□□□	**169 Adam Hall, Nash. RC**	50	25	50
□□□	**170 S. Upshall, Nash. RC**	75	25	75
□□□	**171 Ray Schultz, NYIs. RC**	15	25	35
□□□	172 Mattias Weinhandl, NYIs.	15	25	35
□□□	**173 Jason Spezza, Otta. RC**	200	60	200
□□□	**174 A. Volchenkov, Otta. RC**	25	25	35
□□□	**175 D. Seidenberg, Phil. RC**	25	25	35
□□□	**176 Patrick Sharp, Phil. RC**	15	25	35
□□□	**177 Radovan Somik, Phil. RC**	15	25	35
□□□	**178 Jeff Taffe, Phoe. RC**	50	25	50
□□□	179 Dick Tarnstrom, Pitt.	15	25	35
□□□	**180 Tom Koivisto, SLou. RC**	15	25	35
□□□	**181 C. Sanford (G), SLou. RC**	25	25	35
□□□	**182 A. Svitov, Tamp. RC**	75	25	75
□□□	**183 C. Colaiacovo, Toro. RC**	50	25	50
□□□	**184 S. Eminger, Wash. RC**	25	25	35
□□□	**185 Alex Henry, Wash. RC**	15	25	35

PATCH PARALLEL

	Insert Set (39 cards):	**1600.00**
	Insert	**Patch**
□	102 Dany Heatley, Atla. Patch {*50}	90.00
□	103 Ilya Kovalchuk, Atla. Patch {*50}	90.00
□	104 Joe Thornton, Bost. Patch {*275}	60.00
□	105 Miroslav Satan, Buff. Patch {*275}	20.00
□	106 Jarome Iginla, Calg. Patch {*70}	65.00
□	107 Roman Turek (G), Calg. Patch {*90}	30.00
□	109 Theoren Fleury, Chic. Patch {*275}	30.00
□	112 Marc Denis (G), Colu. Patch {*250}	25.00
□	113 Jason , Dall. Patch {*250}	25.00
□	114 Bill Guerin, Dall. Patch {*100}	25.00
□	115 Mike Modano, Dall. Patch {*150}	60.00
□	116 Sergei Fedorov, Detr. Patch {*150}	60.00
□	119 Nicklas Lidström, Detr. Patch {*275}	30.00
□	121 Steve Yzerman, Detr. Patch {*19}	375.00
□	122 Mike Comrie, Edmo. Patch {*125}	50.00
□	123 Tommy Salo (G), Edmo. Patch {*275}	20.00
□	124 Roberto Luongo (G), Flor. Patch {*150}	50.00
□	125 Félix Potvin (G), LosA. Patch {*250}	30.00
□	126 Marian Gaborik, MinW. Patch {*100}	65.00
□	127 José Théodore (G), Mont. Patch {*50}	105.00
□	128 David Legwand, Nash. Patch {*250}	20.00
□	129 Martin Brodeur (G), NJer. Patch {*150}	100.00
□	130 Patrik Elias, NJer. Patch {*150}	50.00
□	131 Michael Peca, NYIs. Patch {*250}	20.00
□	133 Eric Lindros, NYRa. Patch {*250}	50.00
□	134 Marian Hossa, Otta. Patch {*250}	50.00
□	135 Roman Cechmanek (G), Phil. Patch {*250}	20.00
□	136 Simon Gagné, Phil. Patch {*200}	45.00
□	137 Daymond Langkow, Phoe. Patch {*150}	20.00
□	139 Chris Pronger, SLou. Patch {*250}	30.00
□	140 Keith Tkachuk, SLou. Patch {*150}	35.00
□	141 Evgeni Nabokov (G), SanJ. Patch {*200}	30.00
□	142 Owen Nolan, SanJ. Patch {*250}	30.00
□	143 Nikolai Khabibulin (G), Tamp. Patch {*275}	20.00
□	144 Brad Richards, Tamp. Patch {*275}	20.00
□	145 Ed Belfour (G), Toro. Patch {*245}	50.00
□	147 Todd Bertuzzi, Vanc. Patch {*275}	60.00
□	148 Peter Bondra, Wash. Patch {*275}	30.00
□	150 Robert Lang, Wash. Patch {*250}	20.00

JERSEY RED

	Insert Set (50 cards):	**4,500**
	Insert (#/25)	**Red**
□	101 Adam Oates, Anah. ✂	50.00
□	102 Dany Heatley, Atla. ✂	125.00
□	103 Ilya Kovalchuk, Atla. ✂	125.00
□	104 Joe Thornton, Bost. ✂	150.00
□	105 Miroslav Satan, Buff. ✂	50.00
□	106 Jarome Iginla, Calg. ✂	100.00
□	107 Roman Turek (G), Calg. ✂	60.00
□	108 Ron Francis, Caro. ✂	75.00
□	109 Theoren Fleury, Chic. ✂	75.00
□	110 Patrick Roy (G), Colo. ✂	300.00
□	111 Joe Sakic, Colo. ✂	200.00
□	112 Marc Denis (G), Colu. ✂	60.00
□	113 Jason Arnott, Dall. ✂	60.00
□	114 Bill Guerin, Dall. ✂	50.00
□	115 Mike Modano, Dall. ✂	125.00
□	116 Sergei Fedorov, Detr. ✂	125.00
□	117 Dominik Hasek (G), Detr. ✂	125.00
□	118 Curtis Joseph (G), Detr. ✂	125.00
□	119 Nicklas Lidström, Detr. ✂	75.00
□	120 Luc Robitaille, Detr. ✂	100.00
□	121 Steve Yzerman, Detr. ✂	300.00
□	122 Mike Comrie, Edmo. ✂	100.00
□	123 Tommy Salo (G), Edmo. ✂	50.00
□	124 Roberto Luongo (G), Flor. ✂	100.00
□	125 Félix Potvin (G), LosA. ✂	150.00
□	126 Marian Gaborik, MinW. ✂	125.00
□	127 José Théodore (G), Mont. ✂	150.00
□	128 David Legwand, Nash. ✂	50.00
□	129 Martin Brodeur (G), NJer. ✂	200.00
□	130 Patrik Elias, NJer. ✂	100.00
□	131 Michael Peca, NYIs. ✂	50.00
□	132 Alexei Yashin, NYIs. ✂	75.00
□	133 Eric Lindros, NYRa. ✂	125.00
□	134 Marian Hossa, Otta. ✂	125.00
□	135 Roman Cechmanek (G), Phil. ✂	50.00
□	136 Simon Gagné, Phil. ✂	100.00
□	137 Daymond Langkow, Phoe. ✂	50.00
□	138 Mario Lemieux, Pitt. ✂	375.00
□	139 Chris Pronger, SLou. ✂	75.00
□	140 Keith Tkachuk, SLou. ✂	75.00
□	141 Evgeni Nabokov (G), SanJ. ✂	75.00
□	142 Owen Nolan, SanJ. ✂	75.00
□	143 Nikolai Khabibulin (G), Tamp. ✂	50.00
□	144 Brad Richards, Tamp. ✂	60.00
□	145 Ed Belfour (G), Toro. ✂	125.00
□	146 Mats Sundin, Toro. ✂	125.00
□	147 Todd Bertuzzi, Vanc. ✂	150.00
□	148 Peter Bondra, Wash. ✂	75.00
□	149 Jaromir Jagr, Wash. ✂	125.00
□	150 Robert Lang, Wash. ✂	50.00

CLASS ACT

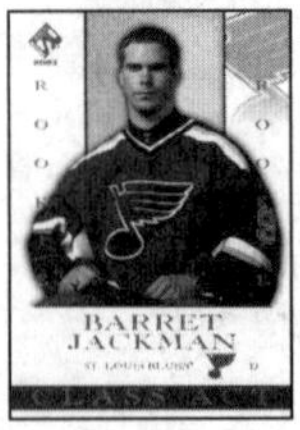

	Insert Set (10 cards):	**65.00**
	Insert (1:9)	**CA**
□	1 Stanislav Chistov, Anah.	9.00
□	2 Alexei Smirnov, Anah.	5.00
□	3 Ivan Huml, Bost.	5.00
□	4 Chuck Kobasew, Calg.	6.00
□	5 Tyler Arnason, Chic.	7.00
□	6 Rick Nash, Colu.	15.00
□	7 Henrik Zetterberg, Detr.	15.00
□	8 Jay Bouwmeester, Flor.	9.00
□	9 Stephen Weiss, Flor.	7.00
□	10 Barret Jackman, SLou.	7.00

IN CREASE SECURITY

	Insert Set (20 cards):	**60.00**
	Insert (1:3)	**ICS**
□	1 Jean-Sébastien Giguère (G), Anah.	4.00
□	2 Roman Turek (G), Calg.	3.00
□	3 Arturs Irbe (G), Caro.	3.00
□	4 Jocelyn Thibault (G), Chic.	3.00
□	5 Patrick Roy (G), Colo.	12.00
□	6 Marc Denis (G), Colu.	3.00
□	7 Marty Turco (G), Dall.	3.00
□	8 Curtis Joseph (G), Detr.	4.00
□	9 Tommy Salo (G), Edmo.	3.00
□	10 Roberto Luongo (G), Flor.	3.00
□	11 Félix Potvin (G), LosA.	3.00
□	12 José Théodore (G), Mont.	5.00
□	13 Martin Brodeur (G), NJer.	6.00
□	14 Chris Osgood (G), NYIs.	3.00
□	15 Mike Richter (G), NYRa.	3.00
□	16 Roman Cechmanek (G), Phil.	3.00
□	17 Sean Burke (G), Phoe.	3.00
□	18 Brent Johnson (G), SLou.	3.00
□	19 Evgeni Nabokov (G), SanJ.	3.00
□	20 Ed Belfour (G), Toro.	4.00

MOMENTS IN TIME

	Insert Set (28 cards):	**45.00**
	Insert (1:9)	**MIT**
□	1 Chuck Kobasew, Calg.	5.00
□	2 Rick Nash, Colu.	15.00
□	3 Jay Bouwmeester, Flor.	8.00
□	4 Stephen Weiss, Flor.	7.00
□	5 Alexander Frolov, LosA.	7.00
□	6 Jamie Lundmark, NYRa.	5.00
□	7 Barret Jackman, SLou.	7.00
□	8 Alexander Svitov, Tamp.	5.00

RESERVE ELITE

	Insert Set (28 cards):	**70.00**
	Insert	**RE**
□	1 Ilya Kovalchuk, Atla.	8.00
□	2 Peter Forsberg, Colo.	10.00
□	3 Patrick Roy (G), Colo.	22.00
□	4 Steve Yzerman, Detr.	18.00
□	5 Mario Lemieux, Pitt.	22.00
□	6 Jaromir Jagr, Wash.	8.00

RETAIL ROOKIES

	Retail Insert (#/1550)	R1550
□	**151 Stanislav Chistov, Anah. RC**	**25.00**
□	**152 Martin Gerber (G), Anah. RC**	**10.00**
□	**153 Alexei Smirnov, Anah. RC**	**10.00**
□	**154 Tim Thomas (G), Bost. RC**	**10.00**
□	**155 Chuck Kobasew, Calg. RC**	**15.00**
□	**156 Jordan Leopold, Calg. RC**	**10.00**
□	**157 Rick Nash, Colu. RC**	**45.00**
□	**158 Lasse Pirjetä, Colu. RC**	**10.00**
□	**159 Dmitri Bykov, Detr. RC**	**10.00**
□	**160 Henrik Zetterberg, Detr. RC**	**45.00**
□	**161 Kari Haakana, Edmo. RC**	**10.00**
□	**162 Ales Hemsky, Edmo. RC**	**25.00**
□	**163 Jay Bouwmeester, Flor. RC**	**25.00**
□	**164 Alexander Frolov, LosA. RC**	**20.00**
□	**165 Pierre-Marc Bouchard, MinW. RC**	**25.00**
□	**166 Stéphane Veilleux, MinW. RC**	**10.00**
□	**167 Sylvain Blouin, Mont. RC**	**10.00**
□	**168 Ron Hainsey, Mont. RC**	**10.00**
□	**169 Adam Hall, Nash. RC**	**10.00**
□	**170 Scottie Upshall, Nash. RC**	**15.00**
□	**171 Ray Schultz, NYIs. RC**	**8.00**
□	172 Mattias Weinhandl, NYIs.	8.00
□	**173 Jason Spezza, Otta. RC**	**30.00**
□	**174 Anton Volchenkov, Otta. RC**	**10.00**
□	**175 Dennis Seidenberg, Phil. RC**	**10.00**
□	**176 Patrick Sharp, Phil. RC**	**10.00**

☐	**177 Radovan Somik, Phil. RC**	**10.00**
☐	**178 Jeff Taffe, Phoe. RC**	**10.00**
☐	179 Dick Tarnstrom, Pitt.	8.00
☐	**180 Tom Koivisto, SLou. RC**	**10.00**
☐	**181 Curtis Sanford (G), SLou. RC**	**10.00**
☐	**182 Alexander Svitov, Tamp. RC**	**15.00**
☐	**183 Carlo Colaiacovo, Toro. RC**	**10.00**
☐	**184 Steve Eminger, Wash. RC**	**10.00**
☐	**185 Alex Henry, Wash. RC**	**10.00**

2002 - 03 PRIVATE STOCK TITANIUM

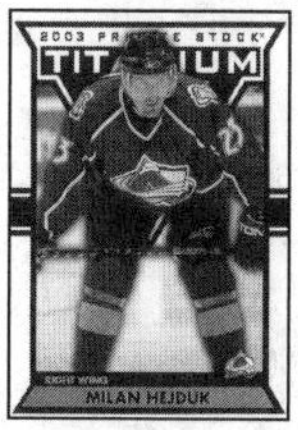

Produced by the Pacific Trading Cards, this series was released in April 2003. In hobby packs, cards 1-100 are availble in two versions: the gold-text base card and the red-text parallel (#/299). Please see the retail listings below.

	Shell Set (100 cards):		**55.00**
	Complete Set (140 cards):	**850.00**	**2000.00**
	Common Player:	**2.00**	**.35**
	Description	**R299**	**H/R**
☐ ☐	1 Jean-Sébastien Giguère (G), Anah.	10.00	1.50
☐ ☐	2 Paul Kariya, Anah.	15.00	2.00
☐ ☐	3 Petr Sykora, Anah.	5.00	.50
☐ ☐	4 Dany Heatley, Atla.	10.00	1.50
☐ ☐	5 Ilya Kovalchuk, Atla.	10.00	1.50
☐ ☐	6 Pasi Nurminen (G), Atla.	2.00	.35
☐ ☐	7 Glen Murray, Bost.	5.00	.50
☐ ☐	8 Brian Rolston, Bost.	2.00	.50
☐ ☐	9 Steve Shields, Bost.	2.00	.35
☐ ☐	10 Joe Thornton, Bost.	15.00	2.00
☐ ☐	11 Martin Biron (G), Buff.	5.00	.50
☐ ☐	12 Chris Gratton, Buff.	2.00	.35
☐ ☐	13 Miroslav Satan, Buff.	2.00	.50
☐ ☐	14 Chris Drury, Calg.	5.00	1.00
☐ ☐	15 Jarome Iginla, Calg.	10.00	1.00
☐ ☐	16 Roman Turek (G), Calg.	5.00	.50
☐ ☐	17 Rod Brind'Amour, Caro.	2.00	.50
☐ ☐	18 Ron Francis, Caro.	5.00	1.00
☐ ☐	19 Jeff O'Neill, Caro.	5.00	.50
☐ ☐	20 Kevin Weekes (G), Caro.	2.00	.35
☐ ☐	21 Tyler Arnason, Chic.	5.00	.50
☐ ☐	22 Theoren Fleury, Chic.	5.00	1.00
☐ ☐	23 Jocelyn Thibault (G), Chic.	5.00	.50
☐ ☐	24 Peter Forsberg, Colo.	15.00	2.00
☐ ☐	25 Milan Hejduk, Colo.	10.00	1.00
☐ ☐	26 Patrick Roy (G), Colo.	40.00	5.00
☐ ☐	27 Joe Sakic, Colo.	20.00	2.50
☐ ☐	28 Andrew Cassels, Colu.	2.00	.35
☐ ☐	29 Marc Denis (G), Colu.	5.00	.50
☐ ☐	30 Geoff Sanderson, Colu.	2.00	.35
☐ ☐	31 Bill Guerin, Dall.	5.00	.50
☐ ☐	32 Mike Modano, Dall.	10.00	1.50
☐ ☐	33 Marty Turco (G), Dall.	5.00	1.00
☐ ☐	34 Pierre Turgeon, Dall.	5.00	.50
☐ ☐	35 Sergei Fedorov, Detr.	10.00	1.50
☐ ☐	36 Brett Hull, Detr.	10.00	1.50
☐ ☐	37 Curtis Joseph (G), Detr.	10.00	1.50
☐ ☐	38 Nicklas Lidström, Detr.	5.00	1.00
☐ ☐	39 Brendan Shanahan, Detr.	10.00	1.50
☐ ☐	40 Steve Yzerman, Detr.	30.00	4.00
☐ ☐	41 Anson Carter, Edmo.	5.00	.50
☐ ☐	42 Mike Comrie, Edmo.	10.00	1.00
☐ ☐	43 Tommy Salo (G), Edmo.	5.00	.50
☐ ☐	44 Ryan Smyth, Edmo.	5.00	.50
☐ ☐	45 Kristian Huselius, Flor.	2.00	.50
☐ ☐	46 Olli Jokinen, Flor.	2.00	.50
☐ ☐	47 Roberto Luongo (G), Flor.	10.00	1.00
☐ ☐	48 Jason Allison, LosA.	5.00	1.00
☐ ☐	49 Éric Bélanger, LosA.	2.00	.35
☐ ☐	50 Zigmund Palffy, LosA.	5.00	1.00
☐ ☐	51 Félix Potvin (G), LosA.	5.00	1.00
☐ ☐	52 Manny Fernandez (G), MinW.	5.00	.50
☐ ☐	53 Marian Gaborik, MinW.	10.00	1.50
☐ ☐	54 Cliff Ronning, MinW.	2.00	.35
☐ ☐	55 Saku Koivu, Mont.	10.00	1.00
☐ ☐	56 Yanic Perreault, Mont.	2.00	.50
☐ ☐	57 José Théodore (G), Mont.	15.00	2.00
☐ ☐	58 Richard Zednik, Mont.	5.00	.50
☐ ☐	59 Andreas Johansson, Nash.	2.00	.35
☐ ☐	60 David Legwand, Nash.	5.00	.50
☐ ☐	61 Tomas Vokoun (G), Nash.	2.00	.35
☐ ☐	62 Martin Brodeur (G), NJer.	20.00	2.50
☐ ☐	63 Scott Gomez, NJer.	5.00	.50
☐ ☐	64 John Madden, NJer.	2.00	.50
☐ ☐	65 Rick DiPietro (G), NYIs.	5.00	.50
☐ ☐	66 Michael Peca, NYIs.	5.00	.50
☐ ☐	67 Alexei Yashin, NYIs.	5.00	1.00
☐ ☐	68 Pavel Bure, NYRa.	10.00	1.00
☐ ☐	69 Eric Lindros, NYRa.	10.00	1.50
☐ ☐	70 Tom Poti, NYRa.	2.00	.35
☐ ☐	71 Daniel Alfredsson, Otta.	5.00	1.00
☐ ☐	72 Marian Hossa, Otta.	10.00	1.50
☐ ☐	73 Patrick Lalime (G), Otta.	5.00	1.00
☐ ☐	74 Roman Cechmanek (G), Phil.	5.00	.50
☐ ☐	75 Simon Gagné, Phil.	10.00	1.00
☐ ☐	76 Jeremy Roenick, Phil.	10.00	1.00
☐ ☐	77 Tony Amonte, Phoe.	5.00	1.00
☐ ☐	78 Brian Boucher (G), Phoe.	2.00	.50
☐ ☐	79 Shane Doan, Phoe.	2.00	.35
☐ ☐	80 Johan Hedberg (G), Pitt.	5.00	.50
☐ ☐	81 Alex Kovalev, Pitt.	5.00	1.00
☐ ☐	82 Mario Lemieux, Pitt.	40.00	5.00
☐ ☐	83 Brent Johnson (G), SLou.	5.00	.50
☐ ☐	84 Cory Stillman, SLou.	2.00	.35
☐ ☐	85 Doug Weight, SLou.	5.00	1.00
☐ ☐	86 Patrick Marleau, SanJ.	5.00	.50
☐ ☐	87 Evgeni Nabokov (G), SanJ.	5.00	1.00
☐ ☐	88 Teemu Selänne, SanJ.	10.00	1.00
☐ ☐	89 Nikolai Khabibulin (G), Tamp.	5.00	.50
☐ ☐	90 Vincent Lecavalier, Tamp.	10.00	1.50
☐ ☐	91 Martin St-Louis, Tamp.	5.00	.50
☐ ☐	92 Ed Belfour (G), Toro.	10.00	1.50
☐ ☐	93 Alexander Mogilny, Toro.	5.00	.50
☐ ☐	94 Mats Sundin, Toro.	10.00	1.50
☐ ☐	95 Todd Bertuzzi, Vanc.	15.00	2.00
☐ ☐	96 Dan Cloutier (G), Vanc.	5.00	.50
☐ ☐	97 Brendan Morrison, Vanc.	2.00	.50
☐ ☐	98 Markus Näslund, Vanc.	10.00	1.50
☐ ☐	99 Jaromir Jagr, Wash.	10.00	1.50
☐ ☐	100 Michael Nylander, Wash.	2.00	.35

ROOKIE

In hobby packs, cards 101-140 are availble in two versions: the gold-text base card (#/99) and the red-text parallel (#/299). Please see below for the retail listings.

	Hobby	**R299**	**H99**
☐ ☐	**101 Stanislav Chistov, Anah. RC**	**25.00**	**150.00**
☐ ☐	**102 Martin Gerber (G), Anah. RC**	**10.00**	**25.00**
☐ ☐	**103 Kurt Sauer, Anah. RC**	**10.00**	**25.00**
☐ ☐	**104 Alexei Smirnov, Anah. RC**	**10.00**	**50.00**
☐ ☐	**105 Shaone Morrisonn, Bost. RC**	**10.00**	**25.00**
☐ ☐	**106 Tim Thomas (G), Bost. RC**	**10.00**	**25.00**
☐ ☐	**107 Ryan Miller (G), Buff. RC**	**20.00**	**125.00**
☐ ☐	**108 Chuck Kobasew, Calg. RC**	**15.00**	**75.00**
☐ ☐	**109 Jordan Leopold, Calg. RC**	**10.00**	**50.00**
☐ ☐	**110 Pascal Leclaire (G), Colu. RC**	**20.00**	**125.00**
☐ ☐	**111 Rick Nash, Colu. RC**	**45.00**	**300.00**
☐ ☐	**112 Steve Ott, Dall. RC**	**10.00**	**50.00**
☐ ☐	**113 Dmitri Bykov, Detr. RC**	**10.00**	**25.00**
☐ ☐	**114 Henrik Zetterberg, Detr. RC**	**45.00**	**400.00**
☐ ☐	**115 Ales Hemsky, Edmo. RC**	**25.00**	**150.00**
☐ ☐	**116 Jay Bouwmeester, Flor. RC**	**25.00**	**150.00**
☐ ☐	**117 Mike Cammalleri, LosA. RC**	**15.00**	**75.00**
☐ ☐	**118 Alexander Frolov, LosA. RC**	**20.00**	**125.00**
☐ ☐	**119 Pierre-Marc Bouchard, MinW. RC**	**25.00**	**150.00**
☐ ☐	**120 Stéphane Veilleux, MinW. RC**	**10.00**	**25.00**
☐ ☐	121 Kyle Wanvig, MinW.	10.00	20.00
☐ ☐	**122 Ron Hainsey, Mont. RC**	**10.00**	**50.00**
☐ ☐	**123 Vernon (G) Fiddler, Nash. RC**	**10.00**	**25.00**
☐ ☐	**124 Adam Hall, Nash. RC**	**10.00**	**50.00**
☐ ☐	**125 Scottie Upshall, Nash. RC**	**15.00**	**75.00**
☐ ☐	**126 Jason Spezza, Otta. RC**	**35.00**	**200.00**
☐ ☐	**127 Anton Volchenkov, Otta. RC**	**10.00**	**25.00**
☐ ☐	**128 Dennis Seidenberg, Phil. RC**	**10.00**	**25.00**
☐ ☐	**129 Radovan Somik, Phil. RC**	**10.00**	**25.00**
☐ ☐	**130 Jeff Taffe, Phoe. RC**	**10.00**	**50.00**
☐ ☐	131 Sébastien Caron (G), Pitt.	10.00	20.00
☐ ☐	**132 Brooks Orpik, Pitt. RC**	**10.00**	**50.00**
☐ ☐	133 Dick Tarnstrom, Pitt.	10.00	20.00
☐ ☐	**134 Tom Koivisto, SLou. RC**	**10.00**	**25.00**
☐ ☐	**135 Curtis Sanford (G), SLou. RC**	**10.00**	**25.00**
☐ ☐	**136 Lynn Loyns, SanJ. RC**	**10.00**	**25.00**
☐ ☐	**137 Alexander Svitov, Tamp. RC**	**15.00**	**75.00**
☐ ☐	**138 Carlo Colaiacovo, Toro. RC**	**10.00**	**50.00**
☐ ☐	**139 Mikael Tellqvist (G), Toro. RC**	**10.00**	**25.00**
☐ ☐	**140 Steve Eminger, Wash. RC**	**10.00**	**25.00**

GAME-WORN JERSEY

	Insert Set (75 cards):	**1150.00**
	Insert (1:1)	**GWJ**
☐	1 Mike Leclerc, Anah. {*375} ✂	12.00
☐	2 Dany Heatley, Atla. {*700} ✂	25.00
☐	3 Ilya Kovalchuk, Atla. {*600} ✂	25.00
☐	4 Patrik Stefan, Atla. {*1200} ✂ Blue	12.00
☐	5 Joe Thornton, Bost. {*150} ✂	65.00
☐	6 Martin Biron (G), Buff. {*1100} ✂	12.00
☐	7 Jean_Pierre Dumont, Buff. {*1000} ✂	12.00
☐	8 Rod Brind'Amour, Caro. {*1225} ✂ Red	12.00
☐	9 Arturs Irbe (G), Caro. {*800} ✂	12.00
☐	10 Jeff O'Neill, Caro. {*275} ✂	15.00
☐	11 Chris Drury, Calg. {*500} ✂	15.00
☐	12 Roman Turek (G), Calg. {*1200} ✂ Blue	12.00
☐	13 Mark Bell, Chic. {*1000} ✂	12.00
☐	14 Sergei Berezin, Chic. {*300} ✂	12.00
☐	15 Steve Sullivan, Chic. {*700} ✂	12.00
☐	16 Rob Blake, Colo. {*1025} ✂	12.00
☐	17 Milan Hejduk, Colo. {*1000} ✂	15.00
☐	18 Patrick Roy (G), Colo. {*150} ✂	165.00
☐	19 Rostislav Klesla, Colu. {*1100} ✂	12.00
☐	20 Geoff Sanderson, Colu. {*1300} ✂	12.00
☐	21 Ron Tugnutt (G), Dall. {*1300} ✂	12.00
☐	22 Marty Turco (G), Dall. {*600} ✂	15.00
☐	23 Sergei Fedorov, Detr. {*600} ✂	25.00
☐	24 Dominik Hasek (G), Detr. {*250} ✂	40.00
☐	25 Brett Hull, Detr. {*900} ✂	20.00
☐	26 Luc Robitaille, Detr. {*800} ✂ Red	15.00
☐	27 Jason Williams, Detr. {*1300} ✂	12.00
☐	28 Mike Comrie, Edmo. {*485} ✂	25.00
☐	29 Tommy Salo (G), Edmo. {*800} ✂	12.00
☐	30 Ryan Smyth, Edmo. {*1050} ✂	12.00
☐	31 Valeri Bure, Flor. {*1300} ✂	12.00
☐	32 Kristian Huselius, Flor. {*1300} ✂	12.00
☐	33 Roberto Luongo (G), Flor. {*1300} ✂	12.00
☐	34 Marian Gaborik, MinW. {*400} ✂	35.00
☐	35 Yanic Perreault, Mont. {*1300} ✂	12.00
☐	36 José Théodore (G), Mont. {*500} ✂	35.00
☐	37 David Legwand, Nash. {*860} ✂	12.00
☐	38 Scott Walker, Nash. {*1300} ✂	12.00
☐	39 Scott Gomez, NJer. {*910} ✂	12.00
☐	40 Scott Stevens, NJer. {*1275} ✂	12.00
☐	41 Michael Peca, NYIs. {*550} ✂	12.00
☐	42 Alexei Yashin, NYIs. {*750} ✂ White	15.00
☐	43 Pavel Bure, NYRa. {*1000} ✂	15.00
☐	44 Eric Lindros, NYRa. {*900} ✂	20.00
☐	45 Mark Messier, NYRa. {*650} ✂	25.00
☐	46 Daniel Alfredsson, Otta. {*570} ✂	15.00
☐	47 Martin Havlat, Otta. {*450} ✂	20.00
☐	48 Patrick Lalime (G), Otta. {*875} ✂	12.00
☐	49 Simon Gagné, Phil. {*1300} ✂	12.00
☐	50 Michal Handzus, Phil. {*700} ✂	12.00
☐	51 Tomi Kallio, Phil. {*925} ✂	12.00
☐	52 John LeClair, Phil. {*1025} ✂	15.00
☐	53 Johan Hedberg (G), Pitt. {*1050} ✂	12.00
☐	54 Mario Lemieux, Pitt. {*350} ✂	115.00
☐	55 Toby Petersen, Pitt. {*1300} ✂	12.00
☐	56 Pavol Demitra, SLou. {*1250} ✂	12.00
☐	57 Ray Ferraro, SLou. {*1300} ✂	12.00
☐	58 Chris Pronger, SLou. {*1200} ✂	12.00
☐	59 Keith Tkachuk, SLou. {*1000} ✂	12.00
☐	60 Sergei Varlamov, SLou. {*1300} ✂	12.00
☐	61 Miikka Kiprusoff (G), SanJ. {*1300} ✂ Teal	12.00
☐	62 Patrick Marleau, SanJ. {*800} ✂ Teal	12.00
☐	63 Owen Nolan, SanJ. {*450} ✂	20.00
☐	64 Nikolai Khabibulin (G), Tamp. {*1000} ✂	12.00
☐	65 Fredrik Modin, Tamp. {*1300} ✂	12.00
☐	66 Alexander Mogilny, Toro. {*900} ✂	12.00
☐	67 Gary Roberts, Toro. {*1300} ✂	12.00
☐	68 Darcy Tucker, Toro. {*1300} ✂	12.00
☐	69 Dan Cloutier (G), Vanc. {*850} ✂	12.00
☐	70 Brendan Morrison, Vanc. {*700} ✂	12.00
☐	71 Daniel Sedin, Vanc. {*1100} ✂	12.00
☐	72 Henrik Sedin, Vanc. {*1100} ✂	12.00
☐	73 Peter Bondra, Wash. {*1300} ✂	12.00
☐	74 Jaromir Jagr, Wash. {*200} ✂	45.00
☐	75 Olaf Kölzig (G), Wash. {*1300} ✂	12.00

GAME-WORN JERSEY PATCH

	Insert Set (63 cards):	**2300.00**
	Insert	**Patch**
☐	1 Mike Leclerc, Anah. ✂ {*10}	60.00
☐	2 Dany Heatley, Atla. ✂ {*20}	125.00
☐	3 Ilya Kovalchuk, Atla. ✂ {*25}	125.00
☐	4 Patrik Stefan, Atla. ✂ {*250}	20.00
☐	5 Joe Thornton, Bost. ✂ {*225}	50.00
☐	6 Martin Biron (G), Buff. ✂ {*65}	40.00
☐	8 Rod Brind'Amour, Caro. ✂ {*125}	20.00
☐	9 Arturs Irbe (G), Caro. ✂ {*15}	50.00
☐	10 Jeff O'Neill, Caro. ✂ {*250}	20.00
☐	11 Chris Drury, Calg. ✂ {*250}	30.00
☐	13 Mark Bell, Chic. ✂ {*225}	20.00
☐	14 Sergei Berezin, Chic. ✂ {*250}	20.00
☐	15 Steve Sullivan, Chic. ✂ {*100}	25.00
☐	16 Rob Blake, Colo. ✂ {*250}	30.00
☐	17 Milan Hejduk, Colo. ✂ {*250}	40.00
☐	19 Rostislav Klesla, Colu. ✂ {*50}	40.00
☐	20 Geoff Sanderson, Colu. ✂ {*25}	40.00
☐	21 Ron Tugnutt (G), Dall. ✂ {*250}	20.00
☐	22 Marty Turco (G), Dall. ✂ {*195}	30.00
☐	23 Sergei Fedorov, Detr. ✂ {*45}	100.00
☐	24 Dominik Hasek (G), Detr. ✂ {*35}	100.00
☐	25 Brett Hull, Detr. ✂ {*85}	75.00
☐	27 Jason Williams, Detr. ✂ {*250}	20.00
☐	28 Mike Comrie, Edmo. ✂ {*150}	50.00
☐	30 Ryan Smyth, Edmo. ✂ {*65}	40.00
☐	31 Valeri Bure, Flor. ✂ {*210}	20.00
☐	32 Kristian Huselius, Flor. ✂ {*250}	20.00
☐	33 Roberto Luongo (G), Flor. ✂ {*250}	40.00
☐	35 Yanic Perreault, Mont. ✂ {*200}	20.00
☐	36 José Théodore (G), Mont. ✂ {*65}	100.00
☐	37 David Legwand, Nash. ✂ {*180}	25.00
☐	38 Scott Walker, Nash. ✂ {*250}	20.00
☐	39 Scott Gomez, NJer. ✂ {*250}	20.00
☐	40 Scott Stevens, NJer. ✂ {*185}	25.00
☐	42 Alexei Yashin, NYIs. ✂ {*30}	50.00
☐	43 Pavel Bure, NYRa. ✂ {*20}	100.00
☐	44 Eric Lindros, NYRa. ✂ {*140}	50.00
☐	45 Mark Messier, NYRa. ✂ {*75}	75.00
☐	46 Daniel Alfredsson, Otta. ✂ {*100}	75.00
☐	47 Martin Havlat, Otta. ✂ {*250}	30.00
☐	48 Patrick Lalime (G), Otta. ✂ {*250}	30.00
☐	49 Simon Gagné, Phil. ✂ {*250}	40.00
☐	50 Michal Handzus, Phil. ✂ {*250}	20.00
☐	53 Johan Hedberg (G), Pitt. ✂ {*250}	20.00
☐	54 Mario Lemieux, Pitt. ✂ {*60}	285.00
☐	55 Toby Petersen, Pitt. ✂ {*250}	20.00
☐	56 Pavol Demitra, SLou. ✂ {*165}	25.00
☐	57 Ray Ferraro, SLou. ✂ {*165}	20.00
☐	58 Chris Pronger, SLou. ✂ {*15}	75.00
☐	59 Keith Tkachuk, SLou. ✂ {*145}	40.00
☐	60 Sergei Varlamov, SLou. ✂ {*250}	20.00
☐	61 Miikka Kiprusoff (G), SanJ. ✂ {*250}	20.00
☐	62 Patrick Marleau, SanJ. ✂ {*175}	30.00
☐	63 Owen Nolan, SanJ. ✂ {*15}	75.00
☐	64 Nikolai Khabibulin (G), Tamp. ✂ {*35}	45.00
☐	65 Fredrik Modin, Tamp. ✂ {*250}	20.00
☐	66 Alexander Mogilny, Toro. ✂ {*70}	40.00
☐	67 Gary Roberts, Toro. ✂ {*140}	25.00
☐	69 Dan Cloutier (G), Vanc. ✂ {*250}	20.00
☐	70 Brendan Morrison, Vanc. ✂ {*40}	40.00
☐	72 Henrik Sedin, Vanc. ✂ {*25}	50.00
☐	74 Jaromir Jagr, Wash. ✂ {*110}	75.00
☐	75 Olaf Kölzig (G), Wash. ✂ {*175}	35.00

MASKED MARAUDERS

	Insert Set (8 cards):	**40.00**
	Insert (1:17)	**MM**
☐	1 Patrick Roy (G), Colo.	15.00
☐	2 Marty Turco (G), Dall.	4.00
☐	3 Curtis Joseph (G), Detr.	5.00
☐	4 José Théodore (G), Mont.	6.00
☐	5 Martin Brodeur (G), NJer.	8.00
☐	6 Nikolai Khabibulin (G), Tamp.	4.00
☐	7 Ed Belfour (G), Toro.	5.00
☐	8 Dan Cloutier (G), Vanc.	4.00

RIGHT ON TARGET

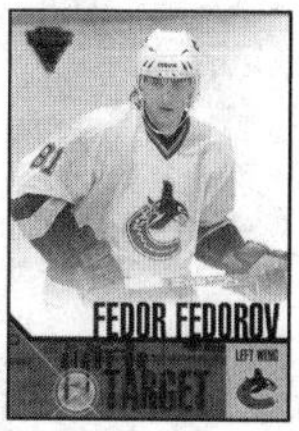

	Insert Set (20 cards):	**70.00**
	Insert (1:5)	**RT**
☐	1 Stanislav Chistov, Anah.	5.00
☐	2 Ivan Huml, Bost.	3.00
☐	3 Chuck Kobasew, Calg.	3.00
☐	4 Jordan Leopold, Calg.	3.00
☐	5 Tyler Arnason, Chic.	4.00
☐	6 Rick Nash, Colu.	9.00
☐	7 Henrik Zetterberg, Detr.	9.00

☐	8 Ales Hemsky, Edmo.	5.00
☐	9 Jay Bouwmeester, Flor.	5.00
☐	10 Stephen Weiss, Flor.	4.00
☐	11 Mike Cammalleri, LosA.	3.00
☐	12 Alexander Frolov, LosA.	4.00
☐	13 Pierre-Marc Bouchard, MinW.	5.00
☐	14 Scottie Upshall, Nash.	3.00
☐	15 Rick DiPietro (G), NYIs.	5.00
☐	16 Jamie Lundmark, NYRa.	3.00
☐	17 Jason Spezza, Otta.	7.00
☐	18 Barret Jackman, SLou.	4.00
☐	19 Jonathan Cheechoo, SanJ.	3.00
☐	20 Fedor Fedorov, Vanc.	3.00

SATURDAY KNIGHTS

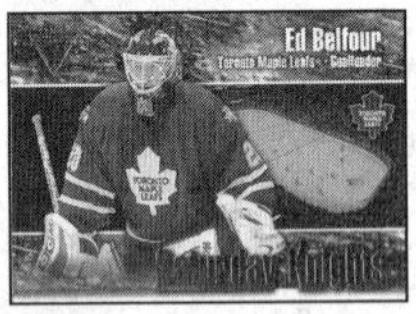

Insert Set (10 cards): 40.00

	Insert (1:9)	SK
☐	1 Jarome Iginla, Calg.	3.00
☐	2 Patrick Roy (G), Colo.	10.00
☐	3 Joe Sakic, Colo.	5.00
☐	4 Steve Yzerman, Detr.	8.00
☐	5 José Théodore (G), Mont.	4.00
☐	6 Marian Hossa, Otta.	3.00
☐	7 Mario Lemieux, Pitt.	10.00
☐	8 Ed Belfour (G), Toro.	3.00
☐	9 Mats Sundin, Toro.	3.00
☐	10 Todd Bertuzzi, Vanc.	4.00

SHADOWS

Insert Set (10 cards): 30.00

	Insert (1:17)	SK
☐	1 Ilya Kovalchuk, Atla.	4.00
☐	2 Joe Thornton, Bost.	4.00
☐	3 Patrick Roy (G), Colo.	12.00
☐	4 Joe Sakic, Colo.	6.00
☐	5 Steve Yzerman, Detr.	9.00
☐	6 Marian Gaborik, MinW.	4.00

RETAIL

In retail packs, cards 1-100 are availble in two versions: the silver-text base card and the blue-text parallel (#/450). Please see the hobby listings above

Shell Set (100 cards): 55.00
Complete Set (140 cards): 550.00 300.00
Common Player: 1.00 .35

	Description	B450	R
☐☐	1 Jean-Sébastien Giguère (G), Anah.	7.00	1.50
☐☐	2 Paul Kariya, Anah.	9.00	2.00
☐☐	3 Petr Sykora, Anah.	2.00	.50
☐☐	4 Dany Heatley, Atla.	7.00	1.50
☐☐	5 Ilya Kovalchuk, Atla.	7.00	1.50
☐☐	6 Pasi Nurminen (G), Atla.	1.00	.35
☐☐	7 Glen Murray, Bost.	3.00	.50
☐☐	8 Brian Rolston, Bost.	2.00	.50
☐☐	9 Steve Shields, Bost.	1.00	.35
☐☐	10 Joe Thornton, Bost.	8.00	2.00
☐☐	11 Martin Biron (G), Buff.	3.00	.50
☐☐	12 Chris Gratton, Buff.	1.00	.35
☐☐	13 Miroslav Satan, Buff.	2.00	.50
☐☐	14 Chris Drury, Calg.	4.00	1.00
☐☐	15 Jarome Iginla, Calg.	5.00	1.00
☐☐	16 Roman Turek (G), Calg.	3.00	.50
☐☐	17 Rod Brind'Amour, Caro.	2.00	.50
☐☐	18 Ron Francis, Caro.	4.00	1.00
☐☐	19 Jeff O'Neill, Caro.	2.00	.50
☐☐	20 Kevin Weekes (G), Caro.	1.00	.35
☐☐	21 Tyler Arnason, Chic.	2.00	.50
☐☐	22 Theoren Fleury, Chic.	4.00	1.00
☐☐	23 Jocelyn Thibault (G), Chic.	2.00	.50
☐☐	24 Peter Forsberg, Colo.	9.00	2.00
☐☐	25 Milan Hejduk, Colo.	5.00	1.00
☐☐	26 Patrick Roy (G), Colo.	21.00	5.00
☐☐	27 Joe Sakic, Colo.	11.00	2.50
☐☐	28 Andrew Cassels, Colu.	1.00	.35
☐☐	29 Marc Denis (G), Colu.	3.00	.50
☐☐	30 Geoff Sanderson, Colu.	1.00	.35
☐☐	31 Bill Guerin, Dall.	2.00	.50
☐☐	32 Mike Modano, Dall.	7.00	1.50
☐☐	33 Marty Turco (G), Dall.	4.00	1.00
☐☐	34 Pierre Turgeon, Dall.	2.00	.50
☐☐	35 Sergei Fedorov, Detr.	7.00	1.50
☐☐	36 Brett Hull, Detr.	7.00	1.50
☐☐	37 Curtis Joseph (G), Detr.	7.00	1.50
☐☐	38 Nicklas Lidström, Detr.	4.00	1.00
☐☐	39 Brendan Shanahan, Detr.	7.00	1.50
☐☐	40 Steve Yzerman, Detr.	16.00	4.00
☐☐	41 Anson Carter, Edmo.	2.00	.50
☐☐	42 Mike Comrie, Edmo.	5.00	1.00
☐☐	43 Tommy Salo (G), Edmo.	2.00	.50
☐☐	44 Ryan Smyth, Edmo.	3.00	.50
☐☐	45 Kristian Huselius, Flor.	2.00	.50
☐☐	46 Olli Jokinen, Flor.	2.00	.50
☐☐	47 Roberto Luongo (G), Flor.	5.00	1.00
☐☐	48 Jason Allison, LosA.	4.00	1.00
☐☐	49 Éric Bélanger, LosA.	1.00	.35
☐☐	50 Zigmund Palffy, LosA.	4.00	1.00
☐☐	51 Félix Potvin (G), LosA.	4.00	1.00
☐☐	52 Manny Fernandez (G), MinW.	2.00	.50
☐☐	53 Marian Gaborik, MinW.	7.00	1.50
☐☐	54 Cliff Ronning, MinW.	1.00	.35
☐☐	55 Saku Koivu, Mont.	5.00	1.00
☐☐	56 Yanic Perreault, Mont.	2.00	.50
☐☐	57 José Théodore (G), Mont.	8.00	2.00
☐☐	58 Richard Zednik, Mont.	2.00	.50
☐☐	59 Andreas Johansson, Nash.	1.00	.35
☐☐	60 David Legwand, Nash.	2.00	.50
☐☐	61 Tomas Vokoun (G), Nash.	1.00	.35
☐☐	62 Martin Brodeur (G), NJer.	11.00	2.50
☐☐	63 Scott Gomez, NJer.	2.00	.50
☐☐	64 John Madden, NJer.	2.00	.50
☐☐	65 Rick DiPietro (G), NYIs.	3.00	.50
☐☐	66 Michael Peca, NYIs.	2.00	.50
☐☐	67 Alexei Yashin, NYIs.	4.00	1.00
☐☐	68 Pavel Bure, NYRa.	5.00	1.00
☐☐	69 Eric Lindros, NYRa.	7.00	1.50
☐☐	70 Tom Poti, NYRa.	1.00	.35
☐☐	71 Daniel Alfredsson, Otta.	4.00	1.00
☐☐	72 Marian Hossa, Otta.	7.00	1.50
☐☐	73 Patrick Lalime (G), Otta.	4.00	1.00
☐☐	74 Roman Cechmanek (G), Phil.	2.00	.50
☐☐	75 Simon Gagné, Phil.	5.00	1.00
☐☐	76 Jeremy Roenick, Phil.	5.00	1.00
☐☐	77 Tony Amonte, Phoe.	4.00	1.00
☐☐	78 Brian Boucher (G), Phoe.	2.00	.50
☐☐	79 Shane Doan, Phoe.	1.00	.35
☐☐	80 Johan Hedberg (G), Pitt.	2.00	.50
☐☐	81 Alex Kovalev, Pitt.	4.00	1.00
☐☐	82 Mario Lemieux, Pitt.	21.00	5.00
☐☐	83 Brent Johnson (G), SLou.	2.00	.50
☐☐	84 Cory Stillman, SLou.	1.00	.35
☐☐	85 Doug Weight, SLou.	4.00	1.00
☐☐	86 Patrick Marleau, SanJ.	3.00	.50
☐☐	87 Evgeni Nabokov (G), SanJ.	4.00	1.00
☐☐	88 Teemu Selänne, SanJ.	5.00	1.00
☐☐	89 Nikolai Khabibulin (G), Tamp.	2.00	.50
☐☐	90 Vincent Lecavalier, Tamp.	7.00	1.50
☐☐	91 Martin St-Louis, Tamp.	3.00	.50
☐☐	92 Ed Belfour (G), Toro.	7.00	1.50
☐☐	93 Alexander Mogilny, Toro.	3.00	.50
☐☐	94 Mats Sundin, Toro.	7.00	1.50
☐☐	95 Todd Bertuzzi, Vanc.	8.00	2.00
☐☐	96 Dan Cloutier (G), Vanc.	2.00	.50
☐☐	97 Brendan Morrison, Vanc.	2.00	.50
☐☐	98 Markus Näslund, Vanc.	7.00	1.50
☐☐	99 Jaromir Jagr, Wash.	7.00	1.50
☐☐	100 Michael Nylander, Wash.	1.00	.35

ROOKIE

In retail packs, cards 101-140 are availble in two versions: the silver-text base card (#/1475) and the blue-text parallel (#/450). Please see hobby listings above.

	Retail	B450	R1475
☐☐	**101 Stanislav Chistov, Anah. RC**	**18.00**	**15.00**
☐☐	**102 Martin Gerber (G), Anah. RC**	**6.00**	**6.00**
☐☐	**103 Kurt Sauer, Anah. RC**	**6.00**	**6.00**
☐☐	**104 Alexei Smirnov, Anah. RC**	**6.00**	**6.00**
☐☐	**105 Shaone Morrisonn, Bost. RC**	**6.00**	**6.00**
☐☐	**106 Tim Thomas (G), Bost. RC**	**6.00**	**6.00**
☐☐	**107 Ryan Miller (G), Buff. RC**	**18.00**	**15.00**
☐☐	**108 Chuck Kobasew, Calg. RC**	**12.00**	**10.00**
☐☐	**109 Jordan Leopold, Calg. RC**	**6.00**	**6.00**
☐☐	**110 Pascal Leclaire (G), Colu. RC**	**18.00**	**15.00**
☐☐	**111 Rick Nash, Colu. RC**	**36.00**	**30.00**
☐☐	**112 Steve Ott, Dall. RC**	**6.00**	**6.00**
☐☐	**113 Dmitri Bykov, Detr. RC**	**6.00**	**6.00**
☐☐	**114 Henrik Zetterberg, Detr. RC**	**36.00**	**30.00**
☐☐	**115 Ales Hemsky, Edmo. RC**	**18.00**	**15.00**
☐☐	**116 Jay Bouwmeester, Flor. RC**	**18.00**	**15.00**
☐☐	**117 Mike Cammalleri, LosA. RC**	**12.00**	**10.00**
☐☐	**118 Alexander Frolov, LosA. RC**	**18.00**	**15.00**
☐☐	**119 Pierre-Marc Bouchard, MinW. RC**	**18.00**	**15.00**
☐☐	**120 Stéphane Veilleux, MinW. RC**	**6.00**	**6.00**
☐☐	121 Kyle Wanvig, MinW.	6.00	6.00
☐☐	**122 Ron Hainsey, Mont. RC**	**6.00**	**6.00**
☐☐	**123 Vernon (G) Fiddler, Nash. RC**	**6.00**	**6.00**
☐☐	**124 Adam Hall, Nash. RC**	**6.00**	**6.00**
☐☐	**125 Scottie Upshall, Nash. RC**	**12.00**	**10.00**
☐☐	**126 Jason Spezza, Otta. RC**	**24.00**	**20.00**
☐☐	**127 Anton Volchenkov, Otta. RC**	**6.00**	**6.00**
☐☐	**128 Dennis Seidenberg, Phil. RC**	**6.00**	**6.00**
☐☐	**129 Radovan Somik, Phil. RC**	**6.00**	**6.00**
☐☐	**130 Jeff Taffe, Phoe. RC**	**6.00**	**6.00**
☐☐	131 Sébastien Caron (G), Pitt.	6.00	6.00
☐☐	**132 Brooks Orpik, Pitt. RC**	**6.00**	**6.00**
☐☐	133 Dick Tarnstrom, Pitt.	6.00	6.00
☐☐	**134 Tom Koivisto, SLou. RC**	**6.00**	**6.00**
☐☐	**135 Curtis Sanford (G), SLou. RC**	**6.00**	**6.00**
☐☐	**136 Lynn Loyns, SanJ. RC**	**6.00**	**6.00**
☐☐	**137 Alexander Svitov, Tamp. RC**	**12.00**	**10.00**
☐☐	**138 Carlo Colaiacovo, Toro. RC**	**6.00**	**6.00**
☐☐	**139 Mikael Tellqvist (G), Toro. RC**	**6.00**	**6.00**
☐☐	**140 Steve Eminger, Wash. RC**	**6.00**	**6.00**

GAME-WORN JERSEY

Insert Set (75 cards): 2300.00

	Insert	GWJ
☐	1 Mike Leclerc, Anah. ✂ {*50}	18.00
☐	2 Dany Heatley, Atla. ✂ {*100}	55.00
☐	3 Ilya Kovalchuk, Atla. ✂ {*90}	60.00
☐	4 Patrik Stefan, Atla. ✂ {*100}	18.00
☐	5 Joe Thornton, Bost. ✂ {*25}	120.00
☐	6 Martin Biron (G), Buff. ✂ {*150}	20.00
☐	7 Jean_Pierre Dumont, Buff. ✂ {*100}	18.00
☐	8 Rod Brind'Amour, Caro. ✂ {*150}	18.00
☐	9 Arturs Irbe (G), Caro. ✂ {*150}	20.00
☐	10 Jeff O'Neill, Caro. ✂ {*100}	20.00
☐	11 Chris Drury, Calg. ✂ {*75}	35.00
☐	12 Roman Turek (G), Calg. ✂ {*100}	25.00
☐	13 Mark Bell, Chic. ✂ {*100}	18.00
☐	14 Sergei Berezin, Chic. ✂ {*75}	30.00
☐	15 Steve Sullivan, Chic. ✂ {*60}	20.00
☐	16 Rob Blake, Colo. ✂ {*150}	30.00
☐	17 Milan Hejduk, Colo. ✂ {*100}	45.00
☐	18 Patrick Roy (G), Colo. ✂ {*25}	300.00
☐	19 Rostislav Klesla, Colu. ✂ {*100}	18.00
☐	20 Geoff Sanderson, Colu. ✂ {*100}	18.00
☐	21 Ron Tugnutt (G), Dall. ✂ {*100}	20.00
☐	22 Marty Turco (G), Dall. ✂ {*80}	35.00
☐	23 Sergei Fedorov, Detr. ✂ {*100}	55.00
☐	24 Dominik Hasek (G), Detr. ✂ {*75}	60.00
☐	25 Brett Hull, Detr. ✂ {*150}	50.00
☐	26 Luc Robitaille, Detr. ✂ {*50}	60.00
☐	27 Jason Williams, Detr. ✂ {*100}	18.00
☐	28 Mike Comrie, Edmo. ✂ {*50}	60.00
☐	29 Tommy Salo (G), Edmo. ✂ {*100}	20.00
☐	30 Ryan Smyth, Edmo. ✂ {*50}	35.00
☐	31 Valeri Bure, Flor. ✂ {*100}	18.00
☐	32 Kristian Huselius, Flor. ✂ {*150}	18.00
☐	33 Roberto Luongo (G), Flor. ✂ {*150}	40.00
☐	34 Marian Gaborik, MinW. ✂ {*75}	60.00
☐	35 Yanic Perreault, Mont. ✂ {*100}	18.00
☐	36 José Théodore (G), Mont. ✂ {*50}	90.00
☐	37 David Legwand, Nash. ✂ {*150}	20.00
☐	38 Scott Walker, Nash. ✂ {*100}	18.00
☐	39 Scott Gomez, NJer. ✂ {*100}	20.00
☐	40 Scott Stevens, NJer. ✂ {*150}	20.00
☐	41 Michael Peca, NYIs. ✂ {*150}	20.00
☐	42 Alexei Yashin, NYIs. ✂ {*125}	30.00
☐	43 Pavel Bure, NYRa. ✂ {*50}	60.00
☐	44 Eric Lindros, NYRa. ✂ {*50}	75.00
☐	45 Mark Messier, NYRa. ✂ {*75}	60.00
☐	46 Daniel Alfredsson, Otta. ✂ {*100}	65.00
☐	47 Martin Havlat, Otta. ✂ {*100}	30.00
☐	48 Patrick Lalime (G), Otta. ✂ {*100}	30.00
☐	49 Simon Gagné, Phil. ✂ {*100}	45.00
☐	50 Michal Handzus, Phil. ✂ {*90}	18.00
☐	51 Tomi Kallio, Phil. ✂ {*150}	18.00
☐	52 John LeClair, Phil. ✂ {*150}	40.00
☐	53 Johan Hedberg (G), Pitt. ✂ {*100}	20.00
☐	54 Mario Lemieux, Pitt. ✂ {*50}	225.00
☐	55 Toby Petersen, Pitt. ✂ {*100}	18.00
☐	56 Pavol Demitra, SLou. ✂ {*100}	20.00
☐	57 Ray Ferraro, SLou. ✂ {*100}	18.00
☐	58 Chris Pronger, SLou. ✂ {*150}	30.00
☐	59 Keith Tkachuk, SLou. ✂ {*50}	45.00
☐	60 Sergei Varlamov, SLou. ✂ {*100}	18.00
☐	61 Miikka Kiprusoff (G), SanJ. ✂ {*100}	18.00
☐	62 Patrick Marleau, SanJ. ✂ {*75}	30.00
☐	63 Owen Nolan, SanJ. ✂ {*125}	30.00
☐	64 Nikolai Khabibulin (G), Tamp. ✂ {*130}	20.00
☐	65 Fredrik Modin, Tamp. ✂ {*100}	18.00
☐	66 Alexander Mogilny, Toro. ✂ {*50}	35.00
☐	67 Gary Roberts, Toro. ✂ {*100}	20.00
☐	68 Darcy Tucker, Toro. ✂ {*100}	18.00
☐	69 Dan Cloutier (G), Vanc. ✂ {*150}	20.00
☐	70 Brendan Morrison, Vanc. ✂ {*85}	18.00
☐	71 Daniel Sedin, Vanc. ✂ {*150}	20.00
☐	72 Henrik Sedin, Vanc. ✂ {*150}	20.00
☐	73 Peter Bondra, Wash. ✂ {*150}	30.00
☐	74 Jaromir Jagr, Wash. ✂ {*25}	100.00
☐	75 Olaf Kölzig (G), Wash. ✂ {*150}	30.00

2002 - 03 QUEST FOR THE CUP

Produced by the Pacific Trading Cards, this series was released in May 2003. There are two variations for each card 1-100: the silver base card and the Gold parallel card (#/325).

Shell Set (100 cards): - 90.00
Complete Set (150 cards): 575.00 425.00
Common Player: 2.00 .50

	Description	G325	QFTC
☐☐	1 Jean-Sébastien Giguère (G), Anah.	6.00	2.50
☐☐	2 Paul Kariya, Anah.	8.00	3.50
☐☐	3 Sandis Ozolinsh, Anah.	2.00	.50
☐☐	4 Dany Heatley, Atla.	6.00	2.50
☐☐	5 Ilya Kovalchuk, Atla.	6.00	2.50
☐☐	6 Jeff Hackett (G), Bost.	2.00	.50
☐☐	7 Glen Murray, Bost.	2.00	1.00
☐☐	8 Joe Thornton, Bost.	6.00	3.00
☐☐	9 Martin Biron (G), Buff.	2.00	1.00
☐☐	10 Miroslav Satan, Buff.	2.00	.50
☐☐	11 Chris Drury, Calg.	2.00	1.50
☐☐	12 Jarome Iginla, Calg.	4.00	2.00
☐☐	13 Roman Turek (G), Calg.	2.00	1.00
☐☐	14 Ron Francis, Caro.	2.00	1.50
☐☐	15 Jeff O'Neill, Caro.	2.00	1.00
☐☐	16 Éric Dazé, Chic.	2.00	1.00
☐☐	17 Theoren Fleury, Chic.	2.00	1.50
☐☐	18 Jocelyn Thibault (G), Chic.	2.00	1.00
☐☐	19 Alexei Zhamnov, Chic.	2.00	.50
☐☐	20 Rob Blake, Colo.	2.00	1.50
☐☐	21 Peter Forsberg, Colo.	8.00	3.50
☐☐	22 Milan Hejduk, Colo.	4.00	2.00
☐☐	23 Patrick Roy (G), Colo.	18.00	7.50
☐☐	24 Joe Sakic, Colo.	10.00	4.00
☐☐	25 Marc Denis (G), Colu.	2.00	1.00
☐☐	26 Ray Whitney, Colu.	2.00	.50
☐☐	27 Bill Guerin, Dall.	2.00	1.00
☐☐	28 Jere Lehtinen, Dall.	2.00	.50
☐☐	29 Mike Modano, Dall.	6.00	2.50
☐☐	30 Marty Turco (G), Dall.	2.00	1.50
☐☐	31 Pierre Turgeon, Dall.	2.00	1.00
☐☐	32 Sergei Fedorov, Detr.	6.00	2.50
☐☐	33 Brett Hull, Detr.	6.00	2.50
☐☐	34 Curtis Joseph (G), Detr.	6.00	2.50
☐☐	35 Nicklas Lidström, Detr.	2.00	1.50
☐☐	36 Brendan Shanahan, Detr.	6.00	2.50
☐☐	37 Steve Yzerman, Detr.	14.00	6.00
☐☐	38 Mike Comrie, Edmo.	4.00	2.00
☐☐	39 Tommy Salo (G), Edmo.	2.00	1.00
☐☐	40 Ryan Smyth, Edmo.	2.00	1.00
☐☐	41 Olli Jokinen, Flor.	2.00	.50
☐☐	42 Roberto Luongo (G), Flor.	4.00	2.00
☐☐	43 Jason Allison, LosA.	2.00	1.50
☐☐	44 Zigmund Palffy, LosA.	2.00	1.50
☐☐	45 Félix Potvin (G), LosA.	2.00	1.50
☐☐	46 Pascal Dupuis, MinW.	2.00	.50
☐☐	47 Manny Fernandez (G), MinW.	2.00	1.00
☐☐	48 Marian Gaborik, MinW.	6.00	2.50
☐☐	49 Cliff Ronning, MinW.	2.00	.50
☐☐	50 Saku Koivu, Mont.	4.00	2.00
☐☐	51 Yanic Perreault, Mont.	2.00	.50
☐☐	52 José Théodore (G), Mont.	6.00	3.00
☐☐	53 Richard Zednik, Mont.	2.00	1.00
☐☐	54 David Legwand, Nash.	2.00	1.00
☐☐	55 Tomas Vokoun (G), Nash.	2.00	.50
☐☐	56 Martin Brodeur (G), NJer.	10.00	4.00
☐☐	57 Patrik Elias, NJer.	4.00	2.00
☐☐	58 Jeff Friesen, NJer.	2.00	.50
☐☐	59 Jamie Langenbrunner, NJer.	2.00	.50
☐☐	60 Rick DiPietro (G), NYIs.	2.00	1.00
☐☐	61 Michael Peca, NYIs.	2.00	1.00
☐☐	62 Alexei Yashin, NYIs.	2.00	1.50
☐☐	63 Pavel Bure, NYRa.	4.00	2.00
☐☐	64 Anson Carter, NYRa.	2.00	1.00
☐☐	65 Alex Kovalev, NYRa.	2.00	1.50
☐☐	66 Eric Lindros, NYRa.	6.00	2.50
☐☐	67 Mark Messier, NYRa.	6.00	2.50
☐☐	68 Daniel Alfredsson, Otta.	2.00	1.50
☐☐	69 Radek Bonk, Otta.	2.00	.50
☐☐	70 Martin Havlat, Otta.	2.00	1.50
☐☐	71 Marian Hossa, Otta.	6.00	2.50
☐☐	72 Patrick Lalime (G), Otta.	2.00	1.50
☐☐	73 Tony Amonte, Phil.	2.00	1.50
☐☐	74 Roman Cechmanek (G), Phil.	2.00	1.00
☐☐	75 Simon Gagné, Phil.	4.00	2.00
☐☐	76 Sami Kapanen, Phil.	2.00	.50
☐☐	77 Jeremy Roenick, Phil.	4.00	2.00
☐☐	78 Sean Burke (G), Phoe.	2.00	1.50
☐☐	79 Johan Hedberg (G), Pitt.	2.00	1.00
☐☐	80 Mario Lemieux, Pitt.	18.00	7.50
☐☐	81 Pavol Demitra, SLou.	2.00	1.00
☐☐	82 Brent Johnson (G), SLou.	2.00	1.00
☐☐	83 Cory Stillman, SLou.	2.00	.50
☐☐	84 Keith Tkachuk, SLou.	2.00	1.50
☐☐	85 Doug Weight, SLou.	2.00	1.50
☐☐	86 Evgeni Nabokov (G), SanJ.	2.00	1.50
☐☐	87 Teemu Selänne, SanJ.	4.00	2.00

□ □	88 Nikolai Khabibulin (G), Tamp.	2.00	1.00
□ □	89 Vincent Lecavalier, Tamp.	6.00	2.50
□ □	90 Martin St-Louis, Tamp.	2.00	1.00
□ □	91 Ed Belfour (G), Toro.	6.00	2.50
□ □	92 Alexander Mogilny, Toro.	2.00	1.00
□ □	93 Mats Sundin, Toro.	6.00	2.50
□ □	94 Todd Bertuzzi, Vanc.	6.00	3.00
□ □	95 Dan Cloutier (G), Vanc.	2.00	1.00
□ □	96 Brendan Morrison, Vanc.	2.00	.50
□ □	97 Markus Näslund, Vanc.	6.00	2.50
□ □	98 Jaromir Jagr, Wash.	6.00	2.50
□ □	99 Olaf Kölzig (G), Wash.	2.00	1.50
□ □	100 Michael Nylander, Wash.	2.00	.50

ROOKIE

There are two variations for each card 101-150: the silver base card (#/950) and the Gold parallel card (#/325).

	Insert	G325	RC950
□ □	101 Stanislav Chistov, Anah. RC	15.00	15.00
□ □	102 Martin Gerber (G), Anah. RC	6.00	6.00
□ □	103 Kurt Sauer, Anah. RC	6.00	6.00
□ □	104 Alexei Smirnov, Anah. RC	6.00	6.00
□ □	105 Shaone Morrisonn, Bost. RC	6.00	6.00
□ □	106 Tim Thomas (G), Bost. RC	6.00	6.00
□ □	107 Ryan Miller (G), Buff. RC	10.00	10.00
□ □	108 Chuck Kobasew, Calg. RC	10.00	10.00
□ □	109 Jordan Leopold, Calg. RC	6.00	6.00
□ □	110 Ryan Bayda, Caro. RC	6.00	6.00
□ □	111 Tomas Malec, Caro. RC	6.00	6.00
□ □	112 Pascal Leclaire (G), Colu. RC	10.00	10.00
□ □	113 Rick Nash, Colu. RC	25.00	25.00
□ □	114 Jason Bacashihua, Dall. RC	6.00	6.00
□ □	115 Steve Ott, Dall. RC	6.00	6.00
□ □	116 Dmitri Bykov, Detr. RC	6.00	6.00
□ □	117 Henrik Zetterberg, Detr. RC	25.00	25.00
□ □	118 Ales Hemsky, Edmo. RC	15.00	15.00
□ □	119 Fernando Pisani, Edmo. RC	6.00	6.00
□ □	120 Jay Bouwmeester, Flor. RC	15.00	15.00
□ □	121 Kip Brennan, LosA. RC	6.00	6.00
□ □	122 Mike Cammalleri, LosA. RC	10.00	10.00
□ □	123 Alexander Frolov, LosA. RC	10.00	10.00
□ □	124 Pierre-Marc Bouchard, MinW. RC	15.00	15.00
□ □	125 Stéphane Veilleux, MinW. RC	6.00	6.00
□ □	126 Ron Hainsey, Mont. RC	6.00	6.00
□ □	127 Mike Komisarek, Mont. RC	6.00	6.00
□ □	128 Vernon (G) Fiddler, Nash. RC	6.00	6.00
□ □	129 Adam Hall, Nash. RC	6.00	6.00
□ □	130 Scottie Upshall, Nash. RC	10.00	10.00
□ □	131 Eric Godard, NYIs. RC	6.00	6.00
□ □	132 Ray Emery, Otta. RC	6.00	6.00
□ □	133 Jason Spezza, Otta. RC	15.00	15.00
□ □	134 Anton Volchenkov, Otta. RC	6.00	6.00
□ □	135 Dennis Seidenberg, Phil. RC	6.00	6.00
□ □	136 Radovan Somik, Phil. RC	6.00	6.00
□ □	137 Jim Vandermeer, Phil. RC	6.00	6.00
□ □	138 Jeff Taffe, Phoe. RC	6.00	6.00
□ □	139 Brooks Orpik, Pitt. RC	6.00	6.00
□ □	140 Tomas Surovy, Pitt. RC	6.00	6.00
□ □	141 Dick Tarnstrom, Pitt.	6.00	6.00
□ □	142 Curtis Sanford (G), SLou. RC	6.00	6.00
□ □	143 Matt Walker, SLou. RC	6.00	6.00
□ □	144 Niko Dimitrakos, SanJ. RC	6.00	6.00
□ □	145 Jim Fahey, SanJ. RC	6.00	6.00
□ □	146 Lynn Loyns, SanJ. RC	6.00	6.00
□ □	147 Alexander Svitov, Tamp. RC	10.00	10.00
□ □	148 Carlo Colaiacovo, Toro. RC	6.00	6.00
□ □	149 Mikael Tellqvist (G), Toro. RC	6.00	6.00
□ □	150 Steve Eminger, Wash. RC	6.00	6.00

AUTOGRAPH

	Autograph
□	Marty Turco, Dall. ✍

CALDER CONTENDERS

Insert Set (10 cards): 90.00

	Insert (1:13)	CC
□	1 Stanislav Chistov, Anah.	6.00
□	2 Ales Kotalik, Buff.	4.00
□	3 Ryan Miller (G), Buff.	6.00
□	4 Tyler Arnason, Chic.	4.00
□	5 Pascal Leclaire (G), Colu.	4.00
□	6 Rick Nash, Colu.	16.00
□	7 Henrik Zetterberg, Detr.	16.00
□	8 Ales Hemsky, Edmo.	4.00
□	9 Jay Bouwmeester, Flor.	8.00
□	10 Jason Spezza, Otta.	12.00

CHASING THE CUP

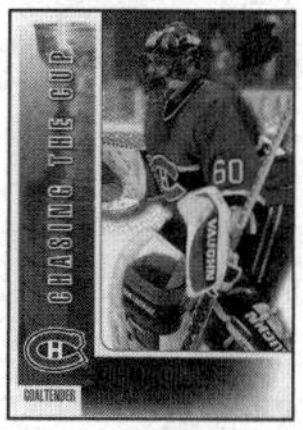

Insert Set (20 cards): 30.00

	Insert (1:5)	CtC
□	1 Paul Kariya, Anah.	4.00
□	2 Dany Heatley, Atla.	2.00
□	3 Ilya Kovalchuk, Atla.	2.00
□	4 Joe Thornton, Bost.	4.00
□	5 Marty Turco (G), Dall.	2.00
□	6 Curtis Joseph (G), Detr.	2.00
□	7 Marian Gaborik, MinW.	2.00
□	8 José Théodore (G), Mont.	4.00
□	9 Alexei Yashin, NYIs.	2.00
□	10 Pavel Bure, NYRa.	2.00
□	11 Eric Lindros, NYRa.	2.00
□	12 Daniel Alfredsson, Otta.	2.00
□	13 Marian Hossa, Otta.	2.00
□	14 Jeremy Roenick, Phil.	2.00
□	15 Teemu Selänne, SanJ.	2.00
□	16 Owen Nolan, Toro.	2.00
□	17 Mats Sundin, Toro.	2.00
□	18 Todd Bertuzzi, Vanc.	4.00
□	19 Brendan Morrison, Vanc.	2.00
□	20 Markus Näslund, Vanc.	2.00

GAME-WORN JERSEY

Insert Set (25 cards): 165.00

	Insert	GWJ
□	1 Dany Heatley, Atla. ✂ {*1000}	20.00
□	2 Glen Murray, Bost. ✂ {*1500}	10.00
□	3 Joe Thornton, Bost. ✂ {*1000}	20.00
□	4 Rob Blake, Colo. ✂ {*1100}	10.00
□	5 Peter Forsberg, Colo. ✂ {*1000}	25.00
□	6 Patrick Roy (G), Colo. ✂ {*1000}	45.00
□	7 Mike Modano, Dall. ✂ {*1250}	15.00
□	8 Marty Turco (G), Dall. ✂ {*1000}	10.00
□	9 Nicklas Lidström, Detr. ✂ {*1125}	10.00
□	10 Rick DiPietro (G), NYIs. ✂ {*1000}	10.00
□	11 Mark Messier, NYRa. ✂ {*625}	25.00
□	12 Daniel Alfredsson, Otta. ✂ {*1250}	10.00
□	13 Marian Hossa, Otta. ✂ {*1000}	20.00
□	14 Jason Spezza, Otta. ✂ {*1000}	10.00
□	15 Roman Cechmanek (G), Phil. ✂ {*1250}	10.00
□	16 Jeremy Roenick, Phil. ✂ {*725}	20.00
□	17 Mario Lemieux, Pitt. ✂ {*525}	90.00
□	18 Brent Johnson (G), SLou. ✂ {*1250}	10.00
□	19 Doug Weight, SLou. ✂ {*1250}	10.00
□	20 Martin St-Louis, Tamp. ✂ {*1500}	10.00
□	21 Ed Belfour (G), Toro. ✂ {*1500}	15.00
□	22 Gary Roberts, Toro. ✂ {*1500}	10.00
□	23 Markus Näslund, Vanc. ✂ {*1000}	20.00
□	24 Jaromir Jagr, Wash. ✂ {*1000}	20.00
□	25 Olaf Kölzig (G), Wash. ✂ {*1500}	10.00

RAISING THE CUP

Insert Set (12 cards): 40.00

	Insert (1:9)	RtC
□	1 Peter Forsberg, Colo.	4.00
□	2 Patrick Roy (G), Colo.	10.00
□	3 Joe Sakic, Colo.	4.00
□	4 Mike Modano, Dall.	2.00
□	5 Sergei Fedorov, Detr.	2.00
□	6 Brett Hull, Detr.	2.00
□	7 Brendan Shanahan, Detr.	2.00
□	8 Steve Yzerman, Detr.	8.00
□	9 Martin Brodeur (G), NJer.	4.00
□	10 Mark Messier, NYRa.	2.00
□	11 Mario Lemieux, Pitt.	10.00
□	12 Jaromir Jagr, Wash.	2.00

2002 - 03 RUSSIAN FUTURE STARS

These cards are said to be produced by A&M Enterprises.

□ 1 Alexander Ovechkin
□ 2 Igor Grigorenko
□ 3 Vladislav Evseev
□ 4 Konstantin Glazachev
□ 5 Fedor Tyutin
□ 6 Denis Grebeshkov
□ 7 Alexander Perezhogin
□ 8 Kiril Koltsov
□ 9 Yuri Trubachev
□ 10 Andrei Taratukhin
□ 11 Igor Mirnov
□ 12 Dmitri Chernykh
□ 13 Dmitri Shitikov
□ 14 Dmirti Semin
□ 15 Andrei Medvedev
□ 16 Alexei Volkov
□ 17 Sergei Zinoviev
□ 18 Sergei Soin
□ 19 Alexei Mikhnov
□ 20 Ilya Nikulin

2002 - 03 SIGNATURE SERIES

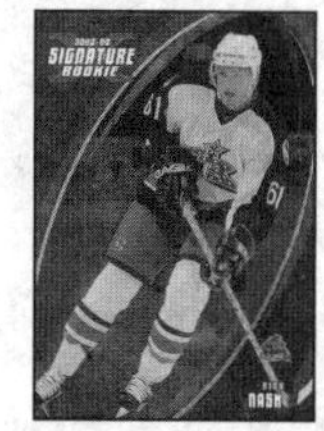

Produced by the In The Game, this series was released in May 2003.

Complete Set (200 cards): 200
Common Player: .50

	Description	BAPS
□	1 Dany Heatley, Atla.	2.50
□	2 Alexei Zhamnov, Chic.	.50
□	3 Mike Comrie, Edmo.	2.00
□	4 Dwayne Roloson (G), MinW.	.50
□	5 Mike Dunham (G), Nash.	1.00
□	6 Simon Gagné, Phil.	2.00
□	7 Evgeni Nabokov (G), SanJ.	1.50
□	8 Bryan McCabe, Toro.	.50
□	9 Todd Bertuzzi, Vanc.	3.00
□	10 Alex Kovalev, Pitt.	1.50
□	11 Dave Andreychuk, Tamp.	.50
□	12 Daniel Alfredsson, Otta.	1.50
□	13 Marian Gaborik, MinW.	2.50
□	14 Jean-Sébastien Aubin (G), Pitt.	.50
□	15 Andy McDonald, Anah.	.50
□	16 Brad Richards, Tamp.	1.00
□	17 Henrik Sedin, Vanc.	1.00
□	18 Mark Bell, Chic.	.50
□	19 Adam Deadmarsh, LosA.	.50
□	20 Marc Denis (G), Colu.	1.00
□	21 Mike York, Edmo.	.50
□	22 Johan Hedberg (G), Pitt.	1.00
□	23 Vincent Damphousse, SanJ.	1.50
□	24 Marian Hossa, Otta.	2.50
□	25 Richard Zednik, Mont.	1.00
□	26 Alexei Yashin, NYIs.	1.50
□	27 Sergei Gonchar, Wash.	.50
□	28 Martin Straka, Pitt.	.50
□	29 Ed Jovanovski, Vanc.	1.00
□	30 Robert Lang, Wash.	.50
□	31 Markus Näslund, Vanc.	2.50
□	32 Mike Sillinger, Colu.	.50
□	33 Jamie Storr (G), LosA.	.50
□	34 Kimmo Timonen, Nash.	.50
□	35 Patrick Lalime (G), Otta.	1.50
□	36 Alyn McCauley, Toro.	.50
□	37 Scott Walker, Nash.	.50
□	38 Trevor Linden, Vanc.	1.00
□	39 Ilya Kovalchuk, Atla.	2.50
□	40 Jarome Iginla, Calg.	2.00
□	41 Alex Tanguay, Colo.	1.50
□	42 Yanic Perreault, Mont.	.50
□	43 Jocelyn Thibault (G), Chic.	1.00
□	44 Eric Brewer, Edmo.	1.00
□	45 Ray Whitney, Colu.	.50
□	46 Ryan Smyth, Edmo.	1.00
□	47 Steven Reinprecht, Colo.	.50
□	48 Phil Housley, Chic.	.50
□	49 Milan Hnilicka (G), Atla.	.50
□	50 Maxim Afinogenov, Buff.	1.00
□	51 Andrew Brunette, MinW.	.50
□	52 Miroslav Satan, Buff.	.50
□	53 Glen Murray, Bost.	1.00
□	54 Mark Parrish, NYIs.	1.00
□	55 Daniel Sedin, Vanc.	1.00
□	56 Brendan Morrison, Vanc.	.50
□	57 Brian Rafalski, NJer.	.50
□	58 Dan Cloutier (G), Vanc.	1.00
□	59 Espen Knutsen, Colu.	.50
□	60 Radim Vrbata, Colo.	.50
□	61 Patrik Stefan, Atla.	.50
□	62 Éric Dazé, Chic.	1.00
□	63 Félix Potvin (G), LosA.	1.50
□	64 Darcy Tucker, Toro.	.50
□	65 José Théodore (G), Mont.	3.00
□	66 Scott Hartnell, Nash.	.50
□	67 Martin Havlat, Otta.	1.50
□	68 Radek Bonk, Otta.	.50
□	69 Patrick Marleau, SanJ.	1.00
□	70 Andy Delmore, Nash.	.50
□	71 Rostislav Klesla, Colu.	.50
□	72 David Aebischer (G), Colo.	.50
□	73 Steve Shields (G), Bost.	.50
□	74 Stu Barnes, Buff.	.50
□	75 Tim Connolly, Buff.	1.00
□	76 Jean-Sébastien Giguère (G), Anah.	2.50
□	77 Shane Doan, Phoe.	.50
□	78 Brian Rolston, Bost.	.50
□	79 Shawn McEachern, Atla.	.50
□	80 Martin Biron (G), Buff.	1.00
□	81 Craig Conroy, Calg.	.50
□	82 Mika Noronen (G), Buff.	1.00
□	83 Brian Boucher, Phoe.	.50
□	84 Kyle Calder, Chic.	.50
□	85 Cliff Ronning, MinW.	.50
□	86 Brian Gionta, NJer.	.50
□	87 Shawn Bates, NYIs.	.50
□	88 Michal Handzus, Phil.	.50
□	89 Daniel Brière, Phoe.	1.00
□	90 Adam Graves, SanJ.	1.00
□	91 Martin St-Louis, Tamp.	1.00
□	92 Ladislav Nagy, Phoe.	.50
□	93 Oleg Tverdovsky, NJer.	.50
□	94 Pavel Brendl, Phil.	.50
□	95 Aleksey Morozov, Pitt.	.50
□	96 Daymond Langkow, Phoe.	.50
□	97 Krys Kolanos, Phoe.	.50
□	98 Sean Burke (G), Phoe.	1.50
□	99 Chris Drury, Calg.	1.50
□	100 Steve Sullivan, Chic.	.50
□	101 Paul Kariya, Anah.	3.50
□	102 Peter Forsberg, Colo.	3.50
□	103 Ron Tugnutt (G), Dall.	1.00
□	104 Manny Legacé (G), Detr.	.50
□	105 Tommy Salo (G), Edmo.	1.00
□	106 Kristian Huselius, Flor.	.50
□	107 Jason Allison, LosA.	1.50
□	108 Mariusz Czerkawski, Mont.	.50
□	109 Jeff Friesen, NJer.	.50
□	110 Chris Osgood (G), NYIs.	1.50
□	111 Martin Prusek (G), Otta.	.50
□	112 Steve Yzerman, Detr.	6.00
□	113 John LeClair, Phil.	2.00
□	114 Jan Hrdina, Pitt.	.50
□	115 Tony Amonte, Phoe.	1.50
□	116 Teemu Selänne, SanJ.	2.00
□	117 Cory Stillman, SLou.	.50
□	118 Nikolai Khabibulin (G), Tamp.	1.00
□	119 Mats Sundin, Toro.	2.50
□	120 Olaf Kölzig (G), Wash.	1.50
□	121 Petr Sykora, Anah.	1.00
□	122 Joe Thornton, Bost.	3.00
□	123 Roman Turek (G), Calg.	1.00
□	124 Derek Morris, Colo.	.50
□	125 Bill Guerin, Dall.	1.00
□	126 Brendan Shanahan, Detr.	2.50
□	127 Roberto Luongo (G), Flor.	2.00

☐	128 Zigmund Palffy, LosA.	1.50
☐	129 Pavol Demitra, SLou.	1.00
☐	130 Saku Koivu, Mont.	2.00
☐	131 Joe Nieuwendyk, NJer.	1.00
☐	132 Michael Peca, NYIs.	1.00
☐	133 Petr Schastlivy, Otta.	.50
☐	134 Jeremy Roenick, Phil.	2.00
☐	135 Mario Lemieux, Pitt.	7.50
☐	136 Petr Cajanek, SLou.	.50
☐	137 Vincent Lecavalier, Tamp.	2.50
☐	138 Peter Bondra, Wash.	1.50
☐	139 Brent Johnson (G), SLou.	1.00
☐	140 Sergei Samsonov, Bost.	1.50
☐	141 Joe Sakic, Colo.	4.00
☐	142 Brenden Morrow, Dall.	.50
☐	143 Arturs Irbe (G), Caro.	1.00
☐	144 Chris Chelios, Detr.	1.50
☐	145 Sandis Ozolinsh, Flor.	.50
☐	146 Doug Gilmour, Mont.	1.50
☐	147 Scott Stevens, NJer.	1.00
☐	148 Sergei Fedorov, Detr.	2.50
☐	149 Keith Primeau, Phil.	1.00
☐	150 Eric Boguniecki, SLou.	.50
☐	151 Shane Willis, Tamp.	.50
☐	152 Rob Blake, Colo.	1.50
☐	153 Luc Robitaille, Detr.	2.00
☐	154 Pierre Turgeon, Dall.	1.00
☐	155 Curtis Joseph (G), Detr.	2.50
☐	156 Stephen Weiss, Flor.	1.00
☐	157 Patrik Elias, NJer.	2.00
☐	158 Mark Recchi, Phil.	1.00
☐	159 Al MacInnis, SLou.	1.00
☐	160 Patrick Roy (G), Colo.	7.50
☐	161 Darryl Sydor, Dall.	.50
☐	162 Nicklas Lidström, Detr.	1.50
☐	163 Doug Weight, SLou.	1.50
☐	164 Roman Cechmanek (G), Phil.	1.00
☐	165 Marty Turco (G), Dall.	1.50
☐	166 Pavel Datsyuk, Detr.	2.00
☐	167 Chris Pronger, SLou.	1.50
☐	168 Scott Young, Dall.	.50
☐	169 Igor Larionov, Detr.	1.50
☐	170 Keith Tkachuk, SLou.	1.50
☐	171 Ron Francis, Caro.	1.50
☐	172 Dan Blackburn (G), NYRa.	1.00
☐	173 Jeff O'Neill, Caro.	1.00
☐	174 Bobby Holik, NYRa.	.50
☐	175 Erik Cole, Caro.	.50
☐	176 Pavel Bure, NYRa.	2.00
☐	177 Brian Leetch, NYRa.	1.50
☐	**178 Curtis Sanford (G), SLou. RC**	**3.00**
☐	**179 Carlo Colaiacovo, Toro. RC**	**4.50**
☐	**180 Dennis Seidenberg, Phil. RC**	**3.00**
☐	**181 Adam Hall (G), Nash. RC**	**4.50**
☐	**182 Ivan Majesky, Flor. RC**	**1.50**
☐	**183 Rick Nash, Colu. RC**	**15.00**
☐	**184 Alexei Smirnov, Anah. RC**	**4.50**
☐	**185 Chuck Kobasew, Calg. RC**	**6.00**
☐	**186 Ron Hainsey, Mont. RC**	**4.50**
☐	**187 Stéphane Veilleux, MinW. RC**	**1.50**
☐	**188 Scottie Upshall, Nash. RC**	**6.00**
☐	**189 Lasse Pirjetä, Colu. RC**	**1.50**
☐	**190 Henrik Zetterberg, Detr. RC**	**15.00**
☐	**191 Jay Bouwmeester, Flor. RC**	**9.00**
☐	**192 Alexander Frolov, LosA. RC**	**7.50**
☐	**193 Dmitri Bykov, Detr. RC**	**3.00**
☐	**194 Stanislav Chistov, Anah. RC**	**9.00**
☐	**195 Jordan Leopold, Calg. RC**	**4.50**
☐	**196 Pierre-Marc Bouchard, MinW. RC**	**9.00**
☐	**197 Mike Cammalleri, LosA. RC**	**6.00**
☐	**198 Anton Volchenkov, Otta. RC**	**3.00**
☐	**199 Lynn Loyns, SanJ. RC**	**1.50**
☐	**200 Steve Eminger, Wash. RC**	**3.00**

ALL-ROOKIE TEAM

Insert Set (12 cards):		400.00
	Insert (#/50)	**AR**
☐	Jay Bouwmeester, Flor. ✂	50.00
☐	Mike Cammalleri, LosA. ✂	30.00
☐	Stanislav Chistov, Anah. ✂	50.00
☐	Marcel Hossa, Mont. ✂	50.00
☐	Barret Jackman, SLou. ✂	50.00
☐	Jan Lasak (G), Nash. ✂	30.00
☐	Jordan Leopold, Calg. ✂	30.00
☐	Ryan Miller, Buff. ✂	50.00
☐	Rick Nash, Colu. ✂	100.00
☐	Dennis Seidenberg, Phil. ✂	30.00
☐	Radovan Somik, Phil. ✂	30.00
☐	Stephen Weiss, Flor. ✂	50.00

AUTOGRAPH

Insert Set (200 cards):		5400.00	3000.00
	Insert	**Gold**	**Aut**
☐☐	1 Dany Heatley, Atla. ✍	35.00	25.00
☐☐	2 Alexei Zhamnov, Chic. ✍	10.00	5.00
☐☐	3 Mike Comrie, Edmo. ✍	30.00	20.00
☐☐	4 Dwayne Roloson (G), MinW. ✍	6.00	5.00
☐☐	5 Mike Dunham (G), Nash. ✍	15.00	10.00
☐☐	6 Simon Gagné, Phil. ✍	30.00	20.00
☐☐	7 Evgeni Nabokov (G), SanJ. ✍	20.00	15.00
☐☐	8 Bryan McCabe, Toro. ✍	6.00	5.00
☐☐	9 Todd Bertuzzi, Vanc. ✍	45.00	30.00
☐☐	10 Alex Kovalev, Pitt. ✍	20.00	15.00
☐☐	11 Dave Andreychuk, Tamp. ✍	10.00	5.00
☐☐	12 Daniel Alfredsson, Otta. ✍	20.00	15.00
☐☐	13 Marian Gaborik, MinW. ✍	35.00	25.00
☐☐	14 Jean-Sébastien Aubin (G), Pitt. ✍	6.00	5.00
☐☐	15 Andy McDonald, Anah. ✍	6.00	5.00
☐☐	16 Brad Richards, Tamp. ✍	15.00	10.00
☐☐	17 Henrik Sedin, Vanc. ✍	15.00	10.00
☐☐	18 Mark Bell, Chic. ✍	6.00	5.00
☐☐	19 Adam Deadmarsh, LosA. ✍	10.00	5.00
☐☐	20 Marc Denis (G), Colu. ✍	15.00	10.00
☐☐	21 Mike York, Edmo. ✍	10.00	5.00
☐☐	22 Johan Hedberg (G), Pitt. ✍	15.00	10.00
☐☐	23 Vincent Damphousse, SanJ. ✍	20.00	15.00
☐☐	24 Marian Hossa, Otta. ✍	35.00	25.00
☐☐	25 Richard Zednik, Mont. ✍	15.00	10.00
☐☐	26 Alexei Yashin, NYIs. ✍	20.00	15.00
☐☐	27 Sergei Gonchar, Wash. ✍	10.00	5.00
☐☐	28 Martin Straka, Pitt. ✍	10.00	5.00
☐☐	29 Ed Jovanovski, Vanc. ✍	15.00	10.00
☐☐	30 Robert Lang, Wash. ✍	6.00	5.00
☐☐	31 Markus Näslund, Vanc. ✍	35.00	25.00
☐☐	32 Mike Sillinger, Colu. ✍	6.00	5.00
☐☐	33 Jamie Storr (G), LosA. ✍	6.00	5.00
☐☐	34 Kimmo Timonen, Nash. ✍	6.00	5.00
☐☐	35 Patrick Lalime (G), Otta. ✍	20.00	15.00
☐☐	36 Alyn McCauley, Toro. ✍	10.00	5.00
☐☐	37 Scott Walker, Nash. ✍	6.00	5.00
☐☐	38 Trevor Linden, Vanc. ✍	15.00	10.00
☐☐	39 Ilya Kovalchuk, Atla. ✍	35.00	25.00
☐☐	40 Jarome Iginla, Calg. ✍	30.00	20.00
☐☐	41 Alex Tanguay, Colo. ✍	20.00	15.00
☐☐	42 Yanic Perreault, Mont. ✍	10.00	5.00
☐☐	43 Jocelyn Thibault (G), Chic. ✍	15.00	10.00
☐☐	44 Eric Brewer, Edmo. ✍	15.00	10.00
☐☐	45 Ray Whitney, Colu. ✍	6.00	5.00
☐☐	46 Ryan Smyth, Edmo. ✍	15.00	10.00
☐☐	47 Steven Reinprecht, Colo. ✍	10.00	5.00
☐☐	48 Phil Housley, Chic. ✍	10.00	5.00
☐☐	49 Milan Hnilicka (G), Atla. ✍	6.00	5.00
☐☐	50 Maxim Afinogenov, Buff. ✍	15.00	10.00
☐☐	51 Andrew Brunette, MinW. ✍	6.00	5.00
☐☐	52 Miroslav Satan, Buff. ✍	10.00	5.00
☐☐	53 Glen Murray, Bost. ✍	15.00	10.00
☐☐	54 Mark Parrish, NYIs. ✍	15.00	10.00
☐☐	55 Daniel Sedin, Vanc. ✍	15.00	10.00
☐☐	56 Brendan Morrison, Vanc. ✍	10.00	5.00
☐☐	57 Brian Rafalski, NJer. ✍	6.00	5.00
☐☐	58 Dan Cloutier (G), Vanc. ✍	15.00	10.00
☐☐	59 Espen Knutsen, Colu. ✍	6.00	5.00
☐☐	60 Radim Vrbata, Colo. ✍	10.00	5.00
☐☐	61 Patrik Stefan, Atla. ✍	10.00	5.00
☐☐	62 Éric Dazé, Chic. ✍	15.00	10.00
☐☐	63 Félix Potvin (G), LosA. ✍	20.00	15.00
☐☐	64 Darcy Tucker, Toro. ✍	6.00	5.00
☐☐	65 José Théodore (G), Mont. ✍	45.00	30.00
☐☐	66 Scott Hartnell, Nash. ✍	6.00	5.00
☐☐	67 Martin Havlat, Otta. ✍	20.00	15.00
☐☐	68 Radek Bonk, Otta. ✍	10.00	5.00
☐☐	69 Patrick Marleau, SanJ. ✍	15.00	10.00
☐☐	70 Andy Delmore, Nash. ✍	6.00	5.00
☐☐	71 Rostislav Klesla, Colu. ✍	10.00	5.00
☐☐	72 David Aebischer (G), Colo. ✍	10.00	5.00
☐☐	73 Steve Shields (G), Bost. ✍	6.00	5.00
☐☐	74 Stu Barnes, Buff. ✍	6.00	5.00
☐☐	75 Tim Connolly, Buff. ✍	15.00	10.00
☐☐	76 Jean-Sébastien Giguère (G), Anah. ✍	35.00	25.00
☐☐	77 Shane Doan, Phoe. ✍	6.00	5.00
☐☐	78 Brian Rolston, Bost. ✍	10.00	5.00
☐☐	79 Shawn McEachern, Atla. ✍	10.00	5.00
☐☐	80 Martin Biron (G), Buff. ✍	15.00	10.00
☐☐	81 Craig Conroy, Calg. ✍	10.00	5.00
☐☐	82 Mika Noronen (G), Buff. ✍	15.00	10.00
☐☐	83 Brian Boucher, Phoe. ✍	10.00	5.00
☐☐	84 Kyle Calder, Chic. ✍	6.00	5.00
☐☐	85 Cliff Ronning, MinW. ✍	6.00	5.00
☐☐	86 Brian Gionta, NJer. ✍	6.00	5.00
☐☐	87 Shawn Bates, NYIs. ✍	6.00	5.00
☐☐	88 Michal Handzus, Phil. ✍	6.00	5.00
☐☐	89 Daniel Brière, Phoe. ✍	15.00	10.00
☐☐	90 Adam Graves, SanJ. ✍	15.00	10.00
☐☐	91 Martin St-Louis, Tamp. ✍	15.00	10.00
☐☐	92 Ladislav Nagy, Phoe. ✍	6.00	5.00
☐☐	93 Oleg Tverdovsky, NJer. ✍	6.00	5.00
☐☐	94 Pavel Brendl, Phil. ✍	10.00	5.00
☐☐	95 Aleksey Morozov, Pitt. ✍	6.00	5.00
☐☐	96 Daymond Langkow, Phoe. ✍	6.00	5.00
☐☐	97 Krys Kolanos, Phoe. ✍	6.00	5.00
☐☐	98 Sean Burke (G), Phoe. ✍	20.00	15.00
☐☐	99 Chris Drury, Calg. ✍	20.00	15.00
☐☐	100 Steve Sullivan, Chic. ✍	10.00	5.00
☐☐	101 Paul Kariya, Anah. ✍ {*}	175.00	85.00
☐☐	102 Peter Forsberg, Colo. ✍ {*}	175.00	85.00
☐☐	103 Ron Tugnutt (G), Dall. ✍ {*}	50.00	25.00
☐☐	104 Manny Legacé (G), Detr. ✍	10.00	5.00
☐☐	105 Tommy Salo (G), Edmo. ✍ {*}	50.00	25.00
☐☐	106 Kristian Huselius, Flor. ✍	10.00	5.00
☐☐	107 Jason Allison, LosA. ✍ {*}	75.00	35.00
☐☐	108 Mariusz Czerkawski, Mont. ✍	6.00	5.00
☐☐	109 Jeff Friesen, NJer. ✍ {*}	40.00	20.00
☐☐	110 Chris Osgood (G), NYIs. ✍ {*}	75.00	35.00
☐☐	111 Martin Prusek (G), Otta. ✍	10.00	5.00
☐☐	112 Steve Yzerman, Detr. ✍ {*}	300.00	150.00
☐☐	113 John LeClair, Phil. ✍ {*}	100.00	50.00
☐☐	114 Jan Hrdina, Pitt. ✍	6.00	5.00
☐☐	115 Tony Amonte, Phoe. ✍ {*}	75.00	35.00
☐☐	116 Teemu Selänne, SanJ. ✍ {*}	100.00	50.00
☐☐	117 Cory Stillman, SLou. ✍	6.00	5.00
☐☐	118 Nikolai Khabibulin (G), Tamp. ✍ {*}	50.00	25.00
☐☐	119 Mats Sundin, Toro. ✍ {*}	125.00	60.00
☐☐	120 Olaf Kölzig (G), Wash. ✍ {*}	75.00	35.00
☐☐	121 Petr Sykora, Anah. ✍	15.00	10.00
☐☐	122 Joe Thornton, Bost. ✍ {*}	150.00	75.00
☐☐	123 Roman Turek (G), Calg. ✍ {*}	60.00	30.00
☐☐	124 Derek Morris, Colo. ✍ {*}	30.00	20.00
☐☐	125 Bill Guerin, Dall. ✍ {*}	50.00	25.00
☐☐	126 Brendan Shanahan, Detr. ✍ {*}	125.00	60.00
☐☐	127 Roberto Luongo (G), Flor. ✍	30.00	20.00
☐☐	128 Zigmund Palffy, LosA. ✍ {*}	75.00	35.00
☐☐	129 Pavol Demitra, SLou. ✍ {*}	50.00	25.00
☐☐	130 Saku Koivu, Mont. ✍ {*}	100.00	50.00
☐☐	131 Joe Nieuwendyk, NJer. ✍ {*}	50.00	25.00
☐☐	132 Michael Peca, NYIs. ✍ {*}	50.00	25.00
☐☐	133 Petr Schastlivy, Otta. ✍	6.00	5.00
☐☐	134 Jeremy Roenick, Phil. ✍ {*}	100.00	50.00
☐☐	135 Mario Lemieux, Pitt. ✍ {**}	6.00	20.00
☐☐	136 Petr Cajanek, SLou. ✍	6.00	5.00
☐☐	137 Vincent Lecavalier, Tamp. ✍ {*}	125.00	60.00
☐☐	138 Peter Bondra, Wash. ✍ {*}	75.00	35.00
☐☐	139 Brent Johnson (G), SLou. ✍ {*}	50.00	25.00
☐☐	140 Sergei Samsonov, Bost. ✍ {*}	75.00	35.00
☐☐	141 Joe Sakic, Colo. ✍ {*}	200.00	100.00
☐☐	142 Brenden Morrow, Dall. ✍	10.00	5.00
☐☐	143 Arturs Irbe (G), Caro. ✍	15.00	10.00
☐☐	144 Chris Chelios, Detr. ✍ {*}	75.00	35.00
☐☐	145 Sandis Ozolinsh, Flor. ✍	6.00	5.00
☐☐	146 Doug Gilmour, Mont. ✍ {*}	75.00	35.00
☐☐	147 Scott Stevens, NJer. ✍ {*}	50.00	25.00
☐☐	148 Sergei Fedorov, Detr. ✍ {*}	125.00	60.00
☐☐	149 Keith Primeau, Phil. ✍ {*}	50.00	25.00
☐☐	150 Eric Boguniecki, SLou. ✍	10.00	5.00
☐☐	151 Shane Willis, Tamp. ✍	6.00	5.00
☐☐	152 Rob Blake, Colo. ✍ {*}	75.00	35.00
☐☐	153 Luc Robitaille, Detr. ✍ {*}	100.00	50.00
☐☐	154 Pierre Turgeon, Dall. ✍ {*}	50.00	25.00
☐☐	155 Curtis Joseph (G), Detr. ✍ {*}	125.00	60.00
☐☐	156 Stephen Weiss, Flor. ✍	20.00	15.00
☐☐	157 Patrik Elias, NJer. ✍ {*}	100.00	50.00
☐☐	158 Mark Recchi, Phil. ✍ {*}	50.00	25.00
☐☐	159 Al MacInnis, SLou. ✍ {*}	50.00	25.00
☐☐	160 Patrick Roy (G), Colo. ✍ {*}	375.00	185.00
☐☐	161 Darryl Sydor, Dall. ✍ {*}	30.00	20.00
☐☐	162 Nicklas Lidström, Detr. ✍ {*}	75.00	35.00
☐☐	163 Doug Weight, SLou. ✍ {*}	75.00	35.00
☐☐	164 Roman Cechmanek (G), Phil. ✍	15.00	10.00
☐☐	165 Marty Turco (G), Dall. ✍	20.00	15.00
☐☐	166 Pavel Datsyuk, Detr. ✍	30.00	20.00
☐☐	167 Chris Pronger, SLou. ✍ {*}	75.00	35.00
☐☐	168 Scott Young, Dall. ✍	10.00	5.00
☐☐	169 Igor Larionov, Detr. ✍ {*}	75.00	35.00
☐☐	170 Keith Tkachuk, SLou. ✍ {*}	75.00	35.00
☐☐	171 Ron Francis, Caro. ✍ {*}	75.00	35.00
☐☐	172 Dan Blackburn (G), NYRa. ✍	15.00	10.00
☐☐	173 Jeff O'Neill, Caro. ✍ {*}	50.00	25.00
☐☐	174 Bobby Holik, NYRa. ✍ {*}	40.00	20.00
☐☐	175 Erik Cole, Caro. ✍	6.00	5.00
☐☐	176 Pavel Bure, NYRa. ✍ {*}	100.00	50.00
☐☐	177 Brian Leetch, NYRa. ✍ {*}	75.00	35.00
☐☐	178 Curtis Sanford (G), SLou. FSC ✍	6.00	5.00
☐☐	179 Carlo Colaiacovo, Toro. FSC ✍	6.00	5.00
☐☐	180 Dennis Seidenberg, Phil. FSC ✍	6.00	5.00
☐☐	181 Adam Hall (G), Nash. FSC ✍	6.00	5.00
☐☐	182 Ivan Majesky, Flor. FSC ✍	6.00	5.00
☐☐	183 Rick Nash, Colu. FSC ✍	60.00	40.00
☐☐	184 Alexei Smirnov, Anah. FSC ✍	6.00	5.00
☐☐	185 Chuck Kobasew, Calg. FSC ✍	10.00	10.00
☐☐	186 Ron Hainsey, Mont. FSC ✍	6.00	5.00
☐☐	187 Stéphane Veilleux, MinW. FSC ✍	6.00	5.00
☐☐	188 Scottie Upshall, Nash. FSC ✍	15.00	10.00
☐☐	189 Lasse Pirjetä, Colu. FSC ✍	6.00	5.00
☐☐	190 Henrik Zetterberg, Detr. FSC ✍	60.00	40.00
☐☐	191 Jay Bouwmeester, Flor. FSC ✍	25.00	15.00
☐☐	192 Alexander Frolov, LosA. FSC ✍	15.00	15.00
☐☐	193 Dmitri Bykov, Detr. FSC ✍	6.00	5.00
☐☐	194 Stanislav Chistov, Anah. FSC ✍	35.00	20.00
☐☐	195 Jordan Leopold, Calg. FSC ✍	6.00	5.00
☐☐	196 Pierre-Marc Bouchard, MinW. FSC ✍	15.00	15.00
☐☐	197 Mike Cammalleri, LosA. FSC ✍	10.00	10.00
☐☐	198 Anton Volchenkov, Otta. FSC ✍	6.00	5.00
☐☐	199 Lynn Loyns, SanJ. FSC ✍	6.00	5.00
☐☐	200 Steve Eminger, Wash. FSC ✍	6.00	5.00

BE A PLAYER GOLF SERIES

Insert Set (100 cards):		100.00
	Insert	**Golf**
☐	GS-1 Adam Foote	1.00
☐	GS-2 Adam Oates	1.00
☐	GS-3 Adrian Aucoin	.75
☐	GS-4 Alex Tanguay	2.00
☐	GS-5 Alexander Mogilny	1.50
☐	GS-6 Alexei Yashin	2.00
☐	GS-7 Alyn McCauley	1.00
☐	GS-8 Andy McDonald	.75
☐	GS-9 Brian Leetch	2.00
☐	GS-10 Bates Battaglia	.75
☐	GS-11 Bobby Holik	1.00
☐	GS-12 Brad Isbister	.75
☐	GS-13 Brendan Morrison	1.00
☐	GS-14 Arturs Irbe (G)	1.00
☐	GS-15 Brian Savage	1.00
☐	GS-16 Bryan Marchment	.75
☐	GS-17 Bryan McCabe	.75
☐	GS-18 Carlo Colaiacovo	.75
☐	GS-19 Chris Drury	2.00
☐	GS-20 Chris Gratton	.75
☐	GS-21 Chris Neil	.75
☐	GS-22 Chris Osgood (G)	2.00
☐	GS-23 Chris Simon	.75
☐	GS-24 Curtis Joseph (G)	3.00
☐	GS-25 Daniel Sedin	1.00
☐	GS-26 Darius Kasparaitis	.75
☐	GS-27 Darren McCarty	1.00
☐	GS-28 Darryl Sittler	2.50
☐	GS-29 David Aebischer (G)	1.00
☐	GS-30 David Legwand	1.00
☐	GS-31 Denis Arkhipov	.75
☐	GS-32 Derek Morris	.75
☐	GS-33 Donald Brashear	.75
☐	GS-34 Doug Gilmour	2.00
☐	GS-35 Ed Belfour (G)	3.00
☐	GS-36 Ed Jovanovski	1.00
☐	GS-37 Erik Cole	.75
☐	GS-38 Eric Lindros	3.00
☐	GS-39 Grant Fuhr (G)	2.00
☐	GS-40 Jaroslav Svoboda	.75
☐	GS-41 Jeff O'Neill	1.00
☐	GS-42 Jarome Iginla	2.50
☐	GS-43 Joe Sakic	5.00
☐	GS-44 Johan Hedberg (G)	1.00
☐	GS-45 Josef Vasicek	.75
☐	GS-46 Jean-Sébastien Giguère (G)	3.00
☐	GS-47 Kenny Jönsson	.75
☐	GS-48 Luc Robitaille	2.50
☐	GS-49 Mario Lemieux	10.00
☐	GS-50 Mark Parrish	1.00
☐	GS-51 Martin Brodeur (G)	5.00
☐	GS-52 Martin Erat	.75
☐	GS-53 Martin Skoula	.75
☐	GS-54 Mats Sundin	3.00
☐	GS-55 Matt Cooke	.75
☐	GS-56 Mattias Öhlund	1.00
☐	GS-57 Mike Dunham (G)	1.00
☐	GS-58 Mike Fisher	.75
☐	GS-59 Mike Keane	.75
☐	GS-60 Michael Peca	1.00
☐	GS-61 Mike Ricci	1.00
☐	GS-62 Milan Hejduk	2.50
☐	GS-63 Miroslav Satan	1.00
☐	GS-64 Nikolai Antropov	.75

- ☐ GS-65 Olaf Kölzig (G) 2.00
- ☐ GS-66 Owen Nolan 2.00
- ☐ GS-67 Pat Verbeek 1.00
- ☐ GS-68 Patrick Marleau 1.50
- ☐ GS-69 Patrick Roy (G) 10.00
- ☐ GS-70 Paul Kariya 4.50
- ☐ GS-71 Peter Bondra 2.00
- ☐ GS-72 Peter Forsberg 4.50
- ☐ GS-73 Petr Sykora 1.00
- ☐ GS-74 Radek Dvorak .75
- ☐ GS-75 Rick DiPietro (G) 1.50
- ☐ GS-76 Rob Blake 2.00
- ☐ GS-77 Robert Lang .75
- ☐ GS-78 Roman Hamrlik .75
- ☐ GS-79 Roman Turek (G) 1.50
- ☐ GS-80 Ron Francis 2.00
- ☐ GS-81 Ryan Smyth 1.50
- ☐ GS-82 Sami Kapanen 1.00
- ☐ GS-83 Scott Hartnell .75
- ☐ GS-84 Scott Stevens 1.00
- ☐ GS-85 Scott Walker .75
- ☐ GS-86 Stan Mikita 2.50
- ☐ GS-87 Stanislav Chistov 1.50
- ☐ GS-88 Steve Konowalchuk .75
- ☐ GS-89 Steve Rucchin .75
- ☐ GS-90 Steve Yzerman 8.00
- ☐ GS-91 Stephen Peat .75
- ☐ GS-92 Steven Reinprecht 1.00
- ☐ GS-93 Teemu Selänne 2.50
- ☐ GS-94 Tie Domi 1.00
- ☐ GS-95 Todd Bertuzzi 4.00
- ☐ GS-96 Todd White .75
- ☐ GS-97 Tom Poti .75
- ☐ GS-98 Trent Klatt .75
- ☐ GS-99 Trevor Kidd (G) 1.00
- ☐ GS-100 Wade Redden 1.00

COMPLETE JERSEY

Insert Set (10 cards): 3700.00
Insert (#/10) CJ

- ☐ Pavel Bure, NYRa. ✂ ✂ ✂ ✂ 225.00
- ☐ Peter Forsberg, Colo. ✂ ✂ ✂ ✂ 400.00
- ☐ Marian Gaborik, MinW. ✂ ✂ ✂ ✂ 300.00
- ☐ Jaromir Jagr, Wash. ✂ ✂ ✂ ✂ 300.00
- ☐ Paul Kariya, Anah. ✂ ✂ ✂ ✂ 400.00
- ☐ Mario Lemieux, Pitt. ✂ ✂ ✂ ✂ 900.00
- ☐ Patrick Roy (G), Colo. ✂ ✂ ✂ ✂ 700.00
- ☐ Joe Sakic, Colo. ✂ ✂ ✂ ✂ 475.00
- ☐ Teemu Selänne, SanJ. ✂ ✂ ✂ ✂ 225.00
- ☐ Steve Yzerman, Detr. ✂ ✂ ✂ ✂ 700.00

DEFENSIVE WALL

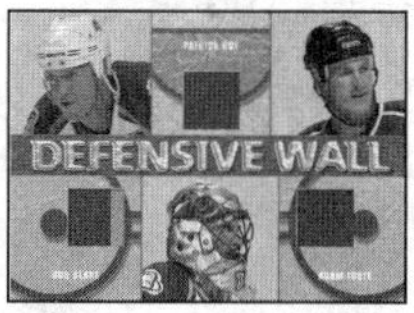

Insert Set (10 cards): 500.00
Insert (#/50) DW

- ☐ DW-1 Blake ✂ / Roy ✂ / Foote ✂ 125.00
- ☐ DW-2 Kaberle ✂ / Belfour (G) ✂ / McCabe ✂ 65.00
- ☐ DW-3 Desjardins ✂ / Cechmanek (G) ✂ / Seidenberg ✂ 40.00
- ☐ DW-4 Leetch ✂ / Blackburn (G) ✂ / Kasparaitis ✂ 50.00
- ☐ DW-5 Zubov ✂ / Turco (G) ✂ / Hatcher ✂ 50.00
- ☐ DW-6 Stevens ✂ / Brodeur (G) ✂ / Niedermayer ✂ 100.00
- ☐ DW-7 Pronger ✂ / Johnson ✂ / MacInnis ✂ 60.00
- ☐ DW-8 Redden ✂ / Lalime (G) ✂ / Phillips ✂ 50.00
- ☐ DW-9 Witt ✂ / Kölzig (G) ✂ / Gonchar ✂ 40.00
- ☐ DW-10 Jovanovski ✂ / Cloutier (G) ✂ / Öhlund ✂ 45.00

FAMOUS SCRAPS

Insert Set (12 cards): 500.00
Insert (#/50) FS

- ☐ FS-1 Dave Schultz ✂ / Tiger Williams ✂ 40.00
- ☐ FS-2 Bob Probert ✂ / Wendel Clark ✂ 60.00
- ☐ FS-3 Ian Laperrière ✂ / Bill Guerin ✂ 40.00
- ☐ FS-4 Peter Worrell ✂ / Chris Gratton ✂ 40.00
- ☐ FS-5 Bill Guerin ✂ / Jarome Iginla ✂ 65.00
- ☐ FS-6 Tie Domi ✂ / Rob Ray ✂ 40.00
- ☐ FS-7 Mike Comrie ✂ / Ilya Kovalchuk ✂ 100.00
- ☐ FS-8 Félix Potvin (G) ✂ / Ron Hextall ✂ 65.00
- ☐ FS-9 Owen Nolan ✂ / Bob Probert ✂ 50.00
- ☐ FS-10 Patrick Roy (G) ✂ / Chris Osgood (G) ✂ 150.00
- ☐ FS-11 Donald Brashear ✂ / Georges Laraque ✂ 40.00
- ☐ FS-12 Matt Johnson ✂ / Sandy McCarthy ✂ 40.00

FOURTH YEAR PHENOMS

Insert Set (12 cards): 300.00
Insert (#/40) FYP

- ☐ Nikolai Antropov, Toro. ✂ 35.00
- ☐ Mike Fisher, Otta. ✂ 35.00
- ☐ Simon Gagné, Phil. ✂ 50.00
- ☐ Scott Gomez, NJer. ✂ 35.00
- ☐ Brent Johnson (G), SLou. ✂ 35.00
- ☐ Espen Knutsen, Colu. ✂ 35.00
- ☐ David Legwand, Nash. ✂ 35.00
- ☐ Roberto Luongo (G), Flor. ✂ 50.00
- ☐ Evgeni Nabokov (G), SanJ. ✂ 35.00
- ☐ Patrik Stefan, Atla. ✂ 35.00
- ☐ Brad Stuart, SanJ. ✂ 35.00
- ☐ Alex Tanguay, Colo. ✂ 35.00

FRANCHISE GAME-USED JERSEY

Insert Set (30 cards): 1400.00
Insert (#/50) FJ

- ☐ Jason Allison, LosA. ✂ 30.00
- ☐ Daniel Brière, Phoe. ✂ 30.00
- ☐ Martin Brodeur (G), NJer. ✂ 100.00
- ☐ Pavel Bure, NYRa. ✂ 50.00
- ☐ Mike Comrie, Edmo. ✂ 50.00
- ☐ Ron Francis, Caro. ✂ 30.00
- ☐ Marian Gaborik, MinW. ✂ 50.00
- ☐ Dany Heatley, Atla. ✂ 50.00
- ☐ Marian Hossa, Otta. ✂ 50.00
- ☐ Jarome Iginla, Calg. ✂ 50.00
- ☐ Jaromir Jagr, Wash. ✂ 50.00
- ☐ Paul Kariya, Anah. ✂ 75.00
- ☐ Vincent Lecavalier, Tamp. ✂ 50.00
- ☐ David Legwand, Nash. ✂ 30.00
- ☐ Mario Lemieux, Pitt. ✂ 200.00
- ☐ Roberto Luongo (G), Flor. ✂ 50.00
- ☐ Mike Modano, Dall. ✂ 50.00
- ☐ Rick Nash, Colu. ✂ 100.00
- ☐ Markus Näslund, Vanc. ✂ 50.00
- ☐ Michael Peca, NYIs. ✂ 30.00
- ☐ Chris Pronger, SLou. ✂ 30.00
- ☐ Jeremy Roenick, Phil. ✂ 50.00
- ☐ Joe Sakic, Colo. ✂ 100.00
- ☐ Miroslav Satan, Buff. ✂ 30.00
- ☐ Teemu Selänne, SanJ. ✂ 50.00
- ☐ Mats Sundin, Toro. ✂ 50.00
- ☐ José Théodore (G), Mont. ✂ 75.00
- ☐ Jocelyn Thibault (G), Chic. ✂ 30.00
- ☐ Joe Thornton, Bost. ✂ 75.00
- ☐ Steve Yzerman, Detr. ✂ 150.00

GAME-USED JERSEY

Insert Set (70 cards): 2000.00
Insert (*90) GJ

- ☐ Daniel Alfredsson, Otta. ✂ 50.00
- ☐ Todd Bertuzzi, Vanc. ✂ 50.00
- ☐ Dan Blackburn (G), NYRa. ✂ 20.00
- ☐ Rob Blake, Colo. ✂ 25.00
- ☐ Peter Bondra, Wash. ✂ 25.00
- ☐ Jay Bouwmeester, Flor. ✂ 40.00
- ☐ Martin Brodeur (G), NJer. ✂ 70.00
- ☐ Pavel Bure, NYRa. ✂ 35.00
- ☐ Mike Cammalleri, LosA. ✂ 25.00
- ☐ Chris Chelios, Detr. ✂ 25.00
- ☐ Stanislav Chistov, Anah. ✂ 40.00
- ☐ Carlo Colaiacovo, Toro. ✂ 20.00
- ☐ Mike Comrie, Edmo. ✂ 35.00
- ☐ Pavel Datsyuk, Detr. ✂ 35.00
- ☐ Sergei Fedorov, Detr. ✂ 40.00
- ☐ Peter Forsberg, Colo. ✂ 60.00
- ☐ Ron Francis, Caro. ✂ 25.00
- ☐ Alexander Frolov, LosA. ✂ 35.00
- ☐ Marian Gaborik, MinW. ✂ 40.00
- ☐ Doug Gilmour, Mont. ✂ 25.00
- ☐ Bill Guerin, Dall. ✂ 20.00
- ☐ Ron Hainsey, Mont. ✂ 20.00
- ☐ Martin Havlat, Otta. ✂ 25.00
- ☐ Dany Heatley, Atla. ✂ 40.00
- ☐ Milan Hejduk, Colo. ✂ 35.00
- ☐ Marian Hossa, Otta. ✂ 40.00
- ☐ Jarome Iginla, Calg. ✂ 35.00
- ☐ Jaromir Jagr, Wash. ✂ 40.00
- ☐ Niko Kapanen, Dall. ✂ 20.00
- ☐ Paul Kariya, Anah. ✂ 60.00
- ☐ Chuck Kobasew, Calg. ✂ 25.00
- ☐ Saku Koivu, Mont. ✂ 35.00
- ☐ Ilya Kovalchuk, Atla. ✂ 40.00
- ☐ Alex Kovalev, Pitt. ✂ 25.00
- ☐ Vincent Lecavalier, Tamp. ✂ 40.00
- ☐ John LeClair, Phil. ✂ 35.00
- ☐ Brian Leetch, NYRa. ✂ 25.00
- ☐ Mario Lemieux, Pitt. ✂ 125.00
- ☐ Jordan Leopold, Calg. ✂ 20.00
- ☐ Nicklas Lidström, Detr. ✂ 25.00
- ☐ Eric Lindros, NYRa. ✂ 40.00
- ☐ Al MacInnis, SLou. ✂ 20.00
- ☐ Mark Messier, NYRa. ✂ 40.00
- ☐ Mike Modano, Dall. ✂ 40.00
- ☐ Alexander Mogilny, Toro. ✂ 20.00
- ☐ Rick Nash, Colu. ✂ 70.00
- ☐ Markus Näslund, Vanc. ✂ 40.00
- ☐ Owen Nolan, SanJ. ✂ 25.00
- ☐ Zigmund Palffy, LosA. ✂ 25.00
- ☐ Chris Pronger, SLou. ✂ 25.00
- ☐ Luc Robitaille, Detr. ✂ 35.00
- ☐ Jeremy Roenick, Phil. ✂ 35.00
- ☐ Patrick Roy (G), Colo. ✂ 100.00
- ☐ Joe Sakic, Colo. ✂ 70.00
- ☐ Sergei Samsonov, Bost. ✂ 25.00
- ☐ Dennis Seidenberg, Phil. ✂ 20.00
- ☐ Teemu Selänne, SanJ. ✂ 35.00
- ☐ Brendan Shanahan, Detr. ✂ 40.00
- ☐ Steve Shields (G), Bost. ✂ 20.00
- ☐ Alexei Smirnov, Anah. ✂ 20.00
- ☐ Jason Spezza, Otta. ✂ 50.00
- ☐ Mats Sundin, Toro. ✂ 40.00
- ☐ José Théodore (G), Mont. ✂ 50.00
- ☐ Joe Thornton, Bost. ✂ 50.00
- ☐ Keith Tkachuk, SLou. ✂ 25.00
- ☐ Marty Turco (G), Dall. ✂ 25.00
- ☐ Scottie Upshall, Nash. ✂ 25.00
- ☐ Doug Weight, SLou. ✂ 25.00
- ☐ Alexei Yashin, NYIs. ✂ 25.00
- ☐ Steve Yzerman, Detr. ✂ 100.00

MAGNIFICENT

Insert Set (10 cards): 900.00
Insert ML

- ☐ Mario Lemieux, Pitt. ✂ (*40) 225.00
- ☐ Mario Lemieux, Pitt. ✂ (*40) 225.00
- ☐ Mario Lemieux, Pitt. ✂ (*40) 225.00
- ☐ Mario Lemieux, Pitt. ✂ (*40) 225.00
- ☐ Mario Lemieux, Pitt. ✂ ✂ (*40) 225.00
- ☐ Mario Lemieux, Pitt. ✂ (*10)
- ☐ Mario Lemieux, Pitt. ✂ (*10)
- ☐ Mario Lemieux, Pitt. ✂ ✂ ✂ (*10)
- ☐ Mario Lemieux, Pitt. ✂ ✂ ✂ ✂ (*10)
- ☐ Mario Lemieux, Pitt. ✂ ✂ ✂ ✂ (*10)

MAGNIFICENT AUTOGRAPHED

Insert Set (10 cards):
Insert ML

- ☐ Mario Lemieux, Pitt. ✍ ✂ (*15)
- ☐ Mario Lemieux, Pitt. ✍ ✂ (*15)
- ☐ Mario Lemieux, Pitt. ✍ ✂ (*15)
- ☐ Mario Lemieux, Pitt. ✍ ✂ (*15)
- ☐ Mario Lemieux, Pitt. ✍ ✂ ✂ (*15)
- ☐ Mario Lemieux, Pitt. ✍ ✂ (*5)
- ☐ Mario Lemieux, Pitt. ✍ ✂ (*5)
- ☐ Mario Lemieux, Pitt. ✍ ✂ ✂ ✂ (*5)
- ☐ Mario Lemieux, Pitt. ✍ ✂ ✂ ✂ ✂ (*5)
- ☐ Mario Lemieux, Pitt. ✍ ✂ ✂ ✂ ✂ (*5)

TEAM QUADS

Insert Set (20 cards): 4000.00
Insert (#/10) TQ

- ☐ TQ-1 Sakic ✂ / Forsberg ✂ / Blake ✂ / Roy ✂ 575.00
- ☐ TQ-2 Belfour (G) ✂ / Sundin ✂ / Mogilny ✂ / Domi ✂ 225.00
- ☐ TQ-3 Roenick ✂ / LeClair ✂ / Recchi ✂ / Cechmanek (G) ✂ 200.00
- ☐ TQ-4 Lindros ✂ / Leetch ✂ / Bure ✂ / Blackburn (G) ✂ 225.00
- ☐ TQ-5 Luongo (G) ✂ / Huselius ✂ / Bouwmeester ✂ / Weiss ✂ 200.00
- ☐ TQ-6 Koivu ✂ / Hossa ✂ / Gilmour ✂ / Théodore (G) ✂ 250.00
- ☐ TQ-7 Stevens ✂ / Niedermayer ✂ / Brodeur (G) ✂ / Elias ✂ 250.00
- ☐ TQ-8 Lemieux ✂ / Kovalev ✂ / Hedberg (G) ✂ / Straka ✂ 375.00
- ☐ TQ-9 Jagr ✂ / Bondra ✂ / Kölzig (G) ✂ / Gonchar ✂ 200.00
- ☐ TQ-10 Potvin ✂ / Deadmarsh ✂ / Frolov ✂ / Allison ✂ 200.00
- ☐ TQ-11 Shields (G) ✂ / Samsonov ✂ / Thornton ✂ / Murray ✂ 200.00
- ☐ TQ-12 Heatley ✂ / Kovalchuk ✂ / Nurminen (G) ✂ / Stefan ✂ 200.00
- ☐ TQ-13 Yzerman ✂ / Fedorov ✂ / Hull ✂ / Lidström ✂ 425.00
- ☐ TQ-14 Bertuzzi ✂ / Näslund ✂ / D. Sedin ✂ / H. Sedin ✂ 250.00
- ☐ TQ-15 Tkachuk ✂ / Pronger ✂ / Weight ✂ / MacInnis ✂ 200.00
- ☐ TQ-16 Turco (G) ✂ / Arnott ✂ / Modano ✂ / Guerin ✂ 200.00
- ☐ TQ-17 Brewer ✂ / Laraque ✂ / Comrie ✂ / Salo ✂ 200.00
- ☐ TQ-18 Damphousse (G) ✂ / Selänne ✂ / Nabokov (G) ✂ / Nolan ✂ 225.00
- ☐ TQ-19 Oates ✂ / Kariya ✂ / Giguère (G) ✂ / Chistov ✂ 275.00
- ☐ TQ-20 Lalime (G) ✂ / Hossa ✂ / Havlat ✂ / Spezza ✂ 225.00

TRIPLE MEMORABILIA

Insert Set (10 cards): 1600.00
Insert (#/30) TM

- ☐ TM-9 Martin Brodeur (G), NJer. ✂ ✂ ✂ 200.00
- ☐ TM-8 Sergei Fedorov, Detr. ✂ ✂ ✂ 125.00
- ☐ TM-7 Brett Hull, Detr. ✂ ✂ ✂ 125.00
- ☐ TM-1 Mario Lemieux, Pitt. ✂ ✂ ✂ 400.00
- ☐ TM-5 Nicklas Lidström, Detr. ✂ ✂ ✂ 75.00
- ☐ TM-6 Patrick Roy (G), Colo. ✂ ✂ ✂ 325.00
- ☐ TM-10 Joe Sakic, Colo. ✂ ✂ ✂ 200.00
- ☐ TM-2 Mats Sundin, Toro. ✂ ✂ ✂ 125.00
- ☐ TM-4 Joe Thornton, Bost. ✂ ✂ ✂ 150.00
- ☐ TM-3 Steve Yzerman, Detr. ✂ ✂ ✂ 325.00

2002 - 03 SLAM CARD

These CD-ROM cards were issued in May 2003.

- ☐ Ed Belfour (G), Toro.
- ☐ Todd Bertuzzi, Vanc.

- Martin Brodeur (G), NJer.
- Pavel Bure, NYRa.
- Roman Cechmanek (G), Phil.
- Chris Chelios, Detr.
- Dan Cloutier (G), Vanc.
- Éric Dazé, Chic.
- Tie Domi, Toro.
- Sergei Fedorov , Detr.
- Theoren Fleury, Chic.
- Adam Foote, Colo.
- Peter Forsberg, Colo.
- Simon Gagné, Phil.
- Milan Hejduk, Colo.
- Bobby Holik, NYRa.
- Phil Housley, Chic.
- Brett Hull, Detr.
- Curtis Joseph (G), Detr.
- Ed Jovanovski, Vanc.
- John LeClair, Phil.
- Brian Leetch, NYRa.
- Trevor Linden, Vanc.
- Eric Lindros, NYRa.
- Al MacInnis, SLou.
- Vladimir Malakhov, NYRa.
- Scott Mellanby, SLou.
- Mark Messier, NYRa.
- Alexander Mogilny, Toro.
- Brendan Morrison, Vanc.
- Glen Murray, Bost.
- Markus Näslund, Vanc.
- Scott Niedermayer, NJer.
- Joe Nieuwendyk, NJer.
- Keith Primeau, Phil.
- Chris Pronger, SLou.
- Brian Rafalski, NJer.
- Markus Recchi, Phil.
- Gary Roberts, Toro.
- Luc Robitaille, Detr.
- Jeremy Roenick, Phil.
- Brian Rolston, Bost.
- Patrick Roy (G), Colo.
- Joe Sakic, Colo.
- Sergei Samsonov, Bost.
- Scott Stevens, NJer.
- Cory Stillman, SLou.
- Steve Sullivan, Chic.
- Mats Sundin, Toro.
- Don Sweeney, Bost.
- Alex Tanguay, Colo.
- Jocelyn Thibault (G), Chic.
- Joe Thornton, Bost.
- Keith Tkachuk, SLou.
- Darcy Tucker, Toro.
- Oleg Tverdovsky, NJer.
- Doug Weight, SLou.
- Steve Yzerman, Detr.
- Rob Zamuner, Bost.
- Alexei Zhamnov, Chic.

2002 - 03 SP AUTHENTIC

Produced by the Upper Deck Company, this series was released in February 2003.

Shell Set (90 cards): 30.00
Complete Set (219 cards): 2300.00
Common Player: .25

Description	Base
1 Jean-Sébastien Giguère (G), Anah.	1.00
2 Paul Kariya, Anah.	1.50
3 Adam Oates, Anah.	.50
4 Dany Heatley, Atla.	1.00
5 Ilya Kovalchuk, Atla.	1.00
6 Joe Thornton, Bost.	1.50
7 Sergei Samsonov, Bost.	.50
8 Steve Shields, Bost.	.25
9 Martin Biron (G), Buff.	.50
10 Miroslav Satan, Buff.	.25
11 Tim Connolly, Buff.	.50
12 Jarome Iginla, Calg.	1.00
13 Roman Turek (G), Calg.	.50
14 Arturs Irbe (G), Caro.	.50
15 Rod Brind'Amour, Caro.	.25
16 Ron Francis, Caro.	.50
17 Alexei Zhamnov, Chic.	.25
18 Éric Dazé, Chic.	.50
19 Jocelyn Thibault (G), Chic.	.50
20 Chris Drury, Calg.	.50
21 Joe Sakic, Colo.	2.00
22 Patrick Roy (G), Colo.	3.50
23 Peter Forsberg, Colo.	1.50
24 Rob Blake, Colo.	.50
25 Ray Whitney, Colu.	.25
26 Marc Denis (G), Colu.	.50
27 Rostislav Klesla, Colu.	.25
28 Bill Guerin, Dall.	.50
29 Marty Turco (G), Dall.	.50
30 Mike Modano, Dall.	1.00
31 Brendan Shanahan, Detr.	1.00
32 Brett Hull, Detr.	1.00
33 Curtis Joseph (G), Detr.	1.00
34 Nicklas Lidström, Detr.	.50
35 Sergei Fedorov, Detr.	1.00
36 Steve Yzerman, Detr.	3.00
37 Mike Comrie, Edmo.	1.00
38 Tommy Salo (G), Edmo.	.50
39 Anson Carter, Edmo.	.50
40 Roberto Luongo (G), Flor.	1.00
41 Olli Jokinen, Flor.	.25
42 Félix Potvin (G), LosA.	.50
43 Zigmund Palffy, LosA.	.50
44 Jason Allison, LosA.	.50
45 Manny Fernandez (G), MinW.	.50
46 Marian Gaborik, MinW.	1.00
47 José Théodore (G), Mont.	1.50
48 Saku Koivu, Mont.	1.00
49 Yanic Perreault, Mont.	.25
50 Tomas Vokoun (G), Nash.	.25
51 David Legwand, Nash.	.50
52 Scott Hartnell, Nash.	.25
53 Martin Brodeur (G), NJer.	2.00
54 Patrik Elias, NJer.	1.00
55 Jeff Friesen, NJer.	.25
56 Alexei Yashin, NYIs.	.50
57 Chris Osgood (G), NYIs.	.50
58 Michael Peca, NYIs.	.50
59 Eric Lindros, NYRa.	1.00
60 Bobby Holik, NYRa.	.25
61 Pavel Bure, NYRa.	1.00
62 Daniel Alfredsson, Otta.	.50
63 Marian Hossa, Otta.	1.00
64 Patrick Lalime (G), Otta.	.50
65 Jeremy Roenick, Phil.	1.00
66 Roman Cechmanek (G), Phil.	.50
67 Simon Gagné, Phil.	1.00
68 John LeClair, Phil.	1.00
69 Sean Burke (G), Phoe.	.50
70 Tony Amonte, Phoe.	.50
71 Daniel Brière, Phoe.	.50
72 Alex Kovalev, Pitt.	.50
73 Mario Lemieux, Pitt.	3.50
74 Evgeni Nabokov (G), SanJ.	.50
75 Owen Nolan, SanJ.	.50
76 Teemu Selänne, SanJ.	1.00
77 Doug Weight, SLou.	.50
78 Pavol Demitra, SLou.	.50
79 Keith Tkachuk, SLou.	.50
80 Nikolai Khabibulin (G), Tamp.	.50
81 Vincent Lecavalier, Tamp.	1.00
82 Alexander Mogilny, Toro.	.50
83 Ed Belfour (G), Toro.	1.00
84 Mats Sundin, Toro.	1.00
85 Markus Näslund, Vanc.	1.00
86 Ed Jovanovski, Vanc.	.50
87 Todd Bertuzzi, Vanc.	1.50
88 Jaromir Jagr, Wash.	1.00
89 Olaf Kölzig (G), Wash.	.50
90 Peter Bondra, Wash.	.50

HAT TRICK PERFORMERS

Insert (*1499)	HTP
91 Paul Kariya, Anah.	8.00
92 Joe Thornton, Bost.	7.00
93 Jarome Iginla, Calg.	5.00
94 Joe Sakic, Colo.	10.00
95 Peter Forsberg, Colo.	8.00
96 Steve Yzerman, Detr.	15.00
97 Brendan Shanahan, Detr.	6.00
98 Brett Hull, Detr.	6.00
99 Wayne Gretzky, LosA.	25.00
100 Eric Lindros, NYRa.	6.00
101 Pavel Bure, All-Star	5.00
102 Mario Lemieux, Pitt.	18.00
103 Keith Tkachuk, SLou.	4.00
104 Todd Bertuzzi, Vanc.	7.00
105 Peter Bondra, Wash.	4.00

FUTURE GREATS

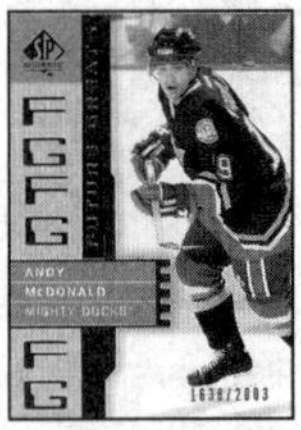

Insert (*2003)	FG
106 Andy McDonald, Anah.	4.00
107 Dany Heatley, Atla.	7.00
108 Ilya Kovalchuk, Atla.	7.00
109 Ivan Huml, Bost.	4.00
110 Maxim Afinogenov, Buff.	4.00
111 Jaroslav Svoboda, Caro.	4.00
112 Kyle Calder, Chic.	4.00
113 Radim Vrbata, Colo.	4.00
114 Rostislav Klesla, Colu.	4.00
115 Pavel Datsyuk, Detr.	6.00
116 Mike Comrie, Edmo.	6.00
117 Marcus Nilson, Flor.	4.00
118 Kristian Huselius, Flor.	4.00
119 Marian Gaborik, MinW.	7.00
120 Mike Ribeiro, Mont.	4.00
121 Scott Hartnell, Nash.	4.00
122 Brian Gionta, NJer.	4.00
123 Raffi Torres, NYIs.	4.00
124 Dan Blackburn (G), NYRa.	4.00
125 Tom Poti, NYRa.	4.00
126 Petr Schastlivy, Otta.	4.00
127 Pavel Brendl, Phil.	4.00
128 Brian Boucher (G), Phoe.	4.00
129 Ville Nieminen, Pitt.	4.00
130 Jeff Jillson, SanJ.	4.00
131 Justin Papineau, SLou.	4.00
132 Brad Richards, Tamp.	4.00
133 Nikita Alexeev, Tamp.	4.00
134 Nikolai Antropov, Toro.	4.00
135 Matt Pettinger, Wash.	4.00

FUTURE WATCH

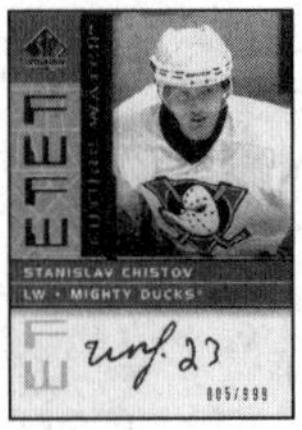

Insert (*900)	FW
136 Martin Gerber (G), Anah. RC	**15.00**
137 Tim Thomas (G), Bost. RC	**15.00**
138 Micki DuPont, Calg. RC	**15.00**
139 Shawn Thornton, Chic. RC	**15.00**
140 Matt Henderson, Chic. RC	**10.00**
141 Jeff Paul, Colo. RC	**10.00**
142 Lasse Pirjetä, Colu. RC	**10.00**
143 Dmitri Bykov, Detr. RC	**15.00**
144 Alex Henry, Wash. RC	**10.00**
145 Kari Haakana, Edmo. RC	**10.00**
146 Ivan Majesky, Flor. RC	**10.00**
147 Sylvain Blouin, Mont. RC	**10.00**
148 Stéphane Veilleux, MinW. RC	**10.00**
149 Greg Koehler, Nash. RC	**10.00**
150 Ray Schultz, NYIs. RC	**10.00**
151 Tomi Pettinen, NYIs. RC	**10.00**
152 Eric Godard, NYIs. RC	**10.00**
153 Dennis Seidenberg, Phil. RC	**15.00**
154 Radovan Somik, Phil. RC	**10.00**
155 Patrick Sharp, Phil. RC	**10.00**
156 Lynn Loyns, SanJ. RC	**10.00**
157 Tom Koivisto, SLou. RC	**10.00**
158 Curtis Sanford (G), SLou. RC	**15.00**
159 Cody Rudkowsky (G), SLou. RC	**15.00**
160 Steve Eminger, Wash. RC	**15.00**
161 Shaone Morrisonn, Bost. RC	**15.00**
162 Anton Volchenkov, Otta. RC	**15.00**
163 Carlo Colaiacovo, Toro. RC	**20.00**
164 Rickard Wallin, MinW. RC	**10.00**
165 Matt Walker, SLou. RC	**10.00**
166 Ryan Miller (G), Buff. RC	**40.00**
167 Levente Szuper (G), Calg. RC	**15.00**
168 Tomas Malec, Caro. RC	**10.00**
169 Jim Fahey, SanJ. RC	**10.00**
170 Jonathan Hedstrom, Anah. RC	**10.00**
171 Michael Leighton (G), Chic. RC	**15.00**
172 Dany Sabourin (G), Calg. RC	**10.00**
173 Mike Cammalleri, LosA. RC	**30.00**
174 Craig Andersson (G), Chic. RC	**20.00**
175 Darren Haydar, Nash. RC	**10.00**
176 Vernon Fiddler, Nash. RC	**10.00**
177 Curtis Murphy, MinW. RC	**10.00**
178 Jared Aulin, LosA. RC	**20.00**
179 Ian MacNeil, Phil. RC	**10.00**
180 Dick Tarnström, Pitt.	10.00

FUTURE WATCH

Insert (*999)	FW
181 Alexei Smirnov, Anah. ✍	30.00
182 Stanislav Chistov, Anah. ✍	100.00
183 Chuck Kobasew, Calg. ✍	30.00
184 Rick Nash, Colu. ✍	225.00
185 Pascal Leclaire (G), Colu. ✍	50.00
186 Henrik Zetterberg, Detr. ✍	250.00
187 Jay Bouwmeester, Flor. ✍	125.00
188 Alexander Frolov, LosA. ✍	50.00
189 Ron Hainsey, Mont. ✍	30.00
190 Adam Hall, Nash. ✍	30.00
191 Jason Spezza, Otta. ✍	175.00
192 Jeff Taffe, Phoe. ✍	30.00
193 Kurt Sauer, Anah. ✍	30.00
194 Alexander Svitov, Tamp. ✍	30.00
195 Mikael Tellqvist (G), Toro. ✍	30.00
196 Jordan Leopold, Calg. ✍	30.00
197 Ales Hemsky, Edmo. ✍	75.00
198 Pierre-Marc Bouchard, MinW. ✍	100.00
199 Scottie Upshall, Nash. ✍	30.00
200 Brooks Orpik, Pitt. ✍	30.00
201 Steve Ott, Dall. ✍	30.00

FUTURE WATCH

These cards were inserted into bonus packs in 2002 - 03 Upper Deck Rookie Update.

Insert (*999)	FW
202 Igor Radulov, Chic. RC	**30.00**
203 Alexei Semenov, Edmo. RC	**15.00**
204 Mike Komisarek, Mont. RC	**20.00**
205 Tomas Surovy, Pitt. RC	**15.00**
206 Jason Bacashihua (G), Dall. RC	**15.00**
207 Ray Emery (G), Otta. RC	**15.00**
208 Fernando Pisani, Edmo. RC	**10.00**
209 Simon Gamache, Atla. RC	**10.00**
210 Ari Ahonen (G), NJer. RC	**20.00**
211 Brandon Reid, Vanc. RC	**30.00**
212 Ryan Bayda, Caro. RC	**10.00**
213 Niko Dimitrakos, SanJ. RC	**10.00**
214 Rob Davison, SanJ. RC	**10.00**
215 Konstantin Koltsov, Pitt. RC	**10.00**
216 Jarret Stoll, Edmo. RC	**20.00**
217 Cristobal Huet, LosA. RC	**15.00**
218 Jason King, Vanc. RC	**10.00**
219 Tomas Kurka, Caro. RC	**10.00**

SIGN OF THE TIMES

Insert Set (33 cards): 1200.00

Insert (1:96)	ST
Maxim Afinogenov, Buff. ✍	15.00
Raymond Bourque, Bost. ✍	40.00
Jay Bouwmeester, Flor. ✍	25.00
Pavel Brendl, Phil. ✍	15.00
Martin Brodeur (G), NJer. ✍	55.00
Pavel Bure, NYRa. ✍	25.00
Erik Cole, Caro. ✍	15.00
Mike Comrie, Edmo. ✍	25.00
Manny Fernandez (G), MinW. ✍	15.00
Alexander Frolov, LosA. ✍	15.00
Simon Gagné, Phil. ✍	25.00
Wayne Gretzky, LosA. ✍	250.00
Martin Havlat, Otta. ✍	20.00
Dany Heatley, Atla. ✍	35.00
Ales Hemsky, Edmo. ✍	25.00
Gordie Howe, Detr. ✍	125.00
Jarome Iginla, Calg. ✍	25.00
Curtis Joseph (G), Detr. ✍	35.00
Nikolai Khabibulin (G), Tamp. ✍	15.00
Milan Kraft, Pitt. ✍	15.00
John LeClair, Phil. ✍	25.00
Evgeni Nabokov (G), SanJ. ✍	20.00
Rick Nash, Colu. ✍	40.00
Markus Näslund, Vanc. ✍	35.00
Bobby Orr, Bost. ✍	225.00
Patrick Roy (G), Colo. ✍	125.00
Sergei Samsonov, Bost. ✍	20.00
Teemu Selänne, SanJ. ✍	25.00
Jason Spezza, Otta. ✍	20.00
Joe Thornton, Bost. ✍	40.00
Justin Williams, Phil. ✍	15.00

☐	Steve Yzerman, Detr. ✍	100.00
☐	Henrik Zetterberg, Detr. ✍	40.00

SIGN OF THE TIMES DUAL

	Insert Set (18 cards):	**2600.00**
	Insert (*99)	**2SotT**
☐	BB B. Orr ✍ / Bouwmeester ✍	275.00
☐	BR P. Roy (G) ✍ / R. Bourque ✍	250.00
☐	CI M. Comrie ✍ / J. Iginla ✍	100.00
☐	GB S.Gagné ✍ / P. Brendl ✍	50.00
☐	GC W. Gretzky ✍ / M. Comrie ✍	325.00
☐	GL S. Gagné ✍ / J. LeClair ✍	100.00
☐	GW W. Gretzky ✍ / G. Howe ✍	600.00
☐	KA I. Kovalchuk ✍ / M. Afinogenov ✍	75.00
☐	KH I. Kovalchuk ✍ / D. Heatley ✍	150.00
☐	KN E. Nabokov (G) ✍ / N. Khabibulin (G) ✍	50.00
☐	LW J. LeClair ✍ / Ju. Williams ✍	50.00
☐	MM M. Brodeur (G) ✍ / M. Ouellet ✍	125.00
☐	OB B. Orr ✍ / R. Bourque ✍	325.00
☐	SN T. Selänne ✍ / E. Nabokov (G) ✍	75.00
☐	ST S.Samsono ✍ / J. Thornton ✍	100.00
☐	SZ J. Spezza ✍ / H. Zetterberg ✍	125.00
☐	YH S. Yzerman ✍ / G. Howe ✍	300.00
☐	YZ S. Yzerman ✍ / H. Zetterberg ✍	200.00

SIGN OF THE TIMES TRIPLE

	Insert Set (5 cards):	**1800.00**
	Insert (*25)	**3SotT**
☐	W. Gretzky ✍ / G. Howe ✍ / B. Orr ✍	1200.00
☐	D. Heatley ✍ / J. Iginla ✍ / M. Comrie ✍	200.00
☐	B. Orr ✍ / R.Bourque ✍ / J. Thornton ✍	500.00
☐	Spezza ✍ / Zetterberg ✍ / Bouwmeester ✍	150.00
☐	J. Thornton ✍ / S.Samsonov ✍ / R. Bourque ✍	250.00

SIGNED FUTURE WATCH PATCH

	Insert Set (15 cards):	**1800.00**
	Insert (*100)	**FWP**
☐	Alexander Frolov, LosA. ✂ ✍	150.00
☐	Ales Hemsky, Edmo. ✂ ✍	175.00
☐	Alexander Svitov, Tamp. ✂ ✍	100.00
☐	Chuck Kobasew, Calg. ✂ ✍	100.00
☐	Adam Hall, Nash. ✂ ✍	75.00
☐	Henrik Zetterberg, Detr. ✂ ✍	300.00
☐	Jay Bouwmeester, Flor. ✂ ✍	175.00
☐	Jordan Leopold, Calg. ✂ ✍	75.00
☐	Jason Spezza, Otta. ✂ ✍	225.00
☐	Pierre-Marc Bouchard, MinW. ✂ ✍	175.00
☐	Ron Hainsey, Mont. ✂ ✍	75.00
☐	Rick Nash, Colu. ✂ ✍	300.00
☐	Stanislav Chistov, Anah. ✂ ✍	175.00
☐	Alexei Smirnov, Anah. ✂ ✍	75.00
☐	Scottie Upshall, Nash. ✂ ✍	100.00

SP LEGENDARY CUTS

	Insert	**Cut**
☐	LC-FB Frank Brlimsek, Bost. ✍	
☐	LC-JA Jack Adams, Detr. ✍	
☐	LC-SA Sid Abel, Detr. ✍	

SUPER PREMIUM

	Insert Set (30 cards):	**300.00**
	Insert (*599)	**SP**
☐	Jason Allison, LosA. ✂	12.00
☐	Martin Biron (G), Buff. ✂	12.00
☐	Daniel Brière, Phoe. ✂	12.00
☐	Martin Brodeur (G), All-Star ✂	20.00
☐	Marc Denis (G), Colu. ✂	12.00
☐	Sergei Fedorov, Detr. ✂	15.00
☐	Peter Forsberg, Colo. ✂	20.00
☐	Simon Gagné, Phil. ✂	12.00
☐	Bill Guerin, Dall. ✂	12.00
☐	Dan Hinote, Colo. ✂	12.00
☐	Jarome Iginla, Calg. ✂	12.00
☐	Jaromir Jagr, Wash. ✂	15.00
☐	Ed Jovanovski, All-Star ✂	12.00
☐	Paul Kariya, Anah. ✂	20.00
☐	Olaf Kölzig (G), Wash. ✂	12.00
☐	Brian Leetch, NYRa. ✂	12.00
☐	Mario Lemieux, Pitt. ✂	45.00
☐	Mike Modano, Dall. ✂	15.00
☐	Aleksey Morozov, Pitt. ✂	12.00
☐	Markus Näslund, Vanc. ✂	15.00
☐	Zigmund Palffy, LosA. ✂	12.00
☐	Jeremy Roenick, Phil. ✂ Black	12.00
☐	Patrick Roy (G), All-Star ✂	35.00
☐	Joe Sakic, Colo. ✂	20.00
☐	Sergei Samsonov, Bost. ✂	12.00
☐	Brendan Shanahan, Detr. ✂	15.00
☐	Mats Sundin, All-Star ✂	15.00
☐	José Théodore (G), Mont. ✂	15.00
☐	Joe Thornton, Bost. ✂	15.00
☐	Steve Yzerman, Detr. ✂	35.00

SUPER PREMIUM DUAL

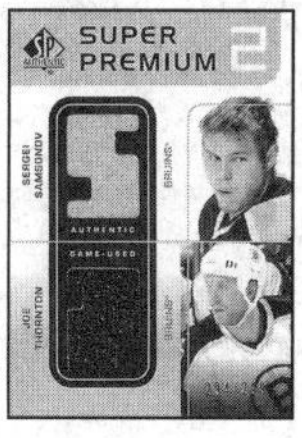

	Insert Set (9 cards):	**300.00**
	Insert (*299)	**2SP**
☐	C/ Drury ✂ / J. Sakic ✂	30.00
☐	P. Forsberg ✂ / P. Roy (G) ✂	55.00
☐	W. Gretzky ✂ / M. Lemieux ✂	200.00
☐	O. Kölzig (G) ✂ / J. Jagr ✂	25.00
☐	M. Modano ✂ / B. Guerin ✂	25.00
☐	J. Roenick ✂ / S. Gagné ✂	25.00
☐	S. Samsonov ✂ Yellow / J. Thornton ✂ Black	25.00
☐	J. Théodore (G) ✂ / S. Koivu ✂	35.00
☐	S. Yzerman ✂ / B. Shanahan ✂	50.00

SUPER PREMIUM TRIPLE

	Insert Set (3 cards):	**1000.00**
	Insert (*15)	**3SP**
☐	W. Gretzky ✂ / M. Lemieux ✂ / S. Yzerman ✂	950.00
☐	P. Roy (G) ✂ / Brodeur (G) ✂ / Belfour (G) ✂	500.00
☐	J. Thornton ✂ / R. Bourque ✂ / C.Neely ✂	350.00

2002 - 03 SP GAME-USED EDITION

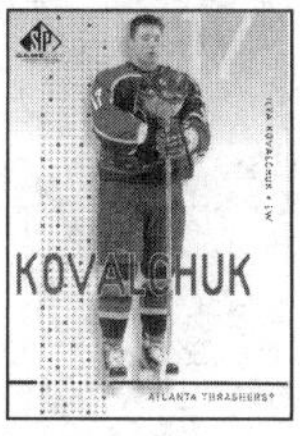

Produced by the Upper Deck Company, this series was released in February 2003.

	Shell Set (50 cards):	**125.00**
	Complete Set (102 cards):	**1,300**
	Common Player:	**1.50**
	Description	**Base**
☐	1 Paul Kariya, Anah.	8.00
☐	2 Ilya Kovalchuk, Atla.	6.00
☐	3 Dany Heatley, Atla.	6.00
☐	4 Joe Thornton, Bost.	7.00
☐	5 Sergei Samsonov, Bost.	3.00
☐	6 Martin Biron (G), Buff.	3.00
☐	7 Jarome Iginla, Calg.	5.00
☐	8 Jeff O_Neill, Caro.	2.00
☐	9 Ron Francis, Caro.	3.00
☐	10 Éric Dazé, Chic.	2.00
☐	11 Peter Forsberg, Colo.	8.00
☐	12 Joe Sakic, Colo.	10.00
☐	13 Patrick Roy (G), Colo.	18.00
☐	14 Marc Denis (G), Colu.	3.00
☐	15 Bill Guerin, Dall.	2.00
☐	16 Mike Modano, Dall.	6.00
☐	17 Steve Yzerman, Detr.	15.00
☐	18 Brendan Shanahan, Detr.	6.00
☐	19 Curtis Joseph (G), Detr.	6.00
☐	20 Mike Comrie, Edmo.	5.00
☐	21 Roberto Luongo (G), Flor.	5.00
☐	22 Félix Potvin (G), LosA.	3.00
☐	23 Zigmund Palffy, LosA.	3.00
☐	24 Marian Gaborik, MinW.	6.00
☐	25 José Théodore (G), Mont.	7.00
☐	26 Saku Koivu, Mont.	5.00
☐	27 Mike Dunham (G), Nash.	2.00
☐	28 Martin Brodeur (G), NJer.	10.00
☐	29 Patrik Elias, NJer.	5.00
☐	30 Michael Peca, NYIs.	2.00
☐	31 Alexei Yashin, NYIs.	3.00
☐	32 Eric Lindros, NYRa.	6.00
☐	33 Pavel Bure, NYRa.	5.00
☐	34 Martin Havlat, Otta.	3.00
☐	35 Daniel Alfredsson, Otta.	3.00
☐	36 Simon Gagné, Phil.	5.00
☐	37 Jeremy Roenick, Phil.	5.00
☐	38 Sean Burke (G), Phoe.	3.00
☐	39 Tony Amonte, Phoe.	3.00
☐	40 Mario Lemieux, Pitt.	18.00
☐	41 Owen Nolan, SanJ.	3.00
☐	42 Evgeni Nabokov (G), SanJ.	3.00
☐	43 Chris Pronger, SLou.	3.00
☐	44 Keith Tkachuk, SLou.	3.00
☐	45 Vincent Lecavalier, Tamp.	6.00
☐	46 Mats Sundin, Toro.	6.00
☐	47 Ed Belfour (G), Toro.	6.00
☐	48 Markus Näslund, Vanc.	6.00
☐	49 Olaf Kölzig (G), Wash.	3.00
☐	50 Jaromir Jagr, Wash.	6.00

ALL-STAR FLASHBACK

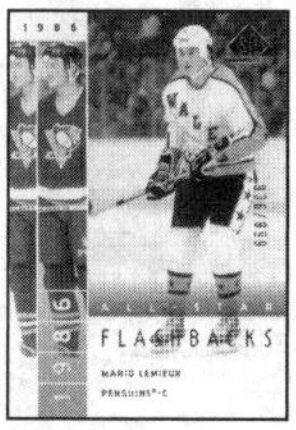

	Insert (*999)	**ASF**
☐	51 Gordie Howe, Detr.	25.00
☐	52 Mario Lemieux, Pitt.	25.00
☐	53 Wayne Gretzky, Edmo.	35.00
☐	54 Mario Lemieux, Pitt.	25.00
☐	55 Wayne Gretzky, LosA.	35.00
☐	56 Vincent Damphousse, Toro.	5.00
☐	57 Brett Hull, SLou.	10.00
☐	58 Mike Richter (G), NYRa.	5.00
☐	59 Raymond Bourque, Bost.	10.00
☐	60 Mark Recchi, Mont.	5.00
☐	61 Teemu Selänne, Anah.	5.00
☐	62 Wayne Gretzky, NYRa.	35.00
☐	63 Pavel Bure, Flor.	5.00
☐	64 Bill Guerin, Bost.	5.00
☐	65 Éric Dazé, Chic.	5.00

NEW GROOVES

	Insert (*750)	**NG**
☐	**66 Alexei Smirnov, Anah. RC**	**25.00**
☐	**67 Stanislav Chistov, Anah. RC**	**50.00**
☐	**68 Martin Gerber (G), Anah. RC**	**15.00**
☐	**69 Kurt Sauer, Anah. RC**	**15.00**
☐	**70 Chuck Kobasew, Calg. RC**	**25.00**
☐	**71 Jordan Leopold, Calg. RC**	**25.00**
☐	**72 Jeff Paul, Colo. RC**	**15.00**
☐	**73 Rick Nash, Colu. RC**	**125.00**
☐	**74 Lasse Pirjetä, Colu. RC**	**15.00**
☐	**75 Henrik Zetterberg, Detr. RC**	**125.00**
☐	**76 Dmitri Bykov, Detr. RC**	**15.00**
☐	**77 Ales Hemsky, Edmo. RC**	**50.00**
☐	**78 Jay Bouwmeester, Flor. RC**	**75.00**
☐	**79 Alexander Frolov, LosA. RC**	**50.00**
☐	**80 Sylvain Blouin, MinW. RC**	**15.00**
☐	**81 Pierre_Marc Bouchard, MinW. RC**	**50.00**
☐	**82 Jason Spezza, Otta. RC**	**100.00**
☐	**83 Ron Hainsey, Mont. RC**	**25.00**
☐	**84 Adam Hall, Nash. RC**	**25.00**
☐	**85 Scottie Upshall, Nash. RC**	**25.00**
☐	**86 Anton Volchenkov, Otta. RC**	**15.00**
☐	**87 Dennis Seidenberg, Phil. RC**	**15.00**
☐	**88 Patrick Sharp, Phil. RC**	**15.00**
☐	**89 Jeff Taffe, Phoe. RC**	**25.00**
☐	**90 Cody Rudkowsky (G), SLou. RC**	**15.00**
☐	**91 Tom Koivisto, SLou. RC**	**15.00**
☐	**92 Curtis Sanford (G), SLou. RC**	**15.00**
☐	**93 Alexander Svitov, Tamp. RC**	**25.00**
☐	**94 Carlo Colaiacovo, Toro. RC**	**25.00**
☐	**95 Steve Eminger, Wash. RC**	**15.00**
☐	**96 Shaone Morrisonn, Bost. RC**	**15.00**
☐	**97 Ryan Miller (G), Buff. RC**	**50.00**
☐	**98 Levente Szuper (G), Calg. RC**	**15.00**
☐	**99 Mike Cammalleri, Calg. RC**	**25.00**
☐	**100 Stéphane Veilleux, MinW. RC**	**15.00**
☐	**101 Lynn Loyns, SanJ. RC**	**15.00**
☐	**102 Mikael Tellqvist (G), Toro. RC**	**15.00**

AUTHENTIC FABRICS

	Insert Set (83 cards):	**1200.00**
	Insert (*225)	**AF**
☐	AF-JA Jason Allison, LosA. ✂	12.00
☐	AF-AM Tony Amonte, Phoe. ✂	12.00

☐	AF-BI Martin Biron (G), Buff. ✂	12.00
☐	AF-BD Peter Bondra, Wash. ✂	12.00
☐	AF-BO Peter Bondra, Wash. ✂	12.00
☐	AF-BB Brian Boucher (G), Phoe. ✂	12.00
☐	AF-BQ Raymond Bourque, Colo. ✂	20.00
☐	AF-RB Raymond Bourque, Colo. ✂	20.00
☐	AF-DB Donald Brashear, Phil. ✂	12.00
☐	AF-MB Martin Brodeur (G), NJer. ✂	35.00
☐	AF-PB Pavel Bure, NYRa. ✂	15.00
☐	AF-CK Roman Cechmanek (G), Phil. ✂	12.00
☐	AF-RC Roman Cechmanek (G), Phil. ✂	12.00
☐	AF-DA Éric Dazé, Chic. ✂	12.00
☐	AF-ED Éric Dazé, Chic. ✂	12.00
☐	AF-PD Pavol Demitra, SLou. ✂	12.00
☐	AF-MD Marc Denis (G), Colu. ✂	12.00
☐	AF-SD Shane Doan, Phoe. ✂	12.00
☐	AF-CD Chris Drury, Calg. ✂	12.00
☐	AF-DR Chris Drury, Calg. ✂	12.00
☐	AF-FV Sergei Fedorov, Detr. ✂	20.00
☐	AF-SF Sergei Fedorov, Detr. ✂	20.00
☐	AF-FO Peter Forsberg, Colo. ✂	30.00
☐	AF-JF Jeff Friesen, NJer. ✂	12.00
☐	AF-GI Jean-Sébastien Giguère (G), Anah. ✂	20.00
☐	AF-JG Jean-Sébastien Giguère (G), Anah. ✂	20.00
☐	AF-GY Wayne Gretzky, NYRa. ✂	80.00
☐	AF-WG Wayne Gretzky, LosA. ✂	80.00
☐	AF-BG Bill Guerin, Bost. ✂	12.00
☐	AF-GU Bill Guerin, Dall. ✂	12.00
☐	AF-HE Milan Hejduk, Colo. ✂	15.00
☐	AF-HO Marian Hossa, Otta. ✂	20.00
☐	AF-MH Marian Hossa, Otta. ✂	20.00
☐	AF-BH Brett Hull, Detr. ✂	20.00
☐	AF-HU Brett Hull, Detr. ✂	20.00
☐	AF-JI Jarome Iginla, Calg. ✂	15.00
☐	AF-JJ Jaromir Jagr, Wash. ✂	20.00
☐	AF-KA Paul Kariya, Anah. ✂	25.00
☐	AF-PK Paul Kariya, Anah. ✂	25.00
☐	AF-SK Saku Koivu, Mont. ✂	15.00
☐	AF-OK Olaf Kölzig (G), Wash. ✂	12.00
☐	AF-IK Ilya Kovalchuk, Atla. ✂	20.00
☐	AF-KK Ilya Kovalchuk, Atla. ✂	20.00
☐	AF-KO Alex Kovalev, Pitt. ✂	12.00
☐	AF-KV Alex Kovalev, Pitt. ✂	12.00
☐	AF-JL John LeClair, Phil. ✂	15.00
☐	AF-BL Brian Leetch, NYRa. ✂	12.00
☐	AF-ML Mario Lemieux, Pitt. ✂	65.00
☐	AF-PM Patrick Marleau, SanJ. ✂	12.00
☐	AF-MM Mike Modano, Dall. ✂	20.00
☐	AF-MO Mike Modano, Dall. ✂	20.00
☐	AF-GM Glen Murray, Bost. ✂	12.00
☐	AF-MN Markus Näslund, Vanc. ✂	20.00
☐	AF-NA Markus Näslund, Vanc. ✂	20.00
☐	AF-ZP Zigmund Palffy, LosA. ✂	12.00
☐	AF-FP Félix Potvin (G), LosA. ✂	12.00
☐	AF-KP Keith Primeau, Phil. ✂	12.00
☐	AF-PU Keith Primeau, Phil. ✂	12.00
☐	AF-MR Mark Recchi, Phil. ✂	12.00
☐	AF-JR Jeremy Roenick, Phil. ✂	15.00
☐	AF-RO Jeremy Roenick, Phil. ✂	15.00
☐	AF-PR Patrick Roy (G), Colo. ✂	45.00
☐	AF-RY Patrick Roy (G), Colo. ✂	45.00
☐	AF-JS Joe Sakic, Colo. ✂	30.00
☐	AF-SC Joe Sakic, Colo. ✂	30.00
☐	AF-SS Sergei Samsonov, Bost. ✂	12.00
☐	AF-SV Sergei Samsonov, Bost. ✂	12.00
☐	AF-SA Miroslav Satan, Buff. ✂	12.00
☐	AF-BS Brendan Shanahan, Detr. ✂	20.00
☐	AF-SN Brendan Shanahan, Detr. ✂	20.00
☐	AF-SH Steve Shields, Bost. ✂	12.00
☐	AF-SU Steve Sullivan, Chic. ✂	12.00
☐	AF-MS Mats Sundin, Toro. ✂	20.00
☐	AF-MT Mats Sundin, Toro. ✂	20.00
☐	AF-AT Alex Tanguay, Colo. ✂	12.00
☐	AF-TA Alex Tanguay, Colo. ✂	12.00
☐	AF-TH José Théodore (G), Mont. ✂	25.00
☐	AF-TT Jocelyn Thibault (G), Chic. ✂	12.00
☐	AF-JT Joe Thornton, Bost. ✂	25.00
☐	AF-RW Ray Whitney, Colu. ✂	12.00
☐	AF-JW Justin Williams, Phil. ✂	12.00
☐	AF-AY Alexei Yashin, NYIs. ✂	12.00
☐	AF-SY Steve Yzerman, Detr. ✂	50.00

AUTHENTIC FABRICS GOLD

	Insert Set (83 cards):	**1700.00**
	Insert (*99)	**AFG99**
☐	AF-JA Jason Allison, LosA. ✂	20.00
☐	AF-AM Tony Amonte, Phoe. ✂	20.00
☐	AF-BI Martin Biron (G), Buff. ✂	20.00
☐	AF-BD Peter Bondra, Wash. ✂	20.00
☐	AF-BO Peter Bondra, Wash. ✂	20.00
☐	AF-BB Brian Boucher (G), Phoe. ✂	20.00

- ☐ AF-BQ Raymond Bourque, Colo. ✂ 25.00
- ☐ AF-RB Raymond Bourque, Colo. ✂ 25.00
- ☐ AF-DB Donald Brashear, Phil. ✂ 20.00
- ☐ AF-MB Martin Brodeur (G), NJer. ✂ 50.00
- ☐ AF-PB Pavel Bure, NYRa. ✂ 25.00
- ☐ AF-CK Roman Cechmanek (G), Phil. ✂ 20.00
- ☐ AF-RC Roman Cechmanek (G), Phil. ✂ 20.00
- ☐ AF-DA Éric Dazé, Chic. ✂ 20.00
- ☐ AF-ED Éric Dazé, Chic. ✂ 20.00
- ☐ AF-PD Pavol Demitra, SLou. ✂ 20.00
- ☐ AF-MD Marc Denis (G), Colu. ✂ 20.00
- ☐ AF-SD Shane Doan, Phoe. ✂ 20.00
- ☐ AF-CD Chris Drury, Calg. ✂ 20.00
- ☐ AF-DR Chris Drury, Calg. ✂ 20.00
- ☐ AF-FV Sergei Fedorov, Detr. ✂ 25.00
- ☐ AF-SF Sergei Fedorov, Detr. ✂ 25.00
- ☐ AF-FO Peter Forsberg, Colo. ✂ 25.00
- ☐ AF-JF Jeff Friesen, NJer. ✂ 20.00
- ☐ AF-GI Jean-Sébastien Giguère (G), Anah. ✂ 25.00
- ☐ AF-JG Jean-Sébastien Giguère (G), Anah. ✂ 25.00
- ☐ AF-GY Wayne Gretzky, NYRa. ✂ 100.00
- ☐ AF-WG Wayne Gretzky, LosA. ✂ 100.00
- ☐ AF-BG Bill Guerin, Bost. ✂ 20.00
- ☐ AF-GU Bill Guerin, Dall. ✂ 20.00
- ☐ AF-HE Milan Hejduk, Colo. ✂ 25.00
- ☐ AF-HO Marian Hossa, Otta. ✂ 25.00
- ☐ AF-MH Marian Hossa, Otta. ✂ 25.00
- ☐ AF-BH Brett Hull, Detr. ✂ 25.00
- ☐ AF-HU Brett Hull, Detr. ✂ 25.00
- ☐ AF-JI Jarome Iginla, Calg. ✂ 25.00
- ☐ AF-JJ Jaromir Jagr, Wash. ✂ 25.00
- ☐ AF-KA Paul Kariya, Anah. ✂ 25.00
- ☐ AF-PK Paul Kariya, Anah. ✂ 25.00
- ☐ AF-SK Saku Koivu, Mont. ✂ 25.00
- ☐ AF-OK Olaf Kölzig (G), Wash. ✂ 20.00
- ☐ AF-IK Ilya Kovalchuk, Atla. ✂ 25.00
- ☐ AF-KK Ilya Kovalchuk, Atla. ✂ 25.00
- ☐ AF-KO Alex Kovalev, Pitt. ✂ 20.00
- ☐ AF-KV Alex Kovalev, Pitt. ✂ 20.00
- ☐ AF-JL John LeClair, Phil. ✂ 25.00
- ☐ AF-BL Brian Leetch, NYRa. ✂ 20.00
- ☐ AF-ML Mario Lemieux, Pitt. ✂ 100.00
- ☐ AF-PM Patrick Marleau, SanJ. ✂ 20.00
- ☐ AF-MM Mike Modano, Dall. ✂ 25.00
- ☐ AF-MO Mike Modano, Dall. ✂ 25.00
- ☐ AF-GM Glen Murray, Bost. ✂ 20.00
- ☐ AF-MN Markus Näslund, Vanc. ✂ 25.00
- ☐ AF-NA Markus Näslund, Vanc. ✂ 25.00
- ☐ AF-ZP Zigmund Palffy, LosA. ✂ 20.00
- ☐ AF-FP Félix Potvin (G), LosA. ✂ 25.00
- ☐ AF-KP Keith Primeau, Phil. ✂ 20.00
- ☐ AF-PU Keith Primeau, Phil. ✂ 20.00
- ☐ AF-MR Mark Recchi, Phil. ✂ 20.00
- ☐ AF-JR Jeremy Roenick, Phil. ✂ 20.00
- ☐ AF-RO Jeremy Roenick, Phil. ✂ 20.00
- ☐ AF-PR Patrick Roy (G), Colo. ✂ 50.00
- ☐ AF-RY Patrick Roy (G), Colo. ✂ 50.00
- ☐ AF-JS Joe Sakic, Colo. ✂ 25.00
- ☐ AF-SC Joe Sakic, Colo. ✂ 25.00
- ☐ AF-SS Sergei Samsonov, Bost. ✂ 20.00
- ☐ AF-SV Sergei Samsonov, Bost. ✂ 20.00
- ☐ AF-SA Miroslav Satan, Buff. ✂ 20.00
- ☐ AF-BS Brendan Shanahan, Detr. ✂ 25.00
- ☐ AF-SN Brendan Shanahan, Detr. ✂ 25.00
- ☐ AF-SH Steve Shields, Bost. ✂ 20.00
- ☐ AF-SU Steve Sullivan, Chic. ✂ 20.00
- ☐ AF-MS Mats Sundin, Toro. ✂ 25.00
- ☐ AF-MT Mats Sundin, Toro. ✂ 25.00
- ☐ AF-AT Alex Tanguay, Colo. ✂ 20.00
- ☐ AF-TA Alex Tanguay, Colo. ✂ 20.00
- ☐ AF-TH José Théodore (G), Mont. ✂ 25.00
- ☐ AF-TT Jocelyn Thibault (G), Chic. ✂ 20.00
- ☐ AF-JT Joe Thornton, Bost. ✂ 25.00
- ☐ AF-RW Ray Whitney, Colu. ✂ 20.00
- ☐ AF-JW Justin Williams, Phil. ✂ 20.00
- ☐ AF-AY Alexei Yashin, NYIs. ✂ 20.00
- ☐ AF-SY Steve Yzerman, Detr. ✂ 75.00

AUTHENTIC FABRICS RAINBOW

Insert (*10) AF10

- ☐ AF-JA Jason Allison, LosA. ✂ 100.00
- ☐ AF-AM Tony Amonte, Phoe. ✂ 100.00
- ☐ AF-BI Martin Biron (G), Buff. ✂ 100.00
- ☐ AF-BD Peter Bondra, Wash. ✂ 100.00
- ☐ AF-BO Peter Bondra, Wash. ✂ 100.00
- ☐ AF-BB Brian Boucher (G), Phoe. ✂ 80.00
- ☐ AF-BQ Raymond Bourque, Colo. ✂ 200.00
- ☐ AF-RB Raymond Bourque, Colo. ✂ 200.00
- ☐ AF-DB Donald Brashear, Phil. ✂ 80.00
- ☐ AF-MB Martin Brodeur (G), NJer. ✂ 350.00
- ☐ AF-PB Pavel Bure, NYRa. ✂ 150.00
- ☐ AF-CK Roman Cechmanek (G), Phil. ✂ 80.00
- ☐ AF-RC Roman Cechmanek (G), Phil. ✂ 80.00
- ☐ AF-DA Éric Dazé, Chic. ✂ 80.00
- ☐ AF-ED Éric Dazé, Chic. ✂ 80.00
- ☐ AF-PD Pavol Demitra, SLou. ✂ 80.00
- ☐ AF-MD Marc Denis (G), Colu. ✂ 100.00
- ☐ AF-SD Shane Doan, Phoe. ✂ 80.00
- ☐ AF-CD Chris Drury, Calg. ✂ 100.00
- ☐ AF-DR Chris Drury, Calg. ✂ 100.00
- ☐ AF-FV Sergei Fedorov, Detr. ✂ 200.00
- ☐ AF-SF Sergei Fedorov, Detr. ✂ 200.00
- ☐ AF-FO Peter Forsberg, Colo. ✂ 300.00
- ☐ AF-JF Jeff Friesen, NJer. ✂ 80.00
- ☐ AF-GI Jean-Sébastien Giguère (G), Anah. ✂ 200.00
- ☐ AF-JG Jean-Sébastien Giguère (G), Anah. ✂ 200.00
- ☐ AF-GY Wayne Gretzky, NYRa. ✂ 800.00
- ☐ AF-WG Wayne Gretzky, LosA. ✂ 800.00
- ☐ AF-BG Bill Guerin, Bost. ✂ 80.00
- ☐ AF-GU Bill Guerin, Dall. ✂ 80.00
- ☐ AF-HE Milan Hejduk, Colo. ✂ 150.00
- ☐ AF-HO Marian Hossa, Otta. ✂ 200.00
- ☐ AF-MH Marian Hossa, Otta. ✂ 200.00
- ☐ AF-BH Brett Hull, Detr. ✂ 200.00
- ☐ AF-HU Brett Hull, Detr. ✂ 200.00
- ☐ AF-JI Jarome Iginla, Calg. ✂ 150.00
- ☐ AF-JJ Jaromir Jagr, Wash. ✂ 200.00
- ☐ AF-KA Paul Kariya, Anah. ✂ 250.00
- ☐ AF-PK Paul Kariya, Anah. ✂ 250.00
- ☐ AF-SK Saku Koivu, Mont. ✂ 250.00
- ☐ AF-OK Olaf Kölzig (G), Wash. ✂ 100.00
- ☐ AF-IK Ilya Kovalchuk, Atla. ✂ 200.00
- ☐ AF-KK Ilya Kovalchuk, Atla. ✂ 200.00
- ☐ AF-KO Alex Kovalev, Pitt. ✂ 100.00
- ☐ AF-KV Alex Kovalev, Pitt. ✂ 100.00
- ☐ AF-JL John LeClair, Phil. ✂ 150.00
- ☐ AF-BL Brian Leetch, NYRa. ✂ 100.00
- ☐ AF-ML Mario Lemieux, Pitt. ✂ 650.00
- ☐ AF-PM Patrick Marleau, SanJ. ✂ 100.00
- ☐ AF-MM Mike Modano, Dall. ✂ 200.00
- ☐ AF-MO Mike Modano, Dall. ✂ 200.00
- ☐ AF-GM Glen Murray, Bost. ✂ 100.00
- ☐ AF-MN Markus Näslund, Vanc. ✂ 200.00
- ☐ AF-NA Markus Näslund, Vanc. ✂ 200.00
- ☐ AF-ZP Zigmund Palffy, LosA. ✂ 100.00
- ☐ AF-FP Félix Potvin (G), LosA. ✂ 250.00
- ☐ AF-KP Keith Primeau, Phil. ✂ 80.00
- ☐ AF-PU Keith Primeau, Phil. ✂ 80.00
- ☐ AF-MR Mark Recchi, Phil. ✂ 80.00
- ☐ AF-JR Jeremy Roenick, Phil. ✂ 150.00
- ☐ AF-RO Jeremy Roenick, Phil. ✂ 150.00
- ☐ AF-PR Patrick Roy (G), Colo. ✂ 450.00
- ☐ AF-RY Patrick Roy (G), Colo. ✂ 450.00
- ☐ AF-JS Joe Sakic, Colo. ✂ 300.00
- ☐ AF-SC Joe Sakic, Colo. ✂ 300.00
- ☐ AF-SS Sergei Samsonov, Bost. ✂ 100.00
- ☐ AF-SV Sergei Samsonov, Bost. ✂ 100.00
- ☐ AF-SA Miroslav Satan, Buff. ✂ 80.00
- ☐ AF-BS Brendan Shanahan, Detr. ✂ 200.00
- ☐ AF-SN Brendan Shanahan, Detr. ✂ 200.00
- ☐ AF-SH Steve Shields, Bost. ✂ 80.00
- ☐ AF-SU Steve Sullivan, Chic. ✂ 80.00
- ☐ AF-MS Mats Sundin, Toro. ✂ 200.00
- ☐ AF-MT Mats Sundin, Toro. ✂ 200.00
- ☐ AF-AT Alex Tanguay, Colo. ✂ 100.00
- ☐ AF-TA Alex Tanguay, Colo. ✂ 100.00
- ☐ AF-TH José Théodore (G), Mont. ✂ 250.00
- ☐ AF-TT Jocelyn Thibault (G), Chic. ✂ 80.00
- ☐ AF-JT Joe Thornton, Bost. ✂ 250.00
- ☐ AF-RW Ray Whitney, Colu. ✂ 80.00
- ☐ AF-JW Justin Williams, Phil. ✂ 80.00
- ☐ AF-AY Alexei Yashin, NYIs. ✂ 100.00
- ☐ AF-SY Steve Yzerman, Detr. ✂ 500.00

AUTHENTIC FABRICS COMBO

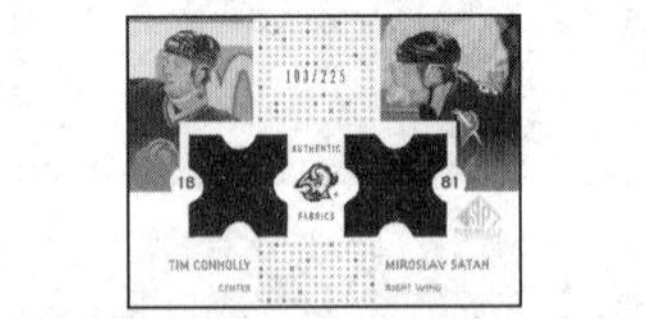

Insert Set (31 cards): 500.00

Insert (*225) 2AFC

- ☐ CF-CS T. Connolly ✂ / M. Satan ✂ 20.00
- ☐ CF-DT P. Demitra ✂ / K.Tkachuk ✂ 20.00
- ☐ CF-JB J. Jagr ✂ / P.Bondra ✂ 20.00
- ☐ CF-LK M. Lemieux ✂ / P. Kariya ✂ 55.00
- ☐ CF-NB J.Nieuwendyk ✂ / M. Brodeur (G) ✂ 25.00
- ☐ CF-SH B.Shanahan ✂ / B. Hull ✂ 25.00
- ☐ CF-TB J.Thibault (G) ✂ / M. Brodeur (G) ✂ 25.00
- ☐ CF-TK J.Théodore (G) ✂ / S.Koivu ✂ 25.00
- ☐ CF-TL K. Tkachuk ✂ / J. LeClair ✂ 20.00
- ☐ CF-TS J. Thornton ✂ / S. Samsonov ✂ 20.00
- ☐ CF-WD D. Weight ✂ / P. Demitra ✂ 20.00
- ☐ CF-YR S. Yzerman ✂ / L. Robitaille ✂ 40.00
- ☐ CF-FO Peter Forsberg, Colo. ✂ ✂ 35.00
- ☐ CF-GR Wayne Gretzky, NYRa. ✂ ✂ 90.00
- ☐ CF-WG Wayne Gretzky, LosA. ✂ ✂ 90.00
- ☐ CF-JJ Jaromir Jagr, Wash. ✂ ✂ 25.00
- ☐ CF-MO Mike Modano, Dall. ✂ ✂ 25.00
- ☐ CF-FP Félix Potvin (G), LosA. ✂ ✂ 20.00
- ☐ CF-JS Joe Sakic, Colo. ✂ ✂ 40.00

AUTHENTIC FABRICS COMBO GOLD

Insert Set (31 cards): 600.00

Insert (*99) 2AFG99

- ☐ CF-CS T. Connolly ✂ / M. Satan ✂ 20.00
- ☐ CF-DT P. Demitra ✂ / K.Tkachuk ✂ 20.00
- ☐ CF-JB J. Jagr ✂ / P.Bondra ✂ 25.00
- ☐ CF-LK M. Lemieux ✂ / P. Kariya ✂ 75.00
- ☐ CF-NB J.Nieuwendyk ✂ / M. Brodeur (G) ✂ 25.00
- ☐ CF-SH B.Shanahan ✂ / B. Hull ✂ 25.00
- ☐ CF-TB J.Thibault (G) ✂ / M. Brodeur (G) ✂ 25.00
- ☐ CF-TK J.Théodore (G) ✂ / S.Koivu ✂ 25.00
- ☐ CF-TL K. Tkachuk ✂ / J. LeClair ✂ 25.00
- ☐ CF-TS J. Thornton ✂ / S. Samsonov ✂ 25.00
- ☐ CF-WD D. Weight ✂ / P. Demitra ✂ 20.00
- ☐ CF-YR S. Yzerman ✂ / L. Robitaille ✂ 50.00
- ☐ CF-FO Peter Forsberg, Colo. ✂ ✂ 50.00
- ☐ CF-GR Wayne Gretzky, NYRa. ✂ ✂ 125.00
- ☐ CF-WG Wayne Gretzky, LosA. ✂ ✂ 125.00
- ☐ CF-JJ Jaromir Jagr, Wash. ✂ ✂ 25.00
- ☐ CF-MO Mike Modano, Dall. ✂ ✂ 25.00
- ☐ CF-FP Félix Potvin (G), LosA. ✂ ✂ 25.00
- ☐ CF-JS Joe Sakic, Colo. ✂ ✂ 50.00

AUTHENTIC FABRICS COMBO RAINBOW

Insert (*10) 2AF10

- ☐ CF-CS T. Connolly ✂ / M. Satan ✂ 80.00
- ☐ CF-DT P. Demitra ✂ / K.Tkachuk ✂ 125.00
- ☐ CF-JB J. Jagr ✂ / P.Bondra ✂ 200.00
- ☐ CF-LK M. Lemieux ✂ / P. Kariya ✂ 550.00
- ☐ CF-NB J.Nieuwendyk ✂ / M. Brodeur (G) ✂ 250.00
- ☐ CF-SH B.Shanahan ✂ / B. Hull ✂ 250.00
- ☐ CF-TB J.Thibault (G) ✂ / M. Brodeur (G) ✂ 250.00
- ☐ CF-TK J.Théodore (G) ✂ / S.Koivu ✂ 300.00
- ☐ CF-TL K. Tkachuk ✂ / J. LeClair ✂ 175.00
- ☐ CF-TS J. Thornton ✂ / S. Samsonov ✂ 225.00
- ☐ CF-WD D. Weight ✂ / P. Demitra ✂ 125.00
- ☐ CF-YR S. Yzerman ✂ / L. Robitaille ✂ 400.00
- ☐ CF-FO Peter Forsberg, Colo. ✂ ✂ 350.00
- ☐ CF-GR Wayne Gretzky, NYRa. ✂ ✂ 900.00
- ☐ CF-WG Wayne Gretzky, LosA. ✂ ✂ 900.00
- ☐ CF-JJ Jaromir Jagr, Wash. ✂ ✂ 250.00
- ☐ CF-MO Mike Modano, Dall. ✂ ✂ 250.00
- ☐ CF-FP Félix Potvin (G), LosA. ✂ ✂ 300.00
- ☐ CF-JS Joe Sakic, Colo. ✂ ✂ 400.00

FIRST ROUNDERS

Insert Set (58 cards): 4000.00

Insert (*30) Patch

- ☐ Jason Allison, LosA. ✂ 80.00
- ☐ Jason Arnott, Dall. ✂ 80.00
- ☐ Martin Biron (G), Buff. ✂ 80.00
- ☐ Dan Blackburn (G), NYRa. ✂ 80.00
- ☐ Brian Boucher (G), Phil. ✂ 80.00
- ☐ Raymond Bourque, Bost. ✂ 100.00
- ☐ Daniel Brière, Phoe. ✂ 80.00
- ☐ Martin Brodeur (G), NJer. ✂ 125.00
- ☐ Tim Connolly, Buff. ✂ 80.00
- ☐ Adam Deadmarsh, LosA. ✂ 80.00
- ☐ Marc Denis (G), Colu. ✂ 80.00
- ☐ Shane Doan, Phoe. ✂ 80.00
- ☐ Jean-Pierre Dumont, Buff. ✂ 80.00
- ☐ Peter Forsberg, Colo. ✂ 100.00
- ☐ Simon Gagné, Phil. ✂ 80.00
- ☐ Jean-Sébastien Giguère (G), Anah. ✂ 80.00
- ☐ Sergei Gonchar, Wash. ✂ 80.00
- ☐ Bill Guerin, Dall. ✂ 80.00
- ☐ Scott Hartnell, Nash. ✂ 80.00
- ☐ Jarome Iginla, Calg. ✂ 80.00
- ☐ Jaromir Jagr, Wash. ✂ 80.00
- ☐ Paul Kariya, Anah. ✂ 100.00
- ☐ Rostislav Klesla, Colu. ✂ 80.00
- ☐ Saku Koivu, Mont. ✂ 100.00
- ☐ Krys Kolanos, Phoe. ✂ 80.00
- ☐ Olaf Kölzig (G), Wash. ✂ 80.00
- ☐ Ilya Kovalchuk, Atla. ✂ 80.00
- ☐ Alex Kovalev, Pitt. ✂ 80.00
- ☐ Vincent Lecavalier, Tamp. ✂ 80.00
- ☐ Brian Leetch, NYRa. ✂ 80.00
- ☐ David Legwand, Nash. ✂ 80.00
- ☐ Mario Lemieux, Pitt. ✂ 250.00
- ☐ Trevor Linden, Anah. ✂ 80.00
- ☐ Eric Lindros, NYRa. ✂ 80.00
- ☐ Roberto Luongo (G), Flor. ✂ 80.00
- ☐ Manny Malhotra, NYRa. ✂ 80.00
- ☐ Patrick Marleau, SanJ. ✂ 80.00
- ☐ Mike Modano, Dall. ✂ 80.00
- ☐ Markus Näslund, Vanc. ✂ 80.00
- ☐ Owen Nolan, SanJ. ✂ 80.00
- ☐ Mika Noronen (G), Buff. ✂ 80.00
- ☐ Keith Primeau, Phil. ✂ 80.00
- ☐ Chris Pronger, SLou. ✂ 80.00
- ☐ Taylor Pyatt, Buff. ✂ 80.00
- ☐ Jeremy Roenick, Phoe. ✂ 80.00
- ☐ Joe Sakic, Colo. ✂ 125.00
- ☐ Sergei Samsonov, Bost. ✂ 80.00
- ☐ Teemu Selänne, SanJ. ✂ 80.00
- ☐ Brendan Shanahan, Detr. ✂ 80.00
- ☐ Patrik Stefan, Atla. ✂ 80.00
- ☐ Mats Sundin, Toro. ✂ 80.00
- ☐ Alex Tanguay, Colo. ✂ 80.00
- ☐ Joe Thornton, Bost. ✂ 100.00
- ☐ Keith Tkachuk, SLou. ✂ 80.00
- ☐ Raffi Torres, NYIs. ✂ 80.00
- ☐ Justin Williams, Phil. ✂ 80.00
- ☐ Alexei Yashin, NYIs. ✂ 80.00
- ☐ Steve Yzerman, Detr. ✂ 200.00

FUTURE FABRICS

Insert Set (31 cards): 300.00

Insert (*225) FF

- ☐ FF-AE David Aebischer (G), Colo. ✂ 12.00
- ☐ FF-MA Maxim Afinogenov, Buff. ✂ 12.00
- ☐ FF-DA Denis (G) Arkhipov, Nash. ✂ 12.00
- ☐ FF-EB Éric Bélanger, LosA. ✂ 12.00
- ☐ FF-MB Mark Bell, Chic. ✂ 12.00
- ☐ FF-PB Pavel Brendl, Phil. ✂ 12.00
- ☐ FF-DB Daniel Brière, Phoe. ✂ 12.00
- ☐ FF-IB Ilja Bryzgalov, Anah. ✂ 12.00
- ☐ FF-CA Kyle Calder, Chic. ✂ 12.00
- ☐ FF-KC Kyle Calder, Chic. ✂ 12.00
- ☐ FF-TC Tim Connolly, Buff. ✂ 12.00
- ☐ FF-ME Martin Erat, Nash. ✂ 12.00
- ☐ FF-SG Simon Gagné, Phil. ✂ 15.00
- ☐ FF-JG Jean-Sébastien Giguère (G), Anah. ✂ 20.00
- ☐ FF-HA Jeff Halpern, Wash. ✂ 12.00
- ☐ FF-JH Jeff Halpern, Wash. ✂ 12.00
- ☐ FF-SH Scott Hartnell, Nash. ✂ 12.00
- ☐ FF-BJ Brent Johnson (G), SLou. ✂ 12.00
- ☐ FF-RK Rostislav Klesla, Colu. ✂ 12.00
- ☐ FF-IK Ilya Kovalchuk, Atla. ✂ 20.00
- ☐ FF-KO Ilya Kovalchuk, Atla. ✂ 20.00
- ☐ FF-MM Manny Malhotra, Dall. ✂ 12.00
- ☐ FF-BM Brenden Morrow, Dall. ✂ 12.00
- ☐ FF-VN Ville Nieminen, Pitt. ✂ 12.00
- ☐ FF-MP Matt Pettinger, Wash. ✂ 12.00
- ☐ FF-TP Taylor Pyatt, Buff. ✂ 12.00
- ☐ FF-SR Steven Reinprecht, Colo. ✂ 12.00
- ☐ FF-MR Mike Ribeiro, Mont. ✂ 12.00
- ☐ FF-RI Mike Ribeiro, Mont. ✂ 12.00
- ☐ FF-AT Alex Tanguay, Colo. ✂ 12.00
- ☐ FF-MT Marty Turco (G), Dall. ✂ 12.00

FUTURE FABRICS GOLD

Insert Set (31 cards): 500.00

Insert (*99) FFG99

- ☐ FF-AE David Aebischer (G), Colo. ✂ 20.00
- ☐ FF-MA Maxim Afinogenov, Buff. ✂ 20.00
- ☐ FF-DA Denis (G) Arkhipov, Nash. ✂ 20.00
- ☐ FF-EB Éric Bélanger, LosA. ✂ 20.00
- ☐ FF-MB Mark Bell, Chic. ✂ 20.00
- ☐ FF-PB Pavel Brendl, Phil. ✂ 20.00
- ☐ FF-DB Daniel Brière, Phoe. ✂ 20.00
- ☐ FF-IB Ilja Bryzgalov, Anah. ✂ 20.00
- ☐ FF-CA Kyle Calder, Chic. ✂ 20.00
- ☐ FF-KC Kyle Calder, Chic. ✂ 20.00
- ☐ FF-TC Tim Connolly, Buff. ✂ 20.00
- ☐ FF-ME Martin Erat, Nash. ✂ 20.00
- ☐ FF-SG Simon Gagné, Phil. ✂ 25.00
- ☐ FF-JG Jean-Sébastien Giguère (G), Anah. ✂ 30.00
- ☐ FF-HA Jeff Halpern, Wash. ✂ 20.00
- ☐ FF-JH Jeff Halpern, Wash. ✂ 20.00
- ☐ FF-SH Scott Hartnell, Nash. ✂ 20.00
- ☐ FF-BJ Brent Johnson (G), SLou. ✂ 20.00
- ☐ FF-RK Rostislav Klesla, Colu. ✂ 20.00
- ☐ FF-IK Ilya Kovalchuk, Atla. ✂ 30.00
- ☐ FF-KO Ilya Kovalchuk, Atla. ✂ 30.00
- ☐ FF-MM Manny Malhotra, Dall. ✂ 20.00
- ☐ FF-BM Brenden Morrow, Dall. ✂ 20.00
- ☐ FF-VN Ville Nieminen, Pitt. ✂ 20.00
- ☐ FF-MP Matt Pettinger, Wash. ✂ 20.00
- ☐ FF-TP Taylor Pyatt, Buff. ✂ 20.00
- ☐ FF-SR Steven Reinprecht, Colo. ✂ 20.00
- ☐ FF-MR Mike Ribeiro, Mont. ✂ 20.00
- ☐ FF-RI Mike Ribeiro, Mont. ✂ 20.00
- ☐ FF-AT Alex Tanguay, Colo. ✂ 20.00
- ☐ FF-MT Marty Turco (G), Dall. ✂ 20.00

FUTURE FABRICS RAINBOW

Insert (*10) AF10

- ☐ FF-AE David Aebischer (G), Colo. ✂ 80.00
- ☐ FF-MA Maxim Afinogenov, Buff. ✂ 80.00
- ☐ FF-DA Denis (G) Arkhipov, Nash. ✂ 80.00
- ☐ FF-EB Éric Bélanger, LosA. ✂ 80.00
- ☐ FF-MB Mark Bell, Chic. ✂ 80.00
- ☐ FF-PB Pavel Brendl, Phil. ✂ 80.00
- ☐ FF-DB Daniel Brière, Phoe. ✂ 100.00
- ☐ FF-IB Ilja Bryzgalov, Anah. ✂ 80.00
- ☐ FF-CA Kyle Calder, Chic. ✂ 80.00
- ☐ FF-KC Kyle Calder, Chic. ✂ 80.00
- ☐ FF-TC Tim Connolly, Buff. ✂ 80.00
- ☐ FF-ME Martin Erat, Nash. ✂ 80.00
- ☐ FF-SG Simon Gagné, Phil. ✂ 150.00

☐ FF-JG Jean-Sébastien Giguère (G), Anah. ✂ 200.00
☐ FF-HA Jeff Halpern, Wash. ✂ 80.00
☐ FF-JH Jeff Halpern, Wash. ✂ 80.00
☐ FF-SH Scott Hartnell, Nash. ✂ 80.00
☐ FF-BJ Brent Johnson (G), SLou. ✂ 80.00
☐ FF-RK Rostislav Klesla, Colu. ✂ 100.00
☐ FF-IK Ilya Kovalchuk, Atla. ✂ 200.00
☐ FF-KO Ilya Kovalchuk, Atla. ✂ 200.00
☐ FF-MM Manny Malhotra, Dall. ✂ 80.00
☐ FF-BM Brenden Morrow, Dall. ✂ 80.00
☐ FF-VN Ville Nieminen, Pitt. ✂ 80.00
☐ FF-MP Matt Pettinger, Wash. ✂ 80.00
☐ FF-TP Taylor Pyatt, Buff. ✂ 80.00
☐ FF-SR Steven Reinprecht, Colo. ✂ 80.00
☐ FF-MR Mike Ribeiro, Mont. ✂ 80.00
☐ FF-RI Mike Ribeiro, Mont. ✂ 80.00
☐ FF-AT Alex Tanguay, Colo. ✂ 100.00
☐ FF-MT Marty Turco (G), Dall. ✂ 100.00

PIECE OF HISTORY

Insert Set (87 cards): 1200.00
Insert (*225) POH225

☐ PH-AL Jason Allison, LosA. ✂ 12.00
☐ PH-JA Jason Allison, LosA. ✂ 12.00
☐ PH-AM Tony Amonte, Phoe. ✂ 12.00
☐ PH-BI Martin Biron (G), Buff. ✂ 12.00
☐ PH-RO Rob Blake, Colo. ✂ 12.00
☐ PH-BD Peter Bondra, Wash. ✂ 12.00
☐ PH-BO Peter Bondra, Wash. ✂ 12.00
☐ PH-BQ Raymond Bourque, Colo. ✂ 20.00
☐ PH-RB Raymond Bourque, Bost. ✂ 20.00
☐ PH-MB Martin Brodeur (G), NJer. ✂ 35.00
☐ PH-PB Pavel Bure, NYRa. ✂ 15.00
☐ PH-SB Sean Burke (G), Phoe. ✂ 12.00
☐ PH-CK Roman Cechmanek (G), Phil. ✂ 12.00
☐ PH-RC Roman Cechmanek (G), Phil. ✂ 12.00
☐ PH-CC Chris Chelios, Detr. ✂ 12.00
☐ PH-TC Tim Connolly, Buff. ✂ 12.00
☐ PH-ED Éric Dazé, Chic. ✂ 12.00
☐ PH-AD Adam Deadmarsh, LosA. ✂ 12.00
☐ PH-MD Marc Denis (G), Colu. ✂ 12.00
☐ PH-CD Chris Drury, Colo. ✂ 12.00
☐ PH-DR Chris Drury, Calg. ✂ 12.00
☐ PH-JD J.P. Dumont, Buff. ✂ 12.00
☐ PH-DU Mike Dunham (G), Nash. ✂ 12.00
☐ PH-FV Sergei Fedorov, Detr. ✂ 20.00
☐ PH-SF Sergei Fedorov, Detr. ✂ 20.00
☐ PH-FO Peter Forsberg, Colo. ✂ 25.00
☐ PH-PF Peter Forsberg, Colo. ✂ 25.00
☐ PH-SG Simon Gagné, Phil. ✂ 15.00
☐ PH-GO Sergei Gonchar, Wash. ✂ 12.00
☐ PH-GY Wayne Gretzky, NYRa. ✂ 90.00
☐ PH-GU Bill Guerin, Dall. ✂ 12.00
☐ PH-MH Milan Hejduk, Colo. ✂ 15.00
☐ PH-BH Brett Hull, Detr. ✂ 20.00
☐ PH-JI Jarome Iginla, Calg. ✂ 15.00
☐ PH-JG Jaromir Jagr, Wash. ✂ 20.00
☐ PH-JJ Jaromir Jagr, Wash. ✂ 20.00
☐ PH-CJ Curtis Joseph (G), Toro. ✂ 20.00
☐ PH-KA Paul Kariya, Anah. ✂ 25.00
☐ PH-PK Paul Kariya, Anah. ✂ 25.00
☐ PH-EK Espen Knutsen, Colu. ✂ 12.00
☐ PH-SK Saku Koivu, Mont. ✂ 20.00
☐ PH-KU Saku Koivu, Mont. ✂ 15.00
☐ PH-KO Steve Konowalchuk, Wash. ✂ 12.00
☐ PH-KK Ilya Kovalchuk, Atla. ✂ 20.00
☐ PH-JL John LeClair, Phil. ✂ 15.00
☐ PH-BL Brian Leetch, NYRa. ✂ 12.00
☐ PH-DL David Legwand, Nash. ✂ 12.00
☐ PH-CL Claude Lemieux, Phoe. ✂ 12.00
☐ PH-ML Mario Lemieux, Pitt. ✂ 60.00
☐ PH-LM Nicklas Lidström, Detr. ✂ 12.00
☐ PH-NL Nicklas Lidström, Detr. ✂ 12.00
☐ PH-EL Eric Lindros, NYRa. ✂ 20.00
☐ PH-PM Patrick Marleau, SanJ. ✂ 12.00
☐ PH-MM Mike Modano, Dall. ✂ 20.00
☐ PH-MO Mike Modano, Dall. ✂ 20.00
☐ PH-MN Markus Näslund, Vanc. ✂ 20.00
☐ PH-NA Markus Näslund, Vanc. ✂ 20.00
☐ PH-JN Joe Nieuwendyk, NJer. ✂ 12.00
☐ PH-ZP Zigmund Palffy, LosA. ✂ 12.00
☐ PH-FP Félix Potvin (G), LosA. ✂ 12.00
☐ PH-KP Keith Primeau, Phil. ✂ 12.00
☐ PH-MR Mark Recchi, Phil. ✂ 12.00
☐ PH-JR Jeremy Roenick, Phil. ✂ 15.00
☐ PH-RK Jeremy Roenick, Phil. ✂ 15.00
☐ PH-PR Patrick Roy (G), Colo. ✂ 45.00
☐ PH-RY Patrick Roy (G), Colo. ✂ 45.00
☐ PH-JS Joe Sakic, Colo. ✂ 30.00
☐ PH-SC Joe Sakic, Colo. ✂ 30.00
☐ PH-SS Sergei Samsonov, Bost. ✂ 12.00
☐ PH-SV Sergei Samsonov, Bost. ✂ 12.00
☐ PH-SA Marc Savard, Calg. ✂ 12.00
☐ PH-TS Teemu Selänne, SanJ. ✂ 15.00
☐ PH-BS Brendan Shanahan, Detr. ✂ 20.00
☐ PH-SH Brendan Shanahan, Detr. ✂ 20.00
☐ PH-MS Mats Sundin, Toro. ✂ 20.00
☐ PH-SU Mats Sundin, Toro. ✂ 20.00
☐ PH-AT Alex Tanguay, Colo. ✂ 12.00
☐ PH-TA Alex Tanguay, Colo. ✂ 12.00
☐ PH-TH José Théodore (G), Mont. ✂ 25.00
☐ PH-JO Jocelyn Thibault (G), Chic. ✂ 12.00
☐ PH-TT Jocelyn Thibault (G), Chic. ✂ 12.00
☐ PH-JT Joe Thornton, Bost. ✂ 25.00
☐ PH-RT Roman Turek (G), Calg. ✂ 12.00
☐ PH-AY Alexei Yashin, NYIs. ✂ 12.00
☐ PH-MY Mike York, Edmo. ✂ 12.00
☐ PH-SY Steve Yzerman, Detr. ✂ 50.00
☐ PH-AZ Alexei Zhamnov, Chic. ✂ 12.00

PIECE OF HISTORY GOLD

Insert Set (87 cards): 1700.00
Insert (*99) POH99

☐ PH-AD Adam Deadmarsh, LosA. ✂ 20.00
☐ PH-AL Jason Allison, LosA. ✂ 20.00
☐ PH-AM Tony Amonte, Phoe. ✂ 20.00
☐ PH-AT Alex Tanguay, Colo. ✂ 20.00
☐ PH-AY Alexei Yashin, NYIs. ✂ 20.00
☐ PH-AZ Alexei Zhamnov, Chic. ✂ 20.00
☐ PH-BD Peter Bondra, Wash. ✂ 20.00
☐ PH-BH Brett Hull, Detr. ✂ 25.00
☐ PH-BI Martin Biron (G), Buff. ✂ 20.00
☐ PH-BL Brian Leetch, NYRa. ✂ 20.00
☐ PH-BO Peter Bondra, Wash. ✂ 20.00
☐ PH-BQ Raymond Bourque, Colo. ✂ 25.00
☐ PH-BS Brendan Shanahan, Detr. ✂ 25.00
☐ PH-CC Chris Chelios, Detr. ✂ 20.00
☐ PH-CD Chris Drury, Colo. ✂ 20.00
☐ PH-CJ Curtis Joseph (G), Toro. ✂ 25.00
☐ PH-CK Roman Cechmanek (G), Phil. ✂ 20.00
☐ PH-CL Claude Lemieux, Phoe. ✂ 20.00
☐ PH-DL David Legwand, Nash. ✂ 20.00
☐ PH-DR Chris Drury, Calg. ✂ 20.00
☐ PH-DU Mike Dunham (G), Nash. ✂ 20.00
☐ PH-ED Éric Dazé, Chic. ✂ 20.00
☐ PH-EK Espen Knutsen, Colu. ✂ 20.00
☐ PH-EL Eric Lindros, NYRa. ✂ 25.00
☐ PH-FO Peter Forsberg, Colo. ✂ 25.00
☐ PH-FP Félix Potvin (G), LosA. ✂ 25.00
☐ PH-FV Sergei Fedorov, Detr. ✂ 25.00
☐ PH-GO Sergei Gonchar, Wash. ✂ 20.00
☐ PH-GU Bill Guerin, Dall. ✂ 20.00
☐ PH-GY Wayne Gretzky, NYRa. ✂ 125.00
☐ PH-JA Jason Allison, LosA. ✂ 20.00
☐ PH-JD J.P. Dumont, Buff. ✂ 20.00
☐ PH-JG Jaromir Jagr, Wash. ✂ 25.00
☐ PH-JI Jarome Iginla, Calg. ✂ 25.00
☐ PH-JJ Jaromir Jagr, Wash. ✂ 25.00
☐ PH-JL John LeClair, Phil. ✂ 25.00
☐ PH-JN Joe Nieuwendyk, NJer. ✂ 20.00
☐ PH-JO Jocelyn Thibault (G), Chic. ✂ 20.00
☐ PH-JR Jeremy Roenick, Phil. ✂ 20.00
☐ PH-JS Joe Sakic, Colo. ✂ 25.00
☐ PH-JT Joe Thornton, Bost. ✂ 25.00
☐ PH-KA Paul Kariya, Anah. ✂ 25.00
☐ PH-KK Ilya Kovalchuk, Atla. ✂ 25.00
☐ PH-KO Steve Konowalchuk, Wash. ✂ 20.00
☐ PH-KP Keith Primeau, Phil. ✂ 20.00
☐ PH-KU Saku Koivu, Mont. ✂ 25.00
☐ PH-LM Nicklas Lidström, Detr. ✂ 20.00
☐ PH-MB Martin Brodeur (G), NJer. ✂ 50.00
☐ PH-MD Marc Denis (G), Colu. ✂ 20.00
☐ PH-MH Milan Hejduk, Colo. ✂ 25.00
☐ PH-ML Mario Lemieux, Pitt. ✂ 75.00
☐ PH-MM Mike Modano, Dall. ✂ 25.00
☐ PH-MN Markus Näslund, Vanc. ✂ 25.00
☐ PH-MO Mike Modano, Dall. ✂ 25.00
☐ PH-MR Mark Recchi, Phil. ✂ 20.00
☐ PH-MS Mats Sundin, Toro. ✂ 25.00
☐ PH-MY Mike York, Edmo. ✂ 20.00
☐ PH-NA Markus Näslund, Vanc. ✂ 25.00
☐ PH-NL Nicklas Lidström, Detr. ✂ 20.00
☐ PH-PB Pavel Bure, NYRa. ✂ 25.00
☐ PH-PF Peter Forsberg, Colo. ✂ 25.00
☐ PH-PK Paul Kariya, Anah. ✂ 25.00
☐ PH-PM Patrick Marleau, SanJ. ✂ 20.00
☐ PH-PR Patrick Roy (G), Colo. ✂ 50.00
☐ PH-RB Raymond Bourque, Bost. ✂ 25.00
☐ PH-RC Roman Cechmanek (G), Phil. ✂ 20.00
☐ PH-RK Jeremy Roenick, Phil. ✂ 20.00
☐ PH-RO Rob Blake, Colo. ✂ 20.00
☐ PH-RT Roman Turek (G), Calg. ✂ 20.00
☐ PH-RY Patrick Roy (G), Colo. ✂ 50.00
☐ PH-SA Marc Savard, Calg. ✂ 20.00
☐ PH-SB Sean Burke (G), Phoe. ✂ 20.00
☐ PH-SC Joe Sakic, Colo. ✂ 25.00
☐ PH-SF Sergei Fedorov, Detr. ✂ 25.00
☐ PH-SG Simon Gagné, Phil. ✂ 25.00
☐ PH-SH Brendan Shanahan, Detr. ✂ 25.00
☐ PH-SK Saku Koivu, Mont. ✂ 25.00
☐ PH-SS Sergei Samsonov, Bost. ✂ 20.00
☐ PH-SU Mats Sundin, Toro. ✂ 25.00
☐ PH-SV Sergei Samsonov, Bost. ✂ 20.00
☐ PH-SY Steve Yzerman, Detr. ✂ 75.00
☐ PH-TA Alex Tanguay, Colo. ✂ 20.00
☐ PH-TC Tim Connolly, Buff. ✂ 20.00
☐ PH-TH José Théodore (G), Mont. ✂ 25.00
☐ PH-TS Teemu Selänne, SanJ. ✂ 25.00
☐ PH-TT Jocelyn Thibault (G), Chic. ✂ 20.00
☐ PH-ZP Zigmund Palffy, LosA. ✂ 20.00

PIECE OF HISTORY RAINBOW

Insert (*10) POH10

☐ PH-AD Adam Deadmarsh, LosA. ✂ 80.00
☐ PH-AL Jason Allison, LosA. ✂ 100.00
☐ PH-AM Tony Amonte, Phoe. ✂ 100.00
☐ PH-AT Alex Tanguay, Colo. ✂ 100.00
☐ PH-AY Alexei Yashin, NYIs. ✂ 100.00
☐ PH-AZ Alexei Zhamnov, Chic. ✂ 80.00
☐ PH-BD Peter Bondra, Wash. ✂ 100.00
☐ PH-BH Brett Hull, Detr. ✂ 200.00
☐ PH-BI Martin Biron (G), Buff. ✂ 100.00
☐ PH-BL Brian Leetch, NYRa. ✂ 100.00
☐ PH-BO Peter Bondra, Wash. ✂ 100.00
☐ PH-BQ Raymond Bourque, Colo. ✂ 200.00
☐ PH-BS Brendan Shanahan, Detr. ✂ 200.00
☐ PH-CC Chris Chelios, Detr. ✂ 100.00
☐ PH-CD Chris Drury, Colo. ✂ 100.00
☐ PH-CJ Curtis Joseph (G), Toro. ✂ 200.00
☐ PH-CK Roman Cechmanek (G), Phil. ✂ 80.00
☐ PH-CL Claude Lemieux, Phoe. ✂ 80.00
☐ PH-DL David Legwand, Nash. ✂ 80.00
☐ PH-DR Chris Drury, Calg. ✂ 100.00
☐ PH-DU Mike Dunham (G), Nash. ✂ 80.00
☐ PH-ED Éric Dazé, Chic. ✂ 80.00
☐ PH-EK Espen Knutsen, Colu. ✂ 80.00
☐ PH-EL Eric Lindros, NYRa. ✂ 200.00
☐ PH-FO Peter Forsberg, Colo. ✂ 250.00
☐ PH-FP Félix Potvin (G), LosA. ✂ 250.00
☐ PH-FV Sergei Fedorov, Detr. ✂ 200.00
☐ PH-GO Sergei Gonchar, Wash. ✂ 80.00
☐ PH-GU Bill Guerin, Dall. ✂ 80.00
☐ PH-GY Wayne Gretzky, NYRa. ✂ 900.00
☐ PH-JA Jason Allison, LosA. ✂ 100.00
☐ PH-JD J.P. Dumont, Buff. ✂ 80.00
☐ PH-JG Jaromir Jagr, Wash. ✂ 200.00
☐ PH-JI Jarome Iginla, Calg. ✂ 150.00
☐ PH-JJ Jaromir Jagr, Wash. ✂ 200.00
☐ PH-JL John LeClair, Phil. ✂ 150.00
☐ PH-JN Joe Nieuwendyk, NJer. ✂ 80.00
☐ PH-JO Jocelyn Thibault (G), Chic. ✂ 80.00
☐ PH-JR Jeremy Roenick, Phil. ✂ 150.00
☐ PH-JS Joe Sakic, Colo. ✂ 300.00
☐ PH-JT Joe Thornton, Bost. ✂ 250.00
☐ PH-KA Paul Kariya, Anah. ✂ 250.00
☐ PH-KK Ilya Kovalchuk, Atla. ✂ 200.00
☐ PH-KO Steve Konowalchuk, Wash. ✂ 80.00
☐ PH-KP Keith Primeau, Phil. ✂ 80.00
☐ PH-KU Saku Koivu, Mont. ✂ 200.00
☐ PH-LM Nicklas Lidström, Detr. ✂ 100.00
☐ PH-MB Martin Brodeur (G), NJer. ✂ 350.00
☐ PH-MD Marc Denis (G), Colu. ✂ 100.00
☐ PH-MH Milan Hejduk, Colo. ✂ 150.00
☐ PH-ML Mario Lemieux, Pitt. ✂ 600.00
☐ PH-MM Mike Modano, Dall. ✂ 200.00
☐ PH-MN Markus Näslund, Vanc. ✂ 200.00
☐ PH-MO Mike Modano, Dall. ✂ 200.00
☐ PH-MR Mark Recchi, Phil. ✂ 80.00
☐ PH-MS Mats Sundin, Toro. ✂ 200.00
☐ PH-MY Mike York, Edmo. ✂ 80.00
☐ PH-NA Markus Näslund, Vanc. ✂ 200.00
☐ PH-NL Nicklas Lidström, Detr. ✂ 100.00
☐ PH-PB Pavel Bure, NYRa. ✂ 150.00
☐ PH-PF Peter Forsberg, Colo. ✂ 250.00
☐ PH-PK Paul Kariya, Anah. ✂ 250.00
☐ PH-PM Patrick Marleau, SanJ. ✂ 100.00
☐ PH-PR Patrick Roy (G), Colo. ✂ 450.00
☐ PH-RB Raymond Bourque, Bost. ✂ 200.00
☐ PH-RC Roman Cechmanek (G), Phil. ✂ 80.00
☐ PH-RK Jeremy Roenick, Phil. ✂ 150.00
☐ PH-RO Rob Blake, Colo. ✂ 100.00
☐ PH-RT Roman Turek (G), Calg. ✂ 100.00
☐ PH-RY Patrick Roy (G), Colo. ✂ 450.00
☐ PH-SA Marc Savard, Calg. ✂ 80.00
☐ PH-SB Sean Burke (G), Phoe. ✂ 100.00
☐ PH-SC Joe Sakic, Colo. ✂ 300.00
☐ PH-SF Sergei Fedorov, Detr. ✂ 200.00
☐ PH-SG Simon Gagné, Phil. ✂ 150.00
☐ PH-SH Brendan Shanahan, Detr. ✂ 200.00
☐ PH-SK Saku Koivu, Mont. ✂ 200.00
☐ PH-SS Sergei Samsonov, Bost. ✂ 100.00
☐ PH-SU Mats Sundin, Toro. ✂ 200.00
☐ PH-SV Sergei Samsonov, Bost. ✂ 100.00
☐ PH-SY Steve Yzerman, Detr. ✂ 500.00
☐ PH-TA Alex Tanguay, Colo. ✂ 100.00
☐ PH-TC Tim Connolly, Buff. ✂ 80.00
☐ PH-TH José Théodore (G), Mont. ✂ 250.00
☐ PH-TS Teemu Selänne, SanJ. ✂ 150.00
☐ PH-TT Jocelyn Thibault (G), Chic. ✂ 80.00
☐ PH-ZP Zigmund Palffy, LosA. ✂ 100.00

SIGNATURE STYLE

Insert Set (32 cards): 1600.00
Insert SigStyle

☐ Alexander Frolov, LosA. ✍ 25.00
☐ Bobby Orr, Bost. ✍ 250.00
☐ Pavel Brendl, Phil. ✍ 20.00
☐ Curtis Joseph (G), Detr. ✍ 50.00
☐ Dany Heatley, Atla. ✍ 50.00
☐ Ed Belfour (G), Toro. ✍ 50.00
☐ Erik Cole, Caro. ✍ 20.00
☐ Gordie Howe, Detr. ✍ 175.00
☐ Ilya Kovalchuk, Atla. ✍ 50.00
☐ Jarome Iginla, Calg. ✍ 50.00
☐ John LeClair, Phil. ✍ 50.00
☐ Joe Thornton, Bost. ✍ 75.00
☐ Justin Williams, Phil. ✍ 20.00
☐ Kristian Huselius, Flor. ✍ 20.00
☐ Maxim Afinogenov, Buff. ✍ 25.00
☐ Martin Brodeur (G), NJer. ✍ 100.00
☐ Mike Comrie, Edmo. ✍ 50.00
☐ Manny Fernandez (G), MinW. ✍ 25.00
☐ Martin Havlat, Otta. ✍ 25.00
☐ Milan Kraft, Pitt. ✍ 20.00
☐ Nikolai Khabibulin (G), Tamp. ✍ 25.00
☐ Pavel Bure, NYRa. ✍ 50.00
☐ Patrick Roy (G), Colo. ✍ 150.00
☐ Raymond Bourque, Bost. ✍ 75.00
☐ Stanislav Chistov, Anah. ✍ 25.00
☐ Simon Gagné, Phil. ✍ 50.00
☐ Scott Hartnell, Nash. ✍ 20.00
☐ Jason Spezza, Otta. ✍ 25.00
☐ Sergei Samsonov, Bost. ✍ 25.00
☐ Steve Yzerman, Detr. ✍ 150.00
☐ Teemu Selänne, SanJ. ✍ 50.00
☐ Wayne Gretzky, Edmo. ✍ 325.00

TOOLS OF THE GAME GLOVE

Insert Set (18 cards): 400.00
Insert (*99) TOGG99

☐ Alex Kovalev, Pitt. ✂ 25.00
☐ Alexander Mogilny, Toro. ✂ 25.00
☐ Brett Hull, Detr. ✂ 35.00
☐ Brendan Shanahan, Detr. ✂ 35.00
☐ Ed Belfour (G), Dall. ✂ 35.00
☐ Jeff Friesen, Anah. ✂ 25.00
☐ Jaromir Jagr, Wash. ✂ 35.00
☐ John LeClair, Phil. ✂ 30.00
☐ Jeremy Roenick, Phil. ✂ 30.00
☐ Joe Thornton, Bost. ✂ 45.00
☐ Keith Primeau, Phil. ✂ 25.00
☐ Keith Tkachuk, SLou. ✂ 25.00
☐ Mats Sundin, Toro. ✂ 35.00
☐ Peter Bondra, Wash. ✂ 25.00
☐ Ron Francis, Caro. ✂ 25.00
☐ Sergei Fedorov, Detr. ✂ 35.00
☐ Sergei Samsonov, Bost. ✂ 25.00
☐ Teemu Selänne, SanJ. ✂ 30.00

TOOLS OF THE GAME LEG PAD

Insert Set (12 cards): 300.00
Insert (*99) TOGL99

☐ Brian Boucher (G), Phil. ✂ 25.00
☐ Byron Dafoe (G), Bost. ✂ 25.00
☐ Ed Belfour (G), Dall. ✂ 35.00
☐ Dominik Hasek (G), Detr. ✂ 35.00
☐ Marc Denis (G), Colu. ✂ 25.00
☐ Olaf Kölzig (G), Wash. ✂ 25.00
☐ Patrick Roy (G), Colo. ✂ 90.00
☐ Roman Cechmanek (G), Phil. ✂ 25.00
☐ Rick DiPietro (G), NYIs. ✂ 25.00
☐ Roberto Luongo (G), Flor. ✂ 30.00
☐ Steve Shields, Anah. ✂ 25.00
☐ José Théodore (G), Mont. ✂ 45.00

2002 - 03 SPORTS VAULT

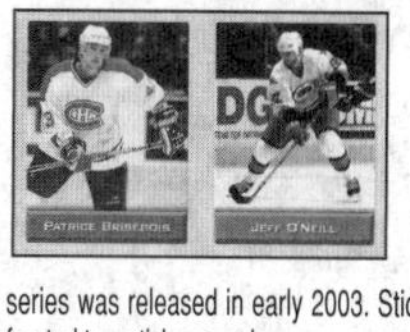

This sticker series was released in early 2003. Stickers were issued in perforated two-sticker panels.

Panels

059 Patrice Brisebois / 037 Jeff O'Neill
073 Shawn Bates / 033 Rod Brind'Amour
086 Mark Messier / 010 Byron Dafoe (G)
087 Petr Nedved / 043 Valeri Bure
108 Éric Desjardins / 143 Peter Bondra
110 Roman Cechmanek (G) / 098 Wade Redden
116 Aleksey Morozov / 252 Predators logo
177 Phil Housley / 170 Roman Turek
191 Blue Jackets logo / 298Ed Jovanovski
290 Evgeni Nabokov (G) / 109 Kim Johnsson

Panel

1 Thrashers logo
2 Thrashers logo
3 Dany Heatley, Atla.
4 Ilya Kovalchuk, Atla.
5 Patrik Stefan, Atla.
6 Frantisek Kaberle, Atla.
7 Yannick Tremblay, Atla.
8 Tony Hrkac, Atla.
9 Shawn McEachern, Atla.
10 Byron Dafoe (G), Atla.
11 Bruins logo
12 Bruins logo
13 Martin Lapointe, Bost.
14 Glen Murray, Bost.
15 Brian Rolston, Bost.
16 Sergei Samsonov, Bost.
17 Joe Thornton, Bost.
18 Jozef Stümpel, Bost.
19 Nick Boynton, Bost.
20 Steve Shields (G), Bost.
21 Sabres logo
22 Sabres logo
23 Stu Barnes, Buff.
24 Curtis Brown, Buff.
25 Miroslav Satan, Buff.
26 Jochen Hecht, Buff.
27 Tim Connolly, Buff.
28 Jay McKee, Buff.
29 Chris Gratton, Buff.
30 Martin Biron (G), Buff.
31 Hurricanes logo
32 Hurricanes logo
33 Rod Brind'Amour, Caro.
34 Erik Cole, Caro.
35 Ron Francis, Caro.
36 Sami Kapanen, Caro.
37 Jeff O'Neill, Caro.
38 Bret Hedican, Caro.
39 Sean Hill, Caro.
40 Kevin Weekes (G), Caro.
41 Panthers logo
42 Panthers logo
43 Valeri Bure, Flor.
44 Olli Jokinen, Flor.
45 Marcus Nilson, Flor.
46 Stephen Weiss, Flor.
47 Kristian Huselius, Flor.
48 Sandis Ozolinsh, Flor.
49 Jay Bouwmeester, Flor.
50 Roberto Luongo (G), Flor.
51 Canadiens logo
52 Canadiens logo
53 Randy McKay, Mont.
54 Richard Zednik, Mont.
55 Doug Gilmour, Mont.
56 Saku Koivu, Mont.
57 Yanic Perreault, Mont.
58 Craig Rivet, Mont.
59 Patrice Brisebois, Mont.
60 José Théodore (G), Mont.
61 Devils logo
62 Devils logo
63 Patrik Elias, NJer.
64 Jeff Friesen, NJer.
65 Joe Nieuwendyk, NJer.
66 Sergei Brylin, NJer.
67 Jamie Langenbrunner, NJer.
68 Scott Stevens, NJer.
69 Scott Niedermayer, NJer.
70 Martin Brodeur (G), NJer.
71 Islanders logo
72 Islanders logo
73 Shawn Bates, NYIs.
74 Brad Isbister, NYIs.
75 Mark Parrish, NYIs.
76 Michael Peca, NYIs.
77 Alexei Yashin, NYIs.
78 Kenny Jönsson, NYIs.
79 Roman Hamrlik, NYIs.
80 Chris Osgood (G), NYIs.
81 Rangers logo
82 Rangers logo
83 Pavel Bure, NYRa.
84 Bobby Holik, NYRa.
85 Eric Lindros, NYRa.
86 Mark Messier, NYRa.
87 Petr Nedved, NYRa.
88 Brian Leetch, NYRa.
89 Darius Kasparaitis, NYRa.
90 Mike Richter (G), NYRa.
91 Senators logo
92 Senators logo
93 Daniel Alfredsson, Otta.
94 Jason Spezza, Otta.
95 Marian Hossa, Otta.
96 Magnus Arvedson, Otta.
97 Martin Havlat, Otta.
98 Wade Redden, Otta.
99 Chris Phillips, Otta.
100 Patrick Lalime (G), Otta.
101 Flyers logo
102 Flyers logo
103 Simon Gagné, Phil.
104 John LeClair, Phil.
105 Keith Primeau, Phil.
106 Mark Recchi, Phil.
107 Jeremy Roenick, Phil.
108 Éric Desjardins, Phil.
109 Kim Johnsson, Phil.
110 Roman Cechmanek (G), Phil.
111 Penguins logo
112 Penguins logo
113 Jan Hrdina, Pitt.
114 Alex Kovalev, Pitt.
115 Mario Lemieux, Pitt.
116 Aleksey Morozov, Pitt.
117 Wayne Primeau, Pitt.
118 Michal Rozsival, Pitt.
119 Dick Tarnström, Pitt.
120 Johan Hedberg (G), Pitt.
121 Lightning logo
122 Lightning logo
123 Dave Andreychuk, Tamp.
124 Vincent Lecavalier, Tamp.
125 Vaclav Prospal, Tamp.
126 Brad Richards, Tamp.
127 Martin St-Louis, Tamp.
128 Pavel Kubina, Tamp.
129 Dan Boyle, Tamp.
130 Nikolai Khabibulin (G), Tamp.
131 Maple Leafs logo
132 Maple Leafs logo
133 Mats Sundin, Toro.
134 Tie Domi, Toro.
135 Darcy Tucker, Toro.
136 Alexander Mogilny, Toro.
137 Gary Roberts, Toro.
138 Tomas Kaberle, Toro.
139 Bryan McCabe, Toro.
140 Ed Belfour (G), Toro.
141 Capitals logo
142 Capitals logo
143 Peter Bondra, Wash.
144 Jaromir Jagr, Wash.
145 Robert Lang, Wash.
146 Jeff Halpern, Wash.
147 Sergei Gonchar, Wash.
148 Dainius Zubrus, Wash.
149 Steve Konowalchuk, Wash.
150 Olaf Kölzig (G), Wash.
151 Mighty Ducks logo
152 Mighty Ducks logo
153 Paul Kariya, Anah.
154 Matt Cullen, Anah.
155 Steve Rucchin, Anah.
156 Mike Leclerc, Anah.
157 Petr1 Sykora, Anah.
158 Stanislav Chistov, Anah.
159 Keith Carney, Anah.
160 Jean-Sébastien Giguère (G), Anah.
161 Flames logo
162 Flames logo
163 Craig Conroy, Calg.
164 Jarome Iginla, Calg.
165 Chris Drury, Calg.
166 Martin Gélinas, Calg.
167 Stéphane Yelle, Calg.
168 Denis (G) Gauthier, Calg.
169 Bob Boughner, Calg.
170 Roman Turek (G), Calg.
171 Blackhawks logo
172 Blackhawks logo
173 Éric Dazé, Chic.
174 Steve Sullivan, Chic.
175 Alexei Zhamnov, Chic.
176 Kyle Calder, Chic.
177 Phil Housley, Chic.
178 Tyler Arnason, Chic.
179 Lyle Odelein, Chic.
180 Jocelyn Thibault (G), Chic.
181 Avalanche logo
182 Avalanche logo
183 Peter Forsberg, Colo.
184 Milan Hejduk, Colo.
185 Joe Sakic, Colo.
186 Alex Tanguay, Colo.
187 Rob Blake, Colo.
188 Adam Foote, Colo.
189 Derek Morris, Colo.
190 Patrick Roy (G), Colo.
191 Blue Jackets logo
192 Blue Jackets logo
193 Rick Nash, Colu.
194 Geoff Sanderson, Colu.
195 Andrew Cassels, Colu.
196 Ray Whitney, Colu.
197 Luke Richardson, Colu.
198 Scott Lachance, Colu.
199 Mike Sillinger, Colu.
200 Marc Denis (G), Colu.
201 Stars logo
202 Stars logo
203 Ulf Dahlén, Dall.
204 Bill Guerin, Dall.
205 Mike Modano, Dall.
206 Pierre Turgeon, Dall.
207 Scott_A Young, Dall.
208 Sergei Zubov, Dall.
209 Darryl Sydor, Dall.
210 Marty Turco (G), Dall.
211 Red Wings logo
212 Red Wings logo
213 Sergei Fedorov, Detr.
214 Brett Hull, Detr.
215 Brendan Shanahan, Detr.
216 Steve Yzerman, Detr.
217 Chris Chelios, Detr.
218 Nicklas Lidström, Detr.
219 Kris Draper, Detr.
220 Curtis Joseph (G), Detr.
221 Oilers logo
222 Oilers logo
223 Anson Carter, Edmo.
224 Mike Comrie, Edmo.
225 Ryan Smyth, Edmo.
226 Mike York, Edmo.
227 Eric Brewer, Edmo.
228 Jason Smith, Edmo.
229 Janne Niinimaa, Edmo.
230 Tommy Salo, Edmo.
231 Kings logo
232 Kings logo
233 Jason Allison, LosA.
234 Adam Deadmarsh, LosA.
235 Bryan Smolinski, LosA.
236 Mathieu Schneider, LosA.
237 Jaroslav Modry, LosA.
238 Zigmund Palffy, LosA.
239 Lubomir Visnovsky, LosA.
240 Félix Potvin (G), LosA.
241 Wild logo
242 Wild logo
243 Andrew Brunette, MinW.
244 Marian Gaborik, MinW.
245 Cliff Ronning, MinW.
246 Sergei Zholtok, MinW.
247 Jim Dowd, MinW.
248 Antti Laaksonen, MinW.
249 Willie Mitchell, MinW.
250 Manny Fernandez (G), MinW.
251 Predators logo
252 Predators logo
253 Andreas Johansson, Nash.
254 Greg Johnson, Nash.
255 Denis Arkhipov, Nash.
256 David Legwand, Nash.
257 Vladimir Orszagh, Nash.
258 Andy Delmore, Nash.
259 Kimmo Timonen, Nash.
260 Tomas Vokoun (G), Nash.
261 Coyotes logo
262 Coyotes logo
263 Tony Amonte, Phoe.
264 Daniel Brière, Phoe.
265 Shane Doan, Phoe.
266 Daymond Langkow, Phoe.
267 Ladislav Nagy, Phoe.
268 Teppo Numminen, Phoe.
269 Danny Markov, Phoe.
270 Sean Burke (G), Phoe.
271 Blues logo
272 Blues logo
273 Pavol Demitra, SLou.
274 Cory Stillman, SLou.
275 Keith Tkachuk, SLou.
276 Doug Weight, SLou.
277 Al MacInnis, SLou.
278 Chris Pronger, SLou.
279 Eric Boguniecki, SLou.
280 Brent Johnson (G), SLou.
281 Sharks logo
282 Sharks logo
283 Vincent Damphouse, SanJ.
284 Adam Graves, SanJ.
285 Patrick Marleau, SanJ.
286 Owen Nolan, SanJ.
287 Teemu Selänne, SanJ.
288 Marco Sturm, SanJ.
289 Mike Ricci, SanJ.
290 Evgeni Nabokov (G), SanJ.
291 Canucks logo
292 Canucks logo
293 Todd Bertuzzi, Vanc.
294 Trevor Linden, Vanc.
295 Brendan Morrison, Vanc.
296 Markus Näslund, Vanc.
297 Henrik Sedin, Vanc.
298 Ed Jovanovski, Vanc.
299 Mattias Öhlund, Vanc.
300 Dan Cloutier (G), Vanc.

2002 - 03 SPX

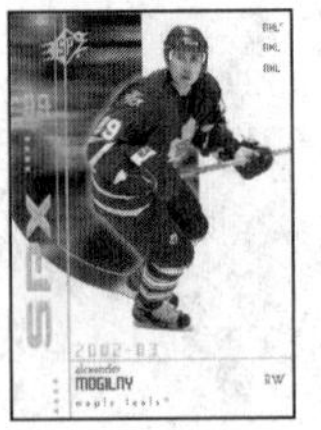

Produced by The Upper Deck Company, this series was released in December 2002. There are three versions for each card 1-100: the base card, the silver parallel (#/199), and the Gold parallel (#/10).

	S199	Base
Shell Set (100 cards):	300.00	55.00
Complete Set (193 cards):		1625.00
Common Player:	3.00	.50
Description	**S199**	**Base**
1 Paul Kariya, Anah.	5.00	1.50
2 J-S Giguère (G), Anah.	5.00	1.00
3 Ilya Kovalchuk, Atla.	5.00	1.00
4 Dany Heatley, Atla.	5.00	1.00
5 Joe Thornton, Bost.	5.00	1.50
6 Sergei Samsonov, Bost.	3.00	.50
7 Miroslav Satan, Buff.	3.00	.50
8 Martin Biron (G), Buff.	3.00	.50
9 Roman Turek (G), Calg.	3.00	.50
10 Jarome Iginla, Calg.	5.00	1.00
11 Jeff O'Neill, Caro.	3.00	.50
12 Ron Francis, Caro.	3.00	.50
13 Arturs Irbe (G), Caro.	3.00	.50
14 Éric Dazé, Chic.	3.00	.50
15 Jocelyn Thibault (G), Chic.	3.00	.50
16 Patrick Roy (G), Colo.	15.00	3.50
17 Chris Drury, Colo.	3.00	.50
18 Joe Sakic, Colo.	10.00	2.00
19 Peter Forsberg, Colo.	5.00	1.50
20 Rob Blake, Colo.	3.00	.50
21 Rostislav Klesla, Colu.	3.00	.50
22 Marc Denis (G), Colu.	3.00	.50
23 Mike Modano, Dall.	5.00	1.00
24 Marty Turco (G), Dall.	3.00	.50
25 Bill Guerin, Dall.	3.00	.50
26 Steve Yzerman, Detr.	15.00	3.00
27 Sergei Fedorov, Detr.	5.00	1.00
28 Nicklas Lidström, Detr.	3.00	.50
29 Brett Hull, Detr.	5.00	1.00
30 Curtis Joseph (G), Detr.	5.00	1.00
31 Brendan Shanahan, Detr.	5.00	1.00
32 Mike Comrie, Edmo.	5.00	1.00
33 Tommy Salo (G), Edmo.	3.00	.50
34 Roberto Luongo (G), Flor.	5.00	1.00
35 Kristian Huselius, Flor.	3.00	.50
36 Félix Potvin (G), LosA.	3.00	.50
37 Zigmund Palffy, LosA.	3.00	.50
38 Marian Gaborik, MinW.	5.00	1.00
39 Manny Fernandez (G), MinW.	3.00	.50
40 José Théodore (G), Mont.	5.00	1.50
41 Saku Koivu, Mont.	5.00	1.00
42 Patrik Elias, NJer.	5.00	1.00
43 Martin Brodeur (G), NJer.	10.00	2.00
44 Scott Hartnell, Nash.	3.00	.50
45 Mike Dunham (G), Nash.	3.00	.50
46 Alexei Yashin, NYIs.	3.00	.50
47 Chris Osgood (G), NYIs.	3.00	.50
48 Michael Peca, NYIs.	3.00	.50
49 Eric Lindros, NYRa.	5.00	1.00
50 Mike Richter (G), NYRa.	3.00	.50
51 Pavel Bure, NYRa.	5.00	1.00
52 Patrick Lalime (G), Otta.	3.00	.50
53 Marian Hossa, Otta.	5.00	1.00
54 Daniel Alfredsson, Otta.	3.00	.50
55 Jeremy Roenick, Phil.	5.00	1.00
56 Simon Gagné, Phil.	5.00	1.00
57 Roman Cechmanek (G), Phil.	3.00	.50
58 Sean Burke (G), Phoe.	3.00	.50
59 Tony Amonte, Phoe.	3.00	.50
60 Alex Kovalev, Pitt.	3.00	.50
61 Mario Lemieux, Pitt.	15.00	3.50
62 Owen Nolan, SanJ.	3.00	.50

☐☐☐	63 Evgeni Nabokov (G), SanJ.	3.00	.50
☐☐☐	64 Keith Tkachuk, SLou.	3.00	.50
☐☐☐	65 Chris Pronger, SLou.	3.00	.50
☐☐☐	66 Brent Johnson (G), SLou.	3.00	.50
☐☐☐	67 Nikolai Khabibulin (G), Tamp.	3.00	.50
☐☐☐	68 Vincent Lecavalier, Tamp.	5.00	1.00
☐☐☐	69 Alexander Mogilny, Toro.	3.00	.50
☐☐☐	70 Mats Sundin, Toro.	5.00	1.00
☐☐☐	71 Ed Belfour (G), Toro.	5.00	1.00
☐☐☐	72 Todd Bertuzzi, Vanc.	5.00	1.50
☐☐☐	73 Markus Näslund, Vanc.	5.00	1.00
☐☐☐	74 Olaf Kölzig (G), Wash.	3.00	.50
☐☐☐	75 Jaromir Jagr, Wash.	5.00	1.00
☐☐☐	76 Paul Kariya, Anah.	5.00	1.00
☐☐☐	77 Adam Oates, Anah.	3.00	.50
☐☐☐	78 Sergei Samsonov, Bost.	3.00	.50
☐☐☐	79 Bobby Orr, Bost.	20.00	4.00
☐☐☐	80 Joe Thornton, Bost.	5.00	1.00
☐☐☐	81 Jeff O'Neill, Caro.	3.00	.50
☐☐☐	82 Ron Francis, Caro.	3.00	.50
☐☐☐	83 Joe Sakic, Colo.	5.00	1.00
☐☐☐	84 Patrick Roy (G), Colo.	15.00	3.00
☐☐☐	85 Peter Forsberg, Colo.	5.00	1.00
☐☐☐	86 Bill Guerin, Dall.	3.00	.50
☐☐☐	87 Mike Modano, Dall.	5.00	1.00
☐☐☐	88 Curtis Joseph (G), Detr.	5.00	1.00
☐☐☐	89 Gordie Howe, Detr.	10.00	2.00
☐☐☐	90 Steve Yzerman, Detr.	10.00	2.00
☐☐☐	91 Mike Comrie, Edmo.	3.00	.50
☐☐☐	92 José Théodore (G), Mont.	5.00	1.00
☐☐☐	93 Martin Brodeur (G), NJer.	5.00	1.00
☐☐☐	94 Pavel Bure, NYRa.	3.00	.50
☐☐☐	95 Wayne Gretzky, NYRa.	20.00	4.00
☐☐☐	96 John LeClair, Phil.	3.00	.50
☐☐☐	97 Mario Lemieux, Pitt.	15.00	3.00
☐☐☐	98 Evgeni Nabokov (G), SanJ.	3.00	.50
☐☐☐	99 Mats Sundin, Toro.	5.00	1.00
☐☐☐	100 Jaromir Jagr, Wash.	5.00	1.00

PROSPECTS

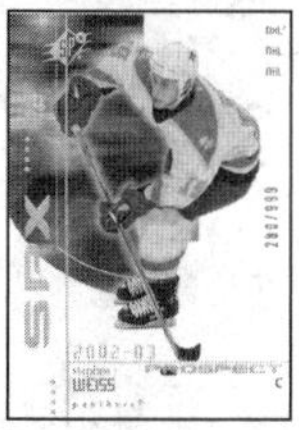

	Insert	P
☐	101 Pasi Nurminen (G), Atla.	1.00
☐	102 Mark Hartigan, Atla.	.50
☐	103 Andy Hilbert, Bost.	1.00
☐	104 Henrik Tallinder, Buff.	.50
☐	105 Jaroslav Svoboda, Caro.	1.00
☐	106 Riku Hahl, Colo.	.50
☐	107 Jordan Krestanovich, Colo.	.50
☐	108 Andrej Nedorost, Colu.	.50
☐	109 Sean Avery, Detr.	.50
☐	110 Jani Rita, Edmo.	1.00
☐	111 Stephen Weiss, Flor.	2.00
☐	112 Lukas Krajicek, Flor.	1.00
☐	113 Tony Virta, MinW.	.50
☐	114 Marcel Hossa, Mont.	2.00
☐	115 Jan Lasak (G), Nash.	1.00
☐	116 Jonas Andersson, Nash.	.50
☐	117 Trent Hunter, NYIs.	.50
☐	118 Martin Prusek (G), Otta.	1.00
☐	119 Bruno St-Jacques, Phil.	.50
☐	120 Branko Radivojevic, Phoe.	1.00
☐	121 Shane Endicott, Pitt.	.50
☐	122 Justin Papineau, SLou.	.50
☐	123 Sébastien Centomo (G), Toro.	1.00
☐	124 Karel Pilar, Toro.	.50
☐	125 Sébastien Charpentier (G), Wash.	.50

CAREER ACHIEVEMENTS

	Insert	CA
☐	126 Mark Messier, NYRa. {*1804}	4.00
☐	127 Ron Francis, Caro. {*1701}	4.00
☐	128 Steve Yzerman, Detr. {*1662}	8.00
☐	129 Mario Lemieux, Pitt. {*1601}	12.00
☐	130 Luc Robitaille, Detr. {*1288}	4.00
☐	131 Joe Sakic, Colo. {*1257}	6.00
☐	132 Brett Hull, Detr. {*1246}	4.00
☐	133 Al MacInnis, SLou. {*1204}	4.00
☐	134 Pierre Turgeon, Dall. {*1192}	4.00
☐	135 Jaromir Jagr, Wash. {*1158}	4.00
☐	136 Mark Recchi, Phil. {*1074}	4.00
☐	137 Brendan Shanahan, Detr. {*1030}	4.00
☐	138 Jeremy Roenick, Phil. {*1014}	4.00
☐	139 Mike Modano, Dall. {*977}	4.00
☐	140 Mats Sundin, Toro. {*942}	4.00
☐	141 Sergei Fedorov, Detr. {*871}	6.00
☐	142 Teemu Selänne, SanJ. {*855}	4.00
☐	143 Pavel Bure, NYRa. {*749}	4.00
☐	144 Peter Bondra, Wash. {*734}	4.00
☐	145 Eric Lindros, NYRa. {*732}	6.00

ROOKIE CARDS

	Insert	Aut.
☐	**146 Alexei Smirnov, Anah. RC ✍ {*1250}**	**35.00**
☐	**147 Kurt Sauer, Anah. RC ✍ {*1250}**	**20.00**
☐	**148 Chuck Kobasew, Calg. RC ✍ {*1250}**	**50.00**
☐	**149 Rick Nash, Colu. RC ✍ {*500}**	**275.00**
☐	**150 Jay Bouwmeester, Flor. RC ✍ {*500}**	**150.00**
☐	**151 Henrik Zetterberg, Detr. RC ✍ {*1250}**	**200.00**
☐	**152 Pierre-Marc Bouchard, MinW. RC ✍ {*1250}**	**75.00**
☐	**153 Ron Hainsey, Mont. RC ✍ {*1250}**	**35.00**
☐	**154 Adam Hall, Nash. RC ✍ {*1250}**	**35.00**
☐	**155 Scottie Upshall, Nash. RC ✍ {*1250}**	**50.00**
☐	**156 Stanislav Chistov, Anah. RC ✍ {*500}**	**150.00**
☐	**157 Jeff Taffe, Phoe. RC ✍ {*1250}**	**35.00**
☐	**158 Mikael Tellqvist (G), Toro. RC ✍ {*1250}**	**25.00**
☐	**159 Alexander Svitov, Tamp. RC ✍ {*1250}**	**50.00**
☐	**160 Ales Hemsky, Edmo. RC {*999}**	**30.00**
☐	**161 Alexander Frolov, LosA. RC {*999}**	**25.00**
☐	**162 Steve Eminger, Wash. RC {*999}**	**10.00**
☐	**163 Anton Volchenkov, Otta. RC {*999}**	**10.00**
☐	**164 Sylvain Blouin, MinW. RC {*999}**	**8.00**
☐	**165 Greg Koehler, Nash. RC {*999}**	**8.00**
☐	**166 Martin Gerber (G), Anah. RC {*999}**	**10.00**
☐	**167 Micki Dupont, Calg. RC {*999}**	**10.00**
☐	**168 Jordan Leopold, Calg. RC {*999}**	**15.00**
☐	**169 Tomi Pettinen, NYIs. RC {*999}**	**8.00**
☐	**170 Lynn Loyns, SanJ. RC {*999}**	**8.00**
☐	**171 Matt Henderson, Chic. RC {*999}**	**8.00**
☐	**172 Radovan Somik, Phil. RC {*999}**	**8.00**
☐	**173 Patrick Sharp, Phil. RC {*999}**	**8.00**
☐	**174 Jeff Paul, Colo. RC {*999}**	**8.00**
☐	**175 Jason Spezza, Otta. RC {*500}**	**200.00**

ROOKIE CARDS

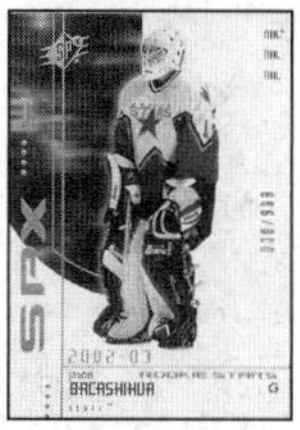

These cards were inserted into bonus packs of 2002 - 03 Upper Deck Rookie Update.

	Insert	R999
☐	**176 Pascal Leclaire (G), Colu. RC**	**25.00**
☐	**177 Steve Ott, Dall. RC**	**15.00**
☐	**178 Brooks Orpik, Pitt. RC**	**15.00**
☐	**179 Jared Aulin, LosA. RC**	**15.00**
☐	**180 Brandon Reid, Vanc. RC**	**20.00**
☐	**181 Ray Emery (G), Otta. RC**	**10.00**
☐	**182 Ari Ahonen (G), NJer. RC**	**15.00**
☐	**183 Niko Dimitrakos, SanJ. RC**	**8.00**
☐	**184 Jarret Stoll, Edmo. RC**	**15.00**
☐	**185 Cristobal Huet, LosA. RC**	**10.00**
☐	**186 Mike Komisarek, Mont. RC**	**15.00**
☐	**187 Ryan Miller (G), Buff. RC**	**25.00**
☐	**188 Jason Bacashihua (G), Dall. RC**	**10.00**
☐	**189 Carlo Colaiacovo, Toro. RC**	**15.00**
☐	**190 Mike Cammalleri, LosA. RC**	**20.00**
☐	**191 Fernando Pisani, Edmo. RC**	**8.00**
☐	**192 Alexei Semenov, Edmo. RC**	**10.00**
☐	**193 Konstantin Koltsov, Pitt. RC**	**8.00**

ROOKIE REDEMPTION

These cards were inserted into packs of 2002 - 03 Upper Deck Rookie Update. These cards cannot be redeemed before the 2003-04 season. As such, the redeemed cards will be listed under "2003 - 04 SPx Rookie".

- ☐ SPx-R1 SPx {*1500}
- ☐ SPx-R2 SPx {*1500}
- ☐ SPx-R3 SPx {*1500}
- ☐ SPx-R4 SPx {*1500}
- ☐ SPx-R5 SPx {*1500}
- ☐ SPx-R6 SPx {*1500}
- ☐ SPx-R7 SPx {*1500}
- ☐ SPx-R8 SPx {*1500}
- ☐ SPx-R9 SPx {*1500}
- ☐ SPx-R10 SPx {*1500}
- ☐ SPx-R11 SPx {*1500}
- ☐ SPx-R12 SPx {*1500}
- ☐ SPx-R13 SPx {*1500}
- ☐ SPx-R14 SPx {*1500}
- ☐ SPx-R15 SPx {*1500}
- ☐ SPx-R16 SPx {*1500}
- ☐ SPx-R17 SPx {*1500}
- ☐ SPx-R18 SPx {*1500}
- ☐ SPx-R19 SPx {*1500}
- ☐ SPx-R20 SPx {*1500}
- ☐ SPx-R21 SPx {*500}
- ☐ SPx-R22 SPx {*500}
- ☐ SPx-R23 SPx {*500}
- ☐ SPx-R24 SPx {*500}
- ☐ SPx-R25 SPx {*500}
- ☐ SPx-R26 SPx {*500}
- ☐ SPx-R27 SPx {*500}
- ☐ SPx-R28 SPx {*500}
- ☐ SPx-R29 SPx {*500}
- ☐ SPx-R30 SPx {*500}

WINNING MATERIALS

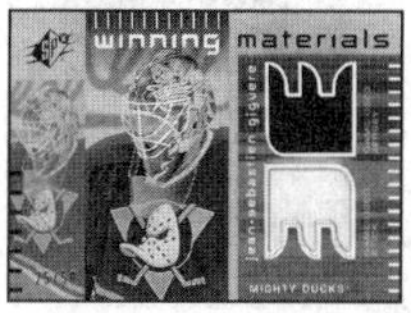

Insert Set (35 cards):		5400	1800	1000
	Insert	G15	S50	M99
☐☐☐	Martin Biron (G), Buff. ✂	75	30	15
☐☐☐	Raymond Bourque, Colo. ✂	225	75	45
☐☐☐	Raymond Bourque, Bost. ✂	225	75	45
☐☐☐	M. Brodeur (G), 2001 AS ✂	300	100	60
☐☐☐	Pavel Bure, NYRa. ✂	150	50	30
☐☐☐	J-P Dumont, Buff. ✂	50	20	15
☐☐☐	Peter Forsberg, Colo. ✂	250	75	50
☐☐☐	Simon Gagné, Phil. ✂	150	50	30
☐☐☐	J-S Giguère (G), Anah. ✂	175	60	35
☐☐☐	Dominik Hasek (G), Detr. ✂	175	50	35
☐☐☐	Jaromir Jagr, Wash. ✂	175	50	35
☐☐☐	Jaromir Jagr, Wash. ✂	175	60	35
☐☐☐	Curtis Joseph (G), Detr. ✂	175	50	35
☐☐☐	Paul Kariya, Anah. ✂	250	75	50
☐☐☐	Paul Kariya, Anah. ✂	250	85	50
☐☐☐	Olaf Kölzig (G), Wash. ✂	100	35	20
☐☐☐	Ilya Kovalchuk, Atla. ✂	175	50	35
☐☐☐	John LeClair, Phil. ✂	150	50	30
☐☐☐	Brian Leetch, NYRa. ✂	100	35	20
☐☐☐	David Legwand, Nash. ✂	75	25	15
☐☐☐	Mario Lemieux, Pitt. ✂	550	175	100
☐☐☐	Eric Lindros, NYRa. ✂	175	60	35
☐☐☐	Mike Modano, Dall. ✂	175	50	35
☐☐☐	Markus Näslund, Vanc. ✂	175	50	35
☐☐☐	Zigmund Palffy, LosA. ✂	100	35	20
☐☐☐	Zigmund Palffy, LosA. ✂	100	35	20
☐☐☐	Félix Potvin (G), LosA. ✂	225	75	45
☐☐☐	Keith Primeau, Phil. ✂	75	25	15
☐☐☐	Jeremy Roenick, Phil. ✂	150	50	30
☐☐☐	Patrick Roy (G), Colo. ✂	550	175	75
☐☐☐	Sergei Samsonov, Bost. ✂	100	35	20
☐☐☐	José Théodore (G), Mont. ✂	225	75	45
☐☐☐	Joe Thornton, Bost. ✂	225	75	45
☐☐☐	Alexei Yashin, NYIs. ✂	100	35	20
☐☐☐	Steve Yzerman, Detr. ✂	450	150	75

MILESTONE JERSEY

Insert Set (15 cards):		2800	900	350
	Insert	G15	S50	M99
☐☐☐	Peter Bondra, Wash. ✂	100	35	15
☐☐☐	Martin Brodeur (G), NJer. ✂	300	100	50
☐☐☐	Pavel Bure, NYRa. ✂	150	50	25
☐☐☐	Sergei Fedorov, Detr. ✂	175	60	25
☐☐☐	Brian Leetch, NYRa. ✂	100	35	15
☐☐☐	Mario Lemieux, Pitt. ✂	550	175	75
☐☐☐	Mike Modano, Dall. ✂	175	50	25
☐☐☐	Mark Recchi, Phil. ✂	75	25	10
☐☐☐	Jeremy Roenick, Phil. ✂	150	50	25
☐☐☐	Patrick Roy (G), Colo. ✂	550	175	50
☐☐☐	Joe Sakic, Colo. ✂	300	100	25
☐☐☐	Teemu Selänne, SanJ. ✂	150	50	25
☐☐☐	Brendan Shanahan, Detr. ✂	175	50	25
☐☐☐	Brendan Shanahan, Detr. ✂	175	60	25
☐☐☐	Steve Yzerman, Detr. ✂	450	150	50

SMOOTH SKATERS

Insert Set (17 cards):		3100	1000	400
	Insert	G15	S50	M99
☐☐☐	Peter Bondra, Wash. ✂	100	35	15
☐☐☐	Éric Dazé, Chic. ✂	75	25	10
☐☐☐	Simon Gagné, Phil. ✂	150	50	20
☐☐☐	Wayne Gretzky, LosA. ✂	750	250	150
☐☐☐	Jarome Iginla, Calg. ✂	150	50	10
☐☐☐	Jaromir Jagr, Wash. ✂	175	50	25
☐☐☐	Paul Kariya, Anah. ✂	250	75	25
☐☐☐	Mario Lemieux, Pitt. ✂	550	175	75
☐☐☐	Mike Modano, Dall. ✂	175	50	25
☐☐☐	Markus Näslund, Vanc. ✂	175	50	25
☐☐☐	Joe Sakic, Colo. ✂	300	100	25
☐☐☐	Sergei Samsonov, Bost. ✂	100	35	15
☐☐☐	Miroslav Satan, Buff. ✂	50	20	10
☐☐☐	Steve Sullivan, Chic. ✂	50	20	10
☐☐☐	Mats Sundin, Toro. ✂	175	50	25
☐☐☐	Joe Thornton, Bost. ✂	225	75	25
☐☐☐	Steve Yzerman, Detr. ✂	450	150	50

XTREME TALENTS

Insert Set (28 cards):		3900	1200	500
	Insert	G15	S50	M99
☐☐☐	Jason Allison, LosA. ✂	100	25	15
☐☐☐	Martin Biron (G), Buff. ✂	75	25	15
☐☐☐	Peter Bondra, Wash. ✂	100	25	15
☐☐☐	Raymond Bourque, Bost. ✂	225	75	25
☐☐☐	Mike Dunham (G), Nash. ✂	75	25	10
☐☐☐	Sergei Fedorov, Detr. ✂	175	50	25
☐☐☐	Peter Forsberg, Colo. ✂	250	75	25
☐☐☐	Simon Gagné, Phil. ✂	150	50	20
☐☐☐	Giguère (G), Anah. ✂	175	50	30
☐☐☐	Jarome Iginla, Calg. ✂	150	50	10
☐☐☐	Jaromir Jagr, Wash. ✂	175	50	25
☐☐☐	Paul Kariya, Anah. ✂	250	75	25
☐☐☐	Saku Koivu, Mont. ✂	225	75	35
☐☐☐	Olaf Kölzig (G), Wash. ✂	100	25	15
☐☐☐	John LeClair, Phil. ✂	150	50	25
☐☐☐	Nicklas Lidström, Detr. ✂	100	25	15
☐☐☐	Mike Modano, Dall. ✂	175	50	25
☐☐☐	Markus Näslund, Vanc. ✂	175	50	25
☐☐☐	Keith Primeau, Phil. ✂	75	25	10
☐☐☐	Patrick Roy (G), Colo. ✂	550	175	50
☐☐☐	Sergei Samsonov, Bost. ✂	100	25	15
☐☐☐	Brendan Shanahan, Detr. ✂	175	50	25
☐☐☐	Mats Sundin, Toro. ✂	175	50	25
☐☐☐	José Théodore (G), Mont. ✂	225	75	25
☐☐☐	Joe Thornton, Bost. ✂	225	75	25
☐☐☐	Marty Turco (G), Dall. ✂	100	25	15
☐☐☐	Roman Turek (G), Calg. ✂	75	25	15
☐☐☐	Steve Yzerman, Detr. ✂	450	150	50

2002 - 03 SP^{X} ROOKIE

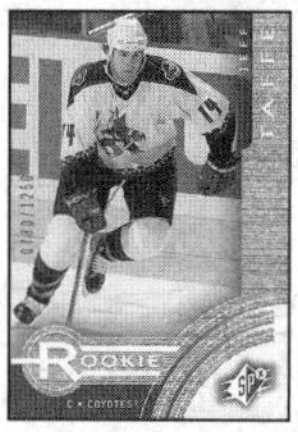

Produced by The Upper Deck Company, this series was released in 2002-03. The original redemption cards were seeded in packs of 2001 - 02 Upper Deck Rookie Update.

	Redemption	SPXR
☐	**R-1 Stanislav Chistov, Anah. RC**	
☐	R-2 Mark Hartigan, Atla.	
☐	**R-3 Tim Thomas (G), Bost. RC**	
☐	R-4 Henrik Tallinder, Buff.	
☐	**R-5 Chuck Kobasew, Calg. RC**	
☐	R-6 Jaroslav Svoboda, Caro.	
☐	**R-7 Shawn Thornton, Chic. RC**	
☐	**R-8 Jeff Paul, Colo. RC**	
☐	**R-9 Rick Nash, Colu. RC**	
☐	**R-10 Steve Ott, Dall. RC**	
☐	**R-11 Henrik Zetterberg, Detr. RC**	
☐	**R-12 Ales Hemsky, Edmo. RC**	
☐	**R-13 Jay Bouwmeester, Flor. RC**	
☐	**R-14 Alexander Frolov, LosA. RC**	
☐	**R-15 Pierre-Marc Bouchard, MinW. RC**	
☐	**R-16 Ron Hainsey, Mont. RC**	
☐	**R-17 Scottie Upshall, Nash. RC**	
☐	R-18 Mike Danton, NJer.	
☐	**R-19 Eric Godard, NYIs. RC**	
☐	R-20 Jamie Lundmark, NYRa.	
☐	**R-21 Jason Spezza, Otta. RC**	
☐	**R-22 Radovan Somik, Phil. RC**	
☐	**R-23 Jeff Taffe, Phoe. RC**	
☐	R-24 Shane Endicott, Pitt.	
☐	**R-25 Lynn Loyns, SanJ. RC**	
☐	**R-26 Curtis Sanford (G), SLou. RC**	

☐ **R-27 Alexander Svitov, Tamp. RC**
☐ **R-28 Carlo Colaiacovo, Toro. RC**
☐ R-29 Fedor Fedorov, Vanc.
☐ **R-30 Steve Eminger, Wash. RC**

2002 - 03 STADIUM CLUB

Produced by The Topps Company, this series was released in November 2002. Each card has three versions: the regular card, the Photographer's Proof parallel, and the thick decoy parallel.

	Decoy	PP	Card
Shell Set (100 cards):			**30.00**
Complete Set (140 cards):	**175.00**	**300.00**	**100.00**
Common Player:	**.75**	**2.00**	**.25**
Description	**Decoy**	**PP**	**Card**
☐☐☐ 1 José Théodore (G), Mont.	1.50	7.50	1.50
☐☐☐ 2 Jarome Iginla, Calg.	1.00	5.00	1.00
☐☐☐ 3 Nicklas Lidström, Detr.	.75	3.50	.50
☐☐☐ 4 Ron Francis, Caro.	.75	3.50	.50
☐☐☐ 5 Jaromir Jagr, Pitt.	1.50	6.00	1.50
☐☐☐ 6 Mario Lemieux, Pitt.	4.50	18.50	4.50
☐☐☐ 7 Owen Nolan, SanJ.	.75	3.50	.50
☐☐☐ 8 Martin Brodeur (G), NJer.	2.00	10.00	2.00
☐☐☐ 9 Joe Sakic, Colo.	2.00	10.00	2.00
☐☐☐ 10 Ilya Kovalchuk, Atla.	1.50	6.00	1.50
☐☐☐ 11 Mike Modano, Dall.	1.50	6.00	1.50
☐☐☐ 12 Jason Allison, LosA.	.75	3.50	.50
☐☐☐ 13 Sean Burke (G), Phoe.	.75	3.50	.50
☐☐☐ 14 Mats Sundin, Toro.	1.50	6.00	1.50
☐☐☐ 15 Markus Näslund, Vanc.	1.50	6.00	1.50
☐☐☐ 16 Jeremy Roenick, Phil.	1.00	5.00	1.00
☐☐☐ 17 Eric Lindros, NYRa.	1.50	6.00	1.50
☐☐☐ 18 Brent Johnson, SLou.	.75	2.50	.50
☐☐☐ 19 Sergei Fedorov, Detr.	1.50	6.00	1.50
☐☐☐ 20 Sergei Samsonov, Bost.	.75	3.50	.50
☐☐☐ 21 Chris Drury, Colo.	.75	3.50	.50
☐☐☐ 22 Ryan Smyth, Edmo.	.75	3.00	.50
☐☐☐ 23 Scott Hartnell, Nash.	.75	2.00	.25
☐☐☐ 24 Simon Gagné, Phil.	1.00	5.00	1.00
☐☐☐ 25 Dan Cloutier (G), Vanc.	.75	2.50	.50
☐☐☐ 26 Vincent Lecavalier, Tamp.	1.50	6.00	1.50
☐☐☐ 27 Martin Havlat, Otta.	.75	3.50	.50
☐☐☐ 28 Patrik Elias, NJer.	1.00	5.00	1.00
☐☐☐ 29 Roberto Luongo (G), Flor.	1.00	5.00	1.00
☐☐☐ 30 Rob Blake, Colo.	.75	3.50	.50
☐☐☐ 31 Jean-Pierre Dumont, Buff.	.75	2.00	.25
☐☐☐ 32 Jeff O'Neill, Caro.	.75	2.50	.50
☐☐☐ 33 Pavel Datsyuk, Detr.	1.00	5.00	1.00
☐☐☐ 34 Dan Blackburn, NYRa.	.75	2.50	.50
☐☐☐ 35 Alexei Kovalev, Pitt.	.75	3.50	.50
☐☐☐ 36 Olaf Kölzig (G), Wash.	.75	3.50	.50
☐☐☐ 37 Milan Hejduk, Colo.	1.00	5.00	1.00
☐☐☐ 38 Steve Yzerman, Detr.	3.50	15.00	3.50
☐☐☐ 39 Marc Denis (G), Colu.	.75	3.00	.50
☐☐☐ 40 Michael Peca, NYIs.	.75	2.50	.50
☐☐☐ 41 Saku Koivu, Mont.	1.00	5.00	1.00
☐☐☐ 42 Marian Gaborik, MinW.	1.50	6.00	1.50
☐☐☐ 43 Brad Richards, Tamp.	.75	3.00	.50
☐☐☐ 44 Alexander Mogilny, Toro.	.75	3.00	.50
☐☐☐ 45 Mike Comrie, Edmo.	1.00	5.00	1.00
☐☐☐ 46 Peter Forsberg, Colo.	2.00	8.50	2.00
☐☐☐ 47 Dany Heatley, Atla.	1.50	6.00	1.50
☐☐☐ 48 Steve Sullivan, Chic.	.75	2.00	.25
☐☐☐ 49 Keith Tkachuk, SLou.	.75	3.50	.50
☐☐☐ 50 Todd Bertuzzi, Vanc.	1.50	7.50	1.50
☐☐☐ 51 Evgeni Nabokov (G), SanJ.	.75	3.50	.50
☐☐☐ 52 David Legwand, Nash.	.75	2.50	.50
☐☐☐ 53 Scott Stevens, NJer.	.75	2.50	.50
☐☐☐ 54 Éric Dazé, Chic.	.75	2.50	.50
☐☐☐ 55 Martin Biron (G), Buff.	.75	3.00	.50
☐☐☐ 56 Zigmund Palffy, LosA.	.75	3.50	.50
☐☐☐ 57 Paul Kariya, Anah.	2.00	8.50	2.00
☐☐☐ 58 Krys Kolanos, Phoe.	.75	2.00	.25
☐☐☐ 59 Pavel Bure, NYRa.	1.00	5.00	1.00
☐☐☐ 60 Darcy Tucker, Toro.	.75	2.00	.25
☐☐☐ 61 Marian Hossa, Otta.	1.50	6.00	1.50
☐☐☐ 62 Roman Cechmanek (G), Phil.	.75	2.50	.50
☐☐☐ 63 Mark Parrish, NYIs.	.75	2.50	.50
☐☐☐ 64 Arturs Irbe (G), Caro.	.75	2.50	.50
☐☐☐ 65 Brian Rolston, Bost.	.75	2.00	.25
☐☐☐ 66 Marty Turco (G), Dall.	.75	3.50	.50
☐☐☐ 67 Peter Bondra, Wash.	.75	3.50	.50
☐☐☐ 68 Johan Hedberg (G), Pitt.	.75	2.50	.50
☐☐☐ 69 Chris Pronger, SLou.	.75	3.50	.50
☐☐☐ 70 Patrick Lalime (G), Otta.	.75	3.50	.50
☐☐☐ 71 Mike Dunham (G), Nash.	.75	2.50	.50
☐☐☐ 72 Kristian Huselius, Flor.	.75	2.00	.25
☐☐☐ 73 Patrick Roy (G), Colo.	4.50	18.50	4.50
☐☐☐ 74 Joe Thornton, Bost.	1.50	7.50	1.50
☐☐☐ 75 Andrew Brunette, MinW.	.75	2.00	.25
☐☐☐ 76 Alexei Yashin, NYIs.	.75	3.50	.50
☐☐☐ 77 John LeClair, Phil.	1.00	5.00	1.00
☐☐☐ 78 Miroslav Satan, Buff.	.75	2.00	.25
☐☐☐ 79 Doug Weight, SLou.	.75	3.50	.50
☐☐☐ 80 Gary Roberts, Toro.	.75	2.50	.50
☐☐☐ 81 Tommy Salo (G), Edmo.	.75	2.50	.50
☐☐☐ 82 Daniel Alfredsson, Otta.	.75	3.50	.50
☐☐☐ 83 Marco Sturm, SanJ.	.75	2.00	.25
☐☐☐ 84 Rostislav Klesla, Colu.	.75	2.00	.25
☐☐☐ 85 Richard Zednik, Mont.	.75	2.50	.50
☐☐☐ 86 Roman Turek (G), Calg.	.75	3.00	.50
☐☐☐ 87 Brian Leetch, NYRa.	.75	3.50	.50
☐☐☐ 88 Chris Osgood (G), NYIs.	.75	3.50	.50
☐☐☐ 89 Brendan Morrison, Vanc.	.75	2.00	.25
☐☐☐ 90 Jocelyn Thibault (G), Chic.	.75	2.50	.50
☐☐☐ 91 Teemu Selänne, SanJ.	1.00	5.00	1.00
☐☐☐ 92 J-S Giguère (G), Anah.	1.50	6.00	1.50
☐☐☐ 93 Nikolai Khabibulin (G), Tamp.	.75	2.50	.50
☐☐☐ 94 Pavol Demitra, SLou.	.75	2.50	.50
☐☐☐ 95 Brendan Shanahan, Detr.	1.50	6.00	1.50
☐☐☐ 96 Mark Recchi, Phil.	.75	2.50	.50
☐☐☐ 97 Félix Potvin (G), LosA.	.75	3.50	.50
☐☐☐ 98 Shane Doan, Phoe.	.75	2.00	.25
☐☐☐ 99 Erik Cole, Caro.	.75	2.00	.25
☐☐☐ 100 Brett Hull, Detr.	1.50	6.00	1.50

SUBSETS

Insert (1:4)	Thick	PP	Subset
☐☐☐ 101 Curtis Joseph (G), Detr.	5.00	6.00	5.00
☐☐☐ 102 Bobby Holik, NYRa.	1.00	2.00	1.00
☐☐☐ 103 Ed Belfour (G), Toro.	5.00	6.00	5.00
☐☐☐ 104 Bill Guerin, Dall.	2.00	2.00	2.00
☐☐☐ 105 Petr1 Sykora, Anah.	2.00	2.00	2.00
☐☐☐ 106 Scott A. Young, Dall.	1.00	2.00	1.00
☐☐☐ 107 Adam Oates, Anah.	2.00	2.00	2.00
☐☐☐ 108 Jeff Friesen, NJer.	1.00	2.00	1.00
☐☐☐ 109 Darius Kasparaitis, NYRa.	1.00	2.00	1.00
☐☐☐ 110 Tony Amonte, Phoe.	3.00	3.00	3.00
☐☐☐ 111 Marcel Hossa, Mont.	2.00	2.00	2.00
☐☐☐ 112 Jamie Lundmark, NYRa.	2.00	2.00	1.00
☐☐☐ 113 Pavel Brendl, Phil.	2.00	2.00	1.00
☐☐☐ 114 Jaroslav Svoboda, Caro.	1.00	2.00	1.00
☐☐☐ 115 Stephen Weiss, Flor.	2.00	2.00	2.00
☐☐☐ 116 Martin Prusek (G), Otta.	2.00	2.00	1.00
☐☐☐ 117 Jani Rita, Edmo.	2.00	2.00	1.00
☐☐☐ 118 Petr Cajanek, SLou.	.75	2.00	1.00
☐☐☐ 119 Trent Hunter, NYIs.	1.00	2.00	1.00
☐☐☐ 120 Jonathan Cheechoo, SanJ.	2.00	2.00	1.00
☐☐☐ **121 S. Chistov, Anah. RC**	**24**	**20**	**10**
☐☐☐ **122 A. Svitov, Tamp. RC**	**18**	**15**	**5**
☐☐☐ **123 A. Frolov, LosA. RC**	**24**	**20**	**10**
☐☐☐ **124 A. Smirnov, Anah. RC**	**12**	**10**	**5**
☐☐☐ **125 C. Kobasew, Calg. RC**	**18**	**15**	**5**
☐☐☐ **126 Rick Nash, Colu. RC**	**48**	**40**	**20**
☐☐☐ **127 H. Zetterberg, Detr. RC**	**48**	**40**	**20**
☐☐☐ **128 J. Bouwmeester, Flor. RC**	**24**	**20**	**10**
☐☐☐ **129 A. Hemsky, Edmo. RC**	**24**	**20**	**10**
☐☐☐ **130 M. Gerber (G), Anah. RC**	**8**	**8**	**5**
☐☐☐ **131 R. Hainsey, Mont. RC**	**12**	**10**	**5**
☐☐☐ **132 PM. Bouchard, MinW. RC**	**24**	**20**	**10**
☐☐☐ **133 J. Spezza, Otta. RC**	**36**	**30**	**15**
☐☐☐ **134 K. Sauer, Anah. RC**	**8**	**8**	**5**
☐☐☐ **135 L. Pirjetä, Colu. RC**	**8**	**8**	**5**
☐☐☐ **136 A. Hall, Nash. RC**	**12**	**10**	**5**
☐☐☐ **137 D. Seidenberg, Phil. RC**	**8**	**8**	**5**
☐☐☐ **138 P. Sharp, Phil. RC**	**8**	**8**	**5**
☐☐☐ **139 S. Eminger, Wash. RC**	**8**	**8**	**5**
☐☐☐ **140 D. Bykov, Detr. RC**	**8**	**8**	**5**

BEAM TEAM

Insert Set (15 cards):	**60.00**
Insert (1:18)	**BT**
☐ BT-1 Steve Yzerman, Detr.	10.00
☐ BT-2 Mario Lemieux, Pitt.	12.00
☐ BT-3 Patrick Roy (G), Colo.	12.00
☐ BT-4 Jarome Iginla, Calg.	3.00
☐ BT-5 José Théodore (G), Mont.	5.00
☐ BT-6 Brendan Shanahan, Detr.	4.00
☐ BT-7 Chris Pronger, SLou.	2.00
☐ BT-8 Dany Heatley, Atla.	4.00
☐ BT-9 Joe Thornton, Bost.	5.00
☐ BT-10 Peter Forsberg, Colo.	5.00
☐ BT-11 Ron Francis, Caro.	2.00
☐ BT-12 Owen Nolan, SanJ.	2.00
☐ BT-13 Todd Bertuzzi, Vanc.	5.00
☐ BT-14 Rob Blake, Colo.	2.00
☐ BT-15 Paul Kariya, Anah.	5.00

FABRIC OF CHAMPIONS

Insert Set (10 cards):	**150.00**
Insert (1:68)	**FC**
☐ FC1 Rob Blake, Colo. ✂	15.00
☐ FC2 Derian Hatcher, Dall. ✂	15.00
☐ FC3 Alex Tanguay, Colo. ✂	15.00
☐ FC4 Martin Brodeur (G), NJer. ✂	40.00
☐ FC5 Milan Hejduk, Colo. ✂	20.00
☐ FC6 Mike Modano, Dall. ✂	25.00
☐ FC7 Scott Niedermayer, NJer. ✂	15.00
☐ FC8 Brian Leetch, NYRa. ✂	15.00
☐ FC9 Sergei Zubov, Dall. ✂	15.00
☐ FC10 Chris Drury, Colo. ✂	15.00

LONE STAR SIGNATURE

Insert Set (12 cards):	**290.00**
Insert (1:56)	**LSS**
☐ Todd Bertuzzi, Vanc. ✍	45.00
☐ Daniel Brière, Phoe. ✍	20.00
☐ Erik Cole, Caro. ✍	20.00
☐ Éric Dazé, Chic. ✍	20.00
☐ Simon Gagné, Phil. ✍	30.00
☐ Brian Gionta, NJer. ✍	20.00
☐ Jarome Iginla, Calg. ✍	30.00
☐ Rostislav Klesla, Colu. ✍	20.00
☐ Ilya Kovalchuk, Atla. ✍	35.00
☐ Patrick Lalime (G), Otta. ✍	20.00
☐ Chris Pronger, SLou. ✍	20.00
☐ Brad Richards, Tamp. ✍	20.00
☐ José Théodore (G), Mont. ✍	45.00
☐ Stephen Weiss, Flor. ✍	20.00

NHL PASSPORT

Insert Set (17 cards):	**55.00**
Insert (1:40)	**NHLP**
☐ NHLP-1 Saku Koivu, Mont. ✂	30.00
☐ NHLP-10 Miroslav Satan, Buff. ✂	15.00
☐ NHLP-12 Zigmund Palffy, LosA. ✂	20.00
☐ NHLP-14 Brian Rolston, Bost. ✂	15.00
☐ NHLP-16 Sergei Samsonov, Bost. ✂	20.00
☐ NHLP-2 Daniel Alfredsson, Otta. ✂	20.00
☐ NHLP-4 Mats Sundin, Toro. ✂	35.00
☐ NHLP-6 Simon Gagné, Phil. ✂	30.00
☐ NHLP-8 Paul Kariya, Anah. ✂	50.00
☐ NHLP-11 Markus Näslund, Vanc. ✂	35.00
☐ NHLP-13 Tony Amonte, Chic. ✂	20.00
☐ NHLP-15 Maxim Afinogenov, Buff. ✂	15.00
☐ NHLP-17 Marco Sturm, SanJ. ✂	15.00
☐ NHLP-3 Eric Lindros, NYRa. ✂	35.00
☐ NHLP-5 Todd Bertuzzi, Vanc. ✂	45.00
☐ NHLP-7 Marian Hossa, Otta. ✂	35.00
☐ NHLP-9 Vincent Lecavalier, Tamp. ✂	35.00

PATCHES OF CHAMPIONS

Insert Set (9 cards):	**35.00**
Insert	**PC**
☐ PC1 Rob Blake, Colo. ✂	45.00
☐ PC2 Derian Hatcher, Dall. ✂	
☐ PC3 Alex Tanguay, Colo. ✂	
☐ PC4 Martin Brodeur (G), NJer. ✂	
☐ PC5 Milan Hejduk, Colo. ✂	
☐ PC6 Mike Modano, Dall. ✂	
☐ PC7 Scott Niedermayer, NJer. ✂	
☐ PC8 Brian Leetch, NYRa. ✂	
☐ PC9 Sergei Zubov, Dall. ✂	

ST. PATRICK

Insert Set (16 cards):	
Insert	**SP**
☐ SP-CA-J Patrick Roy (G), Colo. ✂	
☐ SP-CA-JA Patrick Roy (G), Colo. ✂	
☐ SP-CA-JP Patrick Roy (G), Colo. ✂	
☐ SP-CA-JPA Patrick Roy (G), Colo. ✂	
☐ SP-CA/MC-J Patrick Roy (G), Colo. ✂ Mont. ✂	
☐ SP-CA/MC-J/S Patrick Roy (G), Colo. ✂ Mont. ✂	
☐ SP-CA/MC-J/SA Patrick Roy (G), Colo. ✂ Mont. ✂	
☐ SP-CA/MC-JA Patrick Roy (G), Colo. ✂ Mont. ✂	
☐ SP-CA/MC-JP Patrick Roy (G), Colo. ✂ Mont. ✂	
☐ SP-CA/MC-JPA Patrick Roy (G), Colo. ✂ Mont. ✂	
☐ SP-MC-J Patrick Roy (G), Mont. ✂	
☐ SP-MC-JA Patrick Roy (G), Mont. ✂	
☐ SP-MC-JP Patrick Roy (G), Mont. ✂	
☐ SP-MC-JPA Patrick Roy (G), Mont. ✂	
☐ SP-S Patrick Roy (G), Colo. ✂	
☐ SP-SA Patrick Roy (G), Colo. ✂	

THE PUCK STOPS HERE

Insert Set (15 cards):	**30.00**
Insert (1:6)	**PSH**
☐ PSH-1 Brent Johnson, SLou.	2.00
☐ PSH-2 Roman Cechmanek (G), Phil.	2.00
☐ PSH-3 Evgeni Nabokov (G), SanJ.	2.00
☐ PSH-4 José Théodore (G), Mont.	3.00
☐ PSH-5 Martin Biron (G), Buff.	2.00
☐ PSH-6 Chris Osgood (G), NYIs.	2.00
☐ PSH-7 Marty Turco (G), Dall.	2.00
☐ PSH-8 Nikolai Khabibulin (G), Tamp.	2.00
☐ PSH-9 Roberto Luongo (G), Flor.	2.00
☐ PSH-10 Martin Brodeur (G), NJer.	4.00
☐ PSH-11 Sean Burke (G), Phoe.	2.00
☐ PSH-12 Tommy Salo (G), Edmo.	2.00
☐ PSH-13 Mike Richter, NYRa.	2.00
☐ PSH-14 Patrick Roy (G), Colo.	9.00
☐ PSH-15 Jean-Sébastien Giguère (G), Anah.	3.00

WORLD STAGE

Insert Set (20 cards):	**45.00**
Insert (1:7)	**WS**
☐ WS-1 Sergei Fedorov, Detr.	3.00
☐ WS-2 Chris Drury, Colo.	2.00
☐ WS-3 Martin Brodeur (G), NJer.	6.00
☐ WS-4 Joe Sakic, Colo.	6.00
☐ WS-5 Mike Modano, Dall.	3.00
☐ WS-6 Jeremy Roenick, Phil.	3.00
☐ WS-7 Brett Hull, Detr.	3.00
☐ WS-8 Ilya Kovalchuk, Atla.	3.00
☐ WS-9 Nicklas Lidström, Detr.	2.00
☐ WS-10 Jaromir Jagr, Wash.	3.00
☐ WS-11 Alexei Yashin, NYIs.	2.00
☐ WS-12 Zigmund Palffy, LosA.	2.00
☐ WS-13 Marian Gaborik, MinW.	3.00
☐ WS-14 Teemu Selänne, SanJ.	3.00
☐ WS-15 Alexei Kovalev, Pitt.	2.00
☐ WS-16 Patrik Elias, NJer.	3.00
☐ WS-17 Peter Bondra, Wash.	2.00
☐ WS-18 Pavel Bure, NYRa.	3.00
☐ WS-19 Mats Sundin, Toro.	3.00
☐ WS-20 Daniel Alfredsson, Otta.	2.00

YOUNGSTARS MVP PUCK RELIC AUTOGRAPH

Insert	**MVP**
☐ IK Ilya Kovalchuk, Atla. ✍ ✂	

YOUNGSTARS SOUVENIRS

Insert Set (23 cards):	**295.00**
Insert (1:28)	**YSS**
☐ YSS-1 Ilya Kovalchuk, Atla. ✂	30.00
☐ YSS-2 Pavel Datsyuk, Detr. ✂	25.00
☐ YSS-3 Mike Comrie, Edmo. ✂	25.00
☐ YSS-4 Dan Blackburn, NYRa. ✂	12.00
☐ YSS-5 Dany Heatley, Atla. ✂	30.00
☐ YSS-6 Marian Gaborik, MinW. ✂	30.00
☐ YSS-7 Kristian Huselius, Flor. ✂	12.00
☐ YSS-8 David Legwand, Nash. ✂	12.00
☐ YSS-9 Roberto Luongo (G), Flor. ✂	25.00

YSS-10	Brad Richards, Tamp. ✄	15.00
YSS-11	Justin Williams, Phil. ✄	12.00
YSS-12	Kyle Calder, Chic. ✄	12.00
YSS-13	David Tanabe, Caro. ✄	12.00
YSS-14	Brenden Morrow, Dall. ✄	12.00
YSS-15	Scott Hartnell, Nash. ✄	12.00
YSS-16	Mike Fisher, Otta. ✄	12.00
YSS-17	Tim Connolly, Buff. ✄	12.00
YSS-18	Nick Boynton, Bost. ✄	12.00
YSS-19	Paul Mara, Phoe. ✄	12.00
YSS-20	Mike Ribeiro, Mont. ✄	12.00
YSS-21	Robyn Regehr, Calg. ✄	12.00
YSS-22	Andrew Ference, Pitt. ✄	12.00
YSS-23	Karel Rachunek, Otta. ✄	12.00

YOUNGSTARS SOUVENIRS

Insert Set (6 cards): 180.00

Insert		YSD
YSD-1	D. Heatley ✄ / I. Kovalchuk ✄	60.00
YSD-2	D. Legwand ✄ / S. Hartnell ✄	20.00
YSD-3	K. Huselius ✄ / R. Luongo (G) ✄	35.00
YSD-4	P. Datsyuk ✄ / M. Gaborik ✄	55.00
YSD-5	Ju. Williams ✄ / M. Comrie ✄	35.00
YSD-6	B. Richards ✄ / D. Blackburn ✄	25.00

2002 - 03 STARZ

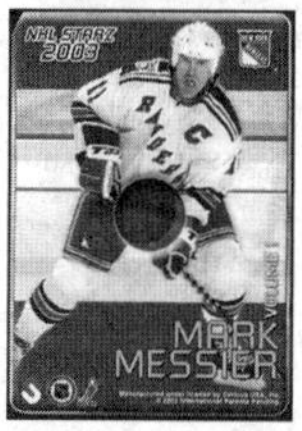

Player
- Brett Hull, Detr.
- Mario Lemieux, Pitt.
- Mark Messier, NYRa.
- Patrick Roy (G), Colo.
- Tony Amonte, Phil.
- Joe Sakic, Colo.
- Mats Sundin, Toro.
- Steve Yzerman, Detr.

2002 - 03 TOPPS & O-PEE-CHEE

Produced by The Topps Company, this series was released in August 2002. There are four versions of each card 1-330: an O-Pee-Chee card, an O-Pee-Chee Premier blue parallel (#/500), an O-Pee-Chee Premier red parallel (#/100), a Topps card, a Topps O-Pee-Chee blue parallel (#/500), and a Topps O-Pee-Chee red parallel (#/100). There are similar values for the Topps and O-Pee-Chee base cards, the blue parallels, and the red parallels.

Complete Set (340 cards): 75.00
Original Set (330 cards): 1250.00 475.00 50.00
Common Player: 3.00 1.00 .20

Description	R100	B500	Topps
1 Patrick Roy (G), Colo.	45	18	3.00
2 Mario Lemieux, Pitt.	45	18	3.00
3 M. Brodeur (G), NJer.	20	9	1.50
4 Steve Yzerman, Detr.	35	14	2.00
5 Jaromir Jagr, Wash.	15	6	1.00
6 Chris Pronger, SLou.	5	3	.50
7 John LeClair, Phil.	10	4	.50
8 Paul Kariya, Anah.	20	8	1.00
9 Tony Amonte, Chic.	5	3	.50
10 Joe Thornton, Bost.	15	7	1.00
11 Ilya Kovalchuk, Atla.	15	6	1.00
12 Jarome Iginla, Calg.	10	4	.50
13 Mike Modano, Dall.	15	6	1.00
14 V. Lecavalier, Tamp.	15	6	1.00
15 Michael Peca, NYIs.	5	2	.20
16 Pavel Bure, NYRa.	10	4	.50
17 Eric Lindros, NYRa.	15	6	1.00
18 Félix Potvin (G), LosA.	15	3	.50
19 Ron Francis, Caro.	5	3	.50
20 Miroslav Satan, Buff.	3	1	.20
21 Rostislav Klesla, Colu.	3	1	.20
22 Mike Comrie, Edmo.	10	4	.50
23 D. Alfredsson, Otta.	15	3	.50
24 Sean Burke (G), Phoe.	5	3	.50
25 David Legwand, Nash.	5	2	.20
26 Marian Gaborik, MinW.	15	6	1.00
27 Saku Koivu, Mont.	15	4	.50
28 Owen Nolan, SanJ.	5	3	.50
29 Mats Sundin, Toro.	15	6	1.00
30 J-P Dumont, Buff.	3	1	.20
31 Chris Drury, Colo.	5	3	.50
32 M. Näslund, Vanc.	15	6	1.00
33 Anson Carter, Edmo.	5	2	.20
34 D. Roloson (G), MinW.	3	1	.20
35 Brad Isbister, NYIs.	3	1	.20
36 Daniel Brière, Phoe.	5	2	.20
37 Martin St-Louis, Tamp.	5	2	.20
38 Shayne Corson, Toro.	3	1	.20
39 Keith Tkachuk, SLou.	5	3	.50
40 Mark Recchi, Phil.	5	2	.20
41 P. Brisebois, Mont.	3	1	.20
42 Niklas Hagman, Flor.	3	1	.20
43 Marc Denis (G), Colu.	5	2	.20
44 Robyn Regehr, Calg.	3	1	.20
45 Byron Dafoe (G), Bost.	5	2	.20
46 Sergei Fedorov, Detr.	15	6	1.00
47 A. Brunette, MinW.	3	1	.20
48 Denis Arkhipov, Nash.	3	1	.20
49 Martin Havlat, Otta.	5	3	.50
50 Mike Rathje, SanJ.	3	1	.20
51 Mattias Öhlund, Vanc.	3	1	.20
52 Ulf Dahlén, Wash.	3	1	.20
53 Tim Connolly, Buff.	5	2	.20
54 Valeri Bure, Flor.	3	1	.20
55 Brian Boucher (G), Phil.	3	1	.20
56 Pascal Dupuis, MinW.	3	1	.20
57 Brian Leetch, NYRa.	5	3	.50
58 Daniel Sedin, Vanc.	5	2	.20
59 Kenny Jönsson, NYIs.	3	1	.20
60 Erik Cole, Caro.	5	2	.20
61 Patrick Lalime (G), Otta.	5	3	.50
62 Mike Leclerc, Anah.	3	1	.20
63 Patrick Marleau, SanJ.	5	2	.20
64 Tom Poti, NYRa.	3	1	.20
65 Lubos Bartecko, Atla.	3	1	.20
66 Tom Barrasso (G), Toro.	5	2	.20
67 Ryan Smyth, Edmo.	5	2	.20
68 Sami Kapanen, Caro.	3	1	.20
69 Michal Handzus, Phoe.	3	1	.20
70 Martin Straka, Pitt.	3	1	.20
71 Peter Forsberg, Colo.	20	8	1.00
72 Marc Savard, Calg.	3	1	.20
73 Jeff Friesen, Anah.	3	1	.20
74 M. Fernandez (G), MinW.	5	2	.20
75 Jason Smith, Edmo.	3	1	.20
76 Mike Ribeiro, Mont.	3	1	.20
77 Stephen Heinze, LosA.	3	1	.20
78 Adam Foote, Colo.	3	1	.20
79 S. McCarthy, NYRa.	3	1	.20
80 Toni Lydman, Calg.	3	1	.20
81 Tie Domi, Toro.	3	1	.20
82 Scott Stevens, NJer.	5	2	.20
83 Radim Vrbata, Colo.	3	1	.20
84 Oleg Petrov, Mont.	3	1	.20
85 Marty Turco (G), Dall.	5	3	.50
86 Kristian Huselius, Flor.	3	1	.20
87 Jeremy Roenick, Phil.	10	4	.50
88 Gary Roberts, Toro.	5	2	.20
89 D. McAmmond, Calg.	3	1	.20
90 Chris Chelios, Detr.	5	3	.50
91 Andy McDonald, Anah.	3	1	.20
92 Brett Hull, Detr.	15	6	1.00
93 Danny Markov, Phoe.	3	1	.20
94 Éric Dazé, Chic.	5	2	.20
95 Alex Tanguay, Colo.	5	3	.50
96 Petr Nedved, NYRa.	3	1	.20
97 Simon Gagné, Phil.	10	4	.50
98 Roman Turek (G), Calg.	5	2	.20
99 Milan Hejduk, Colo.	10	4	.50
100 M. Czerkawski, NYIs.	3	1	.20
101 Jaroslav Modry, LosA.	3	1	.20
102 Dan Cloutier (G), Vanc.	5	2	.20
103 Mark Bell, Chic.	3	1	.20
104 Brendan Witt, Wash.	3	1	.20
105 T. Selänne, SanJ.	10	4	.50
106 Johan Hedberg (G), Pitt.	5	2	.20
107 Mike Ricci, SanJ.	3	1	.20
108 R. Luongo (G), Flor.	10	4	.50
109 V. Prospal, Tamp.	3	1	.20
110 Zigmund Palffy, LosA.	5	3	.50
111 Ed Jovanovski, Vanc.	5	2	.20
112 Scott Gomez, NJer.	5	2	.20
113 Pierre Turgeon, Dall.	5	2	.20
114 N. Sundström, SanJ.	3	1	.20
115 Martin Biron (G), Buff.	5	2	.20
116 Keith Primeau, Phil.	5	2	.20
117 J-S Giguère (G), Anah.	15	6	1.00
118 Filip Kuba, MinW.	3	1	.20
119 David Tanabe, Caro.	3	1	.20
120 Brian Savage, Phoe.	3	1	.20
121 Alexei Zhamnov, Chic.	3	1	.20
122 B. Johnson, SLou.	5	2	.20
123 D. Blackburn, NYRa.	5	2	.20
124 Éric Bélanger, LosA.	3	1	.20
125 J. Niinimaa, Edmo.	3	1	.20
126 Jonas Höglund, Toro.	3	1	.20
127 Marian Hossa, Otta.	15	6	1.00
128 Mike Richter, NYRa.	5	2	.20
129 Peter Bondra, Wash.	5	3	.50
130 R. Brind'Amour, Caro.	3	1	.20
131 Shane Doan, Phoe.	3	1	.20
132 Viktor Kozlov, Flor.	3	1	.20
133 Y. Perreault, Mont.	3	1	.20
134 S. Samsonov, Bost.	5	3	.50
135 N. Khabibulin (G), Tamp.	5	2	.20
136 Rob Ray, Buff.	3	1	.20
137 R. Cechmanek (G), Phil.	5	2	.20
138 Patrik Stefan, Atla.	3	1	.20
139 Matt Cullen, Anah.	3	1	.20
140 Kim Johnsson, Phil.	3	1	.20
141 Jim Dowd, MinW.	3	1	.20
142 Glen Murray, Bost.	5	2	.20
143 Dominik Hasek (G), Detr.	15	6	1.00
144 Brad Richards, Tamp.	5	2	.20
145 Cory Stillman, SLou.	3	1	.20
146 Josef Vasicek, Caro.	3	1	.20
147 Alexei Kovalev, Pitt.	5	3	.50
148 A. Deadmarsh, LosA.	3	1	.20
149 B. Morrison, Vanc.	3	1	.20
150 Eric Brewer, Edmo.	5	2	.20
151 Jason Arnott, Dall.	5	2	.20
152 B. Morrow, Dall.	3	1	.20
153 Manny Legacé (G), Detr.	3	1	.20
154 M. Nylander, Chic.	3	1	.20
155 Pavol Demitra, SLou.	5	2	.20
156 Olaf Kölzig (G), Wash.	5	3	.50
157 Sergei Berezin, Mont.	5	1	.20
158 T. Numminen, Phoe.	3	1	.20
159 V. Orszagh, Nash.	3	1	.20
160 Brian Rafalski, NJer.	3	1	.20
161 Doug Gilmour, Mont.	5	3	.50
162 Jere Lehtinen, Dall.	3	1	.20
163 Mark Parrish, NYIs.	5	2	.20
164 Petr Sykora, NJer.	5	2	.20
165 Sergei Zholtok, MinW.	3	1	.20
166 Wade Redden, Otta.	3	1	.20
167 S. Niedermayer, NJer.	3	1	.20
168 Olli Jokinen, Flor.	3	1	.20
169 Kyle Calder, Chic.	3	1	.20
170 JLangenbrunner, NJer.	3	1	.20
171 Darcy Tucker, Toro.	3	1	.20
172 Aleksey Morozov, Pitt.	3	1	.20
173 Adam Oates, Phil.	5	2	.20
174 Chris Osgood (G), NYIs.	5	3	.50
175 Espen Knutsen, Colu.	3	1	.20
176 Jochen Hecht, Edmo.	3	1	.20
177 M. Afinogenov, Buff.	5	2	.20
178 R. Dvorak, NYRa.	3	1	.20
179 Steve Sullivan, Chic.	3	1	.20
180 Trevor Linden, Vanc.	5	2	.20
181 Tomi Kallio, Atla.	3	1	.20
182 Robert Lang, Pitt.	3	1	.20
183 Milan Hnilicka (G), Atla.	3	1	.20
184 Justin Williams, Phil.	3	1	.20
185 Greg Johnson, Nash.	3	1	.20
186 Craig Conroy, Calg.	3	1	.20
187 A. Mogilny, Toro.	5	2	.20
188 Adrian Aucoin, NYIs.	3	1	.20
189 Fredrik Modin, Tamp.	3	1	.20
190 J. Théodore (G), Mont.	15	7	1.00
191 Ray Whitney, Colu.	3	1	.20
192 Mikael Renberg, Toro.	3	1	.20
193 Mike Sillinger, Colu.	3	1	.20
194 Richard Zednik, Mont.	5	2	.20
195 Mike Dunham (G), Nash.	5	2	.20
196 Joe Sakic, Colo.	20	9	1.50
197 F. Brathwaite (G), SLou.	3	1	.20
198 Chris Simon, Wash.	3	1	.20
199 Al MacInnis, SLou.	5	2	.20
200 G. Laraque, Edmo.	3	1	.20
201 Jozef Stümpel, Bost.	3	1	.20
202 T. Fleury, NYRa.	5	3	.50
203 Rob Blake, Colo.	5	3	.50
204 Todd White, Otta.	3	1	.20
205 Dany Heatley, Atla.	15	6	1.00
206 Scott Hartnell, Nash.	3	1	.20
207 O. Tverdovsky, Anah.	3	1	.20
208 Krys Kolanos, Phoe.	3	1	.20
209 Ian Laperrière, LosA.	3	1	.20
210 Damphousse, SanJ.	5	3	.50
211 Nick Boynton, Bost.	3	1	.20
212 Curtis Joseph (G), Toro.	15	6	1.00
213 Henrik Sedin, Vanc.	5	2	.20
214 Kris Beech, Pitt.	3	1	.20
215 Sandis Ozolinsh, Flor.	3	1	.20
216 Ron Tugnutt (G), Colu.	5	2	.20
217 Todd Bertuzzi, Vanc.	15	7	1.00
218 Tommy Salo (G), Edmo.	5	2	.20
219 Martin Lapointe, Bost.	5	2	.20
220 Derian Hatcher, Dall.	3	1	.20
221 David Vyborny, Colu.	3	1	.20
222 Jocelyn Thibault (G), Chic.	5	2	.20
223 N. Lidström, Detr.	5	3	.50
224 Marcus Nilson, Flor.	3	1	.20
225 Sergei Zubov, Dall.	3	1	.20
226 Bryan McCabe, Toro.	3	1	.20
227 C. Lemieux, Phoe.	3	1	.20
228 Grand-Pierre, Colu.	3	1	.20
229 Bill Guerin, Bost.	5	2	.20
230 Sergei Brylin, NJer.	3	1	.20
231 B. Smolinski, LosA.	3	1	.20
232 Luc Robitaille, Detr.	10	4	.50
233 Alexei Yashin, NYIs.	5	3	.50
234 E. Nabokov (G), SanJ.	5	3	.50
235 P. Datsyuk, Detr.	10	4	.50
236 Martin Erat, Nash.	3	1	.20
237 Stu Barnes, Buff.	3	1	.20
238 Derek Morris, Calg.	3	1	.20
239 Bates Battaglia, Caro.	3	1	.20
240 Jason Allison, LosA.	5	3	.50
241 Peter Worrell, Flor.	3	1	.20
242 M. Messier, NYRa.	15	6	1.00
243 Shawn Bates, NYIs.	3	1	.20
244 D. Langkow, Phoe.	3	1	.20
245 Ed Belfour (G), Dall.	15	6	1.00
246 Jan Hrdina, Pitt.	3	1	.20
247 Pavel Kubina, Tamp.	3	1	.20
248 Scott Young, SLou.	3	1	.20
249 Curtis Brown, Buff.	3	1	.20
250 Brian Rolston, Bost.	3	1	.20
251 Jiri Dopita, Phil.	3	1	.20
252 K. Timonen, Nash.	3	1	.20
253 Marco Sturm, SanJ.	3	1	.20
254 Arturs Irbe (G), Caro.	5	2	.20
255 J. Nieuwendyk, NJer.	5	2	.20
256 S. Gonchar, Wash.	3	1	.20
257 Doug Weight, SLou.	5	3	.50
258 Jeff O'Neill, Caro.	5	2	.20
259 Mike York, Edmo.	3	1	.20
260 Radek Bonk, Otta.	3	1	.20
261 Patrik Elias, NJer.	10	4	.50
262 Phil Housley, Chic.	3	1	.20
263 B. Shanahan, Detr.	15	6	1.00
264 Sheldon Keefe, Tamp.	3	1	.20
265 Rick DiPietro (G), NYIs.	5	2	.20
266 J-F Fortin, Wash.	3	1	.20
267 J. Chimera, Edmo.	3	1	.20
268 Andy Hilbert, Bost.	3	1	.20
269 Brian Gionta, NJer.	3	1	.20
270 S. Varlamov, SLou.	3	1	.20
271 Alex Auld (G), Vanc.	3	1	.20
272 Pavel Brendl, Phil.	3	1	.20
273 B. Radivojevic, Phoe.	3	1	.20
274 Kamil Piros, Atla.	3	1	.20
275 Steve Gainey, Dall.	3	1	.20
276 Mike Mottau, NYRa.	3	1	.20
277 J. Ölvestad, Tamp.	3	1	.20
278 Jeff Jillson, SanJ.	3	1	.20
279 Ilja Bryzgalov, Anah.	3	1	.20
280 Taylor Pyatt, Buff.	3	1	.20
281 A. Raycroft (G), Bost.	3	1	.20
282 C. Berglund, NJer.	3	1	.20
283 P. Desrochers, Phoe.	3	1	.20
284 Lukas Krajicek, Flor.	3	1	.20
285 Riku Hahl, Colo.	3	1	.20
286 Ivan Huml, Bost.	3	1	.20
287 Jani Rita, Edmo.	3	1	.20
288 K. Kudroc, Tamp.	3	1	.20
289 Juraj Kolnik, NYIs.	3	1	.20
290 John Erskine, Dall.	3	1	.20
291 B. Sutherby, Wash.	3	1	.20
292 B. St-Jacques, Phil.	3	1	.20
293 Nick Schultz, MinW.	3	1	.20
294 Pasi Nurminen (G), Atla.	3	1	.20
295 Norm Milley, Buff.	3	1	.20
296 Marcel Hossa, Mont.	5	2	.20
297 Ales Kotalik, Buff.	5	2	.20
298 Bryan Allen, Vanc.	3	1	.20
299 Mika Noronen (G), Buff.	5	2	.20
300 Tyler Arnason, Chic.	5	2	.20
301 Petr Schastlivy, Otta.	3	1	.20
302 Mike Van Ryn, SLou.	3	1	.20
303 S. Montador, Calg.	3	1	.20
304 Denis Shvidki, Flor.	3	1	.20
305 Stephen Weiss, Flor.	10	4	.50
306 N. Alexeev, Tamp.	3	1	.20
307 V. Nedorost, Colo.	3	1	.20

□□□□□□	308 Raffi Torres, NYIs.	3	1	.20
□□□□□□	309 G. Lefebvre, Phil.	3	1	.20
□□□□□□	310 Sean Avery, Detr.	3	1	.20
□□□□□□	311 Shane Endicott, Pitt.	3	1	.20
□□□□□□	312 Ty Conklin, Edmo.	3	1	.20
□□□□□□	313 Damphousse, NJer.	3	1	.20
□□□□□□	314 J. Roenick, Phil.	10	4	.20
□□□□□□	315 Ron Francis, Caro.	5	3	.20
□□□□□□	316 B. Shanahan, Detr.	15	6	.50
□□□□□□	317 Patrick Roy (G), Colo.	45	18	1.50
□□□□□□	318 Luc Robitaille, Detr.	10	4	.20
□□□□□□	319 J. Théodore (G), Mont.	15	7	.50
□□□□□□	320 Patrick Roy (G), Colo.	45	18	1.50
□□□□□□	321 S. Gonchar, Wash.	3	1	.20
□□□□□□	322 Bryan McCabe, Toro.	3	1	.20
□□□□□□	323 Chris Chelios, Detr.	5	3	.20
□□□□□□	324 N. Lidström, Detr.	5	3	.20
□□□□□□	325 Simon Gagné, Phil.	10	4	.20
□□□□□□	326 B. Shanahan, Detr.	15	6	.50
□□□□□□	327 Jaromir Jagr, Wash.	15	6	.50
□□□□□□	328 Jarome Iginla, Calg.	10	4	.20
□□□□□□	329 Mats Sundin, Toro.	15	6	.50
□□□□□□	330 Joe Sakic, Colo.	20	9	.50

ROOKIE REDEMPTION

Cards 331-340 were available via a single redemption card found in packs of 2002-03 O-Pee-Chee or Topps. There are two versions for each card 331-340: the OPC and the Topps card.

	Description	
□□	**331 Henrik Zetterberg, Detr. RC**	**10.00**
□□	**332 Pierre-Marc Bouchard, MinW. RC**	**6.00**
□□	**333 Alexander Frolov, LosA. RC**	**4.00**
□□	**334 Alexander Svitov, Tamp. RC**	**4.00**
□□	**335 Jason Spezza, Otta. RC**	**6.00**
□□	**336 Jay Bouwmeester, Flor. RC**	**6.00**
□□	**337 Ales Hemsky, Edmo. RC**	**6.00**
□□	**338 Rick Nash, Colu. RC**	**10.00**
□□	**339 Chuck Kobasew, Calg. RC**	**4.00**
□□	**340 Stanislav Chistov, Anah. RC**	**6.00**

OVERSIZE

Insert Set (25 cards):

	Insert
□	1 Joe Thornton, Bost.
□	2 Jarome Iginla, Calg.
□	3 Roman Turek (G), Calg.
□	4 Ron Francis, Caro.
□	5 Patrick Roy (G), Colo.
□	6 Joe Sakic, Colo.
□	7 Steve Yzerman, Detr.
□	8 Brendan Shanahan, Detr.
□	9 Mike Comrie, Edmo.
□	10 Ryan Smyth, Edmo.
□	11 Paul Kariya, Anah.
□	12 José Théodore (G), Mont.
□	13 Saku Koivu, Mont.
□	14 Martin Brodeur (G), NJer.
□	15 Michael Peca, NYIs.
□	16 Daniel Alfredsson, Otta.
□	17 Martin Havlat, Otta.
□	18 Sean Burke (G), Phoe.
□	19 Mario Lemieux, Pitt.
□	20 Owen Nolan, SanJ.
□	21 Chris Pronger, SLou.
□	22 Mats Sundin, Toro.
□	23 Curtis Joseph (G), Toro.
□	24 Markus Näslund, Vanc.
□	25 Todd Bertuzzi, Vanc.

UPDATE

These cards were inserted into packs of 2002 - 03 Topps Chrome. There are two versions for each card: an O-Pee-Chee card and a Topps card.

Insert Set (10 cards):		**1020.00**
	Insert	**Update**
□□	9 Tony Amonte, Phoe.	1.50
□□	31 Chris Drury, Calg.	1.50
□□	73 Jeff Friesen, NJer.	.50
□□	100 Mariusz Czerkawski, Mont.	.50
□□	164 Petr Sykora, Anah.	1.00
□□	173 Adam Oates, Anah.	1.00
□□	182 Robert Lang, Wash.	.50
□□	212 Curtis Joseph (G), Detr.	2.50
□□	229 Bill Guerin, Dall.	1.00
□□	245 Ed Belfour (G), Toro.	2.50

CAPTAIN'S CLOTH

Single jerseys are seeded 1:939 packs while triple jerseys are seeded 1:2,686 packs.

Insert Set (17 cards):		**945.00**
	Insert	**Topps**
□	Lemieux ✂ / Sakic ✂ / Francis ✂	200.00
□	Primeau ✂ / LeClair ✂ / Recchi ✂	60.00
□	Hatcher ✂ / Zubov ✂ / Modano ✂	60.00
□	Pronger ✂ / Kariya ✂ / Francis ✂	100.00
□	Koivu ✂ / Näslund ✂ / Sundin ✂	110.00
□	Lemieux ✂ / Sundin ✂ / Primeau ✂	150.00
□	Kariya ✂ / Koivu ✂ / Sakic ✂	125.00
□	CC8 Mario Lemieux, Pitt. ✂	100.00
□	CC9 Keith Primeau, Phil. ✂	20.00
□	CC10 Markus Näslund, Vanc. ✂	35.00
□	CC11 Mats Sundin, Toro. ✂	35.00
□	CC12 Paul Kariya, Anah. ✂	50.00
□	CC13 Joe Sakic, Colo. ✂	50.00
□	CC14 Saku Koivu, Mont. ✂	30.00
□	CC15 Ron Francis, Caro. ✂	20.00
□	CC16 Derian Hatcher, Dall. ✂	20.00
□	CC17 Chris Pronger, SLou. ✂	20.00

COAST TO COAST

Insert Set (10 cards):		**30.00**
	Insert (1:12)	**CC**
□	CC1 Mario Lemieux, Pitt.	10.00
□	CC2 Pavel Bure, NYRa.	3.00
□	CC3 Jarome Iginla, Calg.	3.00
□	CC4 Mats Sundin, Toro.	3.00
□	CC5 Peter Bondra, Wash.	2.00
□	CC6 Ilya Kovalchuk, Atla.	4.00
□	CC7 Joe Thornton, Bost.	4.00
□	CC8 Paul Kariya, Anah.	5.00
□	CC9 Joe Sakic, Colo.	6.00
□	CC10 Patrik Elias, NJer.	3.00

COMMEMORATIVE SERIES

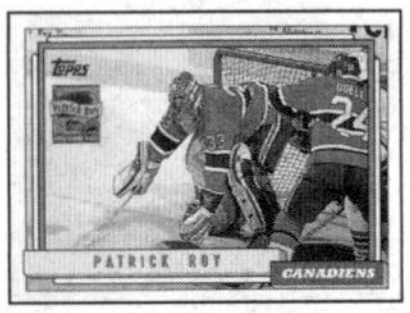

Insert Set (14 cards):		**70.00**
	Insert (1:18)	**MA**
□	1 Patrick Roy (G), Mont. ['86-87]	10.00
□	2 Patrick Roy (G), Mont. ['87-88]	6.00
□	3 Patrick Roy (G), Mont. ['88-89]	6.00
□	4 Patrick Roy (G), Mont. ['89-90]	6.00
□	5 Patrick Roy (G), Mont. ['90-91]	6.00
□	6 Patrick Roy (G), Mont. ['91-92]	6.00
□	7 Patrick Roy (G), Mont. ['92-93]	6.00
□	8 Patrick Roy (G), Mont. ['93-94]	6.00
□	9 Patrick Roy (G), Mont. ['94-95]	6.00
□	10 Patrick Roy (G), Colo. ['95-96]	6.00
□	11 Patrick Roy (G), Colo. ['98-99]	6.00
□	12 Patrick Roy (G), Colo. ['99-00]	6.00
□	13 Patrick Roy (G), Colo. ['00-01]	6.00
□	14 Patrick Roy (G) / Valeri Kamensky ['01-02]	6.00

COMMEMORATIVE SERIES AUTOGRAPH

Insert Set (14 cards):		**4000.00**
	Insert (#33)	**CSA**
□	1 Patrick Roy (G), Mont. ✍ ['86-87]	500.00
□	2 Patrick Roy (G), Mont. ✍ ['87-88]	375.00
□	3 Patrick Roy (G), Mont. ✍ ['88-89]	375.00
□	4 Patrick Roy (G), Mont. ✍ ['89-90]	375.00
□	5 Patrick Roy (G), Mont. ✍ ['90-91]	375.00
□	6 Patrick Roy (G), Mont. ✍ ['91-92]	375.00
□	7 Patrick Roy (G), Mont. ✍ ['92-93]	375.00
□	8 Patrick Roy (G), Mont. ✍ ['93-94]	375.00
□	9 Patrick Roy (G), Mont. ✍ ['94-95]	375.00
□	10 Patrick Roy (G), Colo. ✍ ['95-96]	375.00
□	11 Patrick Roy (G), Colo. ✍ ['98-99]	375.00
□	12 Patrick Roy (G), Colo. ✍ ['99-00]	375.00
□	13 Patrick Roy (G), Colo. ✍ ['00-01]	375.00
□	14 Patrick Roy (G) ✍ / Valeri Kamensky ['01-02]	375.00

FIRST ROUND FABRIC

Insert Set (11 cards):		**190.00**
	Insert (1:216)	**FRF**
□	Martin Biron (G), Buff. ✂	20.00
□	Dan Blackburn, NYRa. ✂	20.00
□	Jean-Pierre Dumont, Buff. ✂	20.00
□	Radek Dvorak, NYRa. ✂	20.00
□	Eric Lindros, NYRa. ✂	25.00
□	Patrick Marleau, SanJ. ✂	20.00
□	Mike Modano, Dall. ✂	25.00
□	Markus Näslund, Vanc. ✂	25.00
□	Scott Niedermayer, NJer. ✂	20.00
□	Keith Primeau, Phil. ✂	20.00
□	Mats Sundin, Toro. ✂	25.00

FIRST ROUND FABRIC AUTOGRAPH

Insert Set (6 cards):		**190.00**
	Insert (1:1191)	**FRFA**
□	Martin Biron (G), Buff. ✍ ✂	30.00
□	Radek Dvorak, NYRa. ✍ ✂	30.00
□	Mike Modano, Dall. ✍ ✂	60.00
□	Scott Niedermayer, NJer. ✍ ✂	30.00
□	Keith Primeau, Phil. ✍ ✂	30.00
□	Mats Sundin, Toro. ✍ ✂	60.00

HOMETOWN HEROES

Insert Set (20 cards):		**50.00**
	Insert (1:12)	**HHC**
□	HHC1 Jarome Iginla, Calg.	4.00
□	HHC2 Ed Jovanovski, Vanc.	2.00
□	HHC3 Ryan Smyth, Edmo.	2.00
□	HHC4 Mike York, Edmo.	1.50
□	HHC5 Mats Sundin, Toro.	5.00
□	HHC6 Todd Bertuzzi, Vanc.	6.00
□	HHC7 Markus Näslund, Vanc.	5.00
□	HHC8 Saku Koivu, Mont.	4.00
□	HHC9 José Théodore (G), Mont.	6.00
□	HHC10 Daniel Alfredsson, Otta.	3.00
□	HHC11 Patrick Lalime (G), Otta.	3.00
□	HHC12 Roman Turek (G), Calg.	2.00
□	HHC13 Mike Comrie, Edmo.	4.00
□	HHC14 Tommy Salo (G), Edmo.	2.00
□	HHC15 Anson Carter, Edmo.	2.00
□	HHC16 Doug Gilmour, Mont.	3.00
□	HHC17 Yanic Perreault, Mont.	1.50
□	HHC18 Radek Bonk, Otta.	1.50
□	HHC19 Darcy Tucker, Toro.	1.50
□	HHC20 Curtis Joseph (G), Toro.	5.00

HOMETOWN HEROES

Insert Set (20 cards):		**75.00**
	Insert	**HHU**
□	HHU1 Martin Brodeur (G), NJer.	7.00
□	HHU2 Joe Sakic, Colo.	7.00
□	HHU3 Mario Lemieux, Pitt.	12.00
□	HHU4 Steve Yzerman, Detr.	10.00
□	HHU5 Paul Kariya, Anah.	6.00
□	HHU6 Mike Modano, Dall.	4.00
□	HHU7 Brett Hull, Detr.	4.00
□	HHU8 Bill Guerin, Bost.	1.50
□	HHU9 Tony Amonte, Chic.	2.00
□	HHU10 Jeremy Roenick, Phil.	3.00
□	HHU11 John LeClair, Phil.	3.00
□	HHU12 Brendan Shanahan, Detr.	4.00
□	HHU13 Owen Nolan, SanJ.	2.00
□	HHU14 Al MacInnis, SLou.	1.50
□	HHU15 Chris Pronger, SLou.	2.00
□	HHU16 Doug Weight, SLou.	2.00
□	HHU17 Ilya Kovalchuk, Atla.	5.00
□	HHU18 Joe Thornton, Bost.	5.00
□	HHU19 Patrick Roy (G), Colo.	12.00
□	HHU20 Ron Francis, Caro.	2.00

OWN THE GAME

Insert Set (20 cards):		**40.00**
	Insert (1:6)	**OTG**
□	OTG1 Jarome Iginla, Calg.	3.00
□	OTG2 Markus Näslund, Vanc.	3.00
□	OTG3 Todd Bertuzzi, Vanc.	4.00
□	OTG4 Mats Sundin, Toro.	3.00
□	OTG5 Jaromir Jagr, Wash.	3.00
□	OTG6 Jarome Iginla, Calg.	3.00
□	OTG7 Mats Sundin, Toro.	3.00
□	OTG8 Bill Guerin, Bost.	1.50
□	OTG9 Glen Murray, Bost.	1.50
□	OTG10 Markus Näslund, Vanc.	3.00
□	OTG11 Dany Heatley, Atla.	3.00
□	OTG12 Ilya Kovalchuk, Atla.	4.00
□	OTG13 Kristian Huselius, Flor.	1.50
□	OTG14 Erik Cole, Caro.	1.50
□	OTG15 Pavel Datsyuk, Detr.	3.00
□	OTG16 Dominik Hasek (G), Detr.	3.00
□	OTG17 Martin Brodeur (G), NJer.	6.00
□	OTG18 Evgeni Nabokov (G), SanJ.	2.00
□	OTG19 Byron Dafoe (G), Bost.	1.50
□	OTG20 Brent Johnson, SLou.	1.50

ROOKIE REPRINT

Insert Set (15 cards):		**25.00**
	Insert (1:18)	**RR**
□	1 Pat LaFontaine, NYIs.	3.00
□	2 Mike Gartner, Wash.	4.00
□	3 Peter Mahovlich, Detr.	2.00
□	4 Andy Bathgate, NYRa.	2.00
□	5 Lorne (Gump) Worsley, NYRa.	4.00
□	6 Danny Gare, Buff.	2.00
□	7 Harry Howell, NYRa.	2.00
□	8 Andy Moog, Edmo.	2.00
□	9 Keith Magnuson, Chic.	2.00
□	10 Milt Schmidt, Bost.	3.00
□	11 Glen Sather	2.00
□	12 Dick Duff, NYRa.	2.00
□	13 Garry Unger	2.00
□	14 Darren Pang, Chic.	2.00
□	15 Glenn Resch, NYIs.	2.00

ROOKIE REPRINT AUTOGRAPH

Insert Set (15 cards):		**425.00**
	Insert (1:1191)	**RRA**
□	1 Pat LaFontaine, NYIs. ✍	35.00
□	2 Mike Gartner, Wash. ✍	50.00
□	3 Peter Mahovlich ✍	35.00
□	4 Andy Bathgate ✍	35.00
□	5 Lorne Worsley ✍	50.00
□	6 Danny Gare ✍	35.00
□	7 Harry Howell ✍	35.00
□	8 Andy Moog, Edmo. ✍	35.00
□	9 Keith Magnuson ✍	35.00
□	10 Milt Schmidt ✍	35.00
□	11 Glen Sather ✍	35.00
□	12 Dick Duff ✍	35.00
□	13 Garry Unger ✍	35.00
□	14 Darren Pang, Chic. ✍	35.00
□	15 Glenn Resch ✍	35.00

STANLEY CUP HEROES

Insert Set (5 cards):		**30.00**
	Insert (1:36)	**SCHA**
□	John Ferguson, Mont.	8.00
□	Reggie Leach, Phil.	8.00
□	Rick MacLeish, Phil.	8.00
□	Derek Sanderson, Bost.	8.00
□	Steve Shutt, Mont.	8.00

STANLEY CUP HEROES AUTOGRAPH

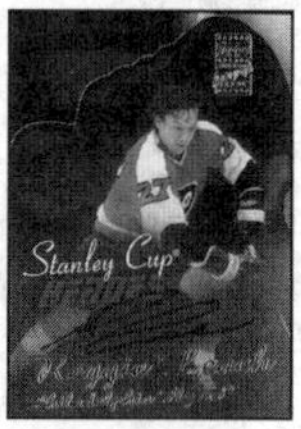

	Insert Set (5 cards):	160.00
	Insert	SCHA
☐	John Ferguson, Mont. ✍	40.00
☐	Reggie Leach, Phil. ✍	40.00
☐	Rick MacLeish, Phil. ✍	40.00
☐	Derek Sanderson, Bost. ✍	40.00
☐	Steve Shutt, Mont. ✍	40.00

SIGNS OF THE FUTURE

	Insert Set (6 cards):	550.00
	Insert (1:1191)	SotF
☐	Mike Comrie, Edmo. ✍	50.00
☐	Martin Havlat, Otta. ✍	40.00
☐	Krys Kolanos, Phoe. ✍	40.00
☐	Ilya Kovalchuk, Atla. ✍	60.00
☐	David Legwand, Nash. ✍	40.00
☐	Radim Vrbata, Colo. ✍	40.00

PRE-PRODUCTION

	Sample Set (6 cards):	.00
	Sample	PP
☐☐	PP1 Simon Gagné, Phil.	1.50
☐☐	PP2 Chris Drury, Calg.	1.00
☐☐	PP3 Jeff Friesen, NJer.	.50
☐☐	PP4 Wade Redden, Otta.	.50
☐☐	PP5 Byron Dafoe (G), Bost.	.50
☐☐	PP6 Patrik Elias, NJer.	1.50

2002 - 03 TOPPS CHROME

Produced by The Topps Company, this series was released in February 2003. Each card has three versions: the regular card, the Refractor parallel, and the Black Border Refractor parallel (#/100).

		BBR100	Refr	Card
	Shell Set (148 cards):			100.00
	Complete Set (182 cards):	975.00	350.00	275.00
	Common Player:	.75	2.00	.25
	Description	BBR100	Refr	Card
☐☐☐	1 Patrick Roy (G), Colo.	45	15	7.50
☐☐☐	2 Mario Lemieux, Pitt.	45	15	7.50
☐☐☐	3 Martin Brodeur (G), NJer.	20	5	4.00
☐☐☐	4 Steve Yzerman, Detr.	35	10	6.00
☐☐☐	5 Jaromir Jagr, Wash.	15	5	2.50
☐☐☐	6 Chris Pronger, SLou.	5	2	1.50
☐☐☐	7 John LeClair, Phil.	10	2	2.00
☐☐☐	8 Paul Kariya, Anah.	20	5	3.50
☐☐☐	9 Tony Amonte, Chic.	5	2	1.50
☐☐☐	10 Joe Thornton, Bost.	15	5	3.00
☐☐☐	11 Ilya Kovalchuk, Atla.	15	5	2.50
☐☐☐	12 Jarome Iginla, Calg.	10	2	2.00
☐☐☐	13 Mike Modano, Dall.	15	5	2.50
☐☐☐	14 Vincent Lecavalier, Tamp.	15	5	2.50
☐☐☐	15 Michael Peca, NYIs.	5	2	1.00
☐☐☐	16 Pavel Bure, NYRa.	10	2	2.00
☐☐☐	17 Eric Lindros, NYRa.	15	5	2.50
☐☐☐	18 Félix Potvin (G), LosA.	5	2	1.50
☐☐☐	19 Ron Francis, Caro.	5	2	1.50
☐☐☐	20 Miroslav Satan, Buff.	4	2	.50
☐☐☐	21 Rostislav Klesla, Colu.	4	2	.50
☐☐☐	22 Mike Comrie, Edmo.	10	2	2.00
☐☐☐	23 Daniel Alfredsson, Otta.	5	2	1.50
☐☐☐	24 Sean Burke (G), Phoe.	5	2	1.50
☐☐☐	25 David Legwand, Nash.	5	2	1.00
☐☐☐	26 Marian Gaborik, MinW.	15	5	2.50
☐☐☐	27 Saku Koivu, Mont.	10	2	2.00
☐☐☐	28 Owen Nolan, SanJ.	5	2	1.50
☐☐☐	29 Mats Sundin, Toro.	15	5	2.50
☐☐☐	30 Jean-Pierre Dumont, Buff.	4	2	.50
☐☐☐	31 Chris Drury, Colo.	5	2	1.50
☐☐☐	32 Markus Näslund, Vanc.	15	5	2.50
☐☐☐	33 Anson Carter, Edmo.	5	2	1.00
☐☐☐	34 Daniel Brière, Phoe.	5	2	1.00
☐☐☐	35 Keith Tkachuk, SLou.	5	2	1.50
☐☐☐	36 Mark Recchi, Phil.	5	2	1.00
☐☐☐	37 Marc Denis (G), Colu.	5	2	1.00
☐☐☐	38 Sergei Fedorov, Detr.	15	5	2.50
☐☐☐	39 Andrew Brunette, MinW.	4	2	.50
☐☐☐	40 Martin Havlat, Otta.	5	2	1.50
☐☐☐	41 Brian Leetch, NYRa.	5	2	1.50
☐☐☐	42 Erik Cole, Caro.	4	2	.50
☐☐☐	43 Patrick Lalime (G), Otta.	5	2	1.50
☐☐☐	44 Patrick Marleau, SanJ.	5	2	1.00
☐☐☐	45 Ryan Smyth, Edmo.	5	2	1.00
☐☐☐	46 Sami Kapanen, Caro.	4	2	.50
☐☐☐	47 Martin Straka, Pitt.	4	2	.50
☐☐☐	48 Peter Forsberg, Colo.	20	5	3.50
☐☐☐	49 Jeff Friesen, NJer.	4	2	.50
☐☐☐	50 Manny Fernandez (G), MinW.	5	2	1.00
☐☐☐	51 Scott Stevens, NJer.	5	2	1.00
☐☐☐	52 Radim Vrbata, Colo.	4	2	.50
☐☐☐	53 Marty Turco (G), Dall.	5	2	1.50
☐☐☐	54 Kristian Huselius, Flor.	4	2	.50
☐☐☐	55 Jeremy Roenick, Phil.	10	2	2.00
☐☐☐	56 Gary Roberts, Toro.	5	2	1.00
☐☐☐	57 Chris Chelios, Detr.	5	2	1.50
☐☐☐	58 Brett Hull, Detr.	15	5	2.50
☐☐☐	59 Éric Dazé, Chic.	5	2	1.00
☐☐☐	60 Alex Tanguay, Colo.	5	2	1.50
☐☐☐	61 Simon Gagné, Phil.	10	2	2.00
☐☐☐	62 Roman Turek (G), Calg.	5	2	1.00
☐☐☐	63 Milan Hejduk, Colo.	10	2	2.00
☐☐☐	64 Mariusz Czerkawski, Mont.	4	2	.50
☐☐☐	65 Dan Cloutier (G), Vanc.	5	2	1.00
☐☐☐	66 Teemu Selänne, SanJ.	10	2	2.00
☐☐☐	67 Johan Hedberg (G), Pitt.	5	2	1.00
☐☐☐	68 Mike Ricci, SanJ.	4	2	.50
☐☐☐	69 Roberto Luongo (G), Flor.	10	2	2.00
☐☐☐	70 Zigmund Palffy, LosA.	5	2	1.50
☐☐☐	71 Ed Jovanovski, Vanc.	5	2	1.00
☐☐☐	72 Scott Gomez, NJer.	5	2	1.00
☐☐☐	73 Pierre Turgeon, Dall.	5	2	1.00
☐☐☐	74 Martin Biron (G), Buff.	5	2	1.00
☐☐☐	75 Keith Primeau, Phil.	5	2	1.00
☐☐☐	76 J-S Giguère (G), Anah.	15	5	2.50
☐☐☐	77 Alexei Zhamnov, Chic.	4	2	.50
☐☐☐	78 Brent Johnson, SLou.	5	2	1.00
☐☐☐	79 Dan Blackburn, NYRa.	5	2	1.00
☐☐☐	80 Mike Richter, NYRa.	5	2	1.00
☐☐☐	81 Peter Bondra, Wash.	5	2	1.50
☐☐☐	82 Rod Brind'Amour, Caro.	4	2	.50
☐☐☐	83 Shane Doan, Phoe.	4	2	.50
☐☐☐	84 Sergei Samsonov, Bost.	5	2	1.50
☐☐☐	85 Nikolai Khabibulin (G), Tamp.	5	2	1.00
☐☐☐	86 Roman Cechmanek (G), Phil.	5	2	1.00
☐☐☐	87 Glen Murray, Bost.	5	2	1.00
☐☐☐	88 Brad Richards, Tamp.	5	2	1.00
☐☐☐	89 Alexei Kovalev, Pitt.	5	2	1.50
☐☐☐	90 Adam Deadmarsh, LosA.	4	2	.50
☐☐☐	91 Brendan Morrison, Vanc.	4	2	.50
☐☐☐	92 Jason Arnott, Dall.	5	2	1.00
☐☐☐	93 Brenden Morrow, Dall.	4	2	.50
☐☐☐	94 Pavol Demitra, SLou.	5	2	1.00
☐☐☐	95 Olaf Kölzig (G), Wash.	5	2	1.50
☐☐☐	96 Doug Gilmour, Mont.	5	2	1.50
☐☐☐	97 Jere Lehtinen, Dall.	4	2	.50
☐☐☐	98 Petr Sykora, Anah.	5	2	1.00
☐☐☐	99 Wade Redden, Otta.	4	2	.50
☐☐☐	100 Adam Oates, Anah.	5	2	1.00
☐☐☐	101 Chris Osgood (G), NYIs.	5	2	1.50
☐☐☐	102 Espen Knutsen, Colu.	4	2	.50
☐☐☐	103 Maxim Afinogenov, Buff.	5	2	1.00
☐☐☐	104 Steve Sullivan, Chic.	4	2	.50
☐☐☐	105 Robert Lang, Wash.	4	2	.50
☐☐☐	106 Milan Hnilicka (G), Atla.	4	2	.50
☐☐☐	107 Craig Conroy, Calg.	4	2	.50
☐☐☐	108 Alexander Mogilny, Toro.	5	2	1.00
☐☐☐	109 José Théodore (G), Mont.	15	5	3.00
☐☐☐	110 Mike Dunham (G), Nash.	5	2	1.00
☐☐☐	111 Joe Sakic, Colo.	20	5	4.00
☐☐☐	112 Al MacInnis, SLou.	5	2	1.00
☐☐☐	113 Marian Hossa, Otta.	15	5	2.50
☐☐☐	114 Rob Blake, Colo.	5	2	1.50
☐☐☐	115 Dany Heatley, Atla.	15	5	2.50
☐☐☐	116 Scott Hartnell, Nash.	4	2	.50
☐☐☐	117 Krys Kolanos, Phoe.	4	2	.50
☐☐☐	118 Vincent Damphousse, SanJ.	5	2	1.50
☐☐☐	119 Curtis Joseph (G), Detr.	15	5	2.50
☐☐☐	120 Todd Bertuzzi, Vanc.	15	5	3.00
☐☐☐	121 Tommy Salo (G), Edmo.	5	2	1.00
☐☐☐	122 Jocelyn Thibault (G), Chic.	5	2	1.00
☐☐☐	123 Nicklas Lidström, Detr.	5	2	1.50
☐☐☐	124 Bryan McCabe, Toro.	4	2	.50
☐☐☐	125 Bill Guerin, Dall.	5	2	1.00
☐☐☐	126 Luc Robitaille, Detr.	10	2	2.00
☐☐☐	127 Alexei Yashin, NYIs.	5	2	1.50
☐☐☐	128 Evgeni Nabokov (G), SanJ.	5	2	1.50
☐☐☐	129 Pavel Datsyuk, Detr.	10	2	2.00
☐☐☐	130 Stu Barnes, Buff.	4	2	.50
☐☐☐	131 Derek Morris, Calg.	4	2	.50
☐☐☐	132 Jason Allison, LosA.	5	2	1.50
☐☐☐	133 Mark Messier, NYRa.	15	5	2.50
☐☐☐	134 Ed Belfour (G), Toro.	15	5	2.50
☐☐☐	135 Scott A. Young, Dall.	4	2	.50
☐☐☐	136 Marco Sturm, SanJ.	4	2	.50
☐☐☐	137 Arturs Irbe (G), Caro.	5	2	1.00
☐☐☐	138 Joe Nieuwendyk, NJer.	5	2	1.00
☐☐☐	139 Sergei Gonchar, Wash.	4	2	.50
☐☐☐	140 Doug Weight, SLou.	5	2	1.50
☐☐☐	141 Jeff O'Neill, Caro.	5	2	1.00
☐☐☐	142 Mike York, Edmo.	4	2	.50
☐☐☐	143 Patrik Elias, NJer.	10	2	2.00
☐☐☐	144 Brendan Shanahan, Detr.	15	5	2.50
☐☐☐	145 Rick DiPietro (G), NYIs.	5	2	1.00
☐☐☐	146 Jani Rita, Edmo.	4	2	.50
☐☐☐	147 Stephen Weiss, Flor.	5	2	1.00
☐☐☐	148 Nikita Alexeev, Tamp.	4	2	.50

ROOKIE

	Insert	BBR100	Refr	Card
☐☐☐	**149 Micki DuPont, Calg. RC**	10	5	4
☐☐☐	**150 Ivan Majesky, Flor. RC**	10	5	3
☐☐☐	**151 Jason Spezza, Otta. RC**	21	18	15
☐☐☐	**152 Eric Godard, NYIs. RC**	10	5	3
☐☐☐	**153 Sh. Thornton, Chic. RC**	10	5	4
☐☐☐	**154 Jeff Paul, Colo. RC**	10	5	3
☐☐☐	**155 Lasse Pirjetä, Colu. RC**	10	5	3
☐☐☐	**156 Adam Hall, Nash. RC**	10	5	6
☐☐☐	**157 M. Tellqvist (G), Toro. RC**	10	5	4
☐☐☐	**158 Tomi Pettinen, NYIs. RC**	10	5	3
☐☐☐	**159 Radovan Somik, Phil. RC**	10	5	3
☐☐☐	**160 Jordan Leopold, Calg. RC**	10	5	5
☐☐☐	**161 Dmitri Bykov, Detr. RC**	10	5	4
☐☐☐	**162 Tim Thomas (G), Bost. RC**	10	5	4
☐☐☐	**163 M. Gerber (G), Anah. RC**	10	5	4
☐☐☐	**164 Tom Koivisto, SLou. RC**	10	5	3
☐☐☐	**165 Patrick Sharp, Phil. RC**	10	5	3
☐☐☐	**166 Steve Eminger, Wash. RC**	10	5	4
☐☐☐	**167 A. Volchenkov, Otta. RC**	10	5	4
☐☐☐	**168 Scottie Upshall, Nash. RC**	10	5	5
☐☐☐	**169 Ron Hainsey, Mont. RC**	10	5	6
☐☐☐	**170 Kurt Sauer, Anah. RC**	10	5	3
☐☐☐	**171 Jeff Taffe, Phoe. RC**	10	5	5
☐☐☐	**172 D. Seidenberg, Phil. RC**	10	5	4
☐☐☐	**173 S. Chistov, Anah. RC**	10	5	10
☐☐☐	**174 Chuck Kobasew, Calg. RC**	10	5	5
☐☐☐	**175 Rick Nash, Colu. RC**	28	24	20
☐☐☐	**176 Ales Hemsky, Edmo. RC**	10	5	10
☐☐☐	**177 J. Bouwmeester, Flor. RC**	10	5	10
☐☐☐	**178 Alexei Smirnov, Anah. RC**	10	5	5
☐☐☐	**179 A. Svitov, Tamp. RC**	10	5	5
☐☐☐	**180 P-M Bouchard, MinW. RC**	10	5	10
☐☐☐	**181 A. Frolov, LosA. RC**	10	5	10
☐☐☐	**182 H. Zetterberg, Detr. RC**	28	24	20

CHROMOGRAPHS

Each card has two versions: the regular Chrome card and the Refractor parallel.

	Insert Set (6 cards):	225.00	110.00
	Insert	Ref.	Aut
☐☐	Erik Cole, Caro. ✍	25.00	15.00
☐☐	Brian Gionta, NJer. ✍	25.00	15.00
☐☐	Curtis Joseph (G), Detr. ✍	100.00	50.00
☐☐	Brad Richards, Tamp. ✍	45.00	20.00
☐☐	Radim Vrbata, Colo. ✍	30.00	15.00
☐☐	Stephen Weiss, Flor. ✍	40.00	20.00

COMMEMORATIVE SERIES

	Insert Set (25 cards):	250.00	125.00
	Insert	CSR	CS
☐☐	1 P. Roy, Mont. [1986-87 Topps]	15.00	8.00
☐☐	2 P. Roy, Mont. [1987-88 Topps]	12.00	6.00
☐☐	3 P. Roy, Mont. [1988-89 Topps]	12.00	6.00
☐☐	4 P. Roy, Mont. [1989-90 Topps]	12.00	6.00
☐☐	5 P. Roy, Mont. [1990-91 Topps]	12.00	6.00
☐☐	6 P. Roy, Mont. [1991-92 Topps]	12.00	6.00
☐☐	7 P. Roy, Mont. [1992-93 Topps]	12.00	6.00
☐☐	8 P. Roy, Mont. [1993-94 Premier]	12.00	6.00
☐☐	9 P. Roy, Mont. [1994-95 Premier]	12.00	6.00
☐☐	10 P. Roy, Colo. [1995-96 Topps]	12.00	6.00
☐☐	11 P. Roy, Colo. [1998-99 Topps]	12.00	6.00
☐☐	12 P. Roy, Colo. [1999-00 Topps]	12.00	6.00
☐☐	13 P. Roy, Colo. [2000-01 Topps]	12.00	6.00
☐☐	14 P. Roy, Colo. [2001-02 Topps]	12.00	6.00
☐☐	15 P. Roy, Mont. [1986-87 OPC]	12.00	6.00
☐☐	16 P. Roy, Mont. [1987-88 OPC]	12.00	6.00
☐☐	17 P. Roy, Mont. [1988-89 OPC]	12.00	6.00
☐☐	18 P. Roy, Mont. [1989-90 OPC]	12.00	6.00
☐☐	19 P. Roy, Mont. [1990-91 OPC]	12.00	6.00
☐☐	20 P. Roy, Mont. [1991-92 OPC]	12.00	6.00
☐☐	21 P. Roy, Mont. [1992-93 OPC]	12.00	6.00
☐☐	22 P. Roy, Colo. [1998-99 OPC]	12.00	6.00
☐☐	23 P. Roy, Colo. [1999-00 OPC]	12.00	6.00
☐☐	24 P. Roy, Colo. [2000-01 OPC]	12.00	6.00
☐☐	25 P. Roy, Colo. [2001-02 OPC]	12.00	6.00

FIRST ROUND FABRIC PATCH

	Insert Set (11 cards):	475.00
	Insert	Relic
☐	Martin Biron (G), Buff. ✂	40.00
☐	Dan Blackburn, NYRa. ✂	35.00
☐	Dumont, Buff. ✂	25.00
☐	Radek Dvorak, NYRa. ✂	25.00
☐	Eric Lindros, NYRa. ✂	85.00
☐	Patrick Marleau, SanJ. ✂	40.00
☐	Mike Modano, Dall. ✂	85.00
☐	Markus Näslund, Vanc. ✂	85.00
☐	Scott Niedermayer, Calg. ✂	25.00
☐	Keith Primeau, Phil. ✂	35.00
☐	Mats Sundin, Toro. ✂	85.00

REPRINT AUTOGRAPH

	Insert (*400)	Aut
☐	COA Patrick Roy (G), Mont. ✍	100.00
☐	CTA Patrick Roy (G), Mont. ✍	100.00

REPRINT AUTOGRAPH REFRACTOR

	Insert (*33)	Aut
☐	COA Patrick Roy (G), Mont. ✍	350.00
☐	CTA Patrick Roy (G), Mont. ✍	350.00

REPRINT JERSEY

	Insert (*250)	Aut
☐	COA Patrick Roy (G), Mont. ✂	50.00
☐	CTA Patrick Roy (G), Mont. ✂	50.00

REPRINT JERSEY REFRACTOR

	Insert (*33)	Aut
☐	COA Patrick Roy (G), Mont. ✂	225.00
☐	CTA Patrick Roy (G), Mont. ✂	225.00

REPRINT JERSEY PATCH

	Insert (*10)	Aut
☐	COA Patrick Roy (G), Mont. ✂	600.00
☐	CTA Patrick Roy (G), Mont. ✂	600.00

2002 - 03 TOPPS HERITAGE

Produced by The Topps Company, this series was released in December 2002.

		C667	Base
	Shell Set (130 cards):		70.00
	Complete Set (180 cards):		400.00
	Chrome Set (100 cards):	375.00	
	Common Player:	2.00	.35
	Description	C667	Base
☐☐	1 Nicklas Lidström, Detr.	4.00	.50
☐☐	2 Jarome Iginla, Calg.	6.00	1.00
☐☐	3 José Théodore (G), Mont.	9.00	1.50
☐☐	4 Ron Francis, Caro.	4.00	.50
☐☐	5 Joe Thornton, Bost.	9.00	1.50
☐☐	6 Jaromir Jagr, Wash.	7.00	1.50
☐☐	7 Mario Lemieux, Pitt.	22.00	4.50
☐☐	8 Roberto Luongo (G), Flor.	6.00	1.00
☐☐	9 Dany Heatley, Atla.	7.00	1.50
☐☐	10 Pavel Bure, NYRa.	6.00	1.00
☐☐	11 Brett Hull, Detr.	7.00	1.50
☐☐	12 Keith Tkachuk, SLou.	4.00	.50
☐☐	13 Mats Sundin, Toro.	7.00	1.50
☐☐	14 Pavel Datsyuk, Detr.	6.00	1.00
☐☐	15 Daniel Alfredsson, Otta.	4.00	.50

☐☐	16 Marian Gaborik, MinW.	7.00	1.50
☐☐	17 Peter Forsberg, Colo.	10.00	2.00
☐☐	18 Miroslav Satan, Buff.	2.00	.35
☐☐	19 Martin Brodeur (G), NJer.	12.00	2.00
☐☐	20 Jeremy Roenick, Phil.	6.00	1.00
☐☐	21 Teemu Selänne, SanJ.	6.00	1.00
☐☐	22 Todd Bertuzzi, Vanc.	9.00	1.50
☐☐	23 Erik Cole, Caro.	2.00	.35
☐☐	24 Jason Allison, LosA.	4.00	.50
☐☐	25 Sean Burke (G), Phoe.	4.00	.50
☐☐	26 Éric Dazé, Chic.	3.00	.50
☐☐	27 Patrick Roy (G), Colo.	22.00	4.50
☐☐	28 Simon Gagné, Phil.	6.00	1.00
☐☐	29 Nikolai Khabibulin (G), Tamp.	3.00	.50
☐☐	30 Alexei Yashin, NYIs.	4.00	.50
☐☐	31 Denis Arkhipov, Nash.	2.00	.35
☐☐	32 Steve Yzerman, Detr.	18.00	3.50
☐☐	33 Mike Modano, Dall.	7.00	1.50
☐☐	34 Joe Sakic, Colo.	12.00	2.00
☐☐	35 Sergei Samsonov, Bost.	4.00	.50
☐☐	36 Saku Koivu, Mont.	6.00	1.00
☐☐	37 Paul Kariya, Anah.	10.00	2.00
☐☐	38 Doug Weight, SLou.	4.00	.50
☐☐	39 Tie Domi, Toro.	2.00	.35
☐☐	40 Kevin Weekes (G), Caro.	2.00	.35
☐☐	41 Rostislav Klesla, Colu.	2.00	.35
☐☐	42 Zigmund Palffy, LosA.	4.00	.50
☐☐	43 Chris Osgood (G), NYIs.	4.00	.50
☐☐	44 Owen Nolan, SanJ.	4.00	.50
☐☐	45 Markus Näslund, Vanc.	7.00	1.50
☐☐	46 Martin Biron (G), Buff.	3.00	.50
☐☐	47 Ryan Smyth, Edmo.	3.00	.50
☐☐	48 Mike Dunham (G), Nash.	3.00	.50
☐☐	49 Martin Havlat, Otta.	4.00	.50
☐☐	50 Patrik Elias, NJer.	6.00	1.00
☐☐	51 Peter Bondra, Wash.	4.00	.50
☐☐	52 Craig Conroy, Calg.	2.00	.35
☐☐	53 Rob Blake, Colo.	4.00	.50
☐☐	54 Mike Richter, NYRa.	3.00	.50
☐☐	55 Stephen Weiss, Flor.	3.00	.50
☐☐	56 Johan Hedberg (G), Pitt.	3.00	.50
☐☐	57 Brendan Morrison, Vanc.	2.00	.35
☐☐	58 Chris Pronger, SLou.	4.00	.50
☐☐	59 Patrick Lalime (G), Otta.	4.00	.50
☐☐	60 David Legwand, Nash.	3.00	.50
☐☐	61 Jocelyn Thibault (G), Chic.	3.00	.50
☐☐	62 Mike Comrie, Edmo.	6.00	1.00
☐☐	63 Sergei Fedorov, Detr.	7.00	1.50
☐☐	64 Michael Peca, NYIs.	3.00	.50
☐☐	65 Tommy Salo (G), Edmo.	3.00	.50
☐☐	66 Scott Stevens, NJer.	3.00	.50
☐☐	67 Mark Recchi, Phil.	3.00	.50
☐☐	68 Vincent Damphousse, SanJ.	4.00	.50
☐☐	69 Vincent Lecavalier, Tamp.	7.00	1.50
☐☐	70 Olaf Kölzig (G), Wash.	4.00	.50
☐☐	71 Shane Doan, Phoe.	2.00	.35
☐☐	72 Marty Turco (G), Dall.	4.00	.50
☐☐	73 Marian Hossa, Otta.	7.00	1.50
☐☐	74 Eric Lindros, NYRa.	7.00	1.50
☐☐	75 Brent Johnson, SLou.	3.00	.50
☐☐	76 John LeClair, Phil.	6.00	1.00
☐☐	77 Dan Cloutier (G), Vanc.	3.00	.50
☐☐	78 Radim Vrbata, Colo.	2.00	.35
☐☐	79 Ilya Kovalchuk, Atla.	7.00	1.50
☐☐	80 Brendan Shanahan, Detr.	7.00	1.50
☐☐	81 Stu Barnes, Buff.	2.00	.35
☐☐	82 Alexander Mogilny, Toro.	3.00	.50
☐☐	83 Félix Potvin (G), LosA.	4.00	.50
☐☐	84 Jeff O'Neill, Caro.	3.00	.50
☐☐	85 Glen Murray, Bost.	3.00	.50
☐☐	86 Marc Denis (G), Colu.	3.00	.50
☐☐	87 Brad Richards, Tamp.	3.00	.50
☐☐	88 Roman Cechmanek (G), Phil.	3.00	.50
☐☐	89 Brian Leetch, NYRa.	4.00	.50
☐☐	90 Roman Turek (G), Calg.	3.00	.50
☐☐	91 Andrew Brunette, MinW.	2.00	.35
☐☐	92 Krys Kolanos, Phoe.	2.00	.35
☐☐	93 Alyn McCauley, Toro.	2.00	.35
☐☐	94 Jean-Sébastien Giguère (G), Anah.	7.00	1.50
☐☐	95 Alexei Kovalev, Pitt.	4.00	.50
☐☐	96 Peter Worrell, Flor.	2.00	.35
☐☐	97 Alexei Zhamnov, Chic.	2.00	.35
☐☐	98 Evgeni Nabokov (G), SanJ.	4.00	.50
☐☐	99 Pavol Demitra, SLou.	3.00	.50
☐☐	100 Chris Drury, Calg.	4.00	.50
☐	101 Jarome Iginla, Calg.		.50
☐	102 Patrick Roy (G), Colo.		3.00
☐	103 Dany Heatley, Atla.		1.00
☐	104 Nicklas Lidström, Detr.		.50
☐	105 José Théodore (G), Mont.		1.00
☐	106 Michael Peca, NYIs.		.35
☐	107 Ron Francis, Caro.		.50
☐	108 Jarome Iginla, Calg.		.50
☐	108 Mats Sundin, Toro.		1.00
☐	109 Jarome Iginla, Calg.		.50
☐	109 Mats Sundin, Toro.		1.00
☐	110 Jason Allison, LosA.		.50
☐	110 Adam Oates, Phil.		.35
☐	111 Pavel Datsyuk, Detr.		.50
☐	111 Dany Heatley, Atla.		1.00
☐	112 Chris Chelios, Detr.		.50
☐	112 Jeremy Roenick, Chic.		.50
☐	113 Nicklas Lidström, Detr.		.50
☐	113 Sergei Gonchar, Wash.		.35
☐	114 Kevin Sawyer, Anah.		.35
☐	114 Peter Worrell, Flor.		.35
☐	115 Martin Brodeur (G), NJer.		1.50
☐	115 Roman Turek (G), Calg.		.35
☐	116 Patrick Roy (G), Colo.		3.00
☐	116 José Théodore (G), Mont.		1.00
☐	117 Patrick Roy (G), Colo.		3.00
☐	117 Roman Cechmanek (G), Phil.		.35
☐	118 Joe Sakic, Colo.		1.50
☐	119 Jarome Iginla, Calg.		.50
☐	120 Markus Näslund, Vanc.		1.00
☐	121 Nicklas Lidström, Detr.		.50
☐	122 Chris Chelios, Detr.		.50
☐	123 Patrick Roy (G), Colo.		3.00
☐	124 Mats Sundin, Toro.		1.00
☐	125 Bill Guerin, Bost.		.35
☐	126 Brendan Shanahan, Detr.		1.00
☐	127 Rob Blake, Colo.		.50
☐	128 Sergei Gonchar, Wash.		.35
☐	129 José Théodore (G), Mont.		1.00
☐	130 Devereaux, Hull, Datsyuk w/ Cup		.50

ROOKIE

	Insert	R
☐	**131 Henrik Zetterberg, Detr. RC**	**40.00**
☐	**132 Martin Gerber (G), Anah. RC**	**8.00**
☐	**133 Alexander Frolov, LosA. RC**	**20.00**
☐	**134 Alexei Smirnov, Anah. RC**	**12.00**
☐	**135 Stanislav Chistov, Anah. RC**	**24.00**
☐	**136 Alexander Svitov, Tamp. RC**	**16.00**
☐	**137 Adam Hall, Nash. RC**	**12.00**
☐	**138 Jay Bouwmeester, Flor. RC**	**24.00**
☐	**139 Ales Hemsky, Edmo. RC**	**24.00**
☐	**140 Rick Nash, Colu. RC**	**50.00**
☐	**141 Chuck Kobasew, Calg. RC**	**16.00**
☐	**142 Shawn Thornton, Chic. RC**	**8.00**
☐	**143 Dennis Seidenberg, Phil. RC**	**8.00**
☐	**144 Ron Hainsey, Mont. RC**	**12.00**
☐	**145 Kurt Sauer, Anah. RC**	**8.00**
☐	**146 Lasse Pirjetä, Colu. RC**	**8.00**
☐	**147 Jason Spezza, Otta. RC**	**30.00**
☐	**148 Tom Koivisto, SLou. RC**	**8.00**
☐	**149 Pierre-Marc Bouchard, MinW. RC**	**24.00**
☐	**150 Patrick Sharp, Phil. RC**	**8.00**
☐	**151 Scottie Upshall, Nash. RC**	**16.00**
☐	**152 Steve Eminger, Wash. RC**	**8.00**
☐	**153 Radovan Somik, Phil. RC**	**8.00**
☐	**154 Anton Volchenkov, Otta. RC**	**8.00**
☐	**155 Dmitri Bykov, Detr. RC**	**8.00**

HIGH NUMBERS

	Insert	TH
☐	156 Bobby Holik, NYRa.	1.50
☐	157 Curtis Joseph (G), Detr.	3.00
☐	158 Jeff Friesen, NJer.	1.50
☐	159 Petr Sykora, Anah.	1.50
☐	160 Ed Belfour (G), Toro.	3.00
☐	161 Darius Kasparaitis, NYRa.	1.50
☐	162 Scott Young, Dall.	1.50
☐	163 Bill Guerin, Dall.	1.50
☐	164 Adam Oates, Anah.	1.50
☐	165 Tony Amonte, Phoe.	2.00
☐	166 Jochen Hecht, Buff.	1.50
☐	167 Randy McKay, Mont.	1.50
☐	168 Jamie Lundmark, NYRa.	1.50
☐	169 Mariusz Czerkawski, Mont.	1.50
☐	170 Bryan Berard, Bost.	1.50
☐	171 Shawn McEachern, Atla.	1.50
☐	172 Brian Boucher (G), Phoe.	1.50
☐	173 Jiri Dopita, Edmo.	1.50
☐	174 Erik Rasmussen, Edmo.	1.50
☐	175 Robert Lang, Wash.	1.50
☐	176 Steve Shields, Bost.	1.50
☐	177 Kelly Buchberger, Phoe.	1.50
☐	178 Andrew Cassels, Colu.	1.50
☐	179 Oleg Tverdovsky, NJer.	1.50
☐	180 Ron Tugnutt (G), Dall.	1.50

LIGHT WOODGRAIN

Insert Set (10 cards): 50.00

	Parallel (1:20)	W
☐	2 Jarome Iginla, Calg.	4.00
☐	3 José Théodore (G), Mont.	5.00
☐	6 Jaromir Jagr, Wash.	4.00
☐	7 Mario Lemieux, Pitt.	13.00
☐	10 Pavel Bure, NYRa.	4.00
☐	13 Mats Sundin, Toro.	4.00
☐	17 Peter Forsberg, Colo.	6.00
☐	27 Patrick Roy (G), Colo.	13.00
☐	32 Steve Yzerman, Detr.	10.00
☐	79 Ilya Kovalchuk, Atla.	4.00

CALDER CLOTH

Insert Set (8 cards): 125.00
Bonus Set (5 cards): 150.00

	Inserts	CCB	CC
☐☐	CC-DA Daniel Alfredsson, Otta.	40.00	15.00
☐☐	CC-MB Martin Brodeur (G), NJer.	40.00	50.00
☐	CC-CD Chris Drury, Calg.		15.00
☐☐	CC-PF Peter Forsberg, Québ.	40.00	40.00
☐	CC-SG Scott Gomez, NJer.		15.00
☐☐	CC-DH Dany Heatley, Atla.	40.00	30.00
☐	CC-BL Brian Leetch, NYRa.		15.00
☐☐	CC-SS Sergei Samsonov, Bost.	40.00	15.00

CHECKLIST

	Insert (1:21)	CL
☐	1 Checklist	.25
☐	2 Checklist	.25
☐	3 Checklist	.25
☐	4 Checklist	.25
☐	5 Checklist	.25
☐	6 Checklist	.25

CREASE PIECE

Insert Set (9 cards): 300.00 75.00

	Inserts	CPB	CP
☐☐	CP-DB Dan Blackburn, NYRa.	35.00	12.00
☐☐	CP-BB Brian Boucher (G), Phoe.	30.00	12.00
☐☐	CP-SB Sean Burke (G), Phoe.	55.00	15.00
☐☐	CP-DC Dan Cloutier (G), Vanc.	35.00	12.00
☐☐	CP-BD Byron Dafoe (G), Bost.	35.00	12.00
☐☐	CP-PL Patrick Lalime (G), Otta.	55.00	15.00
☐☐	CP-ML Manny Legacé (G), Detr.	30.00	12.00
☐☐	CP-FP Félix Potvin (G), LosA.	55.00	15.00
☐☐	CP-MT Marty Turco (G), Dall.	55.00	15.00

GREAT SKATES

Insert Set (10 cards): 125.00
Bonus Set (9 cards): 525.00

	Inserts	GSB	GS
☐☐	GS-TA Tony Amonte, Phoe.	75.00	15.00
☐☐	GS-SG Simon Gagné, Phil.	100.00	25.00
☐☐	GS-MHe Milan Hejduk, Colo.	100.00	25.00
☐☐	GS-MHo Marian Hossa, Otta.	125.00	30.00
☐☐	GS-AK Alexei Kovalev, Pitt.	75.00	15.00
☐	GS-BL Brian Leetch, NYRa.		15.00
☐☐	GS-BM Brendan Morrison, Vanc.	50.00	12.00
☐☐	GS-MR Mark Recchi, Phil.	40.00	12.00
☐☐	GS-MS Marco Sturm, SanJ.	75.00	12.00
☐☐	GS-AT Alex Tanguay, Colo.	40.00	15.00

REAL ONE AUTOGRAPH

Insert Set (9cards): 150.00

	Autograph	Aut
☐	Todd Bertuzzi, Vanc.	45.00
☐	Erik Cole, Caro.	20.00
☐	Chris Drury, Calg.	20.00
☐	Patrik Elias, NJer.	30.00
☐	Krys Kolanos, Phoe.	20.00
☐	Al MacInnis, SLou.	20.00
☐	Bryan McCabe, Toro.	20.00
☐	Michael Peca, NYIs.	20.00
☐	Stephen Weiss, Flor.	20.00

REPRINT

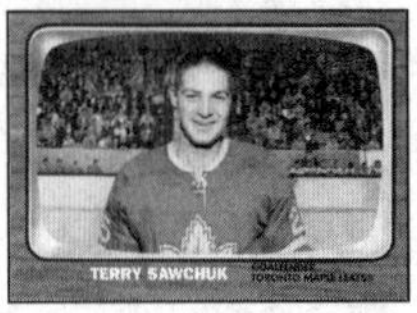

Insert Set (7 cards): 15.00

	Insert (1:21)	R
☐	TML-JB Johnny Bower (G), Toro.	3.00
☐	TML-TH Tim Horton, Toro.	3.00
☐	TML-RK Red Kelly, Toro.	3.00
☐	TML-JP Jim Pappin, Toro.	3.00
☐	TML-RP Bob Pulford, Toro.	3.00
☐	TML-TS Terry Sawchuk (G), Toro.	5.00
☐	TML-ES Eddie Shack, Toro.	3.00

REPRINT AUTOGRAPH

Insert Set (5 cards): 150.00

	Autograph	RA
☐	Johnny Bower (G), Toro.	40.00
☐	Red Kelly, Toro.	40.00
☐	Jim Pappin, Toro.	40.00
☐	Bob Pulford, Toro.	40.00
☐	Eddie Shack, Toro.	40.00

REPRINT RELIC

Insert Set (7 cards): 150.00

	Relic	RR
☐	Johnny Bower (G), Toro. Seat	25.00
☐	Tim Horton, Toro. Seat	35.00
☐	Red Kelly, Toro. Seat	20.00
☐	Jim Pappin, Toro. Seat	20.00
☐	Bob Pulford, Toro. Seat	20.00
☐	Terry Sawchuk (G), Toro. Seat	60.00
☐	Eddie Shack, Toro. Seat	20.00

2002 - 03 TOPPS LIMITED

Produced by The Topps Company, these cards are similar to the regular Topps card but have holographic gold text on the card front.

Original Set (330 cards):
Common Player: .35

	Description	TCS
☐	1 Patrick Roy (G), Colo.	6.00
☐	2 Mario Lemieux, Pitt.	6.00
☐	3 Martin Brodeur (G), NJer.	3.00
☐	4 Steve Yzerman, Detr.	4.50
☐	5 Jaromir Jagr, Wash.	2.00
☐	6 Chris Pronger, SLou.	1.00
☐	7 John LeClair, Phil.	1.50
☐	8 Paul Kariya, Anah.	2.50
☐	9 Tony Amonte, Chic.	1.00
☐	10 Joe Thornton, Bost.	2.00
☐	11 Ilya Kovalchuk, Atla.	2.00
☐	12 Jarome Iginla, Calg.	1.50
☐	13 Mike Modano, Dall.	2.00
☐	14 Vincent Lecavalier, Tamp.	2.00
☐	15 Michael Peca, NYIs.	.50
☐	16 Pavel Bure, NYRa.	1.50
☐	17 Eric Lindros, NYRa.	2.00
☐	18 Félix Potvin (G), LosA.	1.00
☐	19 Ron Francis, Caro.	1.00
☐	20 Miroslav Satan, Buff.	.50
☐	21 Rostislav Klesla, Colu.	.50
☐	22 Mike Comrie, Edmo.	1.50
☐	23 Daniel Alfredsson, Otta.	1.00
☐	24 Sean Burke (G), Phoe.	1.00
☐	25 David Legwand, Nash.	.50
☐	26 Marian Gaborik, MinW.	2.00
☐	27 Saku Koivu, Mont.	1.50
☐	28 Owen Nolan, SanJ.	1.00
☐	29 Mats Sundin, Toro.	2.00
☐	30 Jean-Pierre Dumont, Buff.	.25
☐	31 Chris Drury, Colo.	1.00
☐	32 Markus Näslund, Vanc.	2.00
☐	33 Anson Carter, Edmo.	.50
☐	34 Dwayne Roloson (G), MinW.	.25
☐	35 Brad Isbister, NYIs.	.25
☐	36 Daniel Brière, Phoe.	.50
☐	37 Martin St-Louis, Tamp.	.50
☐	38 Shayne Corson, Toro.	.50
☐	39 Keith Tkachuk, SLou.	1.00
☐	40 Mark Recchi, Phil.	.50
☐	41 Patrice Brisebois, Mont.	.25
☐	42 Niklas Hagman, Flor.	.25
☐	43 Marc Denis (G), Colu.	.50
☐	44 Robyn Regehr, Calg.	.25
☐	45 Byron Dafoe (G), Bost.	.50
☐	46 Sergei Fedorov, Detr.	2.00
☐	47 Andrew Brunette, MinW.	.25
☐	48 Denis Arkhipov, Nash.	.25
☐	49 Martin Havlat, Otta.	1.00
☐	50 Mike Rathje, SanJ.	.25
☐	51 Mattias Öhlund, Vanc.	.50
☐	52 Ulf Dahlén, Wash.	.25

☐	53 Tim Connolly, Buff.	.50
☐	54 Valeri Bure, Flor.	.50
☐	55 Brian Boucher (G), Phil.	.50
☐	56 Pascal Dupuis, MinW.	.25
☐	57 Brian Leetch, NYRa.	1.00
☐	58 Daniel Sedin, Vanc.	.50
☐	59 Kenny Jönsson, NYIs.	.25
☐	60 Erik Cole, Caro.	.50
☐	61 Patrick Lalime (G), Otta.	1.00
☐	62 Mike Leclerc, Anah.	.25
☐	63 Patrick Marleau, SanJ.	.50
☐	64 Tom Poti, NYRa.	.25
☐	65 Lubos Bartecko, Atla.	.25
☐	66 Tom Barrasso (G), Toro.	.50
☐	67 Ryan Smyth, Edmo.	.50
☐	68 Sami Kapanen, Caro.	.50
☐	69 Michal Handzus, Phoe.	.25
☐	70 Martin Straka, Pitt.	.50
☐	71 Peter Forsberg, Colo.	2.50
☐	72 Marc Savard, Calg.	.25
☐	73 Jeff Friesen, Anah.	.50
☐	74 Manny Fernandez (G), MinW.	.50
☐	75 Jason Smith, Edmo.	.25
☐	76 Mike Ribeiro, Mont.	.50
☐	77 Stephen Heinze, LosA.	.25
☐	78 Adam Foote, Colo.	.50
☐	79 Sandy McCarthy, NYRa.	.25
☐	80 Toni Lydman, Calg.	.25
☐	81 Tie Domi, Toro.	.50
☐	82 Scott Stevens, NJer.	.50
☐	83 Radim Vrbata, Colo.	.50
☐	84 Oleg Petrov, Mont.	.50
☐	85 Marty Turco (G), Dall.	1.00
☐	86 Kristian Huselius, Flor.	.50
☐	87 Jeremy Roenick, Phil.	1.50
☐	88 Gary Roberts, Toro.	.50
☐	89 Dean McAmmond, Calg.	.25
☐	90 Chris Chelios, Detr.	1.00
☐	91 Andy McDonald, Anah.	.25
☐	92 Brett Hull, Detr.	2.00
☐	93 Danny Markov, Phoe.	.25
☐	94 Éric Dazé, Chic.	.50
☐	95 Alex Tanguay, Colo.	1.00
☐	96 Petr Nedved, NYRa.	.50
☐	97 Simon Gagné, Phil.	1.50
☐	98 Roman Turek (G), Calg.	.50
☐	99 Milan Hejduk, Colo.	1.50
☐	100 Mariusz Czerkawski, NYIs.	.25
☐	101 Jaroslav Modry, LosA.	.25
☐	102 Dan Cloutier (G), Vanc.	.50
☐	103 Mark Bell, Chic.	.25
☐	104 Brendan Witt, Wash.	.25
☐	105 Teemu Selänne, SanJ.	1.50
☐	106 Johan Hedberg (G), Pitt.	.50
☐	107 Mike Ricci, SanJ.	.50
☐	108 Roberto Luongo (G), Flor.	1.50
☐	109 Vaclav Prospal, Tamp.	.50
☐	110 Zigmund Palffy, LosA.	1.00
☐	111 Ed Jovanovski, Vanc.	.50
☐	112 Scott Gomez, NJer.	.50
☐	113 Pierre Turgeon, Dall.	.50
☐	114 Niklas Sundström, SanJ.	.25
☐	115 Martin Biron (G), Buff.	.50
☐	116 Keith Primeau, Phil.	.50
☐	117 Jean-Sébastien Giguère (G), Anah.	2.00
☐	118 Filip Kuba, MinW.	.25
☐	119 David Tanabe, Caro.	.25
☐	120 Brian Savage, Phoe.	.50
☐	121 Alexei Zhamnov, Chic.	.50
☐	122 Brent Johnson, SLou.	.50
☐	123 Dan Blackburn, NYRa.	.50
☐	124 Éric Bélanger, LosA.	.25
☐	125 Janne Niinimaa, Edmo.	.25
☐	126 Jonas Höglund, Toro.	.25
☐	127 Marian Hossa, Otta.	2.00
☐	128 Mike Richter, NYRa.	.50
☐	129 Peter Bondra, Wash.	1.00
☐	130 Rod Brind'Amour, Caro.	.50
☐	131 Shane Doan, Phoe.	.25
☐	132 Viktor Kozlov, Flor.	.50
☐	133 Yanic Perreault, Mont.	.50
☐	134 Sergei Samsonov, Bost.	1.00
☐	135 Nikolai Khabibulin (G), Tamp.	.50
☐	136 Rob Ray, Buff.	.25
☐	137 Roman Cechmanek (G), Phil.	.50
☐	138 Patrik Stefan, Atla.	.50
☐	139 Matt Cullen, Anah.	.25
☐	140 Kim Johnsson, Phil.	.25
☐	141 Jim Dowd, MinW.	.25
☐	142 Glen Murray, Bost.	.50
☐	143 Dominik Hasek (G), Detr.	2.00
☐	144 Brad Richards, Tamp.	.50
☐	145 Cory Stillman, SLou.	.25
☐	146 Josef Vasicek, Caro.	.25
☐	147 Alexei Kovalev, Pitt.	1.00
☐	148 Adam Deadmarsh, LosA.	.50
☐	149 Brendan Morrison, Vanc.	.50
☐	150 Eric Brewer, Edmo.	.50
☐	151 Jason Arnott, Dall.	.50
☐	152 Brenden Morrow, Dall.	.50
☐	153 Manny Legacé (G), Detr.	.50
☐	154 Michael Nylander, Chic.	.25
☐	155 Pavol Demitra, SLou.	.50
☐	156 Olaf Kölzig (G), Wash.	1.00
☐	157 Sergei Berezin, Mont.	.25
☐	158 Teppo Numminen, Phoe.	.50
☐	159 Vladimir Orszagh, Nash.	.25
☐	160 Brian Rafalski, NJer.	.25
☐	161 Doug Gilmour, Mont.	1.00
☐	162 Jere Lehtinen, Dall.	.50
☐	163 Mark Parrish, NYIs.	.50
☐	164 Petr Sykora, NJer.	.50
☐	165 Sergei Zholtok, MinW.	.25
☐	166 Wade Redden, Otta.	.50
☐	167 Scott Niedermayer, NJer.	.50
☐	168 Olli Jokinen, Flor.	.50
☐	169 Kyle Calder, Chic.	.25
☐	170 Jamie Langenbrunner, NJer.	.25
☐	171 Darcy Tucker, Toro.	.25
☐	172 Aleksey Morozov, Pitt.	.25
☐	173 Adam Oates, Phil.	.50
☐	174 Chris Osgood (G), NYIs.	1.00
☐	175 Espen Knutsen, Colu.	.25
☐	176 Jochen Hecht, Edmo.	.25
☐	177 Maxim Afinogenov, Buff.	.50
☐	178 Radek Dvorak, NYRa.	.25
☐	179 Steve Sullivan, Chic.	.50
☐	180 Trevor Linden, Vanc.	.50
☐	181 Tomi Kallio, Atla.	.25
☐	182 Robert Lang, Pitt.	.25
☐	183 Milan Hnilicka (G), Atla.	.25
☐	184 Justin Williams, Phil.	.50
☐	185 Greg Johnson, Nash.	.25
☐	186 Craig Conroy, Calg.	.50
☐	187 Alexander Mogilny, Toro.	.50
☐	188 Adrian Aucoin, NYIs.	.25
☐	189 Fredrik Modin, Tamp.	.25
☐	190 José Théodore (G), Mont.	2.00
☐	191 Ray Whitney, Colu.	.25
☐	192 Mikael Renberg, Toro.	.50
☐	193 Mike Sillinger, Colu.	.25
☐	194 Richard Zednik, Mont.	.50
☐	195 Mike Dunham (G), Nash.	.50
☐	196 Joe Sakic, Colo.	3.00
☐	197 Fred Brathwaite (G), SLou.	.50
☐	198 Chris Simon, Wash.	.25
☐	199 Al MacInnis, SLou.	.50
☐	200 Georges Laraque, Edmo.	.25
☐	201 Jozef Stümpel, Bost.	.25
☐	202 Theoren Fleury, NYRa.	1.00
☐	203 Rob Blake, Colo.	1.00
☐	204 Todd White, Otta.	.25
☐	205 Dany Heatley, Atla.	2.00
☐	206 Scott Hartnell, Nash.	.25
☐	207 Oleg Tverdovsky, Anah.	.25
☐	208 Krys Kolanos, Phoe.	.25
☐	209 Ian Laperrière, LosA.	.25
☐	210 Vincent Damphousse, SanJ.	1.00
☐	211 Nick Boynton, Bost.	.25
☐	212 Curtis Joseph (G), Toro.	2.00
☐	213 Henrik Sedin, Vanc.	.50
☐	214 Kris Beech, Pitt.	.50
☐	215 Sandis Ozolinsh, Flor.	.25
☐	216 Ron Tugnutt (G), Colu.	.50
☐	217 Todd Bertuzzi, Vanc.	2.00
☐	218 Tommy Salo (G), Edmo.	.50
☐	219 Martin Lapointe, Bost.	.50
☐	220 Derian Hatcher, Dall.	.50
☐	221 David Vyborny, Colu.	.25
☐	222 Jocelyn Thibault (G), Chic.	.50
☐	223 Nicklas Lidström, Detr.	1.00
☐	224 Marcus Nilson, Flor.	.25
☐	225 Sergei Zubov, Dall.	.25
☐	226 Bryan McCabe, Toro.	.25
☐	227 Claude Lemieux, Phoe.	.50
☐	228 Jean-Luc Grand-Pierre, Colu.	.25
☐	229 Bill Guerin, Bost.	.50
☐	230 Sergei Brylin, NJer.	.25
☐	231 Bryan Smolinski, LosA.	.25
☐	232 Luc Robitaille, Detr.	1.50
☐	233 Alexei Yashin, NYIs.	1.00
☐	234 Evgeni Nabokov (G), SanJ.	1.00
☐	235 Pavel Datsyuk, Detr.	1.50
☐	236 Martin Erat, Nash.	.25
☐	237 Stu Barnes, Buff.	.25
☐	238 Derek Morris, Calg.	.25
☐	239 Bates Battaglia, Caro.	.25
☐	240 Jason Allison, LosA.	1.00
☐	241 Peter Worrell, Flor.	.25
☐	242 Mark Messier, NYRa.	2.00
☐	243 Shawn Bates, NYIs.	.25
☐	244 Daymond Langkow, Phoe.	.25
☐	245 Ed Belfour (G), Dall.	2.00
☐	246 Jan Hrdina, Pitt.	.25
☐	247 Pavel Kubina, Tamp.	.25
☐	248 Scott Young, SLou.	.50
☐	249 Curtis Brown, Buff.	.25
☐	250 Brian Rolston, Bost.	.50
☐	251 Jiri Dopita, Phil.	.25
☐	252 Kimmo Timonen, Nash.	.25
☐	253 Marco Sturm, SanJ.	.25
☐	254 Arturs Irbe (G), Caro.	.50
☐	255 Joe Nieuwendyk, NJer.	.50
☐	256 Sergei Gonchar, Wash.	.50
☐	257 Doug Weight, SLou.	1.00
☐	258 Jeff O'Neill, Caro.	.50
☐	259 Mike York, Edmo.	.50
☐	260 Radek Bonk, Otta.	.50
☐	261 Patrik Elias, NJer.	1.50
☐	262 Phil Housley, Chic.	.50
☐	263 Brendan Shanahan, Detr.	2.00
☐	264 Sheldon Keefe, Tamp.	.25
☐	265 Rick DiPietro (G), NYIs.	.50
☐	266 J-F Fortin, Wash.	.25
☐	267 Jason Chimera, Edmo.	.25
☐	268 Andy Hilbert, Bost.	.25
☐	269 Brian Gionta, NJer.	.25
☐	270 Sergei Varlamov, SLou.	.25
☐	271 Alex Auld (G), Vanc.	.25
☐	272 Pavel Brendl, Phil.	.50
☐	273 Branko Radivojevic, Phoe.	.25
☐	274 Kamil Piros, Atla.	.25
☐	275 Steve Gainey, Dall.	.25
☐	276 Mike Mottau, NYRa.	.25
☐	277 Jimmie Ölvestad, Tamp.	.25
☐	278 Jeff Jillson, SanJ.	.25
☐	279 Ilja Bryzgalov, Anah.	.25
☐	280 Taylor Pyatt, Buff.	.25
☐	281 Andrew Raycroft (G), Bost.	.25
☐	282 Christian Berglund, NJer.	.25
☐	283 Patrick Desrochers, Phoe.	.25
☐	284 Lukas Krajicek, Flor.	.25
☐	285 Riku Hahl, Colo.	.25
☐	286 Ivan Huml, Bost.	.25
☐	287 Jani Rita, Edmo.	.50
☐	288 Kristian Kudroc, Tamp.	.25
☐	289 Juraj Kolnik, NYIs.	.25
☐	290 John Erskine, Dall.	.25
☐	291 Brian Sutherby, Wash.	.25
☐	292 Bruno St-Jacques, Phil.	.25
☐	293 Nick Schultz, MinW.	.25
☐	294 Pasi Nurminen (G), Atla.	.25
☐	295 Norm Milley, Buff.	.25
☐	296 Marcel Hossa, Mont.	.50
☐	297 Ales Kotalik, Buff.	.50
☐	298 Bryan Allen, Vanc.	.25
☐	299 Mika Noronen (G), Buff.	.50
☐	300 Tyler Arnason, Chic.	.50
☐	301 Petr Schastlivy, Otta.	.25
☐	302 Mike Van Ryn, SLou.	.25
☐	303 Steve Montador, Calg.	.25
☐	304 Denis Shvidki, Flor.	.25
☐	305 Stephen Weiss, Flor.	1.50
☐	306 Nikita Alexeev, Tamp.	.25
☐	307 Vaclav Nedorost, Colo.	.25
☐	308 Raffi Torres, NYIs.	.25
☐	309 Guillaume Lefebvre, Phil.	.25
☐	310 Sean Avery, Detr.	.25
☐	311 Shane Endicott, Pitt.	.25
☐	312 Ty Conklin, Edmo.	.25
☐	313 Jean-François Damphousse, NJer.	.25
☐	314 Jeremy Roenick, Phil.	1.50
☐	315 Ron Francis, Caro.	1.00
☐	316 Brendan Shanahan, Detr.	2.00
☐	317 Patrick Roy (G), Colo.	6.00
☐	318 Luc Robitaille, Detr.	1.50
☐	319 José Théodore (G), Mont.	2.00
☐	320 Patrick Roy (G), Colo.	6.00
☐	321 Sergei Gonchar, Wash.	.50
☐	322 Bryan McCabe, Toro.	.25
☐	323 Chris Chelios, Detr.	1.00
☐	324 Nicklas Lidström, Detr.	1.00
☐	325 Simon Gagné, Phil.	1.50
☐	326 Brendan Shanahan, Detr.	2.00
☐	327 Jaromir Jagr, Wash.	2.00
☐	328 Jarome Iginla, Calg.	1.50
☐	329 Mats Sundin, Toro.	2.00
☐	330 Joe Sakic, Colo.	3.00

COMMEMORATIVE SERIES

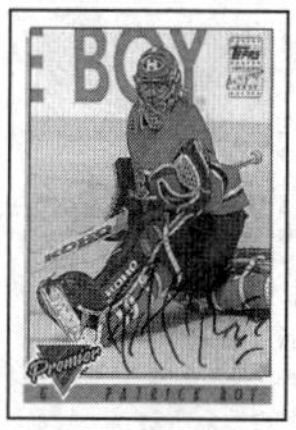

Unlike the reprint cards found in the Topps packs which feature gold text, these cards feature silver text on the card front.

	Insert Set (14 cards):	**100.00**
	Insert (1:box)	**MA**
☐	1 Patrick Roy (G), Mont. ['86-87]	15.00
☐	2 Patrick Roy (G), Mont. ['87-88]	10.00
☐	3 Patrick Roy (G), Mont. ['88-89]	10.00
☐	4 Patrick Roy (G), Mont. ['89-90]	10.00
☐	5 Patrick Roy (G), Mont. ['90-91]	10.00
☐	6 Patrick Roy (G), Mont. ['91-92]	10.00
☐	7 Patrick Roy (G), Mont. ['92-93]	10.00
☐	8 Patrick Roy (G), Mont. ['93-94]	10.00
☐	9 Patrick Roy (G), Mont. ['94-95]	10.00
☐	10 Patrick Roy (G), Colo. ['95-96]	10.00
☐	11 Patrick Roy (G), Colo. ['98-99]	10.00
☐	12 Patrick Roy (G), Colo. ['99-00]	10.00
☐	13 Patrick Roy (G), Colo. ['00-01]	10.00
☐	14 Patrick Roy (G) / Valeri Kamensky ['01-02]	10.00

2002 - 03 TOPPS TOTAL

Produced by the Topps Company, this series was released in February 2003.

	Complete Set (440 cards):	**100.00**
	Common Player:	**.20**
	Description	**Base**
☐	1 Nicklas Lidström, Detr.	.50
☐	2 Mikko Eloranta, LosA.	.20
☐	3 Richard Park, MinW.	.20
☐	4 Eric Lindros, NYRa.	1.00
☐	5 Vincent Lecavalier, Tamp.	1.00
☐	6 Dany Heatley, Atla.	1.00
☐	7 Roman Turek (G), Calg.	.25
☐	8 Rostislav Klesla, Colu.	.25
☐	9 Paul Kariya, Anah.	1.25
☐	10 Marian Hossa, Otta.	1.00
☐	11 Patrick Roy (G), Colo.	3.00
☐	12 Henrik Sedin, Vanc.	.25
☐	13 Adam Graves, SanJ.	.25
☐	14 Ian Laperrière, LosA.	.20
☐	15 Jiri Fischer, Detr.	.20
☐	16 Nick Schultz, MinW.	.20
☐	17 Steve Sullivan, Chic.	.25
☐	18 Sandis Ozolinsh, Flor.	.20
☐	19 Evgeni Nabokov (G), SanJ.	.50
☐	20 Ken Klee, Wash.	.20
☐	21 Danny Markov, Phoe.	.20
☐	22 Adam Foote, Colo.	.25
☐	23 David Vyborny, Colu.	.20
☐	24 Jocelyn Thibault (G), Chic.	.25
☐	25 Mike Leclerc, Anah.	.20
☐	26 Pavol Demitra, SLou.	.25
☐	27 Scott Mellanby, SLou.	.20
☐	28 Brent Sopel, Vanc.	.20
☐	29 Brad Isbister, NYIs.	.20
☐	30 Curtis Leschyshyn, Otta.	.20
☐	31 José Théodore (G), Mont.	1.00
☐	32 Simon Gagné, Phil.	.75
☐	33 Rem Murray, NYRa.	.20
☐	34 Mike Ricci, SanJ.	.25
☐	35 Kim Johnsson, Phil.	.20
☐	36 Adam Oates, Anah.	.25
☐	37 Taylor Pyatt, Buff.	.20
☐	38 Rod Brind'Amour, Caro.	.25
☐	39 Mike Modano, Dall.	1.00
☐	40 Jason Woolley, Buff.	.20
☐	41 Dmitry Yushkevich, Flor.	.20
☐	42 Craig Johnson, LosA.	.20
☐	43 Tony Hrkac, Atla.	.20
☐	44 Scott_A Young, Dall.	.25
☐	45 Marian Gaborik, MinW.	1.00
☐	46 Patrik Stefan, Atla.	.25
☐	47 Jon Klemm, Chic.	.20
☐	48 Andy McDonald, Anah.	.20
☐	49 Chris Pronger, SLou.	.50
☐	50 Frantisek Kaberle, Atla.	.20
☐	51 Jean-Sebastien Giguère (G), Anah.	1.00
☐	52 Luc Robitaille, Detr.	.75
☐	53 Scott Stevens, NJer.	.25
☐	54 Roberto Luongo (G), Flor.	.75
☐	55 Teppo Numminen, Phoe.	.25
☐	56 Alyn McCauley, Toro.	.25
☐	57 John Grahame (G), Bost.	.20
☐	58 David Legwand, Nash.	.25
☐	59 Hal Gill, Bost.	.20
☐	60 Mattias Öhlund, Vanc.	.25
☐	61 Radim Vrbata, Colo.	.25
☐	62 Doug Gilmour, Mont.	.50
☐	63 Vaclav Prospal, Tamp.	.25
☐	64 Brian Leetch, NYRa.	.50
☐	65 Sheldon Keefe, Tamp.	.20
☐	66 Randy McKay, Mont.	.20
☐	67 Mikael Samuelsson, NYRa.	.20

☐ 68 Pavel Bure, NYRa. .75
☐ 69 Zdeno Chara, Otta. .20
☐ 70 PJ Stock, Bost. .25
☐ 71 Shawn McEachern, Atla. .25
☐ 72 Radek Martinek, NYIs. .20
☐ 73 Mike Rathje, SanJ. .20
☐ 74 Kenny Jönsson, NYIs. .20
☐ 75 Jamie Langenbrunner, NJer. .20
☐ 76 Chris Phillips, Otta. .20
☐ 77 Zigmund Palffy, LosA. .50
☐ 78 Stu Barnes, Buff. .20
☐ 79 Robert Reichel, Toro. .25
☐ 80 Jason Allison, LosA. .50
☐ 81 Dimitri Kalinin, Buff. .20
☐ 82 Chris Simon, Chic. .20
☐ 83 Arturs Irbe (G), Caro. .25
☐ 84 Tony Amonte, Phoe. .50
☐ 85 Ruslan Salei, Anah. .20
☐ 86 Pascal Rhéaume, Atla. .20
☐ 87 Marc Denis (G), Colu. .25
☐ 88 Marc Chouinard, Anah. .20
☐ 89 Jim Dowd, MinW. .20
☐ 90 Claude Lemieux, Phoe. .25
☐ 91 Alexei Zhamnov, Chic. .25
☐ 92 Al MacInnis, SLou. .25
☐ 93 Cory Stillman, SLou. .20
☐ 94 Bob Boughner, Calg. .20
☐ 95 Kris Draper, Detr. .20
☐ 96 Mario Lemieux, Pitt. 3.00
☐ 97 Sean Burke (G), Phoe. .50
☐ 98 Wes Walz, MinW. .20
☐ 99 Brenden Morrow, Dall. .25
☐ 100 Dave Andreychuk, Tamp. .25
☐ 101 Jaromir Jagr, Wash. 1.00
☐ 102 Markus Näslund, Vanc. 1.00
☐ 103 Nick Boynton, Bost. .20
☐ 104 Sean Hill, Caro. .20
☐ 105 Trevor Linden, Vanc. .25
☐ 106 Bryan Berard, Bost. .25
☐ 107 Chris Neil, Otta. .20
☐ 108 Marco Sturm, SanJ. .20
☐ 109 Oleg Petrov, Mont. .20
☐ 110 Scott Gomez, NJer. .25
☐ 111 Luke Richardson, Colu. .20
☐ 112 Manny Malhotra, Dall. .20
☐ 113 Valeri Bure, Flor. .25
☐ 114 Marcel Hossa, Mont. .25
☐ 115 Todd Marchant, Edmo. .20
☐ 116 Radek Bonk, Otta. .25
☐ 117 Matt Bradley, SanJ. .20
☐ 118 Jochen Hecht, Buff. .20
☐ 119 Daniel McGillis, Phil. .20
☐ 120 Adrian Aucoin, NYIs. .20
☐ 121 Éric Bélanger, LosA. .20
☐ 122 Peter Forsberg, Colo. 1.25
☐ 123 Aleksey Morozov, Pitt. .20
☐ 124 Jimmie Ölvestad, Tamp. .20
☐ 125 Ed Jovanovski, Vanc. .25
☐ 126 Chris Drury, Calg. .50
☐ 127 Alexander Mogilny, Toro. .25
☐ 128 Stephen Weiss, Flor. .25
☐ 129 Manny Legacé (G), Detr. .25
☐ 130 Jarome Iginla, Calg. .75
☐ 131 Doug Weight, SLou. .50
☐ 132 Martin St-Louis, Tamp. .25
☐ 133 Alexander Khavanov, SLou. .20
☐ 134 Chris Chelios, Detr. .50
☐ 135 Viktor Kozlov, Flor. .25
☐ 136 Bret Hedican, Caro. .20
☐ 137 Denis Arkhipov, Nash. .20
☐ 138 Jere Lehtinen, Dall. .25
☐ 139 Mathieu Schneider, LosA. .20
☐ 140 Tomas Kaberle, Toro. .25
☐ 141 Brian Gionta, NJer. .20
☐ 142 Janne Niinimaa, Edmo. .20
☐ 143 Mark Parrish, NYIs. .25
☐ 144 Todd White, Otta. .20
☐ 145 Geoff Sanderson, Colu. .20
☐ 146 Yanic Perreault, Mont. .25
☐ 147 Roman Hamrlik, NYIs. .20
☐ 148 Mike Fisher, Otta. .20
☐ 149 Jiri Dopita, Edmo. .20
☐ 150 Claude Lapointe, NYIs. .20
☐ 151 Vaclav Nedorost, Colo. .20
☐ 152 Mikael Renberg, Toro. .25
☐ 153 Jozef Stümpel, Bost. .20
☐ 154 Félix Potvin (G), LosA. .50
☐ 155 Chris Gratton, Buff. .20
☐ 156 Adam Deadmarsh, LosA. .25
☐ 157 Sergei Fedorov, Detr. 1.00
☐ 158 Mike Sillinger, Colu. .20
☐ 159 Kris Beech, Pitt. .25
☐ 160 Grant Marshall, Colu. .20
☐ 161 Brent Johnson, SLou. .25
☐ 162 Alex Kovalev, Pitt. .50
☐ 163 Darren McCarty, Detr. .25
☐ 164 Marc Savard, Calg. .20
☐ 165 Janne Laukkanen, Pitt. .20
☐ 166 Phil Housley, Chic. .25
☐ 167 Tomas Holmström, Detr. .20
☐ 168 Bill Guerin, Dall. .25
☐ 169 Darius Kasparaitis, NYRa. .20
☐ 170 Jaroslav Modry, LosA. .20
☐ 171 Martin Gélinas, Calg. .20
☐ 172 Peter Bondra, Wash. .50
☐ 173 Steven Reinprecht, Colo. .25
☐ 174 Anson Carter, Edmo. .25
☐ 175 Eric Brewer, Edmo. .25
☐ 176 Magnus Arvedson, Otta. .20
☐ 177 Patrice Brisebois, Mont. .20
☐ 178 Sergei Brylin, NJer. .20
☐ 179 Vitaly Vishnevski, Anah. .20
☐ 180 Marcus Nilson, Flor. .20
☐ 181 Niklas Sundström, SanJ. .20
☐ 182 Daymond Langkow, Phoe. .20
☐ 183 Craig Conroy, Calg. .25
☐ 184 Gary Roberts, Toro. .25
☐ 185 Justin Williams, Phil. .25
☐ 186 Matt Cooke, Vanc. .20
☐ 187 Pierre Turgeon, Dall. .25
☐ 188 Steve Konowalchuk, Wash. .20
☐ 189 Yannick Tremblay, Atla. .20
☐ 190 Tom Poti, NYRa. .20
☐ 191 Sergei Zholtok, MinW. .20
☐ 192 Robyn Regehr, Calg. .20
☐ 193 Mike Richter, NYRa. .25
☐ 194 Shawn Bates, NYIs. .20
☐ 195 Pavel Trnka, Anah. .20
☐ 196 Martin Straka, Pitt. .25
☐ 197 Jonas Höglund, Toro. .20
☐ 198 Filip Kuba, MinW. .20
☐ 199 Chris Osgood (G), NYIs. .50
☐ 200 Brad May, Phoe. .20
☐ 201 David Aebischer (G), Colo. .25
☐ 202 Fred Brathwaite (G), SLou. .25
☐ 203 Lubos Bartecko, Atla. .20
☐ 204 Marty Turco (G), Dall. .50
☐ 205 Petr Nedved, NYRa. .25
☐ 206 Shayne Corson, Toro. .25
☐ 207 Sergei Samsonov, Bost. .50
☐ 208 Patrik Elias, NJer. .75
☐ 209 Martin Erat, Nash. .20
☐ 210 Krys Kolanos, Phoe. .20
☐ 211 Joe Thornton, Bost. 1.00
☐ 212 Ivan Novoseltsev, Flor. .20
☐ 213 Éric Messier, Colo. .20
☐ 214 Dan Cleary, Edmo. .25
☐ 215 Alex Tanguay, Colo. .50
☐ 216 Robert Lang, Wash. .20
☐ 217 Wade Redden, Otta. .20
☐ 218 Scott Walker, Nash. .20
☐ 219 Milan Hejduk, Colo. .75
☐ 220 Ken Daneyko, NJer. .20
☐ 221 Jean-Pierre Dumont, Buff. .20
☐ 222 Ian Moran, Pitt. .20
☐ 223 Christian Berglund, NJer. .20
☐ 224 Alexei Yashin, NYIs. .50
☐ 225 Brad Stuart, SanJ. .20
☐ 226 Donald Brashear, Phil. .20
☐ 227 Curtis Brown, Buff. .20
☐ 228 John LeClair, Phil. .75
☐ 229 Manny Fernandez (G), MinW. .25
☐ 230 Maxim Afinogenov, Buff. .25
☐ 231 Roman Cechmanek (G), Phil. .25
☐ 232 Tyler Wright, Colu. .20
☐ 233 Vyacheslav Kozlov, Atla. .20
☐ 234 Tyler Arnason, Chic. .25
☐ 235 Sandy McCarthy, NYRa. .20
☐ 236 Pascal Dupuis, MinW. .20
☐ 237 Olaf Kölzig (G), Wash. .50
☐ 238 Kyle Calder, Chic. .20
☐ 239 Jeremy Roenick, Phil. .75
☐ 240 Mathieu Dandenault, Detr. .20
☐ 241 Jeff O'Neill, Caro. .25
☐ 242 David Tanabe, Caro. .20
☐ 243 Calle Johansson, Wash. .20
☐ 244 Greg Vries, Colo. .20
☐ 245 Andrew Brunette, MinW. .20
☐ 246 Dan Hinote, Colo. .20
☐ 247 Jason Smith, Edmo. .20
☐ 248 Mark Bell, Chic. .20
☐ 249 Pavel Kubina, Tamp. .20
☐ 250 Teemu Selänne, SanJ. .75
☐ 251 Vladimir Orszagh, Nash. .20
☐ 252 Brad Ference, Flor. .20
☐ 253 Darryl Sydor, Dall. .20
☐ 254 Vitali Yachmenev, Nash. .20
☐ 255 Scott Hartnell, Nash. .20
☐ 256 Fredrik Modin, Tamp. .20
☐ 257 Alexei Zhitnik, Buff. .20
☐ 258 Brett Hull, Detr. 1.00
☐ 259 Glen Murray, Bost. .25
☐ 260 Michael Peca, NYIs. .25
☐ 261 Owen Nolan, SanJ. .50
☐ 262 Tie Domi, Toro. .25
☐ 263 Ville Nieminen, Pitt. .20
☐ 264 Rob Blake, Colo. .50
☐ 265 Greg Johnson, Nash. .20
☐ 266 Andrei Markov, Mont. .20
☐ 267 Josef Vasicek, Caro. .20
☐ 268 Ryan Smyth, Edmo. .25
☐ 269 Vincent Damphousse, SanJ. .50
☐ 270 Mark Recchi, Phil. .25
☐ 271 Rob Niedermayer, Calg. .20
☐ 272 Mariusz Czerkawski, Mont. .20
☐ 273 Glen Wesley, Caro. .20
☐ 274 Brian Boucher (G), Phoe. .25
☐ 275 Bryan McCabe, Toro. .20
☐ 276 Ron Tugnutt (G), Dall. .25
☐ 277 Daniel Brière, Phoe. .25
☐ 278 Igor Larionov, Detr. .50
☐ 279 Keith Tkachuk, SLou. .50
☐ 280 Mats Sundin, Toro. 1.00
☐ 281 Dwayne Roloson (G), MinW. .20
☐ 282 Andrew Cassels, Colu. .20
☐ 283 Brendan Morrison, Vanc. .25
☐ 284 Bryan Smolinski, LosA. .20
☐ 285 Jan Hlavac, Vanc. .20
☐ 286 Jamal Mayers, SLou. .20
☐ 287 Kevin Weekes (G), Caro. .20
☐ 288 Tim Connolly, Buff. .25
☐ 289 Steve Yzerman, Detr. 2.25
☐ 290 Derek Morris, Colo. .20
☐ 291 Derian Hatcher, Dall. .25
☐ 292 Steve Shields, Bost. .20
☐ 293 Martin Brodeur (G), NJer. 1.50
☐ 294 Marcus Ragnarsson, SanJ. .20
☐ 295 Scott Thornton, SanJ. .20
☐ 296 Oleg Kvasha, NYIs. .20
☐ 297 Mike York, Edmo. .25
☐ 298 Tomi Kallio, Atla. .20
☐ 299 Martin Skoula, Colo. .20
☐ 300 Jeff Halpern, Wash. .20
☐ 301 Ed Belfour (G), Toro. 1.00
☐ 302 Andrew Ference, Pitt. .20
☐ 303 Nikolai Khabibulin (G), Tamp. .25
☐ 304 Bryce Salvador, SLou. .20
☐ 305 Lubomir Visnovsky, LosA. .20
☐ 306 Dan Cloutier (G), Vanc. .25
☐ 307 Andy Delmore, Nash. .20
☐ 308 Martin Lapointe, Bost. .25
☐ 309 Daniel Sedin, Vanc. .25
☐ 310 Kelly Buchberger, Phoe. .20
☐ 311 Darcy Tucker, Toro. .20
☐ 312 Sergei Berezin, Chic. .20
☐ 313 Ruslan Fedotenko, Tamp. .20
☐ 314 Mark Messier, NYRa. 1.00
☐ 315 Mike Comrie, Edmo. .75
☐ 316 Bobby Holik, NYRa. .25
☐ 317 Shane Doan, Phoe. .20
☐ 318 Michal Handzus, Phil. .20
☐ 319 Joe Sakic, Colo. 1.50
☐ 320 Kristian Huselius, Flor. .25
☐ 321 Ben Clymer, Tamp. .20
☐ 322 Mattias Norström, LosA. .20
☐ 323 Pavel Datsyuk, Detr. .75
☐ 324 Richard Matvichuk, Dall. .20
☐ 325 Dainius Zubrus, Wash. .20
☐ 326 Craig Rivet, Mont. .20
☐ 327 Éric Desjardins, Phil. .25
☐ 328 Patrick Marleau, SanJ. .25
☐ 329 Mike Grier, Wash. .20
☐ 330 Steve Rucchin, Anah. .20
☐ 331 Kimmo Timonen, Nash. .20
☐ 332 Brendan Witt, Wash. .20
☐ 333 Sami Kapanen, Caro. .25
☐ 334 Todd Bertuzzi, Vanc. 1.00
☐ 335 Ilya Kovalchuk, Atla. 1.00
☐ 336 Donald Audette, Mont. .25
☐ 337 Georges Laraque, Edmo. .20
☐ 338 Jason Arnott, Dall. .25
☐ 339 John Madden, NJer. .25
☐ 340 Petr Sykora, Anah. .25
☐ 341 Tommy Salo (G), Edmo. .25
☐ 342 Daniel Alfredsson, Otta. .50
☐ 343 Eric Weinrich, Phil. .20
☐ 344 Radek Dvorak, NYRa. .20
☐ 345 Stéphane Yelle, Calg. .20
☐ 346 Sergei Zubov, Dall. .20
☐ 347 Milan Hnilicka (G), Atla. .20
☐ 348 Lubomir Sekeras, MinW. .20
☐ 349 Espen Knutsen, Colu. .20
☐ 350 Travis Green, Toro. .20
☐ 351 Jan Hrdina, Pitt. .20
☐ 352 Paul Laus, Flor. .20
☐ 353 Bates Battaglia, Caro. .20
☐ 354 Miroslav Satan, Buff. .25
☐ 355 Craig Berube, Calg. .20
☐ 356 Sean O'Donnell, Bost. .20
☐ 357 Joe Nieuwendyk, NJer. .25
☐ 358 Patrick Lalime (G), Otta. .50
☐ 359 Brian Rafalski, NJer. .20
☐ 360 Michael Nylander, Wash. .20
☐ 361 Jean-Luc Grand-Pierre, Colu. .20
☐ 362 Ron Francis, Caro. .50
☐ 363 Andrei Nikolishin, Chic. .20
☐ 364 Dallas Drake, SLou. .20
☐ 365 Éric Dazé, Chic. .25
☐ 366 Andreas Dackell, Mont. .20
☐ 367 Scott Niedermayer, NJer. .25
☐ 368 Chris Clark, Calg. .20
☐ 369 Brendan Shanahan, Detr. 1.00
☐ 370 Tomas Vokoun (G), Nash. .20
☐ 371 Johan Hedberg (G), Pitt. .25
☐ 372 Nikita Alexeev, Tamp. .20
☐ 373 Dave Scatchard, NYIs. .20
☐ 374 Matt Cullen, Anah. .20
☐ 375 Steve Thomas, Chic. .20
☐ 376 Brian Rolston, Bost. .25
☐ 377 Richard Zednik, Mont. .25
☐ 378 Sergei Gonchar, Wash. .25
☐ 379 Keith Primeau, Phil. .25
☐ 380 Jeff Friesen, NJer. .25
☐ 381 Keith Carney, Anah. .20
☐ 382 Kirk Maltby, Detr. .20
☐ 383 Erik Cole, Caro. .20
☐ 384 Martin Biron (G), Buff. .25
☐ 385 Jody Shelley, Colu. .20
☐ 386 Brad Richards, Tamp. .25
☐ 387 Michal Rozsival, Pitt. .20
☐ 388 Martin Havlat, Otta. .50
☐ 389 Igor Korolev, Chic. .20
☐ 390 Ladislav Nagy, Phoe. .20
☐ 391 Curtis Joseph (G), Detr. 1.00
☐ 392 Toni Lydman, Calg. .20
☐ 393 Antti Laaksonen, MinW. .20
☐ 394 Jeff Jillson, SanJ. .20
☐ 395 Saku Koivu, Mont. .75
☐ 396 Trevor Letowski, Vanc. .20
☐ 397 Ray Whitney, Colu. .20
☐ 398 Olli Jokinen, Flor. .25
☐ 399 Colin White, NJer. .20
☐ 400 Mike Dunham (G), Nash. .25
☐ 401 Dan Blackburn, NYRa. .25
☐ **402 Ron Hainsey, Mont. RC 2.00**
☐ **403 Scottie Upshall, Nash. RC 3.00**
☐ **404 Anton Volchenkov, Otta. RC 1.50**
☐ **405 Dmitri Bykov, Detr. RC 1.50**
☐ **406 Steve Eminger, Wash. RC 1.50**
☐ **407 Lasse Pirjetä, Colu. RC 1.00**
☐ **408 Tomi Pettinen, NYIs. RC 1.00**
☐ **409 Ales Hemsky, Edmo. RC 4.50**
☐ **410 Chuck Kobasew, Calg. RC 3.00**
☐ **411 Jason Spezza, Otta. RC 6.00**
☐ **412 Jeff Paul, Colo. RC 1.00**
☐ **413 Adam Hall, Nash. RC 2.00**
☐ **414 Rick Nash, Colu. RC 8.00**
☐ **415 Kurt Sauer, Anah. RC 1.00**
☐ **416 Alexander Frolov, LosA. RC 4.00**
☐ **417 Patrick Sharp, Phil. RC 1.00**
☐ **418 Alexei Smirnov, Anah. RC 2.00**
☐ **419 Tom Koivisto, SLou. RC 1.00**
☐ **420 Jay Bouwmeester, Flor. RC 4.50**
☐ **421 Mikael Tellqvist (G), Toro. RC 1.50**
☐ **422 Pierre-Marc Bouchard, MinW. RC 4.50**
☐ **423 Radovan Somik, Phil. RC 1.00**
☐ **424 Ivan Majesky, Flor. RC 1.00**
☐ 425 Jamie Lundmark, NYRa. .50
☐ **426 Henrik Zetterberg, Detr. RC 8.00**
☐ **427 Dennis Seidenberg, Phil. RC 1.50**
☐ **428 Jeff Taffe, Phoe. RC 2.00**
☐ **429 Martin Gerber (G), Anah. RC 1.50**
☐ **430 Lynn Loyns, SanJ. RC 1.00**
☐ **431 Micki DuPont, Calg. RC 1.50**
☐ 432 Jonathan Cheechoo, SanJ. .50
☐ **433 Eric Godard, NYIs. RC 1.00**
☐ **434 Stanislav Chistov, Anah. RC 4.50**
☐ **435 Alexander Svitov, Tamp. RC 3.00**
☐ 436 Fedor Fedorov, Vanc. .20
☐ **437 Stéphane Veilleux, MinW. RC 1.00**
☐ **438 Curtis Sanford (G), SLou. RC 1.50**
☐ **439 Jordan Leopold, Calg. RC 2.00**
☐ **440 Carlo Colaiacovo, Toro. RC 2.00**

CHECKLISTS

Insert Set (30 cards): 15.00
Insert (1:1) TTC

☐ TTC 1 Ilya Kovalchuk, Atla. .50
☐ TTC 2 Joe Thornton, Bost. .50
☐ TTC 3 Miroslav Satan, Buff. .20
☐ TTC 4 Jarome Iginla, Calg. .50
☐ TTC 5 Ron Francis, Caro. .20
☐ TTC 6 Jocelyn Thibault (G), Chic. .20
☐ TTC 7 Patrick Roy (G), Colo. 2.00
☐ TTC 8 Rick Nash, Colu. 3.00
☐ TTC 9 Mike Modano, Dall. .50
☐ TTC 10 Steve Yzerman, Detr. 1.50

☐	TTC 11 Tommy Salo (G), Edmo.	.20
☐	TTC 12 Roberto Luongo (G), Flor.	.50
☐	TTC 13 Jason Allison, LosA.	.20
☐	TTC 14 Paul Kariya, Anah.	1.00
☐	TTC 15 Marian Gaborik, MinW.	.50
☐	TTC 16 José Théodore (G), Mont.	.50
☐	TTC 17 Mike Dunham (G), Nash.	.20
☐	TTC 18 Martin Brodeur (G), Njer.	1.00
☐	TTC 19 Michael Peca, NYIs.	.20
☐	TTC 20 Pavel Bure, NYRa.	.50
☐	TTC 21 Daniel Alfredsson, Otta.	.20
☐	TTC 22 John LeClair, Phil.	.50
☐	TTC 23 Tony Amonte, Phoe.	.20
☐	TTC 24 Mario Lemieux, Pitt.	2.00
☐	TTC 25 Owen Nolan, SanJ.	.20
☐	TTC 26 Keith Tkachuk, Slou.	.20
☐	TTC 27 Nikolai Khabibulin (G), Tamp.	.20
☐	TTC 28 Mats Sundin, Toro.	.50
☐	TTC 29 Todd Bertuzzi, Vanc.	.50
☐	TTC 30 Jaromir Jagr, Wash.	.50

AWARD WINNERS

Insert Set (10 cards):		**15.00**
	Insert (1:36)	**AW**
☐	AW1 Jarome Iginla, Calg.	2.00
☐	AW2 Patrick Roy (G), Colo.	7.50
☐	AW3 Nicklas Lidström, Detr.	1.50
☐	AW4 José Théodore (G), Mont.	3.00
☐	AW5 Dany Heatley, Atla.	2.50
☐	AW6 Ron Francis, Caro.	1.50
☐	AW7 Éric Dazé, Chic.	1.00
☐	AW8 Chris Chelios, Detr.	1.50
☐	AW9 Saku Koivu, Mont.	2.00
☐	AW10 Michael Peca, NYIs.	1.00

SIGNATURES

Insert Set (6 cards):		**110.00**
	Insert (1:926)	**Aut**
☐	TS-BG Brian Gionta, NJer.	20.00
☐	TS-EC Erik Cole, Caro.	20.00
☐	TS-KK Krys Kolanos, Phoe.	20.00
☐	TS-RK Rostislav Klesla, Colu.	30.00
☐	TS-RV Radim Vrbata, Colo.	20.00
☐	TS-SW Stephen Weiss, Flor.	25.00

TOTAL PRODUCTION

Insert Set (15 cards):		**20.00**
	Insert (1:12)	**TP**
☐	TP1 Jarome Iginla, Calg.	1.50
☐	TP2 Joe Sakic, Colo.	3.00
☐	TP3 Mats Sundin, Toro.	2.00
☐	TP4 Peter Forsberg, Colo.	2.50
☐	TP5 Bill Guerin, Dall.	.75
☐	TP6 Brendan Shanahan, Detr.	2.00
☐	TP7 Sergei Fedorov, Detr.	2.00
☐	TP8 Pavel Bure, NYRa.	1.50
☐	TP9 Jeremy Roenick, Phil.	1.50
☐	TP10 Tony Amonte, Phoe.	1.00
☐	TP11 Teemu Selänne, SanJ.	1.50
☐	TP12 Alexander Mogilny, Toro.	.75
☐	TP13 Markus Näslund, Vanc.	2.00
☐	TP14 Todd Bertuzzi, Vanc.	2.00
☐	TP15 Jaromir Jagr, Wash.	2.00

TOTAL TOPPS

Insert Set (20 cards):		**40.00**
	Insert (1:6)	**TT**
☐	TT1 Jarome Iginla, Calg.	1.50
☐	TT2 Patrick Roy (G), Colo.	6.00
☐	TT3 Nicklas Lidström, Detr.	1.00
☐	TT4 José Théodore (G), Mont.	2.00
☐	TT5 Joe Sakic, Colo.	3.00
☐	TT6 Mats Sundin, Toro.	2.00
☐	TT7 Ilya Kovalchuk, Atla.	2.00
☐	TT8 Joe Thornton, Bost.	2.00

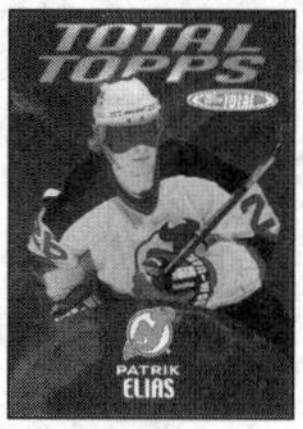

☐	TT9 Mike Modano, Dall.	2.00
☐	TT10 Brett Hull, Detr.	2.00
☐	TT11 Steve Yzerman, Detr.	4.50
☐	TT12 Curtis Joseph (G), Detr.	2.00
☐	TT13 Paul Kariya, Anah.	2.50
☐	TT14 Patrik Elias, NJer.	1.50
☐	TT15 Martin Brodeur (G), NJer.	3.00
☐	TT16 Eric Lindros, NYRa.	2.00
☐	TT17 Daniel Alfredsson, Otta.	1.00
☐	TT18 Mario Lemieux, Pitt.	6.00
☐	TT19 Owen Nolan, SanJ.	1.00
☐	TT20 Jaromir Jagr, Wash.	2.00

2002 - 03 UD SUPERSTARS

Produced by the Upper Deck Company, this series was released in March 2003. There are two versions for each card 1-250: the base card and the Gold parallel (#/250). Only the hockey singles are listed below.

Common Player:		**2.00**	**.35**
	Description	**G250**	**UDS**
☐ ☐	6 Paul Kariya, Anah.	5.00	1.50
☐ ☐	11 Sean Burke (G), Phoe.	2.00	.50
☐ ☐	22 Ilya Kovalchuk, Atla.	5.00	1.00
☐ ☐	36 Bobby Orr, Bost.	25.00	5.00
☐ ☐	37 Raymond Bourque, Bost.	5.00	1.50
☐ ☐	41 Jarome Iginla, Calg.	5.00	1.00
☐ ☐	53 Theoren Fleury, NYRa.	2.00	.50
☐ ☐	67 Patrick Roy (G), Colo.	15.00	3.50
☐ ☐	68 Joe Sakic, Colo.	10.00	2.00
☐ ☐	69 Peter Forsberg, Colo.	5.00	1.50
☐ ☐	75 Mike Modano, Dall.	5.00	1.00
☐ ☐	81 Gordie Howe, Detr.	15.00	3.50
☐ ☐	82 Steve Yzerman, Detr.	15.00	3.00
☐ ☐	83 Curtis Joseph (G), Detr.	5.00	1.00
☐ ☐	84 Wayne Gretzky, Edmo.	25.00	5.00
☐ ☐	123 Zigmund Palffy, LACl.	2.00	.50
☐ ☐	138 José Théodore (G), Mont.	5.00	1.50
☐ ☐	144 Martin Brodeur (G), NJer.	10.00	2.00
☐ ☐	165 Pavel Bure, NYRa.	5.00	1.00
☐ ☐	166 Michael Peca, NYIs.	2.00	.50
☐ ☐	190 Jeremy Roenick, Phil.	5.00	1.00
☐ ☐	197 Mario Lemieux, Pitt.	15.00	3.50
☐ ☐	216 Teemu Selänne, SanJ.	5.00	1.00
☐ ☐	235 Keith Tkachuk, SLou.	2.00	.50
☐ ☐	244 Mats Sundin, Toro.	5.00	1.00
☐ ☐	249 Jaromir Jagr, Wash.	5.00	1.00
☐ ☐	253 Duckett & Kovalchuk	5.00	3.50
☐ ☐	**254 Chistov RC & Ely**	**5.00**	**3.50**
☐ ☐	**255 Heatley & Ennis**	**5.00**	**2.50**
☐ ☐	257 Peppers & Cole	2.00	1.50
☐ ☐	**261 Davis & Nash RC**	**15.00**	**7.00**
☐ ☐	**268 Zetterberg & Edwards**	**10.00**	**5.50**
☐ ☐	**269 Bouwmeester RC & Butler**	**15.00**	**7.00**
☐ ☐	**276 Gooden & Upshall RC**	**15.00**	**6.00**
☐ ☐	**283 Bouchard RC & Radocevic**	**5.00**	**3.50**

CITY ALL-STARS

	Insert (1:32)	**CAS**
☐	T. Helton ✂ / R. Blake ✂	12.00
☐	R. Clemens ✂ / P.Bure ✂	30.00
☐	W. Gretzky ✂ / J. Giambi ✂	55.00
☐	G. Anderson ✂ / P. Kariya ✂	15.00
☐	J. LeClair ✂ / D. Staley ✂	15.00
☐	M. Lemieux ✂ / B.Giles ✂	30.00
☐	M. Piazza ✂ / E. Lindros ✂	25.00
☐	M. Modano ✂ / A. Rodriguez ✂	30.00
☐	A. Beltre ✂ / Z. Palffy ✂	12.00
☐	F. Potvin (G) ✂ / P. Lo Duca ✂	12.00
☐	K. Primeau ✂ / B. Abreu ✂	12.00
☐	B. Griese ✂ / J. Sakic ✂	15.00
☐	S. Samsonov ✂ / A. Walker ✂	15.00
☐	C. Delgado ✂ / M. Sundin ✂	15.00

CITY ALL-STARS TRIPLE

	Insert (*250)	**CAS**
☐	Clemens ✂ / Lindros ✂ / Houston ✂	45.00
☐	Green ✂ / Gretzky ✂ / Bryant ✂	100.00
☐	Giambi ✂ / Sprewell ✂ / Bure ✂	35.00
☐	Johnson ✂ / Marion ✂ / Doan ✂	25.00
☐	Erstad ✂ / Kariya ✂ / Brand ✂	25.00
☐	Kendall ✂ / Stewart ✂ / Kovalev ✂	25.00
☐	I.Rodriguez ✂ / Modano ✂ / Nowitzki ✂	35.00
☐	Drew ✂ / Faulk ✂ / Tkachuk ✂	25.00
☐	Harrington ✂ / Yzerman ✂ / Wallace ✂	40.00

BENCHMARKS

	Insert (1:20)	**B**
☐	DiMaggio & Gretzky	12.00

KEYS TO THE CITY

	Insert (1:6)	**K**
☐	P. Roy (G) / T. Helton	4.00
☐	S. Yzerman / J. Harrington	2.00

LEGENDARY LEADERS

	Insert (1:96)	**L**
☐	Z. Palffy ✂ / S. Green ✂	15.00
☐	S. Yzerman ✂ / J. Harrington ✂	35.00

LEGENDARY LEADERS TRIPLE

	Insert (*250)	**L**
☐	Dazé ✂ / Sosa ✂ / Urlacher ✂	35.00
☐	DiMaggio ✂ / Gretzky ✂ / Bird ✂	150.00
☐	Green ✂ / Gretzky ✂ / Bryant ✂	100.00
☐	Ripken ✂ / Jagr ✂ / Davis ✂	25.00
☐	Clemens ✂ / Rice ✂ / Lemieux ✂	75.00
☐	Gwynn ✂ / Smith ✂ / Lemieux ✂	75.00
☐	Giambi ✂ / Bledsoe ✂ / Messier ✂	25.00
☐	Rodriguez ✂ / Smith ✂ / Modano ✂	50.00
☐	Iverson ✂ / McNabb ✂ / Roenick ✂	25.00
☐	Walker ✂ / Griese ✂ / Roy (G) ✂	50.00
☐	Piazza ✂ / Pennington ✂ / Yashin ✂	25.00
☐	McGwire ✂ / Manning ✂ / Yzerman ✂	75.00

MAGIC MOMENTS

	Insert (1:5)	**MM**
☐	MM17 Bobby Orr, Bost.	8.00
☐	MM18 Wayne Gretzky, LosA.	8.00
☐	MM19 Patrick Roy (G), Colo.	6.00

ROOKIE REWIND

	Insert (1:20)	**RR**
☐	M. Messier / O. Smith	2.00

SPOKESMEN

	Insert	**G25**	**B250**	**S**
☐ ☐ ☐	UD12 Bobby Orr, Bost.	200.00	30.00	10.00
☐ ☐ ☐	UD13 Gordie Howe, Detr.	125.00	20.00	6.00

☐ ☐ ☐	UD14 Wayne Gretzky, LosA.	200.00	30.00	10.00
☐ ☐ ☐	UD27 Bobby Orr, Bost.	200.00	30.00	10.00
☐ ☐ ☐	UD28 Gordie Howe, Detr.	125.00	20.00	6.00
☐ ☐ ☐	UD29 Wayne Gretzky, LosA.	200.00	30.00	10.00

2002 - 03 ULTIMATE MEMORABILIA

Produced by the In The Game, this series was released in May 2003.

Complete Set (100 cards):

	Rookie Card (#/250)
☐	**1 Pierre-Marc Bouchard, MinW. RC**
☐	**2 Rick Nash, Colu. RC**
☐	**3 Dennis Seidenberg, Phil. RC**
☐	**4 Jay Bouwmeester, Flor. RC**
☐	**5 Stanislav Chistov, Anah. RC**
☐	**6 Kurt Sauer, Anah. RC**
☐	**7 Ivan Majesky, Flor. RC**
☐	**8 Chuck Kobasew, Calg. RC**
☐	**9 Jordan Leopold, Calg. RC**
☐	**10 Steve Ott, Dall. RC**
☐	**11 Ales Hemsky, Edmo. RC**
☐	**12 Patrick Sharp, Phil. RC**
☐	**13 Kari Haakana, Edmo. RC**
☐	**14 Dmitri Bykov, Detr. RC**
☐	**15 Alex Henry, Edmo. RC**
☐	**16 Henrik Zetterberg, Detr. RC**
☐	**17 Alexander Frolov, LosA. RC**
☐	**18 Steve Eminger, Wash. RC**
☐	**19 Scottie Upshall, Nash. RC**
☐	**20 Tom Koivisto, SLou. RC**
☐	**21 Ari Ahonen, NJer. RC**
☐	**22 Ron Hainsey, Mont. RC**
☐	**23 Martin Gerber (G), Anah. RC**
☐	**24 Adam Hall (G), Nash. RC**
☐	**25 Lasse Pirjetä, Colu. RC**
☐	**26 Anton Volchenkov, Otta. RC**
☐	**27 Jeff Paul, Colo. RC**
☐	**28 Carlo Colaiacovo, Toro. RC**
☐	**29 Alexander Svitov, Tamp. RC**
☐	**30 Alexei Smirnov, Anah. RC**
☐	**31 Jeff Taffe, Phoe. RC**
☐	**32 Mikael Tellqvist (G), Toro. RC**
☐	**33 Radovan Somik, Phil. RC**
☐	**34 Mike Komisarek, Mont. RC**
☐	**35 Chris Schmidt, LosA. RC**
☐	36 Dick Tarnström, Pitt.
☐	**37 Ryan Bayda, Caro. RC**
☐	**38 Sylvain Blouin, MinW. RC**
☐	**39 Ray Emery, Otta. RC**
☐	**40 Stéphane Veilleux, MinW. RC**
☐	**41 Curtis Sanford (G), SLou. RC**
☐	**42 Eric Godard, NYIs. RC**
☐	**43 Pascal Leclaire (G), Colu. RC**
☐	**44 Patrick Boileau, Detr. RC**
☐	**45 Tim Thomas (G), Bost. RC**
☐	**46 Mike Cammalleri, LosA. RC**
☐	**47 Jason Spezza, Otta. RC**
☐	**48 Cody Rudkowsky (G), SLou. RC**
☐	**49 Darren Haydar, Nash. RC**
☐	**50 Ryan Miller, Buff. RC**
☐	**51 Brandon Reid, Vanc. RC**
☐	**52 Christian Backman, SLou. RC**
☐	**53 Niko Dimitrakos, SanJ. RC**
☐	**54 Garnet Exelby, Atla. RC**
☐	**55 Jason King, Vanc. RC**
☐	**56 Martin Samuelsson, Bost. RC**
☐	**57 Miroslav Zalesak, SanJ. RC**
☐	**58 Tomas Malec, Caro. RC**
☐	**59 Michael Garnett (G), Atla. RC**
☐	**60 Matt Walker, SLou. RC**
☐	**61 Shaone Morrisonn, Bost. RC**
☐	**62 Chad Wiseman, SanJ. RC**
☐	**63 Michael Leighton, Chic. RC**
☐	**64 Tomas Surovy, Pitt. RC**
☐	**65 Jason Bacashihua, Dall. RC**
☐	**66 Jim Vandermeer, Phil. RC**
☐	**67 Konstantin Koltsov, Pitt. RC**
☐	**68 Fernando Pisani, Edmo. RC**
☐	**69 Rickard Wallin, MinW. RC**
☐	**70 Brooks Orpik, Pitt. RC**
☐	**71 Tomas Zizka, LosA. RC**
☐	**72 Jarret Stoll, Edmo. RC**
☐	**73 Cristobal Huet, LosA. RC**
☐	**74 Levente Szuper (G), Calg. RC**
☐	**75 Jared Aulin, LosA. RC**

☐ **76 Simon Gamache, Atla. RC**
☐ **77 Kris Vernarsky, Bost. RC**
☐ **78 Radoslav Hecl, Buff. RC**
☐ **79 Jamie Hodson (G), Toro. RC**
☐ **80 Marc-André Bergeron, Edmo. RC**
☐ **81 Mike Siklenka, Phil. RC**
☐ **82 Igor Radulov, Chic. RC**
☐ **83 Paul Manning, Colu. RC**
☐ **84 John Tripp, NYRa. RC**
☐ **85 Ian MacNeil, Caro. RC**
☐ **86 Jim Fahey, SanJ. RC**
☐ **87 Dany Sabourin (G), Calg. RC**
☐ **88 Alexei Semenov, Edmo. RC**
☐ **89 Curtis Murphy, MinW. RC**
☐ **90 Jerred Smithson, LosA. RC**
☐ **91 François Beauchemin, Mont. RC**
☐ **92 Vernon Fiddler, SanJ. RC**
☐ **93 Cam Severson, Anah. RC**
☐ **94 Burke (G) Henry, Chic. RC**
☐ **95 Brad Defauw, Caro. RC**
☐ **96 Craig Andersson (G), Chic. RC**
☐ **97 Frédéric Cloutier (G), MinW. RC**
☐ **98 Tomas Kurka, Caro. RC**
☐ **99 Jonathan Hedstrom, Anah. RC**
☐ **100 Valeri Kharlamov RC**

500 GOAL SCORERS EMBLEM

Insert Set (3 cards):
Insert (*10)
☐ Jaromir Jagr, Wash. ✂
☐ Joe Nieuwendyk, NJer. ✂
☐ Joe Sakic, Colo. ✂

500 GOAL SCORERS JERSEY

Insert Set (3 cards):
Insert (*30)
☐ Jaromir Jagr, Wash. ✂
☐ Joe Nieuwendyk, NJer. ✂
☐ Joe Sakic, Colo. ✂

500 GOAL SCORERS STICK & JERSEY

Insert Set (3 cards):
Insert (*30)
☐ Jaromir Jagr, Wash. ✂
☐ Joe Nieuwendyk, NJer. ✂
☐ Joe Sakic, Colo. ✂

ACTIVE 8

Insert Set (8 cards):
Insert (*30)
☐ Hull ✂ / Messier ✂ ✂ / Yzerman ✂
☐ Lemieux ✂ / Forsberg ✂ / Oates ✂
☐ Lemieux ✂ / Sakic ✂ / Leetch ✂
☐ Lemieux ✂ / Yzerman ✂ / Oates ✂
☐ Messier ✂ / Francis ✂ / Yzerman ✂
☐ Messier ✂ / Francis ✂ / Yzerman ✂
☐ Roy ✂ / Belfour (G) ✂ / Brodeur (G) ✂
☐ Roy ✂ / Belfour (G) ✂ / Joseph (G) ✂

ALL-STAR MVP

Insert Set (8 cards):
Insert (*40)
☐ 1963 Frank Mahovlich, Toro. ✂
☐ 1964 Jean Béliveau, Mont. ✂
☐ 1967 Henri Richard, Mont. ✂
☐ 1970 Bobby Hull, Chic. ✂
☐ 1971 Bobby Hull, Chic. ✂
☐ 1976 Peter Mahovlich, Mont. ✂
☐ 1980 Reggie Leach, Phil. ✂
☐ 1982 Mike Bossy, NYIs. ✂
☐ 1985 Mario Lemieux, Pitt. ✂
☐ 1986 Grant Fuhr (G), Edmo. ✂
☐ 1988 Mario Lemieux, Pitt. ✂
☐ 1990 Mario Lemieux, Pitt. ✂
☐ 1991 Vincent Damphousse, Toro. ✂
☐ 1992 Brett Hull, SLou. ✂
☐ 1993 Mike Gartner, NYRa. ✂
☐ 1994 Mike Richter (G), NYRa. ✂
☐ 1997 Mark Recchi, Mont. ✂
☐ 1998 Teemu Selänne, Anah. ✂
☐ 2000 Pavel Bure, Flor. ✂
☐ 2001 Bill Guerin, Bost. ✂
☐ 2002 Éric Dazé, Chic. ✂
☐ 2003 Dany Heatley, Atla. ✂

BAP LEGEND

Insert Set (10 cards):
Insert
☐ Maurice Richard ✂ ✍ {*5}
☐ Maurice Richard ✂ ✍ {*5}
☐ Maurice Richard ✂ ✍ {*5}
☐ Maurice Richard ✂ ✍ {*5}
☐ Maurice Richard ✂ ✂ ✂ ✂ ✍ {*5}
☐ Maurice Richard ✂ {*15}
☐ M. Richard ✂ {*15} / J. Plante (G) ✂ {*15}
☐ M. Richard ✂ {*15} / D. Harvey ✂ {*15}
☐ M. Richard ✂ {*15} / J. Béliveau ✂ {*15}
☐ M. Richard ✂ {*15} / H. Richard ✂ {*15}

BLADES OF STEEL

Insert Set (10 cards):
Insert (*10)
☐ Bill Barilko, Toro. Skate ✂
☐ Jean Béliveau, Mont. Skate ✂
☐ Tim Horton, Toro. Skate ✂
☐ Jarome Iginla, Calg. Skate ✂
☐ Aurèle Joliat, Mont. Skate ✂
☐ Mario Lemieux, Pitt. Skate ✂
☐ Jacques Plante (G), Mont. Skate ✂
☐ Maurice Richard, Mont. Skate ✂
☐ Georges Vézina (G), Mont. Skate ✂
☐ Nels Stewart, Skate ✂

CALDER CANDIDATES

Insert Set (20 cards):
Insert (*40)
☐ Tyler Arnason, Chic. ✂
☐ Jay Bouwmeester, Flor. ✂
☐ Stanislav Chistov, Anah. ✂
☐ Alexander Frolov, LosA. ✂
☐ Ron Hainsey, Mont. ✂
☐ Adam Hall (G), Nash. ✂
☐ Ales Hemsky, Edmo. ✂
☐ Ivan Huml, Bost. ✂
☐ Niko Kapanen, Dall. ✂
☐ Chuck Kobasew, Calg. ✂
☐ Jordan Leopold, Calg. ✂
☐ Ryan Miller, Buff. ✂
☐ Rick Nash, Colu. ✂
☐ Dennis Seidenberg, Phil. ✂
☐ Alexei Smirnov, Anah. ✂
☐ Jason Spezza, Otta. ✂
☐ Alexander Svitov, Tamp. ✂
☐ Anton Volchenkov, Otta. ✂
☐ Stephen Weiss, Flor. ✂
☐ Henrik Zetterberg, Detr. ✂

COMPLETE PACKAGE

Insert Set (10 cards):
Insert (*10)
☐ Tim Horton, Toro. ✂ ✂ ✂ ✂
☐ Curtis Joseph (G), Toro. ✂ ✂ ✂ ✂
☐ Guy Lafleur, Mont. ✂ ✂ ✂ ✂
☐ Mario Lemieux, Pitt. ✂ ✂ ✂ ✂
☐ Eric Lindros, NYRa. ✂ ✂ ✂ ✂
☐ Jacques Plante (G), Mont. ✂ ✂ ✂ ✂
☐ Maurice Richard, Mont. ✂ ✂ ✂ ✂
☐ Patrick Roy (G), Mont. ✂ ✂ ✂ ✂
☐ Terry Sawchuk (G), Detr. ✂ ✂ ✂ ✂
☐ Mats Sundin, Toro. ✂ ✂ ✂ ✂

CONN SMYTHE TROPHY WINNER

Insert Set (30 cards):
Insert (*30)
☐ 1965 Jean Béliveau, Mont. ✂
☐ 1966 Roger Crozier (G), Detr. ✂
☐ 1968 Glenn Hall (G), Chic. ✂
☐ 1969 Serge Savard, Mont. ✂
☐ 1973 Yvan Cournoyer, Mont. ✂
☐ 1974 Bernie Parent (G), Phil. ✂
☐ 1975 Bernie Parent (G), Phil. ✂
☐ 1976 Reggie Leach, Phil. ✂
☐ 1977 Guy Lafleur, Mont. ✂
☐ 1978 Larry Robinson, Mont. ✂
☐ 1980 Bryan Trottier, NYIs. ✂
☐ 1982 Mike Bossy, NYIs. ✂
☐ 1983 Billy Smith, NYIs. ✂
☐ 1984 Mark Messier, Edmo. ✂
☐ 1986 Patrick Roy (G), Mont. ✂
☐ 1987 Ron Hextall, Phil. ✂
☐ 1989 Al Macinnis, Calg. ✂
☐ 1990 Bill Ranford, Edmo. ✂
☐ 1991 Mario Lemieux, Pitt. ✂
☐ 1992 Mario Lemieux, Pitt. ✂
☐ 1993 Patrick Roy (G), Colo. ✂
☐ 1994 Brian Leetch, NYRa. ✂
☐ 1995 Claude Lemieux, NJer. ✂
☐ 1996 Joe Sakic, Colo. ✂
☐ 1997 Mike Vernon (G), Detr. ✂
☐ 1998 Steve Yzerman, Detr. ✂
☐ 1999 Joe Nieuwendyk, Dall. ✂
☐ 2000 Scott Stevens, NJer. ✂
☐ 2001 Patrick Roy (G), Colo. ✂
☐ 2002 Nicklas Lidström, Detr. ✂

CORNERSTONES

Insert Set (8 cards):
Insert (*10)
☐ Thompson ✂ / Cheevers (G) ✂ / Neely ✂ / Thornton ✂
☐ Mosienko ✂ / Hull ✂ / Goulet ✂ / Dazé ✂
☐ Lindsay ✂ / Sawchuk (G) ✂ / Delvecchio ✂ / Yzerman ✂
☐ Joliat ✂ / Béliveau ✂ / Lafleur ✂ / Koivu ✂
☐ Potvin ✂ / Trottier ✂ / Bossy ✂ / Yashin ✂
☐ Rayner (G) ✂ / Giacomin (G) ✂ / Esposito ✂ / Messier ✂
☐ Parent ✂ / Clarke ✂ / Lindros ✂ / Gagné ✂
☐ Clancy ✂ / Kennedy ✂ / McDonald ✂ / Sundin ✂

DYNAMIC DUOS

Insert Set (10 cards):
Insert (*30)
☐ P. Bure ✂ / S. Samsonov ✂
☐ P. Forsberg ✂ / M. Sundin ✂
☐ J. Jagr ✂ / M. Gaborik ✂
☐ S. Koivu ✂ / T. Selänne ✂
☐ I. Kovalchuk ✂ / S. Fedorov ✂
☐ M. Lemieux ✂ / J. Thornton ✂
☐ M. Modano ✂ / Br. Hull ✂
☐ J. Sakic ✂ / E. Lindros ✂
☐ P. Kariya ✂ / B. Shanahan ✂
☐ D. Heatley ✂ / S. Yzerman ✂

EMBLEM

Insert Set (30 cards):
Insert (*10)
☐ Martin Brodeur (G), NJer. ✂
☐ Pavel Bure, NYRa. ✂
☐ Chris Chelios, Detr. ✂
☐ Mike Comrie, Edmo. ✂
☐ Sergei Fedorov, Detr. ✂
☐ Peter Forsberg, Colo. ✂
☐ Marian Gaborik, MinW. ✂
☐ Dany Heatley, Atla. ✂
☐ Brett Hull, Detr. ✂
☐ Jaromir Jagr, Wash. ✂
☐ Paul Kariya, Anah. ✂
☐ Valeri Kharlamov, ✂
☐ Saku Koivu, Mont. ✂
☐ Ilya Kovalchuk, Atla. ✂
☐ John LeClair, Phil. ✂
☐ Brian Leetch, NYRa. ✂
☐ Mario Lemieux, Pitt. ✂
☐ Nicklas Lidström, Detr. ✂
☐ Eric Lindros, NYRa. ✂
☐ Mark Messier, NYRa. ✂
☐ Mike Modano, Dall. ✂
☐ Markus Näslund, Vanc. ✂
☐ Luc Robitaille, Detr. ✂
☐ Jeremy Roenick, Phil. ✂
☐ Patrick Roy (G), Colo. ✂
☐ Joe Sakic, Colo. ✂
☐ Brendan Shanahan, Detr. ✂
☐ Mats Sundin, Toro. ✂
☐ Joe Thornton, Bost. ✂
☐ Steve Yzerman, Detr. ✂

EMBLEM GOLD

Insert Set (30 cards):
Insert (*1)
☐ Martin Brodeur (G), NJer. ✂
☐ Pavel Bure, NYRa. ✂
☐ Chris Chelios, Detr. ✂
☐ Mike Comrie, Edmo. ✂
☐ Sergei Fedorov, Detr. ✂
☐ Peter Forsberg, Colo. ✂
☐ Marian Gaborik, MinW. ✂
☐ Dany Heatley, Atla. ✂
☐ Brett Hull, Detr. ✂
☐ Jaromir Jagr, Wash. ✂
☐ Paul Kariya, Anah. ✂
☐ Valeri Kharlamov, ✂
☐ Saku Koivu, Mont. ✂
☐ Ilya Kovalchuk, Atla. ✂
☐ John LeClair, Phil. ✂
☐ Brian Leetch, NYRa. ✂
☐ Mario Lemieux, Pitt. ✂
☐ Nicklas Lidström, Detr. ✂
☐ Eric Lindros, NYRa. ✂
☐ Mark Messier, NYRa. ✂
☐ Mike Modano, Dall. ✂
☐ Markus Näslund, Vanc. ✂
☐ Luc Robitaille, Detr. ✂
☐ Jeremy Roenick, Phil. ✂
☐ Patrick Roy (G), Colo. ✂
☐ Joe Sakic, Colo. ✂
☐ Brendan Shanahan, Detr. ✂
☐ Mats Sundin, Toro. ✂
☐ Joe Thornton, Bost. ✂
☐ Steve Yzerman, Detr. ✂

EMBLEM ATTIC

Insert Set (30 cards):
Insert (*5)
☐ Sid Abel, Detr. ✂
☐ Jean Béliveau, Mont. ✂
☐ Mike Bossy, NYIs. ✂
☐ Frank Brimsek (G) ✂
☐ Johnny Bucyk, Bost. ✂
☐ Gerry Cheevers (G), Bost. ✂
☐ Bobby Clarke, Phil. ✂
☐ Roger Crozier (G), Detr. ✂
☐ Alex Delvecchio, Detr. ✂
☐ Marcel Dionne ✂
☐ Phil Esposito ✂
☐ Tony Esposito (G) ✂
☐ Ed Giacomin (G) ✂
☐ George Hainsworth (G) ✂
☐ Glenn Hall (G) ✂
☐ Doug Harvey, Mont. ✂
☐ Bobby Hull, Chic. ✂
☐ Aurèle Joliat, Mont. ✂
☐ Red Kelly ✂
☐ Guy Lafleur, Mont. ✂
☐ Ted Lindsay, Detr. ✂
☐ Harry Lumley (G) ✂
☐ Frank Mahovlich ✂
☐ Stan Mikita, Chic. ✂
☐ Bernie Parent (G), Phil. ✂
☐ Jacques Plante (G), Mont. ✂
☐ Henri Richard, Mont. ✂
☐ Maurice Richard, Mont. ✂
☐ Terry Sawchuk (G), Detr. ✂
☐ Roy Worters (G), NYAm. ✂

FINAL SHOWDOWN

Insert Set (40 cards):
Insert (*40)
☐ Harvey ✂ / Delvecchio ✂
☐ Geoffrion ✂ / Lindsay ✂
☐ H.Richard ✂ / Horton ✂
☐ M.Richard ✂ / F.Mahovlich ✂
☐ Sawchuk (G) ✂ / Mikita ✂
☐ F.Mahovlich ✂ / Hull ✂
☐ Kelly ✂ / Sawchuk (G) ✂
☐ Horton ✂ / Delvecchio ✂
☐ Béliveau ✂ / Hall (G) ✂
☐ Béliveau ✂ / Crozier (G) ✂
☐ Bower (G) ✂ / Ferguson ✂
☐ P.Mahovlich ✂ / Bo.Hull ✂
☐ Cheevers (G) ✂ / R.Gilbert ✂
☐ Cournoyer ✂ / Hull ✂
☐ Parent ✂ / Bucyk ✂
☐ Clarke ✂ / Perreault ✂
☐ Shutt ✂ / Schultz ✂
☐ Lapointe ✂ / Cheevers (G) ✂
☐ Robinson ✂ / Cheevers (G) ✂
☐ Lafleur ✂ / P.Esposito ✂
☐ Smith ✂ / Clarke ✂
☐ Trottier ✂ / Fuhr (G) ✂
☐ Messier ✂ / Potvin ✂
☐ Roy ✂ / McDonald ✂
☐ Kurri ✂ / Hextall ✂
☐ Lowe ✂ / Neely ✂
☐ MacInnis ✂ / Roy ✂
☐ Messier ✂ / Neely ✂
☐ Lemieux ✂ / Modano ✂
☐ Jagr ✂ / Roenick ✂
☐ Roy ✂ / Robitaille ✂
☐ Messier ✂ / Bure ✂
☐ Brodeur (G) ✂ / Yzerman ✂
☐ Roy ✂ / Niedermayer ✂
☐ Yzerman ✂ / Lindros ✂
☐ Fedorov ✂ / Kölzig (G) ✂
☐ Hull ✂ / Peca ✂
☐ Arnott ✂ / Belfour (G) ✂
☐ Sakic ✂ / Brodeur (G) ✂
☐ Lidström ✂ / Francis ✂

FIRST OVERALL

Insert Set (15 cards):
Insert (*15)
☐ 1988 Mike Modano, Minn. ✂
☐ 1989 Mats Sundin, Québ. ✂
☐ 1990 Owen Nolan, Québ. ✂
☐ 1991 Eric Lindros, Phil. ✂
☐ 1992 Roman Hamrlik, Tamp. ✂
☐ 1993 Alexandre Daigle, Otta. ✂
☐ 1994 Ed Jovanovski, Flor. ✂
☐ 1995 Bryan Berard, NYIs. ✂
☐ 1996 Chris Phillips, Otta. ✂
☐ 1997 Joe Thornton, Bost. ✂
☐ 1998 Vincent Lecavalier, Tamp. ✂
☐ 1999 Patrik Stefan, Atla. ✂
☐ 2000 Rick DiPietro (G), NYIs. ✂
☐ 2001 Ilya Kovalchuk, Atla. ✂
☐ 2002 Rick Nash, Colu. ✂

FIRST OVERALL GOLD

Insert Set (15 cards):
Insert (*1)
☐ 1988 Mike Modano, Minn. ✂
☐ 1989 Mats Sundin, Québ. ✂
☐ 1990 Owen Nolan, Québ. ✂
☐ 1991 Eric Lindros, Phil. ✂
☐ 1992 Roman Hamrlik, Tamp. ✂
☐ 1993 Alexandre Daigle, Otta. ✂
☐ 1994 Ed Jovanovski, Flor. ✂
☐ 1995 Bryan Berard, NYIs. ✂
☐ 1996 Chris Phillips, Otta. ✂
☐ 1997 Joe Thornton, Bost. ✂
☐ 1998 Vincent Lecavalier, Tamp. ✂
☐ 1999 Patrik Stefan, Atla. ✂
☐ 2000 Rick DiPietro (G), NYIs. ✂
☐ 2001 Ilya Kovalchuk, Atla. ✂
☐ 2002 Rick Nash, Colu. ✂

GAME-USED JERSEY

Insert Set (40 cards):

Insert (*50)

☐ Ed Belfour (G), Toro. ✂
☐ Todd Bertuzzi, Vanc. ✂
☐ Jay Bouwmeester, Flor. ✂
☐ Martin Brodeur (G), Njer. ✂
☐ Pavel Bure, NYRa. ✂
☐ Sergei Fedorov, Detr. ✂
☐ Peter Forsberg, Colo. ✂
☐ Marian Gaborik, MinW. ✂
☐ Bill Guerin, Dall. ✂
☐ Dany Heatley, Atla. ✂
☐ Milan Hejduk, Colo. ✂
☐ Marian Hossa, Otta. ✂
☐ Brett Hull, Detr. ✂
☐ Jarome Iginla, Calg. ✂
☐ Jaromir Jagr, Wash. ✂
☐ Paul Kariya, Anah. ✂
☐ Valeri Kharlamov, ✂
☐ Saku Koivu, Mont. ✂
☐ Ilya Kovalchuk, Atla. ✂
☐ Vincent Lecavalier, Tamp. ✂
☐ John LeClair, Phil. ✂
☐ Mario Lemieux, Pitt. ✂
☐ Nicklas Lidström, Detr. ✂
☐ Eric Lindros, NYRa. ✂
☐ Mark Messier, NYRa. ✂
☐ Mike Modano, Dall. ✂
☐ Rick Nash, Colu. ✂
☐ Markus Näslund, Vanc. ✂
☐ Jeremy Roenick, Phil. ✂
☐ Patrick Roy (G), Colo. ✂
☐ Joe Sakic, Colo. ✂
☐ Sergei Samsonov, Bost. ✂
☐ Teemu Selänne, SanJ. ✂
☐ Brendan Shanahan, Detr. ✂
☐ Jason Spezza, Otta. ✂
☐ Mats Sundin, Toro. ✂
☐ José Théodore (G), Mont. ✂
☐ Joe Thornton, Bost. ✂
☐ Marty Turco (G), Dall. ✂
☐ Steve Yzerman, Detr. ✂

GAME-USED STICK & JERSEY

Insert Set (30 cards):

Insert (*50)

☐ Todd Bertuzzi, Vanc. ✂ ✂
☐ Jay Bouwmeester, Flor. ✂ ✂
☐ Martin Brodeur (G), Njer. ✂ ✂
☐ Pavel Bure, NYRa. ✂ ✂
☐ Sergei Fedorov, Detr. ✂ ✂
☐ Peter Forsberg, Colo. ✂ ✂
☐ Marian Gaborik, MinW. ✂ ✂
☐ Dany Heatley, Atla. ✂ ✂
☐ Marian Hossa, Otta. ✂ ✂
☐ Brett Hull, Detr. ✂ ✂
☐ Jaromir Jagr, Wash. ✂ ✂
☐ Paul Kariya, Anah. ✂ ✂
☐ Saku Koivu, Mont. ✂ ✂
☐ Ilya Kovalchuk, Atla. ✂ ✂
☐ Mario Lemieux, Pitt. ✂ ✂
☐ Nicklas Lidström, Detr. ✂ ✂
☐ Roberto Luongo (G), Flor. ✂ ✂
☐ Mark Messier, NYRa. ✂ ✂
☐ Mike Modano, Dall. ✂ ✂
☐ Rick Nash, Colu. ✂ ✂
☐ Markus Näslund, Vanc. ✂ ✂
☐ Patrick Roy (G), Colo. ✂ ✂
☐ Joe Sakic, Colo. ✂ ✂
☐ Teemu Selänne, SanJ. ✂ ✂
☐ Brendan Shanahan, Detr. ✂ ✂
☐ Mats Sundin, Toro. ✂ ✂
☐ José Théodore (G), Mont. ✂ ✂
☐ Joe Thornton, Bost. ✂ ✂
☐ Marty Turco (G), Dall. ✂ ✂
☐ Steve Yzerman, Detr. ✂ ✂

GAME-USED STICK & JERSEY (GOLD)

Insert Set (30 cards):

Insert (*1)

☐ Todd Bertuzzi, Vanc. ✂ ✂
☐ Jay Bouwmeester, Flor. ✂ ✂
☐ Martin Brodeur (G), Njer. ✂ ✂
☐ Pavel Bure, NYRa. ✂ ✂
☐ Sergei Fedorov, Detr. ✂ ✂
☐ Peter Forsberg, Colo. ✂ ✂
☐ Marian Gaborik, MinW. ✂ ✂
☐ Dany Heatley, Atla. ✂ ✂
☐ Marian Hossa, Otta. ✂ ✂
☐ Brett Hull, Detr. ✂ ✂
☐ Jaromir Jagr, Wash. ✂ ✂
☐ Paul Kariya, Anah. ✂ ✂
☐ Saku Koivu, Mont. ✂ ✂
☐ Ilya Kovalchuk, Atla. ✂ ✂
☐ Mario Lemieux, Pitt. ✂ ✂
☐ Nicklas Lidström, Detr. ✂ ✂
☐ Roberto Luongo (G), Flor. ✂ ✂
☐ Mark Messier, NYRa. ✂ ✂
☐ Mike Modano, Dall. ✂ ✂
☐ Rick Nash, Colu. ✂ ✂
☐ Markus Näslund, Vanc. ✂ ✂
☐ Patrick Roy (G), Colo. ✂ ✂
☐ Joe Sakic, Colo. ✂ ✂
☐ Teemu Selänne, SanJ. ✂ ✂
☐ Brendan Shanahan, Detr. ✂ ✂
☐ Mats Sundin, Toro. ✂ ✂
☐ José Théodore (G), Mont. ✂ ✂
☐ Joe Thornton, Bost. ✂ ✂
☐ Marty Turco (G), Dall. ✂ ✂
☐ Steve Yzerman, Detr. ✂ ✂

GLOBAL DOMINATORS

Insert Set (10 cards):

Insert (*30)

☐ Rob Blake, Colo. ✂
☐ Theoren Fleury, Chic. ✂
☐ Peter Forsberg, Colo. ✂
☐ Igor Larionov, Detr. ✂
☐ Mario Lemieux, Pitt. ✂
☐ Al Macinnis, Slou. ✂
☐ Alexander Mogilny, Toro. ✂
☐ Joe Sakic, Colo. ✂
☐ Brendan Shanahan, Detr. ✂
☐ Steve Yzerman, Detr. ✂

GLOBAL DOMINATORS GOLD

Insert Set (10 cards):

Insert (*1)

☐ Rob Blake, Colo. ✂
☐ Theoren Fleury, Chic. ✂
☐ Peter Forsberg, Colo. ✂
☐ Igor Larionov, Detr. ✂
☐ Mario Lemieux, Pitt. ✂
☐ Al Macinnis, Slou. ✂
☐ Alexander Mogilny, Toro. ✂
☐ Joe Sakic, Colo. ✂
☐ Brendan Shanahan, Detr. ✂
☐ Steve Yzerman, Detr. ✂

GLOVES ARE OFF

Insert Set (20 cards):

Insert (*30)

☐ Ace Bailey, Toro. ✂
☐ Chris Chelios, Detr. ✂
☐ King Clancy, Toro. ✂
☐ Sergei Fedorov, Detr. ✂
☐ Bill Gadsby, ✂
☐ Doug Harvey, Mont. ✂
☐ Brett Hull, Detr. ✂
☐ Jarome Iginla, Calg. ✂
☐ Aurèle Joliat, Mont. ✂
☐ Ted Kennedy, Toro. ✂
☐ Guy Lafleur, Mont. ✂
☐ Mario Lemieux, Pitt. ✂
☐ Eric Lindros, NYRa. ✂
☐ Al Macinnis, Slou. ✂
☐ Dickie Moore, Mont. ✂
☐ Maurice Richard, Mont. ✂
☐ Joe Sakic, Colo. ✂
☐ Eddie Shore, Bost. ✂
☐ Mats Sundin, Toro. ✂
☐ Joe Thornton, Bost. ✂

GREAT MOMENTS IN HOCKEY

Insert Set (15 cards):

Insert (*30)

☐ Bill Barilko, Toro. ✂ {*10}
☐ Jean Béliveau, Mont. ✂
☐ George Hainsworth (G), Mont. {*20}
☐ Glenn Hall (G), ✂
☐ Ted Kennedy ✂
☐ Mario Lemieux, Pitt. ✂
☐ Stan Mikita, Chic. ✂
☐ Bill Mosienko, Chic. ✂
☐ Jacques Plante (G), Mont. ✂
☐ M. Richard ✂ / J. Henry
☐ Maurice Richard, Mont. ✂
☐ Maurice Richard, Mont. ✂
☐ Patrick Roy (G), Colo. ✂
☐ Terry Sawchuk (G), Detr. ✂
☐ Teemu Selänne, Winn. ✂
☐ Eddie Shore ✂ / Ace Bailey ✂
☐ Darryl Sittler, Toro. {*27}
☐ AS Game ✂
☐ Canadiens ✂
☐ Mark Messier, NYRa. ✂

HAT TRICKS

Insert Set (20 cards):

Insert (*30)

☐ Rob Blake, Colo. ✂ ✂ ✂
☐ Chris Chelios, Detr. ✂ ✂ ✂
☐ Adam Deadmarsh, LosA. ✂ ✂ ✂
☐ Sergei Fedorov, Detr. ✂ ✂ ✂
☐ Simon Gagné, Phil. ✂ ✂ ✂
☐ Brett Hull, Detr. ✂ ✂ ✂
☐ Jarome Iginla, Calg. ✂ ✂ ✂
☐ John LeClair, Phil. ✂ ✂ ✂
☐ Mario Lemieux, Pitt. ✂ ✂ ✂
☐ Eric Lindros, NYRa. ✂ ✂ ✂
☐ Al Macinnis, Slou. ✂ ✂ ✂
☐ Jeff O'Neill, Caro. ✂ ✂ ✂
☐ Joe Sakic, Colo. ✂ ✂ ✂
☐ Sergei Samsonov, Bost. ✂ ✂ ✂
☐ Mats Sundin, Toro. ✂ ✂ ✂
☐ Joe Thornton, Bost. ✂ ✂ ✂
☐ Keith Tkachuk, Phoe. ✂ ✂ ✂
☐ Doug Weight, Slou. ✂ ✂ ✂
☐ Alexei Yashin, NYIs. ✂ ✂ ✂
☐ Steve Yzerman, Detr. ✂ ✂ ✂

IN THE NUMBERS

Insert Set (30 cards):

Insert (*10)

☐ Martin Brodeur (G), Njer. ✂
☐ Pavel Bure, NYRa. ✂
☐ Chris Chelios, Detr. ✂
☐ Mike Comrie, Edmo. ✂
☐ Sergei Fedorov, Detr. ✂
☐ Peter Forsberg, Colo. ✂
☐ Marian Gaborik, MinW. ✂
☐ Dany Heatley, Atla. ✂
☐ Brett Hull, Detr. ✂
☐ Jaromir Jagr, Wash. ✂
☐ Paul Kariya, Anah. ✂
☐ Valeri Kharlamov, ✂
☐ Saku Koivu, Mont. ✂
☐ Ilya Kovalchuk, Atla. ✂
☐ John LeClair, Phil. ✂
☐ Brian Leetch, NYRa. ✂
☐ Mario Lemieux, Pitt. ✂
☐ Nicklas Lidström, Detr. ✂
☐ Eric Lindros, NYRa. ✂
☐ Mark Messier, NYRa. ✂
☐ Mike Modano, Dall. ✂
☐ Markus Näslund, Vanc. ✂
☐ Luc Robitaille, Detr. ✂
☐ Jeremy Roenick, Phil. ✂
☐ Patrick Roy (G), Colo. ✂
☐ Joe Sakic, Colo. ✂
☐ Brendan Shanahan, Detr. ✂
☐ Mats Sundin, Toro. ✂
☐ Joe Thornton, Bost. ✂
☐ Steve Yzerman, Detr. ✂

JOURNEY EMBLEM

Insert Set (10 cards):

Insert (*10)

☐ Ed Belfour (G), Toro. ✂ Dall. ✂ Chic. ✂
☐ Pavel Bure, NYRa. ✂
☐ Bill Guerin, Dall. ✂
☐ Brett Hull, Detr. ✂ Dall. ✂ SLou. ✂ Calg. ✂
☐ Jaromir Jagr, Wash. ✂ Pitt. ✂
☐ Eric Lindros, NYRa. ✂ Phil. ✂
☐ Alexander Mogilny, Toro. ✂
☐ Adam Oates, Anah. ✂
☐ Jeremy Roenick, Phil. ✂
☐ Patrick Roy (G), Colo. ✂ Mont. ✂

JOURNEY EMBLEM GOLD

Insert Set (10 cards):

Insert (*1)

☐ Ed Belfour (G), ✂
☐ Pavel Bure, ✂
☐ Bill Guerin, ✂
☐ Brett Hull, ✂
☐ Jaromir Jagr, ✂
☐ Eric Lindros, ✂
☐ Alexander Mogilny, ✂
☐ Adam Oates, ✂
☐ Jeremy Roenick, ✂
☐ Patrick Roy (G), ✂

JOURNEY GAME-USED JERSEY

Insert Set (10 cards):

Insert (*50)

☐ Ed Belfour (G), Toro. ✂ Dall. ✂ Chic. ✂
☐ Pavel Bure, NYRa. ✂
☐ Bill Guerin, Dall. ✂
☐ Brett Hull, Detr. ✂ Dall. ✂ SLou. ✂ Calg. ✂
☐ Jaromir Jagr, Wash. ✂ Pitt. ✂
☐ Eric Lindros, NYRa. ✂ Phil. ✂
☐ Alexander Mogilny, Toro. ✂
☐ Adam Oates, Anah. ✂
☐ Jeremy Roenick, Phil. ✂
☐ Patrick Roy (G), Colo. ✂ Mont. ✂

JOURNEY GAME-USED JERSEY GOLD

Insert Set (10 cards):

Insert (*1)

☐ Ed Belfour (G), Toro. ✂ Dall. ✂ Chic. ✂
☐ Pavel Bure, NYRa. ✂
☐ Bill Guerin, Dall. ✂
☐ Brett Hull, Detr. ✂ Dall. ✂ SLou. ✂ Calg. ✂
☐ Jaromir Jagr, Wash. ✂ Pitt. ✂
☐ Eric Lindros, NYRa. ✂ Phil. ✂
☐ Alexander Mogilny, Toro. ✂
☐ Adam Oates, Anah. ✂
☐ Jeremy Roenick, Phil. ✂
☐ Patrick Roy (G), Colo. ✂ Mont. ✂

LIFETIME ACHIEVERS

Insert Set (20 cards):

Insert (*40)

☐ Ed Belfour (G), Toro. ✂
☐ Martin Brodeur (G), NJer. ✂
☐ Pavel Bure, NYRa. ✂
☐ Chris Chelios, Detr. ✂
☐ Sergei Fedorov, Detr. ✂
☐ Ron Francis, Caro. ✂
☐ Doug Gilmour, Toro. ✂
☐ Brett Hull, Detr. ✂
☐ Jaromir Jagr, Wash. ✂
☐ Curtis Joseph (G), Detr. ✂
☐ Brian Leetch, NYRa. ✂
☐ Mario Lemieux, Pitt. ✂
☐ Nicklas Lidström, Detr. ✂
☐ Eric Lindros, NYRa. ✂
☐ Mark Messier, NYRa. ✂
☐ Luc Robitaille, Detr. ✂
☐ Patrick Roy (G), Colo. ✂
☐ Joe Sakic, Colo. ✂
☐ Brendan Shanahan, Detr. ✂
☐ Steve Yzerman, Detr. ✂

MAGNIFICENT

Insert Set (10 cards):

Insert

☐ Mario Lemieux, Pitt. ✂ {*30}
☐ Mario Lemieux, Pitt. ✂ {*30}
☐ Mario Lemieux, Pitt. ✂ {*30}
☐ Mario Lemieux, Pitt. ✂ {*30}
☐ Mario Lemieux, Pitt. ✂ {*30}
☐ Mario Lemieux, Pitt. ✂ {*10}
☐ Mario Lemieux, Pitt. ✂ {*10}
☐ Mario Lemieux, Pitt. ✂ ✂ ✂ {*10}
☐ Mario Lemieux, Pitt. ✂ ✂ ✂ ✂ {*10}
☐ Mario Lemieux, Pitt. ✂ ✂ ✂ ✂ {*10}

MAGNIFICENT AUTOGRAPH

Insert Set (10 cards):

Insert

☐ Mario Lemieux, Pitt. ✍ ✂ {*15}
☐ Mario Lemieux, Pitt. ✍ ✂ {*15}
☐ Mario Lemieux, Pitt. ✍ ✂ {*15}
☐ Mario Lemieux, Pitt. ✍ ✂ {*15}
☐ Mario Lemieux, Pitt. ✍ ✂ {*15}
☐ Mario Lemieux, Pitt. ✍ ✂ {*5}
☐ Mario Lemieux, Pitt. ✍ ✂ {*5}
☐ Mario Lemieux, Pitt. ✍ ✂ ✂ ✂ {*5}
☐ Mario Lemieux, Pitt. ✍ ✂ ✂ ✂ ✂ {*5}
☐ Mario Lemieux, Pitt. ✍ ✂ ✂ ✂ ✂ {*5}

MAGNIFICENT ONES

Insert Set (10 cards):

Insert (*30)

☐ Brodeur (G) ✂ / Lemieux ✂
☐ Bure ✂ / Lemieux ✂
☐ Forsberg ✂ / Lemieux ✂
☐ Jagr ✂ / Lemieux ✂
☐ Kariya ✂ / Lemieux ✂
☐ Modano ✂ / Lemieux ✂
☐ Roy ✂ / Lemieux ✂
☐ Sakic ✂ / Lemieux ✂
☐ Shanahan ✂ / Lemieux ✂
☐ Yzerman ✂ / Lemieux ✂

MAGNIFICENT ONES (AUTOGRAPH)

Insert Set (10 cards):

Insert (*10)

☐ Brodeur (G) ✂ / Lemieux ✂ ✍
☐ Bure ✂ / Lemieux ✂ ✍
☐ Forsberg ✂ / Lemieux ✂ ✍
☐ Jagr ✂ / Lemieux ✂ ✍
☐ Kariya ✂ / Lemieux ✂ ✍
☐ Modano ✂ / Lemieux ✂ ✍
☐ Roy ✂ / Lemieux ✂ ✍
☐ Sakic ✂ / Lemieux ✂ ✍
☐ Shanahan ✂ / Lemieux ✂ ✍
☐ Yzerman ✂ / Lemieux ✂ ✍

NAMEPLATES

Insert Set (20 cards):

Insert (*40)

☐ Ed Belfour (G), Toro. ✂
☐ Jay Bouwmeester, Flor. ✂
☐ Martin Brodeur (G), NJer. ✂
☐ Pavel Bure, NYRa. ✂
☐ Peter Forsberg, Colo. ✂
☐ Marian Gaborik, MinW. ✂
☐ Marian Hossa, Otta. ✂
☐ Jaromir Jagr, Wash. ✂
☐ Curtis Joseph (G), Toro. ✂
☐ Paul Kariya, Anah. ✂
☐ Ilya Kovalchuk, Atla. ✂

☐ Mario Lemieux, Pitt. ✂
☐ Nicklas Lidström, Detr. ✂
☐ Mike Modano, Dall. ✂
☐ Markus Näslund, Vanc. ✂
☐ Patrick Roy (G), Colo. ✂
☐ Joe Sakic, Colo. ✂
☐ Jason Spezza, Otta. ✂
☐ Joe Thornton, Bost. ✂
☐ Steve Yzerman, Detr. ✂

NAMEPLATES GOLD

Insert Set (20 cards):
Insert (*1)

☐ Ed Belfour (G), Toro. ✂
☐ Jay Bouwmeester, Flor. ✂
☐ Martin Brodeur (G), NJer. ✂
☐ Pavel Bure, NYRa. ✂
☐ Peter Forsberg, Colo. ✂
☐ Marian Gaborik, MinW. ✂
☐ Marian Hossa, Otta. ✂
☐ Jaromir Jagr, Wash. ✂
☐ Curtis Joseph (G), Toro. ✂
☐ Paul Kariya, Anah. ✂
☐ Ilya Kovalchuk, Atla. ✂
☐ Mario Lemieux, Pitt. ✂
☐ Nicklas Lidström, Detr. ✂
☐ Mike Modano, Dall. ✂
☐ Markus Näslund, Vanc. ✂
☐ Patrick Roy (G), Colo. ✂
☐ Joe Sakic, Colo. ✂
☐ Jason Spezza, Otta. ✂
☐ Joe Thornton, Bost. ✂
☐ Steve Yzerman, Detr. ✂

NHL SCORING LEADERS

Insert Set (35 cards):
Insert (*40)

☐ 1955 Bernie Geoffrion, Mont. ✂
☐ 1956 Jean Béliveau, Mont. ✂
☐ 1958 Dickie Moore, Mont. ✂
☐ 1959 Dickie Moore, Mont. ✂
☐ 1960 Bobby Hull, Chic. ✂
☐ 1961 Bernie Geoffrion, Mont. ✂
☐ 1962 Bobby Hull, Chic. ✂
☐ 1964 Stan Mikita, Chic. ✂
☐ 1965 Stan Mikita, Chic. ✂
☐ 1966 Bobby Hull, Chic. ✂
☐ 1967 Stan Mikita, Chic. ✂
☐ 1968 Stan Mikita, Chic. ✂
☐ 1969 Phil Esposito, Bost. ✂
☐ 1971 Phil Esposito, Bost. ✂
☐ 1972 Phil Esposito, Bost. ✂
☐ 1973 Phil Esposito, Bost. ✂
☐ 1974 Phil Esposito, Bost. ✂
☐ 1976 Guy Lafleur, Mont. ✂
☐ 1977 Guy Lafleur, Mont. ✂
☐ 1978 Guy Lafleur, Mont. ✂
☐ 1979 Bryan Trottier, NYIs. ✂
☐ 1980 Marcel Dionne, LosA. ✂
☐ 1988 Mario Lemieux, Pitt. ✂
☐ 1989 Mario Lemieux, Pitt. ✂
☐ 1992 Mario Lemieux, Pitt. ✂
☐ 1993 Mario Lemieux, Pitt. ✂
☐ 1995 Jaromir Jagr, Pitt. ✂
☐ 1996 Mario Lemieux, Pitt. ✂
☐ 1997 Mario Lemieux, Pitt. ✂
☐ 1998 Jaromir Jagr, Pitt. ✂
☐ 1999 Jaromir Jagr, Pitt. ✂
☐ 2000 Jaromir Jagr, Pitt. ✂
☐ 2001 Jaromir Jagr, Pitt. ✂
☐ 2002 Jarome Iginla, Calg. ✂
☐ 2003 Peter Forsberg, Colo. ✂

NUMBER ONES

Insert Set (10 cards):
Insert (*10)

☐ Sean Burke (G), Phoe. ✂
☐ Roger Crozier (G), Detr. ✂
☐ Ed Giacomin (G), NYRa. ✂
☐ Glenn Hall (G), Chic. ✂
☐ Johan Hedberg (G), Pitt. ✂
☐ Arturs Irbe (G), Caro. ✂
☐ Roberto Luongo (G), Flor. ✂
☐ Jacques Plante (G), Mont. ✂
☐ Terry Sawchuk (G), Detr. ✂
☐ Roman Turek (G), Calg. ✂

NUMEROLOGY

Insert Set (30 cards):
Insert (*40)

☐ Béliveau ✂ / Lecavalier ✂
☐ Bossy ✂ / Huselius ✂
☐ Bucyk ✂ / Bure ✂
☐ Cournoyer ✂ / Iginla ✂
☐ Delvecchio ✂ / Francis ✂
☐ Dionne ✂ / Linden ✂
☐ Fuhr (G) ✂ / Blackburn (G) ✂
☐ Hall (G) ✂ / Hedberg (G) ✂
☐ Harvey ✂ / Leetch ✂
☐ Hull ✂ / Modano ✂
☐ Kelly ✂ / Blake ✂
☐ Kharlamov ✂ / Kovalchuk ✂
☐ Lafleur ✂ / Gaborik ✂
☐ M.Richard ✂ / Kariya ✂
☐ Mahovlich ✂ / Peca ✂
☐ Mikita ✂ / Forsberg ✂
☐ Nystrom ✂ / Hejduk ✂
☐ P.Esposito ✂ / Tkachuk ✂
☐ Parent ✂ / Luongo (G) ✂
☐ Perreault ✂ / Messier ✂
☐ Plante (G) ✂ / DiPietro (G) ✂
☐ Potvin ✂ / Lidström ✂
☐ R.Gilbert ✂ / Roberts ✂
☐ Robinson ✂ / Yzerman ✂
☐ Savard ✂ / Hossa ✂
☐ Sawchuk (G) ✂ / Turek (G) ✂
☐ Smith ✂ / Joseph (G) ✂
☐ T.Esposito ✂ / Turco (G) ✂
☐ Tretiak (G) ✂ / Belfour (G) ✂
☐ Trottier ✂ / Sakic ✂

PAPER CUTS

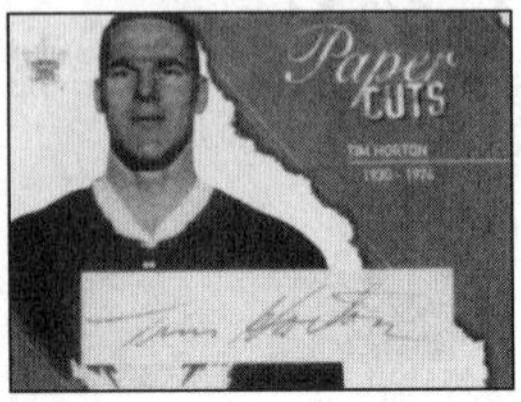

Insert Set (36 cards):
Insert (*1)

☐ Sid Abel ✍
☐ Syl Apps ✍
☐ Ace Bailey ✍
☐ Bill Barilko ✍
☐ Max Bentley ✍
☐ Toe Blake ✍
☐ Frank Boucher ✍
☐ Turk Broda (G) ✍

◆ The Turk Broda one-of-one Paper Cuts card closed at $1,902.77 U.S. (approx. $2,570 Cdn.) in a June Internet auction at eBay.

☐ King Clancy ✍
☐ Neil Colville ✍
☐ Charlie Conacher ✍
☐ Bill Cook ✍

◆ The Bill Cook one-of-one Paper Cuts cut signature card did not receive any bids when it was posted at $2,500 U.S. (approx. $3,375 Cdn.) in a July Internet auction at eBay.

☐ Bun Cook ✍
☐ Baldy Cotton ✍
☐ Bill Cowley ✍
☐ Hap Day ✍
☐ Gordie Drillon ✍
☐ Red Dutton ✍
☐ Ebbie Goodfellow ✍

◆ The Ebbie Goodfellow one-of-one Paper Cuts cut signature card closed at $1,327 U.S. (approx. $1,790 Cdn.) in a June Internet auction at eBay.

☐ Doug Harvey ✍
☐ Bryan Hextall ✍
☐ Flash Hollett ✍
☐ Tim Horton ✍
☐ Busher Jackson ✍

◆ The Busher Jackson one-of-one Paper Cuts cut signature card closed at $1,425 U.S. (approx. $1,925 Cdn.) in a July Internet auction at eBay.

☐ Ching Johnson ✍
☐ Aurèle Joliat ✍
☐ Harry Lumley (G) ✍
☐ Bill Mosienko ✍
☐ Harry Oliver ✍

◆ The Harry Oliver one-of-one Paper Cuts cut signature card closed at $1,324.99 U.S. (approx. $1,790 Cdn.) in a June Internet auction at eBay.

☐ Jacques Plante (G) ✍
☐ Babe Pratt ✍
☐ Joe Primeau ✍
☐ Terry Sawchuk (G) ✍
☐ Sweeney Schriner ✍
☐ Black Stewart ✍

◆ The Jack Stewart one-of-one Paper Cuts cut signature card closed at $1,025 U.S. (approx. $1,385 Cdn.) in a June Internet auction at eBay.

☐ Tiny Thompson (G) ✍

◆ The Cecil Tiny Thompson one-of-one Paper Cuts cut signature card closed at $1,999.95 U.S. (approx. $2,700 Cdn.) in a June Internet auction at eBay.

PLAYOFF SCORERS

Insert Set (30 cards):
Insert (*30)

☐ Jean Béliveau, Mont. ✂
☐ Jean Béliveau, Mont. ✂
☐ Mike Bossy, NYIs. ✂
☐ Phil Esposito, ✂
☐ Phil Esposito, ✂
☐ Sergei Fedorov, Detr. ✂
☐ Peter Forsberg, Colo. ✂
☐ Peter Forsberg, Colo. ✂
☐ Doug Gilmour, Toro. ✂
☐ Bobby Hull, Chic. ✂
☐ Brett Hull, ✂
☐ Brett Hull, ✂
☐ Brett Hull, ✂
☐ Brian Leetch, NYRa. ✂
☐ Mario Lemieux, Pitt. ✂
☐ Mario Lemieux, Pitt. ✂
☐ Mario Lemieux, Pitt. ✂
☐ Eric Lindros, ✂
☐ Mark Messier, ✂
☐ Mark Messier, ✂
☐ Stan Mikita, Chic. ✂
☐ Denis Potvin, NYIs. ✂
☐ Maurice Richard, Mont. ✂
☐ Joe Sakic, Colo. ✂
☐ Joe Sakic, Colo. ✂
☐ Bryan Trottier, NYIs. ✂
☐ Bryan Trottier, NYIs. ✂
☐ Steve Yzerman, Detr. ✂
☐ Steve Yzerman, Detr. ✂
☐ Steve Yzerman, Detr. ✂

PLAYOFF SCORERS GOLD

Insert Set (30 cards):
Insert (*1)

☐ Jean Béliveau, Mont. ✂
☐ Jean Béliveau, Mont. ✂
☐ Mike Bossy, NYIs. ✂
☐ Phil Esposito, ✂
☐ Phil Esposito, ✂
☐ Sergei Fedorov, Detr. ✂
☐ Peter Forsberg, Colo. ✂
☐ Peter Forsberg, Colo. ✂
☐ Doug Gilmour, Toro. ✂
☐ Bobby Hull, Chic. ✂
☐ Brett Hull, ✂
☐ Brett Hull, ✂
☐ Brett Hull, ✂
☐ Brian Leetch, NYRa. ✂
☐ Mario Lemieux, Pitt. ✂
☐ Mario Lemieux, Pitt. ✂
☐ Mario Lemieux, Pitt. ✂
☐ Eric Lindros, ✂
☐ Mark Messier, ✂
☐ Mark Messier, ✂
☐ Stan Mikita, Chic. ✂
☐ Denis Potvin, NYIs. ✂
☐ Maurice Richard, Mont. ✂
☐ Joe Sakic, Colo. ✂
☐ Joe Sakic, Colo. ✂
☐ Bryan Trottier, NYIs. ✂
☐ Bryan Trottier, NYIs. ✂
☐ Steve Yzerman, Detr. ✂
☐ Steve Yzerman, Detr. ✂
☐ Steve Yzerman, Detr. ✂

RETRO ACTIVE TROPHIES

Insert Set (20 cards):
Insert {*40}

☐ Belfour (G) ✂ / Hall (G) ✂
☐ Brodeur (G) ✂ / Brimsek (G) ✂
☐ Forsberg ✂ / Berard ✂
☐ Heatley ✂ / Lemieux ✂
☐ Hull ✂ / Hull ✂
☐ Iginla ✂ / Hull ✂
☐ Jagr ✂ / Mikita ✂
☐ Kariya ✂ / Dionne ✂
☐ Koivu ✂ / H.Richard ✂
☐ Lemieux ✂ / McDonald ✂
☐ Lemieux ✂ / Morenz ✂ {*10}
☐ Lemieux ✂ / P.Esposito ✂
☐ Lidström ✂ / Crozier (G) ✂
☐ Lidström ✂ / Robinson ✂
☐ Messier ✂ / Hextall ✂
☐ Peca ✂ / Clarke ✂
☐ Roy ✂ / Sawchuk (G) ✂
☐ Sakic ✂ / M.Richard ✂
☐ Théodore (G) ✂ / Plante (G) ✂
☐ Yzerman ✂ / Béliveau ✂

RETRO TEAMMATES

Insert Set (10 cards):
Insert (*30)

☐ Gilbert ✂ / Cheevers (G) ✂ / Bucyk ✂
☐ Hull ✂ / Mikita ✂ / Hall (G) ✂
☐ Delvecchio ✂ / Sawchuk (G) ✂ / Abel ✂
☐ Lafleur ✂ / Cournoyer ✂ / S.Savard ✂
☐ M.Richard ✂ / Plante (G) ✂ / Béliveau ✂
☐ R.Gilbert ✂ / Giacomin (G) ✂ / P.Esposito ✂
☐ Schultz ✂ / Clarke ✂ / Parent ✂
☐ Lemieux ✂ / Jagr ✂ / Francis ✂
☐ Sittler ✂ / McDonald ✂ / Williams ✂
☐ Horton ✂ / Bower (G) ✂ / Kelly ✂

SEAMS UNBELIEVABLE

Insert Set (8 cards):
Insert (*10)

☐ Gerry Cheevers (G), Bost. ✂
☐ Bill Durnan (G), Mont. ✂
☐ George Hainsworth (G), Mont. ✂
☐ Glenn Hall (G), Detr. ✂
☐ Guy Lafleur, Mont. ✂
☐ Mario Lemieux, Pitt. ✂
☐ Ted Lindsay, Detr. ✂
☐ Bill Mosienko, Chic. ✂

STANLEY CUP DUELS

Insert Set (20 cards):
Insert {*40}

☐ Hainsworth (G) ✂ / Thompson ✂
☐ Sawchuk (G) ✂ / Plante (G) ✂
☐ Plante (G) ✂ / Bower (G) ✂
☐ Hall (G) ✂ / Sawchuk (G) ✂
☐ Bower (G) ✂ / Sawchuk (G) ✂
☐ Worlsey (G) ✂ / Crozier (G) ✂
☐ Cheevers (G) ✂ / Giacomin (G) ✂
☐ Parent ✂ / Gilbert ✂
☐ Fuhr (G) ✂ / Smith ✂
☐ Roy ✂ / Vernon ✂
☐ Fuhr (G) ✂ / Hextall ✂
☐ Fuhr (G) ✂ / Moog ✂
☐ Vernon ✂ / Roy ✂
☐ Ranford ✂ / Moog ✂
☐ Barrasso (G) ✂ / Belfour (G) ✂
☐ Brodeur (G) ✂ / Vernon ✂
☐ Vanbiesbrouck ✂ / Roy ✂
☐ Osgood (G) ✂ / Kölzig (G) ✂
☐ Brodeur (G) ✂ / Belfour (G) ✂
☐ Roy ✂ / Brodeur (G) ✂

STANLEY CUP DUELS GOLD

Insert Set (20 cards):
Insert (*1)

☐ Hainsworth (G) ✂ / Thompson ✂
☐ Sawchuk (G) ✂ / Plante (G) ✂
☐ Plante (G) ✂ / Bower (G) ✂
☐ Hall (G) ✂ / Sawchuk (G) ✂
☐ Bower (G) ✂ / Sawchuk (G) ✂
☐ Worlsey (G) ✂ / Crozier (G) ✂
☐ Cheevers (G) ✂ / Giacomin (G) ✂
☐ Parent ✂ / Gilbert ✂
☐ Fuhr (G) ✂ / Smith ✂
☐ Roy ✂ / Vernon ✂
☐ Fuhr (G) ✂ / Hextall ✂
☐ Fuhr (G) ✂ / Moog ✂
☐ Vernon ✂ / Roy ✂
☐ Ranford ✂ / Moog ✂
☐ Barrasso (G) ✂ / Belfour (G) ✂
☐ Brodeur (G) ✂ / Vernon ✂
☐ Vanbiesbrouck ✂ / Roy ✂
☐ Osgood (G) ✂ / Kölzig (G) ✂
☐ Brodeur (G) ✂ / Belfour (G) ✂
☐ Roy ✂ / Brodeur (G) ✂

STANLEY CUP DYNASTY EMBLEM

Insert Set (20 cards):
Insert (*10)

☐ Chris Chelios, Detr. ✂
☐ Mathieu Dandenault, Detr. ✂
☐ Pavel Datsyuk, Detr. ✂
☐ Kris Draper, Detr. ✂
☐ Sergei Fedorov, Detr. ✂
☐ Jiri Fischer, Detr. ✂
☐ Tomas Holmström, Detr. ✂
☐ Brett Hull, Detr. ✂
☐ Vyacheslav Kozlov, Detr. ✂
☐ Martin Lapointe, Detr. ✂
☐ Igor Larionov, Detr. ✂
☐ Manny Legacé (G), Detr. ✂
☐ Nicklas Lidström, Detr. ✂
☐ Kirk Maltby, Detr. ✂
☐ Darren McCarty, Detr. ✂
☐ Chris Osgood (G), Detr. ✂
☐ Luc Robitaille, Detr. ✂
☐ Brendan Shanahan, Detr. ✂
☐ Mike Vernon (G), Detr. ✂
☐ Steve Yzerman, Detr. ✂

STANLEY CUP DYNASTY JERSEY

Insert Set (20 cards):
Insert (*50)

☐ Chris Chelios, Detr. ✂
☐ Mathieu Dandenault, Detr. ✂
☐ Pavel Datsyuk, Detr. ✂
☐ Kris Draper, Detr. ✂
☐ Sergei Fedorov, Detr. ✂
☐ Jiri Fischer, Detr. ✂
☐ Tomas Holmström, Detr. ✂
☐ Brett Hull, Detr. ✂

☐ Vyacheslav Kozlov, Detr. ✄
☐ Martin Lapointe, Detr. ✄
☐ Igor Larionov, Detr. ✄
☐ Manny Legacé (G), Detr. ✄
☐ Nicklas Lidström, Detr. ✄
☐ Kirk Maltby, Detr. ✄
☐ Darren McCarty, Detr. ✄
☐ Chris Osgood (G), Detr. ✄
☐ Luc Robitaille, Detr. ✄
☐ Brendan Shanahan, Detr. ✄
☐ Mike Vernon (G), Detr. ✄
☐ Steve Yzerman, Detr. ✄

STANLEY CUP DYNASTY NUMBERS

Insert Set (20 cards):
Insert (*10)
☐ Chris Chelios, Detr. ✄
☐ Mathieu Dandenault, Detr. ✄
☐ Pavel Datsyuk, Detr. ✄
☐ Kris Draper, Detr. ✄
☐ Sergei Fedorov, Detr. ✄
☐ Jiri Fischer, Detr. ✄
☐ Tomas Holmström, Detr. ✄
☐ Brett Hull, Detr. ✄
☐ Vyacheslav Kozlov, Detr. ✄
☐ Martin Lapointe, Detr. ✄
☐ Igor Larionov, Detr. ✄
☐ Manny Legacé (G), Detr. ✄
☐ Nicklas Lidström, Detr. ✄
☐ Kirk Maltby, Detr. ✄
☐ Darren McCarty, Detr. ✄
☐ Chris Osgood (G), Detr. ✄
☐ Luc Robitaille, Detr. ✄
☐ Brendan Shanahan, Detr. ✄
☐ Mike Vernon (G), Detr. ✄
☐ Steve Yzerman, Detr. ✄

STORIED FRANCHISE

Insert Set (25 cards):
Insert {*20}
☐ Georges Vézina (G), Mont. ✄ {*10}
☐ Aurèle Joliat, Mont. ✄
☐ Howie Morenz, Mont. ✄
☐ George Hainsworth (G), Mont. ✄
☐ Maurice Richard, Mont. ✄
☐ Bill Durnan (G), Mont. ✄
☐ Doug Harvey, Mont. ✄
☐ Henri Richard, Mont. ✄
☐ Jean Béliveau, Mont. ✄
☐ Bernie Geoffrion, Mont. ✄
☐ Jacques Plante (G), Mont. ✄
☐ Charlie Hodge (G), Mont. ✄
☐ Gump Worlsey (G), Mont. ✄
☐ Jacques Laperrière, Mont. ✄
☐ Serge Savard, Mont. ✄
☐ Rogatien Vachon (G), Mont. ✄
☐ Frank Mahovlich, Mont. ✄
☐ Yvan Cournoyer, Mont. ✄
☐ Steve Shutt, Mont. ✄
☐ Larry Robinson, Mont. ✄
☐ Guy Lafleur, Mont. ✄
☐ Guy Lapointe, Mont. ✄
☐ Patrick Roy (G), Mont. ✄
☐ John LeClair, Mont. ✄
☐ Henri Richard, Mont. ✄

ULTIMATE AUTOGRAPHS

Insert Set (12 cards):
Insert (*30)
☐ Pavel Bure, NYRa. ✍
☐ Sergei Fedorov, Detr. ✍
☐ Peter Forsberg, Colo. ✍
☐ Dany Heatley, Atla. ✍
☐ Jarome Iginla, Calg. ✍
☐ Saku Koivu, Mont. ✍
☐ Brian Leetch, NYRa. ✍
☐ Mario Lemieux, Pitt. ✍
☐ Patrick Roy (G), Colo. ✍
☐ Joe Sakic, Colo. ✍
☐ José Théodore (G), Mont. ✍
☐ Joe Thornton, Bost. ✍

ULTIMATE AUTOGRAPHS GOLD

Insert Set (12 cards):
Insert (*1)
☐ Pavel Bure, NYRa. ✍
☐ Sergei Fedorov, Detr. ✍
☐ Peter Forsberg, Colo. ✍
☐ Dany Heatley, Atla. ✍
☐ Jarome Iginla, Calg. ✍
☐ Saku Koivu, Mont. ✍
☐ Brian Leetch, NYRa. ✍
☐ Mario Lemieux, Pitt. ✍
☐ Patrick Roy (G), Colo. ✍
☐ Joe Sakic, Colo. ✍
☐ José Théodore (G), Mont. ✍
☐ Joe Thornton, Bost. ✍

ULTIMATE CALDER

☐ Barret Jackman, SLou. ✄ {*10}

ULTIMATE CAPTAINS

Insert Set (8 cards):
Insert (*5)
☐ Paul Kariya, Anah. ✄
☐ Saku Koivu, Mont. ✄
☐ Mario Lemieux, Pitt. ✄
☐ Markus Näslund, Vanc. ✄
☐ Joe Sakic, Colo. ✄
☐ Mats Sundin, Toro. ✄
☐ Joe Thornton, Bost. ✄
☐ Steve Yzerman, Detr. ✄

ULTIMATE MVP

Insert (*10)
☐ Peter Forsberg, Colo. ✄

ULTIMATE ROOKIE AUTOGRAPHS

Insert Set (17 cards):
Insert (*30)
☐ Pierre-autarc Bouchard, autinW. ✍
☐ Jay Bouwauteester, Flor. ✍
☐ Mike Cammalleri, LosA. ✍
☐ Stanislav Chistov, Anah. ✍
☐ Carlo Colaiacovo, Toro. ✍
☐ Alexander Frolov, LosA. ✍
☐ Ron Hainsey, autont. ✍
☐ Adam Hall (G), Nash. ✍
☐ Chuck Kobasew, Calg. ✍
☐ Jordan Leopold, Calg. ✍
☐ Rick Nash, Colu. ✍
☐ Alexei Smirnov, Anah. ✍
☐ Alexander Svitov, Tamp. ✍
☐ Scottie Upshall, Nash. ✍
☐ Stéphane Veilleux, MinW. ✍
☐ Anton Volchenkov, Otta. ✍
☐ Henrik Zetterberg, Detr. ✍

ULTIMATE ROOKIE AUTOGRAPHS GOLD

Insert Set (17 cards):
Insert (*1)
☐ Pierre-autarc Bouchard, autinW. ✍
☐ Jay Bouwauteester, Flor. ✍
☐ Mike Cammalleri, LosA. ✍
☐ Stanislav Chistov, Anah. ✍
☐ Carlo Colaiacovo, Toro. ✍
☐ Alexander Frolov, LosA. ✍
☐ Ron Hainsey, autont. ✍
☐ Adam Hall (G), Nash. ✍
☐ Chuck Kobasew, Calg. ✍
☐ Jordan Leopold, Calg. ✍
☐ Rick Nash, Colu. ✍
☐ Alexei Smirnov, Anah. ✍
☐ Alexander Svitov, Tamp. ✍
☐ Scottie Upshall, Nash. ✍
☐ Stéphane Veilleux, MinW. ✍
☐ Anton Volchenkov, Otta. ✍
☐ Henrik Zetterberg, Detr. ✍

ULTIMATE VÉZINA

Insert (*10)
☐ Martin Brodeur (G), NJer. ✄

VINTAGE GAME-USED JERSEY

Insert Set (40 cards):
Insert (*40)
☐ Sid Abel, Detr. ✄
☐ Bill Barber, Phil. ✄
☐ Jean Béliveau, Mont. ✄
☐ Mike Bossy, NYIs. ✄
☐ Frank Brimsek (G), ✄
☐ Johnny Bucyk, Bost. ✄
☐ Gerry Cheevers (G), Bost. ✄
☐ Bobby Clarke, Phil. ✄
☐ Roger Crozier (G), Detr. ✄
☐ Alex Delvecchio, Detr. ✄
☐ Marcel Dionne, ✄
☐ Phil Esposito, ✄
☐ Tony Esposito (G), ✄
☐ Ed Giacomin (G), NYRa. ✄
☐ George Hainsworth (G), ✄
☐ Glenn Hall (G), ✄
☐ Doug Harvey, Mont. ✄
☐ Tim Horton, Toro. ✄
☐ Bobby Hull, Chic. ✄
☐ Dennis Hull, Chic. ✄
☐ Aurèle Joliat, Mont. ✄
☐ Red Kelly, ✄
☐ Valeri Kharlamov, ✄
☐ Guy Lafleur, Mont. ✄
☐ Ted Lindsay, Detr. ✄
☐ Harry Lumley (G), ✄
☐ Frank Mahovlich, ✄
☐ Peter Mahovlich, ✄
☐ Lanny McDonald, ✄
☐ Stan Mikita, Chic. ✄
☐ Bernie Parent (G), Phil. ✄
☐ Gilbert Perreault, Buff. ✄
☐ Jacques Plante (G), Mont. ✄
☐ Henri Richard, Mont. ✄
☐ Maurice Richard, Mont. ✄
☐ Larry Robinson, Mont. ✄
☐ Terry Sawchuk (G), ✄
☐ Vladislav Tretiak (G), ✄
☐ Bryan Trottier, NYIs. ✄
☐ Roy Worters (G), NYAm. ✄

VINTAGE GAME-USED JERSEY AUTOGRAPH

Insert Set (14 cards):
Insert
☐ Jean Béliveau, Mont. ✄ ✍
☐ Johnny Bucyk, Bost. ✄ ✍
☐ Marcel Dionne, ✄ ✍
☐ Phil Esposito, ✄ ✍
☐ Tony Esposito (G), ✄ ✍
☐ Ed Giacomin (G), NYRa. ✄ ✍
☐ Glenn Hall (G), ✄ ✍
☐ Bobby Hull, Chic. ✄ ✍
☐ Red Kelly, ✄ ✍
☐ Guy Lafleur, Mont. ✄ ✍
☐ Ted Lindsay, Detr. ✄ ✍
☐ Frank Mahovlich, ✄ ✍
☐ Stan Mikita, Chic. ✄ ✍
☐ Henri Richard, Mont. ✄ ✍

VINTAGE GAME-USED JERSEY GOLD

Insert Set (40 cards):
Insert (*1)
☐ Sid Abel, Detr. ✄
☐ Bill Barber, Phil. ✄
☐ Jean Béliveau, Mont. ✄
☐ Mike Bossy, NYIs. ✄
☐ Frank Brimsek (G), ✄
☐ Johnny Bucyk, Bost. ✄
☐ Gerry Cheevers (G), Bost. ✄
☐ Bobby Clarke, Phil. ✄
☐ Roger Crozier (G), Detr. ✄
☐ Alex Delvecchio, Detr. ✄
☐ Marcel Dionne, ✄
☐ Phil Esposito, ✄
☐ Tony Esposito (G), ✄
☐ Ed Giacomin (G), NYRa. ✄
☐ George Hainsworth (G), ✄
☐ Glenn Hall (G), ✄
☐ Doug Harvey, Mont. ✄
☐ Tim Horton, Toro. ✄
☐ Bobby Hull, Chic. ✄
☐ Dennis Hull, Chic. ✄
☐ Aurèle Joliat, Mont. ✄
☐ Red Kelly, ✄
☐ Valeri Kharlamov, ✄
☐ Guy Lafleur, Mont. ✄
☐ Ted Lindsay, Detr. ✄
☐ Harry Lumley (G), ✄
☐ Frank Mahovlich, ✄
☐ Peter Mahovlich, ✄
☐ Lanny McDonald, ✄
☐ Stan Mikita, Chic. ✄
☐ Bernie Parent (G), Phil. ✄
☐ Gilbert Perreault, Buff. ✄
☐ Jacques Plante (G), Mont. ✄
☐ Henri Richard, Mont. ✄
☐ Maurice Richard, Mont. ✄
☐ Larry Robinson, Mont. ✄
☐ Terry Sawchuk (G), ✄
☐ Vladislav Tretiak (G), ✄
☐ Bryan Trottier, NYIs. ✄
☐ Roy Worters (G), NYAm. ✄

VINTAGE HAT TRICKS

Insert Set (6 cards):
Insert (*10)
☐ Jean Béliveau, Mont. ✄ ✄ ✄
☐ Tim Horton, Toro. ✄ ✄ ✄
☐ Aurèle Joliat, Mont. ✄ ✄ ✄
☐ Guy Lafleur, Mont. ✄ ✄ ✄
☐ Maurice Richard, Mont. ✄ ✄ ✄
☐ Eddie Shore, Bost. ✄ ✄ ✄

2002 - 03 UPPER DECK

Produced by The Upper Deck Company, this series was released in November 2002. Each Series One card 1-246 has two versions: the base card and the Exclusive parallel (#/75).

Shell Set 1 (180 cards):			**35.00**
Shell Set 2 (180 cards):			**30.00**
Complete Set (456 cards):		**4500.00**	**1000.00**
Common Player:		**5.00**	**.25**
	Description	**E75**	**Base**
☐ ☐	1 Vitaly Vishnevski, Anah.	5.00	.25
☐ ☐	2 Jean-Sébastien Giguère (G), Anah.	25.00	1.00
☐ ☐	3 Steve Rucchin, Anah.	5.00	.25
☐ ☐	4 Paul Kariya, Anah.	35.00	1.00
☐ ☐	5 Andy McDonald, Anah.	5.00	.25
☐ ☐	6 Lubos Bartecko, Atla.	5.00	.25
☐ ☐	7 Ilya Kovalchuk, Atla.	25.00	1.00
☐ ☐	8 Tomi Kallio, Atla.	5.00	.25
☐ ☐	9 Milan Hnilicka (G), Atla.	5.00	.25
☐ ☐	10 Patrik Stefan, Atla.	5.00	.25
☐ ☐	11 Joe Thornton, Bost.	30.00	1.00
☐ ☐	12 Brian Rolston, Bost.	5.00	.25
☐ ☐	13 Martin Lapointe, Bost.	10.00	.25
☐ ☐	14 Nick Boynton, Bost.	5.00	.25
☐ ☐	15 Andy Hilbert, Bost.	5.00	.25
☐ ☐	16 Glen Murray, Bost.	10.00	.25
☐ ☐	17 Jean-Pierre Dumont, Buff.	5.00	.25
☐ ☐	18 Tim Connolly, Buff.	10.00	.25
☐ ☐	19 Miroslav Satan, Buff.	5.00	.25
☐ ☐	20 Maxim Afinogenov, Buff.	10.00	.25
☐ ☐	21 Taylor Pyatt, Buff.	5.00	.25
☐ ☐	22 Jay McKee, Buff.	5.00	.25
☐ ☐	23 Marc Savard, Calg.	5.00	.25
☐ ☐	24 Roman Turek (G), Calg.	10.00	.25
☐ ☐	25 Dean McAmmond, Calg.	5.00	.25
☐ ☐	26 Craig Conroy, Calg.	5.00	.25
☐ ☐	27 Derek Morris, Calg.	5.00	.25
☐ ☐	28 Rod Brind'Amour, Caro.	5.00	.25
☐ ☐	29 Josef Vasicek, Caro.	5.00	.25
☐ ☐	30 Niclas Wallin, Caro.	5.00	.25
☐ ☐	31 Jaroslav Svoboda, Caro.	5.00	.25
☐ ☐	32 Sami Kapanen, Caro.	5.00	.25
☐ ☐	33 Erik Cole, Caro.	5.00	.25
☐ ☐	34 Jeff O'Neill, Caro.	10.00	.25
☐ ☐	35 Michael Nylander, Chic.	5.00	.25
☐ ☐	36 Alexei Zhamnov, Chic.	5.00	.25
☐ ☐	37 Jon Klemm, Chic.	5.00	.25
☐ ☐	38 Kyle Calder, Chic.	5.00	.25
☐ ☐	39 Éric Dazé, Chic.	10.00	.25
☐ ☐	40 Steve Sullivan, Chic.	5.00	.25
☐ ☐	41 Stéphane Yelle, Colo.	5.00	.25
☐ ☐	42 Rob Blake, Colo.	15.00	.50
☐ ☐	43 Patrick Roy (G), Colo.	75.00	3.00
☐ ☐	44 Radim Vrbata, Colo.	5.00	.25
☐ ☐	45 Chris Drury, Colo.	15.00	.50
☐ ☐	46 Milan Hejduk, Colo.	20.00	.50
☐ ☐	47 Joe Sakic, Colo.	40.00	1.50
☐ ☐	48 Peter Forsberg, Colo.	35.00	1.00
☐ ☐	49 Rostislav Klesla, Colu.	15.00	.25
☐ ☐	50 Marc Denis (G), Colu.	10.00	.25
☐ ☐	51 Grant Marshall, Colu.	5.00	.25
☐ ☐	52 Ray Whitney, Colu.	5.00	.25
☐ ☐	53 Espen Knutsen, Colu.	5.00	.25
☐ ☐	54 Mike Sillinger, Colu.	5.00	.25
☐ ☐	55 Bill Guerin, Dall.	10.00	.25
☐ ☐	56 Mike Modano, Dall.	25.00	1.00
☐ ☐	57 Sergei Zubov, Dall.	5.00	.25
☐ ☐	58 Marty Turco (G), Dall.	15.00	.50
☐ ☐	59 Jason Arnott, Dall.	10.00	.25
☐ ☐	60 Jere Lehtinen, Dall.	5.00	.25
☐ ☐	61 Steve Yzerman, Detr.	60.00	2.00
☐ ☐	62 Sergei Fedorov, Detr.	25.00	1.00
☐ ☐	63 Nicklas Lidström, Detr.	15.00	.50
☐ ☐	64 Curtis Joseph (G), Detr.	25.00	1.00
☐ ☐	65 Igor Larionov, Detr.	15.00	.50
☐ ☐	66 Luc Robitaille, Detr.	20.00	.50
☐ ☐	67 Tomas Holmström, Detr.	5.00	.25
☐ ☐	68 Brett Hull, Detr.	25.00	1.00
☐ ☐	69 Mike Comrie, Edmo.	20.00	.50
☐ ☐	70 Marty Reasoner, Edmo.	5.00	.25
☐ ☐	71 Tommy Salo (G), Edmo.	10.00	.25
☐ ☐	72 Ryan Smyth, Edmo.	10.00	.25
☐ ☐	73 Anson Carter, Edmo.	10.00	.25
☐ ☐	74 Janne Niinimaa, Edmo.	5.00	.25
☐ ☐	75 Sandis Ozolinsh, Flor.	5.00	.25
☐ ☐	76 Roberto Luongo (G), Flor.	20.00	.50
☐ ☐	77 Kristian Huselius, Flor.	5.00	.25
☐ ☐	78 Valeri Bure, Flor.	5.00	.25
☐ ☐	79 Brad Ference, Flor.	5.00	.25
☐ ☐	80 Ian Laperrière, LosA.	5.00	.25
☐ ☐	81 Mattias Norström, LosA.	5.00	.25
☐ ☐	82 Adam Deadmarsh, LosA.	5.00	.25
☐ ☐	83 Jason Allison, LosA.	15.00	.50
☐ ☐	84 Éric Bélanger, LosA.	5.00	.25
☐ ☐	85 Félix Potvin (G), LosA.	30.00	.50
☐ ☐	86 Wes Walz, MinW.	5.00	.25
☐ ☐	87 Darby Hendrickson, MinW.	5.00	.25
☐ ☐	88 Dwayne Roloson (G), MinW.	5.00	.25
☐ ☐	89 Marian Gaborik, MinW.	25.00	1.00
☐ ☐	90 Filip Kuba, MinW.	5.00	.25
☐ ☐	91 Andrei Markov, Mont.	5.00	.25
☐ ☐	92 José Théodore (G), Mont.	30.00	1.00
☐ ☐	93 Mike Ribeiro, Mont.	5.00	.25
☐ ☐	94 Richard Zednik, Mont.	10.00	.25

□ □ 95 Gino Odjick, Mont.	5.00	.25
□ □ 96 Saku Koivu, Mont.	30.00	.50
□ □ 97 Andy Delmore, Nash.	5.00	.25
□ □ 98 Tomas Vokoun (G), Nash.	5.00	.25
□ □ 99 Martin Erat, Nash.	5.00	.25
□ □ 100 Denis (G) Arkhipov, Nash.	5.00	.25
□ □ 101 Scott Hartnell, Nash.	5.00	.25
□ □ 102 Scott Stevens, NJer.	10.00	.25
□ □ 103 Patrik Elias, NJer.	20.00	.50
□ □ 104 Jamie Langenbrunner, NJer.	5.00	.25
□ □ 105 Brian Gionta, NJer.	5.00	.25
□ □ 106 Joe Nieuwendyk, NJer.	10.00	.25
□ □ 107 Martin Brodeur (G), NJer.	40.00	1.50
□ □ 108 Roman Hamrlik, NYIs.	5.00	.25
□ □ 109 Shawn Bates, NYIs.	5.00	.25
□ □ 110 Steve Webb, NYIs.	5.00	.25
□ □ 111 Alexei Yashin, NYIs.	15.00	.50
□ □ 112 Chris Osgood (G), NYIs.	15.00	.50
□ □ 113 Mark Parrish, NYIs.	10.00	.25
□ □ 114 Petr Nedved, NYRa.	5.00	.25
□ □ 115 Eric Lindros, NYRa.	25.00	1.00
□ □ 116 Dan Blackburn (G), NYRa.	10.00	.25
□ □ 117 Radek Dvorak, NYRa.	5.00	.25
□ □ 118 Tom Poti, NYRa.	5.00	.25
□ □ 119 Pavel Bure, NYRa.	20.00	.50
□ □ 120 Todd White, Otta.	5.00	.25
□ □ 121 Patrick Lalime (G), Otta.	15.00	.50
□ □ 122 Marian Hossa, Otta.	25.00	1.00
□ □ 123 Daniel Alfredsson, Otta.	30.00	.50
□ □ 124 Wade Redden, Otta.	5.00	.25
□ □ 125 Mike Fisher, Otta.	5.00	.25
□ □ 126 Keith Primeau, Phil.	10.00	.25
□ □ 127 Jeremy Roenick, Phil.	20.00	.50
□ □ 128 Eric Weinrich, Phil.	5.00	.25
□ □ 129 Roman Cechmanek (G), Phil.	10.00	.25
□ □ 130 Mark Recchi, Phil.	10.00	.25
□ □ 131 Justin Williams, Phil.	5.00	.25
□ □ 132 Brad May, Phoe.	5.00	.25
□ □ 133 Sean Burke (G), Phoe.	15.00	.50
□ □ 134 Paul Mara, Phoe.	5.00	.25
□ □ 135 Shane Doan, Phoe.	5.00	.25
□ □ 136 Tony Amonte, Phoe.	15.00	.50
□ □ 137 Daniel Brière, Phoe.	10.00	.25
□ □ 138 Kris Beech, Pitt.	5.00	.25
□ □ 139 Martin Straka, Pitt.	5.00	.25
□ □ 140 Alex Kovalev, Pitt.	15.00	.50
□ □ 141 Mario Lemieux, Pitt.	75.00	3.00
□ □ 142 Andrew Ference, Pitt.	5.00	.25
□ □ 143 Johan Hedberg (G), Pitt.	10.00	.25
□ □ 144 Patrick Marleau, SanJ.	10.00	.25
□ □ 145 Owen Nolan, SanJ.	15.00	.50
□ □ 146 Mike Rathje, SanJ.	5.00	.25
□ □ 147 Evgeni Nabokov (G), SanJ.	15.00	.50
□ □ 148 Marco Sturm, SanJ.	5.00	.25
□ □ 149 Todd Harvey, SanJ.	5.00	.25
□ □ 150 Pavol Demitra, SLou.	10.00	.25
□ □ 151 Doug Weight, SLou.	15.00	.50
□ □ 152 Al MacInnis, SLou.	10.00	.25
□ □ 153 Brent Johnson (G), SLou.	10.00	.25
□ □ 154 Keith Tkachuk, SLou.	15.00	.50
□ □ 155 Cory Stillman, SLou.	5.00	.25
□ □ 156 Brad Richards, Tamp.	10.00	.25
□ □ 157 Pavel Kubina, Tamp.	5.00	.25
□ □ 158 Nikolai Khabibulin (G), Tamp.	10.00	.25
□ □ 159 Martin St-Louis, Tamp.	10.00	.25
□ □ 160 Vincent Lecavalier, Tamp.	25.00	1.00
□ □ 161 Bryan McCabe, Toro.	5.00	.25
□ □ 162 Gary Roberts, Toro.	10.00	.25
□ □ 163 Ed Belfour (G), Toro.	25.00	1.00
□ □ 164 Mats Sundin, Toro.	25.00	1.00
□ □ 165 Tie Domi, Toro.	5.00	.25
□ □ 166 Alexander Mogilny, Toro.	10.00	.25
□ □ 167 Daniel Sedin, Vanc.	10.00	.25
□ □ 168 Todd Bertuzzi, Vanc.	30.00	1.00
□ □ 169 Mattias Öhlund, Vanc.	5.00	.25
□ □ 170 Dan Cloutier (G), Vanc.	10.00	.25
□ □ 171 Markus Näslund, Vanc.	25.00	1.00
□ □ 172 Jan Hlavac, Vanc.	5.00	.25
□ □ 173 Olaf Kölzig (G), Wash.	15.00	.50
□ □ 174 Peter Bondra, Wash.	15.00	.50
□ □ 175 Sergei Gonchar, Wash.	5.00	.25
□ □ 176 Steve Konowalchuk, Wash.	5.00	.25
□ □ 177 Chris Simon, Wash.	5.00	.25
□ □ 178 Dainius Zubrus, Wash.	5.00	.25
□ □ 179 Patrick Roy (G), Colo.	35.00	1.50
□ □ 180 Steve Yzerman, Detr.	30.00	1.00

SUBSETS

Insert (1:4)	E75	UD
□ □ 181 Paul Kariya, Anah.	35.00	5.00
□ □ 182 Bobby Orr, Bost.	100.00	15.00
□ □ 183 Jarome Iginla, Calg.	20.00	3.00
□ □ 184 Joe Sakic, Colo.	40.00	6.00
□ □ 185 Patrick Roy (G), Colo.	75.00	11.00
□ □ 186 Steve Yzerman, Detr.	60.00	9.00
□ □ 187 Gordie Howe, Detr.	70.00	10.00
□ □ 188 Wayne Gretzky, Edmo.	100.00	15.00
□ □ 189 Wayne Gretzky, LosA.	100.00	15.00
□ □ 190 Martin Brodeur (G), NJer.	40.00	6.00
□ □ 191 Mario Lemieux, Pitt.	75.00	11.00
□ □ 192 Brett Hull, SLou.	25.00	3.00
□ □ 193 Jaromir Jagr, Pitt.	25.00	3.00
□ □ 194 Pavel Bure, Vanc.	20.00	3.00
□ □ 195 Teemu Selänne, Winn.	20.00	3.00
□ □ 196 Mark Hartigan, Atla.	5.00	1.50
□ □ 197 Pasi Nurminen (G), Atla.	5.00	3.00
□ □ 198 Henrik Tallinder, Buff.	5.00	1.50
□ □ **199 Micki Dupont, Calg. RC**	**10.00**	**10.00**
□ □ 200 Tyler Arnason, Chic.	10.00	6.00
□ □ 201 Jordan Krestanovich, Colo.	5.00	2.00
□ □ 202 Kelly Fairchild, Colo.	5.00	1.50
□ □ 203 Andrej Nedorost, Colu.	5.00	1.50
□ □ 204 Sean Avery, Detr.	5.00	2.00
□ □ 205 Stephen Weiss, Flor.	10.00	6.00
□ □ 206 Lukas Krajicek, Flor.	5.00	3.00
□ □ 207 Kyle Rossiter, Flor.	5.00	1.50
□ □ 208 Éric Beaudoin, Flor.	5.00	1.50
□ □ **209 Sylvain Blouin, MinW. RC**	**5.00**	**6.00**
□ □ 210 Marcel Hossa, Mont.	10.00	6.00
□ □ **211 Adam Hall, Nash. RC**	**15.00**	**15.00**
□ □ **212 Greg Koehler, Caro. (Nash.) RC**	**5.00**	**6.00**
□ □ 213 Trent Hunter, NYIs.	5.00	2.00
□ □ **214 Ray Schultz, NYIs. RC**	**5.00**	**6.00**
□ □ 215 Martin Prusek (G), Otta.	5.00	4.00
□ □ 216 Chris Bala, Otta.	5.00	1.50
□ □ 217 Josh Langfeld, Otta.	5.00	1.50
□ □ 218 Bruno St-Jacques, Phil.	5.00	1.50
□ □ 219 Branko Radivojevic, Phoe.	5.00	3.00
□ □ 220 Martin Cibak, Tamp.	5.00	1.50
□ □ 221 Evgeny Konstantinov (G), Tamp.	5.00	2.00
□ □ 222 Karel Pilar, Toro.	5.00	2.00
□ □ 223 Sébastien Centomo (G), Toro.	5.00	3.00
□ □ 224 Sébastien Charpentier (G), Wash.	5.00	2.00
□ □ 225 Jean-François Fortin, Wash.	5.00	1.50

SUBSETS

Insert	E75	UD
□ □ **226 Stanislav Chistov, Anah. RC**	**45.00**	**40.00**
□ □ **227 Alexei Smirnov, Anah. RC**	**20.00**	**20.00**
□ □ **228 Chuck Kobasew, Calg. RC**	**35.00**	**30.00**
□ □ 229 Tony Amonte, Chic.	15.00	6.00
□ □ 230 Peter Forsberg, Colo.	35.00	10.00
□ □ 231 Chris Drury, Colo.	15.00	6.00
□ □ **232 Rick Nash, Colu. RC**	**105.00**	**90.00**
□ □ 233 Brendan Shanahan, Detr.	25.00	10.00
□ □ **234 Henrik Zetterberg, Detr. RC**	**120.00**	**100.00**
□ □ **235 Ales Hemsky, Edmo. RC**	**50.00**	**45.00**
□ □ **236 Jay Bouwmeester, Flor. RC**	**45.00**	**40.00**
□ □ 237 Alexei Yashin, NYIs.	15.00	6.00
□ □ **238 Alexander Frolov, LosA. RC**	**45.00**	**40.00**
□ □ **239 Pierre-Marc Bouchard, MinW. RC**	**50.00**	**45.00**
□ □ **240 Ron Hainsey, Mont. RC**	**20.00**	**20.00**
□ □ 241 Sean Burke (G), Phoe.	15.00	6.00
□ □ 242 Owen Nolan, SanJ.	15.00	6.00
□ □ 243 Chris Pronger, SLou.	15.00	6.00
□ □ 244 Mats Sundin, Toro.	25.00	10.00
□ □ **245 Alexander Svitov, Tamp. RC**	**35.00**	**30.00**
□ □ **246 Steve Eminger, Wash. RC**	**15.00**	**15.00**

SERIES TWO

There are two versions for each Series Two card 247-456: the base card and the Exclusive parallel (#/75).

Insert	E75	UD
□ □ 247 Adam Oates, Anah.	10.00	.25
□ □ 248 Petr Sykora, Anah.	10.00	.25
□ □ 249 Fredrik Olausson, Anah.	5.00	.25
□ □ 250 Matt Cullen, Anah.	5.00	.25
□ □ 251 Ruslan Salei, Anah.	5.00	.25
□ □ 252 Vyacheslav Kozlov, Atla.	5.00	.25
□ □ 253 Dany Heatley, Atla.	25.00	1.00
□ □ 254 Frantisek Kaberle, Atla.	5.00	.25
□ □ 255 Pasi Nurminen (G), Atla.	5.00	.25
□ □ 256 Shawn McEachern, Atla.	5.00	.25
□ □ 257 Sergei Samsonov, Bost.	15.00	.50
□ □ 258 Steve Shields, Bost.	5.00	.25
□ □ 259 Jonathan Girard, Bost.	5.00	.25
□ □ 260 Jozef Stümpel, Bost.	5.00	.25
□ □ 261 Bryan Berard, Bost.	5.00	.25
□ □ 262 Marty McInnis, Bost.	5.00	.25
□ □ 263 Stu Barnes, Buff.	5.00	.25
□ □ 264 Curtis Brown, Buff.	5.00	.25
□ □ 265 Chris Gratton, Buff.	5.00	.25
□ □ 266 Rhett Warrener, Buff.	5.00	.25
□ □ 267 Jochen Hecht, Buff.	5.00	.25
□ □ 268 James Patrick, Buff.	5.00	.25
□ □ 269 Jarome Iginla, Calg.	20.00	.50
□ □ 270 Martin Gélinas, Calg.	5.00	.25
□ □ 271 Chris Drury, Calg.	15.00	.50
□ □ 272 Stéphane Yelle, Calg.	5.00	.25
□ □ 273 Jamie Wright, Calg.	5.00	.25
□ □ 274 Kevin Weekes (G), Caro.	5.00	.25
□ □ 275 Bret Hedican, Caro.	5.00	.25
□ □ 276 Ron Francis, Caro.	15.00	.50
□ □ 277 Kevyn Adams, Caro.	5.00	.25
□ □ 278 Marek Malik, Vanc.	5.00	.25
□ □ 279 Bates Battaglia, Caro.	5.00	.25
□ □ 280 Theoren Fleury, Chic.	15.00	.50
□ □ 281 Sergei Berezin, Chic.	5.00	.25
□ □ 282 Mark Bell, Chic.	5.00	.25
□ □ 283 Alexander Karpovtsev, Chic.	5.00	.25
□ □ 284 Steve Passmore (G), Chic.	5.00	.25
□ □ 285 Bob Probert, Chic.	5.00	.25
□ □ 286 Alex Tanguay, Colo.	15.00	.50
□ □ 287 Steven Reinprecht, Colo.	5.00	.25
□ □ 288 Adam Foote, Colo.	5.00	.25
□ □ 289 David Aebischer (G), Colo.	5.00	.25
□ □ 290 Greg de_Vries, Colo.	5.00	.25
□ □ 291 Dan Hinote, Colo.	5.00	.25
□ □ 292 Derek Morris, Colo.	5.00	.25
□ □ 293 Scott Parker, Colo.	5.00	.25
□ □ 294 Geoff Sanderson, Colu.	5.00	.25
□ □ 295 Andrew Cassels, Colu.	5.00	.25
□ □ 296 Jean-Luc Grand-Pierre, Colu.	5.00	.25
□ □ 297 Luke Richardson, Colu.	5.00	.25
□ □ 298 Tyler Wright, Colu.	5.00	.25
□ □ 299 Jody Shelley, Colu.	5.00	.25
□ □ 300 Ron Tugnutt (G), Dall.	10.00	.25
□ □ 301 Scott Young, Dall.	5.00	.25
□ □ 302 Pierre Turgeon, Dall.	10.00	.25
□ □ 303 Derian Hatcher, Dall.	5.00	.25
□ □ 304 Richard Matvichuk, Dall.	5.00	.25
□ □ 305 Kirk Muller, Dall.	5.00	.25
□ □ 306 Brendan Shanahan, Detr.	25.00	1.00
□ □ 307 Chris Chelios, Detr.	15.00	.50
□ □ 308 Mathieu Dandenault, Detr.	5.00	.25
□ □ 309 Pavel Datsyuk, Detr.	20.00	.50
□ □ 310 Kris Draper, Detr.	5.00	.25
□ □ 311 Boyd Devereaux, Detr.	5.00	.25
□ □ 312 Kirk Maltby, Detr.	5.00	.25
□ □ 313 Manny Legacé (G), Detr.	5.00	.25
□ □ 314 Jani Rita, Edmo.	5.00	.25
□ □ 315 Todd Marchant, Edmo.	5.00	.25
□ □ 316 Dan Cleary, Edmo.	5.00	.25
□ □ 317 Georges Laraque, Edmo.	5.00	.25
□ □ 318 Mike York, Edmo.	5.00	.25
□ □ 319 Jason Smith, Edmo.	5.00	.25
□ □ 320 Viktor Kozlov, Flor.	5.00	.25
□ □ 321 Dmitry Yushkevich, Flor.	5.00	.25
□ □ 322 Olli Jokinen, Flor.	5.00	.25
□ □ 323 Marcus Nilson, Flor.	5.00	.25
□ □ 324 Ivan Novoseltsev, Flor.	5.00	.25
□ □ 325 Aaron Miller, LosA.	5.00	.25
□ □ 326 Zigmund Palffy, LosA.	15.00	.50
□ □ 327 Jamie Storr (G), LosA.	5.00	.25
□ □ 328 Bryan Smolinski, LosA.	5.00	.25
□ □ 329 Mathieu Schneider, LosA.	5.00	.25
□ □ 330 Erik Rasmussen, LosA.	5.00	.25
□ □ 331 Andrew Brunette, MinW.	5.00	.25
□ □ 332 Richard Park, MinW.	5.00	.25
□ □ 333 Manny Fernandez (G), MinW.	10.00	.25
□ □ 334 Matt Johnson, MinW.	5.00	.25
□ □ 335 Ladislav Benysek, MinW.	5.00	.25
□ □ 336 Mariusz Czerkawski, Mont.	5.00	.25
□ □ 337 Sheldon Souray, Mont.	5.00	.25
□ □ 338 Chad Kilger, Mont.	5.00	.25
□ □ 339 Yanic Perreault, Mont.	5.00	.25
□ □ 340 Mathieu Garon (G), Mont.	10.00	.25
□ □ 341 Craig Rivet, Mont.	5.00	.25
□ □ 342 Mike Dunham (G), Nash.	10.00	.25
□ □ 343 David Legwand, Nash.	10.00	.25
□ □ 344 Vladimir Orszagh, Nash.	5.00	.25
□ □ 345 Kimmo Timonen, Nash.	5.00	.25
□ □ 346 Cale Hulse, Nash.	5.00	.25
□ □ 347 Oleg Tverdovsky, NJer.	5.00	.25
□ □ 348 Jeff Friesen, NJer.	5.00	.25
□ □ 349 Brian Rafalski, NJer.	5.00	.25
□ □ 350 Sergei Brylin, NJer.	5.00	.25
□ □ 351 John Madden, NJer.	5.00	.25
□ □ 352 Colin White, NJer.	5.00	.25
□ □ 353 Michael Peca, NYIs.	10.00	.25
□ □ 354 Eric Cairns, NYIs.	5.00	.25
□ □ 355 Dave Scatchard, NYIs.	5.00	.25
□ □ 356 Brad Isbister, NYIs.	5.00	.25
□ □ 357 Oleg Kvasha, NYIs.	5.00	.25
□ □ 358 Mattias Timander, NYIs.	5.00	.25
□ □ 359 Matthew Barnaby, NYRa.	5.00	.25
□ □ 360 Bobby Holik, NYRa.	5.00	.25
□ □ 361 Darius Kasparaitis, NYRa.	5.00	.25
□ □ 362 Vladimir Malakhov, NYRa.	5.00	.25
□ □ 363 Brian Leetch, NYRa.	15.00	.50
□ □ 364 Mark Messier, NYRa.	25.00	1.00
□ □ 365 Mike Richter (G), NYRa.	10.00	.25
□ □ 366 Martin Havlat, Otta.	15.00	.50
□ □ 367 Radek Bonk, Otta.	5.00	.25
□ □ 368 Petr Schastlivy, Otta.	5.00	.25
□ □ 369 Zdeno Chara, Otta.	5.00	.25
□ □ 370 Chris Neil, Otta.	5.00	.25
□ □ 371 Magnus Arvedson, Otta.	5.00	.25
□ □ 372 Pavel Brendl, Phil.	5.00	.25
□ □ 373 Donald Brashear, Phil.	5.00	.25
□ □ 374 Michal Handzus, Phil.	5.00	.25
□ □ 375 Kim Johnsson, Phil.	5.00	.25
□ □ 376 John LeClair, Phil.	20.00	.50
□ □ 377 Simon Gagné, Phil.	20.00	.50
□ □ 378 Claude Lemieux, Phoe.	5.00	.25
□ □ 379 Brian Boucher (G), Phoe.	5.00	.25
□ □ 380 Teppo Numminen, Phoe.	5.00	.25
□ □ 381 Daymond Langkow, Phoe.	5.00	.25
□ □ 382 Ladislav Nagy, Phoe.	5.00	.25
□ □ 383 Brian Savage, Phoe.	5.00	.25
□ □ 384 Ville Nieminen, Pitt.	5.00	.25
□ □ 385 Randy Robitaille, Pitt.	5.00	.25
□ □ 386 Aleksey Morozov, Pitt.	5.00	.25
□ □ 387 Jan Hrdina, Pitt.	5.00	.25
□ □ 388 Michal Rozsival, Pitt.	5.00	.25
□ □ 389 Alexandre Daigle, Pitt.	5.00	.25
□ □ 390 Mike Ricci, SanJ.	5.00	.25
□ □ 391 Vincent Damphousse, SanJ.	15.00	.50
□ □ 392 Teemu Selänne, SanJ.	20.00	.50
□ □ 393 Adam Graves, SanJ.	10.00	.25
□ □ 394 Scott Thornton, SanJ.	5.00	.25
□ □ 395 Scott Hannan, SanJ.	5.00	.25
□ □ 396 Fred Brathwaite (G), SLou.	5.00	.25
□ □ 397 Jamal Mayers, SLou.	5.00	.25
□ □ 398 Reed Low, SLou.	5.00	.25
□ □ 399 Chris Pronger, SLou.	15.00	.50
□ □ 400 Scott Mellanby, SLou.	5.00	.25
□ □ 401 Alexander Khavanov, SLou.	5.00	.25
□ □ 402 Ruslan Fedotenko, Tamp.	5.00	.25
□ □ 403 Fredrik Modin, Tamp.	5.00	.25
□ □ 404 Nikita Alexeev, Tamp.	5.00	.25
□ □ 405 Shane Willis, Tamp.	5.00	.25
□ □ 406 Dave Andreychuk, Tamp.	5.00	.25
□ □ 407 Trevor Kidd (G), Toro.	5.00	.25
□ □ 408 Robert Reichel, Toro.	5.00	.25
□ □ 409 Robert Svehla, Toro.	5.00	.25
□ □ 410 Alyn McCauley, Toro.	5.00	.25
□ □ 411 Tomas Kaberle, Toro.	5.00	.25
□ □ 412 Travis Green, Toro.	5.00	.25
□ □ 413 Henrik Sedin, Vanc.	10.00	.25
□ □ 414 Brendan Morrison, Vanc.	5.00	.25
□ □ 415 Matt Cooke, Vanc.	5.00	.25
□ □ 416 Ed Jovanovski, Vanc.	10.00	.25
□ □ 417 Mattias Öhlund, Vanc.	5.00	.25
□ □ 418 Trevor Linden, Vanc.	10.00	.25
□ □ 419 Jaromir Jagr, Wash.	25.00	1.00
□ □ 420 Robert Lang, Wash.	5.00	.25
□ □ 421 Matt Pettinger, Wash.	5.00	.25
□ □ 422 Ken Klee, Wash.	5.00	.25
□ □ 423 Stephen Peat, Wash.	5.00	.25
□ □ 424 Brian Sutherby, Wash.	5.00	.25
□ □ 425 Joe Thornton, Bost.	15.00	.50
□ □ 426 Wayne Gretzky, NYRa.	50.00	2.00

YOUNG GUNS

Insert	E75	UD
□ □ **427 Martin Gerber (G), Anah. RC**	**12.00**	**10.00**
□ □ **428 Kurt Sauer, Anah. RC**	**12.00**	**5.00**
□ □ **429 Tim Thomas (G), Bost. RC**	**12.00**	**10.00**
□ □ **430 Jordan Leopold, Calg. RC**	**18.00**	**15.00**
□ □ **431 Levente Szuper (G), Calg. RC**	**12.00**	**10.00**
□ □ **432 Shawn Thornton, Chic. RC**	**12.00**	**10.00**
□ □ **433 Jeff Paul, Colo. RC**	**12.00**	**5.00**
□ □ **434 Lasse Pirjetä, Colu. RC**	**12.00**	**5.00**
□ □ **435 Dmitri Bykov, Detr. RC**	**12.00**	**10.00**
□ □ **436 Ryan Miller (G), Buff. RC**	**30.00**	**25.00**
□ □ **437 Kari Haakana, Edmo. RC**	**12.00**	**5.00**
□ □ **438 Ivan Majesky, Flor. RC**	**12.00**	**5.00**
□ □ **439 Stéphane Veilleux, MinW. RC**	**12.00**	**5.00**
□ □ **440 Scottie Upshall, Nash. RC**	**24.00**	**20.00**
□ □ **441 Shaone Morrisonn, Bost. RC**	**12.00**	**10.00**
□ □ **442 Eric Godard, NYIs. RC**	**12.00**	**5.00**
□ □ **443 Jason Spezza, Otta. RC**	**54.00**	**45.00**
□ □ **444 Anton Volchenkov, Otta. RC**	**12.00**	**10.00**
□ □ **445 Dennis Seidenberg, Phil. RC**	**12.00**	**10.00**
□ □ **446 Radovan Somik, Phil. RC**	**12.00**	**5.00**
□ □ **447 Patrick Sharp, Phil. RC**	**12.00**	**5.00**
□ □ **448 Jeff Taffe, Phoe. RC**	**18.00**	**15.00**
□ □ **449 Lynn Loyns, SanJ. RC**	**12.00**	**5.00**
□ □ **450 Mike Cammalleri, LosA. RC**	**24.00**	**20.00**
□ □ **451 Tom Koivisto, SLou. RC**	**12.00**	**5.00**
□ □ **452 Curtis Sanford (G), SLou. RC**	**12.00**	**10.00**
□ □ **453 Cody Rudkowsky (G), SLou. RC**	**12.00**	**10.00**
□ □ **454 Carlo Colaiacovo, Toro. RC**	**18.00**	**15.00**
□ □ **455 Mikael Tellqvist (G), Toro. RC**	**12.00**	**10.00**
□ □ **456 Vernon Fiddler, Nash. RC**	**12.00**	**5.00**

BLOW-UP

Insert	Blow
☐ C1 Paul Kariya, Anah.	
☐ C2 Ilya Kovalchuk, Atla.	
☐ C3 Joe Thornton, Bost.	
☐ C4 Roman Turek (G), Calg.	
☐ C5 Jeff O'Neill, Caro.	
☐ C6 Rob Blake, Colo.	
☐ C7 Patrick Roy (G), Colo.	
☐ C8 Joe Sakic, Colo.	
☐ C9 Peter Forsberg, Colo.	
☐ C10 Marc Denis (G), Colu.	
☐ C11 Mike Modano, Dall.	
☐ C12 Marty Turco (G), Dall.	
☐ C13 Steve Yzerman, Detr.	
☐ C14 Curtis Joseph (G), Detr.	
☐ C15 Nicklas Lidström, Detr.	
☐ C16 Mike Comrie, Edmo.	
☐ C17 Tommy Salo (G), Edmo.	
☐ C18 Roberto Luongo (G), Flor.	
☐ C19 Félix Potvin (G), LosA.	
☐ C20 Marian Gaborik, MinW.	
☐ C21 José Théodore (G), Mont.	
☐ C22 Saku Koivu, Mont.	
☐ C23 Scott Hartnell, Nash.	
☐ C24 Scott Stevens, NJer.	
☐ C25 Martin Brodeur (G), NJer.	
☐ C26 Eric Lindros, NYRa.	
☐ C27 Pavel Bure, NYRa.	
☐ C28 Marian Hossa, Otta.	
☐ C29 Daniel Alfredsson, Otta.	
☐ C30 Keith Primeau, Phil.	
☐ C31 Sean Burke (G), Phoe.	
☐ C32 Tony Amonte, Phoe.	
☐ C33 Mario Lemieux, Pitt.	
☐ C34 Owen Nolan, SanJ.	
☐ C35 Al MacInnis, SLou.	
☐ C36 Brad Richards, Tamp.	
☐ C37 Vincent Lecavalier, Tamp.	
☐ C38 Mats Sundin, Toro.	
☐ C39 Ed Belfour (G), Toro.	
☐ C40 Todd Bertuzzi, Vanc.	
☐ C41 Markus Näslund, Vanc.	
☐ C42 Olaf Kölzig (G), Wash.	

GIFTED GREATS

UD1 Insert Set (14 cards):	65.00
UD1 Insert (1:12)	GG
☐ GG1 Paul Kariya, Anah.	4.00
☐ GG2 Bobby Orr, Bost.	12.00
☐ GG3 Joe Sakic, Colo.	4.00
☐ GG4 Patrick Roy (G), Colo.	9.00
☐ GG5 Peter Forsberg, Colo.	4.00
☐ GG6 Mike Modano, Dall.	3.00
☐ GG7 Dominik Hasek (G), Detr.	3.00
☐ GG8 Steve Yzerman, Detr.	7.00
☐ GG9 Gordie Howe, Detr.	8.00
☐ GG10 Martin Brodeur (G), NJer.	4.00
☐ GG11 Wayne Gretzky, NYRa.	12.00
☐ GG12 Pavel Bure, NYRa.	2.00
☐ GG13 Mario Lemieux, Pitt.	9.00
☐ GG14 Jaromir Jagr, Wash.	3.00

LAST LINE OF DEFENSE

UD2 Insert Set (14 cards):	35.00
UD2 Insert (1:12)	LL
☐ LL1 Jean-Sébastien Giguère (G), Anah.	3.00
☐ LL2 Martin Biron (G), Buff.	3.00
☐ LL3 Patrick Roy (G), Colo.	9.00
☐ LL4 Curtis Joseph (G), Detr.	3.00
☐ LL5 Tommy Salo (G), Edmo.	3.00
☐ LL6 Roberto Luongo (G), Flor.	3.00
☐ LL7 José Théodore (G), Mont.	3.00
☐ LL8 Martin Brodeur (G), NJer.	4.00
☐ LL9 Chris Osgood (G), NYIs.	3.00
☐ LL10 Sean Burke (G), Phoe.	3.00
☐ LL11 Evgeni Nabokov (G), SanJ.	3.00
☐ LL12 Nikolai Khabibulin (G), Tamp.	3.00
☐ LL13 Ed Belfour (G), Toro.	3.00
☐ LL14 Olaf Kölzig (G), Wash.	3.00

NUMBER CRUNCHERS

UD2 Insert Set (14 cards):	30.00
UD2 Insert (1:12)	NC
☐ NC1 Joe Thornton, Bost.	3.00
☐ NC2 Theoren Fleury, Chic.	2.00
☐ NC3 Brenden Morrow, Dall.	2.00
☐ NC4 Gordie Howe, Detr.	8.00
☐ NC5 Brendan Shanahan, Detr.	3.00
☐ NC6 Georges Laraque, Edmo.	2.00
☐ NC7 Scott Hartnell, Nash.	2.00
☐ NC8 Eric Lindros, NYRa.	3.00
☐ NC9 Donald Brashear, Phil.	2.00
☐ NC10 Keith Primeau, Phil.	2.00
☐ NC11 Jeremy Roenick, Phil.	2.00
☐ NC12 Keith Tkachuk, SLou.	2.00
☐ NC13 Ed Jovanovski, Vanc.	2.00
☐ NC14 Todd Bertuzzi, Vanc.	3.00

SHOOTING STARS

UD2 Insert Set (14 cards):	50.00
UD2 Insert (1:12)	SS
☐ SS1 Paul Kariya, Anah.	4.00
☐ SS2 Jarome Iginla, Calg.	2.00
☐ SS3 Joe Thornton, Bost.	3.00
☐ SS4 Joe Sakic, Colo.	4.00
☐ SS5 Mike Modano, Dall.	3.00
☐ SS6 Gordie Howe, Detr.	8.00
☐ SS7 Steve Yzerman, Detr.	7.00
☐ SS8 Mike Comrie, Edmo.	2.00
☐ SS9 Wayne Gretzky, Edmo.	12.00
☐ SS10 Pavel Bure, NYRa.	2.00
☐ SS11 Simon Gagné, Phil.	2.00
☐ SS12 Mario Lemieux, Pitt.	9.00
☐ SS13 Teemu Selänne, SanJ.	2.00
☐ SS14 Jaromir Jagr, Wash.	3.00

SIZZLING SCORERS

UD1 Insert Set (14 cards):	30.00
UD1 Insert (1:12)	SS
☐ SS1 Ilya Kovalchuk, Atla.	3.00
☐ SS2 Joe Thornton, Bost.	3.00
☐ SS3 Jarome Iginla, Calg.	3.00
☐ SS4 Ron Francis, Caro.	3.00
☐ SS5 Joe Sakic, Colo.	4.00
☐ SS6 Mike Modano, Dall.	3.00
☐ SS7 Brendan Shanahan, Detr.	3.00
☐ SS8 Mike Comrie, Edmo.	3.00
☐ SS9 Marian Gaborik, MinW.	3.00
☐ SS10 Patrik Elias, NJer.	3.00
☐ SS11 Pavel Bure, NYRa.	3.00
☐ SS12 Jeremy Roenick, Phil.	3.00
☐ SS13 Mats Sundin, Toro.	3.00
☐ SS14 Todd Bertuzzi, Vanc.	3.00

SUPER SAVERS

UD1 Insert Set (14 cards):	35.00
UD1 Insert (1:12)	SS
☐ SA1 Martin Biron (G), Buff.	3.00
☐ SA2 Roman Turek (G), Calg.	3.00
☐ SA3 Arturs Irbe (G), Caro.	3.00
☐ SA4 Patrick Roy (G), Colo.	9.00
☐ SA5 Marty Turco (G), Dall.	3.00
☐ SA6 Dominik Hasek (G), Detr.	3.00
☐ SA7 José Théodore (G), Mont.	3.00
☐ SA8 Martin Brodeur (G), NJer.	4.00
☐ SA9 Chris Osgood (G), NYIs.	3.00
☐ SA10 Patrick Lalime (G), Otta.	3.00
☐ SA11 Sean Burke (G), Phoe.	3.00
☐ SA12 Evgeni Nabokov (G), SanJ.	3.00
☐ SA13 Brent Johnson (G), SLou.	3.00
☐ SA14 Olaf Kölzig (G), Wash.	3.00

ALL-STAR JERSEY

Insert Set (14 cards):	400.00
UD1 Insert (1:96H)	AS
☐ Rob Blake, AS'02 ✂	15.00
☐ Sean Burke (G), AS'02 ✂	15.00
☐ Chris Chelios, AS'93 ✂	15.00
☐ Vincent Damphousse, AS'02 ✂	15.00
☐ Sergei Fedorov, AS'96 ✂ {*}	30.00
☐ Wayne Gretzky, AS'91 ✂ {*99}	250.00
☐ Ed Jovanovski, AS'02 ✂	15.00
☐ Sami Kapanen, AS'02 ✂	15.00
☐ Paul Kariya, AS'02 ✂	35.00
☐ Markus Näslund, AS'02 ✂	25.00
☐ Sandis Ozolinsh, AS'02 ✂ Burgandy	15.00
☐ Joe Sakic, AS'94 ✂	30.00
☐ Teemu Selänne, AS'99 ✂	15.00
☐ José Théodore (G), AS'02 ✂	25.00

ALL-STAR PERFORMERS

UD2 Insert Set (13 cards):	1700.00
UD2 Insert (1:96)	AS
☐ Rob Blake, All-Star ✂	15.00
☐ Sean Burke (G), All-Star ✂	15.00
☐ Vincent Damphousse, All-Star ✂	15.00
☐ Wayne Gretzky, All-Star ✂	100.00
☐ Ed Jovanovski, All-Star ✂	15.00
☐ Sami Kapanen, All-Star ✂	15.00
☐ Paul Kariya, All-Star ✂	30.00
☐ Mike Modano, All-Star ✂	20.00
☐ Markus Näslund, All-Star ✂	30.00
☐ Sandis Ozolinsh, All-Star ✂	15.00
☐ Patrick Roy (G), All-Star ✂	60.00
☐ Teemu Selänne, All-Star ✂	20.00
☐ José Théodore (G), All-Star ✂	30.00

BRIGHT FUTURES

UD2 Insert Set (21 cards):	1750.00
UD2 Insert (1:72)	BF
☐ Denis (G) Arkhipov, Nash. ✂	15.00
☐ Jaroslav Bednar, LosA. ✂	15.00
☐ Brian Boucher (G), Phoe. ✂	15.00
☐ Pavel Brendl, Phil. ✂	15.00
☐ Ilja Bryzgalov, Anah. ✂	15.00
☐ Tim Connolly, Buff. ✂	15.00
☐ Martin Erat, Nash. ✂	15.00
☐ Simon Gagné, Phil. ✂	20.00
☐ Giguère (G), Anah. ✂	25.00
☐ Rostislav Klesla, Colu. ✂	15.00
☐ David Legwand, Nash. ✂	15.00
☐ Jamie Lundmark, NYRa. ✂	15.00
☐ Manny Malhotra, Dall. ✂	15.00
☐ Aleksey Morozov, Pitt. ✂	15.00
☐ Ville Nieminen, Pitt. ✂	15.00
☐ Timo Pärssinen, Anah. ✂	15.00
☐ Matt Pettinger, Wash. ✂	15.00
☐ Taylor Pyatt, Buff. ✂	15.00
☐ Mike Ribeiro, Mont. ✂	15.00
☐ Patrik Stefan, Atla. ✂	15.00
☐ Mike York, Edmo. ✂	15.00

CHL GRADUATES

There are two versions for each card: the regular insert (1:96H) and the Gold parallel (#/25).

Insert Set (20 cards):	1725.00	450.00
UD1 Insert (1:96H)	G25	CG
☐☐ Jason Arnott, Dall. ✂	50.00	15.00
☐☐ Dan Blackburn (G), NYRa. ✂	50.00	15.00
☐☐ Daniel Brière, Phoe. ✂	50.00	15.00
☐☐ Éric Dazé, Chic. ✂	50.00	15.00
☐☐ Marc Denis (G), Colu. ✂	50.00	15.00
☐☐ Jeff Friesen, Anah. ✂	35.00	15.00
☐☐ David Legwand, Nash. ✂	50.00	15.00
☐☐ Mario Lemieux, Pitt. {*100} ✂	450.00	185.00
☐☐ Trevor Linden, Vanc. ✂	50.00	15.00
☐☐ Eric Lindros, NYRa. ✂	150.00	25.00
☐☐ Mike Modano, Dall. ✂	150.00	20.00
☐☐ Glen Murray, Bost. ✂	50.00	15.00
☐☐ Keith Primeau, Phil. ✂	50.00	15.00
☐☐ Mark Recchi, Phil. ✂	50.00	15.00
☐☐ Joe Sakic, Colo. ✂	225.00	30.00
☐☐ Steve Sullivan, Chic. ✂	25.00	15.00
☐☐ Alex Tanguay, Colo. ✂	75.00	15.00
☐☐ Joe Thornton, Bost. ✂	175.00	30.00
☐☐ Ron Tugnutt (G), Colu. {*100} ✂	50.00	20.00
☐☐ Steve Yzerman, Detr. ✂	350.00	60.00

DIFFERENCE MAKERS

UD2 Insert Set (21 cards):	625.00
UD2 Insert (1:72)	DM
☐ Jason Allison, LosA. ✂	15.00
☐ Rob Blake, Colo. ✂	15.00
☐ Éric Dazé, Chic. ✂	15.00
☐ Mike Dunham (G), Nash. ✂	15.00
☐ Jarome Iginla, Calg. ✂	20.00
☐ Jaromir Jagr, Wash. ✂	25.00
☐ Paul Kariya, Anah. ✂	30.00
☐ Ilya Kovalchuk, Atla. ✂	25.00
☐ Brian Leetch, NYRa. ✂	15.00
☐ Mario Lemieux, Pitt. ✂	75.00
☐ Mike Modano, Dall. ✂	20.00
☐ Zigmund Palffy, LosA. ✂	15.00
☐ Patrick Roy (G), Colo. ✂	60.00
☐ Sergei Samsonov, Bost. ✂	15.00
☐ Miroslav Satan, Buff. ✂	15.00
☐ Brendan Shanahan, Detr. ✂	25.00
☐ Mats Sundin, Toro. ✂	30.00
☐ José Théodore (G), Mont. ✂	30.00
☐ Joe Thornton, Bost. ✂	30.00
☐ Roman Turek (G), Calg. ✂	15.00
☐ Steve Yzerman, Detr. ✂	60.00

FAN FAVORITES

UD2 Insert Set (10 cards):	175.00
UD2 Insert	FF
☐ Martin Brodeur (G), NJer. ✂	40.00
☐ Adam Deadmarsh, LosA. ✂	15.00
☐ Shane Doan, Phoe. ✂	15.00
☐ Peter Forsberg, Colo. ✂	35.00
☐ Jarome Iginla, Calg. ✂	20.00
☐ Jaromir Jagr, Wash. ✂	25.00
☐ Paul Kariya, Anah. ✂	35.00
☐ Saku Koivu, Mont. ✂	20.00
☐ Brian Leetch, NYRa. ✂	15.00
☐ Nicklas Lidström, Detr. ✂	15.00
☐ Mike Modano, Dall. ✂	25.00
☐ Markus Näslund, Vanc. ✂	25.00
☐ Keith Primeau, Phil. ✂	15.00
☐ Sergei Samsonov, Bost. ✂	15.00

GOALTENDER THREADS

UD2 Insert Set (14 cards):	175.00
UD2 Insert (1:96)	GT
☐ Martin Biron (G), Buff. ✂	15.00
☐ Ilja Bryzgalov, Anah. ✂	15.00
☐ Roman Cechmanek (G), Phil. ✂	15.00
☐ Mike Dunham (G), Nash. ✂	15.00
☐ Giguère (G), Anah. ✂	25.00
☐ Olaf Kölzig (G), Wash. ✂	15.00
☐ Roberto Luongo (G), Flor. ✂	20.00
☐ Mika Noronen (G), Buff. ✂	15.00
☐ Félix Potvin (G), LosA. ✂	15.00
☐ Steve Shields, Bost. ✂	15.00
☐ José Théodore (G), Mont. ✂	30.00
☐ Jocelyn Thibault (G), Chic. ✂	15.00
☐ Marty Turco (G), Dall. ✂	15.00
☐ Roman Turek (G), Calg. ✂	15.00

GOALTENDER THREADS GOLD

UD2 Insert Set (14 cards):	875.00
UD2 Insert (#/25)	GTG
☐ Martin Biron (G), Buff. ✂	50.00
☐ Ilja Bryzgalov, Anah. ✂	35.00
☐ Roman Cechmanek (G), Phil. ✂	50.00
☐ Mike Dunham (G), Nash. ✂	50.00
☐ Giguère (G), Anah. ✂	150.00
☐ Olaf Kölzig (G), Wash. ✂	75.00
☐ Roberto Luongo (G), Flor. ✂	100.00

□ Mika Noronen (G), Buff. ✂ 50.00
□ Félix Potvin (G), LosA. ✂ 175.00
□ Steve Shields, Bost. ✂ 35.00
□ José Théodore (G), Mont. ✂ 175.00
□ Jocelyn Thibault (G), Chic. ✂ 50.00
□ Marty Turco (G), Dall. ✂ 75.00
□ Roman Turek (G), Calg. ✂ 50.00

GOOD 'OL DAYS

Insert Set (14 cards): 225.00
UD1 Insert (1:96) GO
□ Pavel Bure, Vanc. ✂ NYRa. ✂ {*} 25.00
□ Theoren Fleury, Calg. ✂ NYRa. ✂ {*} 20.00
□ Bill Guerin, NJer. ✂ Bost. ✂ 15.00
□ Dominik Hasek (G), Chic. ✂ Detr. ✂ 25.00
□ Brett Hull, SLou. ✂ Detr. ✂ {*} 35.00
□ Curtis Joseph (G), SLou. ✂ Toro. ✂ 25.00
□ Al MacInnis, Calg. ✂ SLou. ✂ 15.00
□ Joe Nieuwendyk, Calg. ✂ NJer. ✂ 15.00
□ Keith Primeau, Detr. ✂ Phil. ✂ 15.00
□ Joe Sakic, Québ. ✂ Colo. ✂ 30.00
□ Teemu Selänne, Winn. ✂ SanJ. ✂ 15.00
□ Brendan Shanahan, NJer. ✂ Detr. ✂ 25.00
□ Mats Sundin, Québ. ✂ Toro. ✂ 25.00
□ Keith Tkachuk, Phoe. ✂ SLou. ✂ 15.00

LETTERS OF NOTE

There are two versions for each card: the regular insert (1:144) and the Gold parallel (#/50).

Insert Set (14 cards):	900.00	350.00
Insert	LNG50	LN
□□ Peter Bondra, Wash. ✂	45.00	15.00
□□ Chris Drury, Colo. ✂	45.00	15.00
□□ Jarome Iginla, Calg. ✂	60.00	20.00
□□ Paul Kariya, Anah. ✂	105.00	35.00
□□ Saku Koivu, Mont. ✂	90.00	20.00
□□ Mario Lemieux, Pitt. ✂	225.00	110.00
□□ Mike Modano, Dall. ✂	75.00	25.00
□□ Markus Näslund, Vanc. ✂	75.00	25.00
□□ Owen Nolan, SanJ. ✂	45.00	15.00
□□ Chris Pronger, SLou. ✂	45.00	35.00
□□ Joe Sakic, Colo. ✂	120.00	40.00
□□ Scott Stevens, NJer. ✂	30.00	15.00
□□ Mats Sundin, Toro. ✂	75.00	25.00
□□ Steve Yzerman, Detr. ✂	180.00	60.00

NEW NHL HOT SPOTS

Insert Set (12 cards): 150.00
UD1 Insert (1:96H) HS
□ Denis (G) Arkhipov, Nash. ✂ 15.00
□ Daniel Brière, Phoe. ✂ 15.00
□ Marc Denis (G), Colu. ✂ 15.00
□ Shane Doan, Phoe. ✂ 15.00
□ Mike Dunham (G), Nash. ✂ {*} 15.00
□ Martin Erat, Nash. ✂ 15.00
□ Scott Hartnell, Nash. ✂ 15.00
□ Rostislav Klesla, Colu. ✂ 15.00
□ Ilya Kovalchuk, Atla. ✂ {*} 35.00
□ David Legwand, Nash. ✂ 15.00
□ Claude Lemieux, Phoe. ✂ 15.00
□ Ray Whitney, Colu. ✂ White 15.00

ON THE RISE

Insert Set (7 cards): 100.00
UD1 Insert (1:96H) OR
□ Mark Bell, Chic. ✂ 15.00
□ Dan Blackburn (G), NYRa. ✂ 15.00
□ Rostislav Klesla, Colu. ✂ 15.00
□ Krys Kolanos, Phoe. ✂ 15.00
□ Ilya Kovalchuk, Atla. ✂ 25.00
□ Brenden Morrow, Dall. ✂ {*} 25.00
□ Steven Reinprecht, Colo. ✂ 15.00

PATCH LOGO

UD2 Insert Set (10 cards): 1700.00
UD2 Insert (1:7500) PL
□ Simon Gagné, Phil. ✂ 100.00
□ Wayne Gretzky, LosA. ✂ 600.00
□ Marian Hossa, Otta. ✂ 150.00
□ Jaromir Jagr, Wash. ✂ 150.00
□ Saku Koivu, Mont. ✂ 175.00
□ Ilya Kovalchuk, Atla. ✂ 150.00
□ Markus Näslund, Vanc. ✂ 150.00
□ Patrick Roy (G), Colo. ✂ 350.00
□ Brendan Shanahan, Detr. ✂ 150.00
□ Mats Sundin, Toro. ✂ 150.00

PATCH NAME PLATE

UD2 Insert Set (10 cards): 1825.00
UD2 Insert (1:7500) PP
□ Martin Brodeur (G), NJer. ✂ 225.00
□ Sergei Fedorov, Detr. ✂ 150.00
□ Peter Forsberg, Colo. ✂ 200.00
□ Wayne Gretzky, NYRa. ✂ 600.00
□ Jaromir Jagr, Wash. ✂ 150.00
□ Paul Kariya, Anah. ✂ 200.00
□ Vincent Lecavalier, Tamp. ✂ 150.00
□ Mario Lemieux, Pitt. ✂ 450.00
□ Jeremy Roenick, Phil. ✂ 100.00
□ Sergei Samsonov, Bost. ✂ 75.00

PATCH NUMBERS

UD2 Insert Set (10 cards): 2100.00
UD2 Insert (1:7500) PN
□ Martin Brodeur (G), NJer. ✂ 225.00
□ Wayne Gretzky, NYRa. ✂ 600.00
□ Paul Kariya, Anah. ✂ 200.00
□ Olaf Kölzig (G), Wash. ✂ 75.00
□ Mario Lemieux, Pitt. ✂ 450.00
□ Mike Modano, Dall. ✂ 150.00
□ Joe Sakic, Colo. ✂ 225.00
□ José Théodore (G), Mont. ✂ 175.00
□ Joe Thornton, Bost. ✂ 175.00
□ Steve Yzerman, Detr. ✂ 350.00

PINPOINT ACCURATE

UD2 Insert Set (14 cards): 250.00
UD2 Insert (1:96) PA
□ Pavel Bure, NYRa. ✂ 20.00
□ Éric Dazé, Chic. ✂ 15.00
□ Chris Drury, Calg. ✂ 15.00
□ Sergei Fedorov, Detr. ✂ 25.00
□ Milan Hejduk, Colo. ✂ 20.00
□ Jarome Iginla, Calg. ✂ 20.00
□ Paul Kariya, Anah. ✂ 30.00
□ Mario Lemieux, Pitt. ✂ 75.00
□ Mike Modano, Dall. ✂ 20.00
□ Mark Recchi, Phil. ✂ 15.00
□ Geoff Sanderson, Colu. ✂ 15.00
□ Brendan Shanahan, Detr. ✂ 25.00
□ Alex Tanguay, Colo. ✂ 15.00
□ Joe Thornton, Bost. ✂ 30.00

REACHING FIFTY

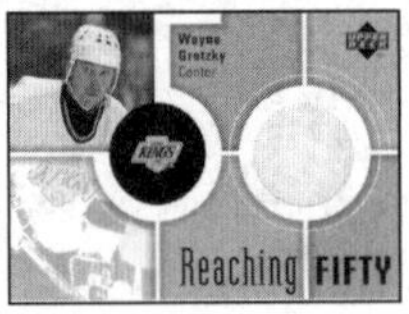

UD2 Insert Set (14 cards): 500.00
UD2 Insert (1:96) 50
□ Peter Bondra, Wash. ✂ 20.00
□ Pavel Bure, Flor. ✂ 25.00
□ Sergei Fedorov, Detr. ✂ 30.00
□ Wayne Gretzky, LosA. ✂ 125.00
□ Brett Hull, SLou. ✂ 35.00
□ Jarome Iginla, Calg. ✂ 25.00
□ Jaromir Jagr, Pitt. ✂ 30.00
□ Paul Kariya, Anah. ✂ 40.00
□ John LeClair, Phil. ✂ 25.00
□ Mario Lemieux, Pitt. ✂ 95.00
□ Mike Modano, Dall. ✂ 30.00
□ Joe Sakic, Colo. ✂ 50.00
□ Keith Tkachuk, Phoe. ✂ 20.00
□ Steve Yzerman, Detr. ✂ 75.00

REACHING FIFTY GOLD

UD2 Insert Set (14 cards): 900.00
UD2 Insert (#/50) 50G
□ Peter Bondra, Wash. ✂ 50.00
□ Pavel Bure, Flor. ✂ 50.00
□ Sergei Fedorov, Detr. ✂ 75.00
□ Wayne Gretzky, LosA. ✂ 350.00
□ Brett Hull, SLou. ✂ 75.00
□ Jarome Iginla, Calg. ✂ 50.00
□ Jaromir Jagr, Pitt. ✂ 75.00
□ Paul Kariya, Anah. ✂ 125.00
□ John LeClair, Phil. ✂ 50.00
□ Mario Lemieux, Pitt. ✂ 250.00
□ Mike Modano, Dall. ✂ 75.00
□ Joe Sakic, Colo. ✂ 125.00
□ Keith Tkachuk, Phoe. ✂ 50.00
□ Steve Yzerman, Detr. ✂ 200.00

SAVIORS

Insert Set (13 cards): 250.00
UD1 Insert (1:96) SV
□ Martin Biron (G), Buff. ✂ 15.00
□ Brian Boucher (G), Phoe. ✂ 15.00
□ Byron Dafoe (G), Bost. ✂ 15.00
□ Mike Dunham (G), Nash. ✂ 15.00
□ Jean-Sébastien Giguère (G), Anah. ✂ 30.00
□ Brent Johnson (G), SLou. ✂ 15.00
□ Olaf Kölzig (G), Wash. ✂ 15.00
□ Patrick Roy (G), Colo. ✂ {*} 105.00
□ José Théodore (G), Mont. ✂ {*} 45.00
□ Jocelyn Thibault (G), Chic. ✂ 15.00
□ Ron Tugnutt (G), Colu. ✂ {*100} 20.00
□ Marty Turco (G), Dall. ✂ 15.00
□ Roman Turek (G), Calg. ✂ 15.00

SPECIALISTS

Insert Set (15 cards): 200.00
UD1 Insert (1:96H) S
□ Éric Bélanger, LosA. ✂ 15.00
□ Peter Bondra, Wash. ✂ 15.00
□ Chris Drury, Colo. ✂ {*} 15.00
□ Sergei Fedorov, Detr. ✂ 25.00
□ Jarome Iginla, Calg. ✂ {*100} 20.00
□ Robert Lang, Pitt. ✂ 15.00
□ Brian Leetch, NYRa. ✂ 15.00
□ Jere Lehtinen, Dall. ✂ 15.00
□ Todd Marchant, Edmo. ✂ 15.00
□ Todd Marchant, Edmo. ✂ White/Blue 15.00
□ Mike Modano, Dall. ✂ 25.00
□ Mark Recchi, Phil. ✂ 15.00
□ Sergei Samsonov, Bost. ✂ 15.00
□ Miroslav Satan, Buff. ✂ {*} 15.00
□ Alexei Zhamnov, Chic. ✂ 15.00

SPEED DEMONS

Insert Set (7 cards): 100.00
UD1 Insert (1:96) SD
□ Daniel Brière, Phoe. ✂ 15.00
□ Pavel Bure, NYRa. ✂ {*} 35.00
□ Sergei Fedorov, Detr. ✂ 25.00
□ Simon Gagné, Phil. ✂ 20.00
□ Todd Marchant, Edmo. ✂ 15.00
□ Zigmund Palffy, LosA. ✂ {*} 30.00
□ Steve Sullivan, Chic. ✂ 15.00

UD FIRST CLASS

There are two versions for each card: the regular insert (1:288 packs) and the Gold parallel (#/75).

Insert Set (7 cards):	1350.00	325.00
UD1 Insert (1:288)	G75	UD
□□ Jaromir Jagr, Wash. ✂	125.00	25.00
□□ Paul Kariya, Anah. ✂	175.00	35.00
□□ Mario Lemieux, Pitt. ✂ {*}	375.00	110.00
□□ Patrick Roy (G), Colo. ✂ {*}	375.00	90.00
□□ Joe Sakic, Colo. ✂ {*}	200.00	60.00
□□ José Théodore (G), Mont. ✂	150.00	30.00
□□ Steve Yzerman, Detr. ✂	300.00	60.00

GAME JERSEY

UD2 Insert Set (14 cards): 2050.00
UD2 Insert (1:96) GJ
□ Ed Belfour (G), Leafs ✂ 30.00
□ Martin Brodeur (G), All-Star ✂ 45.00
□ Pavel Bure, NYRa. ✂ 20.00
□ Simon Gagné, Phil. ✂ 20.00
□ Wayne Gretzky, All-Star ✂ 100.00
□ Scott Hartnell, Nash. ✂ 15.00
□ Ilya Kovalchuk, Atla. ✂ 25.00
□ John LeClair, Phil. ✂ 20.00
□ Patrick Roy (G), Colo. ✂ 60.00
□ Joe Sakic, Colo. ✂ 40.00
□ Sergei Samsonov, Bost. ✂ 15.00
□ Joe Thornton, Bost. ✂ 30.00
□ Steve Yzerman, Detr. ✂ 60.00
□ Henrik Zetterberg, Detr. ✂ 40.00

JERSEY SIGNED

UD2 Insert Set (13 cards): 2050.00
UD2 Insert (#/50) SGJ
□ Ed Belfour (G), Leafs ✍ ✂ 150.00
□ Martin Brodeur (G), All-Star ✍ ✂ 225.00
□ Pavel Bure, NYRa. ✍ ✂ 100.00
□ Simon Gagné, Phil. ✍ ✂ 100.00
□ Wayne Gretzky, All-Star ✍ ✂ 650.00
□ Scott Hartnell, Nash. ✍ ✂ 50.00
□ Ilya Kovalchuk, Atla. ✍ ✂ 150.00
□ John LeClair, Phil. ✍ ✂ 100.00
□ Patrick Roy (G), Colo. ✍ ✂ 350.00
□ Sergei Samsonov, Bost. ✍ ✂ 75.00
□ Joe Thornton, Bost. ✍ ✂ 175.00
□ Steve Yzerman, Detr. ✍ ✂ 350.00
□ Henrik Zetterberg, Detr. ✍ ✂ 100.00

UD PATCHWORK

Insert Set (30 cards): 4,800
UD1 Insert (1:2,500) PW
□ Tony Amonte, Chic. ✂ 100.00
□ Martin Brodeur (G), NJer. ✂ 300.00
□ Sean Burke (G), Phoe. ✂ 100.00
□ Chris Drury, Colo. ✂ 100.00
□ Mike Dunham (G), Nash. ✂ 75.00
□ Sergei Fedorov, Detr. ✂ 200.00
□ Peter Forsberg, Colo. ✂ 275.00
□ Simon Gagné, Phil. ✂ 150.00
□ Bill Guerin, Bost. ✂ 75.00
□ Milan Hejduk, Colo. ✂ 150.00
□ Jaromir Jagr, Wash. ✂ 200.00
□ Paul Kariya, Anah. ✂ 275.00
□ Saku Koivu, Mont. ✂ 225.00
□ Alex Kovalev, Pitt. ✂ 100.00
□ John LeClair, Phil. ✂ 150.00
□ Mario Lemieux, Pitt. ✂ 600.00
□ Nicklas Lidström, Detr. ✂ 100.00
□ Mike Modano, Dall. ✂ 200.00
□ Markus Näslund, Vanc. ✂ 200.00
□ Zigmund Palffy, LosA. ✂ 100.00
□ Keith Primeau, Phil. ✂ 75.00
□ Patrick Roy (G), Colo. ✂ 475.00
□ Joe Sakic, Colo. ✂ 300.00
□ Sergei Samsonov, Bost. ✂ 100.00
□ Brendan Shanahan, Detr. ✂ 200.00
□ Mats Sundin, Toro. ✂ 200.00
□ José Théodore (G), Mont. ✂ 225.00
□ Joe Thornton, Bost. ✂ 225.00
□ Marty Turco (G), Dall. ✂ 100.00
□ Steve Yzerman, Detr. ✂ 475.00

UD PLAYBOOK

Insert Set (14 cards): .00
UD1 Insert PL
□ PL2 Raymond Bourque, Bost. ✂ ✂
□ PL6 Sergei Fedorov, Detr. ✂ ✂
□ PL8 Wayne Gretzky, LosA. ✂ ✂
□ PL9 Wayne Gretzky, LosA. ✂ ✂
□ PL7 Dominik Hasek (G), Chic. ✂ ✂
□ PL13 Curtis Joseph (G), SLou. ✂ ✂
□ PL1 Paul Kariya, Anah. ✂ ✂
□ PL15 Markus Näslund, Vanc. ✂ ✂
□ PL4 Patrick Roy (G), Colo. ✂ ✂
□ PL3 Joe Sakic, Québ. {*15} ✂ ✂
□ PL11 Teemu Selänne, AS'98 ✂ ✂
□ PL5 Brendan Shanahan, NJer. ✂ ✂
□ PL14 Mats Sundin, Québ. {*15} ✂ ✂
□ PL10 José Théodore (G), Mont. {*15} ✂ ✂

UD PLAYBOOK

UD2 Insert Set (28 cards):
UD2 Insert UD
□ Chris Drury, Colo. ✂ ✂
□ Sergei Fedorov, Detr. ✂ ✂
□ Peter Forsberg, Colo. ✂ ✂
□ Giguère (G), Anah. ✂ ✂
□ Milan Hejduk, Colo. ✂ ✂
□ Jaromir Jagr, Wash. ✂ ✂
□ Paul Kariya, Anah. ✂ ✂
□ Saku Koivu, Mont. ✂ ✂
□ Olaf Kölzig (G), Wash. ✂ ✂
□ Alex Kovalev, Pitt. ✂ ✂
□ John LeClair, Phil. ✂ ✂
□ Brian Leetch, NYRa. ✂ ✂
□ Mario Lemieux, Pitt. ✂ ✂
□ Nicklas Lidström, Detr. ✂ ✂
□ Eric Lindros, NYRa. ✂ ✂
□ Mike Modano, Dall. ✂ ✂
□ Keith Primeau, Phil. ✂ ✂
□ Jeremy Roenick, Phil. ✂ ✂
□ Patrick Roy (G), Colo. ✂ ✂
□ Joe Sakic, Colo. ✂ ✂
□ Sergei Samsonov, Bost. ✂ ✂
□ Brendan Shanahan, Detr. ✂ ✂
□ Alex Tanguay, Colo. ✂ ✂
□ José Théodore (G), Mont. ✂ ✂
□ Joe Thornton, Bost. ✂ ✂
□ Marty Turco (G), Dall. ✂ ✂
□ Justin Williams, Phil. ✂ ✂
□ Steve Yzerman, Detr. ✂ ✂

2002 - 03 UPPER DECK ARTISTIC IMPRESSIONS

Produced by The Upper Deck Company, this series was released in April 2003. There are three versions for each card 1-90: a base card, a Gold parallel (#/199), and a UD Promo version.

	Description	G199	Base
Shell Set (90 cards):			40.00
Complete Set (135 cards):		600.00	175.00
Common Player:		2.00	.25
☐☐☐	1 J-S Giguère (G), Anah.	5.00	1.00
☐☐☐	2 Paul Kariya, Anah.	10.00	1.50
☐☐☐	3 Dany Heatley, Atla.	5.00	1.00
☐☐☐	4 Ilya Kovalchuk, Atla.	5.00	1.00
☐☐☐	5 Raymond Bourque, Bost.	5.00	1.50
☐☐☐	6 Joe Thornton, Bost.	5.00	1.50
☐☐☐	7 Bobby Orr, Bost.	30.00	5.00
☐☐☐	8 Sergei Samsonov, Bost.	2.00	.50
☐☐☐	9 Maxim Afinogenov, Buff.	2.00	.50
☐☐☐	10 Martin Biron (G), Buff.	2.00	.50
☐☐☐	11 Miroslav Satan, Buff.	2.00	.25
☐☐☐	12 Roman Turek (G), Calg.	2.00	.50
☐☐☐	13 Jarome Iginla, Calg.	5.00	1.00
☐☐☐	14 Arturs Irbe (G), Caro.	2.00	.50
☐☐☐	15 Ron Francis, Caro.	2.00	.50
☐☐☐	16 Jeff O'Neill, Caro.	2.00	.50
☐☐☐	17 Alexei Zhamnov, Chic.	2.00	.25
☐☐☐	18 Éric Dazé, Chic.	2.00	.50
☐☐☐	19 Jocelyn Thibault (G), Chic.	2.00	.50
☐☐☐	20 Rob Blake, Colo.	2.00	.50
☐☐☐	21 Patrick Roy (G), Colo.	20.00	3.50
☐☐☐	22 Joe Sakic, Colo.	10.00	2.00
☐☐☐	23 Peter Forsberg, Colo.	10.00	1.50
☐☐☐	24 Raymond Bourque, Colo.	5.00	1.50
☐☐☐	25 Marc Denis (G), Colu.	2.00	.50
☐☐☐	26 Espen Knutsen, Colu.	2.00	.25
☐☐☐	27 Rostislav Klesla, Colu.	2.00	.25
☐☐☐	28 Marty Turco (G), Dall.	2.00	.50
☐☐☐	29 Bill Guerin, Dall.	2.00	.50
☐☐☐	30 Mike Modano, Dall.	5.00	1.00
☐☐☐	31 Steve Yzerman, Detr.	15.00	3.00
☐☐☐	32 Nicklas Lidström, Detr.	2.00	.50
☐☐☐	33 Sergei Fedorov, Detr.	5.00	1.00
☐☐☐	34 Curtis Joseph (G), Detr.	5.00	1.00
☐☐☐	35 Brendan Shanahan, Detr.	5.00	1.00
☐☐☐	36 Gordie Howe, Detr.	20.00	3.50
☐☐☐	37 Mike Comrie, Edmo.	5.00	1.00
☐☐☐	38 Tommy Salo (G), Edmo.	2.00	.50
☐☐☐	39 Wayne Gretzky, Edmo.	30.00	5.00
☐☐☐	40 Roberto Luongo (G), Flor.	5.00	1.00
☐☐☐	41 Kristian Huselius, Flor.	2.00	.25
☐☐☐	42 Zigmund Palffy, LosA.	2.00	.50
☐☐☐	43 Félix Potvin (G), LosA.	2.00	.50
☐☐☐	44 Jason Allison, LosA.	2.00	.50
☐☐☐	45 Manny Fernandez (G), MinW.	2.00	.50
☐☐☐	46 Marian Gaborik, MinW.	5.00	1.00
☐☐☐	47 Saku Koivu, Mont.	5.00	1.00
☐☐☐	48 Doug Gilmour, Mont.	2.00	.50
☐☐☐	49 José Théodore (G), Mont.	5.00	1.50
☐☐☐	50 David Legwand, Nash.	2.00	.50
☐☐☐	51 Tomas Vokoun (G), Nash.	2.00	.25
☐☐☐	52 Martin Brodeur (G), NJer.	10.00	2.00
☐☐☐	53 Patrik Elias, NJer.	5.00	1.00
☐☐☐	54 Joe Nieuwendyk, NJer.	2.00	.50
☐☐☐	55 Alexei Yashin, NYIs.	2.00	.50
☐☐☐	56 Michael Peca, NYIs.	2.00	.50
☐☐☐	57 Chris Osgood (G), NYIs.	2.00	.50
☐☐☐	58 Eric Lindros, NYRa.	5.00	1.00
☐☐☐	59 Pavel Bure, NYRa.	5.00	1.00
☐☐☐	60 Brian Leetch, NYRa.	2.00	.50
☐☐☐	61 Martin Havlat, Otta.	2.00	.50
☐☐☐	62 Marian Hossa, Otta.	5.00	1.00
☐☐☐	63 Daniel Alfredsson, Otta.	2.00	.50
☐☐☐	64 John LeClair, Phil.	5.00	1.00
☐☐☐	65 Jeremy Roenick, Phil.	5.00	1.00
☐☐☐	66 Simon Gagné, Phil.	5.00	1.00
☐☐☐	67 Tony Amonte, Phoe.	2.00	.50
☐☐☐	68 Sean Burke (G), Phoe.	2.00	.50
☐☐☐	69 Daniel Brière, Phoe.	2.00	.50
☐☐☐	70 Alex Kovalev, Pitt.	2.00	.50
☐☐☐	71 Johan Hedberg (G), Pitt.	2.00	.50
☐☐☐	72 Mario Lemieux, Pitt.	20.00	3.50
☐☐☐	73 Teemu Selänne, SanJ.	5.00	1.00
☐☐☐	74 Evgeni Nabokov (G), SanJ.	2.00	.50
☐☐☐	75 Owen Nolan, SanJ.	2.00	.50
☐☐☐	76 Chris Pronger, SLou.	2.00	.50
☐☐☐	77 Doug Weight, SLou.	2.00	.50
☐☐☐	78 Keith Tkachuk, SLou.	2.00	.50
☐☐☐	79 Brad Richards, Tamp.	2.00	.50
☐☐☐	80 Nikolai Khabibulin (G), Tamp.	2.00	.50
☐☐☐	81 Vincent Lecavalier, Tamp.	5.00	1.00
☐☐☐	82 Mats Sundin, Toro.	5.00	1.00
☐☐☐	83 Ed Belfour (G), Toro.	5.00	1.00
☐☐☐	84 Alexander Mogilny, Toro.	2.00	.50
☐☐☐	85 Todd Bertuzzi, Vanc.	5.00	1.50
☐☐☐	86 Dan Cloutier (G), Vanc.	2.00	.50
☐☐☐	87 Markus Näslund, Vanc.	5.00	1.00
☐☐☐	88 Jaromir Jagr, Wash.	5.00	1.00
☐☐☐	89 Peter Bondra, Wash.	2.00	.50
☐☐☐	90 Olaf Kölzig (G), Wash.	2.00	.50

ROOKIE IMAGES

There are two versions for each card 91-135: the Rookie Images base insert (1:4 packs) and the Gold parallel (#/75).

	Insert	G75	RI
☐☐	**91 Jonathan Hedstrom, Anah. RC**	**6.00**	**5.00**
☐☐	**92 Henrik Zetterberg, Detr. RC**	**60.00**	**20.00**
☐☐	**93 Steve Ott, Dall. RC**	**15.00**	**5.00**
☐☐	**94 Jay Bouwmeester, Flor. RC**	**35.00**	**10.00**
☐☐	**95 Rick Nash, Colu. RC**	**60.00**	**20.00**
☐☐	**96 Pascal Leclaire (G), Colu. RC**	**30.00**	**10.00**
☐☐	**97 Jason Spezza, Otta. RC**	**45.00**	**15.00**
☐☐	98 Dick Tarnström, Pitt.	15.00	5.00
☐☐	**99 Alexei Smirnov, Anah. RC**	**15.00**	**5.00**
☐☐	**100 Ron Hainsey, Mont. RC**	**15.00**	**5.00**
☐☐	**101 Michael Leighton (G), Chic. RC**	**10.00**	**5.00**
☐☐	**102 Ian MacNeil, Phil. RC**	**6.00**	**5.00**
☐☐	**103 Anton Volchenkov, Otta. RC**	**10.00**	**5.00**
☐☐	**104 Ales Hemsky, Edmo. RC**	**35.00**	**10.00**
☐☐	**105 Steve Eminger, Wash. RC**	**10.00**	**5.00**
☐☐	**106 Shaone Morrisonn, Bost. RC**	**10.00**	**5.00**
☐☐	**107 Levente Szuper (G), Calg. RC**	**10.00**	**5.00**
☐☐	**108 Brooks Orpik, Pitt. RC**	**15.00**	**5.00**
☐☐	**109 Curtis Sanford (G), SLou. RC**	**10.00**	**5.00**
☐☐	**110 Jared Aulin, LosA. RC**	**15.00**	**5.00**
☐☐	**111 Eric Godard, NYIs. RC**	**6.00**	**5.00**
☐☐	**112 Jim Fahey, SanJ. RC**	**6.00**	**5.00**
☐☐	**113 Rickard Wallin, MinW. RC**	**6.00**	**5.00**
☐☐	**114 Mike Cammalleri, LosA. RC**	**20.00**	**5.00**
☐☐	**115 Mikael Tellqvist (G), Toro. RC**	**10.00**	**5.00**
☐☐	**116 Chuck Kobasew, Calg. RC**	**20.00**	**5.00**
☐☐	**117 Scottie Upshall, Nash. RC**	**20.00**	**5.00**
☐☐	**118 Jerred Smithson, LosA. RC**	**6.00**	**5.00**
☐☐	**119 Jeff Taffe, Phoe. RC**	**15.00**	**5.00**
☐☐	**120 Cody Rudkowsky (G), SLou. RC**	**10.00**	**5.00**
☐☐	**121 Alexander Frolov, LosA. RC**	**30.00**	**10.00**
☐☐	**122 Alexander Svitov, Tamp. RC**	**20.00**	**5.00**
☐☐	**123 Stanislav Chistov, Anah. RC**	**35.00**	**10.00**
☐☐	**124 PM. Bouchard, MinW. RC**	**35.00**	**10.00**
☐☐	**125 Patrick Sharp, Phil. RC**	**6.00**	**5.00**
☐☐	**126 Ryan Miller (G), Buff. RC**	**30.00**	**10.00**
☐☐	**127 Tomas Malec, Caro. RC**	**6.00**	**5.00**
☐☐	**128 Curtis Murphy, MinW. RC**	**6.00**	**5.00**
☐☐	**129 Jordan Leopold, Calg. RC**	**15.00**	**5.00**
☐☐	**130 Carlo Colaiacovo, Toro. RC**	**15.00**	**5.00**
☐☐	**131 Alexei Semenov, Edmo. RC**	**10.00**	**5.00**
☐☐	**132 Craig Andersson (G), Chic. RC**	**15.00**	**5.00**
☐☐	**133 Jim Vandermeer, Phil. RC**	**10.00**	**5.00**
☐☐	**134 Ray Emery (G), Otta. RC**	**10.00**	**5.00**
☐☐	**135 Paul Manning, Colu. RC**	**6.00**	**5.00**

RETROSPECTIVES

There are three versions for each card R1-R100: the regular insert (1:1 packs), the Silver parallel (#/99), and the Gold parallel (#/25).

	Insert	G25	S99	R
Insert Set (100 cards):		2175.00	550.00	100.00
☐☐☐	R1 J-S Giguère (G), Anah.	30.00	5.00	1.50
☐☐☐	R2 Paul Kariya, Anah.	40.00	10.00	2.00
☐☐☐	R3 Dany Heatley, Atla.	30.00	5.00	1.50
☐☐☐	R4 Ilya Kovalchuk, Atla.	30.00	5.00	1.50
☐☐☐	R5 Raymond Bourque, Bost.	35.00	10.00	1.50
☐☐☐	R6 Joe Thornton, Bost.	35.00	10.00	1.50
☐☐☐	R7 Bobby Orr, Bost.	120.00	35.00	6.00
☐☐☐	R8 Sergei Samsonov, Bost.	15.00	5.00	.50
☐☐☐	R9 Maxim Afinogenov, Buff.	12.00	4.00	.50
☐☐☐	R10 Martin Biron (G), Buff.	12.00	4.00	.50
☐☐☐	R11 Miroslav Satan, Buff.	12.00	4.00	.50
☐☐☐	R12 Roman Turek (G), Calg.	12.00	4.00	.50
☐☐☐	R13 Jarome Iginla, Calg.	20.00	5.00	1.00
☐☐☐	R14 Arturs Irbe (G), Caro.	12.00	4.00	.50
☐☐☐	R15 Ron Francis, Caro.	15.00	5.00	.50
☐☐☐	R16 Jeff O'Neill, Caro.	12.00	4.00	.50
☐☐☐	R17 Alexei Zhamnov, Chic.	12.00	4.00	.50
☐☐☐	R18 Éric Dazé, Chic.	12.00	4.00	.50
☐☐☐	R19 Jocelyn Thibault (G), Chic.	12.00	4.00	.50
☐☐☐	R20 Rob Blake, Colo.	15.00	5.00	.50
☐☐☐	R21 Patrick Roy (G), Colo.	90.00	25.00	4.50
☐☐☐	R22 Joe Sakic, Colo.	45.00	10.00	2.00
☐☐☐	R23 Peter Forsberg, Colo.	40.00	10.00	2.00
☐☐☐	R24 Raymond Bourque, Colo.	35.00	10.00	1.50
☐☐☐	R25 Marc Denis (G), Colu.	12.00	4.00	.50
☐☐☐	R26 Espen Knutsen, Colu.	12.00	4.00	.50
☐☐☐	R27 Rostislav Klesla, Colu.	12.00	4.00	.50
☐☐☐	R28 Marty Turco (G), Dall.	15.00	5.00	.50
☐☐☐	R29 Bill Guerin, Dall.	12.00	4.00	.50
☐☐☐	R30 Mike Modano, Dall.	30.00	5.00	1.50
☐☐☐	R31 Steve Yzerman, Detr.	70.00	20.00	3.50
☐☐☐	R32 Nicklas Lidström, Detr.	15.00	5.00	.50
☐☐☐	R33 Sergei Fedorov, Detr.	30.00	5.00	1.50
☐☐☐	R34 Curtis Joseph (G), Detr.	30.00	5.00	1.50
☐☐☐	R35 Brendan Shanahan, Detr.	30.00	5.00	1.50
☐☐☐	R36 Gordie Howe, Detr.	80.00	25.00	4.00
☐☐☐	R37 Mike Comrie, Edmo.	20.00	5.00	1.00
☐☐☐	R38 Tommy Salo (G), Edmo.	12.00	4.00	.50
☐☐☐	R39 Wayne Gretzky, Edmo.	120.00	35.00	6.00
☐☐☐	R40 R. Luongo (G), Flor.	20.00	5.00	1.00
☐☐☐	R41 Kristian Huselius, Flor.	12.00	4.00	.50
☐☐☐	R42 Zigmund Palffy, LosA.	15.00	5.00	.50
☐☐☐	R43 Félix Potvin (G), LosA.	15.00	5.00	.50
☐☐☐	R44 Jason Allison, LosA.	15.00	5.00	.50
☐☐☐	R45 M. Fernandez (G), MinW.	12.00	4.00	.50
☐☐☐	R46 Marian Gaborik, MinW.	30.00	5.00	1.50
☐☐☐	R47 Saku Koivu, Mont.	20.00	5.00	1.00
☐☐☐	R48 Doug Gilmour, Mont.	15.00	5.00	.50
☐☐☐	R49 José Théodore (G), Mont.	35.00	10.00	1.50
☐☐☐	R50 David Legwand, Nash.	12.00	4.00	.50
☐☐☐	R51 Tomas Vokoun (G), Nash.	12.00	4.00	.50
☐☐☐	R52 Martin Brodeur (G), NJer.	45.00	10.00	2.00
☐☐☐	R53 Patrik Elias, NJer.	20.00	5.00	1.00
☐☐☐	R54 Joe Nieuwendyk, NJer.	12.00	4.00	.50
☐☐☐	R55 Alexei Yashin, NYIs.	15.00	5.00	.50
☐☐☐	R56 Michael Peca, NYIs.	12.00	4.00	.50
☐☐☐	R57 Chris Osgood (G), NYIs.	15.00	5.00	.50
☐☐☐	R58 Eric Lindros, NYRa.	30.00	5.00	1.50
☐☐☐	R59 Pavel Bure, NYRa.	20.00	5.00	1.00
☐☐☐	R60 Brian Leetch, NYRa.	15.00	5.00	.50
☐☐☐	R61 Martin Havlat, Otta.	15.00	5.00	.50
☐☐☐	R62 Marian Hossa, Otta.	30.00	5.00	1.50
☐☐☐	R63 Daniel Alfredsson, Otta.	15.00	5.00	.50
☐☐☐	R64 John LeClair, Phil.	20.00	5.00	1.00
☐☐☐	R65 Jeremy Roenick, Phil.	20.00	5.00	1.00
☐☐☐	R66 Simon Gagné, Phil.	20.00	5.00	1.00
☐☐☐	R67 Tony Amonte, Phoe.	15.00	5.00	.50
☐☐☐	R68 Sean Burke (G), Phoe.	15.00	5.00	.50
☐☐☐	R69 Daniel Brière, Phoe.	12.00	4.00	.50
☐☐☐	R70 Alex Kovalev, Pitt.	15.00	5.00	.50
☐☐☐	R71 Johan Hedberg (G), Pitt.	12.00	4.00	.50
☐☐☐	R72 Mario Lemieux, Pitt.	90.00	25.00	4.50
☐☐☐	R73 Teemu Selänne, SanJ.	20.00	5.00	1.00
☐☐☐	R74 E. Nabokov (G), SanJ.	15.00	5.00	.50
☐☐☐	R75 Owen Nolan, SanJ.	15.00	5.00	.50
☐☐☐	R76 Chris Pronger, SLou.	15.00	5.00	.50
☐☐☐	R77 Doug Weight, SLou.	15.00	5.00	.50
☐☐☐	R78 Keith Tkachuk, SLou.	15.00	5.00	.50
☐☐☐	R79 Brad Richards, Tamp.	12.00	4.00	.50
☐☐☐	R80 N. Khabibulin (G), Tamp.	12.00	4.00	.50
☐☐☐	R81 V. Lecavalier, Tamp.	30.00	5.00	1.50
☐☐☐	R82 Mats Sundin, Toro.	30.00	5.00	1.50
☐☐☐	R83 Ed Belfour (G), Toro.	30.00	5.00	1.50
☐☐☐	R84 Alexander Mogilny, Toro.	12.00	4.00	.50
☐☐☐	R85 Todd Bertuzzi, Vanc.	35.00	10.00	1.50
☐☐☐	R86 Dan Cloutier (G), Vanc.	12.00	4.00	.50
☐☐☐	R87 Markus Näslund, Vanc.	30.00	5.00	1.50
☐☐☐	R88 Jaromir Jagr, Wash.	30.00	5.00	1.50
☐☐☐	R89 Peter Bondra, Wash.	15.00	5.00	.50
☐☐☐	R90 Olaf Kölzig (G), Wash.	15.00	5.00	.50
☐☐☐	**R91 J. Spezza, Otta. RC**	**70.00**	**15.00**	**5.00**
☐☐☐	**R92 R. Nash, Colu. RC**	**95.00**	**20.00**	**10.00**
☐☐☐	**R93 Bouwmeester, Flor. RC**	**55.00**	**10.00**	**5.00**
☐☐☐	**R94 S. Chistov, Anah. RC**	**55.00**	**10.00**	**5.00**
☐☐☐	**R95 Bouchard, MinW. RC**	**55.00**	**10.00**	**5.00**
☐☐☐	**R96 Leclaire (G), Colu. RC**	**45.00**	**10.00**	**5.00**
☐☐☐	**R97 B. Orpik, Pitt. RC**	**25.00**	**5.00**	**2.00**
☐☐☐	**R98 S. Ott, Dall. RC**	**25.00**	**5.00**	**2.00**
☐☐☐	**R99 A. Frolov, LosA. RC**	**45.00**	**10.00**	**5.00**
☐☐☐	**R100 A. Svitov, Tamp. RC**	**35.00**	**5.00**	**2.00**

COMMON GROUND

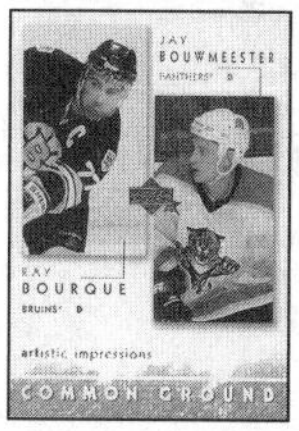

There are two versions for each card CG1-CG22: the regular insert (1:8 packs) and the Gold parallel (#/75).

	Insert	CGG75	CG
Insert Set (22 cards):		200.00	50.00
☐☐	CG1 P. Roy (G) / P. Leclaire (G)	25.00	6.00
☐☐	CG2 J. Jagr / A. Hemsky	8.00	2.00
☐☐	CG3 W. Gretzky / J. Spezza	25.00	8.00
☐☐	CG4 N. Lidström / J. Bouwmeester	8.00	2.00
☐☐	CG5 R. Cechmanek (G) / L. Szuper (G)	8.00	2.00
☐☐	CG6 M. Lemieux / R. Nash	25.00	7.00
☐☐	CG7 R. Bourque / J. Bouwmeester	8.00	2.00
☐☐	CG8 S. Koivu / PM. Bouchard	8.00	2.00
☐☐	CG9 G.Howe / R. Nash	25.00	6.00
☐☐	CG10 P. Bure / A. Frolov	8.00	2.00
☐☐	CG11 R. Blake / B. Orpik	8.00	2.00
☐☐	CG12 M. Sundin / H. Zetterberg	8.00	2.00
☐☐	CG13 S. Samsonov / S. Chistov	8.00	2.00
☐☐	CG14 R. Bourque / J. Leopold	8.00	2.00
☐☐	CG15 B. Guerin / C. Kobasew	8.00	2.00
☐☐	CG16 S. Fedorov / A. Svitov	8.00	2.00
☐☐	CG17 J. Roenick / S. Upshall	8.00	2.00
☐☐	CG18 N. Lidström / C. Colaiacovo	8.00	2.00
☐☐	CG19 S. Yzerman / S. Ott	25.00	3.00
☐☐	CG20 M. Modano / J. Taffe	8.00	2.00
☐☐	CG21 P. Forsberg / H. Zetterberg	8.00	4.00
☐☐	CG22 M. Brodeur (G) / P.Leclaire (G)	8.00	3.00

GREAT DEPICTIONS

There are two versions for each card GD1-GD12: the regular insert (1:20 packs) and the Gold parallel (#/75).

	Insert	GD75	GD
Insert Set (12 cards):		300.00	50.00
☐☐	GD1 Wayne Gretzky, Edmo.	75.00	10.00
☐☐	GD2 Patrick Roy (G), Colo.	50.00	7.00
☐☐	GD3 Martin Brodeur (G), NJer.	25.00	4.00
☐☐	GD4 Bobby Orr, Bost.	75.00	10.00
☐☐	GD5 Ilya Kovalchuk, Atla.	8.00	2.00
☐☐	GD6 Mario Lemieux, Pitt.	50.00	7.00
☐☐	GD7 Raymond Bourque, Bost.	8.00	3.00
☐☐	GD8 Steve Yzerman, Detr.	25.00	6.00
☐☐	GD9 Gordie Howe, Detr.	50.00	7.00
☐☐	GD10 Pavel Bure, NYRa.	8.00	2.00
☐☐	GD11 Marian Gaborik, MinW.	8.00	2.00
☐☐	GD12 Joe Thornton, Bost.	8.00	3.00

UD FLASHBACKS

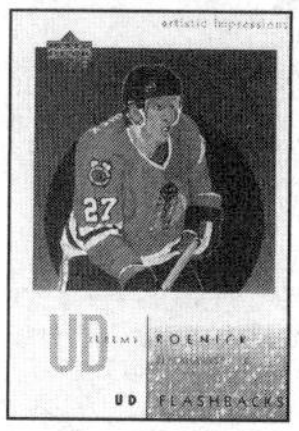

There are two versions for each card UD1-UD11: the regular insert (1:20 packs) and the Gold parallel (#/75).

	Insert	UDG75	UD
Insert Set (11 cards):		150.00	25.00
☐☐	UD1 Joe Sakic, Québ.	25.00	4.00
☐☐	UD2 Mike Modano, Minn..	8.00	2.00
☐☐	UD3 Mario Lemieux, Pitt.	50.00	7.00
☐☐	UD4 Brian Leetch, NYRa.	8.00	2.00
☐☐	UD5 Ron Francis, Hart.	8.00	2.00
☐☐	UD6 Pavel Bure, Vanc.	8.00	2.00
☐☐	UD7 Raymond Bourque, Bost.	8.00	3.00
☐☐	UD8 Sergei Fedorov, Detr.	8.00	2.00
☐☐	UD9 Jaromir Jagr, Pitt.	8.00	2.00
☐☐	UD10 Jeremy Roenick, Chic.	8.00	2.00
☐☐	UD11 Gordie Howe, Detr.	50.00	7.00

ARTIST'S TOUCH

	Insert (#/499)	AT
Insert Set (25 cards):		325.00
☐	Raymond Bourque, Bost. ✂	15.00
☐	Martin Brodeur (G), NJer. ✂	20.00
☐	Sean Burke (G), Phoe. ✂	10.00
☐	Mike Dunham (G), NYRa. ✂	10.00
☐	Sergei Fedorov, Detr. ✂	15.00
☐	Peter Forsberg, Colo. ✂	20.00
☐	Simon Gagné, Phil. ✂	10.00
☐	Dany Heatley, Atla. ✂	15.00
☐	Jarome Iginla, Calg. ✂	10.00
☐	Jaromir Jagr, Wash. ✂	15.00
☐	Curtis Joseph (G), Detr. ✂	15.00
☐	Paul Kariya, Anah. ✂	20.00
☐	Olaf Kölzig (G), Wash. ✂	10.00
☐	Ilya Kovalchuk, Atla. ✂	15.00
☐	Mario Lemieux, Pitt. ✂	45.00
☐	Mike Modano, Dall. ✂	15.00
☐	Zigmund Palffy, LosA. ✂	10.00
☐	Félix Potvin (G), NYIs. ✂	10.00
☐	Jeremy Roenick, Phil. ✂	10.00

Patrick Roy (G), Colo. ✂	45.00
Joe Sakic, Colo. ✂	20.00
Brendan Shanahan, Detr. ✂	15.00
Mats Sundin, Toro. ✂	15.00
José Théodore (G), Mont. ✂	15.00
Joe Thornton, Bost. ✂	15.00

ARTIST'S TOUCH GOLD

Insert Set (25 cards):	625.00
Insert (#/199)	ATG
Raymond Bourque, Bost. ✂	30.00
Martin Brodeur (G), NJer. ✂	40.00
Sean Burke (G), Phoe. ✂	25.00
Mike Dunham (G), NYRa. ✂	25.00
Sergei Fedorov, Detr. ✂ Red	25.00
Peter Forsberg, Colo. ✂	35.00
Simon Gagné, Phil. ✂	25.00
Dany Heatley, Atla. ✂	25.00
Jarome Iginla, Calg. ✂	25.00
Jaromir Jagr, Wash. ✂	25.00
Curtis Joseph (G), Detr. ✂	25.00
Paul Kariya, Anah. ✂	35.00
Olaf Kölzig (G), Wash. ✂	25.00
Ilya Kovalchuk, Atla. ✂	25.00
Mario Lemieux, Pitt. ✂	75.00
Mike Modano, Dall. ✂	25.00
Zigmund Palffy, LosA. ✂	25.00
Félix Potvin (G), NYIs. ✂	25.00
Jeremy Roenick, Phil. ✂	25.00
Patrick Roy (G), Colo. ✂	75.00
Joe Sakic, Colo. ✂	40.00
Brendan Shanahan, Detr. ✂	25.00
Mats Sundin, Toro. ✂	25.00
José Théodore (G), Mont. ✂	30.00
Joe Thornton, Bost. ✂	30.00

ON THE RIGHT TRACK

Insert Set (11 cards):	75.00
Insert (#/299)	RT
Maxim Afinogenov, Buff. ✂	10.00
Jared Aulin, LosA. ✂	10.00
Daniel Brière, Phoe. ✂	10.00
Kyle Calder, Chic. ✂	10.00
Stanislav Chistov, Anah. ✂	10.00
Martin Erat, Nash. ✂	10.00
Alexander Frolov, LosA. ✂	10.00
Dany Heatley, Atla. ✂	20.00
Jamie Lundmark, NYRa. ✂	10.00
Steven Reinprecht, Colo. ✂	10.00
Justin Williams, Phil. ✂	10.00

ON THE RIGHT TRACK GOLD

Insert Set (11 cards):	200.00
Insert (#/175)	RTG
Maxim Afinogenov, Buff. ✂	25.00
Jared Aulin, LosA. ✂	25.00
Daniel Brière, Phoe. ✂	25.00
Kyle Calder, Chic. ✂	25.00
Stanislav Chistov, Anah. ✂	25.00
Martin Erat, Nash. ✂	25.00
Alexander Frolov, LosA. ✂	25.00
Dany Heatley, Atla. ✂	30.00
Jamie Lundmark, NYRa. ✂	25.00
Steven Reinprecht, Colo. ✂	25.00
Justin Williams, Phil. ✂	25.00

SECOND SEASON PERFORMERS

Insert Set (11 cards):	150.00
Insert (#/199)	SSG
Martin Brodeur (G), NJer. ✂	25.00
Jaromir Jagr, Wash. ✂	25.00
John LeClair, Phil. ✂	15.00
Mark Messier, NYRa. ✂	25.00
Patrick Roy (G), Colo. ✂	50.00
Steve Yzerman, Detr. ✂	50.00

SECOND SEASON PERFORMERS GOLD

Insert Set (11 cards):	225.00
Insert (#/75)	SSG
Martin Brodeur (G), NJer. ✂	50.00
Jaromir Jagr, Wash. ✂	35.00
John LeClair, Phil. ✂	35.00
Mark Messier, NYRa. ✂	35.00
Patrick Roy (G), Colo. ✂	75.00
Steve Yzerman, Detr. ✂	75.00

ORIGINAL ARTWORK

These pieces are limited to one copy each.

Insert	Art
1 Alex Kovalev, Pitt.	
2 Alexander Mogilny, Toro.	
3 Alexei Yashin, NYIs.	
4 Alexei Zhamnov, Chic.	
5 Arturs Irbe (G), Caro.	
6 Bill Guerin, Dall.	
7 Brad Richards, Tamp.	
8 Brendan Shanahan, Detr.	
9 Brian Leetch, NYRa.	
10 Chris Osgood (G), NYIs.	
11 Chris Pronger, SLou.	
12 Dan Cloutier (G), Vanc.	
13 Daniel Alfredsson, Otta.	
14 Daniel Brière, Phoe.	
15 David Legwand, Nash.	
16 Doug Gilmour, Mont.	
17 Doug Weight, SLou.	
18 Ed Belfour (G), Toro.	
19 Eric Dazé, Chic.	
20 Eric Lindros, NYRa.	
21 Espen Knutsen, Colu.	
22 Evgeni Nabokov (G), SanJ.	
23 Félix Potvin (G), LosA.	
24 Jarome Iginla, Calg.	
25 Jaromir Jagr, Wash.	
26 Jason Allison, LosA.	
27 Jean-Sébastien Giguère (G), Anah.	
28 Jeff O'Neill, Caro.	
29 Jeremy Roenick, Phil.	
30 Jocelyn Thibault (G), Chic.	
31 Joe Nieuwendyk, NJer.	
32 Joe Sakic, Colo.	
33 Johan Hedberg (G), Pitt.	
34 Keith Tkachuk, SLou.	
35 Kristian Huselius, Flor.	
36 Manny Fernandez (G), MinW.	
37 Marc Denis (G), Colu.	
38 Marian Gaborik, MinW.	
39 Marian Hossa, Otta.	
40 Mario Lemieux, Pitt.	
41 Martin Biron (G), Buff.	
42 Marty Turco (G), Dall.	
43 Mats Sundin, Toro.	
44 Maxim Afinogenov, Buff.	
45 Michael Peca, NYIs.	
46 Mike Modano, Dall.	
47 Miroslav Satan, Buff.	
48 Nicklas Lidström, Detr.	
49 Olaf Kölzig (G), Wash.	
50 Owen Nolan, SanJ.	
51 Patrik Elias, NJer.	
52 Paul Kariya, Anah.	
53 Pavel Bure, NYRa.	
54 Peter Bondra, Wash.	
55 Peter Forsberg, Colo.	
56 Rob Blake, Colo.	
57 Roberto Luongo (G), Flor.	
58 Roman Turek (G), Calg.	
59 Ron Francis, Caro.	
60 Rostislav Klesla, Colu.	
61 Saku Koivu, Mont.	
62 Sean Burke (G), Phoe.	
63 Sergei Fedorov, Detr.	
64 Teemu Selänne, SanJ.	
65 Todd Bertuzzi, Vanc.	
66 Tomas Vokoun (G), Nash.	
67 Tommy Salo (G), Edmo.	
68 Tony Amonte, Phoe.	
69 Vincent Lecavalier, Tamp.	
70 Zigmund Palffy, LosA.	

ORIGINAL ARTWORK SIGNED

Insert	Art
1 Curtis Joseph (G), Detr. ✍	
2 Dany Heatley, Atla. ✍	
3 Gordie Howe, Detr. ✍	
4 Ilya Kovalchuk, Atla. ✍	
5 Jarome Iginla, Calg. ✍	
6 Joe Thornton, Bost. ✍	
7 John LeClair, Phil. ✍	
8 José Théodore (G), Mont. ✍	
9 Markus Näslund, Vanc. ✍	
10 Martin Brodeur (G), NJer. ✍	
11 Martin Havlat, Otta. ✍	
12 Mike Comrie, Edmo. ✍	
13 Nikolai Khabibulin (G), Tamp. ✍	
14 Patrick Roy (G), Colo. ✍	
15 Ray Bourque, Bost. ✍	
16 Ray Bourque, Colo. ✍	
17 Sergei Samsonov, Bost. ✍	
18 Simon Gagné, Phil. ✍	

SAMPLE CARD

Sample Card	SC
SC1 Joe Thornton, Bost.	3.00

SIGNED CASE TOPPER

Insert Set (18 pieces):	.00
Insert	Art
AI1 Ray Bourque, Bost. ✍	
AI2 Martin Brodeur (G), NJer. ✍	
AI3 Pavel Bure, NYRa. ✍	
AI4 Mike Comrie, Edmo. ✍	
AI6 Dany Heatley, Atla. ✍	
AI7 Gordie Howe, Detr. ✍	
AI8 Jarome Iginla, Calg. ✍	
AI9 Curtis Joseph (G), Detr. ✍	
AI10 Ilya Kovalchuk, Atla. ✍	
AI11 John LeClair, Phil. ✍	
AI12 Markus Näslund, Vanc. ✍	
AI13 Bobby Orr, Bost. ✍	
AI14 Patrick Roy (G), Colo. ✍	
AI15 Sergei Samsonov, Bost. ✍	
AI16 José Théodore (G), Mont. ✍	
AI17 Joe Thornton, Bost. ✍	
AI18 Steve Yzerman, Detr. ✍	

2002 - 03 UPPER DECK CLASSIC PORTRAITS

Produced by the Upper Deck Company, this series was released in February 2003.

Shell Set (100 cards):	40.00
Complete Set (130 cards):	225.00
Common Player:	.25
Description	Base
1 Jean-Sébastien Giguère (G), Anah.	1.00
2 Paul Kariya, Anah.	1.50
3 Mike Leclerc, Anah.	.25
4 Dany Heatley, Atla.	1.00
5 Ilya Kovalchuk, Atla.	1.00
6 Milan Hnilicka (G), Atla.	.25
7 Joe Thornton, Bost.	1.50
8 Brian Rolston, Bost.	.25
9 Sergei Samsonov, Bost.	.50
10 Miroslav Satan, Buff.	.25
11 Martin Biron (G), Buff.	.50
12 Tim Connolly, Buff.	.50
13 Roman Turek (G), Calg.	.50
14 Jarome Iginla, Calg.	1.00
15 Craig Conroy, Calg.	.25
16 Arturs Irbe (G), Caro.	.50
17 Ron Francis, Caro.	.50
18 Rod Brind'Amour, Caro.	.25
19 Jeff O'Neill, Caro.	.50
20 Alexei Zhamnov, Chic.	.25
21 Éric Dazé, Chic.	.50
22 Jocelyn Thibault (G), Chic.	.50
23 Rob Blake, Colo.	.50
24 Patrick Roy (G), Colo.	3.50
25 Joe Sakic, Colo.	2.00
26 Peter Forsberg, Colo.	1.50
27 Chris Drury, Calg.	.50
28 Marc Denis (G), Colu.	.50
29 Espen Knutsen, Colu.	.25
30 Rostislav Klesla, Colu.	.25
31 Marty Turco (G), Dall.	.50
32 Brenden Morrow, Dall.	.25
33 Mike Modano, Dall.	1.00
34 Steve Yzerman, Detr.	3.00
35 Nicklas Lidström, Detr.	.50
36 Sergei Fedorov, Detr.	1.00
37 Brendan Shanahan, Detr.	1.00
38 Curtis Joseph (G), Detr.	1.00
39 Mike Comrie, Edmo.	1.00
40 Tommy Salo (G), Edmo.	.50
41 Ryan Smyth, Edmo.	.50
42 Roberto Luongo (G), Flor.	1.00
43 Viktor Kozlov, Flor.	.25
44 Kristian Huselius, Flor.	.25
45 Zigmund Palffy, LosA.	.50
46 Félix Potvin (G), LosA.	.50
47 Jason Allison, LosA.	.50
48 Manny Fernandez (G), MinW.	.50
49 Andrew Brunette, MinW.	.25
50 Marian Gaborik, MinW.	1.00
51 Saku Koivu, Mont.	1.00
52 Yanic Perreault, Mont.	.25
53 José Théodore (G), Mont.	1.50
54 Denis (G) Arkhipov, Nash.	.25
55 Scott Hartnell, Nash.	.25
56 Mike Dunham (G), Nash.	.50
57 Martin Brodeur (G), NJer.	2.00
58 Patrik Elias, NJer.	1.00
59 Joe Nieuwendyk, NJer.	.50
60 Scott Niedermayer, NJer.	.25
61 Alexei Yashin, NYIs.	.50
62 Michael Peca, NYIs.	.50
63 Chris Osgood (G), NYIs.	.50
64 Eric Lindros, NYRa.	1.00
65 Pavel Bure, NYRa.	1.00
66 Brian Leetch, NYRa.	.50
67 Dan Blackburn (G), NYRa.	.50
68 Martin Havlat, Otta.	.50
69 Marian Hossa, Otta.	1.00
70 Daniel Alfredsson, Otta.	.50
71 John LeClair, Phil.	1.00
72 Jeremy Roenick, Phil.	1.00
73 Keith Primeau, Phil.	.50
74 Simon Gagné, Phil.	1.00
75 Tony Amonte, Phoe.	.50
76 Sean Burke (G), Phoe.	.50
77 Daniel Brière, Phoe.	.50
78 Alex Kovalev, Pitt.	.50
79 Johan Hedberg (G), Pitt.	.50
80 Mario Lemieux, Pitt.	3.50
81 Patrick Marleau, SanJ.	.50
82 Teemu Selänne, SanJ.	1.00
83 Evgeni Nabokov (G), SanJ.	.50
84 Owen Nolan, SanJ.	.50
85 Chris Pronger, SLou.	.50
86 Doug Weight, SLou.	.50
87 Keith Tkachuk, SLou.	.50
88 Brad Richards, Tamp.	.50
89 Nikolai Khabibulin (G), Tamp.	.50
90 Vincent Lecavalier, Tamp.	1.00
91 Mats Sundin, Toro.	1.00
92 Gary Roberts, Toro.	.50
93 Ed Belfour (G), Toro.	1.00
94 Alexander Mogilny, Toro.	.50
95 Todd Bertuzzi, Vanc.	1.50
96 Brendan Morrison, Vanc.	.25
97 Markus Näslund, Vanc.	1.00
98 Jaromir Jagr, Wash.	1.00
99 Peter Bondra, Wash.	.50
100 Olaf Kölzig (G), Wash.	.50

PROTÉGÉS

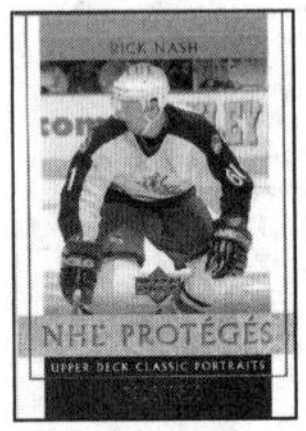

Insert	FW
101 Alexei Smirnov, Anah. RC	**5.00**
102 Stanislav Chistov, Anah. RC	**15.00**
103 Martin Gerber (G), Anah. RC	**5.00**
104 Kurt Sauer, Anah. RC	**5.00**
105 Chuck Kobasew, Calg. RC	**10.00**
106 Micki DuPont, Calg. RC	**5.00**
107 Shawn Thornton, Chic. RC	**5.00**
108 Jeff Paul, Colo. RC	**5.00**
109 Rick Nash, Colu. RC	**30.00**
110 Lasse Pirjetä, Colu. RC	**5.00**
111 Henrik Zetterberg, Detr. RC	**30.00**
112 Dmitri Bykov, Detr. RC	**5.00**
113 Ales Hemsky, Edmo. RC	**15.00**
114 Mike Cammalleri, LosA. RC	**10.00**
115 Ivan Majesky, Flor. RC	**5.00**
116 Jay Bouwmeester, Flor. RC	**15.00**
117 Alexander Frolov, LosA. RC	**15.00**
118 Pierre-Marc Bouchard, MinW. RC	**15.00**
119 Ron Hainsey, Mont. RC	**5.00**
120 Adam Hall, Nash. RC	**5.00**
121 Scottie Upshall, Nash. RC	**10.00**
122 Anton Volchenkov, Otta. RC	**5.00**
123 Dennis Seidenberg, Phil. RC	**5.00**
124 Patrick Sharp, Phil. RC	**5.00**
125 Jeff Taffe, Phoe. RC	**5.00**
126 Jason Spezza, Otta. RC	**20.00**
127 Tom Koivisto, SLou. RC	**5.00**
128 Alexander Svitov, Tamp. RC	**10.00**
129 Carlo Colaiacovo, Toro. RC	**5.00**
130 Steve Eminger, Wash. RC	**5.00**

PROTÉGÉS

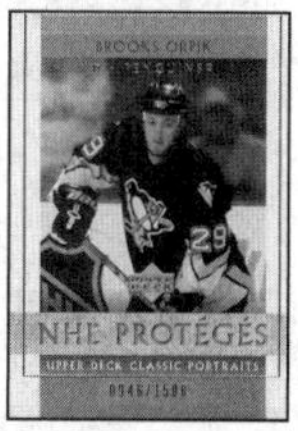

These cards were inserted into bonus packs in 2002 - 03 Upper Deck Rookie Update.

	Insert	FW
☐	131 Jared Aulin, LosA. RC	5.00
☐	132 Pascal Leclaire (G), Colu. RC	15.00
☐	133 Steve Ott, Dall. RC	5.00
☐	134 Brooks Orpik, Pitt. RC	5.00
☐	135 Ari Ahonen (G), NJer. RC	5.00
☐	136 Mike Komisarek, Mont. RC	5.00
☐	137 Ryan Miller (G), Buff. RC	15.00
☐	138 Ray Emery (G), Otta. RC	5.00

CLASSIC STITCHES

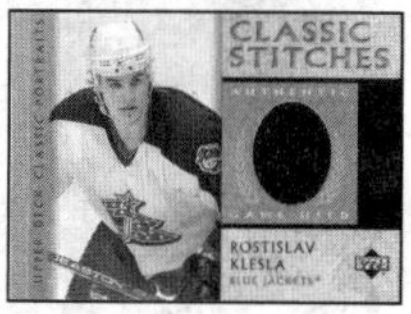

	Insert Set (15 cards):	125.00
	Insert (1:24)	CS
☐	Peter Bondra, Wash. ✂	12.00
☐	Pavel Bure, NYRa. ✂	15.00
☐	Adam Deadmarsh, LosA. ✂	12.00
☐	Chris Drury, Colo. ✂	12.00
☐	Mike Dunham (G), Nash. ✂	12.00
☐	Sergei Fedorov, Detr. ✂	20.00
☐	Jeff Friesen, Anah. ✂	12.00
☐	Simon Gagné, Phil. ✂	15.00
☐	Jarome Iginla, Calg. ✂	15.00
☐	Rostislav Klesla, Colu. ✂	12.00
☐	Krys Kolanos, Phoe. ✂	12.00
☐	Steven Reinprecht, Colo. ✂	12.00
☐	Sergei Samsonov, Bost. ✂	12.00
☐	José Théodore (G), Mont. ✂	20.00
☐	Joe Thornton, Bost. ✂	20.00

CLASSIC STITCHES LIMITED

	Insert Set (15 cards):	2250.00
	Insert (*75)	CSL75
☐	Peter Bondra, Wash. ✂	25.00
☐	Pavel Bure, NYRa. ✂	25.00
☐	Adam Deadmarsh, LosA. ✂	20.00
☐	Chris Drury, Colo. ✂	25.00
☐	Mike Dunham (G), Nash. ✂	20.00
☐	Sergei Fedorov, Detr. ✂	50.00
☐	Jeff Friesen, Anah. ✂	20.00
☐	Simon Gagné, Phil. ✂	25.00
☐	Jarome Iginla, Calg. ✂	25.00
☐	Rostislav Klesla, Colu. ✂	25.00
☐	Krys Kolanos, Phoe. ✂	20.00
☐	Steven Reinprecht, Colo. ✂	20.00
☐	Sergei Samsonov, Bost. ✂	25.00
☐	José Théodore (G), Mont. ✂	50.00
☐	Joe Thornton, Bost. ✂	50.00

ETCHED IN TIME

	Insert Set (15 cards):	30.00
	Insert (1:12)	ET
☐	ET1 Paul Kariya, Anah.	3.00
☐	ET2 Joe Sakic, Colo.	4.00
☐	ET3 Patrick Roy (G), Colo.	7.00
☐	ET4 Mike Modano, Dall.	2.00
☐	ET5 Steve Yzerman, Detr.	6.00
☐	ET6 Brendan Shanahan, Detr.	2.00
☐	ET7 Brett Hull, Detr.	2.00
☐	ET8 Mike Comrie, Edmo.	2.00
☐	ET9 José Théodore (G), Mont.	3.00
☐	ET10 Martin Brodeur (G), NJer.	4.00
☐	ET11 Pavel Bure, NYRa.	2.00
☐	ET12 Simon Gagné, Phil.	2.00
☐	ET13 Mario Lemieux, Pitt.	7.00
☐	ET14 Teemu Selänne, SanJ.	2.00
☐	ET15 Mats Sundin, Toro.	2.00

GENUINE GREATNESS

	Insert Set (7 cards):	15.00
	Insert (1:24)	GG
☐	GG1 Paul Kariya, Anah.	3.00
☐	GG2 Peter Forsberg, Colo.	3.00
☐	GG3 Patrick Roy (G), Colo.	7.00
☐	GG4 Steve Yzerman, Detr.	6.00
☐	GG5 Wayne Gretzky, Edmo.	10.00
☐	GG6 Pavel Bure, NYRa.	2.00
☐	GG7 Jaromir Jagr, Wash.	2.00

HOCKEY HEADLINERS

	Insert Set (12 cards):	170.00
	Insert (1:48)	2HH
☐	P. Kariya ✂ / J. Friesen ✂	20.00
☐	S. Samsonov ✂ / J. Thornton ✂	20.00
☐	É. Dazé ✂ / A. Zhamnov ✂	10.00
☐	P. Forsberg ✂ / J. Sakic ✂	35.00
☐	P. Roy (G) ✂ / D. Aebischer (G) ✂	30.00
☐	N. Lidström ✂ / S. Fedorov ✂	20.00
☐	S. Yzerman ✂ / D. Hasek (G) ✂	40.00
☐	J. Théodore (G) ✂ / S. Koivu ✂	25.00
☐	J. Roenick ✂ / S. Gagné ✂	20.00
☐	C. Lemieux ✂ / K. Kolanos ✂	10.00
☐	M. Lemieux ✂ / A. Morozov ✂	40.00
☐	J. Jagr ✂ / P. Bondra ✂	20.00

HOCKEY HEADLINERS LIMITED

	Insert Set (12 cards):	665.00
	Insert (*25)	2HHL
☐	KF Paul Kariya, Anah. ✂	75.00
☐	ST Sergei Samsonov, Bost. ✂	75.00
☐	DZ Éric Dazé, Chic. ✂	30.00
☐	FS Peter Forsberg, Colo. ✂	150.00
☐	RA Patrick Roy (G), Colo. ✂	125.00
☐	LF Nicklas Lidström, Detr. ✂	75.00
☐	YH Steve Yzerman, Detr. ✂	150.00
☐	TK José Théodore (G), Mont. ✂	100.00
☐	RG Jeremy Roenick, Phil. ✂	75.00
☐	LK Claude Lemieux, Phoe. ✂	30.00
☐	LM Mario Lemieux, Pitt. ✂	150.00
☐	JB Jaromir Jagr, Wash. ✂	75.00

HOCKEY ROYALTY

	Insert Set (30 cards):	800.00
	Insert (*90)	3HR
☐	P. Kariya ✂ / J. Friesen ✂ / J. Giguère (G) ✂	45.00
☐	B. Guerin ✂ / J.Thornton ✂ / G. Murray ✂	40.00
☐	M. Satan ✂ / T. Connolly ✂ / M. Afinogenov ✂	40.00
☐	M. Savard ✂ / J. Iginla ✂ / R. Turek (G) ✂	40.00
☐	É. Dazé ✂ / A. Zhamnov ✂ / J. Thibault (G) ✂	40.00
☐	S. Reinprecht ✂ / C. Drury ✂ / P. Forsberg ✂	40.00
☐	A. Tanguay ✂ / J. Sakic ✂ / D. Hinote ✂	40.00
☐	E. Knutsen ✂ / R. Tugnutt (G) ✂ / R. Klesla ✂	40.00
☐	M. Modano ✂ / B. Morrow ✂ / J. Lehtinen ✂	40.00
☐	B. Shanahan ✂ / S. Yzerman ✂ / N.Lidström ✂	80.00
☐	A. Deadmarsh ✂ / F. Potvin (G) ✂ / Z. Palffy ✂	40.00
☐	M. Dunham (G) ✂ / S. Hartnell ✂ / D. Legwand ✂	40.00
☐	E. Lindros ✂ / P. Bure ✂ / B. Leetch ✂	40.00
☐	J. LeClair ✂ / J. Roenick ✂ / M. Recchi ✂	40.00
☐	K. Primeau ✂ / S. Gagné ✂ / R. Fedotenko ✂	40.00
☐	S. Burke (G) ✂ / C. Lemieux ✂ / D. Brière ✂	40.00
☐	M. Lemieux ✂ / R. Lang ✂ / V.Nieminen ✂	60.00
☐	J.Halpern ✂ / P.Bondra ✂ / O. Kölzig (G) ✂	40.00
☐	S. Konowalchuk ✂ / S. Gonchar ✂ / J. Jagr ✂	40.00
☐	Brodeur (G) ✂ / Potvin (G) ✂ / J. Thibault (G) ✂	55.00
☐	W. Gretzky ✂ / M. Lemieux ✂ / J. Sakic ✂	150.00
☐	S. Gagné ✂ / A. Tanguay ✂ / É. Dazé ✂	25.00
☐	D. Weight ✂ / T. Amonte ✂ / B.Guerin ✂	25.00
☐	J. Jagr ✂ / M. Hejduk ✂ / R. Lang ✂	25.00
☐	S. Fedorov ✂ / P. Bure ✂ / I.Kovalchuk ✂	35.00
☐	P. Kariya ✂ / J. Sakic ✂ / J. Iginla ✂	45.00
☐	M. Lemieux ✂ / E. Lindros ✂ / J.Thornton ✂	65.00
☐	M. Brodeur (G) ✂ / Théodore (G) ✂ / Roy (G) ✂	125.00
☐	T. Selänne ✂ / J.Lehtinen ✂ / V. Nieminen ✂	25.00
☐	M. Näslund ✂ / N. Lidström ✂ / M. Sundin ✂	30.00

HOCKEY ROYALTY LIMITED

	Insert Set (30 cards):	2200.00
	Insert (*25)	3HRLL25
☐	P. Kariya ✂ / J. Friesen ✂ / J. Giguère (G) ✂	125.00
☐	B. Guerin ✂ / J.Thornton ✂ / G. Murray ✂	100.00
☐	M. Satan ✂ / T. Connolly ✂ / M. Afinogenov ✂	100.00
☐	M. Savard ✂ / J. Iginla ✂ / R. Turek (G) ✂	100.00
☐	É. Dazé ✂ / A. Zhamnov ✂ / J. Thibault (G) ✂	100.00
☐	S. Reinprecht ✂ / C. Drury ✂ / P. Forsberg ✂	100.00
☐	A. Tanguay ✂ / J. Sakic ✂ / D. Hinote ✂	125.00
☐	E. Knutsen ✂ / R. Tugnutt (G) ✂ / R. Klesla ✂	100.00
☐	M. Modano ✂ / B. Morrow ✂ / J. Lehtinen ✂	100.00
☐	B. Shanahan ✂ / S. Yzerman ✂ / N.Lidström ✂	200.00
☐	A. Deadmarsh ✂ / F. Potvin (G) ✂ / Z. Palffy ✂	100.00
☐	M. Dunham (G) ✂ / S. Hartnell ✂ / D. Legwand ✂	100.00
☐	E. Lindros ✂ / P. Bure ✂ / B. Leetch ✂	125.00
☐	J. LeClair ✂ / J. Roenick ✂ / M. Recchi ✂	100.00
☐	K. Primeau ✂ / S. Gagné ✂ / R. Fedotenko ✂	100.00
☐	S. Burke (G) ✂ / C. Lemieux ✂ / D. Brière ✂	100.00
☐	M. Lemieux ✂ / R. Lang ✂ / V.Nieminen ✂	175.00
☐	J.Halpern ✂ / P.Bondra ✂ / O. Kölzig (G) ✂	100.00
☐	S. Konowalchuk ✂ / S. Gonchar ✂ / J. Jagr ✂	100.00
☐	Brodeur (G) ✂ / Potvin (G) ✂ / Thibault (G) ✂	125.00
☐	W. Gretzky ✂ / M. Lemieux ✂ / J. Sakic ✂	450.00
☐	S. Gagné ✂ / A. Tanguay ✂ / É. Dazé ✂	80.00
☐	D. Weight ✂ / T. Amonte ✂ / B.Guerin ✂	80.00
☐	J. Jagr ✂ / M. Hejduk ✂ / R. Lang ✂	80.00
☐	S. Fedorov ✂ / P. Bure ✂ / I.Kovalchuk ✂	100.00
☐	P. Kariya ✂ / J. Sakic ✂ / J. Iginla ✂	125.00
☐	M. Lemieux ✂ / E. Lindros ✂ / J.Thornton ✂	200.00
☐	Brodeur (G) ✂ / Théodore (G) ✂ / Roy (G) ✂	250.00
☐	T. Selänne ✂ / J.Lehtinen ✂ / V. Nieminen ✂	80.00
☐	M. Näslund ✂ / N. Lidström ✂ / M. Sundin ✂	100.00

PILLARS OF STRENGTH

	Insert Set (10 cards):	15.00
	Insert (1:9)	PS
☐	PS1 Ilya Kovalchuk, Atla.	2.00
☐	PS2 Jarome Iginla, Calg.	2.00
☐	PS3 Joe Sakic, Colo.	4.00
☐	PS4 Mike Modano, Dall.	2.00
☐	PS5 Brendan Shanahan, Detr.	2.00
☐	PS6 Martin Brodeur (G), NJer.	4.00
☐	PS7 Eric Lindros, NYRa.	2.00
☐	PS8 Mario Lemieux, Pitt.	7.00
☐	PS9 Teemu Selänne, SanJ.	2.00
☐	PS10 Olaf Kölzig (G), Wash.	1.00

PORTRAIT OF A LEGEND

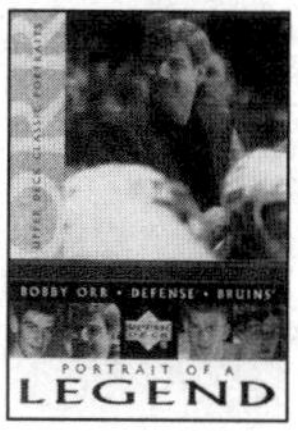

	Insert Set (10 cards):	70.00
	Insert (1:18)	PL
☐	PL1 Bobby Orr, Bost.	12.00
☐	PL2 Bobby Orr, Bost.	12.00
☐	PL3 Bobby Orr, Bost.	12.00
☐	PL4 Bobby Orr, Bost.	12.00
☐	PL5 Bobby Orr, Bost.	12.00
☐	PL6 Bobby Orr, Bost.	12.00
☐	PL7 Bobby Orr, Bost.	12.00
☐	PL8 Bobby Orr, Bost.	12.00
☐	PL9 Bobby Orr, Bost.	12.00
☐	PL10 Bobby Orr, Bost.	12.00

STARRING CAST

	Insert Set (15 cards):	195.00
	Insert (1:48)	SC
☐	Alex Tanguay, Colo. ✂	15.00
☐	Bill Guerin, Bost. ✂	10.00
☐	Brendan Shanahan, Detr. ✂	25.00
☐	Félix Potvin (G), LosA. ✂	15.00
☐	Jeremy Roenick, Phil. ✂	20.00
☐	Keith Tkachuk, SLou. ✂	15.00
☐	Mike Modano, Dall. ✂	25.00
☐	Markus Näslund, Vanc. ✂	25.00
☐	Mats Sundin, Toro. ✂	25.00
☐	Paul Kariya, Anah. ✂	35.00
☐	Miroslav Satan, Buff. ✂	10.00
☐	Sean Burke (G), Phoe. ✂	15.00
☐	Simon Gagné, Phil. ✂	20.00
☐	Steve Yzerman, Detr. ✂	60.00
☐	Zigmund Palffy, LosA. ✂	15.00

STARRING CAST LIMITED

	Insert Set (15 cards):	500.00
	Insert (*50)	SCL50
☐	Alex Tanguay, Colo. ✂	25.00
☐	Bill Guerin, Bost. ✂	25.00
☐	Brendan Shanahan, Detr. ✂	75.00
☐	Félix Potvin (G), LosA. ✂	75.00
☐	Jeremy Roenick, Phil. ✂	50.00
☐	Keith Tkachuk, SLou. ✂	25.00
☐	Mike Modano, Dall. ✂	75.00
☐	Markus Näslund, Vanc. ✂	75.00
☐	Mats Sundin, Toro. ✂	75.00
☐	Paul Kariya, Anah. ✂	100.00
☐	Miroslav Satan, Buff. ✂	25.00
☐	Sean Burke (G), Phoe. ✂	25.00
☐	Simon Gagné, Phil. ✂	50.00
☐	Steve Yzerman, Detr. ✂	175.00
☐	Zigmund Palffy, LosA. ✂	25.00

BUSTS

	Player	Alternate	Marble	Away	Home
☐☐☐	I. Kovalchuk ATLA	–	35	30	25
☐☐☐	D. Heatley ATLA	–	35	30	25
☐☐☐☐	R. Bourque BOST		35	30	25
☐☐☐☐	J. Thornton BOST		40	35	30
☐☐☐☐	P. Roy (G) COLO		65	55	50
☐☐☐	G. Howe DETR	–	50	40	35
☐	G. Howe HART		–	–	–
☐☐☐	B. Shanahan DETR	–	35	30	25
☐☐☐	M. Brodeur (G) NJER	–	35	30	25
☐☐☐☐	P. Bure NYRA	–	35	30	25
☐☐☐	C. Joseph (G) DETR	–	35	30	25
☐☐☐	J. Jagr WASH	–	35	30	25
☐☐☐	P. Kariya ANAH	–	35	30	25
☐☐☐	J. Iginla CALG	–	35	30	25
☐☐☐☐	J. Spezza OTTA		35	30	25
☐☐☐☐	J. Sakic COLO		40	35	30
☐☐☐	D. Hasek (G) DETR	–	35	30	25
☐	D. Hasek (G) BUFF		–	–	–

SIGNED BUSTS

	Player	Home
☐	I. Kovalchuk ATLA ✍	
☐	D. Heatley ATLA ✍	
☐	R. Bourque BOST * ✍	
☐	J. Thornton BOST ✍	
☐	P. Roy (G) COLO * ✍	
☐	G. Howe DETR * ✍	
☐	M. Brodeur (G) NJER ✍	
☐	P. Bure NYRA * ✍	
☐	C. Joseph (G) DETR ✍	
☐	J. Iginla CALG ✍	
☐	J. Spezza OTTA ✍	
☐	J. Sakic COLO ✍	

SIGNED BUSTS

	Player	Away
☐	I. Kovalchuk ATLA blue * 17 ✍	
☐	D. Heatley ATLA blue *15 ✍	
☐	R. Bourque BOST black *77 ✍	
☐	J. Thornton BOST black *19 ✍	
☐	P. Roy COLO burgandy *33 ✍	
☐	G.Howe DETR red *33 ✍	
☐	M. Brodeur NJER red *30 ✍	
☐	P. Bure NYRA blue *9 ✍	
☐	C. Joseph DETR red *31 ✍	
☐	J. Iginla CALG red *12 ✍	
☐	J. Spezza OTTA black *39 ✍	

SIGNED BUSTS

	Player	Alternate
☐	R. Bourque BOST alt. *50 ✍	
☐	J. Thornton BOST alt. *50 ✍	
☐	P. Roy COLO alt. *50 ✍	
☐	G. Howe HART alt. *50 ✍	
☐	P. Bure NYRA alt. *50 ✍	
☐	J. Spezza OTTA alt. *50 ✍	

SIGNED BUSTS

	Player	Marble
☐	I. Kovalchuk marble *25 ✍	
☐	D. Heatley marble *25 ✍	
☐	R. Bourque marble *25 ✍	
☐	J. Thornton marble *25 ✍	
☐	P. Roy marble *25 ✍	
☐	G. Howe marble *25 ✍	
☐	M. Brodeur marble *25 ✍	
☐	P. Bure marble *25 ✍	
☐	C. Joseph marble *25 ✍	
☐	J. Iginla marble *25 ✍	
☐	J. Spezza marble *25 ✍	

SIGNED BUSTS

Player	Glass
I. Kovalchuk glass *10 ✍	
D. Heatley glass *10 ✍	
R. Bourque glass *10 ✍	
J. Thornton glass *10 ✍	
P. Roy glass *10 ✍	
G. Howe glass *10 ✍	
M. Brodeur glass *10 ✍	
P. Bure glass *10 ✍	
C. Joseph glass *10 ✍	
J. Iginla glass *10 ✍	
J. Spezza glass *10 ✍	

2002 - 03 UPPER DECK FOUNDATIONS

Produced by The Upper Deck Company, this series was released in November 2002.

Shell Set (100 cards):	**45.00**
Complete Set (163 cards):	**550.00**
Common Player:	**.25**

Description	Base
1 Andy Moog (G), Bost.	.25
2 Bill Ranford (G), Bost.	.25
3 Cam Neely, Bost.	1.00
4 Bobby Orr, Bost.	4.00
5 Terry O'Reilly, Bost.	.25
6 Raymond Bourque, Bost.	1.00
7 Phil Esposito, Bost.	1.00
8 Clark Gillies, Buff.	.25
9 Grant Fuhr (G), Buff.	.50
10 Dale Hawerchuk, Buff.	.50
11 Kent Nilsson, Calg.	.25
12 Willi Plett, Calg.	.25
13 Al Secord, Chic.	.25
14 Denis Savard, Chic.	.25
15 Bob Probert, Chic.	.25
16 Steve Larmer, Chic.	.25
17 Patrick Roy (G), Colo.	3.00
18 Raymond Bourque, Colo.	1.00
19 Andy Moog (G), Dall.	.25
20 Alex Delvecchio, Detr.	.25
21 Börje Salming, Detr.	.50
22 Dino Ciccarelli, Detr.	.25
23 Gordie Howe, Detr.	2.50
24 John Ogrodnick, Detr.	.25
25 Marcel Dionne, Detr.	1.00
26 Mark Howe, Detr.	.25
27 Ron Duguay, Detr.	.25
28 Steve Yzerman, Detr.	2.00
29 Andy Moog (G), Edmo.	.25
30 Bill Ranford (G), Edmo.	.25
31 Grant Fuhr (G), Edmo.	.50
32 Mark Messier, Edmo.	1.00
33 Marty McSorley, Edmo.	.25
34 Wayne Gretzky, Edmo.	4.00
35 Glenn Anderson, Edmo.	.25
36 Gordie Howe, Hart.	2.50
37 Mark Howe, Hart.	.25
38 Gordie Howe, Houston Aeros	2.50
39 Butch Goring, LosA.	.25
40 Charlie Simmer, LosA.	.25
41 Ron Duguay, LosA.	.25
42 Marcel Dionne, LosA.	1.00
43 Marty McSorley, LosA.	.25
44 Wayne Gretzky, LosA.	4.00
45 Wayne Gretzky, AS'99	4.00
46 Brian Bellows, MinN.	.25
47 Dino Ciccarelli, MinN.	.25
48 Mike Modano, MinN.	1.00
49 Brian Bellows, Mont.	.25
50 Denis Savard, Mont.	.25
51 Guy Lafleur, Mont.	2.00
52 Mats Näslund, Mont.	.25
53 Doug Gilmour, Mont.	.50
54 Patrick Roy (G), Mont.	3.00
55 Rod Langway, Mont.	.25
56 Ryan Walter, Mont.	.25
57 Yvan Cournoyer, Mont.	.50
58 Martin Brodeur (G), NJer.	1.50
59 Bob Nystrom, NYIs.	.25
60 Butch Goring, NYIs.	.25
61 Clark Gillies, NYIs.	.25
62 Mike Bossy, NYIs.	1.50
63 Glenn Anderson, NYRa.	.25
64 Guy Lafleur, NYRa.	2.00
65 Mark Messier, NYRa.	1.00
66 Marcel Dionne, NYRa.	1.00
67 Phil Esposito, NYRa.	1.00
68 Ron Duguay, NYRa.	.25
69 Steve Larmer, NYRa.	.25
70 Wayne Gretzky, NYRa.	4.00
71 Brian Propp, Phil.	.25
72 Jeremy Roenick, Phil.	.50
73 Mark Howe, Phil.	.25
74 Ron Hextall, Phil.	.50
75 Tim Kerr, Phil.	.25
76 Anton Stastny, Québ.	.25
77 Dale Hunter, Québ.	.25
78 Guy Lafleur, Québ.	2.00
79 Ron Hextall, Québ.	.50
80 Wendel Clark, Québ.	.50
81 Wilf Paiement, Québ.	.25
82 Brett Hull, SLou.	1.00
83 Bernie Federko, SLou.	.25
84 Dale Hawerchuk, SLou.	.50
85 Grant Fuhr (G), SLou.	.50
86 Tony Twist, SLou.	.25
87 Wayne Gretzky, SLou.	4.00
88 Börje Salming, Toro.	.50
89 Mats Sundin, Toro.	1.00
90 Glenn Anderson, Toro.	.25
91 Grant Fuhr (G), Toro.	.50
92 Wendel Clark, Toro.	.50
93 Wilf Paiement, Toro.	.25
94 Harold Snepsts, Vanc.	.25
95 Pavel Bure, Vanc.	.50
96 Tony Tanti, Vanc.	.25
97 Dale Hunter, Wash.	.25
98 Dino Ciccarelli, Wash.	.25
99 Rod Langway, Wash.	.25
100 Dale Hawerchuk, Winn.	.50

SUBSETS

Insert (#/1250)	S1250
101 Wayne Gretzky, AS'83	20.00
102 Gordie Howe, Detr.	10.00
103 Bobby Orr, Bost.	20.00
104 Gordie Howe, Hart.	10.00
105 Wayne Gretzky, LosA.	20.00
106 Wayne Gretzky, NYRa.	20.00
107 Cam Neely, Bost.	5.00
108 Raymond Bourque, Colo.	5.00
109 Phil Esposito, Bost.	5.00
110 Grant Fuhr (G), Edmo.	5.00
111 Denis Savard, Chic.	5.00
112 Patrick Roy (G), Colo.	15.00
113 Steve Yzerman, Detr.	10.00
114 Marcel Dionne, LosA.	5.00
115 Guy Lafleur, Mont.	10.00
116 Bernie Federko, SLou.	5.00
117 Wayne Gretzky, SLou.	20.00
118 P. Esposito/ R. Bourque	5.00
119 Mike Bossy, NYIs.	5.00
120 Patrick Roy (G), Mont.	15.00
121 Bob Nystrom, NYIs.	5.00
122 Pasi Nurminen (G), Atla.	5.00
123 Mark Hartigan, Atla.	5.00
124 Henrik Tallinder, Buff.	5.00
125 Micki Dupont, Calg. RC	**10.00**
126 Riku Hahl, Colo.	5.00
127 Andrej Nedorost, Colu.	5.00
128 Ales Pisa, Edmo.	5.00
129 Jani Rita, Edmo.	5.00
130 Stephen Weiss, Flor.	5.00
131 Lukas Krajicek, Flor.	5.00
132 Sylvain Blouin, MinW. RC	**10.00**
133 Marcel Hossa, Mont.	5.00
134 Adam Hall, Nash. RC	**10.00**
135 Jan Lasak (G), Nash.	5.00
136 Ray Schultz, NYIs. RC	**10.00**
137 Trent Hunter, NYIs.	5.00
138 Martin Prusek (G), Otta.	5.00
139 Branko Radivojevic, Phoe.	5.00
140 Sébastien Centomo (G), Toro.	5.00
141 Karel Pilar, Toro.	5.00
142 Sébastien Charpentier (G), Wash.	5.00
143 Stanislav Chistov, Anah. RC	**15.00**
144 Alexei Smirnov, Anah. RC	**10.00**
145 Joe Thornton, Bost.	10.00
146 Chuck Kobasew, Calg. RC	**10.00**
147 Patrick Roy (G), Colo.	15.00
148 Mike Modano, Dall.	10.00
149 Rick Nash, Colu. RC	**30.00**
150 Mike Comrie, Edmo.	10.00
151 Henrik Zetterberg, Detr. RC	**30.00**
152 Ales Hemsky, Edmo. RC	**15.00**
153 Jay Bouwmeester, Flor. RC	**15.00**
154 Pavel Bure, NYRa.	10.00
155 Alexander Frolov, LosA. RC	**15.00**
156 Pierre-Marc Bouchard, MinW. RC	**15.00**
157 Ron Hainsey, Mont. RC	**10.00**
158 Sean Burke (G), Phoe.	10.00
159 Mario Lemieux, Pitt.	15.00
160 Anton Volchenkov, Otta. RC	**10.00**
161 Jeff Taffe, Phoe. RC	**10.00**
162 Alexander Svitov, Tamp. RC	**10.00**
163 Steve Eminger, Wash. RC	**10.00**

SUBSETS

These cards were inserted into bonus packs in 2002 - 03 Upper Deck Rookie Update.

Insert (#/1250)	S1250
164 Jason Spezza, Otta. RC	**20.00**
165 Pascal Leclaire (G), Colu. RC	**15.00**
166 Ari Ahonen (G), NJer. RC	**5.00**
167 Steve Ott, Dall. RC	**5.00**

1000 POINT CLUB JERSEY

Insert Set (11 cards):	2200	450	300
Insert	Jers	Jers	Jers
MB Mike Bossy, NYIs. ✂	225	40	30
JB Johnny Bucyk, Bost. ✂	125	25	15
DC Dino Ciccarelli, Wash. ✂	50	20	15
MG Michel Goulet, Québ. ✂	100	20	15
WG Wayne Gretzky, LosA. ✂	900	175	125
GL Guy Lafleur, NYRa. ✂	250	50	35
LA Guy Lafleur, Québ. ✂	250	50	35
DP Denis Potvin, NYIs. ✂	125	25	15
DE Denis Savard, Chic. ✂	75	20	15
BT Bryan Trottier, NYIs. ✂	175	35	25
SY Steve Yzerman, Detr. ✂	525	105	75

1000 POINT CLUB STICK

Insert Set (28 cards):	700.00
Insert	Stick
AN Glenn Anderson, Edmo. ✂	15.00
AN2 Glenn Anderson, Toro. ✂	15.00
BE Jean Béliveau, Mont. ✂	40.00
BO Mike Bossy, NYIs. ✂	30.00
BO1 Raymond Bourque, Bost. ✂	35.00
BO2 Raymond Bourque, Colo. ✂	35.00
BU Johnny Bucyk, Bost. ✂	15.00
CI Dino Ciccarelli, Minn. ✂	15.00
DI Marcel Dionne, LosA. ✂	25.00
DI2 Marcel Dionne, NYRa. ✂	25.00
ES Phil Esposito, NYRa. ✂	25.00
ES2 Phil Esposito, Bost. ✂	25.00
GA Mike Gartner, Wash. ✂	25.00
GR Wayne Gretzky, NYRa. ✂	125.00
HA Dale Hawerchuk, Buff. ✂	15.00
HA2 Dale Hawerchuk, Winn. ✂	15.00
HO Gordie Howe, Detr. ✂	75.00
KU Jari Kurri, Edmo. ✂	30.00
KU2 Jari Kurri, LosA. ✂	30.00
LA1 Guy Lafleur, NYRa. ✂	35.00
LA2 Guy Lafleur, Mont. ✂	35.00
LA3 Guy Lafleur, Québ. ✂	35.00
MC Lanny McDonald, Calg. ✂	15.00
MI Stan Mikita, Chic. ✂	15.00
PO Denis Potvin, NYIs. ✂	15.00
SA Denis Savard, Chic. ✂	15.00
TR Bryan Trottier, NYIs. ✂	25.00
YZ Steve Yzerman, Detr. ✂	75.00

CALDER TROPHY WINNERS

Insert Set (5 cards):	700	125	100
Insert	CTW	CTW	CTW
T-MB Mike Bossy, NYIs. ✂	225	40	30
T-RB Raymond Bourque, Bost. ✂	250	50	35
T-PB Pavel Bure, Vanc. ✂	175	35	25
T-WP Willi Plett, AtlF. ✂	50	20	15
T-BT Bryan Trottier, NYIs. ✂	175	35	25

CANADIAN HEROES

Insert Set (22 cards):	1125	625	475
Insert	CH	CH	CH
Mike Bossy, NYIs. ✂	50	30	25
Raymond Bourque, Bost. ✂	75	40	30
Johnny Bucyk, Bost. ✂	30	20	15
Dino Ciccarelli, Wash. ✂	30	20	15
Wendel Clark, Toro. ✂	50	25	20
Ron Duguay, NYRa. ✂	30	20	15
Grant Fuhr (G), Edmo. ✂	30	20	15
Michel Goulet, Québ. ✂	30	20	15
Wayne Gretzky, LosA. ✂	250	135	100
Mark Howe, Phil. ✂	30	20	15
Guy Lafleur, NYRa. ✂	75	40	30
Marty McSorley, Pitt. ✂	30	20	15
Cam Neely, Bost. ✂	50	30	25
Willi Plett, Calg. ✂	30	20	15
Patrick Roy (G), Mont. ✂	150	80	60
Patrick Roy (G), Colo. ✂	150	80	60
Denis Savard, Chic. ✂	30	20	15
Harold Snepsts, Detr. ✂	30	20	15
Bryan Trottier, NYIs. ✂	50	25	20
Tony Twist, SLou. ✂	30	20	15
Rick Vaive, Toro. ✂	30	20	15
Steve Yzerman, Detr. ✂	150	80	60

CLASSIC GREATS

Insert Set (17 cards):	750	425	325
Insert	CG	CG	CG
Mike Bossy, NYIs. ✂	50	30	25
Raymond Bourque, Bost. ✂	75	40	30
Raymond Bourque, Colo. ✂	75	40	30
Dino Ciccarelli, Wash. ✂	30	20	15
Wendel Clark, Toro. ✂	50	25	20
Ron Duguay, NYRa. ✂	30	20	15
Grant Fuhr (G), Edmo. ✂	30	20	15
Michel Goulet, Québ. ✂	30	20	15
Wayne Gretzky, LosA. ✂	250	135	100
Mark Howe, Phil. ✂	30	20	15
Guy Lafleur, Québ. ✂	75	40	30
Cam Neely, Bost. ✂	50	30	25
Bob Nystrom, NYIs. ✂	30	20	15
Denis Potvin, NYIs. ✂	30	20	15
Bill Ranford (G) (G), Edmo. ✂	30	20	15
Börje Salming, Toro. ✂	50	25	20
Denis Savard, Chic. ✂	30	20	15

DEFENSE FIRST

Insert Set (8 cards):	900	200	125
Insert	DF	DF	DF
Raymond Bourque, Bost. ✂	250	50	35
Raymond Bourque, Colo. ✂	250	50	35
Grant Fuhr (G), Edmo. ✂	125	25	15
Mark Howe, Phil. ✂	50	20	15
Marty McSorley, Pitt. ✂	50	20	15
Denis Potvin, NYIs. ✂	175	35	15
Börje Salming, Toro. ✂	175	35	15
Harold Snepsts, Detr. ✂	50	20	15

LASTING IMPRESSIONS STICK

Insert Set (8 cards):	225.00
Insert (#/150)	Stick
L-WC Wendel Clark, Toro. ✂	25.00
L-YC Yvan Cournoyer, Mont. ✂	15.00
L-MN Mats Näslund, Mont. ✂	15.00
L-CN Cam Neely, Bost. ✂	30.00
L-BN Bob Nystrom, NYIs. ✂	15.00
L-BO Bobby Orr, Bost. ✂	145.00
L-JP Jacques Plante (G), Mont. ✂	35.00
L-BR Bill Ranford (G), Edmo. ✂	15.00

NHL MILESTONES

Insert Set (9 cards):	725	400	275
Insert	M	M	M
Mike Bossy, NYIs. ✂ Blue	100	50	25
Raymond Bourque, Bost. ✂	75	40	30
Grant Fuhr (G), Edmo. ✂	30	20	15
Wayne Gretzky, LosA. ✂	250	135	100
Cam Neely, Bost. ✂	50	30	25
Denis Potvin, NYIs. ✂	50	25	15
Patrick Roy (G), Colo. ✂	175	100	60
Bryan Trottier, NYIs. ✂	50	30	20
Steve Yzerman, Detr. ✂	150	80	60

PLAYOFF PERFORMERS

Insert Set (16 cards):	1025	575	400
Insert	PP	PP	PP
Mike Bossy, NYIs. ✂ Blue	100	50	25
Raymond Bourque, Colo. ✂	75	40	30

☐☐☐	Johnny Bucyk, Bost. ✂	30	20	15
☐☐☐	Pavel Bure, Vanc. ✂	50	25	20
☐☐☐	Dino Ciccarelli, Wash. ✂	30	20	15
☐☐☐	Grant Fuhr (G), Edmo. ✂	30	20	15
☐☐☐	Michel Goulet, Québ. ✂	30	20	15
☐☐☐	Wayne Gretzky, LosA. ✂	250	135	100
☐☐☐	Marty McSorley, Pitt. ✂	30	20	15
☐☐☐	Cam Neely, Bost. ✂	50	30	25
☐☐☐	Bob Nystrom, NYIs. ✂	30	20	15
☐☐☐	Patrick Roy (G), Mont. ✂	175	100	60
☐☐☐	Patrick Roy (G), Colo. ✂	175	100	60
☐☐☐	Börje Salming, Toro. ✂	50	25	15
☐☐☐	Bryan Trottier, NYIs. ✂	50	30	20
☐☐☐	Steve Yzerman, Detr. ✂	150	80	60

POWER STATIONS

Insert Set (11 cards):		**850**	**225**	**150**
	Insert	**PS**	**PS**	**PS**
☐☐☐	Mike Bossy, NYIs. ✂ Blue	350	70	30
☐☐☐	Dino Ciccarelli, Wash. ✂	50	20	15
☐☐☐	Wendel Clark, Toro. ✂	175	35	25
☐☐☐	Mark Howe, Phil. ✂	50	20	15
☐☐☐	Marty McSorley, Pitt. ✂	50	20	15
☐☐☐	Cam Neely, Bost. ✂	225	40	30
☐☐☐	Bob Nystrom, NYIs. ✂	50	20	15
☐☐☐	Willi Plett, AtlF. ✂	30	20	15
☐☐☐	Harold Snepsts, Detr. ✂	30	20	15
☐☐☐	Tony Twist, SLou. ✂	30	20	15
☐☐☐	Rick Vaive, Toro. ✂	50	20	15

SIGNS OF GREATNESS

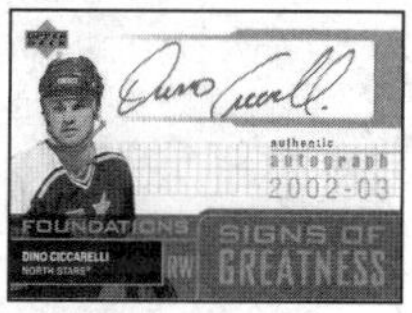

Insert Set (36 cards):		**2000.00**
	Autograph	**SoG**
☐	Glenn Anderson, Edmo. ✍	25.00
☐	Jean Béliveau, Mont. ✍ {*}	50.00
☐	Brian Bellows, Minn. ✍ {*26}	25.00
☐	Mike Bossy, NYIs. ✍	50.00
☐	Raymond Bourque, Colo. ✍ {*23}	250.00
☐	Raymond Bourque, Bost. ✍ {*23}	250.00
☐	Johnny Bucyk, Bost. ✍	25.00
☐	Dino Ciccarelli, Minn. ✍ {*}	25.00
☐	Bobby Clarke, Phil. ✍ {*}	25.00
☐	Marcel Dionne, LosA. ✍ {*}	25.00
☐	Grant Fuhr (G), Edmo. ✍ {*}	25.00
☐	Mike Gartner, Wash. ✍	25.00
☐	Clark Gillies, NYIs. ✍ {*26}	50.00
☐	Michel Goulet, Québ. ✍ {*}	15.00
☐	Wayne Gretzky, Edmo. ✍ {*46}	400.00
☐	Dale Hawerchuk, Winn. ✍	25.00
☐	Ron Hextall, Phil. ✍ {*51}	50.00
☐	Gordie Howe, Detr. ✍ {*43}	225.00
☐	Jari Kurri, Edmo. ✍	50.00
☐	Guy Lafleur, Mont. ✍ {*}	50.00
☐	Steve Larmer, Chic. ✍ {*26}	75.00
☐	Ted Lindsay, Detr. ✍ {*}	25.00
☐	Frank Mahovlich, Toro. ✍ {*}	50.00
☐	Lanny McDonald, Calg. ✍	25.00
☐	Stan Mikita, Chic. ✍ {*}	25.00
☐	Mats Näslund, Mont. ✍ {*87}	15.00
☐	Cam Neely, Bost. ✍ {*}	50.00
☐	Bobby Orr, Bost. ✍ {*48}	400.00
☐	Gilbert Perreault, Buff. ✍ {*}	25.00
☐	Denis Potvin, NYIs. ✍	25.00
☐	Brian Propp, Phil. ✍ {*87}	25.00
☐	Denis Savard, Chic. ✍ {*}	25.00
☐	Al Secord, Chic. ✍ {*26}	25.00
☐	Charlie Simmer, LosA. ✍ {*26}	25.00
☐	Billy Smith (G), NYIs. ✍	25.00
☐	Peter Stastny, Québ. ✍	25.00

2002 - 03 UPPER DECK HONOR ROLL

Produced by the Upper Deck Company, this series was released in April 2003.

Shell Set (100 cards): **40.00**
Complete Set (166 cards): **1000.00**

Common Player:		**.35**
	Description	**UDHR**
☐	1 Paul Kariya, Anah.	1.00
☐	2 Jean-Sébastien Giguère (G), Anah.	1.00
☐	3 Ilya Kovalchuk, Atla.	1.00
☐	4 Dany Heatley, Atla.	1.00
☐	5 Joe Thornton, Bost.	1.00
☐	6 Sergei Samsonov, Bost.	.50
☐	7 Miroslav Satan, Buff.	.25
☐	8 Martin Biron (G), Buff.	.25
☐	9 Chris Drury, Calg.	.50
☐	10 Jarome Iginla, Calg.	.50
☐	11 Ron Francis, Caro.	.50
☐	12 Arturs Irbe (G), Caro.	.25
☐	13 Tyler Arnason, Chic.	.25
☐	14 Jocelyn Thibault (G), Chic.	.25
☐	15 Patrick Roy (G), Colo.	3.00
☐	16 Joe Sakic, Colo.	1.50
☐	17 Peter Forsberg, Colo.	1.00
☐	18 Rob Blake, Colo.	.50
☐	19 Ray Whitney, Colu.	.25
☐	20 Marc Denis (G), Colu.	.25
☐	21 Mike Modano, Dall.	1.00
☐	22 Marty Turco (G), Dall.	.50
☐	23 Bill Guerin, Dall.	.25
☐	24 Steve Yzerman, Detr.	2.00
☐	25 Sergei Fedorov, Detr.	1.00
☐	26 Nicklas Lidström, Detr.	.50
☐	27 Brett Hull, Detr.	1.00
☐	28 Curtis Joseph (G), Detr.	1.00
☐	29 Brendan Shanahan, Detr.	1.00
☐	30 Mike Comrie, Edmo.	.50
☐	31 Tommy Salo (G), Edmo.	.25
☐	32 Roberto Luongo (G), Flor.	.50
☐	33 Kristian Huselius, Flor.	.25
☐	34 Félix Potvin (G), LosA.	.50
☐	35 Zigmund Palffy, LosA.	.50
☐	36 Marian Gaborik, MinW.	1.00
☐	37 Manny Fernandez (G), MinW.	.25
☐	38 José Théodore (G), Mont.	1.00
☐	39 Saku Koivu, Mont.	.50
☐	40 Patrik Elias, NJer.	.50
☐	41 Martin Brodeur (G), NJer.	1.50
☐	42 David Legwand, Nash.	.25
☐	43 Tomas Vokoun (G), Nash.	.25
☐	44 Alexei Yashin, NYIs.	.50
☐	45 Chris Osgood (G), NYIs.	.50
☐	46 Michael Peca, NYIs.	.25
☐	47 Eric Lindros, NYRa.	1.00
☐	48 Mike Richter (G), NYRa.	.25
☐	49 Pavel Bure, NYRa.	.50
☐	50 Marian Hossa, Otta.	1.00
☐	51 Daniel Alfredsson, Otta.	.50
☐	52 Jeremy Roenick, Phil.	.50
☐	53 John LeClair, Phil.	.50
☐	54 Roman Cechmanek (G), Phil.	.25
☐	55 Sean Burke (G), Phoe.	.50
☐	56 Tony Amonte, Phoe.	.50
☐	57 Alex Kovalev, Pitt.	.50
☐	58 Mario Lemieux, Pitt.	3.00
☐	59 Owen Nolan, SanJ.	.50
☐	60 Evgeni Nabokov (G), SanJ.	.50
☐	61 Keith Tkachuk, SLou.	.50
☐	62 Brent Johnson (G), SLou.	.25
☐	63 Nikolai Khabibulin (G), Tamp.	.25
☐	64 Vincent Lecavalier, Tamp.	1.00
☐	65 Mats Sundin, Toro.	1.00
☐	66 Ed Belfour (G), Toro.	1.00
☐	67 Todd Bertuzzi, Vanc.	1.00
☐	68 Markus Näslund, Vanc.	1.00
☐	69 Olaf Kölzig (G), Wash.	.50
☐	70 Jaromir Jagr, Wash.	1.00
☐	71 Paul Kariya, Anah.	1.00
☐	72 Shawn McEachern, Atla.	.25
☐	73 Joe Thornton, Bost.	1.00
☐	74 Stu Barnes, Buff.	.25
☐	75 Craig Conroy, Calg.	.25
☐	76 Ron Francis, Caro.	.50
☐	77 Alexei Zhamnov, Chic.	.25
☐	78 Joe Sakic, Colo.	1.50
☐	79 Ray Whitney, Colu.	.25
☐	80 Derian Hatcher, Dall.	.25
☐	81 Steve Yzerman, Detr.	2.00
☐	82 Jason Smith, Edmo.	.25
☐	83 Valeri Bure, Flor.	.25
☐	84 Mattias Norström, LosA.	.25
☐	85 Andrew Brunette, MinW.	.25
☐	86 Saku Koivu, Mont.	.50
☐	87 Greg Johnson, Nash.	.25
☐	88 Scott Stevens, NJer.	.25
☐	89 Michael Peca, NYIs.	.25
☐	90 Brian Leetch, NYRa.	.50
☐	91 Daniel Alfredsson, Otta.	.50
☐	92 Keith Primeau, Phil.	.25
☐	93 Teppo Numminen, Phoe.	.25
☐	94 Mario Lemieux, Pitt.	3.00
☐	95 Owen Nolan, SanJ.	.50
☐	96 Chris Pronger, SLou.	.50
☐	97 Vincent Lecavalier, Tamp.	1.00
☐	98 Mats Sundin, Toro.	1.00
☐	99 Markus Näslund, Vanc.	1.00
☐	100 Steve Konowalchuk, Wash.	.25

SUBSET

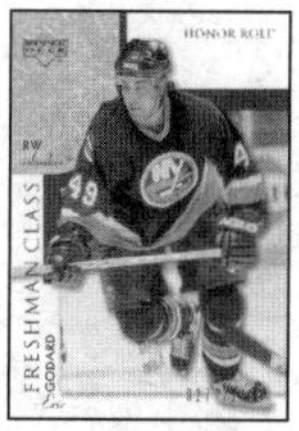

	Insert (*1499)	**R1499**
☐	**101 Alexei Smirnov, Anah. RC**	**10.00**
☐	**102 Martin Gerber (G), Anah. RC**	**5.00**
☐	**103 Kurt Sauer, Anah. RC**	**5.00**
☐	**104 Tim Thomas (G), Bost. RC**	**5.00**
☐	**105 Jordan Leopold, Calg. RC**	**10.00**
☐	**106 Dany Sabourin (G), Calg. RC**	**5.00**
☐	**107 Levente Szuper (G), Calg. RC**	**5.00**
☐	**108 Shawn Thornton, Chic. RC**	**5.00**
☐	**109 Matt Henderson, Chic. RC**	**5.00**
☐	**110 Lasse Pirjetä, Colu. RC**	**5.00**
☐	**111 Pascal Leclaire (G), Colu. RC**	**20.00**
☐	**112 Dmitri Bykov, Detr. RC**	**5.00**
☐	**113 Kari Haakana, Edmo. RC**	**5.00**
☐	**114 Craig Andersson (G), Chic. RC**	**10.00**
☐	**115 Mike Cammalleri, LosA. RC**	**15.00**
☐	**116 Stéphane Veilleux, MinW. RC**	**5.00**
☐	**117 Adam Hall, Nash. RC**	**10.00**
☐	**118 Greg Koehler, Nash. RC**	**5.00**
☐	**119 Vernon Fiddler, Nash. RC**	**5.00**
☐	**120 Ray Emery (G), Otta. RC**	**5.00**
☐	**121 Eric Godard, NYIs. RC**	**5.00**
☐	**122 Dennis Seidenberg, Phil. RC**	**5.00**
☐	**123 Jeff Taffe, Phoe. RC**	**10.00**
☐	**124 Dick Tarnström, Pitt.**	**10.00**
☐	**125 Tom Koivisto, SLou. RC**	**5.00**
☐	**126 Curtis Sanford (G), SLou. RC**	**5.00**
☐	**127 Cody Rudkowsky (G), SLou. RC**	**5.00**
☐	**128 Carlo Colaiacovo, Toro. RC**	**10.00**
☐	**129 Paul Manning, Colu. RC**	**5.00**
☐	**130 Shaone Morrisonn, Bost. RC**	**5.00**
☐	**131 Ryan Miller (G), Buff. RC**	**20.00**
☐	**132 Jerred Smithson, LosA. RC**	**5.00**
☐	**133 Alexei Semenov, Edmo. RC**	**5.00**
☐	**134 Michael Leighton (G), Chic. RC**	**5.00**
☐	**135 Ian MacNeil, Phil. RC**	**5.00**
☐	**136 Jared Aulin, LosA. RC**	**10.00**
☐	**137 Curtis Murphy, MinW. RC**	**5.00**
☐	**138 Jim Vandermeer, Phil. RC**	**5.00**
☐	**139 Steve Ott, Dall. RC**	**10.00**
☐	**140 Brooks Orpik, Pitt. RC**	**10.00**
☐	**141 Jim Fahey, SanJ. RC**	**5.00**
☐	**142 Matt Walker, SLou. RC**	**5.00**
☐	**143 Rickard Wallin, MinW. RC**	**5.00**
☐	**144 Tomas Malec, Caro. RC**	**5.00**
☐	**145 Jonathan Hedstrom, Anah. RC**	**5.00**

DEAN'S LIST

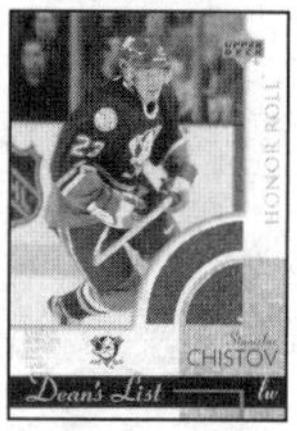

	Insert	**DL**
☐	**146 Stanislav Chistov, Anah. ✂ Teal RC**	**45.00**
☐	**147 Chuck Kobasew, Calg. ✂ RC**	**30.00**
☐	**148 Micki Dupont, Calg. ✂ RC**	**15.00**
☐	**149 Jeff Paul, Colo. ✂ RC**	**15.00**
☐	**150 Rick Nash, Colu. ✂ RC**	**85.00**
☐	**151 Henrik Zetterberg, Detr. ✂ RC**	**100.00**
☐	**152 Ales Hemsky, Edmo. ✂ RC**	**45.00**
☐	**153 Jay Bouwmeester, Flor. ✂ RC**	**45.00**
☐	**154 Alexander Frolov, LosA. ✂ RC**	**40.00**
☐	**155 Pierre-Marc Bouchard, MinW. ✂ RC**	**45.00**
☐	**156 Sylvain Blouin, Mont. ✂ RC**	**15.00**
☐	**157 Ron Hainsey, Mont. ✂ RC**	**20.00**
☐	**158 Scottie Upshall, Nash. ✂ RC**	**30.00**
☐	**159 Tomi Pettinen, NYIs. ✂ RC**	**15.00**
☐	**160 Jason Spezza, Otta. ✂ RC**	**60.00**
☐	**161 Anton Volchenkov, Otta. ✂ RC**	**15.00**
☐	**162 Radovan Somik, Phil. ✂ RC**	**15.00**
☐	**163 Lynn Loyns, SanJ. ✂ RC**	**15.00**
☐	**164 Alexander Svitov, Tamp. ✂ RC**	**30.00**
☐	**165 Mikael Tellqvist (G), Toro. ✂ RC**	**15.00**
☐	**166 Steve Eminger, Wash. ✂ RC**	**15.00**

GRADE A JERSEYS

Insert Set (14 cards):		**175.00**
	Insert	**GA**
☐	Raymond Bourque, Bost. ✂ {**}	10.00
☐	Martin Brodeur (G), NJer. ✂	30.00
☐	Éric Dazé, Chic. ✂ {**}	10.00
☐	Mike Dunham (G), Nash. ✂ {*}	10.00
☐	Peter Forsberg, Colo. ✂	25.00
☐	Simon Gagné, Phil. ✂ {**}	10.00
☐	Jaromir Jagr, Wash. ✂	20.00
☐	Paul Kariya, Anah. ✂	10.00
☐	Saku Koivu, Mont. ✂	15.00
☐	Olaf Kölzig (G), Wash. ✂	10.00
☐	Mike Modano, Dall. ✂ {*}	10.00
☐	Patrick Roy (G), Colo. ✂	45.00
☐	Miroslav Satan, Buff. ✂	10.00
☐	Mats Sundin, Toro. ✂	20.00

GRADE A JERSEYS TRIPLE

Insert Set (5 cards):		**250.00**
	Insert	**3Jers**
☐	T-JKB Jagr ✂ / Bondra ✂ / Kölzig (G) ✂	40.00
☐	Primeau ✂ / Roenick ✂ / Gagné ✂	40.00
☐	Roy (G) ✂ / Forsberg ✂ / Sakic ✂	100.00
☐	Samsonov ✂ Black / Thornton ✂ White / Murray ✂ White	40.00
☐	Yzerman ✂ / Shanahan ✂ / Fedorov ✂	100.00

SIGNATURE CLASS

Insert Set (19 cards):		**1175.00**
	Insert	**SigC**
☐	Maxim Afinogenov, Buff. ✍	20.00
☐	Jay Bouwmeester, Flor. ✍	35.00
☐	Pavel Brendl, Phil. ✍	15.00
☐	Martin Brodeur (G), NJer. ✍	80.00
☐	Pavel Bure, NYRa. ✍	40.00
☐	Stanislav Chistov, Anah. ✍	35.00
☐	Manny Fernandez (G), MinW. ✍	20.00
☐	Wayne Gretzky, NYRa. ✍ {*}	250.00
☐	Dany Heatley, Atla. ✍	50.00
☐	Gordie Howe, Detr. ✍ {*}	175.00
☐	Nikolai Khabibulin (G), Tamp. ✍	20.00
☐	John LeClair, Phil. ✍	40.00
☐	Bobby Orr, Bost. ✍ {*}	250.00
☐	Patrick Roy (G), Colo. ✍	150.00
☐	Teemu Selänne, SanJ. ✍	40.00
☐	Jason Spezza, Otta. ✍	50.00
☐	Alexander Svitov, Tamp. ✍	20.00
☐	Steve Yzerman, Detr. ✍	120.00
☐	Henrik Zetterberg, Detr. ✍	70.00

STUDENTS OF THE GAME

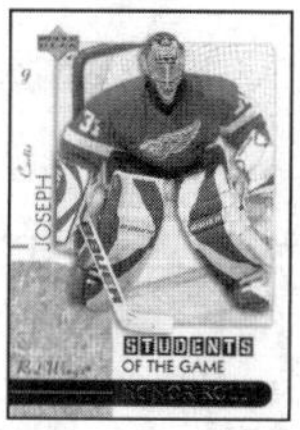

Insert Set (30 cards):		**55.00**
	Insert	**SG**
☐	SG1 Paul Kariya, Anah.	2.00
☐	SG2 Dany Heatley, Atla.	2.00
☐	SG3 Joe Thornton, Bost.	2.00
☐	SG4 Jarome Iginla, Calg.	2.00
☐	SG5 Chris Drury, Calg.	2.00
☐	SG6 Joe Sakic, Colo.	3.00
☐	SG7 Patrick Roy (G), Colo.	6.00
☐	SG8 Peter Forsberg, Colo.	2.00
☐	SG9 Rick Nash, Colu.	2.00
☐	SG10 Mike Modano, Dall.	2.00
☐	SG11 Bill Guerin, Dall.	2.00
☐	SG12 Curtis Joseph (G), Detr.	2.00

□	SG13 Steve Yzerman, Detr.	4.00
□	SG14 Sergei Fedorov, Detr.	2.00
□	SG15 Mike Comrie, Edmo.	2.00
□	SG16 Marian Gaborik, MinW.	2.00
□	SG17 Saku Koivu, Mont.	2.00
□	SG18 Martin Brodeur (G), NJer.	3.00
□	SG19 Alexei Yashin, NYIs.	2.00
□	SG20 Pavel Bure, NYRa.	2.00
□	SG21 Eric Lindros, NYRa.	2.00
□	SG22 Jason Spezza, Otta.	2.00
□	SG23 Jeremy Roenick, Phil.	2.00
□	SG24 Tony Amonte, Phoe.	2.00
□	SG25 Mario Lemieux, Pitt.	6.00
□	SG26 Teemu Selänne, SanJ.	2.00
□	SG27 Keith Tkachuk, SLou.	2.00
□	SG28 Vincent Lecavalier, Tamp.	2.00
□	SG29 Mats Sundin, Toro.	2.00
□	SG30 Jaromir Jagr, Wash.	2.00

TEAM WARRIORS

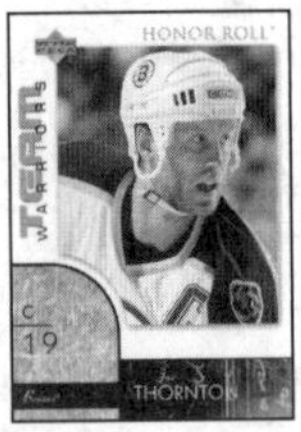

Insert Set (10 cards):		**25.00**
	Insert	**TW**
□	TW1 Joe Thornton, Bost.	2.00
□	TW2 Jarome Iginla, Calg.	2.00
□	TW3 Jeff O_Neill, Caro.	2.00
□	TW4 Peter Forsberg, Colo.	2.00
□	TW5 Mike Modano, Dall.	2.00
□	TW6 Brendan Shanahan, Detr.	2.00
□	TW7 Adam Deadmarsh, LosA.	2.00
□	TW8 Saku Koivu, Mont.	2.00
□	TW9 Michael Peca, NYIs.	2.00
□	TW10 Eric Lindros, NYRa.	2.00
□	TW11 John LeClair, Phil.	2.00
□	TW12 Mario Lemieux, Pitt.	6.00
□	TW13 Owen Nolan, SanJ.	2.00
□	TW14 Mats Sundin, Toro.	2.00
□	TW15 Todd Bertuzzi, Vanc.	2.00

2002 - 03 UPPER DECK MASK COLLECTION

Produced by The Upper Deck Company, this series was released in May 2003. Cards 1-90 have a UD Promo variation.

Complete Set (90 cards):		**25.00**
Complete Set (180 cards):		**275.00**
Common Player:		**.35**
	Description	**UDMC**
□ □	1 Jean-Sébastien Giguère (G), Anah.	1.00
□ □	2 Paul Kariya, Anah.	1.00
□ □	3 Byron Dafoe (G), Atla.	.35
□ □	4 Milan Hnilicka (G), Atla.	.35
□ □	5 Dany Heatley, Atla.	1.00
□ □	6 Ilya Kovalchuk, Atla.	1.00
□ □	7 Pasi Nurminen (G), Atla.	.35
□ □	8 Jeff Hackett (G), Bost.	.35
□ □	9 Steve Shields, Bost.	.35
□ □	10 Joe Thornton, Bost.	1.00
□ □	11 Martin Biron (G), Buff.	.35
□ □	12 Mika Noronen (G), Buff.	.35
□ □	13 Roman Turek (G), Calg.	.35
□ □	14 Jamie McLennan (G), Calg.	.35
□ □	15 Chris Drury, Calg.	.50
□ □	16 Jarome Iginla, Calg.	.50
□ □	17 Kevin Weekes (G), Caro.	.35
□ □	18 Arturs Irbe (G), Caro.	.35
□ □	19 Jocelyn Thibault (G), Chic.	.35
□ □	20 Steve Passmore (G), Chic.	.35
□ □	21 Patrick Roy (G), Colo.	3.00
□ □	22 David Aebischer (G), Colo.	.35
□ □	23 Joe Sakic, Colo.	1.50
□ □	24 Marc Denis (G), Colu.	.35
□ □	25 Jean-François Labbé (G), Colu.	.35
□ □	26 Marty Turco (G), Dall.	.50
□ □	27 Ron Tugnutt (G), Dall.	.35
□ □	28 Mike Modano, Dall.	1.00
□ □	29 Bill Guerin, Dall.	.35
□ □	30 Curtis Joseph (G), Detr.	1.00
□ □	31 Manny Legacé (G), Detr.	.35
□ □	32 Steve Yzerman, Detr.	2.00
□ □	33 Brendan Shanahan, Detr.	1.00
□ □	34 Tommy Salo (G), Edmo.	.35
□ □	35 Jussi Markkanen (G), Edmo.	.35
□ □	36 Mike Comrie, Edmo.	.50
□ □	37 Roberto Luongo (G), Flor.	.50
□ □	38 Jani Hurme (G), Flor.	.35
□ □	39 Félix Potvin (G), LosA.	.50
□ □	40 Jamie Storr (G), LosA.	.35
□ □	41 Zigmund Palffy, LosA.	.50
□ □	42 Manny Fernandez (G), MinW.	.35
□ □	43 Dwayne Roloson (G), MinW.	.35
□ □	44 Marian Gaborik, MinW.	1.00
□ □	45 José Théodore (G), Mont.	1.00
□ □	46 Mathieu Garon (G), Mont.	.35
□ □	47 Saku Koivu, Mont.	.50
□ □	48 Jan Lasak (G), Nash.	.35
□ □	49 Tomas Vokoun (G), Nash.	.35
□ □	50 Martin Brodeur (G), NJer.	1.50
□ □	51 Corey Schwab (G), NJer.	.35
□ □	52 Garth Snow (G), NYIs.	.35
□ □	53 Chris Osgood (G), NYIs.	.50
□ □	54 Mike Dunham (G), NYRa.	.35
□ □	55 Dan Blackburn (G), NYRa.	.35
□ □	56 Jason Labarbera (G), NYRa.	.35
□ □	57 Pavel Bure, NYRa.	.50
□ □	58 Patrick Lalime (G), Otta.	.50
□ □	59 Martin Prusek (G), Otta.	.35
□ □	60 Roman Cechmanek (G), Phil.	.35
□ □	61 Robert Esche (G), Phil.	.35
□ □	62 Jeremy Roenick, Phil.	.50
□ □	63 John LeClair, Phil.	.50
□ □	64 Brian Boucher (G), Phoe.	.35
□ □	65 Sean Burke (G), Phoe.	.50
□ □	66 Jean-Marc Pelletier (G), Phoe.	.35
□ □	67 Tony Amonte, Phoe.	.50
□ □	68 Johan Hedberg (G), Pitt.	.35
□ □	69 Jean-Sébastien Aubin (G), Pitt.	.35
□ □	70 Mario Lemieux, Pitt.	3.00
□ □	71 Sébastien Caron (G), Pitt.	.35
□ □	72 Evgeni Nabokov (G), SanJ.	.50
□ □	73 Vesa Toskala (G), SanJ.	.35
□ □	74 Miikka Kiprusoff (G), SanJ.	.35
□ □	75 Brent Johnson (G), SLou.	.35
□ □	76 Tom Barrasso (G), SLou.	.35
□ □	77 Fred Brathwaite (G), SLou.	.35
□ □	78 Reinhard Divis (G), SLou.	.35
□ □	79 Nikolai Khabibulin (G), Tamp.	.35
□ □	80 Kevin Hodson (G), Tamp.	.35
□ □	81 Evgeny Konstantinov (G), Tamp.	.35
□ □	82 Ed Belfour (G), Toro.	1.00
□ □	83 Trevor Kidd (G), Toro.	.35
□ □	84 Mats Sundin, Toro.	1.00
□ □	85 Dan Cloutier (G), Vanc.	.35
□ □	86 Peter Skudra (G), Vanc.	.35
□ □	87 Jaromir Jagr, Wash.	1.00
□ □	88 Olaf Kölzig (G), Wash.	.50
□ □	89 Craig Billington (G), Wash.	.35
□ □	90 Sébastien Charpentier (G), Wash.	.35

SUBSET

	Insert	**Insert**
□	91 Martin Brodeur (G), NJer. {*1499}	5.00
□	92 Patrick Roy (G), Colo. {*1475}	10.00
□	93 Curtis Joseph (G), Detr. {*1096}	5.00
□	94 Roman Cechmanek (G), Phil. {*1042}	2.00
□	95 Marty Turco (G), Dall. {*590}	2.00
□	96 Jocelyn Thibault (G), Chic. {*1439}	2.00
□	97 José Théodore (G), Mont. {*1836}	2.00
□	98 Jean-Sébastien Giguère (G), Anah. {*1260}	2.00
□	99 Ed Belfour (G), Toro. {*1305}	2.00
□	100 Steve Shields (G), Bost. {*771}	2.00
□	101 Johan Hedberg (G), Pitt. {*1673}	2.00
□	102 Martin Biron (G), Buff. {*1630}	2.00
□	103 Dan Cloutier (G), Vanc. {*1298}	2.00
□	104 Evgeni Nabokov (G), SanJ. {*1669}	2.00
□	105 Sean Burke (G), Phoe. {*1574}	2.00
□	106 Nikolai Khabibulin (G), Tamp. {*1733}	2.00
□	107 Olaf Kölzig (G), Wash. {*1785}	2.00
□	108 Byron Dafoe (G), Atla. {*1379}	2.00
□	109 David Aebischer (G), Colo. {*501}	2.00
□	110 Manny Fernandez (G), MinW. {*1032}	2.00
□	111 Dan Blackburn (G), NYRa. {*840}	2.00
□	112 Félix Potvin (G), LosA. {*1529}	2.00
□	113 Patrick Lalime (G), Otta. {*1373}	2.00
□	114 Brent Johnson (G), SLou. {*1166}	2.00
□	115 Marc Denis (G), Colu. {*1046}	2.00

ROOKIE

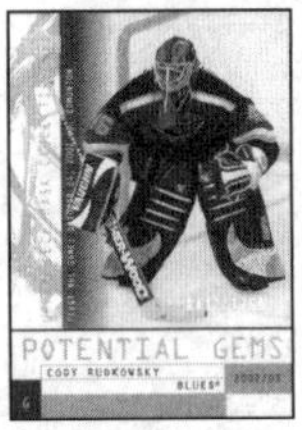

	Insert (*1750)	**R1750**
□	**116 Micki Dupont, Calg. RC**	**5.00**
□	**117 Cody Rudkowsky (G), SLou. RC**	**5.00**
□	**118 Shawn Thornton, Chic. RC**	**5.00**
□	**119 Lasse Pirjetä, Colu. RC**	**5.00**
□	**120 Radovan Somik, Phil. RC**	**5.00**
□	**121 Tomi Pettinen, NYIs. RC**	**5.00**
□	**122 Jonathan Hedstrom, Anah. RC**	**5.00**
□	**123 Sylvain Blouin, Mont. RC**	**5.00**
□	**124 Stéphane Veilleux, MinW. RC**	**5.00**
□	**125 Curtis Sanford (G), SLou. RC**	**5.00**
□	**126 Kurt Sauer, Anah. RC**	**5.00**
□	**127 Vernon Fiddler, Nash. RC**	**5.00**
□	**128 Patrick Sharp, Phil. RC**	**5.00**
□	**129 Greg Koehler, Nash. RC**	**5.00**
□	**130 Dany Sabourin (G), Calg. RC**	**5.00**
□	**131 Dmitri Bykov, Detr. RC**	**5.00**
□	**132 Ivan Majesky, Flor. RC**	**5.00**
□	**133 Ray Schultz, NYIs. RC**	**5.00**
□	**134 Matt Henderson, Chic. RC**	**5.00**
□	**135 Tom Koivisto, SLou. RC**	**5.00**
□	**136 Ian MacNeil, Phil. RC**	**5.00**
□	**137 Eric Godard, NYIs. RC**	**5.00**
□	138 Dick Tarnström, Pitt.	5.00
□	**139 Jeff Paul, Colo. RC**	**5.00**
□	**140 Darren Haydar, Nash. RC**	**5.00**
□	**141 Levente Szuper (G), Calg. RC**	**5.00**
□	**142 Dennis Seidenberg, Phil. RC**	**5.00**
□	**143 Tim Thomas (G), Bost. RC**	**5.00**
□	**144 Fernando Pisani, Edmo. RC**	**5.00**
□	**145 Alex Henry, Wash. RC**	**5.00**
□	**146 Craig Andersson (G), Chic. RC**	**5.00**
□	**147 Kari Haakana, Edmo. RC**	**5.00**
□	**148 Jared Aulin, LosA. RC**	**5.00**
□	**149 Adam Hall, Nash. RC**	**5.00**
□	**150 Carlo Colaiacovo, Toro. RC**	**5.00**
□	**151 Martin Gerber (G), Anah. RC**	**5.00**
□	**152 Jamie Hodson (G), Toro. RC**	**5.00**
□	**153 Ray Emery (G), Otta. RC**	**5.00**
□	**154 Ari Ahonen (G), NJer. RC**	**5.00**
□	**155 Michael Leighton (G), Chic. RC**	**5.00**
□	**156 Kris Vernarsky, Bost. RC**	**5.00**
	Insert (*1250)	**R1250**
□	**157 Jim Vandermeer, Phil. RC**	**5.00**
□	**158 Chuck Kobasew, Calg. RC**	**10.00**
□	**159 Ron Hainsey, Mont. RC**	**5.00**
□	**160 Pierre-Marc Bouchard, MinW. RC**	**15.00**
□	**161 Alexander Frolov, LosA. RC**	**15.00**
□	**162 Henrik Zetterberg, Detr. RC**	**30.00**
□	**163 Alexander Svitov, Tamp. RC**	**10.00**
□	**164 Mike Cammalleri, LosA. RC**	**10.00**
□	**165 Ryan Miller (G), Buff. RC**	**15.00**
□	**166 Anton Volchenkov, Otta. RC**	**5.00**
□	**167 Brooks Orpik, Pitt. RC**	**5.00**
□	**168 Ales Hemsky, Edmo. RC**	**15.00**
□	**169 Stanislav Chistov, Anah. RC**	**15.00**
□	**170 Shaone Morrisonn, Bost. RC**	**5.00**
□	**171 Jason Spezza, Otta. RC**	**20.00**
□	**172 Jay Bouwmeester, Flor. RC**	**15.00**
□	**173 Jordan Leopold, Calg. RC**	**5.00**
□	**174 Jeff Taffe, Phoe. RC**	**5.00**
□	**175 Pascal Leclaire (G), Colu. RC**	**15.00**
□	**176 Scottie Upshall, Nash. RC**	**10.00**
□	**177 Alexei Smirnov, Anah. RC**	**5.00**
□	**178 Rick Nash, Colu. RC**	**30.00**
□	**179 Mikael Tellqvist (G), Toro. RC**	**5.00**
□	**180 Steve Eminger, Wash. RC**	**5.00**

CAREER WINS

Insert Set (17 cards):		**300.00**
	Insert	**CW**
□	Ed Belfour (G), Toro. ✂ {*364}	25.00
□	Martin Brodeur (G), NJer. ✂ {*324}	40.00
□	Sean Burke (G), Phoe. ✂ {*281}	15.00
□	Byron Dafoe (G), Atla. ✂ {*162}	15.00
□	Mike Dunham (G), NYRa. ✂ {*92}	10.00
□	Curtis Joseph (G), Detr. ✂ {*346}	25.00
□	Olaf Kölzig (G), Wash. ✂ {*182}	20.00
□	Andy Moog (G), Bost. ✂ {*372}	10.00
□	Chris Osgood (G), NYIs. ✂ {*253}	15.00
□	Félix Potvin (G), LosA. ✂ {*237}	15.00
□	Mike Richter (G), NYRa. ✂ {*296}	10.00
□	Patrick Roy (G), Mont. ✂ {*232}	75.00
□	Patrick Roy (G), Colo. ✂ {*289}	65.00
□	Tommy Salo (G), Edmo. ✂ {*168}	15.00
□	Jocelyn Thibault (G), Chic. ✂ {*196}	15.00
□	Ron Tugnutt (G), Dall. ✂ {*168}	15.00
□	Roman Turek (G), Calg. ✂ {*126}	20.00

GREAT GLOVES

Photo Photo-need

Insert Set (18 cards):		**175.00**
	Insert (1:60)	**GG**
□	Ed Belfour (G), Toro. ✂	15.00
□	Martin Biron (G), Buff. ✂	10.00
□	Dan Blackburn (G), NYRa. ✂	10.00
□	Brian Boucher (G), Phoe. ✂	10.00
□	Martin Brodeur (G), NJer. ✂	20.00
□	Roman Cechmanek (G), Phil. ✂	10.00
□	Marc Denis (G), Colu. ✂	10.00
□	Mike Dunham (G), Nash. ✂	10.00
□	Jean-Sébastien Giguère (G), Anah. ✂	15.00
□	Curtis Joseph (G), Detr. ✂	15.00
□	Olaf Kölzig (G), Wash. ✂ {*}	20.00
□	Roberto Luongo (G), Flor. ✂	10.00
□	Félix Potvin (G), LosA. ✂	10.00
□	Mike Richter (G), NYRa. ✂	10.00
□	Patrick Roy (G), Colo. ✂	35.00
□	José Théodore (G), Mont. ✂	15.00
□	Marty Turco (G), Dall. ✂	10.00
□	Roman Turek (G), Calg. ✂	10.00

INSTANT OFFENSE

Insert Set (25 cards):		**650.00**
	Insert (*250)	**IO250**
□	Jason Allison, LosA. ✂	20.00
□	Pavel Bure, NYRa. ✂	25.00
□	Éric Dazé, Chic. ✂	15.00
□	Chris Drury, Colo. ✂	20.00
□	Patrik Elias, NJer. ✂	25.00
□	Peter Forsberg, Colo. ✂	45.00
□	Simon Gagné, Phil. ✂	25.00
□	Jarome Iginla, Calg. ✂	25.00
□	Jaromir Jagr, Wash. ✂	30.00
□	Paul Kariya, Anah. ✂	45.00
□	Saku Koivu, Mont. ✂	25.00
□	Mario Lemieux, Pitt. ✂	100.00
□	Eric Lindros, NYRa. ✂	30.00
□	Mike Modano, Dall. ✂	30.00
□	Markus Näslund, Vanc. ✂	30.00
□	Zigmund Palffy, LosA. ✂	20.00
□	Jeremy Roenick, Phil. ✂	25.00
□	Joe Sakic, Colo. ✂	50.00
□	Sergei Samsonov, Bost. ✂	20.00
□	Miroslav Satan, Buff. ✂	15.00
□	Brendan Shanahan, Detr. ✂	30.00
□	Mats Sundin, Toro. ✂	30.00
□	Joe Thornton, Bost. ✂	40.00
□	Alexei Yashin, NYIs. ✂	20.00
□	Steve Yzerman, Detr. ✂	80.00

MASKED MARVELS

Insert Set (17 cards):		**175.00**
	Insert (1:60)	**MM**
□	Martin Biron (G), Buff. ✂	10.00
□	Martin Brodeur (G), NJer. ✂	20.00
□	Roman Cechmanek (G), Phil. ✂	10.00
□	Mike Dunham (G), Nash. ✂	10.00
□	Jean-Sébastien Giguère (G), Anah. ✂	15.00
□	Johan Hedberg (G), Pitt. ✂	10.00
□	Olaf Kölzig (G), Wash. ✂ {*}	15.00
□	Roberto Luongo (G), Flor. ✂	10.00
□	Ryan Miller (G), Buff. ✂	10.00
□	Chris Osgood (G), NYIs. ✂	10.00
□	Félix Potvin (G), LosA. ✂	10.00
□	Mike Richter (G), NYRa. ✂	10.00
□	Patrick Roy (G), Colo. ✂	35.00
□	José Théodore (G), Mont. ✂ {*}	20.00
□	Jocelyn Thibault (G), Chic. ✂	10.00
□	Marty Turco (G), Dall. ✂	10.00
□	Roman Turek (G), Calg. ✂	10.00

MEN BEHIND THE MASK

Insert Set (18 cards):		**175.00**
	Insert (1:60)	**MBM**
□	Ed Belfour (G), Toro. ✂	15.00
□	Martin Biron (G), Buff. ✂	10.00

□	Martin Brodeur (G), NJer. ✄	20.00
□	Roman Cechmanek (G), Phil. ✄	10.00
□	Marc Denis (G), Colu. ✄	10.00
□	Rick DiPietro (G), NYIs. ✄	10.00
□	Mike Dunham (G), Nash. ✄	10.00
□	Jean-Sébastien Giguère (G), Anah. ✄	15.00
□	Johan Hedberg (G), Pitt. ✄	10.00
□	Brent Johnson (G), SLou. ✄	10.00
□	Curtis Joseph (G), Detr. ✄	15.00
□	Olaf Kölzig (G), Wash. ✄	10.00
□	Andy Moog (G), Bost. ✄ {*}	15.00
□	Mika Noronen (G), Buff. ✄	10.00
□	Félix Potvin (G), LosA. ✄	10.00
□	Patrick Roy (G), Colo. ✄	35.00
□	José Théodore (G), Mont. ✄	15.00
□	Marty Turco (G), Dall. ✄	10.00

NATION'S BEST

Insert Set (18 cards):		375.00
	Insert (1:280)	**NB**
□	Ed Belfour (G), Toro. ✄	30.00
□	Martin Biron (G), Buff. ✄	20.00
□	Dan Blackburn (G), NYRa. ✄	20.00
□	Brian Boucher (G), Phoe. ✄	20.00
□	Martin Brodeur (G), NJer. ✄	50.00
□	Sean Burke (G), Detr. ✄	20.00
□	Rick DiPietro (G), NYIs. ✄	20.00
□	Mike Dunham (G), NYRa. ✄	20.00
□	Brent Johnson (G), SLou. ✄	20.00
□	Curtis Joseph (G), Detr. ✄	30.00
□	Roberto Luongo (G), Flor. ✄	25.00
□	Ryan Miller (G), Buff. ✄	20.00
□	Chris Osgood (G), NYIs. ✄	20.00
□	Félix Potvin (G), LosA. ✄	20.00
□	Mike Richter (G), NYRa. ✄	20.00
□	Patrick Roy (G), Colo. ✄	75.00
□	José Théodore (G), Mont. ✄	35.00
□	Marty Turco (G), Detr. ✄	20.00

PATCH CARD

Insert Set (42 cards):		3000.00
	Insert	**Patch**
□	Jason Allison, LosA. ✄ {*19}	75.00
□	Peter Bondra, Wash. ✄ {*39}	50.00
□	Daniel Brière, Phoe. ✄ {*32}	50.00
□	Éric Dazé, Chic. ✄ {*37}	25.00
□	Patrik Elias, NJer. ✄ {*29}	75.00
□	Sergei Fedorov, Detr. ✄ {*30}	100.00
□	Simon Gagné, Phil. ✄ {*33}	75.00
□	Jarome Iginla, Calg. ✄ {*52}	75.00
□	Jaromir Jagr, Wash. ✄ {*31}	100.00
□	Paul Kariya, Anah. ✄ {*32}	150.00
□	Ilya Kovalchuk, Atla. ✄ {*29}	100.00
□	Eric Lindros, NYRa. ✄ {*37}	100.00
□	Mike Modano, Dall. ✄ {*34}	100.00
□	Glen Murray, Bost. ✄ {*41}	50.00
□	Markus Näslund, Vanc. ✄ {*40}	100.00
□	Zigmund Palffy, LosA. ✄ {*31}	50.00
□	Joe Sakic, Colo. ✄ {*26}	200.00
□	Brendan Shanahan, Detr. ✄ {*37}	100.00
□	Mats Sundin, Toro. ✄ {*41}	100.00
□	Steve Yzerman, Detr. ✄ {*13}	375.00
□	Ed Belfour (G), Toro. ✄ {*21}	125.00
□	Martin Biron (G), Buff. ✄ {*31}	50.00
□	Dan Blackburn (G), NYRa. ✄ {*12}	50.00
□	Martin Brodeur (G), NJer. ✄ {*38}	150.00
□	Sean Burke (G), Phoe. ✄ {*33}	50.00
□	Roman Cechmanek (G), Phil. ✄ {*24}	50.00
□	Mike Dunham (G), Nash. ✄ {*23}	50.00
□	Jean-Sébastien Giguère (G), Anah. ✄ {*20}	125.00
□	Johan Hedberg (G), Pitt. ✄ {*25}	50.00
□	Brent Johnson (G), SLou. ✄ {*34}	25.00
□	Curtis Joseph (G), Detr. ✄ {*29}	100.00
□	Olaf Kölzig (G), Wash. ✄ {*31}	50.00
□	Roberto Luongo (G), Flor. ✄ {*16}	100.00
□	Chris Osgood (G), NYIs. ✄ {*31}	50.00
□	Félix Potvin (G), LosA. ✄ {*31}	50.00
□	Mike Richter (G), NYRa. ✄ {*24}	50.00
□	Patrick Roy (G), Colo. ✄ {*32}	275.00
□	Tommy Salo (G), Edmo. ✄ {*30}	25.00
□	José Théodore (G), Mont. ✄ {*31}	125.00
□	Jocelyn Thibault (G), Chic. ✄ {*32}	25.00
□	Marty Turco (G), Dall. ✄ {*15}	75.00
□	Roman Turek (G), Calg. ✄ {*30}	50.00

SUPER STOPPERS

Insert Set (15 cards):		100.00
	Insert (1:60)	**SS**
□	Martin Brodeur (G), NJer. ✄	20.00
□	Roman Cechmanek (G), Phil. ✄	10.00
□	Curtis Joseph (G), Detr. ✄	15.00
□	Olaf Kölzig (G), Wash. ✄	10.00
□	Chris Osgood (G), NYIs. ✄	10.00
□	Patrick Roy (G), Colo. ✄	35.00
□	José Théodore (G), Mont. ✄	15.00
□	Roman Turek (G), Calg. ✄	10.00

VIEW FROM THE CAGE

Insert Set (17 cards):		250.00
	Insert (1:140)	**VC**
□	Ed Belfour (G), Toro. ✄	20.00
□	Martin Biron (G), Buff. ✄	15.00
□	Martin Brodeur (G), NJer. ✄	35.00
□	Sean Burke (G), Phoe. ✄	15.00
□	Roman Cechmanek (G), Phil. ✄	15.00
□	Jean-Sébastien Giguère (G), Anah. ✄	20.00
□	Johan Hedberg (G), Pitt. ✄	15.00
□	Curtis Joseph (G), Detr. ✄	20.00
□	Olaf Kölzig (G), Wash. ✄	15.00
□	Roberto Luongo (G), Flor. ✄	15.00
□	Mike Richter (G), NYRa. ✄	15.00
□	Patrick Roy (G), Colo. ✄	50.00
□	Tommy Salo (G), Edmo. ✄	15.00
□	José Théodore (G), Mont. ✄	25.00
□	Jocelyn Thibault (G), Chic. ✄	15.00
□	Marty Turco (G), Dall. ✄	15.00
□	Roman Turek (G), Calg. ✄	15.00

REPLICA MASK

Insert Set (18 masks):		
	Replica Mask	**Mask**
□	Ed Belfour (G), Toro.	
□	Martin Brodeur (G), NJer.	
□	Gerry Cheevers (G), Bost.	
□	Tony Esposito (G), Chic.	
□	Grant Fuhr (G), SLou.	
□	Grant Fuhr (G), Buff.	
□	Johan Hedberg (G), Pitt.	
□	Curtis Joseph (G), Detr.	
□	Nikolai Khabibulin (G), Tamp.	
□	Andy Moog (G), Bost.	
□	Evgeni Nabokov (G), SanJ.	
□	Jacques Plante (G), Mont.	
□	Jacques Plante (G), Mont.	
□	Félix Potvin (G), LosA.	
□	Chico Resch (G), NYIs.	
□	Patrick Roy (G), Colo.	
□	Terry Sawchuk (G), Detr.	
□	José Théodore (G), Mont.	

REPLICA MASK SIGNED

Insert Set (11 cards):		
	Replica Mask	**Mask**
□	Ed Belfour (G), Toro. ✍	
□	Martin Brodeur (G), NJer. ✍	
□	Gerry Cheevers (G), Bost. ✍	
□	Tony Esposito (G), Chic. ✍	
□	Grant Fuhr (G), SLou. ✍	
□	Grant Fuhr (G), Buff. ✍	
□	Curtis Joseph (G), Detr. ✍	
□	Nikolai Khabibulin (G), Tamp. ✍	
□	Evgeni Nabokov (G), SanJ. ✍	
□	Patrick Roy (G), Colo. ✍	
□	José Théodore (G), Mont. ✍	

2002 - 03 UPPER DECK MVP

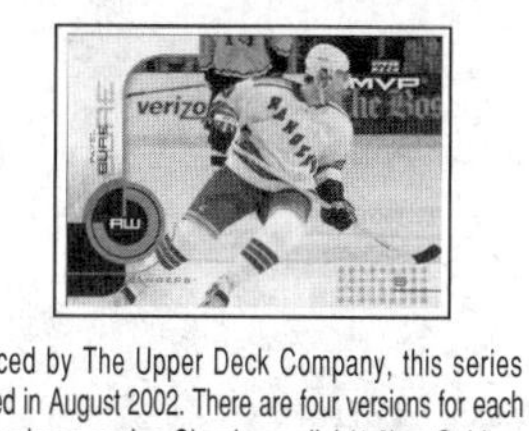

Produced by The Upper Deck Company, this series was released in August 2002. There are four versions for each card 1-220: a base card, a Classic parallel (1:2), a Gold parallel (#/100), and a Golden Classic (#/50).

Complete Set (220 cards):

	GC50	G100	C	Base
Common Player:	**6**	**4**	**.50**	**.20**
Description	**GC50**	**G100**	**C**	**Base**
□□□□ 1 Mike Leclerc	6	4	.50	.20
□□□□ 2 J-S Giguère (G)	20	15	2.00	.50
□□□□ 3 Matt Cullen	6	4	.50	.20
□□□□ 4 Andy McDonald	6	4	.50	.20
□□□□ 5 Jason York	6	4	.50	.20
□□□□ 6 Paul Kariya	30	20	2.50	1.00
□□□□ 7 Frantisek Kaberle	6	4	.50	.20
□□□□ 8 Dany Heatley	30	20	4.00	.50
□□□□ 9 Pasi Nurminen (G)	6	4	.50	.20
□□□□ 10 Ilya Kovalchuk	30	20	4.00	.50
□□□□ 11 Patrik Stefan	6	4	.50	.20
□□□□ 12 Pascal Rhéaume	6	4	.50	.20
□□□□ 13 Sergei Samsonov	10	5	1.00	.20
□□□□ 14 Joe Thornton	25	15	2.00	.50
□□□□ 15 Brian Rolston	6	4	.50	.20
□□□□ 16 Martin Lapointe	6	5	.50	.20
□□□□ 17 Nick Boynton	6	4	.50	.20
□□□□ 18 Jozef Stümpel	6	4	.50	.20
□□□□ 19 Stu Barnes	6	4	.50	.20
□□□□ 20 Jean-Pierre Dumont	6	4	.50	.20
□□□□ 21 Miroslav Satan	6	4	.50	.20
□□□□ 22 Tim Connolly	6	5	.50	.20
□□□□ 23 Maxim Afinogenov	6	5	.50	.20
□□□□ 24 Martin Biron (G)	10	5	.50	.20
□□□□ 25 Craig Conroy	6	4	.50	.20
□□□□ 26 Roman Turek (G)	10	5	.50	.20
□□□□ 27 Derek Morris	6	4	.50	.20
□□□□ 28 Marc Savard	6	4	.50	.20
□□□□ 29 Jarome Iginla	15	10	1.50	.50
□□□□ 30 Igor Kravchuk	6	4	.50	.20
□□□□ 31 Sami Kapanen	6	4	.50	.20
□□□□ 32 Bates Battaglia	6	4	.50	.20
□□□□ 33 Ron Francis	10	5	1.00	.20
□□□□ 34 Erik Cole	6	5	.50	.20
□□□□ 35 Jeff O'Neill	6	5	.50	.20
□□□□ 36 Arturs Irbe (G)	6	5	.50	.20
□□□□ 37 Rod Brind'Amour	6	4	.50	.20
□□□□ 38 Alexei Zhamnov	6	4	.50	.20
□□□□ 39 Michael Nylander	6	4	.50	.20
□□□□ 40 Steve Sullivan	6	4	.50	.20
□□□□ 41 Jocelyn Thibault (G)	6	5	.50	.20
□□□□ 42 Kyle Calder	6	4	.50	.20
□□□□ 43 Éric Dazé	6	5	.50	.20
□□□□ 44 Patrick Roy (G)	65	45	6.00	2.00
□□□□ 45 Milan Hejduk	15	10	1.50	.50
□□□□ 46 Peter Forsberg	30	20	2.50	1.00
□□□□ 47 Rob Blake	10	5	1.00	.20
□□□□ 48 Chris Drury	10	5	1.00	.20
□□□□ 49 Joe Sakic	35	20	3.00	1.00
□□□□ 50 Steven Reinprecht	6	4	.50	.20
□□□□ 51 Brad Moran	6	4	.50	.20
□□□□ 52 Jaroslav Spacek	6	4	.50	.20
□□□□ 53 Marc Denis (G)	10	5	.50	.20
□□□□ 54 Ray Whitney	6	4	.50	.20
□□□□ 55 Rostislav Klesla	6	4	.50	.20
□□□□ 56 Espen Knutsen	6	4	.50	.20
□□□□ 57 Marty Turco (G)	10	5	1.00	.20
□□□□ 58 Jere Lehtinen	6	4	.50	.20
□□□□ 59 Mike Modano	20	15	2.00	.50
□□□□ 60 Derian Hatcher	6	4	.50	.20
□□□□ 61 Brenden Morrow	6	4	.50	.20
□□□□ 62 Jason Arnott	10	5	.50	.20
□□□□ 63 Dominik Hasek (G)	20	15	2.00	.50
□□□□ 64 Brendan Shanahan	20	15	2.00	.50
□□□□ 65 Curtis Joseph (G)	20	15	2.00	.50
□□□□ 66 Brett Hull	20	15	2.00	.50
□□□□ 67 Steve Yzerman	50	35	4.50	1.50
□□□□ 68 Nicklas Lidström	10	5	1.00	.20
□□□□ 69 Pavel Datsyuk	15	10	1.50	.50
□□□□ 70 Ryan Smyth	10	5	.50	.20
□□□□ 71 Anson Carter	6	5	.50	.20
□□□□ 72 Mike Comrie	15	10	1.50	.50
□□□□ 73 Tommy Salo (G)	6	5	.50	.20
□□□□ 74 Eric Brewer	6	5	.50	.20
□□□□ 75 Todd Marchant	6	4	.50	.20
□□□□ 76 Roberto Luongo (G)	15	10	1.50	.50
□□□□ 77 Kristian Huselius	6	4	.50	.20
□□□□ 78 Marcus Nilson	6	4	.50	.20
□□□□ 79 Viktor Kozlov	6	4	.50	.20
□□□□ 80 Sandis Ozolinsh	6	4	.50	.20
□□□□ 81 Valeri Bure	6	4	.50	.20
□□□□ 82 Jason Allison	10	5	1.00	.20
□□□□ 83 Zigmund Palffy	10	5	1.00	.20
□□□□ 84 Adam Deadmarsh	6	4	.50	.20
□□□□ 85 Félix Potvin (G)	25	15	1.00	.20
□□□□ 86 Mathieu Schneider	6	4	.50	.20
□□□□ 87 Bryan Smolinski	6	4	.50	.20
□□□□ 88 Jim Dowd	6	4	.50	.20
□□□□ 89 Marian Gaborik	20	15	2.00	.50
□□□□ 90 Manny Fernandez (G)	6	5	.50	.20
□□□□ 91 Andrew Brunette	6	4	.50	.20
□□□□ 92 Wes Walz	6	4	.50	.20
□□□□ 93 Antti Laaksonen	6	4	.50	.20
□□□□ 94 Yanic Perreault	6	4	.50	.20
□□□□ 95 Richard Zednik	6	5	.50	.20
□□□□ 96 José Théodore (G)	25	15	2.00	.50
□□□□ 97 Oleg Petrov	6	4	.50	.20
□□□□ 98 Donald Audette	6	5	.50	.20
□□□□ 99 Saku Koivu	25	15	1.50	.50
□□□□ 100 Kimmo Timonen	6	4	.50	.20
□□□□ 101 Stu Grimson	6	4	.50	.20
□□□□ 102 Denis (G) Arkhipov	6	4	.50	.20
□□□□ 103 Scott Hartnell	6	4	.50	.20
□□□□ 104 Mike Dunham (G)	6	5	.50	.20
□□□□ 105 Andy Delmore	6	4	.50	.20
□□□□ 106 Brian Rafalski	6	4	.50	.20
□□□□ 107 John Madden	6	4	.50	.20
□□□□ 108 Martin Brodeur (G)	35	20	3.00	1.00
□□□□ 109 Scott Stevens	6	5	.50	.20
□□□□ 110 Patrik Elias	15	10	1.50	.50
□□□□ 111 Scott Niedermayer	6	4	.50	.20
□□□□ 112 Joe Nieuwendyk	6	5	.50	.20
□□□□ 113 Mark Parrish	6	5	.50	.20
□□□□ 114 Michael Peca	6	5	.50	.20
□□□□ 115 Alexei Yashin	10	5	1.00	.20
□□□□ 116 Adrian Aucoin	6	4	.50	.20
□□□□ 117 Chris Osgood (G)	10	5	1.00	.20
□□□□ 118 Steve Webb	6	4	.50	.20
□□□□ 119 Eric Lindros	20	15	2.00	.50
□□□□ 120 Brian Leetch	10	5	1.00	.20
□□□□ 121 Tom Poti	6	4	.50	.20
□□□□ 122 Pavel Bure	15	10	1.50	.50
□□□□ 123 Petr Nedved	6	4	.50	.20
□□□□ 124 Dan Blackburn (G)	6	5	.50	.20
□□□□ 125 Daniel Alfredsson	25	5	1.00	.20
□□□□ 126 Patrick Lalime (G)	10	5	1.00	.20
□□□□ 127 Marian Hossa	20	15	2.00	.50
□□□□ 128 Martin Havlat	10	5	1.00	.20
□□□□ 129 Zdeno Chara	6	4	.50	.20
□□□□ 130 Radek Bonk	6	4	.50	.20
□□□□ 131 Wade Redden	6	4	.50	.20
□□□□ 132 Keith Primeau	6	5	.50	.20
□□□□ 133 John LeClair	15	10	1.50	.50
□□□□ 134 Mark Recchi	6	5	.50	.20
□□□□ 135 Éric Desjardins	6	4	.50	.20
□□□□ 136 Jeremy Roenick	15	10	1.50	.50
□□□□ 137 Justin Williams	6	4	.50	.20
□□□□ 138 Simon Gagné	15	10	1.50	.50
□□□□ 139 Tony Amonte	10	5	1.00	.20
□□□□ 140 Daniel Brière	10	5	.50	.20
□□□□ 141 Sean Burke (G)	10	5	1.00	.20
□□□□ 142 Ladislav Nagy	6	4	.50	.20
□□□□ 143 Shane Doan	6	4	.50	.20
□□□□ 144 Teppo Numminen	6	4	.50	.20
□□□□ 145 Alex Kovalev	10	5	1.00	.20
□□□□ 146 Johan Hedberg (G)	6	5	.50	.20
□□□□ 147 Jan Hrdina	6	4	.50	.20
□□□□ 148 Mario Lemieux	65	45	6.00	2.00
□□□□ 149 Martin Straka	6	4	.50	.20
□□□□ 150 Hans Jonsson	6	4	.50	.20
□□□□ 151 V. Damphousse	10	5	1.00	.20
□□□□ 152 Owen Nolan	10	5	1.00	.20
□□□□ 153 Adam Graves	6	5	.50	.20
□□□□ 154 Evgeni Nabokov (G)	10	5	1.00	.20
□□□□ 155 Mike Ricci	6	4	.50	.20
□□□□ 156 Patrick Marleau	10	5	.50	.20
□□□□ 157 Teemu Selänne	15	10	1.50	.50
□□□□ 158 Brent Johnson (G)	6	5	.50	.20
□□□□ 159 Doug Weight	10	5	1.00	.20
□□□□ 160 Keith Tkachuk	10	5	1.00	.20
□□□□ 161 Al MacInnis	6	5	.50	.20
□□□□ 162 Chris Pronger	10	5	1.00	.20
□□□□ 163 Pavol Demitra	6	5	.50	.20
□□□□ 164 Tyson Nash	6	4	.50	.20
□□□□ 165 Nikolai Khabibulin (G)	6	5	.50	.20
□□□□ 166 Vincent Lecavalier	20	15	2.00	.50
□□□□ 167 Martin St-Louis	10	5	.50	.20
□□□□ 168 Fredrik Modin	6	4	.50	.20
□□□□ 169 Brad Richards	10	5	.50	.20
□□□□ 170 Shane Willis	6	4	.50	.20
□□□□ 171 Alyn McCauley	6	4	.50	.20
□□□□ 172 Gary Roberts	6	5	.50	.20
□□□□ 173 Darcy Tucker	6	4	.50	.20
□□□□ 174 Ed Belfour (G)	20	15	2.00	.50
□□□□ 175 Mats Sundin	20	15	2.00	.50
□□□□ 176 A. Mogilny	10	5	.50	.20
□□□□ 177 Todd Bertuzzi	25	15	2.00	.50
□□□□ 178 Brendan Morrison	6	4	.50	.20
□□□□ 179 Markus Näslund	20	15	2.00	.50
□□□□ 180 Dan Cloutier (G)	6	5	.50	.20
□□□□ 181 Daniel Sedin	6	5	.50	.20
□□□□ 182 Henrik Sedin	6	5	.50	.20
□□□□ 183 Sergei Gonchar	6	4	.50	.20
□□□□ 184 Jaromir Jagr	20	15	2.00	.50
□□□□ 185 Peter Bondra	10	5	1.00	.20
□□□□ 186 Olaf Kölzig (G)	10	5	1.00	.20
□□□□ 187 Robert Lang	6	4	.50	.20
□□□□ 188 S. Konowalchuk	6	4	.50	.20
□□□□ 189 Steve Yzerman	25	15	1.50	1.00
□□□□ 190 Patrick Roy (G)	30	20	1.50	1.50
□□□□ 191 Mark Hartigan	6	4	.50	.20
□□□□ 192 Mike Weaver	6	4	.50	.20
□□□□ 193 Frédéric Cassivi	6	4	.50	.20
□□□□ 194 Andy Hilbert	6	5	1.00	.20
□□□□ 195 Chris Kelleher	6	4	.50	.20
□□□□ 196 Henrik Tallinder	6	4	.50	.20
□□□□ **197 Micki DuPont RC**	**10**	**4**	**1.00**	**.50**
□□□□ 198 Tyler Arnason	10	5	2.00	.50

199 Riku Hahl	6	4	.50	.20
200 Andrej Nedorost	6	4	.50	.20
201 Sean Avery	6	4	.50	.20
202 Stephen Weiss	10	5	2.00	.50
203 Lukas Krajicek	6	5	1.00	.20
204 Kyle Rossiter	6	4	.50	.20
205 Éric Beaudoin	6	4	.50	.20
206 Tony Virta	6	4	.50	.20
207 Marcel Hossa	10	5	2.00	.50
208 Jan Lasak (G)	6	5	1.00	.20
209 Trent Hunter	6	4	.50	.20
210 Ray Schultz RC	**6**	**4**	**.50**	**.20**
211 Martin Prusek (G)	10	5	1.50	.50
212 Chris Bala	6	4	.50	.20
213 Neil Little (G)	6	4	.50	.20
214 Guillaume Lefebvre	6	4	.50	.20
215 Hannes Hyvonen	6	4	.50	.20
216 Gaétan Roy (G)er	6	4	.50	.20
217 Martin Cibak	6	4	.50	.20
218 S. Centomo (G)	6	5	1.00	.20
219 Karel Pilar	6	4	.50	.20
220 S. Charpentier (G)	6	4	.50	.20

BLOW-UP

Insert Set	.00
Insert	Big
26 Roman Turek (G), Calg.	
127 Marian Hossa, Otta.	

HIGHLIGHT NIGHTS

Insert Set (7 cards):	15.00
Insert (1:18)	HN
HN1 Ilya Kovalchuk, Atla.	3.00
HN2 Joe Thornton, Bost.	3.00
HN3 Jarome Iginla, Calg.	2.00
HN4 Brendan Shanahan, Detr.	2.00
HN5 Eric Lindros, NYRa.	2.00
HN6 Mario Lemieux, Pitt.	7.00
HN7 Markus Näslund, Vanc.	2.00

MASKED MEN

Insert Set (7 cards):	15.00
Insert (1:18)	MM
MM1 Patrick Roy (G), Colo.	7.00
MM2 Dominik Hasek (G), Detr.	2.00
MM3 José Théodore (G), Mont.	3.00
MM4 Martin Brodeur (G), NJer.	4.00
MM5 Mike Richter (G), NYRa.	2.00
MM6 Sean Burke (G), Phoe.	2.00
MM7 Olaf Kölzig (G), Wash.	2.00

SHIFTING TO OVERDRIVE

Insert Set (14 cards):	20.00
Insert (1:9)	SO
SO1 Paul Kariya, Anah.	3.00
SO2 Ilya Kovalchuk, Atla.	3.00
SO3 Jarome Iginla, Calg.	2.00
SO4 Sami Kapanen, Caro.	2.00
SO5 Chris Drury, Colo.	2.00
SO6 Peter Forsberg, Colo.	3.00
SO7 Mike Modano, Dall.	2.00
SO8 Sergei Fedorov, Detr.	2.00
SO9 Sandis Ozolinsh, Flor.	2.00
SO10 Marian Hossa, Otta.	2.00
SO11 Simon Gagné, Phil.	2.00
SO12 Alex Kovalev, Pitt.	2.00
SO13 Markus Näslund, Vanc.	2.00
SO14 Peter Bondra, Wash.	2.00

VITAL FORCES

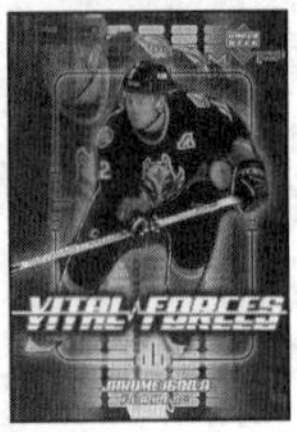

Insert Set (14 cards):	35.00
Insert (1:9)	VF
VF1 Paul Kariya, Anah.	3.00
VF2 Ilya Kovalchuk, Atla.	3.00
VF3 Joe Thornton, Bost.	3.00
VF4 Jarome Iginla, Calg.	2.00
VF5 Patrick Roy (G), Colo.	7.00
VF6 Joe Sakic, Colo.	4.00
VF7 Mike Modano, Dall.	2.00
VF8 Dominik Hasek (G), Detr.	2.00
VF9 Steve Yzerman, Detr.	6.00
VF10 Eric Lindros, NYRa.	2.00
VF11 Jeremy Roenick, Phil.	2.00
VF12 Mario Lemieux, Pitt.	7.00
VF13 Teemu Selänne, SanJ.	2.00
VF14 Jaromir Jagr, Wash.	2.00

PROSIGN

Insert Set (15 cards):	960.00
Insert (1:144)	PrSig
Raymond Bourque, Bost. ✍	85.00
Pavel Bure, NYRa. ✍ {*145}	40.00
Manny Fernandez (G), MinW. ✍	20.00
Wayne Gretzky, NYRa. ✍	250.00
Dany Heatley, Atla. ✍	50.00
Gordie Howe, Detr. ✍	180.00
Kristian Huselius, Flor. ✍	15.00
Curtis Joseph (G), Toro. ✍	50.00
Bobby Orr, Bost. ✍	240.00
Maxime Ouellet, Wash. ✍	20.00
Patrick Roy (G), Colo. ✍ {*48}	150.00
Tommy Salo (G), Edmo. ✍	20.00
Daniel Sedin, Vanc. ✍	20.00
Henrik Sedin, Vanc. ✍	20.00
Teemu Selänne, SanJ. ✍	40.00

SKATE AROUND

Insert Set (15 cards):	255.00
Insert (1:72)	SA
Adam Deadmarsh, LosA.	15.00
Chris Drury, Colo.	15.00
Peter Forsberg, Colo.	25.00
Jarome Iginla, Calg.	15.00
Paul Kariya, Anah.	25.00
Espen Knutsen, Colu.	15.00
Olaf Kölzig (G), Wash.	15.00
John LeClair, Phil.	15.00
Eric Lindros, NYRa.	20.00
Mike Modano, Dall.	20.00
Félix Potvin (G), LosA.	15.00
Keith Primeau, Phil.	15.00
Patrick Roy (G), Colo.	60.00
Joe Sakic, Colo.	30.00
Joe Thornton, Bost.	20.00

SKATE AROUND DOUBLE

Insert Set (30 cards):	825.00
Insert (#/100	SAD
Rob Blake / Rostislav Klesla	30.00
Rod Brind'Amour / Joe Nieuwendyk	20.00
Ed Belfour (G) / Félix Potvin (G)	55.00
Roman Cechmanek (G) / Brian Boucher (G)	20.00
Jean-Pierre Dumont / Martin Biron (G)	20.00
Chris Drury / Simon Gagné	35.00
Chris Drury / Milan Hejduk	35.00
Adam Deadmarsh / John LeClair	25.00
Peter Forsberg / Eric Lindros	60.00
Milan Hejduk / Zigmund Palffy	35.00
Dan Hinote / Steven Reinprecht	20.00
Jaromir Jagr / Mark Messier	50.00
Olaf Kölzig (G) / Roman Cechmanek (G)	25.00
Alex Kovalev / Mark Recchi	25.00
John LeClair / Roman Cechmanek (G)	30.00
Eric Lindros / Theoren Fleury	40.00
John LeClair / Keith Primeau	30.00
Mike Modano / Teemu Selänne	45.00
Mike Modano / Marty Turco (G)	40.00
Joe Nieuwendyk / Eric Lindros	35.00
Félix Potvin (G) / Chris Osgood (G)	45.00
Zigmund Palffy / Félix Potvin (G)	30.00
Patrick Roy (G) / David Aebischer (G)	80.00
Mark Recchi / Simon Gagné	30.00
Joe Sakic / Chris Drury	55.00
Alex Tanguay / Rob Blake	30.00
Marty Turco (G) / Ed Belfour (G)	40.00
Ron Tugnutt (G) / Marc Denis (G)	20.00
Justin Williams / Ruslan Fedotenko	20.00
Justin Williams / Simon Gagné	25.00

SKATE AROUND TRIPLE

Insert Set (12 cards):	560.00
Insert (1:288)	SAT
Adam Deadmarsh / Jason Allison / Zigmund Palffy	40.00
J-P Dumont / Miroslav Satan / Martin Biron (G)	40.00
Alex Kovalev / Theoren Fleury / Miroslav Satan	40.00
Eric Lindros / Joe Nieuwendyk / Joe Thornton	65.00
John LeClair / Keith Primeau / Mark Recchi	40.00
Mark Messier / Mike Modano / Joe Thornton	80.00
Joe Sakic / Peter Forsberg / Patrick Roy (G)	120.00
Teemu Selänne / Milan Hejduk / Zigmund Palffy	55.00
Teemu Selänne / Mike Modano / Jaromir Jagr	70.00
Joe Thornton / Chris Drury / Simon Gagné	65.00
Alex Tanguay / Chris Drury / Milan Hejduk	50.00
Ray Whitney / Rostislav Klesla / Ron Tugnutt (G)	40.00

MVP SOUVENIRS

Insert Set (27 cards):	325.00
Insert (1:48)	Souv.
Ed Belfour (G), Dall.	20.00
Martin Biron (G), Buff.	15.00
Rob Blake, Colo.	15.00
Brian Boucher (G), Phil.	15.00
Rod Brind'Amour, Caro.	15.00
Roman Cechmanek (G), Phil.	15.00
Marc Denis (G), Colu.	15.00
Mike Dunham (G), Nash.	15.00
Theoren Fleury, NYRa.	15.00
Simon Gagné, Phil.	15.00
Dan Hinote, Colo.	15.00
Jaromir Jagr, 2000 All-Star	20.00
Rostislav Klesla, Colu.	15.00
Alex Kovalev, Pitt.	15.00
Mark Messier, 2000 All-Star	20.00
Mike Modano, 2000 All-Star	20.00
Ville Nieminen, Pitt.	15.00
Joe Nieuwendyk, NJer.	15.00
Chris Osgood (G), NYIs.	15.00
Zigmund Palffy, LosA.	15.00
Mark Recchi, Phil.	15.00
Miroslav Satan, Buff.	15.00
Teemu Selänne, 2000 All-Star	15.00
Alex Tanguay, Colo.	15.00
Ron Tugnutt (G), Colu.	15.00
Marty Turco (G), Dall.	15.00
Justin Williams, Phil.	15.00

2002 - 03 UPPER DECK PIECE OF HISTORY

Produced by The Upper Deck Company, this series was released in November 2002.

Shell Set (100 cards):	40.00
Complete Set (150 cards):	400.00
Common Player:	.35
Description	Base
1 Paul Kariya, Anah.	1.50
2 Jean-Sébastien Giguère (G), Anah.	1.00
3 Ilya Kovalchuk, Atla.	1.00
4 Dany Heatley, Atla.	1.00
5 Joe Thornton, Bost.	1.50
6 Sergei Samsonov, Bost.	.50
7 Glen Murray, Bost.	.50
8 Miroslav Satan, Buff.	.35
9 Tim Connolly, Buff.	.50
10 Martin Biron (G), Buff.	.50
11 Jeff O'Neill, Caro.	.50
12 Erik Cole, Caro.	.35
13 Ron Francis, Caro.	.50
14 Arturs Irbe (G), Caro.	.50
15 Roman Turek (G), Calg.	.50
16 Marc Savard, Calg.	.35
17 Jarome Iginla, Calg.	1.00
18 Éric Dazé, Chic.	.50
19 Steve Sullivan, Chic.	.35
20 Jocelyn Thibault (G), Chic.	.50
21 Espen Knutsen, Colu.	.35
22 Rostislav Klesla, Colu.	.35
23 Marc Denis (G), Colu.	.50
24 Patrick Roy (G), Colo.	3.50
25 Chris Drury, Colo.	.50
26 Joe Sakic, Colo.	2.00
27 Peter Forsberg, Colo.	1.50
28 Alex Tanguay, Colo.	.50
29 Mike Modano, Dall.	1.00
30 Marty Turco (G), Dall.	.50
31 Jason Arnott, Dall.	.50
32 Steve Yzerman, Detr.	3.00
33 Sergei Fedorov, Detr.	1.00
34 Nicklas Lidström, Detr.	.50
35 Brett Hull, Detr.	1.00
36 Curtis Joseph (G), Detr.	1.00
37 Brendan Shanahan, Detr.	1.00
38 Mike Comrie, Edmo.	1.00
39 Tommy Salo (G), Edmo.	.50
40 Ryan Smyth, Edmo.	.50
41 Roberto Luongo (G), Flor.	1.00
42 Kristian Huselius, Flor.	.35
43 Jason Allison, LosA.	.50
44 Félix Potvin (G), LosA.	.50
45 Zigmund Palffy, LosA.	.50
46 Marian Gaborik, MinW.	1.00
47 Manny Fernandez (G), MinW.	.50
48 José Théodore (G), Mont.	1.50
49 Saku Koivu, Mont.	1.00
50 Patrik Elias, NJer.	1.00
51 Martin Brodeur (G), NJer.	2.00
52 Joe Nieuwendyk, NJer.	.50
53 Scott Hartnell, Nash.	.35
54 Mike Dunham (G), Nash.	.50
55 Alexei Yashin, NYIs.	.50
56 Chris Osgood (G), NYIs.	.50
57 Michael Peca, NYIs.	.50
58 Eric Lindros, NYRa.	1.00
59 Mike Richter (G), NYRa.	.50
60 Pavel Bure, NYRa.	1.00
61 Brian Leetch, NYRa.	.50
62 Patrick Lalime (G), Otta.	.50
63 Marian Hossa, Otta.	1.00
64 Daniel Alfredsson, Otta.	.50
65 Jeremy Roenick, Phil.	1.00
66 Simon Gagné, Phil.	1.00
67 Roman Cechmanek (G), Phil.	.50
68 Sean Burke (G), Phoe.	.50
69 Daniel Brière, Phoe.	.50
70 Tony Amonte, Phoe.	.50
71 Alex Kovalev, Pitt.	.50
72 Mario Lemieux, Pitt.	3.50
73 Johan Hedberg (G), Pitt.	.50
74 Patrick Marleau, SanJ.	.50
75 Owen Nolan, SanJ.	.50
76 Evgeni Nabokov (G), SanJ.	.50
77 Keith Tkachuk, SLou.	.50
78 Chris Pronger, SLou.	.50
79 Brent Johnson (G), SLou.	.50
80 Nikolai Khabibulin (G), Tamp.	.50
81 Vincent Lecavalier, Tamp.	1.00
82 Alexander Mogilny, Toro.	.50
83 Mats Sundin, Toro.	1.00
84 Ed Belfour (G), Toro.	1.00
85 Todd Bertuzzi, Vanc.	1.50
86 Dan Cloutier (G), Vanc.	.50
87 Markus Näslund, Vanc.	1.00
88 Olaf Kölzig (G), Wash.	.50
89 Peter Bondra, Wash.	.50
90 Jaromir Jagr, Wash.	1.00

SUBSET

Insert (*2999)	S2999
91 Wayne Gretzky, Edmo.	10.00
92 Wayne Gretzky, NYRa.	10.00

☐	93 Mario Lemieux, Pitt.	7.00
☐	94 Patrick Roy (G), Colo.	7.00
☐	95 Steve Yzerman, Detr.	6.00
☐	96 Gordie Howe, Hart.	7.00
☐	97 Bobby Orr, Bost.	10.00
☐	98 Raymond Bourque, Colo.	3.00
☐	99 Brett Hull, SLou.	2.00
☐	100 Teemu Selänne, Winn.	2.00
☐	101 Martin Brodeur (G), NJer.	4.00
☐	102 Jaromir Jagr, Pitt.	2.00
☐	103 Eric Lindros, NYRa.	2.00
☐	104 Joe Sakic, Colo.	4.00
☐	105 Mike Richter (G), NYRa.	2.00
☐	106 Sergei Fedorov, Detr.	2.00
☐	107 Peter Forsberg, Québ.	3.00
☐	108 Mark Messier, NYRa.	2.00
☐	109 Wayne Gretzky, Edmo.	10.00
☐	110 Wayne Gretzky, LosA.	10.00
☐	111 Wayne Gretzky, NYRa.	10.00
☐	112 Gordie Howe, Detr.	7.00
☐	113 Gordie Howe, Houston	7.00
☐	114 Gordie Howe, Hart.	7.00
☐	115 Bobby Orr, Bost.	10.00
☐	116 Bobby Orr, Bost.	10.00
☐	117 Bobby Orr, Bost.	10.00
☐	118 Raymond Bourque, Bost.	3.00
☐	119 Raymond Bourque, AS'96	3.00
☐	120 Raymond Bourque, Colo.	3.00

HISTORY IN THE MAKING

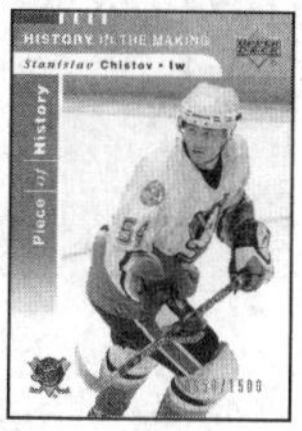

	Insert (#/1500)	**HM1500**
☐	**121 Stanislav Chistov, Anah. RC**	**18.00**
☐	**122 Alexei Smirnov, Anah. RC**	**9.00**
☐	123 Henrik Tallinder, Buff.	2.00
☐	**124 Micki Dupont, Calg. RC**	**6.00**
☐	**125 Chuck Kobasew, Calg. RC**	**12.00**
☐	126 Andrej Nedorost, Colu.	2.00
☐	**127 Rick Nash, Colu. RC**	**30.00**
☐	**128 Henrik Zetterberg, Detr. RC**	**30.00**
☐	**129 Ales Hemsky, Edmo. RC**	**18.00**
☐	130 Jani Rita, Edmo.	3.00
☐	131 Stephen Weiss, Flor.	4.00
☐	**132 Jay Bouwmeester, Flor. RC**	**18.00**
☐	**133 Alexander Frolov, LosA. RC**	**15.00**
☐	**134 Pierre-Marc Bouchard, MinW. RC**	**18.00**
☐	**135 Sylvain Blouin, MinW. RC**	**5.00**
☐	**136 Ron Hainsey, Mont. RC**	**9.00**
☐	**137 Adam Hall, Nash. RC**	**9.00**
☐	138 Jan Lasak (G), Nash.	2.00
☐	**139 Ray Schultz, NYIs. RC**	**5.00**
☐	140 Trent Hunter, NYIs.	2.00
☐	141 Martin Prusek (G), Otta.	3.00
☐	**142 Anton Volchenkov, Otta. RC**	**6.00**
☐	**143 Patrick Sharp, Phil. RC**	**5.00**
☐	**144 Dennis Seidenberg, Phil. RC**	**6.00**
☐	145 Branko Radivojevic, Phoe.	2.00
☐	146 Shane Endicott, Pitt.	2.00
☐	**147 Alexander Svitov, Tamp. RC**	**12.00**
☐	148 Sébastien Centomo (G), Toro.	2.00
☐	149 Karel Pilar, Toro.	2.00
☐	**150 Steve Eminger, Wash. RC**	**6.00**

AWARDS COLLECTION

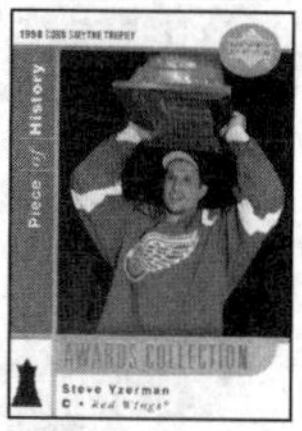

Insert Set (28 cards):		**75.00**
	Insert (1:6)	**AC**
☐	AC1 Paul Kariya, Anah.	4.00
☐	AC2 Raymond Bourque, Bost.	3.00
☐	AC3 Sergei Samsonov, Bost.	2.00
☐	AC4 Jarome Iginla, Calg.	2.00
☐	AC5 Chris Drury, Colo.	2.00
☐	AC6 Joe Sakic, Colo.	4.00
☐	AC7 Rob Blake, Colo.	2.00
☐	AC8 Peter Forsberg, Colo.	4.00
☐	AC9 Patrick Roy (G), Colo.	9.00
☐	AC10 Luc Robitaille, Detr.	2.00
☐	AC11 Brett Hull, Detr.	3.00
☐	AC12 Steve Yzerman, Detr.	7.00
☐	AC13 Dominik Hasek (G), Detr.	3.00
☐	AC14 Nicklas Lidström, Detr.	2.00
☐	AC15 Sergei Fedorov, Detr.	3.00
☐	AC16 Wayne Gretzky, Edmo.	12.00
☐	AC17 Joe Nieuwendyk, NJer.	2.00
☐	AC18 Martin Brodeur (G), NJer.	4.00
☐	AC19 Brian Leetch, NYRa.	2.00
☐	AC20 Pavel Bure, NYRa.	2.00
☐	AC21 Claude Lemieux, Phoe.	2.00
☐	AC22 Mario Lemieux, Pitt.	9.00
☐	AC23 Evgeni Nabokov (G), SanJ.	2.00
☐	AC24 Teemu Selänne, SanJ.	2.00
☐	AC25 Chris Pronger, SLou.	2.00
☐	AC26 Al MacInnis, SLou.	2.00
☐	AC27 Jaromir Jagr, Wash.	3.00
☐	AC28 Olaf Kölzig (G), Wash.	2.00

HOCKEY'S BEGINNINGS

Insert Set (8 cards):		**50.00**
	Insert (1:20)	**HB**
☐	HB1 Bobby Orr, Bost.	12.00
☐	HB2 Raymond Bourque, Bost.	3.00
☐	HB3 Steve Yzerman, Detr.	7.00
☐	HB4 Gordie Howe, Detr.	8.00
☐	HB5 Wayne Gretzky, Edmo.	12.00
☐	HB6 Patrick Roy (G), Mont.	9.00
☐	HB7 Mike Bossy, NYIs.	4.00
☐	HB8 Wayne Gretzky, AS'82	12.00

SIMPLY THE BEST

Insert Set (6 cards):		**25.00**
	Insert (1:24)	**SB**
☐	SB1 Raymond Bourque, Bost.	3.00
☐	SB6 Wayne Gretzky, Edmo.	12.00
☐	SB5 Gordie Howe, Detr.	8.00
☐	SB2 Bobby Orr, Bost.	12.00
☐	SB3 Patrick Roy (G), Colo.	9.00
☐	SB4 Steve Yzerman, Detr.	7.00

EXQUISITE COMBOS

Insert Set (5 cards):		**200.00**
	Insert	**EC**
☐	P. Bure, AS'93 ✄ / M. Messier, NYRa. ✄	30.00
☐	R. Blake, Colo. ✄ / P. Roy (G), Colo. ✄	20.00
☐	M. Lemieux, Pitt. ✄ / A. Kovalev, Pitt. ✄ {*}	130.00
☐	E. Lindros, NYRa. ✄ / M. Messier, NYRa. ✄	35.00
☐	C. Neely, Bost. ✄ / R. Bourque, Bost. ✄	35.00

GRAND MEMORABILIA GIVEAWAY

	Insert	**ARV**
☐	'01-02 Stanley Cup banner	3500
☐	'01-02 Avalanche carpet	4900
☐	Montréal Forum Chair	1050
☐	Raymond Bourque helmet	800
☐	Larry Robinson jersey	2350
☐	Olaf Kölzig (G) stick	400
☐	Brendan Shanahan stick	550
☐	Bobby Smith stick	2100
☐	Dominik Hasek (G) stick	2100
☐	Kevin Lowe jersey	6300
☐	Jason Spezza jersey	700
☐	Raymond Bourque stick	1050
☐	Larry Robinson stick	1050
☐	Keith Tkachuk stick	1050
☐	Marcel Dionne stick	2800
☐	Jari Kurri stick	3500
☐	Ken Dryden (G) stick	4900
☐	Guy Lafleur stick	4900

HEROES OF HOCKEY JERSEY

Insert Set (5 cards):		**75.00**
	Insert (1:48)	**HH**
☐	HH-MG Mike Gartner, Heroes of Hockey	20.00
☐	HH-JK Jari Kurri, Heroes of Hockey	25.00
☐	HH-GP Gilbert Perreault, Heroes of Hockey	20.00
☐	HH-BS Börje Salming, Heroes of Hockey	20.00
☐	HH-PS Peter Stastny, Heroes of Hockey	15.00

HISTORICAL SWATCHES

Insert Set (10 cards):		**425.00**
	Insert (1:96)	**HS**
☐	Mike Bossy, AS'78 ✄ Orange	60.00
☐	Mike Bossy, AS'78 ✄ Orange/Black	75.00
☐	Raymond Bourque, Bost. ✄ {*150}	50.00
☐	Johnny Bucyk, Bost. ✄	20.00
☐	Mike Gartner, Minn. ✄	30.00
☐	Michel Goulet, Québ. ✄	15.00
☐	Wayne Gretzky, LosA. {()50}	150.00
☐	Guy Lafleur, Québ. ✄	75.00
☐	Cam Neely, Bost. ✄ {*}	50.00
☐	Börje Salming, Toro. ✄ {*}	40.00
☐	Bryan Trottier, NYIs. ✄ {*}	50.00

MARKS OF DISTINCTION

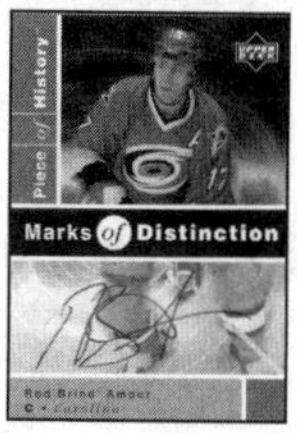

Insert Set (31 cards):		**$3,525**
	Autograph	**MD**
☐	Mike Bossy, NYIs. ✍ {*25}	175.00
☐	Raymond Bourque, Bost. ✍ {*24}	200.00
☐	Pavel Brendl, Phil. ✍	15.00
☐	Rod Brind'Amour, Caro. ✍	15.00
☐	Johnny Bucyk, Bost. ✍ {*25}	75.00
☐	Pavel Bure, NYRa. ✍ {*24}	125.00
☐	Mike Comrie, Edmo. ✍ {*}	50.00
☐	Simon Gagné, Phil. ✍ {*}	50.00
☐	Mike Gartner, Wash. ✍ {*25}	125.00
☐	Michel Goulet, Chic. ✍ {*25}	75.00
☐	Wayne Gretzky, Edmo. ✍ {*24}	675.00
☐	Dany Heatley, Atla. ✍	50.00
☐	Gordie Howe, Detr. ✍ {*24}	375.00
☐	Jarome Iginla, Calg. ✍ {*}	50.00
☐	Jari Kurri, Edmo. ✍ {*25}	150.00
☐	Guy Lafleur, Mont. ✍ {*25}	150.00
☐	Markus Näslund, Vanc. ✍	50.00
☐	Vaclav Nedorost, Colo. ✍	15.00
☐	CN Cam Neely, Bost. ✍ {*25}	150.00
☐	Bobby Orr, Bost. ✍ {*24}	625.00
☐	Gilbert Perreault, Buff. ✍ {*25}	125.00
☐	Mike Richter (G), NYRa. ✍	20.00
☐	Patrick Roy (G), Colo. ✍ {*24}	450.00
☐	Sergei Samsonov, Bost. ✍ {*}	35.00
☐	Daniel Sedin, Vanc. ✍	20.00
☐	Henrik Sedin, Vanc. ✍	20.00
☐	Teemu Selänne, SanJ. ✍	40.00
☐	Peter Stastny, Québ. ✍ {*25}	75.00
☐	Joe Thornton, Bost. ✍ {*24}	175.00
☐	Bryan Trottier, NYIs. ✍ {*25}	150.00
☐	Steve Yzerman, Detr. ✍	120.00

PATCHES OF HISTORY

Insert Set (28 cards):		**3000.00**
	Insert (#/100	**PH**
☐	Maxim Afinogenov, Buff. ✄	60.00
☐	Rob Blake, Colo. ✄	75.00
☐	Raymond Bourque, Bost. ✄	150.00
☐	Sean Burke (G), Phoe. ✄	75.00
☐	Mike Dunham (G), Nash. ✄	60.00
☐	Sergei Fedorov, Detr. ✄	125.00
☐	Simon Gagné, Phil. ✄	100.00
☐	Wayne Gretzky, AS'91 ✄	500.00
☐	Paul Kariya, Anah. ✄	175.00
☐	Brian Leetch, NYRa. ✄	75.00
☐	Eric Lindros, NYRa. ✄	125.00
☐	Mike Modano, Dall. ✄	125.00
☐	Markus Näslund, Vanc. ✄	125.00
☐	Zigmund Palffy, LosA. ✄	75.00
☐	Félix Potvin (G), LosA. ✄	150.00
☐	Keith Primeau, Phil. ✄	60.00
☐	Patrick Roy (G), Colo. ✄	300.00
☐	Joe Sakic, Colo. ✄	200.00
☐	Sergei Samsonov, Bost. ✄	75.00
☐	Teemu Selänne, SanJ. ✄	100.00
☐	Brendan Shanahan, Detr. ✄	125.00
☐	Steve Sullivan, Chic. ✄	60.00
☐	Mats Sundin, Toro. ✄	125.00
☐	José Théodore (G), Mont. ✄	150.00
☐	Joe Thornton, Bost. ✄	150.00
☐	Ron Tugnutt (G), Colu. ✄	60.00
☐	Marty Turco (G), Dall. ✄	75.00
☐	Steve Yzerman, Detr. ✄	300.00

STELLAR STITCHES

Insert Set (6 cards):		**200.00**
	Insert (#/100)	**SS**
☐	SS-PK Paul Kariya, Anah. ✄ {*}	40.00
☐	SS-MM Mike Modano, Dall. ✄ {*}	30.00
☐	SS-JS Joe Sakic, Colo. ✄ {*}	50.00
☐	SS-MS Mats Sundin, Toro. ✄	30.00
☐	SS-JT Joe Thornton, Bost. ✄	35.00
☐	SS-SY Steve Yzerman, Detr. ✄	75.00

THREADS OF TIME

Insert Set (6 cards):		**100.00**
	Insert	**TT**
☐	Chris Drury, Colo. ✄	15.00
☐	Sergei Fedorov, Detr. ✄	25.00
☐	Simon Gagné, Phil. ✄ {*}	25.00
☐	Scott Hartnell, Nash. ✄	15.00
☐	Claude Lemieux, Phoe. ✄	15.00
☐	José Théodore (G), Mont. ✄ {*}	35.00

2002 - 03 UPPER DECK PREMIER COLLECTION

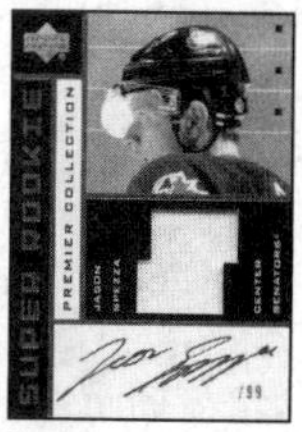

Produced by The Upper Deck Company, this series was released in May 2003.

Shell Set (55 cards):		**155.00**
Complete Set (117 cards):		**3600.00**
	Description	**Base**
☐	1 Paul Kariya, Anah.	6.00
☐	2 Ilya Kovalchuk, Atla.	4.00
☐	3 Dany Heatley, Atla.	4.00
☐	4 Byron Dafoe (G), Atla.	4.00
☐	5 Joe Thornton, Bost.	6.00
☐	6 Jeff Hackett (G), Bost.	4.00
☐	7 Sergei Samsonov, Bost.	4.00
☐	8 Miroslav Satan, Buff.	4.00
☐	9 Jarome Iginla, Calg.	4.00
☐	10 Ron Francis, Caro.	4.00
☐	11 Tyler Arnason, Chic.	4.00
☐	12 Jocelyn Thibault (G), Chic.	4.00
☐	13 Peter Forsberg, Colo.	6.00
☐	14 Joe Sakic, Colo.	8.00
☐	15 Patrick Roy (G), Colo.	15.00
☐	16 Milan Hejduk, Colo.	4.00
☐	17 Marc Denis (G), Colu.	4.00
☐	18 Mike Modano, Dall.	4.00
☐	19 Bill Guerin, Dall.	4.00
☐	20 Marty Turco (G), Dall.	4.00
☐	21 Steve Yzerman, Detr.	10.00
☐	22 Curtis Joseph (G), Detr.	4.00
☐	23 Brendan Shanahan, Detr.	4.00
☐	24 Nicklas Lidström, Detr.	4.00
☐	25 Mike Comrie, Edmo.	4.00
☐	26 Stephen Weiss, Flor.	4.00
☐	27 Roberto Luongo (G), Flor.	4.00
☐	28 Zigmund Palffy, LosA.	4.00
☐	29 Marian Gaborik, MinW.	4.00
☐	30 Saku Koivu, Mont.	4.00
☐	31 José Théodore (G), Mont.	6.00
☐	32 David Legwand, Nash.	4.00
☐	33 Martin Brodeur (G), NJer.	8.00
☐	34 Michael Peca, NYIs.	4.00
☐	35 Alex Kovalev, NYRa.	4.00
☐	36 Eric Lindros, NYRa.	4.00
☐	37 Pavel Bure, NYRa.	4.00
☐	38 Mike Dunham (G), NYRa.	4.00
☐	39 Marian Hossa, Otta.	4.00
☐	40 Jeremy Roenick, Phil.	4.00
☐	41 John LeClair, Phil.	4.00
☐	42 Tony Amonte, Phoe.	4.00
☐	43 Mario Lemieux, Pitt.	15.00
☐	44 Sébastien Caron (G), Pitt.	4.00
☐	45 Evgeni Nabokov (G), SanJ.	4.00
☐	46 Kyle McLaren, SanJ.	4.00
☐	47 Keith Tkachuk, SLou.	4.00
☐	48 Vincent Lecavalier, Tamp.	4.00
☐	49 Nikolai Khabibulin (G), Tamp.	4.00
☐	50 Mats Sundin, Toro.	4.00
☐	51 Ed Belfour (G), Toro.	4.00
☐	52 Todd Bertuzzi, Vanc.	6.00
☐	53 Markus Näslund, Vanc.	4.00
☐	54 Jaromir Jagr, Wash.	4.00
☐	55 Olaf Kölzig (G), Wash.	4.00
☐	56 Wayne Gretzky, NYRa. {*299}	25.00
☐	57 Bobby Orr, Bost. {*299}	25.00
☐	58 Gordie Howe, Detr. {*299}	15.00
☐	59 Raymond Bourque, Bost. {*299}	6.00

SUPER ROOKIE

Some cards have the same number. There are two versions for each card: a base card and a Gold parallel. The three subsets are Super Rookie (#/399, Gold #/199), Signed Super Rookie (#/199, Gold #/25), and Signed Super Rookie Patch (#/99, Gold #/15).

Insert	Gold	Insert
☐☐ 44 Martin Gerber (G), Anah. RC	20.00	20.00
☐☐ 45 Tim Thomas (G), Bost. RC	20.00	20.00
☐☐ 46 Ryan Miller (G), Buff. RC	60.00	50.00
☐☐ 47 Jordan Leopold, Calg. RC	35.00	30.00
☐☐ 48 Shaone Morrisonn, Bost. RC	20.00	20.00
☐☐ 49 Levente Szuper (G), Calg. RC	20.00	20.00
☐☐ 51 Jim Fahey, SanJ. RC	15.00	15.00
☐☐ 52 Dmitri Bykov, Detr. RC	20.00	20.00
☐☐ 56 Mike Cammalleri, LosA. RC	45.00	40.00
☐☐ 57 Stéphane Veilleux, MinW. RC	15.00	15.00
☐☐ 58 Rickard Wallin, MinW. RC	15.00	15.00
☐☐ 59 Vernon Fiddler, Nash. RC	15.00	15.00
☐☐ 60 Darren Haydar, Nash. RC	15.00	15.00
☐☐ 60 Alexei Semenov, Edmo. RC	20.00	20.00
☐☐ 61 Anton Volchenkov, Otta. RC	20.00	20.00
☐☐ 62 Patrick Sharp, Phil. RC	15.00	15.00
☐☐ 63 Dennis Seidenberg, Phil. RC	20.00	20.00
☐☐ 64 Tomas Malec, Caro. RC	15.00	15.00
☐☐ 65 Craig Andersson (G), Chic. RC	35.00	30.00
☐☐ 66 Cody Rudkowsky (G), SLou. RC	20.00	20.00
☐☐ 67 Ari Ahonen (G), NJer. RC	35.00	30.00
☐☐ 67 Curtis Sanford (G), SLou. RC	20.00	20.00
☐☐ 68 Adam Hall, Nash. RC	35.00	30.00
☐☐ 69 Carlo Colaiacovo, Toro. RC	35.00	30.00
☐☐ 70 Steve Eminger, Wash. RC	35.00	20.00
☐☐ 70 Dick Tarnström, Pitt.	15.00	15.00
☐☐ 71 Jamie Hodson (G), Toro. RC	15.00	15.00
☐☐ 71 Alexei Smirnov, Anah. ✍	75.00	60.00
☐☐ 72 Pierre-Marc Bouchard, MinW. ✍	175.00	140.00
☐☐ 72 Jarret Stoll, Edmo. RC	35.00	30.00
☐☐ 73 Ron Hainsey, Mont. ✍	75.00	60.00
☐☐ 74 Pascal Leclaire (G), Colu. ✍	150.00	120.00
☐☐ 75 Scottie Upshall, Nash. ✍	125.00	80.00
☐☐ 76 Jeff Taffe, Phoe. ✍	75.00	60.00
☐☐ 77 Mikael Tellqvist (G), Toro. ✍	50.00	40.00
☐☐ 78 Stanislav Chistov, Anah. ✍ ✂	275.00	225.00
☐☐ 79 Chuck Kobasew, Calg. ✍ ✂	175.00	150.00
☐☐ 80 Rick Nash, Colu. ✍ ✂	475.00	550.00
☐☐ 81 Henrik Zetterberg, Detr. ✍ ✂	475.00	550.00
☐☐ 82 Jay Bouwmeester, Flor. ✍ ✂	275.00	325.00
☐☐ 83 Jason Spezza, Otta. ✍ ✂	350.00	400.00
☐☐ 84 Alexander Svitov, Tamp. ✍ ✂	175.00	175.00
☐☐ 88 Jerred Smithson, LosA. RC	15.00	15.00
☐☐ 89 Jim Vandermeer, Phil. RC	20.00	20.00
☐☐ 90 Michael Leighton (G), Chic. RC	20.00	20.00
☐☐ 91 Ray Emery (G), Otta. RC	20.00	20.00
☐☐ 92 Tomas Zizka, LosA. RC	15.00	15.00
☐☐ 93 Bobby Allen, Edmo. RC	15.00	15.00
☐☐ 94 Kris Vernarsky, Bost. RC	15.00	15.00
☐☐ 95 Cristobal Huet, LosA. RC	20.00	20.00
☐☐ 96 Fernando Pisani, Edmo. RC	15.00	15.00
☐☐ 97 Jonathan Hedstrom, Anah. RC	15.00	15.00
☐☐ 98 Konstantin Koltsov, Pitt. RC	15.00	15.00
☐☐ 99 Ales Hemsky, Edmo. ✍	175.00	140.00
☐☐ 100 Steve Ott, Dall. ✍	75.00	60.00
☐☐ 101 Alexander Frolov, LosA. ✍	150.00	120.00
☐☐ 102 Brooks Orpik, Pitt. ✍	75.00	60.00
☐☐ 103 Jared Aulin, LosA. ✍	75.00	60.00

JERSEY DUAL

Insert Set (14 cards):	375.00
Insert (*99)	NP
☐ B-L Bure ✂ / Lindros ✂	25.00
☐ B-R Blake ✂ / Roy (G) ✂	25.00
☐ F-H Forsberg ✂ / Hejduk ✂	25.00
☐ F-J Fedorov ✂ / Joseph (G) ✂	25.00
☐ G-L Gretzky ✂ / Lemieux ✂	100.00
☐ J-K Jagr ✂ / Kölzig (G) ✂	25.00
☐ N-S Nash ✂ / Spezza ✂	25.00
☐ K-G Kariya ✂ / Gguère ✂	25.00
☐ L-A Leclaire (G) ✂ / Ahonen (G) ✂	25.00
☐ R-G Roenick ✂ / Gagné ✂	25.00
☐ S-R Sakic ✂ / Reinprecht ✂	25.00
☐ S-T Samsonov ✂ / Thornton ✂	25.00
☐ Y-S Yzerman ✂ / Shanahan ✂	50.00
☐ T-K Théodore (G) ✂ / Koivu ✂	25.00

JERSEY DUAL SILVER

Insert Set (14 cards):	500.00
Insert (*50)	JDS
☐ B-L Bure ✂ / Lindros ✂	35.00
☐ B-R Blake ✂ / Roy (G) ✂	50.00
☐ F-H Forsberg ✂ / Hejduk ✂	35.00
☐ F-J Fedorov ✂ / Joseph (G) ✂	35.00
☐ G-L Gretzky ✂ / Lemieux ✂	125.00
☐ J-K Jagr ✂ / Kölzig (G) ✂	35.00
☐ N-S Nash ✂ / Spezza ✂	35.00
☐ K-G Kariya ✂ / Gguère ✂	35.00
☐ L-A Leclaire (G) ✂ / Ahonen (G) ✂	35.00
☐ R-G Roenick ✂ / Gagné ✂	35.00
☐ S-R Sakic ✂ / Reinprecht ✂	35.00
☐ S-T Samsonov ✂ / Thornton ✂	35.00
☐ Y-S Yzerman ✂ / Shanahan ✂	50.00
☐ T-K Théodore (G) ✂ / Koivu ✂	35.00

JERSEY DUAL GOLD

Insert Set (14 cards):	575.00
Insert (*25)	JDS
☐ B-L Bure ✂ / Lindros ✂	40.00
☐ B-R Blake ✂ / Roy (G) ✂	50.00
☐ F-H Forsberg ✂ / Hejduk ✂	40.00
☐ F-J Fedorov ✂ / Joseph (G) ✂	40.00
☐ G-L Gretzky ✂ / Lemieux ✂	150.00
☐ J-K Jagr ✂ / Kölzig (G) ✂	40.00
☐ N-S Nash ✂ / Spezza ✂	40.00
☐ K-G Kariya ✂ / Gguère ✂	50.00
☐ L-A Leclaire (G) ✂ / Ahonen (G) ✂	40.00
☐ R-G Roenick ✂ / Gagné ✂	40.00
☐ S-R Sakic ✂ / Reinprecht ✂	40.00
☐ S-T Samsonov ✂ / Thornton ✂	40.00
☐ Y-S Yzerman ✂ / Shanahan ✂	50.00
☐ T-K Théodore (G) ✂ / Koivu ✂	40.00

NHL PATCH

Insert (*1)
- ☐ Martin Brodeur (G), NJer. ✂
- ☐ Wayne Gretzky, NYRa. ✂
- ☐ Jaromir Jagr, Wash. ✂
- ☐ Paul Kariya, Anah. ✂
- ☐ Mario Lemieux, Pitt. ✂
- ☐ Mike Modano, Dall. ✂
- ☐ Patrick Roy (G), Colo. ✂
- ☐ Joe Sakic, Colo. ✂
- ☐ Mats Sundin, Toro. ✂
- ☐ Steve Yzerman, Detr. ✂

PREMIER JERSEY

Insert Set (44 cards):	600.00
Insert (*299)	PJ
☐ Ari Ahonen (G), NJer. ✂	15.00
☐ Raymond Bourque, Bost. ✂	15.00
☐ Martin Brodeur (G), NJer. ✂	15.00
☐ Pavel Bure, NYRa. ✂	15.00
☐ Mike Comrie, Edmo. ✂	15.00
☐ Chris Drury, Calg. ✂	15.00
☐ Sergei Fedorov, All-Star ✂	15.00
☐ Sergei Fedorov, Detr. ✂	15.00
☐ Theoren Fleury, Chic. ✂	15.00
☐ Peter Forsberg, All-Star ✂	15.00
☐ Peter Forsberg, Colo. ✂	15.00
☐ Simon Gagné, Phil. ✂	15.00
☐ Wayne Gretzky, LosA. ✂	50.00
☐ Milan Hejduk, Colo. ✂	15.00
☐ Jarome Iginla, Calg. ✂	15.00
☐ Jaromir Jagr, All-Star ✂	15.00
☐ Jaromir Jagr, Wash. ✂	15.00
☐ Curtis Joseph (G), Detr. ✂	15.00
☐ Paul Kariya, Anah. ✂	15.00
☐ Saku Koivu, Mont. ✂	15.00
☐ Olaf Kölzig (G), Wash. ✂	15.00
☐ Ilya Kovalchuk, Atla. ✂	15.00
☐ Alex Kovalev, All-Star ✂	15.00
☐ Pascal Leclaire (G), Colu. ✂	15.00
☐ Mario Lemieux, Pitt. ✂	25.00
☐ Eric Lindros, NYRa. ✂	15.00
☐ Mike Modano, All-Star ✂	15.00
☐ Mike Modano, Dall. ✂	15.00
☐ Glen Murray, All-Star ✂	15.00
☐ Brooks Orpik, Pitt. ✂	15.00
☐ Steve Ott, Dall. ✂	15.00
☐ Jeremy Roenick, All-Star ✂	15.00
☐ Jeremy Roenick, Phil. ✂	15.00
☐ Patrick Roy (G), Colo. ✂	25.00
☐ Joe Sakic, Colo. ✂	15.00
☐ Sergei Samsonov, Bost. ✂	15.00
☐ Alexei Semenov, Edmo. ✂	15.00
☐ Brendan Shanahan, Detr. ✂	15.00
☐ Mats Sundin, Toro. ✂	15.00
☐ Alexander Svitov, Tamp. ✂	15.00
☐ José Théodore (G), Mont. ✂	15.00
☐ Joe Thornton, Bost. ✂	15.00
☐ Anton Volchenkov, Otta. ✂	15.00
☐ Steve Yzerman, Detr. ✂	25.00

PREMIER JERSEY GOLD

Insert Set (44 cards):	1500.00
Insert (*25)	PJG

PREMIER JERSEY SILVER

Insert Set (51 cards):	900.00
Insert (*99)	PJS
☐ Ari Ahonen (G), NJer. ✂	15.00
☐ Raymond Bourque, Bost. ✂	25.00
☐ Jay Bouwmeester, Flor. ✂	15.00
☐ Martin Brodeur (G), NJer. ✂	25.00
☐ Martin Brodeur (G), All-Star ✂	25.00
☐ Pavel Bure, NYRa. ✂	15.00
☐ Mike Comrie, Edmo. ✂	15.00
☐ Chris Drury, Calg. ✂	15.00
☐ Sergei Fedorov, All-Star ✂	15.00
☐ Sergei Fedorov, Detr. ✂	15.00
☐ Theoren Fleury, Chic. ✂	15.00
☐ Peter Forsberg, All-Star ✂	25.00
☐ Peter Forsberg, Colo. ✂	25.00
☐ Simon Gagné, Phil. ✂	15.00
☐ Wayne Gretzky, LosA. ✂	75.00
☐ Dany Heatley, All-Star ✂	15.00
☐ Milan Hejduk, Colo. ✂	15.00
☐ Jarome Iginla, Calg. ✂	15.00
☐ Jarome Iginla, All-Star ✂	15.00
☐ Jaromir Jagr, All-Star ✂	15.00
☐ Jaromir Jagr, Wash. ✂	15.00
☐ Curtis Joseph (G), Detr. ✂	15.00
☐ Paul Kariya, Anah. ✂	25.00
☐ Saku Koivu, Mont. ✂	15.00
☐ Olaf Kölzig (G), Wash. ✂	15.00
☐ Ilya Kovalchuk, Atla. ✂	15.00
☐ Alex Kovalev, All-Star ✂	15.00
☐ Pascal Leclaire (G), Colu. ✂	15.00
☐ Mario Lemieux, Pitt. ✂	50.00
☐ Eric Lindros, NYRa. ✂	15.00
☐ Mike Modano, All-Star ✂	15.00
☐ Mike Modano, Dall. ✂	15.00
☐ Glen Murray, All-Star ✂	15.00
☐ Rick Nash, Colu. ✂	15.00
☐ Brooks Orpik, Pitt. ✂	15.00
☐ Steve Ott, Dall. ✂	15.00
☐ Jeremy Roenick, All-Star ✂	15.00
☐ Jeremy Roenick, Phil. ✂	15.00
☐ Patrick Roy (G), Colo. ✂	50.00
☐ Patrick Roy (G), All-Star ✂	50.00
☐ Joe Sakic, Colo. ✂	25.00
☐ Sergei Samsonov, Bost. ✂	15.00
☐ Alexei Semenov, Edmo. ✂	15.00
☐ Brendan Shanahan, Detr. ✂	15.00
☐ Mats Sundin, Toro. ✂	15.00
☐ Alexander Svitov, Tamp. ✂	15.00
☐ José Théodore (G), Mont. ✂	25.00
☐ Joe Thornton, Bost. ✂	25.00
☐ Joe Thornton, All-Star ✂	25.00
☐ Anton Volchenkov, Otta. ✂	15.00
☐ Steve Yzerman, Detr. ✂	50.00
☐ Ari Ahonen (G), NJer. ✂	15.00
☐ Raymond Bourque, Bost. ✂	25.00
☐ Martin Brodeur (G), NJer. ✂	25.00
☐ Pavel Bure, NYRa. ✂	15.00
☐ Mike Comrie, Edmo. ✂	15.00
☐ Chris Drury, Calg. ✂	15.00
☐ Sergei Fedorov, All-Star ✂	25.00
☐ Sergei Fedorov, Detr. ✂	25.00
☐ Theoren Fleury, Chic. ✂	15.00
☐ Peter Forsberg, All-Star ✂	25.00
☐ Peter Forsberg, Colo. ✂	25.00
☐ Simon Gagné, Phil. ✂	15.00
☐ Wayne Gretzky, LosA. ✂	100.00
☐ Milan Hejduk, Colo. ✂	15.00
☐ Jarome Iginla, Calg. ✂	15.00
☐ Jaromir Jagr, All-Star ✂	25.00
☐ Jaromir Jagr, Wash. ✂	25.00
☐ Curtis Joseph (G), Detr. ✂	25.00
☐ Paul Kariya, Anah. ✂	25.00
☐ Saku Koivu, Mont. ✂	15.00
☐ Olaf Kölzig (G), Wash. ✂	15.00
☐ Ilya Kovalchuk, Atla. ✂	25.00
☐ Alex Kovalev, All-Star ✂	15.00
☐ Pascal Leclaire (G), Colu. ✂	15.00
☐ Mario Lemieux, Pitt. ✂	75.00
☐ Eric Lindros, NYRa. ✂	25.00
☐ Mike Modano, All-Star ✂	25.00
☐ Mike Modano, Dall. ✂	25.00
☐ Glen Murray, All-Star ✂	15.00
☐ Brooks Orpik, Pitt. ✂	15.00
☐ Steve Ott, Dall. ✂	15.00
☐ Jeremy Roenick, All-Star ✂	15.00
☐ Jeremy Roenick, Phil. ✂	15.00
☐ Patrick Roy (G), Colo. ✂	50.00
☐ Joe Sakic, Colo. ✂	25.00
☐ Sergei Samsonov, Bost. ✂	15.00
☐ Alexei Semenov, Edmo. ✂	15.00
☐ Brendan Shanahan, Detr. ✂	25.00
☐ Mats Sundin, Toro. ✂	25.00
☐ Alexander Svitov, Tamp. ✂	15.00
☐ José Théodore (G), Mont. ✂	25.00
☐ Joe Thornton, Bost. ✂	25.00
☐ Anton Volchenkov, Otta. ✂	15.00
☐ Steve Yzerman, Detr. ✂	50.00

PREMIER PATCH

Insert Set (32 cards):	2875.00
Insert (*99)	Patch
☐ Raymond Bourque, Colo. ✂	100.00
☐ Raymond Bourque, Bost. ✂	100.00
☐ Martin Brodeur (G), NJer. ✂	125.00
☐ Pavel Bure, NYRa. ✂	50.00
☐ Mike Comrie, Edmo. ✂	50.00
☐ Chris Drury, Colo. ✂	50.00
☐ Sergei Fedorov, Detr. ✂	75.00
☐ Peter Forsberg, Colo. ✂	125.00
☐ Simon Gagné, Phil. ✂	50.00
☐ Wayne Gretzky, NYRa. ✂	350.00
☐ Wayne Gretzky, LosA. ✂	350.00
☐ Milan Hejduk, Colo. ✂	50.00
☐ Jarome Iginla, Calg. ✂	50.00
☐ Jaromir Jagr, Wash. ✂	75.00
☐ Curtis Joseph (G), Detr. ✂	75.00
☐ Paul Kariya, Anah. ✂	125.00
☐ Saku Koivu, Mont. ✂	50.00
☐ Olaf Kölzig (G), Wash. ✂	50.00
☐ Ilya Kovalchuk, Atla. ✂	75.00
☐ Mario Lemieux, Pitt. ✂	250.00
☐ Eric Lindros, NYRa. ✂	75.00
☐ Mike Modano, Dall. ✂	75.00
☐ Jeremy Roenick, Phil. ✂	50.00
☐ Patrick Roy (G), Colo. ✂	200.00
☐ Joe Sakic, Colo. ✂	125.00
☐ Sergei Samsonov, Bost. ✂	50.00
☐ Teemu Selänne, SanJ. ✂	50.00
☐ Brendan Shanahan, Detr. ✂	75.00
☐ Mats Sundin, Toro. ✂	75.00
☐ José Théodore (G), Mont. ✂	100.00
☐ Joe Thornton, Bost. ✂	100.00
☐ Steve Yzerman, Detr. ✂	200.00

PREMIER SIGNATURE

Insert Set (48 cards):	2875.00	1925.00	1275.00
Insert	G50	S125	B
☐☐☐ Maxim Afinogenov, Buff. ✍	30.00	20.00	15.00
☐☐☐ Ed Belfour (G), Toro. ✍	75.00	50.00	25.00
☐☐☐ P-M Bouchard, MinW. ✍	30.00	20.00	15.00
☐☐☐ Raymond Bourque, Colo. ✍	75.00	50.00	30.00
☐☐☐ Raymond Bourque, Bost. ✍	75.00	50.00	30.00
☐☐☐ BM Jay Bouwmeester, Flor. ✍	30.00	20.00	15.00
☐☐☐ JB Jay Bouwmeester, Flor. ✍	30.00	20.00	15.00
☐☐☐ Pavel Brendl, Phil. ✍	30.00	20.00	15.00
☐☐☐ S-MB Brodeur (G), NJer. ✍	100.00	75.00	80.00
☐☐☐ AS-MB Brodeur (G), All-Star ✍	100.00	75.00	40.00
☐☐☐ Pavel Bure, NYRa. ✍	50.00	25.00	40.00
☐☐☐ Stanislav Chistov, Anah. ✍	30.00	20.00	15.00
☐☐☐ Erik Cole, Caro. ✍	30.00	20.00	15.00
☐☐☐ Mike Comrie, Edmo. ✍	50.00	25.00	20.00
☐☐☐ Manny Fernandez (G), MinW. ✍	30.00	20.00	15.00
☐☐☐ Simon Gagné, Phil. ✍	50.00	25.00	20.00
☐☐☐ Wayne Gretzky, NYRa. ✍	300.00	200.00	165.00
☐☐☐ Ron Hainsey, Mont. ✍	30.00	20.00	15.00
☐☐☐ Adam Hall, Nash. ✍	30.00	20.00	15.00
☐☐☐ Scott Hartnell, Nash. ✍	30.00	20.00	15.00
☐☐☐ Martin Havlat, Otta. ✍	30.00	25.00	15.00
☐☐☐ Dany Heatley, Atla. ✍	75.00	50.00	25.00
☐☐☐ Dany Heatley, All-Star ✍	75.00	50.00	25.00
☐☐☐ Gordie Howe, Detr. ✍	200.00	125.00	70.00
☐☐☐ S-JI Jarome Iginla, Calg. ✍	50.00	25.00	20.00
☐☐☐ AS-JI J. Iginla, All-Star ✍	50.00	25.00	20.00
☐☐☐ N. Khabibulin (G), Tamp. ✍	30.00	20.00	15.00
☐☐☐ Chuck Kobasew, Calg. ✍	30.00	20.00	15.00
☐☐☐ Ilya Kovalchuk, Atla. ✍	75.00	50.00	25.00
☐☐☐ John LeClair, Phil. ✍	50.00	25.00	20.00
☐☐☐ NA Rick Nash, Colu. ✍	50.00	50.00	30.00
☐☐☐ RN Rick Nash, Colu. ✍	50.00	50.00	30.00
☐☐☐ Markus Näslund, Vanc. ✍	75.00	50.00	25.00
☐☐☐ Bobby Orr, Bost. ✍	300.00	200.00	100.00
☐☐☐ Patrick Roy (G), Colo. ✍	225.00	150.00	120.00
☐☐☐ Patrick Roy (G), All-Star ✍	225.00	150.00	75.00
☐☐☐ Sergei Samsonov, Bost. ✍	30.00	25.00	15.00
☐☐☐ Alexei Smirnov, Anah. ✍	30.00	20.00	15.00
☐☐☐ Jason Spezza, Otta. ✍	30.00	25.00	15.00
☐☐☐ Alexander Svitov, Tamp. ✍	30.00	20.00	15.00
☐☐☐ Jeff Taffe, Phoe. ✍	30.00	20.00	15.00
☐☐☐ Mikael Tellqvist (G), Toro. ✍	30.00	20.00	15.00
☐☐☐ S-JT Joe Thornton, Bost. ✍	75.00	50.00	30.00
☐☐☐ AS-JT Thornton, All-Star ✍	75.00	50.00	30.00
☐☐☐ Scottie Upshall, Nash. ✍	30.00	20.00	15.00
☐☐☐ Justin Williams, Phil. ✍	30.00	20.00	15.00
☐☐☐ Steve Yzerman, Detr. ✍	175.00	100.00	60.00
☐☐☐ Henrik Zetterberg, Detr. ✍	50.00	50.00	30.00

2002 - 03 UPPER DECK ROOKIE UPDATE

Produced by The Upper Deck Company, this series was released in November 2002.

Shell Set (100 cards):	45.00
Complete Set (204 cards):	1300.00

Common Player: .35

	Description	Base
☐	1 Paul Kariya, Anah.	1.50
☐	2 Adam Oates, Anah.	.50
☐	3 Jean-Sébastien Giguère (G), Anah.	1.00
☐	4 Sandis Ozolinsh, Anah.	.35
☐	5 Dany Heatley, Atla.	1.00
☐	6 Ilya Kovalchuk, Atla.	1.00
☐	7 Patrik Stefan, Atla.	.35
☐	8 Daniel McGillis, Bost.	.35
☐	9 Joe Thornton, Bost.	1.50
☐	10 Sergei Samsonov, Bost.	.50
☐	11 Jeff Hackett (G), Bost.	.35
☐	12 Glen Murray, Bost.	.50
☐	13 Miroslav Satan, Buff.	.35
☐	14 Martin Biron (G), Buff.	.50
☐	15 Daniel Brière, Buff.	.50
☐	16 Chris Drury, Calg.	.50
☐	17 Jarome Iginla, Calg.	1.00
☐	18 Roman Turek (G), Calg.	.50
☐	19 Pavel Brendl, Caro.	.35
☐	20 Rod Brind'Amour, Caro.	.35
☐	21 Ron Francis, Caro.	.50
☐	22 Tyler Arnason, Chic.	.50
☐	23 Jocelyn Thibault (G), Chic.	.50
☐	24 Bryan Marchment, Colo.	.35
☐	25 Joe Sakic, Colo.	2.00
☐	26 Peter Forsberg, Colo.	1.50
☐	27 Patrick Roy (G), Colo.	3.50
☐	28 Rob Blake, Colo.	.50
☐	29 Geoff Sanderson, Colu.	.35
☐	30 Marc Denis (G), Colu.	.50
☐	31 Mike Modano, Dall.	1.00
☐	32 Bill Guerin, Dall.	.50
☐	33 Marty Turco (G), Dall.	.50
☐	34 Steve Yzerman, Detr.	3.00
☐	35 Brendan Shanahan, Detr.	1.00
☐	36 Brett Hull, Detr.	1.00
☐	37 Curtis Joseph (G), Detr.	1.00
☐	38 Nicklas Lidström, Detr.	.50
☐	39 Sergei Fedorov, Detr.	1.00
☐	40 Mathieu Schneider, Detr.	.35
☐	41 Mike Comrie, Edmo.	1.00
☐	42 Tommy Salo (G), Edmo.	.50
☐	43 Olli Jokinen, Flor.	.35
☐	44 Kristian Huselius, Flor.	.35
☐	45 Roberto Luongo (G), Flor.	1.00
☐	46 Adam Deadmarsh, LosA.	.35
☐	47 Zigmund Palffy, LosA.	.50
☐	48 Félix Potvin (G), LosA.	.50
☐	49 Marian Gaborik, MinW.	1.00
☐	50 Mr.& Mrs.Hockey 50th Anniversary	1.50
☐	51 Pascal Dupuis, MinW.	.35
☐	52 Saku Koivu, Mont.	1.00
☐	53 Marcel Hossa, Mont.	.50
☐	54 José Théodore (G), Mont.	1.50
☐	55 David Legwand, Nash.	.50
☐	56 Scott Hartnell, Nash.	.35
☐	57 Tomas Vokoun (G), Nash.	.35
☐	58 John Madden, NJer.	.35
☐	59 Scott Gomez, NJer.	.50
☐	60 Martin Brodeur (G), NJer.	2.00
☐	61 Alexei Yashin, NYIs.	.50
☐	62 Mark Parrish, NYIs.	.50
☐	63 Janne Niinimaa, NYIs.	.35
☐	64 Alex Kovalev, NYRa.	.50
☐	65 Pavel Bure, NYRa.	1.00
☐	66 Mike Dunham (G), NYRa.	.50
☐	67 Mark Messier, NYRa.	1.00
☐	68 Brian Leetch, NYRa.	.50
☐	69 Daniel Alfredsson, Otta.	.50
☐	70 Marian Hossa, Otta.	1.00
☐	71 Patrick Lalime (G), Otta.	.50
☐	72 Jeremy Roenick, Phil.	1.00
☐	73 John LeClair, Phil.	1.00
☐	74 Tony Amonte, Phil.	.50
☐	75 Gordie Howe 75th Birthday	2.50
☐	76 Roman Cechmanek (G), Phil.	.50
☐	77 Brian Boucher (G), Phoe.	.35
☐	78 Shane Doan, Phoe.	.35
☐	79 Mario Lemieux, Pitt.	3.50
☐	80 Martin Straka, Pitt.	.35
☐	81 Sébastien Caron (G), Pitt.	.35
☐	82 Aleksey Morozov, Pitt.	.35
☐	83 Doug Weight, SLou.	.50
☐	84 Keith Tkachuk, SLou.	.50
☐	85 Chris Osgood (G), SLou.	.50
☐	86 Teemu Selänne, SanJ.	1.00
☐	87 Kyle McLaren, SanJ.	.35
☐	88 Evgeni Nabokov (G), SanJ.	.50
☐	89 Martin St-Louis, Tamp.	.50
☐	90 Nikolai Khabibulin (G), Tamp.	.50
☐	91 Doug Gilmour, Toro.	.50
☐	92 Mats Sundin, Toro.	1.00
☐	93 Owen Nolan, Toro.	.50
☐	94 Ed Belfour (G), Toro.	1.00
☐	95 Todd Bertuzzi, Vanc.	1.50
☐	96 Markus Näslund, Vanc.	1.00
☐	97 Dan Cloutier (G), Vanc.	.50
☐	98 Jaromir Jagr, Wash.	1.00
☐	99 Olaf Kölzig (G), Wash.	.50
☐	100 Michael Nylander, Wash.	.35

ROOKIE ROLE MODELS

	Insert (*999)	RI999
☐	101 Gordie Howe, Detr.	14.00
☐	102 Wayne Gretzky, Edmo.	20.00
☐	103 Bobby Orr, Bost.	20.00
☐	104 Patrick Roy (G), Colo.	14.00
☐	105 Mario Lemieux, Pitt.	14.00
☐	106 Joe Thornton, Bost.	6.00
☐	107 Martin Brodeur (G), NJer.	8.00
☐	108 Steve Yzerman, Detr.	12.00
☐	109 Jaromir Jagr, Wash.	4.00
☐	110 Paul Kariya, Anah.	6.00
☐	111 Jarome Iginla, Calg.	4.00
☐	112 Joe Sakic, Colo.	8.00
☐	113 Mats Sundin, Toro.	4.00
☐	114 Ilya Kovalchuk, Atla.	4.00
☐	115 Marian Gaborik, MinW.	4.00
☐	116 Mike Modano, Dall.	4.00

ROOKIE INSPIRATIONS

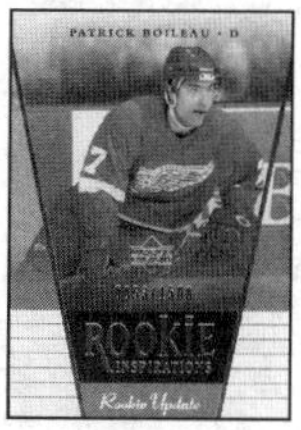

	Insert (*1500)	RI1500
☐	**117 Carlo Colaiacovo, Toro. RC**	**6.00**
☐	**118 Jay Bouwmeester, Flor. RC**	**15.00**
☐	**119 Ari Ahonen (G), NJer. RC**	**6.00**
☐	**120 Patrick Boileau, Detr. RC**	**6.00**
☐	**121 Mike Komisarek, Mont. RC**	**6.00**
☐	**122 Cristobal Huet, LosA. RC**	**6.00**
☐	**123 Josh Harding, MinW. RC**	**6.00**
☐	**124 Chris Schmidt, LosA. RC**	**6.00**
☐	**125 Niko Dimitrakos, SanJ. RC**	**6.00**
☐	**126 Ryan Bayda, Caro. RC**	**6.00**
☐	**127 Radoslav Hecl, Buff. RC**	**6.00**
☐	**128 Burke (G) Henry, Chic. RC**	**6.00**
☐	**129 Frédéric Cloutier (G), MinW. RC**	**6.00**
☐	**130 Tomas Kurka, Caro. RC**	**6.00**
☐	**131 John Tripp, NYRa. RC**	**6.00**
☐	**132 François Beauchemin, Mont. RC**	**6.00**
☐	**133 Brandon Reid, Vanc. RC**	**10.00**
☐	**134 Tomas Surovy, Pitt. RC**	**6.00**
☐	**135 Chad Wiseman, SanJ. RC**	**6.00**
☐	**136 Jason Bacashihua (G), Dall. RC**	**6.00**
☐	**137 Jesse Fibiger, SanJ. RC**	**6.00**
☐	**138 Marc-André Bergeron, Edmo. RC**	**6.00**
☐	**139 Ryan Miller (G), Buff. RC**	**15.00**
☐	**140 Ryan Kraft, SanJ. RC**	**6.00**
☐	**141 Simon Gamache, Atla. RC**	**6.00**
☐	**142 Rob Davison, SanJ. RC**	**6.00**
☐	**143 Jason King, Vanc. RC**	**6.00**
☐	**144 Brad DeFauw, Caro. RC**	**6.00**
☐	**145 Miroslav Zalesak, SanJ. RC**	**6.00**
☐	**146 Sean McMorrow, Buff. RC**	**6.00**
☐	**147 Mike Siklenka, Phil. RC**	**6.00**
☐	**148 Doug Janik, Buff. RC**	**6.00**

ROOKIE INSPIRATIONS

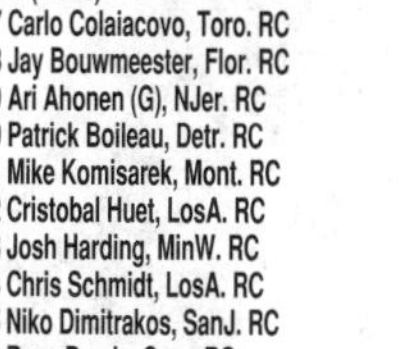

	Insert (*1200)	RI1200
☐	**149a Svitov RC ✄ / Shanahan ✄**	**15.00**
☐	**149b Svitov RC ✄ / Bertuzzi ✄**	**15.00**
☐	**149c Svitov RC ✄ / LeClair ✄**	**10.00**
☐	**150a Smirnov RC ✄ / Yashin ✄**	**10.00**
☐	**150b Smirnov RC ✄ / Bertuzzi ✄**	**15.00**
☐	**150c Smirnov RC ✄ / LeClair ✄**	**10.00**
☐	**151a Orpik RC ✄ / Blake ✄**	**10.00**
☐	**151b Orpik RC ✄ / Jovanovski ✄**	**8.00**
☐	**151c Orpik RC ✄ / Stevens ✄**	**8.00**
☐	**152a Hall (G) RC ✄ / LeClair ✄**	**10.00**
☐	**152b Hall (G) RC ✄ / Deadmarsh ✄**	**8.00**
☐	**152c Hall (G) RC ✄ / Iginla ✄**	**10.00**
☐	**153a Taffe RC ✄ / Drury ✄**	**10.00**
☐	**153b Taffe RC ✄ / York ✄**	**8.00**
☐	**153c Taffe RC ✄ / Roenick ✄**	**10.00**
☐	**154a Eminger RC ✄ / Lidström ✄**	**8.00**
☐	**154b Eminger RC ✄ / Gonchar ✄**	**8.00**
☐	**154c Eminger RC ✄ / Leetch ✄**	**8.00**
☐	**155a Leopold RC ✄ / MacInnis ✄**	**8.00**
☐	**155b Leopold RC ✄ / Leetch ✄**	**10.00**
☐	**155c Leopold RC ✄ / Niedermayer ✄**	**8.00**
☐	**156a Sharp RC ✄ / Reinprecht ✄**	**8.00**
☐	**156b Sharp RC ✄ / Peca ✄**	**8.00**
☐	**156c Sharp RC ✄ / Roenick ✄**	**10.00**
☐	**157a Ott RC ✄ / Kariya ✄**	**20.00**
☐	**157b Ott RC ✄ Green / Samsonov ✄ White**	**10.00**
☐	**157c Ott RC ✄ / Fleury ✄**	**10.00**
☐	**158a Hemsky RC ✄ / Jagr ✄**	**20.00**
☐	**158b Hemsky RC ✄ / Hejduk ✄**	**15.00**
☐	**158c Hemsky RC ✄ Gold / Elias ✄ White**	**15.00**
☐	**159a Frolov RC ✄ / LeClair ✄**	**15.00**
☐	**159b Frolov RC ✄ / Yashin ✄**	**10.00**
☐	**159c Frolov RC ✄ / Jagr ✄**	**15.00**
☐	**160a Stoll RC ✄ / LeClair ✄**	**10.00**
☐	**160b Stoll RC ✄ / Tkachuk ✄**	**10.00**
☐	**160c Stoll RC ✄ / Guerin ✄**	**8.00**
☐	**161a Volchenkov RC ✄ / Blake ✄**	**8.00**
☐	**161b Volchenkov RC ✄ / Stevens ✄**	**8.00**
☐	**161c Volchenkov RC ✄ / Jovanovski ✄**	**8.00**
☐	**162a Bykov RC ✄ / Leetch ✄**	**8.00**
☐	**162b Bykov RC ✄ / Lidström ✄**	**8.00**
☐	**162c Bykov RC ✄ / Gonchar ✄**	**8.00**

ROOKIE INSPIRATIONS

	Insert (*199)	RI199
☐	**163 J. Spezza RC ✍ / W. Gretzky**	**150.00**
☐	**164 PM. Bouchard RC ✍ / S. Samsonov**	**40.00**
☐	**165 R. Hainsey RC ✍ / R. Bourque**	**50.00**
☐	**166 S. Chistov RC ✍ / P. Bure**	**50.00**
☐	**167 C. Kobasew RC ✍ / J. Iginla**	**40.00**
☐	**168 H. Zetterberg RC ✍ / G. Howe**	**150.00**
☐	**169 S. Upshall RC ✍ / M. Comrie**	**40.00**
☐	**170 P. Leclaire (G) RC ✍ / P. Roy (G)**	**100.00**
☐	**171 M. Tellqvist (G) RC ✍ / E. Belfour (G)**	**40.00**
☐	**172 R. Nash RC ✍ / J. Thornton**	**75.00**

ROOKIE INSPIRATIONS

	Insert (*1500)	RI1500
☐	**173 Igor Radulov, Chic. RC**	**10.00**
☐	**174 Paul Gaustad, Buff. RC**	**6.00**
☐	**175 Christian Backman, SLou. RC**	**6.00**
☐	**176 Cam Severson, Anah. RC**	**6.00**

DIGNIFIED JERSEY

Insert Set (36 cards): 575.00

	Insert (*299)	DJ
☐	Todd Bertuzzi, Vanc. ✄	20.00
☐	Pavel Bure, NYRa. ✄	15.00
☐	Roman Cechmanek (G), Phil. ✄	10.00
☐	Pavol Demitra, SLou. ✄	10.00
☐	Mike Dunham (G), NYRa. ✄	10.00
☐	Jean-Sébastien Giguère (G), Anah. ✄	20.00
☐	Bill Guerin, Dall. ✄	10.00
☐	Dany Heatley, Atla. ✄	20.00
☐	Milan Hejduk, Colo. ✄	15.00
☐	Marian Hossa, Otta. ✄	20.00
☐	Jarome Iginla, Calg. ✄	15.00
☐	Jaromir Jagr, Wash. ✄	20.00
☐	Paul Kariya, Anah. ✄	25.00
☐	Saku Koivu, Mont. ✄	15.00
☐	Olaf Kölzig (G), Wash. ✄	10.00
☐	Ilya Kovalchuk, Atla. ✄	20.00
☐	Mario Lemieux, Pitt. ✄	60.00
☐	Eric Lindros, NYRa. ✄	20.00
☐	Roberto Luongo (G), Flor. ✄	15.00
☐	Mike Modano, Dall. ✄	20.00
☐	Chris Osgood (G), SLou. ✄	10.00
☐	Zigmund Palffy, LosA. ✄	10.00
☐	Félix Potvin (G), LosA. ✄	10.00
☐	Keith Primeau, Phil. ✄	10.00
☐	Jeremy Roenick, Phil. ✄	15.00
☐	Patrick Roy (G), Colo. ✄	60.00
☐	Joe Sakic, Colo. ✄	30.00
☐	Tommy Salo (G), Edmo. ✄	10.00
☐	Sergei Samsonov, Bost. ✄	10.00
☐	Brendan Shanahan, Detr. ✄	20.00
☐	Mats Sundin, Toro. ✄	20.00
☐	José Théodore (G), Mont. ✄	20.00
☐	Joe Thornton, Bost. ✄	20.00
☐	Roman Turek (G), Calg. ✄	10.00
☐	Alexei Yashin, NYIs. ✄	10.00
☐	Steve Yzerman, Detr. ✄	45.00

DIGNIFIED JERSEY GOLD

Insert Set (36 cards): 775.00

	Insert (*125)	G125
☐	Todd Bertuzzi, Vanc. ✄	30.00
☐	Pavel Bure, NYRa. ✄	20.00
☐	Roman Cechmanek (G), Phil. ✄	15.00
☐	Pavol Demitra, SLou. ✄	15.00
☐	Mike Dunham (G), NYRa. ✄	15.00
☐	Jean-Sébastien Giguère (G), Anah. ✄	25.00
☐	Bill Guerin, Dall. ✄	15.00
☐	Dany Heatley, Atla. ✄	25.00
☐	Milan Hejduk, Colo. ✄	20.00
☐	Marian Hossa, Otta. ✄	25.00
☐	Jarome Iginla, Calg. ✄	20.00
☐	Jaromir Jagr, Wash. ✄	25.00
☐	Paul Kariya, Anah. ✄	35.00
☐	Saku Koivu, Mont. ✄	20.00
☐	Olaf Kölzig (G), Wash. ✄	15.00
☐	Ilya Kovalchuk, Atla. ✄	25.00
☐	Mario Lemieux, Pitt. ✄	75.00
☐	Eric Lindros, NYRa. ✄	25.00
☐	Roberto Luongo (G), Flor. ✄	20.00
☐	Mike Modano, Dall. ✄	25.00
☐	Chris Osgood (G), SLou. ✄	15.00
☐	Zigmund Palffy, LosA. ✄	15.00
☐	Félix Potvin (G), LosA. ✄	15.00
☐	Keith Primeau, Phil. ✄	15.00
☐	Jeremy Roenick, Phil. ✄	20.00
☐	Patrick Roy (G), Colo. ✄	75.00
☐	Joe Sakic, Colo. ✄	40.00
☐	Tommy Salo (G), Edmo. ✄	15.00
☐	Sergei Samsonov, Bost. ✄	15.00
☐	Brendan Shanahan, Detr. ✄	25.00
☐	Mats Sundin, Toro. ✄	25.00
☐	José Théodore (G), Mont. ✄	30.00
☐	Joe Thornton, Bost. ✄	30.00
☐	Roman Turek (G), Calg. ✄	15.00
☐	Alexei Yashin, NYIs. ✄	15.00
☐	Steve Yzerman, Detr. ✄	60.00

SUPERSTARS JERSEY

Insert Set (6 cards): 225.00

	Insert (*99)	SJ
☐	Jagr ✄ / Kölzig (G) ✄	30.00
☐	Kovalchuk ✄ / Heatley ✄	35.00
☐	Lindros ✄ / Bure ✄	30.00
☐	Roy (G) ✄ / Sakic ✄	85.00
☐	Thornton ✄ / Samsonov ✄	30.00
☐	Yzerman ✄ / Shanahan ✄	60.00

SUPERSTARS JERSEY GOLD

Insert Set (6 cards): 950.00

	Insert (*10)	SJ10
☐	Jagr ✄ / Kölzig (G) ✄	120.00
☐	Kovalchuk ✄ / Heatley ✄	150.00
☐	Lindros ✄ / Bure ✄	135.00
☐	Roy (G) ✄ / Sakic ✄	345.00
☐	Thornton ✄ / Samsonov ✄	135.00
☐	Yzerman ✄ / Shanahan ✄	255.00

TOP DRAWS

Insert Set (29 cards): 1500.00

	Insert (1:144)	TD
☐	Maxim Afinogenov, Buff. ✍	20.00
☐	Pierre-Marc Bouchard, MinW. ✍ {*}	40.00
☐	Raymond Bourque, Bost. ✍ {*}	65.00
☐	Jay Bouwmeester, Flor. ✍ {*}	40.00
☐	Pavel Brendl, Phil. ✍	15.00
☐	Pavel Bure, NYRa. ✍	40.00
☐	Stanislav Chistov, Anah. ✍ {*}	40.00
☐	Erik Cole, Caro. ✍	15.00
☐	Mike Comrie, Edmo. ✍	40.00
☐	Simon Gagné, Phil. ✍	40.00
☐	Wayne Gretzky, Edmo. ✍	220.00
☐	Ron Hainsey, Mont. ✍ {*}	20.00
☐	Martin Havlat, Otta. ✍	30.00
☐	Dany Heatley, Atla. ✍	50.00
☐	Gordie Howe, Detr. ✍ {*}	155.00
☐	Jarome Iginla, Calg. ✍	40.00
☐	Curtis Joseph (G), Detr. ✍	50.00
☐	Chuck Kobasew, Calg. ✍	20.00
☐	Ilya Kovalchuk, Atla. ✍	50.00
☐	John LeClair, Phil. ✍	40.00
☐	Markus Näslund, Vanc. ✍	50.00

☐ Bobby Orr, Bost. ✍ {**}	250.00
☐ Steve Ott, Dall. ✍	15.00
☐ Patrick Roy (G), Colo. ✍ {*}	165.00
☐ Sergei Samsonov, Bost. ✍	30.00
☐ Jason Spezza, Otta. ✍ {*}	50.00
☐ Mikael Tellqvist (G), Toro. ✍ {*}	15.00
☐ Steve Yzerman, Detr. ✍	120.00
☐ Henrik Zetterberg, Detr. ✍ {*}	65.00

2002 - 03 UPPER DECK TOP SHELF

Produced by The Upper Deck Company, this series was released in August 2002.

Shell Set (90 cards):	**65.00**
Complete Set (135 cards):	**925.00**
Common Player:	**.50**
Description	**Base**
☐ 1 Jean-Sébastien Giguère (G), Anah.	2.00
☐ 2 Jeff Friesen, Anah.	.50
☐ 3 Paul Kariya, Anah.	2.50
☐ 4 Ilya Kovalchuk, Atla.	3.00
☐ 5 Dany Heatley, Atla.	3.00
☐ 6 Joe Thornton, Bost.	2.00
☐ 7 Sergei Samsonov, Bost.	1.00
☐ 8 Bill Guerin, Bost.	.50
☐ 9 Martin Biron (G), Buff.	.50
☐ 10 Miroslav Satan, Buff.	.50
☐ 11 Maxim Afinogenov, Buff.	.50
☐ 12 Jarome Iginla, Calg.	1.50
☐ 13 Roman Turek (G), Calg.	.50
☐ 14 Craig Conroy, Calg.	.50
☐ 15 Jeff O'Neill, Caro.	.50
☐ 16 Arturs Irbe (G), Caro.	.50
☐ 17 Sami Kapanen, Caro.	.50
☐ 18 Jocelyn Thibault (G), Chic.	.50
☐ 19 Éric Dazé, Chic.	.50
☐ 20 Alexei Zhamnov, Chic.	.50
☐ 21 Patrick Roy (G), Colo.	6.00
☐ 22 Joe Sakic, Colo.	3.00
☐ 23 Peter Forsberg, Colo.	2.50
☐ 24 Marc Denis (G), Colu.	.50
☐ 25 Espen Knutsen, Colu.	.50
☐ 26 Mike Modano, Dall.	2.00
☐ 27 Jason Arnott, Dall.	.50
☐ 28 Marty Turco (G), Dall.	1.00
☐ 29 Steve Yzerman, Detr.	4.50
☐ 30 Sergei Fedorov, Detr.	2.00
☐ 31 Dominik Hasek (G), Detr.	2.00
☐ 32 Brendan Shanahan, Detr.	2.00
☐ 33 Ryan Smyth, Edmo.	.50
☐ 34 Tommy Salo (G), Edmo.	.50
☐ 35 Mike Comrie, Edmo.	1.50
☐ 36 Roberto Luongo (G), Flor.	1.50
☐ 37 Kristian Huselius, Flor.	.50
☐ 38 Sandis Ozolinsh, Flor.	.50
☐ 39 Zigmund Palffy, LosA.	1.00
☐ 40 Jason Allison, LosA.	1.00
☐ 41 Félix Potvin (G), LosA.	1.00
☐ 42 Manny Fernandez (G), MinW.	.50
☐ 43 Marian Gaborik, MinW.	2.00
☐ 44 Andrew Brunette, MinW.	.50
☐ 45 José Théodore (G), Mont.	2.00
☐ 46 Saku Koivu, Mont.	1.50
☐ 47 Richard Zednik, Mont.	.50
☐ 48 Mike Dunham (G), Nash.	.50
☐ 49 David Legwand, Nash.	.50
☐ 50 Patrik Elias, NJer.	1.50
☐ 51 Joe Nieuwendyk, NJer.	.50
☐ 52 Martin Brodeur (G), NJer.	3.00
☐ 53 Scott Niedermayer, NJer.	.50
☐ 54 Alexei Yashin, NYIs.	1.00
☐ 55 Michael Peca, NYIs.	.50
☐ 56 Chris Osgood (G), NYIs.	1.00
☐ 57 Mike Richter (G), NYRa.	.50
☐ 58 Pavel Bure, NYRa.	1.50
☐ 59 Eric Lindros, NYRa.	2.00
☐ 60 Martin Havlat, Otta.	1.00
☐ 61 Patrick Lalime (G), Otta.	1.00
☐ 62 Marian Hossa, Otta.	2.00
☐ 63 Jeremy Roenick, Phil.	1.50
☐ 64 Roman Cechmanek (G), Phil.	.50
☐ 65 John LeClair, Phil.	1.50
☐ 66 Simon Gagné, Phil.	1.50
☐ 67 Ladislav Nagy, Phoe.	.50
☐ 68 Sean Burke (G), Phoe.	1.00
☐ 69 Daniel Brière, Phoe.	.50
☐ 70 Johan Hedberg (G), Pitt.	.50
☐ 71 Mario Lemieux, Pitt.	6.00
☐ 72 Alex Kovalev, Pitt.	1.00
☐ 73 Evgeni Nabokov (G), SanJ.	1.00
☐ 74 Owen Nolan, SanJ.	1.00
☐ 75 Teemu Selänne, SanJ.	1.50
☐ 76 Brent Johnson (G), SLou.	.50
☐ 77 Keith Tkachuk, SLou.	1.00
☐ 78 Chris Pronger, SLou.	1.00
☐ 79 Brad Richards, Tamp.	.50
☐ 80 Vincent Lecavalier, Tamp.	2.00
☐ 81 Nikolai Khabibulin (G), Tamp.	.50
☐ 82 Alexander Mogilny, Toro.	.50
☐ 83 Mats Sundin, Toro.	2.00
☐ 84 Curtis Joseph (G), Toro.	2.00
☐ 85 Todd Bertuzzi, Vanc.	2.00
☐ 86 Brendan Morrison, Vanc.	.50
☐ 87 Markus Näslund, Vanc.	2.00
☐ 88 Jaromir Jagr, Wash.	2.00
☐ 89 Peter Bondra, Wash.	1.00
☐ 90 Olaf Kölzig (G), Wash.	1.00

ROOKIE

Redemption (*1125)	**R1125**
☐ 91 Tim Thomas (G), Bost.	8.00
☐ 92 Ivan Majesky, Flor.	8.00
☐ 93 Jay Bouwmeester, Flor.	15.00
☐ 94 Ron Hainsey, Mont.	8.00
☐ 95 Ray Schultz, NYIs.	8.00
☐ 96 Tomi Pettinen, NYIs.	8.00
☐ 97 Eric Godard, NYIs.	8.00
☐ 98 Anton Volchenkov, Otta.	8.00
☐ 99 Dennis Seidenberg, Phil.	8.00
☐ 100 Radoslav Somik, Phil.	8.00
☐ 101 Patrick Sharp, Phil.	8.00
☐ 102 Carlo Colaiacovo, Toro.	8.00
☐ 103 Mikael Tellqvist (G), Toro.	8.00
☐ 104 Steve Eminger, Wash.	8.00
☐ 105 Alex Henry, Wash.	8.00
☐ 106 Kurt Sauer, Anah.	8.00
☐ 107 Micki DuPont, Calg.	8.00
☐ 108 Shawn Thornton, Chic.	8.00
☐ 109 Matt Henderson, Chic.	8.00
☐ 110 Jeff Paul, Colo.	8.00
☐ 111 Lasse Pirjetä, Colu.	8.00
☐ 112 Dmitri Bykov, Detr.	8.00
☐ 113 Kari Haakana, Edmo.	8.00
☐ 114 Sylvain Blouin, Mont.	8.00
☐ 115 Stéphane Veilleux, MinW.	8.00
☐ 116 Greg Koehler, Nash.	8.00
☐ 117 Lynn Loyns, SanJ.	8.00
☐ 118 Tomi Koivisto, SLou.	8.00
☐ 119 Curtis Sanford (G), SLou.	8.00
☐ 120 Cody Rudkowsky (G), SLou.	8.00

ROOKIE

Redemption (*500)	**R500**
☐ 121 Martin Gerber (G), Anah. RC	20.00
☐ 122 Alexei Smirnov, Anah. RC	30.00
☐ 123 Stanislav Chistov, Anah. RC	60.00
☐ 124 Jordan Leopold, Calg. RC	30.00
☐ 125 Chuck Kobasew, Calg. RC	40.00
☐ 126 Rick Nash, Colu. RC	120.00
☐ 127 Henrik Zetterberg, Detr. RC	120.00
☐ 128 Ales Hemsky, Edmo. RC	60.00
☐ 129 Alexander Frolov, LosA. RC	50.00
☐ 130 Pierre-Marc Bouchard, MinW. RC	60.00
☐ 131 Adam Hall, Nash. RC	30.00
☐ 132 Scottie Upshall, Nash. RC	40.00
☐ 133 Jason Spezza, Otta. RC	90.00
☐ 134 Jeff Taffe, Phoe. RC	30.00
☐ 135 Alexander Svitov, Tamp. RC	40.00

ALL-STARS

Insert Set (12 cards):	**700.00**
Insert (#/50)	**AS99**
☐ Tony Amonte, 1999 All-Star ✂	40.00
☐ Sergei Fedorov, 1996 All-Star ✂	50.00
☐ Theoren Fleury, 1999 All-Star ✂	40.00
☐ Wayne Gretzky, 1996 All-Star ✂	200.00
☐ Wayne Gretzky, 1991 All-Star ✂	200.00
☐ Jaromir Jagr, 1996 All-Star ✂	50.00
☐ Paul Kariya, 2000 All-Star ✂	50.00
☐ Joe Sakic, 2000 All-Star ✂	75.00
☐ Teemu Selänne, 1999 All-Star ✂	40.00
☐ Scott Stevens, 1999 All-Star ✂	40.00
☐ Mats Sundin, 2000 All-Star ✂	50.00
☐ Keith Tkachuk, 1998 All-Star ✂	40.00

CLUTCH PERFORMERS

Insert Set (42 cards):	**1100.00**
Insert (#/75)	**CP75**
☐ Ed Belfour (G), Dall. ✂	25.00
☐ Peter Bondra, Wash. ✂	20.00
☐ Raymond Bourque, Bost. ✂	25.00
☐ Martin Brodeur (G), NJer. ✂	50.00
☐ Pavel Bure, NYRa. ✂	25.00
☐ Sean Burke (G), Phoe. ✂	20.00
☐ Adam Deadmarsh, LosA. ✂	20.00
☐ Chris Drury, Colo. ✂	20.00
☐ Sergei Fedorov, Detr. ✂	35.00
☐ Simon Gagné, Phil. ✂	30.00
☐ Sergei Gonchar, Wash. ✂	20.00
☐ Wayne Gretzky, LosA. ✂	150.00
☐ Bill Guerin, Bost. ✂	20.00
☐ Milan Hejduk, Colo. ✂	30.00
☐ Jarome Iginla, Calg. ✂	25.00
☐ Jaromir Jagr, Wash. ✂	25.00
☐ Curtis Joseph (G), Toro. ✂	25.00
☐ Paul Kariya, Anah. ✂	50.00
☐ Ilya Kovalchuk, Atla. ✂	25.00
☐ Brian Leetch, NYRa. ✂	20.00
☐ Claude Lemieux, Phoe. ✂	20.00
☐ Mario Lemieux, Pitt. ✂	100.00
☐ Nicklas Lidström, Detr. ✂	20.00
☐ Eric Lindros, NYRa. ✂	35.00
☐ Al MacInnis, SLou. ✂	20.00
☐ Mike Modano, Dall. ✂	35.00
☐ Joe Nieuwendyk, NJer. ✂	20.00
☐ Zigmund Palffy, LosA. ✂	20.00
☐ Mike Richter (G), NYRa. ✂	20.00
☐ Luc Robitaille, Detr. ✂	30.00
☐ Jeremy Roenick, Phil. ✂	30.00
☐ Patrick Roy (G), Colo. ✂	75.00
☐ Joe Sakic, 1993 All-Star ✂	50.00
☐ Sergei Samsonov, Bost. ✂	20.00
☐ Teemu Selänne, SanJ. ✂	30.00
☐ Brendan Shanahan, Detr. ✂	35.00
☐ Steve Sullivan, Chic. ✂	20.00
☐ Mats Sundin, Toro. ✂	25.00
☐ Joe Thornton, Bost. ✂	25.00
☐ Keith Tkachuk, 1998 All-Star ✂	20.00
☐ Doug Weight, SLou. ✂	20.00
☐ Steve Yzerman, Detr. ✂	75.00

GOAL ORIENTED

Insert Set (30 cards):	**625.00**
Insert (#/75)	**GO75**
☐ Tony Amonte, Chic. ✂	20.00
☐ Denis (G) Arkhipov, Nash. ✂	20.00
☐ Peter Bondra, Wash. ✂	20.00
☐ Daniel Brière, Phoe. ✂	20.00
☐ Pavel Bure, NYRa. ✂	30.00
☐ Éric Dazé, Chic. ✂	20.00
☐ Adam Deadmarsh, LosA. ✂	20.00
☐ Radek Dvorak, NYRa. ✂	20.00
☐ Sergei Fedorov, Detr. ✂	35.00
☐ Simon Gagné, Phil. ✂	30.00
☐ Bill Guerin, Bost. ✂	20.00
☐ Milan Hejduk, Colo. ✂	30.00
☐ Jaromir Jagr, Wash. ✂	25.00
☐ Paul Kariya, Anah. ✂	50.00
☐ Ilya Kovalchuk, Atla. ✂	25.00
☐ Robert Lang, Pitt. ✂	20.00
☐ Mike Modano, Dall. ✂	35.00
☐ Glen Murray, Bost. ✂	20.00
☐ Zigmund Palffy, LosA. ✂	20.00
☐ Steven Reinprecht, Colo. ✂	20.00
☐ Joe Sakic, Colo. ✂	50.00
☐ Sergei Samsonov, Bost. ✂	20.00
☐ Miroslav Satan, Buff. ✂	20.00
☐ Teemu Selänne, SanJ. ✂	30.00
☐ Steve Sullivan, Chic. ✂	20.00
☐ Mats Sundin, Toro. ✂	25.00
☐ Alex Tanguay, Colo. ✂	20.00
☐ Joe Thornton, Bost. ✂	25.00
☐ Mike York, Edmo. ✂	20.00
☐ Steve Yzerman, Detr. ✂	75.00

HARDWARE HEROES

Insert Set (10 cards):	**5500.00**
Insert (#/10)	**4HH10**
☐ Belfour (G) ✂ / Roy (G) ✂ / Brodeur (G) ✂ / Dunham (G) ✂	675
☐ Fedorov ✂ / Yzerman ✂ / Gilmour ✂ / Clarke ✂	600
☐ Gretzky ✂ / Kariya ✂ / Sakic ✂ / Demitra ✂	925
☐ Gretzky ✂ / Sakic ✂ / Lemieux ✂ / Jagr ✂	1200
☐ Hasek (G) ✂ / Belfour (G) ✂ / Roy (G) ✂ / Kölzig (G) ✂	625
☐ Howe ✂ / Gretzky ✂ / Lemieux ✂ / Jagr ✂	1300
☐ Pronger ✂ / MacInnis ✂ / Blake ✂ / Lidström ✂	275
☐ Sakic ✂ / Roy (G) ✂ / Blake ✂ / Forsberg ✂	750
☐ Samsonov ✂ / Selänne ✂ / Bure ✂ / Robitaille ✂	375
☐ Yzerman ✂ / Nieuwendyk ✂ / Leetch ✂ / Roy (G) ✂	725

HAT TRICK HEROES

Insert Set (12 cards):	**3200.00**
Insert (#/25)	**HTH**
☐ T. Amonte ✂ / Z. Palffy ✂ / T. Selänne ✂	200.00
☐ P. Bure ✂ / M. Satan ✂ / P. Bondra ✂	175.00
☐ B. Guerin ✂ / M. Hossa ✂ / P. Bondra ✂	200.00
☐ W. Gretzky ✂ / M. Lemieux ✂ / P. Bure ✂	800.00
☐ J. Jagr ✂ / M. Hejduk ✂ / T. Selänne ✂	250.00
☐ P. Kariya ✂ / S. Gagné ✂ / T. Fleury ✂	275.00
☐ P. Kariya ✂ / S. Yzerman ✂ / J. Iginla ✂	475.00
☐ M. Lemieux ✂ / J. Jagr ✂ / J. Thornton ✂	525.00
☐ J. LeClair ✂ / J. Roenick ✂ / M. Recchi ✂	200.00
☐ M. Näslund ✂ / J. Thornton ✂ / M. Hejduk ✂	300.00
☐ B. Shanahan ✂ / B. Hull ✂ / L. Robitaille ✂	275.00
☐ J. Sakic ✂ / J. Iginla ✂ / S. Gagné ✂	325.00

MILESTONES

Insert Set (10 cards):	**2500.00**
Insert (#/25)	**4M25**
☐ Bure ✂ / Bondra ✂ / Recchi ✂ / Roenick ✂	150
☐ Bourque ✂ / Modano ✂ / Bure ✂ / Selänne ✂	225
☐ Gretzky ✂ / Bourque ✂ / Yzerman ✂ / Messier ✂	525
☐ Gretzky ✂ / Howe ✂ / Lemieux ✂ / Yzerman ✂	750
☐ Hasek (G) ✂ / Potvin ✂ / Burke (G) ✂ / Barrasso (G) ✂	200
☐ Lindros ✂ / Nolan ✂ / LeClair ✂ / Amonte ✂	175
☐ Messier ✂ / Hull ✂ / Yzerman ✂ / Robitaille ✂	325
☐ Roy (G) ✂ / Brodeur (G) ✂ / Richter (G) ✂ / Joseph (G) ✂	325
☐ Shanahan ✂ / Fleury ✂ / Roenick ✂ / Messier ✂	200
☐ Shanahan ✂ / Yzerman ✂ / Verbeek ✂ / Robitaille ✂	275

REFLECTIONS

Insert Set (18 cards):	**500.00**
Insert (#/99)	**Refl.**
☐ Ed Belfour (G) ✂ / Marc Denis (G) ✂	40.00
☐ Pavel Bure ✂ / Ilya Kovalchuk ✂	50.00
☐ Rob Blake ✂ / Chris Pronger ✂	30.00
☐ Pavel Bure ✂ / Sergei Samsonov ✂	25.00
☐ Peter Bondra ✂ / Zigmund Palffy ✂	30.00
☐ Sergei Fedorov ✂ / Maxim Afinogenov ✂	35.00
☐ Jarome Iginla ✂ / Justin Williams ✂	25.00
☐ Paul Kariya ✂ / Simon Gagné ✂	50.00
☐ Nicklas Lidström ✂ / Rostislav Klesla ✂	30.00
☐ Mike Modano ✂ / Tim Connolly ✂	35.00
☐ Joe Nieuwendyk ✂ / David Legwand ✂	20.00
☐ Félix Potvin (G) ✂ / Martin Biron (G) ✂	45.00
☐ Keith Primeau ✂ / Joe Thornton ✂	25.00
☐ Patrick Roy (G) ✂ / José Théodore (G) ✂	100.00
☐ Miroslav Satan ✂ / Ruslan Fedotenko ✂	15.00
☐ Brendan Shanahan ✂ / Scott Hartnell ✂	30.00
☐ Steve Sullivan ✂ / Steven Reinprecht ✂	15.00
☐ Steve Yzerman ✂ / Krys Kolanos ✂	50.00

SHOOTING STARS

Insert Set (42 cards):	**700.00**
Insert (#/99)	**SH**
☐ Maxim Afinogenov, Buff. ✂	15.00
☐ Jason Allison, LosA. ✂	15.00
☐ Tony Amonte, Chic. ✂	15.00
☐ Nikolai Antropov, Toro. ✂	15.00
☐ Jason Arnott, Dall. ✂	15.00
☐ Rob Blake, Colo. ✂	15.00
☐ Peter Bondra, Wash. ✂	15.00
☐ Raymond Bourque, Colo. ✂	25.00
☐ Daniel Brière, Phoe. ✂	15.00
☐ Pavel Bure, NYRa. ✂	25.00
☐ Shane Doan, Phoe. ✂	15.00
☐ Sergei Fedorov, Detr. ✂	30.00
☐ Theoren Fleury, NYRa. ✂	15.00
☐ Peter Forsberg, Colo. ✂	25.00
☐ Simon Gagné, Phil. ✂	25.00
☐ Bill Guerin, Bost. ✂	15.00
☐ Scott Hartnell, Nash. ✂	15.00
☐ Milan Hejduk, Colo. ✂	25.00
☐ Brett Hull, Detr. ✂	25.00
☐ Jaromir Jagr, Wash. ✂	25.00
☐ Paul Kariya, Anah. ✂	25.00
☐ Espen Knutsen, Colu. ✂	15.00
☐ Saku Koivu, Mont. ✂	35.00
☐ Krys Kolanos, Phoe. ✂	15.00
☐ Robert Lang, Pitt. ✂	15.00
☐ Brian Leetch, NYRa. ✂	15.00
☐ Mario Lemieux, Pitt. ✂	75.00
☐ Nicklas Lidström, Detr. ✂	15.00
☐ Mike Modano, Dall. ✂	30.00
☐ Brenden Morrow, Dall. ✂	15.00
☐ Glen Murray, Bost. ✂	15.00
☐ Joe Nieuwendyk, NJer. ✂	15.00
☐ Zigmund Palffy, LosA. ✂	15.00
☐ Steven Reinprecht, Colo. ✂	15.00
☐ Miroslav Satan, Buff. ✂	15.00
☐ Teemu Selänne, SanJ. ✂	25.00
☐ Brendan Shanahan, Detr. ✂	30.00
☐ Steve Sullivan, Chic. ✂	15.00
☐ Mats Sundin, Toro. ✂	25.00

□	Alex Tanguay, Colo. ✄	15.00
□	Mike York, Edmo. ✄	15.00
□	Steve Yzerman, Detr. ✄	75.00

SPECIAL TEAMS

Insert Set (42 cards):		1100.00
	Insert (#/99)	**2ST99**
□	Jason Allison ✄ / Éric Bélanger ✄	20.00
□	Raymond Bourque ✄ / Rob Blake ✄	50.00
□	Daniel Brière ✄ / Shane Doan ✄	20.00
□	Pavel Bure ✄ / Brian Leetch ✄	25.00
□	Peter Bondra ✄ / Jaromir Jagr ✄	25.00
□	Valeri Bure ✄ / Roberto Luongo (G) ✄	30.00
□	Martin Biron (G) ✄ / Mika Noronen (G) ✄	20.00
□	Martin Brodeur (G) ✄ / Scott Stevens ✄	50.00
□	Raymond Bourque ✄ / Joe Thornton ✄	50.00
□	Mike Dunham (G) ✄ / Martin Erat ✄	20.00
□	Éric Dazé ✄ / Jocelyn Thibault (G) ✄	20.00
□	Sergei Fedorov ✄ / Nicklas Lidström ✄	25.00
□	Ruslan Fedotenko ✄ / Keith Primeau ✄	20.00
□	Theoren Fleury ✄ / Mike Richter (G) ✄	25.00
□	Simon Gagné ✄ / Brian Boucher (G) ✄	30.00
□	Bill Guerin ✄ / Byron Dafoe (G) ✄	20.00
□	Sergei Gonchar ✄ / Olaf Kölzig (G) ✄	25.00
□	Wayne Gretzky ✄ / Mark Messier ✄	200.00
□	Simon Gagné ✄ / Mark Recchi ✄	30.00
□	Jean-Sébastien Giguère (G) ✄ / Steve Shields ✄	30.00
□	Scott Hartnell ✄ / David Legwand ✄	20.00
□	Milan Hejduk ✄ / Steven Reinprecht ✄	30.00
□	Jarome Iginla ✄ / Marc Savard ✄	25.00
□	Jaromir Jagr ✄ / Olaf Kölzig (G) ✄	25.00
□	Krys Kolanos ✄ / Sean Burke (G) ✄	20.00
□	Paul Kariya ✄ / Jeff Friesen ✄	25.00
□	Saku Koivu ✄ / José Théodore (G) ✄	50.00
□	Rostislav Klesla ✄ / Ray Whitney ✄	20.00
□	Claude Lemieux ✄ / Shane Doan ✄	20.00
□	Mike Modano ✄ / Jason Arnott ✄	25.00
□	Mike Modano ✄ / Brenden Morrow ✄	35.00
□	Markus Näslund ✄ / Trevor Linden ✄	35.00
□	Zigmund Palffy ✄ / Adam Deadmarsh ✄	25.00
□	Miroslav Satan ✄ / Maxim Afinogenov ✄	20.00
□	Joe Sakic ✄ / Dan Hinote ✄	50.00
□	Steve Sullivan ✄ / Tony Amonte ✄	25.00
□	Teemu Selänne ✄ / Owen Nolan ✄	25.00
□	Sergei Samsonov ✄ / Joe Thornton ✄	50.00
□	Ron Tugnutt (G) ✄ / Marc Denis (G) ✄	20.00
□	Joe Thornton ✄ / Bill Guerin ✄	25.00
□	Mike York ✄ / Jochen Hecht ✄	20.00
□	Steve Yzerman ✄ / Brendan Shanahan ✄	100.00

STOPPER SWATCHES

Insert Set (24 cards):		425.00
	Insert (#/99)	**SS99**
□	David Aebischer (G), Colo. ✄	15.00
□	Ed Belfour (G), Dall. ✄	30.00
□	Martin Biron (G), Buff. ✄	15.00
□	Dan Blackburn (G), NYRa. ✄	15.00
□	Brian Boucher (G), Phil. ✄	15.00
□	Martin Brodeur (G), NJer. ✄	50.00
□	Sean Burke (G), Phoe. ✄	15.00
□	Roman Cechmanek (G), Phil. ✄	15.00
□	Byron Dafoe (G), Bost. ✄	15.00
□	Marc Denis (G), Colu. ✄	15.00
□	Mike Dunham (G), Nash. ✄	15.00
□	Jean-Sébastien Giguère (G), Anah. ✄	30.00
□	Dominik Hasek (G), Detr. ✄	30.00
□	Brent Johnson (G), SLou. ✄	15.00
□	Curtis Joseph (G), Toro. ✄	30.00
□	Olaf Kölzig (G), Wash. ✄	15.00
□	Mika Noronen (G), Buff. ✄	15.00
□	Félix Potvin (G), LosA. ✄	35.00
□	Mike Richter (G), NYRa. ✄	15.00
□	Patrick Roy (G), Colo. ✄	75.00
□	Steve Shields, Anah. ✄	15.00
□	José Théodore (G), Mont. ✄	35.00
□	Jocelyn Thibault (G), Chic. ✄	15.00
□	Ron Tugnutt (G), Colu. ✄	15.00

SWEET SWEATERS

Insert Set (42 cards):		1300.00
	Insert (#/50)	**SS50**
□	Maxim Afinogenov, Buff. ✄	25.00
□	Jason Allison, LosA. ✄	30.00
□	Mark Bell, Chic. ✄	25.00
□	Martin Biron (G), Buff. ✄	25.00
□	Raymond Bourque, Bost. ✄	50.00
□	Daniel Brière, Phoe. ✄	25.00
□	Pavel Bure, NYRa. ✄	25.00
□	Adam Deadmarsh, LosA. ✄	25.00
□	Marc Denis (G), Colu. ✄	25.00
□	Chris Drury, Colo. ✄	30.00
□	Mike Dunham (G), Nash. ✄	25.00
□	Sergei Fedorov, Detr. ✄	50.00
□	Jeff Friesen, Anah. ✄	25.00
□	Doug Gilmour, Mont. ✄	30.00
□	Wayne Gretzky, 1996 All-Star ✄	200.00
□	Bill Guerin, Bost. ✄	25.00
□	Brett Hull, Detr. ✄	50.00
□	Jaromir Jagr, Wash. ✄	50.00
□	Curtis Joseph (G), Toro. ✄	50.00
□	Paul Kariya, Anah. ✄	50.00
□	Rostislav Klesla, Colu. ✄	30.00
□	Saku Koivu, Mont. ✄	50.00
□	Olaf Kölzig (G), Wash. ✄	30.00
□	Claude Lemieux, Phoe. ✄	25.00
□	Mike Modano, Dall. ✄	50.00
□	Ville Nieminen, Pitt. ✄	25.00
□	Zigmund Palffy, LosA. ✄	30.00
□	Félix Potvin (G), LosA. ✄	60.00
□	Keith Primeau, Phil. ✄	25.00
□	Steven Reinprecht, Colo. ✄	25.00
□	Joe Sakic, Colo. ✄	75.00
□	Sergei Samsonov, Bost. ✄	30.00
□	Miroslav Satan, Buff. ✄	25.00
□	Teemu Selänne, SanJ. ✄	25.00
□	Steve Sullivan, Chic. ✄	25.00
□	Mats Sundin, Toro. ✄	50.00
□	Alex Tanguay, Colo. ✄	30.00
□	José Théodore (G), Mont. ✄	50.00
□	Jocelyn Thibault (G), Chic. ✄	25.00
□	Joe Thornton, Bost. ✄	50.00
□	Keith Tkachuk, SLou. ✄	30.00
□	Steve Yzerman, Detr. ✄	100.00

THREE STARS

Insert Set (10 cards):		3260.00
	Insert (#/10)	**3TS10**
□	J. Allison ✄ / Z. Palffy ✄ / F. Potvin (G) ✄	400.00
□	M. Afinogenov ✄ / M. Satan ✄ / M. Biron ✄	200.00
□	P. Demitra ✄ / C. Pronger ✄ / B. Johnson (G) ✄	225.00
□	B. Guerin ✄ / J. Thornton ✄ / B. Dafoe (G) ✄	350.00
□	J. Jagr ✄ / P. Bondra ✄ / O. Kölzig (G) ✄	375.00
□	J. LeClair ✄ / S. Gagné ✄ / R. Cechmanek (G) ✄	350.00
□	M. Modano ✄ / B. Morrow ✄ / E. Belfour (G) ✄	400.00
□	S. Sullivan ✄ / T. Amonte ✄ / J. Thibault (G) ✄	225.00
□	B. Shanahan ✄ / S. Yzerman ✄ / D. Hasek (G) ✄	750.00
□	A. Tanguay ✄ / J. Sakic ✄ / P. Roy (G) ✄	800.00

TOP SHELF SIGNATURES

Insert Set (36 cards):		2020.00
	Insert (1:24)	**Sig**
□	Jason Allison, LosA. ✍ {*}	40.00
□	Martin Biron (G), Buff. ✍ {*}	40.00
□	Rob Blake, Colo. ✍	30.00
□	Peter Bondra, Wash. ✍	30.00
□	Brian Boucher (G), Phil. ✍ {*}	40.00
□	Ray Bourque, Bost. ✍ {*}	100.00
□	Pavel Brendl, Phil. ✍	15.00
□	Pavel Bure, NYRa. ✍	25.00
□	Mike Comrie, Edmo. ✍	25.00
□	Rick DiPietro (G), NYIs. ✍	20.00
□	Simon Gagné, Phil. ✍	25.00
□	Wayne Gretzky, Edmo. ✍ {*95}	325.00
□	Bill Guerin, Bost. ✍	20.00
□	Scott Hartnell, Nash. ✍	15.00
□	Martin Havlat, Otta. ✍	30.00
□	Dany Heatley, Atla. ✍	50.00
□	Johan Hedberg (G), Pitt. ✍ {*}	40.00
□	Milan Hejduk, Colo. ✍	40.00
□	Gordie Howe, Detr. ✍ {*27}	450.00
□	Jarome Iginla, Calg. ✍	25.00
□	Rostislav Klesla, Colu. ✍ {*}	40.00
□	Alex Kovalev, Pitt. ✍	30.00
□	John LeClair, Phil. ✍	25.00
□	Markus Näslund, Vanc. ✍	50.00
□	Bobby Orr, Bost. ✍ {*96}	325.00
□	Maxime Ouellet, Wash. ✍	20.00
□	Zigmund Palffy, LosA. ✍	30.00
□	Patrick Roy (G), Colo. ✍ {*}	225.00
□	Tommy Salo (G), Edmo. ✍	20.00
□	Sergei Samsonov, Bost. ✍	30.00
□	Daniel Sedin, Vanc. ✍	20.00
□	Henrik Sedin, Vanc. ✍	20.00
□	José Théodore (G), Mont. ✍	50.00
□	Raffi Torres, NYIs. ✍	15.00
□	Doug Weight, SLou. ✍ {*92}	40.00
□	Steve Yzerman, Detr. ✍ {*53}	200.00

2002 - 03 UPPER DECK VINTAGE

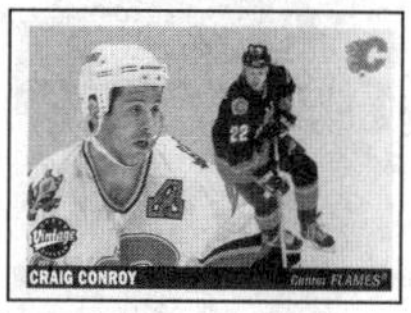

Produced by The Upper Deck Company, this series was released in November 2002. Twenty cards in the base set are short-printed (*).

Shell Set (260 cards):			**50.00**
Complete Set (350 cards):			**120.00**
Parallel Set (100 cards):		**300.00**	
Common Player:		**6.00**	**.25**
	Description	**Green**	**Base**
□	1 Vitaly Vishnevski, Anah.		.25
□	2 Paul Kariya, Anah. *		3.50
□	3 Samuel Påhlsson, Anah.		.25
□	4 Mike LeClerc, Anah.		.25
□	5 Matt Cullen, Anah.		.25
□	6 Ruslan Salei, Anah.		.25
□□	7 Jean-Sébastien Giguère (G), Anah.	10.00	1.00
□	8 Andy McDonald, Anah.		.25
□	9 Patrik Stefan, Atla.		.25
□□	10 Milan Hnilicka (G), Atla.	2.00	.25
□	11 Lubos Bartecko, Atla.		.25
□	12 Jeff Cowan, Atla.		.25
□□	13 Ilya Kovalchuk, Atla.	10.00	2.00
□	14 Frantisek Kaberle, Atla.		.25
□□	15 Dany Heatley, Atla.	10.00	1.00
□	16 Daniel Tjärnqvist, Atla.		.25
□□	17 Sergei Samsonov, Bost.	6.00	.50
□	18 P.J. Stock, Bost.		.25
□	19 Nick Boynton, Bost.		.25
□	20 Martin Lapointe, Bost.		.25
□	21 Jozef Stümpel, Bost.		.25
□	22 John Grahame (G), Bost.		.25
□	23 Joe Thornton, Bost. *		3.00
□□	24 Glen Murray, Bost.	4.00	.25
□□	25 Brian Rolston, Bost.	2.00	.25
□	26 Hal Gill, Bost.		.25
□	27 Stu Barnes, Buff.		.25
□□	28 Tim Connolly, Buff.	4.00	.25
□□	29 Miroslav Satan, Buff.	2.00	.25
□□	30 Maxim Afinogenov, Buff.	4.00	.25
□□	31 Martin Biron (G), Buff.	4.00	.25
□	32 Jay McKee, Buff.		.25
□	33 Jean-Pierre Dumont, Buff.		.25
□	34 Curtis Brown, Buff.		.25
□	35 Alexei Zhitnik, Buff.		.25
□□	36 Roman Turek (G), Calg.	4.00	.25
□	37 Rob Niedermayer, Calg.		.25
□□	38 Marc Savard, Calg.	2.00	.25
□	39 Jarome Iginla, Calg. *		2.00
□	40 Derek Morris, Calg.		.25
□	41 Denis (G) Gauthier, Calg.		.25
□	42 Dave Lowry, Calg.		.25
□	43 Craig Conroy, Calg.		.25
□□	44 Sami Kapanen, Caro.	2.00	.25
□□	45 Ron Francis, Caro.	6.00	.50
□	46 Rod Brind'Amour, Caro.		.25
□	47 Niclas Wallin, Caro.		.25
□	48 Josef Vasicek, Caro.		.25
□□	49 Jeff O'Neill, Caro.	4.00	.25
□□	50 Erik Cole, Caro.	2.00	.25
□	51 David Tanabe, Caro.		.25
□□	52 Arturs Irbe (G), Caro.	4.00	.25
□□	53 Steve Sullivan, Chic.	2.00	.25
□	54 Ryan VandenBussche, Chic.		.25
□	55 Michael Nylander, Chic.		.25
□	56 Mark Bell, Chic.		.25
□	57 Kyle Calder, Chic.		.25
□□	58 Jocelyn Thibault (G), Chic.	4.00	.25
□□	59 Éric Dazé, Chic.	4.00	.25
□	60 Alexei Zhamnov, Chic.		.25
□□	61 Steven Reinprecht, Colo.	2.00	.25
□	62 Stéphane Yelle, Colo.		.25
□□	63 Rob Blake, Colo.	6.00	.50
□□	64 Peter Forsberg, Colo.	14.00	1.00
□	65 Patrick Roy (G), Colo. *		7.50
□□	66 Milan Hejduk, Colo.	8.00	.50
□	67 Joe Sakic, Colo. *		4.00
□	68 Greg de Vries, Colo.		.25
□□	69 Chris Drury, Colo.	6.00	.50
□□	70 Alex Tanguay, Colo.	6.00	.50
□	71 Adam Foote, Colo.		.25
□	72 David Vyborny, Colu.		.25
□□	73 Rostislav Klesla, Colu.	2.00	.25
□□	74 Marc Denis (G), Colu.	4.00	.25
□	75 Ray Whitney, Colu.		.25
□	76 Jody Shelley, Colu.		.25
□	77 Jean-Luc Grand-Pierre, Colu.		.25
□	78 Geoff Sanderson, Colu.		.25
□	79 Espen Knutsen, Colu.		.25
□□	80 Pierre Turgeon, Dall.	4.00	.25
□	81 Mike Modano, Dall. *		2.50
□□	82 Marty Turco (G), Dall.	6.00	.50
□	83 Bill Guerin, Dall.		.25
□	84 Jere Lehtinen, Dall.		.25
□□	85 Jason Arnott, Dall.	4.00	.25
□	86 Derian Hatcher, Dall.		.25
□	87 Brenden Morrow, Dall.		.25
□	88 Steve Yzerman, Detr. *		6.00
□□	89 Sergei Fedorov, Detr.	10.00	1.00
□□	90 Pavel Datsyuk, Detr.	8.00	.50
□□	91 Nicklas Lidström, Detr.	6.00	.50
□	92 Luc Robitaille, Detr.		.50
□	93 Kris Draper, Detr.		.25
□□	94 Curtis Joseph (G), Detr.	10.00	1.00
□	95 Dominik Hasek (G), Detr *.		2.50
□□	96 Brett Hull, Detr.	10.00	1.00
□□	97 Brendan Shanahan, Detr.	10.00	1.00
□	98 Boyd Devereaux, Detr.		.25
□□	99 Tommy Salo (G), Edmo.	4.00	.25
□□	100 Ryan Smyth, Edmo.	4.00	.25
□□	101 Mike York, Edmo.	2.00	.25
□	102 Mike Comrie, Edmo. *		2.00
□	103 Georges Laraque, Edmo.		.25
□	104 Ethan Moreau, Edmo.		.25
□	105 Dan Cleary, Edmo.		.25
□	106 Anson Carter, Edmo.		.25
□	107 Viktor Kozlov, Flor.		.25
□	108 Valeri Bure, Flor.		.25
□□	109 Olli Jokinen, Flor.	2.00	.25
□□	110 Sandis Ozolinsh, Flor.	2.00	.25
□□	111 Roberto Luongo (G), Flor.	8.00	.50
□	112 Peter Worrell, Flor.		.25
□	113 Niklas Hagman, Flor.		.25
□□	114 Kristian Huselius, Flor.	2.00	.25
□□	115 Zigmund Palffy, LosA.	6.00	.50
□	116 Mattias Norström, LosA.		.25
□	117 Mathieu Schneider, LosA.		.25
□□	118 Jason Allison, LosA.	6.00	.50
□□	119 Félix Potvin (G), LosA.	6.00	.50
□	120 Bryan Smolinski, LosA.		.25
□□	121 Adam Deadmarsh, LosA.	2.00	.25
□	122 Aaron Miller, LosA.		.25
□	123 Richard Park, MinW.		.25
□	124 Nick Schultz, MinW.		.25
□	125 Marian Gaborik, MinW. *		2.50
□	126 Jim Dowd, MinW.		.25
□	127 Hnat Domenichelli, MinW.		.25
□	128 Filip Kuba, MinW.		.25
□	129 Manny Fernandez (G), MinW.		.25
□	130 Andrew Brunette, MinW.		.25
□	131 Yanic Perreault, Mont.		.25
□□	132 Saku Koivu, Mont.	8.00	.50
□	133 Richard Zednik, Mont.		.25
□	134 José Théodore (G), Mont. *		3.00
□	135 Donald Audette, Mont.		.25
□	136 Craig Rivet, Mont.		.25
□	137 Andrei Markov, Mont.		.25
□	138 Andreas Dackell, Mont.		.25
□	139 Stu Grimson, Nash.		.25
□□	140 Scott Hartnell, Nash.	2.00	.25
□□	141 Mike Dunham (G), Nash.	4.00	.25
□	142 Martin Erat, Nash.		.25
□	143 Kimmo Timonen, Nash.		.25
□	144 Denis (G) Arkhipov, Nash.		.25
□□	145 David Legwand, Nash.	4.00	.25
□	146 Andy Delmore, Nash.		.25
□	147 Sergei Brylin, NJer.		.25
□	148 Scott Stevens, NJer.		.25
□□	149 Scott Niedermayer, NJer.	2.00	.25
□	150 John Madden, NJer.		.25
□□	151 Patrik Elias, NJer.	8.00	.50
□	152 Martin Brodeur (G), NJer. *		4.00
□□	153 Joe Nieuwendyk, NJer.	4.00	.25
□	154 Brian Rafalski, NJer.		.25
□	155 Roman Hamrlik, NYIs.		.25
□□	156 Raffi Torres, NYIs.	2.00	.25
□□	157 Michael Peca, NYIs.	4.00	.25
□	158 Mark Parrish, NYIs.		.25
□	159 Oleg Kvasha, NYIs.		.25
□	160 Eric Cairns, NYIs.		.25
□	161 Dave Scatchard, NYIs.		.25
□□	162 Chris Osgood (G), NYIs.	6.00	.50
□	163 Alexei Yashin, NYIs. *		1.50
□	164 Tom Poti, NYRa.		.25
□	165 Sandy McCarthy, NYRa.		.25
□	166 Radek Dvorak, NYRa.		.25
□□	167 Petr Nedved, NYRa.	2.00	.25
□	168 Pavel Bure, NYRa. *		2.00
□	169 Matthew Barnaby, NYRa.		.25
□□	170 Mark Messier, NYRa.	10.00	1.00
□□	171 Eric Lindros, NYRa.	10.00	1.00
□□	172 Dan Blackburn (G), NYRa.	4.00	.25
□□	173 Brian Leetch, NYRa.	6.00	.50
□	174 Wade Redden, Otta.		.25
□□	175 Radek Bonk, Otta.	2.00	.25
□□	176 Patrick Lalime (G), Otta.	6.00	.50
□	177 Mike Fisher, Otta.		.25
□□	178 Martin Havlat, Otta.	6.00	.50
□□	179 Marian Hossa, Otta.	10.00	1.00
□	180 Magnus Arvedson, Otta.		.25

☐☐	181 Daniel Alfredsson, Otta.	6.00	.50
☐	182 Simon Gagné, Phil. *		2.00
☐	183 Kim Johnsson, Phil.		.25
☐☐	184 Roman Cechmanek (G), Phil.	4.00	.25
☐☐	185 Mark Recchi, Phil.	4.00	.25
☐☐	186 Keith Primeau, Phil.	4.00	.25
☐☐	187 Justin Williams, Phil.	2.00	.25
☐☐	188 John LeClair, Phil.	8.00	.50
☐☐	189 Jeremy Roenick, Phil.	8.00	.50
☐	190 Eric Weinrich, Phil.		.25
☐	191 Donald Brashear, Phil.		.25
☐	192 Teppo Numminen, Phoe.		.25
☐	193 Shane Doan, Phoe.		.25
☐☐	194 Sean Burke (G), Phoe.	6.00	.50
☐	195 Ladislav Nagy, Phoe.		.25
☐	196 Daymond Langkow, Phoe.		.25
☐	197 Daniel Brière, Phoe.		.25
☐☐	198 Claude Lemieux, Phoe.	2.00	.25
☐☐	199 Tony Amonte, Phoe.	6.00	.50
☐	200 Ville Nieminen, Pitt.		.25
☐☐	201 Martin Straka, Pitt.	2.00	.25
☐	202 Mario Lemieux, Pitt. *		7.50
☐☐	203 Johan Hedberg (G), Pitt.	4.00	.25
☐	204 Jan Hrdina, Pitt.		.25
☐	205 Andrew Ference, Pitt.		.25
☐☐	206 Alex Kovalev, Pitt.	6.00	.50
☐	207 Aleksey Morozov, Pitt.		.25
☐☐	208 Vincent Damphousse, SanJ.	6.00	.50
☐	209 Scott Thornton, SanJ.		.25
☐☐	210 Patrick Marleau, SanJ.	4.00	.25
☐☐	211 Owen Nolan, SanJ.	6.00	.50
☐	212 Mike Ricci, SanJ.		.25
☐	213 Marcus Ragnarsson, SanJ.		.25
☐	214 Marco Sturm, SanJ.		.25
☐	215 Evgeni Nabokov (G), SanJ. *		1.50
☐	216 Brad Stuart, SanJ.		.25
☐	217 Tyson Nash, SLou.		.25
☐	218 Shjon Podein, SLou.		.25
☐☐	219 Pavol Demitra, SLou.	4.00	.25
☐	220 Keith Tkachuk, SLou. *		1.50
☐☐	221 Doug Weight, SLou.	6.00	.50
☐	222 Cory Stillman, SLou.		.25
☐☐	223 Chris Pronger, SLou.	6.00	.50
☐☐	224 Brent Johnson (G), SLou.	4.00	.25
☐☐	225 Al MacInnis, SLou.	4.00	.25
☐☐	226 Vincent Lecavalier, Tamp.	10.00	1.00
☐	227 Vaclav Prospal, Tamp.		.25
☐	228 Shane Willis, Tamp.		.25
☐	229 Pavel Kubina, Tamp.		.25
☐☐	230 Nikolai Khabibulin (G), Tamp.	4.00	.25
☐	231 Martin St-Louis, Tamp.		.25
☐	232 Fredrik Modin, Tamp.		.25
☐☐	233 Brad Richards, Tamp.	4.00	.25
☐	234 Tomas Kaberle, Toro.		.25
☐	235 Tie Domi, Toro.		.25
☐	236 Shayne Corson, Toro.		.25
☐	237 Mats Sundin, Toro. *		2.50
☐	238 Gary Roberts, Toro.		.25
☐	239 Darcy Tucker, Toro.		.25
☐☐	240 Ed Belfour (G), Toro.	10.00	1.00
☐	241 Bryan McCabe, Toro.		.25
☐	242 Alyn McCauley, Toro.		.25
☐☐	243 Alexander Mogilny, Toro.	4.00	.25
☐	244 Trevor Linden, Vanc.		.25
☐	245 Todd Bertuzzi, Vanc.		1.00
☐☐	246 Markus Näslund, Vanc.	10.00	1.00
☐☐	247 Henrik Sedin, Vanc.	4.00	.25
☐	248 Ed Jovanovski, Vanc.		.25
☐☐	249 Daniel Sedin, Vanc.	4.00	.25
☐	250 Dan Cloutier (G), Vanc.		.25
☐	251 Brendan Morrison, Vanc.		.25
☐	252 Brendan Witt, Wash.		.25
☐	253 Steve Konowalchuk, Wash.		.25
☐	254 Sergei Gonchar, Wash.		.25
☐☐	255 Peter Bondra, Wash.	6.00	.50
☐☐	256 Olaf Kölzig (G), Wash.	6.00	.50
☐	257 Jeff Halpern, Wash.		.25
☐	258 Jaromir Jagr, Wash. *		2.50
☐	259 Andrei Nikolishin, Wash.		.25
☐☐	260 Robert Lang, Wash.	2.00	.25

SUBSETS

	Subsets	Card
☐	261 Kariya/ Vishnevski/ Giguère (G)/ Leclerc	2.50
☐	262 Kovalchuk/ Heatley/ Hnilicka (G)/ Stefan	2.00
☐	263 Samsonov/ Thornton/ Boynton/ Murray	2.00
☐	264 Connolly/ Barnes/ Biron/ Satan	1.00
☐	265 Iginla/ Turek (G)/ Savard/ Morris	1.50
☐	266 O'Neill/ Francis/ Irbe (G)/ Cole	1.50
☐	267 Dazé/ Calder/ Thibault (G)/ Zhamnov	1.00
☐	268 Sakic/ Forsberg/ Roy (G)/ Blake	6.00
☐	269 Sanderson/ Denis (G)/ Klesla/ Shelley	1.00
☐	270 Turgeon/ Modano/ Turco (G)/ Hatcher	2.00
☐	271 Yzerman/ Fedorov/ Shanahan/ Lidström	4.50
☐	272 Comrie/ Smyth/ Salo/ Laraque	1.50
☐	273 Kozlov/ Weiss/ Luongo (G)/ Worrell	1.50
☐	274 Palffy/ Allison/ Potvin/ Deadmarsh	1.50
☐	275 Park/ Gaborik/ Fernandez (G)/ Brunette	1.50
☐	276 Perreault/ Audette/ Théodore (G)/ Koivu	2.50
☐	277 Grimson/ Dunham (G)/ Erat/ Hartnell	.50
☐	278 Stevens/ Brodeur (G)/ Rafalski/ Elias	2.50
☐	279 Peca/ Yashin/ Osgood (G)/ Cairns	1.50
☐	280 Bure/ Lindros/ Richter (G)/ Messier	3.00
☐	281 Hossa/ Alfredsson/ Lalime (G)/ Havlat	2.50
☐	282 Gagné/ Roenick/ Cechmanek (G)/ Brashear	2.00
☐	283 Brière/ Numminen/ Amonte/ Burke (G)	1.50
☐	284 Lemieux/ Kovalev/ Hedberg (G)/ Morozov	3.50
☐	285 Marleau/ Nolan/ Nabokov (G)/ Ricci	1.50
☐	286 Demitra/ Pronger/ Johnson/ Nash	1.00
☐	287 Lecavalier/ Richards/ Khabibulin (G)/ Kubina	1.50
☐	288 Sundin/ Mogilny/ Domi/ Belfour (G)	2.50
☐	289 Bertuzzi/ Näslund/ Cloutier (G)/ Linden	2.50
☐	290 Bondra/ Jagr/ Kölzig (G)/ Gonchar	2.00
☐	291 Joe Sakic, Colo.	1.00
☐	292 Patrick Roy (G), Colo.	2.00
☐	293 Mike Modano, Dall.	.50
☐	294 Brendan Shanahan, Detr.	.50
☐	295 Steve Yzerman, Detr.	1.50
☐	296 Red Wings	.25
☐	297 Joe Nieuwendyk, NJer.	.25
☐	298 Martin Brodeur (G), NJer.	1.00
☐	299 Pavel Bure, NYRa.	.50
☐	300 Brian Leetch, NYRa.	.25
☐	301 Jeremy Roenick, Phil.	.50
☐	302 Mark Recchi, Phil.	.25
☐	303 Mario Lemieux, Pitt.	2.00
☐	304 Teemu Selänne, SanJ.	.50
☐	305 Peter Bondra, Wash.	.25
☐	306 Iginla/ Murray/ Sundin	.50
☐	307 Oates/ Allison/ Sakic	.50
☐	308 Iginla/ Näslund/ Bertuzzi	1.00
☐	309 Bondra/ Iginla/ Yashin	.50
☐	310 Gonchar/ Lidström/ Blake	.50
☐	311 Rolston/ Peca/ Satan	.25
☐	312 Chelios/ Roenick/ Gagné	.50
☐	313 Worrell/ Ference/ Neil	.25
☐	314 Brière/ Hrdina/ Deadmarsh	.25
☐	315 Heatley/ Kovalchuk/ Huselius	.50
☐	316 Hasek (G)/ Brodeur (G)/ Nabokov (G)	1.00
☐	317 Roy (G)/ Cechmanek (G)/ Turco (G)	1.00
☐	318 Théodore (G)/ Roy (G)/ Cechmanek (G)	1.50
☐	319 Roy (G)/ Théodore (G)/ Khabibulin (G)	1.50
☐	320 Blackburn (G)/ Kiprusoff (G)/ Biron	.25
☐	321 Pasi Nurminen (G), Atla.	.50
☐	322 Mark Hartigan, Atla.	.25
☐	323 Henrik Tallinder, Buff.	.25
☐	**324 Micki Dupont, Calg. RC**	**1.00**
☐	325 Jaroslav Svoboda, Caro.	.50
☐	326 Jordan Krestanovich, Colo.	.25
☐	327 Kelly Fairchild, Colo.	.25
☐	328 Riku Hahl, Colo.	.25
☐	329 Andrej Nedorost, Colu.	.25
☐	330 Blake Bellefeuille, Colu.	.25
☐	331 Ales Pisa, Edmo.	.25
☐	332 Jani Rita, Edmo.	.50
☐	333 Stephen Weiss, Flor.	1.00
☐	334 Lukas Krajicek, Flor.	.50
☐	**335 Sylvain Blouin, MinW. RC**	**.50**
☐	336 Marcel Hossa, Mont.	1.00
☐	**337 Adam Hall, Nash. RC**	**1.50**
☐	338 Jonas Andersson, Nash.	.25
☐	339 Jan Lasak (G), Nash.	.50
☐	**340 Ray Schultz, NYIs. RC**	**.50**
☐	341 Trent Hunter, NYIs.	.25
☐	342 Martin Prusek (G), Otta.	.50
☐	343 Branko Radivojevic, Phoe.	.50
☐	344 Shane Endicott, Pitt.	.25
☐	345 Sébastien Centomo (G), Toro.	.50
☐	346 Karel Pilar, Toro.	.25
☐	347 Sébastien Charpentier (G), Wash.	.25
☐	348 Jean-François Fortin, Wash.	.25
☐	349 Ales Kotalik, Buff.	1.00
☐	350 Kyle Rossiter, Flor.	.25

EXTRA EFFORT

	Insert Set (10 cards):	400.00	50.00
	Insert	G50	EE
☐☐	Brian Boucher (G), Phil. ✂	45.00	12.00
☐☐	David Aebischer (G), Colo. ✂	45.00	12.00
☐☐	Félix Potvin (G), LosA. ✂	90.00	12.00
☐☐	Martin Biron (G), Buff. ✂	70.00	12.00
☐☐	Mike Dunham (G), Nash. ✂	60.00	12.00
☐☐	Maxime Ouellet, Wash. ✂	60.00	12.00
☐☐	Marty Turco (G), Dall. ✂	90.00	12.00
☐☐	Olaf Kölzig (G), Wash. ✂	90.00	12.00
☐☐	Roman Cechmanek (G), Phil. ✂	60.00	12.00
☐☐	Ron Tugnutt (G), Colu. ✂	60.00	12.00

FRAMED SWEATERS

	Insert Set (6 cards):	475.00	50.00
	Insert	G50	FS
☐☐	Brenden Morrow, Dall. ✂	45.00	12.00
☐☐	Chris Drury, Colo. ✂	90.00	12.00
☐☐	Jaromir Jagr, Wash. ✂	150.00	20.00
☐☐	Keith Primeau, Phil. ✂	60.00	12.00
☐☐	Milan Hejduk, Colo. ✂	120.00	15.00
☐☐	Steve Yzerman, Detr. ✂	360.00	45.00

FUNDAMENTALLY SOUND

	Insert Set (10 cards):	700.00	100.00
	Insert	G50	SO
☐☐	Chris Drury, Colo. ✂	90.00	12.00
☐☐	Eric Lindros, NYRa. ✂	150.00	20.00
☐☐	Jeff Halpern, Wash. ✂	35.00	12.00
☐☐	Jarome Iginla, Calg. ✂ {*}	120.00	20.00
☐☐	Jaromir Jagr, Wash. ✂ {*}	150.00	25.00
☐☐	John LeClair, Phil. ✂	120.00	15.00
☐☐	Keith Primeau, Phil. ✂	60.00	12.00
☐☐	Mark Recchi, Phil. ✂	60.00	12.00
☐☐	Peter Forsberg, Colo. ✂	210.00	25.00
☐☐	Paul Kariya, Anah. ✂	210.00	25.00

HONING THE SKILLS

	Insert Set (9 cards):	375.00	50.00
	Insert	G50	HS
☐☐	Jean-Pierre Dumont, Buff. ✂	35.00	12.00
☐☐	Justin Williams, Phil. ✂	45.00	12.00
☐☐	Marc Denis (G), Colu. ✂	70.00	12.00
☐☐	Peter Bondra, Wash. ✂	90.00	12.00
☐☐	Raymond Bourque, Bost. ✂	180.00	20.00
☐☐	Ruslan Fedotenko, Phil. ✂	20.00	12.00
☐☐	Rostislav Klesla, Colu. ✂	45.00	12.00
☐☐	Simon Gagné, Phil. ✂	120.00	15.00
☐☐	Steve Konowalchuk, Wash. ✂	35.00	12.00
☐☐	Ville Nieminen, Pitt. ✂	35.00	12.00

ORIGINAL SIX

	Insert Set (6 cards):	500.00	75.00
	Insert	G50	OS
☐☐	Éric Dazé, Chic. ✂	60.00	12.00
☐☐	Glen Murray, Bost. ✂	70.00	12.00
☐☐	José Théodore (G), Mont. ✂ {*}	180.00	30.00
☐☐	Mats Sundin, Toro. ✂	150.00	20.00
☐☐	Radek Dvorak, NYRa. ✂	35.00	12.00
☐☐	Steve Yzerman, Detr. ✂	360.00	45.00

TALL BOYS

	Bonus Set (70 cards):	900.00	125.00
	Insert	G99	T
☐☐	T1 Paul Kariya, Anah.	25.00	5.50
☐☐	T2 Jean-Sébastien Giguère (G), Anah.	20.00	4.00
☐☐	T3 Dany Heatley, Atla.	20.00	4.00
☐☐	T4 Ilya Kovalchuk, Atla.	20.00	4.00
☐☐	T5 Joe Thornton, Bost.	20.00	4.50
☐☐	T6 Sergei Samsonov, Bost.	10.00	2.00
☐☐	T7 Miroslav Satan, Buff.	5.00	1.00
☐☐	T8 Maxim Afinogenov, Buff.	5.00	1.50
☐☐	T9 Roman Turek (G), Calg.	5.00	1.50
☐☐	T10 Jarome Iginla, Calg.	15.00	3.00
☐☐	T11 Arturs Irbe (G), Caro.	5.00	1.50
☐☐	T12 Ron Francis, Caro.	10.00	2.00
☐☐	T13 Éric Dazé, Chic.	5.00	1.50
☐☐	T14 Jocelyn Thibault (G), Chic.	5.00	1.50
☐☐	T15 Patrick Roy (G), Colo.	60.00	12.00
☐☐	T16 Peter Forsberg, Colo.	25.00	5.50
☐☐	T17 Joe Sakic, Colo.	30.00	6.00
☐☐	T18 Chris Drury, Colo.	10.00	2.00
☐☐	T19 Alex Tanguay, Colo.	10.00	2.00
☐☐	T20 Espen Knutsen, Colu.	4.00	1.00
☐☐	T21 Rostislav Klesla, Colu.	5.00	1.00
☐☐	T22 Mike Modano, Dall.	20.00	4.00
☐☐	T23 Jason Arnott, Dall.	5.00	1.50
☐☐	T24 Steve Yzerman, Detr.	45.00	9.50
☐☐	T25 Brendan Shanahan, Detr.	20.00	4.00
☐☐	T26 Sergei Fedorov, Detr.	20.00	4.00
☐☐	T27 Curtis Joseph (G), Detr.	20.00	4.00
☐☐	T28 Mike Comrie, Edmo.	15.00	3.00
☐☐	T29 Tommy Salo (G), Edmo.	5.00	1.50
☐☐	T30 Roberto Luongo (G), Flor.	15.00	3.00
☐☐	T31 Stephen Weiss, Flor.	5.00	1.50
☐☐	T32 Jason Allison, LosA.	10.00	2.00
☐☐	T33 Zigmund Palffy, LosA.	10.00	2.00
☐☐	T34 Marian Gaborik, MinW.	20.00	4.00
☐☐	T35 José Théodore (G), Mont.	20.00	4.50
☐☐	T36 Saku Koivu, Mont.	20.00	3.00
☐☐	T37 Mike Dunham (G), Nash.	5.00	1.50
☐☐	T38 Scott Hartnell, Nash.	4.00	1.00
☐☐	T39 Martin Brodeur (G), NJer.	30.00	6.00
☐☐	T40 Patrik Elias, NJer.	15.00	3.00
☐☐	T41 Michael Peca, NYIs.	5.00	1.50
☐☐	T42 Chris Osgood (G), NYIs.	10.00	2.00
☐☐	T43 Eric Lindros, NYRa.	20.00	4.00
☐☐	T44 Pavel Bure, NYRa.	15.00	3.00
☐☐	T45 Daniel Alfredsson, Otta.	10.00	2.00
☐☐	T46 Marian Hossa, Otta.	20.00	4.00
☐☐	T47 Jeremy Roenick, Phil.	15.00	3.00
☐☐	T48 Simon Gagné, Phil.	15.00	3.00
☐☐	T49 Sean Burke (G), Phoe.	10.00	2.00
☐☐	T50 Daniel Brière, Phoe.	5.00	1.50
☐☐	T51 Tony Amonte, Phoe.	10.00	2.00
☐☐	T52 Mario Lemieux, Pitt.	60.00	12.00
☐☐	T53 Johan Hedberg (G), Pitt.	5.00	1.50
☐☐	T54 Owen Nolan, SanJ.	10.00	2.00
☐☐	T55 Evgeni Nabokov (G), SanJ.	10.00	2.00
☐☐	T56 Keith Tkachuk, SLou.	10.00	2.00
☐☐	T57 Chris Pronger, SLou.	10.00	2.00
☐☐	T58 Vincent Lecavalier, Tamp.	20.00	4.00
☐☐	T59 Nikolai Khabibulin (G), Tamp.	5.00	1.50
☐☐	T60 Mats Sundin, Toro.	20.00	4.00
☐☐	T61 Alexander Mogilny, Toro.	5.00	1.50
☐☐	T62 Markus Näslund, Vanc.	20.00	4.00
☐☐	T63 Todd Bertuzzi, Vanc.	20.00	4.50
☐☐	T64 Jaromir Jagr, Wash.	20.00	4.00
☐☐	T65 Olaf Kölzig (G), Wash.	10.00	2.00
☐☐	T66 Gordie Howe, Detr.	40.00	10.00
☐☐	T67 Gordie Howe, Detr.	40.00	10.00
☐☐	T68 Gordie Howe, WHA All-Star	40.00	10.00
☐☐	T69 Gordie Howe, Hart.	40.00	10.00
☐☐	T70 Gordie Howe, Current Photo	40.00	10.00

2002 - 03 VANGUARD

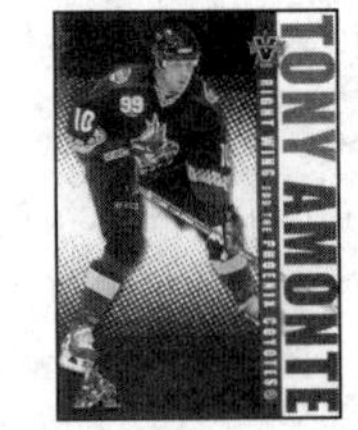

Produced by the Pacific Trading Cards, this series was released in February 2003. There are two versions for each card 1-100: the regular card and the Vanguard Ltd. parallel (#/450).

	Shell Set (100 cards):		**100.00**
	Complete Set (136 cards):	**.00**	**325.00**
	Common Player:	**1.00**	**.50**
	Description	**LTD450**	**V**
☐☐	1 Jean-Sébastien Giguère (G), Anah.	9.00	3.00
☐☐	2 Paul Kariya, Anah.	12.00	4.00
☐☐	3 Steve Rucchin, Anah.	2.00	.50
☐☐	4 Byron Dafoe (G), Atla.	3.00	1.00
☐☐	5 Dany Heatley, Atla.	9.00	3.00
☐☐	6 Ilya Kovalchuk, Atla.	9.00	3.00
☐☐	7 Glen Murray, Bost.	4.00	1.00
☐☐	8 Brian Rolston, Bost.	2.00	.50
☐☐	9 Steve Shields, Bost.	2.00	.50
☐☐	10 Joe Thornton, Bost.	10.00	3.50
☐☐	11 Martin Biron (G), Buff.	4.00	1.00
☐☐	12 Chris Gratton, Buff.	2.00	.50
☐☐	13 Jochen Hecht, Buff.	2.00	.50
☐☐	14 Chris Drury, Calg.	5.00	1.50
☐☐	15 Jarome Iginla, Calg.	7.00	2.00
☐☐	16 Roman Turek (G), Calg.	4.00	1.00
☐☐	17 Rod Brind'Amour, Caro.	2.00	.50
☐☐	18 Ron Francis, Caro.	5.00	1.50
☐☐	19 Jeff O'Neill, Caro.	3.00	1.00
☐☐	20 Kevin Weekes (G), Caro.	2.00	.50
☐☐	21 Tyler Arnason, Chic.	3.00	1.00
☐☐	22 Éric Dazé, Chic.	3.00	1.00
☐☐	23 Theoren Fleury, Chic.	5.00	1.50
☐☐	24 Jocelyn Thibault (G), Chic.	3.00	1.00
☐☐	25 Peter Forsberg, Colo.	12.00	4.00
☐☐	26 Milan Hejduk, Colo.	7.00	2.00
☐☐	27 Patrick Roy (G), Colo.	25.00	9.00
☐☐	28 Joe Sakic, Colo.	14.00	4.00
☐☐	29 Andrew Cassels, Colu.	2.00	.50
☐☐	30 Marc Denis (G), Colu.	4.00	1.00
☐☐	31 Geoff Sanderson, Colu.	2.00	.50
☐☐	32 Bill Guerin, Dall.	3.00	1.00
☐☐	33 Mike Modano, Dall.	9.00	3.00
☐☐	34 Marty Turco (G), Dall.	5.00	1.50
☐☐	35 Sergei Fedorov, Detr.	9.00	3.00
☐☐	36 Brett Hull, Detr.	9.00	3.00
☐☐	37 Curtis Joseph (G), Detr.	9.00	3.00
☐☐	38 Nicklas Lidström, Detr.	5.00	1.50
☐☐	39 Brendan Shanahan, Detr.	9.00	3.00
☐☐	40 Steve Yzerman, Detr.	20.00	7.00
☐☐	41 Anson Carter, Edmo.	3.00	1.00
☐☐	42 Mike Comrie, Edmo.	7.00	2.00
☐☐	43 Tommy Salo (G), Edmo.	3.00	1.00
☐☐	44 Kristian Huselius, Flor.	2.00	.50
☐☐	45 Olli Jokinen, Flor.	2.00	.50
☐☐	46 Roberto Luongo (G), Flor.	7.00	2.00
☐☐	47 Jason Allison, LosA.	5.00	1.50
☐☐	48 Adam Deadmarsh, LosA.	2.00	.50
☐☐	49 Zigmund Palffy, LosA.	5.00	1.50
☐☐	50 Félix Potvin (G), LosA.	5.00	1.50
☐☐	51 Andrew Brunette, MinW.	2.00	.50
☐☐	52 Marian Gaborik, MinW.	9.00	3.00
☐☐	53 Dwayne Roloson (G), MinW.	2.00	.50
☐☐	54 Jeff Hackett (G), Mont.	2.00	.50
☐☐	55 Saku Koivu, Mont.	7.00	2.00
☐☐	56 Yanic Perreault, Mont.	2.00	.50
☐☐	57 José Théodore (G), Mont.	10.00	3.50
☐☐	58 Andreas Johansson, Nash.	2.00	.50
☐☐	59 David Legwand, Nash.	3.00	1.00
☐☐	60 Martin Brodeur (G), NJer.	14.00	4.00
☐☐	61 Patrik Elias, NJer.	7.00	2.00
☐☐	62 Jamie Langenbrunner, NJer.	2.00	.50
☐☐	63 Mark Parrish, NYIs.	3.00	1.00
☐☐	64 Michael Peca, NYIs.	3.00	1.00

☐☐ 65 Alexei Yashin, NYIs.	5.00	1.50
☐☐ 66 Dan Blackburn (G), NYRa.	3.00	1.00
☐☐ 67 Pavel Bure, NYRa.	7.00	2.00
☐☐ 68 Eric Lindros, NYRa.	9.00	3.00
☐☐ 69 Daniel Alfredsson, Otta.	5.00	1.50
☐☐ 70 Marian Hossa, Otta.	9.00	3.00
☐☐ 71 Patrick Lalime (G), Otta.	5.00	1.50
☐☐ 72 Roman Cechmanek (G), Phil.	3.00	1.00
☐☐ 73 Simon Gagné, Phil.	7.00	2.00
☐☐ 74 John LeClair, Phil.	7.00	2.00
☐☐ 75 Jeremy Roenick, Phil.	7.00	2.00
☐☐ 76 Tony Amonte, Phoe.	5.00	1.50
☐☐ 77 Brian Boucher (G), Phoe.	2.00	.50
☐☐ 78 Mike Johnson, Phoe.	2.00	.50
☐☐ 79 Johan Hedberg (G), Pitt.	3.00	1.00
☐☐ 80 Alex Kovalev, Pitt.	5.00	1.50
☐☐ 81 Mario Lemieux, Pitt.	25.00	9.00
☐☐ 82 Eric Boguniecki, SLou.	2.00	.50
☐☐ 83 Cory Stillman, SLou.	2.00	.50
☐☐ 84 Doug Weight, SLou.	5.00	1.50
☐☐ 85 Evgeni Nabokov (G), SanJ.	5.00	1.50
☐☐ 86 Owen Nolan, SanJ.	5.00	1.50
☐☐ 87 Teemu Selänne, SanJ.	7.00	2.00
☐☐ 88 Nikolai Khabibulin (G), Tamp.	3.00	1.00
☐☐ 89 Vincent Lecavalier, Tamp.	9.00	3.00
☐☐ 90 Martin St-Louis, Tamp.	4.00	1.00
☐☐ 91 Ed Belfour (G), Toro.	9.00	3.00
☐☐ 92 Alexander Mogilny, Toro.	4.00	1.00
☐☐ 93 Mats Sundin, Toro.	9.00	3.00
☐☐ 94 Todd Bertuzzi, Vanc.	10.00	3.50
☐☐ 95 Dan Cloutier (G), Vanc.	3.00	1.00
☐☐ 96 Brendan Morrison, Vanc.	2.00	.50
☐☐ 97 Markus Näslund, Vanc.	9.00	3.00
☐☐ 98 Peter Bondra, Wash.	5.00	1.50
☐☐ 99 Jaromir Jagr, Wash.	9.00	3.00
☐☐ 100 Olaf Kölzig (G), Wash.	5.00	1.50

ROOKIE

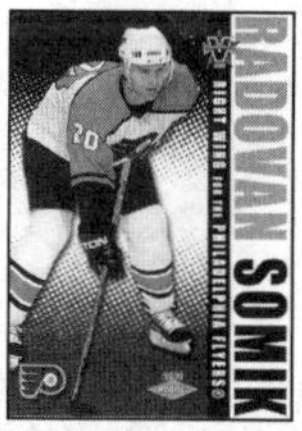

There are two versions for each card 101-136: the regular card (#/1650) and the Vanguard Ltd. parallel (#/450).

Insert	LTD450	V
☐☐ **101 Stanislav Chistov, Anah. RC**	**15.00**	**15.00**
☐☐ **102 Martin Gerber (G), Anah. RC**	**6.00**	**6.00**
☐☐ **103 Alexei Smirnov, Anah. RC**	**6.00**	**6.00**
☐☐ **104 Tim Thomas (G), Bost. RC**	**6.00**	**6.00**
☐☐ **105 Ryan Miller (G), Buff. RC**	**10.00**	**10.00**
☐☐ **106 Chuck Kobasew, Calg. RC**	**10.00**	**10.00**
☐☐ **107 Jordan Leopold, Calg. RC**	**6.00**	**6.00**
☐☐ **108 Pascal Leclaire (G), Colu. RC**	**10.00**	**10.00**
☐☐ **109 Rick Nash, Colu. RC**	**25.00**	**25.00**
☐☐ **110 Lasse Pirjetä, Colu. RC**	**6.00**	**6.00**
☐☐ **111 Steve Ott, Dall. RC**	**6.00**	**6.00**
☐☐ **112 Dmitri Bykov, Detr. RC**	**6.00**	**6.00**
☐☐ **113 Henrik Zetterberg, Detr. RC**	**25.00**	**25.00**
☐☐ **114 Ales Hemsky, Edmo. RC**	**15.00**	**15.00**
☐☐ **115 Jay Bouwmeester, Flor. RC**	**15.00**	**15.00**
☐☐ **116 Mike Cammalleri, LosA. RC**	**10.00**	**10.00**
☐☐ **117 Alexander Frolov, LosA. RC**	**10.00**	**10.00**
☐☐ **118 Pierre-Marc Bouchard, MinW. RC**	**15.00**	**15.00**
☐☐ **119 Stéphane Veilleux, MinW. RC**	**6.00**	**6.00**
☐☐ **120 Sylvain Blouin, Mont. RC**	**6.00**	**6.00**
☐☐ **121 Ron Hainsey, Mont. RC**	**6.00**	**6.00**
☐☐ **122 Adam Hall, Nash. RC**	**6.00**	**6.00**
☐☐ **123 Scottie Upshall, Nash. RC**	**10.00**	**10.00**
☐☐ **124 Jason Spezza, Otta. RC**	**15.00**	**15.00**
☐☐ **125 Anton Volchenkov, Otta. RC**	**6.00**	**6.00**
☐☐ **126 Dennis Seidenberg, Phil. RC**	**6.00**	**6.00**
☐☐ **127 Patrick Sharp, Phil. RC**	**6.00**	**6.00**
☐☐ **128 Radovan Somik, Phil. RC**	**6.00**	**6.00**
☐☐ **129 Jeff Taffe, Phoe. RC**	**6.00**	**6.00**
☐☐ 130 Dick Tarnstrom, Pitt.	6.00	6.00
☐☐ **131 Tom Koivisto, SLou. RC**	**6.00**	**6.00**
☐☐ **132 Curtis Sanford (G), SLou. RC**	**6.00**	**6.00**
☐☐ **133 Lynn Loyns, SanJ. RC**	**6.00**	**6.00**
☐☐ **134 Alexander Svitov, Tamp. RC**	**10.00**	**10.00**
☐☐ **135 Carlo Colaiacovo, Toro. RC**	**6.00**	**6.00**
☐☐ **136 Steve Eminger, Wash. RC**	**6.00**	**6.00**

EAST MEETS WEST

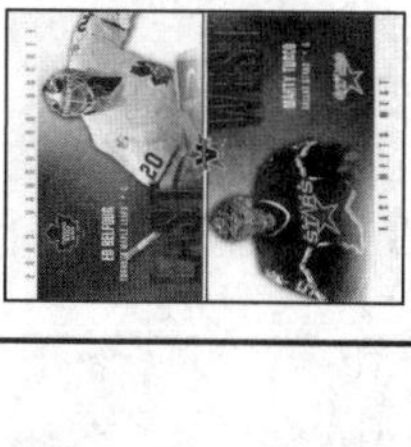

Insert Set (10 cards):	35.00
Insert (1:13)	EMW
☐ 1 Kovalchuk / Näslund	3.00
☐ 2 Thornton / Iginla	3.00
☐ 3 Lemieux / Yzerman	10.00
☐ 4 Bure / Fedorov	3.00
☐ 5 LeClair / Modano	3.00
☐ 6 Sundin / Forsberg	4.00
☐ 7 Lecavalier / Sakic	4.00
☐ 8 Hossa / Gaborik	3.00
☐ 9 Brodeur (G) / Roy	8.00
☐ 10 Belfour (G) / Turco (G)	3.00

GAME-WORN JERSEY

Insert Set (50 cards):	600.00
Insert	GWJ
☐ 1 Adam Oates, Wash. ✂ {*600}	10.00
☐ 2 Dany Heatley, Atla. ✂ {*250}	30.00
☐ 3 Ilya Kovalchuk, Atla. ✂ {*250}	30.00
☐ 4 Patrik Stefan, Atla. ✂ {*600}	10.00
☐ 5 Joe Thornton, Bost. ✂ {*250}	40.00
☐ 6 J-P Dumont, Buff. ✂ {*510}	10.00
☐ 7 Chris Drury, Colo. ✂ {*500}	10.00
☐ 8 Jamie McLennan (G), SLou. ✂ {*500}	10.00
☐ 9 Rod Brind'Amour, Caro. ✂ {*500}	10.00
☐ 10 Sergei Berezin, Chic. ✂ {*510}	10.00
☐ 11 Theoren Fleury, NYRa. ✂ {*275}	15.00
☐ 12 Alexei Zhamnov, Chic. ✂ {*300}	10.00
☐ 13 Joe Sakic, Colo. ✂ {*235}	55.00
☐ 14 Tomi Kallio, Atla. ✂ {*750}	10.00
☐ 15 Rostislav Klesla, Colu. ✂ {*750}	10.00
☐ 16 Mike Modano, Dall. ✂ {*500}	20.00
☐ 17 Pierre Turgeon, Dall. ✂ {*425}	10.00
☐ 18 Sergei Fedorov, Detr. ✂ {*500}	20.00
☐ 19 Brett Hull, Detr. ✂ {*750}	15.00
☐ 20 Curtis Joseph (G), Toro. ✂ {*500}	20.00
☐ 21 Ryan Smyth, Edmo. ✂ {*750}	10.00
☐ 22 Kristian Huselius, Flor. ✂ {*750}	10.00
☐ 23 Zigmund Palffy, LosA. ✂ {*600}	10.00
☐ 24 Yanic Perreault, Mont. ✂ {*750}	10.00
☐ 25 José Théodore (G), Mont. ✂ {*275}	35.00
☐ 26 Scott Walker, Nash. ✂ {*500}	10.00
☐ 27 Martin Brodeur (G), NJer. ✂ {*250}	50.00
☐ 28 Scott Gomez, NJer. ✂ {*750}	10.00
☐ 29 Michael Peca, NYIs. ✂ {*500}	10.00
☐ 30 Pavel Bure, Flor. ✂ {*500}	15.00
☐ 31 Mark Messier, NYRa. ✂ {*500}	20.00
☐ 32 Daniel Alfredsson, Otta. ✂ {*500}	10.00
☐ 33 Patrick Lalime (G), Otta. ✂ {*500}	10.00
☐ 34 John LeClair, Phil. ✂ {*500}	15.00
☐ 35 Krys Kolanos, Phoe. ✂ {*600}	10.00
☐ 36 Johan Hedberg (G), Pitt. ✂ {*500}	10.00
☐ 37 Mario Lemieux, Pitt. ✂ {*500}	60.00
☐ 38 Pavol Demitra, SLou. ✂ {*611}	10.00
☐ 39 Keith Tkachuk, SLou. ✂ {*500}	10.00
☐ 40 Patrick Marleau, SanJ. ✂ {*500}	10.00
☐ 41 Evgeni Nabokov (G), SanJ. ✂ {*500}	10.00
☐ 42 Nikolai Khabibulin (G), Tamp. ✂ {*500}	10.00
☐ 43 Alexander Mogilny, Toro. ✂ {*750}	10.00
☐ 44 Gary Roberts, Toro. ✂ {*750}	10.00
☐ 45 Darcy Tucker, Toro. ✂ {*750}	10.00
☐ 46 Dan Cloutier (G), Vanc. ✂ {*500}	10.00
☐ 47 Brendan Morrison, Vanc. ✂ {*500}	10.00
☐ 48 Markus Näslund, Vanc. ✂ {*500}	20.00
☐ 49 Peter Bondra, Wash. ✂ {*500}	10.00
☐ 50 Jaromir Jagr, Wash. ✂ {*500}	20.00

GAME-WORN JERSEY GOLD

Insert Set (50 cards):	1800.00
Insert (#/50)	GWJG
☐ 1 Adam Oates, Wash. ✂	25.00
☐ 2 Dany Heatley, Atla. ✂	75.00
☐ 3 Ilya Kovalchuk, Atla. ✂	75.00
☐ 4 Patrik Stefan, Atla. ✂	25.00
☐ 5 Joe Thornton, Bost. ✂	75.00
☐ 6 J-P Dumont, Buff. ✂	25.00
☐ 7 Chris Drury, Colo. ✂	25.00
☐ 8 Jamie McLennan (G), SLou. ✂	25.00
☐ 9 Rod Brind'Amour, Caro. ✂	25.00
☐ 10 Sergei Berezin, Phoe. ✂	25.00
☐ 11 Theoren Fleury, NYRa. ✂	25.00
☐ 12 Alexei Zhamnov, Chic. ✂	25.00
☐ 13 Joe Sakic, Colo. ✂	100.00
☐ 14 Tomi Kallio, Atla. ✂	25.00
☐ 15 Rostislav Klesla, Colu. ✂	25.00
☐ 16 Mike Modano, Dall. ✂	75.00
☐ 17 Pierre Turgeon, Dall. ✂	25.00
☐ 18 Sergei Fedorov, Detr. ✂	75.00
☐ 19 Brett Hull, Detr. ✂	75.00
☐ 20 Curtis Joseph (G), Toro. ✂	75.00
☐ 21 Ryan Smyth, Edmo. ✂	25.00
☐ 22 Kristian Huselius, Flor. ✂	25.00
☐ 23 Zigmund Palffy, LosA. ✂	25.00
☐ 24 Yanic Perreault, Mont. ✂	25.00
☐ 25 José Théodore (G), Mont. ✂	75.00
☐ 26 Scott Walker, Nash. ✂	25.00
☐ 27 Martin Brodeur (G), NJer. ✂	100.00
☐ 28 Scott Gomez, NJer. ✂	25.00
☐ 29 Michael Peca, NYIs. ✂	25.00
☐ 30 Pavel Bure, Flor. ✂	50.00
☐ 31 Mark Messier, NYRa. ✂	75.00
☐ 32 Daniel Alfredsson, Otta. ✂	75.00
☐ 33 Patrick Lalime (G), Otta. ✂	25.00
☐ 34 John LeClair, Phil. ✂	50.00
☐ 35 Krys Kolanos, Phoe. ✂	25.00
☐ 36 Johan Hedberg (G), Pitt. ✂	25.00
☐ 37 Mario Lemieux, Pitt. ✂	225.00
☐ 38 Pavol Demitra, SLou. ✂	25.00
☐ 39 Keith Tkachuk, SLou. ✂	25.00
☐ 40 Patrick Marleau, SanJ. ✂	25.00
☐ 41 Evgeni Nabokov (G), SanJ. ✂	25.00
☐ 42 Nikolai Khabibulin (G), Tamp. ✂	25.00
☐ 43 Alexander Mogilny, Toro. ✂	25.00
☐ 44 Gary Roberts, Toro. ✂	25.00
☐ 45 Darcy Tucker, Toro. ✂	25.00
☐ 46 Dan Cloutier (G), Vanc. ✂	25.00
☐ 47 Brendan Morrison, Vanc. ✂	25.00
☐ 48 Markus Näslund, Vanc. ✂	75.00
☐ 49 Peter Bondra, Wash. ✂	25.00
☐ 50 Jaromir Jagr, Wash. ✂	75.00

IN FOCUS

Insert Set (10 cards):	85.00
Insert (1:25)	IF
☐ 1 Paul Kariya, Anah.	8.00
☐ 2 Ilya Kovalchuk, Atla.	6.00
☐ 3 Peter Forsberg, Colo.	8.00
☐ 4 Joe Sakic, Colo.	10.00
☐ 5 Rick Nash, Colu.	20.00
☐ 6 Steve Yzerman, Detr.	15.00
☐ 7 Marian Gaborik, MinW.	6.00
☐ 8 Jason Spezza, Otta.	15.00
☐ 9 Mario Lemieux, Pitt.	18.00
☐ 10 Jaromir Jagr, Wash.	6.00

PRIME PROSPECTS

Insert Set (20 cards):	95.00
Insert (1:7)	PP
☐ 1 Stanislav Chistov, Anah.	7.00
☐ 2 Alexei Smirnov, Anah.	4.00
☐ 3 Ivan Huml, Bost.	4.00
☐ 4 Ryan Miller (G), Buff.	6.00
☐ 5 Chuck Kobasew, Calg.	4.00
☐ 6 Jordan Leopold, Calg.	4.00
☐ 7 Tyler Arnason, Chic.	6.00
☐ 8 Rick Nash, Colu.	12.00
☐ 9 Henrik Zetterberg, Detr.	12.00
☐ 10 Ales Hemsky, Edmo.	7.00
☐ 11 Jay Bouwmeester, Flor.	7.00
☐ 12 Stephen Weiss, Flor.	6.00
☐ 13 Alexander Frolov, LosA.	6.00
☐ 14 Pierre-Marc Bouchard, MinW.	7.00
☐ 15 Scottie Upshall, Nash.	4.00
☐ 16 Justin Mapletoft, NYIs.	4.00
☐ 17 Jamie Lundmark, NYRa.	4.00
☐ 18 Jason Spezza, Otta.	9.00
☐ 19 Petr Cajanek, SLou.	4.00
☐ 20 Barret Jackman, SLou.	6.00

STONEWALLERS

Insert Set (12 cards):	35.00
Insert (1:9)	SW
☐ 1 Patrick Roy (G), Colo.	12.00
☐ 2 Marty Turco (G), Dall.	2.00
☐ 3 Curtis Joseph (G), Detr.	4.00
☐ 4 Roberto Luongo (G), Flor.	3.00
☐ 5 Félix Potvin (G), LosA.	2.00
☐ 6 José Théodore (G), Mont.	4.00
☐ 7 Martin Brodeur (G), NJer.	6.00
☐ 8 Mike Richter (G), NYRa.	2.00
☐ 9 Patrick Lalime (G), Otta.	2.00
☐ 10 Roman Cechmanek (G), Phil.	2.00
☐ 11 Nikolai Khabibulin (G), Tamp.	2.00
☐ 12 Ed Belfour (G), Toro.	4.00

V-TEAM

Insert Set (12 cards):	65.00
Insert (1:25H or 1:25R)	VT
☐ 1 Patrick Roy (G), Colo.	14.00
☐ 2 Marty Turco (G), Dall.	2.00
☐ 3 Curtis Joseph (G), Detr.	4.00
☐ 4 José Théodore (G), Mont.	6.00
☐ 5 Martin Brodeur (G), NJer.	8.00
☐ 6 Ed Belfour (G), Toro.	4.00
☐ 7 Ilya Kovalchuk, Atla.	4.00
☐ 8 Joe Thornton, Bost.	6.00
☐ 9 Joe Sakic, Colo.	8.00
☐ 10 Steve Yzerman, Detr.	12.00
☐ 11 Mario Lemieux, Pitt.	14.00
☐ 12 Jaromir Jagr, Wash.	4.00

2002 - 03 VICTORY

Produced by The Upper Deck Company, this series was released in July 2002. There are four versions for each card 1-220: a base card, a Copper parallel, a Silver parallel, and a sequentially-numbered Gold parallel (#/100). Players are organized by team (from Anaheim to Washington).

Complete Set (220 cards):	1,900	1,800	75.00	45.00
Common Player:	6	5	.50	.20
Description	G100	S	C	Base
☐☐☐☐ 1 Vitaly Vishnevski	6	5	.50	.20
☐☐☐☐ 2 Paul Kariya	55	50	2.00	1.00
☐☐☐☐ 3 Jeff Friesen	10	10	.50	.25
☐☐☐☐ 4 J-S Giguère (G)	40	35	1.50	1.00
☐☐☐☐ 5 Oleg Tverdovsky	6	5	.50	.25
☐☐☐☐ 6 Matt Cullen	6	5	.50	.25
☐☐☐☐ 7 Mike Leclerc	6	5	.50	.25
☐☐☐☐ 8 Pasi Nurminen (G)	6	5	.50	.25
☐☐☐☐ 9 Dany Heatley	40	35	1.50	1.00
☐☐☐☐ 10 Ilya Kovalchuk	40	35	1.50	1.00
☐☐☐☐ 11 Pascal Rhéaume	6	5	.50	.25
☐☐☐☐ 12 Lubos Bartecko	6	5	.50	.25
☐☐☐☐ 13 Mark Hartigan	6	5	.50	.25
☐☐☐☐ 14 Frédéric Cassivi	6	5	.50	.25
☐☐☐☐ 15 Jozef Stümpel	6	5	.50	.25
☐☐☐☐ 16 Sergei Samsonov	20	20	.50	.50
☐☐☐☐ 17 P.J. Stock	10	10	.50	.25
☐☐☐☐ 18 Joe Thornton	45	45	1.50	1.00
☐☐☐☐ 19 Nick Boynton	6	5	.50	.25
☐☐☐☐ 20 Brian Rolston	10	10	.50	.25
☐☐☐☐ 21 Martin Lapointe	15	15	.50	.25
☐☐☐☐ 22 Maxim Afinogenov	15	15	.50	.25
☐☐☐☐ 23 Martin Biron (G)	15	15	.50	.25
☐☐☐☐ 24 Jean-Pierre Dumont	6	5	.50	.25
☐☐☐☐ 25 Stu Barnes	6	5	.50	.25
☐☐☐☐ 26 Tim Connolly	15	15	.50	.25
☐☐☐☐ 27 Miroslav Satan	10	10	.50	.25
☐☐☐☐ 28 Taylor Pyatt	6	5	.50	.25
☐☐☐☐ 29 Craig Conroy	10	10	.50	.25
☐☐☐☐ 30 Roman Turek (G)	15	15	.50	.25
☐☐☐☐ 31 Jarome Iginla	30	30	1.00	.50
☐☐☐☐ 32 Dean McAmmond	6	5	.50	.25
☐☐☐☐ 33 Marc Savard	6	5	.50	.25
☐☐☐☐ 34 Derek Morris	6	5	.50	.25
☐☐☐☐ **35 Micki Dupont RC**	**6**	**5**	**.50**	**.25**

□□□□ 36 Sami Kapanen	10	10	.50	.25
□□□□ 37 Jeff O'Neill	15	15	.50	.25
□□□□ 38 Ron Francis	20	20	.50	.50
□□□□ 39 Rod Brind'Amour	10	10	.50	.25
□□□□ 40 Erik Cole	6	5	.50	.25
□□□□ 41 Bates Battaglia	6	5	.50	.25
□□□□ 42 Arturs Irbe (G)	15	15	.50	.25
□□□□ 43 Alexei Zhamnov	10	10	.50	.25
□□□□ 44 Jocelyn Thibault (G)	15	15	.50	.25
□□□□ 45 Éric Dazé	15	15	.50	.25
□□□□ 46 Steve Sullivan	10	10	.50	.25
□□□□ 47 Phil Housley	10	10	.50	.25
□□□□ 48 Kyle Calder	6	5	.50	.25
□□□□ 49 Bob Probert	10	10	.50	.25
□□□□ 50 Patrick Roy (G)	120	110	4.50	3.00
□□□□ 51 Radim Vrbata	10	10	.50	.25
□□□□ 52 Chris Drury	20	20	.50	.50
□□□□ 53 Joe Sakic	60	60	2.00	1.50
□□□□ 54 Milan Hejduk	30	30	1.00	.50
□□□□ 55 Alex Tanguay	20	20	.50	.50
□□□□ 56 Peter Forsberg	55	50	2.00	1.00
□□□□ 57 Rob Blake	20	20	.50	.50
□□□□ 58 Ray Whitney	6	5	.50	.25
□□□□ 59 Espen Knutsen	6	5	.50	.25
□□□□ 60 Marc Denis (G)	15	15	.50	.25
□□□□ 61 Rostislav Klesla	10	10	.50	.25
□□□□ 62 Ron Tugnutt (G)	15	15	.50	.25
□□□□ 63 Mike Sillinger	6	5	.50	.25
□□□□ 64 Chris Nielsen	6	5	.50	.25
□□□□ 65 Jason Arnott	15	15	.50	.25
□□□□ 66 Marty Turco (G)	20	20	.50	.50
□□□□ 67 Jere Lehtinen	10	10	.50	.25
□□□□ 68 Sergei Zubov	6	5	.50	.25
□□□□ 69 Mike Modano	40	35	1.50	1.00
□□□□ 70 Brenden Morrow	10	10	.50	.25
□□□□ 71 Pierre Turgeon	15	15	.50	.25
□□□□ 72 Derian Hatcher	10	10	.50	.25
□□□□ 73 Brendan Shanahan	40	35	1.50	1.00
□□□□ 74 Dominik Hasek (G)	40	35	1.50	1.00
□□□□ 75 Sergei Fedorov	40	35	1.50	1.00
□□□□ 76 Pavel Datsyuk	30	30	1.00	.50
□□□□ 77 Steve Yzerman	95	90	3.50	2.00
□□□□ 78 Brett Hull	40	35	1.50	1.00
□□□□ 79 Chris Chelios	20	20	.50	.50
□□□□ 80 Luc Robitaille	30	30	1.00	.50
□□□□ 81 Mike Comrie	30	30	1.00	.50
□□□□ 82 Anson Carter	15	15	.50	.25
□□□□ 83 Ryan Smyth	15	15	.50	.25
□□□□ 84 Tommy Salo (G)	15	15	.50	.25
□□□□ 85 Jochen Hecht	6	5	.50	.25
□□□□ 86 Eric Brewer	15	15	.50	.25
□□□□ 87 Mike York	10	10	.50	.25
□□□□ 88 Kristian Huselius	10	10	.50	.25
□□□□ 89 Stephen Weiss	15	15	.50	.25
□□□□ 90 Roberto Luongo (G)	30	30	1.00	.50
□□□□ 91 Sandis Ozolinsh	6	5	.50	.25
□□□□ 92 Valeri Bure	10	10	.50	.25
□□□□ 93 Marcus Nilson	6	5	.50	.25
□□□□ 94 Niklas Hagman	6	5	.50	.25
□□□□ 95 Adam Deadmarsh	10	10	.50	.25
□□□□ 96 Félix Potvin (G)	45	20	.50	.50
□□□□ 97 Jason Allison	20	20	.50	.50
□□□□ 98 Éric Bélanger	6	5	.50	.25
□□□□ 99 Zigmund Palffy	20	20	.50	.50
□□□□ 100 Cliff Ronning	6	5	.50	.25
□□□□ 101 Mathieu Schneider	6	5	.50	.25
□□□□ 102 Andrew Brunette	6	5	.50	.25
□□□□ **103 Sylvain Blouin RC**	**6**	**5**	**.50**	**.25**
□□□□ 104 Marian Gaborik	40	35	1.50	1.00
□□□□ 105 Wes Walz	6	5	.50	.25
□□□□ 106 Filip Kuba	6	5	.50	.25
□□□□ 107 M. Fernandez (G)	15	15	.50	.25
□□□□ 108 Tony Virta	6	5	.50	.25
□□□□ 109 José Théodore (G)	45	45	1.50	1.00
□□□□ 110 Saku Koivu	45	30	1.00	.50
□□□□ 111 Mike Ribeiro	10	10	.50	.25
□□□□ 112 Yanic Perreault	10	10	.50	.25
□□□□ 113 Oleg Petrov	10	10	.50	.25
□□□□ 114 Joé Juneau	6	5	.50	.25
□□□□ 115 Marcel Hossa	15	15	.50	.25
□□□□ 116 Denis (G) Arkhipov	6	5	.50	.25
□□□□ 117 Scott Hartnell	6	5	.50	.25
□□□□ 118 David Legwand	15	15	.50	.25
□□□□ 119 Mike Dunham (G)	15	15	.50	.25
□□□□ 120 Kimmo Timonen	6	5	.50	.25
□□□□ 121 Greg Johnson	6	5	.50	.25
□□□□ 122 Andy Delmore	6	5	.50	.25
□□□□ 123 Petr Sykora	15	15	.50	.25
□□□□ 124 Scott Stevens	15	15	.50	.25
□□□□ 125 Brian Gionta	6	5	.50	.25
□□□□ 126 Scott Niedermayer	10	10	.50	.25
□□□□ 127 Martin Brodeur (G)	60	60	2.00	1.50
□□□□ 128 Patrik Elias	30	30	1.00	.50
□□□□ 129 Joe Nieuwendyk	15	15	.50	.25
□□□□ 130 Scott Gomez	15	15	.50	.25
□□□□ **131 Ray Schultz RC**	**6**	**5**	**.50**	**.25**
□□□□ 132 Mark Parrish	15	15	.50	.25
□□□□ 133 Raffi Torres	6	5	.50	.25
□□□□ 134 Alexei Yashin	20	20	.50	.50
□□□□ 135 Chris Osgood (G)	20	20	.50	.50
□□□□ 136 Michael Peca	15	15	.50	.25
□□□□ 137 Shawn Bates	6	5	.50	.25
□□□□ 138 Pavel Bure	30	30	1.00	.50
□□□□ 139 Mark Messier	40	35	1.50	1.00
□□□□ 140 Eric Lindros	40	35	1.50	1.00
□□□□ 141 Brian Leetch	20	20	.50	.50
□□□□ 142 Petr Nedved	10	10	.50	.25
□□□□ 143 Tom Poti	6	5	.50	.25
□□□□ 144 Dan Blackburn (G)	15	15	.50	.25
□□□□ 145 Mike Richter (G)	15	15	.50	.25
□□□□ 146 Martin Havlat	20	20	.50	.50
□□□□ 147 Patrick Lalime (G)	20	20	.50	.50
□□□□ 148 Daniel Alfredsson	45	20	.50	.50
□□□□ 149 Marian Hossa	40	35	1.50	1.00
□□□□ 150 Radek Bonk	10	10	.50	.25
□□□□ 151 Wade Redden	10	10	.50	.25
□□□□ 152 Magnus Arvedson	6	5	.50	.25
□□□□ 153 Todd White	6	5	.50	.25
□□□□ 154 R. Cechmanek (G)	15	15	.50	.25
□□□□ 155 Mark Recchi	15	15	.50	.25
□□□□ 156 Simon Gagné	30	30	1.00	.50
□□□□ 157 Jeremy Roenick	30	30	1.00	.50
□□□□ 158 John LeClair	30	30	1.00	.50
□□□□ 159 Keith Primeau	15	15	.50	.25
□□□□ 160 Justin Williams	10	10	.50	.25
□□□□ 161 Brian Boucher (G)	10	10	.50	.25
□□□□ 162 Krys Kolanos	6	5	.50	.25
□□□□ 163 Sean Burke (G)	20	20	.50	.50
□□□□ 164 Teppo Numminen	10	10	.50	.25
□□□□ 165 Shane Doan	6	5	.50	.25
□□□□ 166 Ladislav Nagy	6	5	.50	.25
□□□□ 167 Daymond Langkow	6	5	.50	.25
□□□□ 168 Daniel Brière	15	15	.50	.25
□□□□ 169 Kris Beech	10	10	.50	.25
□□□□ 170 Johan Hedberg (G)	15	15	.50	.25
□□□□ 171 Martin Straka	10	10	.50	.25
□□□□ 172 Mario Lemieux	120	110	4.50	3.00
□□□□ 173 Alex Kovalev	20	20	.50	.50
□□□□ 174 Jan Hrdina	6	5	.50	.25
□□□□ 175 Aleksey Morozov	6	5	.50	.25
□□□□ 176 V. Damphousse	20	20	.50	.50
□□□□ 177 Owen Nolan	20	20	.50	.50
□□□□ 178 Patrick Marleau	15	15	.50	.25
□□□□ 179 Evgeni Nabokov (G)	20	20	.50	.50
□□□□ 180 Brad Stuart	15	15	.50	.25
□□□□ 181 Mike Ricci	10	10	.50	.25
□□□□ 182 Scott Thornton	6	5	.50	.25
□□□□ 183 Al MacInnis	15	15	.50	.25
□□□□ 184 Pavol Demitra	15	15	.50	.25
□□□□ 185 Chris Pronger	20	20	.50	.50
□□□□ 186 Brent Johnson (G)	15	15	.50	.25
□□□□ 187 Doug Weight	20	20	.50	.50
□□□□ 188 Keith Tkachuk	20	20	.50	.50
□□□□ 189 Scott Young	10	10	.50	.25
□□□□ 190 Cory Stillman	6	5	.50	.25
□□□□ 191 Sheldon Keefe	6	5	.50	.25
□□□□ 192 Brad Richards	15	15	.50	.25
□□□□ 193 N. Khabibulin (G)	15	15	.50	.25
□□□□ 194 Martin St-Louis	15	15	.50	.25
□□□□ 195 Vincent Lecavalier	40	35	1.50	1.00
□□□□ 196 Fredrik Modin	6	5	.50	.25
□□□□ 197 Pavel Kubina	6	5	.50	.25
□□□□ 198 Alexander Mogilny	15	15	.50	.25
□□□□ 199 Tomas Kaberle	10	10	.50	.25
□□□□ 200 Mats Sundin	40	35	1.50	1.00
□□□□ 201 Gary Roberts	15	15	.50	.25
□□□□ 202 Mikael Renberg	10	10	.50	.25
□□□□ 203 Tie Domi	10	10	.50	.25
□□□□ 204 Darcy Tucker	6	5	.50	.25
□□□□ 205 Brendan Morrison	10	10	.50	.25
□□□□ 206 Brent Sopel	6	5	.50	.25
□□□□ 207 Trevor Linden	15	15	.50	.25
□□□□ 208 Dan Cloutier (G)	15	15	.50	.25
□□□□ 209 Todd Bertuzzi	45	45	1.50	1.00
□□□□ 210 Ed Jovanovski	15	15	.50	.25
□□□□ 211 Markus Näslund	40	35	1.50	1.00
□□□□ 212 Sergei Gonchar	10	10	.50	.25
□□□□ 213 Jaromir Jagr	40	35	1.50	1.00
□□□□ 214 Peter Bondra	20	20	.50	.50
□□□□ 215 Steve Konowalchuk	6	5	.50	.25
□□□□ 216 Dainius Zubrus	6	5	.50	.25
□□□□ 217 Brian Sutherby	6	5	.50	.25
□□□□ 218 Olaf Kölzig (G)	20	20	.50	.50
□□□□ 219 Patrick Roy (G)	60	55	2.00	1.50
□□□□ 220 Pavel Bure	15	15	.50	.25

NATIONAL PRIDE

Insert Set (60 cards):	50.00
Insert (1:12)	NP
□ NP1 Ruslan Salei, Anah.	1.00
□ NP2 Paul Kariya, Anah.	2.50
□ NP3 Jarome Iginla, Calg.	1.50
□ NP4 Joe Sakic, Colo.	3.00
□ NP5 Rob Blake, Colo.	1.00
□ NP6 Steve Yzerman, Detr.	4.50
□ NP7 Brendan Shanahan, Detr.	2.00
□ NP8 Martin Brodeur (G), NJer.	3.00
□ NP9 Eric Lindros, NYRa.	2.00
□ NP10 Simon Gagné, Phil.	1.50
□ NP11 Mario Lemieux, Pitt.	6.00
□ NP12 Chris Pronger, SLou.	1.00
□ NP13 Curtis Joseph (G), Toro.	2.00
□ NP14 Milan Hejduk, Colo.	1.50
□ NP15 Dominik Hasek (G), Detr.	2.00
□ NP16 Patrik Elias, NJer.	1.50
□ NP17 Petr Sykora, NJer.	1.00
□ NP18 Martin Rucinsky, NYRa.	1.00
□ NP19 Martin Havlat, Otta.	1.00
□ NP20 Robert Lang, Pitt.	1.00
□ NP21 Jaromir Jagr, Wash.	2.00
□ NP22 Sami Kapanen, Caro.	1.00
□ NP23 Ville Nieminen, Pitt.	1.00
□ NP24 Jere Lehtinen, Dall.	1.00
□ NP25 Jani Hurme (G), Otta.	1.00
□ NP26 Teppo Numminen, Phoe.	1.00
□ NP27 Teemu Selänne, SanJ.	1.50
□ NP28 Jochen Hecht, Edmo.	1.00
□ NP29 Marco Sturm, SanJ.	1.00
□ NP30 Olaf Kölzig (G), Wash.	1.00
□ NP31 Ilya Kovalchuk, Atla.	2.00
□ NP32 Sergei Samsonov, Bost.	1.00
□ NP33 Alexei Zhamnov, Chic.	1.00
□ NP34 Sergei Fedorov, Detr.	2.00
□ NP35 Pavel Bure, NYRa.	1.50
□ NP36 Alexei Yashin, NYIs.	1.00
□ NP37 Alex Kovalev, Pitt.	1.00
□ NP38 Nikolai Khabibulin (G), Tamp.	1.00
□ NP39 Sergei Gonchar, Wash.	1.00
□ NP40 Miroslav Satan, Buff.	1.00
□ NP41 Zigmund Palffy, LosA.	1.00
□ NP42 Marian Hossa, Otta.	2.00
□ NP43 Pavol Demitra, SLou.	1.00
□ NP44 Nicklas Lidström, Detr.	1.00
□ NP45 Tomas Holmström, Detr.	1.00
□ NP46 Tommy Salo (G), Edmo.	1.00
□ NP47 Daniel Alfredsson, Otta.	1.00
□ NP48 Kim Johnsson, Phil.	1.00
□ NP49 Mats Sundin, Toro.	2.00
□ NP50 Markus Näslund, Vanc.	2.00
□ NP51 Bill Guerin, Bost.	1.00
□ NP52 Tony Amonte, Chic.	1.00
□ NP53 Chris Drury, Colo.	1.00
□ NP54 Mike Modano, Dall.	2.00
□ NP55 Chris Chelios, Detr.	1.00
□ NP56 Mike Dunham (G), Nash.	1.00
□ NP57 Mike Richter (G), NYRa.	1.00
□ NP58 Jeremy Roenick, Phil.	1.50
□ NP59 Keith Tkachuk, SLou.	1.00
□ NP60 Doug Weight, SLou.	1.00

CHAPTER SIX

NHL TEAM ISSUES

ANAHEIM MIGHTY DUCKS

'93 - 94 ANAH.

These blank-back caps are limited to 15,000 copies. Singles start at $1.

Cap Diameter: 1 1/2"
Sponsor: None
Complete Set (6 caps): $6

☐ Mighty Ducks
☐ 1 Tim Sweeney
☐ 2 Bobby Dollas
☐ 3 Stu Grimson
☐ 4 Terry Yake
☐ 5 Bob Corkum

'94 - 95 ANAH.
CARL'S JR.

Paul Kariya is the most expensive single at $12. Singles start at 50¢.

Card Size: 2 1/2" x 3 1/2"
Sponsor: Carl's Jr.
Set (28 cards): $20

☐ 1 Patrick Carnback
☐ 2 Bob Corkum
☐ 3 Robert Dirk
☐ 4 Bobby Dollas
☐ 5 Peter Douris
☐ 6 Todd Ewen
☐ 7 Shaun Van Allen
☐ 8 Garry Valk
☐ 9 Guy Hebert (G)
☐ 10 Paul Kariya
☐ 11 Valeri Karpov
☐ 12 Steven King
☐ 13 Todd Krygier
☐ 14 Tom Kurvers
☐ 15 Randy Ladouceur
☐ 16 Stéphan Lebeau
☐ 17 John Lilley
☐ 18 Don McSween
☐ 19 Steve Rucchin
☐ 20 David Sacco
☐ 21 Joe Sacco
☐ 22 M. Shtalenkov (G)
☐ 23 Jim Thomson
☐ 24 Olef Tverdovsky
☐ 25 David Williams
☐ 26 Mascot Wild Wing
☐ 27 Sponsor Carl Karcher
☐ 28 Sponsor Happy Star

'95 - 96 ANAH.

We have little information on this set. Other singles exist.

Photo Size: 5" x 7"
Sponsor: None

☐ Bobby Dollas
☐ Paul Kariya
☐ David Karpa
☐ Steve Rucchin
☐ Mikhail Shtalenkov (G)
☐ Garry Valk

'96 - 97 ANAH.
UP FRONT SPORTS

The most expenive singles are Paul Kariya at $8 and Teemu Selänne at $4. Regular singles start at 50¢ while pop-up singles (21-24) start at $2. Card number 9 (Garry Valk) is unconfirmed. A 26-card set sells for $25.

Card Size: 2 1/2" x 3 1/2"
Sponsor: Southland Micro Systems

☐ 1 M. Shtalenkov (G)
☐ 2 Bobby Dollas
☐ 3 Roman Oksiuta
☐ 4 Kevin Todd
☐ 5 Ted Drury
☐ 6 Joe Sacco
☐ 7 Dmitri Mironov
☐ 8 Warren Rychel
☐ 10 Shawn Antoski
☐ 11 Steve Rucchin
☐ 12 Ken Baumgartner
☐ 13 Brian Bellows
☐ 14 Nikolai Tsulygin
☐ 15 Jason Marshall
☐ 16 Darren Van Impe
☐ 17 David Karpa
☐ 18 Mascot Wild Wing
☐ 19 J.F. Jomphe
☐ 20 Sean Pronger
☐ 21 Guy Hebert (G)
☐ 22 Paul Kariya
☐ 23 Jari Kurri
☐ 24 Teemu Selänne
☐ 25 Sponsor Southland
☐ 26 Sponsor Southland
☐ 27 Ron Wilson, Coach

'02 - 03 ANAH.

We do not have a checklist for this series of postcards.

ATLANTA FLAMES

'72 - 73 ATLA.
COCA-COLA

The most expensive singles are Bernie Geoffrion at $10 and Pat Quinn at $8 in NM. Singles start at $3.

Card Size: 3 1/2" x 5 1/2"
Sponsor: Coca-Cola
Set (20 cards): $70

☐ Curt Bennett
☐ Dan Bouchard (G)
☐ Rey Comeau
☐ Bernie Geoffrion
☐ Bob Leiter
☐ Kerry Ketter
☐ Billy MacMillan
☐ Randy Manery
☐ Keith McCreary
☐ Lew Morrison
☐ Phil Myre (G)
☐ Bob Paradise
☐ Noel Picard
☐ Bill Plager
☐ Noel Price
☐ Pat Quinn
☐ Jacques Richard
☐ Leon Rochefort
☐ Larry Romanchych
☐ John Stewart

'74 - 75 ATLA.

These cards feature colour photographs and a facsimile signature on the card front. Dan Bouchard and Pat Quinn are the most expensive single at $5-6 in NM. Singles start at $1.50. Other singles may exist.

Sponsor: None

☐ Curt Bennett
☐ Dan Bouchard (G)
☐ Rey Comeau
☐ Tim Ecclestone
☐ Hilliard Graves
☐ Buster Harvey
☐ Bob Leiter
☐ Tom Lysiak
☐ Randy Manery
☐ Phil Myre (G)
☐ Pat Quinn
☐ Larry Romanchych
☐ Eric Vail

'77 - 78 ATLA.

These cards feature colour photographs and a facsimile signature on the card front. Dan Bouchard is the most expensive single at $3-4 in NM. Singles start at $1. Other singles may exist.

Sponsor: None

☐ Dan Bouchard (G)
☐ Guy Chouinard
☐ Bill Clement
☐ Rey Comeau
☐ Tim Ecclestone
☐ John Gould
☐ Ken Houston
☐ Ed Kea
☐ Tom Lysiak
☐ Richard Mulhern
☐ Harold Phillipoff
☐ Willi Plett
☐ Pat Ribble
☐ Dave Shand
☐ Eric Vail

'78 - 79 ATLA.

Dan Bouchard and Réjean Lemelin are the most expensive singles at $3-4 in NM. Singles start at $1.

Card Size: 3 1/2" x 5 1/2"
Sponsors: Coca-Cola, WLTA Radio
Set (20 cards): $35

☐ Dan Bouchard (G)
☐ Guy Chouinard
☐ Bill Clement
☐ Greg Fox
☐ Ken Houston
☐ Ed Kea
☐ Bobby Lalonde
☐ Red Laurence
☐ Réjean Lemelin (G)
☐ Tom Lysiak
☐ Bob MacMillan
☐ Brad Marsh
☐ Bob Murdoch
☐ Harold Phillippoff
☐ Willi Plett
☐ Jean Pronovost
☐ Pat Ribble
☐ Rod Seiling
☐ Dave Shand
☐ Eric Vail

'79 - 80 ATLA.

These cards feature colour photography. Kent Nilsson and Jim Craig are the most expensive cards at $4-5 in NM. Singles start at $1.

Card Size: 3 1/2" x 5 1/2"
Sponsors: Coca-Cola, WLTA Radio, Winn Dixie.
Set (20 cards): $35

☐ Curt Bennett
☐ Dan Bouchard (G)
☐ Guy Chouinard
☐ Bill Clement
☐ Jim Craig (G)
☐ Ken Houston
☐ Don Lever
☐ Bob MacMillan
☐ Brad Marsh
☐ Bob Murdoch
☐ Kent Nilsson
☐ Willi Plett
☐ Jean Pronovost
☐ Pekka Rautakallio
☐ Paul Reinhart
☐ Pat Riggin
☐ Phil Russell
☐ David Shand
☐ Garry Unger
☐ Eric Vail

'79 - 80 ATLA.
BLACK & WHITE

These postcards feature black and white photos and a facsimile signature on the card front. Kent Nilsson and Jim Craig are the most expensive single at $4-5. Singles start at $1.

Card Size: 3 3/4" x 5 1/4"
Sponsor: None
Set (20 cards): $35

☐ Curt Bennett
☐ Ivan Boldirev
☐ Dan Bouchard (G)
☐ Guy Chouinard
☐ Bill Clement
☐ Ken Houston
☐ Bob MacMillan
☐ Al MacNeil, Coach
☐ Brad Marsh
☐ Bob Murdoch
☐ Kent Nilsson
☐ Willi Plett
☐ Jean Pronovost
☐ Pekka Rautakallio
☐ Phil Russell
☐ Paul Reinhart
☐ Darcy Rota
☐ Dave Shand
☐ Garry Unger
☐ Eric Vail

ATLANTA THRASHERS

'02 - 03 ATLA.

We do not have a checklist for this series of postcards.

Card Size: 5" x 7"

☐ Dany Heatley
☐ Ilya Kovalchuk

BOSTON BRUINS

'57 - 58 BOST.

Milt Schmidt is the most expensive single at $20-25 in NM. Singles start at $7. Other singles may exist.

Photo Size: 6 5/8" x 8 1/8"
Sponsor: None

☐ Bob Armstrong
☐ Jack Bionda
☐ Léo Boivin
☐ Real Chevrefils
☐ Fern Flaman
☐ Léo Labine
☐ Fleming Mackell
☐ Don McKenney
☐ Doug Mohns
☐ Johnny Peirson
☐ Larry Regan
☐ Milt Schmidt
☐ Vic Stasiuk
☐ Jerry Toppazzini

'70 - 71 BOST.
STANLEY CUP

This series was issued in two nine-photo packs. The most expensive singles are Bobby Orr at $60 and Phil Esposito at $20 in NM. Commons start at $5.

Card Size: 6" x 8"
Sponsor: None
Set (18 cards): $150

☐ Don Awrey
☐ Garnet Bailey
☐ Johnny Bucyk
☐ Wayne Carleton
☐ Wayne Cashman
☐ Gerry Cheevers (G)
☐ Gary Doak
☐ Phil Esposito
☐ Ken Hodge
☐ Ed Johnston (G)
☐ Don Marcotte
☐ John McKenzie
☐ Bobby Orr
☐ Derek Sanderson
☐ Dallas Smith
☐ Rick Smith
☐ Fred Stanfield
☐ Ed Westfall

'71 - 72 BOST.

This series was originally issued in booklet form. The most expensive singles are Bobby Orr at $50 and Phil Esposito at $15 in NM. Singles start at $2.

Card Size: 3 1/2" x 5 1/2"
Sponsor: None
Set (20 cards): $85

☐ Don Awrey
☐ Garnet Bailey
☐ John Bucyk
☐ Wayne Cashman
☐ Gerry Cheevers (G)
☐ Phil Esposito
☐ Ted Green
☐ Ken Hodge
☐ Ed Johnston (G)
☐ Reggie Leach
☐ Don Marcotte
☐ John McKenzie
☐ Bobby Orr
☐ Garry Peters
☐ Derek Sanderson
☐ Rick Smith
☐ Dallas Smith
☐ Fred Stanfield
☐ Mike Walton
☐ Ed Westfall

'83 - 84 BOST.

Photos are black and white. Raymond Bourque is the most expensive single at $20. Singles start $2.

Card Size: 3 1/8" x 4 1/8"
Sponsor: None
Set (17 cards): $40

☐ Raymond Bourque
☐ Bruce Crowder
☐ Keith Crowder
☐ Luc Dufour
☐ Tom Fergus
☐ Randy Hillier
☐ Steve Kasper
☐ Gord Kluzak
☐ Mike Krushelnyski
☐ Peter McNab
☐ Rick Middleton
☐ Mike Milbury
☐ Mike O'Connell
☐ Terry O'Reilly
☐ Brad Palmer
☐ Barry Pederson
☐ Pete Peeters (G)

'84 - 85 BOST.

Raymond Bourque is the most expensive single at $20. Singles start $2.

Card Size: 3 5/8" x 5 5/8"
Sponsor: None
Set (20 cards): $40

☐ Raymond Bourque
☐ Lyndon Byers
☐ Geoff Courtnall
☐ Keith Crowder
☐ Tom Fergus
☐ Mike Gillis
☐ Steve Kasper
☐ Doug Keans (G)
☐ Gord Kluzak
☐ Ken Linseman
☐ Nevin Markwart
☐ Rick Middleton
☐ Mike Milbury
☐ Mike O'Connell
☐ Terry O'Reilly
☐ Barry Pederson
☐ Pete Peeters (G)
☐ Charlie Simmer
☐ Louis Sleigher
☐ Mats Thelin

'88 - 89 BOST.
SPORTS ACTION

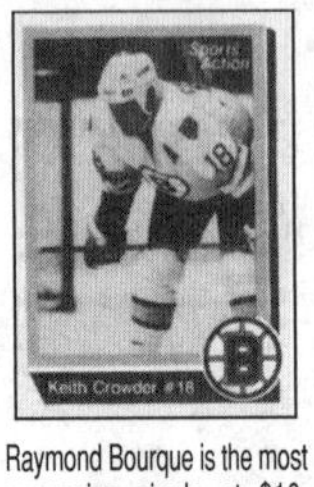

Raymond Bourque is the most expensive single at $10. Singles start at 75¢.

Card Size: 2 1/2" x 3 1/2"
Sponsor: Bruins Pro Shop
Set (24 cards): $25

☐ Raymond Bourque
☐ Randy Burridge
☐ Lyndon Byers
☐ Keith Crowder
☐ Craig Janney
☐ Bob Joyce
☐ Steve Kasper
☐ Gord Kluzak
☐ Reed Larson
☐ Réjean Lemelin (G)
☐ Ken Linseman
☐ Tom McCarthy
☐ Rick Middleton
☐ Jay Miller
☐ Andy Moog (G)
☐ Cam Neely
☐ Terry O'Reilly
☐ Allen Pederson
☐ Willi Plett
☐ Bob Sweeney
☐ Michael Thelvin
☐ Glen Wesley
☐ Janney/ Joyce
☐ Bourque/ Neely

'89 - 90 BOST.
SPORTS ACTION

Raymond Bourque is the most expensive single at $8. Singles start at 75¢.

Card Size: 2 1/2" x 3 1/2"
Sponsor: Bruins Pro Shop
Set (24 cards): $20

☐ Raymond Bourque
☐ Andy Brickley
☐ Randy Burridge
☐ Lyndon Byers
☐ Bob Carpenter
☐ John Carter
☐ Rob Cimetta
☐ Garry Galley
☐ Bob Gould
☐ Greg Hawgood
☐ Craig Janney
☐ Bob Joyce
☐ Réjean Lemelin (G)
☐ Ken Linseman
☐ Andy Moog (G)
☐ Nevin Markwart
☐ Cam Neely
☐ Allen Pederson
☐ Stéphane Quintal
☐ Bob Sweeney
☐ Michael Thelvin
☐ Glen Wesley
☐ Bruins Scorers
☐ Bruins Champions

'89 - 90 BOST.
SPORTS ACTION 2

Raymond Bourque is the most expensive single at $8. Singles start at 75¢.

Card Size: 2 1/2" x 3 1/2"
Sponsor: Bruins Pro Shop
Set (12 cards): $15

☐ Raymond Bourque
☐ Dave Christian
☐ Peter Douris
☐ Gord Kluzak
☐ Brian Lawton
☐ Mike Millar
☐ Dave Poulin
☐ Brian Propp
☐ Don Sweeney
☐ Graeme Townshend
☐ Jim Wiemer
☐ Bourque/ Lemelin/ Neely

'90 - 91 BOST.
SPORTS ACTION

Raymond Bourque is the most expensive single at $8. Singles start at 75¢. Nevin Markwart and Stéphane Quintal are considered short prints and sell at $3-4.

Card Size: 2 1/2" x 3 1/2"
Sponsor: Bruins Pro Shop
Set (26 cards): $30

☐ Bob Beers
☐ Raymond Bourque
☐ Andy Brickley
☐ Randy Burridge
☐ John Byce
☐ Lyndon Byers
☐ Bob Carpenter
☐ John Carter
☐ Dave Christian
☐ Peter Douris
☐ Garry Galley
☐ Ken Hodge, Jr.
☐ Craig Janney
☐ Réjean Lemelin
☐ Nevin Markwart
☐ Andy Moog (G)
☐ Cam Neely
☐ Chris Nilan
☐ Allen Pederson
☐ Dave Poulin
☐ Stéphane Quintal
☐ Bob Sweeney
☐ Don Sweeney
☐ Wes Walz
☐ Glen Wesley
☐ Lemelin/ Moog

'91 - 92 BOST.
SPORTS ACTION

Raymond Bourque is the most expensive single at $6. Singles start at 50¢.

Card Size: 2 1/2" x 3 1/2"
Sponsor: Bruins Pro Shop
Set (24 cards): $20

☐ Brent Ashton
☐ Bob Beers
☐ Daniel Berthiaume (G)
☐ Raymond Bourque
☐ Bob Carpenter
☐ Peter Douris
☐ Glen Featherstone
☐ Ken Hodge, Jr.
☐ Jeff Lazaro
☐ Stephen Leach
☐ Andy Moog (G)
☐ Gord Murphy
☐ Cam Neely
☐ Adam Oates
☐ Dave Poulin
☐ Dave Reid
☐ Vladimir Ruzicka
☐ Bob Sweeney
☐ Don Sweeney
☐ Jim Vesey
☐ Glen Wesley
☐ Jim Wiemer
☐ Chris Winnes
☐ Moog/ Bourque/ Neely

'91 - 92 BOST.
SPORTS ACTION LEGENDS

The most expensive singles are Bobby Orr and Raymond Bourque, each at $6. Singles start at 50¢.

Card Size: 2 1/2" x 3 1/2"
Sponsor: Bruins Pro Shop
Set (36 cards): $20

☐ Bob Armstrong
☐ Léo Boivin

☐ Raymond Bourque
☐ Frank Brimsek (G)
☐ Johnny Bucyk
☐ Wayne Cashman
☐ Gerry Cheevers (G)
☐ Dit Clapper
☐ Bill Cowley
☐ Phil Esposito
☐ Fern Flaman
☐ Lionel Hitchman
☐ Fleming Mackell
☐ Don Marcotte
☐ Don McKenney
☐ Rick Middleton
☐ Doug Mohns
☐ Terry O'Reilly
☐ Bobby Orr
☐ Brad Park
☐ John Pierson
☐ Bill Quackenbush
☐ Jean Ratelle
☐ Art Ross
☐ Ed Sandford
☐ Terry Sawchuk (G)
☐ Milt Schmidt
☐ Eddie Shore
☐ Harry Sinden
☐ Tiny Thompson (G)
☐ Cooney Weiland
☐ Ed Westfall
☐ Hill/ Cowley/ Conacher
☐ Schmidt/ Weiland/ Cowley
☐ Quackenbush/ Armstrong/ Sawchuk/ Flaman/ Boivin
☐ Schmidt/ Dumart/ Bauer

'92 - 93 BOST.

Raymond Bourque is the most expensive single at $8. Singles start at 75¢.

Card Size: 3 1/2" x 5 1/2"
Sponsor: None
Set (12 cards): $20

☐ Raymond Bourque
☐ Ted Donato
☐ Joé Juneau
☐ Dmitri Kvartalnov
☐ Stephen Leach
☐ Andy Moog (G)
☐ Adam Oates
☐ Dave Poulin
☐ Gordie Roberts
☐ Vladimir Ruzicka
☐ Don Sweeney
☐ Glen Wesley

'98 - 99 BOST.
BRUINS ALUMNI

The most expensive single is Bobby Orr at $6. Singles start at 75¢.

Card Size: 2 1/2" x 3 1/2"
Sponsor: None
Set (35 cards): $25

☐ 1 Réjean Lemelin (G)
☐ 2 Harry Sinden
☐ 3 Jim Craig (G)
☐ 4 Bobby Orr
☐ 5 Fern Flaman
☐ 6 Bob Beers
☐ 7 Ken Hodge
☐ 8 Cam Neely
☐ 9 Johnny Bucyk
☐ 10 Jean Ratelle
☐ 11 Bob Miller
☐ 12 Ed Sandford
☐ 13 Ken Linseman
☐ 14 Woody Dumart
☐ 15 Milt Schmidt

☐ 16 Derek Sanderson
☐ 17 Fred Stanfield
☐ 18 Garnet Bailey
☐ 19 John McKenzie
☐ 20 Dallas Smith
☐ 21 Don Marcotte
☐ 22 Brad Park
☐ 23 Matt Glennon
☐ 24 Terry O'Reilly
☐ 25 Garry Doak
☐ 26 Don Awrey
☐ 27 Bill O'Dwyer
☐ 28 Dave Hynes
☐ 29 Ton Songin
☐ 30 Gerry Cheevers
☐ 31 Don McKenney
☐ 32 Frank Simonetti
☐ 33 Bronco Horvath
☐ 34 Doug Mohns
☐ 35 Bobby Orr

'01 - 02 BOST.

Card Size: 5" x 7"

☐ Byron Dafoe (G)
☐ Hal Gill
☐ Martin Lapointe
☐ Kyle McLaren
☐ Brian Rolston
☐ Jozef Stümpel
☐ Don Sweeney

'02 - 03 BOST.

Card Size: 5" x 7"

☐ Per Axelsson
☐ Nick Boynton
☐ Hal Gill
☐ Glen Murray
☐ Brian Rolston
☐ Sergei Samsonov
☐ Joe Thornton
☐ Mascot Blades

BUFFALO SABRES

'72 - 73 BUFF.

Photos by Robert Shaver. The most expensive singles are Gilbert Perreault at $10-12 and Tim Horton at $6-8. Singles start at $3.

Card Size: 3 1/2" x 5 1/2"
Sponsor: None
Set (20 cards): $50

☐ Steve Atkinson
☐ Larry Carriere
☐ Roger Crozier (G)
☐ Butch Deadmarsh
☐ Dave Dryden (G)
☐ Larry Hillman
☐ Tim Horton
☐ Jim Lorentz
☐ Don Luce
☐ Richard Martin
☐ Gerry Meehan
☐ Larry Mickey
☐ Gilbert Perreault
☐ Tracy Pratt
☐ Craig Ramsay
☐ René Robert
☐ Mike Robitaille
☐ Jim Schoenfeld
☐ Paul Terbenche
☐ Randy Wyrozub

'73 - 74 BUFF.

Photos by Robert Shaver. The most expensive singles in NM are Gilbert Perreault at $10-12 and Tim Horton at $6-8. Singles start at $2.

Card Size: 3 1/2" x 5 1/2"
Sponsor: None
Set (23 cards): $50

☐ Steve Atkinson
☐ Larry Carriere
☐ Frank Christie, Trainer
☐ Joe Crozier
☐ Roger Crozier (G)
☐ Dave Dryden (G)
☐ Rick Dudley
☐ John Gould
☐ Tim Horton
☐ Jim Lorentz
☐ Don Luce
☐ Richard Martin
☐ Gerry Meehan
☐ Larry Mickey
☐ Joe Noris
☐ Gilbert Perreault
☐ Tracy Pratt
☐ Craig Ramsay
☐ René Robert
☐ Mike Robitaille
☐ Doug Rombough
☐ Jim Schoenfeld
☐ Paul Terbenche

'73 - 74 BUFF.

BELLS MARKET

The most expensive single is Gilbert Perreault at $12-15 in NM. Singles start at $5.

Card Size: 3 15/16" x 5 1/2"
Sponsor: Bells Market
Set (4 cards): $30

☐ Roger Crozier (G)
☐ Jim Lorentz
☐ Richard Martin
☐ Gilbert Perreault

'74 - 75 BUFF.

The most expensive single is Gilbert Perreault at $10-12 in NM. Singles start at $2.

Card Size: 3 1/2" x 5 1/2"
Sponsor: None
Set (21 cards): $35

☐ Gary Bromley (G)
☐ Larry Carriere
☐ Roger Crozier (G)
☐ Rick Dudley
☐ Rocky Farr (G)
☐ Lee Fogolin
☐ Danny Gare
☐ Norm Gratton
☐ Jocelyn Guevremont
☐ Bill Hajt
☐ Jerry Korab
☐ Jim Lorentz
☐ Don Luce
☐ Richard Martin
☐ Peter McNab
☐ Larry Mickey
☐ Gilbert Perreault
☐ Craig Ramsay
☐ René Robert
☐ Jim Schoenfeld
☐ Brian Spencer

'75 - 76 BUFF.

LINNETT STUDIOS

The most expensive single is Gilbert Perreault at $10-12 in NM. Singles start at $3.

Photo Size: 8 1/2" x 11"
Sponsor: Linnett Studios
Set (12 cards): $35

☐ Roger Crozier (G)
☐ Gerry Desjardins (G)
☐ Dave Dryden (G)
☐ Jim Lorentz
☐ Don Luce
☐ Richard Martin
☐ Peter McNab
☐ Gerry Meehan
☐ Gilbert Perreault
☐ René Robert
☐ Jim Schoenfeld
☐ Fred Stanfield

'79 - 80 BUFF.

BELLS MARKET

The most expensive single is Richard Martin at $5 in NM. Singles start at $2.

Photo Size: 7 1/2" x 10"
Sponsor: Bells Market
Set (9 cards): $25

☐ Don Edwards (G)
☐ Danny Gare
☐ Jerry Korab
☐ Richard Martin
☐ Tony McKegney
☐ Craig Ramsay
☐ Bob Sauvé (G)
☐ Jim Schoenfeld
☐ John Van Boxmeer

'80 - 81 BUFF.

WENDT'S

These two card panels were issued in as many as five different colour tints: Light Blue (1-2, 5-8), Dark Blue (1-8), Red (1-8), Green (1, 3), and Magenta (3). Panels may exist for each colour.

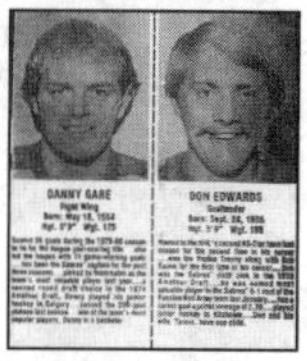

Panel Size: 3 3/4" x 5 1/2"
Sponsor: Wendt

☐ 1 Ramsay/ Schoenfeld
☐ 2 D. Smith/ Van Boxmeer
☐ 3 Edwards/ Gare
☐ 4 Perreault/ Seiling
☐ 5 Luce/ Savard
☐ 6 Dudley/ Dunn
☐ 7 Hajt/ MacKegney
☐ 8 Sauvé/ Martin

'81 - 82 BUFF.

WENDT'S

This series was issued on the backs of milk cartons. Gilbert Perreault is the most expensive single at $25 in NM. Singles start at $10.

Card Size: 3 3/4" x 7 1/2"
Sponsor: Wendt
Set (16 panels): $200

☐ 1 Craig Ramsay
☐ 2 John Van Boxmeer
☐ 3 Don Edwards (G)
☐ 4 Gilbert Perreault
☐ 5 Alan Haworth
☐ 6 Jim Schoenfeld
☐ 7 Richie Dunn
☐ 8 Bob Sauvé (G)
☐ 9 Bill Hajt
☐ 10 Larry Playfair
☐ 11 Tony McKegney
☐ 12 Mike Ramsey
☐ 13 André Savard
☐ 14 Dale McCourt
☐ 15 Ric Seiling
☐ 16 Yvon Lambert

'82 - 83 BUFF.

WENDT'S

This series was issued on the backs of milk cartons. Scotty Bowman, Phil Housley and Gilbert Perreault are the most expensive singles at $25. Singles start at $10.

Card Size: 3 3/4" x 7 1/2"
Sponsor: Wendt
Set (17 panels): $200

☐ 2 Home Schedule
☐ 3 Craig Ramsay
☐ 4 John Van Boxmeer
☐ 5 Lindy Ruff
☐ 6 Bob Sauvé (G)
☐ 7 Gilbert Perreault
☐ 8 Ric Seiling
☐ 9 Jacques Cloutier (G)
☐ 10 Larry Playfair
☐ 11 Phil Housley
☐ 12 Mike Foligno
☐ 13 Tony McKegney
☐ 14 Dale McCourt
☐ 15 Mike Ramsey
☐ 16 Hannu Virta
☐ 17 Brent Peterson
☐ 18 Scotty Bowman

'84 - 85 BUFF.

BLUE SHIELD

There were only 500 sets issued. The most expensive singles are Dave Andreychuk and Tom Barrasso at $20-25. Singles start at $4.

Card Size: 2 1/2" x 3 3/4"
Sponsor: Blue Shield
Set (21 cards): $150

☐ Dave Andreychuk
☐ Tom Barrasso (G)
☐ Adam Creighton
☐ Paul Cyr
☐ Mal Davis
☐ Mike Foligno
☐ Bill Hajt
☐ Gilles Hamel
☐ Phil Housley
☐ Sean McKenna
☐ Mike Moler
☐ Gilbert Perreault
☐ Brent Peterson
☐ Larry Playfair
☐ Craig Ramsay
☐ Mike Ramsey
☐ Lindy Ruff
☐ Bob Sauvé (G)
☐ Ric Seiling
☐ John Tucker
☐ Hannu Virta

'85 - 86 BUFF.

BLUE SHIELD

This series was issued in two forms: standard-size cards and postcards. Pricing is the same for both sets. Daren Puppa is the most expensive card at $6. Singles start at $2. The Jim Schoenfeld card was removed from the set and sells at $20. Sets sold without the Schoenfeld are $40

Postcard Size: 4" x 6"
Card Size: 2 1/2" x 3 1/2"
Sponsor: Blue Shield
Set (28 cards): $50

☐ ☐ Mikael Andersson
☐ ☐ Dave Andreychuk
☐ ☐ Tom Barrasso (G)
☐ ☐ Adam Creighton
☐ ☐ Paul Cyr
☐ ☐ Mal Davis
☐ ☐ Steve Dykstra
☐ ☐ Dave Fenyves
☐ ☐ Mike Foligno
☐ ☐ Bill Hajt
☐ ☐ Bob Halkidis
☐ ☐ Gilles Hamel
☐ ☐ Phil Housley
☐ ☐ Pat Hughes
☐ ☐ Normand Lacombe
☐ ☐ Chris Langevin
☐ ☐ Sean McKenna
☐ ☐ Gaetano Orlando
☐ ☐ Gilbert Perreault
☐ ☐ Larry Playfair
☐ ☐ Daren Puppa (G)
☐ ☐ Craig Ramsay
☐ ☐ Mike Ramsey
☐ ☐ Lindy Ruff
☐ ☐ Ric Seiling
☐ ☐ John Tucker
☐ ☐ Hannu Virta
☐ ☐ Jim Schoenfeld, Coach

'86 - 87 BUFF.

BLUE SHIELD

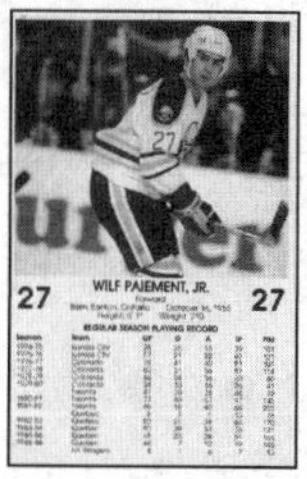

Gilbert Perreault and Dave Andreychuk are the the most expensive single at $7. Singles start at $1.

Postcard Size: 4" x 6"
Sponsor: Blue Shield
Set (28 cards): $35

☐ Shawn Anderson
☐ Dave Andreychuk
☐ Scott Arniel
☐ Tom Barrasso (G)
☐ Jacques Cloutier (G)
☐ Adam Creighton
☐ Paul Cyr
☐ Steve Dykstra
☐ Dave Fenyves
☐ Mike Foligno
☐ Clark Gillies
☐ Bill Hajt
☐ Bob Halkidis
☐ Jim Hofford
☐ Phil Housley
☐ Jim Korn
☐ Uwe Krupp
☐ Tom Kurvers
☐ Normand Lacombe
☐ Gaetano Orlando
☐ Wilf Paiement
☐ Gilbert Perreault
☐ Daren Puppa (G)
☐ Mike Ramsey
☐ Lindy Ruff
☐ Christian Ruuttu
☐ Doug Smith
☐ John Tucker

'87 - 88 BUFF.

BLUE SHIELD

Pierre Turgeon is the the most expensive single at $8. Singles start at $1.

Postcard Size: 4" x 5"
Sponsor: Blue Shield
Set (28 cards): $30

☐ Mikael Andersson
☐ Dave Andreychuk
☐ Scott Arniel
☐ Tom Barrasso (G)
☐ Jacques Cloutier (G)
☐ Adam Creighton
☐ Mike Donnelly
☐ Mike Foligno
☐ Clark Gillies
☐ Bob Halkidis
☐ Mike Hartman
☐ Ed Hospodar
☐ Phil Housley
☐ Calle Johansson
☐ Uwe Krupp
☐ Jan Ludvig
☐ Kevin Maguire
☐ Mark Napier
☐ Ken Priestlay
☐ Daren Puppa (G)
☐ Mike Ramsey
☐ Joe Reekie
☐ Lindy Ruff
☐ Christian Ruuttu
☐ Ray Sheppard
☐ Doug Smith
☐ John Tucker
☐ Pierre Turgeon

'87 - 88 BUFF.

WONDER BREAD / HOSTESS

This set was issued as a three panel album. The first panel is a Sabres team photo. The other two panels can be cut out into 15 cards each measuring 2 5/8" x 3 15/16". The most expensive single is Pierre Turgeon at $8 while other singles start at $1. An uncut, 3-panel set sells at $35.

Panel Size: 10 3/4" x 13 1/2"
Sponsors: Wonder Bread, Hostess
Set (30 cards): $25

☐ 1987-88 Team Photo
☐ Ted Sator
☐ Barry Smith
☐ Don Lever
☐ Jacques Cloutier #1 (G)
☐ Calle Johansson #3
☐ Steve Dykstra #4
☐ Mike Ramsey #5
☐ Phil Housley #6
☐ John Tucker #7
☐ Scott Arniel #9
☐ Mikael Andersson #14
☐ Doug Smith #15
☐ Mike Foligno #17
☐ Kevin Maguire #19
☐ Christian Ruuttu #21
☐ Lindy Ruff #22
☐ Ray Sheppard #23
☐ Ed Hospodar #24
☐ Dave Andreychuk #25
☐ Bob Logan #26
☐ Joe Reekie #27
☐ Tom Barrasso #30 (G)
☐ Daren Puppa #31 (G)
☐ Jan Ludvig #36
☐ Shawn Anderson #37
☐ Adam Creighton #38
☐ Uwe Krupp #40
☐ Mark Napier #65
☐ Pierre Turgeon #77
☐ Clark Gillies #90

'88 - 89 BUFF.

BLUE SHIELD

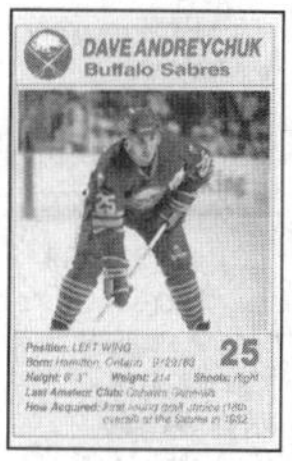

Pierre Turgeon is the the most expensive single at $8. Singles start at 75¢. Benoît Hogue, Jan Ludvig, Mark Napier and Joe Reekie were added late to the set and sell at $2-3. A 24-card set without these four players is $30.

Postcard Size: 4" x 6"
Sponsor: Blue Shield
Set (28 cards): $35

☐ Mikael Andersson #14
☐ Dave Andreychuk #25
☐ Scott Arniel #9
☐ Doug Bodger #8
☐ Jacques Cloutier #1 (G)
☐ Mike Donnelly #16
☐ Mike Foligno #17
☐ Bob Halkidis #18
☐ Mike Hartman #20
☐ Phil Housley #6
☐ Calle Johansson #3
☐ Uwe Krupp #4
☐ Kevin Maguire #19
☐ Jeff Parker #29
☐ Larry Playfair #27
☐ Daren Puppa #31 (G)
☐ Mike Ramsey #5
☐ Lindy Ruff #22
☐ Christian Ruuttu #21
☐ Ray Sheppard #23
☐ John Tucker #7
☐ Pierre Turgeon #77
☐ Rick Vaive #12
☐ Mascot Sabretooth
☐ Benoît Hogue #33
☐ Jan Ludvig #36
☐ Mark Napier #65
☐ Joe Reekie #55

'88 - 89 BUFF.

WONDER BREAD / HOSTESS

This set was issued as a three panel album. The first panel is a Sabres team photo. The other two panels can be cut out into 15 cards each measuring 2 3/4" x 3 3/8". The most expensive single is Pierre Turgeon at $8 while other singles start at 50¢. An uncut, 3-panel set sells at $30.

Panel Size: 10 3/4" x 13 1/2"
Sponsors: Wonder Bread, Hostess
Set (30 cards): $25

☐ 1988-89 Team Photo
☐ Ted Sator
☐ Barry Smith
☐ Don Lever
☐ Jacques Cloutier #1 (G)
☐ Calle Johansson #3
☐ Uwe Krupp #4
☐ Mike Ramsey #5
☐ Phil Housley #6
☐ John Tucker #7
☐ Doug Bodger #8
☐ Scott Arniel #9
☐ Mikael Andersson #14
☐ Mike Foligno #17
☐ Bob Halkidis #18
☐ Kevin Maguire #19
☐ Mike Hartman #20
☐ Christian Ruuttu #21
☐ Lindy Ruff #22
☐ Ray Sheppard #23
☐ Dave Andreychuk #25
☐ Larry Playfair #27
☐ Jeff Parker #29
☐ Daren Puppa #31 (G)
☐ Benoît Hogue #33
☐ Jan Ludvig #36
☐ Adam Creighton #38
☐ Brad Miller #44
☐ Joe Reekie #55
☐ Mark Napier #65
☐ Pierre Turgeon #77

'89 - 90 BUFF.

BLUE SHIELD

Alexander Mogilny is the most expensive single at $7. Singles start at 50¢.

Postcard Size: 4" x 6"
Sponsor: Blue Shield
Set (24 cards): $25

☐ Dave Andreychuk #25
☐ Scott Arniel #9
☐ Doug Bodger #8
☐ Mike Foligno #17
☐ Mike Hartman #20
☐ Benoît Hogue #33
☐ Phil Housley #6
☐ Dean Kennedy #26
☐ Uwe Krupp #4
☐ Grant Ledyard #3
☐ Kevin Maguire #19
☐ Clint Malarchuk #39 (G)
☐ Alexander Mogilny #89
☐ Jeff Parker #29
☐ Larry Playfair #27
☐ Ken Priestlay #56
☐ Daren Puppa #31 (G)
☐ Mike Ramsey #5
☐ Christian Ruuttu #21
☐ Ray Sheppard #23
☐ Dave Snuggerud #18
☐ Pierre Turgeon #77
☐ Rick Vaive #12
☐ Mascot Sabretooth

'89 -90 BUFF.

CAMPBELL'S

This set was issued as a three panel album. The first panel super-imposes three modern day colour photos over a black and white 1970 photo. The other two panels can be cut out into 16 and 12 cards each measuring 2 1/2" x 3 3/8". The most expensive single is Alexander Mogilny at $7 while other singles start at 75¢. An uncut, 3-panel set sells at $35.

Sponsor: Campbell's Chunky Soup
Set (28 cards): $25

☐ 20th Anniversary Photo
☐ Rick Dudley
☐ Don Lever
☐ John Tortorella
☐ Grant Ledyard #3
☐ Uwe Krupp #4
☐ Mike Ramsey #5
☐ Phil Housley #6
☐ Doug Bodger #8
☐ Scott Arniel #9
☐ Mike Foligno #17
☐ Dave Snuggerud #18
☐ Kevin Maguire #19
☐ Mike Hartman #20
☐ Christian Ruuttu #21
☐ Rick Vaive #22
☐ Ray Sheppard #23
☐ Dave Andreychuk #25
☐ Dean Kennedy #26
☐ Larry Playfair #28
☐ Jeff Parker #29
☐ Clint Malarchuk #30 (G)
☐ Daren Puppa #31 (G)
☐ Robert Ray #32
☐ Benoît Hogue #33
☐ Shawn Anderson #37
☐ Pierre Turgeon #77
☐ Alexander Mogilny #89
☐ 20th Anniversary Logo

'89 - 90 BUFF.

BLUE SHIELD

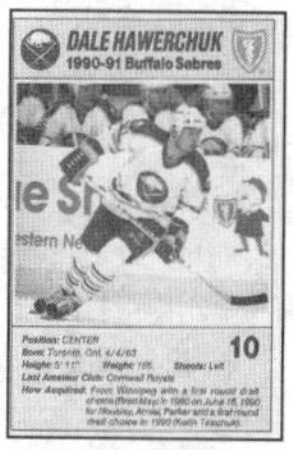

Alexander Mogilny is the most expensive single at $4. Singles start at 50¢.

Postcard Size: 4" x 6"
Sponsor: Blue Shield
Set (26 cards): $20

☐ Dave Andreychuk #25
☐ Donald Audette #28
☐ Doug Bodger #8
☐ Greg Brown #9
☐ Brian Curran #39
☐ Lou Franceschetti #15
☐ Mike Hartman #20
☐ Dale Hawerchuk #10
☐ Benoît Hogue #33
☐ Dean Kennedy #26
☐ Uwe Krupp #4
☐ Grant Ledyard #3
☐ Mikko Mäkelä #42
☐ Clint Malarchuk #30 (G)
☐ Alexander Mogilny #89
☐ Daren Puppa #31 (G)
☐ Mike Ramsey #5
☐ Rob Ray #32
☐ Christian Ruuttu #21
☐ Jiri Sejba #23
☐ Dave Snuggerud #18
☐ John Tucker #7
☐ Pierre Turgeon #77
☐ Rick Vaive #22
☐ Jay Wells #24
☐ Mascot Sabretooth

'90 - 91 BUFF.

CAMPBELL'S

This set was issued as a three panel album. The first panel is a Sabres team photo with a photo of Mikko Makelä on the reverse. The other two panels can be cut out into 16 cards each measuring 2 1/2" x 3 3/8". The most expensive single is Alexander Mogilny at $4 while singles start at 75¢. An uncut, 3-panel set sells at $25.
Panel Size: 10" x 13 1/2"
Sponsor: Campbell's
Set (32 cards): $20
☐ Team/Mikko Mäkelä
☐ Grant Ledyard #3
☐ Uwe Krupp #4
☐ Mike Ramsey #5
☐ John Tucker #7
☐ Doug Bodger #8
☐ Greg Brown #9
☐ Dale Hawerchuk #10
☐ Sabres Logo
☐ Darrin Shannon #16
☐ Mike Foligno #17
☐ Dave Snuggerud #18
☐ Bob Corkum #19
☐ Mike Hartman #20
☐ Christian Ruuttu #21
☐ Rick Vaive #22
☐ Jiri Sejba #23
☐ Jay Wells #24
☐ Dave Andreychuk #25
☐ Dean Kennedy #26
☐ Donald Audette #28
☐ Clint Malarchuk #30 (G)
☐ Daren Puppa #31 (G)
☐ Rob Ray #32
☐ Benoît Hogue #33
☐ Darcy Loewen #36
☐ Mikko Makelä #42
☐ Brad Miller #44
☐ Pierre Turgeon #77
☐ Alexander Mogilny #89
☐ Rick Dudley
☐ John Van Boxmeer
☐ John Tortorella

'91 - 92 BUFF.
BLUE SHIELD

Alexander Mogilny is the most expensive single at $4. Singles start at 50¢.
Postcard Size: 4" x 6"
Sponsor: Blue Shield
Set (26 cards): $20
☐ Dave Andreychuk #25
☐ Donald Audette #28
☐ Doug Bodger #8
☐ Mike Donnelly #34
☐ Tom Draper #35
☐ Kevin Haller #7
☐ Dale Hawerchuk #10
☐ Randy Hillier #23
☐ Pat LaFontaine #16
☐ Grant Ledyard #3
☐ Clint Malarchuk #30 (G)
☐ Brad May #27
☐ Brad Miller #44
☐ Alexander Mogilny #89
☐ Colin Patterson #17
☐ Daren Puppa #31 (G)
☐ Mike Ramsey #5
☐ Rob Ray #32
☐ Christian Ruuttu #21
☐ Dave Snuggerud #18
☐ Ken Sutton #41
☐ Tony Tanti #19
☐ Rick Vaive #22
☐ Jay Wells #24
☐ Randy Wood #15
☐ Mascot Sabretooth

'91 - 92 BUFF.
CAMPBELL'S / PEPSI

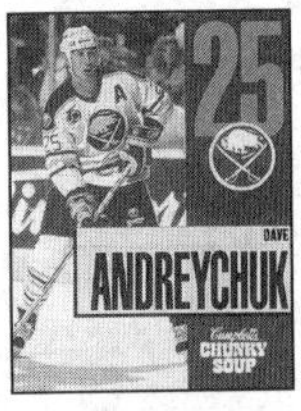

This set was issued as a three panel album. The first panel is a Sabres team photo. The other two panels can be cut out into 16 and 12 cards each measuring 2 1/2" x 3 3/8". Two versions exist: one with the Campbell's Chunky Soup logo and one with the Pepsi logo. Both versions have the same value. The most expensive single is Alexander Mogilny at $4 while singles start at 50¢. An uncut, 3-panel set sells at $25.
Sponsor: Campbell's Chunky Soup or Pepsi
Set (28 cards): $20
☐☐ Team Photo
☐☐ Grant Ledyard #3
☐☐ Mike Ramsey #5
☐☐ Kevin Haller #7
☐☐ Doug Bodger #8
☐☐ Dale Hawerchuk #10
☐☐ Randy Wood #15
☐☐ Pat LaFontaine #16
☐☐ Colin Patterson #17
☐☐ Dave Snuggerud #18
☐☐ Tony Tanti #19
☐☐ Christian Ruuttu #21
☐☐ Rick Vaive #22
☐☐ Randy Hillier #23
☐☐ Jay Wells #24
☐☐ Dave Andreychuk #25
☐☐ Brad May #27
☐☐ Donald Audette #28
☐☐ Clint Malarchuk #30 (G)
☐☐ Daren Puppa #31 (G)
☐☐ Rob Ray #32
☐☐ Mike Donnelly #34
☐☐ Tom Draper #35
☐☐ Ken Sutton #41
☐☐ Brad Miller #44
☐☐ Alexander Mogilny #89
☐☐ Mascot Sabretooth
☐☐ Sabres Logo
☐☐ NHL 75th Ann. Logo

'92 - 93 BUFF.
BLUE SHIELD

Dominik Hasek is the most expensive single at $8-12. Singles start at 50¢.
Postcard Size: 4" x 6"
Sponsor: Blue Shield
Set (26 cards): $30
☐ Dave Andreychuk #25
☐ Donald Audette #28
☐ Doug Bodger #8
☐ Bob Corkum
☐ Mike Donnelly #34
☐ Dave Hannan
☐ D. Hasek #39 (G)
☐ Dale Hawerchuk #10
☐ Yuri Khmylev
☐ Pat LaFontaine #16
☐ Grant Ledyard #3
☐ Brad May #27
☐ Alexander Mogilny #89
☐ Randy Moller
☐ John Muckler, Coach
☐ Colin Patterson #17
☐ Wayne Presley
☐ Daren Puppa #31 (G)
☐ Mike Ramsey #5
☐ Rob Ray #32
☐ Richard Smehlik
☐ Ken Sutton #41
☐ Petr Svoboda
☐ Bob Sweeney
☐ Randy Wood #15
☐ Mascot Sabretooth

'92 - 93 BUFF.
JUBILEE

The most expensive single is the Hasek/ Puppa card at $6. Singles start at 75¢.
Postcard Size: 4" x 7"
Sponsor: Jubilee
Set (16 cards): $22
☐ Dave Andreychuk
☐ Doug Bodger
☐ G. Donnelly/ R. Ray
☐ Hasek (G)/ Puppa (G)
☐ Dale Hawerchuk
☐ Khmylev/ Gordiouk
☐ Pat LaFontaine
☐ Brad May
☐ Alexander Mogilny
☐ R. Moller/ K. Sutton
☐ Wayne Presley
☐ Donald Audette
☐ Mike Ramsey
☐ R. Smehlik/ B. Corkum
☐ Petr Svoboda
☐ Bob Sweeney
☐ Randy Wood

'93 - 94 BUFF.
NOCO EXPRESS

Dominik Hasek is the most expensive single at $6-10. Singles start at 50¢.
Postcard Size: 2 1/2" x 3 1/2"
Sponsor: Noco Express Shop
Set (20 cards): $25
☐ Roger Crozier (G)
☐ Rick Dudley
☐ Mike Foligno
☐ Grant Fuhr (G)
☐ Danny Gare
☐ Dominik Hasek (G)
☐ Dale Hawerchuk
☐ Tim Horton
☐ Pat LaFontaine
☐ Don Luce
☐ Richard Martin
☐ Brad May
☐ Alexander Mogilny
☐ Gilbert Perreault
☐ Craig Ramsay
☐ Mike Ramsey
☐ René Robert
☐ Jim Schoenfeld
☐ Mascot Sabretooth
☐ S. Knox/ P. Imlach
☐ Northrup Knox

'02 - 03 BUFF.

We do not have a checklist for this series of postcards.

CALGARY FLAMES

'80 - 81 CALG.

Kent Nilsson and Reggie Lemelin are the most expensive single at $3-4. Singles start at $1.50.
Postcard Size: 3 3/4" x 5"
Sponsor: None
Set (24 cards): $40
☐ Dan Bouchard (G)
☐ Guy Chouinard
☐ Bill Clement
☐ Denis Cyr
☐ Randy Holt
☐ Ken Houston
☐ Kevin Lavallee
☐ Réjean Lemelin (G)
☐ Don Lever
☐ Bob MacMillan
☐ Brad Marsh
☐ Bob Murdoch
☐ Kent Nilsson
☐ Jim Peplinski
☐ Willi Plett
☐ Pekka Rautakalio
☐ Paul Reinhardt
☐ Pat Riggin (G)
☐ Phil Russell
☐ Brad Smith
☐ Jay Soleway
☐ Eric Vail
☐ Bert Wilson
☐ Team Photo

'81 - 82 CALG.

Lanny McDonald is the most expensive single at $4. Singles start at $1.
Postcard Size: 3 3/4" x 5"
Sponsor: None
Set (21 cards): $30
☐ Charlie Bourgeois
☐ Mel Bridgman
☐ Guy Chouinard
☐ Bill Clement
☐ Denis Cyr
☐ Jamie Hislop
☐ Ken Houston
☐ Steve Konroyd
☐ Dan Labraaten
☐ Kevin Lavallee
☐ Réjean Lemelin (G)
☐ Lanny McDonald
☐ Gary McAdam
☐ Bob Murdoch
☐ Kent Nilsson
☐ Jim Peplinski
☐ Willi Plett
☐ Pekka Rautakallio
☐ Paul Reinhart
☐ Pat Riggin (G)
☐ Phil Russell

'82 - 83 CALG.

Al MacInnis is the most expensive single at $8. Singles start at 75¢.
Postcard Size: 4" x 5 3/4"
Sponsor: None
Set (24 cards): $30
☐ Charlie Bourgeois
☐ Mel Bridgman
☐ Guy Chouinard
☐ Steve Christoff
☐ Richie Dunn
☐ Don Edwards (G)
☐ Kari Eloranta
☐ David Hindmarsh
☐ Jamie Hislop
☐ Tim Hunter
☐ Kari Jalonen
☐ Bob Johnson
☐ Steve Konroyd
☐ Kevin Lavallee
☐ Réjean Lemelin (G)
☐ Al MacInnis
☐ Lanny McDonald
☐ Carl Mokosak
☐ Kent Nilsson
☐ Jim Peplinski
☐ Paul Reinhardt
☐ Pat Ribble
☐ Doug Risebrough
☐ Phil Russell

'85 - 86 CALG.
RED ROOSTER

This set was issued as a six panel set. Panels can be cut out into five cards each measuring 2 3/4" x 3 5/8". Al MacInnis and Mike Vernon are the most expensive singles at $7. Singles start at 75¢. A cut-out 30-card set sells at $20.
Panel Size: 2 3/4" x 18 1/8"
Sponsors: Red Rooster, Old Dutch, Post
Set (6 panels): $30
☐ Bob Johnson
☐ Bob Murdoch
☐ Pierre Pagé
☐ Colin Patterson
☐ Dan Quinn
☐ Paul Baxter
☐ Perry Berezan
☐ Mark D'Amour (G)
☐ Richard Kromm
☐ Al MacInnis
☐ Ed Beers
☐ Charlie Bourgeois
☐ Réjean Lemelin (G)
☐ Joel Otto
☐ Carey Wilson
☐ Steve Bozek
☐ Tim Hunter
☐ Lanny McDonald
☐ Lanny McDonald
☐ Doug Risebrough
☐ Gino Cavallini
☐ Steve Konroyd
☐ Jim Peplinski
☐ Paul Reinhart
☐ Neil Sheehy
☐ Hakan Loob
☐ Jamie Macoun
☐ Doug Risebrough
☐ Gary Suter
☐ Mike Vernon (G)

'86 - 87 CALG.
RED ROOSTER

This set was issued as a six panel set. Panels can be cut out into five cards each measuring 2 3/4" x 3 5/8". The most expensive singles are Gary Roberts and Mike Vernon at $4-5. Singles start at 75¢. A cut-out 30-card set sells at $20.
Panel Size: 2 3/4" x 18 1/8"
Sponsors: Red Rooster, Old Dutch
Set (6 panels): $30
☐ Paul Baxter
☐ Perry Berezan
☐ Steve Bozek
☐ Brian Bradley
☐ Brian Engblom
☐ Nick Fotiu
☐ Tim Hunter
☐ Bob Johnson
☐ Réjean Lemelin (G)
☐ Hakan Loob
☐ Al MacInnis
☐ Jamie Macoun
☐ Lanny McDonald
☐ Lanny McDonald
☐ Joe Mullen
☐ Joe Mullen
☐ Bob Murdoch
☐ Joel Otto
☐ Pierre Pagé
☐ Colin Patterson
☐ Jim Peplinski
☐ Paul Reinhart
☐ Paul Reinhart
☐ Doug Risebrough
☐ Gary Roberts
☐ Neil Sheehy
☐ Gary Suter
☐ John Tonelli
☐ Mike Vernon (G)
☐ Carey Wilson

'87 - 88 CALG.
RED ROOSTER

This set was issued as a six panel set. Panels can be cut out into five cards each measuring 2 3/4" x 3 5/8". Brett Hull is the most expensive single at $20. Singles start at 75¢. A cut-out 30-card set sells at $40.
Panel Size: 2 3/4" x 18 1/8"
Sponsor: Red Rooster

Set (6 panels): $60
☐ Perry Berezan
☐ Steve Bozek
☐ Mike Bullard
☐ Shane Churla
☐ Doug Dadswell
☐ Brian Glynn
☐ Brett Hull
☐ Tim Hunter
☐ Hakan Loob
☐ Hakan Loob
☐ Al MacInnis
☐ Brad McCrimmon
☐ Lanny McDonald
☐ Joe Mullen
☐ Dana Murzyn
☐ Ric Nattress
☐ Joe Nieuwendyk
☐ Joe Nieuwendyk
☐ Joel Otto
☐ Colin Patterson
☐ Jim Peplinski
☐ Paul Reinhart
☐ Gary Roberts
☐ Gary Suter
☐ John Tonelli
☐ Mike Vernon (G)
☐ Terry Crisp, Coach
☐ Pierre Pagé, Coach
☐ D. Risebrough, Coach

'90 - 91 CALG.
IGA

Theoren Fleury and Doug Gilmour are the most expensive singles at $4-5. Singles start at 75¢. Paul Baxter, Guy Charron, Doug Risebrough and the checklist card are supposedly short printed and sell at $2-3. A 26-card set sells for $25.
Card Size: 2 1/2" x 3 1/2"
Sponsors: IGA, McGavin's
Set (30 cards): $35
☐ Theoren Fleury
☐ Doug Gilmour
☐ Jiri Hrdina
☐ Mark Hunter
☐ Tim Hunter
☐ Roger Johansson
☐ Jamie Macoun
☐ Al MacInnis
☐ Brian MacLellan
☐ Sergei Makarov
☐ Stéphane Matteau
☐ Dana Murzyn
☐ Frank Musil
☐ Ric Nattress
☐ Joe Nieuwendyk
☐ Joel Otto
☐ Colin Patterson
☐ Sergei Priakin
☐ Paul Ranheim
☐ Robert Reichel
☐ Gary Roberts
☐ Gary Suter
☐ Tim Sweeney
☐ Mike Vernon (G)
☐ Rick Wamsley (G)
☐ MacInnis/ Makarov
☐ Paul Baxter
☐ Guy Charron
☐ Doug Risebrough
☐ Checklist

'91 - 92 CALG.
RED ROOSTER

Theoren Fleury and Doug Gilmour are the most expensive singles at $3-4. Singles start at 50¢. Paul Baxter, Guy Charron, Doug Risebrough and the checklist card are supposedly short printed and sell at $2-3. A 26-card set sells for $20.

Card Size: 2 1/2" x 3 1/2"
Sponsor: IGA
Set (30 cards): $30
☐ Theoren Fleury
☐ Tomas Forslund
☐ Doug Gilmour
☐ Marc Habscheid
☐ Tim Hunter
☐ Jim Kyte
☐ Al MacInnis
☐ Jamie Macoun
☐ Sergei Makarov
☐ Stéphane Matteau
☐ Frank Musil
☐ Ric Nattress
☐ Joe Nieuwendyk
☐ Mark Osiecki
☐ Joel Otto
☐ Paul Ranheim
☐ Robert Reichel
☐ Gary Roberts
☐ Neil Sheehy
☐ Martin Simard
☐ Ronnie Stern
☐ Gary Suter
☐ Tim Sweeney
☐ Mike Vernon (G)
☐ Rick Wamsley (G)
☐ Carey Wilson
☐ Paul Baxter
☐ Guy Charron
☐ Doug Risebrough
☐ Checklist

'92 - 93 CALG.
IGA

Theoren Fleury is the most expensive single at $3. Singles start at 50¢.
Card Size: 2 1/2" x 3 1/2"
Sponsor: IGA
Set (30 cards): $20
☐ 001 Checklist
☐ 002 Craig Berube
☐ 003 Gary Leeman
☐ 004 Joel Otto
☐ 005 Robert Reichel
☐ 006 Gary Roberts
☐ 007 Greg Smyth
☐ 008 Gary Suter
☐ 009 Jeff Reese (G)
☐ 010 Mike Vernon (G)
☐ 011 Carey Wilson
☐ 012 Trent Yawney
☐ 013 Michel Petit
☐ 014 Paul Ranheim
☐ 015 Sergei Makarov
☐ 016 Frank Musil
☐ 017 Joe Nieuwendyk
☐ 018 Alex. Godynyuk
☐ 019 Roger Johansson
☐ 020 Theoren Fleury
☐ 021 Chris Lindberg
☐ 022 Al MacInnis
☐ 023 Kevin Dahl
☐ 024 Chris Dahlquist
☐ 025 Ronnie Stern
☐ 026 Dave King
☐ 027 Guy Charron
☐ 028 Slavomir Lener
☐ 029 Jamie Hislop
☐ 030 Franchise History

'97 - 98 CALG.
FAMOUS FLAMES

These photos were issued with each game program. Other singles exist.
Photo Size: 6" x 9"
☐ 28 Brett Hull

'99 - 00 CALG.

Other singles exist.
☐ Rocky Thompson

CALIFORNIA GOLDEN SEALS

No sets known.

CAROLINA HURRICANES

'97 - 98 CARO.
SPRINT

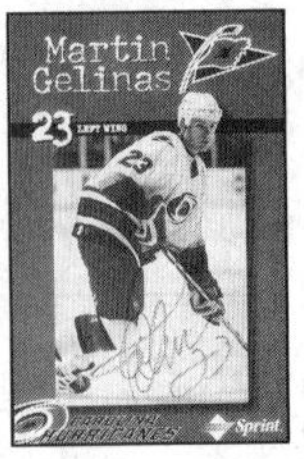

Keith Primeau is the most expensive single at $4. Singles start at $1.
Card Size: 4" x 6"
Sponsor: Sprint
Set (30 cards): $25
☐ Jeff Brown
☐ Sean Burke (G)
☐ Adam Burt
☐ Steve Chiasson
☐ Enrico Ciccone
☐ Kevin Dineen
☐ Nelson Emerson
☐ Martin Gélinas
☐ Stu Grimson
☐ Steven Halko
☐ Kevin Haller
☐ Sean Hill
☐ Sami Kapanen
☐ Trevor Kidd (G)
☐ Robert Kron
☐ Randy Ladouceur
☐ Steve Leach
☐ Curtis Leschyshyn
☐ Kent Manderville
☐ Jeff O'Neill
☐ Nolan Pratt
☐ Keith Primeau
☐ Paul Ranheim
☐ Steven Rice
☐ Gary Roberts
☐ Geoff Sanderson
☐ Glen Wesley
☐ Paul Maurice, Coach
☐ Tom Webster
☐ Mascot Stormy

'98 - 99 CARO.
HIGHWOOD PROPERTIES

Keith Primeau is the most expensive single at $4. Singles start at $1.
Card Size: 4" x 6"
Sponsor: Highwood Properties
Set (25 cards): $25
☐ Bates Battaglia
☐ Adam Burt
☐ Steve Chiasson
☐ Kevin Dineen
☐ Ron Francis
☐ Martin Gélinas
☐ Steven Halko
☐ Sean Hill
☐ Arturs Irbe (G)
☐ Sami Kapanen
☐ Dave Karpa
☐ Trevor Kidd (G)
☐ Curtis Leschyshyn

☐ Marek Malik
☐ Kent Manderville
☐ Jeff O'Neill
☐ Nolan Pratt
☐ Keith Primeau
☐ Paul Ranheim
☐ Byron Ritchie
☐ Gary Roberts
☐ Mike Rucinski
☐ Ray Sheppard
☐ Glen Wesley
☐ Mascot Stormy

'99 - 00 CARO.

We do not have a checklist for this series of postcards.

'00 - 01 CARO.

We do not have a checklist for this series of postcards.

'01 - 02 CARO.

We do not have a checklist for this series of postcards.

'02 - 03 CARO.

PEPSI

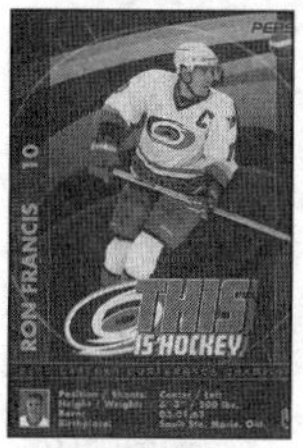

We do not have a checklist for this series of postcards.

CHICAGO BLACKHAWKS

'68 - 68 CHIC.

Stan Mikita is the most expensive single at $20. Singles start at $6.
Card Size: 4" x 6"
Sponsor: None
☐ Dennis Hull
☐ Doug Jarrett
☐ Chico Maki
☐ Gilles Marotte
☐ Stan Mikita
☐ Jim Pappin
☐ Pat Stapleton
☐ Ken Wharram

'70 - 71 CHIC.

The Hull/ Mikita/ Wirtz card is the most expensive single at $25. Singles start at $5.
Card Size: 4" x 6"
Sponsor: None
Set (14 cards): $45
☐ Lou Angotti
☐ Bryan Campbell
☐ Hull/ B. Wirtz/ Mikta
☐ Dennis Hull
☐ T. Ivan/ B. Reay
☐ Doug Jarrett
☐ Keith Magnuson
☐ Hubert Martin
☐ Stan Mikita
☐ Eric Nesterenko
☐ Jim Pappin
☐ Allan Pinder
☐ Paul Schmyr
☐ Bill White

'79 - 80 CHIC.

We have little information on this set. Singles start at $1. in NM. Other singles may exist. There are likely earlier team issued sets as well.
Card Size: 4" x 6"
Sponsor: None
☐ Keith Brown
☐ J.P. Bordeleau
☐ Ted Bulley
☐ Alain Daigle
☐ Tony Esposito (G)
☐ Greg Fox
☐ Tim Higgins
☐ Reg Kerr
☐ Cliff Koroll
☐ Tom Lysiak
☐ Keith Magnuson
☐ John Marks
☐ Stan Mikita
☐ Grant Mulvey
☐ Bob Murray
☐ Mike O'Connell
☐ Rich Preston
☐ Bob Pulford
☐ Terry Ruskowski
☐ Mark Veisor (G)
☐ Doug Wilson

'80 - 81 CHIC.

These cards have a brown back-ground. Denis Savard is the most expensive single at $6 in NM. Singles start at $2.
Card Size: 4" x 6"
Sponsor: None
Set (25 cards): $40
☐ Murray Bannerman (G)
☐ J.P. Bordeleau
☐ Keith Brown
☐ Ted Bulley
☐ Tony Esposito (G)
☐ Greg Fox
☐ Tim Higgins
☐ Dave Hutchinson
☐ Reg Kerr
☐ Cliff Koroll
☐ Doug Lecuyer
☐ Tom Lysiak
☐ Keith Magnuson
☐ John Marks
☐ Grant Mulvey
☐ Bob Murray
☐ Mike O'Connell
☐ Rick Paterson
☐ Rich Preston
☐ Terry Ruskowski
☐ Denis Savard
☐ Rod Sedlbauer
☐ Darryl Sutter
☐ Tim Trimper
☐ Doug Wilson

'80 - 81 CHIC.

WHITE BORDER

These cards have a white border. Denis Savard is the most expensive single at $6 in NM. Singles start at $1.50.
Photo Size: 5 1/2" x 8 1/2"
Sponsor: None
Set (14 cards): $25
☐ Murray Bannerman (G)
☐ J.P. Bordeleau
☐ Keith Brown
☐ Tony Esposito (G)
☐ Greg Fox
☐ Tim Higgins
☐ Doug Lecuyer
☐ John Marks
☐ Grant Mulvey
☐ Rich Preston
☐ Terry Ruskowski
☐ Denis Savard
☐ Darryl Sutter
☐ Tim Trimper

'81 - 82 CHIC.

Denis Savard is the most expensive single at $6. Singles start at $1.
Card Size: 3 1/2" x 5 1/2"
Sponsor: None
Set (26 cards): $35
☐ Murray Bannerman (G)
☐ Keith Brown
☐ Ted Bulley
☐ Doug Crossman
☐ Jerome Dupont
☐ Tony Esposito (G)
☐ Greg Fox
☐ Bill Gardner
☐ Tim Higgins
☐ Dave Hutchinson
☐ Reg Kerr
☐ Tom Lysiak
☐ John Marks
☐ Peter Marsh
☐ Grant Mulvey
☐ Bob Murray
☐ Rick Paterson
☐ Rich Preston
☐ Bob Pulford
☐ Terry Ruskowski
☐ Denis Savard
☐ Al Secord
☐ Glen Sharpley
☐ Darryl Sutter
☐ Tony Tanti
☐ Doug Wilson

'82 - 83 CHIC.

Steve Larmer and Denis Savard are the most expensive singles at $4-6 each. Singles start at $1.
Card Size: 3 1/2" x 5 1/2"
Sponsor: None
Set (23 cards): $30
☐ Murray Bannerman (G)
☐ Keith Brown
☐ Doug Crossman
☐ Dennis Cyr
☐ Tony Esposito (G)
☐ Dave Feamster
☐ Bill Gardner
☐ Greg Fox
☐ Tim Higgins
☐ Steve Larmer
☐ Steve Ludzik
☐ Tom Lysiak
☐ Peter Marsh
☐ Grant Mulvey
☐ Bob Murray
☐ Troy Murray
☐ Rick Paterson
☐ Rich Preston
☐ Denis Savard
☐ Al Secord
☐ Darryl Sutter
☐ Orval Tessier
☐ Doug Wilson

'83 - 84 CHIC.

Steve Larmer and Denis Savard are the most expensive singles at $4-6 each. Singles start at $1. Other singles may exist.
Card Size: 3 1/2" x 5 1/2"
Sponsor: None
☐ Murray Bannerman (G)
☐ Keith Brown
☐ Doug Crossman
☐ Dennis Cyr
☐ Tony Esposito (G)
☐ Dave Feamster
☐ Steve Larmer
☐ Steve Ludzik
☐ Bob Murray
☐ Troy Murray
☐ Rich Preston
☐ Denis Savard
☐ Al Secord
☐ Orval Tessier

'86 - 87 CHIC.

COKE

Steve Larmer and Denis Savard are the most expensive singles at $4-6 each. Singles start $1.
Card Size: 3 1/2" x 6 1/2"
Sponsor: Coke
Set (24 cards): $25
☐ Murray Bannerman (G)
☐ Marc Bergevin
☐ Keith Brown
☐ Dave Donnelly
☐ Curt Fraser
☐ Steve Larmer
☐ Steve Ludzik
☐ Dave Manson
☐ Bob Murray
☐ Troy Murray
☐ Gary Nylund
☐ Jack O'Callahan
☐ Ed Olczyk
☐ Rick Paterson
☐ Wayne Presley
☐ Rich Preston
☐ Bob Sauvé (G)
☐ Denis Savard
☐ Al Secord
☐ Mike Stapleton
☐ Darryl Sutter
☐ Bill Watson
☐ Behn Wilson
☐ Doug Wilson

'86 - 87 CHIC.

COKE

Steve Larmer and Denis Savard are the most expensive singles at $3-5. Singles start at $1.
Card Size: 3 1/2" x 6 1/2"
Sponsor: Coke
Set (30 cards): $30
☐ Murray Bannerman (G)
☐ Marc Bergevin
☐ Keith Brown
☐ Glen Cochrane
☐ Curt Fraser
☐ Steve Larmer
☐ Mark LaVarre
☐ Steve Ludzik
☐ Dave Manson
☐ Bob Mason (G)
☐ Bob McGill
☐ Bob Murdoch
☐ Bob Murray
☐ Troy Murray
☐ Brian Noonan
☐ Gary Nylund
☐ Darren Pang (G)
☐ Wayne Presley
☐ Everett Sanipass
☐ Denis Savard
☐ Mike Stapleton
☐ Darryl Sutter
☐ Duane Sutter
☐ Steve Thomas
☐ Wayne Thomas
☐ Rick Vaive
☐ Dan Vincelette
☐ Bill Watson
☐ Behn Wilson
☐ Doug Wilson

'88 - 89 CHIC.

COKE

Ed Belfour is the most expensive single at $10-15. Singles start at $1.
Card Size: 3 1/2" x 6 1/2"
Sponsor: Coke
Set (25 cards): $40
☐ Ed Belfour (G)
☐ Keith Brown
☐ Bruce Cassidy
☐ Mike Eagles
☐ Dirk Graham
☐ Mike Hudson
☐ Steve Larmer
☐ Dave Manson
☐ Jacques Martin
☐ Bob McGill
☐ E.J. Maguire
☐ Troy Murray
☐ Brian Noonan
☐ Darren Pang (G)
☐ Wayne Presley
☐ Everett Sanipass
☐ Denis Savard
☐ Duane Sutter
☐ Steve Thomas
☐ Rick Vaive
☐ Dan Vincelette
☐ Jimmy Waite (G)
☐ Doug Wilson
☐ Trent Yawney
☐ Mike Keenan, Coach

'89 - 90 CHIC.

COKE

These cards were originally issued in panels. Jeremy Roenick is the most expensive single at $6. Singles start at $1.
Card Size: 4" x 6"
Sponsor: Coke
Set (27 cards): $30
☐ Bob Bassen
☐ Keith Brown
☐ Alain Chevrier (G)
☐ Jacques Cloutier (G)
☐ Adam Creighton
☐ Greg Gilbert
☐ Dirk Graham
☐ Mike Hudson
☐ Steve Konroyd
☐ Steve Larmer
☐ E.J. Maguire
☐ Dave Manson
☐ Jacques Martin
☐ Bob McGill
☐ Bob Murray
☐ Troy Murray
☐ Wayne Presley
☐ Jeremy Roenick
☐ Everett Sanipass
☐ Denis Savard
☐ Al Secord
☐ Duane Sutter
☐ Steve Thomas
☐ Wayne Van Dorp
☐ Doug Wilson
☐ Trent Yawney
☐ Mike Keenan, Coach

'90 - 91 CHIC.

COKE

This set was originally issued in panels. Ed Belfour is the most expensive single at $5. Singles start at 75¢.
Card Size: 3 1/2" x 6"
Sponsor: Coke
Set (28 cards): $25
☐ Ed Belfour (G)
☐ Keith Brown
☐ Chris Chelios
☐ Jacques Cloutier (G)
☐ Adam Creighton
☐ Greg Gilbert
☐ Michel Goulet
☐ Dirk Graham
☐ Stu Grimson
☐ Mike Hudson
☐ Steve Konroyd
☐ Steve Larmer
☐ Jocelyn Lemieux
☐ E.J. Maguire
☐ Dave Manson
☐ Bob McGill
☐ Mike McNeill
☐ Greg Millen (G)
☐ Troy Murray
☐ Mike Peluso
☐ Wayne Presley
☐ Jeremy Roenick
☐ Darryl Sutter
☐ Steve Thomas
☐ Vladislav Tretiak
☐ Doug Wilson
☐ Trent Yawney
☐ Mike Keenan, Coach

'91 - 92 CHIC.

COKE

This set was originally issued in panels. Ed Belfour is the most expensive single at $4. Singles start at 75¢.
Card Size: 3 1/2" x 6"
Sponsor: Coke
Set (28 cards): $25
☐ Ed Belfour (G)
☐ Keith Brown
☐ Rod Buskas
☐ Chris Chelios
☐ Karl Dykhuis
☐ Greg Gilbert
☐ Michel Goulet
☐ Dirk Graham
☐ Stu Grimson
☐ Mike Hudson
☐ Steve Konroyd
☐ Frank Kucera
☐ Steve Larmer
☐ Brad Lauer
☐ Jocelyn Lemieux
☐ Bryan Marchment
☐ Dave McDowall
☐ Brian Noonan
☐ Mike Peluso
☐ Rich Preston
☐ Jeremy Roenick
☐ Steve Smith
☐ Mike Stapleton
☐ Brent Sutter
☐ Darryl Sutter
☐ John Tonelli
☐ Jimmy Waite (G)
☐ Mike Keenan, Coach

'93 - 94 CHIC.

COKE

This set was originally issued in panels. Ed Belfour is the most expensive single at $4. Singles start at 75¢.
Card Size: 3 1/2" x 6"
Sponsor: Coke
Set (30 cards): $25
☐ Paul Baxter
☐ Ed Belfour (G)
☐ Keith Carney
☐ Chris Chelios
☐ Dave Christian
☐ Michel Goulet
☐ Dirk Graham
☐ Jeff Hackett (G)
☐ Darin Kimble
☐ Frank Kucera
☐ Jocelyn Lemieux
☐ Stéphane Matteau
☐ Joe Murphy
☐ Troy Murray
☐ Phil Myre
☐ Brian Noonan
☐ Patrick Poulin
☐ Rich Preston
☐ Bob Pulford
☐ Jeremy Roenick
☐ Cam Russell
☐ Christian Ruuttu
☐ Jeff Shantz
☐ Steve Smith
☐ Darryl Sutter
☐ Rich Sutter
☐ Brent Sutter
☐ Kevin Todd
☐ Eric Weinrich
☐ Neil Wilkinson

'98 - 99 CHIC.

PIZZA HUT

Card Size: 3 1/2" x 6 1/2"
Sponsor: Pizza Hut
Set (5 cards): $15
☐ Tony Esposito (G)
☐ Glenn Hall
☐ Bobby Hull
☐ Steve Larmer
☐ Denis Savard

COLORADO AVALANCHE

'96 - 97 COLO.

We have little information on this set. Other singles exist.
Card Size: 3 1/2" x 5 1/2"
Sponsor: None
☐ Peter Forsberg
☐ Patrick Roy (G)

'98 - 99 COLO.

HOWLER SAYS

Other singles exist.
Sponsor: Howler Says
☐ Milan Hejduk
☐ Shjon Podein
☐ Warren Rychel

'98 - 99 COLO.

KID SMART

Other singles exist.
Sponsor: Kid Smart
☐ Chris Drury

'99 - 00 COLO.

KID SMART

Other singles exist.
Sponsor: Kid Smart
☐ Peter Forsberg
☐ Milan Hejduk
☐ Jeff Odgers
☐ Sandis Ozolinsh
☐ Patrick Roy
☐ Joe Sakic
☐ Stéphane Yelle

'00 - 01 COLO.

We do not have a checklist for this series of postcards.

'01 - 02 COLO.

We do not have a checklist for this series of postcards.

'02 - 03 COLO.

We do not have a checklist for this series of postcards.

COLORADO ROCKIES

'76 - 77 COLO.

HOCKEY TALK

These cards were originally issued as two-card panels. Colin Campbell is the most expensive single at $4-5 in NM. Singles start at $2.
Card Size: 2 9/16" x 2 1/8"
Sponsor: None
Set (20 cards): $75
☐ Ron Andruff
☐ Chuck Arnason
☐ Henry Boucha
☐ Colin Campbell
☐ Gary Croteau
☐ Guy Delparte
☐ Steve Durbano
☐ Tom Edur
☐ Doug Favell (G)
☐ Dave Hudson
☐ Bryan Lefley
☐ Roger Lemelin
☐ Simon Nolet
☐ Wilf Paiement
☐ Michel Plasse (G)
☐ Tracy Pratt
☐ Nelson Pyatt
☐ Phil Roberto
☐ Sean Shanahan
☐ Larry Skinner

'79 - 80 COLO.

Lanny McDonald is the most expensive single at $7 in NM. Singles start at $2.
Card Size: 4" x 6"
Sponsor: None
Set (23 cards): $50
☐ Hardy Astrom (G)
☐ Doug Berry
☐ Nick Beverley
☐ Mike Christie
☐ Gary Croteau
☐ Lucien DeBlois
☐ Ron Delorme
☐ Mike Gillis
☐ Trevor Johansen
☐ Mike Kitchen
☐ Lanny McDonald
☐ Mike McEwen
☐ Bill McKenzie (G)
☐ Kevin Morrison
☐ Bill Oleschuk (G)
☐ Randy Pierce
☐ Michel Plasse (G)
☐ Joel Quenneville
☐ Rob Ramage
☐ René Robert
☐ Don Saleski
☐ Barry Smith
☐ Jack Valiquette

'81 - 82 COLO.

The most expensive singles are Rob Ramage and Glenn Resch at $3. Singles start $1.50.
Postcard Size: 3 1/2" x 5 1/2"
Sponsor: None
Set (30 cards): $35
☐ Brent Ashton
☐ Aaron Broten
☐ Dave Cameron
☐ Joe Cirella
☐ Dwight Foster
☐ Paul Gagné
☐ Marshall Johnston
☐ Veli-Pekka Ketola
☐ Mike Kitchen
☐ Rick Laferriere (G)
☐ Don Lever
☐ Tapio Levo
☐ Bob Lorimer
☐ Bill MacMillan
☐ Bob MacMillan
☐ Merlin Malinowski
☐ Bert Marshall
☐ Kevin Maxwell
☐ Joe Micheletti
☐ Bobby Miller
☐ Phil Myre (G)
☐ Graeme Nicolson
☐ Jukka Porvari
☐ Joel Quenneville
☐ Rob Ramage
☐ Glenn Resch (G)
☐ Steve Tambellini
☐ Yvon Vautour
☐ John Wensink
☐ Team Logo

COLUMBUS BLUE JACKETS

'01 - 02 COLU.
DONATO PIZZA

These perforated cards were issued in four six-card panels through Donato Pizza in Ohio. The most expensive singles are Marc Denis and Rostislav Klesla.

Set (24 cards):

☐ Serge Aubin
☐ Radim Bicanek
☐ Marc Denis
☐ Kevin Dineen
☐ Jean-Luc Grand-Pierre
☐ Jamie Heward
☐ Rostislav Klesla
☐ Espen Knutsen
☐ Robert Kron
☐ Grant Marshall
☐ Chris Neilsen
☐ Lyle Odelein
☐ Jamie Pushor
☐ Deron Quint
☐ Geoff Sanderson
☐ Geoff Sanderson
☐ Mike Sillinger
☐ Blake Sloan
☐ Mattias Timander
☐ Ron Tugnutt
☐ Ron Tugnutt
☐ David Vyborny
☐ Ray Whitney
☐ Tyler Wright

DALLAS STARS

'93 - 94 DALL.
SOUTHWEST AIRLINES

We have very little information on this set. Photos are in black and white. Other singles exist.
Card Size: 3" x 5"
Sponsor: Southwest Airlines

☐ Russ Courtnall

'94 - 95 DALL.
CAPS

Mike Modano is the most expensive single at $2 in NM. Singles start at 50¢.
Diametre: 1 3/4"
Set (25 caps): $12

☐ Dave Barr
☐ Brad Berry
☐ Neal Broten
☐ Paul Broten
☐ Paul Cavallini
☐ Shane Churla
☐ Russ Courtnall
☐ Mike Craig
☐ Ulf Dahlen
☐ Dean Evason
☐ Dave Gagner
☐ Bob Gainey
☐ Brent Gilchrist
☐ Derian Hatcher
☐ Doug Jarvis
☐ Jim Johnson
☐ Trent Klatt
☐ Grant Ledyard
☐ Craig Ludwig
☐ Mike McPhee
☐ Mike Modano
☐ Andy Moog (G)
☐ Mark Tinordi
☐ Darcy Wakaluk (G)
☐ Rick Wilson

'94 - 95 DALL.
SOUTHWEST AIRLINES

Mike Modano is the most expensive single at $4. Singles start at 75¢.
Sponsor: Southwest Airlines
Set (23 cards): $20

☐ Paul Broten
☐ Paul Cavallini
☐ Shane Churla
☐ Gord Donnelly
☐ Mike Donnelly
☐ Dean Evason
☐ Dave Gagner
☐ Brent Gilchrist
☐ Todd Harvey
☐ Derian Hatcher
☐ Kevin Hatcher
☐ Mike Kennedy
☐ Trent Klatt
☐ Mike Lalor
☐ Grant Ledyard
☐ Craig Ludwig
☐ Richard Matvichuk
☐ Corey Millen
☐ Mike Modano
☐ Andy Moog (G)
☐ Darcy Wakaluk (G)
☐ Peter Zezel
☐ Doug Zmolek

'96 - 97 DALL.
SOUTHWEST AIRLINES

Mike Modano is the most expensive single at $3. Singles start at 75¢.
Sponsor: Southwest Airlines
Set (27 cards): $20

☐ Greg Adams
☐ Bob Bassen
☐ Neal Broten
☐ Guy Carbonneau
☐ Brent Gilchrist
☐ Todd Harvey
☐ Derian Hatcher
☐ Benoît Hogue
☐ Bill Huard
☐ Arturs Irbe (G)
☐ Mike Kennedy
☐ Mike Lalor
☐ Jamie Langenbrunner
☐ Grant Ledyard
☐ Jere Lehtinen
☐ Craig Ludwig
☐ Grant Marshall
☐ Richard Matvichuk
☐ Mike Modano
☐ Joe Nieuwendyk
☐ Andy Moog (G)
☐ Dave Reid
☐ Darryl Sydor
☐ Pat Verbeek
☐ Sergei Zubov
☐ Bob Gainey, G.M.
☐ Ken Hitchcock, Coach

'97 - 98 DALL.

These cards were issued as a perforated sheet.
Card Size: 2 1/2" x 3 1/2"
Sponsor: Score
Set (9 cards): $8

☐ 20 Ed Belfour (G)
☐ 92 Mike Modano
☐ 124 Pat Verbeek
☐ 135 Joe Nieuwendyk
☐ 188 Jere Lehtinen
☐ 198 Derian Hatcher
☐ 211 J. Langenbrunner
☐ 217 Benoît Hogue
☐ 238 Darryl Sydor

'99 - 00 DALL.

We do not have a checklist for this series of postcards.

'00 - 01 DALL.
SOUTHWEST AIRLINES

Singles start at 75¢.
Card Size: 4" x 6"

☐ Ed Belfour
☐ Tyler Bouck
☐ Gerlad Diduck
☐ Ted Donato
☐ Derian Hatcher
☐ Sami Helenius
☐ Ken Hitchcock
☐ Brett Hull
☐ Richard Jackman
☐ Mike Keane
☐ Jamie Langenbrunner
☐ Jere Lehtinen
☐ Brad Lukowich
☐ Roman Lyashenko
☐ Grant Marshall
☐ Richard Matvichuk
☐ Mike Modano
☐ Brenden Morrow
☐ Kirk Muller
☐ Joe Nieuwendyk
☐ Jon Sim
☐ Blake Sloan
☐ Darryl Sydor
☐ Marty Turco
☐ Shaun Van Allen
☐ Sergei Zubov

'01 - 02 DALL.
SOUTHWEST AIRLINES

Singles start at 75¢.
Card Size: 4" x 6"

☐ Ed Belfour
☐ Benoît Brunet
☐ Rob DiMaio
☐ John Erskine
☐ Derian Hatcher
☐ Sami Helenius
☐ Ken Hitchcock
☐ Benoît Hogue
☐ Valeri Kamensky
☐ Niko Kapanen
☐ Jamie Langenbrunner
☐ Jere Lehtinen
☐ Brad Lukowich
☐ Roman Lyashenko
☐ Dave Manson
☐ Richard Matvichuk
☐ Mike Modano
☐ Brenden Morrow
☐ Kirk Muller
☐ Joe Nieuwendyk
☐ Martin Rucinsky
☐ Darryl Sydor
☐ Marty Turco
☐ Pierre Turgeon
☐ Pat Verbeek
☐ Sergei Zubov

'02 - 03 DALL.

Other singles exist. Singles start at $1.
Set (21 cards):
Card Size: 4" x 8"

☐ Jason Arnott
☐ Philippe Boucher
☐ Ulf Dahlén
☐ Bill Guerin
☐ Derian Hatcher
☐ Jere Lehtinen
☐ Richard Matvichuk
☐ Mike Modano
☐ Kirk Muller
☐ Stéphane Robidas
☐ Darryl Sydor
☐ Ron Tugnutt
☐ Marty Turco
☐ Pierre Turgeon
☐ Scott A. Young

DETROIT RED WINGS

'70 - 71 DETR.
MARATHON OIL

We have little information on this set. The most expensive singles are Gordie Howe at $60 in NM and Frank Mahovlich and Alex Delvecchio at $12-15. Singles start at $5. Other singles may exist.
Photo Size: 7 1/2" x 14"
Sponsor: Marathon Oil

☐ Gary Bergman
☐ Wayne Connelly
☐ Alex Delvecchio
☐ Roy Edwards (G)
☐ Gordie Howe
☐ Bruce MacGregor
☐ Frank Mahovlich
☐ Dale Rolfe
☐ Jim Rutherford (G)
☐ Garry Unger
☐ Tom Webster

'76 DETR.

We have little information on this black and white photo set. Singles start at $3. Other singles may exist.
Card Size: 2 1/2" x 3 1/2"
Sponsor: None

☐ Gerry Abel
☐ Sid Abel
☐ Doug Barkley
☐ Joe Carveth
☐ Alex Delvecchio
☐ Bill Gadsby
☐ Hal Jackson
☐ Joe Klukay
☐ Ted Lindsay
☐ Jim Orlando
☐ Marty Pavelich
☐ Marcel Pronovost
☐ Marc Reaume
☐ Leo Reise
☐ Glen Skov
☐ Jack Stewart

'79 - 80 DETR.

Rogatien Vachon is the most expensive card at $4 in NM. Singles start at $2.
Card Size: 4" x 5"
Sponsor: None
Set (19 cards): $40

☐ Tommy Bergman
☐ Dan Bolduc
☐ Mike Foligno
☐ Jean Hamel
☐ Glen Hicks
☐ Bill Hogaboam
☐ Greg Joly
☐ Willie Huber
☐ Jim Korn
☐ Dan Labraaten
☐ Barry Long
☐ Reed Larson
☐ Dale McCourt
☐ Vaclav Nedomansky
☐ Jim Rutherford (G)
☐ Dennis Polonich
☐ Errol Thompson
☐ Roggie Vachon (G)
☐ Paul Woods

'80 - 81 DETR.

We have little information on this set. Ted Lindsay is the most expensive single at $3-4 in NM. Singles start at $2.
Photo Size: 8" x 10 1/2"
Sponsor: None
Set (32 photos): $40

☐ Mike Blaisdell
☐ Réjean Cloutier
☐ Mike Foligno
☐ Jody Gage
☐ Gilles Gilbert (G)
☐ Jean Hamel
☐ Glenn Hicks
☐ Bill Hogaboam
☐ Willie Huber
☐ Al Jensen (G)
☐ Greg Joly
☐ Jim Korn
☐ Dan Labraaten
☐ Reed Larson
☐ Ted Lindsay
☐ George Lyle
☐ Peter Mahovlich
☐ Dale McCourt
☐ Perry Miller
☐ Vaclav Nedomansky
☐ Dan Olesevich
☐ John Ogrodnick
☐ Joe Paterson
☐ Brent Peterson
☐ Dennis Polonich
☐ Marcel Pronovost
☐ Jim Rutherford (G)
☐ Jim Skinner
☐ Errol Thompson
☐ Rick Vasko
☐ Russ Wilson
☐ Paul Woods

'84 - 85 DETR.
LITTLE CAESARS

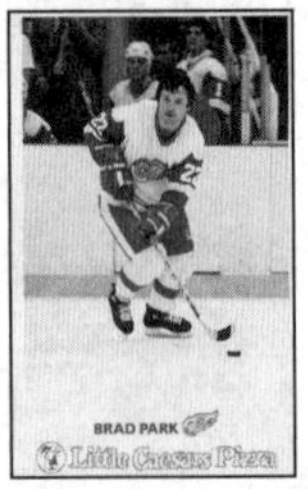

These photos are printed on thin stock and do not mention the photographer's name on the card front. Singles start at $1.50.
Card Size: 3 3/4" x 6"
Sponsor: Little Caesars

☐ Pierre Aubry
☐ John Barrett
☐ Ivan Boldirev
☐ Colin Campbell
☐ Frank Cernik
☐ Milan Chalupa
☐ Ron Duguay
☐ Dwight Foster
☐ Danny Gare
☐ Kelly Kisio
☐ Randy Ladouceur
☐ Lane Lambert
☐ Reed Larson
☐ Bob Manno
☐ Corrado Micalef (G)
☐ Eddy Mio (G)
☐ John Ogrodnick
☐ Brad Park
☐ Nick Polano, Coach
☐ Darryl Sittler
☐ Greg Smith
☐ Larry Trader
☐ Dave Williams
☐ Steve Yzerman

'85 - 86 DETR.
LITTLE CAESARS

These photos are printed on a heavier stock than the 1984-85 photos and do mention the photographer's name to the right of the photo. Seven cards feature the same pose (†) as the 1984-85 card. We have no pricing information on this set.
Card Size: 3 3/4" x 6"
Sponsor: Little Caesars

☐ John Barrett
☐ Chris Cichocki
☐ Jim Devellano
☐ Ron Duguay
☐ Dwight Foster
☐ Tim Friday
☐ Gerard Gallant
☐ (†) Danny Gare
☐ Doug Houda
☐ Kelly Kisio
☐ Petr Klima
☐ Joey Kocur
☐ (†) Randy Ladouceur
☐ (†) Lane Lambert
☐ (†) Reed Larson
☐ Claude Loiselle
☐ Adam Oates
☐ (†) John Ogrodnick
☐ (†) Brad Park
☐ Bob Probert
☐ (†) Greg Smith
☐ Harold Snepsts
☐ Ray Staszak
☐ Greg Stefan (G)
☐ Warren Young
☐ Steve Yzerman

'86 - 87 DETR.
LITTLE CAESARS

These photos are printed on the same stock as the 1985-86 cards but mention the photographer's name to the left of the photo. Nine cards feature the same pose (†) as the 1984-85 or 1985-86 card. Singles start at $1.50.
Card Size: 3 3/4" x 6"
Sponsor: Little Caesars

☐ Brent Ashton
☐ Dave Barr
☐ (†) Shawn Burr
☐ Billy Carroll
☐ Steve Chiasson
☐ Gilbert Delorme
☐ (†) Gerard Gallant
☐ Doug Halward
☐ Glen Hanlon (G)
☐ Tim Higgins
☐ (†) Petr Klima
☐ (†) Joey Kocur
☐ Mark Kumpel
☐ Dave Lewis
☐ Basil McRae
☐ Lee Norwood
☐ Adam Oates
☐ Mike O'Connell
☐ (†) John Ogrodnick
☐ (†) Bob Probert
☐ Sam St. Laurent (G)
☐ Ric Seiling
☐ Doug Shedden
☐ (†) Harold Snepsts
☐ (†) Greg Stefan (G)
☐ Darren Veitch
☐ (†) Steve Yzerman
☐ Rick Zombo
☐ J. Demers, Coach

'87 - 88 DETR.
LITTLE CAESARS

These cards are similar to the 1986-87 cards. The most expensive singles are Steve Yzerman at $15-20 and Adam Oates at $6-8. Singles start $1.50.
Card Size: 3 3/4" x 6"
Sponsor: Little Caesars
Set (25 cards): $45

☐ Brent Ashton
☐ Dave Barr
☐ Mel Bridgman
☐ Shawn Burr
☐ John Chabot
☐ Steve Chiasson
☐ Gilbert Delorme
☐ Gerard Gallant
☐ Adam Graves
☐ Doug Halward
☐ Glen Hanlon (G)
☐ Tim Higgins
☐ Petr Klima
☐ Joe Kocur
☐ Joe Murphy
☐ Lee Norwood
☐ Adam Oates
☐ Mike O'Connell
☐ Bob Probert
☐ Jeff Sharples
☐ Greg Stefan (G)
☐ Darren Veitch
☐ Steve Yzerman
☐ Rick Zombo
☐ J. Demers, Coach

'88 - 89 DETR.
LITTLE CAESARS

These cards are similar to previous Little Caesars issues. Once again, numerous poses from earlier sets were reused in this set. Singles start at $1.50.
Card Size: 3 3/4" x 6"
Sponsor: Little Caesars

☐ Dave Barr
☐ Shawn Burr
☐ John Chabot
☐ Steve Chiasson
☐ Gilbert Delorme
☐ Miroslav Frycer
☐ Gerard Gallant
☐ Adam Graves
☐ Doug Halward
☐ Glen Hanlon (G)
☐ Tim Higgins
☐ Doug Houda
☐ Kris King
☐ Petr Klima
☐ Joey Kocur
☐ Paul MacLean
☐ Joe Murphy
☐ Jim Nill
☐ Lee Norwood
☐ Adam Oates
☐ Mike O'Connell
☐ Jim Pavese
☐ Bob Probert
☐ Jeff Sharples
☐ Greg Stefan (G)
☐ Steve Yzerman
☐ Rick Zombo
☐ J. Demers, Coach

'88 - 89 DETR.
S.A.M.

Steve Yzerman is the most expensive single at $10. Singles start $1.
Card Size: 3 5/8" x 5 1/2"
Sponsor: S.A.M.
Set (10 cards): $20

☐ Shawn Burr
☐ John Chabot
☐ Jacques Demers
☐ Gerard Gallant
☐ Glen Hanlon (G)
☐ Lee Norwood
☐ Mike O'Connell
☐ Jeff Sharples
☐ Steve Yzerman
☐ Rick Zombo

'89 - 90 DETR.
LITTLE CAESARS

These cards feature two photos on the front. We have no pricing information on this set.
Card Size: 3 3/4" x 8 1/2"
Sponsor: Little Caesars

☐ Dave Barr
☐ Shawn Burr
☐ Jimmy Carson
☐ John Chabot
☐ Steve Chiasson
☐ Bernie Federko
☐ Gerard Gallant
☐ Marc Habscheid
☐ Glen Hanlon (G)
☐ Doug Houda
☐ Joey Kocur
☐ Kevin McClelland
☐ Lee Norwood
☐ Mike O'Connell
☐ Borje Salming
☐ Greg Stefan (G)
☐ Steve Yzerman
☐ Rick Zombo
☐ J. Demers, Coach
☐ Lewis/ Myre/ Demers/ Campbell
☐ Team (blank back)

'90 - 91 DETR.
LITTLE CAESARS

These cards feature two photos on the front like the 1989-90 series, but have blank backs instead. Singles start at $1.
Card Size: 3 3/4" x 8 1/2"
Sponsor: Little Caesars

☐ Dave Barr
☐ Shawn Burr
☐ John Chabot
☐ Tim Cheveldae (G)
☐ Per Djoos
☐ Bobby Dollas
☐ Sergei Fedorov
☐ Brent Fedyk
☐ Johan Garpenlov
☐ Rick Green
☐ Sheldon Kennedy
☐ Kevin McClelland
☐ Brad McCrimmon
☐ Randy McKay
☐ Keith Primeau
☐ Bob Probert
☐ Steve Yzerman
☐ Rick Zombo
☐ Mickey Redmond
☐ Bryan Murray, Coach
☐ Team Photo

'91 - 92 DETR.
LITTLE CAESARS

The most expensive singles are Steve Yzerman at $10-12 and Sergei Fedorov at $8-10. Singles start at $1.
Card Size: 8 1/2" x 3 5/8"
Sponsor: Little Caesars
Set (19 cards): $35

☐ Shawn Burr
☐ Jimmy Carson
☐ Steve Chiasson
☐ Sergei Fedorov
☐ Gerard Gallant
☐ Johan Garpenlov
☐ Rick Green
☐ Marc Habscheid
☐ Sheldon Kennedy
☐ Martin Lapointe
☐ Nicklas Lidström
☐ Brad McCrimmon
☐ Bryan Murray, Coach
☐ Keith Primeau
☐ Bob Probert
☐ Dennis Vial
☐ Paul Ysebaert
☐ Steve Yzerman
☐ Red Wings

'98 - 99 DETR.
DETROIT NEWS

These sheets were issued with The Detroit News.
Sponsor: The Detroit News

☐ 1 Howe / Yzerman
☐ 2 Delvecchio / Fedorov
☐ 3 Sawchuk/ Osgood
☐ 4 Mahovlich / Shanahan
☐ 5 Lindsay / McCarty

EDMONTON OILERS

'79 - 80 EDMO.

The most expensive singles in NM are Wayne Gretzky at $60-90 and Mark Messier at $25-35. Singles start at $2. Ed Mio has a variation card with the wrong birthdate. Both the error card and the corrected version have the same value.
Card Size: 3 1/2" x 5 1/4"
Sponsor: None
Set (23 cards): $150

☐ Brett Callighen
☐ Colin Campbell
☐ Ron Chipperfield
☐ Cam Connor
☐ Peter Driscoll
☐ Dave Dryden (G)
☐ Bill Flett
☐ Lee Fogolin
☐ Wayne Gretzky
☐ Al Hamilton
☐ Doug Hicks
☐ Dave Hunter
☐ Kevin Lowe
☐ Dave Lumley
☐ Blair MacDonald
☐ Kari Makkonen
☐ Mark Messier
☐☐ Ed Mio (G)
☐ Pat Price
☐ Dave Semenko
☐ Bobby Schmautz
☐ Risto Siltanen
☐ Stan Weir

'80 - 81 EDMO.
ZELLERS

We have little information on this set. Singles were given out during practices in West Edmonton Mall. Other singles may exist.

Card Size: 5" x 7"
Sponsor: Zellers

☐ Curt Brackenbury
☐ Brett Callighen
☐ Wayne Gretzky
☐ Matti Hagman
☐ Billy Harris
☐ Doug Hicks
☐ John Hughes
☐ Dave Hunter
☐ Jari Kurri
☐ Ron Low (G)
☐ Dave Lumley
☐ Mark Messier
☐ Ed Mio (G)
☐ Don Murdoch
☐ Dave Semenko
☐ Risto Siltanen
☐ Bryan Watson
☐ Stan Weir

'81 - 82 EDMO.
RED ROOSTER

This set was originally issued in panels. Single card prices are listed below. Regional stars may carry a premium.

Card Size: 2 3/4" x 3 5/8"
Sponsors: Red Rooster, Post
Set (23 cards): $100

☐ G. Anderson #9 $3
☐ C. Brackenbury #15 $1
☐ Brett Callighen #18 $1
☐ Paul Coffey #7 $8
☐ Lee Fogolin #2 $1
☐ Mike Forbes #26 $1
☐ Grant Fuhr #1 (G) $6
☐ Ted Green $1
☐ W. Gretzky #99 $15
☐ W. Gretzky #99 $15
☐ W. Gretzky #99 $15
☐ W. Gretzky #99 $15
☐ Matti Hagman #10 $1
☐ Billy Harris $1
☐ Doug Hicks #5 $1
☐ Pat Hughes #16 $1
☐ Dave Hunter #12 $1
☐ Jari Kurri #17 $7
☐ Garry Lariviere #6 $1
☐ Ron Low #30 (G) $2
☐ Kevin Lowe #4 $5
☐ Dave Lumley #20 $1
☐ Mark Messier #11 $10
☐ Andy Moog #35 (G) $6
☐ Glen Sather $3
☐ Dave Semenko #27 $2
☐ Risto Siltanen #8 $1
☐ Garry Unger #77 $1
☐ Stan Weir #21 $1

'81 - 82 EDMO.
WEST EDMO. MALL

Single card prices are listed below. Regional stars may carry a premium. Other singles may exist.

Photo Size: 5" x 7"
Sponsor: West Edmonton Mall

☐ Paul Coffey $20
☐ Lee Fogolin $5
☐ Grant Fuhr (G) $12
☐ Wayne Gretzky $100
☐ Billy Harris $5
☐ Charlie Huddy $5
☐ Gary Larivière $5
☐ Dave Lumley $5
☐ Risto Siltanen $5
☐ Stan Weir $5

'82 - 83 EDMO.
RED ROOSTER

This set was originally issued in panels. Single card prices are listed below. Regional stars may carry a premium.

Card Size: 2 3/4" x 3 5/8"
Sponsors: Red Rooster, Post
Set (23 cards): $60

☐ Glenn Anderson #9 $2
☐ L. Boschman #14 $1
☐ Paul Coffey #7 $6
☐ Lee Fogolin #2 $1
☐ Grant Fuhr #31 (G) $6
☐ Ted Green $1
☐ Randy Gregg #21 $2
☐ W. Gretzky #99 $10
☐ W. Gretzky #99 $12
☐ W. Gretzky #99 $12
☐ W. Gretzky #99 $12
☐ M. Habscheid #23 $1
☐ Charlie Huddy #22 $2
☐ Pat Hughes #16 $1
☐ Dave Hunter #12 $1
☐ Don Jackson #29 $1
☐ Jari Kurri #17 $6
☐ Garry Larivière #6 $1
☐ Ken Linseman #13 $1
☐ Ron Low #30 (G) $2
☐ Kevin Lowe #4 $3
☐ Dave Lumley #20 $1
☐ Mark Messier #11 $8
☐ Andy Moog #35 (G) $5
☐ John Muckler $2
☐ Jaroslav Pouzar #10 $1
☐ Tom Roulston #24 $1
☐ Glen Sather $3
☐ Dave Semenko #27 $2
☐ Garry Unger #77 $1

'83 - 84 EDMO.
RED ROOSTER

There are two versions of this set: a postcard-sized set that was issued in complete sets and a longer size photo edition issued during practices in West Edmonton Mall. We have little pricing information on singles. The longer-sized cards are likely valued at 2-3 times the regular card.

Card Size: 4 1/2" x 6 1/2"
Photo Size Length: 7 1/2"
Sponsor: None
Set (21 cards): $100

☐☐ Glenn Anderson #9
☐☐ Rick Chartraw #6
☐☐ Paul Coffey #7
☐☐ Lee Fogolin #2
☐☐ Grant Fuhr (G) #31
☐☐ Randy Gregg #21
☐☐ Wayne Gretzky #99
☐☐ Charlie Huddy #22
☐☐ Pat Hughes #16
☐☐ Dave Hunter #12
☐☐ Don Jackson #29
☐☐ Jari Kurri #17
☐☐ Willy Lindstrom #19
☐☐ Ken Linseman #13
☐☐ Kevin Lowe #4
☐☐ Dave Lumley #20
☐☐ Kevin McClelland #24
☐☐ Mark Messier #11
☐☐ Andy Moog #35 (G)
☐☐ Jaroslav Pouzar #10
☐☐ Dave Semenko #27

'83 - 84 EDMO.
McDONALD'S

This set was originally issued in panels. The Gretzky panel sells at $12-15. Single panels start at 75¢. Regular stickers measure 1 9/16" x 2 1/2" while the coaches and two goalie stickers measure 3" x 2 1/2".

Panel Size: 3" x 5"
Sponsor: McDonald's
Set (7 panels): $40
Album: $5

☐ Glenn Anderson #9
Jaroslav Pouzar #10
Green/ Sather/ Muckler
☐ Rick Chartraw #6
Wayne Gretzky #99
Dave Lumley #20
Willy Lindstrom #19
☐ Paul Coffey #7
Raimo Summanen #25
Andy Moog #35 (G)
☐ Pat Conacher #15
Lee Fogolin #2
Don Jackson #29
Mark Messier #11
☐ Randy Gregg #21
Charle Huddy #22
Kevin Lowe #4
Emery Edge Award
☐ Pat Hughes #16
Kevin McClelland #24
Grant Fuhr #31 (G)
☐ Dave Hunter #12
Jari Kurri #17
Ken Linseman #13
Dave Semenko #27

'84 - 85 EDMO.

The most expensive singles are Wayne Gretzky at $15 and Mark Messier at $7. Singles start at 75¢.

Card Size: 4 1/2" x 6 1/2"
Set (23 cards): $45

☐ Glenn Anderson
☐ Bill Carroll
☐ Paul Coffey
☐ Lee Fogolin
☐ Grant Fuhr (G)
☐ Randy Gregg
☐ Wayne Gretzky
☐ Charlie Huddy
☐ Pat Hughes
☐ Dave Hunter
☐ Don Jackson
☐ Mike Krushelnyski
☐ Jari Kurri
☐ Willy Lindstrom
☐ Kevin Lowe
☐ Dave Lumley
☐ Kevin McClelland
☐ Larry Melnyk
☐ Mark Messier
☐ Andy Moog (G)
☐ Mark Napier
☐ Jaroslav Pouzar
☐ Dave Semenko

'84 - 85 EDMO.
RED ROOSTER

This series was originally issued in panels. There are four Wayne Gretzky cards each valued at $10. Mark Messier sells at $5 and singles start at 50¢.

Card Size: 2 3/4" x 3 5/8"
Sponsors: Red Rooster, Old Dutch, Post
Set (30 cards): $55

☐ Glenn Anderson
☐ Billy Carroll
☐ Paul Coffey
☐ Lee Fogolin
☐ Grant Fuhr (G)
☐ Ted Green
☐ Randy Gregg
☐ Wayne Gretzky
☐ Wayne Gretzky
☐ Wayne Gretzky
☐ Wayne Gretzky
☐ Marc Habscheid
☐ Charlie Huddy
☐ Pat Hughes
☐ Dave Hunter
☐ Don Jackson
☐ Mike Krushelnyski
☐ Jari Kurri
☐ Willy Lindstrom
☐ Kevin Lowe
☐ Dave Lumley
☐ Kevin McClelland
☐ Larry Melnyk
☐ Mark Messier
☐ Andy Moog (G)
☐ John Muckler
☐ Mark Napier
☐ Jaroslav Pouzar
☐ Glen Sather
☐ Dave Semenko

'85 - 86 EDMO.
RED ROOSTER

This series was originally issued in panels. There are three Wayne Gretzky cards each valued at $10. Mark Messier sells at $5 and singles start at 50¢.

Card Size: 2 3/4" x 3 5/8"
Sponsors: Red Rooster, Old Dutch, Post
Set (30 cards): $50

☐ Glenn Anderson
☐ Paul Coffey
☐ Lee Fogolin
☐ Grant Fuhr (G)
☐ Randy Gregg
☐ Wayne Gretzky
☐ Wayne Gretzky
☐ Wayne Gretzky
☐ Charlie Huddy
☐ Dave Hunter
☐ Don Jackson
☐ Mike Krushelnyski
☐ Jari Kurri
☐ Kevin Lowe
☐ Dave Lumley
☐ Craig MacTavish
☐ Bob McCammon
☐ Kevin McClelland
☐ Marty McSorley
☐ Mark Messier
☐ Andy Moog (G)
☐ John Muckler
☐ Mark Napier
☐ Mike Rogers
☐ Glen Sather
☐ Dave Semenko
☐ Gord Shervan
☐ Steve Smith
☐ Raimo Summanen
☐ Esa Tikkanen

'86 - 87 EDMO.

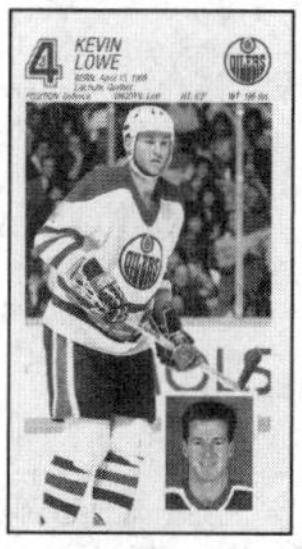

The most expensive singles are Wayne Gretzky at $20 and Mark Messier at $7. Singles start at 75¢.

Card Size: 3 3/4" x 6 5/8"
Sponsor: None
Set (24 cards): $45

☐ Glenn Anderson
☐ Jeff Beukeboom
☐ Paul Coffey
☐ Lee Fogolin
☐ Grant Fuhr (G)
☐ Randy Gregg
☐ Wayne Gretzky
☐ Charlie Huddy
☐ Dave Hunter
☐ Mike Krushelnyski
☐ Stu Kulak
☐ Jari Kurri
☐ Kevin Lowe
☐ Craig MacTavish
☐ Kevin McClelland
☐ Marty McSorley
☐ Mark Messier
☐ Andy Moog (G)
☐ Craig Muni
☐ Mark Napier
☐ Jaroslav Pouzar
☐ Steve Smith
☐ Raimo Summanen
☐ Esa Tikkanen

'86 - 87 EDMO.
RED ROOSTER

This series was originally issued in panels. There are two Wayne Gretzky cards each valued at $10. Mark Messier sells at $5 and singles start at 50¢.

Card Size: 2 3/4" x 3 5/8"
Sponsors: Red Rooster, Old Dutch
Set (30 cards): $40

☐ Glenn Anderson
☐ Jeff Beukeboom
☐ Paul Coffey
☐ Lee Fogolin
☐ Grant Fuhr (G)
☐ Danny Gare
☐ Steve Graves
☐ Ted Green
☐ Randy Gregg
☐ Wayne Gretzky
☐ Wayne Gretzky
☐ Charlie Huddy
☐ Dave Hunter
☐ Mike Krushelnyski
☐ Stu Kulak
☐ Jari Kurri
☐ Kevin Lowe
☐ Craig MacTavish
☐ Kevin McClelland
☐ Marty McSorley
☐ Mark Messier
☐ Andy Moog (G)
☐ Andy Moog (G)
☐ John Muckler
☐ Craig Muni
☐ Mark Napier
☐ Glen Sather
☐ Steve Smith
☐ Raimo Summanen
☐ Esa Tikkanen

'87 - 88 EDMO.

The most expensive singles are Wayne Gretzky at $20 and Mark Messier at $7. Singles start at $1.

Card Size: 3 3/4" x 6 5/8"
Sponsor: None
Set (22 cards): $40

☐ Keith Acton
☐ Glenn Anderson
☐ Jeff Beukeboom
☐ Grant Fuhr (G)
☐ Wayne Gretzky
☐ Dave Hannan
☐ Charlie Huddy
☐ Mike Krushelnyski
☐ Jari Kurri
☐ Normand Lacombe
☐ Kevin Lowe
☐ Craig MacTavish
☐ Kevin McClelland
☐ Marty McSorley
☐ Mark Messier
☐ Craig Muni
☐ Selmar Odelein
☐ Daryl Reaugh (G)
☐ Craig Simpson
☐ Warren Skorodenski (G)
☐ Steve Smith
☐ Esa Tikkanen

'88 - 89 EDMO.

Mark Messier is the most expensive single at $5. Singles start at $1.

Card Size: 3 3/4" x 6 5/8"
Sponsor: None
Set (27 cards): $25

☐ Glenn Anderson
☐ Jeff Beukeboom
☐ Dave Brown
☐ Kelly Buchberger
☐ Jimmy Carson
☐ Miroslav Frycer
☐ Grant Fuhr (G)
☐ Randy Gregg
☐ Doug Halward
☐ Charlie Huddy
☐ Dave Hunter
☐ Tomas Jönsson
☐ Chris Joseph
☐ Jari Kurri
☐ Normand Lacombe
☐ Mark Lamb
☐ John LeBlanc
☐ Kevin Lowe
☐ Craig MacTavish
☐ Kevin McClelland
☐ Mark Messier
☐ Craig Muni
☐ Bill Ranford (G)
☐ Craig Redmond
☐ Craig Simpson
☐ Steve Smith
☐ Esa Tikkanen

'88 - 89 EDMO.
ACTION MAGAZINE

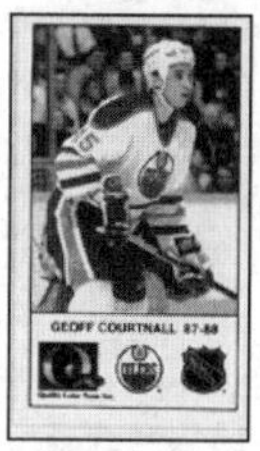

These cards were issued as four-card panels inserted into game programs. Wayne Gretzky's first panel (cards 45-48) sells at $40 while his second panel (cards 53-56) sells at $15-20. Gretzky is also pictured on a third panel with the 1988 Stanley Cup (cards 137-140) which is valued at $10-15. Mark Messier's panel (cards 89-92) sells at $8-10 and single panels start $3. Cut out cards measure 2 9/16" x 4 5/16".

Card Size: 9 1/4" x 7 7/16"
Sponsor: Action Magazine
Set (41 panels): $175

☐ 1 Garry Unger
2 Chris Joseph
3 Raimo Summanen
4 Mike Zanier (G)
☐ 5 Kevin Lowe
6 Dave Semenko
7 Pete Driscoll
8 Ken Solheim
☐ 9 Glenn Anderson
10 Curt Brackenbury
11 Ron Shudra
12 Gord Shervan
☐ 13 Randy Gregg
14 Larry Melnyk
15 Tom Roulston
16 Billy Carroll
☐ 17 Jeff Beukeboom
18 Jaroslav Pouzar
19 Jeff Brubaker
20 Danny Gare
☐ 21 Craig MacTavish
22 Reijo Ruotsalainen
23 Willy Lindstrom
24 Pat Hughes
☐ 25 Jim Wiemer
26 Selmar Odelein
27 Kent Nilsson
28 Mark Napier
☐ 29 Esa Tikkanen
30 John Miner
31 Tom McMurchy
32 Steve Graves
☐ 33 Craig Muni
34 Moe Mantha
35 Dave Lumley
36 Ron Low (G)
☐ 37 Marty McSorley
38 Steve Dykstra
39 Risto Jalo
40 Dave Hunter
☐ 41 Jari Kurri
42 Lee Fogolin
43 Moe Lemay
44 Stu Kulak
☐ 45 Charlie Huddy
46 Wayne Gretzky
47 Ken Linseman
48 Risto Siltanen
☐ 49 Glen Sather
50 Brett Callighen
51 Eddy Mio (G)
52 Ken Hammond
☐ 53 Jimmy Carson
54 Paul Coffey
55 HL: Wayne Gretzky
56 Reed Larson
☐ 57 Ted Green
58 Matti Hagman
59 Marc Habscheid
60 Bill Ranford (G)
☐ 61 Mark Lamb
62 Daryl Reaugh (G)
63 Al Hamilton
64 HL: Paul Coffey
☐ 65 Grant Fuhr (G)
66 Stan Weir
67 Ken Berry
68 John Muckler
☐ 69 Doug Smith
70 Lance Nethery
71 Bill Flett
72 Mike Forbes
☐ 73 Martin Gélinas
74 Ron Chipperfield
75 Reg Kerr
76 Don Jackson
☐ 77 Keith Acton
78 Gary Edwards (G)
79 Mike Krushelnyski
80 L. Kulchisky/ P. Millar/ B. Stafford
☐ 81 Normand Lacombe
82 Pat Price
83 Dave Hannan
84 Garry Lariviere
☐ 85 Greg C. Adams
86 Poul Popiel
87 Tom Gorence
88 Geoff Courtnall
☐ 89 Mark Messier
90 Dave Dryden (G)
91 Andy Moog (G)
92 Jim Ennis
☐ 93 Craig Simpson
94 Laurie Boschman
95 Doug Hicks
96 Rick Chartraw
☐ 97 '84 Cup Champions
98 Ron Carter
99 Blair MacDonald
100 Dean Clark
☐ 101 Glen Cochrane
102 L. Middlebrook (G)
103 Ron Areshenkoff
104 Billy Harris
☐ 105 Mark Messier
106 John Blum
107 Wayne Bianchin
108 Tom Bladon
☐ 109 Kevin McClelland
110 Roy Sommer
111 Mike Toal
112 Don Ashby
☐ 113 Donald Nachbaur
114 '85 Cup Champions
115 Jim Corsi (G)
116 John Hughes
☐ 117 HL: Glen Sather
118 Bob Dupuis
119 Jim Harrison
120 Don Murdoch
☐ 121 Steve Smith
122 Pete LoPresti (G)
123 Colin Campbell
124 Bryan Watson
☐ 125 John Bednarski
126 '87 Cup Champions
127 Scott Metcalfe
128 Mike Rogers
☐ 129 Dan Newman
130 HL: Grant Fuhr (G)
131 W. Skorodenski (G)
132 Todd Strueby
☐ 133 Kelly Buchberger
134 Cam Connor
135 Dean Hopkins
136 Mike Moller
☐ 137 '88 Cup Champions
138 Byron Baltimore
139 Pat Conacher
140 Ray Cote
☐ 141 Walt Poddubny
142 Jim Playfair
143 Nick Fotiu
144 Kari Makkonen
☐ 145 Dave Brown
146 Terry Martin
147 François Leroux
148 Kari Jalonen
☐ 149 Tomas Jönsson
150 Dave Donnelly
151 Mike Ware
152 Don Cutts (G)
☐ 153 Miroslav Frycer
154 Bruce MacGregor
155 Kim Issel
156 Marco Baron (G)
☐ 157 Doug Halward
158 Barry Fraser
159 Alan May
160 Bobby Schmautz
☐ 161 Craig Redmond
162 '89 All-Star Game
163 Alex Tidey
164 Wayne Van Dorp

'90 - 91 EDMO.
IGA

Mark Messier is the most expensive single at $7. Singles start at 50¢. Ted Green, Ron Low, John Muckler and the checklist card are supposedly short printed and sell at $2-3. A 26-card set sells at $30.

Card Size: 2 1/2" x 3 1/2"
Sponsor: McGavin's, IGA
Set (30 cards): $35

- ☐ Glenn Anderson
- ☐ Dave Brown
- ☐ Jeff Beukeboom
- ☐ Kelly Buchberger
- ☐ Martin Gélinas
- ☐ Adam Graves
- ☐ Charlie Huddy
- ☐ Chris Joseph
- ☐ Petr Klima
- ☐ Mark Lamb
- ☐ Ken Linseman
- ☐ Kevin Lowe
- ☐ Craig MacTavish
- ☐ Mark Messier
- ☐ Joey Moss
- ☐ Craig Muni
- ☐ Joe Murphy
- ☐ Bill Ranford (G)
- ☐ Anatoli Semenov
- ☐ Craig Simpson
- ☐ Geoff Smith
- ☐ Steve Smith
- ☐ Kari Takko (G)
- ☐ Esa Tikkanen
- ☐ K. Lowe/ L. Kulchisky/ B. Stafford/ S. Poirier
- ☐ HL: Mark Messier
- ☐ Ted Green
- ☐ Ron Low (G)
- ☐ John Muckler
- ☐ Checklist

'91 - 92 EDMO.
IGA

Bill Ranford is the most expensive single at $2. Singles start at 75¢. Ted Green, Ron Low, Kevin Primeau and the checklist card are supposedly short printed and sell at $3 each. A 26-card set sells at $15.

Card Size: 2 1/2" x 3 1/2"
Sponsor: IGA
Set (30 cards): $25

- ☐ Josef Beranek
- ☐ Kelly Buchberger
- ☐ Vincent Damphousse
- ☐ Louie DeBrusk
- ☐ Martin Gélinas
- ☐ Peter Ing (G)
- ☐ Petr Klima
- ☐ Mark Lamb
- ☐ Kevin Lowe
- ☐ Norm Maciver
- ☐ Craig MacTavish
- ☐ Troy Mallette
- ☐ Dave Manson
- ☐ Scott Mellanby
- ☐ Craig Muni
- ☐ Joe Murphy
- ☐ Bill Ranford (G)
- ☐ Steve Rice
- ☐ Luke Richardson
- ☐ Anatoli Semenov
- ☐ David Shaw
- ☐ Craig Simpson
- ☐ Geoff Smith
- ☐ Scott Thornton
- ☐ Esa Tikkanen
- ☐ IGA logo
- ☐ Ted Green
- ☐ Ron Low (G)
- ☐ Kevin Primeau
- ☐ Checklist

'92 - 93 EDMO.

Doug Weight is the most expensive card at $3. Singles start at 75¢.

Card Size: 3 3/4" x 6 7/8"
Set (22 cards): $18

- ☐ Kelly Buchberger
- ☐ Zdeno Ciger
- ☐ Shayne Corson
- ☐ Louie DeBrusk
- ☐ Todd Elik
- ☐ Brian Glynn
- ☐ Mike Hudson
- ☐ Chris Joseph
- ☐ Igor Kravchuk
- ☐ Francois Leroux
- ☐ Craig MacTavish
- ☐ Dave Manson
- ☐ Shjon Podein
- ☐ Bill Ranford (G)
- ☐ Steve Rice
- ☐ Luke Richardson
- ☐ Craig Simpson
- ☐ Geoff Smith
- ☐ Kevin Todd
- ☐ Vladimir Vujtek
- ☐ Doug Weight
- ☐ Brad Werenka

'92 - 93 EDMO.
IGA

Bill Ranford is the most expensive single at $2. Singles start at 50¢.

Card Size: 2 1/2" x 3 1/2"
Sponsor: IGA
Set (30 cards): $20

- ☐ 001 Checklist
- ☐ 002 Josef Beranek
- ☐ 003 Kelly Buchberger
- ☐ 004 Shayne Corson
- ☐ 005 Dan Currie
- ☐ 006 Louie DeBrusk
- ☐ 007 Martin Gélinas
- ☐ 008 Brent Gilchrist
- ☐ 009 Brian Glynn
- ☐ 010 Greg Hawgood
- ☐ 011 Chris Joseph
- ☐ 012 Petr Klima
- ☐ 013 Craig MacTavish
- ☐ 014 Dave Manson
- ☐ 015 Scott Mellanby
- ☐ 016 Craig Muni
- ☐ 017 Bernie Nicholls
- ☐ 018 Bill Ranford (G)
- ☐ 019 Luke Richardson
- ☐ 020 Craig Simpson
- ☐ 021 Geoff Smith
- ☐ 022 Vladimir Vujtek
- ☐ 023 Esa Tikkanen
- ☐ 024 Ron Tugnutt (G)
- ☐ 025 Shaun Van Allen
- ☐ 026 Glen Sather
- ☐ 027 Ted Green
- ☐ 028 Ron Low (G)
- ☐ 029 Kevin Primeau
- ☐ 030 Oilers

'93 - 94 EDMO.
STARTER LINEUP SHEETS

These photos were issued with game programs. Jason Arnott is the most expensive photo at $10. Singles start at $4. Each card is numbered out of 5,000.

Photo Size: 8" x 10"
Sponsor: Starter
Set (41 cards): $220

- ☐ 06OCT Todd Elik
- ☐ 08OCT Igor Kravchuk
- ☐ 16OCT Dave Manson
- ☐ 20OCT Kelly Buchberger
- ☐ 22OCT Bill Ranford (G)
- ☐ 24OCT Craig MacTavish
- ☐ 29OCT Alexander Kerch
- ☐ 03NOV Chris Joseph
- ☐ 20NOV Geoff Smith
- ☐ 21NOV Ian Herbers
- ☐ 24NOV F. Brathwaite (G)
- ☐ 27NOV Doug Weight
- ☐ 29NOV Ilya Byakin
- ☐ 01DEC Luke Richardson
- ☐ 15DEC Scott Pearson
- ☐ 17DEC Adam Bennett
- ☐ 22DEC Louie DeBrusk
- ☐ 27DEC Brad Werenka
- ☐ 29DEC Shayne Corson
- ☐ 02JAN Steve Rice
- ☐ 07JAN Kirk Maltby
- ☐ 26JAN Shjon Podein
- ☐ 28JAN Peter White
- ☐ 29JAN Vladimir Vujtek
- ☐ 02FEB Scott Thornton
- ☐ 04FEB Roman Oksiuta
- ☐ 06FEB Bob Beers
- ☐ 09FEB Fred Olausson
- ☐ 12FEB Wayne Cowley
- ☐ 13FEB Dean McAmmond
- ☐ 23FEB Jason Arnott
- ☐ 25FEB Ron Low (G)
- ☐ 27FEB Tyler Wright
- ☐ 09MAR Kevin Primeau
- ☐ 11MAR Jozef Cierny
- ☐ 23MAR Gordon Mark
- ☐ 25MAR Brent Grieve
- ☐ 27MAR Brad Zavisha
- ☐ 08APR Mike Stapleton
- ☐ 10APR Glen Sather

'95 - 96 EDMO.

We have little information on this blank-back series. Other singles exist.

Card Size: 3 3/4" x 7 1/8"

- ☐ Curtis Joseph (G)

'96 - 97 EDMO.

This Oilers series can be distinguished from previous years by the new Oilers' shoulder logo. The photos on these blank-back cards were taken by Gerry Thomas. Curtis Joseph is the most expensive single at $4. Singles start at $1.

Card Size: 3 3/4" x 7 1/8"
Set (27 cards): $25

- ☐ Jason Arnott #7
- ☐ Sean Brown #8
- ☐ Kelly Buchberger #16
- ☐ Mariusz Czerkawski #21
- ☐ Louie DeBrusk #29
- ☐ Boyd Devereaux #19
- ☐ Greg de Vries #5
- ☐ Donald Dufresne #34
- ☐ Bob Essensa #30 (G)
- ☐ Mike Grier #25
- ☐ Curtis Joseph #31 (G)
- ☐ Steve Kelly #10
- ☐ Petr Klima #85
- ☐ Andrei Kovalenko #51
- ☐ Mats Lindgren #14
- ☐ Kevin Lowe #4
- ☐ Todd Marchant #26
- ☐ Bryan Marchment #24
- ☐ Daniel McGillis #23
- ☐ Boris Mironov #2
- ☐ Rem Murray #17
- ☐ Jeff Norton #6
- ☐ Dean McAmmond #37
- ☐ Luke Richardson #22
- ☐ Miroslav Satan #18
- ☐ Ryan Smyth #94
- ☐ Doug Weight #39

'97 - 98 EDMO.

The photos on these blank-back cards were taken by Gerry Thomas. Curtis Joseph is the most expensive single at $4. Singles start at $1.

Card Size: 3 3/4" x 7 1/8"
Set (27 cards): $25

- ☐ Jason Arnott #7
- ☐ Drew Bannister #55
- ☐ Sean Brown #23
- ☐ Kelly Buchberger #16
- ☐ Boyd Devereaux #19
- ☐ Greg de Vries #5
- ☐ Bob Essensa #30 (G)
- ☐ Doug Friedman #8
- ☐ Mike Grier #25
- ☐ Bill Huard #28
- ☐ Curtis Joseph #31 (G)
- ☐ Joe Hulbig #12
- ☐ Steve Kelly #10
- ☐ Andrei Kovalenko #51
- ☐ Georges Laraque #27
- ☐ Mats Lindgren #14
- ☐ Kevin Lowe #4
- ☐ Todd Marchant #26
- ☐ Bryan Marchment #24
- ☐ Dean McAmmond #37
- ☐ Daniel McGillis #33
- ☐ Boris Mironov #2
- ☐ Bryan Muir #6
- ☐ Rem Murray #17
- ☐ Ryan Smyth #94
- ☐ Mike Watt #9
- ☐ Doug Weight #39

FLORIDA PANTHERS

'93 - 94 FLOR.

Scott Mellanby is the most expensive single at $3. Singles start at $2. Other cards may exist.

Card Size: 3 3/4" x 7"
Sponsor: None

- ☐ Joe Cirella
- ☐ Tom Fitzgerald
- ☐ Mike Foligno
- ☐ Paul Laus
- ☐ Bill Lindsay
- ☐ Andrei Lomakin
- ☐ Scott Mellanby
- ☐ Brent Severyn

'94 - 95 FLOR.
HEALTH PLAN

John Vanbiesbrouck is the most expensive card at $5. Singles start at $2.

Card Size: 4" x 10"
Sponsor: Health Plan of Florida

- ☐ Brian Skrudland
- ☐ John Vanbiesbrouck (G)
- ☐ Scott Mellanby
- ☐ Stu Barnes
- ☐ Jesse Belanger

'94 - 95 FLOR.
BOSTON ROTISSERIE

We have no pricing information on this set. Other singles may exist.

Card Size: 2 1/2" x 3"
Sponsor: Boston Rotisserie Chicken

- ☐ Dave Lowry
- ☐ Gord Murphy
- ☐ John Vanbiesbrouck (G)
- ☐ Mascot Panther

'96 - 97 FLOR.
WINN-DIXIE ALBUM

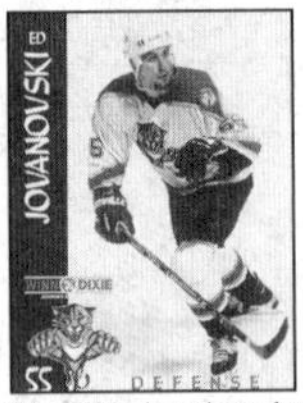

This set was issued as a four panel album. The first panel features a collage of Panthers' photos. The next two panels can be cut out into 12 cards, while the last panel can be cut out into 6 cards plus one Winn-Dixie ad card. The most expensive cut-out single is John Vanbiesbrouck at $3-4. Singles start at 50¢. An uncut album sells at $20.

Card Size: 2 1/2" x 3 1/8"
Sponsor: Winn-Dixie
Set (30 cards): $18

- ☐ Terry Carkner #2
- ☐ Paul Laus #3
- ☐ Per Gustafsson #4
- ☐ Gord Murphy #5
- ☐ Rhett Warrener #7
- ☐ Dave Lowry #10
- ☐ Bill Lindsay #11
- ☐ Jody Hull #12
- ☐ David Nemirovsky #15
- ☐ Jason Podollan #17
- ☐ Mike Hough #18
- ☐ Radek Dvorak #19
- ☐ Brian Skrudland #20
- ☐ Tom Fitzgerald #21
- ☐ Chris Wells #23
- ☐ Robert Svehla #24
- ☐ Ray Sheppard #26
- ☐ Scott Mellanby #27
- ☐ Martin Straka #28
- ☐ Johan Garpenlov #29
- ☐ Mark Fitzpatrick #30 (G)
- ☐ J. Vanbiesbrouck #34 (G)
- ☐ Rob Niedermayer #44
- ☐ Ed Jovanovski #55
- ☐ Doug MacLean, Coach
- ☐ Lindy Ruff, Asst. Coach
- ☐ Duane Sutter, A. Coach
- ☐ Billy Smith, Goal Coach
- ☐ Mascot Stanley Panther
- ☐ Prince of Wales Trophy

'97 - 98 FLOR.
WINN-DIXIE

This set was issued as a four panel album. The first panel features a collage of Panthers' photos. The next two panels can be cut out into 12 cards, while the last panel can be cut out into 6 cards plus one Winn-Dixie/ Broward County Arena ad card. The most expensive cut-out single is John Vanbiesbrouck at $3-4. Singles start at 50¢. An uncut album sells at $20.

Card Size: 2 1/2" x 3 1/8"
Sponsor: Winn-Dixie
Set (30 cards): $18

- ☐ Kevin Weekes #1 (G)
- ☐ J. Vanbiesbrouck #34 (G)
- ☐ Terry Carkner #2
- ☐ Paul Laus #3
- ☐ Gord Murphy #5
- ☐ Jeff Norton #6
- ☐ Rhett Warrener #7
- ☐ Dallas Eakins #8
- ☐ Kirk Muller #9
- ☐ Esa Tikkanen #10
- ☐ Bill Lindsay #11
- ☐ Ray Whitney #14
- ☐ Dave Gagner #15
- ☐ Steve Washburn #17
- ☐ Radek Dvorak #19
- ☐ Tom Fitzgerald #21
- ☐ Dino Ciccarelli #22
- ☐ Chris Wells #23
- ☐ Robert Svehla #24
- ☐ Viktor Kozlov #25
- ☐ Ray Sheppard #26
- ☐ Scott Mellanby #27
- ☐ Johan Garpenlov #29
- ☐ Rob Niedermayer #44
- ☐ Ed Jovanovski #55
- ☐ Bryan Murray, Coach
- ☐ Duane Sutter, A. Coach
- ☐ Joe Cirella, Asst. Coach
- ☐ Billy Smith, Goal Coach
- ☐ Mascot Stanley Panther

'01 - 02 FLOR.

Other singles exist.

- ☐ Valeri Bure
- ☐ Niklas Hagman
- ☐ Kristian Huselius
- ☐ Ryan Johnson
- ☐ Olli Jokinen
- ☐ Mike Keenan
- ☐ Trevor Kidd
- ☐ Viktor Kozlov
- ☐ Roberto Luongo
- ☐ Sandis Ozolinsh
- ☐ Jason Wiemer

'02 - 03 FLOR.

We do not have a checklist for this series of postcards.

HARTFORD WHALERS

'82 - 83 HART.
JUNIOR WHALERS

Ron Francis is the most expensive single at $20. Singles start at $1.50.

Card Size: 3 1/4" x 6 3/8"
Sponsors: Hartford Courant, Junior Whalers Fan Club
Set (22 cards): $50

- ☐ Greg C. Adams
- ☐ Russ Anderson
- ☐ Ron Francis
- ☐ Michel Galarneau
- ☐ Dan Fridgen
- ☐ Archie Henderson
- ☐ Ed Hospodar
- ☐ Mark Johnson
- ☐ Chris Kotsopoulos
- ☐ Pierre Larouche
- ☐ George Lyle
- ☐ Greg Millen (G)
- ☐ Warren Miller
- ☐ Ray Neufeld
- ☐ Mark Renaud
- ☐ Risto Siltanen
- ☐ Stuart Smith
- ☐ Blaine Stoughton
- ☐ Doug Sullivan
- ☐ Bob Sullivan
- ☐ Mike Veisor (G)
- ☐ Mickey Volcan
- ☐ Blake Wesley

'83 - 84 HART.
JUNIOR WHALERS

Ron Francis is the most expensive single at $12. Singles start at $1.50.

Card Size: 3 3/4" x 8 1/4"
Sponsors: Hartford Courant, Junior Whalers Fan Club
Set (22 cards): $45

- ☐ Bob Crawford
- ☐ Mike Crombeen
- ☐ Richie Dunn
- ☐ Normand Dupont
- ☐ Ron Francis
- ☐ Ed Hospodar
- ☐ Marty Howe
- ☐ Mark Johnson
- ☐ Chris Kotsopoulos
- ☐ Pierre Lacroix
- ☐ Greg Malone
- ☐ Greg Millen (G)
- ☐ Ray Neufeld
- ☐ Joel Quenneville
- ☐ Torrie Robertson
- ☐ Risto Siltanen
- ☐ Blaine Stoughton
- ☐ Steve Stoyanovich
- ☐ Doug Sullivan
- ☐ Sylvain Turgeon
- ☐ Mike Veisor (G)
- ☐ Mike Zuke

'84 - 85 HART.
JUNIOR WHALERS

Ron Francis is the most expensive single at $10. Singles start at $1.50.

Card Size: 3 3/4" x 8 1/4"
Sponsors: Wendy's, Junior Whalers Fan Club
lete Set (22 cards): $40

- ☐ Jack Brownschidle
- ☐ Sylvain Côté
- ☐ Bob Crawford
- ☐ Mike Crombeen
- ☐ Tony Currie
- ☐ Ron Francis
- ☐ Mark Fusco
- ☐ Dave Jensen
- ☐ Mark Johnson
- ☐ Chris Kotsopoulos
- ☐ Greg Malone
- ☐ Greg Millen (G)
- ☐ Ray Neufeld
- ☐ Randy Pierce
- ☐ Joel Quenneville
- ☐ Torrie Robertson
- ☐ Ulf Samuelsson
- ☐ Risto Siltanen
- ☐ Dave Tippett
- ☐ Sylvain Turgeon
- ☐ Steve Weeks (G)
- ☐ Mike Zuke

'85 - 86 HART.
JUNIOR WHALERS

Ron Francis is the most expensive single at $7. Singles start at $1.50.

Card Size: 3 3/4" x 8 1/4"
Sponsors: Wendy's, Junior Whalers Fan Club
lete Set (23 cards): $35

- ☐ Jack Brownschidle
- ☐ Sylvain Côté

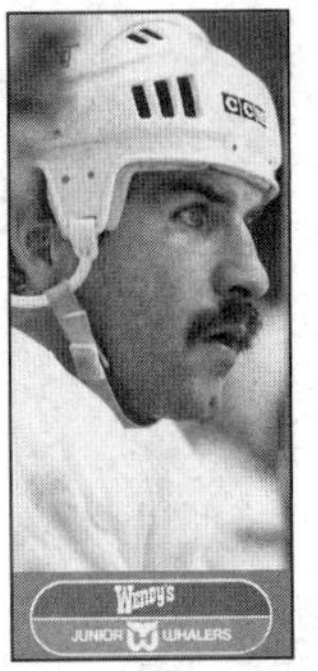

- ☐ Bob Crawford
- ☐ Kevin Dineen
- ☐ Paul Fenton
- ☐ Ray Ferraro
- ☐ Ron Francis
- ☐ Scott Kleinendorst
- ☐ Paul Lawless
- ☐ Mike Liut (G)
- ☐ Paul MacDermid
- ☐ Greg Malone
- ☐ Dana Murzyn
- ☐ Ray Neufeld
- ☐ Jorgen Pettersson
- ☐ Joel Quenneville
- ☐ Torrie Robertson
- ☐ Ulf Samuelsson
- ☐ Risto Siltanen
- ☐ Dave Tippett
- ☐ Sylvain Turgeon
- ☐ Steve Weeks (G)
- ☐ Mike Zuke

'86 - 87 HART.
JUNIOR WHALERS

Ron Francis is the most expensive single at $7. Singles start at $1.50.

Card Size: 3 3/4" x 8 1/4"
Sponsors: Thomas', Junior Whalers Fan Club
Set (23 cards): $35

- ☐ John Anderson
- ☐ Dave Babych
- ☐ Wayne Babych
- ☐ Sylvain Côté
- ☐ Kevin Dineen
- ☐ Dean Evason
- ☐ Ray Ferraro
- ☐ Ron Francis
- ☐ Bill Gardner
- ☐ Stewart Gavin
- ☐ Doug Jarvis
- ☐ Scott Kleinendorst
- ☐ Paul Lawless
- ☐ Mike Liut (G)
- ☐ Paul MacDermid
- ☐ Mike McEwen
- ☐ Dana Murzyn
- ☐ Joel Quenneville
- ☐ Torrie Robertson
- ☐ Ulf Samuelsson
- ☐ Dave Tippett
- ☐ Sylvain Turgeon
- ☐ Steve Weeks (G)

'87 - 88 HART.
JUNIOR WHALERS

Ron Francis is the most expensive single at $6. Singles start at $1.50.

Card Size: 3 3/4" x 8 1/4"
Sponsors: Burger King, Pepsi, Junior Whalers Fan Club
Set (21 cards): $30

- ☐ John Anderson
- ☐ Dave Babych
- ☐ Sylvain Côté
- ☐ Kevin Dineen
- ☐ Dean Evason
- ☐ Ray Ferraro
- ☐ Ron Francis
- ☐ Stewart Gavin
- ☐ Doug Jarvis
- ☐ Scott Kleinendorst
- ☐ Randy Ladouceur
- ☐ Paul Lawless
- ☐ Mike Liut (G)
- ☐ Paul MacDermid
- ☐ Dana Murzyn
- ☐ Joel Quenneville

- ☐ Torrie Robertson
- ☐ Ulf Samuelsson
- ☐ Dave Tippett
- ☐ Sylvain Turgeon
- ☐ Steve Weeks (G)

'88 - 89 HART.
JUNIOR WHALERS

Ron Francis is the most expensive single at $5. Singles start $1.50.
Card Size: 3 11/16" x 8 1/4"
Sponsors: Ground Round, Pepsi, Junior Whalers Fan Club
Set (18 cards): $25

- ☐ John Anderson
- ☐ Dave Babych
- ☐ Sylvain Côté
- ☐ Kevin Dineen
- ☐ Dean Evason
- ☐ Ray Ferraro
- ☐ Ron Francis
- ☐ Scott Kleinendorst
- ☐ Randy Ladouceur
- ☐ Mike Liut (G)
- ☐ Paul MacDermid
- ☐ Brent Peterson
- ☐ Joel Quenneville
- ☐ Torrie Robertson
- ☐ Ulf Samuelsson
- ☐ Dave Tippett
- ☐ Sylvain Turgeon
- ☐ Carey Wilson

'89 - 90 HART.
JUNIOR WHALERS

Ron Francis is the most expensive single at $5. Singles start at $1. Ed Kastelic, Todd Krygier and Mike Tomlak were added late in the season and sell at $2-3. A 21-card set without the three update players sells at $20.
Card Size: 3 11/16" x 8 1/4"
Sponsors: Milk, Junior Whalers Fan Club
Set (24 cards): $25

- ☐ Mikael Andersson
- ☐ Dave Babych
- ☐ Sylvain Côté
- ☐ Randy Cunneyworth
- ☐ Kevin Dineen
- ☐ Dean Evason
- ☐ Ray Ferraro
- ☐ Ron Francis
- ☐ Jody Hull
- ☐ Grant Jennings
- ☐ Randy Ladouceur
- ☐ Brian Lawton
- ☐ Mike Liut (G)
- ☐ Paul MacDermid
- ☐ Joel Quenneville
- ☐ Ulf Samuelsson
- ☐ Brad Shaw
- ☐ Peter Sidorkiewicz (G)
- ☐ Dave Tippett
- ☐ Pat Verbeek
- ☐ Scott Young
- ☐ Ed Kastelic
- ☐ Todd Krygier
- ☐ Mike Tomlak

'90 - 91 HART.
JUNIOR WHALERS

Gordie Howe is the most expensive single at $6. Singles start at $75¢. Rob Brown, Chris Goverdaris, Jim McKenzie and Daryl Reaugh are short printed and sell at $2-3. A 23-card set sells at $15.
Card Size: 3 3/4" x 8 1/4"
Sponsors: 7-Eleven, Junior Whalers Fan Club
Set (27 cards): $22

- ☐ Mikael Andersson
- ☐ Dave Babych
- ☐ Yvon Corriveau
- ☐ Sylvain Côté
- ☐ Doug Crossman
- ☐ Randy Cunneyworth
- ☐ Paul Cyr
- ☐ Kevin Dineen
- ☐ Dean Evason
- ☐ Ron Francis
- ☐ Bobby Holik
- ☐ Gordie Howe
- ☐ Grant Jennings
- ☐ Ed Kastelic
- ☐ Todd Krygier
- ☐ Randy Ladouceur
- ☐ Ulf Samuelsson
- ☐ Brad Shaw
- ☐ Peter Sidorkiewicz (G)
- ☐ Mike Tomlak
- ☐ Pat Verbeek
- ☐ Carey Wilson
- ☐ Scott Young
- ☐ Rob Brown
- ☐ Chris Govedaris
- ☐ Jim McKenzie
- ☐ Daryl Reaugh (G)

'91 - 92 HART.
JUNIOR WHALERS

Geoff Sanderson is the most expensive single at $4. Singles start at 75¢. James Black, Paul Cyr, Paul Gillis, Dan Keczmer, and Steve Konroyd are short printed and sell at $2-3. Andrew Cassels is also short printed and sells at $3-4. A 22-card set sells at $15.
Card Size: 3 3/4" x 8 1/4"
Sponsors: 7-Eleven, Junior Whalers Fan Club
Set (28 cards): $28

- ☐ Mikael Andersson
- ☐ Marc Bergevin
- ☐ Rob Brown
- ☐ Adam Burt
- ☐ Murray Craven
- ☐ John Cullen
- ☐ Randy Cunneyworth
- ☐ Joe Day
- ☐ Mark Greig
- ☐ Bobby Holik
- ☐ Doug Houda
- ☐ Mark Hunter
- ☐ Ed Kastelic
- ☐ Randy Ladouceur
- ☐ Jim McKenzie
- ☐ Michel Picard
- ☐ Geoff Sanderson
- ☐ Brad Shaw
- ☐ Peter Sidorkiewicz (G)
- ☐ Pat Verbeek
- ☐ Kay Whitmore (G)
- ☐ Zarley Zalapski
- ☐ James Black
- ☐ Andrew Cassels
- ☐ Paul Cyr
- ☐ Paul Gillis
- ☐ Dan Keczmer
- ☐ Steve Konroyd

'91 - 93 HART.
DAIRY MART

Sean Burke and Geoff Sanderson are the most expensive singles at $3-4. Singles start at 75¢.
Card Size: 2 3/8" x 3 1/2"
Sponsors: Dairy Mart, Junior Whalers Fan Club
Set (26 cards): $25

- ☐ Jim Agnew
- ☐ Sean Burke (G)
- ☐ Adam Burt
- ☐ Andrew Cassels
- ☐ Murray Craven
- ☐ Randy Cunneyworth
- ☐ Paul Gillis
- ☐ Paul Holmgren
- ☐ Doug Houda
- ☐ Mark Janssens
- ☐ Tim Kerr
- ☐ Steve Konroyd
- ☐ Nick Kypreos
- ☐ Randy Ladouceur
- ☐ Jim McKenzie
- ☐ Michael Nylander
- ☐ Allen Pedersen
- ☐ Robert Petrovicky
- ☐ Frank Pietrangelo (G)
- ☐ Patrick Poulin
- ☐ Geoff Sanderson
- ☐ Pat Verbeek
- ☐ Eric Weinrich
- ☐ Terry Yake
- ☐ Zarley Zalapski

'93 - 94 HART.
COCA-COLA

Chris Pronger is the most expensive single at $5. Singles start at 75¢.
Card Size: 2 3/8" x 3 1/2"
Sponsor: Coca-Cola
Set (24 cards): $25

- ☐ Sean Burke (G)
- ☐ Adam Burt
- ☐ Andrew Cassels
- ☐ Randy Cunneyworth
- ☐ Alexander Godynyuk
- ☐ Mark Greig
- ☐ Mark Janssens
- ☐ Robert Kron
- ☐ Bryan Marchment
- ☐ Brad McCrimmon
- ☐ Pierre McGuire
- ☐ Michael Nylander
- ☐ James Patrick
- ☐ Frank Pietrangelo (G)
- ☐ Marc Potvin
- ☐ Chris Pronger
- ☐ Brian Propp
- ☐ Jeff Reese (G)
- ☐ Geoff Sanderson
- ☐ Jim Sandlak
- ☐ Jim Storm
- ☐ Darren Turcotte
- ☐ Pat Verbeek
- ☐ Zarley Zalapski

'95 - 96 HART.
KIDS CLUB

The most expensive single is Brendan Shanahan at $4. Singles start at 50¢.
Set (26 cards): $22

- ☐ Sean Burke (G)
- ☐ Adam Burt
- ☐ Andrew Cassels
- ☐ Kelly Chase
- ☐ Scott Daniels
- ☐ Gerald Diduck
- ☐ Nelson Emerson
- ☐ Glen Featherstone
- ☐ Brian Glynn
- ☐ Mark Janssens
- ☐ Robert Kron
- ☐ Frantisek Kucera
- ☐ Jocelyn Lemieux
- ☐ Marek Malik
- ☐ Steve Martins
- ☐ Paul Maurice
- ☐ Brad McCrimmon
- ☐ Jason Muzzatti
- ☐ Andrei Nikolishin
- ☐ Jeff O'Neill
- ☐ Paul Ranheim
- ☐ Steven Rice
- ☐ Geoff Sanderson
- ☐ Brendan Shanahan
- ☐ Kevin Smyth
- ☐ Glen Wesley

'96 - 97 HART.
KIDS CLUB

The most expensive single is Keith Primeau at $3. Singles start at 50¢.
Set (26 cards): $20

- ☐ Jeff R. Brown
- ☐ Sean Burke (G)
- ☐ Adam Burt
- ☐ Andrew Cassels
- ☐ Kelly Chase
- ☐ Steve Chiasson
- ☐ Gerald Diduck
- ☐ Kevin Dineen
- ☐ Hnat Domenichelli
- ☐ Nelson Emerson
- ☐ Glen Featherstone
- ☐ Alexander Godynyuk
- ☐ Stu Grimson
- ☐ Mark Janssens
- ☐ Sami Kapanen
- ☐ Robert Kron
- ☐ Curtis Leschyshyn
- ☐ Marek Malik
- ☐ Kent Manderville
- ☐ Jason Muzzatti
- ☐ Jeff O'Neill
- ☐ Nolan Pratt
- ☐ Keith Primeau
- ☐ Paul Ranheim
- ☐ Steven Rice
- ☐ Geoff Sanderson
- ☐ Glen Wesley

LOS ANGELES KINGS

'80 - 81 LOSA.

Marcel Dionne is the most expensive single at $8. Singles start at $1. A total of 5,000 sets were given away at the Kings' "Card Night".
Card Size: 2 1/2" x 3 1/2"
Sponsor: None
Set (14 cards): $22

- ☐ 1 Marcel Dionne
- ☐ 2 Glenn Goldup
- ☐ 3 Doug Halward
- ☐ 4 Billy Harris
- ☐ 5 Steve Jensen
- ☐ 6 Jerry Korab
- ☐ 7 Mario Lessard (G)
- ☐ 8 Dave Lewis
- ☐ 9 Mike Murphy
- ☐ 10 Rob Palmer
- ☐ 11 Charlie Simmer
- ☐ 12 Dave Taylor
- ☐ 13 Garry Unger
- ☐ 14 Jay Wells

'84 - 85 LOSA.
SMOKEY THE BEAR

Marcel Dionne is the most expensive single at $7. Singles start at $1.
Card Size: 2 15/16" x 4 3/8"
Sponsor: Smokey The Bear
Set (23 cards): $22

- ☐ 1 Russ Anderson
- ☐ 2 Marcel Dionne
- ☐ 3 Brian Engblom
- ☐ 4 Daryl Evans
- ☐ 5 Jim Fox
- ☐ 6 Garry Galley
- ☐ 7 Anders Hakansson
- ☐ 8 Mark Hardy
- ☐ 9 Bob Janecyk (G)
- ☐ 10 John P. Kelly
- ☐ 11 Brian MacLellan
- ☐ 12 Bernie Nicholls
- ☐ 13 Craig Redmond
- ☐ 14 Terry Ruskowski
- ☐ 15 Doug Smith
- ☐ 16 Dave Taylor
- ☐ 17 Jay Wells
- ☐ 18 Daren Eliot (G)
- ☐ 19 Rick Lapointe
- ☐ 20 Bob Miller
- ☐ 21 Steve Seguin
- ☐ 22 Phil Sykes
- ☐ 23 Pat Quinn, Coach

'87 - 88 LOSA.

Luc Robitaille is the most expensive single at $12. Singles start $1.
Card Size: 4" x 6"
Sponsor: None
Set (23 cards): $35

- ☐ Bob Bourne
- ☐ Jimmy Carson
- ☐ Steve Duchesne
- ☐ Daren Eliot (G)
- ☐ Bryan Erickson
- ☐ Jim Fox
- ☐ Garry Galley
- ☐ Paul Guay
- ☐ Mark Hardy
- ☐ Bob Janecyk (G)
- ☐ Dean Kennedy
- ☐ Grant Ledyard
- ☐ Morris Lukowich
- ☐ Sean McKenna
- ☐ Roland Melanson (G)
- ☐ Bernie Nicholls
- ☐ Joe Paterson
- ☐ Larry Playfair
- ☐ Luc Robitaille
- ☐ Phil Sykes
- ☐ Dave Taylor
- ☐ Jay Wells
- ☐ Dave Williams

'88 - 89 LOSA.
SOMKEY THE BEAR

The most expensive singles are Wayne Gretzky at $20 and Luc Robitaille at $4-5. Singles start at 75¢.
Card Size: 2 1/2" x 3 1/2"
Sponsor: Smokey The Bear
Set (25 cards): $30

- ☐ Mike Allison
- ☐ Ken Baumgartner
- ☐ Bob Carpenter
- ☐ Doug Crossman
- ☐ Dale DeGray
- ☐ Steve Duchesne
- ☐ Ron Duguay
- ☐ Mark Fitzpatrick (G)
- ☐ Jim Fox
- ☐ Robbie Ftorek
- ☐ Wayne Gretzky
- ☐ Gilles Hamel
- ☐ Glenn Healy (G)
- ☐ Mike Krushelnyski
- ☐ Tom Laidlaw
- ☐ Bryan Maxwell
- ☐ Wayne McBean
- ☐ Marty McSorley
- ☐ Bernie Nicholls
- ☐ Cap Raedar
- ☐ Luc Robitaille
- ☐ Dave Taylor
- ☐ John Tonelli
- ☐ Tim Watters
- ☐ Checklist

'89 - 90 LOSA.
SMOKEY THE BEAR

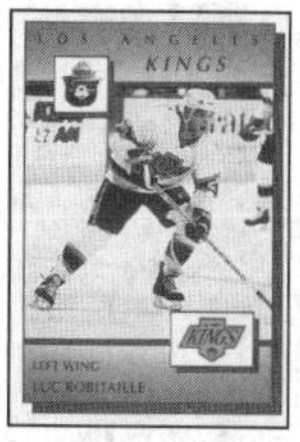

The most expensive singles are Wayne Gretzky at $15 and Luc Robitaille at $3-4. Singles start at 75¢.
Card Size: 2 1/2" x 3 1/2"
Sponsor: Smokey The Bear
Set (25 cards): $30

- ☐ 1 Wayne Gretzky
- ☐ 2 Tim Watters
- ☐ 3 Mikael Lindholm
- ☐ 4 Mike Allison
- ☐ 5 Steve Kasper
- ☐ 6 Dave Taylor
- ☐ 7 Larry Robinson
- ☐ 8 Luc Robitaille
- ☐ 9 Barry Beck
- ☐ 10 Keith Crowder
- ☐ 11 Petr Prajsler
- ☐ 12 Mike Krushelnyski
- ☐ 13 John Tonelli
- ☐ 14 Steve Duchesne
- ☐ 15 Jay Miller
- ☐ 16 Kelly Hrudey
- ☐ 17 Marty McSorley
- ☐ 18 Mario Gosselin (G)
- ☐ 19 Craig Duncanson
- ☐ 20 Bob Kudelski
- ☐ 21 Brian Benning
- ☐ 22 Mikko Mäkelä
- ☐ 23 Tom Laidlaw
- ☐ 24 Checklist

'90 - 91 LOSA.
SMOKEY THE BEAR

The most expensive singles are Wayne Gretzky at $10 and Luc Robitaille at $2. Singles start at 75¢.
Card Size: 2 1/2" x 3 1/2"
Sponsor: Smokey The Bear
Set (25 cards): $25

- ☐ 1 Wayne Gretzky
- ☐ 2 Brian Benning
- ☐ 3 Rob Blake
- ☐ 4 Tim Watters
- ☐ 5 Todd Elik
- ☐ 6 Tomas Sandstrom
- ☐ 7 Steve Kasper
- ☐ 8 Dave Taylor
- ☐ 9 Larry Robinson
- ☐ 10 Luc Robitaille
- ☐ 11 Tony Granato
- ☐ 12 Tom Laidlaw
- ☐ 13 François Breault
- ☐ 14 John Tonelli
- ☐ 15 Steve Duchesne
- ☐ 16 Jay Miller
- ☐ 17 Kelly Hrudey (G)
- ☐ 18 Marty McSorley
- ☐ 19 Daniel Berthiaume (G)
- ☐ 20 Bob Kudelski
- ☐ 21 Brad Jones
- ☐ 22 John McIntyre
- ☐ 23 Rod Buskas
- ☐ 24 Mascot Kingston
- ☐ Kings/ RC challenge

'91 - 92 LOSA.
25th ANNIVERSARY

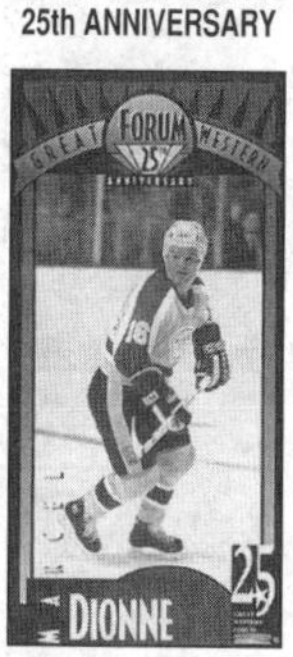

This 25th Anniversary Great Western Forum set features only three hockey players. Wayne Gretzky sells at $15-20, Rogatien Vachon sells at $3-4 and Marcel Dionne sells at $4-5.
Sponsor: None

- ☐ Marcel Dionne
- ☐ Wayne Gretzky
- ☐ Rogatien Vachon (G)

'02 - 03 LOSA.

We do not have a checklist for this series of cards.

MINNESOTA NORTH STARS

'70 - 71 MINN.

Gump Worsley is the most expensive card at $10. Singles start at $3.
Card Size: 3 1/2" x 5 1/2"
Sponsor: None

- ☐ Barry Gibbs
- ☐ Bill Goldsworthy
- ☐ Danny Grant
- ☐ Ted Harris
- ☐ Césare Maniago (G)
- ☐ Jean-Paul Parise
- ☐ Tom Reid
- ☐ Bobby Rousseau
- ☐ Tom Williams
- ☐ Gump Worsley (G)

'73 - 74 MINN.

Gump Worsley is the most expensive single at $6 in NM. Singles start at $1.50.
Card Size: 3 5/8" x 5"
Sponsor: None
Set (20 cards): $30

- ☐ Fred Barrett
- ☐ Gary Bergman
- ☐ Jude Drouin
- ☐ Tony Featherstone
- ☐ Barry Gibbs
- ☐ Bill Goldsworthy
- ☐ Danny Grant
- ☐ Buster Harvey
- ☐ Dennis Hextall
- ☐ Parker MacDonald
- ☐ Césare Maniago (G)
- ☐ Lou Nanne
- ☐ Rod Norrish
- ☐ Dennis O'Brien
- ☐ Murray Oliver
- ☐ Jean-Paul Parise
- ☐ Dean Prentice
- ☐ Tom Reid
- ☐ Fred Stanfield
- ☐ Gump Worsley (G)

'78 - 79 MINN.
CLOVERLEAF DAIRY

These two-card panels were found on the backs of milk cartons and are available with either a red or purple tint. The Bobby Smith/Gary Edwards panel is the most expensive at $25-30 in NM. Singles start at $12.
Panel Size: 3 3/4" x 7 5/8"
Sponsor: Cloverleaf Dairy
Set (9 panels): $150

- ☐ 1 Meloche (G)/ Sargent
- ☐ 2 Barrett/- Brasar
- ☐ 3 Parise/ Smith
- ☐ 4 MacAdam/ Andersson
- ☐ 5 Edwards(G)/ Smith
- ☐ 6 Polich/ Maxwell
- ☐ 7 Payne/ Sharpley
- ☐ 8 Young/ Manery
- ☐ 9 Zanussi/ Younghams

'79 - 80 MINN.

Card fronts are in black & white. Card backs feature a North Stars logo in the top left corner. Bobby Smith is the most expensive single at $5 in NM. Singles start at $1. Other singles may exist.
Postcard Size: 3 1/2" x 5 1/2"
Sponsor: None

- ☐ Kent-Erik Andersson
- ☐ Fred Barrett

- ☐ Gary Edwards (G)
- ☐ Mike Fidler
- ☐ Craig Hartsburg
- ☐ Al MacAdam
- ☐ Kris Manery
- ☐ Brad Maxwell
- ☐ Tom McCarthy
- ☐ Gilles Meloche (G)
- ☐ Steve Payne
- ☐ Mike Polich
- ☐ Gary Sargent
- ☐ Paul Schmyr
- ☐ Bobby Smith
- ☐ Greg Smith
- ☐ Glen Sonmor
- ☐ Tim Young
- ☐ Tom Younghams
- ☐ Ron Zanussi

'80 - 81 MINN.

The most expensive singles are Bobby Smith and Jack Carlson ('70s movie Slap Shot) sell at $3-4. Singles start at $1.

Postcard Size: 3 1/2" x 5 1/2"
Sponsor: None
Set (24 cards): $25

- ☐ Kent-Erik Andersson
- ☐ Fred Barrett
- ☐ Don Beaupré (G)
- ☐ Jack Carlson
- ☐ Steve Christoff
- ☐ Mike Eaves
- ☐ Gary Edwards (G)
- ☐ Curt Giles
- ☐ Craig Hartsburg
- ☐ Al MacAdam
- ☐ Brad Maxwell
- ☐ Tom McCarthy
- ☐ Gilles Meloche (G)
- ☐ Steve Payne
- ☐ Mike Polich
- ☐ Gary Sargent
- ☐ Glen Sharpley
- ☐ Paul Schmyr
- ☐ Bobby Smith
- ☐ Greg Smith
- ☐ Tim Young
- ☐ Tom Younghams
- ☐ Ron Zanussi
- ☐ Oliver/ Parise/ Somner

'81 - 82 MINN.

The most expensive singles are Dino Ciccarelli at $8 and Neal Broten at $4-5 Singles start at $1.

Postcard Size: 3 1/2" x 5 1/2"
Sponsor: None
Set (24 cards): $30

- ☐ Kent-Erik Andersson
- ☐ Fred Barrett
- ☐ Don Beaupré (G)
- ☐ Neal Broten
- ☐ Jack Carlson
- ☐ Steve Christoff
- ☐ Dino Ciccarelli
- ☐ Mike Eaves
- ☐ Anders Hakansson
- ☐ Craig Hartsburg
- ☐ Al MacAdam
- ☐ Brad Maxwell
- ☐ Kevin Maxwell
- ☐ Tom McCarthy
- ☐ Gilles Meloche (G)
- ☐ Bill Nyrop
- ☐ Steve Payne
- ☐ Brad Palmer
- ☐ Gordie Roberts
- ☐ Gary Sargent
- ☐ Bobby Smith
- ☐ Tim Young
- ☐ Oliver/ Parise/ Somner

'82 - 83 MINN.

Dino Ciccarelli is the most expensive single at $5. Singles start $1.

Postcard Size: 3 1/2" x 5 1/2"
Sponsor: None
Set (24 cards): $25

- ☐ Fred Barrett
- ☐ Don Beaupré (G)
- ☐ Brian Bellows
- ☐ Neal Broten
- ☐ Dino Ciccarelli
- ☐ Jordy Douglas
- ☐ Mike Eaves
- ☐ George Ferguson
- ☐ Ron Friest
- ☐ Curt Giles
- ☐ Craig Hartsburg
- ☐ Al MacAdam
- ☐ Dan Mandich
- ☐ Brad Maxwell
- ☐ Tom McCarthy
- ☐ Gilles Meloche (G)
- ☐ Steve Payne
- ☐ Willi Plett
- ☐ Gordie Roberts
- ☐ Gary Sargent
- ☐ Bobby Smith
- ☐ Ken Solheim
- ☐ Tim Young
- ☐ D. Ciccarelli/ B. Wellows
- ☐ Team Photo

'83 - 84 MINN.

Dino Ciccarelli is the most expensive single at $3. Singles start $1.

Postcard Size: 3 1/2" x 5 1/2"
Sponsor: None
Set (27 cards): $25

- ☐ Keith Acton
- ☐ Brent Ashton
- ☐ Don Beaupré (G)
- ☐ Brian Bellows
- ☐ Neal Broten
- ☐ Dino Ciccarelli
- ☐ Jordy Douglas
- ☐ George Ferguson
- ☐ Curt Giles
- ☐ Craig Hartsburg
- ☐ Brian Lawton
- ☐ Craig Levie
- ☐ Lars Lindgren
- ☐ Al MacAdam
- ☐ Bill Mahoney, Coach
- ☐ Dan Mandich
- ☐ Dennis Maruk
- ☐ Brad Maxwell
- ☐ Tom McCarthy
- ☐ Gilles Meloche (G)
- ☐ Mark Napier
- ☐ Steve Payne
- ☐ Willi Plett
- ☐ Dave Richter
- ☐ Gordie Roberts
- ☐ Randy Velischek
- ☐ Team Photo

'84 - 85 MINN.

Dino Ciccarelli is the most expensive single at $3. Singles start at $1.

Postcard Size: 3 1/2" x 5 1/2"
Sponsor: None
Set (25 cards): $20

- ☐ Keith Acton
- ☐ Don Beaupré (G)
- ☐ Brian Bellows
- ☐ Scott Bjugstad
- ☐ Neal Broten
- ☐ Dino Ciccarelli
- ☐ Curt Giles
- ☐ Craig Hartsburg
- ☐ Tom Hirsch
- ☐ Paul Holmgren
- ☐ Brian Lawton
- ☐ Dan Mandich
- ☐ Dennis Maruk
- ☐ Brad Maxwell
- ☐ Tom McCarthy
- ☐ Roland Melanson (G)
- ☐ Gilles Meloche (G)
- ☐ Mark Napier
- ☐ Steve Payne
- ☐ Willi Plett
- ☐ Dave Richter
- ☐ Gordie Roberts
- ☐ Bob Rouse
- ☐ Harold Snepts
- ☐ Ken Solheim

'84 - 85 MINN.
7-ELEVEN

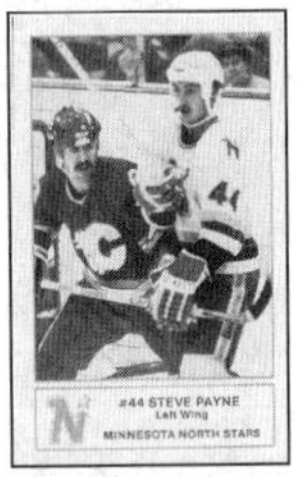

Dino Ciccarelli is the most expensive single at $3. Singles start at $1.

Card Size: 2 5/8" x 4 1/4"
Sponsor: 7-Eleven
Set (12 cards): $15

- ☐ 1 Neal Broten
- ☐ 2 Willi Plett
- ☐ 3 Craig Hartsburg
- ☐ 4 Brian Bellows
- ☐ 5 Gordie Roberts
- ☐ 6 Keith Acton
- ☐ 7 Paul Holmgren
- ☐ 8 Gilles Meloche (G)
- ☐ 9 Dennis Maruk
- ☐ 10 Tom McCarthy
- ☐ 11 Steve Payne
- ☐ 12 Dino Ciccarelli

'85 - 86 MINN.
7-ELEVEN

Dino Ciccarelli is the most expensive single at $2. Singles start at $1.

Postcard Size: 3 1/2" x 5 1/2"
Sponsor: None
Set (27 cards): $20

- ☐ Keith Acton
- ☐ Don Beaupré (G)
- ☐ Brian Bellows
- ☐ Bo Berglund
- ☐ Scott Bjugstad
- ☐ Neal Broten
- ☐ Jon Casey (G)
- ☐ Dino Ciccarelli
- ☐ Tim Coulis
- ☐ Curt Giles
- ☐ Craig Hartsburg
- ☐ Dirk Graham
- ☐ Mats Hallin
- ☐ Craig Hartsburg
- ☐ Tom Hirsch
- ☐ Dave Langevin
- ☐ Brian Lawton
- ☐ Craig Levie
- ☐ Dan Mandich
- ☐ Dennis Maruk
- ☐ Tom McCarthy
- ☐ Tony McKegney
- ☐ Rollie Melanson (G)
- ☐ Steve Payne
- ☐ Gordie Roberts
- ☐ Bob Rouse
- ☐ Gord Shervan

'85 - 86 MINN.
7-ELEVEN

Dino Ciccarelli is the most expensive single at $2. Singles start at $1.

Card Size: 2 1/2" x 3 1/2"
Sponsor: 7-Eleven
Set (12 cards): $12

- ☐ 1 Dino Ciccarelli
- ☐ 2 Scott Bjugstad
- ☐ 3 Curt Giles
- ☐ 4 Don Beaupré (G)

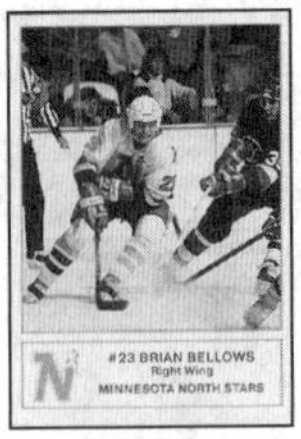

- ☐ 5 Tony McKegney
- ☐ 6 Neal Broten
- ☐ 7 Willi Plett
- ☐ 8 Craig Hartsburg
- ☐ 9 Brian Bellows
- ☐ 10 Keith Acton
- ☐ 11 Dave Langevin
- ☐ 12 Dirk Graham

'86 - 87 MINN.
7-ELEVEN

Dino Ciccarelli is the most expensive single at $2. Singles start at 75¢.

Card Size: 2 1/2" x 3 1/2"
Sponsor: 7-Eleven
Set (12 cards): $15

- ☐ 1 Neal Broten
- ☐ 2 Brian MacLellan
- ☐ 3 Willi Plett
- ☐ 4 Scott Bjugstad
- ☐ 5 Don Beaupré (G)
- ☐ 6 Dino Ciccarelli
- ☐ 7 Craig Hartsburg
- ☐ 8 Dennis Maruk
- ☐ 9 Bob Rouse
- ☐ 10 Gordie Roberts
- ☐ 11 Bob Brooke
- ☐ 12 Brian Bellows

'87 - 88 MINN.

The most expensive singles are Dino Ciccarelli and Dave Gagner at $2-3. Singles start at 75¢.

Postcard Size: 3 1/2" x 5 1/2"
Sponsor: None
Set (31 cards): $20

- ☐ Keith Acton
- ☐ Dave Archibald
- ☐ Warren Babe
- ☐ Don Beaupré (G)
- ☐ Brian Bellows
- ☐ Mike Berger
- ☐ Scott Bjugstad
- ☐ Bob Brooke
- ☐ Herb Brooks
- ☐ Neal Broten
- ☐ Dino Ciccarelli
- ☐ Larry DePalma
- ☐ Dave Gagner
- ☐ Curt Giles
- ☐ Dirk Graham
- ☐ Craig Hartsburg
- ☐ Tom Hirsch
- ☐ Brian Lawton
- ☐ Brian MacLellan
- ☐ Dennis Maruk
- ☐ Basil McRae
- ☐ Frank Musil
- ☐ Steve Payne
- ☐ Pat Price
- ☐ Chris Pryor
- ☐ Gordie Roberts
- ☐ Bob Rouse
- ☐ Terry Ruskowski
- ☐ Kari Takko (G)
- ☐ Ron Wilson
- ☐ Richard Zemlak

'88 - 89 MINN.
AMERICAN DAIRY

Dino Ciccarelli is the most expensive card at $2. Singles start at 75¢.

Card Size: 3 1/2" x 7 1/8"
Sponsor: American Dairy Assoc.

- ☐ Brian Bellows
- ☐ Bob Brooke
- ☐ Neal Broten
- ☐ Jon Casey (G)
- ☐ Shawn Chambers
- ☐ Dino Ciccarelli
- ☐ Larry DePalma
- ☐ Curt Fraser
- ☐ Link Gaetz
- ☐ Dave Gagner
- ☐ Stewart Gavin
- ☐ Curt Giles
- ☐ Marc Habscheid
- ☐ Mark Hardy
- ☐ Craig Hartsburg
- ☐ Brian MacLellan
- ☐ Moe Mantha
- ☐ Basil McRae
- ☐ Frank Musil
- ☐ Dusan Pasek
- ☐ Bob Rouse
- ☐ Terry Ruskowski
- ☐ Kari Takko (G)

MINNESOTA WILD

'01 - 02 MINW.
CRIME PREVENTION

This multi-sport set also features players fromthe Twins and Vikings.

Card Size: 2 1/2" x 3 1/2"
Hockey Set (8 cards): $15

- ☐ 17 Willie Mitchell
- ☐ 18 Marian Gaborik
- ☐ 19 Darby Hendrickson
- ☐ 20 Andrew Brunette
- ☐ 21 Sergei Zholtok
- ☐ 22 Jim Dowd
- ☐ 23 Manny Fernandez
- ☐ 24 Nick Schultz

'01 - 02 MINW.
MARCONI

Other singles exist.

Sponsor: Marconi

- ☐ Marian Gaborik
- ☐ Matt Johnson
- ☐ Nick Schultz
- ☐ Wes Walz

MONTRÉAL CANADIENS

'66 - 67 MONT.
IGA STAMPS

Prices are for stamps in NM. Stamps in EX sell at 50% of NM pricing. Cards intact do command a significant premium.

Stamp Size: 3/4" x 3/4"
Sponsor: IGA
Set (10 stamps): $325

- ☐ Ralph Backstrom #6 30
- ☐ Dick Duff #8 35
- ☐ John Ferguson #22 40
- ☐ Terry Harper #19 30
- ☐ Ted Harris #10 30
- ☐ Claude Larose #11 30
- ☐ Gilles Tremblay #21 30
- ☐ J.C. Tremblay #3 40
- ☐ Bobby Rousseau #15 30
- ☐ G. Worsley #30 (G) 100

'67 - 68 MONT.

These photos are in black and white. Prices are in NM. Regional stars do carry a premium.

Postcard Size: 3 1/2" x 5 3/8"
Sponsor: None
Set (28 cards): $110

- ☐ Toe Blake 8
- ☐ Ralph Backstrom 3
- ☐ Dave Balon 3
- ☐ Jean Béliveau 25
- ☐ Yvan Cournoyer 10
- ☐ Dick Duff 5
- ☐ John Ferguson 5
- ☐ Danny Grant 5
- ☐ Terry Harper 3
- ☐ Ted Harris 3
- ☐ Charlie Hodge (G) 5
- ☐ Jacques Laperrière 5
- ☐ Claude Larose 3
- ☐ Jacques Lemaire 8
- ☐ Gary Monahan 3
- ☐ Claude Provost 3
- ☐ Mickey Redmond 3
- ☐ Henri Richard 8
- ☐ Jim Roberts 3
- ☐ Léon Rochefort 3
- ☐ Bobby Rousseau 3
- ☐ Jean-Guy Talbot 3
- ☐ Gilles Tremblay 3
- ☐ J.C. Tremblay 3
- ☐ Rogatien Vachon (G) 10
- ☐ Carol Vadnais 5
- ☐ Bryan Watson 3
- ☐ Gump Worsley (G) 8

'67 - 68 MONT.
IGA CARDS

Prices are in NM. Regional stars do carry a premium.

Card Size: 1 5/8" x 1 7/8"
Sponsor: IGA
Set (23 cards): $725

- ☐ Ralph Backstrom #6 25
- ☐ Jean Béliveau #4 100
- ☐ Toe Blake 35
- ☐ Yvan Cournoyer #12 55
- ☐ Dick Duff #8 30
- ☐ John Ferguson #22 35
- ☐ Danny Grant #23 30
- ☐ Terry Harper #19 25
- ☐ Ted Harris #10 25
- ☐ Jacques Laperrière #235
- ☐ Claude Larose #11 25
- ☐ Jacques Lemaire #25 55
- ☐ Garry Monahan #20 25
- ☐ Claude Provost #14 30
- ☐ Mickey Redmond #24 35
- ☐ Henri Richard #16 50
- ☐ Bobby Rousseau #15 25
- ☐ Serge Savard #18 45
- ☐ Gilles Tremblay #5 25
- ☐ J.C. Tremblay #3 30
- ☐ R. Vachon #30 (G) 65
- ☐ Carol Vadnais #17 30
- ☐ Gump Worsley #1 (G) 55

'68 - 69 MONT.
IGA CARDS

Prices are in NM. Regional stars do carry a premium.

Card Size: 1 1/4" x 2 1/4"
Sponsor: IGA
Set (19 cards): $575

- ☐ Ralph Backstrom 25
- ☐ Jean Béliveau 90
- ☐ Yvan Cournoyer 50
- ☐ Dick Duff 30
- ☐ John Ferguson 35
- ☐ Terry Harper 25
- ☐ Ted Harris 25
- ☐ Jacques Laperrière 35
- ☐ Jacques Lemaire 50
- ☐ Garry Monahan 25
- ☐ Claude Provost 30
- ☐ Mickey Redmond 35
- ☐ Henri Richard 50
- ☐ Bobby Rousseau 25
- ☐ Serge Savard 35
- ☐ Gilles Tremblay 25
- ☐ J.C. Tremblay 30
- ☐ R. Vachon (G) 50
- ☐ Gump Worsley (G) 50

'69 - 70 MONT.
PROSTAR

Cards have a facsimile autograph on the front. There are numerous variations in this set. Prices are in NM. Regional stars do carry a premium.

Postcard Size: 3 1/2" x 5 1/2"
Sponsor: ProStar Promotions
Set (31 cards): $125

- ☐ Ralph Backstrom 3
- ☐ Jean Béliveau 20
- ☐ Christian Bordeleau 3
- ☐ Pierre Bouchard 3
- ☐ Guy Charron 3
- ☐ Bill Collins 3
- ☐ Yvan Cournoyer 10
- ☐ John Ferguson 5
- ☐ Terry Harper 3
- ☐ Ted Harris 3
- ☐ Réjean Houle 5
- ☐ Jacques Laperrière 6
- ☐ Guy Lapointe 7
- ☐ Claude Larose 3
- ☐ Jacques Lemaire 9
- ☐ Frank Mahovlich 11
- ☐ Peter Mahovlich 5
- ☐ Phil Myre (G) 5
- ☐ Larry Pleau 3
- ☐ Claude Provost 4
- ☐ Mickey Redmond 6
- ☐ Henri Richard 9
- ☐ Phil Roberto 3
- ☐ Jim Roberts 3
- ☐ Bobby Rousseau 3
- ☐ Claude Ruel 3
- ☐ Serge Savard 7
- ☐ Marc Tardif 5
- ☐ Gilles Tremblay 3
- ☐ J.C. Tremblay 4
- ☐ Rogatien Vachon (G) 8

'70 - 71 MONT.

Prices are in NM. Regional stars do carry a premium.

Postcard Size: 3 1/2" x 5 1/2"
Sponsor: None
Complete Set (23 cards): $100

- ☐ Ralph Backstrom 3
- ☐ Jean Béliveau 20
- ☐ Pierre Bouchard 3
- ☐ Guy Charron 3
- ☐ Bill Collins 3
- ☐ Yvan Cournoyer 10
- ☐ John Ferguson 5
- ☐ Terry Harper 3
- ☐ Réjean Houle 5
- ☐ Jacques Laperrière 5
- ☐ Guy Lapointe 7
- ☐ Claude Larose 3
- ☐ Jacques Lemaire 9
- ☐ Frank Mahovlich 11
- ☐ Peter Mahovlich 3
- ☐ Phil Myre (G) 5
- ☐ Larry Pleau 3
- ☐ Mickey Redmond 6
- ☐ Henri Richard 9
- ☐ Serge Savard 7
- ☐ Marc Tardif 5
- ☐ J.C. Tremblay 4
- ☐ Rogatien. Vachon (G) 8

'70 - 72 MONT.
BUTTONS

Please see *The Memorabilia of the Montréal Canadiens* (by Erle Schneidman) for more information on these buttons. Buttons start at $5-10 and go up to $15-20 for Béliveau and $35-50 for Lafleur or Dryden. Please see *Canadian Sports Collector* for more pricing information.

'71 - 72 MONT.
PROSTAR

Prices are in NM. Regional stars do carry a premium.

Card Size: 3 1/2" x 5 1/2"
Sponsor: ProStar Promotions
Set (25 cards): $100

- ☐ Pierre Bouchard 2
- ☐ Scotty Bowman 7
- ☐ Yvan Cournoyer 6
- ☐ Denis DeJordy (G) 3
- ☐ Ken Dryden (G) 45
- ☐ Terry Harper 2
- ☐ Dale Hoganson 2
- ☐ Réjean Houle 3
- ☐ Guy Lafleur 35
- ☐ Jacques Laperrière 4
- ☐ Guy Lapointe 4
- ☐ Claude Larose 2
- ☐ Jacques Lemaire 7
- ☐ Frank Mahovlich 10
- ☐ Peter Mahovlich 3
- ☐ Al MacNeil 2
- ☐ Phil Myre 3
- ☐ Larry Pleau 2
- ☐ Henri Richard 7
- ☐ Phil Roberto 2
- ☐ Jim Roberts 2
- ☐ Serge Savard 4
- ☐ Marc Tardif 3
- ☐ J.C. Tremblay 3
- ☐ Rogatien Vachon (G) 6

'71 - 72 MONT.
PROSTAR UPDATE

Prices are in NM. Regional stars do carry a premium. Bobby Sheehan is considered short printed.

Card Size: 3 1/2" x 5 1/2"
Sponsor: ProStar Promotions
Complete Set (8 cards): $90

- ☐ Jean Béliveau 20
- ☐ Yvan Cournoyer 10
- ☐ Ken Dryden (G) 50
- ☐ Frank Mahovlich 15
- ☐ Phil Roberto 5
- ☐ Léon Rochefort 5
- ☐ Bobby Sheehan 15
- ☐ Rogatien Vachon (G) 12

'72 - 73 MONT.
PROSTAR

Prices are in NM. Regional stars do carry a premium.

Card Size: 3 1/2" x 5 1/2"
Sponsor: ProStar Promotions

Set (22 cards): $100

- ☐ Chuck Arnason 2
- ☐ Pierre Bouchard 2
- ☐ Scotty Bowman 7
- ☐ Yvan Cournoyer 6
- ☐ Ken Dryden (G) 30
- ☐ Réjean Houle 3
- ☐ Guy Lafleur 25
- ☐ Jacques Laperrière 4
- ☐ Guy Lapointe 4
- ☐ Claude Larose 2
- ☐ Chuck Lefley 2
- ☐ Jacques Lemaire 5
- ☐ Frank Mahovlich 7
- ☐ Peter Mahovlich 2
- ☐ Bob Murdoch 2
- ☐ Michel Plasse (G) 4
- ☐ Henri Richard 6
- ☐ Jim Roberts 2
- ☐ Serge Savard 4
- ☐ Steve Shutt 15
- ☐ Marc Tardif 3
- ☐ Murray Wilson 2

'73 - 74 MONT.

PROSTAR

Prices are in NM. Regional stars do carry a premium.

Card Size: 3 1/2" x 5 1/2"

Sponsor: ProStar Promotions

Set (22 cards): $100

- ☐ Jean Béliveau 10
- ☐ Pierre Bouchard 2
- ☐ Scotty Bowman 5
- ☐ Yvan Cournoyer 5
- ☐ Bob Gainey 10
- ☐ Dave Gardner 2
- ☐ Guy Lafleur 18
- ☐ Yvon Lambert 5
- ☐ Jacques Laperrière 4
- ☐ Guy Lapointe 4
- ☐ Michel Larocque (G) 4
- ☐ Claude Larose 2
- ☐ Check Lefley 2
- ☐ Jacques Lemaire 5
- ☐ Frank Mahovlich 7
- ☐ Peter Mahovlich 2
- ☐ Michel Plasse (G) 3
- ☐ Henri Richard 6
- ☐ Jim Roberts 2
- ☐ Larry Robinson 20
- ☐ Serge Savard 4
- ☐ Steve Shutt 8
- ☐ Wayne Thomas (G) 4
- ☐ Murray Wilson 4

'74 - 75 MONT.

Card fronts either do or do not have a facsimile signature. Pierre Bouchard and Yvon Lambert both have variations with and without an autograph. Prices are in NM. Regional stars do carry a premium.

Card Size: 3 1/2" x 5 1/2"

Sponsor: None

Set (27 cards): $100

- ☐☐ Pierre Bouchard 2
- ☐ Scotty Bowman 5
- ☐ Rick Chartraw 2
- ☐ Yvan Cournoyer 5
- ☐ Ken Dryden (G) 20
- ☐ Bob Gainey 7
- ☐ Glenn Goldup 2
- ☐ Guy Lafleur 15
- ☐☐ Yvon Lambert 2
- ☐ Jacques Laperrière 4
- ☐ Guy Lapointe 4
- ☐ Michel Larocque (G) 4
- ☐ Chuck Lefley 2
- ☐ Jacques Lemaire 5
- ☐ Peter Mahovlich 2
- ☐ Henri Richard 5
- ☐ Doug Risebrough 4
- ☐ Jim Roberts 2
- ☐ Larry Robinson 13
- ☐ Glen Sather 5
- ☐ Serge Savard 4
- ☐ Steve Shutt 6
- ☐ Wayne Thomas (G) 4
- ☐ Mario Tremblay 5
- ☐ John Van Boxmeer 2
- ☐ Murray Wilson 2

'75 - 76 MONT.

Prices are in NM. Regional stars do carry a premium.

Card Size: 3 1/2" x 5 1/2"

Sponsor: None

Complete Set (20 cards): $75

- ☐ Don Awrey 2
- ☐ Pierre Bouchard 2
- ☐ Scotty Bowman 5
- ☐ Yvan Cournoyer 5
- ☐ Ken Dryden (G) 18
- ☐ Bob Gainey 6
- ☐ Doug Jarvis 5
- ☐ Guy Lafleur 15
- ☐ Yvon Lambert 2
- ☐ Guy Lapointe 4
- ☐ Michel Larocque (G) 4
- ☐ Jacques Lemaire 5
- ☐ Peter Mahovlich 2
- ☐ Doug Risebrough 3
- ☐ Jim Roberts 2
- ☐ Larry Robinson 10
- ☐ Serge Savard 4
- ☐ Steve Shutt 5
- ☐ Mario Tremblay 4
- ☐ Murray Wilson 2

'76 - 77 MONT.

Prices are in NM. Regional stars do carry a premium.

Card Size: 3 1/2" x 5 1/2"

Sponsor: None

Set (23 cards): $65

- ☐ Pierre Bouchard 2
- ☐ Scotty Bowman 5
- ☐ Rick Chartraw 2
- ☐ Yvan Cournoyer 5
- ☐ Ken Dryden (G) 15
- ☐ Bob Gainey 5
- ☐ Réjean Houle 3
- ☐ Doug Jarvis 2
- ☐ Yvon Lambert 2
- ☐ Guy Lafleur 13
- ☐ Guy Lapointe 4
- ☐ Michel Larocque (G) 3
- ☐ Jacques Lemaire 5
- ☐ Peter Mahovlich 2
- ☐ Bill Nyrop 2
- ☐ Doug Risebrough 3
- ☐ Jim Roberts 2
- ☐ Larry Robinson 7
- ☐ Claude Ruel 2
- ☐ Serge Savard 4
- ☐ Steve Shutt 5
- ☐ Mario Tremblay 4
- ☐ Murray Wilson 2

'77 - 78 MONT.

Prices are in NM. Regional stars do carry a premium.

Card Size: 3 1/2" x 5 1/2"

Sponsor: None

Set (25 cards): $65

- ☐ Pierre Bouchard 2
- ☐ Scotty Bowman 4
- ☐ Rick Chartraw 2
- ☐ Yvan Cournoyer 5
- ☐ Ken Dryden (G) 12
- ☐ Brian Engblom 2
- ☐ Bob Gainey 5
- ☐ Réjean Houle 3
- ☐ Doug Jarvis 2
- ☐ Guy Lafleur 10
- ☐ Yvon Lambert 2
- ☐ Guy Lapointe 4
- ☐ Michel Larocque (G) 3
- ☐ Pierre Larouche 3
- ☐ Jacques Lemaire 5
- ☐ Gilles Lupien 2
- ☐ Pierre Mondou 2
- ☐ Bill Nyrop 2
- ☐ Doug Risebrough 2
- ☐ Larry Robinson 6
- ☐ Claude Ruel 2
- ☐ Serge Savard 4
- ☐ Steve Shutt 5
- ☐ Mario Tremblay 3
- ☐ Murray Wilson 2

'78 - 79 MONT.

Prices are in NM. Regional stars do carry a premium.

Card Size: 3 1/2" x 5 1/2"

Sponsor: None

Set (26 cards): $65

- ☐ Scotty Bowman 4
- ☐ Rick Chartraw 2
- ☐ Cam Conner 2
- ☐ Yvan Cournoyer 5
- ☐ Ken Dryden (G) 10
- ☐ Brian Engblom 2
- ☐ Bob Gainey 4
- ☐ Réjean Houle 3
- ☐ Pat Hughes 2
- ☐ Doug Jarvis 2
- ☐ Guy Lafleur 8
- ☐ Yvon Lambert 2
- ☐ Rod Langway 7
- ☐ Guy Lapointe 4
- ☐ Michel Larocque (G) 3
- ☐ Pierre Larouche 3
- ☐ Jacques Lemaire 5
- ☐ Gilles Lupien 2
- ☐ Pierre Mondou 2
- ☐ Mark Napier 2
- ☐ Doug Risebrough 2
- ☐ Larry Robinson 5
- ☐ Claude Ruel 2
- ☐ Serge Savard 4
- ☐ Steve Shutt 5
- ☐ Mario Tremblay 3

'79 - 80 MONT.

Guy Lafleur is the most expensive single at $6 in NM. Singles start at $1.50. Two cards are supposedly short printed and sell at a premium: Bernie Geoffrion at $5-7 and Richard Sévigny at $3-5.

Card Size: 3 1/2" x 5 1/2"

Sponsor: None

Set (25 cards): $45

- ☐ Rick Chartraw
- ☐ Normand Dupont
- ☐ Brian Engblom
- ☐ Bob Gainey
- ☐ Bernie Geoffrion
- ☐ Danny Geoffrion
- ☐ Denis Herron (G)
- ☐ Réjean Houle
- ☐ Doug Jarvis
- ☐ Guy Lafleur
- ☐ Yvon Lambert
- ☐ Rod Langway
- ☐ Guy Lapointe
- ☐ Michel Larocque (G)
- ☐ Pierre Larouche
- ☐ Gilles Lupien
- ☐ Pierre Mondou
- ☐ Mark Napier
- ☐ Doug Risebrough
- ☐ Larry Robinson
- ☐ Claude Ruel
- ☐ Serge Savard
- ☐ Richard Sévigny (G)
- ☐ Steve Shutt
- ☐ Mario Tremblay

'80 - 81 MONT.

Guy Lafleur is the most expensive single at $7. Singles start at $1.50.

Card Size: 3 1/2" x 5 1/2"

Sponsor: None

Set (26 cards): $45

- ☐ Keith Acton
- ☐ Bill Baker
- ☐ Rick Chartraw
- ☐ Brian Engblom
- ☐ Bob Gainey
- ☐ Gaston Gingras
- ☐ Denis Herron (G)
- ☐ Réjean Houle
- ☐ Doug Jarvis
- ☐ Guy Lafleur
- ☐ Yvon Lambert
- ☐ Rod Langway
- ☐ Guy Lapointe
- ☐ Michel Larocque (G)
- ☐ Pierre Larouche
- ☐ Pierre Mondou
- ☐ Mark Napier
- ☐ Chris Nilan
- ☐ Doug Risebrough
- ☐ Larry Robinson
- ☐ Claude Ruel
- ☐ Serge Savard
- ☐ Richard Sévigny (G)
- ☐ Steve Shutt
- ☐ Mario Tremblay
- ☐ Doug Wickenheiser

'81 - 82 MONT.

Sixteen cards (†) feature the same card photo as the 1980-81 set. Guy Lafleur is the most expensive single at $6. Singles start at $1.50.

Card Size: 3 1/2" x 5 1/2"

Sponsor: None

Set (28 cards): $40

- ☐ (†) Keith Acton
- ☐ Bob Berry
- ☐ Jeff Brubaker
- ☐ Gilbert Delorme
- ☐ Brian Engblom
- ☐ (†) Bob Gainey
- ☐ (†) Gaston Gingras
- ☐ (†) Denis Herron (G)
- ☐ Réjean Houle
- ☐ Mark Hunter
- ☐ (†) Doug Jarvis
- ☐ (†) Guy Lafleur
- ☐ Rod Langway
- ☐ Jacques Laperrière
- ☐ (†) Guy Lapointe
- ☐ Craig Laughlin
- ☐ (†) Pierre Mondou
- ☐ (†) Mark Napier
- ☐ (†) Chris Nilan
- ☐ Robert Picard
- ☐ (†) Doug Risebrough
- ☐ (†) Larry Robinson
- ☐ (†) Richard Sévigny (G)
- ☐ (†) Steve Shutt
- ☐ (†) Mario Tremblay
- ☐ Rick Wamsley (G)
- ☐ (†) Doug Wickenheiser
- ☐ Team Photo

'82 - 83 MONT.

Guy Lafleur is the most expensive single at $6. Singles start at $1.

Card Size: 3 1/2" x 5 1/2"

Sponsor: None

Set (28 cards): $35

- ☐ Keith Acton
- ☐ Bob Berry
- ☐ Guy Carbonneau
- ☐ Dan Daoust
- ☐ Gilbert Delorme
- ☐ Bob Gainey
- ☐ Gaston Gingras
- ☐ Rick Green
- ☐ Réjean Houle
- ☐ Mark Hunter
- ☐ Guy Lafleur
- ☐ Jacques Laperrière
- ☐ Craig Ludwig
- ☐ Pierre Mondou
- ☐ Mark Napier
- ☐ Mats Näslund
- ☐ Ric Nattress
- ☐ Chris Nilan
- ☐ Robert Picard
- ☐ Henri Richard
- ☐ Larry Robinson
- ☐ Bill Root
- ☐ Richard Sévigny (G)
- ☐ Steve Shutt
- ☐ Mario Tremblay
- ☐ Ryan Walter
- ☐ Rick Wamsley (G)
- ☐ Doug Wickenheiser

'82 - 83 MONT.

STEINBERG

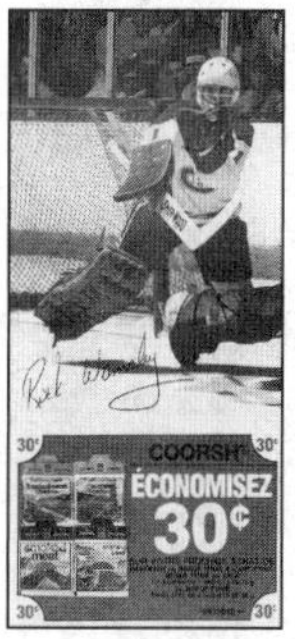

Cards originally measured 3 1/2" x 7 1/2" with a coupon. Guy Lafleur is the most expensive single at $5. Singles start at $1. A cut-out set sells at $20.

Card Size: 3 1/2" x 5 1/2"

Sponsor: Steinberg

Set (24 cards): $30

Album: $7

- ☐ Keith Acton
- ☐ Guy Carbonneau
- ☐ Gilbert Delorme
- ☐ Bob Gainey
- ☐ Rick Green
- ☐ Réjean Houle
- ☐ Mark Hunter
- ☐ Guy Lafleur
- ☐ Craig Ludwig
- ☐ Pierre Mondou
- ☐ Mark Napier
- ☐ Mats Näslund
- ☐ Ric Nattress
- ☐ Chris Nilan
- ☐ Robert Picard
- ☐ Larry Robinson
- ☐ Bill Root
- ☐ Richard Sévigny (G)
- ☐ Steve Shutt
- ☐ Mario Tremblay
- ☐ Ryan Walter
- ☐ Rick Wamsley (G)
- ☐ Doug Wickenheiser
- ☐ Montréal Canadiens

'83 - 84 MONT.

Chris Chelios is the most expensive single at $10. Singles start $1.

Card Size: 3 1/2" x 5 1/2"

Sponsor: None

Set (32 cards): $35

- ☐ Jean Béliveau
- ☐ Bob Berry
- ☐ Guy Carbonneau
- ☐ Kent Carlsson
- ☐ John Chabot
- ☐ Chris Chelios
- ☐ Gilbert Delorme
- ☐ Bob Gainey
- ☐ Rick Green
- ☐ Jean Hamel
- ☐ Mark Hunter
- ☐ Guy Lafleur
- ☐ Jacques Lemaire
- ☐ Jacques Laperrière
- ☐ Craig Ludwig
- ☐ Pierre Mondou
- ☐ Mats Näslund
- ☐ Ric Nattress
- ☐ Chris Nilan
- ☐ Steve Penney (G)
- ☐ Jacques Plante
- ☐ Larry Robinson
- ☐ Bill Root
- ☐ Richard Sévigny (G)
- ☐ Steve Shutt
- ☐ Bobby Smith
- ☐ Mario Tremblay
- ☐ Alfie Turcotte
- ☐ Perry Turnbull
- ☐ Ryan Walter
- ☐ Rick Wamsley (G)
- ☐ Doug Wickenheiser

'84 - 85 MONT.

The most expensive players are at Chris Chelios and Guy Lafleur at $4-6. Singles start $1.

Card Size: 3 1/2" x 5 1/2"

Sponsor: None

Set (28 cards): $30

- ☐ Guy Carbonneau
- ☐ Kent Carlsson
- ☐ Chris Chelios
- ☐ Lucien DeBlois
- ☐ Ron Flockhart
- ☐ Bob Gainey
- ☐ Rick Green
- ☐ Jean Hamel
- ☐ Mark Hunter
- ☐ Tom Kurvers
- ☐ Guy Lafleur
- ☐ Jacques Laperrière
- ☐ Jacques Lemaire
- ☐ Craig Ludwig
- ☐ Pierre Mondou
- ☐ Mats Näslund
- ☐ Ric Nattress
- ☐ Chris Nilan
- ☐ Mike McPhee
- ☐ Steve Penney (G)
- ☐ Jean Perron
- ☐ Larry Robinson
- ☐ Bobby Smith
- ☐ Doug Soetaert (G)
- ☐ Petr Svoboda
- ☐ Mario Tremblay
- ☐ Alfie Turcotte
- ☐ Ryan Walter

'85 - 86 MONT.

Patrick Roy is the most expensive single at $50-60. Claude Lemieux sell at $10. Singles start $1.

Card Size: 3 1/2" x 5 1/2"

Sponsor: None

Set (28 cards): $100

- ☐ Serge Boisvert
- ☐ Randy Bucyk
- ☐ Guy Carbonneau
- ☐ Chris Chelios
- ☐ Kjell Dahlin
- ☐ Bob Gainey
- ☐ Gaston Gingras
- ☐ Rick Green
- ☐ John Kordic
- ☐ Tom Kurvers
- ☐ Mike Lalor
- ☐ Claude Lemieux
- ☐ Craig Ludwig
- ☐ David Maley
- ☐ Mike McPhee
- ☐ Sergio Momesso
- ☐ Mats Näslund
- ☐ Chris Nilan
- ☐ Steve Penney (G)
- ☐ Jean Perron
- ☐ Stéphane Richer
- ☐ Larry Robinson
- ☐ Steve Rooney
- ☐ Patrick Roy (G)
- ☐ Brian Skrudland
- ☐ Bobby Smith
- ☐ Doug Soetaert (G)
- ☐ Petr Svoboda
- ☐ Mario Tremblay
- ☐ Ryan Walter

'85 - 86 MONT.

PROVIGO

Patrick Roy is the most expensive single at $30. Singles start $1.

Sponsor: Provigo

Set (25 cards): $65

Team Binder: $7

- ☐ Guy Carbonneau
- ☐ Chris Chelios
- ☐ Kjell Dahlin
- ☐ Lucien DeBlois
- ☐ Bob Gainey
- ☐ Rick Green
- ☐ Tom Kurvers
- ☐ Mike Lalor
- ☐ Craig Ludwig
- ☐ Mike McPhee
- ☐ Sergio Momesso
- ☐ Mats Näslund
- ☐ Chris Nilan
- ☐ Steve Penney (G)
- ☐ Jean Perron
- ☐ Stéphane Richer
- ☐ Larry Robinson
- ☐ Steve Rooney
- ☐ Patrick Roy (G)
- ☐ Brian Skrudland
- ☐ Bobby Smith
- ☐ Doug Soetaert (G)
- ☐ Petr Svoboda
- ☐ Mario Tremblay
- ☐ Ryan Walter

'86 - 87 MONT.

Patrick Roy is the most expensive single at $25-35. Singles start $1.

Card Size: 3 1/2" x 5 1/2"

Sponsor: None

Set (27 cards): $65

- ☐ Guy Carbonneau
- ☐ Chris Chelios
- ☐ Shayne Corson
- ☐ Kjell Dahlin
- ☐ Bob Gainey
- ☐ Gaston Gingras
- ☐ Rick Green
- ☐ Brian Hayward (G)
- ☐ John Kordic
- ☐ Mike Lalor
- ☐ Jacques Laperrière
- ☐ Claude Lemieux
- ☐ Craig Ludwig
- ☐ David Maley
- ☐ Mike McPhee
- ☐ Sergio Momesso
- ☐ Mats Näslund
- ☐ Chris Nilan
- ☐ Jean Perron
- ☐ Stéphane Richer
- ☐ Larry Robinson
- ☐ Steve Rooney
- ☐ Patrick Roy (G)
- ☐ Brian Skrudland
- ☐ Bobby Smith
- ☐ Petr Svoboda
- ☐ Ryan Walter

'87 - 88 MONT.

Patrick Roy is the most expensive single at $20. Singles start at $1. Stéphane Richer has a version with a moustache as well as without.

Card Size: 3 1/2" x 5 1/2"

Sponsor: None

Set (33 cards): $40

- ☐ François Allaire
- ☐ Guy Carbonneau
- ☐ José Charbonneau
- ☐ Shayne Corson
- ☐ Kjell Dahlin
- ☐ Bob Gainey
- ☐ Gaston Gingras
- ☐ Rick Green
- ☐ Brian Hayward (G)
- ☐ John Kordic
- ☐ Mike Lalor
- ☐ Jacques Laperrière
- ☐ Claude Lemieux
- ☐ Craig Ludwig
- ☐ David Maley
- ☐ Mike McPhee
- ☐ Sergio Momesso
- ☐ Claude Mouton
- ☐ Mats Näslund
- ☐ Chris Nilan
- ☐ Jean Perron
- ☐☐ Stéphane Richer
- ☐ Larry Robinson
- ☐ Steve Rooney
- ☐ Patrick Roy (G)
- ☐ Scott Sandelin
- ☐ Serge Savard
- ☐ Brian Skrudland
- ☐ Bobby Smith
- ☐ Petr Svoboda
- ☐ Gilles Thibodeau
- ☐ Larry Trader
- ☐ Ryan Walter

'87 - 88 MONT.

KODAK PHOTOS

We have no pricing information on this set. These photos may have been issued at an earlier date.

Photo Size: 3 1/2" x 5 1/2"

Sponsor: Kodak

- ☐ Guy Carbonneau
- ☐ Bob Gainey
- ☐ Rick Green
- ☐ Mike McPhee
- ☐ Mats Näslund
- ☐ Chris Nilan
- ☐ Larry Robinson
- ☐ Bobby Smith

'87 - 88 MONT.

VACHON STICKER PANELS

There are 88 stickers in this set. Stickers appear on more than one panel. Other panels may exist. There are sticker variations with or without the sticker number. Panels with Patrick Roy sell at $5-6 while panels with two or more Patrick Roy stickers sells at $6-8. Single panels sell at $1.50.

Panel Size: 2 7/8" x 5 9/16"

Sponsor: Vachon

Album: $7

- ☐ 1 Team Photo TL
  7 Jean Perron
  28 Bobby Smith
  38 Mike McPhee
  57 John Kordic
- ☐ 1 Team Photo TL
  38 Mike McPhee
  41 Bobby Smith
  67 Brian Hayward (G)
  Vachon Logo
- ☐ 2 Team Photo TC
  12 Bob Gainey
  40 Kjell Dahlin
  43 Patrick Roy (G)
  70 Rick Green
- ☐ 2 Team Photo TC

24 Ryan Walter
40 Kjell Dahlin
53 Bob Gainey
82 Chris Chelios
☐ 3 Team Photo TR
7 Jean Perron
28 Bobby Smith
44 Larry Trader
57 John Kordic
☐ 3 Team Photo TR
10 Jean Perron
34 Brian Skrudland
44 Larry Trader
62 Guy Carbonneau
☐ 3 Team Photo TR
41 Bobby Smith
44 Larry Trader
67 Brian Hayward (G)
Vachon
☐ 4 Team Photo BL
12 Bob Gainey
43 Patrick Roy (G)
48 Mats Näslund
70 Rick Green
☐ 4 Team Photo BL
24 Ryan Walter
48 Mats Näslund
53 Bob Gainey
82 Chris Chelios
☐ 5 Team Photo BC
7 Jean Perron
28 Bobby Smith
50 Shayne Corson
57 John Kordic
☐ 5 Team Photo BC
41 Bobby Smith
50 Shayne Corson
67 Brian Hayward (G)
Vachon
☐ 6 Team Photo BR
16 Guy Carbonneau
47 Mats Näslund
52 Stéphane Richer
76 Patrick Roy (G)
☐ 6 Team Photo BR
24 Ryan Walter
52 Stéphane Richer
53 Bob Gainey
82 Chris Chelios
☐ 8 Jacques Laperrière
20 Chris Nilan
29 Mike McPhee
59 Mike Lalor
65 Rick Green
☐ 8 Jacques Laperrière
23 Roy (G)/ Carbonneau
29 Mike McPhee
59 Mike Lalor
71 Patrick Roy (G)
☐ 9 François Allaire
25 Ryan Walter
31 Claude Lemieux
61 Brian Hayward (G)
73 Larry Robinson
☐ 9 François Allaire
30 Bobby Smith
31 Claude Lemieux
61 Brian Hayward (G)
77 Petr Svoboda
☐ 9 François Allaire
31 Claude Lemieux
36 Brian Skrudland
61 Brian Hayward (G)
85 Bobby Smith
☐ 9 François Allaire
31 Claude Lemieux
61 Brian Hayward (G)
33 Claude Lemieux
81 Craig Ludwig
☐ 9 François Allaire
31 Claude Lemieux
61 Brian Hayward (G)
77 Petr Svoboda
86 Bobby Smith
☐ 10 Jean Perron
34 Brian Skrudland
54 Stéphane Richer
62 Guy Carbonneau
86 Bobby Smith
☐ 11 Jacques Laperrière
17 Mike McPhee
37 Mike McPhee
60 Mike Lalor
63 Guy Carbonneau
☐ 11 Jacques Laperrière
23 Roy (G)/ Carbonneau
37 Mike McPhee
63 Guy Carbonneau
71 Patrick Roy (G)
☐ 11 Jacques Laperrière
37 Mike McPhee
56 Sergio Momesso
63 Guy Carbonneau
87 Mats Näslund
☐ 13 Bob Gainey
14 Guy Carbonneau
45 Mats Näslund
58 John Kordic
72 Larry Robinson
☐ 13 Bob Gainey
18 Bob Gainey
45 Mats Näslund
64 Brian Hayward (G)
72 Larry Robinson
☐ 13 Bob Gainey
22 Mike Lalor
45 Mats Näslund
68 Rick Green
72 Larry Robinson
☐ 14 Guy Carbonneau
26 Bobby Smith
55 Sergio Momesso
58 John Kordic
83 Chris Chelios
☐ 14 Guy Carbonneau
19 Chris Nilan
49 Shayne Corson
58 John Kordic
78 Chris Chelios
☐ 15 Guy Carbonneau
35 Craig Ludwig
46 Mats Näslund
75 Petr Svoboda
84 Brian Hayward (G)
☐ 17 Mike McPhee
42 Patrick Roy G()
60 Mike Lalor
69 Patrick Roy (G)
88 Bob Gainey
☐ 19 Chris Nilan
22 Mike Lalor
49 Shayne Corson
68 Rick Green
78 Chris Chelios
☐ 20 Chris Nilan
42 Patrick Roy (G)
65 Rick Green
69 Patrick Roy (G)
88 Bob Gainey
☐ 21 Guy Carbonneau
27 Mats Näslund
51 Stéphane Richer
74 Patrick Roy (G)
80 Craig Ludwig
☐ 21 Guy Carbonneau
32 Bobby Smith
51 Stéphane Richer
79 Chris Chelios
80 Craig Ludwig
☐ 21 Guy Carbonneau
35 Craig Ludwig
51 Stéphane Richer
80 Craig Ludwig
84 Brian Hayward (G)
☐ 22 Mike Lalor
26 Bobby Smith
55 Sergio Momesso
68 Rick Green
83 Chris Chelios
☐ 23 Roy/Carbonneau
42 Patrick Roy (G)
69 Patrick Roy (G)
71 Patrick Roy (G)
88 Bob Gainey
☐ 30 Bobby Smith
39 Kjell Dahlin
66 Rick Green
77 Petr Svoboda
Vachon
☐ 33 Claude Lemieux
39 Kjell Dahlin
66 Rick Green
81 Craig Ludwig
Vachon
☐ 42 Patrick Roy (G)
56 Sergio Momesso
69 Patrick Roy (G)
87 Mats Näslund
88 Bob Gainey
☐ Logo
25 Ryan Walter
39 Kjell Dahlen
66 Rick Green
73 Larry Robinson

'88 - 89 MONT.

Patrick Roy is the most expensive single at $12. Singles start $1.

Card Size: 3 1/2" x 5 1/2"
Sponsor: None
Set (30 cards): $30

☐ François Allaire
☐ Pat Burns
☐ Guy Carbonneau
☐ José Charbonneau
☐ Chris Chelios
☐ Ronald Corey
☐ Shayne Corson
☐ Russ Courtnall
☐ Éric Desjardins
☐ Bob Gainey
☐ Brent Gilchrist
☐ Rick Green
☐ Brian Hayward (G)
☐ Mike Keane
☐ Mike Lalor
☐ Jacques Laperrière
☐ Claude Lemieux
☐ Craig Ludwig
☐ Steve Martinson
☐ Mike McPhee
☐ Mats Näslund
☐ Stéphane Richer
☐ Larry Robinson
☐ Patrick Roy (G)
☐ Serge Savard
☐ Brian Skrudland
☐ Bobby Smith
☐ Petr Svoboda
☐ Gilles Thibodeau
☐ Ryan Walter

'89 - 90 MONT.

Patrick Roy is the most expensive single at $8. Singles start $1.

Card Size: 3 1/2" x 5 1/2"
Sponsor: None
Set (32 cards): $30

☐ François Allaire
☐ Pat Burns
☐ Guy Carbonneau
☐ Chris Chelios
☐ Tom Chorske
☐ Ronald Corey
☐ Shayne Corson
☐ Russ Courtnall
☐ J.J. Daigneault
☐ Éric Desjardins
☐ Martin Desjardins
☐ Donald Dufresne
☐ Brent Gilchrist
☐ Brian Hayward (G)
☐ Mike Keane
☐ Jacques Laperrière
☐ Stéphan Lebeau
☐ Sylvain Lefebvre
☐ Claude Lemieux
☐ Jocelyn Lemieux
☐ Craig Ludwig
☐ Jyrki Lumme
☐ Steve Martinson
☐ Mike McPhee
☐ Mats Näslund
☐ Stéphane Richer
☐ Patrick Roy (G)
☐ Serge Savard
☐ Brian Skrudland
☐ Bobby Smith
☐ Petr Svoboda
☐ Ryan Walter

'89 - 90 MONT.
KRAFT / LE JOURNAL

This set was originally issued in panels. Patrick Roy is the most expensive single at $10. Cut out singles start at $1.

Card Size: 3 3/4" x 5 1/2"
Sponsors: Kraft, Le Journal
Set (24 cards): $30

☐ Pat Burns
☐ Guy Carbonneau #21
☐ Chris Chelios #24
☐ Shayne Corson #27

☐ Russ Courtnall #6
☐ J.J. Daigneault #48
☐ Éric Desjardins #28
☐ Todd Ewen #36
☐ Brent Gilchrist #41
☐ Brian Hayward #1 (G)
☐ Mike Keane #12
☐ Stephane Lebeau #47
☐ Sylvain Lefebvre #3
☐ Claude Lemieux #32
☐ Craig Ludwig #17
☐ Mike McPhee #35
☐ Mats Näslund #26
☐ Stéphane Richer #44
☐ Patrick Roy #33 (G)
☐ Mathieu Schneider #18
☐ Brian Skrudland #39
☐ Bobby Smith #15
☐ Petr Svoboda #25
☐ Ryan Walter #11

'90 - 91 MONT.

Patrick Roy is the most expensive single at $8. Singles start $1.

Card Size: 3 1/2" x 5 1/2"
Sponsor: None
Set (33 cards): $30

☐ François Allaire
☐ J-C Bergeron (G)
☐ Benoît Brunet
☐ Pat Burns
☐ Guy Carbonneau
☐ Andrew Cassels
☐ Tom Chorske
☐ Ronald Corey
☐ Shayne Corson
☐ Russ Courtnall
☐ J.J. Daigneault
☐ Éric Desjardins
☐ Gerald Diduck
☐ Don Dufresne
☐ Todd Ewen
☐ Brent Gilchrist
☐ Mike Keane
☐ Jacques Laperrière
☐ Stéphan Lebeau
☐ Sylvain Lefebvre
☐ Mike McPhee
☐ Lyle Odelein
☐ Mark Pederson
☐ Stephane Richer
☐ Patrick Roy (G)
☐ Denis Savard
☐ Serge Savard
☐ Mathieu Schneider
☐ Brian Skrudland
☐ Petr Svoboda
☐ Charles Thiffault
☐ Sylvain Turgeon
☐ Ryan Walter

'91 - 92 MONT.

Patrick Roy and John LeClair are the most expensive singles at $6-8. Singles start at $1.

Card Size: 3 1/2" x 5 1/2"
Sponsor: None
Set (31 cards): $30

☐ François Allaire
☐ Patrice Brisebois
☐ Pat Burns
☐ Guy Carbonneau
☐ Ron Corey
☐ Shayne Corson
☐ Alain Côté
☐ Russ Courtnall
☐ J.J. Daigneault
☐ Éric Desjardins
☐ Don Dufresne
☐ Todd Ewen
☐ Brent Gilchrist
☐ Mike Keane
☐ Jacques Laperrière
☐ Stéphan Lebeau
☐ John LeClair
☐ Sylvain Lefebvre
☐ Mike McPhee
☐ Kirk Muller
☐ Lyle Odelein
☐ André Racicot (G)
☐ Mario Roberge
☐ Patrick Roy (G)
☐ Denis Savard
☐ Serge Savard
☐ Mathieu Schneider
☐ Brian Skrudland
☐ Petr Svoboda
☐ Charles Thiffault
☐ Sylvain Turgeon

'92 - 93 MONT.

The most expensive singles are Patrick Roy and John LeClair at $4-6. Singles start 75¢.

Card Size: 3 1/2" x 5 1/2"
Sponsor: None
Set (27 cards): $25

☐ Brian Bellows
☐ Patrice Brisebois
☐ Benoît Brunet
☐ Guy Carbonneau
☐ J.J. Daigneault
☐ Vincent Damphousse
☐ Éric Desjardins
☐ Jacques Demers
☐ Gilbert Dionne
☐ Don Dufresne
☐ Todd Ewen
☐ Kevin Haller
☐ Sean Hill
☐ Mike Keane
☐ Patric Kjellberg
☐ Stephan Lebeau
☐ John LeClair
☐ Kirk Muller
☐ Lyle Odelein
☐ Oleg Petrov
☐ André Racicot (G)
☐ Mario Roberge
☐ Ed Ronan
☐ Patrick Roy (G)
☐ Denis Savard
☐ Mathieu Schneider
☐ Brian Skrudland

'92 - 93 MONT.
O-PEE-CHEE

This set was issued in a puck-shaped box for the 1993 All-Star Fanfest in Montréal. A total of 5,000 sets were made. The promo panel features Henri Richard, Jean Béliveau, Yvan Cournoyer and Maurice Richard.

Card Size: 3 1/2" x 5 1/2"
Sponsor: O-Pee-Chee
Set (66 cards): $80.00
Promo Panel: 5.00

☐ 1 Montréal Forum 1.00
☐ 2 Butch Bouchard .75
☐ 3 Henri Richard 1.75
☐ 4 Serge Savard .75
☐ 5 HL: Toe Blake 2.00
☐ 6 HL: M. Richard 5.00
☐ 7 Stéphan Lebeau .50
☐ 8 Kevin Haller .50
☐ 9 Guy Carbonneau .50
☐ 10 Jacques Demers .50
☐ 11 Serge Savard .75
☐ 12 Montréal Forum 1.00
☐ 13 Howie Morenz 5.00
☐ 14 Jean Béliveau 4.00
☐ 15 J. Laperrière 1.00
☐ 16 Bob Gainey 1.25
☐ 17 HL: Guy Lafleur 3.50
☐ 18 J. Raymond .50
☐ 19 Sean Hill .50
☐ 20 Éric Desjardins .50
☐ 21 Aurèle Joliat 3.00
☐ 22 Doug Harvey 2.50
☐ 23 Yvan Cournoyer 1.50
☐ 24 HL: F. Mahovlich 2.00
☐ 25 J.J. Daigneault .50
☐ 26 Kirk Muller .50
☐ 27 Jean Béliveau 4.00
☐ 28 G. Vézina (G) 4.00
☐ 29 Maurice Richard 6.00
☐ 30 Patrick Roy (G) 8.00
☐ 31 Benoît Brunet .50
☐ 32 HL: J. Plante 3.50
☐ 33 Ralph Backstrom .50
☐ 34 Elmer Lach 1.50
☐ 35 Cup Winners 1.00
☐ 36 J. Laperrière 1.00
☐ 37 Statistics .50
☐ 38 V. Damphousse 1.00
☐ 39 Frank Mahovlich 2.00
☐ 40 J. Plante (G) 4.00
☐ 41 Cup Winners 1.00
☐ 42 Kenny Reardon 1.00
☐ 43 Claude Provost .50
☐ 44 HL: J. Béliveau 4.00
☐ 45 Ed Ronan .50
☐ 46 Statistics .50
☐ 47 Bill Durnan 2.50
☐ 48 Stanley Cup 1.00
☐ 49 Patrice Brisebois .50
☐ 50 Denis Savard 1.00
☐ 51 Ken Dryden (G) 6.00
☐ 52 Lou Fontinato .50
☐ 53 Jean-Guy Talbot .50
☐ 54 Bernie Geoffrion 2.50
☐ 55 Joe Malone 1.50
☐ 56 Oleg Petrov .50
☐ 57 Guy Lafleur 4.00
☐ 58 Bert Olmstead 1.00
☐ 59 Dream Team 3.00
☐ 60 Brian Bellows .50
☐ 61 HL: H. Richard 1.75
☐ 62 Jacques Lemaire 1.50
☐ 63 Dickie Moore 1.50
☐ 64 G. Worsley (G) 2.50
☐ 65 Toe Blake 2.00
☐ 66 Checklist .50

'93 - 94 MONT.

Patrick Roy is the most expensive single at $6. Singles start 75¢.

Card Size: 3 1/2" x 5 1/2"
Sponsor: None
Set (26 cards): $20

☐ Brian Bellows
☐ Patrice Brisebois
☐ Benoît Brunet
☐ Guy Carbonneau
☐ J.J. Daigneault
☐ Vincent Damphousse
☐ Jacques Demers
☐ Éric Desjardins
☐ Gilbert Dionne
☐ Paul DiPietro
☐ Kevin Haller
☐ Mike Keane
☐ Stephan Lebeau
☐ John LeClair
☐ Gary Leeman
☐ Kirk Muller
☐ Lyle Odelein
☐ Peter Popovic
☐ André Racicot (G)
☐ Rob Ramage
☐ Mario Roberge
☐ Ed Ronan
☐ Patrick Roy (G)
☐ Matheiu Schneider
☐ Pierre Sévigny
☐ Ron Wilson

'93 - 94 MONT.
MOLSON EXPORT

Singles start at $5. Photos were given out on game nights. Other singles may exist.

Photo Size: 8" x 10 1/2"
Sponsor: Molson

☐ 16OCT93 Carbonneau
☐ 03NOV93 Mike Keane
☐ 20NOV93 Kirk Muller
☐ 12JAN94 Brian Bellows
☐ 17JAN94 Benoît Brunet
☐ 30JAN94 M. Schneider
☐ 23FEB94 Kevin Haller
☐ 16MAR94 Peter Popovic
☐ 21APR94 Mario Roberge

'94 - 95 MONT.

Patrick Roy is the most expensive single at $5. Singles start at 75¢.

Card Size: 3 1/2" x 5 1/2"
Sponsor: None
Set (27 cards): $20

☐ Brian Bellows
☐ Donald Brashear
☐ Patrice Brisebois
☐ Benoît Brunet
☐ J.J. Daigneault
☐ Vincent Damphousse
☐ Jacques Demers
☐ Éric Desjardins
☐ Gilbert Dionne
☐ Paul DiPietro
☐ Gerry Fleming
☐ Bryan Fogarty
☐ Mike Keane
☐ John LeClair
☐ Jim Montgomery
☐ Kirk Muller
☐ Lyle Odelein
☐ Oleg Petrov
☐ Peter Popovic
☐ Yves Racine
☐ Ed Ronan
☐ Patrick Roy (G)
☐ Brian Savage
☐ Mathieu Schneider
☐ Pierre Sévigny
☐ Turner Stevenson
☐ Ron Tugnutt (G)

'94 - 95 MONT.
MOLSON EXPORT

Photos were given out on game nights. Singles start at $5. Other singles exist.

Photo Size: 8" x 10 1/2"
Sponsor: Molson

☐ 18SEP94 Ron Tugnutt
☐ 29JAN95 P. Brisebois
☐ 20FEB95 Lyle Odelein
☐ 25MAR95 Pierre Sévigny
☐ 05APR95 P. Roy (G)
☐ 08APR95 Bryan Fogarty
☐ 29APR95 Yves Racine

'95 - 96 MONT.

Patrick Roy and Saku Koivu are the most expensive singles at $3-5. Singles start at 75¢.

Card Size: 3 1/2" x 5 1/2"
Sponsor: None
Set (20 cards): $20

☐ Donald Brashear
☐ Patrice Brisebois
☐ Benoît Brunet
☐ Valeri Bure
☐ Marc Bureau
☐ Vincent Damphousse
☐ Mike Keane
☐ Saku Koivu
☐ Vladimir Malakhov
☐ Lyle Odelein
☐ Oleg Petrov
☐ Petr Popovic
☐ Stéphane Quintal
☐ Yves Racine
☐ Mark Recchi
☐ Patrick Roy (G)
☐ Brian Savage
☐ Turner Stevenson
☐ Mario Tremblay
☐ Pierre Turgeon

'95 - 96 MONT.
MOLSON EXPORT

Singles start at $5. Photos were given out on game nights. Other singles may exist.

Photo Size: 8" x 11"
Sponsor: Molson

☐ 07OCT95 Benoît Brunet
☐ 25OCT95 V. Malakhov
☐ 20NOV95 S. Quintal
☐ 16DEC95 Brian Savage
☐ 10JAN96 P. Brisebois
☐ 13JAN96 Mark Recchi
☐ 31JAN96 Damphousse
☐ 24FEB96 Pierre Turgeon
☐ 09MAR96 Lyle Odelein
☐ 20MAR96 Lyle Odelein
☐ 25MAR96 T. Stevenson
☐ 01APR96 Peter Popovic
☐ 13APR96 Saku Koivu
☐ 28APR96 Valeri Bure

'96 - 97 MONT.
MOLSON EXPORT

Photos were given out on game nights. Singles start at $5. Other singles exist.

Photo Size: 8" x 11"
Sponsor: Molson

☐ 16SEP96 Peter Popovic
☐ 22SEP96 Mark Recchi
☐ 04DEC96 V. Malakhov
☐ 11DEC96 David Wilkie
☐ 16DEC96 David Wilkie
☐ 21DEC96 S. Quintal
☐ 04JAN97 Scott Thornton
☐ 11JAN97 T. Stevenson
☐ 20JAN97 Saku Koivu
☐ 05APR97 Dave Manson
☐ 07APR97 J. Cullimore
☐ 12APR97 José Théodore

'96 - 98 MONT.

This new series of Canadiens' postcards started with the 1996-97 season. Photos are taken by Robert Laberge. Team sets were available at the Molson Centre as well as through the Canadiens' fan club. Players were added or removed from the team set when they were traded. Team sets sell at $12-15. Saku Koivu is the most expensive single at $3 while singles start at 75¢.

Card Size: 3" x 5 1/2"
Sponsor: None

☐ 96/7 Murray Baron #36
☐ 97/8 S. Bordeleau #71
☐ 96-8 P. Brisebois #43
☐ 96-8 Benoît Brunet #17
☐ 96/7 Valeri Bure #18
☐ 97/8 Valeri Bure #20
☐ 96-8 Marc Bureau #28
☐ 97/8 Brett Clark #29
☐ 96-8 Shayne Corson #27
☐ 96/7 J. Cullimore #35
☐ 96-8 V. Damphousse #25
☐ 97/8 Jonas Hoglund #44
☐ 96/7 P. Jablonski #39 (G)
☐ 96/7 Koivu #11 Cooper
☐ 97/8 Koivu #11 Nike
☐ 96-8 V. Malakhov #18
☐ 97/8 Dave Manson #22
☐ 97/8 Andy Moog #35 (G)
☐ 96/7 Chris Murray #22
☐ 96-8 Peter Popovic #34
☐ 97/8 Patrick Poulin #37
☐ 96/7 S. Quintal #5White
☐ 97/8 S. Quintal #5 Red
☐ 96-8 Mark Recchi #8
☐ 96-8 S. Richer #44
☐ 97/8 Craig Rivet #52
☐ 96-8 Martin Rucinsky #26
☐ 96-8 Brian Savage #49
☐ 96/7 T. Stevenson #30
☐ 97/8 T. Stevenson #23
☐ 96-8 J. Thibault #41 (G)
☐ 96-8 Scott Thornton #24
☐ 96-8 Darcy Tucker #42
☐ 97/8 Igor Ulanov #55

☐ 97/8 Mick Vukota #21
☐ 96/7 David Wilkie #3
☐ 97/8 Zarley Zalapski #3
☐ 96/7 M. Tremblay, Coach
☐ 97/8 A. Vigneault, Coach

'00 - 01 MONT.

This series carries a similar design as the 1996-97 through 1999-00 series. Every photo in this series, however, is new. Singles start at 75¢.
Card Size: 3" x 5 1/2"
Sponsor: None
Set (35 cards): $25

☐ Andrei Bashkirov
☐ F. Bouillon ('00 patch)
☐ Patrice Brisebois
☐ Benoit Brunet
☐ Jim Campbell
☐ Éric Chouinard
☐ Craig Darby
☐ Xavier Delisle
☐ Karl Dykhuis ('00 patch)
☐ Mathieu Garon (G)
☐ Jeff Hackett (G) red
☐ Chad Kilger
☐ Saku Koivu
☐ Christian Laflamme
☐ Éric Landry
☐ Juha Lind
☐ Trevor Linden
☐ Andrei Markov
☐ Gino Odjick
☐ Oleg Petrov #22
☐ Patrick Poulin
☐ Craig Rivet
☐ Robidas #44 ('00 patch)
☐ M. Rucinsky ('00 patch)
☐ Brian Savage
☐ S. Souray ('00 patch)
☐ José Théodore (G)
☐ Eric Weinrich ('00 patch)
☐ Johan Witehall
☐ Dainius Zubrus
☐ Guy Carbonneau
☐ Rick Green
☐ Martin Madden
☐ André Savard
☐ Michel Therrien

'01 - 02 MONT.

While some photos do carry over from the 2000-01 series (†), these cards have a different design on the card back. Specifically, card backs include a facsimile signature below the name and features the team logo/name at the bottom. Singles start at 75¢. Short prints (*) start at $3.
Card Size: 3" x 5 1/2"
Sponsor: None
Set (35 cards): $40

☐ Donald Audette (*)
☐ Francis Bouillon (*)
☐ (†) Patrice Brisebois
☐ (†) Benoit Brunet
☐ Jan Bulis
☐ Andreas Dackell
☐ Karl Dykhuis
☐ (†) Mathieu Garon (G)
☐ Doug Gilmour
☐ (†) Jeff Hackett (G) red
☐ Joé Juneau
☐ (†) Chad Kilger
☐ Saku Koivu
☐ Bill Lindsay (*)
☐ (†) Gino Odjick
☐ Gino Odjick w/ helmet (*)
☐ Yanic Perreault
☐ Oleg Petrov #14
☐ (†) Patrick Poulin
☐ Stéphane Quintal
☐ Mike Ribeiro
☐ Craig Rivet
☐ Stéphane Robidas #56
☐ Martin Rucinsky
☐ (†) Brian Savage
☐ Reid Simpson
☐ Sheldon Souray
☐ (†) José Théodore (G)
☐ Patrick Traverse
☐ Shaun Van Allen (*)
☐ Richard Zednik
☐ (†) Michel Therrien
☐ (†) Guy Carbonneau
☐ (†) Rick Green
☐ Roland Melanson

'02 - 03 MONT.

The Canadiens used new photos for this series. Unlike the 2001-02 card backs which feature the team name under the logo, these card backs say "Tricolore jusqu'au bout! / Habs all the way!" under the logo. Singles start at 75¢. Short prints (*) start at $3.
Card Size: 3" x 5 1/2"
Sponsor: None
Set (36 cards): $40

☐ Donald Audette
☐ Sylvain Blouin
☐ Patrice Brisebois
☐ Francis Bouillon (*)
☐ Jan Bulis
☐ Mariusz Czerkawski
☐ Andreas Dackell
☐ Karl Dykhuis
☐ Mathieu Garon (G)
☐ Doug Gilmour A
☐ Jeff Hackett (G)
☐ RonHainsey
☐ Marcel Hossa (*)
☐ Joé Juneau
☐ Chad Kilger
☐ Saku Koivu
☐ Mike Komisarek (*)
☐ Bill Lindsay
☐ Andrei Markov
☐ Randy McKay
☐ Yanic Perreault
☐ Oleg Petrov
☐ Stéphane Quintal A
☐ Mike Ribeiro
☐ Craig Rivet A
☐ Sheldon Souray
☐ Niklas Sundström (*)
☐ José Théodore (G)
☐ Patrick Traverse
☐ Richard Zednik
☐ Guy Charron
☐ Rick Green
☐ Clément Jodoin
☐ Claude Julien (*)
☐ Roland Melanson
☐ Michel Therrien

NASHVILLE PREDATORS

'98 - 99 NASH.

WENDY'S

Mike Dunham is the most expensive single at $2.
Card Size: 2 1/2" x 3 1/2"
Imprint: © 1998 Pacific Trading Cards
Sponsor: Wendy's
Set (25 cards): $15

☐ 1 Blair Atcheynum
☐ 2 Drake Berehowsky
☐ 3 Sébastien Bordeleau
☐ 4 Joël Bouchard
☐ 5 Bob Boughner
☐ 6 Andrew Brunette
☐ 7 Patrick Côté
☐ 8 Mike Dunham (G)
☐ 9 Éric Fichaud (G)
☐ 10 Tom Fitzgerald
☐ 11 Jamie Heward
☐ 12 Greg Johnson
☐ 13 Patric Kjellberg
☐ 14 Sergei Krivokrasov
☐ 15 Denny Lambert
☐ 16 Jayson More
☐ 17 Ville Peltonen
☐ 18 Cliff Ronning
☐ 19 John Slaney
☐ 20 Kimmo Timonen
☐ 21 Darren Turcotte
☐ 22 Tomas Vokoun (G)
☐ 23 Jan Vopat
☐ 24 Scott Walker
☐ 25 Vitali Yachmenev

NEW JERSEY DEVILS

'83 - 84 NJER.

The most expensive singles are John MacLean and Pat Verbeek at $5-7. Singles start at $1.
Card Size: 3 1/2" x 6"
Sponsor: None
Set (25 cards): $25

☐ Mike Antonovich
☐ Mel Bridgman
☐ Aaron Broten
☐ Murray Bromwell
☐ Dave Cameron
☐ Rich Chernomaz
☐ Joe Cirella
☐ Ken Daneyko
☐ Larry Floyd
☐ Paul Gagné
☐ Mike Kitchen
☐ Jeff Larmer
☐ Don Lever
☐ Dave Lewis
☐ Bob Lorimer
☐ Ron Low (G)
☐ Jan Ludvig
☐ John MacLean
☐ Bob MacMillan
☐ Hector Marini
☐ Rick Meagher
☐ Grant Mulvey
☐ Glenn Resch (G)
☐ Phil Russell
☐ Pat Verbeek

'84 - 85 NJER.

Kirk Muller is the most expensive single at $5. Singles start at $1.
Card Size: 3 1/2" x 6"
Sponsor: None
Set (25 cards): $25

☐ Mel Bridgman #18
☐ Aaron Broten #10
☐ Doug Carpenter
☐ Rich Chernomaz #14
☐ Joe Cirella #2
☐ Bruce Driver #23
☐ Paul Gagne #17
☐ Uli Hiemer #28
☐ Tim Higgins #20
☐ Bob Hoffmeyer #21
☐ Hannu Kamppuri #33 (G)
☐ Don Lever #9
☐ Dave Lewis #25
☐ Bob Lorimer #4
☐ Ron Low #30 (G)
☐ Jan Ludvig #29
☐ John MacLean #15
☐ Rick Meagher #16
☐ Kirk Muller #27
☐ Dave Pichette #8
☐ Rich Preston #19
☐ Glenn Resch #1 (G)
☐ Phil Russell #5
☐ Doug Sulliman #22
☐ Pat Verbeek #12

'85 - 86 NJER.

Reportedly 3,000 sets were produced. Kirk Muller is the most expensive single at $6. Singles start at $1.50.
Card Size: 3 5/8" x 5 1/2"
Sponsor: None
Set (10 cards): $18

☐ 1 Mark Johnson
☐ 2 Craig Billington (G)
☐ 3 Alain Chevrier (G)
☐ 4 Paul Gagné
☐ 5 Greg Adams
☐ 6 Glenn Resch (G)
☐ 7 Craig Wolanin
☐ 8 Perry Anderson
☐ 9 Kirk Muller
☐ 10 Randy Velischek

'86 - 87 NJER.

S.O.B.E.R.

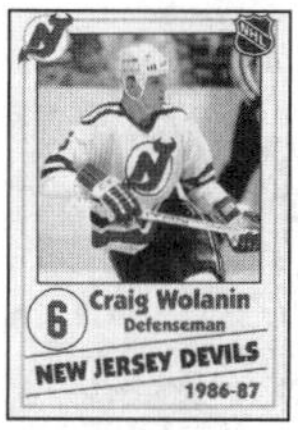

Kirk Muller is the most expensive single at $5. Singles start at $1.
Sponsors: S.O.B.E.R., Howard Bank, Independant Insurance Agents of Bergun County
Set (20 cards): $28

☐ Greg Adams #24
☐ Perry Anderson #25
☐ Timo Blomqvist #5
☐ Andy Brickley #26
☐ Mel Bridgman #18
☐ Aaron Broten #10
☐ Alain Chevrier #30 (G)
☐ Joe Cirella #2
☐ Ken Daneyko #3
☐ Bruce Driver #23
☐ Uli Hiemer #28
☐ Mark Johnson #12
☐ Jan Ludvig #29
☐ John MacLean #15
☐ Peter McNab #7
☐ Kirk Muller #9
☐ Doug Sulliman #22
☐ Randy Velischek #27
☐ Pat Verbeek #16
☐ Craig Wolanin #16

'87 - 88 NJER.

We have little information on this set. Other singles exist.
Card Size: 3 3/4" x 4 3/4"
Sponsor: None

☐ Bob Sauvé #28 (G)

'88 - 89 NJER.

CARETTA TRUCKING

The most expensive singles are Brendan Shanahan at $15 and Sean Burke at $4-5. Singles start at 75¢.
Card Size: 2 7/8" x 4 1/4"
Sponsor: Caretta Trucking
Set (30 cards): $35

☐ Perry Anderson #25
☐ Bob Bellemore
☐ Aaron Broten #10
☐ Doug Brown #24
☐ Sean Burke #1 (G)
☐ Anders Carlsson #20
☐ Joe Cirella #2
☐ Pat Conacher #32
☐ Ken Daneyko #3
☐ Bruce Driver #23
☐ Bob Hoffmeyer
☐ Jamie Huscroft #4
☐ Mark Johnson #12
☐ Jim Korn #14
☐ Tom Kurvers #5
☐ Lou Lamoriello
☐ Claude Loiselle #19
☐ John MacLean #15
☐ David Maley #8
☐ Doug McKay
☐ Kirk Muller #9
☐ Jack O'Callahan #7
☐ Steve Rooney #18
☐ Bob Sauvé #28 (G)
☐ Jim Schoenfeld
☐ Brendan Shanahan #11
☐ Patrik Sundstrom #17
☐ Randy Velischek #27
☐ Pat Verbeek #16
☐ Craig Wolanin #6

'89 - 90 NJER.

CARETTA TRUCKING

There are two variations: cards with the Caretta Trucking logo and cards without the logo. Brendan Shanahan is the most expensive single at $8. Singles start at 75¢.
Card Size: 2 7/8" x 4 1/4"
Sponsor: Caretta Trucking
Set (29 cards): $25

☐ ☐ Tommy Albelin #26
☐ ☐ Bob Bellemore
☐ ☐ Neil Brady #19
☐ ☐ Aaron Broten #10
☐ ☐ Doug Brown #24
☐ ☐ Sean Burke #1 (G)
☐ ☐ Pat Conacher #32
☐ ☐ John Cunniff
☐ ☐ Ken Daneyko #3
☐ ☐ Bruce Driver #23
☐ ☐ Viacheslav Fetisov #2
☐ ☐ Mark Johnson #12
☐ ☐ Jim Korn #14
☐ ☐ Lou Lamoriello
☐ ☐ John MacLean #15
☐ ☐ David Maley #8
☐ ☐ Kirk Muller #9
☐ ☐ Janne Ojanen #22
☐ ☐ Walt Poddubny #21
☐ ☐ Reijo Ruotsalainen #29
☐ ☐ Brendan Shanahan #11
☐ ☐ Sergei Starikov #4
☐ ☐ Patrik Sundstrom #17
☐ ☐ Peter Sundstrom #20
☐ ☐ Chris Terreri #31 (G)
☐ ☐ Sylvain Turgeon #16
☐ ☐ Randy Velischek #27
☐ ☐ Eric Weinrich #7
☐ ☐ Craig Wolanin #6

'90 - 91 NJER.

Brendan Shanahan is the most expensive single at $6. Singles start at 75¢.
Card Size: 2 1/2" x 3 1/2"
Sponsor: None
Set (20 cards): $20

☐ Tommy Albelin
☐ Laurie Boschman
☐ Doug Brown
☐ Sean Burke (G)
☐ Tim Burke
☐ Zdeno Ciger
☐ Pat Conacher
☐ Troy Crowder
☐ John Cunniff
☐ Ken Daneyko
☐ Bruce Driver
☐ Viacheslav Fetisov
☐ Alexei Kasatonov
☐ Lou Lamoriello
☐ Claude Lemieux
☐ David Maley
☐ John MacLean
☐ Jon Morris
☐ Kirk Muller
☐ Lee Norwood
☐ Myles O'Connor
☐ Walt Poddubny
☐ Brendan Shanahan
☐ Peter Stastny
☐ Alan Stewart
☐ Warren Strelow
☐ Doug Sulliman
☐ Patrik Sundstrom
☐ Chris Terreri (G)
☐ Eric Weinrich

'91 - 92 NJER.

Singles start at $3.
Card Size: 2 1/2" x 6"
Sponsor: None
Set (10 cards): $20

☐ 82-83 Devils Photo
☐ 83-84 Devils Photo
☐ 84-85 Devils Photo
☐ 85-86 Devils Photo
☐ 86-87 Devils Photo
☐ 87-88 Devils Photo
☐ 88-89 Devils Photo
☐ 89-90 Devils Photo
☐ 90-91 Devils Photo
☐ 91-92 Devils Photo

'96 - 97 NJER.

SHARP

Martin Brodeur is the most expensive single at $3. Singles start at 50¢.
Card Size: 2 1/2" x 3 1/2"
Sponsor: Sharp Electronics
Set (30 cards): $18

☐ Mike Dunham #1 (G)
☐ Ken Daneyko #3
☐ Scott Stevens #4
☐ Denis Pederson #10
☐ Steve Sullivan #11
☐ Bill Guerin #12
☐ Brian Rolston #14
☐ John MacLean #15
☐ Bobby Holik #16
☐ Petr Sykora #17
☐ Sergei Brylin #18
☐ Bob Carpenter #19
☐ Jay Pandolfo #20
☐ Randy McKay #21
☐ Patrik Elias #22
☐ Dave Andreychuk #23
☐ Lyle Odelein #24
☐ Valeri Zelepukin #25
☐ Jason Smith #26
☐ Scott Niedermayer #27
☐ Kevin Dean #28
☐ Shawn Chambers #29
☐ Martin Brodeur #30 (G)
☐ Steve Thomas #32
☐ Reid Simpson #33
☐ Lou Lamoriello, G.M.
☐ Jacques Lemaire, Coach
☐ J. Caron, Asst. Coach
☐ R. Ftorek, Asst. Coach
☐ J. H. McMullen, Owner

'01 - 02 NJER.

We do not have a checklist for this series of cards.

NEW YORK ISLANDERS

'79 - 80 NYIS.

Prices are in NRMT. Regional stars do carry a premium.

Card Size: 3" x 5"
Sponsor: None
Set (22 cards): $60

☐	Mike Bossy	13
☐	Bob Bourne	2
☐	Curt Giles	2
☐	Billy Harris	2
☐	Lorne Henning	2
☐	Gary Howatt	2
☐	Anders Kallur	2
☐	Mike Kaszycki	2
☐	Dave Langevin	2
☐	Dave Lewis	2
☐	Bob Lorimer	2
☐	Wayne Merrick	2
☐	Bob Nystrom	4
☐	Stefan Persson	2
☐	Denis Potvin	6
☐	Jean Potvin	2
☐	Glenn Resch (G)	5
☐	Billy Smith (G)	7
☐	Steve Tambellini	2
☐	John Tonelli	4
☐	Bryan Trottier	7
☐	Islanders logo	2

'83 - 84 NYIS.

Mike Bossy is the most expensive single at $8. Singles start at $1.50.
Card Size: 2 1/2" x 3 1/2"
Sponsor: None
Set (19 cards): $35

☐ Mike Bossy
☐ Bob Bourne
☐ Billy Carroll
☐ Clark Gillies
☐ Mats Hallin
☐ Kelly Hrudey (G)
☐ Tomas Jönsson
☐ Dave Langevin
☐ Rollie Melanson (G)
☐ Wayne Merrick
☐ Ken Morrow
☐ Bob Nystrom
☐ Denis Potvin
☐ Billy Smith (G)
☐ Brent Sutter
☐ Duane Sutter
☐ John Tonelli
☐ Bryan Trottier
☐ Team Photo

'83 - 84 NYIS.

ISLANDER NEWS

Mike Bossy (card #2) is the most expensive single at $6. Singles start at 75¢.
Card Size: 2 1/2" x 3 1/2"
Sponsor: Islander News
Set (38 cards): $35

☐ 1 Checklist
☐ 2 Mike Bossy
☐ 3 Bob Bourne
☐ 4 Billy Carroll
☐ 5 Greg Gilbert
☐ 6 Clark Gillies
☐ 7 Butch Goring
☐ 8 Mats Hallin
☐ 9 Anders Kallur
☐ 10 Wayne Merrick
☐ 11 Bob Nystrom
☐ 12 Brent Sutter
☐ 13 Duane Sutter
☐ 14 John Tonelli
☐ 15 Bryan Trottier
☐ 16 Tomas Jonsson
☐ 17 Gordie Lane
☐ 18 Dave Langevin
☐ 19 Ken Morrow
☐ 20 Stefan Persson
☐ 21 Denis Potvin
☐ 22 Rollie Melanson (G)
☐ 23 Billy Smith (G)
☐ 24 Stanley Cup
☐ 25 Stanley Cup
☐ 26 Stanley Cup
☐ 27 Lorne Henning
☐ 28 Bill Torrey
☐ 29 Al Arbour
☐ 30 Waske/ Pickard
☐ 31 '79-80 Team Photo
☐ 32 '80-81 Team Photo
☐ 33 '81-82 Team Photo
☐ 34 '82-83 Team Photo
☐ 35 Mike Bossy
☐ 36 Billy Smith (G)
☐ 37 Bryan Trottier
☐ 38 Butch Goring

'84 - 85 NYIS.

ISLANDER NEWS

Pat LaFontaine (card #11) is the most expensive single at $10. Singles start at 75¢.
Card Size: 2 1/2" x 3 1/2"
Sponsor: Islander News
Set (37 cards): $40

☐ 1 Checklist
☐ 2 Mike Bossy
☐ 3 Bob Bourne
☐ 4 Pat Flatley
☐ 5 Greg Gilbert
☐ 6 Clark Gillies
☐ 7 Mats Hallin
☐ 8 Anders Kallur
☐ 9 Alan Kerr
☐ 10 Roger Kortko
☐ 11 Pat LaFontaine
☐ 12 Bob Nystrom
☐ 13 Brent Sutter
☐ 14 Duane Sutter
☐ 15 John Tonelli
☐ 16 Bryan Trottier
☐ 17 Paul Boutilier
☐ 18 Gerald Diduck
☐ 19 Gord Dineen
☐ 20 Tomas Jönsson
☐ 21 Gordie Lane
☐ 22 Dave Langevin
☐ 23 Ken Morrow
☐ 24 Stefan Persson
☐ 25 Denis Potvin
☐ 26 Kelly Hrudey
☐ 27 Billy Smith (G)
☐ 28 Bill Torrey
☐ 29 Al Arbour
☐ 30 Brian Kilrea
☐ 31 Ron Wiske/Jim Pickard
☐ 32 HL: Mike Bossy
☐ 33 HL: Denis Potvin
☐ 34 HL: Billy Smith (G)
☐ 35 HL: Bryan Trottier
☐ 36 '84-85 Team Photo
☐ 37 Wales Conf. Champs

'89 - 90 NYIS.

Pat LaFontaine is the most expensive single at $4. Singles start at $1.
Card Size: 3 7/8" x 7 1/4"
Sponsor: None
Set (22 cards): $30

☐ Al Arbour
☐ Dean Chynoweth
☐ Dave Chyzowski
☐ Doug Crossman
☐ Gerald Diduck
☐ Tom Fitzgerald
☐ Mark Fitzpatrick (G)

☐ Patrick Flatley
☐ Glenn Healy (G)
☐ Alan Kerr
☐ Pat LaFontaine
☐ Mikko Mäkelä
☐ Don Maloney
☐ Jeff Norton
☐ Gary Nylund
☐ Rich Pilon
☐ Brent Sutter
☐ Gilles Thibaudeau
☐ Bryan Trottier
☐ David Volek
☐ Mick Vukota
☐ Randy Wood

'93 - 94 NYIS.

CHEMICAL

Mike Bossy is the most expensive single at $3. Singles start at 75¢.
Card Size: 2 1/2" x 3 1/2"
Sponsor: Chemical Business Bank
Set (10 cards): $15

☐ Mike Bossy
☐ Clark Gillies
☐ Gerry Hart
☐ Wayne Merrick
☐ Bob Nystrom
☐ Denis Potvin
☐ Billy Smith (G)
☐ John Tonelli
☐ Ed Westfall
☐ Islanders

'96 - 97 NYIS.

25th ANNIVERSARY

These postcards feature black and white photos. Zigmund Palffy is the most expensive single at $4. Singles start at $1.
Sponsor: None
Set (23 cards): $25

☐ Niclas Andersson
☐ Derek Armstrong
☐ Todd Bertuzzi
☐ Éric Fichaud (G)
☐ Travis Green
☐ Doug Houda
☐ Brent Hughes
☐ Kenny Jönsson
☐ Derek King
☐ Paul Kruse
☐ Claude Lapointe
☐ Scott Lachance
☐ Bryan McCabe
☐ Marty McInnis
☐ Zigmund Palffy
☐ Dan Plante
☐ Richard Pilon
☐ Tommy Salo (G)
☐ Bryan Smolinski
☐ Dennis Vaske
☐ Mick Vukota
☐ Randy Wood
☐ Mike Milbury, Coach

'99 - 00 NYIS.

UPPER DECK

Card Size: 2 1/2" x 3 1/2"
Sponsor: Upper Deck
Set (11 cards):

☐ NY1 Bryan Trottier
☐ NY2 Billy Smith (G)
☐ NY3 Denis Potvin
☐ NY4 Bob Nystrom
☐ NY5 Clark Gillies
☐ NY6 Lorne Henning
☐ NY7 Al Arbour
☐ NY8 Ken Morrow
☐ NY9 Anders Kallur
☐ NY10 Butch Goring
☐ NY11 John Tonelli

NEW YORK RANGERS

'81 - 82 NYRA.

We have little information on this series. Other singles exist.
Postcard Size: 3 1/2" x 5 1/2"
Sponsor: None

☐ Mark Pavelich #40

'87 - 88 NYRA.

We have little information on this series. Other singles exist.
Card Size: 4 1/2" x 6 1/2"
Sponsor: None

☐ Marcel Dionne

'89 - 90 NYRA.

MARINE MIDLAND

The most expensive singles are Brian Leetch, John Vanbiesbrouck at $6-8 and Mike Richter at $6-8. Singles start at $1.
Card Size: 2 5/8" x 3 5/6"
Sponsor: Marine Midland Bank
Set (30 cards): $35

☐ Jeff Bloemberg #38
☐ Paul Broten #37
☐ Ulf Dahlen #16
☐ Jan Erixon #20
☐ Bob Froese #33 (G)
☐ Ron Greschner #4
☐ Mark Hardy #14
☐ Miloslav Horava #6
☐ Mark Janssens #15
☐ Kris King #12
☐ Kelly Kisio #11
☐ Brian Leetch #2
☐ Troy Mallette #26
☐ Corey Millen #23
☐ Randy Moller #24
☐ Brian Mullen #19
☐ Roger Neilson
☐ Bernie Nicholls #9
☐ Chris Nilan #30
☐ John Ogrodnick #25
☐ James Patrick #3
☐ Rudy Poeschek #29
☐ Mike Richter #35 (G)
☐ Normand Rochefort #5
☐ Lindy Ruff #44
☐ David Shaw #21
☐ Darren Turcotte #8
☐ J. Vanbiesbrouck #34 (G)
☐ Carey Wilson #17
☐ Rangers/ MasterCard

'92 - 93 NYRA.

We have little information on this series. Other singles exist.
Postcard Size: 3 1/2" x 5 1/2"
Sponsor: None

☐ Brian Leetch
☐ Mark Messier

'94 - 95 NYRA.

We have little information on this series. Other singles exist.
Postcard Size: 3 1/2" x 5 1/2"
Sponsor: None

☐ Steve Larmer

'98 - 99 NYRA.

Wayne Gretzky is the most expensive single at $5. Singles start at $1.
Set (24 cards): $40

☐ Jeff Beukeboom
☐ Dan Cloutier (G)
☐ Brent Fedyk
☐ Adam Graves
☐ Wayne Gretzky
☐ Todd Harvey
☐ Mike Knuble
☐ Darren Langdon
☐ Brian Leetch
☐ John MacLean
☐ Manny Malhotra
☐ Stanislav Neckar
☐ Petr Nedved
☐ Peter Popovic
☐ Sean Pronger
☐ Mike Richter (G)
☐ Ulf Samuelsson
☐ Marc Savard
☐ Mathieu Schneider
☐ Kevin Stevens
☐ P.J. Stock
☐ Niklas Sundström
☐ Chris Tamer
☐ Esa Tikkanen

'01 - 02 NYRA.

Other singles exist.

☐ Dan Blackburn (G)
☐ Brian Leetch
☐ Sandy McCarthy
☐ Mike Richter (G)

'02 - 03 NYRA.

We do not have a checklist for this series of cards.

OTTAWA SENATORS

'92 - 93 OTTA.

580 CFRA RADIO

Singles start at $1.50.
Card Size: 4" x 6"
Sponsors: 580 CFRA, Today's Colonial Furniture
Set (21 cards): $20

☐ Dave Archibald
☐ Jamie Baker
☐ Daniel Berthiaume (G)
☐ Laurie Boschman
☐ Neil Brady
☐ Mark Freer
☐ Radek Hamr
☐ Jody Hull
☐ Tomas Jelinek
☐ Bob Kudelski
☐ Mark Lamb
☐ Jeff Lazaro
☐ Chris Luongo
☐ Darcy Loewen
☐ Norm Maciver
☐ Andrew McBain
☐ Mike Peluso
☐ Brad Shaw
☐ Doug Smail
☐ Sylvain Turgeon
☐ Steve Weeks (G)

'93 - 94 OTTA.

KRAFT

Pavol Demitra is the most expensive single at $12. Singles start at $4. 13 of the 26 players are short printed (*) and start at $6.
Photo Size: 8 1/2" x 11"
Sponsor: Kraft
Set (27 photos): $120
Album: $15

☐ Dave Archibald
☐ Craig Billington
☐ Rick Bowness
☐ Robert Burakovsky (*)
☐ Alexandre Daigle
☐ Pavol Demitra (*)
☐ Gord Dineen
☐ Dmitri Filimonov (*)
☐ Brian Glynn (*)
☐ Bill Huard (*)
☐ Jarmo Kekäläinen (*)
☐ Bob Kudelski (*)
☐ Mark Lamb (*)
☐ Darcy Loewen
☐ Norm Maciver
☐ Darrin Madeley (G) (*)
☐ Troy Mallette
☐ Brad Marsh
☐ Dave McLlwain
☐ Darren Rumble (*)
☐ Vladimir Ruzicka (*)
☐ Brad Shaw
☐ Graeme Townshend (*)
☐ Sylvain Turgeon
☐ Dennis Vial (*)
☐ Alexei Yashin
☐ Team Photo

'94 - 95 OTTA.

BELL MOBILITY

Alexei Yashin is the most expensive single at $3. Singles start at $1.
Card Size: 4" x 6"
Sponsor: Bell Mobility
Set (28 cards): $25

☐ Dave Archibald
☐ Don Beaupré (G)
☐ Radim Bicanek
☐ Craig Billington (G)
☐ Claude Boivin
☐ Radek Bonk
☐ Phil Bourque
☐ Rick Bowness
☐ Randy Cunneyworth
☐ Chris Dahlquist
☐ Alexandre Daigle
☐ Pat Elynuik
☐ Rob Gaudreau
☐ Sean Hill
☐ Bill Huard
☐ Kerry Huffman
☐ Scott Levins
☐ Norm Maciver
☐ Darrin Madeley (G)
☐ Troy Mallette
☐ Brad Marsh
☐ Dave McLlwain
☐ Troy Murray
☐ Stanislav Neckar
☐ Jim Paek
☐ Sylvain Turgeon
☐ Dennis Vial
☐ Alexei Yashin

'95 - 96 OTTA.

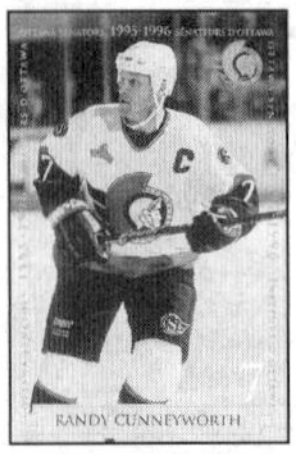

Daniel Alfredsson is the most expensive single at $4. Singles start at $1.
Card Size: 4" x 6"
Sponsor: None
Set (27 cards): $20

☐ Daniel Alfredsson
☐ Dave Archibald
☐ Mike Bales (G)
☐ Don Beaupré (G)
☐ Radek Bonk
☐ Phil Bourque
☐ Tom Chorske
☐ Joe Cirella
☐ Randy Cunneyworth
☐ Alexandre Daigle
☐ Ted Drury
☐ Steve Duchesne
☐ Rob Gaudreau
☐ Sean Hill
☐ Kerry Huffman
☐ Scott Levins
☐ Troy Mallette
☐ Brad Marsh
☐ Trent McCleary
☐ Jaroslav Modry
☐ Frank Musil
☐ Stanislav Neckar
☐ Dan Quinn
☐ Martin Straka
☐ Antti Törmänen
☐ Dennis Vial
☐ Alexei Yashin

'96 - 97 OTTA.

PIZZA HUT

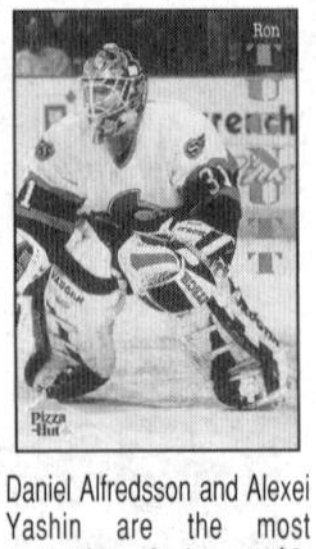

Daniel Alfredsson and Alexei Yashin are the most expensive singles at $3. Singles start at $1.
Card Size: 4" x 6"
Sponsor: Pizza Hut
Set (30 cards): $20

☐ Daniel Alfredsson
☐ Radek Bonk
☐ Tom Chorske
☐ Randy Cunneyworth
☐ Andreas Dackell
☐ Alexandre Daigle
☐ Steve Duchesne
☐ Bruce Gardiner
☐ Dave Hannan
☐ Sean Hill
☐ Denny Lambert
☐ Janne Laukkanen
☐ Jacques Martin
☐ Shawn McEachern
☐ Frank Musil
☐ Phil Myre
☐ Stanislav Neckar
☐ Christer Olsson
☐ Perry Pearn
☐ Lance Pitlick
☐ Craig Ramsay
☐ Wade Redden
☐ Damian Rhodes (G)
☐ Ron Tugnutt (G)
☐ Shaun Van Allen
☐ Dennis Vial
☐ Alexei Yashin
☐ Jason York
☐ Jason Zent
☐ Sergei Zholtok

'97 - 98 OTTA.

The most expensive single is Alexei Yashin at $3. Singles start at 75¢.
Card Size: 3" x 4 1/2"
Sponsor: None
Set (25 cards): $15

☐ Daniel Alfredsson #11
☐ Magnus Arvedsson #20
☐ Radek Bonk #14
☐ Randy Cunneyworth #7
☐ Andreas Dackell #10
☐ Alexandre Daigle #9
☐ Bruce Gardiner #25
☐ Igor Kravchuk #29
☐ Denny Lambert #28
☐ Janne Laukkanen #27
☐ Shawn McEachern #15
☐ Stan Neckar #24
☐ Chris Phillips #5
☐ Lance Pitlick #2
☐ Wade Redden #6
☐ Damian Rhodes #1 (G)
☐ Ron Tugnutt #31 (G)
☐ Shaun Van Allen #22
☐ Dennis Vial #21
☐ Alexei Yashin #19
☐ Jason York #33
☐ Sergei Zholtok #16
☐ Jacques Martin, Coach
☐ Perry Pearn, Asst. Coach
☐ C. Ramsay, Asst. Coach

'98 - 99 OTTA.

Singles start at 75¢.
Sponsor: None
Set (29 cards): $20

☐ Daniel Alfredsson
☐ Magnus Arvedsson
☐ Bill Berg
☐ Radek Bonk
☐ Anders Dackell
☐ Bruce Gardiner
☐ Marian Hossa
☐ Andreas Johansson
☐ Igor Kravchuk
☐ Janne Laukkanen
☐ Jacques Martin
☐ Jacques Martin
☐ Steve Martins
☐ Shawn McEachern
☐ Chris Murray
☐ Chris Phillips
☐ Lance Pitlick
☐ Vaclav Prospal
☐ Wade Redden
☐ Damian Rhodes
☐ Sami Salo
☐ Patrick Traverse
☐ Ron Tugnutt
☐ Shaun Van Allen
☐ Alexei Yashin
☐ Jason York
☐ Mascot Spartacat
☐ Mascot Spartacat
☐ Senators

'99 - 00 OTTA.

CCM

Singles start at $1.50.
Sponsor: CCM
Set (26 cards):

☐ Daniel Alfredsson
☐ Magnus Arvedsson
☐ Radek Bonk
☐ Anders Dackell
☐ Kevin Dineen
☐ Mike Fisher
☐ Bruce Gardiner
☐ Marian Hossa
☐ Joé Juneau
☐ Patrick Lalime
☐ Igor Kravchuk
☐ Janne Laukkanen
☐ Jacques Martin
☐ Shawn McEachern
☐ Chris Phillips
☐ Vaclav Prospal
☐ Wade Redden
☐ André Roy
☐ Lance Pitlick
☐ Patrick Traverse
☐ Ron Tugnutt
☐ Shaun Van Allen
☐ Rob Zamuner
☐ Jason York
☐ Mascot Spartacat
☐ Senators

'00 - 01 OTTA.

Singles start at $1.50.
Set (26 cards):

☐ Daniel Alfredsson
☐ Magnus Arvedsson
☐ Radek Bonk
☐ Andreas Dackell
☐ Mike Fisher
☐ Colin Forbes
☐ Martin Havlat
☐ Marian Hossa
☐ Jani Hurme (G)
☐ Patrick Lalime (G)
☐ Shawn McEachern
☐ Ricard Persson
☐ Chris Phillips
☐ Vaclav Prospal
☐ Karel Rachunek
☐ Wade Redden
☐ Jamie Rivers
☐ André Roy
☐ Sami Salo
☐ Alexei Yashin
☐ Jason York
☐ Rob Zamuner
☐ Jacques Martin
☐ Roger Neilson
☐ Perry Pearn
☐ Mascot Spartacat

'01 - 02 OTTA.

SENS FOUNDATION

Singles start at $1.50.
Set (29 cards):

☐ Daniel Alfredsson
☐ Magnus Arvedsson
☐ Radek Bonk
☐ Zdeno Chara
☐ Ivan Ciernik
☐ Mike Fisher
☐ Martin Havlat
☐ Chris Herperger
☐ Shane Hnidy
☐ Marian Hossa
☐ Jani Hurme (G)
☐ Patrick Lalime (G)
☐ Curtis Leschyshyn
☐ Shawn McEachern
☐ Bill Muckalt
☐ Chris Neil
☐ Ricard Persson
☐ Chris Phillips
☐ Karel Rachunek
☐ Wade Redden
☐ André Roy
☐ Sami Salo
☐ Todd White
☐ Jacques Martin, Coach
☐ Perry Pearn
☐ Roger Neilson
☐ Don Jackson
☐ Mascot Spartacat
☐ Senators 10th year

'02 - 03 OTTA.

Singles start at $1.50.
Set (33 cards):

☐ Daniel Alfredsson
☐ Magnus Arvedsson
☐ Radek Bonk
☐ Dennis Bonvie
☐ Zdeno Chara
☐ Mike Fisher
☐ Martin Havlat
☐ Shane Hnidy
☐ Marian Hossa
☐ Jody Hull
☐ Joel Kwiatkowski
☐ Patrick Lalime (G)
☐ Curtis Leschyshyn
☐ Chris Neil
☐ Chris Phillips
☐ Martin Prusek (G)
☐ Karel Rachunek
☐ Wade Redden
☐ Peter Schaefer
☐ Petr Schastlivy
☐ Brad Smyth
☐ Jason Spezza
☐ Shaun Van Allen
☐ Anton Volchenkov
☐ Peter White
☐ Jacques Martin
☐ Don Jackson
☐ Phil Myre
☐ Roger Neilson
☐ Perry Pearn
☐ Mascot Spartacat
☐ Mascot Spartacat
☐ Mascot Spartacat

PHILADELPHIA FLYERS

'70 - 71 PHIL.

Doug Favell is the most expensive single at $7. Singles start at $4. Other singles may exist.
Card Size: 3 1/2" x 5 1/2"
Sponsor: None

☐ Barry Ashbee
☐ Gary Dornhoefer
☐ W.Elliott/ F.Leurs
☐ Doug Favell (G)
☐ Earl Heiskala
☐ Larry Hillman
☐ André Lacroix
☐ Lew Morrison
☐ Simon Nolet
☐ Garry Peters
☐ Vic Stasiuk
☐ George Swarbrick

'72 - 73 PHIL.

MIGHTY MILK

These cards were issued on the backs of milk cartons. Other singles may exist. Bobby Clarke is the most expensive single at $90 in NRMT. Singles start at $15.
Card Size: 3 5/8" x 7 1/2"
Sponsors: Mighty Milk, Channel 29

☐ Serge Bernier
☐ Bobby Clarke
☐ Gary Dornhoefer
☐ Doug Favell (G)
☐ Jean-Guy Gendron
☐ Bill Lesuk
☐ Lew Morrison
☐ Ed Van Impe

'83 - 84 PHIL.

J.C PENNY

The most expensive singles are Pelle Lindberg at $12 and Bobby Clarke at $6. Singles start at $1.50.
Card Size: 4" x 6"
Sponsor: J.C. Penney
Set (22 cards): $45

☐ Ray Allison
☐ Bill Barber
☐ Frank Bathe
☐ Lindsay Carson
☐ Bobby Clarke
☐ Glen Cochrane
☐ Doug Crossman
☐ Miroslav Dvorak
☐ Thomas Eriksson
☐ Bob Froese (G)
☐ Randy Holt
☐ Mark Howe
☐ Tim Kerr
☐ Pelle Lindberg (G)
☐ Brad Marsh
☐ Brad McCrimmon
☐ Dave Poulin
☐ Brian Propp
☐ Ilkka Sinisalo
☐ Darryl Sittler
☐ Rich Sutter
☐ Ron Sutter

'86 - 87 PHIL.

The most expensive singles are Ron Hextall and Rick Tocchet at $5-7. Singles start at $1. Bob Froese is short printed and sells at $3-5. A 29-card sets sell at $30.
Card Size: 4 1/8" x 6"
Sponsor: None
Set (30 cards): $35

☐ Bill Barber
☐ Dave Brown
☐ Lindsay Carson
☐ Murray Craven
☐ Pat Croce
☐ Doug Crossman
☐ J.J. Daigneault
☐ Per-Erik Eklund
☐ Bob Froese (G)
☐ Ron Hextall (G)
☐ Paul Holmgren
☐ Ed Hospodar
☐ Mark Howe
☐ Mike Keenan
☐ Tim Kerr
☐ Brad Marsh
☐ Brad McCrimmon
☐ E.J. Maguire
☐ Scott Mellanby
☐ Bernie Parent
☐ Dave Poulin
☐ Brian Propp
☐ Glenn Resch (G)
☐ Ilkka Sinisalo
☐ Derrick Smith
☐ Daryl Stanley
☐ Ron Sutter
☐ Rick Tocchet
☐ Peter Zezel
☐ Team Photo

'89 - 90 PHIL.

Bobby Clarke is the most expensive single at $3. Singles start at $1.
Card Size: 4 1/8" x 6"
Sponsor: None
Set (29 cards): $25

☐ Keith Acton
☐ Craig Berube
☐ Mike Bullard
☐ Terry Carkner
☐ Jeff Chychrun
☐ Bob Clarke
☐ Murray Craven
☐ Mike Eaves
☐ Per-Erik Eklund
☐ Ron Hextall (G)
☐ Paul Holmgren
☐ Mark Howe
☐ Kerry Huffman
☐ Tim Kerr
☐ Scott Mellanby
☐ Gord Murphy
☐ Andy Murray
☐ Pete Peeters (G)
☐ Dave Poulin
☐ Brian Propp
☐ Kjell Samuelsson
☐ Ilkka Sinisalo
☐ Derrick Smith
☐ Doug Sulliman
☐ Ron Sutter
☐ Rick Tocchet
☐ Jay Wells
☐ Ken Wregget (G)
☐ Team Photo

'90 - 91 PHIL.

J.C PENNY

Mike Ricci is the most expensive single at $2. Singles start at $1.
Card Size: 4 1/8" x 6"
Sponsor: None
Set (26 cards): $25

☐ Keith Acton
☐ Murray Baron
☐ Craig Berube
☐ Terry Carkner
☐ Jeff Chychrun
☐ Murray Craven
☐ Per-Erik Eklund
☐ Ron Hextall (G)
☐ Tony Horacek
☐ Martin Hostak
☐ Mark Howe
☐ Kerry Huffman
☐ Tim Kerr
☐ Dale Kushner
☐ Norman Lacombe
☐ Jiri Latal
☐ Scott Mellanby
☐ Gord Murphy
☐ Pete Peeters (G)
☐ Mike Ricci
☐ Kjell Samuelsson
☐ Derrick Smith
☐ Ron Sutter
☐ Rick Tocchet
☐ Ken Wregget (G)
☐ Team Photo

'91 - 92 PHIL.

J.C PENNY

Rod Brind'Amour is the most expensive single at $3. Singles start at 75¢.
Card Size: 4 1/8" x 6"
Sponsors: J.C. Penney
Set (26 cards): $25

☐ Keith Acton
☐ Rod Brind'Amour
☐ Dave Brown
☐ Terry Carkner
☐ Kimbi Daniels
☐ Kevin Dineen
☐ Steve Duchesne
☐ Per-Erik Eklund
☐ Corey Foster
☐ Ron Hextall (G)
☐ Tony Horacek
☐ Mark Howe
☐ Kerry Huffman
☐ Brad Jones
☐ Steve Kasper
☐ Dan Kordic
☐ Jiri Latal
☐ Andrei Lomakin
☐ Gord Murphy
☐ Mark Pederson
☐ Dan Quinn
☐ Mike Ricci
☐ Kjell Samuelsson
☐ Rick Tocchet
☐ Ken Wregget (G)
☐ Team Photo

'92 - 93 PHIL.

J.C PENNY

Eric Lindros is the most expensive single at $6-10. Singles start at $1.
Card Size: 4 1/8" x 6"
Sponsor: J.C. Penney
Set (23 cards): $25

☐ Keith Acton
☐ S. Beauregard (G)
☐ Brian Benning
☐ Rod Brind'Amour
☐ Claude Boivin
☐ Dave Brown
☐ Terry Carkner
☐ Shawn Cronin
☐ Kevin Dineen
☐ Per-Erik Eklund
☐ Doug Evans
☐ Brent Fedyk
☐ Garry Galley
☐ Gord Hynes
☐ Eric Lindros
☐ Andrei Lomakin
☐ Ryan McGill
☐ Ric Nattress
☐ Greg Paslawski
☐ Mark Recchi
☐ Dominic Roussel (G)
☐ Dimitri Yushkevich
☐ Team Photo

'92 - 93 PHIL.

UPPER DECK

Eric Lindros (15/11/92) is the most expensive sheet at $25. Lindros' second and third sheet sell at $15. Singles start at $4.
Photo Size: 8 1/2" x 11"
Sponsor: Upper Deck
Set (44 photos): $275

☐ 19SEP Kevin Dineen
☐ 24SEP Brian Benning
☐ 03OCT Mark Recchi
☐ 09OCT Keith Acton
☐ 15OCT Rod Brind'Amour
☐ 18OCT Dave Brown
☐ 22OCT D. Roussel (G)
☐ 24OCT Gord Hynes
☐ 07NOV Claude Boivin
☐ 12NOV D. Yushkevich
☐ 15NOV Eric Lindros
☐ 19NOV Steve Kasper
☐ 22NOV Team Photo
☐ 27NOV Greg Paslawski
☐ 03DEC Terry Carkner
☐ 06DEV Shawn Cronin
☐ 12DEC Brent Fedyk
☐ 17DEC Garry Galley
☐ 19DEC Andrei Lomakin
☐ 23DEC Dineen dad/son
☐ 07JAN Beauregard (G)
☐ 09JAN Mark Recchi
☐ 10JAN Ryan McGill
☐ 14JAN Doug Evans
☐ 17JAN 3 players
☐ 21JAN Ric Nattress
☐ 24JAN Rod Brind'Amour
☐ 26JAN T. Söderström (G)
☐ 28JAN Per-Erik Eklund
☐ 09FEB Dave Brown
☐ 11FEB Soderstrom/ McGill/ Lindros/ Yushkevich/ Roussel
☐ 14FEB Josef Beranek
☐ 25FEB Greg Paslawski
☐ 27FEB Hartsburg/ B.Dineen/ Hitchcock
☐ 02MAR Keith Acton
☐ 11MAR Mark Recchi
☐ 13MAR Garry Galley
☐ 13MAR Team Photo
☐ 16MAR Terry Carkner
☐ 21MAR D. Roussel (G)
☐ 25MAR Greg Hawgood
☐ 03APR V. Butsayev
☐ 04APR Recchi/Lindros/ Fedyk
☐ 08APR Lomakin/ Yushkevich/ Butsayev
☐ 12APR Clarke/ Snider/ Allen, Barber/ Parent/

'93 - 94 PHIL.

GAME LINEUPS

Eric Lindros is the most expensive sheet at $20. Singles start at $5.

Photo Size: 8 1/2" x 11"
Sponsor: None
Set (44 photos): $250

☐ 16SEP Greg Hawgood
☐ 21SEP Brent Fedyk
☐ 26SEP Terry Carkner
☐ 05OCT Mark Recchi
☐ 10OCT Dave Brown
☐ 12OCT Jason Bowen
☐ 16OCT Kevin Dineen
☐ 21OCT Per-Erik Eklund
☐ 23OCT Eric Lindros
☐ 04NOV Mikael Renberg
☐ 07NOV Ryan McGill
☐ 11NOV Garry Galley
☐ 13NOV Yves Racine
☐ 18NOV S. Malgunas
☐ 21NOV Rod Brind'Amour
☐ 24NOV Coaches
☐ 26NOV Al Conroy
☐ 09DEC D. Roussel (G)
☐ 12DEC D. Yushkevich
☐ 16DEC Team Photo
☐ 18DEC Mark Recchi
☐ 21DEC V. Butsayev
☐ 23DEC Rookies
☐ 11JAN Josef Beranek
☐ 13JAN Captains
☐ 16JAN Dave Tippett
☐ 19JAN T. Soderstrom (G)
☐ 29JAN Eric Lindros
☐ 03JAN Claude Boivin
☐ 10FEB D. Yushkevich
☐ 13FEB Jeff Finley
☐ 21FEB Rob Ramage
☐ 24FEB Rob Zettler
☐ 08MAR Tim Kerr
☐ 10MAR Kevin Dineen
☐ 13MAR All-Stars
☐ 19MAR D. Roussel (G)
☐ 24MAR André Faust
☐ 27MAR Rod Brind'Amour
☐ 29MAR Brent Fedyk
☐ 31MAR Mark Lamb
☐ 07APR '73-74 Team
☐ 10APR Eric Lindros
☐ 12APR Players Thanks

'93 - 94 PHIL.

J.C PENNY

Eric Lindros is the most expensive single at $10. Singles start at $1.
Card Size: 4 1/8" x 6"
Sponsor: J.C. Penney
Set (24 cards): $25

☐ Josef Beranek
☐ Claude Boivin
☐ Jason Bowen
☐ Rod Brind'Amour
☐ Viacheslav Butsayev
☐ Dave Brown
☐ Al Conroy
☐ Kevin Dineen
☐ Per-Erik Eklund
☐ Brent Fedyk
☐ Jeff Finley
☐ Garry Galley
☐ Eric Lindros
☐ Stewart Malgunas
☐ Ryan McGill
☐ Rob Ramage
☐ Mark Recchi
☐ Mikael Renberg
☐ Dominic Roussel (G)
☐ Yves Racine
☐ Tommy Soderstrom (G)
☐ Dave Tippett
☐ Dimitri Yushkevich
☐ Team Photo

'94 - 95 PHIL.

GAME LINEUPS

We have little information on this set. Sheets are similar to the 1992-93 and 1993-94 sets. 1995-96 and 1996-97 game sheets were also likely released.
Size: 8 1/2" x 11"
Sponsor: None
Set (35 cards)

☐ Garry Galley
☐ Kevin Dineen
☐ Mark Lamb
☐ Stewart Malgunas
☐ Eric Lindros
☐ Shjon Podein
☐ Rod Brind'Amour
☐ Dominic Roussel (G)
☐ Ron Hextall (G)
☐ Patrik Juhlin
☐ T. Murray/ Acton/ Webster
☐ Mikael Renberg
☐ Kevin Haller
☐ Rob Zettler
☐ Chris Therien
☐ Craig MacTavish
☐ John LeClair
☐ Éric Desjardins
☐ Rob DiMaio
☐ Dimitri Yushkevich
☐ Legion of Doom
☐ Anatoli Semenov
☐ Y.Dupré/Therien/Juhlin
☐ Karl Dykhuis
☐ Gilbert Dionne
☐ Shawn Antoski
☐ Dave Brown
☐ Lindros/ MacT/ B'Amour
☐ Team Photo
☐ Eric Lindros
☐ Brent Fedyk
☐ Ron Hextall (G)
☐ Petr Svoboda
☐ Lindros/LeClair/Renberg
☐ John LeClair

'96 - 97 PHIL.

OCEAN SPRAY

Eric Lindros is the most expensive single at $7. Singles start at 75¢ Other players exist.
Card Size: 4 1/8" x 6"
Sponsor: Ocean Spray Cranberries
Set (24 cards): $20

☐ Rod Brind'Amour
☐ Paul Coffey
☐ Scott Daniels
☐ Éric Desjardins
☐ John Druce
☐ Karl Dykhuis
☐ Pat Falloon
☐ Dale Hawerchuk
☐ Ron Hextall (G)
☐ Trent Klatt
☐ Dan Kordic
☐ Daniel Lacroix
☐ John LeClair
☐ Eric Lindros
☐ Janne Niinimaa
☐ Joel Otto
☐ Shjon Podein
☐ Mikael Renberg
☐ Kjell Samuelsson
☐ Garth Snow
☐ Petr Svoboda
☐ Chris Therien
☐ Dainius Zubrus
☐ Team Photo

'97 - 98 PHIL.

COMCAST

We have little information on these 15-min. phonecards. Other singles exist.
Sponsor: Comcast

☐ Alexandre Daigle
☐ Chris Gratton
☐ John LeClair
☐ Eric Lindros

'01 - 02 PHIL.

Singles start at 75¢.
Size: 4" x 6"

☐ Brian Boucher (G)
☐ Donald Brashear
☐ Roman Cechmanek (G)
☐ Éric Desjardins
☐ Jiri Dopita
☐ Todd Fedoruk
☐ Ruslan Fedotenko
☐ Simon Gagné
☐ Kim Johnsson
☐ Kent Manderville
☐ John LeClair
☐ Chris McAllister
☐ Dan McGillis
☐ Marty Murray
☐ Keith Primeau
☐ Paul Ranheim
☐ Mark Recchi
☐ Luke Richardson
☐ Jeremy Roenick
☐ Chris Therien
☐ Rick Tocchet
☐ Eric Weinrich
☐ Justin Williams
☐ Team Photo
☐ Barber, Stothers, McGuire
☐ Ron Hextall
☐ Bobby Clarke
☐ Broadcasters
☐ Phantoms
☐ Mascot Phlex

'02 - 03 PHIL.

We do not have a checklist for this series of cards.

PHOENIX COYOTES

'96 - 97 PHOE.

COCA-COLA

The most expensive singles are Keith Tkachuk at $4 and Jeremy Roenick at $3. Singles start at $1. The backs of each player's two (or three) cards are identical.
Card Size: 3 1/2" x 6 1/2"
Sponsor: Coca-Cola
Set (35 cards): $25

☐ Bob Corkum #21
☐ Shane Doan #19
☐ Dallas Drake #11
☐ Dallas Eakins #6
☐ Mike Eastwood #32
☐ Jeff Finley #26
☐ Gartner #22 (looking right)
☐ Gartner #22 (facing forward)
☐ Mike Hudson #28
☐ Craig Janney #15
☐ Jim Johnson #8
☐ N. Khabibulin #35 (G) (facing right)
☐ N. Khabibulin #35 (G) (facing left)
☐ Chad Kilger #18
☐ K. King #17 (skating right)
☐ Kris King #17 (facing right)
☐ Igor Korolev #23
☐ Norm Maciver #44
☐ Dave Manson #4
☐ Brad McCrimmon #10
☐ Jim McKenzie #33
☐ Teppo Numminen #27
☐ Deron Quint #5
☐ Jeremy Roenick #97 (referee in background)
☐ Jeremy Roenick #97 (skating forward)
☐ Roenick #97 (looking left)
☐ Cliff Ronning #77
☐ Darrin Shannon #34
☐ Mike Stapleton #14
☐ Tkachuk #7 (looking left)
☐ Tkachuk #7 (looking right)
☐ Oleg Tverdovsky #20
☐ Darcy Wakaluk #43 (G)
☐ Paul MacLean/ Don Hay/ Zinetula Bilyaletdinov
☐ Coyotes Team Photo

'97 - 98 PHOE.

COCA-COLA

The most expensive singles are Keith Tkachuk at $3 and Jeremy Roenick at $2. Singles start at $1. The backs of each player's two or three cards are identical.
Card Size: 3 3/8" x 6 3/8"
Sponsor: Coca-Cola
Set (35 cards): $25

☐ B. Allaire, Goalie Coach
☐ Murray Baron #2
☐ Bob Corkum #21
☐ Gerald Diduck #4
☐ Shane Doan #19
☐ Jason Doig #55
☐ Dallas Drake #11
☐ Mike Gartner #22
☐ Brad Isbister #16
☐ Craig Janney #15
☐ Jim Johnson #8
☐ Nikolai Khabibulin #35 (G)
☐ Chad Kilger #18
☐ Norm Maciver #44
☐ Jocelyn Lemieux #32
☐ Jim McKenzie #33 (helmet)
☐ McKenzie #33 (no helmet)
☐ Jayson More #6
☐ Teppo Numminen #27
☐ Deron Quint #5
☐ Go. Roberts, Asst.Coach
☐ Roenick #97 (facing right)
☐ Roenick #97 (facing front)
☐ Roenick #97 (skating)
☐ Cliff Ronning #77
☐ Jim Schoenfeld, Coach
☐ Darrin Shannon #34
☐ John Slaney #26
☐ Mike Stapleton #14
☐ Keith Tkachuk #7
☐ Rick Tocchet #92
☐ J. Tortorella, Asst.Coach
☐ Jimmy Waite #28 (G)
☐ Darcy Wakaluk #43 (G)
☐ Juha Ylönen #36

'99 - 00 PHOE.

Other singles exist.

☐ Juha Ylönen

'02 - 03 PHOE.

Other singles exist.

☐ Sean Burke (G)

PITTSBURGH PENGUINS

'71 - 72 PITT.

Red Kelly is the most expensive single at $5 in NRMT. Singles start at $2.
Card Size: 3 1/2" x 6"
Sponsor: Sportcolor
Set (21 cards): $50

☐ Syl Apps
☐ Les Binkley (G)
☐ Dave Burrows
☐ Darryl Edestrand
☐ Roy Edwards (G)
☐ Val Fonteyne
☐ Nick Harbaruk
☐ Bryan Hextall
☐ Sheldon Kannegeiser
☐ Red Kelly
☐ Bob Leiter
☐ Keith McCreary
☐ Joe Noris
☐ Greg Polis
☐ Jean Pronovost
☐ René Robert
☐ Jim Rutherford (G)
☐ Ken Schinkel
☐ Ron Schock
☐ Bryan Watson
☐ Bob Woytowich

'74 - 75 PITT.

COCA-COLA

Pierre Larouche is the most expensive single at $5 in NRMT. Singles start at $2.
Postcard Size: 3 1/2" x 5 1/2"
Sponsor: None
Set (22 cards): $35

☐ Syl Apps
☐ Chuck Arnason
☐ Dave Burrows
☐ Colin Campbell
☐ Nelson Debenedet
☐ Steve Durbano
☐ Vic Hadfield
☐ Gary Inness (G)
☐ B.J. Johnson (G)
☐ Rick Kehoe
☐ Bob Kelly
☐ Jean-Guy Lagace
☐ Ron Lalonde
☐ Pierre Larouche
☐ Lowell MacDonald
☐ Dennis Owchar
☐ Bob Paradise
☐ Kelly Pratt
☐ Jean Pronovost
☐ Ron Schock
☐ Ron Stackhouse
☐ Barry Williams

'77 - 78 PITT.

McDONALD'S

Pierre Larouche is the most expensive single at $3 in NRMT. Singles start at $1.50.
Card Size: 2" x 3 1/2"

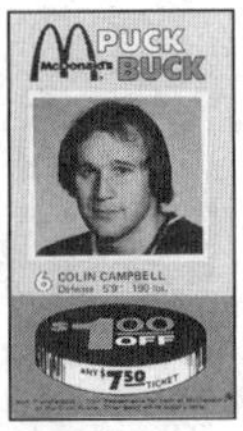

Sponsor: McDonald's
Set (18 cards): $30

☐ Russ Anderson
☐ Syl Apps
☐ Wayne Bianchin
☐ Dave Burrows
☐ Colin Campbell
☐ Blair Chapman
☐ Mike Corrigan
☐ Jim Hamilton
☐ Denis Herron (G)
☐ Rick Kehoe
☐ Pierre Larouche
☐ Lowell MacDonald
☐ Greg Malone
☐ Dennis Owchar
☐ Jean Pronovost
☐ Ron Stackhouse
☐ Dunc Wilson (G)
☐ Johnny Wilson

'83 - 84 PITT.

COKE IS IT!

Marty McSorley is the most expensive single at $5. Singles start at $1.50.

Card Size: 5" x 7"
Sponsor: Coca-Cola
Set (19 cards): $40

☐ Pat Boutette
☐ Andy Brickley
☐ Mike Bullard
☐ Ted Bulley
☐ Rod Buskas
☐ Randy Carlyle
☐ Michel Dion (G)
☐ Bob Errey
☐ Ron Flockhart
☐ Steve Gatzos
☐ Jim Hamilton
☐ Dave Hannan
☐ Denis Herron (G)
☐ Troy Loney
☐ Bryan Maxwell
☐ Marty McSorley
☐ Norm Schmidt
☐ Mark Taylor
☐ Greg Tebbutt

'83 - 84 PITT.

HEINZ

Rick Kehoe is the most expensive single at $3. Singles start at $1.50.

Card Size: 6" x 9"
Sponsor: Heinz
Set (22 cards): $30

☐ Paul Baxter
☐ Pat Boutette
☐ Randy Boyd
☐ Mike Bullard
☐ Randy Carlyle
☐ Marc Chorney
☐ Michel Dion (G)
☐ Bill Gardner
☐ Pat Graham
☐ Anders Hakansson
☐ Dave Hannan
☐ Denis Herron (G)
☐ Greg Hotham
☐ Stan Jonathan
☐ Rick Kehoe
☐ Peter Lee
☐ Greg Malone
☐ Kevin McClelland
☐ Ron Meighan
☐ Doug Shedden
☐ André St. Laurent
☐ Rich Sutter

'84 - 85 PITT.

HEINZ

Marty McSorley is the most expensive single at $5. Singles start at $1.50.

Card Size: 6" x 9"
Sponsor: Heinz
Set (22 cards): $30

☐ Pat Boutette
☐ Andy Brickley
☐ Mike Bullard
☐ Rod Buskas
☐ Randy Carlyle
☐ Michel Dion (G)
☐ Bob Errey
☐ Ron Flockhart
☐ Greg Fox
☐ Steve Gatzos
☐ Denis Herron (G)
☐ Greg Hotham
☐ Rick Kehoe
☐ Bryan Maxwell
☐ Marty McSorley
☐ Tom O'Regan
☐ Gary Rissling
☐ Roberto Romano (G)
☐ Tom Roulston
☐ Rocky Saganiuk
☐ Doug Shedden
☐ Mark Taylor

'86 - 87 PITT.

KODAK

Mario Lemieux is the most expensive single at $40. Singles start at $1.

Card Size: 2 3/16" x 2 1/2"
Sponsor: Kodak
Set (26 cards): $60

☐ Bob Berry
☐ Mike Blaisdell
☐ Doug Bodger
☐ Rod Buskas
☐ John Chabot
☐ Randy Cunneyworth
☐ Ron Duguay
☐ Bob Errey
☐ Dan Frawley
☐ David Hannan
☐ Randy Hillier
☐ Jim Johnson
☐ Kevin LaVallée
☐ Mario Lemieux
☐ Willy Lindstrom
☐ Moe Mantha
☐ Gilles Meloche (G)
☐ Dan Quinn
☐ Jim Roberts
☐ Roberto Romano (G)
☐ Terry Ruskowski
☐ Norm Schmidt
☐ Craig Simpson
☐ Ville Siren
☐ Warren Young (G)
☐ Team Photo

'87 - 88 PITT.

KODAK

Mario Lemieux is the most expensive single at $25. Singles start at $1.

Card Size: 2 3/16" x 2 1/2"
Sponsor: Kodak
Set (26 cards): $40

☐ Doug Bodger
☐ Rob Brown
☐ Rod Buskas
☐ Jock Callander
☐ Paul Coffey
☐ Randy Cunneyworth
☐ Chris Dahlquist
☐ Bob Errey
☐ Dan Frawley
☐ Steve Guenette (G)
☐ Randy Hillier
☐ Dave Hunter
☐ Jim Johnson
☐ Mike Kachowski
☐ Chris Kontos
☐ Mario Lemieux
☐ Troy Loney
☐ Dwight Mathiasen
☐ Dave McLlwain
☐ Gilles Meloche (G)
☐ Dan Quinn
☐ Pat Riggin (G)
☐ Charlie Simmer
☐ Ville Siren
☐ Wayne Van Dorp
☐ Team Photo

'89 - 90 PITT.

ELBY'S BIG BOY

Mario Lemieux is the most expensive single at $12. Singles start at $1. Other singles exist.

Card Size: 4" x 6"
Sponsors: Elby's, Coca-Cola

☐ Phil Bourque
☐ Rob Brown
☐ Mario Lemieux
☐ Kevin Stevens
☐ Zarley Zalapski

'89 - 90 PITT.

FOODLAND

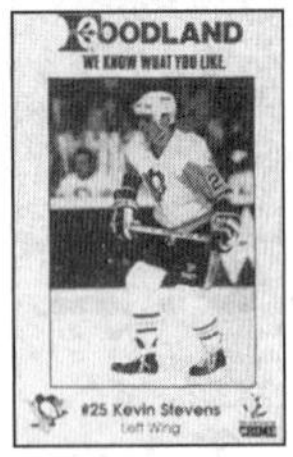

Mario Lemieux is the most expensive single at $12. Singles start at $1. Gilbert Delorme and Troy Loney were late additions and sell at $3-4. A 15-card set sells at $20.

Card Size: 2 5/8" x 4 1/8"
Sponsor: Foodland
Set (17 cards): $25

☐ 1 Rob Brown
☐ 2 Jim Johnson
☐ 3 Zarley Zalapski
☐ 4 Paul Coffey
☐ 5 Phil Bourque
☐ 6 Dan Quinn
☐ 6 Gilbert Delorme
☐ 7 Kevin Stevens
☐ 8 Bob Errey
☐ 9 John Cullen
☐ 10 Mario Lemieux
☐ 11 Randy Hillier
☐ 12 Jay Caufield
☐ 13 Andrew McBain
☐ 13 Troy Loney
☐ 14 Wendell Young (G)
☐ 15 Tom Barrasso (G)

'90 - 91 PITT.

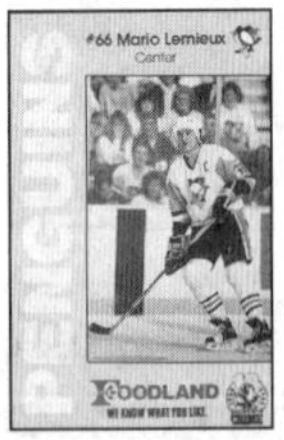

The most expensive singles are Jaromir Jagr at $12 and Mario Lemieux at $10. Singles start at 75¢.

Card Size: 2 11/16" x 4 1/8"
Sponsor: Foodland
Set (15 cards): $25

☐ 1 Phil Bourque
☐ 2 Paul Coffey
☐ 3 Randy Hillier
☐ 4 Barry Pederson
☐ 5 Tom Barrasso (G)
☐ 6 Mark Recchi
☐ 7 Bob Johnson
☐ 8 Joe Mullen
☐ 9 Kevin Stevens
☐ 10 John Cullen
☐ 11 Jaromir Jagr
☐ 12 Zarley Zalapski
☐ 13 Mario Lemieux
☐ 14 Tony Tanti
☐ 15 Bryan Trottier

'91 - 92 PITT.

ELBY'S BIG BOY

Jaromir Jagr and Mario Lemieux are the most expensive singles at $8. Singles start at $1.

Card Size: 4" x 6"
Sponsors: Elby's, Coca-Cola
Set (23 cards): $35

☐ Phil Bourque #29
☐ Scotty Bowman
☐ Jay Caufield #16
☐ Jeff Daniels #43
☐ Ron Francis #10
☐ Jaromir Jagr #68
☐ Grant Jennings #3
☐ Jamie Leach #20
☐ Mario Lemieux #66
☐ Troy Loney #24
☐ Joe Mullen #7
☐ Larry Murphy #55
☐ Jim Paek #2
☐ F. Pietrangelo #40 (G)
☐ Ken Priestlay #18
☐ Mark Recchi #8
☐ Gord Roberts #28
☐ Ulf Samuelsson #5
☐ Paul Stanton #22
☐ Kevin Stevens #25
☐ Peter Taglianetti #32
☐ Rick Tocchet #92
☐ Bryan Trottier #19
☐ Wendell Young #1 (G)

'91 - 92 PITT.

FOODLAND

Jaromir Jagr and Mario Lemieux are the most expensive singles at $8. Singles start at 75¢.

Card Size: 2 1/2" x 3 1/2"
Sponsor: Foodland
Set (15 cards): $20

☐ 1 Jim Paek
☐ 2 Ulf Samuelsson
☐ 3 Ron Francis
☐ 4 Mario Lemieux
☐ 5 Rick Tocchet
☐ 6 Joe Mullen
☐ 7 Troy Loney
☐ 8 Kevin Stevens
☐ 9 Tom Barrasso (G)
☐ 10 Larry Murphy
☐ 11 Jaromir Jagr
☐ 12 Bryan Trottier
☐ 13 Paul Stanton
☐ 14 Peter Taglianetti
☐ 15 Phil Bourque

'91 - 92 PITT.

FOODLAND STICKERS

This series was issued in three-sticker panels. The stickers have the same photos as the 1991-92 Topps set. The Lemieux/ Jagr panel sells at $8. Single panels start at $3.

Panel Size: 2 1/2" x 10 1/2"
Sponsors: Topps, Foodland
Set (4 panels): $20

☐ Bryan Trottier
Joe Mullen
Larry Murphy
☐ Tom Barrasso (G)
Ron Francis
Ulf Samuelsson
☐ Jaromir Jagr
Mario Lemieux
Kevin Stevens
☐ Mark Recchi
Paul Coffey
Frank Pietrangelo (G)

'92 - 93 PITT.

COKE / CLARK

The most expensive singles are Mario Lemieux and Jaromir Jagr at $6-8. Singles start at 75¢.

Card Size: 2 1/2" x 3 1/2"
Sponsors: Coca-Cola, Clark
Set (26 cards): $30

☐ Tom Barrasso (G)
☐ Scotty Bowman
☐ Jay Caufield
☐ Jeff Daniels
☐ Bob Errey
☐ Bryan Fogarty
☐ Ron Francis
☐ Jaromir Jagr
☐ Grant Jennings
☐ Mario Lemieux
☐ Troy Loney
☐ Shawn McEachern
☐ Joe Mullen
☐ Larry Murphy
☐ Mike Needham
☐ Jim Paek
☐ Kjell Samuelsson
☐ Ulf Samuelsson
☐ Paul Stanton
☐ Mike Stapleton
☐ Kevin Stevens
☐ Martin Straka
☐ Dave Tippett
☐ Rick Tocchet
☐ Ken Wregget (G)
☐ Mascot Penguins

'92 - 93 PITT.

FOODLAND

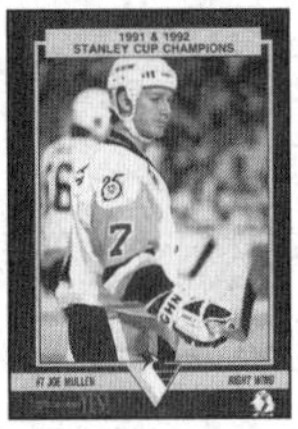

The most expensive singles are Mario Lemieux and Jaromir Jagr at $6-8. Singles start at 75¢.

Card Size: 2 1/2" x 3 1/2"
Sponsor: Foodland
Set (18 cards): $20

☐ 1 Mario Lemieux
☐ 2 Bob Errey
☐ 3 Jaromir Jagr
☐ 4 Rick Tocchet
☐ 5 Tom Barrasso (G)
☐ 6 Joe Mullen
☐ 7 Ron Francis
☐ 8 Troy Loney
☐ 9 Shawn McEachern
☐ 10 Larry Murphy
☐ 11 Jim Paek
☐ 12 Ulf Samuelsson
☐ 13 Paul Stanton
☐ 14 Kjell Samuelsson
☐ 15 Kevin Stevens
☐ 16 Dave Tippett
☐ 17 Martin Straka
☐ 18 Mascot Penguins

'92 - 93 PITT.

FOODLAND STICKERS

This series was issued in three-sticker panels. The Lemieux panel sells at $6-8. Single panels start at $3.

Panel Size: 2 1/2" x 10 1/2"
Sponsor: Foodland
Set (4 panels): $15

☐ Ron Francis
Jim Paek
Kevin Stevens
☐ Tom Barrasso (G)
Mario Lemieux
Troy Loney
☐ Joe Mullen
Ulf Samuelsson
Rick Tocchet
☐ Jaromir Jagr
Shawn McEachern
Larry Murphy

'93 - 94 PITT.

FOODLAND

Mario Lemieux is the most expensive single at $5. Singles start at 75¢.

Card Size: 2 1/2" x 3 1/2"
Sponsor: Foodland
Set (25 cards): $20

☐ 1 Mario Lemieux
☐ 2 Grant Jennings
☐ 3 Ulf Samuelsson
☐ 4 Rick Tocchet
☐ 5 Marty McSorley
☐ 6 Rick Kehoe
☐ 7 Doug Brown
☐ 8 Martin Straka
☐ 9 Jim Paek
☐ 10 Ken Wregget (G)
☐ 11 Jeff Daniels
☐ 12 Bryan Trottier
☐ 13 Larry Murphy
☐ 14 Ron Francis
☐ 15 Mike Needham
☐ 16 Mike Ramsey
☐ 17 Kevin Stevens
☐ 18 Kjell Samuelsson
☐ 19 Ed Johnston
☐ 20 Markus Näslund
☐ 21 Mike Stapleton
☐ 22 Peter Taglianetti
☐ 23 Jaromir Jagr
☐ 24 Tom Barrasso (G)
☐ 25 Joe Mullen

'94 - 95 PITT.

FOODLAND

Jaromir Jagr is the most expensive single at $5. Singles start at 75¢.

Card Size: 2 1/2" x 3 1/2"
Sponsor: Foodland
Set (25 cards): $20

☐ 1 Grant Jennings
☐ 2 Greg Hawgood
☐ 3 Shawn McEachern
☐ 4 Len Barrie
☐ 5 Ulf Samuelsson
☐ 6 Joe Mullen
☐ 7 John Cullen
☐ 8 Mike Hudson
☐ 9 Ron Francis
☐ 10 Tomas Sandstrom
☐ 11 Eddie Johnston
☐ 12 Chris Tamer
☐ 13 François Leroux
☐ 14 Luc Robitaille
☐ 15 Markus Näslund
☐ 16 Ken Wregget (G)
☐ 17 Chris Joseph
☐ 18 Peter Taglianetti
☐ 19 Kevin Stevens
☐ 20 Jim McKenzie
☐ 21 Kjell Samuelsson
☐ 22 Tom Barrasso (G)
☐ 23 Jaromir Jagr
☐ 24 Larry Murphy
☐ 25 Martin Straka

'95 - 96 PITT.

FOODLAND

Mario Lemieux is the most expensive single at $5. Singles start at 50¢.

Card Size: 2 1/2" x 3 1/2"
Sponsor: Foodland
Set (24 cards): $15

☐ 1 Ron Francis
☐ 2 Glen Murray
☐ 3 Chris Wells
☐ 4 Markus Näslund
☐ 5 Jaromir Jagr
☐ 6 François Leroux
☐ 7 Richard Park
☐ 8 Norm Maciver
☐ 9 Ken Wregget (G)
☐ 10 Tom Barrasso (G)
☐ 11 Rick Kehoe, A. Coach
☐ 12 Sergei Zubov
☐ 13 Joe Dziedzic
☐ 14 Ed Patterson
☐ 15 Tomas Sandström
☐ 16 Dave Roche
☐ 17 Petr Nedved
☐ 18 Chris Tamer
☐ 19 Chris Joseph
☐ 20 Ian Moran
☐ 21 Mascot Iceburgh
☐ 22 Ed Johnston, Coach
☐ 23 Mario Lemieux
☐ 24 Bryan Smolinski, Error (Ian Moran)
☐ 25 Dmitri Mironov

'96 - 97 PITT.

TRIBUNE REVIEW

Mario Lemieux is the most expensive single at $15. Singles start at $3.

Card Size: 4" x 5 1/2"
Sponsor: Tribune Review
Set (8 cards): $40

☐ Tom Barrasso (G)
☐ Ron Francis
☐ Jaromir Jagr
☐ Mario Lemieux
☐ Joe Mullen
☐ Ulf Samuelsson
☐ Kevin Stevens
☐ Bryan Trottier

'00 - 01 PITT.

MEDALLIONS

Medallion Diametre: 1 1/4"
Sponsor: None
Set (7 medals): $15

☐ Barrasso/ Binkley
☐ Burrows/ Samuelsson
☐ Coffey/ Murphy
☐ Francis/ Stevens
☐ Jagr/ Kehoe
☐ Johnson/ Patrick
☐ Lemieux/ Pronovost

QUÉBEC NORDIQUES

'80 - 81 QUÉB.

The most expensive player is Peter Stastny at $8. Singles start at $1.50. Michel Bergeron, Ron Grahame, Dave Pichette and Wally Weir are considered short prints and sell at $2-3 each. A 24-card set sells at $35.

Postcard Size: 3 1/2" x 5 1/2"
Sponsor: None
Set (28 cards): $45

☐ Michel Bergeron
☐ Serge Bernier
☐ Ron Chipperfield
☐ Kim Clackson
☐ Réal Cloutier
☐ Alain Côté
☐ Michel Dion (G)
☐ André Dupont
☐ Robbie Ftorek
☐ Michel Goulet
☐ Ron Grahame (G)
☐ Jamie Hislop
☐ Dale Hoganson
☐ Dale Hunter
☐ Pierre Lacroix
☐ Garry Larivière
☐ Richard Leduc
☐ Lee Norwood
☐ John Paddock
☐ Dave Pichette
☐ Michel Plasse (G)
☐ Jacques Richard
☐ Normand Rochefort
☐ Anton Stastny
☐ Peter Stastny
☐ Marc Tardif
☐ Wally Weir
☐ John Wensink

'81 - 82 QUÉB.

The most expensive player is Peter Stastny at $5. Singles start at $1.50.

Postcard Size: 3 1/2" x 5 1/2"
Sponsor: None
Set (21 cards): $30

☐ Pierre Aubry
☐ Michel Bergeron
☐ Dan Bouchard (G)
☐ Réal Cloutier
☐ Alain Côté
☐ André Dupont
☐ Miroslav Frycer
☐ Michel Goulet
☐ Dale Hunter
☐ Pierre Lacroix
☐ Mario Marois
☐ Dave Pichette
☐ Michel Plasse (G)
☐ Jacques Richard
☐ Normand Rochefort
☐ Anton Stastny
☐ Marian Stastny
☐ Peter Stastny
☐ Marc Tardif
☐ Charles Thiffault
☐ Wally Weir

'82 - 83 QUÉB.

The most expensive player is Peter Stastny at $5. Singles start at $1.

Postcard Size: 3 1/2" x 5 1/2"
Sponsor: None
Set (26 cards): $30

☐ Pierre Aubry
☐ Michel Bergeron
☐ Dan Bouchard (G)
☐ Réal Cloutier
☐ Alain Côté
☐ André Dupont
☐ John Garrett (G)
☐ Michel Goulet
☐ Jean Hamel
☐ Dale Hunter
☐ Rick Lapointe
☐ Clint Malarchuk (G)
☐ Mario Marois
☐ Randy Moller
☐ Wilf Paiement
☐ Dave Pichette
☐ Jacques Richard
☐ Normand Rochefort
☐ Louis Sleigher
☐ Anton Stastny
☐ Marian Stastny
☐ Peter Stastny
☐ Marc Tardif
☐ Charles Thiffault
☐ Wally Weir
☐ Title Card

'83 - 84 QUÉB.

The most expensive players is Peter Stastny at $4. Singles start at $1.

Postcard Size: 3 1/2" x 5 1/2"
Sponsor: None
Set (32 cards): $30

☐ Pierre Aubry
☐ Michel Bergeron
☐ Dan Bouchard (G)

☐ Réal Cloutier
☐ Alain Côté
☐ André Doré
☐ André Dupont
☐ John Garrett (G)
☐ Paul Gillis
☐ Mario Gosselin (G)
☐ Michel Goulet
☐ Jean Hamel
☐ Dale Hunter
☐ Rick Lapointe
☐ Clint Malarchuk (G)
☐ Jimmy Mann
☐ Mario Marois
☐ Randy Moller
☐ Wilf Paiement
☐ Dave Pichette
☐ Pat Price
☐ Jacques Richard
☐ Normand Rochefort
☐ Jean-François Sauvé
☐ André Savard
☐ Louis Sleigher
☐ Anton Stastny
☐ Marian Stastny
☐ Peter Stastny
☐ Marc Tardif
☐ Wally Weir
☐ Blake Wesley

'84 - 85 QUÉB.

The most expensive players are Michel Goulet and Peter Stastny at $3-4. Singles start at $1.

Postcard Size: 3 1/2" x 5 1/2"
Sponsor: None
Set (27 cards): $25

☐ Brent Ashton
☐ Bruce Bell
☐ Dan Bouchard (G)
☐ Alain Côté
☐ Gord Donnelly
☐ Luc Dufour
☐ Jean-Marc Gaulin
☐ Paul Gillis
☐ Mario Gosselin (G)
☐ Michel Goulet
☐ Dale Hunter
☐ Jimmy Mann
☐ Mario Marois
☐ Brad Maxwell
☐ Randy Moller
☐ Wilf Paiement
☐ Pat Price
☐ Normand Rochefort
☐ Jean-François Sauvé
☐ André Savard
☐ Richard Sévigny (G)
☐ Anton Stastny
☐ Marian Stastny
☐ Peter Stastny
☐ Michel Bergeron
☐ Guy Lapointe, A. Coach
☐ Simon Nolet, A. Coach

'85 - 86 QUÉB.
GENERAL FOODS

There are two versions of these cards: cards with a Nordiques logo or cards with a General Foods logo. Pricing for both versions is identical. Photos are credited to André Pichette. The most expensive player is Peter Stastny at $4. Singles start at $1.

Card Size: 3 1/2" x 5 1/2"
Sponsor: General Foods
Set (29 cards): $25

☐ ☐ Peter Andersson
☐ ☐ Brent Ashton
☐ ☐ Michel Bergeron
☐ ☐ Jeff Brown
☐ ☐ Alain Côté
☐ ☐ Gilbert Delorme
☐ ☐ Gord Donnelly
☐ ☐ Mike Eagles
☐ ☐ Paul Gillis
☐ ☐ Mario Gosselin (G)
☐ ☐ Michel Goulet
☐ ☐ Ron Harris
☐ ☐ Dale Hunter
☐ ☐ Mark Kumpel
☐ ☐ Jason Lafrenière
☐ ☐ Clint Malarchuk (G)
☐ ☐ Randy Moller
☐ ☐ Simon Nolet
☐ ☐ Robert Picard
☐ ☐ Pat Price
☐ ☐ Ken Quinney
☐ ☐ Normand Rochefort
☐ ☐ Richard Sévigny (G)
☐ ☐ David Shaw
☐ ☐ Risto Siltanen
☐ ☐ Anton Stastny
☐ ☐ Peter Stastny
☐ ☐ Charles Thiffault
☐ ☐ Richard Zemlak

'85 - 86 QUÉB.
McDONALD'S

The most expensive player is Peter Stastny at $4. Singles start at $1.

Postcard Size: 3 1/2" x 5 1/2"
Sponsors: McDonald's, Le Soleil, CHRC80
Set (22 cards): $25

☐ Brent Ashton
☐ Jeff Brown
☐ Alain Côté
☐ Gilbert Delorme
☐ Gord Donnelly
☐ Mike Eagles
☐ Paul Gillis
☐ Mario Gosselin (G)
☐ Michel Goulet
☐ Dale Hunter
☐ Mark Kumpel
☐ Jason Lafrenière
☐ Clint Malarchuk (G)
☐ Randy Moller
☐ Robert Picard
☐ Pat Price
☐ Normand Rochefort
☐ Richard Sévigny (G)
☐ David Shaw
☐ Risto Siltanen
☐ Anton Stastny
☐ Peter Stastny

'85 - 86 QUÉB.
PROVIGO STICKERS

Michel Goulet and Peter Stastny are the most expensive singles at $3-4. Singles start at $1.

Sticker Size: 1 1/8" x 2 1/4"
Sponsor: Provigo
Set (25 cards): $30
Team Poster: $5

☐ John Anderson
☐ Brent Ashton
☐ Wayne Babych
☐ Michel Bergeron
☐ Alain Côté
☐ Gilbert Delorme
☐ Mike Eagles
☐ Steve Finn
☐ Paul Gillis
☐ Mario Gosselin (G)
☐ Michel Goulet
☐ Dale Hunter
☐ Mark Kumpel
☐ Clint Malarchuk (G)
☐ Jimmy Mann
☐ Mario Marois
☐ Randy Moller
☐ Wilf Paiement
☐ Pat Price
☐ Jean-François Sauvé
☐ Richard Sévigny (G)
☐ David Shaw
☐ Anton Stastny
☐ Peter Stastny

'86 - 87 QUÉB.

The most expensive singles are Michel Goulet and Peter Stastny at $3-4. Singles start at $1.

Card Size: 3 1/2" x 5 1/2"
Sponsor: None
Set (30 cards): $25

☐ Michel Bergeron
☐ Jeff Brown
☐ Alain Côté
☐ Bill Derlago
☐ Gord Donnelly
☐ Mike Eagles
☐ Steve Finn
☐ Paul Gillis
☐ Mario Gosselin (G)
☐ Michel Goulet
☐ Mike Hough
☐ Dale Hunter
☐ Jason Lafrenière
☐ Clint Malarchuk (G)
☐ Basil McRae
☐ Randy Moller
☐ Simon Nolet
☐ John Ogrodnick
☐ Robert Picard
☐ Pat Price
☐ Normand Rochefort
☐ Richard Sévigny (G)
☐ David Shaw
☐ Doug Shedden
☐ Risto Siltanen
☐ Anton Stastny
☐ Peter Stastny
☐ Charles Thiffault
☐ Richard Zemlak
☐ Team Photo

'86 - 87 QUÉB.
GENERAL FOODS

These cards have blank backs. Photos are credited to André Pichette. The most expensive singles are Michel Goulet and Peter Stastny at $3-4. Singles start at $1.

Card Size: 3 1/2" x 5 1/2"
Sponsor: General Foods
Set (26 cards): $25

☐ Brent Ashton
☐ Michel Bergeron
☐ Jeff Brown
☐ Alain Côté
☐ Gilbert Delorme
☐ Gord Donnelly
☐ Mike Eagles
☐ Paul Gillis
☐ Mario Gosselin (G)
☐ Mike Hough
☐ Dale Hunter
☐ Mark Kumpel
☐ Jason Lafrenière
☐ Clint Malarchuk (G)
☐ Randy Moller
☐ Simon Nolet
☐ Robert Picard
☐ Ken Quinney
☐ Normand Rochefort
☐ Richard Sévigny (G)
☐ David Shaw
☐ Risto Siltanen
☐ Anton Stastny
☐ Peter Stastny
☐ Charles Thiffault
☐ Richard Zemlak

'86 - 87 QUÉB.
McDONALD'S

The most expensive singles are Michel Goulet and Peter Stastny at $4-5. Singles start at $1.

Card Size: 3 1/2" x 5 1/2"
Sponsors: McDonald's, Le Soleil, CHRC80
Set (25 cards): $25

☐ John Anderson
☐ Brent Ashton
☐ Jeff Brown
☐ Alain Côté
☐ Gilbert Delorme
☐ Mike Eagles
☐ Steve Finn
☐ Paul Gillis
☐ Mario Gosselin (G)
☐ Michel Goulet
☐ Mike Hough
☐ Dale Hunter
☐ Mark Kumpel
☐ Alain Lemieux
☐ Clint Malarchuk (G)
☐ Jimmy Mann
☐ Randy Moller
☐ Wilf Paiement
☐ Pat Price
☐ Normand Rochefort
☐ Jean-François Sauvé
☐ Richard Sévigny (G)
☐ David Shaw
☐ Anton Stastny
☐ Peter Stastny

'86 - 87 QUÉB.
YUM YUM

The most expensive players are Michel Goulet and Peter Stastny at $4-5. Singles start at $2.

Card Size: 2" x 2 1/2"
Sponsor: None
Set (10 cards): $20

☐ Alain Côté
☐ Gilbert Delorme
☐ Paul Gillis
☐ Michel Goulet
☐ Dale Hunter
☐ Clint Malarchuk (G)
☐ Robert Picard
☐ Normand Rochefort
☐ Anton Stastny
☐ Peter Stastny

'87 - 88 QUÉB.
GENERAL FOODS

These cards have blank backs. The most expensive singles are Michel Goulet and Peter Stastny at $3-4. Singles start at $1.

Card Size: 3 3/4" x 5 5/8"
Sponsor: General Foods
Set (32 cards): $25

☐ Tommy Albelin
☐ Jeff Brown
☐ Mario Brunetta (G)
☐ Terry Carkner
☐ Alain Côté
☐ Gord Donnelly
☐ Gaetan Duchesne
☐ Mike Eagles
☐ Steve Finn
☐ Paul Gillis
☐ Mario Gosselin (G)
☐ Michel Goulet
☐ Stéphane Guerard
☐ Alan Haworth
☐ Mike Hough
☐ Jeff Jackson
☐ Stu Kulak
☐ Jason Lafrenière
☐ Lane Lambert
☐ David Latta
☐ Max Middendorf
☐ Randy Moller
☐ Robert Picard
☐ Daniel Poudrier
☐ Ken Quinney
☐ Normand Rochefort
☐ Richard Sévigny (G)
☐ Anton Stastny
☐ Peter Stastny
☐ Ron Tugnutt (G)
☐ Chainey/ Savard/ Lapointe
☐ Mascot Badaboum

'87 - 88 QUÉB.
YUM YUM

The most expensive singles are Michel Goulet and Peter Stastny at $5-6. Singles start at $2.50. Mario Gosselin has a variation with the uniform number 83 on the back and one with the proper uniform number 33.

Card Size: 2" x 2 1/2"
Sponsor: None
Set (10 cards): $20

☐ Alain Côté
☐ Paul Gillis
☐ ☐ Mario Gosselin (G)
☐ Michel Goulet
☐ Alan Haworth
☐ Jason Lafrenière
☐ Robert Picard
☐ Normand Rochefort
☐ Anton Stastny
☐ Peter Stastny

'88 - 89 QUÉB.
GENERAL FOODS

There are two versions of this set: cards with the sponsors' logos and cards without the sponsors' logos. Card backs are blank. Pricing for both versions is identical. Joe Sakic is the most expensive single at $18. Singles start at $1.

Card Size: 3 3/4" x 5 5/8"
Sponsors: General Foods, Le Journal, CHRC80
Set (33 cards): $35

☐ ☐ Tommy Albelin #28
☐ ☐ Joel Baillargeon #38
☐ ☐ Jeff Brown #22
☐ ☐ Mario Brunetta (G) #30
☐ ☐ Alain Côté #19
☐ ☐ Gord Donnelly #34
☐ ☐ Daniel Doré #15
☐ ☐ Gaetan Duchesne #14
☐ ☐ Steve Finn #29
☐ ☐ Marc Fortier #9
☐ ☐ Paul Gillis #23
☐ ☐ Mario Gosselin (G) #33
☐ ☐ Michel Goulet #16
☐ ☐ Jari Grönstrand #5
☐ ☐ Stéphane Guérard #6
☐ ☐ Jeff Jackson #25
☐ ☐ Iiro Jarvi #11
☐ ☐ Lane Lambert #7
☐ ☐ David Latta #27
☐ ☐ Curtis Leschyshyn #46
☐ ☐ Bob Mason (G) #1
☐ ☐ Randy Moller #21
☐ ☐ Robert Picard #24
☐ ☐ Walt Poddubny #75
☐ ☐ Joe Sakic #88
☐ ☐ Greg Smyth #4
☐ ☐ Anton Stastny #20
☐ ☐ Peter Stastny #26
☐ ☐ Trevor Stienburg #17
☐ ☐ Mark Vermette #10
☐ ☐ S.Aubry/ A.Chainey/ G.Lapointe/ R.Lapointe
☐ ☐ Mascot Badaboum
☐ ☐ Team Photo
☐ ☐ Mascot Badaboum

'89 - 90 QUÉB.
GENERAL FOODS

Horizontal photos are used in this set. There are two versions of this set: cards with the General Foods logo and cards without the logo. Pricing for both versions is identical. Joe Sakic is the most expensive single at $12. Guy Lafleur sells at $4-5 and Stéphane Fiset sells at $3-4. Singles start at $1. There are nine players who are not in the General Foods set. A 30-card General Foods set sells at $25.

Card Size: 3 3/4" x 5 5/8"
Sponsor: General Foods
Set (39): $30

☐ Serge Aubry
☐ ☐ Michel Bergeron, Coach
☐ ☐ Jeff Brown
☐ Alain Chainey
☐ ☐ Joe Cirella
☐ ☐ Lucien DeBlois
☐ ☐ Daniel Doré
☐ ☐ Steve Finn
☐ ☐ Stéphane Fiset (G)
☐ Bryan Fogarty
☐ ☐ Marc Fortier
☐ ☐ Paul Gillis
☐ ☐ Michel Goulet
☐ ☐ Jari Grödstrand
☐ ☐ Stéphane Guérard
☐ ☐ Mike Hough
☐ Tony Hrkac
☐ ☐ Jeff Jackson
☐ ☐ Iiro Järvi
☐ ☐ Kevin Kaminski
☐ ☐ Darin Kimble
☐ ☐ Guy Lafleur
☐ Guy Lapointe
☐ ☐ David Latta
☐ Brian Lawton
☐ ☐ Curtis Leschyshyn
☐ ☐ Claude Loiselle
☐ ☐ Mario Marois
☐ Tony McKegney
☐ ☐ Ken McRae
☐ Greg Millen (G)
☐ Randy Moller
☐ ☐ Sergei Mylnikov (G)
☐ ☐ Michel Petit
☐ ☐ Robert Picard
☐ ☐ Joe Sakic
☐ ☐ Peter Stastny
☐ ☐ Ron Tugnutt (G)
☐ ☐ Team Photo

'89 - 90 QUÉB.
POLICE

Horizontal photos are used in this set. Joe Sakic is the most expensive single at $12. Singles start at $1.

Card Size: 2 3/4" x 4"
Sponsor: ville de Vanier
Set (27 cards): $25

☐ Jeff Brown
☐ Joe Cirella
☐ Lucien DeBlois
☐ Daniel Doré
☐ Steve Finn
☐ Stéphane Fiset (G)
☐ Marc Fortier
☐ Paul Gillis
☐ Michel Goulet
☐ Stéphane Guérard
☐ Mike Hough
☐ Jeff Jackson
☐ Iiro Järvi
☐ Darin Kimble
☐ Guy Lafleur
☐ David Latta
☐ Curtis Leschyshyn
☐ Claude Loiselle
☐ Mario Marois
☐ Ken McRae
☐ Sergei Mylnikov (G)
☐ Michel Petit
☐ Robert Picard
☐ Jean-Marc Routhier
☐ Joe Sakic
☐ Peter Stastny
☐ Ron Tugnutt (G)

'90 - 91 QUÉB.

Horizontal photos are used in this set. Joe Sakic is the most expensive single at $6-8. Singles start at $1.

Card Size: 3 3/4" x 5 5/8"
Sponsor: None
Set (26 cards): $25

☐ Joe Cirella
☐ Lucien DeBlois
☐ Daniel Doré
☐ Steve Finn
☐ Stéphane Fiset (G)
☐ Bryan Fogarty
☐ Marc Fortier
☐ Paul Gillis
☐ Michel Goulet
☐ Stéphane Guérard
☐ Mike Hough
☐ Tony Hrkac
☐ Jeff Jackson
☐ Iiro Järvi
☐ Kevin Kaminski
☐ Darin Kimble
☐ David Latta
☐ Curtis Leschyshyn
☐ Claude Loiselle
☐ Mario Marois
☐ Tony McKegney
☐ Ken McRae
☐ Michel Petit
☐ Joe Sakic
☐ Peter Stastny
☐ Ron Tugnutt (G)

'90 - 91 QUÉB.
PETRO CANADA

Joe Sakic and Mats Sundin are the most expensive singles at $5-7. Singles start at $1.

Card Size: 3 3/4" x 5 5/8"
Sponsor: Petro-Canada
Set (28 cards): $25

☐ Aaron Broten
☐ Dave Chambers
☐ Joe Cirella
☐ Lucien DeBlois
☐ Steve Finn
☐ Bryan Fogarty
☐ Marc Fortier
☐ Robbie Ftorek
☐ Paul Gillis
☐ Scott Gordon (G)
☐ Mike Hough
☐ Tony Hrkac
☐ Darin Kimble
☐ Guy Lafleur
☐ Curtis Leschyshyn
☐ Claude Loiselle
☐ Jacques Martin
☐ Tony McKegney
☐ Owen Nolan
☐ Michel Petit
☐ Joe Sakic
☐ Everett Sanipass
☐ Mats Sundin
☐ John Tanner (G)
☐ Ron Tugnutt (G)
☐ Dan Vincelette
☐ Craig Wolanin
☐ Team Photo

'91 - 92 QUÉB.
PETRO CANADA

The most expensive singles are Joe Sakic at $5-6 and Mats Sundin at $4-5. Singles start at $1.

Card Size: 3 3/4" x 5 5/8"
Sponsor: Petro-Canada
Set (35 cards): $25

☐ Don Barber
☐ Jacques Cloutier (G)
☐ Steve Finn
☐ Stéphane Fiset (G)
☐ Bryan Fogarty
☐ Adam Foote
☐ Marc Fortier
☐ Alexei Gusarov
☐ Mike Hough
☐ Don Jackson
☐ Valeri Kamensky
☐ John Kordic
☐ Claude Lapointe
☐ Curtis Leschyshyn
☐ Jacques Martin
☐ Mike McNeill
☐ Ken McRae
☐ Kip Miller
☐ Stéphane Morin
☐ Owen Nolan
☐ Pierre Pagé
☐ Greg Paslawski
☐ Herb Raglan
☐ Joe Sakic
☐ Doug Smail
☐ Greg Smyth
☐ Mats Sundin
☐ Mikhail Tatarinov
☐ Ron Tugnutt (G)
☐ Tony Twist
☐ Wayne Van Dorp
☐ Randy Velischek
☐ Mark Vermette
☐ Craig Wolanin
☐ Mascot Badaboum

'92 - 93 QUÉB.
PETRO CANADA

Joe Sakic is the most expensive single at $5-6. Singles start at 75¢.

Card Size: 3 1/2" x 5 5/8"
Sponsor: Petro-Canada
Set (39 cards): $22

☐ Dan Bouchard
☐ Gino Cavallini
☐ Jacques Cloutier (G)
☐ Steve Duchesne
☐ Steve Finn
☐ Stéphane Fiset (G)
☐ Adam Foote
☐ Alexei Gusarov
☐ Ron Hextall (G)
☐ Mike Hough
☐ Kerry Huffman
☐ Tim Hunter
☐ Don Jackson
☐ Valeri Kamensky
☐ David Karpa
☐ Andrei Kovalenko
☐ Claude Lapointe
☐ Curtis Leschyshyn
☐ Bill Lindsay
☐ Jacques Martin
☐ Owen Nolan
☐ Pierre Pagé
☐ Scott Pearson
☐ Herb Raglan
☐ Mike Ricci
☐ Martin Rucinsky
☐ Joe Sakic
☐ André Savard
☐ Chris Simon
☐ Mats Sundin
☐ John Tanner (G)
☐ Mikhail Tatarinov
☐ Tony Twist
☐ Wayne Van Dorp
☐ Mark Vermette

- ☐ Craig Wolanin
- ☐ Scott Young
- ☐ Mascot Badaboum
- ☐ Team Photo

'94 - 95 QUÉB.
BURGER KING

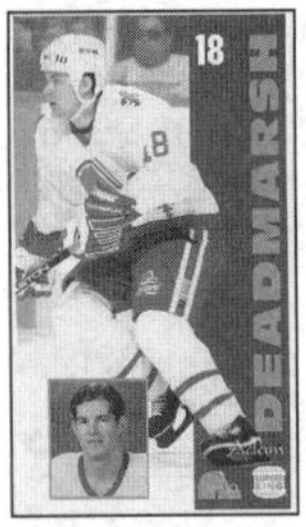

Peter Forsberg is the most expensive single at $6-7. Singles start at $1.
Card Size: 3 1/2" x 6"
Sponsor: Burger King
Set (24 cards): $20

- ☐ Bob Bassen
- ☐ Wendel Clark
- ☐ Adam Deadmarsh
- ☐ Steve Finn
- ☐ Stéphane Fiset (G)
- ☐ Adam Foote
- ☐ Peter Forsberg
- ☐ Alexei Gusarov
- ☐ Valeri Kamensky
- ☐ Andrei Kovalenko
- ☐ Uwe Krupp
- ☐ Claude Lapointe
- ☐ Janne Laukkanen
- ☐ Sylvain Lefebvre
- ☐ Paul MacDermid
- ☐ Owen Nolan
- ☐ Mike Ricci
- ☐ Martin Rucinsky
- ☐ Joe Sakic
- ☐ Chris Simon
- ☐ Jocelyn Thibault (G)
- ☐ Craig Wolanin
- ☐ Scott Young

ST. LOUIS BLUES

'71 - 72 SLOU.

Al Arbour is the most expensive single at $5-6. Singles start at $2.
Card Size: 3 1/2" x 5 1/2"
Sponsor: None
Set (25 cards): $50

- ☐ Al Arbour
- ☐ John Arbour
- ☐ Carl Brewer
- ☐ Jacques Caron (G)
- ☐ Terry Crisp
- ☐ André Dupont
- ☐ Jack Egers
- ☐ Larry Hornung
- ☐ Brian Lavender
- ☐ Mike Murphy
- ☐ Gerry Odrowski
- ☐ Danny O'Shea
- ☐ Mike Parizeau
- ☐ Noel Picard
- ☐ Barclay Plager
- ☐ Bill Plager
- ☐ Bob Plager
- ☐ Phil Roberto
- ☐ Gary Sabourin
- ☐ Frank St. Marseille
- ☐ Floyd Thomson
- ☐ Garry Unger
- ☐ Ernie Wakely (G)
- ☐ Tom Woodcock
- ☐ G.Marchant/ A.McPherson

'72 - 73 SLOU.

Barclay Plager is the most expensive single at $3-4. Singles start at $2.
Card Size: 6 7/8" x 8 3/4"
Sponsor: None
Set (22 cards): $45

- ☐ Jacques Caron (G)
- ☐ Steve Durbano
- ☐ Jack Egers
- ☐ Chris Evans
- ☐ Jean Hamel
- ☐ Fran Huck
- ☐ Brent Hughes
- ☐ Bob Johnson
- ☐ Mike Lampman
- ☐ Bob McCord
- ☐ Wayne Merrick
- ☐ Mike Murphy
- ☐ Danny O'Shea
- ☐ Barclay Plager
- ☐ Bob Plager
- ☐ Pierre Plante
- ☐ Phil Roberto
- ☐ Gary Sabourin
- ☐ Wayne Stephenson (G)
- ☐ Jean-Guy Talbot
- ☐ Floyd Thomson
- ☐ Garry Unger

'72 - 73 SLOU.

Photos are in black and white. Al Arbour is the most expensive single at $4-5. Singles start at $2.
Card Size: 8" x 10"
Sponsor: None
Set (25 cards): $50

- ☐ Al Arbour
- ☐ Jacques Caron (G)
- ☐ André Dupont
- ☐ Steve Durbano
- ☐ Jack Egers
- ☐ Chris Evans
- ☐ Fran Huck
- ☐ Bob Johnson (G)
- ☐ Mike Lampman
- ☐ Wayne Merrick
- ☐ Mike Murphy
- ☐ Danny O'Shea
- ☐ Kevin O'Shea
- ☐ Noel Picard
- ☐ Barclay Plager
- ☐ Bob Plager
- ☐ Phil Roberto
- ☐ Gary Sabourin
- ☐ Frank St. Marseille
- ☐ Wayne Stephenson (G)
- ☐ Floyd Thomson
- ☐ Garry Unger
- ☐ Sid and Sid Jr. Soloman
- ☐ B. McCreary/ J.G. Probstein/ G.Kyle GT. Woocock/ A. Solomon/ T.Madden
- ☐ Lynn Patrick/ Sid Abel

'73 - 74 SLOU.

John Davidson is the most expensive single at $6-7. Singles start at $2. Garry Unger has two cards.
Card Size: 6 7/8" x 8 3/4"
Sponsor: None
Set (24 cards): $50

- ☐ Lou Angotti
- ☐ Don Awrey
- ☐ John Davidson (G)
- ☐ Ab DeMarco
- ☐ Steve Durbano
- ☐ Chris Evans
- ☐ Larry Giroux
- ☐ Jean Hamel
- ☐ Nick Harbaruk
- ☐ J. Bob Kelly
- ☐ Mike Lampman
- ☐ Wayne Merrick
- ☐ Barclay Plager
- ☐ Bob Plager
- ☐ Pierre Plante
- ☐ Phil Roberto
- ☐ Gary Sabourin
- ☐ Glen Sather
- ☐ Wayne Stephenson (G)
- ☐ Jean-Guy Talbot
- ☐ Floyd Thomson
- ☐ Garry Unger
- ☐ Garry Unger
- ☐ Team Photo

'78 - 79 SLOU.

Bernie Federko and Brian Sutter are the most expensive singles at $4-6 in NRMT. Singles start at $1.
Postcard Size: 6 7/8" x 8 3/4"
Sponsor: None
Set (21 cards): $35

- ☐ Wayne Babych
- ☐ Curt Bennett
- ☐ Harvey Bennett
- ☐ Jack Brownschidle
- ☐ Mike Crombeen
- ☐ Tony Currie
- ☐ Bernie Federko
- ☐ Barry Gibbs
- ☐ Larry Giroux
- ☐ Inge Hammarstrom
- ☐ Phil Myre (G)
- ☐ Larry Patey
- ☐ Barclay Plager
- ☐ Rick Shinske
- ☐ John Smrke
- ☐ Ed Staniowski (G)
- ☐ Bob Stewart
- ☐ Brian Sutter
- ☐ Garry Unger
- ☐ Blue Angels
- ☐ Fan Van

'86 - 87 SLOU.

Singles sell at $1.50-2..
Photo Size: 8 1/2" x 11"
Sponsor: None
Set (20 photos): $20

- ☐ 1967-68 Blues
- ☐ 1968-69 Blues
- ☐ 1969-70 Blues
- ☐ 1970-71 Blues
- ☐ 1971-72 Blues
- ☐ 1972-73 Blues
- ☐ 1973-74 Blues
- ☐ 1974-75 Blues
- ☐ 1975-76 Blues
- ☐ 1976-77 Blues
- ☐ 1977-78 Blues
- ☐ 1978-79 Blues
- ☐ 1979-80 Blues
- ☐ 1980-81 Blues
- ☐ 1981-82 Blues
- ☐ 1982-83 Blues
- ☐ 1983-84 Blues
- ☐ 1984-85 Blues
- ☐ 1985-86 Blues
- ☐ 1986-87 Blues

'87 - 88 SLOU.

Brett Hull is the most expensive single at $18. Singles start at $1.
Card Size: 3 1/2" x 5 1/2"
Sponsor: None
Set (24 cards): $40

- ☐ Brian Benning
- ☐ Mike Bullard
- ☐ Gino Cavallini
- ☐ Paul Cavallini
- ☐ Craig Coxe
- ☐ Robert Dirk
- ☐ Doug Evans
- ☐ Todd Ewen
- ☐ Bernie Federko
- ☐ Gaston Gingras
- ☐ Tony Hrkac
- ☐ Brett Hull
- ☐ Tony McKegney
- ☐ Rick Meagher
- ☐ Greg Millen (G)
- ☐ Sergio Momesso
- ☐ Greg Paslawski
- ☐ Herb Raglan
- ☐ Dave Richter
- ☐ Vincent Riendeau (G)
- ☐ Gordie Roberts
- ☐ Brian Sutter
- ☐ Tom Tilley
- ☐ Steve Tuttle

'87 - 88 SLOU.
KODAK

Doug Gilmour is the most expensive single at $8-11. Singles start at $1.
Card Size: 2 3/16" x 3"
Sponsor: Kodak
Set (26 cards): $25

- ☐ Brian Benning #2
- ☐ Tim Bothwell #6
- ☐ Charlie Bourgeois #4
- ☐ Paul Cavallini #14
- ☐ Gino Cavallini #17
- ☐ Michael Dark #26
- ☐ Doug Evans #32
- ☐ Todd Ewen #21
- ☐ Bernie Federko #24
- ☐ Ron Flockhart #12
- ☐ Doug Gilmour #9
- ☐ Gaston Gingras #23
- ☐ Tony Hrkac #18
- ☐ Mark Hunter #20
- ☐ Jocelyn Lemieux #16
- ☐ Tony McKegney #10
- ☐ Rick Meagher #22
- ☐ Greg Millen #29 (G)
- ☐ Robert Nordmark #27
- ☐ Greg Paslawski #28
- ☐ Herb Raglan #25
- ☐ Rob Ramage #5
- ☐ Cliff Ronning #7
- ☐ Brian Sutter #11
- ☐ Perry Turnbull #19
- ☐ Rick Wamsley #30 (G)

'88 - 89 SLOU.
KODAK

Curtis Joseph is the most expensive single at $8. Singles start at $1.
Card Size: 3 1/2" x 4 1/4"
Sponsor: Kodak
Set (24 cards): $35

- ☐ Brian Benning #2
- ☐ Mike Bullard
- ☐ Gino Cavallini #17
- ☐ Paul Cavallini #14
- ☐ Craig Coxe #15
- ☐ Robert Dirk
- ☐ Doug Evans #32
- ☐ Todd Ewen #21
- ☐ Bernie Federko #24
- ☐ Gaston Gingras #23
- ☐ Tony Hrkac #18
- ☐ Brett Hull #16
- ☐ Tony McKegney #10
- ☐ Rick Meagher #22
- ☐ Greg Millen #29 (G)
- ☐ Sergio Momesso #27
- ☐ Greg Paslawski #28
- ☐ Herb Raglan #25
- ☐ Dave Richter #5
- ☐ V. Riendeau #30 (G)
- ☐ Gordie Roberts #4
- ☐ Brian Sutter #11
- ☐ Tom Tilley #20
- ☐ Steve Tuttle #35

'88 - 89 SLOU.
KODAK

Brett Hull is the most expensive single at $8-10. Singles start at $1.
Card Size: 2 3/16" x 3"
Sponsor: Kodak
Set (25 cards): $25

- ☐ Brian Benning #2
- ☐ Tim Bothwell #6
- ☐ Paul Cavallini #14
- ☐ Gino Cavallini #17
- ☐ Craig Coxe #15
- ☐ Doug Evans #32
- ☐ Todd Ewen #21
- ☐ Bernie Federko #24
- ☐ Gaston Gingras #23
- ☐ Tony Hrkac #18
- ☐ Brett Hull #16
- ☐ Mike Lalor #26
- ☐ Tony McKegney #10
- ☐ Rick Meagher #22
- ☐ Greg Millen #29 (G)
- ☐ Sergio Momesso #27
- ☐ Greg Paslawski #28
- ☐ Herb Raglan #25
- ☐ Dave Richter #5
- ☐ V. Riendeau #30 (G)
- ☐ Gordie Roberts #4
- ☐ Cliff Ronning #7
- ☐ Tom Tilley #20
- ☐ Steve Tuttle #35
- ☐ Peter Zezel #9

'89 - 90 SLOU.
KODAK

Curtis Joseph is the most expensive single at $8. Rod Brind'Amour, Adam Oates and Brett Hull sell at $4-6. Singles start at $1.
Card Size: 2 3/8" x 3"
Sponsor: Kodak
Set (25 cards): $25

- ☐ Rod Brind'Amour #19
- ☐ Jeff Brown #21
- ☐ Paul Cavallini #14
- ☐ Gino Cavallini #17
- ☐ Kelly Chase #39
- ☐ Brett Hull #16
- ☐ Pat Jablonski #1 (G)
- ☐ Curtis Joseph #31 (G)
- ☐ Mike Lalor #26
- ☐ Dominic Lavoie #38
- ☐ Dave Lowry #10
- ☐ Paul MacLean #15
- ☐ Rick Meagher #22
- ☐ Sergio Momesso #27
- ☐ Adam Oates #12
- ☐ Adrien Plavsic #23
- ☐ Herb Raglan #25
- ☐ V. Riendeau #30 (G)
- ☐ Gordie Roberts #4
- ☐ Brian Sutter
- ☐ Dave Thomlinson #40
- ☐ Tom Tilley #20
- ☐ Steve Tuttle #35
- ☐ Tony Twist #6
- ☐ Peter Zezel #9

'90 - 91 SLOU.
KODAK

Brett Hull is the most expensive single at $8. Singles start at $1.
Card Size: 2 1/2" x 3 1/2"
Sponsor: Kodak
Set (25 cards): $25

- ☐ Bob Bassen
- ☐ Rod Brind'Amour
- ☐ Jeff Brown
- ☐ Dave Bruce
- ☐ Gino Cavallini
- ☐ Paul Cavallini
- ☐ Geoff Courtnall
- ☐ Robert Dirk
- ☐ Glen Featherstone
- ☐ Brett Hull
- ☐ Curtis Joseph (G)
- ☐ Dave Lowry
- ☐ Paul MacLean
- ☐ Mario Marois
- ☐ Rick Meagher
- ☐ Sergio Momesso
- ☐ Adam Oates
- ☐ Vincent Riendeau (G)
- ☐ Cliff Ronning
- ☐ Harold Snepsts
- ☐ Scott Stevens
- ☐ Brian Sutter
- ☐ Rich Sutter
- ☐ Steve Tuttle
- ☐ Ron Wilson

'91 - 92 SLOU.

Brendan Shanahan is the most expensive single at $6. Singles start at $1.
Postcard Size: 3 1/2" x 5 1/2"
Sponsor: None
Set (22 cards): $25

- ☐ Murray Baron
- ☐ Bob Bassen
- ☐ Jeff Brown
- ☐ Garth Butcher
- ☐ Gino Cavallini
- ☐ Paul Cavallini
- ☐ Kelly Chase
- ☐ Dave Christian
- ☐ Nelson Emerson
- ☐ Brett Hull
- ☐ Pat Jablonski (G)
- ☐ Curtis Joseph (G)
- ☐ Darin Kimble
- ☐ Dave Lowry
- ☐ Michel Mongeau
- ☐ Adam Oates
- ☐ Rob Robinson
- ☐ Brendan Shanahan
- ☐ Rich Sutter
- ☐ Ron Sutter
- ☐ Ron Wilson
- ☐ Rick Zombo

'92 - 93 SLOU.
McDONALD'S

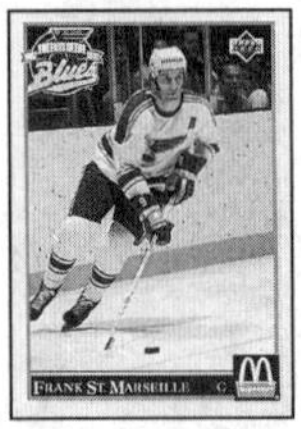

This series was available at McDonald's in six-card packs. Stars sell at $4-6. Singles start at $1. Brett Hull signed 100 cards that were inserted into packs. The Hull autograph sells at $200-225.
Card Size: 2 1/2" x 3 1/2"
Sponsor: McDonald's
Set (28 cards): $30
Album: $15

- ☐ 1 Glenn Hall (G)
- ☐ 2 Doug Gilmour
- ☐ 3 Al Arbour
- ☐ 4 Mike Liut (G)
- ☐ 5 Blake Dunlop
- ☐ 6 Noel Picard
- ☐ 7 Bob Plager
- ☐ 8 Ab McDonald
- ☐ 9 Curtis Joseph (G)
- ☐ 10 Wayne Babych
- ☐ 11 Red Berenson
- ☐ 12 Brett Hull
- ☐ 13 Bob Gassoff
- ☐ 14 Bernie Federko
- ☐ 15 Gary Sabourin
- ☐ 16 Joe Mullen
- ☐ 17 Adam Oates
- ☐ 18 Jorgen Pettersson
- ☐ 19 Frank St. Marseille
- ☐ 20 Scott Stevens
- ☐ 21 Rob Ramage
- ☐ 22 Jacques Plante (G)
- ☐ 23 Rick Meagher
- ☐ 24 Barclay Plager
- ☐ 25 Brian Sutter
- ☐ 26 Perry Turnbull
- ☐ 27 Garry Unger
- ☐ 28 Checklist
- ☐ Brett Hull autograph ✍

'96 - 97 SLOU.
ST. LOUIS DISPATCH

We have no pricing information on this set.
Photo Size: 8 1/2" x 11"
Sponsor: St. Louis Dispatch

- ☐ 1 Brett Hull
- ☐ 2 Al MacInnis
- ☐ 3 Grant Fuhr (G)
- ☐ 4 Tony Twist
- ☐ 5 Chris Pronger

'99 - 00 SLOU.
TACO BELL

These cards were issued in four perforated sheets at Taco Bell restaurants.

Card Size: 2 1/2" x 3 1/2"
Sponsor: Taco Bell
Set (24 cards): $15

- ☐ 1 Marc Bergevin
- ☐ 2 Jochen Hecht
- ☐ 3 Jamie McLennan
- ☐ 4 Pierre Turgeon
- ☐ 5 Scott A. Young
- ☐ 6 Dave Ellett
- ☐ 7 Lubos Bartecko
- ☐ 8 Pavol Demitra
- ☐ 9 Michal Handzus
- ☐ 10 Jeff Finley
- ☐ 11 Ricard Persson
- ☐ 12 Bob Bassen
- ☐ 13 Craig Conroy
- ☐ 14 Mike Eastwood
- ☐ 15 Scott Pellerin
- ☐ 16 Chris Pronger
- ☐ 17 Todd Reirden
- ☐ 18 Roman Turek
- ☐ 19 Kelly Chase
- ☐ 20 Al MacInnis
- ☐ 21 Jamal Mayers
- ☐ 22 Pascal Rhéaume
- ☐ 23 Tyson Nash
- ☐ 24 Stéphane J.J. Richer

SAN JOSE SHARKS

'91 - 92 SANJ.
SPORTS ACTION

Jeff Hackett is the most expensive single at $2. Singles start at $1.
Card Size: 2 1/2" x 3 1/2"
Sponsor: Sports Action
Set (22 cards): $18

- ☐ Perry Anderson
- ☐ Perry Berezan
- ☐ Steve Bozek
- ☐ Dean Evason
- ☐ Pat Falloon
- ☐ Paul Fenton
- ☐ Link Gaetz
- ☐ Jeff Hackett (G)
- ☐ Ken Hammond
- ☐ Brian Hayward (G)
- ☐ Tony Hrkac
- ☐ Kelly Kisio
- ☐ Brian Lawton
- ☐ Pat McLeod
- ☐ Bob McGill
- ☐ Brian Mullen
- ☐ Jarmo Myllys (G)
- ☐ Wayne Presley
- ☐ Neil Wilkinson
- ☐ Doug Wilson
- ☐ Rob Zettler
- ☐ Sharks game action

'92 - 93 SANJ.
PACIFIC BELL

These sheets are limited to 4,500 copies. Sandis Ozolinsh is the most expensive single at $6-8. Singles start at $4.
Photo Size: 8 1/2" x 11"
Sponsor: Pacific Bell
Set (40 photos): $150

- ☐ Jamie Baker
- ☐ Mark Beaufait
- ☐ Viatcheslav Butsayev
- ☐ Dale Craigwell
- ☐ Shawn Cronin
- ☐ Gaetan Duchesne
- ☐ Todd Elik
- ☐ Pat Falloon
- ☐ Wade Flaherty (G)
- ☐ Johan Garpenlov
- ☐ Rob Gaudreau
- ☐ Arturs Irbe (G)
- ☐ AS: Arturs Irbe (G)
- ☐ Viktor Kozlov
- ☐ Vlastimil Kroupa
- ☐ Mike Lalor
- ☐ Igor Larionov
- ☐ Sergei Makarov
- ☐ David Maley
- ☐ Jason More
- ☐ Jeff Norton
- ☐ Jeff Odgers
- ☐ AS: Sandis Ozolinsh
- ☐ Tom Pederson
- ☐ Pete Stemkowski
- ☐ Mike Sullivan
- ☐ Michal Sykora
- ☐ Ray Whitney
- ☐ Dody Wood
- ☐ Jimmy Waite (G)
- ☐ Doug Zmolek
- ☐ Kevin Constantine Du. Sutter/ V. Tikhonov
- ☐ B.Errey/ R.Zettler
- ☐ M.Rathje/ A.Nazarov
- ☐ R.Whitney/ P.Falloon
- ☐ San Jose Arena
- ☐ Sharks Faceoff
- ☐ Sharks Photo
- ☐ Air Shark
- ☐ Zamboni with Fin

TAMPA BAY LIGHTNING

'92 - 93 TAMP.
SHERATON INN

These cards were originally issued as a panel. Roman Hamrlik is the most expensive single at $2-3. Singles start at 75¢.
Card Size: 2 1/2" x 3 1/2"
Sponsor: Sheraton Inn
Set (28 cards): $25

- ☐ Mikael Andersson
- ☐ Bob Beers
- ☐ J.C. Bergeron (G)
- ☐ Marc Bergevin
- ☐ Tim Bergland
- ☐ Brian Bradley
- ☐ Marc Bureau
- ☐ Wayne Cashman
- ☐ Shawn Chambers
- ☐ Danton Cole
- ☐ Adam Creighton
- ☐ Terry Crisp
- ☐ Rob DiMaio

- ☐ Phil Esposito
- ☐ Tony Esposito
- ☐ Roman Hamrlik
- ☐ Pat Jablonski (G)
- ☐ Steve Kasper
- ☐ Chris Kontos
- ☐ Steve Maltais
- ☐ Joe Reekie
- ☐ John Tucker
- ☐ Wendell Young (G)
- ☐ Rob Zamuner
- ☐ Mascot Thunderbug
- ☐ Lightning card
- ☐ Inaugural season
- ☐ Sheraton logo

'93 - 94 TAMP.
KASH N' KARRY

Chris Gratton is the most expensive single at $5. Singles start at $1.50. Other singles may exist.

Card Size: 5" x 7"
Sponsor: Kash n' Karry

- ☐ Brian Bradley
- ☐ Shawn Chambers
- ☐ Chris Gratton
- ☐ Adam Creighton
- ☐ Rob DiMaio
- ☐ Wendell Young (G)

'94 - 95 TAMP.
SKYBOX SPORTS CAFÉ

This set was originally issued as a panel. Chris Gratton is the most expensive single at $2. Singles start at 75¢.

Card Size: 2 1/2" x 3 1/4"
Sponsor: SkyBox Sports Café
Set (28 cards): $20

- ☐ Mikael Andersson
- ☐ Marc Bergevin
- ☐ Brian Bradley
- ☐ Marc Bureau
- ☐ Wayne Cashman
- ☐ Shawn Chambers
- ☐ Enrico Ciccone
- ☐ Danton Cole
- ☐ Adam Creighton
- ☐ Terry Crisp
- ☐ Jim Cummins
- ☐ Pat Elynuik
- ☐ Phil Esposito
- ☐ Tony Esposito
- ☐ Gerard Gallant
- ☐ Danny Gare
- ☐ Chris Gratton
- ☐ Roman Hamrlik
- ☐ Chris Joseph
- ☐ Petr Klima
- ☐ Chris LiPuma
- ☐ Rudy Poeschek
- ☐ Daren Puppa (G)
- ☐ Denis Savard
- ☐ John Tucker
- ☐ Wendell Young (G)
- ☐ Rob Zamuner
- ☐ Mascot Thunderbug

'94 - 95 TAMP.
HEALTH PLAN

We have little information on this set. Other singles may exist.

Card Size: 4" x 5"
Sponsor: Florida Health Plan

- ☐ Daren Puppa (G)
- ☐ Chris Gratton

'95 - 96 TAMP.
SKYBOX SPORTS CAFÉ

Chris Gratton is the most expensive single at $3. Singles start at $1.

Card Size: 3 3/4" x 9"
Sponsors: SkyBox Sports Café, others
Set (21 cards): $25

- ☐ Mikael Andersson
- ☐ Brian Bellows
- ☐ J.C. Bergeron (G)
- ☐ Brian Bradley
- ☐ Shawn Burr
- ☐ Enrico Ciccone
- ☐ Cory Cross
- ☐ John Cullen
- ☐ Aaron Gavey
- ☐ Chris Gratton
- ☐ Roman Hamrlik
- ☐ Bill Houlder
- ☐ Petr Klima
- ☐ Rudy Poeschek
- ☐ Daren Puppa (G)
- ☐ Alexander Selivanov
- ☐ David Shaw
- ☐ John Tucker
- ☐ Jason Wiemer
- ☐ Paul Ysebaert
- ☐ Rob Zamuner

'95 - 96 TAMP.
SKYBOX SPORTS CAFÉ

These cards were originally issued as a panel. Chris Gratton is the most expensive single at $3. Singles start at 75¢.

Card Size: 2 1/2" x 3 1/2"
Sponsor: SkyBox Sports Café
Set (29 cards): $18

- ☐ Mikael Andersson
- ☐ J.C. Bergeron (G)
- ☐ Marc Bergevin
- ☐ Brian Bradley
- ☐ Marc Bureau
- ☐ Wayne Cashman
- ☐ Eric Charron
- ☐ Enrico Ciccone
- ☐ Terry Crisp
- ☐ Cory Cross
- ☐ Phil Esposito
- ☐ Tony Esposito
- ☐ Danny Gare
- ☐ Chris Gratton
- ☐ Bob Halkidis
- ☐ Roman Hamrlik
- ☐ Ben Hankinson
- ☐ Petr Klima
- ☐ Brantt Myhres
- ☐ Adrien Plavsic
- ☐ Rudy Poeschek
- ☐ Daren Puppa (G)
- ☐ Alexander Selivanov
- ☐ Alexander Semak
- ☐ John Tucker
- ☐ Jason Wiemer
- ☐ Paul Ysebaert
- ☐ Rob Zamuner
- ☐ Team Photo

'02 - 03 TAMP.

We do not have a checklist for this series of cards.

TORONTO MAPLE LEAFS

'64 - 65 TORO.
SKYBOX SPORTS CAFÉ

Prices are in NM.

Card Size: 3 1/2" x 5 1/2"
Sponsor: None
Set (23 cards): $150

☐ George Amstrong	10
☐ Andy Bathgate	7
☐ Bob Baun	5
☐ Johnny Bower (G)	12
☐ Carl Brewer	4
☐ Kent Douglas	4
☐ Dick Duff	6
☐ Ron Ellis	5
☐ Billy Harris	4
☐ Tim Horton	18
☐ Punch Imlach	6
☐ Red Kelly	10
☐ Dave Keon	15
☐ Frank Mahovlich	18
☐ Don McKenney	4
☐ Dickie Moore	10
☐ Jim Pappin	4
☐ Bob Pulford	7
☐ Terry Sawchuk (G)	20
☐ Eddie Shack	10
☐ Don Simmons (G)	6
☐ Allan Stanley	7
☐ Ron Stewart	4

'68 - 69 TORO.

Tim Horton is the most expensive single at $15 in NM. Singles start at $2.50. We have no pricing information on complete sets.

Card Size: 3 1/2" x 5 1/2"
Sponsor: None

- ☐ George Armstrong
- ☐ Bob Baun
- ☐ Johnny Bower (G)
- ☐ John Brenneman
- ☐ Brian Conacher
- ☐ Jim Dorey
- ☐ Ron Ellis
- ☐ Bruce Gamble (G)
- ☐ Paul Henderson
- ☐ Larry Hillman
- ☐ Tim Horton
- ☐ Larry Jeffrey
- ☐ Red Kelly
- ☐ Dave Keon
- ☐ Orland Kurtenbach
- ☐ Rick Ley
- ☐ Murray Oliver
- ☐ Jim Pappin
- ☐ Mike Pelyk
- ☐ Pierre Pilote
- ☐ Marcel Pronovost
- ☐ Eddie Shack
- ☐ Darryl Sly
- ☐ Floyd Smith
- ☐ Allan Stanley
- ☐ Bill Sutherland

'69 - 70 TORO.

Tim Horton is the most expensive single at $15 in NM. Singles start at $2.50. We have no pricing information on complete sets.

Card Size: 3 1/2" x 5 1/2"
Sponsor: None

- ☐ George Armstrong
- ☐ Johnny Bower (G)
- ☐ Wayne Carleton
- ☐ King Clancy
- ☐ Terry Clancy
- ☐ Brian Conacher
- ☐ Marv Edwards (G)
- ☐ Ron Ellis
- ☐ Bruce Gamble (G)
- ☐ Brian Glennie
- ☐ Jim Harrison
- ☐ Larry Hillman
- ☐ Tim Horton
- ☐ Dave Keon
- ☐ Rick Ley
- ☐ Frank Mahovlich
- ☐ Jim McKenny
- ☐ Larry Mickey
- ☐ Murray Oliver
- ☐ Jim Pappin
- ☐ Mike Pelyk
- ☐ Marcel Pronovost
- ☐ Bob Pulford
- ☐ Pat Quinn
- ☐ Brit Selby
- ☐ Al Smith
- ☐ Floyd Smith
- ☐ Allan Stanley
- ☐ Norm Ullman
- ☐ Mike Walton
- ☐ Ron Ward

'70 - 71 TORO.

Darryl Sittler is the most expensive single at $35 in NM. Singles start at $2.50. Other singles may exist.

Card Size: 3 1/2" x 5 1/2"
Sponsor: None

- ☐ Jim Dorey
- ☐ Ron Ellis
- ☐ Bruce Gamble (G)
- ☐ Jim Harrison
- ☐ Paul Henderson
- ☐ Rick Ley
- ☐ Bob Liddington
- ☐ Jim McKenny
- ☐ Garry Monahan
- ☐ Mike Pelyk
- ☐ Jacques Plante (G)
- ☐ Brad Selwood
- ☐ Darryl Sittler
- ☐ Guy Trottier
- ☐ Mike Walton

'71 - 72 TORO.

The most expensive singles are Jacques Plante and Darryl Sittler at $12-15 in NM. Singles start at $2.50. Other singles may exist.

Card Size: 3 1/2" x 5 1/2"
Sponsor: None

- ☐ Bob Baun
- ☐ Jim Dorey
- ☐ Denis Dupère
- ☐ Ron Ellis
- ☐ Brian Glennie
- ☐ Jim Harrison
- ☐ Paul Henderson
- ☐ Dave Keon
- ☐ Rick Ley
- ☐ Billy MacMillan
- ☐ Don Marshall
- ☐ Jim McKenny
- ☐ Garry Monahan
- ☐ Bernie Parent (G)
- ☐ Mike Pelyk
- ☐ Jacques Plante (G)
- ☐ Brad Selwood
- ☐ Darryl Sittler
- ☐ Brian Spencer
- ☐ Guy Trottier
- ☐ Norm Ullman

'72 - 73 TORO.

There are several variations in this set. Jacques Plante and Darryl Sittler is the most expensive single at $12-15 in NM. Singles start at $2. We have no pricing information on complete sets.

Card Size: 3 1/2" x 5 1/2"
Sponsor: None

- ☐ Bob Baun
- ☐ Terry Clancy
- ☐ Denis Dupère
- ☐ Ron Ellis
- ☐ George Ferguson
- ☐ Brian Glennie
- ☐ John Grisdale
- ☐ Paul Henderson
- ☐ Pierre Jary
- ☐ Rick Kehoe
- ☐ Dave Keon
- ☐ Ron Low (G)
- ☐ Joe Lundrigan
- ☐ Larry McIntyre
- ☐ Jim McKenny
- ☐ Garry Monahan
- ☐ Randy Osburn
- ☐ Mike Pelyk
- ☐ Jacques Plante (G)
- ☐ Darryl Sittler
- ☐ Errol Thompson
- ☐ Norm Ullman

'73 - 74 TORO.

The most expensive singles in NM are Lanny McDonald at $15 and Borje Salming at $10. Singles start at $2. Variations may exist.

Card Size: 3 1/2" x 5 1/2"
Sponsor: None
Set (25 cards): $90

- ☐ Johnny Bower
- ☐ Willie Brossart
- ☐ Denis Dupère
- ☐ Ron Ellis
- ☐ Doug Favell (G)
- ☐ Brian Glennie
- ☐ Jim Gregory
- ☐ Inge Hammarstrom
- ☐ Paul Henderson
- ☐ Eddie Johnston (G)
- ☐ Rick Kehoe
- ☐ Red Kelly
- ☐ Dave Keon
- ☐ Lanny McDonald
- ☐ Jim McKenny
- ☐ Garry Monahan
- ☐ Bob Neely
- ☐ Mike Pelyk
- ☐ Borje Salming
- ☐ Eddie Shack
- ☐ Darryl Sittler
- ☐ Errol Thompson
- ☐ Ian Turnbull
- ☐ Norm Ullman
- ☐ Dunc Wilson (G)

'74 - 75 TORO.

Lanny McDonald is the most expensive single at $8 in NM. Singles start at $2. Variations may exist.

Card Size: 3 1/2" x 5 1/2"
Sponsor: None
Set (24 cards): $75

- ☐ Claire Alexander
- ☐ Dave Dunn
- ☐ Ron Ellis
- ☐ George Ferguson
- ☐ Bill Flett
- ☐ Brian Glennie
- ☐ Inge Hammarstrom
- ☐ Dave Keon
- ☐ Lanny McDonald
- ☐ Jim McKenny
- ☐ Gord McRae (G)
- ☐ Lyle Moffat
- ☐ Bob Neely
- ☐ Gary Sabourin
- ☐ Borje Salming
- ☐ Rod Seiling
- ☐ Eddie Shack
- ☐ Darryl Sittler
- ☐ Blaine Stoughton
- ☐ Errol Thompson
- ☐ Ian Turnbull
- ☐ Norm Ullman
- ☐ Dave Williams
- ☐ Dunc Wilson (G)

'75 - 76 TORO.

Lanny McDonald and Darryl Sittler are the most expensive single at $5-7 in NM. Singles start at $2. Variations may exist.

Card Size: 3 1/2" x 5 1/2"
Sponsor: None
Set (21 cards): $65

- ☐ Don Ashby
- ☐ Pat Boutette
- ☐ Dave Dunn
- ☐ Doug Favell (G)
- ☐ George Ferguson
- ☐ Brian Glennie
- ☐ Inge Hammarstrom
- ☐ Greg Hubick
- ☐ Lanny McDonald
- ☐ Jim McKenny
- ☐ Gord McRae (G)
- ☐ Bob Neely
- ☐ Borje Salming
- ☐ Rod Seiling
- ☐ Darryl Sittler
- ☐ Blaine Stoughton
- ☐ Wayne Thomas (G)
- ☐ Ian Turnbull
- ☐ Stan Weir
- ☐ Dave Williams

'76 - 77 TORO.

Lanny McDonald and Darryl Sittler are the most expensive singles at $5-6 in NM. Singles start at $2.

Card Size: 3 1/2" x 5 1/2"
Sponsor: None
Set (23 cards): $50

- ☐ Claire Alexander
- ☐ Don Ashby
- ☐ Pat Boutette
- ☐ Randy Carlyle
- ☐ George Ferguson
- ☐ Scott Garland
- ☐ Brian Glennie
- ☐ Inge Hammarstrom
- ☐ Lanny McDonald
- ☐ Jim McKenny
- ☐ Gord McRae (G)
- ☐ Bob Neely
- ☐ Mike Palmateer (G)
- ☐ Mike Pelyk
- ☐ Borje Salming
- ☐ Darryl Sittler
- ☐ Wayne Thomas (G)
- ☐ Errol Thompson
- ☐ Ian Turnbull
- ☐ Jack Valiquette
- ☐ Kurt Walker
- ☐ Stan Weir
- ☐ Dave Williams

'77 - 78 TORO.

Lanny McDonald and Darryl Sittler are the most expensive singles at $5-6 in NM. Singles start at $1.50.

Card Size: 3 1/2" x 5 1/2"
Sponsor: None
Set (21 cards): $35

- ☐ Don Ashby
- ☐ Pat Boutette
- ☐ Randy Carlyle
- ☐ Ron Ellis
- ☐ George Ferguson
- ☐ Brian Glennie
- ☐ Inge Hammarstrom
- ☐ Trevor Johansen
- ☐ Jim Jones
- ☐ Lanny McDonald
- ☐ Jim McKenny
- ☐ Gord McRae (G)
- ☐ Bob Neely
- ☐ Mike Palmateer (G)
- ☐ Borje Salming
- ☐ Darryl Sittler
- ☐ Errol Thompson
- ☐ Ian Turnbull
- ☐ Jack Valiquette
- ☐ Kurt Walker
- ☐ Dave Williams

'78 - 79 TORO.

Lanny McDonald and Darryl Sittler are the most expensive singles at $5-6 in NM. Singles start at $1.50.

Card Size: 3 1/2" x 5 1/2"
Sponsor: None
Set (23 cards): $40

- ☐ John Anderson
- ☐ Bruce Boudreau
- ☐ Dave Burrows
- ☐ Jerry Butler
- ☐ Ron Ellis
- ☐ Paul Harrison
- ☐ Dave Hutchison
- ☐ Trevor Johansen
- ☐ Jimmy Jones
- ☐ Dan Maloney
- ☐ Lanny McDonald
- ☐ Walt McKechnie
- ☐ Garry Monahan
- ☐ Roger Neilson
- ☐ Mike Palmateer (G)
- ☐ Borje Salming
- ☐ Darryl Sittler
- ☐ Lorne Stamler
- ☐ Ian Turnbull
- ☐ Dave Williams
- ☐ Ron Wilson
- ☐ H.Ballard/ K.Clancy
- ☐ Maple Leaf Gardens

'79 - 80 TORO.

Darryl Sittler is the most expensive single at $5 in NM. Singles start at $1.50. Variations may exist.

Card Size: 3 1/2" x 5 1/2"
Sponsor: None
Set (30 cards): $45

- ☐ John Anderson
- ☐ Harold Ballard
- ☐ Laurie Boschman
- ☐ Pat Boutette
- ☐ Carl Brewer
- ☐ Dave Burrows
- ☐ Jiri Crha (G)
- ☐ Ron Ellis
- ☐ Paul Gardner
- ☐ Paul Harrison (G)
- ☐ Pat Hickey
- ☐ Greg Hotham
- ☐ Dave Hutchison
- ☐ Punch Imlach
- ☐ Jimmy Jones
- ☐ Mark Kirton
- ☐ Dan Maloney
- ☐ Terry Martin
- ☐ Lanny McDonald
- ☐ Walt McKechnie
- ☐ Wilf Paiement
- ☐ Mike Palmateer (G)
- ☐ Joel Quenneville
- ☐ Rocky Saganiuk
- ☐ Borje Salming
- ☐ Darryl Sittler
- ☐ Floyd Smith
- ☐ Bob Stephenson
- ☐ Ian Turnbull
- ☐ Ron Wilson

'80 - 81 TORO.

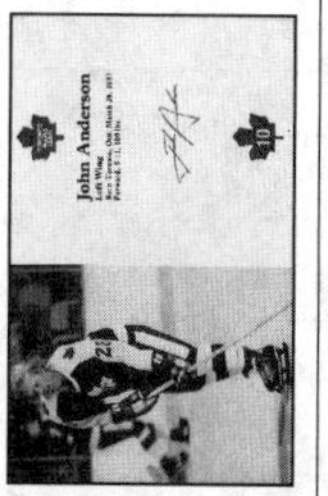

Darryl Sittler is the most expensive single at $4 in NM. Singles start at $1. Variations may exist.

Card Size: 3 1/2" x 5 1/2"
Sponsor: None
Set (26 cards): $35

- ☐ John Anderson
- ☐ Harold Ballard
- ☐ Laurie Boschman
- ☐ Johnny Bower
- ☐ King Clancy
- ☐ Jiri Crha (G)
- ☐ Joe Crozier
- ☐ Bill Derlago
- ☐ Dick Duff
- ☐ Viteslav Duris
- ☐ Dave Farrish
- ☐ Stewart Gavin
- ☐ Paul Harrison (G)
- ☐ Pat Hickey
- ☐ Mark Kirton
- ☐ Terry Martin
- ☐ Gerry McNamara
- ☐ Wilf Paiement
- ☐ Robert Picard
- ☐ Curt Ridley (G)
- ☐ Rocky Saganiuk
- ☐ Borje Salming
- ☐ Dave Shand
- ☐ Darryl Sittler
- ☐ Ian Turnbull
- ☐ Rick Vaive

'81 - 82 TORO.

Darryl Sittler is the most expensive single at $4. Singles start at $1. Variations may exist.

Postcard Size: 3 1/2" x 5 1/2"
Sponsor: None
Set (26 cards): $28

- ☐ John Anderson
- ☐ Harold Ballard
- ☐ Jim Benning
- ☐ Fred Boimistruck
- ☐ Laurie Boschman
- ☐ Bill Derlago
- ☐ Stewart Gavin
- ☐ Michel Larocque (G)
- ☐ Don Luce
- ☐ Bob McGill
- ☐ Dan Maloney
- ☐ Bob Manno
- ☐ Paul Marshall
- ☐ Terry Martin
- ☐ Barry Melrose
- ☐ Mike Nykoluk
- ☐ Wilf Paiement
- ☐ René Robert
- ☐ Rocky Saganiuk
- ☐ Borje Salming
- ☐ Darryl Sittler
- ☐ Vincent Tremblay (G)
- ☐ Rick Vaive
- ☐ Gary Yaremchuk
- ☐ Ron Zanussi
- ☐ H.Ballard/ F.Selke

'82 - 83 TORO.

Borje Salming is the most expensive single at $3. Singles start at $1. Variations may exist.

Postcard Size: 3 1/2" x 5 1/2"
Sponsor: None
Set (27 cards): $25

- ☐ Russ Adams
- ☐ John Anderson
- ☐ Normand Aubin
- ☐ Harold Ballard
- ☐ Jim Benning
- ☐ Serge Boisvert
- ☐ Dan Daoust
- ☐ Bill Derlago
- ☐ Miroslav Frycer
- ☐ Stewart Gavin
- ☐ Gaston Gingras
- ☐ Billy Harris
- ☐ Paul Higgins
- ☐ Peter Ihnacak
- ☐ Jim Korn
- ☐ Dan Maloney
- ☐ Terry Martin
- ☐ Frank Nigro
- ☐ Mike Nykoluk
- ☐ Gary Nylund
- ☐ Mike Palmateer (G)
- ☐ Walt Poddubny
- ☐ Rick St. Croix (G)
- ☐ Borje Salming
- ☐ Greg Terrion
- ☐ Vincent Tremblay (G)
- ☐ Rick Vaive

'83 - 84 TORO.

Borje Salming is the most expensive single at $3. Singles start at $1.

Postcard Size: 3 1/2" x 5 1/2"
Sponsor: None
Set (26 cards): $25

- ☐ John Anderson
- ☐ Jim Benning
- ☐ Dan Daoust
- ☐ Bill Derlago
- ☐ Dave Farrish
- ☐ Miroslav Frycer
- ☐ Stewart Gavin
- ☐ Gaston Gingras
- ☐ Pat Graham
- ☐ Billy Harris
- ☐ Peter Ihnacak
- ☐ Jim Korn
- ☐ Gary Leeman
- ☐ Dan Maloney
- ☐ Terry Martin
- ☐ Basil McRae
- ☐ Frank Nigro
- ☐ Mike Nykoluk
- ☐ Gary Nylund
- ☐ Mike Palmateer (G)
- ☐ Walt Poddubny
- ☐ Rick St. Croix (G)
- ☐ Borje Salming
- ☐ Bill Stewart
- ☐ Greg Terrion
- ☐ Rick Vaive

'84 - 85 TORO.

Russ Courtnall and Al Iafrate are the most expensive singles at $3-4. Singles start at $1.

Postcard Size: 3 1/2" x 5 1/2"
Sponsor: None
Set (24 cards): $25

- ☐ John Anderson
- ☐ Jim Benning
- ☐ Allan Bester (G)
- ☐ John Brophy
- ☐ Jeff Brubaker
- ☐ Russ Courtnall
- ☐ Dan Daoust
- ☐ Bill Derlago
- ☐ Miroslav Frycer
- ☐ Stewart Gavin
- ☐ Al Iafrate
- ☐ Peter Ihnacak
- ☐ Jeff Jackson
- ☐ Jim Korn
- ☐ Gary Leeman
- ☐ Dan Maloney
- ☐ Bob McGill
- ☐ Gary Nylund
- ☐ Walt Poddubny
- ☐ Bill Root
- ☐ Borje Salming
- ☐ Greg Terrion
- ☐ Rick Vaive
- ☐ Ken Wregget (G)

'85 - 86 TORO.

Wendel Clark is the most expensive single at $10. Singles start at $1.

Postcard Size: 3 1/2" x 5 1/2"
Sponsor: None
Set (28 cards): $30

- ☐ Harold Ballard
- ☐ Jim Benning
- ☐ Tim Bernhardt (G)
- ☐ Johnny Bower
- ☐ Jeff Brubaker
- ☐ Wendel Clark
- ☐ Russ Courtnall
- ☐ Dan Daoust
- ☐ Don Edwards (G)
- ☐ Tom Fergus
- ☐ Miroslav Frycer
- ☐ Al Iafrate
- ☐ Peter Ihnacak
- ☐ Jeff Jackson
- ☐ Jim Korn
- ☐ Chris Kotsopoulos
- ☐ Gary Leeman
- ☐ Brad Maxwell
- ☐ Bob McGill
- ☐ Gary Nylund
- ☐ Walt Poddubny
- ☐ Borje Salming
- ☐ Marian Stastny
- ☐ Greg Terrion
- ☐ Steve Thomas
- ☐ Rick Vaive
- ☐ Blake Wesley
- ☐ Ken Wregget (G)

'86 - 87 TORO.

This series has two versions: one regular series and one with the player's name in caps. Wendel Clark and Vincent Damphousse are the most expensive singles at $5-7. Singles start at $1.

Postcard Size: 3 1/2" x 5 1/2"
Sponsor: None
Set (24 cards): $25

- ☐☐ Mike Allison
- ☐☐ Wendel Clark
- ☐☐ Russ Courtnall
- ☐☐ Vincent Damphousse
- ☐☐ Dan Daoust
- ☐☐ Jerome Dupont
- ☐☐ Tom Fergus
- ☐☐ Miroslav Frycer
- ☐☐ Todd Gill
- ☐☐ Dan Hoganson
- ☐☐ Al Iafrate
- ☐☐ Miroslav Ihnacak
- ☐☐ Peter Ihnacak
- ☐☐ Terry Johnson
- ☐☐ Chris Kotsopoulos
- ☐☐ Gary Leeman
- ☐☐ Bob McGill
- ☐☐ Bill Root
- ☐☐ Borje Salming
- ☐☐ Brad Smith
- ☐☐ Greg Terrion
- ☐☐ Steve Thomas
- ☐☐ Rick Vaive
- ☐☐ Ken Wregget (G)

'87 - 88 TORO.

5 x 7

Wendel Clark and Vincent Damphousse are the most expensive singles at $4-5. Singles start at $1.

Postcard Size: 5" x 8"
Sponsor: None
Set (23 cards): $25

- ☐ Allan Bester (G)
- ☐ Wendel Clark
- ☐ Russ Courtnall
- ☐ Vincent Damphousse
- ☐ Dan Daoust
- ☐ Dale DeGray
- ☐ Tom Fergus
- ☐ Miroslav Frycer
- ☐ Al Iafrate
- ☐ Peter Ihnacak
- ☐ Chris Kotsopoulos
- ☐ Rick Lanz
- ☐ Gary Leeman
- ☐ Ed Olczyk
- ☐ Mark Osborne
- ☐ Luke Richardson
- ☐ Borje Salming
- ☐ Al Secord
- ☐ Dave Semenko
- ☐ Brad Smith
- ☐ Greg Terrion
- ☐ Ken Wregget (G)
- ☐ Team Photo

'87 - 88 TORO.

3.5 x 5.5

We have little information on this set. Other singles may exist.

Card Size: 3 1/2" x 5 1/2"
Sponsor: None

- ☐ Russ Courtnall

'87 - 88 TORO.

P.L.A.Y.

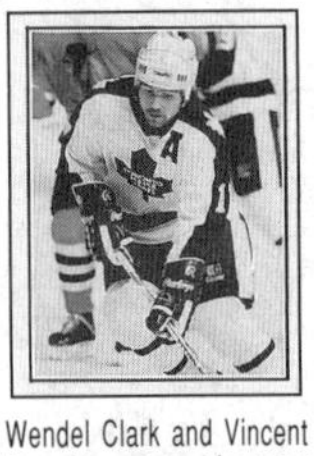

Wendel Clark and Vincent Damphousse are the most expensive singles at $2-3. Singles start at 50¢.

Card Size: 2 3/4" x 3 1/4"
Sponsors: Kelloggs, Salada
Set (30 cards): $20

- ☐ 1 N. LaVerne Shipley
- ☐ 2 Tom Gosnell
- ☐ 3 Checklist
- ☐ 4 Harold Ballard
- ☐ 5 Super. D. Almond
- ☐ 6 Wendel Clark
- ☐ 7 Tom Fergus
- ☐ 8 Borje Salming
- ☐ 9 Ed Olczyk
- ☐ 10 Gary Leeman
- ☐ 11 Rick Lanz
- ☐ 12 Allan Bester (G)
- ☐ 13 Todd Gill
- ☐ 14 Al Secord
- ☐ 15 Miroslav Frycer
- ☐ 16 Chris Kotsopoulos
- ☐ 17 Vincent Damphousse
- ☐ 18 Mike Allison
- ☐ 19 Al Iafrate
- ☐ 20 Dan Daoust
- ☐ 21 Greg Terrion
- ☐ 22 Brad Smith
- ☐ 23 Mark Osborne
- ☐ 24 Peter Ihnacak
- ☐ 25 Dale DeGray
- ☐ 26 Dave Semenko
- ☐ 27 Luke Richardson
- ☐ 28 John Brophy
- ☐ 29 Ken Wregget (G)
- ☐ 30 Russ Courtnall

'88 - 89 TORO.

P.L.A.Y.

Wendel Clark and Vincent Damphousse are the most expensive singles at $2-3. Singles start at 50¢.

Card Size: 2 3/4" x 3 1/2"
Sponsor: Kellogg's
Set (30 cards): $20

- ☐ 1 Police, Law and Youth
- ☐ 2 Wendel Clark
- ☐ 3 Tom Fergus
- ☐ 4 Super. D. Almond
- ☐ 5 Borje Salming
- ☐ 6 Ed Olczyk
- ☐ 7 Checklist
- ☐ 8 Gary Leeman
- ☐ 9 Rick Lanz
- ☐ 10 N. LaVerne Shipley
- ☐ 11 Allan Bester (G)
- ☐ 12 Todd Gill
- ☐ 13 Harold Ballard
- ☐ 14 Al Secord
- ☐ 15 Daniel Marois
- ☐ 16 Chris Kotsopoulos
- ☐ 17 Vincent Damphousse
- ☐ 18 Craig Laughlin
- ☐ 19 Al Iafrate
- ☐ 20 Dan Daoust
- ☐ 21 Derek Laxdal
- ☐ 22 Darren Veitch
- ☐ 23 Mark Osborne
- ☐ 24 David Reid
- ☐ 25 Brad Marsh
- ☐ 26 Brian Curran
- ☐ 27 Sean McKenna
- ☐ 28 John Brophy
- ☐ 29 Ken Wregget (G)
- ☐ 30 Russ Courtnall

'90 - 91 TORO.

We have no pricing information on this set. Other singles may exist.

Card Size: 4" x 6"
Sponsor: None

- ☐ Aaron Broten
- ☐ Vincent Damphousse
- ☐ Dave Ellett
- ☐ Paul Fenton
- ☐ Tom Fergus
- ☐ Lou Franceschetti
- ☐ Al Iafrate
- ☐ Peter Ing (G)
- ☐ Mike Krushelnyski
- ☐ Tom Kurvers
- ☐ Gary Leeman
- ☐ Kevin Maguire
- ☐ Brad Marsh
- ☐ Scott Pearson
- ☐ Michel Petit
- ☐ Rob Ramage
- ☐ Dave Reid
- ☐ Luke Richardson
- ☐ Joe Sacco
- ☐ Doug Shedden
- ☐ Scott Thornton

'90 - 91 TORO.

P.L.A.Y.

Wendel Clark and Grant Fuhr are the most expensive singles at $2-3. Singles start at 75¢.

Sponsor: Kellogg's
Set (30 cards): $20

- ☐ 1 Chief Don Hillock
- ☐ 2 Dep. Chief B. Cousineau
- ☐ 3 Lanny the Police Dog
- ☐ 4 Cliff Fletcher
- ☐ 5 Tom Watt
- ☐ 6 Bob Rouse
- ☐ 7 Dave Ellett
- ☐ 8 Dave Hannan
- ☐ 9 Glenn Anderson
- ☐ 10 Gary Leeman
- ☐ 11 Rob Pearson
- ☐ 12 Claude Loiselle
- ☐ 13 Craig Berube
- ☐ 14 Wendel Clark
- ☐ 15 Tom Fergus
- ☐ 16 Mike Bullard
- ☐ 17 Todd Gill
- ☐ 18 Michel Petit
- ☐ 19 Peter Zezel
- ☐ 20 Mike Krushelnyski
- ☐ 21 Lucien DeBlois
- ☐ 22 Darryl Shannon
- ☐ 23 Grant Fuhr (G)
- ☐ 24 Daniel Marois
- ☐ 25 Rob Cimetta
- ☐ 26 Jeff Reese (G)
- ☐ 27 Bob Halkidis
- ☐ 28 Brian Bradley
- ☐ 29 Mike Foligno
- ☐ 30 Alexander Godynyuk

'92 - 93 TORO.

KODAK

These photos are printed on Kodak paper. The most expensive singles are Félix Potvin at $3 and Doug Gilmour at $2. Singles start at $1.

Card Size: 4" x 6 1/8"
Sponsor: Kodak
Set (21 cards): $20

- ☐ Glenn Anderson
- ☐ Dave Andreychuk
- ☐ Ken Baumgartner
- ☐ Drake Berehowsky
- ☐ Bill Berg
- ☐ Nikolai Borschevsky
- ☐ Wendel Clark
- ☐ John Cullen
- ☐ Mike Eastwood
- ☐ Dave Ellett
- ☐ Doug Gilmour
- ☐ Sylvain Lefebvre
- ☐ Jamie Macoun
- ☐ Kent Manderville
- ☐ Dave McLlwain
- ☐ Dmitri Mironov
- ☐ Mark Osborne
- ☐ Rob Pearson
- ☐ Félix Potvin (G)
- ☐ Bob Rouse
- ☐ Peter Zezel

'93 - 94 TORO.

ABALENE

These singles start at $1. Other singles exist.

Sponsor: Abalene

- ☐ Dave Andreychuk
- ☐ Bill Berg
- ☐ Nikolai Borschevsky
- ☐ Wendel Clark
- ☐ John Cullen
- ☐ Mike Eastwood
- ☐ Dave Ellett
- ☐ Mike Gartner
- ☐ Todd Gill
- ☐ Doug Gilmour
- ☐ Mike Krushelnyski
- ☐ Alexei Kudashov
- ☐ Sylvain Lefebvre
- ☐ Jamie Macoun
- ☐ Kent Manderville
- ☐ Dmitri Mironov
- ☐ Mark Osborne
- ☐ Rob Pearson
- ☐ Félix Potvin (G)
- ☐ Damian Rhodes (G)
- ☐ Bob Rouse
- ☐ Peter Zezel

'93 - 94 TORO.

BLACK'S

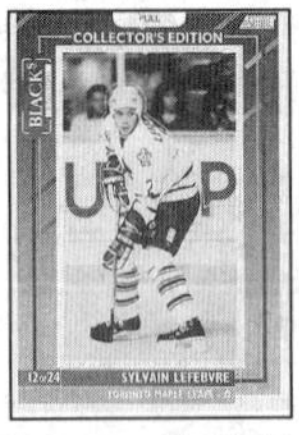

The most expensive single is Félix Potvin at $4. Singles start at 75¢.

Card Size: 2 1/2" x 3 1/2"
Sponsors: Black's, Score
Set (24 cards): $18
Album: $5

- ☐ 1 Wendel Clark
- ☐ 2 Doug Gilmour
- ☐ 3 Glenn Anderson
- ☐ 4 Peter Zezel
- ☐ 5 Bob Rouse
- ☐ 6 Rob Pearson
- ☐ 7 Mark Osborne
- ☐ 8 Dmitri Mironov
- ☐ 9 Dave McLlwain
- ☐ 10 Kent Manderville
- ☐ 11 Jamie Macoun
- ☐ 12 Sylvain Lefebvre
- ☐ 13 Dave Andreychuk
- ☐ 14 Drake Berehowsky
- ☐ 15 Bill Berg
- ☐ 16 John Cullen
- ☐ 17 Ken Baumgartner
- ☐ 18 Nikolai Borschevsky
- ☐ 19 Mike Eastwood
- ☐ 20 Dave Ellett
- ☐ 21 Mike Foligno
- ☐ 22 Todd Gill
- ☐ 23 Mike Krushelnyski
- ☐ 24 Félix Potvin (G)

'93 - 94 TORO.

KODAK

We have little information on this set. Photos are printed on Kodak paper and are practically identical in style to the 1992-93 series. Other singles exist.

Card Size: 4" x 6"
Sponsor: Kodak

- ☐ Damian Rhodes (G)

'94 - 95 TORO.

COKE

Félix Potvin is the most expensive single at $3. Singles start at 75¢.

Card Size: 4 3/4" x 7"
Sponsors: Coca Cola
Set (17 cards): $20

- ☐ Dave Andreychuk
- ☐ Ken Baumgartner
- ☐ Bill Berg
- ☐ Nikolai Borschevsky
- ☐ Mike Eastwood
- ☐ Dave Ellett
- ☐ Mike Gartner
- ☐ Todd Gill
- ☐ Doug Gilmour
- ☐ Alexei Kudashov
- ☐ Jamie Macoun
- ☐ Kent Manderville
- ☐ Dmitri Mironov
- ☐ Mark Osborne
- ☐ Félix Potvin (G)
- ☐ Damian Rhodes (G)
- ☐ Maple Leafs card

'99 - 00 TORO.

PIZZA PIZZA

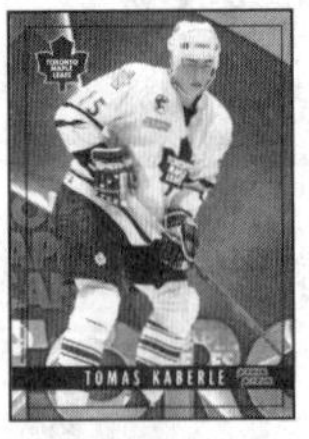

These cards were issued in four perforated sheets at Pizza Pizza restaurants.

Card Size: 2 1/2" x 3 1/2"
Sponsor: Pizza Pizza
Set (20 cards): $15

- ☐ 1 Dmitri Khristich
- ☐ 2 Jonas Höglund
- ☐ 3 Tomas Kaberle
- ☐ 4 Garry Valk
- ☐ 5 Curtis Joseph
- ☐ 6 Danny Markov
- ☐ 7 Bryan Berard
- ☐ 8 Kevyn Adams
- ☐ 9 Alexander Karpovtsev
- ☐ 10 Steve Thomas
- ☐ 11 Alyn McCauley
- ☐ 12 Tie Domi
- ☐ 13 Nikolai Antropov
- ☐ 14 Sergei Berezin
- ☐ 15 Dmitry Yushkevich
- ☐ 16 Igor Korolev
- ☐ 17 Darcy Tucker
- ☐ 18 Glenn Healy
- ☐ 19 Yanic Perreault
- ☐ 20 Mats Sundin

'01 - 02 TORO.

DYNAMIC

Other singles exist.

- ☐ Robert Reichel
- ☐ Mats Sundin

'02 - 03 TORO.

We do not have a checklist for this series of cards.

VANCOUVER CANUCKS

'70 - 71 VANC.

ROYAL BANK

Photos are in black and white on these blank-back cards. Pat Quinn is the most expensive single at $10 in NM. Singles start at $4.

Card Size: 5" x 7"
Sponsor: Royal Bank
Set (20 cards): $80

- ☐ André Boudrias
- ☐ Mike Corrigan
- ☐ Ray Cullen
- ☐ Gary Doak
- ☐ George Gardner (G)
- ☐ Murray Hall
- ☐ Charlie Hodge (G)
- ☐ Dan Johnson
- ☐ Orland Kurtenbach
- ☐ Wayne Maki
- ☐ Rosaire Paiement
- ☐ Poul Popiel
- ☐ Pat Quinn
- ☐ Marc Reaume
- ☐ Darryl Sly
- ☐ Dale Tallon
- ☐ Ted Taylor
- ☐ Barry Wilkins
- ☐ Dunc Wilson (G)
- ☐ Jim Wiste

'71 - 72 VANC.

ROYAL BANK

Photos are in black and white on these blank-back cards. Pat Quinn is the most expensive single at $8 in NM. Singles start at $3. Card #10 was supposedly never issued.

Card Size: 5" x 7"
Sponsor: Royal Bank
Set (20 cards): $65

- ☐ 1 Bobby Lalonde
- ☐ 2 Mike Corrigan
- ☐ 3 Murray Hall
- ☐ 4 Jocelyn Guevremont
- ☐ 5 Pat Quinn
- ☐ 6 Orland Kurtenbach
- ☐ 7 Paul Popiel
- ☐ 8 Ron Ward
- ☐ 9 Rosaire Paiement
- ☐ 11 Dale Tallon
- ☐ 12 Bobby Schmautz
- ☐ 13 Dennis Kearns
- ☐ 14 Barry Wilkins
- ☐ 15 Dunc Wilson (G)
- ☐ 16 André Boudrias
- ☐ 17 Ted Taylor
- ☐ 18 George Gardner (G)
- ☐ 19 John Schella
- ☐ 20 Wayne Maki
- ☐ 21 Gary Doak

'72 - 73 VANC.

ROYAL BANK

These photos are in full colour. Orland Kurtenbach is the most expensive single at $4 in NM. Singles start at $3.

Card Size: 5" x 7"
Sponsor: Royal Bank
Set (21 cards): $50

- ☐ Dale Balon
- ☐ Gregg Boddy
- ☐ Larry Bolonchuk
- ☐ André Boudrias
- ☐ Ed Dyck
- ☐ Jocelyn Guevremont
- ☐ Jim Hargraves
- ☐ Dennis Kearns
- ☐ Orland Kurtenbach
- ☐ Bobby Lalonde
- ☐ Richard Lemieux
- ☐ Don Lever
- ☐ Bryan McSheffrey
- ☐ Wayne Maki
- ☐ Gerry O'Flaherty
- ☐ Bobby Schmautz
- ☐ Dale Tallon
- ☐ Don Tannahill
- ☐ Barry Wilkins
- ☐ Dunc Wilson (G)
- ☐ John Wright

'72 - 73 VANC.

NALLEY'S

These singles were issued on the backs of Nalley's Potato Chip triple packs. Pat Quinn is the most expensive single at $40 in NM. Singles start at $25.

Card Size: 6 3/4" x 5 3/8"
Sponsor: Nalley's Potato Chips
Set (6 cards): $160

- ☐ André Boudrias
- ☐ George Gardner (G)
- ☐ Wayne Maki
- ☐ Rosaire Paiement
- ☐ Pat Quinn
- ☐ Barry Wilkins

'73 - 74 VANC.

ROYAL BANK

Orland Kurtenbach is the most expensive single at $4 in NM. Singles start at $3.

Card Size: 5" x 7"
Sponsor: Royal Bank

Set (21 cards): $50
- □ Paulin Bordeleau
- □ André Boudrias
- □ Jacques Caron (G)
- □ Bob Dailey
- □ Dave Dunn
- □ Jocelyn Guevremont
- □ Dennis Kearns
- □ Jerry Korab
- □ Orland Kurtenbach
- □ Bobby Lalonde
- □ Richard Lemieux
- □ Don Lever
- □ Bill McCreary
- □ Bryan McSheffrey
- □ Gerry O'Flaherty
- □ Bobby Schmautz
- □ Gary Smith (G)
- □ Don Tannahill
- □ Dennis Ververgaert
- □ Barry Wilkins
- □ John Wright

'74 - 75 VANC.
ROYAL BANK

Singles start at $3 in NM.
Card Size: 5" x 7"
Sponsor: Royal Bank
Set (21 cards): $50
- □ Gregg Boddy
- □ Paulin Bordeleau
- □ André Boudrias
- □ Bob Dailey
- □ Ab DeMarco
- □ John Gould
- □ John Grisdale
- □ Dennis Kearns
- □ Bobby Lalonde
- □ Don Lever
- □ Ken Lockett (G)
- □ Gerry Meehan
- □ Garry Monahan
- □ Chris Oddleifson
- □ Gerry O'Flaherty
- □ Tracy Pratt
- □ Mike Robitaille
- □ Léon Rochefort
- □ Gary Smith (G)
- □ Dennis Ververgaert
- □ Jim Wiley

'75 - 76 VANC.
ROYAL BANK

Harold Snepsts is the most expensive single at $4-5 in NM. Singles start at $2.50.
Card Size: 4 3/4" x 7 1/4"
Sponsor: Royal Bank
Set (22 cards): $45
- □ Rick Blight
- □ Gregg Boddy
- □ Paulin Bordeleau
- □ André Boudrias
- □ Bob Dailey
- □ Ab DeMarco
- □ John Gould
- □ John Grisdale
- □ Dennis Kearns
- □ Bobby Lalonde
- □ Don Lever
- □ Ken Lockett (G)
- □ Garry Monahan
- □ Bob Murray
- □ Chris Oddleifson
- □ Gerry O'Flaherty
- □ Tracy Pratt
- □ Mike Robitaille
- □ Ron Sedlbauer
- □ Gary Smith (G)
- □ Harold Snepsts
- □ Dennis Ververgaert

'76 - 77 VANC.
ROYAL BANK

Césare Maniago and Harold Snepsts are the most expensive singles at $4 in NM. Singles start at $2.50.
Card Size: 4 3/4" x 7 1/4"
Sponsor: Royal Bank
Set (23 cards): $45
- □ Rick Blight
- □ Bob Dailey
- □ Dave Fortier
- □ Brad Gassoff
- □ John Gould
- □ John Grisdale
- □ Dennis Kearns
- □ Bobby Lalonde
- □ Don Lever
- □ Césare Maniago (G)
- □ Garry Monahan
- □ Bob Murray
- □ Chris Oddleifson
- □ Gerry O'Flaherty
- □ Curt Ridley (G)
- □ Mike Robitaille
- □ Ron Sedlbauer
- □ Harold Snepsts
- □ Andy Spruce
- □ Ralph Stewart
- □ Dennis Ververgaert
- □ Mike Walton
- □ Jim Wiley

'77 - 78 VANC.
ROYAL BANK

Césare Maniago and Harold Snepsts are the most expensive singles at $3-4 in NM. Singles start at $2.50.
Card Size: 4 1/4" x 5 1/2"
Sponsor: Royal Bank
Set (21 cards): $40
- □ Rick Blight
- □ Larry Carrière
- □ Ron Flockhart
- □ Brad Gassoff
- □ Jere Gillis
- □ Larry Goodenough
- □ Hilliard Graves
- □ John Grisdale
- □ Dennis Kearns
- □ Don Lever
- □ Césare Maniago (G)
- □ Bob Manno
- □ Jack McIlhargey
- □ Garry Monahan
- □ Chris Oddleifson
- □ Gerry O'Flaherty
- □ Curt Ridley (G)
- □ Ron Sedlbauer
- □ Harold Snepsts
- □ Dennis Ververgaert
- □ Mike Walton

'78 - 79 VANC.
ROYAL BANK

The most expensive singles in NM are Stan Smyl at $5 and Glen Hanlon at $4. Singles start at $2.
Card Size: 4 1/4" x 5 1/2"
Sponsor: Royal Bank
Set (23 cards): $40
- □ Rick Blight
- □ Gary Bromley (G)
- □ Bill Derlago
- □ Roland Eriksson
- □ Curt Fraser
- □ Jere Gillis
- □ Thomas Gradin
- □ Hilliard Graves
- □ John Grisdale
- □ Glen Hanlon (G)
- □ Randy Holt
- □ Dennis Kearns
- □ Don Lever
- □ Lars Lindgren
- □ Bob Manno
- □ Pit Martin
- □ Jack McIlhargey
- □ Chris Oddleifson
- □ Ron Sedlbauer
- □ Stan Smyl
- □ Harold Snepsts
- □ Dennis Ververgaert
- □ Lars Zetterstrom

'79 - 80 VANC.
ROYAL BANK

Stan Smyl and Rick Vaive are the most expensive singles at $4-5 in NM. Singles start at $2.
Card Size: 4 1/4" x 5 1/2"
Sponsor: Royal Bank
Set (23 cards): $35
- □ Brent Ashton
- □ Jeff Bandura
- □ Rick Blight
- □ Gary Bromley (G)
- □ Drew Callander
- □ Bill Derlago
- □ Curt Fraser
- □ Jere Gillis
- □ Thomas Gradin
- □ Glen Hanlon (G)
- □ John Hughes
- □ Dennis Kearns
- □ Don Lever
- □ Lars Lindgren
- □ Bob Manno
- □ Kevin McCarthy
- □ Jack McIlhargey
- □ Chris Oddleifson
- □ Curt Ridley (G)
- □ Ron Sedlbauer
- □ Stan Smyl
- □ Harold Snepsts
- □ Rick Vaive

'80 - 81 VANC.

Richard Brodeur is the most expensive single at $5. Singles start at $2.
Card Size: 3 3/4" x 4 7/8"
Sponsor: None
Set (22 cards): $35
- □ Brent Ashton
- □ Ivan Boldirev
- □ Per-Olov Brasar
- □ Richard Brodeur (G)
- □ Gary Bromley (G)
- □ Jerry Butler
- □ Colin Campbell
- □ Curt Fraser
- □ Thomas Gradin
- □ Glen Hanlon (G)
- □ Dennis Kearns
- □ Rick Lanz
- □ Lars Lindgren
- □ Dave Logan
- □ Gary Lupul
- □ Kevin McCarthy
- □ Gerry Minor
- □ Darcy Rota
- □ Bobby Schmautz
- □ Stan Smyl
- □ Harold Snepsts
- □ Tiger Williams

'80 - 81 VANC.
SILVERWOOD DAIRIES

One three-card panel was found in 4L bags of Silverwood Dairies milk. The Hanlon/Brasar/Campbell panel is the most expensive at $5-7. Single panels start at $3. Cut-out singles measure 2 7/16" x 4 1/8" and start at $2. A cut-out 24-card set sells at $40.
Panel Size: 4 1/8" x 7 3/8"
Sponsor: Silverwood Dairies
Set (8 panels): $50
- □ Thomas Gradin
  Dennis Kearns
  Brent Ashton
- □ Glen Hanlon (G)
  Per-Olov Brasar
  Colin Campbell
- □ Rick Lanz
  Darcy Rota
  Gerry Minor
- □ Kevin McCarthy
  Richard Brodeur (G)
  Gary Lupul
- □ Bobby Schmautz
  Curt Fraser
  Dave Logan
- □ Stan Smyl
  Jerry Butler
  Bob Manno
- □ Harold Snepsts
  Ivan Boldirev
  Gary Bromley (G)
- □ David Williams
  Lars Lindgren
  Kevin Primeau

'81 - 82 VANC.

Richard Brodeur is the most expensive single at $4. Singles start at $1.50.
Card Size: 3 3/4" x 4 7/8"
Sponsor: None
Set (20 cards): $30
- □ Ivan Boldirev
- □ Per-Olov Brasar
- □ Richard Brodeur (G)
- □ Jiri Bubla
- □ Jerry Butler
- □ Colin Campbell
- □ Anders Eldebrink
- □ Curt Fraser
- □ Thomas Gradin
- □ Doug Halward
- □ Glen Hanlon (G)
- □ Rick Lanz
- □ Gary Lupul
- □ Blair MacDonald
- □ Kevin McCarthy
- □ Gerry Minor
- □ Lars Molin
- □ Darcy Rota
- □ Stan Smyl
- □ Tiger Williams

'81 - 82 VANC.
SILVERWOOD DAIRIES

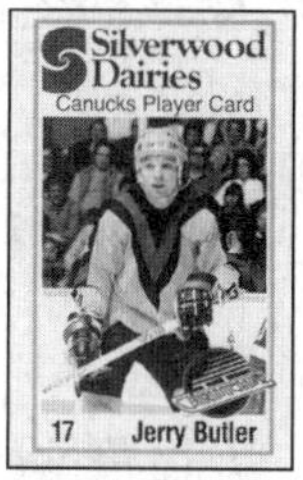

One three-card panel was found in 4L bags of Silverwood Dairies milk. The Lanz/Fraser/Crawford panel is the most expensive at $6-8. Single panels start at $3. Cut-out singles measure 2 7/16" x 4 1/8" and start at $1. A cut-out 24-card set sells at $35.
Panel Size: 4 1/4" x 7 3/8"
Sponsor: Silverwood Dairies
Set (8 panels): $40
- □ Richard Brodeur (G)
  Lars Lindgren
  Darcy Rota
- □ Thomas Gradin
  Jiri Bubla
  Blair MacDonald
- □ Glen Hanlon (G)
  Harold Snepsts
  Gerry Minor
- □ Ivan Hlinka
  Jerry Butler
  Doug Halward
- □ Rick Lanz
  Curt Fraser
  Marc Crawford
- □ Kevin McCarthy
  Ivan Boldirev
  Lars Molin
- □ Stan Smyl
  Colin Campbell
  Per-Olov Brasar
- □ Dave Williams
  Anders Eldebrink
  Gary Lupul

'82 - 83 VANC.

This set was originally issued in panels. Three panels have six cards while the team photo panel has five cards. The team photo measures 4 7/8" x 7 1/2". Richard Brodeur is the most expensive cut-out single at $4. Singles start at $1.50.
Card Size: 4 7/8" x 3 3/4"
Sponsor: None
Set (23 cards): $25
- □ Ivan Boldirev
- □ Richard Brodeur (G)
- □ Jiri Bubla
- □ Garth Butcher
- □ Ron Delorme
- □ Ken Ellacott (G)
- □ Curt Fraser
- □ Thomas Gradin
- □ Doug Halward
- □ Ivan Hlinka
- □ Rick Lanz
- □ Moe Lemay
- □ Lars Lindgren
- □ Kevin McCarthy
- □ Gerry Minor
- □ Lars Molin
- □ Jim Nill
- □ Darcy Rota
- □ Stan Smyl
- □ Harold Snepsts
- □ Patrik Sundström
- □ Dave Williams
- □ Team Photo

'83 - 84 VANC.

This set was originally issued in panels. Three panels have six cards while the team photo panel has five cards. The team photo measures 4 7/8" x 7 1/2". Marc Crawford is the most expensive cut-out single at $5. Singles start at $1.
Card Size: 4 7/8" x 3 3/4"
Sponsor: None
Set (23 cards): $25
- □ Richard Brodeur #35 (G)
- □ Jiri Bubla #29
- □ Garth Butcher #5
- □ Marc Crawford #28
- □ Ron Delorme #19
- □ John Garrett #31(G)
- □ Jere Gillis #4
- □ Thomas Gradin #23
- □ Doug Halward #2
- □ Mark Kirton #16
- □ Rick Lanz #4
- □ Gary Lupul #7
- □ Kevin McCarthy #25
- □ Lars Molin #26
- □ Jim Nill #8
- □ Michel Petit #3
- □ Darcy Rota #18
- □ Stan Smyl #12
- □ Harold Snepsts #27
- □ Patrik Sundström #17
- □ Tony Tanti #9
- □ Dave Williams #22
- □ Team Photo

'84 - 85 VANC.

This set was originally issued in panels. Four panels have six player cards while the last panel features two 4 3/4" x7" photos. Cam Neely is the most expensive cut-out single at $15. Singles start at $1. A cut-out 24-card set sells for $25.
Card Size: 4 1/4" x 3 1/4"
Sponsor: None
Set (26 cards): $30
- □ Neil Belland
- □ Richard Brodeur (G)
- □ Jiri Bubla
- □ Garth Butcher
- □ Frank Caprice (G)
- □ J.J. Daigneault
- □ Ron Delorme
- □ John Garrett (G)
- □ Thomas Gradin
- □ Taylor Hall
- □ Doug Halward
- □ Rick Lanz
- □ Moe Lemay
- □ Doug Lidster
- □ Gary Lupul
- □ Al MacAdam
- □ Peter McNab
- □ Cam Neely
- □ Michel Petit
- □ Darcy Rota
- □ Petri Skriko
- □ Stan Smyl
- □ Patrik Sundström
- □ Tony Tanti
- □ Air Canucks
- □ Team Photo

'85 - 86 VANC.

This set was originally issued in panels. Four panels have six player cards while the last panel features a team photo measuring 4 5/8" x 7". Cam Neely is the most expensive cut-out single at $10. Singles start at $1.
Card Size: 4 1/4" x 3 3/8"
Sponsor: None
Set (25 cards): $25
- □ Richard Brodeur (G)
- □ Jiri Bubla
- □ Garth Butcher
- □ Frank Caprice (G)
- □ Glen Cochrane
- □ Craig Coxe
- □ J.J. Daigneault
- □ Thomas Gradin
- □ Taylor Hall
- □ Doug Halward
- □ Jean-Marc Lanthier
- □ Rick Lanz
- □ Moe Lemay
- □ Doug Lidster
- □ Dave Lowry
- □ Gary Lupul
- □ Cam Neely
- □ Brent Peterson
- □ Jim Sandlak
- □ Petri Skriko
- □ Stan Smyl
- □ Patrik Sundström
- □ Steve Tambellini
- □ Tony Tanti
- □ Team Photo

'86 - 87 VANC.

This set was originally issued in six-card panels. Singles start at 75¢.
Card Size: 2 1/2" x 3 1/2"
Sponsor: None
Set (24 cards): $20
- □ Richard Brodeur #35 (G)
- □ Garth Butcher #5
- □ Frank Caprice #30 (G)
- □ Glen Cochrane #29
- □ Craig Coxe #32
- □ Taylor Hall #8
- □ Stu Kulak #16
- □ Rick Lanz #4
- □ Moe Lemay #14
- □ Doug Lidster #3
- □ Dave Lowry #22
- □ Brad Maxwell #27
- □ Barry Pederson #7
- □ Brent Peterson #10
- □ Michel Petit #24
- □ Dave Richter #6
- □ Jim Sandlak #33
- □ Petri Skriko #26
- □ Stan Smyl #12
- □ Patrik Sundström #17
- □ Rich Sutter #15
- □ Steve Tambellini #20
- □ Tony Tanti #9
- □ Wendell Young #1 (G)

'87 - 88 VANC.
FORMULA SHELL

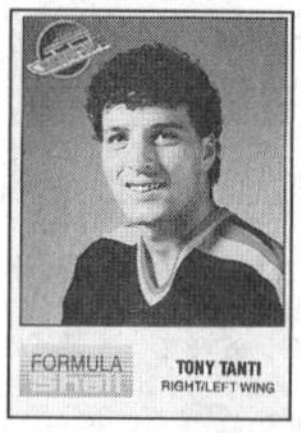

This set was originally issued in four-card panels. One card from each panel was an advertisement card. An eight-panel (32 cards) set sells at $18. Kirk McLean is the most expensive cut-out single at $3. Singles start at 50¢.
Card Size: 2 1/2" x 3 1/2"
Sponsor: Formula Shell
Set (24 cards): $15
- □ Greg Adams
- □ Jim Benning
- □ Randy Boyd
- □ Richard Brodeur (G)
- □ David Bruce
- □ Garth Butcher
- □ Frank Caprice (G)
- □ Craig Coxe
- □ Willie Huber
- □ Doug Lidster
- □ Dave Lowry
- □ Kirk McLean (G)
- □ Larry Melnyk
- □ Barry Pederson
- □ Dave Richter
- □ Jim Sandlak
- □ Dave Saunders
- □ Petri Skriko
- □ Stan Smyl
- □ Daryl Stanley
- □ Rich Sutter
- □ Steve Tambellini
- □ Tony Tanti
- □ Doug Wickenheiser

'88 - 89 VANC.
MOHAWK

This set was originally issued in four-card panels. Trevor Linden is the most expensive single at $6. Singles start at 75¢.
Card Size: 2 1/2" x 3 1/2"
Sponsor: Mohawk
Set (24 cards): $15
- □ Greg Adams #8
- □ Jim Benning #4
- □ Ken Berry #18
- □ Randy Boyd # 29
- □ Steve Bozek #14
- □ Brian Bradley #10
- □ David Bruce #25
- □ Garth Butcher #5
- □ Kevan Guy #2
- □ Doug Lidster #3
- □ Trevor Linden #16
- □ Kirk McLean #1 (G)
- □ Larry Melnyk #24
- □ Robert Nordmark #6
- □ Barry Pederson #7
- □ Paul Reinhart #23
- □ Jim Sandlak #19
- □ Petri Skriko #26
- □ Stan Smyl #12
- □ Harold Snepsts #27
- □ Ronnie Stern #20
- □ Rich Sutter #15
- □ Tony Tanti #9
- □ Steve Weeks #31 (G)

'89 - 90 VANC.
MOHAWK

This set was originally issued in four-card panels. Trevor Linden is the most expensive single at $6. Singles start at 75¢.
Card Size: 2 1/2" x 3 1/2"
Sponsor: Mohawk
Set (24 cards): $15
- □ Greg Adams #8
- □ Jim Benning #4
- □ Steve Bozek #14
- □ Brian Bradley #10
- □ Garth Butcher #5
- □ Craig Coxe #22
- □ Igor Larionov #18
- □ Doug Lidster #3
- □ Trevor Linden #16
- □ Kirk McLean #1 (G)
- □ Larry Melnyk #24
- □ Robert Nordmark #6
- □ Barry Pederson #7
- □ Paul Reinhart #23
- □ Jim Sandlak #19
- □ Petri Skriko #26
- □ Doug Smith
- □ Stan Smyl #12
- □ Harold Snepsts #27
- □ Daryl Stanley #29
- □ Rich Sutter #15
- □ Tony Tanti #9
- □ Steve Weeks #31 (G)

'90 - 91 VANC.
MOHAWK

Trevor Linden and Petr Nedved are the most expensive singles at $2-3. Singles start at 75¢.
Card Size: 2 1/2" x 3 1/2"
Sponsor: Mohawk
Set (29 cards): $15
- □ Greg Adams
- □ Jim Agnew
- □ Steve Bozek
- □ Garth Butcher
- □ Dave Capuano
- □ Craig Coxe
- □ Gerald Diduck
- □ Troy Gamble
- □ Don Gibson
- □ Kevan Guy
- □ Robert Kron
- □ Tom Kurvers
- □ Igor Larionov

☐ Doug Lidster
☐ Trevor Linden
☐ Jyrki Lumme
☐ Jay Mazur
☐ Andrew McBain
☐ Kirk McLean (G)
☐ Rob Murphy
☐ Petr Nedved
☐ Robert Nordmark
☐ Gino Odjick
☐ Adrien Plavsic
☐ Dan Quinn
☐ Jim Sandlak
☐ Stan Smyl
☐ Ronnie Stern
☐ Garry Valk

'90 - 91 VANC.

MOLSON CANADIAN

These photos are entitled Player of the Month. Trevor Linden is the most expensive single at $10. Singles start at $5. Kirk McLean has two photos.

Photo Size: 8" x 10"
Sponsor: Molson Canadian
Set (6 photos): $35

☐ Brian Bradley
☐ Troy Gamble
☐ Doug Lidster
☐ Trevor Linden
☐ Kirk McLean (G)
☐ Kirk McLean (G)

'91 - 92 VANC.

These cards have blank backs. Pavel Bure is the most expensive single at $10. Singles start at $1.

Card Size: 3 3/4" x 8 1/2"
Sponsor: None
Set (23 cards): $30

☐ Greg Adams
☐ Pavel Bure
☐ Dave Babych
☐ Geoff Courtnall
☐ Gerald Diduck
☐ Robert Dirk
☐ Troy Gamble (G)
☐ Randy Gregg
☐ Robert Kron
☐ Igor Larionov
☐ Doug Lidster
☐ Trevor Linden
☐ Jyrki Lumme
☐ Kirk McLean (G)
☐ Sergio Momesso
☐ Rob Murphy
☐ Dana Murzyn
☐ Petr Nedved
☐ Gino Odjick
☐ Adrien Plavsic
☐ Cliff Ronning
☐ Jim Sandlak
☐ Ryan Walter

'91 - 92 VANC.

These cards have player bios on the back. Pavel Bure is the most expensive single at $15. Singles start at $2.50.

Photo Size: 8" x 10"
Sponsor: None
Set (23 cards): $60

☐ Greg Adams
☐ Pavel Bure
☐ Dave Babych
☐ Geoff Courtnall
☐ Gerald Diduck
☐ Robert Dirk
☐ Troy Gamble (G)
☐ Randy Gregg
☐ Robert Kron
☐ Igor Larionov
☐ Doug Lidster
☐ Trevor Linden
☐ Jyrki Lumme
☐ Kirk McLean (G)
☐ Sergio Momesso
☐ Rob Murphy
☐ Dana Murzyn
☐ Petr Nedved
☐ Gino Odjick
☐ Adrien Plavsic
☐ Cliff Ronning
☐ Jim Sandlak
☐ Ryan Walter

'91 - 92 VANC.

MOLSON CANADIAN

These photos are entitled Player of the Month. Pavel Bure has two photos each selling at $20. Singles start at $5.

Photo Size: 8" x 10"
Sponsor: Molson Canadian
Set (6 photos): $55

☐ Greg Adams
☐ Pavel Bure
☐ Pavel Bure
☐ Igor Larionov
☐ Trevor Linden
☐ Kirk McLean (G)
☐ Cliff Ronning

'92 - 93 VANC.

ABALENE PHOTOS

Pavel Bure is the most expensive single at $8. Singles start at $1.

Card Size: 4 3/4" x 7"
Sponsor: Abalene
Set (25 cards): $25

☐ Greg Adams
☐ Shawn Antoski
☐ Dave Babych
☐ Pavel Bure
☐ Geoff Courtnall
☐ Gerald Diduck
☐ Robert Dirk
☐ Tom Fergus
☐ Robert Kron
☐ Doug Lidster
☐ Trevor Linden
☐ Jyrki Lumme
☐ Kirk McLean (G)
☐ Sergio Momesso
☐ Dana Murzyn
☐ Petr Nedved
☐ Gino Odjick
☐ Adrien Plavsic
☐ Cliff Ronning
☐ Jim Sandlak
☐ Jiri Slegr
☐ Garry Valk
☐ Ryan Walter
☐ Dixon Ward
☐ Kay Whitmore (G)

'94 - 95 VANC.

COLLECTOR SERIES

Pavel Bure is the most expensive single at $15. Singles start at $3.50. Other singles may exist. This may, in fact, be a 1993-94 set.

Photo Size: 8" x 10 1/2"
Sponsor: None

☐ Greg Adams
☐ Shawn Antoski
☐ Dave Babych
☐ Jeff Brown
☐ Pavel Bure
☐ Geoff Courtnall
☐ Gerald Diduck
☐ Martin Gelinas
☐ Brian Glynn
☐ Tim Hunter
☐ Nathan Lafayette
☐ Trevor Linden
☐ Jyrki Lumme
☐ Kirk McLean (G)
☐ Dana Murzyn
☐ Gino Odjick
☐ Adrien Plavsic
☐ Cliff Ronning
☐ Jiri Slegr
☐ Kay Whitmore (G)

'95 - 96 VANC.

ABALENE

Pavel Bure is the most expensive single at $7. Singles start at $1.

Card Size: 5" x 7"
Sponsor: Abalene
Set (18 cards): $20

☐ 1 Kirk McLean (G)
☐ 2 Kay Whitmore (G)
☐ 3 Bret Hedican
☐ 4 Tim Hunter
☐ 5 Dana Murzyn
☐ 6 Jyrki Lumme
☐ 7 Cliff Ronning
☐ 8 Jeff Brown
☐ 9 Martin Gelinas
☐ 10 Pavel Bure
☐ 11 Jiri Slegr
☐ 12 Sergio Momesso
☐ 13 Gino Odjick
☐ 14 Geoff Courtnall
☐ 15 John McIntyre
☐ 16 Trevor Linden
☐ 17 Michael Peca
☐ 18 Dave Babych

'96 - 97 VANC.

Pavel Bure is the most expensive single at $5. Singles start at 50¢.

Sponsor: IGA
Set (27 cards): $20

☐ Adrian Aucoin #6
☐ Dave Babych #44
☐ Donald Brashear #8
☐ Pavel Bure #96
☐ Russ Courtnall #9
☐ Troy Crowder #18
☐ Mike Foutain (G) #30
☐ Martin Gelinas #23
☐ Bret Hedican #3
☐ Corey Hirsch (G) #31
☐ Chris Joseph #32
☐ Trevor Linden #16
☐ Jyrki Lumme #21
☐ Kirk McLean (G) #1
☐ Alexander Mogilny #89
☐ Dana Murzyn #5
☐ Markus Näslund #19
☐ Gino Odjick #29
☐ Mike Ridley #17
☐ David Roberts #7
☐ Leif Rohlin #27
☐ Alexander Semak #20
☐ Mike Sillinger #26
☐ Esa Tikkanen #10
☐ Scott Walker #24
☐ Mark Wotton #4
☐ Team Photo

'97 - 98 VANC.

COCA-COLA

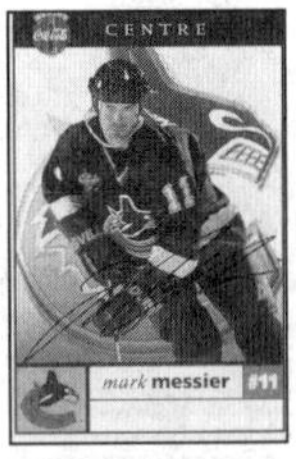

We have little information on this set. Other singles exist.

Card Size: 3 3/4" x 5 1/2"
Sponsor: Coca-Cola

☐ Mark Messier

'00 - 01 VANC.

We have little information on this set. Other singles exist.

☐ Ed Jovanovski
☐ Markus Näslund
☐ Mattias Öhlund

'01 - 02 VANC.

COCA-COLA

Singles star at $1.

Sponsor: Coca-Cola
Set (14 cards):

☐ Murray Baron
☐ Todd Bertuzzi
☐ Donald Brashear
☐ Andrew Cassels
☐ Dan Cloutier (G)
☐ Matt Cooke
☐ Marc Crawford
☐ Ed Jovanovski
☐ Brendan Morrison
☐ Markus Näslund
☐ Mattias Öhlund
☐ Daniel Sedin
☐ Henrik Sedin
☐ Jason Strudwick

'02 - 03 VANC.

We do not have a checklist for this series of cards.

WASHINGTON CAPITALS

'74 - 75 WASH.

These photos are in black and white. Milt Schmidt is the most expensive single at $5 in NM. Singles start at $2.50.

Card Size: 5" x 7"
Sponsor: None
Set (24 cards): $55

☐ John Adams (G)
☐ Jim Anderson, Coach
☐ Ron Anderson
☐ Steve Atkinson
☐ Michel Belhumeur (G)
☐ Mike Bloom
☐ Gord Brooks
☐ Bruce Cowick
☐ Denis Dupère
☐ Jack Egers
☐ Jim Hrycuik
☐ Greg Joly
☐ Dave Kryskow
☐ Yvon Labre
☐ Pete Laframboise
☐ Bill Lesuk
☐ Ron Low (G)
☐ Joe Lundrigan
☐ Mike Marson
☐ Bill Mikkelson
☐ Doug Mohns
☐ André Peloffy
☐ Milt Schmidt, G.M.
☐ Gord Smith

'78 - 79 WASH.

We have no pricing information on this set.

Card Size: 5" x 7"
Sponsor: None

☐ Jim Bedard (G)
☐ Michel Bergeron
☐ Greg Carroll
☐ Guy Charron
☐ Rolf Edberg
☐ Rick Green
☐ Gord Lane
☐ Mark Lofthouse
☐ Jack Lynch
☐ Dennis Maruk
☐ Paul Mulvey
☐ Robert Picard
☐ Bill Riley
☐ Tom Rowe
☐ Bob Sirois
☐ Gord Smith
☐ Leif Svensson
☐ Ryan Walter
☐ Bernie Wolfe

'79 - 80 WASH.

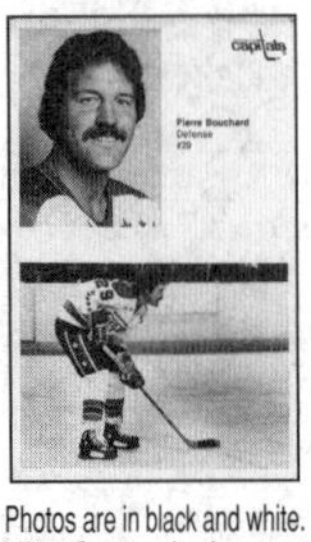

Photos are in black and white. Mike Gartner is the most expensive single at $20-25 in NM. Singles start at $1.50.

Card Size: 5 1/4" x 7 7/8"
Sponsor: None
Set (23 cards): $50

☐ Pierre Bouchard
☐ Guy Charron
☐ Rolf Edberg
☐ Mike Gartner
☐ Rick Green
☐ Bengt Gustafsson
☐ Dennis Hextall
☐ Gary Inness (G)
☐ Yvon Labre
☐ Antero Lehtonen
☐ Mark Lofthouse
☐ Paul McKinnon
☐ Dennis Maruk
☐ Paul Mulvey
☐ Robert Picard
☐ Greg Polis
☐ Errol Rausse
☐ Tom Rowe
☐ Peter Scamurra
☐ Bob Sirois
☐ Wayne Stephenson (G)
☐ Leif Svensson
☐ Ryan Walter

'80 - 81 WASH.

Mike Gartner is the most expensive single at $15-20 in NM. Singles start at $1.50.

Card Size: 5" x 7"
Sponsor: None
Set (24 cards): $45

☐ Pierre Bouchard
☐ Guy Charron
☐ Rolf Edberg
☐ Mike Gartner
☐ Gary Green
☐ Rick Green
☐ Bengt Gustafsson
☐ Alan Hangsleben
☐ Wes Jarvis
☐ Bob Kelly
☐ Yvon Labre
☐ Bill Mahoney
☐ Dennis Maruk
☐ Paul McKinnon
☐ Paul Mulvey
☐ Mike Palmateer (G)
☐ Jean Pronovost
☐ Pat Ribble
☐ Rick Smith
☐ Wayne Stephenson (G)
☐ Darren Veitch
☐ Dennis Ververgaert
☐ Howard Walker
☐ Ryan Walter

'81 - 82 WASH.

Mike Gartner is the most expensive single at $15. Singles start at $1.50.

Card Size: 5" x 7"
Sponsor: None
Set (22 cards): $40

☐ Timo Blomqvist
☐ Bobby Carpenter
☐ Glen Currie
☐ Gaetan Duchesne
☐ Mike Gartner
☐ Bob Gould
☐ Rick Green
☐ Doug Hicks
☐ Randy Holt
☐ Wes Jarvis
☐ Al Jensen (G)
☐ Dennis Maruk
☐ Terry Murray
☐ Lee Norwood
☐ Mike Palmateer (G)
☐ Dave Parro (G)
☐ Torrie Robertson
☐ Greg Theberge
☐ Chris Valentine
☐ Darren Veitch
☐ Howard Walker
☐ Ryan Walter

'82 - 83 WASH.

The most expensive singles are Scott Stevens and Mike Gartner at $12. Singles start at $1.50.

Card Size: 5" x 7"
Sponsor: None
Set (25 cards): $50

☐ Timo Blomqvist
☐ Ted Bulley
☐ Bob Carpenter
☐ Glen Currie
☐ Brian Engblom
☐ Mike Gartner
☐ Bob Gould
☐ Bengt Gustafsson
☐ Alan Haworth
☐ Randy Holt
☐ Ken Houston
☐ Doug Jarvis
☐ Rod Langway
☐ Craig Laughlin
☐ Dennis Maruk
☐ Bryan Murray
☐ Terry Murray
☐ Lee Norwood
☐ Milan Novy
☐ Dave Parro (G)
☐ David Poile
☐ Pat Riggin (G)
☐ Scott Stevens
☐ Chris Valentine
☐ Darren Veitch

'84 - 85 WASH.

Mike Gartner and Scott Stevens are the most expensive singles at $8-10. Singles start at $2.

Card Size: 4 1/2" x 6"
Sponsor: Pizza Hut
Set (15 cards): $45

☐ Bob Carpenter
☐ Dave Christian
☐ Glen Currie
☐ Gaetan Duchesne
☐ Mike Gartner
☐ Bob Gould
☐ Bengt Gustafsson
☐ Alan Haworth
☐ Doug Jarvis
☐ Al Jensen (G)
☐ Rod Langway
☐ Craig Laughlin
☐ Larry Murphy
☐ Pat Riggin (G)
☐ Scott Stevens

'85 - 86 WASH.

Mike Gartner and Scott Stevens are the most expensive singles at $6-8. Singles start at $2.

Card Size: 4 1/2" x 6"
Sponsor: Pizza Hut
Set (15 cards): $40

☐ Bob Carpenter
☐ Dave Christian
☐ Gaetan Duchesne
☐ Mike Gartner
☐ Bob Gould
☐ Bengt Gustafsson
☐ Alan Haworth
☐ Doug Jarvis
☐ Al Jensen (G)
☐ Rod Langway
☐ Craig Laughlin
☐ Larry Murphy
☐ Pat Riggin (G)
☐ Scott Stevens
☐ Darren Veitch

'86 - 87 WASH.

POLICE

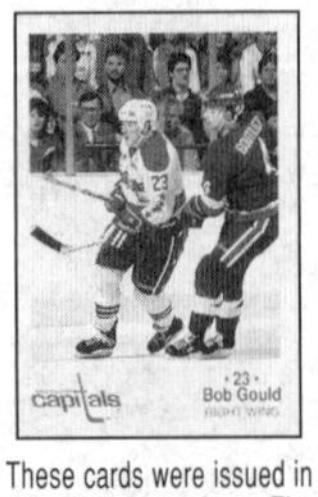

These cards were issued in two-card panels. The Gartner/Gould panel is the most expensive at $5-6. Single panels sell at $1.50. Cut-out cards measure 2 5/8" x 3 3/4" and start at 75¢. A cut-out 24-card set sells at $15.

Panel Size: 2 5/8" x 7 1/2"
Sponsor: Police
Set (12 panels): $22

☐ Greg Adams #22 / John Barrett #6
☐ Bob Carpenter #10 / Dave Christian #27
☐ Yvon Corriveau #26 / Gaetan Duchesne #14
☐ Lou Franceschetti #32 / Mike Gartner #11
☐ Bob Gould #23 / Kevin Hatcher #4
☐ Alan Haworth #15 / Al Jensen #35 (G)
☐ David Jensen #9 / Rod Langway #5
☐ Craig Laughlin #18 / Stephen Leach #21
☐ Larry Murphy #8 / Bryan Murray
☐ Pete Peeters #1 (G) / Jorgen Pettersson #12
☐ Michal Pivonka #17 / David Poile
☐ Greg Smith #19 / Scott Stevens #3

'86 - 87 WASH.

KODAK

These cards were originally issued in panels. The team photo measures 8" x 10". Mike Gartner is the most expensive single at $6. Singles start at $1.

Card Size: 2" x 2 5/8"
Sponsor: Kodak
Set (26 cards): $30

☐ Greg Adams
☐ John Barrett
☐ John Blum
☐ Dave Christian
☐ Bob Crawford
☐ Gaetan Duchesne
☐ Lou Franceschetti
☐ Mike Gartner
☐ Bob Gould
☐ Jeff Greenlaw
☐ Kevin Hatcher
☐ Alan Haworth
☐ David Jensen
☐ Rod Langway
☐ Craig Laughlin
☐ Bob Mason (G)
☐ Kelly Miller
☐ Larry Murphy
☐ Bryan Murray
☐ Pete Peeters (G)
☐ Michal Pivonka
☐ Mike Ridley
☐ Gary Sampson
☐ Greg Smith
☐ Scott Stevens
☐ Team Photo

'87 - 88 WASH.

Mike Gartner is the most expensive single at $5. Singles start at $1.

Panel Size: 5 1/4" x 8"
Sponsor: None
Set (23 cards): $28

☐ Greg Adams
☐ John Barrett
☐ Dave Christian
☐ Lou Franceschetti
☐ Garry Galley
☐ Mike Gartner
☐ Bob Gould
☐ Bengt Gustafsson
☐ Kevin Hatcher
☐ Dale Hunter
☐ David Jensen
☐ Ed Kastelic
☐ Rod Langway
☐ Craig Laughlin
☐ Clint Malarchuk (G)
☐ Kelly Miller
☐ Larry Murphy
☐ Pete Peeters (G)
☐ Michal Pivonka
☐ Mike Ridley
☐ Greg Smith
☐ Scott Stevens
☐ Peter Sundström

'87 - 88 WASH.

KODAK

These cards were originally issued in panels. The team photo measures 8 1/4" x 11". Mike Gartner is the most expensive single at $5. Singles start at $1.

Card Size: 2 3/16" x 2 15/16"
Sponsor: Kodak
Set (26 cards): $25

☐ Greg Adams #22
☐ John Barrett #6
☐ Dave Christian #27
☐ Lou Franceschetti #25
☐ Garry Galley #2
☐ Mike Gartner #11
☐ Bob Gould #23
☐ Bengt Gustafsson #16
☐ Kevin Hatcher #4
☐ Bill Houlder #34
☐ Dale Hunter #32
☐ Ed Kastelic #29
☐ Rod Langway #5
☐ Craig Laughlin #18
☐ Clint Malarchuk #30 (G)
☐ Kelly Miller #10
☐ Larry Murphy #8
☐ Bryan Murray
☐ Pete Peeters #1 (G)
☐ Michal Pivonka #20
☐ David Poile
☐ Mike Ridley #17
☐ Greg Smith #19
☐ Scott Stevens #3
☐ Peter Sundström #12
☐ Team Photo

'88 - 89 WASH.

Mike Gartner is the most expensive single at $4. Singles start at $1.

Card Size: 5" x 7"
Sponsor: None
Set (21 cards): $20

☐ Dave Christian
☐ Yvon Corriveau
☐ Geoff Courtnall
☐ Lou Franceschetti
☐ Mike Gartner
☐ Bob Gould
☐ Bengt Gustafsson
☐ Kevin Hatcher
☐ Dale Hunter
☐ Rod Langway
☐ Stephen Leach
☐ Grant Ledyard
☐ Clint Malarchuk (G)
☐ Kelly Miller
☐ Larry Murphy
☐ Pete Peeters (G)
☐ Michal Pivonka
☐ Mike Ridley
☐ Neil Sheehy
☐ Scott Stevens
☐ Peter Sundström

'88 - 89 WASH.

SMOKEY THE BEAR

Mike Gartner is the most expensive single at $3. Singles start at $1.

Card Size: 2 5/8" x 3 3/4"
Sponsor: Smokey The Bear
Set (24 cards): $15

☐ Dave Christian #27
☐ Yvon Corriveau #26
☐ Geoff Courtnall #14
☐ Lou Franceschetti #25
☐ Mike Gartner #11
☐ Bob Gould #23
☐ Bengt Gustafsson #16
☐ Kevin Hatcher #4
☐ Dale Hunter #32
☐ Rod Langway #5
☐ Stephen Leach #21
☐ Grant Ledyard #6
☐ Clint Malarchuk #30 (G)
☐ Kelly Miller #10
☐ Larry Murphy #8
☐ Bryan Murray
☐ Pete Peeters #1 (G)
☐ Michal Pivonka #20
☐ David Poile
☐ Mike Ridley #17

☐ Neil Sheehy #15
☐ Scott Stevens #3
☐ Peter Sundström #12
☐ Smokey the Bear

'89 - 90 WASH.

Dino Ciccarelli is the most expensive single at $3. Singles start at $1.
Card Size: 5" x 7"
Sponsor: None
Set (23 cards): $20
☐ Don Beaupré (G)
☐ Dave Christian
☐ Dino Ciccarelli
☐ Yvon Corriveau
☐ Geoff Courtnall
☐ Kevin Hatcher
☐ Bill Houlder
☐ Dale Hunter
☐ Calle Johansson
☐ Dimitri Khristich
☐ Scot Kleinendorst
☐ Nick Kypreos
☐ Rod Langway
☐ Stephen Leach
☐ Bob Mason (G)
☐ Alan May
☐ Kelly Miller
☐ Michal Pivonka
☐ Mike Ridley
☐ Bob Rouse
☐ Neil Sheehy
☐ Scott Stevens
☐ Doug Wickenheiser

'89 - 90 WASH.
KODAK

This set was originally issued in panels. Dino Ciccarelli is the most expensive single at $3. Singles start at $1.
Card Size: 2 3/16" x 2 1/2"
Sponsor: Kodak
Set (25 cards): $22
☐ Don Beaupré #33 (G)
☐ Tim Berglund #11
☐ Dino Ciccarelli #22
☐ Geoff Courtnall #14
☐ John Druce #19
☐ Kevin Hatcher #4
☐ Dale Hunter #32
☐ Calle Johansson #6
☐ Bob Joyce #27
☐ Scot Kleinendorst #29
☐ Rob Laird
☐ Rod Langway #5
☐ Stephen Leach #21
☐ Mike Liut #1 (G)
☐ Steve Maltais #26
☐ Alan May #16
☐ Kelly Miller #10
☐ Terry Murray
☐ Michal Pivonka #20
☐ David Poile
☐ Mike Ridley #17
☐ Bob Rouse #8
☐ Neil Sheehy #15
☐ Scott Stevens #3
☐ John Tucker #12

'90 - 91 WASH.
KODAK

This set was originally issued as a three-panel set. Peter Bondra is the most expensive single at $6. Singles start at 75¢.
Card Size: 2" x 2 5/8"
Sponsor: Kodak
Set (25 cards): $20
☐ Don Beaupré (G)
☐ Tim Bergland
☐ Peter Bondra
☐ Dino Ciccarelli
☐ John Druce
☐ Kevin Hatcher
☐ Dale Hunter
☐ Al Iafrate
☐ Calle Johansson
☐ Dimitri Khristich
☐ Nick Kypreos
☐ Mike Lalor
☐ Rod Langway
☐ Stephen Leach
☐ Mike Liut (G)
☐ Alan May
☐ Kelly Miller
☐ Terry Murray
☐ John Perpich
☐ Michal Pivonka
☐ David Poile
☐ Mike Ridley
☐ Ken Sabourin
☐ Mikhail Tatarinov
☐ Dave Tippett

'90 - 91 WASH.
SMOKEY THE BEAR

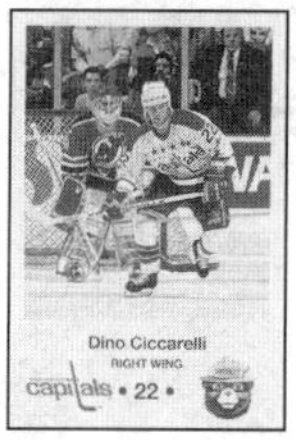

Peter Bondra is the most expensive single at $6. Singles start at 75¢.
Card Size: 2 5/8" x 3 3/4"
Sponsor: Smokey The Bear
Set (22 cards): $18
☐ Don Beaupré (G)
☐ Tim Bergland
☐ Peter Bondra
☐ Dino Ciccarelli
☐ John Druce
☐ Kevin Hatcher
☐ Jim Hrivnak (G)
☐ Dale Hunter
☐ Calle Johansson
☐ Nick Kypreos
☐ Mike Lalor
☐ Rod Langway
☐ Stephen Leach
☐ Mike Liut (G)
☐ Alan May
☐ Kelly Miller
☐ Rob Murray
☐ Michal Pivonka
☐ Mike Ridley
☐ Neil Sheehy
☐ Mikhail Tatarinov
☐ Dave Tippett

'91 - 92 WASH.
SMOKEY THE BEAR

Peter Bondra is the most expensive single at $5. Singles start at 75¢.
Card Size: 5" x 7"
Sponsor: Smokey The Bear
Set (25 cards): $20
☐ Don Beaupré (G)
☐ Tim Bergland
☐ Peter Bondra
☐ Randy Burridge
☐ Shawn Chambers
☐ Dino Ciccarelli
☐ Sylvain Côté
☐ John Druce
☐ Jeff Greenlaw
☐ Kevin Hatcher
☐ Dale Hunter
☐ Al Iafrate
☐ Calle Johansson
☐ Dimitri Khristich
☐ Todd Krygier
☐ Nick Kypreos
☐ Mike Lalor
☐ Rod Langway
☐ Mike Liut (G)
☐ Alan May
☐ Kelly Miller
☐ Michal Pivonka
☐ Mike Ridley
☐ Ken Sabourin
☐ Dave Tippett

'91 - 92 WASH.
KODAK

This set was originally issued as a three-panel set. Each panel measures 11" x 8". The first panel ("Red Hot and Blue") has space for autographs. The second panel has 15 player cards while the third panel has 10 player cards plus a Kodak coupon. Peter Bondra is the most expensive cut-out single at $5. Singles start at 75¢.
Card Size: 2 3/16" x 2 3/4"
Sponsor: Kodak
Set (25 cards): $20
☐ Don Beaupré (G)
☐ Tim Bergland
☐ Peter Bondra
☐ Randy Burridge
☐ Shawn Chambers
☐ Dino Ciccarelli
☐ Sylvain Côté
☐ John Druce
☐ Kevin Hatcher
☐ Jim Hrivnak (G)
☐ Dale Hunter
☐ Al Iafrate
☐ Calle Johansson
☐ Dimitri Khristich
☐ Todd Krygier
☐ Nick Kypreos
☐ Rod Langway
☐ Mike Liut (G)
☐ Paul MacDermid
☐ Alan May
☐ Kelly Miller
☐ Michal Pivonka
☐ Mike Ridley
☐ Brad Schlegel
☐ Dave Tippett

'92 - 93 WASH.
KODAK

This set was originally issued as a three-panel set. Each panel measures 11" x 8". The first panel has room for autographs. The second panel has 15 player cards and the third panel has 10 player cards plus a Kodak coupon. Peter Bondra is the most expensive cut-out single at $3. Singles start at 75¢.
Card Size: 2 3/16" x 2 3/4"
Sponsor: Kodak
Set (25 cards): $15
☐ Shawn Anderson
☐ Don Beaupré (G)
☐ Peter Bondra
☐ Randy Burridge
☐ Bob Carpenter
☐ Paul Cavallini
☐ Sylvain Côté
☐ Pat Elynuik
☐ Kevin Hatcher
☐ Jim Hrivnak (G)
☐ Dale Hunter
☐ Al Iafrate
☐ Calle Johansson
☐ Dimitri Khristich
☐ Steve Konowalchuk
☐ Todd Krygier
☐ Rod Langway
☐ Paul MacDermid
☐ Alan May
☐ Kelly Miller
☐ Michal Pivonka
☐ Mike Ridley
☐ Reggie Savage
☐ Jason Woolley

'95 - 96 WASH.

This series was issued as an album. Peter Bondra is the most expensive single at $3. Singles start at 50¢.
Sponsor: None
Set (28 cards): $15
☐ Jason Allison
☐ Craig Berube
☐ Peter Bondra
☐ Jim Carey (G)
☐ Sylvain Côté
☐ Mike Eagles
☐ Martin Gendron
☐ Sergei Gonchar
☐ Dale Hunter
☐ Calle Johansson
☐ Jim Johnson
☐ Keith Jones
☐ Joé Juneau
☐ Kevin Kaminski
☐ Ken Klee
☐ Olaf Kölzig (G)
☐ Steve Konowalchuk
☐ Kelly Miller
☐ Jeff Nelson
☐ Pat Peake
☐ Michal Pivonka
☐ Joe Reekie
☐ Mark Tinordi
☐ Stefan Ustorf
☐ Brendan Witt
☐ Jim Schoenfeld, Coach
☐ Mascot Slapshot
☐ Mascot Slapshot

'98 - 99 WASH.
KOPS AND KIDS

We have no pricing information on this set.
Sponsor: Washington Police
☐ 1 Olaf Kölzig
☐ 2 Peter Bondra
☐ 3 Adam Oates
☐ 4 Dale Hunter
☐ 5 Calle Johansson
☐ 6 Steve Konowalchuk
☐ 7 Mascot Slapshot

'00 - 01 WASH.

We do not have a checklist for this series of cards.

'01 - 02 WASH.

We do not have a checklist for this series of cards.

'02 - 03 WASH.

We do not have a checklist for this series of cards.

WINNIPEG JETS

'79 - 80 WINN.

Bobby Hull is the most expensive single at $10 in NM. Singles start at $1.
Postcard Size: 3 1/2" x 5 1/2"
Sponsor: None
Set (28 cards): $30
☐ Mike Amodeo
☐ Al Cameron
☐ Scott Campbell
☐ Wayne Dillon
☐ Jude Drouin
☐ John Ferguson
☐ Hillard Graves
☐ Pierre Hamel (G)
☐ Dave Hoyda
☐ Bobby Hull
☐ Bill Lesuk
☐ Willy Lindstrom
☐ Morris Lukowich
☐ Jimmy Mann
☐ Peter Marsh
☐ Gord McTavish
☐ Tom McVie
☐ Barry Melrose
☐ Lyle Moffat
☐ Craig Norwich
☐ Lars-Erik Sjoberg
☐ Gary Smith (G)
☐ Gordon Smith
☐ Lorne Stamler
☐ Peter Sullivan
☐ Bill Sutherland
☐ Ron Wilson
☐ Jets card

'80 - 81 WINN.

Dave Babych is the most expensive single at $3. Singles start at $1.50.
Card Size: 3 1/2" x 5 1/2"
Sponsor: None
Set (23 cards): $22
☐ Dave Babych
☐ Al Cameron
☐ Scott Campbell
☐ Dave Christian
☐ Jude Drouin
☐ Norm Dupont
☐ Danny Geoffrion
☐ Pierre Hamel (G)
☐ Barry Legge
☐ Willy Lindstrom
☐ Barry Long
☐ Morris Lukowich
☐ Kris Manery
☐ Jimmy Mann
☐ Moe Mantha
☐ Markus Mattsson (G)
☐ Richard Mulhern
☐ Doug Smail
☐ Don Spring
☐ Anders Steen
☐ Peter Sullivan
☐ Tim Trimper
☐ Ron Wilson

'81 - 82 WINN.

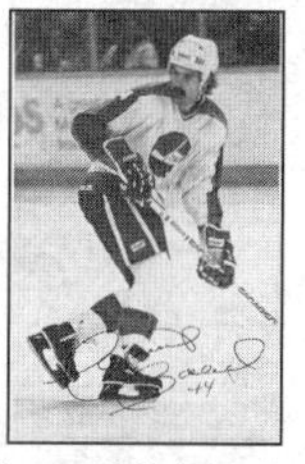

Photos are in black and white on these blank-back cards. Dale Hawerchuk is the most expensive single at $15. Singles start at $1.
Card Size: 3 1/2" x 5 1/2"
Sponsor: None
Set (24 cards): $35
☐ Scott Arniel
☐ Dave Babych
☐ Dave Christian
☐ Lucien DeBlois
☐ Norm Dupont
☐ Larry Hopkins
☐ Dale Hawerchuk
☐ Craig Levie
☐ Willy Lindstrom
☐ Morris Lukowich
☐ Bengt Lundholm
☐ Paul MacLean
☐ Jimmy Mann
☐ Bryan Maxwell
☐ Serge Savard
☐ Doug Smail
☐ Doug Soetaert (G)
☐ Don Spring
☐ Ed Staniowski (G)
☐ Thomas Steen
☐ Bill Sutherland
☐ Tim Trimper
☐ Tim Watters
☐ Tom Watt

'82 - 83 WINN.

Dale Hawerchuk has two singles each selling at $10. Singles start at $1.
Card Size: 3 1/2" x 5 1/2"
Sponsor: None
Set (28 cards): $35
☐ Scott Arniel
☐ Dave Babych
☐ Jerry Butler
☐ Wade Campbell
☐ Dave Christian
☐ Lucien DeBlois
☐ Norm Dupont
☐ Dale Hawerchuk
☐ Dale Hawerchuk
☐ Jim Kyte
☐ Craig Levie
☐ Willy Lindstrom
☐ Morris Lukowich
☐ Bengt Lundholm
☐ Paul MacLean
☐ Jimmy Mann
☐ Bryan Maxwell
☐ Brian Mullen
☐ Serge Savard
☐ Doug Smail
☐ Doug Soetaert (G)
☐ Don Spring
☐ Ed Staniowski (G)
☐ Thomas Steen
☐ Bill Sutherland
☐ Tom Watt
☐ Tim Watters
☐ Team Photo

'83 - 84 WINN.

Dale Hawerchuk is the most expensive single at $6. Singles start at $1.
Card Size: 3 1/4" x 5 1/4"
Sponsor: None
Set (25 cards): $25
☐ Scott Arniel
☐ Dave Babych
☐ Laurie Boschman
☐ Wade Campbell
☐ Lucien DeBlois
☐ John Ferguson
☐ John Gibson
☐ Dale Hawerchuk
☐ Brian Hayward (G)
☐ Jim Kyte
☐ Barry Long
☐ Morris Lukowich
☐ Bengt Lundholm
☐ Paul MacLean
☐ Jimmy Mann
☐ Moe Mantha
☐ Andrew McBain
☐ Brian Mullen
☐ Robert Picard
☐ Doug Smail
☐ Doug Soetaert (G)
☐ Thomas Steen
☐ Tim Watters
☐ Ron Wilson
☐ Tim Young

'84 - 85 WINN.
SAFETY TIPS

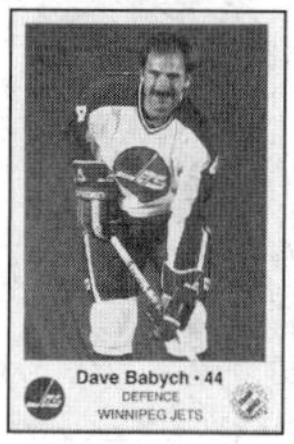

This set was issued in two-card panels. The Hawerchuk/Arniel panel sells at $3-4. Single panels start at $1. Cut-out singles measure 2 5/8" x 3 3/4" and start at 50¢. A cut-out 24-card set sells at $10.
Panel Size: 2 5/8" x 7 1/2"
Sponsor: Police
Set (12 panels): $15
☐ Laurie Boschman #16
Paul Pooley #23
☐ Randy Carlyle #8
Jim Kyte #6
☐ Dave Ellett #2
Dave Babych #44
☐ Dale Hawerchuk #10
Scott Arniel #11
☐ Brian Hayward #1 (G)
Marc Behrend #29 (G)
☐ Bengt Lundholm #22
Ron Wilson #24
☐ Andrew McBain #20
Brian Mullen #19
☐ Robert Picard #3
Tim Watters #7
☐ Doug Smail #29
Paul MacLean #15
☐ Perry Turnbull #27
Morris Lukowich #12
☐ Sutherland/ Long/ Bowness
Thomas Steen #25
☐ John Ferguson
Team Photo

'85 - 86 WINN.

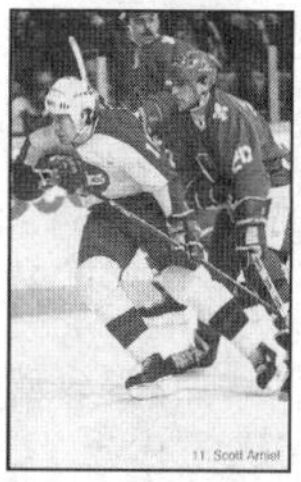

These cards have blank backs. Dale Hawerchuk is the most expensive single at $5. Singles start at $1.
Card Size: 3 1/4" x 5 1/4"
Sponsor: None
Set (22 cards): $20
☐ Scott Arniel
☐ Laurie Boschman
☐ Dan Bouchard (G)
☐ Randy Carlyle
☐ Dave Ellett
☐ Dale Hawerchuk
☐ Brian Hayward (G)
☐ Jim Kyte
☐ Paul MacLean
☐ Andrew McBain
☐ Anssi Melametsa
☐ Brian Mullen
☐ Jim Nill
☐ Dave Silk
☐ Doug Smail
☐ Thomas Steen
☐ Perry Turnbull
☐ Tim Watters
☐ Ron Wilson
☐ John B. Ferguson
☐ Sutherland/ Long/ Bowness
☐ Team Photo

'85 - 86 WINN.
POLICE

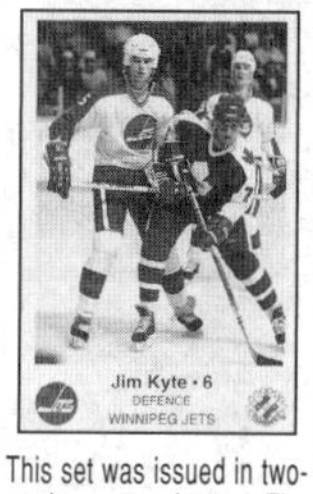

This set was issued in two-card panels. The Hawerchuk/Arniel panel sells at $3-4. Single panels start at $1. cut-out singles measure 2 5/8" x 3 3/4" and start at 50¢. A cut-out 24-card set sells at $10.
Panel Size: 2 5/8" x 7 1/2"
Sponsor: Police
Set (12 panels): $18
☐ Laurie Boschman #16
Jim Nill #17
☐ Randy Carlyle #8
Jim Kyte #6
☐ Dave Ellett #2
Dave Silk #34
☐ Dale Hawerchuk #10
Scott Arniel #11
☐ Brian Hayward #1 (G)
Dan Bouchard #35 (G)
☐ Mario Marois #22
Ron Wilson #24
☐ Andrew McBain #20
Brian Mullen #19
☐ Anssi Melametsa #14
Tim Watters #7
☐ Doug Smail #9
Paul MacLean #15
☐ Perry Turnbull #27
Ray Neufeld #28
☐ Coaches
Thomas Steen #25
☐ John Ferguson
Team Photo

'85 - 86 WINN.
SILVERWOOD

This series was issued on the backs of milk cartons. Dale Hawerchuk is the most expensive panel at $30. Singles start at $10.
Panel Size:
Sponsor: Silverwood Dairies
Set (6 panels): $65
☐ Laurie Boschman
☐ Randy Carlyle
☐ Dave Ellett
☐ Dale Hawerchuk
☐ Paul MacLean
☐ Brian Mullen

'86 - 87 WINN.

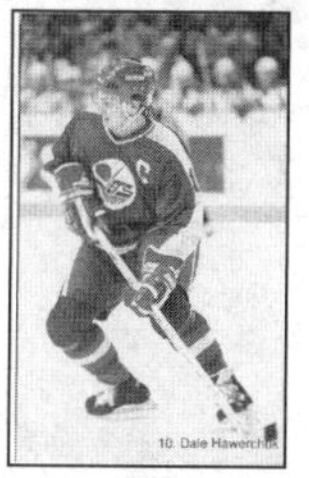

These cards have blank backs. Dale Hawerchuk is the most expensive single at $5. Singles start at $1.
Card Size: 3 1/4" x 5 1/4"
Sponsor: None
Set (26 cards): $22
☐ Brad Berry
☐ Laurie Boschman
☐ Randy Carlyle
☐ Bill Derlago
☐ Dave Ellett
☐ Gilles Hamel
☐ Dale Hawerchuk
☐ Hannu Jarvenpaa
☐ Jim Kyte
☐ Paul MacLean
☐ Andrew McBain
☐ Mario Marois
☐ Brian Mullen
☐ Ray Neufeld
☐ Jim Nill
☐ Fredrik Olausson
☐ Steve Penney (G)
☐ Eldon Reddick (G)
☐ Doug Smail
☐ Thomas Steen
☐ Perry Turnbull
☐ Tim Watters
☐ Ron Wilson
☐ John Ferguson
☐ Bill Sutherland/ Dan Maloney/ R.Bowness
☐ Team Photo

'87 - 88 WINN.

Dale Hawerchuk is the most expensive single at $3. Singles start at 75¢.
Card Size: 3 1/4" x 5 1/4"
Sponsor: None
Set (24 cards): $18
☐ Brad Berry
☐ Daniel Berthiaume (G)
☐ Laurie Boschman
☐ Randy Carlyle
☐ Iain Duncan
☐ Dave Ellett
☐ Pat Elynuik
☐ Gilles Hamel
☐ Dale Hawerchuk
☐ Hannu Jarvenpaa
☐ Jim Kyte
☐ Paul MacLean
☐ Mario Marois
☐ Andrew McBain
☐ Ray Neufeld
☐ Fredrik Olausson

- ☐ Eldon Reddick (G)
- ☐ Steve Rooney
- ☐ Doug Smail
- ☐ Thomas Steen
- ☐ Peter Taglianetti
- ☐ Tim Watters
- ☐ Ron Wilson
- ☐ Team Photo

'88 - 89 WINN.
POLICE

This set was issued in two-card panels. The Hawerchuk/Kyte panel sells at $3-4. Single panels start at $1. cut-out singles measure 2 5/8" x 3 3/46" and start 50¢. A cut-out 24-card set sells at $10.
Panel Size: 2 5/8" x 7 1/2"
Sponsor: Police
Set (12 panels): $18

- ☐ Brent Ashton / Randy Carlyle
- ☐ Laurie Boschman / Andrew McBain
- ☐ Alain Chevrier (G) / Eldon Redddick (G)
- ☐ Iain Duncan / Mario Marois
- ☐ Dave Ellett / Pat Elynuik
- ☐ Randy Gilhen / Suth./ Southern/ St.Croix
- ☐ Dale Hawerchuk / Jim Kyte
- ☐ Dave Hunter / Doug Smail
- ☐ Hannu Jarvenpaa / Fredrik Olausson
- ☐ Ray Neufeld / Teppo Numminen
- ☐ Thomas Steen / Peter Taglianetti
- ☐ Dan Maloney / Team Photo

'89 - 90 WINN.
SAFEWAY

Dale Hawerchuk is the most expensive single at $3. Singles start at 75¢.
Card Size: 3 3/4" x 6 5/8"
Sponsor: Safeway
Set (30 cards): $15

- ☐ Brent Ashton #7
- ☐ Stu Barnes #14
- ☐ Brad Berry #29
- ☐ D. Berthiaume #30 (G)
- ☐ Laurie Boschman #16
- ☐ Randy Carlyle #8
- ☐ Shawn Cronin #44
- ☐ Randy Cunneyworth #18
- ☐ Gord Donnelly #34
- ☐ Tom Draper #37 (G)
- ☐ Iain Duncan #19
- ☐ Dave Ellett #2
- ☐ Pat Elynuik #15
- ☐ Bob Essensa #35 (G)
- ☐ Paul Fenton #11
- ☐ Dale Hawerchuk #10
- ☐ Brent Hughes #46
- ☐ Mark Kumpel #21
- ☐ Moe Mantha #22
- ☐ Dave McLlwain #20
- ☐ Brian McReynolds #26
- ☐ Teppo Numminen #27
- ☐ Fredrik Olausson #4
- ☐ Greg Paslawski #28
- ☐ Doug Smail #12
- ☐ Thomas Steen #25
- ☐ Peter Taglianetti #32
- ☐ Murdoch/ Suhonen/ Drake
- ☐ Mascot Benny
- ☐ Team Photo

'90 - 91 WINN.
IGA

Singles start at 50¢.
Card Size: 3 1/2" x 6 1/2"
Sponsor: IGA
Set (35 cards): $15

- ☐ Scott Arniel
- ☐ Brent Ashton
- ☐ Don Barber
- ☐ S. Beauregard (G)
- ☐ Randy Carlyle
- ☐ Danton Cole
- ☐ Shawn Cronin
- ☐ Gord Donnelly
- ☐ Clare Drake
- ☐ Kris Draper
- ☐ Iain Duncan
- ☐ Pat Elynuik
- ☐ Bob Essensa (G)
- ☐ Doug Evans
- ☐ Phil Housley
- ☐ Sergei Kharin
- ☐ Mark Kumpel
- ☐ Guy Larose
- ☐ Paul MacDermid
- ☐ Moe Mantha
- ☐ Bryan Marchment
- ☐ Dave McLlwain
- ☐ Bob Murdoch
- ☐ Teppo Numminen
- ☐ Fredrik Olausson
- ☐ Ed Olczyk
- ☐ Mark Osborne
- ☐ Greg Paslawski
- ☐ Terry Simpson
- ☐ Thomas Steen
- ☐ Phil Sykes
- ☐ Rick Tabaracci (G)
- ☐ Simon Wheeldon
- ☐ Mascot Benny
- ☐ Team Photo

'91 - 92 WINN.
IGA/CARAMILK

Singles start at 50¢.
Card Size: 3 1/2" x 6 1/2"
Sponsors: IGA, Caramilk
Set (35 cards): $18

- ☐ Stu Barnes
- ☐ S. Beauregard (G)
- ☐ Luciano Borsato
- ☐ Randy Carlyle
- ☐ Danton Cole
- ☐ Shawn Cronin
- ☐ Burton Cummings
- ☐ Mike Eagles
- ☐ Pat Elynuik
- ☐ Bryan Erickson
- ☐ Bob Essensa (G)
- ☐ Doug Evans
- ☐ Mike Hartman
- ☐ Phil Housley
- ☐ Dean Kennedy
- ☐ Paul MacDermid
- ☐ Moe Mantha
- ☐ Rob Murray
- ☐ Troy Murray
- ☐ Teppo Numminen
- ☐ Fredrik Olausson
- ☐ Ed Olczyk
- ☐ Mark Osborne
- ☐ John Paddock
- ☐ Kent Paynter
- ☐ Dave Prior
- ☐ Russ Romaniuk
- ☐ Darrin Shannon
- ☐ Terry Simpson
- ☐ Thomas Steen
- ☐ Phil Sykes
- ☐ Rick Tabaracci (G)
- ☐ Glen Williamson
- ☐ Mascot Benny
- ☐ '90-91 Team Photo

'93 - 94 WINN.
RUFFLES

The most expensive singles are Teemu Selänne at $6 and Keith Tkachuk at $4. Singles start at 50¢.
Card Size: 3 1/2" x 6 1/2"
Sponsor: Ruffles
Set (29 cards): $20

- ☐ Stu Barnes
- ☐ Sergei Bautin
- ☐ S. Beauregard (G)
- ☐ Zinetula Bilyaletdinov
- ☐ Arto Blomsten

- ☐ Luciano Borsato
- ☐ Tie Domi
- ☐ Mike Eagles
- ☐ Nelson Emerson
- ☐ Bryan Erickson
- ☐ Bob Essensa (G)
- ☐ Yan Kaminsky
- ☐ Dean Kennedy
- ☐ Kris King
- ☐ Boris Mironov
- ☐ Andy Murray
- ☐ Teppo Numminen
- ☐ Stéphane Quintal
- ☐ Fredrik Olausson
- ☐ John Paddock
- ☐ Teemu Selänne
- ☐ Darrin Shannon
- ☐ Thomas Steen
- ☐ Keith Tkachuk
- ☐ Igor Ulanov
- ☐ Paul Ysebaert
- ☐ Alexei Zhamnov
- ☐ Mascot Benny
- ☐ Team Photo

'93 - 94 WINN.
READERS CLUB

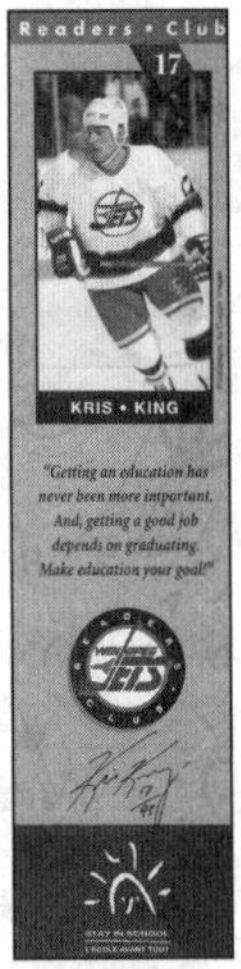

Singles start at 50¢.
Set (22 cards):

- ☐ Stu Barnes
- ☐ Sergei Bautin
- ☐ Arto Blomsten
- ☐ Luciano Borsato
- ☐ Tie Domi
- ☐ Mike Eagles
- ☐ Nelson Emerson
- ☐ Bryan Erickson
- ☐ Bob Essensa
- ☐ Yan Kaminsky
- ☐ Kris King
- ☐ Boris Mironov
- ☐ Teppo Numminen
- ☐ Fredrik Olausson
- ☐ Stéphane Quintal
- ☐ Teemu Selänne
- ☐ Darrin Shannon
- ☐ Thomas Steen
- ☐ Keith Tkachuk
- ☐ Igor Ulanov
- ☐ Paul Ysebaert
- ☐ Alexei Zhamnov

'95 - 96 WINN.
A SEASON TO REMEMBER

The most expensive singles are Teemu Selänne at $5 and Keith Tkachuk at $3. Singles start at 50¢.
Card Size: 3 1/4" x 6 1/2"
Sponsor: None
Set (26 cards): $20

- ☐ Tim Cheveldae #27 (G)
- ☐ Shane Doan #19
- ☐ Jason Doig #55
- ☐ Dallas Drake #18
- ☐ Mike Eastwood #32
- ☐ Randy Gilhen #15
- ☐ N. Khabibulin #35 (G)
- ☐ Kris King #17
- ☐ Igor Korolev #23
- ☐ Stewart Malgunas #36
- ☐ Dave Manson #4
- ☐ Jim McKenzie #33
- ☐ Teppo Numminen #27
- ☐ Ed Olczyk #16
- ☐ Deron Quint #5
- ☐ Ed Ronan #30
- ☐ Teemu Selänne #8
- ☐ Darrin Shannon #34
- ☐ Darryl Shannon #24
- ☐ Mike Stapleton #14
- ☐ Keith Tkachuk #7
- ☐ Darren Turcotte #89
- ☐ Alexei Zhamnov #10
- ☐ Carlyle/ Pearn/ Simpson
- ☐ Team Photo
- ☐ Mascot Benny

'95 - 96 WINN.
READERS CLUB

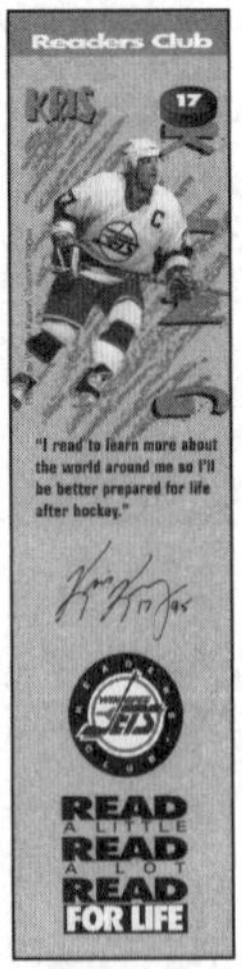

Singles start at 50¢.
Set (12 cards):

- ☐ Tim Cheveldae
- ☐ Dallas Drake
- ☐ Mike Eastwood
- ☐ Nikolai Khabibulin
- ☐ Kris King
- ☐ Alexei Kovalev
- ☐ Dave Manson
- ☐ Teppo Numminen
- ☐ Teemu Selänne
- ☐ Darrin Shannon
- ☐ Keith Tkachuk
- ☐ Alexei Zhamnov

CHAPTER SEVEN

WHA, MINOR & WORLD LEAGUES TEAM ISSUES

WHA TEAM SETS

CINCINNATI STINGERS

'75 - 76 CINCINNATI

KAHN'S WEINERS

We have little information on this set. Each hot dog wrapper featured one player. A 1976-77 set apparently also exists. The most expensive single is Rick Dudley at $25. Singles start at $10.

Size: 1 5/8" x 2 3/4"
Sponsor: Kahn's Weiners

☐ Serge Aubry
☐ Bryan Campbell
☐ Rick Dudley
☐ Pierre Guite
☐ John Hughes
☐ Claude Larose
☐ Jacques Locas
☐ Bernie MacNeil
☐ Mike Pelyk
☐ Ron Plumb
☐ Dale Smedso
☐ Dennis Sobchuk
☐ Gene Sobchuk
☐ Gary Veneruzzo

CLEVELAND CRUSADERS

'72 - 73 CLEVELAND

Gerry Cheevers is the most expensive single at $20 in NRMT. Singles start at $2.

Card Size: 3 1/2" x 5 1/2"
Sponsor: None
Set (19 cards): $50

☐ Paul Andrea
☐ Doug Brindley
☐ Ron Buchanan
☐ G. Cheevers (G)
☐ Ray Clearwater
☐ Bob Dillabough
☐ John Hanna
☐ Joe Hardy
☐ Ted Hodgson
☐ Ralph Hopiavuori
☐ Bill Horton
☐ Gary Jarrett
☐ Skip Krake
☐ Jim McMasters
☐ Wayne Muloin
☐ Gerry Pinder
☐ Richard Pumple
☐ Paul Schmyr
☐ Bob Whidden (G)

'72 - 73 CLEVELAND

CHARLES LINNETT

We have little information on this set. Other singles may exist.

Photo Size: 8 1/2" x 11"
Sponsor: Charles Linnett

☐ Ron Buchanan
☐ Ray Clearwater
☐ Bob Dillabough
☐ Grant Erickson
☐ Ted Hodgson
☐ Ralph Hopiavouri
☐ Billb Horton
☐ Ralph Hopramon
☐ Gary Jarrett
☐ Skip Krake
☐ Jim McMasters
☐ Wayne Muloin
☐ Bill Needham, Coach
☐ Rick Pumple
☐ Paul Shmyr
☐ Robert Whidden (G)
☐ Jim Wiste

HOUSTON AEROS

'75 - 76 HOUSTON

Gordie Howe is the most expensive single at $20 in NRMT. Mark Howe sells at $10 and John Tonelli sells at $8. Singles start at $2.

Set (19 cards): $70

☐ Ron Grahaeme (G)
☐ Larry Hale
☐ Murray Hall
☐ Gordie Howe
☐ Mark Howe
☐ Marty Howe
☐ André Hinse
☐ Frank Hughes
☐ Glen Irwin
☐ Gordon Labossiere
☐ Don Larway
☐ Larry Lund
☐ Poul Popeil
☐ Rich Preston
☐ Terry Ruskowski
☐ Wayne Rutledge (G)
☐ John Schella
☐ Ted Taylor
☐ John Tonelli

LOS ANGELES SHARKS

'72 - 73 LOS ANGELES

Photos are in black and white. Singles sell at $3-5.

Card Size: 2 5/8" x 3 9/16"
Sponsor: None
Set (19 cards): $50

☐ Mike Byers
☐ Bart Crashley
☐ George Gardner (G)
☐ Russ Gillow (G)
☐ Tom Gilmore
☐ Earl Heiskala
☐ J.P. LeBlanc
☐ Ralph MacSweyn
☐ Ted McCaskill
☐ Jim Niekamp
☐ Gerry Odrowski
☐ Tom Serviss
☐ Peter Slater
☐ Steve Sutherland
☐ Joe Szura
☐ Gary Veneruzzo
☐ Jim Watson
☐ Alton White
☐ Bill Young

MINNESOTA FIGHTING SAINTS

'75 - 76 MINNESOTA

We have little information on this set. Other singles likely exist.

Size: 3 1/2" x 5 1/2"
Sponsor: None
Set (25 cards):

☐ Mike Antonovich #12
☐ John Arbour #17
☐ Terry Ball #21
☐ Keith Christiansen #6
☐ Wayne Connelly #7
☐ Mike Curran #1 (G)
☐ Craig Falkman #16
☐ Ted Hampson #10
☐ Jimmy Johnson #20
☐ Bill Klatt #8
☐ George Konik #19
☐ Leonard Lilyholm #15
☐ Bob MacMillan #14
☐ Jack McCartan #30 (G)
☐ Mike McMahon #23
☐ George Morrison #9
☐ Dick Paradise #2
☐ Mel Pearson #26
☐ Terry Ryan #18
☐ Blaine Rydman #22
☐ Frank Sanders #4
☐ Glen Sonmor, Coach
☐ Fred Speck #11
☐ Carl Wetzel (G) #35
☐ Bill Young #24

'74 - 75 MINNESOTA

We have little information on this set. Other singles likely exist.

Size: 3 1/2" x 5 1/2"
Sponsor: None

☐ Mike Antonovich
☐ John Arbour
☐ Ron Busniuk
☐ Wayne Connelly
☐ Mike Curran (G)
☐ Gord Gallant
☐ Ary Gambucci
☐ John Garrett (G)
☐ Ted Hampson
☐ Murray Heatley
☐ Fran Huck
☐ Jim Johnson
☐ Mike McMahon
☐ Rick Smith
☐ Mike Walton

NEW ENGLAND WHALERS

'72 - 73 HARTFORD

Photos are in black and white. Singles sell at $4 in NRMT. The most expensive singles are Ted Green and Rick Ley at $6-7 each.

Card Size: 4 7/8" x 4 5/8"
Sponsor: None
Set (17 cards): $65

☐ Mike Byers
☐ Terry Caffery
☐ John Cunniff
☐ John Danby
☐ Jim Dorey
☐ Tom Earl
☐ John French
☐ Ted Green
☐ Ric Jordan
☐ Bruce Landon
☐ Rick Ley
☐ Larry Pleau
☐ Brad Selwood
☐ Tim Sheehy
☐ Al Smith (G)
☐ Tom Webster
☐ Tom Williams

OTTAWA NATIONALS

'72 - 73 OTTAWA

Photos are in black and white. Singles sell at $5 in NRMT.

Card Size: 4 1/8" x 4 3/4"
Sponsor: None
Set (23 cards): $40

☐ Mike Amodeo
☐ Les Binkley (G)
☐ Mike Boland
☐ Wayne Carleton
☐ Bob Charlebois
☐ Ron Climie
☐ Brian Conacher
☐ Rick Cunningham
☐ John Donnelly
☐ Brian Gibbons
☐ Jack Gibson
☐ Gilles Gratton (G)
☐ Steve King
☐ Gavin Kirk
☐ Bob Leduc
☐ Tom Martin
☐ Chris Meloff
☐ Ron Riley
☐ Rick Sentes
☐ Tom Simpson
☐ Ken Stephenson
☐ Guy Trottier
☐ Steve Warr

PHOENIX ROADRUNNERS

'75 - 76 PHOENIX

Photos are in black and white. Robbie Ftorek is the most expensive single at $5 in NRMT. Singles start at $1.50.

Card Size: 3" x 4"
Sponsor: None
Set (22 cards): $30

☐ Serge Beaudoin
☐ Jim Boyd
☐ Jim Clarke
☐ Cam Connor
☐ Mike Cormier
☐ Barry Dean
☐ Robbie Ftorek
☐ Dave Gorman
☐ John Gray
☐ Del Hall
☐ Ron Huston
☐ Murray Keogan
☐ Gary Kurt (G)
☐ Garry Lariviere
☐ Al McLeod
☐ Peter McNamee
☐ John Migneault
☐ Lauri Mononen
☐ Jim Niekamp
☐ Jack Norris (G)
☐ Pekka Rautakallio
☐ Ron Serafini

'76 - 77 PHOENIX

Robbie Ftorek is the most expensive single at $4 in NRMT. Singles start at $1.50.

Card Size: 3 7/16" x 4 3/8"
Sponsor: None
Set (18 cards): $25

☐ Serge Beaudoin
☐ Mike Cormier
☐ Robbie Ftorek
☐ Del Hall
☐ Clay Hebenton (G)
☐ André Hinse
☐ Mike Hobin
☐ Frank Hughes
☐ Ron Huston
☐ Gary Kurt (G)
☐ Garry Lariviere
☐ Bob Liddington
☐ Lauri Mononen
☐ Jim Niekamp
☐ Pekka Rautakallio
☐ Seppo Repo
☐ Jerry Rollins
☐ Juhani Tamminen

QUÉBEC NORDIQUES

'72 - 74 QUÉBEC

PRO STAR

Richard Brodeur is the most expensive single at $8 in NRMT. Singles start at $2.

Card Size: 3 1/2" x 5 1/2"
Sponsor: ProStar Promotions
Set (29 cards): $45

☐ Mike Archambault
☐ Serge Aubry
☐ Alain Beaule
☐ Yves Bergeron
☐ Serge Bernier
☐ Jacques Blain
☐ Richard Brodeur (G)
☐ Alain Caron
☐ Michel Deguise
☐ Ken Desjardins
☐ Guy Dufour
☐ Maurice Filion, Coach
☐ André Gaudette
☐ Jean-Guy Gendron
☐ Jeannot Gilbert
☐ Réjean Giroux
☐ Frank Golembrosky
☐ Bob Guindon
☐ Pierre Guite
☐ Dale Hoganson
☐ Réjean Houle
☐ François Lacombe
☐ Paul Larose
☐ Rénald Leclerc
☐ Michel Parizeau
☐ Jean Payette
☐ Michel Rouleau
☐ Pierre Roy
☐ Jean-Claude Tremblay

'76 - 77 QUÉBEC

Richard Brodeur is the most expensive single at $6 in NRMT. Singles start at $2.

Postcard Size: 3 1/2" x 5 1/2"
Sponsor: None
Set (20 cards): $40

☐ Serge Aubry
☐ Paul Baxter
☐ Jean Bernier
☐ Serge Bernier
☐ Christian Bordeleau
☐ Paulin Bordeleau
☐ André Boudrias
☐ Curt Brackenbury
☐ Richard Brodeur (G)
☐ Réal Cloutier
☐ Charles Constantin
☐ Jim Dorey
☐ Bob Fitchner
☐ Richard Grenier
☐ François Lacombe
☐ Pierre Roy
☐ Steve Sutherland
☐ Marc Tardif
☐ Jean-Claude Tremblay
☐ Wally Weir

'76 - 77 QUÉBEC

MARIE ANTOINETTE

Artwork is credited to Claude Laroche. Richard Brodeur is the most expensive single at $10 in NRMT. Singles start at $5.

Photo Size: 8" x 10 1/2"
Sponsor: Marie Antoinette
Set (14 cards): $75

☐ Paul Baxter
☐ Serge Bernier
☐ Paulin Bordeleau
☐ André Boudrias
☐ Curt Brackenbury
☐ Richard Brodeur (G)
☐ Réal Cloutier
☐ Charles Constantin
☐ Bob Fitchner
☐ Richard Grenier
☐ Marc Tardif
☐ Jean-Claude Tremblay
☐ Steve Sutherland
☐ Wally Weir

SAN DIEGO MARINERS

'76 - 77 SAN DIEGO

DEAN'S PHOTO

We have no pricing information on this set.

Size: 5" x 8"
Sponsor: Dean's Photo Services
Set (14 cards):

☐ Kevin Devine
☐ Bob Dobek
☐ Norm Ferguson
☐ Brent Hughes
☐ Randy Legge
☐ Ken Lockett (G)
☐ Kevin Morrison
☐ Joe Noris
☐ Gerry Pinder
☐ Brad Rhines
☐ Wayne Rivers
☐ Paul Shmyr
☐ Gary Venneruzzo
☐ Ernie Wakely (G)

VANCOUVER BLAZERS

'73 - 74 VANCOUVER

Colin Campbell is the most expensive single at $5 in NRMT. Singles sell at $2.

Card Size: 3 1/2" x 5"
Sponsor: None
Set (19 cards): $40

☐ Jim Adair
☐ Don Burgess
☐ Bryan Campbell
☐ Colin Campbell
☐ Mike Chernoff
☐ Peter Donnelly
☐ George Gardner (G)
☐ Sam Gellard
☐ Ed Hatoum
☐ Dave Hutchison
☐ Danny Lawton
☐ Ralph MacSweyn
☐ Denis Meloche
☐ John Micneault
☐ Murray Myers
☐ Michel Plante
☐ Ron Plumb
☐ Claude St. Sauveur
☐ Irvin Spencer

WINNIPEG JETS

'78 - 79 WINNIPEG

Kent Nilsson is the most expensive single at $6 in NRMT. Singles start at $1.50.

Postcard Size: 3 1/2" x 5 1/2"
Sponsor: Baker & Sons Ltd.
Set (23 cards): $30

☐ Mike Amodeo
☐ Scott Campbell
☐ Kim Clackson
☐ Joe Daley (G)
☐ John Gray
☐ Ted Green
☐ Robert Guindon
☐ Glenn Hicks
☐ Larry Hillman
☐ Bill Lesuk
☐ Willy Lindstrom
☐ Barry Long
☐ Morris Lukowich
☐ Paul MacKinnon
☐ Markus Mattsson (G)
☐ Lyle Moffat
☐ Kent Nilsson
☐ Rich Preston
☐ Terry Ruskowski
☐ Lars-Erik Sjoberg
☐ Peter Sullivan
☐ Paul Terbenche
☐ Steve West

ADIRONDACK RED WINGS

'95 - 96

ADIRONDACK RED WINGS / SPLIT SECOND

Norm Maracle is one of the more expensive singles at $2-3. Singles start at 50¢.

Card Size: 2 1/2" x 3 1/2"

Set (25 cards): $15

- ☐ Jeff Bloemberg
- ☐ Curtis Bowen
- ☐ Dave Chyzowski
- ☐ Sylvain Cloutier
- ☐ Ryan Duthie
- ☐ Anders Eriksson
- ☐ Yan Golubovsky
- ☐ Ben Hankinson
- ☐ Kevin Hodson (G)
- ☐ Scott Hollis
- ☐ Mike Knuble
- ☐ Jason MacDonald
- ☐ Mark Major
- ☐ Norm Maracle (G)
- ☐ Kurt Miller
- ☐ Mike Needham
- ☐ Troy Neumeier
- ☐ Mark Ouimet
- ☐ Jamie Pushor
- ☐ Stacy Roest
- ☐ Brandon Smith
- ☐ Kerry Toporowski
- ☐ Wes Walz
- ☐ Aaron Ward
- ☐ Macot Hockeye

ALBANY RIVER RATS

'96 - 97

ALBANY RIVER RATS/ SPLIT SECOND

Singles start at 50¢.

Card Size: 2 1/2" x 3 1/2"

Set (28 cards):

Some of the more expensive singles are Patrik Elias and Steve Sullivan. Singles start at 50¢.

Card Size: 2 1/2" x 3 1/2"

Set (26 cards): $30

- ☐ Éric Bertrand
- ☐ Brad Bombardir
- ☐ Steve Brulé
- ☐ John Cunniff
- ☐ Mike Dunham (G)
- ☐ Patrik Elias
- ☐ Dennis Gendron
- ☐ Bryan Helmer
- ☐ Bobby House
- ☐ Geordie Kinnear
- ☐ Chris McAlpine
- ☐ Krzysztof Oliwa
- ☐ Jay Pandolfo
- ☐ Denis Pederson
- ☐ Pascal Rhéaume
- ☐ Vadim Sharifijanov
- ☐ Richard Shulmistra (G)
- ☐ Peter Sidorkiewicz (G)
- ☐ Zdenek Skorepa
- ☐ Sheldon Souray
- ☐ Mark Strobel
- ☐ Steve Sullivan
- ☐ Sergei Vyshedkevich
- ☐ AHL Web Site
- ☐ Mascot Rowdy
- ☐ PHPA

'97 - 98

ALBANY RIVER RATS/ SPLIT SECOND

Some of the more expensive singles are Brendan Morrison and John Madden. Singles start at 50¢.

Card Size: 2 1/2" x 3 1/2"

Set (26 cards): $20

- ☐ Éric Bertrand
- ☐ Jiri Bicek
- ☐ Steve Brulé
- ☐ John Cunniff
- ☐ Dennis Gendron
- ☐ Bryan Helmer
- ☐ Bobby House
- ☐ Judd Lambert
- ☐ Sasha Lakovic
- ☐ Geordie Kinnear
- ☐ John Madden
- ☐ Brendan Morrison
- ☐ Jay Pandolfo
- ☐ Richard Rochefort
- ☐ Vadim Sharifijanov
- ☐ Peter Sidorkiewicz (G)
- ☐ Zdenek Skorepa
- ☐ Rob Skrlac
- ☐ Ken Sutton
- ☐ Paul Traynor
- ☐ Sergei Vyshedkevich
- ☐ Colin White
- ☐ Jeff Williams
- ☐ Peter Zezel
- ☐ AHL Web Site
- ☐ PHPA

'98 - 99

ALBANY RIVER RATS/ SPLIT SECOND

John Madden is one of the more expensive singles. Singles start at 50¢.

Set (25 cards): $15

- ☐ Éric Bertrand
- ☐ Jiri Bicek
- ☐ Steve Brulé
- ☐ Mike Buzak (G)
- ☐ David Cunniff
- ☐ John Cunniff
- ☐ Pierre Dagenais
- ☐ Josh DeWolf
- ☐ Red Gendron
- ☐ Sascha Goc
- ☐ Frédéric Henry
- ☐ Geordie Kinnear
- ☐ John Madden
- ☐ Rob Pattison
- ☐ Henrik Rehnberg
- ☐ Richard Rochefort
- ☐ Alexander Semak
- ☐ Rob Skrlac
- ☐ Ken Sutton
- ☐ Chris Thompson
- ☐ Sergei Vyshedkevich
- ☐ Colin White
- ☐ Jeff Williams
- ☐ AHL Web Site
- ☐ Mascot Rowdy

'99 - 00

ALBANY RIVER RATS/ CHOICE

Willie Mitchell is one of the more expensive singles at $1.50. Singles start at 50¢.

Set (25 cards): $15

- ☐ 1 Steve Brulé
- ☐ 2 Jeff Williams
- ☐ 3 Pierre Dagenais
- ☐ 4 George Awada
- ☐ 5 David Maley
- ☐ 6 Andre Lakos
- ☐ 7 Carlyle Lewis
- ☐ 8 Willie Mitchell
- ☐ 9 Richard Rochefort
- ☐ 10 Steve Kelly
- ☐ 11 Rob Skrlac
- ☐ 12 Jiri Bicek
- ☐ 13 Ken Sutton
- ☐ 14 Colin White
- ☐ 15 Damphousse (G)
- ☐ 16 David Cunniff
- ☐ 17 Sascha Goc
- ☐ 18 F. Henry (G)
- ☐ 19 Josh DeWolf
- ☐ 20 Stanislav Gron
- ☐ 21 Sasha Lakovic
- ☐ 22 Sylvain Cloutier
- ☐ 23 John Cunniff
- ☐ 24 Bob Carpenter
- ☐ 25 Dennis Gendron
- ☐ 26 Mascot Rowdy

'00 - 01

ALBANY RIVER RATS/ CHOICE

Willie Mitchell is one of the more expensive singles at $1.50. Singles start at 50¢.

Set (27 cards): $12

- ☐ 1 Daryl Andrews
- ☐ 2 Jiri Bicek
- ☐ 3 Max Birbraer
- ☐ 4 J. Boumedienne
- ☐ 5 Sylvain Cloutier
- ☐ 6 Mike Commodore
- ☐ 7 Pierre Dagenais
- ☐ 8 Chris Ferraro
- ☐ 9 Sascha Goc
- ☐ 10 Stanislav Gron
- ☐ 11 Mike Jefferson
- ☐ 12 Andre Lakos
- ☐ 13 Jason Lehoux
- ☐ 14 Carlyle Lewis
- ☐ 15 Willie Mitchell
- ☐ 16 Lucas Nehrling
- ☐ 17 Henrik Rehnberg
- ☐ 18 Richard Rochefort
- ☐ 19 Michael Rupp
- ☐ 20 Rob Skrlac
- ☐ 21 Ed Ward
- ☐ 22 J-F Damphousse (G)
- ☐ 23 F. Henry (G)
- ☐ 24 John Cunniff
- ☐ 25 Bob Carpenter
- ☐ 26 Alex Zinevych
- ☐ 27 Checklist

'01 - 02

ALBANY RIVER RATS/ CHOICE

Singles start at 50¢.

Card Size: 2 1/2" x 3 1/2"

Set (28 cards): $15

- ☐ 1 Header Card
- ☐ 2 Sylvain Cloutier
- ☐ 3 J-F Damphousse (G)
- ☐ 4 Mike Commodore
- ☐ 5 Daryl Andrews
- ☐ 6 Andre Lakos
- ☐ 7 Mikko Jokela
- ☐ 8 Joel Dezainde
- ☐ 9 Jiri Bicek
- ☐ 10 Stanislav Gron
- ☐ 11 Brian Gionta
- ☐ 12 Richard Rochefort
- ☐ 13 Michael Rupp
- ☐ 14 Ted Drury
- ☐ 15 Max Birbraer
- ☐ 16 Christian Berglund
- ☐ 17 Scott Cameron
- ☐ 18 Jason Lehoux
- ☐ 19 Brett Clouthier
- ☐ 20 Bruce Gardiner
- ☐ 21 Steve Guolla
- ☐ 22 Victor Uchevatov
- ☐ 23 Joël Bouchard
- ☐ 24 Ari Ahonen
- ☐ 25 S. Clemmensen (G)
- ☐ 26 B. Carpenter, Coach
- ☐ 27 G. Kinnear, A.Coach
- ☐ 28 Mascot Rowdy

'02 - 03

ALBANY RIVER RATS/ CHOICE

Singles start at 50¢.

Set (28 cards): $15

- ☐ 1 Ari Ahonen (G)
- ☐ 2 Alex Brooks
- ☐ 3 Brett Clouthier
- ☐ 4 Christian Berglund
- ☐ 5 Craig Darby
- ☐ 6 Chris Hartsburg
- ☐ 7 Daryl Andrews
- ☐ 8 Dave Roche
- ☐ 9 Eric Johansson
- ☐ 10 Jiri Bicek
- ☐ 11 Joe Hulbig
- ☐ 12 Jason Lehoux
- ☐ 13 Krisjanis Redlihs
- ☐ 14 Ken Sutton
- ☐ 15 Max Birbraer
- ☐ 16 Mikko Jokela
- ☐ 17 Mike Matteucci
- ☐ 18 Michael Rupp
- ☐ 19 Raymond Giroux
- ☐ 20 Rob Skrlac
- ☐ 21 Scott Cameron
- ☐ 22 S. Clemmensen (G)
- ☐ 23 Victor Uchevatov
- ☐ 24 Greg Crozier
- ☐ 25 Dennis Gendron
- ☐ 26 Geordie Kinnear
- ☐ 27 Gates Orlando
- ☐ Mascot / Checklist

ANCHORAGE ACES

'94 - 95

ANCHORAGE ACES

Singles start at 50¢.

Set (27 cards): $10

- ☐ 1 Kevin Fitzgerald
- ☐ 2 Tony Link
- ☐ 3 Zack Westin
- ☐ 4 Kory Wright
- ☐ 5 Kord Cernich
- ☐ 6 Darrin Semeniuk
- ☐ 7 Brian Kraft
- ☐ 8 R. Blackadar
- ☐ 9 Jim Tobin
- ☐ 10 Tracy Link
- ☐ 11 Michael Warde
- ☐ 12 Garvin Federenko
- ☐ 13 Jim Mayes
- ☐ 14 Vern Hickel
- ☐ 15 Derek Donald
- ☐ 16 Brian Majeske
- ☐ 17 Chad Meyhoff
- ☐ 18 Doug Spooner
- ☐ 19 Maurice Hall
- ☐ 20 Pete McEnaney
- ☐ 21 Keith Street
- ☐ 22 Georg Thiele
- ☐ 23 Tim Molle
- ☐ 24 Brian Bethard
- ☐ 25 Dean Trboyevich
- ☐ 26 Aces
- ☐ 27 Team Photo/ CL

'98 - 99

ANCHORAGE ACES / SUBWAY-VIDEO CITY

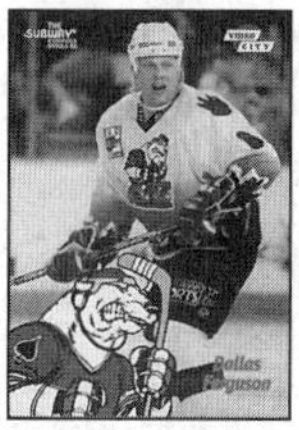

Singles start at 50¢.

Set (26 cards): $10

- ☐ 1 Checklist
- ☐ 2 Dean Trboyevich
- ☐ 3 Kevin Epp
- ☐ 4 Hayden O'Rear
- ☐ 5 Richard Peacock
- ☐ 6 Sean Rowe
- ☐ 7 Mascot Boomer
- ☐ 8 George Wilcox
- ☐ 9 Sergei Tkachenko
- ☐ 10 Frank Jury
- ☐ 11 Walt Poddubny
- ☐ 12 Kent Baumbach
- ☐ 13 Wade Brookbank
- ☐ 14 Keith Street
- ☐ 15 Bob Cunningham
- ☐ 16 Kord Cernich
- ☐ 17 Paul Williams
- ☐ 18 Evgeny Kourilin
- ☐ 19 Jason Gibson
- ☐ 20 Steve MacSwain
- ☐ 21 Dean Larson
- ☐ 22 Dallas Ferguson
- ☐ 23 Derek Gauthier
- ☐ 24 Yvan Corbin
- ☐ 25 Sponsor card
- ☐ 26 Fred Rannard

'99 - 00

ANCHORAGE ACES / GRANDSTAND

Singles start at 50¢.

Set (28 cards): $10

- ☐ Bob Wilkie
- ☐ Fred Rannard
- ☐ Paul Williams
- ☐ Steve MacSwain
- ☐ Marc Charbonneau
- ☐ Chad Power
- ☐ Brian Elder
- ☐ Tim Lozinik
- ☐ Sponsor
- ☐ Kord Cernich
- ☐ George Wilcox
- ☐ Keith Street
- ☐ Derek Gauthier
- ☐ Ruslan Batyrshin
- ☐ Sean Rowe
- ☐ Dean Larson
- ☐ Team photo
- ☐ Sponsor
- ☐ Sponsor
- ☐ Walt Poddubny
- ☐ Dallas Ferguson
- ☐ Chad Richard
- ☐ Denis Pigolitsyn
- ☐ Clayton Read
- ☐ Marc Delmore
- ☐ Lada Hampeis
- ☐ Sponsor

ASHEVILLE SMOKE

'99 - 00

ASHEVILLE SMOKE/ ROOX

Brent and Keith Gretzky are the most expensive singles at $1.50 each. Singles start at 50¢.

Card Size: 2 1/2" x 3 1/2"

Set (29 cards): $10

- ☐ François Bourdeau
- ☐ Dan Brenzavich
- ☐ Peter Cermak
- ☐ Frank DeFrenza
- ☐ Aaron Fackler
- ☐ Paul Giblin
- ☐ Brent Gretzky
- ☐ Keith Gretzky
- ☐ Francois Leroux
- ☐ Dan McIntyre
- ☐ Rob Milliken
- ☐ Hayden O'Rear
- ☐ Vaclav Pazourek
- ☐ Cory Peterson
- ☐ Cory Peterson
- ☐ Jon Pirrong
- ☐ Ken Plaquin
- ☐ Ryan Prentice
- ☐ Josh Tymchak
- ☐ Josh Tymchak
- ☐ Shawn Ulrich
- ☐ Lindsay Vallis
- ☐ Richie Walcott
- ☐ Bruce Watson
- ☐ Bruce Watson
- ☐ Asheville Smoke
- ☐ Mascot Smoky
- ☐ Smoke
- ☐ Zamboni

'00 - 01

ASHEVILLE SMOKE / ROOX

Singles start at 50¢.

Card Size: 2 1/2" x 3 1/2"

Set (18 cards): $10

- ☐ Ryan Aikia
- ☐ Brent Belecki
- ☐ Blue Bennefield
- ☐ Pat Bingham
- ☐ Derek Crimin
- ☐ Alexandre Fomitchev
- ☐ John Hewitt
- ☐ Olaf Kjenstad
- ☐ Dominic Maltais
- ☐ Tyler Prosofsky
- ☐ Bobby Rapoza
- ☐ Bogdan Rudenko
- ☐ J.C. Ruid
- ☐ Lee Svangstu
- ☐ Shawn Ulrich
- ☐ Manager
- ☐ Mascot Smoky
- ☐ Sponsor Ingles Zamboni

ATLANTA KNIGHTS

'92 - 93

ATLANTA KNIGHTS/ SPORT PRINT

Manon Rhéaume is one of the more expensive singles at $6. Singles sell at 50¢.

Size: 2 1/2" x 3 1/2"

Set (24 cards): $15

- ☐ Manon Rhéaume (G)
- ☐ J.C. Bergeron (G)
- ☐ Tim Bergeron
- ☐ Jean Blouin
- ☐ Scott Boston
- ☐ Jeff Buchanan
- ☐ Don Burke
- ☐ Jock Callander
- ☐ Christian Campeau
- ☐ Brent Gretzky
- ☐ Matt Hervey
- ☐ Jason Lafrenière
- ☐ Rick Lanz
- ☐ Chris LiPuma
- ☐ David Littman (G)
- ☐ Steve Maltais
- ☐ Colin Miller
- ☐ Keith Osborne
- ☐ Sergei Ossipov
- ☐ Shawn Rivers
- ☐ Shayne Stevenson
- ☐ Dan Vincelette
- ☐ Gene Ubriaco, Coach
- ☐ Knights/ Checklist

'93 - 94

ATLANTA KNIGHTS / SPORT PRINTS

Manon Rhéaume is one of the more expensive singles at $6. Singles sell at 50¢.

Size: 2 1/2" x 3 1/2"

Sponsor: Sport Print

Set (23 cards): $12

- ☐ J.C. Bergeron
- ☐ Jeff Buchanan
- ☐ Christian Campeau
- ☐ Eric Charron
- ☐ Cory Cross
- ☐ Stan Drulia
- ☐ Eric Dubois
- ☐ Devin Edgerton
- ☐ Mike Greenlay (G)
- ☐ Brent Gretzky
- ☐ Steve Larouche
- ☐ Chris LiPuma
- ☐ Jeff Madill
- ☐ Bill McDougall
- ☐ Colin Miller
- ☐ Manon Rhéaume (G)
- ☐ Shawn Rivers
- ☐ Normand Rochefort
- ☐ Jason Ruff
- ☐ Martin Tanguay
- ☐ Marc Tardif
- ☐ Gene Ubriaco, Coach
- ☐ Knights/ Checklist

'94 - 95

ATLANTA KNIGHTS

Set (27 cards): $12

- ☐ 1 Checklist
- ☐ 2 Mike Greenlay
- ☐ 3 Chris Nelson
- ☐ 4 Derek Mayer
- ☐ 5 Drew Bannister
- ☐ 6 Allen Pedersen
- ☐ 7 Colin Miller
- ☐ 8 Brent Gretzky
- ☐ 9 Peter Ferraro
- ☐ 10 Devin Edgerton
- ☐ 11 Chris Ferraro
- ☐ 12 Jason Ruff
- ☐ 13 Eric Dubois
- ☐ 14 Stan Drulia
- ☐ 15 Allan Egeland
- ☐ 16 Aaron Gavey
- ☐ 17 Yves Heroux
- ☐ 18 Brian Straub
- ☐ 19 Jeff Toms
- ☐ 20 Chris LiPuma
- ☐ 21 Cory Cross
- ☐ 22 C. Campeau
- ☐ 23 Derek Wilkinson
- ☐ 24 Brantt Myhres
- ☐ 25 John Paris
- ☐ 26 Scott Gordon
- ☐ 27 Mascot Sir HT

'95 - 96

ATLANTA KNIGHTS / EDGE ICE

Set (25 cards): $12

- ☐ Drew Bannister
- ☐ Doug Barrault
- ☐ Corey Beaulieu
- ☐ Ryan Brown
- ☐ Christian Campeau
- ☐ Stan Drulia
- ☐ Eric Dubois
- ☐ Allan Egeland
- ☐ Scott Gordon
- ☐ John Paris
- ☐ Brent** Peterson
- ☐ Adrien Plavsic
- ☐ Jeff Toms
- ☐ Derek Wilkinson (G)
- ☐ Mascot Sir Hat Trick
- ☐ Jason Ruff
- ☐ Reggie Savage
- ☐ Corey Spring
- ☐ Alexandre LaPorte
- ☐ Chris LiPuma
- ☐ Tyler Moss (G)
- ☐ Brantt Myhres
- ☐ Mark Greig
- ☐ Bob Halkidis
- ☐ Kurt Harvey

AUSTIN ICE BATS

'00 - 01

AUSTIN ICE BATS / GRANDSTAND

Singles start at 50¢. The last two cards were redemption cards.

Set (30 cards): $15

- ☐ Ryan Anderson
- ☐ David Brosseau
- ☐ Bobby Brown
- ☐ Jonathan Forest
- ☐ Mike Gaffney
- ☐ Jeff Greenlaw
- ☐ Daniel Kletke
- ☐ Jeff Kungle
- ☐ Éric Landry
- ☐ Roger Lewis
- ☐ Josh Maser
- ☐ Bryan McMullen
- ☐ Derek Nicolson
- ☐ Erik Noack
- ☐ Keith O'Brien
- ☐ Tyler Perry
- ☐ Philippe Plante
- ☐ Dan Price
- ☐ Brett Seguin
- ☐ Kelly Smart
- ☐ Troy Stonier
- ☐ Daniel Tetrault
- ☐ Brent Hughes
- ☐ Ken McRae
- ☐ Clint Shuman
- ☐ Sponsor CC Comedy
- ☐ Sponsor Hooters
- ☐ Mascot Fang
- ☐ Mascots Spike & Fang
- ☐ Ice Bats All-Stars

BALTIMORE SKIPJACKS

'91 - 92

BALTIMORE SKIPJACKS / WENDY'S & COKE

Olaf Kölzig is one of the more expensive singles at $5. Singles start at 75¢.

Card Size: 2 1/2" x 3 1/2"

Set (15 cards): $15

- ☐ 1 Tim Taylor
- ☐ 2 Brent Hughes
- ☐ 3 Trevor Halverson
- ☐ 4 Bobby Reynolds
- ☐ 5 Ken Lovsin
- ☐ 6 Olaf Kölzig (G)
- ☐ 7 Reggie Savage
- ☐ 8 Jim Mathieson

- ☐ 9 Todd Hlushko
- ☐ 10 Mark Ferner
- ☐ 11 John Purves
- ☐ 12 Steve Seftel
- ☐ 13 Craig Duncanson
- ☐ 14 Simon Wheeldon
- ☐ 15 Bob Babcock

BC ICEMEN

'98 - 99

BC ICEMEN

Singles start at 50¢.

Set (22 cards): $10

- ☐ 1 Mark Dutiaume
- ☐ 2 Pete Vandermeer
- ☐ 3 Patrice Robitaille
- ☐ 4 Ales Dvorak
- ☐ 5 Shane Dow
- ☐ 6 Scott Ricci
- ☐ 7 Doug Johnson
- ☐ 8 Kearns / Plamondon
- ☐ 9 Chris Grenville
- ☐ 10 Jarno Mensonen
- ☐ 11 Jamie Bird
- ☐ 12 Greg Pajor
- ☐ 13 Derek Knorr
- ☐ 14 Chris Kavanagh
- ☐ 15 Dallas Mann
- ☐ 16 Jon Hillebrandt
- ☐ 17 Dieter Kochan
- ☐ 18 Brad Jones
- ☐ 19 Brian Waselko
- ☐ 20 Mike Thornton
- ☐ 21 Mascot Phantom
- ☐ 22 Mascot Bamboni

'99 - 00

BC ICEMEN / EBK SPORTS

Singles start at 50¢.

Set (27 cards): $10

- ☐ 1 Ales Dvorak
- ☐ 2 Shane Dow
- ☐ 3 Scott Ricci
- ☐ 4 Pete Vandermeer
- ☐ 5 Doug Johnson
- ☐ 6 Mark Dutiaume
- ☐ 7 Justin Kearns
- ☐ 8 Patrice Robitaille
- ☐ 9 Justin Plamondon
- ☐ 10 Chris Grenville
- ☐ 11 Jarno Mensonen
- ☐ 12 Jamie Bird
- ☐ 13 Greg Pajor
- ☐ 14 Dmitri Deryabin
- ☐ 15 Derek Knorr
- ☐ 16 Peter Cermak
- ☐ 17 Chris Kavanagh
- ☐ 18 Jon Hillebrandt
- ☐ 19 Dieter Kochan
- ☐ 20 Brad Jones
- ☐ 21 Brian Weselro
- ☐ 22 Dallas Mann
- ☐ 23 Mike Thornton
- ☐ 24 Mascot Phantom
- ☐ 25 Mascot Bamboni
- ☐ BCIIcemen
- ☐ UHL Web Site

BINGHAMPTON RANGERS

'92 - 93

BINGHAMPTON RANGERS

Sergei Zubov is one of the more expensive singles at $2. Singles start at 50¢.

Card Size: 2 1/2" x 3 1/2"

Set (24 cards): $12

- ☐ 1 Rangers card
- ☐ 2 Mike Hurlbut
- ☐ 3 Michael Stewart
- ☐ 4 Craig Duncanson
- ☐ 5 Rick Bennett
- ☐ 6 Dave Thomlinson
- ☐ 7 Mike Stevens
- ☐ 8 Rob Kenny
- ☐ 9 Chris Cichocki
- ☐ 10 Sergei Zubov
- ☐ 11 Don Biggs
- ☐ 12 Joby Messier
- ☐ 13 Steven King
- ☐ 14 Dave Archibald
- ☐ 15 Brian McReynolds
- ☐ 16 Dave Marcinyshyn
- ☐ 17 Jean-Yves Roy
- ☐ 18 Peter Fiorentino
- ☐ 19 Daniel Lacroix
- ☐ 20 Per Djoos
- ☐ 21 Boris Rousson (G)
- ☐ 22 Corey Hirsch (G)
- ☐ 23 Mascot Rockey
- ☐ 24 Rangers card

'94 - 95

BINGHAMPTON RANGERS / CLASSIC

Darren Langdon is one of the more expensive singles at $1.50. Singles start at 50¢.

Card Size: 2 1/2" x 3 1/2"

Set (23 cards): $12

- ☐ Eric Cairns
- ☐ Craig Duncanson
- ☐ Peter Fiorentino
- ☐ Ken Gernander
- ☐ Jim Hiller
- ☐ Corey Hirsch (G)
- ☐ Rob Kenny
- ☐ Andrei Kudinov
- ☐ Darren Langdon
- ☐ Scott Malone
- ☐ Shawn McCosh
- ☐ Mike McLaughlin
- ☐ Joby Messier
- ☐ Jeff Nielson
- ☐ Mattias Norstrom
- ☐ Jamie Ram (G)
- ☐ Barry Richter
- ☐ Jean-Yves Roy
- ☐ Brad Rubachuk
- ☐ Dave Smith
- ☐ Dmitri Starostenko
- ☐ Michael Stewart
- ☐ Darcy Werenka

'95 - 96

BINGHAMPTON RANGERS / CLASSIC

Singles start at 50¢.

Card Size: 2 1/2" x 3 1/2"

Set (25 cards): $12

- ☐ Sylvain Blouin
- ☐ Eric Cairns
- ☐ Chris Ferraro
- ☐ Peter Ferraro
- ☐ Maxim Galanov
- ☐ Ken Gernander
- ☐ Brad Jones
- ☐ Pavel Komarov
- ☐ Andrei Kudinov
- ☐ Daniel Lacroix
- ☐ Steve Larouche
- ☐ Jon Hillebrandt
- ☐ Scott Malone
- ☐ Cal McGowan
- ☐ Jeff Nielsen
- ☐ Jamie Ram (G)
- ☐ Shawn Reid
- ☐ Barry Richter
- ☐ Andy Silverman
- ☐ Lee Sorochan
- ☐ Dmitri Starostenko
- ☐ Ryan VandenBussche
- ☐ Rick Willis
- ☐ George Burnett, Coach
- ☐ Mike Busniuk, Coach

'96 - 97

BINGHAMPTON RANGERS / SPLIT SECOND

Dan Cloutier is one of the more expensive singles at $2. Singles start at 50¢.

Card Size: 2 1/2" x 3 1/2"

Sponsor: Split Second

Set (24 cards): $12

- ☐ Micah Aivazoff
- ☐ Sylvain Blouin
- ☐ Ed Campbell
- ☐ Dan Cloutier (G)
- ☐ Chris Ferraro
- ☐ Peter Ferraro
- ☐ Peter Fiorentino
- ☐ Eric Flinton
- ☐ Maxim Golanov
- ☐ Ken Gernander
- ☐ Mike Martin
- ☐ Bob Maudie
- ☐ Jeff Nielsen
- ☐ Rocky Raccoon
- ☐ Ken Shepard
- ☐ Andy Silverman
- ☐ Adam Smith
- ☐ Lee Sorochan
- ☐ Ryan VandenBussche
- ☐ Vladimir Vorobiev
- ☐ Rick Willis
- ☐ George Burnett, Coach
- ☐ Mike Busniak, Coach
- ☐ AHL Card

BIRMINGHAM BULLS

'93 - 94

BIRMINGHAM BULLS / FOX-21, WJOX, etal.

Singles start at 50¢.

Card Size: 2 5/8" x 3 5/8"

Set (23 cards): $10

- ☐ 1 Bulls card
- ☐ 2 Jim Larkin
- ☐ 3 Brett Barnett
- ☐ 4 Joe Flanagan
- ☐ 5 Butch Kaebel
- ☐ 6 Scott Matusovich
- ☐ 7 Chuck E. Hughes
- ☐ 8 Dave Craievich
- ☐ 9 Alexander Havanov
- ☐ 10 Paul Marshall
- ☐ 11 Jim Peters
- ☐ 12 Chris Marshall
- ☐ 13 Jerome Bechard
- ☐ 14 Jean-Alain Schneider
- ☐ 15 Kevin Kerr
- ☐ 16 Rob Krauss
- ☐ 17 Greg Burke
- ☐ 18 Mark Romaine
- ☐ 19 Bruce Garber
- ☐ 20 Phil Roberto
- ☐ 21 Dave Cavaliere
- ☐ 22 Tim Woodburn
- ☐ Checklist

'94 - 95

BIRMINGHAM BULLS / 94.5-FM, WB MG-45

Brad Smyth is one of the more expensive singles at $1.50. Singles start at 50¢.

Card Size: 2 3/4" x 3 3/4"

Set (22 cards): $10

- ☐ Greg Bailey
- ☐ Norm Bazin
- ☐ Jerome Bechard
- ☐ Dave Boyd
- ☐ David Craievich
- ☐ Rob Donovan
- ☐ Jon Duval
- ☐ Sandy Galuppo
- ☐ Todd Harris
- ☐ Ian Herbert
- ☐ Craig Johnson
- ☐ John Joyce
- ☐ Chris Kerber
- ☐ Olaf Kjenstad
- ☐ Mike Krassner
- ☐ Jim Larkin
- ☐ Craig Lutes
- ☐ Mark Michaud
- ☐ Jean-Marc Plante
- ☐ Phil Roberto
- ☐ Brad Smyth
- ☐ Checklist

'95 - 96

BIRMINGHAM BULLS / CHEVRON, WJOX

Singles start at 50¢.

Card Size: 2 3/4" x 3 3/4"

Sponsors: Chevron, WJOX

Set (29 cards): $10

- ☐ Phil Roberto
- ☐ Lancy Brady
- ☐ Jeff Wells
- ☐ Brad Prefontaine
- ☐ Mark Raiter
- ☐ Rob Donovan
- ☐ Chris Grenville
- ☐ Colin Gregor
- ☐ Mike Latendresse
- ☐ John Morabito
- ☐ Brendan Creagh
- ☐ Chris Bergeron
- ☐ Jerome Bechard
- ☐ Craig Lutes
- ☐ Ian Herbert
- ☐ John Joyce
- ☐ Jeff Callinan
- ☐ Jason Dexter
- ☐ Olaf Kjenstad
- ☐ Chad Erickson
- ☐ Ray Pack
- ☐ Mascot Toro The Bull
- ☐ Chris Kerber
- ☐ M.Coulter/ S.Giffin
- ☐ Doug Laxton
- ☐ Randy Armstrong
- ☐ Lee Davis
- ☐ Herb Winches
- ☐ Ben Cook

CAPE BRETON OILERS

'94 - 95

CAPE BRETON OILERS / CLASSIC

Todd Marchant is one of the more expensive singles at $2. Singles start at 50¢.

Card Size: 2 1/2" x 3 1/2"

Set (23 cards): $12

- ☐ Scott Allison
- ☐ Martin Bakula
- ☐ Ladislav Benysek
- ☐ Dennis Bonvie
- ☐ Jozef Cierny
- ☐ Duane Dennis
- ☐ Greg DeVries
- ☐ Joaquin Gage (G)
- ☐ Ian Herbers
- ☐ Ralph Intranuovo
- ☐ Claude Jurtras
- ☐ Marc LaForge
- ☐ Todd Marchant
- ☐ Darcy Martini
- ☐ Roman Oksiuta
- ☐ David Oliver
- ☐ Steve Passmore (G)
- ☐ Nick Stajduhar
- ☐ John Van Kessel
- ☐ David Vyborny
- ☐ Peter White
- ☐ Tyler Wright
- ☐ Brad Zavisha

CAROLINA MONARCHS

'96 - 97

CAROLINA MONARCHS / MULTI-AD SERVICES

Kevin Weekes is one of the more expensive singles at $4. Singles start at 50¢.

Set (30 cards): $12

- ☐ Chris Armstrong
- ☐ Drake Berehowsky
- ☐ Ashley Buckberger
- ☐ Chadden Cabana
- ☐ Jon Christiano
- ☐ Gilbert Dionne
- ☐ Trevor Doyle
- ☐ Ivan Droppa
- ☐ Craig Ferguson
- ☐ Craig Fisher
- ☐ Bob Halkidis
- ☐ Ryan Johnson
- ☐ Filip Kuba
- ☐ Richard Kromm
- ☐ David Lemanowicz
- ☐ Craig Martin
- ☐ Eric Montreuil
- ☐ David Nemirovsky
- ☐ Jason Podollan
- ☐ Gaetan Poirier
- ☐ Gairin Smith
- ☐ Geoff Smith
- ☐ Herbert Vasijevs
- ☐ Steve Washburn
- ☐ Kevin Weekes (G)
- ☐ Dean Zayonce
- ☐ Checklist
- ☐ Mascot Monty
- ☐ PHPA
- ☐ Prospect Card

CENTRAL TEXAS STAMPEDE

'97 - 98

CENTRAL TEXAS STAMPEDE SUBWAY

Singles start at 50¢.

Set (20 cards): $8

- ☐ Matt Brenner
- ☐ Mike Dick
- ☐ Darren Duncalfe
- ☐ Larry Dyck
- ☐ Dwayne Gylywoychuk
- ☐ Peter Jas
- ☐ Ricky Jacob
- ☐ Dean Kolstad
- ☐ Jacques Mailhot
- ☐ Don McGrath
- ☐ Derek Nicolson
- ☐ Jeff Rask
- ☐ Layne Roland
- ☐ Alex Rummo
- ☐ Doug Smith
- ☐ Greg Smith
- ☐ Joe Tassone
- ☐ Jason Taylor
- ☐ Peter Zurba
- ☐ Mascot Wild Thing

CHARLOTTE CHECKERS

'96 - 97

CHARLOTTE CHECKERS / SUPER SHOP & SAVE

Singles start at $2.

Set (20 cards): $30

- ☐ J-F Aubé
- ☐ Eric Boulton
- ☐ David Brosseau
- ☐ Jeff Connolly
- ☐ Kimbi Daniels
- ☐ Mickey Elick
- ☐ Eric Fenton
- ☐ Jay Kenney
- ☐ Mick Kempffer
- ☐ Scott Kirton
- ☐ John Marks
- ☐ Darcy Mitani
- ☐ Darryl Noren
- ☐ Kevin Rappana
- ☐ Matt Robbins
- ☐ Evgeny Ryabchikov (G)
- ☐ Kurt Seher
- ☐ Nick Vitucci
- ☐ Shawn Wheeler
- ☐ Mascot Chubby Checker

'97 - 98

CHARLOTTE CHECKERS / HANNAFORD

Singles start at 75¢.

Set (28 cards): $20

- ☐ 1 Matt Alvey
- ☐ 2 Eric Boulton
- ☐ 3 David Brosseau
- ☐ 4 Paxton Schafer (G)
- ☐ 5 Kurt Seher
- ☐ 6 Stéphane Soulliere
- ☐ 7 Derek Crimin
- ☐ 8 Eric Flinton
- ☐ 9 Justin Gould
- ☐ 10 Jason Kelly
- ☐ 11 Mike Hartman
- ☐ 12 Jeff Heil
- ☐ 13 Jay Kenney
- ☐ 14 Milt Mastad
- ☐ 15 Dean Moore
- ☐ 16 Darryl Noren
- ☐ 17 Dale Purinton
- ☐ 18 André Roy
- ☐ 19 P.C. Drouin
- ☐ 20 Bill McCauley
- ☐ 21 Shawn Wheeler
- ☐ 22 John Marks
- ☐ 23 Mascot Chubby
- ☐ 24 Checklist
- ☐ 25 Darryl Noren
- ☐ 25 Kurt Seher
- ☐ 25 Eric Flinton
- ☐ 26 PHPA

'98 - 99

CHARLOTTE CHECKERS / HANNAFORD

Singles start at $1.

Set (24 cards): $20

- ☐ J-F Aubé
- ☐ Shannon Basaraba
- ☐ Doug Battaglia
- ☐ David Brosseau
- ☐ Tom Brown
- ☐ Patrick Brownlee
- ☐ Brooke Chateau
- ☐ Jeff Heil
- ☐ Boyd Kane
- ☐ Kevin Kreutzer
- ☐ Darryl Noren
- ☐ Jason Norrie
- ☐ Nikolai Pronin
- ☐ Kurt Seher
- ☐ Bob Sheehan
- ☐ Ryan Sittler
- ☐ Martin Sychra
- ☐ Shawn Wheeler
- ☐ Dean Zayonce
- ☐ Checklist
- ☐ Mascot Chubby Checker
- ☐ Aubé / Seher / Sittler
- ☐ Aubé / Sheehan
- ☐ Battaglia / Brownlee

'99 - 00

CHARLOTTE CHECKERS / ROOX

Singles start at 50¢.

Card Size: 2 1/2" x 3 1/2"

Set (36 cards): $12

- ☐ 1 Jason Dailey
- ☐ 2 Brooke Chateau
- ☐ 3 Rocky Welsing
- ☐ 4 Kurt Seher
- ☐ 5 Kevin Hilton
- ☐ 6 Reggie Brezeault
- ☐ 7 Lee Hamilton
- ☐ 8 Dave Risk
- ☐ 9 Taras Lendzyk
- ☐ 10 Kurt Mallett
- ☐ 11 Tyler Deis
- ☐ 12 Mike Rucinski
- ☐ 13 Derek Wilkinson
- ☐ 14 Richard Scott
- ☐ 15 David Beauregard
- ☐ 16 Mike Jaros
- ☐ 17 Darryl Noren
- ☐ 18 Marc Tropper
- ☐ 19 Scott Bailey
- ☐ 20 Jeff Brown
- ☐ 21 Boyd Kane
- ☐ 22 Mascot Chubby
- ☐ 23 The Carolina Cup
- ☐ 24 Chateau/ Tropper
- ☐ 25 Mark Burgess
- ☐ 26 Don MacAdam
- ☐ 27 Scott Bailey
- ☐ 28 Dean Mando
- ☐ 29 Kevin Pozzo
- ☐ 30 Martin Cerven
- ☐ 31 Marc Tropper
- ☐ 32 Scott Bailey
- ☐ 33 Mike Rucinski
- ☐ 34 David Beauregard
- ☐ 34 Tyler Deis
- ☐ 35 Darryl Noren
- ☐ 36 Checklist

'00 - 01

CHARLOTTE CHECKERS / MULTI-AD SPORTS

Singles start at 50¢.

Set (36 cards): $12

- ☐ 1 Jason LaBarbera (G)
- ☐ 2 Scott Bailey (G)
- ☐ 3 Scott King
- ☐ 4 Marc Tropper
- ☐ 5 Boyd Kane
- ☐ 6 Justin Harney
- ☐ 7 Kurt Seher
- ☐ 8 Brad Mehalko
- ☐ 9 Kevin Hilton
- ☐ 10 Mathieu Benoit
- ☐ 11 David Oliver
- ☐ 12 Lee Hamilton
- ☐ 13 Wes Jarvis
- ☐ 14 Josh MacNevin
- ☐ 15 Kevin Pozzo
- ☐ 16 Don MacAdam
- ☐ 17 Dave Baseggio
- ☐ 18 Mascot Chubby
- ☐ 19 Paul Giblin
- ☐ 20 Tyler Deis
- ☐ 21 Mark Spence
- ☐ 22 Bob MacIsaac
- ☐ 23 Steve Duke
- ☐ 24 Andre Signoretti
- ☐ 25 Brandon Dietrich
- ☐ 26 Mike Derecola
- ☐ 27 Chris Plumhoff
- ☐ 28 Mascot Chubby
- ☐ 29 Richard Scott
- ☐ 30 Vitali Yeremeyev (G)
- ☐ 31 Ben Carpentier
- ☐ 32 Francois Fortier
- ☐ 33 Scott Wray
- ☐ 34 Mark Moore
- ☐ 35 Bryce Wandler
- ☐ 36 Checklist

CHICAGO WOLVES

'98 - 99

CHICAGO WOLVES / CHUBB INSTITUTE

Wendell Young is one of the more expensive singles at $2. Singles start at 75¢.

Set (25 cards): $20

- ☐ Brent Gretzky
- ☐ Dan Plante
- ☐ Tim Bergland
- ☐ Steve Maltais
- ☐ Steve Gosselin
- ☐ Scott Pearson
- ☐ Niklas Andersson
- ☐ Chris LiPuma
- ☐ Pat Jablonski
- ☐ Mascot Skates
- ☐ Tim Breslin
- ☐ Chris Marinucci
- ☐ Steve Larouche
- ☐ Wendell Young (G)
- ☐ Glen Featherstone
- ☐ Bob Nardella
- ☐ Guy Larose
- ☐ Dennis Vial
- ☐ Kevin Dahl
- ☐ Jeremy Mylymok
- ☐ Paul Koch
- ☐ Tom Tilley
- ☐ John Anderson
- ☐ Kevin Miller
- ☐ PHPA

'98 - 99

CHICAGO WOLVES / TURNER CUP CHAMPS

Wendell Young is one of the more expensive singles at $2. Singles start at 75¢.

Set (24 cards): $20

- ☐ 1 Wendell Young (G)
- ☐ 2 John Anderson
- ☐ 3 David Craievich
- ☐ 3 Alexander Godynyuk
- ☐ 3 Ray LeBlanc
- ☐ 4 Paul Koch
- ☐ 5 Kevin Dahl
- ☐ 6 Jeremy Mylymok
- ☐ 7 Bob Nardella
- ☐ 8 Marc Rodgers
- ☐ 9 Marc Potvin
- ☐ 10 Steve Larouche
- ☐ 11 Steve Maltais
- ☐ 12 Doug Barrault
- ☐ 13 Jamie Baker
- ☐ 14 Chris Marinucci
- ☐ 15 Tim Breslin
- ☐ 16 Dennis Vial
- ☐ 17 Tom Tilley
- ☐ 18 Scott Pearson
- ☐ 19 Steve Martins
- ☐ 20 Mascot Martin
- ☐ 21 Tim Bergland
- ☐ 22 Alexander Semak
- ☐ 23 Ravil Gusmanov
- ☐ 24 S. Beauregard (G)

'99 - 00

CHICAGO WOLVES / CAMPAIGN

Singles start at 75¢.

Set (28 cards): $20

- ☐ 1 Header card
- ☐ 2 Wendell Young (G)
- ☐ 3 Kevin Dahl
- ☐ 4 Dallas Eakins
- ☐ 5 Bob Nardella
- ☐ 6 Niklas Andersson
- ☐ 7 Steve Larouche
- ☐ 8 Steve Maltais
- ☐ 9 Chris Marinucci
- ☐ 10 Brian Noonan
- ☐ 11 Guy Larose
- ☐ 12 Sean Berens
- ☐ 13 Glen Featherstone
- ☐ 14 Tom Tilley
- ☐ 15 Scott Pearson
- ☐ 16 Greg Andrusak
- ☐ 17 Dean Malkoc
- ☐ 18 David Mackey
- ☐ 19 Dan Plante
- ☐ 20 Chris LiPuma
- ☐ 21 Andrei Trefilov (G)
- ☐ 22 Daniel Lacroix
- ☐ 23 J. Anderson, Coach
- ☐ 24 Mart. Howe [A.Coach]
- ☐ 25 Mascot Skates

'00 - 01

CHICAGO WOLVES / CAMPAIGN

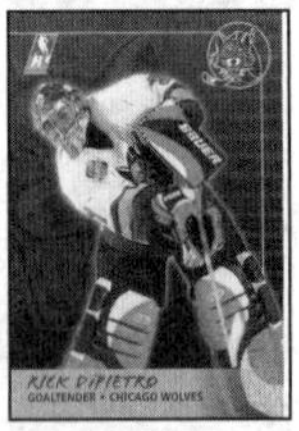

Rick DiPietro is one of the more expensive singles at $10. Singles start at 75¢.

Set (25 cards): $25

- ☐ John Anderson
- ☐ Niklas Andersson
- ☐ Jesse Bélanger
- ☐ Rob Brown
- ☐ Kevin Dahl
- ☐ Rick DiPietro (G)
- ☐ Ted Drury
- ☐ Dallas Eakins
- ☐ Glen Featherstone
- ☐ Eric Houde
- ☐ Paul Kruse
- ☐ Chris LiPuma
- ☐ Steve Maltais
- ☐ Guy Larose
- ☐ Steve Larouche
- ☐ Mark Lawrence
- ☐ Dean Melanson
- ☐ Bob Nardella
- ☐ Brian Noonan
- ☐ Robert Petrovicky
- ☐ Dan Plante
- ☐ Tom Tilley
- ☐ Wendell Young (G)
- ☐ Mascot Skates
- ☐ Wolves

'01 - 02

CHICAGO WOLVES / PERFORMANCE

Singles start at 75¢.

Card Size: 2 5/8" x 3 5/8"

Set (25 cards): $20
☐ Bryan Adams
☐ Zdenek Blatny
☐ Rob Brown
☐ Frédéric Cassivi (G)
☐ Jeff Dessner
☐ Dallas Eakins
☐ Garnet Exelby
☐ Kurtis Foster
☐ Darcy Hordichuk
☐ Derek MacKenzie
☐ Steve Maltais
☐ Norm Maracle (G)
☐ Bob Nardella
☐ Pasi Nurminen (G)
☐ Kamil Piros
☐ Dan Plante
☐ Brian Pothier
☐ Luke Sellars
☐ Ben Simon
☐ Jarrod Skalde
☐ Dan Snyder
☐ Brad Tapper
☐ J.P. Vigier
☐ Mike Weaver
☐ Mascot Skates

'02 - 03
CHICAGO WOLVES / LASALLE

Singles start at 75¢.
Card Size: 2 5/8" x 3 5/8"
Set (25 cards): $20
☐ Mascot Skates
☐ Zdenek Blatny
☐ Rob Brown
☐ Frédéric Cassivi (G)
☐ Joe DiPenta
☐ Dallas Eakins
☐ Garnet Exelby
☐ Jeff Farkas
☐ Kurtis Foster
☐ Simon Gamache
☐ Mark Hartigan
☐ Milan Hnilicka (G)
☐ Andreas Karlsson
☐ Francis Lessard
☐ Norm Maracle (G)
☐ Derek MacKenzie
☐ Kimil Piros
☐ Steve Maltais
☐ Kirill Safronov
☐ Luke Sellars
☐ Ben Simon
☐ Ryan Tobler
☐ Libor Ustrnul
☐ Jean-Pierre Vigier
☐ John Anderson

CINCINNATI CYCLONES

'91 - 92
CINCINNATI CYCLONES / 19-FOX, BELL

Singles start at 50¢.
Card Size: 2 3/8" x 3 1/2"
Set (25 cards): $12
☐ Dan Beaudette
☐ Steve Benoit, Trainer
☐ Steve Cadieux
☐ Craig Charron
☐ David Craievich
☐ Doug Dadswell (G)
☐ S. Desrosiers, Coach
☐ T. Ficorelli, Announcer
☐ Jeff Hogden
☐ Kevin Kerr
☐ Jaan Luik
☐ Scott Luik
☐ Chris Marshall
☐ Daryn McBride
☐ Doug Melnyk
☐ David Moore
☐ Tom Neziol
☐ Mark Romaine
☐ Jay Rose
☐ Martin St. Amour
☐ Kevin Scott
☐ Peter Schure
☐ Steve Shaunessy
☐ B. Stoughton, A. Coach
☐ Bobby Wallwork

'92 - 93
CINCINNATI CYCLONES / BELL

Singles start at 50¢.
Size: 2 1/2" x 3 1/2"
Set (30 cards): $12
☐ Bill Armstrong #27
☐ Ralph Barahona #16
☐ Steve Benoît, Trainer
☐ Mike Bodarchuk #14
☐ Craig Charron #7
☐ Todd Copeland #33
☐ Doug Dadswell #35 (G)
☐ Mike Dagenais #6
☐ Kevin Dean #20
☐ D. Desrosiers, Coach
☐ Chad Erickson #34 (G)
☐ Todd Flichel #3
☐ Alan Hepple #23
☐ Dennis Holland #18
☐ Sergei Kharin #15
☐ David Latta #29
☐ Jeff Madill #12
☐ Jon Morris #10
☐ Dean Morton #21
☐ Chris Nelson #2
☐ Darcy Norton #25
☐ Alex Ochoa, Trainer
☐ Howie Rosenblatt #24
☐ Scott Shaunessy #5
☐ B. Stoughton, A.Coach
☐ Mario Thyer #28
☐ Al Tuer #4
☐ T. Ficorelli, Announcer
☐ Wildman Walker, Ann.
☐ Mascot Mr. Cyclone

'93 - 94
CINCINNATI CYCLONES / BELL

Singles start at 50¢.
Set (32 cards): $12
☐ Doug Barrault
☐ Len Barrie
☐ Don Biggs
☐ Chris Cichocki
☐ Jason Cirone
☐ Dallas Eakins
☐ Daniel Gauthier
☐ Jeff Greenlaw
☐ Rick Hayward
☐ Gord Hynes
☐ Ian Kidd
☐ Marc Labelle
☐ Paul Lawless
☐ Jamie Leach
☐ Patrick Lebeau
☐ Ray LeBlanc
☐ Jamie Linden
☐ Jaroslav Nedved
☐ D'Arcy Norton
☐ E. (Pokey) Reddick (G)
☐ 21 Stéphane J.G. Richer
☐ 22 Jeff Serowik
☐ 23 Scott Shaunessy
☐ 24 Brad Smyth
☐ 25 Dennis Desrosiers
☐ 26 Richard Kromm
☐ 27 Wildman Walker
☐ 28 Mascot Mr. Cyclone
☐ 29 Mike Spilman
☐ 30 Steve Benoit
☐ 31 Terry Ficorelli
☐ Header Card/Checklist

'94 - 95
CINCINNATI CYCLONES

Singles start at 50¢.
Set (29 cards): $12
☐ Doug Barrault
☐ Chris Bergeron
☐ Don Biggs
☐ Bob Boughner
☐ Frédéric Chabot
☐ Chris Cichocki
☐ Jason Cirone
☐ Trevor Doyle
☐ Dallas Eakins
☐ Terry Ficorelli
☐ Ray Pack
☐ Dave Tomlinson
☐ Mascot Snowbird
☐ Radio Announcers
☐ Stéphane J.G. Richer
☐ Mike Stevens
☐ Marc Laniel
☐ Paul Lawless
☐ Jamie Linden
☐ Danny Lorenz
☐ Sean McCann
☐ Mark Mills
☐ Jeff Greenlaw
☐ Nick Kenney
☐ Don Jackson
☐ Marc Labelle
☐ Richard Kromm
☐ Yuri Krivokhija
☐ Sergei Kharin

'95 - 96
CINCINNATI CYCLONES / EDGE ICE

Singles start at 50¢.
Set (25 cards): $12
☐ Don Biggs
☐ Frédéric Chabot
☐ Chris Cichocki
☐ Chris Dahlquist
☐ Dale (Digger) DeGray
☐ Brian Dobbin
☐ Len Esau
☐ Scott Thomas
☐ Dave Tomlinson
☐ Jeff Wells
☐ Bob Wilkie
☐ Mascot Snowbird
☐ Ron Smith
☐ Paul Lawless
☐ Danny Lorenz
☐ Doug MacDonald
☐ Dave Marcinyshyn
☐ Mark Mills
☐ Jeff Greenlaw
☐ Todd Hawkins
☐ Al Hill
☐ Nick Kenney
☐ Duane Joyce
☐ Marc Labelle
☐ Chris Kontos

'96 - 97
CINCINNATI CYCLONES / SPLIT SECOND

Singles start at 50¢.
Size: 2 1/2" x 3 1/2"
Set (25 cards): $12
☐ Don Biggs #22
☐ Mike Casselman #17
☐ Chris Cichocki #33
☐ Ted Crowley #4
☐ Eric Dandenault #37
☐ Dale DeGray #51
☐ Jeff Greenlaw #29
☐ Todd Hawkins #12
☐ Al Hill, Asst.Coach
☐ Tony Horacek #24
☐ Duane Joyce #3
☐ Nick Kenney, Trainer
☐ Marc Laniel #26
☐ Paul Lawless #13
☐ Doug MacDonald #44
☐ Todd MacDonald #1 (G)
☐ Dave Marcinyshyn #27
☐ Mark Mills, Equipment
☐ Scott Morrow #28
☐ Myles O'Connor #6
☐ Geoff Sarjeant #31 (G)
☐ Ron Smith, Coach
☐ Scott Thomas #19
☐ Jeff Wells #5
☐ Mascot Snowbird

'97 - 98
CINCINNATI CYCLONES / BELL

Singles start at 50¢.
Set (23 cards): $12
☐ Don Biggs
☐ Paul Broten
☐ Mike Casselman
☐ Chris Cichocki
☐ Éric Dandenault
☐ Gilbert Dionne
☐ Jeff Greenlaw
☐ Todd Hawkins
☐ Burt Henderson
☐ Nick Kenney
☐ Marc Labelle
☐ Steven* King
☐ Doug MacDonald
☐ Todd MacDonald
☐ Pat MacLeod
☐ Mark Mills
☐ Scott Morrow
☐ Geoff Sarjeant
☐ Todd Simon
☐ Jeff Sirkka
☐ Ron Smith
☐ Jeff Wells
☐ David* Williams
☐ Mascot Snowbird

'98 - 99
CINCINNATI CYCLONES / BELL

Jani Hurme is one of the more expensive singles at $4.
Singles start at 50¢.
Set (30 cards): $15
☐ 1 Todd Hawkins
☐ 2 Kirk Nielsen
☐ 3 Ed Patterson
☐ 4 Fred Knipscheer
☐ 5 Doug MacDonald
☐ 6 Todd Simon
☐ 7 Phil Crowe
☐ 8 Gilbert Dionne
☐ 9 Scott Morrow
☐ 10 Rastislav Pavlikovsky
☐ 11 Jeff Shevalier
☐ 12 Kaspars Astashenko
☐ 13 Éric Dandenault
☐ 14 Burt Henderson
☐ 15 Chris Joseph
☐ 16 Pat MacLeod
☐ 17 Geoff Smith
☐ 18 Jeff Wells
☐ 19 Frédéric Cassivi
☐ 20 Jani Hurme (G)
☐ 21 Tom Nemeth
☐ 22 Olaf Kjenstadt
☐ 23 Team Photo
☐ 24 Ron Smith
☐ 25 Chris Cichocki
☐ 26 Scott MacPherson
☐ 27 Mark Mills
☐ 28 Nick Kenney
☐ 29 Mascot Snowbird
☐ 30 PHPA

'99 - 00
CINCINNATI CYCLONES / MULTI-AD SPORTS

Shane Willis is one of the more expensive singles at $5.
Singles start at 50¢.
Size: 2 1/2" x 3 1/2"
Set (26 cards): $15
☐ 1 Pat MacLeod
☐ 2 Nikos Tselios
☐ 3 Steve Bancroft
☐ 4 Greg Kuznik
☐ 5 Todd Simon
☐ 6 Craig MacDonald
☐ 7 Greg Koehler
☐ 8 Todd Hawkins
☐ 9 Stefan Ustorf
☐ 10 Mike Rucinski
☐ 11 Craig Adams
☐ 12 Ian MacNeil
☐ 13 Gilbert Dionne
☐ 14 Len Esau
☐ 15 Shane Willis
☐ 16 Gilbert Dionne
☐ 17 Mark Fitzpatrick (G)
☐ 18 Randy Petruk (G)
☐ 19 Dave Karpa
☐ 20 Eric Dandenault
☐ 21 Ron Smith
☐ 22 Chris Cichocki
☐ 23 Mark Mills
☐ 24 Nick Kenney
☐ 25 Mascot Snowbird
☐ 26 PHPA Web card

'00 - 01
CINCINNATI CYCLONES / MULTI-AD SPORTS

Erik Cole and Jaroslav Svoboda are the most expensive singles. Singles start at 50¢.
Size: 2 1/2" x 3 1/2"
Set (30 cards): $20
☐ 1 Nikos Tselios
☐ 2 Jeremiah McCarthy
☐ 3 Greg Kuznik

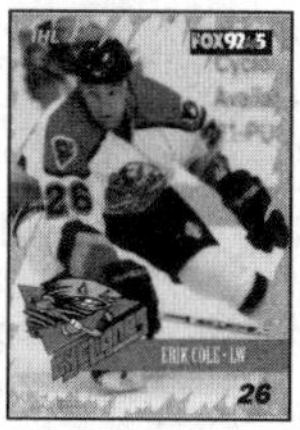

☐ 4 Byron Ritchie
☐ 5 Craig MacDonald
☐ 6 Greg Koehler
☐ 7 Stefan Ustorf
☐ 8 Jeff Heerema
☐ 9 Mike Rucinski
☐ 10 Ian MacNeil
☐ 11 Gilbert Dionne
☐ 12 Erik Cole
☐ 13 Reggie Berg
☐ 14 Jon Rohloff
☐ 15 Len Esau
☐ 16 Brian Felsner
☐ 17 Brad DeFauw
☐ 18 Harlan Pratt
☐ 19 Jaroslav Svoboda
☐ 20 J-M Pelletier (G)
☐ 21 Corey Hirsch (G)
☐ 22 Marc Magliarditi
☐ 23 Ron Smith
☐ 24 Mark Mills
☐ 25 Nick Kenney
☐ 26 Mascot Snowbird
☐ 27 GMC Zamboni
☐ 28 Cyclones team picture
☐ 29 The Firstar Center
☐ 30 PHPA.com

CINCINNATI MIGHTY DUCKS

'98 - 99
CINCINNATI MIGHTY DUCKS

Singles start at 75¢.
Set (29 cards): $20
☐ 1 Mascot Buster
☐ 2 Marc Andreozzi
☐ 3 Gary Linquist
☐ 4 John Walton
☐ 5 Eddie Johnstone
☐ 6 Moe Mantha
☐ 7 Frank Banham
☐ 8 Mike Leclerc
☐ 9 Byron Briske
☐ 10 Éric Lecompte
☐ 11 Terran Sandwith
☐ 12 Jamie Ram (G)
☐ 13 Craig Reichert
☐ 14 Joel Kwiatkowski
☐ 15 Mike Crowley
☐ 16 Matt Loen
☐ 17 Jeremy Stevenson
☐ 18 Dan Trebil
☐ 19 Bob Wren
☐ 20 Lloyd Shaw
☐ 21 Igor Nikulin
☐ 22 Jeff Winter
☐ 23 Tony Mohagen
☐ 24 Tony Tuzzolino
☐ 25 Peter LeBoutilier
☐ 26 Tom Askey (G)
☐ 27 Marc Chouinard
☐ 28 Scott Ferguson
☐ 29 PHPA

'99 - 00
CINCINNATI MIGHTY DUCKS / ARNOLD

Vitaly Vishnevski is one of the more expensive singles at $3.
Singles start at 75¢.
Set (32 cards): $20
☐ 1 Ducks / Wings
☐ 2 Moe Mantha
☐ 3 Jason Payne
☐ 4 Antti Aalto
☐ 4 Jeff Nielsen
☐ 4 Ruslan Salei
☐ 5 Joel Kwiatkowski
☐ 6 Lloyd Shaw
☐ 7 Philippe Audet
☐ 8 Aren Miller
☐ 9 Dan Trebil
☐ 10 Rastislav Pavlikovsky
☐ 11 Frank Banham
☐ 12 Scott Ferguson
☐ 13 Maxim Balmockhnykh
☐ 14 Darryl Laplante
☐ 15 Johan Davidsson
☐ 16 Peter Leboutillier
☐ 17 Jesse Wallin
☐ 18 Alexandre Jacques
☐ 19 B.J. Young
☐ 20 Ed Johnstone
☐ 21 Ryan Hoople
☐ 22 Matt Cullen
☐ 22 Mike Leclerc
☐ 22 Pavel Trnka
☐ 23 Mascot Buster
☐ 24 Jeremy Stevenson
☐ 25 Jay Legault
☐ 26 Marc Chouinard
☐ 27 Torrey DiRoberto
☐ 28 Maxim Kuznetsov
☐ 29 Shane Hnidy
☐ 30 Vitaly Vishnevski
☐ 31 Bob Wren
☐ 32 Gregg Naumenko (G)

'01 - 02
CINCINNATI MIGHTY DUCKS / ARNOLD

Singles start at 75¢.
Card Size: 2 1/2" x 3 1/2"
Set (27 cards): $20
☐ Sean Avery
☐ Maxim Balmochnykh
☐ Drew Bannister
☐ Ryan Barnes
☐ Travis Brigley
☐ Aris Brimanis
☐ Steve Brûlé
☐ Ilja Bryzgalov (G)
☐ Garrett Burnett
☐ Yuri Butsayev
☐ Josh DeWolf
☐ Jason Elliott
☐ Ryan Gaucher
☐ Andy McDonald
☐ Antti-Jussi Niemi
☐ Timo Pärssinen
☐ Peter Podhradsky
☐ Bruce Richardson
☐ Bert Robertsson
☐ David Roche
☐ Jonas Rönnqvist
☐ Jarrett Smith
☐ Brian White
☐ Jason Williams
☐ Dwayne Zinger
☐ Mike Babcock, Coach
☐ Kevin Kaminski, A.Coach
☐ Mascot Buster the Duck

CLEVELAND BARONS

'01 - 02
CLEVELAND BARONS

Singles start at 75¢.
Set (24): $20
☐ Steve Bancroft
☐ Matt Carkner
☐ Jonathan Cheechoo
☐ Adam Colagiacomo
☐ Mike Craig
☐ Rob Davison
☐ Jesse Fibiger
☐ Hannes Hyvonen
☐ Jeff Jillson
☐ Seamus Kotyk
☐ Ryan Kraft
☐ Eric Laplante
☐ Lynn Loyns
☐ Andy Lundholm
☐ Graig Mischler
☐ Robert Mulick
☐ Adam Nittel
☐ Joel Prpic
☐ Brandon Smith
☐ Vesa Toskala
☐ Chad Wiseman
☐ Miroslav Zalesak
☐ Roy Sommer
☐ Nick Fotiu

CLEVELAND LUMBERJACKS

'92 - 93
CLEVELAND LUMBERJACKS / WKNR, RUSTERMINATOR

Singles start at 50¢.
Card Size: 2 3/8" x 3 1/2"
Set (25 cards): $12
☐ 1 Lumberjacks
☐ 2 Larry Gordon, G.M.
☐ 3 Paul Laus
☐ 4 Travis Thiessen
☐ 5 Phil Russell, Coach
☐ 6 Gilbert Delorme
☐ 7 Jamie Heward
☐ 8 Greg Andrusak
☐ 9 David Quinn
☐ 10 Perry Ganchar
☐ 11 George Zajankala
☐ 12 Todd Nelson
☐ 13 Dave Michayluk
☐ 14 Bruce Racine (G)
☐ 15 Rob Dopson (G)
☐ 16 Bert Godin (G)
☐ 17 Ed Patterson
☐ 18 Justin Duberman
☐ 19 Sandy Smith
☐ 20 Jason Smart
☐ 21 Ken Priestlay
☐ 22 Daniel Gauthier
☐ 23 Robert Melanson
☐ 24 Mark Major
☐ 25 Paul Dyck

'93 - 94
CLEVELAND LUMBERJACKS / WMMS, PEAK

Singles start at 50¢.
Card Size: 2 3/8" x 3 1/2"
Set (21 cards): $12
☐ Greg Andrusak
☐ Steve Bancroft
☐ Jamie Black
☐ Jock Callander
☐ Mike Dagenais
☐ Gilbert Delorme
☐ Rob Dopson (G)
☐ Justin Duberman
☐ Paul Dyck
☐ Perry Ganchar
☐ Todd Hawkins
☐ Jamie Heward
☐ Ladislav Karabin
☐ Dave Michayluk
☐ Pat Neaton
☐ Rick Paterson, Coach
☐ Ed Patterson
☐ Olie Sundstrom (G)
☐ Chris Tamer
☐ Travis Thiessen
☐ Leonid Toropchenko

'95 - 96
CLEVELAND LUMBERJACKS / HUNTINGTON BANK

Patrick Lalime is one of the more expensive at $8. Singles start at 50¢.
Card Size: 2 3/8" x 3 1/2"
Set (24 cards): $20
☐ Peter Allen
☐ Bill Armstrong
☐ Len Barrie
☐ Dave Baseggio
☐ Oleg Belov
☐ Drake Berehowsky
☐ Stefan Bergkvist
☐ Jock Callander
☐ Jeff Christian
☐ Philippe DeRouville (G)
☐ Corey Foster
☐ Perry Ganchar
☐ Victor Gervais
☐ Rick Hayward
☐ Patrick Lalime (G)
☐ Brad Laur
☐ Dave McLlwain
☐ Dave Michayluk
☐ Mark Osborne
☐ Rick Paterson
☐ Domenic Pittis
☐ Ryan Savoia
☐ Mike Stevens
☐ Lumberjacks cards

'96 - 97
CLEVELAND LUMBERJACKS / MULTI-AD SERVICES

Patrick Lalime ($6) and Jan Hrdina ($4) are the most expenisve singles.Singles start at 50¢.
Set (30 cards): $20
☐ Checklist
☐ Peter Allen
☐ Bill Armstrong
☐ Serge Aubin
☐ Stefan Bergkvist
☐ Brian Bonin
☐ Sven Butenschon
☐ Jock Callander
☐ Jeff Christian
☐ Rusty Fitzgerald
☐ Corey Foster
☐ Perry Ganchar, A.Coach
☐ Rick Hayward
☐ Jan Hrdina
☐ Patrick Lalime (G)
☐ Lane Lambert
☐ Brad Lauer
☐ Dave McLlwain
☐ Dave Michayluk
☐ Ian Moran
☐ Mark Osborne
☐ Jim Paek
☐ Richard Park
☐ Rick Paterson, Coach
☐ Ed Patterson
☐ Mike Tamburro
☐ Derek Wilkinson
☐ Mascot Buzz
☐ Heritage Night
☐ PHPA Website Card

'97 - 98
CLEVELAND LUMBERJACKS / NABISCO

Martin St-Louis is one of the more expensive singles at $5.
Singles start at 50¢.
Set (30 cards): $15
☐ Dave Baseggio
☐ Stefan Bergkvist
☐ Jock Callander
☐ Mark Cornforth
☐ John Craighead
☐ Joe Dziedzic
☐ Vadim Epantchisev
☐ Rusty Fitzgerald
☐ Brett Harkins
☐ Rick Hayward
☐ Pat Jablonski (G)
☐ Alexei Krivchenkov
☐ Lane Lambert
☐ Brad Lauer
☐ Chris Longo
☐ Jason McBain
☐ Ryan Mougenel
☐ Jim Paek
☐ Rob Pearson
☐ Eric Perrin
☐ Martin St. Louis
☐ Mike Tamburro
☐ Darren Wetherill
☐ Derek Wilkinson (G)
☐ Perry Ganchar, Coach
☐ Mark Osborne, A.Coach
☐ M. St-Louis/ E. Perrin
☐ Team Photo
☐ Mascot Buzz
☐ PHPA Website card

'98 - 99
CLEVELAND LUMBERJACKS

Zac Bierk and Corey Schwab are the most expensive singles at $1.50 each. Singles start at 50¢.

Set (24 cards): $10
☐ Header Card
☐ Perry Ganchar, Coach
☐ Dave Baseggio
☐ Jesse Bélanger
☐ Karel Betik
☐ Zac Bierk (G)
☐ Jason Bonsignore
☐ Jock Callander
☐ John Cullen
☐ Xavier Delisle
☐ Brett Harkins
☐ Lane Lambert
☐ Mario Larocque
☐ Eric Lavigne
☐ Chris Longo
☐ Jim Paek
☐ Eduard Pershin
☐ Brent Peterson
☐ Jason Ruff
☐ Corey Schwab (G)
☐ Andrei Skopintsev
☐ Corey Spring
☐ Derek Wilkinson (G)
☐ Mascot Buzz

'99 - 00

CLEVELAND LUMBERJACKS / THE PEAK

Singles start at 50¢.
Set (24 cards): $18
☐ Radim Bicanek
☐ Kyle Calder
☐ Jock Callander
☐ Jeff Christian
☐ Ted Crowley
☐ Casey Hankinson
☐ Brett Harkins
☐ Chris Herperger
☐ Ty Jones
☐ Marc Lamothe
☐ Eric Lavigne
☐ Chris Longo
☐ Cleveland Lumberjacks
☐ Evgeni Nabokov (G)
☐ Jim Paek
☐ Jeff Paul
☐ Nathan Perrott
☐ Geoff Peters
☐ Todd Rohloff
☐ Remi Royer
☐ Reid Simpson
☐ Dmitri Tolkunov
☐ Todd White
☐ Mascot Buzz

'00 - 01

CLEVELAND LUMBERJACKS / THE PEAK

Derek Gustafson is one of the more expensive singles. Singles start at 50¢.
Set (25 cards): $15
☐ 1 Christian Matte
☐ 2 Brian Bonin
☐ 3 Mike Matteucci
☐ 4 Eric Charron
☐ 5 Nick Naumenko
☐ 6 Brett McLean
☐ 7 Pavel Patera
☐ 8 Chris Longo
☐ 9 Ian Herbers
☐ 10 Pascal Dupuis
☐ 11 Kai Nurminen
☐ 12 David Brumby
☐ 13 Zac Bierk (G)
☐ 14 Jonathon Shocke
☐ 15 Darryl Laplante
☐ 16 J-J Daigneault
☐ 17 Garrett Burnett
☐ 18 Chris Armstrong
☐ 19 Richard Park
☐ 20 Todd McLellan
☐ 21 Jock Callander
☐ 22 Ray Schultz
☐ 23 Steve Aronson
☐ 24 D. Gustafson (G)
☐ 25 Mascot Buzz

COLORADO GOLD KINGS

'99 - 00

COLORADO GOLD KINGS

Singles start at 50¢.
Set (26 cards): $12
☐ Travis Thiessen
☐ R.J. Enga
☐ Tom Perry
☐ Corey Lyons
☐ Bogdan Rudenko
☐ Don Lester
☐ Stéphane Madore
☐ Steve Dowhy
☐ Greg Eisler
☐ Jean-François Picard
☐ Mascot King Midas
☐ Steve Vézina
☐ Kevin McKinnon
☐ Craig Lyons
☐ Aaron Schweitzer
☐ Carl LeBlanc
☐ Daniel Olers
☐ Dean Ewen
☐ Frederik Beaubien
☐ Kirk Tomlinson
☐ Wade Fennig
☐ Kristoffer Eriksson
☐ Rob McCaig
☐ Greg Gatto
☐ Gold Kings
☐ Sponsor Taco Bell

COLUMBUS CHECKERS

'67 - 68

COLUMBUS CHECKERS

These cards feature black and white photography and a facsimile signature. Singles start at $5.
Size: 8 3/4" x 10 3/4"
Set (16 cards): $60
☐ Moe Bartoli
☐ Bill Bond
☐ Serge Boudreault
☐ Gord Dibley (G)
☐ Bret Fizzell
☐ Chuck Kelly
☐ Ted Leboda
☐ Nelson Leclair
☐ R. Paquette
☐ Dick Proceviat
☐ Hartley Stakowski
☐ Ken Sutvla
☐ Nelson Tremblay
☐ Jack Turner
☐ Al White
☐ Team Photo

'69

COLUMBUS CHECKERS

These cards feature black and white photography and the player's name at the bottom of the photo. Singles start at $5.
Size: 4" x 7 1/4"
Set (16 cards): $60
☐ John Bailey
☐ Moe Bartoli
☐ Kerry Bond
☐ André Daoust (G)
☐ Bert Fizzell
☐ Marcel Goudreau
☐ Jim Graham
☐ Paul Jackson
☐ Ken Laidlaw
☐ Noel Lirette
☐ Gary Longman
☐ Garry MacMillan
☐ Gary Mork
☐ Matt Thorp (G)
☐ Jack Turner
☐ Al White

DAYTON BOMBERS

'92 - 93

DAYTON BOMBERS / WTUE 104.7

Darren Langdon is one of the more expensive singles at $4. Singles start at 50¢.
Card Size: 2 1/2" x 3 1/2"
Set (21 cards): $12
☐ Steve Bogoyevac
☐ Darren Colbourne
☐ Derek Crawford
☐ Derek Donald
☐ Ray Edwards
☐ Doug Evans
☐ Sandy Galuppo
☐ Shayne Green
☐ Rod Houck
☐ Peter Kasowski
☐ Steve Kerrigan
☐ Frank Kovacs
☐ Darren Langdon
☐ Denis Larocque
☐ Darwin MacPherson
☐ Tom Nemeth
☐ Claude Noel
☐ Tony Peters
☐ Marshall Phillip
☐ Mike Reier
☐ Steve Wilson

'93 - 94

DAYTON BOMBERS / WTUE 104.7

Singles start at 50¢.
Card Size: 2 1/2" x 3 1/2"
Set (18 cards): $10
☐ 1 Checklist
☐ 2 Jeff Levy
☐ 3 Steve Wilson
☐ 4 Jason Downey
☐ 5 Jim Peters
☐ 6 Ondrej Kriz
☐ 7 Steve Bogoyevac
☐ 8 Jason Disiewich
☐ 9 Marc Savard
☐ 10 Dan O'Shea
☐ 11 Tom Nemeth
☐ 12 Guy Prince
☐ 13 Ray Edwards
☐ 14 Sergei Kharin
☐ 15 Derek Donald
☐ 16 Darwin McPherson
☐ 17 Jeff Stolp
☐ 18 Mascot Adam Bomber

'94 - 95

DAYTON BOMBERS

Singles start at 50¢.
Card Size: 2 1/2" x 3 1/2"
Set (24 cards): $10
☐ 1 Checklist
☐ 2 Paul Taylor
☐ 3 Steve Wilson
☐ 4 Jason Downey
☐ 5 Craig Charron
☐ 6 Jim Lessard
☐ 7 Karson Karbel
☐ 8 Jamie Steer
☐ 9 Rob Hartnell
☐ 10 Mike Doers
☐ 11 Sean Gagnon
☐ 12 Kevin Brown
☐ 13 John Brill
☐ 14 Dean Fedorchuk
☐ 15 Tony Gruba
☐ 16 Steve Lingren
☐ 17 Brandon Smith
☐ 18 Jeff Stolp
☐ 19 Mike Vandeberghe
☐ 20 Jim Playfair
☐ 21 Action card
☐ 22 Jamie Steer
☐ 23 Steve Wilson
☐ 24 Jeff Stolp

'95 - 96

DAYTON BOMBERS

Singles start at 50¢.
Card Size: 5" x 7"
Sponsor: None
Set (32 cards): $10
☐ Paul Andrea
☐ Brent Brekke
☐ John Brill
☐ Kevin Brown
☐ Jeff Buckley
☐ Greg Burke
☐ Jason Downey
☐ Sean Gagnon
☐ Dwayne Gylywoychuk
☐ Derek Herlofsky
☐ Chris Johnston
☐ Sergei Kharin
☐ Steve Lingren
☐ Matt McElwee
☐ Colin Miller
☐ Mike Murray
☐ Mike Naylor
☐ Sean Ortiz
☐ Rob Peters
☐ Jeff Petric
☐ Jim Playfair
☐ Nick Poole
☐ Brian Renfrew
☐ Steve Roberts
☐ Ted Russell
☐ Jeremy Stasiuk
☐ George Zajankala
☐ Mascot Adam Bomber
☐ AS: Steve Lingren
☐ AS: Jim Playfair
☐ Sean Gagnon
☐ Sergei Kharin

'96 - 97

DAYTON BOMBERS / WTUE 104.7

Singles start at 50¢.
Set (24 cards): $10
☐ 1 Steve Roberts
☐ 2 Chris Sullivan
☐ 3 Steve Lingren
☐ 4 Jordan Shields
☐ 5 Ildar Yubin
☐ 6 Dwight Parrish
☐ 7 Brian Ridolfi
☐ 8 Jordan Willis
☐ 9 Dale Hooper
☐ 10 Will Clarke
☐ 11 Tavis Morrison
☐ 12 Trent Schachle
☐ 13 John Emmons
☐ 14 Sam McKenney
☐ 15 Bryan Richardson
☐ 16 Ryan Gillis
☐ 17 Marty Flichel
☐ 18 Jason Downey
☐ 19 Troy Christensen
☐ 20 Derek Herlofsky
☐ 21 Sal Manganaro
☐ 22 Tom Nemeth
☐ 23 Evgeny Ryabchikov
☐ 24 Colin Miller

'98 - 99

DAYTON BOMBERS / EBK SPORTS

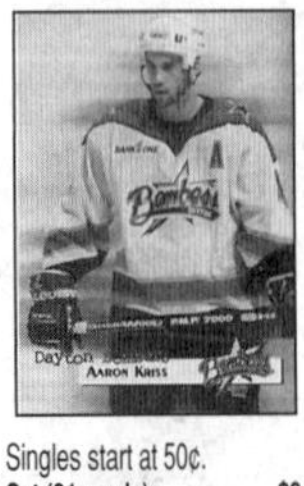

Singles start at 50¢.
Set (21 cards): $9
☐ 1 Frédéric Bouchard
☐ 2 Aaron Kriss
☐ 3 Brian Secord
☐ 4 Colin Miller
☐ 5 Jamie Ling
☐ 6 Bobby" Brown
☐ 7 Tom Nemeth
☐ 8 Brian Ridolfi
☐ 9 Travis Dillabough
☐ 10 Justin Krall
☐ 11 Dan Hendrickson
☐ 12 Ed Gingher
☐ 13 Brian Regan
☐ 14 Trevor Koenig
☐ 15 Greg Ireland
☐ 16 C. Miller / Nemeth
☐ 17 Mascot Bucky
☐ 18 Brandon Sugden
☐ 19 Norman Dezainde
☐ 20 Kiley Hill
☐ Checklist

'98 - 99

DAYTON BOMBERS / SPLIT SECOND

Singles start at 50¢.
Set (21 cards): $9
☐ John Beaulieu
☐ Frédéric Bouchard
☐ Bobby" Brown
☐ Dale Coulthard
☐ Norman Dezainde
☐ Travis Dillabough
☐ Ryan Furness
☐ Dan Hendrickson
☐ Greg Ireland
☐ Aaron Kriss
☐ Justin Krall
☐ Trevor Koenig
☐ Jamie Ling
☐ Jim Logan
☐ Colin Miller
☐ Tom Nemeth
☐ Brian Regan
☐ Brian Ridolfi
☐ Brian Secord
☐ Lee Stieg
☐ Larry Thornton
☐ Chris Wismer
☐ Bombers Team Photo
☐ Kerrigan & Christopher
☐ Mascot Buddy

DAYTON ICE BANDITS

'96 - 97

DAYTON ICE BANDITS / MULTI-AD SERVICES

Singles start at 50¢.
Size: 2 1/2" x 3 1/2"
Set (29 cards): $10
☐ 1 Checklist
☐ 2 Jesse Austin
☐ 3 Mike Bajurny
☐ 4 Dan Belisle
☐ 5 Dan Carter
☐ 6 Cosmo Clarke
☐ 7 Bob Clouston
☐ 8 Tom Colasanto
☐ 9 Brad Cook
☐ 10 Richard Fatrola
☐ 11 Jack Greig
☐ 12 Kelly Melton
☐ 13 Andrew Plumb
☐ 14 Brian Renfrew
☐ 15 Bobby Rapoza
☐ 16 Jacque Rodrigue
☐ 17 Fred Scott
☐ 18 Troy Stevens
☐ 19 Larry Thornton
☐ 20 Mike Thornton
☐ 21 Scott Vettraino
☐ 22 Marty Wells
☐ 23 Kevin Young
☐ 24 Mascot The Phantom
☐ 25 The Famous Chicken
☐ 26 WTUE Employees
☐ 27 WTUE Employees
☐ 28 WTUE Employees
☐ 29 WTUE Employees

DES MOINES BUCCANEERS

'99 - 00

DES MOINES BUCCANEERS / ROOX SPORTS

Singles start at 50¢.
Card Size: 2 1/2" x 3 1/2"
Set (24 cards): $9
☐ 1 Dominic Torretti
☐ 2 Felipe Larranaga
☐ 3 Paul Baumgartner
☐ 4 Nathan Berry
☐ 5 Matt Weber
☐ 6 Troy Riddle
☐ 7 Nick Dimella
☐ 8 Jesse Lane
☐ 9 Peter Sejna
☐ 10 Landon Bathe
☐ 11 Travis Doan
☐ 12 Mark Murphy
☐ 13 Rob Novak
☐ 14 Alex Kim
☐ 15 Wade Chiodo
☐ 16 Jerrid Reinholz
☐ 17 Miroslav Durak
☐ 18 Ryan Kirchhoff
☐ 19 Mark Mullen
☐ 20 Ryan Bennett
☐ 21 Jeff Ronkoske
☐ 22 Mike Mantua
☐ 23 Paul Morrissey
☐ 24 Mascot Winger

DETROIT VIPERS

'96 - 97

DETROIT VIPERS / AMERITECH

Segei Samsonov is the most expensive single at $15. Singles start at 50¢.
Set (20 cards): $30
☐ 1 Peter Ciavaglia
☐ 2 Bob Jay
☐ 3 Brad Shaw
☐ 4 Stan Drulia
☐ 5 Sergei Samsonov
☐ 6 Rich Parent (G)
☐ 7 Todd Simon
☐ 8 Ian Herbers
☐ 9 Yvon Corriveau
☐ 10 Dan Kesa
☐ 11 Mike Donnelly
☐ 12 Wayne Presley
☐ 13 Jeff Reese (G)
☐ 14 Darren Banks
☐ 15 Jeff Parrott
☐ 16 Phil Crowe
☐ 17 Patrice Tardif
☐ 18 Phil Von Stefenelli
☐ 19 Steve Walker
☐ 20 Len Esau

'97 - 98

DETROIT VIPERS / AMERITECH

This series was handed out over 20 home games. Johan Hedberg is one of the more expensive singles. Singles start at 50¢.
Set (20 cards): $18
☐ 1 Peter Ciavaglia
☐ 2 Phil Crowe
☐ 3 Dan Kesa
☐ 4 Stan Drulia
☐ 5 Bob Jay
☐ 6 Ian Herbers
☐ 7 Brad Shaw
☐ 8 Steve Walker
☐ 9 Trent McCleary
☐ 10 Scott Thomas
☐ 11 Johan Hedberg (G)
☐ 12 Jimmy Carson
☐ 13 Clayton Beddoes
☐ 14 Tim Murray
☐ 15 John Gruden
☐ 16 Jeff Reese (G)
☐ 17 Keith Aldridge
☐ 18 Brent Fedyk
☐ 19 Darren Banks
☐ 20 Mascot Vipe-Bear

'98 - 99

DETROIT VIPERS / EBK SPORTS

Jani Hurme and Kevin Weekes are two of the more expensive singles at $2-4 each. Singles start at 50¢.
Set (26 cards): $15
☐ 1 Keith Aldridge
☐ 2 Brad Shaw
☐ 3 Tim Murray
☐ 4 Brian Felsner
☐ 5 Peter Ciavaglia
☐ 6 Andy Bezeau
☐ 7 Mike Gaffney
☐ 8 Phil Crowe
☐ 9 John Emmons
☐ 10 Kory Karlander
☐ 11 Mike Prokopec
☐ 12 Stan Drulia
☐ 13 Bob Jay
☐ 14 Darren Banks
☐ 15 Jeff Whittle
☐ 16 Steve Walker
☐ 17 Ian Herbers
☐ 18 Jani Hurme (G)
☐ 19 John Gruden
☐ 20 Kevin Weekes (G)
☐ 21 Mascot Vipe-Bear
☐ 22 Steve Ludzik
☐ 23 John Blum
☐ 24 Dave Boyer
☐ 25 Mike Astalos
☐ 26 Checklist

'99 - 00

DETROIT VIPERS / OMNIPOINT

Singles start at 50¢.
Set (15 cards): $12
☐ Dave Baseggio
☐ Andy Bezeau
☐ Zac Bierk (G)
☐ Peter Ciavaglia
☐ Nils Ekman
☐ Matt Elich
☐ Kyle Freadrich
☐ Kyle Kos
☐ Mario Larocque
☐ Dale Rominski
☐ Jeff Shevalier
☐ Samuel St-Pierre
☐ Alex Stojanov
☐ Tim Thomas
☐ Steve Walker

ERIE PANTHERS

'94 - 95

ERIE PANTHERS / C&J SPORTS

Singles start at 50¢.
Card Size: 2 1/2" x 3 1/2"
Set (20 cards): $8
☐ Cam Brown
☐ S. Charbonneau
☐ Scott Burfoot
☐ Ian DeCorby
☐ Vassili Demin
☐ Larry Empey
☐ Vern Guetens (G)
☐ Ron Hansis, Coach
☐ Brad Harrison
☐ Andrei Kozlov
☐ P. Laughlin, Trainer
☐ Kevin McKinnon
☐ Francis Ouellette (G)
☐ Justin Peca
☐ V. Polikarkin
☐ Barry Smith, Coach
☐ Jason Smith
☐ Sergei Stas
☐ Chris Tschupp
☐ Checklist

FLINT GENERALS

'93 - 94

FLINT GENERALS / RISING STAR

Singles start at 50¢.
Set (20 cards): $8
☐ 1 Header Card
☐ 2 Brent Stickney
☐ 3 Brett Strot
☐ 4 Brian Sakic
☐ 5 Chris O'Rourke
☐ 6 Dan Elsener
☐ 7 Darcy Austin
☐ 8 Dominic Niro
☐ 9 Jim Duhart
☐ 10 John Heasty
☐ 11 Keith Whitmore
☐ 12 Ken Spangler
☐ 13 Kevin Kerr
☐ 14 Larry Bernard
☐ 15 Lorne Knauft
☐ 16 Marc Vachon
☐ 17 Mark Gowens
☐ 18 Peter Horachek
☐ 19 Stéphane Brochu
☐ 20 Todd Humphrey

'94 - 95

FLINT GENERALS

Singles start at 50¢.
Set (24 cards): $9
☐ Kevin Barrett
☐ Larry Bernard
☐ Ken Blum
☐ Stéphane Brochu
☐ Keith Carney
☐ Ryan Douglas
☐ Jim Duhart
☐ Ray Gallagher
☐ Mark Gowens
☐ Keith Whitmore
☐ Jeff Whittle
☐ Checklist
☐ Kyle Reeves
☐ Brian Sakic
☐ Stefan Simoes
☐ Ken Spangler
☐ Petr Leska
☐ Stan Matwijiw
☐ Glen Mears
☐ Peter Horachek
☐ Todd Humphrey
☐ Doug Jones
☐ Fredrik Jax
☐ Kevin Kerr

'95 - 96

FLINT GENERALS / BOOSTER CLUB

Set (25 cards): $10
☐ 1 Erin Whitten
☐ 2 Kevin Kerr
☐ 3 Sverre Sears
☐ 4 Scott Burfoot
☐ 5 John Batten
☐ 6 Chad Grills
☐ 7 Lady Generals
☐ 8 Mascot General Rally
☐ 9 Rob Nichols
☐ 10 Mikhail Nemirovsky
☐ 11 Robin Bouchard
☐ 12 D. Grandmaison
☐ 13 Andrei Mezin
☐ 14 Steve Beadle
☐ 15 Darryl LaFrance
☐ 16 Chris Gotziaman
☐ 17 Gerry St-Cyr
☐ 18 Derek Knorr
☐ 19 Chris Gordon
☐ 20 Brett MacDonald
☐ 21 Brian Sakic
☐ 22 Jamie Hearn
☐ 23 Jeff Whittle
☐ 24 Stéphane Brochu
☐ 25 Jim Duhart

'96 - 97

FLINT GENERALS / DORT FEDERAL CREDIT

Singles start at 50¢.
Set (26 cards): $8
☐ Steve Beadle
☐ Pascal Bélanger
☐ Robin Bouchard
☐ Stéphane Brochu
☐ Neil Eisenhut
☐ Nick Forbes
☐ Igor Galkin
☐ Jason Glover
☐ Chad Grills
☐ John Heasty
☐ Lorne Knauft
☐ Kevin Kerr
☐ Karl Lawson
☐ Brett MacDonald
☐ Andrei Mezin

☐ Rob Nichols
☐ Jason Payne
☐ Jason Ralph
☐ Dmitri Rodine
☐ Zdenek Sikl
☐ Ken Spangler
☐ Matt Weder
☐ Jeff Whittle
☐ Ross Wilson
☐ Checklist
☐ Generals
☐ Generals
☐ Mascot General Rally

'98 - 99
FLINT GENERALS / DORT FEDERAL CREDIT

Singles start at 50¢.
Set (22 cards): $8

☐ 1 Generals
☐ 2 Chad Grills
☐ 3 Jason Payne
☐ 4 Jeremy Sladovnik
☐ 5 Stéphane Brochu
☐ 6 Jeff Whittle
☐ 7 Rob Nichols
☐ 8 Brian Sakic
☐ 9 Checklist
☐ 10 Nick Forbes
☐ 11 Mike Bondy
☐ 12 Peter Ambroziak
☐ 13 Luciano Nasato
☐ 14 Mikhail Nemirovsky
☐ 15 Bobby Reynolds
☐ 16 Generals
☐ 17 Lorne Knauft
☐ 18 Rob Laurie
☐ 19 Ross** Wilson
☐ 20 Jason Glover
☐ 21 Brett MacDonald
☐ 22 Kahlil Thomas

FLINT SPIRITS

'87 - 88
FLINT SPIRITS

John Cullen is one of the more expensive singles at $3. Singles start at 50¢.
Card Size: 2 1/2" x 3 1/2"
Set (20 cards): $10

☐ Mark Chitaroni
☐ John Cullen
☐ Bob Fleming
☐ Keith Gretzky
☐ Todd Hawkins
☐ Mike Hoffman
☐ Curtis Hunt
☐ Dwaine Hutton
☐ Trent Kaese
☐ Tom Karalis
☐ Ray LeBlanc (G)
☐ Darren Lowe
☐ Brett MacDonald
☐ Chris McSorley
☐ Mike Mersch
☐ Victor Posa
☐ Kevin Schamehorn
☐ Ron Stern
☐ Don Waddell
☐ Dan Woodley

1988 - 89 SPIRITS

Singles start at 50¢.
Card Size: 2 1/2" x 3 1/2"
Sponsor: None
Set (22 cards): $12

☐ Dean Anderson
☐ Rob Bryden
☐ John Devereaux
☐ Stéphane Giguère
☐ Steve Harrison
☐ Yves Heroux
☐ Mike Hoffman
☐ Peter Horachek
☐ Guy Jacob
☐ Bob Kennedy
☐ Gary Kruzich (G)
☐ Lonnie Loach
☐ Brett MacDonald
☐ Mike MacWilliam
☐ Moe Mansi
☐ Mike Mersch
☐ Michel Mongeau
☐ Ken Spangler
☐ Mark Vichorek
☐ Troy Vollhoffer
☐ Don Waddell
☐ Harrison/ Mersch/ Hoffman

FLORIDA EVERBLADES

'98 - 99
FLORIDA EVERBLADES / MULTI-AD SPORTS

Singles start at 50¢.
Set (27 cards): $8

☐ 1 Brett Bruininks
☐ 2 Matt Brush
☐ 3 Nick Checco
☐ 4 Matt Demarski
☐ 5 Sergei Fedotov
☐ 6 Tim Ferguson
☐ 7 Hugh Hamilton
☐ 8 Mike Jickling
☐ 9 Greg Koehler
☐ 10 Greg Kuznik
☐ 11 Dane Litke
☐ 12 Marc Magliarditi
☐ 13 Kevin McDonald
☐ 14 Pat Mikesch
☐ 15 Randy Petruk (G)
☐ 16 Jason Prokepetz
☐ 17 Dan Reimann
☐ 18 Eric Ricard
☐ 19 Eric Rud
☐ 20 Steve Tardif
☐ 21 Andrew Taylor
☐ 22 P.K. O'Handley
☐ 23 Josh Penn
☐ 24 Bob Ferguson
☐ 25 Mascot Swampee
☐ 26 PHPA
☐ 27 Todd Wisocki

'99 - 00
FLORIDA EVERBLADES / ROOX SPORTS

Singles start at 50¢.
Card Size: 2 1/2" x 3 1/2"
Set (26 cards): $10

☐ Reggie Berg
☐ Tom Buckley
☐ Joe Cardarelli
☐ Brent Cullaton
☐ Matt Demarski
☐ Bob Ferguson
☐ Tim Ferguson
☐ Hugh Hamilton
☐ Peter Kasper
☐ Ty Jones
☐ Greg Kuznik
☐ Terry Lindgren
☐ Dane Litke
☐ Andy MacIntyre
☐ Marc Magliarditi
☐ Jeff Maund
☐ Steve Moffatt
☐ Jason Morgan
☐ P.K. O'Handley
☐ Cellular One
☐ Harlan Pratt
☐ Jason Prokopetz
☐ Eric Rud
☐ Steve Tardif
☐ John Varga
☐ Mascot Swampy

'00 - 01
FLORIDA EVERBLADES / ROOX SPORTS

Singles start at 50¢.
Card Size: 2 1/2" x 3 1/2"
Set (26 cards): $10

☐ 1 Marc Magliarditi
☐ 2 Sandy Cohen
☐ 3 Bob Ferguson, Coach
☐ 4 John Jennings, Eq.Mgr.
☐ 5 Todd Wisocki, Trainer
☐ 6 P.O'Handley, A.Coach
☐ 7 Reggie Berg
☐ 8 Darrell Hay
☐ 9 Brent Pope
☐ 10 Brent McDonald
☐ 11 Devin Hartnell
☐ 12 Hugh Hamilton
☐ 13 Peter Hogan
☐ 14 Terry Lindgren
☐ 15 Mike Jickling
☐ 16 Randy Copley
☐ 17 Sean Blanchard
☐ 18 David Vallieres
☐ 19 Jason Metcalfe
☐ 20 Jason Morgan
☐ 21 Mascot Swampee
☐ 22 Sponsor TTI
☐ 23 Matt Demarski
☐ 24 Andy MacIntyre
☐ 25 Tom Buckley
☐ 26 Bujar Amidovski (G)

'01 - 02
FLORIDA EVERBLADES / CHOICE

Singles start at 50¢.
Card Size: 2 1/2" x 3 1/2"
Set (23 cards): $10

☐ 1 Checklist
☐ 2 Gerry Fleming, Coach
☐ 3 P. O'Handley, A.Coach
☐ 4 Vince Williams
☐ 5 Terry Lindgren
☐ 6 Duane Harmer
☐ 7 Andrew Long
☐ 8 Reggie Berg
☐ 9 Brent McDonald
☐ 10 Tom Buckley
☐ 11 Briane Thompson
☐ 12 Mike Cirillo
☐ 13 Don Smith
☐ 14 Joe Blaznek
☐ 15 Peter Reynolds
☐ 16 Paul Spadafora
☐ 17 Keith Anderson
☐ 18 Shaun Fisher
☐ 19 Randy Petruk (G)
☐ 20 Ryan Murphy
☐ 21 Mascot Swampee
☐ Sponsor card
☐ Sponsor card

FORT WAYNE KOMETS

'92 - 93
FORT WAYNE KOMETS

Singles start at 50¢.
Set (32 cards): $10

☐ 1 Team
☐ 2 Ralph Barahona
☐ 3 Ian Boyce
☐ 4 Igor Chibirev
☐ 5 Colin Chin
☐ 6 Sylvain Couturier
☐ 7 Lee Davidson
☐ 8 Guy Dupuis
☐ 9 Steven Fletcher
☐ 10 David Gagnon
☐ 11 Scott Gruhl
☐ 12 Peter Hankinson
☐ 13 Kelly Hurd
☐ 14 Bob Jay
☐ 15 Kory Kocur
☐ 16 Bob Lakso
☐ 17 Carey Lucyk
☐ 18 Kevin MacDonald
☐ 19 Dan Ratushny
☐ 20 Pokey Reddick (G)
☐ 21 Jean-Marc Richard
☐ 22 Grant Richison
☐ 23 Joel Savage
☐ 24 Dave Smith
☐ 25 Bob Wilkie
☐ 26 Paul Willett
☐ 27 Steve Wilson
☐ 28 Al Sims
☐ 29 Derek Ray
☐ 30 Franke Brothers
☐ 31 Kurt Skinner
☐ 32 Eddie Sink

'93 - 94
FORT WAYNE KOMETS / KEEBLER

Singles start at 50¢.
Set (27 cards): $10

☐ 1 Team
☐ 2 Ian Boyce
☐ 3 Colin Chin
☐ 4 Lee Davidson
☐ 5 Guy Dupuis
☐ 6 Steven Fletcher
☐ 7 Sean Gauthier
☐ 8 Darryl Gilmour
☐ 9 Kelly Hurd
☐ 10 Dan Lambert
☐ 11 Carey Lucyk
☐ 12 Kevin MacDonald
☐ 13 Igor Malykhin
☐ 14 Brian McKee
☐ 15 Mitch Messier
☐ 16 Max Middendorf
☐ 17 John Purves
☐ 18 Grant Richison
☐ 19 Dave Smith
☐ 20 Shayne Stevenson
☐ 21 Dave Tretowicz
☐ 22 Vladimir Tsyplakov
☐ 23 Doug Wickenheiser
☐ 24 Bruce Boudreau
☐ 25 Derek Ray
☐ 26 Joe Franke
☐ 27 Galen Head

'94 - 95
FORT WAYNE KOMETS

Singles start at 50¢.
Set (29 cards): $10

☐ 1 Colin Chin
☐ 2 Igor Malykhin
☐ 3 Steven Fletcher
☐ 4 Shawn Reid
☐ 5 Vladimir Tsyplakov
☐ 6 John Purves
☐ 7 Dan Ratushny
☐ 8 Scott Burfoot
☐ 9 Chris Rowland
☐ 10 Peter Ing (G)
☐ 11 Guy Dupuis
☐ 12 Paul Willett
☐ 13 Peter Sidorkiewicz (G)
☐ 14 Ian Boyce
☐ 15 Steve Bancroft
☐ 16 Jeff Rohlicek
☐ 17 Grant Richison
☐ 18 Jason Renard
☐ 19 Radek Hamr
☐ 20 Kelly Hurd
☐ 21 Carey Lucyk
☐ 22 Rob Doyle
☐ 23 Dave Smith
☐ 24 Kevin Miehm
☐ 25 Igor Chibirev
☐ 26 Derek Ray
☐ 27 Joe Franke
☐ 28 Galen Head
☐ 29 Mascot Icy

'95 - 96
FORT WAYNE KOMETS / EDGE ICE

Singles start at 50¢.
Set (25 cards): $10

☐ 1 Andy Bezeau
☐ 2 Colin Chin
☐ 3 Shawn Cronin
☐ 4 Guy Dupuis
☐ 5 Pat Elynuik
☐ 6 Bob Essensa (G)
☐ 7 Shawn Evans
☐ 8 Steven Fletcher
☐ 9 Peter Ing (G)
☐ 10 Andrew McBain
☐ 11 Mitch Messier
☐ 12 Rob Murphy
☐ 13 Alex Nikolic
☐ 14 Grant Richison
☐ 15 Jeff Rohlicek
☐ 16 Konstatin Shafronov
☐ 17 Darin Smith
☐ 18 Sergei Stas
☐ 19 Brian Straub
☐ 20 Chris Tok
☐ 21 Paul Willett
☐ 22 Kevin Wortman
☐ 23 Oleg Yashin
☐ 24 Derek Ray
☐ 25 Mascot Icy

'97 - 98
FORT WAYNE KOMETS / ACORDIA-O'ROURKE

Kevin Weekes is one of the more expensive singles at $2. Singles start at 50¢.
Set (21 cards): $12

☐ 1 Guy Dupuis
☐ 2 Ian Boyce
☐ 3 Lee Davidson
☐ 4 Bruce Racine
☐ 5 Dan Currie
☐ 6 Robin Bawa
☐ 7 Tom Nemeth
☐ 8 Ed Campbell
☐ 9 Viacheslav Butsayev
☐ 10 Steffon Walby
☐ 11 Derek Eberle
☐ 12 Chris Armstrong
☐ 13 Norm Batherson
☐ 14 Konstatin Shafronov
☐ 15 Tom Pederson
☐ 16 Andrei Bashkirov
☐ 17 Carlin Nordstrom
☐ 18 Trevor Doyle
☐ 19 Eric Boguniecki
☐ 20 Kevin Weekes (G)
☐ 21 Mascot Icy D. Eagle

'98 - 99
FORT WAYNE KOMETS / EBK SPORTS

Singles start at 50¢.
Set (28 cards): $10

☐ 1 Ed Campbell
☐ 2 Viacheslav Butsayev
☐ 3 Ian Boyce
☐ 4 Eric Boguniecki
☐ 5 Robin Bawa
☐ 6 Gerard Gallant
☐ 7 Mascot Icy D. Eagle
☐ 8 Guy Dupuis
☐ 9 Dion Darling
☐ 10 Bob Chase
☐ 11 Brad Purdie
☐ 12 Andrei Petrakov
☐ 13 David Nemirovsky
☐ 14 Mike Martin
☐ 15 Tero Lehterä
☐ 16 Oleg Shargorodsky
☐ 17 Shawn Selmser
☐ 18 André Roy
☐ 19 Pokey Reddick (G)
☐ 20 Bruce Racine
☐ 21 Memorial Coliseum
☐ 22 Derek Wood
☐ 23 Lee Sorochan
☐ 24 Grant Sonier
☐ 25 Checklist
☐ 26 PHPA
☐ 27 IHL Web Site
☐ 28 Andrei Bashkirov

'99 - 00
FORT WAYNE KOMETS / ROOX SPORTS

Singles start at 50¢.
Card Size: 2 1/2" x 3 1/2"
Set (27 cards): $10

☐ 1 Jon Austin
☐ 2 Ryan Black
☐ 3 Frédéric Bouchard
☐ 4 Keli Corpse
☐ 5 Jason Goulet
☐ 6 John Gurskis
☐ 7 Kelly Hurd
☐ 8 Richard Keyes
☐ 9 Charlie Lawson
☐ 10 Dave Lemay
☐ 11 Jim Logan
☐ 12 Igor Malykhin
☐ 13 Milt Mastad
☐ 14 Trevor Matter
☐ 15 Jeff McKercher
☐ 16 Sacha Molin
☐ 17 Steve Parsons
☐ 18 Dennis Pinfold
☐ 19 Bruce Ramsay
☐ 20 Dan Ronan
☐ 21 Petr Sachl
☐ 22 Konstatin Shafronov
☐ 23 Vadim Sharapov
☐ 24 Kevin Slota
☐ 25 Doug Teskey
☐ 26 Dave Allison
☐ 27 Mascot Icy D. Eagle

FORT WORTH BRAHMAS

'97 - 98
FORT WORTH BRAHAMAS

Singles start at 50¢.
Set (21 cards): $8

☐ Chris Albert
☐ Steve Carter
☐ Brian Caruso
☐ Cosmo DuPaul
☐ David Graff
☐ Craig Hayden
☐ Murray Hogg
☐ Alex Kholomeyev
☐ Stéphane Larocque
☐ Rob Laurie
☐ Mike McCormick
☐ Bill McDonald
☐ Nolan McDonald
☐ Terry Menard
☐ Max Middendorf
☐ Dwight Mullins
☐ Mark O'Donnell
☐ Adam Robbins
☐ Todd St-Louis
☐ Mark Strohack
☐ Gatis Tsepils

'98 - 99
FORT WORTH BRAHAMAS / ROOX

Singles start at 50¢.
Card Size: 2 1/2" x 3 1/2"
Set (20 cards): $9

☐ Terry Menard
☐ Steve Plouffe
☐ Tim Green
☐ Scott Shaunessy
☐ Jim Dinneen
☐ Martin Machacek
☐ François Albert
☐ Sean Brady
☐ Murray Hogg
☐ Ryan Black
☐ Mark Strohack
☐ Richie Walcott
☐ Stéphane Larocque
☐ Barry Cummins
☐ Phil Miaskowski
☐ Martin Lamarche
☐ Cosmo DuPaul
☐ Jon Olofson
☐ Craig Hayden
☐ Steve Carter

'99 - 00
FORT WORTH BRAHAMAS / ROOX SPORTS

Singles start at 50¢.
Card Size: 2 1/2" x 3 1/2"
Set (20 cards): $9

☐ 1 Cosmo Dupaul
☐ 2 Terry Menard
☐ 3 Mascot Bruiser
☐ 4 Dennis Shiryaev
☐ 5 Murray Hogg
☐ 6 Louis Bernard
☐ 7 Derek Kups
☐ 8 Gatis Tsepils
☐ 9 Alex Kholomeyev
☐ 10 Robert Pochyly
☐ 11 Martin Lamarche
☐ 12 Jon Olofson
☐ 13 Mike Sanderson
☐ 14 Al Rooney
☐ 15 Stéphane Larocque
☐ 16 Michael Tilson
☐ 17 Cory Evans
☐ 18 Steve Plouffe
☐ 19 Jason Disher
☐ 20 Ross Harris

FREDERICTON CANADIENS

'92 - 93
FREDERICTON CANADIENS / BEN'S BAKERY

Oleg Petrov is one of the more expensive singles at $2. Singles start at 50¢.
Card Size: 2 1/2" x 3 3/4"
Set (28 cards): $15

☐ Jesse Bélanger
☐ Paulin Bordeleau, Coach
☐ Donald Brashear
☐ Patrik Carnback
☐ Frédéric Chabot (G)
☐ Eric Charron
☐ Alain Côté
☐ Paul DiPietro
☐ Craig Ferguson
☐ Gerry Fleming
☐ Luc Gauthier, A.Coach
☐ Robert Guillet
☐ Patric Kjellberg
☐ Les Kuntar (G)
☐ Patrick Langois, Equip.
☐ Ryan Kuwabara
☐ Steve Larouche
☐ Jacques Parent, Therap.
☐ Charles Paulin
☐ Oleg Petrov
☐ Yves Sarault
☐ Pierre Sévigny
☐ Darcy Simon
☐ Turner Stevenson
☐ Lindsay Vallis
☐ Steve Veilleux
☐ Mascot Tricolo
☐ Fredericton card

'93 - 94
FREDERICTON CANADIENS / BEN'S BAKERY, PEPSI

Oleg Petrov is one of the more expensive singles at $2. Singles start at 50¢.
Card Size: 2 1/2" x 3 1/2"
Set (30 cards): $15

☐ Brent Bilodeau #5
☐ Paulin Bordeleau, Coach
☐ Donald Brashear #24
☐ Martin Brochu (G) #1
☐ Craig Darby#10
☐ Kevin Darby #20
☐ Mario Doyon #19
☐ Craig Ferguson #11
☐ Craig Flander #30 (G)
☐ Gerry Fleming #28
☐ Luc Gauthier, A.Coach
☐ Robert Guillet #12
☐ Les Kuntar #29 (G)
☐ Ryan Kuwabara #21
☐ Patrick Langlois, Equip.
☐ Marc Laniel #26
☐ Christian Larivière #8
☐ Kevin O'Sullivan #32
☐ Denis Ouellete, Trainer
☐ Jacques Parent, Therap.
☐ Oleg Petrov #6
☐ Charles Poulin #16
☐ Christian Proulx #3
☐ Tony Prpic #27
☐ Yves Sarault #22
☐ Turner Stevenson #23
☐ Lindsay Vallis #18
☐ Mascot Tricolo
☐ Fredericton card
☐ Donald Brashear (fight)

'94 - 95
FREDERICTON CANADIENS / BEN'S BAKERY

Valeri Bure is one of the more expensive singles at $3. Singles start at 50¢.
Card Size: 2 1/2" x 3 1/2"
Set (30 cards): $18

☐ Louis Bernard
☐ Brent Bilodeau
☐ Paulin Bordeleau, Coach
☐ Donald Brashear
☐ Martin Brochu (G)
☐ Valeri Bure
☐ Jim Campbell
☐ Paul Chagnon
☐ Craig Conroy
☐ Craig Darby
☐ Dion Darling
☐ Craig Ferguson
☐ Scott Fraser
☐ Luc Gauthier, A.Coach
☐ Patrick Labrecque (G)
☐ Marc Lamothe
☐ Patrick Langlois, Equip.
☐ Brad Layzelle
☐ Derek Maguire
☐ Chris Murray
☐ Kevin O'Sullivan
☐ Jacques Parent, Therap.
☐ Christian Proulx
☐ Craig Rivet
☐ Yves Sarault
☐ Turner Stevenson
☐ Martin Sychra
☐ Tim Tisdale
☐ David Wilkie
☐ Mascot Tricolo

'95 - 96
FREDERICTON CANADIENS / BEN'S BAKERY

Darcy Tucker is one of the more expensive singles at $1.50. Singles start at 50¢.
Card Size: 2 1/2" x 3 1/2"
Set (29 cards): $15

☐ Louis Bernard
☐ Paulin Bordeleau, Coach
☐ Sébastien Bordeleau
☐ Martin Brochu (G)
☐ Jim Campbell
☐ Paul Chagnon
☐ Craig Conroy
☐ Keli Corpse
☐ Dion Darling
☐ Rory Fitzpatrick
☐ Scott Fraser
☐ Luc Gauthier, A.Coach
☐ Gaston Gingras
☐ David Grenier
☐ Harold Hersh
☐ Patrick Labrecque (G)
☐ Marc Lamothe
☐ Patrick Langlois, Equip.
☐ Alan Letang
☐ Alexei Lojkin
☐ Xavier Majic
☐ Chris Murray
☐ Jacques Parent, Therap.
☐ Craig Rivet
☐ Mario Roberge
☐ Pierre Sévigny
☐ Darcy Tucker
☐ Adam Wiesel
☐ Mascot Tricolo

'96 - 97
FREDERICTON CANADIENS / JOLLY RANCHER

José Théodore is the more expensive single at $20-25. Other singles start at 50¢.
Card Size: 2 1/2" x 3 1/2"
Set (29 cards): $30

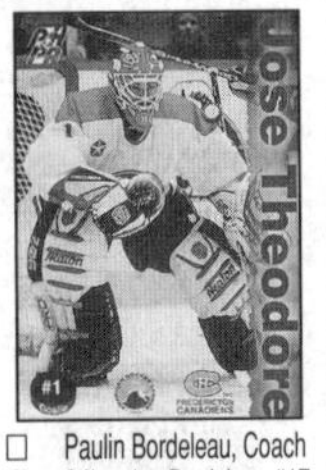

- ☐ Paulin Bordeleau, Coach
- ☐ Sébastien Bordeleau #17
- ☐ Brad Brown #24
- ☐ Paul Chagnon
- ☐ Earl Cronan #40
- ☐ Dion Darling #4
- ☐ Jimmy Drolet #8
- ☐ Gerry Fleming #28
- ☐ Scott Fraser #21
- ☐ L. Gauthier, A. Coach
- ☐ François Groleau #38
- ☐ Miloslav Guren #19
- ☐ Harold Hersh #22
- ☐ Eric Houde #32
- ☐ Patrick Langlois, Equip.
- ☐ Alan Letang #31
- ☐ David Ling #27
- ☐ Alexei Lojkin #23
- ☐ Boyd Olson #10
- ☐ Jacques Parent, Therap.
- ☐ Tony Prpic #12
- ☐ Jessie Rezansoff #14
- ☐ Craig Rivet #26
- ☐ Pierre Sévigny #25
- ☐ Todd Sparks #41
- ☐ José Théodore #1 (G)
- ☐ Tomas Vokoun #29 (G)
- ☐ Adam Wiesel #5
- ☐ Mascot Tricolo

FREDERICTON EXPRESS

'82 - 83

FREDERICTON EXPRESS / POLICE

Marc Crawford and Jacques Demers are the most expensive singles sell at $3. Singles start at 50¢.

Card Size: 2 1/2" x 3 3/4"

Set (26 cards): $20

- ☐ 1 Team Photo
- ☐ 2 B.J. MacDonald
- ☐ 3 Sylvain Côté
- ☐ 4 Michel Bolduc
- ☐ 5 Gary Lupul
- ☐ 6 Clint Malarchuk (G)
- ☐ 7 Tony Currie
- ☐ 8 Tim Tookey
- ☐ 9 Anders Eldebrink
- ☐ 10 Basil McRae
- ☐ 11 Kelly Elcombe
- ☐ 12 Jacques Demers
- ☐ 13 Frank Caprice (G)
- ☐ 14 Terry Johnson
- ☐ 15 Grant Martin
- ☐ 16 André Chartrain
- ☐ 17 Marc Crawford
- ☐ 18 Gaston Therrien
- ☐ 19 Andy Schliebener
- ☐ 20 Christian Tanguay
- ☐ 21 Art Rutland
- ☐ 22 Jean-Marc Gaulin
- ☐ 23 Noil Bolland
- ☐ 24 André Côté
- ☐ 25 Jim McRae
- ☐ 26 S.Beckingham/ Flynn

'83 - 84

FREDERICTON EXPRESS / POLICE

Mike Eagles is one of the more expensive singles at $2. Singles start at 50¢.

Card Size: 2 1/2" x 3 3/4"

Set (27 cards): $15

- ☐ 1 Team Photo
- ☐ 2 Frank Caprice (G)
- ☐ 3 Michael Dufour (G)
- ☐ 4 Brian Ford (G)
- ☐ 5 Jean-Marc Lanthier
- ☐ 6 Jim Dobson
- ☐ 7 Mike Hough
- ☐ 8 Rick Lapointe
- ☐ 9 Michel Bolduc
- ☐ 10 Christian Tanguay
- ☐ 11 Tony Currie
- ☐ 12 Moe Lemay
- ☐ 13 Bruce Halloway
- ☐ 14 Neil Belland
- ☐ 15 Richard Turmel
- ☐ 16 Claude Julien
- ☐ 17 André Chartrain
- ☐ 18 Grant Martin
- ☐ 19 Réjean Vignola
- ☐ 20 André Côté
- ☐ 21 Jean-Marc Gaulin
- ☐ 22Andy Schliebener
- ☐ 23 Stu Kulak
- ☐ 24 Mike Eagles
- ☐ 25 Earl Jessiman
- ☐ 26 M. Flynn S. Beckingham
- ☐ Checklist

'84 - 85

FREDERICTON EXPRESS / POLICE

Marc Crawford is one of the more expensive singles at $3. Mike Hough and Clint Malarchuk sell at $2. Singles start at 50¢.

Card Size: 2 1/2" x 3 3/4"

Set (28 cards): $18

- ☐ 1 Dave Morrison
- ☐ 2 David Shaw
- ☐ 3 Bruce Halloway
- ☐ 4 Roger Haegglund
- ☐ 5 Neil Belland
- ☐ 6 Gord Donnelly
- ☐ 7 David Bruce
- ☐ 8 Claude Julien
- ☐ 9 Dan Wood
- ☐ 10 Clint Malarchuk (G)
- ☐ 11 Jere Gillis
- ☐ 12 Mike Hough
- ☐ 13 Michel Bolduc
- ☐ 14 Peter Loob
- ☐ 15 Steve Driscoll
- ☐ 16 Newll Brown
- ☐ 17 Jim Dobson
- ☐ 18 Wendell Young (G)
- ☐ 19 Mark Kumpel
- ☐ 20 Mike Eagles
- ☐ 21 Tom Thornbury
- ☐ 22 Grant Martin
- ☐ 23 Marc Crawford
- ☐ 24 Andy Schliebener
- ☐ 25 Earl Jeesiman
- ☐ 26 Yvon Vautour
- ☐ 27 Craig Coxe
- ☐ 28 Blake Wesley

'85 - 86

FREDERICTON EXPRESS / POLICE

Marc Crawford is one of the more expensive singles at $3. Singles start at 50¢.

Card Size: 2 1/2" x 3 3/4"

Set (28 cards): $15

- ☐ 1 Scott Tottle
- ☐ 2 David Bruce
- ☐ 3 Team Photo
- ☐ 4 Marc Crawford
- ☐ 5 Mike Stevens
- ☐ 6 Gary Lupul
- ☐ 7 Alain Lemieux
- ☐ 8 Mike Hough
- ☐ 9 Tony Currie
- ☐ 10 Dunc MacIntyre
- ☐ 11 Jere Gillis
- ☐ 12 W. Young (G)
- ☐ 13 Jean-Marc Lanthier
- ☐ 14 Ken Quinney
- ☐ 15 Claude Julien
- ☐ 16 Michel Petit
- ☐ 17 Luc Guenette
- ☐ 18 Andy Schliebener
- ☐ 19 Mark Kirton
- ☐ 20 Gord Donnelly
- ☐ 21 Tom Karalis
- ☐ 22 Daniel Poudrier
- ☐ 23 Neil Belland
- ☐ 24 Dale Dunbar
- ☐ 25 M. Flynn/ S.Beckingham
- ☐ 26 Jean-Marc Gaulin
- ☐ 27 Al MacAdam
- ☐ 28 André Savard

'86 - 87

FREDERICTON EXPRESS / POLICE

Marc Crawford is one of the more expensive singles at $3. Singles start at 50¢.

Card Size: 2 1/2" x 3 3/4"

Set (26 cards): $15

- ☐ Jim Agnew
- ☐ Brian Bertuzzi
- ☐ David Bruce
- ☐ Frank Caprice (G)
- ☐ Marc Crawford
- ☐ Steven Finn
- ☐ Jean-Marc Gaulin
- ☐ Scott Gordon (G)
- ☐ Taylor Hall
- ☐ Yves Heroux
- ☐ Mike Hough
- ☐ Tom Karalis
- ☐ Mark Kirton
- ☐ Jean-Marc Lanthier
- ☐ Jean LeBlanc
- ☐ Brett MacDonald
- ☐ Duncan MacIntyre
- ☐ Greg Malone
- ☐ Terry Perkins
- ☐ Daniel Poudrier
- ☐ Jeff Rohlicek
- ☐ André Savard
- ☐ Mike Stevens
- ☐ Trevor Stienburg
- ☐ M.Flynn/S.Beckingham
- ☐ Team Photo

GRAND RAPIDS GRIFFINS

'96 - 97

GRAND RAPIDS GRIFFINS / MEIER-KODAK

Pavol Demitra is one of the more expensive singles at $2. Singles start at 50¢.

Set (30 cards): $15

- ☐ Kevyn Adams
- ☐ Dave Allison
- ☐ Danton Cole
- ☐ Keli Corpse
- ☐ Pavol Demitra
- ☐ Ben Hankinson
- ☐ Cory Johnson
- ☐ Stanislav Jasecko
- ☐ Jamie Linden
- ☐ Sean McCann
- ☐ Don McSween
- ☐ Tyler Moss (G)
- ☐ Jeff Nelson
- ☐ Todd Nelson
- ☐ Michel Picard
- ☐ Bruce Ramsay
- ☐ Pokey Reddick (G)
- ☐ Chad Remackel
- ☐ Travis Richards
- ☐ Matt Ruchty
- ☐ Darcy Simon
- ☐ Griffins
- ☐ Header Card 1
- ☐ Header Card 2
- ☐ Header Card 3
- ☐ Header Card 4
- ☐ Header Card 5
- ☐ Mascot Griff
- ☐ Team Photo
- ☐ Van Andel Arena 1

'97 - 98

GRAND RAPIDS GRIFFINS / SPLIT SECOND

Glen Metropolit is one of the more expensive singles at $1.50. Singles start at 50¢.

Card Size: 2 1/2" x 3 1/2"

Set (24 cards): $12

- ☐ 1 Michel Picard
- ☐ 2 Tom Ashe
- ☐ 3 Greg Clancy
- ☐ 4 Danton Cole
- ☐ 5 Ian Gordon
- ☐ 6 Mark Greig
- ☐ 7 Shane Hnidy
- ☐ 8 Kerry Huffman
- ☐ 9 Glen Metropolit
- ☐ 10 Todd Nelson
- ☐ 11 Ed Patterson
- ☐ 12 Bruce Ramsay
- ☐ 13 Pokey Reddick (G)
- ☐ 14 Travis Richards
- ☐ 15 Matt Ruchty
- ☐ 16 Darcy Simon
- ☐ 17 Brian Sullivan
- ☐ 18 Sean Tallaire
- ☐ 19 Dean Trboyevich
- ☐ 20 Jason Weaver
- ☐ 21 Dave Allison
- ☐ 22 Curtis Hunt
- ☐ 23 Mascot Griff
- ☐ 24 PHPA

'98 - 99

GRAND RAPIDS GRIFFINS / SPLIT SECOND

Glen Metropolit is one of the more expensive singles at $1.50. Singles start at 50¢.

Card Size: 2 1/2" x 3 1/2"

Set (24 cards): $12

- ☐ Jared Bednar
- ☐ Radim Bicanek
- ☐ Anders Bjork
- ☐ Aris Brimanis
- ☐ Guy Charron
- ☐ Danton Cole
- ☐ Curtis Hunt
- ☐ Jed Fiebelkorn
- ☐ Ian Gordon
- ☐ Todd Hlushko
- ☐ Kerry Huffman
- ☐ Neil Little (G)
- ☐ Glen Metropolit
- ☐ Vaclav (Jr.) Nedomansky
- ☐ Robert Petrovicky
- ☐ Bruce Ramsay
- ☐ Travis Richards
- ☐ Gaetan Royer
- ☐ Darren Rumble
- ☐ Maxim Spiridonov
- ☐ Andrei Vasilyev
- ☐ Mascot Griff
- ☐ PHPA
- ☐ The Zone

'99 - 00

GRAND RAPIDS GRIFFINS / SPLIT SECOND

Janie Hurme is one of the more expensive singles at $2. Singles start at 50¢.

Card Size: 2 1/2" x 3 1/2"

Set (25 cards): $12

- ☐ Vyacheslav Butsayev
- ☐ Guy Charron
- ☐ Ivan Ciernik
- ☐ Danton Cole
- ☐ John Emmons
- ☐ Mike Fountain (G)
- ☐ Erich Goldmann
- ☐ Konstantin Gorovikov
- ☐ John Gruden
- ☐ Curtis Hunt
- ☐ Jani Hurme (G)
- ☐ Derek King
- ☐ Kevin Miller
- ☐ Chris Neil
- ☐ Todd Nelson
- ☐ Ed Patterson
- ☐ Michel Picard
- ☐ Philippe Plante
- ☐ Karel Rachunek
- ☐ Travis Richards
- ☐ Yves Sarault
- ☐ Petr Schastlivy
- ☐ Andrei Srubko
- ☐ Chris Szysky
- ☐ David Van Drunen

'00 - 01

GRAND RAPIDS GRIFFINS / SPLIT SECOND

Singles start at 50¢.

Card Size: 2 1/2" x 3 1/2"

Set (25 cards): $12

- ☐ Keith Aldridge
- ☐ Sean Berens
- ☐ Vyacheslav Butsayev
- ☐ Mathieu Chouinard (G)
- ☐ Ivan Ciernik
- ☐ Ilja Demidov
- ☐ Mike Fountain (G)
- ☐ Sean Gagnon
- ☐ Konstantin Gorovikov
- ☐ John Gruden
- ☐ Derek King
- ☐ Joel Kwiatkowski
- ☐ Marty McSorley
- ☐ Kip Miller
- ☐ Chris Neil
- ☐ David Oliver
- ☐ Ed Patterson
- ☐ Travis Richards
- ☐ David Roberts
- ☐ Petr Schastlivy
- ☐ Chris Szysky
- ☐ Todd White
- ☐ Bruce Cassidy, Coach
- ☐ Danton Cole, A.Coach
- ☐ Mascot Griff

'01 - 02

GRAND RAPIDS GRIFFINS / CHOICE

Singles start at 50¢.

Card Size: 2 1/2" x 3 1/2"

Set (26 cards): $12

- ☐ 1 Julien Vauclair
- ☐ 2 John Gruden
- ☐ 3 Wade Brookbank
- ☐ 4 Kip Miller
- ☐ 5 Alexandre Giroux
- ☐ 6 Hugo Boisvert
- ☐ 7 James Black
- ☐ 8 Steve Martins
- ☐ 9 David Hymovitz
- ☐ 10 Chris Szysky
- ☐ 11 Petr Schastlivy
- ☐ 12 Jeff Ulmer
- ☐ 13 Josh Langfeld
- ☐ 14 Chris Kelly
- ☐ 15 Joe Murphy
- ☐ 16 Travis Richards
- ☐ 17 Martin Prusek (G)
- ☐ 18 Chris Bala
- ☐ 19 David Van Drunen
- ☐ 20 Jason Doig
- ☐ 21 Joel Kwiatkowski
- ☐ 22 Mat. Chouinard (G)
- ☐ 23 Toni Dahlman
- ☐ 24 Bruce Cassidy, Coach
- ☐ 25 Gene Reilly
- ☐ 26 Mascot Griff

'02 - 03

GRAND RAPIDS GRIFFINS / CHOICE

Singles start at 50¢.

Card Size: 2 1/2" x 3 1/2"

Set (27 cards): $12

- ☐ Bryan Adams
- ☐ Sean Avery
- ☐ Paul Ballantyne
- ☐ Ryan Barnes
- ☐ Gregor Baumgartner
- ☐ Patrick Boileau
- ☐ Hugo Boisvert
- ☐ Sheldon Brookbank
- ☐ Ed Campbell
- ☐ Danton Cole
- ☐ Rob Collins
- ☐ Nick Greenough
- ☐ Danny Groulx
- ☐ Derek King
- ☐ Tomas Kopecky
- ☐ Marc Lamothe
- ☐ Joey MacDonald
- ☐ Mark Mowers
- ☐ Todd Nelson
- ☐ Michel Picard
- ☐ Travis Richards
- ☐ Nathan Robinson
- ☐ Stacy Roest
- ☐ Tim Skarperud
- ☐ Dave Van Drunen
- ☐ Advertising Card
- ☐ Mascot Griff

GREENSBORO GENERALS

'99 - 00

GREENSBORO GENERALS / ROOX SPORTS

- ☐ Clay Awe
- ☐ Igor Boiko
- ☐ Van Burgess
- ☐ Justin Cardwell
- ☐ Aniket Dhadphale
- ☐ Tracy Egeland
- ☐ Matt Eisler
- ☐ Martin Galik
- ☐ Joel Irwin
- ☐ Alexei Krovopuskov
- ☐ Francis Larivée
- ☐ Sal Manganaro
- ☐ Keith O'Connell
- ☐ Dean Shmyr
- ☐ Juraj Slovak
- ☐ Wes Swinson
- ☐ T.J. Tanberg
- ☐ Oleg Timchenko
- ☐ Ian Walterson
- ☐ David Whitworth
- ☐ Dean Zayonce
- ☐ 40th Anniversary
- ☐ Checklist
- ☐ Group Celebrates
- ☐ Radio Bill Flynn
- ☐ Settling Differences

GREENSBORO MONARCHS

'91 - 92

GREENSBORO MONARCHS / RBI SPORTS

Singles start at 50¢.

Card Size: 2 1/2" x 3 1/2"

Set (19 cards): $8

- ☐ Rob Bateman
- ☐ Phil Berger
- ☐ Mike Butters
- ☐ John Devereaux
- ☐ Eric Dubois
- ☐ Todd Gordon
- ☐ Chris Laganas
- ☐ Eric LeMarque
- ☐ Timo Makela
- ☐ Greg Menges
- ☐ Daryl Noren
- ☐ Peter Sentner
- ☐ Boyd Sutton
- ☐ Nick Vitucci
- ☐ Shawn Wheeler
- ☐ Scott White
- ☐ Chris Wolanin
- ☐ Dean Zayonce
- ☐ Team Photo

'92 - 93

GREENSBORO MONARCHS / RBI SPORTS

Dan Bylsma is one of the more expensive singles at $1.50. Singles start at 50¢.

Card Size: 2 1/2" x 3 1/2"

Set (19 cards): $10

- ☐ 1 Team
- ☐ 2 Chris Wolanin
- ☐ 3 Bill Horn
- ☐ 4 Brock Woods
- ☐ 5 Phil Berger
- ☐ 6 Dan Bylsma
- ☐ 7 Davis Payne
- ☐ 8 Wayne Muir
- ☐ 9 Andrei Iakovenko
- ☐ 10 Roger Larche
- ☐ 11 Jamie Nicholls
- ☐ 12 Darryl Noren
- ☐ 13 Todd Gordon
- ☐ 14 Claude Maillet
- ☐ 15 Dave Burke
- ☐ 16 Jamie Steer
- ☐ 17 Greg Capson
- ☐ 18 Chris Lappin
- ☐ 19 Greg Menges

'93 - 94

GREENSBORO MONARCHS / RBI SPORTS

Dan Bylsma is one of the more expensive singles at $1.50. Singles start at 50¢.

Card Size: 2 1/2" x 3 1/2"

Set (16 cards): $10

- ☐ Phil Berger
- ☐ Trevor Burgess
- ☐ Dan Bylsma
- ☐ Greg Capson
- ☐ Brendan Creagh
- ☐ Dan Gravelle
- ☐ Sébastien LaPlante
- ☐ Savo Mitrovic
- ☐ Tom Newman
- ☐ Jamie Nicolls
- ☐ Davis Payne
- ☐ Stig Salomonsson
- ☐ Sverre Sears
- ☐ Chris Valicevic
- ☐ John Young
- ☐ Dean Zayonce

'94 - 95

GREENSBORO MONARCHS / RBI SPORTS

Peter Skudra is one of the more expensive singles at $2. Singles start at 50¢.

Card Size: 2 1/2" x 3 1/2"

Set (20 cards): $10

- ☐ Phil Berger
- ☐ Brendan Creagh
- ☐ Mark DeSantis
- ☐ Doug Evans
- ☐ Jeff Gabriel
- ☐ Dwayne Gylywoychuk
- ☐ Bill Horn
- ☐ Artur Kupacs
- ☐ Scott McKay
- ☐ Ron Pasco
- ☐ David Payne
- ☐ Hugo Proulx
- ☐ Howie Rosenblatt
- ☐ Sverre Sears
- ☐ Chad Seibel
- ☐ Peter Skudra (G)
- ☐ Jeremy Stevenson
- ☐ Glenn Stewart
- ☐ Dean Zayonce
- ☐ Mascot Monte

HALIFAX CITADELS

'89 - 90

HALIFAX CITADELS / FARMER'S CO-OP

Robbie Ftorek is one of the more expensive singles at $1.50. Singles start at 75¢.

Card Size: 2 1/2" x 4 1/2"

Set (26 cards): $15

- ☐ Jason Baillargeon
- ☐ Jamie Baker
- ☐ Mario Brunetta
- ☐ Gerald Bzdel
- ☐ David Espe
- ☐ Bryan Fogarty
- ☐ Robbie Ftorek
- ☐ Scott Gordon (G)
- ☐ Dean Hopkins
- ☐ Miroslav Ihnacak
- ☐ Claude Julien
- ☐ Kevin Kaminski
- ☐ Claude Lapointe
- ☐ Max Middendorf
- ☐ Stéphane Morin
- ☐ Dave Pichette
- ☐ Ken Quinney
- ☐ Jean-Marc Richard
- ☐ Jean-Marc Routhier
- ☐ Jaroslav Sevcik
- ☐ Brent Severyn
- ☐ Greg Smyth
- ☐ Trevor Stienburg
- ☐ Mark Vermette
- ☐ Ladislav Tresl
- ☐ C.McQuaid/ Brent Smith

'90 - 91

HALIFAX CITADELS / FARMER'S CO-OP

Stéphane Fiset is one of the more expensive singles at $3. Singles start at 75¢.

Card Size: 2 3/4" x 4 1/4"

Set (28 cards): $15

- ☐ Jamie Baker
- ☐ Mike Bishop (G)
- ☐ Gerald Bzdel
- ☐ Daniel Doré
- ☐ Mario Doyon
- ☐ David Espe
- ☐ Stéphane Fiset (G)
- ☐ Scott Gordon (G)
- ☐ Stéphane Guérard
- ☐ Dean Hopkins
- ☐ Miroslav Ihnacak
- ☐ Jeff Jackson
- ☐ Clement Jodoin
- ☐ Claude Lapointe
- ☐ Dave Latta
- ☐ Chris McQuaid
- ☐ Kip Miller
- ☐ Stéphane Morin
- ☐ Ken Quinney
- ☐ Jean-Marc Richard
- ☐ Serge Roberge
- ☐ Jaroslav Sevcik
- ☐ Brent Severyn
- ☐ Mike Shuman
- ☐ Greg Smyth
- ☐ Jim Sprott
- ☐ Trevor Stienburg
- ☐ Mark Vermette

HAMILTON BULLDOGS

'99 - 00

HAMILTON BULLDOGS / SPLIT SECOND

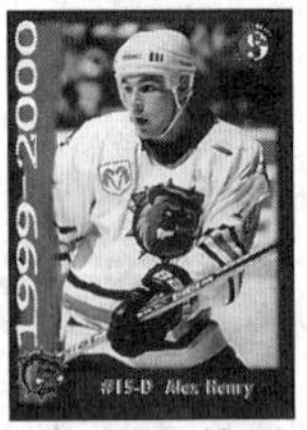

Dan Cleary is one of the more expensive singles at $4. Singles start at 50¢.

Card Size: 2 1/2" x 3 1/2"

Set (25 cards): $12

- ☐ Mike Minard (G)
- ☐ Chris Hajt
- ☐ Brad Norton
- ☐ Walt Kyle
- ☐ Éric Houde
- ☐ Kevin Bolibruck
- ☐ Dan Cleary
- ☐ Vladimir Vorobiev
- ☐ Dan LaCouture
- ☐ Brian Swanson
- ☐ Martin Laitre
- ☐ Peter Sarno
- ☐ Alex Zhurik
- ☐ Chad Hinz
- ☐ Kevin Brown
- ☐ Matthieu Descoteaux

☐ Jason Chimera
☐ Alex Henry
☐ Sean Selmser
☐ Ryan Risidore
☐ Michel Riesen
☐ Sergei Yerkovich
☐ Elias Abrahamsson
☐ Eric Heffler
☐ Mascot Bruiser

'99 - 00
HAMILTON BULLDOGS / STAZ COMMUNICATIONS

Singles start at $1. Other singles exist.
Card Size: 8" x 10"

☐ 11 Mike Minard (G)
☐ 15 Elias Abrahamsson
☐ 16 Alex Henry
☐ 18 Martin Laitre
☐ 19 Ryan Risidore
☐ 20 Kevin Bolibruck
☐ 26 Sergei Yerkovich
☐ 27 Alex Zhurik
☐ 28 Rob Murray
☐ 29 After the goal
☐ 33 Daniel Cleary All-Star
☐ 34 Brad Norton All-Star
☐ 35 Boyd Devereaux Grad
☐ 37 Chad Kilger Grad
☐ 39 Daw/ Sandwith/ Murray
☐ 40 Mascot Bruiser

'00 - 01
HAMILTON BULLDOGS / CHOICE

Singles start at 50¢.
Card Size: 2 1/2" x 3 1/2"
Set (28 cards): $12

☐ 1 Chris Madden (G)
☐ 2 Terran Sandwith
☐ 3 Ryan Risidore
☐ 4 Kurt Drummond
☐ 5 Chris Hajt
☐ 6 Brad Norton
☐ 7 Maxim Spiridonov
☐ 8 Patrick* Côté
☐ 9 Alex Henry
☐ 10 Paul Healey
☐ 11 Jason Chimera
☐ 12 Peter Sarno
☐ 13 Brian Urick
☐ 14 Michael Henrich
☐ 15 Brian Swanson
☐ 16 Martin Laitre
☐ 17 Chris Albert
☐ 18 Fernando Pisani
☐ 19 Lloyd Shaw
☐ 20 Scott Ferguson
☐ 21 Michel Riesen
☐ 22 Alain Nasreddine
☐ 23 Chad Hinz
☐ 24 Joaquin Gage (G)
☐ 25 Claude Julien, Coach
☐ 26 Morey Gare
☐ 27 Mascot Bruiser
☐ 28 Checklist

'00 - 01
HAMILTON BULLDOGS / STAZ COMMUNICATIONS

Singles start at $1. Other singles exist.
Card Size: 8" x 10"

☐ 4 Peter Sarno
☐ 5 Terran Sandwith
☐ 6 Ryan Risidore
☐ 7 Max Spiridonov
☐ 32 Terran Sandwith

'01 - 02
HAMILTON BULLDOGS / CARTES, TIMBRES, MONNAIES STE-FOY

Singles start at 50¢.

Card Size: 2 1/2" x 3 1/2"
Set (26 cards): $12

☐ 1 Ales Pisa
☐ 2 Chris Hajt
☐ 3 Alex Henry
☐ 4 Jan Horacek
☐ 5 Kevin Brown
☐ 6 Jason Chimera
☐ 7 Peter Sarno
☐ 8 Craig Reichert
☐ 9 Greg Leeb
☐ 10 Marc-André Bergeron
☐ 11 Brian Swanson
☐ 12 Jani Rita
☐ 13 Fernando Pisani
☐ 14 Michael Henrich
☐ 15 Sean Selmser
☐ 16 Ty Conklin (G)
☐ 17 Alain Nasreddine
☐ 18 Alexei Semenov
☐ 19 Adam Dewan
☐ 20 Marc Lamothe
☐ 21 Sven Butenschon
☐ 22 Chad Hinz
☐ 23 Claude Julien, Coach
☐ 24 Geoff Ward, A.Coach
☐ 25 Mascot Bruiser
☐ 26 Checklist

'01 - 02
HAMILTON BULLDOGS / STAZ COMMUNICATIONS

Singles start at $1. Other singles exist.
Card Size: 8" x 10"

☐ 2 Alain Nasreddine
☐ 5 Brian Swanson
☐ 6 Chris Hajt
☐ 7 Peter Sarno
☐ 23 Jani Rita
☐ 26 Marc Lamothe (G) The Save
☐ 31 C. Julien / G. Ward
☐ 33 Hamilton Red Wings
☐ 36 Adam Dewan

'02 - 03
HAMILTON BULLDOGS / CARTES, TIMBRES, MONNAIES STE-FOY

Singles start at 50¢.
Card Size: 2 1/2" x 3 1/2"
Set (20 cards): $12

☐ 1 Bobby Allen
☐ 2 Benjamin Carpentier
☐ 3 Ron Hainsey
☐ 4 Tony Salmelainen
☐ 5 Chad Hinz
☐ 6 Nate DiCasmirro
☐ 7 Tomas Plekanec
☐ 8 Jason Ward
☐ 9 Jarret Stoll
☐ 10 Matt O'Dette
☐ 11 Marc-André Bergeron
☐ 12 Jani Rita
☐ 13 François Beauchemin
☐ 14 Fernando Pisani
☐ 15 Michael Ryder
☐ 16 Michael Henrich
☐ 17 Ty Conklin
☐ 18 Éric Fichaud
☐ 19 Alexei Smirnov
☐ 20 Adam Dewan
☐ 21 Mathieu Garon
☐ 22 Benoît Gratton
☐ 23 Francis Bouillon
☐ 24 Mike Komisarek
☐ 25 Jozef Balej
☐ 26 Marcel Hossa
☐ 27 Mascot Bruiser
☐ 28 Checklist

HAMILTON CANUCKS

'92 - 93
HAMILTON CANUCKS / Y95 RADIO & DIAMOND MEMORIES

Some of the most expensive singles are Rick Vaive and Mike Fountain at $1-2 each. Singles start at 50¢.
Card Size: 2 1/2" x 3 1/2"
Set (30 cards): $12

☐ Shawn Antoski
☐ Robin Bawa
☐ Jamie Carlson
☐ Jassen Cullimore
☐ Alain Deeks
☐ Neil Eisenhut
☐ Mike Fountain (G)
☐ Troy Gamble (G)
☐ Jason Herter
☐ Pat Hickey
☐ Dane Jackson
☐ Dan Kesa
☐ Mario Marois (Marios)
☐ Bob Mason (G)
☐ Mike Maurice
☐ Jay Mazur
☐ Jack McIlhargey
☐ Sandy Moger
☐ Stéphane Morin
☐ Eric Murano
☐ Troy Neumeier
☐ Matt Newson
☐ Libor Polasek
☐ Phil von Stefenelli
☐ Doug Torrel
☐ Doug Tretiak
☐ Rick Vaive
☐ Mario Marois/ Pat Hickey
☐ Jeff Lumby
☐ Team Photo

HAMPTON ROADS ADMIRALS

'91 - 92
HAMPTON ROADS ADMIRALS / PEARLE VISION, WGNT

Singles start at 50¢.
Set (20 cards): $18

☐ Mark Bernard
☐ John Brophy
☐ Mike Chighisola
☐ John East
☐ Victor Gervais
☐ Randy Pearce
☐ Steve Poapst
☐ Murray Hood
☐ Darcy Kaminski
☐ Scott Johnson
☐ Paul Krepelka
☐ Olaf Kölzig (G)
☐ Al MacIsaac
☐ Brian Martin
☐ Dennis McEwen
☐ Dave Morissette
☐ Billy Nolan
☐ Pete Siciliano
☐ Shawn Snesar
☐ Keith Whitmore

'92 - 93
HAMPTON ROADS ADMIRALS / WARD'S SPORTING GOODS

Singles start at 50¢.
Card Size: 2 1/2" x 3 1/2"
Set (20 cards): $8

☐ Claude Barthe
☐ Mark Bernard
☐ John Brophy, Coach
☐ Trevor Duhaime
☐ Victor Gervais
☐ Kurt Kabat
☐ Paul Krepelka
☐ Al MacIsaac
☐ Steve Martell
☐ Brian Martin
☐ Harry Mews
☐ Steve Mirabile
☐ Dave Morisette
☐ Steve Poapst
☐ Jason Rathbone
☐ Chris Scarlata
☐ Shawn Snesar
☐ Kelly Sorenson
☐ Rod Taylor
☐ Nick Vitucci

'93 - 94
HAMPTON ROADS ADMIRALS / WARD'S SPORTING GOODS

Singles start at 50¢.
Card Size: 2 1/2" x 3 1/2"
Set (20 cards): $8

☐ John Brophy, Coach
☐ Rick Burrell
☐ Daniel Chaput
☐ Brendan Curley
☐ Victor Gervais
☐ Brian Goudie
☐ Shamus Gregga
☐ Al MacIsaac
☐ Kevin Malgunas
☐ Dennis McEwen
☐ Jason MacIntyre
☐ Mark Michaud
☐ Ron Pascucci
☐ Darren Perkins
☐ Steven Perkovic
☐ Shawn Snesar
☐ Kelly Sorenson
☐ Rod Taylor
☐ Richie Walcott
☐ Shawn Wheeler

'94 - 95
HAMPTON ROADS ADMIRALS

Patrick Lalime is one of the more expensive singles at $5. Singles start at 50¢.
Card Size: 2 1/2" x 3 1/2"
Set (22 cards): $15

☐ 1 John Brophy, Coach
☐ 2 Al MacIsaac
☐ 3 Patrick Lalime (G)
☐ 4 Colin Gregor
☐ 5 Ron Pascucci
☐ 6 John Porco
☐ 7 Trevor Halverson
☐ 8 Rod Taylor
☐ 9 Brian Goudie
☐ 10 Chris Phelps
☐ 11 Tom Menicci
☐ 12 Anthony MacAulay
☐ 13 Rick Kowalsky
☐ 14 Dennis McEwen
☐ 15 Kelly Sorenson
☐ 16 Brendan Curely
☐ 17 Jason MacIntyre
☐ 18 Jim Brown
☐ 19 Matt Mallgrave
☐ 20 Ron Majic
☐ 21 Corwin Saurdiff
☐ 22 Team Photo

'95 - 96
HAMPTON ROADS ADMIRALS / WARD'S SPORTING GOODS

Serge Aubin is one of the more expensive singles at $1.50. Singles start at 50¢.
Card Size: 2 1/2" x 3 1/2"
Set (25 cards): $10

☐ HRA-1 Team Photo
☐ HRA-2 John Brophy
☐ HRA-3 Al MacIsaac
☐ HRA-4 D. Paquette
☐ HRA-5 Mark Bernard
☐ HRA-6 Ron Pascucci
☐ HRA-7 D. Maltais
☐ HRA-8 J. MacIntyre
☐ HRA-9 Serge Aubin
☐ HRA-10 R. Kowalsky
☐ HRA-11 C. Fillion
☐ HRA-12 Rod Taylor
☐ HRA-13 Krivchenkov
☐ HRA-14 D. St. Pierre
☐ HRA-15 S. Richards
☐ HRA-16 T. Halverson
☐ HRA-17 Chris Phelps
☐ HRA-18 Jeff Kostuch
☐ HRA-19 S. Selmser
☐ HRA-20 A. Downey
☐ HRA-21 Bob Woods
☐ HRA-22 S. Voronov
☐ HRA-23 C. Saurdiff
☐ HRA-24 Rick Burrell
☐ HRA-25 G. Mansfield

'96 - 97
HAMPTON ROADS ADMIRALS / Q-CARDS

Singles start at 50¢.
Set (25 cards): $10

☐ 1 Darryl Paquette
☐ 2 Mike Larkin
☐ 3 Chris Phelps
☐ 4 Alexander Alexeev
☐ 5 Joel Thériault
☐ 6 Neal Martin
☐ 7 Ryan Mulhern
☐ 8 Darryl Shedden
☐ 9 Victor Gervais
☐ 10 Rod Taylor
☐ 11 Andy Weidenbach
☐ 12 Alain Savage
☐ 13 Randy Pearce
☐ 14 Chad Ackerman
☐ 15 Alexei Krivchenkov
☐ 16 Rick Kowalsky
☐ 17 Dominic Maltais
☐ 18 Joel Poirier
☐ 19 Marc Seliger
☐ 20 Aaron Downey
☐ 21 John Brophy
☐ 22 Al MacIsaac
☐ 23 Kevin (Stu) Bender
☐ 23 Gary Mansfield
☐ 24 Mascot Salty
☐ Team Photo

'97 - 98
HAMPTON ROADS ADMIRALS

Singles start at 50¢.
Set (24 cards): $10

☐ Chad Ackerman
☐ Alexander Alexeev
☐ Rob Bonneau
☐ John Brophy
☐ Dan Carney
☐ Dan Ceman
☐ Sébastien Charpentier
☐ Marty Clapton
☐ Victor Gervais
☐ Rick Kowalsky
☐ Alexander Kharlamov
☐ Mike Larkin
☐ Bill Lincoln
☐ Al MacIsaac
☐ Ron Majic
☐ Jason Mansoff
☐ Chris Phelps
☐ Joel Poirier
☐ Jason Saal
☐ Kayle Short
☐ Rod Taylor
☐ Joel Thériault
☐ Yuri Yuresko
☐ Bender / Mansfield

'98 - 99
HAMPTON ROADS ADMIRALS / Q-CARDS

Singles start at 50¢.
Set (25 cards): $10

☐ 1 Mascot Salty
☐ 2 John Brophy
☐ 3 Al MacIsaac
☐ 4 Chris Phelps
☐ 5 Trevor Johnson
☐ 6 Jami Yoder
☐ 7 Joel Poirier
☐ 8 Alexander Kharlamov
☐ 9 Bobby Russell
☐ 10 Trever Fraser
☐ 11 Jason Deleurme
☐ 12 Henry Higdon
☐ 13 Rod Taylor
☐ 14 Jeff Corbett
☐ 15 Derek Ernest
☐ 16 Charlie Retter
☐ 17 Chad Ackerman
☐ 18 Boris Zelenko
☐ 19 Dan Ceman
☐ 20 Marty Clapton
☐ 21 Milt Mastad
☐ 22 Dominic Maltais
☐ 23 Stephen Valiquette
☐ 24 Jason Saal
☐ 25 Bender / Boggs

'98 - 99
HAMPTON ROADS ADMIRALS / Q-CARDS 10-YEAR ANNIVERSARY

Olaf Kölzig and Byron Dafoe are the most expensive singles at $4 each. Singles start at 50¢.
Set (30 cards): $12

☐ 1 John Brophy
☐ 2 Rod Taylor
☐ 3 Victor Gervais
☐ 4 Brian Martin
☐ 5 Dennis McEwen
☐ 6 Chris Phelps
☐ 7 Randy Pearce
☐ 8 Murray Hood
☐ 9 Olaf Kölzig (G)
☐ 10 Kelly Sorenson
☐ 11 Mark Bernard
☐ 12 Andrew Brunette
☐ 13 Trevor Halverson
☐ 14 Rick Kowalsky
☐ 15 Aaron Downey
☐ 16 Patrick Lalime (G)
☐ 17 Steve Poapst
☐ 18 Alexander Alexeev
☐ 19 Harry Mews
☐ 20 Al MacIsaac
☐ 21 John Porco
☐ 22 Kent Hawley
☐ 23 Dave Flanagan
☐ 24 Billy Nolan
☐ 25 Brendan Curley
☐ 26 Ron Pascucci
☐ 27 Mark Michaud
☐ 28 Shawn Snesar
☐ 29 Byron Dafoe (G)
☐ 30 Séb. Charpentier (G)

'99 - 00
HAMPTON ROADS ADMIRALS / Q-CARDS

Singles start at 50¢.
Set (30 cards): $10

☐ 1 Chad Ackerman
☐ 2 Gerad Adams
☐ 3 Louis Bedard
☐ 4 Brad Church
☐ 5 Marty Clapton
☐ 6 Curtis Cruickshank
☐ 7 Derek Ernest
☐ 8 Ryan Gillis
☐ 9 Trevor Johnson
☐ 10 Rick Kowalsky
☐ 11 Jan Lasak (G)
☐ 12 Dominic Maltais
☐ 13 Mike Omicioli
☐ 14 John Parco
☐ 15 Dwight Parrish
☐ 16 Colin Pepperall
☐ 17 Richard Pitirri
☐ 18 Bobby Russell
☐ 19 Mike Siklenka
☐ 20 Dean Stork
☐ 21 Rod Taylor
☐ 22 John Brophy
☐ 23 Al MacIsaac
☐ 24 Bender / Boggs
☐ Checklist

HARTFORD WOLF PACK

'97 - 98
HARTFORD WOLF PACK / KID'S CLUB

Marc Savard and Dan Cloutier are the most expensive singles at $2 each. Singles start at 50¢.
Set (29 cards): $12

☐ Derek Armstrong
☐ Sylvain Blouin
☐ Eric Cairns
☐ Dan Cloutier (G)
☐ Christian Dubé
☐ Peter Ferraro
☐ Maxim Galanov
☐ Ken Gernander
☐ Daniel Goneau
☐ Todd Hall
☐ Johan Lindbom
☐ Mike Martin
☐ Jason Muzzatti (G)
☐ Dale Purinton
☐ Marc Savard
☐ Pierre Sévigny
☐ Adam Smith
☐ Geoff Smith
☐ Brad Smyth
☐ Lee Sorochan
☐ Robb Stauber (G)
☐ P.J. Stock
☐ Ronnie Sundin
☐ Tim Sweeney
☐ Brent Thompson
☐ Ryan VandenBussche
☐ Vladimir Vorobiev
☐ Chris Winnes
☐ Mascot Sonar

'98 - 99
HARTFORD WOLF PACK / KID'S CLUB

Marc Savard is one of the more expensive singles at $2. Singles start at 50¢.
Set (28 cards): $12

☐ Derek Armstrong
☐ Rich Brennan
☐ Jeff* Brown
☐ Ed Campbell
☐ Ben Carpentier
☐ Stefan Cherneski
☐ Christian Dubé
☐ Bob Errey
☐ Jeff Finley
☐ Ken Gernander
☐ Daniel Goneau
☐ Todd Hall
☐ Boyd Kane
☐ Jean-François Labbé (G)
☐ Mike Martin
☐ Dale Purinton
☐ Ryan Risidore
☐ Marc Savard
☐ Adam Smith
☐ Lee Sorochan
☐ P.J. Stock
☐ Brent Thompson
☐ Alexei Vasilyev
☐ Vladimir Vorobiev
☐ Kay Whitmore (G)
☐ Chris Winnes
☐ Johan Witehall
☐ Mascot Sonar

'99 - 00
HARTFORD WOLF PACK / KID'S CLUB

Milan Hnilicka is one of the more expensive singles at $2. Singles start at 50¢.
Set (23 cards): $12

☐ Derek Armstrong
☐ Drew Bannister
☐ Ben Carpentier
☐ Stefan Cherneski
☐ Jason Doig
☐ Francois Fortier
☐ Ken Gernander
☐ Daniel Goneau
☐ Todd Hall
☐ Mike Harder
☐ Burke Henry
☐ Milan Hnilicka (G)
☐ Chris Kenady
☐ Jean-Francois Labbé (G)
☐ Alexander Korobolin
☐ Tomas Kloucek
☐ Dale Purinton
☐ Brad Smyth
☐ P.J. Stock
☐ Tony Tuzzolino
☐ Alexei Vasiliev
☐ Terry Virtue
☐ Johan Witehall

'00 - 01
HARTFORD WOLF PACK / KID'S CLUB

Singles start at 50¢.
Set (29 cards): $12

☐ Derek Armstrong
☐ Drew Bannister
☐ Ryan Bast
☐ Ben Carpentier
☐ Jason Dawe
☐ Brandon Dietrich
☐ Jason Doig
☐ Dave Duerden
☐ Ken Gernander
☐ Michal Grosek
☐ Todd Hall
☐ Burke Henry
☐ Johan Holmqvist (G)
☐ Boyd Kane
☐ Chris Kenady
☐ Tomas Kloucek
☐ Jason Labarbera (G)
☐ Manny Malhotra
☐ Brad Mehalko
☐ Mike Mottau
☐ Dale Purinton
☐ Bert Robertsson
☐ Richard Scott
☐ Brad Smyth
☐ Tony Tuzzolino
☐ Jeff Ulmer
☐ Terry Virtue
☐ Vitali Yeremeyev (G)
☐ Mascot Sonar

'01 - 02
HARTFORD WOLF PACK / KID'S CLUB

Singles start at 50¢.
Set (26 cards): $12

☐ Jason Dawe
☐ Benoit Dusablon
☐ Rico Fata
☐ Sean Gagnon
☐ Ken Gernander
☐ Christian Gosselin
☐ Michal Grosek
☐ Barrett Heisten
☐ Johan Holmqvist (G)
☐ Wes Jarvis
☐ Boyd Kane
☐ Matt Kinch
☐ Jason Labarbera (G)
☐ Jamie Lundmark
☐ Dave MacIsaac
☐ Brad Mehalko
☐ Scott Meyer
☐ Mike Mottau
☐ Cam Severson
☐ Peter Smrek
☐ Brad Smyth
☐ Chris St. Croix
☐ John Tripp
☐ Igor Ulanov
☐ Terry Virtue
☐ Mascot Sonar

'02 - 03
HARTFORD WOLF PACK

We do not have a checklist for this series.

HERSHEY BEARS

'94 - 95
HERSHEY BEARS

Vaclav Prospal is one of the more expensive singles at $1.50. Singles start at 50¢.
Set (24 cards): $12

☐ Vladislav Boulin
☐ Aris Brimanis
☐ Bruce Coles
☐ Brad Dibeler
☐ Yanick Dupré
☐ Tracy Egeland
☐ André Faust
☐ Jeff Finley
☐ Václav Prospal
☐ Bob Wilkie

☐ Chris Winnes
☐ Terran Sandwith
☐ Ryan Sittler
☐ Mike Stothers
☐ Dan Stuck
☐ Jay Leach
☐ Neil Little (G)
☐ Mike McHugh
☐ Clayton Norris
☐ Milos Holán
☐ Paul Jerrard
☐ Mitch Lamoureux
☐ Les Kuntar (G)
☐ Dan Kordic

'98 - 99

HERSHEY BEARS / LEBANON DAILY NEWS

The most expensives singles are Marc Denis, David Aebischer and Ville Nieminen at $2 each. Singles start at 50¢.

Set (40 cards): $20

☐ 1 Lamoureux / Lazarev
☐ 2 Marc Denis (G)
☐ 3 Jeff Buchanan
☐ 4 Ted Crowley
☐ 5 Yuri Babenko
☐ 6 Evgeny Lazarev
☐ 7 Scott Parker
☐ 8 Mike Foligno
☐ 9 Rob Shearer
☐ 10 Brad Larsen
☐ 11 Bears
☐ 12 Rick Berry
☐ 13 Troy Crowder
☐ 14 Dan Hinote
☐ 15 Serge Aubin
☐ 16 Bears
☐ 17 Bears
☐ 18 Bears
☐ 19 David Aebischer (G)
☐ 20 Mitch Lamoureux
☐ 21 Christian Matte
☐ 22 Dan Smith
☐ 23 Jay Wells
☐ 24 Bears
☐ 25 Ville Nieminen
☐ 26 Nick Bootland
☐ 27 Bears
☐ 28 Bruce Richardson
☐ 29 Brian Willsie
☐ 30 Hershey Park Arena
☐ 31 Brian White
☐ 32 Bears
☐ 33 Bears
☐ 34 Dan (Beak) Stock
☐ 35 Bears
☐ 36 Frank Mathers
☐ 37 Arnie Kullman
☐ 38 Mike Nykoluk
☐ 39 Tim Tookey
☐ 40 Hershey

'00 - 01

HERSHEY BEARS / THE PATRIOT NEWS

Villie Nieminen is one of the more expensive singles at $3-4. Singles start at 50¢.

Card Size: 2 1/2" x 3 1/2"

Set (20 cards): $12

☐ Yuri Babenko
☐ Rick Berry
☐ Nick Bootland
☐ Frédéric Cassivi (G)
☐ Mike Craig
☐ Kelly Fairchild
☐ Stewart Malgunas
☐ Brad Larsen
☐ Evgeny Lazarev
☐ Ville Nieminen
☐ Joel Prpic
☐ Alexandr Ryazantsev
☐ Philippe Sauvé (G)
☐ Matt Scorsune
☐ Rob Shearer
☐ Dan Smith
☐ Ben Storey
☐ K.C. Timmons
☐ Stefton Walby
☐ Brian White

'01 - 02

HERSHEY BEARS / THE PATRIOT NEWS

Singles start at 50¢.

Card Size: 2 1/2" x 3 1/2"

Set (28 cards): $12

☐ Yuri Babenko
☐ Frédéric Cassivi (G)
☐ Mike Cirillo
☐ Larry Courville
☐ Jeff Daw
☐ Kelly Fairchild
☐ Riku Hahl
☐ Matt Herr
☐ Jordan Krestanovich
☐ Mikhail Kuleshov
☐ Evgeny Lazarev
☐ Dave MacIsaac
☐ Bryan Muir
☐ Brad Norton
☐ Jeff Paul
☐ Alexander Riazantsev
☐ Philippe Sauvé (G)
☐ Matt Scorsune
☐ Brent Thompson
☐ K.C. Timmons
☐ Steve Moore
☐ Vaclav Nedorost
☐ Jaroslav Obsut
☐ Rocky Thompson
☐ Radim Vrbata
☐ Mike Foligno, Coach
☐ Paul Fixter, A.Coach
☐ Mascot Coco the Bear

'02 - 03

HERSHEY BEARS

Singles start at 50¢.

Card Size: 2 1/2" x 3 1/2"

Set (20 cards): $12

☐ Philippe Sauvé (G)
☐ Peter Budaj (G)
☐ Tim Wedderburn
☐ Éric Bertrand
☐ Pierre-Luc Émond
☐ Mark Freer
☐ Mark Busenburg
☐ Charlie Stephens
☐ Rob Voltera
☐ Brian Willsie
☐ Agris Saviels
☐ Jordan Krestanovich
☐ Cail MacLean
☐ Bryan Muir
☐ Mikhail Kuleshov
☐ Riku Hahl
☐ KC Timmons
☐ Alexander Ryazantsev
☐ Brent Thompson
☐ Giant Center

HOUSTON AEROS

'95 - 96

HOUSTON AEROS / EDGE ICE

Singles start at 50¢.

Card Size: 2 1/2" x 3 1/2"

Set (24 cards): $12

☐ Scott Arniel
☐ Allan Conroy
☐ Paul DiPietro

☐ Gord Donnelly
☐ Rob Dopson
☐ Mark Freer
☐ Troy Gamble
☐ Kevin Grant
☐ Curtis Hunt
☐ Steve Jaques
☐ Gord Kruppke
☐ Mark Lamb
☐ Marc Laniel
☐ Kevin Malgunas
☐ Mike Maurice
☐ Scott McCrory
☐ Myles O'Connor
☐ Jim Paek
☐ Vadim Slivchenko
☐ Graeme Townshend
☐ Sylvain Turgeon
☐ Carl Valimont
☐ Michael Yeo
☐ Dave Tippett
☐ Terry Ruskowski

'99 - 00

HOUSTON AEROS / ALL-STAR GAME

Singles start at 50¢.

Set (24 cards): $12

☐ 1 Paul Dyck
☐ 2 Marty Wilford
☐ 3 Scott Swanson
☐ 4 Mark Lamb
☐ 5 Jeff Daw
☐ 6 Brian Wiseman
☐ 7 Lane Lambert
☐ 8 Brian Felsner
☐ 9 Terry Marchant
☐ 10 Lee Jinman
☐ 11 Rudy Poeschek
☐ 12 David Oliver
☐ 13 Brad Williamson
☐ 14 Mark Major
☐ 15 David Wilkie
☐ 16 Maxime Gingras
☐ 17 Greg Pankewicz
☐ 18 Greg Walters
☐ 19 Sandy Moger
☐ 20 Frédéric Chabot
☐ 21 Ron Low, Coach
☐ 22 Dave Barr
☐ 23 Steve Sumner
☐ 24 Jerry Meins
☐ 25 Mascot Chill E. Dog
☐ 26 Aeros
☐ 27 PHPA

HUMBERSIDE HAWKS

'93 - 94

HUMBERSIDE HAWKS

Singles start at 50¢.

Set (18 cards): $8

☐ 1 Kenny Johnson
☐ 2 Gavin De Jonge
☐ 3 Chris Hobson
☐ 4 Mike Bishop
☐ 5 Paul Simpson
☐ 6 Stewart Carvil
☐ 7 Shaun Johnson
☐ 8 Arren Burn
☐ 9 Anthony Johnson
☐ 10 Stephen Johnson
☐ 11 Anthony Payne
☐ 12 Andy Giles
☐ 13 Mike O'Connor
☐ 14 Andy Steel
☐ 15 Frank Killen
☐ 16 Dan Dorion
☐ 17 Alexandr Koulikov
☐ 18 Peter Johnson

'94 - 95

HUMBERSIDE HAWKS

Singles start at 50¢.

Set (18 cards): $8

☐ 1 Malcolm Bell
☐ 2 Mike Bishop
☐ 3 Scott' Young
☐ 4 Paul Simpson
☐ 5 Shaun Johnson
☐ 6 Wayne Anchikoski
☐ 7 Stephen Johnson
☐ 8 Anthony Johnson
☐ 9 Tony Saxby
☐ 10 Darcy Cahill
☐ 11 Chris Hobson
☐ 12 Danny Parkin
☐ 13 Scott Morrison
☐ 14 Danny Thompson
☐ 15 David Standing
☐ 16 Andy Port
☐ 17 Paul Cast
☐ 18 Peter Johnson

HUNTINGTON BLIZZARD

'93 - 94

HUNTINGTON BLIZZARD / WCHS

2500 sets were available. Singles start at 50¢.

Card Size: 2 1/2" x 3 1/2"

Set (27 cards): $12

☐ Ray Alcindor
☐ Shayne Antoski
☐ Greg Bailey
☐ Jared Bednar
☐ Andy Borggaard
☐ Malcolm Cameron
☐ Dave Dimitri
☐ Mark Franks
☐ Ray Gallagher
☐ Murray Garbutt
☐ Brad Harrison
☐ Todd Huyber
☐ Ron Majic
☐ Bob May
☐ Jim Mill
☐ Jim Mirabello
☐ Dave Persigehl
☐ Paul Pickard
☐ Scott Roberts
☐ Greg Scott
☐ Geoff Simpson
☐ Doug Stromback
☐ Dave Weekley
☐ Misty Zambito
☐ Mascot Klondike Bear
☐ Blizzard Babes
☐ Blizzards Card

'94 - 95

HUNTINGTON BLIZZARD / WSAZ

Singles start at 50¢.

Card Size: 2 1/2" x 3 1/2"

Set (26 cards): $10

☐ 1 Checklist
☐ 2 Steve Barnes
☐ 3 Jared Bednar
☐ 4 Jim Bermingham
☐ 5 Todd Brost
☐ 6 Andy Brown
☐ 7 Ray Edwards
☐ 8 Trent Eigner
☐ 9 Dan Fournel
☐ 10 Mark Franks
☐ 11 Gord Frantti
☐ 12 Chris Gordon
☐ 13 Kelly Harper
☐ 14 J.C. Ihrig
☐ 15 Mitch Kean
☐ 16 Jeff Levy
☐ 17 Chris Morque
☐ 18 Derek Schooley
☐ 19 Jim Solly
☐ 20 Mike Stone
☐ 21 Jason Weinrich
☐ 22 Mark Woolf
☐ 23 Paul Pickard
☐ 24 Mascot Klondike Bear
☐ 25 Blizzard Babes
☐ 32 Blizzards card

'98 - 99

HUNTINGTON BLIZZARD / EBK SPORTS

Singles start at 50¢.

Set (27 cards): $10

☐ 1 Bill Baaki
☐ 2 Mike Perna
☐ 3 Chad Lang
☐ 4 Jamie Sokolsky
☐ 5 D.J. Harding
☐ 6 Jan Slavik
☐ 7 Karson Kaebel
☐ 8 Jason Bermingham
☐ 9 Kelly Harper
☐ 10 Derek Smith
☐ 11 Jim Bermingham
☐ 12 Tracy Egeland
☐ 13 Brodie Coffin
☐ 14 Rob Stanfield
☐ 15 Kevin Paden
☐ 16 Michael Schultz
☐ 17 Rich Bronilla
☐ 18 Jake Deadmarsh
☐ 19 Butch Kaebel
☐ 20 Blaine Russell
☐ 21 Ray Edwards
☐ 22 Chris Plumhoff
☐ 23 Dave Allen
☐ 24 Mascot Klondike
☐ 25 Checklist
☐ 26 Blizzard Pro Shop
☐ 27 PHPA/ECHL

'99 - 00

HUNTINGTON BLIZZARD / ROOX SPORTS

Singles start at 50¢.

Card Size: 2 1/2" x 3 1/2"

Set (24 cards): $9

☐ 1 Anthony Cappelletti
☐ 2 Mike Perna
☐ 3 Jamie Pegg
☐ 4 Jamie Sokolsky
☐ 5 Andrew Pearsall
☐ 6 Jason Bermingham
☐ 7 Peter Brearley
☐ 8 Jim Bermingham
☐ 9 Jim Moss
☐ 10 Bill Baaki
☐ 11 Anthony Terzo
☐ 12 David Oliver
☐ 13 Keith Cassidy
☐ 14 Mark Spence
☐ 15 Ryan Hoople
☐ 16 Butch Kaebel
☐ 17 Blaine Russell
☐ 18 WRVC AM390
☐ 19 Action Blizzard
☐ 20 Mascot Klondike
☐ 21 Ray Edwards
☐ 22 Dave Allen
☐ 23 Kelly Harper
☐ 24 Curtis Bois

INDIANAPOLIS CHECKERS

'81 - 82

INDIANAPOLIS CHECKERS / PIZZA HUT

Kelly Hrudey is one of the more expensive singles at $15. Singles start at $1.

Card Size: 2 3/8" x 3 1/2"

Set (20 cards): $30

☐ 1 Mike Hordy
☐ 2 Randy Johnston
☐ 3 John Marks
☐ 4 Tim Lockridge
☐ 5 Darcey Regier
☐ 6 Garth MacGuigan
☐ 7 Charlie Skjodt
☐ 8 Mats Hallin
☐ 9 Frank Beaton
☐ 10 Kevin Devine
☐ 11 Steve Stoyanovich
☐ 12 Lorne Stamler
☐ 13 Red Laurence
☐ 14 Monty Trottier
☐ 15 Neil Hawryliw
☐ 16 Kelly Davis
☐ 17 Glen Duncan
☐ 18 Kelly Hrudey (G)
☐ 19 Bob Holland
☐ 20 Bruce Andres

'82 - 83

INDIANAPOLIS CHECKERS / PIZZA HUT

Kelly Hrudey is one of the more expensive singles at $12. Singles start at $1.

Card Size: 2 3/8" x 3 1/2"

Set (21 cards): $25

☐ Kelly Davis
☐ Kevin Devine
☐ Gord Dineen
☐ Glen Duncan
☐ Greg Gilbert
☐ Mike Greeder
☐ Mats Hallin
☐ Dave Hanson
☐ Rob Holland
☐ Scott Howson
☐ Kelly Hrudey (G)
☐ Randy Johnston
☐ Red Laurence
☐ Tim Lockridge
☐ Garth MacGuigan
☐ Darcy Regier
☐ Dan Revell
☐ Dave Simpson
☐ Lorne Stamler
☐ Steve Stoyanovich
☐ Monty Trottier

INDIANAPOLIS ICE

'92 - 93

INDIANAPOLIS ICE

Kevin Hodson is one of the more expensive singles at $2. Singles start at 50¢.

Card Size: 2 1/2" x 3 1/2"

Set (26 cards): $12

☐ Alexander Andrijevski
☐ Steve Bancroft
☐ Zac Boyer
☐ Rod Buskas
☐ Shawn Byram
☐ Joe Cleary
☐ Ron Conn
☐ Joe Cowley
☐ Trevor Dam
☐ Ivan Droppa
☐ Tracy Egeland
☐ Dave Hakstol
☐ Kevin Hodson (G)
☐ Tony Horacek
☐ Tony Hrkac
☐ Sergei Krivokrasov
☐ Brad Lauer
☐ Ray LeBlanc (G)
☐ Owen Lessard
☐ Kevin St. Jacques
☐ Mike Speer
☐ Milan Tichy
☐ Kerry Toporowski
☐ Sean Williams
☐ Craig Woodcroft
☐ Jim Playfair/ J.Marks

'93 - 94

INDIANAPOLIS ICE / MJ'S COLLECTIBLES

Singles start at 50¢.

Set (25 cards): $12

☐ 1 Hugo Belanger
☐ 2 Zac Boyer
☐ 3 Shawn Byram
☐ 4 Robert Cimetta
☐ 5 Rob Conn
☐ 6 Joe Crowley
☐ 7 Ivan Droppa
☐ 8 Steve Dubinsky
☐ 9 Karl Dykhuis
☐ 10 Dino Grossi
☐ 11 Dave Hakstol
☐ 12 Yves Heroux
☐ 13 Bobby House
☐ 14 Tony Horacek
☐ 15 Bob Kellogg
☐ 16 Sergei Krivokrasov
☐ 17 Jeff Ricciardi
☐ 18 Chris Rogles
☐ 19 Kevin St-Jacques
☐ 20 Christian Soucy (G)
☐ 21 Mike Speer
☐ 22 Kerry Toporowski
☐ 23 Duane Sutter
☐ 24 Gene Van Parfet
☐ 25 Mascot Polar Bear

'94 - 95

INDIANAPOLIS ICE / CLASSIC

Sergei Krivokrasov is one of the more expensive singles at $1.50. Singles start at 50¢.

Card Size: 2 1/2" x 3 1/2"

Set (26 cards): $15

☐ Hugo Belanger
☐ Bruce Cassidy
☐ Rob Conn
☐ Ivan Droppa
☐ Steve Dubinsky
☐ Karl Dykhuis
☐ Craig Fisher
☐ Daniel Gauthier
☐ Tony Horacek
☐ Bobby House
☐ Bob Kellogg
☐ Sergei Klimovich
☐ Sergei Krivokrasov
☐ Andy MacIntyre
☐ Dean Malkoc
☐ Matt Oates
☐ Mike Pomichter
☐ Mike Prokopec
☐ Jeff Ricciardi
☐ Chris Rogles
☐ Bogdan Savenko
☐ Jeff Shantz
☐ Christian Soucy (G)
☐ Duane Sutter
☐ Travis Thiessen
☐ Team Photo

'95 - 96

INDIANAPOLIS ICE / EDGE ICE

Ethan Moreau is one of the more expensive singles at $2. Singles start at 50¢.

Card Size: 2 1/2" x 3 1/2"

Set (23 cards): $12

☐ Bill H. Armstrong
☐ James H. Black
☐ Jeff Buchanan
☐ Bruce Cassidy
☐ Ivan Droppa
☐ Steve Dubinsky
☐ Bob Ferguson
☐ Dmitri Filimonov
☐ Daniel Gauthier
☐ Mike Prokopec
☐ André Racicot (G)
☐ Jimmy Waite (G)
☐ Brad Werenka
☐ Jeff Serowik
☐ Christian Soucy (G)
☐ Éric Lecompte
☐ Andy Macintyre
☐ Eric Manlow
☐ Steve McLaren
☐ Kip Miller
☐ Ethan Moreau
☐ Ryan Huska
☐ Sergei Klimovich

'97 - 98

INDIANAPOLIS ICE

Jani Hurme is one of the more expensive singles at $1.50. Singles start at 50¢.

Set (30 cards): $12

☐ 1 Bob Ferguson
☐ 2 Chris Mizer
☐ 3 Jim Stucky
☐ 4 Kory Cooper
☐ 5 Kirk Daubenspeck
☐ 6 Glen Featherstone
☐ 7 Brian Felsner
☐ 8 Martin Gendron
☐ 9 Jani Hurme (G)
☐ 10 Ryan Huska
☐ 11 Marc Hussey
☐ 12 David Hymovitz
☐ 13 Marc Lamothe
☐ 14 Éric Lecompte
☐ 15 Eric Manlow
☐ 16 Steve McLaren
☐ 17 Kevin Miller
☐ 18 Craig Mills
☐ 19 Frantisek Musil
☐ 20 Dimitri Nabokov
☐ 21 Alain Nasreddine
☐ 22 Ryan Risidore
☐ 23 Michal Sykora
☐ 24 Steve Tardif
☐ 25 Alfie Turcotte
☐ 26 Petri Varis
☐ 27 Todd White
☐ 28 Marty Wilford
☐ 29 M.J.'s Collectibles
☐ 30 PHPA

'98 - 99

INDIANAPOLIS ICE / EBK SPORTS

Singles start at 50¢.

Set (29 cards): $12

☐ 1 Brian Noonan
☐ 2 Matt Cooney
☐ 3 Ryan VandenBussche
☐ 4 Marty Wilford
☐ 5 Nathan Perrott
☐ 6 Mike Vukonich
☐ 7 Rémi Royer
☐ 8 Marc Dupuis
☐ 9 Mike Hall
☐ 10 Sylvain Cloutier
☐ 11 Andrei Trefilov (G)
☐ 12 Andrei Kozyrev
☐ 13 Chris Herperger
☐ 14 Marc Lamothe
☐ 15 Erik Andersson
☐ 16 Bryan Fogarty
☐ 17 Mascot Slapshot
☐ 18 Bob Lachance
☐ 19 Kirk Daubenspeck
☐ 20 Barrie Moore
☐ 21 Bruce Cassidy
☐ 22 David Hymovitz
☐ 23 Justin Hocking
☐ 24 Crowd Favorite
☐ 25 Dale (Digger) DeGray
☐ 26 Jeff Paul
☐ 27 IHL Web Site
☐ 28 MJ Collectibles
☐ 29 PHPA

'99 - 00

INDIANAPOLIS ICE / ROOX SPORTS

Singles start at 50¢.

Card Size: 2 1/2" x 3 1/2"

Set (21 cards): $12

☐ 1 Mike Berger
☐ 2 Ken Boone
☐ 3 Jason Carriere
☐ 4 Yvan Corbin
☐ 5 Dan Cousineau
☐ 6 Robert Davidson
☐ 7 Jay Hern
☐ 8 Peter Jas
☐ 9 Bernie John
☐ 10 Lubos Krajcovic
☐ 11 Eric Landry
☐ 12 Chris MacKenzie
☐ 12 Mascot Slapshot
☐ 13 Jason Mansoff
☐ 14 Jamie Morris
☐ 15 Sebastian Pajerski
☐ 16 Tom Stewart
☐ 17 Benoit Thibert
☐ 18 Steven Toll
☐ 20 Rod Davidson
☐ 21 Joe Trotta

JOHNSTOWN CHIEFS

'89 - 90

JOHNSTOWN CHIEFS / SHEETZ, 850 WJAC

Steve Carlson is one of the more expensive singles at $5. Singles start at 50¢. Cards 1-18 were likely part of a 1988-89 issue.

Card Size: 2 1/2" x 3 1/2"

Set (18 cards): $10

☐ 19 Rick Burchill
☐ 20 Bob Goulet
☐ 21 John Messuri
☐ 22 Darren Servatius
☐ 23 Rick Boyd
☐ 24 Bob Kennedy
☐ 25 Mike Rossetti
☐ 26 Dan Williams
☐ 27 Mark Bogoslowski
☐ 28 Dean Hall
☐ 29 Mitch Molloy

☐ 30 Darren Schwartz
☐ 31 Doug Weiss
☐ 32 Marc Vachon
☐ 33 Mike Jeffrey
☐ 34 Frank Dell
☐ 35 Sean Finn
☐ 36 Steve Carlson

'93 - 94
JOHNSTOWN CHIEFS / PONDEROSA

Singles start at 50¢.
Card Size: 2 1/2" x 3 1/2"
Set (23 cards): **$10**

☐ 1 John Bradley
☐ 2 Campbell Blair
☐ 3 François Bourdeau
☐ 4 Bob Woods
☐ 5 Ted Dent
☐ 6 Matt Hoffman
☐ 7 Gord Christian
☐ 8 Tim Hanus
☐ 9 Phil Soukoroff
☐ 10 Jason Jennings
☐ 11 Dusty McLellan
☐ 12 Dennis Purdie
☐ 13 Chuck Wiegand
☐ 14 Jamie Adams
☐ 15 Jan Beran
☐ 16 Rob Laurie
☐ 17 Cory Banika
☐ 18 Perry Florio
☐ 19 Rob Leask
☐ 20 Ed Johnstone
☐ 21 John Daley
☐ 22 Matt Koeck
☐ Chiefs card

'94 - 95
JOHNSTOWN CHIEFS / PONDEROSA

Patrick Lalime is one of the more expensive singles at $3. Singles start at 50¢.
Card Size: 2 1/2" x 3 1/2"
Set (24 cards): **$10**

☐ 1 Checklist
☐ 2 Jason Brousseau
☐ 3 Brandon Christian
☐ 4 Gord Christian
☐ 5 Bruce Coles
☐ 6 Ted Dent
☐ 7 Martin D'Orsonnens
☐ 8 Perry Florio
☐ 9 Rod Hinks
☐ 10 Matt Hoffman
☐ 11 Aaron Israel
☐ 12 Jason Jennings
☐ 13 Rob Laurie
☐ 14 Rob Leask
☐ 15 Dennis Purdie
☐ 16 Kevin Quinn
☐ 17 Jason Richard
☐ 18 Dan Sawyer
☐ 19 Ben Wyzansky
☐ 20 Matt Yingst
☐ 21 Trainers
☐ 22 Ed Johnstone
☐ 23 WHMTZ-FM
☐ 24 WHMTZ-FM

'96 - 97
JOHNSTOWN CHIEFS / BIG LEAGUE CARDS

Singles start at 50¢.
Set (30 cards): **$10**

☐ 1 Greg Callahan
☐ 2 Brandon Christian
☐ 3 Alexander Chunchukov
☐ 4 Trevor Converse
☐ 5 Chad Dameworth
☐ 6 Carl Fleury
☐ 7 Dan Harrison
☐ 8 Jim Krayer
☐ 9 Denis Lamoureux
☐ 10 Kelly Leroux
☐ 11 Martin Masa
☐ 12 Klemen Mohoric
☐ 13 Sean Perry
☐ 14 Ryan Petz
☐ 15 Dan Reimann
☐ 16 Beau Riedel
☐ 17 Ted Russell
☐ 18 Ryan Savoia
☐ 19 Marc Siegel
☐ 20 Lukas Smital
☐ 21 Olie Sundström
☐ 22 Kam White
☐ 23 Martin Woods
☐ 24 Nick Fotiu
☐ 25 Scott Allen
☐ 26 Heinze/ Midderhoff
☐ 27 Office Staff
☐ 28 Mascot The Iron Dog
☐ 29 Home Schedule
☐ 30 Chiefs

KALAMAZOO WINGS

'77 - 78
KALAMAZOO WINGS / ISB BANK

These cards feature black and white photography. Ron Wilson is one of the more expensive singles at $4. Singles start at $1. Other singles may exist although the set is believed to be complete at 15 cards.
Size: 2 1/2" x 3 1/2"
Set (15 cards): **$15**

☐ 1 George Klasons
☐ 2 Ron Wilson
☐ 3 Bob Lemieux, Coach
☐ 4 Len Ircandia
☐ 5 Ron Kennedy
☐ 6 Daniel Poulin
☐ 7 Terry Ryan
☐ 8 Yvon Dupuis
☐ 9 Tom Milani
☐ 10 Mike Wanchuk
☐ 11 Steve Lee
☐ 12 Yves Guilmette (G)
☐ 13 Al Genovy
☐ 15 Jim Baxter (G)
☐ 18 Alvin White

KANSAS CITY BLADES

'90 - 91
KANSAS CITY BLADES / JONES STORE CO.

Wade Flaherty is one of the more expensive singles at $1.50. Singles start at 50¢.
Card Size: 2 1/2" x 3 1/2"
Set (20 cards): **$10**

☐ 1 Claudio Scremin
☐ 2 Jeff Odgers
☐ 3 Wade Flaherty (G)
☐ 4 Rick Barkovich
☐ 5 Ron Handy
☐ 6 Kevin Sullivan
☐ 7 Randy Exelby
☐ 8 Darin Smith
☐ 9 Stu Kulak
☐ 10 Andrew Akervik
☐ 11 Scott White
☐ 12 Claude Julien
☐ 13 Mike Hitner
☐ 14 Mike Colman
☐ 15 Kury Semandel
☐ 16 Mike Kelfer
☐ 17 Mark Karpen
☐ 18 Lee Giffin
☐ 19 Cam Plante
☐ 20 Jim Latos

'92 - 93
KANSAS CITY BLADES / JONES STORE CO.

Wade Flaherty is one of the more expensive singles at $1.50. Singles start at 50¢.
Set (20 cards): **$10**

☐ 1 Wade Flaherty (G)
☐ 2 David Williams
☐ 3 Duane Joyce
☐ 4 Jeff Sharples
☐ 5 Victor Ignatjov
☐ 6 Jeff McLean
☐ 7 Brian Lawton
☐ 8 Troy Frederick
☐ 9 Jaroslav Otevrel
☐ 10 Gary Emmons
☐ 11 Dody Wood
☐ 12 Ed Courtenay
☐ 13 Mark Beaufait
☐ 14 Jean-François Quintin
☐ 15 Dale Craigwell
☐ 16 Mikhail Kravets
☐ 17 John Weisbrod
☐ 18 Mike Colman
☐ 19 Claudio Scremin
☐ 20 Dean Kolstad

'93 - 94
KANSAS CITY BLADES / JONES STORE CO.

Wade Flaherty is one of the more expensive singles at $1.50. Singles start at 50¢.
Set (20 cards): **$10**

☐ 1 Duane Joyce
☐ 2 Sean Gorman
☐ 3 Victor Ignatjov
☐ 4 Jeff McLean
☐ 5 Kip Miller
☐ 6 Jaroslav Otevrel
☐ 7 David Bruce
☐ 8 Gary Emmons
☐ 9 Dody Wood
☐ 10 Lee J. Leslie
☐ 11 Alexander Cherbayev
☐ 12 Jean-François Quintin
☐ 13 Ed Courtenay
☐ 14 Andrei Nazarov
☐ 15 Mikhail Kravets
☐ 16 Mike Colman
☐ 17 Vlastimil Kroupa
☐ 18 Andrei Buschan
☐ 19 Trevor Robins
☐ 20 Wade Flaherty (G)

'94 - 95
KANSAS CITY BLADES / JONES STORE CO.

Singles start at 50¢.
Set (20 cards): **$12**

☐ 1 Duane Joyce
☐ 2 Ken Hammond
☐ 3 Michal Sykora
☐ 4 Kevin Wortman
☐ 5 Andrei Buschan
☐ 6 Chris Tancill
☐ 7 Ken (Jr.) Hodge
☐ 8 David Bruce
☐ 9 Jan Caloun
☐ 10 Gary Emmons
☐ 11 Dody Wood
☐ 12 Lee J. Leslie
☐ 13 Alexander Cherbayev
☐ 14 Jean-François Quintin
☐ 15 Claudio Scremin
☐ 16 Dean Grillo
☐ 17 Andrei Nazarov
☐ 18 Todd Holt
☐ 19 Vlastimil Kroupa
☐ 20 Trevor Robins

'95 - 96
KANSAS CITY BLADES / ARGOSY CASINO

Singles start at 50¢.
Set (25 cards): **$12**

☐ Jeff Batters
☐ Sergei Bautin
☐ David Bruce
☐ Jan Caloun
☐ Alexander Cherbayev
☐ Larry Dyck
☐ Paul Dyck
☐ Gary Emmons
☐ Dean Ewen
☐ Pat Ferschweiler
☐ Jean-François Quintin
☐ Chris Tancill
☐ Vasily Tikhonov
☐ Alexei Yegorov
☐ Mascot Chilly
☐ Drew Remenda
☐ Geoff Sarjeant
☐ Claudio Scremin
☐ Jeff McLean
☐ Fredrik Nilsson
☐ Fredrik Oduya
☐ Alexander Osadchy
☐ Dean Grillo
☐ Ken Hammond
☐ Viktor Kozlov

'96 - 97
KANSAS CITY BLADES / STATION CASINO

Singles start at 50¢.
Set (25 cards): **$12**

☐ 1 Ian Boyce
☐ 2 David Bruce
☐ 3 Jason Cirone
☐ 4 Dale Craigwell
☐ 5 Brent Cullaton
☐ 6 Philippe DeRouville (G)
☐ 7 Larry Dyck
☐ 8 Paul Dyck
☐ 9 Gary Emmons
☐ 10 Dean Ewen
☐ 11 Bryan Fogarty
☐ 12 Jason Herter
☐ 13 Jim Kyte
☐ 14 Jeff Madill
☐ 15 Jeff McLean
☐ 16 John Purves
☐ 17 Jean-François Quintin
☐ 18 Normand Rochefort
☐ 19 Claudio Scremin
☐ 20 Brian Stacey
☐ 21 Dean Sylvester
☐ 22 Don Jackson
☐ 23 Lucien DeBlois
☐ 24 KC Blades
☐ 25 PHPA

'98 - 99
KANSAS CITY BLADES

Patrick Lalime is one of the more expensive singles at $3. Singles start at 50¢.
Set (30 cards): **$12**

☐ 1 Checklist
☐ 2 Brian Leitza
☐ 3 Dan Ratushny
☐ 4 Trevor Sherban
☐ 5 Eric Rud
☐ 6 Tuomas Grönman
☐ 7 Eric Perrin
☐ 8 Brendan Yarema
☐ 9 Brian Bonin
☐ 10 Pat Ferschweiler
☐ 11 Dody Wood
☐ 12 David Ling
☐ 13 Rocky Welsing
☐ 14 Jean-Guy Trudel
☐ 15 Vlastimil Kroupa
☐ 16 Steven Low
☐ 17 Ryan Mulhern
☐ 18 Brent Bilodeau
☐ 19 Grant Richison
☐ 20 Dave Chyzowski
☐ 21 David Vallieres
☐ 22 Patrick Lalime (G)
☐ 23 J-S Aubin (G)
☐ 24 Jason Cirone
☐ 25 Paul MacLean, Coach
☐ 26 G. Emmons, A.Coach
☐ 27 John Doolan, Eq. Mgr.
☐ 28 Jeff Kreuser, Trainer
☐ 29 Mascot Scrapper
☐ 30 PHPA Sponsor

'99 - 00
KANSAS CITY BLADES / GREAT MOMENTS

Singles start at $1.
Set (4 cards): **$6**

☐ Gary Emmons
☐ Wade Flaherty (G)
☐ Claudio Scremin
☐ Dody Wood

'99 - 00
KANSAS CITY BLADES / MULTI-AD SPORTS

Singles start at 50¢.
Set (30 cards): **$10**

☐ 1 Tom Askey (G)
☐ 2 Joe Blaznek
☐ 3 Aris Brimanis
☐ 4 Dave Chyzowski
☐ 5 Jason Cirone
☐ 6 Pat Ferschweiler
☐ 7 Forrest Gore
☐ 8 Sean Haggerty
☐ 9 David Ling
☐ 10 Steve Lingren
☐ 11 Tyler Moss
☐ 12 Nick Naumenko
☐ 13 Eric Perrin
☐ 14 Michal Pivonka
☐ 15 Bruce Racine
☐ 16 Grant Richison
☐ 17 Jon Rohloff
☐ 18 Ray Schultz
☐ 19 David Vallieres
☐ 20 Jan Vodrazka
☐ 21 Dody Wood
☐ 22 Brendan Yarema
☐ 23 Mascot Scrapper
☐ 24 Jeff Kreuser
☐ 25 John Doolan
☐ 26 Gary Emmons
☐ 27 Paul MacLean
☐ 28 PHPA
☐ 29 Sponsor Supercuts
☐ 30 Checklist

'00 - 01
KANSAS CITY BLADES / DICK'S SPORT. GOODS

Singles start at 50¢.
Set (27 cards): **$12**

☐ 1 Ryan Bonni
☐ 2 Jan Vodrazka
☐ 3 Bryan Allen
☐ 4 Zenith Komarniski
☐ 5 Sean Tallaire
☐ 6 Ryan Ready
☐ 7 Regan Darby
☐ 8 Dody Wood
☐ 9 Harold Druken
☐ 10 Darrell Hay
☐ 11 Vadim Sharifijanov
☐ 12 Steve Lingren
☐ 13 Josh Holden
☐ 14 Mike Brown
☐ 15 Jeff Scissons
☐ 16 Jarkko Ruutu
☐ 17 Pat Kavanagh
☐ 18 Brad Leeb
☐ 19 Bryan Helmer
☐ 20 Artem Chubarov
☐ 21 Corey Schwab (G)
☐ 22 Alfie Michaud
☐ 23 Stan Smyl
☐ 24 Barry Smith
☐ 25 Sponsor Ryno
☐ 26 Dick's Sporting goods
☐ 27 PHPA web site

KENTUCKY THOROUGHBLADES

'96 - 97
KENTUCKY THOROUGHBLADES / SPLIT SECOND

Singles start at 50¢.
Card Size: 2 1/2" x 3 1/2"
Set (26 cards): **$10**

☐ Ken Belanger
☐ Alexandre Boikov
☐ Jan Caloun
☐ Denis Chervyakov
☐ Jarrett Deuling
☐ Iain Fraser
☐ Dean Grillo
☐ Stephen Guolla
☐ Sean Haggerty
☐ Jason Holland
☐ Lance Leslie
☐ Chris LiPuma
☐ Pat Mikesch
☐ Fredrik Oduya
☐ Jamie Ram (G)
☐ Jason Strudwick
☐ Chris Tancill
☐ Steve Webb
☐ Jason Widmer
☐ Jim Wiley
☐ Alexei Yegorov
☐ AHL Web Site
☐ Mascot Lucky
☐ PHPA
☐ Arena Opening Night
☐ Team Photo

'97 - 98
KENTUCKY THOROUGHBLADES / SPLIT SECOND

Evgeny Nabokov is one of the more expensive singles at $5. Singles start at 50¢.
Card Size: 2 1/2" x 3 1/2"
Set (25 cards): **$15**

☐ Peter Allen
☐ Niklas Andersson
☐ Alexandre Boikov
☐ Zdeno Chara
☐ Stephen Guolla
☐ Sean Haggerty
☐ Jason Holland
☐ Alexander Korolyuk
☐ Evgeni Nabokov (G)
☐ Fredrik Oduya
☐ Chad Penney
☐ Jamie Ram
☐ Peter Roed
☐ Jason Strudwick
☐ Tony Tuzzolino
☐ Steve Webb
☐ Jason Widmer
☐ Jim Wiley
☐ Brendan Yarema
☐ Alexei Yegorov
☐ Andrei Zyuzin
☐ AHL Web Site
☐ Mascot Lucky
☐ PHPA
☐ Team Photo

'98 - 99
KENTUCKY THOROUGHBLADES / SPLIT SECOND

Evgeni Nabokov is one of the more expensive singles at $1.50. Singles start at 50¢.
Card Size: 2 1/2" x 3 1/2"
Sponsor: Split Second
Set (25 cards): **$15**

☐ Peter Allen
☐ Eric Boulton
☐ Dan Boyle
☐ Matt Bradley
☐ Mike Craig
☐ Jarrett Deuling
☐ Curtis Doell
☐ Dave Duerden
☐ Sean Gauthier
☐ Christian Gosselin
☐ Stephen Guolla
☐ Harold Hersh
☐ Filip Kuba
☐ Alexander Korolyuk
☐ Steve Lingren
☐ Andy MacIntyre
☐ Evgeni Nabokov (G)
☐ Jarrod Skalde
☐ Mark Smith
☐ Roy Sommer
☐ Herbert Vasiljevs
☐ Eric Veilleux
☐ Andrei Zyuzin
☐ AHL Web Site
☐ Mascot Lucky

'99 - 00
KENTUCKY THOROUGHBLADES / WKYT TV27

Johan Hedberg is one of the more expensive singles at $4-8. Singles start at 50¢.
Set (25 cards): **$15**

☐ Chris Armstrong
☐ Matt Bradley
☐ Garrett Burnett
☐ Adam Colagiacomo
☐ Jon Coleman
☐ Larry Courville
☐ Mike Craig
☐ Jarrett Deuling
☐ Doug Friedman
☐ Christian Gosselin
☐ Scott Hannan
☐ Johan Hedberg (G)
☐ Shawn Heins
☐ Robert Jindrich
☐ Miikka Kiprusoff
☐ Éric Landry
☐ Chris Lipsett
☐ Andy Lundbohm
☐ Robert Mulick
☐ Adam Nittel
☐ Peter Roed
☐ Mark Smith
☐ Coaching Staff
☐ Mascot Lucky
☐ Thoroughblades

'00 - 01
KENTUCKY THOROUGHBLADES

Singles start at 50¢.
Set (27 cards): **$18**

☐ Ryan Kraft
☐ SP1 Ryan Kraft
☐ SP2 Evgeni Nabokov (G)
☐ Greg Andrusak
☐ Steve Bancroft
☐ Zoltan Batovsky
☐ Matt Bradley
☐ Jonathan Cheechoo
☐ Adam Colagiacomo
☐ Larry Courville
☐ Rob Davison
☐ Jarrett Deuling
☐ Christian Gosselin
☐ Robert Jindrich
☐ Miikka Kiprusoff (G)
☐ Chris Lipsett
☐ Andy Lundbohm
☐ Dave MacIsaac
☐ Eric Laplante
☐ Jim Montgomery
☐ Robert Mulick
☐ Adam Nittel
☐ Mikael Samuelsson
☐ Mark Smith
☐ Vesa Toskala
☐ Miroslav Zalesak
☐ Thoroughblades
☐ Fotiu / Sommer
☐ Promo J. Cheechoo
☐ Promo Adam Nittel

KNOXVILLE CHEROKEES

'91 - 92
KNOXVILLE CHEROKEES / THE NEWS SENTINEL

Singles start at 50¢.
Card Size: 2 1/2" x 3 1/2"
Set (20 cards): **$8**

☐ Dean Anderson
☐ Karl Clauss
☐ Jamie Dabanovich
☐ Trevor Forsythe
☐ Joel Gardner
☐ Mike Gober
☐ Mike Greenlay
☐ Galen Head
☐ Roman Hubalek
☐ Brett Lawrence
☐ Shawn Lillie
☐ Dean McDonald
☐ Robert Melanson
☐ Troy Mick
☐ Bill Nyrop
☐ Greg Pankewicz
☐ Steve Ryding
☐ David Shute
☐ Chad Thompson
☐ Bruno Villeneuve

'93 - 94
KNOXVILLE CHEROKEES

Manon Rhéaume is one of the more expensive singles at $6. Singles start at 50¢.
Card Size: 2 1/2" x 3 1/2"
Set (20 cards): **$15**

☐ Scott Boston
☐ Cory Cadden
☐ Tim Chase
☐ Steven Flomenhoft
☐ Scott Gordon (G)
☐ Jon Larson
☐ Carl LeBlanc
☐ Kim Maier
☐ Wes McCauley
☐ Scott Mercalfe
☐ Mike Murray
☐ Hayden O'Rear
☐ Jeff Reid
☐ Manon Rhéaume (G)
☐ Marc Rodgers
☐ Doug Searle
☐ Barry Smith
☐ Martin Tanguay
☐ Nicholas Vachon
☐ Bruno Villeneuve

'94 - 95
KNOXVILLE CHEROKEES / AMERICAN CLOTHING

Singles start at 50¢.
Card Size: 2 1/2" x 3 1/2"
Set (24 cards): **$10**

☐ 1 Checklist
☐ 2 Barry Smith
☐ 3 Aaron Fackler
☐ 4 Andy Davis
☐ 5 Stéphane Ménard
☐ 6 Doug Searle
☐ 7 Hayden O'Rear
☐ 8 Sean Brown
☐ 9 Mike Murray
☐ 10 Jon Jenkins
☐ 11 Sean Pronger
☐ 12 Steven Flomenhoft
☐ 13 David Neilson
☐ 14 Jack Callahan
☐ 15 Carl LeBlanc
☐ 16 Alain Deeks
☐ 17 George Zajankala
☐ 18 Chris Fess
☐ 19 Michel Gaul
☐ 20 Pat Murray
☐ 21 Rob McIntyre
☐ 22 V. Nedomansky, Jr
☐ 23 Cory Cadden
☐ 24 Michael Burman

'96 - 97
KNOXVILLE CHEROKEES / SPLIT SECOND

Singles start at 50¢.
Card Size: 2 1/2" x 3 1/2"
Set (24 cards): **$10**

☐ 1 Team Photo
☐ 2 Barry Smith
☐ 3 Sean Halifax
☐ 4 Daniel Chaput
☐ 5 Jamie Bird
☐ 6 Matt Turek
☐ 7 Chris Fess
☐ 8 Kelly Hollingshead
☐ 9 Darren Johnson
☐ 10 V. (Jr.) Nedomansky
☐ 11 Kent Fearns
☐ 12 Martin Tanguay
☐ 13 Wayne Anchikoski
☐ 14 Jim Brown
☐ 15 Garrett Burnett
☐ 16 Stéphane Soulliere
☐ 17 Dean Moore
☐ 18 David Neilson
☐ 19 Mike Vandenberghe
☐ 20 Brad Guzda
☐ 21 Olaf Kjenstadt
☐ 22 PHPA
☐ P1 Brad Guzda
☐ P2 Jim Brown

LAS VEGAS THUNDER

'93 - 94
LAS VEGAS THUNDER / SATURN

Butch Goring is one of the more expensive singles at $1. Singles start at 50¢.
Card Size: 2 1/2" x 3 1/2"
Set (32 cards): **$10**

☐ Brent Ashton
☐ Bob Bourne
☐ Rod Buskas
☐ Lyndon Byers
☐ Rich Campbell
☐ Colin Cowherd
☐ Butch Goring
☐ Steve Gotaas
☐ Marc Habscheid
☐ Brett Hauer
☐ Shawn Heaphy
☐ Scott Hollis
☐ Peter Ing (G)
☐ Steve Jaques
☐ Bob Joyce
☐ Jim Kyte
☐ Patrice Lefebvre
☐ Clint Malarchuk (G)
☐ Ken Quinney
☐ Jean-Marc Richard

☐ Todd Richards
☐ Marc Rodgers
☐ Jeff Sharples
☐ Randy Smith
☐ Greg Spenrath
☐ Bob Strumm
☐ Kirk Tomlinson
☐ Kerry Toporowski
☐ Mark Vermette
☐ Steve Wissman
☐ Thunder card
☐ Mascot Boom Boom

'94 - 95

LAS VEGAS THUNDER / CHEVROLET

Manon Rhéaume and Radek Bonk are the most expensive singles at $4 each. Singles start at 50¢.
Card Size: 2 1/2" x 3 1/2"
Set (29 cards): $18

☐ James Black
☐ Radek Bonk
☐ Rich Campbell
☐ Frank Evans
☐ Marc Habscheid
☐ Alex Hicks
☐ Bob Joyce
☐ Jim Kyte
☐ Patrice Lefebvre
☐ Darcy Loewen
☐ Sal Lombardi
☐ Clint Malarchuk (G)
☐ Andrew McBain
☐ Chris McSorley
☐ David Neilson
☐ Jerry Olenyn
☐ Ken Quinney
☐ Eldon Reddick (G)
☐ Jeff Reid
☐ Manon Rhéaume (G)
☐ Jean-Marc Richard
☐ Todd Richards
☐ Marc Rodgers
☐ Jeff Sharples
☐ Jarrod Skalde
☐ Bob Strumm
☐ Kerry Toporowski
☐ Morning Radio
☐ Mascot Boom Boom

'95 - 96

LAS VEGAS THUNDER / EDGE ICE

Singles start at 50¢.
Card Size: 2 1/2" x 3 1/2"
Set (25 cards): $12

☐ Bill Bowler
☐ Peter Fiorentino
☐ Greg Hawgood
☐ Sasha Lakovic
☐ Patrice Lefebvre
☐ Darcy Loewen
☐ Clint Malarchuk (G)
☐ Gord Marx
☐ Chris McSorley
☐ Blaine Moore
☐ Vaclav Nedomansky, Jr.
☐ Eldon Reddick (G)
☐ Jeff Roccoardo
☐ Jean-Marc Richard
☐ Marc Rodgers
☐ Ken Quinney
☐ Ruslan Salei
☐ Jeff Sharples
☐ Daniel Shank
☐ Todd Simon
☐ Bob Strumm
☐ Rhett Trombley
☐ Vladimir Tsyplakov
☐ Sergei Zholtok
☐ Mascot Boom Boom

'96 - 97

LAS VEGAS THUNDER / HEINEKIN

Pavol Demitra is one of the more expensive singles at $3. Singles start at 50¢.
Card Size: 2 1/2" x 3 1/2"
Set (24 cards): $12

☐ Igor Bashkatov
☐ Kevin Dahl
☐ Chris Dahlquist
☐ Pavol Demitra
☐ Parris Duffus (G)
☐ Martin Gendron
☐ Brent Gretzky
☐ Kerry Huffman
☐ Igor Karpenko
☐ Don Larner
☐ Patrice Lefebvre
☐ Darcy Loewen
☐ Blaine Moore
☐ Ken Quinney
☐ Jeff Serowik
☐ Jason Simon
☐ Rhett Trombley
☐ Sergei Yerkowich
☐ Sergei Zholtok
☐ Bob Strumm, G.M.
☐ Clint Malarchuk, A.G.M.
☐ Chris McSorley, Coach
☐ Mascot Boom Boom
☐ IHL Card

'97 - 98

LAS VEGAS THUNDER

Manny Legacé is one of the more expensive singles at $2. Singles start at 50¢.
Set (28 cards): $12

☐ 1 Ken Quinney
☐ 2 Manny Legacé
☐ 3 Jesse Bélanger
☐ 4 Joe Day
☐ 5 Darcy Loewen
☐ 6 Trevor Roenick
☐ 7 Steve Bancroft
☐ 8 Thom Cullen
☐ 9 John Slaney
☐ 10 Sergei Yerkovich
☐ 11 Bob Strumm, G.M.
☐ 12 C. McSorley, Coach
☐ 13 D. Tretiak, Eq. Mgr.
☐ 14 Sponsor KKLZ
☐ 15 Patrice Lefebvre
☐ 16 Tim Cheveldae
☐ 17 Jeff Christian
☐ 18 Sergei Klimovich
☐ 19 Rob Pattison
☐ 20 Dan Shermerhorn
☐ 21 Ilya Byakin
☐ 22 Justin Kurtz
☐ 23 Radoslav Suchy
☐ 24 Mascot Boom Boom
☐ 25 Malarchuk, Asst. G.M.
☐ 26 Van Parfet, Trainer
☐ 27 D. McCann
☐ 28 PHPA Web Site

'98 - 99

LAS VEGAS THUNDER

Petr Nedved is one of the more expensive singles at $2.Singles start at 50¢.
Set (30 cards): $10

☐ 1 Sami Helenius
☐ 2 Nick Naumenko
☐ 3 Patrice Lefebvre
☐ 4 Trevor Roenick
☐ 5 Shawn Wansborough
☐ 6 Taj Melson
☐ 7 Stefan Ustorf
☐ 8 Sean Berens
☐ 9 Russ Romaniuk
☐ 10 Scott Hollis
☐ 11 Dean Ewen
☐ 12 Jason McBain
☐ 13 Andrei Srubko
☐ 14 Petr Franek
☐ 15 Dampy Brar
☐ 16 Brad Guzda
☐ 17 Kevin Kaminski
☐ 18 Brad Miller
☐ 19 Petr Nedved
☐ 20 Mike Wilson
☐ 21 Drew Bannister
☐ 22 Bryan Helmer
☐ 23 Konstantin Simchuk
☐ 24 Bob Strumm, G.M.
☐ 25 Bob Bourne, Coach
☐ 26 R. Buskas, A.Coach
☐ 27 Van Parfet, Trainer
☐ 28 Kennedy/ Krouse, Eq.
☐ 29 Mascot Boom Boom
☐ 30 PHPA Web Site

LONG BEACH ICE DOGS

'97 - 98

LONG BEACH ICE DOGS / ICE BREAKERS

Singles start at 50¢.
Set (20 cards): $8

☐ Doug Ast
☐ Patrik Augusta
☐ Collin Bauer
☐ Mike Buzak (G)
☐ John Byce
☐ Brian Chapman
☐ Mark Ferner
☐ Victor Ignatjev
☐ Rob Kenny
☐ Dan Lambert
☐ Mike Matteucci
☐ Joby Messier
☐ Stéphane Morin
☐ Shawn Penn
☐ Russ Romaniuk
☐ Nicholas Vachon
☐ Andrei Vasilyev
☐ Kay Whitmore (G)
☐ Darryl Williams
☐ Mascot Spike

'98 - 99

LONG BEACH ICE DOGS / ICE BREAKERS

Patrik Stefan is one of the more expensive singles at $10. Singles start at 50¢.
Set (20 cards): $18

☐ Doug Ast
☐ Patrik Augusta
☐ John Byce
☐ Dan Bylsma
☐ Mark Ferner
☐ Mike Jickling
☐ Frédérick Jobin
☐ Claude Jutras
☐ Dan Lambert
☐ Manny Legacé (G)
☐ Jocelyn Lemieux
☐ Mike Matteucci
☐ Sacha Molin
☐ Jan Nemecek
☐ Andy Roach
☐ Pavel Rosa
☐ Patrik Stefan
☐ Darryl Williams
☐ J. Van Boxmeer, Coach
☐ Mascot Spike

LOUISIANA ICE GATORS

'95 - 96

LOUISIANA ICE GATORS

Rob Valicevic is one of the more expensive singles at $1. Singles start at 50¢.
Card Size: 2 1/2" x 3 1/2
Sponsor: None
Set (21 cards): $10

☐ Bob Berg
☐ John Depourcq
☐ Wade Fournier
☐ Fred Goltz
☐ Ron Handy
☐ Mike Heany
☐ Dean Hulett
☐ Jim Latos
☐ George Maneluk
☐ Rob McCaig
☐ Jason McQuat
☐ Rod Pasma
☐ Sean Rowe
☐ Bryan Schoen
☐ Darryl Shedden
☐ Doug Shedden
☐ Fred Spoltore
☐ Chris Valicevic
☐ Rob Valicevic
☐ John Vary
☐ Marty Yewchuk

'95 - 96

LOUISIANA ICE GATORS / CHEVROLET

Singles start at 50¢.
Card Size: 2 1/2" x 3 1/2"
Set (21 cards): $10

☐ Bob Berg
☐ Aaron Boh
☐ Eric Cloutier
☐ John DePourcq
☐ Wade Fournier
☐ Ron Handy
☐ Mike Heaney
☐ Dean Hulett
☐ Jim Latos
☐ George Maneluk
☐ Rob McCaig
☐ Jason McQuat
☐ Chad Nelson
☐ Dan O'Rourke
☐ Rod Pasma
☐ Darryl Shedden
☐ Doug Shedden
☐ John Spoltore
☐ Chuck Thuss
☐ C.Valicevic/ R.Valicevic
☐ John Vary

'96 - 97

LOUISIANA ICE GATORS / STARZSPORTS

Singles start at 50¢.
Set (22 cards): $10

☐ Aaron Boh
☐ Marc Delorme
☐ John DePourcq
☐ Louis Dumont
☐ Ron Handy
☐ Mikhail Kravets
☐ Jim Latos
☐ Rob McCaig
☐ Jason McQuat
☐ Stan Melanson
☐ Joey Mittelsteadt
☐ Chad Nelson
☐ Dan O'Rourke
☐ Ken Ruddick
☐ Dean Seymour
☐ Ryan Shanahan
☐ Darryl Shedden
☐ Doug Shedden
☐ Sergei Tkachenko
☐ Chris Valicevic
☐ Rob Weingartner
☐ Jack Williams

'97 - 98

LOUISIANA ICE GATORS / STARZSPORTS

Singles start at 50¢.
Set (22 cards): $10

☐ 1 Louis Dumont
☐ 2 Jason McQuat
☐ 3 Mascot Alphonse
☐ 4 Matt Pagnutti
☐ 5 Richard Smit
☐ 6 John Varga
☐ 7 Jay Murphy
☐ 8 Darrell Woodley
☐ 9 Scott McKay
☐ 10 Jack Williams
☐ 11 Stan Melanson
☐ 12 Brad Toporowski
☐ 13 John Jennings
☐ 14 Éric Cloutier
☐ 15 Ryan Pisiak
☐ 16 John Spoltore
☐ 17 Mikhail Kravets
☐ 18 Paul Rushforth
☐ 19 Doug Bonner
☐ 20 Chad Nelson
☐ 21 Doug Shedden
☐ 22 Don Parsons

'98 - 99

LOUISIANA ICE GATORS / STARZSPORTS

Singles start at 50¢.
Set (23 cards): $9

☐ Bujar Amidovski
☐ Doug Bonner
☐ Éric Cloutier
☐ Mark DeSantis
☐ Louis Dumont
☐ Blair Manning
☐ Roger Maxwell
☐ Jason McQuat
☐ Stan Melanson
☐ Jay Murphy
☐ Mike Murray
☐ Matt Pagnutti
☐ Don Parsons
☐ Gary Roach
☐ Ryan Shanahan
☐ Doug Shedden
☐ John Spoltore
☐ Chris Valicevic
☐ John Varga
☐ Rob Weingartner
☐ Mascot Alphonse
☐ Team Photo
☐ Thurlow / Livin

'99 - 00

LOUISIANA ICE GATORS / ROOX SPORTS

Singles start at 50¢.
Card Size: 2 1/2" x 3 1/2"
Set (25 cards): $10

☐ Dave Arsenault
☐ Chris Bogas
☐ Mark Cadotte
☐ John DePourcq
☐ Sean Gauthier
☐ Dennis Holland
☐ John Jennings
☐ Mike Kucsulain
☐ Hugo Marchand
☐ Shawn McNeil
☐ Jason McQuat
☐ Stan Melanson
☐ Don Murdoch
☐ Jay Murphy
☐ Michael Murray
☐ Vaclav (Jr.) Nedomansky
☐ Corey Neilson
☐ Mike Oliveira
☐ Matt Pagnutti
☐ Jesse Rezansoff
☐ Jason Sessa
☐ Ryan Shanahan
☐ John Spoltore
☐ Chris Valicevic
☐ Mascot Claw'd

'00 - 01

LOUISIANA ICE GATORS

Singles start at 50¢.
Set (24 cards):

☐ Stan Melanson
☐ Jay Murphy
☐ Nathan Borega
☐ Shawn McNeil
☐ Ryan Shanahan
☐ Roman Marakhovski
☐ Mike Kucsulain
☐ Dalen Hrooshkin
☐ Kevin Karlander
☐ Corey Neilson
☐ Bruce Richardson
☐ Jason Saal
☐ Michael Murray
☐ Jason McQuat
☐ John Spoltore
☐ Mike Valley
☐ Magnus Nilsson
☐ Dan Tessier
☐ Matt Pagnutti
☐ Roger Maxwell
☐ D. Farrish & J.DePourq
☐ Johnny Gomez
☐ Greg Sieg
☐ Andy Davis

'01 - 02

LOUISIANA ICE GATORS

Singles start at 50¢.
Set (25 cards):

☐ Header
☐ Steve Aronson
☐ Frédéric Cloutier
☐ Cory Cyrenne
☐ Dominic Forget
☐ Russell Hewson
☐ Konstantin Kalmikov
☐ Branislav Kvetan
☐ Greg Labenski
☐ Marc Magliarditi
☐ Ryan Marsh
☐ Shawn McNeil
☐ Kevin Mitchell
☐ Jay Murphy
☐ Corey Neilson
☐ Randy Perry
☐ Nathan Rempel
☐ Ryan Shanahan
☐ Dennis Shiryaev
☐ Chris Valicevic
☐ Dave Farrish
☐ John DePourcq
☐ Andy Davis
☐ R.Casataneda & G.Sieg
☐ Mascot Alphonse

'02 - 03

LOUISIANA ICE GATORS

Singles start at 50¢.
Set (25 cards):

☐ Semir Ben-Amor
☐ Cal Benazic
☐ Bobby Brown
☐ Frédéric Cloutier
☐ Kenny Corupe
☐ John DePourcq
☐ Daniel Goneau
☐ Kyle Kettles
☐ Branislav Kvetan
☐ Louis Mass
☐ Shawn McNeil
☐ Kevin Mitchell
☐ J_P Morin
☐ Nathan Rempel
☐ Bruce Richardson
☐ Rod Sarich
☐ Dennis Shiryaev
☐ Shawn Skiehar
☐ Chris Taliercio
☐ Tony Tuzzolino
☐ Jeff Worlton
☐ Dave Farrish
☐ Andy Davis
☐ Greg Sieg
☐ Ice Gators

LOUISVILLE PANTHERS

'99 - 00

LOUISVILLE PANTHERS / ROOX SPORTS

Ivan Novoseltsev is one of the more expensive singles at $1.50. Singles start at 50¢.
Card Size: 2 1/2" x 3 1/2"
Set (33 cards): $15

☐ 1 Craig Ferguson
☐ 2 Brent Thompson
☐ 3 Craig Reichert
☐ 4 Eric Boguniecki
☐ 5 Dan Boyle
☐ 6 Ivan Novoseltsev
☐ 7 Dave Duerden
☐ 8 Curtis Doell
☐ 9 Sean Gauthier
☐ 10 Peter Ratchuk
☐ 11 John Jakopin
☐ 12 Marcus Nilson
☐ 13 Mascot Paws
☐ 14 Chris Wells
☐ 15 Kirby Law
☐ 16 Chris Allen
☐ 17 Chad Cabana
☐ 18 R. Shulmistra (G)
☐ 19 Dwayne Hay
☐ 20 Joey Tetarenko
☐ 21 Paul Brousseau
☐ 22 Nick Smith
☐ 23 Brad Ference
☐ 24 Lance Ward
☐ 25 Jeff Ware
☐ 26 Paul Harvey
☐ 27 Andrew Long
☐ 28 Joe Paterson
☐ 29 Gerard Gallant
☐ 30 Tamer Afr
☐ 31 Chuck Fletcher
☐ 32 UPS
☐ 33 Indiana Casino

'00 - 01

LOUISVILLE PANTHERS / CHOICE

Denis Shvidki is one of the more expensive singles at $2. Singles start at 50¢.
Set (13 cards): $12

☐ 1 Checklist
☐ 2 Brent Thompson
☐ 3 Paul Brousseau
☐ 4 David Emma
☐ 5 Joey Tetarenko
☐ 6 Peter Ratchuk
☐ 7 Dave Duerden
☐ 8 Sean Gauthier
☐ 9 Kyle Rossiter
☐ 10 Rocky Thompson
☐ 11 Denis Shvidki
☐ 12 Brad Ference
☐ 13 Joe Paterson

LOWELL LOCK MONSTERS

'99 - 00

LOWELL LOCK MONSTERS / JCDU

Singles start at 50¢.
Set (27 cards): $10

☐ 1 Ray Giroux
☐ 2 Dave MacIsaac
☐ 3 Richard Seeley
☐ 4 Nathan LaFayette
☐ 5 Rich Brennan
☐ 6 Petr Mika
☐ 7 Donald MacLean
☐ 8 Cody Bowtell
☐ 9 Vladimir Chebaturkin
☐ 10 David Hymovitz
☐ 11 Sean Blanchard
☐ 12 Éric Bélanger
☐ 13 Dimitri Nabokov
☐ 14 Vladimir Országh
☐ 15 Greg Phillips
☐ 16 Jason Krog
☐ 17 Eric Brewer
☐ 18 Travis Scott
☐ 19 Evgeny Korolev
☐ 20 S. Valiquette (G)
☐ 21 Jason Podollan
☐ 22 Jockey Jack Baldwin
☐ 23 Lock Monsters
☐ 24 Mascot Louie
☐ 25 Bruce Boudreau
☐ 26 Steve Stirling
☐ 27 Tom Rowe

'00 - 01

LOWELL LOCK MONSTERS / JCDU

Singles start at 50¢.
Set (30 cards): $12

☐ 1 Joe Corvo
☐ 2 Andreas Lilja
☐ 3 Joe Rullier
☐ 4 Jeff Daw
☐ 5 Petr Mika
☐ 6 Rich Brennan
☐ 7 Brad Chartrand
☐ 8 Marko Tuomainen
☐ 9 Eric Veilleux
☐ 10 Éric Bélanger
☐ 11 Peter Leboutillier
☐ 12 David Hymovitz
☐ 13 Juraj Kolnik
☐ 14 Chris Schmidt
☐ 15 Kevin Baker
☐ 16 Steve Passmore
☐ 17 Richard Seeley
☐ 18 Jason Krog
☐ 19 Travis Scott
☐ 20 Marcel Cousineau (G)
☐ 21 Nate Miller
☐ 22 Branislav Mezei
☐ 23 Mathieu Biron
☐ 24 Kip Brennan
☐ 25 Greg Phillips
☐ 26 Mascot Louie
☐ 27 Mike Pudlick
☐ 28 Bruce Boudreau
☐ 29 Steve Stirling
☐ 30 Tom Rowe

MANCHESTER MONARCHS

'01 - 02

MANCHESTER MONARCHS / CHOICE

Each series was numbered cards 1-15.
Set (30 cards):

☐ 1 Randy Robitaille
☐ 2 Derek Bekar
☐ 3 Brad Chartrand
☐ 4 Nate Miller
☐ 5 Andre Payette
☐ 6 Brett Hauer
☐ 7 Chris Schmidt
☐ 8 Mike Pudlick
☐ 9 Kip Brennan
☐ 10 Tomas Zizka
☐ 11 Jerred Smithson
☐ 12 Joe Corvo
☐ 13 Stéphane Fiset (G)
☐ 14 Marcel Cousineau (G)
☐ 15 B. Boudreau, Coach
☐ 1 Dane Jackson
☐ 2 Travis Scott (G)
☐ 3 Ted Donato
☐ 4 Joe Rullier
☐ 5 Rich Brennan
☐ 6 Eric Healey
☐ 7 Jason Holland
☐ 8 Richard Seeley
☐ 9 Jaroslav Bednar
☐ 10 Ryan Flinn
☐ 11 Rob Valicevic
☐ 12 Steve Kelly
☐ 13 Dan Riva
☐ 14 Scott Thomas
☐ 15 Mascot Maximillian

'02 - 03

MANCHESTER MONARCHS / CHOICE

Cards start at 50¢.
Set (15 cards):

☐ 1 Chris Aldous
☐ 2 Scott Barney
☐ 3 Bruce Boudreau
☐ 4 Kip Brennan
☐ 5 Mike Cammalleri
☐ 6 Joe Corvo
☐ 7 Eric Healey
☐ 8 Steve Heinze
☐ 9 Dane Jackson
☐ 10 Steve Kelly
☐ 10 Yanick Lehoux
☐ 10 Mike Pudlick
☐ 13 Joe Rullier
☐ 14 Travis Scott
☐ 15 Richard Seeley

MANITOBA MOOSE

'97 - 98

MANITOBA MOOSE / GRAPE'S

Cards A1-A6 and B1-B6 were inserted in game programs

while cards A7-A8 and B7-A8 were available at Grape's Leons' Centre. Fred Brathwaite is one of the more expensive singles at $2.

Set (16 cards): $10

- ☐ A1 Ralph Intranuovo
- ☐ A2 Russ Romaniuk
- ☐ A3 Randy Gilhen
- ☐ A4 Dave Thomlinson
- ☐ A5 Fred Brathwaite (G)
- ☐ A6 Mascot MickE. Moose
- ☐ A7 Scott Arniel
- ☐ A8 Randy Carlyle, Coach
- ☐ B1 Brian Chapman
- ☐ B2 Radim Bicanek
- ☐ B3 Michael Stewart
- ☐ B4 Jason Christie
- ☐ B5 Greg Pankewicz
- ☐ B6 Brad Purdie
- ☐ B7 Kent Fearns
- ☐ B8 Mike Ruark

'98 - 99

MANITOBA MOOSE / GRAPE'S

Cards C1-C6 and D1-D6 were inserted in game programs while cards C7-C8 and D7-D8 were available at Grape's Leons' Centre.

Set (16 cards): $10

- ☐ C1 Scott Arniel
- ☐ C2 Bill Bowler
- ☐ C3 Kent Fearns
- ☐ C4 Brett Hauer
- ☐ C5 Ralph Intranuovo
- ☐ C6 Mike Ruark
- ☐ C7 Michael Stewart
- ☐ C8 Scott Thomas
- ☐ D1 Jason MacDonald
- ☐ D2 Christian Bronsard
- ☐ D3 Jeff Parrott
- ☐ D4 Brian Chapman
- ☐ D5 R. Shulmistra (G)
- ☐ D6 Jimmy Roy
- ☐ D7 Rhett Gordon
- ☐ D8 Patrice Tardif

'99 - 00

MANITOBA MOOSE / GRAPE'S

Manny Legacé is one of the more expensive singles at $2. Singles start at 50¢.

Set (22 cards): $12

- ☐ 1 Manny Legacé (G)
- ☐ 2 Michael Stewart
- ☐ 3 Vlad Serov
- ☐ 4 Lonny Bohonos
- ☐ 5 Mike Prokopec
- ☐ 6 Jeff Parrott
- ☐ 7 Bill Bowler
- ☐ 8 Mike Ruark
- ☐ 9 Eric Veilleux
- ☐ 10 Brett Hauer
- ☐ 11 Jason Elliott
- ☐ 12 Cory Cyrenne
- ☐ 13 Justin Kurtz
- ☐ 14 Patrice Tardif
- ☐ 15 Jimmy Roy
- ☐ 16 Jason MacDonald
- ☐ 17 Larry Shapley
- ☐ 18 Brian Chapman
- ☐ 19 Marc Rodgers
- ☐ 20 Jim Montgomery
- ☐ 21 Moose vs. Grizzlies
- ☐ 22 Checklist

'00 - 01

MANITOBA MOOSE / HUSKY'S MOHAWK

Johan Hedberg is one of the more expensive singles at $5. Singles start at 50¢.

Card Size: 2 1/2" x 3 3/4"

Set (23 cards): $18

- ☐ Mel Angelstad
- ☐ Doug Ast
- ☐ Cal Benazic
- ☐ Philippe Boucher
- ☐ Steve Brûlé
- ☐ Brian Chapman
- ☐ Dion Darling
- ☐ Bobby Dollas
- ☐ Rusty Fitzgerald
- ☐ Daniel Goneau
- ☐ Brett Hauer
- ☐ Johan Hedberg (G)
- ☐ Dan Kesa
- ☐ Justin Kurtz
- ☐ John MacLean
- ☐ Dmitri Leonov
- ☐ Sean Pronger
- ☐ Bruce Richardson
- ☐ Jimmy Roy
- ☐ Mike Ruark
- ☐ Scott Thomas
- ☐ Ken Wregget
- ☐ Mascot Mick E. Moose

'01 - 02

MANITOBA MOOSE / MOHAWK

Singles start at 50¢.

Set (23 cards):

- ☐ Regan Darby
- ☐ Ryan Bonni
- ☐ Bryan Allen
- ☐ Darrell Hay
- ☐ Zenith Komarniski
- ☐ Brandon Reid
- ☐ Artem Chubarov
- ☐ Ryan Ready
- ☐ Pat Kavanagh
- ☐ Justin Kurtz
- ☐ Steve Kariya
- ☐ André Savage
- ☐ Jimmy Roy
- ☐ Brian Chapman
- ☐ Bryan Helmer
- ☐ Alfie Michaud
- ☐ Justin Morrison
- ☐ Brad Leeb
- ☐ Jason Cipolla
- ☐ Josh Holden
- ☐ Fedor Fedorov
- ☐ Mascot Mick E. Moose
- ☐ Checklist

'02 - 03

MANITOBA MOOSE

Singles start at 50¢.

Set (26 cards): $15

- ☐ Header
- ☐ Mascot Mick E. Moose
- ☐ Bryan Allen
- ☐ Alex Auld
- ☐ Nolan Baumgartner
- ☐ Tyler Bouck
- ☐ Brian Chapman
- ☐ Regan Darby
- ☐ Fedor Fedorov
- ☐ Jason Goulet
- ☐ Darrell Hay
- ☐ Bryan Helmer
- ☐ Steve Kariya
- ☐ Pat Kavanagh
- ☐ Jason King
- ☐ Zenith Komarniski
- ☐ Justin Kurtz
- ☐ Tyler Moss
- ☐ Jaroslav Obsut
- ☐ Ryan Ready
- ☐ Brandon Reid
- ☐ Jimmy Roy
- ☐ Jason Shmyr
- ☐ Nathan Smith
- ☐ Herbert Vasiljevs
- ☐ René Vydareny

MICHIGAN K-WINGS

'96 - 97

MICHIGAN K-WINGS / B.J. SPORTS

Some of the more expensive singles are Roman Turek and Manny Fernandez at $3-5 each. Singles start at 50¢.

Set (27 cards): $20

- ☐ 1 Dan Keczmer
- ☐ 2 Dennis Smith
- ☐ 3 Brad Berry
- ☐ 4 Shane Peacock
- ☐ 5 Jason Lafrenière
- ☐ 6 Collin Bauer
- ☐ 7 Sergey Gusev
- ☐ 8 Igor Korolev
- ☐ 9 Brent Fedyk
- ☐ 10 Pat Elynuik
- ☐ 11 Jamie Wright
- ☐ 12 Lee Jinman
- ☐ 13 Jeff Mitchell
- ☐ 14 Brad Lukowich
- ☐ 15 Derrick Smith
- ☐ 16 Petr Buzek
- ☐ 17 Patrick Côté
- ☐ 18 Mark Lawrence
- ☐ 19 Jim Storm
- ☐ 20 Roman Turek (G)
- ☐ 21 Neil Brady
- ☐ 22 Manny Fernandez (G)
- ☐ 23 Claude Noël
- ☐ 24 Jim Playfair
- ☐ 25 Checklist
- ☐ 26 PHPA
- ☐ 27 BJ Sports Card

'98 - 99

MICHIGAN K-WINGS / EBK SPORTS

Marty Turco is one of the more expensive singles at $4. Singles start at 50¢.

Set (21 cards): $10

- ☐ 1 David Roberts
- ☐ 2 Doug Doull
- ☐ 3 Brad Lukowich
- ☐ 4 Brad Berry
- ☐ 5 Aaron Gavey
- ☐ 6 Jonathan Sim
- ☐ 7 Jeff Mitchell
- ☐ 8 Jason Botterill
- ☐ 9 Greg Leeb
- ☐ 10 Evgeny Tsybuk
- ☐ 11 Matt Martin
- ☐ 12 Marty Flichel
- ☐ 13 Mike Bales (G)
- ☐ 14 Mel Angelstad
- ☐ 15 Kelly Fairchild
- ☐ 16 Marty Turco (G)
- ☐ 17 Ryan Christie
- ☐ 18 Richard Jackman
- ☐ 19 Petr Buzek
- ☐ 20 Logo Card
- ☐ 21 PHPA Web Card

'99 - 00

MICHIGAN K-WINGS / EBK SPORTS

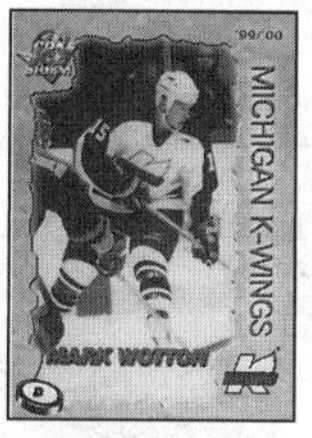

Marty Turco is one of the more expensive singles at $4. Singles start at 50¢.

Set (21 cards): $18

- ☐ 1 Jamie Wright
- ☐ 2 Keith Aldridge
- ☐ 3 Steve Gainey
- ☐ 4 Jonathan Sim
- ☐ 5 Mike Martin
- ☐ 6 Gaetan Royer
- ☐ 7 Jeff MacMillan
- ☐ 8 Aaron Gavey
- ☐ 9 Evgeny Tsybouk
- ☐ 10 Marty Turco (G)
- ☐ 11 Matt Martin
- ☐ 12 Ryan Christie
- ☐ 13 Greg Leeb
- ☐ 14 Mark Wotton
- ☐ 15 Kelly Fairchild
- ☐ 16 Gregor Baumgartner
- ☐ 17 Brenden Morrow
- ☐ 18 Mel Angelstad
- ☐ 19 Mike Bales
- ☐ 20 Richard Jackman
- ☐ 21 Roman Lyashenko

MILWAUKEE ADMIRALS

'81 - 82

MILWAUKEE ADMIRALS / TCMA

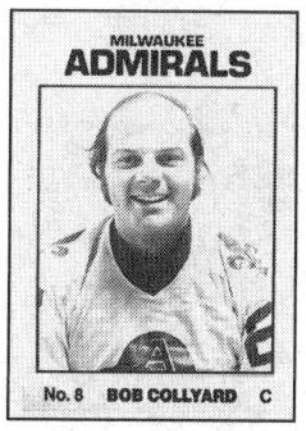

These cards feature black and white photography. Singles start at $1.

Card Size: 2 1/2" x 3 1/2"

Set (15 cards): $15

- ☐ 1 Pat Rabbitt
- ☐ 2 Réal Paiement
- ☐ 3 Fred Berry
- ☐ 4 Blaine Peerless
- ☐ 5 John Flesch
- ☐ 6 Yves Preston
- ☐ 7 Bruce McKay
- ☐ 8 Dale Yakiwchuk
- ☐ 9 Lorne Bokshowan
- ☐ 10 Danny Lecours
- ☐ 11 Sheldon Currie
- ☐ 12 Doug Robb
- ☐ 13 Rob Polman Tuin (G)
- ☐ 14 Bob Collyard
- ☐ 15 Tim Ringler

'93 - 94

MILWAUKEE ADMIRALS / UNSIGNERS

Singles start at 50¢.

Set (31 cards): $12

- ☐ 1 Header Card
- ☐ 2 Curt Fraser
- ☐ 3 Peter Bakovic
- ☐ 4 Doug Agnew
- ☐ 5 Jergus Baca
- ☐ 6 Matt Hervey
- ☐ 7 Carl Valimont
- ☐ 8 Steve Strunk
- ☐ 9 Jason Lafrenière
- ☐ 10 Richard Zemlak
- ☐ 11 Sylvain Couturier
- ☐ 12 Brian Dobbin
- ☐ 13 Mike McNeill
- ☐ 14 Jeff Larmer
- ☐ 15 Scott Robinson
- ☐ 16 Randy Velischek
- ☐ 17 Yuri Krivokhija
- ☐ 18 Jim Johannson
- ☐ 19 Don Gibson
- ☐ 20 Scott Gruhl
- ☐ 21 Steve Tuttle
- ☐ 22 Dale Henry
- ☐ 23 Pat MacLeod
- ☐ 24 Bob Mason
- ☐ 25 Ladislav Tresl
- ☐ 26 Duane Derksen
- ☐ 27 Larry Dyck
- ☐ 28 Gino Cavallini
- ☐ 29 Ken Sabourin
- ☐ 30 Alex. Galchenyuk
- ☐ 31 Dave Marcinyshyn

'94 - 95

MILWAUKEE ADMIRALS / CLASSIC

Singles start at 50¢.

Card Size: 2 1/2" x 3 1/2"

Set (28 cards): $12

- ☐ Doug Agnew
- ☐ Peter Bakovic
- ☐ Matt Block
- ☐ Gino Cavallini
- ☐ Sylvain Couturier
- ☐ Brian Dobbin
- ☐ Shawn Evans
- ☐ Chris Govedaris
- ☐ Jim Hrivnak (G)
- ☐ Tony Hrkac
- ☐ Fabian Joseph
- ☐ Mark LaForest (G)
- ☐ Don MacAdam
- ☐ Dave Mackey
- ☐ Pat MacLeod
- ☐ Dave Marcinyshyn
- ☐ Bob Mason (G)
- ☐ Mike McNeill
- ☐ Kent Paynter
- ☐ Ken Sabourin
- ☐ Trevor Sim
- ☐ Martin Simard
- ☐ Mike Tomlak
- ☐ Steve Tuttle
- ☐ Randy Velischek
- ☐ Brad Werenka
- ☐ Phil Wittliff
- ☐ Fabulous Fritz

'95 - 96

MILWAUKEE ADMIRALS / EDGE ICE

Singles start at 50¢.

Set (25 cards): $12

- ☐ 1 Shawn Anderson
- ☐ 2 Jergus Baca
- ☐ 3 Gino Cavallini
- ☐ 4 Joe Cirella
- ☐ 5 Sylvain Couturier
- ☐ 6 Tom Draper (G)
- ☐ 7 Robert Guillet
- ☐ 8 Tony Hrkac
- ☐ 9 Fabian Joseph
- ☐ 10 Mark LaForest (G)
- ☐ 11 Dave MacIsaac
- ☐ 12 Mike McNeill
- ☐ 13 David Mackey
- ☐ 14 Kent Paynter
- ☐ 15 Ken Sabourin
- ☐ 16 Andrew Shier
- ☐ 17 Tom Tilley
- ☐ 18 Mike Tomlak
- ☐ 19 Steve Tuttle
- ☐ 20 Terry Yake
- ☐ 21 Phil Wittliff
- ☐ 22 Peter Bakovic
- ☐ 23 Rob Kirsch
- ☐ 24 Doug Agnew
- ☐ 25 Dream Ride Song

'96 - 97

MILWAUKEE ADMIRALS / BANK ONE

Singles start at 50¢.

Set (27 cards): $12

- ☐ 1 Sylvain Couturier
- ☐ 2 Larry DePalma
- ☐ 3 Peter Douris
- ☐ 4 Denny Felsner
- ☐ 5 Eric Fenton
- ☐ 6 Shannon Finn
- ☐ 7 Tony Hrkac
- ☐ 8 Jacques Joubert
- ☐ 9 Rick Knickle
- ☐ 10 Brad Layzelle
- ☐ 11 Danny Lorenz
- ☐ 12 Chris Luongo
- ☐ 13 David Mackey
- ☐ 14 Mike McNeill
- ☐ 15 Michel Mongeau
- ☐ 16 Kent Paynter
- ☐ 17 Christian Proulx
- ☐ 18 Patrice Robitaille
- ☐ 19 Ken Sabourin
- ☐ 20 Steve Strunk
- ☐ 21 Tom Tilley
- ☐ 22 Mike Tomlak
- ☐ 23 Steve Tuttle
- ☐ 24 Phil Wittliff
- ☐ 25 Peter Bakovic
- ☐ 26 Fabian Joseph
- ☐ 27 Doug Agnew

'97 - 98

MILWAUKEE ADMIRALS / BANK ONE

Singles start at 50¢.

Set (25 cards): $10

- ☐ Jason Cipolla
- ☐ Kerry Clark
- ☐ Jarrett Deuling
- ☐ Kelly Fairchild
- ☐ Eric Fenton
- ☐ Shannon Finn
- ☐ Martin Gendron
- ☐ Mike Harder
- ☐ Marc Hussey
- ☐ Danny Lorenz
- ☐ Dave MacIntyre
- ☐ Mike McNeill
- ☐ Don McSween
- ☐ Jeff Nelson
- ☐ Brent Peterson
- ☐ Christian Proulx
- ☐ Ken Sabourin
- ☐ Mike Tomlak
- ☐ Mike Torchia (G)
- ☐ Steve Tuttle
- ☐ Mark Visheau
- ☐ Al Sims, Coach
- ☐ Peter Bakovic, A.Coach
- ☐ Fabian Joseph, A.Coach
- ☐ Doug Agnew, Trainer

'98 - 99

MILWAUKEE ADMIRALS / BANK ONE

Singles start at 50¢.

Set (24 cards): $10

- ☐ 1 Al Sims, Coach
- ☐ 2 Jeff Daniels
- ☐ 3 Sergei Klimentiev
- ☐ 4 Chris Mason (G)
- ☐ 5 Eric Fenton
- ☐ 6 Shannon Finn
- ☐ 7 Jason Cipolla
- ☐ 8 Jeff Kealty
- ☐ 9 Bobby Russell
- ☐ 10 David Gosselin
- ☐ 11 Richard Lintner
- ☐ 12 Jeff Nelson
- ☐ 13 Kay Whitmore (G)
- ☐ 14 C. Noe, A.Coach
- ☐ 15 Karlis Skrastins
- ☐ 16 Mark Mowers
- ☐ 17 Craig Darby
- ☐ 18 Mascot Roscoe
- ☐ 19 Doug Friedman
- ☐ 20 Matt Henderson
- ☐ 21 Marc Moro
- ☐ 22 Petr Sykora
- ☐ 23 Jeff Staples
- ☐ 24 Marian Cisar

'99 - 00

MILWAUKEE ADMIRALS / KEEBLER

Singles start at 50¢.

Set (20 cards): $12

- ☐ 2 Marc Moro
- ☐ 3 Jason Dawe
- ☐ 4 Mark Mowers
- ☐ 5 Jayme Filipowicz
- ☐ 6 Alexandre Boikov
- ☐ 7 Chris Mason
- ☐ 8 Andrew Berenzweig
- ☐ 9 Dan Keczmer
- ☐ 10 David Gosselin
- ☐ 11 Dan Riva
- ☐ 12 Brent Peterson
- ☐ 13 Ryan Tobler
- ☐ 14 Matt Eldred
- ☐ 15 Paul Healey
- ☐ 16 Eric Fenton
- ☐ 17 Al Sims
- ☐ 18 Claude Noel
- ☐ 19 Marián Cisar
- ☐ 20 Corey Hirsch (G)

'00 - 01

MILWAUKEE ADMIRALS / KEBBLER

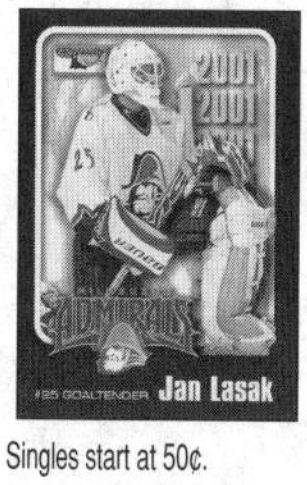

Singles start at 50¢.

Set (20 cards): $12

- ☐ 1 Chris Mason (G)
- ☐ 2 Jeremy Stevenson
- ☐ 3 Jayme Filipowicz
- ☐ 4 Mark Eaton
- ☐ 5 Evgeny Namestnikov
- ☐ 6 Jan Lasak
- ☐ 7 Marc Moro
- ☐ 8 Pavel Skrbek
- ☐ 9 Greg Classen
- ☐ 10 Dan Riva
- ☐ 11 Andrew Berenzweig
- ☐ 12 Mike Watt
- ☐ 13 Sean Haggerty
- ☐ 14 Alexei Vasiliev
- ☐ 15 Petr Sachl
- ☐ 16 Ryan Tobler
- ☐ 17 Mark Mowers
- ☐ 18 Denis Arkhipov
- ☐ 19 Ville Peltonen
- ☐ 20 Jonas Andersson

'01 - 02

MILWAUKEE ADMIRALS / KEEBLER

Singles start at 50¢.

Set (25 cards): $15

- ☐ Erik Anderson
- ☐ Jonas Andersson
- ☐ Martin Bartek
- ☐ Andrew Berenzweig
- ☐ Alexandre Boikov
- ☐ Frédéric Bouchard
- ☐ Marian Cisar
- ☐ Kevin Dean
- ☐ Steve Dubinsky
- ☐ David Gosselin
- ☐ Jason Goulet
- ☐ Chris Mason (G)
- ☐ Brett Hauer
- ☐ Tmo Hebling
- ☐ Jan Lasak (G)
- ☐ Jayme Legault
- ☐ Bryan Lundbohm
- ☐ Marc Moro
- ☐ Mark Mowers
- ☐ Konstantin Panov
- ☐ Nathan Perrot
- ☐ Petr Sachl
- ☐ Yves Sarault
- ☐ Robert Schnabel
- ☐ Jeremy Stevenson

'02 - 03

MILWAUKEE ADMIRALS / KEBBLER

We do not have the checklist for this series.

MINNESOTA MOOSE

'94 - 95

MINNESOTA MOOSE / HARDEE'S

Singles start at 50¢.

Set (16 cards): $10

- ☐ 1 Dave Christian
- ☐ 2 Kris Miller
- ☐ 3 John Young
- ☐ 4 Tom Draper (G)
- ☐ 5 Daniel Shank
- ☐ 6 Dean Kolstad
- ☐ 7 Yvon Corriveau
- ☐ 8 Frank Serratore
- ☐ 9 Dave Snuggerud
- ☐ 10 Mark Osiecki
- ☐ 11 Brad Miller
- ☐ 12 Frank Pietrangelo (G)
- ☐ 13 Stéphane Morin
- ☐ 14 Sean Williams
- ☐ 15 Dave Hakstol
- ☐ 16 Mascot Mick Moose

'95 - 96

MINNESOTA MOOSE / HARDEE'S

Singles start at 50¢.

Set (16 cards): $10

- ☐ 1 Dave Christian
- ☐ 2 Chris Jensen
- ☐ 3 Sandy Smith
- ☐ 4 Stéphane Morin
- ☐ 5 David Gagnon
- ☐ 6 Sean Williams
- ☐ 7 Yvon Corriveau
- ☐ 8 Chris Govedaris
- ☐ 9 Mike Hurlbut
- ☐ 10 Dave Hakstol
- ☐ 11 Bryan Fogarty
- ☐ 12 Dave Morissette
- ☐ 13 Brad Miller
- ☐ 14 Kris Miller
- ☐ 15 Frank Serratore
- ☐ 16 Mascot Mick Moose

MISSISSIPPI SEA WOLVES

'96 - 97

MISSISSIPPI SEA WOLVES

Singles start at 50¢.

Set (22 cards): $9

- ☐ Frederick Beaubien
- ☐ Alexei Budayev
- ☐ Sylvain Daigle
- ☐ Kevin Evans
- ☐ Quinn Fair
- ☐ Shawn Frappier
- ☐ Kevin HIlton
- ☐ Kelly Huard
- ☐ Derek Innanen
- ☐ Yanick Jean
- ☐ John Kosobud
- ☐ Troy Mann
- ☐ Roger Maxwell
- ☐ Mike Muller
- ☐ Simon Oliver
- ☐ Patrick Rochon
- ☐ Jeff Rohlicek
- ☐ Mark Rupnow
- ☐ Joaikin Wassberger
- ☐ Steven Yule
- ☐ Bruce Boudreau
- ☐ Mascot Hook

'99 - 00

MISSISSIPPI SEA WOLVES / KELLY CUP CHAMPS

Singles start at 50¢.

Set (25 cards): $9

- ☐ 1 Bruce Boudreau
- ☐ 2 Mascot Hook
- ☐ 3 Jim Carey
- ☐ 4 Cynthia Dedeaux
- ☐ 5 Karl Infanger
- ☐ 6 Sean Blanchard
- ☐ 7 Bob Woods
- ☐ 8 Cody Bowtell
- ☐ 9 V. (Jr.) Nedomansky
- ☐ 10 Patrick Rochon
- ☐ 11 John Kosobud
- ☐ 12 Brad Essex
- ☐ 13 Andrew Dale
- ☐ 14 Dean Mando
- ☐ 15 Kevin Hilton
- ☐ 16 Quinn Fair
- ☐ 17 Chris Schmidt
- ☐ 18 Mike Martone
- ☐ 19 Kelly Hurd
- ☐ 20 Mikhail Kravets
- ☐ 21 Travis Scott
- ☐ 22 Mark Rupnow
- ☐ 23 Troy Mann
- ☐ 24 Chuck Thuss
- ☐ 25 Sea Wolves

'99 - 00

MISSISSIPPI SEA WOLVES / ROOX SPORTS

Singles start at 50¢.

Card Size: 2 1/2" x 3 1/2"

Set (25 cards): $10

- ☐ 1 Rob Flahiff
- ☐ 2 Marc Potvin

☐ 3 Mascot Hook
☐ 4 Sea Wolves
☐ 5 Cynthia Dedeaux
☐ 6 Trevor Gillies
☐ 7 Steve Duke
☐ 8 Sean Gillam
☐ 9 Bob Woods
☐ 10 Cody Bowtell
☐ 11 Patrick Rochon
☐ 12 Jonathan Weaver
☐ 13 John Kosobud
☐ 14 Brad Essex
☐ 15 Scott King
☐ 16 Ryan Gaucher
☐ 17 Brad Goulet
☐ 18 Mike Martone
☐ 19 J-F Aubé
☐ 20 Dave Paradise
☐ 21 John Evangelista
☐ 22 Mikhail Kravets
☐ 23 Chuck Thuss
☐ 24 Sylvain Daigle
☐ 25 Mark Rupnow

MISSOURI RIVEROTTERS

'99 - 00

MISSOURI RIVEROTTERS / ROOX SPORTS

Singles start at 50¢.
Card Size: 2 1/2" x 3 1/2"
Sponsor: Roox
Set (29 cards): $9

☐ 1 RiverOtters
☐ 2 Tomas Baluch
☐ 3 Chris Bernard
☐ 4 Charlie Blyth
☐ 5 Colin Chaulk
☐ 6 Randy Gallatin
☐ 7 Forrest Gore
☐ 8 Ben Gorewich
☐ 9 Jay Hebert
☐ 10 Kiley Hill
☐ 11 Jan Kobezda
☐ 12 Lonnie Loach
☐ 13 Jeremiah McCarthy
☐ 14 Jeremy Rebek
☐ 15 Brian Regan
☐ 16 Allan Roulette
☐ 17 Alain St. Hilaire
☐ 18 Curtis Sayler
☐ 19 Trevor Sherban
☐ 20 Marty Standish
☐ 21 Michal Stastny
☐ 22 Chris Tok
☐ 23 Dan Tompkins
☐ 24 Mark Reeds
☐ 25 Scott Bell
☐ 26 Mascot Oscar
☐ 27 Otter Mobile
☐ 28 Checklist
☐ RiverOtters

MOBILE MYSTICKS

'99 - 00

MOBILE MYSTICS / ROOX SPORTS

Singles start at 50¢.
Card Size: 2 1/2" x 3 1/2"
Set (23 cards): $10

☐ Dave Craievich
☐ David Van Drunen
☐ Mitch Vig
☐ Benoit Cotnoir
☐ Bobby Stewart
☐ John McCabe
☐ Hugues Gervais
☐ Tom Nolan

☐ Chad Onufrechuk
☐ Jason Elders
☐ B.J. Kilbourne
☐ Mark Turner
☐ Jeff Kozakowski
☐ Josh Harrold
☐ Russ Guzior
☐ Anders Sorensen
☐ Jason Clarke
☐ Chad Alban
☐ Steve Debus
☐ Scott Cherrey
☐ Jeff Pyle
☐ Tom Neziol
☐ Southern Ford

MONCTON ALPINES

'83 - 84

MONCTON ALPINES / POLICE

Steve Smith is one of the more expensive singles at $5. Singles start at 75¢.
Card Size: 2 1/2" x 3 3/4"
Set (27 cards): $20

☐ 1 Doug Messier
☐ 2 Chris Smith (G)
☐ 3 Marc Baron (G)
☐ 4 Mark Zanier (G)
☐ 5 Dwayne Boettger
☐ 6 Lowell Loveday
☐ 7 Joe McDonnell
☐ 8 Peter Dineen
☐ 9 John Blum
☐ 10 Steve Smith
☐ 11 Reg Kerr
☐ 12 Tom Rowe
☐ 13 Ross Lambert
☐ 14 Pat Conacher
☐ 15 Paul Miller
☐ 16 Bert Yachimel
☐ 17 Tom Gorence
☐ 18 Jeff Crawford
☐ 19 Serge Boisvert
☐ 20 Todd Strueby
☐ 21 Todd Bidner
☐ 22 Dean Dachyshyn
☐ 23 Ray Cote
☐ 24 Shawn Babcock
☐ 25 Shawn Dineen
☐ 26 Marc Habscheid
☐ Checklist

MONCTON GOLDEN FLAMES

'84 - 85

MONCTON GOLDEN FLAMES / POLICE

Mike Vernon is one of the more expensive singles at $12. Singles start at 75¢.
Card Size: 2 12" x 3 3/4"
Set (26 cards): $25

☐ 1 Brian Patafie
☐ 2 Mike Bianni
☐ 3 Pierre Pagé
☐ 4 Neil Sheehy
☐ 5 George White
☐ 6 Mark Lamb
☐ 7 Dan Kane
☐ 8 Dan Bolduc
☐ 9 Lou Kiriakou
☐ 10 Joel Otto
☐ 11 Dale DeGray
☐ 12 Mike Clayton
☐ 13 Mickey Volcan
☐ 14 Ted Pearson
☐ 15 Mario Simioni
☐ 16 Keith Hanson
☐ 17 Yves Courteau
☐ 18 Dan Cormier
☐ 19 Todd Hooey
☐ 20 Mike Vernon (G)
☐ 21 Dave Meszaros (G)
☐ 22 Bruce Eakin
☐ 23 Tony Stiles
☐ 24 Ed Kastelic
☐ 25 Pierre Rioux
☐ 26 Gino Cavallini

'85 - 86

MONCTON GOLDEN FLAMES / POLICE

Geoff Courtnall is one of the more expensive singles at $5. Singles start at 75¢.
Card Size: 2 12" x 3 3/4"
Set (28 cards): $20

☐ 1 Terry Crisp
☐ 2 Dan Bolduc
☐ 3 Terry Crisp/ D. Bolduc
☐ 4 Al Pedersen
☐ 5 Dave Meszaros (G)
☐ 6 George White
☐ 7 Mark Lamb
☐ 8 Doug Kostynski
☐ 9 Brian Bradley
☐ 10 Ron Kivell
☐ 11 Geoff Courtnall
☐ 12 Tony Stiles
☐ 13 Jim Buettgen
☐ 14 Cleon Daskelakis (G)
☐ 15 Rick Kosti (G)
☐ 16 Kevan Guy
☐ 17 John Blum
☐ 18 Patafie/ Bianni/ Druet
☐ 19 Greg Johnston
☐ 20 Dale DeGray
☐ 21 John Meulenbroeks
☐ 22 Dave Reid
☐ 23 Jay Miller
☐ 24 Yves Courteau
☐ 25 Robin Bartel
☐ 26 Benoît Doucet
☐ 27 Pete Bakovic
☐ 28 Team Photo

'86 - 87

MONCTON GOLDEN FLAMES / POLICE

Brett Hull is one of the more expensive singles at $35. Bill Ranford and Gary Roberts sells at $10. Singles start at 75¢.
Card Size: 2 12" x 3 3/4"
Set (28 cards): $65

☐ 1 Terry Crisp
☐ 2 Danny Bolduc
☐ 3 Doug Dadswell (G)
☐ 4 Doug Kostynski
☐ 5 Bill Ranford (G)
☐ 6 Brian Patafie
☐ 7 Dave Pasin
☐ 8 Darwin McCutcheon
☐ 9 Team Photo
☐ 10 Kevan Guy
☐ 11 Kraig Nienhuis
☐ 12 Gary Roberts
☐ 13 Ken Sabourin
☐ 14 Marc D'Amour (G)
☐ 15 Don Mercier
☐ 16 Wade Campbell
☐ 17 Mark Peterson
☐ 18 Cleon Daskelakis (G)
☐ 19 Lyndon Byers
☐ 20 Brett Hull
☐ 21 Bob Sweeney
☐ 22 Gord Hynes
☐ 23 Peter Bakovic
☐ 24 Dave Reid
☐ 25 Mike Rucinski
☐ 26 Ray Podloski
☐ 27 Bob Bodak
☐ 28 John Carter

MONCTON HAWKS

'87 - 88

MONCTON HAWKS / POLICE

Bob Essensa is one of the more expensive singles at $1.50-2. Singles start at 75¢.
Card Size: 2 1/2" x 3 5/8"
Set (25 cards): $15

☐ Joel Baillargeon
☐ Rick Bowness
☐ Bobby Dollas
☐ Peter Douris
☐ Iain Duncan
☐ Bob Essensa (G)
☐ Todd Flichel
☐ Rob Fowler
☐ Randy Gilhen
☐ Matt Hervey
☐ Brent Hughes
☐ Jamie Husgen
☐ Mike Jeffrey
☐ Guy Larose
☐ Chris Levasseur
☐ Len Nielson
☐ Roger Ohman
☐ Dave Quigley (G)
☐ Ron Pesetti
☐ Steve Penney (G)
☐ Scott Schneider
☐ Ryan Stewart
☐ Gord Whitaker
☐ Team Photo
☐ R. Carrano/ W. Flemming

'89 - 90

MONCTON HAWKS / POLICE

Singles start at 75¢. Other singles exist.
Card Size: 2 1/2" x 3 5/8"

☐ Iain Duncan
☐ Matt Hervey
☐ Sergei Kharin
☐ Denis Laroque
☐ Tyler Larter
☐ Chris Norton

'90 - 91

MONCTON HAWKS / POLICE

Rick Tabaracci is one of the more expensive singles at $2. Singles start at 50¢.
Card Size: 2 1/2" x 3 5/8"
Set (26 cards): $15

☐ Larry Bernard
☐ Lee Davidson
☐ Iain Duncan
☐ Craig Duncanson
☐ Dallas Eakins
☐ Dave Farrish
☐ Wayne Flemming
☐ Todd Flichel
☐ Peter Hankinson
☐ Matt Hervey
☐ Brent Hughes
☐ Anthony Joseph
☐ Sergei Kharin
☐ Denis Larocque
☐ Guy Larose
☐ Tyler Larter
☐ Scott Levins
☐ Bryan Marchment
☐ Chris Norton
☐ Mike O'Neill
☐ Grant Richison
☐ Scott Schneider
☐ Rob Snitzer
☐ Rick Tabaracci (G)
☐ Simon Wheeldon
☐ Team Card

'91 - 92

MONCTON HAWKS / POLICE

Rick Tabaracci is one of the more expensive singles at $2. Singles start at 50¢.
Card Size: 2 1/2" x 3 5/8"
Set (28 cards): $15

☐ Luciano Borsato
☐ Jason Cirone
☐ Rob Cowie
☐ Lee Davidson
☐ Kris Draper
☐ Dallas Eakins
☐ Dave Farrish
☐ Wayne Flemming
☐ Sean Gauthier
☐ Ken Gernander
☐ Tod Hartje
☐ Bob Joyce
☐ Claude Julien
☐ Chris Kiene
☐ Mark Kumpel
☐ Derek Langille
☐ Tyler Larter
☐ John LeBlanc
☐ Scott Levins
☐ Rob Murray
☐ Kent Paynter
☐ Rudy Poeschek
☐ Dave Prior
☐ Warren Rychel
☐ Rob Snitzer
☐ Rick Tabaracci (G)
☐ Darren Veitch
☐ Mascot The Hawk

MUSKEGON FURY

'93 - 94

MUSKEGON FURY / RISING STAR

Singles start at 50¢.
Set (20 cards): $10

☐ 1 Header Card
☐ 2 Steve Ludzik
☐ 3 Bob Jones
☐ 4 Darrel Newman
☐ 5 Brett Seguin
☐ 6 Dan Woodley
☐ 7 Jodi Murphy
☐ 8 Mark Karpen
☐ 9 Rob Melanson
☐ 10 Paul Kelly
☐ 11 Joey Simon
☐ 12 Scott Feasby
☐ 13 Scott Campbell
☐ 14 Joe Hawley
☐ 15 Justin Morrison
☐ 16 Roch Belley
☐ 17 Todd Charlesworth
☐ 18 Kevin Barrett
☐ 19 Mark Turner
☐ 20 Steve Herniman

'94 - 95

MUSKEGON FURY / RISING STAR

Singles start at 50¢.
Set (18 cards): $10

☐ Andy Bezeau
☐ Jamie Black
☐ Grant Block
☐ Scott Campbell
☐ Todd Charlesworth
☐ Scott Feasby
☐ Darryl Gilmour
☐ Rich Parent
☐ Mark Vilneff
☐ Steve Walker
☐ Header Card
☐ Marc Saumier
☐ Brett Seguin
☐ Wes McCauley
☐ Justin Morrison
☐ Steve Herniman
☐ Paul Kelly
☐ Norm Krumpschmid

'95 - 96

MUSKEGON FURY / RISING STAR

Singles start at 50¢.
Set (20 cards): $10

☐ Richard Fatrola
☐ Scott Feasby
☐ Terry Ficorelli
☐ Rick Girhiny
☐ Rich Parent
☐ Mark Turner
☐ Mark Vilneff
☐ Steve Walker
☐ Bobby Wallwork
☐ Steve Webb
☐ McDonald's Sponsor
☐ Fury Team Photo
☐ Brett Seguin
☐ Rob Melanson
☐ Brian Greer
☐ Kyle Haviland
☐ Jamie Hearn
☐ Steve Herniman
☐ Paul Kelly
☐ Cory Johnson

'98 - 99

MUSKEGON FURY / GINMAN TIRE

Singles start at 50¢.
Set (25 cards): $10

☐ 1 Terry Ficorelli
☐ 2 Jason Pain
☐ 3 Mascot Furious Fred
☐ 4 Lubos Krajcovic
☐ 5 Chris Maillet
☐ 6 Robin Bouchard
☐ 7 Randy Cantu
☐ 8 Francis Nault
☐ 9 Checklist
☐ 10 Richard Kromm
☐ 11 Joe Dimaline
☐ 12 Richard Kromm
☐ 13 David Bouskill
☐ 14 Cory Banika
☐ 15 Rob Melanson
☐ 16 John Vary
☐ 17 Ginman Tire
☐ 18 Andy Bezeau
☐ 19 Paul Willett
☐ 20 Mike Feasby
☐ 21 Sergei Kharin
☐ 22 Denis Khlopotnov
☐ 23 David Beauregard
☐ 24 Dmitri Emilyantsev
☐ 25 Mark Vilneff

'99 - 00

MUSKEGON FURY / ROOX SPORTS

Singles start at 50¢.
Card Size: 2 1/2" x 3 1/2"
Set (36 cards): $12

☐ 1 Sergei Kharin
☐ 2 Vadim Podrezov
☐ 3 Andrei Petrunin
☐ 4 Scott Feasby
☐ 5 Joe Dimaline
☐ 6 Rob Melanson
☐ 7 Robin Bouchard
☐ 8 Colonial Cup celebration
☐ 9 Quinn Hancock
☐ 10 Francis Nault
☐ 11 Alex Vasilevskii
☐ 12 Mark Vilneff
☐ 13 Andrew Luciuk
☐ 14 Bob Janosz
☐ 15 Chris Maillet
☐ 16 Tomas Kapusta
☐ 17 Mike McCourt
☐ 18 Brian Tucker
☐ 19 Aaron Porter
☐ 20 Jason Rose
☐ 21 Alain LaPlante
☐ 22 Mike Feasby
☐ 23 Terry Ficorelli
☐ 24 Furious Fred
☐ 25 Richard Kromm
☐ 26 Phil Kopinski
☐ 27 Mikhail Nemirovsky
☐ 28 Don McSween
☐ 29 Dalen Hrooshkin
☐ 30 Lucas Nehrling
☐ 31 Fury All-Stars
☐ 32 Tony Lisman
☐ 33 Checklist
☐ 34 Rob Hutson
☐ 35 Joel Gardner
☐ 36 Fury

NASHVILLE KNIGHTS

'89 - 90

NASHVILLE KNIGHTS / LEE'S COUNTRY CHICKEN

Singles start at 50¢.
Card Size: 2 1/2" x 3 1/2"
Set (23 cards): $10

☐ Pat Bingham
☐ André Brassard
☐ Mike Bukta
☐ Chris Cambio
☐ Glen Engevik
☐ Archie Henderson
☐ Billy Huard
☐ Todd Jenkins
☐ Brock Kelly
☐ Eddie Krayer
☐ Garth Lamb
☐ Rob Levasseur
☐ Dan O'Brien
☐ John Reid (G)
☐ John Reid (G)
☐ Jeff Salzbrunn
☐ Mike Schwalb
☐ Ron Servatius
☐ Jason Simon
☐ D. Cavaliere/ C. Jenkins
☐ Matt Gallagher/ S. Greer
☐ Rob Polk/ Ron Fuller
☐ Chick-E-Lee

NEW HAVEN BEAST

'98 - 99

NEW HAVEN BEAST / RISING STAR

Singles start at 50¢.
Set (20 cards): $10

☐ 1 Craig Ferguson
☐ 2 Ian MacNeil
☐ 3 Marek Malik
☐ 4 Craig MacDonald
☐ 5 Byron Ritchie
☐ 6 Steven Halko
☐ 7 Shane Willis
☐ 8 Todd MacDonald
☐ 9 Scott Levins
☐ 10 Dwayne Hay
☐ 11 Chadden Cabana
☐ 12 Tom Buckley
☐ 13 Ryan Johnson
☐ 14 Mike Fountain
☐ 15 Ashlin Halfnight
☐ 16 John Jakopin
☐ 17 C. Allen/ P. Ratchuk
☐ 18 Tetarenko/ L. Ward
☐ 19 Koehler/ A. Long
☐ 20 M. Nilson/ T. Weslund

NEW HAVEN NIGHTHAWKS

'89 - 90

NEW HAVEN NIGHTHAWKS / CASIO

Ken Baumgartner is one of the more expensive singles at $2. Singles start at 50¢.
Card Size: 2 1/2" x 3 1/2"
Set (15 cards): $15

☐ Ken Baumgartner
☐ Jon Bednarski
☐ Tom Colley
☐ Rick Dudley
☐ Daryl Evans
☐ Ed Johnstone
☐ Alain Langlais
☐ Mark Lofthouse
☐ Parker McDonald
☐ Hubie McDonough
☐ Bill Plager
☐ Ron Scott
☐ Bobby Sheehan
☐ Doug Soetaert (G)
☐ Jim Wiemer

NEWMARKET SAINTS

'90 - 91

NEWMARKET SAINTS / POLICE

Damian Rhodes is one of the more expensive singles at $2. Singles start at 50¢.
Card Size: 2 1/2" x 3 3/4"
Set (26 cards): $15

☐ Frank Anzalone
☐ Tim Bean
☐ Brian Blad
☐ Alan Hepple
☐ Robert Horyna
☐ Kent Hulst
☐ Mike Jackson
☐ Greg Johnston
☐ Derek Langille
☐ Mike Millar
☐ Mike Moes
☐ Bill Purcell
☐ Bobby Reynolds
☐ Damian Rhodes (G)
☐ Bill Root
☐ Joe Sacco
☐ Darryl Shannon
☐ Doug Shedden
☐ Mike Stevens
☐ Darren Veitch
☐ Greg Walters
☐ Bryan Cousineau
☐ Donald Hillock
☐ Eldred King
☐ Frank Kovacs
☐ Police Dog Lanny

NEW MEXICO SCORPIONS

'97 - 98

NEW MEXICO SCORPIONS / CELLULAR ONE

Singles start at 50¢.
Set (30 cards): $10

☐ 1 Team Photo
☐ 2 Regan Harper
☐ 3 Eric Ricard
☐ 4 Darren Wright
☐ 5 Derek Crawford
☐ 6 Sylvain Naud
☐ 7 Mike Sanderson
☐ 8 Brian Barnes
☐ 9 Craig Hamelin
☐ 10 Darcy Pengelly
☐ 11 Todd Marcellus
☐ 12 George Dupont
☐ 13 Jordan Shields
☐ 14 François Chaput
☐ 15 Nick Hriczov
☐ 16 Frederick Beaubien
☐ 17 David Lessard
☐ 18 Hugo Bertrand
☐ 19 Kelly Morel
☐ 20 Derek Shybunka
☐ 21 Tony Martino
☐ 22 Marc Siegel
☐ 23 Brad Wingfield
☐ 24 Tyler Boucher
☐ 25 Carl Paradis
☐ 26 Aldo Iaquinta
☐ 27 Garry Unger
☐ 28 Mascot Spencer
☐ 29 Stingers Cheerleaders
☐ 30 New Year's Celebration

NEW ORLEANS BRASS

'97 - 98

NEW ORLEANS BRASS / STARZSPORTS

Singles start at 50¢.

Set (21 cards): $9

☐ 1 Jeff Lazaro
☐ 2 Darryl LaFrance
☐ 3 Eric Montreuil
☐ 4 Steve Cheredaryk
☐ 5 Brad Symes
☐ 6 Bill McKay
☐ 7 Martin Villeneuve
☐ 8 Martin Woods
☐ 9 Joe Seroski
☐ 10 Russ Guzior
☐ 11 Mascot Scratch Mo
☐ 12 Kevin Pozzo
☐ 13 Pierre Gendron
☐ 14 Mike Minard
☐ 15 Scott Allegrino
☐ 16 Mikhail Nemirovsky
☐ 17 Kyle Peterson
☐ 18 Ted Sator
☐ 19 Scott King
☐ 20 Jason Downey
☐ 21 Éric Brulé

NORFOLK ADMIRALS

'01 - 02

NORFOLK ADMIRALS / CHOICE

Singles start at 50¢.

Card Size: 2 1/2" x 3 1/2"

Set (27 cards): $12

☐ 1 Ajay Baines
☐ 2 Bill Bowler
☐ 3 Bobby Russell
☐ 4 Casey Hankinson
☐ 5 Chris McAlpine
☐ 6 Craig Andersson
☐ 7 Dmitri Tolkunov
☐ 8 Jean-Yves Leroux
☐ 9 Jeff Helperl
☐ 10 Jim Campbell
☐ 11 Kent Huskins
☐ 12 Matt Henderson
☐ 13 Mike Leighton
☐ 14 Mike** Peluso
☐ 15 Mike Souza
☐ 16 Nolan Baumgartner
☐ 17 Peter White
☐ 18 Quintin Laing
☐ 19 Rumun Ndur
☐ 20 Shawn Thornton
☐ 21 Steve McCarthy
☐ 22 Ty Jones
☐ 23 Tyler Arnason
☐ 24 Valeri Zelepukin
☐ 25 Vladimir Chebaturkin
☐ 26 Trent Yawney, Coach
☐ Header / Admirals

NOVA SCOTIA OILERS

'84 - 85

NOVA SCOTIA OILERS / POLICE

Steve Smith is one of the more expensive singles at $4. Singles start at 75¢.

Card Size: 2 1/2" x 3 5/8"

Set (26 cards): $18

☐ 1 Mark Holden (G)
☐ 2 Dave Allison
☐ 3 Dwayne Boettger
☐ 4 Lowell Loveday
☐ 5 Réjean Cloutier
☐ 6 Ray Cote
☐ 7 Pat Conacher
☐ 8 Ken Berry
☐ 9 Steve Graves
☐ 10 Todd Strueby
☐ 11 Steve Smith
☐ 12 Archie Henderson
☐ 13 Dean Dachyshyn
☐ 14 Marc Habscheid
☐ 15 Larry Melnyk
☐ 16 R. Summanen
☐ 17 Jim Playfair
☐ 18 Mike Zanier (G)
☐ 19 Ian Wood (G)
☐ 20 Dean Hopkins
☐ 21 Norm Aubin
☐ 22 Tony Currie
☐ 23 Ross Lambert
☐ 24 Terry Martin
☐ 25 Chadwick/ Kish/ Boucher
☐ 26 L. Christian/ K. Farris

'85 - 86

NOVA SCOTIA OILERS / POLICE

Jeff Beukeboom is one of the more expensive singles at $4-5. Singles start at 50¢.

Card Size: 2 1/2" x 3 5/8"

Set (28 cards): $18

☐ 1 Dean Hopkins
☐ 2 Jeff Larmer
☐ 3 Mike Moller
☐ 4 Dean Dachyshyn
☐ 5 Bruce Boudreau
☐ 6 Ken Solheim
☐ 7 Jeff Beukeboom
☐ 8 Mark Lavarre
☐ 9 John Ollson
☐ 10 Lou Crawford
☐ 11 W. Skorodenski (G)
☐ 12 Dwayne Boettger
☐ 13 Daryl Reaugh (G)
☐ 14 John Miner
☐ 15 Jim Ralph (G)
☐ 16 Wayne Presley
☐ 17 Steve Graves
☐ 18 Tom McMurchy
☐ 19 Darin Sceviour
☐ 20 Kent Paynter
☐ 21 Larry Kish
☐ 22 Jim Playfair
☐ 23 K. Farris/ R. Mosher
☐ 24 Mickey Volcan
☐ 25 Ron Low
☐ 26 Don Biggs
☐ 27 Bruce Eakin
☐ 28 Team Photo

NOVA SCOTIA VOYAGEURS

'77 - 78

NOVA SCOTIA VOYAGEURS / FARMER'S CO-OP

Pat Hughes and Rick Meagher are the most expensive singles at $2-3. Singles start at $1.50.

Card Size: 2 1/8" x 4 1/2"

Set (24 cards): $25

☐ Bruce Baker
☐ Maurice Barrette
☐ Barry Borrett
☐ Tim Burke
☐ Jim Cahoon
☐ Norm Dupont
☐ Greg Fox
☐ Mike Hobin
☐ Bob Holland
☐ Don Howse
☐ Pat Hughes
☐ Chuck Luksa
☐ Dave Lumley
☐ Al MacNeil
☐ Gord MacTavish
☐ Rick Meagher
☐ Mike Polich
☐ Moe Robinson
☐ Gaeton Rochette
☐ Pierre Roy
☐ Frank St. Marseille
☐ Derrick St. Marseille
☐ Rod Schutt
☐ Ron Wilson

'83 - 84

NOVA SCOTIA VOYAGEURS / POLICE

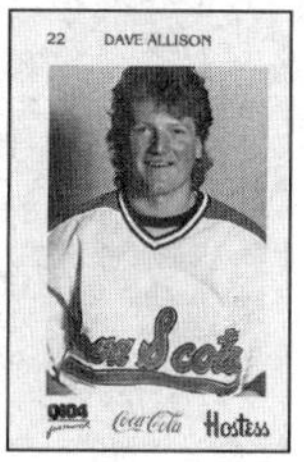

Brian Skrudland is most expensive single at $3. Singles start at 75¢.

Card Size: 2 1/8" x 4 1/2"

Set (24 cards): $20

☐ 1 Mark Holden (G)
☐ 2 Bill Kitchen
☐ 3 Dave Allison
☐ 4 Stéphane Lefebvre
☐ 5 Stan Hennigar
☐ 6 Steve Marengère
☐ 7 John Goodwin
☐ 8 John Newberry
☐ 9 Bill Rilay
☐ 10 Norman Baron
☐ 11 Brian Skrudland
☐ 12 Mike Lalor
☐ 13 Blair Barnes
☐ 14 Rémi Gagné
☐ 15 Steve Penney (G)
☐ 16 Michel Therrien
☐ 17 Dave Stoyanovich
☐ 18 B. Patafie/ L. Christian
☐ 19 Mike McPhee
☐ 20 Wayne Thompson
☐ 21 Ted Fauss
☐ 22 Jeff Teal
☐ 23 Larry Landon
☐ 24 Greg Moffett

ODESSA JACKALOPES

'98 - 99

ODESSA JACKALOPES

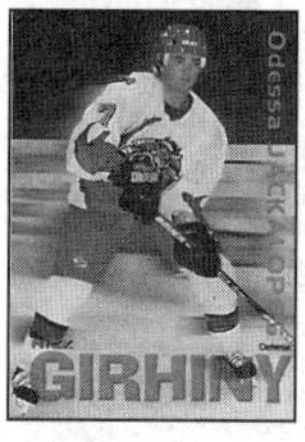

Singles start at 50¢.

Card Size: 2 1/2" x 3 1/2"

Set (22 cards):

☐ Carl Boudreau
☐ 1 Jacque Rodrigue
☐ 2 Rob Lukacs
☐ 3 Ryan Equale
☐ 4 Rick Girhiny
☐ 5 Terry Flynn
☐ 6 Paul Fioroni
☐ 7 Mike Ross
☐ 8 Johan Hagman
☐ 9 Sami Laine
☐ 10 Anders Lindberg
☐ 11 Dan Lavergne
☐ 12 Bo Andersen
☐ 13 Shayne LeBreton
☐ 14 Michael Tornquist
☐ 15 Christian Wibner
☐ 16 Chris Morque
☐ 17 Bill Pye
☐ 18 Martin Ohrstedt
☐ 19 Joe Clark
☐ 20 Pat Kerin
☐ 21 Greg Andis
☐ 22 Sponsor Golden Corral

'99 - 00

ODESSA JACKALOPES

Singles start at 50¢.

Card Size: 2 1/2" x 3 1/2"

Set (21 cards):

☐ Michael Tornquist
☐ Paul Vincent
☐ Chris Morque
☐ Fredrik Lindh
☐ Bill Pye
☐ Sami Laine
☐ Jason Pellerin
☐ Eric Perricone
☐ Karson Kaebel
☐ Roy Gray
☐ Rick Girhiny
☐ Mark Smith
☐ John Bossio
☐ Mike Vandenberghe
☐ Gary Coupal
☐ Jacque Rodrigue
☐ Savo Mitrovic
☐ George Umunna
☐ Greg Andis
☐ Joe Harrell
☐ Sponsor KFC

OKLAHOMA CITY BLAZERS

'92 - 93

OKLAHOMA CITY BLAZERS / TD SPORTS CARDS

Singles start at 50¢.

Card Size: 2 1/2" x 3 1/2"

Set (18 cards): $8

☐ Carl Boudreau
☐ Joel Burton
☐ Sylvain Fleury
☐ Brendan Garvey
☐ Guy Girouard
☐ Sean Gorman
☐ Jamie Hearn
☐ Craig Johnson
☐ Paul Krake
☐ Chris Laganas
☐ Daniel Larin
☐ Mark McGinn
☐ Alan Perry
☐ Steve Simoni
☐ Jim Solly
☐ Boyd Sutton
☐ Team Photo
☐ Blazers card

'98 - 99

OKLAHOMA CITY BLAZERS / EBK SPORTS

Singles start at 50¢.

Sponsor: EBK Sports

Set (23 cards): $9

☐ 1 Peter Arvanitis
☐ 2 Dan Fournel
☐ 3 Dominic Fafard
☐ 4 Craig Willard
☐ 5 Simon Olivier
☐ 6 Joe Burton
☐ 7 Craig Johnson
☐ 8 Tom Gomes
☐ 9 Steve Moore
☐ 10 Jim Jensen
☐ 11 Brad Preston
☐ 12 Rod Butler
☐ 13 Michael Pozzo
☐ 14 Chris Johnston
☐ 15 Hardy Sauter
☐ 16 Jean-Ian Filiatrault
☐ 17 Mike Williams
☐ 18 Doug Sauter
☐ 19 Corey MacIntyre
☐ 20 Daniel Larin
☐ 21 Brandon Rose
☐ 22 Blazers
☐ 23 Blazers

ORLANDO SOLAR BEARS

'98 - 99

ORLANDO SOLAR BEARS / EBK SPORTS

Singles start at 50¢.

Set (19 cards): $8

☐ 1 CL: Logo Card
☐ 2 Patrick Neaton
☐ 3 Sean McCann
☐ 4 Clayton Norris
☐ 5 Hubie McDonough
☐ 6 Shawn Carter
☐ 7 Grigori Panteleyev
☐ 8 Todd Richards
☐ 9 Shawn Wansborough
☐ 10 Mark Beaufait
☐ 11 Scott Hollis
☐ 12 David Mackey
☐ 13 David Littman
☐ 14 AS: G. Panteleyev
☐ 15 AS: Mark Beaufait
☐ 16 Curt Fraser, Coach
☐ 17 Horachek, A. Coach
☐ 18 Orlando Arena
☐ 19 Mascot Shades

'98 - 99

ORLANDO SOLAR BEARS / GEICO DIRECT

These cards were issued in sheets.

Set (22 cards): $8

☐ David Littman
☐ Mark Beaufait
☐ Shawn Carter
☐ David Mackey
☐ Sean McCann
☐ Hubie McDonough
☐ Patrick Neaton
☐ Clayton Norris
☐ Grigori Panteleyev
☐ Todd Richards
☐ Curt Fraser, Coach
☐ Scott Bailey
☐ Rob Bonneau
☐ Allan Egeland
☐ Todd Krygier
☐ Kirby Law
☐ Curtis Murphy
☐ Mike Nicholishen
☐ Fredrik Oduyan
☐ Ken Sabourin
☐ Pierre Sévigny
☐ Peter Horachek, A.Coach

PENSACOLA ICE PILOTS

'96 - 97

PENSACOLA ICE PILOTS / DLUX PRINTING

2,000 sets were produced. Brent Gretzky is one of the more expensive singles at $1.50. Singles start at 50¢.

Card Size: 2 1/2" x 3 1/2"

Set (24 cards): $12

☐ 1 Craig Brown
☐ 2 Stéphane Julien
☐ 3 David Barozzino
☐ 4 Jeremy Mylymok
☐ 5 Patrik Allvin
☐ 6 Rostislav Saglo
☐ 7 Glen Metropolit
☐ 8 Chad Quenneville
☐ 9 Trevor Buchanan
☐ 10 Brandon Gray
☐ 11 Jon Pirrong
☐ 12 Brent Gretzky
☐ 13 Martin LaChaine
☐ 14 Brian Secord
☐ 15 Hugo Belanger
☐ 16 Christian Sbrocca
☐ 17 Tony Prpic
☐ 18 Shane Calder
☐ 19 Nick Stajduhar
☐ 20 Brendan Concannon
☐ 21 Sean Gauthier
☐ 22 Al Pederson
☐ 23 George Kozak
☐ Information Card

'97 - 98

PENSACOLA ICE PILOTS / DLUX PRINTING

Singles start at 50¢.

Set (25 cards): $10

☐ Team Photo
☐ J-F Aubé
☐ Craig Brown
☐ Michael Burkett
☐ Shane Calder
☐ Martin Chouinard
☐ Brendan Concannon
☐ Jon Dunmar
☐ Sean Gauthier
☐ Christian Gosselin
☐ Brian LaFleur
☐ Steven Low
☐ Scott Malone
☐ Mike Mayhew
☐ Keith O'Connell
☐ Val Passarelli
☐ Mark Polak
☐ Chad Quenneville
☐ Andrew Rodgers
☐ Nick Stajduhar
☐ Mike Sullivan
☐ Kelly Hultgren
☐ George Kozak
☐ Allen Pedersen
☐ D-Lux Printing Sponsor

PEORIA RIVERMEN

'92 - 93

PEORIA RIVERMEN / COKE, KROGER

Doug Wickenheiser is one of the more expensive singles at $1.50. Singles start at 50¢.

Card Size: 2 1/2" x 3 1/2"

Set (30 cards): $12

☐ Jeff Batters
☐ Parris Duffus (G)
☐ Greg Eberle
☐ John Faginkrantz
☐ Denny Felsner
☐ Derek Frenette
☐ Ron Handy
☐ Joe Hawley
☐ Terry Hollinger
☐ Ron Hoover
☐ Dan Laperrière
☐ Lee J. Leslie
☐ Dave Mackey
☐ Jason Marshall
☐ Brian McKee
☐ Rick Meagher
☐ Kevin Miehm
☐ Brian Pellerin
☐ Richard Pion
☐ Mark Reeds
☐ Kyle Reeves
☐ Rob Robinson
☐ Jason Ruff
☐ Geoff Sarjeant (G)
☐ Darren Veitch
☐ Doug Wickenheiser
☐ Shawn Wheeler
☐ Coke Coupon
☐ Rivermen card
☐ Checklist

'93 - 94

PEORIA RIVERMEN / HAT TRICKS

Singles start at 50¢.

Card Size: 2 1/2" x 3 1/2"

Set (31 cards): $10

☐ Mark Bassen
☐ Jeff Batters
☐ René Chapdelaine
☐ Doug Crossman
☐ Parris Duffus (G)
☐ Greg Eberle
☐ Doug Evans
☐ Kevin Evans
☐ John Faginkrantz
☐ Denny Felsner
☐ Derek Frenette
☐ Terry Hollinger
☐ Ron Hoover
☐ Butch Kaebel
☐ Nathan Lafayette
☐ Dan Laperrière
☐ Dave Mackey
☐ Paul MacLean
☐ Michel Mongeau
☐ Brian Pellerin
☐ Richard Pion
☐ Vitali Prokhorov
☐ Mark Reeds
☐ John Roderick
☐ Geoff Sarjeant (G)
☐ Steve Staios
☐ Darren Veitch
☐ Nick Vitucci
☐ Rivermen card
☐ Alcohol awareness
☐ Checklist

'94 - 95

PEORIA RIVERMEN / COKE, KROGER

Singles start at 50¢.

Set (24 cards): $8

☐ 1 David Roberts
☐ 2 Steve Tuttle
☐ 3 Terry Hollinger
☐ 4 Sportscaster Lee Hall
☐ 5 Ian Laperrière
☐ 6 Doug Evans
☐ 7 Jeff Batters
☐ 8 M. Reeds, A.Coach
☐ 9 Greg Paslawski
☐ 10 Daniel Laperrière
☐ 11 Kirk Tomlinson
☐ 12 Martin Hamrlik
☐ 13 Geoff Sarjeant
☐ 14 Steve Staios
☐ 15 Kevin Evans
☐ 16 René Chapdelaine
☐ 17 Michel Mongeau
☐ 18 Ron Hoover
☐ 19 Dave MacIntyre
☐ 20 Parris Duffus (G)
☐ 21 Patrice Tardif
☐ 22 Darren Veitch
☐ 23 Butch Kaebel
☐ 24 Glenn Mulvenna

'95 - 96

PEORIA RIVERMEN / COKE, KROGER

This series was issued in four-card strips. Singles start at 50¢.

Set (24 cards): $10

☐ 1 Jon Casey (G)
☐ 2 Shannon Finn
☐ 3 Ron Hoover
☐ 4 Jacques Joubert
☐ 5 Paul Taylor
☐ 6 Jon Pratt
☐ 7 Keith Osborne
☐ 8 Michel Mongeau
☐ 9 Dan Ratushny
☐ 10 Eric Murano
☐ 11 Steve Thornton
☐ 12 Eric Fenton
☐ 13 Dave MacIntyre
☐ 14 Martin Hamrlik
☐ 15 Lee Leslie
☐ 16 René Chapdelaine
☐ 17 Greg Paslawski
☐ 18 Travis Thiessen
☐ 19 Glenn Mulvenna
☐ 20 Kirk Tomlinson
☐ 21 Doug Evans
☐ 22 Patrice Robitaille
☐ 23 Steve Wilson
☐ 24 Jason Miller

'96 - 97

PEORIA RIVERMEN / MULTI-AD SPORTS

Singles start at 50¢.

Set (25 cards): $9

☐ 1 Rivermen
☐ 2 Mark Reeds
☐ 3 Doug Evans
☐ 4 Mike Barrie
☐ 5 Doug Bonner
☐ 6 Brad Essex
☐ 7 Liam Garvey
☐ 8 Trevor Hanas
☐ 9 Jon Hillebrandt
☐ 10 Dan Hodge
☐ 11 Butch Kaebel
☐ 12 Karson Kaebel
☐ 13 Justin Krall
☐ 14 Jeff Kungle
☐ 15 Kevin Lune
☐ 16 Darren Maloney
☐ 17 Dustin McArthur
☐ 18 Jon Pratt
☐ 19 Brad Purdie
☐ 20 Jason Saal
☐ 21 Jan Slavik
☐ 22 Marc Terris
☐ 23 Jean-Guy Trudel
☐ 24 Paul Vincent
☐ 25 Greg Eberle

'97 - 98

PEORIA RIVERMEN / MULTI-AD SPORTS

Singles start at 50¢.

Set (29 cards): $10

☐ 1 Garry Gruber
☐ 2 Derek Diener
☐ 3 Samy Nasreddine
☐ 4 Doug Evans
☐ 5 Darren Maloney
☐ 6 Joe Craigen
☐ 7 Rob Phillips
☐ 8 Brian Clifford
☐ 9 Darcy Smith
☐ 10 Butch Kaebel
☐ 11 Jean-Guy Trudel
☐ 12 Brad Essex
☐ 13 Justin Krall
☐ 14 John Dance
☐ 15 Marc Terris

☐ 16 Trevor Hanas
☐ 17 Dave Paradise
☐ 18 David Vallieres
☐ 19 Scott Roche
☐ 20 Marcel Kuris
☐ 21 Jon Pratt
☐ 22 Rob Giffin
☐ 23 Mark Reeds
☐ 24 Greg Eberle
☐ 25 John Krouse
☐ 26 Rocky & Lil' Rocky
☐ 27 PHPA
☐ 28 Merchandise Disc
☐ 29 Checklist

'98 - 99
PEORIA RIVERMEN / EBK SPORTS

Singles start at 50¢.
Set (28 cards): $10

☐ 1 Darren Maloney
☐ 2 Dan Hodge
☐ 3 Doug Evans
☐ 4 Dan Carney
☐ 5 Chris Coveny
☐ 6 Alexandre Couture
☐ 7 Jamie Thompson
☐ 8 Jay Kenney
☐ 9 J.F. Boutin
☐ 10 Joe Craigen
☐ 11 Darcy Smith
☐ 12 Dan Murphy
☐ 13 Quinn Hancock
☐ 14 Mark Reeds
☐ 15 Marek Ivan
☐ 16 Kory Karlander
☐ 17 Ken Boone
☐ 18 Jeff Trembecky
☐ 19 Steve MacKinnon
☐ 20 Josef Rybár
☐ 21 Rivermen Photo
☐ 22 Scott Roche
☐ 23 Chad Lang
☐ 24 Rivermen
☐ 25 Blaine Fitzpatrick
☐ 26 Michael Schultz
☐ 27 Maloney/ Thompson
☐ Checklist

'99 - 00
PEORIA RIVERMEN / ROOX SPORTS

Singles start at 50¢.
Card Size: 2 1/2" x 3 1/2"
Set (36 cards): $10

☐ 1 Mascot Rocky
☐ 2 Don Granato
☐ 3 Greg Eberle
☐ 4 Jamie Healy
☐ 5 Trevor Baker
☐ 6 Duane Derksen
☐ 7 Darren Clark
☐ 8 Jason Christie
☐ 9 Blaine Fitzpatrick
☐ 10 John Gurskis
☐ 11 Alexandre Couture
☐ 12 Darren Maloney
☐ 13 Blaz Emersic
☐ 14 Cody Rudkowsky
☐ 15 J.F. Boutin
☐ 16 Joe Rybar
☐ 17 Matt Smith
☐ 18 Tomaz Razinger
☐ 19 Craig Anderson
☐ 20 Jason Lawmaster
☐ 21 Bret Meyers
☐ 22 Sean Farmer
☐ 23 Darin Kimble
☐ 24 Dan Hodge
☐ 25 Luke Gruden
☐ 26 Tyler McMillan
☐ 27 Kenzie Homer
☐ 28 James Desmarais
☐ 29 John Butler
☐ 30 Mike Nelson
☐ 31 Bart Rogers
☐ 32 Michael Sauers
☐ 33 Jim Small
☐ 34 Norm Ulrich
☐ 35 Manda Girard
☐ 36 B.J. Stone

'00 - 01
PEORIA RIVERMEN / ROOX SPORTS

Singles start at 50¢.
Card Size: 2 1/2" x 3 1/2"
Set (21 cards): $9

☐ 1 Curtis Sanford
☐ 2 Didier Tremblay
☐ 3 Luke Gruden
☐ 4 J.F. Boutin
☐ 5 Lauri Kinos
☐ 6 Darren Maloney
☐ 7 Trevor Baker
☐ 8 Tyler Willis
☐ 9 Bret Meyers
☐ 10 Dustin Kuk
☐ 11 Dan Hodge
☐ 12 Joe Rybar
☐ 13 Blaine Fitzpatrick
☐ 14 Darren Clark
☐ 15 Matt Golden
☐ 16 Kenric Exner
☐ 17 Jason Lawmaster
☐ 18 Arvid Rekis
☐ 19 Tomaz Razinger
☐ 20 Joe Trotta
☐ 21 Jason Christie

'01 - 02
PEORIA RIVERMEN / CHOICE

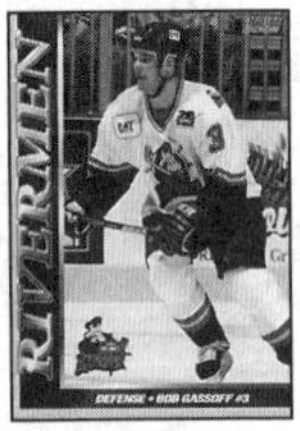

Singles start at 50¢.
Card Size: 2 1/2" x 3 1/2"
Set (24 cards): $10

☐ 1 Header Card
☐ 2 Jason Christie, Coach
☐ 3 Curtis Sanford
☐ 4 Bob Gassoff
☐ 5 Chad Starling
☐ 6 Blake Evans
☐ 7 Kevin Tucker
☐ 8 Trevor Baker
☐ 9 Jonathan Fauteux
☐ 10 Randy Rowe
☐ 11 Dustin Kuk
☐ 12 Bret Meyers
☐ 13 Kevin Granato
☐ 14 Dan Hodge
☐ 15 Tyler Rennette
☐ 16 Ryan Finnerty
☐ 17 Brad Voth
☐ 18 Joe Rybar
☐ 19 Darren Clark
☐ 20 Matt Golden
☐ 21 Phil Osaer
☐ 22 Jason Lawmaster
☐ 23 Arvid Rekis
☐ 24 Kevin Cloutier

'02 - 03
PEORIA RIVERMEN / CHOICE

Singles start at 50¢.
Set (25 cards):
These cards are slightly oversize. Singles start at 50¢.
Set (25)

☐ 1 Jason Christie
☐ 2 Simon Lajeunesse
☐ 3 Trevor Gillies
☐ 4 Lauri Kinos
☐ 5 Darren Clark
☐ 6 Trevor Baker
☐ 7 Greg Day
☐ 8 Bret DeCecco
☐ 9 Randy Rowe
☐ 10 Randy Copley
☐ 11 Duane Derksen
☐ 12 Kevin Granato
☐ 13 Tyler Rennette
☐ 14 Ryan Finnerty
☐ 15 Brad Voth
☐ 16 Brendan Brooks
☐ 17 Derek Booth
☐ 18 Scott Crawford
☐ 19 Jeremy Yablonski
☐ 20 Jason Lawmaster
☐ 21 Josh Kern
☐ 22 Arvid Rekis
☐ 23 Anthony Belza
☐ 24 Alfie Michaud
☐ Checklist

PHILADELPHIA PHANTOMS

'02 - 03
PHILADELPHIA PHANTOMS / CHOICE

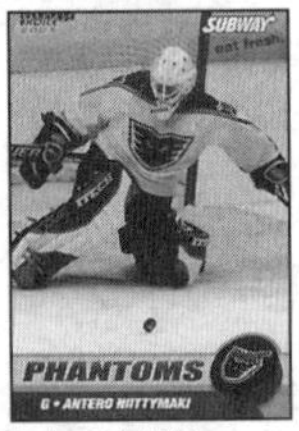

Singles start at 50¢.
Set (26 cards):

☐ 1 Antero Niittymaki
☐ 2 Bruno St-Jacques
☐ 3 Dan Peters
☐ 4 Mark Greig
☐ 5 Kirby Law
☐ 6 Peter White
☐ 7 Eric Betournay
☐ 8 Jack Baker
☐ 9 Patrick Sharp
☐ 10 Guillaume Lefebvre
☐ 11 Peter Vandermeer
☐ 12 André Savage
☐ 13 Jim Vandermeer
☐ 14 Mike Siklenka
☐ 15 Ian MacNeil
☐ 16 Ben Stafford
☐ 17 John Slaney
☐ 18 Mike Lephart
☐ 19 Brad Tiley
☐ 20 Wade Skolney
☐ 21 Neil Little
☐ 22 David Harlock
☐ 23 John Stevens
☐ 24 Mascot Phlex
☐ 25 Subway coupon
☐ Checklist

PHOENIX MUSTANGS

'98 - 99
PHOENIX MUSTANGS

Singles start at 50¢.
Set (25 cards): $9

☐ 1 Hugo Belanger
☐ 2 David Goverde
☐ 3 Dana G. Seltzer
☐ 4 Iannique Renaud
☐ 5 Mark Spence
☐ 6 Daniel Shank
☐ 7 Stu Kulak
☐ 8 Rusty McKie
☐ 9 Gene Bono
☐ 10 Jamie Allan
☐ 11 Michel Couvrette
☐ 12 Sebastien Fortier
☐ 13 Corey Laniuk
☐ 14 Doug McCarthy
☐ 15 Tom Menicci
☐ 16 Savo Mitrovic
☐ 17 Matt Oliver
☐ 18 Teemu Numminen
☐ 19 Bobby Rapoza
☐ 20 Jason Rose
☐ 21 Darren Veitch
☐ 22 Sean Whyte
☐ 23 Brad McCaughey
☐ 24 Dick Earle
☐ 25 Mascot Rusty

PHOENIX ROADRUNNERS

'92 - 93
PHOENIX ROADRUNNERS / SAFEWAY

Singles start at 50¢.
Card Size: 2 1/2" x 3 1/2"
Set (28 cards): $10

☐ Tim Bothwell
☐ François Breault
☐ Tim Breslin
☐ René Chapdelaine
☐ Sylvain Couturier
☐ Phil Crowe
☐ Darryl Gilmour (G)
☐ David Goverde
☐ Ed Kastelic
☐ Rick Kozuback
☐ Ted Kramer
☐ Robert Lang
☐ Guy Lévêque
☐ Jim Maher
☐ Brad McCaughey
☐ Shawn McCosh
☐ John Mokosak
☐ Keith Redmond
☐ Mike Ruark
☐ Brandy Semchuk
☐ Dave Stewart
☐ Brad Tiley
☐ Dave Tretowicz
☐ Mike Vukonich
☐ Tim Watters
☐ Sean Whyte
☐ Darryl Williams
☐ Mascot Rocky Roadrunner

'93 - 94
PHOENIX ROADRUNNERS / JESSEN

Singles start at 50¢.
Card Size: 2 1/2" x 3 1/2"
Set (25 cards): $10

☐ Tim Breslin
☐ Brian Chapman
☐ Stéphane Charbonneau
☐ Dan Currie
☐ Rick Dudley
☐ Marc Fortier
☐ David Goverde
☐ Kevin Grant
☐ Mark Hardy
☐ Dean Hulett
☐ Pauli Jaks (G)
☐ Bob Jay
☐ Rick Knickle (G)
☐ Guy Lévêque
☐ Eric Lavigne
☐ Dominic Lavoie
☐ Jim Maher
☐ Brian McReynolds
☐ Rob Murphy
☐ Keith Redmond
☐ Dave Stewart
☐ Dave Tomlinson
☐ Brad Tiley
☐ Jim Vesey
☐ Darryl Williams

'94 - 95
PHOENIX ROADRUNNERS / POGs

Yanic Perreault is one of the more expensive singles at $2.
Singles start at 50¢.
Set (24 POGs): $15

☐ 1 Rob Laird
☐ 2 Chris Snell
☐ 3 Barry Potomski
☐ 4 Brian McReynolds
☐ 5 Jeff Shevalier
☐ 6 André Racicot (G)
☐ 7 Dan Currie
☐ 8 Brian Chapman
☐ 9 Dan Bylsma
☐ 10 Dave Thomlinson
☐ 11 Rob Cowie
☐ 12 Sean O'Donnell
☐ 13 Mascot Rocky
☐ 14 Yanic Perreault
☐ 15 Pauli Jaks
☐ 16 Kevin Brown
☐ 17 Tim Watters
☐ 18 Éric Lacroix
☐ 19 Byron Dafoe
☐ 20 Rob (Jr.) Brown
☐ 21 Jim Vesey
☐ 22 Justin Hocking
☐ 23 Nicholas Vachon
☐ 24 Éric Lavigne

'95 - 96
PHOENIX ROADRUNNERS / SAFEWAY

Jamie Storr is one of the more expensive singles at $2.
Singles start at 50¢.
Card Size: 2 1/2" x 3 1/2"
Set (24 cards): $15

☐ Ruslan Batyrshin
☐ Frederik Beaubien
☐ John Blue
☐ Mike Boback
☐ Kevin Brown
☐ Jim Burton
☐ Dan Bylsma
☐ Brian Chapman
☐ Rob Cowie
☐ Devin Edgerton
☐ Rob Laird
☐ Ken McRae
☐ Barry Potomski
☐ Daniel Rydmark
☐ Jeff Shevalier
☐ Gary Shuchuk
☐ Chris Snell
☐ Jamie Storr (G)
☐ Dave Thomlinson
☐ Nicholas Vachon
☐ Jan Vopat
☐ Steve Wilson
☐ Phoenix Trainers
☐ Mascot Rocky Roadrunner

PORTLAND PIRATES

'93 - 94
PORTLAND PIRATES / PEPSI

Byron Dafoe and Olaf Kölzig are the most expensive singles at $4 each. Singles start at 50¢.
Card Size: 2 1/2" x 3 1/2"
Set (25 cards): $20

☐ Mike Boback
☐ Kerry Clark
☐ Byron Dafoe (G)
☐ Eric Fenton
☐ Paul Gardner
☐ Kent Hulst
☐ Chris Jensen
☐ Martin Jiranek
☐ Kevin Kaminski
☐ Ken Klee
☐ Olaf Kölzig (G)
☐ Chris Longo
☐ Jim Mathieson
☐ Darren McAusland
☐ Todd Nelson
☐ Jeff Nelson
☐ Randy Pearce
☐ Michel Picard
☐ Steve Poapst
☐ Jeff Sirkka
☐ John Slaney
☐ Barry Trotz
☐ Jason Woolley
☐ Mascot Checkers
☐ Pirates Card

'94 - 95
PORTLAND PIRATES / CLASSIC

Jim Carey is one of the more expensive singles at $1.50.
Singles start at 50¢.
Card Size: 2 1/2" x 3 1/2"
Set (23 cards): $10

☐ Norm Batherson
☐ Mike Boback
☐ Andrew Brunette
☐ Jim Carey (G)
☐ Jason Christie
☐ Kerry Clark
☐ Brian Curran
☐ Martin Gendron
☐ Sergei Gonchar
☐ Kent Hulst
☐ Chris Jensen
☐ Kevin Kaminski
☐ Ken Klee
☐ Chris Longo
☐ Jim Mathieson
☐ Darren McAusland
☐ Jeff Nelson
☐ Todd Nelson
☐ Mike Parson
☐ Steve Poapst
☐ André Racicot (G)
☐ Sergei Tertyshny
☐ Stefan Ustorf

'95 - 96
PORTLAND PIRATES / DUNKIN' DONUTS

Jason Allison is one of the more expensive singles at $5. The Ron Tugnutt singles sells at $2. Singles start at 50¢.
Card Size: 2 1/2" x 3 1/2"
Set (24 cards): $15

☐ Alexander Alexeyev
☐ Jason Allison
☐ Norm Batherson
☐ Frank Bialowas
☐ Patrick Boileau
☐ Andrew Brunette
☐ Stéphane Charbonneau
☐ Jason Christie
☐ Brian Curran
☐ Martin Gendron
☐ Kent Hulst
☐ Alexander Kharlamov
☐ Jim Mathieson
☐ Darren McAusland
☐ Jeff Nelson
☐ Darryl Paquette
☐ Rob Pearson
☐ Steve Poapst
☐ Joel Poirier
☐ Sergei Tertyshny
☐ Ron Tugnutt (G)
☐ Stefan Ustorf
☐ Barry Trotz, Coach
☐ Mascot Crackers

'96 - 97
PORTLAND PIRATES / SPLIT SECOND

Anson Carter is one of the more expensive singles at $2.
Singles start at 50¢.
Card Size: 2 1/2" x 3 1/2"
Set (25 cards): $12

☐ Stewart Malguna #4
☐ Norm Batherson #7
☐ Nolan Baumgartner #5
☐ Patrick Boileau #27
☐ Martin Brochu (G) #30
☐ Andrew Brunette #19
☐ Anson Carter #33
☐ Jason Christie #21
☐ Brad Church #12
☐ Miika Elomo #20
☐ Benoît Gratton #25
☐ Trevor Halverson #28
☐ Kent Hulst #10
☐ A. Kharlamov #22
☐ Daniel Laperriere #24
☐ Darren McAusland #16
☐ Ron Pascucci #6
☐ Steve Poapst #3
☐ Marc Potvin #9
☐ Robb Stauber (G) #1
☐ Jaroslav Svejkovsky #15
☐ Richard Zednik #14
☐ Barry Trotz, Coach
☐ Paul Gardner, A.Coach
☐ AHL Card

'97 - 98
PORTLAND PIRATES / SPLIT SECOND

Singles start at 50¢.
Card Size: 2 1/2" x 3 1/2"
Set (26 cards): $12

☐ Mark Major
☐ Stewart Malgunas
☐ Rick Mrozik
☐ Ryan Mulhern
☐ Mike O'Neill
☐ Steve Poapst
☐ Kayle Short

☐ Bryan Trottier
☐ Alexandre (Jr.) Volchkov
☐ Jay Wells
☐ AHL Web Site
☐ PHPA
☐ Nolan Baumgartner
☐ Jan Benda
☐ Patrick Boileau
☐ Martin Brochu
☐ Andrew Brunette
☐ Sébastien Charpentier
☐ Jason Christie
☐ Brad Church
☐ Miika Elomo
☐ Benoît Gratton
☐ David Harlock
☐ Dwayne Hay
☐ Kent Hulst
☐ Kevin Kaminski

'98 - 99
PORTLAND PIRATES / SPLIT SECOND

J-P Dumont is one of the more expensive singles at $2.
Singles start at 50¢.
Card Size: 2 1/2" x 3 1/2"
Set (25 cards): $15

☐ 1 Jean-Pierre Dumont
☐ 2 Patrick Boileau
☐ 3 Martin Brochu (G)
☐ 4 Trevor Halverson
☐ 5 Matt Herr
☐ 6 Benoît Gratton
☐ 7 Nolan Baumgartner
☐ 8 Casey Hankinson
☐ 9 Kent Hulst
☐ 10 Rick Kowalsky
☐ 11 Dan Cleary
☐ 12 Todd Rohloff
☐ 13 Jeff Toms
☐ 14 Steve Poapst
☐ 15 Mike Peluso
☐ 16 Soutuyo / Young
☐ 17 Mike Rosati
☐ 18 Trent Whitfield
☐ 19 Neil Belland
☐ 19 Mark Kumpel
☐ 20 Craig Mills
☐ 21 Stewart Malgunas
☐ 22 Rick Mrozik
☐ 23 Dwight Parrish
☐ 24 Mark Major
☐ 25 AHL Web Site

'99 - 00
PORTLAND PIRATES / SPLIT SECOND

Singles start at 50¢.
Card Size: 2 1/2" x 3 1/2"
Sponsor: Split Second
Set (24 cards): $15

☐ 1 Kent Hulst
☐ 2 Glen Metropolit
☐ 3 Patrick Boileau
☐ 4 Jean-Francois Fortin
☐ 5 Ryan Mulhern
☐ 6 Seb. Charpentier (G)
☐ 7 Jamie Huscroft
☐ 8 Mike Peluso
☐ 9 Jakub Ficenec
☐ 10 A. (Jr.) Volchkov
☐ 11 Steve Poapst
☐ 12 Martin Brochu
☐ 13 Jeff Nelson
☐ 14 Nolan Baumgartner
☐ 15 Alexei Tezikov
☐ 16 Steve Shirreffs
☐ 17 Barrie Moore
☐ 18 Trent Whitfield
☐ 19 Miika Elomo
☐ 20 Jason Shmyr
☐ 21 Rob Zettler
☐ 22 Matt Herr
☐ 23 Glen Hanlon, Coach
☐ 23 Mark Kumpel
☐ 24 Young/ Soutuyo
☐ 24 Mascot

'00 - 01
PORTLAND PIRATES / CHOICE

Singles start at 50¢.
Card Size: 2 1/2" x 3 1/2"
Set (20 cards): $10

☐ 1 Kent Hulst
☐ 2 Jeff Nelson
☐ 3 Krys Barch
☐ 4 Mark Murphy
☐ 5 Patrick Boileau
☐ 6 Todd Rohloff
☐ 7 Jean-François Fortin
☐ 8 Sébastien Charpentier
☐ 9 Glen Metropolit
☐ 10 Rémi Royer
☐ 11 Derek Bekar
☐ 12 Martin Hlinka
☐ 13 Corey Hirsch (G)
☐ 14 Alexei Tezikov
☐ 15 Rob Zettler
☐ 16 Mike Farrell
☐ 17 Jakub Ficenec
☐ 18 Matt Pettinger
☐ 19 Jason Shmyr
☐ 20 Brad Church

PROVIDENCE BRUINS

'96 - 97
PROVIDENCE BRUINS / SPLIT SECOND

Singles start at 50¢.
Card Size: 2 1/2" x 3 1/2"
Set (26 cards): $15

☐ Bob Beers
☐ Mark Cornforth
☐ P.C. Drouin
☐ David Emma
☐ Bob Francis
☐ Justin Gould
☐ John Gruden
☐ Brett Harkins
☐ Mitch Lamoureux
☐ Brad Konik
☐ Peter Laviolette
☐ Milt Mastad
☐ Bill McCauley
☐ Jay Moser
☐ Kirk Nielsen
☐ Charles Paquette
☐ Davis Payne
☐ André Roy
☐ Jean-Yves Roy
☐ Kevin Sawyer
☐ Yevgeny Shaldybin
☐ Martin Simard
☐ Tim Sweeney
☐ Robbie Tallas (G)
☐ AHL Web Site
☐ PHPA

'97 - 98
PROVIDENCE BRUINS / SPLIT SECOND

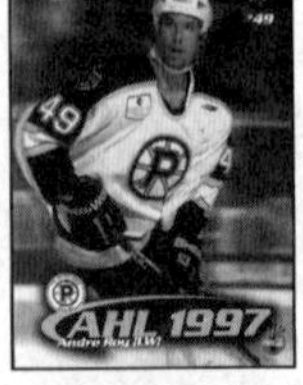

Singles start at 50¢.
Card Size: 2 1/2" x 3 1/2"
Set (26 cards): $15

☐ 1 Robbie Tallas
☐ 2 Elias Abrahamsson
☐ 3 Bill C. Armstrong

☐ 4 Dean Chynoweth
☐ 5 Aaron Downey
☐ 6 Hal Gill
☐ 7 John Grahame
☐ 8 Antti Laaksonen
☐ 9 Cameron Mann
☐ 10 Anders Myrvold
☐ 11 Éric Naud
☐ 12 Kirk Nielsen
☐ 13 Charles Paquette
☐ 14 Joel Prpic
☐ 15 Barry Richter
☐ 16 Randy Robitaille
☐ 17 Jon Rohloff
☐ 18 André Roy
☐ 19 Jean-Yves Roy
☐ 20 Yevgeny Shaldybin
☐ 21 Landon Wilson
☐ 22 Andrei Yakhanov
☐ 23 Tom McVie
☐ 24 Rod Langway
☐ 25 PHPA
☐ 26 AHL Web Site

'98 - 99
PROVIDENCE BRUINS / SPLIT SECOND

Singles start at 50¢.
Card Size: 2 1/2" x 3 1/2"
Set (25 cards): $12

☐ 1 Peter Laviolette
☐ 2 Elias Abrahamsson
☐ 3 Johnathan Aitken
☐ 4 Bill C. Armstrong
☐ 5 Steve Bancroft
☐ 6 Shawn Bates
☐ 7 Jim Carey (G)
☐ 8 Aaron Downey
☐ 9 John Grahame
☐ 10 Joe Harney
☐ 11 Jay Henderson
☐ 12 Antti Laaksonen
☐ 13 Cameron Mann
☐ 14 Marquis Mathieu
☐ 15 Eric Nickulas
☐ 16 Peter Nordström
☐ 17 Joel Prpic
☐ 18 Randy Robitaille
☐ 19 André Savage
☐ 20 Brandon Smith
☐ 21 Mattias Timander
☐ 22 Joel Trottier
☐ 23 Terry Virtue
☐ 24 Landon Wilson
☐ 25 AHL Web Site

'99 - 00
PROVIDENCE BRUINS / SPLIT SECOND

Singles start at 50¢.
Card Size: 2 1/2" x 3 1/2"
Set (25 cards): $12

☐ 1 Elias Abrahamsson
☐ 2 Johnathan Aitken
☐ 3 Shane Belter
☐ 4 Nick Boynton
☐ 5 Jeremy Brown
☐ 6 Vratislav Cech
☐ 7 Jassen Cullimore
☐ 8 Aaron Downey
☐ 9 Peter Ferraro
☐ 10 Maxime Gingras
☐ 11 John Grahame
☐ 12 Jay Henderson
☐ 13 Joe Hulbig
☐ 14 Antti Laaksonen
☐ 15 Tim Lovell
☐ 16 Cameron Mann
☐ 17 Marquis Mathieu
☐ 18 Keith McCambridge
☐ 19 Eric Nickulas
☐ 20 Joel Prpic
☐ 21 Andre Savage
☐ 22 Brandon Smith
☐ 23 Denis Timofeev
☐ 24 Jeff Wells
☐ 25 Kay Whitmore

'00 - 01
PROVIDENCE BRUINS / CHOICE

Singles start at 50¢.
Card Size: 2 1/2" x 3 1/2"
Set (22 cards): $12

☐ Checklist
☐ Peter Ferraro
☐ Jonathan Girard
☐ Jon Coleman
☐ Mattias Karlin
☐ Brandon Smith
☐ Jeremy Brown
☐ Elias Abrahamsson
☐ Terry Hollinger
☐ Ivan Huml
☐ Marquis Mathieu
☐ Pete Vandermeer
☐ Lee Goren
☐ Jay Henderson
☐ Pavel Kolarik
☐ Eric Nickulas
☐ Cameron Mann
☐ Zdenek Kutlák
☐ Eric Manlow
☐ Nick Boynton
☐ Keith McCambridge
☐ Kay Whitmore (G)

'01 - 02
PROVIDENCE BRUINS / CHOICE

Singles start at 50¢.
Card Size: 2 1/2" x 3 1/2"
Set (22 cards): $12

☐ 1 Andrew Raycroft (G)
☐ 2 Jeff Maund
☐ 3 Keith McCambridge
☐ 4 Bobby Allen
☐ 5 Chris Kelleher
☐ 6 Eric Manlow
☐ 7 Zdenek Kutlak
☐ 8 Tony Tuzzolino
☐ 9 Pavel Kolarik
☐ 10 Lee Goren
☐ 11 John Emmons
☐ 12 Andy Hilbert
☐ 13 Joe Hulbig
☐ 14 Carl Corazzini
☐ 15 Ivan Huml
☐ 16 Sean Haggerty
☐ 17 Dennis Bonvie
☐ 18 Mattias Karlin
☐ 19 Martin Wilde
☐ 20 Greg Crozier
☐ 21 Jonathan Girard
☐ Checklist

QUAD CITY MALLARDS

'97 - 98
QUAD CITY MALLARDS / ROOX SPORTS

Singles start at 50¢.
Card Size: 2 1/2" x 3 1/2"
Set (23 cards): $10

☐ 1 Glenn Stewart
☐ 2 Rick Emmett
☐ 3 Sergei Zvyagin
☐ 4 Howie Rosenblatt
☐ 5 Brad Barton
☐ 6 Kirk Llano
☐ 7 Wayne Muir
☐ 8 Hugo Proulx
☐ 9 Mark McFarlane
☐ 10 Steve Chelios
☐ 11 Travis Tucker
☐ 12 Carl LeBlanc
☐ 13 Stas Tkatch
☐ 14 Andy Faulkner
☐ 15 Steve Gibson
☐ 16 Tom Perry
☐ 17 Matt Mullin
☐ 18 Bogdan Rudenko
☐ 19 Ryan Gelinas
☐ 20 Jim Brown
☐ 21 Kerry Toporowski
☐ 22 Corey Neilson
☐ 23 Mallards City

'98 - 99
QUAD CITY MALLARDS / ROOX SPORTS

Singles start at 50¢.
Card Size: 2 1/2" x 3 1/2"
Set (23 cards): $9

☐ 1 Sergei Zvyagin
☐ 2 Brendan Brooks
☐ 3 Scott Burfoot
☐ 4 Matt Carey
☐ 5 Rick Emmett
☐ 6 Martin Fillion
☐ 7 Rusty Fitzgerald
☐ 8 Chad Ford
☐ 9 Robert Frid
☐ 10 Steve Gibson
☐ 11 Garry Gulash
☐ 12 Kevin Kerr
☐ 13 Brian LaFleur
☐ 14 Carl LeBlanc
☐ 15 Mark McFarlane
☐ 16 Stéphane Madore
☐ 17 Mike Melas
☐ 18 Hugo Proulx
☐ 19 Bruce Richardson
☐ 20 Howie Rosenblatt
☐ 21 Scott Thompson
☐ 22 Bill Weir
☐ 23 Glenn Stewart

'99 - 00
QUAD CITY MALLARDS / ROOX SPORTS

Singles start at 50¢.
Card Size: 2 1/2" x 3 1/2"
Set (24 cards): $10

☐ 1 Iannique Renaud
☐ 1 Mascot Moe Mallard
☐ 2 Yannick Latour
☐ 3 Steve Gibson
☐ 4 Garry Gulash
☐ 5 Mike Melas
☐ 6 Rick Emmett
☐ 7 Ryan Lindsay
☐ 8 Patrick Nadeau
☐ 9 Hugo Proulx
☐ 10 Paul Johnson
☐ 11 Brendan Buckley
☐ 12 Martin Hlinka
☐ 13 Brendan Brooks
☐ 14 Rusty Fitzgerald
☐ 15 Kelly Hultgren
☐ 16 Mark McFarlane
☐ 17 Glenn Stewart
☐ 18 Martin Villeneuve
☐ 19 Brian LaFleur
☐ 20 Robert DeCiantis
☐ 21 Kevin Kerr
☐ 22 Scott Buhler
☐ 24 Mallards

'00 - 01
QUAD CITY MALLARDS / ROOX SPORTS

Singles start at 50¢.
Card Size: 2 1/2" x 3 1/2"
Set (27 cards): $10

☐ 1 Mallards City
☐ 2 Andy Fermoyle
☐ 3 Garry Gulash
☐ 4 Frederick Jobin
☐ 5 Vlad Serov
☐ 6 Dan Bjornlie
☐ 7 Peter Armbrust
☐ 8 Patrick Nadeau
☐ 9 Ryan Lindsay
☐ 10 Jason Ulmer
☐ 11 Hugo Proulx
☐ 12 Mike Sim
☐ 13 Chad Power
☐ 14 Paul Johnson
☐ 15 Kelly Perrault
☐ 16 Mark McFarlane
☐ 17 Etienne Drapeau
☐ 18 Martin Hlinka
☐ 19 Rick Emmett
☐ 20 Martin Villeneuve
☐ 21 Scott Myers
☐ 22 Cam Severson
☐ 23 Steve Gibson
☐ 24 Kerry Toporowski
☐ 25 Paul MacLean
☐ 26 Mo Mallard
☐ 27 Ima Duck

QUÉBEC CITADELLES

'99 - 00
QUÉBEC CITADELLES

Mathieu Garon is one of the more expensive singles at $2.
Singles start at 50¢.
Card Size: 2 1/2" x 3 1/2"
Set (26 cards): $12

☐ 1 Mike McBain
☐ 2 Gennady Razin
☐ 3 Chris Albert
☐ 4 Xavier Delisle
☐ 5 Darcy Harris
☐ 6 Marc Beaucage
☐ 7 Stéphane Robidas
☐ 8 Jason Ward
☐ 9 François Groleau
☐ 10 Jonathan Delisle
☐ 11 Stéphane Roy
☐ 12 Patrice Tardif
☐ 13 Pierre Sévigny
☐ 14 Jesse Bélanger
☐ 15 Éric Fichaud
☐ 16 Andrei Bashkirov
☐ 17 Mathieu Garon (G)
☐ 18 Dave Morissette
☐ 19 Miloslav Guren
☐ 20 Matthieu Descoteaux
☐ 21 Jeff Shevalier
☐ 22 Josh DeWolf
☐ 23 Boyd Olson
☐ 24 Matt Higgins
☐ 25 Arron Asham
☐ Québec Citadelles

'00 - 01
QUÉBEC CITADELLES / CARTES, TIMBRES, MONNAIES STE-FOY

Mathieu Garon is one of the more expensive singles at $2.
Singles start at 50¢.
Card Size: 2 1/2" x 3 1/2"
Set (24 cards): $12

☐ 1 Gennady Razin
☐ 2 Éric Chouinard
☐ 3 François Beauchemin
☐ 4 Xavier Delisle
☐ 5 Marc Beaucage
☐ 6 Jason Ward
☐ 7 Matt Higgins
☐ 8 Mike McBain
☐ 9 Miloslav Guren
☐ 10 Pierre Sévigny
☐ 11 Michael Ryder
☐ 12 Jonathan Delisle
☐ 13 Éric Fichaud (G)
☐ 14 Andrei Bashkirov
☐ 15 Mathieu Garon (G)
☐ 16 Matt O'Dette
☐ 17 Mathieu Raby
☐ 18 Barry Richter
☐ 19 Mathieu Descôteaux
☐ 20 Josh DeWolf
☐ 21 Éric Bertrand
☐ 22 Arron Asham
☐ 23 Mike Ribeiro
☐ 24 Checklist

'00 - 01
QUÉBEC CITADELLES / CARTES, TIMBRES, MONNAIES STE-FOY

Mathieu Garon is one of the more expensive singles at $2.
Singles start at 50¢.
Card Size: 2 1/2" x 3 1/2"
Set (28 cards): $12

☐ 1 Gennady Razin
☐ 2 Éric Chouinard
☐ 3 Éric Landry
☐ 4 Ron Hainsey
☐ 5 Jason Ward
☐ 6 Craig Darby
☐ 7 Marc-André Thinel
☐ 8 Martti Järventie
☐ 9 Francis Bouillon
☐ 10 Francis Bélanger
☐ 11 François Beauchemin
☐ 12 Pierre Sévigny
☐ 13 Michael Ryder
☐ 14 Jonathan Delisle
☐ 15 Vadim Tarasov (G)
☐ 16 Mathieu Garon (G)
☐ 17 Matt O'Dette
☐ 18 Luc Bélanger (G)
☐ 19 Jayme Filipowicz
☐ 20 Matthieu Descôteaux
☐ 21 Benoît Gratton
☐ 22 Timo Vertala
☐ 23 Arron Asham
☐ 24 Andrei Markov
☐ 25 Xavier Delisle
☐ 26 Mike Ribeiro
☐ 27 Marcel Hossa
☐ 28 Checklist

RALEIGH ICECAPS

'93 - 94
RALEIGH ICECAPS / RBI SPORTS

Singles start at 50¢.
Card Size: 2 1/2" x 3 1/2"
Set (20 cards): $10

☐ Ralph Barahona
☐ Rick Barkovich
☐ Matt Delguidice
☐ Martin d'Orsonnens
☐ Jamie Erb
☐ Chad Erickson
☐ Donevan Hextall
☐ Shaune Kane
☐ Al Leggett
☐ Derek Linnell
☐ Joe McCarthy
☐ Chris Nelson
☐ Barry Nieckar
☐ Jim Powers
☐ Stan Reddick
☐ Kevin Riehl
☐ Jeff Robison
☐ David Shute
☐ Lyle Wildgoose
☐ Kurt Kleinendorst

'94 - 95
RALEIGH ICECAPS / RBI SPORTS

Singles start at 50¢.
Card Size: 2 1/2" x 3 1/2"
Set (19 cards): $10

☐ Jon Blessman
☐ Rick Barkovich
☐ Alexander Chunchukov
☐ Frank Cirone
☐ Brett Duncan
☐ Anton Fedorov
☐ Todd Hunter
☐ Rodrigo Lavinsh
☐ Derek Linnell
☐ Eric Long
☐ Scott MacNair
☐ Brad Mullahy
☐ Lenny Pereira
☐ Jimmy Powers
☐ Chris Pojar
☐ Kevin Riehl
☐ Todd Reirden
☐ Justin Tomlinson
☐ Lyle Wildgoose

RICHMOND RENEGADES

'91 - 92
RICHMOND RENEGADES / DOMINO'S PIZZA

Jamie McLennan is one of the more expensive singles at $2.
Singles start at 50¢.
Card Size: 2 1/2" x 3 1/2"
Set (20 cards): $10

☐ 1 Rob Vanderydt
☐ 2 Larry Rooney
☐ 3 Brendan Flynn
☐ 4 Scott Drevitch
☐ 5 Jouni Lehto
☐ 6 Todd Drevitch
☐ 7 Paul Rutherford
☐ 8 Dave Aiken
☐ 9 Pat Bingham
☐ 10 Trevor Jobe
☐ 11 Bob Berg
☐ 12 Mark Kuntz
☐ 13 Joe Capprini
☐ 14 Trevor Converse
☐ 15 Steve Scheifele
☐ 16 Jon Gustafson
☐ 17 Marco Fuster
☐ 18 Guy Gadowsky
☐ 19 Dave Allison
☐ 20 Jamie McLennan (G)

'92 - 93
RICHMOND RENEGADES / KELLOGG'S

Singles start at 50¢.
Card Size: 2 1/2" x 3 1/2"
Set (20 cards): $8

☐ Will Averill
☐ Frank Bialowas
☐ Scott Drevitch
☐ Brendan Flynn
☐ Guy Gadowsky
☐ Jon Gustafson
☐ Phil Huber
☐ Mike James
☐ Jeffrey Kampersal
☐ Mark Kuntz
☐ Sean LeBrun
☐ Kevin Malgunas
☐ Jim McGeough
☐ Ed Sabo
☐ Jeff Saterdalen
☐ Alan Schuler
☐ Martin Smith
☐ Roy Sommer
☐ Jeff Torrey
☐ Ben Wyzansky

'93 - 94
RICHMOND RENEGADES / BLEACHERS

Singles start at 50¢.
Card Size: 2 1/2" x 3 1/2"
Set (20 cards): $8

☐ 1 Ken Weiss
☐ 2 Guy Phillips
☐ 3 Alexander Zhdan
☐ 4 Alan Schuler
☐ 5 John Craighead
☐ 6 Colin Gregor
☐ 7 Rob MacInnis
☐ 8 Devin Derksen
☐ 9 John Renard
☐ 10 Peter Allen
☐ 11 Roy Sommer
☐ 12 Milan Hnilicka
☐ 13 Oleg Santurian
☐ 14 Brendan Flynn
☐ 15 Ken Blum
☐ 16 Steve Bogoyevac
☐ 17 Eric Germain
☐ 18 Chris Foy
☐ 19 Darren Colbourne
☐ 20 Jon Gustafson

'94 - 95
RICHMOND RENEGADES / Q94

Jan Benda is one of the more expensive singles at $1-1.50.
Singles start at 50¢.
Card Size: 2 1/2" x 3 1/2"
Set (20 cards): $10

☐ Jan Benda
☐ Lou Body
☐ Steve Bogoyevac
☐ Jason Currie
☐ Chris Foy
☐ Scott Gruhl
☐ Shane Henry
☐ Don Lester
☐ Garrett MacDonald
☐ Kurt Mallett
☐ Blaine Moore
☐ Jay Murphy
☐ Sean O'Brien
☐ Andrew Shier
☐ Grant Sjervin
☐ Shawn Snesar
☐ Roy Sommer
☐ Mike Taylor
☐ Chris Tucker
☐ Darren Wetherill

'95 - 96
RICHMOND RENEGADES / BLEACHER BUM

Singles start at 50¢.
Card Size: 2 1/2" x 3 1/2"
Set (25 cards): $8

☐ Sandy Allan (G)
☐ Lou Body
☐ Michael Burman
☐ Steve Carpenter
☐ Andy Davis
☐ Brendan Flynn
☐ Brian Goudie
☐ Scott Gruhl
☐ Greg Hadden
☐ Rob Jones
☐ Garrett MacDonald
☐ Kurt Mallett
☐ Jason Mallon
☐ Mike Morin
☐ Jay Murphy
☐ Dmitri Pankov
☐ Martin Roy
☐ Trevor Senn
☐ Grant Sjervin
☐ Roy Sommer
☐ Todd Sparks
☐ Mike Taylor
☐ Darren Wetherill
☐ C. Laughlin/ H.Feuerstein
☐ Mascot The Gade

'96 - 97
RICHMOND RENEGADES / POWERPLAY

Singles start at 50¢.
Set (25 cards): $10

☐ 1 Tripp Tracy
☐ 2 Grant Sjervin
☐ 3 Jason Wright
☐ 4 P.J. Lepler
☐ 5 Garry Gulash
☐ 6 Brian Goudie
☐ 7 Brian Secord
☐ 8 Andrew Shier
☐ 9 Chris Pittman
☐ 10 Tom Holmes
☐ 11 Mike Taylor
☐ 12 Taylor Clarke
☐ 13 Mike Harding
☐ 14 Scott Burfoot
☐ 15 Mike Rucinski
☐ 16 David Dartsch
☐ 17 Craig Paterson
☐ 18 Trevor Senn
☐ 19 Jay McNeill
☐ 20 Matt Garzone
☐ 21 Scott Gruhl
☐ 22 Rod Langway
☐ 23 Mascot The Glade
☐ 24 The Freezer Arena
☐ 25 PHPA

ROANOKE EXPRESS

'93 - 94
ROANOKE EXPRESS / VIRGINIA BANK

Singles start at 50¢.
Card Size: 2 1/2" x 3 1/2"
Set (25 cards): $8

☐ Frank Anzalone
☐ Will Averill
☐ Claude Barthe
☐ Lev Berdichevsky
☐ Hughes Bouchard
☐ Reggie Brezeault
☐ Ilja Dubkov
☐ Pat Ferschweiler
☐ Kyle Galloway
☐ Jeff Jestadt
☐ Roger Larche
☐ Dana McGuane
☐ Jim Mill
☐ Dave Morissette
☐ HL: Dave Morissette
☐ Chris Potter
☐ Dan Ryder
☐ Gairin Smith
☐ Michael Smith
☐ Tony Szabo
☐ Stephen Tepper
☐ Oleg Yashin
☐ Team Photo
☐ Sponsor Logo
☐ Sponsor Logo

'94 - 95
ROANOKE EXPRESS / RALLY'S

Singles start at 50¢.
Card Size: 2 1/2" x 3 1/2"
Set (23 cards): $8

☐ Frank Anzalone
☐ Robin Bouchard
☐ Jason Clarke
☐ Stéphane Desjardins
☐ Ilja Dubukov
☐ Pat Ferschweiler
☐ Carl Fleury
☐ Dave Gagnon
☐ Jeff Jestadt
☐ Jon Larson
☐ Derek Laxdal
☐ Mark Luger
☐ Dana McGuane
☐ Chris Potter
☐ Dan Ryder
☐ Marty Schriner
☐ Michael Smith
☐ Dave Stewart
☐ Rouslan Toujikov
☐ Oleg Yashin
☐ Mascot Loco
☐ Team Photo
☐ Board of Directors

'95 - 96
ROANOKE EXPRESS

Singles start at 50¢.
Card Size: 2 1/2" x 3 1/2"
Sponsor: None
Set (25 cards): $8

☐ Frank Anzalone
☐ Daniel Berthiaume
☐ L.P. Charbonneau
☐ Ted Christian
☐ Jason Clarke
☐ Paul Crôteau
☐ Matt DelGuidice (G)
☐ Ilja Dubukov
☐ Brian Gallentine
☐ Tim Hanley
☐ Duane Harmer
☐ Craig Herr
☐ Dave Holum
☐ Jeff Jablonski
☐ Jeff Jestadt
☐ Nick Jones
☐ Jon Larson
☐ Chris Pollack
☐ Chris Potter
☐ Marty Schriner
☐ Michael Smith
☐ Mike Stacchi
☐ Dave Stewart
☐ Mascot Loco
☐ Team Photo

'96 - 97
ROANOKE EXPRESS

Singles start at 50¢.
Set (24 cards): $9

☐ 1 David Gagnon
☐ 2 Dave Stewart
☐ 3 Éric Landry
☐ 4 Mike Smith
☐ 5 Jeff Loder
☐ 6 Duane Harmer
☐ 7 Bobby Brown
☐ 8 J.F. Tremblay
☐ 9 Ryan Equale
☐ 10 Doug Searle
☐ 11 Jeff Jablonski
☐ 12 Jeff Cowan
☐ 13 Sean Brown
☐ 14 Ilja Dubkov
☐ 15 Matt O'Dette
☐ 16 Chris Lipsett
☐ 17 Tim Christian
☐ 18 Larry Moberg
☐ 19 Frank Anzalone
☐ 20 Mike Holden
☐ 21 Mascot Loco
☐ 22 Mascot Elmer
☐ 23 Team Photo
☐ 24 Checklist

'98 - 99
ROANOKE EXPRESS / ROOX SPORTS

Singles start at 50¢.
Card Size: 2 1/2" x 3 1/2"

Set (14 cards): $9

- ☐ 1 Scott Gordon
- ☐ 2 Mike Mader
- ☐ 3 Peter Brearley
- ☐ 4 Nic Beaudoin
- ☐ 5 Chris Wismer
- ☐ 6 Daniel Berthiaume
- ☐ 7 Dru Burgess
- ☐ 8 Kris Cantu
- ☐ 9 Jason Dailey
- ☐ 10 Perry Florio
- ☐ 11 Tim Christian
- ☐ 12 Doug Searle
- ☐ 13 Chris Lipsett
- ☐ 14 Mascot Loco

ROCHESTER AMERICANS

'91 - 92

ROCHESTER AMERICANS / DUNKIN' DONUTS

Lindy Ruff is one of the more expensive singles at $2. Singles start at 50¢.

Card Size: 2 1/2" x 3 1/2"

Set (16 cards): $10

- ☐ Greg Brown
- ☐ Peter Ciavaglia
- ☐ Bob Corkum
- ☐ Brian Curren
- ☐ David DiVita
- ☐ Tom Draper (G)
- ☐ Jody Gage
- ☐ Dan Frawley
- ☐ Dave Littman (G)
- ☐ Darcy Loewen
- ☐ Don McSween
- ☐ Brad Rubachuk
- ☐ Lindy Ruff
- ☐ Joel Savage
- ☐ Jiri Sejba
- ☐ Chris Snell

'91 - 92

ROCHESTER AMERICANS / KODAK, WEGMON'S

Keith Carney is one of the more expensive singles at $1.50. Singles start at 50¢.

Card Size: 2 1/4" x 3 1/8"

Set (26 cards): $12

- ☐ Ian Boyce
- ☐ John Bradley
- ☐ Greg Brown
- ☐ Keith Carney
- ☐ Peter Ciavaglia
- ☐ Bob Corkum
- ☐ Brian Curran
- ☐ David DiVita
- ☐ Lou Franceschetti
- ☐ Dan Frawley
- ☐ Jody Gage
- ☐ Kevin Haller
- ☐ Don Lever
- ☐ Dave Littman (G)
- ☐ Darcy Loewen
- ☐ Steve Ludzik
- ☐ Terry Martin
- ☐ Don McSween
- ☐ Brad Miller
- ☐ Sean O'Donnell
- ☐ Brad Rubachuk
- ☐ Lindy Ruff
- ☐ Joel Savage
- ☐ Jiri Sejba
- ☐ Chris Snell
- ☐ Jason Winch

'91 - 92

ROCHESTER AMERICANS / GENNY LIGHT

Keith Carney is one of the more expensive singles at $1.50 Singles start at 50¢.

Postcard Size: 3 1/2" x 5 1/2"

Sponsor: Genny Light

Set (21 cards): $10

- ☐ Dave Baseggio
- ☐ John Bradley
- ☐ Greg Brown
- ☐ Keith Carney
- ☐ Peter Ciavaglia
- ☐ Bob Corkum
- ☐ David DiVita
- ☐ Tom Draper (G)
- ☐ Lou Franceschetti
- ☐ Dan Frawley
- ☐ Bill Houlder
- ☐ Don Lever
- ☐ David Littman (G)
- ☐ Terry Martin
- ☐ Don McSween
- ☐ Sean O'Donnell
- ☐ Lindy Ruff
- ☐ Joel Savage
- ☐ Jiri Sejba
- ☐ Chris Snell
- ☐ Ed Zawatsky

'92 - 93

ROCHESTER AMERICANS / DUNKIN' DONUTS

Olaf Kölzig is one of the more expensive singles at $3. Singles start at 50¢.

Card Size: 2 1/2" x 3 1/2"

Set (20 cards): $10

- ☐ Peter Ambroziak
- ☐ Greg Brown
- ☐ Peter Ciavaglia
- ☐ Jozef Cierny
- ☐ David DiVita
- ☐ Dan Frawley
- ☐ Jody Gage
- ☐ Andrei Jakovenko
- ☐ Olaf Kölzig (G)
- ☐ Doug MacDonald
- ☐ Mike McLaughin
- ☐ Sean O'Donnell
- ☐ Bill Pye
- ☐ Brad Rubachuk
- ☐ Bruce Shoebottom
- ☐ Todd Simon
- ☐ Jeff Sirkka
- ☐ Chris Snell
- ☐ Scott Thomas
- ☐ Jason Young

'92 - 93

ROCHESTER AMERICANS / WEGMONS PHOTO

Olaf Kölzig is one of the more expensive singles at $3. Singles start at 50¢.

Card Size: 2 1/4" x 3 1/8"

Set (26 cards): $12

- ☐ Peter Ambroziak
- ☐ Greg Brown
- ☐ Peter Ciavaglia
- ☐ Jozef Cierny
- ☐ David DiVita
- ☐ Dan Frawley
- ☐ Jody Gage
- ☐ Tony Iob
- ☐ Olaf Kölzig (G)
- ☐ Doug MacDonald
- ☐ Terry Martin
- ☐ Mike McLaughlin
- ☐ Sean O'Donnell
- ☐ Brad Pascall
- ☐ Bill Pye
- ☐ Brad Rubachuk
- ☐ Joel Savage
- ☐ Bruce Shoebottom
- ☐ Todd Simon
- ☐ Jeff Sirkka
- ☐ Chris Snell
- ☐ Scott Thomas
- ☐ John Van Boxmeer
- ☐ Jason Winch
- ☐ Jason Young
- ☐ Mascot The Moose

'93 - 94

ROCHESTER AMERICANS / KODAK, WEGMON'S

Singles start at 50¢.

Card Size: 2 1/2" x 3 1/2"

Set (25 cards): $12

- ☐ Peter Ambroziak
- ☐ Mike Bavis
- ☐ James Black
- ☐ Derek Booth
- ☐ Philippe Boucher
- ☐ David Cooper
- ☐ Todd Flichel
- ☐ Jody Gage
- ☐ Viktor Gordiouk
- ☐ Bill Horn
- ☐ Markus Ketterer (G)
- ☐ Mark Krys
- ☐ Doug MacDonald
- ☐ Terry Martin
- ☐ Dean Melanson
- ☐ Sean O'Donnell
- ☐ Brad Pascall
- ☐ Sergei Petrenko
- ☐ Brad Rubachuk
- ☐ Todd Simon
- ☐ Scott Thomas
- ☐ John Van Boxmeer
- ☐ Mikhail Volkov
- ☐ Jason Young
- ☐ Mascot The Moose

'95 - 96

ROCHESTER AMERICANS / SPLIT SECOND

Steve Shields is one of the more expensive singles at $4. Singles start at 50¢.

Card Size: 2 1/2" x 3 1/2"

Set (25 cards): $15

- ☐ Craig Charron
- ☐ David Cooper
- ☐ Dan Frawley
- ☐ Jody Gage
- ☐ Terry Hollinger
- ☐ Dane Jackson
- ☐ Ladislav Karabin
- ☐ Sergei Klimentiev
- ☐ Jamie Leach
- ☐ Jay Mazur
- ☐ Dean Melanson
- ☐ Scott Metcalfe
- ☐ Barrie Moore
- ☐ Scott Nichol
- ☐ Roman Ndur
- ☐ Scott Pearson
- ☐ Serge Roberge
- ☐ Steve Shields (G)
- ☐ Robb Stauber (G)
- ☐ John Tortorella
- ☐ Mikhail Volkov
- ☐ Dixon Ward
- ☐ Bob Westerby
- ☐ Mike Wilson
- ☐ Shayne Wright

'96 - 97

ROCHESTER AMERICANS / SPLIT SECOND

Singles start at 50¢.

Card Size: 2 1/2" x 3 1/2"

Set (26 cards): $15

- ☐ 1 Americans
- ☐ 2 Sergei Klimentiev
- ☐ 3 Craig Charron
- ☐ 4 Craig Millar
- ☐ 5 Scott Metcalfe
- ☐ 6 Ed Ronan
- ☐ 7 Terry Hollinger
- ☐ 8 Shayne Wright
- ☐ 9 Barrie Moore
- ☐ 10 Scott Nichol
- ☐ 11 Charlie Huddy
- ☐ 12 Václav Varada
- ☐ 13 Wayne Primeau
- ☐ 14 Terry Yake
- ☐ 15 Dan Frawley
- ☐ 16 Frederic Deschenes
- ☐ 17 Steve Shields
- ☐ 18 Paul Rushforth
- ☐ 19 Dane Jackson
- ☐ 20 Rumun Ndur
- ☐ 21 Greg Walters
- ☐ 22 Éric Lavigne
- ☐ 23 John Tortorella
- ☐ 24 Mascot Moose
- ☐ 25 AHL Web Site
- ☐ 26 PHPA

'97 - 98

ROCHESTER AMERICANS / PEPSI

Singles start at 50¢.

Set (25 cards): $15

- ☐ Mike McKee
- ☐ Dean Melanson
- ☐ Martin Menard
- ☐ Scott Metcalfe
- ☐ Rumun Ndur
- ☐ Scott Nichol
- ☐ Erik Rasmussen
- ☐ Patrice Tardif
- ☐ Václav Varada
- ☐ Greg Walters
- ☐ Shayne Wright
- ☐ Mike Zanutto
- ☐ Mike Bales
- ☐ Daniel Bienvenue
- ☐ Martin Biron
- ☐ Craig Charron
- ☐ Matt Davidson
- ☐ Mark Dutiaume
- ☐ Dan Frawley
- ☐ Jean-Luc Grand-Pierre
- ☐ Denis Hamel
- ☐ Mike Hurlbut
- ☐ Dane Jackson
- ☐ Sergei Klimentiev
- ☐ Éric Lavigne

'98 - 99

ROCHESTER AMERICANS / PEPSI

Singles start at 50¢.

Set (25 cards): $15

- ☐ 1 Craig Fisher
- ☐ 2 Greg Walters
- ☐ 3 Matt Davidson
- ☐ 4 Randy Cunneyworth
- ☐ 5 Martin Biron
- ☐ 6 Mike Hurlbut
- ☐ 7 Tom Draper
- ☐ 8 Mike Harder
- ☐ 9 Denis Hamel
- ☐ 10 J-L Grand-Pierre
- ☐ 11 Scott Nichol
- ☐ 12 François Méthot
- ☐ 13 Dean Melanson
- ☐ 14 Jason Mansoff
- ☐ 15 Jason Holland
- ☐ 16 Darren Van Oene
- ☐ 17 Dean Sylvester
- ☐ 18 Cory Sarich
- ☐ 19 Erik Rasmussen
- ☐ 20 Domenic Pittis
- ☐ 21 Mascot The Moose
- ☐ 22 Darwin McCutcheon
- ☐ 23 Jody Gage
- ☐ 24 Shane Kenny
- ☐ 25 Steffon Walby

'00 - 01

ROCHESTER AMERICANS / CHOICE

Singles start at 50¢.

Card Size: 2 1/2" x 3 1/2"

Set (29 cards): $18

- ☐ 1 Jeremy Adduono
- ☐ 2 Tom Askey (G)
- ☐ 3 Martin Biron (G)
- ☐ 4 Kevin Bolibruck
- ☐ 5 Craig Brunel
- ☐ 6 Brian Campbell
- ☐ 7 Craig Charron
- ☐ 8 Jason Cipolla
- ☐ 9 Jason Holland
- ☐ 10 Doug Houda
- ☐ 11 Mike Hurlbut
- ☐ 12 Dane Jackson
- ☐ 13 Jaroslav Kristek
- ☐ 14 Mike Mader
- ☐ 15 François Méthot
- ☐ 16 Norm Milley
- ☐ 17 Joe Murphy
- ☐ 18 Todd Nelson
- ☐ 19 Mika Noronen (G)
- ☐ 20 Andrew Peters
- ☐ 21 Chris Taylor
- ☐ 22 Paul Traynor
- ☐ 23 Darren Van Oene
- ☐ 24 Randy Cunneyworth
- ☐ 25 Jon Christiano
- ☐ 26 Dave Williams
- ☐ 27 Kent
- ☐ 28 Mascot the Moose
- ☐ 28 Mascot the Moose
- ☐ Americans

'02 - 03

ROCHESTER AMERICANS / CHOICE

Singles start at 50¢.

Card Size: 2 1/2" x 3 1/2"

Set (26 cards):

- ☐ 1 Tom Askey
- ☐ 2 Milan Bartovic
- ☐ 3 Jason Botterill
- ☐ 4 Rory Fitzpatrick
- ☐ 5 Paul Gaustad
- ☐ 6 Denis Hamel
- ☐ 7 Radoslav Hecl
- ☐ 8 Doug Houda
- ☐ 9 Doug Janik
- ☐ 10 Ryan Jorde
- ☐ 11 Jaroslav Kristek
- ☐ 12 Sean McMorrow
- ☐ 13 François Méthot
- ☐ 14 Ryan Miller
- ☐ 15 Norm Milley
- ☐ 16 Karel Mosovsky
- ☐ 17 Jiri Novotny
- ☐ 18 Andrew Peters
- ☐ 19 Jason Pominville
- ☐ 20 Peter Ratchuk
- ☐ 21 Chris Taylor
- ☐ 22 Ryan Miller
- ☐ 23 Randy Cunneyworth
- ☐ 24 Jon Christiano
- ☐ 25 Mascot The Moose
- ☐ Checklist

ROCKFORD ICEHOGS

'99 - 00

ROCKFORD ICEHOGS / ROOX

Singles start at 50¢.

Card Size: 2 1/2" x 3 1/2"

Set (24 cards): $9

- ☐ 1 Brant Blackned
- ☐ 2 Peter Cava
- ☐ 3 Patrice Charbonneau
- ☐ 4 Mike Correia
- ☐ 5 Dan Davies
- ☐ 6 Raymond Delarosbil
- ☐ 7 Mike Figliomeni
- ☐ 8 Jason Firth
- ☐ 9 Sheldon Gorski
- ☐ 10 Jeff Kostuch
- ☐ 11 Yevgeny Krivomaz
- ☐ 12 Derek Landmesser
- ☐ 13 Alexandre Makombo
- ☐ 14 Barry McKinlay
- ☐ 15 Normand Paquet
- ☐ 16 Jean-Francois Rivard
- ☐ 17 Shawn Smith
- ☐ 18 Carlos Soke
- ☐ 19 Wayne Strachan
- ☐ 20 Curtis Tipler
- ☐ 21 Jesse Welling
- ☐ 22 Scott Burfoot
- ☐ 23 Dale (Digger) DeGray
- ☐ 24 Mascot Ham. E. Hog

'00 - 01

ROCKFORD ICEHOGS

Singles start at 50¢.

Card Size: 2 1/2" x 3 1/2"

Set (25 cards):

- ☐ Curtis Bois
- ☐ Patrice Charbonneau
- ☐ Nick Checco
- ☐ Curtis Cruickshank
- ☐ Jeff DaCosta
- ☐ Dan Davies
- ☐ Steve Dumonski
- ☐ Chris Fattey
- ☐ Mike Figiomeni
- ☐ Justin Kearns
- ☐ Evgeny Krivomaz
- ☐ Jocelyn Langlois
- ☐ Michel Periard
- ☐ Jean-François Rivard
- ☐ David Runge
- ☐ François Sasseville
- ☐ Shawn Smith
- ☐ Mike Tobin
- ☐ Yan Turgeon
- ☐ Eduard Zankovets
- ☐ Dale (Digger) DeGray
- ☐ Scott Burfoot
- ☐ Mascot Hamilton E. Hog
- ☐ Logo
- ☐ Header

'01 - 02

ROCKFORD ICEHOGS / CHOICE

Singles start at 50¢.

Card Size: 2 1/2" x 3 1/2"

Set (25 cards):

- ☐ 1 Ben Christopherson
- ☐ 2 Clint Wensley
- ☐ 3 Dan Davies
- ☐ 4 Darwin Murray
- ☐ 5 David Hoogsteen
- ☐ 6 Ernie Thorp
- ☐ 7 Forrest Gore
- ☐ 8 Mascot Hamilton..
- ☐ 9 Harold Hersh
- ☐ 10 Jean_François Rivard
- ☐ 11 Jared Reigstad
- ☐ 12 Jeff Antonovich
- ☐ 13 Jeff DaCosta
- ☐ 14 Jeremy Vokes
- ☐ 15 Joe Statkus
- ☐ 16 Mike Sgroi
- ☐ 17 Nick Checco
- ☐ 18 Oak Hewer
- ☐ 19 Quinten Van Horlick
- ☐ 20 Scott Bell
- ☐ 21 Sergei Petrov
- ☐ 22 Steve Debus
- ☐ 23 TJ Guidarelli
- ☐ 24 Wes Belvins
- ☐ Checklist

SAGINAW GEARS

'78 - 79

SAGINAW GEARS

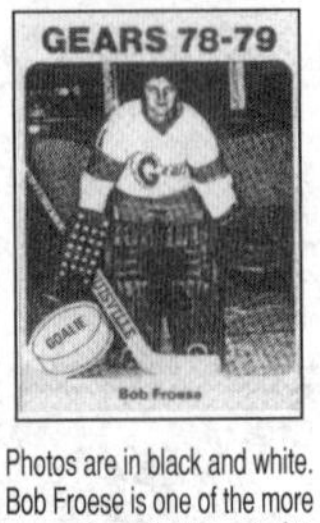

Photos are in black and white. Bob Froese is one of the more expensive singles at $5. Singles start at $1.

Card Size: 2 1/2" x 3 1/2"

Sponsor: None

Set (20 cards): $25

- ☐ Wren Blair
- ☐ Marcel Comeau
- ☐ Dennis Desrosiers
- ☐ Jon Fontas
- ☐ Bob Froese (G)
- ☐ Gunner Garrett
- ☐ Bob Gladney
- ☐ Warren Holmes
- ☐ Larry Hopkins
- ☐ Stu Irving
- ☐ Scott Jesse
- ☐ Lynn Jorgenson
- ☐ Doug Keans (G)
- ☐ Claude Larochelle
- ☐ Paul McIntosh
- ☐ Don Perry
- ☐ Greg Steel
- ☐ Mark Suzor
- ☐ Mark Toffolo
- ☐ Dave Westner

SAINT JOHN FLAMES

'94 - 95

SAINT JOHN FLAMES / CLASSIC

The most expensive single is Cory Stillman. Singles start at 50¢.

Card Size: 2 1/2" x 3 1/2"

Set (26 cards): $12

- ☐ Joel Bouchard
- ☐ Rick Carrière
- ☐ Ryan Duthie
- ☐ Neil Eisenhut
- ☐ Léonard Esau
- ☐ Bob Francis
- ☐ Mark Greig
- ☐ François Groleau
- ☐ Sami Helenius
- ☐ Todd Hlushko
- ☐ Dan Kushner
- ☐ Bobby Maxwell
- ☐ Scott Morrow
- ☐ Mike Murray
- ☐ Jason Muzzatti (G)
- ☐ Barry Nieckar
- ☐ Nicolas Perreault
- ☐ Jeff Perry
- ☐ Dwayne Roloson (G)
- ☐ Todd Simpson
- ☐ Cory Stillman
- ☐ David Struch
- ☐ Niklas Sundblad
- ☐ Andrei Trefilov (G)
- ☐ Vesa Viitakoski
- ☐ Harbour Station

'95 - 96

SAINT JOHN FLAMES

Singles start at 50¢.

Card Size: 2 1/2" x 3 1/2"

Sponsor: None

Set (25 cards): $12

- ☐ Jamie Allison
- ☐ Paul Baxter
- ☐ Joel Bouchard
- ☐ Tom Coolen
- ☐ Brett Duncan
- ☐ Ian Gordon
- ☐ Sami Helenius
- ☐ Todd Hlushko
- ☐ Marc Hussey
- ☐ Ladislav Kohn
- ☐ Frank Kovacs
- ☐ David Ling
- ☐ Jesper Mattson
- ☐ Keith McCambridge
- ☐ Marty Murray
- ☐ Mike Murray
- ☐ David Neilson
- ☐ Jeff Perry
- ☐ Darren Ritchie
- ☐ Dwayne Roloson (G)
- ☐ Todd Simpson
- ☐ Jarrod Skalde
- ☐ David Struch
- ☐ Niklas Sundblad
- ☐ Vesa Viitakoski

'96 - 97

SAINT JOHN FLAMES / SPLIT SECOND

Singles start at 50¢.

Card Size: 2 1/2" x 3 1/2"

Set (26 cards): $12

- ☐ Jesper Mattsson
- ☐ Keith McCambridge
- ☐ Dale McTavish
- ☐ Burke Murphy
- ☐ Marty Murray
- ☐ Jeff Perry
- ☐ Paxton Schulte
- ☐ Jarrod Skalde
- ☐ Jason Smith
- ☐ Clarke Wilm
- ☐ Ravil Yakubov
- ☐ AHL Web Site
- ☐ Mascot Fleaburn
- ☐ PHPA
- ☐ Jamie Allison
- ☐ Paul Baxter
- ☐ Chris Dingman
- ☐ Scott Fraser
- ☐ Denis Gauthier
- ☐ Ian Gordon
- ☐ Patrik Haltia
- ☐ Sami Helenius
- ☐ Marc Hussey
- ☐ Marko Jantunen
- ☐ Martin Lamarche
- ☐ Ladislav Kohn

'97 - 98

SAINT JOHN FLAMES

Singles start at 50¢.

Set (25 cards): $15

- ☐ Jesper Mattsson (G)
- ☐ Keith McCambridge
- ☐ Tyler Moss (G)
- ☐ Burke Murphy
- ☐ Marty Murray
- ☐ Chris O'Sullivan
- ☐ Jeff Perry
- ☐ Paxton Schulte
- ☐ Bill Stewart
- ☐ Rocky Thompson
- ☐ John Tripp
- ☐ Clarke Wilm
- ☐ Jamie Allison
- ☐ Erik Andersson
- ☐ Ryan Bast
- ☐ Travis Brigley
- ☐ Éric Charron
- ☐ Jeff Cowan
- ☐ Hnat Domenichelli
- ☐ Jim Dowd
- ☐ Denis Gauthier
- ☐ Jean-Sébastien Giguère
- ☐ Sami Helenius
- ☐ Ladislav Kohn
- ☐ Éric Landry

ST. JOHN'S MAPLE LEAFS

'92 - 93

ST. JOHN'S MAPLE LEAFS

Yanic Perreault is one of the more expensive singles at $4. Singles start at 50¢.

Card Size: 2 1/2" x 3 3/4"

Sponsor: None

Set (25 cards): $15

- ☐ Patrik Augusta
- ☐ Drake Berehowsky
- ☐ Robert Cimetta
- ☐ Marc Crawford
- ☐ Ted Crowley
- ☐ Mike Eastwood
- ☐ Todd Hawkins
- ☐ Curtis Hunt
- ☐ Eric Lacroix
- ☐ Guy Lehoux
- ☐ Kent Manderville
- ☐ Kevin McClelland
- ☐ Ken McRae
- ☐ Brad Miller
- ☐ Yanic Perreault
- ☐ Rudy Poeschek
- ☐ Joel Quenneville
- ☐ Damian Rhodes (G)
- ☐ Joe Sacco
- ☐ Jeff Serowik
- ☐ Scott Sharples (G)
- ☐ Dave Tomlinson
- ☐ Nick Wohlers
- ☐ Mascot Buddy
- ☐ Team Photo

'93 - 94
ST. JOHN'S MAPLE LEAFS

Marc Crawford, Damian Rhodes and Yanic Perreault are the most expensive single at $2-3. Singles start at 50¢.
Card Size: 2 1/2" x 3 3/4"
Sponsor: None
Set (25 cards): $15

☐ Patrik Augusta
☐ Frank Bialowas
☐ Rich Chernomaz
☐ Terry Chitaroni
☐ Marcel Cousineau (G)
☐ Marc Crawford
☐ Todd Gillingham
☐ Chris Govedaris
☐ Paul Holden
☐ Curtis Hunt
☐ Alexei Kudashov
☐ Eric Lacroix
☐ Guy Lehoux
☐ Matt Mallgrave
☐ Grant Marshall
☐ Ken McRae
☐ Yanic Perreault
☐ Bruce Racine (G)
☐ Damian Rhodes (G)
☐ Chris Snell
☐ Dan Stiver
☐ Andy Sullivan
☐ Ryan Vandenbussche
☐ Steffon Walby
☐ Mascot Buddy

'94 - 95
ST. JOHN'S MAPLE LEAFS / CLASSIC

Kenny Jönsson is one of the more expensive singles at $3. Singles start at 50¢.
Card Size: 2 1/2" x 3 3/4"
Set (24 cards): $12

☐ Patrik Augusta
☐ Ken Belanger
☐ Frank Bialowas
☐ Rich Chernomaz
☐ Brandon Convery
☐ Marcel Cousineau (G)
☐ Trent Cull
☐ Nathan Dempsey
☐ Kelly Fairchild
☐ Janne Gronvall
☐ David Harlock
☐ Darby Hendrickson
☐ Marc Hussey
☐ Kenny Jönsson
☐ Mark Kolesar
☐ Alexei Kudashov
☐ Guy Lehoux
☐ Guy Lévêque
☐ Matt Martin
☐ Robb McIntyre
☐ Bruce Racine (G)
☐ Ryan Vandenbussche
☐ Steffon Walby
☐ Todd Warriner

'95 - 96
ST. JOHN'S MAPLE LEAFS / CLASSIC

Brent Gretzky and Todd Warriner are the most expensive single at $1-1.50. Singles start at 50¢.
Card Size: 2 1/2" x 3 3/4"
Sponsor: Classic
Set (25 cards): $12

☐ Ken Belanger
☐ Rob Butz
☐ Brandon Convery
☐ Marcel Cousineau (G)
☐ Trent Cull
☐ Nathan Dempsey
☐ Kelly Fairchild
☐ Mike Foligno
☐ Brent Gretzky
☐ Janne Gronvall
☐ David Harlock
☐ Jamie Heward
☐ Mark Kolesar
☐ Guy Lehoux
☐ Kent Manderville
☐ Kory Mullin
☐ Jason Saal (G)
☐ Shayne Toporowski
☐ Paul Vincent
☐ Steffon Walby
☐ Mike Ware
☐ Todd Warriner
☐ Tom Watt
☐ Mascot Buddy
☐ Team Photo

'96 - 97
ST. JOHN'S MAPLE LEAFS / ULTRAMAR

Singles start at 50¢.
Set (25 cards): $12

☐ Jason Saal
☐ Greg Smyth
☐ Shayne Toporowski
☐ Yannick Tremblay
☐ Brian Wiseman
☐ Mascot Buddy
☐ Sgt. Randy Mercer
☐ Don Beaupré (G)
☐ Jared Bednar
☐ Aaron Brand
☐ Rich Brown
☐ Greg Bullock
☐ Rob Butz
☐ Shawn Carter
☐ Jason Cipolla
☐ Brandon Convery
☐ David Cooper
☐ John Craighead
☐ Trent Cull
☐ Nathan Dempsey
☐ Mark Deyell
☐ Jamie Heward
☐ Mark Hunter
☐ Mark Kolesar
☐ Guy Lehoux

'97 - 98
ST. JOHN'S MAPLE LEAFS / ULTRAMAR

Singles start at 50¢.
Sponsor: Ultramar
Set (25 cards): $12

☐ Al MacAdam
☐ Danny Markov
☐ Zdenek Nedved
☐ Clayton Norris
☐ Warren Norris
☐ Ryan Pepperall
☐ Jason Podollan
☐ Denis (D.J.) Smith
☐ Greg Smyth
☐ Shawn Thornton
☐ Jeff Ware
☐ Mascot Buddy the Puffin
☐ Kevyn Adams
☐ Lonny Bohonos
☐ Aaron Brand
☐ Rich Brown
☐ Shawn Carter
☐ David Cooper
☐ Marcel Cousineau
☐ Nathan Dempsey
☐ Mark Deyell
☐ Todd Gillingham
☐ Per' Gustafsson
☐ Mike Kennedy
☐ Francis Larivée

'99 - 00
ST. JOHN'S MAPLE LEAFS / MARIE'S DELI

Singles start at 50¢.
Set (25 cards): $15

☐ Al MacAdam
☐ Adam Mair
☐ Dennis Maxwell
☐ David Nemirovsky
☐ Ryan Pepperall
☐ Marek Posmyk
☐ Marc Robitaille
☐ Terry Ryan
☐ Terran Sandwith
☐ Darrin Shannon
☐ D.J. Smith
☐ Shawn Thornton
☐ Jimmy Waite
☐ Dmitriy Yakushin
☐ Kevyn Adams
☐ Vladimir Antipov
☐ Syl (III) Apps
☐ Jason Bonsignore
☐ Aaron Brand
☐ Craig Charron
☐ Nathan Dempsey
☐ Tyler Harlton
☐ Justin Hocking
☐ Bobby House
☐ Konstantin Kalmikov

'00 - 01
ST. JOHN'S MAPLE LEAFS / MARIE'S DELI

Singles start at 50¢.
Set (30 cards): $12

☐ 1 Morgan Warren
☐ 2 D.J. Smith
☐ 3 Tyler Harlton
☐ 4 Syl (III) Apps
☐ 5 Donald MacLean
☐ 6 Mikhail Travnicek
☐ 7 Mikael Hakansson
☐ 8 Jeff Farkas
☐ 9 Konstantin Kalmikov
☐ 10 Dmitry Yakushin
☐ 11 Adam Mair
☐ 12 Alexei Ponikarovsky
☐ 13 Jacques Larivière
☐ 14 Frank Mrazek
☐ 15 Allan Rourke
☐ 16 Bobby House
☐ 17 Jimmy Waite
☐ 18 Shawn Thornton
☐ 19 David Cooper
☐ 20 Mike Minard
☐ 21 Chad Allan
☐ 22 Kevin McClelland
☐ 23 Lou Crawford
☐ 24 Mascot Buddy Puffin
☐ 25 Nathan Dempsey
☐ 26 Félix Potvin
☐ 27 Patrik Augusta
☐ 28 Yanic Perreault
☐ 29 Chris Snell
☐ 30 Rich Chernomaz

'01 - 02
ST. JOHN'S MAPLE LEAFS / CLARENVILLE POLICE

Each card features a Maple Leafs player and a Clarenville policeman. The cards were handed out in the Clarenville area (north-west of St. John's).
Set (16 cards):

☐ Luca Cereda
☐ Christian Chartier
☐ Nathan Dempsey
☐ Doug Doull
☐ Jeff Farkas
☐ Paul Healey
☐ Bobby House
☐ Donald MacLean
☐ Craig Mills
☐ Mike Minard (G)
☐ Alexei Ponikarovsky
☐ Allan Rourke
☐ D.J. Smith
☐ Petr Svoboda
☐ Morgan Warren
☐ Marty Wilford

'01 - 02
ST. JOHN'S MAPLE LEAFS / NEWTEL, ALLANT

Singles start at 50¢.
Card Size: 2 1/2" x 3 1/2"
Set (30 cards): $10

☐ Nikolai Antropov
☐ François Bouchard

☐ Luca Cereda
☐ Christian Chartier
☐ Nathan Dempsey
☐ Doug Doull
☐ Jeff Farkas
☐ Paul Healey
☐ Bobby House
☐ Jacques Larivière
☐ Donald MacLean
☐ Craig Mills
☐ Mike Minard (G)
☐ Frank Mrazek
☐ Karel Pilar
☐ Alexei Ponikarovsky
☐ Allan Rourke
☐ D.J. Smith
☐ Petr Svoboda
☐ Mikael Tellqvist (G)
☐ Mihail Travnicek
☐ Morgan Warren
☐ Marty Wilford
☐ Bob Wren
☐ Lou Crawford, Coach
☐ Russ Adam, A.Coach
☐ K.McClelland, A.Coa.
☐ Mile One Stadium
☐ Mascot Buddy Puffin
☐ AHL All-Star Game

'02 - 03
ST. JOHN'S MAPLE LEAFS / ALLANT

A Bob Wren card may exist. These are oversized cards.
Set (6 cards):

☐ Brad Boyes
☐ Doug Doull
☐ Aaron Gavey
☐ Josh Holden
☐ Craig Mills
☐ Mikael Tellqvist

SALT LAKE GOLDEN EAGLES

'88 - 89
SALT LAKE GOLDEN EAGLES / SMOKEY THE BEAR

Theoren Fleury is one of the more expensive singles at $12. Singles start at $1.
Card Size: 2 1/2" x 3 1/2"
Set (24 cards): $25

☐ 1 Rick Barkovich
☐ 2 Michael Dark
☐ 3 Terry Perkins
☐ 4 Peter Lappin
☐ 5 Wayne Cowley
☐ 6 Rich Chernomaz
☐ 7 Steve Smith
☐ 8 Theoren Fleury
☐ 9 Dave Reierson
☐ Smokey The Bear (no#)
☐ 11 Martin Simard
☐ 12 Stu Grimson
☐ 13 Darwin McCutcheon
☐ 14 Doug Clarke
☐ 15 Doug Pickell
☐ 16 Randy Bucyk
☐ 17 Jim Johannson
☐ 18 Rick Lessard
☐ 19 Ken Sabourin
☐ 20 Chris Biotti
☐ 21 Jeff Wenaas
☐ 22 Mark Holmes
☐ 23 Bob Bodak
☐ 24 Marc Bureau

'92 - 93
SALT LAKE GOLDEN EAGLES / WHEATIES

Singles start at 50¢.
Set (25 cards): $12

☐ Todd Brost
☐ Rod Buskas
☐ Rich Chernomaz
☐ Kerry Clark
☐ Tomas Forslund
☐ Bob Francis
☐ Todd Gillingham
☐ Brian Patafie
☐ Todd Harkins
☐ Tim Harris
☐ Shawn Heaphy
☐ Paul Holden
☐ Paul Kruse
☐ Trevor Kidd
☐ Patrick Lebeau
☐ Sandy McCarthy
☐ Kris Miller
☐ Jason Muzzatti
☐ Alex Nikolic
☐ Ken Sabourin
☐ David St-Pierre
☐ Darren Stolk
☐ David Struch
☐ Andrei Trefilov (G)
☐ Kevin Wortman

SAN ANGELO OUTLAWS

'99 - 00
SAN ANGELO OUTLAWS / ROOX SPORTS

Singles start at 50¢.
Card Size: 2 1/2" x 3 1/2"
Set (32 cards): $10

☐ Adam Lord
☐ Dave Lylyk
☐ Kevin McKinnon
☐ Skeeter Moore
☐ Erik Noack
☐ Carl Paradis
☐ Inflatable Rusty
☐ Robby Sandrock
☐ Jeff Smith
☐ Kris Waltze
☐ Dion Wandler
☐ Jay Willman
☐ Darren Wright
☐ Action
☐ Booster Club
☐ Coliseum
☐ Mascot Ransom
☐ Mascot Rusty
☐ Off ice officials
☐ Outlaws
☐ Mike Bajurny
☐ Scott Chartier
☐ Mike Collins
☐ Pavel Evstigneev
☐ Frank Froio
☐ Jamie Garrick
☐ Sandis Girvitch
☐ Jeff Havard
☐ Kyle Henry
☐ Corey Isen
☐ Kevin Kreutzer
☐ Ed Kowalski

SAN DIEGO GULLS

'92 - 93
SAN DIEGO GULLS

Lindy Ruff is one of the more expensive singles at $1.50.Singles start at 50¢.
Card Size: 2 1/2" x 3 1/2"
Sponsor: None
Set (24 cards): $12

☐ John Anderson
☐ Perry Anderson
☐ Scott Arniel
☐ Michael Brewer
☐ Dale DeGray
☐ Gord Dineen
☐ Rick Dudley
☐ Larry Floyd
☐ Keith Gretzky
☐ Peter Hankinson
☐ Bill Houlder
☐ Andrei Jakovenko
☐ Rick Knickle (G)
☐ Denny Lambert
☐ Mitch Lamoureux
☐ Clint Malarchuk (G)
☐ Steve Martinson
☐ Hubie McDonough
☐ Don McSween
☐ Mitch Molloy
☐ Robbie Nichols
☐ Lindy Ruff
☐ Daniel Shank
☐ Sergei Starikov

'93 - 94
SAN DIEGO GULLS / CARL'S JR.

Singles start at 50¢.
Set (20 cards): $12

☐ 1 John Anderson
☐ 2 Scott Arniel
☐ 3 Allan Bester (G)
☐ 4 Greg Brown
☐ 5 Scott Chartier
☐ 6 Dale (Digger) DeGray
☐ 7 Mark DeSantis
☐ 8 Barry Dreger
☐ 9 Larry Floyd
☐ 10 Trevor Halverson
☐ 11 J-F Jomphe
☐ 12 Denny Lambert
☐ 13 Lonnie Loach
☐ 14 Hubie McDonough
☐ 15 Scott McKay
☐ 16 Don McSween
☐ 17 Antoine Mindjimba
☐ 18 Daniel Shank
☐ 19 Jarrod Skalde
☐ 20 Harold Snepsts

SHERBROOKE CANADIENS

'86 - 87
SHERBROOKE CANADIENS

The most expensive card is a group shot that includes Patrick Roy. Singles start at 50¢.
Card Size: 2 1/2" x 3 1/2"
Set (30 cards): $25

☐ 1 Entraineurs
☐ 2 Soigneurs 1986-87
☐ 3 Stanley Cup
☐ 4 Joel Baillargeon
☐ 5 Daniel Berthiaume
☐ 6 Serge Boisvert
☐ 7 Graeme Bonar
☐ 8 Randy Bucyk
☐ 9 Bill Campbell
☐ 10 J. Charbonneau
☐ 11 Réjean Cloutier
☐ 12 Bobby Dollas
☐ 13 Peter Douris
☐ 14 Steven Fletcher
☐ 15 Perry Ganchar
☐ 16 Luc Gauthier
☐ 17 Randy Gilhen
☐ 18 Scott Harlow
☐ 19 Rick Hayward
☐ 20 Kevin Houle
☐ 21 Rick Knickle (G)
☐ 22 Vincent Riendeau (G)
☐ 23 Guy Rouleau
☐ 24 Scott Sandelin
☐ 25 Karel Svoboda
☐ 26 Peter Taglianetti
☐ 27 Gilles Thibaudeau
☐ 28 Ernie Vargas
☐ 29 Andre Villeneuve
☐ 30 Brian Williams

SIOUX CITY MUSKETEERS

'74 - 75
SIOUX CITY MUSKETEERS

These cards are printed on yellow stock with green ink. Singles start at $1.
Size: 2 1/2" x 3 3/4"
Sponsor: None
Set (20 cards): $15

☐ Steve Boyle #8
☐ Dave Davies #12
☐ Steve Desloges #6
☐ Greg Gilbert #5
☐ Barry Head #9
☐ Steve Heathwood #16
☐ Dave Kartio #7
☐ Ralph Kloiber (G) #30
☐ Pete Maxwell (G) #27
☐ Randy McDonald #19
☐ Terry Mulroy (G) #1
☐ Sam Nelligan #11
☐ Julian Nixon #15
☐ Mike Noel #20
☐ Jim Peck #3
☐ Bogdan Podwysocki #18
☐ John Saville #10
☐ Alex Shibicky #17
☐ Bob Thomerson #4
☐ Jim White #2

SPRINGFIELD FALCONS

'96 - 97
SPRINGFIELD FALCONS / SPLIT SECOND

Manny Legacé is one of the more expensive singles at $2. Singles start at 50¢.
Card Size: 2 1/2" x 3 1/2"
Set (24 cards): $15

☐ Chris Longo
☐ Kent Manderville
☐ Steve Martins
☐ Jason McBain
☐ Rob Murray
☐ Nolan Pratt
☐ Deron Quint
☐ Ryan Risidore
☐ Reggie Savage
☐ Brent Thompson
☐ Juha Ylönen
☐ AHL Web Site
☐ PHPA
☐ Kevin Brown
☐ Tom Buckley
☐ Steve Cheredaryk
☐ Jeff Daniels
☐ Hnat Domenichelli
☐ Rhett Gordon
☐ Steven Halko
☐ Tavis Hansen
☐ Scott Langkow (G)
☐ Manny Legacé (G)
☐ Scott Levins

'97 - 98
SPRINGFIELD FALCONS / SPLIT SECOND

Singles start at 50¢.
Card Size: 2 1/2" x 3 1/2"
Set (26 cards): $15

☐ Jason Morgan
☐ Rob Murray
☐ Mike Pomichter
☐ Jeff Shevalier
☐ Martin Simard
☐ Brad Tiley
☐ Ron' Wilson
☐ AHL Web Site
☐ PHPA
☐ Ruslan Batyrshin
☐ Daniel Brière
☐ Ted Crowley
☐ Sylvain Daigle
☐ Andrew Dale
☐ Shane Doan
☐ Jason Doig
☐ Dave Farrish
☐ Dan Focht
☐ Sean Gagnon
☐ Rhett Gordon
☐ Tavis Hansen
☐ Chad Kilger
☐ Scott Langkow (G)
☐ Trevor Letowski
☐ Scott Levins
☐ Richard Lintner

SPRINGFIELD INDIANS

'83 - 84
SPRINGFIELD INDIANS

Singles start at $1.
Card Size: 2 1/2" x 3 1/2"
Sponsor: None
Set (25 cards): $15

☐ 1 Gil Hudon (G)
☐ 2 Jim Ralph (G)
☐ 3 Todd Bergen
☐ 4 Len Hachborn
☐ 5 John Olsson
☐ 6 Steve Tsujira
☐ 7 Gordie Williams
☐ 8 Dave Brown
☐ 9 Dan Frawley
☐ 10 Tom McMurchy
☐ 11 Dave Michayluk
☐ 12 Bob Mormina
☐ 13 Perry Pelensky
☐ 14 Andy Brickley
☐ 15 Ross Fitzpatrick
☐ 16 Florent Robidoux
☐ 17 Jeff Smith
☐ 18 Rod Willard
☐ 19 Darrell Anholt
☐ 20 Steve Blyth
☐ 21 Don Dietrich
☐ 22 Steve Smith
☐ 23 Daryl Stanley
☐ 24 Taras Zytynsky
☐ 25 Doug Sauter

'84 - 85
SPRINGFIELD INDIANS

Dirk Graham is one of the

more expensive singles at $2.50.Singles start at $1.
Card Size: 2 1/2" x 3 1/2"
Sponsor: None
Set (25 cards): $15

☐ 1 Mike Sands (G)
☐ 2 Lorne Molleken (G)
☐ 3 Todd Lumbard (G)
☐ 4 Randy Velischek
☐ 5 David Jensen
☐ 6 Ken Leiter
☐ 7 Vern Smith
☐ 8 Alan Kerr
☐ 9 Scott Howson
☐ 10 Tim Coulis
☐ 11 Terry Tait
☐ 12 Tim Trimper
☐ 13 Ron Flockhart
☐ 14 Ron Handy
☐ 15 Jim Poner
☐ 16 Chris Pryor
☐ 17 Dale Henry
☐ 18 Mark Hamway
☐ 19 Monty Trottier
☐ 20 Miroslav Mally
☐ 21 Dirk Graham
☐ 22 Roger Kortko
☐ 23 Bob Bodak
☐ 24 Lorne Henning
☐ 25 Checklist

SYRACUSE CRUNCH

'96 - 97

SYRACUSE CRUNCH / SPLIT SECOND

Singles start at 50¢.
Card Size: 2 1/2" x 3 1/2"
Set (25 cards): $12

☐ Brian Loney
☐ Chris McAllister
☐ Jack McIlhargey
☐ Ian McIntyre
☐ Yevgeny Namestnikov
☐ Tyson Nash
☐ Bert Robertsson
☐ Bogdan Savenko
☐ Dave Scatchard
☐ Darren Sinclair
☐ Rod Stevens
☐ Brent Tully
☐ Mark Wotton
☐ AHL Web Site
☐ Mascot Crunchman
☐ PHPA
☐ Chad Allan
☐ Doug Ast
☐ John Badduke
☐ Lonny Bohonos
☐ Frédéric Cassivi
☐ Larry Courville
☐ Mike Fountain
☐ Rick Girard
☐ Robb Gordon
☐ Mark Krys

'00 - 01

SYRACUSE CRUNCH / CHOICE

Singles start at 50¢.
Card Size: 2 1/2" x 3 1/2"
Set (25 cards): $12

☐ 1 Marc Lamothe (G)
☐ 2 J-F Labbé (G)
☐ 3 Andrei Sryubko
☐ 4 J. Andersson-Junkka
☐ 5 Michael Gaul
☐ 6 Dan Watson
☐ 7 Bill Bowler
☐ 8 Chris Nielsen
☐ 9 Jody Shelley
☐ 10 Mathieu Darche
☐ 11 Blake Bellefeuille
☐ 12 Jeremy Reich
☐ 13 Jeff Williams
☐ 14 Martin Spanhel
☐ 15 Brad Moran
☐ 16 Scott Hollis
☐ 17 Jeff Ware
☐ 18 Matt Davidson
☐ 19 Sean Selmser
☐ 20 Radim Bicanek
☐ 21 Reggie Savage
☐ 22 Gary Agnew, Coach
☐ 23 Ross Yates, A.Coach
☐ 24 Mascot Al
☐ Tully's Restaurant

'01 - 02

SYRACUSE CRUNCH / CHOICE

Singles start at 50¢.
Card Size: 2 1/2" x 3 1/2"
Set (25 cards): $12

☐ 1 J-F Labbé (G)
☐ 2 Andrei Sryubko
☐ 3 Dan Watson
☐ 4 Paul Manning
☐ 5 Matt Davidson
☐ 6 Duvie Westcott
☐ 7 Jody Shelley
☐ 8 Mathieu Darche
☐ 9 Blake Bellefeuille
☐ 10 Jeremy Reich
☐ 11 Martin Spanhel
☐ 12 David Ling
☐ 13 Sean Pronger
☐ 14 Brad Moran
☐ 15 Derrick Walser
☐ 16 Jeff Ware
☐ 17 Martin Paroulek
☐ 18 Darrel Scoville
☐ 19 Kent McDonell
☐ 20 Adam Borzecki
☐ 21 Andrej Nedorost
☐ 22 Brett Harkins
☐ 23 Jonathan Schill
☐ 24 Tully's Restaurant
☐ 25 Mascot Al

'02 - 03

SYRACUSE CRUNCH / CHOICE

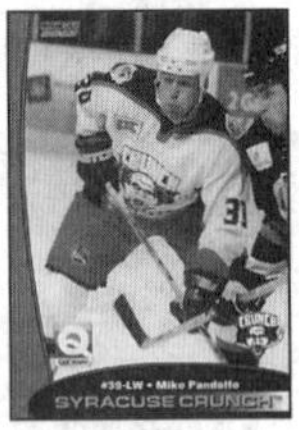

Singles start at 50¢.
Card Size: 2 1/2" x 3 1/2"
Set (24 cards):

☐ 1 Karl Goehring
☐ 2 Pasal Leclaire (G)
☐ 3 Tyler Sloan
☐ 4 Dan Watson
☐ 5 Paul Manning
☐ 6 Matt Davidson
☐ 7 Mathieu Darche
☐ 8 Blake Bellefeuille
☐ 9 Jeremy Reich
☐ 10 Tim Jackman
☐ 11 David Ling
☐ 12 Jonathan Schill
☐ 13 Brad Moran
☐ 14 Pauli Levokari
☐ 15 Darrel Scoville
☐ 16 Kent McDonell
☐ 17 Adam Borzecki
☐ 18 Andrej Nedorost
☐ 19 Radim Bicanek
☐ 20 Trevor Ettinger
☐ 21 Matt Dzieduszycki
☐ 22 Mike Pandolfo
☐ 23 Trent Cull
☐ 24 Mascot Al
☐ Quickway coupon

TALLAHASSEE TIGER SHARKS

'95 - 96

TALLAHASSE TIGER SHARKS / BURGER KING

Singles start at 50¢.
Card Size: 2 1/2" x 3 1/2"
Set (27 cards): $12

☐ 1 Rodrigo Lavinsh
☐ 2 Jon Engfer
☐ 3 Rod Aldoff
☐ 4 Aaron Kriss
☐ 5 Ron Pasco
☐ 6 Mark Deazley
☐ 7 Sean O'Brien
☐ 8 Kevin Paden
☐ 9 Darren Schwartz
☐ 10 Jim Paradise
☐ 11 John Uniac
☐ 12 Cal Ingraham
☐ 13 Matt Osiecki
☐ 14 Greg Geldart
☐ 15 A. Savchenkov
☐ 16 Casey Hungle
☐ 17 Mark Richards
☐ 18 Bob Bell
☐ 19 Mascot Frenzy
☐ 20 Jim Mirabello
☐ 21 M. Richards/ Bob Bell
☐ 22 Terry Christensen
☐ 23 Jack Capuano
☐ 24 Jerry Hilker
☐ 25 Walter Edwards
☐ 26 Tony Mancuso
☐ 27 John Summers

THUNDER BAY SENATORS

'93 - 94

THUNDER BAY SENATORS / RISING STAR

Trent McLeary is one of the more expensive singles at $1-1.50. Singles start at 50¢.
Card Size: 2 1/2" x 3 1/2"
Set (19 cards): $8

☐ Mel Angelstad
☐ Richard Borgo
☐ Brian Downey
☐ Jamie Hayden
☐ Tommi Hietalal
☐ Todd Howarth
☐ Chris Hynnes
☐ Jean-François Labbé (G)
☐ Trent McCleary
☐ Barry McKinley
☐ Terry Menard
☐ Llew NcWana
☐ Don Osborne
☐ Bruce Ramsay
☐ Vern Ray
☐ Gerry St. Cyr
☐ Ron Talakowki
☐ Tom Warden
☐ Bryan Wells

'94 - 95

THUNDER BAY SENATORS / RISING STAR

Singles start at 50¢.
Card Size: 2 1/2" x 3 1/2"
Set (19 cards): $8

☐ Mel Angelstad
☐ Jean Blouin
☐ Alain Côté
☐ Jason Firth
☐ Rival Fullum
☐ Jake Grimes
☐ Todd Howarth
☐ Lance Leslie
☐ Mike McCourt
☐ Barry McKinley
☐ Llew NcWana
☐ Don Osborne
☐ Steve Parson
☐ Darren Perkins
☐ Neal Purdon
☐ Bruce Ramsay
☐ Chris Rowland
☐ Derek Scanlan
☐ Pat Szturm

'95 - 96

THUNDER BAY SENATORS / RISING STAR

Singles start at 50¢.
Card Size: 2 1/2" x 3 1/2"
Set (20 cards): $9

☐ Mel Angelstad
☐ Omer Belisle
☐ Frédéric Cassivi (G)
☐ Brandon Christian
☐ Jason Disher
☐ Jason Firth
☐ Rival Fullum
☐ Todd Howarth
☐ Chris Hynnes
☐ Barry McKinley
☐ Terry Menard
☐ Derek Nicolson
☐ Llew NcWana
☐ Steve Parson
☐ Darren Perkins
☐ Dan Poirier
☐ Neal Purdon
☐ Bruce Ramsay
☐ Pat Szturm
☐ Team Photo

TOLEDO STORM

'92 - 93

TOLEDO STORM / WIOT-104

Singles start at 50¢.
Card Size: 2 3/8" x 3 1/2"
Set 1 (30 cards): $10

☐ Wade Bartley
☐ Derek Booth
☐ Rick Corriveau
☐ Mark Deazeley
☐ Iain Duncan
☐ Jeff Gibbons
☐ Alex Hicks
☐ Jeff Jablonski
☐ Rick Judson
☐ Scott King (G)
☐ Scott Luhrmann
☐ Bruce MacDonald
☐ Chris McSorley
☐ Tim Mouser
☐ Greg Puhalski
☐ Pat Pylypuik
☐ Alex Roberts
☐ Brent Sapergia
☐ Barry Soskin
☐ Jason Stos
☐ Andy Suhy
☐ Mike Williams
☐ Distillery Crew
☐ Checklist
☐ Beth Daniels
☐ Don Davis
☐ Dennis O'Brien
☐ Becky Shock
☐ Wil Worster
☐ The Dawbusters

Set 2 (25 cards): $10

☐ Derek Booth #23
☐ Rick Corriveau #24
☐ Mark Deazeley #12
☐ Iain Duncan #19
☐ Jeff Gibbons, P.R. #6
☐ Alex Hicks #21
☐ Jeff Jablonski #16
☐ John Johnson #13
☐ Rick Judson #20
☐ Scott King #8 (G)
☐ Scott Luhrmann, Equip.
☐ Bruce MacDonald #18
☐ Chris McSorley, Coach
☐ Tim Mouser, P.R. #5
☐ Barry Potomskin #22
☐ Greg Puhalski #17
☐ Pat Pylypuik #10
☐ Alex Roberts #11
☐ Jeff Rohlicek #14
☐ Claude Scott, Fan #7
☐ Barry Soskin, G.M.
☐ Andy Suhy #9
☐ Dan Wiebe #15
☐ Checklist
☐ Mark Richards #25

'93 - 94

TOLEDO STORM

Erin Whitten is one of the more expensive singles at $5. Singles start at 50¢.
Card Size: 2 3/8" x 3 1/2"
Sponsor: None
Set (29 cards): $15

☐ 1 Checklist
☐ 2 Chris McSorley, Coach
☐ 3 Barry Soskin, G.M.
☐ 4 Tim Mouser, P.R.
☐ 5 Jeff Gibbons, P.R.
☐ 6 Scott Luhrmann
☐ 7 Nick Vitucci
☐ 8 Andy Suhy
☐ 9 Pat Pylypuik
☐ 10 Chris Belanger
☐ 11 Mike Markovich
☐ 12 Darren Perkins
☐ 13 Dennis Snedden
☐ 14 Mark Deazeley
☐ 15 Mark McCreary
☐ 16 Jeff Rohlicek
☐ 17 Chris Bergeron
☐ 18 John Hendry
☐ 19 Greg Puhalski
☐ 20 Bruce MacDonald
☐ 21 Marc Lyons
☐ 22 Rick Judson
☐ 23 Alex Hicks
☐ 24 Barry Potomski
☐ 25 Rick Corriveau
☐ 26 Kyle Reeves
☐ 27 Erin Whitten (G)
☐ 28 Brian Schoen
☐ 29 Riley Cup Champs

'94 - 95

TOLEDO STORM

Singles start at 50¢.
Card Size: 2 1/2" x 3 1/2"
Sponsor: None
Set (24 cards): $10

☐ Dave Bankoske
☐ Wyatt Buckland
☐ Rick Corriveau
☐ Norm Dezainde
☐ Iain Duncon
☐ Jeff Gibbons
☐ Alain Harvey
☐ John Hendry
☐ Ed Henrich
☐ Rick Judson
☐ Mike Latendress
☐ Scott Luhrmann
☐ B.J. MacPherson
☐ Jim Maher
☐ Jay Neal
☐ Marquis Mathieu
☐ Shawn Penn
☐ Darren Perkins
☐ Greg Puhalski
☐ Gerry St. Cyr
☐ Barry Soskin
☐ Rhett Trombley
☐ Nick Vitucci
☐ Riley Cup Champions

'95 - 96

TOLEDO STORM / FRITO LAY

Singles start at 50¢.
Card Size: 2 1/2" x 3 1/2"
Set (26 cards): $10

☐ Wade Bartley
☐ Brandon Carper
☐ Dan Carter
☐ Norman Dezainde
☐ Jason Gladney
☐ Patrick Gladu
☐ David Goverde
☐ Chuck Imburgia
☐ Rick Judson
☐ Mark Kelly
☐ Paul Koch
☐ Mike Kolenda
☐ Rob Laurie
☐ Scott Luhrmann
☐ B.J. MacPherson
☐ Glen Mears
☐ Shawn Penn
☐ Nicolas Perreault
☐ Greg Puhalski
☐ Dennis Purdie
☐ Jason Smart
☐ Barry Soskin
☐ Mark Stitt
☐ Todd Wetzel
☐ Mike Whitton
☐ Frito Lay

'96 - 97

TOLEDO STORM / SPLIT SECOND

Card Size: 2 1/2" x 3 1/2"
Set (24 cards): $9

☐ Scott Luhrmann
☐ Alex Matvichuk
☐ Jeremy Mylymok
☐ Dan Pawlaczyk
☐ Greg Puhalski
☐ Dennis Purdie
☐ Barry Soskin
☐ Mike Sullivan
☐ Robert Thorpe
☐ Mike Whitton
☐ PHPA
☐ Ryan Bach
☐ Ryan Bast
☐ Chris Bergeron
☐ Brian Clifford
☐ Norman Dezainde
☐ Jason Gladney
☐ David Goverde
☐ Mark Kelly
☐ Rick Judson
☐ Arturs Kupaks
☐ Mike Kolenda
☐ Paul Koch
☐ Don Larner

'97 - 98

TOLEDO STORM / GRANDSTAND

Singles start at 50¢.
Set (30 cards): $9

☐ 1 Louis Bernard
☐ 2 Robert Thorpe
☐ 3 Greg Lakovic
☐ 4 Alexandre Jacques
☐ 5 Gordy Hunt
☐ 6 Andrei Srubko
☐ 7 Sean Venedam
☐ 8 Jeremy Rebek
☐ 9 Sean Ortiz
☐ 10 Tony Prpic
☐ 11 Brian Blad
☐ 12 Ron Newhook
☐ 13 Nick Vitucci
☐ 14 Dennis Holland
☐ 15 Mark Deazeley
☐ 16 Rick Judson
☐ 17 Lee Cole
☐ 18 Mike Kolenda
☐ 19 Dave Arsenault
☐ 20 Jason Gladney
☐ 21 Bruce MacDonald
☐ 22 Kevin Brown
☐ 23 Andrew Williamson
☐ 24 Shawn Maltby
☐ 25 Mike Loach
☐ 26 Greg Puhalski
☐ 27 Barry Soskin
☐ 28 Team Staff
☐ 29 Mark Kelly
☐ 30 Matt Bresnan

TOPEKA SCARECROWS

'98 - 99

TOPEKA SCARECROWS / EBK SPORTS

Singles start at 50¢.
Set (22 cards): $9

☐ 1 Scarecrows Checklist
☐ 2 Michal Podolka (G)
☐ 3 Shawn Randall
☐ 4 Mike Rusk
☐ 5 Brett Seguin
☐ 6 Tom Stewart
☐ 7 Andy Adams
☐ 8 Chad Antonishyn
☐ 9 Chris Bowen
☐ 10 Joe Coombs
☐ 11 Scott Dickson
☐ 12 Troy Frederick
☐ 13 Dave Gregory
☐ 14 Trevor Hanas
☐ 15 Kyle Haviland
☐ 16 Mascot Haywire
☐ 17 Kevin Lune
☐ 18 Sergei Olympiev
☐ 19 Ryan Phillips
☐ 20 Paul Kelly
☐ 21 Podolka (G)/ Adams
☐ 22 Scarecrows Photo

'99 - 00

TOPEKA SCARECROWS / ROOX SPORTS

Singles start at 50¢.
Card Size: 2 1/2" x 3 1/2"
Set (21 cards): $10

☐ 1 Scarecrows
☐ 2 John Vary
☐ 3 Oleg Tsirkounov
☐ 4 Bill Monkman
☐ 5 Sergei Deschevvy
☐ 6 Randy Best
☐ 7 Blair Manning
☐ 8 Steve Moore
☐ 9 Kirk Llano
☐ 10 Joey Beaudry
☐ 11 Trevor Hanas
☐ 12 David Duke Bouskill
☐ 13 Rod Branch
☐ 14 Joe Coombs
☐ 15 Mike Rusk
☐ 16 Scot Bell
☐ 17 Michal Podolka (G)
☐ 18 Brett Seguin
☐ 19 Mascot Haywire
☐ 20 Paul Kelly
☐ 21 Scarecrows

UTAH GRIZZLIES

'99 - 00

UTAH GRIZZLIES / VOLKSWAGON

Singles start at 50¢.
Set (35 cards): $15

☐ 1 Sponsor Volkswagon
☐ 2 Rich Parent (G)
☐ 3 Richard Park
☐ 4 John Purves
☐ 5 Jarrod Skalde
☐ 6 Bob Bourne
☐ 7 Checklist
☐ 8 Sponsor Volkswagon
☐ 9 Gord Dineen
☐ 10 Sean Tallaire
☐ 11 Micah Aivazoff
☐ 12 Shawn Penn
☐ 13 Larry Ness
☐ 14 1995 - 96 Turner Cup
☐ 15 Sponsor Volkswagon
☐ 16 Joe Frederick
☐ 17 Stewart Malgunas
☐ 18 Mick Vukota
☐ 19 Patrick Neaton
☐ 20 Dean Chynoweth
☐ 21 Aivazoff/ G. Dineen
☐ 22 Sponsor Volkswagon
☐ 23 Rob Bonneau
☐ 24 Ian Gordon
☐ 25 Brad Lauer
☐ 26 Neil Brady
☐ 27 Mascot Grizbee
☐ 28 Mick Vukota
☐ 29 Sponsor card
☐ 30 Brad Miller
☐ 31 Jeff Sharples
☐ 32 Darcy Werenka
☐ 33 Zarley Zalapski
☐ 34 Greg Payette
☐ 35 Utah Freezz

'00 - 01

UTAH GRIZZLIES / DAVE'S STRONG

Singles start at 50¢.

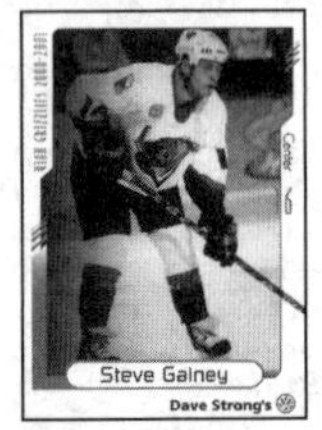

Perforated Card Size: 2 1/2" x 3 1/2"
Set (21 cards): $12

☐ 1 Sponsor Volkswagon
☐ 2 Mike Bales (G)
☐ 3 Steve Gainey
☐ 4 Brad Lauer
☐ 5 Jeff MacMillan
☐ 6 Bob Bourne
☐ 7 Checklist
☐ 8 Sponsor Passat
☐ 9 Patrick Neaton
☐ 10 John Erskine
☐ 11 John Purves
☐ 12 Greg Leeb
☐ 13 Jason Taylor
☐ 14 Grizzlies
☐ 15 Sponsor card
☐ 16 R. Tabaracci (G)
☐ 17 Chris Wells
☐ 18 Ryan Christie
☐ 19 Alan Letang
☐ 20 Craig Ludwig
☐ 21 Grizzlies

'01 - 02

UTAH GRIZZLIES / DAVE'S STRONG

Singles start at 50¢.
Perforated Card Size: 2 1/2" x 3 1/2"
Set (35 cards): $12

☐ 1 Paul Elliott
☐ 2 John Erskine
☐ 3 Gregor Baumgartner
☐ 4 Jonathan Sim
☐ 5 Tommy Salo (G) [Then & Now]
☐ 6 Mascot Grizzbee K
☐ 7 Sponsor card
☐ 8 Greg Hawgood
☐ 9 John Purves
☐ 10 Steve Gainey
☐ 11 Serge Payer
☐ 12 Zigmund Palffy [Then & Now]
☐ 13 Eq. Assistants
☐ 14 Sponsor card
☐ 15 Mark Wotton
☐ 16 Mark Kristofferson
☐ 17 Éric Beaudoin
☐ 18 Roman Lyashenko
☐ 19 Vladimir Orszagh [Then & Now]
☐ 20 Bob Bassen, A.Coach
☐ 21 Sponsor card
☐ 22 Jeff MacMillan
☐ 23 Cameron Mann
☐ 24 Ryan Jardine
☐ 25 Jim Montgomery
☐ 26 Chad Alban (G)
☐ 27 Eq. Mgrs. & Trainer
☐ 28 Sponsor card
☐ 29 Dan Jancevski
☐ 30 Justin Cox
☐ 31 Kyle Rossiter
☐ 32 Gavin Morgan
☐ 33 Wade Flaherty (G)
☐ 34 Don Hay, Coach
☐ 35 Sponsor card

WHEELING THUNDERBIRDS

'92 - 93

WHEELING THUNDERBIRDS / THOSE GUYS

Singles start at 50¢.
Card Size: 2 1/2" x 3 1/2"
Set (24 cards): $10

☐ 1 Thunderbirds Card
☐ 2 Claude Barthe
☐ 3 Joel Blain
☐ 4 Derek DeCosty
☐ 5 Marc Deschamps
☐ 6 Tom Dion
☐ 7 Devin Edgerton
☐ 8 Pete Heine
☐ 9 Kim Maier
☐ 10 Mike Millham (G)
☐ 11 Cory Paterson
☐ 12 T. Pochipinski
☐ 13 Tim Roberts
☐ 14 Mark Rodgers
☐ 15 Darren Schwartz
☐ 16 Trevor Senn
☐ 17 Tim Tisdale
☐ 18 John Uniac
☐ 19 Denny Magruder
☐ 20 C. Greenwood/ J. Smith
☐ 21 Larry Kish
☐ 22 Doug Sauter
☐ 23 Mascot T-Bird
☐ 24 Doug Bacon

'93 - 94

WHEELING THUNDERBIRDS / THOSE GUYS

Singles start at 50¢.
Card Size: 2 1/2" x 3 1/2"
Set (21 cards): $8

☐ 1 Checklist
☐ 2 Darren Schwartz
☐ 3 Cory Paterson
☐ 4 Derek DeCosty
☐ 5 Jim Bermingham
☐ 6 Brock Woods
☐ 7 Tim Roberts
☐ 8 Eric Raymond
☐ 9 Brett Abel
☐ 10 Sébastien Fortier
☐ 11 John Johnson
☐ 12 Brent Pope
☐ 13 Marquis Mathieu
☐ 14 Terry Virtue
☐ 15 Vadim Silvchenko
☐ 16 Clayton Gainer
☐ 17 Sylvain Lapointe
☐ 18 Douig Sauter
☐ 19 Larry Kish
☐ 20 Denny Magruder
☐ 21 Bill Cordery

'94 - 95

WHEELING THUNDERBIRDS / THOSE GUYS

Singles start at 50¢.
Card Size: 2 1/2" x 3 1/2"
Set (12 cards): $6

☐ 1 Checklist
☐ 2 Tim Tisdale
☐ 3 Brock Woods
☐ 4 Vadim Silvchenko
☐ 5 Tim Roberts
☐ 6 Derek DeCosty
☐ 7 Steve Gibson
☐ 8 Xavier Majic
☐ 9 Peter Marek
☐ 10 Greg Loder
☐ 11 Gairin Smith
☐ 12 Darren McAusland

WICHITA THUNDER

'98 - 99

WICHITA THUNDER / GM GOODWRENCH

Singles start at 50¢.
Set (25 cards): $12

☐ 1 Checklist
☐ 2 Vernon Beardy
☐ 3 Travis Clayton
☐ 4 Chris Dashney
☐ 5 Mike Donaghue
☐ 6 Jason Duda
☐ 7 Rhett Dudley
☐ 8 Trevor Folk
☐ 9 Todd Howarth
☐ 10 John Kachur
☐ 11 Mark Karpen
☐ 12 Lance Leslie
☐ 13 Brad Link
☐ 14 Mark Macera
☐ 15 Walker McDonald
☐ 16 Jim McGeough
☐ 17 Thomas Migdal
☐ 18 Aaron Novak
☐ 19 Sean O'Reilly
☐ 20 Kevin Powell
☐ 21 Greg Smith
☐ 22 Travis Tipler
☐ 23 Troy Yarosh
☐ 24 Bryan Wells
☐ 25 Goodwrench Dealer

WILKES-BARRE/ SCRANTON PENGUINS

'00 - 01

WILKES-BARRE/ SCRANTON PENGUINS / CHOICE

Singles start at 50¢.
Set (28 cards): $12

☐ Dennis Bonvie
☐ Brendan Buckley
☐ Sven Butenschon
☐ Sébastien Caron
☐ Greg Crozier
☐ Trent Cull
☐ Andrew Ference
☐ Dylan Gyori
☐ Chris Kelleher
☐ Tom Kostopoulos
☐ Joel Laing
☐ Jason MacDonald
☐ Alexander Mathieu
☐ Jim Leger
☐ Josef Melichar
☐ Eric Meloche
☐ Rich Parent (G)
☐ Glenn Patrick
☐ Toby Petersen
☐ John Slaney
☐ Martin Sonnenberg
☐ Jean-Philippe Soucy
☐ Billy Tibbetts
☐ Darcy Verot
☐ Mike Yeo
☐ Alexander Zevakhin
☐ Checklist
☐ Mascot Tux

'01 - 02

WILKES-BARRE/ SCRANTON PENGUINS / CHOICE

Singles start at 50¢.
Set (26 cards): $12

☐ 1 Rob Tallas (G)
☐ 2 Rob Scuderi
☐ 3 David Koci
☐ 4 Brooks Orpik
☐ 5 Darcy Robinson
☐ 6 Mike Wilson
☐ 7 Darcy Verot
☐ 8 Ross Lupaschuk
☐ 9 Martin Sonnenberg
☐ 10 Jan Fadrny
☐ 11 Alexander Zevakhin
☐ 12 Shane Endicott
☐ 13 Brendan Buckley
☐ 14 Jason MacDonald
☐ 15 Tomas Surovy
☐ 16 Tom Kostopoulos
☐ 17 Alexandre Mathieu
☐ 18 Peter Ratchuk
☐ 19 Sebastien Caron
☐ 20 Steve Parsons
☐ 21 Robert Dome
☐ 22 Éric Meloche
☐ 23 Glenn Patrick, Coach
☐ 24 Mike Yeo, A.Coach
☐ 25 Mascot Tux
☐ Header card

'02 - 03

WILKES-BARRE/ SCRANTON PENGUINS / CHOICE

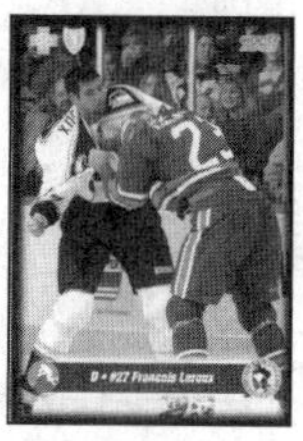

Singles start at 50¢.
Card Size: 2 1/2" x 3 1/2"
Set (27 cards):

☐ Checklist
☐ 1 Rob Scuderi
☐ 2 Brooks Orpik
☐ 3 Darcy Robinson
☐ 4 Mike Wilson
☐ 5 Michel Ouellet
☐ 6 Ross Lupaschuk
☐ 7 Matt Hussey
☐ 8 Milan Kraft
☐ 9 Alexander Zevakhin
☐ 10 Kris Beech
☐ 11 Shane Endicott
☐ 12 Toby Petersen
☐ 13 Colby Armstrong
☐ 14 Michal Sivek
☐ 15 Matt Murley
☐ 16 Brendan Buckley
☐ 17 Jason MacDonald
☐ 18 Tomas Surovy
☐ 19 François Leroux
☐ 20 Konstantin Koltsov
☐ 21 Tom Kostopoulos
☐ 22 Robbie Tallas
☐ 23 Sébastien Caron
☐ 24 Éric Meloche
☐ 25 Glenn Patrick
☐ 26 Mike Yeo
☐ Checklist

WORCESTER ICECATS

'00 - 01

WORCESTER ICECATS / CHOICE

Singles start at 50¢.
Card Size: 2 1/2" x 3 1/2"
Set (30 cards): $12

☐ 1 Ed Campbell
☐ 2 Daniel Corso
☐ 3 Justin Papineau
☐ 4 Jaroslav Obsut
☐ 5 Ladislav Nagy
☐ 6 Marc Brown
☐ 7 Pascal Rhéaume
☐ 8 Mike Van Ryn
☐ 9 Cody Rudkowsky
☐ 10 Andrei Troschinsky
☐ 11 Mark Rycroft
☐ 12 Matt Walker
☐ 13 Jamie Thompson
☐ 14 Darren Rumble
☐ 15 Mascot Scratch
☐ 16 Checklist
☐ 17 Dwayne Roloson (G)
☐ 18 Jame Pollock
☐ 19 Eric Boguniecki
☐ 20 Chris Murray
☐ 21 Tyler Rennette
☐ 22 Marty Reasoner
☐ 23 Dale Clarke
☐ 24 Tyler Willis
☐ 25 Jan Horacek
☐ 26 Peter Smrek
☐ 27 Mike Peluso
☐ 28 Doug Friedman
☐ 29 Shawn Mamane
☐ 30 Don Granato, Coach

'01 - 02

WORCESTER ICECATS / CHOICE

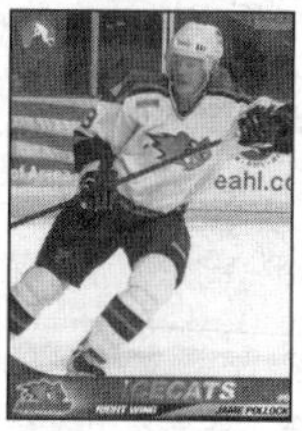

Singles start at 50¢.
Card Size: 2 1/2" x 3 1/2"
Set (30 cards): $12

☐ 1 Darren Rumble
☐ 2 Marc Brown
☐ 3 Ed Campbell
☐ 4 Jeff Panzer
☐ 5 Cody Rudkowsky
☐ 6 Igor Valeev
☐ 7 Dale Clarke
☐ 8 Mike Van Ryn
☐ 9 Barret Jackman
☐ 10 Jame Pollock
☐ 11 Daniel Tkaczuk
☐ 12 Greg Davis
☐ 13 Jamie Thompson
☐ 14 Tyson Nash
☐ 15 Mascot Scratch
☐ 16 Checklist
☐ 17 Reinhard Divis (G)
☐ 18 Andrei Troschinsky
☐ 19 Steve Halko
☐ 20 Matt Walker
☐ 21 Eric Boguniecki
☐ 22 Justin Papineau
☐ 23 Christian Laflamme
☐ 24 Brad Voth
☐ 25 Mark Rycroft
☐ 26 Steve McLaren
☐ 27 Eric Nickulas
☐ 28 All-Time All-Stars
☐ 29 Brent Johnson (G) [Alumni]
☐ 30 Don Granato, Coach

'02 - 03

WORCESTER ICECATS / CHOICE

Singles start at 50¢.
Card Size: 2 1/2" x 3 1/2"
Set (28 cards):

☐ 1 Team Photo
☐ 2 Terry Virtue
☐ 3 Steve Bancroft
☐ 4 Aris Brimanis
☐ 5 John Pohl
☐ 6 Jame Pollock
☐ 7 Eric Nickulas
☐ 8 Jason Dawe
☐ 9 Blake Evans
☐ 10 Greg Davis
☐ 11 Marc Brown
☐ 12 Steve Dubinsky
☐ 13 Steve McLaren
☐ 14 Brett Scheffelmaier
☐ 15 Mark Rycroft
☐ 16 Christian Laflamme
☐ 17 Justin Papineau
☐ 18 Igor Valeev
☐ 19 Matt Walker
☐ 20 Jeff Panzer
☐ 21 Sergei Varlamov
☐ 22 Christian Backman
☐ 23 Curtis Sanford
☐ 24 Phil Osaer
☐ 25 Reinhard Divis
☐ 26 Eric Bognuniecki
☐ 27 Don Granato Coach
☐ 28 Mascot Scratch

BELFAST GIANTS

'01 - 02

BELFAST GIANTS / CARDTRADERS

Card 13 does not exist. Singles start at 50¢.
Set (21 cards):

☐ 1 Mike Bales (G)
☐ 2 Terran Sandwith
☐ 3 Dave Whistle
☐ 4 Shane Johnson
☐ 5 Colin Ward
☐ 6 Kevin Riehl
☐ 7 Rob Stewart
☐ 8 Jason Ruff
☐ 9 Sean Berens
☐ 10 Jeff Hoad
☐ 11 David Matsos
☐ 12 Curtis Bowen
☐ 14 Chad Allen
☐ 15 Rod Stevens
☐ 16 Paxton Schulte
☐ 17 Jason Bowen
☐ 18 Mark Cavallin (G)
☐ 19 Todd Kelman
☐ 20 Checklist
☐ 21 Tom Blatchford
☐ 22 Redemption

'01 - 02

BELFAST GIANTS / CARDTRADERS SUPPLEMENTARY

Singles start at 50¢.
Set (13 cards):

☐ 23 Shayne Toporowski
☐ 24 Derek Wilkinson
☐ 25 Paul Ferone
☐ 26 Todd Goodwin
☐ 27 Kory Karlander
☐ 28 Doug Searle
☐ 29 Jerry Keefe
☐ 30 Jason Wright
☐ 31 Steve Roberts
☐ 32 Mark Cavallin (G)
☐ 33 Mike Bales (G)
☐ 34 Directors
☐ 35 Checklist

CARDIFF DEVILS

'01 - 02

CARDIFF DEVILS / CARDTRADERS

Singles start at 50¢.
Set (19 cards):

☐ 1 Clayton Norris
☐ 2 Rick Strachan
☐ 3 Alan Schuler
☐ 4 Kim Ahlroos
☐ 5 John Parco
☐ 6 Frank Evans
☐ 7 Denis Chassé
☐ 8 Steve Thornton
☐ 9 Dwight Parrish
☐ 10 Steve Moria
☐ 11 Jonathan Phillips
☐ 12 Ian McIntyre
☐ 13 Ivan Matulik
☐ 14 Mike Ware
☐ 15 Vezio Sacratini
☐ 16 Stevie Lyle (G)
☐ 17 Derek Herlofsky (G)
☐ 18 Kip Noble
☐ 19 Checklist

COVENTRY BLAZE

'02 - 03

COVENTRY BLAZE / CARDTRADERS

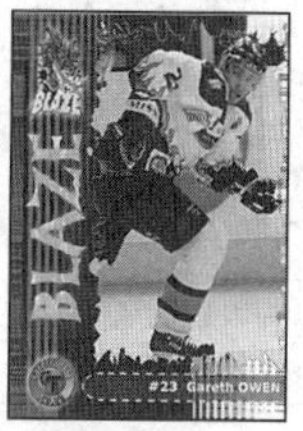

Singles start at 50¢.
Set (24 cards):

☐ 1 Greg Rockman (G)
☐ 2 Jody Lehman (G)
☐ 3 Steve Carpenter
☐ 4 Alan Levers (G)
☐ 5 James Pease
☐ 6 Andreas Moborg
☐ 7 Mathias Söderström
☐ 8 Adam Radmall
☐ 9 Ron Shudra
☐ 10 Shaun Johnson
☐ 11 Steve Chartrand
☐ 12 Kurt Irvine
☐ 13 Russ Cowley
☐ 14 Tom Watkins
☐ 15 Ashley Tait
☐ 16 Gareth Owen
☐ 17 Joel Poirier
☐ 18 Hilton Ruggles
☐ 19 Lee Richardson
☐ 20 Michael Tasker
☐ 21 Paul Thompson
☐ 22 Hadley, Crook, Small
☐ 23 Dancing Geoff Phillips, Dancing crew
☐ 24 Checklist

DUNDEE TEXOL STARS

'02 - 03

DUNDEE TEXOL STARS / CARDTRADERS

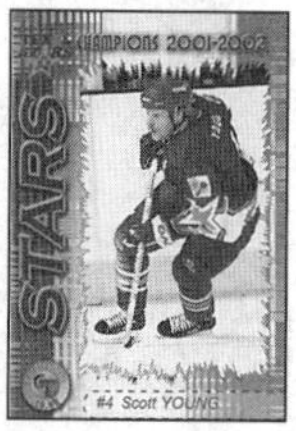

Singles start at 50¢.
Set (18 cards):

☐ 1 Checklist
☐ 2 Nate Leslie
☐ 3 Scott Young
☐ 4 Tony Hand
☐ 5 Paul Berrington
☐ 6 Gary Dowd
☐ 7 Teeder Wynne
☐ 8 Mikko Inkinen
☐ 9 Andy Findlay
☐ 10 Jan Mikel
☐ 11 Craig Nelson
☐ 12 Dominic Hopkins
☐ 13 Stewart Rugg (G)
☐ 14 Patric Lochi
☐ 15 Stephen Murphy (G)
☐ 16 Viacheslav Koulikov
☐ 17 Martin Wiita
☐ 18 Scott Kirton

GUILDFORD FLAMES

'94 - 95

GUILDFORD FLAMES

Singles start at 50¢.
Set (25 cards): $15

☐ 1 Checklist
☐ 2 Ben Challice
☐ 3 Peter Morley
☐ 4 Wayne Trunchion
☐ 5 Andy Allan
☐ 6 Terry Kurtenbach
☐ 7 Ryan Campbell
☐ 8 Fred Perlini
☐ 9 Ronnie Evans-Harvey
☐ 10 Andrew Sparks
☐ 11 Paul Thompson
☐ 12 Rob Friesen
☐ 13 Bill Rawles
☐ 14 Drew Chapman
☐ 15 Nicky Iandoli
☐ 16 Kevin Parish
☐ 17 Elliot Andrews
☐ 18 John Noctor
☐ 19 D. Russell-Samways
☐ 20 5 Imports
☐ 21 Guildford Away Kit
☐ 22 Guildford Home Kit
☐ 23 3 Letters
☐ 24 Spectrum
☐ 25 Ron Charbonneau

'95 - 96

GUILDFORD FLAMES

Singles start at 50¢.
Set (30 cards): $15

☐ 1 Celebration
☐ 2 Checklist
☐ 3 Future
☐ 4 Flames
☐ 5 Home Action
☐ 6 Barrie Aisbitt
☐ 7 Andy Allan
☐ 8 Elliot Andrews
☐ 9 Ryan Campbell
☐ 10 Drew Chapman
☐ 11 Ronnie Evans-Harvey
☐ 12 Dave Graham
☐ 13 Dave Gregory
☐ 14 Troy Kennedy
☐ 15 Terry Kurtenbach
☐ 16 Fred Perlini
☐ 17 Team Photo
☐ 18 Team Photo
☐ 19 Nick Rothwell
☐ 20 D. Russell-Samways
☐ 21 Andrew Sparks
☐ 22 Guildford Spectrum
☐ 23 Paul Thompson
☐ 24 Wayne Trunchion
☐ 25 Darrin Zinger
☐ 26 Paul Thompson
☐ 27 Terry Kurtenbach
☐ 28 Ivan Brown
☐ 29 Jim Bennett
☐ 30 Fred Perlini

'96 - 97

GUILDFORD FLAMES

Singles start at 50¢.
Set (29 cards): $15

☐ 1 Spectrum Checklist
☐ 2 John Wolfe
☐ 3 Rob Lamey
☐ 4 Wayne Crawford
☐ 5 Terry Kurtenbach
☐ 6 Ryan Campbell
☐ 7 Fred Perlini
☐ 8 Paul Thompson
☐ 9 Mike Bettens
☐ 10 Mark Finney
☐ 11 Rylan Ferster
☐ 12 Nick Cross
☐ 13 Damian Smith
☐ 14 Mike Mowbray
☐ 15 Elliot Andrews
☐ 16 Celebration
☐ 17 Darrin Zinger
☐ 18 Brad Kirkwood
☐ 19 Derek DeCosty
☐ 20 Mike Hazlehurst
☐ 21 Lee Saunders
☐ 22 Barrie Aisbitt
☐ 23 Paul McCallion
☐ 24 Flames
☐ 25 Captains
☐ 26 Home Jerseys
☐ 27 Pep Talk
☐ 28 Valerie Vassie
☐ 29 Goalies

'97 - 98

GUILDFORD FLAMES / ARCO

Singles start at 50¢.
Set (30 cards): $15

☐ 1 Checklist
☐ 2 Peter Morley
☐ 3 Rob Lamey
☐ 4 Andy Hannah
☐ 5 Joe Johnston
☐ 6 Terry Kurtenbach
☐ 7 Ryan Campbell
☐ 8 Scott Adair
☐ 9 Paul Thompson
☐ 10 Ricky Plant
☐ 11 Peter Kasowski
☐ 12 Andrew Einhorn
☐ 13 Bobby Brown
☐ 14 Anthony Page
☐ 15 Nick Rothwell
☐ 16 Mike Harding
☐ 17 Darrin Zinger
☐ 18 Jamey Organ
☐ 19 Barclay Pearce
☐ 20 Simon Smith
☐ 21 Russ Plant
☐ 22 Stan Marple
☐ 23 Team photo
☐ 24 Flames
☐ 25 Dressing Room
☐ 26 Captain & Assistants
☐ 27 Celebration
☐ 28 Spectrum Home Rink
☐ 29 Mascot Sizzler
☐ 30 Training Staff

'98 - 99

GUILDFORD FLAMES / ARCO

Singles start at 50¢.
Set (30 cards): $15

☐ 1 Checklist
☐ 2 Peter Morley
☐ 3 Sam Mager
☐ 4 Rob Lamey
☐ 5 Derek DeCosty
☐ 6 Dominic Hopkins
☐ 7 Terry Kurtenbach
☐ 8 Ryan Campbell
☐ 9 Kirk Humphreys
☐ 10 Greg Randall
☐ 11 Scott Stephenson
☐ 12 Paul Thompson
☐ 13 Robin Davison
☐ 14 Andy Johnston
☐ 15 Peter Kasowski
☐ 16 Andy Pickles
☐ 17 Brian Mason
☐ 18 Robert Johnston
☐ 19 Jamey Organ
☐ 20 Barclay Pearce
☐ 21 Simon Smith
☐ 22 Simon Howard
☐ 23 Adrian Lomonaco
☐ 24 Stan Marple
☐ 25 Captain & Assistants
☐ 26 Paul Thompson
☐ 27 Trophies
☐ 28 Home Kit
☐ 29 Flames
☐ 30 Mascot Sizzler

HANOVER SCORPIONS

'01 - 02

HANNOVER SCORPIONS

Other singles exist. Singles start at $1.

- ☐ Egor Bashkatov
- ☐ Igor Chibirev
- ☐ Jakob Karlsson

HV 71 JONKOPING

'01 - 02

HV 71 JONKOPING

Other singles exist. Singles start at $1.

- ☐ Johan Hult #28
- ☐ Fredrik Johnsson #33
- ☐ Mikael Lindman #44
- ☐ Anttti Törmänen #15

LONDON KNIGHTS

'02 - 03

LONDON KNIGHTS / CARDTRADERS

Singles start at 50¢.
Set (24 cards):

- ☐ 1 Checklist
- ☐ 2 Åke Lilljebjörn (G)
- ☐ 3 Gerad Adams
- ☐ 4 Kim Ahlroos
- ☐ 5 Nathan Leslie
- ☐ 6 Moe Mansi
- ☐ 7 Mark Kolesar
- ☐ 8 A.J. Kelham
- ☐ 9 Jeff Hoad
- ☐ 10 Chris Slater
- ☐ 11 Ian McIntyre
- ☐ 12 Greg Burke
- ☐ 13 Steve Aronson
- ☐ 14 Rich Bronilla
- ☐ 15 Vezio Sacratini
- ☐ 16 Dave Trofimenkoff (G)
- ☐ 17 Paul Rushforth
- ☐ 18 Sean Blanchard
- ☐ 19 Dennis Maxwell
- ☐ 20 Ed Patterson
- ☐ 21 Bob Leslie
- ☐ 22 Mascot Mighty Knight
- ☐ 23 Jim Brithén
- ☐ 24 Jason Ellery

METALLURG MAGNITOGORSK

'99 - 00

METALLURG MAGNITOGORSK / MIR

Set (29 cards):

- ☐ 27 Sergei Gomolyako
- ☐ 28 Vadim Glovatski
- ☐ 29 Sergei Tertyshny
- ☐ 30 Igor Zemlyanoi
- ☐ 31 Valeri Nikulin
- ☐ 32 Andrei Sapozhnikov
- ☐ 33 Boris Tortunov
- ☐ 34 Sergei Zemchenok
- ☐ 35 Oleg Mikulchik
- ☐ 36 Andrei Razin
- ☐ 37 Ravil Gusmanov
- ☐ 38 Maxim Bets
- ☐ 39 Andrei Petrakov
- ☐ 40 Andrei Andrei
- ☐ 41 Mikhail Borodulin
- ☐ 42 Sergei Osipov
- ☐ 43 Valeri Karpov
- ☐ 44 Evgueni Koreshkov
- ☐ 45 Alexander Koreshkov
- ☐ 46 Dmitri Popov
- ☐ 47 Andrei Sokolov
- ☐ 48 Oleg Leontiev
- ☐ 49 Vladimir Antipin
- ☐ 50 Alexei Stepanov
- ☐ 51 Vitali Prokhorov
- ☐ 52 Alexander Goltz
- ☐ 53 Konstantin Shafranov
- ☐ Team Photo

MANCHESTER STORM

'01 - 02

MANCHESTER STORM / CARDTRADERS

This series is limited to 495 copies. Card 13 does not exist. Singles start at 50¢.
Set (24 cards):

- ☐ 1 Paul Ferone
- ☐ 2 Dan Preston
- ☐ 3 Trevor Gallant
- ☐ 4 Mike Morin
- ☐ 5 Dwight Parrish
- ☐ 6 Mark Bultje
- ☐ 7 Joe Busillo
- ☐ 8 Ivan Matulik
- ☐ 9 Pierre Allard
- ☐ 10 Russ Romaniuk
- ☐ 11 Joe Cardarelli
- ☐ 12 Stevie Lyle (G)
- ☐ 14 Mike Torchia (G)
- ☐ 15 Kayle Short
- ☐ 16 Justin Hocking
- ☐ 17 Chris Miller
- ☐ 18 Russ Richardson
- ☐ 19 Daryl Lipsey
- ☐ 20 Mike Torchia (G)
- ☐ 21 Stevie Lyle
- ☐ 22 Mascot Lightning Jack
- ☐ 23 Rob Wilson
- ☐ 24 Redemption
- ☐ 25 Checklist

'02 - 03

MANCHESTER STORM / CARDTRADERS

Singles start at 50¢.
Set (21 cards):

- ☐ 1 Colin Pepperall
- ☐ 2 Dan Preston
- ☐ 3 Shawn Maltby
- ☐ 4 Geoff Peters
- ☐ 5 Mike Perna
- ☐ 6 Pasi Nielikainen
- ☐ 7 Dwight Parrish
- ☐ 8 Mark Bultje
- ☐ 9 Rob Wilson
- ☐ 10 Ivan Matulik
- ☐ 11 Pierre Allard
- ☐ 12 David Longstaff
- ☐ 13 Ryan Stewart
- ☐ 14 Joe Cardarelli
- ☐ 15 Stevie Lyle (G)
- ☐ 16 Mike Torchia (G)
- ☐ 17 Dan Hodge
- ☐ 18 Daryl Lipsey
- ☐ 19 Mike Torchia (G)
- ☐ 20 Stevie Lyle (G)
- ☐ 21 Checklist

DYNAMO MOSCOW

'99 - 00

DYANMO MOSCOW

Set (27 cards):

- ☐ 1 Alexei Tereshenko
- ☐ 2 Igor Shadilov
- ☐ 3 Alexei Panikarovski
- ☐ 4 Alexei Litvinenko
- ☐ 5 Roman Zolotov
- ☐ 6 Andrei Markov
- ☐ 7 Alexander Khavanov
- ☐ 8 Vitali Proshkin
- ☐ 9 Alexei Troshinski
- ☐ 10 Oleg Orekhovsky
- ☐ 11 Marat Davidov
- ☐ 12 Dmitri Kokorev
- ☐ 13 Alexander Kharitonov
- ☐ 14 Alexander Prokopiev
- ☐ 15 Mikhail Ivanov
- ☐ 16 Alexei Kudashov
- ☐ 17 Alexander Kuvaldin
- ☐ 18 Denis Kartsev
- ☐ 19 Stanislav Romanov
- ☐ 20 A. Savchenkov
- ☐ 21 Lev Berdichevsky
- ☐ 22 Alexei Zalyukhny
- ☐ 23 Alexander Stepanov
- ☐ 24 Boris Zelenko
- ☐ 25 Vitali Eremeev
- ☐ 26 Alexei Egorov
- ☐ Team Photo

NOTTINGHAM PANTHERS

'00 - 01

NOTTINGHAM PANTHERS / CARDTRADERS

This series is limited to 495 copies. Card 13 does not exist. Singles start at 50¢.
Set (30 cards):

- ☐ 1 Checklist
- ☐ 2 Jordan Willis (G)
- ☐ 3 Paul Moran
- ☐ 4 Duncan Paterson
- ☐ 5 Kevin Hoffman
- ☐ 6 David Struch
- ☐ 7 Randall Weber
- ☐ 8 Greg Hadden
- ☐ 9 Daryl Lavoie
- ☐ 10 PC Drouin
- ☐ 11 Marc Levers
- ☐ 12 Darryl Moxam
- ☐ 14 Greg Burke
- ☐ 15 Ashley Tait
- ☐ 16 Ryan Gillis
- ☐ 17 Jim Paek
- ☐ 18 Chris Baxter
- ☐ 19 Jamie Leach
- ☐ 20 Eoin McInerney (G)
- ☐ 21 Robert Nordmark
- ☐ 22 Graham Garden
- ☐ 23 Casson Masters
- ☐ 24 Barry Nieckar
- ☐ 25 Éric Lavigne
- ☐ 26 Peter Woods
- ☐ 27 Redemption
- ☐ 28 Alex Dampier
- ☐ 29 Gary Moran
- ☐ 30 Information
- ☐ 31 Player awards

'01 - 02

NOTTINGHAM PANTHERS / CARDTRADERS

This series is limited to 495 copies. Card 13 does not exist. Singles start at 50¢.
Set (31 cards):

- ☐ 1 Checklist
- ☐ 2 Brent Pope
- ☐ 3 Clayton Norris
- ☐ 4 Patrick Wallenburg
- ☐ 5 Randall Weber
- ☐ 6 Greg Hadden
- ☐ 7 Frank Evans
- ☐ 8 Claude Savoie
- ☐ 9 PC Drouin
- ☐ 10 Steve Moria
- ☐ 11 Ashley Tait
- ☐ 12 Paul Adey
- ☐ 14 Jimmy Drolet
- ☐ 15 Danny Lorenz (G)
- ☐ 16 Joel Poirier
- ☐ 17 Paul Moran
- ☐ 18 Barry Nieckar
- ☐ 19 Darren Maloney
- ☐ 20 Calle Carlsson
- ☐ 21 Pasi Hakkinen (G)
- ☐ 22 AJ Kelham
- ☐ 23 Alex Dampier
- ☐ 24 Lee Jinman
- ☐ 25 Gary Moran
- ☐ 26 Mascot Paws
- ☐ 27 Equipment
- ☐ 28 Physiotherapists
- ☐ 29 Office
- ☐ 30 Christian Sjögren
- ☐ 31 Jim Paek
- ☐ 32 Danny Lorenz (G)

'02 - 03

NOTTINGHAM PANTHERS / CARDTRADERS

Singles start at 50¢.
Set (22 cards):

- ☐ 1 Mika Pietila (G)
- ☐ 2 Jimmy Paek
- ☐ 3 Marc Hussey
- ☐ 4 Éric Charron
- ☐ 5 Greg Hadden
- ☐ 6 Dody Wood
- ☐ 7 Briane Thompson
- ☐ 8 Jason Elders
- ☐ 9 Kristian Taubert
- ☐ 10 Scott Allison
- ☐ 11 Mark Cadotte
- ☐ 12 Petter Sandström (G)
- ☐ 13 John Purves
- ☐ 14 Paul Moran
- ☐ 15 Barry Nieckar
- ☐ 16 Jason Clarke
- ☐ 17 Lee Jinman
- ☐ 18 Paul Adey
- ☐ 19 Mascot Paws
- ☐ 20 Gary Moran
- ☐ 21 Checklist
- ☐ 22 Equipment & Office

PETERBOROUGH PHANTOMS

'02 - 03

PETERBOROUGH PHANTOMS / CARDTRADERS

Singles start at 50¢.
Set (18 cards):

- ☐ 1 Luc Chabot
- ☐ 2 James Moore (G)
- ☐ 3 David Whitwell (G)
- ☐ 4 Craig Britton
- ☐ 5 Jon Fone
- ☐ 6 Pete Morley
- ☐ 7 Jessie Hammill
- ☐ 8 Jason Buckman
- ☐ 9 Lewis Buckman
- ☐ 10 Russell Coleman
- ☐ 11 Duncan Cook
- ☐ 12 Darren Cotton
- ☐ 13 Joe Cotton
- ☐ 14 James Ellwood
- ☐ 15 Grant Hendry
- ☐ 16 Doug McEwen
- ☐ 17 Shaun Yardley
- ☐ 18 Checklist

SHEFFIELD STEELERS

'93 - 94

SHEFFIELD STEELERS

Singles start at 50¢.
Set (23 cards): $15

- ☐ 1 Andy Havenhand
- ☐ 2 Alan Hague
- ☐ 3 Tim Cranston
- ☐ 4 Neil Abel
- ☐ 5 Scott Neil
- ☐ 6 Steve Nemeth
- ☐ 7 Steve Nemeth
- ☐ 8 Tommy Plommer
- ☐ 9 Ivan Matulik
- ☐ 10 Danny Boome
- ☐ 11 Mark Wright
- ☐ 12 Chris Kelland
- ☐ 13 Lee Mills
- ☐ 14 Les Millie
- ☐ 15 Selmar Odelein
- ☐ 16 Ron Shudra
- ☐ 17 Ron Shudra
- ☐ 18 Martin McKay
- ☐ 19 Martin McKay
- ☐ 19 Andy Havenhand
- ☐ 20 Alex Dampier
- ☐ 20 Clyde Tuil
- ☐ 21 Sheffield Steelers
- ☐ 22 Sheffield Scimtars
- ☐ 23 Sheffield Arena

'94 - 95

SHEFFIELD STEELERS

Singles start at 50¢.
Set (25 cards): $10

- ☐ 1 Martin McKay
- ☐ 2 Chris Kelland
- ☐ 3 Scott Heaton
- ☐ 4 Dean Smith
- ☐ 5 Perry Doyle
- ☐ 6 Tommy Plommer
- ☐ 7 Scott Neil
- ☐ 8 Ron Shudra
- ☐ 9 Mike O'Connor
- ☐ 10 Andy Havenhand
- ☐ 11 Neil Abel
- ☐ 12 Mascot Steeler Dan
- ☐ 13 Patrick O'Connor
- ☐ 14 Paul Jackson
- ☐ 15 Tim Cranston
- ☐ 16 Ron Handy
- ☐ 17 Office Staff
- ☐ 18 Mark Wright
- ☐ 19 Team Card
- ☐ 20 Alan Hague
- ☐ 21 Rob Wilson
- ☐ 22 Les Millie
- ☐ 23 Clyde Tuyl
- ☐ 24 Alex Dampier
- ☐ Steve Nemeth

'95 - 96

SHEFFIELD STEELERS / POLICE

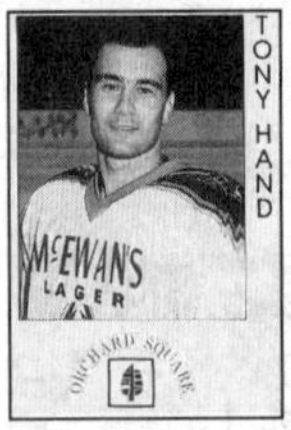

The arena and team photo cards measure 3 5/8" x 5 1/4" while the trophy card measures 2 3/4" x 5 1/4".
Card Size: 2 3/8" x 3 1/2"
Sponsor: Sheffield Police
Set (24 cards): $12

- ☐ Neil Abel
- ☐ Nicky Chinn
- ☐ Tim Cranston
- ☐ Alex Dampier
- ☐ Perry Doyle
- ☐ Tony Hand
- ☐ Scott Heaton
- ☐ Chris Kelland
- ☐ Andre Malo
- ☐ Martin McKay
- ☐ Les Millie
- ☐ Scott Neil
- ☐ Steve Nemeth
- ☐ Mike O'Connor
- ☐ Tommy Plummer
- ☐ Ken Priestlay
- ☐ Ron Shudra
- ☐ Clyde Tuyl
- ☐ Mark Wright
- ☐ S. Lawley/ A. Weston/ Hayley Roach/ A. Akers
- ☐ Mascot Foggy Dan
- ☐ Arena
- ☐ Team Photo
- ☐ Trophies

'97 - 98

SHEFFIELD STEELERS / POLICE

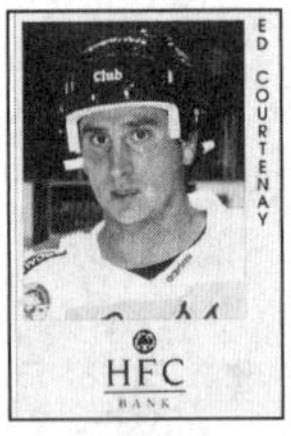

We have no pricing information on this 24-card set. An album was also available.
Card Sizes: 2 3/8" x 3 1/2"; 3 5/8" x 5 3/16"
Set (24 cards): $12

- ☐ Scott Allison
- ☐ Corey Beaulieu
- ☐ Nicky Chinn
- ☐ Ed Courtenay
- ☐ Tim Cranston
- ☐ Dion Del Monte
- ☐ Piero Greco (G)
- ☐ Tony Hand
- ☐ James Hibbert (G)
- ☐ Chris Kelland
- ☐ Frank Kovacs
- ☐ David Longstaff
- ☐ André Malo
- ☐ Tom Plommer
- ☐ Ken Priestlay
- ☐ Ron Shudra
- ☐ Jamie Van der Horst
- ☐ Mike Ware
- ☐ Rob Wilson
- ☐ Alex Dampier, Mgr.
- ☐ Clyde Tuyl, Coach
- ☐ Mascot Steeler Foggy Dan
- ☐ Arena (3 5/8" x 5 3/16")
- ☐ Team (3 5/8" x 5 3/16")

'01 - 02

SHEFFIELD STEELERS / CARDTRADERS CENTURIONS

Singles start at 50¢.
Set (18 cards):

- ☐ 1 Ed Courtenay
- ☐ 2 Tommy Plommer
- ☐ 3 David Longstaff
- ☐ 4 Rob Wilson
- ☐ 5 Ron Shudra
- ☐ 6 Tim Cranston
- ☐ 7 Chris Kelland
- ☐ 8 André Malo
- ☐ 9 Ken Priestlay
- ☐ 10 Scott Neil
- ☐ 11 Tony Hand
- ☐ 12 Kayle Short
- ☐ 13 Mike O'Connor
- ☐ 14 Scott Allison
- ☐ 15 Neil Abel
- ☐ 16 Steve Nemeth
- ☐ 17 Checklist
- ☐ 18 Ron Shudra

'01 - 02

SHEFFIELD STEELERS / CARDTRADERS GRAND SLAM

Singles start at 50¢.
Set (27 cards):

- ☐ 1 Mascot Steeler Dan
- ☐ 2 Steve Carpentier
- ☐ 3 Dale Craigwell
- ☐ 4 Jeff Sebastian
- ☐ 5 Shayne McCosh
- ☐ 6 Scott Metcalfe
- ☐ 7 Jason Weaver
- ☐ 8 Scott Allison
- ☐ 9 Rick Brebant
- ☐ 10 Paul Adey
- ☐ 11 Paul Beraldo
- ☐ 12 Warren Norris
- ☐ 13 Adam Smith
- ☐ 14 Kayle Short
- ☐ 15 Dennis Vial
- ☐ 16 David Longstaff
- ☐ 17 Kent Simpson
- ☐ 18 Mike O'Neill (G)
- ☐ 19 Mike Torchia (G)
- ☐ 20 Steve Roberts
- ☐ 21 Brent Bobyck
- ☐ 22 Redemption
- ☐ 23 Supporters Club
- ☐ 24 Backroom staff
- ☐ 25 Checklist
- ☐ 26 David Simms
- ☐ 27 Mike Blaisdell

ZUG SWISS

'01 - 02

ZUG SWISS / MOTOROLA

Other singles exist. Singles start at $1.

- ☐ Paul DiPietro
- ☐ Todd Elik

CHAPTER EIGHT

JUNIOR & COLLEGE TEAM ISSUES

U. ARIZONA ICECATS

'85 - 86

U. ARIZONA ICECATS / CHOICE

These cards were originally issued as a sheet. Glenn Hall is the most expensive single at $5. Singles start at $1.

Card Size: 2 5/8" x 4 1/8"

Sponsor: None

Set (20 cards): $15

☐ Arizona Icecats
☐ Dan Anderson
☐ Don Carlson (G)
☐ Dan Divjak
☐ Shane Fausel
☐ Flavio Gentile
☐ Leo Golembiewski
☐ Jeremy Goltz
☐ Glenn Hall
☐ Steve Hutchings
☐ Aaron Joffe
☐ Greg Mithcell
☐ Cory Oleson
☐ Ricky Rope
☐ Drew Sibr
☐ Dean Sives
☐ Tommy Smith
☐ Nate Soules
☐ Kelly Walker
☐ Icecat Leaders

BAIE-COMEAU DRAKKAR

'00 - 01

BAIE-COMEAU DRAKKAR / CARTES, TIMBRES, MONNAIES STE-FOY

Singles start at 50¢.

Set (25 cards): $12

☐ 1 Jonathan Walsh
☐ 2 Joël Perrault
☐ 3 Pierre-André Leblanc
☐ 4 Dominic Périard
☐ 5 Maxime Fortunus
☐ 6 Pascal Pelletier
☐ 7 Robin Leblanc
☐ 8 Luis Tremblay
☐ 9 Thierry Douville
☐ 10 Marco Charpentier
☐ 11 Premysl Duben
☐ 12 Yanick Lehoux
☐ 13 Duilio Grande
☐ 14 Kevin Deslauriers
☐ 15 Matthew Hyde
☐ 16 Guy Turmel
☐ 17 Evgeny Gusakov
☐ 18 Ghyslain Rousseau
☐ 19 David St-Germain
☐ 20 Jonathan Jolette
☐ 21 Martin Mandeville
☐ 22 Daniel Bergeron
☐ 23 Charles Linglet
☐ 24 Jonathan Gautier
☐ 25 Ricahrd Martel
☐ 26 Mascot Snorri

'01 - 02

BAIE-COMEAU DRAKKAR / CARTES, TIMBRES, MONNAIES STE-FOY

Singles start at 50¢.

Set (25 cards): $12

☐ 1 Joël Perrault
☐ 2 Louis-Philippe Martin
☐ 3 Jonathan Lachance
☐ 4 Maxime Fortunus
☐ 5 Pascal Pelletier
☐ 6 Robin Leblanc
☐ 7 Luis Tremblay
☐ 8 Thierry Douville
☐ 9 Martin Kuna
☐ 10 Yanick Lehoux
☐ 11 Duilio Grande
☐ 12 Kevin Deslauriers
☐ 13 Matthew Hyde
☐ 14 Jean Junior Morin
☐ 15 Ghyslain Rousseau
☐ 16 Jonathan Dupras
☐ 17 Caleb Moffat
☐ 18 Marc-André Roy
☐ 19 Martin Manderville
☐ 20 Daniel Bergeron
☐ 21 Charles Linglet
☐ 22 J-F Savage
☐ 23 Benoît Mondou
☐ 24 J-F Jacques
☐ 25 Richard Martel

'02 - 03

BAIE-COMEAU DRAKKAR / CARTES, TIMBRES, MONNAIES STE-FOY

Singles start at 50¢.

Set (26 cards): $12

☐ 1 Maxime Bélanger
☐ 2 Joël Perrault
☐ 3 A. Lamarche-Froelich
☐ 4 Jean-Philippe Gauthier
☐ 5 Louis-Philippe Martin
☐ 6 Maxime Fortunas
☐ 7 Pascal Pelletier
☐ 8 Robin Leblanc
☐ 9 Luis Tremblay
☐ 10 Thierry Douville
☐ 11 Jimmy Arsenault
☐ 12 Travis Antler
☐ 13 Kevin Deslauriers
☐ 14 Patrick Lepage (G)
☐ 15 Sébastien Leonard
☐ 16 Philip Lacroix (G)
☐ 17 M. Bergevin-Robinson (G)
☐ 18 Caleb Moffat
☐ 19 Marc-André Roy
☐ 20 Patrick Thoresen
☐ 21 Martin Mandeville
☐ 22 Charles Linglet
☐ 23 Benoit Mondou
☐ 24 J-F Jacques
☐ 25 Checklist
☐ Mascot Snorri

BARRIE COLTS

'95 - 96

BARRIE COLTS

We do not yet have a checklist for this series.

'96 - 97

BARRIE COLTS

We do not yet have a checklist for this series.

'97 - 98

BARRIE COLTS

We do not yet have a checklist for this series.

'98 - 99

BARRIE COLTS / COCA-COLA

The most expensive singles are Brian Finley, Sheldon Keefe, Denis Shvidki, Martin Skoula and Daniel Tkaczuk. Singles start at 50¢.

Set (25 cards): $15

☐ Ryan Barnes
☐ Scott Cameron
☐ Shawn Cation
☐ Mike Christian
☐ Jerry Connell
☐ Joel Dezainde
☐ Chris Feil
☐ Brian Finley (G)
☐ Michael Henrich
☐ Ed Hill
☐ Rick Hwodeky
☐ Sheldon Keefe
☐ Mike Jefferson
☐ Andre Lakos
☐ Ryan O'Keefe
☐ Denis Shvidki
☐ Martin Skoula
☐ Nick Smith
☐ Bert Templeton
☐ Jeff Tetzlaff
☐ Daniel Tkaczuk
☐ Ben Vanderklok
☐ Tim Verbeek
☐ Mascot Charlie Horse
☐ D. Keily / G. Scott

'00 - 01

BARRIE COLTS

We do not yet have a checklist for this series.

BELLEVILLE BULLS

'83 - 84

BELLEVILLE BULLS / POLICE

Team owner Wayne Gretzky is the most expensive single at $75. Al Iafrate sells at $7 while Craig Billington and Dan Quinn sell at $2-4. Singles start at $1.

Card Size: 2 5/8" x 4 1/8"

Set (30 cards): 90.00

☐ 1 Bulls Logo
☐ 2 Quinte Sports Centre
☐ 3 Dan Quinn
☐ 4 Dave MacLean
☐ 5 Scott Gardiner
☐ 6 Mike Knuude
☐ 7 Brian Martin
☐ 8 Dr. R. Vaughn
☐ 9 John MacDonald (G)
☐ 10 Brian Small
☐ 11 Mike Savage
☐ 12 Dunc MacIntyre
☐ 13 Charlie Moore
☐ 14 Jim Andanoff
☐ 15 Mario Martini
☐ 16 Rick Adolfi
☐ 17 Mike Vellucci
☐ 18 Scott McMichael
☐ 19 Ali Butorac
☐ 20 Al Iafrate
☐ 21 Rob Crocock
☐ 22 Craig Coxe
☐ 23 Grant Robertson
☐ 24 Craig Billington (G)
☐ 25 Darren Gani
☐ 26 Tim Bean
☐ 27 Wayne Gretzky
☐ 28 Russ Soule
☐ 29 Larry Mavety
☐ 30 Team Photo

'84 - 85

BELLEVILLE BULLS / POLICE

Craig Billington is the most expensive single at $3. Singles start at $1.

Card Size: 2 5/8" x 4 1/8"

Set (30 cards): $25

☐ 1 Team Photo
☐ 2 Dr. R. Vaughan
☐ 3 Larry Mavety
☐ 4 Dunc MacIntyre
☐ 5 Bulls Logo
☐ 6 Mike Knuude
☐ 7 John Purves
☐ 8 Charlie Moore
☐ 9 Stan Drulia
☐ 10 Craig Billington (G)
☐ 11 Dave MacLean
☐ 12 Darren Moxam
☐ 13 Shane Doyle
☐ 14 Larry Vanherzele
☐ 15 Tim Bean
☐ 16 Kent Brimmer
☐ 17 Angelo Catenaro
☐ 18 Steve Linseman
☐ 19 Grant Robertson
☐ 20 John Reid
☐ 21 Dean Whyte
☐ 22 Darren Gani
☐ 23 Roger Robertson
☐ 24 Gary Callaghan
☐ 25 John Tamer
☐ 26 Todd Hawkins
☐ 27 Jim Andanoff
☐ 28 Chris Rutledge
☐ 29 Matt Taylor
☐ 30 Mike Hartman

'00 - 01

BELLEVILLE BULLS

We do not yet have a checklist for this series.

'01 - 02

BELLEVILLE BULLS

The original release (29 cards) are bigger than the update cards (standard size). Singles start at 50¢.

Set (29 cards):

☐ Title card
☐ Jan Chovan
☐ Paulo Colaiacovo
☐ Matt Coughlin
☐ Adam Sturgeon
☐ Malcolm Hutt
☐ Michael Knight
☐ Oliver Maron
☐ Dan Growden
☐ Rane Carnegie
☐ Cody McCormick
☐ Michael Renzi
☐ Andrew Brown
☐ Andre Deveaux
☐ Matthew Stajan
☐ Alex White
☐ David Silverstone
☐ Jake Gilmour
☐ Adam Paiement
☐ Neill MacInnis
☐ Nathan Robinson
☐ Marc Rancourt
☐ Kyle Wellwood
☐ Jim Hulton
☐ James Boyd
☐ Bulls action
☐ Bulls action
☐ Renzi
☐ Mascot Bullie

Update Set (9 cards):

☐ Jason Spezza
☐ Michael Mole
☐ Glenn Ridler
☐ Neil Smith
☐ David Clarkson
☐ Jason Spezza
☐ Jason Spezza
☐ Steve Cooke
☐ Lubos Velebny

BRAMPTON BATALLION

'99 - 00

BRAMPTON BATALLION / FIRST CHOICE

The most expensive single is Jason Spezza. Other expensive singles are Rostislav Klesla and Raffi Torres. Singles start at 50¢.

Card Size: 2 1/2" x 3 1/2"

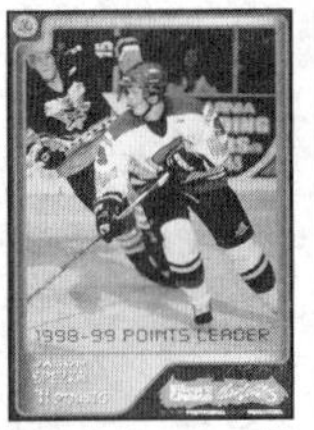

Set (32 cards): $30

☐ 1 Checklist
☐ 2 Battalion
☐ 3 David Chant
☐ 4 Scott Della Vedova
☐ 5 Tyler Hanchuck
☐ 6 Jason Maleyko
☐ 7 Paul Flache
☐ 8 Cam McLaughlin
☐ 9 Rostislav Klesla
☐ 10 Brad Woods
☐ 11 Raffi Torres
☐ 12 Matt Reynolds
☐ 13 Chris Rowan
☐ 14 Lukas Havel
☐ 15 Mike Rice
☐ 16 Tyler Dukelow
☐ 17 Jay McClement
☐ 18 Matt Grennier
☐ 19 Kurt MacSweyn
☐ 20 Aaron Van Leusen
☐ 21 Chris Cook
☐ 22 Jay Harrison
☐ 23 Richard Kearns
☐ 24 Jeff Bateman
☐ 25 Blair McLaughlin
☐ 26 Scott Thompson
☐ 27 Jason Spezza
☐ 28 Stan Butler
☐ 30 Bobby Jones
☐ 31 Jason Maleyko
☐ 32 Batallion

'00 - 01

BRAMPTON BATALLION

We do not yet have a checklist for this series.

BRANDON WHEAT KINGS

'82 - 83

BRANDON WHEAT KINGS / POLICE

Ron Hextall is the most expensive single at $15. Singles start at $1.

Card Size: 2 3/8" x 4"

Set (24 cards): $25

☐ 1 Wheat Kings Logo
☐ 2 Kevin Pylypow
☐ 3 Dean Kennedy
☐ 4 Sonny Sodke
☐ 5 Darren Schmidt
☐ 6 Cam Plante
☐ 7 Sid Cranston
☐ 8 Brue Thomson
☐ 9 Dave McDowall
☐ 10 Bill Vince
☐ 11 Kelly Glowa
☐ 12 Tom McMurchy
☐ 13 Ed Palichuk
☐ 14 Roy Caswell
☐ 15 Allan Tarasuk
☐ 16 Brent Jessiman
☐ 17 Randy Slawson
☐ 18 Gord Smith
☐ 19 Mike Sturgeon
☐ 20 Larry Blumstead
☐ 21 Kirk Blomquist
☐ 22 Ron Loustel
☐ 23 Ron Hextall (G)
☐ 24 Brandon Police

'83 - 84

BRANDON WHEAT KINGS / POLICE

Ron Hextall is the most expensive single at $10. Ray Ferraro sells at $6. Singles start at $1.

Card Size: 2 1/4" x 4"

Set (24 cards): $25

☐ 1 Brian Wells
☐ 2 Jim Agnew
☐ 3 Gord Paddock
☐ 4 John Dzikowski
☐ 5 Kelly Kozack
☐ 6 Brian Lomow
☐ 7 Pat Loyer
☐ 8 Rob Ordman
☐ 9 Brad Wells
☐ 10 Dave Thomlinson
☐ 11 Cam Plante
☐ 12 Jay Palmer (G)
☐ 13 Boyd Lomow
☐ 14 Brent Jessiman
☐ 15 Paul More
☐ 16 Stacy Pratt
☐ 17 Brandon Police
☐ 18 Jack Sangster
☐ 19 Derek Laxdal
☐ 20 Ray Ferraro
☐ 21 Allan Tarasuk
☐ 22 Randy Cameron
☐ 23 Dave Curry
☐ 24 Ron Hextall (G)

'84 - 85

BRANDON WHEAT KINGS / POLICE

Eldon Reddick is the most expensive single at $2. Singles start at $1.

Card Size: 2 1/4" x 4"

Set (24 cards): $15

☐ 1 Garnet Kazuik
☐ 2 Brent Mireau
☐ 3 Bryan Lomow
☐ 4 Dean Shaw (G)
☐ 5 Dean Sexsmith
☐ 6 Brad Mueller
☐ 7 John Dzikowski
☐ 8 Artie Feher (G)
☐ 9 Pat Loyer
☐ 10 Murray Rice
☐ 11 Derek Laxdal
☐ 12 Perry Fafard
☐ 13 Lee Trim
☐ 14 Dan Hart
☐ 15 Trent Ciprick
☐ 16 Jeff Waver
☐ 17 Brandon Police
☐ 18 Jack Sangster
☐ 19 Darwin MacPherson
☐ 20 Eldon Reddick (G)
☐ 21 Boyd Lomow
☐ 22 Dave Thomlinson
☐ 23 Paul More
☐ 24 Brent Severyn

'85 - 86

BRANDON WHEAT KINGS / POLICE

Terry Yake is the most expensive single at $2. Singles start at $1.

Card Size: 2 1/4" x 4"

Set (24 cards): $15

☐ 1 Kelly Hitchins
☐ 2 Brent Mireau
☐ 3 Byron Lomow
☐ 4 Bob Heeney
☐ 5 Dean Sexsmith
☐ 6 Dave Curry
☐ 7 John Dzikowski
☐ 8 Artie Feher (G)
☐ 9 Kevin Mayo
☐ 10 Murray Rice
☐ 11 Derek Laxdal
☐ 12 Al Cherniwchan
☐ 13 Lee Trim
☐ 14 Terry Yake
☐ 15 Trent Ciprick
☐ 16 Jeff Waver
☐ 17 Team Photo
☐ 18 Jack Sangster
☐ 19 Mike Morin
☐ 20 Jason Phillips
☐ 21 Rod Williams
☐ 22 Dave Thomlinson
☐ 23 Shane Eirickson
☐ 24 Randy Hoffart

'88 - 89

BRANDON WHEAT KINGS / POLICE

Trevor Kidd is the most expensive single at $4. Singles start at $1.

Card Size: 2 1/4" x 4"

Set (24 cards): $18

☐ 1 Kevin Cheveldayoff
☐ 2 Bob Woods
☐ 3 Dwayne Newman
☐ 4 Mike Vandenberghe
☐ 5 Brad Woods
☐ 6 Gary Audette
☐ 7 Mark Bassen
☐ 8 Troy Frederick
☐ 9 Troy Kennedy
☐ 10 Barry Dreger
☐ 11 Bill Whistle
☐ 12 Jeff Odgers
☐ 13 Sheldon Kowalchuk
☐ 14 Chris Robertson
☐ 15 Don Laurin
☐ 16 Curtis Folkett
☐ 17 Team Photo
☐ 18 Kelly McCrimmon
☐ 19 Doug Sauter
☐ 20 Kelly Hitchins
☐ 21 Trevor Kidd (G)
☐ 22 Pryce Wood
☐ 23 Cam Brown
☐ 24 Greg Hutchings

'89 - 90

BRANDON WHEAT KINGS / POLICE

Trevor Kidd is the most expensive single at $3. Singles start at $1.

Card Size: 2 1/4" x 4"

Set (24 cards): $16

☐ 1 Trevor Kidd (G)
☐ 2 Troy Frederick
☐ 3 Kelly Thiessen
☐ 4 Pryce Wood
☐ 5 Mike Vandenberghe
☐ 6 Chris Constant
☐ 7 Hardy Sauter
☐ 8 Cam Brown
☐ 9 Bart Cote
☐ 10 Jeff Hoad
☐ 11 Kevin Robertson
☐ 12 Dwayne Newman
☐ 13 Calvin Flint
☐ 14 Glen Webster
☐ 15 Greg Hutchings
☐ 16 Rob Puchniak
☐ 17 Gary Audette
☐ 18 Kevin Schmalz
☐ 19 Dwayne Gylywoychuk
☐ 20 Jeff Odgers
☐ 21 Brian Purdy
☐ 22 Merv Priest
☐ 23 Doug Sauter
☐ 24 Team Photo

'90 - 91

BRANDON WHEAT KINGS / POLICE

Trevor Kidd is the most expensive single at $3. Singles start at 75¢.

Card Size: 2 1/4" x 4"

Set (24 cards): $16

☐ 1 Jeff Hoad
☐ 2 Merv Priest
☐ 3 Mike Vandenberghe
☐ 4 Bart Côté
☐ 5 Hardy Sauter
☐ 6 Mark Johnston
☐ 7 Kelly McCrimmon
☐ 8 Team Photo
☐ 9 Kevin Robertson
☐ 10 Glen Webster
☐ 11 Greg Hutchings
☐ 12 Dan Kopec
☐ 13 Dwayne Gylywoychuk
☐ 14 Brian Purdy
☐ 15 Trevor Kidd (G)
☐ 16 Johan Skillgard
☐ 17 Stu Scantlebury
☐ 18 Byron Penstock
☐ 19 Rob Puchniak
☐ 20 Gary Audette
☐ 21 Calvin Flint
☐ 22 Jason White
☐ 23 Chris Constant
☐ 24 Glen Gulutzan

'92 - 93

BRANDON WHEAT KINGS / POLICE

Singles start at 75¢.

Card Size: 2 1/4" x 4"

Set (24 cards): $12

☐ Aris Brimanis
☐ Colin Cloutier (G)
☐ Chris Dingman
☐ Mike Dubinsky
☐ Todd Dutiaume
☐ Mark Franks
☐ Craig Geekie
☐ Dwayne Gylywoychuk
☐ Scott Hlady
☐ Jeff Hoad
☐ Bobby House
☐ Chris Johnston
☐ Mark Kolesar
☐ Scott Laluk
☐ Mike Maneluk
☐ Sean McFatridge
☐ Marty Murray
☐ Byron Penstock
☐ Darren Ritchie
☐ Trevor Robins
☐ Ryan Smith
☐ Jeff Staples
☐ Darcy Werenka
☐ Mascot Willie

'93 - 94

BRANDON WHEAT KINGS / POLICE

We do not yet have a checklist for this series.

'95 - 96

BRANDON WHEAT KINGS / POLICE

Mike Leclerc is the most expensive single. Singles start at 50¢.

Set (24 cards): $15

- ☐ 1 Andrei Lupandin
- ☐ 2 Daniel Tetrault
- ☐ 3 Gerhard Unterluggauer
- ☐ 4 Wade Redden
- ☐ 5 Kelly Smart
- ☐ 6 Bobby" Brown
- ☐ 7 Jason Skilnick
- ☐ 8 Mike Leclerc
- ☐ 9 Cory Cyrenne
- ☐ 10 Dean Kletzel
- ☐ 11 David Darguzas
- ☐ 12 Jeff Temple
- ☐ 13 Justin Kurtz
- ☐ 14 Mark Dutiaume
- ☐ 15 Sven Butenschon
- ☐ 16 Vinnie Jonasson
- ☐ 17 Ryan Robson
- ☐ 18 Chris Dingman
- ☐ 19 Darren Van Oene
- ☐ 20 Stefan Cherneski
- ☐ 21 Daryl Stockham
- ☐ 22 Peter Schaefer
- ☐ 23 Burke Henry
- ☐ 24 Brian Elder

'96 - 97
BRANDON WHEAT KINGS / POLICE

We do not yet have a checklist for this series.

'97 - 98
BRANDON WHEAT KINGS / POLICE

We do not yet have a checklist for this series.

'98 - 99
BRANDON WHEAT KINGS / McDONALD'S

Singles start at 50¢.
Set (25 cards): $12

- ☐ Alex Argyriou
- ☐ Ryan Craig
- ☐ Jomar Cruz
- ☐ Jan Fadrny
- ☐ Brett Girard
- ☐ Aaron Goldade
- ☐ Burke Henry
- ☐ Jamie Hodson
- ☐ J.D. Kehler
- ☐ Andrew Kaminsky
- ☐ Ryan Johnston
- ☐ Peter Kudrna
- ☐ Andrei Lupandin
- ☐ Scott McCallum
- ☐ Richard Mueller
- ☐ Randy Ponte
- ☐ Ryan Robson
- ☐ Wade Skolney
- ☐ Daniel Tetrault
- ☐ Brett Thurston
- ☐ Brad Twordik
- ☐ Cory Unser
- ☐ Mike Wirll
- ☐ Justin Yeoman

'99 - 00
BRANDON WHEAT KINGS / POLICE

Singles start at 50¢.
Set (24 cards):

- ☐ Mark Ardelan
- ☐ Milan Bartovic
- ☐ Les Borsheim
- ☐ Ryan Craig
- ☐ Brett Dickie
- ☐ Ryan Diduck
- ☐ Jan Fadrny
- ☐ Brett Girard
- ☐ Aaron Goldade
- ☐ Kevin Harris
- ☐ Jamie Hodson
- ☐ J.D. Kehler
- ☐ Colin McRae
- ☐ Robert McVicar
- ☐ Richard Mueller
- ☐ Randy Ponte
- ☐ Bart Rushmer
- ☐ Wade Skolney
- ☐ Daniel Tetrault
- ☐ Brett Thurston
- ☐ Jordin Tootoo
- ☐ Brad Twordik
- ☐ Cory Unser
- ☐ Mike Wirll

'01 - 02
BRANDON WHEAT KINGS / POLICE

We do not yet have a checklist for this series.

'02 - 03
BRANDON WHEAT KINGS / POLICE

We do not yet have a checklist for this series.

BRANTFORD ALEXANDERS

'83 - 84
BRANTFORD ALEXANDERS / POLICE

Bob Probert is the most expensive single at $10. Shayne Corson sells at $6.
Singles start at $1.
Card Size: 2 3/4" x 3 1/2"
Set (30 cards): $40

- ☐ 1 Ken Gratton
- ☐ 2 Shayne Corson
- ☐ 3 Bob Probert
- ☐ 4 Bruce Bell
- ☐ 5 Warren Bechard
- ☐ 6 Jason Lafrenière
- ☐ 7 Ron Moffat
- ☐ 8 Jack Calbeck
- ☐ 9 Marc West
- ☐ 10 Larry Van Herzele
- ☐ 11 Doug Stewart
- ☐ 12 Brian MacDonald
- ☐ 13 Dave Draper
- ☐ 14 Jeff Jackson
- ☐ 15 Steve Linseman
- ☐ 16 Steve Short
- ☐ 17 Allan Bester (G)
- ☐ 18 John Weir
- ☐ 19 Chris Pusey
- ☐ 20 Mike Millar
- ☐ 21 Chris Glover
- ☐ 22 Bob Pierson
- ☐ 23 Phil Priddle
- ☐ 24 Grant Anderson
- ☐ 25 Ken Gagner
- ☐ 26 Andy Alway
- ☐ 27 Todd Francis
- ☐ 28 John Meulenbroeks
- ☐ 29 Mike Chettleburgh
- ☐ 30 Bill Dynes

BROCKVILLE BRAVES

'87 - 88
BROCKVILLE BRAVES / POLICE

Singles start at 75¢.
Card Size: 2 5/8" x 3 5/8"
Set (25 cards): $10

- ☐ 1 Police Logo
- ☐ 2 Steve Harper
- ☐ 3 Peter Kelly
- ☐ 4 Mac MacLean
- ☐ 5 Mike McCourt
- ☐ 6 Paul MacLean
- ☐ 7 Mark Michaud (G)
- ☐ 8 Alain Marchessault
- ☐ 9 Tom Roman
- ☐ 10 Darren Burns
- ☐ 11 Scott Halpenny (G)
- ☐ 12 Ray Gallagher
- ☐ 13 Bob Lindsay
- ☐ 14 Brett Harkins
- ☐ 15 Dave Hyrsky
- ☐ 16 Richard Marchessault
- ☐ 17 Scott Boston
- ☐ 18 Steve Hogg (G)
- ☐ 19 Chris Webster
- ☐ 20 Stuart Birnie
- ☐ 21 Brett Dunk
- ☐ 22 Charles Cusson
- ☐ 23 Pat Gooley
- ☐ 24 Andy Rodman
- ☐ 25 Peter Radlein

'88 - 89
BROCKVILLE BRAVES / POLICE

Singles start at 75¢.
Card Size: 2 5/8" x 3 5/8"
Set (25 cards): $10

- ☐ 1 Ray Gallagher
- ☐ 2 Peter Kelly
- ☐ 3 Steve Harper
- ☐ 4 Winston Jones
- ☐ 5 Mac MacLean
- ☐ 6 Kevin Doherty
- ☐ 7 Stuart Birnie
- ☐ 8 Charles Cusson
- ☐ 9 Paul MacLean
- ☐ 10 Bob Lindsay
- ☐ 11 Darren Burns
- ☐ 12 Rick Pracey (G)
- ☐ 13 Mike Malloy
- ☐ 14 Dave Hyrsky
- ☐ 15 Rob Percival
- ☐ 16 Jarrett Eligh
- ☐ 17 Pat Gooley
- ☐ 18 Michael Bracco (G)
- ☐ 19 Ken Crook
- ☐ 20 Brad Osborne
- ☐ 21 Todd Reynolds
- ☐ 22 Mike McCourt
- ☐ 23 Chris Webster
- ☐ 24 Kevin Lune
- ☐ 25 Police Logo

CALGARY HITMEN

'98 - 99
CALGARY HITMEN

The most expensive singles are Pavel Brendl, Kris Beech and Brad Moran. Singles start at 50¢.
Set (26 cards): $20

- ☐ 1 Matt Kinch
- ☐ 2 Ryan Shannon
- ☐ 3 Jeff Feniak
- ☐ 4 Kenton Smith
- ☐ 5 Rod Sarich
- ☐ 6 Pavel Brendl
- ☐ 7 Chris Nielsen
- ☐ 8 Sean McAslan
- ☐ 9 Jordan Krestanovich
- ☐ 10 Michael Bubnick
- ☐ 11 Kris Beech
- ☐ 12 Ryan Geremia
- ☐ 13 Wade Davis
- ☐ 14 Brad Moran
- ☐ 15 Lyle Steenbergen
- ☐ 16 Curtis Rich
- ☐ 17 Ryan Andres
- ☐ 18 Brent Dodginghorse
- ☐ 19 Jerred Smithson
- ☐ 20 Peter Bergman
- ☐ 21 Alexandre Fomitchev
- ☐ 22 Eric Clark
- ☐ 23 Donald Choukalos
- ☐ 24 Dean Clark
- ☐ 25 Jeff Maher
- ☐ 26 Mascot Vulk

'99 - 00
CALGARY HITMEN / TOYS 'R' US

Singles start at 50¢.
Card Size: 2 1/2" x 3 1/2"

Set (25 cards):

- ☐ Mascot The Vulk
- ☐ Matt Kinch
- ☐ Kenton Smith
- ☐ Rod Sarich
- ☐ Robin Gomez
- ☐ Pavel Brendl
- ☐ Chris Nielsen
- ☐ Sean McAslan
- ☐ Jordan Krestanovich
- ☐ Michael Bubnick
- ☐ Kris Beech
- ☐ Shaun Norrie
- ☐ Wade Davis
- ☐ Brad Moran
- ☐ Owen Fussey
- ☐ Anders Lovdahl
- ☐ Jerred Smithson
- ☐ Brandon Segal
- ☐ Jared Carli
- ☐ Sean Connors
- ☐ Brent Krahn
- ☐ Dean Clark
- ☐ Jeff Maher
- ☐ Jeff Feniak
- ☐ Eric Clark

'00 - 01
CALGARY HITMEN / TOYS 'R' US

Singles start at 50¢.
Card Size: 2 1/2" x 3 1/2"
Set (28 cards):

- ☐ Toni Bader
- ☐ Kris Beech
- ☐ Brady Block
- ☐ Johnny Boychuk
- ☐ Pavel Brendl
- ☐ Michael Bubnick
- ☐ Adam Breitkreuz
- ☐ Jared Carli
- ☐ Wade Davis
- ☐ Mike Egener
- ☐ Danny Ehrmen
- ☐ Owen Fussey
- ☐ Robin Gomez
- ☐ Matt Kinch
- ☐ Brent Krahn
- ☐ Jordan Krestanovich
- ☐ Sean McAslan
- ☐ Shaun Norrie
- ☐ Rod Sarich
- ☐ Brandon Segal
- ☐ Shaun Sutter
- ☐ David Vrbata
- ☐ Chad Wolkowski
- ☐ Dean Clark
- ☐ Jeff Maher
- ☐ Mascot The Vulk
- ☐ Calgary Herald
- ☐ "Toys "R" Us"

'01 - 02
CALGARY HITMEN / MOHAWK

Singles start at 50¢.
Set (26 cards):

- ☐ Paul Albers
- ☐ Kyle Annesley
- ☐ Tyler Beechey
- ☐ Johnny Boychuk
- ☐ Adam Breitkreuz
- ☐ Michael Bubnick
- ☐ Jared Carli
- ☐ Waade Davis
- ☐ Mike Egener
- ☐ Dan Ehrman
- ☐ Owen Fussey
- ☐ Sébastien Laplante
- ☐ Ryan Martin
- ☐ Lance Morrison
- ☐ Ryan Papaioannou
- ☐ Wes Rypien
- ☐ Rod Sarich
- ☐ Brandon Segal
- ☐ Denis Sergaev
- ☐ Mark Shetchyk
- ☐ Fredrik Sjöstrom
- ☐ Rob Smith
- ☐ Chad Wolkowski
- ☐ Richard Kromm
- ☐ Jeff Maher
- ☐ Mascot The Vulk

CAPE BRETON SCREAMING EAGLES

'01 - 02
CAPE BRETON SCREAMING EAGLES / CARTES, TIMBRES, MONNAIES STE-FOY

Singles start at 50¢.
Card Size: 2 1/2" x 3 1/2"
Set (24 cards): $12

- ☐ 1 Steve Villeneuve
- ☐ 2 Maxime Lessard
- ☐ 3 Pierre-Luc Laprise
- ☐ 4 David Cloutier
- ☐ 5 Stuart MacRae
- ☐ 6 Dominic Noel
- ☐ 7 Jean-Philippe Côté
- ☐ 8 Martin Kasik
- ☐ 9 Steve Dixon
- ☐ 10 Marc-Olivier Vary
- ☐ 11 Justin Hawco
- ☐ 12 Pierre-Luc Emond
- ☐ 13 Guillaume Demers
- ☐ 14 Rodrigue Boucher
- ☐ 15 George Davis
- ☐ 16 André Martineau
- ☐ 17 Carl McLean
- ☐ 18 Pascal Morency
- ☐ 19 Mathieu Dumas
- ☐ 20 Jean-François Dufort
- ☐ 21 Marc-André Fleury
- ☐ 22 Jasen Awalt
- ☐ 23 Kevin Asselin
- ☐ 24 Checklist

CHICOUTIMI SAGUENÉENS

'84 - 85
CHICOUTIMI SAGUENÉENS

Stéphane Richer is the most expensive single at $6.
Singles start at $1.50.
Photo Size: 8 1/2" x 11"
Sponsor: None
Set (24 photos): $30

- ☐ Mario Barbe
- ☐ Mario Bazinet
- ☐ Daniel Berthiaume (G)
- ☐ Francis Breault
- ☐ Gregg Choules
- ☐ Christian Duperron
- ☐ Luc Dufour
- ☐ Luc Duval
- ☐ Patrick Emond
- ☐ Marc Fortier
- ☐ Steve Gauthier
- ☐ Yves Heroux
- ☐ Daniel Jomphe
- ☐ Gilles Laberge
- ☐ Claude Lajoie
- ☐ Serge Lauzon
- ☐ Roch Marinier
- ☐ Pierre Millier
- ☐ Marc Morin
- ☐ Scott Rettew
- ☐ Jean-Marc Richard
- ☐ Stéphane Richer
- ☐ Pierre Sévigny
- ☐ Bedard/ M.Boivin/ Byatt J.M.Couture/ P.Gosselin/ J.Y. Laberge/ R.Riverin

'00 - 01
CHICOUTIMI SAGUENÉENS / CARTES, TIMBRES, MONNAIES STE-FOY

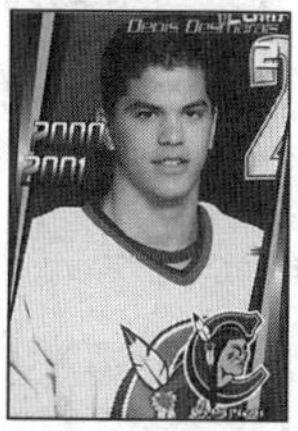

Singles start at 50¢.
Card Size: 2 1/2" x 3 1/2"
Set (24 cards): $12

- ☐ 1 Olivier Dannel
- ☐ 2 Alex Turcotte
- ☐ 3 Mathieu Bétournay
- ☐ 4 Michel Finn
- ☐ 5 Éric Bétournay
- ☐ 6 Jonathan Francoeur
- ☐ 7 Sébastien Laprise
- ☐ 8 Sylvain Watt
- ☐ 9 Sébastien Laprise
- ☐ 10 Stanislav Hudec
- ☐ 11 Christian Larivée
- ☐ 12 François Caron
- ☐ 13 Éric Beaudin
- ☐ 14 Alain Chenard
- ☐ 15 Karl St-Pierre
- ☐ 16 Michael Parent
- ☐ 17 D. Ouellet Beaudry
- ☐ 18 J-F Demers
- ☐ 19 Dave Verville
- ☐ 20 Guillaume Karrer
- ☐ 21 Martin Beauchesne
- ☐ 22 Jean-Michel Martin
- ☐ 23 Pierre-Marc Bouchard
- ☐ 24 Checklist

CLARKSON GOLDEN KNIGHTS

'92 - 93
CLARKSON GOLDEN KNIGHTS

Todd Marchant is the most expensive single at $3.
Singles start at 75¢.
Card Size: 2 1/2" x 3 1/2"
Sponsor: None
Set (24 cards): $15

- ☐ Josh Bartell
- ☐ Hugo Belanger
- ☐ Craig Conroy
- ☐ Jason Currie
- ☐ Steve Dubinsky
- ☐ Shawn Fotheringham
- ☐ Dave Green
- ☐ Ed Henrihc
- ☐ Chris Lipsett
- ☐ Todd Marchant
- ☐ Brian Mueller
- ☐ Kevin Murphy
- ☐ Martin d'Orsonnens
- ☐ Steve Palmer
- ☐ Patrice Robitaille
- ☐ Chris Rogles
- ☐ Jerry Rosenheck
- ☐ Chris de Ruiter
- ☐ Guy Sanderson
- ☐ David Seitz
- ☐ Mikko Tavi
- ☐ Patrick Theriault
- ☐ Marko Tuomainen
- ☐ d'Orsonnens/ Dubinsky

'93 - 94
CLARKSON KNIGHTS

We do not yet have a checklist for this series.

CORNWALL ROYALS

'91 - 92
CORNWALL ROYALS / POLICE

Singles start at 50¢.
Card Size: 2 5/8" x 3 3/4"
Set (29 cards): $12

- ☐ 1 Jason Meloche
- ☐ 2 Mark DeSantis
- ☐ 3 Richard Raymond
- ☐ 4 Gord Pell
- ☐ 5 Dave Lemay
- ☐ 6 John Lovell
- ☐ 7 Ryan VandenBussche
- ☐ 8 David Babcock
- ☐ 9 Sam Oliveira
- ☐ 10 Jeremy Stevenson
- ☐ 11 Todd Walker
- ☐ 12 Jean-Alain Schneider
- ☐ 13 Ilpo Kauhanen (G)
- ☐ 14 Guy Lévêque
- ☐ 15 Shayne Gaffar
- ☐ 16 Rival Fullum
- ☐ 17 Mike Prokopec
- ☐ 18 Nathan Lafayette
- ☐ 19 Larry Courville
- ☐ 20 Chris Clancy
- ☐ 21 Tom Nemeth
- ☐ 22 Jeff Reid
- ☐ 23 Paul Andrea
- ☐ 24 John Slaney
- ☐ 25 Alan Letang
- ☐ 26 Rob Dykeman (G)
- ☐ 27 P.Fixter/ B.O'Leary
- ☐ 28 Chief Claude Shaver
- ☐ 29 Checklist

DRUMMONDVILLE VOLTIGEURS

'01 - 02
DRUMMONDVILLE VOLTIGEURS / CARTES, TIMBRES, MONNAIES STE-FOY

Singles start at 50¢. This series is sponsored by Collecto Sports.
Card Size: 2 1/2" x 3 1/2"
Set (25 cards): $12

- ☐ 1 Francis Breault
- ☐ 2 Evgeni Nourislamov
- ☐ 3 Todd Paul
- ☐ 4 André Joanisse
- ☐ 5 Jules Melanson
- ☐ 6 André Vincent
- ☐ 7 Dominic Fiset
- ☐ 8 Kevin Lacombe
- ☐ 9 Alexandre Demers
- ☐ 10 Laurent Lanoie
- ☐ 11 Yannick Riendeau
- ☐ 12 Patrick Lévesque
- ☐ 13 Sébastien Laprise
- ☐ 14 Benoît Duhamel
- ☐ 15 Jonathan Dick
- ☐ 16 Kevin Mailhot
- ☐ 17 Jason D'Ascanio
- ☐ 18 Thomas Bellemare
- ☐ 19 Samuel Villeneuve
- ☐ 20 Kevin Duchaîne
- ☐ 21 Éric Dagenais
- ☐ 22 Sylvain Michaud (G)
- ☐ 23 P-O Girouard (G)
- ☐ 24 Pier Olivier Bégin (G)
- ☐ 25 Checklist

FERRIS STATE BULLDOGS

'91 - 92
FERRIS STATE BULLDOGS

Singles start at 50¢.
Card Size: 2 1/2" x 3 1/2"
Sponsor: None
Set (30 cards): $10

- ☐ Aaron Asp
- ☐ Seth Appert
- ☐ J.J. Bamberger
- ☐ Kevin Beals
- ☐ Scott Bell
- ☐ Brad Burnham
- ☐ Dan Chaput
- ☐ Tim Christian
- ☐ Bob Daniels
- ☐ Colin Dodunski
- ☐ Mick Dolan
- ☐ John Duff
- ☐ Daryl Filipek
- ☐ John Gruden
- ☐ Luke Harvey
- ☐ Jeff Jestadt
- ☐ Dave Karpa
- ☐ Gary Kitching
- ☐ Mike Kolenda
- ☐ Craig Lisko
- ☐ Mike May
- ☐ Pat Mazzoli
- ☐ Robb McIntyre
- ☐ Kevin Moore
- ☐ Greg Paine
- ☐ Dwight Parrish
- ☐ Val Passarelli
- ☐ Keith Sergott
- ☐ Doug Smith
- ☐ Mascot The Bulldog

GUELPH STORM

'95 - 96
GUELPH STORM / AXIOM, BURGER KING

Dan Cloutier is the most expensive single at $2.
Singles start at 50¢.
Card Size: 2 1/2" x 3 1/2"
Set (30 cards): $10

- ☐ 1 Checklist
- ☐ 2 Andrew Clark
- ☐ 3 Dwayne Hay
- ☐ 4 Jason Jackman
- ☐ 5 Burger King ad
- ☐ 6 Nick Bootland
- ☐ 7 Andrew Long
- ☐ 8 Todd Norman
- ☐ 9 Michael Pittman
- ☐ 10 Herbert Vasilijevs
- ☐ 11 Jeff Williams
- ☐ 12 Joel Cort
- ☐ 13 Chris Hajt
- ☐ 14 Brian Willsie
- ☐ 15 Brian Wesenberg
- ☐ 16 Mike Lankshear
- ☐ 17 Darryl McArthur
- ☐ 18 Bryan McKinney
- ☐ 19 Regan Stocco
- ☐ 20 Ryan Risidore

- ☐ 21 Mike Vellinga
- ☐ 22 Dan Cloutier (G)
- ☐ 23 Bryan McMullen
- ☐ 24 Brett Thompson
- ☐ 25 Ryan Robichaud
- ☐ 26 Kid's Club
- ☐ 27 Jamie Wright
- ☐ 28 Guelph Police
- ☐ 29 Mike Galati
- ☐ 30 Domino's Pizza

'96 - 97

GUELPH STORM / BURGER KING

Manny Malhotra is the most expensive single at $3. Singles start at 50¢.

Card Size: 2 1/2" x 3 1/2"

Set (36 cards): $15

- ☐ 1 Checklist
- ☐ 2 Brett Thompson
- ☐ 3 David MacDonald
- ☐ 4 John Zubyck
- ☐ 5 Denis Ivanov
- ☐ 6 Joel Cort
- ☐ 7 Chris Hajt
- ☐ 8 Manny Malhotra
- ☐ 9 Mike Dombkiewicz
- ☐ 10 Ryan Robichaud
- ☐ 11 Kent McDonell
- ☐ 12 Joe Gerbe
- ☐ 13 Mike Christian
- ☐ 14 Brian Wesenberg
- ☐ 15 Todd Norman
- ☐ 16 Darryl McArthur
- ☐ 17 Richard Irwin
- ☐ 18 Brian Willsie
- ☐ 19 Mike Vellinga
- ☐ 20 Jason Jackman
- ☐ 21 Chris Madden
- ☐ 22 Dwayne Hay
- ☐ 23 Joey Bartley
- ☐ 24 Mike Lankshear
- ☐ 25 Andrew Long
- ☐ 26 Matt Bell
- ☐ 27 Nick Bootland
- ☐ 28 E.J. McGuire
- ☐ 29 Rick Allain
- ☐ 30 Burger King
- ☐ 31 Kid's Club
- ☐ 32.Malhotra/ Norman
- ☐ 33 Domino's Pizza
- ☐ 34 Domino's Pizza
- ☐ 35 C.Hajt/ D.Hay
- ☐ 36 Team Photo

'96 - 97

GUELPH STORM / PREMIER

We do not yet have a checklist for this series.

'97 - 98

GUELPH STORM

We do not yet have a checklist for this series.

'98 - 99

GUELPH STORM

We do not yet have a checklist for this series.

'99 - 00

GUELPH STORM / POLICE

Singles start at 50¢.

Set (36 cards): $12

- ☐ 1 Checklist
- ☐ 2 Craig Andersson (G)
- ☐ 3 Chris Madden
- ☐ 4 Kevin Mitchell
- ☐ 5 Kevin Dallman
- ☐ 6 Matt Rock
- ☐ 7 Jon Hedberg
- ☐ 8 Radek Matalik
- ☐ 9 Joe Gerbe
- ☐ 10 Bo Subr
- ☐ 11 Lindsay Plunkett
- ☐ 12 Kent McDonnell
- ☐ 13 Peter Flache
- ☐ 14 Charlie Stephens
- ☐ 15 Colt King
- ☐ 16 Nick Jones
- ☐ 17 Brent Kelly
- ☐ 18 Jon Peters
- ☐ 19 Derek Hennessey
- ☐ 20 Andrew Brown
- ☐ 21 Aran Myers
- ☐ 22 Matt House
- ☐ 23 Éric Beaudoin
- ☐ 24 Ian Forbes
- ☐ 25 Morgan McCormick
- ☐ 26 Paul Gillis
- ☐ 27 Bart Crashley
- ☐ 28 Shane Mabey
- ☐ 29 Russ Hammond
- ☐ 30 Mascot Spyke
- ☐ 31 Storm
- ☐ 32 Guelph Police
- ☐ 33 Burger King
- ☐ 34 Burger King
- ☐ 35 Domino's
- ☐ 36 Domino's

'00 - 01

GUELPH STORM

We do not yet have a checklist for this series.

'01 - 02

GUELPH STORM

Singles start at 50¢.

Set (35 cards):

- ☐ 1 Fedor Tjutin
- ☐ 2 Frank Burgio
- ☐ 3 Kevin Dallman
- ☐ 4 Leonid Zvachkin
- ☐ 5 Tim Branham
- ☐ 6 George Bradley
- ☐ 7 Martin St-Pierre
- ☐ 8 Malcolm MacMillan
- ☐ 9 Michael Krelove
- ☐ 10 Colin Power
- ☐ 11 Aaron Lobb
- ☐ 12 Daniel Paille
- ☐ 13 Alex Butkus
- ☐ 14 Ryan Thompson
- ☐ 15 Luc Chiasson
- ☐ 16 Derek Hennessey
- ☐ 17 Evan Kotsopoulos
- ☐ 18 Matt Puntureri
- ☐ 19 Andrew Archer
- ☐ 20 Morgan McCormick
- ☐ 21 Chris Beckford-Tseu
- ☐ 22 Andrew Penner
- ☐ 23 Dustin Brown
- ☐ 24 Dwight LaBrosse
- ☐ 25 Jeff Jackson
- ☐ 26 Shawn Camp
- ☐ 27 M&T Printing
- ☐ 28 Mascot Spyke
- ☐ 29 Shane Mabey
- ☐ 30 Russ Hammond
- ☐ 31 Guelph Police
- ☐ 32 Domino's Pizza
- ☐ 33 Thomas McKinnon
- ☐ 34 Ian McNally
- ☐ 35 Goal card / Checklist

'01 - 02

GUELPH STORM / MEMORIAL CUP

Singles start at 50¢.

Set (35 cards):

- ☐ 1 Fedor Tjutin
- ☐ 2 Kevin Dallman
- ☐ 3 Leonid Zvachkin
- ☐ 4 Tim Branham
- ☐ 5 Eric Larochelle
- ☐ 6 George Bradley
- ☐ 7 Martin St-Pierre
- ☐ 8 Malcolm MacMillan
- ☐ 9 Michael Krelove
- ☐ 10 Colin Power
- ☐ 11 Aaron Lobb
- ☐ 12 Daniel Paille
- ☐ 13 Alex Butkus
- ☐ 14 Ryan Thompson
- ☐ 15 Luc Chiasson
- ☐ 16 Derek Hennessey
- ☐ 17 Lou Dickenson
- ☐ 18 Matt Puntureri
- ☐ 19 Scott Rozendal
- ☐ 20 Andrew Archer
- ☐ 21 Morgan McCormick
- ☐ 22 Andrew Penner
- ☐ 23 Dustin Brown
- ☐ 24 Dwight LaBrosse
- ☐ 25 Jeff Jackson
- ☐ 26 Shawn Camp
- ☐ 27 Mascot Spyke
- ☐ 28 Shane Mabey
- ☐ 29 Russ Hammond
- ☐ 30 M&T Printing
- ☐ 31 Memorial Cup card
- ☐ 32 Storm team photo
- ☐ 33 Storm the community
- ☐ 34 Storm the community
- ☐ 35 Checklist / goal card

HALIFAX MOOSEHEAD

'95 - 96

HALIFAX MOOSEHEADS / SOBEYS

This was the first year that Halifax produced a team set. As with later series, the team set could be bought at Halifax's home arena, the MetroCentre, or at Moosehead Cold Beer Stores. Jean-Sébastien Giguère is the most expensive single at $20. Singles sell at 50¢.

Size: 2 1/2" x 3 1/2"

Set (26 cards): $30

- ☐ Elias Abrahamsson #6
- ☐ Frédéric Belanger #22
- ☐ Jamie Brown #7
- ☐ David Carson #20
- ☐ Étienne Drapeau #9
- ☐ J-S Giguère #47 (G)
- ☐ Chris Halverson #5
- ☐ Harlin Hayes #31 (G)
- ☐ Eric Houde #33
- ☐ Patrick Lafleur #27
- ☐ Mark Lynk #10
- ☐ Nicolas Maheux #19
- ☐ Billy Manley #16
- ☐ Jan Melichercik #18
- ☐ Steve Mongrain #15
- ☐ Danielle Payette #26
- ☐ Chris Peyton #23
- ☐ Derrick Pyke #11
- ☐ Jody Shelley #25
- ☐ Brian Surette #12
- ☐ Joel Theriault #53
- ☐ Didier Tremblay #4
- ☐ Clement Jodoin, Coach
- ☐ S. MacKenzie, A. Coach
- ☐ C. McQuaid, Ath. Trainer
- ☐ Title Card

'96 - 97

HALIFAX MOOSEHEADS / SOBEYS

J-S Giguère is the most expensive single at $15. Singles start at 50¢. The first edition features players in their home uniforms, while the second edition features players in their away uniforms.

Card Size: 2 1/2" x 3 1/2"

Set 1 (28 cards): $30

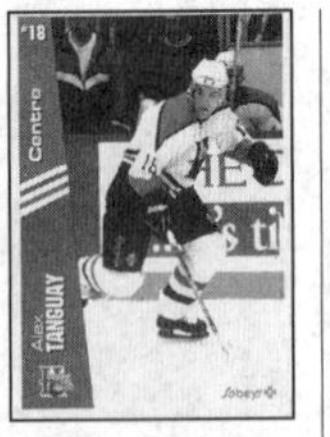

- ☐ Elias Abrahamsson #6
- ☐ Frédéric Belanger #22
- ☐ Martin Bilodeau #1 (G)
- ☐ Jamie Brown #7
- ☐ Marc Chouinard #55
- ☐ Benoît Dusablon #19
- ☐ J-S Giguère #47 (G)
- ☐ Andrew Gilby #26
- ☐ Clement Jodoin
- ☐ Alex Johnstone #34
- ☐ Eric Laplante #11
- ☐ Jean-Simon Lemay #44
- ☐ Mark Lynk #10
- ☐ Shawn Mackenzie
- ☐ Billy Manley #16
- ☐ Alexandre Mathieu #15
- ☐ Chris McQuaid
- ☐ Todd Row #9
- ☐ Ryan Rowell #23
- ☐ François Sasseville #40
- ☐ Jody Shelley #25
- ☐ Jeffrey Sullivan #27
- ☐ Alex Tanguay #18
- ☐ Didier Tremblay #4
- ☐ Jason Troini #33
- ☐ Clark Udle #19
- ☐ Team Photo
- ☐ Checklist

Set 2 (28 cards): $20

- ☐ Elias Abrahamsson #6
- ☐ Frédéric Bélanger #22
- ☐ Martin Bilodeau #1 (G)
- ☐ Jamie Brown #7
- ☐ Marc Chouinard #55
- ☐ Benoît Dusablon #19
- ☐ J-S Giguère #47 (G)
- ☐ Andrew Gilby #26
- ☐ Clement Jodoin
- ☐ Alex Johnstone #34
- ☐ Eric Laplante #11
- ☐ Jean-Simon Lemay #44
- ☐ Mark Lynk #10
- ☐ Shawn Mackenzie
- ☐ Billy Manley #16
- ☐ Alexandre Mathieu #15
- ☐ Chris McQuaid
- ☐ Martin Pouiot
- ☐ Todd Row #9
- ☐ Ryan Rowell #23
- ☐ François Sasseville #40
- ☐ Jody Shelley #25
- ☐ Jeffrey Sullivan #27
- ☐ Alex Tanguay #18
- ☐ Didier Tremblay #4
- ☐ Jason Troini #33
- ☐ Shelley/ JS. Giguère (G)
- ☐ Checklist

'97 - 98

HALIFAX MOOSEHEADS / SOBEYS

Alex Tanguay is the most expensive single at $4. Singles sell at 50¢. The first edition features players in their home uniforms while the second edition feature players in their away uniforms.

Size: 2 1/2" x 3 1/2"

Set 1 (28 cards): $15

- ☐ Frédéric Belanger #22
- ☐ Martin Bilodeau #1 (G)
- ☐ Marc-André Binette #17
- ☐ Alexandre Couture #41
- ☐ Andrew Gilby #2
- ☐ Alex Johnstone #34
- ☐ Eric Laplante #11
- ☐ P.J. Lynch #44
- ☐ Mark Lynk #77
- ☐ Joey MacDonald (G)
- ☐ Ali MacEachern #36
- ☐ Billy Manley #16
- ☐ Alexandre Mathieu #32
- ☐ Steve Mongrain #31 (G)
- ☐ Ryan Power #19
- ☐ Brandon Reid #55
- ☐ Todd Row #20
- ☐ Dean Stock #10
- ☐ Jeff Sullivan #27
- ☐ Alex Tanguay #18
- ☐ Didier Tremblay #4
- ☐ Jason Troini #33
- ☐ Dwight Wolfe #23
- ☐ Danny Grant, Coach
- ☐ S. MacKenzie, A. Coach
- ☐ C. McQuaid, Ath. Trainer
- ☐ Team Photo
- ☐ Checklist

Set 2 (28 cards): $15

- ☐ Frédéric Belanger #22
- ☐ Martin Bilodeau #1 (G)
- ☐ Marc-André Binette #17
- ☐ Alexandre Couture #41
- ☐ Mauro Di Paolo #45
- ☐ Alex Johnstone #34
- ☐ P.J. Lynch #44
- ☐ Joey MacDonald #31 (G)
- ☐ Al MacEachern #36
- ☐ Boris Majesky #5
- ☐ Bill Manley #16
- ☐ Alexandre Mathieu #32
- ☐ Ryan Power #19
- ☐ Stephen Quirk #20
- ☐ Brandon Reid #55
- ☐ A.J. Rivers #7
- ☐ Dean Stock #10
- ☐ Jeffrey Sullivan #27
- ☐ Alex Tanguay #18
- ☐ Alex Tanguay (Canada)
- ☐ Jason Troini #33
- ☐ Andrew Warr #40
- ☐ Dwight Wolfe #23
- ☐ Danny Grant, Coach
- ☐ S. MacKenzie, A. Coach
- ☐ C. McQuaid, Ath. Trainer
- ☐ Mascot Moosemaniac
- ☐ Checklist

'98 - 99

HALIFAX MOOSEHEADS / SOBEYS

The most expensive singles are Pascal Leclaire, Alex Tanguay and Alexei Volkov. Singles start at 50¢.

Sizes: 2 1/2" x 3 1/2"

Set (23 cards): $22

- ☐ Alexei Volkov (G)
- ☐ Pascal Leclaire (G)
- ☐ Mathieu Paul
- ☐ Samuel Seguin
- ☐ Bill Manley
- ☐ Ladislav Nagy
- ☐ Alex Tanguay
- ☐ Mike Bray
- ☐ Carlyle Lewis
- ☐ Frederic Belanger
- ☐ David McCutcheron
- ☐ Jeff Sullivan
- ☐ Alexandre Mathieu
- ☐ Jason Troini
- ☐ Alex Johnstone
- ☐ Al McEachern
- ☐ Brandon Benedict
- ☐ Tyler Reid
- ☐ Jasmin Gelinas
- ☐ P.J. Lynch
- ☐ Mauro Lapaole
- ☐ Brandon Reid
- ☐ Marc-André Binette

'99 - 00

HALIFAX MOOSEHEADS / SOBEYS

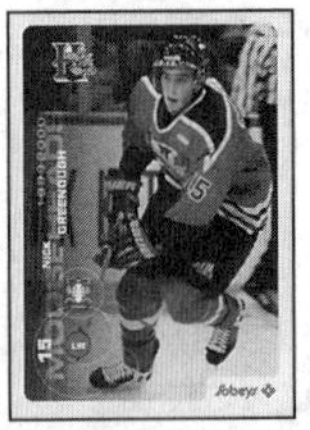

The most expensive singles are Ramzi Abid, Pascal Leclaire and Alexei Volkov. Singles start at 50¢.

Size: 2 1/2" x 3 1/2"

Set (30 cards): $18

- ☐ Ramzi Abid
- ☐ Brandon Benedict
- ☐ Jonathan Boone
- ☐ Joe DiPenta
- ☐ Benoit Dusablon
- ☐ Ryan Flinn
- ☐ Jasmin Gelinas
- ☐ Nick Greenough
- ☐ Joe Groleau
- ☐ Darrell Jerrett
- ☐ Jason King
- ☐ Jules-Edy Laraque
- ☐ Pascal Leclaire (G)
- ☐ Hugo Lehoux
- ☐ Shawn Lewis
- ☐ Ali MacEachern
- ☐ Brandon Reid
- ☐ Carlos Sayde
- ☐ Andrei Shefer
- ☐ Jonathan St-Louis
- ☐ Robbie Sutherland
- ☐ Alexei Volkov (G)
- ☐ Gary Zinck
- ☐ Checklist
- ☐ Checklist
- ☐ Checklist
- ☐ Checklist
- ☐ Checklist
- ☐ Mascot Hal
- ☐ Mooseheads

'00 - 01

HALIFAX MOOSEHEADS / SOBEYS

Singles start at 50¢.

Set (26 cards): $12

- ☐ Brandon Benedict
- ☐ Jonathan Boone
- ☐ Michael Couch
- ☐ Dany Dallaire
- ☐ Bruce Gillis
- ☐ Nick Greenough
- ☐ Milan Jurcina
- ☐ Derrick Kent
- ☐ Jason King
- ☐ Sergei Klyazmin
- ☐ Sébastien Laprise
- ☐ Jules-Edy Laraque
- ☐ Pascal Leclaire (G)
- ☐ Hugo Lehoux
- ☐ Ali McEachern
- ☐ A.J. Maclean
- ☐ Ryan MacPherson
- ☐ Louis Mandeville
- ☐ Connor McGuire
- ☐ Jules Saulnier
- ☐ Giulio Scandella
- ☐ Robbie Sutherland
- ☐ Randy Upshall
- ☐ Ryan White
- ☐ Gary Zinck
- ☐ Checklist

HAMILTON FINCUPS

'75 - 76

HAMILTON FINCUPS

Dale McCourt is the most expensive single at $5. Singles start at $2.

Card Size: 2 1/2" x 3 1/2"

Sponsor: None

Set (18 cards): $22

- ☐ Jack Anderson
- ☐ Mike Clarke
- ☐ Greg Clause
- ☐ Joe Contini
- ☐ Mike Fedorko
- ☐ Paul Foley
- ☐ Greg Hickey
- ☐ Tony Harvath
- ☐ Mike Keating
- ☐ Archie King
- ☐ Ted Long
- ☐ Dale McCourt
- ☐ Dave Norris
- ☐ Greg Redquest
- ☐ Glenn Richardson
- ☐ Ron Roscoe
- ☐ Ric Seiling
- ☐ Danny Shearer

HULL OLYMPIQUES

'87 - 88

HULL OLYMPIQUES / POLICE

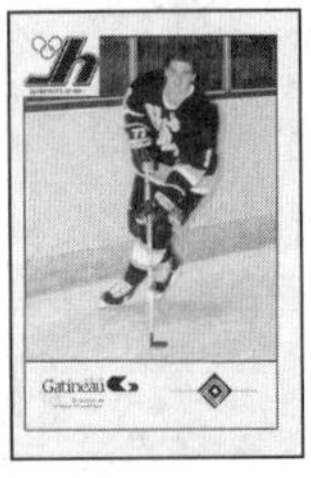

Team President Wayne Gretzky is the most expensive single at $70. Singles start at $1

Card Size: 2 3/4" x 4"

Set (24 cards): $90

- ☐ Joe Aloi
- ☐ Joel Bain
- ☐ Christian Breton
- ☐ Benoît Brunet
- ☐ Guy Dupuis
- ☐ Martin Gelinas
- ☐ Jason Glickman (G)
- ☐ Wayne Gretzky, Owner
- ☐ Denis Heon
- ☐ Herbie Hohenberger
- ☐ Ken MacDermid
- ☐ Craig Martin
- ☐ Mark McLane
- ☐ Stéphane Matteau
- ☐ Kelly Nester
- ☐ Jacques Parent
- ☐ Marc Saumier
- ☐ Claude-Charles Sauriol
- ☐ Joe Suk
- ☐ Alain Vigneault
- ☐ George Wilcox
- ☐ Olympiques Card
- ☐ Olympiques Card
- ☐ Olympiques Card

'99 - 00

HULL OLYMPIQUES / CARTES, TIMBRES, MONNAIES STE-FOY

Singles start at 50¢.

Card Size: 2 1/2" x 3 1/2"

Set (24 cards):

- ☐ 1 Erich Parochy
- ☐ 2 Andrew Carver
- ☐ 3 Bobby** Clarke
- ☐ 4 Donald Johnstone
- ☐ 5 Bruno Lemire
- ☐ 6 Derick Martin
- ☐ 7 Alexandre Giroux
- ☐ 8 Dustin Russell
- ☐ 9 Daniel Hudgin
- ☐ 10 Roberto Bissonnette
- ☐ 11 Daniel Clermont
- ☐ 12 Radim Vrbata
- ☐ 13 Mario Joly
- ☐ 14 Jason Lehoux
- ☐ 15 Brock Boucher
- ☐ 16 Philippe Lacasse
- ☐ 17 Paul Spadarofa
- ☐ 18 Ryan Lauzon
- ☐ 19 Michael Ryder
- ☐ 20 Adam Rivet
- ☐ 21 Patrick Lafrenière
- ☐ 22 Éric Lafrance
- ☐ 23 Philippe Sauvé
- ☐ 24 Checklist

'99 - 00

HULL OLYMPIQUES / BANQUE NATIONALE

The most expensive singles are Philippe Sauvé, Michael Ryder and Luc Robitaille. Singles start at 50¢.

Set (25 cards): $15

- ☐ 1 Erich Parashy
- ☐ 2 Andrew Carver
- ☐ 3 Bobby Clarke
- ☐ 4 Donald Johnstone
- ☐ 5 Bruno Lemire
- ☐ 6 Derick Martin
- ☐ 7 Alexandre Giroux
- ☐ 8 Dustin Russell
- ☐ 9 Daniel Hudgin
- ☐ 10 Roberto Bissonette
- ☐ 11 Daniel Clermont
- ☐ 12 Radim Vrbata
- ☐ 13 Mario Joly
- ☐ 14 Jason Lehoux
- ☐ 15 Brock Boucher
- ☐ 16 Philippe Lacasse
- ☐ 17 Paul Spadafora
- ☐ 18 Ryan Lauzon
- ☐ 19 Michael Ryder
- ☐ 20 Adam Rivet
- ☐ 21 Patrick Lafrenière
- ☐ 22 Éric Lafrance
- ☐ 23 Philippe Sauvé
- ☐ 24 Hull Olympiques
- ☐ Luc Robitaille

'00 - 01

HULL OLYMPIQUES / CARTES, TIMBRES, MONNAIES STE-FOY

Singles start at 50¢.

Card Size: 2 1/2" x 3 1/2"

Set (24 cards):

- ☐ 1 Chris Moher
- ☐ 2 Andrew Carver
- ☐ 3 Bobby Clarke
- ☐ 4 Doug O'Brien
- ☐ 5 Bruno Lemire
- ☐ 6 John Cilladi
- ☐ 7 Derick Martin
- ☐ 8 Roberto Bissonnette
- ☐ 9 Ales Hemsky
- ☐ 10 Philippe Choinière
- ☐ 11 Jonathan Labelle
- ☐ 12 Mario Joly
- ☐ 13 Jason Kostadine

- ☐ 14 Carle Rochon
- ☐ 15 Philippe Lacasse
- ☐ 16 Maxime Talbot
- ☐ 17 Jean-Michel Daoust
- ☐ 18 Brent G. Roach
- ☐ 19 Dale Sullivan
- ☐ 20 Adam Rivet
- ☐ 21 Éric Lafrance
- ☐ 22 Olivier Dannel
- ☐ 23 Ian Courville
- ☐ 24 Checklist

'01 - 02
HULL OLYMPIQUES / CARTES, TIMBRES, MONNAIES STE-FOY

Singles start at 50¢.
Card Size: 2 1/2" x 3 1/2"
Set (24 cards): $15

- ☐ 1 Chris Moher
- ☐ 2 Bryan Riddell
- ☐ 3 Charles Fontaine
- ☐ 4 Dominic D'Amour
- ☐ 5 Doug O'Brien
- ☐ 6 Francis Wathier
- ☐ 7 Derick Martin
- ☐ 8 Philippe Dupuis
- ☐ 9 Scott Gibson
- ☐ 10 Ales Hemsky
- ☐ 11 Nick Fugère
- ☐ 12 Jonathan Labelle
- ☐ 13 Martin Vagner
- ☐ 14 Jason Kostadine
- ☐ 15 Jesse Lane
- ☐ 16 Philippe Lacasse
- ☐ 17 Brent Roach
- ☐ 18 Maxime Talbot
- ☐ 19 Jean-Michel Daoust
- ☐ 20 Dale Sullivan
- ☐ 21 Éric Lafrance
- ☐ 22 Michael Dilorenzo
- ☐ 23 Jean-Junior Morin
- ☐ 24 Checklist

'02 - 03
HULL OLYMPIQUES / CARTES, TIMBRES, MONNAIES STE-FOY

Singles start at 50¢.
Set (24 cards): $12

- ☐ 1 Christopher Pottie
- ☐ 2 Jeff Smith
- ☐ 3 Charles Fontaine
- ☐ 4 Dominic D'Amour
- ☐ 5 Doug O'Brien
- ☐ 6 Sam Roberts
- ☐ 7 Francis Wathier
- ☐ 8 Jonathan Bellemare
- ☐ 9 Philippe Dupuis
- ☐ 10 Guillaume Labrecque
- ☐ 11 Nick Fugère
- ☐ 12 Olivier Labelle
- ☐ 13 Martin Vagner
- ☐ 14 Renaud Des Alliers
- ☐ 15 Andrew Hayes
- ☐ 16 Brent Roach
- ☐ 17 Maxime Talbot
- ☐ 18 Jean-Michel Daoust
- ☐ 19 Dale Sullivan
- ☐ 20 Mathieu Brunelle
- ☐ 21 Éric Lafrance (G)
- ☐ 22 David Tremblay (G)
- ☐ 23 Tyler Reid
- ☐ 24 Checklist

KAMLOOPS BLAZERS

'84 - 85
KAMLOOPS BLAZERS / POLICE

Ken Hitchcock is the most expensive single at $4.
Singles start at $1.
Card Size: 2 3/4" x 4"
Set (24 cards): $25

- ☐ Will Anderson
- ☐ Brian Benning
- ☐ Brian Bertuzzi
- ☐ Rob Brown
- ☐ Todd Carnelley
- ☐ Dean Clark
- ☐ Rob DiMaio
- ☐ Greg Evtuschevski
- ☐ Mark Ferner
- ☐ Greg Hawgood
- ☐ Ken Hitchcock
- ☐ Mark Kachowski
- ☐ Bob Labrier
- ☐ Pat Mangold
- ☐ Gord Mark
- ☐ Len Mark
- ☐ Rob McKinley (G)
- ☐ Mike Nottingham
- ☐ Neil Pilon
- ☐ Rudy Poeschek
- ☐ Daryl Reaugh (G)
- ☐ Ryan Stewart
- ☐ Mark Thietke
- ☐ Gord Walker

'85 - 86
KAMLOOPS BLAZERS / POLICE

Ken Hitchcock is the most expensive single at $4.
Singles start at $1.
Card Size: 2 3/4" x 4"
Set (26 cards): $25

- ☐ Robin Bawa
- ☐ Craig Berube
- ☐ Rob Brown
- ☐ Pat Bingham
- ☐ Todd Carnelley
- ☐ Randy Hansch (G)
- ☐ Greg Hawgood
- ☐ Ken Hitchcock
- ☐ Mark Kachowski
- ☐ Troy Kennedy
- ☐ R.T. Labrier
- ☐ Dave Marcinyshyn
- ☐ Len Mark
- ☐ Rob McKinley (G)
- ☐ Ken Morrison
- ☐ Pat Nogier (G)
- ☐ Mike Nottingham
- ☐ Doug Pickell
- ☐ Rudy Poeschek
- ☐ Mike Ragot
- ☐ Don Schmidt
- ☐ Ron Shudra
- ☐ Peter Soberlak
- ☐ Lonnie Spink
- ☐ Chris Tarnowski
- ☐ Greg Wallace

'86 - 87
KAMLOOPS BLAZERS / POLICE

Cards were originally issued in panels. Mark Recchi is the most expensive single at $20.
Singles start at $1.
Card Size: 2 1/2" x 4"
Set (24 cards): $40

- ☐ Warren Babe
- ☐ Robin Bawa
- ☐ Rob Brown
- ☐ Dean Cook (G)
- ☐ Scott Daniels
- ☐ Mario Desjardins
- ☐ Bill Harrington
- ☐ Greg Hawgood
- ☐ Serge Lajoie
- ☐ Dave Marcinyshyn
- ☐ Len Mark
- ☐ Rob McKinley (G)
- ☐ Casey McMillan
- ☐ Darcy Norton
- ☐ Kelly Para
- ☐ Doug Pickell
- ☐ Rudy Poeschek
- ☐ Mark Recchi
- ☐ Don Schmidt
- ☐ Ron Shudra
- ☐ Chris Tarnowski
- ☐ Steve Wienke
- ☐ Rich Wiest
- ☐ Team Photo

'87 - 88
KAMLOOPS BLAZERS / POLICE

Mark Recchi is the most expensive single at $15.
Singles start at $1.
Card Size: 2 1/2" x 3 1/2"
Set (24 cards): $30

- ☐ Warren Babe
- ☐ Paul Checknita
- ☐ Dave Chyzowski
- ☐ Dean Cook (G)
- ☐ Greg Davies
- ☐ Kim Deck
- ☐ Todd Decker
- ☐ Bill Harrington
- ☐ Greg Hawgood
- ☐ Phil Huber
- ☐ Steve Kloepzig
- ☐ Willie MacDonald (G)
- ☐ Pat MacLeod
- ☐ Casey McMillan
- ☐ Glenn Mulvenna
- ☐ Mike Needham
- ☐ Darcy Norton
- ☐ Devon Oleniuk
- ☐ Doug Pickell
- ☐ Garth Premak
- ☐ Mark Recchi
- ☐ Don Schmidt
- ☐ Alec Shelfo
- ☐ Team Photo

'88 - 89
KAMLOOPS BLAZERS / POLICE

Cards were originally issued in panels. Corey Hirsch and Darryl Sydor are the most expensive singles at $4. Singles start at $1. There are also 12 ad cards that came with the panels.
Card Size: 2 1/2" x 3 1/2"
Set (24 cards): $22

- ☐ Cory Anderson
- ☐ Pat Bingham
- ☐ Ed Bertuzzi
- ☐ Zac Boyer
- ☐ Trevor Buchanan
- ☐ Dave Chyzowski
- ☐ Dean Cook (G)
- ☐ Cory Crichton
- ☐ Kim Deck
- ☐ Ryan Harrison
- ☐ Brad Heschuk
- ☐ Corey Hirsch (G)
- ☐ Phil Huber
- ☐ Len Jorgenson
- ☐ Paul Kruse
- ☐ Dave Linford
- ☐ Pat MacLeod
- ☐ Darwin McClelland
- ☐ Cal McGowan
- ☐ Mike Needham
- ☐ Don Schmidt
- ☐ Brian Shantz
- ☐ Darryl Sydor
- ☐ Steve Yule

'89 - 90
KAMLOOPS BLAZERS / POLICE

Scott Niedermayer is the most expensive single at $5.
Singles start at $1.
Card Size: 2 1/2" x 3 1/2"
Set (24 cards): $20

- ☐ Len Barrie
- ☐ Craig Bonner
- ☐ Jarrett Bousquet
- ☐ Zac Boyer
- ☐ Murray Duval
- ☐ Shea Esselmont
- ☐ Todd Esselmont
- ☐ Todd Harris
- ☐ Corey Hirsch (G)
- ☐ Phil Huber
- ☐ Lance Johnson
- ☐ Paul Kruse
- ☐ Dean Malkoc
- ☐ Dale Mason
- ☐ Cal McGowan
- ☐ Joey Mittelsteadt
- ☐ Mike Needham
- ☐ Scott Niedermayer
- ☐ Brian Shantz
- ☐ Trevor Sim
- ☐ Darryl Sydor
- ☐ Jeff Watchorn
- ☐ Clayton Young
- ☐ Steve Yule

'93 - 94
KAMLOOPS BLAZERS / POLICE

Jarome Iginla is the most expensive single at $15.
Singles start at 75¢.
Card Size: 2 1/2" x 3 1/2"
Sponsors: Police, NL Radio
Set (24 cards): $30

- ☐ Nolan Baumgartner
- ☐ Rod Branch
- ☐ Jarret Deuling
- ☐ Shane Doan
- ☐ Hnat Domenichelli
- ☐ Scott Ferguson
- ☐ Greg Hart
- ☐ Jason Holland
- ☐ Ryan Huska
- ☐ Jarome Iginla
- ☐ Mike Josephson
- ☐ Aaron Keller
- ☐ Mike Kroopshoop
- ☐ Scott Loucks
- ☐ Brad Lukowich
- ☐ Bob Maudie
- ☐ Chris Murray
- ☐ Tyson Nash
- ☐ Steve Passmore (G)
- ☐ Rod Stevens
- ☐ Jason Strudwick
- ☐ Darcy Tucker
- ☐ Bob Westerby
- ☐ David Wilkie

'95 - 96
KAMLOOPS BLAZERS

We do not yet have a checklist for this series.

'96 - 97
KAMLOOPS BLAZERS

Singles start at 50¢.
Set (28 cards):

- ☐ Jeff Ainsworth
- ☐ Steve Albrecht
- ☐ Nils Antons
- ☐ Ajay Baines
- ☐ Konrad Brand
- ☐ Wade Burt
- ☐ Jake Deadmarsh
- ☐ Micki DuPont
- ☐ Steve Gainey
- ☐ Jonathan Hobson
- ☐ Drew Kehler
- ☐ Donnie Kinney
- ☐ Alan Manness
- ☐ Shawn McNeil
- ☐ Randy Petruk
- ☐ Clayton Pool
- ☐ Gennady Razin
- ☐ Robyn Regehr
- ☐ Blair Rota
- ☐ Thomas Scantlebury
- ☐ Steve Shrum
- ☐ Rob Skrlac
- ☐ Darcy Smith
- ☐ Chris St. Croix
- ☐ Darren Wright
- ☐ Ed Dempsey
- ☐ Spike Wallace
- ☐ Mascot Digger

'97 - 98
KAMLOOPS BLAZERS

Singles start at 50¢.
Set (24 cards):

- ☐ Nils Antons
- ☐ Ajay Baines
- ☐ Shane Belter
- ☐ Mike Brown
- ☐ Wade Burt
- ☐ Adam Dombrowski
- ☐ Brett Draney
- ☐ Micki DuPont
- ☐ Steve Gainey
- ☐ Gable Gross
- ☐ Jonathan Hobson
- ☐ Donnie Kinney
- ☐ Kevin Mackie
- ☐ Alan Manness
- ☐ Tyler Perry
- ☐ Randy Petruk
- ☐ Clayton Pool
- ☐ Gennady Razin
- ☐ Robyn Regehr
- ☐ Mark Scott
- ☐ Steve Shrum
- ☐ Chris St. Croix
- ☐ Shawn Thompson
- ☐ Ryan Thorpe

'98 - 99
KAMLOOPS BLAZERS

'98-99 Kamloops Blazers
Singles start at 50¢.
Set (24 cards):

- ☐ Jared Aulin
- ☐ Ajay Baines
- ☐ Anton Borodkin
- ☐ Mike Brown
- ☐ Paul Deniset
- ☐ Adam Dombrowski
- ☐ Brett Draney
- ☐ Micki DuPont
- ☐ Kenric Exner
- ☐ Jordon Flodell
- ☐ Steve Gainey
- ☐ Aaron Gionet
- ☐ Gable Gross
- ☐ Jonathan Hobson
- ☐ Donnie Kinney
- ☐ David Klatt
- ☐ Kevin Mackie
- ☐ Alan Manness
- ☐ Konstantin Panov
- ☐ Robyn Regehr
- ☐ Steve Shrum
- ☐ Chad Starling
- ☐ Chris St. Croix
- ☐ Ryan Thorpe

'99 - 00
KAMLOOPS BLAZERS

Singles start at 50¢.
Set (24 cards):

- ☐ Jared Aulin
- ☐ Jason Bone
- ☐ Anton Borodkin
- ☐ Erik Christensen
- ☐ Paul Deniset
- ☐ Blaine Depper
- ☐ Brett Draney
- ☐ Micki DuPont
- ☐ Aaron Gionet
- ☐ Gable Gross
- ☐ Jonathan Hobson
- ☐ Kyle Ladobruk
- ☐ Kevin Mackie
- ☐ Grant McCune
- ☐ Shaone Morrisonn
- ☐ Mike Munro
- ☐ Konstantin Panov
- ☐ Davis Parley
- ☐ Mark Rooneem
- ☐ Chad Schockenmaier
- ☐ Steve Shrum
- ☐ Chad Starling
- ☐ Jordan Walker
- ☐ Mascot Digger

'00 - 01
KAMLOOPS BLAZERS

Singles start at 50¢.
Set (24 cards):

- ☐ Jared Aulin
- ☐ Steve Belanger
- ☐ Tyler Boldt
- ☐ Josh Bonar
- ☐ Patrick Brandreth
- ☐ Erik Christensen
- ☐ Paul Elliott
- ☐ Aaron Gionet
- ☐ Gable Gross
- ☐ Jonathan Hobson
- ☐ Nikita Korovkin
- ☐ Derek Krestanovich
- ☐ Kyle Ladobruk
- ☐ Jarret Lukin
- ☐ Shaone Morrisonn
- ☐ Colton Orr
- ☐ Konstantin Panov
- ☐ Davis Parley
- ☐ Mark Rooneem
- ☐ Chad Schockenmaier
- ☐ Conlan Seder
- ☐ Tyler Sloan
- ☐ Scottie Upshall
- ☐ Mascot Digger

'01 - 02
KAMLOOPS BLAZERS

Singles start at 50¢.
Set (24 cards):

- ☐ Ryan Annesley
- ☐ Jared Aulin
- ☐ Steve Belanger
- ☐ Tyler Boldt
- ☐ Paul Brown
- ☐ Jonathan Bubnick
- ☐ Erik Christensen
- ☐ Aaron Gionet
- ☐ Scott Henkelman
- ☐ Ben Knopp
- ☐ Nikita Korovkin
- ☐ Casey Lee
- ☐ Jarret Lukin
- ☐ Keegan McAvoy
- ☐ Cam McCaffrey
- ☐ Shaone Morrisonn
- ☐ Colton Orr
- ☐ Davis Parley
- ☐ Josh Pokol
- ☐ Mark Rooneem
- ☐ Conlan Seder
- ☐ Alex Shelkunov
- ☐ Tyler Sloan
- ☐ Scottie Upshall

'02 - 03
KAMLOOPS BLAZERS

Singles start at 50¢.
Set (24 cards):

- ☐ Tyler Boldt
- ☐ Paul Brown
- ☐ Erik Christensen
- ☐ Cam Cunning
- ☐ Wade Davis
- ☐ Devon Dubnyk
- ☐ Aaron Gionet
- ☐ Moises Gutierrez
- ☐ Kris Hogg
- ☐ Grant Jacobsen
- ☐ Jonas Johansson
- ☐ Reid Jorgensen
- ☐ Nikita Korovkin
- ☐ Casey Lee
- ☐ Jason Lloyd
- ☐ Jarret Lukin
- ☐ Cam McCaffrey
- ☐ Josh Morrow
- ☐ Davis Parley
- ☐ Josh Pokol
- ☐ Jeff Schmidt
- ☐ Conlan Seder
- ☐ Scottie Upshall
- ☐ Mascot Digger

KELOWNA ROCKETS

'98 - 99
KELOWNA ROCKETS

Singles start at 50¢.
Set (28 cards):

- ☐ Ryan Cuthbert
- ☐ Jan Dusanek
- ☐ B.J. Fehr
- ☐ Vernon Fiddler
- ☐ Mitch Fritz
- ☐ Carsen Germyn
- ☐ Scott Hannan
- ☐ Bruce Harrison
- ☐ Trevor Hitchings
- ☐ J.J. Hunter
- ☐ Justin Jack
- ☐ Clint Keichinger
- ☐ Kevin Korol
- ☐ Corey Koski
- ☐ Quintin Laing
- ☐ Lindsey Materi
- ☐ Rory McDade
- ☐ Brett McLean
- ☐ Gavin McLeod
- ☐ Kiel McLeod
- ☐ Lubomir Pistek
- ☐ Robby Sandrock
- ☐ David Selthun
- ☐ Joe Suderman
- ☐ Kevin Swanson
- ☐ Ryan Wade
- ☐ Nolan Yonkman
- ☐ Mascot Rocky Raccoon

'00 - 01
KELOWNA ROCKETS

Singles start at 50¢.
Set (22 cards):

- ☐ Kiel McLeod
- ☐ Rory McDade
- ☐ Tomas Oravec
- ☐ Carsen Germyn
- ☐ Chris Di Ubaldo
- ☐ Ryan Cuthbert
- ☐ Randall Gelech
- ☐ Blaine Depper
- ☐ Gavin McLeod
- ☐ Bart Rushmer
- ☐ Tyler Mosienko
- ☐ Josh Gorges
- ☐ Jason Stone
- ☐ Brett Palin
- ☐ Richie Regehr
- ☐ David Selthun
- ☐ Seth Leonard
- ☐ Jan Fadrny
- ☐ Joe Suderman
- ☐ Kevin Swanson
- ☐ Mascot Rocky Raccoon
- ☐ Marc Habscheid

KELOWNA WINGS

'83 - 84
KELOWNA WINGS / ESSO

Brent Gilchrist is the most expensive single at $3.
Singles start at $1.
Photo Size: 8" x 10 3/4"
Set (23 cards): $22

- ☐ Craig Butz
- ☐ Bruno Campese (G)
- ☐ Grant Delcourt
- ☐ R.J. Dundas
- ☐ Rocky Dundas
- ☐ Jeff Fenton
- ☐ Mark Fioretti
- ☐ Brent Gilchrist
- ☐ Mikael Jonsson
- ☐ Cam Lozoruk
- ☐ Dave MacDonald
- ☐ Dave McLay
- ☐ Darwein Moeller
- ☐ Ed Palichuk
- ☐ Jeff Sharples
- ☐ Bob Shaw
- ☐ Shawn Vincent
- ☐ Tod Voshell
- ☐ Darcy Wakaluk
- ☐ Chad Walker
- ☐ Stuart Wenaas
- ☐ Terry Zaporkan
- ☐ Greg Zuk

KINGSTON CANADIANS

'81 - 82
KINGSTON CANADIANS / POLICE

Kirk Muller is the most expensive single at $15.
Singles start at $1.
Card Size: 2 5/8" x 4"
Set (25 cards): $30

- ☐ 1 Canadians Logo
- ☐ 2 Scott MacLellan
- ☐ 3 Dave Courtemanche
- ☐ 4 Mark Reade
- ☐ 5 Shawn Babcock
- ☐ 6 Phil Bourque
- ☐ 7 Ian MacInnis
- ☐ 8 Neail Trineer
- ☐ 9 Syl Grandmaitre
- ☐ 10 Carmine Vani
- ☐ 11 Chuck Brimmer
- ☐ 12 Mike Linseman
- ☐ 13 Steve Seguin
- ☐ 14 Dan Wood
- ☐ 15 Kirk Muller
- ☐ 16 Jim Aldred
- ☐ 17 Rick Wilson
- ☐ 18 Mike Siltala
- ☐ 19 Howie Scruton
- ☐ 20 Mike Stothers
- ☐ 21 Dennis Smith
- ☐ 22 Steve Richey (G)
- ☐ 23 Mike Moffat (G)
- ☐ 24 Jim Morrison
- ☐ 25 Randy Plumb

'82 - 83
KINGSTON CANADIANS / POLICE

Singles start at $1.
Card Size: 2 5/8" x 4"
Set (27 cards): $15

- ☐ 1 Jim Morrison
- ☐ 2 Dennis Smith
- ☐ 3 Curtis Collin
- ☐ 4 Joel Brown
- ☐ 5 Ron Handy
- ☐ 6 Carmine Vani
- ☐ 7 Al Andrews (G)
- ☐ 8 Mike Siltala
- ☐ 9 Syl Grandmaitre
- ☐ 10 Steve Seguin
- ☐ 11 Brian Dobbin
- ☐ 12 Mark Reade
- ☐ 13 John Kemp (G)
- ☐ 14 Dan Mahon
- ☐ 15 Keith Knight
- ☐ 16 Ron Sanko
- ☐ 17 John Landry
- ☐ 18 Chris Brant
- ☐ 19 Dave Simurda
- ☐ 20 Mike Lafoy
- ☐ 21 Scott MacLellan
- ☐ 22 Brad Walcot
- ☐ 23 Steve Richey (G)
- ☐ 24 Rod Graham
- ☐ 25 Ben Levesque
- ☐ 26 Checklist/Logo
- ☐ 27 Int. Hall of Fame

'83 - 84
KINGSTON CANADIANS / POLICE

Singles start at $1.
Card Size: 2 5/8" x 3 5/8"
Set (30 cards): $15

- ☐ 1 Checklist
- ☐ 2 Dennis Smith
- ☐ 3 Ben Lévesque
- ☐ 4 Constable Arie Moraal
- ☐ 5 Tom Allen
- ☐ 6 Mike Plesh
- ☐ 7 Roger Belanger
- ☐ 8 Jeff Chychrun
- ☐ 9 Mike King
- ☐ 10 Scott Metcalfe
- ☐ 11 David Lundmark
- ☐ 12 Tim Salmon
- ☐ 13 Ted Linseman

☐ 14 Chris Clifford (G)
☐ 15 Todd Elik
☐ 16 Kevin Conway
☐ 17 Barry Burkholder
☐ 18 Joel Brown
☐ 19 Steve King
☐ 20 Craig Kales
☐ 21 John Humphries
☐ 22 David James
☐ 23 Dave Simurda
☐ 24 Allen Bishop
☐ 25 Jeff Hogg (G)
☐ 26 Rick Cornacchia
☐ 27 Ken Slater
☐ 28 Constable B. Dextater
☐ 29 Checklist/ Logo
☐ 30 Int. Hall of Fame

'84 - 85
KINGSTON CANADIANS / POLICE

Singles start at $1.
Card Size: 2 5/8" x 3 5/8"
Set (30 cards): $15

☐ 1 Kington Police logo
☐ 2 Rick Cornaccia
☐ 3 Constable Arie Moraal
☐ 4 Ken Slater
☐ 5 Checklist/Logo
☐ 6 Scott Metcalfe
☐ 7 Chris Clifford (G)
☐ 8 Todd Elik
☐ 9 Len Spratt (G)
☐ 10 Mike Plesh
☐ 11 Marc Lyons
☐ 12 Barry Burkholder
☐ 13 Rick Fera
☐ 14 David Hoover
☐ 15 Andy Rivers
☐ 16 Marc Laforge
☐ 17 Peter Viscovich
☐ 18 Jeff Chychrun
☐ 19 Wayne Erskine
☐ 20 Todd Clarke
☐ 21 Darren Wright
☐ 22 Tony Rocca
☐ 23 Brian Verbeek
☐ 24 Herb Raglan
☐ 25 Daril Holmes
☐ 26 Len Coyle
☐ 27 Ted Linseman
☐ 28 Int. Hall of Fame
☐ 29 Troy MacNevin
☐ 30 Peter Campbell

'85 - 86
KINGSTON CANADIANS / POLICE

Singles start at $1.
Card Size: 2 5/8" x 3 5/8"
Set (30 cards): $15

☐ 1 Kingston Police
☐ 2 Dale Sandles
☐ 3 Constable Arie Moraal
☐ 4 Fred O'Donnell
☐ 5 Checklist/ Logo
☐ 6 Scott Metcalfe
☐ 7 Chris Clifford (G)
☐ 8 Steve Seftel
☐ 9 Andy Pearson (G)
☐ 10 Jeff Cornelius
☐ 11 Marc Lyons
☐ 12 Barry Burkholder
☐ 13 Bryan Fogarty
☐ 14 Jeff Sirkka
☐ 15 Scott Pearson
☐ 16 Marc Laforge
☐ 17 Peter Viscovich
☐ 18 Chychrun (Chycren)
☐ 19 Wayne Erskine
☐ 20 Todd Clarke
☐ 21 Darren Wright
☐ 22 Mike Maurice
☐ 23 Brian Verbeek
☐ 24 Mike Fiset
☐ 25 Daril Holmes
☐ 26 Len Coyle
☐ 27 Ted Linseman
☐ 28 Int. Hall of Fame
☐ 29 Troy MacNevin
☐ 30 Peter Campbell

'86 - 87
KINGSTON CANADIANS / POLICE

Singles start at 50¢.
Card Size: 2 5/8" x 3 5/8"
Set (30 cards): $10

☐ 1 Checklist/ Logo
☐ 2 Fred O'Donnell
☐ 3 Constable Arie Moraal
☐ 4 Dale Sandles
☐ 5 Kingston Police
☐ 6 Brian Tessier (G)
☐ 7 Franco Giammarco (G)
☐ 8 Peter Liptrott
☐ 9 Chris Clifford (G)
☐ 10 Scott Metcalfe
☐ 11 Scott Pearson
☐ 12 Bryan Fogarty
☐ 13 Daril Holmes
☐ 14 Andy Rivers
☐ 15 Troy MacNevin
☐ 16 Marc Laforge
☐ 17 Wayne Erskine
☐ 18 Peter Viskovich
☐ 19 Mike Maurice
☐ 20 Steve Seftel
☐ 21 Chad Badaway
☐ 22 Marc Lyons
☐ 23 Jeff Sirkka
☐ 24 Mike Fiset
☐ 25 John Battice
☐ 26 Len Coyle
☐ 27 Sloan Torti
☐ 28 Alain Laforge
☐ 29 Ted Linseman
☐ 30 Peter Campbell

'87 - 88
KINGSTON CANADIANS / POLICE

Singles start at 50¢.
Card Size: 2 5/8" x 3 5/8"
Set (30 cards): $12

☐ 1 Constable Arie Moraal
☐ 2 Gord Wood
☐ 3 Kingston Police
☐ 4 Jacques Tremblay
☐ 5 Rhonda Sheridan
☐ 6 Jeff Wilson (G)
☐ 7 Franco Giammarco (G)
☐ 8 Peter Liptrott
☐ 9 David Weiss (G)
☐ 10 Joel Morin
☐ 11 Mark Turner
☐ 12 Jeff Sirkka
☐ 13 James Henckle
☐ 14 Mike Bodnarchuk
☐ 15 Mike Cavanaugh
☐ 16 Darcy Cahill
☐ 17 Kevin Falesy
☐ 18 Dean Pella
☐ 19 Brad Gratton
☐ 20 Steve Seftel
☐ 21 Bryan Fogarty
☐ 22 Scott Pearson
☐ 23 Tyler Pella
☐ 24 Mike Fiset
☐ 25 John Baddice
☐ 26 Len Coyle
☐ 27 Geoff Schneider
☐ 28 Chris Lukey
☐ 29 Trevor Smith
☐ 30 Peter Campbell

KINGSTON FRONTENACS

'97 - 98
KINGSTON FRONTENACS

We do not yet have a checklist for this series.

'98 - 99
KINGSTON FRONTENACS

We do not yet have a checklist for this series.

'99 - 00
KINGSTON FRONTENACS

The most expensive singles are Andrew Raycroft and Michael Zigomanis. Singles start at 50¢.
Set (23 cards): $12

☐ Sean Avery
☐ Eric Braff
☐ Brett Clouthier
☐ Chris Cook
☐ Sean Griffin
☐ Brad Horan
☐ Andrew Ianiero
☐ Matt Junkins
☐ Darryl Knight
☐ Travis Lisabeth
☐ Doug MacIver
☐ Shaun Peet
☐ Jason Polera
☐ Andrew Raycroft (G)
☐ Jonathan Schill
☐ Jean-Francois Seguin
☐ Tomas Skvaridlo
☐ Mike Smith
☐ Cory** Stillman
☐ Nathan Tennant
☐ Darryl Thomson
☐ Michael Zigomanis
☐ Checklist

'00 - 01
KINGSTON FRONTENACS

Singles start at 50¢.
Set (26 cards):

☐ 1 Header Card
☐ 2 Mascot Frontenac
☐ 3 Bignell / Mavety
☐ 4 Eric Braff
☐ 5 Derek Campbell
☐ 6 Brett Clouthier
☐ 7 Chris Cook
☐ 8 Peter Hamerlik
☐ 9 Brad Horan
☐ 10 Andrew Ianiero
☐ 11 Travis Lisabeth
☐ 12 Doug MacIver
☐ 13 Justin McCutcheon
☐ 14 Sean McMorrow
☐ 15 Shane O'Brien
☐ 16 Glenn Ridler
☐ 17 Corey Sabourin
☐ 18 Jean-Francois Seguin
☐ 19 Tomas Skvaridlo
☐ 20 Cory Stillman
☐ 21 Nathan Tennant
☐ 22 Darryl Thomson
☐ 23 Brody Todd
☐ 24 Michael Zigomanis
☐ 25 Coca-Cola

'01 - 02
KINGSTON FRONTENACS

Singles start at 50¢.
Set (25 cards):

☐ 1 Header Card
☐ 2 Chris Cook
☐ 3 Lou Dickenson
☐ 4 Josh Gratton
☐ 5 Peter Hamerlik
☐ 6 Chris Hardill
☐ 7 Brad Horan
☐ 8 Andrew Ianiero
☐ 9 Drew Kivell
☐ 10 Sean Langdon
☐ 11 Doug MacIver
☐ 12 Brandon McBride
☐ 13 Justin McCutcheon
☐ 14 Kyle Neufeld
☐ 15 Shane O'Brien
☐ 16 Scott Sheppard
☐ 17 Mike Smith
☐ 18 Sean Stefanski
☐ 19 Anthony Stewart
☐ 20 Cory Stillman
☐ 21 Justin Suda
☐ 22 Nathan Tennant
☐ 23 Ed Van Herpt
☐ 24 Nick Van Herpt
☐ 25 Sponsor Coca-Cola

KITCHENER RANGERS

'82 - 83
KITCHENER RANGERS / POLICE

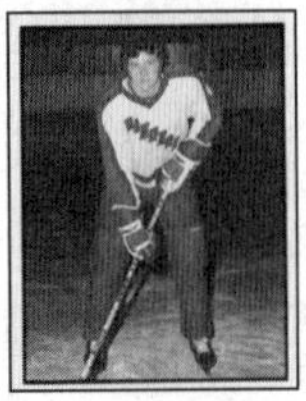

Al MacInnis is the most expensive single at $20. Singles start at $1.
Card Size: 2 3/4" x 3 1/2"
Set (30 cards): $35

☐ 1 Waterloo Police
☐ 2 Chief Harold Basse
☐ 3 Sponsor Logo
☐ 4 Joe Crozier
☐ 5 Checklist/ Logo
☐ 6 Kerry Kerch (G)
☐ 7 Tom St. James
☐ 8 Wendell Young (G)
☐ 9 David Shaw
☐ 10 Darryl Boudreau (G)
☐ 11 David Bruce
☐ 12 Wayne Presley
☐ 13 Garnet McKechney
☐ 14 Kevin Petendra
☐ 15 Brian Wilks
☐ 16 Jim Quinn
☐ 17 Al MacInnis
☐ 18 Dave Nicholls
☐ 19 Mike Eagles
☐ 20 Mike Hough
☐ 21 Greg Puhalski
☐ 22 Darren Wright
☐ 23 Todd Steffan
☐ 24 John Tucker
☐ 25 Kent Paynter
☐ 26 Andy O'Brien
☐ 27 Les Bradley
☐ 28 Scott Biggs
☐ 29 Chris Martin
☐ 30 Dave Webster

'83 - 84
KITCHENER RANGERS / POLICE

Singles start at $1.
Card Size: 2 3/4" x 3 1/2"
Set (30 cards): $15

☐ 1 Joe Mantione (G)
☐ 2 Jim Quinn
☐ 3 Checklist/Logo
☐ 4 Rob MacInnis
☐ 5 Louie Berardicurti
☐ 6 Neil Sandilands
☐ 7 Darren Wright
☐ 8 Tom Barrett
☐ 9 Brian Wilks
☐ 10 Garnet McKechney
☐ 11 David Bruce
☐ 12 Kent Paynter
☐ 13 Sponsor Logos
☐ 14 Scott Kerr
☐ 15 Greg Puhalski
☐ 16 Wayne Presley
☐ 17 Carmine Vani
☐ 18 Shawn Burr
☐ 19 Dave Latta
☐ 20 John Tucker
☐ 21 Mike Stevens
☐ 22 Chief Harold Basse
☐ 23 Waterloo Police
☐ 24 Peter Bakovic
☐ 25 Brian Ross
☐ 26 Brad Balshin
☐ 27 David Shaw
☐ 28 Chris Trainer
☐ 29 Les Bradley
☐ 30 Ray LeBlanc (G)

'84 - 85
KITCHENER RANGERS / POLICE

Singles start at $1.
Card Size: 2 3/4" x 3 1/2"
Set (30 cards): $15

☐ 1 Waterloo Police
☐ 2 Chief Harold Basse
☐ 3 Garnet McKechney
☐ 4 Tom Barrett
☐ 5 Checklist/ Logo
☐ 6 Mike Bishop (G)
☐ 7 Craig Wolanin
☐ 8 Steve Marcolini
☐ 9 Peter Langlois
☐ 10 Dave Weiss (G)
☐ 11 Ken Alexander
☐ 12 Ian Pound
☐ 13 Doug Stromback
☐ 14 Joel Brown
☐ 15 Brian Wilks
☐ 16 Robert Rubic
☐ 17 Kent Paynter
☐ 18 Jon Helsinki
☐ 19 Greg Puhalski
☐ 20 Wayne Presley
☐ 21 Dave McLlwain
☐ 22 Shawn Burr
☐ 23 Dave Latta
☐ 24 John Keller
☐ 25 Mike Stevens
☐ 26 Sponsor Logos
☐ 27 Richard Adolfi
☐ 28 Grant Sanders
☐ 29 Les Bradley
☐ 30 Sponsor Logos

'85 - 86
KITCHENER RANGERS / POLICE

Singles start at $1.
Card Size: 2 3/4" x 3 1/2"
Set (30 cards): $15

☐ 1 Waterloo Police
☐ 2 Chief Harold Basse
☐ 3 Sponsor Logo
☐ 4 Tom Barrett
☐ 5 Checklist/ Logo
☐ 6 Dave Weiss (G)
☐ 7 Steve Marcolini
☐ 8 Kevin Grant
☐ 9 Ken Alexander
☐ 10 Mike Volpe (G)
☐ 11 Ian Pound
☐ 12 Brett MacDonald
☐ 13 Scott Taylor
☐ 14 Greg Hankkio
☐ 15 Mike Morrison
☐ 16 Mike Wolak
☐ 17 Craig Booker
☐ 18 Jeff Noble
☐ 19 Shawn Tyers
☐ 20 Peter Lisy
☐ 21 Shawn Burr
☐ 22 David Latta
☐ 23 Ron Sanko
☐ 24 Doug Jones
☐ 25 Paul Penelton
☐ 26 Blair MacPherson
☐ 27 Richard Hawkins
☐ 28 Brad Sparkes
☐ 29 Ron Goodall
☐ 30 Kevin Duguay

'86 - 87
KITCHENER RANGERS / POLICE

Singles start at 75¢.
Card Size: 2 3/4" x 3 1/2"
Set (30 cards): $12

☐ 1 Waterloo Police
☐ 2 Chief Harold Basse
☐ 3 Sponsor Logo
☐ 4 Tom Barrett
☐ 5 Checklist/ Logo
☐ 6 Dave Weiss (G)
☐ 7 Darren Rumble
☐ 8 Kevin Garnett
☐ 9 Len Fawcett
☐ 10 Darren Beals (G)
☐ 11 Ed Kister
☐ 12 Scott Taylor
☐ 13 Darren Moxam
☐ 14 Paul Epoch
☐ 15 Richard Borgo
☐ 16 Allan Lake
☐ 17 Jeff Noble
☐ 18 Mark Montanari
☐ 19 Jim Hutton
☐ 20 Kelly Cain
☐ 21 Craig Booker
☐ 22 David Latta
☐ 23 Doug Jones
☐ 24 Gary Callahan
☐ 25 Bruno Lapensee
☐ 26 Scott Montgomery
☐ 27 Ron Goodall
☐ 28 Discount Card
☐ 29 Steve Ewing
☐ 30 Joe McDonnell

'87 - 88
KITCHENER RANGERS / POLICE

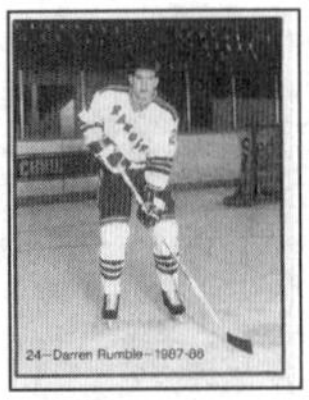

Singles start at 75¢.
Card Size: 2 3/4" x 3 1/2"
Set (30 cards): $12

☐ 1 Waterloo Police
☐ 2 Chief Harold Basse
☐ 3 hildren's Bonus Card
☐ 4 Joe McDonnell
☐ 5 Checklist/ Logo
☐ 6 Gus Morschauser (G)
☐ 7 Rick Allain
☐ 8 Kevin Grant
☐ 9 Rob Thiel
☐ 10 Darren Beals (G)
☐ 11 Cory Keenan
☐ 12 Rival Fullum
☐ 13 Tony Crisp
☐ 14 Tyler Ertel
☐ 15 Richard Borgo
☐ 16 Steven Rice
☐ 17 Rob Sangster
☐ 18 Jeff Noble
☐ 19 Mark Montanari
☐ 20 Jim Mutton
☐ 21 Craig Booker
☐ 22 Doug Jones
☐ 23 Randy Pearce
☐ 24 Darren Rumble
☐ 25 Joe Ranger
☐ 26 Sponsor
☐ 27 Ron Goodall
☐ 28 Allan Lake
☐ 29 Scott Montgomery
☐ 30 Sponsor Card

'88 - 89
KITCHENER RANGERS / POLICE

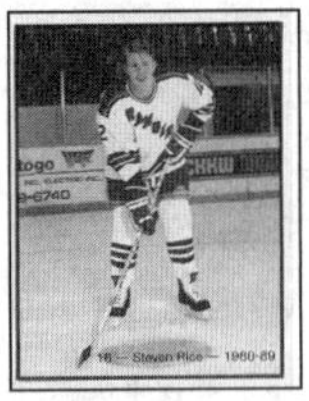

Singles start at 75¢.
Card Size: 2 3/4" x 3 1/2"
Set (30 cards): $10

☐ 1 Waterloo Police
☐ 2 Chief Harold Basse
☐ 3 Bonus Card
☐ 4 Joe McDonnell
☐ 5 Checklist/ Logo
☐ 6 Mike Torchia (G)
☐ 7 Rick Allain
☐ 8 John Uniac
☐ 9 Rob Thiel
☐ 10 Gus Morschauser (G)
☐ 11 Cory Keenan
☐ 12 Rival Fullum
☐ 13 Jason Firth
☐ 14 Joey St. Aubin
☐ 15 Richard Borgo
☐ 16 Steven Rice
☐ 17 Rob Sangster
☐ 18 Gilbert Dionne
☐ 19 Mark Montanari
☐ 20 Shayne Stevenson
☐ 21 Pierre Gagnon
☐ 22 Kirk Tomlinson
☐ 23 Randy Pearce
☐ 24 Brad Barton
☐ 25 Chris LiPuma
☐ 26 Sponsor Logo
☐ 27 Steve Herniman
☐ 28 Darren Rumble
☐ 29 Rick Chambers
☐ 30 Sponsor Logo

'89 - 90
KITCHENER RANGERS / POLICE

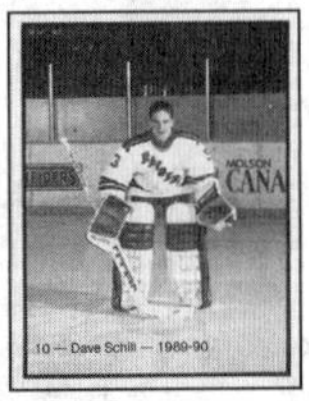

Singles start at 50¢.
Card Size: 2 3/4" x 3 1/2"
Set (30 cards): $10

☐ 1 Waterloo Police
☐ 2 Chief Harold Basse
☐ 3 Children's Bonus Card
☐ 4 Joe McDonnell
☐ 5 Checklist/ Logo
☐ 6 Mike Torchia (G)
☐ 7 Rick Allain
☐ 8 John Uniac
☐ 9 Jack Williams
☐ 10 Dave Schill (G)
☐ 11 John Copley
☐ 12 Cory Keenan
☐ 13 Rival Fullum
☐ 14 Jason Firth
☐ 15 Joey St. Aubin
☐ 16 Richard Borgo
☐ 17 Steven Rice
☐ 18 Rob Sangster
☐ 19 Gilbert Dionne
☐ 20 Jamie Israel
☐ 21 Shayne Stevenson
☐ 22 Gib Tucker
☐ 23 Randy Pearce
☐ 24 Brad Barton
☐ 25 Chris LiPuma
☐ 26 Sponsor Logos
☐ 27 Kevin Falesy
☐ 28 Steve Smith
☐ 29 Rick Chambers
☐ 30 Sponsor Logos

'90 - 91
KITCHENER RANGERS / POLICE

Singles start at 50¢.
Card Size: 2 3/4" x 3 1/2"
Set (30 cards): $10

☐ 1 Waterloo Police
☐ 2 Chief Harold Basse
☐ 3 Joe McDonnell
☐ 4 Rick Chambers
☐ 5 Checklist
☐ 6 Mike Torchia (G)
☐ 7 Len DeVuono
☐ 8 John Uniac
☐ 9 Steve Smith
☐ 10 Rob Stopar (G)
☐ 11 Tony McCabe
☐ 12 Jason Firth
☐ 13 Joey St. Aubin
☐ 14 Richard Borgo
☐ 15 Norm Dezainde
☐ 16 Jeff Szeryk
☐ 17 Derek Gauthier
☐ 18 Jamie Israel
☐ 19 Shayne McCosh
☐ 20 Gib Tucker
☐ 21 Paul McCallion
☐ 22 Mike Allen
☐ 23 Brad Barton
☐ 24 Chris LiPuma
☐ 25 Justin Cullen
☐ 26 Sponsor Logos
☐ 27 Rod Saarinen
☐ 28 Jack Williams
☐ 29 Steve Rice
☐ 30 Sponsor Logos

'96 - 97
KITCHENER RANGERS

We do not yet have a checklist for this series.

'97 - 98
KITCHENER RANGERS

We do not yet have a checklist for this series.

'98 - 99
KITCHENER RANGERS

We do not yet have a checklist for this series.

'99 - 00
KITCHENER RANGERS

We do not yet have a checklist for this series.

'00 - 01
KITCHENER RANGERS

We do not yet have a checklist for this series.

'01 - 02
KITCHENER RANGERS

Singles start at 50¢.
Card Size: 2 1/2" x 3 1/2"
Set (30 cards):

☐ Roster (richards
☐ Cober Printing
☐ TD Canada Trust
☐ Scott Dickie
☐ Nick Policelli

☐ Thomas Harrison
☐ Ryan Ramsay
☐ Steve Eminger
☐ Petr Kanko
☐ Mike Amodeo
☐ Matt Grenier
☐ Derek Roy
☐ André Benoit
☐ Mike Richards
☐ Petr Hemsky
☐ John Osborne
☐ Rafa Martynowski
☐ Marcus Smith
☐ T.J. Eason
☐ Adam Keefe
☐ Matt Harpwood
☐ Bill Kinkel
☐ Jeff Szwez
☐ Chad McCaffrey
☐ Peter DeBoer
☐ Steve Spott
☐ Dan Lebold
☐ Derek Roy
☐ Steve Eminger
☐ Mascot Tex

LAKE SUPERIOR STATE LAKERS

'91 - 92
LAKE SUPERIOR STATE LAKERS

Brian Rolston is the most expensive single at $2. Singles start at 50¢.
Card Size: 2 1/2" x 3 1/2"
Sponsor: None
Set (33 cards): $15

☐ Keith Aldridge
☐ Dan Angelelli
☐ Mark Astley
☐ Mike Bachusz
☐ Steve Barnes
☐ Clayton Beddoes
☐ David Gartshore
☐ Tim Hanley
☐ Matt Hanson
☐ John Hendry
☐ Dean Hulett
☐ Jeff Jackson
☐ Blaine Lacher (G)
☐ Darrin Madeley (G)
☐ Mike Matteucci
☐ Scott McCabe
☐ Kurt Miller
☐ Mike Morin
☐ Jay Ness
☐ Gino Pulente
☐ Brian Rolston
☐ Paul Sass
☐ Michael Smith
☐ Wayne Strachan
☐ Sean Tallaire
☐ Adam Thompson
☐ Jason Trzcinski
☐ Rob Valicevic
☐ Jason Welch
☐ Darren Wetherill
☐ Brad Willner
☐ Team Photo
☐ Team Photo

'92 - 93
LAKE SUPERIOR STATE LAKERS

We do not yet have a checklist for this series.

LETHBRIDGE HURRICANES

'88 - 89
LETHBRIDGE HURRICANES / POLICE

This set was originally issued in three-card panels. One card from each panel was an ad/coupon card. Singles start at 75¢.
Card Size: 2 1/2" x 3 1/2"
Set (24 cards): $10

☐ Mark Bassen

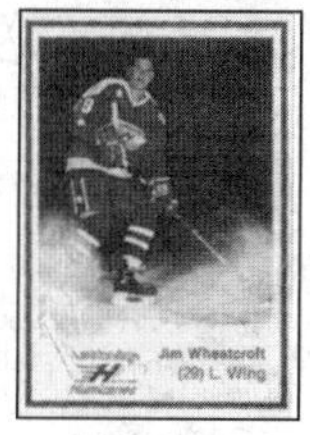

☐ Pete Berthelsen
☐ Bryan Bosch
☐ Paul Checknita
☐ Kelly Ens
☐ Jeff Ferguson (G)
☐ Scott Fukami
☐ Colin Gregor
☐ Mark Greig
☐ Rob Hale
☐ Ted Hutchings
☐ Dusty Imoo (G)
☐ Ivan Jessey
☐ Mark Kuntz
☐ Corey Lyons
☐ Shane Mazutinec
☐ Casey McMillan
☐ Pat Pylypuik
☐ Brad Rubachuk
☐ Jason Ruff
☐ Chad Seibel
☐ Wes Walz
☐ Jim Wheatcroft
☐ Team Photo

'89 - 90
LETHBRIDGE HURRICANES / POLICE

This set was originally issued in three-card panels. One card from each panel was an ad/coupon card. Singles start at 50¢.
Card Size: 2 1/2" x 3 1/2"
Set (24 cards): $10

☐ Doug Barrault
☐ Pete Berthelsen
☐ Bryan Bosch
☐ Kelly Ens
☐ Mark Greig
☐ Ron Gunville
☐ Rob Hale
☐ Neil Hawryluk
☐ David Holzer
☐ Dusty Imoo (G)
☐ Darcy Kaminski
☐ Bob Loucks
☐ Corey Lyons
☐ Duane Maruschak
☐ Jamie McLennan (G)
☐ Shane Peacock
☐ Pat Pylypuik
☐ Gary Reilly
☐ Brad Rubachuk
☐ Jason Ruff
☐ Kevin St. Jacques
☐ Wes Walz
☐ Darcy Werenka
☐ Brad Zimmer

'93 - 94
LETHBRIDGE HURRICANES / POLICE

This set was originally issued in three-card panels. One card from each panel was an ad/coupon card. Singles start at 50¢.
Card Size: 2 1/2" x 3 1/2"
Set (24 cards): $10

☐ Rob Daun
☐ Derek Diener
☐ Kirk DeWalle
☐ Scott Giuco
☐ David Jesiolowski
☐ Todd MacIsaac
☐ Stan Matwijiw
☐ Larry McMorran
☐ Brad Mehalko
☐ Shane Peacock
☐ Randy Perry
☐ Byron Ritchie
☐ Domenic Rittis
☐ Bryce Salvador
☐ Lee Sorochan
☐ Ryan Smith
☐ Mark Szoke
☐ Scott Townsend
☐ David Trofimenkoff
☐ Ivan Vologjaninov
☐ Jason Widmer
☐ Derek Wood
☐ Aaron Zarowny
☐ Mascot Twister

'99 - 00
LETHBRIDGE HURRICANES

Singles start at 50¢.
Set (25 cards):

☐ Derek Atkinson
☐ Brian Ballman
☐ Nathan Barrett
☐ Brady Block
☐ Scott Borders
☐ Phil Cole
☐ Radek Duda
☐ Simon Ferguson
☐ Jordon Flodell
☐ Eric Godard
☐ Jason Hegberg
☐ Brandon Janes
☐ Ryan Jorde
☐ Dustin Kazak
☐ Angel Krstev
☐ Petr Kudrna
☐ Darren Lynch
☐ Warren McCutcheon
☐ Justin Ossachuk
☐ Derek Parker
☐ Brian Patterson
☐ Derrick Ruck
☐ Thomas Scantlebury
☐ Eric Sonnenberg
☐ Chad Yaremko

LONDON KNIGHTS

'85 - 86
LONDON KNIGHTS / POLICE

Brendan Shanahan is the most expensive single at $45. Singles start at $1.
Card Size: 2 3/4" x 3 1/2"
Set (30 cards): $55
Album: $5

☐ 1 Chief LaVerne Shipley
☐ 2 Joe Ranger
☐ 3 Checklist/ Logo
☐ 4 Don Boyd
☐ 5 Harry E. Sparling
☐ 6 Murray Nystrom
☐ 7 Bob Halkidis
☐ 8 Morgan Watts
☐ 9 Brendan Shanahan
☐ 10 Brian Dobbin
☐ 11 Ed Kister
☐ 12 Darin Smith
☐ 13 Greg Puhalski
☐ 14 Dave Haas
☐ 15 Pete McLeod
☐ 16 Frank Tremblay
☐ 17 Matthew Smyth
☐ 18 Glen Leslie
☐ 19 Mike Zombo
☐ 20 Jamie Groke
☐ 21 Brad Schlegel
☐ 22 Kelly Cain
☐ 23 Tom Allen
☐ 24 Rod Gerow
☐ 25 Pat Vachon
☐ 26 Paul Cook
☐ 27 Jeff Reese (G)
☐ 28 Fred Kean
☐ 29 Scott Cumming (G)
☐ 30 John Williams

'86 - 87
LONDON KNIGHTS / POLICE

Brendan Shanahan is the most expensive single at $30. Singles start at $1.
Card Size: 2 3/4" x 3 1/2"
Set (30 cards): $45
Album: 5.00

☐ 1 Chief LaVerne Shipley
☐ 2 Mayor Tom Gosnell
☐ 3 Checklist/ Logo
☐ 4 Wayne Maxner
☐ 5 Harry E. Sparling
☐ 6 Brendan Shanahan
☐ 7 Pat Vachon
☐ 8 Brad Schlegel
☐ 9 Barry Earhart
☐ 10 Jean Marc MacKenzie
☐ 11 Jason Simon
☐ 12 Jim Sprott
☐ 13 Bill Long
☐ 14 Murray Nystrom
☐ 15 Shayne Stevenson
☐ 16 Don Martin
☐ 17 Ian Pound
☐ 18 Peter Lisy
☐ 19 Steve Marcolini
☐ 20 Craig Majaury
☐ 21 Trevor Dam
☐ 22 Dave Akey
☐ 23 Dennis McEwen
☐ 24 Shane Whelan
☐ 25 Greg Hankkio
☐ 26 Pat Kelly
☐ 27 Stephen Titus (G)
☐ 28 Fred Kean
☐ 29 Chris Somers (G)
☐ 30 Gord Clark

'00 - 01
LONDON KNIGHTS / BANK OF MONTRÉAL

Singles start at 50¢.
Set (35 cards):

☐ 1 Mark & Dale Hunter
☐ 2 Bobby Turner
☐ 3 Matt Cooper
☐ 4 Aaron Lobb
☐ 5 Lou Dickenson
☐ 6 Lindsay Hofford
☐ 7 Kyle Neufeld
☐ 8 Petr Hemsky
☐ 9 Rick Nash
☐ 10 Brent Varty
☐ 11 Daniel Bois
☐ 12 Joel Scherban
☐ 13 Brian Dobbin
☐ 14 Aaron Molnar
☐ 15 Mike Clarke
☐ 16 Ian Turner
☐ 17 John Eminger
☐ 18 Daniel Jancevski
☐ 19 Jason Davies
☐ 20 Logan Hunter
☐ 21 Checklist
☐ 22 Don Brankley
☐ 23 Josh Chambers
☐ 24 Chris Kelly
☐ 25 Matthew Albiani
☐ 26 Matt Junkins
☐ 27 Mike Stathopulos
☐ 1A Chris Kelly
☐ 2A Mark Hunter
☐ 3A Daniel Jancevski
☐ 4A Logan Hunter
☐ 5A Dale Hunter
☐ 6A Daniel Bois
☐ 7A Mascot Scorch
☐ 8A Rick Nash

'01 - 02
LONDON KNIGHTS

Singles start at 50¢.
Set (30 cards):

☐ Checklist
☐ Sean Dixon
☐ Dennis Wideman
☐ Patrick Barbieri
☐ Bryan Thompson
☐ Chris Bain
☐ Mike Stathopoulos
☐ Danny Bois
☐ Matt Iannetta
☐ Charlie Stephens
☐ Dylan Hunter
☐ Logan Hunter
☐ Sean McMorrow
☐ Chad Thompson
☐ Rick Steadman
☐ Matt Junkins
☐ Dan Buccella
☐ Rick Nash
☐ Robbie Colangelo
☐ Matt Iorianni
☐ Ian Turner
☐ Corey Perry
☐ Jan Chovan
☐ Matt Weir
☐ Alex White
☐ Jacques Beaulieu
☐ Lindsay Hofford
☐ Dale Hunter
☐ Don Brankley
☐ Mission hockey ad

'02 - 03
LONDON KNIGHTS / CHARTER HOUSE

Singles start at 50¢.
Set (30 cards):

☐ 1 Team photo
☐ 2 Dennis Wideman
☐ 3 Logan Hunter
☐ 4 Corey Perry
☐ 5 Mike Stathopoulos
☐ 6 Danny Bois
☐ 7 Ryan Hare
☐ 8 Dylan Hunter
☐ 9 Rick Steadman
☐ 10 Matt Weir
☐ 11 David Bolland
☐ 12 Kyle Piwowarczyk
☐ 13 Brandon Prust
☐ 14 Chris Bain
☐ 15 Adam Nemeth
☐ 16 Zach Tranmer
☐ 17 Danny Syvret
☐ 18 Jimmy Ball
☐ 19 Kyle Quincey
☐ 20 Marc Méthot
☐ 21 Gerald Coleman
☐ 22 Chris Houle
☐ 23 Jayme Helmer
☐ 24 Robbie Drummond
☐ 25 Tomas Linhart
☐ 26 Matt Iorianni
☐ 27 Dale Hunter
☐ 28 Don Brankley
☐ 29 Jacques Beaulieu
☐ 30 Danny Bois

MAINE BLACK BEARS

'92 - 93
MAINE BLACK BEARS / IRVING

Paul Kariya is the most expensive single at $30. Garth Snow has two cards each at $2-3. Singles start at 50¢.
Card Size: 2 1/2" x 3 1/2"
Series One Set (1-16): $10
Series Two Set (17-36): $35

☐ 1 Black Bears Card
☐ 2 Mike Dunham (G)
☐ 3 Andy Silverman
☐ 4 Matt Martin
☐ 5 Chris Imes
☐ 6 Jason Weinrich
☐ 7 Scott Pellerin
☐ 8 Dan Murphy
☐ 9 Dave LaCouture
☐ 10 Patrice Tardif
☐ 11 Eric Fenton
☐ 12 Jim Montgomery
☐ 13 Kent Salfi
☐ 14 Jean-Yves Roy
☐ 15 Garth Snow (G)
☐ 16 Cal Ingram
☐ 17 Black Bears card
☐ 18 Mike Dunham (G)
☐ 19 Chris Imes
☐ 20 Paul Kariya
☐ 21 Mike Latendresse
☐ 22 Dan Murphy
☐ 23 Dave MacIsaac
☐ 24 Dave LaCouture
☐ 25 Chris Ferraro
☐ 26 Peter Ferraro
☐ 27 Jim Montgomery
☐ 28 Brad Purdie
☐ 29 Lee Saunders
☐ 30 Justin Tomberlin
☐ 31 Chuck Texeira
☐ 32 Martin Mercier
☐ 33 Garth Snow (G)
☐ 34 Cal Ingraham
☐ 35 Greg Hirsch
☐ 36 Jamie Thompson

'93 - 94
MAINE BLACK BEARS / IRVING

Paul Kariya has two cards (#s 41, 60) at $15. Kariya also has two multiple single cards (#s 37, 61) at $6. Singles start at 50¢.
Card Size: 2 1/2" x 3 1/2"
Series Three Set (37-61): $45

☐ 37 P. Kariya/ L.Wlasow
☐ 38 Andy Silverman
☐ 39 Jason Weinrich
☐ 40 Jason Mansoff
☐ 41 Paul Kariya
☐ 42 Mike Latendresse
☐ 43 Barry Clukey
☐ 44 Wayne Conlan
☐ 45 Dave MacIsaac
☐ 46 Patrice Tardif
☐ 47 Brad Purdie
☐ 48 Dan Shermerhorn
☐ 49 Lee Saunders
☐ 50 Justin Tomberlin
☐ 51 Chuck Texeira
☐ 52 Tim Lovell
☐ 53 Cal Ingraham
☐ 54 Leo Wlasow
☐ 55 Blair Allison
☐ 56 Blair Marsh
☐ 57 Marcel Pineau
☐ 58 Trevor Roenick
☐ 59 Reg Cardinal
☐ 60 Paul Kariya
☐ 61 Montgomery/ P.Kariya

MEDICINE HAT TIGERS

'82 - 83
MEDICINE HAT TIGERS

Murray Craven is the most expensive single at $5. Singles start at $1.
Card Size: 3" x 4"
Sponsor: None
Set (21 cards): $20

☐ Al Conroy
☐ Murray Craven
☐ Mark Frank
☐ Kevan Guy
☐ Jim Hougen
☐ Ken Jorgenson
☐ Matt Kabayama
☐ Brent Kisilivich
☐ Mark Lamb
☐ Mike Lay
☐ Dean McArthur
☐ Brent Meckling
☐ Shawn Nagurny
☐ Kodie Nelson
☐ Al Pedersen
☐ Todd Pederson
☐ Jay Reid
☐ Gord Shmyrko
☐ Brent Steblyk
☐ Rocky Trottier
☐ Dan Turner

'83 - 84
MEDICINE HAT TIGERS / POLICE

Murray Craven is the most expensive single at $4. Singles start at $1.
Card Size: 2 3/4" x 5"
Set (23 cards): $22

☐ 1 Murray Craven
☐ 2 Shane Churla
☐ 3 Don Herczeg
☐ 4 Gary Johnson
☐ 5 Brent Kisilivich
☐ 6 Blair MacDonald
☐ 7 Terry Knight
☐ 8 Mark Lamb
☐ 9 Al Pedersen
☐ 10 Trevor Semeniuk
☐ 11 Dan Turner
☐ 12 Brent Steblyk
☐ 13 Rocky Trottier
☐ 14 Kevan Guy
☐ 15 Bobby Bassen
☐ 16 Brent Meckling
☐ 17 Matt Kabayama
☐ 18 Gord Hynes
☐ 19 Daryl Henry
☐ 20 Jim Kambeitz
☐ 21 Mike Lay
☐ 22 Gord Shmyrko
☐ 23 Al Conroy

'85 - 86
MEDICINE HAT TIGERS / POLICE

Mark Fitzpatrick is the most expensive single at $5. Singles start at $1.
Card Size: 2 1/4" x 4"
Set (24 cards): $22

☐ 1 MikeClaringbull
☐ 2 Doug Houda
☐ 3 Mark Kuntz
☐ 4 Guy Phillips
☐ 5 Rob DiMaio
☐ 6 Al Conroy
☐ 7 Craig Berube
☐ 8 Doug Sauter
☐ 9 Dean Chynoweth
☐ 10 Scott McCrady
☐ 11 Neil Brady
☐ 12 Dale Kushner
☐ 13 Jeff Wenaas
☐ 14 Wayne Hynes
☐ 15 Troy Gamble (G)
☐ 16 Bryan Maxwell
☐ 17 Gord Hynes
☐ 18 Wayne McBean
☐ 19 Mark Pederson
☐ 20 Darren Cota
☐ 21 Randy Siska
☐ 22 Dave Mackey
☐ 23 Mark Fitzpatrick (G)
☐ 24 Doug Ball

'95 - 96
MEDICINE HAT TIGERS

We do not yet have a checklist for this series.

'97 - 98
MEDICINE HAT TIGERS

We do not yet have a checklist for this series.

'99 - 00
MEDICINE HAT TIGERS

Singles start at 50¢.
Set (25 cards):

☐ Checklist
☐ Jay Bouwmeester
☐ Konrad Brand
☐ Berkeley Buchko
☐ Martin Cibak
☐ Ken Davis
☐ Paul Elliott
☐ Chris Ferguson
☐ Ryan Hollweg
☐ Cody Jensen
☐ Denny Johnston
☐ Kyle Kettles
☐ Ryan Kinasewich
☐ Kevin Labbe
☐ Josh Maser
☐ Ben McMullin
☐ Josh Morrow
☐ Tyson Mulock
☐ Brett Scheffelmaier
☐ Vladimir Sicak
☐ Chris St. Jacques
☐ Shaun Sutter
☐ Justin Taylor
☐ Ben Thomson
☐ Brad Voth

'00 - 01
MEDICINE HAT TIGERS

Singles start at 50¢.
Set (26 cards):

☐ Ryan Olynyk
☐ Petr Chivojka
☐ Jay Bowmeester
☐ B.J. Fehr
☐ Josh Morrow
☐ Tyson Mulock
☐ Ryan Hollweg
☐ Chris St. Jacques
☐ Joffrey Lupul
☐ Ben Thomson
☐ Brad Voth
☐ Brett Draney
☐ Denny Johnston
☐ Vernon Fiddler
☐ Ken Davis
☐ Ryan Kinasewich
☐ Jeremy Goetzinger
☐ David Ullmann
☐ Brett Scheffelmaier
☐ Ryan Chieduch
☐ Ben McMullin
☐ Kyle Kettles
☐ Bob Loucks
☐ Randy Wong
☐ Bryan Ellerman
☐ Mascot

'01 - 02
MEDICINE HAT TIGERS

We do not yet have a checklist for this series.

'02 - 03
MEDICINE HAT TIGERS

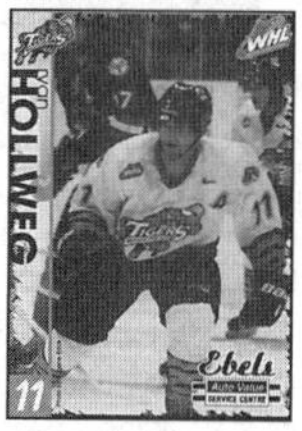

We do not yet have a checklist for this series.

MICHIGAN STATE SPARTANS

'93 - 94
MICHIGAN STATE SPARTANS

Bryan Smolinski and Anson Carter are the most expensive singles at $4-5. Singles start at 50¢.
Card Size: 2 1/2" x 3 1/2"

Sponsor: None
Set (32 cards): $22

☐ Matt Abers
☐ Michael Burkett
☐ Mike Buzak
☐ Anson Carter
☐ Brian Clifford
☐ Brian Crane
☐ Steve Ferranti
☐ Ryan Fleming
☐ Steve Guolla
☐ Kelly Harper
☐ Eric Kruse
☐ Ron Mason
☐ Mike Mattis
☐ Rem Murray
☐ Steve Norton
☐ Nicolas Perreault
☐ Tom Ross
☐ Chris Slater
☐ Chris Smith
☐ Bryan Smolinski
☐ Chris Sullivan
☐ Steve Suk
☐ Bart Turner
☐ Tony Tuzzolino
☐ Bart Vanstaalduinen
☐ Mike Ware
☐ John Weidenbach
☐ John Wiegand
☐ Scott Worden
☐ Mascot Sparty
☐ Spartans Arena
☐ Spartans Logo

MICHIGAN TECH HUSKIES

'90 - 91

MICHIGAN TECH HUSKIES / DAILY MINING GAZETTE

Damian Rhodes is the most expensive single at $3. Singles start at 75¢.

Card Size: 2 1/2" x 3 1/2"
Set (31 cards): $13

☐ Jim Bonner
☐ Newell Brown
☐ Dwight DeGiacomo
☐ Rod Ewacha
☐ Peter Grant
☐ Tim Hartnett
☐ Mike Hauswirth
☐ Kelly Hurd
☐ Kelly Hurd
☐ Randy Lewis
☐ Jay Luknowsky
☐ Darcy Martini
☐ Reid MacDonald
☐ Don Osborne
☐ Greg Parnell
☐ Davis Payne
☐ Kent Plaquin
☐ Damian Rhodes (G)
☐ Geoff Sarjeant (G)
☐ Jamie Steer
☐ Rob Tustian
☐ Tim Watters
☐ John Young
☐ Layne Lebel/ Jeff Hill
☐ Ken Martel/ Mark Leach
☐ McEwen/ Storm/ Manninen
☐ Perreault/ Brkic
☐ S. Vetteraino/ J. Ram
☐ John Young/Kelly Hurd
☐ Huskies Photo
☐ Huskies Photo

'91 - 92

MICHIGAN TECH HUSKIES / DAILY MINING GAZETTE

Singles start at 75¢.

Card Size: 2 1/2" x 3 1/2"
Set (36 cards): $15

☐ Jim Bonner
☐ Darren Brkic
☐ Rod Ewacha
☐ Tim Hartnett
☐ Mike Hauswirth
☐ Jeff Hill
☐ Layne Lebel
☐ Randy Lewis
☐ AS: Randy Lewis
☐ John MacInnes
☐ Darcy Martini
☐ AS: Darcy Martini
☐ Reid MacDonald
☐ Hugh McEwen
☐ Bob Olson
☐ Don Osborne
☐ Greg Parnell
☐ Davis Payne
☐ Kirby Perreault
☐ Ken Plaquin
☐ Jamie Ram (G)
☐ Geoff Sarjeant (G)
☐ AS: Geoff Sarjeant (G)
☐ Jamie Steer
☐ AS: Jamie Steer
☐ Jim Sotrm
☐ Scott Vettraino
☐ John Young
☐ Peca/ Gavey/ Stevens Peterson/ Seale
☐ Martini/ Payne/ Sarjeant Plaquin/ Storm/ Ram Steer/ Bonner
☐ Team Photo
☐ Huskies Players
☐ Huskies Players
☐ Huskies Players
☐ Huskies Players
☐ Huskies Players

MINNESOTA GOLDEN GOPHERS

'91 - 92

MINNESOTA GOLDEN GOPHERS / MCI

Trent Klatt is the most expensive single at $2. Singles start at 50¢.

Card Size: 2 1/2" x 3 1/2"
Set (26 cards): $15

☐ Scott Bell
☐ Tony Bianchi
☐ John Brill
☐ Jeff Callinan (G)
☐ Joe Dziedzic
☐ Sean Fabian
☐ Jed Fiebelkorn
☐ Nick Gerebi
☐ Darby Hendrickson
☐ Craig Johnson
☐ Trent Klatt
☐ Cory Laylin
☐ Steve Magnusson
☐ Chris McAlpine
☐ Justin McHugh
☐ Eric Means
☐ Mike Muller
☐ Tom Newman (G)
☐ Jeff Nielsen
☐ John O'Connell
☐ Larry Olimb
☐ Travis Richards
☐ Brandon Steege
☐ Jeff Stolp
☐ Todd Westlund
☐ Doug Zmolek

'92 - 93

MINNESOTA GOLDEN GOPHERS

Singles start at 50¢.

Card Size: 2 1/2" x 3 1/2"
Sponsor: None
Set (25 cards): $10

☐ Scott Bell
☐ Tony Bianchi
☐ John Brill
☐ Jeff Callinan (G)
☐ Joe Dziedzic
☐ Jed Fiebelkorn
☐ Darby Hendrickson
☐ Craig Johnson
☐ Steve Magnusson
☐ Chris McAlpine
☐ Justin McHugh
☐ Eric Means
☐ Jeff Moen (G)
☐ Tom Newman (G)
☐ Jeff Nielsen
☐ Travis Richards
☐ Brandon Steege
☐ Todd Westlund
☐ Doug Woog
☐ J. Bertogliat/ Brian Bonin
☐ Dustin/ Larson
☐ Stelljes/ Alstead
☐ Trebil/ Zwakman
☐ Wasley/ McAlpine
☐ Woog/ Hillman

'93 - 94

MINNESOTA GOLDEN GOPHERS

Singles start at 50¢.

Card Size: 2 1/2" x 3 1/2"
Sponsor: None
Set (30 cards): $12

☐ Brett Abrahamson
☐ Jesse Bertogliat
☐ Tony Bianchi
☐ Brian Bonin
☐ Andy Brink
☐ Jeff Callinan (G)
☐ Nick Checco
☐ Bobby Dustin
☐ Joe Dziedzic
☐ Jed Fiebelkorn
☐ Brent Godbout
☐ Dan Hendrickson
☐ Jim Hillman
☐ John Hillman
☐ Brian LaFleur
☐ Dave Larson
☐ Steve Magnusson
☐ Chris McAlpine
☐ Mike McAlpiune
☐ Justin McHugh
☐ Eric Means
☐ Jeff Moen (G)
☐ Jeff Nielsen
☐ Brandon Steege
☐ Dan Trebil
☐ Charlie Wasley
☐ Dan Woog
☐ Doug Woog
☐ Greg Zwakman
☐ Golden Gophers Card

'94 - 95

MINNESOTA GOLDEN GOPHERS

The Broten brothers card is the most expensive single at $2. Singles start at 50¢.

Card Size: 2 1/2" x 3 1/2"
Sponsor: None
Set (31 cards): $12

☐ Will Anderson
☐ Scott Bell
☐ Jesse Bertogliat
☐ Brian Bonin
☐ Andy Brink
☐ Jeff Callinan (G)
☐ Nick Checco
☐ Mike Crowley
☐ Steve DeBus
☐ Bobby Dustin
☐ Jed Fiebelkorn
☐ Brent Godbout
☐ Jason Godbout
☐ Casey Hankinson
☐ Dan Hendrickson
☐ Ryan Kraft
☐ Brian LaFleur
☐ Dave Larson
☐ Justin McHugh
☐ Jeff Moen (G)
☐ Jay Moser
☐ Lou Nanne
☐ Joe Pakratz
☐ Jason Seils
☐ Brandon Steege
☐ Dan Trebil
☐ Charlie Wasley
☐ Dan Woog
☐ Doug Woog
☐ Greg Zwakman
☐ Broten Brothers

MINN.-DULUTH BULLDOGS

'84 - 85

MINN.-DULUTH BULLDOGS

These cards say 1984-85 WCHA Champions on the card front. Brett Hull is the most expensive single in the set. We do not yet have a checklist for this series.

'85 - 86

MINN.-DULUTH BULLDOGS / TIM & LARRY'S SPORTSCARDS

These cards say 1984-85 WCHA Champions on the card front. Brett Hull is the most expensive single at $25. Singles start at 75¢.

Card Size: 2 1/2" x 3 1/5"
Set (36 cards): $35

☐ 1 Skeeter Moore
☐ 2 Terry Shold
☐ 3 Mike DeAngelis
☐ 4 Rob Pallin
☐ 5 Norm Maciver
☐ 6 Wayne Smith
☐ 7 Dave Cowan
☐ 8 Darin Illikainen
☐ 9 Rick Hayko (G)
☐ 10 Guy Gosselin
☐ 11 Paul Roff
☐ 12 Jim Toninato
☐ 13 Tom Hanson
☐ 14 Mike Cortes (G)
☐ 15 Matt Christensen
☐ 16 Bruce Fishback
☐ 17 Mark Odnokon
☐ 18 Brian Johnson
☐ 19 Bob Alexander
☐ 20 Tom Lorentz
☐ 21 Roman Sindelar
☐ 22 Jim Spregner
☐ 23 Dan Tousignant
☐ 24 Sean Toomey
☐ 25 Brian Durand
☐ 26 John Hyduke (G)
☐ 27 Brian Nelson
☐ 28 Brett Hull
☐ 29 John DeLisle
☐ 30 Pat Janostin
☐ 31 Ben Duffy
☐ 32 Sean Krakiwsky
☐ 33 Mike Sertich
☐ 34 Knapp/ Kulyk/ Menz/ McDonald/ Valesano/ Hoganson/ Feissner
☐ 35 Cheerleaders
☐ 36 Mascot Maroon Loon

'93 - 94

MINN.-DULUTH BULLDOGS

Singles start at 50¢.

Card Size: 2 1/2" x 3 1/5"
Sponsor: None
Set (30 cards): $12

☐ Rod Aldoff
☐ Niklas Axelson
☐ David Buck
☐ Jerome Butler
☐ Brian Caruso
☐ Marc Christian
☐ Joe Ciccarello
☐ Brad Federenko
☐ Rusty Fitzgerald
☐ Jason Garatti
☐ Greg Hanson
☐ Don Jablonic
☐ Kraig Karakas
☐ Brett Larson
☐ Taras Lendzyk
☐ Derek Locker
☐ Chris Marinucci
☐ Rod Miller
☐ Rick Mrozik
☐ Aaron Novak
☐ Corey Osmak
☐ Sergei Petrov
☐ Jeff Romfo
☐ Mike Sertich
☐ Chris Sittlow
☐ Joe Tamminen
☐ M.Christian/C.Culic
☐ Kyle Erickson/ A.Roy
☐ T.Mickolajak/ C.Snell
☐ Bulldogs Card

MISSISSAUGA ICEDOGS

'00 - 01

MISSISSAUGA ICEDOGS / ACTION CARDS

The most expensive single is Jason Spezza. Singles start at 50¢.

Set (28 cards): $15

☐ Brett Angel
☐ Grant Buckley
☐ Don Cherry
☐ Steve Cherry
☐ Fraser Clair
☐ Mark Cranley
☐ David Dalliday
☐ Andrew Davis
☐ Justin Dumont
☐ Omar Ennaffati
☐ John Jarram
☐ Patrick Jarrett
☐ Brent Labre
☐ Brian McGrattan
☐ Sean McMorrow
☐ Michael Mole
☐ Chris Osborne
☐ Jeff Paisley
☐ Brandon Robinson
☐ Adam Solnik
☐ Jason Spezza
☐ Dan Sullivan
☐ Chris Thaler
☐ Rick Vaive
☐ Mike Wehrstedt
☐ Chad Wiseman
☐ IceDogs
☐ Mascots Blue&Baby Blue

'01 - 02

MISSISSAUGA ICEDOGS / ACTION CARDS

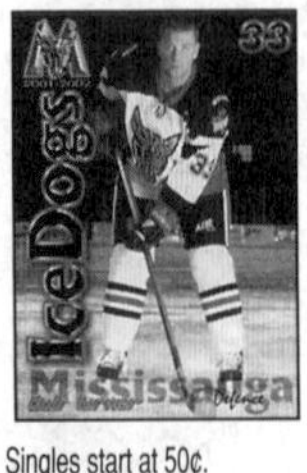

Singles start at 50¢.

Card Size: 2 1/2" x 3 1/2"
Set (26 cards):

☐ Team Lineup
☐ Matt Tanel
☐ T.J. Reynolds
☐ Travis Parent
☐ Nathan O'Nabigon
☐ Patrick O'Sullivan
☐ Chris Churran
☐ Dan Rudisuela
☐ Mike Wehrstedt
☐ Tyler Eady
☐ John Kozoriz
☐ Adam Sturgeon
☐ Chris Hawley
☐ Alexander Skorohod
☐ Miguel Beaudry
☐ Andrew Smale
☐ Bob Turner
☐ John Eminger
☐ Igor Radulov
☐ Greg Jacina
☐ Mike Barrett
☐ Daniel Sisca
☐ Don Cherry
☐ Steve Cherry
☐ Joe Washkurak
☐ Mascot Blue

'01 - 02

MONCTON WILDCATS / CARTES, TIMBRES, MONNAIES STE-FOY

Singles start at 50¢.

Card Size: 2 1/2" x 3 1/2"
Set (23 cards): $12

☐ 1 Travis Parent
☐ 2 Ian Maracle
☐ 3 Scott Hotham
☐ 4 Derek Lyons
☐ 5 Chris Curran
☐ 6 Dan Rudisuela
☐ 7 Tyler Eady
☐ 8 Tomas Linhart
☐ 9 Chris Hawley
☐ 10 Pavel Voroshnin
☐ 11 Wes Rypien
☐ 12 Miguel Beaudry
☐ 13 Matt Harpwood
☐ 14 Daniel Buccella
☐ 15 Rob Schremp
☐ 16 Salvatore Malandrino
☐ 17 Greg Jacina
☐ 18 Ryan Stokes
☐ 19 Patrick O_Sullivan
☐ 20 Dany Revelle
☐ 21 Blair Jarrett
☐ 22 Daniel Sisca
☐ Checklist

MONCTON WILDCATS

'01 - 02

MONCTON WILDCATS / CARTES, TIMBRES, MONNAIES STE-FOY

Singles start at 50¢.

Card Size: 2 1/2" x 3 1/2"
Set (26 cards): $12

☐ 1 Bill Ruggiero
☐ 2 Andrew Carver
☐ 3 James Sanford
☐ 4 Kyle Murnaghan
☐ 5 Daniel Hudgin
☐ 6 Mathieu Bétournay
☐ 7 Karl Gagné
☐ 8 Ian Séguin
☐ 9 Michel Dubé
☐ 10 François Caron
☐ 11 Nathan Saunders
☐ 12 Brad Larter
☐ 13 Teddy Kyres
☐ 14 Kevin Glode
☐ 15 David Philpott
☐ 16 Ryan Salvis
☐ 17 Collin Circelli
☐ 18 Corey Crawford
☐ 19 Matt Davis
☐ 20 Patrick Thoresen
☐ 21 Maxime Desruisseaux
☐ 22 Julien Lavoie
☐ 23 Scott English
☐ 24 Luke Pelham
☐ 25 Steve Bernier
☐ 26 Checklist

MONTRÉAL JUNIORS

'79 - 80

MONTRÉAL JUNIORS / SAUVÉ STUDIOS BLACK & WHITE

Photos are in black and white. Denis Savard is the most expensive single at $25. Mike Krushelnyski sells at $3. Singles start at $1.

Card Size: 3 3/4" x 5 5/8"
Set (29 cards): $40

☐ Jeff Barratt
☐ André Bégin
☐ Denis Champagne
☐ Denis Cyr
☐ Ghyslain Cyr
☐ Roland Diotte
☐ Pierre Dubois
☐ Sylvaine Gagné
☐ Guy Jacob
☐ Mike Krushelnyski
☐ Ron Lapointe
☐ Richard Lavallée
☐ Daniel Laxton
☐ François Laxton
☐ François Lecompte
☐ Eikke Leime
☐ Pierre Martin
☐ Bill Mulcahy
☐ Gaetano Orlando
☐ Patrice Pare
☐ Mario Patry
☐ Fabian Pavlin
☐ Roger Poitras
☐ Constant Prindolo
☐ Denis Savard
☐ Eric Taylor
☐ Denis Tremblay
☐ J. Jacques Vézina
☐ Taras Zytynsky

'79 - 80

MONTRÉAL JUNIORS / SAUVÉ STUDIOS COLOUR

Photos are in colour. Denis Savard is the most expensive single at $25. Mike Krushelnyski sells at $3. Singles start at $1.

Card Size: 3 3/4" x 5 5/8"
Set (24 cards): $40

☐ Jeff Barratt
☐ André Bégin
☐ Alain Bouchard
☐ Denis Champagne
☐ Denis Cyr
☐ Roland Diotte
☐ Pierre Dubois
☐ Sylvain Gagné
☐ Guy Jacob
☐ Mike Klassen
☐ Mike Krushelnyski
☐ Richard Lavallée
☐ François Lecompte
☐ Eikke Leime
☐ Pierre Martin
☐ Eric Morin
☐ Bill Mulcahy
☐ Gaetano Orlando
☐ Patrice Pare
☐ Constant Prindolo
☐ Denis Savard
☐ Jacques St. Jean
☐ J. Jacques Vézina
☐ Taras Zytynsky

MOOSE JAW WARRIORS

'01 - 02

MOOSE JAW WARRIORS / CARTES, TIMBRES, MONNAIES STE-FOY

Singles start at 50¢.

Card Size: 2 1/2" x 3 1/2"
Set (23 cards): $12

☐ 1 Ryan Jorde
☐ 2 Jarad Bourassa
☐ 3 Deryk Engelland
☐ 4 Nathan Paetsch
☐ 5 Bobby-Chad Mitchell
☐ 6 Kyle Brodziak
☐ 7 Derek Krestanovich
☐ 8 Steve Crampton
☐ 9 Sean O'Connor
☐ 10 Brian Sutherby
☐ 11 Tim Plett
☐ 12 Shawn Limpright
☐ 13 Lee Zalasky
☐ 14 Harlan Anderson
☐ 15 Tyler Johnson
☐ 16 David Bararuk
☐ 17 Mark Kitts
☐ 18 Craig Olynick
☐ 19 Lane Manson
☐ 20 Shaun Landolt
☐ 21 Kyle Kettles
☐ 22 Blake Grenier
☐ 23 Checklist

'02 - 03

MOOSE JAW WARRIORS / CARTES, TIMBRES, MONNAIES STE-FOY

Singles start at 50¢.

Card Size: 2 1/2" x 3 1/2"
Set (22 cards): $12

☐ 1 John Boychuk
☐ 2 Jarad Bourassa
☐ 3 Deryk Engelland
☐ 4 Nathan Paetsch
☐ 5 Michael Busto
☐ 6 Kyle Brozdiak
☐ 7 Tomas Fleischmann
☐ 8 Derek Krestanovich
☐ 9 Owen Fussey
☐ 10 Petr Jelinek
☐ 11 Jonathan Kress
☐ 12 Harlan Anderson
☐ 13 Tyler Johnson
☐ 14 David Bararuk
☐ 15 Troy Brouwer
☐ 16 Ashton Rome
☐ 17 Lane Manson
☐ 18 Dustin Boyd
☐ 19 Cam Lilley
☐ 20 Blake Grenier (G)
☐ 21 Steve Belanger (G)
☐ 22 Checklist

NANAIMO CLIPPERS

'91 - 92

NANAIMO CLIPPERS / DEC PRODUCTIONS

Singles start at 50¢.
Card Size: 3 3/8" x 4 7/8"
Set (22 cards): $10

☐ Glenn Calder
☐ Wade Dayley
☐ Jason Disiewich
☐ Andy Faulkener
☐ Darren Holme
☐ Casey Hungle
☐ Jim Ingram
☐ Chris Jones
☐ Ryan Keller
☐ Jade Kersey
☐ Scott Kowalski
☐ Sean Krause
☐ Jim Lessard
☐ Ryan Loxam
☐ Mickey McGuire
☐ Dan Murphy (G)
☐ Jason Northard
☐ Trevor Pest
☐ Brian Schiebel (G)
☐ Sjon Wynia
☐ Shawn York
☐ Geordie Young

NIAGARA FALLS THUNDER

'88 - 89

NIAGARA FALLS THUNDER / POLICE

Keith Primeau is the most expensive single at $8. Singles start at $1.
Card Size: 2 5/8" x 4 1/8"
Set (25 cards): $25

☐ 1 Thunder Logo
☐ 2 Brad May
☐ 3 Paul Wolanski
☐ 4 Keith Primeau
☐ 5 Mark Lawrence
☐ 6 Michael Rosati (G)
☐ 7 Dennis Vial
☐ 8 Shawn McCosh
☐ 9 Jason Soules
☐ 10 Rob Fournier
☐ 11 Scott Pearson
☐ 12 Jamie Leach
☐ 13 Colin Millar
☐ 14 Bryan Fogarty
☐ 15 Keith Osborne
☐ 16 Stan Drulia
☐ 17 Paul Laus
☐ 18 Adrian Vanderslot
☐ 19 Greg Allen
☐ 20 Don Pancoe
☐ 21 Alain LaForge
☐ 22 Bill LaForge
☐ 23 Steve Locke
☐ 24 Benny Rogano
☐ 25 Heavy Evason

'89 - 90

NIAGARA FALLS THUNDER / POLICE

Keith Primeau is the most expensive single at $6. Singles start at $1.
Card Size: 2 5/8" x 4 1/8"
Set (25 cards): $20

☐ Greg Allen
☐ Roch Belley (G)
☐ David Benn
☐ Andy Bezeau
☐ George Burnett
☐ Rodd Coopman
☐ Randy Hall
☐ John Johnson
☐ Paul Laus
☐ Mark Lawrence
☐ Brad May
☐ Don McConnell
☐ Brian Mueggler
☐ Don Pancoe
☐ Keith Primeau
☐ Geoff Rawson
☐ Ken Ruddick
☐ Greg Suchan
☐ Steve Udvari (G)
☐ Jeff Walker
☐ Jason Winch
☐ Paul Wolanski
☐ P.Bruneau/ D.Scott
☐ Thunder Logo
☐ Checklist

NORTH BAY CENTENNIALS

'82 - 83

NORTH BAY CENTENNIALS / AUNT MAY'S

Andrew McBain is the most expensive single at $2. Singles start at $1.50.
Card Size: 2 1/2" x 3 3/8"
Set (24 cards): $22

☐ Allen Bishop
☐ John Capel
☐ Rob Degagne
☐ Phil Drouillard
☐ Jeff Eatough
☐ Tony Gillard
☐ Paul Gillis
☐ Pete Handley
☐ Mark Hatcher
☐ Tim Helmer
☐ Craig Kales
☐ Bob Laforest
☐ Mark Laforest (G)
☐ Bill Maguire
☐ Andrew McBain
☐ Ron Meighan
☐ Rick Morocco
☐ Alain Raymond
☐ Joe Reekie
☐ Joel Smith (G)
☐ Bert Templeton
☐ Kevin Vescio
☐ Peter Woodgate
☐ Don Young

'83 - 84

NORTH BAY CENTENNIALS / AUNT MAY'S

Kevin Hatcher is the most expensive single at $6. Singles start at $1.
Card Size: 2 1/2" x 3 3/8"
Set (25 cards): $25

☐ Peter Abric
☐ Richard Benoit
☐ Scott Birnie
☐ John Capel
☐ Curtis Collin
☐ Ron Degagne
☐ Kevin Hatcher
☐ Mark Hatcher
☐ Tim Helmer
☐ Jim Hunter
☐ Kevin Kerr
☐ Nick Kypreos
☐ Mike Larouche
☐ Greg Larsen
☐ Mark Lavarre
☐ Brett MacDonald
☐ Wayne Macphee
☐ Peter McGrath
☐ Rob Nichols
☐ Ron Sanko
☐ Bert Templeton
☐ Kevin Vescio
☐ Mike Webber
☐ Peter Woodgate
☐ Sponsor Logos

N. MICHIGAN WILDCATS

'93 - 94

N. MICHIGAN WILDCATS

☐ Brian Barker
☐ Keith Bartholomaus
☐ Steve Carpenter
☐ Rick Comley
☐ Darcy Dallas
☐ Chad Dameworth
☐ Pat Ford
☐ Bryan Ganz
☐ Morey Gare
☐ Justin George
☐ Paul Taylor
☐ Shayne Tomlinson
☐ Jason Welch
☐ Steve Woog
☐ Brent Riplinger
☐ Dean Seymour
☐ Scott Smith
☐ Roger Lewis
☐ Garett MacDonald
☐ Bill MacGillivray
☐ Don McCusker
☐ Scott Green
☐ Greg Hadden
☐ Steve Hamilton
☐ Patrik Hansson
☐ Mike Harding
☐ Jason Hehr
☐ Mike Hillock
☐ Kory Karlander
☐ Karson Kaebel
☐ Trevor Janicki
☐ Dieter Kochan

OSHAWA GENERALS

'80 - 81

OSHAWA GENERALS / POLICE

Bobby Orr is the most expensive single at $100. Dave Andreychuk sells at $25. Singles start at $2.
Card Size: 2 5/8" x 4 1/8"
Set (25 cards): $135

☐ 1 Generals Logo
☐ 2 Ray Flaherty
☐ 3 Craig Kitchener
☐ 4 Dan Revell
☐ 5 Bob Kucheran
☐ 6 Pat Poulin
☐ 7 Dave Andreychuk
☐ 8 Barry Tabobondung
☐ 9 Steve Konroyd
☐ 10 Paul Edwards
☐ 11 Dale DeGray
☐ 12 Joe Cirella
☐ 13 Norm Schmidt
☐ 14 Markus Lehto
☐ 15 Mitch Lamoureux
☐ 16 Tony Tanti
☐ 17 Bill Laforge
☐ 18 Greg Gravel
☐ 19 Mike Lekum
☐ 20 Chris Smith (G)
☐ 21 Peter Sidorkiewicz (G)
☐ 22 Greg Stefan (G)
☐ 23 Tom McCarthy
☐ 24 Rick Lanz
☐ 25 Bobby Orr

'81 - 82

OSHAWA GENERALS / POLICE

Dave Andreychuk and John MacLean are the most expensive single at $15-20. Singles start at $2.
Card Size: 2 5/8" x 4 1/8"
Set (25 cards): 55.00

☐ 1 Generals Logo
☐ 2 Chris Smith (G)
☐ 3 Peter Sidorkiewicz (G)
☐ 4 Ali Butorac
☐ 5 Dan Revell
☐ 6 Mitch Lamoureux
☐ 7 Norm Schmidt
☐ 8 Paul Edwards
☐ 9 Dan Nicholson
☐ 10 John Hutchings
☐ 11 Dave Gans
☐ 12 Dave Andreychuk
☐ 13 Mike Stern
☐ 14 Dale DeGray
☐ 15 Mike Lekun
☐ 16 Greg Gravel
☐ 17 Dave MacLean
☐ 18 Tony Tanti
☐ 19 John MacLean
☐ 20 Jim Uens
☐ 21 Guy Jacob
☐ 22 Jeff Steffan
☐ 23 Paul Theriault
☐ 24 Sherry Bassen
☐ 25 Durham Police

'82 - 83

OSHAWA GENERALS / POLICE

John MacLean is the most expensive single at $8. Singles start at $1.
Card Size: 2 5/8" x 4 1/8"
Set (25 cards): $30

☐ 1 Generals Logo
☐ 2 Jeff Hogg (G)
☐ 3 Peter Sidorkiewicz (G)
☐ 4 Dale DeGray
☐ 5 Joe Cirella
☐ 6 Todd Smith
☐ 7 Scott Brydges
☐ 8 Jeff Steffan
☐ 9 Don Biggs
☐ 10 Todd Hooey
☐ 11 Tony Tanti
☐ 12 Danny Gratton
☐ 13 Steve King
☐ 14 Dan Defazio
☐ 15 John MacLean
☐ 16 Tim Burgess
☐ 17 Mike Stern
☐ 18 Dan Nicholson
☐ 19 David Gans
☐ 20 John Hutchings
☐ 21 Norm Schmidt
☐ 22 Todd Charlesworth
☐ 23 Paul Theriault
☐ 24 Sherry Bassen
☐ 25 Durham Police

'83 - 84

OSHAWA GENERALS / POLICE

Kirk McLean is the most expensive single at $15. Singles start at $1.
Card Size: 2 5/8" x 4 1/8"
Set (30 cards): $35

☐ 1 Peter Sidorkiewicz (G)
☐ 2 Kirk McLean (G)
☐ 3 Todd Charlesworth
☐ 4 Ian Ferguson
☐ 5 John Hutchings
☐ 6 Generals Logo
☐ 7 Mark Haarmann
☐ 8 Joel Curtis
☐ 9 Dan Gratton
☐ 10 Steve Hedington
☐ 11 Scott Brydges
☐ 12 CKAR Radio
☐ 13 Brad Walcot
☐ 14 Paul Theriault
☐ 15 Jon Jenkins
☐ 16 Sherry Bassen
☐ 17 Craig Morrison
☐ 18 Sponsor Logo
☐ 19 Bruce Melanson
☐ 20 Mike Stern
☐ 21 Gary McColgan
☐ 22 Lee Giffin
☐ 23 Brent Maki
☐ 24 Ronald McDonald
☐ 25 Jeff Steffan
☐ 26 John Stevens
☐ 27 David Gans
☐ 28 Don Biggs
☐ 29 Chris Crandall
☐ 30 Durham Police

'89 - 90

OSHAWA GENERALS / POLICE

Eric Lindros is the most expensive single at $25-30. Singles start at 75¢.
Card Size: 2 5/8" x 4 1/8"
Set (35 cards): $35

☐ 1 Cory Banika
☐ 2 David Craievich
☐ 3 Scott Hollis
☐ 4 Mike Decoff
☐ 5 Joe Busillo
☐ 6 Matt Hoffman
☐ 7 Craig Donaldson
☐ 8 Jason Denomme
☐ 9 Brian Grieve
☐ 10 Wade Simpson
☐ 11 Dale Craigwell
☐ 12 Mike Lenarduzzi
☐ 13 Rick Cornaccia
☐ 14 Dan Edwards
☐ 15 Kevin Butt (G)
☐ 16 Oshawa Generals
☐ 17 Clair Cornish
☐ 18 Jarrod Skalde
☐ 19 Mark Deazeley
☐ 20 Jean-Paul Davis
☐ 21 Todd Coopman
☐ 22 Trevor McIvor
☐ 23 Mike Craig
☐ 24 Paul O'Hagan
☐ 25 Iain Fraser
☐ 26 Sponsor Logo
☐ 27 Sponsor Logo
☐ 28 Sponsor Logo
☐ 29 Durham Police
☐ 30 Generals Logo
☐ 31 Eric Lindros
☐ 32 Bill Armstrong
☐ 33 Chris Vanclief
☐ 34 Scott Luik
☐ 35 Fred Brathwaite (G)

'90 - 91

OSHAWA GENERALS / POLICE

Eric Lindros is the most expensive single at $15-20. Singles start at 75¢.
Card Size: 2 5/8" x 3 3/4"
Set (30 cards): $30

☐ 1 Sponsor Logo
☐ 2 Mike Côté
☐ 3 Fred Brathwaite (G)
☐ 4 Scott Luik
☐ 5 Sponsor Logo
☐ 6 Mike Fountain (G)
☐ 7 Rick Cornacchia
☐ 8 David Edwards
☐ 9 Tony Sweet
☐ 10 Jan Benda
☐ 11 David Dorosh
☐ 12 Craig Lutes
☐ 13 Eric Lindros
☐ 14 David Craievich
☐ 15 Wade Simpson
☐ 16 Dale Craigwell
☐ 17 Generals Logo
☐ 18 Matt Hoffman
☐ 19 Rob Pearson
☐ 20 Paul O'Hagan
☐ 21 Brent Grieve
☐ 22 Mark Deazeley
☐ 23 Clair Cornish
☐ 24 B.J. MacPherson
☐ 25 Jason Weaver
☐ 26 Markus Brunner
☐ 27 Trevor Burgess
☐ 28 Jean-Paul Davis
☐ 29 Durham Police
☐ 30 Scott Hollis

'91 - 92

OSHAWA GENERALS / DOMINO'S PIZZA

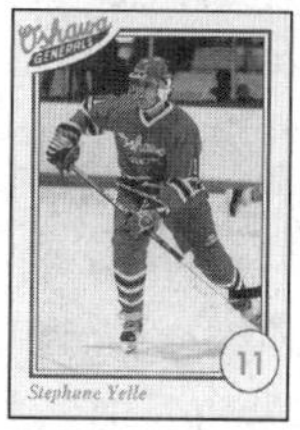

Eric Lindros is the most expensive single at $12. Jason Arnott sells at $6. Singles start at 50¢.
Card Size: 2 1/2" x 3 1/2"
Set (31 cards): $25

☐ 1 Mike Fountain (G)
☐ 2 Brian Grieve
☐ 3 Trevor Burgess
☐ 4 Wade Simpson
☐ 5 Ken Sheppard
☐ 6 Stéphane Yelle
☐ 7 Matt Hoffman
☐ 8 Neil Iserhoff
☐ 9 Rob Leask
☐ 10 Kevin Spero
☐ 11 Scott Hollis
☐ 12 Sean Brown
☐ 13 Todd Bradley
☐ 14 Darryl LaFrance
☐ 15 Markus Brunner
☐ 16 B.J. MacPherson
☐ 17 Jason Campeau
☐ 18 Jason Weaver
☐ 19 Jan Benda
☐ 20 Jason Arnott
☐ 21 Eric Lindros
☐ 22 Wayne Daniels
☐ 23 Joe Cook
☐ 24 Coke Sponsor
☐ 25 Domino's Pizza
☐ 26 Mark Deazeley
☐ 27 Jean-Paul Davis
☐ 28 Brian Grieve
☐ 29 Team Photo
☐ 30 Young/ Marson/ Cornacchia
☐ 31 Prosport's Action

'91 - 92

OSHAWA GENERALS

This set was originally issued as a 26-card sheet. Eric Lindros is the most expensive single at $12. Jason Arnott sells at $5. Singles start at 50¢.
Card Size: 2 1/2" x 3 1/2"
Sponsor: None
Set (26 cards): $20

☐ David Anderson
☐ Jason Arnott
☐ Jan Benda
☐ Todd Bradley
☐ Fred Brathwaite (G)
☐ Markus Brunner
☐ Trevor Burgess
☐ Jason Campeau
☐ Joe Cook
☐ Mike Côté
☐ Jean-Paul Davis
☐ Mark Deazeley
☐ Mike Fountain (G)
☐ Brian Grieve
☐ Matt Hoffman
☐ Scott Hollis
☐ Neil Iserhoff
☐ Darryl LaFrance
☐ Eric Lindros
☐ Craig Lutes
☐ B.J. MacPherson
☐ Wade Simpson
☐ Kevin Spero
☐ Troy Sweet
☐ Jason Weaver
☐ Stéphane Yelle

'92 - 93

OSHAWA GENERALS

This set was originally issued as a 26-card sheet. Jason Arnott is the most expensive single at $5. Singles start at 50¢.
Card Size: 2 1/2" x 3 1/2"
Sponsor: None
Set (26 cards): $20

☐ Aaron Albright
☐ Jason Arnott
☐ Todd Bradley
☐ Mark Brooks
☐ Sean Brown
☐ Trevor Burgess
☐ Jason Campeau
☐ Joe Cook
☐ Serge Dunphy
☐ Joel Gagnon
☐ Steve Haight
☐ Chris Hall
☐ Scott Hollis
☐ Neil Iserhoff
☐ Billy-Jay Johnston
☐ Jason Julian
☐ Brian Kent
☐ Jamie Kress
☐ Darryl Lafrance
☐ B.J. MacPherson
☐ Jason McQuat
☐ Rob McQuat
☐ Wade Simpson
☐ Stéphane Soullière
☐ Kevin Spero
☐ Stéphane Yelle

OTTAWA 67'S

'81 - 82

OTTAWA 67'S

We have little pricing information on these cards.
Card Size: 5 1/2" x 8 1/2"
Sponsor: None
Set (25 cards):

☐ James Allison
☐ John Boland
☐ Randy Boyd
☐ Adam Creighton
☐ Bill Dowd
☐ Dwayne Davison
☐ Alan Hepple
☐ Mike James
☐ Brian Kilrea
☐ Moe Lemay
☐ Banny Longe
☐ Paul Louttit
☐ Don MacLaren
☐ John Ollson
☐ Brian Patafie
☐ Mark Paterson
☐ Phil Patterson
☐ Larry Power
☐ Jim Ralph (G)
☐ Darcy Roy
☐ Brad Shaw
☐ Brian Small
☐ Doug Stewart
☐ Jeff Vaive
☐ Fraser Wood

'82 - 83

OTTAWA 67'S / M.O.M. PRINTING

Gary Roberts is the most expensive single at $7. Singles start at $1.
Card Size: 2 5/8" x 4 1/8"
Set (25 cards): $30

☐ Bruce Cassidy
☐ Greg Coram (G)
☐ Adam Creighton
☐ Bill Dowd
☐ Gord Hamilton
☐ Scott Hammond
☐ Alan Hepple
☐ Alan Hepple
☐ Jim Jackson
☐ Mike James
☐ Brian Kilrea
☐ Paul Louttit
☐ Brian McKinnon
☐ Don MacLaren
☐ John Ollson
☐ Darren Pang (G)
☐ Mark Paterson
☐ Phil Patterson
☐ Larry Power
☐ Gary Roberts
☐ Brian Rome
☐ Darcy Roy
☐ Brad Shaw
☐ Doug Stewart
☐ Jeff Vaive

'83 - 84

OTTAWA 67'S / M.O.M. PRINTING

Gary Roberts is the most expensive single at $6. Singles start at $1.
Card Size: 2 5/8" x 4 1/8"
Set (27 cards): $25

☐ Richard Adolfi
☐ Bill Bennett
☐ Bruce Cassidy
☐ Todd Clarke
☐ Greg Coram (G)
☐ Adam Creighton
☐ Bob Giffin
☐ Gord Hamilton
☐ Gord Hamilton Jr.
☐ Scott Hammond
☐ John Hanna
☐ Tim Helmer
☐ Steve Hrynewich
☐ Jim Jackson
☐ Mike James
☐ Brian Kilrea
☐ Larry MacAndrew
☐ Brian McKinnon
☐ Don McLaren
☐ Ron Myllari
☐ Darren Pang (G)
☐ Mark Paterson
☐ Phil Patterson
☐ Gary Roberts
☐ Darcy Roy
☐ Brad Shaw
☐ Steve Simoni

'84 - 85

OTTAWA 67'S

Gary Roberts is the most expensive single at $6. Singles start at $1.
Card Size: 2 5/8" x 4 1/8"
Set (28 cards): $30

☐ Tom Allen
☐ Graydon Almstedt
☐ Bill Bennett
☐ Bruce Cassidy
☐ Greg Coram (G)
☐ Bob Ellett
☐ Tony Geesink
☐ Bob Giffin
☐ John Hanna
☐ Tim Helmer
☐ Andy Helmuth
☐ Steve Hrynewich
☐ Rob Hudson

- ☐ Jim Jackson
- ☐ Steve Kayser
- ☐ Bill Kuchma
- ☐ Mike Larouche
- ☐ Tom Lawson
- ☐ Rick Lessard
- ☐ Gary Roberts
- ☐ Jerry Scott
- ☐ John Sheppard
- ☐ Steve Simoni
- ☐ Greg Sliz
- ☐ Gord Thomas
- ☐ Chris Vickers
- ☐ Bert Weir
- ☐ Dennis Wigle

'92 - 93

OTTAWA 67'S / OTTAWA CITIZEN

This set was originally issued as a sheet. Michael Peca is the most expensive single at $3. Singles start at 50¢.
Card Size: 2 1/2" x 3 1/2"
Set (24 cards): $12

- ☐ Ken Belanger
- ☐ Curt Bowen
- ☐ Rich Bronilla
- ☐ Mathew Burnett
- ☐ Shawn Caplice
- ☐ Mike Carr
- ☐ Chris Coveny
- ☐ Howard Darwin
- ☐ Shean Donovan
- ☐ Mark Edmundson
- ☐ Billy Hall
- ☐ Mike Johnson
- ☐ Brian Kilrea
- ☐ Grayson Lafoley
- ☐ Grant Marshall
- ☐ Cory Murphy
- ☐ Michael Peca
- ☐ Greg Ryan
- ☐ Jeff Salajko (G)
- ☐ Gerry Skrypec
- ☐ Sean Spencer
- ☐ Steve Washburn
- ☐ Mark Yakabuski
- ☐ 67's card

'99 - 00

OTTAWA 67'S / JOGO

Singles start at 50¢.
Card Size: 2 1/2" x 3 1/2"
Set (30 cards): $12

- ☐ 1 Mark Bell
- ☐ 2 Matt Zultek
- ☐ 3 Adam Chapman
- ☐ 4 Miguel Delisle
- ☐ 5 Randy Davidson
- ☐ 6 Lance Galbraith
- ☐ 7 Ian Jacobs
- ☐ 8 Mike James
- ☐ 9 Zenon Konopka
- ☐ 10 Marc Lefebvre
- ☐ 11 Joe Talbot
- ☐ 12 Josh Tataryn
- ☐ 13 Dan Tessier
- ☐ 14 Vincent Grant
- ☐ 15 Brendan Bell
- ☐ 16 Chris Cava
- ☐ 17 Kevin Malcolm
- ☐ 18 Mike Cresdal
- ☐ 19 Russ Moyer
- ☐ 20 Luke Sellars
- ☐ 21 Jeremy Van Hoof
- ☐ 22 Jonathon Zion
- ☐ 23 Seamus Kotyk
- ☐ 24 Lavente Szuper
- ☐ 25 Jeff Hunt
- ☐ 26 Brian Kilrea
- ☐ 27 Bert O'Brien
- ☐ 28 Vince Mallette
- ☐ 29 Jeff Keech
- ☐ 30 Memorial Cup Champions

'00 - 01

OTTAWA 67'S / JOGO

Singles start at 50¢.
Card Size: 2 1/2" x 3 1/2"
Set (30 cards): $12

- ☐ 1 Joe Talbot
- ☐ 2 Lance Galbraith
- ☐ 3 Jeremy Van Hoof
- ☐ 4 Jon Zion
- ☐ 5 Russ Moyers
- ☐ 6 Pierre Mitsou
- ☐ 7 Brendan Bell
- ☐ 8 Adam Snyth
- ☐ 9 Marc Lefebvre
- ☐ 10 Sean Scully
- ☐ 11 Brett McGrath
- ☐ 12 Zenon Kenopka
- ☐ 13 Rodney Bauman
- ☐ 14 Luke Sellars
- ☐ 15 Miguel Delisle
- ☐ 16 Vadim Sozinov
- ☐ 17 Adam Chapman
- ☐ 18 Bryan Rodney
- ☐ 19 Sébastien Savage
- ☐ 20 Seamus Kotyk
- ☐ 21 John Ceci
- ☐ 22 Vince Mallette
- ☐ 23 Bert O'Brien
- ☐ 24 Brian Kilrea
- ☐ 25 Jeff Hunt
- ☐ 26 Riley & Killer Puck
- ☐ 27 Brian Kilrea 900 Wins
- ☐ 28 Doug Wilson Alumni
- ☐ 29 67's
- ☐ 30 67's Dance Team

'01 - 02

OTTAWA 67'S / JOGO

Singles start at 50¢.
Card Size: 2 1/2" x 3 1/2"
Set (30 cards): $12

- ☐ 1 J.F. Perras
- ☐ 2 Jon Ceci
- ☐ 3 Karol Sloboda
- ☐ 4 Carter Trevisani
- ☐ 5 Jon Zion
- ☐ 6 Russ Moyer
- ☐ 7 Pierre Mitsou
- ☐ 8 Adam Smyth
- ☐ 9 Brendan Bell
- ☐ 10 Mathew Albiani
- ☐ 10 Lane Moodie
- ☐ 12 Sean Scully
- ☐ 13 Brett McGrath
- ☐ 14 Zenon Kenopka
- ☐ 15 Rodney Bauman
- ☐ 16 Miguel Delisle
- ☐ 17 Jeremy Akeson
- ☐ 18 Mark Mancari
- ☐ 19 Adam Chapman
- ☐ 20 Bryan Rodney
- ☐ 21 Corey Locke
- ☐ 22 Vince Mallette
- ☐ 23 Bert O'Brien
- ☐ 24 Brian Kilrea
- ☐ 25 Jeff Hunt
- ☐ 26 Banner ceremony
- ☐ 27 Brad Marsh Alumni
- ☐ 28 Rily & Riley Jr.
- ☐ 29 Killer Puck
- ☐ 30 67's Dance Team

'02 - 03

OTTAWA 67'S

We do not yet have a checklist for this series.

OWEN SOUND ATTACK

'00 - 01

OWEN SOUND ATTACK

Singles start at 50¢.
Set (27 cards):

- ☐ 1 Cory Roberts
- ☐ 2 Agris Saviels
- ☐ 3 Dene Poulin
- ☐ 4 Josh Legge
- ☐ 5 Greg Jancina
- ☐ 6 Brandon Verner
- ☐ 7 Bryan Kazarian
- ☐ 8 Shawn Snider
- ☐ 9 Richard Colwill
- ☐ 10 Trevor Blanchard
- ☐ 11 Ryan Sharp
- ☐ 12 Kris Fraser
- ☐ 13 Justin Hodgins
- ☐ 14 Daniel Sisca
- ☐ 15 Kyle McAllister
- ☐ 16 Mike Barrett
- ☐ 17 Joel Ward
- ☐ 18 Bill Zalba
- ☐ 19 Luc Chaisson
- ☐ 20 Nick Vukovic
- ☐ 21 Richard Power
- ☐ 22 Dan Sullivan
- ☐ 23 Justin Day
- ☐ 24 Attack Sound
- ☐ 25 Brian O'Leary
- ☐ 26 Paul MacDermid
- ☐ 27 Jason Nobili

'01 - 02

OWEN SOUND ATTACK

Singles start at 50¢.
Set (24 cards):

- ☐ Rob Chapman
- ☐ Richard Colwill
- ☐ Ryan Courtney
- ☐ David Dalliday
- ☐ Justin Day
- ☐ Jesse Gimblett
- ☐ Fred Hatziioannou
- ☐ Greg Jacina
- ☐ Michael Jacobsen
- ☐ Ladislav Kolda
- ☐ Jeff MacDermid
- ☐ Kyle McAllister
- ☐ Richard Power
- ☐ Justin Renner
- ☐ Brad Richardson
- ☐ Cory Roberts
- ☐ Dan Rogers
- ☐ Agris Saviels
- ☐ Ryan Sharp
- ☐ Daniel Sisca
- ☐ Sean Stefanski
- ☐ Dan Sullivan
- ☐ John Wheaton
- ☐ Tom Zanoski

'02 - 03

OWEN SOUND ATTACK / CARTES, TIMBRES, MONNAIES STE-FOY

Singles start at 50¢.
Set (26 cards): $12

- ☐ 1 Mascot Cubby
- ☐ 2 Brett Howden
- ☐ 3 Pat Sutton
- ☐ 4 Jiri Paska
- ☐ 5 Mark Giordano
- ☐ 6 Patrick Jarrett
- ☐ 7 Dan Rogers
- ☐ 8 Matt Passfield
- ☐ 9 Tom Zanoski
- ☐ 10 Jesse Gimblett
- ☐ 11 Michael Gough
- ☐ 12 Brad Richardson
- ☐ 13 Andrew Maksym
- ☐ 14 Steve Hanwood
- ☐ 15 Brett McGrath
- ☐ 16 Justin Renner
- ☐ 17 Ladislav Kolda
- ☐ 18 John Wheaton
- ☐ 19 Fred Hatziioannou
- ☐ 20 Jeff MacDermid
- ☐ 21 Miguel Delisle
- ☐ 22 David Edgeworth
- ☐ 23 Mike Angelidis
- ☐ 24 Dan LaCosta (G)
- ☐ 25 Marty Magers (G)
- ☐ 26 Checklist

OWEN SOUND PLATERS

'93 - 94

OWEN SOUND PLATERS

Jamie Storr has three singles each selling at $3. Singles start at 50¢.
Card Size: 2 1/2" x 3 1/2"
Set (36 cards): $18

- ☐ Craig Binns
- ☐ Jim Brown
- ☐ Andrew Brunette
- ☐ Luigi Calce
- ☐ Jason Campbell
- ☐ Paddy Flynn
- ☐ Kirk Furey
- ☐ Jerry Harrigan
- ☐ Joe Harris
- ☐ Rod Hinks
- ☐ Marian Kacir
- ☐ Shane Kenny
- ☐ Jeff Kostuch
- ☐ Dave Lemay
- ☐ Jason MacDonald
- ☐ Rick Mancini
- ☐ Kirk Maltby
- ☐ Brian Medeiros
- ☐ Mike Morrone
- ☐ Ryan Mougenel
- ☐ Scott Penton
- ☐ Wayne Primeau
- ☐ Jeremy Rebek
- ☐ Rob Schweyer
- ☐ Willie Skilliter
- ☐ Jamie Storr (G)
- ☐ Jamie Storr (G) (Gold)
- ☐ Jamie Storr (Mask)
- ☐ Scott Walker
- ☐ Kevin Weekes (G)
- ☐ Kevin Weekes (Mask)
- ☐ Shayne Wright
- ☐ R.Hinks/ J.MacDonald K.Weekes/ M.Kacir
- ☐ Jamie Storr/ W.Primeau
- ☐ Domino's Ad
- ☐ Eastwood Ad

PETERBOROUGH PETES

'88 - 89

PETERBOROUGH PETES / COKE

We have little information on this set. Other singles exist.

- ☐ Tie Domi

'91 - 92

PETERBOROUGH PETES / POLICE

Chris Pronger is the most expensive single at $5. Singles start at 75¢.
Card Size: 2 1/2" x 3 3/4"
Set (30 cards): $22

- ☐ 1 Jason Dawe
- ☐ 2 Chris Pronger
- ☐ 3 Scott Turner
- ☐ 4 Chad Grills
- ☐ 5 Brent Tully
- ☐ 6 Mike Harding
- ☐ 7 Chris Longo
- ☐ 8 Mascot Slapshot
- ☐ 9 Doug Searle
- ☐ 10 Mike Tomlinson
- ☐ 11 Bryan Gendron
- ☐ 12 Andrew Verner (G)
- ☐ 13 Ryan Black
- ☐ 14 Don O'Neill
- ☐ 15 Jeff Twohey
- ☐ 16 Dale McTavish
- ☐ 17 Jeff Walker
- ☐ 18 Matt St. Germain
- ☐ 19 Dave Roche
- ☐ 20 Colin Wilson
- ☐ 21 Cullimore (Err: Jason)
- ☐ 22 Chad Lang
- ☐ 23 Dick Todd
- ☐ 24 Geordie Kinnear
- ☐ 25 Shawn Heins
- ☐ 26 Jay Johnson
- ☐ 27 Kelly Vipond
- ☐ Kiwanis Sponsor
- ☐ Quaker Sponsor
- ☐ Peterborough Police

'01 - 02

PETERBOROUGH PETES

Singles start at 50¢.
Set (20 cards):

- ☐ Matt Armstrong
- ☐ Ryan Card
- ☐ Greg Chambers
- ☐ David Currie
- ☐ James Edgar
- ☐ Adam Elzinga
- ☐ Mark Flood
- ☐ Jim Gagnon
- ☐ Bryan Hammond
- ☐ Trevor Hendrix
- ☐ Matt Herneisen
- ☐ Jon Howse
- ☐ Lukas Krajicek
- ☐ Josh Patterson
- ☐ Jason Penner
- ☐ Brad Seif
- ☐ Cody Spicer
- ☐ Eric Staal
- ☐ Jamie Tardif
- ☐ Dustin Wood

PLYMOUTH WHALERS

'01 - 02

PLYMOUTH WHALERS

We do not yet have a checklist for this series.

'02 - 03

PLYMOUTH WHALERS / MCDONALD FORD

Singles start at 50¢.
Set (30 cards):

- ☐ Cole Jarrett
- ☐ Nate Kiser
- ☐ Karl Stewart
- ☐ John Mitchell
- ☐ Jimmy Gagnon
- ☐ Sean Thompson
- ☐ Chad LaRose
- ☐ John Vigilante
- ☐ Taylor Raszka
- ☐ Ryan Ramsay
- ☐ Mike Letizia
- ☐ Steve Phillips
- ☐ Paul Drew
- ☐ Jonas Fiedler
- ☐ Bernt Mahon
- ☐ Cole Jarrett
- ☐ Tim Sestito
- ☐ Martin Cizek
- ☐ Chad LaRose
- ☐ Chris Thorburn
- ☐ James Wisniewski
- ☐ Mike Nelson
- ☐ Nick Vernelli
- ☐ Jeff Weber
- ☐ Erik Lundmark
- ☐ David Liffiton
- ☐ David Liffiton
- ☐ Mascot Shooter
- ☐ Pat Peake
- ☐ Whalers photo

PORTLAND WINTER HAWKS

'86 - 87

PORTLAND WINTER HAWKS / AM/PM MINI MARKET

Glen Wesley is the most expensive single at $4. Singles start at $1.
Card Size: 2 1/2" x 3 1/2"
Set (24 cards): $18

- ☐ Dave Archibald
- ☐ Bruce Basken
- ☐ Thomas Bjuhr
- ☐ Shaun Clouston
- ☐ Jeff Finley
- ☐ Bob Foglietta
- ☐ Brian Gerrits
- ☐ Darryl Gilmour (G)
- ☐ Dennis Holland
- ☐ Steve Kloepzig
- ☐ Jim Latos
- ☐ Dave McLay
- ☐ Scott Melnyk
- ☐ Troy Mick
- ☐ Roy Mitchell
- ☐ Jamie Nicolls
- ☐ Trevor Pohl
- ☐ Troy Pohl
- ☐ Glen Seymour (G)
- ☐ Jeff Sharples
- ☐ Jay Stark
- ☐ Jim Swan
- ☐ Glen Wesley
- ☐ Dan Woodley

'88 - 89

PORTLAND WINTER HAWKS / FRED MAYER PEPSI

Byron Dafoe is the most expensive single at $5. Singles start at $1.
Card Size: 2 1/2" x 3 1/2"
Set (21 cards): $15

- ☐ Wayne Anchikoski
- ☐ Eric Badzgon (G)
- ☐ Chad Biafore
- ☐ James Black
- ☐ Terry Black
- ☐ Shaun Clouston
- ☐ Byron Dafoe (G)
- ☐ Brent Fleetwood
- ☐ Rob Flintoft
- ☐ Bryan Gourdie
- ☐ Mark Greyeyes
- ☐ Dennis Holland
- ☐ Kevin Jorgenson
- ☐ Greg Leahy
- ☐ Troy Mick
- ☐ Roy Mitchell
- ☐ Joey Mittelsteadt
- ☐ Mike Moore
- ☐ Scott Mydan
- ☐ Calvin Thudiun
- ☐ Sponsor Pepsi

'89 - 90

PORTLAND WINTER HAWKS / FRED MAYER PEPSI

Byron Dafoe is the most expensive single at $4. Singles start at $1.
Card Size: 2 1/2" x 3 1/2"
Set (21 cards): $15

- ☐ James Black
- ☐ Vince Cocciolo
- ☐ Byron Dafoe (G)
- ☐ Cam Danyluk
- ☐ Kim Deck
- ☐ Dean Dorchak
- ☐ Brent Fleetwood
- ☐ Rick Fry
- ☐ Bryan Gourlie
- ☐ Brad Harrison
- ☐ Juson Innes
- ☐ Dean Intwert (G)
- ☐ Kevin Jorgenson
- ☐ Todd Kinniburgh
- ☐ Greg Leahy
- ☐ Jamie Linden
- ☐ Scott Mydan
- ☐ Mike Ruark
- ☐ Jeff Sebastian
- ☐ Brandon Smith
- ☐ Steve Young

'93 - 94

PORTLAND WINTER HAWKS / FRED MAYER PEPSI

Adam Deadmarsh is the most expensive single at $5. Singles start at 50¢.
Card Size: 2 1/2" x 3 1/2"
Set (24 cards): $18

- ☐ Mike Arbulic
- ☐ Lonny Bohonos
- ☐ Shannon Briske
- ☐ Dave Cammock
- ☐ Shawn Collins
- ☐ Matt Davidson
- ☐ Adam Deadmarsh
- ☐ Jake Deadmarsh
- ☐ Brett Fizzell
- ☐ Colin Foley
- ☐ Brad Isbister
- ☐ Scott Langkow (G)
- ☐ Mike Little
- ☐ Dmitri Markovsky
- ☐ Jason McBain
- ☐ Scott Nichol
- ☐ Brent Peterson
- ☐ Nolan Pratt
- ☐ Scott Rideout (G)
- ☐ Layne Roland
- ☐ Dave Scratchard
- ☐ Brandon Smith
- ☐ Brad Swanson
- ☐ Brad Symes
- ☐ Jason Wiemer
- ☐ Mike Williamson
- ☐ Hawks Action
- ☐ Hawks Action
- ☐ Hawks Action
- ☐ Hawks Action

'97 - 98

PORTLAND WINTER HAWKS / TACO BELL

Singles start at 50¢.
Sponsor: Taco Bell
Set (25 cards):

- ☐ 1 Checklist
- ☐ 2 Brent Belecki
- ☐ 3 Mike Muzechka
- ☐ 4 Marian Hossa
- ☐ 5 Ken Davis
- ☐ 6 Jerad Smith
- ☐ 7 Josh Green
- ☐ 8 Bobby Russell
- ☐ 9 Kyle Chant
- ☐ 10 Brenden Morrow
- ☐ 11 Derek MacLean
- ☐ 12 Todd Hornung
- ☐ 13 Andrej Podkonicky
- ☐ 14 Bobby Duncan
- ☐ 15 Todd Robinson
- ☐ 16 Chris Jacobson
- ☐ 17 Shon Jones-Parry
- ☐ 18 Kevin Haupt
- ☐ 19 Ryan Thrussell
- ☐ 20 Marty Standish
- ☐ 21 Jason LaBarbera
- ☐ 22 Matt Walker
- ☐ 23 Andrew Ference
- ☐ 24 Joey Tetarenko
- ☐ 25 Coaches

PRINCE ALBERT RAIDERS

'84 - 85

PRINCE ALBERT RAIDERS / POLICE

Photos are in black and white. Ken Baumgartner is the most expensive single at $8. Singles start at $1.50.
Sticker Size: 2" x 1 3/4"
Set (22 stickers): $25

- ☐ Ken Baumgartner
- ☐ Brad Bennett
- ☐ Dean Braham
- ☐ Rod Dallman
- ☐ Neil Davey
- ☐ Pat Elynuik
- ☐ Collin Feser
- ☐ Dave Goertz
- ☐ Steve Gotaas
- ☐ Tony Grenier
- ☐ Roydon Gunn
- ☐ Doug Hobson
- ☐ Dan Hodgson
- ☐ Curtis Hunt
- ☐ Kim Issel
- ☐ Ward Komonosky
- ☐ David Manson
- ☐ Dale McFee
- ☐ Ken Morrison
- ☐ Dave Pasin
- ☐ Don Schmidt
- ☐ Emanuel Viveiros

'90 - 91

PRINCE ALBERT RAIDERS / HIGH NOON OPTIMIST

Singles start at 50¢.
Card Size: 2 1/2" x 3 1/2"
Set (22 cards): $12

- ☐ Scott Allison
- ☐ Laurie Billeck
- ☐ Jeff Gorman
- ☐ Donevan Hextall
- ☐ Troy Hjertaas
- ☐ Don Kesa
- ☐ Jason Kwiatkowski
- ☐ Travis Laycock
- ☐ Lee J. Leslie
- ☐ Jamie Linden
- ☐ Dean McAmmond
- ☐ Dave Nelson
- ☐ Troy Neumeier
- ☐ Pat Odnokon
- ☐ Brian Pellerin
- ☐ Darren Perkins
- ☐ Curt Regnier
- ☐ Chad Seibel
- ☐ Mark Stowe
- ☐ Darren Van Impe
- ☐ Shane Zulyniak
- ☐ Raiders card

'91 - 92
PRINCE ALBERT RAIDERS / HIGH NOON OPTIMIST
Singles start at 50¢.
Card Size: 2 1/2" x 3 1/2"
Set (23 cards): $12
☐ Mike Fedorko
☐ Jeff Gorman
☐ Merv Haney
☐ Donevan Hextall
☐ Troy Hjertaas
☐ Dan Kesa
☐ Jason Klassen
☐ Jason Kwiatkowski
☐ Jeff Lank
☐ Travis Laycock
☐ Lee J. Leslie
☐ Stan Matwijiw
☐ Dean McAmmond
☐ David Nelson
☐ Mark Odnokon
☐ Darren Perkins
☐ Ryan Pisiak
☐ Nick Polychronopoulos
☐ Curt Regnier
☐ Jason Renard
☐ Barkley Swenson
☐ Darren Van Impe
☐ Shane Zulyniak

'93 - 94
PRINCE ALBERT RAIDERS / HIGH NOON OPTIMIST
Singles start at 50¢.
Card Size: 2 1/2" x 3 1/2"
Set (21 cards): $10
☐ Ryan Bast
☐ Rodney Bowers
☐ Van Burgess
☐ Brad Church
☐ Joaquin Gage (G)
☐ Jeff Gorman
☐ Merv Haney
☐ Greg Harvey
☐ Paul Healey
☐ Shane Hnidy
☐ Russell Hogue
☐ Jason Issel
☐ Steve Kelly
☐ Jeff Lank
☐ Mike McGhan
☐ Denis Pederson
☐ Mitch Shawara
☐ Shayne Toporowski
☐ Dean Whitney
☐ Darren Wright
☐ Shane Zulyniak

'95 - 96
PRINCE ALBERT RAIDERS / HIGH NOON OPTIMIST
Chris Phillips is the most expensive single at $3.
Singles start at 50¢.
Card Size: 2 1/2" x 3 1/2"
Set (22 cards): $12
☐ Rod Branch
☐ Curtis Brown
☐ Brad Church
☐ Kris Fizzell
☐ Dallas Flaman
☐ Don Halverson
☐ Shane Hnidy
☐ Russell Hogue
☐ Jason Issel
☐ Garnet Jacobson
☐ Kevin Kellett
☐ Steve Kelly
☐ Dylan Kemp
☐ Michael McGhan
☐ Marian Menhart
☐ Chris Phillips
☐ Blaine Russell
☐ Mitch Shawara
☐ Dave Van Drunen
☐ Roman Vopat
☐ Shane Willis
☐ Darren Wright

PRINCE GEORGE COUGARS

'99 - 00
PRINCE GEORGE COUGARS
Singles start at 50¢.
Set (25 cards):
☐ Scott Myers
☐ Tim Wedderburn
☐ Ryan Chieduch
☐ Jeff Zorn
☐ Dan Hamhuis
☐ Kevin Seibel
☐ Garry Toor
☐ Devin Wilson
☐ Jozef Mrena
☐ Aaron Foster
☐ Tyler Bouck
☐ Jonathan Parker
☐ Shon Jones-Parry
☐ Roman Takac
☐ Chris Falloon
☐ Justin Hansen
☐ Trent Hunter
☐ Blair Betts
☐ Travis Eagles
☐ Dempsey / Thompson
☐ Paul Valaitis
☐ Billy Thompson
☐ Justin Cox
☐ Dan Baum

'00 - 01
PRINCE GEORGE COUGARS / DAIRY QUEEN
Singles start at 50¢.
Card Size: 2 1/2" x 3 1/2"
Set (25 cards):
☐ Header
☐ Billy Thompson
☐ Tim Wedderburn
☐ David Koci
☐ Dan Hamhuis
☐ Gary Gladue
☐ Joey Hope
☐ Devin Wilson
☐ Chris Falloon
☐ Nathan Brice
☐ Christian Chartier
☐ Berkeley Buchko
☐ Scott Lynch
☐ Aaron Foster
☐ Jonathan Filewich
☐ Tomas Tesarek
☐ Dan Baum
☐ Adam Stefishen
☐ Mark Kitts
☐ Willy Glover
☐ Brett Allan
☐ Travis Eagles
☐ Justin Cox
☐ Duane Perillat
☐ Derek Boogaard

QUÉBEC REMPARTS

'80 - 81
QUÉBEC REMPARTS
Gaetan Duchesne is the most expensive single at $3.
Singles start at $1.
Card Size: 2" x 3"
Sponsor: None
Set (22 cards): $20
☐ Marc Bertrand
☐ Jacques Chouinard
☐ Roger Côté
☐ Gaston Drapeau
☐ Claude Drouin
☐ Gaetan Duchesne
☐ Scott Fraser
☐ Jean-Paul Larivière
☐ André Larocque
☐ Roberto Lavoie
☐ Stéphane Lessard
☐ Marc Lemay
☐ Paul Lévesque
☐ Richard Linteau
☐ Patrice Massé
☐ Jean-Marc Lanthier
☐ David Pretty
☐ Guy Riel
☐ Daniel Rioux
☐ Roberto Romano (G)
☐ Michel Therrien
☐ Gilles Tremblay

'98 - 99
QUÉBEC REMPARTS / CARTES, TIMBRES, MONNAIES STE-FOY
Singles start at 50¢.
Set (25 cards):
☐ Daniel Archambault
☐ David Bernier
☐ Nicholas Bilotto
☐ Tommy Bolduc
☐ Éric Chouinard
☐ Ray Dalton
☐ Joey Fetta
☐ Simon Gagné
☐ Martin Grenier
☐ Éric Laplante
☐ Jeff Leblanc
☐ Pierre Loiselle
☐ Jérôme Marois
☐ André Martineau
☐ Martin Moïse
☐ Alexandre Morel
☐ Maxime Ouellet
☐ Sylvain Plamondon
☐ Wesley Scanzano
☐ Dmitri Tolkunov
☐ Simon Tremblay
☐ Antoine Vermette
☐ Jonathan Wilhelmy
☐ Travis Zachary
☐ Checklist

'99 - 00
QUÉBEC REMPARTS / CARTES, TIMBRES, MONNAIES STE-FOY
Singles start at 50¢.
Card Size: 2 1/2" x 3 1/2"
Set (25 cards):
☐ 1 Jean Mallette
☐ 2 Patrick Chouinard
☐ 3 Kirill Safronov
☐ 4 Éric Chouinard
☐ 5 Patrick Grandmaître
☐ 6 Éric Laplante
☐ 7 Wesley Scanzano
☐ 8 Chris Lyness
☐ 9 Tommy Bolduc
☐ 10 J-F Touchette
☐ 11 Philippe Paris
☐ 12 Karl Morin
☐ 13 André Martineau
☐ 14 Sylvain Plamondon
☐ 15 Martin Moise
☐ 16 Martin Grenier
☐ 17 André Hart
☐ 18 Maxime Ouellet
☐ 19 Martin Paré
☐ 20 Éric Cloutier
☐ 21 Kristian Kudroc
☐ 22 Casey Leggett
☐ 23 Shawn Collymore
☐ 24 Mike Ribeiro
☐ 25 Checklist

'00 - 01
QUÉBEC REMPARTS / CARTES, TIMBRES, MONNAIES STE-FOY

Singles start at 50¢.
Card Size: 2 1/2" x 3 1/2"
Set (23 cards): $12
☐ 1 Jean Mallette
☐ 2 Sébastien Bourgon
☐ 3 Richard Paul
☐ 4 David Boilard
☐ 5 Jeff Hadley
☐ 6 Rémi Bergeron
☐ 7 Sébastien Morissette
☐ 8 Philippe Paris
☐ 9 Justin Stewart
☐ 10 Yannick Searles
☐ 11 Mike Bray
☐ 12 Guillaume Fournier
☐ 13 Robert Pearce
☐ 14 Petr Preucil
☐ 15 Philippe Parent
☐ 16 Didier Bochatay
☐ 17 Scott Della Vedova
☐ 18 Alexandre Reuben
☐ 19 David Massé
☐ 20 Shawn Collymore
☐ 21 Guillaume Bérubé
☐ 22 Kevin Lachance
☐ 23 Cory Urquhart

'01 - 02
QUÉBEC REMPARTS / CARTES, TIMBRES, MONNAIES STE-FOY

Singles start at 50¢.
Card Size: 2 1/2" x 3 1/2"
Set (25 cards): $12
☐ 1 Jean-Michel Bolduc
☐ 2 Sébastien Bourgon
☐ 3 Yan Turcotte
☐ 4 Jeff Hadley
☐ 5 Josh Hennessy
☐ 6 Mark Hurtubise
☐ 7 Mathieu Déry
☐ 8 Robert Pearce
☐ 9 Yannick Searles
☐ 10 Mike Bray
☐ 11 Tomas Spila
☐ 12 Samuel Duplain
☐ 13 Petr Preucil
☐ 14 Daniel Houle
☐ 15 Didier Bochatay
☐ 16 Guillaume Bérubé
☐ 17 Jeff Macaulay
☐ 18 Mario Joly
☐ 19 David Massé
☐ 20 Shawn Collymore
☐ 21 Denis Bérubé
☐ 22 Kevin Lachance
☐ 23 Sébastien Thinel
☐ 24 Cory Urquhart
☐ 25 Checklist

'02 - 03
QUÉBEC REMPARTS / CARTES, TIMBRES, MONNAIES STE-FOY

Singles start at 50¢.
Card Size: 2 1/2" x 3 1/2"
Set (23 cards): $12
☐ 1 Jean-Michel Bolduc
☐ 2 Sébastien Bourgon
☐ 3 Colin Leclaire
☐ 4 Josh Hennessy
☐ 5 Mark Hurtubise
☐ 6 Vladimir Kutny
☐ 7 Robert Pearce
☐ 8 Jordan LaVallée
☐ 9 Timofei Shishkanov
☐ 10 Jason Kostadine
☐ 11 Curtis Tidball
☐ 12 Frédéric Faucher
☐ 13 Karl St-Pierre
☐ 14 Didier Bochatsay
☐ 15 B. McMullin (G)
☐ 16 David Massé
☐ 17 Shawn Collymore
☐ 18 Guillaume Bérubé
☐ 19 Steve Pelletier
☐ 20 Kevin Lachance (G)
☐ 21 P-O Beaulieu
☐ 22 Chris Montgomery
☐ 22 Checklist
Set (9 cards):
☐ 12 Evan Shaw
☐ 14 J-M Filiatrault (G)
☐ 15 Alexandre Rouleau
☐ 16 Aaron Johnson
☐ 17 Pierre Morvan
☐ 20 Benoît Beauchemin
☐ 21 Rémy Tremblay
☐ 22 Checklist
☐ 23 Jamie McCabe

RAYSIDE-BALFOUR JR. CANADIENS

'89 - 90
RAYSIDE-BALFOUR JR. CANADIENS / LOEB-IGA
Singles start at 50¢.
Card Size: 2 3/8" x 3 3/8"
Set (20 cards): $10
☐ Dave Barrett
☐ Dan Baston
☐ Rick Chartrand
☐ Simon Chartrand
☐ Ron Clark
☐ Brian Dickison
☐ Trevor Duncan
☐ Don Gauthier
☐ Shawn Hawkins
☐ Roy Hildebrandt
☐ Al Laginski
☐ Eric Lanteigne
☐ Mike Leblanc
☐ Kevin MacDonald
☐ Mike Mooney
☐ Rick Potvin
☐ Rick Poulin
☐ Steve Prior
☐ Scott Sutton
☐ Team Photo

'90 - 91
RAYSIDE-BALFOUR JR. CANADIENS / BELANGER
Troy Mallette is the most expensive single at $1.
Singles start at 50¢.
Card Size: 2 3/8" x 3 3/8"
Construction Ltd.
Set (23 cards): $10
☐ Dan Baston
☐ Jon Boeve (G)
☐ Jordan Boyle
☐ Serge Coulombe
☐ Mike Dore
☐ Denis Gosselin
☐ Mike Gratton
☐ Jason Hall
☐ Grant Healey
☐ Marc Lafrenière
☐ Alain Leclair
☐ Mike Longo
☐ Matthew Mooney
☐ Virgil Nose
☐ Trevor Oystrick (G)
☐ Steve Proceviat
☐ Chris Puskas
☐ Yvon Quenneville
☐ Michael Sullivan
☐ Trevor Tremblay
☐ Sean Van Amburg
☐ Troy Mallette
☐ Canadians card

'91 - 92
RAYSIDE-BALFOUR JR. CANADIENS / KLS ERECTORS
Singles start at 50¢.
Card Size: 2 3/8" x 3 3/8"
Set (23 cards): $10
☐ Dan Baston
☐ Don Cuckey
☐ Dean Cull
☐ Mike Dore
☐ Denis Gosselin
☐ Jason Hall (G)
☐ Grant Healey
☐ Marc Lafrenière
☐ Mike Longo
☐ Scott Maclellan
☐ Matt Mooney
☐ Rob Moxness (G)
☐ Virgil Nose
☐ Trent Oystrick
☐ Jon Stewart
☐ Jon Stos
☐ Dave Sutton
☐ Scott Sutton
☐ Trevor Tremblay
☐ Jaak Valiots
☐ Sean Van Amburg
☐ Jason Young, Stickboy
☐ Canadians Card

RED DEER REBELS

'93 - 94
RED DEER REBELS
Singles start at 50¢.
Card Size: 2 1/2" x 3 1/2"
Sponsor: None
Set (30 cards): $10
☐ Peter Anholt
☐ Byron Briske
☐ Curtis Cardinal
☐ Jason Clague
☐ Dale Donaldson
☐ Dave Greenway
☐ Scott Grimwood
☐ Sean Halifax
☐ Chris Kibermanis
☐ Pete LeBoutilier
☐ Pete LeBoutilier (Action)
☐ Terry Lindgren
☐ Chris Maillet
☐ Eddie Marchant
☐ Mike McBain
☐ Mike Moller
☐ Andy Nowicki
☐ Berkley Pennock
☐ Tyler Quiring
☐ Craig Reichert
☐ Ken Richardson
☐ Sean Selmser
☐ Vaclav Slansky
☐ Mark Toljanich
☐ Darren Van Impe
☐ Pete Vandermeer
☐ Chris Wickenheiser
☐ Brad Zimmer
☐ Jonathan Zukiwsky
☐ Rebels Arena

'95 - 96
RED DEER REBELS
Singles start at 50¢.
Card Size: 2 1/2" x 3 1/2"
Sponsor: None
Set (23 cards): $10
☐ Arron Asham
☐ Bryan Boorman
☐ Aleksei Boudaev
☐ Mike Broda
☐ Mike Brown
☐ Jay Henderson
☐ David Hruska
☐ Chris Kibermanis
☐ Brad Leeb
☐ Terry Lindgren
☐ Mike McBain
☐ Brent McDonald
☐ Ken MacKay
☐ Harlan Pratt
☐ Greg Schmidt
☐ Pete Vendermeer
☐ Jesse Wallin
☐ Lance Ward
☐ Mike Whitney (G)
☐ Chris Wickenheiser
☐ B.J. Young
☐ Jonathan Zukiwsky
☐ Team Photo

'00 - 01
RED DEER REBELS
Singles start at 50¢.
Set (24 cards):
☐ Checklist
☐ Colby Armstrong
☐ Shane Bendera
☐ Andrew Bergen
☐ Devin Francon
☐ Michael Garnett
☐ Boyd Gordon
☐ Shane Grypiuk
☐ Diarmuid Kelly
☐ Ladislav Kouba
☐ Ross Lupaschuk
☐ Doug Lynch
☐ Justin Mapletoft
☐ Derek Meech
☐ Donovan Rattray
☐ Jeff Smith
☐ Shay Stephenson
☐ Joel Stepp
☐ Bryce Thoma
☐ Jim Vandermeer
☐ Martin Vymazal
☐ Justin Wallin
☐ Kyle Wanvig
☐ Jeff Woywitka

REGINA PATS

'81 - 82
REGINA PATS / POLICE
Garth Butcher and Gary Leeman are the most expensive singles at $3-4.
Singles start at $1.
Card Size: 2 5/8" x 4 1/8"
Set (25 cards): $25
☐ 1 Pats Logo
☐ 2 Garth Butcher
☐ 3 Lyndon Byers
☐ 4 Jock Callander
☐ 5 Marc Centrone
☐ 6 Dave Goertz
☐ 7 Evans Dobni
☐ 8 Dale Derkatch
☐ 9 Jeff Crawford
☐ 10 Jim Clarke
☐ 11 Jason Meyer
☐ 12 Gary Leeman
☐ 13 Bruce Holloway
☐ 14 Ken Heppner
☐ 15 Taylor Hall
☐ 16 Wally Schrieber
☐ 17 Kevin Pylypow
☐ 18 Ray Plamondon
☐ 19 Brent Pascal
☐ 20 Dave Michayluk
☐ 21 Barry Trotz
☐ 22 Al Tuer
☐ 23 Tony Vogel
☐ 24 Marty Wood
☐ 25 Regina Police Logo

'82 - 83
REGINA PATS / POLICE
Gary Leeman and Stu Grimson are the most expensive singles at $2-3.
Singles start at $1.
Card Size: 2 5/8" x 4 1/8"
Set (25 cards): $18
☐ 1 Regina Police
☐ 2 Todd Lumbard (G)
☐ 3 Jamie Reeve (G)
☐ 4 Dave Goertz
☐ 5 John Miner
☐ 6 Doug Trapp
☐ 7 R.J. Dundas
☐ 8 Stu Grimson
☐ 9 Al Tuer
☐ 10 Rick Herbert
☐ 11 Tony Vogel
☐ 12 John Bekkers
☐ 13 Dale Derkatch
☐ 14 Gary Leeman
☐ 15 Nevin Markwart
☐ 16 Kurt Wickenheiser
☐ 17 Jeff Frank
☐ 18 Marc Centrone
☐ 19 Taylor Hall
☐ 20 Lyndon Byers
☐ 21 Jason Meyer
☐ 22 Jeff Crawford
☐ 23 Don Boyd
☐ 24 Barry Trapp
☐ 25 Mascot K-9 Blue

'83 - 84
REGINA PATS / POLICE
Gary Leeman and Stu Grimson are the most expensive singles at $2-3.
Singles start at $1.
Card Size: 2 5/8" x 4 1/8"
Set (25 cards): $18
☐ 1 Regina Pats Logo
☐ 2 Todd Lumbard (G)
☐ 3 Jamie Reeve (G)

☐ 4 Dave Goertz
☐ 5 John Miner
☐ 6 Doug Trapp
☐ 7 R.J. Dundas
☐ 8 Stu Grimson
☐ 9 Al Tuer
☐ 10 Rick Herbert
☐ 11 Tony Vogel
☐ 12 John Bekkers
☐ 13 Dale Derkatch
☐ 14 Gary Leeman
☐ 15 Nevin Markwart
☐ 16 Kurt Wickenheiser
☐ 17 Jeff Frank
☐ 18 Marc Centrone
☐ 19 Taylor Hall
☐ 20 Lyndon Byers
☐ 21 Jayson Meyer
☐ 22 Jeff Crawford
☐ 23 Don Boyd
☐ 24 Barry Trapp
☐ 25 Mascot K-9 Big Blue

'86 - 87
REGINA PATS / ROYALS STUDIOS
Mark Janssens is the most expensive single at $1.
Singles start at 75¢.
Card Size: 2 1/2" x 3 1/2"
Set (30 cards): $13
☐ Troy Bakogeorge
☐ Grant Chorney
☐ Gary Dickie
☐ Milan Dragicevic
☐ Mike Dyck
☐ Craig Endean
☐ Mike Gibson
☐ Erin Ginnell
☐ Brad Hornung
☐ Mark Janssens
☐ Trent Kachur
☐ Craig Kalawsky
☐ Dan Logan
☐ Jim Mathieson
☐ Darin McInnes
☐ Darrin McKechnie
☐ Rob McKinley (G)
☐ Brad Miller
☐ Stacy Nickel
☐ Cregg Nicol
☐ Len Nielsen
☐ Darren Parsons
☐ Doug Sauter
☐ Ray Savard
☐ Dennis Sobchuk
☐ Chris Tarnowski
☐ Mike Van Slooten
☐ Brian Wilkie
☐ Rod Williams
☐ Mascot K-9 Big Blue

'87 - 88
REGINA PATS / ROYALS STUDIOS
Mike Sillinger and Mark Janssens are the most expensive singles at $1.
Singles start at 50¢.
Card Size: 2 1/2" x 3 1/2"
Set (28 cards): $13
☐ Kevin Clemens
☐ Gary Dickie
☐ Milan Dragicevic
☐ Mike Dyck
☐ Craig Endean
☐ Kevin Gallant
☐ Jamie Heward
☐ Rod Houk (G)
☐ Mark Janssens
☐ Trent Kachur
☐ Craig Kalawsky
☐ Frank Kovacs
☐ Darren Kwiatkowski

- ☐ Brian Leibel
- ☐ Tim Logan
- ☐ Jim Mathieson
- ☐ Darrin McKechnie
- ☐ Rob McKinely
- ☐ Brad Miller
- ☐ Cregg Nicol
- ☐ Doug Sauter
- ☐ Dan Sexton
- ☐ Mike Sillinger
- ☐ Dennis Sobchuk
- ☐ Stanley Szumlak
- ☐ Mike Van Slooten
- ☐ Mascot K-9 Big Blue
- ☐ Team Photo

'88 - 89

REGINA PATS / ROYALS STUDIOS

Kevin Haller is the most expensive single at $2.
Singles start at 75¢.
Card Size: 2 1/2" x 3 1/2"
Set (22 cards): $12

- ☐ Shane Bogden
- ☐ Cam Braver
- ☐ Scott Daniels
- ☐ Gary Dickie
- ☐ Mike Dyck
- ☐ Dave Gerse
- ☐ Kevin Haller
- ☐ Rod Houck
- ☐ Frank Kovacs
- ☐ Brian Leibel
- ☐ Bernie Lynch
- ☐ Kelly Markwart
- ☐ Jim Mathieson
- ☐ Brad Miller
- ☐ Dwayne Monteith
- ☐ Curtis Nykyforuk
- ☐ Darren Parsons
- ☐ Cory Paterson
- ☐ Jeff Sebastian
- ☐ Mike Sillinger
- ☐ Chad Silver
- ☐ Jamie Splett

'89 - 90

REGINA PATS / MR. LUBE

Singles start at 50¢.
Card Size: 2 1/2" x 3 1/2"
Set (19 cards): $10

- ☐ Kelly Chotowetz
- ☐ Hal Christiansen
- ☐ Scott Daniels
- ☐ Wade Fennig
- ☐ Jason Glickman
- ☐ Jamie Heward
- ☐ Terry Hollinger
- ☐ Frank Kovacs
- ☐ Kelly Markwart
- ☐ Jim Mathieson
- ☐ Cam McLellan
- ☐ Troy Mick
- ☐ Greg Pankewicz
- ☐ Cory Paterson
- ☐ Garry Pearce
- ☐ Mike Risdale
- ☐ Colin Ruck
- ☐ Mike Sillinger
- ☐ Jamie Splett

'96 - 97

REGINA PATS / VANTAGE POINT

Singles start at 50¢.
Set (25 cards):

- ☐ Gerald Adams
- ☐ Andy Adams
- ☐ Dean Arsene
- ☐ Joey Bouvier
- ☐ Kyle Calder
- ☐ Josh Dobbyn
- ☐ Kyle Freadrich
- ☐ Josh Holden

- ☐ Cody Jensen
- ☐ Perry Johnson
- ☐ Boyd Kane
- ☐ Shane Lanigan
- ☐ Brett Lysak
- ☐ David Maruca
- ☐ Chad Mercier
- ☐ Aaron Mori
- ☐ Derek Morris
- ☐ Dmitri Nabokov
- ☐ Clint Orr
- ☐ Lars Pattersen
- ☐ Rich Preston
- ☐ Bryan Randall
- ☐ Brad Stuart
- ☐ Curtis Tipler
- ☐ Team photo

'97 - 98

REGINA PATS / VANTAGE POINT

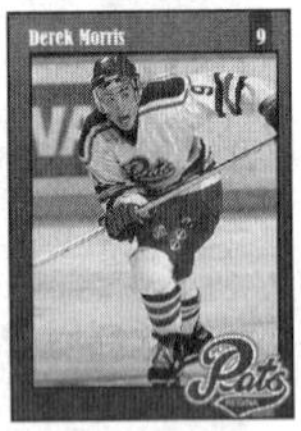

Singles start at 50¢.
Set (25 cards):

- ☐ Gerald Adams
- ☐ Dean Arsene
- ☐ Dennis Bassett
- ☐ Joey Bouvier
- ☐ Kyle Calder
- ☐ Travis Churchman
- ☐ John Cirjak
- ☐ Kyle Freadrich
- ☐ Josh Holden
- ☐ Barret Jackman
- ☐ Cody Jensen
- ☐ Boyd Kane
- ☐ Drew Kehler
- ☐ Chris Kwas
- ☐ Shane Lanigan
- ☐ Brett Lysak
- ☐ David Maruca
- ☐ Aaron Mori
- ☐ Derek Morris
- ☐ Ronald Petrovicky
- ☐ Bryan Randall
- ☐ Scott Roles
- ☐ Kevin Saurette
- ☐ Brad Stuart
- ☐ Mark Thompson

'01 - 02

REGINA PATS / CANADIAN TIRE

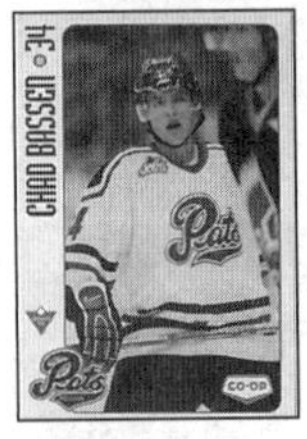

Singles start at 50¢.
Card Size: 2 1/2" x 3 1/2"
Set (25 cards):

- ☐ 1 Darryl Yacboski
- ☐ 2 Matej Trojovsky
- ☐ 3 Filip Novak
- ☐ 4 Jeff Feniak
- ☐ 5 Brennan Chapman
- ☐ 6 Dean Beuker
- ☐ 7 Garth Murray
- ☐ 8 Grant Jacobsen
- ☐ 9 David McDonald
- ☐ 10 Kevin Korol
- ☐ 11 Daniel Waschuk
- ☐ 12 Matt Hubbauer
- ☐ 13 Chris Schlenker
- ☐ 14 Codey Becker
- ☐ 15 Eric Sonnenberg
- ☐ 16 Kyle Ladobruk
- ☐ 17 Curtis Austring
- ☐ 18 Chad Davidson
- ☐ 19 Tyson Moulton
- ☐ 20 Chad Bassen
- ☐ 21 Josh Harding
- ☐ 22 Zack Roe
- ☐ 23 Chad Mercier
- ☐ 24 Drew Callander
- ☐ 25 Bob Lowes

RICHELIEU RIVERAINS

'84 - 85

RICHELIEU RIVERAINS

Stéphane Quintal is the most expensive single at $4.
Singles start at $1.
Card Size: 4" x 5 1/2"
Sponsor: None
Set (19 cards): $20

- ☐ Miguel Baldris
- ☐ Nicolas Beaulieu
- ☐ Martin Côté
- ☐ Sylvain Coutourier
- ☐ Dominic Edmond
- ☐ Yves Gaucher
- ☐ Eric Gobel
- ☐ Carl Lemieux
- ☐ Michel Lévesque
- ☐ Brad Loi
- ☐ Eric Primeau
- ☐ Stéphane Quintal
- ☐ Jean-Michel Ray
- ☐ Serge Richard
- ☐ Stéphane Robinson
- ☐ Danny Rochefort
- ☐ Martin Savaria
- ☐ Sylvain Senecal
- ☐ Eric Charron

'88 - 89

RICHELIEU RIVERAINS

Singles start at 50¢.
Card Size: 2 7/8" x 4"
Sponsor: None
Set (30 cards): $10

- ☐ Marc Beaurivage
- ☐ Denis Benoît
- ☐ Jonathan Black
- ☐ Richard Boisvert
- ☐ Hughes Bouchard
- ☐ François Bourdeau
- ☐ Guy Caplette
- ☐ Bertrand Cournoyer
- ☐ Yves Cournoyer
- ☐ Michel Deguise
- ☐ Patrick Grise
- ☐ Robert Guillet
- ☐ Jimmy Lachance
- ☐ Roger Laporte
- ☐ Frédéric Lefebvre
- ☐ Frédéric Maltais
- ☐ André Millette
- ☐ Joseph Napolitano
- ☐ Rémy Patoine
- ☐ Jean Plamondon
- ☐ Steve Plasse
- ☐ Jean-François Poirier
- ☐ Jacques Provencal
- ☐ Alain Rancourt
- ☐ Frédéric Savard
- ☐ François St-Germain
- ☐ Martin Tanguay
- ☐ Richard Valois
- ☐ Stéphane Valois
- ☐ Team Photo

RIMOUSKI OCÉANIC

'96 - 97

RIMOUSKI OCÉANIC

Vincent Lecavalier is the most expensive single at $15.
Singles start at 50¢.
Card Size: 2 1/2" x 3 1/2"
Sponsor: None
Set 1 (28 cards): $20

- ☐ Jonathan Beaulieu
- ☐ Martin Bédard
- ☐ Eric Belzile
- ☐ Denis Boily
- ☐ Dave Bolduc
- ☐ Yan Bouchard
- ☐ Nicolas Chabot
- ☐ Eryc Collin
- ☐ Eric Drouin
- ☐ Yannick Dupont
- ☐ Frédéric Girard
- ☐ Jimmy Grondin
- ☐ Vincent Lecavalier
- ☐ Frédéric Levac
- ☐ François Lévesque
- ☐ Philippe Lord
- ☐ David Malenfant
- ☐ Eric Normandin
- ☐ Mathieu Normandin
- ☐ Philippe Plante
- ☐ Martin Poitras
- ☐ David St. Onge
- ☐ Philippe Sauvé
- ☐ Sébastien Simard
- ☐ Mathieu Sunderland
- ☐ Bobby Lebel
- ☐ Gaston Thérien
- ☐ Team Photo

Set 2 (10 cards): $5

- ☐ Eric Bélanger
- ☐ Eric Bélanger
- ☐ Philippe Grondin
- ☐ Jason Lehoux
- ☐ Jonathan Lévesque
- ☐ Guillaume Rodrigue
- ☐ Joé Rullier
- ☐ Russell Smith
- ☐ Derrick Walser
- ☐ Mascot Louky

'97 - 98

RIMOUSKI OCÉANIC

Singles start at 50¢.
Card Size: 2 1/2" x 3 1/2"
Set (26 cards):

- ☐ Jonathan Beaulieu
- ☐ Éric? Bélanger
- ☐ Francis Bélanger
- ☐ David Bilodeau
- ☐ Kevin Bolduc
- ☐ Adam Borzecki
- ☐ Guillaume Couture
- ☐ Julien Desrosiers
- ☐ François Drainville
- ☐ Éric Drouin
- ☐ Jimmy Grondin
- ☐ Philippe Grondin
- ☐ Alexandre Jacques
- ☐ Vincent Lecavalier
- ☐ Casey Leggett
- ☐ Dave Malenfant
- ☐ Jean-Marc Pelletier
- ☐ Brad Richards
- ☐ Sébastien Roy
- ☐ Joe Rullier
- ☐ Philippe Sauvé
- ☐ Jonathan St-Louis
- ☐ David St-Onge
- ☐ Yannick Tremblay
- ☐ Derrick Walser
- ☐ Header

'99 - 00

RIMOUSKI OCÉANIC / CARTES, TIMBRES, MONNAIES STE-FOY

Singles start at 50¢.
Card Size: 2 1/2" x 3 1/2"
Set (23 cards):

- ☐ 1 Nicolas Pilote
- ☐ 2 Joé Rullier
- ☐ 3 Jonathan Beaulieu
- ☐ 4 Nicolas Poirier
- ☐ 5 Thatcher Bell
- ☐ 6 Brent Maclellan
- ☐ 7 Alexandre Tremblay
- ☐ 8 Jean-François Babin
- ☐ 9 Benoît Martin
- ☐ 10 Jan Philippe Cadieux
- ☐ 11 Jean-Philippe Brière
- ☐ 12 Alexis Castonguay
- ☐ 13 René Vydareny
- ☐ 14 Ronnie Decontie
- ☐ 15 Shawn Scanzano
- ☐ 16 Michel Ouellet
- ☐ 17 Jacques Larivière
- ☐ 18 Éric Salvail
- ☐ 19 Sébastien Caron
- ☐ 20 Brad Richards
- ☐ 21 Aaron Johnson
- ☐ 22 Juraj Kolnik
- ☐ 23 Michel Périard

'00 - 01

RIMOUSKI OCÉANIC / CARTES, TIMBRES, MONNAIES STE-FOY

Singles start at 50¢.
Card Size: 2 1/2" x 3 1/2"
Set (25 cards): $12

- ☐ 1 Philippe Lauzé
- ☐ 2 Tim Sinasac
- ☐ 3 Jonathan Beaulieu
- ☐ 4 Nicolas Pilote
- ☐ 5 Nicolas Poirier
- ☐ 6 Thatcher Bell
- ☐ 7 Tomas Malec
- ☐ 8 Brent MacLellan
- ☐ 9 Jean-François Plourde
- ☐ 10 Jean-François Babin
- ☐ 11 Benoit Martin
- ☐ 12 Daniel Petiquay
- ☐ 13 Jean-Philippe Brière
- ☐ 14 Ryan Clowe
- ☐ 15 Mathieu Fournier
- ☐ 16 Gabriel Balasescu
- ☐ 17 Mathieu Simard
- ☐ 18 Samuel Gibbons
- ☐ 19 Michel Ouellet
- ☐ 20 Jonathan Pelletier
- ☐ 21 Éric Salvail
- ☐ 22 Aaron Johnson
- ☐ 23 Sébastien Bolduc
- ☐ 24 Mascot Louky
- ☐ 25 Doris Labonté

'01 - 02

RIMOUSKI OCÉANIC / CARTES, TIMBRES, MONNAIES STE-FOY

Singles start at 50¢.
Card Size: 2 1/2" x 3 1/2"
Set (24 cards): $12

- ☐ 1 Chaz Johnson
- ☐ 2 Philippe Lauze
- ☐ 3 Dany Stewart
- ☐ 4 Michal Gavalier
- ☐ 5 Nicolas Poirier
- ☐ 6 Thatcher Bell
- ☐ 7 Thomas Malec
- ☐ 8 Brent MacLellan
- ☐ 9 Jean-François Plourde
- ☐ 10 Benoît Martin
- ☐ 11 Daniel Petiquay
- ☐ 12 Jean-Philippe Brière
- ☐ 13 Ryan Clowe
- ☐ 14 Mathieu Fournier
- ☐ 15 Gabriel Balasescu
- ☐ 16 Samuel Gibbons
- ☐ 17 Michel Ouellet
- ☐ 18 Éric Neilson
- ☐ 19 Patrick Lepage
- ☐ 20 Éric Salvail
- ☐ 21 Aaron Johnson
- ☐ 22 Sébastien Bolduc
- ☐ 23 Marc-Antoine Pouliot
- ☐ 24 Checklist

ROUYN-NORANDA HUSKIES

'99 - 00

ROUYN-NORANDA HUSKIES

Singles start at 50¢.
Set (40 cards):

- ☐ Éric L'Italien
- ☐ Michel Marcoux
- ☐ François Méthot
- ☐ Éric Naud
- ☐ André Parke
- ☐ Patrick Pelchat
- ☐ Jonathan Pelletier
- ☐ Bertand-Pierre Plouffe
- ☐ Jean Pronovost
- ☐ Matthew Quinn
- ☐ Mike Ribeiro
- ☐ Mike Ribeiro
- ☐ Rémi Royer
- ☐ Shawn Scanzano
- ☐ Jason Tessier
- ☐ Jérôme Tremblay
- ☐ Jérôme Tremblay
- ☐ Alain Turcotte
- ☐ Steeve Vandal
- ☐ Steeve Vandal
- ☐ Jimmy Verdule
- ☐ Martin Villeneuve
- ☐ Kirill Alexeev
- ☐ Marc-André Binette
- ☐ Maxime Bouchard
- ☐ Guy Boucher
- ☐ Bruno Cadieux
- ☐ Sébastien Centomo
- ☐ Marco Cimon
- ☐ Kevin Cloutier
- ☐ Gabrile Côté
- ☐ Pierre Dagenais
- ☐ James Desmarais
- ☐ Jonathan Gauthier
- ☐ Patrick Gilbert
- ☐ André Hart
- ☐ Robert Horak
- ☐ Mathieu Leclerc
- ☐ Jason Lehoux
- ☐ Jason Lehoux

'00 - 01

ROUYN-NORANDA HUSKIES / CARTES, TIMBRES, MONNAIES STE-FOY

Singles start at 50¢.
Card Size: 2 1/2" x 3 1/2"
Set (28 cards): $12

- ☐ 1 Dominic D'Amour
- ☐ 2 Jonathan Gauthier
- ☐ 3 Matthew Quinn
- ☐ 4 Kirill Alexeev
- ☐ 5 Sébastien Strozynski
- ☐ 6 Bertrand Pierre Plouffe
- ☐ 7 Maxime Talbot
- ☐ 8 Guillaume Lefebvre
- ☐ 9 Alexandre Morel
- ☐ 10 Michal Pinc
- ☐ 11
- ☐ 12 Mathieu Leclerc
- ☐ 13 Jérome Marois
- ☐ 14 Patrice Thériault
- ☐ 15 Patrick Gilbert
- ☐ 16 Maxime Ouellet
- ☐ 17 Louis Mandeville
- ☐ 18 Wesley Scanzano
- ☐ 19 Sébastien Centomo
- ☐ 20 Maxime Bouchard
- ☐ 21 Bruno Cadieux
- ☐ 22 Jean-Philippe Hamel
- ☐ 23 Shawn Scanzano
- ☐ 24 Jonathan Gagnon
- ☐ 25 Marc-André Binette
- ☐ 26 Jean Pronovost
- ☐ 27 Mascot Lappy
- ☐ 28 Checklist

SASKATOON BLADES

'81 - 82

SASKATOON BLADES / POLICE

Brian Skrudland is the most expensive single at $4.
Singles start at $1.
Card Size: 2 1/2" x 3 7/8"
Set (25 cards): $20

- ☐ 1 Team Photo
- ☐ 2 Daryl Stanley
- ☐ 3 Leroy Gorski
- ☐ 4 Donn Clark
- ☐ 5 Brad Duggen
- ☐ 6 Dave Chartier
- ☐ 7 Dave Brown
- ☐ 8 Adam Thompson
- ☐ 9 Bruce Eakin
- ☐ 10 Brian Skrudland
- ☐ 11 Roger Kortko
- ☐ 12 Ron Dreger
- ☐ 13 Daryl Lubiniecki
- ☐ 14 Marc Habscheid
- ☐ 15 Saskatoon Police
- ☐ 16 Todd Strueby
- ☐ 17 Craig Hurley
- ☐ 18 Bill Hlynsky
- ☐ 19 Lane Lambert
- ☐ 20 Mike Bloski
- ☐ 21 Bruce Gordon
- ☐ 22 Perry Ganchar
- ☐ 23 Ron Loustel
- ☐ 24 Blades Logo
- ☐ 25 Checklist

'83 - 84

SASKATOON BLADES / POLICE

Wendel Clark is the most expensive single at $10.
Singles start at $1.
Card Size: 2 1/2"x 3 3/4"
Set (24 cards): $28

- ☐ 1 Team Photo
- ☐ 2 Trent Yawney
- ☐ 3 Grant Jennings
- ☐ 4 Duncan MacPherson
- ☐ 5 Greg Holtby
- ☐ 6 Dan Leier
- ☐ 7 Dwaine Hutton
- ☐ 8 Wendel Clark
- ☐ 9 Kerry Laviolette
- ☐ 10 Dave Chartier
- ☐ 11 Dale Henry
- ☐ 12 Randy Smith
- ☐ 13 Kevin Kowalchuk
- ☐ 14 Todd MacLellan
- ☐ 15 Saskatoon Police
- ☐ 16 Larry Korchinski
- ☐ 17 Curtis Chamberlain
- ☐ 18 Greg Lebsack
- ☐ 19 Ron Dreger
- ☐ 20 Doug Kyle
- ☐ 21 Rick Smith
- ☐ 22 Joey Kocur
- ☐ 23 Allan Larouchelle
- ☐ 24 Mark Thietke

'84 - 85

SASKATOON BLADES / POLICE

Photos are in black and white. Wendel Clark is the most expensive single at $10.
Singles start at $1.50.
Sticker Size: 2" x 1 3/4"
Set (20 stickers): $28

- ☐ Jack Bowkus
- ☐ Curtis Chamberlain
- ☐ Wendel Clark
- ☐ Ron Dreger
- ☐ Randy Hoffart
- ☐ Mark Holick
- ☐ Greg Holtby
- ☐ Grant Jennings
- ☐ Kevin Kowalchuk
- ☐ Bryan Larkin
- ☐ James Latos
- ☐ Duncan MacPherson
- ☐ Rod Matechuk
- ☐ Todd McLellan
- ☐ Darren Moren
- ☐ Mike Morin
- ☐ Devon Oleniuk
- ☐ Grant Tkachuk
- ☐ Troy Vollhoffer
- ☐ Trent Yawney

'86 - 87

SASKATOON BLADES / SHELL

Singles start at $2.
Photo Size: 8 1/2" x 11"
Set (25 photos): $35

- ☐ Blair Atcheynum
- ☐ Colin Bayer
- ☐ Jack Bowkus
- ☐ Mike Butka
- ☐ Kelly Chase
- ☐ Tim Cheveldae (G)
- ☐ Blaine Chrest
- ☐ Kerry Clark
- ☐ Brian Glynn
- ☐ Mark Holick
- ☐ Kevin Kaminski
- ☐ Tracy Katelnikoff
- ☐ Kory Kocur
- ☐ Brian Larkin
- ☐ Curtis Leschyshyn
- ☐ Dan Logan
- ☐ Todd MacLellan
- ☐ Devon Oleniuk
- ☐ Marty Prazma
- ☐ Mary Reimer
- ☐ Walter Shutter
- ☐ Grant Tkachuk
- ☐ Tony Twist
- ☐ Shaun Van Allen

'89 - 90

SASKATOON BLADES / POLICE

Richard Matvichuk is the most expensive single at $2.
Singles start at $1.
Card Size: 2 3/4" x 4"
Set (25 cards): $18

- ☐ 1 Chief Joe Penkala
- ☐ 2 Saskatoon Police Logo
- ☐ 3 Marcel Comeau
- ☐ 4 Dean Kuntz
- ☐ 5 Mike Greenlay
- ☐ 6 Jody Praznik
- ☐ 7 Ken Sutton
- ☐ 8 Shawn Snesar
- ☐ 9 Shane Langager
- ☐ 10 Dean Holoien
- ☐ 11 Rob Lelacheur
- ☐ 12 David Struch
- ☐ 13 Collin Bauer
- ☐ 14 Kevin Yellowaga
- ☐ 15 Drew Sawtell
- ☐ 16 Brian Gerrits
- ☐ 17 Kirk Roworth
- ☐ 18 Tracey Katelnikoff
- ☐ 19 Scott Scissons
- ☐ 20 Jason Smart
- ☐ 21 Jason Christie
- ☐ 22 Darin Bader
- ☐ 23 Kevin Kaminsky
- ☐ 24 Kory Kocur
- ☐ 25 Darwin MacPherson

'90 - 91

SASKATOON BLADES / POLICE

Singles start at 75¢.
Card Size: 2 1/2" x 3 1/2"
Set (27 cards): $15

- ☐ 1 Terry Ruskowski
- ☐ 2 Trevor Robins
- ☐ 3 Cam Moon
- ☐ 4 Jeff Buchanan
- ☐ 5 Mark Raiter
- ☐ 6 Trevor Sherban

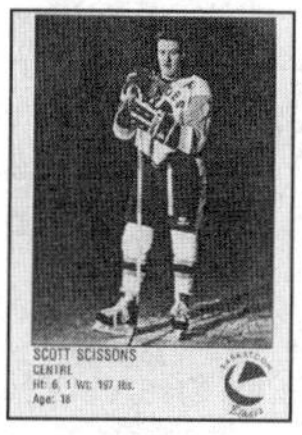

☐ 7 Jason Knox
☐ 8 Dean Rambo
☐ 9 Rob LeCacheur
☐ 10 David Struch
☐ 11 Greg Leahy
☐ 12 Derek Tibbatts
☐ 13 Shane Calder
☐ 14 Richard Matvichuk
☐ 15 Trent Coghill
☐ 16 Mark Wotton
☐ 17 Kelly Markwart
☐ 18 Mark Franks
☐ 19 Scott Scissons
☐ 20 Tim Cox
☐ 21 Gaetan Blouin
☐ 22 Darin Bader
☐ 23 Shawn Yakimishyn
☐ 24 Ryan Strain
☐ 25 Jason Peters
☐ 26 Blades Card
☐ 27 Blades Card

'91 - 92
SASKATOON BLADES / POLICE

Singles start at 50¢.
Card Size: 2 1/2" x 3 1/2"
Sponsor: Saskatoon Police
Set (25 cards): $10

☐ 1 Lorne Molleken
☐ 2 Trevor Robins (G)
☐ 3 Norm Maracle
☐ 4 Jeff Buchanan
☐ 5 Mark Raiter
☐ 6 Bryce Goebel
☐ 7 Rhett Trombley
☐ 8 Chad Rusnak
☐ 9 Jason Knight
☐ 10 David Struch
☐ 11 Shane Calder
☐ 12 Derek Tibbatts
☐ 13 Glen Gulutzan
☐ 14 Richard Matvichuk
☐ 15 Chad Michalchuk
☐ 16 Mark Wotton
☐ 17 Mark Franks
☐ 18 Andy McIntyre
☐ 19 Ryan Fujita
☐ 20 Sean McFatridge
☐ 21 Jason Becker
☐ 22 Shawn Yakimishyn
☐ 23 James Startup
☐ 24 Paul Buczkowski
☐ Crime Dog McGruff

'93 - 94
SASKATOON BLADES / COCA-COLA

Singles start at 75¢.
Card Size: 5 1/2" x 8 1/2"
Set (25 cards): $15

☐ Chad Allan
☐ Frank Banham
☐ Wade Belak
☐ Paul Buczkowski
☐ Shane Calder
☐ Mark Deyell
☐ Jason Duda
☐ Trevor Ethier
☐ Mike Gray
☐ Trevor Hanas
☐ Devon Hanson
☐ Andrew Kemper
☐ Kirby Law
☐ Andy Macintyre
☐ Norm Maracle
☐ Ivan Salon
☐ Todd Simpson
☐ Derek Tibbatts
☐ Rhett Warrener
☐ Clark Wilm
☐ Mark Wotton
☐ Banham/ Deyell/ Salon
☐ Tibbatts/ Wilm/ Macintyre
☐ Team Photo

'00 - 01
SASKATOON BLADES

Singles start at 50¢.
Card Size: 2 1/2" x 3 1/2"
Set (32 cards):

☐ Blades
☐ Blades
☐ Kevin Dickie
☐ Bruno Baseotto
☐ Tim Cheveldae
☐ Jason Goulet
☐ Matt Suderman
☐ Scotty Balan
☐ Ryan Stempfle
☐ Kane Ludwar
☐ Adrian Foster
☐ Martin Erat
☐ Garrett Bembridge
☐ Davin Heintz
☐ Justin Wallin
☐ Trent Adamus
☐ Jeff Coulter
☐ Chris Manchakowski
☐ Justin Kanigan
☐ David Cameron
☐ Derek Halldorson
☐ Aaron Starr
☐ Ryan Kehrig
☐ Rob Woods
☐ Warren Peters
☐ Petr Prochazka
☐ Justin Kelly
☐ Michael Garnett
☐ Tony Kolewaski
☐ Martin Vymazal
☐ Mascot Helmutt
☐ D.J. Jay Richards

SAULT STE. MARIE GREYHOUNDS

'80 - 81
SOO GREYHOUNDS / 920-CKCY

John Vanbiesbrouck and Ron Francis are the most expensive singles at $40-45. Singles start at $1.
Card Size: 2 1/2" x 4"
Set (25 cards): 90.00

☐ Tony Butorac
☐ Tony Cella
☐ Terry Crisp
☐ Marc D'Amour (G)
☐ Gord Dineen
☐ Ron Francis
☐ Steve Gatzos
☐ John Goodwin
☐ Ron Handy
☐ Huey Larkin
☐ Ken Latta
☐ Vic Morin
☐ Rick Morocco
☐ Jim Pavese
☐ Brian Petterle
☐ Ken Porteous
☐ Dirk Rueter
☐ Doug Shedden
☐ Steve Smith
☐ Terry Tait
☐ John Vanbiesbrouck (G)
☐ Tim Zwijack
☐ S.S. Marie Police
☐ OMJHL Logo
☐ Greyhounds Logo

'81 - 82
SOO GREYHOUNDS / 920-CKCY

John Vanbiesbrouck and Ron Francis are the most expensive singles at $30-35. Rick Tocchet sells at $15. Singles start at $1.
Card Size: 2 1/2" x 4"
Set (28 cards): 80.00

☐ Jim Alfred
☐ Dave Andreoli
☐ Richard Beaulne
☐ Bruce Bell
☐ Chuck Brimmer
☐ Tony Cella
☐ Kevin Conway
☐ Terry Crisp
☐ Marc D'Amour (G)
☐ Gord Dineen
☐ Chris Felix
☐ Ron Francis
☐ Steve Graves
☐ Wayne Groulx
☐ Huey Larkin
☐ Ken Latta
☐ Mike Lococo
☐ Jim Pavese
☐ Dirk Rueter
☐ Steve Smith
☐ Terry Tait
☐ Rick Tocchet
☐ John Vanbiesbrouck (G)
☐ Harry Wolfe
☐ J.D. Yari
☐ Bluebird Bakery Logo
☐ Canadian Tire Logo
☐ Coke Logo

'82 - 83
SOO GREYHOUNDS / 920-CKCY

John Vanbiesbrouck is the most expensive single at $25. Rick Tocchet sells at $10. Singles start at $1.
Card Size: 2 1/2" x 4"
Set (25 cards): $45

☐ Jim Aldred
☐ John Armelin
☐ Richard Beaulne
☐ Jeff Beukeboom
☐ Tony Cella
☐ Kevin Conway
☐ Terry Crisp
☐ Chris Felix
☐ Steve Graves
☐ Gus Greco
☐ Wayne Groulx
☐ Sam Haidy
☐ Tim Hoover
☐ Pat Lahey
☐ Huey Larkin
☐ Mike Lococo
☐ Mike Neill
☐ Ken Sabourin
☐ Steve Smith
☐ Terry Tait
☐ Rick Tocchet
☐ John Vanbiesbrouck (G)
☐ Harry Wolfe
☐ Bluebird Bakery Logo
☐ Station Mall Logo

'83 - 84
SOO GREYHOUNDS / 920-CKCY

Rick Tocchet is the most expensive single at $8. Singles start at $1.
Card Size: 2 1/2" x 4"
Set (25 cards): $25

☐ Jeff Beukeboom
☐ Grame Bonar
☐ Chris Brant
☐ John English
☐ Chris Felix
☐ Rick Fera
☐ Marc Fournier
☐ Steve Graves
☐ Gus Greco
☐ Wayne Groulx
☐ Sam Haidy
☐ Tim Hoover
☐ Jerry Iuliano
☐ Pat Lahey
☐ Mike Lococo
☐ Jean-Marc MacKenzie
☐ Mike Oliverio
☐ Brit Peer
☐ Joey Rampton
☐ Ken Sabourin
☐ Jim Samec
☐ Rick Tocchett
☐ Harry Wolfe
☐ Coke Logo
☐ IGA Logo

'84 - 85
SOO GREYHOUNDS / 920-CKCY

Bob Probert is the most expensive single at $8. Derek King sells at $3. Singles start at $1.
Card Size: 2 1/2" x 4"
Set (25 cards): $25

☐ Marty Abrams
☐ Jeff Beukeboom
☐ Chris Brant
☐ Terry Crisp
☐ Chris Felix
☐ Scott Green
☐ Wayne Groulx
☐ Steve Hollett
☐ Tim Hoover
☐ Derek King
☐ Tyler Larter
☐ Jean-Marc MacKenzie
☐ Scott Mosey
☐ Mike Oliverio
☐ Grit Peer
☐ Wayne Presley
☐ Bob Probert
☐ Brian Rome
☐ Ken Sabourin
☐ Ron Veccia
☐ Harry Wolfe
☐ Coke Logo
☐ IGA Logo

'87 - 88
SOO GREYHOUNDS / POLICE

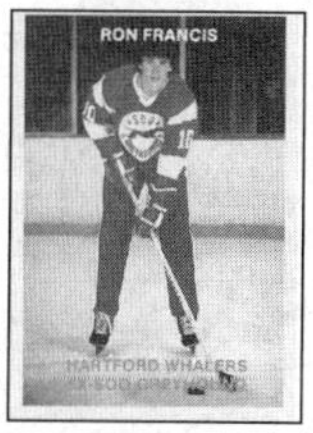

Regional stars do carry a premium.
Card Size: 2 1/2" x 4"
Set (35 cards): 1$30

☐ 1 Chief Barry King 1.00
☐ 2 Dan Currie 1.00
☐ 3 Mike Glover 1.00
☐ 4 Tyler Larter 1.00
☐ 5 Bob Jones 1.00
☐ 6 Singer Slewidge 1.00
☐ 7 Brad Jones 1.00
☐ 8 Ron Francis $12
☐ 9 Dale Turnbull 1.00
☐ 10 Don McConnell 1.00
☐ 11 Chris Felix 1.00
☐ 12 Steve Udvari 1.00
☐ 13 Shawn Simpson 1.00
☐ 14 Rob Zettler 2.00
☐ 15 Phil Esposito $10
☐ 16 J. V'b'sbrouck (G) $12
☐ 17 Mike Oliverio 1.00
☐ 18 Colin Ford 1.00
☐ 19 Steve Herniman 1.00
☐ 20 Troy Mallette 2.00
☐ 21 Craig Hartsburg 4.00
☐ 22 Don Boyd 1.00
☐ 23 Peter Fiorentino 1.00
☐ 24 Jeff Columbus 1.00
☐ 25 Brad Stepan 1.00
☐ 26 Rick Tocchet 6.00
☐ 27 Shane Sargant 1.00
☐ 28 Wayne Muir 1.00
☐ 29 Wayne Gretzky 1$25
☐ 30 Gary Luther 1.00
☐ 31 Harry Wolfe 1.00
☐ 32 Rod Thacker 1.00
☐ 33 Terry Tait 1.00
☐ 34 Brian Howard 1.00
☐ 35 Greg Johnston 1.00

'89 - 90
SOO GREYHOUNDS / POLICE

Ron Francis is the most expensive single at $8. Adam Foote sells at 2. Singles start at 75¢.
Card Size: 2 3/4" x 3 1/2"
Set (30 cards): $25

☐ 1 CL: Chief Barry King
☐ 2 S.S. Marie Police
☐ 3 Ted Nolan
☐ 4 Greyhounds Logo
☐ 5 Sherry Bassin
☐ 6 Jim Ritchie
☐ 7 Bob Boughner
☐ 8 Denny Lambert
☐ 9 Doug Minor
☐ 10 Rick Pracey
☐ 11 Colin Miller
☐ 12 Kevin King
☐ 13 Ron Francis
☐ 14 Rick Kowalsky
☐ 15 Adam Foote
☐ 16 Wade Whitten
☐ 17 Dale Turnbull
☐ 18 Bob Jones
☐ 19 David Carrie
☐ 20 Brad Tuley
☐ 21 Wayne Muir
☐ 22 Dave Babcock
☐ 23 David Matsos
☐ 24 Dan Ferguson
☐ 25 Jeff Szeryk
☐ 26 Mike Zuke
☐ 27 Dave Doucette
☐ 28 John Campbell
☐ 29 Graeme Harvey
☐ 30 John Fuselli

'93 - 94
SOO GREYHOUNDS / POLICE

The most expensive singles are Dan Cloutier and Kevin Hodson at $2. Singles start at 75¢.
Card Size: 2 1/2" x 3 1/2"
Set (32 cards): $20

☐ 1 Memorial Cup
☐ 2 Dan Tanevski
☐ 3 Mark Matier
☐ 4 Oliver Pastinsky
☐ 5 Peter MacKeller
☐ 6 Drew Bannister
☐ 7 Sean Gagnon
☐ 8 Joe Clarke
☐ 9 Chad Penney
☐ 10 Neal Martin
☐ 11 Perry Pappas
☐ 12 David Matsos
☐ 13 Rick Kowalsky
☐ 14 Gary Roach
☐ 15 Jarret Reid
☐ 16 Steve Sullivan
☐ 17 Tom MacDonald
☐ 18 Jodie Murphy
☐ 19 Ralph Intranuovo
☐ 20 Brad Baber
☐ 21 Blaine Thompson
☐ 22 Aaron Gavey
☐ 23 Wade Gibson
☐ 24 Kiley Hill
☐ 25 Jeff Toms
☐ 26 Joe Van Volsen
☐ 27 Dan Cloutier (G)
☐ 28 Kevin Hodson (G)
☐ 29 D.Mayville/S.Bassin
☐ 30 Ted Nolan/D.Flynn
☐ 31 Greyhounds Staff
☐ 32 M.Zuke/ F.Varcoe/ J.Mayne/ M.Sicard

'96 - 97
SOO GREYHOUNDS / TD BANK

Joe Thornton has two cards each at $10. Singles start at 50¢. An autographed set was also available.
Card Size: 2 1/2" x 3 1/2"
Set (28 cards): $35

☐ Wes Booker #24
☐ Bill Browne #3
☐ Peter Cava #14
☐ Justin Davis #15
☐ J.J. Dickie #26
☐ Oak Hewer #7
☐ Richard Jackman #23
☐ Richard Jackman
☐ Matt Lahey #22
☐ David Mayville
☐ Jake McCracken #30 (G)
☐ Marc Moro #21
☐ Robert Mulick #28
☐ Daniel Passero #5
☐ Joe Paterson
☐ Nathan Perrot #18
☐ Michal Podolka #33 (G)
☐ Nick Robinson #6
☐ Ben Schust #12
☐ Joe Seroski #11
☐ Chad Spurr #25
☐ Brian Stewart #29
☐ Joe Thornton #19
☐ Joe Thornton
☐ Trevor Tokarczyk #16
☐ Richard Uniacke #9
☐ David Wight #20
☐ Chad Woollard #17
☐ Bob Jones/ Mike Zuke
☐ Team Photo

'02 - 03
SOO GREYHOUNDS

We do not yet have a checklist for this series.

SEATTLE THUNDERBIRDS

'93 - 94
SEATTLE THUNDERBIRDS

Brendan Witt and Deron Quint are the most expensive singles at $1.50-2. Singles start at 50¢.
Card Size: 2 1/2"x 3 1/2"
Sponsor: None
Set (30 cards): $15

☐ Mike Barrie
☐ Doug Bonner
☐ David Carson
☐ Jeff Dewar
☐ Brett Duncan
☐ Shawn Gervais
☐ Chris Herperger
☐ Troy Hyatt
☐ Curt Kamp
☐ Olaf Kjenstadt
☐ Walt Kyle
☐ Milt Mastad
☐ Alexandre Matvichuk
☐ Larry McMorran
☐ Jim McTaggart
☐ Regan Mueller
☐ Kevin Mylander
☐ Drew Palmer
☐ Jeff Peddigrew
☐ Darryl Plandowski
☐ Deron Quint
☐ Darrell Sandback
☐ Chris Schmidt
☐ Lloyd Shaw
☐ Darcy Smith
☐ Rob Tallas (G)
☐ Paul Vincent
☐ Chris Wells
☐ Brendan Witt
☐ Team Photo

SHAWINIGAN CATARACTES

'99 - 00
SHAWINIGAN CATARACTES / CARTES, TIMBRES, MONNAIES STE-FOY

Singles start at 50¢.
Card Size: 2 1/2" x 3 1/2"
Set (24 cards): $12

☐ 1 Jonathan Lessard
☐ 2 Philippe Gélinas
☐ 3 Jonathan Bellemare
☐ 4 Anthony Quessy
☐ 5 Alexandre Blackburn
☐ 6 Pascal Dupuis
☐ 7 Marc-André Bergeron
☐ 8 Francis Deslauriers
☐ 9 J-S Trudelle
☐ 10 Jean-Philippe Paré
☐ 11 Jean-François David
☐ 12 Philippe Deblois
☐ 13 Dave Verville
☐ 14 Mathieu Chouinard
☐ 15 Gilbert Lefrançois
☐ 16 Denis Desmarais
☐ 17 Yannick Noiseaux
☐ 18 Dominic Fourget
☐ 19 Conor McGuire
☐ 20 Jean-François Dufort
☐ 21 André Landry
☐ 22 David Chicoine
☐ 23 Jason Pominville
☐ 24 Checklist

'00 - 01
SHAWINIGAN CATARACTES / CARTES, TIMBRES, MONNAIES STE-FOY

Singles start at 50¢.
Card Size: 2 1/2" x 3 1/2"
Set (24 cards): $12

☐ 1 Denis Desmarais
☐ 2 Michalek Zbynek
☐ 3 Jonathan Beaulieu
☐ 4 Jonathan Lessard
☐ 5 Jonathan Bellemare
☐ 6 Patrick Bolduc
☐ 7 Anthony Quessy
☐ 8 David Chicoine
☐ 9 Gilbert Lefrançois
☐ 10 Radim Vrbata
☐ 11 Yannick Noiseaux
☐ 12 Marc-André Bergeron
☐ 13 Jimmy Cuddihy
☐ 14 Kevin Bergin
☐ 15 François Gagnon
☐ 16 Olivier Michaud
☐ 17 Frédéric Cloutier
☐ 18 J-F Cloutier
☐ 19 A. Ménard Burrows
☐ 20 Jason Pominville
☐ 21 Dominic Forget
☐ 22 Trevor Ettinger
☐ 23 Jean-François Dufort
☐ 24 Checklist

'01 - 02
SHAWINIGAN CATARACTES / CARTES, TIMBRES, MONNAIES STE-FOY

Singles start at 50¢.
Card Size: 2 1/2" x 3 1/2"
Set (24 cards):

☐ 1 Denis Desmarais
☐ 2 Zbynek Michalek
☐ 3 Paul-André Bourgoin
☐ 4 Jimmy Fillion
☐ 5 Jonathan Lessard
☐ 6 Jonathan Bellemare
☐ 7 Mathieu Gravel
☐ 8 Jonathan Villeneuve
☐ 9 David Chicoine
☐ 10 Armands Berzins
☐ 11 Philippe Bastarache
☐ 12 Jimmy Cuddihy
☐ 13 Chris Hodgson
☐ 14 Thiery Poudrier
☐ 15 Olivier Michaud
☐ 16 Guillaume Lavallée
☐ 17 David Leroux
☐ 18 Jean-François David
☐ 19 Jonathan Boutin
☐ 20 Alexandre Burrows
☐ 21 Mathieu Payette
☐ 22 Jason Pominville
☐ 23 Jean-François Dufort
☐ 24 Checklist

'02 - 03
SHAWINIGAN CATARACTES / CARTES, TIMBRES, MONNAIES STE-FOY

Singles start at 50¢.
Card Size: 2 1/2" x 3 1/2"
Set (25 cards):

☐ 1 Julian Ellis (G)
☐ 2 Dave Grenier
☐ 3 Paul-André Bourgoin
☐ 4 Frédéric Gariépy
☐ 5 Mathieu Gravel
☐ 6 Karl Morin
☐ 7 Armands Berzins

☐ 8 Danick Bouchard
☐ 9 Jimmy Cuddihy
☐ 10 Mathieu Fournier
☐ 11 Kévin Deslauriers
☐ 12 Thiery Poudrier
☐ 13 David Leroux
☐ 14 Sébastien Gauthier
☐ 15 Jonathan Villeneuve
☐ 16 M. B.-Robinson (G)
☐ 17 Jonathan Boutin
☐ 18 Justin Vinneau
☐ 19 Marek Hascak
☐ 20 Simon-Pierre Sauvé
☐ 21 Dominic Plante
☐ 22 Benoît Mondou
☐ 23 Nicolas Désilets
☐ 24 Charles Gauthier
☐ 25 Checklist

SHERBROOKE CASTORS

'00 - 01
SHERBROOKE CASTORS / CARTES, TIMBRES, MONNAIES STE-FOY

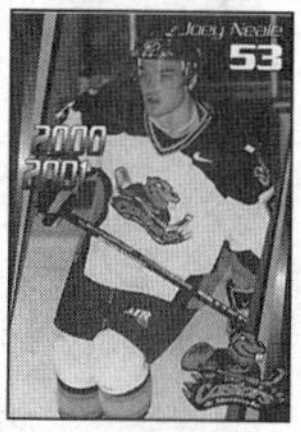

Singles start at 50¢.
Card Size: 2 1/2" x 3 1/2"
Set (20 cards):

☐ 1 Drew MacIntyre
☐ 2 Sébastien Courcelles
☐ 3 Simon Tremblay
☐ 4 Éric Lavigne
☐ 5 Patrick Gosselin
☐ 6 Steve Morency
☐ 7 Francis Trudel
☐ 9 Jonathan Robert
☐ 11 Éric Dagenais
☐ 12 Louis-Philip Lemay
☐ 13 Artem Ternavski
☐ 14 Joey Neale
☐ 15 Benoît Genesse
☐ 16 P-L Courchesne
☐ 17 Mathieu Thibodeau
☐ 18 Nicolas Corbeil
☐ 21 François Bélanger
☐ 22 Mascot Cajou
☐ 23 Joe Canale
☐ 24 Checklist

'01 - 02
SHERBROOKE CASTORS / CARTES, TIMBRES, MONNAIES STE-FOY

Singles start at 50¢.
Card Size: 2 1/2" x 3 1/2"
Set (23 cards):

☐ 1 Drew MacIntyre
☐ 2 Éric Dagenais

- ☐ 3 Dany Roussin
- ☐ 4 Juha-Pekka (Jr.) Ketola
- ☐ 5 Patrik Lévesque
- ☐ 6 David Chicoine
- ☐ 7 Jonathan Paiement
- ☐ 8 Cédrick Duhamel
- ☐ 9 Yan Gaudette
- ☐ 10 Francis Trudel
- ☐ 11 Maxime Boisclair
- ☐ 12 Jonathan Robert
- ☐ 13 Mathieu Wathier
- ☐ 14 Louis-Philip Lemay
- ☐ 15 B.-Pierre Plouffe
- ☐ 16 Sébastien Courcelles
- ☐ 17 Patrick Mbaraga
- ☐ 18 P-L Courchesne
- ☐ 19 Nicolas Corbeil
- ☐ 20 Bruno D'Amico
- ☐ 21 François Bélanger
- ☐ 22 Jean Pronovost
- ☐ 23 Checklist

SPOKANE CHIEFS

'89 - 90

SPOKANE CHIEFS / TEACHERS CREDIT UNION

Pat Falloon and Travis Green are the most expensive singles at $3-4. Ray Whitney and Jon Klemm sell at $1-2. Singles start at 75¢.

Card Size: 2 1/2" x 3 1/2"

Set (20 cards): $16

- ☐ Mike Chrun
- ☐ Shawn Dietrich
- ☐ Milan Dragicevic
- ☐ Frank Evans
- ☐ Pat Falloon
- ☐ Jeff Ferguson
- ☐ Travis Green
- ☐ Bobby House
- ☐ Mick Jickling
- ☐ Jon Klemm
- ☐ Steve Junker
- ☐ Chris Rowland
- ☐ Dennis Saharchuk
- ☐ Kerry Toporowski
- ☐ Trevor Tovell
- ☐ Bram Vanderkracht
- ☐ Ray Whitney

'95 - 96

SPOKANE CHIEFS

Jason Podollan is the most expensive single at $1.50. Singles start at 50¢.

Card Size: 2 1/2" x 3 1/2"

Sponsor: None

Set (30 cards): $15

- ☐ 1 David Lemanowicz
- ☐ 2 Scott Fletcher
- ☐ 3 Hugh Hamilton
- ☐ 4 Chris Lane
- ☐ 5 Dmitri Leonov
- ☐ 6 Darren Sinclair
- ☐ 7 Ty Jones
- ☐ 8 Kris Graf
- ☐ 9 Trent Whitfield
- ☐ 10 Martin Cerven
- ☐ 11 Randy Favaro
- ☐ 12 Jason Podollan
- ☐ 13 Joel Boschman
- ☐ 14 Jared Hope
- ☐ 15 Greg Leeb
- ☐ 16 John Cirjak
- ☐ 17 Mike Haley
- ☐ 18 Ryan Berry
- ☐ 19 Sean Gillam
- ☐ 20 Derek Schutz
- ☐ 21 Joe Cardarelli
- ☐ 22 Adam Magarrell
- ☐ 23 Jay Bertsch
- ☐ 24 John Shockey
- ☐ 25 Mike Babcock
- ☐ 26 Parry Shockey
- ☐ 27 T.D. Forss
- ☐ 28 Ted Schott
- ☐ 29 Dan Mitchell
- ☐ 30 Aren Miller

'97 - 98

SPOKANE CHIEFS

Singles start at 50¢.

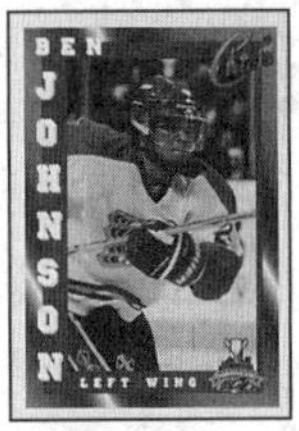

Set (30 cards):

- ☐ Aren Miller (G)
- ☐ Brad Ference
- ☐ Perry Johnson
- ☐ Mark Forth
- ☐ Zenith Komarniski
- ☐ Justin Ossachuk
- ☐ Cole Fischer
- ☐ Brandin Côté
- ☐ Ty Jones
- ☐ Kris Graf
- ☐ Trent Whitfield
- ☐ Jared Smyth
- ☐ Marc Brown
- ☐ Greg Leeb
- ☐ Justin Kelly
- ☐ Ben Johnson
- ☐ Kyle Rossiter
- ☐ Derek Schultz
- ☐ Marian Cisar
- ☐ Lynn Loyns
- ☐ Kris Waltze
- ☐ Curtis Suter
- ☐ Josh Maser
- ☐ Ron Grimard
- ☐ Dan Vandermeer
- ☐ Shaun Fleming
- ☐ Mike Babcock
- ☐ Mike Pelino
- ☐ T.D. Forss
- ☐ Dan Mitchell

'98 - 99

SPOKANE CHIEFS

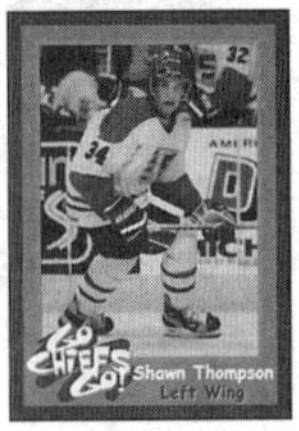

We do not yet have a checklist for this series.

'99 - 00

SPOKANE CHIEFS

We do not yet have a checklist for this series.

SUDBURY WOLVES

'84 - 85

SUDBURY WOLVES / PEPSI

Jeff Brown is the most expensive single at $5. Singles start at $1.

Card Size: 3 1/2" x 6"

Set (16 cards): $15

- ☐ 1 Andy Spruce
- ☐ 2 Sean Envoy (G)
- ☐ 3 Mario Martini
- ☐ 4 Brent Daugherty
- ☐ 5 Mario Chitaroni
- ☐ 6 Dan Chiasson
- ☐ 7 Jeff Brown

- ☐ 8 Todd Sepkowski
- ☐ 9 Brad Belland
- ☐ 10 Glenn Greenough
- ☐ 11 John Landry
- ☐ 12 Max Middendorf
- ☐ 13 David Moylan
- ☐ 14 Jamie Nadjiwan
- ☐ 15 Warren Rychel
- ☐ 16 Ed Smith

'85 - 86

SUDBURY WOLVES / POLICE

Jeff Brown is the most expensive single at $3. Singles start at $1.

Card Size: 2 3/4" x 4"

Imprint: Journal Printing

Set (26 cards): $15

- ☐ 1 Sudbury Police
- ☐ 2 Sponsor Logos
- ☐ 3 Checklist
- ☐ 4 Chief R. Zanibbi
- ☐ 5 Wayne Maxner
- ☐ 6 Sean Envoy (G)
- ☐ 7 Todd Lalonde
- ☐ 8 Costa Papista
- ☐ 9 Robin Rubic
- ☐ 10 David Moylan
- ☐ 11 Brent Daugherty
- ☐ 12 Glenn Greenough
- ☐ 13 Mario Chitaroni
- ☐ 14 Ken McRae
- ☐ 15 Mike Hudson
- ☐ 16 Andy Paquette
- ☐ 17 Ed Lemaire
- ☐ 18 Mark Turner
- ☐ 19 Craig Duncanson
- ☐ 20 Jeff Brown
- ☐ 21 Team Photo
- ☐ 22 Max Middendorf
- ☐ 23 Keith Van Rooyen
- ☐ 24 Brad Walcot
- ☐ 25 Ron Wilson
- ☐ 26 Bill White

'86 - 87

SUDBURY WOLVES / POLICE

Photos are credited to Rigo Peloso. Singles start at $1.

Card Size: 3" x 4 1/8"

Set (33 cards): $15

- ☐ 1 Anders Hoberg (G)
- ☐ 1 Ted Mielczarek (G)
- ☐ 2 Todd Lalonde
- ☐ 3 Costa Papista
- ☐ 4 Justin Corbeil
- ☐ 5 Dave Moylan
- ☐ 6 Brent Daugherty
- ☐ 8 Mario Chitaroni
- ☐ 9 Jim Way
- ☐ 10 Dean Jalbert
- ☐ 11 President J. Drago
- ☐ 12 Ken McRae
- ☐ 14 Steve Hedington
- ☐ 15 Mike Hudson
- ☐ 16 Pierre Gagnon
- ☐ 17 Peter Hughes
- ☐ 18 Mark Turner
- ☐ 19 Sudbury Police
- ☐ 20 Wayne Doucet
- ☐ 21 Paul DiPietro
- ☐ 22 Max Middendorf
- ☐ 23 Phil Paquette
- ☐ 25 Rob Wilson
- ☐ 26 Checklist
- ☐ 27 Chief R. Zanibbi
- ☐ 28 Claude D'Amour
- ☐ 29 Guy Blanchard
- ☐ 30 Joe Desrosiers
- ☐ 31 Jake Bisschops
- ☐ 33 Bill White

'87 - 88

SUDBURY WOLVES / POLICE

Singles start at $1.

Card Size: 3" x 4 1/8"

Set (26 cards): $12

- ☐ 1 Checklist
- ☐ 2 Ted Mielczarek (G)
- ☐ 3 Dan Gatenby
- ☐ 4 Todd Lalonde
- ☐ 5 Justin Corbeil
- ☐ 6 Jordan Fois
- ☐ 7 Rodney Lapointe
- ☐ 8 Dave Akey
- ☐ 9 Jim Smith
- ☐ 10 Fred Pennell
- ☐ 11 Joey Simon
- ☐ 12 Luciano Fagioli
- ☐ 13 Robb Graham
- ☐ 14 John Uniac
- ☐ 15 Dave Carrie
- ☐ 16 Pierre Gagnon
- ☐ 17 Peter Hughes
- ☐ 18 Scott McCullough
- ☐ 19 Dean Guitard
- ☐ 20 Pat Holley
- ☐ 21 Chad Bradaway
- ☐ 22 Paul DiPietro
- ☐ 23 Derek Thompson
- ☐ 24 Scott Luce
- ☐ 25 Rob Wilson
- ☐ 26 Chief R. Zanibbi

'88 - 89

SUDBURY WOLVES / POLICE

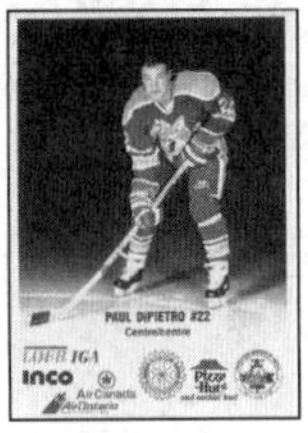

Singles start at 75¢.

Card Size: 3" x 4 1/8"

Set (26 cards): $12

- ☐ 1 Checklist
- ☐ 2 David Goverde (G)
- ☐ 3 Ted Mielczarek (G)
- ☐ 4 Adam Bennett
- ☐ 5 Kevin Grant
- ☐ 6 Jordan Fois
- ☐ 7 Sean O'Donnell
- ☐ 8 Kevin Meisner
- ☐ 9 Jim Smith
- ☐ 10 Fred Pennell
- ☐ 11 Tyler Pella
- ☐ 12 Dean Pella
- ☐ 13 Darren Bell
- ☐ 14 Derek Thompson
- ☐ 15 Terry Chitaroni
- ☐ 16 Sean Stansfield
- ☐ 17 Alastair Still
- ☐ 18 Jim Sonmez
- ☐ 19 Shannon Bolton
- ☐ 20 Andy Paquette
- ☐ 21 Mark Turner
- ☐ 22 Paul DiPietro
- ☐ 23 Robert Knesaurek
- ☐ 24 Todd Lalonde
- ☐ 25 Scott Herniman
- ☐ 26 Chief R. Zanibbi

'89 - 90

SUDBURY WOLVES / POLICE

Glen Murray is the most expensive single at $8. Singles start at 75¢.

Card Size: 3" x 4 1/8"

Set (25 cards): $20

- ☐ 1 Checklist
- ☐ 2 Alastair Still
- ☐ 3 Bill Kovacs
- ☐ 4 Darren Bell
- ☐ 5 Scott Mahoney
- ☐ 6 Glen Murray
- ☐ 7 Iain Laforge
- ☐ 8 Jamie Matthews
- ☐ 9 Jon Boeve (G)
- ☐ 10 Adam Bennett
- ☐ 11 Derek Etches
- ☐ 12 Marcus Middleton
- ☐ 13 Jim Sonmez
- ☐ 14 Leonard MacDonald
- ☐ 15 Paul DiPietro
- ☐ 16 Neil Ethier
- ☐ 17 Sean O'Donnell
- ☐ 18 Andy MacVicar
- ☐ 19 David Goverde (G)
- ☐ 20 Jason Young
- ☐ 21 Wade Bartley
- ☐ 22 Barry Young
- ☐ 23 Chief R. Zanibbi
- ☐ 24 Terry Chitaroni
- ☐ 25 Rob Knesaurek

'90 - 91

SUDBURY WOLVES / POLICE

Michael Peca is the most expensive single at $3. Singles start at 75¢.

Card Size: 3" x 4 1/8"

Set (25 cards): $15

- ☐ 1 Darryl Paquette
- ☐ 2 Adam Bennett
- ☐ 3 Barry Young
- ☐ 4 Jon Boeve
- ☐ 5 Kyle Blacklock
- ☐ 6 Sean O'Donnell
- ☐ 7 Dan Ryder
- ☐ 8 Wade Bartley
- ☐ 9 Jamie Matthews
- ☐ 10 Rod Hinks
- ☐ 11 Derek Etches
- ☐ 12 Brandon Convery
- ☐ 13 Glen Murray
- ☐ 14 Bill Kovacs
- ☐ 15 Terry Chitaroni
- ☐ 16 Jason Young
- ☐ 17 Alastair Still
- ☐ 18 Shawn Rivers
- ☐ 19 Alain Laforge
- ☐ 20 J.D. Eaton
- ☐ 21 Michael Peca
- ☐ 22 Mascot Howler
- ☐ 23 Mike Yeo
- ☐ 24 Checklist
- ☐ 25 Chief R. Zanibbi

'91 - 92

SUDBURY WOLVES / POLICE

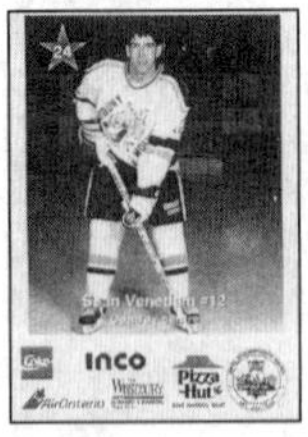

Michael Peca is the most expensive single at $3. Singles start at 75¢.

Card Size: 3" x 4 1/8"

Set (25 cards): $15

- ☐ 1 Chief R. Zanibbi
- ☐ 2 Mascot Howler
- ☐ 3 Team Photo
- ☐ 4 Kyle Blacklock
- ☐ 5 Sean Gagnon
- ☐ 6 Bernie John
- ☐ 7 Bob MacIsaac
- ☐ 8 Jamie Rivers
- ☐ 9 Shawn Rivers
- ☐ 10 Joel Sandie
- ☐ 11 Barry Young
- ☐ 12 George Dourian (G)
- ☐ 13 Dan Ryder
- ☐ 14 Derek Armstrong
- ☐ 15 Terry Chitaroni
- ☐ 16 Brandon Convery
- ☐ 17 Tim Favot
- ☐ 18 Rod Hinks
- ☐ 19 Jamie Matthews
- ☐ 20 Barrie Moore
- ☐ 21 Glen Murray
- ☐ 22 Michael Peca
- ☐ 23 Michael Yeo
- ☐ 24 Jason Young
- ☐ 25 Jason Zohil

'92 - 93

SUDBURY WOLVES / POLICE

Singles start at 75¢.

Card Size: 3" x 4 1/8"

Set (27 cards): $15

- ☐ 1 Mascot Howler
- ☐ 2 Chief R. Zanibbi
- ☐ 3 Bob MacIsaac
- ☐ 4 Joel Sandie
- ☐ 5 Rory Fitzpatrick
- ☐ 6 Mike Wilson
- ☐ 7 Shawn Frappier
- ☐ 8 Bernie John
- ☐ 9 Jamie Rivers
- ☐ 10 Jamie Matthews
- ☐ 11 Zdenek Nedved
- ☐ 12 Ryan Shanahan
- ☐ 13 Corey Crane
- ☐ 14 Matt Kiereck
- ☐ 15 Rick Bodkin
- ☐ 16 Derek Armstrong
- ☐ 17 Barrie Moore
- ☐ 18 Rod Hinks
- ☐ 19 Kayle Short
- ☐ 20 Michael Yeo
- ☐ 21 Gary Coupal
- ☐ 22 Dennis Maxwell
- ☐ 23 Steve Potvin
- ☐ 24 Joel Poirier
- ☐ 25 Greg Dreveng (G)
- ☐ 26 Mark Gowan
- ☐ 27 Steve Staios

'93 - 94

SUDBURY WOLVES / POLICE

Singles start at 75¢.

Card Size: 3" x 4 1/8"

Set (26 cards): $15

- ☐ 1 Chief R. Zanibbi
- ☐ 2 Mascot The Howler
- ☐ 3J ay McKee
- ☐ 4 Chris McMurtry
- ☐ 5 Rory Fitzpatrick
- ☐ 6 Mike Wilson
- ☐ 7 Shawn Frappier
- ☐ 8 Jamie Rivers
- ☐ 9 Jamie Matthews
- ☐ 10 Zdenek Nedved
- ☐ 11 Ryan Shanahan
- ☐ 12 Andrew Dole
- ☐ 13 Mark Giannetti
- ☐ 14 Rick Bodkin
- ☐ 15 Barrie Moore
- ☐ 16 Gary Coupal
- ☐ 17 Ilya Lysenko
- ☐ 18 Simon Sherry
- ☐ 19 Steve Potvin
- ☐ 20 Joel Poirier
- ☐ 21 Shawn Silver (G)
- ☐ 22 Michael Yeo
- ☐ 23 Jeff Melnechuk (G)
- ☐ 24 Sean Venedam
- ☐ 25 Bob MacIsaac
- ☐ 26 Sponsors Logos

'96 - 97

SUDBURY WOLVES / POLICE

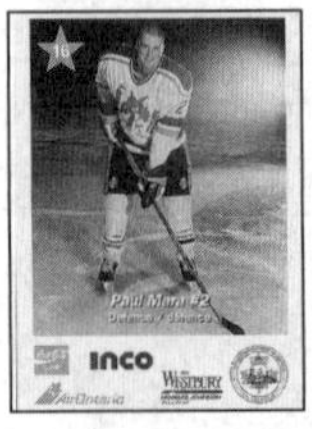

Paul Mara is the most expensive single at $2. Singles start at 75¢.

Card Size: 3" x 4 1/8"

Set (25 cards): $13

- ☐ 1 Alex McCauley
- ☐ 2 Mascot The Howler
- ☐ 3 Wolves Logo
- ☐ 4 Jeremy Adduono #10
- ☐ 5 Louie Blackbird #21
- ☐ 6 Tom Brown #23
- ☐ 7 Peter Campbell #14
- ☐ 8 Brad Domonsky #27
- ☐ 9 Tyson Flinn #4
- ☐ 10 Jason Gaggi #30 (G)
- ☐ 11 Luc Gagne #18
- ☐ 12 Kevin Hansen #7
- ☐ 13 Kon. Kalmikov #96
- ☐ 14 Robin Lacour #25
- ☐ 15 Joe Lombardo #8
- ☐ 16 Paul Mara #2
- ☐ 17 Norm Milley #9
- ☐ 18 Scott Page #24
- ☐ 19 R. Rochefort #19
- ☐ 20 Brian Scott #20
- ☐ 21 Chris Shanahan #11
- ☐ 22 Ryan Sly #5
- ☐ 23 Jonas Soling #15
- ☐ 24 Tim Swartz #3
- ☐ 25 S. Valiquette #1 (G)

'98 - 99

SUDBURY WOLVES / POLICE

Singles start at 50¢.

Set (25 cards): $12

- ☐ 1 Alex McCauley
- ☐ 2 Ken MacKenzie
- ☐ 3 Alexei Salashchenko
- ☐ 4 Kevin Beaumont
- ☐ 5 Norm Milley
- ☐ 6 Derek MacKenzie
- ☐ 7 Reg Higgs
- ☐ 8 Matt Barnhardt
- ☐ 9 Mike Fisher
- ☐ 10 Tom Kotsopoulos
- ☐ 11 Marc Long
- ☐ 12 Kyle Dafoe
- ☐ 13 Jason Jaspers
- ☐ 14 Glenn Crawford
- ☐ 15 Ryan McKie
- ☐ 16 Corey Sabourin
- ☐ 17 Kip Brennan
- ☐ 18 Serge Dube
- ☐ 19 Brad Morgan
- ☐ 20 Brian McGrattan
- ☐ 21 Taylor Pyatt
- ☐ 22 Abe Herbst
- ☐ 23 Kevin Mota
- ☐ 24 Mark Aggio
- ☐ 25 Andrew Raycroft (G)

'99 - 00

SUDBURY WOLVES / POLICE

Singles start at 50¢.

Set (26 cards): $12

- ☐ 1 Alex McCauley
- ☐ 2 Bert Templeton
- ☐ 3 Darren Keily
- ☐ 4 Corey Sabourin
- ☐ 5 Kyle Dafoe
- ☐ 6 Abe Herbst
- ☐ 7 Dennis Wideman
- ☐ 8 Kevin Mota
- ☐ 9 Norm Milley
- ☐ 10 Taylor Pyatt
- ☐ 11 Mike Fisher
- ☐ 12 Alexei Semenov
- ☐ 13 Alexei Salashchenko
- ☐ 14 Derek MacKenzie
- ☐ 15 Steven Ellis
- ☐ 16 Warren Hefford
- ☐ 17 Jason Jaspers
- ☐ 18 Brian McGrattan
- ☐ 19 Drew Kivell
- ☐ 20 Tom Kotsopoulos
- ☐ 21 Brad Morgan
- ☐ 22 Scott Smith
- ☐ 23 R.A. Mobile
- ☐ 24 Mike Vaillancourt
- ☐ 25 Mike Gorman
- ☐ 26 Miguel Beaudry

'00 - 01

SUDBURY WOLVES / POLICE

Singles start at 50¢.

Set (25 cards):

- ☐ 1 Alex McCauley
- ☐ 2 Bert Templeton
- ☐ 3 Darren Keily
- ☐ 4 T.J. Warkus
- ☐ 5 Dave Csumrik
- ☐ 6 Jason Hicks
- ☐ 7 Walter Prawdzik
- ☐ 8 Dennis Wideman
- ☐ 9 Mike Vaillancourt
- ☐ 10 Troy Duncan
- ☐ 11 Ladislav Reznicek
- ☐ 12 Alexei Semenov
- ☐ 13 Chad Starling
- ☐ 14 Nathan Harrington
- ☐ 15 Derek MacKenzie
- ☐ 16 Jerry Connell
- ☐ 17 Steven Ellis
- ☐ 18 Adam Keefe
- ☐ 19 Jaspers / Bone
- ☐ 20 Drew Kivell
- ☐ 21 Tom Kotsopoulos
- ☐ 22 Fedor Fedorov
- ☐ 23 Mike Smith
- ☐ 24 Miguel Beaudry
- ☐ 25 Mascot Howler

SWIFT CURRENT BRONCOS

'95 - 96

SWIFT CURRENT BRONCOS / ZELLERS

Singles start at 75¢.

Card Size: 2 1/2" x 3 1/2"

Set (20 cards): $10

- ☐ Aaron MacDonald
- ☐ Brad Larsen
- ☐ Brent Sopel
- ☐ Chad Beagle
- ☐ Chris Szysky
- ☐ Colin O'Hara
- ☐ Craig Millar
- ☐ Derek Arbez
- ☐ Jaroslav Obsut
- ☐ Jeff Kirwan
- ☐ Jeff Schaeffer
- ☐ Jeff Henkelman
- ☐ Jeremy Rondeau
- ☐ Jesse Rezansoff
- ☐ Josh St. Louis
- ☐ Kurt Drummond
- ☐ Ryan Gernemia
- ☐ Sergei Varlamov
- ☐ Terry Friesen
- ☐ Tyler Willis

TACOMA ROCKETS

'92 - 93

TACOMA ROCKETS

Singles start at 75¢.

Card Size: 2 1/2" x 3 1/2"

Sponsor: None

Set (30 cards): $15

- ☐ Alexander Alexeev
- ☐ Jamie Black
- ☐ Jamie Butt
- ☐ Jeff Calvert
- ☐ Don Clark
- ☐ Marcel Comeau
- ☐ Duane Crouse
- ☐ Allan Egeland
- ☐ Marty Flichel
- ☐ Trever Fraser
- ☐ Jason Kwiatkowski
- ☐ Todd MacDonald
- ☐ Dave McMillen
- ☐ Tony Penchthalt
- ☐ Ryan Phillips
- ☐ Mike Piersol
- ☐ Dennis Pinfold
- ☐ Kevin Powell
- ☐ Tyler Prosofsky
- ☐ Stu Scantlebury
- ☐ Drew Schoneck
- ☐ Adam Smith
- ☐ Corey Stock
- ☐ Barkley Swenson
- ☐ Michal Sykora
- ☐ Dallas Thompson
- ☐ John Varga
- ☐ Toby Weishaar
- ☐ Michal Sykora (Action)
- ☐ Rockets Logo

'93 - 94

TACOMA ROCKETS

Kyle McLaren is the most expensive single at $3. Singles start at 75¢.

Card Size: 2 1/2" x 3 1/2"

Sponsor: None

Set (30 cards): $15
- ☐ Alexander Alexeev
- ☐ Jamie Butt
- ☐ Trevor Cairns
- ☐ Jeff Calvert (G)
- ☐ Marcel Comeau
- ☐ Jason Deleurme
- ☐ Allan Egeland
- ☐ Marty Flichel
- ☐ Trever Fraser
- ☐ Lada Hampeis
- ☐ Tavis Hansen
- ☐ Burt Henderson
- ☐ Jeff Jubenville
- ☐ Todd MacDonald
- ☐ Kyle McLaren
- ☐ Kory Mullin
- ☐ Steve Oviatt
- ☐ Ryan Phillips
- ☐ Mike Piersol
- ☐ Dennis Pinfold
- ☐ Tyler Prosofsky
- ☐ Jamie Reeve
- ☐ Adam Smith
- ☐ Corey Stock
- ☐ Michal Sykora
- ☐ Dallas Thompson
- ☐ John Varga
- ☐ Team Photo
- ☐ Tacoma Dome
- ☐ Tacome Rockets

TORONTO ST. MIKE'S MAJORS

'00 - 01

TORONTO ST. MIKE'S MAJORS / PRESIDENT'S CHOICE

Singles start at 75¢.
Card Size: 2 1/2" x 3 1/2"
Set (27 cards):
- ☐ Checklist
- ☐ Team Photo
- ☐ Peter Budaj (G)
- ☐ Andy Chiodo
- ☐ Tyler Cook
- ☐ Chris Boucher
- ☐ TJ Reynolds
- ☐ Kevin Klein
- ☐ Mark Popovic
- ☐ Tim Brent
- ☐ Drew Fata
- ☐ Lindsay Plunkett
- ☐ Michael Gough
- ☐ Ryan Walsh
- ☐ Matt Bacon
- ☐ Frantisek Lukes
- ☐ Matt Ellis
- ☐ Mike Sellan
- ☐ Adam DeLeeuw
- ☐ Ryan Robert
- ☐ Darryl Bootland
- ☐ Steve Farquharson
- ☐ Matt Bannan
- ☐ Lorne Misita
- ☐ Dave Cameron
- ☐ Bob Jones
- ☐ Division Conference

TRI-CITY AMERICANS

'95 - 96

TRI-CITY AMERICANS

Singles start at 50¢.
Set (31 cards):
- ☐ 1 Header
- ☐ 2 Mascot Eddie Eagle
- ☐ 3 Terry Ryan
- ☐ 4 Brian Boucher
- ☐ 5 Daymond Langkow
- ☐ 6 Eric Schneider
- ☐ 7 Mark Hurley
- ☐ 8 Zenith Komarniski
- ☐ 9 Dylan Gyori
- ☐ 10 Brent Ascroft
- ☐ 11 Tom Zavediuk
- ☐ 12 Mike Hurley
- ☐ 13 Byron Briske
- ☐ 14 Scott McCallum
- ☐ 15 Gary Toor
- ☐ 16 Jaroslav Svejkovsky
- ☐ 17 Dan Smith
- ☐ 18 Jody Lapeyre
- ☐ 19 Jeremy Thompson
- ☐ 20 Boyd Olson
- ☐ 21 Craig Stahl
- ☐ 22 Dan Focht
- ☐ 23 Aaron Baker
- ☐ 24 Alexandre Boikov
- ☐ 25 Chris Anderson
- ☐ 26 Dorian Anneck
- ☐ 27 Bob Brown
- ☐ 28 Bob Loucks
- ☐ 29 Warren Renden
- ☐ 30 Jerry Fredricksen
- ☐ 31 Boucher/ Ryan/ Langkow

VAL D'OR FOREURS

'00 - 01

VAL D'OR FOREURS / CARTES, TIMBRES, MONNAIES STE-FOY

Singles start at 50¢.
Card Size: 2 1/2" x 3 1/2"
Set (25 cards):
- ☐ 1 Mathieu Roy
- ☐ 2 Yan Hallé
- ☐ 3 Chris Lyness
- ☐ 4 Hugo Lévesque
- ☐ 5 Luc Girard
- ☐ 6 David Cloutier
- ☐ 7 Tomas Psenka
- ☐ 8 Nicolas Pelletier
- ☐ 9 Kory Baker
- ☐ 10 Steve Pelletier
- ☐ 11 Alex Turcot
- ☐ 12 Simon Gamache
- ☐ 13 Simon Lajeunesse
- ☐ 14 Alexandre Rouleau
- ☐ 15 Samuel Duplain
- ☐ 16 Pierre Morvan
- ☐ 17 Brandon Reid
- ☐ 18 Mathieu Bastien
- ☐ 19 Maxime Daigneault
- ☐ 20 Jérôme Bergeron
- ☐ 21 Frédéric Bédard
- ☐ 22 Éric Fortier
- ☐ 23 Stéphane Veilleux
- ☐ 24 Sénèque Hyacinthe
- ☐ 25 Checklist

'01 - 02

VAL D'OR FOREURS / CARTES, TIMBRES, MONNAIES STE-FOY

Singles start at 50¢.
Card Size: 2 1/2" x 3 1/2"
Set (25 cards):
- ☐ 1 Philippe Séguin
- ☐ 2 Hugo Lévesque
- ☐ 3 Chaz Johnson
- ☐ 4 Rémy Tremblay
- ☐ 5 Steve Richards
- ☐ 6 Jonathan Gauthier
- ☐ 7 Vincent Duriau
- ☐ 8 Jeff Cotton
- ☐ 9 Patrice Bilodeau
- ☐ 10 Frédéric Bédard
- ☐ 11 Nicolas Pelletier
- ☐ 12 François Gagnon
- ☐ 13 Alexandre Rouleau
- ☐ 14 Pierre Morvan
- ☐ 15 Mathieu Roy
- ☐ 16 Samuel Gibbons
- ☐ 17 Jonathan Charette
- ☐ 18 Kyle Schutte
- ☐ 19 Steve Pelletier
- ☐ 20 Maxime Daigneault
- ☐ 21 Éric Fortier
- ☐ 22 Mathieu Simard
- ☐ 23 Adam Morneau
- ☐ 24 David Rodman
- ☐ 25 Checklist

'02 - 03

VAL D'OR FOREURS / CARTES, TIMBRES, MONNAIES STE-FOY

Singles start at 50¢.
Card Size: 2 1/2" x 3 1/2"
Set (24 cards): $12
- ☐ 1 Éric Glaude
- ☐ 2 Pierre-Luc Laprise
- ☐ 3 Patrice Bilodeau
- ☐ 4 Vincent Duriau
- ☐ 5 Mark Hurtubise
- ☐ 6 Frédéric Bédard
- ☐ 7 Artem Kozitsyn
- ☐ 8 Mathieu Curadeau
- ☐ 9 François Gagnon
- ☐ 10 Érick Lajoie
- ☐ 11 Mathieu Dumas
- ☐ 12 Denis Bérubé (G)
- ☐ 13 Olivier Latendresse
- ☐ 14 Mathieu Roy
- ☐ 15 Benoît Genesse
- ☐ 16 Jonathan Charette
- ☐ 17 Shawn Collymore
- ☐ 18 Didier Bochatay
- ☐ 19 M. Daigneault (G)
- ☐ 20 Jeff Cotton
- ☐ 21 Dominic Lachaine
- ☐ 22 David Rodman
- ☐ 23 Chaz Johnson
- ☐ 24 Checklist

VICTORIA COUGARS

'81 - 82

VICTORIA COUGARS / POLICE

Geoff Courtnall is the most expensive single at $8. Singles start at $1.
Card Size: 3" x 5"
Set (16 cards): $20
- ☐ Bob Bales
- ☐ Greg Barber
- ☐ Ray Benik
- ☐ Rich Chernomaz
- ☐ Daryl Coldwell
- ☐ Geoff Courtnall
- ☐ Paul Cyr
- ☐ Wade Jenson (G)
- ☐ Stu Kulak
- ☐ Peter Martin
- ☐ John Mokosak
- ☐ Mark Morrison
- ☐ Bryant Seaton
- ☐ Jack Shupe
- ☐ Eric Thurston
- ☐ Randy Wickware

'82 - 83

VICTORIA COUGARS / POLICE

Grant Fuhr is the most expensive single at $20. Russ Courtnall and Geoff Courtnall sells at $6. Singles start at $1.
Card Size: 3" x 5"
Set (23 cards): $45
- ☐ Steve Bayliss
- ☐ Ray Beink

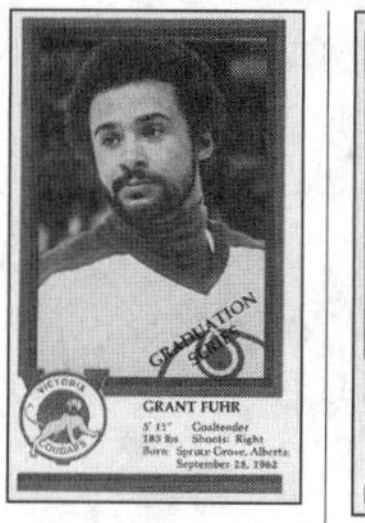

- ☐ Rich Chernomaz
- ☐ Geoff Courtnall
- ☐ Russ Courtnall
- ☐ Paul Cyr
- ☐ Shawn Green
- ☐ Fabian Joseph
- ☐ Stu Kulak
- ☐ Brenn Leach
- ☐ Jack MacKeigan
- ☐ Dave Mackey
- ☐ Mark McLeary
- ☐ Dan Moberg
- ☐ John Mokosak
- ☐ Mark Morrison
- ☐ Eric Thurston
- ☐ Ron Viglasi
- ☐ Curt Fraser
- ☐ Grant Fuhr (G)
- ☐ Gary Lupul
- ☐ Brad Palmer
- ☐ Barry Pederson

'83 - 84

VICTORIA COUGARS / POLICE

Russ Courtnall is the most expensive single at $5. Singles start at $1.
Card Size: 3" x 5"
Set (24 cards): $20
- ☐ Misko Antisin
- ☐ Steve Baylis
- ☐ Paul Bifano
- ☐ Russ Courtnall
- ☐ Greg Davies
- ☐ Dean Drozdiak
- ☐ Jim Gunn
- ☐ Richard Hajdu
- ☐ Randy Hansch (G)
- ☐ Matt Hervey
- ☐ Fabian Joseph
- ☐ Ron Kivell
- ☐ Brenn Leach
- ☐ Jack Mackeigan
- ☐ Dave Mackey
- ☐ Tom Martin
- ☐ Darren Moren (G)
- ☐ Adam Morrison
- ☐ Dan Sexton
- ☐ Randy Siska
- ☐ Eric Thurston
- ☐ Simon Wheeldon
- ☐ Murray Bannerman (G)
- ☐ Gord Roberts

'84 - 85

VICTORIA COUGARS / POLICE

The most expensive singles are Russ and Geoff Courtnall at $4. Singles start at $1.
Card Size: 3" x 5"
Set (24 cards): $20
- ☐ Misko Antisin
- ☐ Greg Batters
- ☐ Chris Calverly
- ☐ Darin Choquette
- ☐ Russ Courtnall
- ☐ Rick Davidson
- ☐ Bill Gregoir
- ☐ Richard Hajdu

- ☐ Randy Hansch (G)
- ☐ Rob Kivell
- ☐ Brad Melin
- ☐ Jim Mentis
- ☐ Adam Morrison
- ☐ Mark Morrison
- ☐ Kodie Nelson
- ☐ Ken Priestlay
- ☐ Bruce Pritchard
- ☐ Trevor Semeniuk
- ☐ Dan Sexton
- ☐ Randy Siska
- ☐ Chris Tarnowski
- ☐ Mel Bridgman
- ☐ Geoff Courtnall
- ☐ Torrie Robertson

'89 - 90

VICTORIA COUGARS / FLYNN PRINTING

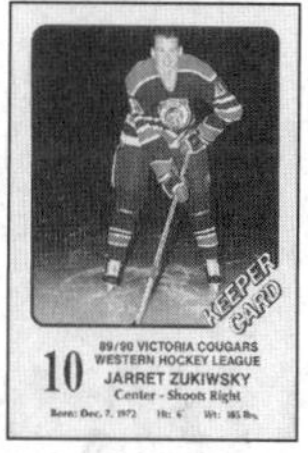

Singles start at 75¢.
Card Size: 2 3/4" x 4"
Set (21 cards): $12
- ☐ John Badduke
- ☐ Terry Bendera
- ☐ Trevor Buchanan
- ☐ Jarret Burgoyne (G)
- ☐ Dino Caputo
- ☐ Chris Catellier
- ☐ Mark Cipriano
- ☐ Milan Drag
- ☐ Dean Dyer
- ☐ Shayne Green
- ☐ Ryan Harrison
- ☐ Corey Jones (G)
- ☐ Terry Klapstein
- ☐ Jason Knox
- ☐ Curtis Nykyforuk
- ☐ Jason Peters
- ☐ Blair Scott
- ☐ Mike Seaton
- ☐ Rob Sumner
- ☐ Larry Woo
- ☐ Jarret Zukiwsky

VANCOUVER GIANTS

'01 - 02

VANCOUVER GIANTS

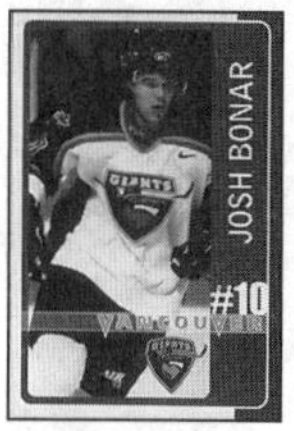

Singles start at 50¢.
Card Size: 2 1/2" x 3 1/2"
Set (25 cards):
- ☐ Team card
- ☐ Don Choukalos
- ☐ Brett Jaeger
- ☐ Pat Brandreth
- ☐ Nick Marach
- ☐ Tyson Marsh
- ☐ Ryan Thomas
- ☐ Jeff Beatch
- ☐ Robin Big Snake
- ☐ Josh Bonar
- ☐ Andrew Davidson
- ☐ Jeff Coulter
- ☐ Mark Ardelan
- ☐ Andrew Desousa
- ☐ Marian Havel
- ☐ Jeremy Jackson
- ☐ Mark Ashton
- ☐ Robin Kovar
- ☐ Darren Lynch
- ☐ Chad Bassen
- ☐ T.J. Mulock
- ☐ Jack Redlick
- ☐ Dave Selthun
- ☐ Chris Stubel
- ☐ Clay Thoring

VICTORIAVILLE TIGRES

'00 - 01

VICTORIAVILLE TIGRES / CARTES, TIMBRES, MONNAIES STE-FOY

Singles start at 50¢.
Card Size: 2 1/2" x 3 1/2"
Set (25 cards): $12
- ☐ 1 James Sanford
- ☐ 2 Carl Mallette
- ☐ 3 Matthew Lombardi
- ☐ 4 Teddy Kyres
- ☐ 5 Martin Autotte
- ☐ 6 Simon St-Pierre
- ☐ 7 Pierre-Luc Daneau
- ☐ 8 Antoine Vermette
- ☐ 9 Marc-André Thinel
- ☐ 10 Mathieu Wathier
- ☐ 11 Pierre-Luc Sleigher
- ☐ 12 Sandros Sbrocca
- ☐ 13 Jonathan Fauteux
- ☐ 14 Sergei Kaltygen
- ☐ 15 Adam Wojcik
- ☐ 16 J-F Nogues
- ☐ 17 Richard Paul
- ☐ 18 David Massé
- ☐ 19 Luc Lévesque
- ☐ 20 Mathieu Brunelle
- ☐ 21 Sébastien Morissette
- ☐ 22 Sébastien Thinel
- ☐ 23 Danny Groulx
- ☐ 24 Mario Durocher
- ☐ 25 Checklist

'01 - 02

VICTORIAVILLE TIGRES / CARTES, TIMBRES, MONNAIES STE-FOY

Singles start at 50¢.
Card Size: 2 1/2" x 3 1/2"
Set (23 cards): $12
- ☐ 1 Jean-François Racine
- ☐ 2 Patrick Turbide
- ☐ 3 Evgueni Nourislamov
- ☐ 4 Jean-Philippe Glaude
- ☐ 5 Thierry Kaszap
- ☐ 6 Éric Jean
- ☐ 7 Louis-Philippe Lessard
- ☐ 8 André Vincent
- ☐ 9 Steve Proulx
- ☐ 10 Olivier Proulx
- ☐ 11 Martin Autotte
- ☐ 12 Yanick Riendeau
- ☐ 13 Michael Stacey
- ☐ 14 Frédéric Faucher
- ☐ 15 Benoît Paris
- ☐ 16 Vincent Tougas
- ☐ 17 Kirill Alexeev
- ☐ 18 Jean-François Cyr
- ☐ 19 Carl Zacharie
- ☐ 20 Kevin Rainville
- ☐ 21 Sylvain Michaud
- ☐ 22 Maxime Bouchard
- ☐ 23 Checklist

W. MICHIGAN BRONCOS

'92 - 93

WESTERN MICHIGAN BRONCOS

Singles start at 50¢.
Card Size: 2 1/2" x 3 1/2"
Sponsor: None
Set (30 cards): $10
- ☐ Chris Belanger
- ☐ Joe Bonnett
- ☐ Brent Brekke
- ☐ Chris Brooks
- ☐ Jeremy Brown
- ☐ Tom Carriere
- ☐ Scott Chartier
- ☐ Ryan D'Arcy
- ☐ Pat Ferschweiler
- ☐ Brian Gallentine
- ☐ Jim Holman
- ☐ Derek Innanen
- ☐ Jason Jennings
- ☐ Mikail Lapin
- ☐ François Leroux
- ☐ Jamal Mayers
- ☐ Kevin McCaffrey
- ☐ Dave Mitchell
- ☐ Brian Renfrew
- ☐ Mike Schafer
- ☐ Derek Schooley
- ☐ Neil Smith
- ☐ Colin Ward
- ☐ Dave Weaver
- ☐ Mike Whitton
- ☐ Bill Wilkinson
- ☐ Peter Wilkinson
- ☐ Byron Witkowski
- ☐ Lawson Arena

'93 - 94

WESTERN MICHIGAN BRONCOS

Singles start at 50¢.
Card Size: 2 1/2" x 3 1/2"
Sponsor: None
Set (30 cards): $10
- ☐ David Agnew
- ☐ Brent Brekke
- ☐ Chris Brooks
- ☐ Craig Brown
- ☐ Jeremy Brown
- ☐ Justin Caldwell
- ☐ Tom Carriere
- ☐ Tony Code
- ☐ Matt Cressman
- ☐ Jim Culhane
- ☐ Ryan D'Arcy
- ☐ Brian Gallentine
- ☐ Matt Greene
- ☐ Rob Hodge
- ☐ Jim Holman
- ☐ Derek Innanen
- ☐ Mark Jodoin
- ☐ Brendan Kenny
- ☐ Misha Lapin
- ☐ Darren Maloney
- ☐ Jamal Mayers
- ☐ Dave Mitchell
- ☐ Brian Renfrew
- ☐ Mike Schafer
- ☐ Derek Schooley
- ☐ Colin Ward
- ☐ Mike Whitton
- ☐ Bill Wilkinson
- ☐ Peter Wilkinson
- ☐ Shawn Zimmerman

WINDSOR SPITFIRES

'89 - 90

WINDSOR SPITFIRES

Singles start at $1.
Card Size: 2 1/2" x 3 1/2"
Sponsor: None
Set (22 cards): $10
- ☐ Sean Burns
- ☐ Glen Craig
- ☐ Brian Forestell
- ☐ Chris Fraser
- ☐ Trent Gleason
- ☐ Jon Hartley
- ☐ Ron Jones
- ☐ Bob Leeming
- ☐ Kevin MacKay
- ☐ Kevin McDougall
- ☐ Ryan Merritt
- ☐ David Myles
- ☐ Sean O'Hagan (G)
- ☐ Mike Polano
- ☐ Jason Snow
- ☐ Brad Smith
- ☐ Jason Stos
- ☐ Jon Stos
- ☐ Jamie Vargo
- ☐ Trevor Walsh
- ☐ K.J. White
- ☐ Jason Zohil

'92 - 93

WINDSOR SPITFIRES / DEVONSHIRE MALL

Photos are credited to Sean Murphy. Adam Graves is the most expensive single at $4. Singles start at 50¢.
Card Size: 2 5/8" x 3 5/8"
Set (31 cards): $15
- ☐ 1 Checklist
- ☐ 2 Matt Martin
- ☐ 3 Luke Clowes
- ☐ 4 Jason Haelzle
- ☐ 5 Adam Graves
- ☐ 6 Craig Lutes
- ☐ 7 David Pluck
- ☐ 8 Colin Wilson
- ☐ 9 Bill Bowler
- ☐ 10 Ryan O'Neill
- ☐ 11 Adam Young
- ☐ 12 Gerrard Masse
- ☐ 13 Daryl Lavoie
- ☐ 14 Peter Allison
- ☐ 15 Ernie Godden
- ☐ 16 Brady Blain
- ☐ 17 Todd Warriner
- ☐ 18 Rick Marshall
- ☐ 19 Craig Johnson
- ☐ 20 Kelly Vipond
- ☐ 21 Mascot Devy Bear
- ☐ 22 Stephen Webb
- ☐ 23 Scott Miller
- ☐ 24 Dennis Purdie
- ☐ 25 Steve Gibson
- ☐ 26 Mike Hartwick
- ☐ 27 Shawn Heins
- ☐ 28 David Benn
- ☐ 29 Matt Mullin
- ☐ 30 David Mitchell
- ☐ 31 T.Warriner/ C.Stillman

CHAPTER NINE

INDEX OF PLAYERS

A

AAB, VITALIJ
01/2 UD DEL 266

AABY,
92/3 Semic Nordisk 208

AABY, HENRIK
95 Panini Worlds 255
96 Wien 208

AALTO, ANTTI
99/0 Cardset AH 7-risti
00/1 Cardset 359
02/3 Cardset 151
93/4 Classic 35
93/4 Cla. 4 Sport 224
98/9 Omega 9
00/1 Pa. Paramount 1
94/5 Parkie SE227
95 Semic 238
93/4 Sisu 43, 394
94/5 Sisu 129
95/6 Sisu 328
96/7 Sisu 147
94/5 SP 161
99/0 Topps 225
99/0 To. Chrome 225
94/5 Topps Finest 122
98/9 UD Choice 9
94/5 Upper Deck 511
98/9 Upper Deck 1
98/9 UD G. Reserve 1
99/0 UD G. Reserve 336
00/1 UD MVP 1
99/0 Cincinnati M'Ducks

AALTO, TEEMU
99/0 Cardset 238
00/1 Cardset 26
02/3 Cardset 152

AALTONEN, JUHANI
70/1 Kuvajulkaisut 276
71/2 Williams Finnish 147
72/3 Williams Finnish 100
73/4 Williams Finnish 194

AALTONEN, LASSE
70/1 Kuvajulkaisut 225

AALTONEN, PETRI
93/4 Jyvas Hyva 294
93/4 Sisu 80

AASS, ANDRE
92/3 Semic Nordisk 171

ABBOTT, REGGIE
48-52 Exhibits [Canadiens]

ABBOTT, T.
89/0 ProCards AHL 311

ABEL, BRETT
93/4 Wheeling Thund'birds

ABEL, CLARENCE
33/4 Canadian Gum
33-35 Diamond Match Silv.

ABEL, GERRY
76 DETR

ABEL, NEIL
01/2 Sheffield Steelers
93/4 Sheffield Steelers 4
94/5 Sheffield Steelers 11
95/6 Sheffield Steelers

ABEL, SID
01/2 BAP Update ✂ PTT3
34-43 BeeHive-1 [Detr.]
45-64 BeeHive-2 [Detr.]
51 Berk Ross
48-52 Exhibits [Red Wings]
83 HHOF Postcard A1
83&87 HHOF 2
92/3 Legends 12
39/0 O-Pee-Chee 68
51/2 Parkhurst 64
60/1 Parkhurst 23
62/3 Parkhurst 34
02/3 Parkie - Reprint 160, 252, 280, ✂ VT6
94/5 Parkie Tall 65
52 Royal Desserts 4
60/1 Shirriff 80
61/2 Shirriff 61
02/3 SP Authentic ✍ Cut
01/2 SP Game Used ✍ Sig
64/5 Topps 93
65/6 Topps 41
66/7 Topps 42
01/2 Ultimate Mem. ✂ BL, ✂ PL, ✂ RN
02/3 Ultimate Memorabilia ✂ EA, ✂ RT, ✂ VGJ, ✍ Cut
91/2 Ultimate Original Six 66, ✍ Aut. 66
92/3 Upper Deck HH 21
01/2 Upper Deck ✍ Cut
01/2 UD Legends 18
76 DETR

ÅBERG, MAGNUS
89/0 Semic Elitserien 48

ÅBERG, PATRIC
94/5 Leaf Elit Set 181
95/6 Leaf Elit Set 7
91/2 Semic Elitserien 286
92/3 Semic Elitserien 302
95/6 UD Elitserien 8

ABERS, MATT
93/4 Michigan State

ABID, RAMZI
98 Bowman 110, 121, ✍ A18
98 Bowman Chrome 110, 121
98/9 Bowman's Best 141
02/3 Calder 88
02/3 Choice Prospects 1
98/9 OPC Chrome 221
02/3 Pacific Complete 555
94 Québec Pee Wee 418
98/9 Topps 221
99/0 Halifax Mooseheads

ÅBLAD, TOBIAS
98/9 Cardset 143

ABRAHAMSON, BRETT
93/4 Minnesota G'Gophers

ABRAHAMSSON, CHRISTER
74 Hellas MM-Jenkki 22
94/5 Leaf Elit Set 304
75/6 OPC WHA 28
76/7 OPC WHA 67
76/7 OPC WHA 110
72 Panda MM-Toronto
92/3 Semic Elitserien 333
72 Semic Sticker 43
74 Semic Sticker 1
77-79 Sports. FIN 43-1031
71/2 Williams Finnish 40
72/3 Williams Finnish 41
73/4 Williams Finnish 22

ABRAHAMSSON, ELIAS
99/0 Hamilton Bulldogs
99/0 Hamilton Bulldogs/ Staz
97/8 Providence Bruins
98/9 Providence Bruins
99/0 Providence Bruins
00/1 Providence Bruins
95/6 Halifax Moosehead
96/7 Halifax Moosehead
96/7 Halifax Moosehead

ABRAHAMSSON, HANS
98/9 DEL 307
94/5 Leaf Elit Set 123
95/6 Leaf Elit Set 51
95/6 UD Elitserien 78

ABRAHAMSSON, THOMMY
72 Hellas MM-Jenkki 24
70/1 Kuvajulkaisut 21
75/6 OPC WHA 127
76/7 OPC WHA 79
72 Panda MM-Toronto
72 Semic Sticker 49
74 Semic Sticker 6
77-79 Sports. FIN 43-1031
71/2 Williams Finnish 41
72/3 Williams Finnish 42
73/4 Williams Finnish 23

ABRAMOV, SERGEI
96 Wien 130

ABRAMS, MARTY
84/5 Soo Greyhounds

ABRIC, PETER
83/4 North Bay Centennials

ABSTREITER, PETER
99/0 Eishockey 320
01/2 UD DEL 262

ABSTREITER, TOBIAS
94/5 DEL 316
95/6 DEL 215
96/7 DEL 358
98/9 DEL 63
99/0 Eishockey 186, 386
92 Semic Sticker 190
00/1 UD DEL 233, ✂ GJ
01/2 UD DEL 121

ACKERMAN, CHAD
96/7 Hampton Roads
97/8 Hampton Roads
98/9 Hampton Roads
99/0 Hampton Roads

ACKERSTRÖM,
97/8 Hockey-Box

ACKERSTRÖM, OSCAR
98/9 Cardset 79
99/0 Cardset 239
94/5 Leaf Elit Set 120
95/6 Leaf Elit Set 208
90/1 Semic Elitserien 36
91/2 Semic Elitserien 284
92/3 Semic Elitserien 304
00/1 UD DEL 89
01/2 UD DEL 91, SS5

ACTON, KEITH
90/1 Bowman 113
91/2 Bowman 244
92/3 Bowman 184
80/1 Dernière Heure
92/3 Fleer Ultra 368
93/4 Leaf 420
81/2 O-Pee-Chee 181
82/3 O-Pee-Chee 179
83/4 O-Pee-Chee 180
83/4 O-Pee-Chee 184
84/5 O-Pee-Chee 93
85/6 OPC/Topps 82
86/7 OPC/Topps 172
90/1 OPC/Topps 355
91/2 O-Pee-Chee 19
92/3 O-Pee-Chee 368
89/0 O-Pee-Chee 254
82/3 OPC/Topps Sticker 42
82/3 OPC/Topps Sticker 43
85/6 OPC Sticker 38
87/8 Panini Sticker 299
89/0 Panini Sticker 76, 301
91/2 Panini Sticker 237
93/4 Panini Sticker 50
80/1 Pepsi Bottle Cap
92/3 Pinnacle 363
82/3 Post [Mont.]
93/4 Premier 407
90/1 Pro Set 497
90/1 Score 301
91/2 Score 133
91/2 Score CAN 133
92/3 Score 341
93/4 Score 301
83/4 Souhaits Keychain [Canadiens]
92/3 Topps 199
91/2 To. Stadium 247
92/3 T. Stadium Club 223
93/4 To. Stadium 205
90/1 Upper Deck 445
87/8 EDMO
88/9 EDMO / Action 77
83/4 MINS
84/5 MINS
84/5 MINS / 7-Eleven 6
85/6 MINS
85/6 MINS / 7-Eleven 10
87/8 MINS
80/1 MONT
81/2 MONT
82/3 MONT
82/3 MONT / Steinberg
89/0 PHIL
90/1 PHIL
91/2 PHIL / J.C. Penney
92/3 PHIL / UD Sheet
92/3 PHIL / UD Sheet
92/3 PHIL / J.C. Penney
94/5 PHIL / Sheet

ADAIR, JIM
73/4 Vancouver Blazers

ADAIR, SCOTT
90/1 7th..Sketch WHL 140
97/8 Guildford Flames

ADAM, DIETRICH
94/5 DEL 21

ADAM, RICHARD
95/6 APS 204
98/9 OFS 133, 306

ADAM, RUSS
82/3 TORO
01/2 St. John's Maple Leafs

ADAMCIK, DUSAN
95/6 APS 240

ADAMEC, VACLAV
97/8 APS 309
98/9 OFS 62
99/0 Score 4

ADAMIEC, JANUSZ
89 Semic Sticker 143
92 Semic Sticker 277

ADAMIK, PETER
74 Hellas MM-Jenkki 65
73/4 Williams Finnish 43

ADAMS, AKIL
93/4 Slapshot / Windsor 24

ADAMS, ANDY
93/4 Slapshot / Guelph 22
94/5 Slapshot / Guelph 3
95/6 Slapshot 82, 379
98/9 Topeka Scarecrows
98/9 Topeka Scarecrows
96/7 Regina Pats

ADAMS, BRYAN
00/1 BAP Mem. 81
00/1 Pacific 27
00/1 SP Authentic 135
00/1 SPx 175
00/1 UD Ice 82
01/2 Chicago Wolves
02/3 Grand Rapids Griffins

ADAMS, CHARLES
83 HHOF Postcard D1
83&87 HHOF 47

ADAMS, CRAIG
00/1 PS Titanium Draft 155
01/2 Signature 33, ✍ Aut. 33
00/1 SP Authentic 140
00/1 UD Ice 46
99/0 Cincinnati Cyclones

ADAMS, GERAD
99/0 Hampton Roads
02/3 London Knights

ADAMS, GERALD
96/7 Regina Pats
97/8 Regina Pats

ADAMS, GREG A.
99/0 BAP Mem. 34
00/1 BAP Mem. 374
90/1 Bowman 59
91/2 Bowman 311
92/3 Bowman 333
93/4 Donruss 350
94/5 Donruss 101
95/6 Donruss 158
96/7 Donruss 82
94/5 Flair 187
95/6 Fleer Metal 37
92/3 Fleer Ultra 217
93/4 Fleer Ultra 19
94/5 Fleer Ultra 380
95/6 Fleer Ultra 227
93/4 Leaf 192
94/5 Leaf 222
95/6 Leaf 112
96/7 Leaf 103
86/7 OPC/Topps 10
86/7 OPC/Topps Box A
87/8 OPC/Topps 135
88/9 OPC/Topps 162
90/1 OPC/Topps 106
91/2 O-Pee-Chee 340
92/3 O-Pee-Chee 365
89/0 OPC/Topps 178
86/7 OPC Sticker 196
88/9 OPC Sticker 66
97/8 Omega 66
98/9 Pacific 171
99/0 Pacific 315
97/8 Pa. Invincible R-59
99/0 Pa. Paramount 177
87/8 Panini Sticker 84
88/9 Panini Sticker 136
89/0 Panini Sticker 154
90/1 Panini Sticker 303
90/1 Panini/VAN 2
91/2 Panini Sticker 39
93/4 Panini Sticker 173
96/7 Panini Sticker 176
91/2 Parkhurst 183
92/3 Parkhurst 195
93/4 Parkhurst 480
95/6 Parkhurst 327
94/5 Parkie SE185
91/2 Pinnacle 218
92/3 Pinnacle 28
93/4 Pinnacle 247
94/5 Pinnacle 240
96/7 Pinnacle 194
97/8 Pi. Be A Player 164, ✍ Aut. 164
96/7 Pi. Summit 95
94/5 POG 96
95/6 POG 91
93/4 Power Play 247
94/5 Premier 414
90/1 Pro Set 291
91/2 Pro Set 243
91/2 Pro Set Platinum 125
90/1 Score 240
91/2 Score 44
91/2 Score CAN 44
92/3 Score 146
93/4 Score 196
95/6 Score 89
96/7 Score 39
92/3 Topps 507
00/1 Topps 228
91/2 To. Stadium 52
92/3 T. Stadium Club 232
94/5 T. Stadium Club 156
90/1 Upper Deck 342
91/2 Upper Deck 426
92/3 Upper Deck 192
93/4 Upper Deck 77, SP-161
94/5 Upper Deck 211
95/6 Upper Deck 26, SE-113
97/8 Upper Deck 265
98/9 Upper Deck 344
95/6 UD Be A Player 22, ✍ S22
96/7 UD Black Diam. 23
95/6 UD CC 286
97/8 UD Coll. Choice 71
98/9 UD G. Reserve 344
96/7 UD Ice 14
99/0 UD MVP 163
99/0 Victory 229
96/7 DALL / Southwest
85/6 NJER 5
86/7 NJER / S.O.B.E.R.
98/9 PHOE / Coca-Cola
87/8 VANC / Shell
88/9 VANC / Mohawk
89/0 VANC / Mohawk
90/1 VANC / Mohawk
90/1 VANC
91/2 VANC / Photo
91/2 VANC / PotM
92/3 VANC / Road Trip
94/5 VANC

ADAMS, GREG C.
86/7 O-Pee-Chee 253
87/8 OPC/Topps 139
88/9 O-Pee-Chee 199
90/1 O-Pee-Chee 518
87/8 Panini Sticker 185
88/9 EDMO / Action 85
82/3 HART / Jr. Whalers
86/7 WASH / Kodak
86/7 WASH / Police
87/8 WASH
87/8 WASH / Kodak

ADAMS, JACK
02/3 SP Authentic ✍ Cut

ADAMS, JACK E.
34-43 BeeHive-1 [Mont.]
40/1 O-Pee-Chee 104

ADAMS, JACK J.
24/5 Champ's Cigarettes
83 HHOF Postcard J1
83&87 HHOF 182
93/4 Legends of Hockey 21
23/4 William Paterson 24
24/5 William Paterson 53
37/8 World Wide Gum 99

ADAMS, JAMIE
93/4 Johnstown Chiefs 14

ADAMS, JOHN
74/5 WASH

ADAMS, KEVYN
99/0 BAP Mem. 365
00/1 BAP Mem. 352
01/2 BAP Memor. 178
93/4 Donruss USA1
01/2 Pacific 168
02/3 Pacific Complete 187
00/1 Pa. Paramount 66
01/2 Parkhurst 169
93/4 Pinnacle 488
97/8 Pinnacle 22
00/1 Revolution 41
94/5 Score 211
97/8 Score 60
97/8 Score Toro. 15
00/1 Signature 129, ✍ Aut. 38
00/1 Stadium 207
00/1 To. Chrome 227
93/4 Upper Deck 568
00/1 Upper Deck 52
01/2 Upper Deck 76
02/3 Upper Deck 277
01/2 UD MVP 81
00/1 UD Vintage 105, 110
01/2 Victory 147
99/0 TORO / Pizza Pizza 8
96/7 Grand Rapids Griffins
97/8 St. John's Maple Leafs
99/0 St. John's Maple Leafs

ADAMS, WESTON W. (SR.)
83 HHOF Postcard I1
83&87 HHOF 122

ADAMSON, IAN
92/3 MPS SJHL 114

ADAMUS, DAMIAN
94/5 DEL 290
95/6 DEL 281
96/7 DEL 90

ADAMUS, TRENT
00/1 Saskatoon Blades

ADDUONO, JEREMY
98 Bowman 29
98 Bowman Chrome 29
95/6 Slapshot 391
00/1 Rochester Americans
96/7 Sudbury Wolves

ADEY, PAUL
01/2 Nottingham Panthers
02/3 Nottingham Panthers
01/2 Sheffield Steelers GS

ADOLFI, RICHARD
83/4 Belleville Bulls
84/5 Kitchener Rangers

ADOLFSON, MARCUS
98/9 DEL 12

AEBISCHER, DAVID
01/2 Adrenaline 44
00/1 BAP Mem. 479
01/2 BAP Memor. 194
01/2 BT Pipes 23, 164, ✂ Jers., ✂ S&J, ✂ GT
02/3 Between the Pipes 22, ✂ GUE6, ✂ GUJ6, ✂ GSJ6, ✂ ITN6, ✂ T2
02/3 Bowman 109, ✂ FFDS, ✂ FFJ, ✂ FFP, ✂ FFR, ✂ FFRP, ✂ FFS, ✂ FFTS, ✍ YSA, / ✍ Puck
00/1 Crown Royale 118, 21CR-7
00/1 Crown Royale CC
02/3 First Edition 13, ✂ Jers.
01/2 Heads Up - BTI 5
01/2 O-Pee-Chee 46
01/2 Pacific 95, ✍ 444
02/3 Pacific 86
02/3 Pacific Complete 47
00/1 Premier Plus 122
00/1 Private Stock 111, PSR-6
01/2 Pr. Stock -PS 15
00/1 PS Titanium 111
00/1 PS Titanium Draft 111
92 Québec Pee Wee 1403
01/2 Signature 180, ✍ Aut. 180
02/3 Signature Series 72, -GS 29, ✍ 72
00/1 SP Authentic 98
00/1 SP GU 65
02/3 SP Game-Used ✂ FF
00/1 SPx 157
00/1 Stadium 257
01/2 Stadium Club NR2, ✍ NR
01/2 Topps 46
00/1 To. Chrome 244
01/2 To. Chrome 46
00/1 To. Gold Label 103
00/1 To. Heritage 78
00/1 To. Stars 117
02/3 T. Total 201
00/1 UD Heroes 161
00/1 UD Reserve 91
00/1 Upper Deck 433
02/3 Upper Deck 289
00/1 UD ASG PP6, HH1
00/1 UD Black Diam. 114
02/3 UD Classic ✂ HH
00/1 UD Ice 85
01/2 UD Mask ✂ GJ, ✂ JP, ✂ DP, ✂ MM, ✂ ST
02/3 UD Mask 21, 22, 109
02/3 UD MVP - SD
00/1 UD Pros&Prosp. 99
01/2 UD SCup Champs 34
02/3 UD Top Shelf ✂ SS
02/3 UD Vintage ✂ EE
00/1 Vanguard 111
01/2 Victory 88
98/9 Hershey Bears

AESCHLIMANN, PETER
72 Semic Sticker 145

AFANASENKOV, DMITRY
00/1 Upper Deck 200
00/1 UD Black Diam. 65
00/1 UD Ice 45
00/1 UD MVP 214
01/2 Victory 388

AFFLECK, BRUCE
74/5 Loblaws
76/7 O-Pee-Chee 305
77/8 O-Pee-Chee 376
78/9 O-Pee-Chee 279

AFINOGENOV, DENIS
97/8 APS 97
97/8 DS Sticker 100
00/1 Mir 167, 337

AFINOGENOV, MAXIM
00/1 Aurora 16
99/0 BAP Mem. 350
00/1 BAP Mem. 64
01/2 BAP Memor. 9
02/3 BAP Memorabilia 55
99/0 Crown Royale 16
02/3 First Edition 70, ✂ Jers.
99/0 Millenium C-24
00/1 Mir Fetisov 7
99/0 NHL Power Play [x3]
01/2 O-Pee-Chee 74
02/3 O-Pee-Chee 177
99/0 Omega 24
00/1 Pacific 46
01/2 Pacific 42
02/3 Pacific 36
00/1 Pa. Paramount 24
00/1 Parkhurst P-12
01/2 Parkhurst 64
02/3 Parkhurst 153
00/1 Premier Plus PA3
99/0 Prism 16
00/1 Private Stock 10, AC-4, PS-5, PSNW-3
00/1 Revolution 14
00/1 Signature 83, ✍ Aut. 81
01/2 Signature 176, ✍ Aut. 176
02/3 Signature Series 50, ✍ 50
99/0 SP Authentic 12, TH3
00/1 SP Authentic 11
02/3 SP Authentic 110, ✍ SotT, ✍ SotTD
00/1 SP GU 7
01/2 SP Game Used ✂ AF, ✂ AFD
02/3 SP Game-Used ✂ FF, ✍ Sig
01/2 SPx 159, ✂ DT, ✂ TT
98/9 SPx Prospects 76
00/1 Stadium 154
99/0 Stadium 168
00/1 Stadium 121
01/2 Stadium Club 23
02/3 Stadium ✂ NHLP-15
00/1 Topps 180, OTG28
01/2 Topps 74
02/3 Topps 177
00/1 To. Chrome 120
01/2 To. Chrome 74
02/3 T. Chrome 103
00/1 To. Gold Label 30
00/1 To. Heritage 64
02/3 T. Limited 177
99/0 To. Prmr. Plus 120
02/3 T. Total 230
98/9 UD Choice 282
00/1 UD Heroes PI3
01/2 UD PlayMakers Ltd ✂ PCCJ, ✂ PCJ
00/1 Upper Deck 23, P2
01/2 Upper Deck 22
02/3 Upper Deck 20
02/3 UD Artistic 9, R9, ✂ RT, / Art
97/8 UD Black Diam. 43
98/9 UD Black Diam. 108
00/1 UD Black Diam. 7
02/3 UD Classic ✂ HR
02/3 UD Honor ✍ SC
01/2 UD Mask ✂ GJ, ✂ JP, ✂ DP
00/1 UD MVP 25
01/2 UD MVP 17
02/3 UD MVP 23
02/3 UD Piece ✂ PH
01/2 UD Premier ✂ D
02/3 UD Premier ✍ Sig.
00/1 UD Pros&Prosp. 12, NA1
02/3 UD Rookie ✍ TD
02/3 UD Top Shelf 11, ✂ R, ✂ SH, ✂ ST, ✂ SW, ✂ TS
00/1 UD Vintage 48
01/2 UD Vintage 28
02/3 UD Vintage 30, GB 30, T8
00/1 Vanguard 11
00/1 Victory 32
01/2 Victory 40
02/3 Victory 26

AFR, TAMER
99/0 Louisville Panthers

AGARKOV, PAVEL
98/9 Mir 85
99/0 Mir 195
00/1 Mir 264

AGEEV, ALEXANDER
00/1 Mir 244

AGEIKIN, SERGEI
87/8 Soviet Stars

AGGATTS, J.P.
25 Dominion Chocolates 68

AGGIO, MARK
98/9 Sudbury Wolves 24

AGNEL, BENJAMIN
94 Semic 221

AGNEVSHIKOV, ALEXANDER
00/1 Mir 183

AGNEW, DAVID
93/4 W. Michigan Broncos

AGNEW, DOUG
93/4 Milwaukee Admirals
94/5 Milwaukee Admirals
95/6 Milwaukee Admirals
96/7 Milwaukee Admirals
97/8 Milwaukee Admirals

AGNEW, GARY
89/0 7th..Sketch OHL 47
90/1 7th..Sketch OHL 148
91/2 7th...Sketch OHL 369
95/6 Slapshot 130
00/1 Syracuse Crunch

AGNEW, JIM
90/1 Panini/VAN 1
89/0 ProCards IHL 185
92/3 HART / Dairymart
90/1 VANC / Mohawk
86/7 Fredericton Express
83/4 Brandon Wheat Kings

AGUADO, BIEVENIDO
79 Panini Sticker 373

AHEARN, KEVIN
72 Semic Sticker 129

AHEARN, T. FRANKLIN
83 HHOF Postcard E1
83&87 HHOF 62

AHEARNE, J. FRANK
83 HHOF Postcard J2
83&87 HHOF 183

AHENAKEW, JASON
92/3 MPS SJHL 27

AHERN, FRED
76/7 O-Pee-Chee 298
77/8 O-Pee-Chee 280
78/9 O-Pee-Chee 386

AHL, BOO
94/5 Leaf Elit Set 186
95/6 Leaf Elit Set 49, S-6
91/2 Semic Elitserien 105
92/3 Semic Elitserien 126
95/6 UD Elitserien 75
00/1 UD Elitserien 165, M7, ✍ Sig.
96 Wien 41

AHLBERG, MATS
74 Hellas MM-Jenkki 40
79 Panini Sticker 165
73/4 Williams Finnish 42

AHLBERG, SAKARI
74 Hellas MM-Jenkki 1
70/1 Kuvajulkaisut 118
72 Panda MM-Toronto
74 Semic Sticker 96
78/9 SM-Liiga 53
71/2 Williams Finnish 167
72/3 Williams Finnish 118
73/4 Williams Finnish 172

AHLBERG, SAMI
98/9 Cardset 95
99/0 Cardset 54
00/1 Cardset 327
97/8 Hockey-Box
93/4 Sisu 132
94/5 Sisu 117
95/6 Sisu 40

ÅHLBERG, LENNART
92/3 Semic Nordisk 36

ÅHLBERG, MARTIN
92/3 Semic Nordisk 26

ÅHLBERG, MATS
74 Semic Sticker 11

AHLEN, THOMAS
89/0 Semic Elitserien 5

AHLQVIST, TIMO
65/6 Hellas 150

AHLROOS, KIM
97/8 Hockey-Box
93/4 Jyvas Hyva 29
93/4 Sisu 94
94/5 Sisu 51
95/6 Sisu 344
01/2 Cardiff Devils
02/3 London Knights

AHLSTRÖM, BJÖRN
94/5 Leaf Elit Set 84
95/6 Leaf Elit Set 162
91/2 Semic Elitserien 26
92/3 Semic Elitserien 45
95/6 UD Elitserien 16
97/8 UD Elitserien 16
98/9 UD Elitserien 10
99/0 UD Elitserien 10
00/1 UD Elitserien 13, 181, T1

ÅHLUND, HÅKAN
98/9 DEL 276
99/0 Eishockey 158
97/8 Hockey-Box
94/5 Leaf Elit Set 115
95/6 Leaf Elit Set 91
95 Panini Worlds 159
90/1 Semic Elitserien 140
91/2 Semic Elitserien 190
92/3 Semic Elitserien 218
91 Semic Sticker 40
95/6 UD Elitserien 148

AHMAOJA, TIMO
98/9 Cardset 147
99/0 Cardset 226
00/1 Cardset 144
96/7 Sisu 61
98/9 UD Choice 280
97/8 UD Black Diam. 102

AHNE, MANFRED
94/5 DEL 163

AHO,
97/8 Hockey-Box

AHO, HARRI
00/1 Cardset 53

AHO, JUHA-PEKKA
70/1 Kuvajulkaisut 308
72/3 Williams Finnish 299

AHO, KALEVI
80/1 Mallasjuoma 191
78/9 SM-Liiga 217

AHOKAINEN, SEPPO
72 Hellas MM-Jenkki 1
74 Hellas MM-Jenkki 2
80/1 Mallasjuoma 175
79 Panini Sticker 175
71/2 Williams Finnish 168
72/3 Williams Finnish 61
72/3 Williams Finnish 119
73/4 Williams Finnish 63
73/4 Williams Finnish 173

AHOKAS, PERTTI
70/1 Kuvajulkaisut 172
80/1 Mallasjuoma 138
78/9 SM-Liiga 204
71/2 Williams Finnish 96
72/3 Williams Finnish 137

AHOLA, PETER
92/3 Bowman 353
98/9 Cardset 235, Leij. 4
99/0 Cardset 208, -Aces/2-r
00/1 Cardset 5
02/3 Cardset 1
92/3 Fleer Ultra 78, 376
97/8 Hockey-Box
92/3 O-Pee-Chee 268
91/2 Parkhurst 65
91/2 Pinnacle 312
92/3 Pinnacle 243
91/2 Pro Set 540
92/3 Pro Set 73
91/2 Pro Set Platinum 257
92/3 Score 310
93 Semic Sticker 48
94/5 Sisu 270, H-5
95/6 Sisu 205, DT-5, SS-8
96/7 Sisu 3
95/6 Sisu Limited 57, LG-5
92/3 Topps 73
92/3 T. Stadium Club 192
91/2 Upper Deck 543
92/3 Upper Deck 41
92/3 Upper Deck 526
92/3 Upper Deck E5
92/3 Upper Deck ERT4

AHONEN, ARI
02/3 BAP Memorabilia 337
99/0 Cardset 219, MW10
00/1 Cardset 13, MM, NG5
02/3 Cardset 153
02/3 In The Game-Used 185
02/3 Parkhurst Retro 233
02/3 SP Authentic 210
02/3 SPx 182
02/3 Ultimate Memorabilia 21
02/3 UD Classic 135
02/3 UD Foundations 166 [*1250]
02/3 UD Mask 154
02/3 UD Premier 67, ✂ Jers, ✂ JD
02/3 UD Rookie 119
01/2 Albany River Rats
02/3 Albany River Rats

AHONEN, ASKO
73/4 Williams Finnish 240

AHONEN, JUKKA
72/3 Williams Finnish 341

AHONEN, MARKO
99/0 Cardset 94

AHONEN, OLLI
99/0 Cardset 19

AHONEN, VELI-PEKKA
94/5 Sisu 351
95/6 Sisu 101
96/7 Sisu 106

AHRENS, CHRIS
74/5 Loblaws
74/5 O-Pee-Chee 346
75/6 O-Pee-Chee 371

AHRENS, FABIAN
96/7 DEL 214

AHRGREN, JOHAN
92/3 BCJHL 39

AHVENHARJU, MATTI
70/1 Kuvajulkaisut 277
71/2 Williams Finnish 148

AHXNER, MATHIAS
98/9 DEL 280

AIKAA, SAMI
92/3 Jyvas Hyva 104

AIKAS, LEO
71/2 Williams Finnish 166
72/3 Williams Finnish 117
73/4 Williams Finnish 215

AIKEN, DAVE
91/2 Richmond Renegades

AIKIA, RYAN
00/1 Asheville Smoke

AIMONETTE, RICHARD
90/1 7th..Sketch LHJMQ 253

AIMONETTO, RICHARD
95 Panini Worlds 115

AINSWORTH, JEFF
94/5 Slapshot Memorial 11
96/7 Kamloops Blazers

AIR, SANDY
59/60 Whitby Dunlops

AIRAKSINEN, ERKKI
71/2 Williams Finnish 276

AIRAKSINEN, JUKKA
80/1 Mallasjuoma 23
78/9 SM-Liiga 44

AISBITT, BARRIE
95/6 Guildford Flames 6
96/7 Guildford Flames 22

AITKEN, BRAD
88/9 ProCards / Muskegon
89/0 ProCards IHL 155
90/1 ProCards 388
91/2 ProCards 340

AITKEN, JOHNATHAN
96/7 All-Sport PPF 75
00/1 BAP Mem. 157
95/6 Bowman P1
95/6 Classic 56
95/6 Cla. Vis. Signings 74, ✍ Aut.
00/1 Pacific 45
00/1 SPx 113
00/1 Upper Deck 218
98/9 Providence Bruins
99/0 Providence Bruins

AITKENHEAD, ANDY
36-39 Diamond Match TT1

AIVAZOFF, MICAH
93/4 Cla. Prospects 72
93/4 Donruss 421
93/4 Fleer Ultra 303
93/4 Parkhurst 253
93/4 Premier 345
94/5 Premier 104
89/0 ProCards AHL 6
90/1 ProCards 417
91/2 ProCards 131
93/4 To. Stadium 263
93/4 Upper Deck 432
94/5 UD Be A Player ✍ 173
01/2 UD DEL 226
96/7 Binghampton Rangers
99/0 Utah Grizzlies
99/0 Utah Grizzlies

ÅKERBLOM, BENGT
89/0 Semic Elitserien 70

ÅKERBLOM, BJORN
89/0 Semic Elitserien 258
90/1 Semic Elitserien 168

ÅKERBLOM, MARKUS
94/5 Leaf Elit Set 53
95/6 Leaf Elit Set 240, FTF-15
90/1 Semic Elitserien 216
91/2 Semic Elitserien 144
92/3 Semic Elitserien 96
95/6 UD Elitserien 108,NA13
97/8 UD Elitserien 115
98/9 UD Elitserien 131
99/0 UD Elitserien 117

AKERMAN, JOHAN
94/5 Leaf Elit Set 240
95/6 Leaf Elit Set 8

AKERS, ANDY
95/6 Sheffield Steelers

AKERSTRÖM, ROGER
95/6 Leaf Elit Set 78, FTF-8
89/0 Semic Elitserien 153
90/1 Semic Elitserien 233
91/2 Semic Elitserien 258
92/3 Semic Elitserien 294

ÅKERSTRÖM, ROGER
94/5 Leaf Elit Set 278
95/6 UD Elitserien 120
98/9 UD Elitserien 137
99/0 UD Elitserien 139
00/1 UD Elitserien 124

AKERVIK, ANDY
88/9 ProCards / Kalamazoo
90/1 ProCards 593
91/2 ProCards 526
90/1 Kansas City Blades

AKESON, JEREMY
01/2 Ottawa 67's 17

AKEY, DAVE
86/7 London Knights
87/8 Sudbury Wolves

AKHMETOV, EVGENI
00/1 Mir 390

AKULININ, IGOR
90/1 O-Pee-Chee 491

ALAIN, GABRIEL
52/3 Anonymous 71

ALALAURI, SAMI
00/1 Cardset 298

ALANEN, JOHANNES
98/9 Cardset 225
99/0 Cardset 126
00/1 Cardset 91

ALANKO, RAMI
98/9 Cardset 103
99/0 Cardset 57
00/1 Cardset 42
02/3 Cardset 154

ALATALO, ILKKA
78/9 SM-Liiga 149

ALATALO, MIKA
01/2 Atomic ✂ GWJ 42
00/1 BAP Mem. 215
98/9 Cardset 249, Leij. 19
99/0 Cardset AH J-risti, PA-1
00/1 Cardset 360
02/3 Cardset 2
94/5 Classic T76
01/2 Crown Royale ✂ TT 14
01/2 Heads Up ✂ JQ 16
92/3 Jyvas Hyva 126
93/4 Jyvas Hyva 234
01/2 Pacific ✂ GWJ 23
99/0 Panini Sticker 274
95 Panini Worlds 177
99/0 Prism 106
00/1 PS Titanium ✂ GUG 123
00/1 PS Titanium Draft ✂ 74

ALATALO, MIKA
94 Semic 21

ALATALO, MIKA
95 Semic 15
93 Semic Sticker 62
94/5 SR Auto-Phonex 1, ✍ 1
00/1 Signature 188, ✍ Aut. 128
93/4 Sisu 202
94/5 Sisu 165, 279, H-20, SS-1
95/6 Sisu 128, P-2
99/0 SP Authentic 113
99/0 Stadium 180
99/0 To. Prmr. Plus 114
00/1 Upper Deck 362
99/0 UD Black Diam. 67
97/8 UD Elitserien 131
99/0 WGretzky 134

ALAVAARA, JAN-AXEL
95/6 Leaf Elit Set 278,R-2
97/8 UD Elitserien 151
98/9 UD Elitserien 169
99/0 UD Elitserien 171
00/1 UD Elitserien 153

ALBAN, CHAD
99/0 Mobile Mysticks
01/2 Utah Grizzlies

ALBELIN, TOMMY
95 Globe 10
88/9 O-Pee-Chee 210
90/1 OPC/Topps 323
89/0 O-Pee-Chee 241
88/9 OPC Sticker 184-53
01/2 Pacific 56
02/3 Pacific Complete 291
97/8 Pa. Invincible R-26
88/9 Panini Sticker 348
89/0 Panini Sticker 257
90/1 Panini Sticker 76
96/7 Panini Sticker 242
97/8 Panini Sticker 195
98/9 Panini Sticker 182
99/0 Panini Sticker 187
95/6 Parkhurst 126
94/5 Pinnacle 508
96/7 Pi. Be A Player 161, ✍ Aut. 161
94/5 Premier 251
90/1 Pro Set 162
90/1 Score 378
91/2 Score CAN 393
94 Semic 60
89 Semic Sticker 6
93 Semic Sticker 28
99/0 Topps 217
99/0 To. Chrome 217
00/1 To. Gold Label 97
90/1 Upper Deck 88
97/8 Upper Deck 237
95/6 UD Elitserien 248
96 Wien 43
89/0 NJER
89/0 NJER / Caretta
90/1 NJER
87/8 QUÉB / Gene. Foods
88/9 QUÉB
88/9 QUÉB / Gene. Foods

ALBERS, PAUL
01/2 Calgary Hitmen

ALBERT, CHRIS
97/8 Fort Worth Brahmas
00/1 Hamilton Bulldogs
99/0 Québec Citadelles 3

ALBERT, FRANÇOIS
98/9 Fort Worth Brahmas

ALBIANI, MATTHEW
00/1 London Knights
01/2 Ottawa 67's 10

ALBRECHT, STEVE
96/7 Kamloops Blazers

ALBRECHT, ZDENEK
92/3 Semic Nordisk 68

ALBRIGHT, AARON
92/3 Oshawa Generals

ALBRIGHT, CLINT
45-64 BeeHive-2 [NYRa.]

ALCINDOR, RAY
93/4 Huntington Blizzard

ALDCORN, GARY
45-64 BeeHive-2 [Toro.]
57/8 Parkhurst [Toro.] 24
58/9 Parkhurst 18
60/1 Parkhurst 33
93/4 Parkie 56-57 122
60/1 Shirriff 39

ALDOFF, ROD
95/6 Tallahasee Tiger Sharks
93/4 Minnesota-Duluth

ALDOUS, CHRIS
02/3 Manchester Monarchs

ALDRED, JIM
81/2 Kingston Canadians
82/3 Soo Greyhounds

ALDRIDGE, KEITH
98/9 EBK IHL All-Star
00/1 SPx 114
00/1 Upper Deck 183
00/1 UD DEL 87
01/2 UD DEL 31
00/1 UD MVP 192
00/1 Victory 263
97/8 Detroit Vipers
98/9 Detroit Vipers
00/1 Grand Rapids Griffins
99/0 Michigan K-Wings
91/2 L. Superior State Lakers

ALEKSEEV, ALEXEI
00/1 Mir 188

ALENIUS, ANTTI
66/7 Champion 147

ALEXANDER, BOB
85/6 Minnesota-Duluth 19

ALEXANDER, CLAIRE
76/7 O-Pee-Chee 321
74/5 TORO
76/7 TORO

ALEXANDER, KEN
84/5 Kitchener Rangers
85/6 Kitchener Rangers

ALEXANDRE, ARTHUR
31/2 La Presse

ALEXANDROV, BORIS
92/3 Future Trends C76 150

ALEXANDROV, IGOR
98/9 DEL 90
99/0 Eishockey 240
92/3 Upper Deck 611
01/2 UD DEL 1

ALEXEEV, ALEXANDER
92/3 Classic 54
96/7 Hampton Roads
97/8 Hampton Roads
98/9 Hampton Roads
95/6 Portland Pirates
92/3 Tacoma Rockets
93/4 Tacoma Rockets

ALEXEEV, KIRILL
99/0 Rouyn-Noranda Huskies
00/1 Rouyn-Noranda Huskies 4
01/2 Victoriaville Tigres 17

ALEXEEV, NIKITA
01/2 Adrenaline 224, RR19
01/2 Atomic 124, RR10
01/2 BAP Memor. 375
01/2 Bowman 157
01/2 Crown Royale 178, RR20
02/3 First Edition 240
01/2 Heads Up 119
01/2 O-Pee-Chee 346
02/3 O-Pee-Chee 306
01/2 Pacific 462
02/3 Pacific 345
01/2 Parkhurst 283
01/2 Pr. Stock 139, RR10, -PS 90
01/2 PS Titanium 181
01/2 PS Titanium Draft 167
01/2 Signature 248, ✍ Aut. 248
01/2 SP Authentic 172
02/3 SP Authentic 133
01/2 SP Game Used 98
01/2 SPx 128
01/2 SPx Rookie RR27
01/2 Topps 346
02/3 Topps 306
01/2 To. Chrome 164
02/3 T. Chrome 148
01/2 To. Heritage 148
02/3 T. Limited 306
01/2 To. Reserve 120
02/3 T. Total 372
01/2 UD PlayMakers Ltd 142
01/2 Upper Deck 227
02/3 Upper Deck 404
01/2 UD Challenge 133
01/2 UD Honor Roll 88
01/2 UD Ice 69

01/2 UD Mask 167
01/2 UD Premier 107
99/0 UD Prospects 12, IN7
00/1 UD Prospects 5, ✍ Sig
01/2 UD Top Shelf 75
01/2 UD Vintage 297
01/2 Vanguard 129, PP18

ALFORS, PEKKA
65/6 Hellas 120

ALFRED, JIM
81/2 Soo Greyhounds

ALFREDSSON, DANIEL
01/2 Adrenaline 131
01/2 Atomic 67
02/3 Atomic 70, -CF 18
98/9 Aurora 128, -CF 32, -FL 6
00/1 Aurora 99
02/3 BAP All-Star 1, ✂ ASJ
98/9 Be A Player 98, ✍ Aut. 98
99/0 BAP Mem. 287
00/1 BAP Mem. 195, ✂ J-27
01/2 BAP Memor. 62, ✂ ASJ, ✂ ASE, ✂ ASN, ✂ CoO, ✂ SCP
02/3 BAP Memorabilia 22, ✂ ASJ1, ✂ SC20
96/7 Bic.Sports Aces 7-C
97/8 Bicycle 6-Heart
95/6 Bowman 110, BB16
01/2 Bowman 27
02/3 Bowman 85
98/9 Bowman's Best 16
02/3 Calder 13, ✂ GWJ 15
99/0 Crown Royale 94
00/1 Crown Royale 73, ✂ JR-7
01/2 Crown Royale 99
02/3 Crown Royale 66
95/6 Donruss 299, RR-14
96/7 Donruss RR 10
97/8 Donruss 17
96/7 Do. Canadian 34
97/8 Do. Canadian 112
95/6 Do. Elite 25, R-3
96/7 Do. Elite 100, A-2
97/8 Do. Elite 104
97/8 Do. Preferred 90
97/8 Do. Priority 113, DD-27
97/8 Do. Studio 94
98/9 Dynagon Ice 126
99/0 Dynagon Ice 136
97/8 Esso 44
02/3 eTopps 29
02/3 Exclusive 119
02/3 First Edition 140, ✂ Jers., ✂ TSL 13
96/7 Flair 63
96/7 Fleer 73, 136, RS-1
95/6 Fleer Metal 169
96/7 Fl. Picks 78, F50-1, DL-3, JE-1
95/6 Fleer Ultra 329, HS-1
96/7 Fl. Ultra 113
00 Gatorade Sticker
95 Globe 47
01/2 Heads Up 67, ✂ JQ 19
02/3 Heads Up 84, -ITN 16, ✂ GWQ 19, ✂ GWQ 31
02/3 In The Game-Used 52, 152, ✂ E23, ✂ GUJ23, ✂ SJ23
96/7 Kraft / TT
96/7 Leaf 210, S-14
97/8 Leaf 145
94/5 Leaf Elit Set 82, ND-6
95/6 L. Limited 25, RP-2
96/7 Leaf Limited 73
96/7 L. Preferred 48, LS-35
97/8 Limited 22, 186, FG-46
96/7 McDonald's McD-9
01/2 McDonald's ✂ JPatch 14
02/3 McDonald's 28, -CC5, ✂ JP 12
96/7 Metal Univ. 103
98/9 NHL Power Play
01/2 O-Pee-Chee 102
02/3 O-Pee-Chee 23
98/9 OPC Chrome 130
97/8 Omega 152
98/9 Omega 163
99/0 Omega 156
98/9 Pacific 305
99/0 Pacific 283
00/1 Pacific 273, 443
01/2 Pacific 269
02/3 Pacific 260, -MA 14
02/3 Pacific Complete 419
97/8 Pacific CC 58
97/8 Pa. Crown Roy. 89
98/9 Pa. Crown Roy. 92
97/8 Pa. Dynagon 83, T-71
97/8 Pa. Invincible 92
97/8 Pa. Paramount 122
98/9 Pa. Paramount 160
99/0 Pa. Paramount 158
00/1 Pa. Paramount 169
97/8 Pa. Revolution 92, TC-17
98/9 Pa. Revolution 98
98/9 Panini Photocard
96/7 Panini Sticker 46, 152
97/8 Panini Sticker 41
98/9 Panini Sticker 42
99/0 Panini Sticker 112
00/1 Panini Sticker 70
95 Panini Worlds 160
95/6 Parkhurst 257, 507, CCP-15, PP-38
00/1 Parkhurst P-65
01/2 Parkhurst 81, ✂ PJ10, ✂ PS10, ✂ T16
02/3 Parkhurst 95, ✂ GJ42, ✂ SJ42, ✂ TT11
02/3 Parkhurst Retro 25
96/7 Pinnacle 205, BTN-10, T-4
97/8 Pinnacle 155
96/7 Pi. Be A Player BB-23
97/8 Pi. BeeHive 48
97/8 Pi. Certified 114
97/8 Pi. Inside 26
96/7 Pi. Mint 10
95/6 Pi. Summit 182
96/7 Pi. Summit 167, HV-4
97/8 Pi. Totally 114
95/6 Pi. Zenith 149, RRC-10
96/7 Pi. Zenith 103, ZT-13
96/7 Playoff 341
00/1 Premier Plus 62
99/0 Prism 94
00/1 Private Stock 68
01/2 Pr. Stock 66
02/3 Private Stock Reserve 70
00/1 PS Titanium ✂ GUG 41, ✂ 119
01/2 PS Titanium 98, SK 15, ✂ DSJ 30, ✂ DSJ 48, ✂ DSJ 58
01/2 PS Titanium Draft ✂ 64
02/3 Private Stock Titanium 71, ✂ GWJ 46
00/1 PS Titanium Draft ✂ 70
02/3 Quest for the Cup 68, -CTC 12, ✂ GWJ 12
00/1 Revolution 101
96/7 Score 240
97/8 Score 131
95/6 Select CE 122
96/7 Select CE 47
92/3 Semic Elitserien 319
96/7 SB 7-Eleven Phonecard
00/1 Signature 19, ✍ Aut. 196
01/2 Signature 191, ✍ Aut. 191, ✂ FP21, ✂ GUE44, ✂ GU78, ✂ HSHSJers, ✂ ITN44, ✂ TM21
02/3 Signature Series 12, ✍ 12, ✂ SGJ23
95/6 SBx Impact 214
96/7 SBx Impact 86, 164, F-1
95/6 SP 100, FX-15
96/7 SP 107, GF-20, HC-9
97/8 SP Authentic 106, I30
98/9 SP Authentic 60, ✍ SotT
01/2 SP Authentic 59
02/3 SP Authentic 62
02/3 SP Game-Used Edition 35
02/3 Sports Vault 93
96/7 SPx 32, GF-1
97/8 SPx 34
99/0 SPx 103
02/3 SPx 54
00/1 Stadion 117
99/0 Stadium 98, -Chrome 32
00/1 Stadium 34, ✍ CO3, ✍ LS4
01/2 Stadium Club 47
02/3 Stadium 82, -WS-20, ✂ NHLP2
97/8 SLU
96/7 Team Out!
95/6 Topps 369
98/9 Topps 130
99/0 Topps 157
00/1 Topps 105
01/2 Topps 102
02/3 Topps 23, -HHC10
99/0 To. Chrome 157
00/1 To. Chrome 82
01/2 To. Chrome 102
02/3 T. Chrome 23
95/6 To. Finest 116
98/9 To. Finest 13, C19
98/9 T. Gold Label 69
99/0 To. Gold Label 37, QC7
00/1 To. Gold Label 34
00/1 To. Heritage 55
01/2 To. Heritage 63
02/3 To. Heritage 15, ✂ CC, ✂ CCB
02/3 T. Limited 23
96/7 Topps Picks RS1
99/0 To. Prmr. Plus 73, CAC3
01/2 To. Reserve 41
95/6 To. Stadium ER206
95/6 TSC Members Only 38
00/1 To. Stars 22
95/6 T. Super Skills SR12
02/3 T. Total 342, TTC21, TT17
98/9 UD Choice 144
00/1 Ultimate Mem. ✍ U-14
01/2 Ultimate Mem. ✂ CT, ✂ DD, ✂ UC, ✍ Aut.
95/6 Upper Deck 504, AS-12, H-23, SE-145
96/7 Upper Deck 113, X6, SS18A
97/8 Upper Deck 112, SS27, T14A
98/9 Upper Deck 327
99/0 Upper Deck 265
00/1 Upper Deck 121
01/2 Upper Deck 121, LP10
02/3 Upper Deck 123
02/3 UD Artistic 63, R63, / Art
95/6 UD Be A Player 171, LL6, ✍ S171
96/7 UD Black Diam. 141
97/8 UD Black Diam. 73
98/9 UD Black Diam. 61
02/3 UD Classic 70
95/6 UD CC 406
96/7 UD CC 177, 344, UD39, C13, CR13
97/8 UD Coll. Choice 172, SQ51, S11
98/9 UD G. Reserve 327
99/0 UD G. Reserve 265
02/3 UD Honor 51, 91
96/7 UD Ice 95
97/8 UD Ice 11, L4A
01/2 UD Ice 109
01/2 UD Mask 67
98/9 UD MVP 141
99/0 UD MVP 140
00/1 UD MVP 122
01/2 UD MVP 129, ✂ C
02/3 UD MVP 125
99/0 UD MVP Cup 126
99/0 UD Ovation 40
02/3 UD Piece 64
02/3 UD Rookie 69
00/1 UD Vintage 253
01/2 UD Vintage 177, 182
02/3 UD Vintage 181, 281, GB 181, T45
00/1 Vanguard 68
01/2 Vanguard 67
02/3 Vanguard 69, ✂ GWJ 32
99/0 Victory 204
00/1 Victory 163
01/2 Victory 245
02/3 Victory 148, NP47
99/0 WGretzky 121
96 Wien 72
97/8 Zenith 43, Z25
95/6 OTTA
96/7 OTTA
97/8 OTTA
98/9 OTTA
99/0 OTTA
00/1 OTTA
01/2 OTTA
02/3 OTTA

ALGOTSSON, HÅKAN
99/0 Eishockey 243
95 Globe 4
94/5 Leaf Elit Set 2, CS-10, GC-7
95/6 Leaf Elit Set 137, S-4
94 Semic 51
89/0 Semic Elitserien 264
90/1 Semic Elitserien 28
91/2 Semic Elitserien 278
92/3 Semic Elitserien 300
93 Semic Sticker 2
95/6 UD Elitserien 202

ALHO, RISTO
66/7 Champion 140

ALINC, JAN
94/5 APS 224
95/6 APS 171, 376, 440
97/8 APS 364
99/0 DS 66
00/1 DS 116
97/8 Hockey-Box
99/0 OFS 337
00/1 OFS 94
01/2 OFS 5
95 Semic 164

ALINIC, JAN
98/9 UD Elitserien 179

ALIPOV, JEVGENIJ
99/0 Score 101

ALKULA, JUKKA
66/7 Champion 205
74 Hellas MM-Jenkki 3
78/9 SM-Liiga 184
71/2 Williams Finnish 128
72/3 Williams Finnish 191
73/4 Williams Finnish 149

ALKUNEN, KAUKO
71/2 Williams Finnish 277

ALLAIN, RICK
90/1 ProCards 139
91/2 ProCards 51
90 7th..Sketch Mem.Cup 41
96/7 Guelph Storm
88/9 Kitchener Rangers
89/0 Kitchener Rangers

ALLAIRE, BENOÎT
97/8 PHOE / Coca-Cola

ALLAIRE, FRANÇOIS
87/8 MONT
87/8 MONT / Vachon 9
88/9 MONT
89/0 MONT
90/1 MONT
91/2 MONT

ALLAN, ANDY
94/5 Guildford Flames 5
95/6 Guildford Flames 7

ALLAN, BRETT
98 Bowman 122, ✍ A26
98 Bowman Chrome 122
00/1 Prince George Cougars

ALLAN, CHAD
95/6 Donruss C3TWC 4
95/6 Do. Elite WJ 3
94/5 SR Auto-Phonex 2, ✍ 2
95/6 Topps 17CJ
94/5 Topps Finest 147
94/5 Upper Deck 499
95/6 Upper Deck 532
00/1 St. John's Maple Leafs
96/7 Syracuse Crunch
93/4 Saskatoon Blades

ALLAN, JAMIE
98/9 Phoenix Mustangs 10

ALLAN, SANDY
92/3 Classic 19
91/2 7th...Sketch OHL 51
93/4 Slapshot / North Bay 2
95/6 Richmond Renegades

ALLAN, SIR MONTAGU
83 HHOF Postcard I2
83&87 HHOF 123
94/5 Legends 52

ALLARD, ANDRÉ
79 Panini Sticker 381

ALLARD, PIERRE
00/1 Kudos 97
90/1 7th..Sketch LHJMQ 227
91/2 7th...Sketch LHJMQ 14
01/2 Manchester Storm
02/3 Manchester Storm

ALLEGRINO, SCOTT
97/8 New Orleans Brass

ALLEN, BOBBY
02/3 BAP Memorabilia 323
02/3 UD Premier 93
02/3 Hamilton Bulldogs
01/2 Providence Bruins

ALLEN, BRYAN
00/1 BAP Mem. 514
01/2 BAP Memor. 299
97/8 Bell
98 Bowman 25, 133, SC1, ✍ A12
98 Bowman Chrome 25, 133
01/2 O-Pee-Chee 305
02/3 O-Pee-Chee 298
98/9 OPC Chrome 226
02/3 Pacific Complete 391
01/2 Parkhurst 297
01/2 Pr. Stock 110, -PS 91
01/2 Signature 77, ✍ Aut. 77
01/2 Stadium Club 118
98/9 Topps 226
01/2 Topps 305
02/3 Topps 298
98/9 To. Finest F5
02/3 T. Limited 298
97/8 Upper Deck 401
00/1 Kansas City Blades 3
01/2 Manitoba Moose
02/3 Manitoba Moose

ALLEN, CHAD
01/2 Belfast Giants

ALLEN, CHRIS
95/6 Bowman P2
95/6 Cla. Vis. Signings 69, ✍ Aut.
95/6 Future Legends ✍ SSD-2
95/6 Slapshot 109, 433
99/0 Upper Deck 61
99/0 UD G. Reserve 61
99/0 UD MVP 91
99/0 Louisville Panthers
98/9 New Haven Beast 17

ALLEN, DAVE
98/9 Huntington Blizzard
99/0 Huntington Blizzard

ALLEN, GEORGE
34-43 BeeHive-1 [Chic.]
39/0 O-Pee-Chee 79
43-47 Parade Sportive
45-54 Quaker Oats

ALLEN, GREG
89/0 7th..Sketch OHL 145
90/1 7th..Sketch OHL 251
88/9 Niagara Falls Thunder
89/0 Niagara Falls Thunder

ALLEN, JASON
94/5 Slapshot / Sudbury 25

ALLEN, KEITH
96/7 Legends 81
54/5 Parkhurst 47

ALLEN, MARKO
92/3 Jyvas Hyva 25
93/4 Jyvas Hyva 55
93/4 Sisu 236
94/5 Sisu 4
95/6 Sisu 20

ALLEN, MIKE
90/1 7th..Sketch OHL 226
90/1 Kitchener Rangers

ALLEN, PETER
00/1 UD DEL 212
01/2 UD DEL 227
95/6 Cleveland Lumberjacks
96/7 Cleveland Lumberjacks
97/8 Kentucky Tho'blades
98/9 Kentucky Tho'blades
93/4 Richmond Renegades

ALLEN, RICK
87/8 Kitchener Rangers

ALLEN, SANDY
92/3 Classic Four Sport 168

ALLEN, SCOTT
91/2 ProCards 444
96/7 Johnstown Chiefs

ALLEN, SQUEE
34-43 BeeHive-1 [NYAm.]

ALLEN, TOM
83/4 Kingston Canadians
85/6 London Knights
84/5 Ottawa 67's

ALLISON, BLAIR
92/3 MPS SJHL 4
93/4 Maine Black Bears

ALLISON, DAVE
88/9 ProCards / Indianapolis
93/4 Slapshot / Kingston 24
99/0 Fort Wayne Komets
96/7 Grand Rapids Griffins
97/8 Grand Rapids Griffins
84/5 Nova Scotia Oilers
83/4 Nova Scotia Voyageurs
91/2 Richmond Renegades

ALLISON, JAMES**
81/2 Ottawa 67's

ALLISON, JAMIE*
00/1 BAP Mem. 10
01/2 BAP Memor. 464
95/6 Edge Ice 75
97/8 Pacific CC 315
91/2 7th...Sketch OHL 189
01/2 Signature 90, ✍ Aut. 90
93/4 Slapshot / Detroit 15
94/5 Slapshot / Detroit Jr. 17
94/5 Slapshot Memorial 91
94/5 Upper Deck 464
95/6 Saint John Flames
96/7 Saint John Flames
97/8 Saint John Flames

ALLISON, JASON
01/2 Adrenaline 85
01/2 Atomic 5
02/3 Atomic 48, -PC 9, -SC 8
98/9 Aurora 7
99/0 Aurora 9
00/1 Aurora 8, Pin. 8
98/9 Be A Player 156, ✍ Aut. 156
99/0 BAP Mem. 50
00/1 BAP Mem. 265
01/2 BAP Memor. 197, 314
02/3 BAP Memorabilia 102, 242
01/2 BAP Update ✂ H26
01/2 Bowman 8
02/3 Bowman 30
98/9 Bowman's Best 51
93/4 Classic 13
94/5 Classic 110, C1, CP14, R1, T73
93/4 Cla. 4 Sport 200
94/5 Classic 4 Sport 160
94/5 Cla. Images 4 Sport 114
99/0 Crown Royale 10
00/1 Crown Royale 8, JotC-4, NP-3
01/2 Crown Royale 66, JotC 15
02/3 Crown Royale 44
93/4 Donruss CAN1
95/6 Donruss 75, C3TWC-12
97/8 Donruss 131
97/8 Do. Priority 122
98/9 Dynagon Ice 7
99/0 Dynagon Ice 20
02/3 Exclusive 79
02/3 First Edition 216, 373, 410R
94/5 Flair 195
94/5 Fleer 231
94/5 Fleer Ultra 386
01/2 Heads Up 6
02/3 Heads Up 55, ✂ GWQ 1, ✂ GWQ 13, /Bobble
02/3 In The Game-Used 36, 136
94/5 Leaf 511, GLR-13
95/6 Leaf 103
94/5 L. Limited 98
95/6 L. Limited 5
02/3 McDonald's 18
01/2 O-Pee-Chee 26
02/3 O-Pee-Chee 240
98/9 OPC Chrome 125, SB27
97/8 Omega 10
98/9 Omega 10
99/0 Omega 16
98/9 Pacific 41
99/0 Pacific 17
00/1 Pacific 29
01/2 Pacific 27, 403, 426
02/3 Pacific 164, -MA 9, ✂ GWJ 21
02/3 Pacific Complete 4
97/8 Pa. Crown Roy. 6
98/9 Pa. Crown Roy. 6
97/8 Pa. Dynagon 6, T-29
97/8 Pa. Invincible 6
98/9 Pa. Paramount 8
99/0 Pa. Paramount 16
00/1 Pa. Paramount 16
97/8 Pa. Revolution 6
98/9 Pa. Revolution 6
98/9 Panini Photocard
98/9 Panini Sticker 14
99/0 Panini Sticker 27, 326
95/6 Parkhurst 494
00/1 Parkhurst P-191
01/2 Parkhurst 232, ✂ T4
02/3 Parkhurst 20, ✂ TT6
02/3 Parkhurst Retro 7, ✂ RF14
94/5 Parkie SE194, SE208
93/4 Pinnacle 466
94/5 Pinnacle 247, 474, RTP-7
97/8 Pinnacle 147
96/7 Pi. Be A Player 36, ✍ Aut. 36
97/8 Pi. Inside 147
96/7 Pi. Zenith 125
95/6 Playoff 106
94/5 Premier 467
00/1 Premier Plus 33
99/0 Prism 10
01/2 Pr. Stock 44, -PS 35
02/3 Pr. Stock Reserve 44
00/1 PS Titanium 4
01/2 PS Titanium 63, ✂ DSJ 75
01/2 PS Titanium Draft ✂ 41
02/3 Private Stock Titanium 48
95/6 Pro Magnet 29
02/3 Quest for the Cup 43
99/0 Revolution 10, / CSC 10
94/5 Score 206, 231
95/6 Score 128
97/8 Score 233
97/8 Score Bost. 7
94/5 Select 193,YE-8
91/2 7th...Sketch OHL 381
00/1 Signature 102, ✍ Aut. 19
01/2 Signature C-15, ✍ Aut. LJAL
02/3 Signature Series 107, ✍ 107, ✂ FJ14, ✂ TQ10
95/6 SBx Emotion 185
94/5 SP 151
96/7 SP 168
97/8 SP Authentic 10
98/9 SP Authentic 6, ✍ SotT
00/1 SP Authentic 8
01/2 SP Authentic 38, ✍ SotT, ✍ SotTD
02/3 SP Authentic 44, ✂ SP
02/3 SP Game-Used ✂ AF, ✂ PC, ✂ PH (x2)
02/3 Sports Vault 233
99/0 SPx 12
00/1 SPx 4
01/2 SPx 176, ✂ DT
02/3 SPx ✂ X
98/9 SPx Finite 6
99/0 Stadium 88, EG7
00/1 Stadium 38
01/2 Stadium Club 7, ✂ SCST
02/3 Stadium 12
95/6 Topps 4CJ
98/9 Topps 125, I6, SB27, ✍ CAI
99/0 Topps 109
00/1 Topps 193
01/2 Topps 26, OTG4, ✂ CC3
02/3 Topps 240
99/0 To. Chrome 109
00/1 To. Chrome 128
01/2 To. Chrome 26
02/3 T. Chrome 132
94/5 Topps Finest 55, 154
98/9 To. Finest 141, C8, R13
98/9 T. Gold Label 50
99/0 To. Gold Label 31
00/1 To. Gold Label 36
00/1 To. Heritage 44, ✂ OSS
01/2 To. Heritage 7
02/3 To. Heritage 24, 110
02/3 T. Limited 240
99/0 To. Prmr. Plus 30
01/2 To. Reserve 30, ✂ TR
94/5 T. Stadium Club 118
00/1 To. Stars 24, ✂ GG
02/3 T. Total 80, TTC13
98/9 UD Choice 14
00/1 UD Heroes 8
01/2 UD PlayMakers Ltd 47
00/1 UD Reserve 7
00/1 Ultimate Mem. ✂ J-31, ✂ J-27, ✂ JJ-16, ✂ S-31
93/4 Upper Deck 537
94/5 Upper Deck 242, 535, C4, SP-174
95/6 Upper Deck 59
97/8 Upper Deck 8
98/9 Upper Deck 41, FF26
99/0 Upper Deck 185
00/1 Upper Deck 16
01/2 Upper Deck 309
02/3 Upper Deck 83, ✂ DM
02/3 UD Artistic 44, R44, / Art
94/5 UD Be A Player R155
97/8 UD Black Diam. 32
98/9 UD Black Diam. 6
01/2 UD Challenge 39, ✂ FP, ✂✍ FPS, ✂✍ UCS
02/3 UD Classic 47
97/8 UD Coll. Choice 16
98/9 UD G. Reserve 41
99/0 UD G. Reserve 185
01/2 UD Ice 100
01/2 UD Mask 43, ✂ GJ, ✂ JP, ✂ DP
02/3 UD Mask ✂ IO, ✂ PG
98/9 UD MVP 13, ✍ PS
99/0 UD MVP 15
00/1 UD MVP 16, ✂ GS
01/2 UD MVP 11, ✂ S
02/3 UD MVP 82, ST
02/3 UD Piece 43
00/1 UD Pros&Prosp. 8
01/2 UD Top Shelf 97, ✂ J, ✂✍ SJ
02/3 UD Top Shelf 40, ✂ SH, ✂ ST, ✂ SW, ✂ TW, ✍ Sig
00/1 UD Vintage 31
02/3 UD Vintage 118, 274, 307, GB 118, T32
00/1 Vanguard 7, HV-7, IF-3
01/2 Vanguard 44, QTH 12, ✂ DGM 48
02/3 Vanguard 47
99/0 Victory 27
00/1 Victory 22
01/2 Victory 30
02/3 Victory 97
99/0 WGretzky 17
97/8 Zenith 80, Z28
95/6 WASH
95/6 Portland Pirates

ALLISON, MIKE
81/2 O-Pee-Chee 221
90/1 O-Pee-Chee 417
89/0 OPC/Topps 141
88/9 Panini Sticker 73
82/3 Post [NYRa.]
93/4 Slapshot / Kingston 24
81/2 Topps 94 [East]
88/9 LOSA / Smokey
89/0 LOSA / Smokey 4
86/7 TORO
86/7 TORO
87/8 TORO / P.L.A.Y. 18

ALLISON, PETER
92/3 Windsor Spitfires

ALLISON, RAY
84/5 Kelowna Wings &...
80/1 O-Pee-Chee 126
83/4 O-Pee-Chee 259
89/0 ProCards AHL 338
80/1 Topps 126
83/4 PHIL / J.C. Penney

ALLISON, SCOTT
99/0 Eishockey 157
00/1 Kudos 150
90/1 Score 424
90/1 7th..Sketch WHL 273
91/2 7th...Sketch WHL 276
94/5 Cape Breton Oilers
02/3 Nottingham Panthers
01/2 Sheffield Steelers
01/2 Sheffield Steelers GS
97/8 Sheffield Steelers
90/1 Prince Albert Raiders

ALLMAN, STEVEN
92 Semic Sticker 28

ALLMANN, STEVE
92/3 Semic Nordisk 51

ALLVIN, PATRIK
99/0 UD Elitserien 109
96/7 Pensacola Ice Pilots

ALMASY, PETER
92 Semic Sticker 239

ALMSTEDT, GRAYDON
84/5 Ottawa 67's

ALOI, JOE
87/8 Hull Olympiques

ALSETH,
92/3 Semic Nordisk 205

ALSTEAD, RYAN
92/3 Minnesota G'Gophers

ALSTON, JAN
98/9 DEL 246
99/0 Eishockey 20
00/1 UD DEL 14, P1

ALTAREV, DMITRI
00/1 Mir 201

ALTHOFF, CHRISTIAN
94/5 DEL 357

ALTRICHTER, MARTIN
94/5 APS 250
95/6 APS 125
96/7 APS 288
97/8 APS 148
96/7 DS Sticker 208
97/8 DS Sticker 188
99/0 Score 132

ALTRICHTER, PETR
99/0 Score 36

ALVAREZ, MAURICIO
95/6 Slapshot 21

ALVEY, MATT
97/8 Charlotte Checkers

ALWAY, ANDY
83/4 Brantford Alexanders

AMADIO, DAVE
68/9 O-Pee-Chee 157
70/1 O-Pee-Chee 33
68/9 Shirriff / LosA. 10
70/1 Topps 33

AMADIO, LEO
52/3 Anonymous 75

AMANN, RICK
94/5 DEL 89
95/6 DEL 83
98/9 DEL
99/0 Eishockey 400
95 Globe 219
94 Semic 273
93 Semic Sticker 155

AMBROSIO, JEFF
94/5 Parkie SE266
94/5 Sig. Rookies FF1, ✍ FF1
95/6 Slapshot 143

AMBROZIAK, PETER
89/0 7th..Sketch OHL 60
90/1 7th..Sketch OHL 76
91/2 7th...Sketch OHL 291
98/9 Flint Generals
92/3 Rochester Americans DD
92/3 Rochester Americans WPC
93/4 Rochester Americans

AMBRUZ, MARTIN
00/1 DS 59
98/9 OFS 279
99/0 OFS 457
00/1 OFS 364
01/2 OFS 77

AMBURG, SEAN
90/1 Rayside-Balfour
91/2 Rayside-Balfour

AMIDOVSKI, BUJAR
98 Bowman 32, SC4
98 Bowman Chrome 32
98/9 EBK ECHL All-Star
98/9 OPC Chrome 239
95/6 Slapshot 106
98/9 Topps 239
00/1 Florida Everblades
98/9 Louisiana Ice Gators

AMIROV, RUSTEM
99/0 Mir 132

AMODEO, DOMINIC
92/3 Canada Nationals

AMODEO, MIKE
72/3 O-Pee-Chee 291
79/0 O-Pee-Chee 268
82 Semic Sticker 126
79/0 WINN
72/3 Ottawa Nationals
78/9 Winnipeg Jets
01/2 Kitchener Rangers

AMONTE, TONY
01/2 Adrenaline 38, ✂ GWJ 38
01/2 Atomic 19, PP 7, ✂ GWJ 8
02/3 Atomic 76, -NPU 8
98/9 Aurora 38
99/0 Aurora 30, Stripe 30
00/1 Aurora 31, Pin. 31
02/3 BAP All-Star 2, ✂ ASJ, ✂ HSHSJers
98/9 Be A Player 28, P-11, ✍ Aut. 28, ✂ G-22
99/0 BAP Mem. 94, SL9, ✂ J-27, ✂ TM-27, ✂ TM-33
00/1 BAP Mem. 264, ✂ J-11, ✂ TM-4, ✂ TM-25
01/2 BAP Memor. 257, ✂ ASJ, ✂ ASE, ✂ ASN, ✂ ASD, ✂ AST, ✂ CoO
02/3 BAP Memorabilia 144, 270, 309, ✂ ASJ2, ✂ AST 19
01/2 BAP Update ✂ PTT2
97/8 Bicycle 7-Club
92/3 Bowman 389
01/2 Bowman 13
02/3 Bowman 3
98/9 Bowman's Best 77
02/3 Calder 48
99/0 Crown Royale 30, IE-5
00/1 Crown Royale 23
01/2 Crown Royale 29
02/3 Crown Royale 73
93/4 Donruss 217
93/4 Donruss 411
94/5 Donruss 107
95/6 Donruss 121
96/7 Donruss 80
97/8 Donruss 102
97/8 Do. Canadian 34
97/8 Do. Elite 97
97/8 Do. Preferred 64
97/8 Do. Priority 151
97/8 Do. Studio 99
98/9 Dynagon Ice 38
99/0 Dynagon Ice 46, CM-19
02/3 Exclusive 130
02/3 First Edition 101, ✂ Jers.
96/7 Flair 14
94/5 Fleer 37
92/3 Fleer Ultra 133, -UR 1
93/4 Fleer Ultra 202
94/5 Fleer Ultra 273
95/6 Fleer Ultra 216
96/7 Fl. Ultra 28
95 Globe 121
01/2 Heads Up 18, ✂ JQ 6
02/3 Heads Up 24, ✂ GWQ 7
93/4 Hockey Wit 2
99/0 HoloGrFX 12
02/3 In The Game-Used 80, 180, ✂ IE16
00/1 Kraft 24
93/4 Leaf 17
94/5 Leaf 2
95/6 Leaf 17
96/7 Leaf 92
97/8 Leaf 139
97/8 Limited 105
99/0 McDonald's ✂ GJ, ✍ SS
96/7 Metal Univ. 24
99/0 Millenium 56, ✍ Aut. 56, ✂ J22, ✂ JS22
98/9 NHL Power Play
91/2 O-Pee-Chee 26
92/3 O-Pee-Chee 155
92/3 O-Pee-Chee 255
92/3 OPC - Anniv. 24
01/2 O-Pee-Chee 5
02/3 O-Pee-Chee 9, Update 9
98/9 OPC Chrome 204
91/2 OPC Premier 11
97/8 Omega 46
98/9 Omega 48
99/0 Omega 51
98/9 Pacific 142
99/0 Pacific 84
00/1 Pacific 92, GCDC-6
01/2 Pacific 82, ✂ GWJ 6
02/3 Pacific 73, ✂ GWJ 7
02/3 Pacific Complete 207
97/8 Pacific CC 264
97/8 Pa. Crown Roy. 27
98/9 Pa. Crown Roy. 27
97/8 Pa. Dynagon 24, T-33
97/8 Pa. Invincible 27
97/8 Pa. Paramount 40
98/9 Pa. Paramount 43
99/0 Pa. Paramount 52, IAI-7, PB-7
00/1 Pa. Paramount 48, FF-6, ✂ J&P-2
97/8 Pa. Revolution 27
98/9 Pa. Revolution 28, -ASG 1, -Show. 7
98/9 Panini Photocard
92/3 Panini Sticker 270
92/3 Panini Sticker T
93/4 Panini Sticker 90
94/5 Panini Sticker 128
95/6 Panini Sticker 160
96/7 Panini Sticker 160
97/8 Panini Sticker 131
98/9 Panini Sticker 118
99/0 Panini Sticker 203, 319
00/1 Panini Sticker 126
91/2 Parkhurst 114
91/2 Parkhurst 443
92/3 Parkhurst 107
92/3 Parkhurst 235
93/4 Parkhurst 132
94/5 Parkhurst V56
95/6 Parkhurst 311
00/1 Parkhurst P-2
01/2 Parkhurst 76, ✂ PJ25, ✂ PS25, ✂ HSHSJers, ✂ T9
02/3 Parkhurst 148, -CR 10, ✂ CRM10
02/3 Parkhurst Retro 46
94/5 Parkie SE36
91/2 Pinnacle 301
91/2 Pinnacle 390
92/3 Pinnacle 55
92/3 Pinnacle T2K 4
93/4 Pinnacle 6
93/4 Pinnacle T2K1 19
94/5 Pinnacle 16
96/7 Pinnacle 54
97/8 Pinnacle 148
96/7 Pi. Be A Player 66, ✍ Aut. 66
97/8 Pi. Certified 68
97/8 Pi. Inside 53
95/6 Pi. Summit 165
97/8 Pi. Totally 68
95/6 Playoff 235
94/5 POG 65
95/6 POG 63
94/5 Post
93/4 Power Play 156
93/4 Premier 70
94/5 Premier 5
00/1 Premier Plus 27, MB4, PP4
99/0 Prism 32
00/1 Private Stock 19, ✂ GUG-15
01/2 Pr. Stock 17, ✂ GUG 20
02/3 Pr. Stock Reserve 76
00/1 PS Titanium 16, ✂ GUG-5
01/2 PS Titanium 28, ✂ DSJ 8
01/2 PS Titanium Draft ✂ 20
02/3 Private Stock Titanium 77
00/1 PS Titanium Draft ✂ 16
91/2 Pro Set 550
92/3 Pro Set 118
92/3 Pro Set RGL 1
91/2 Pro Set Platinum 262
02/3 Quest for the Cup 73
99/0 Revolution 32, SS-7, TL-24, / CSC 32
00/1 Revolution 29, HD-7, SM-22, ✂ GWJ-4
91/2 Score 398
91/2 Score CAN 288
92/3 Score 389
92/3 Score 415
92/3 Score 506
93/4 Score 215
94/5 Score 92
95/6 Score 133
96/7 Score 169
97/8 Score 114
92/3 Score Young Stars 2
92/3 Seasons 27
94/5 Select 115
93 Semic Sticker 188
00/1 Signature 220, HSHS, F-7, ✍ Aut. 198, ✂ J-22, ✂ GSJ-22
01/2 Signature C-45, ✍ Aut., ✂ FP7, ✂ GUE12, ✂ GJ12, ✂ GSJ12, ✂ HSHSJers, ✂ ITN12, ✂ IS2, ✂ TM7
02/3 Signature Series 115, ✍ 115
96/7 SBx Impact 16
94/5 SP 26
95/6 SP 28
96/7 SP 32, HC-18
97/8 SP Authentic 29, I29, ✍ SotT
98/9 SP Authentic 17
99/0 SP Authentic 19
00/1 SP Authentic 20
01/2 SP Authentic 14, ✍ SotT, ✍ SotTT
02/3 SP Authentic 70
00/1 SP GU 11, ✂ TotG, ✂ P
01/2 SP Game Used 8, ✂✍ ISD, ✂ Patch, ✂✍ PatchSig., ✂ PatchC, ✂✍ PatchCSig
02/3 SP Game-Used Edition 39, ✂ AF, ✂ PH
02/3 Sports Vault 263
97/8 SPx 8
99/0 SPx 35
00/1 SPx 12, X3, ✂ WM
01/2 SPx 11, ✂ DT, ✂ TT
02/3 SPx 59
98/9 SPx Finite 18, 106
98/9 SPx Prospects 9, PS20
99/0 Stadium 6, -Chrome 6
00/1 Stadium 59, BT23
01/2 Stadium Club 13, G32, P15
02/3 Stadium 110, ✂ NHLP13
98/9 SLU
02/3 Starz
92/3 Topps 6
92/3 Topps 229
95/6 Topps 79, 4PL
98/9 Topps 204
99/0 Topps 187, FF3
00/1 Topps 17, TC3, OTG7, ✍ CAI
01/2 Topps 5, -SM8, ✂ CC2
02/3 Topps 9, Update 9, HHU9
99/0 To. Chrome 187, FF3
00/1 To. Chrome 17, TC3, RF7
01/2 To. Chrome 5
02/3 T. Chrome 9
98/9 To. Finest 29
98/9 T. Gold Label 33, GR9
99/0 To. Gold Label 8
00/1 To. Gold Label 74
00/1 To. Heritage 18, 234, HH16, ✍ CAI, OSA
01/2 To. Heritage 12
02/3 To. Heritage 165, ✂ GS, ✂ GSB
02/3 T. Limited 9
96/7 Topps Picks 133
99/0 To. Prmr. Plus 31
01/2 To. Reserve 16, ✂ TR
92/3 T. Stadium Club 32
92/3 T. Stadium Club 250
93/4 To. Stadium 226
93/4 To. Stadium 458
95/6 To. Stadium 117
00/1 To. Stars 12, ✂ GG
02/3 T. Total 84, TTC23, TP10
98/9 UD Choice 51, SQ26
00/1 UD Heroes 24
01/2 UD PlayMakers Ltd 22
00/1 UD Reserve 20, OS2
00/1 Ultimate Mem. ✍ U-22, ✂ J-22, ✂ Jers. 20, ✂ S-22, ✂ TM-18
01/2 Ultimate Mem. ✂ Cor., ✂ DD, ✂ WTF, ✍ Aut.
99/0 Ult. Victory 19
91/2 Upper Deck 440
91/2 Upper Deck 450
92/3 Upper Deck 13
92/3 Upper Deck 138
92/3 Upper Deck 359
92/3 Upper Deck 453
92/3 Upper Deck 635
92/3 Upper Deck AR1
93/4 Upper Deck 64, SP-97
94/5 Upper Deck 4, SP-105
95/6 Upper Deck 18, SE-18
96/7 Upper Deck 32
97/8 Upper Deck 208
97/8 Upper Deck 245, SS18, SG10, S23, T9A, ✂ GJ6
98/9 Upper Deck 243, FF16
99/0 Upper Deck 37, 168, CT25, FF12
00/1 Upper Deck 266, UDF-UD2, ✍ SG
01/2 Upper Deck 38, 222, FC12, LP2, SS20, ✂ PoaN, ✂ PoaND, ✂ PoaNT
02/3 Upper Deck 136, 229, ✂ PW
96/7 UD All-Star YCTG AR1
02/3 UD Artistic 67, R67, / Art
93/4 Upper Deck Be A Player 1
94/5 UD Be A Player R17, ✍ 97
96/7 UD Black Diam. 173
97/8 UD Black Diam. 101
98/9 UD Black Diam. 20
99/0 UD Black Diam. 22
00/1 UD Black Diam. 12
01/2 UD Challenge 14, ✂ FP
02/3 UD Classic 75, ✂ HR
95/6 UD CC 206
96/7 UD CC 49
97/8 UD Coll. Choice 44, SQ65, C10, CR10
97/8 UD Diam. Vision 19
98/9 UD G. Reserve 243
99/0 UD G. Reserve 37, 168
01/2 UD Honor Roll 91
02/3 UD Honor 56, -SG24
96/7 UD Ice 13
97/8 UD Ice 63
00/1 UD Ice 9
01/2 UD Ice 7
00/1 UD Legends 29, 30
92/3 UD Locker 51
01/2 UD Mask 17, ✂ GJ, ✂ JP, ✂ DP, ✂ PM
02/3 UD Mask 67
98/9 UD MVP 45
99/0 UD MVP 46
00/1 UD MVP 46
01/2 UD MVP 38, ✂ S
02/3 UD MVP 139
99/0 UD MVP Cup 43
99/0 UD Ovation 13
02/3 UD Piece 70
01/2 UD Premier ✂ B, ✂ D, ✍ Sig
02/3 UD Premier 42
00/1 UD Pros&Prosp. 21
99/0 UD Retro 17, ✍ Ink.
02/3 UD Rookie 74
01/2 UD Top Shelf 7
02/3 UD Top Shelf ✂ AS, ✂ GO, ✂ HT, ✂ M, ✂ SH, ✂ ST, ✂ TS
00/1 UD Vintage 75, 85-86, NH7
01/2 UD Vintage 57, 61
02/3 UD Vintage 199, 283, GB 199, T51
00/1 Vanguard 22
01/2 Vanguard 18, ✂ DGM 8
02/3 Vanguard 76
99/0 Victory 64, 65, 327
00/1 Victory 50, 51, 290
01/2 Victory 73
02/3 Victory -NP52
01/2 Waving the Flag 23
99/0 WGretzky 43, ✂ TG
97/8 Zenith 78

AMORE, ANGELO
91/2 7th...Sketch OHL 358

ANCHIKOSKI, WAYNE
91/2 Avant Garde BCJHL 156
91/2 Avant Garde BCJHL 167
94/5 Humberside Hawks 6
96/7 Knoxville Cherokees
88/9 Portland Winter Hawks

ANCICKA, MARTIN
94/5 APS 55
95/6 APS 347

ANDANOFF, JIM
83/4 Belleville Bulls
84/5 Belleville Bulls

ANDELMIN, TEUVO
66/7 Champion 81

ANDERSEN, BO
98/9 Odessa Jackalopes

ANDERSEN, CARL OSCAR BOE
95 Panini Worlds 240

ANDERSEN, CARL_OSCAR
92/3 Semic Nordisk 25

ANDERSEN, CATO
92/3 Semic Nordisk 44

ANDERSEN, CATO TOM
95 Globe 192
94 Semic 253
95 Semic 181
92 Semic Sticker 34
93 Semic Sticker 232

ANDERSEN, CATO_TOM
92/3 Semic Nordisk 46

ANDERSEN, LARS_H
92/3 Semic Nordisk 61

ANDERSEN, MARTIN
92/3 Semic Nordisk 42

ANDERSEN, MORGAN
92/3 Semic Nordisk 92

ANDERSEN, RICHARD
79 Panini Sticker 364

ANDERSEN, VIDAR
92/3 Semic Nordisk 57

ANDERSON, CHRIS
95/6 Tri-City Americans 25

ANDERSON, CORY
88/9 Kamloops Blazers

ANDERSON, CRAIG
99/0 Peoria Rivermen

ANDERSON, DAN
85/6 U. of Arizona Ice Cats

ANDERSON, DAVID
89/0 7th..Sketch OHL 39
90/1 7th..Sketch OHL 126
91/2 Oshawa Generals

ANDERSON, DEAN
89/0 ProCards AHL 105
90/1 ProCards 166
88/9 Flint Spirits
91/2 Knoxville Cherokees

ANDERSON, EARL
77/8 O-Pee-Chee 114
77/8 Topps 114

ANDERSON, ERIK
01/2 Milwaukee Admirals

ANDERSON, ERNIE
23/4 Paulins Candy 66

ANDERSON, EVAN
91/2 Air Canada SJHL 28
91/2 Air Canada SJHL A45

ANDERSON, GLENN
90/1 Bowman 195
91/2 Bowman 116
92/3 Bowman 104
95/6 DEL 441
93/4 Donruss 340
93/4 Donruss 460
94/5 Donruss 254
83/4 Esso Stars
01/2 Fleer Greats 32, ✍ Aut.
92/3 Fleer Ultra 207
93/4 Fleer Ultra 9
94/5 Fleer Ultra 135
88/9 Frito Lay
83/4 Funmate Puffy 2 [w/]
93/4 Hockey Wit 50
89/0 Kraft 10
86/7 Kraft Sports 11
93/4 Leaf 41
94/5 Leaf 14
81/2 O-Pee-Chee 108
82/3 O-Pee-Chee 100
83/4 O-Pee-Chee 24
84/5 O-Pee-Chee 238
85/6 O-Pee-Chee 168
86/7 OPC/Topps 80
87/8 O-Pee-Chee 199
88/9 OPC/Topps 189
90/1 OPC/Topps 145
91/2 O-Pee-Chee 124
92/3 O-Pee-Chee 134
89/0 O-Pee-Chee 226
87/8 OPC Leaders 1
91/2 OPC Premier 10
81/2 OPC Sticker 7
81/2 OPC Sticker 8
81/2 OPC Sticker 9
81/2 OPC Sticker 10
81/2 OPC Sticker 217
82/3 OPC/Topps Sticker 99
82/3 OPC/Topps Sticker 100
83/4 OPC/Topps Sticker 92
83/4 OPC/Topps Sticker 93
83/4 OPC/Topps Sticker 158
84/5 OPC Sticker 247
84/5 OPC Sticker 248
85/6 OPC Sticker 227-94
86/7 OPC Sticker 78
87/8 OPC Sticker 95
88/9 OPC Sticker 229
89/0 opcSticker 218
87/8 Panini Sticker 265
88/9 Panini Sticker 57
89/0 Panini Sticker 77
90/1 Panini Sticker 227
90/1 Panini/EDM 1
91/2 Panini Sticker 120
92/3 Panini Sticker 76
93/4 Panini Sticker 225
91/2 Parkhurst 177
92/3 Parkhurst 178
93/4 Parkhurst 201
80/1 Pepsi Bottle Cap
91/2 Pinnacle 12
92/3 Pinnacle 355
93/4 Pinnacle 398
96/7 Pinnacle 171
82/3 Post [Edmo.]
93/4 Power Play 237
93/4 Premier 104
94/5 Premier 270
90/1 Pro Set 81
91/2 Pro Set 75
92/3 Pro Set 185
90/1 Score 114
90/1 Sco. Hot Cards 54
91/2 Score 47
91/2 Score 61T
91/2 Score CAN 47
91/2 Score CAN 611
92/3 Score 241
93/4 Score 180
93/4 Score 449
84/5 7-Eleven
83/4 Souhaits Keychain [Oilers]
92/3 Topps 162
91/2 To. Stadium 116
92/3 T. Stadium Club 124
93/4 To. Stadium 168
90/1 Upper Deck 284
91/2 Upper Deck 250
95/6 UD CC 46
02/3 UD Foundations 35, 63, 90, ✂ 1000Stick (x2), ✍ SG
01/2 UD Legends 21
83/4 Vachon 21-101
81/2 EDMO / Red Rooster
82/3 EDMO / Red Rooster
83/4 EDMO / Button
83/4 EDMO / McDonald's
83/4 EDMO / West Mall
83/4 EDMO
84/5 EDMO
84/5 EDMO / Red Rooster
85/6 EDMO / Red Rooster
86/7 EDMO
86/7 EDMO / Red Rooster
87/8 EDMO
88/9 EDMO
88/9 EDMO / Action 9
90/1 EDMO / IGA
91/2 TORO / P.L.A.Y. 9
92/3 TORO / Kodak
93/4 TORO / Black's 3

ANDERSON, GRANT
83/4 Brantford Alexanders

ANDERSON, HARLAN
01/2 Moose Jaw Warriors 14
02/3 Moose Jaw Warriors

ANDERSON, JIM
74/5 O-Pee-Chee 118
74/5 Topps 118
74/5 WASH

ANDERSON, JOHN
83/4 Esso Stars
83/4 Funmate Puffy 4 [w/]
84/5 Kellogg's 3
80/1 O-Pee-Chee 79
81/2 O-Pee-Chee 313
82/3 O-Pee-Chee 315
83/4 O-Pee-Chee 325
84/5 O-Pee-Chee 295
85/6 OPC/Topps 20
86/7 OPC/Topps 13
87/8 OPC/Topps 45
88/9 OPC/Topps 190
89/0 OPC/Topps 124
81/2 OPC Sticker 107
82/3 OPC/Topps Sticker 73
82/3 OPC/Topps Sticker 74
83/4 OPC/Topps Sticker 30
83/4 OPC/Topps Sticker 31
84/5 OPC Sticker 18
85/6 OPC Sticker 10-138
86/7 OPC Sticker 54-192
87/8 OPC Sticker 204-63
88/9 OPC Sticker 270-134
87/8 Panini Sticker 45
88/9 Panini Sticker 239
80/1 Pepsi Bottle Cap
82/3 Post [Toro.]
90/1 ProCards 543
91/2 ProCards 361
84/5 7-Eleven
83/4 Souhaits Keychain [Maple Leafs]
80/1 Topps 79
84/5 Topps 136
83/4 Vachon 81-36
86/7 HART / Jr. Whalers
87/8 HART / Jr. Whalers
88/9 HART / Jr. Whalers
85/6 QUÉB / Provigo
86/7 QUÉB / McDonald's
78/9 TORO
79/0 TORO
80/1 TORO
81/2 TORO
82/3 TORO
83/4 TORO
84/5 TORO
98/9 Chicago Wolves
98/9 Chicago Wolves Champs
98/9 Chicago Wolves Champs
00/1 Chicago Wolves
02/3 Chicago Wolves
92/3 San Diego Gulls
93/4 San Diego Gulls

ANDERSON, KEITH
01/2 Florida Everblades

ANDERSON, OLE
95/6 Slapshot 234

ANDERSON, PERRY
91/2 O-Pee-Chee 501
92/3 O-Pee-Chee 38
91/2 Parkhurst 164
91/2 Pro Set 481
89/0 ProCards AHL 216
90/1 ProCards 561
91/2 Score 99T
91/2 Score CAN 649
92/3 Topps 286
92/3 T. Stadium Club 89
85/6 NJER 8
86/7 NJER / S.O.B.E.R.
88/9 NJER / Caretta
91/2 SANJ / Sports Action
92/3 San Diego Gulls

ANDERSON, RON C.
70/1 Colgate 48
70/1 Eddie Sargent 18
71/2 Eddie Sargent 18
70/1 Esso Power Player
69/0 O-Pee-Chee 14
71/2 O-Pee-Chee 163
72/3 O-Pee-Chee 298

ANDERSON, RON H.
74/5 Loblaws
74/5 O-Pee-Chee 314
74/5 WASH

ANDERSON, RUSS
78/9 O-Pee-Chee 156
79/0 O-Pee-Chee 264
78/9 Topps 156
79/0 Topps 264
82/3 HART / Jr. Whalers
84/5 LOSA / Smokey 1
77/8 PITT / McDonald's

ANDERSON, RYAN
00/1 Austin Ice Bats

ANDERSON, SHAWN
91/2 Bowman 147
94/5 Leaf 346
90/1 Pro Set 513
88/9 ProCards / Rochester
91/2 To. Stadium 358
00/1 UD DEL 111, A9
01/2 UD DEL 196
86/7 BUFF / Blue Shield
87/8 BUFF / Won. Bread
89/0 BUFF / Campbell's
92/3 WASH / Kodak
95/6 Milwaukee Admirals

ANDERSON, TOM
34-43 BeeHive-1 [NYAm.]
36-39 Diamond Match TT2
36-39 Diamond Match TT3
39/0 O-Pee-Chee 61

ANDERSON, VERN
91/2 Air Canada SJHL C13

ANDERSON, WILL
84/5 Kamloops Blazers
94/5 Minnesota G'Gophers

ANDERSSON, CHRISTER
72 Semic Sticker 44

ANDERSSON, CRAIG
02/3 BAP Memorabilia 318
02/3 Between the Pipes 90
02/3 Parkhurst 227
02/3 Parkhurst Retro 236
02/3 SP Authentic 174
02/3 Ultimate Memorabilia 96
02/3 UD Artistic 132
02/3 UD Honor 114
02/3 UD Mask 146
02/3 UD Premier 65
01/2 Norfolk Admirals
99/0 Guelph Storm

ANDERSSON, DICK
89/0 Semic Elitserien 193

ANDERSSON, ERIK
90/1 Semic Elitserien 97
91/2 Semic Elitserien 25
99/0 UD Elitserien 17
00/1 UD Elitserien 12
98/9 Indianapolis Ice
97/8 Saint John Flames

ANDERSSON, FREDRIK
94/5 Leaf Elit Set 17, CS-9
95/6 Leaf Elit Set 271
89/0 Semic Elitserien 169, 215
90/1 Semic Elitserien 3
91/2 Semic Elitserien 201
92/3 Semic Elitserien 223
92 Semic Sticker 52

ANDERSSON, HENRIK
89/0 Semic Elitserien 246
90/1 Semic Elitserien 156
99/0 UD Elitserien 125, 210

ANDERSSON, J-A
91/2 Semic Elitserien 310

ANDERSSON, JESPER
99/0 UD Elitserien 124

ANDERSSON, JONAS
90/1 Semic Elitserien 47
02/3 SPx 116
00/1 Upper Deck 202
00/1 UD Black Diam. 67
00/1 UD Ice 47
00/1 UD MVP 216
02/3 UD Vintage 338
00/1 Milwaukee Admirals
01/2 Milwaukee Admirals

ANDERSSON, KENNETH
90/1 Semic Elitserien 196

ANDERSSON, KENT-ERIK
78/9 O-Pee-Chee 17
80/1 O-Pee-Chee 383
81/2 O-Pee-Chee 158
82/3 O-Pee-Chee 218
79 Panini Sticker 200
82/3 Post [Minn.]
78/9 Topps 17
81/2 Topps 102 [West]
78/9 MINS / Cloverleaf 4
79/0 MINS
80/1 MINS
81/2 MINS

ANDERSSON, MATTIAS
89/0 Semic Elitserien 81
90/1 Semic Elitserien 206
91/2 Semic Elitserien 134
92/3 Semic Elitserien 155

ANDERSSON, MIKAEL
00/1 BAP Mem. 139
91/2 Bowman 11
92/3 Bowman 158
93/4 Donruss 322
94/5 Donruss 14
93/4 EA Sports 130
92/3 Fleer Ultra 406
93/4 Fleer Ultra 421
94/5 Fleer Ultra 370
95 Globe 42
93/4 Leaf 285
94/5 Leaf 347
90/1 OPC/Topps 35
91/2 O-Pee-Chee 197
92/3 O-Pee-Chee 214
92/3 OPC Premier 55
98/9 Pacific 395
97/8 Pa. Invincible R-182
90/1 Panini Sticker 47
92/3 Panini Sticker 258
93/4 Panini Sticker 216
94/5 Panini Sticker 186
96/7 Panini Sticker 132
97/8 Panini Sticker 104
98/9 Panini Sticker 102
91/2 Parkhurst 63
92/3 Parkhurst 169
93/4 Parkhurst 198
94/5 Parkhurst 226
95/6 Parkhurst 196
92/3 Pinnacle 384
93/4 Pinnacle 329
94/5 Pinnacle 451
96/7 Pi. Be A Player 65, ✍ Aut. 65
94/5 POG 220
93/4 Power Play 440
93/4 Premier 150
94/5 Premier 287
90/1 Pro Set 98
91/2 Pro Set 394
92/3 Pro Set 65
91/2 Pro Set Platinum 180
88/9 ProCards / Rochester
92/3 Score 215
93/4 Score 427
95 Semic 72
89/0 Semic Elitserien 274
90/1 Semic Elitserien 45
91/2 Semic Elitserien 290
93 Semic Sticker 37
92/3 Topps 151
95/6 Topps 123
91/2 To. Stadium 39
92/3 T. Stadium Club 348
93/4 To. Stadium 427
93/4 To. Stadium 97
94/5 T. Stadium Club 75
91/2 Upper Deck 238
92/3 Upper Deck 103
94/5 Upper Deck 297
96/7 Upper Deck 155
95/6 UD CC 182
00/1 UD Elitserien 75, 194, ✍ Sig.
85/6 BUFF / Blue Shield
87/8 BUFF / Blue Shield
87/8 BUFF / Won. Bread
88/9 BUFF / Blue Shield
88/9 BUFF / Won. Bread
89/0 HART / Jr. Whalers
90/1 HART / Jr. Whalers
92/3 TAMP / Sheraton Inn
94/5 TAMP / Sky Box
95/6 TAMP / Sky Box

ANDERSSON, NIKLAS
95/6 Bowman 126
92/3 Classic Prospects 120
96/7 Donruss 214
96/7 Do. Elite 89
98/9 EBK IHL All-Star
95/6 Future Legends 2
95 Globe 51
97/8 Pacific CC 144
96/7 Panini Sticker 98
97/8 Panini Sticker 75
95/6 Parkhurst 398
96/7 Pi. Be A Player 98, ✍ Aut. 98
96/7 Pi. Summit 172
91/2 ProCards 533
93/4 Score 460
96/7 Score 248
96/7 Select CE 57
89/0 Semic Elitserien 281
90/1 Semic Elitserien 39
91/2 Semic Elitserien 317
93 Semic Sticker 44
96/7 SBx Impact 165
00/1 To. Heritage 202
91/2 Upper Deck 29
93/4 Upper Deck 239
96/7 Upper Deck 292
96/7 UD CC 165
97/8 UD Coll. Choice 156
96/7 NYIS
98/9 Chicago Wolves
99/0 Chicago Wolves
00/1 Chicago Wolves
97/8 Kentucky Tho'blades

ANDERSSON, OLA
89/0 Semic Elitserien 68
90/1 Semic Elitserien 66
91/2 Semic Elitserien 246

ANDERSSON, PAUL
94/5 Leaf Elit Set 107
95/6 Leaf Elit Set 131
89/0 Semic Elitserien 283
91/2 Semic Elitserien 265
92/3 Semic Elitserien 298
95/6 UD Elitserien 200

ANDERSSON, PENTTI
66/7 Champion 119

ANDERSSON, PETER*
91/2 Semic Elitserien 343
82 Semic Sticker 12
89 Semic Sticker 11
85/6 QUÉB
85/6 QUÉB / Gene. Foods

ANDERSSON, PETER
96/7 DEL 276
95 Globe 11
94/5 Leaf Elit Set 267
95/6 Leaf Elit Set 87, 304, FTF-14
94/5 Parkhurst 88
94/5 Premier 212
95 Semic 60
90/1 Semic Elitserien 128
91/2 Semic Elitserien 180
92/3 Semic Elitserien 345
93 Semic Sticker 27
92/3 Upper Deck 481
93/4 Upper Deck 71
95/6 UD Elitserien 138, 231, 257

ANDERSSON, PETER?
91 Semic Sticker 35, 36
92 Semic Sticker 54
92 Semic Sticker 55

ANDERSSON, STEFAN
95/6 Leaf Elit Set 155
95/6 UD Elitserien 12

ANDERSSON-EVERBERG, PAUL
98/9 UD Elitserien 193
99/0 UD Elitserien 197

ANDERSSON-JUNKKA, JONAS
98/9 Cardset 11
99/0 Cardset 32
00/1 Cardset 23
94/5 Leaf Elit Set 184, RR-2
95/6 Leaf Elit Set 138
94/5 Parkie SE238
94/5 SR Auto-Phonex 3, ✍ 3
00/1 Syracuse Crunch

ANDIS, GREG
98/9 Odessa Jackalopes
99/0 Odessa Jackalopes

ANDRASOVSKY, DUSAN
00/1 OFS 79
01/2 OFS 209

ANDREA, PAUL
70/1 Esso Power Player
70/1 O-Pee-Chee 77
91/2 7th...Sketch OHL 24
68/9 Shirriff / Pitt. 8
70/1 Topps 77
72/3 Cleveland Crusaders
95/6 Dayton Bombers
91/2 Cornwall Royals

ANDREOLI, DAVE
81/2 Soo Greyhounds

ANDREOZZI, MARC
98/9 Cincinnati M'Ducks 2

ANDRES, BRUCE
81/2 Indianapolis Checkers

ANDRES, RYAN
98/9 Calgary Hitmen 17

ANDREWS, AL
82/3 Kingston Canadians

ANDREWS, DARYL
00/1 Albany River Rats
01/2 Albany River Rats
02/3 Albany River Rats

ANDREWS, ELLIOT
94/5 Guildford Flames 17
95/6 Guildford Flames 8
96/7 Guildford Flames 15

ANDREWS, JEFF
93/4 Slapshot / Oshawa 9

ANDREWS, LLOYD
24/5 Champ's Cigarettes
23/4 William Paterson 21
24/5 William Paterson 59

ANDREYCHUK, DAVE
94 At The Pinnacle
98/9 Aurora 106
98/9 Be A Player 77, M-5, M-21, ✍ Aut. 77
00/1 BAP Mem. 385, 418
01/2 BAP Memor. ✂ 500GS
02/3 BAP Memorabilia 258
01/2 BAP Update ✂ TP15
90/1 Bowman 246
91/2 Bowman 22
92/3 Bowman 44
95/6 Bowman 7
83 Canada Juniors
93/4 Donruss 342
94/5 Donruss 323
95/6 Donruss 98
96/7 Donruss 109
97/8 Donruss 61
97/8 Do. Canadian 105, 148
97/8 Do. Preferred 66
97/8 Do. Priority 152
98/9 Dynagon Ice 106
93/4 EA Sports 136
02/3 Exclusive 154
02/3 First Edition 222
94/5 Flair 177
94/5 Fleer 212
95/6 Fleer Metal 141
92/3 Fleer Ultra 12
93/4 Fleer Ultra 57
93/4 Fleer Ultra RLS 1
94/5 Fleer Ultra 211, RLS-1, UP-1
95/6 Fleer Ultra 158
96/7 Fl. Ultra 92
95/6 Hoyle / West. 2-Heart
94/5 Kraft / Heroes
93/4 Leaf 63
93/4 Leaf GLAS 4
94/5 Leaf 72
95/6 Leaf 270
96/7 Leaf 24
97/8 Leaf 116
94/5 L. Limited 34
95/6 L. Limited 21
96/7 L. Preferred 51
97/8 Limited 22, 74
94/5 McDonald's McD-18
96/7 Metal Univ. 85
84/5 O-Pee-Chee 17
84/5 O-Pee-Chee 353
85/6 OPC/Topps 143
86/7 OPC/Topps 16
87/8 OPC/Topps 3
88/9 OPC/Topps 163
88/9 OPC/Topps Box M
90/1 OPC/Topps 169
91/2 O-Pee-Chee 38
92/3 O-Pee-Chee 141
89/0 OPC/Topps 106
84/5 OPC Sticker 209
84/5 OPC Sticker 210
85/6 OPC Sticker 187-61
86/7 OPC Sticker 49
87/8 OPC Sticker 147-8
88/9 OPC Sticker 261
89/0 opcSticker 258-137
99/0 Omega 17
98/9 Pacific 260
00/1 Pacific 106
01/2 Pacific 43
02/3 Pacific 346
02/3 Pacific Complete 264
97/8 Pacific CC 84
97/8 Pa. Dynagon 67, T-37
97/8 Pa. Invincible 75
97/8 Pa. Paramount 100
98/9 Pa. Paramount 130
87/8 Panini Sticker 19
87/8 Panini Sticker 27
88/9 Panini Sticker 223
89/0 Panini Sticker 215
90/1 Panini Sticker 29
91/2 Panini Sticker 309
92/3 Panini Sticker 249
93/4 Panini Sticker 223
94/5 Panini Sticker 194, 236b, JJ
95/6 Panini Sticker 203
96/7 Panini Sticker 82
97/8 Panini Sticker 71
98/9 Panini Sticker 66
99/0 Panini Sticker 24
91/2 Parkhurst 17
91/2 Parkhurst 437
92/3 Parkhurst 10
92/3 Parkhurst 409
93/4 Parkhurst 200
94/5 Parkhurst 303,V89
95/6 Parkhurst 470
01/2 Parkhurst ✂ 500GS
94/5 Parkie SE182
91/2 Pinnacle 122
92/3 Pinnacle 58
93/4 Pinnacle 42
93/4 Pinnacle NF 11
94/5 Pinnacle 5
95/6 Pinnacle 31
96/7 Pinnacle 177
97/8 Pinnacle 131
96/7 Pi. Be A Player 2, ✍ Aut. 2
97/8 Pi. Certified 69
97/8 Pi. Inside 118
95/6 Pi. Summit 36
96/7 Pi. Summit 124
97/8 Pi. Totally 69
95/6 Pi. Zenith 41, GG-13
95/6 Playoff 93
96/7 Playoff 348
94/5 POG 229
95/6 POG 260
93/4 Power Play 238
93/4 Power Play SA 1
93/4 Premier 235
94/5 Premier 38, 510, TF-4
99/0 Prism 11
02/3 Pr. Stock Reserve 90
95/6 Pro Magnet 71
90/1 Pro Set 17, 363
91/2 Pro Set 23
92/3 Pro Set 15
92/3 Pro Set 249
91/2 Pro Set Platinum 8
90/1 Score 189
90/1 Sco. Hot Cards 87
91/2 Score 277
91/2 Score CAN 497
92/3 Score 204
93/4 Score 343
93/4 Score 481
93/4 Score/CAN DD1
94/5 Score DT11, NP10
95/6 Score 109
96/7 Score 44
97/8 Score 115
97/8 Score NJer. 3
94/5 Select 99
95/6 Select CE 28
01/2 Signature ✂ 500GS
02/3 Signature Series 11, ✍ 11
95/6 SBx Emotion 168
95/6 SBx Impact 158, 246
96/7 SBx Impact 67
94/5 SP 119
02/3 Sports Vault 123
99/0 Stadium 164
00/1 Stadium 215
95/6 Super Sticker 119
84/5 Topps 13
92/3 Topps 164
95/6 Topps 175
00/1 Topps 157, PC-9
00/1 To. Chrome 111, PC-9
94/5 Topps Finest 39
95/6 To. Finest 6
98/9 To. Finest 11
01/2 To. Heritage 184
96/7 Topps Picks 127
91/2 To. Stadium 93
92/3 T. Stadium Club 132
93/4 To. Stadium 23
94/5 T. Stadium Club 58, 140
95/6 To. Stadium 5
93/4 TSC Members Only 13
00/1 To. Stars 95
95/6 T. Super Skills 52
02/3 T. Total 100
01/2 Ultimate Mem. ✂ 500GS
90/1 Upper Deck 41
91/2 Upper Deck 124
92/3 Upper Deck 269
92/3 Upper Deck 456
93/4 Upper Deck 86, SP-155
94/5 Upper Deck 313, R6, R35, SP-77
95/6 Upper Deck 367, SE-79
96/7 Upper Deck 89
97/8 Upper Deck 96
99/0 Upper Deck 182
01/2 Upper Deck 390
02/3 Upper Deck 406
94/5 UD Be A Player R33, ✍ 52
93/4 UD BAP Roots 18
95/6 UD CC 20
96/7 UD CC 153
97/8 UD Coll. Choice 142
99/0 UD G. Reserve 182
99/0 UD MVP Cup ✍ PS
00/1 UD Vintage 47
84/5 BUFF / Blue Shield
85/6 BUFF / Blue Shield
86/7 BUFF / Blue Shield
87/8 BUFF / Blue Shield
87/8 BUFF / Won. Bread
88/9 BUFF / Blue Shield
88/9 BUFF / Won. Bread
89/0 BUFF / Blue Shield
89/0 BUFF / Campbell's
90/1 BUFF / Blue Shield
90/1 BUFF / Campbell's
91/2 BUFF / Blue Shield
91/2 BUFF / Campbell's
91/2 BUFF / Pepsi
92/3 BUFF / Blue Shield
92/3 BUFF / Jubilee
96/7 NJER / Sharp
92/3 TORO / Kodak
93/4 TORO / Abalene
93/4 TORO / Black's 13
94/5 TORO / Coca-Cola
80/1 Oshawa Generals
81/2 Oshawa Generals

ANDRIAENSEN, GEORGES
79 Panini Sticker 340

ANDRIJEVSKI, ALEXANDER
92/3 Classic Prospects 75
97/8 Hockey-Box
91/2 O-Pee-Chee 31R
95/6 Sisu 225, 367
96/7 Sisu 20, MA-3
92/3 Upper Deck 342
93/4 Upper Deck 26
00/1 UD DEL 203
92/3 Indianapolis Ice

ANDRIYASHEV, IVAN
99/0 Mir 57

ANDRUFF, RON
77/8 O-Pee-Chee 288
78/9 O-Pee-Chee 315
76/7 COLR / Hockey Talk

ANDRUSAK, GREG
90/1 Canada Nationals 3
94/5 Classic T52
94/5 Classic 4 Sport 156
92/3 Classic Prospects 110
93/4 Cla. Prospects 156
96/7 DEL 28
98/9 DEL 174
00/1 SP Authentic 160
00/1 SPx 109
00/1 Upper Deck 194
01/2 UD DEL 27
00/1 UD MVP 206
00/1 Victory 270
99/0 Chicago Wolves
92/3 Cleveland Lumberjacks
93/4 Cleveland Lumberjacks
00/1 Kentucky Tho'blades

ANDRYUSHENKO, IGOR
98/9 Mir 57
99/0 Mir 96
00/1 Mir 8

ANGEL, BRETT
00/1 Mississauga IceDogs

ANGELELLI, DAN
91/2 L. Superior State Lakers

ANGELIDIS, MIKE
02/3 Owen Sound Attack

ANGELSTAD, MEL
00/1 Manitoba Moose
98/9 Michigan K-Wings
99/0 Michigan K-Wings
93/4 Thunder Bay Senators
94/5 Thunder Bay Senators
95/6 Thunder Bay Senators

ANGER, NIKLAS
95/6 Upper Deck 561
95/6 UD CC 344
97/8 UD Elitserien 49
98/9 UD Elitserien 15
99/0 UD Elitserien 15

ANGLEHART, SERGE
90/1 ProCards 485
91/2 ProCards 124
90 7th..Sketch Mem.Cup 74

ANGNEL, BENJAMIN
95 Panini Worlds 106

ANGOTTI, LOU
64-67 BeeHive-3 [Chic.]
64-67 BeeHive-3 [NYRa.]
64/5 Coke/Sprite [NYRa.]
70/1 Colgate 8
70/1 Dad's Cookies
70/1 Eddie Sargent 40
71/2 Eddie Sargent 38
72/3 Eddie Sargent 65
70/1 Esso Power Player
72/3 Post 16
68/9 O-Pee-Chee 103
68/9 O-Pee-Chee PS 11
69/0 O-Pee-Chee 134
70/1 O-Pee-Chee 12
71/2 O-Pee-Chee 212
72/3 O-Pee-Chee 243
73/4 O-Pee-Chee 224
74/5 O-Pee-Chee 63
95/6 Parkie 66-67 28
94/5 Parkie Tall 96
68/9 Shirriff / Pitt. 11
64/5 Topps 66
66/7 Topps 116
68/9 Topps 103
70/1 Topps 12
74/5 Topps 63
71/2 Toronto Sun Photo
70/1 CHIC
73/4 SLOU

ANHOLT, DARRELL
83/4 Springfield Indians 19

ANHOLT, PETER
90/1 7th..Sketch WHL 22
91/2 7th...Sketch WHL 140
93/4 Red Deer Rebels

ANISIMOV, ANDREI
00/1 Mir 133

ANISIMOV, ARTEM
98/9 Mir 120
99/0 Mir 55

ANISIN, VYACHESLAV
91/2 Future Trends C72 90
72 Hellas MM-Jenkki 73
74 Hellas MM-Jenkki 42
73/4 Soviet Stars 14
74/5 Soviet Stars 18
72/3 Williams Finnish 21
73/4 Williams Finnish 1

ANKEN, OLIVIER
79 Panini Sticker 258

ANNECK, DORIAN
94/5 Sig. Rookies 45, ✍ 45
95/6 Tri-City Americans 26

ANNESLEY, KYLE
01/2 Calgary Hitmen

ANNESLEY, RYAN
01/2 Kamloops Blazers

ANNING, LES
49 Carreras Cigarettes 44

ANONSEN, HANS_M
92/3 Semic Nordisk 233

ANSAKORPI, PERTTI
66/7 Champion 157
65/6 Hellas 157
70/1 Kuvajulkaisut 208
71/2 Williams Finnish 129
72/3 Williams Finnish 192
73/4 Williams Finnish 150

ANTAL, ELOD
79 Panini Sticker 313

ANTILA, KRISTIAN
99/0 Cardset 43
00/1 Cardset 343, Mask-9
02/3 Cardset 3

ANTIPIN, VLADIMIR
96/7 APS 249
96/7 DS Sticker 80
98/9 Mir 12
99/0 Mir 4
00/1 Mir 124
00/1 Metallurg 49

ANTIPOV, VLADIMIR
99/0 St. John's Maple Leafs

ANTISIN, MISKO
95 Panini Worlds 125
83/4 Victoria Cougars
84/5 Victoria Cougars

ANTLER, TRAVIS
02/3 Baie-Comeau

ANTONENKO, OLEG
00/1 Mir 85
99/0 OFS 441

ANTONIK, MIKI
92/3 BCJHL 127

ANTONIN, JIRI
95/6 APS 322

ANTONISHYN, CHAD
98/9 Topeka Scarecrows

ANTONOVICH, JEFF
94/5 Slapshot Memorial 16
01/2 Rockford IceHogs

ANTONOVICH, MIKE
79/0 O-Pee-Chee 349
74/5 OPC WHA 37
75/6 OPC WHA 111
76/7 OPC WHA 23
77/8 OPC WHA 34
83/4 NJER
72/3 Minn. Fight. Saints
74/5 Minn. Fight. Saints

ANTONS, NILS
96/7 Kamloops Blazers
97/8 Kamloops Blazers

ANTOS, DEAN
91/2 ProCards 232

ANTOS, MILAN
94/5 APS 269
95/6 APS 140
96/7 APS 330
97/8 APS 308
00/1 DS 36
96/7 DS Sticker 167
97/8 DS Sticker 122
98/9 OFS 42
99/0 OFS 117
00/1 OFS 73
01/2 OFS 13

ANTOSKI, SHAWN
93/4 Donruss 498
93/4 Fleer Ultra 437
94/5 Fleer Ultra 381
93/4 Leaf 368
91/2 O-Pee-Chee 98
92/3 OPC Premier 10
93/4 Parkhurst 479
94/5 Parkhurst 248
96/7 Pi. Be A Player 120, ✍ Aut. 120
93/4 Premier 31
94/5 Premier 226
91/2 ProCards 595
90/1 Score 429
91/2 Score 323
91/2 Score CAN 353
97/8 Score Anah. 15
89/0 7th..Sketch OHL 152
93/4 To. Stadium 288
91/2 Upper Deck 351
92/3 Upper Deck 81
93/4 Upper Deck 325
96/7 Upper Deck 318
96/7 ANAH / Up Front 10
94/5 PHIL / Sheet
92/3 VANC / Road Trip
94/5 VANC
92/3 Hamilton Canucks

ANTOSKI, SHAYNE
91 7th..Sketch Mem.Cup 118
89/0 7th..Sketch OHL 161
90/1 7th..Sketch OHL 301
91/2 7th...Sketch OHL 120
93/4 Huntington Blizzard

ANTROPOV, NIKOLAI
00/1 Aurora 136, Pin. 136, ✍ Aut.
99/0 BAP Mem. 302
00/1 BAP Mem. 158
01/2 BAP Memor. 106
99/0 Crown Royale 131
99/0 Dynagon Ice 184
00/1 McDonald's 31
99/0 Millenium 224, C-16, ✍ Aut. 224
98/9 Mir 160
99/0 NHL Power Play [x3]
01/2 O-Pee-Chee 240
99/0 Omega 221
00/1 Pacific 384, ✍ Aut.
02/3 Pacific Complete 363
00/1 Pa. Paramount 226
00/1 Parkhurst P-32
01/2 Parkhurst 160
02/3 Parkhurst Retro 196
99/0 Prism 134, IP-8
00/1 Private Stock 92, PSNW-24
00/1 Revolution 136, HD-33
00/1 Signature 176, ✍ Aut. 3
02/3 Signature Series GS-64
99/0 SP Authentic 118
01/2 SP Authentic 120
02/3 SP Authentic 134
00/1 SPx 64
99/0 Stadium 171
00/1 Stadium 163, ✍ CO3, ✍ LS5
00/1 Topps 163
01/2 Topps 240
99/0 To. Chrome 297
00/1 To. Chrome 113
99/0 To. Gold Label 98
00/1 To. Heritage 181
99/0 To. Prmr. Plus 117
00/1 To. Stars 65
99/0 Ult. Victory 103
01/2 Upper Deck 397, ✂ PotL
99/0 UD Black Diam. 83
00/1 UD MVP 168
01/2 UD MVP 176
99/0 UD MVP Cup 178
02/3 UD Top Shelf ✂ SH
00/1 UD Vintage 336
01/2 UD Vintage 239
00/1 Vanguard 91
00/1 Victory 222
01/2 Victory 333
99/0 TORO / Pizza Pizza 13
01/2 St. John's Maple Leafs

ANTROPOV, NIKOLAIOLAI
02/3 Signature Series ✂ YP11

ANTTI, PETTER
89/0 Semic Elitserien 167

ANTTILA, KARI
70/1 Kuvajulkaisut 327

ANTTILA, PEKKA
70/1 Kuvajulkaisut 365

ANZALONE, FRANK
90/1 Newmarket Saints
93/4 Roanoke Express
94/5 Roanoke Express
95/6 Roanoke Express
96/7 Roanoke Express 19

APEL, THORSTEN
98/9 DEL 142

APPEL, DAVID
98/9 OFS 192
99/0 OFS 411
00/1 OFS 232
01/2 OFS 186

APPEL, FRANK
01/2 UD DEL 61

APPEL, JOACHIM
94/5 DEL 273
95/6 DEL 264
96/7 DEL 158
99/0 Eishockey 77
00/1 UD DEL 123

APPERT, SETH
91/2 Ferris State Bulldogs

APPLETON, JOEL
91/2 Air Canada SJHL D2

APPS, SYL
02/3 Canada Post
02/3 Ultimate Memorabilia ✍ Cut

APPS, SYL (III)
99/0 St. John's Maple Leafs
00/1 St. John's Maple Leafs

APPS, SYL (JR.)
77/8 Coke
70/1 Colgate 26
70/1 Eddie Sargent 113
71/2 Eddie Sargent 161
72/3 Eddie Sargent 169
74/5 Lipton Soup 49
74/5 Loblaws
71/2 O-Pee-Chee 77
72/3 O-Pee-Chee 115
73/4 O-Pee-Chee 76
74/5 O-Pee-Chee 13
74/5 O-Pee-Chee 183
75/6 O-Pee-Chee 130
76/7 O-Pee-Chee 50
76/7 O-Pee-Chee 218
76/7 OPC 392
77/8 O-Pee-Chee 248
78/9 O-Pee-Chee 56
79/0 O-Pee-Chee 366
80/1 O-Pee-Chee 362
71/2 Topps 77
72/3 Topps 11
73/4 Topps 160
74/5 Topps 13
74/5 Topps 183
75/6 Topps 130
76/7 Topps 50
76/7 Topps 218
76/7 Topps NS 13
77/8 Topps 248
78/9 Topps 56
71/2 Toronto Sun Photo
01/2 UD Legends 56
71/2 PITT / Sportcolor
74/5 PITT
77/8 PITT / McDonald's

APPS, SYL (SR.)
34-43 BeeHive-1 [Toro.]
45-64 BeeHive-2 [Toro.]
83 HHOF Postcard O1
83&87 HHOF 212
91/2 Kraft 50
91/2 Kraft 83
36/7 O-Pee-Chee 101
37/8 O-Pee-Chee 141
39/0 O-Pee-Chee 6
40/1 O-Pee-Chee 118, 146
55/6 Parkhurst 28
93/4 Parkie 56-57 P-5
38/9 Quaker Oats
45-54 Quaker Oats
99/0 UD C. Legends 33
00/1 UD Legends 121
37/8 World Wide Gum 23

AQUINO, ANTHONY
96 Québec Pee Wee 1179

ARABSKI, ROB
94/5 Slapshot / Brantford 7

ARAVIRTA, HANNU
92/3 Jyvas Hyva 69
94/5 Sisu 392
95/6 Sisu 386

ARBELIUS, PEKKA
80/1 Mallasjuoma 110
82 Semic Sticker 46
82 Skopbank
71/2 Williams Finnish 297

ARBEZ, DEREK
95/6 Swift Current Broncos

ARBOUR, AL
52/3 Anonymous 5
45-64 BeeHive-2 [Detr.]
45-64 BeeHive-2 [Chic.]
45-64 BeeHive-2 [Toro.]
62/3 Cowan Tile
93/4 Kraft / PB
68/9 O-Pee-Chee 128
69/0 O-Pee-Chee 178
69/0 O-Pee-Chee 4in1
74/5 O-Pee-Chee 91
53/4 Parkhurst 37
53/4 Parkhurst 38
93/4 Parkie 56-57 158
93/4 Parkie 56-57 61
90/1 Pro Set 671
60/1 Shirriff 67
61/2 Shirriff 60
62/3 Shirriff 20
68/9 Shirriff / SLou. 3
57/8 Topps 38
58/9 Topps 64
59/0 Topps 35
60/1 Topps 64
74/5 Topps 91
01/2 To. Heritage S2, ✍ CAI
71/2 Toronto Sun Photo
61/2 York 33
83/4 NYIS / News 29
84/5 NYIS / News 29
89/0 NYIS
99/0 NYIS / UD NY7
71/2 SLOU
92/3 SLOU / McDon. 3

ARBOUR, AMOS
23/4 William Paterson 20

ARBOUR, JOHN
68/9 O-Pee-Chee 189
75/6 OPC WHA 54
71/2 Toronto Sun Photo
71/2 SLOU
72/3 Minn. Fight. Saints
74/5 Minn. Fight. Saints

ARBOUR, TY
23/4 Paulins Candy 44

ARBULIC, MIKE
93/4 Portland Winter Hawks

ARCAND, BILLY
51/2 Laval Dairy 54
52/3 St. Lawrence 99

ARCANGELONI, STÉPHANE
95 Panini Worlds 107
94 Semic 222

ARCELLA, GERRY
91/2 7th...Sketch OHL 379

ARCHALOUS, JAN
99/0 OFS 359

ARCHAMBAULT, DANIEL
98/9 Québec Remparts

ARCHAMBAULT, MICHEL
72/3 O-Pee-Chee 320
72/3 Québec Nordiques

ARCHER, ANDREW
01/2 Guelph Storm
01/2 Guelph Storm M-Cup

ARCHIBAL, GEORGES
51/2 Lac St-Jean 47

ARCHIBALD, DAVE
92 C.O.A. Winter Olympics 180
90/1 Canada Nationals 9
91/2 Canada Nationals
96/7 DEL 65
93/4 Donruss 231
94/5 Leaf 432
88/9 OPC/Topps 112
89/0 OPC/Topps 10
88/9 OPC Sticker 53-184
89/0 opcSticker 201-59
88/9 Panini Sticker 88
94/5 Panini Sticker 102
94/5 Parkie SE118
93/4 Power Play 168
93/4 Premier 458
90/1 Score 162
92/3 Score COH 3
94/5 Score 133
93/4 To. Stadium 399
92/3 Upper Deck 473
93/4 Upper Deck 105
94/5 Upper Deck 383
87/8 MINS
92/3 OTTA
93/4 OTTA
94/5 OTTA
95/6 OTTA
92/3 Binghampton Rangers
86/7 Portland Winter Hawks

ARCHIBALD, DENNIS
91/2 Avant Garde BCJHL 130
92/3 BCJHL 44

ARDASHEV, ALEXANDER
00/1 Mir 58

ARDELAN, MARK
99/0 Brandon Wheat Kings
01/2 Vancouver Giants

AREKAEB, SERGEI
99/0 Mir 194

ARENDT, RONNY
01/2 UD DEL 18

ARESHENKOFF, RON
88/9 EDMO / Action 103

ARGENTOS, GUISEPPE
91/2 7th...Sketch LHJMQ 41

ARGIROPOULOS, JOHN
95/6 Slapshot 291

ARGOKOV, ARTEM
99/0 Mir 113
00/1 Mir 177

ARGYRIOU, ALEX
98/9 Brandon Wheat Kings

ARIAL, SIMON
91/2 7th...Sketch LHJMQ 150

ARIMA, TONY
80/1 Mallasjuoma 54
94/5 Sisu 281
95/6 Sisu 173

ARKHIPOV, DENIS
02/3 Atomic 58
01/2 BAP Memor. 211
02/3 BAP Memorabilia 30
02/3 Exclusive 96
02/3 First Edition 251
02/3 Heads Up 67
98/9 Mir 45
99/0 Mir 72
02/3 O-Pee-Chee 48
02/3 Pacific 205
02/3 Pacific Complete 123
02/3 Parkhurst 178
02/3 Pr. Stock Reserve 56
01/2 Signature 42, ✍ Aut. 42
02/3 Signature Series GS-31
02/3 SP Game-Used ✂ FF
02/3 Sports Vault 255
98/9 SPx Prospects 75
02/3 Topps 48
02/3 To. Heritage 31
02/3 T. Limited 48
02/3 T. Total 137
01/2 Upper Deck 101
02/3 Upper Deck 100, ✂ BF, ✂ HS
98/9 UD Black Diam. 105
02/3 UD Classic 54
02/3 UD MVP 102
02/3 UD Top Shelf ✂ GO
02/3 UD Vintage 144
02/3 Victory 116
00/1 Milwaukee Admirals

ARKIOMAA, TERO
98/9 Cardset 269
99/0 Cardset 155
96/7 DEL 13
92/3 Jyvas Hyva 136
93/4 Jyvas Hyva 232
00/1 Kudos 117
95 Panini Worlds 184
94 Semic 23
95 Semic 31
93/4 Sisu 198
94/5 Sisu 85, 173, FOI-14
95/6 Sisu 170, 307
95/6 Sisu Limited 33

ARMBRUST, PETER
00/1 Quad City Mallards

ARMELIN, JOHN
82/3 Soo Greyhounds

ARMITAGE, SCOTT
97/8 Pi. CBC Sports 1

ARMSTRONG, BILL C.
90/1 ProCards 45
91/2 ProCards 289
90 7th..Sketch Mem.Cup 82
89/0 7th..Sketch OHL 20, 199
95/6 Cleveland Lumberjacks
96/7 Cleveland Lumberjacks
97/8 Providence Bruins
98/9 Providence Bruins
89/0 Oshawa Generals

ARMSTRONG, BILL H.
91/2 O-Pee-Chee 36
89/0 ProCards AHL 349
90/1 ProCards 50
91/2 ProCards 266
92/3 Cincinnati Cyclones
95/6 Indianapolis Ice

ARMSTRONG, BOB
02/3 Parkie - Reprint 194

ARMSTRONG, BOB R.
45-64 BeeHive-2 [Bost.]
52/3 Parkhurst 84
54/5 Parkhurst 55
93/4 Parkie 56-57 7
60/1 Shirriff 118
61/2 Shirriff 12
54/5 Topps 7
57/8 Topps 3
58/9 Topps 1
59/0 Topps 39
60/1 Topps 56
61/2 Topps 13
59/0 Toronto Star Photo
57-58 BOST
91/2 BOST / SA Legends
91/2 BOST / SA Legends

ARMSTRONG, BOB*
23/4 Paulins Candy 56

ARMSTRONG, CHRIS
94/5 Classic 32, T25
93/4 Donruss CAN2
95/6 Edge Ice 22
93/4 Pinnacle 459
93/4 Upper Deck 546
96/7 Carolina Monarchs
00/1 Cleveland Lumberjacks
97/8 Fort Wayne Komets
99/0 Kentucky Tho'blades

ARMSTRONG, COLBY
01 UD Prospects GU 32, ✂ TPJ, ✂ JC
02/3 WBS Penguins
00/1 Red Deer Rebels

ARMSTRONG, DEREK
93/4 Cla. Prospects 178
94/5 Leaf 51
02/3 Pacific Complete 430
97/8 Pacific CC 300
96/7 Pi. Be A Player 179, ✍ Aut. 179
91/2 7th...Sketch OHL 246
96/7 NYIS
97/8 Hartford Wolf Pack
98/9 Hartford Wolf Pack
99/0 Hartford Wolf Pack
00/1 Hartford Wolf Pack
91/2 Sudbury Wolves
92/3 Sudbury Wolves

ARMSTRONG, GEORGE
45-64 BeeHive-2 [Toro.]
45-64 BeeHive-2 [Toro.]
45-64 BeeHive-2 [Toro.]
64-67 BeeHive-3 [Toro.]
63-65 Chex
64/5 Coke/Sprite [Toro.]
65/6 Coca-Cola
02/3 Cowan Tile
83 HHOF Postcard N1
83&87 HHOF 197
96/7 Legends 76
70/1 O-Pee-Chee 113
52/3 Parkhurst 51
53/4 Parkhurst 11
54/5 Parkhurst 24
55/6 Parkhurst 4
57/8 Parkhurst [Toro.] 1
58/9 Parkhurst 7
58/9 Parkhurst 48
59/0 Parkhurst 7
60/1 Parkhurst 17
61/2 Parkhurst 17
62/3 Parkhurst 13
63/4 Parkhurst 13
63/4 Parkhurst 73
92/3 Parkhurst PR-17
93/4 Parkhurst PR38
02/3 Parkie - Reprint 218
93/4 Parkie 56-57 125
95/6 Parkie 66-67 116
94/5 Parkie Tall 122, 178
67/8 Post Tips 9
45-54 Quaker Oats
60/1 Shirriff 9
61/2 Shirriff 51
62/3 Shirriff 10
68/9 Shirriff / Toro. 1
64/5 Topps 69
65/6 Topps 19
66/7 Topps 84
66/7 Topps / Test 17
67/8 Topps 83
70/1 Topps 113
57/8 Toronto Star Photo
58/9 Toronto Star Photo
63/4 Toronto Star Action
63/4 Toronto Star Photo
60/1 Toronto Star Weekend
60/1 York Glass [Toro.]
60/1 York
61/2 York 37
62/3 York Transfer 17
63/4 York 16
67/8 York
67/8 York
64/5 TORO
68/9 TORO
69/0 TORO
72/3 MONT / Pro Star
74/5 PITT

ARNASON, TYLER
01/2 BAP Memor. 387
02/3 Bowman 140, ✂ FFDS, ✂ FFJ, ✂ FFP, ✂ FFR, ✂ FFRP, ✂ FFS, ✂ FFTS, ✍ YSA, / ✍ Puck
02/3 Calder 63, -CR 6
02/3 Crown Royale -RR 6
02/3 O-Pee-Chee 300
02/3 Pacific Complete 198
01/2 Parkhurst 309
02/3 Parkhurst Retro 65, ✂ CH1
02/3 Pr. Stock Reserve -CA 5
01/2 PS Titanium Draft 114
02/3 Private Stock Titanium 21, -ROT 5
02/3 Quest for the Cup -CC 4
02/3 Sports Vault 178
02/3 Topps 300
02/3 T. Limited 300
02/3 T. Total 234
02/3 Ultimate Memorabilia ✂ CC
02/3 Upper Deck 200
02/3 UD Honor 13
02/3 UD MVP 198
01/2 UD Premier 92
02/3 UD Premier 11
02/3 UD Rookie 22
02/3 Vanguard 21, -PP 7
01/2 Norfolk Admirals

ARNESEN, SVEIN H
92/3 Semic Nordisk 31

ARNHOLT, P.M.
95/6 DEL 333

ARNIEL, SCOTT
90/1 Bowman 243
91/2 Bowman 206
95/6 Edge Ice 129
83/4 Funmate Puffy 2 [w/]
83/4 O-Pee-Chee 379
84/5 O-Pee-Chee 333
86/7 OPC/Topps 194
87/8 OPC/Topps 194
88/9 OPC/Topps 90
90/1 OPC/Topps 324
91/2 O-Pee-Chee 137
89/0 OPC/Topps 187
90/1 OPC Premier 1
84/5 OPC Sticker 286
86/7 OPC Sticker 58
88/9 OPC Sticker 258-126
88/9 Panini Sticker 224
89/0 Panini Sticker 213
90/1 Panini Sticker 30
90/1 Panini/WPG 1
91/2 Panini Sticker 74
82/3 Post [Winn.]
90/1 Pro Set 18, 557
90/1 Score 251, 68T
91/2 Score CAN 256
84/5 7-Eleven
83/4 Souhaits Keychain [Jets]
91/2 To. Stadium 30
90/1 Upper Deck 397
83/4 Vachon 121-1
86/7 BUFF / Blue Shield
87/8 BUFF / Blue Shield
87/8 BUFF / Won. Bread
88/9 BUFF / Blue Shield
88/9 BUFF / Won. Bread
89/0 BUFF / Blue Shield
89/0 BUFF / Campbell's
81/2 WINN
82/3 WINN
83/4 WINN
84/5 WINN / Safety Tips
85/6 WINN
85/6 WINN / Safety Tips
90/1 WINN / IGA
95/6 Houston Aeros
97/8 Manitoba Moose
98/9 Manitoba Moose
92/3 San Diego Gulls
93/4 San Diego Gulls

ARNMARK, GORAN
89/0 Semic Elitserien 170
90/1 Semic Elitserien 4
91/2 Semic Elitserien 202

ARNOST, TOMAS
94/5 APS 258
95/6 APS 155

ARNOTT, JASON
01/2 Adrenaline 110
01/2 Atomic 56, PP20, TN8
02/3 Atomic 31, -SC5, ✂ GWJ 3
98/9 Aurora 107
99/0 Aurora 83
00/1 Aurora 80
98/9 Be A Player 78, ✍ Aut. 78
99/0 BAP Mem. 64
00/1 BAP Mem. 262, ✂ TM-21, ✂ TM-27
01/2 BAP Memor. 53, 467, ✂ SCP
02/3 BAP Memorabilia 81, 247, 257
96/7 Bic.Sports Aces 3-D
97/8 Bicycle J-Spade
95/6 Bicycle Sports Aces 6-Diamond
01/2 Bowman 89
02/3 Bowman 60
02/3 Calder 17
93/4 Classic 7
93/4 Classic - Top Ten DP7
94/5 Classic AR2
93/4 Cla. 4 Sport 191
93/4 Cla. Images 4 Sport 142
93/4 Cla. Images 4 Sport 62
93/4 Cla. Prospects 11
01/2 Crown Royale 84
93/4 Donruss 120
93/4 Donruss H
93/4 Donruss RR 12
94/5 Donruss 25, ES-1
95/6 Donruss 44
96/7 Donruss 143, D-5
97/8 Donruss 145
96/7 Do. Canadian 68
97/8 Do. Canadian 117, NP-12
95/6 Do. Elite 101
96/7 Do. Elite 46, 150
97/8 Do. Elite 95
97/8 Do. Preferred 31
97/8 Do. Priority 97, DD-30
97/8 Do. Studio 35, P-29
98/9 Dynagon Ice 107
99/0 Dynagon Ice 113
02/3 Exclusive 54
02/3 First Edition 242, 409H
94/5 Flair 56, CIS-1
96/7 Flair 32
94/5 Fleer 68, FF-1
96/7 Fleer 36
95/6 Fleer Metal 52, IW-1
96/7 Fl. Picks 58
93/4 Fleer Ultra 312
93/4 Fleer Ultra WotF 1
94/5 Fleer Ultra 68, ARS-1, PP-1, UP-2
95/6 Fleer Ultra 52, CC-1, HS-2, RS-1
96/7 Fl. Ultra 57
95 Globe 95
01/2 Heads Up 55, SM10
02/3 Heads Up 37
95/6 Hoyle / West. 3-Heart
93/4 Kraft / KD
94/5 Kraft / SS
95/6 Kraft / IP
93/4 Leaf 382
93/4 Leaf FP 7
94/5 Leaf 133, GLR-2, GLS-10, LL-8
95/6 Leaf 119
96/7 Leaf 179
97/8 Leaf 61
94/5 L. Limited 66
95/6 L. Limited 22
96/7 Leaf Limited 43
96/7 L. Preferred 20, LS-19
97/8 Limited 27, 79
96/7 Maggers 66
94/5 McDonald's McD-37
95/6 McDonald's McD-14
01/2 McDonald's 23
96/7 Metal Univ. 52
99/0 Millenium 148, ✍ Aut. 148
01/2 O-Pee-Chee 31
02/3 O-Pee-Chee 151
98/9 OPC Chrome 199
97/8 Omega 125
98/9 Omega 135
99/0 Omega 132
98/9 Pacific 261
99/0 Pacific 234
00/1 Pacific 231
01/2 Pacific 225
02/3 Pacific 110, ✂ GWJ 14
02/3 Pacific Complete 322
97/8 Pacific CC 79
97/8 Pa. Crown Roy. 52
98/9 Pa. Crown Roy. 77
97/8 Pa. Invincible 54
97/8 Pa. Paramount 72
98/9 Pa. Paramount 131
99/0 Pa. Paramount 130
00/1 Pa. Paramount 141
98/9 Pa. Revolution 82
98/9 Panini Photocard
94/5 Panini Sticker W
95/6 Panini Sticker 255
96/7 Panini Sticker 258
97/8 Panini Sticker 210
99/0 Panini Sticker 84
95 Panini Worlds 11
93/4 Parkhurst 261
93/4 Parkhurst C6
93/4 Parkhurst W8
94/5 Parkhurst 271,V84, YCTG-8
95/6 Parkhurst 73
00/1 Parkhurst P-39
01/2 Parkhurst 99, 375, ✂ PS47, ✂ T15
02/3 Parkhurst 155
02/3 Parkhurst Retro 103
94/5 Parkie SE59
93/4 Pinnacle 441
93/4 Pinnacle SR7
94/5 Pinnacle 124, 463, NL-14
95/6 Pinnacle 16, FC-8
96/7 Pinnacle 118
97/8 Pinnacle 61
96/7 Pi. Be A Player LTH5B, BB-21, ✍ Aut. LTH5B
97/8 Pi. Certified 124
95/6 Pi. FANtasy 22
97/8 Pi. Inside 55
95/6 Pi. Summit 18, MH-6
96/7 Pi. Summit 103
97/8 Pi. Totally 124
95/6 Pi. Zenith 23, GG-15
96/7 Pi. Zenith 65, A-3
95/6 Playoff 37
94/5 POG 97
94/5 POG / Western 1
95/6 POG 106
94/5 Post
97/8 Pi. Post 6, F4
93/4 Power Play 337
93/4 Power Play RooS 1
94/5 Premier 193, 530, OF-10
00/1 Premier Plus 22
00/1 Private Stock 56
01/2 Pr. Stock 54, -PS 43
02/3 Pr. Stock Reserve ✂ 113
00/1 PS Titanium 53
01/2 PS Titanium 81, ✂ DSJ 68
01/2 PS Titanium Draft ✂ 32
95/6 Pro Magnet 81
99/0 Revolution 83, / CSC 83
00/1 Revolution 84
93/4 Score 594
93/4 Score/CAN DD7
94/5 Score 254, TF8
95/6 Score 8, GB-20
96/7 Score 55
97/8 Score 136
94/5 Select 87
96/7 Select CE 9, DS-8
96/7 Select CE 38
91/2 7th...Sketch OHL 148
00/1 Signature 232, ✍ Aut. 64, ✂ J-38, ✂ HSHSJers
01/2 Signature C-16, ✂ GUE35, ✂ GJ36, ✂ GSJ36, ✂ ITN35, ✂ TM17
02/3 Signature Series ✂ TQ16
95/6 SBx Emotion 61
95/6 SBx Impact 59, 237
96/7 SBx Impact 41
95/6 SP 40
95/6 SP 51, FX-8
96/7 SP 55, HC-4
97/8 SP Authentic 59
00/1 SP Authentic 54
02/3 SP Authentic 49
02/3 SP Game-Used ✂ PC
97/8 SPx 18
01/2 SPx 39
00/1 Stadium 99, BT21
01/2 Stadium Club 77
97/8 SLU
95/6 Super Sticker 44, DC-13
96/7 Team Out!
95/6 Topps 17, 340, 3CG, YS10
98/9 Topps 199
99/0 Topps 194
00/1 Topps 142
01/2 Topps 31, ✂ GWJ, ✍ CA
02/3 Topps 151
99/0 To. Chrome 194
00/1 To. Chrome 104, 165
01/2 To. Chrome 31
02/3 T. Chrome 92
94/5 Topps Finest 21
95/6 To. Finest 139
00/1 To. Gold Label 96, B1
00/1 To. Heritage 247
01/2 To. Heritage 75
02/3 T. Limited 151
01/2 To. Reserve 82, ✂ TR
93/4 To. Stadium 345
94/5 T. Stadium Club 7, 115
95/6 To. Stadium EC171, -MP
93/4 TSC Members Only 49
94/5 TSC Members Only 31
00/1 To. Stars 91, PP1
95/6 T. Super Skills 67
02/3 T. Total 338
98/9 UD Choice 118
01/2 UD PlayMakers Ltd 60
00/1 Ultimate Mem. ✍ U-46, ✂ Jer. 37, ✂ J-45, ✂ S-45, ✂ T-30
01/2 Ultimate Mem. ✂ NP
02/3 Ultimate Memorabilia ✂ FS
93/4 Upper Deck 423, R9, SP-48
94/5 Upper Deck 305, IG2, SP-26
95/6 Upper Deck 29, SE-119
96/7 Upper Deck 57, X12, P6, SS19B
97/8 Upper Deck 66, T17A
98/9 Upper Deck 120
00/1 Upper Deck 106
01/2 Upper Deck 103, T5
02/3 Upper Deck 59, ✂ CG
93/4 Upper Deck Be A Player 19
94/5 UD Be A Player R34, R93, R134, ✍ 110
96/7 UD Black Diam. 97
97/8 UD Black Diam. 117
00/1 UD Black Diam. 101
95/6 UD CC 41, C19
96/7 UD CC 92, 317, C23, CR23
97/8 UD Coll. Choice 95, SQ7
98/9 UD G. Reserve 120
96/7 UD Ice 20, S9
01/2 UD Mask ✂ PM
98/9 UD MVP 122, ✍ PS
99/0 UD MVP 120
01/2 UD MVP 115
02/3 UD MVP 62
02/3 UD Piece 31
95/6 UD Post 20
01/2 UD SCup Champs 72
01/2 UD Top Shelf 90
02/3 UD Top Shelf 27, ✂ SH, ✂ ST
00/1 UD Vintage 212
01/2 UD Vintage 151, 157
02/3 UD Vintage 85, Gb 85, T23
00/1 Vanguard 56
01/2 Vanguard 55
99/0 Victory 172
00/1 Victory 140
01/2 Victory 209
02/3 Victory 65
96 Wien 97
02/3 DALL / Southwest
93/4 EDMO / Sheet
96/7 EDMO
97/8 EDMO
91/2 Oshawa Generals
91/2 Oshawa Generals
92/3 Oshawa Generals

ARNOULD, PATRICK
79 Panini Sticker 343

ARO, JORMA
74 Hellas MM-Jenkki 4
70/1 Kuvajulkaisut 119
80/1 Mallasjuoma 25
72 Panda MM-Toronto
78/9 SM-Liiga 46
71/2 Williams Finnish 169
72/3 Williams Finnish 120
73/4 Williams Finnish 174

ARO, KARI
65/6 Hellas 7

ARO, SEPPO
70/1 Kuvajulkaisut 309
72/3 Williams Finnish 322

AROMAKI, JUHANI
66/7 Champion 204

ARONSON, STEVE
00/1 Cleveland Lumberjacks
01/2 Louisiana Ice Gators
02/3 London Knights

ARS, STEVE
90/1 7th...Sketch LHJMQ 75
91/2 7th...Sketch LHJMQ 109

ARSENAULT, DANIEL
90 7th..Sketch Mem.Cup 72

ARSENAULT, DAVE
99/0 Louisiana Ice Gators
97/8 Toledo Storm 19

ARSENAULT, JIMMY
02/3 Baie-Comeau

ARSENAULT, YAN
90/1 7th...Sketch LHJMQ 237
91/2 7th...Sketch LHJMQ 142

ARSENE, DEAN
96/7 Regina Pats
97/8 Regina Pats

ARTHUR, FRED
82/3 O-Pee-Chee 245
82/3 Post [Phil.]

ARTURSSON, GREGER
95/6 Leaf Elit Set 216
89/0 Semic Elitserien 83
90/1 Semic Elitserien 256
91/2 Semic Elitserien 89
98/9 UD Elitserien 86
99/0 UD Elitserien 55
00/1 UD Elitserien 80, ✍ Sig.

ARTYUKHIN, EVGENI
00/1 Mir 393

ARUNDEL, JOHN
52/3 Laval Dairy Update 99
52/3 St. Lawrence 63

ARVAJA, MIKA
98/9 Cardset 85
99/0 Cardset 56
92/3 Jyvas Hyva 45
93/4 Jyvas Hyva 144
93/4 Sisu 149
93/4 Sisu 321
94/5 Sisu 133
95/6 Sisu 244
96/7 Sisu 33
00/1 UD DEL 200

ARVAJA, PERTTI
71/2 Williams Finnish 97
72/3 Williams Finnish 138
73/4 Williams Finnish 105

ARVANITIS, PETER
92/3 BCJHL 57
98/9 Oklahoma City Blazers

ARVEDSON, MAGNUS
99/0 Aurora 98
99/0 BAP Mem. 102
00/1 BAP Mem. 185
99/0 Dynagon Ice 137
02/3 First Edition 161
94/5 Leaf Elit Set 196
95/6 Leaf Elit Set 43
99/0 Millenium 171, ✍ 171
97/8 Omega 153
99/0 Omega 157
98/9 Pacific 306
99/0 Pacific 284
00/1 Pacific 274
01/2 Pacific 270
02/3 Pacific 261
02/3 Pacific Complete 50
98/9 Pa. Paramount 161
99/0 Pa. Paramount 159
00/1 Pa. Paramount 170
98/9 Panini Sticker 44
99/0 Panini Sticker 115
00/1 Panini Sticker 67
00/1 Parkhurst P-206
01/2 Parkhurst 183
97/8 Pinnacle 16
97/8 Pi. Be A Player 225, ✍ Aut. 225
99/0 Revolution 101, / CSC 101
97/8 Score 70
01/2 Signature 67, ✍ Aut.
02/3 Sports Vault 96
99/0 SPx 105
99/0 Stadium 52
99/0 Topps 135, PP4
00/1 Topps 264
99/0 To. Chrome 135, PP4
99/0 To. Prmr. Plus 65
02/3 T. Total 176
97/8 Upper Deck 324
98/9 Upper Deck 138
00/1 Upper Deck 353
01/2 Upper Deck 123
02/3 Upper Deck 371
95/6 UD Elitserien 67
98/9 UD G. Reserve 138
97/8 UD Ice 37
98/9 UD MVP 142
99/0 UD MVP 139
01/2 UD MVP 135
01/2 UD Vintage 178, 182
02/3 UD Vintage 180
99/0 Victory 205
00/1 Victory 164
01/2 Victory 249
02/3 Victory 152
97/8 Zenith RR-5
97/8 OTTA
98/9 OTTA
99/0 OTTA
00/1 OTTA
01/2 OTTA
02/3 OTTA

ARVEDSSON, GREGER
97/8 UD Elitserien 56

ARVSELL, HENRIK
94/5 Leaf Elit Set CS 8

ASCROFT, BRENT
95/6 Tri-City Americans 10

ASHAM, ARRON
00/1 BAP Mem. 306
97 Bowman 107
99/0 Millenium 130, ✍ Aut. 130
95/6 Upper Deck 509
99/0 Upper Deck 70
99/0 UD G. Reserve 70
99/0 UD MVP 105
99/0 Victory 144
99/0 Québec Citadelles
00/1 Québec Citadelles
01/2 Québec Citadelles
95/6 Red Deer Rebels

ASHBEE, BARRY
65/6 Coca-Cola
70/1 Esso Power Player
72/3 Post 21
71/2 O-Pee-Chee 104
72/3 O-Pee-Chee 206
71/2 Toronto Sun Photo
70/1 PHIL

ASHBY, DON
77/8 O-Pee-Chee 365
78/9 O-Pee-Chee 351
88/9 EDMO / Action 112
75/6 TORO
76/7 TORO
77/8 TORO

ASHE, TOM
97/8 Grand Rapids Griffins

ASHLEY, JOHN
83 HHOF Postcard O2 [Referee]
83&87 HHOF 213

ASHTON, BRENT
90/1 Bowman 130
91/2 Bowman 211
92/3 Bowman 357
92/3 Fleer Ultra 1
89/0 Kraft 46
86/7 Kraft Sports 42
81/2 O-Pee-Chee 330
82/3 O-Pee-Chee 135
83/4 O-Pee-Chee 225
85/6 O-Pee-Chee 170
86/7 OPC/Topps 181
87/8 OPC/Topps 100
88/9 OPC/Topps 128
90/1 OPC/Topps 24
91/2 O-Pee-Chee 240
89/0 OPC/Topps 181
82/3 OPC/Topps Sticker 227
85/6 OPC Sticker 153-24
86/7 OPC Sticker 25
87/8 OPC Sticker 108
88/9 OPC Sticker 250-120
89/0 opcSticker 138
87/8 Panini Sticker 244
88/9 Panini Sticker 40
89/0 Panini Sticker 164
90/1 Panini Sticker 321
90/1 Panini/WPG 2
91/2 Panini Sticker 70
92/3 Parkhurst 258
80/1 Pepsi Bottle Cap
91/2 Pinnacle 280
82/3 Post [Colo.]
90/1 Pro Set 323
91/2 Pro Set 272
91/2 Pro Set 352
91/2 Pro Set Platinum 155
90/1 Score 31
91/2 Score 78
91/2 Score 22T
91/2 Score CAN 78
92/3 Score 164
93/4 Score 434
83/4 Souhaits Keychain [Devils]
92/3 Topps 191
91/2 To. Stadium 90
92/3 T. Stadium Club 146
93/4 To. Stadium 51
90/1 Upper Deck 220
91/2 Upper Deck 303
91/2 BOST / Sports Action
81/2 COLR
86/7 DETR / Little Caesars
87/8 DETR / Little Caesars
83/4 MINS
84/5 QUÉB
85/6 QUÉB
85/6 QUÉB / Gene. Foods
85/6 QUÉB / McDonald's
85/6 QUÉB / Provigo
86/7 QUÉB / Gene. Foods
86/7 QUÉB / McDonald's
79/0 VANC / Royal Bank
80/1 VANC
80/1 VANC / Silverwood
88/9 WINN / Safety Tips
89/0 WINN / Safeway
90/1 WINN / IGA
93/4 Las Vegas Thunder

ASHTON, MARK
01/2 Vancouver Giants

ASIKAINEN, MIKA
99/0 Cardset 98
95/6 Sisu 255

ASKAROV, MARAT
99/0 Mir 262

ASKEY, TOM
98/9 Pacific 67
98/9 Upper Deck 36
98/9 UD G. Reserve 36
98/9 Cincinnati M'Ducks 26
99/0 Kansas City Blades
00/1 Rochester Americans
02/3 Rochester Americans

ÅSLAND, GLENN
92/3 Semic Nordisk 89

ÅSLIN, PETER
94/5 Leaf Elit Set 54, CS-5
89/0 Semic Elitserien 121
90/1 Semic Elitserien 100
91/2 Semic Elitserien 104
92/3 Semic Elitserien 125
93 Semic Sticker 1

ASP, AARON
91/2 Ferris State Bulldogs

ASPLUND, JOHAN
00/1 UD Elitserien 29

ASSELIN, KEVIN
99 Québec Pee Wee 25
01/2 Cape Breton Eagles 23

ASSELSTINE, RON
90/1 Pro Set 681

ASSELTINE, JACK
23/4 Paulins Candy 25

AST, DOUG
91/2 Avant Garde BCJHL 135
92/3 BCJHL 24
01/2 UD DEL 106
97/8 Long Beach Ice Dogs
98/9 Long Beach Ice Dogs
00/1 Manitoba Moose
96/7 Syracuse Crunch

ASTALOS, MIKE
98/9 Detroit Vipers

ASTASHENKO, KASPARS
00/1 Pacific 382
00/1 SPx 116
00/1 Upper Deck 225
98/9 Cincinnati Cyclones

ASTLEY, MARK
92/3 Canada Nationals
94/5 Cla. Images 68
93/4 Donruss 44
95/6 Edge Ice 62
95/6 Fleer Ultra 209
93/4 Parkhurst 295
93/4 Premier 342
94/5 Score CT13
93/4 To. Stadium 311
93/4 Upper Deck 494
91/2 L. Superior State Lakers

ASTRAHANTSEV, KONSTANTIN
94 Panini Olympics 280
94 Semic 149
93 Semic Sticker 138
94/5 Sisu 339

ASTASHENKO, HARDY
80/1 O-Pee-Chee 269
79 Panini Sticker 185
79/0 COLR

ATANASOV, IVAN
79 Panini Sticker 350

ATCHEYNUM, BLAIR
98/9 Pacific 361
99/0 Pacific 351
98/9 Pa. Paramount 120
97/8 Pa. Revolution 116
97/8 Pi. Be A Player 210, ✍ Aut. 210
89/0 ProCards AHL 288
90/1 ProCards 178
91/2 ProCards 107
98/9 Upper Deck 300
98/9 UD G. Reserve 300
99/0 UD MVP Cup 45
98/9 NASH / Wendy's 1
86/7 Saskatoon Blades

ATCHINSON, A.
12/3 Imperial 4

ATKINS, SCOTT
95/6 Slapshot 209

ATKINSON, DEREK
99/0 Lethbridge Hurricanes

ATKINSON, STEVE
72/3 Eddie Sargent 40
70/1 Esso Power Player
74/5 Loblaws
71/2 O-Pee-Chee 162
72/3 O-Pee-Chee 40
73/4 O-Pee-Chee 245
74/5 O-Pee-Chee 192
72/3 Topps 47
74/5 Topps 192
72/3 BUFF
73/4 BUFF
74/5 WASH

ATTERSLEY, BOB
52/3 Anonymous 84
59/60 Whitby Dunlops

ATTWELL, RON
60/1 Cleveland Barons

AUBÉ, J.F.
98/9 EBK ECHL All-Star
96/7 Charlotte Checkers
99/0 Mississippi S'Wolves
97/8 Pensacola Ice Pilots

AUBÉ, JEAN-FRANÇOIS
98/9 Charlotte Checkers

AUBIN, JEAN-SEBASTIEN
00/1 Aurora 114, Pin. 114, ✍ Aut., TPS-9B
00/1 BAP Mem. 54
01/2 BAP Memor. ✂ GJ
01/2 BT Pipes 6, 96, ✂ Jers., ✂ S&J, ✂ GG, ✂ GT, ✂ HSHSJers
02/3 Between the Pipes 30, ✂ DM17, ✂ GUE10, ✂ GUJ10, ✂ GP11, ✂ GSJ10, ✂ ITN10, ✂ T7
01/2 Heads Up ✂ JQ 18
02/3 In The Game-Used ✂ GP7
01/2 O-Pee-Chee 121
98/9 Omega 192
99/0 Omega 194
99/0 Pacific 350
00/1 Pacific 324
01/2 Pacific 310
02/3 Pacific 305
02/3 Pacific Complete 55
00/1 Pa. Paramount 195, GS-15
98/9 Pa. Revolution 115
00/1 Parkhurst P-142
01/2 Parkhurst ✂ T2
00/1 Premier Plus 32
99/0 Prism 112
00/1 Private Stock 78, PSNW-19
01/2 Pr. Stock ✂ GUG 75
00/1 PS Titanium ✂ GUG 130
00/1 PS Titanium Draft ✂ 80
00/1 Revolution 116
00/1 Signature 170, ✍ Aut. 200
02/3 Signature Series 14, ✍ 14
98/9 SP Authentic 105
00/1 SP Authentic ✍ SotT
00/1 SPx 55
00/1 Stadium 98
99/0 Topps 33
00/1 Topps 238
01/2 Topps 121
99/0 To. Chrome 33
00/1 To. Chrome 148
00/1 To. Gold Label 84
00/1 To. Heritage 107
00/1 UD Heroes 96
00/1 Ultimate Mem. ✂ G-24
98/9 Upper Deck 350
01/2 Upper Deck 142
00/1 UD Black Diam. ✂ GG
98/9 UD G. Reserve 350
02/3 UD Mask 68, 69
99/0 UD MVP 172
00/1 UD MVP 144
00/1 UD Vintage 285, 295, 296, GG14
00/1 Vanguard 78
99/0 Victory 240
01/2 Victory 287
98/9 Kansas City Blades 23

AUBIN, NORMAND
82/3 O-Pee-Chee 316
82/3 Post [Toro.]
82/3 TORO
84/5 Nova Scotia Oilers

AUBIN, SERGE
01/2 BAP Memor. 130
00/1 Crown Royale 119
01/2 O-Pee-Chee 211
00/1 Pacific 125
01/2 Pacific 109
00/1 Pa. Paramount 67
00/1 Private Stock 112
00/1 PS Titanium 112
00/1 PS Titanium Draft 112
94/5 SR Auto-Phonex 4, ✍ 4
01/2 Signature 58, ✍ Aut.58
00/1 SP Authentic 100, ✍ SotT
00/1 SPx 95
00/1 Topps 307
01/2 Topps 211
00/1 To. Chrome 202
00/1 Upper Deck 182
01/2 Upper Deck 52, ✂ GN
00/1 UD Ice 56
01/2 UD Ice ✂ GJ
00/1 UD MVP 190
00/1 UD Pros&Prosp. 100
00/1 UD Vintage 377
00/1 Vanguard 112
00/1 Victory 261
01/2 Victory 98
01/2 COLU
96/7 Cleveland Lumberjacks
95/6 Hampton Roads
98/9 Hershey Bears

AUBRY, PIERRE
81/2 Dernière Heure
82/3 O-Pee-Chee 277
83/4 O-Pee-Chee 289
91/2 7th...Sketch LHJMQ 273
83/4 Souhaits Keychain [Nordiques]
84/5 DETR / Little Caesars
81/2 QUÉB
82/3 QUÉB
83/4 QUÉB

AUBRY, SERGE
75/6 OPC WHA 3
88/9 QUÉB
88/9 QUÉB / Gene. Foods
89/0 QUÉB
75/6 Cincinnati Stingers
72/3 Québec Nordiques
73/4 Québec Nordiques
76/7 Québec Nordiques

AUCOIN, ADRIAN
99/0 BAP Mem. 292, SL23
00/1 BAP Mem. 362
02/3 BAP Memorabilia 26
98/9 Bowman's Best 36
92/3 Canada Nationals
93/4 Canada Nationals
93/4 Cla. Prospects IA1
93/4 Cla. Prospects LP11
02/3 First Edition 294, 385
93/4 Fleer Ultra 458
99/0 Millenium 238, ✍ Aut. 238
02/3 O-Pee-Chee 188
98/9 Omega 234
99/0 Pacific 419
00/1 Pacific 403
02/3 Pacific 232
02/3 Pacific Complete 167
97/8 Pa. Invincible R-198
99/0 Pa. Paramount 232
99/0 Panini Sticker 312, 343
01/2 Parkhurst 355
02/3 Parkhurst 179, -HHN 8
96/7 Pi. Be A Player 79, ✍ Aut. 79
93/4 Power Play 478
93/4 Premier - Canada 3
94/5 Score CT14
97/8 Score Vanc. 14
02/3 Signature Series GS-3
99/0 Topps 180
00/1 Topps 269
02/3 Topps 188
99/0 To. Chrome 180
02/3 T. Limited 188
02/3 T. Total 120
92/3 Upper Deck 584
93/4 Upper Deck 251
95/6 Upper Deck 56
00/1 Upper Deck 398
02/3 UD MVP 116
99/0 UD MVP Cup 184
00/1 UD Vintage 350
96/7 VANC / IGA

AUDET, GERARD
51/2 Lac St-Jean 23

AUDET, PHILIPPE
97 Bowman 52
95/6 Classic 44
99/0 Cincinnati M'Ducks

AUDETTE, DONALD
01/2 Adrenaline 57
99/0 Aurora 67
99/0 BAP Mem. 92
00/1 BAP Mem. 290
02/3 BAP Memorabilia 32
92/3 Bowman 288
00/1 Crown Royale 4
93/4 Donruss 32
94/5 Donruss 305
95/6 Donruss 141
97/8 Donruss 44
95/6 Do. Elite 49
97/8 Do. Priority 126
94/5 Flair 15
94/5 Fleer 19
95/6 Fleer Metal 12
92/3 Fleer Ultra - UR2
93/4 Fleer Ultra 273
94/5 Fleer Ultra 19
95/6 Fleer Ultra 15
96/7 Fl. Ultra 13
02/3 Heads Up 62
93/4 Leaf 272
94/5 Leaf 64
95/6 Leaf 274
97/8 Leaf 99
95/6 L. Limited 12
97/8 Limited 118
96/7 Metal Univ. 12
99/0 Millenium 121, ✍ Aut. 121
91/2 O-Pee-Chee 273
92/3 O-Pee-Chee 117
01/2 O-Pee-Chee 210
98/9 Pacific 103
99/0 Pacific 186
00/1 Pacific 14
01/2 Pacific 44
02/3 Pacific 190
02/3 Pacific Complete 115
97/8 Pacific CC 184
99/0 Pa. Paramount 107
00/1 Pa. Paramount 9
92/3 Panini Sticker U
93/4 Panini Sticker 103
94/5 Panini Sticker 93
95/6 Panini Sticker 19
96/7 Panini Sticker 17
97/8 Panini Sticker 16
98/9 Panini Sticker 17
91/2 Parkhurst 11
92/3 Parkhurst 18
92/3 Parkhurst 231
93/4 Parkhurst 26
94/5 Parkhurst 23
95/6 Parkhurst 292
00/1 Parkhurst P-171
01/2 Parkhurst 245, 381
91/2 Pinnacle 330
92/3 Pinnacle 38
93/4 Pinnacle 274
94/5 Pinnacle 244
95/6 Pinnacle 104
96/7 Pinnacle 59
97/8 Pinnacle 102
96/7 Pi. Be A Player 73, ✍ Aut. 73
97/8 Pi. Inside 105
95/6 Playoff 11
94/5 POG 48
93/4 Power Play 295
93/4 Premier 61
94/5 Premier 289
00/1 PS Titanium 3
95/6 Pro Magnet 110
91/2 Pro Set 524
92/3 Pro Set 18
92/3 Pro Set RGL 3
91/2 Pro Set Platinum 249
89/0 ProCards AHL 265
90/1 ProCards 289
99/0 Revolution 67
91/2 Score 389
91/2 Score CAN 279
92/3 Score 393
92/3 Score SS 19
93/4 Score 77
94/5 Score 157
95/6 Score 101
96/7 Score 233
97/8 Score 179
97/8 Score Buff. 4
92/3 Seasons 43
94/5 Select 26
01/2 Signature C-11, ✍ Aut. LDA
95/6 SBx Emotion 14
95/6 SBx Impact 14
00/1 SP Authentic 5
01/2 SPx 179
92/3 Topps 12
92/3 Topps 206
95/6 Topps 214
99/0 Topps 89
00/1 Topps 148
01/2 Topps 210
99/0 To. Chrome 89
95/6 To. Finest 71
00/1 To. Gold Label 53
00/1 To. Heritage 115
01/2 To. Heritage 175
92/3 T. Stadium Club 112
93/4 To. Stadium 213
94/5 T. Stadium Club 87
95/6 To. Stadium 54
95/6 T. Super Skills 3
02/3 T. Total 336
98/9 UD Choice 28
00/1 UD Heroes 6
90/1 Upper Deck 519
91/2 Upper Deck 585
92/3 Upper Deck 2
92/3 Upper Deck 306
93/4 Upper Deck 5
94/5 Upper Deck 30, SP-97
95/6 Upper Deck 2, SE-9
96/7 Upper Deck 18
97/8 Upper Deck 20
98/9 Upper Deck 227
99/0 Upper Deck 64

00/1 Upper Deck 10
01/2 Upper Deck 60
94/5 UD Be A Player ✍ 31
96/7 UD Black Diam. 30
95/6 UD CC 217
97/8 UD Coll. Choice 28, C12, CR12
98/9 UD G. Reserve 227
99/0 UD G. Reserve 64
01/2 UD Ice 102
01/2 UD Mask 50
98/9 UD MVP 96
99/0 UD MVP 95, ✍ PS
00/1 UD MVP 11
02/3 UD MVP 98
00/1 UD Pros&Prosp. 4
00/1 UD Vintage 15
01/2 UD Vintage 85
02/3 UD Vintage 135, 276
99/0 Victory 133
00/1 Victory 12
90/1 BUFF / Blue Shield
90/1 BUFF / Campbell's
91/2 BUFF / Blue Shield
91/2 BUFF / Campbell's
91/2 BUFF / Pepsi
92/3 BUFF / Blue Shield
92/3 BUFF / Jubilee
01/2 MONT
02/3 MONT

AUDETTE, GARY
91/2 Avant Garde BCJHL 20
90/1 7th..Sketch WHL 235
88/9 Brandon Wheat Kings
89/0 Brandon Wheat Kings
90/1 Brandon Wheat Kings

AUGER, DOMINIC
98 Bowman 112
98 Bowman Chrome 112

AUGUSTA, JOSEF
94/5 APS 276
95/6 APS 98
97/8 APS 289
92/3 Future Trends C76 136
98/9 OFS 49, 443
99/0 OFS 251

AUGUSTA, PATRIK
92/3 Classic Prospects 36
98/9 EBK IHL All-Star
95/6 Edge Ice 148
99/0 Eishockey 206
00/1 UD DEL 220
01/2 UD DEL 151
97/8 Long Beach Ice Dogs
98/9 Long Beach Ice Dogs
92/3 St. John's Maple Leafs
93/4 St. John's Maple Leafs
94/5 St. John's Maple Leafs
00/1 St. John's Maple Leafs

AUGUSTA, PAVEL
94/5 APS 231
95/6 APS 25
96/7 APS 146
97/8 APS 251
97/8 DS 68
96/7 DS Sticker 247
97/8 DS Sticker 130
99/0 Eishockey 345
98/9 OFS 19, 292
00/1 OFS 332

AUHUBER, KLAUS
79 Panini Sticker 101

AULD, ALEX
01/2 BAP Memor. 386
01/2 BT Pipes 152
02/3 Between the Pipes 74, ✂ FW11, ✂ T12
99 Bowman 1, ✍ BA21
02/3 Choice Prospects 2
02/3 First Edition 250
02/3 O-Pee-Chee 271
02/3 Pacific Complete 502
01/2 Parkhurst 376
99/0 Topps 262
02/3 Topps 271
99/0 To. Chrome 262
02/3 T. Limited 271
02/3 Manitoba Moose

AULIN, JARED
02/3 BAP Memorabilia 393
02/3 Calder 120
02/3 Choice Prospects 3
02/3 Pacific Complete 588
02/3 Parkhurst 206
02/3 Parkhurst Retro 207
96 Québec Pee Wee 245
99/0 UD Sobey's 13
02/3 SP Authentic 178
02/3 SPx 179
02/3 Ultimate Memorabilia 75
02/3 UD Artistic 110, ✂ RT
02/3 UD Classic 131
02/3 UD Honor 136
02/3 UD Mask 148
02/3 UD Premier ✍ 103
99/0 UD Prospects 46, 70
00/1 UD Prospects 51
98/9 Kamloops Blazers
99/0 Kamloops Blazers
98/9 Kamloops Blazers
00/1 Kamloops Blazers
01/2 Kamloops Blazers

AURIE, LARRY
33/4 Anonymous 19
34-43 BeeHive-1 [Detr.]
33/4 Canadian Gum
33/4 Hamilton Gum 44
33/4 O-Pee-Chee 51
36/7 O-Pee-Chee 131
34/5 Sweet Caporal
33/4 WWGum 59

AUSTIN, COLIN
89/0 7th..Sketch OHL 163

AUSTIN, DARCY
90/1 7th..Sketch WHL 121
91/2 7th...Sketch WHL 336
93/4 Flint Generals

AUSTIN, JESSE
96/7 Dayton Ice Bandits

AUSTIN, JON
99/0 Fort Wayne Komets

AUSTMAN, J.
24/5 Holland Creameries 10

AUSTRING, CURTIS
01/2 Regina Pats

AUTERE, ANTTI
91/2 ProCards 448

AUTOTTE, MARTIN
00/1 Victoriaville Tigres 5
01/2 Victoriaville Tigres 11

AUVINEN, HANNU
70/1 Kuvajulkaisut 278
71/2 Williams Finnish 149

AVDEJEV, IVAN
89/0 Semic Elitserien 111

AVERCHENKOV, IGOR
99/0 Mir 68

AVERILL, WILL
92/3 Richmond Renegades
93/4 Roanoke Express

AVERKIN, VADIM
00/1 Mir 91

AVERY, SEAN
01/2 BAP Memor. 368
98 Bowman 35
98 Bowman Chrome 35
02/3 O-Pee-Chee 310
02/3 Pacific Complete 290
01/2 Parkhurst 334
01/2 PS Titanium Draft 125
01/2 SPx 204
02/3 SPx 109
02/3 Topps 310
02/3 T. Limited 310
02/3 Upper Deck 204
01/2 UD Honor Roll 72
01/2 UD Mask 143
02/3 UD MVP 201
01/2 UD Premier 96
01/2 Cincinnati Mighty Ducks
02/3 Grand Rapids Griffins
99/0 Kingston Frontenacs

AWADA, GEORGE
99/0 Albany River Rats

AWALT, JASEN
01/2 Cape Breton Eagles 22

AWE, CLAY
99/0 Greensboro Generals

AWIZUS, FRANK
99/0 Eishockey 406

AWREY, DON
65/6 Coca-Cola
70/1 Dad's Cookies
70/1 Eddie Sargent 2
71/2 Eddie Sargent 13
72/3 Eddie Sargent 23
70/1 Esso Power Player
91/2 Future Trends C72 17, ✍ 17
72/3 Post 8
74/5 Loblaws
74/5 Loblaws Update
74/5 Nabisco 22
68/9 O-Pee-Chee 3
68/9 O-Pee-Chee 43
69/0 O-Pee-Chee 203
70/1 O-Pee-Chee 4
71/2 O-Pee-Chee 3
72/3 O-Pee-Chee 170
72/3 O-Pee-Chee TC
73/4 O-Pee-Chee 240
74/5 O-Pee-Chee 80
75/6 O-Pee-Chee 344
76/7 O-Pee-Chee 311
77/8 O-Pee-Chee 137
78/9 O-Pee-Chee 383
95/6 Parkie 66-67 12
94/5 Parkie Tall 19
68/9 Shirriff / Bost. 3
65/6 Topps 99
67/8 Topps 37
67/8 Topps 93
68/9 Topps 3
70/1 Topps 4
74/5 Topps 80
77/8 Topps 137
71/2 Toronto Sun Photo
70/1 BOST
71/2 BOST
98/9 BOST / Alumni 26
75/6 MONT
73/4 SLOU

AXELSON, NIKLAS
93/4 Minnesota-Duluth

AXELSSON, MAGNUS
92/3 Semic Elitserien 146

AXELSSON, PER
01/2 Heads Up ✂ JQ 3
94/5 Leaf Elit Set 248
95/6 Leaf Elit Set 204
97/8 Omega 11
98/9 Pacific 69
99/0 Pacific 18
00/1 Pacific 30
01/2 Pacific 28
02/3 Pacific Complete 182
98/9 Pa. Paramount 9
98/9 Panini Sticker 9
99/0 Panini Sticker 28
00/1 Panini Sticker 12
94/5 Parkie SE240
97/8 Pi. Be A Player 238, ✍ Aut. 238
01/2 Pr. Stock ✂ GUG 7
00/1 PS Titanium ✂ GUG 55
00/1 PS Titanium Draft ✂ 3
97/8 Upper Deck 220
99/0 UD MVP Cup 15

AXELSSON, STEFAN
94/5 Leaf Elit Set 130
95/6 Leaf Elit Set 201
89/0 Semic Elitserien 269
90/1 Semic Elitserien 33
91/2 Semic Elitserien 283
92/3 Semic Elitserien 306
95/6 UD Elitserien 206

AXINTE, DIMITRU
79 Panini Sticker 316

AYERS, VERNON
33/4 O-Pee-Chee 65
33/4 WWGum 51

AYRES, VERN
36-39 Diamond Match TT1
36-39 Diamond Match TT2
36-39 Diamond Match TT3

B

BAAKI, BILL
98/9 Huntington Blizzard
99/0 Huntington Blizzard

BABANDO, PETE
45-64 BeeHive-2 [Bost.]
45-64 BeeHive-2 [Detr.]
45-64 BeeHive-2 [Chic.]
51/2 Parkhurst 51
52/3 Parkhurst 16

BABCOCK, BOBBY
92/3 OPC Premier 56
89/0 ProCards AHL 84
90/1 ProCards 209
91/2 ProCards 569
91/2 Baltimore Skipjacks

BABCOCK, DAVID
90/1 7th..Sketch OHL 151
91/2 7th...Sketch OHL 197
91/2 Cornwall Royals
89/0 Soo Greyhounds

BABCOCK, MIKE
91/2 7th...Sketch WHL 275
01/2 Cincinnati Mighty Ducks
95/6 Spokane Chiefs 25
97/8 Spokane Chiefs

BABCOCK, SHAWN
83/4 Moncton Alpines
81/2 Kingston Canadians

BABE, WARREN
88/9 ProCards / Kalamazoo
90/1 ProCards 101
87/8 MINS
86/7 Kamloops Blazers
87/8 Kamloops Blazers

BABENKO, NIKOLAI
99/0 Mir 178
00/1 Mir 369

BABENKO, YURI
00/1 UD Black Diam. 115
01/2 Victory 367
98/9 Hershey Bears
00/1 Hershey Bears
01/2 Hershey Bears

BABER, BRAD
91/2 7th...Sketch OHL 338
93/4 Slapshot / S.S.Marie 12
93/4 Soo Greyhounds 20

BABIC, MAREK
95/6 Slapshot 286

BABIN, JEAN-FRANÇOIS
99/0 Rimouski Océanic 8
00/1 Rimouski Océanic 10

BABIN, MICHAEL
95 Panini Worlds 105
94 Semic 226
92 Semic Sticker 228
93 Semic Sticker 257

BABINOV, SERGEI
82 Semic Sticker 54
83/4 Soviet Stars

BABY, JOHN
78/9 O-Pee-Chee 366
79/0 O-Pee-Chee 357

BABYCH, DAVE
90/1 Bowman 256
92/3 Bowman 119
83/4 Esso Stars
92/3 Fleer Ultra 218
95/6 Fleer Ultra 315
83/4 Funmate Puffy 1 [w/]
84/5 Kellogg's 11
90/1 Kraft 1
94/5 Leaf 430
81/2 O-Pee-Chee 358
82/3 O-Pee-Chee 375
82/3 O-Pee-Chee 376
83/4 O-Pee-Chee 380
84/5 O-Pee-Chee 334
85/6 OPC/Topps 10
86/7 OPC/Topps 73
87/8 OPC/Topps 5
88/9 OPC/Topps 164
90/1 OPC/Topps 328
92/3 O-Pee-Chee 213
89/0 OPC/Topps 46
81/2 OPC Sticker 137
82/3 OPC/Topps Sticker 207
83/4 OPC/Topps Sticker 163
83/4 OPC/Topps Sticker 285
83/4 OPC/Topps Sticker 286
84/5 OPC Sticker 287
85/6 OPC Sticker 249-129
86/7 OPC Sticker 50
87/8 OPC Sticker 208-75
88/9 OPC Sticker 267-131
89/0 opcSticker 265-146
97/8 Pa. Invincible R-199
87/8 Panini Sticker 40
88/9 Panini Sticker 236
89/0 Panini Sticker 225
90/1 Panini Sticker 40
92/3 Panini Sticker 35
91/2 Parkhurst 187
92/3 Parkhurst 424
93/4 Parkhurst 481
80/1 Pepsi Bottle Cap
91/2 Pinnacle 270
92/3 Pinnacle 201
94/5 Pinnacle 353
97/8 Pi. Be A Player 49, ✍ Aut. 49
81/2 Post 26
82/3 Post [Winn.]
93/4 Power Play 456
93/4 Premier 428
94/5 Premier 256
90/1 Pro Set 99
91/2 Pro Set 503
92/3 Pro Set 200
90/1 Score 172
91/2 Score 34T
91/2 Score CAN 584
92/3 Score 212
97/8 Score Vanc. 20
84/5 7-Eleven
83/4 Souhaits Keychain [Jets]
83/4 Stater Mint H8
81/2 Topps 1
84/5 Topps 150
92/3 Topps 138
92/3 T. Stadium Club 120
90/1 Upper Deck 194
93/4 Upper Deck 376
95/6 UD Be A Player 94, ✍ S94
83/4 Vachon 122-2
83/4 Vachon 122-99
86/7 HART / Jr. Whalers
87/8 HART / Jr. Whalers
88/9 HART / Jr. Whalers
89/0 HART / Jr. Whalers
90/1 HART / Jr. Whalers
91/2 VANC
91/2 VANC / Photo
92/3 VANC / Road Trip
94/5 VANC
95/6 VANC / Abalene 18
96/7 VANC / IGA
80/1 WINN
81/2 WINN
82/3 WINN
83/4 WINN
84/5 WINN / Safety Tips

BABYCH, WAYNE
79/0 O-Pee-Chee 142
80/1 O-Pee-Chee 281
81/2 O-Pee-Chee 290
82/3 O-Pee-Chee 299
83/4 O-Pee-Chee 310
84/5 O-Pee-Chee 181
85/6 OPC/Topps 108
86/7 O-Pee-Chee 213
81/2 OPC Sticker 130
82/3 OPC/Topps Sticker 201
85/6 OPC Sticker 103-236
82/3 Post [SLou.]
79/0 Topps 142
81/2 Topps 114 [West]
86/7 HART / Jr. Whalers
85/6 QUÉB / Provigo
78/9 SLOU
92/3 SLOU / McDon. 10

BACA, JERGUS
96/7 APS 270, 421
96/7 DS Sticker 174
99/0 Eishockey 294
94/5 Leaf Elit Set 168, FA-9
91/2 O-Pee-Chee 131
90/1 OPC Premier 2
91/2 ProCards 94
90/1 Score 101T
94 Semic 199
89 Semic Sticker 185
92 Semic Sticker 130
92/3 Topps 64
91/2 Upper Deck 425
00/1 UD DEL 211, ✂ GJ
01/2 UD DEL 212
96 Wien 224
93/4 Milwaukee Admirals
95/6 Milwaukee Admirals

BACASHIHUA, JASON
02/3 BAP Memorabilia 399
02/3 Calder 113
02/3 Choice Prospects 4
02/3 Pacific Complete 554
02/3 Quest for the Cup 114
02/3 SP Authentic 206
02/3 SPx 188
02/3 Ultimate Memorabilia 65
02/3 UD Rookie 136

BACCARI, AL
52/3 Laval Dairy Update 10
52/3 St. Lawrence 44

BACH, RYAN
91/2 Air Canada SJHL B28
96/7 Toledo Storm

BACHO, PAVEL
98/9 OFS 76
99/0 OFS 419

BACHUSZ, MIKE
91/2 L. Superior State Lakers

BACIK, TIM
91/2 7th...Sketch OHL 331

BACKLUND, JOAKIM
89/0 Semic Elitserien 144
95/6 UD Elitserien 127
97/8 UD Elitserien 126
98/9 UD Elitserien 190

BACKLUND, PATRICK
95/6 Leaf Elit Set 282

BACKMAN, CHRISTIAN
02/3 BAP Memorabilia 331
02/3 Ultimate Memorabilia 52
02/3 UD Rookie 175
02/3 Worcester IceCats

BACKMAN, GUNNAR
70/1 Kuvajulkaisut 22

BÄCKMAN, CHRISTIAN
99/0 UD Elitserien 74, 216
00/1 UD Elitserien 62, 213, ✍ Sig.

BACKSTROM, RALPH
71/2 Bazooka Panel
45-64 BeeHive-2 [Mont.]
64-67 BeeHive-3 [Mont.]
63-65 Chex
64/5 Coke/Sprite [Mont.]
65/6 Coca-Cola
70/1 Colgate 21
71/2 Eddie Sargent 79
72/3 Eddie Sargent 88
62/3 Cowan Tile
68/9 O-Pee-Chee 60
69/0 O-Pee-Chee 166
70/1 O-Pee-Chee 54
71/2 O-Pee-Chee 108
72/3 O-Pee-Chee 131
74/5 OPC WHA 47
75/6 OPC WHA 23
76/7 OPC WHA 124
58/9 Parkhurst 16
59/0 Parkhurst 29
60/1 Parkhurst 41
60/1 Parkhurst 56
61/2 Parkhurst 39
62/3 Parkhurst 44
63/4 Parkhurst 24
63/4 Parkhurst 83
92/3 Parkhurst PR-18
93/4 Parkie 56-57 77
95/6 Parkie 66-67 64
94/5 Parkie Tall 73
68/9 Post Marble
67/8 Post Tips 11
90/1 ProCards 367
91/2 ProCards 405
60/1 Shirriff 31
61/2 Shirriff 114
62/3 Shirriff 26
68/9 Shirriff / Mont. 8
64/5 Topps 78
65/6 Topps 73
66/7 Topps 75
66/7 Topps / Test 6
67/8 Topps 67
68/9 Topps 60
70/1 Topps 54
71/2 Topps 108
72/3 Topps 133
60/1 Toronto Star Photo
59/0 Toronto Star Weekend
71/2 Toronto Sun Photo
91/2 Ultimate Original Six 7, ✍ Aut. 7
60/1 York
61/2 York 24
62/3 York Transfer 16
63/4 York 27
67/8 York 14
67/8 York 27
67/8 York 34
67/8 York
66/7 MONT / IGA Stamp
67/8 MONT
67/8 MONT / IGA Card
68/9 MONT / IGA Card
69/0 MONT / Pro Star
70/1 MONT
92/3 MONT / OPC 33

BÄCKSTRÖM, NIKLAS
98/9 Cardset 29
99/0 Cardset 218
00/1 Cardset 200, Mask. 4
02/3 Cardset 148, 160

BACON, DOUG
92/3 Wheeling Thund'birds 24

BACON, MATT
00/1 Toronto St. Mike's

BACUL, ROBIN
98/9 OFS 255
99/0 OFS 392
00/1 OFS 101
01/2 OFS 234

BADAL, ALES
94/5 APS 129

BADAWAY, CHAD
86/7 Kingston Canadians

BADDICE, JOHN
87/8 Kingston Canadians

BADDUKE, JOHN
94/5 Classic E4
90/1 7th..Sketch WHL 241
91/2 7th...Sketch WHL 49
96/7 Syracuse Crunch
89/0 Victoria Cougars

BADER, DARIN
90/1 7th..Sketch WHL 94
89/0 Saskatoon Blades
90/1 Saskatoon Blades

BADER, MIKE
94/5 DEL 431
95/6 DEL 398
96/7 DEL 303

BADER, TONI
00/1 Calgary Hitmen

BADYUKOV, ALEXEI
00/1 Mir 225

BADZGON, ERIC
88/9 Portland Winter Hawks

BAGU, BRAD
92/3 MPS SJHL 48
90/1 7th..Sketch WHL 243
91/2 7th...Sketch WHL 239

BAHENSKY, MILOSLAV
00/1 OFS 189

BAILEY, ACE
02/3 In The Game-Used ✂ VM5
02/3 Parkhurst ✂ VT18
02/3 Parkhurst ✂ NN13
02/3 Ultimate Memorabilia ✂ GAO, ✂ GMIH, ✍ Cut

BAILEY, BOB
45-64 BeeHive-2 [Toro.]
51/2 Cleveland Barons
54/5 Parkhurst 28
57/8 Topps 19

BAILEY, CHRISTINA
94/5 Classic W38

BAILEY, GARNET (ACE)
70/1 Eddie Sargent 13
72/3 Eddie Sargent 28
70/1 Esso Power Player
70/1 O-Pee-Chee 10
72/3 O-Pee-Chee 191
74/5 O-Pee-Chee 332
75/6 O-Pee-Chee 284
75/6 O-Pee-Chee 330
76/7 O-Pee-Chee 304
77/8 O-Pee-Chee 196
78/9 O-Pee-Chee 276
70/1 Topps 10
75/6 Topps 284
75/6 Topps 330
77/8 Topps 196
71/2 Toronto Sun Photo
70/1 BOST
71/2 BOST
98/9 BOST / Alumni 18

BAILEY, GREG
90/1 7th..Sketch OHL 351
91/2 7th...Sketch OHL 121
94/5 Birmingham Bulls
93/4 Huntington Blizzard

BAILEY, IRVINE (ACE)
33/4 Anonymous 3
35-40 Canada Starch
33/4 Canadian Gum
33 Goudey Sport Kings 29
33/4 Hamilton Gum 11
83 HHOF Postcard N2
83&87 HHOF 198
93/4 Legends of Hockey 32
74/5 Loblaws
32/3 Maple Leafs O'Keefe
33/4 O-Pee-Chee 13
55/6 Parkhurst 30
94/5 Parkie Tall 1
01/2 Ultimate Mem. ✂ Corn., ✂ Gloves
33/4 WWGum 22

BAILEY, JOHN
69 Columbus Checkers

BAILEY, REID
82/3 Post [Phil.]

BAILEY, SCOTT
95/6 Bowman 158
95/6 Edge Ice 58
95/6 Parkhurst 524
96/7 Pinnacle 215
96/7 Pi. Zenith 143
91 7th..Sketch Mem.Cup 73
90/1 7th..Sketch WHL 202
91/2 7th...Sketch WHL 4
99/0 Charlotte Checkers
00/1 Charlotte Checkers
98/9 Orlando Solar Bears Geico

BAILLARGEON, JASON
89/0 Halifax Citadels

BAILLARGEON, JOEL
88/9 ProCards / Halifax
89/0 ProCards AHL 178
88/9 QUÉB
88/9 QUÉB / Gene. Foods
87/8 Moncton Hawks
86/7 Sherb. Canadiens 4

BAIN, CHRIS
01/2 London Knights

BAIN, DONALD
83 HHOF Postcard B1
83&87 HHOF 227

BAIN, JOEL
87/8 Hull Olympiques

BAINES, AJAY
99 Bowman 103
01/2 Norfolk Admirals
96/7 Kamloops Blazers
97/8 Kamloops Blazers
98/9 Kamloops Blazers

BAIRD, BOB
94/5 Slapshot / Brantford 21

BAIRD, KEN
75/6 OPC WHA 37
77/8 OPC WHA 46

BAIRD, MARK
91/2 Air Canada SJHL B11

BAJURNY, MIKE
96/7 Dayton Ice Bandits
99/0 San Angelo Outlaws

BAKER, AARON
95/6 Tri-City Americans 23

BAKER, BILL
83/4 O-Pee-Chee 240
82/3 Post [SLou.]
94/5 SR Miracle 1,2, ✍ 1,2
80/1 MONT

BAKER, BRUCE
77/8 Nova Scotia Voyageurs

BAKER, DARIN
88/9 ProCards / Kalamazoo

BAKER, HOBEY
83 HHOF Postcard B2
83&87 HHOF 17
92/3 Legends 6

BAKER, JACK
02/3 Philadelphia Phantoms

BAKER, JAMIE
91/2 Bowman 136
92/3 Bowman 436
93/4 EA Sports 93
92/3 Fleer Ultra 360
93/4 Fleer Ultra 6
93/4 Leaf 134
94/5 Leaf 421
92/3 O-Pee-Chee 41
97/8 Pa. Invincible R-190
93/4 Panini Sticker 113
92/3 Parkhurst 353
93/4 Parkhurst 459
91/2 Pinnacle 348
93/4 Pinnacle 378
94/5 Pinnacle 502
96/7 Pi. Be A Player 17, ✍ Aut. 17
96/7 Pi. Summit 74
95/6 Playoff 301
96/7 Playoff 402
95/6 POG 232
93/4 Premier 22
89/0 ProCards AHL 156
90/1 ProCards 449
91/2 ProCards 541
93/4 Score 546
93/4 Score 57
97/8 Score Toro. 19
92/3 Topps 506
92/3 T. Stadium Club 136
93/4 To. Stadium 461
94/5 T. Stadium Club 249
92/3 Upper Deck 130
92/3 Upper Deck 464
94/5 Upper Deck 439
92/3 OTTA
92/3 SANJ / Pacific Bell
98/9 Chicago Wolves Champs
89/0 Halifax Citadels
90/1 Halifax Citadels

BAKER, KEVIN
00/1 Lowell Lock Monsters

BAKER, KORY
00/1 Val d'Or Foreurs 9

BAKER, STEVE
80/1 O-Pee-Chee 346
81/2 O-Pee-Chee 231

BAKER, TREVOR
99/0 Peoria Rivermen
00/1 Peoria Rivermen
01/2 Peoria Rivermen
02/3 Peoria Rivermen

BAKHMUTOV, IGOR
99/0 Mir 98
00/1 Mir 298

BAKOGEORGE, TROY
86/7 Regina Pats

BAKOS, MICHAEL
96/7 DEL 10
98/9 DEL 282, 335
99/0 Eishockey 161

BAKOVIC, PETER
89/0 ProCards IHL 168
90/1 ProCards 330
91/2 ProCards 596
93/4 Milwaukee Admirals
94/5 Milwaukee Admirals
95/6 Milwaukee Admirals
96/7 Milwaukee Admirals
97/8 Milwaukee Admirals

BAKOVIC, PETER G.
85/6 Moncton G'Flames
86/7 Moncton G'Flames

BAKOVIC, PETER*
83/4 Kitchener Rangers

BAKRLIK, FRANTISEK
01 UD Prospects GU 38, ✂ TPJ

BAKULA, MARTIN
95/6 APS 110
96/7 APS 102
97/8 APS 154
93/4 Cla. Prospects 158
97/8 DS 75
98/9 DS 70
99/0 DS 118
96/7 DS Sticker 267
97/8 DS Sticker 192
98/9 OFS 213
99/0 OFS 42
94/5 Cape Breton Oilers

BAKUS, OLDRICH
99/0 Score 161

BAL, JAG
91/2 Avant Garde BCJHL 144
92/3 BCJHL 37

BALA, CHRIS
01/2 BAP Memor. 410
02/3 Pacific 262
01/2 Parkhurst 331
92 Québec Pee Wee 1120
02/3 Upper Deck 216
01/2 UD Mask 157
02/3 UD MVP 212
01/2 Grand Rapids Griffins

BALAN, SCOTTY
00/1 Saskatoon Blades

BALASESCU, GABRIEL
00/1 Rimouski Océanic 16
01/2 Rimouski Océanic 15

BALASTIK, JAROSLAV
00/1 DS 57
98/9 OFS 278
99/0 OFS 207
01/2 OFS 95

BALAZ, RADOSLAV
91/2 7th...Sketch LHJMQ 196

BALAZS, DAVID
94/5 APS 227
95/6 APS 162
96/7 APS 184
97/8 APS 94
99/0 OFS 147
01/2 OFS 197

BALCOMBE, DARREN
92/3 MPS SJHL 59

BALDERIS, HELMUT
92/3 Future Trends C76 130
79 Panini Sticker 152
82 Semic Sticker 70
79/0 Soviet Stars 20
83/4 Soviet Stars
77-79 Sports. FIN 47-1113

BALDRIS, MIGUEL
84/5 Richelieu Riverains

BALDWIN, DOUG
45-54 Quaker Oats

BALEJ, JOSEF
00/1 UD Prospects 72

BALEJ, JOZEF
02/3 Hamilton Bulldogs

BALES, BOB
81/2 Victoria Cougars

BALES, MIKE
92/3 Classic 73
93/4 Classic 126
93/4 Cla. 4 Sport 230
95/6 Parkhurst 419
95/6 OTTA
98/9 Michigan K-Wings
99/0 Michigan K-Wings
97/8 Rochester Americans
00/1 Utah Grizzlies
01/2 Belfast Giants
01/2 Belfast Giants

BALFOUR, EARL
45-64 BeeHive-2 [Toro.]
45-64 BeeHive-2 [Chic.]
54/5 Parkhurst 25
60/1 Shirriff 68
58/9 Topps 37
59/0 Topps 50
61/2 Topps 3
61/2 Topps 21

BALFOUR, MURRAY
45-64 BeeHive-2 [Chic.]
64-67 BeeHive-3 [Bost.]
64/5 Coke/Sprite [Bost.]
62/3 Cowan Tile
94/5 Parkie Tall 17
60/1 Shirriff 65
61/2 Shirriff 30
59/0 Topps 33
60/1 Topps 12
61/2 Topps 33
61/2 Topps - Stamp
62/3 Topps 36
63/4 Topps 35
64/5 Topps 90

BALKOVEC, MACO
92/3 BCJHL 236

BALL, DOUG
84/5 Medicine Hat Tigers

BALL, MATT
93/4 Slapshot / Detroit 8
94/5 Slapshot / Detroit Jr. 7
95/6 Slapshot 66
94/5 Slapshot Memorial 81

BALL, TERRY
78/9 SM-Liiga 28
72/3 Minn. Fight. Saints

BALLANTYNE, PAUL
02/3 Grand Rapids Griffins

BALLARD, HAROLD
83 HHOF Postcard E2
83&87 HHOF 63
78/9 TORO
79/0 TORO
80/1 TORO
81/2 TORO
81/2 TORO
82/3 TORO
85/6 TORO
87/8 TORO / P.L.A.Y. 4
88/9 TORO / P.L.A.Y. 13

BALLEUX, MARTIN
90/1 7th..Sketch LHJMQ 63
91/2 7th...Sketch LHJMQ 37

BALLMAN, BRIAN
99/0 Lethbridge Hurricanes

BALMIN, DMITRI
98/9 Mir 123
99/0 Mir 53
00/1 Mir 35

BALMOCHNYKH, MAXIM
99/0 BAP Mem. 362
00/1 BAP Mem. 180
00/1 Pacific 1
00/1 Pa. Paramount 2
00/1 Premier Plus ✂ GP
00/1 Topps 284
00/1 To. Chrome 179
98/9 UD Choice 283
97/8 UD Black Diam. 47
00/1 UD MVP 7
00/1 Victory 272
99/0 Cincinnati M'Ducks
01/2 Cincinnati Mighty Ducks

BALOG, TYSON
91/2 Air Canada SJHL A3
92/3 MPS SJHL 143

BALOGH, JANOS
79 Panini Sticker 267

BALON, DAVE
45-64 BeeHive-2 [NYRa.]
45-64 BeeHive-2 [Mont.]
64-67 BeeHive-3 [Mont.]
63-65 Chex
64/5 Coke/Sprite [Mont. #20]
70/1 Colgate 33
70/1 Eddie Sargent 119
71/2 Eddie Sargent 125
72/3 Eddie Sargent 220
70/1 Esso Power Player
62/3 Cowan Tile
68/9 O-Pee-Chee 169
69/0 O-Pee-Chee 191
70/1 O-Pee-Chee 61
71/2 O-Pee-Chee 229
72/3 O-Pee-Chee 162
63/4 Parkhurst 38
63/4 Parkhurst 97
95/6 Parkie 66-67 62
94/5 Parkie Tall 68
60/1 Shirriff 94
68/9 Shirriff / NYRa. 15
62/3 Topps 56
62/3 Topps Dollar
64/5 Topps 37
65/6 Topps 72
66/7 Topps 74
70/1 Topps 61
72/3 Topps 117
64/5 Toronto Star Action
63/4 Toronto Star Weekend
71/2 Toronto Sun Photo
63/4 York 33
67/8 MONT
72/3 VANC / Royal Bank

BALSHIN, BRAD
83/4 Kitchener Rangers

BALTIMORE, BYRON
75/6 OPC WHA 9
88/9 EDMO / Action 138

BALUCH, TOMAS
99/0 Missouri RiverOtters

BAMBERGER, J.J.
91/2 Ferris State Bulldogs

BANCROFT, STEVE
92/3 Classic Prospects 48
90/1 ProCards 159
91/2 ProCards 49
89/0 7th..Sketch OHL 85
01/2 UD Ice 148
99/0 Cincinnati Cyclones
01/2 Cleveland Barons
93/4 Cleveland Lumberjacks
94/5 Fort Wayne Komets 15
92/3 Indianapolis Ice
00/1 Kentucky Tho'blades
97/8 Las Vegas Thunder 7
98/9 Providence Bruins
02/3 Worcester IceCats

BANDURA, JEFF
79/0 VANC / Royal Bank

BANHAM, FRANK
00/1 Cardset 130
02/3 Cardset 4
97/8 Donruss 203
98/9 Pacific 43
98/9 Cincinnati M'Ducks 7
99/0 Cincinnati M'Ducks
93/4 Saskatoon Blades
93/4 Saskatoon Blades

BANIKA, CORY
90 7th..Sketch Mem.Cup 87
89/0 7th..Sketch OHL 17
93/4 Johnstown Chiefs 17
98/9 Muskegon Fury
89/0 Oshawa Generals

BANKOSKE, DAVE
94/5 Toledo Storm

BANKS, DARREN
92/3 OPC Premier 118
93/4 Parkhurst 286
90/1 ProCards 622
91/2 ProCards 582
96/7 Detroit Vipers
97/8 Detroit Vipers
98/9 Detroit Vipers

BANNAN, MATT
00/1 Toronto St. Mike's

BANNERMAN, MURRAY
01/2 BT Pipes -Mask
81/2 O-Pee-Chee 68
82/3 O-Pee-Chee 61
83/4 O-Pee-Chee 97
84/5 O-Pee-Chee 32
85/6 OPC/Topps 27
86/7 OPC/Topps 180
83/4 OPC/Topps Sticker 113
83/4 OPC/Topps Sticker 164
84/5 OPC Sticker 32
84/5 OPC Sticker 135
85/6 OPC Sticker 27-155
89/0 opcSticker 124
87/8 Panini Sticker 218
87/8 Panini Sticker 221
84/5 Topps 27
80/1 CHIC / Colour
80/1 CHIC / Brown
81/2 CHIC
82/3 CHIC
83/4 CHIC
86/7 CHIC / Coke
87/8 CHIC / Coke
83/4 Victoria Cougars

BANNISTER, DARIN
90/1 ProCards 298
91/2 ProCards 136

BANNISTER, DREW
95/6 Bowman 104
02/3 Cardset 155
94/5 Classic 64
93/4 Donruss CAN3
95/6 Edge Ice 99
95/6 Parkhurst 467
93/4 Pinnacle 460
96/7 Pi. Be A Player 219, ✍ Aut. 219
90/1 7th..Sketch OHL 152
91/2 7th...Sketch OHL 327
93/4 Slapshot / S.S.Marie 6
97/8 UD Coll. Choice 94
97/8 EDMO
94/5 Atlanta Knights 5
95/6 Atlanta Knights
01/2 Cincinnati Mighty Ducks
99/0 Hartford Wolf Pack
00/1 Hartford Wolf Pack
98/9 Las Vegas Thunder
93/4 Soo Greyhounds 6

BANVILLE, GILLES
65/6 Québec Aces

BARADA, STANISLAV
99/0 OFS 460

BARAHONA, RALPH
90/1 ProCards 132
91/2 Upper Deck 496
92/3 Cincinnati Cyclones
92/3 Fort Wayne Komets 2
93/4 Raleigh Icecaps

BARANOV, ALEXEI
99/0 Mir 230

BARANOV, ROMAN
98/9 Mir 119
99/0 Mir 105

BARARUK, DAVID
01/2 Moose Jaw Warriors 16
02/3 Moose Jaw Warriors

BARBE, MARLO
88/9 ProCards / Cape Breton
89/0 ProCards AHL 132
90/1 ProCards 228
84/5 Chicoutimi Saguenéens

BARBER, BILL
01/2 Fleer Greats 38, ✍ Aut.
83/4 Funmate Puffy 9 [w/]
92/3 Future Trends C76 169
75/6 Hockey Heroes
93/4 Hockey Wit 13
95/6 Legends of Hockey 55
74/5 Lipton Soup 31
74/5 Loblaws
82/3 McDonald's Les Étoiles 11
73/4 O-Pee-Chee 81
74/5 O-Pee-Chee 8
75/6 O-Pee-Chee 226
76/7 O-Pee-Chee 178
76/7 O-Pee-Chee 215
76/7 OPC 391
77/8 O-Pee-Chee 227
78/9 OPC 69
78/9 O-Pee-Chee 176
79/0 O-Pee-Chee 140
80/1 O-Pee-Chee 200
81/2 O-Pee-Chee 238
81/2 O-Pee-Chee 247
81/2 O-Pee-Chee 253
82/3 O-Pee-Chee 244
82/3 O-Pee-Chee 246
82/3 O-Pee-Chee 247
83/4 O-Pee-Chee 260
84/5 O-Pee-Chee 156
81/2 OPC Sticker 155
81/2 OPC Sticker 174
82/3 OPC/Topps Sticker 110
82/3 OPC/Topps Sticker 170
83/4 OPC/Topps Sticker 5
83/4 OPC/Topps Sticker 194
92/3 Parkhurst 469
01/2 Parkhurst ✍ PA53
02/3 Parkhurst ✂ VT12
82/3 Post [Phil.]
90/1 Score 356
83/4 Souhaits Keychain [Flyers]
73/4 Topps 81
74/5 Topps 8
75/6 Topps 226
76/7 Topps 178
76/7 Topps 215
76/7 Topps NS 12
77/8 Topps 227
78/9 Topps 69
78/9 Topps 176
79/0 Topps 140
80/1 Topps 200
81/2 Topps 2
81/2 Topps 59
81/2 Topps 123 [East]
01/2 Ultimate Mem. ✂ RN, ✂ RT, ✂ SCD
02/3 Ultimate Memorabilia ✂ VGJ
01/2 UD Legends 55, ✂ M, ✂ TT
83/4 PHIL / J.C. Penney
86/7 PHIL

BARBER, DON
90/1 Bowman 179
90/1 OPC/Topps 53
90/1 Panini Sticker 259
90/1 Pro Set 558
91/2 Pro Set 464
90/1 Score 284, 14T
90/1 Upper Deck 28
91/2 QUÉB / Petro-Canada
90/1 WINN / IGA

BARBER, GREG
81/2 Victoria Cougars

BARBIERI, PATRICK
01/2 London Knights

BARCH, KRYS
00/1 Portland Pirates

BAREK, MARTIN
99/0 OFS 87
00/1 OFS 33

BARICA, DUSAN
99/0 Score 153

BARIL, TONY
24/5 Selkirks Crescent 3

BARILKO, BILL
45-64 BeeHive-2 [Toro.]
48-52 Exhibits [Maple Leafs]
51/2 Parkhurst 52
93/4 Parkhurst PR35
02/3 Parkie - Reprint 157
91/2 Pro Set 340
45-54 Quaker Oats
02/3 Ultimate Memorabilia ✂ BOS, ✂ GMIH, ✍ Cut

BARIN, STÉPHANE
98/9 DEL 38
99/0 Eishockey 140
94 Panini Olympics 327
94 Semic 228
92 Semic Sticker 229
93 Semic Sticker 258
00/1 UD DEL 235
01/2 UD DEL 152
96 Wien 191

BARKER, BRIAN
95/6 Slapshot 20
93/4 N. Michigan Wildcats

BARKER, ELDON
92/3 MPS SJHL 93

BARKER, RANDY
92/3 BCJHL 223

BARKLEY, DOUG
45-64 BeeHive-2 [Detr.]
45-64 BeeHive-2 [Detr.]
64-67 BeeHive-3 [Detr.]
64/5 Coke/Sprite [Detr.]
65/6 Coca-Cola
62/3 Cowan Tile
63/4 Parkhurst 60

94/5 Parkie Tall 49
64/5 Topps 9
65/6 Topps 43
62/3 York Transfer 24
63/4 York 46
76 DETR

BARKLUND, NIKLAS
91/2 7th...Sketch WHL 231

BARKOV, ALEXANDER
98/9 Cardset 219
99/0 Cardset 125, 174
00/1 Cardset 335
02/3 Cardset 156
97/8 Hockey-Box
92/3 Red Ace Violet 1
94/5 Sisu 215
95/6 Sisu 117, 368
96/7 Sisu 132
95/6 Sisu Limited 80

BARKOVICH, RICK
88/9 ProCards / Indianapolis
89/0 ProCards IHL 193
90/1 ProCards 588
90/1 Kansas City Blades
93/4 Raleigh Icecaps
94/5 Raleigh Icecaps
88/9 Salt Lake G'Eagles

BARKUNOV, ALEXANDER
00/1 Mir 308

BARLIE,
92/3 Semic Nordisk 203 [Draften Av NHL]

BARLIE, VEGAR
94 Semic 267
92/3 Semic Nordisk 93

BARLOW, BOB
70/1 Eddie Sargent 93
69/0 O-Pee-Chee 196
70/1 O-Pee-Chee 45
70/1 Topps 45

BARLOW, HUGH
52/3 Anonymous 33

BARNABY, MATTHEW
98/9 Aurora 15
99/0 Aurora 114
98/9 Be A Player 14, ✍ Aut. 14
99/0 BAP Mem. 74
01/2 BAP Memor. 475
01/2 BAP Update ✂ TC14, ✂ TC38
93/4 Cla. Prospects 179
93/4 Donruss 42
94/5 Donruss 289
95/6 Donruss 383
96/7 Donruss 152
97/8 Donruss 170
97/8 Do. Canadian 84
98/9 Dynagon Ice 16
99/0 Dynagon Ice 157, -CM 13
93/4 Fleer Ultra 13
01/2 Heads Up ✂ JQ 27
93/4 Leaf 362
94/5 Leaf 285
97/8 Limited 68
01/2 O-Pee-Chee 143
98/9 OPC Chrome 213
98/9 Omega 20
98/9 Pacific 36
99/0 Pacific 333
00/1 Pacific 325
01/2 Pacific 349, 422
02/3 Pacific 246
02/3 Pacific Complete 293
97/8 Pacific CC 210
98/9 Pa. Crown Roy. 11
97/8 Pa. Paramount 17
98/9 Pa. Paramount 17
99/0 Pa. Paramount 186
00/1 Pa. Paramount 196
97/8 Pa. Revolution 12
98/9 Pa. Revolution 12, -TPA 1
96/7 Panini Sticker 20
99/0 Panini Sticker 140
92/3 Parkhurst 483
93/4 Parkhurst 296
01/2 Parkhurst 389
93/4 Pinnacle 216
97/8 Pinnacle 108
96/7 Pi. Be A Player 147, ✍ Aut. 147
97/8 Pi. Inside 176
93/4 Premier 346
00/1 PS Titanium ✂ GUG 143
96/7 Score 188
97/8 Score 216
97/8 Score Buff. 5
91/2 7th...Sketch LHJMQ 189
98/9 SP Authentic ✍ SotT
99/0 SPx 125
98/9 SPx Finite 11
98/9 Topps 213
99/0 Topps 131
00/1 Topps 39
01/2 Topps 143
99/0 To. Chrome 131
00/1 To. Heritage 167
93/4 To. Stadium 321
93/4 Upper Deck 439, SP-13
95/6 Upper Deck 341
97/8 Upper Deck 16, 393
98/9 Upper Deck 228
99/0 Upper Deck 107
00/1 Upper Deck 141
01/2 Upper Deck 160
02/3 Upper Deck 359
96/7 UD CC 33
97/8 UD Coll. Choice 27
98/9 UD G. Reserve 228
99/0 UD G. Reserve 107
98/9 UD MVP 22
99/0 UD MVP 171
00/1 UD MVP 146
01/2 UD Vintage 266
02/3 UD Vintage 169
99/0 Victory 236
00/1 Victory 185
01/2 Victory 323

BARNES, BLAIR
83/4 Nova Scotia Voyageurs

BARNES, BRIAN
91/2 Avant Garde BCJHL 102
92/3 BCJHL 121
97/8 New Mexico Scorpions

BARNES, JAMIE
90/1 7th..Sketch WHL 303
91/2 7th...Sketch WHL 293

BARNES, NORM
80/1 O-Pee-Chee 308
81/2 OPC Sticker 67

BARNES, ROBERT
78/9 SM-Liiga 72

BARNES, RYAN
01/2 Cincinnati Mighty Ducks
02/3 Grand Rapids Griffins
98/9 Barrie Colts

BARNES, STEVE
94/5 Huntington Blizzard
91/2 L. Superior State Lakers

BARNES, STU
01/2 Adrenaline 18
98/9 Aurora 151
98/9 Be A Player 114, ✍ Aut. 114
99/0 BAP Mem. 128
00/1 BAP Mem. 393
01/2 BAP Memor. 158
02/3 BAP Memorabilia 119
92/3 Bowman 26
01/2 Bowman 84
02/3 Bowman 81
90/1 Canada Nationals 10
00/1 Crown Royale ✂ JR 1
01/2 Crown Royale 14
93/4 Donruss 377
93/4 Donruss 432
94/5 Donruss 306
95/6 Donruss 132
96/7 Donruss 68
99/0 Dynagon Ice 27
94/5 Fleer 76
95/6 Fleer Metal 58
94/5 Fleer Ultra 78
95/6 Fleer Ultra 59
01/2 Heads Up ✂ JQ 4
99/0 Kraft / PB
93/4 Leaf 350
94/5 Leaf 73
95/6 Leaf 36
96/7 Leaf 30
98/9 NHL Power Play
92/3 O-Pee-Chee 39
01/2 O-Pee-Chee 153
02/3 O-Pee-Chee 237
98/9 OPC Chrome 98
91/2 OPC Premier 109
97/8 Omega 181
98/9 Omega 193
98/9 Pacific 348
99/0 Pacific 33
00/1 Pacific 47
01/2 Pacific 45
02/3 Pacific 37
02/3 Pacific Complete 86
97/8 Pacific CC 175
98/9 Pa. Paramount 189
99/0 Pa. Paramount 25
00/1 Pa. Paramount 25
97/8 Pa. Revolution 110
98/9 Pa. Revolution 116
98/9 Panini Photocard
95/6 Panini Sticker 69
99/0 Panini Sticker 40
91/2 Parkhurst 419
93/4 Parkhurst 226
95/6 Parkhurst 86
00/1 Parkhurst P-211
01/2 Parkhurst 179
02/3 Parkhurst Retro 80
94/5 Parkie SE66
91/2 Pinnacle 319
93/4 Pinnacle 426
94/5 Pinnacle 47
95/6 Pinnacle 40
96/7 Pinnacle 135
95/6 Pi. Summit 47
96/7 Pi. Summit 131
95/6 Playoff 152
94/5 POG 104
95/6 POG 115
93/4 Power Play 345
93/4 Premier 351
94/5 Premier 458
01/2 Pr. Stock -PS 6, ✂ GUG 9
00/1 PS Titanium ✂ GUG 58
01/2 PS Titanium 12
00/1 PS Titanium Draft ✂ 10
91/2 Pro Set 566
91/2 Pro Set Platinum 273
90/1 Score 391
91/2 Score 80T
91/2 Score CAN 630
92/3 Score 319
93/4 Score 380
93/4 Score 644
94/5 Score 138
95/6 Score 22
96/7 Score 180
97/8 Score 237
97/8 Score Pitt. 9
00/1 Signature 118, ✍ Aut. 182
02/3 Signature Series 74, ✍ 74
95/6 SBx Emotion 68
95/6 SBx Impact 66
94/5 SP 43
02/3 Sports Vault 23
98/9 SPx Finite 69
95/6 Super Sticker 48
92/3 Topps 210
95/6 Topps 110
98/9 Topps 98
00/1 Topps 122
01/2 Topps 153
02/3 Topps 237
01/2 To. Chrome 116
02/3 T. Chrome 130
94/5 Topps Finest 66
95/6 To. Finest 68
98/9 To. Finest 131
98/9 T. Gold Label 52
02/3 To. Heritage 81
02/3 T. Limited 237
92/3 T. Stadium Club 285
94/5 T. Stadium Club 261
95/6 To. Stadium 73
95/6 T. Super Skills 38
02/3 T. Total 78
98/9 UD Choice 167
01/2 UD PlayMakers Ltd 12
91/2 Upper Deck 53
92/3 Upper Deck 426
93/4 Upper Deck 94
94/5 Upper Deck 493
95/6 Upper Deck 345, SE-33
96/7 Upper Deck 64
98/9 Upper Deck 347
00/1 Upper Deck 249
01/2 Upper Deck 21
02/3 Upper Deck 263
95/6 UD Be A Player 127, ✍ S127
95/6 UD CC 209
96/7 UD CC 110
97/8 UD Coll. Choice 212
98/9 UD G. Reserve 347
02/3 UD Honor 74
01/2 UD Mask 11
98/9 UD MVP 167
99/0 UD MVP W25
00/1 UD MVP 22
01/2 UD MVP 18
02/3 UD MVP 19
00/1 UD Vintage 40
02/3 UD Vintage 27, 264
01/2 Victory 41
02/3 Victory 25
99/0 WGretzky 24
94/5 FLOR / Health Plan
89/0 WINN / Safeway
91/2 WINN / IGA
93/4 WINN / Ruffles
93/4 WINN Readers

BARNETT, BRETT
89/0 ProCards IHL 92
90/1 ProCards 107
93/4 Birmingham Bulls

BARNEY, SCOTT
99 Bowman 123, 164
97 Bowman 150, BB14, ✍ Aut.
98 Bowman 39
98 Bowman Chrome 39
95/6 Slapshot 328
96/7 Upper Deck 379
96/7 UD Black Diam. 14
97/8 UD Coll. Choice 310
02/3 Manchester Monarchs

BARNHARDT, MATT
98/9 Sudbury Wolves 8

BARNSTABLE, SCOTT
90/1 7th..Sketch WHL 153

BARON, MARCO
88/9 EDMO / Action 156
83/4 Moncton Alpines

BARON, MURRAY
91/2 Bowman 243
92/3 Bowman 409
93/4 Fleer Ultra 407
91/2 O-Pee-Chee 373
01/2 Pacific 376
97/8 Pa. Dynagon BKS-73
91/2 Pinnacle 204
92/3 Pinnacle 144
91/2 Pro Set 472
89/0 ProCards AHL 334
90/1 ProCards 35
90/1 Score 399
91/2 Score 183
91/2 Score 66T
91/2 Score CAN 183
91/2 Score CAN 616
92/3 Score 176
93/4 Score 294
91/2 Score Young Stars 27
99/0 Stadium 68
92/3 Topps 354
91/2 To. Stadium 334
92/3 T. Stadium Club 194
94/5 T. Stadium Club 168
90/1 Upper Deck 275
91/2 Upper Deck 497
96/7 Upper Deck 143, 198
95/6 UD Be A Player 158, ✍ S158
00/1 UD Vintage 352
96/7 MONT
90/1 PHIL
97/8 PHOE / Coca-Cola
91/2 SLOU
01/2 VANC / Coke

BARON, NORMAND
83/4 Nova Scotia Voyageurs

BAROZZINO, DAVID
96/7 Pensacola Ice Pilots

BARR, DAVE
90/1 Bowman 231
91/2 Bowman 49
86/7 O-Pee-Chee 237
90/1 OPC/Topps 308
91/2 O-Pee-Chee 147
89/0 OPC/Topps 13
91/2 OPC Premier 54
89/0 opcSticker 250-113
89/0 Panini Sticker 60
93/4 Power Play 320
90/1 Pro Set 65
91/2 Pro Set 65
91/2 Score 187
91/2 Score 47T
91/2 Score CAN 187
91/2 Score CAN 597
92/3 Score 315
92/3 Topps 197
91/2 To. Stadium 141
92/3 T. Stadium Club 291
90/1 Upper Deck 257
94/5 DALL / Cap
86/7 DETR / Little Caesars
87/8 DETR / Little Caesars
88/9 DETR / Little Caesars
89/0 DETR / Little Caesars
90/1 DETR / Little Caesars
99/0 Houston Aeros

BARR, DON
92/3 BCJHL 4
92/3 BCJHL 18

BARRASSO, TOM
02/3 Atomic -NPU 10, ✂ GWJ 22
98/9 Aurora 152, -CF 39
99/0 Aurora 115
99/0 BAP Mem. 77
00/1 BAP Mem. ✂ V-15
01/2 BAP Memor. 493
01/2 BT Pipes 78, 116
02/3 Between the Pipes 69, ✂ GN10
98/9 Bicycle Sports Q-S
90/1 Bowman 209
91/2 Bowman 80
92/3 Bowman 250
95/6 Bowman 47
01/2 Bowman 100
98/9 Bowman's Best 56
99/0 Crown Royale 111
93/4 Donruss 260
94/5 Donruss 208
95/6 Donruss 291
96/7 Donruss 67
96/7 Do. Canadian 70
96/7 Do. Elite 63
97/8 Do. Priority 139, PG-17
98/9 Dynagon Ice 148
99/0 Dynagon Ice 158
93/4 EA Sports 108
94/5 Flair 133
96/7 Fleer 84
95/6 Fleer Metal 115
92/3 Fleer Ultra 162
93/4 Fleer Ultra 26
94/5 Fleer Ultra 162
x95/6 Fleer Ultra 364
96/7 Fl. Ultra 138
88/9 Frito Lay
95 Globe 102
93/4 High Liner 6
93/4 Hockey Wit 25
92/3 Kraft / PB
93/4 Kraft / JELL-O
94/5 Kraft / KD
95/6 Kraft / PS
93/4 Leaf 196
93/4 Leaf GLAS 5
93/4 Leaf PW 9
94/5 Leaf 103
96/7 Leaf 26
96/7 L. Preferred 46, LS-27
96/7 Maggers 122
96/7 Metal Univ. 124
98/9 NHL Power Play
84/5 O-Pee-Chee 18
84/5 O-Pee-Chee 212
84/5 O-Pee-Chee 375
84/5 O-Pee-Chee 379
85/6 OPC/Topps 105
85/6 O-Pee-Chee 263
86/7 OPC/Topps 91
87/8 OPC/Topps 78
88/9 OPC/Topps 107
90/1 OPC/Topps 65
91/2 O-Pee-Chee 372
91/2 O-Pee-Chee 402
92/3 O-Pee-Chee 340
02/3 O-Pee-Chee 66
89/0 OPC/Topps 36
98/9 OPC Chrome 209,SB6
91/2 OPC Premier 103
88/9 OPC Stars 1
84/5 OPC Sticker 205
x84/5 OPC Sticker 206
x84/5 OPC Sticker 227-226
x84/5 OPC Sticker 228-229
85/6 OPC Sticker 114
85/6 OPC Sticker 179
85/6 OPC Sticker 189-62
85/6 OPC Sticker 55-203
86/7 OPC Sticker 62
86/7 OPC Sticker 45-186
87/8 OPC Sticker 148
88/9 OPC Sticker 259-127
89/0 opcSticker 235-98
97/8 Omega 182
98/9 Omega 194
98/9 Pacific 35, -GCDC 28
99/0 Pacific 334, ITCNF-16
00/1 Pacific 275
02/3 Pacific 357
97/8 Pa. Crown Roy. 108, FO-16
98/9 Pa. Crown Roy. 108
97/8 Pa. Invincible R-157
97/8 Pa. Paramount 147, GSL-17
98/9 Pa. Paramount 190, -GS 16
99/0 Pa. Paramount 187, GS-17
97/8 Pa. Revolution 111, RTS-16
98/9 Pa. Revolution 117
98/9 Panini Photocard
87/8 Panini Sticker 22
88/9 Panini Sticker 219
89/0 Panini Sticker 312, 313
90/1 Panini Sticker 134
91/2 Panini Sticker 271
92/3 Panini Sticker 219
93/4 Panini Sticker 141
93/4 Panini Sticker 88
94/5 Panini Sticker 81
96/7 Panini Sticker 60
98/9 Panini Sticker 51
99/0 Panini Sticker 137
91/2 Parkhurst 139
92/3 Parkhurst 134
93/4 Parkhurst 157
94/5 Parkhurst 182
95/6 Parkhurst 435
01/2 Parkhurst 213, 397
91/2 Pinnacle 44
92/3 Pinnacle 298
93/4 Pinnacle 3
93/4 Pinnacle TP 7
94/5 Pinnacle 20, GT-17
95/6 Pinnacle 97
96/7 Pinnacle 95
97/8 Pinnacle 76
97/8 Pi. Inside SU-1
95/6 Pi. Summit 88
96/7 Pi. Summit 93
95/6 Pi. Zenith 90
96/7 Pi. Zenith 98
94/5 POG 291
95/6 POG 221
93/4 Power Play 187
93/4 Power Play Netm. 1
93/4 Premier 175
93/4 Premier 204
93/4 Premier 446
93/4 Premier 501
93/4 Prmr. - BG-OPC 9
93/4 Prmr. - BG-Top. 11
94/5 Premier 84, 206, 311
01/2 PS Titanium 23, TSS 2, ✂ DSJ 44, ✂ DSJ 59
01/2 PS Titanium Draft ✂ 89
90/1 Pro Set 227
91/2 Pro Set 186
92/3 Pro Set 145
91/2 Pro Set Platinum 96
91/2 Pro Set Platinum PC3
90/1 Pro Set PotM P1
91/2 Puck / Pro Set 22
99/0 Revolution 116, / CSC 116
90/1 Score 121
91/2 Score 225
91/2 Score CAN 225
92/3 Score 70
92/3 Score 518
93/4 Score 225
93/4 Score 483
93/4 Score DT 1
94/5 Score 31
95/6 Score 152
96/7 Score 124, NW-12, SD-10
97/8 Score 17
97/8 Score Pitt. 1
92/3 Seasons 36
94/5 Select 88
95/6 Select CE 95
95 Semic 215
89 Semic Sticker 153
93 Semic Sticker 169
84/5 7-Eleven
85/6 7-Eleven Superstars 2
96/7 SBx Impact 99
95/6 SP 119
91/2 SI For Kids 9
98/9 SPx Finite 70
99/0 Stadium 99, GC7
94/5 Starting Lineup
95/6 SLU
96/7 SLU
84/5 Topps 14
84/5 Topps 158
85/6 OPC/Topps-Stick. 12
92/3 Topps 503
95/6 Topps 262
98/9 Topps 209, SB6
99/0 Topps 169
00/1 Topps 151
02/3 Topps 66
99/0 To. Chrome 169
94/5 Topps Finest RL-19
95/6 To. Finest 129
98/9 To. Finest 142
98/9 T. Gold Label 78
02/3 T. Limited 66
91/2 To. Stadium 155
92/3 T. Stadium Club 416
93/4 To. Stadium 79, -MP
94/5 T. Stadium Club DAD 1
95/6 To. Stadium 158, M6
95/6 T. Super Skills 79
98/9 UD Choice 165, 250
00/1 Ultimate Mem. ✂ D-9
01/2 Ultimate Mem. ✂ A8, ✂ CT
02/3 Ultimate Memorabilia ✂ SCD
90/1 Upper Deck 121
91/2 Upper Deck 116
92/3 Upper Deck 243
93/4 Upper Deck 45, SP-120
94/5 Upper Deck 70
95/6 Upper Deck 115, SE-68
96/7 Upper Deck 132
98/9 Upper Deck 162
99/0 Upper Deck 105
95/6 UD Be A Player 124, ✍ S124
00/1 UD Black Diam. ✂ GG
01/2 UD Challenge ✂ T200
95/6 UD CC 53
96/7 UD CC 213
98/9 UD G. Reserve 162
99/0 UD G. Reserve 105
02/3 UD Mask 76
98/9 UD MVP 164
99/0 UD MVP 168, LL8
99/0 UD MVP Cup 148
02/3 UD Top Shelf ✂ M
99/0 Victory 237
97/8 Zenith 77
84/5 BUFF / Blue Shield
85/6 BUFF / Blue Shield
86/7 BUFF / Blue Shield
87/8 BUFF / Blue Shield
87/8 BUFF / Won. Bread
89/0 PITT / Foodland 15
90/1 PITT / Foodland 5
91/2 PITT / Foodland 9
91/2 PITT / Food. Stickers
92/3 PITT / Coke-Clark
92/3 PITT / Foodland 5
92/3 PITT / Food. Stickers
93/4 PITT / Foodland 24
94/5 PITT / Foodland 22
95/6 PITT / Foodland 10
96/7 PITT / Tribune

BARRATT, JEFF
79/0 Montréal Juniors B&W
79/0 Montréal Jrs. Colour

BARRAULT, DOUG
92/3 Classic Prospects 61
94/5 Fleer Ultra 294
93/4 Power Play 88
91/2 ProCards 158
93/4 Score 457
95/6 Atlanta Knights
98/9 Chicago Wolves Champs
93/4 Cincinnati Cyclones
94/5 Cincinnati Cyclones
89/0 Lethbridge Hurricanes

BARRETT, DAVE
89/0 Rayside-Balfour

BARRETT, FRED
70/1 Esso Power Player
74/5 Loblaws
71/2 O-Pee-Chee 128
73/4 O-Pee-Chee 264
74/5 O-Pee-Chee 234
75/6 O-Pee-Chee 124
76/7 O-Pee-Chee 249
77/8 O-Pee-Chee 291
78/9 O-Pee-Chee 185
80/1 O-Pee-Chee 253
82/3 Post [Minn.]
83/4 Souhaits Keychain [North Stars]
74/5 Topps 234
75/6 Topps 124
76/7 Topps 249
78/9 Topps 185
80/1 Topps 253
71/2 Toronto Sun Photo
73/4 MINS
78/9 MINS / Cloverleaf 2
79/0 MINS
80/1 MINS
81/2 MINS
82/3 MINS

BARRETT, JOHN
82/3 O-Pee-Chee 80
83/4 O-Pee-Chee 117
84/5 O-Pee-Chee 49
82/3 Post [Detr.]
84/5 DETR / Little Caesars
85/6 DETR / Little Caesars
86/7 WASH / Kodak
86/7 WASH / Police
87/8 WASH
87/8 WASH / Kodak

BARRETT, KEVIN
94/5 Flint Generals
93/4 Muskegon Fury

BARRETT, MIKE
01/2 Mississauga IceDogs
00/1 Owen Sound Attack 16

BARRETT, NATHAN
99/0 Lethbridge Hurricanes

BARRETT, TOM
95/6 Slapshot 180
83/4 Kitchener Rangers
84/5 Kitchener Rangers
85/6 Kitchener Rangers
86/7 Kitchener Rangers

BARRETTE, MAURICE
77/8 Nova Scotia Voyageurs

BARRIE, DOUG
71/2 Eddie Sargent 28
70/1 Esso Power Player
71/2 O-Pee-Chee 22
75/6 OPC WHA 117
76/7 OPC WHA 119
71/2 Topps 22
71/2 Toronto Sun Photo

BARRIE, LEN
00/1 BAP Mem. 188
92/3 Classic Prospects 53
98/9 DEL 135
94/5 Fleer 161
94/5 Leaf 491
93/4 Parkhurst 351
90/1 ProCards 49
91/2 ProCards 274
90 7th..Sketch Mem.Cup 1
95/6 Topps 66
91/2 Upper Deck 459
94/5 PITT / Foodland 4
93/4 Cincinnati Cyclones
95/6 Cleveland Lumberjacks
89/0 Kamloops Blazers

BARRIE, MIKE
91/2 7th...Sketch WHL 60
94/5 Sig. Rookies 40, ✍ 40
96/7 Peoria Rivermen
93/4 Seattle Thunderbirds

BARRY, KEVIN
95/6 Slapshot 168

BARRY, MARTY J.
35/6 Amalgamated Press
33/4 Anonymous 38
34-43 BeeHive-1 [Detr.]
34-43 BeeHive-1 [Mont.]
35-40 Canada Starch
33-35 Diamond Match Silv.
83 HHOF Postcard O3
83&87 HHOF 214
35/6 O-Pee-Chee 81
39/0 O-Pee-Chee 57
33/4 WWGum 27
37/8 World Wide Gum 4

BARRY, MIKE
98/9 Halifax Moosehead

BARRY, RAY
45-64 BeeHive-2 [Bost.]
51/2 Parkhurst 32

BARTA, LIBOR
95/6 APS 200
96/7 APS 143
97/8 APS 244
97/8 DS 67
98/9 DS 16
99/0 DS 71, G6
00/1 DS 85
97/8 DS Sticker 127
98/9 OFS 375
99/0 OFS 1
00/1 OFS 31, -Star 10
01/2 OFS 207, -H14

BARTANUS, KAROL
97 Bowman 59, 130, ✍ Aut.
98 Bowman 98, SC11
98 Bowman Chrome 98
01/2 OFS 94

BARTECKO, LUBOS
99/0 NHL Power Play
02/3 O-Pee-Chee 65
98/9 Omega 208
99/0 Pacific 352
00/1 Pacific 339
02/3 Pacific 12
02/3 Pacific Complete 183
00/1 Pa. Paramount 203
01/2 Signature 174, ✍ 174
00/1 SP Authentic ✍ SotT
00/1 Topps 175
02/3 Topps 65
02/3 T. Limited 65
02/3 T. Total 203
99/0 Upper Deck 115
01/2 Upper Deck 240
02/3 Upper Deck 6
99/0 UD G. Reserve 115
01/2 UD Mask 5
99/0 UD MVP 187
00/1 UD Pros&Prosp. ✂✍ GJS
00/1 UD Vintage 316
02/3 UD Vintage 11
99/0 Victory 261
00/1 Victory 202
01/2 Victory 312
02/3 Victory 12
99/0 SLOU / Taco Bell 7

BARTEK, MARTIN
01/2 Milwaukee Admirals

BARTEL, ROBIN
85/6 Moncton G'Flames

BARTELL, JOSH
92/3 Clarkson G'Knights

BARTH, TODD
92/3 MPS SJHL 112

BARTHE, CLAUDE
90/1 7th..Sketch LHJMQ 268
92/3 Hampton Roads
93/4 Roanoke Express
92/3 Wheeling Thund'birds 2

BARTHELSON, TONY
94/5 Leaf Elit Set 204
89/0 Semic Elitserien 198

BARTHELSSON, TONY
95/6 Leaf Elit Set 6
95/6 UD Elitserien 6

BARTHOLOMAUS, KEITH
93/4 N. Michigan Wildcats

BARTLETT, JIM
60/1 Shirriff 113
58/9 Topps 26
59/0 Topps 51

BARTLEY, JOEY
96/7 Guelph Storm

BARTLEY, WADE
92/3 Toledo Storm WIOT
95/6 Toledo Storm
89/0 Sudbury Wolves
90/1 Sudbury Wolves

BARTMAN, JAMIE
95/6 DEL 316

BARTOLI, MOE
67/8 Columbus Checkers
69 Columbus Checkers

BARTOLONE, CHRIS
96/7 DEL 188
98/9 DEL 27
99/0 Eishockey 139
00/1 UD DEL 53
01/2 UD DEL 46

BARTON, BRAD
90 7th..Sketch Mem.Cup 45
90/1 7th..Sketch OHL 227
91/2 7th...Sketch OHL 93
94/5 Slapshot / Brantford 10
97/8 Quad City Mallards
88/9 Kitchener Rangers
89/0 Kitchener Rangers
90/1 Kitchener Rangers

BARTON, PAT
94/5 Slapshot / Guelph 14

BARTON, PATRICK
91/2 7th...Sketch OHL 71

BARTOS, PETER
01/2 BAP Memor. 271
99/0 DS 37
98/9 OFS 208
99/0 OFS 278, 491
01/2 OFS 141
00/1 SP Authentic 111
00/1 UD Reserve 99
00/1 UD Black Diam. 122

BARTOVIC, MILAN
99/0 UD Prospects 45
02/3 Rochester Americans
99/0 Brandon Wheat Kings

BARUS, MIROSLAV
94/5 APS 247
95/6 APS 12
96/7 APS 262
97/8 APS 286
98/9 DS 36
99/0 DS 25
00/1 DS 54
96/7 DS Sticker 91
97/8 DS Sticker 81
98/9 OFS 205
99/0 OFS 312
00/1 OFS 366

BASALGIN, ANDREI
91/2 O-Pee-Chee 49R

BASANTA, MARK
91/2 Avant Garde BCJHL 41
91/2 Avant Garde BCJHL 122
92/3 BCJHL 221

BASARABA, SHANNON
98/9 Charlotte Checkers

BASEGGIO, DAVE
89/0 ProCards AHL 277
90/1 ProCards 270
91/2 ProCards 9
00/1 Charlotte Checkers
95/6 Cleveland Lumberjacks
97/8 Cleveland Lumberjacks
98/9 Cleveland Lumberjacks
99/0 Detroit Vipers
91/2 Rochester Americans GL

BASEOTTO, BRUNO
00/1 Saskatoon Blades

BASHKATOV, EGOR
99/0 Eishockey 224

BASHKATOV, IGOR
00/1 UD DEL 91
01/2 UD DEL 92
96/7 Las Vegas Thunder

BASHKIROV, ANDREI
00/1 MONT
97/8 Fort Wayne Komets
98/9 Fort Wayne Komets
99/0 Québec Citadelles 16
00/1 Québec Citadelles

BASILIO, SEAN
89/0 7th..Sketch OHL 31, 177
90/1 7th..Sketch OHL 127
91/2 7th...Sketch OHL 271

BASKEN, BRUCE
86/7 Portland Winter Hawks

BASQUE, CLAUDE
51/2 Lac St-Jean 48

BASSEN, BOB
91/2 Bowman 379
92/3 Bowman 378
93/4 Donruss 476
94/5 Donruss 257
99/0 Eishockey 81
92/3 Fleer Ultra 182
93/4 Fleer Ultra 408
91/2 O-Pee-Chee 51
92/3 O-Pee-Chee 139
91/2 Panini Sticker 29
93/4 Panini Sticker 163
91/2 Parkhurst 379
93/4 Parkhurst 445
94/5 Parkhurst 184
92/3 Pinnacle 203
93/4 Pinnacle 169
94/5 Pinnacle 327
96/7 Pi. Be A Player 89, ✍ Aut. 89
96/7 Pi. Summit 122
95/6 Playoff 245
95/6 POG 83
90/1 Pro Set 520
91/2 Pro Set 221
89/0 ProCards IHL 53
91/2 Score 179
91/2 Score CAN 179
92/3 Score 132
93/4 Score 279
93/4 Score 643
95/6 Score 216
96/7 Score 218
95/6 SBx Emotion 44
95/6 SBx Impact 43
00/1 Stadium 124
92/3 Topps 454
91/2 To. Stadium 367
92/3 T. Stadium Club 176
91/2 Upper Deck 319
92/3 Upper Deck 181
93/4 Upper Deck 2
94/5 Upper Deck 481
89/0 CHIC / Coke
96/7 DALL / Southwest
94/5 QUÉB / Burger King
90/1 SLOU / Kodak
91/2 SLOU
99/0 SLOU / Taco Bell 12
01/2 Utah Grizzlies
83/4 Medicine Hat Tigers

BASSEN, BOB
02/3 Fleer Throwbacks 88, ✂ 3SC, ✂ 3SCTD

BASSEN, CHAD
01/2 Regina Pats
01/2 Vancouver Giants

BASSEN, HANK
45-64 BeeHive-2 [Detr.]
64-67 BeeHive-3 [Detr.]
65/6 Coca-Cola
62/3 Parkhurst 19
61/2 Shirriff 80
65/6 Topps 106
66/7 Topps 107

BASSEN, MARK
92/3 Canada Nationals
94/5 DEL 364, 366
95/6 DEL 239
96/7 DEL 306
98/9 DEL 219
99/0 Eishockey 96
89/0 ProCards AHL 355
90/1 ProCards 43
91/2 ProCards 33
93/4 Peoria Rivermen
88/9 Brandon Wheat Kings
88/9 Lethbridge Hurricanes

BASSETT, DENNIS
97/8 Regina Pats

BASSIN, SHERRY
92 7th...Sketch Awards 9
81/2 Oshawa Generals
82/3 Oshawa Generals
83/4 Oshawa Generals
89/0 Soo Greyhounds
93/4 Soo Greyhounds 29

BAST, RYAN
99/0 UD MVP 153
99/0 Victory 217
00/1 Hartford Wolf Pack
97/8 Saint John Flames
96/7 Toledo Storm
93/4 Prince Albert Raiders

BASTARACHE, PHILIPPE
01/2 Shawinigan Cataractes 11

BASTIANSEN, HARALD
92/3 Semic Nordisk 223

BASTIEN, BAZ
43-47 Parade Sportive
45-54 Quaker Oats

BASTIEN, MATHIEU
00/1 Val d'Or Foreurs 18

BASTIEN, MORRIS
37/8 World Wide Gum 131

BASTON, DAN
89/0 Rayside-Balfour
90/1 Rayside-Balfour
91/2 Rayside-Balfour

BATCHVAROV, MARIN
79 Panini Sticker 352

BATEMAN, JEFF
95 Québec Pee Wee 684
00/1 SP Authentic 132
00/1 SP GU 87
00/1 SPx ✂ 129
00/1 UD Reserve 118
00/1 Upper Deck 438
00/1 UD Pros&Prosp. 129
00/1 UD Vintage 400
99/0 Brampton Batallion 24

BATEMAN, ROB
91/2 Greensboro Monarchs

BATES, L.
37 British Sporting Personalities 36

BATES, SHAWN
99/0 BAP Mem. 246
97/8 Do. Preferred 156
02/3 O-Pee-Chee 243
99/0 Pacific 19
02/3 Pacific 233
02/3 Pacific Complete 146
97/8 Pa. Dynagon Rookie
01/2 Parkhurst 388
02/3 Parkhurst Retro 178
00/1 Private Stock ✂ GUG 4
01/2 Pr. Stock ✂ GUG 61
97/8 Score Bost. 1
02/3 Signature Series 87, ✍ 87
02/3 Sports Vault 73
99/0 Topps 39
02/3 Topps 243
99/0 To. Chrome 39
02/3 T. Limited 243
02/3 T. Total 194
98/9 UD Choice 18
99/0 Upper Deck 20
00/1 Upper Deck 247
02/3 Upper Deck 109
99/0 UD G. Reserve 20
99/0 UD MVP 18
01/2 Vanguard ✂ DGM 18
99/0 Victory 24
02/3 Victory 137
98/9 Providence Bruins

BATHE, FRANK
80/1 O-Pee-Chee 389
91/2 ProCards 68
83/4 PHIL / J.C. Penney

BATHE, LANDON
99/0 Des Moines Buc's

BATHERSON, NORM
93/4 Cla. Prospects 157
98/9 DEL 5
97/8 Fort Wayne Komets
94/5 Portland Pirates
95/6 Portland Pirates
96/7 Portland Pirates Hershey
96/7 Portland Pirates

BATHGATE, ANDY
68/9 Bauer Photo
99/0 BAP Mem. AH-8, ✍ AH-8
45-64 BeeHive-2 [NYRa.]
45-64 BeeHive-2 [NYRa.]
45-64 BeeHive-2 [Toro.]
64-67 BeeHive-3 [Toro.]
64-67 BeeHive-3 [Detr.]
64/5 Coke/Sprite [Toro. #9]
65/6 Coca-Cola
70/1 Eddie Sargent 173
70/1 Esso Power Player
01/2 Fleer Greats 65, ✍ Aut.
62/3 Cowan Tile
83 HHOF Postcard O4
83&87 HHOF 215
68/9 O-Pee-Chee 104
70/1 O-Pee-Chee 207
53/4 Parkhurst 56
92/3 Parkhurst PR-22
02/3 Parkie - Reprint 182
93/4 Parkie 56-57 173
93/4 Parkie 56-57 90
95/6 Parkie 66-67 44
94/5 Parkie Tall 124, 174
97/8 Pi. BeeHive 62, ✍ Aut. 62
60/1 Shirriff 89
61/2 Shirriff 88
62/3 Shirriff 48
68/9 Shirriff / Pitt. 5
81/2 TCMA 8
54/5 Topps 11
57/8 Topps 60
58/9 Topps 21
59/0 Topps 34
60/1 Topps 45
61/2 Topps 22
61/2 Topps 53
61/2 Topps - Stamp
62/3 Topps 52, -Dollar
63/4 Topps 52
64/5 Topps 86
65/6 Topps 48
66/7 Topps 44
68/9 Topps 104
02/3 Topps - Reprint 4, ✍ Reprint 4
00/1 To. Heritage ✍ CAI
01/2 T/O Archives 1
58/9 Toronto Star Photo
60/1 Toronto Star Photo
63/4 Toronto Star Action
63/4 Toronto Star Photo
64/5 Toronto Star Action
58/9 Toronto Star Weekend
62/3 Toronto Star Weekend
91/2 Ultimate Original Six 18, 74, ✍ Aut. 18
93/4 Zellers, ✍ Aut.
64/5 TORO

BATHGATE, FRANK
52/3 Laval Dairy Update 89

BATIANI, ALESSANDRO
92 Semic Sticker 251

BATIRSHIN, RUSLAN
00/1 Mir 139

BATKIEWICZ, JOSEF
74 Hellas MM-Jenkki 92
79 Panini Sticker 126
73/4 Williams Finnish 85

BATOVSKY, ZOLTAN
00/1 Kentucky Tho'blades

BATTAGLIA, BATES
02/3 BAP Memorabilia 51
02/3 Exclusive 25
02/3 First Edition 295
02/3 O-Pee-Chee 239
02/3 Pacific 62
02/3 Pacific Complete 463
02/3 Parkhurst 10
02/3 Parkhurst Retro 136
02/3 Signature Series GS-10
02/3 Topps 239
02/3 T. Limited 239
02/3 T. Total 353
02/3 Upper Deck 279
02/3 UD MVP 32
02/3 Victory 41

BATTAGLIA, DOUG
98/9 Charlotte Checkers
98/9 Charlotte Checkers

BATTAGLIA, JON (BATES)
00/1 BAP Mem. 288
98/9 Bowman's Best F1
99/0 NHL Power Play
97/8 Omega 38
99/0 Pacific 67
00/1 Pacific 78
01/2 Pacific 69
99/0 Panini Sticker 52
99/0 Prism 27
01/2 Signature 178, ✍ Aut. 178
98/9 SP Authentic ✍ SotT
98/9 SPx Finite 17, 137
00/1 Stadium 111
00/1 Topps 250
98/9 UD Choice 38
98/9 UD3 17, 77, 137
98/9 Upper Deck 62
99/0 Upper Deck 34
00/1 Upper Deck 33
01/2 Upper Deck 266
98/9 UD G. Reserve 62
99/0 UD G. Reserve 34
99/0 UD MVP 43
00/1 UD Vintage 63
99/0 Victory 55
01/2 Victory 70
99/0 WGretzky 35
98/9 CARO / Highwoods

BATTEN, JOHN
95/6 Flint Generals

BATTERS, GREG
84/5 Victoria Cougars

BATTERS, JEFF
95/6 Kansas City Blades
92/3 Peoria Rivermen
93/4 Peoria Rivermen
94/5 Peoria Rivermen

BATTERSBY, BROOKE
92/3 MPS SJHL 10

BATTICE, JOHN
89/0 7th..Sketch OHL 29
86/7 Kingston Canadians

BATYRSHIN, RUSLAN
99/0 Anchorage Aces
95/6 Phoenix Roadrunners
97/8 Springfield Falcons

BAUER, BOBBY
34-43 BeeHive-1 [Bost.]
39/0 O-Pee-Chee 99
43-47 Parade Sportive

BAUER, COLLIN
90/1 ProCards 238
91/2 ProCards 220
91/2 BOST / SA Legends
97/8 Long Beach Ice Dogs
96/7 Michigan K-Wings
89/0 Saskatoon Blades

BAUER, FR. DAVID
96/7 Legends 75

BAUER, LUBOMIR
96/7 APS 73
97/8 APS 194
98/9 OFS 395
99/0 OFS 324

BAUER, REINHOLD
72 Semic Sticker 113
BAUER, STEPHAN
94/5 DEL 340
95/6 DEL 296
BAUM, DAN
99/0 Prince George Cougars
00/1 Prince George Cougars
BAUMAN, GARY
68/9 O-Pee-Chee 145
65/6 Québec Aces
BAUMAN, RODNEY
00/1 Ottawa 67's 13
01/2 Ottawa 67's 15
BAUMBACH, KENT
98/9 Anchorage Aces
BAUMGARTNER, GREGOR
99 Bowman 60
97 Bowman 151, ✍ Aut.
98/9 Collection Souvenir 20
02/3 Grand Rapids Griffins
99/0 Michigan K-Wings
01/2 Utah Grizzlies
BAUMGARTNER, KEN
98/9 Be A Player 160, ✍ Aut. 160
94/5 Donruss 288
96/7 Donruss 9
92/3 Fleer Ultra 416
93/4 Fleer Ultra 429
94/5 Fleer Ultra 212
90/1 O-Pee-Chee 414
91/2 O-Pee-Chee 316
98/9 OPC Chrome 201
98/9 Pacific 70
97/8 Pa. Invincible R-1
92/3 Panini Sticker 85
92/3 Parkhurst 413
93/4 Parkhurst 207
95/6 Parkhurst 476
91/2 Pinnacle 239
96/7 Pi. Be A Player 32, ✍ Aut. 32
95/6 Playoff 201, 314
96/7 Playoff 393
93/4 Power Play 448
90/1 Pro Set 178
91/2 Pro Set 432
88/9 ProCards / New Haven
90/1 Score 265
91/2 Score 148
91/2 Score CAN 148
92/3 Score 35
96/7 Score 206
97/8 Score Bost. 15
92/3 Topps 217
98/9 Topps 201
92/3 T. Stadium Club 103
94/5 T. Stadium Club 98
90/1 Upper Deck 439
91/2 Upper Deck 402
94/5 UD Be A Player R140, R166, ✍ 149
93/4 UD BAP Roots 29
96/7 ANAH / Up Front 12
88/9 LOSA / Smokey
92/3 TORO / Kodak
93/4 TORO / Black's 17
94/5 TORO / Coca-Cola
89/0 New Haven Nighthawks
84/5 Prince Albert Raiders
BAUMGARTNER, KEN
02/3 Fleer Throwbacks 61, ✍ Aut.
BAUMGARTNER, NOLAN
94/5 Classic 9, CP6
95/6 Classic AST, BK20
95/6 Cla. 5 Sport 126, S-73, SFF-10, ✍ Aut.
94/5 Classic 4 Sport 124
94/5 Cla. Images 4 Sport 102
95/6 Donruss C3TWC 3
96/7 Donruss 235
95/6 Do. Elite WJ 4
96/7 Fleer 121
96/7 Fl. Picks 168
96/7 Leaf GLR-6
94/5 L. Limited CAN 1
96/7 Metal Univ. 169
99/0 Pacific 450
95/6 Parkhurst 491
94/5 Pinnacle 525
96/7 Pinnacle 245
96/7 Pi. Summit 173
96/7 Score 251
94/5 Sig. Rookies 25, ✍ 25
94/5 SR Auto-Phonex B4, ✍ B4
94/5 SR Gold Standard 76, GS2
95/6 SR Tetrad F1
95/6 SR Tetrad Autobilia 38
96/7 SBx Impact 144
94/5 Slapshot Memorial 4
95/6 SP 174
95/6 Topps 11CJ
94/5 Topps Finest 148
94/5 Upper Deck 505
95/6 Upper Deck 353
98/9 Upper Deck 387
98/9 UD G. Reserve 387
99/0 Victory 313
02/3 Manitoba Moose
01/2 Norfolk Admirals
96/7 Portland Pirates Hershey
96/7 Portland Pirates
97/8 Portland Pirates
98/9 Portland Pirates
99/0 Portland Pirates
93/4 Kamloops Blazers
BAUMGARTNER, PAUL
99/0 Des Moines Buc's
BAUN, BOB
45-64 BeeHive-2 [Toro.]
64-67 BeeHive-3 [Toro.]
64-67 BeeHive-3 [Toro.]
63-65 Chex
64/5 Coke/Sprite [Toro.]
65/6 Coca-Cola
70/1 Colgate 66
70/1 Dad's Cookies
70/1 Eddie Sargent 64
71/2 Eddie Sargent 196
72/3 Eddie Sargent 199
70/1 Esso Power Player
71/2 Frito Lay
62/3 Cowan Tile
91/2 Kraft 28
91/2 Kraft 78
72/3 Post 9
68/9 O-Pee-Chee 24
69/0 O-Pee-Chee 57
69/0 O-Pee-Chee 4in1
70/1 O-Pee-Chee 223
71/2 O-Pee-Chee 196
72/3 O-Pee-Chee 66
57/8 Parkhurst [Toro.] 20
58/9 Parkhurst 15
59/0 Parkhurst 21
60/1 Parkhurst 11
61/2 Parkhurst 11
62/3 Parkhurst 3
63/4 Parkhurst 18
63/4 Parkhurst 78
92/3 Parkhurst PR-12
02/3 Parkie - Reprint 222, 227, 239, 247, 260, 272
93/4 Parkie 56-57 123
95/6 Parkie 66-67 117
94/5 Parkie Tall 120
60/1 Shirriff 7
61/2 Shirriff 50
62/3 Shirriff 19
68/9 Shirriff / Detr. 13
64/5 Topps 57
65/6 Topps 13
66/7 Topps 83
68/9 Topps 24
69/0 Topps 57
72/3 Topps 134
62/3 Toronto Star Photo
63/4 Toronto Star Action
64/5 Toronto Star Action
65/6 Toronto Star Photo
71/2 Toronto Sun Photo
91/2 Ultimate Original Six 30
91/2 Ultimate Original Six 93
60/1 York
61/2 York 1
63/4 York 7
64/5 TORO
68/9 TORO
71/2 TORO
72/3 TORO
BAUTIN, SERGEI
93/4 Donruss 378
99/0 Eishockey 38
92/3 Fleer Ultra 440
93/4 Fleer Ultra 10
93/4 Leaf 242
98/9 Mir 49
92/3 OPC Premier 84
92/3 Parkhurst 435
93/4 Pinnacle 197
93/4 Power Play 268
93/4 Premier 332
92/3 Red Ace Blue 16
92/3 Red Ace Violet 2
93/4 Score 351
92/3 Upper Deck 337
92/3 Upper Deck 499
93/4 Upper Deck 514
97/8 UD Elitserien 119
93/4 WINN / Ruffles
93/4 WINN Readers
95/6 Kansas City Blades
BAUYBA, DAINIUS
00/1 Kudos 12
BAVAUDIN, DENIS
73/4 Williams Finnish 304
BAVIS, MARK
93/4 Classic 60
BAVIS, MIKE
93/4 Classic 60
94/5 Classic ✍ Aut.
93/4 Cla. Prospects 66
93/4 Rochester Americans
BAWA, ROBIN
95/6 Edge Ice 187
88/9 ProCards / Baltimore
89/0 ProCards AHL 99
90/1 ProCards 536
91/2 ProCards 597
93/4 To. Stadium 445
97/8 Fort Wayne Komets
98/9 Fort Wayne Komets
92/3 Hamilton Canucks
85/6 Kamloops Blazers
86/7 Kamloops Blazers
BAWLF, NICK
10/1 Imperial 18
BAXTER, CHRIS
00/1 Nottingham Panthers
BAXTER, JIM
99 Bowman 135
77/8 Kalamazoo Wings
BAXTER, PAUL
78/9 Dernière Heure
78/9 Dernière Heure
79/0 O-Pee-Chee 372
82/3 O-Pee-Chee 238
82/3 Post [Pitt.]
83/4 Vachon 1-121
85/6 CALG / Red Rooster
86/7 CALG / Red Rooster
90/1 CALG / McGavin's
91/2 CALG / IGA
93/4 CHIC / Coke
83/4 PITT / Heinz
76/7 Québec Nordiques
76/7 Québ. / Antoinette
95/6 Saint John Flames
96/7 Saint John Flames
BAXTER, PAUL
02/3 Fleer Throwbacks 25
BAYDA, RYAN
02/3 BAP Memorabilia 302
02/3 Calder 109
02/3 Pacific Complete 514
02/3 Quest for the Cup 110
02/3 SP Authentic 212
02/3 Ultimate Memorabilia 37
02/3 UD Rookie 126
BAYER, COLIN
86/7 Saskatoon Blades
BAYER, MARCO
95 Panini Worlds 118
BAYLIS, STEVE
82/3 Victoria Cougars
83/4 Victoria Cougars
BAYRACK, MIKE
95/6 Lethbridge Hurricanes
BAZIN, NORM
94/5 Birmingham Bulls
BAZINET, MARIO
84/5 Chicoutimi Saguenéens
BAZINET, MICHAEL
90/1 7th..Sketch LHJMQ 217
BEACH, GEORGE
30s A&BC Chewing Gum 40
BEADLE, STEVE
90/1 ProCards 37
95/6 Flint Generals
96/7 Flint Generals
BEAGAN, BETH
94/5 Classic W36
BEAGLE, CHAD
95/6 Swift Current Broncos
BEALS, DARREN
88/9 ProCards / Cape Breton
86/7 Kitchener Rangers
87/8 Kitchener Rangers
BEALS, KEVIN
91/2 Ferris State Bulldogs
BEAMIN, RYAN
92/3 BCJHL 92
BEAN, TIM
89/0 ProCards AHL 116
90/1 ProCards 163
90/1 Newmarket Saints
83/4 Belleville Bulls
84/5 Belleville Bulls
BEAR, ROBBY
91/2 Air Canada SJHL D24
BEARDSMORE, COLIN
95/6 Slapshot 62
00/1 UD DEL 102
01/2 UD DEL 107
BEARDY, VERNON
98/9 Wichita Thunder
BEATCH, JEFF
99 Bowman 4, ✍ BA24
01/2 Vancouver Giants
BEATON, FRANK
81/2 Indianapolis Checkers
BEATON, JASON
89/0 7th..Sketch OHL 168
90/1 7th..Sketch OHL 302
BEATON, JOE
37 British Sporting Personalities 37
BEATTIE, DONALD
52/3 Anonymous 56
BEATTIE, RED
33/4 Anonymous 35 [Error: Beatty]
34-43 BeeHive-1 [Bost.]
39/0 Bruins Magazine
33-35 Diamond Match Silv.
28/9 Paulins Candy 46
33/4 WWGum 29
BEATTIE, SCOTT
91/2 Air Canada SJHL B25
96/7 DEL 201
BEAUBIEN, FREDERICK
95/6 Edge Ice 181
96/7 Mississippi S'Wolves
BEAUBIEN, FREDERICK
97/8 New Mexico Scorpions
95/6 Phoenix Roadrunners
BEAUBIEN, FREDERIK
99/0 Colorado Gold Kings
BEAUCAGE, MARC
90/1 7th..Sketch LHJMQ 47
91/2 7th...Sketch LHJMQ 231
01/2 UD DEL 2
99/0 Québec Citadelles 6
00/1 Québec Citadelles
BEAUCHAMP, DENIS
90/1 7th..Sketch LHJMQ 262
91/2 7th...Sketch LHJMQ 263
BEAUCHEMIN, BENOIT
02/3 Québec Remparts
BEAUCHEMIN, FRANÇOIS
02/3 BAP Memorabilia 357
98 Bowman 92, 153, ✍ A13
98 Bowman Chrome 92, 153
02/3 Ultimate Memorabilia 91
02/3 UD Rookie 132
02/3 Hamilton Bulldogs
00/1 Québec Citadelles
01/2 Québec Citadelles
BEAUCHESNE, MARTIN
00/1 Chicoutimi Saguenéens 21
BEAUCHESNE, SERGE
92/3 BCJHL 197
BEAUDETTE, DAN
91/2 Cincinnati Cyclones
BEAUDIN, ÉRIC
00/1 Chicoutimi Saguenéens 13
BEAUDIN, NORM
70/1 O-Pee-Chee 48
72/3 O-Pee-Chee 290
74/5 OPC WHA 11
73/4 Quaker Oats 9
70/1 Topps 48
BEAUDOIN, CARL
94/5 Slapshot Memorial 60
BEAUDOIN, ÉRIC
01/2 BAP Memor. 418
02/3 Pacific 151
96 Québec Pee Wee 839
02/3 Upper Deck 208
02/3 UD MVP 205
01/2 Utah Grizzlies
99/0 Guelph Storm
BEAUDOIN, NIC
95/6 Classic 43
93/4 Slapshot / Detroit 22
94/5 Slapshot / Detroit Jr. 24
95/6 Slapshot 76
94/5 Slapshot Memorial 98
98/9 Roanoke Express
BEAUDOIN, ROGER
51/2 Lac St-Jean 46
BEAUDOIN, SERGE
75/6 Phoenix Roadrunners
76/7 Phoenix Roadrunners
BEAUDRY, DAVID OUELLET
00/1 Chicoutimi Saguenéens 17
BEAUDRY, JOEY
99/0 Topeka Scarecrows
BEAUDRY, MIGUEL
01/2 Mississauga IceDogs
02/3 Mississauga IceDogs
99/0 Sudbury Wolves 26
00/1 Sudbury Wolves 24
BEAUFAIT, MARK
92/3 Classic Prospects 24
98/9 EBK IHL All-Star
93/4 Fleer Ultra 417
95 Panini Worlds 234
93/4 Pinnacle 206
93/4 Power Play 498
93/4 Premier - USA Hockey 6
93/4 To. Stadium - Team U.S.A. 1
92/3 SANJ / Pacific Bell
93/4 Kansas City Blades
98/9 Orlando Solar Bears
98/9 Orlando Solar Bears
98/9 Orlando Solar Bears Geico
BEAULE, ALAIN
73/4 Québec Nordiques
BEAULIEU, COREY
89/0 ProCards AHL 286
95/6 Atlanta Knights
97/8 Sheffield Steelers
BEAULIEU, JACQUES
01/2 London Knights
BEAULIEU, JOHN2
98/9 Dayton Bombers
BEAULIEU, JONATHAN
96/7 Rimouski Océanic
97/8 Rimouski Océanic
99/0 Rimouski Océanic 3
00/1 Rimouski Océanic 3
00/1 Shawinigan Cataractes 3
BEAULIEU, NICOLAS
88/9 ProCards / Cape Breton
89/0 ProCards IHL 109
90/1 ProCards 521
84/5 Richelieu Riverains
BEAULIEU, PIERRE-OLIVIER
02/3 Québec Remparts
BEAULNE, RICHARD
81/2 Soo Greyhounds
82/3 Soo Greyhounds
BEAUMONT, KEVIN
98/9 Sudbury Wolves 4
BEAUPRÉ, CLAUDE
52/3 Anonymous 166
BEAUPRÉ, DON
90/1 Bowman 72
91/2 Bowman 304
92/3 Bowman 222
92/3 Bowman 297
95/6 Donruss 286
93/4 EA Sports 156
94/5 Fleer 141
95/6 Fleer Metal 103
92/3 Fleer Ultra 229
93/4 Fleer Ultra 28
94/5 Fleer Ultra 387
95/6 Fleer Ultra 109
92/3 Kraft / PB
94/5 Kraft / KD
95/6 Kraft / PS
95/6 Leaf 52
92/3 McDonald's McD-15
81/2 O-Pee-Chee 159
82/3 O-Pee-Chee 163
83/4 O-Pee-Chee 166
84/5 O-Pee-Chee 94
85/6 OPC/Topps 142
86/7 OPC/Topps 89
87/8 OPC/Topps 132
88/9 OPC/Topps 42
90/1 OPC/Topps 253
91/2 O-Pee-Chee 505
92/3 O-Pee-Chee 28
90/1 OPC/Topps O
81/2 OPC Sticker 89
81/2 OPC Sticker 146
82/3 OPC/Topps Sticker 193
83/4 OPC/Topps Sticker 122
87/8 OPC Sticker 51-190
88/9 OPC Sticker 196-61
87/8 Panini Sticker 289
88/9 Panini Sticker 84
90/1 Panini Sticker 158
91/2 Panini Sticker 201
92/3 Panini Sticker 159
93/4 Panini Sticker 33
94/5 Panini Sticker 27
95/6 Panini Sticker 57
91/2 Parkhurst 416
92/3 Parkhurst 197
93/4 Parkhurst 225
95/6 Parkhurst 152
91/2 Pinnacle 148
92/3 Pinnacle 48
92/3 Pinnacle 268
93/4 Pinnacle 292
94/5 Pinnacle 355
95/6 Pinnacle 87
95/6 Pi. Summit 35
95/6 Playoff 177
96/7 Playoff 381
94/5 POG 298
95/6 POG 200
93/4 Power Play 463
93/4 Premier 304
90/1 Pro Set 307
91/2 Pro Set 257
91/2 Pro Set 501
92/3 Pro Set 206
91/2 Pro Set Platinum 139
90/1 Score 215
91/2 Score 185
91/2 Score CAN 185
92/3 Score 320
93/4 Score 58
95/6 Score 246
92/3 Seasons 49
94/5 Select 12
95/6 Select CE 104
95/6 SBx Emotion 121
95/6 SBx Impact 118
83/4 Souhaits Keychain [North Stars]
94/5 SP 82
81/2 Topps 103 [West]
84/5 Topps 70
92/3 Topps 195
95/6 Topps 142
91/2 To. Stadium 246
92/3 T. Stadium Club 270
93/4 To. Stadium 71
95/6 To. Stadium 44
90/1 Upper Deck 217
91/2 Upper Deck 197
92/3 Upper Deck 23
92/3 Upper Deck 310
93/4 Upper Deck 123
94/5 Upper Deck 389, SP-143
95/6 Upper Deck 402, SE-61
95/6 UD Be A Player 96, ✍ S96
95/6 UD CC 11
96/7 UD CC 264
01/2 UD Legends 75
80/1 MINS
81/2 MINS
82/3 MINS
83/4 MINS
84/5 MINS
85/6 MINS
85/6 MINS / 7-Eleven 4
86/7 MINS / 7-Eleven 5
87/8 MINS
94/5 OTTA
95/6 OTTA
89/0 WASH
89/0 WASH / Kodak
90/1 WASH / Kodak
90/1 WASH / Smokey
91/2 WASH / Kodak
91/2 WASH / Smokey
92/3 WASH / Kodak
96/7 St. John's Maple Leafs
BEAUPRÉ, MARTIN
90/1 7th..Sketch LHJMQ 41
91/2 7th...Sketch LHJMQ 94
91 7th..Sketch Mem.Cup 44
BEAUREGARD, DANNY
90/1 7th..Sketch LHJMQ 31
91/2 7th...Sketch LHJMQ 89
91 7th..Sketch Mem.Cup 39
BEAUREGARD, DAVID
99/0 Charlotte Checkers
98/9 Muskegon Fury
BEAUREGARD, STEPHANE
92/3 Bowman 405
95/6 Edge Ice 188
99/0 Eishockey 212
92/3 Fleer Ultra 369
93/4 Fleer Ultra 451
95/6 Future Legends 26
90/1 OPC/Topps 180, 223
92/3 OPC Premier 88
90/1 Panini/WPG 3
91/2 Parkhurst 426
90/1 Pro Set 648
88/9 ProCards / Moncton
89/0 ProCards IHL 139
90/1 Score 282
91/2 Score CAN 638
92/3 Score 402
92/3 Topps 62
92/3 To. Stadium 304
90/1 Upper Deck 415
92/3 Upper Deck 536
92/3 PHIL / UD Sheet
92/3 PHIL / J.C. Penney
90/1 WINN / IGA
91/2 WINN / IGA
93/4 WINN / Ruffles
98/9 Chicago Wolves Champs
BEAURIVAGE, MARC
88/9 Richelieu Riverains
BEAUTLER, ANDREAS
93 Semic Sticker 112
BEAUVAIS, ÉRIC
90/1 7th..Sketch LHJMQ 188
91/2 7th...Sketch LHJMQ 57
BEAZLEY, PAUL
94/5 Slapshot / Windsor 4
BÉCHARD, JÉRÔME
93/4 Cla. Prospects 229
90/1 ProCards 356
91/2 ProCards 363
93/4 Birmingham Bulls
94/5 Birmingham Bulls
95/6 Birmingham Bulls
BÉCHARD, WARREN
83/4 Brantford Alexanders
BECK, BARRY
01/2 Fleer Greats 15, ✍ Aut.
83/4 Funmate Puffy 20 [w]
84/5 Kellogg's 6
82/3 McDonald's Les Étoiles 27
78/9 O-Pee-Chee 121
79/0 O-Pee-Chee 35
80/1 O-Pee-Chee 90
80/1 O-Pee-Chee 170
81/2 O-Pee-Chee 220
81/2 O-Pee-Chee 230
82/3 O-Pee-Chee 219, 220
83/4 O-Pee-Chee 241
84/5 O-Pee-Chee 140
85/6 OPC/Topps 138
81/2 OPC Sticker 168
82/3 OPC/Topps Sticker 135
83/4 OPC/Topps Sticker 210
84/5 OPC Sticker 100
85/6 OPC Sticker 82-213
81/2 Post 14
82/3 Post [NYRa.]
84/5 7-Eleven
85/6 7-Eleven Superstars 13
83/4 Souhaits Keychain [Rangers]
78/9 Topps 121
79/0 Topps 35
80/1 Topps 90
80/1 Topps 170
81/2 Topps 3
81/2 Topps 124 [East]
84/5 Topps 105
01/2 UD Legends 73
89/0 LOSA / Smokey 9
BECK, BARRY
02/3 Fleer Throwbacks 2, 5SO, ✂ 5SO
BECK, BRAD
88/9 ProCards / Indianapolis
91/2 ProCards 429
BECK, ROB
91/2 Air Canada SJHL 13
91/2 Air Canada SJHL A40
92/3 MPS SJHL 22
BECKER, BARRY
91/2 7th...Sketch WHL 228
BECKER, CODEY
01/2 Regina Pats
BECKER, JASON
91/2 7th...Sketch WHL 118
91/2 Saskatoon Blades
BECKER, TROY
91/2 Avant Garde BCJHL 10
BECKETT, BOB
93/4 Parkie 56-57 13
BECKFORD-TSEU, CHRIS
01/2 Guelph Storm
BECKINGHAM, S
82/3 Fredericton Express
83/4 Fredericton Express
85/6 Fredericton Express
86/7 Fredericton Express
BEDARD, CAMILLE
52/3 Anonymous 41
BEDARD, JIM*
80/1 Mallasjuoma 198
78/9 O-Pee-Chee 243
79/0 O-Pee-Chee 62
78/9 Topps 243
79/0 Topps 62
78/9 WASH
BEDARD, JIM**
45-64 BeeHive-2 [Chic.]
BEDARD, LOUIS
00/1 Kudos 118
99/0 Hampton Roads
BEDARD, ROGER
52/3 Laval Dairy Update 115
52/3 St. Lawrence 105
BÉDARD, FRÉDÉRIC
00/1 Val d'Or Foreurs 21
01/2 Val d'Or Foreurs 10
02/3 Val d'Or Foreurs
BÉDARD, MARTIN
96/7 Rimouski Océanic
BEDDOES, CLAYTON
95/6 Bowman 102
94/5 Classic 50
98/9 DEL 112
95/6 Edge Ice 59
99/0 Eishockey 5
95/6 Parkhurst 286
97/8 Detroit Vipers
91/2 L. Superior State Lakers
BEDNAR, JARED
91/2 7th...Sketch WHL 11
98/9 Grand Rapids Griffins
93/4 Huntington Blizzard
94/5 Huntington Blizzard
96/7 St. John's Maple Leafs
BEDNAR, JAROSLAV
01/2 Adrenaline 211, RR10
95/6 APS 145
96/7 APS 22
97/8 APS 14
01/2 Atomic 111
01/2 BAP Memor. 363
01/2 Bowman 130
02/3 Calder 71
99/0 Cardset 280
00/1 Cardset 140, MB-4
02/3 Cardset 5
01/2 Crown Royale 163, RR11
97/8 DS 88
98/9 DS 96
01/2 DS 24
96/7 DS Sticker 126
97/8 DS Sticker 217
01/2 Heads Up 108
01/2 O-Pee-Chee 358
98/9 OFS 139
01/2 Pacific 457
02/3 Pacific Complete 527
01/2 PTC Calder 6
01/2 Parkhurst 255
01/2 Pr. Stock 124, MiT, RR5, -PS 82
01/2 PS Titanium 162
01/2 PS Titanium Draft 134
01/2 Signature 235, ✍ 235
01/2 SP Authentic 151
01/2 SP Game Used 80, ✂ AF
01/2 SPx 149, -RT
01/2 SPx Rookie RR14
01/2 Topps 358
01/2 To. Chrome 176
01/2 To. Heritage 152
01/2 To. Reserve 106
01/2 Upper Deck 427
01/2 Upper Deck 427
02/3 Upper Deck ✂ BF
01/2 UD Challenge 109
01/2 UD Honor Roll 93
01/2 UD Ice 56
01/2 UD Premier 64
01/2 UD Vintage 282
01/2 Vanguard 115, PP8, RR15
01/2 Manchester Monarchs
BEDNAR, VLADIMIR
72 Hellas MM-Jenkki 97
74 Hellas MM-Jenkki 66
70/1 Kuvajulkaisut 41
69/0 Mästar Serien 9
98/9 OFS 291
72 Semic Sticker 41
74 Semic Sticker 68
72/3 Williams Finnish 1
BEDNARIK, LUKAS
99/0 OFS 341
00/1 OFS 156
99/0 Score 87
BEDNARSKI, JOHN
76/7 O-Pee-Chee 231
76/7 Topps 231
88/9 EDMO / Action 125
89/0 New Haven Nighthawks
BEECH, KRIS
01/2 Adrenaline RR15
01/2 Atomic 121, RR8
00/1 BAP Mem. 398
02/3 BAP Memorabilia 237 [w/ Jagr]
99 Bowman 34, SC9, ✍ BA7
01/2 Bowman 164
02/3 Choice Prospects 5
01/2 Crown Royale RR16
02/3 First Edition 237
02/3 Heads Up ✂ GWQ 22
01/2 O-Pee-Chee 273
02/3 O-Pee-Chee 214
02/3 Pacific 306
00/1 Parkhurst P-134
01/2 Parkhurst 292
00/1 Premier Plus 88, ✂ GP
00/1 Private Stock 150
01/2 Pr. Stock 107, RR9, -PS 86
01/2 PS Titanium Draft ✂ 77
00/1 Signature 284, ✍ Aut. 246
01/2 Signature 194, ✍ Aut. 194
99/0 UD Sobey's 4
98/9 SP Authentic 123, ✍ SotT
01/2 SP Authentic 119
99/0 SPx 175
00/1 SPx 151
00/1 Stadium 230
01/2 Stadium Club 116
99/0 Topps 260
01/2 Topps 273
02/3 Topps 214
99/0 To. Chrome 260
01/2 To. Chrome 140
01/2 To. Heritage 174
02/3 T. Limited 214
00/1 To. Stars 143
02/3 T. Total 159
98/9 Upper Deck 400
99/0 Upper Deck 324
01/2 Upper Deck 373
02/3 Upper Deck 138
99/0 UD Black Diam. 93
98/9 UD G. Reserve 400
99/0 UD G. Reserve 324
99/0 UD MVP Cup 214, ✂ GU, ✍ PS
99/0 UD Ovation 73
99/0 UD Prospects 32, C4, DS8, ✂ GJ, ✍ Sig.
01/2 Vanguard 78
01/2 Victory 390
02/3 Victory 169
02/3 WBS Penguins
98/9 Calgary Hitmen 11
99/0 Calgary Hitmen
00/1 Calgary Hitmen
BEECHEY, TYLER
01/2 Calgary Hitmen
BEERS, BOB
90/1 Bowman 34
93/4 Donruss 426
93/4 EA Sports 127
92/3 Fleer Ultra 407
93/4 Fleer Ultra 18
94/5 Fleer Ultra 69
94/5 Leaf 43, 537
90/1 OPC/Topps 113
97/8 Pa. Invincible R-9
93/4 Panini Sticker 217
95 Panini Worlds 220
92/3 Parkhurst 401
93/4 Pinnacle 262
93/4 Pinnacle 186
94/5 Pinnacle 419
93/4 Power Play 227
93/4 Power Play 338
93/4 Premier 44
94/5 Premier 41
91/2 Pro Set 520
89/0 ProCards AHL 68
90/1 ProCards 140
90/1 Score 385
93/4 Score 369
93/4 Score 575
94/5 Score 7
90/1 Upper Deck 125
91/2 Upper Deck 490
95/6 UD CC 107
90/1 BOST / Sports Action
91/2 BOST / Sports Action
98/9 BOST / Alumni 6
93/4 EDMO / Sheet
92/3 TAMP / Sheraton Inn
96/7 Providence Bruins
BEERS, ED
83/4 O-Pee-Chee 76
84/5 O-Pee-Chee 219
84/5 O-Pee-Chee 354
85/6 OPC/Topps 144
86/7 O-Pee-Chee 238
83/4 OPC/Topps Sticker 141
84/5 OPC Sticker 243
85/6 OPC Sticker 214-83
84/5 Topps 24
83/4 Vachon 2-122
85/6 CALG / Red Rooster
BEGG, GARY
69/0 Mästar Serien 16
BÉGIN, ANDRÉ
79/0 Montréal Juniors B&W
79/0 Montréal Jrs. Colour
BÉGIN, PIER OLIVIER
01/2 Drummondville
BÉGIN, STEVE
97 Bowman 58
98/9 Collection Souvenir 13
97/8 Pa. Paramount 25
92 Québec Pee Wee 836
01/2 Signature 228, ✍ Aut. 228
00/1 Topps 299
00/1 To. Chrome 194
98/9 UD Choice 267
98/9 Upper Deck 49
98/9 UD G. Reserve 49
BEHM, DANIEL
91/2 Semic Elitserien 162
BEHREND, MARC
84/5 WINN / Safety Tips
BEINK, RAY
82/3 Victoria Cougars
BEKAR, DEREK
00/1 Pacific 355
01/2 Manchester Monarchs
00/1 Portland Pirates
BEKBULATOV, VADIM
98/9 OFS 13
BEKKEN, HANS
92/3 Semic Nordisk 134
BEKKEN, JAN
92/3 Semic Nordisk 135
BEKKERS, JOHN
82/3 Regina Pats
83/4 Regina Pats
BEKKERUD, BJØRN_F
92/3 Semic Nordisk 77
BELAK, WADE
00/1 BAP Mem. T-8
01/2 BAP Update ✂ TC15, ✂ TC25
94/5 Classic 11
94/5 Classic 4 Sport 126
94/5 Cla. Images 20
94/5 Cla. Images 4 Sport 104
97/8 Donruss 222
98/9 Omega 66
98/9 Pacific 158
02/3 Pacific Complete 496
94/5 Sig. Rookies 18, ✍ 18
94/5 SR Gold Standard 77
01/2 Signature 198, ✍ Aut. 198
98/9 SPx Finite 25
01/2 UD PlayMakers Ltd 91
97/8 Upper Deck 186
98/9 Upper Deck 252
98/9 UD G. Reserve 252
99/0 UD MVP 33
93/4 Saskatoon Blades
BELANGER, CHRIS
93/4 Cla. Prospects 246
93/4 Toledo Storm 10
92/3 W. Michigan Broncos
BELANGER, ERIC
02/3 Pacific Complete 271
BELANGER, HUGO
93/4 Cla. Prospects 147
93/4 Indianapolis Ice
94/5 Indianapolis Ice
96/7 Pensacola Ice Pilots
98/9 Phoenix Mustangs 1
92/3 Clarkson G'Knights
BELANGER, KEN
01/2 BAP Update ✂ TC5, ✂ TC37
99/0 Millenium 21, ✍ Aut. 21
98/9 Omega 11
01/2 Pacific 403
97/8 Pacific CC 351
97/8 Pi. Be A Player 145, ✍ Aut. 145
91/2 7th...Sketch OHL 312
93/4 Slapshot / Guelph 14
00/1 To. Heritage 169
97/8 Upper Deck 190
96/7 Kentucky Tho'blades
94/5 St. John's Maple Leafs
95/6 St. John's Maple Leafs
92/3 Ottawa 67's
BELANGER, RAY
29/0 La Presse
BELANGER, ROGER
83/4 Kingston Canadians
BELANGER, STEVE
00/1 Kamloops Blazers
01/2 Kamloops Blazers
02/3 Moose Jaw Warriors
BELANGER, DOMINIC
91/2 7th...Sketch OHL 107
BÉLANGER, ÉRIC
97 Bowman 73
01/2 O-Pee-Chee 132
02/3 O-Pee-Chee 124
01/2 Pacific 279
00/1 Premier Plus 125
00/1 Private Stock 121, PSR-9
02/3 PS Titanium 49
00/1 PS Titanium Draft 161
93 Québec Pee Wee 387
01/2 Signature 186, ✍ Aut. 186
00/1 SP Authentic 107
01/2 SP Authentic 127
02/3 SP Game-Used ✂ FF
00/1 SPx 162
01/2 Stadium Club 52
01/2 Topps 132
02/3 Topps 124
00/1 To. Heritage 98
01/2 To. Heritage 82
02/3 T. Limited 124
00/1 To. Stars 121
02/3 T. Total 121
00/1 UD Reserve 96
00/1 Upper Deck 436
01/2 Upper Deck 80
02/3 Upper Deck 84, ✂ S
00/1 UD Ice 89
01/2 UD MVP 89
00/1 UD Pros&Prosp. 106
02/3 UD Top Shelf ✂ ST
00/1 UD Vintage 380
01/2 UD Vintage 118
00/1 Vanguard 123
01/2 Victory 168
02/3 Victory 98
99/0 Lowell Lock Monsters
00/1 Lowell Lock Monsters
96/7 Rimouski Océanic
BÉLANGER, ÉRIC*
96/7 Rimouski Océanic
BÉLANGER, ÉRIC?
94 Québec Pee Wee 604
97/8 Rimouski Océanic
BÉLANGER, FRANCIS
01/2 Pacific 202
01/2 Pr. Stock 127
01/2 SP Authentic 154
01/2 SPx 108
01/2 Upper Deck 194
01/2 UD MVP 205
01/2 UD Top Shelf 57
01/2 Victory 377
01/2 Québec Citadelles
97/8 Rimouski Océanic
BÉLANGER, FRANÇOIS
90/1 7th..Sketch LHJMQ 32
91 7th..Sketch Mem.Cup 40
00/1 Sherbrooke Castors 21
01/2 Sherbrooke Castors 21
BÉLANGER, FREDERIC
95/6 Halifax Moosehead
96/7 Halifax Moosehead
96/7 Halifax Moosehead
97/8 Halifax Moosehead
97/8 Halifax Moosehead
98/9 Halifax Moosehead
BÉLANGER, JESSE
93/4 Cla. Images 4 Sport 32
92/3 Classic Prospects 115
92/3 Classic Prospects BC11
93/4 Donruss 123
94/5 Donruss 321
95/6 Donruss 204
96/7 Donruss 70
94/5 Flair 63
94/5 Fleer 77
93/4 Fleer Ultra 320
94/5 Fleer Ultra 79
95/6 Fleer Ultra 60
95/6 Kraft / KD
93/4 Leaf 278
94/5 Leaf 145
95/6 Leaf 62
94/5 L. Limited 19
95/6 Panini Sticker 70
92/3 Parkhurst 488
93/4 Parkhurst 346
93/4 Parkhurst C15
94/5 Parkhurst 86, 284, V31
95/6 Parkhurst 87
94/5 Pinnacle 122
95/6 Pinnacle 18
95/6 Pi. Summit 20
95/6 Playoff 40, 153
96/7 Playoff 339
94/5 POG 368
95/6 POG 114
93/4 Power Play 89
93/4 Power Play RooS 2
93/4 Premier 451
94/5 Premier 197, 544, OF-12
90/1 ProCards 75
91/2 ProCards 83
93/4 Score 454
93/4 Score 585
94/5 Score 257
95/6 Score 155
96/7 Score 222
95/6 SBx Emotion 69
95/6 SBx Impact 67
95/6 Topps 159
94/5 To. Stadium 63
95/6 To. Stadium 133
94/5 Upper Deck 72, SP-119
95/6 Upper Deck 209
95/6 UD Be A Player 143, ✍ S143
95/6 UD CC 66
94/5 FLOR / Health Plan
00/1 Chicago Wolves
98/9 Cleveland Lumberjacks
92/3 Fredericton Canadiens
97/8 Las Vegas Thunder 3
99/0 Québec Citadelles 14
BÉLANGER, LUC
01/2 Québec Citadelles
BÉLANGER, MAXIME
02/3 Baie-Comeau
BÉLANGER, PASCAL
96/7 Flint Generals
BÉLANGER, YVES
76/7 O-Pee-Chee 168
77/8 O-Pee-Chee 367
78/9 O-Pee-Chee 44
76/7 Topps 168
78/9 Topps 44
BELASTIK, JAROSLAV
00/1 OFS 362
BELECKI, BRENT
98 Bowman 41, 162
98 Bowman Chrome 41, 162
00/1 Asheville Smoke
97/8 Portland Winter Hawks
BELFOUR, ED
01/2 Adrenaline 58, CL 5, PP12, ✂ GWJ 11
01/2 Atomic 31, Stat. 2, TN5, ✂ GWJ 16
02/3 Atomic 91, -D 20
98/9 Aurora 53, -CF 14
99/0 Aurora 43, Stripe 43, CF-10, GU-7, ST-7
00/1 Aurora 43, Pin. 43, CF-7, SR-8
02/3 BAP All-Star 3, ✂ ASJ, ✂ HSHSJers
98/9 Be A Player 190, P-6, ✍ Aut. 190, ✂ G-19, ✂ AS-24, ✂ S-22
99/0 BAP Mem. 174, H-17, ✂ J-24, ✂ D-8, ✂ TM-11, ✂ TM-47, ✂ TM-48
00/1 BAP Mem. 242, ✂ J-33, ✂ G-4, ✂ G-21, ✂ G-22, ✂ H-6, ✂ TM-14, ✂ TM-36, ✂ V-8, ✂ V-10
01/2 BAP Memor. 36, ✂ AST, ✂ GJ, ✂ SCP
02/3 BAP Memorabilia 266, 301, ✂ ASJ3
01/2 BAP Update HSHS, ✂ HSHSJers, ✂ H11
01/2 BT Pipes 10, 101, 112, HSHS, -Mask, ✂ ASJ, ✂ Jers., ✂ S&J, ✂ GR, ✂ GT, ✂ TW, ✂ HSHSJers
02/3 Between the Pipes 33, 148, M-28, ✂ ASJ1, ✂ BM19, ✂ GUJ32, ✂ GP5, ✂ I6, ✂ RB14, ✂ T14
98/9 Bicycle Sports J-H
95/6 Bicycle Sports Aces 5-Club
90/1 Bowman 7
91/2 Bowman 390
92/3 Bowman 90
92/3 Bowman 199
95/6 Bowman 53
01/2 Bowman 43
02/3 Bowman 94
98/9 Bowman's Best 34
02/3 Calder 21, -CG 9, ✂ GWJ 21
99/0 Challenger 25
99/0 Crown Royale 42, IE-9
00/1 Crown Royale 34, ✂ GWJ-7
01/2 Crown Royale 46
02/3 Crown Royale 90, -COA 10
93/4 Donruss 64
94/5 Donruss 275, D-7, IM-1, MM-1
95/6 Donruss 108,BTP-10, D-8
96/7 Donruss 62, BTP-6
97/8 Donruss 164
96/7 Do. Canadian 113, OC-6
97/8 Do. Canadian 26, NP-22
95/6 Do. Elite 20, PW-4
96/7 Do. Elite 91, PW-7
97/8 Do. Elite 102
97/8 Do. Preferred 54, CG-16
97/8 Do. Priority 71, PG-7
97/8 Do. Studio 58
98/9 Dynagon Ice 53, -IW 3
99/0 Dynagon Ice 63, ASP-9
93/4 EA Sports 187
93/4 EA Sports 30
01/2 eTopps 22
02/3 Exclusive 159, -EA 15
02/3 First Edition 184, ✂ DGJ 5
94/5 Flair 31
96/7 Flair 83, HG-1
94/5 Fleer 38, N-1
96/7 Fleer 15, VT-1
95/6 Fleer Metal 23, IW-2
96/7 F. Picks DL-8
92/3 Fleer Ultra 32, -AS 9
93/4 Fleer Ultra 22
93/4 Fleer Ultra AS 10
93/4 Fleer Ultra AW 1
94/5 Fleer Ultra 39
95/6 Fleer Ultra 30, 365, PPM-1
96/7 Fl. Ultra 29
91/2 Gillette 18

95 Globe 74
96/7 Got-Um
01/2 Heads Up 29, HD 12, SS 5
02/3 Heads Up 114, ✂ GWQ 11
92/3 High Five / Promo P6
93/4 High Liner 2
93/4 Hockey Wit 18
99/0 HoloGrFX 20
95/6 Hoyle / West. 4-Heart
02/3 In The Game-Used 71, 171, ✂ GP6
92/3 Kraft / PB
93/4 Kraft / KD
94/5 Kraft / KD
95/6 Kraft / PS, PB
96/7 Kraft / KD
98/9 Kraft / OML
99/0 Kraft / JELL-O
94/5 Kraft Mask
93/4 Leaf 175
93/4 Leaf 62
93/4 Leaf GLAS 10
93/4 Leaf PW 6
94/5 Leaf 296, CP-2, GLS-7
95/6 Leaf 329
96/7 Leaf 199, SD-4
97/8 Leaf 87
94/5 L. Limited 3
95/6 L. Limited 15, SS-8
96/7 Leaf Limited 53, S-6
96/7 L. Preferred 30, MM-12, VP-14
97/8 Limited 28, 164, FG-33
96/7 Maggers 26
92/3 McDonald's McD-01
93/4 McDonald's McH-06
95/6 McDonald's McD-29
96/7 McDonald's McD-37
98/9 McDonald's McD21
99/0 McDonald's McD-8, ✍ SS
01/2 McDonald's 8, -HP 6, ✂ JPatch 5
02/3 McDonald's -SLG 1
96/7 Metal Univ. 25, AP-1
99/0 Millenium 79, ✍ Aut. 79, ✂ J-24, ✂✍ J-24, ✂ JS-24
95/6 Cool Trade 14
98/9 NHL Power Play
91/2 O-Pee-Chee 4
91/2 O-Pee-Chee 20
91/2 O-Pee-Chee 263
91/2 O-Pee-Chee 271
91/2 O-Pee-Chee 288
91/2 O-Pee-Chee 425
91/2 O-Pee-Chee 518
91/2 O-Pee-Chee 519
92/3 O-Pee-Chee 81
01/2 O-Pee-Chee 90
02/3 O-Pee-Chee 245, Update 245
98/9 OPC Chrome 123, SB3
91/2 OPC Premier 19
97/8 Omega 67, 246, NSZ-3, TL-6
98/9 Omega 68, -Onl. 11, -PI 7
99/0 Omega 70, 5ST-27
98/9 Pacific 20, GCDC 11, -Time. 6
99/0 Pacific 117, GC-13, ITCNF-6, PAP-9
00/1 Pacific 126, ✍ Aut.
01/2 Pacific 122, IZ8, SC6
02/3 Pacific 111
02/3 Pacific Complete 25
97/8 Pacific CC 20, ITC-19
97/8 Pa. Crown Roy. 39, FO-6
98/9 Pa. Crown Roy. 37, -PotG 9
97/8 Pa. Invincible 123, R-174
97/8 Pa. Paramount 56, GSL-6
98/9 Pa. Paramount 62, -GS 7
99/0 Pa. Paramount 69, GS-7, PB-12
00/1 Pa. Paramount 73, FF-11, GS-8, ✂ GUS-8
97/8 Pa. Revolution 40, ASG-9, RTS-6
98/9 Pa. Revolution 40, -ASG 2, -TPA 13
98/9 Panini Photocard
89/0 Panini Sticker 46
91/2 Panini Sticker 9
91/2 Panini Sticker 337
92/3 Panini Sticker 3
92/3 Panini Sticker 284
93/4 Panini Sticker 140
93/4 Panini Sticker 155
94/5 Panini Sticker 135
95/6 Panini Sticker 166
96/7 Panini Sticker 156
98/9 Panini Sticker 6, 122
99/0 Panini Sticker 227
91/2 Parkhurst 30
91/2 Parkhurst 218
92/3 Parkhurst 28
92/3 Parkhurst 461
93/4 Parkhurst 44
94/5 Parkhurst 41
95/6 Parkhurst 41, AS-6, GP-6
00/1 Parkhurst P-118
01/2 Parkhurst 70, ✂ PJ51, ✂ PSJ7, ✂ M5, ✂ M44, ✂ H11, ✂ T12, ✂ T21, ✂ HSHSJers
02/3 Parkhurst 138, -CR18, ✂ CRM18, ✂ MS3
95/6 Parkhurst 24-karat Gold
95 Parkhurst Phonecard
02/3 Parkhurst Retro 150, ✂ RJ8, ✂ HSHSJers, ✂ VH1
94/5 Parkie SE seV14
91/2 Pinnacle 127
91/2 Pinnacle 388
91/2 Pinnacle 400
92/3 Pinnacle 118
92/3 Pinnacle 265
92/3 Pinnacle TP 1
93/4 Pinnacle 224
93/4 Pinnacle 227
93/4 Pinnacle 255
93/4 Pinnacle TP 1
94/5 Pinnacle 42, GT-4
95/6 Pinnacle 153, FS-7
96/7 Pinnacle 94
97/8 Pinnacle 51
97/8 Pi. Be A Player 249, STP-5, TN-3, ✍ Aut. 249
97/8 Pi. BeeHive 10
97/8 Pi. Certified 9
96/7 Pi. FANtasy 20
97/8 Pi. Inside 74, S-24
95/6 Pi. Summit 120, ITC-4
96/7 Pi. Summit 97, ITC-3
97/8 Pi. Totally 9
95/6 Pi. Zenith 95
96/7 Pi. Zenith 25
95/6 Playoff 21
96/7 Playoff 394
94/5 POG 276
95/6 POG 16, 17, I-020
93/4 Power Play 46
93/4 Power Play Netm. 2
93/4 Premier 60
93/4 Premier 95
93/4 Prmr. - BG-OPC 16
93/4 Prmr. - BG-Top. 14
94/5 Premier 285
00/1 Premier Plus 41, MB13, TT6, ✂ GP
99/0 Prism 43, SGDC-8
00/1 Private Stock 30, EA-6, PS-16, ✂ GUG-34
01/2 Pr. Stock 28, GR 3, -PS 22, ✂ GUG 34
02/3 Pr. Stock Reserve -ICS 20, ✂ 145
00/1 PS Titanium 27, 3SS-3, ✂ GUG-81
01/2 PS Titanium 43, SK 4, ✂ DSJ 53, ✂ DSJ 65
02/3 Private Stock Titanium 92, -MM 7, -SK 8
00/1 PS Titanium Draft ✂ 28
95/6 Pro Magnet 1, IC1
90/1 Pro Set 598
91/2 Pro Set 43
91/2 Pro Set 321
91/2 Pro Set 600
92/3 Pro Set 33
91 Pro Set Awards AC1,AC19
91/2 Pro Set Platinum 26
88/9 ProCards / Saginaw
02/3 Quest for the Cup 91, ✂ GWJ 21
99/0 Revolution 44, O-8, SS-12, / CSC 44
00/1 Revolution 45, HD-12, II-7, SM-14
90/1 Score 103T
91/2 Score 290
91/2 Score 348
91/2 Score 410
91/2 Score 411
91/2 Score 430
91/2 Score 431
91/2 Score 433
91/2 Score - Hot Card 9
91/2 Score CAN 300
91/2 Score CAN 301
91/2 Score CAN 320
91/2 Score CAN 321
91/2 Score CAN 323
91/2 Score CAN 378
91/2 Score CAN 510
92/3 Score 178
93/4 Score 485
93/4 Score 70
93/4 Score PiAS 42
94/5 Score 149
95/6 Score 87, 318
96/7 Score 123, NW-5, SD-4
97/8 Score 20, NW-18
91/2 Score Shows 6
91/2 Score Young Stars 32
92/3 Score Young Stars 25
92/3 Seasons 3
93/4 Seasons 1
94/5 Select 53
95/6 Select CE 93
96/7 Select CE 11, F-6
95 Semic 78
91 Semic Sticker 53
92 Semic Sticker 76
00/1 Signature 158, ✍ Aut. 78, ✂ J-24, ✂ HSHSJers
01/2 Signature C-13, ✂ GU73, ✂ TM10
02/3 Signature Series GS-35, ✂ DW2, ✂ TQ2
95/6 SBx Emotion 27
95/6 SBx Impact 27, D-9
96/7 SBx Impact 17, ZH-1
02/3 Slam Card
94/5 SP 24
95/6 SP 27
96/7 SP 28,GF-11
97/8 SP Authentic 44, I13
98/9 SP Authentic 26
99/0 SP Authentic 29
00/1 SP Authentic 28, SS3
01/2 SP Authentic 24, 96, ✍ SotT, ✍ SotTD, ✍ SotTT
02/3 SP Authentic 83, ✂ TP
00/1 SP GU 20, ✂ C
01/2 SP Game Used 15, ✂ AF, ✂ AFD, ✂ AFT, ✂✍ IS2, ✂ Patch, ✂✍ PatchSig, ✂✍ PatchCSig, ✂ PatchT
02/3 SP Game-Used Edition 47, ✂ TG (x2), ✍ Sig
02/3 Sports Vault 140
99/0 SPx 50, XT18
00/1 SPx 20, ✂ WM
01/2 SPx 20
02/3 SPx 71
98/9 SPx Finite 29
98/9 SPx Prospects 20
00/1 Stadion 92
99/0 Stadium 77, Chrome 28, ✍ CS10, ✍ CS12, ✍ LS8, ✂ SCS
00/1 Stadium 7, BT17, CA4, GS2
01/2 Stadium Club 44, G13, P10, ✂ SCSD (x2), SCST
02/3 Stadium 103
91/2 Star Pics 20
93/4 SLU / Card-A
93/4 SLU / Card-B
93/4 Starting Lineup
98/9 SLU
00/1 SLU 20
95/6 Super Sticker 20, 23
96/7 Team Out!
92/3 Topps 22
95/6 Topps 130, 378, HGC24, PF16
98/9 Topps 123, SB3
99/0 Topps 153, IM16, PM4, SC19
00/1 Topps 49, OTG17
01/2 Topps 90, OTG29, ✂ GWJ
02/3 Topps 245, Update 245
99/0 To. Chrome 153, IM16, PM4
00/1 To. Chrome 40, 162
01/2 To. Chrome 90
02/3 T. Chrome 134
94/5 Topps Finest 51, DF-11
95/6 To. Finest 108
98/9 To. Finest 3
98/9 T. Gold Label 24
99/0 To. Gold Label 18
00/1 To. Gold Label 73, BTM2, B2
00/1 To. Heritage 23, 233, HH17
01/2 To. Heritage 30
02/3 To. Heritage 160
02/3 T. Limited 245
96/7 Topps Picks 179
99/0 To. Prmr. Plus 48, CAC8, IG1
01/2 To. Reserve 15, ✂ TR
91/2 To. Stadium 333
92/3 To. Stadium 243
92/3 To. Stadium 333
93/4 To. Stadium 144
93/4 To. Stadium 150
93/4 To. Stadium 99
93/4 To. Stadium - All-Stars
94/5 To. Stadium 155, 180
95/6 To. Stadium 55, M5
91/2 TSC Charter
91/2 TSC Charter
94/5 TSC Members Only 35
95/6 TSC Members Only 6
00/1 To. Stars 32, P6
95/6 T. Super Skills 90
02/3 T. Total 301
98/9 UD Choice 63, 249, BH26, SQ17
00/1 UD Heroes 38, SS4
01/2 UD PlayMakers Ltd 31, -PCPJ
00/1 UD Reserve 29
98/9 UD3 45, 105, 165
00/1 Ultimate Mem. ✍ U-24, ✂ A8-6, ✂ G-10, ✂ PJ-2, ✂ J-24, ✂ Jer.22, ✂ RA-4, ✂ S-24, ✂ TM-25, ✂ TM-26, ✂ TM-27, ✂ TM-35, ✂ GM-5, ✂ GM-11, ✂ GM-13
01/2 Ultimate Mem. ✂ BAPL, ✂ CT, ✂ JE, ✂ JJ
02/3 Ultimate Memorabilia ✂ A8 (x2), ✂ FS, ✂ GUJ, ✂ JE, ✂ JGUJ, ✂ LA, ✂ NP, ✂ Num, ✂ RAT, ✂ SCD (x2)
99/0 Ult. Victory 29, NW4
90/1 Upper Deck 55
91/2 Upper Deck 39
91/2 Upper Deck 81
91/2 Upper Deck 164
91/2 Upper Deck 625
91/2 Upper Deck AW2, AW4, AW7
92/3 Upper Deck 203
93/4 Upper Deck 147, AW3, SP-27
94/5 Upper Deck 290, H27, SP-15
95/6 Upper Deck 216, 455, AS-6, H-18, SE-19
96/7 Upper Deck 234, X18, SS22A
97/8 Upper Deck 259
98/9 Upper Deck 80, FT26, LS23, ✂ GJ7
99/0 Upper Deck 44, AS14, UD5, ✂ GJ, ✂✍ GJS
00/1 Upper Deck 287, SS7, TT2, ✂ DGJ
01/2 Upper Deck 56, GL2, LL2, ✂ CJers, ✂ SCFJers, ✂ SCFJersT, ✂✍ SigJers
02/3 Upper Deck 163, -LL13, ✂ GJ, ✂✍ SGJ
02/3 UD Artistic 83, R83, / Art
95/6 UD Be A Player 194, ✍ S194
96/7 UD Black Diam. 34
97/8 UD Black Diam. 134
98/9 UD Black Diam. 26, WF9
99/0 UD Black Diam. 31, ✂ APOH
00/1 UD Black Diam. 19
01/2 UD Challenge 24, ✂ T200, ✂ UC, ✂✍ T200S, ✂✍ TNS
02/3 UD Classic 93
95/6 UD CC 109, 387
96/7 UD CC 55
97/8 UD Coll. Choice 216, SQ36, S20
98/9 UD G. Reserve 80
99/0 UD G. Reserve 44, / Backup 167
01/2 UD Honor Roll ✂ GAJ
02/3 UD Honor 66
96/7 UD Ice 11
01/2 UD Ice 13
00/1 UD Legends 38, 40, LC5
92/3 UD Locker 19
01/2 UD Mask 110, 176, ✂ GG, ✂ GJ, ✂ JP, ✂ DP, ✂✍ SP, ✂ MB, ✂ ST, ✂ VC, / Mask
02/3 UD Mask 82, 83, 84, 99, ✂ CW, ✂ GG, ✂ BM, ✂ NB, ✂ PW, ✂ VC, / Mask, ✍ Mask
98/9 UD MVP 60
99/0 UD MVP 62, LL5
00/1 UD MVP 59, MM3, ✂ CG
01/2 UD MVP 61, MM2, ✂ GS
02/3 UD MVP 174, SD (x2), Souv.
99/0 UD MVP Cup 59
99/0 UD Ovation 20, LP19
02/3 UD Piece 84
01/2 UD Premier 18, ✂ B, ✂ D
02/3 UD Premier 51, ✍ Sig.
00/1 UD Pros&Prosp. 29
99/0 UD Retro 26
02/3 UD Rookie 94, 171
01/2 UD SCup Champs 50, ✂ G
01/2 UD Top Shelf ✂ J, ✂✍ SJ
02/3 UD Top Shelf ✂ CP, ✂ HH (x2), ✂ R, ✂ SS, ✂ TS
00/1 UD Vintage 118, 123, 124, GG7
01/2 UD Vintage 80, 87
02/3 UD Vintage 240, 288, GB 240
00/1 Vanguard 33, HV-10
01/2 Vanguard 31, SW 6, VT 3
02/3 Vanguard 91, -EMW 10, -SW 12, -VT 6
99/0 Victory 86, 347, 377
00/1 Victory 71, 296
01/2 Victory 108, 114, 403
99/0 WGretzky 55, ✂ TG
96 Wien 75, SG2
97/8 Zenith 49, CTC-10, Z10
88/9 CHIC / Coke
90/1 CHIC / Coke
91/2 CHIC / Coke
93/4 CHIC / Coke
97/8 DALL / Score 20
00/1 DALL / Southwest
01/2 DALL / Southwest

BELHUMEUR, MICHEL
72/3 O-Pee-Chee 273
74/5 O-Pee-Chee 153
75/6 O-Pee-Chee 232
76/7 O-Pee-Chee 296
74/5 Topps 153
75/6 Topps 232
74/5 WASH

BELIAVSKI, ALEXANDER
94/5 Leaf Elit Set 274
95/6 Leaf Elit Set 145
98/9 UD Elitserien 25
00/1 UD Elitserien 21, 182, ✍ Sig.

BELISLE, DAN
96/7 Dayton Ice Bandits

BELISLE, OMER
95/6 Thunder Bay Senators

BELISLE, PATRICK
91/2 7th...Sketch LHJMQ 9

BELITSKI, DAVID
95/6 Classic 87
94/5 Parkie SE251
94/5 SR Auto-Phonex 5, ✍ 5
93/4 Slapshot / Kitchener 2
93/4 Slapshot / Kitchener 29
94/5 Slapshot / Promo
94/5 Slapshot / Kitchener 2
95/6 Slapshot 131

BÉLIVEAU, JEAN
01/2 ASG History
01/2 BAP Memor. ✂ 500GS, ✂ RM
02/3 BAP Memorabilia / Cup
45-64 BeeHive-2 [Mont.]
64-67 BeeHive-3 [Mont.]
02/3 Canada Post, ✍ Aut.
63-65 Chex
63-65 Chex
64/5 Coke/Sprite [Mont.]
65/6 Coca-Cola
00 CSAS Signat. Series
70/1 Dad's Cookies
72/3 Dernière Heure
77/8 Dernière Heure
96/7 Duracell JB21-22
70/1 Eddie Sargent 108
62/3 El Producto
70/1 Esso Power Player
88/9 Esso All-Star
48-52 Exhibits [Canadiens]
48-52 Exhibits [Québec Aces]
01/2 Fleer Greats 3, -RC 2, ✍ Aut.
01/2 Fleer Legacy 6, 9, ✂ HK, ✍✂ HKA
83 HHOF Postcard C1
83&87 HHOF 31
93/4 Hockey Wit 23
02/3 In The Game-Used ✂ VM6
91/2 Kraft 68
51/2 La Patrie
51/2 Laval Dairy 1
94/5 Legends 46
68/9 O-Pee-Chee 166
68/9 O-Pee-Chee PS 7
69/0 O-Pee-Chee 10
69/0 O-Pee-Chee 220
69/0 O-Pee-Chee 4in1
69/0 O-Pee-Chee Stamp
70/1 O-Pee-Chee 55
70/1 O-Pee-Chee DE 21
71/2 O-Pee-Chee 263
53/4 Parkhurst 27
54/5 Parkhurst 3
55/6 Parkhurst 44
55/6 Parkhurst 74
55/6 Parkhurst 77
57/8 Parkhurst [Mont.] 3
58/9 Parkhurst 34
59/0 Parkhurst 6
60/1 Parkhurst 49
60/1 Parkhurst 59
61/2 Parkhurst 45
62/3 Parkhurst 39
63/4 Parkhurst 30
63/4 Parkhurst 89
92/3 Parkhurst PR-30
01/2 Parkhurst HSHS, PR9, PR16, PR33, PR80, PR82, PR107, PR110, PR118, PR130, P136, ✂ 500GS, ✂ Hero., ✍ PA3, ✍ PA6, ✍ PA27, ✂ PV, ✂ HSHSJers
02/3 Parkhurst ✂ VM7, ✂ VT8
93/4 Parkie 56-57 64, 138, 149, 150, 156, 157, 162, 164, 172, ✍ A-5
02/3 Parkhurst Retro ✂ NN20
95/6 Parkie 66-67 73, 125
94/5 Parkie Tall 85, 142, 146, 159, 172
68/9 Post Marble
67/8 Post Tips 7
67/8 Post Tips 8
45-54 Quaker Oats
72 Semic Sticker 207
60/1 Shirriff 30
61/2 Shirriff 102
62/3 Shirriff 32
68/9 Shirriff / Mont. 6
01/2 Signature ✂ 500GS, ✍ VA5, ✍ VA6
Sport Flash 4
Sport Flash 4
77-79 Sportscaster 10-14
77-79 Sports. FIN 33-785
52/3 St. Lawrence 39
91/2 Star Pics 4
95/6 SLU Cdn. Legend
97/8 SLU Cdn. Leg.
81/2 TCMA 11
64/5 Topps 33
65/6 Topps 6
66/7 Topps 73
66/7 Topps 127
66/7 Topps / Test 31
67/8 Topps 74
68/9 Topps 61
69/0 Topps 10
70/1 Topps 55
01/2 To. Heritage S7, ✂ Relic, ✍ CAI
57/8 Toronto Star Photo
58/9 Toronto Star Photo
62/3 Toronto Star Photo
63/4 Toronto Star Action
64/5 Toronto Star Action
64/5 Toronto Star Photo
65/6 Toronto Star Photo
60/1 Toronto Star Weekend
66/7 Toronto Star Weekend
00/1 UD Heroes 130, ✍ SG
01/2 Ultimate Mem. ✂ 500GS, ✂ ASG, ✂ Corn., ✂ EA, ✂ LC, ✂ PP, ✂ RN, ✂ SCW, ✂ UC, ✍ Aut.
02/3 Ultimate Memorabilia ✂ ASMVP, ✂ BOS, ✂ CSTW, ✂ Cor, ✂ EA, ✂ FS (x2), ✂ GMIH, ✂ SL, ✂ Num, ✂ PS (x2), ✂ RAT, ✂ RT, ✂ SF, ✂ VGJ, ✂ VHT
00 ✂ UD APOH 500, ✂✍ 500
99/0 UD C. Legends 6, ✍ ES
02/3 UD Foundations ✂ 1000Stick, ✍ SG
00/1 UD Legends 64, ✍ ES
01/2 UD Legends 31, ✂ PoH, ✍ ES
99/0 UD Retro 85, G5A, ✍ Ink.
01/2 UD SCup Champs 13
71/2 Williams Finnish 379
60/1 York Glass [Mont.]
60/1 York
61/2 York 10
62/3 York Transfer 8
63/4 York 26
67/8 York 23
67/8 York 25
67/8 York 28
67/8 York
94/5 Zellers, ✍ Aut.
67/8 MONT
67/8 MONT / IGA Card
68/9 MONT / IGA Card
69/0 MONT / Pro Star
70/1 MONT
71/2 MONT / Pro Star
73/4 MONT / Pro Star
83/4 MONT
92/3 MONT / OPC 14
92/3 MONT / OPC 27
92/3 MONT / OPC 44

BELKIN, OLEG
00/1 Mir 163

BELL, BOB
91/2 Avant Garde BCJHL 118
95/6 Tallahasee Tiger Sharks
95/6 Tallahasee Tiger Sharks

BELL, BRENDAN
01 UD Prospects GU 39, ✂ TPJ
99/0 Ottawa 67's
00/1 Ottawa 67's 7
01/2 Ottawa 67's 9

BELL, BRUCE
85/6 O-Pee-Chee 231
85/6 OPC Sticker 142
87/8 Panini Sticker 308
89/0 ProCards AHL 135
90/1 ProCards 234
91/2 ProCards 338
84/5 QUÉB
83/4 Brantford Alexanders
81/2 Soo Greyhounds

BELL, DARREN
90/1 7th..Sketch OHL 26
88/9 Sudbury Wolves
89/0 Sudbury Wolves

BELL, DAVID
95/6 Slapshot 259

BELL, GORDIE
45-54 Quaker Oats

BELL, MALCOLM
94/5 Humberside Hawks 1

BELL, MARK
01/2 Adrenaline RR5
02/3 Atomic 19
00/1 BAP Mem. 508
01/2 BAP Memor. 252
02/3 BAP Memorabilia 111
98 Bowman 36, 123, ✍ A8
98 Bowman Chrome 36, 123
98/9 Bowman's Best 138
01/2 Crown Royale 30, CA4, RR4
02/3 Exclusive 34
02/3 First Edition 8, 419R, ✂ Jers.
02/3 Heads Up ✂ GWQ 7
01/2 O-Pee-Chee 278
02/3 O-Pee-Chee 103
98/9 OPC Chrome 222
01/2 Pacific 83
02/3 Pacific 74
02/3 Pacific Complete 260
01/2 PTC Draft 3
01/2 PTC Collectibles 3
01/2 PTC Rookie 3
01/2 Parkhurst 289
02/3 Parkhurst 136
01/2 Pr. Stock 102, -PS 79
02/3 Pr. Stock Reserve 19
01/2 PS Titanium 29, TSS 24, TRT 4, ✂ DSJ 24, ✂ DSJ 73
01/2 PS Titanium Draft 115
02/3 PS Titanium ✂ GWJ 13
01/2 Signature 230, ✍ Aut. 230
02/3 Signature Series 18, ✍ 18
99/0 UD Sobey's 5
02/3 SP Game-Used ✂ FF
01/2 SPx 165
98/9 Topps 222
01/2 Topps 278
02/3 Topps 103
01/2 To. Chrome 143
98/9 To. Finest F7
02/3 T. Limited 103
02/3 T. Total 248
99/0 Upper Deck 318
02/3 Upper Deck 282, ✂ OR
99/0 UD Black Diam. 106
99/0 UD G. Reserve 318
01/2 UD Mask 18, ✂ GJ, ✂ JP, ✂ DP
99/0 UD Ovation 79
99/0 UD Prospects 4, C3, ✍ Sig.
01/2 UD Top Shelf 85
02/3 UD Top Shelf ✂ SW
02/3 UD Vintage 56
01/2 Vanguard 19
01/2 Victory 366
99/0 Ottawa 67's

BELL, MATT
96/7 Guelph Storm

BELL, SCOTT
99/0 Missouri RiverOtters
01/2 Rockford IceHogs
99/0 Topeka Scarecrows
91/2 Ferris State Bulldogs
91/2 Minnesota G'Gophers
92/3 Minnesota G'Gophers
94/5 Minnesota G'Gophers

BELL, THATCHER
99/0 UD Sobey's 11
99/0 UD Prospects 55, 68, C10, ✂ GJ
00/1 UD Prospects 82
99/0 Rimouski Océanic 5
00/1 Rimouski Océanic 6
01/2 Rimouski Océanic 6

BELL, TIM
92/3 BCJHL 11

BELLA, TONY
90/1 7th..Sketch OHL 51
91/2 7th...Sketch OHL 222

BELLAND, BRAD
84/5 Sudbury Wolves

BELLAND, NEIL
84/5 VANC
82/3 Fredericton Express
83/4 Fredericton Express
84/5 Fredericton Express
85/6 Fredericton Express
98/9 Portland Pirates

BELLAVANCE, JEAN-ROCH
51/2 Bas du Fleuve 33

BELLAVANCE, NORMAND
51/2 Bas du Fleuve 40
52/3 Bas du Fleuve 11

BELLEFEUILLE, BLAKE
01/2 BAP Memor. 362
95/6 Classic 57
01/2 SPx 203
01/2 UD PlayMakers Ltd 113
01/2 UD Ice 134
01/2 UD Premier 61
02/3 UD Vintage 330
00/1 Syracuse Crunch
01/2 Syracuse Crunch
02/3 Syracuse Crunch

BELLEFEUILLE, PETE
25-27 Anonymous 61

BELLEFONTAINE, SCOTT
91/2 Air Canada SJHL 42
91/2 Air Canada SJHL C41
90/1 7th..Sketch WHL 20

BELLEMARE, JONATHAN
02/3 Hull Olympiques
99/0 Shawinigan Cataractes 3
00/1 Shawinigan Cataractes 5
01/2 Shawinigan Cataractes 6

BELLEMARE, THOMAS
01/2 Drummondville

BELLEMORE, BOB
88/9 NJER / Caretta
89/0 NJER
89/0 NJER / Caretta

BELLEROSE, ERIC
92/3 Canada Nationals
90/1 7th..Sketch LHJMQ 135

BELLEROSE, ÉRIC
91/2 7th...Sketch LHJMQ 118

BELLEY, ROCH
91/2 ProCards 497
89/0 7th..Sketch OHL 139
90/1 7th..Sketch OHL 252
93/4 Muskegon Fury
89/0 Niagara Falls Thunder

BELLIO, JOHN
82 Semic Sticker 127

BELLIVEAU, LUC
95/6 Slapshot 210

BELLIVEAU, RÉMI
90/1 7th..Sketch LHJMQ 78

BÉLLIVEAU, DAVE
90/1 7th..Sketch LHJMQ 207
91/2 7th...Sketch LHJMQ 164

BELLOWS, BRIAN
98/9 Aurora 193
98/9 Be A Player 145, ✍ Aut. 145
90/1 Bowman 182
91/2 Bowman 129
92/3 Bowman 200
92/3 Bowman 260
93/4 Donruss 170
94/5 Donruss 203
95/6 Donruss 341
96/7 Donruss 64
93/4 EA Sports 71
94/5 Flair 84
94/5 Fleer 101
01/2 Fleer Greats 54, ✍ Aut.
92/3 Fleer Ultra 100, 324
93/4 Fleer Ultra 4
94/5 Fleer Ultra 105
95/6 Fleer Ultra 307
88/9 Frito Lay
83/4 Funmate Puffy 17 [w/]
93/4 Hockey Wit 11
90/1 Kraft 2
91/2 Kraft 38
93/4 Leaf 76
94/5 Leaf 301
96/7 Leaf 10
92/3 McDonald's McD-02
83/4 O-Pee-Chee 165
83/4 O-Pee-Chee 167
84/5 O-Pee-Chee 95
84/5 O-Pee-Chee 359
85/6 OPC/Topps 50
85/6 OPC/Topps Box A
86/7 OPC/Topps 75
87/8 OPC/Topps 94
88/9 OPC/Topps 95
90/1 OPC/Topps 70, 200
90/1 Topps-TL 15
91/2 O-Pee-Chee 44
91/2 O-Pee-Chee 110
92/3 O-Pee-Chee 384
89/0 OPC/Topps 177
98/9 OPC Chrome 133
90/1 OPC Premier 3
92/3 OPC Premier 75
83/4 OPC/Topps Sticker 142
84/5 OPC Sticker 44
84/5 OPC Sticker 45
85/6 OPC Sticker 41
86/7 OPC Sticker 167-28
87/8 OPC Sticker 53-194
88/9 OPC Sticker 203
89/0 opcSticker 200-58
98/9 Omega 243
98/9 Pacific 23
99/0 Pacific 435
97/8 Pacific CC 70
97/8 Pa. Dynagon 1, T-29
97/8 Pa. Invincible 1
98/9 Pa. Paramount 241
99/0 Pa. Paramount 241
87/8 Panini Sticker 286
87/8 Panini Sticker 296
88/9 Panini Sticker 89
89/0 Panini Sticker 105
90/1 Panini Sticker 257
91/2 Panini Sticker 108
92/3 Panini Sticker 88
93/4 Panini Sticker 15
95/6 Panini Sticker 128
96/7 Panini Sticker 130
97/8 Panini Sticker 190
91/2 Parkhurst 79
92/3 Parkhurst 87
93/4 Parkhurst 371
94/5 Parkhurst 112
95/6 Parkhurst 466
91/2 Pinnacle 129
92/3 Pinnacle 325
93/4 Pinnacle 22
94/5 Pinnacle 290
97/8 Pi. Inside 140
95/6 Pi. Summit 11
95/6 Playoff 91
94/5 POG 132
95/6 POG 253
93/4 Power Play 124
93/4 Premier 202
94/5 Premier 219
90/1 Pro Set 130
91/2 Pro Set 109
91/2 Pro Set Platinum 59
91/2 Puck / Pro Set 13
90/1 Score 7, 322
90/1 Sco. Hot Cards 3
91/2 Score 160
91/2 Score CAN 160
92/3 Score 335
93/4 Score 4
93/4 Score/CAN DD6
93/4 Score / Promo 4
94/5 Score 73
95/6 Score 231
96/7 Score 221
94/5 Select 91
84/5 7-Eleven
85/6 7-Eleven Superstars 9
83/4 Souhaits Keychain [North Stars]
91/2 SI For Kids 20
95/6 Super Sticker 115
84/5 Topps 71
92/3 Topps 240
95/6 Topps 253
98/9 Topps 133
94/5 Topps Finest 105
91/2 To. Stadium 87
92/3 To. Stadium 293
93/4 To. Stadium 156
90/1 Upper Deck 126,3 08
91/2 Upper Deck 236
92/3 Upper Deck 172
92/3 Upper Deck 471
92/3 Upper Deck 636
92/3 Upper Deck G1
93/4 Upper Deck 390, SP-76
94/5 Upper Deck 309, SP-130
95/6 Upper Deck 404
98/9 Upper Deck 204
95/6 UD Be A Player 32, ✍ S32
96/7 UD Black Diam. 104
95/6 UD CC 84
02/3 UD Foundations 46, 49, ✍ SG
98/9 UD G. Reserve 204
98/9 UD MVP 213, ✍ PS
96/7 ANAH / Up Front 13
82/3 MINS
82/3 MINS
83/4 MINS
84/5 MINS
84/5 MINS / 7-Eleven 4
85/6 MINS
85/6 MINS / 7-Eleven 9
86/7 MINS / 7-Eleven 12
87/8 MINS
88/9 MINS / ADA
92/3 MONT
92/3 MONT / OPC 60
93/4 MONT
93/4 MONT / Export
94/5 MONT

BELLRINGER, DON
51/2 Bas du Fleuve 50

BELOBRAGIN, MIKHAIL
00/1 Mir 97

BELOHLAV, RADEK
94/5 APS 110
95/6 APS 64, 374, 433
96/7 APS 255, 343
97/8 APS 43
97/8 DS 62
98/9 DS 85
99/0 DS 134
00/1 DS 81
96/7 DS Sticker 8, 90
97/8 DS Sticker 177
98/9 OFS 108, 426, 481
99/0 OFS 256, 438
00/1 OFS 18
01/2 OFS 14
96 Wien 123

BELOHLAVEK, PETR
99/0 OFS 72

BELOSHEIKIN, EUGENY
91/2 ProCards 223
89 Semic Sticker 78
87/8 Soviet Stars

BELOUSOV, MATVEI
99/0 Mir 133

BELOUSOV, VALERI
98/9 Mir 162

BELOV, OLEG
95 Panini Worlds 41
93/4 Upper Deck 274
99/0 UD Elitserien 92
00/1 UD Elitserien 98, 198, ✍ Sig., T6
95/6 Cleveland Lumberjacks

BELOV, VALERI
96/7 APS 115
96/7 DS Sticker 283
99/0 Mir 161

BELTER, SHANE
99/0 Providence Bruins
97/8 Kamloops Blazers

BELVINS, LOGO
00/1 Rockford IceHogs

BELVINS, WES
01/2 Rockford IceHogs

BELYAVSKI, IGOR
98/9 Mir 86
99/0 Mir 213

BELZA, ANTHONY
02/3 Peoria Rivermen

BELZILE, ERIC
96/7 Rimouski Océanic

BEMBRIDGE, GARRETT
00/1 Saskatoon Blades

BEMSTRÖM, JÖRGEN
97/8 UD Elitserien 174
98/9 UD Elitserien 144
99/0 UD Elitserien 146
00/1 UD Elitserien 163

BEN-AMOR, SEMIR
00/1 Cardset 131
02/3 Louisiana Ice Gators

BENAK, JAROSLAV
94/5 APS 168

BENAK, VACLAV
98/9 OFS 365
00/1 OFS 12
01/2 OFS 202
99/0 Score 115

BENAQUEZ, FERNAND
51/2 Lac St-Jean 17

BENARD, LEO
23/4 Paulins Candy 10
23/4 Selkirks Crescent 2
24/5 Selkirks Crescent 11

BENAZIC, CAL
92/3 BCJHL 185
02/3 Louisiana Ice Gators
00/1 Manitoba Moose

BENDA, JAN
95/6 APS 399
96/7 APS 140
98/9 Cardset 268
99/0 Cardset 171, 266, AH J-hertta
00/1 Cardset 44
02/3 Cardset 6
95/6 DEL 435
96/7 DS Sticker 63
99/0 Eishockey 365
95 Panini Worlds 62
90/1 7th..Sketch OHL 326
91/2 7th...Sketch OHL 149
97/8 Portland Pirates
94/5 Richmond Renegades
90/1 Oshawa Generals
91/2 Oshawa Generals

BENDELIN, TORGNY
94/5 Leaf Elit Set 295

BENDER, KEVIN (STU)
96/7 Hampton Roads
97/8 Hampton Roads
98/9 Hampton Roads
99/0 Hampton Roads

BENDERA, SHANE
00/1 UD Prospects 73
00/1 Red Deer Rebels

BENDERA, TERRY
90/1 7th..Sketch WHL 170
91/2 7th...Sketch WHL 224
89/0 Victoria Cougars

BENEDICT, BRANDON
98/9 Halifax Moosehead
00/1 Halifax Moosehead
99/0 Halifax Mooseheads

BENEDICT, CLINT
25-27 Anonymous 95
24/5 Champ's Cigarettes
83 HHOF Postcard H1
83&87 HHOF 107
12/3 Imperial 3
28/9 La Presse
24/5 Maple Crispette [V130] 2
23/4 William Paterson 7
24/5 William Paterson 32

BENES, STANISLAV
94/5 APS 141
95/6 APS 250

BENIC, GEOFF
88/9 ProCards / Indianapolis

BENIK, RAY
81/2 Victoria Cougars

BENN, DAVID
89/0 7th..Sketch OHL 126
90/1 7th..Sketch OHL 123
91/2 7th...Sketch OHL 39
89/0 Niagara Falls Thunder
92/3 Windsor Spitfires

BENNEFIELD, BLUE
00/1 Asheville Smoke

BENNETT, ADAM
94/5 Leaf 389
93/4 Parkhurst 334
94/5 Parkhurst 77
91/2 ProCards 501
90/1 7th..Sketch OHL 378
93/4 Upper Deck 237
94/5 Upper Deck 202
93/4 EDMO / Sheet
88/9 Sudbury Wolves
89/0 Sudbury Wolves
90/1 Sudbury Wolves

BENNETT, BILL
83/4 Ottawa 67's
84/5 Ottawa 67's

BENNETT, BRAD
90/1 Canada Nationals 11
84/5 Prince Albert Raiders

BENNETT, CURT
74/5 Loblaws
73/4 O-Pee-Chee 149
74/5 O-Pee-Chee 33
75/6 O-Pee-Chee 8
76/7 O-Pee-Chee 202
76/7 OPC 379
77/8 O-Pee-Chee 97
78/9 O-Pee-Chee 31
79/0 O-Pee-Chee 344
79 Panini Sticker 214
73/4 Topps 152
74/5 Topps 33
75/6 Topps 8
76/7 Topps 202
77/8 Topps 97
78/9 Topps 31
72/3 ATLF
74/5 ATLF
79/0 ATLF / B&W
79/0 ATLF / Colour
78/9 SLOU

BENNETT, HARVEY
77/8 O-Pee-Chee 282
78/9 O-Pee-Chee 163
79 Panini Sticker 219
78/9 Topps 163
78/9 SLOU

BENNETT, JIM
95/6 Guildford Flames 29

BENNETT, RICK
90/1 OPC/Topps 252
90/1 ProCards 21
91/2 ProCards 198
90/1 Score 400
90/1 Upper Deck 540
92/3 Binghampton Rangers

BENNETT, RYAN
99/0 Des Moines Buc's

BENNING, BRIAN
92/3 Bowman 39
93/4 Donruss 129
92/3 Fleer Ultra 151
93/4 Fleer Ultra 3, 321
93/4 Leaf 328
94/5 Leaf 379
87/8 OPC/Topps 122
88/9 OPC/Topps 174
90/1 OPC/Topps 365
91/2 O-Pee-Chee 283
91/2 O-Pee-Chee 359
92/3 O-Pee-Chee 68
89/0 OPC/Topps 86
87/8 OPC Leaders 2
87/8 OPC Sticker 124-112
88/9 OPC Sticker 18-151
89/0 opcSticker 24-162
88/9 Panini Sticker 101
89/0 Panini Sticker 124
92/3 Parkhurst 125
92/3 Parkhurst 284
93/4 Parkhurst 343
94/5 Parkie SE65
91/2 Pinnacle 402
92/3 Pinnacle 45
93/4 Pinnacle 341
94/5 Pinnacle 414
94/5 POG 111
93/4 Power Play 90
94/5 Premier 389
90/1 Pro Set 114
91/2 Pro Set 398
92/3 Pro Set 135
91/2 Pro Set Platinum 182
90/1 Score 306
91/2 Score 186
91/2 Score CAN 186
92/3 Score 133
93/4 Score 512
93/4 Score 64
92/3 Topps 250
92/3 To. Stadium 91
94/5 To. Stadium 157
91/2 Upper Deck 415
92/3 Upper Deck 301
93/4 Upper Deck 496
94/5 Upper Deck 217
89/0 LOSA / Smokey 21
90/1 LOSA / Smokey 2
92/3 PHIL / UD Sheet
92/3 PHIL / J.C. Penney
87/8 SLOU
87/8 SLOU / Kodak
88/9 SLOU
88/9 SLOU / Kodak
84/5 Kamloops Blazers

BENNING, JIM
84/5 Kelowna Wings &...
82/3 O-Pee-Chee 317
83/4 O-Pee-Chee 326
84/5 O-Pee-Chee 296
85/6 O-Pee-Chee 250
87/8 O-Pee-Chee 260
90/1 O-Pee-Chee 455
82/3 OPC/Topps Sticker 64
84/5 OPC Sticker 21
85/6 OPC Sticker 16-146
87/8 OPC Sticker 197-56
88/9 OPC Sticker 58-191
88/9 Panini Sticker 133
82/3 Post [Toro.]
90/1 Pro Set 292
92/3 Pro Set 181
90/1 ProCards 329
83/4 Vachon 82-31
81/2 TORO
82/3 TORO
83/4 TORO
84/5 TORO
85/6 TORO
87/8 VANC / Shell
88/9 VANC / Mohawk
89/0 VANC / Mohawk

BENOIT, ANDRÉ
01/2 Kitchener Rangers

BENOIT, JOE
34-43 BeeHive-1 [Mont.]
40/1 O-Pee-Chee 121
43-47 Parade Sportive
45-54 Quaker Oats

BENOIT, MARCEL
52/3 Bas du Fleuve 21

BENOIT, MAURICE
51/2 Bas du Fleuve 19

BENOÎT, DENIS
88/9 Richelieu Riverains

BENOÎT, MATHIEU
99 Bowman 61
00/1 Charlotte Checkers

BENOÎT, RICHARD
83/4 North Bay Centennials

BENOÎT, STEVE
91/2 Cincinnati Cyclones
92/3 Cincinnati Cyclones
93/4 Cincinnati Cyclones

BENSON, BILL
34-43 BeeHive-1 [NYAm.]
40/1 O-Pee-Chee 135

BENSON, BOBBIE
23/4 Paulins Candy 65

BENSON, R.J.
24/5 Holland Creameries 6

BENTHAM,
91/2 Avant Garde BCJHL 160

BENTLEY, DOUG
34-43 BeeHive-1 [Chic.]
34-43 BeeHive-1 [xM.Bentley's card]
45-64 BeeHive-2 [Chic.]
48-52 Exhibits [Blackhawks]
83 HHOF Postcard F1
83&87 HHOF 77
96/7 Legends 83
43-47 Parade Sportive
51/2 Parkhurst 48
93/4 Parkie 56-57 P-11

BENTLEY, MAX
34-43 BeeHive-1 [Chic.]
45-64 BeeHive-2 [Toro.]
45-64 BeeHive-2 [NYRa.]
48-52 Exhibits [Blackhawks]
83 HHOF Postcard C2
83&87 HHOF 32
96/7 Legends 84
40/1 O-Pee-Chee 131
43-47 Parade Sportive
51/2 Parkhurst 81
52/3 Parkhurst 95
53/4 Parkhurst 55
02/3 Parkie - Reprint 181
45-54 Quaker Oats
02/3 Ultimate Memorabilia ✍ Cut
99/0 UD C. Legends 49

BENYSEK, LADISLAV
95/6 APS 342
96/7 APS 271
97/8 APS 23, 349
00/1 BAP Mem. 481
98/9 DS 89
99/0 DS 144
96/7 DS Sticker 173
98/9 OFS 132, 423, 449
99/0 OFS 257, 395, 494
02/3 Upper Deck 335
94/5 Cape Breton Oilers

BERALDO, PAUL
95/6 DEL 321
96/7 DEL 179
00/1 Kudos 151
88/9 ProCards / Maine
89/0 ProCards AHL 55
01/2 Sheffield Steelers GS

BERAN, JAN
93/4 Johnstown Chiefs 15

BERAN, KAREL
95/6 APS 203

BERANEK, JIRI
94/5 APS 157
95/6 APS 87
96/7 APS 90
97/8 APS 207
96/7 DS Sticker 139
97/8 DS Sticker 238

BERANEK, JOSEF
94/5 APS 243
96/7 APS 165, 384, 407, 412
97/8 APS 47, 359
98/9 Be A Player 203, ✍ Aut. 203
99/0 BAP Mem. 129, 382
00/1 BAP Mem. 356
98 Bonaparte 3A
98 Bonaparte Pexeso 8
94/5 Donruss 13
95/6 Donruss 356
97/8 DS 3
99/0 DS NS18
01/2 DS 38, -IH 4
96/7 DS Sticker 12, 30
97/8 DS Sticker 183
94/5 Fleer 221
94/5 Fleer Ultra 153
95 Globe 158
01/2 Heads Up ✂ JQ 28
94/5 Leaf 31
95/6 Leaf 232
98/9 OFS 242, 331, OW 18
99/0 OFS 18, 381
00/1 OFS 411
01/2 OFS 6, -RE2 D
98/9 Omega 90
99/0 Pacific 152
97/8 Pa. Invincible R-158
99/0 Pa. Paramount 89
95/6 Panini Sticker 291
96/7 Panini Sticker 298
95 Panini Worlds 203
94/5 Parkhurst 166
95/6 Parkhurst 208
94/5 Pinnacle 148
95/6 Pinnacle 140
94/5 POG 356
94/5 Premier 141
01/2 PS Titanium ✂ DSJ 33
94/5 Score 77
95/6 Score 118
99/0 Score JT11
95 Semic 154
95/6 SBx Emotion 176
95/6 Topps 149
94/5 Upper Deck 117, SP-56
95/6 Upper Deck 67
00/1 Upper Deck 370
95/6 UD CC 312
99/0 UD MVP 77
00/1 UD Vintage 288
01/2 Vanguard ✂ DGM 23
99/0 Victory 114
96 Wien 127
91/2 EDMO / IGA
92/3 EDMO / IGA 002
92/3 PHIL / UD Sheet
93/4 PHIL / Sheet
93/4 PHIL / J.C. Penney

BERANEK, JOSEF (SR.)
95/6 APS 148

BERANEK, MILAN
95/6 APS 324

BERÁNEK, JIRI
91/2 7th...Sketch WHL 39

BERÁNEK, JOSEF
92/3 Bowman 100
92/3 Classic Prospects 81
93/4 Donruss 247
92/3 Fleer Ultra 56
93/4 Fleer Ultra 17
93/4 Leaf 103
92/3 O-Pee-Chee 178
91/2 OPC Premier 149
92/3 Panini Sticker I
91/2 Parkhurst 47
92/3 Parkhurst 360
93/4 Parkhurst 153
91/2 Pinnacle 303
92/3 Pinnacle 208
93/4 Pinnacle 424
93/4 Power Play 177
93/4 Premier 467
91/2 Pro Set 534
91/2 Pro Set Platinum 255
92/3 Score 105
93/4 Score 439
94 Semic 176
92 Semic Sticker 137
93 Semic Sticker 105
92/3 Topps 177
92/3 To. Stadium 214
93/4 To. Stadium 69
91/2 Upper Deck 17
91/2 Upper Deck 595
92/3 Upper Deck 196
92/3 Upper Deck E11
93/4 Upper Deck 15, SP-113

BERARD, BRYAN
96/7 All-Sport PPF 97
98/9 Aurora 114
98/9 Be A Player 85, ✍ Aut. 85
99/0 BAP Mem. 267
02/3 BAP Memorabilia 259 [w/ Potvin]
97/8 Bicycle A-Diamond
98/9 Bowman's Best 80
02/3 Calder 11
95/6 Classic 1, 84, 99, AS8, BK1, SP4
95/6 Cla. Clear Assets 56
95/6 Cla. 5 Sport 123, S-70, CS-5, FT-5
94/5 Cla. Images 1, CE1, PD1
95/6 Cla. Visions 82
95/6 Cla. Vis. Signings 77, ✍ Aut.
97/8 Donruss 163, L2L-9
96/7 Do. Canadian 131
97/8 Do. Canadian 92
95/6 Do. Elite WJ 25
96/7 Do. Elite 147, A-23
97/8 Do. Elite 29, 124, C-26
97/8 Do. Preferred 79, 186
97/8 Do. Priority 54, 194, OD-20, Post-25, Stamp-25
97/8 Do. Studio 27, HH-4, P-24
98/9 Dynagon Ice 113
02/3 First Edition 54, ✂ Jers.
96/7 Flair 114
96/7 Fl. Ultra 98, UR-1
97/8 Leaf 30, 183, BS-18
94/5 L. Limited USA 1
96/7 L. Limited LR-3
96/7 L. Preferred 129
97/8 Limited 70, 181, 182, FG-31
97/8 McDonald's McD-10
96/7 Metal Univ. 170
99/0 Millenium 229, ✍ Aut. 229
99/0 NHL Power Play
98/9 OPC Chrome 198
97/8 Omega 136
98/9 Omega 225
98/9 Pacific 275
99/0 Pacific 401
02/3 Pacific 247
02/3 Pacific Complete 212
97/8 Pacific CC 222
97/8 Pa. Crown Roy. 78, BOS-13
98/9 Pa. Crown Roy. 82
97/8 Pa. Dynagon 72, DD-9A, T-71, BKS-107
97/8 Pa. Invincible 80, AZ-12
97/8 Pa. Paramount 106
98/9 Pa. Paramount 140
99/0 Pa. Paramount 221
97/8 Pa. Revolution 80
98/9 Panini Photocard
97/8 Panini Sticker 80, 119, 247
98/9 Panini Sticker 78
99/0 Panini Sticker 160
01/2 Parkhurst 247
94/5 Parkie SE250
97/8 Pinnacle 145
97/8 Pi. Be A Player 18, TN-9
97/8 Pi. BeeHive 8
97/8 Pi. Certified 40
97/8 Pi. Inside 80
97/8 Pi. Totally 40
96/7 Pi. Zenith 126
97/8 Score 137, 267,CI-12
94/5 Select 149
96/7 Select CE 114
94/5 Sig. Rookies 60, ✍ 60
94/5 SR Auto-Phonex 29, P1, ✍ 29, ✍ P1
95/6 SR Draft / Promo FF1
95/6 SR Tetrad F2
95/6 SR Tetrad Autobilia 39
94/5 Slapshot / Detroit Jr. 18
95/6 Slapshot 75
94/5 Slapshot Memorial 92
94/5 SP 174
96/7 SP 182, SF-4
97/8 SP Authentic 92, ✍ SotT, ✍ T4
98/9 SP Authentic 53
99/0 SP Authentic 82
97/8 SPx 29, D-SPX8
99/0 SPx 146
98/9 SPx Finite 51
99/0 Stadium 35
98/9 SLU
98/9 Topps 198
99/0 Topps 78
99/0 To. Chrome 78
94/5 Topps Finest 114
98/9 To. Finest 107, C2
02/3 To. Heritage 170
02/3 T. Total 106
98/9 UD Choice 123
01/2 Ultimate Mem. ✂ CT
02/3 Ultimate Memorabilia ✂ FO
94/5 Upper Deck 522
96/7 Upper Deck 294, X23
97/8 Upper Deck 98, SS28, SG34, S29, T4A
98/9 Upper Deck 21, 127, LS19
99/0 Upper Deck 293
02/3 Upper Deck 261
96/7 UD Black Diam. 161
97/8 UD Black Diam. 12, PC16
96/7 UD CC 359
97/8 UD Coll. Choice 155, SQ1
98/9 UD G. Reserve 21, 127
99/0 UD G. Reserve 293
96/7 UD Ice 93
97/8 UD Ice 54
98/9 UD MVP 200
99/0 UD MVP 201
99/0 UD Retro G1C
99/0 Victory 282
99/0 WGretzky 165
97/8 Zenith 53, Z32
99/0 TORO / Pizza Pizza 7

BERARDICURTI, LOUIE
83/4 Kitchener Rangers

BERDICHEVSKY, LEV
00/1 Mir 65
91/2 O-Pee-Chee 50R
92/3 Red Ace Blue 32
93/4 Roanoke Express
00/1 Dynamo 21

BERDNIKOV, SERGEI
98/9 Mir 135
99/0 Mir 147
00/1 Mir 103

BEREHOWSKY, DRAKE
92/3 Classic Prospects 59
93/4 Donruss 336
92/3 Fleer Ultra 417
93/4 Fleer Ultra 90
92/3 Humpty Dumpty
94/5 Leaf 410
91/2 O-Pee-Chee 70
98/9 OPC Chrome 137
92/3 OPC Premier 131
99/0 Pacific 217
90/1 Panini/TOR 1
93/4 Parkhurst 199
94/5 Parkie SE177
92/3 Pinnacle 231
95/6 POG 218
93/4 Power Play 239
93/4 Premier 69
90/1 Score 434
91/2 Score 385
91/2 Score CAN 275
93/4 Score 355
90/1 7th..Sketch OHL 52
91/2 7th...Sketch OHL 70
98/9 Topps 137
00/1 Topps 36
93/4 To. Stadium 331
90/1 Upper Deck 361
92/3 Upper Deck 415
93/4 Upper Deck 20
94/5 Upper Deck 458
00/1 Upper Deck 327
94/5 UD Be A Player ✍ 55
01/2 UD Mask 97
00/1 UD MVP 99
99/0 UD MVP Cup 101
00/1 UD Vintage 200
00/1 Victory 133
98/9 NASH / Wendy's 2
92/3 TORO / Kodak
93/4 TORO / Black's 14
96/7 Carolina Monarchs
95/6 Cleveland Lumberjacks
92/3 St. John's Maple Leafs

BEREK, MIROSLAV
94/5 DEL 415
95/6 DEL 218
96/7 DEL 68

BERENS, SEAN
99/0 Chicago Wolves
00/1 Grand Rapids Griffins
98/9 Las Vegas Thunder
01/2 Belfast Giants

BERENSON, RED
45-64 BeeHive-2 [Black script]
45-64 BeeHive-2 [Mont.]
64-67 BeeHive-3 [Mont.]
63-65 Chex
70/1 Colgate 24
70/1 Dad's Cookies
70/1 Eddie Sargent 177
71/2 Eddie Sargent 51
72/3 Eddie Sargent 73
70/1 Esso Power Player
91/2 Future Trends C72 48, ✍ 48
62/3 Cowan Tile
74/5 Lipton Soup 25
74/5 Loblaws
74/5 Loblaws Update
68/9 O-Pee-Chee 114
69/0 O-Pee-Chee 20
69/0 O-Pee-Chee 4in1
69/0 O-Pee-Chee Stamp
70/1 O-Pee-Chee 103
70/1 O-Pee-Chee DE 25
71/2 O-Pee-Chee 91
72/3 O-Pee-Chee 123
72/3 O-Pee-Chee Crest 7
72/3 O-Pee-Chee TC
73/4 O-Pee-Chee 10
74/5 O-Pee-Chee 19
75/6 O-Pee-Chee 22
76/7 O-Pee-Chee 236
77/8 O-Pee-Chee 107
78/9 O-Pee-Chee 218
71/2 O-Pee-Chee Poster 10
63/4 Parkhurst 26
63/4 Parkhurst 85
95/6 Parkie 66-67 92
94/5 Parkie Tall 80
72 Semic Sticker 183
62/3 Shirriff 42
68/9 Shirriff / SLou. 4
64/5 Topps 61
65/6 Topps 9
66/7 Topps 92
66/7 Topps / Test 10
67/8 Topps 24
68/9 Topps 114
69/0 Topps 20
70/1 Topps 103
71/2 Topps 91
72/3 Topps 95
73/4 Topps 174
74/5 Topps 19
75/6 Topps 22
76/7 Topps 236
77/8 Topps 107
78/9 Topps 218
64/5 Toronto Star Action
71/2 Toronto Sun Photo
63/4 York 36
92/3 SLOU / McDon. 11

BERENZWEIG, ANDREW (BUBBA)
01/2 BAP Memor. 262
94/5 Classic DP1
01/2 PS Titanium Draft 141
94/5 Select 151
00/1 Upper Deck 187
99/0 Milwaukee Admirals
00/1 Milwaukee Admirals
01/2 Milwaukee Admirals

BEREZAN, PERRY
92/3 Bowman 105
90/1 OPC/Topps 357
91/2 O-Pee-Chee 485
92/3 O-Pee-Chee 182
89/0 Panini Sticker 110
91/2 Parkhurst 381
91/2 Pinnacle 287
92/3 Pinnacle 148
90/1 Pro Set 459
91/2 Pro Set 487
90/1 Score 379
91/2 Score 94T
91/2 Score CAN 527
92/3 Score 169
92/3 Topps 342
91/2 To. Stadium 227
92/3 To. Stadium 441
92/3 Upper Deck 451
85/6 CALG / Red Rooster
86/7 CALG / Red Rooster
87/8 CALG / Red Rooster
91/2 SANJ / Sports Action

BEREZIN, SERGEI
01/2 Adrenaline 145
98/9 Aurora 179
99/0 Aurora 134
98/9 Be A Player 285, ✍ Aut. 285
99/0 BAP Mem. 273
00/1 BAP Mem. 205
01/2 BAP Memor. 188, 488
94/5 Classic 67
99/0 Crown Royale 132
00/1 Crown Royale 99
94/5 DEL 221
95/6 DEL 217
97/8 Donruss 165
96/7 Do. Canadian 119
96/7 Do. Elite 138, A-17
97/8 Do. Elite 55
97/8 Do. Preferred 77
97/8 Do. Priority 28
97/8 Do. Studio 104, HH-14
98/9 Dynagon Ice 177
99/0 Dynagon Ice 185
96/7 Flair 124
96/7 Fl. Ultra 161, UR-2
96/7 Got-Um
02/3 Heads Up ✂ GWQ 15
99/0 HoloGrFX 56
97/8 Leaf 66,BS-21
96/7 L. Limited LR-7
96/7 L. Preferred 123
97/8 Limited 8, 13, 154, FG-57
96/7 Metal Univ. 171
99/0 Millenium 232, ✍ Aut. 232
01/2 O-Pee-Chee 159
02/3 O-Pee-Chee 157
98/9 OPC Chrome 55
97/8 Omega 217
99/0 Omega 222
98/9 Pacific 410
99/0 Pacific 402,GC-33
00/1 Pacific 385
01/2 Pacific 361
02/3 Pacific 191, ✂ GWJ 25
02/3 Pacific Complete 409
97/8 Pacific CC 36, SS-10C
97/8 Pa. Crown Roy. 128
98/9 Pa. Crown Roy. 128
97/8 Pa. Dynagon 120, 144, T-10, T-27, BKS-91
97/8 Pa. Invincible 135, FP-32, OTG-19, R-191
97/8 Pa. Paramount 178
98/9 Pa. Paramount 224
99/0 Pa. Paramount 222
00/1 Pa. Paramount 227
97/8 Panini Sticker 180, 250
98/9 Panini Sticker 166
99/0 Panini Sticker 161
00/1 Parkhurst P-182
01/2 Parkhurst 358
97/8 Pinnacle 162
96/7 Pi. Be A Player LTH3A, ✍ Aut. LTH3A
97/8 Pi. Certified 127
97/8 Pi. Inside 120
97/8 Pi. Totally 127
96/7 Pi. Zenith 127
97/8 Pi. Post 15
99/0 Prism 135
00/1 PS Titanium 90
01/2 PS Titanium ✂ DSJ 72
01/2 PS Titanium Draft ✂ 48
02/3 PS Titanium ✂ GWJ 14
99/0 Revolution 135, / CSC 135
97/8 Score 145
97/8 Score Toro. 6
96/7 Select CE 98
95 Semic 135
00/1 Signature 150
01/2 Signature 193, ✍ Aut. 193
96/7 SP 188, SF-4
97/8 SP Authentic 153, ✍ SotT
99/0 SPx 145
01/2 SPx 178
99/0 Stadium 53
98/9 Topps 55
99/0 Topps 236
00/1 Topps 55
01/2 Topps 159
02/3 Topps 157
99/0 To. Chrome 236
99/0 To. Gold Label 62
01/2 To. Heritage 185
02/3 T. Limited 157
99/0 To. Prmr. Plus 35
02/3 T. Total 312
98/9 UD Choice 201
00/1 UD Heroes 110
00/1 UD Reserve 82
96/7 Upper Deck 346, X31
97/8 Upper Deck 161, SG51, T19A
98/9 Upper Deck 186
99/0 Upper Deck 123
00/1 Upper Deck 165
01/2 Upper Deck 363, ✂ PotL
02/3 Upper Deck 281
96/7 UD Black Diam. 94
96/7 UD CC 350
97/8 UD Coll. Choice 247, SQ48
98/9 UD G. Reserve 186
99/0 UD G. Reserve 123
96/7 UD Ice 103
97/8 UD Ice 4
01/2 UD Mask 49
99/0 UD MVP 199
00/1 UD MVP 169
99/0 UD MVP Cup 176
99/0 UD Retro 73
00/1 UD Vintage 335
02/3 Vanguard ✂ GWJ 10
99/0 Victory 283
00/1 Victory 219
99/0 WGretzky 162
96 Wien 153, AS4
99/0 TORO / Pizza Pizza 14

BEREZNIUK, CHAD
90/1 7th..Sketch WHL 305

BERG, AKI
99/0 BAP Mem. 221
00/1 BAP Mem. 309
95/6 Bowman 146
98/9 Cardset 233
99/0 Cardset 181, MW-1, AH 5-ruutu
00/1 Cardset 112
02/3 Cardset 157
94/5 Classic DP2
95/6 Classic 3,BK3
95/6 Cla. 5 Sport 125, S-72, SFF-Q
95/6 Donruss 325
97/8 Donruss 129
96/7 Do. Elite 108
97/8 Do. Preferred 112
95/6 Fleer Metal 170
95/6 Fleer Ultra 330
95/6 Future Legends 27
95/6 L. Limited 20
97/8 Limited 85
96/7 Metal Univ. 72
99/0 NHL Power Play
00/1 Pacific 192
02/3 Pacific Complete 480
97/8 Pa. Dynagon BKS-44
98/9 Panini Sticker 202
95/6 Parkhurst 253, 510
97/8 Pi. Be A Player 155, ✍ Aut. 155
95/6 Pi. Summit 175
96/7 Pi. Summit 164
95/6 Pi. Zenith 146, RRC-6
96/7 Score 264
95/6 Select CE 127
94/5 SR Auto-Phonex 6, P4, ✍ 6, ✍ P4
95/6 SR Tetrad F3
95/6 SR Tetrad Autobilia 40
93/4 Sisu 38
94/5 Sisu 335
95/6 Sisu DD 1
95/6 Sisu Limited SAS 4
95/6 SBx Impact 203
95/6 SP 69
99/0 SPx 77
95/6 Topps 267
95/6 To. Finest 138
95/6 To. Stadium ER201
95/6 T. Super Skills SR6
95/6 Upper Deck 267, H-25
99/0 Upper Deck 235
95/6 UD CC 337, 410
96/7 UD CC 128
97/8 UD Coll. Choice 121
99/0 UD G. Reserve 235
01/2 Victory 335
99/0 WGretzky 83
96 Wien 30

BERG, BILL
91/2 Bowman 216
93/4 Leaf 287
91/2 O-Pee-Chee 122
93/4 Parkhurst 472
94/5 Parkie SE181
94/5 Pinnacle 57
96/7 Pi. Be A Player 84, ✍ Aut. 84
94/5 Premier 136
91/2 Pro Set 145
88/9 ProCards / Springfield
89/0 ProCards AHL 232
91/2 Score CAN 541
97/8 Score NYRa. 9
91/2 To. Stadium 385
94/5 UD Be A Player ✍ 57
98/9 OTTA
92/3 TORO / Kodak
93/4 TORO / Abalene
93/4 TORO / Black's 15
94/5 TORO / Coca-Cola

BERG, BOB
90/1 ProCards 432
91/2 ProCards 384
89/0 7th..Sketch OHL 72
90/1 7th..Sketch OHL 400
95/6 Louisiana Ice Gators
95/6 Louisiana Ice Gators-2
91/2 Richmond Renegades

BERG, REG
95/6 Do. Elite WJ 32
95/6 Upper Deck 567

BERG, REGGIE
00/1 Cincinnati Cyclones
99/0 Florida Everblades
00/1 Florida Everblades
01/2 Florida Everblades

BERG, STÅLE
92/3 Semic Nordisk 109

BERGE, DAVID
96/7 DEL 248
98/9 DEL 129
99/0 Eishockey 286, 360

BERGEN, ANDREW
00/1 Red Deer Rebels

BERGEN, BRAD
94/5 DEL 234
95/6 DEL 81
96/7 DEL 272
98/9 DEL 270, 330
00/1 UD DEL 6
01/2 UD DEL 166

BERGEN, BRADLEY
99/0 Eishockey 156

BERGEN, TODD
83/4 Springfield Indians 3

BERGENHEIM, CHRISTER
72/3 Williams Finnish 139

BERGENHEIM, SEAN
02/3 Cardset 158, -BG 1, -DD 10, ✍ BFG

BERGER, JURG
79 Panini Sticker 264

BERGER, MIKE
88/9 ProCards / Kalamazoo
89/0 ProCards AHL 285
87/8 MINS
99/0 Indianapolis Ice

BERGER, PHIL
91/2 Greensboro Monarchs
92/3 Greensboro Monarchs 5
93/4 Greensboro Monarchs
94/5 Greensboro Monarchs

BERGER, STANISLAV
94/5 APS 284
95/6 APS 268
96/7 APS 407

BERGERON, CHRIS
95/6 Birmingham Bulls
94/5 Cincinnati Cyclones
93/4 Toledo Storm 17
96/7 Toledo Storm

BERGERON, DANIEL
00/1 Baie-Comeau 22
01/2 Baie-Comeau 20

BERGERON, DAVID
91/2 7th...Sketch LHJMQ 172

BERGERON, GERARD
52/3 Anonymous 37

BERGERON, GERMAIN
51/2 Lac St-Jean 44

BERGERON, J. MICHEL
80/1 QUÉB
81/2 QUÉB
82/3 QUÉB
83/4 QUÉB
84/5 QUÉB
85/6 QUÉB
85/6 QUÉB / Gene. Foods
85/6 QUÉB / Provigo
86/7 QUÉB
86/7 QUÉB / Gene. Foods
89/0 QUÉB
89/0 QUÉB / Gene. Foods

BERGERON, J-C
91/2 Bowman 335
95/6 Donruss 241
90/1 OPC Premier 4
90/1 Panini/MTL 1
93/4 Panini Sticker 220
95/6 Parkhurst 465
90/1 Pro Set 614
89/0 ProCards AHL 181
91/2 ProCards 77
95/6 Topps 174
90/1 Upper Deck 408
90/1 MONT
92/3 TAMP / Sheraton Inn
95/6 TAMP / Sky Box
92/3 Atlanta Knights
93/4 Atlanta Knights

BERGERON, JÉRÔME
00/1 Val d'Or Foreurs 20

BERGERON, MARC-ANDRÉ
02/3 BAP Memorabilia 316
02/3 Ultimate Memorabilia 80
02/3 UD Rookie 138
01/2 Hamilton Bulldogs
02/3 Hamilton Bulldogs
99/0 Shawinigan Cataractes 7
00/1 Shawinigan Cataractes

BERGERON, MARTIN
90/1 ProCards 17

BERGERON, MICHEL
81/2 Dernière Heure
78/9 WASH

BERGERON, MICHEL*
76/7 O-Pee-Chee 71
76/7 OPC 385
77/8 O-Pee-Chee 159
78/9 O-Pee-Chee 273
76/7 Topps 71
77/8 Topps 159

BERGERON, RÉMI
98 Bowman 102
98 Bowman Chrome 102
00/1 Québec Remparts 6

BERGERON, TIM
92/3 Atlanta Knights

BERGERON, YVAN
90/1 7th..Sketch LHJMQ 101

BERGERON, YVES
72/3 Québec Nordiques

BERGEVIN, MARC
92/3 Durivage 30
92/3 Fleer Ultra 200
94/5 Leaf 384
01/2 O-Pee-Chee 253
89/0 O-Pee-Chee 249
00/1 Pacific 340
97/8 Pa. Invincible R-166
99/0 Panini Sticker 289
95 Panini Worlds 9
92/3 Pinnacle 385
93/4 Pinnacle 304
93/4 Pinnacle CA22
94/5 Pinnacle 183
96/7 Pi. Be A Player 85, ✍ Aut. 85
93/4 Premier 373
94/5 Premier 507
91/2 Pro Set 397
91/2 Pro Set Platinum 176
89/0 ProCards AHL 251
92/3 Score 404
93/4 Score 363
97/8 Score SLou. 19
92/3 Topps 61
99/0 Topps 242
01/2 Topps 253
99/0 To. Chrome 242
92/3 To. Stadium 174
93/4 To. Stadium 154
94/5 To. Stadium 101
97/8 Upper Deck 351
94/5 UD Be A Player ✍ 10
86/7 CHIC / Coke
87/8 CHIC / Coke
91/2 HART / Jr. Whalers
99/0 SLOU / Taco Bell 1
92/3 TAMP / Sheraton Inn
94/5 TAMP / Sky Box
95/6 TAMP / Sky Box

BERGEVIN-ROBINSON, MICHEL
02/3 Baie-Comeau
02/3 Shawinigan Cataractes

BERGGREN, BO
74 Semic Sticker 22

BERGIN, KEVIN
00/1 Shawinigan Cataractes 14

BERGIN, TONY
92/3 MPS SJHL 109

BERGKVIST, JONAS
95 Globe 34
94/5 Leaf Elit Set 250, GC-9, SS-6
95/6 Leaf Elit Set 69, LM-2
95 Panini Worlds 154
94 Semic 73
95 Semic 63
91/2 Semic Elitserien 149
91/2 Semic Elitserien 356
92/3 Semic Elitserien 167
89 Semic Sticker 17
95/6 UD Elitserien 105
97/8 UD Elitserien 113, 202, 221, UDS10, S15, C10
96 Wien 71

BERGKVIST, PER RAGNAR
95/6 Leaf Elit Set 235
95/6 Upper Deck 564

BERGKVIST, STEFAN
94/5 Classic 28
95/6 Classic 88
96/7 Upper Deck 323
98/9 UD Elitserien 122
99/0 UD Elitserien 108, S8
00/1 UD Elitserien 109
95/6 Cleveland Lumberjacks
96/7 Cleveland Lumberjacks
97/8 Cleveland Lumberjacks

BERGLAND, TIM
91/2 Bowman 297
90/1 O-Pee-Chee 507
91/2 O-Pee-Chee 34
91/2 Parkhurst 409
90/1 Pro Set 550
91/2 Pro Set 507
88/9 ProCards / Baltimore
89/0 ProCards AHL 95
92/3 Topps 244
91/2 To. Stadium 351
92/3 To. Stadium 127
92/3 TAMP / Sheraton Inn
90/1 WASH / Kodak
90/1 WASH / Smokey
91/2 WASH / Kodak
91/2 WASH / Smokey
98/9 Chicago Wolves
98/9 Chicago Wolves Champs

BERGLUND, ANDERS
94/5 Leaf Elit Set 9
95/6 Leaf Elit Set 284
89/0 Semic Elitserien 80, 255
90/1 Semic Elitserien 6, 163
91/2 Semic Elitserien 208
91/2 Semic Elitserien 268
92/3 Semic Elitserien 225
92/3 Semic Elitserien 294
95/6 UD Elitserien 171

BERGLUND, ART
89 Semic Sticker 152

BERGLUND, BO
84/5 O-Pee-Chee 276
89/0 Semic Elitserien 14
89 Semic Sticker 14
83/4 Vachon 61-41
85/6 MINS

BERGLUND, CHARLES
95 Globe 37
94/5 Leaf Elit Set 183, GC-3
95 Panini Worlds 149
95 Semic 67
89/0 Semic Elitserien 65
90/1 Semic Elitserien 284
91/2 Semic Elitserien 66
91/2 Semic Elitserien 351
92/3 Semic Elitserien 86
91 Semic Sticker 42
97/8 UD Elitserien 41, 210
98/9 UD Elitserien 59
99/0 UD Elitserien 44, L3
00/1 UD Elitserien 50

BERGLUND, CHRISTIAN
01/2 BAP Memor. 330
01/2 Bowman 114
02/3 Calder 78
02/3 Exclusive 101
02/3 O-Pee-Chee 282
02/3 Pacific Complete 509
01/2 Parkhurst 327
02/3 Pr. Stock Reserve 60
01/2 PS Titanium Draft 145
01/2 SPx 209
02/3 Topps 282
02/3 T. Limited 282
02/3 T. Total 223
01/2 UD PlayMakers Ltd 126
99/0 UD Elitserien 68, 206
00/1 UD Elitserien 85, 190, S2
01/2 UD Honor Roll 79
01/2 UD Ice 145
01/2 UD Mask 153
01/2 UD MVP 227
01/2 UD Premier 101
01/2 UD Top Shelf 132
01/2 Victory 447
01/2 Albany River Rats
02/3 Albany River Rats

BERGLUND, TIM
89/0 WASH / Kodak

BERGLUND, TOMAS
94/5 Leaf Elit Set 78
95/6 Leaf Elit Set 81
89/0 Semic Elitserien 165
90/1 Semic Elitserien 239
91/2 Semic Elitserien 169
92/3 Semic Elitserien 189
95/6 UD Elitserien 129
98/9 UD Elitserien 141
99/0 UD Elitserien 143
00/1 UD Elitserien 128

BERGMAN, ANDERS
89/0 Semic Elitserien 74
90/1 Semic Elitserien 248
91/2 Semic Elitserien 79
92/3 Semic Elitserien 101

BERGMAN, GARY
68/9 Bauer Photo
64-67 BeeHive-3 [Detr.]
64/5 Coke/Sprite [Detr.]
65/6 Coca-Cola
70/1 Colgate 73
70/1 Dad's Cookies
70/1 Eddie Sargent 49
71/2 Eddie Sargent 54
72/3 Eddie Sargent 79
70/1 Esso Power Player
91/2 Future Trends C72 87, ✍ 87
72/3 Post 19
74/5 Loblaws
74/5 Loblaws Update
73/4 Mac's Milk
68/9 O-Pee-Chee 25
69/0 O-Pee-Chee 58
70/1 O-Pee-Chee 154
71/2 O-Pee-Chee 119
72/3 O-Pee-Chee 164
72/3 O-Pee-Chee Crest 8
72/3 O-Pee-Chee TC
73/4 O-Pee-Chee 65
75/6 O-Pee-Chee 236
95/6 Parkie 66-67 41
94/5 Parkie Tall 57
71/2 Pro Star Promotions
68/9 Shirriff / Detr. 1
64/5 Topps 8
65/6 Topps 107
66/7 Topps 47
66/7 Topps / Test 47
67/8 Topps 47
68/9 Topps 25
69/0 Topps 58
71/2 Topps 119
72/3 Topps 49
73/4 Topps 65
75/6 Topps 236
76/7 Topps 159
71/2 Toronto Sun Photo
91/2 Ultimate Original Six 67, ✍ Aut. 67
70/1 DETR / Marathon Oil
73/4 MINS

BERGMAN, JAN
89/0 Semic Elitserien 223
90/1 Semic Elitserien 57
91/2 Semic Elitserien 230

BERGMAN, PETER
98/9 Calgary Hitmen 20

BERGMAN, SUNE
94/5 Leaf Elit Set 299

BERGMAN, THOMMIE
72 Hellas MM-Jenkki 25
74 Hellas MM-Jenkki 23
74/5 Loblaws
73/4 O-Pee-Chee 204
74/5 O-Pee-Chee 265
74/5 O-Pee-Chee 365
79/0 O-Pee-Chee 148
75/6 OPC WHA 29
76/7 OPC WHA 51
72 Semic Sticker 55
79/0 Topps 148
71/2 Williams Finnish 42
72/3 Williams Finnish 43
79/0 DETR

BERGQVIST, FREDRIK
94/5 Leaf Elit Set 294
91/2 Semic Elitserien 211
92/3 Semic Elitserien 234
95/6 UD Elitserien DS17
98/9 UD Elitserien 21

BERGQVIST, KENNETH
99/0 UD Elitserien 31, 202
00/1 UD Elitserien 42

BERGSENG, ARNE
92/3 Semic Nordisk 97

BERGSENG, LARS
92/3 Semic Nordisk 101

BERGSTRÖM, ERIK
94/5 Leaf Elit Set 169
95/6 Leaf Elit Set 127
92/3 Semic Elitserien 276

BERGSTRÖM, LARS
94/5 Leaf Elit Set 301

BERLINQUETTE, LOUIS
25-27 Anonymous 47
24/5 Champ's Cigarettes
24/5 Maple Crispette [V130] 30
23/4 Paulins Candy 32
24/5 William Paterson 41

BERMINGHAM, JASON
98/9 Huntington Blizzard
99/0 Huntington Blizzard

BERMINGHAM, JIM
98/9 EBK ECHL All-Star
90/1 7th..Sketch LHJMQ 49
91/2 7th...Sketch LHJMQ 226
90 7th..Sketch Mem.Cup 71
94/5 Huntington Blizzard
98/9 Huntington Blizzard
99/0 Huntington Blizzard
93/4 Wheeling Thund'birds

BERNAQUEZ, BERNIE
51/2 Bas du Fleuve 46

BERNAQUEZ, FERNAND
52/3 Bas du Fleuve 26

BERNARD, CHRIS
99/0 Missouri RiverOtters

BERNARD, LARRY
89/0 ProCards AHL 32
90/1 ProCards 245
93/4 Flint Generals
94/5 Flint Generals
90/1 Moncton Hawks

BERNARD, LOUIS
91/2 7th...Sketch LHJMQ 276
93/4 Slapshot / Drummondville 11
99/0 Fort Worth Brahmas
94/5 Fredericton Canadiens
95/6 Fredericton Canadiens
97/8 Toledo Storm 1

BERNARD, MARK
91/2 Hampton Roads
92/3 Hampton Roads
95/6 Hampton Roads
98/9 Hampton Roads

BERNDANER, IGNAZ
79 Panini Sticker 98

BERNDTSSON, PETER
94/5 Leaf Elit Set 70
95/6 Leaf Elit Set 143
89/0 Semic Elitserien 279
90/1 Semic Elitserien 44
91/2 Semic Elitserien 295
95/6 UD Elitserien 213
97/8 UD Elitserien 80
98/9 UD Elitserien 77
99/0 UD Elitserien 82

BERNHARDT, TIM
85/6 O-Pee-Chee 166
85/6 OPC Sticker 9-137
88/9 ProCards / Newmarket
89/0 ProCards AHL 110
85/6 TORO

BERNIE, JOHN
90/1 7th..Sketch OHL 61

BERNIER, ART
91 C55 Reprint 37
10/1 Imperial
10/1 Imperial 25
11/2 Imperial 37
12/3 Imperial 6

BERNIER, DAVID
98/9 Québec Remparts

BERNIER, JEAN
77/8 OPC WHA 2
76/7 Québec Nordiques

BERNIER, PASCAL
91/2 7th...Sketch LHJMQ 265

BERNIER, SERGE
71/2 Bazooka Panel
76/7 Dernière Heure
78/9 Dernière Heure
71/2 Eddie Sargent 155
72/3 Eddie Sargent 97
70/1 Esso Power Player
71/2 O-Pee-Chee 19
72/3 O-Pee-Chee 152
79/0 O-Pee-Chee 47
80/1 O-Pee-Chee 309
74/5 OPC WHA 5
75/6 OPC WHA 60
75/6 OPC WHA 70
76/7 OPC WHA 109
77/8 OPC WHA 60
80/1 Pepsi Bottle Cap
71/2 Topps 19
72/3 Topps 36
79/0 Topps 47
71/2 Toronto Sun Photo
72/3 PHIL / Milk
80/1 QUÉB
73/4 Québec Nordiques
76/7 Québec Nordiques
76/7 Québ. / Antoinette

BERNIER, STEVE
98 Québec Pee Wee 907
99 Québec Pee Wee 671
01/2 Moncton Wildcats 25

BERNIKOV, RUSLAN
99/0 Mir 118
00/1 Mir 13

BERRA, ANDRÉ
72 Semic Sticker 142

BERRINGTON, PAUL
02/3 Dundee Texol Stars

BERRY, BOB
72/3 Eddie Sargent 98
70/1 Esso Power Player
93/4 Kraft / PB
74/5 Loblaws
71/2 O-Pee-Chee 76
72/3 O-Pee-Chee 9
73/4 O-Pee-Chee 175
74/5 O-Pee-Chee 18
75/6 O-Pee-Chee 196
75/6 O-Pee-Chee 320
76/7 O-Pee-Chee 300
77/8 O-Pee-Chee 268
71/2 Topps 76
72/3 Topps 21
73/4 Topps 172
74/5 Topps 18
75/6 Topps 196
75/6 Topps 320
81/2 MONT
82/3 MONT
83/4 MONT
86/7 PITT / Kodak

BERRY, BRAD
92/3 Parkhurst 312
91/2 ProCards 147
90/1 Semic Elitserien 178
94/5 DALL / Cap
86/7 WINN
87/8 WINN
89/0 WINN / Safeway
96/7 Michigan K-Wings
98/9 Michigan K-Wings

BERRY, BRENT
92/3 BCJHL 156

BERRY, DOUG
79/0 COLR

BERRY, FRED
81/2 Milwaukee Admirals

BERRY, KEN
83/4 EDMO / Button
88/9 EDMO / Action 67
88/9 VANC / Mohawk
84/5 Nova Scotia Oilers

BERRY, NATHAN
99/0 Des Moines Buc's

BERRY, RICK
01/2 BAP Memor. 237, 485
01/2 O-Pee-Chee 303
01/2 Pacific 96
01/2 Parkhurst 288
01/2 Signature 231, ✍ Aut. 231
00/1 SPx 156
01/2 Topps 303
98/9 Hershey Bears
00/1 Hershey Bears

BERRY, RYAN
95/6 Spokane Chiefs 18

BERTAGGIA, SANDRO
95 Globe 213
95 Panini Worlds 119
91 Semic Sticker 184
92 Semic Sticker 200
93 Semic Sticker 116

BERTELL, KRISTEN
66/7 Champion 112

BERTHELSEN, PETE
88/9 Lethbridge Hurricanes
89/0 Lethbridge Hurricanes

BERTHIAUME, DANIEL
91/2 Bowman 190
92/3 Bowman 140
92/3 Fleer Ultra 361
93/4 Fleer Ultra 54
87/8 O-Pee-Chee 217
88/9 OPC/Topps 142
90/1 OPC/Topps 247
91/2 O-Pee-Chee 313
89/0 O-Pee-Chee 296
87/8 OPC Leaders 3
90/1 OPC Premier 5
87/8 OPC Sticker 249-139
88/9 OPC Sticker 149
87/8 Panini Sticker 356
88/9 Panini Sticker 148
92/3 Parkhurst 359
91/2 Pinnacle 165
90/1 Pro Set 454
90/1 Score 73T
91/2 Score 132
91/2 Score CAN 132
91 Semic Sticker 54
92/3 Topps 505
91/2 To. Stadium 290
92/3 To. Stadium 101
90/1 Upper Deck 381, 412
91/2 Upper Deck 150
91/2 BOST / Sports Action
90/1 LOSA / Smokey 19
92/3 OTTA
87/8 WINN
89/0 WINN / Safeway
95/6 Roanoke Express
98/9 Roanoke Express
86/7 Sherb. Canadiens 5
84/5 Chicoutimi Saguenéens

BERTI, CHRIS
99/0 UD Prospects 15

BERTOGLIAT, JESSE
93/4 Minnesota G'Gophers
94/5 Minnesota G'Gophers

BERTRAND, ÉRIC
02/3 BAP Memorabilia 360
02/3 Parkhurst 237
96/7 Albany River Rats
97/8 Albany River Rats
98/9 Albany River Rats
02/3 Hershey Bears
00/1 Québec Citadelles

BERTRAND, HUGO
97/8 New Mexico Scorpions

BERTRAND, MARC
80/1 Québec Remparts

BERTRAND, RON
89/0 7th..Sketch OHL 172
90/1 7th..Sketch OHL 303
91/2 7th...Sketch OHL 52

BERTSCH, JAY
95/6 Spokane Chiefs 23

BERTUZZI, BRIAN
86/7 Fredericton Express
84/5 Kamloops Blazers

BERTUZZI, ED
88/9 Kamloops Blazers

BERTUZZI, TODD
01/2 Adrenaline 187
02/3 Atomic 95, -PC 18, -SC 16
98/9 Aurora 186
98/9 Be A Player 292, ✍ Aut. 292
99/0 BAP Mem. 23
00/1 BAP Mem. 299
01/2 BAP Memor. 100
02/3 BAP Memorabilia 114, 245, ✄ HSHSJers, ✄ SC13
01/2 BAP Update HSHS, ✄ HSHSJers
95/6 Bowman 156, BB30
02/3 Bowman 4
93/4 Classic 14
94/5 Classic 103, T40
95/6 Classic 85
93/4 Cla. 4 Sport 204
94/5 Cla. Images 37
02/3 Crown Royale 94
95/6 Donruss 346, RR-2
96/7 Donruss RR 9
97/8 Donruss 12
96/7 Do. Canadian 28
95/6 Do. Elite 57, R-4
96/7 Do. Elite 18, A-4
97/8 Do. Priority 155
98/9 Dynagon Ice 185
02/3 eTopps 23
02/3 Exclusive 165
02/3 First Edition 73, 371, 411H, ✄ Jers.
96/7 Fleer 63, RS-2
95/6 Fleer Metal 171
95/6 Fleer Ultra 331, HS-3
96/7 Fl. Ultra 99
02/3 Heads Up 119, -ITN 22, -SM 14, ✄ GWQ 27
02/3 In The Game-Used 76, 176, ✄ GUJ32, ✄ SJ32, ✄ T19
96/7 Leaf 205
97/8 Leaf 134
95/6 L. Limited 19, RP-10
96/7 L. Limited 19, S-9
96/7 L. Preferred 93, LS-20
97/8 Limited 10
02/3 McDonald's 39, -CA 6
96/7 Metal Univ. 91
01/2 O-Pee-Chee 178
02/3 O-Pee-Chee 217
99/0 Omega 231
98/9 Pacific 424
99/0 Pacific 420
00/1 Pacific 404
01/2 Pacific 377
02/3 Pacific 373, -L 13
02/3 Pacific Complete 102
97/8 Pa. Invincible R-115
97/8 Pa. Paramount 107
98/9 Pa. Paramount 232
00/1 Pa. Paramount 236
96/7 Panini Sticker 89
00/1 Panini Sticker 211
95/6 Parkhurst 264, PP-44
x95/6 Parkhurst PP44
00/1 Parkhurst P-20
01/2 Parkhurst 174, ✄ T17
02/3 Parkhurst 35, ✄ GJ29, ✄ SJ29, ✄ PP8, ✄ TT18
02/3 Parkhurst Retro 5, ✄ RJ29, ✄ RSJ20, ✄ HSHSJers
96/7 Pinnacle 208
97/8 Pi. Be A Player 168, ✍ Aut. 168
95/6 Pi. Summit 193
96/7 Pi. Summit 154
95/6 Pi. Zenith 140, RRC-9
96/7 Pi. Zenith 81, A-6
02/3 Pr. Stock Reserve ✄ 147
01/2 PS Titanium 134, ✄ DSJ 55
01/2 PS Titanium Draft ✄ 92
02/3 Private Stock Titanium 95, -SK 10
02/3 Quest for the Cup 94, -CTC 18
00/1 Revolution 142
96/7 Score 244
95/6 Select CE 123
96/7 Select CE 80
91/2 7th...Sketch OHL 357
00/1 Signature 81, ✍ Aut. 60
01/2 Signature ✄ GJ68, ✄ GSJ68
02/3 Signature Series 9, GS95, ✍ 9, ✄ SGJ32, ✄ TQ14
95/6 SBx Emotion 103, GN-8
95/6 SBx Impact 208
96/7 SBx Impact 74, 166, F-2
02/3 Slam Card
93/4 Slapshot / Guelph 23
94/5 Slapshot / Guelph 22
96/7 SP 88
96/7 SP 96
97/8 SP Authentic 96
02/3 SP Authentic 87
02/3 SP Authentic 104
02/3 Sports Vault 293
96/7 SPx 30
02/3 SPx 72
98/9 SPx Finite 85
00/1 Stadium 110
01/2 Stadium Club 65
02/3 Stadium 50, -BT-13, ✄ NHLP5, ✍ LSS
95/6 Topps 339
99/0 Topps 30
00/1 Topps 99
01/2 Topps 178
02/3 Topps 217, HHC6, OTG3
99/0 To. Chrome 38
02/3 T. Chrome 120
95/6 To. Finest 146
02/3 To. Heritage 22, ✍ Aut
02/3 T. Limited 217
96/7 Topps Picks 121, RS10
95/6 To. Stadium ER204
95/6 T. Super Skills SR7
02/3 T. Total 334, TTC29, TP14
98/9 UD Choice 212
02/3 Ultimate Memorabilia ✄ GUJ, ✄ GUSJ
x95/6 Upper Deck SE53
96/7 Upper Deck 291, X14, P7
97/8 Upper Deck 103
98/9 Upper Deck 194
00/1 Upper Deck 169
01/2 Upper Deck 401
02/3 Upper Deck 168, -NC14, -SS14
02/3 UD Artistic 85, R85, / Art
95/6 UD Be A Player 168, ✍ S168
96/7 UD Black Diam. 84
02/3 UD Classic 95
96/7 UD CC 164, 323, 338
97/8 UD Coll. Choice 154
98/9 UD G. Reserve 194
02/3 UD Honor 67, -TW15
01/2 UD Mask 94
00/1 UD MVP 176
01/2 UD MVP 181
02/3 UD MVP 177
02/3 UD Piece 85
02/3 UD Premier 52
02/3 UD Rookie 95, ✄ 149b, ✄ 150b, ✄ DJ
02/3 UD Top Shelf 85
00/1 UD Vintage 349
01/2 UD Vintage 249, 251
02/3 UD Vintage 245, 289, 308, T63
02/3 Vanguard 94
99/0 Victory 301
01/2 Victory 341
02/3 Victory 209
96/7 NYIS
01/2 VANC / Coke

BERUBE, CRAIG
98/9 Be A Player 298, ✍ Aut. 298
00/1 BAP Mem. ✄ T-25
01/2 BAP Update ✄ TC4, ✄ TC22
93/4 Leaf 314
94/5 Leaf 343
90/1 O-Pee-Chee 448
92/3 O-Pee-Chee 147
91/2 OPC Premier 47
98/9 Omega 244
98/9 Pacific 437
00/1 Pacific 292
97/8 Pa. Dynagon BKS-99
91/2 Parkhurst 246
94/5 Pinnacle 515
96/7 Pi. Be A Player 115, ✍ Aut. 115
94/5 Premier 433
00/1 Private Stock ✄ GUG 100
90/1 Pro Set 498
91/2 Pro Set 495
91/2 Score 28T
91/2 Score CAN 578
92/3 Score 258
92/3 Topps 208
92/3 To. Stadium 458
02/3 T. Total 355
99/0 Ult. Victory 63
90/1 Upper Deck 450
94/5 UD Be A Player ✍ 64
92/3 CALG / IGA 002
89/0 PHIL
90/1 PHIL
91/2 TORO / P.L.A.Y. 13
95/6 WASH
85/6 Kamloops Blazers
84/5 Medicine Hat Tigers

BÉRUBÉ, DENIS
02/3 Québec Remparts 21
02/3 Val d'Or Foreurs

BÉRUBÉ, GUILLAUME
00/1 Québec Remparts 21
01/2 Québec Remparts 16
02/3 Québec Remparts

BÉRUBÉ, SÉBASTIEN
91/2 7th...Sketch LHJMQ 6

BERWANGER, MARKUS
94/5 DEL 259
95/6 DEL 345

BERZINS, ARMANDS
01/2 Shawinigan Cataractes 10
02/3 Shawinigan Cataractes

BES, JEFF
93/4 Cla. Prospects 144
90/1 7th..Sketch OHL 201, 209
90/1 7th..Sketch OHL 209
91/2 7th...Sketch OHL 346
93/4 Upper Deck 265

BESSETTE, MARCEL
51/2 Laval Dairy 68

BESSETTE, ROGER
51/2 Laval Dairy 48
52/3 St. Lawrence 78

BEST, RANDY
99/0 Topeka Scarecrows

BESTER, ALLAN
90/1 Bowman 154
95/6 Edge Ice 170
84/5 O-Pee-Chee 297
87/8 O-Pee-Chee 236
90/1 OPC/Topps 32
89/0 O-Pee-Chee 271
84/5 OPC Sticker 20
87/8 OPC Sticker 162
89/0 opcSticker 169
87/8 Panini Sticker 323
88/9 Panini Sticker 116
89/0 Panini Sticker 139
90/1 Panini/TOR 2
90/1 Pro Set 275
91/2 ProCards 118
90/1 Score 27
90/1 Upper Deck 241
84/5 TORO
87/8 TORO / 5x8
87/8 TORO / P.L.A.Y. 12
88/9 TORO / P.L.A.Y. 11
93/4 San Diego Gulls
83/4 Brantford Alexanders

BETHARD, BRIAN
94/5 Anchorage Aces 24

BETIK, KAREL
99/0 Pa. Paramount 213
98/9 Cleveland Lumberjacks

BETOGLIAT, JESSE
92/3 Minnesota G'Gophers

BETOURNAY, ERIC
02/3 Philadelphia Phantoms

BÉTOURNAY, ÉRIC
00/1 Chicoutimi Saguenéens 5

BÉTOURNAY, MATHIEU
00/1 Chicoutimi Saguenéens
01/2 Moncton Wildcats 6

BETS, MAXIM
93/4 Classic 15
94/5 Classic 92
93/4 Cla. 4 Sport 208
94/5 Classic 4 Sport 127
94/5 Donruss 33
99/0 Mir 23
94/5 Parkhurst 10, V37
93/4 Pinnacle 502
94/5 Pinnacle 483, RTP-6
94/5 Score 232
94/5 Upper Deck 353, SP-1
00/1 Metallurg 38

BETTENS, MIKE
96/7 Guildford Flames 9

BETTIOL, FRANK
52/3 Anonymous 53

BETTS, BLAIR
99 Bowman 104
98 Bowman 124, ✍ A32
98 Bowman Chrome 124
97/8 Upper Deck 407
99/0 Prince George Cougars

BETY, SÉBASTIEN
94/5 Sig. Rookies 19, ✍ 19
93/4 Slapshot / Drummondville 4

BEUKEBOOM, JEFF
98/9 Be A Player 242, ✍ Aut. 242
91/2 Bowman 110
92/3 Bowman 347
92/3 Do. Elite 87
94/5 Flair 110
94/5 Fleer 131
92/3 Fleer Ultra 351
94/5 Fleer Ultra 136
94/5 Leaf 528
90/1 O-Pee-Chee 471
91/2 O-Pee-Chee 284
92/3 O-Pee-Chee 237
98/9 OPC Chrome 87
98/9 Pacific 290
97/8 Pacific CC 57
88/9 Panini Sticker 56
90/1 Panini/EDM 2
91/2 Parkhurst 341
94/5 Parkhurst 148
95/6 Parkhurst 410
91/2 Pinnacle 229
92/3 Pinnacle 112
93/4 Pinnacle 309
94/5 Pinnacle 195
95/6 Pinnacle 112
96/7 Pi. Be A Player 158, ✍ Aut. 158
96/7 Pi. Summit 71
95/6 POG 185
93/4 Power Play 389
93/4 Premier 54
94/5 Premier 138
90/1 Pro Set 439
91/2 Pro Set 444
91/2 Pro Set Platinum 206
91/2 Score CAN 253
92/3 Score 137
93/4 Score 94
94/5 Score 66
97/8 Score NYRa. 20
92/3 Topps 57
95/6 Topps 63
98/9 Topps 87
94/5 Topps Finest RL-9
91/2 To. Stadium 350
92/3 To. Stadium 129
93/4 To. Stadium 7
98/9 UD Choice 136
91/2 Upper Deck 394
92/3 Upper Deck 161
94/5 Upper Deck 339
95/6 Upper Deck 203
96/7 Upper Deck 105
97/8 Upper Deck 314
98/9 Upper Deck 326
94/5 UD Be A Player ✍ 107
95/6 UD CC 317
98/9 UD G. Reserve 326
86/7 EDMO
86/7 EDMO / Red Rooster
87/8 EDMO
88/9 EDMO
88/9 EDMO / Action 17
90/1 EDMO / IGA
98/9 NYRA
85/6 Nova Scotia Oilers
82/3 Soo Greyhounds
83/4 Soo Greyhounds
84/5 Soo Greyhounds

BEUKEBOOM, JEFF
02/3 Fleer Throwbacks 31

BEUKER, DEAN
01/2 Regina Pats

BEVERIDGE, BILL
33/4 Anonymous 25
34-43 BeeHive-1 [Maroons]
35-40 Canada Starch
36-39 Diamond Match TT1
33/4 O-Pee-Chee 54
37/8 O-Pee-Chee 181
33/4 WWGum 60
37/8 World Wide Gum 82

BEVERLEY, NICK
72/3 O-Pee-Chee 281
73/4 O-Pee-Chee 239
75/6 O-Pee-Chee 279
76/7 O-Pee-Chee 41
77/8 O-Pee-Chee 198
78/9 O-Pee-Chee 111
75/6 Topps 279
76/7 Topps 41
77/8 Topps 198
78/9 Topps 111
79/0 COLR

BEZBORODOV, KONSTANTIN
99/0 Mir 27
00/1 Mir 135

BEZEAU, ANDY
95/6 Edge Ice 125
89/0 7th..Sketch OHL 147
90/1 7th..Sketch OHL 253
98/9 Detroit Vipers
99/0 Detroit Vipers
95/6 Fort Wayne Komets
94/5 Muskegon Fury
98/9 Muskegon Fury
89/0 Niagara Falls Thunder

BEZPALEC, ROMAN
99/0 Score 116

BEZRUKOV, DMITRI
98/9 Mir 76
99/0 Mir 100

BEZUKLADNIKOV, VYACHESLAV
00/1 Mir 122

BIAFORE, CHAD
96/7 DEL 32
98/9 DEL 179
88/9 Portland Winter Hawks

BIAGINI, CHRIS
95/6 Slapshot 284

BIALOWAS, DWIGHT
74/5 O-Pee-Chee 372
75/6 O-Pee-Chee 106
76/7 O-Pee-Chee 198
77/8 O-Pee-Chee 271
75/6 Topps 106
76/7 Topps 198

BIALOWAS, FRANK
94/5 Parkhurst 237
95/6 Portland Pirates
92/3 Richmond Renegades
93/4 St. John's Maple Leafs
94/5 St. John's Maple Leafs

BIALYNICKI, KRZYSZTOF
73/4 Williams Finnish 86

BIANCHI, TONY
91/2 Minnesota G'Gophers
92/3 Minnesota G'Gophers
93/4 Minnesota G'Gophers

BIANCHIN, WAYNE
74/5 Loblaws
77/8 O-Pee-Chee 188
78/9 O-Pee-Chee 103
79/0 O-Pee-Chee 290
77/8 Topps 188
78/9 Topps 103
88/9 EDMO / Action 107
77/8 PITT / McDonald's

BIANNI, MIKE
84/5 Moncton G'Flames
85/6 Moncton G'Flames

BIBEAULT, PAUL
34-43 BeeHive-1 [Mont.]
43-47 Parade Sportive

BICANEK, RADIM
93/4 Classic 36
94/5 Classic 111, T46
95/6 Classic 83
94/5 Cla. Images 43
95/6 Donruss 15
95/6 Leaf 69
97/8 Pa. Dynagon BKS-64
00/1 Panini Sticker 139
95/6 Pinnacle 217
95/6 Score 306
93/4 Upper Deck 262
01/2 COLU
94/5 OTTA
99/0 Cleveland Lumberjacks
98/9 Grand Rapids Griffins
97/8 Manitoba Moose
00/1 Syracuse Crunch
02/3 Syracuse Crunch

BICEK, JIRI
02/3 Calder 79
01/2 O-Pee-Chee 309
01/2 Pacific 226
02/3 Pacific Complete 507
01/2 Parkhurst 273
01/2 Signature 239, ✍ Aut. 239
01/2 Topps 309
00/1 UD Ice 115
97/8 Albany River Rats
98/9 Albany River Rats
99/0 Albany River Rats
00/1 Albany River Rats
01/2 Albany River Rats
02/3 Albany River Rats

BICKELL, J.P.
83 HHOF Postcard J3
83&87 HHOF 184

BIDNER, TODD
83/4 Moncton Alpines

BIEGL, RADOV
01/2 OFS G5

BIEGL, RADOVAN
94/5 APS 24
95/6 APS 316
96/7 APS 50
97/8 APS 315
97/8 DS 110
98/9 DS 25
00/1 DS 145, G13
96/7 DS Sticker 227
97/8 DS Sticker 267
98/9 OFS 178
00/1 OFS 264, Star-32
01/2 OFS 62, -CL 7

BIELAS, ROLF
74 Hellas MM-Jenkki 119
70/1 Kuvajulkaisut 81
79 Panini Sticker 253

BIELKE, RENÉ
94/5 DEL 245
95/6 DEL 220

BIENVENUE, DANIEL
97/8 Rochester Americans

BIERK, ZAC
97 Bowman 19
98/9 EBK IHL All-Star
98/9 Omega 224
98/9 Pacific 396
02/3 Pacific Complete 488
94/5 SR Auto-Phonex 7, ✍ 7
93/4 Slapshot / Peterborough 10
95/6 Slapshot 307, P, ✍ Aut.
98/9 SPx Finite 79, 148
00/1 Topps 314
98/9 Upper Deck 181
98/9 UD G. Reserve 181
98/9 Cleveland Lumberjacks
00/1 Cleveland Lumberjacks
99/0 Detroit Vipers

BIETTE, KERRY
90/1 7th..Sketch WHL 177
91/2 7th...Sketch WHL 227

BIFANO, PAUL
83/4 Victoria Cougars

BIG SNAKE, ROBIN
01/2 Vancouver Giants

BIGGS, DON
93/4 Cla. Prospects 83
95/6 Edge Ice 110
88/9 ProCards / Hershey
89/0 ProCards AHL 331
91/2 ProCards 205
92/3 Binghampton Rangers
93/4 Cincinnati Cyclones
94/5 Cincinnati Cyclones
95/6 Cincinnati Cyclones
96/7 Cincinnati Cyclones
97/8 Cincinnati Cyclones
85/6 Nova Scotia Oilers
82/3 Oshawa Generals
83/4 Oshawa Generals

BIGGS, KENNETH
51/2 Laval Dairy 40

BIGGS, SCOTT
82/3 Kitchener Rangers

BIGNELL, GREG
89/0 7th..Sketch OHL 86
00/1 Kingston Frontenacs 3

BILEK, MARTIN
97/8 APS 196
99/0 DS 155, G12
97/8 DS Sticker 228
98/9 OFS 396
99/0 OFS 2

BILES, C.
28/9 Paulins Candy 59

BILL, ROBERT
88/9 ProCards / Utica
89/0 ProCards AHL 228

BILLECK, LAURIE
90/1 7th..Sketch WHL 261
91/2 7th...Sketch WHL 152
90/1 Prince Albert Raiders

BILLINGTON, CRAIG
98/9 Be A Player 185, ✍ Aut. 185
01/2 BT Pipes 7
02/3 Between the Pipes 60
98/9 Bicycle Sports 8-S
92/3 Bowman 102
90/1 Canada Nationals 1
93/4 Donruss 226
94/5 Donruss 209
95/6 Donruss 381
94/5 Flair 119
92/3 Fleer Ultra 334
93/4 Fleer Ultra 378
94/5 Fleer Ultra 145
94/5 Kraft / KD
93/4 Leaf 354
94/5 Leaf 84
92/3 O-Pee-Chee 372
97/8 Omega 54
98/9 Pacific 157
99/0 Pacific 100
01/2 Pacific 389
02/3 Pacific 387
02/3 Pacific Complete 61
97/8 Pa. Dynagon BKS-23
98/9 Pa. Paramount 52
87/8 Panini Sticker 72
94/5 Panini Sticker 108
91/2 Parkhurst 320
92/3 Parkhurst 330
93/4 Parkhurst 138
94/5 Parkhurst 158
95/6 Parkhurst 285
93/4 Pinnacle 352
94/5 Pinnacle 320
97/8 Pi. Be A Player 138, ✍ Aut. 138
94/5 POG 289
93/4 Power Play 169
93/4 Premier 374
94/5 Premier 482
91/2 Pro Set Platinum 197
88/9 ProCards / Utica
89/0 ProCards AHL 224
92/3 Score 228
93/4 Score 207
93/4 Score 521, -PiAS 1
94/5 Score 167
96/7 Score 231
97/8 Score 19
97/8 Score Colo. 2
94/5 Select 49
92/3 Topps 48
92/3 To. Stadium 343
93/4 To. Stadium - All-Stars
91/2 Upper Deck 559
92/3 Upper Deck 315
93/4 Upper Deck 424, SP-105
94/5 Upper Deck 370, SP-53
95/6 Upper Deck 112
95/6 UD Be A Player 151, ✍ S151
02/3 UD Mask 88, 89
85/6 NJER 2
93/4 OTTA
94/5 OTTA
83/4 Belleville Bulls
84/5 Belleville Bulls

BILLKVAM, ARNE
94 Semic 268
92/3 Semic Nordisk 49
92 Semic Sticker 35
93 Semic Sticker 245

BILODEAU, BRENT
91/2 Arena 13
91/2 Classic 14
91/2 Classic Four Sport 14
93/4 Cla. Prospects 58
91 7th..Sketch Mem.Cup 99
90/1 7th..Sketch WHL 1, 346
91/2 7th...Sketch WHL 180
91/2 Star Pics 53
91/2 Ultimate Draft Pick 14, 70, ✍ Aut.
91/2 Upper Deck 694
91/2 Upper Deck WJC 81
93/4 Fredericton Canadiens
94/5 Fredericton Canadiens
98/9 Kansas City Blades 18

BILODEAU, DAVID
97/8 Rimouski Océanic

BILODEAU, MARTIN
96/7 Halifax Moosehead
97/8 Halifax Moosehead
98/9 Halifax Moosehead
97/8 Halifax Moosehead

BILODEAU, PATRICE
01/2 Val d'Or Foreurs 9
02/3 Val d'Or Foreurs

BILODEAU, ROLAND
51/2 Bas du Fleuve 17
52/3 Bas du Fleuve 56

BILOTTO, NICHOLAS
98/9 Québec Remparts

BILOUS, JASON
91/2 Avant Garde BCJHL 136

BILYALETDINOV, ZINETULA
82 Semic Sticker 58
79/0 Soviet Stars 11
83/4 Soviet Stars
87/8 Soviet Stars
96/7 PHOE / Coca-Cola
93/4 WINN / Ruffles

BINETTE, MARC-ANDRE
97/8 Halifax Moosehead
97/8 Halifax Moosehead
98/9 Halifax Moosehead
99/0 Rouyn-Noranda Huskies
00/1 Rouyn-Noranda Huskies 25

BINGHAM, PAT
00/1 Asheville Smoke
89/0 Nashville Knights
91/2 Richmond Renegades
85/6 Kamloops Blazers
88/9 Kamloops Blazers

BINKLEY, LES
52/3 Anonymous 174
60/1 Cleveland Barons
70/1 Colgate 75
70/1 Dad's Cookies
70/1 Eddie Sargent 175
71/2 Eddie Sargent 166
70/1 Esso Power Player
68/9 O-Pee-Chee 100
69/0 O-Pee-Chee 110
69/0 O-Pee-Chee 4in1
69/0 O-Pee-Chee Stamp
70/1 O-Pee-Chee 200, DE-10
71/2 O-Pee-Chee 192
72/3 O-Pee-Chee 300
72 Semic Sticker 215
68/9 Shirriff / Pitt. 6
68/9 Topps 100
69/0 Topps 110
71/2 Toronto Sun Photo
71/2 PITT / Sportcolor
72/3 Ottawa Nationals

BINNIE, TROY
89/0 7th..Sketch OHL 52
90/1 7th..Sketch OHL 77

BINNS, CRAIG
00/1 Kudos 111
91/2 7th...Sketch OHL 179
93/4 Owen Sound Platers

BIONDA, JACK
45-64 BeeHive-2 [Toro.]
93/4 Parkie 56-57 14
57/8 Topps 2
57-58 BOST

BIOTTI, CHRIS
89/0 ProCards IHL 202
88/9 Salt Lake G'Eagles

BIRBRAER, MAX
00/1 Albany River Rats
01/2 Albany River Rats
02/3 Albany River Rats

BIRCH, JOE
95/6 Slapshot 151

BIRD, JAMIE
91/2 7th...Sketch LHJMQ 178
94/5 Slapshot Memorial 56
98/9 BC Icemen 11
98/9 BC Icemen
96/7 Knoxville Cherokees

BIRK, HARALD
94/5 DEL 318
95/6 DEL 23
98/9 DEL 269, 334
99/0 Eishockey 165

BIRK, KLAUS
94/5 DEL 328
95/6 DEL 324

BIRNIE, SCOTT
83/4 North Bay Centennials

BIRNIE, STUART
87/8 Brockville Braves
88/9 Brockville Braves

BIRON, MARTIN
01/2 Adrenaline 19, CL 1, PP 5
01/2 Atomic 10
02/3 Atomic 9
00/1 Aurora 17
99/0 BAP Mem. 137
00/1 BAP Mem. 204
02/3 BAP Memorabilia 9
01/2 BT Pipes 13, 95, -Mask, ✄ DM, ✄ FW, ✄ Jers., ✄ S&J, ✄ GG, ✄ HSHSJers
02/3 Between the Pipes 15, 124, M4, ✄ GUE16, ✄ FW9, ✄ GUJ16, ✄ GSJ16, ✄ ITN16, ✄ T6, ✍ Aut.
95/6 Classic 16, BK13
99/0 Crown Royale 17
01/2 Crown Royale 15
02/3 Crown Royale 10, ✄ GWDP 2
96/7 Do. Canadian LG 9
99/0 Dynagon Ice 28
02/3 Exclusive 16
02/3 First Edition 36, 414R, ✄ Jers.
96/7 Fleer 122
02/3 Heads Up 12, ✄ GWQ 4
96/7 Leaf 213
99/0 Millenium 35, C-22, ✍ Aut. 35
99/0 NHL Power Play
02/3 O-Pee-Chee 115
99/0 Omega 25
99/0 Pacific 34
00/1 Pacific 48, IO-3
01/2 Pacific 46
02/3 Pacific 38
02/3 Pacific Complete 459
00/1 Pa. Paramount 26, GS-2
96/7 Panini Sticker 299
95/6 Parkhurst 295
00/1 Parkhurst P-247
01/2 Parkhurst 39, ✄ T11
02/3 Parkhurst 139
02/3 Parkhurst Retro 119
96/7 Pinnacle 224
96/7 Pi. Summit 179
99/0 Prism 17, -IP 2
01/2 Pr. Stock 8, GR 1, -PS 7
02/3 Pr. Stock Reserve 10
01/2 PS Titanium 13, ✄ DSJ 66
01/2 PS Titanium Draft ✄ 12
02/3 Private Stock Titanium 11, ✄ GWJ 6
02/3 Quest for the Cup 9
99/0 Revolution 16, / CSC 16
00/1 Revolution 15, SM-11
00/1 Signature 183, ✍ Aut. 77
01/2 Signature 150, ✍ Aut., ✄ TM4
02/3 Signature Series 80, ✍ 80
96/7 SBx Impact 145
00/1 SP Authentic ✍ SotT
01/2 SP Authentic 9, 126, ✍ SotT
02/3 SP Authentic 9, ✄ SP
01/2 SP Game Used ✄ AFD, ✄✍ IS, ✄✍ ISD, ✄ Patch, ✄✍ PatchSig, ✄✍ PatchCSig (x2)
02/3 SP Game-Used Edition 6, ✄ AF, ✄ PC, ✄ PH
02/3 Sports Vault 30
99/0 SPx 19
00/1 SPx ✄ WM W-BI
01/2 SPx 6, ✄ TT
02/3 SPx 8, ✄ WM, ✄ X
00/1 Stadion 155
99/0 Stadium 191
00/1 Stadium 53
02/3 Stadium 55, -PSH-5
00/1 Topps 192
02/3 Topps 115, ✄ FRF, ✄✍ FRF
01/2 To. Chrome 130
02/3 T. Chrome 74, ✄ FRF
99/0 To. Gold Label 95, FG8
01/2 To. Heritage 107
02/3 To. Heritage 46
02/3 T. Limited 115
99/0 To. Prmr. Plus 129
01/2 To. Reserve 71
02/3 T. Total 384
01/2 UD PlayMakers Ltd 13
99/0 Upper Deck 188
00/1 Upper Deck 19, ✄ GJ
01/2 Upper Deck 250, ✄ GN
02/3 Upper Deck -LL2, -SA1, ✄ GT, ✄ SV
02/3 UD Artistic 10, R10, / Art
99/0 UD Black Diam. 14
00/1 UD Black Diam. ✄ GG
01/2 UD Challenge 8
02/3 UD Classic 11
99/0 UD G. Reserve 188
02/3 UD Honor 8
96/7 UD Ice 118
01/2 UD Ice 4
01/2 UD Mask 104, 172, ✄ GP, ✄ GJ, ✄ JP, ✄ DP, ✄✍ SP, ✄ PM, ✄ SuS
02/3 UD Mask 11, 12, 102, ✄ GG, ✄ MM, ✄ BM, ✄ NB, ✄ PW, ✄ VC
99/0 UD MVP 25
00/1 UD MVP ME6, ✍ ME
01/2 UD MVP 21
02/3 UD MVP 24, SD, ST, Souv.
99/0 UD MVP Cup 25, ✍ PS
02/3 UD Piece 10
01/2 UD Premier ✍ Sig
02/3 UD Rookie 14
01/2 UD Top Shelf 81, ✄ GG-LP
02/3 UD Top Shelf 9, ✄ R, ✄ ST, ✄ SS, ✄ SW, ✄ TS, ✍ Sig
01/2 UD Vintage 27
02/3 UD Vintage 31, 264, 320, GB 31, ✄ EE
01/2 Vanguard 9, SW 3
02/3 Vanguard 11
99/0 Victory 37
01/2 Victory 43
02/3 Victory 23
97/8 Rochester Americans
98/9 Rochester Americans
00/1 Rochester Americans

BIRON, MATHIEU
99/0 BAP Mem. 305
00/1 BAP Mem. 62
99 Bowman 69
98 Bowman 154, ✍ A21
98 Bowman Chrome 154
98/9 Collection Souvenir 27
99/0 Dynagon Ice 121
99/0 Millenium C-35
98/9 OPC Chrome 238
94 Québec Pee Wee 1752
00/1 Signature 80, ✍ Aut. 50
98/9 Topps 238
00/1 Topps 158
00/1 UD MVP 113
99/0 WGretzky 105
00/1 Lowell Lock Monsters

BISAILLON, J.P.
51/2 Laval Dairy 71
52/3 St. Lawrence 30

BISAILLON, PATRICK
90/1 7th..Sketch LHJMQ 34
91/2 7th...Sketch LHJMQ 264
91 7th..Sketch Mem.Cup 32

BISHOP, ALLEN
83/4 Kingston Canadians
82/3 North Bay Centennials

BISHOP, MIKE
90/1 ProCards 465
90/1 Halifax Citadels
93/4 Humberside Hawks 4
94/5 Humberside Hawks 12
84/5 Kitchener Rangers

BISSCHOPS, JAKE
86/7 Sudbury Wolves

BISSETT, TOM
02/3 Cardset 159
95 Panini Worlds 232
90/1 ProCards 480
91/2 Semic Elitserien 52
92/3 Semic Elitserien 63
98/9 UD Elitserien 46
99/0 UD Elitserien 30, H2
00/1 UD Elitserien 37, 183, ✍ Sig.

BISSON, STEVE
88/9 ProCards / Sherbrooke
89/0 ProCards IHL 130

BISSONNETTE, ÉRIC
90/1 7th..Sketch LHJMQ 205
90 7th..Sketch Mem.Cup 60

BISSONNETTE, ROBERTO
99/0 Hull Olympiques BN
99/0 Hull Olympiques 10
00/1 Hull Olympiques 8

BJORK, ANDERS
92/3 Semic Elitserien 41
98/9 Grand Rapids Griffins

BJORK, STEFAN
92/3 Semic Elitserien 350

BJÖRKLÖF, ANN
99/0 Cardset AH Q-hertta

BJORKMAN, HENRIC
89/0 Semic Elitserien 131
90/1 Semic Elitserien 207
91/2 Semic Elitserien 135
92/3 Semic Elitserien 154
97/8 UD Elitserien 196, S9, C29

BJÖRKMAN, HENRIC
99/0 UD Elitserien 190

BJÖRN, LARS
98/9 UD Elitserien 199

BJORNLIE, DAN
00/1 Quad City Mallards

BJORNOFT, NIKLAS
92/3 Semic Elitserien 179

BJØRNSTAD, SVENN ERIK
92/3 Semic Nordisk 13

BJUGSTAD, SCOTT
86/7 OPC/Topps 23
86/7 OPC Sticker 168-29
88/9 Panini Sticker 90
90/1 Pro Set 455
88/9 ProCards / Kalamazoo
89/0 ProCards AHL 15
91/2 ProCards 404
84/5 MINS
85/6 MINS
85/6 MINS / 7-Eleven 2
86/7 MINS / 7-Eleven 4
87/8 MINS

BJUHR, THOMAS
89/0 Semic Elitserien 20
90/1 Semic Elitserien 87
91/2 Semic Elitserien 16
92/3 Semic Elitserien 37
86/7 Portland Winter Hawks

BLACK, CLINT
91/2 Avant Garde BCJHL 133
92/3 BCJHL 27

BLACK, JAMES H.
92/3 Bowman 252
93/4 Donruss 85
95/6 Future Legends 48
92/3 O-Pee-Chee 388
99/0 Pacific 436
97/8 Pa. Dynagon BKS-19
97/8 Pi. Be A Player 186, ✍ Aut. 186
89/0 ProCards AHL 292
90/1 ProCards 191
91/2 ProCards 101
92/3 Topps 232
92/3 To. Stadium 303
91/2 Upper Deck 580
92/3 Upper Deck 323
93/4 Upper Deck 517
91/2 HART / Jr. Whalers
01/2 Grand Rapids Griffins
95/6 Indianapolis Ice
94/5 Las Vegas Thunder
93/4 Rochester Americans
88/9 Portland Winter Hawks
89/0 Portland Winter Hawks

BLACK, JAMIE*
93/4 Cla. Prospects 122
90/1 7th..Sketch WHL 318
91/2 7th...Sketch WHL 172
93/4 Cleveland Lumberjacks
94/5 Muskegon Fury
92/3 Tacoma Rockets

BLACK, JESSE
95/6 Slapshot 187

BLACK, JONATHAN
88/9 Richelieu Riverains

BLACK, RYAN
90/1 7th..Sketch OHL 352, 362
91/2 7th...Sketch OHL 144
99/0 Fort Wayne Komets
98/9 Fort Worth Brahmas
91/2 Peterborough Petes

BLACK, STEVE
45-64 BeeHive-2 [Detr.]

BLACK, TERRY
88/9 Portland Winter Hawks

BLACKADAR, RAYMOND
94/5 Anchorage Aces 8

BLACKBIRD, LOUIE
96/7 Sudbury Wolves

BLACKBURN, ALEXANDRE
99/0 Shawinigan Cataractes 5

BLACKBURN, BOB
70/1 Esso Power Player
69/0 O-Pee-Chee 113

BLACKBURN, DAN
01/2 Adrenaline 217, RR12
02/3 Atomic 66
01/2 BAP Draft Florida 10
01/2 BAP Memor. 305
02/3 BAP Memorabilia 54, ✄ FG2
01/2 BT Pipes 57, ✄ FW
02/3 Between the Pipes 6, ✄ GUE4, ✄ FW5, ✄ GUJ4, ✄ GSJ4, ✄ GN1, ✄ HSHSJers 6, ✄ ITN4, ✄ I7, ✄ T1, ✍ Aut.
01/2 Bowman 140, ✄ FFJ, ✄ FFS, ✄ FFDS, ✄ FFR, ✍ YSA
02/3 Bowman 131
01/2 Crown Royale 171, CA15, RR14
02/3 Exclusive 112, -GE 13
02/3 First Edition 254, 425H
01/2 Heads Up 112
02/3 Heads Up 77, -HF 10
01/2 O-Pee-Chee 332
02/3 O-Pee-Chee 123
01/2 Pacific 458
02/3 Pacific 248, -SM 9
02/3 Pacific Complete 168
01/2 PTC Calder 8
01/2 PTC Draft 8
01/2 PTC High Voltage 7
01/2 PTC Collectibles 8
01/2 PTC Rookie 9
01/2 Parkhurst 281
02/3 Parkhurst 51
02/3 Parkhurst Retro 174
01/2 Pr. Stock 131, MiT, RR, -PS 100
02/3 Pr. Stock Reserve 65
01/2 PS Titanium 171
01/2 PS Titanium Draft 152
01/2 Signature 201, ✍ Aut. 201
02/3 Signature Series 172, ✍ 172, ✄ DW4, ✄ SGJ50, ✄ TQ4
01/2 SP Authentic ✍ 178
02/3 SP Authentic 124
01/2 SP Game Used 88
02/3 SP Game-Used ✄ PC
01/2 SPx 117
01/2 SPx Rookie RR20
01/2 Stadium Club 131
02/3 Stadium 34, ✄ YSS4, ✄ YSD6
01/2 Topps 332
02/3 Topps 123, ✄ FRF
01/2 To. Chrome 150
02/3 T. Chrome 79, ✄ FRF
01/2 To. Heritage 147
02/3 To. Heritage ✄ CP, ✄ CPB
02/3 T. Limited 123
01/2 To. Reserve 116
02/3 T. Total 401
01/2 UD PlayMakers Ltd 131
02/3 Ultimate Memorabilia ✄ Num
01/2 Upper Deck 434
02/3 Upper Deck 116, ✄ CG, ✄ OR
01/2 UD Challenge 121
02/3 UD Classic 67
01/2 UD Collectors
01/2 UD Honor Roll 96
01/2 UD Ice 62
01/2 UD Mask 155
02/3 UD Mask 54, 55, 56, 111, ✄ GG, ✄ NB, ✄ PW
01/2 UD MVP 229
02/3 UD MVP 124
01/2 UD Premier 113, ✍ SigG
00/1 UD Prospects 53, 91, CC7, D2, ✄ GJ, ✄ GJC (x3), ✄✍ GJS, ✍ Sig.
01 UD Prospects GU 2, ✄ TPJ, ✄✍ TPJS, ✄ JC (x4), ✄ SoT
01/2 UD Top Shelf 72
02/3 UD Top Shelf ✄ SS
02/3 UD Vintage 172, 320, GB 172
01/2 Vanguard 122, PP12
02/3 Vanguard 66
01/2 Victory 449
02/3 Victory 144

BLACKBURN, DON
63/4 Québec Aces
65/6 Québec Aces
68/9 Shirriff / Phil. 8

BLACKBURN, JOE
93 Québec Pee Wee 1756
98/9 SPx Prospects 89
98/9 UD Black Diam. 119

BLACKLOCK, KYLE
90/1 7th..Sketch OHL 379
91/2 7th...Sketch OHL 254
90/1 Sudbury Wolves
91/2 Sudbury Wolves

BLACKNED, BRANT
91/2 7th...Sketch LHJMQ 244
99/0 Rockford IceHogs

BLAD, BRIAN
88/9 ProCards / Newmarket
89/0 ProCards AHL 107
90/1 ProCards 164
91/2 ProCards 608
94/5 Slapshot / Brantford 14
90/1 Newmarket Saints
97/8 Toledo Storm 11

BLADON, TOM
74/5 Loblaws

74/5 O-Pee-Chee 396
75/6 O-Pee-Chee 74
76/7 O-Pee-Chee 164
77/8 O-Pee-Chee 131
78/9 O-Pee-Chee 152
79/0 O-Pee-Chee 204
80/1 O-Pee-Chee 135
75/6 Topps 74
76/7 Topps 164
77/8 Topps 131
78/9 Topps 152
79/0 Topps 204
80/1 Topps 135
88/9 EDMO / Action 108

BLAHA, JAN
94/5 APS 60

BLAHA, MICHAEL
91/2 Upper Deck 669
91/2 Upper Deck WJC 30

BLAHA, PAVEL
94/5 APS 255
97/8 APS 225
97/8 DS 16
97/8 DS Sticker 31
98/9 OFS 84

BLAIN, BRADY
91/2 7th...Sketch OHL 194
93/4 Slapshot / Windsor 12
92/3 Windsor Spitfires

BLAIN, JACQUES
72/3 Québec Nordiques

BLAIN, JOEL
90/1 7th...Sketch LHJMQ 149
91/2 7th...Sketch LHJMQ 212
92/3 Wheeling Thund'birds 3

BLAIN, ROBERT
95/6 Slapshot 412

BLAIR, ANDY
33/4 Anonymous 11
34-43 BeeHive-1 [Toro.]
36-39 Diamond Match Chic.
33/4 Hamilton Gum 9
29/0 La Presse
32/3 Maple Leafs O'Keefe
33/4 O-Pee-Chee 70
33/4 WWGum 4
37/8 World Wide Gum 56

BLAIR, CAMPBELL
93/4 Johnstown Chiefs 2

BLAIR, DANNY
52/3 Anonymous 50

BLAIR, SCOTT
94/5 Slapshot / Detroit Jr. 14
95/6 Slapshot 64
94/5 Slapshot Memorial 88

BLAIR, WREN
59/60 Whitby Dunlops

BLAISDELL, MIKE
00/1 Kudos 142
82/3 O-Pee-Chee 81
83/4 O-Pee-Chee 242
82/3 Post [Detr.]
88/9 ProCards / Newmarket
83/4 Souhaits Keychain [Red Wings]
80/1 DETR
86/7 PITT / Kodak
01/2 Sheffield Steelers GS

BLAKE, HECTOR (TOE)
34-43 BeeHive-1 [Mont.]
35-40 Canada Starch
63-65 Chex
77/8 Dernière Heure
48-52 Exhibits [Canadiens]
83 HHOF Postcard G1
83&87 HHOF 92
51/2 Laval Dairy 76
37/8 O-Pee-Chee 160
40/1 O-Pee-Chee 101
43-47 Parade Sportive
55/6 Parkhurst 67
57/8 Parkhurst [Mont.] 16
58/9 Parkhurst 9
59/0 Parkhurst 27
63/4 Parkhurst 34
63/4 Parkhurst 93
93/4 Parkhurst PR47
93/4 Parkie 56-57 84
94/5 Parkie Tall 87
91/2 Pro Set 337
38/9 Quaker Oats
45-54 Quaker Oats
60/1 Shirriff 40
61/2 Shirriff 101
62/3 Shirriff 31
64/5 Topps 43
65/6 Topps 1
66/7 Topps 1
61/2 York 22
67/8 MONT
67/8 MONT / IGA Card
92/3 MONT / OPC 5
92/3 MONT / OPC 65

BLAKE, JASON
00/1 BAP Mem. 364
99/0 Dynagon Ice 94
99/0 Millenium 126, ✍ Aut. 126
02/3 Pacific Complete 305
99/0 SP Authentic 105
99/0 To. Prmr. Plus 102
99/0 Ult. Victory 100
99/0 Upper Deck 240
99/0 UD G. Reserve 240

BLAKE, ROB
01/2 Adrenaline 45
01/2 Atomic 22
02/3 Atomic 22, -NPC 3
98/9 Aurora 85, -CF 23
99/0 Aurora 68
00/1 Aurora 65
02/3 BAP All-Star 4, ✄ ASJ
98/9 Be A Player 212, ✍ Aut. 212
99/0 BAP Mem. 297, ✄ TM2
00/1 BAP Mem. 22, 500, ✄ J-39
01/2 BAP Memor. 278, ✄ ASJ, ✄ ASE, ✄ ASN, ✄ ASD, ✄ ASS, ✄ AST, ✄ CoO
02/3 BAP Memorabilia 33, 251, ✄ ASJ4, ✄ ASTJ1, ✄ AS3, ✄ TM5
01/2 BAP Update ✄ H29, ✄ TP6
90/1 Bowman 142
91/2 Bowman 182
92/3 Bowman 367
01/2 Bowman 34
02/3 Bowman 70
98/9 Bowman's Best 9
99/0 Crown Royale 64
01/2 Crown Royale 35, ASH3
93/4 Donruss 158
95/6 Donruss 22
96/7 Donruss 100
96/7 Do. Canadian 42
97/8 Do. Canadian 57
96/7 Do. Elite 48
97/8 Do. Priority 49
98/9 Dynagon Ice 86, -TC 12
99/0 Dynagon Ice 95
93/4 EA Sports 61
97/8 Esso 16, ✍ Aut.
02/3 Exclusive 39
02/3 First Edition 157, 391, ✄ Jers.
94/5 Flair 77
96/7 Flair 45
94/5 Fleer 93, FF-2
95/6 Fleer Metal 69
92/3 Fleer Ultra 79
93/4 Fleer Ultra 24
94/5 Fleer Ultra 96
95/6 Fleer Ultra 73
96/7 Fl. Ultra 77
91/2 Gillette 6
95 Globe 82
01/2 Heads Up 21, ASGUN 2
02/3 Heads Up 28, ✄ GWQ 9
95/6 Hoyle / West. 5-Heart
02/3 In The Game-Used 17, 117, ✄ GUJ35, ✄ SJ35, ✄ T10, ✄ TM18
91/2 Kellogg's / Score 22
97/8 Kraft / PB
98/9 Kraft / PB
93/4 Leaf 172
94/5 Leaf 12, GLS-12
95/6 Leaf 148
96/7 Leaf 177
94/5 L. Limited 32
95/6 L. Limited 71
94/5 McDonald's McD-17
98/9 McDonald's T11
02/3 McDonald's -SLG 2
96/7 Metal Univ. 73
99/0 Millenium 118, ✍ Aut. 118
01/2 Nextel
98/9 NHL Power Play
91/2 O-Pee-Chee 6
91/2 O-Pee-Chee 112
92/3 O-Pee-Chee 243
01/2 O-Pee-Chee 71
02/3 O-Pee-Chee 203
98/9 OPC Chrome 63, B11
90/1 OPC Premier 6
91/2 OPC Premier 44
97/8 Omega 106
98/9 Omega 109
99/0 Omega 106
98/9 Pacific 4
99/0 Pacific 187
00/1 Pacific 193
01/2 Pacific 97
02/3 Pacific 87, ✄ GWJ 9
02/3 Pacific Complete 493
97/8 Pacific CC 193, TC-12
97/8 Pa. Crown Roy. 62
98/9 Pa. Crown Roy. 62
97/8 Pa. Dynagon 58, T-45
98/9 Pa. Invincible 65
97/8 Pa. Paramount 87
98/9 Pa. Paramount 102, -TC 12
99/0 Pa. Paramount 108
00/1 Pa. Paramount 110
98/9 Pa. Revolution 65
98/9 Panini Photocard [x2]
91/2 Panini Sticker 86
91/2 Panini Sticker 339
92/3 Panini Sticker 71
93/4 Panini Sticker 209
94/5 Panini Sticker 177
95/6 Panini Sticker 272
96/7 Panini Sticker 268
97/8 Panini Sticker 220
98/9 Panini Sticker 205, 224
99/0 Panini Sticker 252
00/1 Panini Sticker 165
95 Panini Worlds 8
91/2 Parkhurst 293
92/3 Parkhurst 302
93/4 Parkhurst 94
94/5 Parkhurst 105, V85
95/6 Parkhurst 106
00/1 Parkhurst P-55
01/2 Parkhurst 73, ✄ PS33, ✄ HSHSJers
02/3 Parkhurst 112, -CR5, -HHN3, ✄ CRM5, ✄ GJ38, ✄ SJ38
02/3 Parkhurst Retro 66, ✄ NH2
91/2 Pinnacle 201
91/2 Pinnacle 382
92/3 Pinnacle 32
92/3 Pinnacle T2K 16
93/4 Pinnacle 46
94/5 Pinnacle 9, BR-10, TP-4
95/6 Pinnacle 198
97/8 Pinnacle 64
97/8 Pi. Certified 77
97/8 Pi. Inside 71
95/6 Pi. Summit 86
97/8 Pi. Totally 77
95/6 Pi. Zenith 88
95/6 Playoff 48
94/5 POG 129
95/6 POG 138
93/4 Power Play 113
93/4 Premier 56
94/5 Premier 498
00/1 Premier Plus 51, WP8
99/0 Prism 65
00/1 Private Stock ✄ GUG 54
01/2 Pr. Stock 20
02/3 Pr. Stock Reserve 23
00/1 PS Titanium 41, ✄ GUG-19, ✄ GUG-20
01/2 PS Titanium 34, TAS 5, ✄ DSJ 13, ✄ DSJ 19
01/2 PS Titanium Draft ✄ 25
02/3 PS Titanium ✄ GWJ 16
95/6 Pro Magnet 61
90/1 Pro Set 611
91/2 Pro Set 92
92/3 Pro Set 67
91/2 Pro Set Platinum 51
91/2 Pro Set Platinum PC8
02/3 Quest for the Cup 20, ✄ GWJ 4
99/0 Revolution 68
00/1 Revolution 66
90/1 Score 421
91/2 Score 27
92/3 Score 349
91/2 Score CAN 27
92/3 Score CAN 379
92/3 Score 177
93/4 Score 236
94/5 Score 47
95/6 Score 11, CI-9
96/7 Score 130
97/8 Score 148
91/2 Score Young Stars 8
92/3 Score Young Stars 38
94/5 Select 98
95/6 Select CE 74
95 Semic 79
00/1 Signature 151, F-14, ✍ Aut. 4, ✄ DD-20
01/2 Signature C-35, ✍ Aut. LRB, ✄ DD1, ✄ GJ19, ✄ GSJ19, ✄ HSHSJers, ✄ IG2
02/3 Signature Series 152, GS-76, ✍ 152, ✄ DW1, ✄ SGJ35, ✄ TQ1
95/6 SBx Emotion 80
95/6 SBx Impact 78
94/5 SP 53
96/7 SP 74
97/8 SP Authentic 72
98/9 SP Authentic 39, ✍ SotT
99/0 SP Authentic 42
00/1 SP Authentic 21
01/2 SP Authentic 19, ✍ SotT, ✍ SotTT (x2)
02/3 SP Authentic 24
01/2 SP Game Used 9
02/3 SP Game-Used ✄ PH
02/3 Sports Vault 187
97/8 SPx 23
99/0 SPx 73
00/1 SPx 31
01/2 SPx ✄ DT (x2), ✄ TT
02/3 SPx 20
98/9 SPx Finite 42, 108
98/9 SPx Prospects 30
00/1 Stadium 145
99/0 Stadium 101
00/1 Stadium 95
01/2 Stadium Club 57
02/3 Stadium 30, -BT14, ✄ FC, ✄ PC
95/6 SLU
95/6 Super Sticker 56, 58
96/7 Team Out!
92/3 Topps 211
95/6 Topps 307
98/9 Topps 63, B11
99/0 Topps 22
00/1 Topps 103
01/2 Topps 71
02/3 Topps 203
99/0 To. Chrome 22
00/1 To. Chrome 81
01/2 To. Chrome 71
02/3 T. Chrome 114
94/5 Topps Finest 45
98/9 To. Finest 7
98/9 T. Gold Label 96
99/0 To. Gold Label 32
00/1 To. Gold Label 72
00/1 To. Heritage 60, 224
01/2 To. Heritage 69, 117
02/3 To. Heritage 53, 127
02/3 T. Limited 203
96/7 Topps Picks 159
99/0 To. Prmr. Plus 50
01/2 To. Reserve 91
91/2 To. Stadium 348
92/3 To. Stadium 23
93/4 To. Stadium 246
94/5 To. Stadium 135
95/6 To. Stadium 56
93/4 TSC Members Only 8
00/1 To. Stars 47
02/3 T. Total 264
98/9 UD Choice 95, 227, 234, BH20
00/1 UD Heroes 55
01/2 UD PlayMakers Ltd 27, ✄ PCCJ
02/3 UD Superstars ✄ CAS
00/1 Ultimate Mem. ✍ U-43, ✄ Jer. 38, ✄ J-46, ✄ N-3, ✄ S-46
01/2 Ultimate Mem. ✄ Emb., ✄ Jers., ✄ S&J, ✄ ITN, ✄ JE, ✄ JJ, ✄ NP, ✄ PP, ✍ Aut.
02/3 Ultimate Memorabilia ✄ GD, ✄ HT, ✄ Num
99/0 Ult. Victory 43
90/1 Upper Deck 45
91/2 Upper Deck 43
91/2 Upper Deck 148
92/3 Upper Deck 140
93/4 Upper Deck 317, SP-68
94/5 Upper Deck 488, 564, C32, SP-35
95/6 Upper Deck 478, SE-42
96/7 Upper Deck 278, X35
98/9 Upper Deck 285, FT7
99/0 Upper Deck 62
00/1 Upper Deck 82, TT8
01/2 Upper Deck 275
02/3 Upper Deck 42, ✄ ASJ, ✄ ASP, ✄ DM
02/3 UD Artistic 20, R20, -CG11, / Art
94/5 UD Be A Player R40, G3
95/6 UD Be A Player 113, ✍ S113
93/4 UD BAP Roots 20
96/7 UD Black Diam. 144
97/8 UD Black Diam. 103
98/9 UD Black Diam. 41
00/1 UD Black Diam. 28
01/2 UD Challenge 16, ✄ ✍ UCS
02/3 UD Classic 23
95/6 UD CC 160
97/8 UD Coll. Choice 125, S4, W13
98/9 UD G. Reserve 285
99/0 UD G. Reserve 62
99/0 UD Gretzky Excl. 70
01/2 UD Honor Roll 11, 41, TC2
02/3 UD Honor 18
96/7 UD Ice 29
00/1 UD Ice 102
01/2 UD Mask 23, ✄ GJ, ✄ JP, ✄ DP
98/9 UD MVP 94
99/0 UD MVP 92
00/1 UD MVP 88
01/2 UD MVP 47
02/3 UD MVP 47, SD (x2), Souv.
99/0 UD MVP Cup 87
02/3 UD Piece -AC7, ✄ EC, ✄ PH
95/6 UD Post 24
01/2 UD Premier ✄ D (x2), ✍ SigS
02/3 UD Premier ✄ JD
00/1 UD Pros&Prosp. 40
99/0 UD Retro 37
02/3 UD Rookie 28, ✄ 151a, ✄ 161a
01/2 UD SCup Champs 36
01/2 UD Top Shelf 86
02/3 UD Top Shelf ✄ HH (x2), ✄ R, ✄ SH, ✄ ST, ✍ Sig
00/1 UD Vintage 165, 172
01/2 UD Vintage 63
02/3 UD Vintage 63, 268, 310, GB 63
97/8 Valu-net, ✍ Aut.
01/2 Vanguard 23, ✄ DGM 49
99/0 Victory 130, 131
00/1 Victory 108, 109, 306
01/2 Victory 57, -NP5
99/0 WGretzky 78
90/1 LOSA / Smokey 3

BLAKE, TOE
02/3 Parkie - Reprint 211, 213, 225, 241, 290, 299
02/3 Ultimate Memorabilia ✍ Cut

BLANCHARD, GUY
86/7 Sudbury Wolves

BLANCHARD, SEAN
97/8 Bell
97 Bowman 13
98 Bowman 24
98 Bowman Chrome 24
95/6 Slapshot 277
98/9 UD Choice 264
00/1 Florida Everblades
99/0 Lowell Lock Monsters
99/0 Mississippi S'Wolves
02/3 London Knights

BLANCHARD, TREVOR
00/1 Owen Sound Attack 10

BLANK, BORIS
01/2 UD DEL 244

BLASKO, DAN
91/2 Avant Garde BCJHL 19
92/3 BCJHL 81

BLATAK, MIROSLAV
00/1 OFS 376
01/2 OFS 116

BLATCHFORD, TOM
01/2 Belfast Giants

BLATNY, ZDENEK
00/1 SP Authentic 126
00/1 SP GU 86
00/1 SPx ✄ 122
00/1 UD Heroes 177
00/1 UD Reserve 116
00/1 Upper Deck 208
00/1 UD Black Diam. 73
00/1 UD Ice 53
00/1 UD Pros&Prosp. 128
00/1 UD Prospects D5
00/1 UD Vintage 395
01/2 Chicago Wolves
02/3 Chicago Wolves

BLAZEK, JAKUB
01/2 OFS 78

BLAZEK, LADISLAV
94/5 APS 2
95/6 APS 102
96/7 APS 265
97/8 APS 149
97/8 DS 74
98/9 DS 19
99/0 DS 113, G9
00/1 DS 109
96/7 DS Sticker 170
97/8 DS Sticker 187
98/9 OFS 251
99/0 OFS 3, -CL
00/1 OFS 83, 399, -Star 35

BLAZEK, ROMAN
94/5 APS 264
95/6 APS 141
96/7 APS 66
96/7 DS Sticker 239

BLAZEK, TOMAS
94/5 APS 41
95/6 APS 331
96/7 APS 156
97/8 APS 254
97/8 DS 69
98/9 DS 52
99/0 DS 81
00/1 DS 92
96/7 DS Sticker 257
97/8 DS Sticker 137
99/0 OFS 153
99/0 OFS 88, 495
00/1 OFS 44
01/2 OFS 246
94/5 SP 156

BLAZEK, TOMÁS
93/4 Parkhurst 517

BLAZNEK, JOE
98/9 EBK ECHL All-Star
01/2 Florida Everblades
99/0 Kansas City Blades

BLEICHER, MARCUS
94/5 DEL 149
95/6 DEL 143
98/9 DEL 153

BLESSMAN, JOHN
88/9 ProCards / Utica
94/5 Raleigh Icecaps

BLIGHT, RICK
76/7 O-Pee-Chee 238
77/8 O-Pee-Chee 259
78/9 O-Pee-Chee 7
79/0 O-Pee-Chee 395
80/1 O-Pee-Chee 372
76/7 Topps 238
77/8 Topps 259
78/9 Topps 7
75/6 VANC / Royal Bank
76/7 VANC / Royal Bank
77/8 VANC / Royal Bank
78/9 VANC / Royal Bank
79/0 VANC / Royal Bank

BLINCO, RUSS
34-43 BeeHive-1 [Maroons]
35-40 Canada Starch
35/6 O-Pee-Chee 75
36/7 O-Pee-Chee 127
37/8 O-Pee-Chee 169
34/5 Sweet Caporal
37/8 World Wide Gum 30

BLINOV, YURI
91/2 Future Trends C72 34
72 Hellas MM-Jenkki 69
74 Hellas MM-Jenkki 62
72/3 Williams Finnish 22

BLISHEN, DON
90/1 7th...Sketch WHL 116

BLOCK, BRADY
99 Bowman 102
00/1 Calgary Hitmen
99/0 Lethbridge Hurricanes

BLOCK, GRANT
94/5 Muskegon Fury

BLOCK, KEN
73/4 Quaker Oats 37

BLOCK, MATT
94/5 Milwaukee Admirals

BLOEM, DIETER
95/6 DEL 249
96/7 DEL 99

BLOEMBERG, JEFF
90/1 O-Pee-Chee 483
89/0 ProCards IHL 38
90/1 ProCards 10
91/2 ProCards 210
90/1 Upper Deck 370
89/0 NYRA / Marine
95/6 Adirondack Red Wings

BLOMQUIST, KIRK
82/3 Brandon Wheat Kings

BLOMQVIST, ARI
80/1 Mallasjuoma 64
78/9 SM-Liiga 83

BLOMQVIST, TIMO
99/0 Cardset AH 2-ruutu
80/1 Mallasjuoma 70
89/0 Semic Elitserien 171
90/1 Semic Elitserien 127
91/2 Semic Elitserien 179
92/3 Semic Elitserien 203
89 Semic Sticker 32
94/5 Sisu 262
95/6 Sisu 86, DT-6
95/6 Sisu Limited 58
78/9 SM-Liiga 67
86/7 NJER / S.O.B.E.R.
81/2 WASH
82/3 WASH

BLOMSTEN, ARTO
93/4 Donruss 506
95 Globe 20
94/5 Leaf 125
93/4 Parkhurst 232
95/6 Parkhurst 373
93/4 Premier 453
89/0 Semic Elitserien 53
90/1 Semic Elitserien 276
91/2 Semic Elitserien 59
92/3 Semic Elitserien 78
93 Semic Sticker 4
92/3 Upper Deck 369
92/3 Upper Deck 376
93/4 Upper Deck 505, SP-174
97/8 UD Elitserien 72
98/9 UD Elitserien 187
93/4 WINN / Ruffles
93/4 WINN Readers

BLONDIN, CARL
91/2 7th...Sketch LHJMQ 99

BLOOM, MIKE
74/5 Loblaws
74/5 O-Pee-Chee 369
75/6 O-Pee-Chee 376
76/7 O-Pee-Chee 56
77/8 O-Pee-Chee 375
76/7 Topps 56
74/5 WASH

BLOSKI, MIKE
81/2 Saskatoon Blades

BLOUIN, GAETAN
90/1 7th...Sketch WHL 95
90/1 Saskatoon Blades

BLOUIN, JACQUES
91/2 7th...Sketch LHJMQ 136

BLOUIN, JEAN
91/2 ProCards 290
90/1 7th...Sketch LHJMQ 56
92/3 Atlanta Knights
94/5 Thunder Bay Senators

BLOUIN, SYLVAIN
02/3 Atomic 114
02/3 BAP Memorabilia 359
02/3 Crown Royale 121
02/3 First Edition 270
02/3 Heads Up 126
02/3 Parkhurst 238
02/3 Pr. Stock Reserve 167
91/2 7th...Sketch LHJMQ 238
94/5 Sig. Rookies 59, ✍ 59
02/3 SP Authentic 147
02/3 SP Game-Used Edition 80
02/3 SPx 164
02/3 Ultimate Memorabilia 38
02/3 Upper Deck 209
02/3 UD Foundations 132
02/3 UD Honor 156
02/3 UD Mask 123
02/3 UD Piece 135
02/3 UD Top Shelf 114
02/3 UD Vintage 335
02/3 Vanguard 120
02/3 Victory 103
02/3 MONT
95/6 Binghampton Rangers
96/7 Binghampton Rangers
97/8 Hartford Wolf Pack

BLOYE, DAMIAN
93/4 Slapshot / North Bay 16
94/5 Slapshot / North Bay 19

BLUE, JOHN
92/3 Parkhurst 245
92/3 Parkhurst CP19
93/4 Pinnacle 335
94/5 POG 271
93/4 Power Play 287
93/4 Premier 209
90/1 ProCards 103
91/2 ProCards 50
93/4 Score 399
93/4 To. Stadium 334
93/4 Upper Deck 74
95/6 Phoenix Roadrunners

BLUM, JOHN
88/9 ProCards / Adirondack
89/0 ProCards AHL 73
90/1 ProCards 128
88/9 EDMO / Action 106
86/7 WASH / Kodak
98/9 Detroit Vipers
83/4 Moncton Alpines
85/6 Moncton G'Flames

BLUM, KEN
90/1 7th...Sketch OHL 202
94/5 Flint Generals
93/4 Richmond Renegades

BLUMSTEAD, LARRY
82/3 Brandon Wheat Kings

BLYTH, CHARLIE
99/0 Missouri RiverOtters

BLYTH, STEVE
83/4 Springfield Indians 20

BOAKE, PETER
91/2 Air Canada SJHL B8

BOBACK, MIKE
92/3 Classic 83
93/4 Cla. Prospects 46
95/6 Phoenix Roadrunners
93/4 Portland Pirates
94/5 Portland Pirates

BOBARIKO, EVGENI
00/1 Mir 362, 363

BOBILLIER, FRÉDY
95 Panini Worlds 120

BOBROV, VSEVOLD
91/2 Future Trends C72 10
73/4 Soviet Stars 23
74/5 Soviet Stars 22

BOBYCK, BRENT
00/1 Kudos 39, 160
90/1 ProCards 59
01/2 Sheffield Steelers GS

BOCHATAY, DIDIER
00/1 Québec Remparts 16
01/2 Québec Remparts 15
02/3 Val d'Or Foreurs

BOCHATSAY, DIDIER
02/3 Québec Remparts

BOCHENSKY, BRETISLAV
94/5 APS 288

BODAK, BOB
89/0 ProCards AHL 295
90/1 ProCards 3
86/7 Moncton G'Flames
88/9 Salt Lake G'Eagles
84/5 Springfield Indians 23

BODARCHUK, MIKE
92/3 Cincinnati Cyclones

BODDY, GREGG
72/3 Eddie Sargent 223
74/5 Loblaws
73/4 O-Pee-Chee 235
74/5 O-Pee-Chee 349
75/6 O-Pee-Chee 285
75/6 Topps 285
72/3 VANC / Royal Bank
74/5 VANC / Royal Bank
75/6 VANC / Royal Bank

BODDY, LOU
94/5 SR Auto-Phonex 8, ✍ 8
94/5 Richmond Renegades
95/6 Richmond Renegades

BODGER, DOUG
90/1 Bowman 245
91/2 Bowman 21
92/3 Bowman 13
93/4 Donruss 33
95/6 Donruss 226
93/4 EA Sports 13
94/5 Flair 16
96/7 Fl. Picks 164
92/3 Fleer Ultra 258
93/4 Fleer Ultra 31
94/5 Fleer Ultra 20
93/4 Leaf 19
94/5 Leaf 357
85/6 OPC/Topps 38
86/7 OPC/Topps 24
87/8 OPC/Topps 125
88/9 OPC/Topps 96
90/1 OPC/Topps 282
91/2 O-Pee-Chee 207
92/3 O-Pee-Chee 146
89/0 OPC/Topps 154
85/6 OPC Sticker 99-230
86/7 OPC Sticker 232-103
87/8 OPC Sticker 234-102
89/0 opcSticker 257-136
97/8 Pa. Invincible R-175
87/8 Panini Sticker 141
88/9 Panini Sticker 332
89/0 Panini Sticker 209
90/1 Panini Sticker 33
91/2 Panini Sticker 307
92/3 Panini Sticker 245
93/4 Panini Sticker 109
97/8 Panini Sticker 229
91/2 Parkhurst 15
92/3 Parkhurst 253
95/6 Parkhurst 454
91/2 Pinnacle 8
92/3 Pinnacle 97
93/4 Pinnacle 82
94/5 Pinnacle 357
96/7 Pi. Be A Player 208, ✍ Aut. 208
94/5 POG 49
93/4 Power Play 26
93/4 Premier 29
90/1 Pro Set 19
91/2 Pro Set 19
92/3 Pro Set 17
91/2 Pro Set Platinum 12
91/2 Puck / Pro Set 3
90/1 Score 211
91/2 Score 297
91/2 Score CAN 517
92/3 Score 126
93/4 Score 21
94/5 Score 198
95/6 Score 171
95/6 SP 134
92/3 Topps 247
99/0 Topps 149
99/0 To. Chrome 149
91/2 To. Stadium 114
92/3 To. Stadium 147
93/4 To. Stadium 354
94/5 To. Stadium 148
90/1 Upper Deck 50
91/2 Upper Deck 477
92/3 Upper Deck 207
93/4 Upper Deck 187
94/5 Upper Deck 494
95/6 Upper Deck 165, SE-8
94/5 UD Be A Player ✍ 39
95/6 UD CC 77
88/9 BUFF / Blue Shield
88/9 BUFF / Won. Bread
89/0 BUFF / Blue Shield
89/0 BUFF / Campbell's
90/1 BUFF / Blue Shield
90/1 BUFF / Campbell's
91/2 BUFF / Blue Shield
91/2 BUFF / Campbell's
91/2 BUFF / Pepsi
92/3 BUFF / Blue Shield
92/3 BUFF / Jubilee
86/7 PITT / Kodak
87/8 PITT / Kodak

BODKIN, RICK
93/4 Slapshot / Sudbury 14
94/5 Slapshot / Sudbury 12
92/3 Sudbury Wolves
93/4 Sudbury Wolves

BODNAR, GUS
45-64 BeeHive-2 [Chic.]
45-64 BeeHive-2 [Bost.]
51/2 Parkhurst 40
52/3 Parkhurst 37
53/4 Parkhurst 75
54/5 Parkhurst 62
45-54 Quaker Oats
91/2 Ultimate Original Six 31, ✍ Aut. 31

BODNARCHUK, MIKE
90/1 ProCards 574
91/2 ProCards 419
87/8 Kingston Canadians

BODUNOV, ALEXANDER
91/2 Future Trends C72 32
74 Hellas MM-Jenkki 43
74 Semic Sticker 41
73/4 Soviet Stars 16
74/5 Soviet Stars 19
73/4 Williams Finnish 3

BOE, VINCE
90/1 7th...Sketch WHL 15

BOESCH, GARTH
45-64 BeeHive-2 [Toro.]
45-54 Quaker Oats

BOETTGER, DWAYNE
83/4 Moncton Alpines
84/5 Nova Scotia Oilers
85/6 Nova Scotia Oilers

BOEVE, JON
90/1 Rayside-Balfour
89/0 Sudbury Wolves
90/1 Sudbury Wolves

BOGAS, CHRIS
95/6 Do. Elite WJ 26
99/0 Louisiana Ice Gators

BOGDANOV, ANATOLI
92/3 Jyvas Hyva 35
94/5 Sisu 394
95/6 Sisu 392

BOGDEN, SHANE
88/9 Regina Pats

BOGELSACK, FRIEDHELM
94/5 DEL 132
95/6 DEL 124
79 Panini Sticker 255

BOGGS, SCOTT
98/9 Hampton Roads
99/0 Hampton Roads

BOGOSLOWSKI, MARK
89/0 Johnstown Chiefs

BOGOYEVAC, STEVE
92/3 Dayton Bombers
93/4 Dayton Bombers
93/4 Richmond Renegades
94/5 Richmond Renegades

BOGUNIECKI, ERIC
99/0 BAP Mem. 389
02/3 Bowman 73
00/1 Pacific 191
02/3 Pacific Complete 190
02/3 Signature Series 150, ✍ 150
02/3 Sports Vault 279
02/3 Vanguard 82
97/8 Fort Wayne Komets
98/9 Fort Wayne Komets
99/0 Louisville Panthers
00/1 Worcester IceCats
01/2 Worcester IceCats
02/3 Worcester IceCats

BOGUSEVICH, YURI
00/1 Mir 344

BOH, AARON
91/2 7th...Sketch WHL 16
95/6 Louisiana Ice Gators-2
96/7 Louisiana Ice Gators

BOHAC, DANIEL
00/1 DS 153
00/1 OFS 276
01/2 OFS 276

BOHAC, JAN
00/1 DS 119
99/0 OFS 387
00/1 OFS 97
01/2 OFS 260

BOHACEK, JAN
94/5 APS 72
95/6 APS 180
96/7 APS 124
97/8 APS 273
00/1 DS 138
96/7 DS Sticker 59
97/8 DS Sticker 72
00/1 OFS 115
01/2 OFS 176
99/0 Score 91

BÖHM, RICHARD
94/5 DEL 374
95/6 DEL 371
95 Semic 170

BOHONOS, LONNY
95/6 Bowman 93
94/5 Cla. Images 69
97/8 Donruss 15
95/6 Edge Ice 87
99/0 Pacific 403
97/8 Pacific CC 310
97/8 Pi. Be A Player 148, ✍ Aut. 148
97/8 Score 78
97/8 Score Vanc. 9
97/8 Upper Deck 172
99/0 Manitoba Moose
97/8 St. John's Maple Leafs
96/7 Syracuse Crunch
93/4 Portland Winter Hawks

BOHUN, BRYCE
91/2 Air Canada SJHL 14
91/2 Air Canada SJHL A6

BOHUNICKY, PETR
99/0 OFS 325
00/1 OFS 180
01/2 OFS 114

BOICHENKO, PAVEL
00/1 Mir 325

BOIGER, ELMAR
94/5 DEL 178
95/6 DEL 180

BOIJ, PATRIK
95/6 UD Elitserien 151

BOIKO, IGOR
99/0 Greensboro Generals

BOIKOV, ALEXANDRE
00/1 Mir 277
00/1 Pacific 229
00/1 Upper Deck 424
96/7 Kentucky Tho'blades
97/8 Kentucky Tho'blades
99/0 Milwaukee Admirals
01/2 Milwaukee Admirals
95/6 Tri-City Americans 24

BOILARD, DAVID
00/1 Québec Remparts 4

BOILEAU, CLAUDE
52/3 Anonymous 136

BOILEAU, MARC
52/3 Anonymous 116
74/5 O-Pee-Chee 49
62/3 Parkhurst 29
74/5 Topps 49

BOILEAU, PATRICK
02/3 BAP Memorabilia 358
95/6 Edge Ice 51
02/3 Parkhurst 243
02/3 Ultimate Memorabilia 44
02/3 UD Rookie 120
02/3 Grand Rapids Griffins
95/6 Portland Pirates
96/7 Portland Pirates
97/8 Portland Pirates
98/9 Portland Pirates
99/0 Portland Pirates
00/1 Portland Pirates

BOILY, DENIS
96/7 Rimouski Océanic

BOIMISTRUCK, FRED
82/3 O-Pee-Chee 318
82/3 Post [Toro.]
81/2 TORO

BOIS, CURTIS
99/0 Huntington Blizzard
00/1 Rockford IceHogs

BOIS, DANNY
00/1 London Knights
01/2 London Knights

BOISCLAIR, DANIEL
96 Québec Pee Wee 16
01 UD Prospects GU 3, ✄ TPJ, ✄ JC

BOISCLAIR, MAXIME
98 Québec Pee Wee 238
99 Québec Pee Wee 36
01/2 Sherbrooke Castors 11

BOISVERT, ANDRÉ
51/2 Lac St-Jean 18

BOISVERT, GILLES
52/3 Anonymous 118

BOISVERT, HUGO
01/2 Grand Rapids Griffins
02/3 Grand Rapids Griffins

BOISVERT, RICHARD
88/9 Richelieu Riverains

BOISVERT, SERGE
89/0 Semic Elitserien 277
90/1 Semic Elitserien 40
91/2 Semic Elitserien 288
92/3 Semic Elitserien 310
85/6 MONT
82/3 TORO
83/4 Moncton Alpines
86/7 Sherb. Canadiens 6

BOITEAU, JEAN-SEBASTIEN
91/2 7th...Sketch LHJMQ 50

BOIVIN, CLAUDE
93/4 Parkhurst 146
94/5 Parkhurst 159
92/3 Pro Set 130
91/2 Pro Set Platinum 264
90/1 ProCards 48
91/2 ProCards 273
92/3 Score 352
90 7th...Sketch Mem.Cup 69
92/3 Topps 427
92/3 To. Stadium 16
91/2 Upper Deck 475
92/3 Upper Deck 57
94/5 Upper Deck 146
94/5 OTTA
92/3 PHIL / UD Sheet
92/3 PHIL / J.C. Penney
93/4 PHIL / Sheet
93/4 PHIL / J.C. Penney

BOIVIN, FRÉDÉRIC
90/1 7th...Sketch LHJMQ 140
91/2 7th...Sketch LHJMQ 220

BOIVIN, LEO
45-64 BeeHive-2 [Toro.]
45-64 BeeHive-2 [Bost.]
64-67 BeeHive-3 [Bost.]
64-67 BeeHive-3 [Detr.]
64/5 Coke/Sprite [Bost.]
65/6 Coca-Cola
62/3 Cowan Tile
83&87 HHOF 252
68/9 O-Pee-Chee 101
69/0 O-Pee-Chee 122
69/0 O-Pee-Chee 4in1
70/1 O-Pee-Chee 42
70/1 O-Pee-Chee DE 15
52/3 Parkhurst 34
53/4 Parkhurst 6
54/5 Parkhurst 26
02/3 Parkie - Reprint 170, 175, 191
93/4 Parkie 56-57 11
95/6 Parkie 66-67 48
94/5 Parkie Tall 9
45-54 Quaker Oats
60/1 Shirriff 107
61/2 Shirriff 5
68/9 Shirriff / Pitt. 7
57/8 Topps 18
58/9 Topps 20
59/0 Topps 26
60/1 Topps 62
61/2 Topps 7, Stamp
62/3 Topps 5
62/3 Topps Dollar
63/4 Topps 5
64/5 Topps 50
65/6 Topps 32
66/7 Topps 50
68/9 Topps 101
69/0 Topps 122
70/1 Topps 42
62/3 Toronto Star Photo
63/4 Toronto Star Action
64/5 Toronto Star Action
59/0 Toronto Star Weekend
57-58 BOST
91/2 BOST / SA Legends
91/2 BOST / SA Legends

BOJCUN, TODD
89/0 7th...Sketch OHL 122
90/1 7th...Sketch OHL 353

BOKENFOHR, MURRAY
90/1 7th...Sketch WHL 325

BOKSHOWAN, LORNE
81/2 Milwaukee Admirals

BOLAN, EDDY
51/2 Bas du Fleuve 52

BOLAND, JOHN
81/2 Ottawa 67's

BOLAND, MIKE
72/3 Ottawa Nationals

BOLDIN, IGOR
99/0 Mir 41
00/1 Mir 6, 364
92/3 Red Ace Blue 12
92/3 Red Ace Violet 3
94/5 Sisu 32, 167, FOI-3

BOLDIREV, IVAN
72/3 Eddie Sargent 51
74/5 Loblaws
72/3 O-Pee-Chee 41
73/4 O-Pee-Chee 68
74/5 O-Pee-Chee 16
75/6 O-Pee-Chee 12
76/7 O-Pee-Chee 251
77/8 O-Pee-Chee 61
78/9 O-Pee-Chee 135
79/0 O-Pee-Chee 127
80/1 O-Pee-Chee 52
81/2 O-Pee-Chee 329
82/3 O-Pee-Chee 338
83/4 O-Pee-Chee 118
84/5 O-Pee-Chee 50
85/6 OPC/Topps 92
82/3 OPC/Topps Sticker 241
83/4 OPC/Topps Sticker 132
84/5 OPC Sticker 39
85/6 OPC Sticker 34-164
80/1 Pepsi Bottle Cap
82/3 Post [Vanc.]
72/3 Topps 146
73/4 Topps 68
74/5 Topps 16
75/6 Topps 12
76/7 Topps 251
77/8 Topps 61
78/9 Topps 135
79/0 Topps 127
80/1 Topps 52
84/5 Topps 38
71/2 Toronto Sun Photo
79/0 ATLF / B&W
84/5 DETR / Little Caesars
80/1 VANC
80/1 VANC / Silverwood
81/2 VANC
81/2 VANC / Silverwood
82/3 VANC

BOLDT, MAX
96/7 DEL 19

BOLDT, TYLER
00/1 Kamloops Blazers
01/2 Kamloops Blazers
02/3 Kamloops Blazers

BOLDUC, ALEX
37/8 World Wide Gum 119

BOLDUC, DAN
79/0 O-Pee-Chee 173
79/0 Topps 173
79/0 DETR
84/5 Moncton G'Flames
85/6 Moncton G'Flames
85/6 Moncton G'Flames
86/7 Moncton G'Flames

BOLDUC, DAVE
96/7 Rimouski Océanic

BOLDUC, J-M
01/2 Québec Remparts 1
02/3 Québec Remparts

BOLDUC, KEVIN
97/8 Rimouski Océanic

BOLDUC, MICHEL
82/3 Fredericton Express
83/4 Fredericton Express
84/5 Fredericton Express

BOLDUC, PATRICK
00/1 Shawinigan Cataractes 6

BOLDUC, SÉBASTIEN
00/1 Rimouski Océanic 23
01/2 Rimouski Océanic 22

BOLDUC, TOMMY
98/9 Québec Remparts
99/0 Québec Remparts 9

BOLIBRUCK, KEVIN
97 Bowman 14
95/6 Classic 94
94/5 SR Auto-Phonex 9, ✍ 9
95/6 Slapshot 280
99/0 Hamilton Bulldogs
99/0 Hamilton Bulldogs/ Staz
00/1 Rochester Americans

BOLKOV, OLEG
99/0 Mir 186

BOLL, BUZZ
33/4 Anonymous 4
34-43 BeeHive-1 [Toro.]
35/6 O-Pee-Chee 90
36/7 O-Pee-Chee 119
37/8 O-Pee-Chee 140
39/0 O-Pee-Chee 21
38/9 Quaker Oats
37/8 World Wide Gum 40

BOLONCHUK, LARRY
76/7 O-Pee-Chee 322
78/9 O-Pee-Chee 387
72/3 VANC / Royal Bank

BOLTON, HUGH
45-64 BeeHive-2 [Toro.]
51/2 Parkhurst 79
55/6 Parkhurst 14

55/6 Parkhurst 69
57/8 Parkhurst [Toro.] 13
93/4 Parkie 56-57 124
45-54 Quaker Oats

BOLTON, SHANNON
88/9 Sudbury Wolves

BOLTUNOV, OLEG
99/0 Mir 229
00/1 Mir 368

BOMAN, JOHAN
00/1 UD Elitserien 24

BOMBARDIR, BRAD
94/5 Cla. Images 51
02/3 First Edition 260
95/6 Future Legends 1
97/8 Omega 126
97/8 Pi. Be A Player 214, ✍ Aut. 214
94/5 Sig. Rookies 66, ✍ 66
99/0 Topps 178
99/0 To. Chrome 178
91/2 Upper Deck WJC 55
00/1 UD Vintage 181
01/2 UD Vintage 125
96/7 Albany River Rats

BOMBIC, FRANTISEK
02/3 Cardset 7

BONAR, DAN
82/3 O-Pee-Chee 150

BONAR, GRAEME
88/9 ProCards / Indianapolis
86/7 Sherb. Canadiens 7
83/4 Soo Greyhounds

BONAR, JOSH
00/1 Kamloops Blazers
01/2 Vancouver Giants

BOND, BILL
67/8 Columbus Checkers

BOND, KERRY
69 Columbus Checkers

BOND, ROLAND
74 Hellas MM-Jenkki 24
74 Semic Sticker 15
73/4 Williams Finnish 24

BONDRA, PETER
01/2 Adrenaline 194
01/2 Atomic 97, PP35, TN15
02/3 Atomic 98, -PC 20
98/9 Aurora 194, -ALC 20, -CF 49, -MACF 20, -Cube 19
99/0 Aurora 146, Stripe 146
00/1 Aurora 146, ✂ GWJ-10, ✂ GWJ-14
02/3 BAP All-Star 5, ✂ ASJ
98/9 Be A Player 146, ✍ Aut. 146
99/0 BAP Mem. 72, ✂ J-28, ✂ TM-13
00/1 BAP Mem. 74
01/2 BAP Memor. 195, ✂ ASJ, ✂ ASE, ✂ ASN, ✂ AST, ✂ CoO
02/3 BAP Memorabilia 142, ✂ ASJ5, ✂ TM1
01/2 BAP Update ✂ HSHSJers
95/6 Bicycle Sports Aces 7-Diamond
91/2 Bowman 299
92/3 Bowman 248
95/6 Bowman 55
01/2 Bowman 48
02/3 Bowman 61
98/9 Bowman's Best 21, F13, ✍ A3A, ✍ A3B
99/0 Crown Royale 141
00/1 Crown Royale 106
01/2 Crown Royale 141, ✂ TT 20
02/3 Crown Royale 98, ✂ GWDP 23, ✂ GWJ 24
93/4 Donruss 366
94/5 Donruss 31
95/6 Donruss 19, M-1
96/7 Donruss 147
97/8 Donruss 135, RA-10
96/7 Do. Canadian 24
97/8 Do. Canadian 25
95/6 Do. Elite 48
96/7 Do. Elite 11
97/8 Do. Preferred 78
97/8 Do. Priority 47
97/8 Do. Studio 60
98/9 Dynagon Ice 193, -FT 20, -TC 27
99/0 Dynagon Ice 199, ASP-20
93/4 EA Sports 155
95/6 Edge Ice 120, C15
02/3 eTopps 26
02/3 Exclusive 170
02/3 First Edition 143, 387, ✂ Jers.
94/5 Flair 196
96/7 Flair 97
94/5 Fleer 232
96/7 Fleer 115, 138
95/6 Fleer Metal 156
96/7 Fl. Picks 44, F50-2
92/3 Fleer Ultra 230
93/4 Fleer Ultra 46
94/5 Fleer Ultra 231
95/6 Fleer Ultra 172, 319, EA-1, RLS-1
96/7 Fl. Ultra 172, MM-1
01/2 Heads Up 97
02/3 Heads Up 123, ✂ GWQ 34
99/0 HoloGrFX 59
95/6 Hoyle / East. 2-Heart
02/3 In The Game-Used 79, 179, ✂ GUJ45, ✂ SJ45
95/6 Kraft / KD
96/7 Kraft / PB
97/8 Kraft / KD
98/9 Kraft / KD
00/1 Kraft 7
93/4 Leaf 79
94/5 Leaf 277
95/6 Leaf 136
96/7 Leaf 200
97/8 Leaf 91
95/6 L. Limited 30
96/7 L. Limited 63
96/7 L. Preferred 29
97/8 Limited 129
96/7 Maggers 162
99/0 McDonald's ✂ GJ
96/7 Metal Univ. 161, LW-1
99/0 Millenium 245, ✍ Aut. 245, ✂ J-17, ✂✍ J-17, ✂ JS-17
98/9 NHL Power Play
91/2 O-Pee-Chee 362
92/3 O-Pee-Chee 106
01/2 O-Pee-Chee 34
02/3 O-Pee-Chee 129
98/9 OPC Chrome 126, SB14
90/1 OPC Premier 7
97/8 Omega 236, GF-20
98/9 Omega 245, -Onl. 36, -PI 8
99/0 Omega 242
98/9 Pacific 12, -DI 19, -GCDC 35
99/0 Pacific 437, TL-28
00/1 Pacific 418
01/2 Pacific 390, 425, 443
02/3 Pacific 388
02/3 Pacific Complete 14
97/8 Pacific CC 18, SS-12C, TC-26
97/8 Pa. Crown Roy. 138, HT-20
98/9 Pa. Crown Roy. 140, -MP 20, -PotG 25, -PP 24
97/8 Pa. Dynagon 130, T-15, BKS-100
97/8 Pa. Invincible 145, FP-36, R-206
97/8 Pa. Paramount 193
98/9 Pa. Paramount 242, -SD 20, -TC 27
99/0 Pa. Paramount 242, IAI-28
00/1 Pa. Paramount 243
97/8 Pa. Revolution 145, ASG-20, TC-26
98/9 Pa. Revolution 146, -ASG 3, -CTLC 20, -Show. 36
98/9 Panini Photocard [x2]
92/3 Panini Sticker 164
93/4 Panini Sticker 24
94/5 Panini Sticker 24
95/6 Panini Sticker 139, 151
96/7 Panini Sticker 133
97/8 Panini Sticker 109
98/9 Panini Sticker 2, 104
99/0 Panini Sticker 167
00/1 Panini Sticker 102
91/2 Parkhurst 188
92/3 Parkhurst 204
93/4 Parkhurst 222
94/5 Parkhurst 251
95/6 Parkhurst 490
00/1 Parkhurst P-236
01/2 Parkhurst 30, ✂ PJ7, ✂ PS7, ✂ M32, ✂ T6
02/3 Parkhurst 98, ✂ GJ45, ✂ SJ45, ✂ TT17
02/3 Parkhurst Retro 24
94/5 Parkie SE seV13
91/2 Pinnacle 87
92/3 Pinnacle 82
93/4 Pinnacle 164
94/5 Pinnacle 281
95/6 Pinnacle R20-14
96/7 Pinnacle 109
97/8 Pinnacle 181
97/8 Pi. Be A Player 92, OT-13, ✍ Aut. 92
97/8 Pi. Certified 46
97/8 Pi. Inside 83
95/6 Pi. Summit 63, MH-11
96/7 Pi. Summit 62
97/8 Pi. Totally 46
95/6 Pi. Zenith 49
96/7 Pi. Zenith 71
95/6 Playoff 212, 320
96/7 Playoff 391
94/5 POG 242
95/6 POG 281
97/8 Pi. Post 22
93/4 Power Play 258
93/4 Premier 12
94/5 Premier 283
99/0 Prism 146
00/1 Private Stock PS-59, ✂ GUG 101
01/2 Pr. Stock 97, -PS 74, ✂ GUG 99
02/3 Pr. Stock Reserve ✂ 148
00/1 PS Titanium 98
01/2 PS Titanium 140
01/2 PS Titanium Draft ✂ 99
02/3 PS Titanium ✂ GWJ 73
00/1 PS Titanium Draft ✂ 98
90/1 Pro Set 645
91/2 Pro Set 511
92/3 Pro Set 209
91/2 Pro Set Platinum 244
99/0 Revolution 147, SS-36, TL-30, / CSC 147
00/1 Revolution 146, ✂ GUG-10
90/1 Score 71T
91/2 Score 216
91/2 Score CAN 216
92/3 Score 165
93/4 Score 344
93/4 Score IS 4
93/4 Score PiAS 12
94/5 Score 12
95/6 Score 53, GB-4, L-7
96/7 Score 185
97/8 Score 103
94/5 Select 89
95/6 Select CE 51
96/7 Select CE 78
00/1 Signature 121, ✍ Aut. 213, ✂ HSHSJers
01/2 Signature C-31, ✍ Aut. LPBO, ✂ GUE32, ✂ GJ64, ✂ GSJ64, ✂ HSHSJers, ✂ ITN32, ✂ TM30
02/3 Signature Series 138, GS-71, ✍ 138, ✂ SGJ45, ✂ TQ9
95/6 SBx Impact 174, 242
96/7 SBx Impact 136
94/5 SP 129
95/6 SP 155
96/7 SP 163, HC-14
97/8 SP Authentic 164, ✍ SotT
98/9 SP Authentic 88, -SS28, -SO18, ✍ SotT
99/0 SP Authentic 90
00/1 SP Authentic 88
01/2 SP Authentic 88
02/3 SP Authentic 90, 105
01/2 SP Game Used 60, ✂ AF, ✂ AFD, ✂✍ ISD, ✂ Patch, ✂✍ PatchSig, ✂ PatchC, ✂✍ PatchCSig, ✂ TotGSig
02/3 SP Game-Used ✂ AF (x2), ✂ CF, ✂ PH (x2), ✂ TG
02/3 Sports Vault 143
96/7 SPx 49
97/8 SPx 50
99/0 SPx 159
00/1 SPx ✂ WM PBo
01/2 SPx 69, ✂ DT, ✂ TT
02/3 SPx 144, ✂ M, ✂ SS, ✂ X
98/9 SPx Finite 87, 110, 168, H30, L15, PS15
98/9 SPx Prospects 60, H30, L15, PS15
99/0 Stadium 100, Chrome 33
00/1 Stadium 160
01/2 Stadium Club 9
02/3 Stadium 67, -WS-17
97/8 SLU
98/9 SLU
95/6 Super Sticker 130
96/7 Team Out!
92/3 Topps 294
95/6 Topps 6, 310, 6HG
98/9 Topps 126, M14, SB14
99/0 Topps 67, TW18
00/1 Topps 44
01/2 Topps 34, SM12
02/3 Topps 129, -CC5
99/0 To. Chrome 67
00/1 To. Chrome 36
01/2 To. Chrome 34
02/3 T. Chrome 81
95/6 To. Finest 73
98/9 To. Finest 52, R5
98/9 T. Gold Label 16
99/0 To. Gold Label 9
00/1 To. Gold Label 43
00/1 To. Heritage 16
01/2 To. Heritage 35
02/3 To. Heritage 51
02/3 T. Limited 129
99/0 To. Prmr. Plus 2, CR7
01/2 To. Reserve 11
91/2 To. Stadium 37
92/3 To. Stadium 286
93/4 To. Stadium 82
93/4 To. Stadium - All-Stars
94/5 To. Stadium 247
95/6 To. Stadium 209
95/6 TSC Members Only 31
02/3 T. Total 172
98/9 UD Choice 213, SQ14
00/1 UD Heroes ✍ SG
01/2 UD PlayMakers Ltd 98
00/1 UD Reserve 87
98/9 UD3 38, 98, 158
01/2 Ultimate Mem. ✂ DD, ✂ GSL, ✍ Aut.
99/0 Ult. Victory 90
90/1 Upper Deck 536
91/2 Upper Deck 131
91/2 Upper Deck E12
92/3 Upper Deck 115
93/4 Upper Deck 95, 308, SP-168
94/5 Upper Deck 135, SP-85
95/6 Upper Deck 232, 249, 339, AS-11, SE-177
96/7 Upper Deck 180, 364, X26
x97/8 Upper Deck S12
98/9 Upper Deck 200, FF2
99/0 Upper Deck 132, 151, CT30
00/1 Upper Deck 407, ✂ GJ
01/2 Upper Deck 173, CT15, SS20
02/3 Upper Deck 174, ✂ LN, ✂ R50, ✂ S
95/6 UD ASG MVP26
96/7 UD All-Star YCTG AR18
02/3 UD Artistic 89, R89, / Art
95/6 UD Be A Player 210, ✍ S210
96/7 UD Black Diam. 133
97/8 UD Black Diam. 87
98/9 UD Black Diam. 88, M15, WF29
99/0 UD Black Diam. 89, D17
99/0 UD C. Legends 69
01/2 UD Challenge 90
02/3 UD Classic 99, ✂ CS, ✂ HH, ✂ HR
95/6 UD CC 58, C13
96/7 UD CC 279, 334, UD23, C4, CR4
97/8 UD Coll. Choice 270, SQ58, C25, CR25
98/9 UD G. Reserve 200
99/0 UD G. Reserve 132, 151
01/2 UD Honor Roll - DPuck, ✂ GAJ
02/3 UD Honor ✂ GA
97/8 UD Ice 12
01/2 UD Ice 125, ✍ CCA
00/1 UD Legends ✍ ES
92/3 UD Locker 1
01/2 UD Mask 99
02/3 UD Mask ✂ PG
98/9 UD MVP 209, -Snip. S9
99/0 UD MVP 215, DR6
00/1 UD MVP 182
01/2 UD MVP 184, ✂ S
02/3 UD MVP 185, SO14
99/0 UD MVP Cup 188, SC20
99/0 UD Ovation 59
02/3 UD Piece 89
01/2 UD Premier ✂ B, ✂ D, ✍ SigS
00/1 UD Pros&Prosp. 87
99/0 UD Retro 79
01/2 UD Top Shelf 120, ✂ J, ✂ S
02/3 UD Top Shelf 89, ✂ CP, ✂ GO, ✂ HT (x2), ✂ M, ✂ R, ✂ SH, ✂ ST, ✂ TS, ✍ Sig
00/1 UD Vintage 364, 369
01/2 UD Vintage 255, 260, 264
02/3 UD Vintage 255, 290, 305, 309, ✂ GB 255, ✂ HS
00/1 Vanguard 98, HV-36
01/2 Vanguard 98, ✂ DGM 33
02/3 Vanguard 98, ✂ GWJ 49
99/0 Victory 303, 304
00/1 Victory 234, 329
01/2 Victory 350, 430
02/3 Victory 214
99/0 WGretzky 173, EG13
96 Wien 228
97/8 Zenith 42, Z43
90/1 WASH / Kodak
90/1 WASH / Smokey
91/2 WASH / Kodak
91/2 WASH / Smokey
92/3 WASH / Kodak
95/6 WASH
98/9 WASH / Kids 'n 2

BONDY, MIKE
98/9 Flint Generals

BONE, JASON
99/0 Kamloops Blazers
99/0 Kamloops Blazers
00/1 Sudbury Wolves 19

BONELLO, FRANK
52/3 Anonymous 172
59/60 Whitby Dunlops

BONIN, BRIAN
95/6 Future Legends ✍ SSD-3
99/0 Pacific 350
96/7 Cleveland Lumberjacks
00/1 Cleveland Lumberjacks
98/9 Kansas City Blades 9
92/3 Minnesota G'Gophers
93/4 Minnesota G'Gophers
94/5 Minnesota G'Gophers

BONIN, MARCEL
45-64 BeeHive-2 [Detr.]
45-64 BeeHive-2 [Mont.]
51/2 Laval Dairy 15
57/8 Parkhurst [Mont.] 18
58/9 Parkhurst 32
59/0 Parkhurst 12
60/1 Parkhurst 51
61/2 Parkhurst 47
62/3 Parkhurst 45
02/3 Parkie - Reprint 232, 256, 269
93/4 Parkie 56-57 19
60/1 Shirriff 29
61/2 Shirriff 115
62/3 Shirriff 27
92/3 Sport Flash 7
54/5 Topps 59
61/2 Toronto Star Weekend
60/1 York Glass [Mont.]
60/1 York
61/2 York 29

BONK, RADEK
01/2 Adrenaline 132
96/7 APS 342
94/5 Assets 20, 45
00/1 Aurora 100
02/3 BAP All-Star 6, ✂ ASJ
98/9 Be A Player 94, ✍ Aut. 94
99/0 BAP Mem. 136
00/1 BAP Mem. 105
01/2 BAP Memor. 3, ✂ ASJ, ✂ ASE, ✂ ASN, ✂ CoO
02/3 BAP Memorabilia 177
01/2 Bowman 97
02/3 Bowman 28
93/4 Classic 98
93/4 Classic - Class of '94 CL4
93/4 Classic N10
94/5 Classic 3, CP13, R2, T47, ✍ Aut.
94/5 Classic Draft Day
94/5 Classic 4 Sport 117, BC18, T4, HV12
94/5 Cla. Images 25, CE13, PR6, ✍ Aut.
93/4 Cla. Images 4 Sport CC16
94/5 Cla. Images 4 Sport 96
93/4 Cla. Prospects 1, 2, 3, 100, 200, LP21, ✍ Aut.
99/0 Crown Royale 95
00/1 Crown Royale 74
95/6 Donruss 194
96/7 Donruss 128
95/6 Do. Elite 62
99/0 DS 79
99/0 Dynagon Ice 138
95/6 Edge Ice 158
02/3 Exclusive 120
02/3 First Edition 15, ✂ Jers.
94/5 Fleer 142, RS-1
96/7 Fleer 74
95/6 Fleer Metal 102
95/6 Fleer Ultra 110, HS-4
96/7 Fl. Ultra 114
02/3 Heads Up 85
95/6 Hoyle / East. 3-Heart
02/3 In The Game-Used ✂ IE21
00/1 Kraft 9
95/6 Leaf 263, SR-20
96/7 Leaf 129
97/8 Limited 12
96/7 Metal Univ. 104
01/2 O-Pee-Chee 36
02/3 O-Pee-Chee 260
99/0 Omega 158
98/9 Pacific 307
99/0 Pacific 285
00/1 Pacific 276
01/2 Pacific 271
02/3 Pacific 263
02/3 Pacific Complete 309
97/8 Pacific CC 331
97/8 Pa. Paramount 123
99/0 Pa. Paramount 160
00/1 Pa. Paramount 171
95/6 Panini Sticker 50
96/7 Panini Sticker 49
97/8 Panini Sticker 37
98/9 Panini Sticker 41
99/0 Panini Sticker 116
00/1 Panini Sticker 72
95/6 Parkhurst 147
00/1 Parkhurst P-115
01/2 Parkhurst 130, ✂ PJ47, ✂ T16
02/3 Parkhurst 121
02/3 Parkhurst Retro 31
95/6 Pinnacle 43, GG-6
96/7 Pinnacle 50
95/6 Pi. Summit 123
95/6 Playoff 72
95/6 POG 194
99/0 Prism 95
00/1 Private Stock 69
01/2 Pr. Stock -PS 51
02/3 Pr. Stock Reserve 71
00/1 PS Titanium 64
95/6 Pro Magnet 111
02/3 Quest for the Cup 69
00/1 Revolution 102
95/6 Score 190
96/7 Score 97
94/5 Select 186
94/5 Sig. Rookies CF1, ✍ CF1
94/5 SR Gold Standard 78, GS3
00/1 Signature 166, ✍ Aut. 160
01/2 Signature 164, ✍ Aut. 164, ✂ GJ44, ✂ GSJ44
02/3 Signature Series 68, ✍ 68
95/6 SBx Emotion 122
95/6 SBx Impact 117
96/7 SBx Impact 87
94/5 SP 80, P-6
95/6 SP 102
96/7 SP 105
99/0 SP Authentic 59
01/2 SP Authentic 58
01/2 SP Game Used 37, ✂ AF
00/1 SPx 47
01/2 SPx 45
00/1 Stadium 72
95/6 Super Sticker 84, 88
95/6 Topps 64
00/1 Topps 134, PP4
01/2 Topps 36
02/3 Topps 260, HHC18
00/1 To. Chrome 101
01/2 To. Chrome 36
94/5 Topps Finest 3, BBM-3, BBR-11
99/0 To. Gold Label 73
00/1 To. Heritage 132
02/3 T. Limited 260
96/7 Topps Picks 147
95/6 To. Stadium 101
02/3 T. Total 116
00/1 UD Heroes 84
01/2 UD PlayMakers Ltd 68
94/5 Upper Deck 304, 538, 542, SP-144
95/6 Upper Deck 124, SE-62
96/7 Upper Deck 301
97/8 Upper Deck 320
99/0 Upper Deck 266
00/1 Upper Deck 349
01/2 Upper Deck 120, T6, ✂ GN
02/3 Upper Deck 367
95/6 UD Be A Player 31, ✍ S31
99/0 UD Black Diam. 60
00/1 UD Black Diam. 41
95/6 UD CC 110
96/7 UD CC 181
99/0 UD G. Reserve 266
00/1 UD Legends 94, 95
01/2 UD Mask 69
00/1 UD MVP 127
01/2 UD MVP 130
02/3 UD MVP 130
99/0 UD MVP Cup 125
00/1 UD Pros&Prosp. 61
00/1 UD Vintage 248
01/2 UD Vintage 175, 181, 182
02/3 UD Vintage 175, GB 175
00/1 Victory 160
01/2 Victory 246, 432
02/3 Victory 150
99/0 WGretzky 117
94/5 OTTA
95/6 OTTA
96/7 OTTA
97/8 OTTA
98/9 OTTA
99/0 OTTA
00/1 OTTA
01/2 OTTA
02/3 OTTA
94/5 Las Vegas Thunder

BONNEAU, ROB
97/8 Hampton Roads
98/9 Orlando Solar Bears Geico
99/0 Utah Grizzlies

BONNER, CRAIG
90 7th..Sketch Mem.Cup 23
90/1 7th..Sketch WHL 298
91/2 7th...Sketch WHL 91
89/0 Kamloops Blazers

BONNER, DOUG
94/5 L. Limited USA 2
94/5 Sig. Rookies 62, ✍ 62
94/5 Topps Finest 113
97/8 Louisiana Ice Gators
98/9 Louisiana Ice Gators
96/7 Peoria Rivermen
93/4 Seattle Thunderbirds

BONNER, JIM
90/1 Michigan Tech Huskies
91/2 Michigan Tech Huskies
91/2 Michigan Tech Huskies

BONNETT, JOE
92/3 W. Michigan Broncos

BONNEY, WAYNE
90/1 Pro Set 682

BONNEYMAN, ART
28/9 Paulins Candy 41

BONNI, RYAN
99/0 BAP Mem. 374
97 Bowman 135, BB11, ✍ Aut.
99/0 Omega 238
00/1 Topps 312
00/1 To. Chrome 207
00/1 Kansas City Blades 1
01/2 Manitoba Moose

BONO, GENE
98/9 Phoenix Mustangs 9

BONSIGNORE, JASON
95/6 Bowman 101
93/4 Classic 99
93/4 Classic - Class of '94 CL2
93/4 Classic N4
94/5 Classic 4, R3, T22, ✍ Aut.
95/6 Classic 97, BK17
94/5 Classic Draft Day
95/6 Cla. 5 Sport 127, S-74, SFF-6
94/5 Classic 4 Sport 118, HV16
94/5 Cla. Images 45, ✍ Aut.
94/5 Cla. Images 4 Sport 97
93/4 Cla. Prospects 201, ✍ Aut.
93/4 Donruss USA2
95/6 Donruss 249, PP-3
96/7 Fleer 123
95/6 Fleer Metal 172
95/6 Fleer Ultra 332
95/6 Leaf 229, SR-12
94/5 L. Limited USA 3
95/6 L. Limited 59
98/9 OPC Chrome 129
98/9 Pacific 64
95/6 Panini Sticker 256
96/7 Panini Sticker 301
93/4 Parkhurst 510
95/6 Parkhurst 80
93/4 Pinnacle 489
95/6 Pinnacle 207
95/6 Pi. Zenith 136
95/6 Playoff 256
95/6 Pro Magnet 82
94/5 Score 209
95/6 Score 308
95/6 Select CE 113
95/6 SBx Emotion gN 3
95/6 SBx Impact 196
96/7 SBx Impact 146
93/4 Slapshot / Niagara Falls 23
93/4 Slapshot / Niagara Falls 28
94/5 Slapshot / Promo
94/5 Slapshot / Sudbury 17
94/5 SP 173
98/9 Topps 129
94/5 Topps Finest 117
95/6 To. Stadium ER191
95/6 T. Super Skills SR2
93/4 Upper Deck 560
94/5 Upper Deck 523
95/6 Upper Deck 266
96/7 Upper Deck 62
98/9 Upper Deck 180
95/6 UD Be A Player 179, ✍ S179
98/9 UD G. Reserve 180
98/9 Cleveland Lumberjacks
99/0 St. John's Maple Leafs

BONVIE, DENNIS
95/6 Leaf 306
91/2 7th...Sketch OHL 54
00/1 Stadium 107
95/6 Upper Deck 393
97/8 Upper Deck 277
02/3 OTTA
94/5 Cape Breton Oilers
01/2 Providence Bruins
00/1 WBS Penguins

BONVIE, HERB
95/6 Slapshot 225

BOOGAARD, DEREK
00/1 Prince George Cougars

BOOKER, CRAIG
85/6 Kitchener Rangers
86/7 Kitchener Rangers
87/8 Kitchener Rangers

BOOKER, WES
96/7 Soo Greyhounds

BOOME, DANNY
93/4 Sheffield Steelers 10

BOOMER, RON
52/3 Anonymous 180

BOON, RICHARD (DICKIE)
83 HHOF Postcard H2
83&87 HHOF 108
60/1 Topps 17
61/2 Topps - Stamp

BOONE, JONATHAN
00/1 Halifax Moosehead
99/0 Halifax Mooseheads

BOONE, KEN
93/4 Slapshot / Kingston 11
99/0 Indianapolis Ice
98/9 Peoria Rivermen

BOORK, LEIF
94/5 Leaf Elit Set 303
91/2 Semic Elitserien 313
92/3 Semic Elitserien 335

BOORMAN, BRYAN
95/6 Red Deer Rebels

BOOS, TINO
94/5 DEL 171
95/6 DEL 167
96/7 DEL 243
98/9 DEL 62
99/0 Eishockey 190, 382
00/1 UD DEL 138
01/2 UD DEL 136

BOOTH, DEREK
90/1 7th..Sketch OHL 254
02/3 Peoria Rivermen
93/4 Rochester Americans
92/3 Toledo Storm WIOT
92/3 Toledo Storm

BOOTHMAN, GEORGE
34-43 BeeHive-1 [Toro.]

BOOTLAND, DARRYL
99/0 UD Prospects 7
00/1 Toronto St. Mike's

BOOTLAND, NICK
95/6 Slapshot 104
98/9 Hershey Bears
00/1 Hershey Bears
95/6 Guelph Storm
96/7 Guelph Storm

BORDELEAU, CHRISTIAN
70s Dernière Heure
70/1 Eddie Sargent 185
71/2 Eddie Sargent 187
70/1 Esso Power Player
72/3 Post 24
71/2 O-Pee-Chee 51
72/3 O-Pee-Chee 299
75/6 OPC WHA 116
76/7 OPC WHA 49
73/4 OPC WHA Poster 17
73/4 Quaker Oats 15
71/2 Topps 51
71/2 Toronto Sun Photo
69/0 MONT / Pro Star
76/7 Québec Nordiques

BORDELEAU, J.P.
79/0 Dernière Heure
74/5 Loblaws
73/4 O-Pee-Chee 258
74/5 O-Pee-Chee 69
74/5 O-Pee-Chee 309
75/6 O-Pee-Chee 369
76/7 O-Pee-Chee 208
77/8 O-Pee-Chee 156
78/9 O-Pee-Chee 101
79/0 O-Pee-Chee 212
80/1 O-Pee-Chee 339
74/5 Topps 69
76/7 Topps 208
77/8 Topps 156
78/9 Topps 101
79/0 Topps 212
79/0 CHIC
80/1 CHIC / Colour
80/1 CHIC / Brown

BORDELEAU, PAULIN
74/5 Loblaws
74/5 O-Pee-Chee 340
75/6 O-Pee-Chee 151
76/7 OPC WHA 98
77/8 OPC WHA 32
90/1 ProCards 74
91/2 ProCards 91
75/6 Topps 151
73/4 VANC / Royal Bank
74/5 VANC / Royal Bank
75/6 VANC / Royal Bank
76/7 Québec Nordiques
76/7 Québ. / Antoinette
92/3 Fredericton Canadiens
93/4 Fredericton Canadiens
94/5 Fredericton Canadiens
95/6 Fredericton Canadiens
96/7 Fredericton Canadiens

BORDELEAU, SÉBASTIEN
95/6 Edge Ice 38
97/8 Limited 195
99/0 Pacific 218
00/1 Pacific 219
01/2 Pacific 320
97/8 Pacific CC 194
97/8 Pi. Be A Player 211, ✍ Aut. 211
97/8 Score Mont. 14
91/2 7th...Sketch LHJMQ 210
94/5 Slapshot Memorial 69
99/0 Topps 204
99/0 To. Chrome 204
96/7 Upper Deck 193
97/8 Upper Deck 87
98/9 Upper Deck 298
98/9 UD G. Reserve 298
98/9 UD MVP 115
97/8 MONT
98/9 NASH / Wendy's 3
95/6 Fredericton Canadiens
96/7 Fredericton Canadiens

BORDERS, SCOTT
99/0 Lethbridge Hurricanes

BORDKIN, ANTON
99/0 Kamloops Blazers

BOREGA, NATHAN
00/1 Louisiana Ice Gators

BORGGAARD, ANDY
93/4 Huntington Blizzard

BORGO, RICHARD
92/3 Classic Prospects 103
90 7th..Sketch Mem.Cup 35
90/1 7th..Sketch OHL 228
93/4 Thunder Bay Senators
86/7 Kitchener Rangers
87/8 Kitchener Rangers
88/9 Kitchener Rangers
89/0 Kitchener Rangers
90/1 Kitchener Rangers

BORGQVIST, ROBERT
95/6 UD CC 348

BORGSTROM, JORMA
65/6 Hellas 52
70/1 Kuvajulkaisut 279
71/2 Williams Finnish 150
72/3 Williams Finnish 140

BORISKOV, IGOR
00/1 Mir 310

BORLAND, BILL
23/4 Paulins Candy 1
28/9 Paulins Candy 77
24/5 Selkirks Crescent 14

BORODKIN, ANTON
98/9 Kamloops Blazers
99/0 Kamloops Blazers

BORODULIN, MIKHAIL
98/9 Mir 10
99/0 Mir 3
00/1 Metallurg 41

BORRETT, BARRY
77/8 Nova Scotia Voyageurs

BORSATO, LUCIANO
92/3 Bowman 52
98/9 Cardset 44
99/0 Cardset 30
95/6 DEL 207
96/7 DEL 350
92/3 Fleer Ultra 239
93/4 Fleer Ultra 452
92/3 O-Pee-Chee 149
92/3 Panini Sticker E
93/4 Panini Sticker 195
91/2 Parkhurst 425
92/3 Parkhurst 439
93/4 Parkhurst 501
94/5 Parkie SE200
91/2 Pinnacle 353
92/3 Pinnacle 218
93/4 Power Play 471
93/4 Premier 234
94/5 Premier 148
92/3 Pro Set RGL 8
92/3 Pro Set TL 15
91/2 Pro Set Platinum 275
89/0 ProCards AHL 35
91/2 ProCards 186
92/3 Score 256
93/4 Score 401
92/3 Topps 239
92/3 To. Stadium 81
93/4 To. Stadium 317
91/2 Upper Deck 599
92/3 Upper Deck 77
00/1 UD DEL 185
01/2 UD DEL 197
91/2 WINN / IGA
93/4 WINN / Ruffles
93/4 WINN Readers
91/2 Moncton Hawks

BORSCHEVSKY, NIKOLAI
92/3 Classic 52
93/4 Donruss 332
93/4 EA Sports 137
92/3 Fleer Ultra 418, -U 11
93/4 Fleer Ultra 99
94/5 Fleer Ultra 375
93/4 Leaf 137
94/5 Leaf 279
92/3 OPC Premier 100
93/4 Panini Sticker 224
94/5 Panini Sticker 192
92/3 Parkhurst 186
92/3 Parkhurst 216
93/4 Parkhurst 203
94/5 Parkhurst 231
92/3 Pinnacle 397
93/4 Pinnacle 12
94/5 Pinnacle 160
94/5 POG 230
93/4 Power Play 240
93/4 Premier 107
92/3 Red Ace Blue 11
92/3 Red Ace Violet 4
93/4 Score 41
93/4 Score IS 12
94/5 Score 30
93/4 To. Stadium 375
94/5 To. Stadium 209
92/3 Upper Deck 572
93/4 Upper Deck 164, SP-156
94/5 Upper Deck 405
95/6 Upper Deck 173
95/6 UD CC 300
92/3 TORO / Kodak
93/4 TORO / Abalene
93/4 TORO / Black's 18
94/5 TORO / Coca-Cola

BORSHEIM, LES
99/0 Brandon Wheat Kings

BORYS, CORY
91/2 Air Canada SJHL D35

BORZECKI, ADAM
98 Bowman 120
98 Bowman Chrome 120
01/2 Syracuse Crunch
02/3 Syracuse Crunch
97/8 Rimouski Océanic

BOSCH, BRYAN
88/9 Lethbridge Hurricanes
89/0 Lethbridge Hurricanes

BOSCHER, RICHARD
91/2 Air Canada SJHL B1
92/3 MPS SJHL 130

BOSCHMAN, JOEL
95/6 Spokane Chiefs 13

BOSCHMAN, LAURIE
91/2 Bowman 282
86/7 Kraft Sports 72
80/1 O-Pee-Chee 179
81/2 O-Pee-Chee 314
83/4 O-Pee-Chee 381
84/5 O-Pee-Chee 335
85/6 O-Pee-Chee 251
86/7 OPC/Topps 184
87/8 O-Pee-Chee 222
88/9 O-Pee-Chee 200
90/1 OPC/Topps 39
91/2 O-Pee-Chee 202
90/1 OPC Premier 8
81/2 OPC Sticker 103
84/5 OPC Sticker 288
85/6 OPC Sticker 254-134
86/7 OPC Sticker 111
88/9 OPC Sticker 139-10
89/0 opcSticker 147-266
87/8 Panini Sticker 368
88/9 Panini Sticker 153
89/0 Panini Sticker 169
90/1 Panini Sticker 320
91/2 Panini Sticker 215
91/2 Parkhurst 316
92/3 Parkhurst 122
80/1 Pepsi Bottle Cap
92/3 Pinnacle 375
90/1 Pro Set 324, 476
91/2 Pro Set 426
90/1 Score 63T
91/2 Score CAN 436
92/3 Score 374
92/3 Score 513
93/4 Score 289
84/5 7-Eleven
80/1 Topps 179
84/5 Topps 151
92/3 Topps 246
91/2 To. Stadium 292
92/3 To. Stadium 310
93/4 To. Stadium 3
90/1 Upper Deck 103
91/2 Upper Deck 279
83/4 Vachon 123-3
82/3 EDMO / Red Rooster
88/9 EDMO / Action 94
90/1 NJER
92/3 OTTA
79/0 TORO
80/1 TORO
81/2 TORO
83/4 WINN
84/5 WINN / Safety Tips
85/6 WINN
85/6 WINN / Safety Tips
85/6 WINN / Silverwood
86/7 WINN
87/8 WINN
88/9 WINN / Safety Tips
89/0 WINN / Safeway

BOSCHMAN, LAURIE
02/3 Fleer Throwbacks 55

BOSSIO, JOHN
99/0 Odessa Jackalopes

BOSSON, MATHIAS
99/0 Cardset 301
94/5 Leaf Elit Set 252
95/6 Leaf Elit Set 94
95/6 UD Elitserien 142
97/8 UD Elitserien 143
00/1 UD Elitserien 26

BOSSY, MIKE
01/2 ASG History
01/2 BAP Memor. ✂ 500GS
02/3 BAP Memorabilia / Stanley Cup
02/3 Canada Post
93/4 Classic 116, ✍ Aut.
77/8 Dernière Heure
80/1 Dernière Heure
82/3 Dernière Heure
88/9 Esso All-Star
01/2 Fleer Greats 72, -BC 4, ✍ Aut.
01/2 Fleer Legacy 32
83/4 Funmate Puffy 19 [w/]
84/5 Kellogg's 17
96/7 Legends 87
82/3 McDonald's Les Étoiles 6
82/3 McDonald's Les Étoiles 21
78/9 O-Pee-Chee 1
78/9 O-Pee-Chee 63
78/9 O-Pee-Chee 67
78/9 O-Pee-Chee 115
79/0 O-Pee-Chee 1
79/0 OPC 5
79/0 OPC 7
79/0 O-Pee-Chee 161
79/0 O-Pee-Chee 230
80/1 O-Pee-Chee 25
80/1 O-Pee-Chee 204
80/1 O-Pee-Chee 262
81/2 O-Pee-Chee 198
81/2 O-Pee-Chee 208
81/2 O-Pee-Chee 219
81/2 O-Pee-Chee 382
81/2 O-Pee-Chee 386
81/2 O-Pee-Chee 388
81/2 O-Pee-Chee 390
82/3 O-Pee-Chee 2
82/3 O-Pee-Chee 197
82/3 O-Pee-Chee 199
83/4 O-Pee-Chee 1
83/4 O-Pee-Chee 3
83/4 O-Pee-Chee 205
83/4 O-Pee-Chee 210
84/5 O-Pee-Chee 122
84/5 O-Pee-Chee 209
84/5 O-Pee-Chee 362
84/5 O-Pee-Chee 376
85/6 OPC/Topps 130
86/7 OPC/Topps 90
86/7 OPC/Topps Box B
87/8 OPC/Topps 105
92/3 O-Pee-Chee 391
92/3 OPC - Anniv. 11
81/2 OPC Sticker 150
81/2 OPC Sticker 158
81/2 OPC Sticker 253
82/3 OPC/Topps Sticker 1
82/3 OPC/Topps Sticker 50
82/3 OPC/Topps Sticker 51
82/3 OPC/Topps Sticker 165
83/4 OPC/Topps Sticker 10
83/4 OPC/Topps Sticker 78
83/4 OPC/Topps Sticker 79
83/4 OPC/Topps Sticker 176
83/4 OPC/Topps Sticker 306
83/4 OPC/Topps Sticker 321
83/4 OPC/Topps Sticker 322
84/5 OPC Sticker 82, 83
84/5 OPC Sticker 235-234
85/6 OPC Sticker 66
85/6 OPC Sticker 118
86/7 OPC Sticker 217
86/7 OPC Sticker 117-131
86/7 OPC Sticker 194-56
87/8 OPC Sticker 244
80/1 O-Pee-Chee Super 12
87/8 Panini Sticker 97
01/2 Parkhurst ✂ 500GS, ✍ PA29
02/3 Parkhurst ✂ VT10
92/3 Pinnacle 245
81/2 Post 6
82/3 Post [NYIs.]
90/1 Pro Set 650
91/2 Pro Set HHOF 1
87/8 Pro Sport CW6
84/5 7-Eleven
85/6 7-Eleven Superstars 12
01/2 Signature ✂ 500GS, ✍ VA30
83/4 Souhaits Keychain [Islanders]
97/8 SLU Cdn. Leg.
98/9 SLU -CL
78/9 Topps 1
78/9 Topps 63
78/9 Topps 67
78/9 Topps 115
79/0 Topps 1
79/0 Topps 5
79/0 Topps 7
79/0 Topps 161
79/0 Topps 230
80/1 Topps 25
80/1 Topps 204
80/1 Topps 262
81/2 Topps 4
81/2 Topps 57
81/2 Topps 125 [East]
84/5 Topps 91
84/5 Topps 155
85/6 OPC/Topps-Stick. 9
86/7 OPC/Topps - Stick. 4
99/0 Topps SC2, ✍ SCH
01/2 T/O Archives 63
00/1 UD Heroes 133, ✂ GT, ✂ GC
01/2 Ultimate Mem. ✂ 500GS, ✂ ASGH, ✂ CT, ✂ RN, ✂ RT, ✂ RA, ✂ SCD, ✂ SCP
02/3 Ultimate Memorabilia ✂ ASMVP, ✂ CSTW, ✂ Cor, ✂ EA, ✂ Num, ✂ PS, ✂ VGJ
00 ✂ UD APOH 500, ✂✍ 500
99/0 UD C. Legends 20, ✂ JC2, ✍ ES
02/3 UD Foundations 62, 119, ✂ 1000Jers, ✂ 1000Stick, ✂ CTW, ✂ CH, ✂ CH, ✂ CG, ✂ MS, ✂ PP, ✂ PS, ✍ SG
00/1 UD Legends 81, ES8, EG3, SM12, ✍ ES, ✂ LGJ
01/2 UD Legends 42, 96, FC, ✂ M, ✂ PoH, ✍ ES
02/3 UD Piece -HB7, ✂ HS, ✍ MD
01/2 UD Premier ✍ SigS
99/0 UD Retro 96, ✍ Ink.
01/2 UD SCup Champs 19, ✂ S, ✂ G, ✂ T
00/1 UD Vintage ✂ D-POH
01/2 UD Vintage ✂ SC, ✂ SD
96 Wien HL3
95/6 Zellers
79/0 NYIS
83/4 NYIS
83/4 NYIS / News 2
83/4 NYIS / News 35
84/5 NYIS / News 2
84/5 NYIS / News 32
93/4 NYIS / Bank

BOSTON, SCOTT
89/0 7th..Sketch OHL 87
90/1 7th..Sketch OHL 340
91/2 7th...Sketch OHL 115
92/3 Atlanta Knights
93/4 Knoxville Cherokees
87/8 Brockville Braves

BOSTROM, HELGE
33/4 Canadian Gum

BOSTROM, JUHANI
70/1 Kuvajulkaisut 101
72 Panda MM-Toronto
78/9 SM-Liiga 38
71/2 Williams Finnish 111
72/3 Williams Finnish 81
73/4 Williams Finnish 126

BOTHWELL, TIM
84/5 O-Pee-Chee 182
85/6 OPC/Topps 161
87/8 OPC/Topps 29
85/6 OPC Sticker 49-180
87/8 OPC Sticker 26-167

88/9 ProCards / Peoria
89/0 ProCards AHL 23
90/1 7th..Sketch WHL 42
91/2 7th...Sketch WHL 328
87/8 SLOU / Kodak
88/9 SLOU / Kodak
92/3 Phoenix Roadrunners

BOTTERI, STÉPHANE
94 Semic 217
92 Semic Sticker 221
93 Semic Sticker 251

BOTTERILL, JASON
99/0 BAP Mem. 252
93/4 Donruss CAN4
95/6 Donruss C3TWC 18
95/6 Do. Elite WJ 10
98/9 McDonald's McD25
99/0 Millenium 18, ✍ Aut. 18
98/9 Pacific 172
99/0 Pa. Paramount 9
93/4 Pinnacle 467
94/5 Score 202
94/5 SP 143
95/6 SP 175
95/6 Topps 14CJ
94/5 Topps Finest 144
93/4 Upper Deck 534
98/9 Upper Deck 260
98/9 UD G. Reserve 260
99/0 Victory 17
98/9 Michigan K-Wings
02/3 Rochester Americans

BOUCCHARD, FREDERIC
01/2 Milwaukee Admirals

BOUCHA, HENRY
72/3 Eddie Sargent 84
74/5 Lipton Soup 32
74/5 Loblaws
73/4 O-Pee-Chee 33
74/5 O-Pee-Chee 38
76/7 O-Pee-Chee 209
75/6 OPC WHA 79
72 Semic Sticker 126
73/4 Topps 33
74/5 Topps 38
76/7 Topps 209
76/7 COLR / Hockey Talk

BOUCHARD,
97/8 Hockey-Box

BOUCHARD, ALAIN
79/0 Montréal Jrs. Colour

BOUCHARD, DAN
79/0 Dernière Heure
81/2 Dernière Heure
70s Dernière Heure

BOUCHARD, DANICK
02/3 Shawinigan Cataractes

BOUCHARD, DANIEL
72/3 Eddie Sargent 14
83/4 Funmate Puffy 18 [w/]
74/5 Lipton Soup 44
74/5 Loblaws
72/3 O-Pee-Chee 203
73/4 O-Pee-Chee 45
74/5 O-Pee-Chee 15
75/6 O-Pee-Chee 268
76/7 O-Pee-Chee 111
77/8 O-Pee-Chee 37
78/9 O-Pee-Chee 169
79/0 O-Pee-Chee 28
80/1 O-Pee-Chee 68
81/2 O-Pee-Chee 270
82/3 O-Pee-Chee 278
83/4 O-Pee-Chee 290
84/5 O-Pee-Chee 277
85/6 O-Pee-Chee 246
81/2 OPC Sticker 73
81/2 OPC Sticker 84
82/3 OPC/Topps Sticker 27
83/4 OPC/Topps Sticker 245
84/5 OPC Sticker 172
84/5 OPC Sticker 173
85/6 OPC Sticker 143-13
79 Panini Sticker 53
80/1 Pepsi Bottle Cap
83/4 Souhaits Keychain [Nordiques]
73/4 Topps 45
74/5 Topps 15
75/6 Topps 268
76/7 Topps 111
77/8 Topps 37
78/9 Topps 169
79/0 Topps 28
80/1 Topps 68
84/5 Topps 128
83/4 Vachon 62-42
72/3 ATLF
74/5 ATLF
77/8 ATLF
78/9 ATLF / Colour
79/0 ATLF / B&W
79/0 ATLF / Colour
80/1 CALG
81/2 QUÉB
82/3 QUÉB
83/4 QUÉB
84/5 QUÉB
92/3 QUÉB / Petro-Canada
85/6 WINN
85/6 WINN / Safety Tips

BOUCHARD, EDMOND
24/5 Champ's Cigarettes
23/4 William Paterson 37
24/5 William Paterson 19

BOUCHARD, EMILE (BUTCH)
01/2 BAP Memor. ✄ RM
34-43 BeeHive-1 [Mont.]
45-64 BeeHive-2 [Mont.]
77/8 Dernière Heure
48-52 Exhibits [Canadiens]
83 HHOF Postcard M1
83&87 HHOF 228
51/2 La Patrie
43-47 Parade Sportive
51/2 Parkhurst 3
52/3 Parkhurst 13
53/4 Parkhurst 32
54/5 Parkhurst 6
54/5 Parkhurst 97
55/6 Parkhurst 46
55/6 Parkhurst 71
01/2 Parkhurst PR50, PR63, PR70, PR73, PR105, ✍ PA25
45-54 Quaker Oats
01/2 Signature ✍ VA19
54 Toronto Star Weekend
91/2 Ultimate Original Six 8, ✍ Aut. 8
92/3 MONT / OPC 2

BOUCHARD, ERIC*
91/2 7th...Sketch WHL 137

BOUCHARD, FRANÇOIS
99/0 UD Elitserien 173
00/1 UD Elitserien 46
01/2 St. John's Maple Leafs

BOUCHARD, FREDERIC
98/9 Dayton Bombers
98/9 Dayton Bombers
99/0 Fort Wayne Komets

BOUCHARD, GILLES
90/1 7th..Sketch LHJMQ 38
91 7th..Sketch Mem.Cup 34

BOUCHARD, HUGHES
91/2 7th...Sketch LHJMQ 152
93/4 Roanoke Express
88/9 Richelieu Riverains

BOUCHARD, JOËL
93/4 Donruss CAN5
01/2 Pacific 297
97/8 Pacific CC 338
97/8 Panini Sticker 197
98/9 Panini Sticker 141
93/4 Pinnacle 461
97/8 Pi. Be A Player 129, ✍ Aut. 129
90/1 7th..Sketch LHJMQ 244
91/2 7th...Sketch LHJMQ 143
99/0 Topps 220
99/0 To. Chrome 220
93/4 Upper Deck 541
96/7 UD Ice 8
98/9 NASH / Wendy's 4
01/2 Albany River Rats
94/5 Saint John Flames
95/6 Saint John Flames

BOUCHARD, LEON
52/3 Bas du Fleuve 57
52/3 Laval Dairy Update 25
52/3 St. Lawrence 41

BOUCHARD, MAXIME
99/0 Rouyn-Noranda Huskies
00/1 Rouyn-Noranda Huskies 20
01/2 Victoriaville Tigres 22

BOUCHARD, PIERRE
71/2 Bazooka Panel
72/3 Dernière Heure
73/4 Dernière Heure
79/0 Dernière Heure
71/2 Eddie Sargent 111
72/3 Eddie Sargent 116
74/5 Loblaws
71/2 O-Pee-Chee 2
72/3 O-Pee-Chee 165
73/4 O-Pee-Chee 261
74/5 O-Pee-Chee 178
74/5 O-Pee-Chee 254
75/6 O-Pee-Chee 304
76/7 O-Pee-Chee 177
77/8 O-Pee-Chee 20
78/9 O-Pee-Chee 116
79/0 O-Pee-Chee 289
80/1 O-Pee-Chee 373
74/5 Topps 178
74/5 Topps 254
75/6 Topps 304
76/7 Topps 177
77/8 Topps 20
78/9 Topps 116
71/2 Toronto Sun Photo
69/0 MONT / Pro Star
70/1 MONT
71/2 MONT / Pro Star
72/3 MONT / Pro Star
73/4 MONT / Pro Star
74/5 MONT
74/5 MONT
75/6 MONT
76/7 MONT
77/8 MONT
79/0 WASH
80/1 WASH

BOUCHARD, PIERRE-MARC
02/3 Atomic 113
02/3 BAP All-Star 126
02/3 BAP Draft Toronto 4
02/3 BAP Memorabilia 271
02/3 Bowman 161
02/3 Calder 124, -CR 15
02/3 Crown Royale 118
02/3 eTopps 46
02/3 Exclusive 180
02/3 First Edition 440H
02/3 Heads Up 126
02/3 In The Game-Used 81
02/3 O-Pee-Chee 332
02/3 Pacific 126
02/3 Pacific Complete 516
02/3 PTC/ ASG 8
02/3 Parkhurst 201
02/3 Parkhurst Retro 201
02/3 Pr. Stock Reserve 165
02/3 Private Stock Titanium 119, -ROT 13
98 Québec Pee Wee 1376
02/3 Quest for the Cup 124
02/3 Signature Series 196, ✍ 196
02/3 SP Authentic ✍ 198, ✍ ✄ Patch
02/3 SP Game-Used Edition 81
02/3 SPx ✍ 152
02/3 Stadium 132
02/3 Topps 332
02/3 T. Chrome 180
02/3 To. Heritage 149
02/3 T. Total 422
02/3 UD Superstars 283
02/3 Ultimate Memorabilia 1, ✍ RAut
02/3 Upper Deck 239
02/3 UD Artistic 124, CG8
02/3 UD Classic 118
02/3 UD Foundations 156
02/3 UD Honor 155
02/3 UD Mask 160
02/3 UD Piece 134
02/3 UD Premier ✍ 72, ✍ Sig.
02/3 UD Rookie ✍ 164, ✍ TD
02/3 UD Top Shelf 130
02/3 Vanguard 118, -PP 14
00/1 Chicoutimi Saguenéens 23

BOUCHARD, ROBIN
91/2 7th...Sketch LHJMQ 48
95/6 Flint Generals
96/7 Flint Generals
98/9 Muskegon Fury
99/0 Muskegon Fury
94/5 Roanoke Express

BOUCHARD, YAN
96/7 Rimouski Océanic

BOUCHER, BILLY*
25-27 Anonymous 1
25-27 Anonymous 2
25-27 Anonymous 19
24/5 Champ's Cigarettes
24/5 Maple Crispette [V130] 11
23/4 William Paterson 16
24/5 William Paterson 46

BOUCHER, BILLY2
84/5 Nova Scotia Oilers

BOUCHER, BRIAN
00/1 Aurora 104, Pin. 104, CF-16, SR-16, TPS-8B
99/0 BAP Mem. 336
00/1 BAP Mem. 143
01/2 BAP Memor. ✄ GoalJ
02/3 BAP Memorabilia 261 [w/ Handzus]
01/2 BT Pipes 61, 93, HSHS, ✄ DM, ✄ FW, ✄ Jers., ✄ JE, ✄ S&J, ✄ GG, ✄ GT, ✄ ITN, ✄ HSHSJers
02/3 Between the Pipes 56
97 Bowman 81
00/1 Crown Royale 78
01/2 Crown Royale 104
95/6 Do. Elite WJ 23
99/0 Dynagon Ice 144
02/3 Exclusive 131
02/3 First Edition 79, 415R, ✄ Jers.
02/3 In The Game-Used ✄ GP17
00/1 McDonald's 24, GSNF-5
99/0 Millenium C-27
02/3 O-Pee-Chee 55
99/0 Omega 167
00/1 Pacific 293, IO-17, GCDC-22, ITC-9
01/2 Pacific 283
02/3 Pacific 275
02/3 Pacific Complete 460
00/1 Pa. Paramount 177, ES-15, FF-25, GS-14
00/1 Parkhurst P-89
02/3 Parkhurst 154
02/3 Parkhurst Retro 90
00/1 Premier Plus 2, MB18
99/0 Prism 100
00/1 Private Stock 71, PS-41, PSNW-17
00/1 PS Titanium 68, 3SS-6
02/3 Private Stock Titanium 78
00/1 Revolution 106, HD-24, SM-17
94/5 Select 155
94/5 SR Auto-Phonex 10, ✍ 10
95/6 SR Tetrad 69
95/6 SR Tetrad Autobilia 94
00/1 Signature 217, ✍ Aut. 168
01/2 Signature 192, ✍ Aut. 192, ✄ GUE49, ✄ GJ50, ✄ GSJ50, ✄ ITN49, ✄ TM23
02/3 Signature Series 83, ✍ 83
02/3 SP Authentic 128
00/1 SP GU 44, ✄ TotG, ✄ C, ✄ P
01/2 SP Game Used ✄ AF, ✄ AFD, ✄ ToG, ✄ ToGC (x3), ✄ ToGT
02/3 SP Game-Used ✄ AF, ✄ PC, ✄ TG
00/1 SPx 49, HH10, ✄ WM
01/2 SPx 188
99/0 Stadium 196
00/1 Stadium 190, BT22, GS5
00/1 Topps 63
01/2 Topps ✄ GWJ
02/3 Topps 55
99/0 To. Chrome 289
00/1 To. Chrome 51
01/2 To. Chrome 135
00/1 To. Gold Label 46, BTM5, NG13, ✍ GLA
00/1 To. Heritage 101, 237, NT8
02/3 To. Heritage 172, ✄ CP, ✄ CPB
02/3 T. Limited 55
99/0 To. Prmr. Plus 140
01/2 To. Reserve ✄ TR
00/1 To. Stars 80, P6, ✍ CAI
02/3 T. Total 274
00/1 UD Heroes 87, TM8
00/1 Ultimate Mem. ✄ G-22, ✄ PJ-15, ✄ GM-7
00/1 Upper Deck 128, A7, P9, RP6
01/2 Upper Deck 357, ✄ GoalJ, ✄ TendThre
02/3 Upper Deck 379, ✄ BF, ✄ SV
00/1 UD Black Diam. 42
00/1 UD Challenge 60, ✄ UC
01/2 UD Honor Roll ✄ GAJ
96/7 UD Ice 148
00/1 UD Ice 29
01/2 UD Ice 113
00/1 UD Legends 99
01/2 UD Mask ✄ GJ, ✄ JP, ✄ DP, ✄ MM, ✄ MB, ✄ SIS, ✄ SY
02/3 UD Mask 64, 65, 66, ✄ GG, ✄ NB
00/1 UD MVP 130, MM6, ✍ PS
01/2 UD MVP -J, ✍ SJ
02/3 UD MVP SD, Souv.
99/0 UD MVP Cup 137
01/2 UD Premier ✄ D
01/2 UD Rookie 77
01/2 UD Top Shelf ✄ GG-LP
02/3 UD Top Shelf ✄ ST, ✄ SS, ✍ Sig
00/1 UD Vintage 266, 271, 272, GG13, S5B
02/3 UD Vintage ✄ EE
00/1 Vanguard 71
02/3 Vanguard 77
00/1 Victory 172, 254
01/2 Victory 264
02/3 Victory 161
01/2 PHIL
95/6 Tri-City Americans 4
95/6 Tri-City Americans 31

BOUCHER, BROCK
95/6 Slapshot 22
99/0 Hull Olympiques BN
99/0 Hull Olympiques 15

BOUCHER, CHARLIE
91/2 7th...Sketch LHJMQ 174

BOUCHER, CHRIS
00/1 Toronto St. Mike's

BOUCHER, DENIS
52/3 Anonymous 135

BOUCHER, FRANK
34-43 BeeHive-1 [NYRa.]
35-40 Canada Starch
34/5 CCM [Green]
33-35 Diamond Match Silv.
36-39 Diamond Match TT2
36-39 Diamond Match TT2
36-39 Diamond Match TT3
83 HHOF Postcard G2
83&87 HHOF 93
28/9 La Presse
60/1 Topps 29
61/2 Topps - Stamp
02/3 Ultimate Memorabilia ✍ Cut
37/8 World Wide Gum 16

BOUCHER, GEORGE (BUCK)
83 HHOF Postcard L1
83&87 HHOF 229
28/9 La Presse
23/4 William Paterson 6
24/5 William Paterson 2

BOUCHER, GUY
99/0 Rouyn-Noranda Huskies

BOUCHER, PHILIPPE
91/2 Arena 10
91/2 Classic 11
91/2 Classic Four Sport 11
92/3 Classic Prospects 68
93/4 Durivage 4
93/4 Fleer Ultra 70
93/4 Fleer Ultra ARS 1
94/5 Leaf 539
92/3 OPC Premier 72
02/3 Pacific Complete 364
97/8 Pa. Invincible R-92
92/3 Parkhurst 16
93/4 Parkhurst 24
93/4 Parkhurst C11
94/5 Parkie SE16
93/4 Pinnacle 213
96/7 Pi. Be A Player 74, ✍ Aut. 74
93/4 Power Play 296
94/5 Premier 371
93/4 Score 455
92 7th...Sketch Awards 21
92 7th...Sketch Awards 25
90/1 7th..Sketch LHJMQ 50
91/2 7th...Sketch LHJMQ 43
91 7th..Sketch Mem.Cup 103
91/2 Star Pics 28
91/2 Star Pics 36
95/6 Topps 136
01/2 To. Reserve 56
94/5 To. Stadium 64
91/2 Ultimate Draft Pick 11, 67, 75, 82, ✍ Aut.
91/2 Upper Deck 68
92/3 Upper Deck 484
93/4 Upper Deck 82, SP-14
94/5 Upper Deck 71
98/9 UD MVP 99
02/3 DALL / Southwest
00/1 Manitoba Moose
93/4 Rochester Americans

BOUCHER, ROBERT
24/5 Champ's Cigarettes

BOUCHER, RODRIGUE
01/2 Cape Breton Eagles 14

BOUCHER, SCOTT
92/3 BCJHL 167

BOUCHER, TYLER
91/2 Avant Garde BCJHL 90
91/2 Avant Garde BCJHL 159
92/3 BCJHL 119
97/8 New Mexico Scorpions

BOUCK, TYLER
00/1 BAP Mem. 430
01/2 BAP Memor. 227
99 Bowman 105
00/1 Premier Plus 117
00/1 Private Stock 115
00/1 PS Titanium Draft 159
00/1 SP Authentic 103
00/1 SP GU 68
00/1 SPx 160
00/1 To. Gold Label 114
00/1 To. Stars 125
00/1 UD Heroes 163
01/2 UD PlayMakers Ltd - PCPJ
00/1 UD Reserve 94
00/1 Upper Deck 201
01/2 Upper Deck 365
00/1 UD Black Diam. 66, 96
00/1 UD Ice 46
00/1 UD MVP 215
00/1 UD Pros&Prosp. 103
00/1 UD Vintage 378
00/1 Vanguard 116
00/1 DALL / Southwest
02/3 Manitoba Moose
99/0 Prince George Cougars

BOUDAEV, ALEXEI
95/6 Red Deer Rebels

BOUDRAIS, ANDRÉ
71/2 Eddie Sargent 215

BOUDREAU, BRUCE
78/9 O-Pee-Chee 280
79/0 O-Pee-Chee 354
88/9 ProCards / Springfield
89/0 ProCards IHL 108
90/1 ProCards 541
91/2 ProCards 260
78/9 TORO
93/4 Fort Wayne Komets 24
99/0 Lowell Lock Monsters
00/1 Lowell Lock Monsters
01/2 Manchester Monarchs
02/3 Manchester Monarchs
96/7 Mississippi S'Wolves
99/0 Mississippi S'Wolves
85/6 Nova Scotia Oilers

BOUDREAU, CARL
90/1 7th..Sketch LHJMQ 97
91/2 7th...Sketch LHJMQ 116
90 7th..Sketch Mem.Cup 56
92/3 Oklahoma City Blazers

BOUDREAU, DARRYL
82/3 Kitchener Rangers

BOUDREAU, DAVID
90/1 7th..Sketch LHJMQ 119

BOUDREAU, RENÉ
37/8 World Wide Gum 117

BOUDREAULT, DAVE*
91/2 7th...Sketch LHJMQ 117

BOUDREAULT, SERGE
67/8 Columbus Checkers

BOUDRIAS, ANDRÉ
71/2 Bazooka Panel
70/1 Dad's Cookies
70/1 Eddie Sargent 219
72/3 Eddie Sargent 214
70/1 Esso Power Player
74/5 Lipton Soup 14
74/5 Loblaws
68/9 O-Pee-Chee 53
69/0 O-Pee-Chee 16
70/1 O-Pee-Chee 121
71/2 O-Pee-Chee 12
72/3 O-Pee-Chee 93
73/4 O-Pee-Chee 19
74/5 OPC 117
74/5 O-Pee-Chee 191
75/6 O-Pee-Chee 60
75/6 O-Pee-Chee 329
76/7 OPC WHA 87
72 Semic Sticker 210
68/9 Shirriff / Minn. 3
68/9 Topps 53
69/0 Topps 16
70/1 Topps 121
71/2 Topps 12
72/3 Topps 158
73/4 Topps 19
74/5 Topps 117
74/5 Topps 191
75/6 Topps 60
75/6 Topps 329
71/2 Toronto Sun Photo
70/1 VANC / Royal Bank
71/2 VANC / Royal Bank 15
72/3 VANC / Nalley's
72/3 VANC / Royal Bank
73/4 VANC / Royal Bank
74/5 VANC / Royal Bank
75/6 VANC / Royal Bank
76/7 Québec Nordiques
76/7 Québ. / Antoinette

BOUGHNER, BOB
00/1 BAP Mem. ✄ T-21
01/2 Heads Up ✄ JQ 28
01/2 O-Pee-Chee 223
99/0 Pacific 219
02/3 Pacific 50
02/3 Pacific Complete 433
97/8 Pa. Dynagon BKS-9
96/7 Pi. Be A Player 178, ✍ Aut. 178
01/2 PS Titanium ✄ DSJ 6
91 7th..Sketch Mem.Cup 4
90/1 7th..Sketch OHL 153
02/3 Sports Vault 169
99/0 Topps 173
01/2 Topps 223
99/0 To. Chrome 173
02/3 T. Total 94
99/0 UD Retro 42
01/2 Vanguard ✄ DGM 24
99/0 Victory 160
98/9 NASH / Wendy's 5
94/5 Cincinnati Cyclones
89/0 Soo Greyhounds

BOUGIE, GEORGES
51/2 Laval Dairy 77
52/3 St. Lawrence 32

BOUILLON, FRANCIS
99/0 BAP Mem. 331
99/0 Omega 124
99/0 Prism 70
01/2 Signature 188, ✍ Aut. 188
99/0 To. Prmr. Plus 83
99/0 UD G. Reserve 343
01/2 UD Mask 51
99/0 UD MVP Cup 96
00/1 MONT
01/2 MONT
02/3 MONT
02/3 Hamilton Bulldogs
01/2 Québec Citadelles

BOULANGER, B.
88/9 ProCards / Sherbrooke

BOULERICE, JESSE
01/2 Parkhurst 251
01/2 Signature 242, ✍ Aut. 242
95/6 Slapshot 74
98/9 UD Choice 305
97/8 UD Black Diam. 98

BOULIANE, ANDRÉ
90/1 7th..Sketch LHJMQ 264
91/2 7th...Sketch LHJMQ 149

BOULIN, VLADISLAV
99/0 Eishockey 149
94/5 Flair 125
94/5 Fleer Ultra 342
94/5 Leaf 456
94/5 Parkie SE125
94/5 Premier 434
94/5 Upper Deck 266
94/5 Hershey Bears

BOULTON, ERIC
00/1 BAP Mem. 438
00/1 Crown Royale 112, 21CR-3
02/3 Pacific Complete 440
00/1 Premier Plus 137
00/1 Private Stock 104
93/4 Slapshot / Oshawa 21
95/6 Slapshot 339
00/1 SP Authentic 137
00/1 SPx 177
00/1 UD Black Diam. 92
00/1 UD Ice 111
96/7 Charlotte Checkers
97/8 Charlotte Checkers
98/9 Kentucky Tho'blades

BOUMEDIENNE, JOSEF
01/2 BAP Memor. 346
98/9 Cardset 207
99/0 Cardset 120
01/2 Parkhurst 298
01/2 SP Authentic 160
01/2 SP Game Used 85
01/2 SPx 112
01/2 UD PlayMakers Ltd 141
01/2 Upper Deck 432
01/2 UD Challenge 117
97/8 UD Elitserien 171
01/2 UD Ice 82
01/2 UD Premier 82
01/2 UD Vintage 284
00/1 Albany River Rats

BOURASSA, BERTRAND
51/2 Laval Dairy 81

BOURASSA, JARAD
01/2 Moose Jaw Warriors 2
02/3 Moose Jaw Warriors

BOURBONNAIS,
69/0 Mästär Serien 36

BOURBONNAIS, RICK
77/8 O-Pee-Chee 312

BOURDEAU, FRANÇOIS
90/1 7th..Sketch LHJMQ 104
91/2 7th...Sketch LHJMQ 68
99/0 Asheville Smoke
93/4 Johnstown Chiefs 3
88/9 Richelieu Riverains

BOURDON, ARMAND
51/2 Lac St-Jean 9

BOURGEAULT, LEO
29/0 La Presse
33/4 O-Pee-Chee 28

BOURGEOIS, CHARLIE
86/7 O-Pee-Chee 239
86/7 OPC Sticker 178-41
87/8 Panini Sticker 309
88/9 ProCards / Binghampton
81/2 CALG
82/3 CALG
85/6 CALG / Red Rooster
87/8 SLOU / Kodak

BOURGEOIS, SHAWN
91/2 Avant Garde BCJHL 15
92/3 BCJHL 202

BOURGET, STÉPH.
90/1 7th..Sketch LHJMQ 99

BOURGOIN, PAUL-ANDRE
01/2 Shawinigan Cataractes 3
02/3 Shawinigan Cataractes

BOURGON, SEBASTIEN
00/1 Québec Remparts 2
01/2 Québec Remparts 2
02/3 Québec Remparts

BOURNE, BOB
84/5 Kelowna Wings &...
75/6 O-Pee-Chee 163
77/8 O-Pee-Chee 93
78/9 OPC 69
78/9 O-Pee-Chee 126
79/0 O-Pee-Chee 56
80/1 O-Pee-Chee 276
81/2 O-Pee-Chee 201
82/3 O-Pee-Chee 198
83/4 O-Pee-Chee 4
84/5 O-Pee-Chee 123
85/6 OPC/Topps 97
86/7 OPC/Topps 14
87/8 OPC/Topps 167
88/9 OPC/Topps 101
88/9 OPC Stars 2
81/2 OPC Sticker 163
82/3 OPC/Topps Sticker 53
83/4 OPC/Topps Sticker 80
83/4 OPC/Topps Sticker 174
84/5 OPC Sticker 89
85/6 OPC Sticker 67-191
86/7 OPC Sticker 208-82
88/9 OPC Sticker 213-84
88/9 Panini Sticker 399
82/3 Post [NYIs.]
83/4 Souhaits Keychain [Islanders]
75/6 Topps 163
77/8 Topps 93
78/9 Topps 69
78/9 Topps 126
79/0 Topps 56
81/2 Topps 87 [East]
84/5 Topps 92
00/1 UD Vintage ✄ D-POH
87/8 LOSA
79/0 NYIS
83/4 NYIS
83/4 NYIS / News 3
84/5 NYIS / News 3
93/4 Las Vegas Thunder
98/9 Las Vegas Thunder
99/0 Utah Grizzlies
00/1 Utah Grizzlies

BOURQUE, CLAUDE
34-43 BeeHive-1 [Mont.]
35-40 Canada Starch
39/0 O-Pee-Chee 28

BOURQUE, DAVE
95/6 Slapshot 351

BOURQUE, PHIL
90/1 Bowman 205
91/2 Bowman 94
92/3 Bowman 293
92/3 Fleer Ultra 352
95 Globe 126
90/1 OPC/Topps 41
91/2 O-Pee-Chee 33
89/0 OPC/Topps 19
92/3 OPC Premier 73
89/0 Panini Sticker 317
90/1 Panini Sticker 129
91/2 Panini Sticker 272
92/3 Panini Sticker 225
95 Panini Worlds 223
91/2 Parkhurst 136
91/2 Pinnacle 227
92/3 Pinnacle 353
93/4 Pinnacle 331
94/5 Pinnacle 112
90/1 Pro Set 228
91/2 Pro Set 189
90/1 Score 234
91/2 Score 69
91/2 Score CAN 69
92/3 Score 223
93/4 Score 308
92/3 Topps 442
91/2 To. Stadium 168
92/3 To. Stadium 282
90/1 Upper Deck 31
91/2 Upper Deck 398
92/3 Upper Deck 141
92/3 Upper Deck 452
95/6 UD CC 86
94/5 OTTA
95/6 OTTA
89/0 PITT / Elby's
89/0 PITT / Foodland 5
90/1 PITT / Foodland 1
91/2 PITT / Elby's
91/2 PITT / Foodland 15
81/2 Kingston Canadians

BOURQUE, RAYMOND
98/9 Aurora 8, -CF 3, -MACF 3
99/0 Aurora 10, -Stripe 10, -CF 3
00/1 Aurora 36, Pin. 36, CF-4, TPS-4B
98/9 Be A Player 8, M13, P-13, ✍ Aut. 8, ✄ G-13, ✄ AS-16, ✄ S-15
00/1 BAP All-Star AS-3
99/0 BAP Mem. 38, 309, ✄ J-9, ✄ D-7, ✄ TM-6, ✄ TM-15, ✄ TM-24
00/1 BAP Mem. 284, ✄ J-37, ✄ H-16
01/2 BAP Memor. 216, ✄ ASJ, ✄ ASE, ✄ ASN, ✄ ASD, ✄ ASS, ✄ AST, ✄ CoO, ✄ SCC, ✄ SCP
96/7 Bic.Sports Aces 5-H
97/8 Bicycle 2-Spade
95/6 Bicycle Sports Aces 8-Diamond
90/1 Bowman 31
91/2 Bowman 356
92/3 Bowman 3
92/3 Bowman 223
95/6 Bowman 2
98/9 Bowman's Best 33, F17, SB10, ✍ A5A, ✍ A5B
02/3 Canada Post
99/0 Crown Royale 11, -TC 2
00/1 Crown Royale 26, JotC-7, NP-4
79/0 Dernière Heure
82/3 Dernière Heure
93/4 Donruss 24
94/5 Donruss 68, D-2
95/6 Donruss 127, D-3
96/7 Donruss 132, D-3
97/8 Donruss 66, L2L-21
96/7 Do. Canadian 21, 150
97/8 Do. Canadian 11, NP-11
95/6 Do. Elite 9
96/7 Do. Elite 17
97/8 Do. Elite 21
97/8 Do. Preferred 24, 174
97/8 Do. Priority 20, Post-35, Stamp-35
97/8 Do. Studio 28
96/7 Duracell JB19
92/3 Durivage 31
93/4 Durivage 26
98/9 Dynagon Ice 8, TC2
99/0 Dynagon Ice 21, -ASP 3, -CM 10
93/4 EA Sports 7
93/4 EA Sports 185
88/9 Esso All-Star
94/5 Flair 8
96/7 Flair 4, HN-1
94/5 Fleer 9
96/7 Fleer 4, 140, NT-1
95/6 Fleer Metal 6
96/7 Fl. Picks 14, F50-3
92/3 Fleer Ultra 2, -AS 2, -AW 8
93/4 Fleer Ultra 1
93/4 Fleer Ultra AS 2
94/5 Fleer Ultra 10, ASG-1, AW-1
95/6 Fleer Ultra 8
96/7 Fl. Ultra 8, PL-1, UP-1
88/9 Frito Lay
83/4 Funmate Puffy 11 [w/]
91/2 Gillette 26
95 Globe 77
96/7 Got-Um
92/3 High Five / Promo P1
93/4 Hockey Wit 77
99/0 HoloGrFX 5, ✍ Aut.
95/6 Hoyle / East. 4-Heart
92/3 Humpty Dumpty
94 Koululainen
89/0 Kraft 52
90/1 Kraft 3, 80
91/2 Kraft 57
92/3 Kraft / Kraft Singles
93/4 Kraft / PB
94/5 Kraft / PB [x2]
95/6 Kraft / PB
96/7 Kraft / AS, PB
97/8 Kraft / PB
98/9 Kraft / PB
99/0 Kraft / OML, / PB
89/0 Kraft Stickers 4
93/4 Leaf 215
93/4 Leaf GLAS 7
94/5 Leaf 77, GLS-6
95/6 Leaf 106, GLS-3
96/7 Leaf 122
97/8 Leaf 13
94/5 L. Limited 84
95/6 L. Limited 16
96/7 L. Limited 49
96/7 L. Preferred 83, LS-4
97/8 Limited 92, 125, 139, FG-29
96/7 Maggers 17
82/3 McDonald's Les Étoiles 28
91/2 McDonald's Mc-10
91/2 McDonald's McH3
92/3 McDonald's McH-04
93/4 McDonald's McH-04
94/5 McDonald's McD-5
96/7 McDonald's McD-31
97/8 McDonald's McD-17, F7
99/0 McDonald's ✍ SS
00/1 McDonald's 7
01/2 McDonald's 4, -HG 1
96/7 Metal Univ. 7
99/0 Millenium 20, D-19, ✍ Aut. 20, ✍ D-9, ✄ J-13, ✄ JS-13
95/6 Cool Trade 6
00/1 Nortel Networks All-Star 10
80/1 O-Pee-Chee 2
80/1 O-Pee-Chee 140
81/2 O-Pee-Chee 1
x81/2 O-Pee-Chee 17
82/3 O-Pee-Chee 7
x82/3 O-Pee-Chee 24
83/4 O-Pee-Chee 45
84/5 O-Pee-Chee 1
x84/5 O-Pee-Chee 211
85/6 OPC/Topps 40
85/6 OPC/Topps Box B
86/7 OPC/Topps 1
87/8 OPC/Topps 87
87/8 OPC/Topps Box F
88/9 OPC/Topps 73
88/9 OPC/Topps Box I
90/1 OPC/Topps 43, 196
90/1 O-Pee-Chee 475
91/2 O-Pee-Chee 66
91/2 O-Pee-Chee 170
91/2 O-Pee-Chee 261
91/2 O-Pee-Chee 517
91/2 Topps - Team Leader 19
92/3 O-Pee-Chee 126
92/3 O-Pee-Chee 348
01/2 O-Pee-Chee 89, 317
89/0 OPC/Topps 110
89/0 Topps - Sticker 7
90/1 OPC/Topps I
98/9 OPC Chrome 206, B4, -Reprint 3
87/8 OPC Leaders 4
90/1 OPC Premier 9
91/2 OPC Premier 119
91/2 OPC Premier 192
88/9 OPC Stars 3
81/2 OPC Sticker 49
82/3 OPC/Topps Sticker 86
x82/3 OPC/Topps Sticker 87
x82/3 OPC/Topps Sticker 166
83/4 OPC/Topps Sticker 46
x83/4 OPC/Topps Sticker 47
x83/4 OPC/Topps Sticker 173
84/5 OPC Sticker 143
x84/5 OPC Sticker 183
85/6 OPC Sticker 115
x85/6 OPC Sticker 157
86/7 OPC Sticker 34
x86/7 OPC Sticker 119-133
87/8 OPC Sticker 67
x87/8 OPC Sticker 140
x87/8 OPC Sticker 116-128
x87/8 OPC Sticker 178-33
88/9 OPC Sticker 23
x88/9 OPC Sticker 38
x88/9 OPC Sticker 117-247
x88/9 OPC Sticker 208-79
89/0 opcSticker 32, 162-24, / AS 33
97/8 Omega 12, TL-2
98/9 Omega 12, -Onl. 3, -PI 1
99/0 Omega 18, -NAAS 2
98/9 Pacific 77
99/0 Pacific 20, -GC 3, -PAP 3, -TL 3
00/1 Pacific 107, GCDC-7, PR-4, ✄ GWJ-1
01/2 Pacific 98, CCA 2, GCDC 4, IZ 6, NAAS 3
97/8 Pacific CC 1, TC-2
97/8 Pa. Crown Roy. 7
98/9 Pa. Crown Roy. 7, -PotG 2
97/8 Pa. Dynagon 7, DD-2A, T-28, BKS-5
97/8 Pa. Invincible 7, FP-3, R-10
97/8 Pa. Paramount 9
98/9 Pa. Paramount 10
99/0 Pa. Paramount 17, -HOFB 2, -IAI 3, -PB 3
00/1 Pa. Paramount 56, ES-4, FF-7, HOFB-3, ✄ J&P-3, ✄ GUS-2
97/8 Pa. Revolution 7, ASG-2
98/9 Pa. Revolution 7, -ASG 4, -Show. 3, -TPA 10
01/2 PTC Collectors 1
98/9 Panini Photocard [x2]
87/8 Panini Sticker 6
x87/8 Panini Sticker 381
88/9 Panini Sticker 204
x88/9 Panini Sticker 405
89/0 Panini Sticker 187, 201
90/1 Panini Sticker 17, 322
91/2 Panini Sticker 171
91/2 Panini Sticker 335
92/3 Panini Sticker 144
92/3 Panini Sticker 279
93/4 Panini Sticker 10
94/5 Panini Sticker 8
95/6 Panini Sticker 9
96/7 Panini Sticker 1
97/8 Panini Sticker 9
98/9 Panini Sticker 12
99/0 Panini Sticker 21, 342
91/2 Parkhurst 9
91/2 Parkhurst 221
91/2 Parkhurst 469
91/2 Parkhurst 472
92/3 Parkhurst 1
92/3 Parkhurst 464
93/4 Parkhurst 14
94/5 Parkhurst 13, 304, YCTG-2
95/6 Parkhurst 11, AS-5, CCP-9, PP-22
00/1 Parkhurst P-103
01/2 Parkhurst ✄ M19, ✄ M21
94/5 Parkie SE seV18
91/2 Pinnacle 15
91/2 Pinnacle 368
91/2 Pinnacle B-2
92/3 Pinnacle 2
92/3 Pinnacle TP 2
93/4 Pinnacle 250
93/4 Pinnacle CA2
93/4 Pinnacle TP 8
94/5 Pinnacle 190, BR-7, TP-3
95/6 Pinnacle 56
96/7 Pinnacle 199
97/8 Pinnacle 38
97/8 Pi. Be A Player 248, TN-1 ✍ Aut. 248
97/8 Pi. BeeHive 17
97/8 Pi. Certified 41
95/6 Pi. FANtasy 2
96/7 Pi. FANtasy 1
97/8 Pi. Inside 16
95/6 Pi. Summit 33, GMC-13
96/7 Pi. Summit 141
97/8 Pi. Totally 41
95/6 Pi. Zenith 29
96/7 Pi. Zenith 4
95/6 Playoff 5, 116, 226
96/7 Playoff 371
94/5 POG 42, 263, 327
95/6 POG 36, I-004, I-018
81/2 Post 1
82/3 Post [Bost.]
94/5 Post
93/4 Power Play 16
93/4 Power Play SA 2
93/4 Premier 93
93/4 Premier 350
93/4 Premier 383
93/4 Prmr. - BG-OPC 21
93/4 Prmr. - BG-Top. 15
94/5 Premier 36, 420, 454, 490
00/1 Premier Plus 42, TT8, WP6
99/0 Prism 12, -SGDC 3
00/1 Private Stock 22, PS-8, PSS-5, ✄ GUG-18, ✄ GUG-19
00/1 PS Titanium 19, NAAS-3
95/6 Pro Magnet 11
90/1 Pro Set 1, 357
91/2 Pro Set 9
91/2 Pro Set 296
91/2 Pro Set 322
91/2 Pro Set 567
92/3 Pro Set 4
92/3 Pro Set 261
91 Pro Set Awards AC7
91/2 Pro Set Platinum 2
91/2 Pro Set Platinum 278
91/2 Puck / Pro Set 1
99/0 Revolution 11, -NI 2, SS-3
00/1 Revolution 34, II-4, NI-5, SM-23
90/1 Score 200, 313, 363, / Promo 200
90/1 Sco. Hot Cards 35
91/2 Score 50
91/2 Score 344
91/2 Score 415
91/2 Score 429
91/2 Score / Promo 50
91/2 Score CAN 50
91/2 Score CAN 319
91/2 Score CAN 331
91/2 Score CAN 374
92/3 Score 100
92/3 Score 419
92/3 Score 447
92/3 Score 490
92/3 Score 520
93/4 Score 29
93/4 Score DT 7
93/4 Score PiAS 21
93/4 Score PiAS 48
93/4 Score TF 1
94/5 Score 180, DT3, NP21
95/6 Score 199
96/7 Score 53, S-7
97/8 Score 89
97/8 Score Bost. 4
91/2 Score Shows 3
92/3 Seasons 17
94/5 Select 18, FL-2
95/6 Select CE 34, DS-3
96/7 Select CE 5
89 Semic Sticker 57
91 Semic Sticker 55
92 Semic Sticker 80
93 Semic Sticker 192
84/5 7-Eleven
85/6 7-Eleven Superstars 1
96/7 SB 7-Eleven Phonecard
00/1 Signature 13, ✍ Aut. 135, ✄ DD-2
95/6 SBx Emotion 6
95/6 SBx Impact 7
96/7 SBx Impact 5, F-3
83/4 Souhaits Keychain [Bruins]
94/5 SP 6, P-20
95/6 SP 5, E3
96/7 SP 7, HC-23, Inside
97/8 SP Authentic 8, I28, ✍ SotT, ✍ T6
98/9 SP Authentic 7, SS15, SO20
99/0 SP Authentic 7
00/1 SP Authentic 22, ✍ SotT, ✍ SotTD
01/2 SP Authentic 92, ✄ NN, ✄ PP, ✍ SotTT
02/3 SP Authentic ✍ SotT, ✍ SotTD (x2), ✍ SotTT (x2), ✄ TP
00/1 SP GU 16, ✄ TotG, ✄ P, ✄✍ A
01/2 SP Game Used ✄ AF, ✄ AFQ, ✄✍ IS, ✄✍ IS2, ✄✍ ISD, ✄ TotGSig., ✄ TotGCSig.
02/3 SP Game-Used Edition 59, ✄ AF (x2), ✄ PC, ✄ PH (x2), ✍ Sig
96/7 SPx 3, HH-1
97/8 SPx 3
99/0 SPx 9, P14, XT15, ✄ WM
00/1 SPx 17, 84, P2, ✄ WM, ✄✍ WM
01/2 SPx 15, ✄✍ HTSig
02/3 SPx ✄ WM (x2), ✄ X
98/9 SPx Finite 117, 158, 177
98/9 SPx Prospects 3, H3, L17, PS3, ✄ WM
99/0 Stadium 5, -Chrome 5, -Big 5, CA21, ✍ CS13, ✍ CS15, ✍ LS4
00/1 Stadium 23, BT18
93/4 SLU / Card 504087
93/4 SLU / Card 504109
93/4 Starting Lineup
94/5 Starting Lineup
00/1 SLU 4
95/6 Super Sticker 6, DC-6
96/7 Team Out!
80/1 Topps 2
80/1 Topps 140
81/2 Topps 5
x81/2 Topps 126 [East]
84/5 Topps 1
x84/5 Topps 157
85/6 OPC/Topps-Stick. 5
86/7 OPC/Topps - Stick. 11
87/8 OPC/Topps - Stick. 1
88/9 OPC/Topps - Stick. 5
92/3 Topps 221
92/3 Topps 262
95/6 Topps 50, HGC9, 3RL
98/9 Topps 206, B4, -Reprint 3
99/0 Topps 11, 276, AT3, IM7
00/1 Topps 67, 327, PC-5, TC6, ✍ CAI
01/2 Topps 89, 317
99/0 To. Chrome 11, 276, AT3, IM7
00/1 To. Chrome 54, PC-5, TC6
94/5 Topps Finest 35, BBB-1, DF-2
95/6 To. Finest 2, 77
98/9 To. Finest 101, M12, M15, M18, M19
96 Topps Finest Bronze 20
98/9 T. Gold Label 9
99/0 To. Gold Label 26, PG9
00/1 To. Gold Label 1, B4, ✍

GLA
00/1 To. Heritage 1, HH1
00/1 To. Heritage ASG 1
96/7 Topps Picks FT4,ID2
99/0 To. Prmr. Plus 6, FP8, ✍ CS
91/2 To. Stadium 233
92/3 To. Stadium 249
92/3 To. Stadium 267
93/4 To. Stadium 160
93/4 To. Stadium - Master Photo-1 3
93/4 To. Stadium - All-Stars
93/4 To. Stadium - Finest 12
94/5 To. Stadium 77, 267, F-8
95/6 To. Stadium 2, M4, N5
91/2 TSC Charter
93/4 TSC Members Only 25
94/5 TSC Members Only 2
95/6 TSC Members Only 28
00/1 To. Stars 19, AS1, PS8
95/6 T. Super Skills 57
98/9 UD Choice 15, 222, BH3, SQ21
00/1 UD Heroes 144, L2, ✂ GT
00/1 UD Reserve 21, BT3
02/3 UD Superstars 37
98/9 UD3 55, 115, 175
00/1 Ultimate Mem. ✍ U-13, ✂MO-6, ✂RE-8, ✂N-7, ✂N-10, ✂TM-40
99/0 Ult. Victory 8, S12
90/1 Upper Deck 64, 204, 320, 489
91/2 Upper Deck 255
91/2 Upper Deck 633
91/2 Upper Deck AW5
92/3 Upper Deck 265
92/3 Upper Deck 626
93/4 Upper Deck 116, NL4, SP-7
94/5 Upper Deck 296, C26, R14, SP-4
95/6 Upper Deck 230, 250, 300, AS-1, F-10, H-32, R-48, SE-4
96/7 Upper Deck 14, 366, X8, SS7A, ✂ GJ4
97/8 Upper Deck 9, SS7, S27, T11A
98/9 Upper Deck 38, FT25, GN16-18, P23
99/0 Upper Deck 17, 156, AS16, CT20, HOF3, MA1, SB2, ✂ GJ, ✂✍ GJS
00/1 Upper Deck 44, D2, EC11, FT2, GA8, TT8, ✂ GJ
01/2 Upper Deck 212, SS14, ✂ JPatch, ✂ SCFJersD., ✂ SupSwe., ✂✍ JerSig., ✂✍ SigJer.
02/3 Upper Deck ✂ PL2
95/6 UD ASG MVP21
96/7 UD All-Star YCTG AR12
00/1 UD ASG CA1, HH3
02/3 UD Artistic 5, 24, R5, R24, CG7, CG14, GD7, UD7, ✂ AT, / Art
94/5 UD Be A Player R32, ✍ 32
96/7 UD Black Diam. 177
97/8 UD Black Diam. 60, PC4
98/9 UD Black Diam. 4, M17
99/0 UD Black Diam. 9, ✂ APOH
00/1 UD Black Diam. 15, FP13
99/0 UD C. Legends 16, 57, AC11, E2, ✍ ES, ✂ JC4
01/2 UD Challenge AT5, ✂ FP, ✂ TN, ✂ UC, ✂✍ FPS, ✂✍ T200S
95/6 UD CC 216, 385, C24
96/7 UD CC 13, 304, 310, UD27, C22, CR22
97/8 UD Coll. Choice 12, SQ77, S27, C7, CR7
01/2 UD Collectors
97/8 UD Diam. Vision 8
02/3 UD Foundations 6, 18, 108, ✂ 1000Stick (x2), ✂ CTW, ✂ CH, ✂ CG (x2), ✂ DF (x2), ✂ MS, ✂ PP, ✍ SG (x2)
98/9 UD G. Reserve 38
99/0 UD G. Reserve 17, 156
99/0 UD Gretzky Excl. 67
01/2 UD Honor Roll 5, 35, ✂ GAJ
02/3 UD Honor ✂ GA
96/7 UD Ice 106
97/8 UD Ice 77
00/1 UD Ice 11, FP3, ✂ IGJ
01/2 UD Ice 10
00/1 UD Legends 32, EG7, SM15, ✂ LGJ
01/2 UD Legends 50, ✂ PoH
92/3 UD Locker 39
01/2 UD Mask ✂ GG, ✂ GJ, ✂ JP, ✂ DP
98/9 UD MVP 9, OT4, -Souv.
99/0 UD MVP 11, W6, MVP5, ✍ PS
00/1 UD MVP 52, ME10, M3, ✂ GS
01/2 UD MVP 48, ✂ S
02/3 UD MVP ✍ PSig
99/0 UD MVP Cup 55, CP2, SC3, ✂ GU
99/0 UD Ovation 5, LP11
02/3 UD Piece 98, 118, 119, 120, AC2, HB2, SB1, ✂ EC, ✂ HS, ✂ PH, ✍ MD, / Giveaway
95/6 UD Post 1
96/7 UD Post
99/0 UD PowerDeck 4
01/2 UD Premier 4, ✂ B, ✂ G, ✂ D (x2), ✍ SigS
02/3 UD Premier 59, ✂ Jers, ✂ Patch (x2), ✍ Sig (x2)
00/1 UD Pros&Prosp. 22, NP1, ✂ GJ
99/0 UD Retro 4, DR1, G4C, TC6, ✍ Ink.
02/3 UD Rookie 165, ✍ TD
01/2 UD SCup Champs 5, ✂ S, ✂ G, ✂ T
01/2 UD Top Shelf 10, ✂ J, ✂✍ SJ, ✂ S, ✂ ST
02/3 UD Top Shelf ✂ CP, ✂ M (x2), ✂ SH, ✂ ST (x2), ✂ SW, ✍ Sig
00/1 UD Vintage 91, 98, UD4
01/2 UD Vintage 66, ✂ NL
02/3 UD Vintage ✂ HS
97/8 Valu-net, ✍ Aut.
00/1 Vanguard 25, HV-5, IF-4
99/0 Victory 20, 21, 317, 343
00/1 Victory 63, 246, 294
01/2 Victory 85, 411
99/0 WGretzky 20, W7, ✂ TG, ✍ SG
96 Wien 78
97/8 Zenith 11, Z40
83/4 BOST
84/5 BOST
88/9 BOST / Sports Action [x2]
89/0 BOST / Sports Action [x3]
90/1 BOST / Sports Action
91/2 BOST / Sports Action [x2]
91/2 BOST / SA Legends
92/3 BOST / Postcard

BOUSEK, LADISLAV
99/0 Score 28

BOUSKILL, DAVID
98/9 Muskegon Fury
99/0 Topeka Scarecrows

BOUSQUET, JARRETT
90 7th..Sketch Mem.Cup 14
90/1 7th..Sketch WHL 285
91/2 7th...Sketch WHL 80
89/0 Kamloops Blazers

BOUSTEDT, TOMMY
94/5 Leaf Elit Set 297

BOUTETTE, PAT
76/7 O-Pee-Chee 367
77/8 O-Pee-Chee 284
78/9 O-Pee-Chee 374
79/0 O-Pee-Chee 319
80/1 O-Pee-Chee 14
81/2 O-Pee-Chee 255
82/3 O-Pee-Chee 263
83/4 O-Pee-Chee 276
84/5 O-Pee-Chee 171
82/3 OPC/Topps Sticker 148
83/4 OPC/Topps Sticker 233
82/3 Post [Pitt.]
83/4 Souhaits Keychain [Penguins]
80/1 Topps 14
81/2 Topps 81 [East]
83/4 PITT / Coke Is It!
83/4 PITT / Heinz
84/5 PITT / Heinz
75/6 TORO
76/7 TORO
77/8 TORO
79/0 TORO

BOUTILIER, PAUL
84/5 NYIS / News 17

BOUTIN, J.F.
98/9 Peoria Rivermen
99/0 Peoria Rivermen
00/1 Peoria Rivermen

BOUTIN, JONATHAN
01/2 Shawinigan Cataractes 19
02/3 Shawinigan Cataractes

BOUVIER, JOEY
96/7 Regina Pats
97/8 Regina Pats

BOUVRETTE, LIONEL
43-47 Parade Sportive

BOUWMEESTER, JAY
02/3 Atomic 111
02/3 BAP All-Star 142
02/3 BAP Draft Toronto 2
02/3 BAP Memorabilia 274
02/3 Bowman 133, ✂ FFDS, ✂ FFJ, ✂ FFP, ✂ FFR, ✂ FFRP, ✂ FFS, ✂ FFTS, ✍ YSA, / ✍ Puck
02/3 Calder 119, -CR 11
02/3 Crown Royale 114, -RR 11
02/3 eTopps 43
02/3 Exclusive 198, ✍ 198
02/3 First Edition 438R
02/3 Heads Up 126
02/3 In The Game-Used 84, ✂ C3, ✂ E39
02/3 O-Pee-Chee 336
02/3 Pacific 126
02/3 Pacific Complete 568
02/3 PTC/ ASG 6
02/3 PTC/ Collections 5
02/3 PTC/ Spring Expo 5
02/3 Parkhurst 204, -HHC 4, ✂ GJ51, ✂ NH10
02/3 Parkhurst Retro 204, ✂ CH8, ✂ RJ12, ✂ RM26
02/3 Pr. Stock Reserve 163, -CA 8, -MIT 3
02/3 Private Stock Titanium 116, -ROT 9
96 Québec Pee Wee 720
02/3 Quest for the Cup 120, -CC 9
02/3 Signature Series 191, ✍ 191, ✂ AR2, ✂ SGJ55, ✂ TQ5
02/3 SP Authentic ✍ 187, ✍ SotT, ✍ SotTD, ✍ SotTT, , ✍✂ Patch
02/3 SP Game-Used Edition 78
02/3 Sports Vault 49
02/3 SPx ✍ 150
02/3 Stadium 128
02/3 Topps 336
02/3 T. Chrome 177
02/3 To. Heritage 138
02/3 T. Total 420
02/3 UD Superstars 269
02/3 Ultimate Memorabilia 4, ✂ CC, ✂ GUJ, ✂ GUSJ, ✂ NP, ✍ Raut
02/3 Upper Deck 236
02/3 UD Artistic 94, R93, CG4, CG7
02/3 UD Classic 116
02/3 UD Foundations 153
02/3 UD Honor 153, ✍ SC
02/3 UD Mask 172
02/3 UD Piece 132
02/3 UD Premier ✍✂ 82, ✂ Jers., ✍ Sig. (x2)
99/0 UD Prospects 50, 74, C5, DS10, ✂ GJ, ✍ Sig.
00/1 UD Prospects 56, 100, CC4, CS9, D4, ✂ GJ, ✂ GJC, ✂✍ GJS, ✍ Sig
01 UD Prospects GU ✍ SoT
02/3 UD Rookie 118, ✍ TD
02/3 UD Top Shelf 93
02/3 Vanguard 115, -PP 11
99/0 Medicine Hat Tigers
00/1 Medicine Hat Tigers

BOVAIR,
89/0 7th..Sketch OHL 118

BOWEN, CHRIS
98/9 Topeka Scarecrows

BOWEN, CURTIS
92/3 Classic 12
92/3 Classic LP8
93/4 Classic 16
94/5 Classic 26, T19
92/3 Classic Four Sport 161
93/4 Cla. 4 Sport 256
93/4 Donruss CAN6
95/6 Edge Ice 1
00/1 Kudos 91
93/4 Pinnacle 468
90/1 7th..Sketch OHL 78
91/2 7th...Sketch OHL 305
93/4 Upper Deck 547
95/6 Adirondack Red Wings
01/2 Belfast Giants
92/3 Ottawa 67's

BOWEN, JASON
92/3 Classic 9
92/3 Classic Four Sport 158
93/4 Donruss 241
94/5 Donruss 32
93/4 Fleer Ultra 35
94/5 Fleer Ultra 154
94/5 Leaf 248
93/4 Parkhurst 418
93/4 Pinnacle 215
94/5 Pinnacle 111
93/4 Power Play 404
94/5 Premier 234
93/4 Score 471
90/1 7th..Sketch WHL 97
91/2 7th...Sketch WHL 288
93/4 Upper Deck 240
93/4 PHIL / Sheet
93/4 PHIL / J.C. Penney
01/2 Belfast Giants

BOWER, JOHNNY
01/2 ASG History
99/0 BAP Mem. CH-5, ✍ CH-5
00/1 BAP Mem. ✂ G-13, ✂ G-19, ✂ G-24, ✂ G-29
01/2 BAP Memor. ✂ GT2, ✂ GT20, ✂ GT21, ✂ GT37
02/3 BAP Memorabilia / Stanley Cup
01/2 BAP Update ✂ RR3
45-64 BeeHive-2 [NYRa.]
45-64 BeeHive-2 [Toro.]
64-67 BeeHive-3 [Toro.]
64-67 BeeHive-3 [Toro.]
01/2 BT Pipes 123, 149, ✂ VM12
02/3 Between the Pipes ✂ RB13, ✂ VM1, ✍ Aut.
63-65 Chex
51/2 Cleveland Barons
64/5 Coke/Sprite [Toro.]
65/6 Coca-Cola
65/6 Coke How To... A
65/6 Coke How To... W
88/9 Esso All-Star
01/2 Fleer Greats 14, ✍ Aut.
62/3 Cowan Tile
93/4 High Liner 9
83 HHOF Postcard O5
83&87 HHOF 211
02/3 In The Game-Used ✂ VM15
93/4 Legends of Hockey 23
68/9 O-Pee-Chee 122
68/9 O-Pee-Chee PS 17
69/0 O-Pee-Chee 187
54/5 Parkhurst 65
58/9 Parkhurst 46
59/0 Parkhurst 25
59/0 Parkhurst 32
60/1 Parkhurst 3
61/2 Parkhurst 3
62/3 Parkhurst 16
63/4 Parkhurst 5, 65
92/3 Parkhurst PR-3
93/4 Parkhurst DPR-8
01/2 Parkhurst PR26, PR55, PR91, PR125, PR139, PR148, ✂ PV30
93/4 Parkie 56-57 103
02/3 Parkhurst Retro ✂ NN8
95/6 Parkie 66-67 119
94/5 Parkie Tall 129, 152, 177, TW-4
97/8 Pi. BeeHive 57, ✍ Aut. 57
68/9 Post Marble
67/8 Post Tips 1
67/8 Post Tips 2
60/1 Shirriff 1
61/2 Shirriff 41
62/3 Shirriff 1
68/9 Shirriff / Toro. 6
00/1 Signature ✂ GLS-1
01/2 Signature ✍ VA10
64/5 Topps 40
65/6 Topps 77
66/7 Topps 12
66/7 Topps / Test 12
67/8 Topps 76
68/9 Topps 122
02/3 To. Heritage - Reprint TML, ✂ Reprint, ✍ Reprint
99/0 To. Prmr. Plus ✍ CS4, ✍ CSC2
01/2 T/O Archives 52
59/0 Toronto Star Photo
63/4 Toronto Star Action
61/2 Toronto Star Weekend
00/1 Ultimate Mem. ✂ UG-4, ✂GM-6, ✂GM-19
01/2 Ultimate Mem. ✂ 01/2 ASG History
01/2 Ultimate Mem. ✂ Cornerstones [w/ Bailey, ✂ McDonald, ✂ Sundin]
01/2 Ultimate Mem. ✂ Retro Teammates [w/ Horton, ✂ Sawchuk]
01/2 Ultimate Mem. ✂ Stanley Cup Winners [Pads] BGS-8.5
02/3 Ultimate Memorabilia ✂ FS, ✂ RT, ✂ SCD (x2)
91/2 Ultimate Original Six 32, 80, ✍ Aut. 32
60/1 York Glass [Toro.]
60/1 York
61/2 York 8
62/3 York Transfer 1
63/4 York 2
67/8 York 16
67/8 York 23
67/8 York 25
67/8 York 26
67/8 York 27
67/8 York 29
67/8 York 30
67/8 York 34
67/8 York 36
92/3 Zellers
64/5 TORO
68/9 TORO
69/0 TORO
73/4 TORO
80/1 TORO
85/6 TORO

BOWERS, RODNEY
93/4 Prince Albert Raiders

BOWIE, RUSSELL
83 HHOF Postcard D2
83&87 HHOF 48

BOWKUS, JACK
84/5 Saskatoon Blades
86/7 Saskatoon Blades

BOWLER, BILL
98/9 EBK IHL All-Star
91/2 7th...Sketch OHL 188
93/4 Slapshot / Windsor 8
94/5 Slapshot / Windsor 10
01/2 SPx 110
01/2 Upper Deck 195
01/2 UD Top Shelf 51
01/2 Victory 371
95/6 Las Vegas Thunder
98/9 Manitoba Moose
99/0 Manitoba Moose
01/2 Norfolk Admirals
00/1 Syracuse Crunch
92/3 Windsor Spitfires

BOWMAN, BILL
24/5 Selkirks Crescent 4

BOWMAN, KIRK
77/8 O-Pee-Chee 309
78/9 O-Pee-Chee 61
78/9 Topps 61

BOWMAN, RALPH
34-43 BeeHive-1 [Detr.]
36-39 Diamond Match TT1

BOWMAN, SCOTTY
98/9 Bowman's Best SB1-11, ✍ SB11
72/3 Dernière Heure
93/4 Hockey Wit 49
93/4 Kraft / PB
96/7 Kraft / TT
00/1 Mir Fetisov 41
74/5 O-Pee-Chee 261
91/2 Pro Set HHOF 4
77-79 Sportscaster 82-05 [Coach]
77-79 Sports. FIN 90-2162 [Coach]
74/5 Topps 261
96/7 UD CC 308
82/3 BUFF / Wendt's 18
71/2 MONT / Pro Star
72/3 MONT / Pro Star
73/4 MONT / Pro Star
74/5 MONT
75/6 MONT
76/7 MONT
77/8 MONT
78/9 MONT
91/2 PITT / Elby's
92/3 PITT / Coke-Clark

BOWNASS, JACK
51/2 Laval Dairy 61
52/3 St. Lawrence 98

BOWNESS, RICK
77/8 O-Pee-Chee 265
78/9 O-Pee-Chee 173
81/2 O-Pee-Chee 361
88/9 ProCards / Moncton
89/0 ProCards AHL 75
90/1 ProCards 143
78/9 Topps 173
93/4 OTTA
94/5 OTTA
84/5 WINN / Safety Tips
85/6 WINN
85/6 WINN / Safety Tips
86/7 WINN
87/8 Moncton Hawks

BOWTELL, CODY
99/0 Lowell Lock Monsters
99/0 Mississippi S'Wolves
99/0 Mississippi S'Wolves

BOYCE, ARTHUR
12/3 Imperial 40

BOYCE, IAN
90/1 ProCards 268
91/2 ProCards 249
92/3 Fort Wayne Komets 3
93/4 Fort Wayne Komets 2
94/5 Fort Wayne Komets 14
97/8 Fort Wayne Komets
98/9 Fort Wayne Komets
96/7 Kansas City Blades
91/2 Rochester Americans WPC

BOYCHUK, JOHN
02/3 Moose Jaw Warriors

BOYCHUK, JOHNNY
00/1 Calgary Hitmen
01/2 Calgary Hitmen

BOYD, DAVE
94/5 Birmingham Bulls

BOYD, DON
85/6 London Knights
82/3 Regina Pats
83/4 Regina Pats
87/8 Soo Greyhounds 22

BOYD, DUSTIN
02/3 Moose Jaw Warriors

BOYD, JAMES
01/2 Belleville Bulls

BOYD, JAMES*
93/4 Slapshot / Kitchener 14
95/6 Slapshot 43

BOYD, JIM**
75/6 Phoenix Roadrunners

BOYD, KEVIN
95/6 Slapshot 167

BOYD, RANDY
83/4 O-Pee-Chee 283
91/2 ProCards 609
83/4 PITT / Heinz
87/8 VANC / Shell
88/9 VANC / Mohawk
81/2 Ottawa 67's

BOYD, RICK
88/9 ProCards / Indianapolis
89/0 Johnstown Chiefs

BOYD, STEPHANIE
94/5 Classic W33

BOYD, STEVE
89/0 7th..Sketch OHL 37

BOYD, YANK
34-43 BeeHive-1 [Bost.]

BOYER, DAVE
98/9 Detroit Vipers

BOYER, WALLY
64-67 BeeHive-3 [Toro.]
64-67 BeeHive-3 [Chic.]
70/1 Dad's Cookies
70/1 Eddie Sargent 171
70/1 Esso Power Player
68/9 O-Pee-Chee 105
69/0 O-Pee-Chee 118
70/1 O-Pee-Chee 203
72/3 O-Pee-Chee 308
68/9 Shirriff / Pitt. 12
66/7 Topps 55
68/9 Topps 105
69/0 Topps 118
71/2 Toronto Sun Photo

BOYER, ZAC
93/4 Cla. Prospects 114
90 7th..Sketch Mem.Cup 2
90/1 7th..Sketch WHL 284
91/2 7th...Sketch WHL 84
92/3 Indianapolis Ice
93/4 Indianapolis Ice
88/9 Kamloops Blazers
89/0 Kamloops Blazers

BOYES, BRAD
02/3 Choice Prospects 6
99/0 UD Sobey's 15
99/0 UD Prospects 10, 69
00/1 UD Prospects 6, FL3
02/3 St. John's Maple Leafs

BOYKO, DARREN
92/3 Jyvas Hyva 7
93/4 Sisu 96
94/5 Sisu 10
95/6 Sisu 13, 174, 369
95/6 Sisu Limited 44

BOYKO, ROB
95/6 Classic 82

BOYLE, DAN
99/0 BAP Mem. 285
99/0 Millenium 114, ✍ Aut. 114
99/0 Pacific 185
02/3 Pacific Complete 250
02/3 Sports Vault 129
01/2 Upper Deck 77
98/9 Kentucky Tho'blades
99/0 Louisville Panthers

BOYLE, JORDAN
90/1 Rayside-Balfour

BOYLE, STEVE
74/5 Sioux City Musketeers

BOYNTON, NICK
00/1 BAP Mem. 274
01/2 BAP Memor. 223
01/2 Bowman 127, ✂ FFJ, ✂ FFS, ✂ FFDS, ✂ FFR, ✍ YSA
97 Bowman 15, 154, BB6, ✍ Aut.
98 Bowman 27
98 Bowman Chrome 27
95/6 Classic 92
02/3 Exclusive 10
02/3 First Edition 35, ✂ Jers.
02/3 O-Pee-Chee 211
00/1 Pacific 45
02/3 Pacific 23
02/3 Pacific Complete 35
00/1 Parkhurst P-86
01/2 Parkhurst 278
02/3 Parkhurst Retro 198
92 Québec Pee Wee 343
01/2 Signature 227, ✍ Aut. 227
95/6 Slapshot 262, -P
02/3 Sports Vault 19
99/0 SPx 173
02/3 Stadium ✂ YSS18
02/3 Topps 211
02/3 T. Limited 211
02/3 T. Total 103
96/7 Upper Deck 373
99/0 Upper Deck 162
02/3 Upper Deck 14
96/7 UD Black Diam. 22
97/8 UD Coll. Choice 309
99/0 UD G. Reserve 162
02/3 UD MVP 17
02/3 UD Vintage 19, 263
99/0 Victory 372
02/3 Victory 19
99/0 Providence Bruins
00/1 Providence Bruins

BOZEK, DARWIN
89/0 ProCards AHL 11

BOZEK, ROMAN
94/5 APS 112
95/6 APS 70

BOZEK, STEVE
90/1 Bowman 64
91/2 Bowman 325
82/3 O-Pee-Chee 151
83/4 O-Pee-Chee 77
84/5 O-Pee-Chee 220
87/8 O-Pee-Chee 216
90/1 OPC/Topps 76
91/2 O-Pee-Chee 242
91/2 O-Pee-Chee 397
82/3 OPC/Topps Sticker 233
89/0 opcSticker 67-207
90/1 Panini Sticker 301
90/1 Panini/VAN 3
91/2 Panini Sticker 48
91/2 Pinnacle 61
82/3 Post [LosA.]
90/1 Pro Set 293
91/2 Pro Set 486
90/1 Score 89T
91/2 Score 6T
91/2 Score CAN 252, 556
92/3 Score 37
91/2 To. Stadium 28
83/4 Vachon 3-123
85/6 CALG / Red Rooster
86/7 CALG / Red Rooster
87/8 CALG / Red Rooster
91/2 SANJ / Sports Action
88/9 VANC / Mohawk
89/0 VANC / Mohawk
90/1 VANC / Mohawk

BOZIK, MOJMIR
89 Semic Sticker 188

BOZON, PHILIPPE
98/9 DEL 226
94/5 Donruss 261
92/3 Fleer Ultra 392
93/4 Fleer Ultra 210
95 Globe 205
94/5 Leaf 321
92/3 O-Pee-Chee 257
92/3 OPC Premier 25
95 Panini Worlds 112
91/2 Parkhurst 375
92/3 Parkhurst 159
92/3 Parkhurst 452
93/4 Parkhurst 179
94/5 Parkie SE153
93/4 Premier 68
92 Semic Sticker 230
92/3 Topps 433
92/3 To. Stadium 8
93/4 To. Stadium 214
94/5 To. Stadium 233
92/3 Upper Deck 283
93/4 Upper Deck 113, SP-134
96 Wien 188

BRABEC, JAROSLAV
94/5 APS 105
95/6 APS 71, 266

BRABENEC, KAMIL
96/7 APS 261
99/0 DS 42
00/1 DS 84
01/2 DS 12
98/9 OFS 413
99/0 OFS 177
00/1 OFS 20
01/2 OFS 135

BRACCO, JON
92/3 MPS SJHL 102

BRACCO, MICHAEL
88/9 Brockville Braves

BRACKENBURY, CURT
78/9 Dernière Heure
79/0 O-Pee-Chee 308
81/2 O-Pee-Chee 109
76/7 O-Pee-Chee WHA 4
80/1 Pepsi Bottle Cap
80/1 EDMO / Zellers
81/2 EDMO / Red Rooster
88/9 EDMO / Action 10
76/7 Québec Nordiques
76/7 Québ. / Antoinette

BRACKENBURY, CURT
02/3 Fleer Throwbacks 89, ✂ 3SW

BRADAWAY, CHAD
87/8 Sudbury Wolves

BRADFORD, BRENT
92/3 BCJHL 63

BRADLEY, BRIAN
95/6 Bicycle Sports Aces 4-Club
90/1 Bowman 58
91/2 Bowman 159
92/3 Bowman 283
93/4 Donruss 324
94/5 Donruss 40
95/6 Donruss 139
96/7 Donruss 116
95/6 Do. Elite 82
93/4 EA Sports 129
94/5 Flair 170
94/5 Fleer 203
96/7 Fleer 103
95/6 Fleer Metal 135
92/3 Fleer Ultra 408
93/4 Fleer Ultra 36
94/5 Fleer Ultra 202
95/6 Fleer Ultra 308
96/7 Fl. Ultra 155
95/6 Hoyle / East. 5-Heart
93/4 Kraft / KD
95/6 Kraft / KD
93/4 Leaf 209
94/5 Leaf 42
95/6 Leaf 159
96/7 Leaf 58
96/7 L. Limited 76
96/7 L. Preferred 18
93/4 McDonald's McD-01
96/7 Metal Univ. 142
90/1 OPC/Topps 59, 115
91/2 O-Pee-Chee 234
92/3 O-Pee-Chee 27
89/0 O-Pee-Chee 287
91/2 OPC Premier 185
91/2 OPC Premier 190
89/0 opcSticker 63-205
97/8 Pacific CC 64
89/0 Panini Sticker 152
90/1 Panini Sticker 302
90/1 Panini/VAN 4
91/2 Panini Sticker 93
93/4 Panini Sticker T
94/5 Panini Sticker 182
95/6 Panini Sticker 124
96/7 Panini Sticker 122
91/2 Parkhurst 171
92/3 Parkhurst 174
93/4 Parkhurst 465
94/5 Parkhurst 221, V71
95/6 Parkhurst 190
91/2 Pinnacle 90
92/3 Pinnacle 387
93/4 Pinnacle 60
94/5 Pinnacle 278
96/7 Pinnacle 17
95/6 Pi. Summit 146
96/7 Pi. Summit 18
96/7 Pi. Zenith 59
95/6 Playoff 197
94/5 POG 221
95/6 POG 246
93/4 Power Play 228
93/4 Premier 117
94/5 Premier 247
95/6 Pro Magnet 66
90/1 Pro Set 294
91/2 Pro Set 489
92/3 Pro Set 174
91/2 Pro Set Platinum 231
90/1 Score 198
91/2 Score CAN 255
92/3 Score 259
93/4 Score 230
93/4 Score PiAS 33
93/4 Score PiAS 50
93/4 Score TF 20
94/5 Score 179
95/6 Score 232
96/7 Score 45
94/5 Select 43
95/6 Select CE 83
95/6 SBx Emotion 162
95/6 SBx Impact 153
96/7 SBx Impact 120, BR-1
94/5 SP 114
96/7 SP 149
96/7 SLU
95/6 Super Sticker 111, 113
92/3 Topps 291
95/6 Topps 148
95/6 To. Finest 143
96/7 Topps Picks 71
91/2 To. Stadium 257
92/3 To. Stadium 163
93/4 To. Stadium 212
93/4 To. Stadium - All-Stars
95/6 To. Stadium 39
93/4 TSC Members Only 41
95/6 T. Super Skills 59
90/1 Upper Deck 79
92/3 Upper Deck 544
93/4 Upper Deck 121, 305, SP-148
94/5 Upper Deck 118, SP-74
95/6 Upper Deck 83, SE-166
95/6 UD Be A Player 117, ✍ S117
95/6 UD CC 128
96/7 UD CC 250
92/3 UD Locker 20
86/7 CALG / Red Rooster
92/3 TAMP / Sheraton Inn
93/4 TAMP / Kash N' Karry
94/5 TAMP / Sky Box
95/6 TAMP / Sky Box
91/2 TORO / P.L.A.Y. 28
88/9 VANC / Mohawk
89/0 VANC / Mohawk
90/1 VANC / PotM
85/6 Moncton G'Flames

BRADLEY, GEORGE
01/2 Guelph Storm
01/2 Guelph Storm M-Cup

BRADLEY, JOHN
93/4 Johnstown Chiefs 1
91/2 Rochester Americans GL
91/2 Rochester Americans WPC
95/6 Lethbridge Hurricanes

BRADLEY, LES
82/3 Kitchener Rangers
83/4 Kitchener Rangers
84/5 Kitchener Rangers

BRADLEY, MATT
00/1 BAP Mem. 435
95/6 Bowman P3
98 Bowman 28
98 Bowman Chrome 28
02/3 Pacific Complete 261
01/2 PS Titanium Draft 164
00/1 Signature 256, ✍ Aut. 218
95/6 Slapshot 113
02/3 T. Total 117
98/9 UD Choice 274
98/9 Kentucky Tho'blades
99/0 Kentucky Tho'blades
00/1 Kentucky Tho'blades

BRADLEY, TODD
91/2 7th...Sketch OHL 150
93/4 Slapshot / Oshawa 13
91/2 Oshawa Generals
91/2 Oshawa Generals
92/3 Oshawa Generals

BRADY, FRED
52/3 Anonymous 60

BRADY, LANCY
95/6 Birmingham Bulls

BRADY, NEIL
90/1 Bowman 88
92/3 OPC Premier 82
93/4 Panini Sticker 119
92/3 Parkhurst 124
93/4 Premier 17
88/9 ProCards / Utica
90/1 ProCards 568
93/4 Score 293
93/4 To. Stadium 199
92/3 To. Stadium Members Only
93/4 Upper Deck 81
89/0 NJER
89/0 NJER / Caretta
92/3 OTTA
96/7 Michigan K-Wings
99/0 Utah Grizzlies
84/5 Medicine Hat Tigers

BRADY, SEAN
98/9 Fort Worth Brahmas

BRAFF, ERIC
99/0 Kingston Frontenacs
00/1 Kingston Frontenacs 4

BRAGNALO, RICK
77/8 O-Pee-Chee 296
78/9 O-Pee-Chee 308
82 Semic Sticker 134

BRAHAM, DEAN
84/5 Prince Albert Raiders

BRAKIN, WALLY
59/60 Whitby Dunlops

BRANCH, DAVID
90/1 7th..Sketch OHL 300
95/6 Slapshot 5

BRANCH, ROD
94/5 Slapshot Memorial 1
99/0 Topeka Scarecrows
93/4 Kamloops Blazers
95/6 Prince Albert Raiders

BRANCIK, RICHARD
94/5 APS 21
95/6 APS 118
97/8 APS 120
99/0 Score 106

BRAND, AARON
95/6 Classic 96
94/5 Slapshot / Sarnia 9
95/6 Slapshot 338
96/7 St. John's Maple Leafs
97/8 St. John's Maple Leafs
99/0 St. John's Maple Leafs

BRAND, KONRAD
96/7 Kamloops Blazers
99/0 Medicine Hat Tigers

BRANDA, DANIEL
00/1 DS 115
98/9 OFS 14
99/0 OFS 342
00/1 OFS 93
01/2 OFS 11m -UHI 21

BRANDL, THOMAS
94/5 DEL 202
95/6 DEL 205, 430
96/7 DEL 289
98/9 DEL 21
95 Globe 221
95 Panini Worlds 63
94 Semic 280
91 Semic Sticker 165
93 Semic Sticker 166
00/1 UD DEL 155, S5
01/2 UD DEL 153
96 Wien 197

BRANDL, TOMAS
99/0 Eishockey 127

BRANDNER, CHRISTOPH
95 Panini Worlds 275
00/1 UD DEL 151

BRANDOW, HOWARD
23/4 Paulins Candy 7
23/4 Selkirks Crescent 4
24/5 Selkirks Crescent 1

BRANDRETH, PAT
01/2 Vancouver Giants

BRANDRETH, PATRICK
00/1 Kamloops Blazers

BRANHAM, TIM
01/2 Guelph Storm
01/2 Guelph Storm M-Cup

BRANKLEY, DON
00/1 London Knights
01/2 London Knights

BRANNARE, STEFAN
92/3 BCJHL 154

BRANNSTROM, NIKLAS
99/0 Eishockey 257

BRÄNNSTRÖM, FABIAN
94/5 DEL 74
95/6 DEL 71
01/2 UD DEL 167

BRÄNNSTRÖM, NIKLAS
94/5 Leaf Elit Set 275
89/0 Semic Elitserien 210
91/2 Semic Elitserien 98
92/3 Semic Elitserien 120
95/6 UD Elitserien DS7
97/8 UD Elitserien 179

BRANT, CHRIS
00/1 Kudos 40
88/9 ProCards / Binghampton
82/3 Kingston Canadians
83/4 Soo Greyhounds
84/5 Soo Greyhounds

BRAR, DAMPY
98/9 Las Vegas Thunder

BRASAR, PER-OLOV
78/9 O-Pee-Chee 99
79/0 O-Pee-Chee 192
80/1 O-Pee-Chee 291
81/2 O-Pee-Chee 330
81/2 OPC Sticker 244
79 Panini Sticker 195
80/1 Pepsi Bottle Cap
78/9 Topps 99
79/0 Topps 192
78/9 MINS / Cloverleaf 2
80/1 VANC
80/1 VANC / Silverwood
81/2 VANC
81/2 VANC / Silverwood

BRASEY, PATRICE
91 Semic Sticker 182
92 Semic Sticker 198
93 Semic Sticker 113

BRASHEAR, DONALD
98/9 Aurora 187
98/9 Be A Player 143, ✍ Aut. 143
00/1 BAP Mem. ✂ T-6
01/2 BAP Memor. 462
01/2 BAP Update ✂ TC16, ✂ TC19
94/5 Classic E1
93/4 Cla. Prospects 146
94/5 Donruss 146
98/9 Dynagon Ice 186
02/3 First Edition 247
94/5 Fleer Ultra 310
94/5 Leaf 227
01/2 O-Pee-Chee 190
97/8 Omega 227
98/9 Pacific 425
99/0 Pacific 421
00/1 Pacific 405
01/2 Pacific 378, 424
02/3 Pacific 276
02/3 Pacific Complete 68
98/9 Pa. Crown Roy. 133
97/8 Pa. Invincible R-200
98/9 Pa. Paramount 233
99/0 Pa. Paramount 233
97/8 Pa. Revolution 138
98/9 Pa. Revolution -3PA
01/2 Parkhurst 354
02/3 Parkhurst 177
96/7 Pi. Be A Player 181, ✍ Aut. 181
97/8 Score Vanc. 17
90/1 7th..Sketch LHJMQ 245
91/2 7th...Sketch LHJMQ 139
02/3 Signature Series GS-33, ✂ FS11
02/3 SP Game-Used ✂ AF
01/2 Topps 190
00/1 To. Heritage 164
01/2 To. Reserve ✂ TR
02/3 T. Total 226
95/6 Upper Deck 411
97/8 Upper Deck 376
00/1 Upper Deck 401
01/2 Upper Deck 403
02/3 Upper Deck 373, -NC9
01/2 UD Ice 110
00/1 UD Vintage 351, 357
02/3 UD Vintage 191, 282
01/2 Victory 339
94/5 MONT
95/6 MONT
01/2 PHIL
96/7 VANC / IGA
01/2 VANC / Coke
92/3 Fredericton Canadiens
93/4 Fredericton Canadiens
93/4 Fredericton Canadiens
94/5 Fredericton Canadiens

BRASSARD, ANDRÉ
89/0 Nashville Knights

BRASSARD, CHRIS
94/5 Slapshot / Kitchener 19

BRASSARD, JOEL
91/2 7th...Sketch LHJMQ 38

BRATASH, OLEG
98/9 Mir 141
90/1 O-Pee-Chee 525

BRATHWAITE, FRED
01/2 Adrenaline 157, PP29, ✂ GWJ 39
00/1 Aurora 22, Pin. 22
99/0 BAP Mem. 360
00/1 BAP Mem. 190
01/2 BAP Memor. 33
02/3 BAP Memorabilia 141, 256
01/2 BT Pipes 67
02/3 Between the Pipes 58, ✂ GUJ40, ✂ T15
93/4 Donruss 119
94/5 Donruss 320
95/6 Edge Ice 31
93/4 Fleer Ultra 313
94/5 Fleer Ultra 289
01/2 Heads Up 79
94/5 Leaf 26
01/2 McDonald's 32
01/2 O-Pee-Chee 217
02/3 O-Pee-Chee 197
99/0 Omega 34
99/0 Pacific 51
00/1 Pacific 61, ITC 2
01/2 Pacific 57, ✂ GWJ 4
02/3 Pacific 319
02/3 Pacific Complete 159
00/1 Pa. Paramount 33, GS 4
00/1 Parkhurst P-28
93/4 Power Play 339
00/1 Private Stock 14, ✂ GUG-64
01/2 Pr. Stock -PS 60, ✂ GUG 86
00/1 PS Titanium ✂ GUG 64
01/2 PS Titanium ✂ DSJ 37
00/1 PS Titanium Draft ✂ 13
99/0 Revolution 23
00/1 Revolution 20
93/4 Score 618
90 7th..Sketch Mem.Cup 77
89/0 7th..Sketch OHL 23
90/1 7th..Sketch OHL 327
91/2 7th...Sketch OHL 169
00/1 Signature 182, ✍ Aut. 66
01/2 Signature 196, ✍ Aut. 196
99/0 SP Authentic 15
00/1 SPx 8
00/1 Stadium 120, GS10
99/0 Topps 108
00/1 Topps 51, ✍ CAI
01/2 Topps 217
02/3 Topps 197
99/0 To. Chrome 108
00/1 To. Chrome 41
00/1 To. Gold Label 52
00/1 To. Heritage 156
01/2 To. Heritage 177
02/3 T. Limited 197
00/1 To. Stars 61
02/3 T. Total 202
00/1 UD Heroes 16
93/4 Upper Deck 435
00/1 Upper Deck 30
01/2 Upper Deck 382
02/3 Upper Deck 396
02/3 UD Mask 75, 77
00/1 UD MVP 30
99/0 UD MVP Cup 32
00/1 UD Vintage 56, 61, 62, GG4
01/2 Vanguard ✂ DGM 5
00/1 Victory 36
01/2 Victory 48, 51
93/4 EDMO / Sheet
97/8 Manitoba Moose
89/0 Oshawa Generals
90/1 Oshawa Generals
91/2 Oshawa Generals

BRAUER, CAM
90/1 ProCards 173
91/2 ProCards 98

BRAULT, BOB
51/2 Bas du Fleuve 22
52/3 Bas du Fleuve 61

BRAUN, FRANK
74 Hellas MM-Jenkki 113
70/1 Kuvajulkaisut 82

BRAVER, CAM
88/9 Regina Pats

BRAY, MIKE
00/1 Québec Remparts 11
01/2 Québec Remparts 10

BRAZDA, RADOMIR
94/5 APS 256
95/6 APS 320
96/7 APS 145
96/7 DS Sticker 251
99/0 Score 130

BREARLEY, PETER
93/4 Slapshot / Kitchener 17
99/0 Huntington Blizzard
98/9 Roanoke Express

BREAULT, FRANCIS
01/2 Drummondville

BREAULT, FRANCIS*
84/5 Chicoutimi Saguenéens

BREAULT, FRANÇOIS
91/2 O-Pee-Chee 496
90/1 Pro Set 612
91/2 Pro Set 541
88/9 ProCards / New Haven
89/0 ProCards AHL 2
90/1 LOSA / Smokey 13
92/3 Phoenix Roadrunners

BREBANT, RICK
00/1 Kudos 152
01/2 Sheffield Steelers GS

BREEN, GEORGE
95/6 Classic 70, ✍ Aut.
95/6 Cla. 5 Sport 129, 189

BREILIN, MATTI
66/7 Champion 69

BREISTROFF, MICHEL
94 Semic 218

BREITENBACH, KEN
77/8 O-Pee-Chee 279

BREITKREUZ, ADAM
00/1 Calgary Hitmen
01/2 Calgary Hitmen

BREKKE, BRENT
95/6 Dayton Bombers
92/3 W. Michigan Broncos
93/4 W. Michigan Broncos

BRENDL, PAVEL
01/2 Adrenaline 219, RR13
01/2 Atomic 118, RR6
01/2 BAP Memor. 380
02/3 BAP Memorabilia 50, 236
99 Bowman 5, 83, SC3, ✍ BA25
02/3 Bowman 111, ✄ FFDS, ✄ FFJ, ✄ FFP, ✄ FFR, ✄ FFRP, ✄ FFS, ✄ FFTS, ✍ YSA, / ✍ Puck
02/3 Calder 60
02/3 Exclusive 124
02/3 First Edition 82, ✄ Jers.
01/2 Heads Up 114
02/3 O-Pee-Chee 272
02/3 Pacific Complete 532
01/2 Parkhurst 275
02/3 Parkhurst Retro 188
01/2 Pr. Stock 106, MiT 8, RR 7, -PS 84, ✄ GUG 70
01/2 PS Titanium ✄ DSJ 31, ✄ DSJ 33
01/2 PS Titanium Draft 155
01/2 Signature 220, ✍ Aut. 220
02/3 Signature Series 94, ✍ 94
99/0 UD Sobey's 7
99/0 SP Authentic 122
00/1 SP Authentic ✍ SotT, ✍ SotTD
01/2 SP Authentic 124
02/3 SP Authentic 127, ✍ SotT, ✍ SotTD
01/2 SP GU 40
02/3 SP Game-Used ✄ FF, ✍ Sig
99/0 SPx 166
00/1 SPx ✄ 123
01/2 SPx 120
01/2 Stadium 113
02/3 Stadium 113
99/0 Topps 271
02/3 Topps 272
99/0 To. Chrome 271
02/3 T. Limited 272
00/1 UD Heroes ✍ SG
99/0 Ult. Victory 109
99/0 Upper Deck 306
00/1 Upper Deck 212, ✍ SG
01/2 Upper Deck 358
02/3 Upper Deck 372, ✄ BF
99/0 UD Black Diam. 91
99/0 UD G. Reserve 306, / Backup 164
02/3 UD Honor ✍ SC
00/1 UD MVP ME2, ✍ ME
99/0 UD MVP Cup 194, ✄ GU, ✄ SGU, ✍ PS
99/0 UD Ovation 61
02/3 UD Piece ✍ MD
02/3 UD Premier ✍ Sig.
99/0 UD Prospects 33, C7, DS2, IN3, ✄ GJ, ✍ Sig.
00/1 UD Prospects 46, CC6, CS5, D3, ✄ GJ, ✄✍ GJS, ✍ Sig
02/3 UD Rookie 19, ✍ TD
02/3 UD Top Shelf ✍ Sig
01/2 Vanguard 71, PP 14, ✄ DGM 19
99/0 Victory 358
98/9 Calgary Hitmen 6
99/0 Calgary Hitmen
00/1 Calgary Hitmen

BRENNAN, DOUG
33-35 Diamond Match Silv.
33/4 WWGum 45

BRENNAN, KIP
01/2 BAP Memor. 329
02/3 Pacific Complete 569
02/3 Quest for the Cup 121
01/2 UD PlayMakers Ltd 121
00/1 Lowell Lock Monsters
01/2 Manchester Monarchs
02/3 Manchester Monarchs
98/9 Sudbury Wolves 17

BRENNAN, LESTER
37/8 World Wide Gum 106

BRENNAN, MICHAEL
91/2 Air Canada SJHL B50

BRENNAN, RICH
98/9 Pacific 377
97/8 Pi. Be A Player 236, ✍ Aut. 236
91/2 Upper Deck WJC 76
98/9 Hartford Wolf Pack
99/0 Lowell Lock Monsters
00/1 Lowell Lock Monsters
01/2 Manchester Monarchs

BRENNEMAN, JOHN
64-67 BeeHive-3 [Toro.]
64/5 Coke/Sprite [Chic.]
68/9 O-Pee-Chee 83
68/9 Shirriff / Oakl. 2
68/9 Topps 83
68/9 TORO

BRENNER, MATT
97/8 Central Texas

BRENT, STEVE
91/2 Air Canada SJHL D42
92/3 MPS SJHL 6

BRENT, TIM
00/1 Toronto St. Mike's

BRENZAVICH, DAN
99/0 Asheville Smoke

BRESAGK, MICHAEL
94/5 DEL 249
95/6 DEL 244
98/9 DEL 143, 319
99/0 Eishockey 76, 383
95 Panini Worlds 59
00/1 UD DEL 74
01/2 UD DEL 76

BRESAGK, THOMAS
94/5 DEL 409
95/6 DEL 407

BRESLIN, TIM
91/2 ProCards 395
98/9 Chicago Wolves
98/9 Chicago Wolves Champs
92/3 Phoenix Roadrunners
93/4 Phoenix Roadrunners

BRESNAN, MATT
97/8 Toledo Storm 30

BRETON, CHRISTIAN
87/8 Hull Olympiques

BREWER, CARL
45-64 BeeHive-2 [Toro.]
64-67 BeeHive-3 [Toro.]
64/5 Coke/Sprite [Toro.]
62/3 Cowan Tile
69/0 O-Pee-Chee 59
69/0 O-Pee-Chee 4in1
70/1 O-Pee-Chee 243
71/2 O-Pee-Chee 222
59/0 Parkhurst 3
60/1 Parkhurst 18
61/2 Parkhurst 18
62/3 Parkhurst 8
63/4 Parkhurst 8
63/4 Parkhurst 68
92/3 Parkhurst PR-13
93/4 Parkie 56-57 FS-1
94/5 Parkie Tall 114
60/1 Shirriff 3
61/2 Shirriff 45
62/3 Shirriff 5
62/3 Shirriff 51
64/5 Topps 75
65/6 Topps 78
69/0 Topps 59
61/2 Toronto Star Photo
63/4 Toronto Star Action
64/5 Toronto Star Action
59/0 Toronto Star Weekend
63/4 Toronto Star Weekend
71/2 Toronto Sun Photo
60/1 York Glass [Toro.]
60/1 York
61/2 York 13
62/3 York Transfer 5
63/4 York 17
71/2 SLOU
64/5 TORO
79/0 TORO

BREWER, ERIC
01/2 Adrenaline 71
98/9 Be A Player 235, ✍ Aut. 235
02/3 BAP Memorabilia 39
97 Bowman 153, BB8, ✍ Aut.
98/9 Bowman's Best 115, F17
98/9 Dynagon Ice 114
02/3 First Edition 198, 417R
99/0 HoloGrFX 36
02/3 McDonald's -SLG 4
02/3 O-Pee-Chee 150
98/9 Omega 153
99/0 Pacific 251
02/3 Pacific 138
02/3 Pacific Complete 63
99/0 Pa. Paramount 140
02/3 Parkhurst 182
01/2 Signature 184, ✍ Aut. 184
02/3 Signature Series 44, ✍ 44, ✄ TQ17
98/9 SP Authentic 102, SS21
02/3 Sports Vault 227
99/0 SPx 92
98/9 SPx Prospects 37
99/0 Stadium 110, CA8
99/0 Topps 97
02/3 Topps 150
99/0 To. Chrome 97
98/9 T. Gold Label 68
02/3 T. Limited 150
02/3 T. Total 175
98/9 UD Choice 256
98/9 Upper Deck 417, GN18, P5, ✄ GJ12
99/0 Upper Deck 82, CT10, N18
00/1 Upper Deck 297
01/2 Upper Deck 301
97/8 UD Black Diam. 90
98/9 UD Black Diam. 52, M29
98/9 UD G. Reserve 417
99/0 UD G. Reserve 82
98/9 UD MVP 124, ✍ PS
99/0 UD MVP 126, DR4
02/3 UD MVP 74
99/0 UD Retro 53
00/1 UD Vintage 140
99/0 Victory 176, 177
02/3 Victory 86
99/0 Lowell Lock Monsters

BREWER, MIKE
92/3 Canada Nationals
92/3 San Diego Gulls

BRÉZEAULT, REGINALD
90/1 7th..Sketch LHJMQ 182
91/2 7th...Sketch LHJMQ 157
99/0 Charlotte Checkers
93/4 Roanoke Express

BREZGUNOV, VADIM
00/1 Mir 316
91/2 O-Pee-Chee 11R
98/9 OFS 353

BREZIK, DAVID
98/9 OFS 276
99/0 Score 150

BREZINA, ROBERT
94/5 DEL 426
95/6 DEL 395
96/7 DEL 304

BRIAND, ARNAUD
94 Semic 229
92 Semic Sticker 231
93 Semic Sticker 259
00/1 UD DEL 20

BRICE, NATHAN
00/1 Prince George Cougars

BRICKER, HARRY
89/0 ProCards AHL 357
90/1 ProCards 52

BRICKLEY, ANDY
90/1 Bowman 27
92/3 Bowman 17
90/1 OPC/Topps 88
89/0 OPC/Topps 29
87/8 Panini Sticker 86
89/0 Panini Sticker 194
90/1 Panini Sticker 16
90/1 Pro Set 406
92/3 Score 296
92/3 Topps 109
92/3 To. Stadium 208
90/1 Upper Deck 84
89/0 BOST / Sports Action
90/1 BOST / Sports Action
86/7 NJER / S.O.B.E.R.
83/4 PITT / Coke Is It!
84/5 PITT / Heinz
83/4 Springfield Indians 14

BRICKNELL, COREY
93/4 Slapshot / Niagara Falls 20

BRIDGMAN, MEL
84/5 Kelowna Wings &...
76/7 O-Pee-Chee 26
77/8 O-Pee-Chee 121
78/9 O-Pee-Chee 26
79/0 O-Pee-Chee 201
80/1 O-Pee-Chee 189
81/2 O-Pee-Chee 248
82/3 O-Pee-Chee 39
82/3 O-Pee-Chee 40
83/4 O-Pee-Chee 226
84/5 O-Pee-Chee 109
84/5 O-Pee-Chee 361
85/6 OPC/Topps 42
86/7 OPC/Topps 136
87/8 OPC/Topps 17
82/3 OPC/Topps Sticker 213
83/4 OPC/Topps Sticker 265
84/5 OPC Sticker 71
85/6 OPC Sticker 57
86/7 OPC Sticker 203
87/8 Panini Sticker 249
82/3 Post [Calg.]
84/5 7-Eleven
85/6 7-Eleven Superstars 11
83/4 Souhaits Keychain [Flames]
82/3 Stater Mint 1
76/7 Topps 26
77/8 Topps 121
78/9 Topps 26
79/0 Topps 201
80/1 Topps 189
84/5 Topps 84
81/2 CALG
82/3 CALG
87/8 DETR / Little Caesars
83/4 NJER
84/5 NJER
86/7 NJER / S.O.B.E.R.
84/5 Victoria Cougars

BRIEEL, LARS
00/1 UD Elitserien 23

BRIÈRE, DANIEL
96/7 All-Sport PPF 172
02/3 Atomic 77, -PC 15
02/3 BAP Memorabilia 16, 223, 340, ✄ FP 23
95/6 Bowman P4
97 Bowman 50
98/9 Bowman's Best 108, BP8
95/6 Classic 58, AS17
95/6 Cla. Vis. Signings 68, ✍ Aut.
01/2 Crown Royale 110
02/3 Crown Royale 74
02/3 Exclusive 132
02/3 First Edition 64, 363, 388, ✄ Jers.
02/3 Heads Up 94
02/3 In The Game-Used ✄ F23
98/9 McDonald's McD27
02/3 O-Pee-Chee 36
98/9 OPC Chrome 149
98/9 Omega 182
01/2 Pacific 298
02/3 Pacific 291
02/3 Pacific Complete 406
98/9 Pa. Crown Roy. RC 7
98/9 Pa. Revolution 109
02/3 Parkhurst 16, ✄ FP23, ✄ TT20
02/3 Parkhurst Retro 56, ✄ RF23
94/5 Parkie SE261
02/3 Pr. Stock Reserve 77
02/3 Signature Series 89, ✍ 89, ✄ FJ23
98/9 SP Authentic 104
02/3 SP Authentic 71, ✄ SP
02/3 SP Game-Used ✄ PC, ✄ FF
02/3 Sports Vault 264
98/9 SPx Finite 143
98/9 SPx Prospects 48
02/3 Stadium ✍ LSS
98/9 Topps 149
99/0 Topps 144
02/3 Topps 36
99/0 To. Chrome 144
02/3 T. Chrome 34
02/3 T. Limited 36
01/2 To.Reserve ✄ TR
02/3 T. Total 277
98/9 UD Choice 163
98/9 Upper Deck 7, GN19
99/0 Upper Deck 272
02/3 Upper Deck 137, ✄ CG, ✄ HS, ✄ SD
02/3 UD Artistic 69, R69, ✄ RT, / Art
98/9 UD Black Diam. 67
02/3 UD Classic 77, ✄ HR
98/9 UD G. Reserve 7
99/0 UD G. Reserve 272
96/7 UD Ice 120
01/2 UD Mask ✄ GJ, ✄ JP, ✄ DP
02/3 UD Mask ✄ PG
98/9 UD MVP 157
99/0 UD MVP 162
02/3 UD MVP 140
02/3 UD Piece 69
02/3 UD Rookie 15
02/3 UD Top Shelf 69, ✄ GO, ✄ SH, ✄ ST, ✄ SW
02/3 UD Vintage 197, 283, 314, T50
99/0 Victory 230
01/2 Victory 273
02/3 Victory 168
99/0 WGretzky 131
98/9 PHOE / Coca-Cola
97/8 Springfield Falcons

BRIÈRE, JEAN-PHILIPPE
99/0 Rimouski Océanic 11
00/1 Rimouski Océanic 13
01/2 Rimouski Océanic 12

BRIGHT, CHRIS
93/4 Cla. Prospects 245
90/1 ProCards 188
91/2 ProCards 110

BRIGLEY, TRAVIS
97 Bowman 110
99/0 Omega 42
99/0 To. Prmr. Plus 87
99/0 UD G. Reserve 339
01/2 Cincinnati Mighty Ducks
97/8 Saint John Flames
95/6 Lethbridge Hurricanes

BRIIMSEK, FRANK
02/3 SP Authentic ✍ Cut

BRILL, JOHN
93/4 Cla. Prospects 232
94/5 Dayton Bombers 13
95/6 Dayton Bombers
91/2 Minnesota G'Gophers
92/3 Minnesota G'Gophers

BRILLANT, PIERRE
51/2 Bas du Fleuve 36
52/3 Laval Dairy Update 13
52/3 St. Lawrence 50

BRIMANIS, ARIS
94/5 Cla. Images 76, ✍ Aut.
93/4 Cla. Prospects 138
94/5 Donruss 65
94/5 Leaf 123
00/1 UD Heroes 76
01/2 Cincinnati Mighty Ducks
98/9 Grand Rapids Griffins
94/5 Hershey Bears
99/0 Kansas City Blades
02/3 Worcester IceCats
92/3 Brandon Wheat Kings

BRIMMER, CHUCK
81/2 Kingston Canadians
81/2 Soo Greyhounds

BRIMMER, KENT
84/5 Belleville Bulls

BRIMSEK, FRANK
01/2 ASG History
00/1 BAP Mem. ✄ G-10, ✄ G-14, ✄ G-26
01/2 BAP Memor. GT
01/2 BAP Update ✄ RR5
34-43 BeeHive-1 [Bost.]
45-64 BeeHive-2 [Bost.]
45-64 BeeHive-2 [Chic.]
01/2 BT Pipes 128, 148, ✄ TW, ✄ VM
02/3 Between the Pipes 112, ✄ VM17
83 HHOF Postcard I3
83&87 HHOF 124
02/3 In The Game-Used ✄ VM19
39/0 O-Pee-Chee 97
43-47 Parade Sportive
02/3 Parkhurst Retro ✄ NN1
94/5 Parkie Tall 7
00/1 Ultimate Mem. ✄ GM-18
01/2 Ultimate Mem. ✄ ASGH, ✄ CT, ✄ Corn.
02/3 Ultimate Memorabilia ✄ EA, ✄ RAT, ✄ VGJ
91/2 BOST / SA Legends

BRIND'AMOUR, ROD
01/2 Adrenaline 31
91/2 Air Canada SJHL D51
98/9 Aurora 135
99/0 Aurora 103
00/1 Aurora 27
98/9 Be A Player 251, ✍ Aut. 251
99/0 BAP Mem. 59, 394
00/1 BAP Mem. 200
01/2 BAP Memor. 246
02/3 BAP Memorabilia 192
96/7 Bic.Sports Aces 8-S
90/1 Bowman 23
91/2 Bowman 374
92/3 Bowman 224
92/3 Bowman 268
98/9 Bowman's Best 67
02/3 Crown Royale 16, ✄ GWDP 3
93/4 Donruss 248
94/5 Donruss 80
95/6 Donruss 188
96/7 Donruss 155
97/8 Donruss 157
97/8 Do. Canadian 113
95/6 Do. Elite 91
96/7 Do. Elite 93
97/8 Do. Preferred 67
97/8 Do. Priority 33
98/9 Dynagon Ice 133
99/0 Dynagon Ice 145
93/4 EA Sports 100
97/8 Esso 11, ✍ Aut.
02/3 Exclusive 26
02/3 First Edition 278, 386
94/5 Flair 126
94/5 Fleer 150
96/7 Fleer 78
95/6 Fleer Metal 108
96/7 Fl. Picks 54
92/3 Fleer Ultra 152
93/4 Fleer Ultra 74
94/5 Fleer Ultra 155
95/6 Fleer Ultra 115, CC-2
96/7 Fl. Ultra 121
02/3 Heads Up ✄ GWQ 6
93/4 Hockey Wit 59
95/6 Hoyle / East. 6-Heart
92/3 Humpty Dumpty
97/8 Kraft / PB
93/4 Leaf 26
94/5 Leaf 150
95/6 Leaf 154
96/7 Leaf 41
97/8 Leaf 125
94/5 L. Limited 78
95/6 L. Limited 69
96/7 L. Preferred 64
97/8 Limited 82
92/3 McDonald's McD-16
96/7 Metal Univ. 109
99/0 Millenium 181, ✍ Aut. 181
98/9 NHL Power Play
90/1 OPC/Topps 332
91/2 O-Pee-Chee 490
92/3 O-Pee-Chee 49
01/2 O-Pee-Chee 216
02/3 O-Pee-Chee 130
98/9 OPC Chrome 116
91/2 OPC Premier 94
92/3 OPC Premier SP9
97/8 Omega 160, TL-15
98/9 Omega 172
98/9 Pacific 17
99/0 Pacific 299
00/1 Pacific 79
01/2 Pacific 70
02/3 Pacific 63
02/3 Pacific Complete 317
97/8 Pacific CC 31, SS6A
97/8 Pa. Crown Roy. 95
98/9 Pa. Crown Roy. 97
97/8 Pa. Dynagon 88, T-20, BKS-68
97/8 Pa. Invincible 98, R-139
97/8 Pa. Paramount 130
98/9 Pa. Paramount 169
99/0 Pa. Paramount 168
00/1 Pa. Paramount 41
97/8 Pa. Revolution 97
98/9 Pa. Revolution 103
98/9 Panini Photocard
90/1 Panini Sticker 266, 343
91/2 Panini Sticker 30
92/3 Panini Sticker 187
93/4 Panini Sticker 47
94/5 Panini Sticker 37
95/6 Panini Sticker 114
96/7 Panini Sticker 111
97/8 Panini Sticker 93
98/9 Panini Sticker 90
99/0 Panini Sticker 124
95 Panini Worlds 19
91/2 Parkhurst 124
92/3 Parkhurst 126
93/4 Parkhurst 152
94/5 Parkhurst 167
95/6 Parkhurst 158
00/1 Parkhurst P-24
01/2 Parkhurst 104
02/3 Parkhurst 1
02/3 Parkhurst Retro 99
94/5 Parkie SE seV25
91/2 Pinnacle 9
92/3 Pinnacle 26
92/3 Pinnacle T2K 18
93/4 Pinnacle 170
93/4 Pinnacle T2K1 11
94/5 Pinnacle 273
95/6 Pinnacle 109
96/7 Pinnacle 123
97/8 Pinnacle 111
96/7 Pi. Be A Player 21, ✍ Aut. 21
97/8 Pi. Certified 93
97/8 Pi. Inside 92
95/6 Pi. Summit 79
96/7 Pi. Summit 123
97/8 Pi. Totally 93
95/6 Pi. Zenith 68
95/6 Playoff 291
94/5 POG 373
95/6 POG 202
93/4 Power Play 178
93/4 Premier 115
94/5 Premier 17
00/1 Premier Plus 76
00/1 Pr. Stock ✄ GUG 12
01/2 Pr. Stock ✄ GUG 18
02/3 Pr. Stock Reserve 15
01/2 PS Titanium ✄ DSJ 46
02/3 Private Stock Titanium 17, ✄ GWJ 8
95/6 Pro Magnet 46
90/1 Pro Set 259
91/2 Pro Set 211
91/2 Pro Set 453
92/3 Pro Set 132
91/2 Pro Set Platinum 90
91/2 Puck / Pro Set 20
99/0 Revolution 106, / CSC 106
00/1 Revolution 25
90/1 Score 131, 328
90/1 Sco. Hot Cards 98
91/2 Score 85
91/2 Score 68T
91/2 Score CAN 85
91/2 Score CAN 618
92/3 Score 324
93/4 Score 45
94/5 Score 132, NP13
95/6 Score 244
96/7 Score 102
97/8 Score 127, CI-16
97/8 Score Phil. 5
90/1 Sco. Young Stars 31
92/3 Score Young Stars 26
92/3 Seasons 39
94/5 Select 119
95/6 Select CE 59
95 Semic 90
00/1 Signature 16, ✍ Aut. 166
01/2 Signature 152, ✍ Aut. 152
95/6 SBx Emotion 129
95/6 SBx Impact 123
96/7 SBx Impact 92
94/5 SP 86
95/6 SP 110
97/8 SP Authentic 115
98/9 SP Authentic 64
01/2 SP Authentic ✍ SotT
02/3 SP Authentic 15
02/3 Sports Vault 33
99/0 SPx 111
98/9 SPx Finite 62
99/0 Stadium 33, EG10, PP4
00/1 Stadium 8
01/2 Stadium 95
00/1 SLU 10
95/6 Super Sticker 94
92/3 Topps 90
95/6 Topps 39
98/9 Topps 116
99/0 Topps 238
00/1 Topps 57
01/2 Topps 216
02/3 Topps 130
99/0 To. Chrome 238
00/1 To. Chrome 45
02/3 T. Chrome 82
94/5 Topps Finest 85
95/6 To. Finest 44
98/9 To. Finest 17
98/9 T. Gold Label 99
99/0 To. Gold Label 59
00/1 To. Heritage 110
02/3 T. Limited 130
99/0 To. Prmr. Plus 62
01/2 To.Reserve 25
91/2 To. Stadium 184
92/3 To. Stadium 202
93/4 To. Stadium 78
95/6 To. Stadium 36
00/1 To. Stars 38
02/3 T. Total 38
98/9 UD Choice 149
01/2 UD PlayMakers Ltd - PCPJ
90/1 Upper Deck 36, 347
91/2 Upper Deck 189
91/2 Upper Deck 547
92/3 Upper Deck 15
92/3 Upper Deck 264
93/4 Upper Deck 361, SP-114
94/5 Upper Deck 111, SP-57
95/6 Upper Deck 324, SE-64
96/7 Upper Deck 121, P26
97/8 Upper Deck 121, T17C
98/9 Upper Deck 334
99/0 Upper Deck 96
00/1 Upper Deck 36
01/2 Upper Deck 264
02/3 Upper Deck 28
94/5 UD Be A Player ✍ 175
96/7 UD Black Diam. 117
97/8 UD Black Diam. 61
98/9 UD Black Diam. 65
02/3 UD Classic 18
95/6 UD CC 29
96/7 UD CC 192
97/8 UD Coll. Choice 192, W8
98/9 UD G. Reserve 334
99/0 UD G. Reserve 96
96/7 UD Ice 48
98/9 UD MVP 155
99/0 UD MVP 149, ✍ PS
00/1 UD MVP 38
01/2 UD MVP 32 , -J, ✍ SJ
02/3 UD MVP 37, SD, Souv.
02/3 UD Piece ✍ MD
02/3 UD Rookie 20
00/1 UD Vintage 71
01/2 UD Vintage 48, 52
02/3 UD Vintage 46
97/8 Valu-net, ✍ Aut.
00/1 Vanguard 18
02/3 Vanguard 17, ✄ GWJ 9
99/0 Victory 214
00/1 Victory 45
01/2 Victory 60
02/3 Victory 39
99/0 WGretzky 127
96 Wien 98
97/8 Zenith 74, Z49
91/2 PHIL / J.C. Penney
92/3 PHIL / UD Sheet
92/3 PHIL / UD Sheet
92/3 PHIL / J.C. Penney
93/4 PHIL / Sheet
93/4 PHIL / Sheet
93/4 PHIL / J.C. Penney
94/5 PHIL / Sheet
94/5 PHIL / Sheet
96/7 PHIL / Ocean Spray
89/0 SLOU / Kodak
90/1 SLOU / Kodak

BRINDLEY, DOUG
72/3 Cleveland Crusaders

BRINK, ANDY
93/4 Donruss USA3
93/4 Pinnacle 490
93/4 Minnesota G'Gophers
94/5 Minnesota G'Gophers

BRISEBOIS, PATRICE
98/9 Be A Player 216, ✍ Aut. 216
99/0 BAP Mem. 182
00/1 BAP Mem. 240
92/3 Bowman 435
93/4 Donruss 171
94/5 Donruss 250
92/3 Durivage 32
93/4 Durivage 7
94/5 Flair 85
94/5 Fleer 102
96/7 Fl. Picks 160
92/3 Fleer Ultra 325
93/4 Fleer Ultra 52
94/5 Fleer Ultra 106
95/6 Fleer Ultra 254
98/9 Kraft / PB
93/4 Leaf 191
94/5 Leaf 325
92/3 O-Pee-Chee 239
02/3 O-Pee-Chee 41
98/9 OPC Chrome 80
00/1 Pacific 205
01/2 Pacific 203
02/3 Pacific 192
02/3 Pacific Complete 65
92/3 Panini Sticker 155
95/6 Panini Sticker 44
91/2 Parkhurst 309
92/3 Parkhurst 320
93/4 Parkhurst 105
94/5 Parkhurst 116
95/6 Parkhurst 380
92/3 Pinnacle 153
93/4 Pinnacle 253
94/5 Pinnacle 191
95/6 Playoff 272
95/6 POG 152
93/4 Power Play 125
93/4 Premier 59
91/2 ProCards 80
91/2 Score 382
91/2 Score CAN 272
92/3 Score 388
93/4 Score 163
95/6 Score 148
97/8 Score Mont. 20
92 7th...Sketch Awards 24
90/1 7th..Sketch LHJMQ 8
90 7th..Sketch Mem.Cup 59
91 7th..Sketch Mem.Cup 62
95/6 SP 77
02/3 Sports Vault 59
00/1 Stadium 147
92/3 Topps 189
95/6 Topps 199
98/9 Topps 80
02/3 Topps 41
02/3 T. Limited 41
92/3 To. Stadium 238
93/4 To. Stadium 27
02/3 T. Total 177
90/1 Upper Deck 454
91/2 Upper Deck 442
92/3 Upper Deck 277
93/4 Upper Deck 318
94/5 Upper Deck 193
95/6 Upper Deck 6
96/7 Upper Deck 88
97/8 Upper Deck 295
98/9 Upper Deck 293
01/2 Upper Deck 93
95/6 UD Be A Player 44, ✍ S44
95/6 UD CC 61
96/7 UD CC 142
98/9 UD G. Reserve 293
01/2 UD MVP 99
01/2 Victory 189
91/2 MONT
92/3 MONT
92/3 MONT / OPC 49
93/4 MONT
94/5 MONT
94/5 MONT / Export
95/6 MONT
95/6 MONT / Export
96-98 MONT
00/1 MONT
01/2 MONT
02/3 MONT

BRISKE, BYRON
94/5 Sig. Rookies 58, ✍ 58
98/9 Cincinnati M'Ducks 9
93/4 Red Deer Rebels
95/6 Tri-City Americans 13

BRISKE, SHANNON
93/4 Portland Winter Hawks

BRISSON, SYLVAIN
91/2 7th...Sketch LHJMQ 42

BRISSON, THÉRÈSE
94/5 Classic W4
97/8 UD Coll. Choice 286

BRISTOW, CAM
91/2 Air Canada SJHL D41
00/1 Kudos 13
92/3 MPS SJHL 49
90/1 7th..Sketch WHL 246

BRITHÉN, JIM
02/3 London Knights

BRITTIG, CHRISTIAN
94/5 DEL 307
95/6 DEL 65
96/7 DEL 261
98/9 DEL 120

BRITTON, CRAIG
02/3 Peterborough Phantoms

BRIZA, PETR
95/6 APS 355
96/7 APS 359
94/5 DEL 260
95/6 DEL 242
96/7 DEL 135
98/9 DEL 65
99/0 DS 141, G11
00/1 DS 1, G1, TS1, Star 7
01/2 DS 51, - G3
95 Globe 146
99/0 OFS 4, 487, -CL
00/1 OFS 290
01/2 OFS 16, -CL 11, -H15
94 Panini Olympics 319
95 Panini Worlds 186
94 Semic 165
95 Semic 140, 213
93/4 Sisu 366
96 Wien 104

BRÍZA, PETR
91/2 Jyvas Hyva 43
92/3 Jyvas Hyva 121
89 Semic Sticker 180
91 Semic Sticker 102
93 Semic Sticker 89

BRIZGALOV, VLADISLAV
99/0 Mir 189, 234

BRKIC, DARREN
90/1 Michigan Tech Huskies
91/2 Michigan Tech Huskies

BRKLACICH, STEVE
52/3 Laval Dairy Update 61

BROADBELT, DAVE
52/3 Anonymous 163

BROADBENT, HARRY (PUNCH)
24/5 Champ's Cigarettes
83 HHOF Postcard A2
83&87 HHOF 3
12/3 Imperial 2
24/5 Maple Crispette [V130] 18
23/4 William Paterson 9
24/5 William Paterson 39

BROCHU, MARTIN
01/2 BT Pipes 80
02/3 Between the Pipes 61
99/0 Choice 1
93/4 Cla. Prospects 94
95/6 Edge Ice 39, QM-11
00/1 Pacific 419, G-18, G-19, G-27
90/1 7th..Sketch LHJMQ 67
91/2 7th...Sketch LHJMQ 44
00/1 SP Authentic 139
00/1 UD Ice 83
93/4 Fredericton Canadiens
94/5 Fredericton Canadiens
95/6 Fredericton Canadiens
96/7 Portland Pirates
97/8 Portland Pirates
98/9 Portland Pirates
99/0 Portland Pirates

BROCHU, STÉPHANE
90/1 ProCards 546
91/2 ProCards 445
93/4 Flint Generals
94/5 Flint Generals
95/6 Flint Generals
96/7 Flint Generals
98/9 Flint Generals

BROCKLEHURST, CRAIG
90/1 7th..Sketch OHL 27

BROCKMANN, ANDREAS
94/5 DEL 93
95/6 DEL 95, 436
96/7 DEL 282
98/9 DEL 176
91 Semic Sticker 167
93 Semic Sticker 156

BRODA, MIKE
95/6 Red Deer Rebels

BRODA, WALTER (TURK)
01/2 ASG History
00/1 BAP Mem. ✄ G18, ✄ G19, ✄ G27
01/2 BAP Memor. ✄ GT3, ✄ GT19, ✄ GT21, ✄ GT37
01/2 BAP Update ✄ RR6
34-43 BeeHive-1 [Toro.]
45-64 BeeHive-2 [Toro.]
64-67 BeeHive-3 [Toro.]
01/2 BT Pipes 127, 147, ✄ TW, ✄ VM
02/3 Between the Pipes 118
48-52 Exhibits [Maple Leafs]
83 HHOF Postcard G3
83&87 HHOF 94
91/2 Kraft 37
96/7 Legends 74
36/7 O-Pee-Chee 97
37/8 O-Pee-Chee 133
39/0 O-Pee-Chee 2
40/1 O-Pee-Chee 108
40/1 O-Pee-Chee 130
43-47 Parade Sportive
51/2 Parkhurst 75
55/6 Parkhurst 23
92/3 Parkhurst PR-6
01/2 Parkhurst PR106, ✄ PV20
93/4 Parkie 56-57 P-6
02/3 Parkhurst Retro ✄ NN18
38/9 Quaker Oats
45-54 Quaker Oats
00/1 Ultimate Mem. ✄ GM-6, ✄ GM-19
01/2 Ultimate Mem. ✄ ASGH, ✄ SCW
02/3 Ultimate Memorabilia ✍ Cut

BRODAHL, ERIK
92/3 Semic Nordisk 131

BRODEN, CONNIE
93/4 Parkie 56-57 82
59/60 Whitby Dunlops

BRODERICK, KEN
69/0 O-Pee-Chee 197
75/6 O-Pee-Chee 340
76/7 OPC WHA 44
77/8 OPC WHA 4

BRODERICK, LEN
57/8 Parkhurst [Mont.] 21, 23
02/3 Parkie - Reprint 216

BRODEUR, DENIS
51/2 Bas du Fleuve 2
52/3 Bas du Fleuve 17

BRODEUR, MARTIN
01/2 Adrenaline 111, BR 7, CL 11, PP 22, ✄ GWJ 25
01/2 Atomic 57, CP, Stat., TN
02/3 Atomic 60, -D 11, -NPC 8
98/9 Aurora 108, ALC-12, CF-26, NC-7, ✍ CFA 26, / Cube 11
99/0 Aurora 84, Stripe 84, CF-15, GU-11, ST-12
00/1 Aurora 81, Pin. 81, CC-7, CF-14, SR-13, TPS-7B
02/3 BAP All-Star 7-9, ✄ ASJ, ✄ HSHSJers, Bobble
98/9 Be A Player 79, H-4, P-19, ✍ Aut. 79, ✄ G-9, ✄ AS-8, ✄ S-8, ✄✍ G-9
99/0 BAP Mem. 61, SL-12, ✄ J-8, ✄ D-19, ✄ TM-9, ✄ TM-17, ✄ TM-35
00/1 BAP Mem. 40, ✄ J-4, ✄ TM-1, ✄ TM-10
01/2 BAP Memor. 40, ✄ ASJ, ✄ ASE, ✄ ASN, ✄ ASD, ✄ AST, ✄ CoO, ✄ Jers., HSHS, ✄ SCP
02/3 BAP Memorabilia 89, 218, ✄ ASJ6, ✄ ASE1, ✄ ASN1, ✄ AST9, ✄ AST18, ✄ AST25, ✄ FP18, ✄ HSHSJers, ✄ SC8, ✄ TM14, / Cup
01/2 BAP Update HSHS, ✄ HSHSJers
01/2 BT Pipes 36, 98, HSHS, ✄ ASJ, ✄ DM, ✄ Jers., ✄ S&J, ✄ GG, ✄ GR, ✄ TW, ✄ -HSHSJers.
02/3 Between the Pipes 8, 138, ✄ ASJ3, ✄ BM2, ✄ DM1, ✄ GUE18, ✄ GUJ18, ✄ GP1, ✄ GSJ18, ✄ HSHSJers 16, ✄ ITN18, ✄ I8, ✄ RB9
96/7 Bic.Sports Aces 9-C
97/8 Bicycle Q-Club
98/9 Bicycle.. K-S
95/6 Bicycle Sports Aces 9-Club
95/6 Bowman 70, BB8
01/2 Bowman 80
02/3 Bowman 2
98/9 Bowman's Best 8, F19, SB2
02/3 Calder 16, -CG 6, -HS 6
99/0 Challenger 8
94/5 Classic AR1
93/4 Cla. Images 4 Sport 101
93/4 Cla. Prospects 12
99/0 Crown Royale 78, IE-16, IG-14, CS-13, CCA-8, GC-5
00/1 Crown Royale 62, JotC-17, Land.-7, NP-11
01/2 Crown Royale 85, ASH, CW, JotC, LH
02/3 Crown Royale 56, -COA 6, -RP 7, ✄ GWDP 14, ✄ GWJ 10
93/4 Donruss 195
93/4 Donruss RR 10
94/5 Donruss 24, ES-2, MM-2
95/6 Donruss 149, BTP-5,D-4
96/7 Donruss 148, BTP-2, D-1
97/8 Donruss 126, BTP-2, ES-10
98/9 Donruss ES 13
96/7 Do. Canadian 46, LG-4
97/8 Do. Canadian 42, LG-3, SCS-24
95/6 Do. Elite 43, PW-3
96/7 Do. Elite 16, PW-8
97/8 Do. Elite 8, 137, BF-7, C-8, ✍ BF-7
97/8 Do. Preferred 16, 185, CG-2, PM-6, / Tin-10, WideTin 9
97/8 Do. Priority 7, 196, OD-7, PG-10, Post-24, Stamp-24
97/8 Do. Studio 20, S-4, P-20, ✍ Aut.
96/7 Duracell JB6
93/4 Durivage 5
98/9 Dynagon Ice 108, -IW 5, -PP 7, -TC 15
99/0 Dynagon Ice 114, 205, -ASP 13, -GM 2,7, -LotR 8
95/6 Edge Ice L11
01/2 eTopps 10
02/3 eTopps 6, -Intro
02/3 Exclusive 102, -EIS 7, -EA 11
02/3 First Edition 141, 330, 358, 380, 405H, ✄ Jers., ✄ DGJ 7, HSHSJers 24
94/5 Flair 92
96/7 Flair 52, HG-2
94/5 Fleer 111, N-2
96/7 Fleer 58, 145, 146
95/6 Fleer Metal 81
96/7 Fl. Picks F50-4, DL-3, FF-8
93/4 Fleer Ultra 357
93/4 Fleer Ultra WotF 2
94/5 Fleer Ultra 115, ARS-2, AW-2
95/6 Fleer Ultra 86, 186, 366, HS-5, PPM-3
96/7 Fl. Ultra 93
01/2 Heads Up 56, ASGUN 2, HD 17, RI 8, SS 12, / Bobble
02/3 Heads Up 70, -EIT 11, -ITN 13, -S 13, ✄ GWQ 17, ✄ GWQ 28
99/0 HoloGrFX 33
95/6 Hoyle / East. 7-Heart
02/3 In The Game-Used 41, 141, ✄ E15, ✄ F18, ✄ GP3, ✄ IE20, ✄ GUJ15, ✄ SJ15, ✄ T14
94/5 Kraft / KD, PB
95/6 Kraft / PS
96/7 Kraft / KD
97/8 Kraft / PB
98/9 Kraft / OML, / Post 2
99/0 Kraft / JELL-O, / PB
93/4 Leaf 345
94/5 Leaf 56, CP-9, GLR-1, GLS-8, LL-13
95/6 Leaf 66, RTTC-2
96/7 Leaf 6, SD-6, S-6
97/8 Leaf 7, 174, PD-6
94/5 L. Limited 70
95/6 L. Limited 18, SS-2
96/7 L. Limited 87, S-11
96/7 L. Preferred 81, LS-2, MM-2
97/8 Limited 74, 127, 149, 150, FG-2
96/7 Maggers 91
94/5 McDonald's McD-35
95/6 McDonald's McD-27
96/7 McDonald's McD-33
97/8 McDonald's McD-25
98/9 McDonald's McD17
00/1 McDonald's 20, GWJ-7, GSNF-4
01/2 McDonald's 24, -GSNF 4
02/3 McDonald's 23, -SLG 1, ✄ JP 9
96/7 Metal Univ. 86, AP-2, IC-1
99/0 Millenium 143, ✍ Aut. 143, ✄ J-25, ✄✍ J-25, ✄ JS-25
00/1 Mir Fetisov 33
96/7 NJER / Sharp
95/6 Cool Trade 18
98/9 NHL Power Play
92/3 O-Pee-Chee 59
01/2 O-Pee-Chee 3
02/3 O-Pee-Chee 3
98/9 OPC Chrome 20, SB2
97/8 Omega 127, 249, NSZ-7, S-7, TL-13
98/9 Omega 136, -CS 6, -EOP 13, -FTF 1, -Onl. 19, -PI 19, -Prism 12
99/0 Omega 133, 5ST-28, CC-12, EOP-11, NAAS-7, ✄ GWJ
98/9 Pacific 30, -CCA 6, -DI 12, -GCDC 18, -TC 15, -TW 1
99/0 Pacific 235, -CI 14, -GC 21, -ITCNF 10, -PAP 15, -TL 16
00/1 Pacific 232, IO-12, CCA-7, GCDC-18, ITC-7, NAS-7
01/2 Pacific 227, CCA 7, GCDC 12, IZ 12, NAAS 9, SC 11
02/3 Pacific 218, -CCA 8, -MA 11, -MI 5
02/3 Pacific Complete 465
97/8 Pacific CC 30, GS-10, GCDC-14, ITC-12,TC-14
97/8 Pa. Crown Roy. 73, FO-11
98/9 Pa. Crown Roy. 78, -CCA 7, -LL 7, -MP 13, -PotG 16, -PP 14
97/8 Pa. Dynagon 68, S-12, T-12, BKS-52, BKS-106
97/8 Pa. Invincible 76, FP-19, R-108
97/8 Pa. Paramount 101, GSL-11, CG-9, BN-12
98/9 Pa. Paramount 132, -GS 10, -HOFB 6, -IG 6, -TC 15
99/0 Pa. Paramount 131, GS-11, HOFB-7, IAd-14, IAI-16, PB-21
00/1 Pa. Paramount 142, ES-13, FF-21, GS-12, HOFB-8, SZ-7
97/8 Pa. Revolution 75, ASG-13, I-6, RTS-11, TC-14
98/9 Pa. Revolution 83, -ASG 5, -TPA 15, -NI 7, -Show. 21
01/2 PTC Collectors 6
02/3 PTC/ Les Gardiens 6
98/9 Panini Photocard [x2]
94/5 Panini Sticker 35
95/6 Panini Sticker 90
96/7 Panini Sticker 79
97/8 Panini Sticker 64, 124
98/9 Panini Sticker 67
99/0 Panini Sticker 79, 347
00/1 Panini Sticker 48
93/4 Parkhurst 380
94/5 Parkhurst 126, 278
95/6 Parkhurst 122, AS-6, CCB-11, GP-1, PP-32, ✍ Aut.
00/1 Parkhurst P-99
01/2 Parkhurst 98, ✄ PJ46, ✄ PS31, ✄ PSJ8, HSHSJers, ✄ M2, ✄ M16, ✄ M47, ✄ H9, ✄ T14, ✄ T28
02/3 Parkhurst 96, -HHV4, ✄ FP18, ✄ GJ43, ✄ SJ43, ✄ HSHSJers, ✄ MM4, ✄ MS2, ✄ TT5
02/3 Parkhurst Retro 70, ✄ RF18, ✄ RJ6, ✄ RSJ6, ✄ HSHSJers, ✄ RM9, ✄ VH3
94/5 Parkie SE seV8
94/5 Pinnacle 145, 462, GT-7
95/6 Pinnacle CS 1, M-2, R20-3
96/7 Pinnacle 92, M-4, TP-9
97/8 Pinnacle 43, M-3, TP1, P-7, / Tin 1
96/7 Pi. Be A Player SP-5
97/8 Pi. Be A Player 2, STP-11, ✍ Aut. 2
97/8 Pi. BeeHive 45, BHT-6
97/8 Pi. Certified 3, CT-1
97/8 Pi. Epix E8
95/6 Pi. FANtasy 19
97/8 Pi. Inside 7, IT-6, SU-2, S-4, / Can 2, LargeCan
96/7 Pi. Mint 23
97/8 Pi. Mint 16
95/6 Pi. Summit 27, GMC-2, ITC-1
96/7 Pi. Summit 114, ITC-8, U-16
97/8 Pi. Totally 3
97/8 Pi. Uncut 1
95/6 Pi. Zenith 12, ZT-2

96/7 Pi. Zenith 2, CS-15
95/6 Playoff 57, 275
96/7 Playoff 440
94/5 POG 284, 326
95/6 POG 167
94/5 Post
97/8 Pi. Post 8
93/4 Power Play 374
93/4 Premier 401
94/5 Premier 83, 190, 380, 470, OF-14
00/1 Premier Plus 36, MB11, PT5, WP2, ✍ PS
99/0 Prism 79, CA-12, SGDC-13
00/1 Pr. Stock 57, AC-14, EA-13, Res. 14, PS-31, PSS-17
01/2 Pr. Stock 55, GR 7, -PS 44
02/3 Pr. Stock Reserve -ICS 13, ✄ 129
00/1 PS Titanium 54, 3SS-4, NAAS-7, ✄ GUG-105
01/2 PS Titanium 82, SK 12, TSS 5, ✄ DSJ 68
01/2 PS Titanium Draft ✄ 51
02/3 Private Stock Titanium 62, -MM 5
95/6 Pro Magnet 31, IC2
02/3 Quest for the Cup 56, -RTC 9
99/0 Revolution 84, IS-7, NI-12, O-13, SS-21, / CSC 84
00/1 Revolution 85, HD-20, II-13, NI-15, SM-16
90/1 Score 439
92/3 Score 480
93/4 Score 648
95/6 Score 25, 323
96/7 Score 10, NW-2, SD-1, / Promo 10
97/8 Score 30, 269, NW-14
97/8 Score NJer. 16
94/5 Select 78
95/6 Select CE 24, GT-9
96/7 Select CE 6, F-1
90/1 7th..Sketch LHJMQ 222
91/2 7th...Sketch LHJMQ 1
95/6 SR Tetrad F6
95/6 SR Tetrad Autobilia 95
00/1 Signature 164, HSHS, F-18, ✍ Aut. 139, ✄ J-25,✄ HSHSJers
01/2 Signature C-24, ✄ FP18, ✄ GUE34, ✄ GJ35, ✄ GSJ35, ✄ ITN34, ✄ IG1, ✄ TM17
02/3 Signature Series GS-51, ✄ DW6, ✄ FJ18, ✄ SGJ15, ✄ TQ7, ✄ TM9
95/6 SBx Emotion 94, Xci-18
95/6 SBx Impact 90, D-11
96/7 SBx Impact 68
02/3 Slam Card
94/5 SP 63
95/6 SP 79, E18, FX12
96/7 SP 86, SF-3, SF-5, ✍ Aut.
97/8 SP Authentic 87, I14, ✍ SotT
98/9 SP Authentic 48, SS13, SO13
99/0 SP Authentic 49, HR4, SS7
00/1 SP Authentic 53, PS5, SP4, SS4, ✍ SotT, ✍ SotTD, ✍ SotTT
01/2 SP Authentic 48, 102, ✄ PP, ✍ SotT, ✍ SotTD, ✍ SotTT
02/3 SP Authentic 53, ✍ SotT, ✍ SotTD, ✄ SP, ✄ TP
00/1 SP GU 36, ✄ TotG, ✄ C, ✄ P
01/2 SP GU 31, ✄ AF, ✄ AFD, ✄✍ IS, ✄✍ IS2, ✄ Patch, ✄✍ PatchSig, ✄ PatchC, ✄✍ PatchCSig, ✄ PatchT
02/3 SP Game-Used Edition 28, ✄ AF, ✄ CF (x2), ✄ PC, ✄ PH, ✍ Sig
02/3 Sports Vault 70
96/7 SPx 25
97/8 SPx 27, DV, ✍ DVS
99/0 SPx 85, ✄ WM
00/1 SPx 37, 88, X8, S4, ✄ WM, ✄✍ WM
01/2 SPx 37, 87, ✄ TT
02/3 SPx 43, 93, ✄ WM, ✄ M
98/9 SPx Finite 46, 105, 161, 176
98/9 SPx Prospects 35, H17, L21, PS5
00/1 Stadion 65, 156
99/0 Stadium 16, Chrome 15, Big 9, CA14, GC2
00/1 Stadium 16, BT13, CA2, ✍ CO2, GS1, ✍ LS2, SF17
01/2 Stadium 1, G23, P3, ✄ SCS, ✄ SCSD (x2), ✄ SCST
02/3 Stadium 8, -PSH-10, -W-3, ✄ FC4, ✄ FC5, ✄ PC4, ✄ PC5
95/6 SLU
97/8 SLU
98/9 SLU
95/6 Super Sticker 70, DC-16
96/7 Team Out!
92/3 Topps 513
95/6 Topps 9, 325, M21, PF6, YS2
98/9 Topps 20, L6, M12, SB2
99/0 Topps 20, AT2, IM11, PM6, SC14, TW15
00/1 Topps 131, 326, TC8, HM1, OTG11
01/2 Topps 3, OTG21
02/3 Topps 3, HHU1, OTG17
99/0 To. Chrome 20, AT2, IM11, PM6
00/1 To. Chrome 98, 163, TC8, HM1
01/2 To. Chrome 3
02/3 T. Chrome 3
94/5 Topps Finest 71
95/6 To. Finest 45, 178
98/9 To. Finest 35, C11, M21-24, -Big 3
95 Topps Finest Bronze 12
98/9 T. Gold Label 10
99/0 To. Gold Label 24, QC5
00/1 To. Gold Label 71, BTM4, B1, ✄ GLJ
00/1 To. Heritage 2, 231, HH6
01/2 To. Heritage 46, 128, ✄ GWJ
02/3 To. Heritage 19, 115, ✄ CC, ✄ CCB
02/3 T. Limited 3
96/7 Topps Picks 27, FT3, ID6
99/0 To. Prmr. Plus 66, CAC5, IG3, PT9
01/2 To.Reserve 40, ✄ TR
92/3 To. Stadium 233
93/4 To. Stadium 352
94/5 To. Stadium 119, 186, 264
95/6 To. Stadium 85, GT5, N6
93/4 TSC Members Only 46
95/6 TSC Members Only 29
00/1 To. Stars 17, 126, P5, WF10
95/6 T. Super Skills 80
02/3 T. Total 293, TTC18, TT15
98/9 UD Choice 116, 245, BH7, SQ23
00/1 UD Heroes 149, PI2, SS7, TM6, ✄ GT, ✄ GC
01/2 UD PlayMakers Ltd 58, ✄ PCJ, / PM
00/1 UD Reserve 52, GG7, PP4, BT7
02/3 UD Superstars 144
98/9 UD3 36, 96, 156
00/1 Ultimate Mem. ✍ U-25, ✄A8-7, ✄A8-8, ✄G-18, ✄PJ-3, ✄J-25, ✄Jer. 23, ✄MO-3, ✄S-25, ✄TM-30, ✄GM-14
01/2 Ultimate Mem. ✄ BAPL, ✄ CT, ✄ Emb., ✄ Jers., ✄ S&J, ✄ ITN, ✄ NP, ✄ PP, ✄ RA, ✄ WTF
02/3 Ultimate Memorabilia ✄ A8, ✄ Emb, ✄ FS (x2), ✄ GUJ, ✄ GUSJ, ✄ ITN, ✄ LA, ✄ MO, ✄ NP, ✄ RAT, ✄ SCD (x3), ✄ UV
99/0 Ult. Victory 50, FF7, NW10, S7, TV6
92/3 Upper Deck 408
93/4 Upper Deck 334
94/5 Upper Deck 96, H12, H29, IG11, SP-43
95/6 Upper Deck 211, AS-6, F-15, H-5, R57, SE-135
96/7 Upper Deck 91, X18, HH10,LS5, SS12A
97/8 Upper Deck 300, SG4, S30, T10A
98/9 Upper Deck 118, FT4, LS5, P6, ✄ GJ6
99/0 Upper Deck 77, 148, AS19, CT24, N7, SS15, UD9, ✄ GJ
00/1 Upper Deck 335, EC7, GA8, L6, P6, SS13, TT2, ✄ GJ, ✄ DGJ, ✍ SG
01/2 Upper Deck 221, 332, 411, FC8, GL3, LL5, SS1, -PatchL, ✄ PoaN, ✄ PoaND, ✄ SCFJers., ✄ SCFJersD, ✄ SupSwe, ✄ TendThr, ✄✍ SigJers
02/3 Upper Deck 107, 190, -GG10, -LL8, -SA8, ✄ FF, ✄ PP, ✄ PN, ✄ GJ, ✄✍ SGJ, ✄ PW
95/6 UD ASG MVP29
02/3 UD Artistic 52, R52, CG22, GD3, ✄ AT, ✄ SS, ✍ / Art
94/5 UD Be A Player R58, R130, ✍ 3
96/7 UD Black Diam. 134
97/8 UD Black Diam. 122, PC24
98/9 UD Black Diam. 50, M21, WF15
99/0 UD Black Diam. 51, D10, DS8, ✄ APOH
00/1 UD Black Diam. 33, 89, FP7, IC4
99/0 UD C. Legends 63
01/2 UD Challenge 50, BB6, ✄ T200, ✄✍ T200S
02/3 UD Classic 57, ET10, PS6, ✄ HR (x2)
95/6 UD CC 204
96/7 UD CC 144, 306, 322, UD21, S24
97/8 UD Coll. Choice 141, SQ50, S3, W20
01/2 UD Collectors
97/8 UD Diam. Vision 5
02/3 UD Foundations 58
98/9 UD G. Reserve 118
99/0 UD G. Reserve 77, 148
01/2 UD Honor Roll 12, 42, ✄ GAJ, ✄ HS, ✄ PPM
02/3 UD Honor 41, -SG18, ✄ GA, ✍ SC
96/7 UD Ice 92
97/8 UD Ice 7, IC7
00/1 UD Ice 24, IC4, FP7, ✄ IGJ
01/2 UD Ice 27, ✍ CCA
00/1 UD Legends 76, 79, EG5, LC2, ✍ ES, ✄ LGJ
01/2 UD Mask 118, 181, ✄ CG, ✄✍ SP, ✄ MB, ✄ PM, ✄ StS, ✄ VC, / Mask
02/3 UD Mask 50, 51, 91, ✄ CW, ✄ GG, ✄ MM, ✄ BM, ✄ NB, ✄ PW, ✄ SS, ✄ VC, / Mask, ✍ Mask
98/9 UD MVP 117, F9
99/0 UD MVP 115, W9, LL2, MVP9
00/1 UD MVP 106, MM5, M10, VC6, ✄ CG
01/2 UD MVP 110, -MM1, -MT14, -VC4, ✄ GS
02/3 UD MVP 108, MM4
99/0 UD MVP Cup 104, CP6, GM6, PH7, SC10
99/0 UD Ovation 33, LP17, ST8, APOH
02/3 UD Piece 51, 101, AC18
95/6 UD Post 2
99/0 UD PowerDeck 14
01/2 UD Premier 32, ✄ S, ✄ D
02/3 UD Premier 33, ✄ NHLP, ✄ Jers, ✄ Patch, ✄ Sig (x2)
00/1 UD Pros&Prosp. 52, CR6, PM7
99/0 UD Retro 45, DR2, TC2
02/3 UD Rookie 60, 107
01/2 UD SCup Champs 78, ✄ S, ✄ G
01/2 UD Top Shelf 25, -ASGN, ✄ P, ✄ S
02/3 UD Top Shelf 52, ✄ CP, ✄ HH, ✄ M, ✄ ST, ✄ SS
00/1 UD Vintage 211, 221, 222, UD2, NH14, S4B
01/2 UD Vintage 149, 157, 267, 270
02/3 UD Vintage 152, 278, 298, 316, T39
97/8 Valu-net, ✍ Aut.
00/1 Vanguard 57, CF-7, HV-19, IF-12, VP-14
01/2 Vanguard 56, EMW 4, IF 7, SW 11, VT 5, ✄ DGM 50
02/3 Vanguard 60, -EMW 9, SW 7, VT 5, ✄ GWJ 27
99/0 Victory 165, 166, 346, 386
00/1 Victory 134, 135, 309
01/2 Victory 205, 215, 402
02/3 Victory 127, -NP8
01/2 Waving the Flag 6
99/0 WGretzky 100, EG10
97/8 Zenith 21, CTC-11, ZT-8, Z5

BRODEUR, RICHARD
78/9 Dernière Heure
82/3 Dernière Heure
83/4 Esso Stars
01/2 Fleer Greats 48, ✍ Aut.
83/4 Funmate Puffy 1 [w/]
84/5 Kellogg's 16
86/7 Kraft Sports 62
82/3 McDonald's Les Étoiles 2
79/0 O-Pee-Chee 176
81/2 O-Pee-Chee 331
82/3 O-Pee-Chee 339
82/3 O-Pee-Chee 340
83/4 O-Pee-Chee 346
84/5 O-Pee-Chee 314
85/6 O-Pee-Chee 180
86/7 O-Pee-Chee 246
87/8 O-Pee-Chee 257
82/3 OPC/Topps Sticker 7
82/3 OPC/Topps Sticker 247
83/4 OPC/Topps Sticker 276
83/4 OPC/Topps Sticker 277
84/5 OPC Sticker 277
86/7 OPC Sticker 98-228
87/8 OPC Sticker 189-50
75/6 OPC WHA 44
76/7 OPC WHA 12
77/8 OPC WHA 38
87/8 Panini Sticker 340
80/1 Pepsi Bottle Cap
82/3 Post [Vanc.]
88/9 ProCards / Binghampton
72/3 Québec Nordiques
73/4 Québec Nordiques
76/7 Québec Nordiques
76/7 Québ. / Antoinette
84/5 7-Eleven
83/4 Souhaits Keychain [Canucks]
79/0 Topps 176
00/1 UD Legends 127, 128
83/4 Vachon 101-21
83/4 Vachon 101-94
80/1 VANC
80/1 VANC / Silverwood
81/2 VANC
81/2 VANC / Silverwood
82/3 VANC
83/4 VANC
84/5 VANC
85/6 VANC
86/7 VANC
87/8 VANC / Shell

BRODIE, ANDREW
89/0 7th..Sketch OHL 68
90/1 7th..Sketch OHL 79

BRODMAN, MARIO
93 Semic Sticker 120

BRODNICKE, RICHARD
94/5 DEL 350

BRODZIAK, KYLE
01/2 Moose Jaw Warriors 6

BROMLEY, GARY
74/5 BUFF
74/5 Loblaws
74/5 O-Pee-Chee 7
75/6 O-Pee-Chee 368
79/0 O-Pee-Chee 167
80/1 O-Pee-Chee 330
77/8 OPC WHA 45
74/5 Topps 7
79/0 Topps 167
78/9 VANC / Royal Bank
79/0 VANC / Royal Bank
80/1 VANC
80/1 VANC / Silverwood

BROMS, ANDERS
89/0 Semic Elitserien 143

BRONILLA, RICH
98/9 Huntington Blizzard
00/1 Kudos 72
02/3 London Knights
92/3 Ottawa 67's
95/6 Slapshot 260

BRONSARD, CHRISTIAN
98/9 Manitoba Moose

BROOKBANK, LEIGH
91/2 Air Canada SJHL B30
92/3 MPS SJHL 157

BROOKBANK, SHELDON
02/3 Grand Rapids Griffins

BROOKBANK, WADE
98/9 Anchorage Aces
01/2 Grand Rapids Griffins

BROOKE, BOB
90/1 Bowman 79
86/7 MINS / 7-Eleven 11
87/8 MINS
88/9 MINS / ADA
85/6 O-Pee-Chee 202
86/7 OPC/Topps 48
87/8 OPC/Topps 64
88/9 OPC/Topps 61
90/1 OPC/Topps 105
89/0 O-Pee-Chee 215
86/7 OPC Sticker 219-89
87/8 Panini Sticker 301
88/9 Panini Sticker 91
89 Semic Sticker 171

BROOKS, ALEX
02/3 Albany River Rats

BROOKS, BRENDAN
02/3 Peoria Rivermen
98/9 Quad City Mallards
99/0 Quad City Mallards

BROOKS, CHRIS
92/3 W. Michigan Broncos
93/4 W. Michigan Broncos

BROOKS, GORD
74/5 Loblaws
74/5 WASH

BROOKS, HERB
87/8 MINS
80 Olympic USA
94/5 SR Miracle 41,42, ✍ 42

BROOKS, JASON
95/6 Slapshot 171

BROOKS, MARK
92/3 Oshawa Generals

BROOKS, ROSS
74/5 Loblaws
74/5 O-Pee-Chee 376

BROOKS, W.
28/9 Paulins Candy 80

BROPHY, JOHN
91/2 Hampton Roads
92/3 Hampton Roads
93/4 Hampton Roads
94/5 Hampton Roads
95/6 Hampton Roads
96/7 Hampton Roads
97/8 Hampton Roads
98/9 Hampton Roads
98/9 Hampton Roads
99/0 Hampton Roads
84/5 TORO
87/8 TORO / P.L.A.Y. 28
88/9 TORO / P.L.A.Y. 28

BROS, MICHAL
95/6 APS 120
96/7 APS 278
97/8 APS 33
97/8 DS 65
98/9 DS 81
99/0 DS 151
00/1 DS 11, WCH-11
01/2 DS 13
96/7 DS Sticker 181
97/8 DS Sticker 180
98/9 OFS 110, 432
99/0 OFS 102, 472
00/1 OFS 306
01/2 OFS 15
95/6 Upper Deck 541

BROSSART, WILLIE
74/5 Loblaws
74/5 Loblaws Update
73/4 TORO

BROSSEAU, DAVID
00/1 Austin Ice Bats
96/7 Charlotte Checkers
97/8 Charlotte Checkers
98/9 Charlotte Checkers

BROST, TODD
92 C.O.A. Winter Olympics 191
90/1 Canada Nationals 12
91/2 Canada Nationals
93/4 Canada Nationals
93/4 Fleer Ultra 459
94/5 Huntington Blizzard
93/4 Power Play 479
93/4 Premier - Canada 8
92/3 Salt Lake G'Eagles

BROTEN, AARON
90/1 Bowman 185
91/2 Bowman 162
81/2 COLR
94/5 Minnesota G'Gophers
83/4 NJER
84/5 NJER
86/7 NJER / S.O.B.E.R.
88/9 NJER / Caretta
89/0 NJER
89/0 NJER / Caretta
82/3 O-Pee-Chee 136
83/4 O-Pee-Chee 227
85/6 O-Pee-Chee 249
87/8 OPC/Topps 46
88/9 OPC/Topps 138
90/1 OPC/Topps 118
89/0 OPC/Topps 180
90/1 OPC Premier 10
83/4 OPC/Topps Sticker 226
85/6 OPC Sticker 62-189
87/8 OPC Sticker 62
88/9 OPC Sticker 76
89/0 opcSticker 88-229
87/8 Panini Sticker 78
88/9 Panini Sticker 271
89/0 Panini Sticker 254
90/1 Panini Sticker 247
91/2 Panini Sticker 105
90/1 Pro Set 131, 530
90/1 QUÉB / Petro-Canada
90/1 Score 162, 21T
90/1 Sco. Hot Cards 72
91/2 Score 307
91/2 Score CAN 250
91/2 Score CAN 337
90/1 TORO
90/1 Upper Deck 210

BROTEN, NEAL
90/1 Bowman 178
91/2 Bowman 121
92/3 Bowman 81
94/5 DALL / Cap
96/7 DALL / Southwest
94/5 Donruss 67
95/6 Donruss 259
94/5 Flair 39
01/2 Fleer Greats 71, ✍ Aut.
01/2 Fleer Legacy 29
95/6 Fleer Metal 82
92/3 Fleer Ultra 89
93/4 Fleer Ultra 296
94/5 Fleer Ultra 48
95/6 Fleer Ultra 87, 187
88/9 Frito Lay
83/4 Funmate Puffy 13 [w/]
94/5 Leaf 246
95/6 Leaf 286, RTTC-7
94/5 Minnesota G'Gophers
81/2 MINS
82/3 MINS
83/4 MINS
84/5 MINS
84/5 MINS / 7-Eleven 1
85/6 MINS
85/6 MINS / 7-Eleven 6
86/7 MINS / 7-Eleven 1
87/8 MINS
88/9 MINS / ADA
82/3 O-Pee-Chee 164
83/4 O-Pee-Chee 168
84/5 O-Pee-Chee 96
85/6 OPC/Topps 124
86/7 OPC/Topps 99
87/8 OPC/Topps 11
88/9 OPC/Topps 144
90/1 OPC/Topps 90
91/2 O-Pee-Chee 420
92/3 O-Pee-Chee 62
89/0 OPC/Topps 87
82/3 OPC/Topps Sticker 190
83/4 OPC/Topps Sticker 120
84/5 OPC Sticker 46
85/6 OPC Sticker 40-169
86/7 OPC Sticker 166
87/8 OPC Sticker 52-193
88/9 OPC Sticker 201-72
89/0 opcSticker 202
97/8 Pa. Dynagon BKS-28
87/8 Panini Sticker 297
88/9 Panini Sticker 92
89/0 Panini Sticker 107
90/1 Panini Sticker 261
91/2 Panini Sticker 107
92/3 Panini Sticker 89
93/4 Panini Sticker 272
95/6 Panini Sticker 80
91/2 Parkhurst 80
92/3 Parkhurst 313
93/4 Parkhurst 54
94/5 Parkhurst 53
95/6 Parkhurst 120
91/2 Pinnacle 161
92/3 Pinnacle 209
93/4 Pinnacle 334
94/5 Pinnacle 293
95/6 Pinnacle 117
95/6 Playoff 276
94/5 POG 76
95/6 POG 157
93/4 Power Play 57
93/4 Premier 131
94/5 Premier 74
90/1 Pro Set 132
91/2 Pro Set 112
91/2 Pro Set Platinum 188
90/1 Score 144
91/2 Score 280
91/2 Score 307
91/2 Score CAN 337
91/2 Score CAN 500
92/3 Score 32
93/4 Score 166
94/5 Score 113
95/6 Score 265
89 Semic Sticker 165
91 Semic Sticker 140
94/5 SR Miracle 3,4, ✍ 3,4
94/5 SR Miracle 49
95/6 SBx Emotion 95
95/6 SBx Impact 91
84/5 Topps 72
92/3 Topps 309
01/2 To. Chrome -CA5, ✍ CA5
91/2 To. Stadium 99
92/3 To. Stadium 90
93/4 To. Stadium 28
01/2 T/O Archives 15, -Seat
90/1 Upper Deck 48
91/2 Upper Deck 232
92/3 Upper Deck 206
93/4 Upper Deck 109, SP-34
94/5 Upper Deck 273, SP-18
95/6 Upper Deck 114
95/6 UD Be A Player 42, ✍ S42
95/6 UD CC 285
96/7 UD CC 152
01/2 UD Legends ✄ M

BROTEN, PAUL
90/1 Bowman 224
92/3 Bowman 265
97/8 Cincinnati Cyclones
94/5 DALL / Southwest
94/5 DALL / Cap
98/9 DEL 110
92/3 Fleer Ultra 134, 353
94/5 Leaf 409
94/5 Minnesota G'Gophers
89/0 NYRA / Marine
92/3 O-Pee-Chee 364
91/2 Parkhurst 336
93/4 Parkhurst 324
94/5 Parkhurst 60
92/3 Pinnacle 212
94/5 Pinnacle 433
94/5 Premier 261
89/0 ProCards IHL 28
90/1 Score 41T
92/3 Score 353
93/4 Score 297
93/4 Score 658
92/3 Topps 355
91/2 To. Stadium 376
92/3 To. Stadium 109
91/2 Upper Deck 550
92/3 Upper Deck 148
93/4 Upper Deck 468
94/5 Upper Deck 15

BROUGHTON, G.
12/3 Imperial 39

BROUSSEAU, JASON
94/5 Johnstown Chiefs 2
90/1 7th..Sketch LHJMQ 57
91/2 7th...Sketch LHJMQ 230
90 7th..Sketch Mem.Cup 67

BROUSSEAU, PAUL
93/4 Cla. Prospects 152
99/0 Louisville Panthers
00/1 Louisville Panthers
97/8 Pi. Inside 141
90/1 7th..Sketch LHJMQ 177
91/2 7th...Sketch LHJMQ 206

BROUWER, TROY
02/3 Moose Jaw Warriors

BROWER, SCOTT
89/0 ProCards IHL 36
90/1 ProCards 302
93/4 Sisu 256

BROWN, ADAM
34-43 BeeHive-1 [Detr.]
45-64 BeeHive-2 [Chic.]
51/2 Parkhurst 30

BROWN, ANDREW
01/2 Belleville Bulls
99/0 Guelph Storm

BROWN, ANDY
72/3 Eddie Sargent 83
74/5 OPC WHA 58

BROWN, ANDY?
94/5 Huntington Blizzard

BROWN, ARNIE
64-67 BeeHive-3 [NYRa.]
64/5 Coke/Sprite [NYRa.]
65/6 Coca-Cola
70/1 Colgate 76
70/1 Dad's Cookies
70/1 Eddie Sargent 116
71/2 Eddie Sargent 57
72/3 Eddie Sargent 72
70/1 Esso Power Player
74/5 Loblaws
68/9 O-Pee-Chee 68
69/0 O-Pee-Chee 34
70/1 O-Pee-Chee 66
71/2 O-Pee-Chee 14
72/3 O-Pee-Chee 144
73/4 O-Pee-Chee 225
95/6 Parkie 66-67 86
94/5 Parkie Tall 97
68/9 Shirriff / NYRa. 6
64/5 Topps 34
65/6 Topps 90
66/7 Topps 90
66/7 Topps / Test 48
67/8 Topps 89
68/9 Topps 68
69/0 Topps 34
70/1 Topps 66
71/2 Topps 14
72/3 Topps 111
71/2 Toronto Sun Photo

BROWN, BOB
95/6 Tri-City Americans 27

BROWN, BOB**
52/3 Anonymous 15

BROWN, BOBBY
00/1 Austin Ice Bats
02/3 Louisiana Ice Gators

BROWN, BOBBY*
95/6 Brandon Wheat Kings
98/9 Dayton Bombers
98/9 Dayton Bombers
98/9 EBK ECHL All-Star
97/8 Guildford Flames
96/7 Roanoke Express 7
92 7th...Sketch Awards 19
94/5 Slapshot Memorial 36

BROWN, BRAD
00/1 BAP Mem. 475, ✄ T-15
01/2 BAP Update ✄ TC9
93/4 Classic 100
94/5 Classic 16
95/6 Classic 90
94/5 Classic 4 Sport 132
94/5 Cla. Images 4 Sport 109
98/9 Dynagon Ice 93
96/7 Fredericton Canadiens
99/0 Millenium 55, ✍ Aut. 55
98/9 Omega 57
97/8 Pa. Invincible R-100
91/2 7th...Sketch OHL 53
94/5 Sig. Rookies FF2, ✍ FF2
94/5 SR Gold Standard 79
93/4 Slapshot / North Bay 1
93/4 Slapshot / North Bay 25
94/5 Slapshot / North Bay 4
00/1 To. Gold Label 99
97/8 Upper Deck 296
98/9 Upper Deck 292
98/9 UD G. Reserve 292

BROWN, CAL
90/1 ProCards 171

BROWN, CAM
88/9 Brandon Wheat Kings
89/0 Brandon Wheat Kings
94/5 Erie Panthers
90/1 ProCards 336
91/2 ProCards 598

BROWN, CONNY
34-43 BeeHive-1 [Detr.]

BROWN, CRAIG
96/7 Pensacola Ice Pilots
97/8 Pensacola Ice Pilots
93/4 W. Michigan Broncos

BROWN, CURTIS
99/0 Aurora 15
99/0 BAP Mem. 243
00/1 BAP Mem. 332
95/6 Do. Elite WJ 11
99/0 Dynagon Ice 29
96/7 Fl. Picks 150
95/6 Fleer Ultra 333
96/7 Fl. Ultra 14, UR-3
99/0 Kraft / PB
96/7 L. Preferred 142
96/7 Metal Univ. 172
02/3 O-Pee-Chee 249
98/9 OPC Chrome 185
98/9 Omega 21
99/0 Omega 26
98/9 Pacific 104
99/0 Pacific 35
00/1 Pacific 49
02/3 Pacific 39
02/3 Pacific Complete 243
99/0 Pa. Paramount 26
00/1 Pa. Paramount 27
00/1 Panini Sticker 19
02/3 Parkhurst 197
96/7 Pinnacle 227
97/8 Pi. Be A Player 53, ✍ Aut. 53
96/7 Pi. Summit 185
96/7 Pi. Zenith 145
95/6 Prince Albert Raiders
99/0 Prism 18
99/0 Revolution 17
94/5 Sig. Rookies 63, ✍ 63
96/7 SP 14
02/3 Sports Vault 24
98/9 Topps 185
99/0 Topps 86
00/1 Topps 137
02/3 Topps 249
99/0 To. Chrome 86
02/3 T. Limited 249
02/3 T. Total 227
95/6 Upper Deck 531
96/7 Upper Deck 226
97/8 Upper Deck 230
99/0 Upper Deck 190
00/1 Upper Deck 250
01/2 Upper Deck 20, ✄ NG
02/3 Upper Deck 264
99/0 UD G. Reserve 190
00/1 UD MVP 21, CB
99/0 UD MVP Cup 24
00/1 UD Vintage 43
01/2 UD Vintage 33, 35
02/3 UD Vintage 34
00/1 Victory 31
01/2 Victory 37
99/0 WGretzky 25

BROWN, DAN
89/0 7th..Sketch OHL 99

BROWN, DAVE
88/9 EDMO
88/9 EDMO / Action 145
90/1 EDMO / IGA
94/5 Leaf 428
88/9 Panini Sticker 319
90/1 Panini/EDM 3
86/7 PHIL
91/2 PHIL / J.C. Penney
92/3 PHIL / UD Sheet
92/3 PHIL / UD Sheet
92/3 PHIL / J.C. Penney
93/4 PHIL / Sheet
93/4 PHIL / J.C. Penney
94/5 PHIL / Sheet
90/1 Pro Set 440
91/2 Pro Set 452
81/2 Saskatoon Blades
91/2 Score 84T
91/2 Score CAN 634
83/4 Springfield Indians 8

BROWN, DAVE
02/3 Fleer Throwbacks 32, 8SO, ✄ 8SO, ✍ Aut.

BROWN, DOUG
91/2 Bowman 285
92/3 Bowman 126
93/4 Donruss 258
94/5 Donruss 213
93/4 Fleer Ultra 393
95 Globe 114
93/4 Leaf 378
94/5 Leaf 116
00/1 Mir Fetisov 30
88/9 NJER / Caretta
89/0 NJER
89/0 NJER / Caretta
90/1 NJER
88/9 OPC/Topps 115
90/1 OPC/Topps 117
91/2 O-Pee-Chee 42
92/3 O-Pee-Chee 333
89/0 O-Pee-Chee 242
88/9 OPC Sticker 80-209
88/9 OPC Sticker 23
98/9 Pacific 187
99/0 Pacific 134
00/1 Pacific 144
97/8 Pa. Invincible R-67
88/9 Panini Sticker 272
90/1 Panini Sticker 67
93/4 Parkhurst 424
94/5 Parkie SE135
91/2 Pinnacle 363
94/5 Pinnacle 197
96/7 Pi. Be A Player 43, ✍ Aut. 43
93/4 PITT / Foodland 7
93/4 Power Play 411
94/5 Premier 263
90/1 Pro Set 163
91/2 Pro Set 138
91/2 Score 163
91/2 Score CAN 163
92/3 Score 118
93/4 Score 582
94/5 Score 15
95/6 Score 193
97/8 Score Detr. 13
94 Semic 117
92 Semic Sticker 165
92/3 Topps 139
95/6 Topps 81, 8PL
98/9 To. Finest 10
91/2 To. Stadium 47
92/3 To. Stadium 331
98/9 UD Choice RW10
90/1 Upper Deck 159
91/2 Upper Deck 214
93/4 Upper Deck 459
94/5 Upper Deck 422
95/6 Upper Deck 79
98/9 Upper Deck 267
94/5 UD Be A Player ✍ 28
95/6 UD CC 47
98/9 UD G. Reserve 267
98/9 UD MVP 76

BROWN, DUSTIN
01/2 Guelph Storm
01/2 Guelph Storm M-Cup

BROWN, GEORGE ALLAN
34-43 BeeHive-1 [Mont.]
37/8 O-Pee-Chee 157

BROWN, GEORGE V.
83 HHOF Postcard L2
83&87 HHOF 152

BROWN, GREG
90/1 BUFF / Blue Shield
90/1 BUFF / Campbell's
98/9 DEL 94
99/0 Eishockey 120
95/6 Leaf Elit Set 287
90/1 OPC Premier 11
90/1 Pro Set 590
91/2 ProCards 18
91/2 Rochester Americans DD
91/2 Rochester Americans GL
91/2 Rochester Americans WPC
92/3 Rochester Americans DD
92/3 Rochester Americans WPC
93/4 San Diego Gulls
90/1 Score 96T
91/2 Score CAN 518
95/6 UD Elitserien 176

BROWN, IVAN
95/6 Guildford Flames 28

BROWN, JAMIE
95/6 Halifax Moosehead
96/7 Halifax Moosehead
96/7 Halifax Moosehead

BROWN, JASON
91/2 Air Canada SJHL B46
92/3 MPS SJHL 18

BROWN, JEFF R.
90/1 Bowman 25
91/2 Bowman 385
92/3 Bowman 247
97/8 CARO / Sprint
93/4 Donruss 293
93/4 Donruss 499
94/5 Donruss 109
95/6 Donruss 183
95/6 Do. Elite 78
93/4 EA Sports 121
94/5 Flair 188
94/5 Fleer 222
95/6 Fleer Metal 148
96/7 Fl. Picks 64
92/3 Fleer Ultra 183
93/4 Fleer Ultra 223
94/5 Fleer Ultra 221
95/6 Fleer Ultra 165
96/7 Fl. Ultra 72
96/7 HART / Kids Club
95/6 Hoyle / West. 6-Heart
89/0 Kraft 28
93/4 Leaf 29
94/5 Leaf 247
95/6 Leaf 245
94/5 L. Limited 18
96/7 Metal Univ. 65
88/9 O-Pee-Chee 201
90/1 OPC/Topps 295
91/2 O-Pee-Chee 222
89/0 OPC/Topps 28
88/9 OPC Sticker 192
89/0 opcSticker 193
98/9 Pacific 438
97/8 Pa. Dynagon BKS-16
98/9 Pa. Paramount 243
88/9 Panini Sticker 349
89/0 Panini Sticker 325
90/1 Panini Sticker 274
91/2 Panini Sticker 23
92/3 Panini Sticker 25
93/4 Panini Sticker 165
94/5 Panini Sticker 152
95/6 Panini Sticker 297
96/7 Panini Sticker 27
91/2 Parkhurst 156
93/4 Parkhurst 173
94/5 Parkhurst 244, V45
95/6 Parkhurst 365
91/2 Pinnacle 72
92/3 Pinnacle 13
93/4 Pinnacle 39
94/5 Pinnacle 34
95/6 Pinnacle 29
96/7 Pinnacle 12
97/8 Pi. Be A Player 89, ✍ Aut. 89
95/6 Playoff 206
96/7 Playoff 396
94/5 POG 313
94/5 POG / Western 17
95/6 POG 276
93/4 Power Play 207
93/4 Premier 363
93/4 Premier 381
94/5 Premier 272, 487
90/1 Pro Set 260
91/2 Pro Set 212
92/3 Pro Set 158
91/2 Pro Set Platinum 114
85/6 QUÉB
85/6 QUÉB / Gene. Foods
85/6 QUÉB / McDonald's
86/7 QUÉB
86/7 QUÉB / Gene. Foods
86/7 QUÉB / McDonald's
87/8 QUÉB / Gene. Foods
88/9 QUÉB
88/9 QUÉB / Gene. Foods
89/0 QUÉB
89/0 QUÉB / Gene. Foods
89/0 QUÉB / Police
90/1 Score 41
91/2 Score 276
91/2 Score CAN 496
92/3 Score 220
93/4 Score 194
95/6 Score 23
96/7 Score 87
94/5 Select 110
95/6 SBx Emotion 177
95/6 SBx Impact 166
96/7 SBx Impact 51
94/5 SP 123
89/0 SLOU / Kodak
90/1 SLOU / Kodak
91/2 SLOU
84/5 Sudbury Wolves
85/6 Sudbury Wolves
95/6 Super Sticker 126
96/7 Team Out!
92/3 Topps 174
95/6 Topps 268
91/2 To. Stadium 148
92/3 To. Stadium 263
93/4 To. Stadium 188
93/4 To. Stadium - Finest 2
94/5 TSC Members Only 23
90/1 Upper Deck 191
91/2 Upper Deck 211
93/4 Upper Deck 130, SP-135
94/5 Upper Deck 34, SP-81
95/6 Upper Deck 352, SE-84
96/7 Upper Deck 73
95/6 UD CC 301
96/7 UD CC 120
94/5 VANC
95/6 VANC / Abalene 8

BROWN, JEFF*
95/6 Bowman P5
98 Bowman 4
98 Bowman Chrome 4
99/0 Charlotte Checkers
95/6 Classic 96
98/9 Hartford Wolf Pack
94/5 Slapshot / Sarnia 21
95/6 Slapshot 347, 439

BROWN, JEREMY
99/0 Providence Bruins
00/1 Providence Bruins
92/3 W. Michigan Broncos
93/4 W. Michigan Broncos

BROWN, JERRY
34-43 BeeHive-1 [Detr.]

BROWN, JIM
94/5 Hampton Roads
96/7 Knoxville Cherokees
96/7 Knoxville Cherokees
93/4 Owen Sound Platers
97/8 Quad City Mallards
90/1 7th..Sketch OHL 298
91/2 7th...Sketch OHL 288

BROWN, JOEL
82/3 Kingston Canadians
83/4 Kingston Canadians
84/5 Kitchener Rangers

BROWN, KEITH
90/1 Bowman 10
92/3 Bowman 4
79/0 CHIC
80/1 CHIC / Colour
80/1 CHIC / Brown
81/2 CHIC
82/3 CHIC
83/4 CHIC
86/7 CHIC / Coke
87/8 CHIC / Coke
88/9 CHIC / Coke
89/0 CHIC / Coke
90/1 CHIC / Coke
91/2 CHIC / Coke
94/5 Fleer 78
93/4 Fleer Ultra 322
94/5 Fleer Ultra 295
80/1 O-Pee-Chee 98
81/2 O-Pee-Chee 55
82/3 O-Pee-Chee 62
83/4 O-Pee-Chee 98
84/5 O-Pee-Chee 33
85/6 OPC/Topps 59
86/7 O-Pee-Chee 206
87/8 OPC/Topps 47
90/1 OPC/Topps 276
92/3 O-Pee-Chee 48
81/2 OPC Sticker 115
84/5 OPC Sticker 28
87/8 Panini Sticker 233
90/1 Panini Sticker 192
91/2 Panini Sticker 21
92/3 Panini Sticker 13
91/2 Parkhurst 261
92/3 Parkhurst 274
91/2 Pinnacle 154
91/2 Pinnacle 370
92/3 Pinnacle 92
93/4 Pinnacle 422
94/5 Pinnacle 368
90/1 Pro Set 49
91/2 Pro Set 371
90/1 Score 161
91/2 Score 76
91/2 Score CAN 76
92/3 Score 68
93/4 Score 384
93/4 Score 569
80/1 Topps 98
81/2 Topps 67 [West]
84/5 Topps 28
92/3 Topps 52
92/3 To. Stadium 274
93/4 To. Stadium 281
93/4 To. Stadium 58

BROWN, KEVIN
93/4 Classic 17
93/4 Classic 33
94/5 Classic 36, T31
93/4 Cla. 4 Sport 257
94/5 Cla. Images 28
94/5 Dayton Bombers 12
95/6 Dayton Bombers
95/6 Donruss 168
95/6 Edge Ice 182
99/0 Hamilton Bulldogs
01/2 Hamilton Bulldogs
00/1 Kudos 98
94/5 Leaf 457
95/6 Leaf 38
94/5 L. Limited 7
94/5 Parkie SE77
94/5 Phoenix Roadrunners
95/6 Phoenix Roadrunners
95/6 Pinnacle 215
95/6 Score 301
90/1 7th..Sketch OHL 255
91/2 7th...Sketch OHL 108
91/2 7th...Sketch OHL 218
93/4 Slapshot / Detroit 17
96/7 Springfield Falcons
97/8 Toledo Storm 22
94/5 Topps Finest 15
94/5 Upper Deck 249
98/9 UD MVP 84

BROWN, LARRY
71/2 Eddie Sargent 159
72/3 Eddie Sargent 95
70/1 Esso Power Player
74/5 O-Pee-Chee 271
75/6 O-Pee-Chee 377
76/7 O-Pee-Chee 355
77/8 O-Pee-Chee 289
78/9 O-Pee-Chee 361
79/0 O-Pee-Chee 323
71/2 Toronto Sun Photo

BROWN, LISA
94/5 Classic W24

BROWN, MARC
97/8 Spokane Chiefs
00/1 Worcester IceCats
01/2 Worcester IceCats
02/3 Worcester IceCats

BROWN, MIKE
99 Bowman 106
97 Bowman 126, BB13, ✍ Aut.
97/8 Kamloops Blazers
98/9 Kamloops Blazers
00/1 Kansas City Blades 14
01/2 O-Pee-Chee 297
00/1 PS Titanium Draft 174
95/6 Red Deer Rebels
01/2 SPx 130
01/2 Topps 297
01/2 Upper Deck 210
01/2 UD MVP 218
01/2 UD Top Shelf 65

BROWN, NEWELL
84/5 Fredericton Express
90/1 Michigan Tech Huskies

BROWN, PAUL
01/2 Kamloops Blazers
02/3 Kamloops Blazers

BROWN, RICH
94/5 Slapshot / Sarnia 27
95/6 Slapshot 354
96/7 St. John's Maple Leafs
97/8 St. John's Maple Leafs

BROWN, ROB
02/3 Chicago Wolves

BROWN, ROB (JR.)
98/9 Be A Player 265, ✍ Aut. 265
90/1 Bowman 202, -HT3
91/2 Bowman 16
92/3 Bowman 168
00/1 Chicago Wolves
01/2 Chicago Wolves
95/6 Edge Ice 104, QM-4
92/3 Fleer Ultra 33
94/5 Fleer Ultra 304
95/6 Future Legends 13
90/1 HART / Jr. Whalers
91/2 HART / Jr. Whalers
84/5 Kamloops Blazers
85/6 Kamloops Blazers
86/7 Kamloops Blazers
94/5 Leaf 540
88/9 OPC/Topps 109
90/1 OPC/Topps 19
91/2 O-Pee-Chee 83
92/3 O-Pee-Chee 170
89/0 OPC/Topps 193
89/0 Topps - Sticker 8
88/9 OPC Sticker 131-267

88/9 OPC Sticker 237-107
88/9 OPC Sticker 63
89/0 opcSticker 163-25, 236-99, / AS 31
97/8 Omega 183
98/9 Pacific 349
99/0 Pacific 335
88/9 Panini Sticker 336
89/0 Panini Sticker 186, 310
90/1 Panini Sticker 128
91/2 Panini Sticker 315
92/3 Panini Sticker 10
91/2 Parkhurst 60
91/2 Parkhurst 258
94/5 Phoenix Roadrunners
91/2 Pinnacle 141
92/3 Pinnacle 331
97/8 Pi. Be A Player 48, ✍ Aut. 48
87/8 PITT / Kodak
89/0 PITT / Elby's
89/0 PITT / Foodland 1
90/1 Pro Set 229
91/2 Pro Set 80
91/2 Pro Set 606
91/2 Pro Set Platinum 42
90/1 Score 105
90/1 Sco. Hot Cards 51
91/2 Score 246
91/2 Score CAN 466
92/3 Score 244
92/3 Score SS 22
97/8 Score Pitt. 19
90/1 Sco. Young Stars 5
92/3 Topps 72
91/2 To. Stadium 200
92/3 To. Stadium 295
99/0 Ult. Victory 71
90/1 Upper Deck 142
91/2 Upper Deck 198
92/3 Upper Deck 387
94/5 Upper Deck 403

BROWN, RYAN
95/6 Atlanta Knights
93/4 Cla. 4 Sport 218
91/2 7th...Sketch WHL 127

BROWN, SEAN
01/2 BAP Memor. 486
95/6 Classic 20, 83
97/8 Donruss 208
96/7 EDMO
97/8 EDMO
94/5 Knoxville Cherokees
99/0 Millenium 101, ✍ Aut. 101
98/9 Omega 91
91/2 Oshawa Generals
92/3 Oshawa Generals
02/3 Pacific 24
96/7 Roanoke Express 13
90/1 7th..Sketch OHL 203
93/4 Slapshot / Oshawa 8
95/6 Slapshot 352
00/1 UD Heroes 50
98/9 Upper Deck 276
98/9 UD G. Reserve 276

BROWN, TOM
98/9 Charlotte Checkers
94/5 Slapshot / Sarnia 6
95/6 Slapshot 335
96/7 Sudbury Wolves

BROWN, WALTER
83 HHOF Postcard F2
83&87 HHOF 78

BROWNE, BILL
96/7 Soo Greyhounds

BROWNE, CECIL
25 Dominion Chocolates 103
23/4 Paulins Candy 5
28/9 Paulins Candy 63
23/4 Selkirks Crescent 7
24/5 Selkirks Crescent 6

BROWNLEE, BRENT
90/1 7th..Sketch OHL 128
91/2 7th...Sketch OHL 364

BROWNLEE, PATRICK
98/9 Charlotte Checkers
98/9 Charlotte Checkers

BROWNSCHIDLE, JACK
84/5 HART / Jr. Whalers
85/6 HART / Jr. Whalers
78/9 O-Pee-Chee 379
79/0 O-Pee-Chee 278
80/1 O-Pee-Chee 101
81/2 O-Pee-Chee 302
82/3 O-Pee-Chee 300
83/4 O-Pee-Chee 311
82/3 Post [SLou.]
78/9 SLOU
80/1 Topps 101

BROZ, JIRI
98/9 OFS 415
99/0 OFS 279
00/1 OFS 25
01/2 OFS 136

BROZDIAK, KYLE
02/3 Moose Jaw Warriors

BRUBAKER, JEFF
88/9 EDMO / Action 19
81/2 MONT
88/9 ProCards / Adirondack
84/5 TORO
85/6 TORO

BRUCE, DAVID
92/3 Bowman 358
98/9 DEL 69
92/3 Fleer Ultra 191
84/5 Fredericton Express
85/6 Fredericton Express
86/7 Fredericton Express
93/4 Kansas City Blades
94/5 Kansas City Blades 8
95/6 Kansas City Blades
96/7 Kansas City Blades
82/3 Kitchener Rangers
83/4 Kitchener Rangers
92/3 O-Pee-Chee 246
88/9 Panini Sticker 137
92/3 Panini Sticker 126
91/2 Parkhurst 384
92/3 Pinnacle 159
91/2 Pro Set 485
92/3 Pro Set 170
91/2 Pro Set Platinum 227
89/0 ProCards IHL 173
90/1 ProCards 86
91/2 Score CAN 644
92/3 Score 301
90/1 SLOU / Kodak
92/3 Topps 448
92/3 To. Stadium 284
92/3 Upper Deck 102
87/8 VANC / Shell
88/9 VANC / Mohawk

BRUGGEMANN, LARS
99/0 Eishockey 135

BRÜGGEMANN, LARS
94/5 DEL 284
95/6 DEL 297
96/7 DEL 324
98/9 DEL 29
01/2 UD DEL 62

BRUGGERMANN, LARS
99/0 Eishockey 378

BRUININKS, BRETT
98/9 Florida Everblades

BRUK, DAVID
94/5 APS 86
95/6 APS 44, 419
96/7 APS 36
97/8 APS 279
96/7 DS Sticker 106
97/8 DS Sticker 78
95 Semic 157

BRULÉ, ÉRIC
91/2 ProCards 302
90/1 7th..Sketch LHJMQ 26
91 7th..Sketch Mem.Cup 28

BRÛLÉ, ÉRIC
97/8 New Orleans Brass

BRÛLÉ, STEVE
96/7 Albany River Rats
97/8 Albany River Rats
98/9 Albany River Rats
99/0 Albany River Rats
01/2 Cincinnati Mighty Ducks
00/1 Manitoba Moose
00/1 SPx 101
00/1 Upper Deck 221

BRUMBY, DAVID
00/1 Cleveland Lumberjacks
95/6 Lethbridge Hurricanes

BRUMMER, JOHAN
94/5 Leaf Elit Set 95
95/6 Leaf Elit Set 229
89/0 Semic Elitserien 44
90/1 Semic Elitserien 194
92/3 Semic Elitserien 296
95/6 UD Elitserien 93

BRUMWELL, MURRAY
83/4 NJER
83/4 O-Pee-Chee 228
83/4 OPC/Topps Sticker 179
88/9 ProCards / Utica
89/0 ProCards AHL 9
90/1 ProCards 435

BRUNA, MIROSLAV
95/6 APS 197
96/7 APS 332
96/7 DS Sticker 158
98/9 OFS 60

BRUNCHK, BEDRICH
72 Semic Sticker 35
74 Semic Sticker 74
71/2 Williams Finnish 21

BRUNEAU, PAUL
89/0 Niagara Falls Thunder
89/0 7th..Sketch OHL 141

BRUNEL, CRAIG
00/1 Rochester Americans

BRUNELLE, MATHIEU
02/3 Hull Olympiques
97 Québec Pee Wee 0088
00/1 Victoriaville Tigres 20

BRUNET, BENOÎT
01/2 Atomic ✂ GWJ 31
98/9 Be A Player 70, ✍ Aut. 70
01/2 BAP Memor. 456
92/3 Bowman 414
01/2 DALL / Southwest
93/4 Donruss 166
95/6 Donruss 367
92/3 Durivage 19
93/4 Durivage 8
95/6 Fleer Metal 75
92/3 Fleer Ultra 101
93/4 Fleer Ultra 349
95/6 Fleer Ultra 255
01/2 Heads Up ✂ JQ 12
87/8 Hull Olympiques
93/4 Leaf 363
94/5 Leaf 401
96/7 Maggers 84
90/1 MONT
92/3 MONT
92/3 MONT / OPC 31
93/4 MONT
93/4 MONT / Export
94/5 MONT
95/6 MONT / Export
95/6 MONT
96-98 MONT
00/1 MONT
01/2 MONT
92/3 O-Pee-Chee 352
98/9 Omega 118
98/9 Pacific 248
99/0 Pacific 201
00/1 Pacific 206
99/0 Pa. Paramount 114
93/4 Panini Sticker 20
95/6 Panini Sticker 39
93/4 Parkhurst 375
95/6 Parkhurst 116
94/5 Pinnacle 452
95/6 Playoff 162
95/6 POG 146
93/4 Power Play 366
93/4 Premier 84
94/5 Premier 94
00/1 PS Titanium ✂ GUG 100
00/1 PS Titanium Draft ✂ 49
88/9 ProCards / Sherbrooke
89/0 ProCards AHL 186
97/8 Score Mont. 18
92/3 Topps 137
95/6 Topps 87
00/1 Topps 260
92/3 To. Stadium 134
93/4 To. Stadium 422
94/5 To. Stadium 227
91/2 Upper Deck 469
92/3 Upper Deck 80
93/4 Upper Deck 415
95/6 Upper Deck 156
00/1 Upper Deck 324
95/6 UD Be A Player 86, ✍ S86
95/6 UD CC 35

BRUNET, GERRY
51/2 Lac St-Jean 58

BRUNET, LUCIEN
28/9 La Presse

BRUNETEAU, EDDIE
43-47 Parade Sportive

BRUNETEAU, MUD
34-43 BeeHive-1 [Detr.]
39/0 O-Pee-Chee 43
40/1 O-Pee-Chee 138
43-47 Parade Sportive
37/8 World Wide Gum 47

BRUNETTA, MARIO
96/7 DEL 24
98/9 DEL 163
89/0 Halifax Citadels
90/1 Panini Sticker 152
89/0 ProCards AHL 159
87/8 QUÉB / Gene. Foods
88/9 QUÉB
88/9 QUÉB / Gene. Foods
99/0 UD Elitserien 69

BRUNETTE, ANDREW
02/3 Atomic 51, -PC 11
98/9 Aurora 99
99/0 Aurora 6
00/1 Aurora 5
99/0 BAP Mem. 258
00/1 BAP Mem. 211
01/2 BAP Memor. 255, 334
02/3 BAP Memorabilia 31
99/0 Crown Royale 5
00/1 Crown Royale 5
01/2 Crown Royale 71
98/9 Dynagon Ice 100
02/3 Exclusive 84
02/3 First Edition 219
96/7 Fleer 124, CC-1
96/7 Fl. Ultra 173
95/6 Future Legends 47
98/9 Hampton Roads
02/3 Heads Up 59
00/1 Kraft 19
99/0 Millenium 15, ✍ Aut. 15
01/2 MINW / Crime 20
98/9 NASH / Wendy's 6
01/2 O-Pee-Chee 170
02/3 O-Pee-Chee 47
97/8 Omega 237
98/9 Omega 127
99/0 Omega 9
93/4 Owen Sound Platers
98/9 Pacific 439
99/0 Pacific 220
00/1 Pacific 15
01/2 Pacific 14
02/3 Pacific 177
02/3 Pacific Complete 315
98/9 Pa. Crown Roy. 72
97/8 Pa. Invincible R-207
98/9 Pa. Paramount 121
99/0 Pa. Paramount 10
00/1 Pa. Paramount 10
98/9 Pa. Revolution 77
98/9 Panini Photocard
96/7 Panini Sticker 141, 304
99/0 Panini Sticker 18
00/1 Panini Sticker 6
00/1 Parkhurst P-22
01/2 Parkhurst 379
02/3 Parkhurst 158
97/8 Pi. Inside 111
94/5 Portland Pirates
95/6 Portland Pirates
96/7 Portland Pirates Hershey
96/7 Portland Pirates
97/8 Portland Pirates
00/1 Premier Plus 64
99/0 Prism 6
02/3 Pr. Stock Reserve 48
01/2 PS Titanium 68
00/1 Revolution 5
90/1 7th..Sketch OHL 277
91/2 7th...Sketch OHL 284
00/1 Signature 63, ✍ Aut. 133
02/3 Signature Series 51, ✍ 51
96/7 SBx Impact 147
98/9 SP Authentic 46
99/0 SP Authentic 5
02/3 Sports Vault 243
01/2 SPx 177
00/1 Stadium 85
02/3 Stadium 75
00/1 Topps 52
01/2 Topps 170
02/3 Topps 47
00/1 To. Chrome 42
02/3 T. Chrome 39
99/0 To. Gold Label 68
00/1 To. Heritage 197
01/2 To. Heritage 158
02/3 To. Heritage 91
02/3 T. Limited 47
00/1 To. Stars 60
02/3 T. Total 245
00/1 UD Heroes 7
01/2 UD PlayMakers Ltd 51
96/7 Upper Deck 184
97/8 Upper Deck 382
98/9 Upper Deck 301
00/1 Upper Deck 8
01/2 Upper Deck 317
02/3 Upper Deck 331
01/2 UD Challenge 43
02/3 UD Classic 49
98/9 UD G. Reserve 301
02/3 UD Honor 85
01/2 UD Mask 45
98/9 UD MVP 113
00/1 UD MVP 8
02/3 UD MVP 91
02/3 UD Top Shelf 44
00/1 UD Vintage 21
02/3 UD Vintage 130, 275
02/3 Vanguard 51
00/1 Victory 10
01/2 Victory 14
02/3 Victory 102
99/0 WGretzky 10

BRUNNER, GERHARD
96/7 DEL 225
98/9 DEL 314
99/0 Eishockey 265

BRUNNER, MARKUS
90/1 Oshawa Generals
91/2 Oshawa Generals
91/2 Oshawa Generals
90/1 7th..Sketch OHL 328
91/2 7th...Sketch OHL 151

BRUNS, ROGER
94/5 DEL 437

BRUNSING, FRANK
94/5 DEL 224

BRUNVOLL,
92/3 Semic Nordisk 212 [Rookie]

BRUS, KJELL
72 Semic Sticker 63

BRUSELINCK, DEREK
92/3 MPS SJHL 151

BRUSH, MATT
98/9 Florida Everblades

BRUUN, ANTTI
99/0 Cardset 248
00/1 Cardset 152

BRUX, ARNO
94/5 DEL 333
95/6 DEL 237

BRYAM, SHAWN
00/1 Kudos 14

BRYAN, TIM
95/6 Slapshot 430

BRYDEN, ROB
88/9 Flint Spirits
88/9 ProCards / Sherbrooke

BRYDGE, BILL
33/4 Anonymous 22
33/4 Canadian Gum
33-35 Diamond Match Silv.
36-39 Diamond Match TT1
36-39 Diamond Match TT2
36-39 Diamond Match TT3
25 Dominion Chocolates 101
23/4 Paulins Candy 19
33/4 WWGum 2

BRYDGES, PAUL
88/9 ProCards / Rochester
89/0 ProCards AHL 27
93/4 Slapshot / Guelph 27
94/5 Slapshot / Guelph 28

BRYDGES, SCOTT
82/3 Oshawa Generals
83/4 Oshawa Generals

BRYDSON, GLENN
34-43 BeeHive-1 [Chic.]
33/4 Canadian Gum
36-39 Diamond Match TT1
36-39 Diamond Match BH TT
36-39 Diamond Match Chic.
36-39 Diamond Match BH BT
33/4 O-Pee-Chee 64
33/4 WWGum 39

BRYLIN, SERGEI
01/2 Adrenaline 112
98/9 Be A Player 231, ✍ Aut. 231
99/0 BAP Mem. 83
00/1 BAP Mem. 66
01/2 BAP Memor. 166
92/3 Classic 47
92/3 Classic Four Sport 188
95/6 Donruss 52
95/6 Fleer Ultra 88
95/6 Leaf 40
00/1 Mir Fetisov 14
96/7 NJER / Sharp
02/3 O-Pee-Chee 230
01/2 Pacific 228
02/3 Pacific 219
02/3 Pacific Complete 300
95/6 Parkhurst 119
00/1 Parkhurst P-194
01/2 Parkhurst 182
93/4 Pinnacle 509
95/6 Pinnacle 120, GG-18
95/6 Playoff 277
92/3 Red Ace Blue 23
92/3 Red Ace Violet 5
95/6 Score 274
97/8 Score NJer. 19
00/1 Signature 100
02/3 Sports Vault 66
00/1 Stadion 119
95/6 Topps 35, 2NG
02/3 Topps 230
02/3 T. Limited 230
02/3 T. Total 178
93/4 Upper Deck 276
94/5 Upper Deck 329
95/6 Upper Deck 31
98/9 Upper Deck 311
00/1 Upper Deck 107, 336
01/2 Upper Deck 336
02/3 Upper Deck 350
95/6 UD CC 296
98/9 UD G. Reserve 311
99/0 UD MVP Cup 110
01/2 UD SCup Champs 76
02/3 UD Vintage 147
01/2 Victory 213

BRYZGALOV, ILJA
01/2 Adrenaline 201, RR 1
01/2 Atomic 101
01/2 BAP Memor. 301
01/2 BT Pipes 84
02/3 Between the Pipes 83
01/2 Bowman 161
01/2 Cincinnati Mighty Ducks
01/2 Crown Royale 145
02/3 First Edition 264
01/2 Heads Up 101
00/1 Mir 155
01/2 O-Pee-Chee 350
02/3 O-Pee-Chee 279
01/2 Parkhurst 285
01/2 Pr. Stock 111, -PS 76
01/2 PS Titanium 145
01/2 PS Titanium Draft 101
01/2 SP Authentic 131
01/2 SP GU 61
02/3 SP Game-Used ✂ FF
01/2 SPx 92
01/2 SPx Rookie RR1
01/2 Topps 350
02/3 Topps 279
01/2 To. Chrome 168
02/3 T. Limited 279
01/2 UD PlayMakers Ltd 102
01/2 Upper Deck 413
01/2 Upper Deck 413
02/3 Upper Deck ✂ BF, ✂ GT
01/2 UD Challenge 91
01/2 UD Honor Roll 61
01/2 UD Ice 43
01/2 UD Premier 88
01/2 UD Top Shelf 67
01/2 UD Vintage 272
01/2 Vanguard 101

BUBLA, JIRI
72 Hellas MM-Jenkki 95
74 Hellas MM-Jenkki 67
82/3 O-Pee-Chee 346
83/4 O-Pee-Chee 347
84/5 O-Pee-Chee 315
83/4 OPC/Topps Sticker 143
79 Panini Sticker 76
72 Semic Sticker 38
74 Semic Sticker 53
83/4 Souhaits Keychain [Canucks]
83/4 Vachon 102-22
81/2 VANC
81/2 VANC / Silverwood
82/3 VANC
83/4 VANC
84/5 VANC
85/6 VANC
71/2 Williams Finnish 22
72/3 Williams Finnish 2
73/4 Williams Finnish 44

BUBNICK, JONATHAN
01/2 Kamloops Blazers

BUBNICK, MICHAEL
98/9 Calgary Hitmen 10
99/0 Calgary Hitmen
00/1 Calgary Hitmen
01/2 Calgary Hitmen
99/0 UD Prospects 53

BUBNIK, VLASTIMIL
97/8 APS 378
01/2 DS L3

BUBOLA, ADRIAN
91/2 Avant Garde BCJHL 9

BUCCELLA, DAN
01/2 London Knights

BUCCELLA, DANIEL
02/3 Mississauga IceDogs

BUCCIARELLI, B.
88/9 ProCards / Hershey

BUCHAL, JAROSLAV
95/6 APS 164
96/7 APS 187
97/8 APS 239
96/7 DS Sticker 50
01/2 OFS 162

BUCHANAN, BUCKY
51/2 Laval Dairy 56

BUCHANAN, GREG
91/2 Avant Garde BCJHL 6
92/3 BCJHL 211

BUCHANAN, JEFF
92/3 Atlanta Knights
93/4 Atlanta Knights
98/9 Hershey Bears
95/6 Indianapolis Ice
90/1 Saskatoon Blades
91/2 Saskatoon Blades
90/1 7th..Sketch WHL 89
91/2 7th...Sketch WHL 102

BUCHANAN, KIRK
92/3 BCJHL 188

BUCHANAN, RON
72/3 Cleveland Crusaders
72/3 Clev. WHA / Linnett
74/5 OPC WHA 23
75/6 OPC WHA 39
73/4 Quaker Oats 36

BUCHANAN, TREVOR
88/9 Kamloops Blazers
96/7 Pensacola Ice Pilots
89/0 Victoria Cougars

BUCHANEN, BUCKY
52/3 Laval Dairy Update 29

BUCHBERGER, KELLY
98/9 Aurora 70
99/0 Aurora 7
98/9 Be A Player 201, ✍ Aut. 201
92/3 Bowman 393
94/5 Donruss 18
99/0 Dynagon Ice 14
93/4 EDMO / Sheet
88/9 EDMO
88/9 EDMO / Action 133
90/1 EDMO / IGA
91/2 EDMO / IGA
92/3 EDMO
92/3 EDMO / IGA 003
96/7 EDMO
97/8 EDMO
92/3 Fleer Ultra 291
93/4 Fleer Ultra 314
94/5 Fleer Ultra 290
96/7 Kraft / PB
98/9 Kraft / Post 13
94/5 Leaf 333
99/0 Millenium 19, ✍ Aut. 19
98/9 NHL Power Play
92/3 O-Pee-Chee 125
01/2 O-Pee-Chee 229
98/9 OPC Chrome 22
97/8 Omega 89
98/9 Pacific 205
00/1 Pacific 194
02/3 Pacific Complete 381
97/8 Pacific CC 268
97/8 Pa. Dynagon 47, T-49
98/9 Pa. Paramount 84
99/0 Pa. Paramount 11
90/1 Panini/EDM 4
93/4 Panini Sticker 241
94/5 Panini Sticker 201
95/6 Panini Sticker 261
99/0 Panini Sticker 10
95 Panini Worlds 15
91/2 Parkhurst 275
95/6 Parkhurst 77
92/3 Pinnacle 95
93/4 Pinnacle 58
94/5 Pinnacle 332
97/8 Pi. Be A Player 150, ✍ Aut. 150
94/5 POG 98
94/5 POG / Western 13
95/6 POG 111
93/4 Power Play 340
94/5 Premier 404
90/1 Pro Set 441
91/2 Pro Set 385
92/3 Pro Set 48
99/0 Revolution 6
91/2 Score CAN 429
92/3 Score 126
92/3 Score SS 11
93/4 Score 317
97/8 SP Authentic 64
99/0 Stadium 158
92/3 Topps 455
95/6 Topps 298
98/9 Topps 22
99/0 Topps 216
00/1 Topps 259
01/2 Topps 229
99/0 To. Chrome 216
02/3 To. Heritage 177
92/3 To. Stadium 235
94/5 To. Stadium 121
02/3 T. Total 310
99/0 Ult. Victory 6
92/3 Upper Deck 123
93/4 Upper Deck 197
94/5 Upper Deck 134
95/6 Upper Deck 121
97/8 Upper Deck 278
98/9 Upper Deck 93
99/0 Upper Deck 179
00/1 Upper Deck 86
95/6 UD CC 310
96/7 UD CC 94
98/9 UD G. Reserve 93
99/0 UD G. Reserve 179
99/0 Victory 14
99/0 WGretzky 9

BUCHER, LAURENT
91/2 Upper Deck 668
91/2 Upper Deck WJC 29

BUCHKO, BERKELEY
99/0 Medicine Hat Tigers
00/1 Prince George Cougars

BUCHWIESER, HUBERT
95/6 DEL 352

BUCK, DAVID
93/4 Minnesota-Duluth

BUCKBERGER, ASHLEY
96/7 Carolina Monarchs
91/2 7th...Sketch WHL 193
94/5 Slapshot Memorial 18

BUCKLAND, FRANK
83 HHOF Postcard O6
83&87 HHOF 216

BUCKLAND, WYATT
90/1 7th..Sketch OHL 278
91/2 7th...Sketch OHL 287
94/5 Toledo Storm

BUCKLE, CHAD
92/3 BCJHL 196

BUCKLEY, BRENDAN
99/0 Quad City Mallards
00/1 WBS Penguins
01/2 WBS Penguins
02/3 WBS Penguins

BUCKLEY, GRANT
00/1 Mississauga IceDogs

BUCKLEY, JEFF
95/6 Dayton Bombers

BUCKLEY, TOM
99/0 Florida Everblades
00/1 Florida Everblades
01/2 Florida Everblades
98/9 New Haven Beast 12
94/5 Slapshot / Detroit Jr. 10
95/6 Slapshot 77
94/5 Slapshot Memorial 84
96/7 Springfield Falcons

BUCKMAN, CHRIS
92/3 BCJHL 139

BUCKMAN, JASON
02/3 Peterborough Phantoms

BUCKMAN, LEWIS
02/3 Peterborough Phantoms

BUCYK, JOHNNY
01/2 ASG History
99/0 BAP Mem. AH-5, ✍ AH-5
01/2 BAP Memor. ✂ 500GS
02/3 BAP Memorabilia 233
01/2 BAP Update ✂ PTT1
45-64 BeeHive-2 [Detr.]
45-64 BeeHive-2 [Bost.]
64-67 BeeHive-3 [Bost.]
70/1 BOST
71/2 BOST
91/2 BOST / SA Legends
98/9 BOST / Alumni 9
64/5 Coke/Sprite [Bost.]
65/6 Coca-Cola
70/1 Colgate 46
70/1 Dad's Cookies
70/1 Eddie Sargent 8
71/2 Eddie Sargent 9
72/3 Eddie Sargent 16
70/1 Esso Power Player
01/2 Fleer Greats 76, ✍ Aut.
01/2 Fleer Legacy 22
62/3 Cowan Tile
83 HHOF Postcard J4
83&87 HHOF 181
74/5 Loblaws
73/4 Mac's Milk
68/9 O-Pee-Chee 5
68/9 O-Pee-Chee 210
69/0 O-Pee-Chee 26
70/1 O-Pee-Chee 2
71/2 O-Pee-Chee 35
71/2 O-Pee-Chee 249
71/2 O-Pee-Chee 255
72/3 O-Pee-Chee 1
73/4 O-Pee-Chee 147
74/5 O-Pee-Chee 28
74/5 O-Pee-Chee 239
74/5 O-Pee-Chee 245
75/6 O-Pee-Chee 9
76/7 O-Pee-Chee 95
76/7 O-Pee-Chee 381
77/8 O-Pee-Chee 155
01/2 Parkhurst ✂ 500GS, ✍ PA21
02/3 Parkhurst ✂ VM1, ✂ VT3
93/4 Parkie 56-57 56
02/3 Parkhurst Retro ✂ NN7
95/6 Parkie 66-67 5, SL1
94/5 Parkie Tall 1, SL-1
97/8 Pi. BeeHive 58, ✍ Aut. 58
70/1 Post Shooters
71/2 Pro Star Promotions
60/1 Shirriff 104
61/2 Shirriff 7
68/9 Shirriff / Bost. 6
01/2 Signature ✂ 500GS, ✍ VA31
81/2 TCMA 5
57/8 Topps 10
58/9 Topps 40
59/0 Topps 23
60/1 Topps 11
61/2 Topps 8
61/2 Topps - Stamp
62/3 Topps 11
62/3 Topps Dollar
63/4 Topps 11
64/5 Topps 100
65/6 Topps 101
66/7 Topps 39
66/7 Topps / Test 39
67/8 Topps 42
68/9 Topps 5
69/0 Topps 26
70/1 Topps 2
71/2 Topps 1
71/2 Topps 2
71/2 Topps 3
71/2 Topps 35
72/3 Topps 60
73/4 Topps 26
74/5 Topps 28
74/5 Topps 239
74/5 Topps 245
75/6 Topps 9
76/7 Topps 95
76/7 Topps NS 14
77/8 Topps 155
01/2 To. Heritage S1, ✂ Relic
01/2 T/O Archives 17, -Seat, ✍ CAI
63/4 Toronto Star Action
63/4 Toronto Star Photo
60/1 Toronto Star Weekend
71/2 Toronto Sun Photo
01/2 Ultimate Mem. ✂ 500GS, ✂ ASGH, ✂ Cor., ✂ RN, ✂ UC
02/3 Ultimate Memorabilia ✂ EA, ✂ FS, ✂ Num, ✂ RT, ✂ VGJ
99/0 UD C. Legends 46, ✍ ES
02/3 UD Foundations ✂ 1000Jers, ✂ 1000Stick, ✂ CH, ✂ PP, ✍ SG
00/1 UD Legends 8, ✍ ES
01/2 UD Legends 4
02/3 UD Piece ✂ HS, ✍ MD
99/0 UD Retro 105, ✍ Ink.
93/4 Zellers, ✍ Aut.

BUCYK, JOHNNY
02/3 Fleer Throwbacks 18

BUCYK, RANDY
85/6 MONT
89/0 ProCards IHL 205
90/1 ProCards 608
88/9 Salt Lake G'Eagles
86/7 Sherb. Canadiens 8

BUCZKOWSKI, PAUL
91/2 Saskatoon Blades
93/4 Saskatoon Blades
91/2 7th...Sketch WHL 105

BUDA, DAVE
89/0 ProCards AHL 54

BUDAI, JEFF
91/2 7th...Sketch WHL 269

BUDAJ, PETER
02/3 Hershey Bears
00/1 Toronto St. Mike's

BUDAYEV, ALEXEI
96/7 Mississippi S'Wolves

BUDEAU, DENNIS
91/2 Air Canada SJHL D18

BUDY, TIM
89/0 ProCards AHL 226
92/3 Semic Nordisk 106

BUETOW, JASON
90/1 7th..Sketch OHL 279
91/2 7th...Sketch OHL 286

BUETTGEN, JIM
85/6 Moncton G'Flames

BUHLER, SCOTT
99/0 Quad City Mallards

BUIE, CHRIS
92/3 BCJHL 107

BUJAR, KRZYSZTOF
89 Semic Sticker 142
92 Semic Sticker 280

BUKAC, LUDEK
95/6 APS 351
96/7 APS 334
94/5 DEL 369
98/9 OFS Leg. 10
92 Semic Sticker 170

BUKNA, MATEJ
00/1 Kudos 33

BUKTA, MIKE
89/0 Nashville Knights

BULATOV, ALEXEI
99/0 Mir 151

BULDAKOV, ANDREI
99/0 Mir 136

BULIS, JAN
00/1 BAP Mem. 350
01/2 BAP Memor. 135
95/6 Bowman P6
97 Bowman 1
99/0 Crown Royale 142
97/8 Do. Priority 174
99/0 Dynagon Ice 200
99/0 Millenium 250, ✍ Aut. 250
01/2 MONT
02/3 MONT
99/0 NHL Power Play
99/0 Omega 241
98/9 Pacific 440
99/0 Pacific 438
00/1 Pacific 420
01/2 Pacific 204
02/3 Pacific Complete 199
99/0 Pa. Paramount 243
01/2 Parkhurst 201
97/8 Pinnacle 24
99/0 Prism 147
95/6 Slapshot 24
97/8 SP Authentic 198
99/0 SPx 162
98/9 SPx Finite 89, 131
98/9 UD Choice 216
98/9 UD3 29, 89, 149
97/8 Upper Deck 381
98/9 Upper Deck 202
99/0 Upper Deck 133
01/2 Upper Deck 95
97/8 UD Black Diam. 89
98/9 UD G. Reserve 202
99/0 UD G. Reserve 133
97/8 UD Ice 59
99/0 UD MVP 218
99/0 Victory 306
00/1 Victory 236
99/0 WGretzky 177

BULJIN, VLADISLAV
91/2 Upper Deck WJC 2

BULLARD, MIKE
90/1 Bowman 114
87/8 CALG / Red Rooster
94/5 DEL 258
95/6 DEL 256
96/7 DEL 144
98/9 DEL 156
99/0 Eishockey 73
83/4 Funmate Puffy 9 [w/]
82/3 O-Pee-Chee 262
82/3 O-Pee-Chee 264
83/4 O-Pee-Chee 277
84/5 O-Pee-Chee 172
84/5 O-Pee-Chee 365
85/6 OPC/Topps 67
86/7 OPC/Topps 83
87/8 O-Pee-Chee 210
88/9 OPC/Topps 152
90/1 OPC/Topps 274
89/0 OPC/Topps 21
82/3 OPC/Topps Sticker 149
83/4 OPC/Topps Sticker 235
84/5 OPC Sticker 118
85/6 OPC Sticker 104-237
86/7 OPC Sticker 228-98
87/8 OPC Sticker 37-180
88/9 OPC Sticker 93
88/9 OPC Sticker 119-249
89/0 opcSticker 104-241
88/9 Panini Sticker 8
90/1 Panini Sticker 119
91/2 Parkhurst 397
89/0 PHIL
91/2 Pinnacle 69
83/4 PITT / Coke Is It!
83/4 PITT / Heinz
84/5 PITT / Heinz
82/3 Post [Pitt.]
90/1 Pro Set 211
91/2 Pro Set 496
91/2 Pro Set Platinum 233
91/2 Score 40T
91/2 Score CAN 590
92/3 Score 218
84/5 7-Eleven
85/6 7-Eleven Superstars 15
83/4 Souhaits Keychain [Penguins]
87/8 SLOU
88/9 SLOU
84/5 Topps 123
92/3 Topps 146
92/3 To. Stadium 494
91/2 TORO / P.L.A.Y. 16
90/1 Upper Deck 230
00/1 UD DEL 225, P6
01/2 UD DEL 228

BULLER, HYMAN
45-64 BeeHive-2 [NYRa.]
51/2 Parkhurst 91
52/3 Parkhurst 98
53/4 Parkhurst 58

BULLEY, TED
79/0 CHIC
80/1 CHIC / Brown
81/2 CHIC
78/9 O-Pee-Chee 217
79/0 OPC 7
79/0 O-Pee-Chee 128
80/1 O-Pee-Chee 229
81/2 O-Pee-Chee 56
82/3 O-Pee-Chee 360
83/4 PITT / Coke Is It!
82/3 Post [Chic.]
78/9 Topps 217
79/0 Topps 7
79/0 Topps 128
80/1 Topps 229
81/2 Topps 68 [West]
82/3 WASH

BULLOCK, GREG
95/6 Classic 71, ✍ Aut.
95/6 Cla. 5 Sport 131, ✍ Aut.
98/9 DEL 290
00/1 Kudos 99
96/7 St. John's Maple Leafs

BÜLOW, JOHAN
99/0 UD Elitserien 134

BULTJE, MARK
00/1 Kudos 41
01/2 Manchester Storm
02/3 Manchester Storm

BURAKOVSKY, MIKAEL
95/6 Leaf Elit Set 263, R-7
97/8 UD Elitserien 148

BURAKOVSKY, ROBERT
93/4 Cla. Prospects 166
93/4 Fleer Ultra 379
93/4 Leaf 429
95/6 Leaf Elit Set 262, FTF-9
93/4 OTTA
93/4 Parkhurst 144
89/0 Semic Elitserien 16
90/1 Semic Elitserien 85
91/2 Semic Elitserien 189
92/3 Semic Elitserien 221
91 Semic Sticker 44
93/4 Upper Deck 498, SP-106
95/6 UD Elitserien 149
00/1 UD Elitserien 119, 199

BURAS, MIROSLAV
99/0 OFS 508

BURCH, BILLY
25-27 Anonymous 79
25-27 Anonymous 79
24/5 Champ's Cigarettes
83 HHOF Postcard E3
83&87 HHOF 64
24/5 Maple Crispette [V130] 21
23/4 William Paterson 35
24/5 William Paterson 13

BURCHELL, FRED (SKIPPY)
52/3 La Patrie
63/4 Québec Aces
52/3 St. Lawrence 6

BURCHILL, RICK
89/0 Johnstown Chiefs

BURDA, VACLAV
95/6 APS 272, 431
96/7 APS 127, 393
97/8 APS 21
97/8 DS 81
98/9 DS 88
96/7 DS Sticker 60
97/8 DS Sticker 210
98/9 OFS 364
99/0 UD Elitserien 136

BURE, PAVEL
94/5 Action Packed
01/2 Adrenaline 79, BR 6, WB 7
01/2 ASG History
01/2 Atomic 44, AB 6, CP6, PP 16, Stat. 14
02/3 Atomic 67, -CF 17, -PC 13, ✂ GWJ 15
98/9 Aurora 188, ALC-18, CF-47, MACF-18, / Cube 17
99/0 Aurora 61, Stripe 61, CC-7, CF-14, -ST-11
00/1 Aurora 60, Pin. 60, CC-6, CF-13, SR-11
02/3 BAP All-Star 11-12, ✂ ASJ, ✂ HSHSJes, Bobble
98/9 Be A Player 211, H-12, P-4, ✍ Aut. 211, ✂ G-10, ✂ AS-19, ✂✍ G-10
99/0 BAP Mem. 126, H-19, ✂ J-19, ✂ D-13, ✂ TM-14, ✂ TM-19, ✂ TM-30
00/1 BAP Mem. 161, ✂ J-3, ✂ H-2, ✂ PP-3, ✂ BB-1, ✂ TM-8
01/2 BAP Memor. 104, 480, ✂ ASJ, ✂ ASE, ✂ ASN, ✂ ASS, ✂ AST, ✂ CoO, HSHS, ✂ PP
02/3 BAP Memorabilia 166, 220, 238, ✂ ASJ7, ✂ ASE2, ✂ ASN2, ✂ ASTJ3, , ✂ AST10, ✂ AST 24, ✂ FP20, ✂ HSHSJers, ✂ TM6
01/2 BAP Update HSHS, ✂ HSHSJers (x2), ✂ H9
02/3 Between the Pipes ✂ GN5
96/7 Bic.Sports Aces 2-H
97/8 Bicycle 9-Heart
95/6 Bicycle Sports Aces 9-Diamond
92/3 Bowman 154
95/6 Bowman 65, BB13
01/2 Bowman 16
02/3 Bowman 92
98/9 Bowman's Best 58, F14
02/3 Calder 19
92/3 Classic - Autograph
93/4 Classic 117, N6, ✍ Aut.
94/5 Cla. Images 10, 100, CE10, PL1
93/4 Cla. Prospects LP22
99/0 Crown Royale 59, IG-11, CS-12, C21-5, CCA-7
00/1 Crown Royale 45, JotC-16, Land. 6, NP-9
01/2 Crown Royale 63, ASH, CA, JotC
02/3 Crown Royale 63, -LOR 14
95/6 DEL 442
93/4 Donruss 351
93/4 Donruss X
93/4 Donruss IK 8
94/5 Donruss 19, D-8, ES-3
95/6 Donruss 170, D-6
96/7 Donruss 65, D-7, ES-1
97/8 Donruss 187, L2L-11, RA-6
98/9 Donruss ES 8
96/7 Do. Canadian 59
97/8 Do. Canadian 18
95/6 Do. Elite 77
96/7 Do. Elite 103, S-1
97/8 Do. Elite 4, 118, C-20, PN-12
97/8 Do. Preferred 25, 194, LT-4A, / Tin 17, WideTin 5
97/8 Do. Priority 15, 211,DD-3, OD-13, Post-5, Stamp-5
97/8 Do. Studio 14, HH-18, S-9, P-14
98/9 Dynagon Ice 187
99/0 Dynagon Ice 87, -ASP 12, -CM 25, -LL 6
93/4 EA Sports 143
97/8 Esso 38
01/2 eTopps 17
02/3 eTopps 2, -Intro
02/3 Exclusive 113, -MO 14
02/3 First Edition 120, 338, 360, ✂ Jers., ✂ DGJ 1, ✂ HSHSJers 5
94/5 Flair 189, HN-1, SP-1
96/7 Flair 93, CIS-1
94/5 Fleer 223, H-1
96/7 Fleer 111, ART-1, PA-1
95/6 Fleer Metal 149, HM-1, IS-1
96/7 Fl. Picks F50-5, DL-4
92/3 Fleer Ultra 219, -AW 9, -UI 2, -UR 3
93/4 Fleer Ultra 37
93/4 Fleer Ultra AS 17
93/4 Fleer Ultra RLS 2
93/4 Fleer Ultra SM 1
94/5 Fleer Ultra 222, ASG-7, RLS-2, SK-1, SM-1
95/6 Fleer Ultra 166, 379
96/7 Fl. Ultra 167, MM-2
91/2 Gillette 10
95 Globe 174
96/7 Got-Um
01/2 Heads Up 43, ASGUN 4, HD 6, RI 7, SM 8, ✂ JQ 21
02/3 Heads Up 78, -SM 10, ✂ GWQ 30, / Bobble
93/4 Hockey Wit 7
99/0 HoloGrFX 26, ✍ Aut.
95/6 Hoyle / West. A-Diamond
02/3 In The Game-Used 51, 151, ✂ E6, ✂ F20, ✂ GUJ6, ✂ SJ6, ✂ T4
93/4 Kraft / JELL-O
93/4 Kraft / KD
94/5 Kraft / PB
95/6 Kraft / KD
98/9 Kraft / KD
99/0 Kraft / OML
00/1 Kraft 15
93/4 Leaf 10
93/4 Leaf GLAS 8
94/5 Leaf 10, FOI-3, GLS-4, LL-24
95/6 Leaf 135, FOI-1
96/7 Leaf 15, LL-9, S-13
97/8 Leaf 60, FOI-8
94/5 L. Limited 100, G-10
95/6 L. Limited 17
96/7 L. Limited 32, S-10
96/7 L. Preferred 94, SP-3, VP-9
97/8 Limited 7, 104, 154, FG-66
96/7 Maggers 156
93/4 McDonald's McD-02
94/5 McDonald's McD-23
95/6 McDonald's McD-8
96/7 McDonald's McD-27
97/8 McDonald's McD-3
98/9 McDonald's McD14
00/1 McDonald's 17, DAS-3, GWJ-6
01/2 McDonald's 18, -CF2
02/3 McDonald's 26, ✂ JP 10

96/7 Metal Univ. 155, IC-2, LW-2
99/0 Millenium 106, ✍ Aut. 106, ✂ J-10, ✂✍ J-10, ✂ JS-10
00/1 Mir Fetisov 2
95/6 Cool Trade 10
98/9 NHL Power Play
00/1 Nortel Networks All-Star 3
92/3 O-Pee-Chee 25
92/3 O-Pee-Chee 324
92/3 OPC - Anniv. 25
92/3 O-Pee-Chee Box
01/2 O-Pee-Chee 8
02/3 O-Pee-Chee 16
98/9 OPC Chrome 180, SB15
91/2 OPC Premier 67
92/3 OPC Premier SP10
97/8 Omega 228, GF-18, S-11, SHLC-19, TL-19
98/9 Omega 99, -CS 5, -EOP 12, -FTF 4, -Onl. 17, -PI 20, -Prism 11
99/0 Omega 97, 250, 5ST-15, CC-11, EOP-10, G-7, WAS-4
98/9 Pacific 10, -CCA 10, -DI 17, -GCDC 33, -TC 26, -Time. 19
99/0 Pacific 169, GC-19, PAP-14, TL-12
00/1 Pacific 177, IO-10, CCA-6, ES-5, GCDC-16, PR-11, ✂ GWJ-9
01/2 Pacific 169, 412, 431, CCA 6, GCDC 11, WAS 4
02/3 Pacific 249, -L 9, -MA 13, ✂ GWJ 34
02/3 Pacific Complete 301
97/8 Pacific CC 96, SS-20, GCDC-20, SS11A, TC-25
97/8 Pa. Crown Roy. 133, BOS-19, CCA-10, HT-18, L-19
98/9 Pa. Crown Roy. 134
97/8 Pa. Dynagon 125, DD-15A, KN-10, T-14, BKS-95
97/8 Pa. Invincible 140, AZ-23, OTG-20, R-201
97/8 Pa. Paramount 186, P-19, BN-19
98/9 Pa. Paramount 234, -SD 18
99/0 Pa. Paramount 98, IAd-12, IAl-12, PB-19
00/1 Pa. Paramount 102, ES-12, FF-18, HOFB-7, SZ-6
97/8 Pa. Revolution 139, ASG-18, I-10, TC-25
98/9 Pa. Revolution 59, -TPA 30
98/9 Panini Photocard
92/3 Panini Sticker 271
92/3 Panini Sticker 290
92/3 Panini Sticker C
93/4 Panini Sticker O
94/5 Panini Sticker 146, 235b, GG
95/6 Panini Sticker 293
96/7 Panini Sticker 289
97/8 Panini Sticker 236
98/9 Panini Sticker 216
99/0 Panini Sticker 56
00/1 Panini Sticker 37
95 Panini Worlds 281
91/2 Parkhurst 404
91/2 Parkhurst 446
91/2 Parkhurst 462
92/3 Parkhurst 188
92/3 Parkhurst 234
92/3 Parkhurst 460
92/3 Parkhurst 506
93/4 Parkhurst 211
93/4 Parkhurst G7
93/4 Parkhurst W2
94/5 Parkhurst 297, V18, YCTG-24
95/6 Parkhurst 248, 482, AS-3, CCB-5
00/1 Parkhurst P-1
01/2 Parkhurst 13, 390, HSHS, ✂ PJ19, ✂ PS19, ✂ PSJ2, ✂ HSHSJers, ✂ M30, ✂ H4, ✂ T10, ✂ T20
02/3 Parkhurst 7, -HHH7, -HHP6, -HHR 6, ✂ FP20, ✂ GJ35, ✂ SJ35, ✂ HSHSJers, ✂ MS10, ✂ PP6, ✂ TT1
02/3 Parkhurst Retro 13, ✂ RF20, ✂ RJ9, ✂ RSJ10, ✂ HSHSJers, ✂ NN28, ✂ RM16
94/5 Parkie SE187, ES15
91/2 Pinnacle 315
92/3 Pinnacle 110
92/3 Pinnacle T2K 8
92/3 Pinnacle TP 4
93/4 Pinnacle 320
93/4 Pinnacle NF 6
93/4 Pinnacle T2K1 3
93/4 Pinnacle TP 10
94/5 Pinnacle 140, BR-13. GR-4, MVPC, NL17, TP-12
95/6 Pinnacle 1, GG-1, CS-12, R20-8
96/7 Pinnacle 175, 248, BTN-15
97/8 Pinnacle 41, P-14
96/7 Pi. Be A Player LTH4B, BB-18, ✍ Aut. LTH4B
97/8 Pi. Be A Player OT 12
97/8 Pi. BeeHive 15
97/8 Pi. Certified 45
97/8 Pi. Epix E21
95/6 Pi. FANtasy 12
96/7 Pi. FANtasy 14
97/8 Pi. Inside 11, IT-12, / Can 20
96/7 Pi. Mint 7
97/8 Pi. Mint 17, M-6
95/6 Pi. Summit 7, GMC-7, MH-7
96/7 Pi. Summit 42, 200
97/8 Pi. Totally 45
95/6 Pi. Zenith 9, ZT-12
96/7 Pi. Zenith 3, ZT-8
95/6 Playoff 100, 207, 316
96/7 Playoff 438
94/5 POG 266, 341, 376
94/5 POG / Western 7
95/6 POG 274, I-021
94/5 Post
97/8 Pi. Post 17
93/4 Power Play 248
93/4 Power Play GG 1
93/4 Power Play PL 1
93/4 Premier 260
93/4 Premier 440
93/4 Prmr. - BG-OPC 7
94/5 Premier 39, 151, 325, 415, TF-1, GTG-5
00/1 Premier Plus 60, MB3, PT6, TT13, WP17
99/0 Prism 60, CA-10, SGDC-12
00/1 Pr. Stock 42, AC-13, Res. 11, PS-25, PSS-14
01/2 Pr. Stock 42, Res. 7, -PS 33
02/3 Pr. Stock Reserve 66
00/1 PS Titanium 39, WAS-5
01/2 PS Titanium 59, SK 9
02/3 Private Stock Titanium 68, ✂ GWJ 43
00/1 PS Titanium Draft ✂ 46
95/6 Pro Magnet 21
91/2 Pro Set 564
92/3 Pro Set 192
92/3 Pro Set CC3
92/3 Pro Set RGL 2
92/3 Pro Set TL 13
91/2 Pro Set Platinum 272
02/3 Quest for the Cup 63, -CTC 10
91/2 Red Ace
99/0 Revolution 62, IS-6, O-12, SS-19, TL-4, / CSC 62
00/1 Revolution 61, HD-16, II-12, NI-13, SM-6
91/2 Score 49T
92/3 Score 14
92/3 Score 504
92/3 Score 523
93/4 Score 333
93/4 Score DT 19
93/4 Score IS 1
93/4 Score PiAS 31
93/4 Score TF 22
94/5 Score 190, DT24, NP5, TF24
95/6 Score 135, BB-11, DT-10, L-2
96/7 Score 35, DT-10, SD-6
97/8 Score 96, 261
97/8 Score Vanc. 1
92/3 Score Young Stars 30
92/3 Seasons 31
93/4 Seasons 2
94/5 Select 92, FL-6
95/6 Select CE 16, GT-5
96/7 Select CE 34, C-7
91 Semic Sticker 89
92 Semic Sticker 116
96/7 SB 7-Eleven Phonecard
00/1 Signature 226, HSHS, F-13, ✍ Aut. 1, ✂ J-10, ✂ HSHSJers
01/2 Signature C-32, ✍ Aut. LPBU, ✂ FP13, ✂ GUE26, ✂ GJ28, ✂ GSJ28, ✂ IRN26, ✂ IB6, ✂ TM13
02/3 Signature Series 176, ✍ 176, ✂ CJ8, ✂ FJ20, ✂ SGJ6, ✂ TQ4
95/6 SBx Emotion 178, Xci-16
95/6 SBx Impact 167, CTI-9, IQ-3
96/7 SBx Impact 131, CTI-1, VT-1
02/3 Slam Card
94/5 SP 121, P-16
95/6 SP 149, E29, FX20
96/7 SP 157, CW-16, SF-2
97/8 SP Authentic 156, I36
98/9 SP Authentic 86, SO17, ✍ SotT
99/0 SP Authentic 37, SF6, SS6, ✍ SotT
00/1 SP Authentic 38, ST4, SP3, SF4, ✍ SotT, ✍ SotTD, ✍ SotTT
01/2 SP Authentic 35, ✍ SotT, ✍ SotTD, ✍ SotTT
02/3 SP Authentic 61, 101, ✍ SotT
00/1 SP GU 27, ✂ TotG, ✂ C, ✂ P, ✂ A
01/2 SP GU 23, ✂ AF, ✂ Patch, ✂✍ PatchSig, ✂ PatchC, ✂✍ PatchCSig (x2), ✂ PatchT
02/3 SP Game-Used Edition 33, 63, ✂ AF, ✂ PH, ✍ Sig
02/3 Sports Vault 83
96/7 SPx 46
97/8 SPx 47, D-SPX6
99/0 SPx 69, HH7, X3, S3
00/1 SPx 28, 87, HH8, X7
01/2 SPx 29, 76, 86, 183
02/3 SPx 51, 94, 143, ✂ WM, ✂ M
98/9 SPx Finite 84, 91, 170
98/9 SPx Prospects 58, H29, L10
00/1 Stadion 99
99/0 Stadium 9, Chrome 9, Big 7, CA18, OE10
00/1 Stadium 1, CL, BT5, CA7, ✍ CO1, ✍ LS1, SF7
01/2 Stadium 16, G24, NHLP4, P1, ✂ SCS, ✂ SCSD (x2)
02/3 Stadium 59, -WS-18
91/2 Star Pics 25
94/5 Starting Lineup
95/6 SLU
00/1 SLU Classic Doubles 6
95/6 Super Sticker 123, DC-14
96/7 Team Out!
92/3 Topps 8
92/3 Topps 353
95/6 Topps 20, 300, 5CG, 5HG, M15, PF11
98/9 Topps 180, L14, M3, SB15
98/9 Topps SB15
99/0 Topps 10, AT15, TW9
00/1 Topps 6, 328, TC1, HM2, NHLD8, OTG2
01/2 Topps 8, OTG7, SM2, SG3
02/3 Topps 16, -CC2
99/0 To. Chrome 10, AT15
00/1 To. Chrome 6, TC1, HM2, RF1
01/2 To. Chrome 8
02/3 T. Chrome 16
94/5 Topps Finest 24, BBB-11, DF-20
95/6 To. Finest 75, 187
98/9 To. Finest 105, MA43, MA46, MA48, MA49, R4
94 Topps Finest Bronze 4
98/9 T. Gold Label 74
99/0 To. Gold Label 10, PG14
00/1 To. Gold Label 8, GG1
00/1 To. Heritage 9, 220, 230, 243, HH11
01/2 To. Heritage 11, 121, 124, 132
02/3 To. Heritage 10, -Light 10
02/3 T. Limited 16
96/7 Topps Picks 15, FT13
99/0 To. Prmr. Plus 71, CAC7, CR8, FP6
01/2 To.Reserve 8, ✂ TR
92/3 To. Stadium 246
92/3 To. Stadium 489
93/4 To. Stadium 480
93/4 To. Stadium - All-Stars
94/5 To. Stadium 10, DAD-3, F-5
95/6 To. Stadium EC186, EN1, N4
92 TSC Members Only
93/4 TSC Members Only 4
94/5 TSC Members Only 41
00/1 To. Stars 34, 127, AS10, WF1
95/6 T. Super Skills 30
02/3 T. Total 68, TTC20, TP8
91/2 Tri Globe From... 5-6
91/2 Tri Globe Mag. Five 6-10
98/9 UD Choice 208, BH30, SQ2
00/1 UD Heroes 148, PI3, TM5, TS3, ✍ SG
01/2 UD PlayMakers Ltd 45, / PM
00/1 UD Reserve 36, GS5, OS4, BT5
02/3 UD Superstars 165, ✂ CAS, ✂ CAST
00/1 Ultimate Mem. ✍ U-10, ✂ A8-3, ✂ J-10, ✂ Jer. 8, ✂ JJ-3, ✂ S-10, ✂ TM-19
01/2 Ultimate Mem. ✂ ASGH, ✂ BL, ✂ CT, ✂ DD, ✂ Emb., ✂ Jers., ✂ S&J, ✂ GSL, ✂ ITN, ✂ JE, ✂ JJ, ✂ NP, ✂ PP, ✂ WTF, ✍ Aut.
02/3 Ultimate Memorabilia ✂ ASMVP, ✂ DD, ✂ Emb, ✂ FS, ✂ GUJ, ✂ GUSJ, ✂ ITN, ✂ JE, ✂ JGUJ, ✂ LA, ✂ MO, ✂ NP, ✂ Num, ✍ Uaut
99/0 Ult. Victory 38, FF-3, sg-9, S6, UV-3
90/1 Upper Deck 526
91/2 Upper Deck 54
91/2 Upper Deck 555
91/2 Upper Deck 647
92/3 Upper Deck 156
92/3 Upper Deck 362
92/3 Upper Deck 431
92/3 Upper Deck SP2
92/3 Upper Deck E2
92/3 Upper Deck ERT1
92/3 Upper Deck WG5
93/4 Upper Deck 35, 307, FH-30, HB5, H2, SP-162
94/5 Upper Deck 227, 469, H2, H19, R1, R25, R31, R53, SP-171
95/6 Upper Deck 214, 406, AS-4, F-10, R-9, R-26, SE-172
96/7 Upper Deck 347, HH14, LS18, SS1A, ✂ GJ10
97/8 Upper Deck 168, SS24, SG58, S10, T5C
98/9 Upper Deck 18, 193, FF13, FT24, GN28-30, LS26
99/0 Upper Deck 59, 149, AS7, CT28, FF9, IG10, MA10, SB7, SS13
00/1 Upper Deck 74, A5, D6, EC4, FF6, F6, GA7, P5, RP2, SS11, TT7, ✂ DGJ, ✂ GJ
01/2 Upper Deck 73, 180, 230, FF1, FC2, LP6, SS8, SS6, T4
02/3 Upper Deck 119, 194, -GG12, -SS10, -SS11, ✂ GO, ✂ PA, ✂ R50, ✂ SD, ✂ GJ, ✂✍ SGJ
96/7 UD All-Star YCTG AR8
02/3 UD Artistic 59, R59, CG10, GD10, UD6, / Art
93/4 Upper Deck Be A Player 20
94/5 UD Be A Player R35, R177, UC3
95/6 UD Be A Player LL7
93/4 UD BAP Roots 15
96/7 UD Black Diam. 176, RC14
97/8 UD Black Diam. 115, PC9
98/9 UD Black Diam. 37, M10, WF28
99/0 UD Black Diam. 41, D8, DS4, M6, ✂ APOH
00/1 UD Black Diam. 26, 88, IG4, FP6, CC3
99/0 UD C. Legends 58, E6, ✍ ES
01/2 UD Challenge 37, CM10, CR6, ✂✍ FPS
02/3 UD Classic 65m ET11, GC6, ✂ CS, ✂ HR (x2)
95/6 UD CC 45, C1
96/7 UD CC 266, 333, UD22, S16, C17, CR17
97/8 UD Coll. Choice 255, SQ59, S25, C24, CR24
01/2 UD Collectors
97/8 UD Diam. Vision 10
02/3 UD Foundations 95, 154, ✂ CTW, ✂ PP
98/9 UD G. Reserve 18, 193
99/0 UD G. Reserve 59, 149, ✂ GR, ✍ UDA
99/0 UD Gretzky Excl. 76
01/2 UD Honor Roll 15, 45, SS4, -DPuck, ✂ HS
02/3 UD Honor 49, -SG20, ✍ SC
96/7 UD Ice 105
97/8 UD Ice 86
00/1 UD Ice 20, CC3, IG4, FP6, ✍ CCA, ✂ IGJ
01/2 UD Ice 20
00/1 UD Legends 55, 57, EG3, ✍ ES, ✂ LGJ
92/3 UD Locker 21
01/2 UD Mask 64
02/3 UD Mask 57, ✂ IO
98/9 UD MVP 85, OT11, -Snip. S8
99/0 UD MVP 85, 21st-9, S10, H3, GUS, ✂ GU18, ✍ PS
00/1 UD MVP 79, 219, ME2, M8, TD5, TP6, ✂ GS, ✍ PS, ✍ ME
01/2 UD MVP 78,MT7, VC2, ✂ C
02/3 UD MVP 122, ✍ PSig
99/0 UD MVP Cup 77, PH6, SS5, SC8, GC, ✂ GU, ✍ PS
99/0 UD Ovation 27, 88, LP5, ST9, APOH, ✍ APOH
02/3 UD Piece 60, AC20, ✂ EC, ✍ MD
99/0 UD PowerDeck 12
01/2 UD Premier 35, ✂ B, ✂ D (x2), ✍ SigG
02/3 UD Premier 37, ✂ Jers, ✂ JD, ✂ Patch, ✍ Sig
00/1 UD Pros&Prosp. 36, GS5, PM6, ✂ GJ
99/0 UD Retro 35, G6B, ✍ Ink.
02/3 UD Rookie 65, 166, ✂ DJ, ✂ S, ✍ TD
01/2 UD Top Shelf 19, 109, ✂ S, ✂ ST
02/3 UD Top Shelf 58, ✂ CP, ✂ GO, ✂ HH, ✂ HT (x2), ✂ M (x2), ✂ R, ✂ SH, ✂ ST, ✂ SW, ✍ Sig
00/1 UD Vintage 150, 160, 161, UD10, NH12
01/2 UD Vintage 106, 112, 113, 261, 264
02/3 UD Vintage 168, 280, 299, T44
91/2 VANC
91/2 VANC / Photo
91/2 VANC / PotM
91/2 VANC / PotM
92/3 VANC / Road Trip
94/5 VANC
95/6 VANC / Abalene 10
96/7 VANC / IGA
00/1 Vanguard 45, CF-6, HV-16, IF-10, VP-13
01/2 Vanguard 42, EMW 8, IF 6, VT 15, ✂ DGM 46
02/3 Vanguard 67, EMW 4, ✂ GWJ 30
99/0 Victory 119, 120
00/1 Victory 100, 101, 241, 251, 304, www.
01/2 Victory 151, 395
02/3 Victory 138, 220, -NP35
01/2 Waving the Flag 30
99/0 WGretzky 72, CG9, EG8, GH10, ✍ SG, ✂ TG
96 Wien 142
97/8 Zenith 34, Z59

BURE, VALERI

01/2 Adrenaline 80, ✂ GWJ 18
01/2 Atomic 45, ✂ GWJ 27
99/0 Aurora 20
00/1 Aurora 23, Pin. 23, ✍ Aut.
02/3 BAP All-Star 10, ✂ ASJ
98/9 Be A Player 170, ✍ Aut. 170
99/0 BAP Mem. 239
00/1 BAP Mem. 138, ✂ BB-1
01/2 BAP Memor. 244, 379, ✂ ASJ, ✂ ASE, ✂ ASN, ✂ AST, ✂ CoO
02/3 BAP Memorabilia 145, 260
95/6 Bowman 160, BB28
02/3 Calder ✂ GWJ 19
92/3 Classic 14
92/3 Classic - Autograph
92/3 Classic LP9
93/4 Classic 18
94/5 Classic 30, R4, T34
92/3 Classic Four Sport 163
92/3 Classic Four Sport BC8
92/3 Classic Four Sport LP24
93/4 Cla. 4 Sport 258
94/5 Cla. Images 77
99/0 Crown Royale 21
00/1 Crown Royale 17, ✂ GWJ-2
01/2 Crown Royale ✂ TT 3
02/3 Crown Royale ✂ GWDP 11, ✂ GWJ 7
95/6 Donruss 102
96/7 Donruss RR-3
97/8 Donruss 8
96/7 Do. Canadian 69
96/7 Do. Elite 119, A-8
97/8 Do. Elite 57
97/8 Do. Preferred 75
97/8 Do. Priority 95
99/0 Dynagon Ice 34
95/6 Edge Ice 40, C-11, QM-10
02/3 Exclusive 75
02/3 First Edition 74, ✂ Jers.
94/5 Flair 86
96/7 Fleer 52, 136, RS-3
96/7 Fl. Picks 124
94/5 Fleer Ultra 311
95/6 Fleer Ultra 256
01/2 FLOR
94/5 Fredericton Canadiens
01/2 Heads Up ✂ JQ 5
02/3 Heads Up ✂ GWQ 25
00/1 Kraft 14
94/5 Leaf 471
95/6 Leaf 39
96/7 Leaf 207
96/7 L. Limited 62
96/7 L. Preferred 88, LS-43
97/8 Limited 7
95/6 McDonald's McD-34
00/1 McDonald's 6, CL1
99/0 Millenium 40, ✍ Aut. 40
95/6 MONT
95/6 MONT / Export
96/7 MONT
97/8 MONT
98/9 NHL Power Play
01/2 O-Pee-Chee 48
02/3 O-Pee-Chee 54
98/9 Omega 30
99/0 Omega 35, 250, -WAS 2
99/0 Pacific 52
00/1 Pacific 62, GCDC-5
01/2 Pacific 58
02/3 Pacific 152
02/3 Pacific Complete 217
97/8 Pacific CC 116
99/0 Pa. Paramount 35
00/1 Pa. Paramount 34, FF-5
96/7 Panini Sticker 34
97/8 Panini Sticker 31
99/0 Panini Sticker 189
00/1 Panini Sticker 116
93/4 Parkhurst 509
93/4 Parkhurst 528
95/6 Parkhurst 114, 511
00/1 Parkhurst P-44
01/2 Parkhurst 237
02/3 Parkhurst 36
02/3 Parkhurst Retro 130
94/5 Parkie SE87
93/4 Pinnacle 501
94/5 Pinnacle 492
95/6 Pinnacle 174, GG-22
96/7 Pinnacle 209
95/6 Pi. Summit 197
96/7 Pi. Summit 160
95/6 Pi. Zenith 125
96/7 Pi. Zenith 9, A-15
95/6 POG 147
94/5 Premier 337
00/1 Premier Plus 26, ✂ GP
99/0 Prism 22
00/1 Pr. Stock 15, PSNW-5
01/2 Pr. Stock ✂ GUG 49
02/3 Pr. Stock Reserve 41
00/1 PS Titanium ✂ GUG 65
02/3 PS Titanium ✂ GWJ 31
00/1 PS Titanium Draft ✂ 14
95/6 Pro Magnet 20
99/0 Revolution 22, / CSC 22
00/1 Revolution 21
94/5 Score 215
95/6 Score 138
96/7 Score 245
97/8 Score 231
97/8 Score Mont. 10
94/5 Select 187
95/6 Select CE 131
96/7 Select CE 18
95 Semic 134
91/2 7th...Sketch WHL 1
00/1 Signature 201, ✍ Aut. 2, ✂ J-35
01/2 Signature ✂ IB14
96/7 SBx Impact 60, 167, F-4
94/5 SP P-11
95/6 SP 74
96/7 SP 80, HC-16
97/8 SP Authentic 78
99/0 SP Authentic 13
00/1 SP Authentic 13
01/2 SP Authentic 36
00/1 SP GU 8
01/2 SP GU 24
02/3 Sports Vault 43
99/0 SPx 21
00/1 SPx 9, HH4, ✂ WM
98/9 SPx Finite 14
99/0 Stadium 142
00/1 Stadium 135, BT16
95/6 Topps 358
99/0 Topps 31, PP4
00/1 Topps 96, 328, TC1, ✍ CAI
01/2 Topps 48
02/3 Topps 54
99/0 To. Chrome 31
00/1 To. Chrome 76, TC1
01/2 To. Chrome 48
94/5 Topps Finest 48
95/6 To. Finest 34
99/0 To. Gold Label 47
00/1 To. Gold Label 6
00/1 To. Heritage 114
01/2 To. Heritage 172
02/3 T. Limited 54
96/7 Topps Picks RS8
99/0 To. Prmr. Plus 29
95/6 To. Stadium 220
00/1 To. Stars 33
02/3 T. Total 113
98/9 UD Choice 31
00/1 UD Heroes 17
01/2 UD PlayMakers Ltd 43
00/1 UD Reserve 14
00/1 Ultimate Mem. ✍ U-37, ✂ J-36
01/2 Ultimate Mem. ✂ BL
99/0 Ult. Victory 13
91/2 Upper Deck 647
93/4 Upper Deck 571
94/5 Upper Deck 255, C8, SP-131
95/6 Upper Deck 304, SE-46
96/7 Upper Deck 283, X29
98/9 Upper Deck 52
99/0 Upper Deck 26
00/1 Upper Deck 26, A2, SS4
01/2 Upper Deck 302, T4
02/3 Upper Deck 78
94/5 UD Be A Player R159
95/6 UD Be A Player 34, ✍ S34
97/8 UD Black Diam. 6
99/0 UD Black Diam. 16
00/1 UD Black Diam. 8
01/2 UD Challenge 36
95/6 UD CC 119
96/7 UD CC 141
97/8 UD Coll. Choice 132
98/9 UD G. Reserve 52
99/0 UD G. Reserve 26
01/2 UD Honor Roll ✂ HS
02/3 UD Honor 83
00/1 UD Ice 7
00/1 UD Legends 20, 21
98/9 UD MVP 30
99/0 UD MVP 29
00/1 UD MVP 34
02/3 UD MVP 81
99/0 UD MVP Cup 29
99/0 UD Ovation 10
00/1 UD Pros&Prosp. 14
99/0 UD Retro 11
01/2 UD Top Shelf ✂ J
02/3 UD Top Shelf ✂ ST
00/1 UD Vintage 51, 61, 62, NH6
02/3 UD Vintage 108
00/1 Vanguard 15
99/0 Victory 44
00/1 Victory 34, 35, 241, 288
01/2 Victory 55
02/3 Victory 92
99/0 WGretzky 29

BUREAU, MARC

91/2 Bowman 126
92/3 Bowman 382
95/6 MONT
96-98 MONT
91/2 O-Pee-Chee 93
92/3 O-Pee-Chee 78
98/9 OPC Chrome 140
91/2 Parkhurst 302
92/3 Parkhurst 400
93/4 Parkhurst 461
91/2 Pinnacle 335
93/4 Pinnacle 321
96/7 Pi. Be A Player 82, ✍ Aut. 82
93/4 Premier 344
91/2 Pro Set 544
89/0 ProCards IHL 208
90/1 ProCards 603
88/9 Salt Lake G'Eagles
90/1 Score 423
91/2 Score CAN 476
97/8 Score Mont. 19
92/3 TAMP / Sheraton Inn
94/5 TAMP / Sky Box
95/6 TAMP / Sky Box
92/3 Topps 179
91/2 To. Stadium 322
92/3 To. Stadium 30
93/4 To. Stadium 134
91/2 Upper Deck 274
99/0 WGretzky 124

BURES, JIRI

99/0 Score 134

BURFOOT, SCOTT

94/5 Erie Panthers
95/6 Flint Generals
94/5 Fort Wayne Komets 8
98/9 Quad City Mallards
96/7 Richmond Renegades
99/0 Rockford IceHogs
00/1 Rockford IceHogs

BURGER, JIRI

95/6 APS 88
96/7 APS 92
97/8 APS 210
00/1 Cardset 132
98/9 DS 101
99/0 DS 164
01/2 DS 14
96/7 DS Sticker 149
97/8 DS Sticker 242
98/9 OFS 170
99/0 OFS 326, 497
01/2 OFS 75

BURGESS, DON

74/5 OPC WHA 32
77/8 OPC WHA 66
73/4 Vancouver Blazers

BURGESS, DRU

98/9 EBK ECHL All-Star
98/9 Roanoke Express

BURGESS, MARK

99/0 Charlotte Checkers

BURGESS, TIM

82/3 Oshawa Generals

BURGESS, TREVOR

96/7 DEL 132
99/0 Eishockey 244
93/4 Greensboro Monarchs
90/1 Oshawa Generals
91/2 Oshawa Generals
91/2 Oshawa Generals
92/3 Oshawa Generals
90/1 7th..Sketch OHL 329
91/2 7th...Sketch OHL 162

BURGESS, VAN

99/0 Greensboro Generals
93/4 Prince Albert Raiders
90/1 7th..Sketch WHL 45
91/2 7th...Sketch WHL 170

BURGIO, FRANK

01/2 Guelph Storm

BURGOYNE, JARRET

89/0 Victoria Cougars

BURGOYNE, RYAN

95/6 Slapshot 162

BURKE, CLAUDE

37/8 World Wide Gum 112

BURKE, DAVE

92/3 Greensboro Monarchs 15

BURKE, DON

92/3 Atlanta Knights

BURKE, EDDIE

33-35 Diamond Match Silv.
36-39 Diamond Match TT1

BURKE, GREG

93/4 Birmingham Bulls
95/6 Dayton Bombers
00/1 Kudos 127
02/3 London Knights
00/1 Nottingham Panthers

BURKE, GREGORY

96/7 DEL 111

BURKE, JIM

90/1 ProCards 174
91/2 ProCards 111

BURKE, JUSTIN

90/1 7th..Sketch WHL 63

BURKE, MARTY

34-43 BeeHive-1 [Chic.]
35-40 Canada Starch
33/4 Canadian Gum
33-35 Diamond Match Silv.
36-39 Diamond Match TT1
36-39 Diamond Match TT2
36-39 Diamond Match TT3
36-39 Diamond Match BH TT
36-39 Diamond Match Chic.
36-39 Diamond Match BH BT
33/4 Hamilton Gum 3
27/8 La Patrie
28/9 La Presse
33/4 WWGum 14
37/8 World Wide Gum 72

BURKE, SEAN

01/2 Adrenaline 146, CL, PP 27
01/2 Atomic 75
02/3 Atomic 78, -D 16
99/0 Aurora 62
02/3 BAP All-Star 13, ✂ ASJ
98/9 Be A Player 209, ✍ Aut. 209
99/0 BAP Mem. 216
00/1 BAP Mem. 354
01/2 BAP Memor. 83
02/3 BAP Memorabilia 110, ✂ SC10
01/2 BT Pipes 31, HSHS, -Mask, ✂ DM, ✂ Jers., ✂ S&J, ✂ GG, ✂ GT, ✂ HSHSJers
02/3 Between the Pipes 31, 143, M22, ✂ ASJ13, ✂ BM7, ✂ CP7, ✂ DM2, ✂ GUE29, ✂ GB18, ✂ GUJ29, ✂ GP7, ✂ GSJ29, ✂ GT17, ✂ HSHSJers 8, ✂ ITN29, ✂ I5, ✍ Aut.
98/9 Bicycle.. 7-D
91/2 Bowman 275
95/6 Bowman 26
01/2 Bowman 31
02/3 Bowman 37
92 C.O.A. Winter Olympics 185
91/2 Canada Nationals
97/8 CARO / Sprint
92/3 Classic 117
00/1 Crown Royale 82
01/2 Crown Royale 111
02/3 Crown Royale 75
93/4 Donruss 141
94/5 Donruss 158
95/6 Donruss 28, BTP-8
96/7 Donruss 121
97/8 Donruss 128
96/7 Do. Canadian 66
97/8 Do. Canadian 99
95/6 Do. Elite 107
96/7 Do. Elite 51
97/8 Do. Elite 39
97/8 Do. Preferred 104
97/8 Do. Priority 44
97/8 Do. Studio 62
98/9 Dynagon Ice 78
99/0 Dynagon Ice 88
93/4 EA Sports 60
02/3 Exclusive 133
02/3 First Edition 10, ✂ Jers.
94/5 Flair 70
94/5 Fleer 84
96/7 Fleer 45, VT-2
95/6 Fleer Metal 63
92/3 Fleer Ultra 68
93/4 Fleer Ultra 15
94/5 Fleer Ultra 87
95/6 Fleer Ultra 65, 367, PPM-2
96/7 Fl. Ultra 73
88/9 Frito Lay
92/3 HART / Dairymart
93/4 HART / Coke
95/6 HART / Kids Club
96/7 HART / Kids Club
01/2 Heads Up 75, ✂ JQ 16, ✂ JQ 26
02/3 Heads Up 95, -S 16
02/3 In The Game-Used 60, 160, ✂ GP13
89/0 Kraft 53
90/1 Kraft 4
92/3 Kraft / PB
94/5 Kraft / KD
95/6 Kraft / PS
89/0 Kraft Stickers 6
93/4 Leaf 132
94/5 Leaf 85
95/6 Leaf 63
96/7 Leaf 85
97/8 Leaf 63
95/6 L. Limited 14
96/7 L. Preferred 85
97/8 Limited 119, 194
96/7 Maggers 73
96/7 Metal Univ. 66
88/9 NJER / Caretta
89/0 NJER
89/0 NJER / Caretta
90/1 NJER
88/9 OPC/Topps 94
90/1 OPC/Topps 140
91/2 O-Pee-Chee 67
01/2 O-Pee-Chee 56
02/3 O-Pee-Chee 24
89/0 OPC/Topps 92
98/9 OPC Chrome 19
92/3 OPC Premier 92
88/9 OPC Sticker 82-211
88/9 OPC Sticker 158
89/0 opcSticker 86, 34-174, / FS 8
97/8 Omega 229
98/9 Omega 100
98/9 Pacific 321
99/0 Pacific 170
00/1 Pacific 311
01/2 Pacific 299, 438, SC 16
02/3 Pacific 292, -MI 6
02/3 Pacific Complete 177
97/8 Pacific CC 81
98/9 Pa. Crown Roy. 56
97/8 Pa. Dynagon 20, T-37
97/8 Pa. Invincible 22
99/0 Pa. Paramount 99
97/8 Pa. Revolution 140
98/9 Pa. Revolution 60
88/9 Panini Sticker 267
89/0 Panini Sticker 185, 256
90/1 Panini Sticker 77
91/2 Panini Sticker 212
93/4 Panini Sticker 131
94/5 Panini Sticker 117
95/6 Panini Sticker 35
96/7 Panini Sticker 24
98/9 Panini Sticker 91
99/0 Panini Sticker 54
92/3 Parkhurst 57
95/6 Parkhurst 96
00/1 Parkhurst P-246
01/2 Parkhurst 144
02/3 Parkhurst 166, ✂ TT20
02/3 Parkhurst Retro 140
94/5 Parkie SE71
92/3 Pinnacle 295
93/4 Pinnacle 31
94/5 Pinnacle 114, GT-12
95/6 Pinnacle 124, M-9
96/7 Pinnacle 37
97/8 Pinnacle 42
96/7 Pi. Be A Player 18, ✍ Aut. 18
97/8 Pi. Certified 25
97/8 Pi. Inside 30
95/6 Pi. Summit 125, ITC-13
96/7 Pi. Summit 109
97/8 Pi. Totally 25
95/6 Pi. Zenith 100
95/6 Playoff 45
94/5 POG 281
95/6 POG 131
93/4 Power Play 103
93/4 Premier 241
94/5 Premier 542
01/2 Pr. Stock 75, -PS 56, ✂ GUG 73
02/3 Pr. Stock Reserve 78, -ICS 17
00/1 PS Titanium 72, ✂ GUG-124
01/2 PS Titanium 108
00/1 PS Titanium Draft ✂ 75
95/6 Pro Magnet 126
90/1 Pro Set 164
91/2 Pro Set 132
92/3 Pro Set PV2
02/3 Quest for the Cup 78
99/0 Revolution 63
90/1 Score 34
90/1 Sco. Hot Cards 17
91/2 Score 245
91/2 Score CAN 465
92/3 Score COH 13
93/4 Score 126
93/4 Score TF 8
94/5 Score 84
95/6 Score 32, 320
96/7 Score 46
97/8 Score 1
90/1 Sco. Young Stars 11
94/5 Select 127
95/6 Select CE 100
96/7 Select CE 44
00/1 Signature 74
01/2 Signature 22, ✍ Aut. 22, ✂ FP23, ✂ GU80
02/3 Signature Series 98, ✍ 98
95/6 SBx Emotion 73
95/6 SBx Impact 71, D-4
96/7 SBx Impact 52, ZH-2
94/5 SP 51
95/6 SP 65
96/7 SP 70
01/2 SP Authentic 65
02/3 SP Authentic 69
01/2 SP GU 42
02/3 SP Game-Used Edition 38, ✂ PH
02/3 Sports Vault 270
01/2 SPx 50
02/3 SPx 58
00/1 Stadium 102
01/2 Stadium 45, ✂ SCS
02/3 Stadium 13, -PSH-11
95/6 Super Sticker 54
95/6 Topps 135
98/9 Topps 19
99/0 Topps 230
00/1 Topps 30
01/2 Topps 56, SG2
02/3 Topps 24
99/0 To. Chrome 230
00/1 To. Chrome 28
01/2 To. Chrome 56
02/3 T. Chrome 24
95/6 To. Finest 132
00/1 To. Heritage 125
01/2 To. Heritage 15
02/3 To. Heritage 25, ✂ CP, ✂ CPB
02/3 T. Limited 24
01/2 To.Reserve 20, ✂ TR
91/2 To. Stadium 76
93/4 To. Stadium 207
94/5 To. Stadium 171
95/6 To. Stadium 29
95/6 T. Super Skills 76
02/3 T. Total 97
98/9 UD Choice 147, 252
00/1 UD Heroes 93
01/2 UD PlayMakers Ltd 77
00/1 UD Reserve 66
02/3 UD Superstars 11
02/3 Ultimate Memorabilia ✂ NO
90/1 Upper Deck 66
91/2 Upper Deck 183
92/3 Upper Deck 518
94/5 Upper Deck 158
95/6 Upper Deck 130, SE-39
96/7 Upper Deck 72
97/8 Upper Deck 31
00/1 Upper Deck 366
01/2 Upper Deck 132
02/3 Upper Deck 133, 241, -LL10, -SA11, ✂ ASJ, ✂ ASP, ✂ PW
02/3 UD Artistic 68, R68, ✂ AT, / Art
94/5 UD Be A Player ✍ 53
00/1 UD Black Diam. ✂ GG
01/2 UD Challenge 66, ✂ T200
02/3 UD Classic 76, ✂ HR, ✂ SC
95/6 UD CC 199
96/7 UD CC 119, 319
97/8 UD Coll. Choice 111
02/3 UD Foundations 158
02/3 UD Honor 55
96/7 UD Ice 26
01/2 UD Ice 34
01/2 UD Mask 123, 185, ✂ CG, ✂ MM, ✂ VC
02/3 UD Mask 64, 65, 67, 105, ✂ CW, ✂ NB, ✂ PW, ✂ VC
01/2 UD MVP 147, MM10
02/3 UD MVP 141, MM6
99/0 UD MVP Cup 145
02/3 UD Piece 68, ✂ PH
01/2 UD Premier 40, ✂ D
01/2 UD Top Shelf 32, -ASGN
02/3 UD Top Shelf 68, ✂ CP, ✂ M, ✂ ST, ✂ SS
00/1 UD Vintage 281, 283, 284
01/2 UD Vintage 192, 198, 199, 269
02/3 UD Vintage 194, 283, GB 194, T49
01/2 Vanguard 75
00/1 Victory 178
01/2 Victory 265, 272
02/3 Victory 163
96 Wien 77

BURKE, TIM

90/1 NJER
77/8 Nova Scotia Voyageurs

BURKETT, MICHAEL

93/4 Michigan State
97/8 Pensacola Ice Pilots

BURKHARD, ALFRED

94/5 DEL 25

BURKHOLDER, BARRY

83/4 Kingston Canadians
84/5 Kingston Canadians
85/6 Kingston Canadians

BURKHOLDER, DAVE

95/6 Slapshot 204

BURKITT, NOËL

95/6 Slapshot 400

BURKITT, TOBY

90/1 7th..Sketch OHL 354
91/2 7th...Sketch OHL 356

BURLIN, DICK

89/0 Semic Elitserien 201

BURLUTSKI, OLEG

98/9 Mir 140

BURMAN, MICHAEL

94/5 Knoxville Cherokees
95/6 Richmond Renegades
90/1 7th..Sketch OHL 304
91/2 7th...Sketch OHL 62
93/4 Slapshot / North Bay 11

BURN, ARREN

93/4 Humberside Hawks 8

BURNETT, GARRETT

01/2 Cincinnati Mighty Ducks
00/1 Cleveland Lumberjacks
99/0 Kentucky Tho'blades
96/7 Knoxville Cherokees
94/5 Slapshot / Kitchener 35

BURNETT, GEORGE

95/6 Binghampton Rangers
96/7 Binghampton Rangers
89/0 Niagara Falls Thunder
92 7th...Sketch Awards 7
89/0 7th..Sketch OHL 124
91/2 7th...Sketch OHL 203

BURNETT, MATHEW

92/3 Ottawa 67's

BURNHAM, BRAD

91/2 Ferris State Bulldogs

BURNIE, STUART

88/9 ProCards / Springfield
90/1 ProCards 531

BURNS,

91/2 Avant Garde BCJHL 159

BURNS, BOB

94/5 DEL 416
96/7 DEL 291

BURNS, CHARLIE

68/9 Bauer Photo
45-64 BeeHive-2 [Bost.]
70/1 Colgate 19
70/1 Dad's Cookies
70/1 Eddie Sargent 87
71/2 Eddie Sargent 87
72/3 Eddie Sargent 106
70/1 Esso Power Player
62/3 Cowan Tile
68/9 O-Pee-Chee 108
69/0 O-Pee-Chee 129
70/1 O-Pee-Chee 44
70/1 O-Pee-Chee DE 13
71/2 O-Pee-Chee 238
72/3 O-Pee-Chee 178
61/2 Shirriff 4
58/9 Topps 43
59/0 Topps 40
60/1 Topps 24
61/2 Topps 11
61/2 Topps - Stamp
62/3 Topps 15
63/4 Topps 9
68/9 Topps 108
69/0 Topps 129
70/1 Topps 44
71/2 Topps 21
62/3 Toronto Star Photo
71/2 Toronto Sun Photo
59/60 Whitby Dunlops

BURNS, DARREN

87/8 Brockville Braves
88/9 Brockville Braves

BURNS, LANCE

90/1 7th..Sketch WHL 130
91/2 7th...Sketch WHL 346

BURNS, NORMAN

34-43 BeeHive-1 [NYRa.]

BURNS, PAT

93/4 Kraft / PB
88/9 MONT
89/0 MONT
89/0 MONT / Kraft
90/1 MONT
91/2 MONT
90/1 Pro Set 669

BURNS, R.R.

95/6 DEL 383

BURNS, ROBIN

74/5 Loblaws
75/6 O-Pee-Chee 104
75/6 Topps 104

BURNS, SEAN

90/1 7th..Sketch OHL 177
89/0 Windsor Spitfires

BURR, SHAWN

98/9 Be A Player 121, ✍ Aut. 121
90/1 Bowman 232
91/2 Bowman 43
92/3 Bowman 122
86/7 DETR / Little Caesars
87/8 DETR / Little Caesars
88/9 DETR / Little Caesars
88/9 DETR / S.A.M.
89/0 DETR / Little Caesars
90/1 DETR / Little Caesars
91/2 DETR / Little Caesars
92/3 Fleer Ultra 44
83/4 Kitchener Rangers
84/5 Kitchener Rangers
85/6 Kitchener Rangers
93/4 Leaf 296
94/5 Leaf 368
87/8 OPC/Topps 164
88/9 OPC/Topps 78
90/1 OPC/Topps 74
91/2 O-Pee-Chee 184
92/3 O-Pee-Chee 24
89/0 OPC/Topps 101
87/8 OPC Leaders 5
87/8 OPC Sticker 125-113
89/0 opcSticker 252-115
97/8 Pacific CC 152
97/8 Pa. Paramount 163
87/8 Panini Sticker 247
88/9 Panini Sticker 41
89/0 Panini Sticker 63
90/1 Panini Sticker 213
91/2 Panini Sticker 135
91/2 Parkhurst 45
93/4 Parkhurst 328
94/5 Parkhurst 62
95/6 Parkhurst 461
91/2 Pinnacle 86
92/3 Pinnacle 171
93/4 Pinnacle 93
94/5 Pinnacle 318
96/7 Pi. Be A Player 191, ✍ Aut. 191
93/4 Premier 83
90/1 Pro Set 66

91/2 Pro Set 58
92/3 Pro Set 45
90/1 Score 49
90/1 Sco. Hot Cards 21
91/2 Score 54
91/2 Score CAN 54
92/3 Score 207
93/4 Score 175
95/6 Score 13
94/5 Slapshot / Sarnia 29
92/3 Topps 178
91/2 To. Stadium 101
92/3 To. Stadium 126
93/4 To. Stadium 313
90/1 Upper Deck 111
91/2 Upper Deck 315
93/4 Upper Deck 91
94/5 Upper Deck 484
95/6 Upper Deck 355
94/5 UD Be A Player ✍ 93
96/7 UD CC 254

BURRELL, RICK
93/4 Hampton Roads
95/6 Hampton Roads

BURRIDGE, RANDY
88/9 BOST / Sports Action
89/0 BOST / Sports Action
90/1 BOST / Sports Action
91/2 Bowman 349
91/2 Bowman 410
92/3 Bowman 29
92/3 Bowman 225
93/4 Donruss 503
94/5 Donruss 66
96/7 Donruss 127
94/5 Flair 197
95/6 Fleer Metal 13
93/4 Fleer Ultra 444
95/6 Fleer Ultra 210
94/5 Leaf 291
96/7 Leaf 121
86/7 OPC/Topps 70
88/9 OPC/Topps 33
90/1 OPC/Topps 190
91/2 O-Pee-Chee 358
92/3 O-Pee-Chee 370
89/0 OPC/Topps 121
91/2 OPC Premier 43
88/9 OPC Sticker 159
88/9 OPC Sticker 29-169
89/0 opcSticker 28-166
97/8 Pa. Invincible R-18
88/9 Panini Sticker 208
89/0 Panini Sticker 197
91/2 Panini Sticker 174
92/3 Panini Sticker 163
91/2 Parkhurst 190
93/4 Parkhurst 492
95/6 Parkhurst 293
91/2 Pinnacle 55
92/3 Pinnacle 115
93/4 Pinnacle 418
94/5 Pinnacle 110
96/7 Pinnacle 198
97/8 Pi. Be A Player 79, ✍ Aut. 79
96/7 Pi. Summit 26
94/5 POG 243, 343
93/4 Power Play 464
90/1 Pro Set 2
91/2 Pro Set 4
91/2 Pro Set 510
92/3 Pro Set 207
91/2 Pro Set Platinum 241
90/1 Score 72
91/2 Score 102
91/2 Score 14T
91/2 Score CAN 102
91/2 Score CAN 564
92/3 Score 297
93/4 Score 370
94/5 Score 90
95/6 Score 164
96/7 Score 52
97/8 Score Buff. 6
92/3 Topps 83
95/6 To. Finest 21
91/2 To. Stadium 119
92/3 To. Stadium 61
93/4 To. Stadium 416
94/5 To. Stadium 163
90/1 Upper Deck 196
91/2 Upper Deck 567
92/3 Upper Deck 153
93/4 Upper Deck 504
95/6 Upper Deck 320, SE-99
95/6 UD Be A Player 114, ✍ S114
96/7 UD CC 28
91/2 WASH / Kodak
91/2 WASH / Smokey
92/3 WASH / Kodak

BURROWS, ALEXANDRE
01/2 Shawinigan 20

BURROWS, DAVE
77/8 Coke
72/3 Eddie Sargent 182
74/5 Loblaws
72/3 O-Pee-Chee 133
73/4 O-Pee-Chee 140
74/5 O-Pee-Chee 137
74/5 O-Pee-Chee 241
75/6 O-Pee-Chee 186
76/7 O-Pee-Chee 83
77/8 O-Pee-Chee 66
78/9 O-Pee-Chee 254
80/1 O-Pee-Chee 147
71/2 PITT / Sportcolor
74/5 PITT
77/8 PITT / McDonald's
72/3 Topps 82
73/4 Topps 27
74/5 Topps 137
74/5 Topps 241
75/6 Topps 186
76/7 Topps 83
77/8 Topps 66
78/9 Topps 254
80/1 Topps 147
78/9 TORO
79/0 TORO

BURSTRÖM, ANDERS
94/5 Leaf Elit Set 173
95/6 Leaf Elit Set 250
97/8 UD Elitserien 129
98/9 UD Elitserien 143
99/0 UD Elitserien 145
00/1 UD Elitserien 130

BURT, ADAM
90/1 Bowman 252
97/8 CARO / Sprint
98/9 CARO / Highwoods
93/4 Donruss 139
92/3 Fleer Ultra 69
91/2 HART / Jr. Whalers
92/3 HART / Dairymart
93/4 HART / Coke
95/6 HART / Kids Club
96/7 HART / Kids Club
93/4 Leaf 280
90/1 O-Pee-Chee 431
99/0 Pacific 300
97/8 Pa. Invincible R-34
91/2 Panini Sticker 318
92/3 Panini Sticker 264
91/2 Parkhurst 291
91/2 Pinnacle 77
93/4 Pinnacle 313
94/5 Pinnacle 356
95/6 Pinnacle 200
96/7 Pi. Be A Player 117, ✍ Aut. 117
95/6 Playoff 155
90/1 Pro Set 447
90/1 Score 370
91/2 Score CAN 449
92/3 Score 261
93/4 Score 307
92/3 Topps 283
95/6 Topps 184
92/3 To. Stadium 139
90/1 Upper Deck 324
95/6 Upper Deck 303
00/1 UD Pros&Prosp. 5

BURT, WADE
96/7 Kamloops Blazers
97/8 Kamloops Blazers

BURTON, ARCHIE
52/3 Anonymous 16

BURTON, CUMMING
52/3 Anonymous 8

BURTON, JAMES
95 Globe 188
95 Semic 184
96 Wien 213

BURTON, JIM
95/6 Phoenix Roadrunners

BURTON, JOE
92/3 Oklahoma City Blazers
98/9 Oklahoma City Blazers

BUSCH, ROBERT
95/6 DEL 238

BUSCHAN, ANDREI
94/5 Classic 4 Sport 152
93/4 Kansas City Blades
94/5 Kansas City Blades 5

BUSENBURG, MARK
02/3 Hershey Bears

BUSH, EDDIE
34-43 BeeHive-1 [Detr.]

BUSHAN, ANDREI
99/0 Mir 144

BUSILLO, GIUSEPPE
98/9 DEL 105
99/0 Eishockey 56

BUSILLO, JOE
96/7 DEL 354
01/2 Manchester Storm
89/0 Oshawa Generals
90 7th..Sketch Mem.Cup 86
91 7th..Sketch Mem.Cup 16
89/0 7th..Sketch OHL 3
90/1 7th..Sketch OHL 154

BUSKAS, ROD
91/2 CHIC / Coke
92/3 Indianapolis Ice
93/4 Las Vegas Thunder
98/9 Las Vegas Thunder
90/1 LOSA / Smokey 23
90/1 O-Pee-Chee 509
87/8 Panini Sticker 144
91/2 Pinnacle 417
83/4 PITT / Coke Is It!
84/5 PITT / Heinz
86/7 PITT / Kodak
87/8 PITT / Kodak
90/1 Pro Set 456
92/3 Salt Lake G'Eagles
90/1 Score 12T
91/2 Score CAN 427

BUSKOVEN, HENRIK
92/3 Semic Nordisk 63

BUSNIAK, MIKE
91/2 7th...Sketch WHL 306

BUSNIUK, MIKE
95/6 Binghampton Rangers
96/7 Binghampton Rangers
80/1 O-Pee-Chee 326
81/2 O-Pee-Chee 249

BUSNIUK, RON
74/5 Minn. Fight. Saints

BUSTO, MICHAEL
02/3 Moose Jaw Warriors

BUSWELL, WALTER
34-43 BeeHive-1 [Mont.]
35-40 Canada Starch
36-39 Diamond Match TT3
37/8 O-Pee-Chee 174
39/0 O-Pee-Chee 32
38/9 Quaker Oats
37/8 World Wide Gum 32

BUTCHER, GARTH
91/2 Bowman 383
92/3 Bowman 124
93/4 Donruss 289
93/4 Donruss 477
93/4 EA Sports 122
92/3 Fleer Ultra 184
93/4 Fleer Ultra 27
84/5 Kelowna Wings &...
93/4 Leaf 239
94/5 Leaf 466
88/9 O-Pee-Chee 202
90/1 OPC/Topps 150
91/2 O-Pee-Chee 204
92/3 O-Pee-Chee 280
87/8 OPC Sticker 200-59
88/9 OPC Sticker 54-185
89/0 opcSticker 72-210
87/8 Panini Sticker 343
88/9 Panini Sticker 134
89/0 Panini Sticker 158
90/1 Panini/VAN 5
91/2 Panini Sticker 28
92/3 Panini Sticker 24
93/4 Panini Sticker 164
91/2 Parkhurst 374
92/3 Parkhurst 390
93/4 Parkhurst 449
94/5 Parkhurst 188
91/2 Pinnacle 85
91/2 Pinnacle 409
92/3 Pinnacle 72
93/4 Pinnacle 66
94/5 Pinnacle 394
95/6 Pinnacle 53
93/4 Power Play 208
93/4 Premier 316
94/5 Premier 441
90/1 Pro Set 295
91/2 Pro Set 210
91/2 Pro Set 583
92/3 Pro Set 160
91/2 Pro Set Platinum 223
81/2 Regina Pats
90/1 Score 18
91/2 Score 24
91/2 Score CAN 24
92/3 Score 65
93/4 Score 173
93/4 Score 657
93/4 Score PiAS 24
94/5 Score 13
91/2 SLOU
92/3 Topps 281
91/2 To. Stadium 223
92/3 To. Stadium 287
93/4 To. Stadium 21
93/4 To. Stadium - All-Stars
90/1 Upper Deck 98
91/2 Upper Deck 397
83/4 Vachon 103-23
82/3 VANC
83/4 VANC
84/5 VANC
85/6 VANC
86/7 VANC
87/8 VANC / Shell
88/9 VANC / Mohawk
89/0 VANC / Mohawk
90/1 VANC / Mohawk

BUTCHER, GARTH
02/3 Fleer Throwbacks 74

BUTENSCHON, SVEN
95/6 Brandon Wheat Kings
96/7 Cleveland Lumberjacks
01/2 Hamilton Bulldogs
94/5 SR Tetrad CIV, ✍ Aut.
94/5 Slapshot Memorial 33
98/9 Upper Deck 10
98/9 UD G. Reserve 10
00/1 WBS Penguins

BUTKA, MIKE
86/7 Saskatoon Blades

BUTKO, SERGEI
95/6 APS 158
96/7 APS 174
96/7 DS Sticker 40
00/1 Mir 24
98/9 OFS 6

BUTKUS, ALEX
01/2 Guelph Storm
01/2 Guelph Storm M-Cup

BUTLER, JEROME
93/4 Minnesota-Duluth

BUTLER, JERRY
74/5 Loblaws
74/5 O-Pee-Chee 393
75/6 O-Pee-Chee 167
76/7 O-Pee-Chee 336
77/8 O-Pee-Chee 349
78/9 O-Pee-Chee 304
79/0 O-Pee-Chee 393
80/1 O-Pee-Chee 351
81/2 O-Pee-Chee 332
80/1 Pepsi Bottle Cap
75/6 Topps 167
78/9 TORO
80/1 VANC
80/1 VANC / Silverwood
81/2 VANC
81/2 VANC / Silverwood
82/3 WINN

BUTLER, JOHN
99/0 Peoria Rivermen

BUTLER, ROB
95/6 Slapshot 395

BUTLER, ROD
98/9 Oklahoma City Blazers

BUTLER, STAN
99/0 Brampton Batallion 28
95/6 Slapshot 255

BUTORAC, ALI
83/4 Belleville Bulls
81/2 Oshawa Generals

BUTORAC, TONY
80/1 Soo Greyhounds

BUTSAYEV, VIACHESLAV
93/4 Classic 87
92/3 Classic Prospects 131
92/3 Classic Prospects BC14
98/9 EBK IHL All-Star
92/3 Fleer Ultra 153
93/4 Fleer Ultra 385
97/8 Fort Wayne Komets
98/9 Fort Wayne Komets
99/0 Grand Rapids Griffins
00/1 Grand Rapids Griffins
93/4 Leaf 307
91/2 O-Pee-Chee 12R
92/3 OPC Premier 31
92/3 Parkhurst 363
93/4 Parkhurst 151
94/5 Parkhurst 213
92/3 PHIL / UD Sheet
93/4 PHIL / Sheet
93/4 PHIL / J.C. Penney
94/5 Pinnacle 498
93/4 Premier 79
92/3 Red Ace Blue 14
92/3 Red Ace Violet 6
92/3 SANJ / Pacific Bell
93/4 Score 656
94 Semic 148
91 Semic Sticker 90
92 Semic Sticker 114
93/4 To. Stadium 94
92/3 Upper Deck 503
93/4 Upper Deck 406
94/5 Upper Deck 417

BUTSAYEV, YURI
99/0 BAP Mem. 317
01/2 Cincinnati Mighty Ducks
99/0 Dynagon Ice 71
99/0 Millenium 94, ✍ Aut. 94
99/0 NHL Power Play
99/0 Stadium 175
99/0 To. Prmr. Plus 107

BUTSENKO, KONSTANTIN
98/9 Mir 112

BUTT, JAMIE
92/3 Tacoma Rockets
93/4 Tacoma Rockets

BUTT, KEVIN
89/0 Oshawa Generals
90 7th..Sketch Mem.Cup 76
89/0 7th..Sketch OHL 18
90/1 7th..Sketch OHL 101

BUTTERFIELD, JACK
83 HHOF Postcard M2
83&87 HHOF 167

BUTTERS, MIKE
91/2 Greensboro Monarchs
90/1 ProCards 551

BUTURLIN, ALEXANDER
00/1 Mir 292
99/0 SP Authentic 128
99/0 Upper Deck 322
99/0 UD G. Reserve 322
99/0 UD MVP Cup 200

BUTURLIN, MIKHAIL
99/0 Mir 205

BUTZ, CRAIG
83/4 Kelowna Wings

BUTZ, ROB
95/6 St. John's Maple Leafs
96/7 St. John's Maple Leafs

BUZAK, MIKE
98/9 Albany River Rats
95/6 Edge Ice 91
97/8 Long Beach Ice Dogs
93/4 Michigan State

BUZAS, GYORGY
79 Panini Sticker 273

BUZEK, PETR
94/5 APS 167
99/0 BAP Mem. 353
00/1 BAP Mem. 245
95/6 Classic 52, ✍ Aut.
95/6 Cla. 5 Sport 133
96/7 Michigan K-Wings
98/9 Michigan K-Wings
99/0 Millenium C-25
99/0 NHL Power Play
99/0 Omega 15
00/1 Pacific 16
00/1 Panini Sticker 9
99/0 Prism 7
00/1 Signature 130, ✍ Aut. 48
94/5 SP 155
00/1 Stadium 133
00/1 Topps 184
00/1 To. Chrome 123
99/0 To. Prmr. Plus 122
98/9 Upper Deck 82
98/9 UD G. Reserve 82
00/1 UD Vintage 20

BYAKIN, ILYA
93/4 Donruss 427
93/4 EDMO / Sheet
94/5 Fleer Ultra 70
97/8 Las Vegas Thunder 21
95/6 Leaf Elit Set 261
00/1 Mir 157
90/1 O-Pee-Chee 1R
91/2 O-Pee-Chee 13R
93/4 Parkhurst 341
93/4 Power Play 341
94/5 Premier 223
93/4 Score 619
95 Semic 124
91 Semic Sticker 83
93 Semic Sticker 131
89/0 Soviet Stars
95/6 UD Elitserien 136
96 Wien 138

BYCE, JOHN
90/1 BOST / Sports Action
90/1 Bowman 38
97/8 Long Beach Ice Dogs
98/9 Long Beach Ice Dogs
91/2 ProCards 59
90/1 Score 62T
90/1 Upper Deck 25

BYE, CARLOS
91/2 7th...Sketch WHL 217

BYE, GUNNAR
92/3 Semic Nordisk 123

BYE, KARYN
94/5 Classic W27

BYERS, JERRY
74/5 Loblaws
74/5 O-Pee-Chee 273

BYERS, LYNDON
84/5 BOST
88/9 BOST / Sports Action
89/0 BOST / Sports Action
90/1 BOST / Sports Action
93/4 Las Vegas Thunder
86/7 Moncton G'Flames
90/1 O-Pee-Chee 464
90/1 Pro Set 3
81/2 Regina Pats
82/3 Regina Pats
83/4 Regina Pats

BYERS, MIKE
70/1 Colgate 55
71/2 Eddie Sargent 80
70/1 Esso Power Player
72/3 Los Angeles Sharks
72/3 New England Whalers
70/1 O-Pee-Chee 160
71/2 O-Pee-Chee 34
68/9 Shirriff / Toro. 17
71/2 Topps 34
71/2 Toronto Sun Photo

BYFUGLIEN, JAMIE
91/2 Air Canada SJHL C21

BYKOV, DMITRI
02/3 Atomic 106
02/3 BAP All-Star 146
02/3 BAP Memorabilia 284
02/3 Bowman 158
02/3 Calder 115
02/3 Crown Royale 110
02/3 Exclusive 177
02/3 Heads Up 126
02/3 In The Game-Used 91
99/0 Mir 50
00/1 Mir 31, 267
02/3 Pacific Complete 537
02/3 Parkhurst 214
02/3 Parkhurst Retro 214
02/3 Pr. Stock Reserve 159
02/3 Private Stock Titanium 113
02/3 Quest for the Cup 116
02/3 Signature Series 193, ✍ 193
02/3 SP Authentic 143
02/3 SP Game-Used Edition 76
02/3 Stadium 140
02/3 T. Chrome 161
02/3 To. Heritage 155
02/3 T. Total 405
02/3 Ultimate Memorabilia 14
02/3 Upper Deck 435
02/3 UD Classic 112
02/3 UD Honor 112
02/3 UD Mask 131
02/3 UD Premier 52
02/3 UD Rookie ✂ 162
02/3 UD Top Shelf 112
02/3 Vanguard 112

BYKOV, VYACHESLAV
95 Globe 180
00/1 Mir Fetisov 22
90/1 O-Pee-Chee 10R
94 Panini Olympics 281
95 Panini Worlds 49
94 Semic 145
95 Semic 138
89 Semic Sticker 92
91 Semic Sticker 100
93 Semic Sticker 147
83/4 Soviet Stars
87/8 Soviet Stars
89/0 Soviet Stars
96 Wien 151

BYLSMA, DAN
92/3 Greensboro Monarchs 6
93/4 Greensboro Monarchs
98/9 Long Beach Ice Dogs
99/0 Millenium 124, ✍ Aut. 124
02/3 Pacific Complete 282
97/8 Pacific CC 323
94/5 Phoenix Roadrunners
95/6 Phoenix Roadrunners
97/8 Pi. Be A Player 29, ✍ Aut. 29
96/7 Upper Deck 276
01/2 UD Vintage 7

BYLSMA, SHELDON
91/2 Air Canada SJHL D29
92/3 MPS SJHL 167

BYRAM, SHAWN
92/3 Indianapolis Ice
93/4 Indianapolis Ice
88/9 ProCards / Springfield
89/0 ProCards AHL 235
90/1 ProCards 496
91/2 ProCards 482

BYRNES, JASON
94/5 Slapshot / Kitchener 7
95/6 Slapshot 146

BYRON, WALLY
24/5 Falcons Crescent 2
24/5 Holland Creameries 8

BYSTRÖM, LARS
94/5 Leaf Elit Set 92, SS-9
95/6 Leaf Elit Set 109
89/0 Semic Elitserien 182
90/1 Semic Elitserien 17
91/2 Semic Elitserien 216
92/3 Semic Elitserien 245
95/6 UD Elitserien 169

BZDEL, GERALD
89/0 Halifax Citadels
90/1 Halifax Citadels
88/9 ProCards / Halifax
89/0 ProCards AHL 174
90/1 ProCards 444
91/2 ProCards 529

BZDEL, MIKE
92/3 BCJHL 150

C

CABANA, CHADDEN
96/7 Carolina Monarchs
99/0 Louisville Panthers
98/9 New Haven Beast 11
91/2 7th...Sketch WHL 298

CACHNIN, RICHARD
98/9 OFS 63
99/0 Score 48

CADDEN, CORY
93/4 Knoxville Cherokees
94/5 Knoxville Cherokees

CADIEUX, BRUNO
99/0 Rouyn-Noranda
00/1 Rouyn-Noranda 21

CADIEUX, JAN PHILIPPE
99/0 Rimouski Océanic 10

CADIEUX, STEVE
91/2 Cincinnati Cyclones

CADOTTE, MARK
99/0 Louisiana Ice Gators
02/3 Nottingham Panthers
95/6 Slapshot 78

CAFFERY, JACK
52/3 Anonymous 154
45-64 BeeHive-2 [Bost.]
55/6 Parkhurst 19
93/4 Parkie 56-57 12
57/8 Topps 8

CAFFERY, TERRY
72/3 New England Whalers
69/0 O-Pee-Chee 135

CAGAS, PAVEL
94/5 APS 1
95/6 APS 101
96/7 DEL 226
98/9 DS 18
99/0 DS 43, G4
98/9 OFS 313
99/0 OFS 531
01/2 OFS 240, -CL3, -H12
00/1 UD DEL 96

CAGE, JOAQUIN
91/2 7th...Sketch WHL 46

CAHAN, LARRY
45-64 BeeHive-2 [Toro.]
45-64 BeeHive-2 [NYRa.]
45-64 BeeHive-2 [NYRa.]
64-67 BeeHive-3 [NYRa.]
70/1 Dad's Cookies
70/1 Eddie Sargent 79
70/1 Esso Power Player
62/3 Cowan Tile
68/9 O-Pee-Chee 35
70/1 O-Pee-Chee 164
72/3 O-Pee-Chee 307
55/6 Parkhurst 16
93/4 Parkie 56-57 87
61/2 Shirriff 95
57/8 Topps 59
58/9 Topps 23
61/2 Topps 52
62/3 Topps 48
63/4 Topps 51
68/9 Topps 35
71/2 Toronto Sun Photo

CAHILL, DARCY
94/5 Humberside Hawks 10
87/8 Kingston Canadians
90/1 7th..Sketch OHL 204

CAHOON, JIM
77/8 Nova Scotia Voyageurs

CAHTINEN, TIMO
92/3 Semic Elitserien 331

CAIN, AARON
91/2 Air Canada SJHL A39
92/3 MPS SJHL 23

CAIN, DUTCH
25-27 Anonymous 91 [No Border]
25-27 Anonymous 91

CAIN, HERBERT
34-43 BeeHive-1 [Maroons]
35-40 Canada Starch
35-40 Canada Starch
35/6 O-Pee-Chee 77
36/7 O-Pee-Chee 110
37/8 O-Pee-Chee 172
39/0 O-Pee-Chee 42
38/9 Quaker Oats
34/5 Sweet Caporal
37/8 World Wide Gum 46

CAIN, JIM
24/5 Champ's Cigarettes
24/5 Maple Crispette [V130] 16
24/5 William Paterson 35

CAIN, KELLY
86/7 Kitchener Rangers
85/6 London Knights

CAIRNS, ERIC
00/1 BAP Mem. 58, ✂ T-4
01/2 BAP Update ✂ TC30, ✂TC40
94/5 Binghampton Rangers
95/6 Binghampton Rangers
97/8 Hartford Wolf Pack
97/8 Pacific CC 301
97/8 Pi. Be A Player 28, ✍ Aut. 28
91/2 7th...Sketch OHL 31
93/4 Slapshot / Detroit 7
02/3 Upper Deck 354
02/3 UD Vintage 160, 279

CAIRNS, TREVOR
93/4 Tacoma Rockets

CAISSIE, JEREMY
91/2 7th...Sketch LHJMQ 279

CAJANEK, PETR
94/5 APS 202
95/6 APS 46
96/7 APS 45
97/8 APS 66
02/3 Crown Royale -RR 18
97/8 DS 108
98/9 DS 111
99/0 DS 7
00/1 DS 56, TS3, VP6
01/2 DS 15, 60, -BB 4
96/7 DS Sticker 111
97/8 DS Sticker 298
02/3 Exclusive 189
98/9 OFS 29, 488
99/0 OFS 258, 451, 511
00/1 OFS 361, -Star 5
01/2 OFS 93, -RE18D, -UHI 6
94/5 Parkie SE214
02/3 Signature Series 136, ✍ 136
02/3 Stadium 118
94/5 Upper Deck 507
02/3 Vanguard - PP 19

CAJKA, LUDEK
97/8 APS 377
98/9 OFS Leg. 9

CALBECK, JACK
83/4 Brantford Alexanders

CALCE, LUIGI
93/4 Owen Sound Platers
91/2 7th...Sketch OHL 282

CALDER, FRANK
83 HHOF Postcard B3
83&87 HHOF 18
93/4 Legends of Hockey 36
01/2 UD Legends 51

CALDER, GLENN
91/2 Avant Garde BCJHL 79
92/3 BCJHL 98
91/2 Nanaimo Clippers

CALDER, KYLE
99/0 BAP Mem. 335
01/2 BAP Memor. 236
02/3 BAP Memorabilia ✂ FG16
99 Bowman 84
01/2 Bowman 149, ✂ FFJ, ✂ FFS, ✂ FFDS, ✂ FFR, ✍ YSA
99/0 Cleveland Lumberjacks
99/0 Crown Royale 31
01/2 Crown Royale 31, ✂ TT 6
02/3 First Edition 232
01/2 Heads Up ✂ JQ 6
99/0 Millenium C-3
01/2 O-Pee-Chee 172
02/3 O-Pee-Chee 169
02/3 Pacific 75
02/3 Pacific Complete 132
02/3 Parkhurst Retro 86
01/2 Pr. Stock ✂ GUG 21
01/2 PS Titanium 30, ✂ DSJ 9
01/2 PS Titanium Draft ✂ 21
96/7 Regina Pats
97/8 Regina Pats
01/2 Signature 98, ✍ Aut. 98
02/3 Signature Series 84, ✍ 84
99/0 SP Authentic 99
02/3 SP Authentic 112
02/3 SP Game-Used ✂ FF (x2)
02/3 Sports Vault 176
01/2 SPx 166
02/3 Stadium ✂ YSS12
00/1 Topps 317
01/2 Topps 172
02/3 Topps 169
00/1 To. Chrome 212
02/3 T. Limited 169
99/0 To. Prmr. Plus 103
02/3 T. Total 238
99/0 Ult. Victory 95
99/0 Upper Deck 203
02/3 Upper Deck 38
02/3 UD Artistic ✂ RT
99/0 UD Black Diam. 21
99/0 UD G. Reserve 203
02/3 UD MVP 42
02/3 UD Vintage 57, 267
01/2 Vanguard 20
00/1 Victory 275
01/2 Victory 80
02/3 Victory 48
99/0 WGretzky 45

CALDER, PIERRE
90/1 7th..Sketch LHJMQ 61

CALDER, SHANE
98/9 EBK ECHL All-Star
96/7 Pensacola Ice Pilots
97/8 Pensacola Ice Pilots
90/1 Saskatoon Blades
91/2 Saskatoon Blades
93/4 Saskatoon Blades
90/1 7th..Sketch WHL 73
91/2 7th...Sketch WHL 109

CALDR, VLADIMIR
94/5 APS 286
95/6 APS 51, 445
96/7 APS 237
97/8 APS 264
98/9 OFS 307
99/0 OFS 41

CALDWELL, JUSTIN
93/4 W. Michigan Broncos

CALLAHAN, GARY
84/5 Belleville Bulls
86/7 Kitchener Rangers
88/9 ProCards / Binghampton

CALLAHAN, GREG
96/7 Johnstown Chiefs

CALLAHAN, JACK
94/5 Knoxville Cherokees
94/5 SR Auto-Phonex 11, ✍ 11

CALLANDER, DREW
01/2 Regina Pats
79/0 VANC / Royal Bank

CALLANDER, JOCK
92/3 Atlanta Knights
93/4 Cleveland Lumberjacks
95/6 Cleveland Lumberjacks
96/7 Cleveland Lumberjacks
97/8 Cleveland Lumberjacks
98/9 Cleveland Lumberjacks
99/0 Cleveland Lumberjacks
00/1 Cleveland Lumberjacks
95/6 Edge Ice 115
87/8 PITT / Kodak
92/3 Pro Set 175
88/9 ProCards / Muskegon
91/2 ProCards 291
81/2 Regina Pats
93/4 Upper Deck 10

CALLANDER, JOHN
90/1 ProCards 371

CALLIGHEN, BRETT
79/0 EDMO
80/1 EDMO / Zellers
81/2 EDMO / Red Rooster
88/9 EDMO / Action 50
79/0 O-Pee-Chee 315
80/1 O-Pee-Chee 114
81/2 O-Pee-Chee 110
82/3 O-Pee-Chee 103
81/2 OPC Sticker 212
80/1 Pepsi Bottle Cap
81/2 Post 20
82/3 Post [Edmo.]
80/1 Topps 114

CALLINAN, JEFF
95/6 Birmingham Bulls
91/2 Minnesota G'Gophers
92/3 Minnesota G'Gophers
93/4 Minnesota G'Gophers
94/5 Minnesota G'Gophers

CALOUN, JAN
98 Bonaparte 4C
98 Bonaparte Pexeso 14
98/9 Cardset 40
99/0 Cardset 4, 26, 158, AH 6-ruutu
00/1 Cardset 262, MB-2
02/3 Cardset 8
92/3 Classic 38
94/5 Cla. Images 23, PR10
95/6 Edge Ice 144
95/6 Future Legends 16
97/8 Hockey-Box
94/5 Kansas City Blades 9
95/6 Kansas City Blades
96/7 Kentucky Tho'blades
96/7 Leaf 217
96/7 Metal Univ. 173
98/9 OFS 244
99/0 OFS 259
96/7 Pinnacle 229
96/7 Pi. Summit 187
99/0 Score N 13
95 Semic 159
96/7 Upper Deck 195
91/2 Upper Deck WJC 91
00/1 UD Vintage 109

CALVANESE, R.
88/9 ProCards / Springfield

CALVERLY, CHRIS
84/5 Victoria Cougars

CALVERT, JEFF
90/1 7th..Sketch WHL 159
91/2 7th...Sketch WHL 153
92/3 Tacoma Rockets
93/4 Tacoma Rockets

CAMAZZOLA, JIM
98/9 DEL 272
99/0 Eishockey 163
95 Globe 234
92 Semic Sticker 247
93 Semic Sticker 212
00/1 UD DEL 28

CAMBELL, TERRY
94/5 DEL 407

CAMBIO, CHRIS
89/0 Nashville Knights

CAMERON, AL
77/8 O-Pee-Chee 48
78/9 O-Pee-Chee 396
80/1 Pepsi Bottle Cap
77/8 Topps 48
79/0 WINN
80/1 WINN

CAMERON, CRAIG
74/5 Loblaws
74/5 Loblaws Update
72/3 O-Pee-Chee 13
73/4 O-Pee-Chee 42
74/5 O-Pee-Chee 263
75/6 O-Pee-Chee 239
76/7 O-Pee-Chee 327
72/3 Topps 22
73/4 Topps 147
74/5 Topps 263
75/6 Topps 239

CAMERON, DAVE
00/1 Toronto St. Mike's

CAMERON, DAVE**
81/2 COLR
83/4 NJER
82/3 Post [Colo.]

CAMERON, DAVID
00/1 Saskatoon Blades

CAMERON, DAVID*
98 Bowman 141, ✍ A29
98 Bowman Chrome 141

CAMERON, DON
26 Dominion Chocolates 25

CAMERON, HARRY
83 HHOF Postcard G4
83&87 HHOF 95

CAMERON, JULIAN
25 Dominion Chocolates 70
90 7th..Sketch Mem.Cup 52

CAMERON, MALCOLM
93/4 Huntington Blizzard

CAMERON, RANDY
83/4 Brandon Wheat Kings
84/5 Kelowna Wings &...

CAMERON, SCOTT
01/2 Albany River Rats
02/3 Albany River Rats
98/9 Barrie Colts
99 Bowman 30, ✍ BA11
99/0 Topps 257
99/0 To. Chrome 257
00/1 UD Prospects 36

CAMMALLERI, MICHAEL
96 Québec Pee Wee 1174

CAMMALLERI, MIKE
02/3 BAP All-Star 145
02/3 BAP Memorabilia 395
02/3 Bowman 148
02/3 Calder 121, -CR 13
02/3 Crown Royale 116
02/3 In The Game-Used 184, ✂ C20
02/3 Manchester Monarchs
02/3 Pacific Complete 504
02/3 PTC/ Spring Expo 6
02/3 Parkhurst 245
02/3 Parkhurst Retro 246
02/3 Private Stock Titanium 117, -ROT 11
02/3 Quest for the Cup 122
02/3 Signature Series 197, ✍ 197, ✂ AR10, ✂ SGJ64
02/3 SP Authentic 173
02/3 SP Game-Used Edition 99
02/3 SPx 190
02/3 Ultimate Memorabilia 46, ✍ Raut
02/3 Upper Deck 450
02/3 UD Artistic 114
02/3 UD Classic 114
02/3 UD Honor 115
02/3 UD Mask 164
02/3 UD Premier 56
02/3 Vanguard 116

CAMMOCK, DAVE
93/4 Portland Winter Hawks
91/2 7th...Sketch WHL 36

CAMP, SHAWN
01/2 Guelph Storm
01/2 Guelph Storm M-Cup

CAMPBELL, AARON
91/2 Air Canada SJHL A33

CAMPBELL, ANGUS
83 HHOF Postcard I4
83&87 HHOF 125
10/1 Imperial 9

CAMPBELL, BILL
86/7 Sherb. Canadiens 9

CAMPBELL, BRIAN
99/0 BAP Mem. 104
00/1 BAP Mem. 92
01/2 BAP Memor. 192
99 Bowman 137
98 Bowman 23
98 Bowman Chrome 23
99/0 HoloGrFX 7
99/0 Millenium 32, ✍ Aut. 32
01/2 O-Pee-Chee 311
99/0 Omega 27
01/2 Parkhurst 236
00/1 Rochester Americans
95/6 Slapshot 275
99/0 SP Authentic 94, ✍ SotT
00/1 Topps 285
01/2 Topps 311
00/1 To. Chrome 180
99/0 To. Prmr. Plus 119
99/0 Ult. Victory 92
99/0 Upper Deck 189
99/0 UD G. Reserve 189
99/0 Victory 367
99/0 WGretzky 26

CAMPBELL, BRYAN
70/1 CHIC
75/6 Cincinnati Stingers
70/1 Esso Power Player
69/0 O-Pee-Chee 106
71/2 O-Pee-Chee 214
74/5 OPC WHA 6
75/6 OPC WHA 31
76/7 OPC WHA 16
77/8 OPC WHA 22
73/4 OPC WHA Poster 19
73/4 Quaker Oats 13
71/2 Toronto Sun Photo
73/4 Vancouver Blazers

CAMPBELL, CAMERON
92/3 BCJHL 28

CAMPBELL, CASSIE
94/5 Classic W5
97/8 Esso 59, ✍ Aut.
97/8 Game of Her Life
97/8 General Mills
97/8 UD Coll. Choice 281

CAMPBELL, CLARENCE
83 HHOF Postcard A3
83&87 HHOF 4
01/2 SP GU ✍ Sig
01/2 Upper Deck ✍ Cut

CAMPBELL, COLIN
76/7 COLR / Hockey Talk
84/5 DETR / Little Caesars
89/0 DETR / Little Caesars
79/0 EDMO
88/9 EDMO / Action 123
75/6 O-Pee-Chee 346
76/7 O-Pee-Chee 372
78/9 O-Pee-Chee 269
79/0 O-Pee-Chee 339
80/1 O-Pee-Chee 380
81/2 O-Pee-Chee 333
82/3 O-Pee-Chee 82
83/4 O-Pee-Chee 119
84/5 O-Pee-Chee 51
80/1 Pepsi Bottle Cap
74/5 PITT
77/8 PITT / McDonald's
83/4 Souhaits Keychain [Red Wings]
84/5 Topps 39
73/4 Vancouver Blazers
80/1 VANC
80/1 VANC / Silverwood
81/2 VANC
81/2 VANC / Silverwood

CAMPBELL, DEREK
00/1 Kingston Frontenacs 5

CAMPBELL, DUKE
49 Carreras Cigarettes 37

CAMPBELL, ED
96/7 Binghampton Rangers
97/8 Fort Wayne Komets
98/9 Fort Wayne Komets
02/3 Grand Rapids Griffins
98/9 Hartford Wolf Pack
00/1 Worcester IceCats
01/2 Worcester IceCats

CAMPBELL, GREGORY
96 Québec Pee Wee 578

CAMPBELL, JASON
93/4 Owen Sound Platers
95/6 Slapshot 292

CAMPBELL, JIM
91/2 Arena 21
98/9 Aurora 158
98/9 Be A Player 125, ✍ Aut. 125
97/8 Bicycle 9-Spade
91/2 Classic 25
91/2 Classic Four Sport 25
93/4 Cla. Images 4 Sport 46
93/4 Cla. Prospects IA12
93/4 Cla. Prospects LP1
97/8 Donruss 111
96/7 Do. Canadian 132
97/8 Do. Canadian 9
96/7 Do. Elite 142, A-7
97/8 Do. Elite 78
97/8 Do. Preferred 98
97/8 Do. Priority 94
97/8 Do. Studio 34
98/9 Dynagon Ice 155
96/7 Flair 123
93/4 Fleer Ultra 479
96/7 Fl. Ultra 144, UR-4
94/5 Fredericton Canadiens
95/6 Fredericton Canadiens
96/7 Got-Um
97/8 Leaf 54
96/7 L. Preferred 147
97/8 Limited 51, 67, 99
00/1 MONT
01/2 Norfolk Admirals
97/8 Omega 189
98/9 Pacific 362
97/8 Pacific CC 332
97/8 Pa. Crown Roy. 113
98/9 Pa. Crown Roy. 113
97/8 Pa. Dynagon 105, 143, DD-14A, T-18, T-58
97/8 Pa. Invincible 117, FP-30
97/8 Pa. Paramount 155
98/9 Pa. Paramount 198
97/8 Pa. Revolution 117
97/8 Panini Sticker 248
95 Panini Worlds 233
97/8 Pinnacle 130
96/7 Pi. Be A Player LTH7A, ✍ Aut. LTH7A
97/8 Pi. Certified 52
97/8 Pi. Inside 66
96/7 Pi. Mint 30
97/8 Pi. Totally 52
96/7 Pi. Zenith 129
93/4 Power Play 499
93/4 Premier - USA Hockey 17
97/8 Score 215
97/8 Score SLou. 4
96/7 Select CE 106
91/2 7th...Sketch LHJMQ 209
96/7 SP 187
97/8 SP Authentic 137
91/2 Star Pics 62
98/9 SLU
98/9 To. Finest 118
93/4 To. Stadium - Team U.S.A. 2
98/9 UD Choice 189
91/2 Ultimate Draft Pick 19, ✍ Aut.
92/3 Upper Deck 605
96/7 Upper Deck 328
97/8 Upper Deck 143, SG46, T15A
98/9 Upper Deck 178
99/0 Upper Deck 285
96/7 UD Black Diam. 142
96/7 UD CC 360
97/8 UD Coll. Choice 228
91/2 Upper Deck WJC 71
98/9 UD G. Reserve 178
99/0 UD G. Reserve 285
96/7 UD Ice 64
97/8 UD Ice 13
98/9 UD MVP 183
99/0 Victory 267

CAMPBELL, JOHN
89/0 Soo Greyhounds

CAMPBELL, PETER
84/5 Kingston Canadians
85/6 Kingston Canadians
86/7 Kingston Canadians
87/8 Kingston Canadians
96/7 Sudbury Wolves

CAMPBELL, RICH
93/4 Las Vegas Thunder
94/5 Las Vegas Thunder

CAMPBELL, RYAN
94/5 Guildford Flames 7
95/6 Guildford Flames 9
96/7 Guildford Flames 6
97/8 Guildford Flames 8
98/9 Guildford Flames

CAMPBELL, SCOTT
94/5 DEL 7
95/6 DEL 4
96/7 DEL 4
93/4 Muskegon Fury
94/5 Muskegon Fury
80/1 Pepsi Bottle Cap
89/0 7th..Sketch OHL 103
90/1 7th..Sketch OHL 355
91/2 7th...Sketch OHL 201
78/9 Winnipeg Jets
79/0 WINN
80/1 WINN

CAMPBELL, SPIFF (EARL)
24/5 Champ's Cigarettes
24/5 William Paterson 8

CAMPBELL, TERENCE
96/7 DEL 16
00/1 UD DEL 107

CAMPBELL, TERRY
99/0 Eishockey 351, 381

CAMPBELL, WADE
86/7 Moncton G'Flames
83/4 O-Pee-Chee 382
84/5 O-Pee-Chee 356
87/8 Tallahasee Tiger Sharks
89/0 ProCards AHL 130
90/1 ProCards 221
83/4 Vachon 124-4
82/3 WINN
83/4 WINN

CAMPEAU, CHRISTIAN
92/3 Atlanta Knights
93/4 Atlanta Knights
94/5 Atlanta Knights 22
95/6 Atlanta Knights
90/1 7th..Sketch LHJMQ 72
91/2 7th...Sketch LHJMQ 35

CAMPEAU, JASON
91/2 Oshawa Generals
91/2 Oshawa Generals
92/3 Oshawa Generals
91/2 7th...Sketch OHL 152
93/4 Slapshot / North Bay 7
94/5 Slapshot / North Bay 8

CAMPEAU, JEAN-CLAUDE (TOD)
45-64 BeeHive-2 [Mont.]
52/3 La Patrie
51/2 Laval Dairy 43
43-47 Parade Sportive
45-54 Quaker Oats
52/3 St. Lawrence 77

CAMPESE, BRUNO
96/7 DEL 2
95 Globe 227
83/4 Kelowna Wings
95 Panini Worlds 76
96 Wien 175

CANALE, JOE
92 7th...Sketch Awards 27
90/1 7th..Sketch LHJMQ 43
91/2 7th...Sketch LHJMQ 97
91 7th..Sketch Mem.Cup 46
00/1 Sherbrooke Castors 23

CANIELSSON, MARTIN
92/3 Semic Elitserien 134

CANNON, JASON
95/6 Slapshot 15

CANTU, KRIS
98/9 Roanoke Express
94/5 Slapshot / North Bay 13
95/6 Slapshot 219

CANTU, RANDY
98/9 Muskegon Fury

CAPEK, IVO
94/5 APS 71
95/6 APS 269, 429
96/7 APS 311
99/0 DS 29, G3
00/1 DS 74, G7
96/7 DS Sticker 151
99/0 OFS 5
00/1 OFS 7

CAPEL, JOHN
82/3 North Bay Centennials
83/4 North Bay Centennials

CAPELLO, JEFF
88/9 ProCards / Rochester

CAPILLAS, ANTONIO
79 Panini Sticker 375

CAPLA, BORIS
94/5 DEL 391

CAPLETTE, GUY
88/9 Richelieu Riverains

CAPLICE, SHAWN
92/3 Ottawa 67's
90/1 7th..Sketch OHL 28
91/2 7th...Sketch OHL 223

CAPPELLETTI, ANTHONY
99/0 Huntington Blizzard

CAPPRINI, JOE
91/2 Richmond Renegades

CAPRICE, FRANK
82/3 Fredericton Express
83/4 Fredericton Express
86/7 Fredericton Express
87/8 Panini Sticker 339
89/0 ProCards AHL 72
84/5 VANC
85/6 VANC
86/7 VANC
87/8 VANC / Shell

CAPSON, GREG
92/3 Greensboro Monarchs 17
93/4 Greensboro Monarchs

CAPUANO, DAVE
91/2 Bowman 323
90/1 OPC/Topps 170
91/2 O-Pee-Chee 318
90/1 Panini/VAN 6
91/2 Panini Sticker 41
90/1 Pro Set 543
91/2 Pro Set 237
89/0 ProCards IHL 145
90/1 Score 105T
91/2 Score 86
91/2 Score CAN 86
91/2 To. Stadium 53
91/2 Upper Deck 202
90/1 VANC / Mohawk

CAPUANO, JACK
88/9 ProCards / Newmarket
91/2 ProCards 55
95/6 Tallahasee Tiger Sharks

CAPUTO, DINO
90/1 7th..Sketch WHL 245
89/0 Victoria Cougars

CARBONNEAU, GUY
98/9 Be A Player 39, ✍ Aut. 39
90/1 Bowman 44
91/2 Bowman 338
92/3 Bowman 38
96/7 DALL / Southwest
93/4 Donruss 450
92/3 Durivage 1
93/4 Durivage 9
92/3 Fleer Ultra 102, -AW 3
93/4 Fleer Ultra 350
95/6 Fleer Ultra 228
89/0 Kraft 19
91/2 Kraft 79
93/4 Kraft / PB
99/0 Kraft / PB
86/7 Kraft Sports 21
94/5 Leaf 23
82/3 MONT
82/3 MONT / Steinberg
83/4 MONT
84/5 MONT
85/6 MONT
85/6 MONT / Provigo
86/7 MONT
87/8 MONT
87/8 MONT / Kodak Poster
87/8 MONT / Vachon 14-16, 21,23, 62, 63
88/9 MONT
89/0 MONT
89/0 MONT / Kraft
90/1 MONT
91/2 MONT
92/3 MONT
92/3 MONT / OPC 9
93/4 MONT / Export
93/4 MONT
00/1 MONT
01/2 MONT
83/4 O-Pee-Chee 185
84/5 O-Pee-Chee 257
85/6 O-Pee-Chee 233
86/7 OPC/Topps 176
87/8 O-Pee-Chee 232
88/9 O-Pee-Chee 203
90/1 OPC/Topps 93
91/2 O-Pee-Chee 54
92/3 O-Pee-Chee 206
89/0 OPC/Topps 53
98/9 OPC Chrome 106
91/2 OPC Premier 152
88/9 OPC Stars 4
83/4 OPC/Topps Sticker 180
84/5 OPC Sticker 160
85/6 OPC Sticker 135-255
86/7 OPC Sticker 7-152
87/8 OPC Sticker 7-146
88/9 OPC Sticker 209-80
88/9 OPC Sticker 41-172
89/0 opcSticker 213-74, 48-194
98/9 Pacific 173
00/1 Pacific 127
97/8 Pacific CC 292
99/0 Pa. Paramount 70
87/8 Panini Sticker 64
88/9 Panini Sticker 256
88/9 Panini Sticker 407
89/0 Panini Sticker 241, 381
90/1 Panini Sticker 58
90/1 Panini/MTL 2
91/2 Panini Sticker 197
92/3 Panini Sticker 149
93/4 Panini Sticker 19
94/5 Panini Sticker 10
99/0 Panini Sticker 220
91/2 Parkhurst 92
91/2 Parkhurst 466
92/3 Parkhurst 485
93/4 Parkhurst 372
95/6 Parkhurst 332
94/5 Parkie SE155
91/2 Pinnacle 130
91/2 Pinnacle 374
92/3 Pinnacle 43
93/4 Pinnacle 280
93/4 Pinnacle CA12
94/5 Pinnacle 372
95/6 Pinnacle 144
97/8 Pi. Be A Player 194, ✍ Aut. 194
93/4 Power Play 126
93/4 Premier 250
94/5 Premier 282
90/1 Pro Set 146
91/2 Pro Set 130
91/2 Pro Set 345
91/2 Pro Set 576
92/3 Pro Set 88
92/3 Pro Set CC5
91/2 Pro Set Platinum 63
87/8 Pro Sport CW2
91/2 Puck / Pro Set 15
90/1 Score 93
90/1 Sco. Hot Cards 43
91/2 Score 19
91/2 Score CAN 19
92/3 Score 269
92/3 Score 524
93/4 Score 51
94/5 Score 46
95/6 Score 280
85/6 7-Eleven Superstars 10
92/3 Topps 125
98/9 Topps 106
91/2 To. Stadium 41
92/3 To. Stadium 260
92/3 To. Stadium 289
93/4 To. Stadium 1
94/5 To. Stadium 174
x95/6 To. Stadium M12
92 TSC Members Only
90/1 Upper Deck 188
91/2 Upper Deck 265
92/3 Upper Deck 260
93/4 Upper Deck 439
95/6 Upper Deck 273
94/5 UD Be A Player R67, ✍ 106
93/4 UD BAP Roots 2
95/6 UD CC 302
96/7 UD CC 73
83/4 Vachon 41-61

CARD, HEADER
00/1 Kingston Frontenacs 1
01/2 Kingston Frontenacs 1

CARD, RYAN
01/2 Peterborough Petes

CARDARELLI, JOE
99/0 Florida Everblades
00/1 Kudos 42
01/2 Manchester Storm
02/3 Manchester Storm
95/6 Spokane Chiefs 21

CARDIFF, JIM
73/4 Quaker Oats 31

CARDIFF, MARK
90/1 7th..Sketch OHL 256
91/2 7th...Sketch OHL 207

CARDINAL, CARSON
92/3 MPS SJHL 13

CARDINAL, CURTIS
93/4 Red Deer Rebels

CARDINAL, ERIC
90/1 7th..Sketch LHJMQ 110
91/2 7th...Sketch LHJMQ 232

CARDINAL, REG
93/4 Maine Black Bears

CARDWELL, JUSTIN
99/0 Greensboro Generals

CAREAU, SYLVAIN
91/2 7th...Sketch LHJMQ 93

CAREY, J.
91/2 7th...Sketch WHL 285

CAREY, JIM
00/1 BAP Mem. ✂ V-5
96/7 Bic.Sports Aces J-S
95/6 Bicycle Sports Aces 6-Spade
95/6 Bowman 74
94/5 Cla. Images 4, 99, CE4, PR2
95/6 Donruss 189, BTP-6, D-4, RT-1
96/7 Donruss 33, BTP-3, D-1
97/8 Donruss 22
96/7 Do. Canadian 79
97/8 Do. Canadian 59
95/6 Do. Elite 69, PW-10
96/7 Do. Elite 19, PW-3
97/8 Do. Preferred 43, CG-13
97/8 Do. Studio 45
95/6 Edge Ice 52, C-5, QM-8, TW-7
96/7 Flair 98, HG-3
94/5 Fleer 233
96/7 Fleer 116, 144, 145, 146, VT-3
95/6 Fleer Metal 157
96/7 Fl. Picks F50-6, JE-12
95/6 Fleer Ultra 173, 320, 368, AR-1, PPM-4
96/7 Fl. Ultra 174, CTI-1
95/6 Kraft / PS
96/7 Kraft / TT
95/6 Leaf 78, FF-1, GLS-1, SR-1
96/7 Leaf 68, SD-10, S-9
97/8 Leaf 71, PD-10
95/6 L. Limited 55, SS-1
96/7 L. Limited 16, S-5
96/7 L. Preferred 23, LS-21, MM-1
97/8 Limited 14, 131, FG-54
96/7 Maggers 167
95/6 McDonald's McD-40
96/7 McDonald's McD-32
96/7 Metal Univ. 162, AP-3, IC-3
97/8 Pacific CC 23
97/8 Pa. Dynagon 8, DD-2B, S-2, T-17, BKS-6
97/8 Pa. Invincible 8, R-11
97/8 Pa. Paramount 10
95/6 Panini Sticker 145, 303
96/7 Panini Sticker 134, 154
97/8 Panini Sticker 8
95/6 Parkhurst 492, CCB-16, GP-5, PP-36
95/6 Pinnacle 138, M-3, R20-9
96/7 Pinnacle 105, M-2, T-5
97/8 Pinnacle 83
96/7 Pi. Be A Player SP-8
97/8 Pi. Certified 15
95/6 Pi. FANtasy 20
97/8 Pi. Inside 62, SU-3, S-7
96/7 Pi. Mint 28
95/6 Pi. Summit 51, ITC-6
96/7 Pi. Summit 94, ITC-6, U-14
97/8 Pi. Totally 15
95/6 Pi. Zenith 5, ZT-18
96/7 Pi. Zenith 7, ZT-15
95/6 Playoff 104, 213
96/7 Playoff 426
95/6 POG 287, I-028
94/5 Portland Pirates
95/6 Pro Magnet 26
98/9 Providence Bruins
96/7 Score 78, 317, DT-12
96/7 Score 74, NW-3, SD-2
97/8 Score 14, NW-2
97/8 Score Bost. 2
95/6 Select CE 12, CF-2
96/7 Select CE 29, F-3
94/5 Sig. Rookies 44, ✍ 44
95/6 SR Draft / Promo JC1-JC5
95/6 SR Tetrad F7
95/6 SBx Emotion 186, Xci-19
95/6 SBx Impact 175, 228, D-2
96/7 SBx Impact 137, ZH-3
94/5 SP 128
95/6 SP 156
96/7 SP 164, GF-13
96/7 SPx 48
96/7 SLU
95/6 Super Sticker 128, 131
96/7 Team Out!
95/6 Topps 210, 383, 1NG, YS8
95/6 To. Finest 66
96/7 Topps Picks 13, ID9
95/6 To. Stadium 115, GT6
94/5 TSC Members Only 48
95/6 T. Super Skills 73
95/6 Upper Deck 344, F-20, H-16, SE-77
96/7 Upper Deck 174, SS14A
95/6 UD Be A Player 189, ✍ S189
96/7 UD Black Diam. 147
95/6 UD CC 30, 369, 375
96/7 UD CC 278, 334, S17
97/8 UD Coll. Choice 17, SQ57
96/7 UD Ice 72
95/6 WASH
96 Wien 157, SG5

CAREY, JIM**
99/0 Mississippi S'Wolves

CAREY, MATT
98/9 Quad City Mallards

CARIGNAN, PATRICK
91/2 7th...Sketch LHJMQ 160

CARKNER, MATT
99 Bowman 23, ✍ BA18
01/2 Cleveland Barons
99/0 Topps 273
99/0 To. Chrome 273

CARKNER, TERRY
98/9 Be A Player 207, ✍ Aut. 207
91/2 Bowman 232
92/3 Bowman 129
93/4 Donruss 422
92/3 Fleer Ultra 370
93/4 Fleer Ultra 304
96/7 FLOR / Winn-Dixie
97/8 FLOR / Winn-Dixie
90/1 OPC/Topps 381
91/2 O-Pee-Chee 291
92/3 O-Pee-Chee 180
89/0 OPC/Topps 3
97/8 Pa. Invincible R-84
89/0 Panini Sticker 297
90/1 Panini Sticker 114
91/2 Panini Sticker 235
92/3 Panini Sticker 190
93/4 Panini Sticker 54
91/2 Parkhurst 342
92/3 Parkhurst 362
93/4 Parkhurst 332
94/5 Parkhurst 69
95/6 Parkhurst 354
89/0 PHIL
90/1 PHIL
91/2 PHIL / J.C. Penney
92/3 PHIL / UD Sheet
92/3 PHIL / UD Sheet
92/3 PHIL / J.C. Penney
93/4 PHIL / Sheet
91/2 Pinnacle 51
92/3 Pinnacle 63
93/4 Pinnacle 286
94/5 Pinnacle 221
97/8 Pi. Be A Player 195, ✍ Aut. 195
93/4 Power Play 328
93/4 Premier 152
94/5 Premier 359
90/1 Pro Set 212
91/2 Pro Set 173
92/3 Pro Set 269
91/2 Pro Set Platinum 212
87/8 QUÉB / Gene. Foods
90/1 Score 47
91/2 Score 64
91/2 Score CAN 64
92/3 Score 66
93/4 Score 233
93/4 Score 508
92/3 Topps 465
91/2 To. Stadium 219
92/3 To. Stadium 463
93/4 To. Stadium 252
90/1 Upper Deck 398
91/2 Upper Deck 204
94/5 Upper Deck 467
95/6 Upper Deck 286
97/8 Upper Deck 283
94/5 UD Be A Player R167, ✍ 144
95/6 UD CC 113
96/7 UD CC 109

CARLETON, WAYNE
70/1 BOST
70/1 Eddie Sargent 6
71/2 Eddie Sargent 131
70/1 Esso Power Player
72/3 Post 18
69/0 O-Pee-Chee 184
70/1 O-Pee-Chee 9
71/2 O-Pee-Chee 178
72/3 O-Pee-Chee 337
74/5 OPC WHA 45
75/6 OPC WHA 43
73/4 OPC WHA Poster 8
72/3 Ottawa Nationals
68/9 Post Marble
68/9 Shirriff / Toro. 2
67/8 Topps 77
70/1 Topps 9
69/0 TORO
71/2 Toronto Sun Photo
91/2 Ultimate Original Six 47, ✍ Aut. 47

CARLI, JARED
99/0 Calgary Hitmen
00/1 Calgary Hitmen
01/2 Calgary Hitmen

CARLSON, DON
85/6 U. of Arizona Ice Cats

CARLSON, JACK
80/1 MINS
81/2 MINS

CARLSON, JACK
02/3 Fleer Throwbacks 87

CARLSON, JAMIE
92/3 Hamilton Canucks

CARLSON, KENT
83/4 MONT
84/5 MONT
83/4 Vachon 42-62

CARLSON, STEVE
89/0 Johnstown Chiefs

CARLSSON, ANDERS
94/5 Leaf Elit Set 210
95/6 Leaf Elit Set 236, C-5
88/9 NJER / Caretta
88/9 ProCards / Utica
89/0 Semic Elitserien 38
90/1 Semic Elitserien 185
91/2 Semic Elitserien 354
92/3 Semic Elitserien 61
91 Semic Sticker 48
95/6 UD Elitserien 102
97/8 UD Elitserien 109, C9
98/9 UD Elitserien 126
99/0 UD Elitserien 112, H8, L6

CARLSSON, ARNE
70/1 Kuvajulkaisut 23
72 Panda MM-Toronto
72 Semic Sticker 50
74 Semic Sticker 3
71/2 Williams Finnish 43
73/4 Williams Finnish 25

CARLSSON, BJORN
89/0 Semic Elitserien 228
90/1 Semic Elitserien 65
91/2 Semic Elitserien 240

CARLSSON, CALLE
01/2 Nottingham Panthers
92/3 Upper Deck 208
00/1 UD DEL 103

CARLSSON, DANIEL
97/8 UD Elitserien 35

CARLSSON, LEIF
96/7 DEL 29
98/9 DEL 175
99/0 Eishockey 65
95/6 Leaf Elit Set 219
89/0 Semic Elitserien 23
90/1 Semic Elitserien 29
91/2 Semic Elitserien 84
92/3 Semic Elitserien 106
95/6 UD Elitserien 63

CARLSSON, PER-OLOF
89/0 Semic Elitserien 133
90/1 Semic Elitserien 212
91/2 Semic Elitserien 141
92/3 Semic Elitserien 168

CARLSSON, ROBERT
00/1 UD Elitserien 170

CARLSSON, ROLAND
98/9 Cardset 171
99/0 Cardset 296
00/1 Cardset 320
95/6 Sisu 5

CARLSSON, THOMAS
94/5 Leaf Elit Set 129
89/0 Semic Elitserien 224
91/2 Semic Elitserien 233

CARLYLE, RANDY
91/2 Bowman 199
92/3 Bowman 287
98/9 EBK IHL All-Star
83/4 Funmate Puffy 12 [w]
89/0 Kraft 47
86/7 Kraft Sports 73
97/8 Manitoba Moose
78/9 O-Pee-Chee 312
79/0 O-Pee-Chee 124
80/1 O-Pee-Chee 367
81/2 O-Pee-Chee 256
82/3 O-Pee-Chee 265
82/3 O-Pee-Chee 266
83/4 O-Pee-Chee 278
84/5 O-Pee-Chee 337
85/6 OPC/Topps 57
86/7 OPC/Topps 144
87/8 OPC/Topps 9
88/9 O-Pee-Chee 204
90/1 OPC/Topps 51
91/2 O-Pee-Chee 72
92/3 O-Pee-Chee 12
89/0 O-Pee-Chee 291
81/2 OPC Sticker 183
82/3 OPC Sticker 255
82/3 OPC/Topps Sticker 144
83/4 OPC/Topps Sticker 227
84/5 OPC Sticker 291
85/6 OPC Sticker 251
86/7 OPC Sticker 107-237
87/8 OPC Sticker 248-138
88/9 OPC Sticker 148
89/0 opcSticker 143-264
87/8 Panini Sticker 360
88/9 Panini Sticker 149
89/0 Panini Sticker 166, 168
90/1 Panini Sticker 314
90/1 Panini/WPG 4
91/2 Panini Sticker 76
91/2 Parkhurst 418
91/2 Pinnacle 288
92/3 Pinnacle 67
83/4 PITT / Coke Is It!
83/4 PITT / Heinz
84/5 PITT / Heinz
81/2 Post 8
82/3 Post [Pitt.]
93/4 Premier 86
90/1 Pro Set 325
91/2 Pro Set 273
92/3 Pro Set 265
90/1 Score 136
91/2 Score 125
91/2 Score CAN 125
92/3 Score 167
93/4 Score PiAS 27
83/4 Souhaits Keychain [Penguins]
79/0 Topps 124
81/2 Topps 112 [East]
92/3 Topps 147
91/2 To. Stadium 94
92/3 To. Stadium 332
93/4 To. Stadium - All-Stars
76/7 TORO
77/8 TORO
90/1 Upper Deck 331
84/5 WINN / Safety Tips
85/6 WINN
85/6 WINN / Safety Tips
85/6 WINN / Silverwood
86/7 WINN
87/8 WINN
88/9 WINN / Safety Tips
89/0 WINN / Safeway
90/1 WINN / IGA
91/2 WINN / IGA
95/6 WINN

CARNBÄCK, PATRIK
94/5 ANAH / Carl's Jr. 1
92/3 Classic Prospects 105
96/7 DEL 359
93/4 Donruss 6
94/5 Donruss 29
94/5 Fleer 1
93/4 Fleer Ultra 251
92/3 Fredericton Canadiens
95 Globe 41
95/6 Hoyle / West. 7-Heart
94/5 Leaf 102
94/5 Leaf Elit Set 270
94/5 Panini Sticker N
95/6 Panini Sticker 224
95 Panini Worlds 152
93/4 Parkhurst 8
94/5 Parkhurst 7, V28
95/6 Parkhurst 1
94/5 Pinnacle 189
95/6 Playoff 111
93/4 Power Play 281
93/4 Premier 379
94/5 Premier OF-1
95/6 Pro Magnet 36
93/4 Score 615
95 Semic 74
89/0 Semic Elitserien 276
90/1 Semic Elitserien 37
91/2 Semic Elitserien 287
91 Semic Sticker 46
93 Semic Sticker 43
95/6 Topps 335
93/4 To. Stadium 434
94/5 To. Stadium 53
93/4 Upper Deck 463
94/5 Upper Deck 475
95/6 Upper Deck 180
95/6 UD CC 42
95/6 UD Elitserien 241
97/8 UD Elitserien 78, S13
98/9 UD Elitserien 76
99/0 UD Elitserien 81, L12
00/1 UD Elitserien 68, 195, S3, ✍ Sig., T4
96 Wien 63

CARNEGIE, HERBIE
52/3 La Patrie
51/2 Laval Dairy 16
52/3 St. Lawrence 53

CARNEGIE, OSSIE
51/2 Bas du Fleuve 13

CARNEGIE, RANE
01/2 Belleville Bulls

CARNELLEY, TODD
84/5 Kamloops Blazers
85/6 Kamloops Blazers

CARNEY, DAN
97/8 Hampton Roads
98/9 Peoria Rivermen

CARNEY, KEITH
93/4 CHIC / Coke
92/3 Classic 102
93/4 Donruss 412
92/3 Fleer Ultra 13
94/5 Flint Generals
94/5 Leaf 359
92/3 OPC Premier 81
97/8 Omega 47
99/0 Pacific 316
00/1 Pacific 311
01/2 Pacific 300
02/3 Pacific Complete 80
97/8 Pa. Invincible R-41
96/7 Panini Sticker 166
92/3 Parkhurst 15
94/5 Parkhurst 50
98/9 PHOE / Coca-Cola
92/3 Pinnacle 229
92/3 Pro Set 223
91/2 Rochester Americans GL
91/2 Rochester Americans WPC
92/3 Score 461
02/3 Sports Vault 159
02/3 T. Total 381
98/9 UD Choice 155
92/3 Upper Deck 402
93/4 Upper Deck 516
94/5 Upper Deck 449
95/6 Upper Deck 435
98/9 Upper Deck 343
95/6 UD Be A Player 9, ✍ S9
98/9 UD G. Reserve 343

CARON, ALAIN
72/3 O-Pee-Chee 324
73/4 Quaker Oats 38
72/3 Québec Nordiques
73/4 Québec Nordiques

CARON, CHRISTIAN
91/2 7th...Sketch LHJMQ 92

CARON, EDDIE
96 Québec Pee Wee 1417

CARON, FRANÇOIS
00/1 Chicoutimi Saguenéens 12
01/2 Moncton Wildcats 10
97 Québec Pee Wee 0486

CARON, JACQUES
72/3 Eddie Sargent 193
96/7 NJER / Sharp
72/3 O-Pee-Chee 140
72/3 O-Pee-Chee Crest 18
89/0 ProCards AHL 301
71/2 SLOU
72/3 SLOU
72/3 Topps 86
73/4 VANC / Royal Bank

CARON, MARTIN
90/1 7th..Sketch LHJMQ 203

CARON, PAT
90 7th..Sketch Mem.Cup 64

CARON, SÉBASTIEN
02/3 Calder 89
02/3 Pacific Complete 517
02/3 Private Stock Titanium 131
99/0 Rimouski Océanic 19
00/1 Upper Deck 209
00/1 UD Black Diam. 74
00/1 UD Ice 54
02/3 UD Mask 71
02/3 UD Premier 44
02/3 UD Rookie 81
00/1 WBS Penguins
01/2 WBS Penguins
02/3 WBS Penguins

CARON, SÉBASTIEN>
93 Québec Pee Wee 432

CARON, SÉBASTIEN?
93 Québec Pee Wee 15

CARONE, NICK
92/3 Semic Nordisk 5

CARPANO, ANDREA
93/4 Slapshot / S.S.Marie 1

CARPENTER, BOB
99/0 Albany River Rats
00/1 Albany River Rats
98/9 Be A Player 228, ✍ Aut. 228
89/0 BOST / Sports Action
90/1 BOST / Sports Action
91/2 BOST / Sports Action
90/1 Bowman 30
92/3 Bowman 10
95/6 Fleer Ultra 188
83/4 Funmate Puffy 20 [w]
93/4 Hockey Wit 68
93/4 Leaf 421
94/5 Leaf 436
88/9 LOSA / Smokey
00/1 Mir Fetisov 23
96/7 NJER / Sharp
82/3 O-Pee-Chee 361
83/4 O-Pee-Chee 366
84/5 O-Pee-Chee 194
85/6 OPC/Topps 26
85/6 OPC/Topps Box C
86/7 OPC/Topps 150
87/8 OPC/Topps 30
88/9 OPC/Topps 72
90/1 OPC/Topps 139
91/2 O-Pee-Chee 404
92/3 O-Pee-Chee 131
89/0 OPC/Topps 167
91/2 OPC Premier 148
92/3 OPC Premier 78
82/3 OPC/Topps Sticker 154
83/4 OPC/Topps Sticker 206
84/5 OPC Sticker 132
85/6 OPC Sticker 112
86/7 OPC Sticker 250-140
88/9 OPC Sticker 153-24
97/8 Pa. Invincible R-109
88/9 Panini Sticker 74
89/0 Panini Sticker 196
90/1 Panini Sticker 7
91/2 Panini Sticker 181
92/3 Panini Sticker 140
91/2 Parkhurst 226
94/5 Parkie SE96
91/2 Pinnacle 99
91/2 Pinnacle 396
92/3 Pinnacle 315
94/5 Pinnacle 201
96/7 Pi. Be A Player 125, ✍ Aut. 125
95/6 POG 156
82/3 Post [Wash.]
93/4 Premier 413
90/1 Pro Set 4
91/2 Pro Set 349
91/2 Pro Set Platinum 154
90/1 Score 16
91/2 Score 162
91/2 Score CAN 162
92/3 Score 142
93/4 Score 267
93/4 Score 578
97/8 Score NJer. 18
89 Semic Sticker 168
83/4 Souhaits Keychain [Capitals]
92/3 Topps 378
91/2 To. Stadium 161
92/3 To. Stadium 122
93/4 To. Stadium 175
94/5 To. Stadium 158
90/1 Upper Deck 158
92/3 Upper Deck 478
95/6 Upper Deck 183
95/6 UD Be A Player 11, ✍ S11
81/2 WASH
82/3 WASH
84/5 WASH / Pizza Hut
85/6 WASH / Pizza Hut
86/7 WASH / Police
92/3 WASH / Kodak

CARPENTER, BOBBY
01/2 Albany River Rats

CARPENTER, DAVE
88/9 ProCards / Halifax

CARPENTER, DOUG
84/5 NJER
91/2 ProCards 382

CARPENTER, STEVE
02/3 Coventry Blaze
00/1 Kudos 144
93/4 N. Michigan Wildcats
95/6 Richmond Renegades
94/5 Slapshot / North Bay 9
95/6 Slapshot 214

CARPENTIER, BEN
00/1 Charlotte Checkers
98/9 Hartford Wolf Pack
99/0 Hartford Wolf Pack
00/1 Hartford Wolf Pack

CARPENTIER, BENJAMIN
02/3 Hamilton Bulldogs

CARPENTIER, STEVE
01/2 Sheffield Steelers GS

CARPER, BRANDON
95/6 Toledo Storm

CARR, ALLAN
95/6 Slapshot 334

CARR, GENE
74/5 Loblaws
74/5 O-Pee-Chee 320
75/6 O-Pee-Chee 343
76/7 O-Pee-Chee 290
77/8 O-Pee-Chee 298
78/9 O-Pee-Chee 14
78/9 Topps 14
71/2 Toronto Sun Photo

CARR, LORNE
34-43 BeeHive-1 [NYAm.]
34-43 BeeHive-1 [Toro.]
36-39 Diamond Match TT1
36-39 Diamond Match TT2
36-39 Diamond Match TT3
39/0 O-Pee-Chee 62
45-54 Quaker Oats
37/8 World Wide Gum 26

CARR, MIKE
92/3 Ottawa 67's

CARRANO, RICK
87/8 Moncton Hawks

CARRIE, DAVE
87/8 Sudbury Wolves

CARRIE, DAVID
89/0 Soo Greyhounds

CARRIER, MARIO
93/4 Slapshot / Drummondville 26

CARRIERE, JASON
99/0 Indianapolis Ice

CARRIERE, LARRY
74/5 BUFF

CARRIERE, TOM
92/3 W. Michigan Broncos
93/4 W. Michigan Broncos

CARRIÈRE, LARRY
72/3 BUFF
73/4 BUFF
74/5 Loblaws
72/3 O-Pee-Chee 282
73/4 O-Pee-Chee 260
74/5 O-Pee-Chee 43
75/6 O-Pee-Chee 154
76/7 O-Pee-Chee 297
77/8 O-Pee-Chee 304
78/9 O-Pee-Chee 272
Sport Flash 2
Sport Flash 2
74/5 Topps 43
75/6 Topps 154
77/8 VANC / Royal Bank

CARRIÈRE, RICK
94/5 Saint John Flames

CARROL, LORNE
24/5 Falcons Crescent 9

CARROLL, BILLY
86/7 DETR / Little Caesars
84/5 EDMO
84/5 EDMO / Red Rooster
88/9 EDMO / Action 16
83/4 NYIS
83/4 NYIS / News 4
83/4 O-Pee-Chee 5
85/6 O-Pee-Chee 203
85/6 OPC Sticker 224-91
00/1 UD Vintage ✂ D-POH

CARROLL, GEORGE
24/5 Champ's Cigarettes
24/5 Maple Crispette [V130] 20
24/5 William Paterson 42

CARROLL, GREG
79/0 O-Pee-Chee 184
79/0 Topps 184
78/9 WASH

CARROLL, KEN
94/5 Slapshot / Sarnia 2
95/6 Slapshot 181

CARSE, BILL
34-43 BeeHive-1 [Chic.]
39/0 O-Pee-Chee 80

CARSE, BOB
34-43 BeeHive-1 [Chic.]
43-47 Parade Sportive
45-54 Quaker Oats

CARSON, DAVID
95/6 Halifax Moosehead
93/4 Seattle Thunderbirds

CARSON, GERRY
34-43 BeeHive-1 [Maroons]
33/4 Canadian Gum
33-35 Diamond Match Silv.
36-39 Diamond Match TT1
34/5 Sweet Caporal
33/4 WWGum 24

CARSON, JIMMY
90/1 Bowman 229
91/2 Bowman 62
92/3 Bowman 108
89/0 DETR / Little Caesars
91/2 DETR / Little Caesars
97/8 Detroit Vipers
93/4 Donruss 159
93/4 Donruss 500
95/6 Donruss 359
88/9 EDMO
88/9 EDMO / Action 53
94/5 Fleer 85
92/3 Fleer Ultra 45
93/4 Fleer Ultra 42
94/5 Fleer Ultra 299
93/4 Hockey Wit 62
90/1 Kraft 5
93/4 Leaf 149
95/6 Leaf 308
87/8 LOSA
87/8 OPC/Topps 92
88/9 OPC/Topps 9
90/1 OPC/Topps 231
91/2 O-Pee-Chee 104
92/3 O-Pee-Chee 152
89/0 OPC/Topps 127
87/8 OPC Leaders 6
90/1 OPC Premier 12
91/2 OPC Premier 167
88/9 OPC Stars 5
87/8 OPC Sticker 126-114
87/8 OPC Sticker 210-76
88/9 OPC Sticker 158
89/0 opcSticker 222
87/8 Panini Sticker 279
88/9 Panini Sticker 75
89/0 Panini Sticker 72
90/1 Panini Sticker 214
91/2 Panini Sticker 139
92/3 Panini Sticker 114
93/4 Panini Sticker 204
95/6 Panini Sticker 26
91/2 Parkhurst 43
92/3 Parkhurst 308
93/4 Parkhurst 368
94/5 Parkhurst 239
94/5 Parkie SE61
91/2 Pinnacle 173
92/3 Pinnacle 329
93/4 Pinnacle 285
94/5 Pinnacle 436
93/4 Power Play 114
93/4 Premier 376
94/5 Premier 326
90/1 Pro Set 67
91/2 Pro Set 55
91/2 Pro Set Platinum 33
90/1 Score 64
90/1 Sco. Hot Cards 28
91/2 Score 224
91/2 Score CAN 224
92/3 Score 9
92/3 Score SS 9
93/4 Score 109
93/4 Score 572
89 Semic Sticker 163
91 Semic Sticker 150
93 Semic Sticker 187
92/3 Topps 398
91/2 To. Stadium 121
92/3 To. Stadium 277
93/4 To. Stadium 118
90/1 Upper Deck 132
91/2 Upper Deck 161
92/3 Upper Deck 253
94/5 Upper Deck 198
95/6 UD CC 180

CARSON, LINDSAY
83/4 O-Pee-Chee 261
83/4 OPC/Topps Sticker 181
83/4 PHIL / J.C. Penney
86/7 PHIL
88/9 ProCards / Binghampton

CARTELLI, MARIO
00/1 DS 64
01/2 DS 4
98/9 OFS 388
99/0 OFS 192
00/1 OFS 214
01/2 OFS 49, -UHI 9

CARTER, ANSON
01/2 Adrenaline 72
98/9 Aurora 9
99/0 Aurora 11
00/1 Aurora 10
99/0 BAP Mem. 26
00/1 BAP Mem. 43
01/2 BAP Memor. 16
02/3 BAP Memorabilia 25, 346
01/2 Bowman 105
02/3 Bowman 59
01/2 Crown Royale 58
02/3 Crown Royale 38
93/4 Donruss CAN7
97/8 Donruss 118
97/8 Do. Canadian 73
97/8 Do. Preferred 29
97/8 Do. Priority 89
97/8 Do. Studio 33
98/9 Dynagon Ice 10
99/0 Dynagon Ice 22
02/3 Exclusive 69
02/3 First Edition 197
97/8 Leaf 85
96/7 L. Preferred 146
97/8 Limited 107
02/3 McDonald's 18
93/4 Michigan State
01/2 O-Pee-Chee 198
02/3 O-Pee-Chee 33
97/8 Omega 13
98/9 Omega 13
99/0 Omega 19
98/9 Pacific 73
99/0 Pacific 21
00/1 Pacific 31
01/2 Pacific 153
02/3 Pacific 139
02/3 Pacific Complete 319
97/8 Pacific CC 131
97/8 Pa. Crown Roy. 8
97/8 Pa. Paramount 11
98/9 Pa. Paramount 11
99/0 Pa. Paramount 18
00/1 Pa. Paramount 17
98/9 Pa. Revolution 8
99/0 Panini Sticker 22
00/1 Panini Sticker 13
00/1 Parkhurst P-159
01/2 Parkhurst 107
02/3 Parkhurst 30, -CR15, ✂ CRM15
02/3 Parkhurst Retro 71
93/4 Pinnacle 469
97/8 Pi. Be A Player 67, ✍ Aut. 67
97/8 Pi. Inside 171
96/7 Pi. Zenith 122
96/7 Portland Pirates
00/1 Pr. Stock ✂ GUG 48
01/2 Pr. Stock ✂ GUG 46
02/3 Pr. Stock Reserve 38
01/2 PS Titanium 55
02/3 Private Stock Titanium 41
00/1 PS Titanium Draft ✂ 43
02/3 Quest for the Cup 64
99/0 Revolution 12
00/1 Revolution 9, ✂ GWJ-2
97/8 Score 226
97/8 Score Bost. 8
96/7 Select CE 94
00/1 Signature 72
01/2 Signature 11, ✍ Aut. 11
00/1 SP Authentic ✍ SotT
02/3 SP Authentic 39
01/2 SP GU ✂ TotG, ✂ TotGC, ✂ TotGT
02/3 Sports Vault 223
00/1 SPx ✂ WM
99/0 Stadium 138, -Chrome 38
00/1 Stadium 119, ✍ CO4, ✍ LS7
00/1 SLU 3
99/0 Topps 203, NS1
00/1 Topps 40, NHLD9
01/2 Topps 198
02/3 Topps 33, HHC15
99/0 To. Chrome 203, FG7
00/1 To. Chrome 32
01/2 To. Chrome 125
02/3 T. Chrome 33
98/9 To. Finest 21
99/0 To. Gold Label FG7
00/1 To. Gold Label 90
00/1 To. Heritage 215
01/2 To. Heritage 80
02/3 T. Limited 33
99/0 To. Prmr. Plus 69
02/3 T. Total 174
01/2 UD PlayMakers Ltd 42
93/4 Upper Deck 531
96/7 Upper Deck 358
97/8 Upper Deck 11
99/0 Upper Deck 187
01/2 Upper Deck 296
02/3 Upper Deck 73
00/1 UD Black Diam. 98
97/8 UD Coll. Choice 13
99/0 UD G. Reserve 187
00/1 UD Ice ✂ IGJ
01/2 UD Mask 38
98/9 UD MVP 18
99/0 UD MVP 14
01/2 UD MVP 73
02/3 UD MVP 71
01/2 UD Vintage 103
02/3 UD Vintage 106
00/1 Vanguard 42
02/3 Vanguard 41
99/0 Victory 28
00/1 Victory 23
01/2 Victory 135
02/3 Victory 82

CARTER, BILLY
63/4 Québec Aces
60/1 Shirriff 115

CARTER, DAN
96/7 Dayton Ice Bandits
95/6 Toledo Storm

CARTER, JOHN
89/0 BOST / Sports Action
90/1 BOST / Sports Action
90/1 Bowman 39
92/3 Fleer Ultra 399
86/7 Moncton G'Flames
91/2 O-Pee-Chee 300
90/1 Panini Sticker 8
90/1 Pro Set 5
88/9 ProCards / Maine
90/1 Score 283
91/2 Score 7T
91/2 Score CAN 557
90/1 Upper Deck 211

CARTER, LYLE
71/2 Toronto Sun Photo

CARTER, RON
88/9 EDMO / Action 98

CARTER, SHAWN
91/2 Avant Garde BCJHL 97
98/9 Orlando Solar Bears
98/9 Orlando S' Bears Geico
96/7 St. John's Maple Leafs
97/8 St. John's Maple Leafs

CARTER, STEVE
97/8 Fort Worth Brahmas
98/9 Fort Worth Brahmas

CARUSO, BRIAN
97/8 Fort Worth Brahmas
93/4 Minnesota-Duluth

CARUSO, JAMIE
89/0 7th..Sketch OHL 156
90/1 7th..Sketch OHL 305
91/2 7th...Sketch OHL 88

CARVER, ANDREW
99 Bowman 65
99/0 Hull Olympiques BN
99/0 Hull Olympiques 2
00/1 Hull Olympiques 2
01/2 Moncton Wildcats 2

CARVER, ORRIN
52/3 Anonymous 97

CARVETH, JOE
34-43 BeeHive-1 [Detr.]
45-64 BeeHive-2 [Mont.]
51/2 Cleveland Barons
76 DETR
40/1 O-Pee-Chee 123
43-47 Parade Sportive
45-54 Quaker Oats

CARVIL, STEWART
93/4 Humberside Hawks 6

CASALE, AGOSTINO
96/7 DEL 122

CASATANEDA, RICKY
01/2 Louisiana Ice Gators

CASAVANT, DENYS
43-47 Parade Sportive

CASEY, DAVE
88/9 ProCards / Adirondack
89/0 ProCards AHL 316

CASEY, GERALD
52/3 Anonymous 95

CASEY, JON
90/1 Bowman 183
91/2 Bowman 119
92/3 Bowman 269
93/4 Donruss 16
96/7 Donruss 37
93/4 EA Sports 36
95/6 Edge Ice 176
92/3 Fleer Ultra 90
93/4 Fleer Ultra 266
93/4 Fleer Ultra 91
91/2 Kraft 75
92/3 Kraft / PB
93/4 Leaf 322
96/7 Leaf 89
93/4 McDonald's McD-03
85/6 MINS
88/9 MINS / ADA
90/1 OPC/Topps 269
91/2 O-Pee-Chee 237
92/3 O-Pee-Chee 16
89/0 OPC/Topps 48
90/1 OPC/Topps B
91/2 OPC Premier 112
92/3 OPC Premier SP7
89/0 opcSticker 197-53
97/8 Pa. Invincible R-167
89/0 Panini Sticker 114
90/1 Panini Sticker 254
91/2 Panini Sticker 118
92/3 Panini Sticker 87
93/4 Panini Sticker 276
94/5 Panini Sticker 9
95/6 Panini Sticker 199
91/2 Parkhurst 77
92/3 Parkhurst 73
93/4 Parkhurst 12
95/6 Parkhurst 177
94/5 Parkie SE158
95/6 Peoria Rivermen
91/2 Pinnacle 144
92/3 Pinnacle 42
93/4 Pinnacle 357
94/5 Pinnacle 393
96/7 Pi. Be A Player 63, ✍ Aut. 63
95/6 Playoff 194
93/4 Power Play 17
93/4 Premier 437
94/5 Premier 229
90/1 Pro Set 133
91/2 Pro Set 111
92/3 Pro Set 82
91/2 Pro Set Platinum 56
90/1 Score 182
90/1 Sco. Hot Cards 80
91/2 Score 191
91/2 Score CAN 191
92/3 Score 249
93/4 Score 193
93/4 Score 526
93/4 Score PiAS 41
93/4 Score PiAS 49
94/5 Score 111
95/6 Score 290
96/7 Score 214
92/3 Seasons 64
92/3 Topps 379
91/2 To. Stadium 138
92/3 To. Stadium 198
93/4 To. Stadium 303
93/4 To. Stadium 456
93/4 To. Stadium - All-Stars
94/5 To. Stadium 184
90/1 Upper Deck 385
91/2 Upper Deck 205
92/3 Upper Deck 190
93/4 Upper Deck 507, SP-8
94/5 Upper Deck 206
95/6 Upper Deck 70
92/3 UD Locker 40

CASHMAN, WAYNE
99/0 BAP Mem. AH-6, ✍ AH-6
70/1 BOST
71/2 BOST
91/2 BOST / SA Legends
71/2 Eddie Sargent 14
72/3 Eddie Sargent 18
70/1 Esso Power Player
91/2 Future Trends C72 25, ✍ 25
74/5 Lipton Soup 9
74/5 Loblaws
73/4 Mac's Milk
70/1 O-Pee-Chee 7
70/1 O-Pee-Chee 233
71/2 O-Pee-Chee 129
72/3 O-Pee-Chee 68
72/3 O-Pee-Chee TC
73/4 O-Pee-Chee 85
74/5 O-Pee-Chee 206
75/6 O-Pee-Chee 63
76/7 O-Pee-Chee 165
77/8 O-Pee-Chee 234
77/8 O-Pee-Chee NS 1
78/9 O-Pee-Chee 124
79/0 O-Pee-Chee 79
80/1 O-Pee-Chee 318
81/2 O-Pee-Chee 11
82/3 O-Pee-Chee 8
94/5 Parkie Tall 18
82/3 Post [Bost.]
92/3 TAMP / Sheraton Inn
94/5 TAMP / Sky Box
95/6 TAMP / Sky Box
70/1 Topps 7
71/2 Topps 129
72/3 Topps 29
73/4 Topps 166
74/5 Topps 206
75/6 Topps 63
76/7 Topps 165
77/8 Topps 234
77/8 ToppsNS 1
78/9 Topps 124
79/0 Topps 79
01/2 To. Chrome -CA2, ✍ CA2
01/2 T/O Archives 31, -Seat
71/2 Toronto Sun Photo

CASHMAN, WAYNE
02/3 Fleer Throwbacks 56

CASLAVA, PETR
98/9 OFS 378
99/0 OFS 367
01/2 OFS 226

CASPARSSON, PETER
99/0 UD Elitserien 130

CASSELMAN, MIKE
96/7 Cincinnati Cyclones
97/8 Cincinnati Cyclones
98/9 DEL 74
99/0 Eishockey 318
00/1 UD DEL 228, A7
01/2 UD DEL 63

CASSELS, ANDREW
01/2 Adrenaline 188, ✂ GWJ 49
98/9 Aurora 23
00/1 Aurora 142
98/9 Be A Player 20, ✍ Aut. 20
00/1 BAP Mem. 178
01/2 BAP Memor. 254
91/2 Bowman 340
92/3 Bowman 387
95/6 Bowman 4
02/3 Bowman 39
00/1 Crown Royale 103
01/2 Crown Royale ✂ TT 9
02/3 Crown Royale 27
93/4 Donruss 142
94/5 Donruss 178
95/6 Donruss 148
96/7 Donruss 162
97/8 Donruss 146
97/8 Do. Canadian 66
97/8 Do. Elite 48
97/8 Do. Preferred 94
97/8 Do. Priority 64
98/9 Dynagon Ice 23
99/0 Dynagon Ice 192
93/4 EA Sports 57
02/3 Exclusive 49
94/5 Flair 71
96/7 Flair 41
94/5 Fleer 86
96/7 Fleer 46
95/6 Fleer Metal 64
96/7 Fl. Picks 104
92/3 Fleer Ultra 70
93/4 Fleer Ultra 33
94/5 Fleer Ultra 300
95/6 Fleer Ultra 66
91/2 HART / Jr. Whalers
92/3 HART / Dairymart
93/4 HART / Coke
95/6 HART / Kids Club
96/7 HART / Kids Club
95/6 Kraft / KD
93/4 Leaf 50
94/5 Leaf 276
95/6 Leaf 147
96/7 Leaf 78
97/8 Leaf 106
97/8 Limited 45
90/1 MONT
91/2 O-Pee-Chee 176
92/3 O-Pee-Chee 222
01/2 O-Pee-Chee 212
91/2 OPC Premier 72
97/8 Omega 28
99/0 Omega 232
98/9 Pacific 115
99/0 Pacific 53
00/1 Pacific 406
01/2 Pacific 379, IZ 20
02/3 Pacific 374
02/3 Pacific Complete 399
97/8 Pacific CC 166
98/9 Pa. Crown Roy. 16
97/8 Pa. Dynagon 21, T-39
97/8 Pa. Invincible 23
97/8 Pa. Paramount 26
98/9 Pa. Paramount 26
00/1 Pa. Paramount 237
90/1 Panini/MTL 3
93/4 Panini Sticker 123
94/5 Panini Sticker 110
95/6 Panini Sticker 25
96/7 Panini Sticker 28
97/8 Panini Sticker 21
99/0 Panini Sticker 311
00/1 Panini Sticker 207
91/2 Parkhurst 285
92/3 Parkhurst 298
93/4 Parkhurst 359
94/5 Parkhurst 97, V58
95/6 Parkhurst 364
00/1 Parkhurst P-202
01/2 Parkhurst 115
02/3 Parkhurst 181
93/4 Pinnacle 103
94/5 Pinnacle 319
96/7 Pinnacle 82
97/8 Pinnacle 178
97/8 Pi. Be A Player 8, ✍ Aut. 8
97/8 Pi. Certified 130
97/8 Pi. Inside 106
95/6 Pi. Summit 158
96/7 Pi. Summit 44
97/8 Pi. Totally 130
95/6 Playoff 46
94/5 POG 113
95/6 POG 124
93/4 Power Play 104
93/4 Premier 65
94/5 Premier 227
01/2 Pr. Stock ✂ GUG 98
02/3 Pr. Stock Reserve 30
00/1 PS Titanium 94, ✂ GUG-48
01/2 PS Titanium Draft ✂ 93
02/3 Private Stock Titanium 28
95/6 Pro Magnet 127
90/1 Pro Set 615
91/2 Pro Set 395
89/0 ProCards AHL 191
90/1 Score 422
91/2 Score 57T
91/2 Score CAN 238
91/2 Score CAN 607
92/3 Score 323
93/4 Score 164
94/5 Score 34
95/6 Score 136
96/7 Score 146
97/8 Score 134
94/5 Select 141
95/6 SBx Emotion 74
95/6 SBx Impact 72
96/7 SBx Impact 53
94/5 SP 50
95/6 SP 61
96/7 SP 72
02/3 Sports Vault 195
92/3 Topps 23
95/6 Topps 30
00/1 Topps 270
01/2 Topps 212
00/1 To. Chrome 160
95/6 To. Finest 74
98/9 To. Finest 82
02/3 To. Heritage 178
91/2 To. Stadium 329
92/3 To. Stadium 39
93/4 To. Stadium 74
95/6 To. Stadium 61
95/6 T. Super Skills 4
02/3 T. Total 282
90/1 Upper Deck 265
91/2 Upper Deck 379
91/2 Upper Deck 551
92/3 Upper Deck 288
93/4 Upper Deck 346
94/5 Upper Deck 317, SP-32
95/6 Upper Deck 492, SE-36
96/7 Upper Deck 74
98/9 Upper Deck 231
00/1 Upper Deck 168
01/2 Upper Deck 398
02/3 Upper Deck 295
95/6 UD Be A Player 30, ✍ S30
96/7 UD Black Diam. 123
95/6 UD CC 52
96/7 UD CC 115
97/8 UD Coll. Choice 113
98/9 UD G. Reserve 231
99/0 UD MVP Cup 185
00/1 UD Vintage 354
01/2 UD Vintage 247
01/2 VANC / Coke
00/1 Vanguard 95
01/2 Vanguard ✂ DGM 34
02/3 Vanguard 29
00/1 Victory 227
01/2 Victory 340

CASSELSTAHL, DANIEL
94/5 Leaf Elit Set 178
00/1 UD Elitserien 168

CASSIDY, BRUCE
88/9 CHIC / Coke
98/9 EBK IHL All-Star
00/1 Grand Rapids Griffins
01/2 Grand Rapids Griffins
94/5 Indianapolis Ice
95/6 Indianapolis Ice
98/9 Indianapolis Ice
82/3 Ottawa 67's
83/4 Ottawa 67's
84/5 Ottawa 67's
88/9 ProCards / Saginaw
89/0 ProCards IHL 51

CASSIDY, KEITH
99/0 Huntington Blizzard

CASSIVI, FRÉDÉRIC
01/2 BAP Memor. 421
01/2 BT Pipes 161
02/3 Between the Pipes 35
01/2 Chicago Wolves
02/3 Chicago Wolves
98/9 Cincinnati Cyclones
02/3 First Edition 262
00/1 Hershey Bears
01/2 Hershey Bears
01/2 Parkhurst 301
96/7 Syracuse Crunch
95/6 Thunder Bay Senators
01/2 UD Mask 131
02/3 UD MVP 193
01/2 UD Premier 53
02/3 Victory 14

CAST, PAUL
94/5 Humberside Hawks 17

CASTELLA, REUBEN
91/2 7th...Sketch OHL 174

CASTELLAN, JASON
90/1 7th..Sketch OHL 280

CASTONGUAY, ALEXIS
99/0 Rimouski Océanic 12

CASWELL, ROY
82/3 Brandon Wheat Kings

CATELLIER, CHRIS
90/1 7th..Sketch WHL 238
91/2 7th...Sketch WHL 53
89/0 Victoria Cougars

CATENACCI, MAURIZIO
96/7 DEL 100

CATENARO, ANGELO
84/5 Belleville Bulls

CATION, SHAWN
98/9 Barrie Colts

CATON, MURRAY
91/2 Avant Garde BCJHL 8

CATTARINCH, JOSEPH
10/1 Imperial 16
27/8 La Presse

CATTARINICH, JOSEPH
83 HHOF Postcard M3
83&87 HHOF 168

CAUFIELD, JAY
89/0 PITT / Foodland 12
91/2 PITT / Elby's
92/3 PITT / Coke-Clark
90/1 Pro Set 504

CAUSEY, CAREY
91/2 Avant Garde BCJHL 113

CAVA, CHRIS
99/0 Ottawa 67's

CAVA, PETER
98 Bowman 18
98 Bowman Chrome 18
99/0 Rockford IceHogs
96/7 Soo Greyhounds
95/6 Slapshot 365

CAVALIERE, DAVE
93/4 Birmingham Bulls
89/0 Nashville Knights

CAVALLIN, MARK
01/2 Belfast Giants
01/2 Belfast Giants
00/1 Kudos 23

CAVALLINI, GINO
91/2 Bowman 368
85/6 CALG / Red Rooster
96/7 DEL 152
95/6 Edge Ice 159
93/4 Milwaukee Admirals
94/5 Milwaukee Admirals
95/6 Milwaukee Admirals
84/5 Moncton G'Flames
87/8 OPC/Topps 146
88/9 OPC/Topps 149
90/1 OPC/Topps 36
91/2 O-Pee-Chee 281
89/0 OPC/Topps 176
87/8 Panini Sticker 315
88/9 Panini Sticker 103
89/0 Panini Sticker 123
90/1 Panini Sticker 265
91/2 Panini Sticker 24
91/2 Pinnacle 216
93/4 Premier 232
90/1 Pro Set 261
91/2 Pro Set 218
92/3 QUÉB / Petro-Canada
90/1 Score 63
90/1 Sco. Hot Cards 27
91/2 Score 258
91/2 Score 308
91/2 Score CAN 338
91/2 Score CAN 478
92/3 Score 42
93/4 Score 414
87/8 SLOU
87/8 SLOU / Kodak
88/9 SLOU
88/9 SLOU / Kodak
89/0 SLOU / Kodak
90/1 SLOU / Kodak
91/2 SLOU
92/3 Topps 234
91/2 To. Stadium 34
92/3 To. Stadium 480
93/4 To. Stadium 152
90/1 Upper Deck 38
91/2 Upper Deck 187
91/2 Upper Deck 646

CAVALLINI, PAUL
90/1 Bowman 22
91/2 Bowman 378
92/3 Bowman 193
94/5 DALL / Southwest
94/5 DALL / Cap
93/4 Donruss 88
94/5 Donruss 135
92/3 Fleer Ultra 185, 432
94/5 Fleer Ultra 49
93/4 Leaf 397
94/5 Leaf 79
90/1 OPC/Topps 57
91/2 O-Pee-Chee 328
92/3 O-Pee-Chee 379
89/0 O-Pee-Chee 269
89/0 opcSticker 19-159
89/0 Panini Sticker 127
90/1 Panini Sticker 276
91/2 Panini Sticker 35
92/3 Panini Sticker 23
91/2 Parkhurst 154
93/4 Parkhurst 50
94/5 Parkhurst V12
94/5 Parkie SE42
91/2 Pinnacle 182
91/2 Pinnacle 411
92/3 Pinnacle 319
93/4 Pinnacle 370
94/5 Pinnacle 81
94/5 POG 82
93/4 Power Play 321
94/5 Premier 246
90/1 Pro Set 262, 353
91/2 Pro Set 214
92/3 Pro Set 159
91/2 Pro Set Midwest
91/2 Pro Set Platinum 224
90/1 Score 185, 349
91/2 Score 107
91/2 Score 308
91/2 Score CAN 107
91/2 Score CAN 338
92/3 Score 22
93/4 Score 172
93/4 Score 538
94/5 Score 94
91 Semic Sticker 59
87/8 SLOU
87/8 SLOU / Kodak
88/9 SLOU
88/9 SLOU / Kodak
89/0 SLOU / Kodak
90/1 SLOU / Kodak
91/2 SLOU
92/3 Topps 233
91/2 To. Stadium 48
92/3 To. Stadium 447
90/1 Upper Deck 281
91/2 Upper Deck 184
91/2 Upper Deck 646
92/3 Upper Deck 212
93/4 Upper Deck 441, SP-35
94/5 Upper Deck 311, SP-108
92/3 WASH / Kodak

CAVANAGH, CHAD
95/6 Slapshot 164

CAVANAGH, MIKE
87/8 Kingston Canadians
90/1 7th..Sketch OHL 29

CECH, FILIP
00/1 OFS 371

CECH, MARTIN
97/8 APS 192
02/3 Cardset 9
99/0 DS 89
00/1 DS 28
97/8 DS Sticker 152
98/9 OFS 288
99/0 OFS 118, 473
00/1 OFS 60

CECH, MICHAL
98/9 OFS 322
99/0 OFS 237
00/1 OFS 282

CECH, ROMAN
94/5 APS 165
95/6 APS 181
96/7 APS 171
97/8 APS 85
99/0 DS 34
96/7 DS Sticker 41
97/8 DS Sticker 92
98/9 OFS 198
99/0 OFS 178

CECH, VRATISLAV
97 Bowman 155, ✍ Aut.
99/0 Providence Bruins

CECH, ZDENEK
94/5 APS 294
95/6 APS 28
97/8 APS 52

CECHMANEK, ROMAN
01/2 Adrenaline 138, CL 15, PP 26
94/5 APS 228
95/6 APS 3, 353, 388, 400
96/7 APS 214, 337, 365, 415
97/8 APS 28, 342, 370
01/2 Atomic 71, Stat. 7
02/3 Atomic 73, -D 15
02/3 BAP All-Star 14, ✂ ASJ
00/1 BAP Mem. 424
01/2 BAP Memor. 42, ✂ ASJ, ✂ ASE, ✂ ASN, ✂ AST, ✂ CoO, ✂ GoalJ, HSHS, ✂ SCP
02/3 BAP Memorabilia 196, ✂ SC1, ✂ TM0
01/2 BT Pipes 19, 103, -Mask, ✂ ASJ, ✂ Jers., ✂ S&J, ✂ GT, ✂ -HSHSJers.
02/3 Between the Pipes 39, 142, M21, ✂ ASJ14, ✂ CP12, ✂ GUE27, ✂ GB10, ✂ GUJ27, ✂ GUJ27, ✂ HSHSJers 9, ✂ ITN27, ✂ T8
98 Bonaparte 4B
98 Bonaparte Pexeso 11
01/2 Bowman 98
02/3 Bowman 87
02/3 Calder ✂ GWJ 17
01/2 Crown Royale 105
02/3 Crown Royale 69
00/1 Crown Royale G-5
97/8 DS 1
98/9 DS 20
99/0 DS 127, G10, P3
00/1 DS NT2, WCH1
01/2 DS G4
96/7 DS Sticker 1, 18
97/8 DS Sticker 8, 167
01/2 eTopps 27
02/3 Exclusive 125
02/3 First Edition 55, 376, 377, ✂ Jers.
01/2 Heads Up 71, ASGUN 1, HD 19, SS 16
02/3 Heads Up 89, ✂ GWQ 20
02/3 In The Game-Used ✂ GP12, ✂ IE27
01/2 McDonald's 28
01/2 O-Pee-Chee 59, 315
02/3 O-Pee-Chee 137
98/9 OFS 99, 228, 438, 470, -OW 17
99/0 OFS 6, 254, 489, -CL
01/2 Pacific 284, 437, IZ 15, SC 15, WAS 7
02/3 Pacific 277
02/3 Pacific Complete 119
00/1 Parkhurst P-230
01/2 Parkhurst 71, ✂ PH44, ✂ PSJ17, ✂ T13
02/3 Parkhurst 150
02/3 Parkhurst Retro 123
01/2 PHIL
00/1 Premier Plus 136
01/2 Pr. Stock 70, GR 8, -PS 53
02/3 Pr. Stock Reserve -ICS 16, ✂ 135
01/2 PS Titanium 103, ✂ DSJ 49, ✂ DSJ 60
01/2 PS Titanium Draft ✂ 67
02/3 Private Stock Titanium 74
00/1 PS Titanium Draft 169
02/3 Quest for the Cup 74, ✂ GWJ 15
00/1 Signature 297
01/2 Signature 165, ✍ Aut. 165, ✂ GUE46, ✂ GJ47, ✂ GSJ47, ✂ ITN46
02/3 Signature Series 164, ✍ 164, ✂ DW4, ✂ TQ3
02/3 Slam Card
00/1 SP Authentic 119
01/2 SP Authentic 64
02/3 SP Authentic 66
00/1 SP GU 77
01/2 SP GU 41, ✂ TotG, ✂ TotGC, ✂ TotGT
02/3 SP Game-Used ✂ AF (x2), ✂ PH (x2), ✂ TG
02/3 Sports Vault 110
00/1 SPx 169
01/2 SPx 47, ✂ HT
02/3 SPx 57
01/2 Stadium 30, G12, NR8, ✍ NR, NHLP9
02/3 Stadium 62, -PSH-2
01/2 Topps 59 , 315, OTG28
02/3 Topps 137
01/2 To. Chrome 59
02/3 T. Chrome 86
00/1 To. Gold Label 115
00/1 To. Heritage 88
01/2 To. Heritage 59, 119, 129
02/3 To. Heritage 88, 117
02/3 T. Limited 137
01/2 To.Reserve 85
00/1 To. Stars 105
02/3 T. Total 231
00/1 UD Heroes 175
01/2 UD PlayMakers Ltd 73
00/1 UD Reserve 111
01/2 Ultimate Mem. ✂ NP
00/1 Upper Deck 435
01/2 Upper Deck 130, 224, LL6, SS16, ✂ CJers., ✂ TendThr.
02/3 Upper Deck 129, ✂ GT
02/3 UD Artistic CG5
00/1 UD Black Diam. 128
01/2 UD Challenge BB7
01/2 UD Honor Roll ✂ HS
02/3 UD Honor 54
00/1 UD Ice 96
01/2 UD Mask 122, 184, ✂ SY, ✂ VC, ✂ MB
02/3 UD Mask 60, 61, 62, 63, 94, ✂ GG, ✂ MM, ✂ BM, ✂ PW, ✂ SS, ✂ VC
01/2 UD MVP 138, -MM13, ✂ GS
02/3 UD MVP SD (x3), Souv.
02/3 UD Piece 67
01/2 UD Premier ✂ D (x2)
00/1 UD Pros&Prosp. 120
02/3 UD Rookie 76, ✂ DJ
01/2 UD Top Shelf 31, -ASGN, ✂ GG-LP
02/3 UD Top Shelf 64, ✂ SS, ✂ TS
01/2 UD Vintage 184, 191, 268, 269, 270, ✂ NL
02/3 UD Vintage 184, 282, 317, 318, GB 184, ✂ EE
00/1 Vanguard 137
01/2 Vanguard 72, SW 15, VT 7
02/3 Vanguard 72, -SW 10
01/2 Victory 253, 259
02/3 Victory 154

CECI, JON
00/1 Ottawa 67's 21
01/2 Ottawa 67's 2

CEJ, JEFF
91/2 7th...Sketch WHL 305

CELIO, MANUELE
91 Semic Sticker 192
92 Semic Sticker 211
93 Semic Sticker 124

CELIO, NICOLA
91/2 Upper Deck 665
91/2 Upper Deck WJC 26

CELLA, TONY
80/1 Soo Greyhounds
81/2 Soo Greyhounds
82/3 Soo Greyhounds

CELY, ZDENEK
94/5 APS 180
95/6 APS 213

CEMAN, DAN
98/9 EBK ECHL All-Star
97/8 Hampton Roads
98/9 Hampton Roads
00/1 Kudos 43

CENTOMO, SÉBASTIEN
01/2 BAP Memor. 333
01/2 BT Pipes 158
02/3 Between the Pipes 95, ✂ GUJ44
02/3 First Edition 266
01/2 Parkhurst 348
99/0 Rouyn-Noranda
00/1 Rouyn-Noranda 19
01/2 SPx 215
02/3 SPx 123
02/3 Upper Deck 223
02/3 UD Foundations 140
02/3 UD MVP 218
02/3 UD Piece 148
01/2 UD Premier 84
02/3 UD Vintage 345

CENTRONE, MARC
81/2 Regina Pats
82/3 Regina Pats
83/4 Regina Pats

CEOTE, FRANK
52/3 Bas du Fleuve 36

CERBAJEV, ALEXANDER
97/8 APS 136
98/9 DS 106
97/8 DS Sticker 261
98/9 OFS 120

CEREDA, LUCA
01/2 St. John's Maple Leafs
01/2 St. John's / Clarenville

CERESINO, RAY
45-64 BeeHive-2 [Toro.]
51/2 Cleveland Barons

CERMAK, DAVID
94/5 APS 61
95/6 APS 89
96/7 APS 86
96/7 DS Sticker 150

CERMAK, LEOS
00/1 OFS 102
01/2 OFS 273

CERMAK, PETER
99/0 Asheville Smoke
98/9 BC Icemen

CERNICH, KORD
94/5 Anchorage Aces 5
98/9 Anchorage Aces
99/0 Anchorage Aces
90/1 ProCards 6
91/2 ProCards 211
91/2 ProCards 330

CERNIK, FRANTISEK
97/8 APS 376
84/5 DETR / Little Caesars
98/9 OFS Leg. 14
79 Panini Sticker 91
82 Semic Sticker 91

CERNOSEK, MAREK
96/7 APS 273
96/7 DS Sticker 172
97/8 DS Sticker 34
98/9 OFS 333
99/0 OFS 119, 343
00/1 OFS 140
01/2 OFS 235

CERNY, FRANTISEK
82 Semic Sticker 88

CERNY, JOSEF
70/1 Kuvajulkaisut 42
72 Panda MM-Toronto
72 Semic Sticker 34
74 Semic Sticker 70
71/2 Williams Finnish 23

CERNY, MICHAL
94/5 APS 126
97/8 APS 229
97/8 DS Sticker 36
99/0 Score 124
92/3 Upper Deck 603

CERNY, MILAN
94/5 APS 150

CERNY, OTAKAR
94/5 APS 54

CERVEN, MARTIN
97 Bowman 90
99/0 Charlotte Checkers
95/6 Spokane Chiefs 10

CERVENY, PETR
99/0 Score 56

CHABADA, MARTIN
00/1 DS 9
98/9 OFS 143
99/0 OFS 397
00/1 OFS 304
01/2 OFS 19

CHABOT, FRÉDÉRIC
94/5 Cincinnati Cyclones
95/6 Cincinnati Cyclones
92/3 Fredericton Canadiens
95/6 Future Legends 17
99/0 Houston Aeros
97/8 Pi. Be A Player 169, ✍ Aut. 169
89/0 ProCards IHL 135
90/1 ProCards 66
01/2 UD DEL 198, ✂ GJ

CHABOT, JOHN
90/1 Bowman 236
94/5 DEL 67
95/6 DEL 67
96/7 DEL 263
98/9 DEL 134
87/8 DETR / Little Caesars
88/9 DETR / Little Caesars
88/9 DETR / S.A.M.
89/0 DETR / Little Caesars
90/1 DETR / Little Caesars
99/0 Eishockey 82
83/4 MONT
84/5 O-Pee-Chee 258
85/6 O-Pee-Chee 244
87/8 OPC/Topps 32
88/9 OPC/Topps 39
90/1 OPC/Topps 163
89/0 O-Pee-Chee 225
85/6 OPC Sticker 101-233
86/7 OPC Sticker 230-101
87/8 OPC Sticker 169-29
87/8 Panini Sticker 151
88/9 Panini Sticker 42
90/1 Panini Sticker 216
86/7 PITT / Kodak
90/1 Pro Set 68
90/1 ProCards 488
90/1 Score 277
90/1 Upper Deck 113
91/2 Upper Deck 393
00/1 UD DEL 65, P3

CHABOT, LORNE
33/4 Anonymous 45
34-43 BeeHive-1 [Chic.]
33/4 Canadian Gum
34/5 CCM [Green]
33-35 Diamond Match Silv.
36-39 Diamond Match TT1
36-39 Diamond Match TT2
36-39 Diamond Match TT3
33/4 Hamilton Gum 30
32/3 Maple Leafs O'Keefe
33/4 O-Pee-Chee 18
55/6 Parkhurst 21
02/3 Parkie - Reprint 202
23/4 Paulins Candy 15
34/5 Sweet Caporal
33/4 WWGum 71

CHABOT, LUC
02/3 Peterborough Phantoms

CHABOT, NICOLAS
96/7 Rimouski Océanic

CHAD, JOHNNY
34-43 BeeHive-1 [Chic.]

CHADNEY, RANDY
91/2 7th...Sketch WHL 55

CHADWICK, BILL
83 HHOF Postcard E4
83&87 HHOF 65
77-79 Sportscaster 67-21

CHADWICK, ED
52/3 Anonymous 157
45-64 BeeHive-2 [Toro.]
84/5 Nova Scotia Oilers
57/8 Parkhurst [Mont.] 24
57/8 Parkhurst [Mont.] 25
57/8 Parkhurst [Toro.] 2
58/9 Parkhurst 12
59/0 Parkhurst 5
93/4 Parkie 56-57 128
93/4 Parkie 56-57 155
93/4 Parkie 56-57 157
93/4 Parkie 56-57 160
61/2 Shirriff 20
57/8 Toronto Star Photo

CHAGNON, PAUL
94/5 Fredericton Canadiens
95/6 Fredericton Canadiens
96/7 Fredericton Canadiens

CHAGODAEV, ALEXANDER
00/1 Mir 291

CHAINEY, ALAIN
87/8 QUÉB / Gene. Foods
88/9 QUÉB
88/9 QUÉB / Gene. Foods
89/0 QUÉB
91/2 7th...Sketch LHJMQ 182

CHAISSON, LUC
00/1 Owen Sound Attack 19

CHALANEK, MIROSLAV
94/5 APS 15

CHALIFOUX, DENIS
91/2 ProCards 106
90/1 7th..Sketch LHJMQ 51
90 7th..Sketch Mem.Cup 70

CHALK, DAVE
78/9 SM-Liiga 119

CHALLICE, BEN
94/5 Guildford Flames 2

CHALMERS, WILLIAM (CHICK)
52/3 Anonymous 52

CHALONER, KANE
91/2 7th...Sketch WHL 58

CHALUPA, MILAN
84/5 DETR / Little Caesars
98/9 OFS 145
99/0 OFS 349
00/1 OFS 185
79 Panini Sticker 79
82 Semic Sticker 80

CHAMBERLAIN, CURTIS
83/4 Saskatoon Blades
84/5 Saskatoon Blades

CHAMBERLAIN, JAMIE
99 Bowman 6, ✍ BA26
95 Québec Pee Wee 617
99/0 Topps 255
99/0 To. Chrome 255

CHAMBERLAIN, MURPH
34-43 BeeHive-1 [Mont.]
34-43 BeeHive-1 [Toro.]
45-64 BeeHive-2 [Mont.]
37/8 O-Pee-Chee 147
39/0 O-Pee-Chee 12
43-47 Parade Sportive
38/9 Quaker Oats
45-54 Quaker Oats

CHAMBERS, DAVE
90/1 Pro Set 675
90/1 QUÉB / Petro-Canada

CHAMBERS, GREG
01/2 Peterborough Petes

CHAMBERS, JOSH
00/1 London Knights

CHAMBERS, RICK
88/9 Kitchener Rangers
89/0 Kitchener Rangers
90/1 Kitchener Rangers
90 7th..Sketch Mem.Cup 27
93/4 Slapshot / Kitchener 28
94/5 Slapshot / Kitchener 29

CHAMBERS, SHAWN
90/1 Bowman 180
93/4 Donruss 325
94/5 Donruss 72
95/6 Donruss 126
94/5 Flair 171
94/5 Fleer 204
93/4 Fleer Ultra 75
94/5 Fleer Ultra 203
95/6 Fleer Ultra 259
93/4 Leaf 40
94/5 Leaf 332
95/6 Leaf 234
99/0 Millenium 83, ✍ Aut. 83
88/9 MINS / ADA
96/7 NJER / Sharp
90/1 OPC/Topps 192
89/0 OPC/Topps 142
98/9 Pacific 174
89/0 Panini Sticker 111
90/1 Panini Sticker 252
93/4 Panini Sticker 219
94/5 Panini Sticker 187
95/6 Panini Sticker 86
95 Panini Worlds 213
92/3 Parkhurst 406
94/5 Parkhurst 223
95/6 Parkhurst 392
93/4 Pinnacle 87
94/5 Pinnacle 97
96/7 Pi. Be A Player 75, ✍ Aut. 75
94/5 POG 227
93/4 Power Play 229
93/4 Premier 101
94/5 Premier 174
90/1 Pro Set 134
90/1 Score 57
91/2 Score CAN 572
92/3 Score 508
93/4 Score 391
94/5 Score 153
95/6 Score 86
95 Semic 109
95/6 SBx Emotion 96
95/6 SBx Impact 92
92/3 TAMP / Sheraton Inn
93/4 TAMP / Kash N' Karry
94/5 TAMP / Sky Box
93/4 To. Stadium 412
90/1 Upper Deck 106
92/3 Upper Deck 104
93/4 Upper Deck 68
95/6 Upper Deck 148
96/7 Upper Deck 287
91/2 WASH / Kodak
91/2 WASH / Smokey

CHAMPAGNE, DENIS
79/0 Montréal Juniors B&W
79/0 Montréal Jrs. Colour

CHAN, CARISSA
99/0 Cardset AH Q-ruutu

CHANNELL, CRAIG
89/0 ProCards IHL 134

CHANT, DAVID
99/0 Brampton Batallion 3

CHANT, KYLE
97/8 Portland Winter Hawks

CHAPDELAINE, RENÉ
93/4 Peoria Rivermen
94/5 Peoria Rivermen
95/6 Peoria Rivermen
92/3 Phoenix Roadrunners
89/0 ProCards AHL 21
90/1 ProCards 429

CHAPMAN, ADAM
99/0 Ottawa 67's
00/1 Ottawa 67's 17
01/2 Ottawa 67's 19

CHAPMAN, ART
34-43 BeeHive-1 [NYAm.]
33-35 Diamond Match Silv.
36-39 Diamond Match TT1
36-39 Diamond Match TT2
36-39 Diamond Match TT3
35/6 O-Pee-Chee 94
39/0 O-Pee-Chee 18
33/4 WWGum 32
37/8 World Wide Gum 42

CHAPMAN, BLAIR
77/8 O-Pee-Chee 174
78/9 O-Pee-Chee 33
79/0 O-Pee-Chee 21
80/1 O-Pee-Chee 48
81/2 O-Pee-Chee 291
77/8 PITT / McDonald's
77/8 Topps 174
78/9 Topps 33
79/0 Topps 21
80/1 Topps 48
81/2 Topps 115 [West]

CHAPMAN, BRENNAN
01/2 Regina Pats

CHAPMAN, BRIAN
97/8 Long Beach Ice Dogs
97/8 Manitoba Moose
98/9 Manitoba Moose
99/0 Manitoba Moose
00/1 Manitoba Moose
01/2 Manitoba Moose
02/3 Manitoba Moose
93/4 Phoenix Roadrunners
94/5 Phoenix Roadrunners
95/6 Phoenix Roadrunners
88/9 ProCards / Binghampton
89/0 ProCards AHL 299
90/1 ProCards 190
91/2 ProCards 109

CHAPMAN, CRAIG
90/1 7th..Sketch WHL 2
91/2 7th...Sketch WHL 122

CHAPMAN, DREW
94/5 Guildford Flames 14
95/6 Guildford Flames 10

CHAPMAN, PHIL
52/3 Anonymous 89

CHAPMAN, ROB
01/2 Owen Sound Attack

CHAPPOT, ROGER
72 Semic Sticker 149

CHAPUT, DANIEL
91/2 Ferris State Bulldogs
93/4 Hampton Roads
96/7 Knoxville Cherokees

CHAPUT, FRANÇOIS
97/8 New Mexico Scorpions

CHAPUT, MARTIN
90/1 7th..Sketch LHJMQ 46
91/2 7th...Sketch LHJMQ 233

CHARA, ZDENO
01/2 Adrenaline ✂ GWJ 31
01/2 BAP Memor. 498
02/3 BAP Memorabilia 130
97/8 Kentucky Tho'blades
99/0 Millenium 155, ✍ Aut. 155
01/2 OTTA
02/3 OTTA
98/9 Pacific 276
99/0 Pacific 252
01/2 Pacific 242, 415
02/3 Pacific 264
02/3 Pacific Complete 56
99/0 Panini Sticker 89
01/2 Parkhurst 392
02/3 Parkhurst Retro 182
00/1 Pr. Stock ✂ GUG 67
00/1 Revolution ✂ GWJ 7
97/8 SP Authentic 186
98/9 SPx Finite 52
00/1 Stadium 167
99/0 Topps 29
00/1 Topps 263
99/0 To. Chrome 29
02/3 T. Total 69
98/9 UD Choice 124
98/9 UD3 20, 80, 140
98/9 Upper Deck 126
99/0 Upper Deck 85
00/1 Upper Deck 111
02/3 Upper Deck 369
98/9 UD G. Reserve 126
99/0 UD G. Reserve 85
99/0 UD MVP 130
02/3 UD MVP 129
99/0 Victory 178

CHARBONNEAU, JOSE
90/1 Canada Nationals 13
95/6 DEL 257
96/7 DEL 145
98/9 DEL 141
99/0 Eishockey 86
93/4 Fleer Ultra 438
87/8 MONT
88/9 MONT
93/4 Parkhurst 484
93/4 Power Play 457
88/9 ProCards / Sherbrooke
89/0 ProCards IHL 181
86/7 Sherb. Canadiens 10
93/4 Upper Deck 503
00/1 UD DEL 82

CHARBONNEAU, LOUIS-PHILIPPE
95/6 Roanoke Express
94/5 Slapshot Memorial 72

CHARBONNEAU, MARC
99/0 Anchorage Aces

CHARBONNEAU, PATRICE
99/0 Rockford IceHogs
00/1 Rockford IceHogs

CHARBONNEAU, PATRICE*
93/4 Slapshot / Drummondville 17

CHARBONNEAU, PATRICK
93/4 Cla. 4 Sport 255
91/2 7th...Sketch LHJMQ 251

CHARBONNEAU, RON
94/5 Guildford Flames 25

CHARBONNEAU, STEPHANE
94/5 Erie Panthers
93/4 Phoenix Roadrunners
95/6 Portland Pirates
91/2 ProCards 536
90/1 7th..Sketch LHJMQ 40
91 7th..Sketch Mem.Cup 43

CHARETTE, JONATHAN
01/2 Val d'Or Foreurs 17
02/3 Val d'Or Foreurs

CHARLAND, CARL
94/5 Slapshot Memorial 63

CHARLEBOIS, BOB
72/3 O-Pee-Chee 309
72/3 Ottawa Nationals
73/4 Quaker Oats 23

CHARLESWORTH, TODD
93/4 Muskegon Fury
94/5 Muskegon Fury
82/3 Oshawa Generals
83/4 Oshawa Generals
88/9 ProCards / Muskegon
89/0 ProCards AHL 139
90/1 ProCards 2

CHARPENTIER, MARCO
00/1 Baie-Comeau 10

CHARPENTIER, SÉBASTIEN
01/2 BAP Memor. 328
02/3 Between the Pipes 97,

✂ GUJ33
02/3 Calder 98
97/8 Hampton Roads
98/9 Hampton Roads
02/3 Pacific Complete 505
01/2 Parkhurst 350
97/8 Portland Pirates
99/0 Portland Pirates
00/1 Portland Pirates
02/3 SPx 125
02/3 Upper Deck 224
02/3 UD Foundations 142
02/3 UD Mask 90
02/3 UD MVP 220
02/3 UD Vintage 347

CHARROIS, MARTIN
90/1 7th..Sketch LHJMQ 9
91 7th..Sketch Mem.Cup 52

CHARROIS, YVAN
90/1 7th..Sketch LHJMQ 105

CHARRON, CRAIG
91/2 Cincinnati Cyclones
92/3 Cincinnati Cyclones
94/5 Dayton Bombers 5
95/6 Rochester Americans
96/7 Rochester Americans
97/8 Rochester Americans
00/1 Rochester Americans
99/0 St. John's Maple Leafs

CHARRON, ÉRIC
93/4 Atlanta Knights
00/1 Cleveland Lumberjacks
94/5 Fleer 205
94/5 Fleer Ultra 371
92/3 Fredericton Canadiens
02/3 Nottingham Panthers
94/5 Premier 343
90/1 ProCards 56
91/2 ProCards 89
84/5 Richelieu Riverains
97/8 Saint John Flames
95/6 TAMP / Sky Box
94/5 Upper Deck 489

CHARRON, GUY
90/1 CALG / McGavin's
91/2 CALG / IGA
92/3 CALG / IGA 027
79/0 Dernière Heure
71/2 Eddie Sargent 60
72/3 Eddie Sargent 80
98/9 Grand Rapids Griffins
99/0 Grand Rapids Griffins
74/5 Loblaws
74/5 Loblaws Update
69/0 MONT / Pro Star
70/1 MONT
02/3 MONT
72/3 O-Pee-Chee 223
73/4 O-Pee-Chee 220
74/5 O-Pee-Chee 57
75/6 O-Pee-Chee 32
75/6 O-Pee-Chee 319
76/7 O-Pee-Chee 186
76/7 O-Pee-Chee 384
77/8 O-Pee-Chee 145
78/9 O-Pee-Chee 22
79/0 O-Pee-Chee 152
80/1 O-Pee-Chee 352
79 Panini Sticker 62
74/5 Topps 57
75/6 Topps 32
75/6 Topps 319
76/7 Topps 186
77/8 Topps 145
78/9 Topps 22
79/0 Topps 152
71/2 Toronto Sun Photo
78/9 WASH
79/0 WASH
80/1 WASH

CHARRON, YVES
91/2 7th...Sketch LHJMQ 31

CHARTIER, CHRISTIAN
00/1 Prince George Cougars
01/2 St. John's Maple Leafs
01/2 St. John's / Clarenville
97/8 Upper Deck 402

CHARTIER, DAVE
81/2 Saskatoon Blades
83/4 Saskatoon Blades

CHARTIER, SCOTT
91/2 Avant Garde BCJHL 35
91/2 Avant Garde BCJHL 158
93/4 Classic 61
94/5 Classic ✍ Aut.
99/0 San Angelo Outlaws
93/4 San Diego Gulls
92/3 W. Michigan Broncos

CHARTRAIN, ANDRÉ
82/3 Fredericton Express
83/4 Fredericton Express

CHARTRAND, BRAD
99/0 BAP Mem. 373
00/1 Lowell Lock Monsters
01/2 Manchester Monarchs
99/0 NHL Power Play
99/0 Omega 115
99/0 To. Prmr. Plus 90
99/0 UD G. Reserve 342
00/1 UD MVP 194
00/1 Victory 264

CHARTRAND, JACQUES
52/3 St. Lawrence 27

CHARTRAND, RICK
89/0 Rayside-Balfour

CHARTRAND, SIMON
89/0 Rayside-Balfour

CHARTRAND, STEVE
02/3 Coventry Blaze

CHARTRAW, RICK
83/4 EDMO / McDonald's
83/4 EDMO / West Mall
83/4 EDMO
88/9 EDMO / Action 96
74/5 MONT
76/7 MONT
77/8 MONT
78/9 MONT
79/0 MONT
80/1 MONT
75/6 O-Pee-Chee 388
76/7 O-Pee-Chee 244
77/8 O-Pee-Chee 363
78/9 O-Pee-Chee 238
79/0 O-Pee-Chee 243
80/1 O-Pee-Chee 364
82/3 Post [LosA.]
76/7 Topps 244
78/9 Topps 238
79/0 Topps 243

CHASE, BOB
98/9 Fort Wayne Komets

CHASE, KELLY
98/9 Be A Player 276, ✍ Aut. 276
00/1 BAP Mem. ✂ T-9
90/1 Bowman 14
93/4 Donruss 483
94/5 Donruss 157
95/6 HART / Kids Club
96/7 HART / Kids Club
94/5 Leaf 396
90/1 O-Pee-Chee 432
91/2 O-Pee-Chee 23
98/9 Pacific 363
97/8 Pa. Paramount 156
98/9 Pa. Paramount 199
96/7 Pi. Be A Player 60, ✍ Aut. 60
88/9 ProCards / Peoria
90/1 ProCards 87
86/7 Saskatoon Blades
89/0 SLOU / Kodak
91/2 SLOU
99/0 SLOU / Taco Bell 19
96/7 UD CC 122

CHASE, KELLY
02/3 Fleer Throwbacks 63, ✂ 1SW, ✍ Aut.

CHASE, TIM
93/4 Knoxville Cherokees

CHASLE, YVON
52/3 Anonymous 134

CHASSÉ, DENIS
01/2 Cardiff Devils
92/3 Classic Prospects 79
95/6 Donruss 164
94/5 Fleer 184
95/6 Fleer Ultra 137
00/1 Kudos 59
95/6 Leaf 132
91/2 ProCards 535
90/1 7th..Sketch LHJMQ 13
91 7th..Sketch Mem.Cup 54
95/6 SBx Impact Fox 5
94/5 Topps Finest BBR-15
94/5 Upper Deck 414
95/6 Upper Deck 416

CHATEAU, BROOKE
98/9 Charlotte Checkers
99/0 Charlotte Checkers
99/0 Charlotte Checkers

CHATTINGTON, TERRANCE
52/3 Anonymous 57

CHAULK, COLIN
99/0 Missouri RiverOtters
95/6 Slapshot 123

CHEBATURKIN, VLADIMIR
93/4 Classic 37
93/4 Cla. 4 Sport 212
99/0 Lowell Lock Monsters
01/2 Norfolk Admirals
98/9 Pacific 277
00/1 Stadion 194

CHECCO, NICK
98/9 Florida Everblades
93/4 Minnesota G'Gophers
94/5 Minnesota G'Gophers
00/1 Rockford IceHogs
01/2 Rockford IceHogs

CHECKNITA, PAUL
87/8 Kamloops Blazers
88/9 Lethbridge Hurricanes

CHEECHOO, JONATHAN
02/3 Bowman 120
98 Bowman 142, 164, -SC18, ✍ A25
98 Bowman Chrome 142, 164
02/3 Calder 93, -CR 20
01/2 Cleveland Barons
02/3 Crown Royale -RR 19
02/3 Exclusive 190, -DFG 10
00/1 Kentucky Tho'blades
x00/1 Kentucky Tho'blades
98/9 OPC Chrome 230
02/3 Pacific Complete 539
02/3 Private Stock Titanium -ROT 19
02/3 Stadium 120
98/9 Topps 230
02/3 T. Total 432
99/0 Upper Deck 317
99/0 UD G. Reserve 317
99/0 UD Ovation 78

CHEEVERS, GERRY
99/0 BAP Mem. AH-4, ✍ AH-4
00/1 BAP Mem. ✂ G-8, ✂ G-14, ✂ G-25, ✂ G-26, ✂ G-30
01/2 BAP Memor. GT
02/3 BAP Memorabilia / Cup
01/2 BT Pipes 146, -Mask, ✂ DM, ✂ GR, ✂ VM
02/3 Between the Pipes ✂ HSHSJers 26, ✂ I9, ✂ RB8, ✂ VM7, ✍ Aut.
70/1 BOST
71/2 BOST
91/2 BOST / SA Legends
98/9 BOST / Alumni 30
72/3 Cleveland Crusaders
65/6 Coca-Cola
70/1 Colgate 71
70/1 Dad's Cookies
70/1 Eddie Sargent 15
71/2 Eddie Sargent 16
70/1 Esso Power Player
01/2 Fleer Greats 60, ✍ Aut.
01/2 Fleer Legacy 36
83&87 HHOF 250
75/6 Hockey Heroes
93/4 Hockey Wit 81
02/3 In The Game-Used ✂ GP15
72/3 Post 8
68/9 O-Pee-Chee 140
69/0 O-Pee-Chee 22
69/0 O-Pee-Chee 4in1
70/1 O-Pee-Chee 1
71/2 O-Pee-Chee 54
72/3 O-Pee-Chee 340
76/7 O-Pee-Chee 120
77/8 O-Pee-Chee 260
77/8 O-Pee-Chee NS 2
78/9 O-Pee-Chee 140
78/9 O-Pee-Chee 263
79/0 O-Pee-Chee 85
80/1 O-Pee-Chee 168
92/3 O-Pee-Chee 343
92/3 OPC - Anniv. 5
74/5 OPC WHA 30
75/6 OPC WHA 20
75/6 OPC WHA 67
73/4 OPC WHA Poster 6
01/2 Parkhurst ✍ PA33
02/3 Parkhurst ✂ VM18, ✂ VT3
02/3 Parkhurst Retro ✂ NN6
95/6 Parkie 66-67 16
94/5 Parkie Tall FS-2
73/4 Quaker Oats 8
72 Semic Sticker 188
68/9 Shirriff / Bost. 4
00/1 Signature ✂ GLS-2
01/2 Signature ✍ VA17
01/2 SP GU ✂ TotGC (x2), ✂ TotGT
77-79 Sportscaster 44-20
77-79 Sports. FIN 49-1174
91/2 Star Pics 61
65/6 Topps 31
67/8 Topps 99
68/9 Topps 1
69/0 Topps 22
70/1 Topps 1
71/2 Topps 4
71/2 Topps 54
76/7 Topps 120
77/8 Topps 260
77/8 ToppsNS 2
78/9 Topps 140
78/9 Topps 263
79/0 Topps 85
80/1 Topps 168
01/2 Topps -SCH, -Reprint, ✍ SCHA, ✍ Reprint
01/2 T/O Archives 23, -Seat, ✍ CAI
71/2 Toronto Sun Photo
00/1 Ultimate Mem. ✂ UG-1, ✂GM-8, ✂GM-9, ✂GM-18
02/3 Ultimate Memorabilia ✂ Cor, ✂ EA, ✂ FS (x3), ✂ RT, ✂ SU, ✂ SCD, ✂ VGJ
x99/0 UD C. Legends ✍ ES
01/2 UD Legends 6, 79, ✂ PoH, ✂ TT
02/3 UD Mask / Mask, ✍ Mask
99/0 UD Retro 92, ✍ Ink.
01/2 UD Top Shelf ✂ GG-LP
01/2 UD Vintage ✂ GG, ✂ NL
94/5 Zellers, ✍ Aut.

CHELIOS, CHRIS
94/5 Action Packed
01/2 Adrenaline 63
92/3 American Licorice 3
02/3 Atomic -NPU 3
98/9 Aurora 39, CF-10
99/0 Aurora 49, Stripe 49
00/1 Aurora 48, Pin. 48
02/3 BAP All-Star 15, ✂ ASJ, ✂ HSHSJers
98/9 Be A Player 180, H-14, ✍ Aut. 180, ✂ AS-21, ✂ S-19
99/0 BAP Mem. 30, H-20, ✂ J-21, ✂ TM-11, ✂ TM-24, ✂ TM-39
00/1 BAP Mem. 212, ✂ H-12, ✂ TM-12
01/2 BAP Memor. 124, ✂ AST
02/3 BAP Memorabilia 84, 241, ✂ ASJ8, ✂ SCC 3
96/7 Bic.Sports Aces 5-C
97/8 Bicycle 3-Diamond
95/6 Bicycle Sports Aces 9-Spade
90/1 Bowman 42, 46
91/2 Bowman 398
92/3 Bowman 43
92/3 Bowman 201
95/6 Bowman 12
98/9 Bowman's Best 29
02/3 Calder 28
90/1 CHIC / Coke
91/2 CHIC / Coke
93/4 CHIC / Coke
93/4 Classic 118, ✍ Aut.
99/0 Crown Royale 48
00/1 Crown Royale ✂ GWJ 13
93/4 Donruss 65
93/4 Donruss IK 5
94/5 Donruss 118, D-6
95/6 Donruss 91, D-7, PP-4
96/7 Donruss 71, D-3, HL-6
97/8 Donruss 37, L2L-13
96/7 Do. Canadian 56
97/8 Do. Canadian 120, SCS-4
95/6 Do. Elite 61
96/7 Do. Elite 20, P-11
97/8 Do. Elite 31
97/8 Do. Preferred 127, 171
97/8 Do. Priority 99, OD-24, Post-23, Stamp-23
97/8 Do. Studio 30, P-28
96/7 Duracell DC8
98/9 Dynagon Ice 39, -TC 6
99/0 Dynagon Ice 72, CM-7
93/4 EA Sports 186
93/4 EA Sports 25
97/8 Esso 30
02/3 Exclusive 60
02/3 First Edition 185, 339, 374
94/5 Flair 32
96/7 Flair 15
94/5 Fleer 39
96/7 Fleer 16, 140, NT-2
95/6 Fleer Metal 24, IS-2
96/7 Fl. Picks F50-7, DL-2
92/3 Fleer Ultra 34, -AS 7
93/4 Fleer Ultra 40
93/4 Fleer Ultra AS 14
93/4 Fleer Ultra AW 2
94/5 Fleer Ultra 40, ASG-8
95/6 Fleer Ultra 31, 380
96/7 Fl. Ultra 30, PL-2, UP-2
91/2 Gillette 16
95 Globe 107
96/7 Got-Um
01/2 Heads Up ✂ JQ 11, ✂ JQ 22
93/4 Hockey Wit 12
95/6 Hoyle / West. 8-Heart
92/3 Humpty Dumpty
02/3 In The Game-Used 24, 124, ✂ IE18, ✂ GUJ34, ✂ SJ34, ✂ T5, ✂ TM7
89/0 Kraft 20
90/1 Kraft 6, 81
91/2 Kraft 18
92/3 Kraft / Kraft Singles
93/4 Kraft / KD
94/5 Kraft / HH
95/6 Kraft / PB
96/7 Kraft / AS, TT, PB
97/8 Kraft / Jrs. to Pros.
98/9 Kraft / PB, / Post 22
86/7 Kraft Sports 22
93/4 Leaf 290
93/4 Leaf 51
93/4 Leaf GLAS 2
94/5 Leaf 7
95/6 Leaf 142, GLS-2, RTTC-6
96/7 Leaf 46
97/8 Leaf 64
94/5 L. Limited 83
95/6 L. Limited 40
96/7 L. Limited 1
96/7 L. Preferred 19, LS-7
97/8 Limited 16, 87, 166, 175, FG-58
96/7 Maggers 27
91/2 McDonald's Mc-22
91/2 McDonald's McH2
92/3 McDonald's McD-03
93/4 McDonald's McH-05
94/5 McDonald's McD-16
95/6 McDonald's McD-23
96/7 McDonald's McD-8
96/7 Metal Univ. 26, CS-1
99/0 Millenium 91, ✍ Aut. 91, ✂ J-14, ✂ JS-14
83/4 MONT
84/5 MONT
85/6 MONT
85/6 MONT / Provigo
86/7 MONT
87/8 MONT / Vachon 78
87/8 MONT / Vachon 79
87/8 MONT / Vachon 82
87/8 MONT / Vachon 83
88/9 MONT
89/0 MONT
89/0 MONT / Kraft
95/6 Cool Trade 11
98/9 NHL Power Play
84/5 O-Pee-Chee 259
85/6 OPC/Topps 51
85/6 OPC/Topps Box D
86/7 OPC/Topps 171
87/8 OPC/Topps 106
88/9 OPC/Topps 49
90/1 OPC/Topps 29
91/2 O-Pee-Chee 233
91/2 O-Pee-Chee 268
92/3 O-Pee-Chee 13
02/3 O-Pee-Chee 90, 323
89/0 OPC/Topps 174
89/0 O-Pee-Chee 323
89/0 Topps - Sticker 1
98/9 OPC Chrome 166, B2
90/1 OPC Premier 13
91/2 OPC Premier 17
91/2 OPC Premier 150
85/6 OPC Sticker 125
86/7 OPC Sticker 6-151
87/8 OPC Sticker 9
88/9 OPC Sticker 51
89/0 opcSticker 56, 156-14, 212-73, / AS 26
97/8 Omega 48, 245, SHLC-4
98/9 Omega 49, -Onl. 6, -PI 2
99/0 Omega 80
98/9 Pacific 7, GCDC 7, -TC 6
99/0 Pacific 135, CG-16
00/1 Pacific 145
01/2 Pacific 138
02/3 Pacific 123
02/3 Pacific Complete 442
97/8 Pacific CC 7, GCDC-6, TC-6
97/8 Pa. Crown Roy. 28, BOS-4
98/9 Pa. Crown Roy. 28, -PotG 5
97/8 Pa. Dynagon 25, T-35, BKS-20
97/8 Pa. Invincible 28, FP-6, R-42
97/8 Pa. Paramount 41
98/9 Pa. Paramount 44, -TC 6
99/0 Pa. Paramount 79
00/1 Pa. Paramount 83, ✂ GUS-9
97/8 Pa. Revolution 28, ASG-5, TC-6
98/9 Pa. Revolution 29, -TPA 3, -Show. 8
94 Panini Olympics 324
98/9 Panini Photocard
87/8 Panini Sticker 58
88/9 Panini Sticker 253
89/0 Panini Sticker 237, 238, 379
90/1 Panini Sticker 49
91/2 Panini Sticker 10
91/2 Panini Sticker 329
92/3 Panini Sticker 11
92/3 Panini Sticker 286
93/4 Panini Sticker 153
94/5 Panini Sticker 134
95/6 Panini Sticker 164
96/7 Panini Sticker 151, 157
97/8 Panini Sticker 129
98/9 Panini Sticker 114
99/0 Panini Sticker 238
91/2 Parkhurst 32
92/3 Parkhurst 29
92/3 Parkhurst 457
92/3 Parkhurst CP16
93/4 Parkhurst 45
94/5 Parkhurst 45
95/6 Parkhurst 38, AS-4, CCP-13, PP-20
00/1 Parkhurst P-128
01/2 Parkhurst 146, ✂ PJ42, ✂ PS32
02/3 Parkhurst 54, -CR7, -HHN7, ✂ CRM7
02/3 Parkhurst Retro 160
91/2 Pinnacle 58
91/2 Pinnacle B-9
92/3 Pinnacle 109
92/3 Pinnacle TP 2
93/4 Pinnacle 181
93/4 Pinnacle 223
93/4 Pinnacle 233
93/4 Pinnacle TP 2
94/5 Pinnacle 94, BR-4, TP-3
95/6 Pinnacle 50, FS-9, FC-6
96/7 Pinnacle 34, T-8
97/8 Pinnacle 65, TP-3
97/8 Pi. Be A Player 11, ✍ Aut. 11
97/8 Pi. BeeHive 25
97/8 Pi. Certified 74, CT-5
96/7 Pi. FANtasy 11
97/8 Pi. Inside 18
96/7 Pi. Mint 22
95/6 Pi. Summit 39, GMC-3
96/7 Pi. Summit 43
97/8 Pi. Totally 74
95/6 Pi. Zenith 37
96/7 Pi. Zenith 68, CS-12
95/6 Playoff 22
96/7 Playoff 370
94/5 POG 73
95/6 POG 70, I-012
94/5 Post
97/8 Pi. Post 12
93/4 Power Play 47
93/4 Premier 237
93/4 Premier 94
94/5 Premier 475, 486
99/0 Prism 49
00/1 Pr. Stock ✂ GUG 43, PS-19
02/3 Pr. Stock Reserve 35
00/1 PS Titanium ✂ GUG-16, ✂ GUG-94
00/1 PS Titanium Draft ✂ 36
95/6 Pro Magnet 2
90/1 Pro Set 147, 368, 427
91/2 Pro Set 48
91/2 Pro Set 278
92/3 Pro Set 34
91 Pro Set Awards AC15
91/2 Pro Set Platinum 25
87/8 Pro Sport CW3
99/0 Revolution 50
00/1 Revolution 50
90/1 Score 15, 4T
90/1 Sco. Hot Cards 9
91/2 Score 235
91/2 Score CAN 455
92/3 Score 2
92/3 Score 497
92/3 Score USAG 2
93/4 Score 101
93/4 Score DT 3
93/4 Score PiAS 26
94/5 Score 189, CI17, DT8
95/6 Score 3
96/7 Score 36, CI-15, S-8
97/8 Score 90, CI-9
92/3 Seasons 4
94/5 Select 31, FL-9
95/6 Select CE 2, DS-4
96/7 Select CE 27
94 Semic 111
94 Semic 338
95 Semic 104
89 Semic Sticker 157
91 Semic Sticker 130
92 Semic Sticker 153
93 Semic Sticker 172
00/1 Signature DD-3
01/2 Signature ✂ GU79, ✂ IS3
02/3 Signature Series 144, ✍ 144, ✂ SGJ34
95/6 SBx Emotion 28, Xci-20
95/6 SBx Impact 28
96/7 SBx Impact 18, BR-2, F-5
02/3 Slam Card
94/5 SP 23
95/6 SP 23, FX3
96/7 SP 27,CW-18, HC-6
97/8 SP Authentic 30, I3, ✍ SotT
98/9 SP Authentic 19
01/2 SP Authentic ✂ NN
02/3 SP Game-Used ✂ PH
02/3 Sports Vault 217
96/7 SPx 6
97/8 SPx 9, D-SPX10
99/0 SPx 60
98/9 SPx Finite 120
98/9 SPx Prospects 12
99/0 Stadium 122
00/1 Stadium 115
95/6 SLU
97/8 SLU
95/6 Super Sticker 22, DC-10
96/7 Team Out!
92/3 Topps 98
95/6 Topps 8, 230, HGA6, M18, 9RL
98/9 Topps 166, B2, M17
99/0 Topps 219
00/1 Topps 182
02/3 Topps 90, 323
99/0 To. Chrome 219
00/1 To. Chrome 121
02/3 T. Chrome 57
94/5 Topps Finest 34
95/6 To. Finest 19, 121
98/9 To. Finest 127
98/9 T. Gold Label 3
02/3 To. Heritage 112, 122
02/3 T. Limited 90, 323
96/7 Topps Picks 19, FT6, ID3
99/0 To. Prmr. Plus 67
91/2 To. Stadium 6
92/3 To. Stadium 87
93/4 To. Stadium 147
93/4 To. Stadium 420
93/4 To. Stadium 459
93/4 To. Stadium - All-Stars
94/5 To. Stadium 70, DAD-5
95/6 To. Stadium 10,F2
93/4 TSC Members Only 2
94/5 TSC Members Only 38
95/6 TSC Members Only 4
00/1 To. Stars 87
95/6 T. Super Skills 50
02/3 T. Total 134, AW8
98/9 UD Choice 46, 223, BH23
00/1 Ultimate Mem. ✂ JJ-13, ✂N-5, ✂N-8, ✂TM-3, ✂TM-35
01/2 Ultimate Mem. ✂ Gloves
02/3 Ultimate Memorabilia ✂ Emb, ✂ GAO, ✂ HT, ✂ ITN, ✂ LA, ✂ SCDE, ✂ SCDGJ, ✂ SCDN
90/1 Upper Deck 174, 422, 491
91/2 Upper Deck 37
91/2 Upper Deck 354
92/3 Upper Deck 159
92/3 Upper Deck 629
92/3 Upper Deck WG3
93/4 Upper Deck 129, AW5, GG2, SP-28
94/5 Upper Deck 26, C29, H7, SP-16
95/6 Upper Deck 170, 238, AS-2, H-34, SE-17
96/7 Upper Deck 31, X11, P15, SS27A
97/8 Upper Deck 36, 394, SG7, T4C
98/9 Upper Deck 65, FT21
99/0 Upper Deck 223, HOF14
00/1 Upper Deck 291
01/2 Upper Deck ✂ ASJ
02/3 Upper Deck 307, ✂ ASJ
95/6 UD ASG MVP9
93/4 Upper Deck Be A Player 2
94/5 UD Be A Player R97, R109
95/6 UD Be A Player 211, ✍ S211
96/7 UD Black Diam. 145
97/8 UD Black Diam. 29
98/9 UD Black Diam. 19
99/0 UD C. Legends 42
95/6 UD CC 37, 380
96/7 UD CC 47, 301, 313, UD31
97/8 UD Coll. Choice 46, SQ11, S7
98/9 UD G. Reserve 65
99/0 UD G. Reserve 223
96/7 UD Ice 10
97/8 UD Ice 67
92/3 UD Locker 22
98/9 UD MVP 44
99/0 UD MVP 73
00/1 UD MVP 65, ✂ GS
95/6 UD Post 15
96/7 UD Post, SU-3
99/0 UD Retro 30
00/1 UD Vintage 132
02/3 UD Vintage 312
00/1 Vanguard ✂ DGJ 5
01/2 Vanguard ✂ DGM 3
99/0 Victory 99
00/1 Victory 84
02/3 Victory 79, -NP55
99/0 WGretzky 64
96 Wien 159
97/8 Zenith 14, Z39

CHELIOS, STEVE
97/8 Quad City Mallards

CHELODI, ARMANDO
95 Panini Worlds 92
94 Semic 309

CHEMOMAZ, RICH
98/9 DEL 205

CHENARD, ALAIN
00/1 Chicoutimi Saguenéens 14

CHERBAYEV, ALEXANDER
92/3 Classic 49
93/4 Classic 38
92/3 Classic Four Sport 190
93/4 Cla. Prospects 194
99/0 Eishockey 34
93/4 Kansas City Blades
94/5 Kansas City Blades 13
95/6 Kansas City Blades
94/5 Leaf 465
92/3 Red Ace Violet 7
93 Semic Sticker 137
94/5 Topps Finest 14
91/2 Upper Deck 657
93/4 Upper Deck 279
94/5 Upper Deck 263
91/2 Upper Deck WJC 18
00/1 UD DEL 188
01/2 UD DEL 16

CHEREDARYK, STEVE
97/8 New Orleans Brass
94/5 Sig. Rookies 43, ✍ 43
96/7 Springfield Falcons

CHERNESKI, STEFAN
97 Bowman 117, BB10
98 Bowman 76
98 Bowman Chrome 76
95/6 Brandon Wheat Kings
98/9 Hartford Wolf Pack
99/0 Hartford Wolf Pack
97/8 Pi. BeeHive 63, ✍ Aut. 63
92 Québec Pee Wee 1202

CHERNIK, ALEXANDER
89/0 Soviet Stars

CHERNIKOV, ALEXEI
00/1 Mir 254

CHERNIN, VALERI
00/1 Mir 56

CHERNIWCHAN, AL
85/6 Brandon Wheat Kings

CHERNOFF, MIKE
73/4 Vancouver Blazers

CHERNOMAZ, RICH
95/6 DEL 403
96/7 DEL 311
99/0 Eishockey 217
83/4 NJER
84/5 NJER
89/0 ProCards IHL 198
90/1 ProCards 607
91/2 ProCards 586
88/9 Salt Lake G'Eagles
92/3 Salt Lake G'Eagles
93/4 St. John's Maple Leafs
94/5 St. John's Maple Leafs
00/1 St. John's Maple Leafs
81/2 Victoria Cougars
82/3 Victoria Cougars

CHERNOSKUTOV, ANDREI
99/0 Mir 245

CHERNOV, ARTEM
00/1 Mir 82, 289

CHERNY, VALERI
98/9 Mir 157

CHERNYAVSKI, SERGEI
99/0 Mir 216

CHERNYKH, DMITRI
02/3 Russian Future Stars 12

CHERREY, SCOTT
99/0 Mobile Mysticks
94/5 Sig. Rookies 5, ✍ 5
93/4 Slapshot / North Bay 15
94/5 Slapshot / North Bay 18
95/6 Slapshot 371

CHERRY, DICK
69/0 O-Pee-Chee 173

CHERRY, DON
52/3 Anonymous 100
96/7 Duracell DC2122
00/1 Mississauga IceDogs
01/2 Mississauga IceDogs
92 National Game 22
74/5 O-Pee-Chee 161
92/3 Parkhurst CP
92/3 Parkhurst PR 101, Aut.
93/4 Parkhurst D20
97/8 Pi. CBC Sports 2
74/5 Topps 161
00/1 To. Stars GG, ✍ GGA

CHERRY, STEVE
00/1 Mississauga IceDogs
01/2 Mississauga IceDogs

CHERVYAKOV, ALEXEI
99/0 Mir 142
00/1 Mir 358
93 Semic Sticker 130

CHERVYAKOV, DENIS
92/3 Classic Prospects 69
96/7 Kentucky Tho'blades
99/0 UD Elitserien 187, S14

CHETTLEBURGH, MIKE
83/4 Brantford Alexanders

CHEVALIER, ROBERT
52/3 Anonymous 68

CHEVELDAE, TIM
91/2 Bowman 47
92/3 Bowman 202
92/3 Bowman 420
94/5 Cla. Images PL8
90/1 DETR / Little Caesars
93/4 Donruss 507
93/4 Donruss 96
94/5 Donruss 325
93/4 EA Sports 42
94/5 Flair 205
92/3 Fleer Ultra 46
93/4 Fleer Ultra 14
94/5 Fleer Ultra 240
95/6 Hoyle / West. 9-Heart
92/3 Kraft / PB
94/5 Kraft / KD
95/6 Kraft / PS
97/8 Las Vegas Thunder 16
93/4 Leaf 195
94/5 Leaf 81
90/1 O-Pee-Chee 430
91/2 O-Pee-Chee 35
92/3 O-Pee-Chee 128
91/2 OPC Premier 175
90/1 Panini Sticker 212
91/2 Panini Sticker 136
92/3 Panini Sticker 111
93/4 Panini Sticker 254
94/5 Panini Sticker 171
91/2 Parkhurst 39
91/2 Parkhurst 441
92/3 Parkhurst 37
93/4 Parkhurst 59
95/6 Parkhurst 234
94/5 Parkie SE203
91/2 Pinnacle 21
92/3 Pinnacle 37
92/3 Pinnacle 269
92/3 Pinnacle T2K 20
93/4 Pinnacle 282
94/5 Pinnacle 130
95/6 Pinnacle 136
95/6 Playoff 325
96/7 Playoff 406
94/5 POG 297
95/6 POG 296
93/4 Power Play 67
93/4 Premier 66
94/5 Premier 502
95/6 Pro Magnet 56
90/1 Pro Set 602
91/2 Pro Set 57
92/3 Pro Set 43
92/3 Pro Set 251
91/2 Pro Set Platinum 31
88/9 ProCards / Adirondack
89/0 ProCards AHL 326
91/2 Puck / Pro Set 7
86/7 Saskatoon Blades
00/1 Saskatoon Blades
90/1 Score 87
91/2 Score 272
91/2 Score CAN 492
92/3 Score 275
92/3 Score 417
93/4 Score 68
95/6 Score 212
91/2 Score Young Stars 25
92/3 Score Young Stars 21
92/3 Seasons 7
94/5 Select 102
92/3 Topps 225
92/3 Topps 310
95/6 Topps 291
91/2 To. Stadium 224
92/3 To. Stadium 199
93/4 To. Stadium 166
94/5 To. Stadium 217
90/1 Upper Deck 393
91/2 Upper Deck 129
92/3 Upper Deck 5
92/3 Upper Deck 197
93/4 Upper Deck 9
94/5 Upper Deck 75, SP-178
95/6 Upper Deck 452, SE-179
95/6 UD Be A Player 76, ✍ S76
95/6 UD CC 319
95/6 WINN
95/6 WINN Readers

CHEVELDAYOFF, KEVIN
88/9 Brandon Wheat Kings
90/1 ProCards 507
91/2 ProCards 459

CHEVREFILS, RÉAL
45-64 BeeHive-2 [Bost.]
57-58 BOST
52/3 Parkhurst 80
53/4 Parkhurst 89
54/5 Parkhurst 63
93/4 Parkie 56-57 8
54/5 Topps 6
57/8 Topps 1
57/8 Toronto Star Photo

CHEVRIER, ALAIN
89/0 CHIC / Coke
85/6 NJER 3
86/7 NJER / S.O.B.E.R.
86/7 O-Pee-Chee 225
87/8 OPC/Topps 58
90/1 O-Pee-Chee 436
89/0 OPC/Topps 132
87/8 OPC Sticker 72
87/8 OPC Sticker 63-204
88/9 OPC Sticker 162
87/8 Panini Sticker 73
89/0 Panini Sticker 54
90/1 Pro Set 230
88/9 WINN / Safety Tips

CHEYNE, TRAVIS
92/3 MPS SJHL 25

CHIARELLO, GENE
99 Bowman 161

CHIASSON, DAN
84/5 Sudbury Wolves

CHIASSON, LUC
01/2 Guelph Storm
01/2 Guelph Storm M-Cup

CHIASSON, PASCAL
91/2 7th...Sketch LHJMQ 253

CHIASSON, STEVE
99/0 BAP Mem. SC-3
90/1 Bowman 234
92/3 Bowman 91
97/8 CARO / Sprint
98/9 CARO / Highwoods
86/7 DETR / Little Caesars
87/8 DETR / Little Caesars
88/9 DETR / Little Caesars
89/0 DETR / Little Caesars
91/2 DETR / Little Caesars
93/4 Donruss 97
95/6 Donruss 69
96/7 Donruss 120
93/4 EA Sports 38
94/5 Fleer 28
92/3 Fleer Ultra 282
93/4 Fleer Ultra 305
94/5 Fleer Ultra 268
95/6 Fleer Ultra 23
96/7 HART / Kids Club
93/4 Leaf 111
94/5 Leaf 487
95/6 Leaf 193
96/7 Maggers 22
90/1 OPC/Topps 94
91/2 O-Pee-Chee 508
92/3 O-Pee-Chee 160
89/0 OPC/Topps 164
98/9 Pacific 129
89/0 Panini Sticker 62
90/1 Panini Sticker 207
91/2 Panini Sticker 143
92/3 Panini Sticker 120
93/4 Panini Sticker 251
95/6 Panini Sticker 239
91/2 Parkhurst 268
92/3 Parkhurst 282
93/4 Parkhurst 55
94/5 Parkhurst 68
95/6 Parkhurst 298
91/2 Pinnacle 298
92/3 Pinnacle 339
93/4 Pinnacle 194
94/5 Pinnacle 376
95/6 Pinnacle 189
97/8 Pi. Be A Player 202, ✍ Aut. 202
95/6 Playoff 15
94/5 POG / Western 24
95/6 POG 57
93/4 Power Play 68
93/4 Premier 196
94/5 Premier 327, 348
90/1 Pro Set 69
90/1 Score 214
91/2 Score 293
91/2 Score CAN 513
92/3 Score 185
93/4 Score 221
93/4 Score PiAS 23
94/5 Score 45
95/6 Score 146
96/7 Score 235
95/6 SBx Emotion 20
95/6 SBx Impact 20
96/7 SP 22
92/3 Topps 37
95/6 Topps 129
96/7 Topps Picks 125
92/3 To. Stadium 105
93/4 To. Stadium 247
93/4 To. Stadium - All-Stars
90/1 Upper Deck 96
91/2 Upper Deck 283
92/3 Upper Deck 546
93/4 Upper Deck 345
94/5 Upper Deck 197, SP-101
95/6 Upper Deck 10
96/7 Upper Deck 26
94/5 UD Be A Player R83, ✍ 130
95/6 UD CC 43
96/7 UD CC 44

CHIBIREV, IGOR
93/4 Cla. 4 Sport 228
92/3 Classic Prospects 98
93/4 Cla. Prospects 61
93/4 Donruss 436
99/0 Eishockey 234
92/3 Fort Wayne Komets 4
94/5 Fort Wayne Komets 25
90/1 O-Pee-Chee 8R
91/2 O-Pee-Chee 14R
94/5 Parkhurst 98
93/4 Power Play 350
00/1 UD DEL 97
01/2 UD DEL 93

CHICOINE, DAVID
99/0 Shawinigan 22
00/1 Shawinigan 8
01/2 Shawinigan 9
01/2 Sherbrooke Castors 6

CHIEDUCH, RYAN
00/1 Medicine Hat Tigers
99/0 Prince George Cougars

CHIGHISOLA, MIKE
91/2 Hampton Roads

CHIKIN, DIMITRI
00/1 Mir 348
99/0 UD Elitserien 188

CHIMERA, JASON
01/2 BAP Memor. 218
99 Bowman 85
02/3 Calder 68
01/2 Crown Royale 158
99/0 Hamilton Bulldogs
00/1 Hamilton Bulldogs
01/2 Hamilton Bulldogs
01/2 O-Pee-Chee 277
02/3 O-Pee-Chee 267
01/2 Pacific 154
02/3 Pacific Complete 383
01/2 Parkhurst 315
01/2 Pr. Stock 121
01/2 PS Titanium 157
01/2 PS Titanium Draft 128
01/2 SP Authentic 148
01/2 SP GU 77
01/2 SPx 140, -RT
01/2 Stadium 136
01/2 Topps 277
02/3 Topps 267
01/2 To. Heritage 156
02/3 T. Limited 267
01/2 UD PlayMakers Ltd 118
01/2 Upper Deck 190
01/2 UD MVP 201
01/2 UD Top Shelf 54
01/2 Vanguard 110
01/2 Victory 370

CHIN, COLIN
93/4 Cla. Prospects 81
92/3 Fort Wayne Komets 5
93/4 Fort Wayne Komets 3
94/5 Fort Wayne Komets 1
95/6 Fort Wayne Komets
89/0 ProCards IHL 123
90/1 ProCards 540
91/2 ProCards 250

CHING, HSIANG SHU
79 Panini Sticker 360

CHINN, NICKY
00/1 Kudos 76
94 Semic 318
95/6 Sheffield Steelers
97/8 Sheffield Steelers

CHIODO, ANDY
00/1 Toronto St. Mike's

CHIODO, WADE
99/0 Des Moines Buc's

CHIPMAN, JASON
92/3 BCJHL 208
90/1 7th..Sketch OHL 53

CHIPPERFIELD, RON
79/0 EDMO
88/9 EDMO / Action 74
80/1 O-Pee-Chee 280
74/5 OPC WHA 42
75/6 OPC WHA 4
76/7 OPC WHA 32
77/8 OPC WHA 10
80/1 QUÉB

CHISHOLM, LEX
34-43 BeeHive-1 [Toro.]
40/1 O-Pee-Chee 148

CHISTOKLETOV, VASILI
00/1 Mir 94

CHISTOV, STANISLAV
02/3 Atomic 101
02/3 BAP All-Star 133
02/3 BAP Draft Florida 5
02/3 BAP Memorabilia 275
02/3 Bowman 116, ✂ FFDS, ✂ FFJ, ✂ FFP, ✂ FFR, ✂ FFRP, ✂ FFS, ✂ FFTS, ✍ YSA, / ✍ Puck
02/3 Calder 101, -CR 1
02/3 Crown Royale 101, -RR 1
02/3 eTopps 40
02/3 Exclusive 193, DFG 1, ✍ 193
02/3 First Edition 436R
02/3 Heads Up 126
02/3 In The Game-Used 85, ✂ C10
00/1 Mir 307
02/3 O-Pee-Chee 340
02/3 Pacific 126
02/3 Pacific Complete 506
02/3 PTC/ ASG 1
02/3 PTC/ Collections 1
02/3 PTC/ Spring Expo 1
02/3 Parkhurst 205, -HHC 8
02/3 Parkhurst Retro 205, ✂ CH6
02/3 Pr. Stock Reserve 151, -CA 1
02/3 Private Stock Titanium 101, -ROT 1
02/3 Quest for the Cup 101, -CC 1
02/3 Signature Series 194, GS87, ✍ 194, ✂ AR11, ✂ SGJ57, ✂ TQ19
02/3 SP Authentic ✍ 182, ✍ ✂ Patch
02/3 SP Game-Used Edition 67, ✍ Sig
02/3 Sports Vault 158
02/3 SPx ✍ 156
02/3 Stadium 121
02/3 Topps 340
02/3 T. Chrome 173
02/3 To. Heritage 135
02/3 T. Total 434
02/3 UD Superstars 254
02/3 Ultimate Memorabilia 5, ✂ CC, ✍ RAut
02/3 Upper Deck 226
02/3 UD Artistic 123, R94, CG13, ✂ RT
02/3 UD Classic 102
02/3 UD Foundations 143
02/3 UD Honor 146, ✍ SC
02/3 UD Mask 169
02/3 UD Piece 121
02/3 UD Premier ✍ ✂ 78, ✍ Sig
02/3 UD Rookie ✍ 166, ✍ TD
02/3 UD Top Shelf 123
02/3 Vanguard 101, -PP 1

CHISTOV, VICTOR
00/1 Mir 234, 340

CHISTYAKOV, ALEXEI
99/0 Mir 202

CHITARONI, MARIO
96/7 DEL 44
98/9 DEL 178
99/0 Eishockey 64
88/9 ProCards / New Haven
94 Semic 307
93 Semic Sticker 224
84/5 Sudbury Wolves
85/6 Sudbury Wolves
86/7 Sudbury Wolves
00/1 UD DEL 191
01/2 UD DEL 199
96 Wien 181

CHITARONI, MARK
87/8 Flint Spirits

CHITARONI, TERRY
92/3 Classic Prospects 92
91 7th..Sketch Mem.Cup 121
90/1 7th..Sketch OHL 380
91/2 7th...Sketch OHL 250
94/5 Slapshot / Brantford 11
93/4 St. John's Maple Leafs
91/2 Star Pics 15
88/9 Sudbury Wolves
89/0 Sudbury Wolves

90/1 Sudbury Wolves
91/2 Sudbury Wolves
91/2 Ultimate Draft Pick 49, ✍ Aut.
CHIVOJKA, PETR
00/1 Medicine Hat Tigers
CHLAD, MARTIN
94/5 APS 47
95/6 APS 77
96/7 APS 75
99/0 Score 85
CHLUBNA, TOMAS
94/5 APS 132
95/6 APS 310
96/7 APS 204
97/8 APS 330
02/3 Cardset 10
97/8 DS 115
98/9 DS 122
99/0 DS 109
00/1 DS 128
96/7 DS Sticker 203
97/8 DS Sticker 276
98/9 OFS 392
99/0 OFS 320, 406
00/1 OFS 173
CHOINIÈRE, PHILIPPE
00/1 Hull Olympiques 10
CHOKAN, DALE
90/1 7th..Sketch OHL 205
91/2 7th...Sketch OHL 116
CHOLETTE, JULES
37/8 World Wide Gum 127
CHOLEWA, MAREK
89 Semic Sticker 132
92 Semic Sticker 272
CHOQUETTE, DARIN
84/5 Victoria Cougars
CHORNEY, GRANT
86/7 Regina Pats
CHORNEY, MARC
83/4 PITT / Heinz
82/3 Post [Pitt.]
83/4 Souhaits Keychain [Penguins]
CHORSKE, TOM
91/2 Bowman 345
92/3 Fleer Ultra 112
94/5 Leaf 262
89/0 MONT
90/1 MONT
90/1 O-Pee-Chee 490
91/2 O-Pee-Chee 287
91/2 OPC Premier 91
95/6 OTTA
96/7 OTTA
98/9 Pacific 278
97/8 Pa. Invincible R-132
90/1 Panini/MTL 4
91/2 Parkhurst 95
93/4 Parkhurst 384
91/2 Pinnacle 295
92/3 Pinnacle 293
94/5 Pinnacle 182
96/7 Pinnacle 26
97/8 Pi. Be A Player 207, ✍ Aut. 207
94/5 POG 349
93/4 Power Play 375
93/4 Premier 524
94/5 Premier 131
90/1 Pro Set 616
91/2 Score 63T
91/2 Score CAN 613
92/3 Score 184
95/6 Score 284
92/3 Topps 313
91/2 To. Stadium 276
92/3 To. Stadium 351
91/2 Upper Deck 427
93/4 Upper Deck 416
94/5 Upper Deck 191
95/6 UD Be A Player 43, ✍ S43
95/6 UD CC 237
CHOTEBORSKY, JAN
00/1 OFS 66
01/2 OFS 201
CHOTOWETZ, KELLY
89/0 Regina Pats
90/1 7th..Sketch WHL 172
CHOUINARD, DAVE
90/1 7th..Sketch LHJMQ 240
91/2 7th...Sketch LHJMQ 134
CHOUINARD, ÉRIC
00/1 BAP Mem. 512
01/2 BAP Memor. 273
99 Bowman 50
98 Bowman 104, 143, ✍ A15
98 Bowman Chrome 104, 143
98/9 Bowman's Best 139
02/3 Calder 87
98/9 Collection Souvenir 26
00/1 MONT
01/2 O-Pee-Chee 280
02/3 Pacific Complete 561
00/1 Québec Citadelles
01/2 Québec Citadelles
93 Québec Pee Wee 116
94 Québec Pee Wee 345
98/9 Québec Remparts
99/0 Québec Remparts 4
01/2 Topps 280
98/9 To. Finest F13
97/8 Upper Deck 408
CHOUINARD, GUY
77/8 ATLF
78/9 ATLF / Colour
79/0 ATLF / B&W
79/0 ATLF / Colour
80/1 CALG
81/2 CALG
82/3 CALG
98/9 Collection Souvenir 02
79/0 Dernière Heure
76/7 O-Pee-Chee 316
77/8 O-Pee-Chee 237
78/9 O-Pee-Chee 340
79/0 O-Pee-Chee 60
80/1 O-Pee-Chee 45
81/2 O-Pee-Chee 33
82/3 O-Pee-Chee 41
83/4 O-Pee-Chee 78
81/2 OPC Sticker 219
82/3 OPC/Topps Sticker 215
80/1 Pepsi Bottle Cap
82/3 Post [Calg.]
83/4 Souhaits Keychain [Flames]
77/8 Topps 237
79/0 Topps 60
80/1 Topps 45
81/2 Topps 6
CHOUINARD, JACQUES
80/1 Québec Remparts
CHOUINARD, MARC
01/2 BAP Memor. 233
98/9 Cincinnati M'Ducks 27
99/0 Cincinnati M'Ducks
95/6 Classic 29, AS18
95/6 Cla. 5 Sport 153
96/7 Halifax Moosehead
96/7 Halifax Moosehead
02/3 Pacific Complete 288
00/1 PS Titanium Draft 151
01/2 Signature 18, ✍ Aut. 18
00/1 SP Authentic 133
00/1 SPx 173
02/3 T. Total 88
00/1 UD Ice 81
CHOUINARD, MARTIN
97/8 Pensacola Ice Pilots
CHOUINARD, MATHIEU
99 Bowman 64
98 Bowman 82, 159, ✍ A9
98 Bowman Chrome 82, 159
98/9 Collection Souvenir 25
00/1 Grand Rapids Griffins
01/2 Grand Rapids Griffins
94 Québec Pee Wee 497
99/0 Shawinigan 14
98/9 To. Finest F12
97/8 Upper Deck 399
99/0 Upper Deck 330
99/0 UD Black Diam. 105
99/0 UD G. Reserve 330
99/0 UD Ovation 75
99/0 UD Prospects 64, ✍ Sig.
CHOUINARD, PATRICK
99/0 Québec Remparts 2
CHOUKALOS, DON
98/9 Calgary Hitmen 23
01/2 Vancouver Giants
CHOULES, GREGG
84/5 Chicoutimi Saguenéens
CHOVAN, JAN
01/2 Belleville Bulls
01/2 London Knights
CHOWANIEC, STEFAN
74 Hellas MM-Jenkki 93
79 Panini Sticker 127
73/4 Williams Finnish 87
CHREST, BLAINE
86/7 Saskatoon Blades
CHRÉTIEN, CLAUDE
51/2 Lac St-Jean 19
CHRISTENSEN, ERIK
99/0 Kamloops Blazers
99/0 Kamloops Blazers
00/1 Kamloops Blazers
01/2 Kamloops Blazers
02/3 Kamloops Blazers
00/1 UD Prospects 50
CHRISTENSEN, MATT
85/6 Minnesota-Duluth 15
CHRISTENSEN, TED
95/6 UD CC 349
CHRISTENSEN, TERRY
95/6 Tallahassee Tiger Sharks
CHRISTENSEN, TROY
96/7 Dayton Bombers
CHRISTIAN, BRANDON
94/5 Johnstown Chiefs 3
96/7 Johnstown Chiefs
95/6 Thunder Bay Senators
CHRISTIAN, DAVE
89/0 BOST / Sports Action
90/1 BOST / Sports Action
80/1 Bowman 40
91/2 Bowman 358
92/3 Bowman 6
93/4 CHIC / Coke
94/5 Cla. Images 26
95/6 Edge Ice 164
92/3 Fleer Ultra 273
94/5 Minnesota Moose
95/6 Minnesota Moose
80/1 O-Pee-Chee 176
81/2 O-Pee-Chee 359, 360
81/2 O-Pee-Chee 378
82/3 O-Pee-Chee 377
83/4 O-Pee-Chee 367
84/5 O-Pee-Chee 195
85/6 OPC/Topps 99
86/7 OPC/Topps 21
86/7 OPC/Topps Box C
87/8 OPC/Topps 88
88/9 OPC/Topps 14
90/1 OPC/Topps 263
91/2 O-Pee-Chee 276
92/3 O-Pee-Chee 289
89/0 OPC/Topps 159
91/2 OPC Premier 53
92/3 OPC Premier 1
81/2 OPC Sticker 136
82/3 OPC/Topps Sticker 206
84/5 OPC Sticker 133
85/6 OPC Sticker 110-243
86/7 OPC Sticker 248
87/8 OPC Sticker 235-102
88/9 OPC Sticker 70-199
89/0 opcSticker 78-219
80 Olympic USA
87/8 Panini Sticker 184
88/9 Panini Sticker 192
88/9 Panini Sticker 369
89/0 Panini Sticker 345
90/1 Panini Sticker 18
91/2 Panini Sticker 173
91/2 Parkhurst 159
80/1 Pepsi Bottle Cap
91/2 Pinnacle 244
92/3 Pinnacle 193
82/3 Post [Winn.]
93/4 Premier 118
90/1 Pro Set 6
91/2 Pro Set 11
91/2 Pro Set 297
91/2 Pro Set 471
91/2 Pro Set Platinum 110
90/1 Score 295
91/2 Score 292
91/2 Score 39T
91/2 Score CAN 589
92/3 Score 198
93/4 Score 440
94 Semic 127
89 Semic Sticker 166
91 Semic Sticker 142
92 Semic Sticker 164
94/5 SR Miracle 5,6, ✍ 5,6
83/4 Souhaits Keychain [Jets]
91/2 SLOU
80/1 Topps 176
81/2 Topps 7
81/2 Topps 66
84/5 Topps 142
92/3 Topps 21
91/2 To. Stadium 95
92/3 To. Stadium 216
90/1 Upper Deck 61
91/2 Upper Deck 541
92/3 Upper Deck 194
84/5 WASH / Pizza Hut
85/6 WASH / Pizza Hut
86/7 WASH / Kodak
86/7 WASH / Police
87/8 WASH
87/8 WASH / Kodak
88/9 WASH
88/9 WASH / Smokey
89/0 WASH
80/1 WINN
81/2 WINN
82/3 WINN
CHRISTIAN, GORD
93/4 Johnstown Chiefs 7
94/5 Johnstown Chiefs 4
CHRISTIAN, JEFF
95/6 Cleveland Lumberjacks
96/7 Cleveland Lumberjacks
99/0 Cleveland Lumberjacks
97/8 Las Vegas Thunder 17
90/1 ProCards 572
91/2 ProCards 415
00/1 UD DEL 153
01/2 UD DEL 156
CHRISTIAN, LOU
84/5 Nova Scotia Oilers
83/4 Nova Scotia Voyageurs
CHRISTIAN, MARC
93/4 Minnesota-Duluth
93/4 Minnesota-Duluth
CHRISTIAN, MIKE
98/9 Barrie Colts
96/7 Guelph Storm
CHRISTIAN, TED
95/6 Roanoke Express
CHRISTIAN, TIM
91/2 Ferris State Bulldogs
96/7 Roanoke Express 17
98/9 Roanoke Express
CHRISTIANO, JON
96/7 Carolina Monarchs
00/1 Rochester Americans
02/3 Rochester Americans
CHRISTIANSEN,
92/3 Semic Nordisk 214 [Rookie]
CHRISTIANSEN, HAL
89/0 Regina Pats
90/1 7th..Sketch WHL 164
91/2 7th...Sketch WHL 225
CHRISTIANSEN, KEITH
72/3 Minn. Fight. Saints
72 Semic Sticker 124
CHRISTIE, FRANK
73/4 BUFF
CHRISTIE, JASON
97/8 Manitoba Moose
99/0 Peoria Rivermen
00/1 Peoria Rivermen
01/2 Peoria Rivermen
02/3 Peoria Rivermen
94/5 Portland Pirates
95/6 Portland Pirates
96/7 Portland Pirates Hershey
96/7 Portland Pirates
97/8 Portland Pirates
89/0 Saskatoon Blades
CHRISTIE, MIKE
79/0 COLR
74/5 Loblaws
74/5 O-Pee-Chee 278
75/6 O-Pee-Chee 366
76/7 O-Pee-Chee 333
76/7 OPC 383
77/8 O-Pee-Chee 357
78/9 O-Pee-Chee 291
79/0 O-Pee-Chee 345
80/1 O-Pee-Chee 358
82/3 OPC/Topps Sticker 194
80 Olympic USA
82/3 Post [Minn.]
94/5 SR Miracle 7,8, ✍ 7,8
80/1 Topps 103
81/2 Topps 104 [West]
CHRISTIE, RYAN
99/0 Crown Royale 43
98/9 Michigan K-Wings
99/0 Michigan K-Wings
98/9 Omega 78
95/6 Slapshot 293
00/1 Utah Grizzlies
00/1 Victory 263
CHRISTION, SCOTT
91/2 Air Canada SJHL 16
91/2 Air Canada SJHL B18
CHRISTOF, STEVE
82/3 CALG
80/1 MINS
81/2 MINS
80/1 O-Pee-Chee 103
81/2 O-Pee-Chee 160
82/3 O-Pee-Chee 42
83/4 O-Pee-Chee 169
84/5 O-Pee-Chee 81
CHRISTOFFER, JUSTIN
91/2 Air Canada SJHL C37
CHRISTOFFERSEN, M
92/3 Semic Nordisk 65
CHRISTOPHER, DES
90/1 7th..Sketch WHL 207
CHRISTOPHERSON, BEN
01/2 Rockford IceHogs
CHRUN, MIKE
90/1 7th..Sketch WHL 188
91/2 7th...Sketch WHL 203
89/0 Spokane Chiefs
CHRYSTAL, BOB
45-64 BeeHive-2 [NYRa.]
51/2 Cleveland Barons
54/5 Parkhurst 69
54/5 Topps 2
CHUBAROV, ARTEM
99/0 BAP Mem. 310
99/0 Dynagon Ice 193
00/1 Kansas City Blades 20
01/2 Manitoba Moose
99/0 Millenium 233, ✍ Aut. 233
98/9 Mir 163
02/3 Pacific Complete 180
00/1 Panini Sticker 208
98/9 UD Choice 284
97/8 UD Black Diam. 69
99/0 UD MVP Cup 186
CHUKANOV, MAXIM
98/9 Mir 30
CHUMICHEV, VITALI
00/1 Mir 81, 351
CHUN, WAN TA
79 Panini Sticker 357
CHUNCHUKOV, ALEXANDER
96/7 Johnstown Chiefs
94/5 Raleigh Icecaps
CHUPIN, ALEXEI
98/9 Mir 53
99/0 Mir 54
00/1 Mir 37
CHURCH, BRAD
95/6 Classic 17, BK15
95/6 Cla. 5 Sport 134, S-78, SFF-3
94/5 Cla. Images 82, PD5
99/0 Hampton Roads
96/7 Portland Pirates
97/8 Portland Pirates
00/1 Portland Pirates
93/4 Prince Albert Raiders
95/6 Prince Albert Raiders
95/6 SR Tetrad 68
95/6 SR Tetrad Autobilia 96
CHURCH, JACK
34-43 BeeHive-1 [Toro.]
39/0 O-Pee-Chee 52
CHURCHMAN, TRAVIS
97/8 Regina Pats
CHURLA, SHANE
87/8 CALG / Red Rooster
94/5 DALL / Southwest
94/5 DALL / Cap
92/3 Fleer Ultra 315
94/5 Fleer Ultra 278
94/5 Leaf 364
83/4 Medicine Hat Tigers
97/8 Pa. Invincible R-123
92/3 Parkhurst 316
93/4 Parkhurst 316
95/6 Parkhurst 61
94/5 Parkie SE41
94/5 Pinnacle 516
96/7 Pinnacle 191
97/8 Pi. Be A Player 182, ✍ Aut. 182
95/6 Playoff 246
96/7 Playoff 365
93/4 Premier 368
95/6 Pro Magnet 121
90/1 Pro Set 135
91/2 Score CAN 542
93/4 Score 425
94/5 To. Stadium 21
94/5 Upper Deck 186
95/6 Upper Deck 458
97/8 Upper Deck 317
94/5 UD Be A Player ✍ 169
CHURLA, SHANE
02/3 Fleer Throwbacks 79
CHURRAN, CHRIS
01/2 Mississauga IceDogs
CHVATAL, PETR
99/0 Eishockey 405
CHVOJKA, PETR
99/0 OFS 120
CHYCHRUN, JEFF
92/3 Bowman 257
92/3 Durivage 33
83/4 Kingston Canadians
84/5 Kingston Canadians
85/6 Kingston Canadians
90/1 O-Pee-Chee 465
89/0 PHIL
90/1 PHIL
90/1 Pro Set 213
90/1 Score 138
91/2 Score CAN 626
92/3 Score 364
92/3 Topps 196
92/3 To. Stadium 298
90/1 Upper Deck 446
CHYNOWETH, DEAN
84/5 Medicine Hat Tigers
89/0 NYIS
97/8 Pacific CC 340
97/8 Pi. Be A Player 246, ✍ Aut. 246
94/5 Premier 45
90/1 ProCards 511
91/2 ProCards 463
97/8 Providence Bruins
97/8 Upper Deck 222
99/0 Utah Grizzlies
CHYNOWETH, ED
91/2 7th...Sketch WHL 120
CHYZOWSKI, BARRY
89/0 ProCards IHL 42
CHYZOWSKI, DAVE
95/6 Adirondack Red Wings
91/2 Bowman 229
87/8 Kamloops Blazers
88/9 Kamloops Blazers
98/9 Kansas City Blades 20
99/0 Kansas City Blades
89/0 NYIS
90/1 OPC/Topps 146
91/2 O-Pee-Chee 435
91/2 Panini Sticker 253
90/1 Pro Set 483
90/1 ProCards 509
91/2 ProCards 471
90/1 Score 372
91/2 Score CAN 443
90/1 Sco. Young Stars 12
90 7th..Sketch Mem.Cup 3
91/2 To. Stadium 250
90/1 Upper Deck 228
91/2 Upper Deck 281
00/1 UD DEL 19
01/2 UD DEL 229
CHYZOWSKI, RON
88/9 ProCards / Sherbrooke
CIARCIA, JERRY
82 Semic Sticker 142
CIAVAGLIA, PETER
92/3 Classic 103
92/3 Classic Four Sport 215
96/7 Detroit Vipers
97/8 Detroit Vipers
98/9 Detroit Vipers
98/9 EBK IHL All-Star
95/6 Edge Ice 121
95 Panini Worlds 222
91/2 ProCards 12
91/2 Rochester Americans DD
91/2 Rochester Americans GL
92/3 Rochester Americans WPC
92/3 Rochester Americans DD
92/3 Rochester Americans WPC
93/4 Score 474
CIBAK, MARTIN
01/2 BAP Memor. 323
99/0 Medicine Hat Tigers
01/2 Parkhurst 346
02/3 Upper Deck 220
01/2 UD Ice 149
02/3 UD MVP 217
01/2 UD Premier 81
CICCARELLI, DINO
98/9 Aurora 78, CF-22
98/9 Be A Player M3, M9
01/2 BAP Memor. ✂ 500GS
90/1 Bowman 69, -HT 15
91/2 Bowman 302
92/3 Bowman 176
98/9 Bowman's Best 68
93/4 Donruss 98
94/5 Donruss 86
95/6 Donruss 30
96/7 Donruss 150
97/8 Donruss 177
97/8 Do. Canadian 77
97/8 Do. Elite 43
97/8 Do. Preferred 51
97/8 Do. Priority 66
97/8 Do. Studio 65
98/9 Dynagon Ice 79, -TC 11
93/4 EA Sports 41
94/5 Flair 46
96/7 Flair 86
94/5 Fleer 57
01/2 Fleer Greats 28, ✂ O6, ✍ Aut.
01/2 Fleer Legacy 31, ✂ ITC, ✂ TM
92/3 Fleer Ultra 47, 283
93/4 Fleer Ultra 32
94/5 Fleer Ultra 58
95/6 Fleer Ultra 232
96/7 Fl. Ultra 156
97/8 FLOR / Winn-Dixie
83/4 Funmate Puffy 15 [w/]
84/5 Kellogg's 18
90/1 Kraft 7
91/2 Kraft 14
93/4 Leaf 18
94/5 Leaf 44
95/6 Leaf 100
96/7 Leaf 16
97/8 Leaf 83
97/8 Limited 25
96/7 Maggers 57
82/3 McDonald's Les Étoiles 7
96/7 Metal Univ. 143
81/2 MINS
82/3 MINS
82/3 MINS
83/4 MINS
84/5 MINS
84/5 MINS / 7-Eleven 12
85/6 MINS
85/6 MINS / 7-Eleven 1
86/7 MINS / 7-Eleven 6
87/8 MINS
88/9 MINS / ADA
81/2 O-Pee-Chee 161
82/3 O-Pee-Chee 162
82/3 O-Pee-Chee 165
83/4 O-Pee-Chee 164
83/4 O-Pee-Chee 170
84/5 O-Pee-Chee 97
85/6 OPC/Topps 13
86/7 OPC/Topps 138
87/8 OPC/Topps 81
88/9 OPC/Topps 175
90/1 OPC/Topps 100
90/1 Topps-TL 6
91/2 O-Pee-Chee 429
92/3 O-Pee-Chee 249
89/0 OPC/Topps 41
98/9 OPC Chrome 119
87/8 OPC Leaders 7
90/1 OPC Premier 14
92/3 OPC Premier 44
82/3 OPC/Topps Sticker 189
83/4 OPC/Topps Sticker 118
83/4 OPC/Topps Sticker 119
84/5 OPC Sticker 47
85/6 OPC Sticker 39-168
86/7 OPC Sticker 169
87/8 OPC Sticker 57
87/8 OPC Sticker 118-130
88/9 OPC Sticker 202
89/0 opcSticker 75-214
97/8 Omega 97
98/9 Omega 101
98/9 Pacific 22
99/0 Pacific 171
97/8 Pacific CC 15, TC-23
97/8 Pa. Crown Roy. 124
98/9 Pa. Crown Roy. 57
97/8 Pa. Dynagon 115, T-57, BKS-77
97/8 Pa. Invincible 129, AZ-22, R-183
97/8 Pa. Paramount 171
98/9 Pa. Paramount 94, -TC 11
97/8 Pa. Revolution 58
98/9 Pa. Revolution 61
87/8 Panini Sticker 293
88/9 Panini Sticker 93
89/0 Panini Sticker 342
90/1 Panini Sticker 161
91/2 Panini Sticker 207
92/3 Panini Sticker 160
93/4 Panini Sticker 245
95/6 Panini Sticker 182
97/8 Panini Sticker 100
91/2 Parkhurst 193
92/3 Parkhurst 45
93/4 Parkhurst 60
93/4 Parkhurst D5
94/5 Parkhurst 65
95/6 Parkhurst 339
01/2 Parkhurst ✂ 500GS, ✍ PA34
94/5 Parkie SE seV2
91/2 Pinnacle 128
92/3 Pinnacle 311
93/4 Pinnacle 127
93/4 Pinnacle 239
94/5 Pinnacle 241
95/6 Pinnacle 74
96/7 Pinnacle 31
97/8 Pinnacle 68
97/8 Pi. BeeHive 29
97/8 Pi. Certified 105
97/8 Pi. Inside 134
95/6 Pi. Summit 65
97/8 Pi. Totally 105
95/6 Pi. Zenith 51, GG-16
96/7 Pi. Zenith 87
95/6 Playoff 251
94/5 POG 86
95/6 POG 99
82/3 Post [Minn.]
93/4 Power Play 69
93/4 Premier 49
94/5 Premier 541
90/1 Pro Set 308
91/2 Pro Set 258
91/2 Pro Set Platinum 131
90/1 Score 230
90/1 Sco. Hot Cards 94
91/2 Score 128
91/2 Score CAN 128
92/3 Score 395
93/4 Score 214
94/5 Score 19, 243, 246
95/6 Score 247
96/7 Score 101
97/8 Score 119, CI-15
94/5 Select 118
95/6 Select CE 102
84/5 7-Eleven
85/6 7-Eleven Superstars 9
01/2 Signature ✂ 500GS, ✍ VA28
95/6 SBx Emotion 51
95/6 SBx Impact 50
94/5 Slapshot / Sarnia 29
83/4 Souhaits Keychain [North Stars]
96/7 SP 147
97/8 SP Authentic 148, I27
81/2 Topps 105 [West]
84/5 Topps 73
92/3 Topps 318
95/6 Topps 77
98/9 Topps 119
98/9 To. Finest 5
96/7 Topps Picks FC4
91/2 To. Stadium 118
92/3 To. Stadium 399
93/4 To. Stadium 294
94/5 To. Stadium 191
95/6 To. Stadium 150, PS7
98/9 UD Choice 93
01/2 Ultimate Mem. ✂ 500GS
90/1 Upper Deck 76
91/2 Upper Deck 276
92/3 Upper Deck 461
93/4 Upper Deck 136, SP-41
94/5 Upper Deck 5, SP-112
95/6 Upper Deck 431, SE-28
96/7 Upper Deck 154, 336, P22
97/8 Upper Deck 154, 199
00 ✂ UD APOH 500, ✍ 500
96/7 UD All-Star YCTG AR17
94/5 UD Be A Player R39, R129
95/6 UD Be A Player 49, ✍ S49
96/7 UD Black Diam. 148
97/8 UD Black Diam. 21
95/6 UD CC 88
96/7 UD CC 88
97/8 UD Coll. Choice 237, SQ22, S22, C2, CR22
02/3 UD Foundations 22, 47, 98, ✂ 1000Jers, ✂ 1000Stick, ✂ CH, ✂ CG, ✂ PP, ✂ PS, ✍ SG
96/7 UD Ice 66
97/8 UD Ice 22
00/1 UD Legends 62
89/0 WASH
89/0 WASH / Kodak
90/1 WASH / Kodak
90/1 WASH / Smokey
91/2 WASH / Kodak
91/2 WASH / Smokey
97/8 Zenith 47
CICCARELLI, DINO
02/3 Fleer Throwbacks 80
CICCARELLO, JOE
00/1 Kudos 44
93/4 Minnesota-Duluth
CICCONE, ENRICO
00/1 BAP Mem. ✂ T-19
97/8 CARO / Sprint
99/0 Eishockey 359
93/4 Leaf 375
92/3 OPC Premier 122
98/9 Pacific 397
97/8 Pa. Invincible R-43
93/4 Parkhurst 219
96/7 Pi. Be A Player 129, ✍ Aut. 129
95/6 POG 254
90/1 ProCards 120
94/5 TAMP / Sky Box
95/6 TAMP / Sky Box
91/2 Upper Deck 51
92/3 Upper Deck 90
93/4 Upper Deck 528
94/5 Upper Deck 460
95/6 Upper Deck 382
96/7 Upper Deck 238
94/5 UD Be A Player R16, ✍ 132
95/6 UD CC 152
CICCONE, ENRICO
02/3 Fleer Throwbacks 69, ✂ 2SC, ✂ 2SCTD, ✂ 8SW
CICHOCKI, CHRIS
92/3 Binghampton Rangers
93/4 Cincinnati Cyclones
94/5 Cincinnati Cyclones
95/6 Cincinnati Cyclones
96/7 Cincinnati Cyclones
97/8 Cincinnati Cyclones
98/9 Cincinnati Cyclones
99/0 Cincinnati Cyclones
85/6 DETR / Little Caesars
86/7 OPC/Topps 41
86/7 OPC Sticker 124-184
88/9 ProCards / Utica
90/1 ProCards 14
91/2 ProCards 206
CIERNIK, IVAN
01/2 Atomic 116
01/2 BAP Memor. 232
99/0 Grand Rapids Griffins
00/1 Grand Rapids Griffins
01/2 O-Pee-Chee 357
01/2 OTTA
01/2 Parkhurst 253, 400
01/2 Signature 241, ✍ Aut. 241
01/2 SP Authentic 165
01/2 SP GU 90
01/2 SPx 119
01/2 SPx Rookie RR21
01/2 Stadium 133
01/2 Topps 357
01/2 To. Chrome 175
01/2 Upper Deck 437
01/2 UD Challenge 125
01/2 UD Honor Roll 83
01/2 UD Ice 63
01/2 UD Premier 86
01/2 UD Vintage 290
CIERNY, JOZEF
94/5 Cape Breton Oilers
92/3 Classic 35
93/4 Classic 127
92/3 Classic Four Sport 182
93/4 Cla. 4 Sport 231
93/4 Cla. Prospects 86
98/9 DEL 255
93/4 EDMO / Sheet
99/0 Eishockey 39
92/3 Rochester Americans DD
92/3 Rochester Americans WPC
94/5 Score 217
CIERNY, LADISLAV
00/1 OFS 13
01/2 OFS 124
CIESLA, HANK
52/3 Anonymous 32
45-64 BeeHive-2 [Chic.]
63/4 Parkhurst 51
93/4 Parkie 56-57 29
58/9 Topps 49
CIGER, ZDENO
91/2 Bowman 280
93/4 Donruss 113
94/5 Donruss 274
95/6 Donruss 360
96/7 Donruss 203
95/6 Do. Elite 24
92/3 EDMO
95/6 Fleer Metal 53
96/7 Fl. Picks 96
92/3 Fleer Ultra 113
93/4 Fleer Ultra 315
94/5 Fleer Ultra 71
95/6 Fleer Ultra 237
93/4 Leaf 197
94/5 Leaf 65
96/7 Leaf 76
96/7 Maggers 65
90/1 NJER
91/2 O-Pee-Chee 352
92/3 O-Pee-Chee 88
90/1 OPC Premier 15
00/1 OFS 415
92/3 Panini Sticker 175
93/4 Panini Sticker 239
94/5 Panini Sticker 200
96/7 Panini Sticker 259
92/3 Parkhurst 283
93/4 Parkhurst 336
94/5 Parkhurst 76
95/6 Parkhurst 79
01/2 Parkhurst 209
92/3 Pinnacle 302
94/5 Pinnacle 70
96/7 Pinnacle 148
96/7 Pi. Summit 19
93/4 Power Play 78
93/4 Premier 456
01/2 Pr. Stock -PS 47
90/1 Pro Set 619
90/1 Score 82T
91/2 Score CAN 405
92/3 Score 534
93/4 Score 388
94/5 Score 122
96/7 Score 20
94 Semic 198
92 Semic Sticker 144
95/6 SP 53
92/3 Topps 496
95/6 To. Finest 107
91/2 To. Stadium 379
92/3 To. Stadium 228
93/4 To. Stadium 73
94/5 To. Stadium 229
95/6 To. Stadium 127
90/1 Upper Deck 429
91/2 Upper Deck 385
92/3 Upper Deck 245
93/4 Upper Deck 330
94/5 Upper Deck 28
01/2 Upper Deck 349
95/6 UD Be A Player 137, ✍ S137
96/7 UD CC 95
96 Wien 229
CIHAL, MIROSLAV
95/6 APS 230
96/7 APS 57
97/8 APS 318
98/9 OFS 182
CIHLAR, JIRI
94/5 APS 177
95/6 APS 189
97/8 APS 303
97/8 DS 38
98/9 DS 40
97/8 DS Sticker 117
98/9 OFS 57
99/0 Score 43
CIKL, IGOR
95/6 APS 113, 344
CILLADI, JOHN
00/1 Hull Olympiques 6
CIMELLARO, TONY
96/7 DEL 109
90/1 7th..Sketch OHL 54
91/2 7th...Sketch OHL 109
CIMETTA, ROBERT
89/0 BOST / Sports Action
91/2 Bowman 160
94/5 DEL 280
95/6 DEL 276
96/7 DEL 181
98/9 DEL 113
99/0 Eishockey 275
93/4 Indianapolis Ice
90/1 OPC/Topps 288
91/2 O-Pee-Chee 256
91/2 OPC Premier 160
92/3 St. John's Maple Leafs
92/3 Topps 181
91/2 To. Stadium 9
92/3 To. Stadium 93
91/2 TORO / P.L.A.Y. 25
CIMON, MARCO
99/0 Rouyn-Noranda
CINIBULK, MARTIN
96/7 APS 122
97/8 APS 4
98/9 DS 22
97/8 DS Sticker 208
98/9 OFS 162
CIPOLLA, JASON
01/2 Manitoba Moose
97/8 Milwaukee Admirals
98/9 Milwaukee Admirals
00/1 Rochester Americans
96/7 St. John's Maple Leafs
CIPRIANO, MARK
90/1 7th..Sketch WHL 242
89/0 Victoria Cougars
CIPRICK, TRENT
84/5 Brandon Wheat Kings
85/6 Brandon Wheat Kings
CIPRUSS, AIGARS
98/9 Cardset 183
99/0 Cardset 90
00/1 Cardset 167
02/3 Cardset 161
97/8 Hockey-Box
CIRCELLI, ANTHONY
96/7 DEL 223
95 Globe 229
95 Panini Worlds 82
95 Semic 173
92 Semic Sticker 248
93 Semic Sticker 215
CIRCELLI, COLLIN
01/2 Moncton Wildcats 17
CIRELLA, JOE
83 Canada Juniors
81/2 COLR
96/7 DEL 346
93/4 EA Sports 49
93/4 FLOR
97/8 FLOR / Winn-Dixie
93/4 Leaf 269
95/6 Milwaukee Admirals
83/4 NJER
84/5 NJER
86/7 NJER / S.O.B.E.R.
88/9 NJER / Caretta
82/3 O-Pee-Chee 137
84/5 O-Pee-Chee 110
85/6 OPC/Topps 98
86/7 OPC/Topps 163
87/8 OPC/Topps 170
88/9 OPC/Topps 188
90/1 OPC/Topps 107
91/2 O-Pee-Chee 502
89/0 OPC/Topps 130
84/5 OPC Sticker 74
86/7 OPC Sticker 198-67
87/8 OPC Sticker 61-203
88/9 OPC Sticker 79-208
89/0 opcSticker 77
80/1 Oshawa Generals
82/3 Oshawa Generals
95/6 OTTA
87/8 Panini Sticker 75
88/9 Panini Sticker 268
90/1 Panini Sticker 141
90/1 Panini/QUE 1
91/2 Parkhurst 340
93/4 Parkhurst 347
93/4 Pinnacle 346
93/4 Pinnacle Expa. 3
94/5 Pinnacle 308
82/3 Post [Colo.]
93/4 Power Play 91
93/4 Premier 41
93/4 Premier 414
90/1 Pro Set 243
89/0 QUÉB
89/0 QUÉB / Gene. Foods
89/0 QUÉB / Police
90/1 QUÉB
90/1 QUÉB / Petro-Canada
91/2 Score CAN 441
92/3 Score 369
93/4 Score 515
84/5 Topps 85
92/3 Topps 163
92/3 To. Stadium 479
93/4 To. Stadium 2
90/1 Upper Deck 293
93/4 Upper Deck 65
CIRILLO, MIKE
01/2 Florida Everblades
01/2 Hershey Bears
CIRILLO, RYAN
95/6 Slapshot 191
CIRJAK, JOHN
97 Bowman 95
97/8 Regina Pats
95/6 Spokane Chiefs 16
CIRONE, FRANK
94/5 Raleigh Icecaps
CIRONE, JASON
93/4 Cincinnati Cyclones
94/5 Cincinnati Cyclones
96/7 Kansas City Blades
98/9 Kansas City Blades 24
99/0 Kansas City Blades
91/2 Moncton Hawks
91/2 ProCards 183
90/1 7th..Sketch OHL 30, 178
91/2 Upper Deck 605
00/1 UD DEL 81
CISAR, MARIAN
01/2 BAP Memor. 274
98 Bowman 58
98 Bowman Chrome 58
98/9 Milwaukee Admirals
99/0 Milwaukee Admirals
00/1 Milwaukee Admirals
01/2 Milwaukee Admirals
01/2 Pacific 215
01/2 Parkhurst 158
97/8 Pi. BeeHive 67, ✍ Aut. 67
00/1 PS Titanium 131
00/1 PS Titanium Draft 131
97/8 Spokane Chiefs
98/9 Upper Deck 303
98/9 UD G. Reserve 303
CISAR, MARIÁN
92 Québec Pee Wee 1719
CITY, MALLARDS
97/8 Quad City Mallards
00/1 Quad City Mallards
CIZEK, MARTIN
02/3 Plymouth Whalers
CLACKSON, KIM
81/2 O-Pee-Chee 271
80/1 Pepsi Bottle Cap
80/1 QUÉB
78/9 Winnipeg Jets
CLACKSON, KIM
02/3 Fleer Throwbacks 39
CLAESSON, STEFAN
89/0 Semic Elitserien 9
90/1 Semic Elitserien 82
91/2 Semic Elitserien 234
CLAGUE, JASON
93/4 Red Deer Rebels
CLAIR, FRASER
00/1 Mississauga IceDogs
CLANCY, CHRIS
91/2 Cornwall Royals
90/1 7th..Sketch OHL 31
91/2 7th...Sketch OHL 16
CLANCY, FRANCIS (KING)
35/6 Amalgamated Press
25-27 Anonymous 17
25-27 Anonymous 18 [No Border]
33/4 Anonymous 8
01/2 BAP Update ✂ PTT6
34-43 BeeHive-1 [Toro.]
35-40 Canada Starch
33/4 Canadian Gum
24/5 Champ's Cigarettes
33/4 Hamilton Gum 17
83 HHOF Postcard C3
83&87 HHOF 33
02/3 In The Game-Used ✂ VM20
29/0 La Presse
92/3 Legends 8
32/3 Maple Leafs O'Keefe
33/4 O-Pee-Chee 31
36/7 O-Pee-Chee 125
55/6 Parkhurst 33
59/0 Parkhurst 50
63/4 Parkhurst 20
93/4 Parkie 56-57 P-4
94/5 Parkie Tall 132
02/3 Parkie - Reprint 206, 245, ✂ VT18
02/3 Parkhurst Retro ✂ NN14
34/5 Sweet Caporal
60/1 Topps 47
61/2 Topps - Stamp
69/0 TORO
78/9 TORO
80/1 TORO
01/2 Ultimate Mem. ✂ Gloves
02/3 Ultimate Memorabilia ✂ Cor, ✂ GAO, ✍ Cut
01/2 Upper Deck ✍ Cut
01/2 UD Legends 64
23/4 William Paterson 3
24/5 William Paterson 3
33/4 WWGum Premium 1
33/4 WWGum 13
37/8 World Wide Gum 29
61/2 York 39
CLANCY, GREG
97/8 Grand Rapids Griffins
89/0 7th..Sketch OHL 59
90/1 7th..Sketch OHL 81
CLANCY, TERRY
69/0 TORO
72/3 TORO
CLANTARA, ROLAND
51/2 Lac St-Jean 52
CLAPPER, DIT
33/4 Anonymous 36
34-43 BeeHive-1 [Bost.]
91/2 BOST / SA Legends
33/4 Canadian Gum
33-35 Diamond Match Silv.
83 HHOF Postcard F3
83&87 HHOF 79
33/4 O-Pee-Chee 8
39/0 O-Pee-Chee 95
94/5 Parkie Tall 8
60/1 Topps 26
61/2 Topps - Stamp
99/0 UD C. Legends 44
33/4 WWGum 1
37/8 World Wide Gum 38
CLAPTON, MARTY
97/8 Hampton Roads
98/9 Hampton Roads
99/0 Hampton Roads
CLARINGBULL, MIKE
84/5 Medicine Hat Tigers
CLARK, ANDREW
96/7 DEL 307
95/6 Guelph Storm
93/4 Slapshot / S.S.Marie 18
94/5 Slapshot / Guelph 10
95/6 Slapshot 90
CLARK, BRETT
98/9 Be A Player 220, ✍ Aut. 220
97/8 MONT
01/2 O-Pee-Chee 247
01/2 Topps 247
98/9 UD MVP 105
CLARK, CHRIS
99/0 BAP Mem. 391
01/2 BAP Memor. 225
02/3 First Edition 162
00/1 Pacific 77
02/3 Pacific 51
02/3 Pacific Complete 285
02/3 T. Total 368
CLARK, DARREN
99/0 Peoria Rivermen
00/1 Peoria Rivermen
01/2 Peoria Rivermen
02/3 Peoria Rivermen
CLARK, DEAN
98/9 Calgary Hitmen 24
99/0 Calgary Hitmen
00/1 Calgary Hitmen
88/9 EDMO / Action 100
84/5 Kamloops Blazers
CLARK, DON
91/2 7th...Sketch WHL 149
92/3 Tacoma Rockets
CLARK, DONN*
81/2 Saskatoon Blades

CLARK, ERIC
98/9 Calgary Hitmen 22
99/0 Calgary Hitmen

CLARK, GARY
95/6 DEL 359
96/7 DEL 182

CLARK, GEORGE
23/4 Selkirks Crescent 5

CLARK, GORD
86/7 London Knights

CLARK, JASON
98/9 DEL 3

CLARK, JOE
98/9 Odessa Jackalopes

CLARK, KERRY
94/5 Classic E7
95/6 Edge Ice 171
97/8 Milwaukee Admirals
93/4 Portland Pirates
94/5 Portland Pirates
88/9 ProCards / Springfield
89/0 ProCards AHL 248
90/1 ProCards 620
91/2 ProCards 584
92/3 Salt Lake G'Eagles
86/7 Saskatoon Blades

CLARK, NOBERT
51/2 Lac St-Jean 20

CLARK, RON
89/0 Rayside-Balfour

CLARK, WENDEL
98/9 Be A Player 280, ✍ Aut. 280
99/0 BAP Mem. 268
01/2 BAP Update ✂ TC34
90/1 Bowman 159
91/2 Bowman 156
92/3 Bowman 325
95/6 Bowman 45
98/9 Bowman's Best 19
93/4 Donruss 337
95/6 Donruss 193, 389
96/7 Donruss 98, D-6, HL-2
97/8 Donruss 57
96/7 Do. Canadian 29
97/8 Do. Canadian 80
95/6 Do. Elite 27
96/7 Do. Elite 98
97/8 Do. Priority 150
98/9 Dynagon Ice 171
99/0 Dynagon Ice 47
94/5 Flair 142
96/7 Flair 89
94/5 Fleer 173, SA-1
01/2 Fleer Greats 34, ✍ Aut.
95/6 Fleer Metal 89
96/7 Fl. Picks 130
92/3 Fleer Ultra 208
93/4 Fleer Ultra 146
94/5 Fleer Ultra 172, 354
95/6 Fleer Ultra 129, 265
96/7 Fl. Ultra 162
88/9 Frito Lay
91/2 Gillette 11
95/6 Hoyle / East. 8-Heart
92/3 Humpty Dumpty
91/2 Kellogg's / Score 3
89/0 Kraft 34
91/2 Kraft 42
93/4 Kraft / PB
94/5 Kraft / HH
95/6 Kraft / IP
86/7 Kraft Sports 52
93/4 Leaf 166
94/5 Leaf 542
95/6 Leaf 207
96/7 Leaf 166
94/5 L. Limited 31
95/6 L. Limited 70
96/7 L. Limited 12, S-20
96/7 L. Preferred 87, LS-48
97/8 Limited 40
96/7 Maggers 153
94/5 McDonald's McD-24
96/7 Metal Univ. 148
98/9 NHL Power Play
86/7 OPC/Topps 149
87/8 OPC/Topps 12
90/1 OPC/Topps 79
91/2 O-Pee-Chee 464
92/3 O-Pee-Chee 96
98/9 OPC Chrome 142
91/2 OPC Premier 116
91/2 OPC Premier 177
86/7 OPC Sticker 141
x86/7 OPC Sticker 125-185
87/8 OPC Sticker 152
88/9 OPC Sticker 172-41
97/8 Omega 218
98/9 Omega 217
98/9 Pacific 411
99/0 Pacific 136
00/1 Pacific 386
97/8 Pacific CC 17, SS-10A
97/8 Pa. Crown Roy. 129
98/9 Pa. Crown Roy. 123
97/8 Pa. Dynagon 121, T-27
97/8 Pa. Invincible 136
97/8 Pa. Paramount 179
97/8 Pa. Revolution 133
98/9 Pa. Revolution 131
87/8 Panini Sticker 320
x87/8 Panini Sticker 330
88/9 Panini Sticker 121
89/0 Panini Sticker 144
90/1 Panini Sticker 286
90/1 Panini/TOR 3
91/2 Panini Sticker 102
92/3 Panini Sticker 79
93/4 Panini Sticker 227
94/5 Panini Sticker 195
95/6 Panini Sticker 247
96/7 Panini Sticker 213
97/8 Panini Sticker 174
99/0 Panini Sticker 205
91/2 Parkhurst 170
92/3 Parkhurst 179
92/3 Parkhurst CP11
93/4 Parkhurst 475
93/4 Parkhurst F9
95/6 Parkhurst 399
94/5 Parkie SE146
91/2 Pinnacle 250
92/3 Pinnacle 276
93/4 Pinnacle 157
93/4 Pinnacle CA23
94/5 Pinnacle 385, GR13, NL5
95/6 Pinnacle FS 8
95/6 Pinnacle 196
97/8 Pinnacle 185
97/8 Pi. Certified 71
95/6 Pi. FANtasy 21
97/8 Pi. Inside 89
95/6 Pi. Summit 131, MH-8
96/7 Pi. Summit 140
97/8 Pi. Totally 71
95/6 Pi. Zenith 94, GG-3
96/7 Pi. Zenith 24
95/6 Playoff 279
96/7 Playoff 411
94/5 POG 194
95/6 POG 174
93/4 Power Play 241
93/4 Premier 359
93/4 Premier - Finest 9
94/5 Premier 55, 297, 345, TF-10
95/6 Pro Magnet 54
90/1 Pro Set 276
91/2 Pro Set 225
91/2 Pro Set 585
92/3 Pro Set 189
91/2 Pro Set Platinum 120
87/8 Pro Sport CW10
94/5 QUÉB / Burger King
83/4 Saskatoon Blades
84/5 Saskatoon Blades
90/1 Score 171
91/2 Score 116
91/2 Score CAN 116
92/3 Score 110
93/4 Score 137
94/5 Score 3, CI3
95/6 Score 57
96/7 Score 42, CI-7
97/8 Score 128
97/8 Score Toro. 5
92/3 Seasons 70
94/5 Select 20
95/6 Select CE 82
96/7 Select CE 65, / Promo 65
02/3 Signature Series ✂ FS2
95/6 SBx Impact 99
96/7 SBx Impact 125
94/5 SP 97
96/7 SP 150
97/8 SP Authentic 152
98/9 SP Authentic 79
99/0 SPx 32
95/6 Super Sticker 77
92/3 Topps 325
95/6 Topps 269, HGC2
98/9 Topps 142
94/5 Topps Finest 103
95/6 To. Finest 87
91/2 To. Stadium 124
92/3 To. Stadium 204
93/4 To. Stadium 192
95/6 To. Stadium 155, F8, PS8
94/5 TSC Members Only 18
95/6 T. Super Skills 45
85/6 TORO
86/7 TORO
x86/7 TORO
87/8 TORO / 5x8
87/8 TORO / P.L.A.Y. 6
88/9 TORO / P.L.A.Y. 2
91/2 TORO / P.L.A.Y. 14
92/3 TORO / Kodak
93/4 TORO / Abalene
93/4 TORO / Black's 1
98/9 UD Choice 202
90/1 Upper Deck 3
91/2 Upper Deck 386
92/3 Upper Deck 89
93/4 Upper Deck 340
94/5 Upper Deck 115, SP-154
95/6 Upper Deck 325, SE-139
96/7 Upper Deck 342, X15
97/8 Upper Deck 164
98/9 Upper Deck 188, 369
99/0 Upper Deck 205
01/2 Upper Deck ✂ PotL
94/5 UD Be A Player R72, R142
95/6 UD Be A Player 55, ✍ S55
93/4 UD BAP Roots 6
96/7 UD Black Diam. 107
98/9 UD Black Diam. 79
95/6 UD CC 103
96/7 UD CC 258
97/8 UD Coll. Choice 246
02/3 UD Foundations 80, 92, ✂ CH, ✂ CG, ✂ LI, ✂ PS
98/9 UD G. Reserve 188, 369
99/0 UD G. Reserve 205
98/9 UD MVP 190
99/0 UD MVP ✍ PS

CLARKE, BOBBY
01/2 ASG History
02/3 BAP Memorabilia / Cup
77/8 Coke
70/1 Dad's Cookies
79/0 Dernière Heure
82/3 Dernière Heure
70/1 Eddie Sargent 148
71/2 Eddie Sargent 152
72/3 Eddie Sargent 162
70/1 Esso Power Player
88/9 Esso All-Star
01/2 Fleer Greats 33, -RC 10
01/2 Fleer Legacy 39
83/4 Funmate Puffy 7 [w/]
91/2 Future Trends C72 57, ✍ 57
92/3 Future Trends C76 177
92/3 Future Trends C76 - Autograph
83&87 HHOF 258
75/6 Hockey Heroes
93/4 Hockey Wit 80
84/5 Kelowna Wings &...
91/2 Kraft 54
91/2 Kraft 67
92/3 Legends 16
74/5 Lipton Soup 21
74/5 Loblaws
73/4 Mac's Milk
99/0 Millenium P-15, ✍ P-15
70/1 O-Pee-Chee 195
71/2 O-Pee-Chee 114
71/2 O-Pee-Chee Book. 10
72/3 O-Pee-Chee 14
72/3 O-Pee-Chee TC
73/4 O-Pee-Chee 50
73/4 O-Pee-Chee 134
73/4 O-Pee-Chee 135
74/5 O-Pee-Chee 3
74/5 O-Pee-Chee 135
74/5 O-Pee-Chee 154
74/5 O-Pee-Chee 260
75/6 O-Pee-Chee 209
75/6 O-Pee-Chee 250
75/6 O-Pee-Chee 286
75/6 O-Pee-Chee 325
76/7 O-Pee-Chee 2
76/7 O-Pee-Chee 3
76/7 O-Pee-Chee 70
76/7 O-Pee-Chee 215
76/7 OPC 391
77/8 O-Pee-Chee 115
77/8 O-Pee-Chee NS 3
78/9 O-Pee-Chee 215
79/0 O-Pee-Chee 125
80/1 O-Pee-Chee 55
81/2 O-Pee-Chee 240
82/3 O-Pee-Chee 248
83/4 O-Pee-Chee 262
02/3 O-Pee-Chee 43
92/3 OPC - Anniv. 3
81/2 OPC Sticker 178
82/3 OPC/Topps Sticker 115
83/4 OPC/Topps Sticker 12
83/4 OPC/Topps Sticker 198
83/4 OPC/Topps Sticker 302
80/1 O-Pee-Chee Super 16
92/3 Parkhurst 468
01/2 Parkhurst ✍ PA42, ✂ HSHSJers
02/3 Parkhurst ✂ VT12
72/3 PHIL / Milk
83/4 PHIL / J.C. Penney
89/0 PHIL
01/2 PHIL
91/2 Pinnacle 386
81/2 Post 7
82/3 Post [Phil.]
00/1 Premier Plus ✍ CS
90/1 Pro Set 651, 657
83/4 Souhaits Keychain [Flyers]
77-79 Sportscaster 31-03
77-79 Sportscaster 60-12
77-79 Sports. FIN 38-891
77-79 Sports. FIN 69-1649
98/9 SLU -CL
71/2 Topps 114
72/3 Topps 90
73/4 Topps 2
73/4 Topps 3
73/4 Topps 50
74/5 Topps 3
74/5 Topps 135
74/5 Topps 154
74/5 Topps 260
75/6 Topps 209
75/6 Topps 250
75/6 Topps 286
75/6 Topps 325
76/7 Topps 2
76/7 Topps 3
76/7 Topps 70
76/7 Topps 215
76/7 Topps NS 1
77/8 Topps 115
77/8 ToppsNS 3
78/9 Topps 215
79/0 Topps 125
80/1 Topps 55
81/2 Topps 103 [East]
01/2 TO Archives 19, ✂ Stick, ✂ Jers, ✍ CAI
71/2 Toronto Sun Photo
00/1 UD Heroes 134, ✍ SG
01/2 Ultimate Mem. ✂ ASGH, ✂ RN, ✂ RT, ✂ RA, ✂ SCD
02/3 Ultimate Memorabilia ✂ Cor, ✂ EA, ✂ FS (x2), ✂ RAT, ✂ RT, ✂ VGJ
90/1 Upper Deck 509
00/1 Upper Deck ✂ DGJ
99/0 UD C. Legends 24, ✍ ES, ✂ JC1
02/3 UD Foundations ✍ SG
00/1 UD Legends 96, 101, ES9, ✍ ES
01/2 UD Legends 53, FC, ✂ M, ✂ PoH, ✍ ES
99/0 UD Retro 99, G2B, TC10, ✍ Ink.
01/2 UD SCup Champs 23
02/3 UD Top Shelf ✂ HH
01/2 UD Vintage ✂ SD

CLARKE, BOBBY
02/3 Fleer Throwbacks 3, 6SO, ✂ 6SO, ✂ 12SW, ✍ Aut.

CLARKE, BOBBY**
99/0 Hull Olympiques BN
99/0 Hull Olympiques 3
00/1 Hull Olympiques 3

CLARKE, CHRIS
95/6 DEL 363
91/2 ProCards 560

CLARKE, COSMO
96/7 Dayton Ice Bandits

CLARKE, DALE
92 Québec Pee Wee 416
01/2 Upper Deck 206
01/2 UD MVP 216
00/1 Worcester IceCats
01/2 Worcester IceCats

CLARKE, DOUG
88/9 Salt Lake G'Eagles

CLARKE, GEORGE
26 Dominion Chocolates 26

CLARKE, HERB
10/1 Imperial 11

CLARKE, JASON
99/0 Mobile Mysticks
02/3 Nottingham Panthers
94/5 Roanoke Express
95/6 Roanoke Express
91/2 7th...Sketch OHL 202

CLARKE, JIM
75/6 Phoenix Roadrunners
81/2 Regina Pats

CLARKE, JOE
93/4 Soo Greyhounds 8
92/3 Semic Nordisk 162

CLARKE, MIKE
00/1 London Knights

CLARKE, TAYLOR
96/7 Richmond Renegades

CLARKE, TODD
84/5 Kingston Canadians
85/6 Kingston Canadians
83/4 Ottawa 67's

CLARKE, WILL
96/7 Dayton Bombers

CLARKSON, DAVID
01/2 Belleville Bulls Update

CLASSEN, GREG
00/1 BAP Mem. 442
01/2 BAP Memor. 230
00/1 Milwaukee Admirals
00/1 Premier Plus 135
00/1 PS Titanium Draft 164
00/1 SP Authentic 149
00/1 SP GU 72
00/1 To. Heritage 94
00/1 UD Reserve 101
00/1 Upper Deck 427
00/1 UD Ice 114
00/1 UD Pros&Prosp. 110
00/1 UD Vintage 383

CLAUSS, KARL
91/2 Knoxville Cherokees

CLAYTON, MIKE
84/5 Moncton G'Flames

CLAYTON, TRAVIS
98/9 Wichita Thunder

CLEARWATER, RAY
72/3 Cleveland Crusaders
72/3 Clev. WHA / Linnett

CLEARY, DAN
01/2 Adrenaline 73
96/7 All-Sport PPF 178
96/7 Autograph Coll. 46, ✍ Aut.
99/0 BAP Mem. 120
00/1 BAP Mem. 388
01/2 BAP Memor. 153
97 Bowman 2, 121, BB7, ✍ Aut.
98/9 Bowman's Best 103
95/6 Classic 83, AS11
01/2 Crown Royale 59
97/8 Do. Elite 37, 123, BF-4, C-10, ✍ BF-4
97/8 Do. Preferred 152, 199, LT-6C
97/8 Do. Priority 166, 217
99/0 Hamilton Bulldogs
99/0 Hamilton Bulldogs/ Staz
97/8 Leaf 159, 200
97/8 Limited FotG 68
97/8 McDonald's McD-36
01/2 McDonald's -HP 8
01/2 Pacific 155
02/3 Pacific 140
02/3 Pacific Complete 155
97/8 Pa. Dynagon Rookie
97/8 Pa. Paramount 42
97/8 Pinnacle 10
97/8 Pi. Be A Player 224, ✍ Aut. 224
97/8 Pi. Certified E
98/9 Portland Pirates
97/8 Score 61
94/5 SR Auto-Phonex 15, P3, ✍ 15, ✍ P3
95/6 SR Tetrad Autobilia 41
00/1 Signature 103, ✍ Aut. 29
95/6 Slapshot 39
97/8 SP Authentic 177
99/0 SPx 67
98/9 SPx Finite 20, 128
98/9 To. Finest F17
98/9 T. Gold Label 38
00/1 To. Heritage 179
02/3 T. Total 214
98/9 UD Choice 44
95/6 Upper Deck 507
97/8 Upper Deck 247
98/9 Upper Deck 4
00/1 Upper Deck 72
01/2 Upper Deck 298
02/3 Upper Deck 316
97/8 UD Coll. Choice 307
98/9 UD G. Reserve 4
97/8 UD Ice 38
98/9 UD MVP 47
01/2 UD Vintage 146
02/3 UD Vintage 105
01/2 Victory 142
97/8 Visions Signings 42

CLEARY, JOE
92/3 Indianapolis Ice

CLEGHORN, ODIE
25-27 Anonymous 46 [No Border]
25-27 Anonymous 46 [No Border]
25-27 Anonymous 46
25-27 Anonymous 57
91 C55 Reprint 25
24/5 Champ's Cigarettes
25 Dominion Chocolates 117 [Error: Ogie]
10/1 Imperial
11/2 Imperial 25
12/3 Imperial 50
23/4 William Paterson 18
24/5 William Paterson 45

CLEGHORN, SPRAGUE
25-27 Anonymous 31
25-27 Anonymous 41 [No Border]
91 C55 Reprint 24
24/5 Champ's Cigarettes
83 HHOF Postcard E5
83&87 HHOF 66
10/1 Imperial
11/2 Imperial 24
12/3 Imperial 15
24/5 Maple Crispette [V130] 15
61/2 Topps - Stamp
23/4 William Paterson 11
24/5 William Paterson 49

CLEMENS, KEVIN
87/8 Regina Pats

CLEMENT, BILL
77/8 ATLF
78/9 ATLF / Colour
79/0 ATLF / B&W
79/0 ATLF / Colour
80/1 CALG
81/2 CALG
72/3 Eddie Sargent 168
74/5 Loblaws
74/5 O-Pee-Chee 357
75/6 O-Pee-Chee 189
76/7 O-Pee-Chee 82
77/8 O-Pee-Chee 292
78/9 O-Pee-Chee 364
79/0 O-Pee-Chee 295
80/1 O-Pee-Chee 376
81/2 O-Pee-Chee 39
82/3 O-Pee-Chee 44
92/3 Parkhurst 478
80/1 Pepsi Bottle Cap
75/6 Topps 189
76/7 Topps 82
01/2 To. Chrome -CA6, ✍ CA6
01/2 TO Archives 38

CLEMENT, PATRICK
91/2 7th...Sketch LHJMQ 85
91 7th..Sketch Mem.Cup 31

CLEMENT, SEAN
88/9 ProCards / Moncton

CLEMENTS, SCOTT
88/9 ProCards / Indianapolis

CLEMMENSEN, SCOTT
01/2 Adrenaline 214
01/2 Albany River Rats
02/3 Albany River Rats
01/2 Atomic 114
01/2 BAP Memor. 374
01/2 BT Pipes 79
02/3 Between the Pipes 88
02/3 Choice Prospects 7
02/3 First Edition 279
01/2 Heads Up 111
01/2 O-Pee-Chee 343
01/2 Parkhurst 281
01/2 Pr. Stock 129, -PS 83
01/2 PS Titanium Draft 146
01/2 Signature 216, ✍ Aut. 216
01/2 SP Authentic 159
01/2 SP GU 84
01/2 SPx 111
01/2 Stadium 134
01/2 Topps 343
01/2 To. Chrome 161
01/2 To. Heritage 157
01/2 To.Reserve 102
01/2 Upper Deck 433
01/2 Upper Deck 433
01/2 UD Challenge 119
01/2 UD Ice 79
01/2 UD Premier 69
01/2 UD Vintage 285

CLERMONT, DANIEL
99/0 Hull Olympiques BN
99/0 Hull Olympiques 11

CLIFFORD, BRIAN
93/4 Michigan State
97/8 Peoria Rivermen
96/7 Toledo Storm

CLIFFORD, CHRIS
83/4 Kingston Canadians
84/5 Kingston Canadians
85/6 Kingston Canadians
86/7 Kingston Canadians
88/9 ProCards / Saginaw
89/0 ProCards IHL 144
90/1 ProCards 372

CLIMIE, RON
72/3 O-Pee-Chee 318
74/5 OPC WHA 15
75/6 OPC WHA 52
73/4 OPC WHA Poster 12
72/3 Ottawa Nationals

CLINE, BRUCE
52/3 Laval Dairy Update 70
93/4 Parkie 56-57 106
52/3 St. Lawrence 23

CLOCH, IVANO
92 Semic Sticker 263

CLOUSTON, BOB
96/7 Dayton Ice Bandits

CLOUSTON, SHAUN
86/7 Portland Winter Hawks
88/9 Portland Winter Hawks
89/0 ProCards IHL 166
90/1 ProCards 333

CLOUTHIER, BRETT
01/2 Albany River Rats
02/3 Albany River Rats
99/0 Kingston Frontenacs
00/1 Kingston Frontenacs 6

CLOUTIER, COLIN
92/3 Brandon Wheat Kings
94/5 Sig. Rookies 4, ✍ 4
94/5 Slapshot Memorial 45

CLOUTIER, DAN
01/2 Adrenaline 189, PP 35
02/3 Atomic 96
00/1 Aurora 131
99/0 BAP Mem. 90
00/1 BAP Mem. 145
02/3 BAP Memorabilia 36
01/2 BAP Update ✂ TP16
01/2 BT Pipes 14, 108, ✂ FW, ✂ Jers., ✂ S&J, ✂ GG, ✂ HSHSJers
02/3 Between the Pipes 11, 149, ✂ BM17, ✂ DM3, ✂ GUE5, ✂ FW8, ✂ GUI5, ✂ GP8, ✂ GSJ5, ✂ GT3, ✂ HSHSJers 19, ✂ ITN5, ✂ T12, ✍ Aut.
96/7 Binghampton Rangers
01/2 Bowman 38
02/3 Bowman 44
98/9 Bowman's Best 116, F9
94/5 Classic 23
95/6 Classic 95
94/5 Classic 4 Sport 139
94/5 Cla. Images 49
94/5 Cla. Images 4 Sport 113
99/0 Crown Royale 127
01/2 Crown Royale 136
02/3 Crown Royale 95
95/6 Donruss C3TWC 2
99/0 Dynagon Ice 179
02/3 Exclusive 166
02/3 First Edition 84, 413H, ✂ Jers.
95/6 Guelph Storm
97/8 Hartford Wolf Pack
01/2 Heads Up 93, ✂ JQ 19
02/3 Heads Up 120, -S 20, ✂ GWQ 27
02/3 In The Game-Used ✂ GP8
01/2 McDonald's 40
99/0 Millenium 219, ✍ Aut. 219
98/9 NYRA
01/2 O-Pee-Chee 233
02/3 O-Pee-Chee 102
98/9 Omega 154
99/0 Omega 213
98/9 Pacific 291
99/0 Pacific 267
00/1 Pacific 369
01/2 Pacific 380
02/3 Pacific 375, ✂ GWJ 49
02/3 Pacific Complete 446
98/9 Pa. Paramount 150
99/0 Pa. Paramount 214
00/1 Pa. Paramount 219
97/8 Pa. Revolution 85
99/0 Panini Sticker 150
00/1 Parkhurst P-121
01/2 Parkhurst 164
02/3 Parkhurst 43, ✂ TT18
02/3 Parkhurst Retro 152
94/5 Parkie SE210
94/5 Pinnacle 522
99/0 Prism 129
00/1 Pr. Stock 90, PSNW-22
01/2 Pr. Stock 93
02/3 Pr. Stock Reserve 95
00/1 PS Titanium ✂ GUG 144
01/2 PS Titanium 135, ✂ DSJ 56
01/2 PS Titanium Draft ✂ 94
02/3 Private Stock Titanium 96, -MM 8, ✂ GWJ 69
02/3 Quest for the Cup 95
00/1 Revolution 132
93/4 Soo Greyhounds 27
94/5 SR Gold Standard 80
94/5 SR Tetrad CV, ✍ Aut.
00/1 Signature 51, ✍ Aut. 10
01/2 Signature ✂ GU94
02/3 Signature Series 58, ✍ 58, ✂ DW10
02/3 Slam Card
93/4 Slapshot / S.S.Marie 3
95/6 Slapshot 95, 357
94/5 SP 146
99/0 SP Authentic 79
02/3 Sports Vault 300
99/0 SPx 139
00/1 SPx 62
98/9 SPx Finite 125
99/0 Stadium 161
00/1 Stadium 27
02/3 Stadium 25
95/6 Topps 18CJ
00/1 Topps 35
01/2 Topps 233
02/3 Topps 102
00/1 To. Chrome 30
01/2 To. Chrome 75
02/3 T. Chrome 65
94/5 Topps Finest 145
02/3 To. Heritage 77, ✂ CP, ✂ CPB
02/3 T. Limited 102
02/3 T. Total 306
98/9 UD Choice 131
00/1 UD Heroes 106
98/9 UD3 25, 85, 145
00/1 Ultimate Mem. ✂ G-27
99/0 Ult. Victory 80
00/1 Upper Deck 498
98/9 Upper Deck 134
99/0 Upper Deck 120
00/1 Upper Deck 159
01/2 Upper Deck 399
02/3 Upper Deck 170
02/3 UD Artistic 86, R86, / Art
97/8 UD Black Diam. 78
99/0 UD Black Diam. 79
00/1 UD Black Diam. 54
98/9 UD G. Reserve 134
99/0 UD G. Reserve 120
01/2 UD Mask 129
02/3 UD Mask 85, 86, 103
00/1 UD MVP 159
01/2 UD MVP 180
99/0 UD MVP Cup 168
02/3 UD Piece 86
02/3 UD Rookie 97
00/1 UD Vintage 325, 332, 333, GG17
02/3 UD Vintage 250, 289
01/2 VANC / Coke
01/2 Vanguard 95, ✂ DGM 35
02/3 Vanguard 95, ✂ GWJ 46
99/0 Victory 273, 387
00/1 Victory 212
01/2 Victory 337, 346
02/3 Victory 208

CLOUTIER, DAVID
01/2 Cape Breton Eagles 4
00/1 Val d'Or Foreurs 6

CLOUTIER, DENIS
90/1 7th..Sketch LHJMQ 111

CLOUTIER, ÉRIC
95/6 Louisiana Ice Gators-2
97/8 Louisiana Ice Gators
98/9 Louisiana Ice Gators
99/0 Québec Remparts 20

CLOUTIER, FRANÇOIS
94/5 Slapshot Memorial 65

CLOUTIER, FRÉDÉRIC
02/3 BAP Memorabilia 373
01/2 Louisiana Ice Gators
02/3 Louisiana Ice Gators
02/3 Parkhurst Retro 240
00/1 Shawinigan 17
02/3 Ultimate Memorabilia 97
02/3 UD Rookie 129

CLOUTIER, JACQUES
90/1 Bowman 11
91/2 Bowman 146
92/3 Bowman 332
82/3 BUFF / Wendt's 9
86/7 BUFF / Blue Shield
87/8 BUFF / Blue Shield
88/9 BUFF / Won. Bread
88/9 BUFF / Blue Shield
88/9 BUFF / Won. Bread
89/0 CHIC / Coke
90/1 CHIC / Coke
92/3 Durivage 46
93/4 Durivage 18
90/1 OPC/Topps 378
91/2 O-Pee-Chee 286
92/3 O-Pee-Chee 113
87/8 Panini Sticker 21
90/1 Panini Sticker 197
91/2 Parkhurst 368
90/1 Pro Set 428
91/2 Pro Set Platinum 219
88/9 ProCards / Rochester
91/2 QUÉB / Petro-Canada
92/3 QUÉB / Petro-Canada
91/2 Score CAN 236
92/3 Score 378
83/4 Souhaits Keychain [Sabres]
92/3 Topps 66
91/2 To. Stadium 166
92/3 To. Stadium 118
90/1 Upper Deck 114
91/2 Upper Deck 374
92/3 Upper Deck 324

CLOUTIER, JEAN-FRANÇOIS
00/1 Shawinigan 18

CLOUTIER, KEVIN
01/2 Peoria Rivermen
99/0 Rouyn-Noranda

CLOUTIER, NICHOL
90/1 7th..Sketch LHJMQ 243

CLOUTIER, PATRICK
90/1 7th..Sketch LHJMQ 216

CLOUTIER, RÉAL
76/7 Dernière Heure
76/7 Dernière Heure
78/9 Dernière Heure
81/2 Dernière Heure
70s Dernière Heure
83/4 Funmate Puffy 10 [w/]
79/0 O-Pee-Chee 239
80/1 O-Pee-Chee 178
80/1 O-Pee-Chee 238
82/3 O-Pee-Chee 279
82/3 O-Pee-Chee 280
83/4 O-Pee-Chee 62
84/5 O-Pee-Chee 19
81/2 OPC Sticker 74
82/3 OPC/Topps Sticker 23
83/4 OPC/Topps Sticker 246
74/5 OPC WHA 63
75/6 OPC WHA 16
76/7 OPC WHA 1
76/7 OPC WHA 3
76/7 OPC WHA 76
77/8 OPC WHA 8
80/1 Pepsi Bottle Cap
81/2 Post 17
82/3 Post [Québ.]
76/7 Québec Nordiques
76/7 Québ. / Antoinette
80/1 QUÉB
81/2 QUÉB
82/3 QUÉB
83/4 QUÉB
83/4 Souhaits Keychain [Nordiques]
77-79 Sportscaster 78-04
77-79 Sports. FIN 90-2139
79/0 Topps 239
80/1 Topps 178
80/1 Topps 238
84/5 Topps 15

CLOUTIER, RÉJEAN
80/1 DETR
84/5 Nova Scotia Oilers
86/7 Sherb. Canadiens 11

CLOUTIER, SYLVAIN
95/6 Adirondack Red Wings
99/0 Albany River Rats
00/1 Albany River Rats
01/2 Albany River Rats
92/3 Classic 22
92/3 Classic Four Sport 171
98/9 Indianapolis Ice
91/2 7th...Sketch OHL 350
93/4 Slapshot / Guelph 9

CLOWE, RYAN
00/1 Rimouski Océanic 14
01/2 Rimouski Océanic 13

CLOWES, LUKE
93/4 Slapshot / Windsor 22
94/5 Slapshot / Windsor 24
92/3 Windsor Spitfires

CLUKEY, BARRY
93/4 Maine Black Bears

CLUNE, ART
52/3 Anonymous 152

CLUNE, WALTER
51/2 Laval Dairy 96
52/3 Laval Dairy Update 96
52/3 St. Lawrence 12

CLYMER, BEN
95/6 Do. Elite WJ 27
99/0 NHL Power Play
99/0 Omega 220
02/3 Pacific 347
02/3 Pacific Complete 268
99/0 Prism 130
01/2 Signature 197, ✍ Aut. 197
02/3 T. Total 321
99/0 UD G. Reserve 348

CMUNT, JIRI
99/0 Score 7

COALTER, BRANDON
95/6 Slapshot 237

COALTER, GARY
74/5 Loblaws
74/5 O-Pee-Chee 17
75/6 O-Pee-Chee 334
74/5 Topps 17

COATES, BRANDON
91/2 7th...Sketch WHL 35

COCCIOLO, VINCE
89/0 Portland Winter Hawks

COCHRANE, GLEN
87/8 CHIC / Coke
88/9 EDMO / Action 101
86/7 Kraft Sports 63
83/4 PHIL / J.C. Penney
82/3 Post [Phil.]
83/4 Souhaits Keychain [Flyers]
85/6 VANC
86/7 VANC

COCHRANE, GLEN
02/3 Fleer Throwbacks 41

COCKBURN, BILL
24/5 Falcons Crescent 1
31/2 La Presse

CODE, CHRIS
90/1 7th..Sketch OHL 206

CODE, TONY
93/4 W. Michigan Broncos

COFFEY, PAUL
01/2 ASG History
00/1 Aurora 11, ✂ GWJ-11
98/9 Be A Player 177, H-9, M14, ✍ Aut. 177, ✂ AS-11
99/0 BAP Mem. H-15, ✂ TM-17
00/1 BAP Mem. 221, 467, ✂ J-28, ✂ H-3
95/6 Bicycle Sports Aces A-Club
90/1 Bowman 211
91/2 Bowman 81
92/3 Bowman 181
92/3 Bowman 226
95/6 Bowman 41
91 Canada Cup
93/4 Donruss 99
94/5 Donruss 54, D-6
95/6 Donruss 119, D-7, E-5, I-2
96/7 Donruss 140, 238, D-3
97/8 Donruss 63, L2L-15
96/7 Do. Canadian 4, 149
97/8 Do. Canadian 64, NP-23, SCS-30
95/6 Do. Elite 85, CE-13
96/7 Do. Elite 72, P-5
97/8 Do. Elite 63
97/8 Do. Preferred 12
97/8 Do. Priority 110
97/8 Do. Studio 85
96/7 Duracell DC1,JB1
93/4 EA Sports 37
81/2 EDMO / Red Rooster
81/2 EDMO / West Mall
82/3 EDMO / Red Rooster
83/4 EDMO / Button
83/4 EDMO / McDonald's
83/4 EDMO / West Mall
83/4 EDMO
84/5 EDMO
84/5 EDMO / Red Rooster
85/6 EDMO / Red Rooster
86/7 EDMO
86/7 EDMO / Red Rooster
88/9 EDMO / Action 54
88/9 EDMO / Action 64
88/9 Esso All-Star
83/4 Esso Stars
94/5 Flair 47
96/7 Flair 66, HN-2
94/5 Fleer 58
96/7 Fleer 29, 140, NT-3
95/6 Fleer Metal 44
96/7 Fl. Picks 20, F50-8, JE-18
92/3 Fleer Ultra 80, -AS 1
93/4 Fleer Ultra 71
94/5 Fleer Ultra 59, ASG-9
95/6 Fleer Ultra 44
96/7 Fl. Ultra 122, PL-3, UP-3
88/9 Frito Lay
83/4 Funmate Puffy 3 [w/]
91/2 Gillette 37
95 Globe 76
93/4 Hockey Wit 46
95/6 Hoyle / West. 10-Heart
84/5 Kellogg's 1
89/0 Kraft 54
90/1 Kraft 8, 82
91/2 Kraft 74
92/3 Kraft / Kraft Singles
93/4 Kraft / KD
95/6 Kraft / KD, PB
86/7 Kraft Sports 12
89/0 Kraft Stickers 3
93/4 Leaf 67
93/4 Leaf GLAS 7
94/5 Leaf 168, FOI-8
95/6 Leaf 144, FOI-4, GLS-2, RTTC-5
96/7 Leaf 164, LL-4
97/8 Leaf 21
94/5 L. Limited 75
95/6 L. Limited 24
96/7 L. Limited 18, S-4
96/7 L. Preferred 101
97/8 Limited 6, 100, 108, FG-12
96/7 Maggers 62
91/2 McDonald's Mc-11
92/3 McDonald's McD-17
93/4 McDonald's McD-04
94/5 McDonald's McD-19
95/6 McDonald's McD-4
97/8 McDonald's McD-1
98/9 McD's T10
96/7 Metal Univ. 67, IC-4
99/0 Millenium J-32, ✂ ✍ J-32, ✂ JS-32
81/2 O-Pee-Chee 111
82/3 O-Pee-Chee 101
82/3 O-Pee-Chee 102
83/4 O-Pee-Chee 25
84/5 O-Pee-Chee 217
84/5 O-Pee-Chee 239
85/6 OPC/Topps 85
86/7 OPC/Topps 137
87/8 OPC/Topps 99
88/9 OPC/Topps 179
90/1 OPC/Topps 116, 202
91/2 O-Pee-Chee 183
91/2 O-Pee-Chee 504
92/3 O-Pee-Chee 5
92/3 O-Pee-Chee 187
92/3 O-Pee-Chee 318
92/3 OPC - Anniv. 14
89/0 OPC/Topps 95
90/1 OPC/Topps C
98/9 OPC Chrome 10
87/8 OPC Leaders 8
90/1 OPC Premier 16
91/2 OPC Premier 79
92/3 OPC Premier SP4
88/9 OPC Stars 6
82/3 OPC/Topps Sticker 104
82/3 OPC/Topps Sticker 105
82/3 OPC/Topps Sticker 160
83/4 OPC/Topps Sticker 94
83/4 OPC/Topps Sticker 95
84/5 OPC Sticker 134
84/5 OPC Sticker 251
84/5 OPC Sticker 252
85/6 OPC Sticker 124
85/6 OPC Sticker 217
85/6 OPC Sticker 191-67
85/6 OPC Sticker 56-204
86/7 OPC Sticker 68
86/7 OPC Sticker 112-126
86/7 OPC Sticker 188-47
87/8 OPC Sticker 89
88/9 OPC Sticker 233-101
89/0 opcSticker 237
97/8 Omega 161
98/9 Omega 39
98/9 Pacific 322
99/0 Pacific 68
00/1 Pacific 80
97/8 Pacific CC 77
97/8 Pa. Invincible 99, R-140
98/9 Pa. Paramount 45
97/8 Pa. Revolution 98
87/8 Panini Sticker 256
88/9 Panini Sticker 333
89/0 Panini Sticker 183, 311
90/1 Panini Sticker 135, 324
91/2 Panini Sticker 276
91/2 Panini Sticker 336
92/3 Panini Sticker 72
92/3 Panini Sticker 278
93/4 Panini Sticker 134
93/4 Panini Sticker 252
94/5 Panini Sticker 215
95/6 Panini Sticker 147, 184
96/7 Panini Sticker 179
00/1 Panini Sticker 26
95 Panini Worlds 10
91/2 Parkhurst 140
91/2 Parkhurst 212
91/2 Parkhurst 225
91/2 Parkhurst 297
92/3 Parkhurst 63
92/3 Parkhurst 276
92/3 Parkhurst 458
93/4 Parkie 56
93/4 Parkhurst D8
94/5 Parkhurst 63
95/6 Parkhurst 66, AS-5, CCB-8, PP-19, TW-4
00/1 Parkhurst P-102
94/5 Parkie SE seV15
80/1 Pepsi Bottle Cap
96/7 PHIL / Ocean Spray
91/2 Pinnacle 186
91/2 Pinnacle 377
92/3 Pinnacle 50
92/3 Pinnacle TP 3
93/4 Pinnacle 80
93/4 Pinnacle TP 8
94/5 Pinnacle 429, TP5
95/6 Pinnacle 14
96/7 Pinnacle 14, TP-7
97/8 Pinnacle 153
97/8 Pi. Be A Player 12, TN-11, ✍ Aut. 12
97/8 Pi. Certified 102
96/7 Pi. FANtasy 2
97/8 Pi. Inside 160
96/7 Pi. Mint 20
95/6 Pi. Summit 16, 198, GMC-9
96/7 Pi. Summit 3
97/8 Pi. Totally 102
95/6 Pi. Zenith 2
96/7 Pi. Zenith 48, CS-4
87/8 PITT / Kodak
89/0 PITT / Foodland 4
90/1 PITT / Foodland 2
91/2 PITT / Food. Stickers
95/6 Playoff 33, 143, 252
94/5 POG 93
95/6 POG 10, 102, I-013
82/3 Post [Edmo.]
93/4 Power Play 70
93/4 Premier 145
93/4 Prmr. - BG-Top. 6
94/5 Premier 15, 489
00/1 Pr. Stock ✂ GUG-5, ✂ GUG-6
95/6 Pro Magnet 101
90/1 Pro Set 231, 361
91/2 Pro Set 190
91/2 Pro Set 312
92/3 Pro Set 71
91/2 Pro Set Platinum 94
91/2 Pro Set Platinum PC12
87/8 Pro Sport CW14
91/2 Puck / Pro Set 21
90/1 Score 6, 319, 322
90/1 Sco. Hot Cards 65
91/2 Score 115
91/2 Score 372
91/2 Score CAN 115
91/2 Score CAN 262
92/3 Score 265
92/3 Score 441
93/4 Score 106
93/4 Score DT 8
93/4 Score PiAS 43
94/5 Score DT6
95/6 Score 24, GB-5
96/7 Score 142, S-6
97/8 Score 166
97/8 Score Phil. 11
91/2 Score Shows 9
93/4 Seasons 3
94/5 Select 72
95/6 Select CE 21
96/7 Select CE 89
94 Semic 337
94 Semic 86
95 Semic 82
89 Semic Sticker 59
91 Semic Sticker 58
92 Semic Sticker 81
93 Semic Sticker 197
84/5 7-Eleven
85/6 7-Eleven Superstars 6
96/7 SB 7-Eleven Phonecard
00/1 Signature 120, ✍ Aut. 202, ✂ DD-13, ✂ D-4, ✂ D-7, ✂ MO-10, ✂ N-6
95/6 SBx Emotion 52
95/6 SBx Impact 51
96/7 SBx Impact 33, F-6
83/4 Souhaits Keychain [Oilers]
94/5 SP 36
95/6 SP 45, E13, FX6
96/7 SP CW-13, GF-19
97/8 SP Authentic 113
96/7 SPx 15, Hh-4
00/1 Stadion 157
99/0 Stadium CA27
00/1 Stadium 219
96/7 SLU
97/8 SLU
95/6 Super Sticker 39, DC-5
96/7 Team Out!
84/5 Topps 50
84/5 Topps 163
85/6 OPC/Topps-Stick. 4
86/7 OPC/Topps - Stick. 5
92/3 Topps 5
92/3 Topps 182
95/6 Topps 4, 265, HGC-11, PF-12
98/9 Topps 10
00/1 Topps 133, PC-4
00/1 To. Chrome 100, PC-4
94/5 Topps Finest 68, RL-6
95/6 To. Finest 137
96/7 Topps Picks FT7
91/2 To. Stadium 212
92/3 To. Stadium 169
93/4 To. Stadium 450
93/4 To. Stadium - All-Stars
93/4 To. Stadium - Finest 4
95/6 To. Stadium 34, M11, PS4
91/2 TSC Charter
92 TSC Members Only
93/4 TSC Members Only 3
94/5 TSC Members Only 30
95/6 TSC Members Only 5
00/1 To. Stars 96
95/6 T. Super Skills 29
98/9 UD Choice 151
00/1 Ultimate Mem. ✂ D-4, ✂ D-7, ✂ MO-10
01/2 Ultimate Mem. ✂ ASGH, ✂ RT
90/1 Upper Deck 124, 498
91/2 Upper Deck 11
91/2 Upper Deck 177
91/2 Upper Deck 501
91/2 Upper Deck 615
92/3 Upper Deck 116
93/4 Upper Deck 315, GG6, SP-42
94/5 Upper Deck 24, C31, SP-22

95/6 Upper Deck 226, 248, 396, AS-1, F-17, H-3, H-31, R-12, SE-118
96/7 Upper Deck 268, X9, LS10, SS20A
97/8 Upper Deck 329
98/9 Upper Deck 66
00/1 Upper Deck 244
95/6 UD ASG MVP8
94/5 UD Be A Player R91, G2
96/7 UD Black Diam. 151
99/0 UD C. Legends 29
95/6 UD CC 18, 379, 390, C29
96/7 UD CC 85, 316, UD28
97/8 UD Coll. Choice 189
98/9 UD G. Reserve 66
99/0 UD Gretzky Excl. 63
00/1 UD Legends 52
92/3 UD Locker 23
95/6 UD Post 16
96/7 UD Post
00/1 UD Vintage 29
83/4 Vachon 22-102
83/4 Vachon 22-83
99/0 Victory 60
00/1 Victory 48
96 Wien 79

COFFIN, BRODIE
98/9 Huntington Blizzard

COGHILL, TRENT
90/1 Saskatoon Blades
90/1 7th..Sketch WHL 81

COHEN, PAUL
98/9 DEL 56
90/1 ProCards 505

COHEN, SANDY
00/1 Florida Everblades

COLAGIACOMO, ADAM
96/7 All-Sport PPF 74
96/7 Autograph Coll. 49, ✍ Aut.
99 Bowman 143
97 Bowman 145, BB12, ✍ Aut.
95/6 Classic 88
01/2 Cleveland Barons
99/0 Kentucky Tho'blades
00/1 Kentucky Tho'blades
92 Québec Pee Wee 497
93 Québec Pee Wee 1408
95/6 Slapshot 170, -P
96/7 Upper Deck 369
96/7 UD Black Diam. 24

COLAIACOVO, CARLO
02/3 BAP All-Star 137
02/3 BAP Memorabilia 289
02/3 Calder 147
02/3 Crown Royale 138
02/3 First Edition 438H
02/3 In The Game-Used 98
02/3 Pacific Complete 575
02/3 PTC/ Spring Expo 8
02/3 Parkhurst 242
02/3 Parkhurst Retro 228
02/3 Pr. Stock Reserve 183
02/3 Private Stock Titanium 138
02/3 Quest for the Cup 148
02/3 Signature Series 179, GS18, ✍ 179, ✂ SGJ67
02/3 SP Authentic 163
02/3 SP Game-Used Edition 94
02/3 SPx 189
02/3 T. Total 440
02/3 Ultimate Memorabilia 28, ✍ RAut
02/3 Upper Deck 454
02/3 UD Artistic 130, CG18
02/3 UD Classic 129
02/3 UD Honor 128
02/3 UD Mask 150
02/3 UD Premier 69
00/1 UD Prospects 4
02/3 UD Rookie 117
02/3 UD Top Shelf 102
02/3 Vanguard 135

COLAIACOVO, PAULO
01/2 Belleville Bulls

COLAIAICOVO, CARLO
01 UD Prospects GU 26

COLANGELO, ROBBIE
01/2 London Knights

COLASANTO, TOM
96/7 Dayton Ice Bandits

COLBORNE, BRETT
92/3 MPS SJHL 105

COLBOURNE, DARREN
93/4 Cla. Prospects 243
92/3 Dayton Bombers
93/4 Richmond Renegades

COLDWELL, DARYL
81/2 Victoria Cougars

COLE, BOB
97/8 Pi. CBC Sports 3

COLE, DANTON
91/2 Bowman 202
96/7 DEL 88
93/4 Donruss 491
94/5 Donruss 172
94/5 Fleer Ultra 204
96/7 Grand Rapids Griffins
97/8 Grand Rapids Griffins
98/9 Grand Rapids Griffins
99/0 Grand Rapids Griffins
00/1 Grand Rapids Griffins
02/3 Grand Rapids Griffins
94/5 Leaf 259
91/2 O-Pee-Chee 27
90/1 OPC Premier 17
90/1 Panini/WPG 5
91/2 Panini Sticker 72
92/3 Panini Sticker 56
94/5 Panini Sticker 184
92/3 Parkhurst 408
93/4 Parkhurst 464
94/5 Parkie SE169
94/5 Pinnacle 45
94/5 POG 222
93/4 Power Play 441
94/5 Premier 11
91/2 Pro Set 263
89/0 ProCards AHL 30
91/2 Score CAN 240
93/4 Score 655
94/5 Score 131
92/3 TAMP / Sheraton Inn
94/5 TAMP / Sky Box
91/2 To. Stadium 342
93/4 To. Stadium 239
90/1 Upper Deck 517
91/2 Upper Deck 210
94/5 Upper Deck 126
90/1 WINN / IGA
91/2 WINN / IGA

COLE, ERIK
01/2 Adrenaline 205, RR4
01/2 Atomic 106
02/3 Atomic 15, -SC 4
01/2 BAP Memor. 302
02/3 BAP Memorabilia 73
01/2 Bowman 156
02/3 Bowman 113
00/1 Cincinnati Cyclones
01/2 Crown Royale 150, RR3
02/3 Crown Royale ✂ GWDP 3
02/3 eTopps 17
02/3 Exclusive 27, -GE 4
02/3 First Edition 183
02/3 Heads Up 104
02/3 Heads Up 19, -PSP 1, ✂ GWQ 35
02/3 In The Game-Used 32, 132
01/2 O-Pee-Chee 348
02/3 O-Pee-Chee 60
02/3 Pacific 64, -SM 3
02/3 Pacific Complete 5
01/2 PTC Calder 3
01/2 PTC Draft 2
01/2 PTC High Voltage 3
01/2 Parkhurst 308
02/3 Parkhurst 52, -CR2, ✂ CRM2
02/3 Parkhurst Retro 179
01/2 Pr. Stock 117, -PS 78
02/3 Pr. Stock Reserve 16
01/2 PS Titanium 152, TSS 23, TRT 3, ✂ DSJ 46, ✂ DSJ 62
01/2 PS Titanium Draft 113, ✂ 18
01/2 Signature 229, ✍ Aut. 229
02/3 Signature Series 175, GS-37, ✍ 175
01/2 SP Authentic 139
02/3 SP Authentic ✍ SotT EC
01/2 SP GU 69
02/3 SP Game-Used ✍ Sig
02/3 Sports Vault 34
01/2 SPx 99
01/2 SPx Rookie RR6
01/2 Stadium 137
02/3 Stadium 99, ✍ LSS
01/2 Topps 348
02/3 Topps 60, OTG14
01/2 To. Chrome 166
02/3 T. Chrome 42, ✍ Graph
01/2 To. Heritage 154
02/3 To. Heritage 23, ✍ Aut.
02/3 T. Limited 60
01/2 To.Reserve 104
02/3 T. Total 383, ✍ Sig
01/2 UD PlayMakers Ltd 109
02/3 UD Superstars 257
01/2 Upper Deck 419
02/3 Upper Deck 33
01/2 UD Challenge 100
01/2 UD Ice 48
01/2 UD Mask 138
01/2 UD MVP 222
02/3 UD MVP 34
02/3 UD Piece 12
01/2 UD Premier 91
02/3 UD Premier ✍ Sig.
02/3 UD Rookie ✍ TD
01/2 UD Top Shelf 124
02/3 UD Vintage 50, 266, GB 50
01/2 Vanguard 106
01/2 Victory 442
02/3 Victory 40

COLE, JEFF
91/2 Air Canada SJHL 5
91/2 Air Canada SJHL C36

COLE, LEE
95/6 Slapshot 373
97/8 Toledo Storm 17

COLE, MIKE
92/3 BCJHL 217

COLE, PHIL
99/0 Lethbridge Hurricanes

COLEMAN, JON
93/4 Donruss USA4
99/0 Kentucky Tho'blades
93/4 Pinnacle 481
00/1 Providence Bruins
93/4 Upper Deck 563

COLEMAN, RUSSELL
02/3 Peterborough Phantoms

COLES, BRUCE
94/5 Hershey Bears
94/5 Johnstown Chiefs 5

COLES, JASON
90/1 7th..Sketch OHL 257
91/2 7th...Sketch OHL 209

COLLETT, ERNIE (E.J.)
25 Dominion Chocolates 15
23 Willards Chocolates 45

COLLEY, KEVIN
99 Bowman 124
98 Bowman 37
98 Bowman Chrome 37

COLLEY, TOM
89/0 New Haven Nighthawks

COLLIN, CURTIS
82/3 Kingston Canadians
83/4 North Bay Centennials

COLLIN, ERYC
96/7 Rimouski Océanic

COLLINS,
91/2 Avant Garde BCJHL 163

COLLINS, BILL
70/1 Eddie Sargent 104
71/2 Eddie Sargent 49
72/3 Eddie Sargent 71
70/1 Esso Power Player
74/5 Loblaws
69/0 MONT / Pro Star
70/1 MONT
69/0 O-Pee-Chee 126
71/2 O-Pee-Chee 139
72/3 O-Pee-Chee 265
73/4 O-Pee-Chee 163
74/5 O-Pee-Chee 364
77/8 O-Pee-Chee 369
68/9 Shirriff / Minn. 7
73/4 Topps 158
71/2 Toronto Sun Photo

COLLINS, GARY
52/3 Anonymous 121
57/8 Parkhurst [Toro.] 23

COLLINS, KEN S.
52/3 Anonymous 115

COLLINS, KEVIN
90/1 Pro Set 683

COLLINS, KIM
95/6 DEL 7

COLLINS, MAURICE
52/3 Anonymous 65

COLLINS, MIKE
99/0 San Angelo Outlaws

COLLINS, ROB
02/3 Grand Rapids Griffins

COLLINS, SEAN
97 Québec Pee Wee 0800

COLLINS, SHAWN
93/4 Portland Winter Hawks

COLLYARD, BOB
74/5 Loblaws
81/2 Milwaukee Admirals
79 Panini Sticker 216

COLLYMORE, SHAWN
99/0 Québec Remparts 23
00/1 Québec Remparts 20
01/2 Québec Remparts 20
02/3 Québec Remparts
01 UD Prospects GU 20, ✂ TPJ
02/3 Val d'Or Foreurs

COLMAN, MIKE
90/1 Kansas City Blades
92/3 Kansas City Blades
93/4 Kansas City Blades
90/1 ProCards 599
91/2 ProCards 510

COLOMBI, CARLO
91/2 7th...Sketch LHJMQ 4

COLUMBUS, JEFF
87/8 Soo Greyhounds 24

COLVILLE, MAC
34-43 BeeHive-1 [NYRa.]
39/0 O-Pee-Chee 90
37/8 World Wide Gum 89

COLVILLE, NEIL
34-43 BeeHive-1 [NYRa.]
83 HHOF Postcard A4
83&87 HHOF 5
36/7 O-Pee-Chee 105
39/0 O-Pee-Chee 39
02/3 Ultimate Memorabilia ✍ Cut
37/8 World Wide Gum 91

COLWILL, LES
58/9 Topps 19

COLWILL, RICHARD
00/1 Owen Sound Attack 9
01/2 Owen Sound Attack

COMBE, BERNARD
79 Panini Sticker 380

COMEAU, MARCEL
90/1 ProCards 440
78/9 Saginaw Gears
89/0 Saskatoon Blades
91/2 7th...Sketch WHL 148
92/3 Tacoma Rockets
93/4 Tacoma Rockets

COMEAU, REY
72/3 ATLF
74/5 ATLF
77/8 ATLF
74/5 Loblaws
72/3 O-Pee-Chee 239
73/4 O-Pee-Chee 29
74/5 O-Pee-Chee 296
75/6 O-Pee-Chee 248
76/7 O-Pee-Chee 343
77/8 O-Pee-Chee 346
78/9 O-Pee-Chee 293
79/0 O-Pee-Chee 385
73/4 Topps 29
75/6 Topps 248

COMFORT, FRED
23/4 Paulins Candy 8
24/5 Selkirks Crescent 9

COMLEY, RICK
93/4 N. Michigan Wildcats

COMMODORE, MIKE
00/1 Albany River Rats
01/2 Albany River Rats
01/2 BAP Memor. 240
01/2 O-Pee-Chee 300
00/1 PS Titanium Draft 165
01/2 SP Authentic 151
00/1 SPx 181
01/2 Topps 300

COMPLOI, GEORG
95 Panini Worlds 79
94 Semic 296
92 Semic Sticker 252
93 Semic Sticker 216

COMRIE, MIKE
01/2 Adrenaline 74, PM
01/2 Atomic 41, AB, PP, TN
02/3 Atomic 42, -CF 13
02/3 BAP All-Star 105
00/1 BAP Mem. 505
01/2 BAP Memor. 38
02/3 BAP Memorabilia 99, 212, ✂ FP12, ✂ FG7
01/2 Bowman 153, ✂ FFJ, ✂ FFS, ✂ FFDS, ✂ FFR, ✍ YSA
02/3 Bowman 135
02/3 Calder 40
01/2 Crown Royale 60
02/3 Crown Royale 39, ✂ GWJ 6
00/1 Crown Royale G-2
01/2 eTopps 19
02/3 eTopps 38
02/3 Exclusive 70, -GE 7
02/3 First Edition 187, 352
01/2 Heads Up 40, BTI 10, PP 1
02/3 Heads Up 49, ✂ GWQ 5, / Bobble
02/3 In The Game-Used 31, 131, ✂ F12, ✂ GUJ46, ✂ SJ46
01/2 McDonald's - FL 1, -HP 4
02/3 McDonald's 15, -CA 4, ✂ JP 6
01/2 O-Pee-Chee 293
02/3 O-Pee-Chee 22
01/2 Pacific 156
02/3 Pacific 141, -MA 8
02/3 Pacific Complete 302
01/2 Parkhurst 100
02/3 Parkhurst 56, ✂ FP12
02/3 Parkhurst Retro 67, ✂ RF12
01/2 Pr. Stock 39, Res. 6, -PS 30
02/3 Pr. Stock Reserve ✂ 122
00/1 PS Titanium 118
01/2 PS Titanium 56, SK 8
01/2 PS Titanium Draft 118
02/3 Private Stock Titanium 42, ✂ GWJ 28
00/1 PS Titanium Draft 118
02/3 Quest for the Cup 38
01/2 Signature 38, ✍ Aut. 38
02/3 Signature Series 3, ✍ 3, ✂ FS7, ✂ FJ12, ✂ SGJ46, ✂ TQ17
00/1 SP Authentic 106
02/3 SP Authentic 34, 112, ✍ SotT, ✍ SotTD
02/3 SP Authentic 37, 116, ✍ SotT, ✍ SotTD (x2), ✍ SotTT
01/2 SP GU 42
02/3 SP Game-Used Edition 20, ✍ Sig
02/3 Sports Vault 224
00/1 SPx 161
01/2 SPx 28, ✍ Sig
02/3 SPx 32, 91
01/2 Stadium 76,G25
02/3 Stadium 45, ✂ YSS3, ✂ YSD5
01/2 Topps 293
02/3 Topps 22, HHC13, ✍ SF
01/2 To. Chrome 145
02/3 T. Chrome 22
00/1 To. Heritage 80
01/2 To. Heritage 62
02/3 To. Heritage 62
02/3 T. Limited 22
01/2 To.Reserve 14
02/3 T. Total 315
01/2 UD PlayMakers Ltd 39
02/3 Ultimate Memorabilia ✂ Emb., ✂ ITN
01/2 Upper Deck 67
02/3 Upper Deck 69, -SS8, -SS8
02/3 UD Artistic 37, R37, ✍ / Art
00/1 UD Black Diam. 97
01/2 UD Challenge 32
02/3 UD Classic 39, ET8
02/3 UD Foundations 150
02/3 UD Honor 30, -SG15
00/1 UD Ice 88
01/2 UD Ice 19, ✍ CCA
01/2 UD Mask 36
02/3 UD Mask 36
01/2 UD MVP 76
02/3 UD MVP 72
02/3 UD Piece 38, ✍ MD
01/2 UD Premier ✍ Sig
02/3 UD Premier 25, ✂ Jers, ✂ Patch, ✍ Sig
00/1 UD Prospects 70, CC8, CS8, FL7, GD3
02/3 UD Rookie 41, 169, ✍ TD
01/2 UD Top Shelf 94
02/3 UD Top Shelf 35, ✍ Sig
01/2 UD Vintage 98, 105
02/3 UD Vintage 102, 272, T28
01/2 Vanguard 39, PP 6
02/3 Vanguard 42
01/2 Victory 370
02/3 Victory 81

COMRIE, PAUL
99/0 BAP Mem. 392
99/0 Dynagon Ice 80
99/0 Millenium 105, C-26, ✍ Aut. 105
99/0 NHL Power Play [x3]
99/0 Omega 89
99/0 SP Authentic 103
99/0 Stadium 184
99/0 To. Prmr. Plus 108
99/0 Ult. Victory 98
99/0 Upper Deck 226
99/0 UD Black Diam. 38
99/0 UD G. Reserve 226

CONACHER, BRIAN
64-67 BeeHive-3 [Toro.]
71/2 O-Pee-Chee 138
72/3 Ottawa Nationals
68/9 Shirriff / Detr. 14
67/8 Topps 17
68/9 TORO
69/0 TORO
71/2 Toronto Sun Photo
67/8 York
67/8 York

CONACHER, CHARLIE
35/6 Amalgamated Press
33/4 Anonymous 5
34-43 BeeHive-1 [Toro.]
33/4 Canadian Gum
34/5 CCM [Green]
33/4 Hamilton Gum 49
83 HHOF Postcard A5
83&87 HHOF 6
30/1 La Presse
92/3 Legends 14
32/3 Maple Leafs O'Keefe
33/4 O-Pee-Chee 34
36/7 O-Pee-Chee 123
37/8 O-Pee-Chee 138
39/0 O-Pee-Chee 59
55/6 Parkhurst 26
91/2 Pro Set 338
34/5 Sweet Caporal
02/3 Ultimate Memorabilia ✍ Cut
99/0 UD C. Legends 38
37/8 World Wide Gum 1

CONACHER, JIM
45-64 BeeHive-2 [Detr.]
45-64 BeeHive-2 [Chic.]
51/2 Parkhurst 105
52/3 Parkhurst 103

CONACHER, LIONEL
35/6 Amalgamated Press
33/4 Canadian Gum
33-35 Diamond Match Silv.
25 Dominion Chocolates 118
27/8 La Presse
36/7 O-Pee-Chee 102
94/5 Parkie Tall 12
34/5 Sweet Caporal
37/8 World Wide Gum 10

CONACHER, PAT
93/4 Donruss 153
83/4 EDMO / Button
83/4 EDMO / McDonald's
88/9 EDMO / Action 139
93/4 Fleer Ultra 342
93/4 Leaf 380
83/4 Moncton Alpines
88/9 NJER / Caretta
89/0 NJER
89/0 NJER / Caretta
90/1 NJER
84/5 Nova Scotia Oilers
92/3 OPC Premier 49
89/0 Panini Sticker 253
93/4 Parkhurst 363
94/5 Parkhurst 107
94/5 Pinnacle 403
95/6 Playoff 268
94/5 POG 122
95/6 POG 136
93/4 Power Play 358
93/4 Premier 252
90/1 Pro Set 477
91/2 Pro Set 427
89/0 ProCards AHL 219
91/2 Score CAN 654
92/3 Score 544
91/2 To. Stadium 387
93/4 To. Stadium 179
94/5 To. Stadium 237
94/5 UD Be A Player G4
95/6 UD Be A Player 92, ✍ S92

CONACHER, PETE
45-64 BeeHive-2 [Chic.]
45-64 BeeHive-2 [Toro.]
52/3 Parkhurst 33
53/4 Parkhurst 70
54/5 Parkhurst 86
57/8 Parkhurst [Toro.] 14
54/5 Topps 33

CONACHER, ROY
34-43 BeeHive-1 [Bost.]
45-64 BeeHive-2 [Chic.]
91/2 BOST / SA Legends
48-52 Exhibits [Blackhawks]
39/0 O-Pee-Chee 91
51/2 Parkhurst 50

CONCANNON, BRENDAN
96/7 Pensacola Ice Pilots
97/8 Pensacola Ice Pilots

CONKLIN, TY
01/2 Adrenaline 208
01/2 BAP Memor. 388
01/2 BT Pipes 82
02/3 Between the Pipes 45
01/2 Bowman 154
02/3 Choice Prospects 8
01/2 Crown Royale 159, RR 9
02/3 First Edition 284
01/2 Hamilton Bulldogs
02/3 Hamilton Bulldogs
01/2 O-Pee-Chee 359
02/3 O-Pee-Chee 312
01/2 Parkhurst 314
01/2 PS Titanium 158
01/2 PS Titanium Draft 129
01/2 SP Authentic 146
01/2 SP GU 76
01/2 SPx Rookie RR12
01/2 Topps 359
02/3 Topps 312
01/2 To. Chrome 177
02/3 T. Limited 312
01/2 UD PlayMakers Ltd 117
01/2 Upper Deck 423
01/2 UD Challenge 106
01/2 UD Ice 54
01/2 UD Premier 62
01/2 Vanguard 111

CONLAN, WAYNE
93/4 Maine Black Bears

CONN, HUGH (RED)
33-35 Diamond Match Silv.
36-39 Diamond Match TT1

CONN, JOE
45-64 BeeHive-2 [Chic.]

CONN, ROB
92/3 Indianapolis Ice
93/4 Indianapolis Ice
94/5 Indianapolis Ice
91/2 ProCards 494

CONNELL, ALEX
25-27 Anonymous 16
34-43 BeeHive-1 [Maroons]
33/4 Canadian Gum
24/5 Champ's Cigarettes
83 HHOF Postcard M4
83&87 HHOF 169
34/5 Sweet Caporal
61/2 Topps - Stamp
24/5 William Paterson 10

CONNELL, JERRY
98/9 Barrie Colts
00/1 Sudbury Wolves 16

CONNELLY, JACK
23/4 Selkirks Crescent 8

CONNELLY, JIM
52/3 Anonymous 51

CONNELLY, WAYNE
45-64 BeeHive-2 [Bost.]
45-64 BeeHive-2 [Bost.]
64-67 BeeHive-3 [Bost.]
70/1 Dad's Cookies
70/1 DETR / Marathon Oil
70/1 Eddie Sargent 54
71/2 Eddie Sargent 186
70/1 Esso Power Player
62/3 Cowan Tile
72/3 Minn. Fight. Saints
74/5 Minn. Fight. Saints
68/9 O-Pee-Chee 50
69/0 O-Pee-Chee 60
70/1 O-Pee-Chee 159
71/2 O-Pee-Chee 237
72/3 O-Pee-Chee 296
74/5 OPC WHA 54
76/7 OPC WHA 122
61/2 Parkhurst 44
95/6 Parkie 66-67 20
73/4 Quaker Oats 35
68/9 Shirriff / Minn. 1
62/3 Topps 18
66/7 Topps 40
68/9 Topps 50
69/0 Topps 60
71/2 Topps 127
71/2 Toronto Sun Photo

CONNER, CAM
78/9 MONT

CONNOLLY, BERT
36-39 Diamond Match TT1
36-39 Diamond Match TT2
36-39 Diamond Match TT3

CONNOLLY, JEFF
96/7 Charlotte Checkers

CONNOLLY, TIM
01/2 Adrenaline 20
01/2 Atomic 11
00/1 Aurora 87
99/0 BAP Mem. 229
00/1 BAP Mem. 15
01/2 BAP Memor. 61, 366
02/3 BAP Memorabilia 174, 253
99 Bowman 11, 144, SC1, ✍ BA31
01/2 Bowman 111, ✂ FFJ, ✂ FFS, ✂ FFDS, ✂ FFR, ✍ YSA
99/0 Crown Royale 84
00/1 Crown Royale 66
01/2 Crown Royale 16
99/0 Dynagon Ice 122
02/3 Exclusive 17
02/3 First Edition 210
99/0 HoloGrFX 37
00/1 McDonald's GCDC 5
99/0 Millenium 153, C-21, ✍ Aut. 153
99/0 NHL Power Play [x2]
01/2 O-Pee-Chee 141
02/3 O-Pee-Chee 53
99/0 Omega 146
00/1 Pacific 247
01/2 Pacific 243
02/3 Pacific 40
02/3 Pacific Complete 318
00/1 Pa. Paramount 152, FF-23
99/0 Panini Sticker 93
00/1 Panini Sticker 56
00/1 Parkhurst P-47
01/2 Parkhurst 44
02/3 Parkhurst 163, ✂ TT12
02/3 Parkhurst Retro 147
00/1 Premier Plus 5, PA10
99/0 Prism 85
00/1 Pr. Stock 61, EA-14, PS-35, PSNW-15, ✂ GUG-68
01/2 Pr. Stock 9
02/3 Pr. Stock Reserve 11
00/1 PS Titanium 57
01/2 PS Titanium 14
93 Québec Pee Wee 664
94 Québec Pee Wee 649
95 Québec Pee Wee 516
00/1 Revolution 90
00/1 Signature 142, ✍ Aut. 171
01/2 Signature 127, ✍ Aut. 127
02/3 Signature Series 75, ✍ 75
99/0 SP Authentic 52, ✍ SotT
00/1 SP Authentic 58
02/3 SP Authentic 11
00/1 SP GU 38
02/3 SP Game-Used ✂ CF, ✂ PC, ✂ FF, ✂ PH
02/3 Sports Vault 27
99/0 SPx 174
00/1 SPx 42
01/2 SPx ✂ DT
98/9 SPx Prospects 86
99/0 Stadium 199, Chrome 49
00/1 Stadium 83, CA15
02/3 Stadium ✂ YSS17
99/0 Topps 259
00/1 Topps 217, OTG129
01/2 Topps 141
02/3 Topps 53
99/0 To. Chrome 259
00/1 To. Chrome 139
99/0 To. Gold Label 88, FG15
99/0 To. Gold Label 15, NG15
00/1 To. Heritage 21
01/2 To. Heritage 173
02/3 T. Limited 53
99/0 To. Prmr. Plus 137
00/1 To. Stars 28
02/3 T. Total 288
00/1 UD Heroes 75
00/1 UD Reserve 53
99/0 Upper Deck 255, SS12
00/1 Upper Deck 109, P6, SS14, UD5, ✂ GJ, ✂ DGJ
01/2 Upper Deck 251
02/3 Upper Deck 18, ✂ BF
98/9 UD Black Diam. 117
99/0 UD Black Diam. 54, ✂ APOH
00/1 UD Black Diam. 36
02/3 UD Classic 12, ✂ HR
99/0 UD G. Reserve 255
02/3 UD Honor Roll ✂ GAJ
00/1 UD Ice 26, ✍ CCA, ✂ IGJ
01/2 UD Ice 88
00/1 UD Legends 87, 88
01/2 UD Mask 12, ✂ GJ, ✂ JP, ✂ DP
00/1 UD MVP 114
02/3 UD MVP 22
99/0 UD MVP Cup 111
99/0 UD Ovation 35, APOH
02/3 UD Piece 9
01/2 UD Premier 7
00/1 UD Pros&Prosp. 53
02/3 UD Top Shelf ✂ R
00/1 UD Vintage 223, 233, 234
02/3 UD Vintage 28, 264, GB 28
00/1 Vanguard 61
01/2 Vanguard 10
99/0 Victory 374
00/1 Victory 142, 144, 311
01/2 Victory 222
02/3 Victory 26
99/0 WGretzky 103

CONNOR, CAM
79/0 EDMO
88/9 EDMO / Action 134
79/0 O-Pee-Chee 138
80/1 O-Pee-Chee 387
75/6 OPC WHA 48
76/7 OPC WHA 89
75/6 Phoenix Roadrunners
79/0 Topps 138

CONNORS, BOBBY
23/4 Paulins Candy 12

CONNORS, SEAN
99/0 Calgary Hitmen

CONROY, ALLAN
95/6 Houston Aeros
82/3 Medicine Hat Tigers
83/4 Medicine Hat Tigers
84/5 Medicine Hat Tigers
93/4 PHIL / Sheet
93/4 PHIL / J.C. Penney
93/4 Premier 352
89/0 ProCards AHL 314
90/1 ProCards 473
91/2 ProCards 267
92/3 Topps Gold 525

CONROY, CRAIG
02/3 Atomic 12
98/9 Be A Player 277, ✍ Aut. 277
02/3 BAP Memorabilia 11
01/2 Bowman 92
02/3 Bowman 90
92/3 Clarkson G'Knights
94/5 Classic 51, AA1
94/5 Cla. Images 64, ✍ Aut.
01/2 Crown Royale 19, ✂ TT 2
95/6 Donruss 169
95/6 Edge Ice 41
02/3 Exclusive 21
02/3 First Edition 253
94/5 Fredericton Canadiens
95/6 Fredericton Canadiens
02/3 Heads Up 15
95/6 Leaf 85
02/3 O-Pee-Chee 186
98/9 OPC Chrome 47
98/9 Pacific 364
99/0 Pacific 353
01/2 Pacific 59
02/3 Pacific 52
02/3 Pacific Complete 310
97/8 Pa. Invincible R-168
98/9 Pa. Paramount 200
99/0 Pa. Paramount 194
99/0 Panini Sticker 289
02/3 Parkhurst 200
02/3 Parkhurst Retro 197
95/6 Pinnacle 218
97/8 Pi. Be A Player 59, ✍ Aut. 59
01/2 Pr. Stock ✂ GUG 14
02/3 Pr. Stock Reserve 13
01/2 PS Titanium 17
95/6 Score 297
02/3 Signature 81, ✍ 81
02/3 SP Authentic 13
02/3 Sports Vault 163
01/2 SPx 161
99/0 SLOU / Taco Bell 13
95/6 Topps 187
98/9 Topps 47
99/0 Topps 145
02/3 Topps 186
99/0 To. Chrome 145
02/3 T. Chrome 107
02/3 To. Heritage 52
02/3 T. Limited 186
02/3 T. Total 183
01/2 Upper Deck 30
02/3 Upper Deck 26
01/2 UD Challenge 11
02/3 UD Classic 15
02/3 UD Honor 75
01/2 UD Mask 14
01/2 UD MVP 24
02/3 UD MVP 25
02/3 UD Top Shelf 14
01/2 UD Vintage 41
02/3 UD Vintage 43
01/2 Vanguard ✂ DGM 6
01/2 Victory 54
02/3 Victory 29

CONSTANT, CHRIS
89/0 Brandon Wheat Kings
90/1 Brandon Wheat Kings
90/1 7th..Sketch WHL 229
91/2 7th...Sketch WHL 209

CONSTANTIN, CHARLES
76/7 Québec Nordiques
76/7 Québ. / Antoinette

CONSTANTINE, KEVIN
90/1 ProCards 121

CONTE, DAVID
78/9 SM-Liiga 74

CONTE, GIOVANNI
79 Panini Sticker 261

CONTI, LEONARDO
96/7 DEL 3
98/9 DEL 278
99/0 Eishockey 189
00/1 UD DEL 75
01/2 UD DEL 248

CONVERSE, TREVOR
96/7 Johnstown Chiefs
91/2 Richmond Renegades

CONVERY, BRANDON
92/3 CSC 10
94/5 Classic 82, T67
93/4 Cla. Prospects 59
93/4 Donruss CAN8
97/8 Donruss 85
96/7 Do. Canadian 144
95/6 Edge Ice 78
96/7 Fl. Picks 146
94/5 Leaf 483
x96/7 Leaf GLR-7
96/7 L. Preferred 132
97/8 Limited 167
97/8 Pa. Invincible R-192
93/4 Pinnacle 470
96/7 Pinnacle 241
97/8 Pi. Inside 152
96/7 Pi. Summit 174
96/7 Pi. Zenith 132
94/5 Premier 386
97/8 Score 164
97/8 Score Toro. 14
90/1 7th..Sketch OHL 381
91/2 7th...Sketch OHL 258
93/4 Slapshot / Niagara Falls 11
93/4 Slapshot / Niagara Falls 28
94/5 St. John's Maple Leafs
95/6 St. John's Maple Leafs
96/7 St. John's Maple Leafs
90/1 Sudbury Wolves
91/2 Sudbury Wolves
93/4 Upper Deck 548
94/5 Upper Deck 259
96/7 Upper Deck 186

CONWAY, KEVIN
83/4 Kingston Canadians
81/2 Soo Greyhounds
82/3 Soo Greyhounds
94 Semic 324

COOK, BEN
95/6 Birmingham Bulls

COOK, BILL
35/6 Amalgamated Press
33/4 Anonymous 31
34-43 BeeHive-1 [NYRa.]
33-35 Diamond Match Silv.
36-39 Diamond Match TT2
36-39 Diamond Match TT2
36-39 Diamond Match TT3
83 HHOF Postcard I5
83&87 HHOF 126
33/4 O-Pee-Chee 38
94/5 Parkie 56-57 P-8
23/4 Paulins Candy 35
34/5 Sweet Caporal
60/1 Topps 10
61/2 Topps - Stamp
02/3 Ultimate Memorabilia ✍ Cut
99/0 UD C. Legends 45
24/5 William Paterson 24
33/4 WWGum 30

COOK, BRAD
96/7 Dayton Ice Bandits
93/4 Slapshot / Detroit 13

COOK, BUN
02/3 Ultimate Memorabilia ✍ Cut

COOK, CAM
92/3 MPS SJHL 150

COOK, CHRIS
99/0 Brampton Batallion 21
99/0 Kingston Frontenacs
00/1 Kingston Frontenacs 7
01/2 Kingston Frontenacs 2

COOK, DEAN
86/7 Kamloops Blazers
87/8 Kamloops Blazers
88/9 Kamloops Blazers
89/0 ProCards IHL 187

COOK, DUNCAN
02/3 Peterborough Phantoms

COOK, FRED (BUN)
35/6 Amalgamated Press
33/4 Anonymous 46
34-43 BeeHive-1 [Bost.]
33/4 Canadian Gum
51/2 Cleveland Barons
33-35 Diamond Match Silv.
36-39 Diamond Match TT1
36-39 Diamond Match TT2
36-39 Diamond Match TT3
28/9 La Presse
33/4 O-Pee-Chee 72
94/5 Parkie Tall 10
34/5 Sweet Caporal
33/4 WWGum 66
37/8 World Wide Gum 68

COOK, JOE
93/4 Cla. Prospects 231
91/2 Oshawa Generals
91/2 Oshawa Generals
92/3 Oshawa Generals
91/2 7th...Sketch OHL 163

COOK, LLOYD
25-27 Anonymous 41
24/5 Maple Crispette [V130] 6
19 Vancouver Millionaires

COOK, MICHEL
91/2 Air Canada SJHL 32
91/2 Air Canada SJHL B42
92/3 MPS SJHL 156

COOK, PAUL
85/6 London Knights

COOK, TOM
34-43 BeeHive-1 [Maroons]
33-35 Diamond Match Silv.
36-39 Diamond Match TT1
36-39 Diamond Match TT2
36-39 Diamond Match TT3
36-39 Diamond Match BH TT
36-39 Diamond Match Chic.
36-39 Diamond Match BH BT
31/2 La Presse
37/8 O-Pee-Chee 180
37/8 World Wide Gum 43

COOK, TYLER
00/1 Toronto St. Mike's

COOKE, JAMIE
91/2 ProCards 282

COOKE, MATT
97 Bowman 22
98 Bowman 11
98 Bowman Chrome 11
98/9 Bowman's Best 134
98/9 Dynagon Ice 188
02/3 First Edition 165
98/9 Omega 242
02/3 Pacific 376
02/3 Pacific Complete 151
92 Québec Pee Wee 421
02/3 Signature Series GS-55
95/6 Slapshot 415
00/1 Stadium 192
00/1 To. Heritage 121
02/3 T. Total 186
98/9 UD Choice 268
98/9 Upper Deck 381
02/3 Upper Deck 415
98/9 UD G. Reserve 381
01/2 VANC / Coke

COOKE, STEVE
01/2 Belleville Bulls Update

COOL, ERIC
90/1 7th..Sketch LHJMQ 128
91/2 7th...Sketch LHJMQ 192

COOLEN, TOM
96/7 DEL 112
95/6 Saint John Flames

COOMBS, JOE
95/6 Slapshot 49
98/9 Topeka Scarecrows
99/0 Topeka Scarecrows

COONEY, MATT
98/9 Indianapolis Ice

COOPER, CARSON
25-27 Anonymous 31
25-27 Anonymous 32
24/5 Champ's Cigarettes
24/5 Maple Crispette [V130] 9
24/5 William Paterson 21

COOPER, DAVID
94/5 Classic T7
94/5 Classic 4 Sport 151
93/4 Cla. Prospects 210
99/0 Eishockey 172
93/4 Rochester Americans
95/6 Rochester Americans
90/1 7th..Sketch WHL 38
91/2 7th...Sketch WHL 319
96/7 St. John's Maple Leafs
97/8 St. John's Maple Leafs
00/1 St. John's Maple Leafs
97/8 Upper Deck 193
01/2 UD DEL 32, SS2

COOPER, JEFF
88/9 ProCards / Muskegon

COOPER, JOE
34-43 BeeHive-1 [NYRa.]

COOPER, JOHN
93/4 Slapshot / Windsor 23
94/5 Slapshot / Windsor 25

COOPER, KORY
97 Bowman 20
97/8 Indianapolis Ice 4
95/6 Slapshot 31

COOPER, LAN
94 Semic 330

COOPER, MATT
00/1 London Knights

COOPER, STEPHEN
94 Semic 314

COOPMAN, TODD
89/0 Niagara Falls Thunder
89/0 Oshawa Generals
89/0 7th..Sketch OHL 128
90/1 7th..Sketch OHL 258

COPELAND, TODD
92/3 Cincinnati Cyclones
90/1 ProCards 573
91/2 ProCards 418

COPIJA, MIROSLAV
89 Semic Sticker 141
92 Semic Sticker 278

COPLEY, JOHN
89/0 Kitchener Rangers
90 7th..Sketch Mem.Cup 42
90/1 7th..Sketch OHL 179
91/2 7th...Sketch OHL 178

COPLEY, RANDY
98 Bowman 114, 125, ✍ A34
98 Bowman Chrome 114, 125
00/1 Florida Everblades
02/3 Peoria Rivermen

COPP, ROBERT
34-43 BeeHive-1 [Toro.]

CORAM, GREG
82/3 Ottawa 67's
83/4 Ottawa 67's
84/5 Ottawa 67's

CORAZZINI, CARL
01/2 Providence Bruins

CORBEAU, BERT
25-27 Anonymous 64
24/5 Champ's Cigarettes
23/4 William Paterson 25
24/5 William Paterson 58

CORBEIL, JUSTIN
86/7 Sudbury Wolves
87/8 Sudbury Wolves

CORBEIL, NICOLAS
00/1 Sherbrooke Castors 18
01/2 Sherbrooke Castors 19
01 UD Prospects GU 13, ✂ TPJ

CORBET, RENÉ
91/2 Arena 18
01/2 Atomic ✂ GWJ 43
91/2 Classic 21
94/5 Classic 98, T55
91/2 Classic Four Sport 21
94/5 Cla. Images 78
93/4 Cla. Prospects 130
95/6 Donruss 371
95/6 Edge Ice 27
94/5 Flair 143
99/0 Millenium 42, ✍ Aut. 42
98/9 Pacific 158
99/0 Pacific 54
97/8 Pa. Invincible R-50
99/0 Pa. Paramount 36
93/4 Parkhurst 433
94/5 Parkhurst 193
93/4 Pinnacle 448
94/5 Pinnacle 460, RTP6
97/8 Pi. Be A Player 205, ✍ Aut. 205
00/1 PS Titanium ✂ GUG 131
94/5 Score 236
97/8 Score Colo. 14
94/5 Select 197
91/2 7th...Sketch LHJMQ 287
91 7th..Sketch Mem.Cup 63, 105
95/6 SBx Emotion 35
91/2 Star Pics 31
94/5 Topps Finest 97
91/2 Ultimate Draft Pick 20, ✍ Aut.
93/4 Upper Deck 339
94/5 Upper Deck 179
95/6 Upper Deck 100
95/6 UD Be A Player 78, ✍ S78
99/0 UD MVP 36
99/0 Victory 49
01/2 Victory 286

CORBETT, JEFF
98/9 Hampton Roads

CORBETT, PETER
91/2 ProCards 437

CORBETT, SCOTT
95/6 Slapshot 350

CORBIN, VICTOR
52/3 Bas du Fleuve 14
51/2 Lac St-Jean 36

CORBIN, YVAN
98/9 Anchorage Aces
99/0 Indianapolis Ice
90/1 7th..Sketch LHJMQ 179
91/2 7th...Sketch OHL 81

CORDERY, BILL
93/4 Wheeling Thund'birds

COREY, RONALD
88/9 MONT
89/0 MONT
90/1 MONT
91/2 MONT

CORKUM, BOB
93/4 ANAH / Cap 5
94/5 ANAH / Carl's Jr. 2
90/1 BUFF / Campbell's
92/3 BUFF / Blue Shield
92/3 BUFF / Jubilee
93/4 Donruss 10
94/5 Donruss 96
95/6 Donruss 112
94/5 Flair 1
94/5 Fleer 2
94/5 Fleer Ultra 1
94/5 Leaf 299
95/6 Leaf 300
01/2 O-Pee-Chee 259

98/9 Pacific 334
99/0 Pacific 317
97/8 Pacific CC 226
91/2 Parkhurst 238
93/4 Parkhurst 6
94/5 Parkie SE2
96/7 PHOE / Coca-Cola
97/8 PHOE / Coca-Cola
98/9 PHOE / Coca-Cola
94/5 Pinnacle 144
95/6 Pinnacle 121
97/8 Pi. Be A Player 117, ✍ Aut. 117
95/6 Playoff 221
96/7 Playoff 415
94/5 POG 28
93/4 Power Play 282
94/5 Premier 31
89/0 ProCards AHL 278
90/1 ProCards 280
91/2 ProCards 8
91/2 Rochester Americans DD
91/2 Rochester Americans GL
91/2 Rochester Americans WPC
93/4 Score 637
94/5 Score 158
95/6 Score 42
94/5 SP 4
95/6 SLU
92/3 Topps 74
95/6 Topps 59
01/2 Topps 259
94/5 Topps Finest 72
92/3 To. Stadium 179
93/4 To. Stadium 284
90/1 Upper Deck 35
94/5 Upper Deck 413
95/6 Upper Deck 149
95/6 UD Be A Player 112, ✍ S112
95/6 UD CC 14

CORMIER, DAN
84/5 Moncton G'Flames

CORMIER, DEREK
98/9 DEL 293
99/0 Eishockey 252
00/1 UD DEL 66
01/2 UD DEL 213

CORMIER, MICHEL
75/6 OPC WHA 74
75/6 Phoenix Roadrunners
76/7 Phoenix Roadrunners

CORMIER, SYLVAIN
90/1 7th..Sketch LHJMQ 197

CORNACCHIA, RICK
83/4 Kingston Canadians
84/5 Kingston Canadians
89/0 Oshawa Generals
90/1 Oshawa Generals
91/2 Oshawa Generals
90 7th..Sketch Mem.Cup 75
90/1 7th..Sketch OHL 349
91/2 7th...Sketch OHL 171
93/4 Slapshot / Oshawa 26

CORNELIUS, JEFF
85/6 Kingston Canadians

CORNFORTH, MARK
97/8 Cleveland Lumberjacks
96/7 Providence Bruins

CORNISH, CLAIR
89/0 Oshawa Generals
90/1 Oshawa Generals
90 7th..Sketch Mem.Cup 98
89/0 7th..Sketch OHL 5
90/1 7th..Sketch OHL 330

CORPSE, KELI
99/0 Fort Wayne Komets
95/6 Fredericton Canadiens
96/7 Grand Rapids Griffins
90/1 7th..Sketch OHL 11, 55
91/2 7th...Sketch OHL 224
93/4 Slapshot / Kingston 22

CORREIA, MIKE
99/0 Rockford IceHogs

CORRIGAN, JASON
89/0 7th..Sketch OHL 153

CORRIGAN, MIKE
71/2 Eddie Sargent 224
72/3 Eddie Sargent 94
70/1 Esso Power Player
74/5 Loblaws
70/1 O-Pee-Chee 227
71/2 O-Pee-Chee 157
72/3 O-Pee-Chee 74
73/4 O-Pee-Chee 48
74/5 O-Pee-Chee 37
75/6 O-Pee-Chee 361
76/7 O-Pee-Chee 268
76/7 OPC 386
77/8 O-Pee-Chee 236
77/8 PITT / McDonald's
72/3 Topps 89
73/4 Topps 48
74/5 Topps 37
77/8 Topps 236
70/1 VANC / Royal Bank
71/2 VANC / Royal Bank 2

CORRINET, CHRIS
01/2 BAP Memor. 352
01/2 Crown Royale 179
01/2 PS Titanium 183
01/2 PS Titanium Draft 169
01/2 SP GU 99
01/2 Upper Deck 441
01/2 UD Challenge 135
01/2 UD Honor Roll 90
01/2 UD Ice 84
01/2 UD Premier 87

CORRIVEAU, ANDRÉ
51/2 La Patrie
51/2 Laval Dairy 74
52/3 St. Lawrence 24

CORRIVEAU, RICK
90/1 Score 396
89/0 7th..Sketch OHL 40
90/1 7th..Sketch OHL 129
91/2 7th...Sketch OHL 200
92/3 Toledo Storm WIOT
92/3 Toledo Storm
93/4 Toledo Storm 25
94/5 Toledo Storm

CORRIVEAU, YVON
98/9 DEL 170
96/7 Detroit Vipers
99/0 Eishockey 57
90/1 HART / Jr. Whalers
94/5 Minnesota Moose
95/6 Minnesota Moose
90/1 OPC/Topps 364
92/3 OPC Premier 74
92/3 Panini Sticker 259
92/3 Parkhurst 295
93/4 Premier 208
90/1 Pro Set 100
90/1 Score 302
92/3 Score 541
92/3 Topps 474
92/3 To. Stadium 476
93/4 To. Stadium 9
91/2 Upper Deck 407
92/3 Upper Deck 460
01/2 UD DEL 29
86/7 WASH / Police
88/9 WASH
88/9 WASH / Smokey
89/0 WASH

CORSI, JIM
78/9 Dernière Heure
88/9 EDMO / Action 115
82 Semic Sticker 122

CORSO, DANIEL
01/2 BAP Memor. 23
95/6 Bowman P7
97 Bowman 71
98 Bowman 89
98 Bowman Chrome 89
98/9 Collection Souvenir 14
01/2 O-Pee-Chee 270
92 Québec Pee Wee 604
01/2 Topps 270
01/2 To. Chrome 148
98/9 UD Choice 269
95/6 Upper Deck 510
01/2 Upper Deck 385
00/1 Worcester IceCats

CORSON, SHAYNE
01/2 Adrenaline ✂ GWJ 46
98/9 Aurora 92, MACF-11
99/0 Aurora 73
99/0 BAP Mem. 29
00/1 BAP Mem. 426
02/3 BAP Memorabilia 120
90/1 Bowman 41
91/2 Bowman 328
92/3 Bowman 82
95/6 Bowman 11
98/9 Bowman's Best 98
83/4 Brantford Alexanders
91 Canada Cup
99/0 Challenger 13
93/4 Donruss 114
94/5 Donruss 221
95/6 Donruss 376
96/7 Donruss 55
97/8 Donruss 42
96/7 Do. Canadian 43
96/7 Do. Elite 58
98/9 Dynagon Ice 94
99/0 Dynagon Ice 100
93/4 EA Sports 46
93/4 EDMO / Sheet
92/3 EDMO
92/3 EDMO / IGA 004
94/5 Flair 57
94/5 Fleer 69
96/7 Fleer 95
95/6 Fleer Metal 122
92/3 Fleer Ultra 57, 292
93/4 Fleer Ultra 51
94/5 Fleer Ultra 291
95/6 Fleer Ultra 53, 296
96/7 Fl. Ultra 85
95/6 Hoyle / West. J-Heart
92/3 Humpty Dumpty
89/0 Kraft 21
91/2 Kraft 29
97/8 Kraft / PB
99/0 Kraft / KD
93/4 Leaf 46
94/5 Leaf 164
95/6 Leaf 123
96/7 Leaf 163
96/7 L. Limited 66
96/7 L. Preferred 26
97/8 Limited 172
96/7 Maggers 143
96/7 Metal Univ. 130
86/7 MONT
87/8 MONT
87/8 MONT / Vachon 49
87/8 MONT / Vachon 50
88/9 MONT
89/0 MONT
89/0 MONT / Kraft
90/1 MONT
91/2 MONT
96-98 MONT
90/1 OPC/Topps 58
91/2 O-Pee-Chee 157
92/3 O-Pee-Chee 231
02/3 O-Pee-Chee 38
89/0 O-Pee-Chee 248
91/2 OPC Premier 161
87/8 OPC Sticker 127-115
89/0 opcSticker 49-195
97/8 Omega 116, 248, TL-11
98/9 Omega 119
99/0 Omega 116
98/9 Pacific 249
99/0 Pacific 202
00/1 Pacific 207
01/2 Pacific 362
02/3 Pacific 358
02/3 Pacific Complete 64
97/8 Pacific CC 246
97/8 Pa. Crown Roy. 67
98/9 Pa. Crown Roy. 67
97/8 Pa. Paramount 93
98/9 Pa. Paramount 111
99/0 Pa. Paramount 115
97/8 Pa. Revolution 69
98/9 Pa. Revolution 71
89/0 Panini Sticker 242
90/1 Panini Sticker 54
90/1 Panini/MTL 5
91/2 Panini Sticker 196
92/3 Panini Sticker 150
93/4 Panini Sticker 236
94/5 Panini Sticker 202
95/6 Panini Sticker 260
96/7 Panini Sticker 204
95 Panini Worlds 13
91/2 Parkhurst 86
92/3 Parkhurst 53
93/4 Parkhurst 338
94/5 Parkhurst 75, V3
95/6 Parkhurst 174
91/2 Pinnacle 102
92/3 Pinnacle 323
93/4 Pinnacle 249
94/5 Pinnacle 44
96/7 Pinnacle 104
96/7 Pi. Be A Player 62, ✍ Aut. 62
95/6 Pi. Summit 151
96/7 Pi. Summit 137
95/6 Pi. Zenith 98
96/7 Pi. Zenith 107
95/6 Playoff 86
94/5 POG 99
94/5 POG / Western 9
95/6 POG 241
93/4 Power Play 79
93/4 Premier 38
94/5 Premier 210
00/1 Pr. Stock ✂ GUG 95
00/1 PS Titanium Draft ✂ 94
90/1 Pro Set 148, 369
91/2 Pro Set 413
92/3 Pro Set 89
99/0 Revolution 73, / CSC 73
90/1 Score 213
90/1 Sco. Hot Cards 91
91/2 Score 65
91/2 Score CAN 65
92/3 Score 158
93/4 Score 108
93/4 Score/CAN DD7
94/5 Score 174
95/6 Score 245
96/7 Score 78
97/8 Score Mont. 12
94/5 Select 47
95/6 Select CE 101
96/7 Select CE 73
94 Semic 93
95 Semic 91
92 Semic Sticker 93
00/1 Signature 171, ✍ Aut. 211
95/6 SBx Emotion 145
95/6 SBx Impact 138
96/7 SBx Impact 110
94/5 SP 42
95/6 SP 122, FX19
96/7 SP 84
97/8 SP Authentic 84
99/0 Stadium 49
96/7 Team Out!
92/3 Topps 201
95/6 Topps 55, 229
99/0 Topps 126
00/1 Topps 240
02/3 Topps 38
99/0 To. Chrome 126
00/1 To. Chrome 150
94/5 Topps Finest 74
95/6 To. Finest 18
02/3 T. Limited 38
96/7 Topps Picks 139
91/2 To. Stadium 5
92/3 To. Stadium 221
93/4 To. Stadium 40
95/6 To. Stadium 7
93/4 TSC Members Only 12
02/3 T. Total 206
98/9 UD Choice 103
90/1 Upper Deck 280
91/2 Upper Deck 282
91/2 Upper Deck 505
92/3 Upper Deck 330
92/3 Upper Deck 541
93/4 Upper Deck 132, SP-49
94/5 Upper Deck 351, SP-116
95/6 Upper Deck 101, SE-159
96/7 Upper Deck 139
97/8 Upper Deck 298
98/9 Upper Deck 291
00/1 Upper Deck 394
01/2 Upper Deck 166
94/5 UD Be A Player ✍ 172
93/4 UD BAP Roots 13
96/7 UD Black Diam. 119
97/8 UD Black Diam. 107
95/6 UD CC 146
96/7 UD CC 225
97/8 UD Coll. Choice 137
98/9 UD G. Reserve 291
98/9 UD MVP 109
01/2 UD Vintage 237
02/3 UD Vintage 236
97/8 Valu-net, ✍ Aut.
00/1 Vanguard ✂ DGJ 18
99/0 Victory 151
00/1 Victory 124
97/8 Zenith 67, Z34

CORT, JOEL
95/6 Guelph Storm
96/7 Guelph Storm
94/5 Slapshot / Guelph 6
95/6 Slapshot 86

CORTES, MIKE
85/6 Minnesota-Duluth 14

CORUPE, KENNY
02/3 Louisiana Ice Gators

CORVO, JOE
02/3 Calder 73
00/1 Lowell Lock Monsters
01/2 Manchester Monarchs
02/3 Manchester Monarchs
02/3 Pacific Complete 545
96/7 UD Ice 145

COSSETTE, BRYAN
91/2 Air Canada SJHL D44
92/3 MPS SJHL 9

COSSETTE, J.M.
52/3 Anonymous 39

COSTEA, MARIAN
79 Panini Sticker 317

COSTELLO, LES
45-64 BeeHive-2 [Toro.]
45-54 Quaker Oats

COSTELLO, MURRAY
52/3 Anonymous 156
45-64 BeeHive-2 [Chic.]
45-64 BeeHive-2 [Bost.]
93/4 Parkie 56-57 60

COSTELLO, RICH
84/5 O-Pee-Chee 298

COTA, DARREN
84/5 Medicine Hat Tigers

COTE, BART
89/0 Brandon Wheat Kings
90/1 Brandon Wheat Kings
91 7th..Sketch Mem.Cup 94
90/1 7th..Sketch WHL 219

COTE, FRANK
51/2 Bas du Fleuve 51

COTE, MIKE
90/1 Oshawa Generals
91/2 Oshawa Generals
90/1 7th..Sketch OHL 325, 331
91/2 7th...Sketch OHL 344

COTE, RAY
88/9 EDMO / Action 140
83/4 Moncton Alpines
84/5 Nova Scotia Oilers

COTÉ, ALAIN
81/2 Dernière Heure

CÔTÉ, ALAIN
78/9 Dernière Heure
86/7 Kraft Sports 43
79/0 O-Pee-Chee 324
81/2 O-Pee-Chee 272
82/3 O-Pee-Chee 281
83/4 O-Pee-Chee 291
84/5 O-Pee-Chee 278
85/6 O-Pee-Chee 205
86/7 O-Pee-Chee 233
87/8 O-Pee-Chee 254
88/9 O-Pee-Chee 205
85/6 OPC Sticker 149-18
86/7 OPC Sticker 20-161
88/9 OPC Sticker 186-55
87/8 Panini Sticker 169
88/9 Panini Sticker 352
82/3 Post [Québ.]
80/1 QUÉB
81/2 QUÉB
82/3 QUÉB
83/4 QUÉB
84/5 QUÉB
85/6 QUÉB
85/6 QUÉB / Gene. Foods
85/6 QUÉB / McDonald's
85/6 QUÉB / Provigo
86/7 QUÉB
86/7 QUÉB / Gene. Foods
86/7 QUÉB / McDonald's
86/7 QUÉB / Yum Yum
87/8 QUÉB / Gene. Foods
87/8 QUÉB / Yum Yum
88/9 QUÉB
88/9 QUÉB / Gene. Foods
83/4 Vachon 63-43

CÔTÉ, ALAIN G.
93/4 Durivage 19
92/3 Fredericton Canadiens
91/2 MONT
91/2 OPC Premier 188
91/2 Pro Set 417
89/0 ProCards AHL 102
90/1 ProCards 54

CÔTÉ, ALAIN*
90/1 7th..Sketch LHJMQ 89
91/2 7th...Sketch LHJMQ 25

CÔTÉ, ALAIN**
90/1 7th..Sketch LHJMQ 190
91/2 7th...Sketch LHJMQ 54

CÔTÉ, ALAIN?
00/1 Cardset 210
94/5 Thunder Bay Senators

CÔTÉ, ALAIN_G
99/0 Eishockey 45

CÔTÉ, ANDRÉ
82/3 Fredericton Express
83/4 Fredericton Express

CÔTÉ, BENOÎT
97 Bowman 128, ✍ Aut.

CÔTÉ, BRANDIN
98/9 SP Authentic 124
97/8 Spokane Chiefs
98/9 Upper Deck 401
98/9 UD G. Reserve 401

CÔTÉ, GABRILE
99/0 Rouyn-Noranda

CÔTÉ, JEAN-PHILIPPE
01/2 Cape Breton Eagles 7

CÔTÉ, MARTIN
84/5 Richelieu Riverains

CÔTÉ, PATRICK*
95/6 Classic 33
00/1 Hamilton Bulldogs
96/7 Michigan K-Wings
98/9 NASH / Wendy's 7
98/9 Omega 134
99/0 Pacific 221
97/8 Pi. Be A Player 235, ✍ Aut. 235
98/9 Upper Deck 304
98/9 UD G. Reserve 304
99/0 Victory 162

CÔTÉ, PATRICK**
90/1 7th..Sketch LHJMQ 252

CÔTÉ, ROGER
80/1 Québec Remparts

CÔTÉ, SYLVAIN
00/1 BAP Mem. 307, 486
91/2 Bowman 17
92/3 Bowman 115
93/4 Donruss 367
94/5 Donruss 153
92/3 Durivage 34
93/4 Durivage 35
94/5 Flair 198
94/5 Fleer 234
95/6 Fleer Metal 158
92/3 Fleer Ultra 433
93/4 Fleer Ultra 445
94/5 Fleer Ultra 232
95/6 Fleer Ultra 321
84/5 HART / Jr. Whalers
85/6 HART / Jr. Whalers
86/7 HART / Jr. Whalers
87/8 HART / Jr. Whalers
88/9 HART / Jr. Whalers
89/0 HART / Jr. Whalers
90/1 HART / Jr. Whalers
93/4 Leaf 52
94/5 Leaf 140
95/6 Leaf 218
91/2 O-Pee-Chee 249
92/3 O-Pee-Chee 277
89/0 OPC/Topps 162
98/9 Pacific 412
99/0 Pacific 404
00/1 Pacific 128
97/8 Pacific CC 207
88/9 Panini Sticker 237
89/0 Panini Sticker 229
94/5 Panini Sticker 25
96/7 Panini Sticker 137
92/3 Parkhurst 431
93/4 Parkhurst 489
95/6 Parkhurst 222
94/5 Parkie SE193
91/2 Pinnacle 221
92/3 Pinnacle 182
93/4 Pinnacle 258
94/5 Pinnacle 33
95/6 Pinnacle 65
95/6 Playoff 321
94/5 POG 249
93/4 Power Play 259
93/4 Premier 138
94/5 Premier 208
00/1 Pr. Stock ✂ GUG 102
90/1 Pro Set 448
91/2 Pro Set 82
91/2 Pro Set 512
90/1 Score 83
91/2 Score 129
91/2 Score 46T
91/2 Score CAN 129
91/2 Score CAN 596
92/3 Score 78
93/4 Score 450
93/4 Score 92
95/6 Score 183
94/5 Select 128
96/7 SBx Impact 138
92/3 Topps 428
95/6 Topps 151
95/6 To. Finest 37
96/7 Topps Picks 153
91/2 To. Stadium 183
92/3 To. Stadium 145
93/4 To. Stadium 66
95/6 To. Stadium 23
94/5 Upper Deck 354
95/6 Upper Deck 133, SE-176
94/5 UD Be A Player ✍ 166
95/6 UD CC 284
96/7 UD CC 287
91/2 WASH / Kodak
91/2 WASH / Smokey
92/3 WASH / Kodak
95/6 WASH

CÔTÉ, SYLVAIN**
82/3 Fredericton Express

COTNOIR, BENOÎT
99/0 Mobile Mysticks

COTTON, BALDY
02/3 Ultimate Memorabilia ✍ Cut

COTTON, DARREN
02/3 Peterborough Phantoms

COTTON, HAROLD
02/3 Parkie - Reprint 205

COTTON, HAROLD (BALDY)
33/4 Anonymous 12
34-43 BeeHive-1 [Toro.]
33/4 Hamilton Gum 39
32/3 Maple Leafs O'Keefe
33/4 O-Pee-Chee 35
55/6 Parkhurst 32
33/4 WWGum 33
37/8 World Wide Gum 35

COTTON, JEFF
01/2 Val d'Or Foreurs 8
02/3 Val d'Or Foreurs

COTTON, JOE
02/3 Peterborough Phantoms

COUCH, MICHAEL
00/1 Halifax Moosehead

COUGHLIN, MATT
01/2 Belleville Bulls

COULIS, TIM
85/6 MINS
84/5 Springfield Indians 10

COULOMBE, SERGE
90/1 Rayside-Balfour

COULTER, ART
34-43 BeeHive-1 [NYRa.]
36-39 Diamond Match TT1
36-39 Diamond Match TT2
36-39 Diamond Match TT3
83 HHOF Postcard J5
83&87 HHOF 185
35/6 O-Pee-Chee 93
39/0 O-Pee-Chee 34

COULTER, JEFF
00/1 Saskatoon Blades
01/2 Vancouver Giants

COULTER, M
95/6 Birmingham Bulls

COULTHARD, DALE
98/9 Dayton Bombers

COUPAL, GARY
99/0 Odessa Jackalopes
93/4 Slapshot / Sudbury 17
92/3 Sudbury Wolves
93/4 Sudbury Wolves

COURCELLES, SÉBASTIEN
00/1 Sherbrooke Castors 2
01/2 Sherbrooke Castors 16

COURCHESNE, PIERRE-LUC
00/1 Sherbrooke Castors 16
01/2 Sherbrooke Castors 18

COURNOYER, BERTRAND
88/9 Richelieu Riverains

COURNOYER, YVAN
01/2 AGF
71/2 Bazooka Panel
99/0 BAP Mem. CH-11, ✍ CH-11
02/3 BAP Memorabilia / Cup
64-67 BeeHive-3 [Mont.]
64/5 Coke/Sprite [Mont.]
65/6 Coca-Cola
77/8 Coke
71/2 Colgate Head
70/1 Colgate 60
70/1 Dad's Cookies
72/3 Dernière Heure
73/4 Dernière Heure
70/1 Eddie Sargent 109
71/2 Eddie Sargent 102
72/3 Eddie Sargent 117
70/1 Esso Power Player
88/9 Esso All-Star
01/2 Fleer Greats 25, ✍ Aut.
71/2 Frito Lay
91/2 Future Trends C72 82, ✍ 82
83 HHOF Postcard K1
83&87 HHOF 136
75/6 Hockey Heroes
91/2 Kraft 79
72/3 Post 15
74/5 Lipton Soup 13
74/5 Loblaws
73/4 Mac's Milk
67/8 MONT
67/8 MONT / IGA Card
68/9 MONT / IGA Card
69/0 MONT / Pro Star
70/1 MONT
71/2 MONT / Pro Star
71/2 MONT / Pro Star
72/3 MONT / Pro Star
73/4 MONT / Pro Star
74/5 MONT
75/6 MONT
76/7 MONT
77/8 MONT
78/9 MONT
92/3 MONT / OPC 23
68/9 O-Pee-Chee 62
69/0 O-Pee-Chee 6
69/0 O-Pee-Chee 221
69/0 O-Pee-Chee 4in1
69/0 O-Pee-Chee Stamp
70/1 O-Pee-Chee 50
70/1 O-Pee-Chee DE 23
71/2 O-Pee-Chee 15
71/2 O-Pee-Chee 260
72/3 O-Pee-Chee 29
72/3 O-Pee-Chee 44
72/3 O-Pee-Chee 250
72/3 O-Pee-Chee TC
73/4 O-Pee-Chee 157
74/5 O-Pee-Chee 124
74/5 O-Pee-Chee 140
75/6 O-Pee-Chee 70
76/7 O-Pee-Chee 30
77/8 O-Pee-Chee 230
78/9 O-Pee-Chee 60
71/2 O-Pee-Chee Poster 4
95/6 Parkie 66-67 60
94/5 Parkie Tall 75, 160, ✍ A2
68/9 Post Marble
71/2 Pro Star Promotions
71/2 Pro Star Promotions
71/2 Pro Star Promotions
72 Semic Sticker 204
68/9 Shirriff / Mont. 13
Sport Flash 12
Sport Flash 12
77-79 Sportscaster 02-13
77-79 Sportscaster 15-13
77-79 Sports. FIN 58-1392
65/6 Topps 76
66/7 Topps 72
66/7 Topps / Test 13
67/8 Topps 70
68/9 Topps 62
69/0 Topps 6
70/1 Topps 50
71/2 Topps 15
72/3 Topps 10
72/3 Topps 131
73/4 Topps 115
74/5 Topps 124
74/5 Topps 140
75/6 Topps 70
76/7 Topps 30
77/8 Topps 230
78/9 Topps 60
01/2 Topps -SCH, -Reprint, ✍ SCHA, ✍ Reprint
01/2 T/O Archives 29, -Seat, ✍ CAI
71/2 Toronto Sun Photo
01/2 Ultimate Mem. ✂ LC, ✂ RT, ✂ SCD, ✂ SCW
02/3 Ultimate Memorabilia ✂ CSTW, ✂ FS, ✂ Num, ✂ RT, ✂ SF
02/3 UD Foundations 57, ✂ LI
01/2 UD Legends 35
01/2 UD SCup Champs 14
67/8 York 28-30
93/4 Zellers, ✍ Aut.

COURNOYER, YVES*
88/9 Richelieu Riverains

COURNOYER, YVON
01/2 Parkhurst ✍ PA52

COURTEAU, MAURICE
51/2 Lac St-Jean 59

COURTEAU, YVES
84/5 Moncton G'Flames
85/6 Moncton G'Flames

COURTEMANCHE, DAVE
81/2 Kingston Canadians

COURTENAY, ED
93/4 Fleer Ultra 8
92/3 Kansas City Blades
93/4 Kansas City Blades
00/1 Kudos 15
93/4 Leaf 145
92/3 OPC Premier 8
93/4 Panini Sticker 261
93/4 Power Play 217
89/0 ProCards IHL 80
90/1 ProCards 116
91/2 ProCards 507
97/8 Sheffield Steelers
01/2 Sheffield Steelers
93/4 To. Stadium 72
91/2 Upper Deck 517
92/3 Upper Deck 507

COURTNALL, GEOFF
98/9 Aurora 159
98/9 Be A Player 124, ✍ Aut. 124
99/0 BAP Mem. 183
84/5 BOST
90/1 Bowman 73
91/2 Bowman 318
92/3 Bowman 345
93/4 Donruss 352
94/5 Donruss 50
95/6 Donruss 238
96/7 Donruss 54
97/8 Donruss 47
96/7 Do. Elite 43
98/9 Dynagon Ice 156
93/4 EA Sports 142
88/9 EDMO / Action 88
94/5 Fleer 224
92/3 Fleer Ultra 220
93/4 Fleer Ultra 76
94/5 Fleer Ultra 382
95/6 Fleer Ultra 167, 297
95/6 Hoyle / West. Q-Heart
90/1 Kraft 9
91/2 Kraft 15
93/4 Leaf 72
94/5 Leaf 53
95/6 Leaf 233
96/7 Leaf 158
94/5 L. Limited 69
95/6 L. Limited 3
97/8 Limited 24
85/6 Moncton G'Flames
90/1 OPC/Topps 273
91/2 O-Pee-Chee 305
92/3 O-Pee-Chee 176
89/0 OPC/Topps 111
89/0 Topps - Sticker 9
98/9 OPC Chrome 139
90/1 OPC Premier 18
91/2 OPC Premier 101
88/9 OPC Sticker 222-98
89/0 opcSticker 80, 164-26, / AS 29
97/8 Omega 190
98/9 Pacific 365
99/0 Pacific 354
97/8 Pacific CC 62, SS-9A
97/8 Pa. Invincible 118
97/8 Pa. Paramount 157
98/9 Pa. Paramount 201
97/8 Pa. Revolution 118
88/9 Panini Sticker 172
88/9 Panini Sticker 183
88/9 Panini Sticker 184
88/9 Panini Sticker 185
88/9 Panini Sticker 186
89/0 Panini Sticker 340
90/1 Panini Sticker 159
91/2 Panini Sticker 38
92/3 Panini Sticker 29
93/4 Panini Sticker 170
94/5 Panini Sticker 149
95/6 Panini Sticker 193
96/7 Panini Sticker 205
97/8 Panini Sticker 167
98/9 Panini Sticker 156
91/2 Parkhurst 186
92/3 Parkhurst 189
93/4 Parkhurst 216
94/5 Parkhurst 240
95/6 Parkhurst 448
91/2 Pinnacle 263
92/3 Pinnacle 187
93/4 Pinnacle 132
94/5 Pinnacle 276
96/7 Pinnacle 146
95/6 Pi. Summit 119
95/6 Pi. Zenith 58
95/6 Playoff 87, 305
94/5 POG 329
95/6 POG 240
94/5 Post
93/4 Power Play 249
93/4 Premier 337
94/5 Premier 186, 525
95/6 Pro Magnet 10
90/1 Pro Set 309, 521
91/2 Pro Set 245
92/3 Pro Set 198
91/2 Pro Set Platinum 123
90/1 Score 124, 5T
91/2 Score 150
91/2 Score 380
91/2 Score CAN 150
91/2 Score CAN 270
92/3 Score 234
93/4 Score 78
94/5 Score 161
95/6 Score 255
96/7 Score 32
97/8 Score 184
97/8 Score SLou. 15
92/3 Seasons 33
94/5 Select 137
95/6 SBx Emotion 146
95/6 SBx Impact 139
96/7 SBx Impact 111
94/5 SP 125
95/6 SP 128
90/1 SLOU / Kodak
92/3 Topps 472
95/6 Topps 276
98/9 Topps 139
94/5 Topps Finest 83
95/6 To. Finest 49
96/7 Topps Picks 149
91/2 To. Stadium 149
92/3 To. Stadium 265
93/4 To. Stadium 413
98/9 UD Choice 190
90/1 Upper Deck 238, 438
91/2 Upper Deck 467
92/3 Upper Deck 39
92/3 Upper Deck 240
93/4 Upper Deck 114, SP-163
94/5 Upper Deck 286, SP-82
95/6 Upper Deck 120
96/7 Upper Deck 327
98/9 Upper Deck 357
94/5 UD Be A Player R6, ✍ 135
95/6 UD CC 31
96/7 UD CC 229
97/8 UD Coll. Choice 227
98/9 UD G. Reserve 357
91/2 VANC
91/2 VANC / Photo
92/3 VANC / Road Trip
94/5 VANC
95/6 VANC / Abalene 14
81/2 Victoria Cougars
82/3 Victoria Cougars
84/5 Victoria Cougars
88/9 WASH
88/9 WASH / Smokey
89/0 WASH
89/0 WASH / Kodak

COURTNALL, RUSS
90/1 Bowman 47
91/2 Bowman 346
91/2 Bowman 414
92/3 Bowman 45
91 Canada Cup
94/5 DALL / Cap
93/4 Donruss 80
94/5 Donruss 167
95/6 Donruss 199
96/7 Donruss 194
93/4 EA Sports 35
94/5 Flair 40
94/5 Fleer 48
95/6 Fleer Metal 150
92/3 Fleer Ultra 91, 316
93/4 Fleer Ultra 50
93/4 Fleer Ultra SM 2
94/5 Fleer Ultra 279, SM-2
95/6 Fleer Ultra 168
95/6 Hoyle / West. K-Heart
92/3 Humpty Dumpty
84/5 Kelowna Wings &...
89/0 Kraft 22
91/2 Kraft 49
93/4 Kraft / KD
86/7 Kraft Sports 53
93/4 Leaf 65
94/5 Leaf 126
95/6 Leaf 51
96/7 Leaf 29
94/5 L. Limited 35
96/7 Metal Univ. 156
88/9 MONT
89/0 MONT
89/0 MONT / Kraft
90/1 MONT
91/2 MONT
86/7 OPC/Topps 174
87/8 OPC/Topps 62
87/8 OPC/Topps Box P
88/9 OPC/Topps 183
90/1 OPC/Topps 124
91/2 O-Pee-Chee 119
91/2 Topps - Team Leader 18
92/3 O-Pee-Chee 284
89/0 O-Pee-Chee 239
98/9 OPC Chrome 188
91/2 OPC Premier 58
91/2 OPC Premier 194
92/3 OPC Premier 20
85/6 OPC Sticker 20-151
86/7 OPC Sticker 149
87/8 OPC Sticker 156
88/9 OPC Sticker 175
89/0 opcSticker 53-197
98/9 Pacific 233
99/0 Pacific 188
97/8 Pacific CC 275
98/9 Pa. Paramount 103
97/8 Pa. Revolution 64
87/8 Panini Sticker 327
88/9 Panini Sticker 122
90/1 Panini Sticker 56
90/1 Panini/MTL 6
91/2 Panini Sticker 186
92/3 Panini Sticker 154
93/4 Panini Sticker 268
94/5 Panini Sticker 230
95/6 Panini Sticker 296
96/7 Panini Sticker 292
91/2 Parkhurst 308
92/3 Parkhurst 78
93/4 Parkhurst 53
94/5 Parkhurst 52
95/6 Parkhurst 210
94/5 Parkie SE seV30
91/2 Pinnacle 254
92/3 Pinnacle 337
93/4 Pinnacle 268
94/5 Pinnacle 133
96/7 Pinnacle 75
95/6 Pi. Summit 128
96/7 Pi. Summit 22
95/6 Pi. Zenith 115
94/5 POG 77
95/6 POG 275
94/5 Post
93/4 Power Play 58
93/4 Premier 153
94/5 Premier 395
90/1 Pro Set 149
91/2 Pro Set 126
91/2 Pro Set Platinum 62
90/1 Score 148
91/2 Score 42
91/2 Score 380
91/2 Score CAN 42
91/2 Score CAN 270
92/3 Score 4
93/4 Score 130
94/5 Score 43
95/6 Score 242
96/7 Score 109
94/5 Select 70
94 Semic 98
95 Semic 95
92 Semic Sticker 95
95/6 SBx Emotion 179
95/6 SBx Impact 168
96/7 SBx Impact 132
96/7 SP 161
92/3 Topps 276
95/6 Topps 194
98/9 Topps 188
94/5 Topps Finest 54
96/7 Topps Picks 107
91/2 To. Stadium 43
92/3 To. Stadium 152
93/4 To. Stadium 55
94/5 To. Stadium 170
95/6 To. Stadium 9
93/4 TSC Members Only 19
95/6 T. Super Skills 11
84/5 TORO
85/6 TORO
86/7 TORO
86/7 TORO
87/8 TORO / 3x5
87/8 TORO / 5x8
87/8 TORO / P.L.A.Y. 30
88/9 TORO / P.L.A.Y. 30
90/1 Upper Deck 259
91/2 Upper Deck 87
91/2 Upper Deck 168
92/3 Upper Deck 39
92/3 Upper Deck 94
92/3 Upper Deck 441
93/4 Upper Deck 32, SP-36
94/5 Upper Deck 31, SP-19
95/6 Upper Deck 317
96/7 Upper Deck 350
94/5 UD Be A Player R27, G5
95/6 UD Be A Player 65, ✍ S65
95/6 UD CC 267
96/7 UD CC 276
97/8 UD Coll. Choice 166
96/7 VANC / IGA
82/3 Victoria Cougars
83/4 Victoria Cougars
84/5 Victoria Cougars

#VALUE!
94/5 POG / Western 3

#VALUE!
94/5 POG / Western 11

#VALUE!
52/3 Anonymous 93

COURTNEY, RYAN
01/2 Owen Sound Attack

COURTURIER, FRANCIS
90/1 7th..Sketch LHJMQ 95

COURVILLE, IAN
00/1 Hull Olympiques 23

COURVILLE, LARRY
95/6 Classic 50
91/2 Cornwall Royals
95/6 Donruss C3TWC 11
95/6 Edge Ice 88
01/2 Hershey Bears
99/0 Kentucky Tho'blades
00/1 Kentucky Tho'blades
94/5 Pinnacle 540
96/7 Pinnacle 235
97/8 Score 57
97/8 Score Vanc. 13
91/2 7th...Sketch OHL 15
94/5 SP 150
96/7 Syracuse Crunch
95/6 Topps 3CJ
94/5 Topps Finest 156

COUSINEAU, BRYAN
90/1 Newmarket Saints

COUSINEAU, DAN
99/0 Indianapolis Ice

COUSINEAU, MARCEL
98/9 Bicycle.. 2-H
91/2 Classic 50
91/2 Classic Four Sport 50
93/4 Cla. Prospects 111
97/8 Donruss 198, RR-7
97/8 Do. Canadian 147, LG-10
97/8 Do. Preferred 158
97/8 Leaf 114
97/8 Limited 86, 116, 160, FG-39
00/1 Lowell Lock Monsters
01/2 Manchester Monarchs
97/8 Omega 219
96/7 Pi. Be A Player 213, ✍ Aut. 213
97/8 Pi. Inside 69, SU-4, -S22
97/8 Score 23
97/8 Score Toro. 3
90/1 7th..Sketch LHJMQ 133
93/4 St. John's Maple Leafs
94/5 St. John's Maple Leafs
95/6 St. John's Maple Leafs
97/8 St. John's Maple Leafs
91/2 Star Pics 47
91/2 Ultimate Draft Pick 45, 57, ✍ Aut.
96/7 UD Black Diam. 63

COUTOURIER, SYLVAIN
84/5 Richelieu Riverains

COUTU, BILLY
25-27 Anonymous 2, 42
24/5 Champ's Cigarettes
25 Dominion Chocolates 89
23/4 William Paterson 17
24/5 William Paterson 44

COUTURE, ALEXANDRE
97/8 Halifax Moosehead
97/8 Halifax Moosehead
98/9 Peoria Rivermen
99/0 Peoria Rivermen

COUTURE, GERRY
45-64 BeeHive-2 [Detr.]
45-64 BeeHive-2 [Mont.]
45-64 BeeHive-2 [Chic.]
51/2 Parkhurst 17
52/3 Parkhurst 41
53/4 Parkhurst 84
45-54 Quaker Oats

COUTURE, GUILLAUME
97/8 Rimouski Océanic

COUTURE, JERRY
45-64 BeeHive-2 [Detr.]

COUTURE, ROSARIO (LOLO)
33-35 Diamond Match Silv.
36-39 Diamond Match TT1
36-39 Diamond Match TT2
36-39 Diamond Match TT3
31/2 La Presse

COUTURIER, SYLVAIN
98/9 DEL 127
99/0 Eishockey 281
92/3 Fort Wayne Komets 6
93/4 Milwaukee Admirals
94/5 Milwaukee Admirals
95/6 Milwaukee Admirals
96/7 Milwaukee Admirals
92/3 Phoenix Roadrunners
88/9 ProCards / New Haven
89/0 ProCards AHL 7
90/1 ProCards 360
91/2 Upper Deck 491

COUVRETTE, MICHEL
98/9 Phoenix Mustangs 11

COVENY, CHRIS
92/3 Ottawa 67's
98/9 Peoria Rivermen
91/2 7th...Sketch OHL 302

COVENY, MICHAEL
94/5 Slapshot Memorial 51

COWAN, DAVE
85/6 Minnesota-Duluth 7

COWAN, JEFF
00/1 BAP Mem. 18
01/2 BAP Memor. 449
95/6 Classic 82
00/1 PS Titanium 107
00/1 PS Titanium Draft 107
96/7 Roanoke Express 12
97/8 Saint John Flames
01/2 Signature 75, ✍ Aut. 75
93/4 Slapshot / Guelph 20
94/5 Slapshot / Guelph 23
95/6 Slapshot 23
00/1 SPx 94
00/1 UD Heroes 160
00/1 Upper Deck 220
00/1 UD Black Diam. 77
00/1 UD Pros&Prosp. 96
00/1 UD Vintage 375
02/3 UD Vintage 12

COWHERD, COLIN
93/4 Las Vegas Thunder

COWICK, BRUCE
74/5 O-Pee-Chee 386
74/5 WASH

COWIE, ROB
94/5 Cla. Images 57
95/6 Edge Ice 183
99/0 Eishockey 69
91/2 Moncton Hawks
94/5 Phoenix Roadrunners
95/6 Phoenix Roadrunners
91/2 ProCards 174
00/1 UD DEL 71

COWLEY, BILL (COWBOY)
34-43 BeeHive-1 [Bost.]
91/2 BOST / SA Legends
91/2 BOST / SA Legends
91/2 BOST / SA Legends
36-39 Diamond Match TT1
83 HHOF Postcard M5
83&87 HHOF 170
39/0 O-Pee-Chee 98
43-47 Parade Sportive
02/3 Ultimate Mem. ✍ Cut

COWLEY, JOE
92/3 Indianapolis Ice

COWLEY, RUSS
02/3 Coventry Blaze

COWLEY, WAYNE
96/7 DEL 204
93/4 EDMO / Sheet
89/0 ProCards IHL 206
90/1 ProCards 609
88/9 Salt Lake G'Eagles

COX, ALLAN
90/1 7th..Sketch OHL 306
91/2 7th...Sketch OHL 56

COX, DANNY
33/4 Anonymous 48
33/4 Canadian Gum
33/4 O-Pee-Chee 1
23/4 Paulins Candy 18
33/4 WWGum 69

COX, JUSTIN
99/0 Prince George Cougars
00/1 Prince George Cougars
01/2 Utah Grizzlies

COX, PETER
90/1 7th..Sketch WHL 158
91/2 7th...Sketch WHL 45

COX, TIM
90/1 Saskatoon Blades
90/1 7th..Sketch WHL 91

COXE, CRAIG
83/4 Belleville Bulls
84/5 Fredericton Express
90/1 OPC/Topps 339
91/2 O-Pee-Chee 447
90/1 Panini/VAN 7
90/1 Pro Set 544
91/2 Pro Set 329
91/2 ProCards 520
91/2 Score 96T
91/2 Score CAN 646
87/8 SLOU
88/9 SLOU
88/9 SLOU / Kodak
91/2 Upper Deck 60
85/6 VANC
86/7 VANC
87/8 VANC / Shell
89/0 VANC / Mohawk
90/1 VANC / Mohawk

COYLE, LEN
84/5 Kingston Canadians
85/6 Kingston Canadians
86/7 Kingston Canadians
87/8 Kingston Canadians

COYNE, COLLEEN
94/5 Classic W26

CRABB, KEN
94/5 Slapshot / Brantford 21

CRAIEVICH, DAVID
93/4 Birmingham Bulls
94/5 Birmingham Bulls
98/9 Chicago Wolves Champs
91/2 Cincinnati Cyclones
99/0 Mobile Mysticks
89/0 Oshawa Generals
90/1 Oshawa Generals
91/2 ProCards 422
90 7th..Sketch Mem.Cup 84
89/0 7th..Sketch OHL 13
90/1 7th..Sketch OHL 332

CRAIG, GLEN
90/1 7th..Sketch OHL 102
91/2 7th...Sketch OHL 30
89/0 Windsor Spitfires

CRAIG, JIM
79/0 ATLF / Colour
98/9 BOST / Alumni 3
80/1 O-Pee-Chee 22
80 Olympic USA
94/5 SR Miracle 9,10, ✍ 9,10
80/1 Topps 22

CRAIG, MIKE
91/2 Bowman 130
92/3 Bowman 334
01/2 Cleveland Barons
94/5 DALL / Cap
93/4 Donruss 81
92/3 Fleer Ultra 317
93/4 Fleer Ultra 297
00/1 Hershey Bears
98/9 Kentucky Tho'blades
99/0 Kentucky Tho'blades
93/4 Leaf 88
94/5 Leaf 510
91/2 O-Pee-Chee 187
92/3 O-Pee-Chee 103
90/1 OPC Premier 19
89/0 Oshawa Generals
97/8 Pacific CC 105
92/3 Panini Sticker 95
93/4 Panini Sticker 271
94/5 Panini Sticker 228
91/2 Parkhurst 301
92/3 Parkhurst 314
93/4 Parkhurst 323
94/5 Parkhurst 54
91/2 Pinnacle 219
92/3 Pinnacle 99
93/4 Pinnacle 314
94/5 Pinnacle 399
94/5 POG 231
93/4 Power Play 322
93/4 Premier 309
94/5 Premier 538
90/1 Pro Set 613
91/2 Pro Set 405
91/2 Pro Set Platinum 189
90/1 Score 59T
91/2 Score 181
91/2 Score CAN 181
92/3 Score 271
93/4 Score 156
97/8 Score Toro. 11
90 7th..Sketch Mem.Cup 90
89/0 7th..Sketch OHL 9
92/3 Topps 238
91/2 To. Stadium 344
92/3 To. Stadium 268
93/4 To. Stadium 355
90/1 Upper Deck 472
91/2 Upper Deck 125
92/3 Upper Deck 65
93/4 Upper Deck 191
94/5 Upper Deck 213
95/6 UD Be A Player 17, ✍ S17

CRAIG, RYAN
98/9 Brandon Wheat Kings
99/0 Brandon Wheat Kings
99/0 UD Prospects 31
00/1 UD Prospects 47

CRAIGDALLIE, MARTY
92/3 BCJHL 66

CRAIGEN, JOE
97/8 Peoria Rivermen
98/9 Peoria Rivermen

CRAIGHEAD, JOHN
91/2 Avant Garde BCJHL 165
02/3 BAP Memorabilia 332
97/8 Cleveland Lumberjacks
99/0 Eishockey 47
93/4 Richmond Renegades
96/7 St. John's Maple Leafs
00/1 UD DEL 238
01/2 UD DEL 214

CRAIGWELL, DALE
92/3 Bowman 198
98/9 DEL 285
95/6 Edge Ice 189
92/3 Fleer Ultra 192
92/3 Kansas City Blades
96/7 Kansas City Blades
00/1 Kudos 153
92/3 O-Pee-Chee 271
89/0 Oshawa Generals
90/1 Oshawa Generals
92/3 Panini Sticker 133
91/2 Parkhurst 389
92/3 Parkhurst 168
93/4 Premier 348
91/2 ProCards 516
92/3 SANJ / Pacific Bell
92/3 Score 466
92 7th...Sketch Awards 2
90 7th..Sketch Mem.Cup 85
89/0 7th..Sketch OHL 4
90/1 7th..Sketch OHL 333
01/2 Sheffield Steelers GS
92/3 Topps 60
92/3 To. Stadium 464
90/1 Upper Deck 464
92/3 Upper Deck 40
93/4 Upper Deck 56
94/5 Upper Deck 380

CRAMERI, GIAN-MARCO
95 Panini Worlds 126

CRAMPTON, STEVE
01/2 Moose Jaw Warriors 8

CRANDALL, CHRIS
83/4 Oshawa Generals

CRANE, BRIAN
93/4 Michigan State

CRANE, COREY
92/3 Sudbury Wolves

CRANE, DERRICK
90/1 7th..Sketch OHL 130
91/2 7th...Sketch OHL 375

CRANE, TODD
95/6 Slapshot 163

CRANLEY, MARK
00/1 Mississauga IceDogs

CRANSTON, SID
82/3 Brandon Wheat Kings

CRANSTON, TIM
94 Semic 320
93/4 Sheffield Steelers 3
94/5 Sheffield Steelers 15
95/6 Sheffield Steelers
97/8 Sheffield Steelers
01/2 Sheffield Steelers

CRASHLEY, BART
99/0 Guelph Storm
72/3 Los Angeles Sharks
72/3 O-Pee-Chee 295
67/8 Topps 105

CRAVEN, MURRAY
98/9 Be A Player 118, ✍ Aut. 118
90/1 Bowman 109
91/2 Bowman 239
92/3 Bowman 280
93/4 Donruss 353
94/5 Donruss 131
95/6 Donruss 46
92/3 Fleer Ultra 71
93/4 Fleer Ultra 439
94/5 Fleer Ultra 223
91/2 HART / Jr. Whalers
92/3 HART / Dairymart
84/5 Kelowna Wings &...
93/4 Leaf 5
94/5 Leaf 121
95/6 Leaf 6
82/3 Medicine Hat Tigers
83/4 Medicine Hat Tigers
83/4 O-Pee-Chee 120
85/6 OPC/Topps 50
86/7 OPC/Topps 167
87/8 OPC/Topps 22
88/9 OPC/Topps 79
88/9 OPC/Topps Box J
90/1 OPC/Topps 318
91/2 O-Pee-Chee 254
92/3 O-Pee-Chee 127
89/0 OPC/Topps 44
92/3 OPC Premier SP3
85/6 OPC Sticker 95-228
86/7 OPC Sticker 244-136
87/8 OPC Sticker 69
88/9 OPC Sticker 98-222
98/9 Pacific 378
97/8 Pacific CC 238
87/8 Panini Sticker 133
88/9 Panini Sticker 130
90/1 Panini Sticker 116
91/2 Panini Sticker 234
92/3 Panini Sticker 262
93/4 Panini Sticker 169
91/2 Parkhurst 288
92/3 Parkhurst 55
92/3 Parkhurst 495
93/4 Parkhurst 208
94/5 Parkhurst 242
95/6 Parkhurst 313
86/7 PHIL
89/0 PHIL
90/1 PHIL
91/2 Pinnacle 177
92/3 Pinnacle 281
93/4 Pinnacle 88
94/5 Pinnacle 291
95/6 Pinnacle 179
96/7 Pinnacle 162
93/4 Power Play 458
93/4 Premier 400
94/5 Premier 47
90/1 Pro Set 214
91/2 Pro Set 175
91/2 Pro Set 393
92/3 Pro Set 60
91/2 Pro Set Platinum 179
90/1 Score 56
92/3 Score 262
91/2 Score CAN 482
92/3 Score 18
93/4 Score 49
94/5 Score 109
95/6 Score 214
96/7 Team Out!
92/3 Topps 248
95/6 Topps 52
91/2 To. Stadium 176
92/3 To. Stadium 442
93/4 To. Stadium 264
94/5 To. Stadium 255
90/1 Upper Deck 6
91/2 Upper Deck 306
92/3 Upper Deck 49
93/4 Upper Deck 410
94/5 Upper Deck 45
95/6 Upper Deck 151
95/6 UD Be A Player 46, ✍ S46
95/6 UD CC 120

CRAWFORD, BOB
83/4 HART / Jr. Whalers
84/5 HART / Jr. Whalers
85/6 HART / Jr. Whalers
84/5 O-Pee-Chee 68
85/6 OPC/Topps 162
84/5 OPC Sticker 197
85/6 OPC Sticker 167-36
84/5 Topps 53
86/7 WASH / Kodak

CRAWFORD, COREY
01/2 Moncton Wildcats 18

CRAWFORD, DEREK
92/3 Dayton Bombers
98/9 New Mexico Scorpions

CRAWFORD, FLOYD
52/3 Bas du Fleuve 45
51/2 Laval Dairy 25

CRAWFORD, GLENN
95/6 Classic 98
94/5 Slapshot / Windsor 8
95/6 Slapshot 411, 438
98/9 Sudbury Wolves 14
95/6 Upper Deck 520

CRAWFORD, JEFF
83/4 Moncton Alpines
81/2 Regina Pats
82/3 Regina Pats
83/4 Regina Pats

CRAWFORD, JOHN
34-43 BeeHive-1 [Bost.]
45-64 BeeHive-2 [Bost.]
40/1 O-Pee-Chee 134

CRAWFORD, KENNETH
52/3 Anonymous 181

CRAWFORD, LOU
85/6 Nova Scotia Oilers
88/9 ProCards / Adirondack
89/0 ProCards AHL 56
90/1 ProCards 138
91/2 ProCards 62
00/1 St. John's Maple Leafs
01/2 St. John's Maple Leafs

CRAWFORD, MARC
97/8 COLO / Denver Post
82/3 Fredericton Express
84/5 Fredericton Express
85/6 Fredericton Express
86/7 Fredericton Express
96/7 Kraft / TT
97/8 Kraft / PB
82/3 O-Pee-Chee 342
95/6 POG 9
82/3 Post [Vanc.]
91/2 ProCards 357
90/1 7th..Sketch OHL 50
92/3 St. John's Maple Leafs
93/4 St. John's Maple Leafs
97/8 Valu-net, ✍ Aut.
81/2 VANC / Silverwood
83/4 VANC
01/2 VANC / Coke

CRAWFORD, RUSTY
83 HHOF Postcard E6
83&87 HHOF 67
23/4 Paulins Candy 70

CRAWFORD, SCOTT
02/3 Peoria Rivermen

CRAWFORD, WAYNE
96/7 Guildford Flames 4

CREAGH, BRENDAN
95/6 Birmingham Bulls
93/4 Greensboro Monarchs
94/5 Greensboro Monarchs

CREAMER, PIERRE
90 7th..Sketch Mem.Cup 50

CREIGHTNEY, NIGEL
92/3 BCJHL 239

CREIGHTON, ADAM
90/1 Bowman 9
91/2 Bowman 394
92/3 Bowman 88
84/5 BUFF / Blue Shield
85/6 BUFF / Blue Shield
86/7 BUFF / Blue Shield
87/8 BUFF / Blue Shield
87/8 BUFF / Won. Bread
88/9 BUFF / Won. Bread
89/0 CHIC / Coke
90/1 CHIC / Coke
93/4 Donruss 326
95/6 Donruss 336
94/5 Fleer 185
92/3 Fleer Ultra 409
91/2 Kraft 47
93/4 Leaf 85
90/1 OPC/Topps 83
91/2 O-Pee-Chee 314
92/3 O-Pee-Chee 85
89/0 O-Pee-Chee 218
91/2 OPC Premier 171
92/3 OPC Premier 61
81/2 Ottawa 67's
82/3 Ottawa 67's
83/4 Ottawa 67's
87/8 Panini Sticker 31
88/9 Panini Sticker 225
89/0 Panini Sticker 51
90/1 Panini Sticker 193
91/2 Panini Sticker 13
92/3 Panini Sticker 204
93/4 Panini Sticker 215
96/7 Panini Sticker 209
91/2 Parkhurst 113
92/3 Parkhurst 172
94/5 Parkhurst 222
95/6 Parkhurst 444
91/2 Pinnacle 82
92/3 Pinnacle 199
93/4 Pinnacle 272
96/7 Pinnacle 80
95/6 POG 234
90/1 Pro Set 50
91/2 Pro Set 42
92/3 Pro Set 437
92/3 Pro Set 103
91/2 Puck / Pro Set 17
90/1 Score 82
92/3 Score 265
91/2 Score 21T
91/2 Score CAN 485
92/3 Score 144
93/4 Score 86
95/6 Score 283
92/3 TAMP / Sheraton Inn
93/4 TAMP / Kash N' Karry
94/5 TAMP / Sky Box
92/3 Topps 451
91/2 To. Stadium 89
92/3 To. Stadium 45
93/4 To. Stadium 5
94/5 To. Stadium 23
90/1 Upper Deck 4
91/2 Upper Deck 254
92/3 Upper Deck 311
94/5 Upper Deck 348
95/6 Upper Deck 375
95/6 UD Be A Player 142, ✍ S142
95/6 UD CC 229

CREIGHTON, DAVE
45-64 BeeHive-2 [Bost.]
45-64 BeeHive-2 [Bost.]
45-64 BeeHive-2 [Toro.]
52/3 Parkhurst 76
53/4 Parkhurst 85
54/5 Parkhurst 58
60/1 Parkhurst 10
93/4 Parkie 56-57 99
57/8 Topps 66

CRESDAL, MIKE
99/0 Ottawa 67's

CRESSMAN, GLEN
52/3 Anonymous 127

CRESSMAN, MATT
93/4 W. Michigan Broncos

CRETTENAND, YVES
92 Semic Sticker 232
93 Semic Sticker 260

CRHA, JIRI
81/2 O-Pee-Chee 315
81/2 OPC Sticker 106
79 Panini Sticker 75
80/1 Pepsi Bottle Cap
79/0 TORO
80/1 TORO
73/4 Williams Finnish 45

CRICHTON, CORY
88/9 Kamloops Blazers

CRIMIN, DEREK
91/2 Air Canada SJHL 27
91/2 Air Canada SJHL B45
00/1 Asheville Smoke
97/8 Charlotte Checkers
92/3 MPS SJHL 65

CRISP, TERRY
77/8 CALG / Red Rooster
91/2 Canada Nationals
70/1 Eddie Sargent 182
71/2 Eddie Sargent 179
72/3 Eddie Sargent 128
70/1 Esso Power Player
74/5 Loblaws
85/6 Moncton G'Flames
85/6 Moncton G'Flames
86/7 Moncton G'Flames
71/2 O-Pee-Chee 127
72/3 O-Pee-Chee 88
74/5 O-Pee-Chee 352
75/6 O-Pee-Chee 337
80/1 Soo Greyhounds
81/2 Soo Greyhounds
82/3 Soo Greyhounds
83/4 Soo Greyhounds
84/5 Soo Greyhounds
68/9 Shirriff / SLou. 10
71/2 SLOU
92/3 TAMP / Sheraton Inn
94/5 TAMP / Sky Box
95/6 TAMP / Sky Box
72/3 Topps 103
71/2 Toronto Sun Photo

CRISP, TONY
87/8 Kitchener Rangers

CRISTENSEN, TERRY
00/1 Kudos 87

CRISTOFOLI, ED
89/0 ProCards AHL 194
90/1 ProCards 72

CROCE, PAT
86/7 PHIL

CROCKER, COREY
95/6 Slapshot 312

CROCKETT, KEN
91/2 Avant Garde BCJHL 31

CROCOCK, ROB
83/4 Belleville Bulls

CROGHAN, MAURICE
37/8 World Wide Gum 103

CROMBEEN, MIKE
83/4 HART / Jr. Whalers
84/5 HART / Jr. Whalers
83/4 O-Pee-Chee 312
83/4 OPC/Topps Sticker 126
82/3 Post [SLou.]
78/9 SLOU

CROMBIE, CHRIS
89/0 7th..Sketch OHL 30
90/1 7th..Sketch OHL 131
91/2 7th...Sketch OHL 374

CRONAN, EARL
96/7 Fredericton Canadiens

CRONIN, SHAWN
90/1 Bowman 128
95/6 Fort Wayne Komets
92/3 OPC Premier 42
90/1 Panini/WPG 6
91/2 Parkhurst 423
92/3 PHIL / UD Sheet
92/3 PHIL / J.C. Penney
90/1 Pro Set 559
91/2 Pro Set 268
88/9 ProCards / Baltimore
92/3 SANJ / Pacific Bell
91/2 Score CAN 423
92/3 Score 366
92/3 Topps 489
92/3 To. Stadium 471
91/2 Upper Deck 478
89/0 WINN / Safeway
90/1 WINN / IGA
91/2 WINN / IGA

CROOK, KEN
88/9 Brockville Braves

CROOP, J.
88/9 ProCards / Utica

CROSS, CORY
93/4 Atlanta Knights
94/5 Atlanta Knights 21
98/9 Be A Player 128, ✍ Aut. 128
94/5 Cla. Images 88
95/6 Leaf 275
99/0 Pacific 386
01/2 Pacific 363
97/8 Pa. Invincible R-184
96/7 Pi. Be A Player 143, ✍ Aut. 143
95/6 TAMP / Sky Box
95/6 Topps 44
94/5 Upper Deck 340
97/8 Upper Deck 365
00/1 Upper Deck 396

CROSS, NICK
96/7 Guildford Flames 12

CROSSMAN, DOUG
90/1 Bowman 115
81/2 CHIC
82/3 CHIC
83/4 CHIC
92/3 Fleer Ultra 410
90/1 HART / Jr. Whalers
90/1 Kraft 10
88/9 LOSA / Smokey
90/1 NYIS
82/3 O-Pee-Chee 63
83/4 O-Pee-Chee 263
84/5 O-Pee-Chee 157
87/8 OPC/Topps 182
88/9 OPC/Topps 197
90/1 OPC/Topps 72
91/2 O-Pee-Chee 341
92/3 OPC Premier 59
86/7 OPC Sticker 237-107
88/9 OPC Sticker 100-226
87/8 Panini Sticker 125
90/1 Panini Sticker 91
92/3 Parkhurst 388
93/4 Peoria Rivermen
83/4 PHIL / J.C. Penney
86/7 PHIL
82/3 Post [Chic.]
93/4 Premier 159
90/1 Pro Set 179
92/3 Pro Set 180
90/1 Score 59, 52T
91/2 Score 38
91/2 Score CAN 38
93/4 Score 25
83/4 Souhaits Keychain [Blackhawks]
90/1 Upper Deck 7, 419

CROTEAU, GARY
76/7 COLR / Hockey Talk
79/0 COLR
70/1 Eddie Sargent 141
71/2 Eddie Sargent 133
72/3 Eddie Sargent 48
70/1 Esso Power Player
72/3 Post 12
74/5 Loblaws
70/1 O-Pee-Chee 189
71/2 O-Pee-Chee 17
72/3 O-Pee-Chee 3
73/4 O-Pee-Chee 228
74/5 O-Pee-Chee 36
76/7 O-Pee-Chee 283
77/8 O-Pee-Chee 52
78/9 O-Pee-Chee 362
79/0 O-Pee-Chee 158
72 Semic Sticker 180
71/2 Topps 17
72/3 Topps 83
74/5 Topps 36
77/8 Topps 52
79/0 Topps 158
71/2 Toronto Sun Photo

CROTEAU, PAUL
95/6 Roanoke Express

CROUSE, DUANE
92/3 Tacoma Rockets

CROWDER, BRUCE
83/4 BOST
82/3 O-Pee-Chee 9
83/4 O-Pee-Chee 46
82/3 Post [Bost.]
83/4 Souhaits Keychain [Bruins]

CROWDER, KEITH
83/4 BOST
84/5 BOST
88/9 BOST / Sports Action
89/0 LOSA / Smokey 10
82/3 O-Pee-Chee 10
83/4 O-Pee-Chee 47
84/5 O-Pee-Chee 2
85/6 OPC/Topps 159
86/7 OPC/Topps 130
87/8 OPC/Topps 194
88/9 O-Pee-Chee 206
90/1 O-Pee-Chee 476
89/0 O-Pee-Chee 199
82/3 OPC/Topps Sticker 80
83/4 OPC/Topps Sticker 56
85/6 OPC Sticker 163-33
86/7 OPC Sticker 37
87/8 OPC Sticker 136-245
88/9 OPC Sticker 30
87/8 Panini Sticker 14
88/9 Panini Sticker 178
88/9 Panini Sticker 209
84/5 Topps 2

CROWDER, TROY
98/9 Hershey Bears
90/1 NJER
91/2 O-Pee-Chee 374
91/2 OPC Premier 169
97/8 Pa. Dynagon BKS-96
90/1 Pro Set 620
90/1 Score 43T
91/2 Score 52T
91/2 Score CAN 602
90/1 Upper Deck 441
91/2 Upper Deck 342
96/7 VANC / IGA

CROWDER, TROY
02/3 Fleer Throwbacks 33

CROWE, PHIL
98/9 Cincinnati Cyclones
96/7 Detroit Vipers
97/8 Detroit Vipers
98/9 Detroit Vipers
93/4 Donruss 446
99/0 Milwaukee Admirals
97/8 Pa. Dynagon BKS-65
92/3 Phoenix Roadrunners

CROWE, RICK
91/2 Avant Garde BCJHL 3

CROWIE, ROB
98/9 DEL 155

CROWLEY, JOE
93/4 Indianapolis Ice
91/2 7th...Sketch LHJMQ 203

CROWLEY, MIKE
98/9 Cincinnati M'Ducks 15
94/5 Minnesota G'Gophers
98/9 Pacific 47
98/9 Upper Deck 8
98/9 UD G. Reserve 8
98/9 UD MVP 5

CROWLEY, TED
96/7 Cincinnati Cyclones
92/3 Classic Prospects 112
99/0 Cleveland Lumberjacks
93/4 Fleer Ultra 480
98/9 Hershey Bears
94/5 Parkhurst 93
93/4 Power Play 500
93/4 Premier - USA Hockey 12
94/5 Score 233
97/8 Springfield Falcons
92/3 St. John's Maple Leafs
93/4 To. Stadium - Team U.S.A. 3
94/5 Upper Deck 442
00/1 UD DEL 116
01/2 UD DEL 64

CROWTHER, CORY
92/3 BCJHL 103

CROZIER, GREG
02/3 Albany River Rats
01/2 Providence Bruins
01/2 SPx 96
01/2 Upper Deck 204
01/2 Victory 385
00/1 WBS Penguins

CROZIER, JOE
73/4 BUFF
82/3 Kitchener Rangers
51/2 Laval Dairy 3
52/3 St. Lawrence 43
80/1 TORO

CROZIER, ROGER
71/2 Bazooka Panel
01/2 BAP Memor. GT
64-67 BeeHive-3 [Detr.]
02/3 Between the Pipes ✂ DM20, ✂ GT16, HSHSJers 23, VM3
72/3 BUFF
73/4 BUFF
73/4 BUFF / Bells Market
74/5 BUFF
75/6 BUFF / Linnett
93/4 BUFF / Noco
64/5 Coke/Sprite [Detr.]
65/6 Coca-Cola
70/1 Colgate 83
70/1 Dad's Cookies
70/1 Eddie Sargent 26
71/2 Eddie Sargent 27
72/3 Eddie Sargent 32
70/1 Esso Power Player
72/3 Post 3
74/5 Loblaws
68/9 O-Pee-Chee 23
68/9 O-Pee-Chee PS 10
69/0 O-Pee-Chee 55
69/0 O-Pee-Chee 4in1
70/1 O-Pee-Chee 145
70/1 O-Pee-Chee DE 11
71/2 O-Pee-Chee 36
71/2 O-Pee-Chee Book. 5
72/3 O-Pee-Chee 50
73/4 O-Pee-Chee 153
75/6 O-Pee-Chee 350
02/3 Parkhurst ✂ VT17
95/6 Parkie 66-67 56
94/5 Parkie Tall 53, 155, 157, 158, AS-1, TW-5
72 Semic Sticker 165
68/9 Shirriff / Detr. 2
64/5 Topps 47
65/6 Topps 42
66/7 Topps 43
66/7 Topps / Test 43
67/8 Topps 48
68/9 Topps 23
69/0 Topps 55
71/2 Topps 36
72/3 Topps 31
73/4 Topps 108
66/7 Toronto Star Weekend
71/2 Toronto Sun Photo
02/3 Ultimate Memorabilia ✂ CSTW, ✂ EA, ✂ FS, ✂ NO, ✂ RAT, ✂ SCD, ✂ VGJ

CRUICKSHANK, CURTIS
97/8 Bell
97 Bowman 139, BB19, ✍ Aut.
99/0 Hampton Roads
00/1 Rockford IceHogs

CRUICKSHANK, GORD
89/0 ProCards AHL 62

CRUMLEY, CHAD
92/3 MPS SJHL 66

CRUTCHFIELD, NELS
34/5 Sweet Caporal

CRUZ, JOMAR
98/9 Brandon Wheat Kings

CSIPKA, PAVEL
00/1 OFS 162

CSUMRIK, DAVE
00/1 Sudbury Wolves 5

CUCKSEY, DON
91/2 Rayside-Balfour

CUCUZ, SASHA
94/5 Slapshot / Sarnia 26
95/6 Slapshot 179

CUDDIHY, JIMMY
00/1 Shawinigan 13
01/2 Shawinigan 12
02/3 Shawinigan Cataractes

CUDE, WILF
34-43 BeeHive-1 [Mont.]
35-40 Canada Starch
36-39 Diamond Match TT1
36-39 Diamond Match TT2
36-39 Diamond Match TT3
35/6 O-Pee-Chee 73
36/7 O-Pee-Chee 120
37/8 O-Pee-Chee 149
38/9 Quaker Oats
34/5 Sweet Caporal
37/8 World Wide Gum 9

CULHANE, JIM
88/9 ProCards / Binghampton
89/0 ProCards AHL 298
90/1 ProCards 504
91/2 ProCards 454
93/4 W. Michigan Broncos

CULIC, CHET
93/4 Minnesota-Duluth

CULL, DEAN
91/2 Rayside-Balfour
90/1 7th..Sketch OHL 389

CULL, TRENT
90/1 7th..Sketch OHL 281
91/2 7th...Sketch OHL 177
93/4 Slapshot / Kingston 19
94/5 St. John's Maple Leafs
95/6 St. John's Maple Leafs
96/7 St. John's Maple Leafs
02/3 Syracuse Crunch
00/1 WBS Penguins

CULLATON, BRENT
99/0 Florida Everblades
96/7 Kansas City Blades
01/2 UD DEL 77

CULLEN, BARRY
45-64 BeeHive-2 [Toro.]
45-64 BeeHive-2 [Toro.]
45-64 BeeHive-2 [xBrian Cullen's card]
57/8 Parkhurst [Toro.] 21
58/9 Parkhurst 31
58/9 Parkhurst 36
60/1 Parkhurst 32
93/4 Parkie 56-57 120
91/2 Pinnacle 391
60/1 Shirriff 47
59/0 Topps 25
57/8 Toronto Star Photo

CULLEN, BRANDON
00/1 UD Prospects 16

CULLEN, BRIAN
52/3 Anonymous 25
45-64 BeeHive-2 [Toro.]
45-64 BeeHive-2 [NYRa.]
55/6 Parkhurst 13
57/8 Parkhurst [Mont.] 22
57/8 Parkhurst [Toro.] 9
58/9 Parkhurst 50
93/4 Parkie 56-57 118
60/1 Shirriff 99
59/0 Topps 55

CULLEN, DAVID
01/2 BAP Memor. 414
01/2 Crown Royale 164
01/2 Pr. Stock 135
01/2 PS Titanium 163
01/2 PS Titanium Draft 135
01/2 SP Authentic 169
01/2 SPx 121
01/2 Upper Deck 203
01/2 UD Challenge 129
01/2 UD MVP 212
01/2 UD Vintage 293
01/2 Vanguard 125
01/2 Victory 384

CULLEN, JOHN
90/1 Bowman 210
91/2 Bowman 1
92/3 Bowman 194
92/3 Bowman 227
98/9 Cleveland Lumberjacks
93/4 Donruss 334
95/6 Donruss 156
98/9 Dynagon Ice 172
96/7 Flair 87
92/3 Fleer Ultra 72, 419
93/4 Fleer Ultra 20
94/5 Fleer Ultra 348
95/6 Fleer Ultra 309
87/8 Flint Spirits
91/2 HART / Jr. Whalers
91/2 Kraft 24
93/4 Leaf 245
94/5 Leaf 412
95/6 Leaf 181
92/3 McDonald's McD-18
90/1 OPC/Topps 208
91/2 O-Pee-Chee 226
92/3 O-Pee-Chee 104
89/0 OPC/Topps 145
90/1 OPC Premier 20
91/2 OPC Premier 127
89/0 opcSticker 231-92, / FS 13
97/8 Pacific CC 282
97/8 Pa. Dynagon 116, T-53
97/8 Pa. Invincible 130
89/0 Panini Sticker 316
90/1 Panini Sticker 125
91/2 Panini Sticker 314
92/3 Panini Sticker 257
93/4 Panini Sticker 226
97/8 Panini Sticker 107
91/2 Parkhurst 59
92/3 Parkhurst 180
93/4 Parkhurst 473
95/6 Parkhurst 463
94/5 Parkie SE140
91/2 Pinnacle 125
91/2 Pinnacle 391
92/3 Pinnacle 285
93/4 Pinnacle 388
94/5 Pinnacle 397
89/0 PITT / Foodland 9
90/1 PITT / Foodland 10
94/5 PITT / Foodland 7
95/6 POG 248
93/4 Power Play 242
93/4 Premier 479
94/5 Premier 423
90/1 Pro Set 232
91/2 Pro Set 85
91/2 Pro Set 302
91/2 Pro Set CC9
92/3 Pro Set 57
91/2 Pro Set Platinum 175
90/1 Score 164
90/1 Sco. Hot Cards 73
91/2 Score 7
92/3 Score 421
91/2 Score CAN 7
91/2 Score CAN 311
92/3 Score 150
93/4 Score 425
93/4 Score 189
95/6 Score 105
97/8 Score 155
91/2 Score Young Stars 5
92/3 Seasons 45
91 Semic Sticker 72
94/5 SP 91
92/3 Topps 132
95/6 Topps 74
91/2 To. Stadium 289
92/3 To. Stadium 160
93/4 To. Stadium 209
92/3 TORO / Kodak
93/4 TORO / Abalene
93/4 TORO / Black's 16
90/1 Upper Deck 12, 492
91/2 Upper Deck 84
91/2 Upper Deck 235
92/3 Upper Deck 304
92/3 Upper Deck 465
93/4 Upper Deck 395
94/5 Upper Deck 281
95/6 Upper Deck 358
98/9 Upper Deck 365
94/5 UD Be A Player ✍ 105
95/6 UD CC 181
98/9 UD G. Reserve 365

CULLEN, JUSTIN
90/1 Kitchener Rangers
90/1 7th..Sketch OHL 229
91/2 7th...Sketch OHL 95

CULLEN, MATT
99/0 BAP Mem. 159
00/1 BAP Mem. 357
99/0 Cincinnati M'Ducks
01/2 Crown Royale 1
95/6 Do. Elite WJ 33
02/3 First Edition 171
99/0 Millenium 9, ✍ Aut. 9
99/0 NHL Power Play
02/3 O-Pee-Chee 139
97/8 Omega 1
99/0 Omega 1
98/9 Pacific 45
99/0 Pacific 1
00/1 Pacific 2
01/2 Pacific 1
02/3 Pacific 1
02/3 Pacific Complete 157
99/0 Pa. Paramount 1
00/1 Pa. Paramount 3
99/0 Panini Sticker 177
97/8 Score Anah. 5
00/1 Signature 32, ✍ Aut. 73
02/3 Sports Vault 154
00/1 Stadium 91
00/1 Topps 211
02/3 Topps 139
98/9 To. Finest 53
02/3 T. Limited 139
02/3 T. Total 374
98/9 UD Choice 7
98/9 UD3 16, 76, 136
98/9 Upper Deck 32
99/0 Upper Deck 12
00/1 Upper Deck 232
01/2 Upper Deck 234
02/3 Upper Deck 250
98/9 UD G. Reserve 32
99/0 UD G. Reserve 12
01/2 UD Mask 3
99/0 UD MVP 7, ✍ PS
00/1 UD MVP 2
02/3 UD MVP 3
00/1 UD Vintage 3
02/3 UD Vintage 5
99/0 Victory 4
01/2 Victory 4
02/3 Victory 6
99/0 WGretzky 6

CULLEN, RAY
68/9 Bauer Photo
70/1 Colgate 15
70/1 Dad's Cookies
70/1 Eddie Sargent 216
70/1 Esso Power Player
68/9 O-Pee-Chee 54
69/0 O-Pee-Chee 130
69/0 O-Pee-Chee 4in1
69/0 O-Pee-Chee Stamp
70/1 O-Pee-Chee 228
70/1 O-Pee-Chee DE 31
68/9 Shirriff / Minn. 9
68/9 Topps 54
69/0 Topps 130
70/1 VANC / Royal Bank

CULLEN, THOM
97/8 Las Vegas Thunder 8

CULLIMORE, JASSEN
91/2 Arena 22
91/2 Classic 26
91/2 Classic Four Sport 26
94/5 Cla. Images 53
95/6 Donruss 175
95/6 Edge Ice 89
92/3 Hamilton Canucks
94/5 Leaf 488
95/6 Leaf 25
96/7 MONT
96/7 MONT / Export
97/8 Pa. Invincible R-101
99/0 Pa. Paramount 215
94/5 Parkie SE191
91/2 Peterborough Petes
94/5 Premier 477
99/0 Providence Bruins
89/0 7th..Sketch OHL 116
90/1 7th..Sketch OHL 356
91/2 7th...Sketch OHL 146
91/2 Star Pics 71
95/6 Topps 101
91/2 Ultimate Draft Pick 23, ✍ Aut.
91/2 Upper Deck 72
91/2 Upper Deck 690
94/5 Upper Deck 247
01/2 Upper Deck 388
94/5 UD Be A Player ✍ 80
91/2 Upper Deck WJC 64
00/1 UD Vintage 329

CUMMING, SCOTT
85/6 London Knights

CUMMINGS, BURTON
91/2 WINN / IGA

CUMMINGS, DON
28/9 Paulins Candy 52

CUMMINS, BARRY
98/9 Fort Worth Brahmas

CUMMINS, JIM
92/3 Classic 94
92/3 Classic Four Sport 209
94/5 Leaf 434
98/9 Pacific 335
99/0 Pacific 318
01/2 Pacific 2, 401
97/8 Pa. Invincible R-44
98/9 PHOE / Coca-Cola
97/8 Pi. Be A Player 80, ✍ Aut. 80
94/5 TAMP / Sky Box
00/1 To. Heritage 174
93/4 To. Stadium 448

CUMMINS, JIM
02/3 Fleer Throwbacks 45, ✂ 5DTG, ✂ 5SW

CUNNEYWORTH, RANDY
93/4 Donruss 413
92/3 Fleer Ultra 73
94/5 Fleer Ultra 336
89/0 HART / Jr. Whalers
90/1 HART / Jr. Whalers
91/2 HART / Jr. Whalers
92/3 HART / Dairymart
93/4 HART / Coke
89/0 Kraft 48
96/7 Kraft / PB
87/8 OPC/Topps 150
88/9 OPC/Topps 19
90/1 OPC/Topps 67
89/0 OPC/Topps 63
88/9 OPC Sticker 231
94/5 OTTA
95/6 OTTA
96/7 OTTA
97/8 OTTA
97/8 Pacific CC 198
87/8 Panini Sticker 148
88/9 Panini Sticker 337
91/2 Panini Sticker 320
92/3 Panini Sticker 260
96/7 Panini Sticker 55
91/2 Parkhurst 284
95/6 Parkhurst 421
94/5 Pinnacle 406
97/8 Pi. Be A Player 175, ✍ Aut. 175
86/7 PITT / Kodak
87/8 PITT / Kodak
93/4 Premier 423
95/6 Pro Magnet 115
90/1 Pro Set 101
91/2 Pro Set 392
98/9 Rochester Americans
00/1 Rochester Americans
02/3 Rochester Americans
90/1 Score 276
91/2 Score CAN 424
97/8 Score 161
99/0 Topps 142
99/0 To. Chrome 142
93/4 To. Stadium 341
94/5 To. Stadium 38
90/1 Upper Deck 268
96/7 Upper Deck 111
95/6 UD Be A Player 81, ✍ S81
96/7 UD CC 178
89/0 WINN / Safeway

CUNNIFF, DAVID
98/9 Albany River Rats
99/0 Albany River Rats

CUNNIFF, JOHN
96/7 Albany River Rats
97/8 Albany River Rats
98/9 Albany River Rats
99/0 Albany River Rats
00/1 Albany River Rats
72/3 New England Whalers
89/0 NJER
89/0 NJER / Caretta
90/1 NJER
90/1 Pro Set 670

CUNNING, CAM
02/3 Kamloops Blazers

CUNNINGHAM, BOB
98/9 Anchorage Aces
61/2 Shirriff 96

CUNNINGHAM, LES
34-43 BeeHive-1 [Chic.]
39/0 O-Pee-Chee 78

CUNNINGHAM, RICK
72/3 Ottawa Nationals

CURADEAU, MATHIEU
02/3 Val d'Or Foreurs

CURCIO, PATRICK
98/9 DEL 199

CURLEY, BRENDAN
93/4 Hampton Roads
94/5 Hampton Roads
98/9 Hampton Roads

CURLEY, CINDY
94/5 Classic W31

CURRAN, BRIAN
90/1 BUFF / Blue Shield
87/8 OPC/Topps 90
87/8 Panini Sticker 95
90/1 Panini/TOR 4
94/5 Portland Pirates
95/6 Portland Pirates
90/1 Pro Set 277
91/2 ProCards 2
91/2 Rochester Americans DD
91/2 Rochester Americans WPC
88/9 TORO / P.L.A.Y. 26

CURRAN, CHRIS
02/3 Mississauga IceDogs

CURRAN, MIKE
69/0 Mästär Serien 15
72/3 Minn. Fight. Saints
74/5 Minn. Fight. Saints
72 Semic Sticker 118

CURRIE, ALEX
91 C55 Reprint 13
10/1 Imperial
11/2 Imperial 13
12/3 Imperial 32

CURRIE, DAN
92/3 Classic Prospects 150
98/9 DEL 198
95/6 Edge Ice 105
92/3 EDMO / IGA 005
97/8 Fort Wayne Komets
93/4 Phoenix Roadrunners
94/5 Phoenix Roadrunners
88/9 ProCards / Cape Breton
89/0 ProCards AHL 136
90/1 ProCards 222
91/2 ProCards 228
87/8 Soo Greyhounds 2
91/2 Upper Deck 347

CURRIE, DAVID
01/2 Peterborough Petes

CURRIE, GLEN
82/3 Post [Wash.]
83/4 Souhaits Keychain [Capitals]
81/2 WASH
82/3 WASH
84/5 WASH / Pizza Hut

CURRIE, JASON
92/3 Clarkson G'Knights
94/5 Richmond Renegades

CURRIE, SHELDON
81/2 Milwaukee Admirals

CURRIE, TONY
82/3 Fredericton Express
83/4 Fredericton Express
85/6 Fredericton Express
84/5 HART / Jr. Whalers
84/5 Nova Scotia Oilers
80/1 O-Pee-Chee 384
81/2 O-Pee-Chee 292
82/3 O-Pee-Chee 341
78/9 SLOU
81/2 Topps 116 [West]

CURRY, DAVE
83/4 Brandon Wheat Kings
85/6 Brandon Wheat Kings

CURRY, FLOYD
02/3 Parkie - Reprint 151, 164, 188, 215

CURRY, FLOYD (BUSHER)
45-64 BeeHive-2 [Mont.]
77/8 Dernière Heure
48-52 Exhibits [Canadiens]
51/2 La Patrie
43-47 Parade Sportive
51/2 Parkhurst 12
52/3 Parkhurst 7
53/4 Parkhurst 35
54/5 Parkhurst 15
54/5 Parkhurst 89
55/6 Parkhurst 40
55/6 Parkhurst 76
57/8 Parkhurst [Mont.] 20
93/4 Parkie 56-57 78
45-54 Quaker Oats
63/4 Québec Aces

CURTH, CHRISTIAN
94/5 DEL 15
95/6 DEL 130
96/7 DEL 320

CURTIN, LUKE
95/6 Bowman P8
95/6 Cla. Vis. Signings 64, ✍ Aut.
98/9 EBK ECHL All-Star
94/5 Select 153

CURTIS, ?
98/9 Grand Rapids Griffins

CURTIS, JOEL
83/4 Oshawa Generals

CURTIS, PAUL
71/2 Eddie Sargent 77
72/3 Eddie Sargent 85
70/1 Esso Power Player
71/2 O-Pee-Chee 4
72/3 O-Pee-Chee 266
71/2 Toronto Sun Photo

CUSHENAN, IAN
45-64 BeeHive-2 [Mont.]
45-64 BeeHive-2 [NYRa.]
58/9 Parkhurst 24
63/4 Parkhurst 49

CUSSON, CHARLES
87/8 Brockville Braves
88/9 Brockville Braves

CUSTER, HENRY
95/6 Classic ✍ Aut.

CUTHBERT, CHRIS
97/8 Pi. CBC Sports 4

CUTHBERT, RYAN
98/9 Kelowna Rockets
00/1 Kelowna Rockets

CUTTA, JAKUB
00/1 BAP Mem. 406
01/2 O-Pee-Chee 267
00/1 PS Titanium Draft 175
00/1 SPx 172
01/2 Topps 267
00/1 UD Pros&Prosp. 125
99/0 UD Prospects 47

CUTTS, DON
88/9 EDMO / Action 152

CUVELIER, CHRISTIAN
79 Panini Sticker 341

CYPLJAKOV, ALEXANDER
98/9 OFS 376

CYR, DENIS
80/1 CALG
81/2 CALG
82/3 CHIC
83/4 CHIC
79/0 Montréal Juniors B&W
79/0 Montréal Jrs. Colour
82/3 O-Pee-Chee 43
82/3 Post [Calg.]

CYR, GHYSLAIN
79/0 Montréal Juniors B&W

CYR, JEAN-FRANÇOIS
01/2 Victoriaville Tigres 18

CYR, PAUL
91/2 Bowman 20
84/5 BUFF / Blue Shield
85/6 BUFF / Blue Shield
86/7 BUFF / Blue Shield
83 Canada Juniors
90/1 HART / Jr. Whalers
91/2 HART / Jr. Whalers
84/5 Kelowna Wings &...
86/7 O-Pee-Chee 200
91/2 O-Pee-Chee 73
85/6 OPC Sticker 183-52
87/8 Panini Sticker 33
91/2 Panini Sticker 321
90/1 Pro Set 449
91/2 Pro Set 88
91/2 ProCards 100
90/1 Score 72T
91/2 Score CAN 413
91/2 To. Stadium 279
81/2 Victoria Cougars
82/3 Victoria Cougars

CYR, RAYMOND
52/3 Anonymous 81

CYRENNE, CORY
98 Bowman 74
98 Bowman Chrome 74
95/6 Brandon Wheat Kings
01/2 Louisiana Ice Gators
99/0 Manitoba Moose

CYRWUS, STANISLAW
92 Semic Sticker 276

CZACHOVSKI, LUDWIK
74 Hellas MM-Jenkki 94
73/4 Williams Finnish 88

CZAPKA, LUDWIK
89 Semic Sticker 137
92 Semic Sticker 281

CZEPNISHEV, ANDREI
74 Hellas MM-Jenkki 95
69/0 Soviet Stars
70/1 Soviet Stars
71/2 Soviet Stars
73/4 Williams Finnish 89

CZERKAWSKI, MARIUSZ
01/2 Adrenaline 118
01/2 Atomic 59, ✂ GWJ 38
99/0 Aurora 89
00/1 Aurora 88
99/0 BAP Mem. 178
00/1 BAP Mem. 269
01/2 BAP Memor. 289
99/0 Crown Royale 85
01/2 Crown Royale ✂ TT 14
94/5 Donruss 138
95/6 Donruss 21
96/7 Do. Canadian 96
99/0 Dynagon Ice 123
96/7 EDMO
02/3 Exclusive 89, ✂ GWJ 14
94/5 Flair 9
94/5 Fleer 10
94/5 Fleer Ultra 11
95/6 Fleer Ultra 9, AR-2
01/2 Heads Up 59, ✂ JQ 4
00/1 Kraft 25
94/5 Leaf 82
95/6 Leaf 55, SR-17
94/5 L. Limited 29
95/6 McDonald's McD-37
99/0 Millenium 157, ✍ Aut. 157
02/3 MONT
01/2 O-Pee-Chee 10
02/3 O-Pee-Chee 100, Update 100
99/0 Omega 140
98/9 Pacific 279
99/0 Pacific 253
00/1 Pacific 248
01/2 Pacific 244, 415, 434, ✂ GWJ 19
02/3 Pacific 234
02/3 Pacific Complete 220
97/8 Pacific CC 216
98/9 Pa. Paramount 141
99/0 Pa. Paramount 141
00/1 Pa. Paramount 153
95/6 Panini Sticker 5
96/7 Panini Sticker 261
97/8 Panini Sticker 211
99/0 Panini Sticker 94
00/1 Panini Sticker 54
94/5 Parkhurst 20, V55
95/6 Parkhurst 18, 345
00/1 Parkhurst P-105
01/2 Parkhurst 173
02/3 Parkhurst 191
94/5 Parkie SE ES-5
94/5 Pinnacle 246, 467, RTP12
95/6 Pinnacle 185, GG-24
96/7 Pinnacle 167
97/8 Pinnacle 122
96/7 Pi. Be A Player 166, ✍ Aut. 166
95/6 Pi. FANtasy 4
97/8 Pi. Inside 158
95/6 Playoff 117
96/7 Playoff 368
95/6 POG 34
94/5 Premier 293
00/1 Premier Plus 29
99/0 Prism 86
00/1 Pr. Stock 62, ✂ GUG-69
01/2 Pr. Stock ✂ GUG 62
02/3 Pr. Stock Reserve 51
00/1 PS Titanium 58, ✂ GUG 31, ✂ GUG 108
01/2 PS Titanium 86
00/1 PS Titanium Draft ✂ 61
99/0 Revolution 90
00/1 Revolution 91
94/5 Score 227
95/6 Score 143
97/8 Score 208
94/5 Select 190, YE-11
91/2 Semic Elitserien 73
92 Semic Sticker 288
00/1 Signature 86, F-19, ✍ Aut. 111
01/2 Signature 190, ✍ Aut. 190
02/3 Signature Series 108, ✍ 108
95/6 Sisu Limited 63
95/6 SBx Impact Fox 1
94/5 SP 10
96/7 SP 59
00/1 SPx 41
00/1 Stadion 158
99/0 Stadium 130
00/1 Stadium 132, CA9
95/6 Topps 153, 19NG, 7PL
00/1 Topps 114, PP1
01/2 Topps 10
02/3 Topps 100, Update 100
00/1 To. Chrome 88
01/2 To. Chrome 10
02/3 T. Chrome 64
94/5 Topps Finest BBR-20
00/1 To. Heritage 232
02/3 To. Heritage 169
02/3 T. Limited 100
01/2 To.Reserve ✂ TR
00/1 To. Stars 57, ✂ GG
02/3 T. Total 272
00/1 UD Heroes 74
99/0 Ult. Victory 54
94/5 Upper Deck 239, 534, 543, C5, SP-5
95/6 Upper Deck 189, SE-6
99/0 Upper Deck 256
00/1 Upper Deck 110
01/2 Upper Deck 113
02/3 Upper Deck 336
96/7 UD Black Diam. 122
00/1 UD Black Diam. 37
95/6 UD CC 50
96/7 UD CC 93
97/8 UD Coll. Choice 93
99/0 UD G. Reserve 256
99/0 UD MVP 123
00/1 UD MVP 112
01/2 UD MVP 120
00/1 UD Vintage 226
01/2 UD Vintage 160, 165
00/1 Vanguard 62, ✂ DGJ-8
01/2 Vanguard ✂ DGM 18
99/0 Victory 181
00/1 Victory 147
01/2 Victory 219

CZERLINSKI, JAN
95/6 APS 345

D

D'ALESSIO, CORRIE
91/2 ProCards 616

D'AMICO, BRUNO
01/2 Sherbrooke Castors 20

D'AMICO, JOHN
93/4 Action Packed 5

D'AMOUR, CLAUDE
86/7 Sudbury Wolves

D'AMOUR, DOMINIC
01/2 Hull Olympiques 4
02/3 Hull Olympiques
00/1 Rouyn-Noranda 1

D'AMOUR, MARC
85/6 CALG / Red Rooster
86/7 Moncton G'Flames
88/9 ProCards / Hershey
89/0 ProCards AHL 352
91/2 ProCards 264
80/1 Soo Greyhounds
81/2 Soo Greyhounds

D'ARCY, RYAN
92/3 W. Michigan Broncos
93/4 W. Michigan Broncos

D'ASCANIO, JASON
01/2 Drummondville

D'ORSONNENS, MARTIN
92/3 Clarkson G'Knights
92/3 Clarkson G'Knights
94/5 Johnstown Chiefs 7
93/4 Raleigh Icecaps

DABANOVICH, JAMIE
91/2 Knoxville Cherokees

DACHYSHYN, DEAN
83/4 Moncton Alpines
84/5 Nova Scotia Oilers
85/6 Nova Scotia Oilers

DACKELL, ANDREAS
98/9 Aurora 129
99/0 BAP Mem. 111
00/1 BAP Mem. 107
97/8 Donruss 113
96/7 Do. Canadian 134
96/7 Flair 117
96/7 Fl. Ultra 115
95 Globe 44
94/5 Leaf Elit Set 49, GC=2
95/6 Leaf Elit Set 18, C-10
97/8 Limited 137
96/7 Metal Univ. 174
01/2 MONT
02/3 MONT
97/8 Omega 154
96/7 OTTA
97/8 OTTA
98/9 OTTA
99/0 OTTA
00/1 OTTA
98/9 Pacific 308
99/0 Pacific 286
00/1 Pacific 444
02/3 Pacific 193
02/3 Pacific Complete 60
97/8 Pacific CC 278
98/9 Pa. Paramount 162
99/0 Pa. Paramount 161
99/0 Panini Sticker 110
95 Panini Worlds 147
01/2 Parkhurst 219
96/7 Pi. Be A Player 109, ✍ Aut. 109
96/7 Pi. Zenith 121
00/1 Private Stock ✂ GUG 80
00/1 Revolution ✂ GWJ 9
97/8 Score 203
96/7 Select CE 118
95 Semic 70
91/2 Semic Elitserien 51
92/3 Semic Elitserien 64
96/7 SP 109
97/8 SP Authentic 109
99/0 Topps 245
99/0 To. Chrome 245
02/3 T. Total 366
98/9 UD Choice 146
99/0 Ult. Victory 60
96/7 Upper Deck 303
97/8 Upper Deck 323
98/9 Upper Deck 331
00/1 Upper Deck 352
01/2 Upper Deck 323
97/8 UD Coll. Choice 175
95/6 UD Elitserien 36, NA3
98/9 UD G. Reserve 331
00/1 UD MVP 129
02/3 UD Vintage 138
00/1 Vanguard ✂ DGJ 17
01/2 Victory 251
96 Wien 68

DACOSTA, JEFF
00/1 Rockford IceHogs
01/2 Rockford IceHogs
93/4 Slapshot / Kingston 6
95/6 Slapshot 111

DADSWELL, DOUG
87/8 CALG / Red Rooster
90/1 Canada Nationals 2
91/2 Cincinnati Cyclones
92/3 Cincinnati Cyclones
86/7 Moncton G'Flames

DAFFNER, THOMAS
00/1 UD DEL 125
01/2 UD DEL 122

DAFOE, BYRON
01/2 Adrenaline 12, PP
01/2 Atomic 6, ✂ GWJ 3
98/9 Aurora 10, -CF 4
99/0 Aurora 12, Stripe 12, GU-2
00/1 Aurora 12
98/9 Be A Player 6, ✍ Aut. 6
99/0 BAP Mem. 41, H-16
00/1 BAP Mem. 186, ✂ TM-11
01/2 BAP Memor. 47, ✂ GoalJ, ✂ GT
01/2 BT Pipes 8, 106, HSHS, -Mask, ✂ Jers., ✂ S&J, ✂ GT, ✂ HSHSJers
02/3 Between the Pipes 72, ✂ GT4
98/9 Bicycle.. J-C
95/6 Bowman 97, BB23
01/2 Bowman 63
92/3 Classic Prospects 73
99/0 Crown Royale 12
00/1 Crown Royale 9, ✂ GWJ-1
01/2 Crown Royale 9
94/5 Donruss 175
95/6 Donruss 362
96/7 Donruss 221
97/8 Donruss 20
95/6 Do. Elite R-5
97/8 Do. Elite 60
97/8 Do. Preferred 71
97/8 Do. Priority 104, PG-14
98/9 Dynagon Ice 9
99/0 Dynagon Ice 23
02/3 First Edition 7, ✂ Jers.
95/6 Fleer Metal 173
95/6 Fleer Ultra 334
98/9 Hampton Roads
01/2 Heads Up 7, SS 2, ✂ JQ 2
02/3 Heads Up 7, -S 2
99/0 Kraft / JELL-O
94/5 Leaf 283
96/7 Leaf 211
97/8 Limited 63
99/0 Millenium 23, ✍ Aut. 23
01/2 O-Pee-Chee 183
02/3 O-Pee-Chee 45
98/9 OPC Chrome 3
97/8 Omega 14
98/9 Omega 14
99/0 Omega 20
98/9 Pacific 74
99/0 Pacific 22,GC-4, ITCNF-2
00/1 Pacific 32
01/2 Pacific 29, IZ 2, SC 2
02/3 Pacific 25
02/3 Pacific Complete 327
97/8 Pacific CC 141
97/8 Pa. Crown Roy. 9, FO-2
98/9 Pa. Crown Roy. 8
98/9 Pa. Paramount 12, -GS 2
99/0 Pa. Paramount 19, GS-2
00/1 Pa. Paramount 18, GS-1
97/8 Pa. Revolution 8, RTS-2
98/9 Pa. Revolution 9
96/7 Panini Sticker 267
98/9 Panini Sticker 10
99/0 Panini Sticker 23, 351
95/6 Parkhurst 375
00/1 Parkhurst P-163
01/2 Parkhurst 117, ✂ PJ48, ✂ PSJ19, ✂ T4
02/3 Parkhurst 149
02/3 Parkhurst Retro 106
94/5 Phoenix Roadrunners
96/7 Pi. Be A Player 30, ✍ Aut. 30
97/8 Pi. Be A Player STP 15
95/6 Pi. Summit 192
95/6 Pi. Zenith 133
93/4 Portland Pirates
88/9 Portland Winter Hawks
89/0 Portland Winter Hawks
94/5 Premier 42
00/1 Premier Plus 78
99/0 Prism 13
00/1 Private Stock 7
01/2 Pr. Stock -PS 4, ✂ GUG 8
00/1 PS Titanium 5, ✂ GUG-56
01/2 PS Titanium 7
00/1 PS Titanium Draft ✂ 4
91/2 ProCards 548
99/0 Revolution 13, SS-4, / CSC 13
00/1 Revolution 10
96/7 Score 260
97/8 Score 47
97/8 Score Bost. 13
95/6 Select CE 120
00/1 Signature 87, ✍ Aut. 122
01/2 Signature C-3, ✍ Aut. LBD, ✂ GUE5, ✂ GJ5, ✂ GSJ5, ✂ ITN5, ✂ TM3
96/7 SBx Impact 56
95/6 SP 70
98/9 SP Authentic ✍ SotT
00/ 1 SP Authentic ✍ SotT
00/1 SP GU 4, ✂ TotG
01/2 SP GU ✂ TotG (x3), ✂ TotGC (x4), ✂ TotGT
02/3 SP Game-Used ✂ TG
02/3 Sports Vault 10
99/0 SPx 13
98/9 SPx Finite 7
99/0 Stadium 93, GC3
00/1 Stadium 18
95/6 Topps 293
98/9 Topps 3
99/0 Topps 186, NS7, PM2
00/1 Topps 53
01/2 Topps 183
02/3 Topps 45, OTG19, PP5
99/0 To. Chrome 186, PM2
00/1 To. Chrome 43
01/2 To. Chrome 122
99/0 To. Gold Label 52
00/1 To. Gold Label 18
00/1 To. Heritage 140
01/2 To. Heritage 90
02/3 To. Heritage ✂ CP, ✂ CPB
02/3 T. Limited 45
96/7 Topps Picks RS14
99/0 To. Prmr. Plus 37, IG8
00/1 To. Stars 75
98/9 UD Choice 10
00/1 UD Heroes 11
01/2 UD PlayMakers Ltd 9
00/1 UD Reserve 6
00/1 Ultimate Mem. ✂ G-3, ✂GM-18
01/2 Ultimate Mem. ✂ BAPL
94/5 Upper Deck 447
95/6 Upper Deck 460
98/9 Upper Deck 221
99/0 Upper Deck 21, UD1
00/1 Upper Deck 242
01/2 Upper Deck 18
02/3 Upper Deck ✂ SV
96/7 UD Black Diam. 65
99/0 UD Black Diam. 8
00/1 UD Black Diam. ✂ GG
97/8 UD Coll. Choice 128
98/9 UD G. Reserve 221
99/0 UD G. Reserve 21
96/7 UD Ice 31
01/2 UD Mask 103, 171, ✂ GP, ✂ GG, ✂ MM, ✂ SuS
02/3 UD Mask 3, 4, 5, 6, 7, 108, ✂ CW
98/9 UD MVP 14
99/0 UD MVP 17, LL4
00/1 UD MVP 19
01/2 UD MVP ✂ GS
99/0 UD MVP Cup 19
02/3 UD Premier 4
01/2 UD Top Shelf 80, ✂ GG-LP
02/3 UD Top Shelf ✂ ST, ✂ SS, ✂ TS
00/1 UD Vintage 33, 36, 37, GG2
01/2 UD Vintage 20, 26
00/1 Vanguard ✂ DGJ 13
01/2 Vanguard 5, SW 2
02/3 Vanguard 4
99/0 Victory 25, 382
00/1 Victory 21
01/2 Victory 24, 33
97/8 Zenith 40

DAFOE, KYLE
98/9 Sudbury Wolves 12
99/0 Sudbury Wolves 5

DAGENAIS, EMILE
52/3 Laval Dairy Update 106
52/3 St. Lawrence 67

DAGENAIS, ÉRIC
01/2 Drummondville
00/1 Sherbrooke Castors 11
01/2 Sherbrooke Castors 2

DAGENAIS, MIKE
92/3 Cincinnati Cyclones
93/4 Cleveland Lumberjacks
90/1 ProCards 407
91/2 ProCards 528
89/0 7th..Sketch OHL 102

DAGENAIS, PIERRE
98/9 Albany River Rats
99/0 Albany River Rats
00/1 Albany River Rats
00/1 BAP Mem. 517
01/2 BAP Memor. 155, ✂ 481
98 Bowman 100
98 Bowman Chrome 100
01/2 O-Pee-Chee 281
01/2 Parkhurst 378
97/8 Pi. BeeHive 74, ✍ Aut. 74
99/0 Rouyn-Noranda
01/2 Signature 250, ✍ Aut. 250
01/2 Stadium 117
01/2 Topps 281
01/2 Victory 379

DAHL,
92/3 Semic Nordisk 187 [Årets Rookie]

DAHL, BJÖRN ANDERS
95 Panini Worlds 245

DAHL, BJØRN_A
92/3 Semic Nordisk 110

DAHL, GEIR_TORE
92/3 Semic Nordisk 111

DAHL, KEVIN
92 C.O.A. Winter Olympics 174
92/3 CALG / IGA 023
91/2 Canada Nationals
98/9 Chicago Wolves
98/9 Chicago Wolves Champs
99/0 Chicago Wolves
00/1 Chicago Wolves
92/3 Fleer Ultra 266
93/4 Fleer Ultra 23
96/7 Las Vegas Thunder
92/3 OPC Premier 22
92/3 Parkhurst 261
93/4 Parkhurst 298
93/4 Premier 362
93/4 Score 423
93/4 To. Stadium 432
92/3 Upper Deck 493
01/2 UD DEL 200

#VALUE!
92/3 Semic Nordisk 215 [Rookie]

#VALUE!
90/1 Bowman 176
91/2 Bowman 127
92/3 Bowman 143
94/5 DALL / Cap
02/3 DALL / Southwest
93/4 Donruss 488
93/4 Donruss 78
94/5 Donruss 57
95/6 Donruss 92
96/7 Donruss 115
02/3 First Edition 285
94/5 Flair 161
94/5 Fleer 194
95/6 Fleer Metal 128
92/3 Fleer Ultra 92
93/4 Fleer Ultra 81
94/5 Fleer Ultra 192
95/6 Fleer Ultra 144
95 Globe 48
01/2 Heads Up ✂ JQ 12
95/6 Hoyle / West. 2-Spade
95/6 Kraft / KD
93/4 Leaf 198
94/5 Leaf 25
95/6 Leaf 157
96/7 Leaf 55
94/5 L. Limited 76
89/0 NYRA / Marine
88/9 OPC/Topps 47
90/1 OPC/Topps 12
91/2 O-Pee-Chee 177
92/3 O-Pee-Chee 129
02/3 O-Pee-Chee 52
89/0 OPC/Topps 2
88/9 OPC Stars 7
88/9 OPC Sticker 128-260
88/9 OPC Sticker 126-258
00/1 Pacific 450
01/2 Pacific 391
02/3 Pacific 389
02/3 Pacific Complete 475
97/8 Pacific CC 74
88/9 Panini Sticker 305
89/0 Panini Sticker 288
91/2 Panini Sticker 110
92/3 Panini Sticker 92
93/4 Panini Sticker 270
94/5 Panini Sticker 221
95/6 Panini Sticker 281
96/7 Panini Sticker 283
97/8 Panini Sticker 130
99/0 Panini Sticker 164
00/1 Panini Sticker 105
95 Panini Worlds 286
91/2 Parkhurst 76
92/3 Parkhurst 310
93/4 Parkhurst 322
94/5 Parkhurst 215
95/6 Parkhurst 245, 452
94/5 Parkie SE ES-6
91/2 Pinnacle 152
92/3 Pinnacle 68
93/4 Pinnacle 248
94/5 Pinnacle 48, WE4
95/6 Pinnacle 13
96/7 Pi. Be A Player 35, ✍ Aut. 35
95/6 Pi. Summit 15
95/6 Pi. Zenith 7
95/6 Playoff 190
94/5 POG 63
95/6 POG 228
93/4 Power Play 59
93/4 Premier 75
94/5 Premier 299
00/1 Private Stock ✂ GUG 103
00/1 PS Titanium Draft ✂ 99
95/6 Pro Magnet 118
90/1 Pro Set 136
91/2 Pro Set 106
91/2 Pro Set 607
92/3 Pro Set 80
91/2 Pro Set Platinum 186
90/1 Score 22
91/2 Score 164
91/2 Score CAN 164
92/3 Score 330
93/4 Score 107
93/4 Score IS 13
95/6 Score 137
96/7 Score 234
97/8 Score 252
94/5 Select 123
95/6 Select CE 25
93 Semic Sticker 34
95/6 SBx Emotion 154
95/6 SBx Impact 146
02/3 Sports Vault 203
95/6 Super Sticker 109
92/3 Topps 28
95/6 Topps 227
00/1 Topps 270
02/3 Topps 52
02/3 T. Limited 52
91/2 To. Stadium 55
92/3 To. Stadium 207
93/4 To. Stadium 238
93/4 To. Stadium 428
94/5 TSC Members Only 42
90/1 Upper Deck 283
91/2 Upper Deck 348
92/3 Upper Deck 250
93/4 Upper Deck 360
94/5 Upper Deck 16, SP-70
95/6 Upper Deck 381, SE-72
95/6 UD CC 297
96/7 UD CC 243
97/8 UD Coll. Choice 48
98/9 UD Elitserien 116
01/2 UD Mask 98
00/1 Vanguard ✂ DGJ 17
96 Wien 60

DAHLENE, OLE_P
92/3 Semic Nordisk 82

DAHLIN, KJELL
86/7 Kraft Sports 23
85/6 MONT
85/6 MONT / Provigo
86/7 MONT
87/8 MONT
87/8 MONT / Vachon 39
87/8 MONT / Vachon 40
86/7 OPC/Topps 15
86/7 O-Pee-Chee 262
86/7 OPC Sticker 18
86/7 OPC Sticker 126-112
87/8 OPC Sticker 14-153
89/0 Semic Elitserien 88
90/1 Semic Elitserien 262
91/2 Semic Elitserien 95
92/3 Semic Elitserien 123

DAHLMAN, TONI
01/2 BAP Memor. 335
02/3 Calder 86
00/1 Cardset 156
02/3 Cardset 11
01/2 Grand Rapids Griffins
02/3 Pacific Complete 526
01/2 SPx 211
01/2 UD PlayMakers Ltd 132
01/2 UD Premier 74

DAHLQUIST, CHRIS
91/2 Bowman 128
92/3 Bowman 359
92/3 CALG / IGA 024
95/6 Cincinnati Cyclones
92/3 Fleer Ultra 267
96/7 Las Vegas Thunder
94/5 Leaf 386
90/1 O-Pee-Chee 528
91/2 O-Pee-Chee 142
92/3 O-Pee-Chee 22
92/3 OPC Premier 38
94/5 OTTA
92/3 Pinnacle 167
93/4 Pinnacle 414
94/5 Pinnacle 402
87/8 PITT / Kodak
95/6 POG 197
90/1 Pro Set 464
91/2 Pro Set 408
91/2 Score 365
91/2 Score CAN 404
92/3 Score 294
93/4 Score 314
92/3 Topps 231
91/2 To. Stadium 314
92/3 To. Stadium 57
93/4 To. Stadium 266
91/2 Upper Deck 307

DAHLSTROM, CULLY
34-43 BeeHive-1 [Chic.]
36-39 Diamond Match BH TT
36-39 Diamond Match BH BT
39/0 O-Pee-Chee 46
40/1 O-Pee-Chee 137

DAHLSTRÖM, LARS
94/5 Leaf Elit Set 94
91/2 Semic Elitserien 293
92/3 Semic Elitserien 321
97/8 UD Elitserien 178

DAHLSTRÖM, OLE ESKILD
94 Semic 259
92 Semic Sticker 41
93 Semic Sticker 240

DAHLSTRØM,
92/3 Semic Nordisk 201 [Draften Av NHL]

DAHLSTRØM, OLE_ESKILD
92/3 Semic Nordisk 34

DAHLSTRØM, PÅL
92/3 Semic Nordisk 41

DAIGLE, ALEXANDRE
98/9 Aurora 136
00/1 BAP Mem. 349
02/3 BAP Memorabilia 140
95/6 Bicycle Sports Aces 4-Diamond
93/4 Classic 1
93/4 Classic 114
93/4 Classic 34
93/4 Classic 50
93/4 Classic 51
93/4 Classic 52
93/4 Classic 53
93/4 Classic 54
93/4 Classic N1
93/4 Classic - Top Ten DP1
93/4 Cla. 4 Sport 185
93/4 Cla. 4 Sport - Acetate 11
93/4 Cla. 4 Sport DS58
93/4 Cla. 4 Sport LP22
93/4 Cla. 4 Sport PP18
93/4 Cla. 4 Sport TC4
93/4 Cla. Images 4 Sport 4
93/4 Cla. Images 4 Sport CC14
93/4 Cla. Prospects 13
93/4 Donruss 237
93/4 Donruss 393
93/4 Donruss P
93/4 Donruss ES 2
93/4 Donruss RR 1
94/5 Donruss 211
95/6 Donruss 160, C3TWC-16
96/7 Donruss 204
97/8 Donruss 78
96/7 Do. Canadian 104
97/8 Do. Canadian 122, NP-15
96/7 Do. Elite 84
97/8 Do. Elite 24
97/8 Do. Preferred 48
97/8 Do. Priority 22
97/8 Do. Studio 92
93/4 Durivage 1
98/9 Dynagon Ice 134
94/5 Flair 120, SP-2
94/5 Fleer 143
95/6 Fleer Metal 104
93/4 Fleer Ultra 380
93/4 Fleer Ultra WotF 3
94/5 Fleer Ultra 146, ARS-3
95/6 Fleer Ultra 111, HS-6, RS-2
96/7 Fl. Ultra 116
93/4 Hockey Wit 91
95/6 Hoyle / East. 9-Heart
93/4 Kraft / KD
95/6 Kraft / IP, KD
93/4 Leaf 311
93/4 Leaf FP 1
93/4 Leaf SSS 9
94/5 Leaf 119, GLR-5
95/6 Leaf 179
96/7 Leaf 80
97/8 Leaf 26
94/5 L. Limited 87
95/6 L. Limited 38
97/8 Limited 161
96/7 Maggers 110
94/5 McDonald's McD-36
95/6 McDonald's McD-38
96/7 Metal Univ. 105
99/0 Omega 147
93/4 OTTA
94/5 OTTA
95/6 OTTA
96/7 OTTA
97/8 OTTA
98/9 Pacific 323
99/0 Pacific 387
00/1 Pacific 258
02/3 Pacific Complete 398
97/8 Pacific CC 250, TC-17
97/8 Pa. Crown Roy. 90
97/8 Pa. Dynagon 84, T-54
97/8 Pa. Invincible 93, FP-23
97/8 Pa. Paramount 124
98/9 Pa. Paramount 170
97/8 Pa. Revolution 99
94/5 Panini Sticker 101
95/6 Panini Sticker 47
96/7 Panini Sticker 45
97/8 Panini Sticker 38
98/9 Panini Sticker 93
93/4 Parkhurst 244
93/4 Parkhurst C1
93/4 Parkhurst D11
93/4 Parkhurst F1
93/4 Parkhurst G6
93/4 Parkhurst E3
94/5 Parkhurst 285, V42
95/6 Parkhurst 150
94/5 Parkie SE119
97/8 PHIL / Comcast
93/4 Pinnacle 236, SR1, ✍ 236
94/5 Pinnacle 2, 461, 531, GR6, NL6
95/6 Pinnacle 7
96/7 Pinnacle 133
97/8 Pinnacle 159
97/8 Pi. Certified 98
95/6 Pi. FANtasy 3
97/8 Pi. Inside 109
95/6 Pi. Summit 21
96/7 Pi. Summit 106
97/8 Pi. Totally 98
95/6 Pi. Zenith 22
95/6 Playoff 73, 178
94/5 POG 353
95/6 POG 190
93/4 Power Play 396
93/4 Power Play RooS 3
93/4 Premier 405
93/4 Premier - Finest 1
94/5 Premier 140, 195, OF-7
95/6 Pro Magnet 112
93/4 Score 496
93/4 Score 587
93/4 Score/CAN DD3
94/5 Score 248, DT21, TF16
95/6 Score 18
96/7 Score 66
97/8 Score 101
94/5 Select 3
95/6 Select CE 22
91/2 7th...Sketch LHJMQ 270
95/6 SBx Emotion 123
95/6 SBx Impact 118
96/7 SBx Impact 88
94/5 SP 81, 136
95/6 SP 103
96/7 SP 106
97/8 SP Authentic 107
98/9 SPx Finite 61
95/6 Super Sticker 86
95/6 Topps 342, 5CJ, HGC14
94/5 Topps Finest 88, 155
98/9 To. Finest 24
93/4 To. Stadium 300
94/5 To. Stadium 110
95/6 To. Stadium 97
93/4 TSC Members Only 50
95/6 T. Super Skills 24
98/9 UD Choice 148
02/3 Ultimate Memorabilia ✂ FO
92/3 Upper Deck 587
93/4 Upper Deck 170, 250, E15, R3, SP-107
94/5 Upper Deck 87, IG10, SP-54
95/6 Upper Deck 271, SE-60
96/7 Upper Deck 302
97/8 Upper Deck 117
98/9 Upper Deck 144
02/3 Upper Deck 389
93/4 Upper Deck Be A Player 3
94/5 UD Be A Player R30
95/6 UD Be A Player 188, ✍ S188
96/7 UD Black Diam. 91
94/5 UD Canada Junior 4
95/6 UD CC 208
96/7 UD CC 180, 324
97/8 UD Coll. Choice 174, SQ25
98/9 UD G. Reserve 144
98/9 UD MVP 189
99/0 Victory 277

DAIGLE, CHRISTIAN
99 Bowman 79
97 Bowman 79

DAIGLE, R. ALAIN
79/0 CHIC
75/6 O-Pee-Chee 394
76/7 O-Pee-Chee 156
77/8 O-Pee-Chee 208
78/9 O-Pee-Chee 117
79/0 O-Pee-Chee 227
76/7 Topps 156
77/8 Topps 208
78/9 Topps 117
79/0 Topps 227

DAIGLE, SYLVAIN
96/7 Mississippi S'Wolves
99/0 Mississippi S'Wolves
97/8 Springfield Falcons

DAIGNEAULT, J-J
98/9 Be A Player 76, ✍ 76
92/3 Bowman 371
00/1 Cleveland Lumberjacks
92/3 Durivage 35
93/4 Durivage 10
92/3 Fleer Ultra 326
93/4 Fleer Ultra 351
93/4 Leaf 437
94/5 Leaf 407
89/0 MONT
89/0 MONT / Kraft
90/1 MONT
91/2 MONT
92/3 MONT
92/3 MONT / OPC 25
93/4 MONT
94/5 MONT
91/2 O-Pee-Chee 456
92/3 O-Pee-Chee 304
97/8 Pa. Dynagon BKS-1
90/1 Panini/MTL 7
91/2 Panini Sticker 192
91/2 Parkhurst 312
92/3 Parkhurst 324
93/4 Parkhurst 377
95/6 Parkhurst 442
86/7 PHIL
93/4 Pinnacle 311
94/5 Pinnacle 224
96/7 Pi. Be A Player 34, ✍ Aut. 34
95/6 Playoff 163
96/7 Playoff 377
95/6 POG 153
93/4 Power Play 367
93/4 Premier 372
90/1 Pro Set 466
91/2 Pro Set 124
88/9 ProCards / Hershey
88/9 ProCards / Sherbrooke
91/2 Score CAN 520
92/3 Score 311
93/4 Score 299
97/8 Score 254
97/8 Score Anah. 8
92/3 Topps 334
92/3 To. Stadium 308
93/4 To. Stadium 475
94/5 To. Stadium 52
91/2 Upper Deck 170
92/3 Upper Deck 331
94/5 Upper Deck 341
97/8 Upper Deck 212
98/9 Upper Deck 305
98/9 UD G. Reserve 305
84/5 VANC
85/6 VANC
99/0 WGretzky 133

DAIGNEAULT, MAXIME
00/1 Val d'Or Foreurs 19
01/2 Val d'Or Foreurs 20
02/3 Val d'Or Foreurs

DAIGNEAULT, PAUL
90/1 7th..Sketch LHJMQ 171

DAILEY, BOB
74/5 Loblaws
74/5 O-Pee-Chee 240
75/6 O-Pee-Chee 231
76/7 O-Pee-Chee 350
77/8 O-Pee-Chee 98
78/9 O-Pee-Chee 131
79/0 O-Pee-Chee 226
80/1 O-Pee-Chee 131
81/2 O-Pee-Chee 241
74/5 Topps 240
75/6 Topps 231
77/8 Topps 98
78/9 Topps 131
79/0 Topps 226
80/1 Topps 131
81/2 Topps 104 [East]
73/4 VANC / Royal Bank
74/5 VANC / Royal Bank
75/6 VANC / Royal Bank
76/7 VANC / Royal Bank

DAILEY, JASON
99/0 Charlotte Checkers
98/9 Roanoke Express

DAINVILLE, BOB
52/3 St. Lawrence 89

DAIRON, MICHAEL
92/3 BCJHL 123

DALE, ANDREW
99/0 Mississippi S'Wolves
93/4 Slapshot / Sudbury 12
94/5 Slapshot / Sudbury 11
95/6 Slapshot 142, 394
97/8 Springfield Falcons
93/4 Sudbury Wolves

DALENE, GEIR
92/3 Semic Nordisk 228

DALEY, JOE
70/1 Eddie Sargent 17
71/2 Eddie Sargent 62
68/9 O-Pee-Chee 188
69/0 O-Pee-Chee 152
71/2 O-Pee-Chee 137
74/5 OPC WHA 38
75/6 OPC WHA 101
76/7 O-Pee-Chee WHA 5
76/7 OPC WHA 20
76/7 OPC WHA 61
77/8 OPC WHA 9
71/2 Toronto Sun Photo
78/9 Winnipeg Jets

DALEY, JOHN
93/4 Johnstown Chiefs 21

DALEY, TREVOR
00/1 UD Prospects 26

DALGARNO, BRAD
93/4 Donruss 197
93/4 Fleer Ultra 364
93/4 Leaf 320
89/0 O-Pee-Chee 246
92/3 Parkhurst 336
93/4 Parkhurst 393
93/4 Pinnacle 333
94/5 Pinnacle 238
94/5 POG 153
93/4 Premier 223
90/1 Pro Set 482
93/4 Score 374
91/2 To. Stadium 371
93/4 To. Stadium 167
94/5 To. Stadium 259
93/4 Upper Deck 219
95/6 UD Be A Player 10, ✍ S10

DALLAIRE, DANY
00/1 Halifax Moosehead

DALLAIRE, STACY
90/1 7th..Sketch LHJMQ 172
91/2 7th...Sketch LHJMQ 147

DALLAS, DARCY
93/4 N. Michigan Wildcats

DALLIDAY, DAVID
00/1 Mississauga IceDogs
01/2 Owen Sound Attack

DALLMAN, KEVIN
99/0 Guelph Storm
01/2 Guelph Storm
01/2 Guelph Storm M-Cup

DALLMAN, MARTY
95 Globe 187
88/9 ProCards / Newmarket
94 Semic 250

DALLMAN, ROD
84/5 Prince Albert Raiders
88/9 ProCards / Springfield
89/0 ProCards AHL 245
91/2 ProCards 278

DALMAD, DUNCAN
95/6 Slapshot 159

DALMAN, DADDY
23/4 Paulins Candy 13

DALPIAZ, KLAUS
95/6 DEL 361
96/7 DEL 184
98/9 DEL 308
95 Globe 181
94 Panini Olympics 326
95 Panini Worlds 257
94 Semic 231
93 Semic Sticker 270
96 Wien 210

DALTON, RAY
98/9 Québec Remparts

DAM, TREVOR
92/3 Indianapolis Ice
86/7 London Knights
90/1 ProCards 403
91/2 ProCards 483
89/0 7th..Sketch OHL 25

DAME, BUNNY
34-43 BeeHive-1 [Mont.]

DAME, GEORGE
28/9 Paulins Candy 83

DAMEWORTH, CHAD
96/7 Johnstown Chiefs
93/4 N. Michigan Wildcats

DAMGAARD, JESPER
01/2 UD DEL 215
97/8 UD Elitserien 138
98/9 UD Elitserien 153

DAMPHOUSSE, JEAN-FRANÇOIS
99/0 Albany River Rats
00/1 Albany River Rats
01/2 Albany River Rats
01/2 BT Pipes 90
02/3 Between the Pipes 79
97 Bowman 160, ✍ Aut.
98/9 Collection Souvenir 18
02/3 O-Pee-Chee 313
01/2 PS Titanium 83
01/2 PS Titanium Draft 147
02/3 Topps 313
02/3 T. Limited 313
99/0 Victory 375

DAMPHOUSSE, VINCENT
98/9 Aurora 93
99/0 Aurora 119, Stripe 119
00/1 Aurora 126
02/3 BAP All-Star 16, ✂ ASJ
98/9 Be A Player 217, ✍ Aut. 217
99/0 BAP Mem. 269
00/1 BAP Mem. 270
01/2 BAP Memor. 29
02/3 BAP Memorabilia 167, ✂ AS4
96/7 Bic.Sports Aces 9-H
97/8 Bicycle 8-Diamond
90/1 Bowman 163, -HT 6
91/2 Bowman 170
92/3 Bowman 203, 329
01/2 Bowman 104
02/3 Bowman 57
98/9 Bowman's Best 14
99/0 Crown Royale 122
01/2 Crown Royale 123

02/3 Crown Royale 84
95/6 DEL 443
93/4 Donruss 172
94/5 Donruss 226
95/6 Donruss 202
96/7 Donruss 35
97/8 Donruss 173
96/7 Do. Canadian 53
97/8 Do. Canadian 115, NP-29
95/6 Do. Elite 96
97/8 Do. Elite 81
97/8 Do. Preferred 140
97/8 Do. Priority 164
97/8 Do. Studio 76
96/7 Duracell JB15
92/3 Durivage 20
93/4 Durivage 11
98/9 Dynagon Ice 95
99/0 Dynagon Ice 171
93/4 EA Sports 70
91/2 EDMO / IGA
02/3 Exclusive 148
02/3 First Edition 122, 392, ✂ Jers.
94/5 Flair 87
96/7 Flair 47
94/5 Fleer 103
96/7 Fleer 53
95/6 Fleer Metal 76
96/7 Fl. Picks 36
92/3 Fleer Ultra 103
93/4 Fleer Ultra 79
94/5 Fleer Ultra 107
95/6 Fleer Ultra 80
96/7 Fl. Ultra 86
00 Gatorade Sticker
96/7 Got-Um
93/4 Hockey Wit 72
95/6 Hoyle / East. 10-Heart
89/0 Kraft 35
91/2 Kraft 84
94/5 Kraft / SS
96/7 Kraft / PB
97/8 Kraft / KD, Casecard
98/9 Kraft / KD
93/4 Leaf 4
94/5 Leaf 69
95/6 Leaf 302
96/7 Leaf 79
97/8 Leaf 109
94/5 L. Limited 90
95/6 L. Limited 4
96/7 L. Limited 84
96/7 L. Preferred 25
97/8 Limited 137
96/7 Maggers 88
91/2 McDonald's Mc-16
92/3 McDonald's McD-04
94/5 McDonald's McD-29
97/8 McDonald's McD-21
96/7 Metal Univ. 79
92/3 MONT
92/3 MONT / OPC 38
93/4 MONT
94/5 MONT
95/6 MONT
95/6 MONT / Export
96-98 MONT
01/2 Nextel
98/9 NHL Power Play
87/8 O-Pee-Chee 243
88/9 O-Pee-Chee 207
90/1 OPC/Topps 121, 241
91/2 O-Pee-Chee 299
91/2 Topps - Team Leader 9
92/3 O-Pee-Chee 192
01/2 O-Pee-Chee 222, 323
02/3 O-Pee-Chee 210
89/0 O-Pee-Chee 272
98/9 OPC Chrome 118
90/1 OPC Premier 21
91/2 OPC Premier 104
92/3 OPC Premier 3
87/8 OPC Sticker 128-116
88/9 OPC Sticker 171-40
89/0 opcSticker 179
97/8 Omega 117
98/9 Omega 120
99/0 Omega 204
98/9 Pacific 250
99/0 Pacific 369
00/1 Pacific 356
01/2 Pacific 336, ✂ GWJ 33
02/3 Pacific 332
02/3 Pacific Complete 214
97/8 Pacific CC 25, SS-4B
97/8 Pa. Crown Roy. 68
98/9 Pa. Crown Roy. 68
97/8 Pa. Dynagon 62, T-46, BKS-48
97/8 Pa. Invincible 70, R-102
97/8 Pa. Paramount 94
98/9 Pa. Paramount 112
99/0 Pa. Paramount 203, IAI-24
00/1 Pa. Paramount 212
97/8 Pa. Revolution 70
98/9 Pa. Revolution 72
98/9 Panini Photocard
87/8 Panini Sticker 333
88/9 Panini Sticker 123
89/0 Panini Sticker 134
90/1 Panini Sticker 291
90/1 Panini/TOR 5
91/2 Panini Sticker 92
92/3 Panini Sticker 104
93/4 Panini Sticker 13
94/5 Panini Sticker 14
95/6 Panini Sticker 38
96/7 Panini Sticker 35
97/8 Panini Sticker 29
99/0 Panini Sticker 303
00/1 Panini Sticker 200
91/2 Parkhurst 48
92/3 Parkhurst 86
92/3 Parkhurst 496
93/4 Parkhurst 104
94/5 Parkhurst 115, V23
95/6 Parkhurst 110
00/1 Parkhurst P-40
01/2 Parkhurst 175
02/3 Parkhurst 9, ✂ MS6
02/3 Parkhurst Retro 77
91/2 Pinnacle 91
92/3 Pinnacle 261
92/3 Pinnacle 349
93/4 Pinnacle 232
93/4 Pinnacle 85
93/4 Pinnacle TP 10
94/5 Pinnacle 4, NL3
95/6 Pinnacle 84
96/7 Pinnacle 72
97/8 Pinnacle 85
97/8 Pi. Be A Player 157, ✍ Aut. 157
97/8 Pi. Certified 72
97/8 Pi. Inside 36
95/6 Pi. Summit 64
96/7 Pi. Summit 136
97/8 Pi. Totally 72
95/6 Pi. Zenith 77
96/7 Pi. Zenith 100
95/6 Playoff 53
94/5 POG 133
95/6 POG 148
97/8 Pi. Post 9
93/4 Power Play 127
93/4 Premier 233
93/4 Prmr. - BG-OPC 2
94/5 Premier 65, TF-22
99/0 Prism 123
00/1 Private Stock 87, ✂ GUG-91, ✂ GUG-92
01/2 Pr. Stock ✂ GUG 91
02/3 Pr. Stock Reserve 86
00/1 PS Titanium 84
01/2 PS Titanium 121
00/1 PS Titanium Draft ✂ 91
95/6 Pro Magnet 16
90/1 Pro Set 278
91/2 Pro Set 224
91/2 Pro Set 293
91/2 Pro Set 381
92/3 Pro Set TL 5
91/2 Pro Set Platinum 35
99/0 Revolution 126
00/1 Revolution 127
90/1 Score 95
90/1 Sco. Hot Cards 47
91/2 Score 300
91/2 Score 338
91/2 Score 59T
91/2 Score CAN 368
91/2 Score CAN 609
92/3 Score 170
93/4 Score 244
94/5 Score 165, NP20
95/6 Score 36
96/7 Score 50
97/8 Score 112, CI-11
97/8 Score Mont. 4
94/5 Select 59
95/6 Select CE 75
96/7 Select CE 37
96/7 SB 7-Eleven Phonecard
00/1 Signature 161, ✍ Aut. 108
01/2 Signature 195, ✍ Aut. 195
02/3 Signature 23, ✍ 23, ✂ TQ18
95/6 SBx Emotion 87
95/6 SBx Impact 84
96/7 SBx Impact 61
94/5 SP 58
95/6 SP 75
97/8 SP Authentic 82
98/9 SP Authentic 43
01/2 SP Authentic 74
02/3 SP GU 56
99/0 SPx 126
98/9 SPx Prospects 32
02/3 Sports Vault 283
99/0 Stadium 123
00/1 Stadium 183
98/9 SLU
95/6 Super Sticker 62, 67
92/3 Topps 55
95/6 Topps 270, 9PL
98/9 Topps 118
00/1 Topps 178
01/2 Topps 222, 323
02/3 Topps 210
00/1 To. Chrome 119
01/2 To. Chrome 77
02/3 T. Chrome 118
94/5 Topps Finest 98
95/6 To. Finest 52
98/9 To. Finest 9
98/9 T. Gold Label 67
99/0 To. Gold Label 79
02/3 To. Heritage 68
02/3 T. Limited 210
91/2 To. Stadium 146
92/3 To. Stadium 191
93/4 To. Stadium 240
95/6 To. Stadium 159
02/3 T. Total 269
86/7 TORO
86/7 TORO
87/8 TORO / 5x8
87/8 TORO / P.L.A.Y. 17
88/9 TORO / P.L.A.Y. 17
90/1 TORO
98/9 UD Choice 110
00/1 UD Heroes 98
01/2 Ultimate Mem. ✂ DD
02/3 Ultimate Mem. ✂ ASMVP
90/1 Upper Deck 224, 484
91/2 Upper Deck 136
91/2 Upper Deck 535
92/3 Upper Deck 6
92/3 Upper Deck 307
92/3 Upper Deck 476
93/4 Upper Deck 295,380, HT8, SP-77
94/5 Upper Deck 280, SP-39
95/6 Upper Deck 66, SE-133
96/7 Upper Deck 86
97/8 Upper Deck 86
98/9 Upper Deck 110
99/0 Upper Deck 108
00/1 Upper Deck 373
01/2 Upper Deck 378
02/3 Upper Deck 391, ✂ ASJ, ✂ ASP
94/5 UD BAP R102, R112, ✍ 120
93/4 UD BAP Roots 25
96/7 UD Black Diam. 25
98/9 UD Black Diam. 43
95/6 UD CC 320
96/7 UD CC 138
97/8 UD Coll. Choice 130, SQ32
98/9 UD G. Reserve 110
99/0 UD G. Reserve 108
96/7 UD Ice 32
01/2 UD Mask 80
98/9 UD MVP 101
99/0 UD MVP 173
00/1 UD MVP 152
01/2 UD MVP 157
02/3 UD MVP 151
99/0 UD MVP Cup 156
95/6 UD Post 4
96/7 UD Post, SU-1
99/0 UD Retro 67
00/1 UD Vintage 300
01/2 UD Vintage 214, 217
02/3 UD Vintage 208, GB 208
00/1 Vanguard 86
99/0 Victory 247
00/1 Victory 192
01/2 Victory 296
02/3 Victory 176
99/0 WGretzky 152
97/8 Zenith 39, Z57

DAMPIER, ALEX
00/1 Kudos 124
00/1 Nottingham Panthers
01/2 Nottingham Panthers
93/4 Sheffield Steelers 20
94/5 Sheffield Steelers 24
95/6 Sheffield Steelers
97/8 Sheffield Steelers

DANBY, JOHN
72/3 New England Whalers

DANCE, JOHN
97/8 Peoria Rivermen

DANDENAULT, ÉRIC
96/7 Cincinnati Cyclones
97/8 Cincinnati Cyclones
98/9 Cincinnati Cyclones
99/0 Cincinnati Cyclones
91/2 ProCards 277
90/1 7th..Sketch LHJMQ 10
91 7th..Sketch Mem.Cup 53

DANDENAULT, MATHIEU
01/2 Atomic ✂ GWJ 21
02/3 BAP Memorabilia ✂ SCC2
95/6 Bowman 114
01/2 Crown Royale ✂ TT 6
95/6 Donruss 234
01/2 Heads Up ✂ JQ 11, ✂ JQ 22
95/6 L. Limited 37
99/0 Millenium 95, ✍ Aut. 95
99/0 NHL Power Play
01/2 Pacific ✂ GWJ 13
02/3 Pacific Complete 371
00/1 Pa. Paramount 84
95/6 Parkhurst 335
96/7 Pi. Be A Player 95, ✍ Aut. 95
00/1 PS Titanium ✂ GUG 95
00/1 PS Titanium Draft ✂ 37
95/6 SP 43
99/0 Topps 165
99/0 To. Chrome 165
95/6 To. Stadium 213
02/3 T. Total 240
02/3 Ultimate Mem. ✂ SCDE, ✂ SCDGJ, ✂ SCDN
95/6 Upper Deck 497
98/9 Upper Deck 84
01/2 Upper Deck 293
02/3 Upper Deck 308
98/9 UD G. Reserve 84
01/2 UD SCup Champs 59
01/2 Victory 125

DANDURAND, LÉO
25-27 Anonymous 15
83 HHOF Postcard G5
83&87 HHOF 96
27/8 La Patrie
27/8 La Presse

DANEAU, PIERRE-LUC
00/1 Victoriaville Tigres 7

DANEYKO, KEN
91/2 Bowman 284
92/3 Fleer Ultra 335
93/4 Fleer Ultra 358
94/5 Fleer Ultra 318
95/6 Fleer Ultra 189
94/5 Leaf 336
00/1 Mir Fetisov 25
83/4 NJER
86/7 NJER / S.O.B.E.R.
88/9 NJER / Caretta
89/0 NJER
89/0 NJER / Caretta
90/1 NJER
96/7 NJER / Sharp
91/2 O-Pee-Chee 118
89/0 O-Pee-Chee 243
98/9 OPC Chrome 101
99/0 Pacific 236
97/8 Pacific CC 325
87/8 Panini Sticker 76
89/0 Panini Sticker 258
91/2 Panini Sticker 218
99/0 Panini Sticker 85
91/2 Parkhurst 317
92/3 Parkhurst 332
93/4 Parkhurst 387
94/5 Parkhurst 131
91/2 Pinnacle 142
92/3 Pinnacle 354
93/4 Pinnacle 134
94/5 Pinnacle 330
95/6 Pinnacle 177
93/4 Premier 236
94/5 Premier 79
90/1 Pro Set 165
91/2 Pro Set 139
90/1 Score 178
91/2 Score 46
91/2 Score CAN 46
92/3 Score 53
93/4 Score 286
94/5 Score 142
97/8 Score NJer. 20
92/3 Topps 357
95/6 Topps 188
98/9 Topps 101
91/2 To. Stadium 103
93/4 To. Stadium 206
02/3 T. Total 220
90/1 Upper Deck 427
91/2 Upper Deck 435
92/3 Upper Deck 259
97/8 Upper Deck 305
95/6 UD BAP 48, ✍ S48

DANIEL, JARROD
91/2 7th...Sketch WHL 184

DANIELS, BETH
92/3 Toledo Storm WIOT

DANIELS, BOB
91/2 Ferris State Bulldogs

DANIELS, JEFF
00/1 BAP Mem. 90
92/3 Fleer Ultra 377
93/4 Leaf 251
98/9 Milwaukee Admirals
92/3 OPC Premier 58
92/3 Parkhurst 492
93/4 Parkhurst 429
91/2 PITT / Elby's
92/3 PITT / Coke-Clark
93/4 PITT / Foodland 11
93/4 Premier 343
88/9 ProCards / Muskegon
89/0 ProCards IHL 146
91/2 ProCards 298
91/2 Score 400
91/2 Score CAN 290
96/7 Springfield Falcons
93/4 To. Stadium 483
91/2 Upper Deck 564
92/3 Upper Deck 506
93/4 Upper Deck 87

DANIELS, KIMBI
96/7 Charlotte Checkers
91/2 Parkhurst 346
91/2 PHIL / J.C. Penney
91/2 Pinnacle 336
91/2 Score 399
91/2 Score CAN 289
90/1 7th...Sketch WHL 46, 72
92/3 To. Stadium 453
91/2 Upper Deck 492
91/2 Upper Deck 687
92/3 Upper Deck 75
91/2 Upper Deck WJC 61

DANIELS, MARK
91/2 Air Canada SJHL D21

DANIELS, SCOTT
98/9 Be A Player 229, ✍ Aut. 229
95/6 HART / Kids Club
86/7 Kamloops Blazers
96/7 PHIL / Ocean Spray
96/7 Pi. Be A Player 170, ✍ Aut. 170
97/8 Pi. Be A Player 116, ✍ Aut. 116
90/1 ProCards 192
91/2 ProCards 112
88/9 Regina Pats
89/0 Regina Pats
95/6 Upper Deck 328

DANIELS, WAYNE
91/2 Oshawa Generals
93/4 Slapshot / Oshawa 26

DANIELSMEIER, COLIN
01/2 UD DEL 117

DANIELSSON, BJORN
95/6 UD CC 342
00/1 UD Elitserien 11

DANILOV, ALEXEI
98/9 Mir 167

DANNEL, OLIVIER
00/1 Chicoutimi Saguenéens 1
00/1 Hull Olympiques 22

DANO, JOZEF
96/7 APS 68
97/8 APS 328
97/8 DS 113
98/9 DS 121
00/1 DS 69
96/7 DS Sticker 238
97/8 DS Sticker 279
98/9 OFS 390
99/0 OFS 404
00/1 OFS 225
96 Wien 236

DANTON, MIKE
00/1 Albany River Rats
02/3 Atomic 118
98/9 Barrie Colts
01/2 BAP Memor. 217
02/3 Exclusive 184
02/3 Heads Up 126
94 Québec Pee Wee 1710
01/2 SPx 114
01/2 Upper Deck 196
01/2 UD MVP 206
01/2 UD Top Shelf 58
01/2 Victory 379

DANYLUK, CAM
89/0 Portland Winter Hawks
91 7th..Sketch Mem.Cup 84
90/1 7th..Sketch WHL 210, 320
91/2 7th...Sketch WHL 335

DAOUST, ANDRÉ
69 Columbus Checkers

DAOUST, DAN
82/3 Dernière Heure
86/7 Kraft Sports 54
82/3 MONT
83/4 O-Pee-Chee 328
84/5 O-Pee-Chee 299
85/6 OPC/Topps 164
86/7 O-Pee-Chee 241
89/0 O-Pee-Chee 277
83/4 OPC/Topps Sticker 28
83/4 OPC/Topps Sticker 29
84/5 OPC Sticker 9
84/5 OPC Sticker 10
85/6 OPC Sticker 11-139
86/7 OPC Sticker 146-254
88/9 OPC Sticker 169-29
89/0 opcSticker 177-37
88/9 Panini Sticker 124
83/4 Souhaits Keychain [Maple Leafs]
84/5 Topps 137
82/3 TORO
83/4 TORO
84/5 TORO
85/6 TORO
86/7 TORO
86/7 TORO
87/8 TORO / 5x8
87/8 TORO / P.L.A.Y. 20
88/9 TORO / P.L.A.Y. 20
83/4 Vachon 83-22

DAOUST, EDDY
51/2 Lac St-Jean 1

DAOUST, JEAN-MICHEL
00/1 Hull Olympiques 17
01/2 Hull Olympiques 19
02/3 Hull Olympiques

DAPUZZO, PAT
90/1 Pro Set 684

DARBY, CRAIG
02/3 Albany River Rats
00/1 BAP Mem. 17
93/4 Classic 62
94/5 Classic 86, ✍ Aut.
94/5 Classic 4 Sport 134
94/5 Cla. Images 33
93/4 Cla. Prospects 110
95/6 Edge Ice 92
93/4 Fredericton Canadiens
94/5 Fredericton Canadiens
98/9 Milwaukee Admirals
00/1 MONT
99/0 Omega 117
95/6 Pinnacle 213
01/2 Québec Citadelles
95/6 Score 305
00/1 Signature 245, ✍ Aut. 197
94/5 Upper Deck 452
00/1 Upper Deck 95
01/2 Victory 191

DARBY, KEVIN
93/4 Fredericton Canadiens

DARBY, REGAN
00/1 Kansas City Blades 7
01/2 Manitoba Moose
02/3 Manitoba Moose

DARCHE, MATHIEU
01/2 BAP Memor. 238
01/2 Crown Royale 153
01/2 O-Pee-Chee 310
01/2 Pacific 110
01/2 PS Titanium Draft 119
01/2 SP GU 72
01/2 SPx 137, -RT
00/1 Syracuse Crunch
01/2 Syracuse Crunch
02/3 Syracuse Crunch
01/2 Topps 310
01/2 Upper Deck 187
01/2 UD MVP 197
01/2 UD Premier 59
01/2 UD Top Shelf 53
01/2 Victory 372

DARGUZAS, DAVID
95/6 Brandon Wheat Kings

DARK, MICHAEL
88/9 Salt Lake G'Eagles
87/8 SLOU / Kodak

DARLING, DION
93/4 Cla. 4 Sport 222
98/9 Fort Wayne Komets
94/5 Fredericton Canadiens
95/6 Fredericton Canadiens
96/7 Fredericton Canadiens
00/1 Manitoba Moose

DARRAGH, HARRY
32/3 Maple Leafs O'Keefe

DARRAGH, JACK
91 C55 Reprint 17
83 HHOF Postcard N3
83&87 HHOF 199
10/1 Imperial
11/2 Imperial 17
12/3 Imperial 29
23/4 William Paterson 4

DARTSCH, DAVID
96/7 Richmond Renegades

DARVEAU, GUY
89/0 ProCards AHL 193

DARWIN, HOWARD
92/3 Ottawa 67's

DASHNEY, CHRIS
98/9 Wichita Thunder

DASKALAKIS, CLEON
85/6 Moncton G'Flames
86/7 Moncton G'Flames

DATSYUK, PAVEL
01/2 Adrenaline 207, RR8
01/2 Atomic 108
02/3 Atomic 35, -CF 10
01/2 BAP Memor. 303
02/3 BAP Memorabilia 116, ✂ FG1, ✂ HSHSJers 24, ✂ SCC13
01/2 Bowman 165, ✂ FFJ, ✂ FFS, ✂ FFDS, ✂ FFR, ✍ YSA
02/3 Bowman 123
01/2 Crown Royale 157, RR8
02/3 eTopps 13
02/3 Exclusive 61, -DFG 6, -GE 6
02/3 First Edition 186
01/2 Heads Up 106
02/3 In The Game-Used 28, 128
00/1 Mir 334
01/2 O-Pee-Chee 349
02/3 O-Pee-Chee 235
02/3 Pacific 124, -SM 5
02/3 Pacific Complete 23
01/2 PTC Rookie 6
01/2 Parkhurst 254
02/3 Parkhurst 55
02/3 Parkhurst Retro 173
01/2 Pr. Stock 120, RR 4, -PS 80
01/2 PS Titanium 156
01/2 PS Titanium Draft 126
01/2 Signature 233, ✍ Aut. 233
02/3 Signature 166, ✍ 166, ✂ SGJ47
01/2 SP Authentic 145
02/3 SP Authentic 115
01/2 SP GU 75
01/2 SPx 104
01/2 SPx Rookie RR11
01/2 Stadium 139
02/3 Stadium 33, ✂ YSS2, ✂ YSD4
01/2 Topps 349
02/3 Topps 235, OTG15
01/2 To. Chrome 167
02/3 T. Chrome 129
01/2 To. Heritage 151
02/3 To. Heritage 14, 111, 130
02/3 T. Limited 235
01/2 To. Reserve 117
02/3 T. Total 323
01/2 UD PlayMakers Ltd 116
02/3 Ultimate Mem. ✂ SCDE, ✂ SCDGJ, ✂ SCDN
01/2 Upper Deck 422
02/3 Upper Deck 309
01/2 UD Challenge 105
01/2 UD Honor Roll 71
01/2 UD Ice 53
01/2 UD Mask 144
01/2 UD MVP 223
02/3 UD MVP 69
01/2 UD Premier 95
01/2 UD Top Shelf 127
02/3 UD Vintage 90, GB 90
01/2 Vanguard 109, PP 5
01/2 Victory 443
02/3 Victory 76

DAUBENSPECK, KIRK
97/8 Indianapolis Ice 5
98/9 Indianapolis Ice

DAUGHERTY, BRENT
84/5 Sudbury Wolves
85/6 Sudbury Wolves
86/7 Sudbury Wolves

DAUM, ROB
93/4 Lethbridge Hurricanes
90/1 7th..Sketch WHL 262

DAVEY, NEIL
84/5 Prince Albert Raiders

DAVID, JEAN-FRANÇOIS
99/0 Shawinigan 11
01/2 Shawinigan 18

DAVID, JIRI
99/0 OFS 452

DAVID, RICHARD
78/9 Dernière Heure
92/3 Semic Nordisk 144

DAVIDOV, MARAT
00/1 Dynamo 11

DAVIDSON,
91/2 Avant Garde BCJHL 159

DAVIDSON, ANDREW
01/2 Vancouver Giants

DAVIDSON, BOB
34-43 BeeHive-1 [Toro.]
36/7 O-Pee-Chee 100
37/8 O-Pee-Chee 136
39/0 O-Pee-Chee 5
38/9 Quaker Oats
45-54 Quaker Oats
91/2 Ultimate Original Six 33, ✍ Aut. 33
37/8 World Wide Gum 48

DAVIDSON, CHAD
01/2 Regina Pats

DAVIDSON, GORD
34-43 BeeHive-1 [NYRa.]

DAVIDSON, JOHN
99/0 BAP Mem. AH-11, ✍ AH-11
02/3 Between the Pipes ✍ Aut.
77/8 Coke
01/2 Fleer Greats 10, ✍ Aut.
74/5 Loblaws
74/5 O-Pee-Chee 11
75/6 O-Pee-Chee 183
76/7 O-Pee-Chee 204
77/8 O-Pee-Chee 28
78/9 O-Pee-Chee 211
79/0 O-Pee-Chee 110
80/1 O-Pee-Chee 190
81/2 O-Pee-Chee 222
77-79 Sportscaster 80-18
73/4 SLOU
74/5 Topps 11
75/6 Topps 183
76/7 Topps 204
77/8 Topps 28
78/9 Topps 211
79/0 Topps 110
80/1 Topps 190
81/2 Topps 95 [East]

DAVIDSON, LEE
98/9 DEL 189
92/3 Fort Wayne Komets 7
93/4 Fort Wayne Komets 4
97/8 Fort Wayne Komets
90/1 Moncton Hawks
91/2 Moncton Hawks
90/1 ProCards 256
91/2 ProCards 166

DAVIDSON, MATT
01/2 BAP Memor. 438
01/2 Pacific 111
01/2 Parkhurst 200
93/4 Portland Winter Hawks
97/8 Rochester Americans
98/9 Rochester Americans
01/2 SP Authentic 143
01/2 SP GU 73
01/2 SPx 138, -RT
00/1 Syracuse Crunch
01/2 Syracuse Crunch
02/3 Syracuse Crunch
01/2 Upper Deck 188
01/2 UD Honor Roll 92
01/2 UD MVP 198
01/2 UD Premier 58
01/2 Victory 372

DAVIDSON, RANDY
99/0 Ottawa 67's

DAVIDSON, RICK
84/5 Victoria Cougars

DAVIDSON, ROBERT
99/0 Indianapolis Ice

DAVIDSON, ROD
99/0 Indianapolis Ice

DAVIDSON, SCOTTY
83 HHOF Postcard K2
83&87 HHOF 137

DAVIDSON, SHAWNA
94/5 Classic W25

DAVIDSON, TY
92/3 BCJHL 126

DAVIDSSON, JOHAN
00/1 BAP Mem. 131
98/9 Bowman's Best 125
00/1 Cardset 251
02/3 Cardset 12
99/0 Cincinnati M'Ducks
95 Globe 62
97/8 Hockey-Box
94/5 Leaf Elit Set 242, ND-2
95/6 Leaf Elit Set 53
98/9 Omega 9
99/0 Pacific 2
93/4 Parkhurst 538
94/5 Parkie SE236
92/3 Semic Elitserien 353
94/5 Sig. Rookies 57, ✍ 57
94/5 SR Gold Standard 81
98/9 SP Authentic 91
98/9 Upper Deck 211
98/9 UD Black Diam. 3
95/6 UD Elitserien 86, NA10
98/9 UD G. Reserve 211
98/9 UD MVP 4
99/0 UD MVP 10

DAVIE, BOB
33-35 Diamond Match Silv.

DAVIES, CURLY
52/3 Anonymous 128

DAVIES, DAN
92/3 BCJHL 29
99/0 Rockford IceHogs
00/1 Rockford IceHogs
01/2 Rockford IceHogs

DAVIES, DAVE
74/5 Sioux City Musketeers

DAVIES, GREG
87/8 Kamloops Blazers
88/9 ProCards / Muskegon
83/4 Victoria Cougars

DAVIES, JASON
00/1 London Knights

DAVIES, MARK
92/3 BCJHL 194

DAVIS, ANDREW
00/1 Mississauga IceDogs

DAVIS, ANDY
94/5 Knoxville Cherokees
00/1 Louisiana Ice Gators
01/2 Louisiana Ice Gators
02/3 Louisiana Ice Gators
95/6 Richmond Renegades

DAVIS, BOB
23/4 Paulins Candy 54

DAVIS, DON
92/3 Toledo Storm WIOT

DAVIS, GEORGE
01/2 Cape Breton Eagles 15

DAVIS, GREG
01/2 Worcester IceCats
02/3 Worcester IceCats

DAVIS, JEAN-PAUL
89/0 Oshawa Generals
90/1 Oshawa Generals
91/2 Oshawa Generals
91/2 Oshawa Generals
90 7th..Sketch Mem.Cup 80
89/0 7th..Sketch OHL 6
90/1 7th..Sketch OHL 334
91/2 7th...Sketch OHL 164

DAVIS, JUSTIN
96/7 Soo Greyhounds
95/6 Slapshot 115

DAVIS, KELLY
81/2 Indianapolis Checkers
82/3 Indianapolis Checkers

DAVIS, KEN
99/0 Medicine Hat Tigers
00/1 Medicine Hat Tigers
97/8 Portland Winter Hawks

DAVIS, LEE
95/6 Birmingham Bulls

DAVIS, LORNE
45-64 BeeHive-2 [Mont.]

DAVIS, MAL
84/5 BUFF / Blue Shield
85/6 BUFF / Blue Shield
85/6 OPC Sticker 186-60

DAVIS, MATT
01/2 Moncton Wildcats 19

DAVIS, RYAN
95/6 Slapshot 290

DAVIS, SCOTT
90/1 7th..Sketch WHL 16

DAVIS, WAADE
01/2 Calgary Hitmen

DAVIS, WADE
98/9 Calgary Hitmen 13
99/0 Calgary Hitmen
00/1 Calgary Hitmen
02/3 Kamloops Blazers

DAVISON, DWAYNE
81/2 Ottawa 67's

DAVISON, ROB
02/3 BAP Memorabilia 307
01/2 Cleveland Barons
00/1 Kentucky Tho'blades
02/3 SP Authentic 214
02/3 UD Rookie 142

DAVISON, ROBIN
98/9 Guildford Flames

DAVYDKIN, NIKOLAI
89/0 Semic Elitserien 31
91/2 Semic Elitserien 32
92/3 Semic Nordisk 35

DAVYDOV, EVGENY (GENE)
93/4 Donruss 127
92/3 Fleer Ultra 441
93/4 Fleer Ultra 323
93/4 Fleer Ultra 58
94/5 Fleer Ultra 147
93/4 Leaf 24
90/1 O-Pee-Chee 18R
92/3 OPC Premier 66
93/4 Panini Sticker 194
91/2 Parkhurst 422
92/3 Parkhurst 211
92/3 Parkhurst 226
93/4 Parkhurst 78
94/5 Parkhurst 161
92/3 Pinnacle 226
93/4 Pinnacle 109
94/5 Pinnacle 202
93/4 Power Play 269
93/4 Power Play 397
93/4 Premier 200
93/4 Premier 444
94/5 Premier 518
92/3 Pro Set 244
91/2 Red Ace
92/3 Score 456
93/4 Score 114
93/4 Score 499
91 Semic Sticker 92
92/3 Topps 115
93/4 To. Stadium 34
93/4 To. Stadium 487
94/5 To. Stadium 66
92/3 Upper Deck 420
92/3 Upper Deck CC19
92/3 Upper Deck ER17
92/3 Upper Deck E8
93/4 Upper Deck 443, SP-55
94/5 Upper Deck 49
97/8 UD Elitserien 29, C17

DAVYDOV, MORAT
95 Panini Worlds 30

DAVYDOV, OLEG
95 Panini Worlds 32

DAVYDOV, VITALY
70/1 Kuvajulkaisut 1
72 Panda MM-Toronto
72 Semic Sticker 2
74 Semic Sticker 43
69/0 Soviet Stars
70/1 Soviet Stars
71/2 Soviet Stars
71/2 Williams Finnish 1

DAW, JEFF
01/2 BAP Memor. 427
99/0 Hamilton Bulldogs/ Staz
01/2 Hershey Bears
99/0 Houston Aeros
00/1 Lowell Lock Monsters
01/2 UD Mask 141

DAWE, JASON
91/2 Arena 26
98/9 Aurora 115
91/2 Classic 31
93/4 Classic 19
91/2 Classic Four Sport 31
93/4 Cla. Prospects 88
93/4 Donruss 404
94/5 Donruss 245
95/6 Donruss 315
96/7 Donruss 165
95/6 Edge Ice C20
96/7 Fleer 9
95/6 Fleer Metal 14
96/7 Fl. Picks 122
94/5 Fleer Ultra 21
95/6 Fleer Ultra 16, 211
96/7 Fl. Ultra 15
00/1 Hartford Wolf Pack
01/2 Hartford Wolf Pack
94/5 Leaf 48
96/7 Leaf 93
95/6 L. Limited 111
96/7 Metal Univ. 13
99/0 Milwaukee Admirals
98/9 OPC Chrome 202
97/8 Omega 20
98/9 Pacific 280
97/8 Pacific CC 314
97/8 Pa. Crown Roy. 12
97/8 Pa. Invincible 11
97/8 Pa. Paramount 18
98/9 Pa. Paramount 142
97/8 Pa. Revolution 13
95/6 Panini Sticker 18
96/7 Panini Sticker 16
95/6 Parkhurst 24
94/5 Parkie SE20
91/2 Peterborough Petes
94/5 Pinnacle 366
95/6 Pinnacle 123
96/7 Pinnacle 10
95/6 Playoff 230
96/7 Playoff 421
95/6 POG 43
94/5 Premier 149
96/7 Score 59
97/8 Score 204
97/8 Score Buff. 7
91 7th..Sketch Mem.Cup 113
89/0 7th..Sketch OHL 106
90/1 7th..Sketch OHL 357
91/2 7th...Sketch OHL 145
93/4 Slapshot / Peterborough 27
97/8 SP Authentic 13
91/2 Star Pics 59
95/6 Topps 128, 6PL
98/9 Topps 202
95/6 To. Finest 158
95/6 To. Stadium 147
91/2 Ultimate Draft Pick 27, 86, ✍ Aut.
91/2 Upper Deck 75
93/4 Upper Deck 254
94/5 Upper Deck 167
95/6 Upper Deck 61, SE-100
96/7 Upper Deck 19
97/8 Upper Deck 19
98/9 Upper Deck 129
95/6 UD BAP 50, ✍ S50
96/7 UD Black Diam. 139
97/8 UD Black Diam. 30
96/7 UD CC 31
97/8 UD Coll. Choice 32
98/9 UD G. Reserve 129
02/3 Worcester IceCats

DAWE, WADE
95/6 Slapshot 317

DAWES, BOB
45-64 BeeHive-2 [Toro.]

DAWKINS, MARK
91/2 7th...Sketch WHL 310

DAWSON, MIKE
90/1 7th..Sketch OHL 56
91/2 7th...Sketch OHL 233

DAWSON, W.
91/2 ProCards 162

DAY, GREG
02/3 Peoria Rivermen

DAY, HAP
33/4 Anonymous 2
34-43 BeeHive-1 [Toro.]
33/4 Canadian Gum
24/5 Champ's Cigarettes
33/4 Hamilton Gum 33
83 HHOF Postcard F4
83&87 HHOF 80
28/9 La Presse
32/3 Maple Leafs O'Keefe
33/4 O-Pee-Chee 32
55/6 Parkhurst 34
02/3 Parkie - Reprint 207, 223
93/4 Parkie 56-57 134
02/3 Ultimate Mem. ✍ Cut
33/4 WWGum Premium 2
33/4 WWGum 10
37/8 World Wide Gum 52

DAY, JOE
91/2 HART / Jr. Whalers
97/8 Las Vegas Thunder 4
94/5 Parkhurst 138
90/1 ProCards 181
91/2 ProCards 103
91/2 Upper Deck 516

DAY, JUSTIN
00/1 Owen Sound Attack 23
01/2 Owen Sound Attack

DAYLEY, CORY
92/3 BCJHL 112

DAYLEY, WADE
91/2 Avant Garde BCJHL 47
92/3 BCJHL 116
91/2 Nanaimo Clippers

DAYMAN, RYAN
92/3 BCJHL 31

DAZÉ, ÉRIC
01/2 Adrenaline 39
01/2 Atomic ✂ GWJ 9
02/3 Atomic 20, -CF 7
98/9 Aurora 40
00/1 Aurora 32
02/3 BAP All-Star 17, ✂ ASJ
98/9 Be A Player 179, ✍ Aut. 179
99/0 BAP Mem. 97
00/1 BAP Mem. 144, ✂ TM-25
01/2 BAP Memor. 167
02/3 BAP Memorabilia 49, 207, 240, ✂ ASJ9, ✂ FP7, ✂ SC15
96/7 Bic.Sports Aces 7-S
95/6 Bowman 125, BB18
01/2 Bowman 51
02/3 Calder 14
94/5 Cla. Images 14
99/0 Crown Royale 32
01/2 Crown Royale 32, ✂ TT 6
02/3 Crown Royale 20
95/6 Donruss 345, C3TWC-15, RR-6
96/7 Donruss D-10, HL-12, RR-1
97/8 Donruss 192
96/7 Do. Canadian 20, OC-14
97/8 Do. Canadian 21
95/6 Do. Elite 63, R-1
96/7 Do. Elite 71, A-1
97/8 Do. Preferred 116
97/8 Do. Priority 26
96/7 Duracell JB4
98/9 Dynagon Ice 40
99/0 Dynagon Ice 48
02/3 Exclusive 35
02/3 First Edition 78, 317, 347, ✂ Jers., ✂ TSL 6
96/7 Flair 16, HN-3
96/7 Fleer 17, 136, RS-4
95/6 Fleer Metal 174
96/7 Fl. Picks F50-9, FF-4, JE-19
95/6 Fleer Ultra 32, 335, EA-2
96/7 Fl. Ultra 31
01/2 Heads Up ✂ JQ 6
02/3 Heads Up 25, ✂ GWQ 7
02/3 In The Game-Used ✂ F7, ✂ GUJ39, ✂ SJ39
95/6 Leaf 226, SR-11
96/7 Leaf 202, S-7, TBO-2
97/8 Leaf 97
94/5 L. Limited CAN 2
95/6 L. Limited 65, RP-6
96/7 L. Limited 37, BTB-10
96/7 L. Preferred 61, 149, LS-25
97/8 Limited 65
96/7 Maggers 32
96/7 McDonald's McD-3
96/7 Metal Univ. 27
99/0 Millenium 62, ✍ Aut. 62
99/0 NHL Power Play
01/2 O-Pee-Chee 234
02/3 O-Pee-Chee 94
98/9 OPC Chrome 195
97/8 Omega 49
98/9 Omega 50
99/0 Omega 52
98/9 Pacific 143
99/0 Pacific 85
00/1 Pacific 93
01/2 Pacific 84
02/3 Pacific 76
02/3 Pacific Complete 497
97/8 Pacific CC 108
97/8 Pa. Crown Roy. 29
98/9 Pa. Crown Roy. 29
97/8 Pa. Dynagon 26, T-31
97/8 Pa. Invincible 29
97/8 Pa. Paramount 43
98/9 Pa. Paramount 46
99/0 Pa. Paramount 53
97/8 Pa. Revolution 29
98/9 Pa. Revolution 30
01/2 PTC National 3
98/9 Panini Photocard
95/6 Panini Sticker 159
96/7 Panini Sticker 159
97/8 Panini Sticker 136
98/9 Panini Sticker 113
99/0 Panini Sticker 198
95/6 Parkhurst 45, CCP-16, PP-40
00/1 Parkhurst P-243
01/2 Parkhurst 235, ✂ PJ50, ✂ T9
02/3 Parkhurst 38, ✂ FP7, ✂ GJ6, ✂ SJ6, ✂ HSHSJers 26, ✂ TT13
02/3 Parkhurst Retro 32
94/5 Pinnacle 529
95/6 Pinnacle 203
96/7 Pinnacle 212, BTN-11, TP-10
97/8 Pinnacle 121
97/8 Pi. Be A Player TN2
97/8 Pi. Certified 122
97/8 Pi. Inside 88
95/6 Pi. Summit 190
96/7 Pi. Summit 151, HV-7
97/8 Pi. Totally 122
95/6 Pi. Zenith 122, RRC-13
96/7 Pi. Zenith 99, ZT-14
95/6 Playoff 234
00/1 Private Stock ✂ GUG 16
01/2 Pr. Stock -PS 13, ✂ GUG 22
02/3 Pr. Stock Reserve 20
01/2 PS Titanium 31, TAS 4, ✂ DSJ 24
00/1 PS Titanium Draft ✂ 17
02/3 Quest for the Cup 16
95/6 Score 312
96/7 Score 236, CI-16, / Promo 236
97/8 Score 193
95/6 Select CE 132
96/7 Select CE 79
01/2 Signature 68, ✍ Aut. 68, ✂ GU81, ✂ HSHSJers, ✂ TM7
02/3 Signature 62, ✍ 62
95/6 SBx Emotion gN 2
95/6 SBx Impact 193, F-17
96/7 SBx Impact 19, 168, F-7
02/3 Slam Card
95/6 SP 22
96/7 SP 26, CW-20, HC-2
97/8 SP Authentic 31
02/3 SP Authentic 18
02/3 SP GU 10, 65, ✂ AF (x2), ✂ PH
02/3 Sports Vault 173
96/7 SPx 50
96/7 SPx GF1
01/2 SPx ✂ TT
02/3 SPx 14, ✂ SS
99/0 Stadium 50
00/1 Stadium 84
02/3 Stadium 54, ✍ LSS
96/7 Team Out!
95/6 Topps 26, 19CJ
98/9 Topps 195
99/0 Topps 231
00/1 Topps 113
01/2 Topps 234
02/3 Topps 94
99/0 To. Chrome 231
01/2 To. Chrome 67
02/3 T. Chrome 59
94/5 Topps Finest 157
95/6 To. Finest 3
98/9 To. Finest 66
98/9 T. Gold Label 98
01/2 To. Heritage 64
02/3 To. Heritage 26
02/3 T. Limited 94
96/7 Topps Picks 77, RS4
95/6 To. Stadium ER195
95/6 TSC Members Only 50
02/3 T. Total 365, AW7
98/9 UD Choice 45
02/3 UD Superstars ✂ LLT
02/3 Ultimate Mem. ✂ ASMVP, ✂ Cor
94/5 Upper Deck 497
95/6 Upper Deck 268, H-29
96/7 Upper Deck 29, 359, X19, LS15, SS18B
97/8 Upper Deck 41
98/9 Upper Deck 68
00/1 Upper Deck 39
01/2 Upper Deck 40, ✂ NG
02/3 Upper Deck 39, ✂ CG, ✂ DM, ✂ PA
02/3 UD Artistic 18, R18, / Art
95/6 UD BAP 170, LL4, ✍ S170
97/8 UD Black Diam. 63
02/3 UD Classic 21, ✂ HH, ✂ HR (x2)
95/6 UD CC 411
96/7 UD CC 45, 313, UD37, C20
97/8 UD Coll. Choice 53, SQ15
98/9 UD G. Reserve 68
02/3 UD Honor ✂ GA
96/7 UD Ice 79
01/2 UD Ice ✂ GJ
02/3 UD Mask ✂ IO, ✂ PG
98/9 UD MVP 48
00/1 UD MVP 42
01/2 UD MVP 40
02/3 UD MVP 43
02/3 UD Piece 18
02/3 UD Top Shelf 19, ✂ GO, ✂ ST
00/1 UD Vintage 77
01/2 UD Vintage 53, 61
02/3 UD Vintage 59, 267, GB 59, T13, ✂ OS
00/1 Vanguard ✂ DGJ 16
01/2 Vanguard 21
02/3 Vanguard 22
99/0 Victory 73
00/1 Victory 57
01/2 Victory 74
02/3 Victory 45
99/0 WGretzky 42
97/8 Zenith 55, Z54

DE ANGELIS, MICHAEL
85/6 Minnesota-Duluth 3
95 Panini Worlds 85
95 Semic 172
92 Semic Sticker 249
93 Semic Sticker 214

DE CORTE, LUIGI
95 Panini Worlds 80
94 Semic 293

DE HEER, JACK
79 Panini Sticker 282

DE JONGE, GAVIN
93/4 Humberside Hawks 2

DE MARCHI, PAT
79 Panini Sticker 392

DE PIERO, BOB
82 Semic Sticker 140

DE RAAF, HELMUT
95/6 DEL 76
91 Semic Sticker 152
93 Semic Sticker 149

DE RUITER, CHRIS
92/3 Clarkson G'Knights

DE TONI, LINO
94 Semic 306
93 Semic Sticker 223

DE TONI, RENATO
79 Panini Sticker 390

DE VRIES, GREG
02/3 BAP Memorabilia 77
94/5 Cape Breton Oilers
01/2 Crown Royale ! TT 7
96/7 EDMO
97/8 EDMO
01/2 Heads Up ! JQ 9
00/1 Pacific 110
02/3 Pacific Complete 358
97/8 Pa. Invincible R-76
97/8 Pi. Be A Player 78, ✍ Aut. 78
00/1 Private Stock ! GUG 20
93/4 Slapshot / Niagara Falls 5
96/7 Upper Deck 191
01/2 Upper Deck 277
02/3 Upper Deck 290
98/9 UD MVP 56
02/3 UD Vintage 68
01/2 Vanguard ! DGM 37

DEA, BILLY
45-64 BeeHive-2 [NYRa.]
45-64 BeeHive-2 [Detr.]
70/1 Eddie Sargent 53
70/1 Esso Power Player
68/9 O-Pee-Chee 190
70/1 O-Pee-Chee 30
93/4 Parkie 56-57 47
57/8 Topps 39
70/1 Topps 30

DEACON, DON
39/0 O-Pee-Chee 70

DEADMARSH, ADAM
01/2 Adrenaline 58
98/9 Aurora 45
99/0 Aurora 35
98/9 Be A Player 36, ✍ Aut. 36
00/1 BAP All-Star AS-9
99/0 BAP Mem. 169
00/1 BAP Mem. 46
01/2 BAP Memor. 267
02/3 BAP Memorabilia 29, 251
01/2 Bowman 44
99/0 Challenger 10
93/4 Classic 20
94/5 Classic T56
93/4 Cla. 4 Sport 197, ✍ Aut.
94/5 Cla. Images 60, ✍ Aut.
01/2 Crown Royale 67
02/3 Crown Royale ✄ GWDP 12
93/4 Donruss USA5
95/6 Donruss 145
96/7 Donruss 145
97/8 Donruss 161, RA-1
97/8 Do. Canadian 126
97/8 Do. Elite 75
97/8 Do. Preferred 53
97/8 Do. Priority 163
97/8 Do. Studio 70
98/9 Dynagon Ice 45
99/0 Dynagon Ice 54
02/3 Exclusive 80
02/3 First Edition 29, 388, 410H, ✄ Jers.
94/5 Flair 144
94/5 Fleer 174
95/6 Fleer Metal 30
94/5 Fleer Ultra 355
95/6 Fleer Ultra 130
96/7 Fl. Ultra 34
02/3 Heads Up 56, ✄ GWQ 1
02/3 In The Game-Used ✄ TM20
94/5 Leaf 442
95/6 Leaf 72
97/8 Leaf 57
94/5 L. Limited USA 4
97/8 Limited 95, 132, 161
96/7 Metal Univ. 30
98/9 NHL Power Play
01/2 O-Pee-Chee 110
02/3 O-Pee-Chee 148
97/8 Omega 55
98/9 Omega 58
99/0 Omega 60
98/9 Pacific 18
99/0 Pacific 101
00/1 Pacific 108
01/2 Pacific 180
02/3 Pacific 165
02/3 Pacific Complete 111
97/8 Pacific CC 47
97/8 Pa. Crown Roy. 32
97/8 Pa. Invincible 33
97/8 Pa. Paramount 48
98/9 Pa. Paramount 53
99/0 Pa. Paramount 60
00/1 Pa. Paramount 57, ✄ GUS-3
98/9 Pa. Revolution 33
99/0 Panini Sticker 214
95/6 Parkhurst 54
00/1 Parkhurst P-192
01/2 Parkhurst 238
02/3 Parkhurst 130
02/3 Parkhurst Retro 43
94/5 Parkie SE144, SE246
93/4 Pinnacle 491
94/5 Pinnacle 253
95/6 Pinnacle 72
96/7 Pinnacle 43
97/8 Pinnacle 114
97/8 Pi. Be A Player 52, ✍ Aut. 52
97/8 Pi. Certified 112
97/8 Pi. Inside 170
97/8 Pi. Totally 112
95/6 Playoff 136
95/6 POG 81
93/4 Portland Winter Hawks
94/5 Premier 449
02/3 Pr. Stock Reserve 45
01/2 PS Titanium 64, ✄ DSJ 18
01/2 PS Titanium Draft ✄ 42
94/5 QUÉB / Burger King
99/0 Revolution 37
95/6 Score 168, CI-6
96/7 Score 93
97/8 Score 146
97/8 Score Colo. 8
94/5 Select 179
91/2 7th...Sketch WHL 32
01/2 Signature 25, ✍ Aut. 25
02/3 Signature 19, ✍ 19, ✄ TQ10
95/6 SBx Impact Fox 4
94/5 SP P-15
95/6 SP 33
96/7 SP 36, CW-17
97/8 SP Authentic 40
98/9 SP Authentic 23, ✍ SotT
00/1 SP Authentic 41
01/2 SP GU 25
02/3 SP Game-Used ✄ PC, ✄ PH
02/3 Sports Vault 234
99/0 SPx 45
01/2 SPx 32
01/2 SPx ✄ DT, ✄ TT
99/0 Stadium 97
01/2 Stadium 41
00/1 SLU 10
95/6 Topps 288, 6NG
99/0 Topps 28
00/1 Topps 152
01/2 Topps 110
02/3 Topps 148
99/0 To. Chrome 28
01/2 To. Chrome 110
02/3 T. Chrome 90
94/5 Topps Finest 31, 118, BBR-13
98/9 To. Finest 79
01/2 To. Heritage 50
02/3 T. Limited 148
96/7 Topps Picks 103
99/0 To. Prmr. Plus 38
01/2 To. Reserve 59
02/3 T. Total 156
98/9 UD Choice 57
00/1 UD Heroes 32
02/3 Ultimate Mem. ✄ HT
92/3 Upper Deck 609
93/4 Upper Deck 562
94/5 Upper Deck 261, 562, SP-155
95/6 Upper Deck 65, SE-22
96/7 Upper Deck 41, X25, P23
97/8 Upper Deck 46, T13A
98/9 Upper Deck 72
99/0 Upper Deck 214
00/1 Upper Deck 276
01/2 Upper Deck 84
02/3 Upper Deck 82, ✄ FF
00/1 UD ASG CA3
94/5 UD BAP R165
95/6 UD BAP 186, ✍ S186
96/7 UD Black Diam. 81
97/8 UD Black Diam. 75
01/2 UD Challenge - UC
02/3 UD Classic ✄ CS, ✄ HR
95/6 UD CC 294, 360
96/7 UD CC 58
97/8 UD Coll. Choice 57, SQ45
98/9 UD G. Reserve 72
99/0 UD G. Reserve 214
02/3 UD Honor -TW7
97/8 UD Ice 18
00/1 UD Ice 71
01/2 UD Ice 21
01/2 UD Mask 42, ✄ GJ, ✄ JP, ✄ DP
98/9 UD MVP 58
99/0 UD MVP 57
00/1 UD MVP 53
01/2 UD MVP 86
02/3 UD MVP 84, SA, SD, ST
01/2 UD Premier ✄ D
02/3 UD Rookie 46, ✄ 152b
01/2 UD SCup Champs 42
02/3 UD Top Shelf ✄ CP, ✄ GO, ✄ ST, ✄ SW
00/1 UD Vintage 90
01/2 UD Vintage 116, 122
02/3 UD Vintage 121, 274, 314, GB 121
02/3 Vanguard 48
99/0 Victory 81
00/1 Victory 64
01/2 Victory 165
02/3 Victory 95
99/0 WGretzky 49

DEADMARSH, BUTCH
72/3 BUFF
74/5 O-Pee-Chee 73
75/6 OPC WHA 59
76/7 OPC WHA 53

DEADMARSH, JAKE
98/9 Huntington Blizzard
96/7 Kamloops Blazers
93/4 Portland Winter Hawks
94/5 SR Auto-Phonex 12, ✍ 12

DEAN, BARRY
77/8 O-Pee-Chee 183
78/9 O-Pee-Chee 142
79/0 O-Pee-Chee 318
75/6 Phoenix Roadrunners
77/8 Topps 183
78/9 Topps 142

DEAN, KEVIN
98/9 Be A Player 82, ✍ Aut. 82
92/3 Cincinnati Cyclones
01/2 Milwaukee Admirals
96/7 NJER / Sharp
00/1 Pacific 94
99/0 Panini Sticker 14
97/8 Pi. Be A Player 57, ✍ Aut. 57
91/2 ProCards 417
95/6 Topps 208
01/2 UD Vintage 59

DEASLEY, BRYAN
90/1 ProCards 619
91/2 ProCards 580

DEAZELEY, MARK
89/0 Oshawa Generals
90/1 Oshawa Generals
91/2 Oshawa Generals
91/2 Oshawa Generals
90 7th..Sketch Mem.Cup 97
89/0 7th..Sketch OHL 10
90/1 7th..Sketch OHL 335
91/2 7th...Sketch OHL 153
92/3 Toledo Storm WIOT
92/3 Toledo Storm
93/4 Toledo Storm 14
97/8 Toledo Storm 15

DEAZLEY, MARK
95/6 Tallahasee Tiger Sharks

DEBENEDET, NELSON
74/5 Loblaws
74/5 O-Pee-Chee 293
74/5 PITT

DEBLOIS, LUCIEN
79/0 COLR
77/8 Dernière Heure
92/3 Durivage 2
96/7 Kansas City Blades
84/5 MONT
85/6 MONT / Provigo
78/9 O-Pee-Chee 136
80/1 O-Pee-Chee 146
81/2 O-Pee-Chee 74
82/3 O-Pee-Chee 379
83/4 O-Pee-Chee 378
83/4 O-Pee-Chee 383
84/5 O-Pee-Chee 260
90/1 O-Pee-Chee 441
91/2 O-Pee-Chee 102
81/2 OPC Sticker 232
82/3 OPC/Topps Sticker 212
83/4 OPC/Topps Sticker 284
84/5 OPC Sticker 290
90/1 Panini Sticker 140
91/2 Panini Sticker 100
82/3 Post [Winn.]
90/1 Pro Set 244, 531
91/2 Pro Set 491
89/0 QUÉB
89/0 QUÉB / Gene. Foods
89/0 QUÉB / Police
90/1 QUÉB
90/1 QUÉB / Petro-Canada
91/2 Score CAN 395
92/3 Score 371
83/4 Souhaits Keychain [Jets]
83/4 Stater Mint H11
78/9 Topps 136
80/1 Topps 146
81/2 Topps 79 [West]
91/2 TORO / P.L.A.Y. 21
90/1 Upper Deck 363
83/4 Vachon 125-100
83/4 Vachon 125-5
81/2 WINN
82/3 WINN
83/4 WINN

DEBLOIS, PHILIPPE
99/0 Shawinigan 12

DEBOER, PETER
01/2 Kitchener Rangers
89/0 ProCards IHL 169
90/1 ProCards 326
93/4 Slapshot / Detroit 24
95/6 Slapshot 80
94/5 Slapshot Memorial 100

DEBOL, DAVE
79/0 O-Pee-Chee 363
80/1 O-Pee-Chee 381
79 Panini Sticker 215

DEBRIE, DARREN
95/6 Slapshot 270

DEBRUSK, LOUIE
92/3 Bowman 318
93/4 Donruss 108
93/4 EDMO / Sheet
91/2 EDMO / IGA
92/3 EDMO
92/3 EDMO / IGA 006
96/7 EDMO
93/4 Leaf 225
94/5 Leaf 532
98/9 Pacific 398
00/1 Pacific 313
01/2 Pacific 418
97/8 Pa. Dynagon BKS-37
91/2 Parkhurst 281
93/4 Parkhurst 337
95/6 Parkhurst 81
91/2 Pinnacle 347
93/4 Premier 319
91/2 Pro Set 535
89/0 7th..Sketch OHL 28
90/1 7th..Sketch OHL 132
92/3 Topps 392
92/3 T. Stadium Club 290
91/2 Upper Deck 249
91/2 Upper Deck 526
92/3 Upper Deck 467
93/4 Upper Deck 79
94/5 Upper Deck 485
00/1 Upper Deck 365
94/5 UD BAP R89, ✍ 29
95/6 UD CC 87
96/7 UD CC 100

DEBUS, STEVE
94/5 Minnesota G'Gophers
99/0 Mobile Mysticks

DEBUS, STEVE
01/2 Rockford IceHogs

DEBUSSCHERE, DAVE
91/2 Air Canada SJHL D46
92/3 MPS SJHL 8

DECAEN, STEVE
91/2 7th...Sketch LHJMQ 153

DECARIE, ED
10/1 Imperial 13

DECARLE, MIKE
89/0 ProCards IHL 104

DECECCO, BRET
02/3 Peoria Rivermen

DECECCO, BRETT
99 Bowman 107, 163
98 Bowman 59
98 Bowman Chrome 59
98/9 Bowman's Best 149
97/8 Upper Deck 409

DECELLES, LUC
93/4 Slapshot / Drummondville 20

DECHAINE, CHRIS
92/3 MPS SJHL 107

DECIANTIS, ROB
95/6 Classic 87
99/0 Quad City Mallards
94/5 Slapshot / Kitchener 21
95/6 Slapshot 141

DECK, KIM
87/8 Kamloops Blazers
88/9 Kamloops Blazers
89/0 Portland Winter Hawks
90/1 7th..Sketch WHL 156, 323

DECKER, TODD
87/8 Kamloops Blazers

DECOFF, MIKE
89/0 Oshawa Generals
91 7th..Sketch Mem.Cup 15
90/1 7th..Sketch OHL 155

DECOMMIRE, BOB
94/5 Slapshot / Brantford 2

DECONTIE, RONNIE
99/0 Rimouski Océanic 14

DECORBY, IAN
94/5 Erie Panthers

DECOSTY, DEREK
96/7 Guildford Flames 19
98/9 Guildford Flames
92/3 Wheeling Thund'birds 4
93/4 Wheeling Thund'birds
94/5 Wheeling Thund'birds

DEDEAUX, CYNTHIA
99/0 Mississippi S'Wolves
99/0 Mississippi S'Wolves

DEEKS, ALAIN
92/3 Hamilton Canucks
93/4 Knoxville Cherokees

DEEV, YAKOV
99/0 Mir 49

DEFAUW, BRAD
02/3 BAP Memorabilia 348

DEFAUW, BRAD
00/1 Cincinnati Cyclones

DEFAUW, BRAD
02/3 Ultimate Mem. 95

DEFAUW, BRAD
02/3 UD Rookie 144

DEFAZIO, DAN
82/3 Oshawa Generals

DEFAZIO, JERRETT
89/0 7th..Sketch OHL 57
90/1 7th..Sketch OHL 82

DEFELICE, NORM
52/3 Anonymous 18
45-64 BeeHive-2 [Bost.]

DEFRENZA, FRAN
90/1 7th..Sketch WHL 98
91/2 7th...Sketch WHL 54

DEFRENZA, FRANK
99/0 Asheville Smoke

DEGAETANO, PHIL
88/9 ProCards / Maine

DEGAGNE, RON
82/3 North Bay Centennials
83/4 North Bay Centennials

DEGERSTEDT, PATRIK
98/9 DEL 289

DEGIACOMO, DWIGHT
90/1 Michigan Tech Huskies

DEGNER, TERRY
90/1 7th..Sketch WHL 99
91/2 7th...Sketch WHL 290

DEGRACE, YANICK
90/1 7th..Sketch LHJMQ 170
91/2 7th...Sketch LHJMQ 208

DEGRAY, DALE (DIGGER)
95/6 Cincinnati Cyclones
96/7 Cincinnati Cyclones
95/6 Edge Ice 111
98/9 Indianapolis Ice
88/9 LOSA / Smokey
84/5 Moncton G'Flames
85/6 Moncton G'Flames
89/0 OPC/Topps 18
80/1 Oshawa Generals
81/2 Oshawa Generals
82/3 Oshawa Generals
90/1 ProCards 279
99/0 Rockford IceHogs
00/1 Rockford IceHogs
92/3 San Diego Gulls
93/4 San Diego Gulls
87/8 TORO / 5x8
87/8 TORO / P.L.A.Y. 25

DEGUISE, MICHEL
73/4 Québec Nordiques
88/9 Richelieu Riverains

DEHART, JOHN
91/2 Avant Garde BCJHL 99
91/2 Avant Garde BCJHL 159
91/2 Avant Garde BCJHL 164

DEIS, TYLER
99/0 Charlotte Checkers
99/0 Charlotte Checkers
00/1 Charlotte Checkers
92/3 MPS SJHL 52

DEITER, THOMAS
94/5 DEL 432

DEJORDY, DENIS
71/2 Bazooka Panel
64-67 BeeHive-3 [Chic.]
63-65 Chex
64/5 Coke/Sprite [Chic.]
70/1 Colgate 84
70/1 Dad's Cookies
70/1 Eddie Sargent 73
72/3 Eddie Sargent 130
70/1 Esso Power Player
71/2 MONT / Pro Star
68/9 O-Pee-Chee 12
69/0 O-Pee-Chee 66
69/0 O-Pee-Chee 4in1
70/1 O-Pee-Chee 31
71/2 O-Pee-Chee 63
72/3 O-Pee-Chee 184
95/6 Parkie 66-67 39, TW6
94/5 Parkie Tall 28
68/9 Shirriff / Chic. 4
61/2 Topps 37
62/3 Topps 25
63/4 Topps 24
64/5 Topps 22
65/6 Topps 113
66/7 Topps 115
66/7 Topps / Test 50
67/8 Topps 65
67/8 Topps 115
68/9 Topps 12
69/0 Topps 66
70/1 Topps 31
71/2 Topps 63
72/3 Topps 144
71/2 Toronto Sun Photo

DEL MONACO, PASCAL
79 Panini Sticker 379

DEL MONTE, DAN
94/5 Slapshot / Sarnia 17

DEL MONTE, DION
96/7 DEL 331
97/8 Sheffield Steelers

DELARONDE, SHANE
95/6 Slapshot 10

DELAROSBIL, RAYMOND
99/0 Rockford IceHogs
90/1 7th..Sketch LHJMQ 178
91/2 7th...Sketch LHJMQ 155
93/4 Slapshot / Drummondville 18

DELCOURT, GRANT
83/4 Kelowna Wings
84/5 Kelowna Wings &...

DELEEUW, ADAM
00/1 Toronto St. Mike's

DELESOY, JASON
92/3 BCJHL 16

DELEURME, JASON
98 Bowman 49
98 Bowman Chrome 49
98/9 Hampton Roads
93/4 Tacoma Rockets
01/2 UD DEL 238

DELFINO, DAVID
94 Semic 291
92 Semic Sticker 243
93 Semic Sticker 209

DELGUIDICE, MATT
91/2 OPC Premier 96
91/2 Parkhurst 1
91/2 Pro Set 521
90/1 ProCards 125
93/4 Raleigh Icecaps
95/6 Roanoke Express
91/2 Upper Deck 463

DELIANEDLS, DAN
88/9 ProCards / Utica

DELISLE, GUY
51/2 Bas du Fleuve 12

DELISLE, JOHN*
85/6 Minnesota-Duluth 29

DELISLE, JONATHAN
97 Bowman 55
99/0 Québec Citadelles 10
00/1 Québec Citadelles
01/2 Québec Citadelles
94/5 Slapshot Memorial 70

DELISLE, MIGUEL
99/0 Ottawa 67's
00/1 Ottawa 67's 15
01/2 Ottawa 67's 16
02/3 Owen Sound Attack
99/0 UD Sobey's 16
99/0 UD Prospects 21
00/1 UD Prospects 18

DELISLE, XAVIER
98/9 Cleveland Lumberjacks
00/1 MONT
94/5 Parkie SE255
00/1 PS Titanium Draft 163
99/0 Québec Citadelles 4
00/1 Québec Citadelles
01/2 Québec Citadelles
94/5 SP 178

DELIVA, JOEY
91/2 7th...Sketch LHJMQ 204

DELL, FRANK
89/0 Johnstown Chiefs

DELL'JANNONE, PATRICK
82 Semic Sticker 133

DELLA VEDOVA, SCOTT
99/0 Brampton Batallion 4

DELLAIRE, HENRI
91 C55 Reprint 39
10/1 Imperial
11/2 Imperial 39
12/3 Imperial 7

DELLSPERGER, ROLAND
79 Panini Sticker 262

DELMONTE, DAN
93/4 Slapshot / Peterborough 24

DELMORE, ANDY
99/0 BAP Mem. 318
00/1 BAP Mem. 60
97 Bowman 34
02/3 First Edition 293
99/0 Omega 177
00/1 Pacific 294
02/3 Pacific 206
02/3 Pacific Complete 148
00/1 Pa. Paramount 178
01/2 Parkhurst 383
94/5 SR Auto-Phonex 13, ✍ 13
00/1 Signature 162, ✍ Aut. 119
02/3 Signature 70, ✍ 70
93/4 Slapshot / North Bay 5
95/6 Slapshot 336
02/3 Sports Vault 258
00/1 Stadium 71
00/1 Topps 301
00/1 To. Chrome 196
02/3 T. Total 307
00/1 Upper Deck 358
01/2 Upper Deck 327
02/3 Upper Deck 97
99/0 UD G. Reserve 346
00/1 UD MVP 201
02/3 UD MVP 105
00/1 UD Vintage 267
02/3 UD Vintage 146
00/1 Victory 277
02/3 Victory 122

DELMORE, MARC
99/0 Anchorage Aces

DELORME, GILBERT
92/3 Cleveland Lumberjacks
93/4 Cleveland Lumberjacks
86/7 DETR / Little Caesars
87/8 DETR / Little Caesars
88/9 DETR / Little Caesars
81/2 MONT
82/3 MONT
82/3 MONT / Steinberg
83/4 MONT
83/4 O-Pee-Chee 186
86/7 O-Pee-Chee 234
90/1 O-Pee-Chee 517
83/4 OPC/Topps Sticker 70
86/7 OPC Sticker 28-167
89/0 PITT / Foodland 6
91/2 ProCards 300
85/6 QUÉB
85/6 QUÉB / Gene. Foods
85/6 QUÉB / McDonald's
85/6 QUÉB / Provigo
86/7 QUÉB / Gene. Foods
86/7 QUÉB / McDonald's
86/7 QUÉB / Yum Yum
83/4 Souhaits Keychain [Canadiens]
83/4 Vachon 43-63

DELORME, MARC
96/7 Louisiana Ice Gators
94/5 Slapshot / Brantford 19

DELORME, RON
79/0 COLR
84/5 Kelowna Wings &...
78/9 O-Pee-Chee 323
79/0 O-Pee-Chee 284
80/1 O-Pee-Chee 231
81/2 O-Pee-Chee 82
82/3 O-Pee-Chee 347
83/4 O-Pee-Chee 348
84/5 O-Pee-Chee 316
81/2 OPC Sticker 231
82/3 Post [Vanc.]
83/4 Vachon 104-24
82/3 VANC
83/4 VANC
84/5 VANC

DELORME, RON
02/3 Fleer Throwbacks 47

DELPARTE, GUY
76/7 COLR / Hockey Talk

DELVECCHIO, ALEX
71/2 Bazooka Panel
99/0 BAP Mem. R-7, ✍ R-7
45-64 BeeHive-2 [Detr.]
64-67 BeeHive-3 [Detr.]
64-67 BeeHive-3 [Detr.]
63-65 Chex
64/5 Coke/Sprite [Detr. #10]
65/6 Coca-Cola
70/1 Colgate 4
70/1 Dad's Cookies
70/1 DETR / Marathon Oil
76 DETR
99/0 DETR / News 2
70/1 Eddie Sargent 59
71/2 Eddie Sargent 55
72/3 Eddie Sargent 76
70/1 Esso Power Player
01/2 Fleer Greats 40, ✍ Aut.
01/2 Fleer Legacy 60
62/3 Cowan Tile
83 HHOF Postcard E7
83&87 HHOF 230
02/3 In The Game-Used ✄ VM11
68/9 O-Pee-Chee 28
69/0 O-Pee-Chee 157
69/0 O-Pee-Chee 206
69/0 O-Pee-Chee 4in1
70/1 O-Pee-Chee 157
71/2 O-Pee-Chee 37
71/2 O-Pee-Chee Book. 12
72/3 O-Pee-Chee 26
73/4 O-Pee-Chee 1
74/5 O-Pee-Chee 222
51/2 Parkhurst 63
52/3 Parkhurst 53
53/4 Parkhurst 47
54/5 Parkhurst 36
54/5 Parkhurst 90
60/1 Parkhurst 36
61/2 Parkhurst 25
62/3 Parkhurst 32
63/4 Parkhurst 50
91/2 Parkhurst PHC2
92/3 Parkhurst PR-19
02/3 Parkie - Reprint 159, 173, 180, 193, 255, 265, 278, 292, ✄ VT17
93/4 Parkie 56-57 59
95/6 Parkie 66-67 53, 127
94/5 Parkie Tall 56
90/1 Pro Set 652, 658
72 Semic Sticker 193
60/1 Shirriff 44
61/2 Shirriff 70
68/9 Shirriff / Detr. 4
91/2 Star Pics 10
54/5 Topps 39
57/8 Topps 34
58/9 Topps 52
59/0 Topps 8
64/5 Topps 95
65/6 Topps 47
66/7 Topps 102
66/7 Topps / Test 63
67/8 Topps 51
68/9 Topps 28
69/0 Topps 64
71/2 Topps 37
72/3 Topps 141
73/4 Topps 141
74/5 Topps 222
00/1 To. Heritage ✍ CAI
01/2 Topps Archives 13, -Seat, ✄ Jers, ✍ CAI
57/8 Toronto Star Photo
58/9 Toronto Star Photo
63/4 Toronto Star Action[Error: Alec]
64/5 Toronto Star Action
58/9 Toronto Star Weekend
62/3 Toronto Star Weekend
71/2 Toronto Sun Photo
02/3 Ultimate Mem. ✄ Cor, ✄ EA, ✄ FS (x2), ✄ Num, ✄ RT, ✄ VGJ
91/2 Ultimate Original Six 68, ✍ Aut. 68
02/3 UD Foundations 20
01/2 UD Legends 20, ✍ ES
99/0 UD Retro 89, ✍ Ink.
60/1 York Glass [Detr.]
62/3 York Transfer 21
63/4 York 50

DELVECCHIO, BILL
45-64 BeeHive-2 [Detr.]

DEMARCO, AB (JR.)
74/5 Loblaws
74/5 Loblaws Update
69/0 Mästär Serien 32
71/2 O-Pee-Chee 90
73/4 O-Pee-Chee 118
74/5 O-Pee-Chee 89
75/6 O-Pee-Chee 78
76/7 O-Pee-Chee 374
77/8 O-Pee-Chee 283
73/4 SLOU
73/4 Topps 118
74/5 Topps 89
75/6 Topps 78
74/5 Toronto Sun Photo
74/5 VANC / Royal Bank
75/6 VANC / Royal Bank

DEMARCO, AB (SR.)
39/0 O-Pee-Chee 82

DEMARSKI, MATT
98/9 Florida Everblades
99/0 Florida Everblades
00/1 Florida Everblades

DEMEL, TOMAS
97/8 APS 44
98/9 OFS 345
00/1 OFS 344

DEMERES, TONY
40/1 O-Pee-Chee 144

DEMERS, ALEXANDRE
01/2 Drummondville

DEMERS, GUILLAUME
01/2 Cape Breton Eagles 13

DEMERS, JACQUES
78/9 Dernière Heure
86/7 DETR / Little Caesars
87/8 DETR / Little Caesars
88/9 DETR / Little Caesars
88/9 DETR / S.A.M.
89/0 DETR / Little Caesars
89/0 DETR / Little Caesars
82/3 Fredericton Express
93/4 Kraft / PB
92/3 MONT
92/3 MONT / OPC 10
93/4 MONT
94/5 MONT

DEMERS, JEAN-FRANCOIS
00/1 Chicoutimi Saguenéens 18

DEMERS, NORMAND
90/1 7th..Sketch LHJMQ 83
90 7th..Sketch Mem.Cup 73

DEMERS, TONY
34-43 BeeHive-1 [Mont.]
43-47 Parade Sportive

DEMIDOV, ILJA
00/1 Grand Rapids Griffins

DEMIN, VASSILI
94/5 Erie Panthers

DEMITRA, PAVOL
01/2 Adrenaline 158
02/3 Atomic -PC 16, ✄ GWJ 20
99/0 Aurora 124
00/1 Aurora 119
02/3 BAP All-Star 18, ✄ ASJ
98/9 Be A Player 126, ✍ Aut. 126
99/0 BAP Mem. 164, SL-2, H-23
00/1 BAP Mem. 129
01/2 BAP Memor. 45, ✄ ASJ, ✄ ASE, ✄ ASN, ✄ CoO
02/3 BAP Memorabilia 190, ✄ ASJ10
01/2 Bowman 66
02/3 Bowman 50
99/0 Crown Royale 115, -IG 22
01/2 Crown Royale 118
02/3 Crown Royale 80, ✄ GWDP 18
93/4 Donruss 240
94/5 Donruss 133
99/0 Dynagon Ice 165
95/6 Edge Ice 48
02/3 Exclusive 141
02/3 First Edition 66, 378, ✄ Jers.
94/5 Fleer 144
94/5 Fleer Ultra 337
96/7 Grand Rapids Griffins
02/3 Heads Up 102, -ITN 18, ✄ GWQ 23, ✄ GWQ 34
99/0 HoloGrFX 51
96/7 Las Vegas Thunder
93/4 Leaf 366
94/5 Leaf 115
99/0 Millenium 204, ✍ Aut. 204
98/9 NHL Power Play
01/2 O-Pee-Chee 61
02/3 O-Pee-Chee 155
97/8 Omega 191
98/9 Omega 201
99/0 Omega 195, -WAS 7
93/4 OTTA
98/9 Pacific 38
99/0 Pacific 355
00/1 Pacific 341, ES-7
01/2 Pacific 321
02/3 Pacific 320, ✄ GWJ 43
02/3 Pacific Complete 437
97/8 Pa. Crown Roy. 114
98/9 Pa. Paramount 202
99/0 Pa. Paramount 195, -PB 32
00/1 Pa. Paramount 204
98/9 Pa. Revolution 121
95/6 Panini Sticker 53
96/7 Panini Sticker 52
98/9 Panini Sticker 157
99/0 Panini Sticker 293, 328
00/1 Panini Sticker 195
93/4 Parkhurst 140
95/6 Parkhurst 149
00/1 Parkhurst P-114
01/2 Parkhurst 16, ✄ PS35
02/3 Parkhurst 18
02/3 Parkhurst Retro 20
94/5 Parkie SE121
93/4 Pinnacle 446
97/8 Pi. Be A Player 146, ✍ Aut. 146
95/6 POG 195
94/5 Premier 336
00/1 Premier Plus 45
99/0 Prism 117
00/1 Private Stock 82, PS-51
02/3 Pr. Stock Reserve 82
00/1 PS Titanium 80
01/2 PS Titanium 115
02/3 PS Titanium ✄ GWJ 56
02/3 Quest for the Cup 81
99/0 Revolution 121, SS-30, TL-9
00/1 Revolution 121
93/4 Score 624
97/8 Score SLou. 18
94/5 Select 185
00/1 Signature 124
01/2 Signature 169, ✍ Aut. 169
02/3 Signature 129, ✍ 129
97/8 SP Authentic 142
98/9 SP Authentic 74
99/0 SP Authentic 75
01/2 SP Authentic 75
02/3 SP Authentic 78
00/1 SP GU 53, ✄ TotG
01/2 SP GU 50, ✄ AF
02/3 SP Game-Used ✄ AF, ✄ CF (x2)
02/3 Sports Vault 273
99/0 SPx 132
00/1 SPx 60, ✄ WM
01/2 SPx 61
98/9 SPx Finite 76
99/0 SLOU / Taco Bell 8
99/0 Stadium 70, EG9
00/1 Stadium 28, ✍ CO1, ✍ LS8, SF13
01/2 Stadium 36
02/3 Stadium 94
99/0 Topps 205, NS15
00/1 Topps 43, NHLD10
01/2 Topps 61
02/3 Topps 155
99/0 To. Chrome 205
00/1 To. Chrome 35
01/2 To. Chrome 61
02/3 T. Chrome 94
94/5 Topps Finest 111
98/9 To. Finest 62
98/9 T. Gold Label 29
99/0 To. Gold Label 21
00/1 To. Gold Label 67, B5
00/1 To. Heritage 51, 242
01/2 To. Heritage 102
02/3 To. Heritage 99
02/3 T. Limited 155
99/0 To. Prmr. Plus 64
00/1 To. Stars 54
02/3 T. Total 26
98/9 UD Choice 186
00/1 UD Heroes 103
01/2 UD PlayMakers Ltd 85
99/0 Ult. Victory 76
92/3 Upper Deck 602
93/4 Upper Deck 372, SP-108
94/5 Upper Deck 216, SP-145
97/8 Upper Deck 146
98/9 Upper Deck 173
99/0 Upper Deck 113
00/1 Upper Deck 150, 383
01/2 Upper Deck 151, FF2, T9
02/3 Upper Deck 150
99/0 UD Black Diam. 72
01/2 UD Challenge 76
97/8 UD Coll. Choice 232
98/9 UD G. Reserve 173
99/0 UD G. Reserve 113
01/2 UD Honor Roll 98, ✄ GAJ
00/1 UD Ice ✄ IGJ
01/2 UD Ice 117
00/1 UD Legends 117
01/2 UD Mask 86, ✄ GJ, ✄ JP, ✄ DP
98/9 UD MVP 185
99/0 UD MVP 182, ✍ PS
00/1 UD MVP 156
01/2 UD MVP 165
02/3 UD MVP 163
99/0 UD MVP Cup 160
99/0 UD Ovation 48
99/0 UD Retro 69
02/3 UD Rookie ✄ DJ
01/2 UD Top Shelf 115, ✄ J
02/3 UD Top Shelf ✄ HH, ✄ TS
00/1 UD Vintage 310, 320
01/2 UD Vintage 221, 226
02/3 UD Vintage 219, 286, GB 219
02/3 Vanguard ✄ GWJ 38
99/0 Victory 259
00/1 Victory 200, 322
01/2 Victory 307
02/3 Victory 184, -NP43
99/0 WGretzky 145

DEMMANS, TREVOR
92/3 MPS SJHL 118

DEMMEL, FRANZ
94/5 DEL 220
95/6 DEL 216
96/7 DEL 360

DEMPSEY, ED
96/7 Kamloops Blazers
99/0 Prince George Cougars

DEMPSEY, NATHAN
99/0 BAP Mem. 306
90/1 7th..Sketch WHL 221
01/2 Signature 71, ✍ Aut. 71
94/5 St. John's Maple Leafs
95/6 St. John's Maple Leafs
96/7 St. John's Maple Leafs
97/8 St. John's Maple Leafs
98/9 St. John's Maple Leafs
99/0 St. John's Maple Leafs
00/1 St. John's Maple Leafs
01/2 St. John's / Clarenville
99/0 UD MVP Cup 177
00/1 Victory 270

DENHAM, JEFF
91/2 Avant Garde BCJHL 37

DENIS, LOUIS (LULU)
51/2 Laval Dairy 97
52/3 Laval Dairy Update 97
52/3 St. Lawrence 13
37/8 World Wide Gum 125

DENIS, MARC
01/2 Adrenaline 52, PP10
01/2 Atomic 29
02/3 Atomic 28
99/0 BAP Mem. 86, SL-24
00/1 BAP Mem. 75
01/2 BAP Memor. 163
02/3 BAP Memorabilia 19
01/2 BT Pipes 25, ✄ Jers.
02/3 Between the Pipes 25, 129, M9, ✄ BM13, ✍ Aut.
01/2 Bowman 88
02/3 Bowman 24
97 Bowman 61
01/2 COLU
99/0 Crown Royale 35
00/1 Crown Royale 120, 21CR-8
01/2 Crown Royale 42
02/3 Crown Royale 28, ✄ GWDP 7
97/8 Donruss 202, RR-4
97/8 Do. Canadian 145, LG-12
95/6 Do. Elite WJ 1
97/8 Do. Elite BF-2, ✍ BF-2
97/8 Do. Preferred 145, 187, CG-10
97/8 Do. Priority PG 18
97/8 Do. Studio 25, P-26
02/3 Exclusive 50, -EA 5
02/3 First Edition 233, 416H
01/2 Heads Up 27, BTI 8
02/3 Heads Up 34, ✄ GWQ 10
98/9 Hershey Bears
97/8 Leaf 105, 148
97/8 Limited 47, 127, FG-47
99/0 Millenium 72, C-43, ✍ Aut. 72
99/0 NHL Power Play
01/2 O-Pee-Chee 218
02/3 O-Pee-Chee 43
98/9 Omega 59
99/0 Omega 68
00/1 Pacific 109
01/2 Pacific 112
02/3 Pacific 99, ✄ GWJ 12
02/3 Pacific Complete 385
99/0 Pa. Paramount 61
00/1 Pa. Paramount 68
00/1 Parkhurst P-164
01/2 Parkhurst 69
02/3 Parkhurst 88
02/3 Parkhurst Retro 164
97/8 Pi. Inside 64
00/1 Private Stock 27, PS-15, PSNW-9, ✄ GUG-33
01/2 Pr. Stock -PS 20
02/3 Pr. Stock Reserve -ICS 6, ✄ 112
00/1 PS Titanium 113, ✄ GUG-11
01/2 PS Titanium 39
01/2 PS Titanium Draft ✄ 29
02/3 PS Titanium 29
00/1 PS Titanium Draft 113
02/3 Quest for the Cup 25
00/1 Revolution 42
97/8 Score Colo. 3
01/2 Signature 35, ✍ Aut. 35
02/3 Signature 20, ✍ 20
00/1 SP Authentic ✍ SotT
02/3 SP Authentic 26, ✄ SP
02/3 SP GU 14, ✄ AF, ✄ PC, ✄ PH, ✄ TG
02/3 Sports Vault 200
02/3 SPx 22
00/1 Stadium 209
01/2 Stadium 100, NR5, ✍ NR
02/3 Stadium 39
99/0 Topps 214
00/1 Topps 273
01/2 Topps 218
02/3 Topps 43
99/0 To. Chrome 214
00/1 To. Chrome 168
01/2 To. Chrome 89
02/3 T. Chrome 37
01/2 To. Heritage 86
02/3 To. Heritage 86
02/3 T. Limited 43
02/3 T. Total 87
00/1 UD Heroes 33, ✍ SG
01/2 UD PlayMakers Ltd 28
00/1 Ultimate Mem. ✄ G-09
95/6 Upper Deck 529
97/8 Upper Deck T12B
98/9 Upper Deck 25, 75, GN9
00/1 Upper Deck 53
01/2 Upper Deck 229
02/3 Upper Deck 50, ✄ CG, ✄ HS
02/3 UD Artistic 25, R25, / Art
96/7 UD Black Diam. 130
00/1 UD Black Diam. ✄ GG
02/3 UD Classic 28
96/7 UD CC 363
97/8 UD Coll. Choice 302
98/9 UD G. Reserve 25, 75
02/3 UD Honor 20
96/7 UD Ice 117
97/8 UD Ice 31
00/1 UD Ice 68
01/2 UD Mask ✄ GP, ✄ GJ, ✄ JP, ✄ DP
02/3 UD Mask 24, 25, 115, ✄ GG, ✄ BM
99/0 UD MVP W17
00/1 UD MVP 55
02/3 UD MVP 53, SD, Souv.
99/0 UD MVP Cup 56
02/3 UD Piece 23
02/3 UD Premier 17
00/1 UD Pros&Prosp. 25
02/3 UD Rookie 30
02/3 UD Top Shelf 24, ✄ R, ✄ ST, ✄ SS, ✄ SW
00/1 UD Vintage 100, 110
02/3 UD Vintage 74, 269, GB 74, ✄ HS
00/1 Vanguard 113
02/3 Vanguard 30
01/2 Victory 104
02/3 Victory 60

DENISET, PAUL
98/9 Kamloops Blazers
99/0 Kamloops Blazers
99/0 Kamloops Blazers

DENISOV, DENIS
00/1 Mir 284

DENISOV, DMITRI
97/8 APS 99
97/8 DS Sticker 102
99/0 Mir 165
00/1 Mir 372
95 Panini Worlds 38
96 Wien 155

DENNENY, CORBETT
23/4 William Paterson 40

DENNENY, CY
25-27 Anonymous 17
24/5 Champ's Cigarettes
83 HHOF Postcard K3
83&87 HHOF 138
60/1 Topps 8
61/2 Topps - Stamp
23/4 William Paterson 10
24/5 William Paterson 7

DENNIS, DANIEL
92/3 MPS SJHL 20

DENNIS, DUANE
94/5 Cape Breton Oilers

DENNISON, HEATH
92/3 BCJHL 158

DENNISON, JOE
12/3 Imperial 42

DENOMME, C.JAY
91/2 7th...Sketch OHL 74

DENOMME, JASON
89/0 Oshawa Generals
91 7th..Sketch Mem.Cup 9
90/1 7th..Sketch OHL 156
91/2 7th...Sketch OHL 328

DENT, TED
93/4 Johnstown Chiefs 5
94/5 Johnstown Chiefs 6

DEOBALD, LONNY
92/3 MPS SJHL 56

DEPALMA, LARRY
96/7 Milwaukee Admirals
87/8 MINS
88/9 MINS / ADA
89/0 ProCards IHL 79
90/1 ProCards 111
91/2 ProCards 524

DEPOURCQ, JOHN
95/6 Louisiana Ice Gators
95/6 Louisiana Ice Gators-2
96/7 Louisiana Ice Gators
99/0 Louisiana Ice Gators
00/1 Louisiana Ice Gators
01/2 Louisiana Ice Gators
02/3 Louisiana Ice Gators

DEPPER, BLAINE
99/0 Kamloops Blazers
99/0 Kamloops Blazers
00/1 Kelowna Rockets

DERAAF, HELMUT
94/5 DEL 78

DERECOLA, MIKE
00/1 Charlotte Checkers

DERKATCH, DALE
83 Canada Juniors
94/5 DEL 305
95/6 DEL 191
81/2 Regina Pats
82/3 Regina Pats
83/4 Regina Pats

DERKSEN, DEVIN
93/4 Richmond Renegades
90/1 7th..Sketch WHL 100

DERKSEN, DUANE
92/3 Classic 91
92/3 Classic Four Sport 208
93/4 Milwaukee Admirals
99/0 Peoria Rivermen
02/3 Peoria Rivermen
00/1 UD DEL 108

DERLAGO, BILL
83/4 Esso Stars
83/4 Funmate Puffy 1 [w/]
84/5 Kelowna Wings &...
86/7 Kraft Sports 74
80/1 O-Pee-Chee 11
81/2 O-Pee-Chee 305
81/2 O-Pee-Chee 319
82/3 O-Pee-Chee 320
83/4 O-Pee-Chee 327
84/5 O-Pee-Chee 300
85/6 OPC/Topps 71
86/7 O-Pee-Chee 254
81/2 OPC Sticker 99
81/2 OPC Sticker 108
82/3 OPC/Topps Sticker 67
82/3 OPC/Topps Sticker 68
83/4 OPC/Topps Sticker 35
84/5 OPC Sticker 14
85/6 OPC Sticker 7
86/7 OPC Sticker 105-234
87/8 OPC Sticker 224-91
80/1 Pepsi Bottle Cap
82/3 Post [Toro.]
86/7 QUÉB
84/5 7-Eleven
83/4 Souhaits Keychain [Maple Leafs]
80/1 Topps 11
81/2 Topps 8
80/1 TORO
81/2 TORO
82/3 TORO
83/4 TORO
84/5 TORO
83/4 Vachon 84-47
78/9 VANC / Royal Bank
79/0 VANC / Royal Bank
86/7 WINN

DERNDTSSON, PETER
92/3 Semic Elitserien 314

DERNESTAL, STEFAN
91/2 Semic Elitserien 227

DEROUVILLE, PHILIPPE
95/6 Cleveland Lumberjacks
95/6 Donruss 206
97/8 Donruss 197
97/8 Do. Canadian LG 11
95/6 Edge Ice 116

96/7 Kansas City Blades
00/1 Kudos 4
95/6 Leaf 111
95/6 Pinnacle 214
95/6 Score 291
91/2 7th...Sketch LHJMQ 131
93/4 Upper Deck 260

DERRAUGH, DOUG
95/6 DEL 375
96/7 DEL 196
99/0 Eishockey 277
01/2 UD DEL 123

DÉRY, MATHIEU
01/2 Québec Remparts 7

DERYABIN, DMITRI
98/9 BC Icemen

DES ALLIERS, RENAUD
02/3 Hull Olympiques

DESANTIS, MARK
94/5 Classic E10
94/5 Classic 4 Sport 150
93/4 Cla. Prospects 77
91/2 Cornwall Royals
94/5 Greensboro Monarchs
98/9 Louisiana Ice Gators
93/4 San Diego Gulls
90/1 7th..Sketch OHL 32
91/2 7th...Sketch OHL 3

DESAULNIERS, GERRY
51/2 Laval Dairy 93
52/3 Laval Dairy Update 93
52/3 St. Lawrence 4

DESBIENS, GUILLAUME
99 Québec Pee Wee 777

DESBIENS, ROBERT
51/2 Lac St-Jean 4

DESCHAMPS, MARC
92/3 Wheeling Thund'birds 5

DESCHAMPS, ROBERT
89/0 7th..Sketch OHL 158
90/1 7th..Sketch OHL 282

DESCHAUME, LAURENT
95 Panini Worlds 108
93 Semic Sticker 261

DESCHENES, FRÉDÉRIC
96/7 Rochester Americans

DESCHESNE, DONAT
52/3 Bas du Fleuve 41
51/2 Laval Dairy 20

DESCHEVVY, SERGEI
99/0 Topeka Scarecrows

DESCÔTEAUX, MATTHIEU
95/6 Bowman P9
99/0 Hamilton Bulldogs
99/0 Québec Citadelles 20
00/1 Québec Citadelles
01/2 Québec Citadelles

DESGAGNE, MARC
91/2 7th...Sketch LHJMQ 7

DESILETS, JOFFRE
34-43 BeeHive-1 [Mont.]
35-40 Canada Starch
36/7 O-Pee-Chee 114
37/8 O-Pee-Chee 156
39/0 O-Pee-Chee 44

DESILETS, MIKE
52/3 Anonymous 158

DÉSILETS, NICOLAS
99 Québec Pee Wee 887
02/3 Shawinigan Cataractes

DESJARDINE, KEN
72/3 Québec Nordiques
73/4 Québec Nordiques

DESJARDINS, ÉRIC
98/9 Aurora 137
99/0 Aurora 104
00/1 Aurora 105
98/9 Be A Player 253, ✍ Aut. 253
99/0 BAP Mem. 189
00/1 BAP Mem. 53
01/2 BAP Memor. 159
91/2 Bowman 329
92/3 Bowman 228
92/3 Bowman 311
91 Canada Cup
00/1 Crown Royale ✂ GWJ 19
93/4 Donruss 173
94/5 Donruss 177
95/6 Donruss 151
96/7 Donruss 25
97/8 Donruss 141
92/3 Durivage 36
93/4 Durivage 12
93/4 EA Sports 67
97/8 Esso 13, ✍ Aut.
02/3 First Edition 175
94/5 Flair 88
94/5 Fleer 151
96/7 Fleer 79, NT-4
95/6 Fleer Metal 109
92/3 Fleer Ultra 104
93/4 Fleer Ultra 94
94/5 Fleer Ultra 108
95/6 Fleer Ultra 116
96/7 Fl. Ultra 123
97/8 General Mills
91/2 Gillette 27
01/2 Heads Up ✂ JQ 15
97/8 Kraft / PB
99/0 Kraft / KD
93/4 Leaf 203
94/5 Leaf 433
95/6 Leaf 70
96/7 Leaf 27
96/7 L. Preferred 32
97/8 Limited 80
96/7 Metal Univ. 110
99/0 Millenium 180, ✍ Aut. 180
88/9 MONT
89/0 MONT
89/0 MONT / Kraft
90/1 MONT
91/2 MONT
92/3 MONT
92/3 MONT / OPC 20
93/4 MONT
94/5 MONT
90/1 O-Pee-Chee 425
91/2 O-Pee-Chee 14
92/3 O-Pee-Chee 360
01/2 O-Pee-Chee 245
98/9 OPC Chrome 35
91/2 OPC Premier 157
97/8 Omega 162
98/9 Omega 173
99/0 Omega 168
98/9 Pacific 324
99/0 Pacific 301
00/1 Pacific 295, ✂ GWJ-10
01/2 Pacific 285
02/3 Pacific 278
02/3 Pacific Complete 348
97/8 Pacific CC 121
98/9 Pa. Paramount 171
99/0 Pa. Paramount 169
00/1 Pa. Paramount 179, ✂ J&P-8
90/1 Panini/MTL 8
91/2 Panini Sticker 189
92/3 Panini Sticker 156
93/4 Panini Sticker 21
94/5 Panini Sticker 17
95/6 Panini Sticker 119
96/7 Panini Sticker 115
99/0 Panini Sticker 127
91/2 Parkhurst 85
92/3 Parkhurst 80
93/4 Parkhurst 102
94/5 Parkhurst 118
95/6 Parkhurst 428
00/1 Parkhurst P-36
01/2 Parkhurst 111
94/5 PHIL / Sheet
96/7 PHIL / Ocean Spray
01/2 PHIL
91/2 Pinnacle 73
92/3 Pinnacle 16
92/3 Pinnacle T2K 9
93/4 Pinnacle 59
94/5 Pinnacle 106
95/6 Pinnacle 110
96/7 Pinnacle 169
96/7 Pi. Be A Player 40, ✍ Aut. 40
95/6 Playoff 75
94/5 POG 139
95/6 POG 209
93/4 Power Play 128
93/4 Premier 32
00/1 Private Stock ✂ GUG-81, ✂ GUG-121
00/1 PS Titanium ✂ GUG 121
00/1 PS Titanium Draft ✂ 72
90/1 Pro Set 467
91/2 Pro Set 118
92/3 Pro Set 86
91/2 Pro Set Platinum 193
00/1 Revolution 107
90/1 Score 58T
91/2 Score 119
91/2 Score CAN 119
92/3 Score 23
93/4 Score 128
94/5 Score 110
95/6 Score 207
96/7 Score 159
97/8 Score 196
97/8 Score Phil. 7
91/2 Score Young Stars 23
92/3 Score Young Stars 28
94/5 Select 113
94 Semic 87
93 Semic Sticker 195
00/1 Signature 15, ✍ Aut. 156, ✂ DD-17
02/3 Signature ✂ DW3
95/6 SBx Emotion 130
95/6 SBx Impact 124
96/7 SBx Impact 93, F-8
95/6 SP 112
96/7 SP 113
02/3 Sports Vault 108
99/0 SPx 113
00/1 Stadium 169
95/6 Super Sticker 93
96/7 Team Out✂
92/3 Topps 192
95/6 Topps 290
98/9 Topps 35
99/0 Topps 158
00/1 Topps 167
01/2 Topps 245
99/0 To. Chrome 158
00/1 To. Chrome 115
95/6 To. Finest 174
98/9 To. Finest 102
00/1 To. Heritage 225, 236
01/2 To. Heritage ✂ CC
96/7 Topps Picks 93
01/2 To. Reserve ✂ TR
91/2 To. Stadium 214
92/3 T. Stadium Club 326
93/4 To. Stadium 170
94/5 T. Stadium Club 263
95/6 To. Stadium 125
95/6 TSC Members Only 41
00/1 To. Stars 53
02/3 T. Total 327
00/1 Ultimate Mem. ✂ TM-29
90/1 Upper Deck 428
91/2 Upper Deck 360
91/2 Upper Deck 504
92/3 Upper Deck 268
93/4 Upper Deck 184
94/5 Upper Deck 279
95/6 Upper Deck 186, AS-9, SE-150
96/7 Upper Deck 123
97/8 Upper Deck 332
98/9 Upper Deck 150
99/0 Upper Deck 98
00/1 Upper Deck 130
01/2 Upper Deck 126
94/5 UD BAP R105, ✍ 111
96/7 UD Black Diam. 37
95/6 UD CC 105
96/7 UD CC 195
97/8 UD Coll. Choice W15
98/9 UD G. Reserve 150
99/0 UD G. Reserve 98
96/7 UD Ice 47
98/9 UD MVP 154
99/0 UD MVP 152
00/1 UD MVP 133
01/2 UD MVP 142
02/3 UD MVP 135
95/6 UD Post 5
01/2 UD SCup Champs 68
00/1 UD Vintage 265
01/2 UD Vintage 189
97/8 Valu-net, ✍ Aut.
99/0 Victory 215
00/1 Victory 171
01/2 Victory 263
96 Wien 83

DESJARDINS, GERRY
75/6 BUFF / Linnett
70/1 Colgate 67
70/1 Eddie Sargent 45
72/3 Eddie Sargent 129
70/1 Esso Power Player
69/0 O-Pee-Chee 99
69/0 O-Pee-Chee 4in1
69/0 O-Pee-Chee Stamp
70/1 O-Pee-Chee 152
72/3 O-Pee-Chee 119
73/4 O-Pee-Chee 178
75/6 O-Pee-Chee 125
76/7 O-Pee-Chee 230
77/8 O-Pee-Chee 150
69/0 Topps 99
72/3 Topps 38
73/4 Topps 114
75/6 Topps 125
76/7 Topps 230
77/8 Topps 150

DESJARDINS, MARIO
86/7 Kamloops Blazers

DESJARDINS, MARTIN
89/0 MONT
88/9 ProCards / Sherbrooke
90/1 ProCards 410
91/2 ProCards 484

DESJARDINS, NORMAN
89/0 ProCards AHL 189
90/1 ProCards 69
91/2 ProCards 75

DESJARDINS, STÉPHANE
94/5 Roanoke Express
90/1 7th..Sketch LHJMQ 5
91/2 7th...Sketch LHJMQ 286
91 7th..Sketch Mem.Cup 61

DESLAURIERS, FRANCIS
99/0 Shawinigan 8

DESLAURIERS, JACQUES
51/2 Laval Dairy 82
52/3 St. Lawrence 25

DESLAURIERS, KEVIN
00/1 Baie-Comeau 14
01/2 Baie-Comeau 12
02/3 Baie-Comeau

DESLAURIERS, KÉVIN
02/3 Shawinigan Cataractes

DESLOGES, STEVE
74/5 Sioux City Musketeers

DESMARAIS, DENIS
99/0 Shawinigan 16
00/1 Shawinigan 1
01/2 Shawinigan 1

DESMARAIS, JAMES
99 Bowman 82
99/0 Peoria Rivermen
99/0 Rouyn-Noranda

DESMARAIS, MATT
92/3 MPS SJHL 46

DESNOYERS, DAVID
91/2 7th...Sketch LHJMQ 3

DESOUSA, ANDREW
01/2 Vancouver Giants

DESPATIS, CHRIS
95/6 Slapshot 276

DESROCHERS, ÉRIC
90/1 7th..Sketch LHJMQ 191

DESROCHERS, PATRICK
97/8 Bell
01/2 BT Pipes 88

DESROCHERS, PATRICK
02/3 Between the Pipes 93

DESROCHERS, PATRICK
97 Bowman 40
98 Bowman 139, SC5, ✍ A20
98 Bowman Chrome 139
02/3 O-Pee-Chee 283
95/6 Slapshot 332
02/3 Topps 283
98/9 To. Finest F11
02/3 T. Limited 283
96/7 Upper Deck 371

DESROSIERS, DENNIS
91/2 Cincinnati Cyclones
92/3 Cincinnati Cyclones
93/4 Cincinnati Cyclones
78/9 Saginaw Gears

DESROSIERS, GILLES
52/3 Bas du Fleuve 53
51/2 Lac St-Jean 3

DESROSIERS, JOE
89/0 7th..Sketch OHL 95
86/7 Sudbury Wolves

DESROSIERS, JULIEN
97/8 Rimouski Océanic

DESROSIERS, LOUIS
52/3 Anonymous 47
52/3 Bas du Fleuve 65

DESRUISSEAUX, MAXIME
01/2 Moncton Wildcats 21

DESSNER, JEFF
01/2 Chicago Wolves

DESSUREAULT, GAËTAN
53/4 La Patrie

DESYATKOV, PAVEL
00/1 Mir 194
93/4 Pinnacle 505

DEUBERT, HARALD
99/0 Eishockey 404

DEULING, JARRETT
93/4 Kamloops Blazers
96/7 Kentucky Tho'blades
98/9 Kentucky Tho'blades
99/0 Kentucky Tho'blades
00/1 Kentucky Tho'blades
97/8 Milwaukee Admirals
90/1 7th..Sketch WHL 308
91/2 7th...Sketch WHL 93

DEUTSCHER, TORSTEN
94/5 DEL 36
95/6 DEL 29

DEVEAUX, ANDRE
01/2 Belleville Bulls

DEVELLANO, JIM
85/6 DETR / Little Caesars

DEVEREAUX, BOYD
96/7 All-Sport PPF 79
00/1 BAP Mem. 450
95/6 Bowman P10
97 Bowman 23
95/6 Classic 87
95/6 Cla. Vis. Signings 61, ✍ Aut.
97/8 Do. Elite 90
97/8 Do. Priority 184
96/7 EDMO
97/8 EDMO
95/6 Future Legends ✍ HS-2
99/0 Hamilton Bulldogs/ Staz
97/8 Leaf 149
99/0 NHL Power Play
98/9 OPC Chrome 21
00/1 Pacific 163
02/3 Pacific 125
02/3 Pacific Complete 98
97/8 Pa. Paramount 73
97/8 Pinnacle 13
97/8 Pi. Be A Player 237, ✍ Aut. 237
97/8 Pi. Certified J
97/8 Score 73
95/6 Slapshot 149, 432
97/8 SP Authentic 181
00/1 Stadium 224
98/9 Topps 21
02/3 To. Heritage 130
02/3 Upper Deck 311
96/7 UD Black Diam. 86
97/8 UD Black Diam. 146
97/8 UD Coll. Choice 311
96/7 UD Ice 122
99/0 UD MVP Cup 75
02/3 UD Vintage 98
01/2 Victory 130
97/8 Zenith 93

DEVEREAUX, JOHN
88/9 Flint Spirits
91/2 Greensboro Monarchs

DEVINE, KEVIN
81/2 Indianapolis Checkers
82/3 Indianapolis Checkers
76/7 San Diego Mariners

DEVLIN, VINCE
92/3 BCJHL 216
92/3 BCJHL 227

DEVUONO, LENNY
90/1 Kitchener Rangers
90/1 7th..Sketch OHL 93, 230

DEWALLE, KIRK
93/4 Lethbridge Hurricanes

DEWAN, ADAM
01/2 Hamilton Bulldogs
01/2 Hamilton Bulldogs/ Staz
02/3 Hamilton Bulldogs

DEWAR, JEFF
93/4 Seattle Thunderbirds

DEWITZ, DIETER
74 Hellas MM-Jenkki 109
70/1 Kuvajulkaisut 83

DEWOLF, JOSH
98/9 Albany River Rats
99/0 Albany River Rats
01/2 Cincinnati Mighty Ducks
95/6 Classic 59
99/0 Québec Citadelles 22
00/1 Québec Citadelles

DEWSBURY, AL
45-64 BeeHive-2 [Chic.]
51/2 Parkhurst 38
52/3 Parkhurst 17
53/4 Parkhurst 78
54/5 Parkhurst 78
02/3 Parkie - Reprint 156, 165, 198
93/4 Parkie 56-57 22

DEXHEIMER, ALEXANDER
98/9 DEL 218

DEXTER, JASON
95/6 Birmingham Bulls

DEY, EDGAR
10/1 Imperial 6

DEYELL, MARK
93/4 Saskatoon Blades
93/4 Saskatoon Blades
96/7 St. John's Maple Leafs
97/8 St. John's Maple Leafs

DEZAINDE, JOEL
01/2 Albany River Rats
98/9 Barrie Colts
95/6 Slapshot 158

DEZAINDE, NORMAN
98/9 Dayton Bombers
98/9 Dayton Bombers
90/1 Kitchener Rangers
90/1 7th..Sketch OHL 231
91/2 7th...Sketch OHL 82
94/5 Sig. Rookies 24, ✍ 24
93/4 Slapshot / Kitchener 8
94/5 Toledo Storm
95/6 Toledo Storm
96/7 Toledo Storm

DHADPHALE, ANIKET
99/0 Greensboro Generals

DI FAZIO, ALBERTO
82 Semic Sticker 136

DI FIORE, RALPH
94 Semic 295

DI MUZIO, FRANK
98/9 DEL 201
88/9 ProCards / Baltimore
94 Semic 300
93 Semic Sticker 217

DI PAOLO, MAURO
97/8 Halifax Moosehead
98/9 Halifax Moosehead

DI UBALDO, CHRIS
00/1 Kelowna Rockets

DIBELER, BRAD
94/5 Hershey Bears

DIBLEY, GORD
67/8 Columbus Checkers

DICAIRE, GERARD
00/1 UD Prospects 65

DICASMIRRO, NATE
02/3 Hamilton Bulldogs

DICK, JONATHAN
01/2 Drummondville

DICK, MIKE
97/8 Central Texas

DICKENS, ERNIE
34-43 BeeHive-1 [Toro.]
45-64 BeeHive-2 [Chic.]

DICKENSON, HERB
52/3 Parkhurst 57

DICKENSON, LOU
01/2 Guelph Storm M-Cup
01/2 Kingston Frontenacs 3
00/1 London Knights
99/0 UD Prospects 25, ✂ GJ

DICKIE, BRETT
99/0 Brandon Wheat Kings

DICKIE, GARY
86/7 Regina Pats
87/8 Regina Pats
88/9 Regina Pats

DICKIE, GORD
91/2 7th...Sketch OHL 289
93/4 Slapshot / Kitchener 6

DICKIE, J.J.
96/7 Soo Greyhounds

DICKIE, KEVIN
91/2 Air Canada SJHL 3
00/1 Saskatoon Blades

DICKIE, SCOTT
01/2 Kitchener Rangers

DICKISON, BRIAN
89/0 Rayside-Balfour

DICKSON, DARRYL
91/2 Air Canada SJHL D47
92/3 MPS SJHL 24

DICKSON, SCOTT
98/9 Topeka Scarecrows

DIDMON,
91/2 Avant Garde BCJHL 160

DIDUCK, GERALD
92/3 Bowman 65
93/4 Donruss 360
92/3 Fleer Ultra 424
93/4 Fleer Ultra 440
95/6 Fleer Ultra 245
95/6 HART / Kids Club
96/7 HART / Kids Club
93/4 Leaf 387
94/5 Leaf 402
95/6 Leaf 313
90/1 MONT
84/5 NYIS / News 18
89/0 NYIS
90/1 O-Pee-Chee 421
91/2 O-Pee-Chee 280
92/3 O-Pee-Chee 309
89/0 OPC/Topps 182
90/1 OPC Premier 22
89/0 opcSticker 117-256
00/1 Pacific 388
88/9 Panini Sticker 198
89/0 Panini Sticker 274
90/1 Panini Sticker 85
90/1 Panini/MTL 9
91/2 Parkhurst 407
92/3 Parkhurst 419
95/6 Parkhurst 368
97/8 PHOE / Coca-Cola
98/9 PHOE / Coca-Cola
91/2 Pinnacle 211
92/3 Pinnacle 81
93/4 Pinnacle 291
94/5 Pinnacle 359
96/7 Pi. Be A Player 167, ✍ Aut. 167
97/8 Pi. Be A Player 55, ✍ Aut. 55
93/4 Power Play 250
90/1 Pro Set 180, 468
91/2 Pro Set 502
90/1 Score 139, 23T
91/2 Score CAN 243
92/3 Score 34
93/4 Score 356
92/3 Topps 44
95/6 Topps 247
92/3 T. Stadium Club 97
94/5 T. Stadium Club 91
90/1 Upper Deck 390
90/1 VANC / Mohawk
91/2 VANC
91/2 VANC / Photo
92/3 VANC / Road Trip
94/5 VANC

DIDUCK, GERLAD
00/1 DALL / Southwest

DIDUCK, JUDY
94/5 Classic W12
97/8 UD Coll. Choice 283

DIDUCK, RYAN
99/0 Brandon Wheat Kings

DIENER, DEREK
93/4 Lethbridge Hurricanes
95/6 Lethbridge Hurricanes
97/8 Peoria Rivermen

DIETRICH, BRANDON
00/1 Charlotte Checkers
00/1 Hartford Wolf Pack

DIETRICH, DON
83/4 Springfield Indians 21

DIETRICH, LOU
52/3 Anonymous 13

DIETRICH, SHAWN
90/1 7th..Sketch WHL 198
91/2 7th...Sketch WHL 200
89/0 Spokane Chiefs

DIETSCH, ANDRE
94/5 DEL 34
95/6 DEL 26

DIFRONZE, MICHELE
94/5 Classic W32

DIJAN, JEAN-MARC
92 Semic Sticker 219

DILIO, FRANK
83 HHOF Postcard F5
83&87 HHOF 81

DILLABOUGH, BOB
64-67 BeeHive-3 [Bost.]
72/3 Cleveland Crusaders
72/3 Clev. WHA / Linnett
65/6 Coca-Cola
70/1 Dad's Cookies
70/1 Eddie Sargent 217
68/9 O-Pee-Chee 191
69/0 O-Pee-Chee 150
63/4 Parkhurst 47
65/6 Topps 39
66/7 Topps 98

DILLABOUGH, TRAVIS
98/9 Dayton Bombers
98/9 Dayton Bombers

DILLON, CECIL
33/4 Anonymous 32
34-43 BeeHive-1 [NYRa.]
33/4 Canadian Gum
33-35 Diamond Match Silv.
36-39 Diamond Match TT2
36-39 Diamond Match TT2
36-39 Diamond Match TT3
33/4 O-Pee-Chee 71
33/4 WWGum 15

DILLON, WAYNE
75/6 O-Pee-Chee 363
76/7 O-Pee-Chee 9
77/8 O-Pee-Chee 166
78/9 O-Pee-Chee 73
79/0 O-Pee-Chee 359
74/5 OPC WHA 3
76/7 Topps 9
77/8 Topps 166
78/9 Topps 73
79/0 WINN

DILORENZO, MICHAEL
01/2 Hull Olympiques 22

DIMAIO, ROB
98/9 Be A Player 7, ✍ Aut. 7
92/3 Bowman 403
01/2 DALL / Southwest
84/5 Kamloops Blazers
94/5 Leaf 549
84/5 Medicine Hat Tigers
90/1 OPC Premier 27
92/3 OPC Premier 62
98/9 Pacific 75
02/3 Pacific Complete 289
97/8 Pacific CC 287
93/4 Panini Sticker 218
97/8 Panini Sticker 1
99/0 Panini Sticker 30
91/2 Parkhurst 325
92/3 Parkhurst 402
93/4 Parkhurst 196
95/6 Parkhurst 431
94/5 PHIL / Sheet
94/5 Pinnacle 360
97/8 Pi. Be A Player 6, ✍ Aut. 6
93/4 Premier 242
94/5 Premier 114
90/1 Pro Set 625
91/2 Pro Set 430
88/9 ProCards / Springfield
89/0 ProCards AHL 234
90/1 ProCards 512
97/8 Score Bost. 9
92/3 TAMP / Sheraton Inn
93/4 TAMP / Kash N' Karry
92/3 Topps 488
95/6 Topps 92
98/9 To. Finest 61
92/3 T. Stadium Club 33
93/4 To. Stadium 182
90/1 Upper Deck 225
91/2 Upper Deck 481
92/3 Upper Deck 529
93/4 Upper Deck 176
95/6 Upper Deck 336
00/1 Upper Deck 265
01/2 Upper Deck 288
95/6 UD BAP 105, ✍ S105
99/0 WGretzky 19

DIMALINE, JOE
98/9 Muskegon Fury
99/0 Muskegon Fury

DIMBAT, ANDREAS
95/6 DEL 68
96/7 DEL 264

DIMELLA, NICK
99/0 Des Moines Buc's

DIMITRAKOS, NIKO
02/3 BAP Memorabilia 365
02/3 Calder 143
02/3 Choice Prospects 9
02/3 Pacific Complete 513
02/3 Quest for the Cup 144
02/3 SP Authentic 213
02/3 SPx 183
02/3 Ultimate Mem. 53
02/3 UD Rookie 125

DIMITRI, DAVE
93/4 Huntington Blizzard

DIMME, BIRLEY
52/3 Anonymous 55

DIMMERS, RALPH
99/0 Eishockey 403

DINEEN, BILL
52/3 Anonymous 147
45-64 BeeHive-2 [Detr.]
60/1 Cleveland Barons
53/4 Parkhurst 37
53/4 Parkhurst 38
54/5 Parkhurst 48
93/4 Parkhurst PR62
93/4 Parkie 56-57 50
92/3 PHIL / UD Sheet
88/9 ProCards / Adirondack
63/4 Québec Aces
92/3 Score 517
54/5 Topps 57
57/8 Topps 49

DINEEN, GORD
92/3 Durivage 37
95/6 Edge Ice 192
82/3 Indianapolis Checkers
84/5 NYIS / News 19
90/1 O-Pee-Chee 470
89/0 O-Pee-Chee 256
93/4 OTTA
94/5 Panini Sticker 106
90/1 Pro Set 233
91/2 ProCards 306
92/3 San Diego Gulls
80/1 Soo Greyhounds
81/2 Soo Greyhounds
94/5 T. Stadium Club 219
90/1 Upper Deck 369
99/0 Utah Grizzlies
99/0 Utah Grizzlies

DINEEN, KEVIN
98/9 Aurora 30
90/1 Bowman 261, -HT 7
91/2 Bowman 6
92/3 Bowman 121
97/8 CARO / Sprint
98/9 CARO / Highwoods
94/5 Cla. Images 21, PL3
01/2 COLU
93/4 Donruss 249
94/5 Donruss 36
95/6 Donruss 212
92/3 Durivage 12
93/4 Durivage 37
98/9 Dynagon Ice 30
95/6 Edge Ice 130, C-3
92/3 Fleer Ultra 154
93/4 Fleer Ultra 107
94/5 Fleer Ultra 156
88/9 Frito Lay
85/6 HART / Jr. Whalers
86/7 HART / Jr. Whalers
87/8 HART / Jr. Whalers
88/9 HART / Jr. Whalers
89/0 HART / Jr. Whalers
90/1 HART / Jr. Whalers
96/7 HART / Kids Club
91/2 Kellogg's / Score 11
90/1 Kraft 11
91/2 Kraft 86
93/4 Kraft / PB
96/7 Kraft / PB
93/4 Leaf 156
93/4 Leaf HTA 6
94/5 Leaf 167
95/6 Leaf 205
98/9 NHL Power Play
85/6 OPC/Topps 34
86/7 OPC/Topps 88
87/8 OPC/Topps 124
88/9 OPC/Topps 36
90/1 OPC/Topps 213
91/2 O-Pee-Chee 285
92/3 O-Pee-Chee 200
89/0 OPC/Topps 20, / Box M
98/9 OPC Chrome 173
90/1 OPC Premier 23
85/6 OPC Sticker 168-39
86/7 OPC Sticker 56-194
87/8 OPC Sticker 202-60
88/9 OPC Sticker 269-133
89/0 opcSticker 270
99/0 OTTA
98/9 Pacific 130
99/0 Pacific 69
02/3 Pacific Complete 178
97/8 Pacific CC 218
97/8 Pa. Crown Roy. 22
97/8 Pa. Paramount 33
98/9 Pa. Paramount 34
87/8 Panini Sticker 44
88/9 Panini Sticker 240
89/0 Panini Sticker 219
90/1 Panini Sticker 43
91/2 Panini Sticker 323
92/3 Panini Sticker 186
93/4 Panini Sticker 49
94/5 Panini Sticker 41
91/2 Parkhurst 348
92/3 Parkhurst 127
93/4 Parkhurst 421
94/5 Parkhurst 172
95/6 Parkhurst 366
91/2 PHIL / J.C. Penney
92/3 PHIL / UD Sheet
92/3 PHIL / UD Sheet
92/3 PHIL / J.C. Penney
93/4 PHIL / Sheet
93/4 PHIL / Sheet
93/4 PHIL / J.C. Penney
94/5 PHIL / Sheet
91/2 Pinnacle 246
91/2 Pinnacle 366
92/3 Pinnacle 14
93/4 Pinnacle 276
93/4 Pinnacle CA17
94/5 Pinnacle 426
95/6 Pinnacle 150
94/5 POG 357
95/6 POG 207
93/4 Power Play 179
93/4 Premier 167
94/5 Premier 207
00/1 PS Titanium ✂ GUG 12
90/1 Pro Set 102
91/2 Pro Set 89
91/2 Pro Set 451
92/3 Pro Set 134
91 Pro Set Awards AC17
91/2 Pro Set Platinum 46
90/1 Score 212
90/1 Sco. Hot Cards 90
91/2 Score 118
91/2 Score CAN 118
92/3 Score 284
92/3 Score 517
93/4 Score 122
94/5 Score 197
95/6 Score 277
94/5 Select 142
91 Semic Sticker 71
96/7 SP 71
92/3 Topps 131
95/6 Topps 143
98/9 Topps 173
00/1 To. Chrome 226
91/2 To. Stadium 162
92/3 T. Stadium Club 365
93/4 To. Stadium 43
90/1 Upper Deck 266
91/2 Upper Deck 105
91/2 Upper Deck 530
92/3 Upper Deck 256
93/4 Upper Deck 212
94/5 Upper Deck 431
96/7 Upper Deck 270
97/8 Upper Deck 241
00/1 Upper Deck 283
96/7 UD Black Diam. 72
97/8 UD Coll. Choice 109

DINEEN, PETER
83/4 Moncton Alpines
88/9 ProCards / Adirondack
89/0 ProCards AHL 327
90/1 ProCards 306

DINEEN, SHAWN
83/4 Moncton Alpines
89/0 ProCards IHL 120

DINGMAN, CHRIS
00/1 BAP All-Star AS-10
00/1 BAP Mem. 277, ✂ T-18
01/2 BAP Mem.SCC
01/2 BAP Update ✂ TC26, ✂ TC39
92/3 Brandon Wheat Kings
95/6 Brandon Wheat Kings
94/5 Classic 17, T10
94/5 Classic 4 Sport 133
94/5 Cla. Images 4 Sport 110
01/2 Heads Up ✂ JQ 9
97/8 Leaf 158
01/2 Pacific ✂ GWJ 8
97/8 Pa. Crown Roy. 17
97/8 Pa. Paramount 27
97/8 Pinnacle 7
97/8 Pi. Be A Player 216, ✍ Aut. 216
00/1 Private Stock ✂ GUG 21
00/1 PS Titanium Draft ✂ 23
96/7 Saint John Flames
97/8 Score 55
94/5 Sig. Rookies 20, ✍ 20
94/5 Slapshot Memorial 43
97/8 Upper Deck 234
01/2 Upper Deck 267

DINNEEN, JIM
98/9 Fort Worth Brahmas

DINSMORE, CHUCK
24/5 Champ's Cigarettes
24/5 Maple Crispette [V130] 17
24/5 William Paterson 40

DION, CONNIE
43-47 Parade Sportive

DION, MICHEL
83/4 Funmate Puffy 11 [w/]
79/0 O-Pee-Chee 316
80/1 O-Pee-Chee 223
82/3 O-Pee-Chee 267
83/4 O-Pee-Chee 279
84/5 O-Pee-Chee 173
82/3 OPC/Topps Sticker 146
82/3 OPC/Topps Sticker 168
83/4 OPC/Topps Sticker 234
76/7 O-Pee-Chee WHA 5
76/7 OPC WHA 114
77/8 OPC WHA 62
83/4 PITT / Coke Is It✂
83/4 PITT / Heinz
84/5 PITT / Heinz
82/3 Post [Pitt.]
80/1 QUEB
83/4 Souhaits Keychain [Penguins]
80/1 Topps 223

DION, STEVEN
91/2 7th...Sketch LHJMQ 221

DION, TOM
92/3 Wheeling Thund'birds 6

DIONL, STEVEN
90/1 7th..Sketch LHJMQ 141

DIONNE, GILBERT
92/3 Bowman 439
96/7 Carolina Monarchs
97/8 Cincinnati Cyclones
98/9 Cincinnati Cyclones
99/0 Cincinnati Cyclones
99/0 Cincinnati Cyclones
00/1 Cincinnati Cyclones
92/3 Classic Prospects 87
93/4 Donruss 174
92/3 Durivage 21
93/4 Durivage 13
98/9 EBK IHL All-Star
94/5 Fleer 152
92/3 Fleer Ultra 105, -UR 4
93/4 Fleer Ultra 141
94/5 Fleer Ultra 109
92/3 Humpty Dumpty
88/9 Kitchener Rangers
89/0 Kitchener Rangers
93/4 Leaf 117
92/3 MONT
93/4 MONT
94/5 MONT
92/3 O-Pee-Chee 307
92/3 Panini Sticker 272
92/3 Panini Sticker M
93/4 Panini Sticker 18
94/5 Panini Sticker 15
91/2 Parkhurst 313
91/2 Parkhurst 447
92/3 Parkhurst 81
92/3 Parkhurst 237
93/4 Parkhurst 101
94/5 Parkhurst V14
94/5 Parkie SE91
94/5 PHIL / Sheet
92/3 Pinnacle 5
92/3 Pinnacle T2K 29
93/4 Pinnacle 199
94/5 Pinnacle 422
94/5 POG 134
93/4 Power Play 368
93/4 Premier 480
94/5 Premier 366
92/3 Pro Set 92
92/3 Pro Set PV3
92/3 Pro Set RGL 6
90/1 ProCards 62
91/2 ProCards 73
92/3 Score 331
92/3 Score SS 7
93/4 Score 178
92/3 Score Young Stars 6
92/3 Seasons 24
90 7th..Sketch Mem.Cup 39
92/3 Topps 13
92/3 Topps 19
92/3 T. Stadium Club 403
93/4 To. Stadium 115
91/2 Upper Deck 448
92/3 Upper Deck 356
92/3 Upper Deck 427
92/3 Upper Deck 625
92/3 Upper Deck AR2
93/4 Upper Deck 117
94/5 Upper Deck 57, 384
94/5 UD BAP R22
01/2 UD DEL 157, GA8

DIONNE, MARCEL
01/2 ASG History
01/2 BAP Memor. ✂ 500GS
77/8 Coke
71/2 Colgate Head
79/0 Dernière Heure
83/4 Dernière Heure
70s Dernière Heure
88/9 Esso All-Star
01/2 Fleer Greats 16, -RC 8, ✂ O6, R✍ Aut.
01/2 Fleer Legacy 16, ✂ HK
88/9 Frito Lay
83/4 Funmate Puffy 11 [w/]
91/2 Future Trends C72 91, ✍ 91
92/3 Future Trends C76 179
84/5 Kellogg's 23
91/2 Kraft 85
94/5 Legends 54
74/5 Loblaws
80/1 LOSA 1
84/5 LOSA / Smokey 2
91/2 LOSA / GW Forum
99/0 Millenium P-11, ✍ P-11
87/8 NYRA
87/8 NYRA
71/2 O-Pee-Chee 133
72/3 O-Pee-Chee 8
73/4 O-Pee-Chee 17
74/5 O-Pee-Chee 72
74/5 O-Pee-Chee 84
75/6 O-Pee-Chee 140
75/6 O-Pee-Chee 210
75/6 O-Pee-Chee 318
76/7 O-Pee-Chee 91
76/7 OPC 386
77/8 O-Pee-Chee 1
77/8 OPC 2
77/8 O-Pee-Chee 3
77/8 O-Pee-Chee 240
77/8 O-Pee-Chee NS 4
78/9 O-Pee-Chee 120
79/0 O-Pee-Chee 1
79/0 OPC 2
79/0 O-Pee-Chee 3
79/0 OPC 5
79/0 O-Pee-Chee 160
80/1 O-Pee-Chee 20
80/1 O-Pee-Chee 81
80/1 O-Pee-Chee 162
80/1 O-Pee-Chee 163
80/1 O-Pee-Chee 165
81/2 O-Pee-Chee 141
81/2 O-Pee-Chee 150
81/2 O-Pee-Chee 156
81/2 O-Pee-Chee 391
82/3 O-Pee-Chee 149
82/3 O-Pee-Chee 152
82/3 O-Pee-Chee 153
83/4 O-Pee-Chee 150
83/4 O-Pee-Chee 151
83/4 O-Pee-Chee 152
83/4 O-Pee-Chee 211
84/5 O-Pee-Chee 82
85/6 OPC/Topps 90
85/6 OPC/Topps Box E
86/7 OPC/Topps 30
87/8 OPC/Topps 129
88/9 OPC/Topps 13
92/3 O-Pee-Chee 294
92/3 OPC - Anniv. 4
88/9 OPC Stars 8
81/2 OPC Sticker 147
81/2 OPC Sticker 235
81/2 OPC Sticker 267
82/3 OPC/Topps Sticker 230
83/4 OPC/Topps Sticker 1
83/4 OPC/Topps Sticker 294
83/4 OPC/Topps Sticker 295
83/4 OPC/Topps Sticker 323
83/4 OPC/Topps Sticker 324
84/5 OPC Sticker 264
84/5 OPC Sticker 265
85/6 OPC Sticker 235
86/7 OPC Sticker 88
87/8 OPC Sticker 34-179
88/9 OPC Sticker 244-114
80/1 O-Pee-Chee Super 8
79 Panini Sticker 61
87/8 Panini Sticker 113
88/9 Panini Sticker 190
01/2 Parkhurst ✂ 500GS, ✍ PA31
02/3 Parkhurst ✂ VM5
91/2 Pinnacle 385
81/2 Post 12
82/3 Post [LosA.]
00/1 Premier Plus ✍ CS
90/1 Pro Set 653
84/5 7-Eleven
85/6 7-Eleven Superstars 8
01/2 Signature ✂ 500GS, ✍ VA37
83/4 Souhaits Keychain [Kings]
97/8 SLU Cdn. Leg.
98/9 SLU -CL
72/3 Topps 18
73/4 Topps 17
74/5 Topps 72, 84
75/6 Topps 140
75/6 Topps 210
75/6 Topps 318
76/7 Topps 91
76/7 Topps NS 4
77/8 Topps 1-3
77/8 Topps 240
77/8 ToppsNS 4
78/9 Topps 120
79/0 Topps 1-3, 5
79/0 Topps 160
80/1 Topps 20
80/1 Topps 81
80/1 Topps 162
80/1 Topps 163
80/1 Topps 165
81/2 Topps 9
81/2 Topps 54
81/2 Topps 125 [West]
84/5 Topps 64
01/2 Topps Archives 27, -Seat, ✍ CAI
71/2 Toronto Sun Photo
00/1 UD Heroes 127, ✍ SG
01/2 Ultimate Mem. ✂ 500GS, ✂ ASGH, ✂ NP, ✂ RN, ✍ Aut.
02/3 Ultimate Mem. ✂ EA, ✂ SL, ✂ Num, ✂ RAT, ✂ VGJ
91/2 Upper Deck 636
00 ✂ UD APOH 500, ✂✍ 500
99/0 UD C. Legends 39, ✍ ES
02/3 UD Foundations 25, 42, 66, 114, ✂ 1000Stick (x2), ✍ SG
00/1 UD Legends 58, ES5, ✍ ES, ✂ LGJ
01/2 UD Legends 27, 93, FC, ✂ M, ✂ PoH, ✍ ES
02/3 UD Piece / Giveaway
99/0 UD Retro 103, ✂ RM2, ✍ Ink.
93/4 Zellers, ✍ Aut.

DIONNE, VINCENT
99 Bowman 52

DIOTTE, ROLAND
79/0 Montréal Juniors B&W
79/0 Montréal Jrs. Colour

DIPENTA, JOE
02/3 Chicago Wolves
99/0 Halifax Mooseheads

DIPIETRO, PAUL
92/3 Classic Prospects 104
93/4 Fleer Ultra 159
92/3 Fredericton Canadiens
95/6 Houston Aeros
93/4 Leaf 248
93/4 MONT
94/5 MONT
92/3 Parkhurst 489
93/4 Parkhurst 108
91/2 Pinnacle 350
93/4 Pinnacle 114
94/5 Pinnacle 443
93/4 Power Play 369
93/4 Premier 288
94/5 Premier 252
91/2 Pro Set 546
90/1 ProCards 68
91/2 ProCards 70
93/4 Score 494
93/4 Slapshot / Sudbury 24
86/7 Sudbury Wolves
87/8 Sudbury Wolves
88/9 Sudbury Wolves
89/0 Sudbury Wolves
92/3 Topps 361
92/3 T. Stadium Club 98
93/4 To. Stadium 194
93/4 Upper Deck 108

DIPIETRO, RICK
01/2 Adrenaline 119, CL 12, PP23, RR11
01/2 Atomic 60, RR5, Stat. 5, TN 9
00/1 BAP Mem. 497
01/2 BAP Memor. 1
02/3 BAP Memorabilia 146, ✂ FG15
01/2 BT Pipes 4, ✂ FW, ✂ GG
02/3 Between the Pipes 14, M19, ✂ BM12, ✂ GUE3, ✂ FW4, ✂ GUJ3, ✂ GSJ3, ✂ ITN3, ✂ I10, ✂ T16
02/3 Calder 81, -CR 17, ✂ GWJ 14
00/1 Chicago Wolves
02/3 Choice Prospects 10
00/1 Crown Royale 132, 21CR-15
01/2 Crown Royale 89, CA, RR13
00/1 Crown Royale CC, G-3
01/2 eTopps 26
02/3 Exclusive 106, -GE 12
02/3 First Edition 192, 421R
01/2 Heads Up 60, BTI 14, PP 4, SS 13
02/3 Heads Up -HF 8
02/3 In The Game-Used 46, 146
01/2 McDonald's 25, -FL 2
01/2 O-Pee-Chee 39
02/3 O-Pee-Chee 265
01/2 Pacific 245, 434, GCDC 13, SC 12, TDP 1
02/3 Pacific 235
02/3 Pacific Complete 19
01/2 PTC Draft 6
00/1 Parkhurst P-225
01/2 Parkhurst 42, ✂ PS68
02/3 Parkhurst 78, -CR4, ✂ CRM4
00/1 Premier Plus 127
00/1 Private Stock 151, PSNW-26, PSR-26
01/2 Pr. Stock 105, MiT 6, -PS 99
00/1 PS Titanium 133, 3SS-24
01/2 PS Titanium 87, TSS 28, TRT 8
02/3 PS Titanium 65, -ROT 15
00/1 PS Titanium Draft 133
94 Québec Pee Wee 1211
02/3 Quest for the Cup 60, ✂ GWJ 10
00/1 Signature 296
01/2 Signature 1, ✍ Aut.
02/3 Signature GS-75
00/1 SP Authentic 114, ✍ SotT
01/2 SP Authentic 129, ✍ SotT, ✍ SotTD, ✍ SotTT
00/1 SP GU 73
01/2 SP GU 32, ✂ TotG
02/3 SP Game-Used ✂ TG
00/1 SPx 166
01/2 SPx 41
01/2 Stadium 19, G34, NR11
01/2 Topps 39
02/3 Topps 265
00/1 To. Chrome 251
01/2 To. Chrome 39
02/3 T. Chrome 145
00/1 To. Gold Label 112
00/1 To. Heritage 96

01/2 To. Heritage 25
02/3 T. Limited 265
01/2 To. Reserve 58
00/1 UD Heroes 170
00/1 UD Reserve 104
02/3 Ultimate Mem. ✂ FO, ✂ Num
00/1 Upper Deck 411
01/2 Upper Deck 108
00/1 UD Black Diam. 125
01/2 UD Honor Roll 30, 60
00/1 UD Ice 94
01/2 UD Ice 29
01/2 UD Mask ✂ GG
02/3 UD Mask ✂ BM, ✂ NB
01/2 UD MVP 117, ✂ GS
00/1 UD Pros&Prosp. 114, NA5
01/2 UD Top Shelf 27
02/3 UD Top Shelf ✍ Sig
01/2 UD Vintage 159, 165
00/1 Vanguard 133, HV-21
01/2 Vanguard 58, PP 11, QTH 20
01/2 Victory 218, 223

DIRK, ROBERT
94/5 ANAH / Carl's Jr. 3
92/3 Fleer Ultra 425
91/2 O-Pee-Chee 493
91/2 Parkhurst 403
92/3 Parkhurst 425
93/4 Pinnacle 327
94/5 Pinnacle 405
93/4 Premier 284
90/1 Pro Set 522
89/0 ProCards IHL 8
91/2 Score CAN 508
92/3 Score 279
93/4 Score 288
87/8 SLOU
88/9 SLOU
90/1 SLOU / Kodak
92/3 Topps 437
95/6 Upper Deck 432
95/6 UD BAP 159, ✍ S159
91/2 VANC
91/2 VANC / Photo
92/3 VANC / Road Trip

DIROBERTO, TORREY
99/0 Cincinnati M'Ducks

DISHER, JASON
99/0 Fort Worth Brahmas
93/4 Slapshot / Kingston 9
95/6 Thunder Bay Senators

DISIEWICH, JASON
91/2 Avant Garde BCJHL 55
91/2 Avant Garde BCJHL 153
92/3 BCJHL 94
92/3 BCJHL 111
93/4 Dayton Bombers
91/2 Nanaimo Clippers

DIVIS, REINHARD
01/2 BAP Memor. 341
02/3 Between the Pipes 98, ✂ GUJ49
99/0 UD Elitserien 103
00/1 UD Elitserien 106, M4, ✍ Sig.
02/3 UD Mask 78
01/2 Worcester IceCats
02/3 Worcester IceCats

DIVISEK, MICHAL
96/7 APS 223
97/8 APS 45
99/0 DS 21
97/8 DS Sticker 172
98/9 OFS 53
99/0 OFS 313
00/1 OFS 39

DIVISEK, TOMAS
01/2 BAP Memor. 121
01/2 O-Pee-Chee 289
98/9 OFS 222
01/2 Parkhurst 336
01/2 SPx 147, -RT
01/2 Topps 289
01/2 UD PlayMakers Ltd 134
01/2 Upper Deck 201
01/2 UD Honor Roll 97
01/2 UD MVP 211
01/2 UD Premier 76
01/2 UD Top Shelf 62
01/2 UD Top Shelf 62

DIVITA, DAVID
91/2 ProCards 17
91/2 Rochester Americans DD
91/2 Rochester Americans GL
91/2 Rochester Americans WPC
92/3 Rochester Americans DD
92/3 Rochester Americans WPC

DIVJAK, DAN
85/6 U. of Arizona Ice Cats

DIXON, SEAN
01/2 London Knights

DIXON, STEVE
01/2 Cape Breton Eagles 9

DJELLOUL, SERGE
95 Panini Worlds 98

DJOOS, PÄR
92/3 Binghampton Rangers
90/1 DETR / Little Caesars
90/1 OPC Premier 24
90/1 Pro Set 603
90/1 Score 107T
89/0 Semic Elitserien 29
98/9 UD Elitserien 37, -DL2
99/0 UD Elitserien 22, L2
00/1 UD Elitserien 31, 211, ✍ Sig.

DJOOS, PER
94/5 Leaf Elit Set 164
95/6 Leaf Elit Set 140
92/3 Score 372
93 Semic Sticker 30
92/3 Topps 93
92/3 T. Stadium Club 492
95/6 UD Elitserien 203
97/8 UD Elitserien 18

DLOUHY, JAN
94/5 APS 53
95/6 APS 79
96/7 APS 79
97/8 APS 202
99/0 DS 160
96/7 DS Sticker 134
97/8 DS Sticker 234
98/9 OFS 164
99/0 OFS 162
00/1 OFS 117
01/2 OFS 182

DMITRIEV, EDUARD
99/0 Mir 265

DMITRIEV, IGOR
89/0 Soviet Stars

DOAK, GARY
70/1 BOST
98/9 BOST / Alumni 25
70/1 Dad's Cookies
70/1 Eddie Sargent 218
71/2 Eddie Sargent 214
70/1 Esso Power Player
68/9 O-Pee-Chee 138
69/0 O-Pee-Chee 202
70/1 O-Pee-Chee 114
71/2 O-Pee-Chee 87
72/3 O-Pee-Chee 73
74/5 O-Pee-Chee 361
75/6 O-Pee-Chee 358
76/7 O-Pee-Chee 7
77/8 O-Pee-Chee 181
78/9 O-Pee-Chee 305
80/1 O-Pee-Chee 374
68/9 Shirriff / Bost. 14
67/8 Topps 97
70/1 Topps 114
71/2 Topps 87
72/3 Topps 81
76/7 Topps 7
77/8 Topps 181
70/1 VANC / Royal Bank
71/2 VANC / Royal Bank 20

DOAN, SHANE
01/2 Adrenaline 147, ✂ GWJ 33
00/1 Aurora 110
00/1 BAP Mem. 192
01/2 BAP Memor. 293
02/3 BAP Memorabilia 137
95/6 Bowman 149, BB24
02/3 Bowman 95
95/6 Classic 7, AS5, BK7
94/5 Cla. Images 85
00/1 Crown Royale 83
01/2 Crown Royale 112
95/6 Donruss 210, RR-8
95/6 Do. Elite 109, R-13
02/3 First Edition 49, ✂ Jers.
95/6 Fleer Metal 175
95/6 Fleer Ultra 336, HS-7
01/2 Heads Up ✂ JQ 16
02/3 Heads Up ✂ GWQ 21
93/4 Kamloops Blazers
95/6 L. Limited 7
99/0 NHL Power Play
01/2 O-Pee-Chee 156
02/3 O-Pee-Chee 131
99/0 Omega 178
99/0 Pacific 319
00/1 Pacific 314, ✂ GWJ-12
01/2 Pacific 301, ✂ GWJ 24
02/3 Pacific 293
02/3 Pacific Complete 469
97/8 Pacific CC 330
97/8 Pa. Invincible R-149
00/1 Pa. Paramount 187, ✂ J&P-9
99/0 Panini Sticker 283
95/6 Parkhurst 267
00/1 Parkhurst P-195
01/2 Parkhurst 124
02/3 Parkhurst 65
02/3 Parkhurst Retro 118
96/7 PHOE / Coca-Cola
97/8 PHOE / Coca-Cola
98/9 PHOE / Coca-Cola
95/6 Pi. Summit 188
95/6 Pi. Zenith 132, RRC-15
00/1 Private Stock ✂ GUG 87, ✂ GUG-125
01/2 Pr. Stock -PS 57, ✂ GUG 74
00/1 PS Titanium ✂ GUG 125
02/3 PS Titanium 79
00/1 PS Titanium Draft ✂ 76
00/1 Revolution 112
96/7 Score 262
95/6 Select CE 114
94/5 SR Auto-Phonex 14
95/6 SR Tetrad 67
95/6 SR Tetrad Autobilia 97
01/2 Signature 47, ✍ Aut. 47
02/3 Signature 77, ✍ 77
95/6 SBx Impact 226
94/5 Slapshot Memorial 15
00/1 SP Authentic 69
01/2 SP Authentic 67
02/3 SP Game-Used ✂ AF, ✂ PC
02/3 Sports Vault 265
97/8 Springfield Falcons
00/1 Stadium 187
02/3 Stadium 98
95/6 Topps 314
00/1 Topps 166
01/2 Topps 156
02/3 Topps 131
02/3 T. Chrome 83
95/6 To. Finest 22
00/1 To. Heritage 183
02/3 To. Heritage 71
02/3 T. Limited 131
01/2 To. Reserve 88
95/6 To. Stadium ER207
95/6 T. Super Skills SR8
02/3 T. Total 317
00/1 UD Heroes 91
01/2 UD PlayMakers Ltd 76
02/3 UD Superstars ✂ CAST
95/6 Upper Deck 269, H-27
96/7 Upper Deck 314
97/8 Upper Deck 131
00/1 Upper Deck 136
01/2 Upper Deck 133, ✂ NG
02/3 Upper Deck 135, ✂ FF, ✂ HS
95/6 UD BAP 172, ✍ S172
95/6 UD CC 403
96/7 UD CC 205
01/2 UD Mask 76, ✂ GJ, ✂ JP, ✂ DP
00/1 UD MVP 138
01/2 UD MVP 145
02/3 UD MVP 143
99/0 UD MVP Cup 144
00/1 UD Pros&Prosp. 66
02/3 UD Rookie 78
02/3 UD Top Shelf ✂ SH, ✂ ST (x2)
00/1 UD Vintage 278
01/2 UD Vintage 193, 199
02/3 UD Vintage 193
00/1 Vanguard 75
01/2 Vanguard 76
00/1 Victory 180
01/2 Victory 266
02/3 Victory 165
95/6 WINN

DOAN, TRAVIS
99/0 Des Moines Buc's

DOBBIN, BRIAN
95/6 Cincinnati Cyclones
82/3 Kingston Canadians
85/6 London Knights
00/1 London Knights
93/4 Milwaukee Admirals
94/5 Milwaukee Admirals
89/0 ProCards AHL 341
90/1 ProCards 33
91/2 ProCards 375

DOBBYN, JOSH
96/7 Regina Pats

DOBEK, BOB
76/7 San Diego Mariners

DOBES, ZDENEK
97/8 APS 126
97/8 DS Sticker 248

DOBNI, EVANS
81/2 Regina Pats

DOBRESCU, JAY
92/3 MPS SJHL 7

DOBRISHKIN, YURI
98/9 Mir 158

DOBRON, MICHAL
00/1 DS 6
98/9 OFS 366
99/0 OFS 132
00/1 OFS 296
01/2 OFS 194

DOBROTA, ANDREI
91/2 7th...Sketch LHJMQ 132

DOBROVOLNY, JIRI
98/9 OFS 308
99/0 OFS 369
00/1 OFS 65

DOBRYSHKIN, YURI
99/0 Mir 46

DOBRZYNSKI, RALF
94/5 DEL 209

DOBSON, JIM
83/4 Fredericton Express
84/5 Fredericton Express

DODGINGHORSE, BRENT
98/9 Calgary Hitmen 18

DODUNSKI, COLIN
91/2 Ferris State Bulldogs

DOELL, CURTIS
98/9 Kentucky Tho'blades
99/0 Louisville Panthers

DOERS, MIKE
94/5 Dayton Bombers 10

DOHERTY, KEVIN
88/9 Brockville Braves

DOHERTY, PAUL
90/1 7th..Sketch OHL 103
93/4 Slapshot / Oshawa 20

DOHLER, UDO
94/5 DEL 111
95/6 DEL 27
96/7 DEL 25
99/0 Eishockey 59, 388
00/1 UD DEL 36

DOIG, JASON
95/6 Bowman 120
97 Bowman 48
94/5 Classic CP4
95/6 Classic 31, AS15
95/6 Cla. 5 Sport 154, ✍ Aut.
94/5 Cla. Images 12, CE18, PD9
95/6 Donruss 253
96/7 Fleer 125, CC-2
95/6 Fleer Ultra 337
01/2 Grand Rapids Griffins
99/0 Hartford Wolf Pack
00/1 Hartford Wolf Pack
99/0 NHL Power Play
98/9 Pacific 336
95/6 Parkhurst 529
94/5 Parkie SE254
97/8 PHOE / Coca-Cola
98/9 PHOE / Coca-Cola
94/5 Select 161
96/7 SBx Impact 148
94/5 SP 177
97/8 Springfield Falcons
95/6 Topps 355
95/6 To. Stadium 222
95/6 Upper Deck 499
95/6 UD CC 407
96/7 UD Ice 119
95/6 WINN

DOIRON, SHANE
90/1 7th..Sketch LHJMQ 130
91/2 7th...Sketch LHJMQ 201

DOKSHIN, ILIA
00/1 Mir 73

DOLAK, THOIMAS
99/0 Eishockey 387

DOLAK, THOMAS
98/9 DEL 61, 331
99/0 Eishockey 173
00/1 UD DEL 180

DOLAN, MICK
91/2 Ferris State Bulldogs

DOLANA, LIBOR
94/5 APS 174
95/6 APS 186
96/7 APS 321
91 Semic Sticker 120

DOLEZAL, JIRI
96/7 APS 13
97/8 APS 160
94/5 DEL 334
95/6 DEL 304
97/8 DS 77
98/9 DS 75
99/0 DS 122
96/7 DS Sticker 125
97/8 DS Sticker 197
98/9 OFS 217
99/0 OFS 382
95 Panini Worlds 206
95 Semic 153
89 Semic Sticker 193

DOLEZAL, JIRI
91/2 Jyvas Hyva 28

DOLLARD, DAID
92/3 BCJHL 52

DOLLAS, BOBBY
93/4 ANAH / Cap 2
94/5 ANAH / Carl's Jr. 4
95/6 ANAH / Photo
96/7 ANAH / Up Front 2
98/9 Be A Player 266, ✍ Aut. 266
90/1 DETR / Little Caesars
94/5 Flair 2
94/5 Leaf 383
00/1 Manitoba Moose
87/8 Moncton Hawks
00/1 Pacific 63
97/8 Pacific CC 41
95/6 Panini Sticker 228
96/7 Panini Sticker 227
94/5 Pinnacle 41
96/7 Pinnacle 157
96/7 Pi. Be A Player 96, ✍ Aut. 96
95/6 Playoff 112
94/5 POG 366
95/6 POG 25
93/4 Power Play 283
93/4 Premier 491
94/5 Premier 264
88/9 ProCards / Halifax
86/7 Sherb. Canadiens 12
95/6 SBx Emotion 1
95/6 SBx Impact 1
93/4 To. Stadium 463
94/5 Upper Deck 13
95/6 Upper Deck 395
95/6 UD CC 289

DOMBKIEWICZ, MIKE
96/7 Guelph Storm

DOMBROWSKI, ADAM
97/8 Kamloops Blazers
98/9 Kamloops Blazers

DOME, ROBERT
96/7 All-Sport PPF 175
96/7 Autograph Coll. 47, ✍ Aut.
00/1 BAP Mem. 316
98/9 Collection Souvenir 08
97/8 Do. Preferred 163
97/8 Do. Priority 169
98/9 Pacific 350
97/8 Pinnacle 21
92 Québec Pee Wee 1741
93 Québec Pee Wee 1560
97/8 Score Pitt. 16
97/8 SP Authentic 128
98/9 SPx Finite 67, 147
98/9 UD Choice 171
98/9 UD3 9, 69, 129
97/8 Upper Deck 346
98/9 Upper Deck 164, -GN22
97/8 UD Black Diam. 88
98/9 UD G. Reserve 164
98/9 UD MVP 166
99/0 UD MVP Cup 151
01/2 WBS Penguins

DOMENICHELLI, HNAT
00/1 BAP Mem. 369
01/2 BAP Memor. 405
97/8 Donruss 196
96/7 Do. Canadian 122
97/8 Do. Canadian 131
95/6 Do. Elite WJ 12
96/7 Fl. Ultra 74
96/7 HART / Kids Club
93/4 Kamloops Blazers
97/8 Leaf 79
96/7 L. Limited LR-4
96/7 L. Preferred 121
97/8 Limited 45
96/7 Metal Univ. 175
98/9 Pacific 116
00/1 Pacific 17
01/2 Pacific 15
02/3 Pacific 178
97/8 Pacific CC 237
97/8 Pi. Inside 93
97/8 Saint John Flames
97/8 Score 68
01/2 Signature 74, ✍ Aut. 74
94/5 Slapshot Memorial 13
96/7 Springfield Falcons
95/6 Upper Deck 539
96/7 Upper Deck 272
97/8 Upper Deck 22
98/9 Upper Deck 53
00/1 Upper Deck 237
01/2 Upper Deck 243
97/8 UD Coll. Choice 33
98/9 UD G. Reserve 53
01/2 UD MVP 10
00/1 UD Vintage 17
02/3 UD Vintage 127
01/2 Victory 15

DOMI, TIE
01/2 Adrenaline 179
98/9 Aurora 180, -FL 10
00/1 Aurora 137
00/1 BAP Mem. ✂ TM-9, ✂ TM-37, ✂ T-2
01/2 BAP Update ✂ TC2, ✂ TC18
99/0 Crown Royale 133
93/4 Donruss 381
94/5 Donruss 60
95/6 Donruss 225
96/7 Duracell DC13
98/9 Dynagon Ice 178
99/0 Dynagon Ice 186, CM-15
02/3 First Edition 228
94/5 Fleer Ultra 392
95/6 Fleer Ultra 159
00 Gatorade Sticker
01/2 Heads Up ✂ JQ 19
93/4 Leaf 216
94/5 Leaf 318
96/7 Maggers 152
99/0 McDonald's ✍ SS TD
98/9 NHL Power Play
01/2 O-Pee-Chee 204
02/3 O-Pee-Chee 81
90/1 OPC Premier 25
97/8 Omega 220
98/9 Omega 226
99/0 Omega 223
98/9 Pacific 28
99/0 Pacific 405
00/1 Pacific 387
01/2 Pacific 364, 423, IZ 17
02/3 Pacific 359
02/3 Pacific Complete 166
97/8 Pacific CC 65
98/9 Pa. Crown Roy. 129
98/9 Pa. Paramount 225
99/0 Pa. Paramount 223
00/1 Pa. Paramount 228
97/8 Pa. Revolution 134
98/9 Pa. Revolution 136, -TPA 9
94/5 Panini Sticker 167
96/7 Panini Sticker 221
97/8 Panini Sticker 176
98/9 Panini Sticker 162
99/0 Panini Sticker 162
91/2 Parkhurst 333
92/3 Parkhurst 434
93/4 Parkhurst 230
95/6 Parkhurst 205
02/3 Parkhurst 180
94/5 Parkie SE202
93/4 Pinnacle 295
94/5 Pinnacle 344
95/6 Pinnacle 159, FC-9
96/7 Pi. Be A Player 47, ✍ Aut. 47
95/6 Playoff 94
94/5 POG 250, 344
95/6 POG 263
93/4 Premier 513
94/5 Premier 444
99/0 Prism 136
01/2 Pr. Stock ✂ GUG 94
00/1 PS Titanium ✂ GUG 145
00/1 PS Titanium Draft ✂ 95
91/2 Pro Set 440
89/0 ProCards AHL 127
90/1 ProCards 22
99/0 Revolution 136, / CSC 136
00/1 Revolution 137
92/3 Score 408
93/4 Score 312
94/5 Score 123
95/6 Score 275
97/8 Score 219
97/8 Score Toro. 8
00/1 Signature 143, ✍ Aut. 181, ✂ TM-13, ✂ TM-14
02/3 Signature GS-94, ✂ FW6, ✂ TQ2
02/3 Slam Card
01/2 SP Authentic ✂ NN
02/3 Sports Vault 134
00/1 Stadium ✂ SCS-8
01/2 Stadium 78, ✂ SCS, ✂ SCSD
92/3 Topps 395
99/0 Topps 192
00/1 Topps 244, ✂ GWS
01/2 Topps 204
02/3 Topps 81
99/0 To. Chrome 192
00/1 To. Chrome 153
00/1 To. Gold Label B6
00/1 To. Heritage 170, OSJ
02/3 To. Heritage 39
02/3 T. Limited 81
01/2 To. Reserve ✂ TR
02/3 T. Total 262
99/0 TORO / Pizza Pizza 12
98/9 UD Choice 204
00/1 Ultimate Mem. ✂ TM-13, ✂ TM-14
92/3 Upper Deck 99
94/5 Upper Deck 409
96/7 Upper Deck 201
97/8 Upper Deck 196, 368
98/9 Upper Deck 189
01/2 Upper Deck ✂ PotL
02/3 Upper Deck 165
94/5 UD BAP R65, R168, ✍ 143
95/6 UD CC 242
96/7 UD CC 261
97/8 UD Coll. Choice 253
98/9 UD G. Reserve 189
96/7 UD Ice 68
99/0 UD MVP ✍ PS
00/1 UD Vintage 344, 345
02/3 UD Vintage 235, 288
00/1 Vanguard 92
99/0 Victory 289
00/1 Victory 224
01/2 Victory 334
02/3 Victory 203
93/4 WINN / Ruffles
93/4 WINN Readers

DOMI, TIE
02/3 Fleer Throwbacks 11, ✍ Aut.

DOMIN, PETR
00/1 OFS 182
01/2 OFS 200

DOMKE, HENRY
95/6 DEL 348

DOMONSKY, BRAD
95/6 Slapshot 402
96/7 Sudbury Wolves

DONAGHUE, MIKE
98/9 Wichita Thunder

DONAHUE, MARK
90/1 7th..Sketch OHL 104
93/4 Slapshot / Kitchener 16

DONALD, DEREK
94/5 Anchorage Aces 15
92/3 Dayton Bombers
93/4 Dayton Bombers

DONALD, DOUG
01/2 UD DEL 71

DONALDSON, CRAIG
89/0 Oshawa Generals
90 7th..Sketch Mem.Cup 79
89/0 7th..Sketch OHL 7

DONALDSON, DALE
93/4 Red Deer Rebels

DONATELLI, CLARK
90/1 Bowman 181
90/1 O-Pee-Chee 458
90/1 ProCards 316

DONATO, TED
98/9 Aurora 11
99/0 BAP Mem. 69
92/3 BOST / Postcard
00/1 DALL / Southwest
93/4 Donruss 25
94/5 Donruss 155
95/6 Donruss 263
96/7 Donruss 211
97/8 Donruss 108
99/0 Dynagon Ice 7
92/3 Fleer Ultra 251
93/4 Fleer Ultra 267
94/5 Fleer Ultra 12
95/6 Fleer Ultra 204
93/4 Leaf 54
94/5 Leaf 49
95/6 Leaf 326
97/8 Limited 118
01/2 Manchester Monarchs
92/3 OPC Premier 30
97/8 Omega 15
98/9 Omega 145
98/9 Pacific 76
00/1 Pacific 3
97/8 Pacific CC 209
97/8 Pa. Crown Roy. 10
97/8 Pa. Invincible 9
97/8 Pa. Paramount 12
98/9 Pa. Paramount 13
97/8 Pa. Revolution 9
93/4 Panini Sticker 8
94/5 Panini Sticker 2
95/6 Panini Sticker 4
96/7 Panini Sticker 10
97/8 Panini Sticker 4
98/9 Panini Sticker 11
99/0 Panini Sticker 178
91/2 Parkhurst 230
92/3 Parkhurst 8
93/4 Parkhurst 283
95/6 Parkhurst 17
94/5 Parkie SE14
93/4 Pinnacle 102
94/5 Pinnacle 146
96/7 Pi. Be A Player 37, ✍ Aut. 37
97/8 Pi. Certified 87
97/8 Pi. Inside 101
97/8 Pi. Totally 87
94/5 POG 43
95/6 POG 30
93/4 Power Play 18
93/4 Premier 146
94/5 Premier 88
00/1 PS Titanium ✂ GUG 14
92/3 Pro Set 221
92/3 Score 479
93/4 Score 262
94/5 Score 27
95/6 Score 28
96/7 Score 30
97/8 Score 171
97/8 Score Bost. 6
94/5 Sisu 357, GS-1
95/6 Sisu Limited 97
96/7 SP 13
97/8 SP Authentic 7
99/0 SPx 8
95/6 Topps 324
92/3 T. Stadium Club 271
93/4 To. Stadium 83
98/9 UD Choice 11
92/3 Upper Deck 202
92/3 Upper Deck 393
92/3 Upper Deck G20
93/4 Upper Deck 143
94/5 Upper Deck 61
95/6 Upper Deck 80, SE-97
96/7 Upper Deck 221
97/8 Upper Deck 221
98/9 Upper Deck 217
00/1 Upper Deck 289
94/5 UD BAP ✍ 141
95/6 UD CC 76
96/7 UD CC 19
97/8 UD Coll. Choice 14
98/9 UD G. Reserve 217
99/0 Victory 9

DONIKA, MIKHAIL
00/1 Mir 313

DONLEVY, JACK
59/60 Whitby Dunlops

DONNELLY, DAVE
86/7 CHIC / Coke
88/9 EDMO / Action 150
90/1 ProCards 131

DONNELLY, GORD
92/3 BUFF / Blue Shield
92/3 BUFF / Jubilee
94/5 DALL / Southwest
92/3 Durivage 13
92/3 Fleer Ultra 259
84/5 Fredericton Express
85/6 Fredericton Express
95/6 Houston Aeros
90/1 Panini/WPG 7
90/1 Pro Set 560
91/2 Pro Set 357
84/5 QUÉB
85/6 QUÉB
85/6 QUÉB / Gene. Foods
85/6 QUÉB / McDonald's
86/7 QUÉB
86/7 QUÉB / Gene. Foods
87/8 QUÉB / Gene. Foods
88/9 QUÉB
88/9 QUÉB / Gene. Foods
93/4 To. Stadium 396
91/2 Upper Deck 305
89/0 WINN / Safeway
90/1 WINN / IGA

DONNELLY, GORD
02/3 Fleer Throwbacks 49

DONNELLY, JOHN
72/3 Ottawa Nationals

DONNELLY, MIKE
92/3 Bowman 342
87/8 BUFF / Blue Shield
88/9 BUFF / Blue Shield
91/2 BUFF / Blue Shield
91/2 BUFF / Campbell's
91/2 BUFF / Pepsi
94/5 DALL / Southwest
96/7 Detroit Vipers
93/4 Donruss 155
94/5 Donruss 282
95/6 Donruss 232
94/5 Flair 78
92/3 Fleer Ultra 81
94/5 Fleer Ultra 97
93/4 Leaf 282
94/5 Leaf 106
95/6 Leaf 217
92/3 O-Pee-Chee 151
95/6 Panini Sticker 170
91/2 Parkhurst 294
93/4 Parkhurst 369
95/6 Parkhurst 57
91/2 Pinnacle 299
92/3 Pinnacle 98
93/4 Pinnacle 172
94/5 Pinnacle 223
95/6 Pinnacle 156
94/5 POG 123
95/6 POG 87
93/4 Power Play 359
93/4 Premier 33
94/5 Premier 308
91/2 Pro Set 399
91/2 Pro Set Platinum 183
88/9 ProCards / Rochester
89/0 ProCards AHL 274
90/1 ProCards 428
91/2 Score CAN 499
92/3 Score 67
93/4 Score 176
95/6 Score 147
92/3 Topps 121
92/3 T. Stadium Club 411
93/4 To. Stadium 374
94/5 T. Stadium Club 14
91/2 Upper Deck 420
94/5 Upper Deck 199
95/6 Upper Deck 87
95/6 UD BAP 80, ✍ S80
95/6 UD CC 263

DONNELLY, PETE
73/4 Quaker Oats 29
73/4 Vancouver Blazers

DONNELLY, TRUMAN
37/8 World Wide Gum 134

DONOVAN, ROB
94/5 Birmingham Bulls
95/6 Birmingham Bulls

DONOVAN, RYAN
91/2 Avant Garde BCJHL 109
92/3 BCJHL 171

DONOVAN, SHEAN
95/6 Bowman 140
95/6 Classic 92
94/5 Cla. Images 46, ✍ Aut.
95/6 Donruss 77, C3TWC-19
95/6 Leaf 47
99/0 Millenium 63, ✍ Aut. 63
99/0 NHL Power Play
92/3 Ottawa 67's
98/9 Pacific 159
97/8 Pa. Invincible R-176
00/1 Pa. Paramount 11
96/7 Panini Sticker 287
95/6 Parkhurst 458
01/2 Parkhurst 194
94/5 Pinnacle 539
95/6 Pinnacle 211
97/8 Pi. Be A Player 142, ✍ Aut. 142
95/6 Pi. Summit 177
95/6 Score 307
94/5 SP 149
95/6 Topps 42, 13CJ
94/5 Topps Finest 158
95/6 To. Finest 163
95/6 To. Stadium 114
94/5 Upper Deck 366
95/6 Upper Deck 131
96/7 Upper Deck 149
97/8 Upper Deck 152
98/9 Upper Deck 251
95/6 UD BAP 3, ✍ S3
96/7 UD CC 234
98/9 UD G. Reserve 251

DONTIGNY, STEVE
90/1 7th..Sketch LHJMQ 193
91/2 7th...Sketch LHJMQ 60

DOOLAN, JOHN
98/9 Kansas City Blades 27
99/0 Kansas City Blades

DOPITA, JIRI
01/2 Adrenaline 220
95/6 APS 20, 369, 405
96/7 APS 230, 355, 364, 413
97/8 APS 39, 358, 369
01/2 Atomic 119, RR
01/2 BAP Memor. 345
98 Bonaparte 5A
98 Bonaparte Pexeso 16
01/2 Bowman 110
01/2 Crown Royale 173
94/5 DEL 43
97/8 DS 7
98/9 DS 1
99/0 DS 133, NS22, P10
00/1 DS 20, NT6, TS4, VP5
01/2 DS 58, -BB 9
96/7 DS Sticker 10, 32
97/8 DS Sticker 175
02/3 First Edition 226
01/2 Heads Up 115
02/3 Heads Up ✂ GWQ 20, ✂ GWQ 36
01/2 O-Pee-Chee 355
02/3 O-Pee-Chee 251
98/9 OFS 105, 241, 478, -OW 1
99/0 OFS 57, 260, 512
00/1 OFS 334, -Star 2
01/2 OFS -UHI 5
01/2 Pacific 459
02/3 Pacific 279, ✂ GWJ 38
01/2 Parkhurst 263
01/2 PHIL
01/2 Pr. Stock 134, -PS 85
01/2 PS Titanium 174, ✂ DSJ 49, ✂ DSJ 63
01/2 PS Titanium Draft 158, ✂ 68
01/2 Signature 206, ✍ Aut. 206
01/2 SP Authentic 167
01/2 SP GU 93
01/2 SPx 150, -RT
01/2 SPx Rookie RR22
01/2 Stadium 123
01/2 Topps 355
02/3 Topps 251
01/2 To. Chrome 173
01/2 To. Heritage 142
02/3 To. Heritage 173
02/3 T. Limited 251
01/2 To. Reserve 108
02/3 T. Total 149
01/2 UD PlayMakers Ltd 135
01/2 Upper Deck 438
01/2 UD Challenge 126
01/2 UD Honor Roll 98
01/2 UD Ice 64
01/2 UD Mask 159
01/2 UD MVP 230
01/2 UD Premier 103
01/2 UD Top Shelf 74
01/2 UD Vintage 292
01/2 Vanguard 124
01/2 Victory 450
96 Wien 122

DOPITA, LUBOS
94/5 APS 267

DOPSON, ROB
92/3 Cleveland Lumberjacks
93/4 Cleveland Lumberjacks
95/6 Edge Ice 131
95/6 Houston Aeros
90/1 ProCards 370
91/2 ProCards 301

DORATY, KEN
33/4 Anonymous 14
26 Dominion Chocolates 28
32/3 Maple Leafs O'Keefe
33/4 O-Pee-Chee 4
33/4 WWGum 49

DORCHAK, DEAN
89/0 Portland Winter Hawks
90/1 7th..Sketch WHL 321

DORE, MIKE
90/1 Rayside-Balfour
91/2 Rayside-Balfour

DORÉ, ANDRÉ
83/4 O-Pee-Chee 313
84/5 O-Pee-Chee 279
82/3 Post [NYRa.]
83/4 QUÉB

DORÉ, DANIEL
90/1 Halifax Citadels
90/1 Panini/QUE 2
91/2 ProCards 539
88/9 QUÉB
88/9 QUÉB / Gene. Foods
89/0 QUÉB
89/0 QUÉB / Gene. Foods
89/0 QUÉB / Police
90/1 QUÉB
90/1 Upper Deck 255

DOREY, JIM
70/1 Colgate 79
78/9 Dernière Heure
70/1 Eddie Sargent 197
71/2 Eddie Sargent 201
70/1 Esso Power Player
72/3 New England Whalers
69/0 O-Pee-Chee 45
70/1 O-Pee-Chee 106
71/2 O-Pee-Chee 57
72/3 O-Pee-Chee 339
75/6 OPC WHA 94
76/7 OPC WHA 24
73/4 Quaker Oats 47
76/7 Québec Nordiques
72 Semic Sticker 168
70/1 Topps 106
71/2 Topps 57
68/9 TORO
70/1 TORO
71/2 TORO
71/2 Toronto Sun Photo

DORION, DAN
93/4 Humberside Hawks 16
88/9 ProCards / Utica

DORNHOEFER, GARY
68/9 Bauer Photo
64-67 BeeHive-3 [Bost.]
64/5 Coke/Sprite [Bost.]
70/1 Colgate 40
70/1 Dad's Cookies
70/1 Eddie Sargent 149
71/2 Eddie Sargent 151
72/3 Eddie Sargent 161
70/1 Esso Power Player
72/3 Post 3
74/5 Loblaws
68/9 O-Pee-Chee 94
69/0 O-Pee-Chee 94
70/1 O-Pee-Chee 85
70/1 O-Pee-Chee DE 33
71/2 O-Pee-Chee 202
72/3 O-Pee-Chee 146
72/3 O-Pee-Chee 268
73/4 O-Pee-Chee 182
74/5 O-Pee-Chee 44
75/6 O-Pee-Chee 129
76/7 O-Pee-Chee 256
77/8 O-Pee-Chee 202
94/5 Parkie Tall 20
70/1 PHIL
72/3 PHIL / Milk
72 Semic Sticker 179
68/9 Shirriff / Phil. 4
64/5 Topps 72
65/6 Topps 38
68/9 Topps 94
69/0 Topps 94
70/1 Topps 85
71/2 Topps 89
72/3 Topps 41
72/3 Topps 65
73/4 Topps 167
74/5 Topps 44
75/6 Topps 129
76/7 Topps 256
77/8 Topps 202
71/2 Toronto Sun Photo

DOROCHIN, IGOR
95/6 DEL 46

DOROFEYEV, IGOR
98/9 Mir 48
91/2 O-Pee-Chee 32R
92/3 Upper Deck 352

DOROHOY, EDDIE
45-64 BeeHive-2 [Mont.]
45-54 Quaker Oats

DOROSH, DAVID
90/1 Oshawa Generals

DOROSHUK, ROB
92/3 Semic Nordisk 120

DOSDALL, CORY
90/1 7th..Sketch WHL 169
91/2 7th...Sketch WHL 308

DOSTAL, DAVID
96/7 APS 118

DOUCET, BENOÎT
94/5 DEL 86
95/6 DEL 91, 431
96/7 DEL 279
85/6 Moncton G'Flames
95 Panini Worlds 66
94 Semic 281
96 Wien 196

DOUCET, DAVE
91/2 Air Canada SJHL C6
92/3 MPS SJHL 81

DOUCET, WAYNE
90/1 ProCards 497
91/2 ProCards 461
90/1 Score 397
86/7 Sudbury Wolves

DOUCETTE, DAVE
89/0 Soo Greyhounds

DOUGLAS, JORDY
82/3 MINS
83/4 MINS
79/0 O-Pee-Chee 335
80/1 O-Pee-Chee 97
84/5 O-Pee-Chee 338
81/2 OPC Sticker 65
82/3 Post [Hart.]
83/4 Souhaits Keychain [North Stars]
80/1 Topps 97

DOUGLAS, KENT
68/9 Bauer Photo
45-64 BeeHive-2 [Toro.]
64-67 BeeHive-3 [Toro.]
63-65 Chex
64/5 Coke/Sprite [Toro.]
65/6 Coca-Cola
68/9 O-Pee-Chee 26
63/4 Parkhurst 7
63/4 Parkhurst 67
95/6 Parkie 66-67 105
94/5 Parkie Tall 109
68/9 Shirriff / Detr. 6
65/6 Topps 14
66/7 Topps 82
68/9 Topps 26
64/5 TORO
62/3 Toronto Star Photo
63/4 Toronto Star Action
62/3 York Transfer 13
63/4 York 13

DOUGLAS, LAYNE
91/2 Air Canada SJHL 19
91/2 Air Canada SJHL A22

DOUGLAS, LES
34-43 BeeHive-1 [Detr.]
51/2 Laval Dairy 100
52/3 Laval Dairy Update 100
40/1 O-Pee-Chee 129
52/3 St. Lawrence 5

DOUGLAS, RYAN
92/3 BCJHL 157
94/5 Flint Generals
93/4 Slapshot / Peterborough 21
93/4 Slapshot / S.S.Marie 2

DOULL, DOUG
00/1 Kudos 100
98/9 Michigan K-Wings
91/2 7th...Sketch OHL 114
01/2 St. John's Maple Leafs
01/2 St. John's / Clarenville
02/3 St. John's Maple Leafs

DOURIAN, GEORGE
89/0 7th..Sketch OHL 71
90/1 7th..Sketch OHL 207
91/2 7th...Sketch OHL 266
91/2 Sudbury Wolves

DOURIS, PETER
94/5 ANAH / Carl's Jr. 5
89/0 BOST / Sports Action
90/1 BOST / Sports Action
91/2 BOST / Sports Action
98/9 DEL 70
99/0 Eishockey 323
94/5 Leaf 397
96/7 Milwaukee Admirals
87/8 Moncton Hawks
90/1 OPC Premier 26
91/2 OPC Premier 141
92/3 Panini Sticker 141
95/6 Panini Sticker 225
95/6 Parkhurst 278
95/6 Playoff 222
94/5 POG 30
95/6 POG 18
93/4 Power Play 284
93/4 Premier 265
94/5 Premier 184
90/1 Pro Set 407
91/2 Pro Set 347
88/9 ProCards / Peoria
91/2 ProCards 64
91/2 Score CAN 633
92/3 Score 384
86/7 Sherb. Canadiens 13
92/3 Topps 190
92/3 T. Stadium Club 402
91/2 Upper Deck 403
91/2 Upper Deck 601
95/6 UD BAP 25, ✍ S25
00/1 UD DEL 177, A3
01/2 UD DEL 193

DOUVILLE, THIERRY
00/1 Baie-Comeau 9
01/2 Baie-Comeau 8
02/3 Baie-Comeau

DOW, SHANE
98/9 BC Icemen 5
98/9 BC Icemen

DOWD, BILL
81/2 Ottawa 67's
82/3 Ottawa 67's

DOWD, GARY
02/3 Dundee Texol Stars

DOWD, JIM
92/3 Classic Prospects 22
93/4 Cla. Prospects 44
00/1 Crown Royale 52
01/2 Crown Royale 72
94/5 Donruss 47
02/3 First Edition 298
94/5 Fleer Ultra 116
95/6 Fleer Ultra 260
94/5 Leaf 307
01/2 MINW / Crime 22
01/2 O-Pee-Chee 155
02/3 O-Pee-Chee 141
00/1 Pacific 164
01/2 Pacific 192
02/3 Pacific 179
02/3 Pacific Complete 96
94/5 Parkhurst 279
95/6 Parkhurst 485
94/5 Parkie SE98
94/5 Pinnacle 439
97/8 Pi. Be A Player 111, ✍ Aut. 111
93/4 Power Play 376
94/5 Premier 321
01/2 PS Titanium 69
91/2 ProCards 423
97/8 Saint John Flames
02/3 Sports Vault 247
95/6 Topps 316
01/2 Topps 155
02/3 Topps 141
00/1 To. Chrome 235
01/2 To. Chrome 117
02/3 T. Limited 141
94/5 T. Stadium Club 194
95/6 To. Stadium 91
02/3 T. Total 89
00/1 UD Reserve 43
94/5 Upper Deck 410
00/1 Upper Deck 91
01/2 Upper Deck 314
94/5 UD BAP ✍ 91
01/2 UD Mask 47
02/3 UD MVP 88
00/1 UD Vintage 176
02/3 UD Vintage 126

DOWHY, STEVE
99/0 Colorado Gold Kings

DOWNEY, AARON
00/1 BAP Mem. 230
95/6 Hampton Roads
96/7 Hampton Roads
98/9 Hampton Roads
97/8 Providence Bruins
98/9 Providence Bruins
99/0 Providence Bruins

DOWNEY, BRIAN
93/4 Thunder Bay Senators

DOWNEY, JASON
93/4 Dayton Bombers
94/5 Dayton Bombers 4
95/6 Dayton Bombers
96/7 Dayton Bombers
97/8 New Orleans Brass
90/1 7th..Sketch LHJMQ 176
91/2 7th...Sketch LHJMQ 154

DOYLE, JASON
95/6 Bowman P11
95/6 Classic 88
92 Québec Pee Wee 1112
95/6 Slapshot 375, 434

DOYLE, JOE
94/5 Slapshot / Sarnia 5

DOYLE, PAUL
95/6 Slapshot 144

DOYLE, PERRY
94/5 Sheffield Steelers 5
95/6 Sheffield Steelers

DOYLE, ROB
98/9 DEL 139
94/5 Fort Wayne Komets 22
88/9 ProCards / Adirondack
01/2 UD DEL 78

DOYLE, ROBIN
99/0 Eishockey 79
94 Semic 233
93 Semic Sticker 272
00/1 UD DEL 76
96 Wien 212

DOYLE, SHANE
84/5 Belleville Bulls
88/9 ProCards / Indianapolis

DOYLE, TREVOR
96/7 Carolina Monarchs
94/5 Cincinnati Cyclones
97/8 Fort Wayne Komets
00/1 Kudos 6
93/4 Slapshot / Kingston 5

DOYON, MARIO
99/0 Eishockey 103
93/4 Fredericton Canadiens
90/1 Halifax Citadels
88/9 ProCards / Saginaw
89/0 ProCards IHL 66
90/1 ProCards 443
91/2 ProCards 364
91/2 Upper Deck 411
01/2 UD DEL 158

DRABEK, ADAM
96/7 APS 285

DRABEK, JOSEF
99/0 Score 139

DRABEK, VACLAV
99/0 Score 10

DRAG, MILAN
89/0 Victoria Cougars

DRAGAN, JAROMIR
96 Wien 220

DRAGICEVIC, MILAN
86/7 Regina Pats
87/8 Regina Pats
89/0 Spokane Chiefs

DRAGON, JOE
93/4 Cla. Prospects 237

DRAINVILLE, FRANÇOIS
97/8 Rimouski Océanic

DRAINVILLE, ROBERT
52/3 Laval Dairy Update 39

DRAISAITL, PETER
94/5 DEL 208
95/6 DEL 209, 437
96/7 DEL 353
98/9 DEL 323
99/0 Eishockey 349
91 Semic Sticker 166
92 Semic Sticker 182
00/1 UD DEL 209
DRAISATL, PETER
89 Semic Sticker 124
DRAKE, CLARE
89/0 WINN / Safeway
90/1 WINN / IGA
DRAKE, DALLAS
00/1 Aurora 120
98/9 Be A Player 257, ✍ Aut. 257
99/0 BAP Mem. 282
00/1 BAP Mem. 147, 405
92/3 Classic 86
94/5 Classic ✍ Aut.
92/3 Classic Four Sport 206
92/3 Classic Four Sport BC9
92/3 Classic Prospects 15
92/3 Classic Prospects BC19
92/3 Classic Prospects LP5
93/4 Donruss 100
93/4 Donruss 508
94/5 Flair 206
93/4 Fleer Ultra 104
94/5 Fleer Ultra 241
95/6 Fleer Ultra 326
93/4 Leaf 148
94/5 Leaf 380
95/6 Leaf 268
98/9 OPC Chrome 107
97/8 Omega 172
98/9 Omega 183
99/0 Omega 179
98/9 Pacific 337
99/0 Pacific 320
00/1 Pacific 315
01/2 Pacific 322
02/3 Pacific 321
02/3 Pacific Complete 92
97/8 Pa. Invincible R-150
98/9 Pa. Paramount 180
99/0 Pa. Paramount 178
95/6 Panini Sticker 211
93/4 Parkhurst 61
94/5 Parkhurst 261, V90
95/6 Parkhurst 503
00/1 Parkhurst P-221
96/7 PHOE / Coca-Cola
97/8 PHOE / Coca-Cola
98/9 PHOE / Coca-Cola
93/4 Pinnacle 28
94/5 Pinnacle 225
95/6 Pinnacle 25
95/6 Playoff 326
96/7 Playoff 405
94/5 POG 251
95/6 POG 288
93/4 Power Play 71
93/4 Premier 365
94/5 Premier 64
00/1 Private Stock ✂ GUG 90
00/1 PS Titanium Draft ✂ 89
95/6 Pro Magnet 57
93/4 Score 246
95/6 Topps 328
98/9 Topps 107
00/1 Topps 171
93/4 To. Stadium 484
02/3 T. Total 364
99/0 Ult. Victory 66
93/4 Upper Deck 50, HB-4, SP-43
94/5 Upper Deck 360
95/6 Upper Deck 17, SE-178
97/8 Upper Deck 338
98/9 Upper Deck 342
01/2 Upper Deck 383
95/6 UD BAP 83, ✍ S83
95/6 UD CC 269
97/8 UD Coll. Choice 197
98/9 UD G. Reserve 342
99/0 UD MVP Cup 142
00/1 UD Vintage 318
01/2 Vanguard ✂ DGM 28
95/6 WINN
95/6 WINN Readers
DRANEY, BRETT
97/8 Kamloops Blazers
98/9 Kamloops Blazers
99/0 Kamloops Blazers
99/0 Kamloops Blazers
00/1 Medicine Hat Tigers
DRAPEAU, ÉTIENNE
95/6 Bowman P12
95/6 Classic AS16
95/6 Halifax Moosehead
00/1 Quad City Mallards
92 Québec Pee Wee 1271
95/6 Upper Deck 514
DRAPEAU, GASTON
80/1 Québec Remparts
90/1 7th..Sketch LHJMQ 180
91/2 7th...Sketch LHJMQ 124
DRAPER, DAVE
83/4 Brantford Alexanders
DRAPER, KRIS
98/9 BAP 200, ✍ Aut. 200
02/3 BAP Memorabilia 184
93/4 Donruss 423
94/5 Donruss 182
96/7 Donruss 169
96/7 Do. Canadian 92
94/5 Leaf 28
96/7 Leaf 119
91/2 Moncton Hawks
92/3 O-Pee-Chee 374
98/9 OPC Chrome 168
92/3 OPC Premier 27
98/9 Pacific 188
99/0 Pacific 137
00/1 Pacific 146
02/3 Pacific 126
02/3 Pacific Complete 176
97/8 Pa. Invincible R-68
90/1 Panini/WPG 8
97/8 Pi. Be A Player 20, ✍ Aut. 20
95/6 POG 94
91/2 ProCards 177
90/1 Score 404
96/7 Score 192
97/8 Score Detr. 12
90/1 7th..Sketch OHL 83
02/3 Sports Vault 219
92/3 Topps 249
98/9 Topps 168
94/5 T. Stadium Club 72
02/3 T. Total 95
98/9 UD Choice RW12
02/3 Ultimate Mem. ✂ SCDE, ✂ SCDGJ, ✂ SCDN
90/1 Upper Deck 466, 473
94/5 Upper Deck 492
95/6 Upper Deck 459
97/8 Upper Deck 62
98/9 Upper Deck 268
02/3 Upper Deck 310
94/5 UD BAP ✍ 25
96/7 UD Black Diam. 33
98/9 UD G. Reserve 268
00/1 UD Vintage 133
02/3 UD Vintage 93
99/0 Victory 106
90/1 WINN / IGA
DRAPER, TOM
92/3 Bowman 56
91/2 BUFF / Blue Shield
91/2 BUFF / Campbell's
91/2 BUFF / Pepsi
99/0 Cardset 201, 281
00/1 Cardset 244, Mask. 8
02/3 Cardset 13
95/6 Edge Ice 160
92/3 Fleer Ultra 14
95/6 Milwaukee Admirals
94/5 Minnesota Moose
92/3 O-Pee-Chee 376
92/3 Panini Sticker 243
91/2 Parkhurst 240
91/2 Parkhurst 448
91/2 Pinnacle 341
92/3 Pro Set 14
88/9 ProCards / Moncton
90/1 ProCards 554
91/2 ProCards 20
91/2 Rochester Americans DD
91/2 Rochester Americans GL
98/9 Rochester Americans
92/3 Score 530
92/3 Topps 278
92/3 T. Stadium Club 395
91/2 Upper Deck 552
92/3 Upper Deck 201
92/3 Upper Deck 361
89/0 WINN / Safeway
DRASP, PATRICK
91/2 7th...Sketch LHJMQ 185
DRAXLER, MARKUS
95/6 DEL 377
DREGER, BARRY
88/9 Brandon Wheat Kings
93/4 San Diego Gulls
DREGER, RON
81/2 Saskatoon Blades
83/4 Saskatoon Blades
84/5 Saskatoon Blades
DREVENY, GREG
89/0 7th..Sketch OHL 92
90/1 7th..Sketch OHL 2
91/2 7th...Sketch OHL 112
92/3 Sudbury Wolves
DREVITCH, SCOTT
88/9 ProCards / Maine
89/0 ProCards AHL 76
91/2 Richmond Renegades
92/3 Richmond Renegades
DREVITCH, TODD
91/2 Richmond Renegades
DREW, PAUL
02/3 Plymouth Whalers
DRILLON, GORDIE
34-43 BeeHive-1 [Mont.]
34-43 BeeHive-1 [Toro.]
83 HHOF Postcard H3
83&87 HHOF 109
37/8 O-Pee-Chee 142
39/0 O-Pee-Chee 4
40/1 O-Pee-Chee 110
55/6 Parkhurst 25
38/9 Quaker Oats
02/3 Ultimate Mem. ✍ Cut
DRINKWATER, CHARLIE
96/7 Legends 85
DRINKWATER, GRAHAM
83 HHOF Postcard J6
83&87 HHOF 186
DRISCOLL, CHRIS
90/1 7th..Sketch OHL 283
DRISCOLL, PETER
79/0 EDMO
88/9 EDMO / Action 7
76/7 OPC WHA 45
DRISCOLL, STEVE
84/5 Fredericton Express
DRIVER, BRUCE
90/1 Bowman 87
91/2 Bowman 281
93/4 Donruss 185
96/7 Fl. Picks 156
92/3 Fleer Ultra 336
93/4 Fleer Ultra 214
95/6 Fleer Ultra 190
93/4 Leaf 56
94/5 Leaf 377
84/5 NJER
86/7 NJER / S.O.B.E.R.
88/9 NJER / Caretta
89/0 NJER
89/0 NJER / Caretta
90/1 NJER
85/6 OPC/Topps 127
86/7 OPC/Topps 19
87/8 OPC/Topps 79
88/9 OPC/Topps 157
90/1 OPC/Topps 172
91/2 O-Pee-Chee 294
98/9 OPC Chrome 41
87/8 OPC Sticker 60-202
88/9 OPC Sticker 77-206
98/9 Pacific 292
97/8 Pa. Invincible R-124
87/8 Panini Sticker 74
88/9 Panini Sticker 269
90/1 Panini Sticker 69
91/2 Panini Sticker 225
92/3 Panini Sticker 178
93/4 Panini Sticker 44
91/2 Parkhurst 322
92/3 Parkhurst 333
95/6 Parkhurst 413
91/2 Pinnacle 63
92/3 Pinnacle 278
93/4 Pinnacle 277
94/5 Pinnacle 126
97/8 Pi. Be A Player 87, ✍ Aut. 87
94/5 POG 150
93/4 Power Play 135
93/4 Premier 377
94/5 Premier 292
90/1 Pro Set 166
91/2 Pro Set 140
91/2 Pro Set 577
92/3 Pro Set 99
91/2 Pro Set Platinum 69
90/1 Score 109
91/2 Score 89
91/2 Score CAN 89
92/3 Score 251
93/4 Score 263
94/5 Score 115
95/6 Score 257
97/8 Score NYRa. 11
92/3 Topps 384
98/9 Topps 41
91/2 To. Stadium 122
92/3 T. Stadium Club 376
93/4 To. Stadium 126
94/5 T. Stadium Club 35
90/1 Upper Deck 373
91/2 Upper Deck 292
92/3 Upper Deck 200
97/8 Upper Deck 110
95/6 UD BAP 147, ✍ S147
DROLET, JIMMY
96/7 Fredericton Canadiens
00/1 Kudos 34
01/2 Nottingham Panthers
DROLET, NANCY
94/5 Classic W18
97/8 Esso 56, ✍ Aut.
97/8 General Mills
97/8 UD Coll. Choice 277
DRONOV, VICTOR
99/0 Mir 93
DROPPA, IVAN
96/7 Carolina Monarchs
93/4 Classic 128
93/4 Cla. 4 Sport 232
92/3 Classic Prospects 149
98/9 DEL 267
93/4 Donruss 414
99/0 Eishockey 185
93/4 Fleer Ultra 288
92/3 Indianapolis Ice
93/4 Indianapolis Ice
94/5 Indianapolis Ice
95/6 Indianapolis Ice
94/5 Leaf 112
93/4 Parkhurst 42
94/5 Parkhurst 49
94/5 T. Stadium Club 252
94/5 Upper Deck 435
91/2 Upper Deck WJC 98
00/1 UD DEL 52, S1
01/2 UD DEL 48, GA7
DROUILLARD, PHIL
82/3 North Bay Centennials
DROUIN, CLAUDE
80/1 Québec Remparts
DROUIN, ÉRIC
97 Bowman 67
98 Bowman 111
98 Bowman Chrome 111
96/7 Rimouski Océanic
97/8 Rimouski Océanic
DROUIN, FINDME
00/1 Nottingham Panthers
DROUIN, JUDE
70/1 Colgate 18
70/1 Eddie Sargent 88
71/2 Eddie Sargent 82
72/3 Eddie Sargent 100
72/3 Post 21
74/5 Loblaws
74/5 Loblaws Update
73/4 MINS
70/1 O-Pee-Chee 171
71/2 O-Pee-Chee 68
71/2 O-Pee-Chee Book. 21
72/3 O-Pee-Chee 47
73/4 O-Pee-Chee 125
74/5 O-Pee-Chee 255
75/6 O-Pee-Chee 224
76/7 O-Pee-Chee 106
77/8 O-Pee-Chee 182
78/9 O-Pee-Chee 93
79/0 O-Pee-Chee 329
80/1 O-Pee-Chee 285
80/1 Pepsi Bottle Cap
71/2 Topps 68
72/3 Topps 153
73/4 Topps 125
74/5 Topps 255
75/6 Topps 224
76/7 Topps 106
77/8 Topps 182
78/9 Topps 93
71/2 Toronto Sun Photo
79/0 WINN
80/1 WINN
DROUIN, P.C.
97/8 Charlotte Checkers
96/7 Providence Bruins
DROUIN, PC
00/1 Nottingham Panthers
01/2 Nottingham Panthers
DROUIN, PIERRE
00/1 Kudos 133
DROUIN, POLLY
34-43 BeeHive-1 [Mont.]
35-40 Canada Starch
37/8 O-Pee-Chee 158
39/0 O-Pee-Chee 24
38/9 Quaker Oats
37/8 World Wide Gum 50
DROZDETSKIJ, NIKOLAI
82 Semic Sticker 63
DROZDETSKIN, ALEXANDER
99/0 Mir 240
DROZDIAK, DEAN
83/4 Victoria Cougars
DRUCE, JOHN
90/1 Bowman-HT 16
91/2 Bowman 293
92/3 Bowman 180
94/5 Donruss 223
92/3 Fleer Ultra 442
94/5 Fleer Ultra 98
94/5 Leaf 131
95/6 Leaf 107
90/1 OPC/Topps 298
91/2 O-Pee-Chee 206
92/3 O-Pee-Chee 105
92/3 OPC Premier 80
97/8 Pa. Dynagon BKS-69
91/2 Panini Sticker 200
95/6 Panini Sticker 269
91/2 Parkhurst 415
92/3 Parkhurst 437
96/7 PHIL / Ocean Spray
91/2 Pinnacle 395
92/3 Pinnacle 185
94/5 Pinnacle 304
95/6 Pinnacle 113
94/5 POG 124
95/6 POG 135
93/4 Power Play 360
94/5 Premier SFX 549
90/1 Pro Set 310
91/2 Pro Set 251
91/2 Pro Set Platinum 129
89/0 ProCards AHL 100
90/1 Score 246
91/2 Score 180
91/2 Score CAN 180
92/3 Score 121
97/8 Score Phil. 19
90/1 Sco. Young Stars 25
92/3 Topps 188
95/6 Topps 111
91/2 To. Stadium 331
92/3 T. Stadium Club 405
94/5 T. Stadium Club 71
90/1 Upper Deck 371
91/2 Upper Deck 151
92/3 Upper Deck 205
95/6 UD CC 135
89/0 WASH / Kodak
90/1 WASH / Kodak
90/1 WASH / Smokey
91/2 WASH / Kodak
91/2 WASH / Smokey
DRUET, J
85/6 Moncton G'Flames
DRUKEN, HAROLD
99/0 BAP Mem. 383
00/1 BAP Mem. 137
01/2 BAP Memor. 224
99 Bowman 145
97 Bowman 146, ✍ Aut.
00/1 Kansas City Blades 9
01/2 McDonald's -HP 8
99/0 Omega 239
00/1 Pacific 407
02/3 Pacific Complete 295
00/1 Signature 163, ✍ Aut. 129
98/9 SPx Prospects 64
00/1 Topps 272
00/1 To. Chrome 167
96/7 Upper Deck 380
01/2 Upper Deck 172
98/9 UD Black Diam. 91
99/0 UD G. Reserve 350
00/1 UD MVP 175
00/1 Victory 232
01/2 Victory 348
DRULIA, STAN
93/4 Atlanta Knights
94/5 Atlanta Knights 14
95/6 Atlanta Knights
00/1 BAP Mem. 336
84/5 Belleville Bulls
96/7 Detroit Vipers
97/8 Detroit Vipers
98/9 Detroit Vipers
98/9 EBK IHL All-Star
95/6 Edge Ice 100, QM-6
88/9 Niagara Falls Thunder
92/3 OPC Premier 105
99/0 Omega 214
00/1 Pacific 370
92/3 Parkhurst 177
93/4 Parkhurst 191
89/0 ProCards AHL 138
91/2 ProCards 379
99/0 Ult. Victory 81
92/3 Upper Deck 487
DRUMM, BRIAN
93/4 Slapshot / Oshawa 26
DRUMMOND, KURT
99 Bowman 95
00/1 Hamilton Bulldogs
95/6 Swift Current Broncos
DRURY, BRYAN
90/1 7th..Sketch OHL 284
DRURY, CHRIS
01/2 Adrenaline 46, WB 2
01/2 Atomic 23
02/3 Atomic 23
99/0 Aurora 36, Stripe 36
00/1 Aurora 37, Pin.
00/1 BAP All-Star AS-5
99/0 BAP Mem. 184, SL-19
00/1 BAP Mem. 162
01/2 BAP Memor. 49, ✂ SCC, ✂ SCP
02/3 BAP Memorabilia 47, 255, ✂ SC18
01/2 Bowman 69
02/3 Bowman 17
98/9 Bowman's Best 102, BP7, ✍ A8A, ✍ A8B
02/3 Calder 7
93/4 Classic 101
98/9 COLO / Kid Smart
99/0 Crown Royale 36, IG-5, C21-3
00/1 Crown Royale 27
01/2 Crown Royale 36
02/3 Crown Royale 13
95/6 Do. Elite WJ 34
98/9 Dynagon Ice 46, -IR 1
99/0 Dynagon Ice 55, CM-20
02/3 Exclusive 22
02/3 First Edition 93, ✂ Jers.
01/2 Heads Up 22, BTI 6
02/3 Heads Up 29, ✂ GWQ 8
99/0 HoloGrFX 16, ✍ Aut.
99/0 McDonald's McD-18
99/0 Millenium 69, ✍ Aut. 69
99/0 NHL Power Play
01/2 O-Pee-Chee 35
02/3 O-Pee-Chee 31, Update 31
98/9 Omega 67
99/0 Omega 61, G-3
99/0 Pacific 102, GC-7
00/1 Pacific 111, IO-5
01/2 Pacific 99
02/3 Pacific 88, ✂ GWJ 10
02/3 Pacific Complete 121
98/9 Pa. Crown Roy. 32, -RC-1
99/0 Pa. Paramount 62, PB-8
00/1 Pa. Paramount 58, ✂ GUS-4
98/9 Pa. Revolution 34
99/0 Panini Sticker 4, 215
00/1 Parkhurst P-51
01/2 Parkhurst 91, ✂ PJ30, ✂ PS30, ✂ HSHSJers, ✂ T5, ✂ T22
02/3 Parkhurst 49, -CR1, ✂ CRM1
02/3 Parkhurst Retro 137
00/1 Premier Plus 82
99/0 Prism 37
00/1 Private Stock PS-9, ✂ GUG 22
01/2 Pr. Stock 21, -PS 16, ✂ GUG 28
02/3 Pr. Stock Reserve 14
01/2 PS Titanium ✂ DSJ 11
02/3 PS Titanium 14, ✂ GWJ 11
02/3 Quest for the Cup 11
99/0 Revolution 38, SS-8, TL-11, / CSC 38
00/1 Revolution 35
00/1 Signature 82, ✍ Aut. 70
01/2 Signature C-7, ✍ Aut. LCD, ✂ GUE17, ✂ GJ18, ✂ GSJ18, ✂ HSHSJers, ✂ ITN17, ✂ IS11, ✂ TM9
02/3 Signature 99, GS-19, ✍ 99
98/9 SP Authentic 96, SS20
99/0 SP Authentic 25
01/2 SP Authentic 20
02/3 SP Authentic 20, ✂ DP
01/2 SP GU 11
02/3 SP Game-Used ✂ AF (x2), ✂ PH (x2)
02/3 Sports Vault 165
99/0 SPx 42
01/2 SPx 82, 169, ✂ DT, ✂ TT
02/3 SPx 17
98/9 SPx Prospects 17
99/0 Stadium 121, CA2, Chrome 36, ✍ CS1, ✍ CS3, ✍ LS11
00/1 Stadium 87
01/2 Stadium 93, G8, NHLP13, ✂ SCSD, ✂ SCST
02/3 Stadium 21, -WS-2, ✂ FC10
99/0 Topps 106, NS6, IF2, ✍ TA6
00/1 Topps 77
01/2 Topps 35, ✂ GWJ, ✍ CA
02/3 Topps 31, Update 31, PP2
99/0 To. Chrome 106, IF2
00/1 To. Chrome 60
01/2 To. Chrome 35
02/3 T. Chrome 31
99/0 To. Gold Label 48, FG4
00/1 To. Gold Label 29, NG14
00/1 To. Heritage 72, NT7
01/2 To. Heritage 66
02/3 To. Heritage 100, ✂ CC, ✍ Aut.
00/1 To. Heritage ASG 6
02/3 T. Limited 31
99/0 To. Prmr. Plus 8, CAC1, TN3, ✂ GP, / PP5
01/2 To. Reserve 70, ✂ TR
02/3 T. Total 126
00/1 UD Heroes 28
01/2 UD PlayMakers Ltd 25
00/1 Ultimate Mem. ✍ U-40
01/2 Ultimate Mem. ✂ CT
99/0 Ult. Victory 25
95/6 Upper Deck 569
98/9 Upper Deck 415, GN21, P26
99/0 Upper Deck 41, 142, N15
00/1 Upper Deck 274
01/2 Upper Deck 46, CT3, GA7, ✂ SCFJers., ✂ SCFJersD, ✂ SupSwe
02/3 Upper Deck 45, 231, 271, ✂ LN, ✂ PA, ✂ S, ✂ PW, UDPL
00/1 UD ASG PP4
98/9 UD Black Diam. 24, M11, WF16
99/0 UD Black Diam. 27
00/1 UD Black Diam. ✂ GG
99/0 UD C. Legends 74
01/2 UD Challenge 19
02/3 UD Classic 27, ✂ CS, ✂ HR
98/9 UD G. Reserve 415
99/0 UD G. Reserve 41, 142, ✍ UDA
99/0 UD Gretzky Excl. 86
01/2 UD Honor Roll 92, ✂ GAJ
02/3 UD Honor 9, -SG5
00/1 UD Legends 33
01/2 UD Mask 20, ✂ GG, ✂ GJ, ✂ JP, ✂ DP
02/3 UD Mask 15, ✂ IO
98/9 UD MVP 54, ✍ PS
99/0 UD MVP 54, 21st-10, ✍ PS
00/1 UD MVP 47
01/2 UD MVP 46
02/3 UD MVP 48, SO5, SA, SD (x3), ST (x2)
99/0 UD MVP Cup 53, CC4
02/3 UD Piece 25, AC5, ✂ TT
01/2 UD Premier 14, ✂ B, ✂ D (x2)
02/3 UD Premier ✂ Jers, ✂ Patch
99/0 UD Retro 23
02/3 UD Rookie 16, ✂ 153a
01/2 UD SCup Champs 35
01/2 UD Top Shelf 88, ✂ J
02/3 UD Top Shelf ✂ CP, ✂ SW
00/1 UD Vintage 94
01/2 UD Vintage 62
02/3 UD Vintage 69, GB 69, T18, ✂ FS, ✂ SO
00/1 Vanguard 26
01/2 Vanguard 24, QTH 13
02/3 Vanguard 14, ✂ GWJ 7
99/0 Victory 76, 353
00/1 Victory 59
01/2 Victory 89
02/3 Victory 52, -NP53
99/0 WGretzky 47, ✂ SG
DRURY, TED
01/2 Albany River Rats
96/7 ANAH / Up Front 5
98/9 Be A Player 5, ✍ Aut. 5
00/1 Chicago Wolves
93/4 Classic 63
94/5 Classic ✍ Aut.
93/4 Cla. Images 4 Sport 38
93/4 Cla. Prospects 14
93/4 Cla. Prospects LP2
93/4 Donruss 437
93/4 Donruss 58
93/4 Donruss RR 14
94/5 Donruss 186
93/4 Fleer Ultra 280
93/4 Fleer Ultra WotF 4
94/5 Fleer Ultra 88
93/4 Leaf 424
94/5 Leaf 22
98/9 OPC Chrome 212
95/6 OTTA
97/8 Pacific CC 312
00/1 Pa. Paramount 69
93/4 Parkhurst 35
94/5 Parkhurst 96
95/6 Parkhurst 422
93/4 Pinnacle 447
94/5 Pinnacle 187
97/8 Pi. Be A Player 84, ✍ Aut. 84
93/4 Power Play 303
94/5 Premier 157
00/1 Private Stock 28
93/4 Score 608
97/8 Score Anah. 11
98/9 Topps 212
93/4 To. Stadium 443
92/3 Upper Deck 396
93/4 Upper Deck 466, SP-20
94/5 Upper Deck 205
95/6 Upper Deck 298
96/7 Upper Deck 115
94/5 UD BAP ✍ 34
96/7 UD CC 183
97/8 UD Coll. Choice 6
99/0 UD MVP Cup 116
DRYDEN, DAVE
64-67 BeeHive-3 [Chic.]
72/3 BUFF
73/4 BUFF
75/6 BUFF / Linnett
65/6 Coca-Cola
70/1 Colgate 80
71/2 Eddie Sargent 32
72/3 Eddie Sargent 34
79/0 EDMO
88/9 EDMO / Action 90
68/9 O-Pee-Chee 150
71/2 O-Pee-Chee 159
72/3 O-Pee-Chee 241
73/4 O-Pee-Chee 63
79/0 O-Pee-Chee 71
74/5 OPC WHA 20
75/6 OPC WHA 104
76/7 OPC WHA 85
77/8 OPC WHA 28
68/9 Shirriff / Chic. 13
77-79 Sportscaster 82-23
77-79 Sports. FIN 85-2024
67/8 Topps 57
73/4 Topps 187
79/0 Topps 71
71/2 Toronto Sun Photo
DRYDEN, KEN
71/2 Colgate Head
72/3 Dernière Heure
72/3 Eddie Sargent 124
88/9 Esso All-Star
71/2 Frito Lay
91/2 Future Trends C72 31
91/2 Future Trends C72 85, ✍ 85
83 HHOF Postcard N4
83&87 HHOF 196
72/3 Post 2
72/3 Post 22
74/5 Lipton Soup 19
74/5 Loblaws
69/0 Mästär Serien 26
71/2 MONT / Pro Star
71/2 MONT / Pro Star
72/3 MONT / Pro Star
74/5 MONT
75/6 MONT
76/7 MONT
77/8 MONT
78/9 MONT
92/3 MONT / OPC 51
71/2 O-Pee-Chee 45
71/2 O-Pee-Chee Book. 17
72/3 O-Pee-Chee 134
72/3 O-Pee-Chee 145
72/3 O-Pee-Chee 247
72/3 O-Pee-Chee Crest 12
72/3 O-Pee-Chee TC
73/4 O-Pee-Chee 136
74/5 O-Pee-Chee 155
75/6 O-Pee-Chee 35
75/6 O-Pee-Chee 213
76/7 O-Pee-Chee 6
76/7 O-Pee-Chee 200
77/8 O-Pee-Chee 6
77/8 OPC 8
77/8 O-Pee-Chee 100
77/8 O-Pee-Chee NS 5
78/9 O-Pee-Chee 50
78/9 O-Pee-Chee 68
78/9 OPC 70
78/9 O-Pee-Chee 330
79/0 O-Pee-Chee 6
79/0 OPC 8
79/0 O-Pee-Chee 150
71/2 O-Pee-Chee Poster 22
71/2 Pro Star Promotions
71/2 Pro Star Promotions
71/2 Pro Star Promotions
71/2 Pro Star Promotions
91 Semic Sticker 236
77-79 Sportscaster 14-23
77-79 Sports. FIN 48-1145
71/2 Topps 45
72/3 Topps 127
72/3 Topps 160
72/3 Topps 174
73/4 Topps 4
73/4 Topps 10
74/5 Topps 155
75/6 Topps 35
75/6 Topps 213
76/7 Topps 6
76/7 Topps 200
76/7 Topps NS 5
77/8 Topps 6
77/8 Topps 8
77/8 Topps 100
77/8 ToppsNS 5
78/9 Topps 50
78/9 Topps 68
78/9 Topps 70
79/0 Topps 6
79/0 Topps 8
79/0 Topps 150
71/2 Toronto Sun Photo
02/3 UD Piece / Giveaway
99/0 UD Retro 101, ✂ RM5
96 Wien HL1
DRYNDIN, VITALI
00/1 Mir 49
DUBA, LUKAS
96/7 APS 236
DUBA, TOMAS
02/3 Cardset 14, 150, -DD 8, -Nimik.
99/0 OFS 539
00/1 OFS 292
DUBÉ, CHRISTIAN
99/0 BAP Mem. 46
95/6 Classic 34
96/7 Do. Canadian 146
95/6 Do. Elite WJ 13
96/7 Do. Elite 137, A-25
96/7 Fl. Ultra 104, UR-5
97/8 Hartford Wolf Pack
98/9 Hartford Wolf Pack
96/7 L. Preferred 135
97/8 Limited 46
96/7 Metal Univ. 176
97/8 Pa. Paramount 113
94/5 Parkie SE258
96/7 Pi. Zenith 135
97/8 Score NYRa. 14
94/5 Select 166
96/7 Select CE 95
94/5 SP 179
95/6 SP 171
96/7 SP 183
96/7 Upper Deck 296
97/8 Upper Deck 105
96/7 UD Black Diam. 79
96/7 UD CC 357
96/7 UD Ice 136
DUBÉ, DANIELLE
97/8 UD Coll. Choice 288
DUBÉ, DANY
92/3 Canada Nationals
93/4 Canada Nationals
DUBÉ, GILLES
45-64 BeeHive-2 [Mont.]
52/3 Laval Dairy Update 50
52/3 St. Lawrence 75
DUBÉ, MICHEL
01/2 Moncton Wildcats 9
DUBÉ, NORMAND
78/9 Dernière Heure
77/8 OPC WHA 54
DUBÉ, ROGER
93 Semic Sticker 262
DUBÉ, SERGE
98/9 Sudbury Wolves 18
DUBÉ, YANNICK
94/5 Classic C2
93/4 Donruss CAN9
93/4 Parkhurst 512
93/4 Pinnacle 471
91/2 7th...Sketch LHJMQ 227
94/5 Sig. Rookies 3, ✍ 3
94/5 SR Gold Standard 82
93/4 Upper Deck 533
DUBEN, MIROSLAV
97/8 APS 300
98/9 DS 37
97/8 DS Sticker 114
98/9 OFS 298, 477
00/1 OFS 37
99/0 Score 42
DUBEN, PREMYSL
00/1 Baie-Comeau 11
DUBERMAN, JUSTIN
92/3 Classic Prospects 116
92/3 Cleveland Lumberjacks
93/4 Cleveland Lumberjacks
93/4 Donruss 471
DUBINSKY, MIKE
92/3 Brandon Wheat Kings
94/5 Sig. Rookies 42, ✍ 42
94/5 Slapshot Memorial 37
DUBINSKY, STEVE
92/3 Clarkson G'Knights
92/3 Clarkson G'Knights
93/4 Classic 64
93/4 Cla. Prospects 7
93/4 Donruss 70
94/5 Donruss 26
93/4 Indianapolis Ice
94/5 Indianapolis Ice
95/6 Indianapolis Ice
94/5 Leaf 426
99/0 Millenium 45, ✍ Aut. 45
01/2 Milwaukee Admirals
01/2 Pacific 85
97/8 Pa. Dynagon BKS-21
93/4 Parkhurst 40
97/8 Pi. Be A Player 166, ✍ Aut. 166
94/5 Premier 233
99/0 Stadium 32
93/4 Upper Deck 477
02/3 Worcester IceCats
DUBKOV, ILJA
93/4 Roanoke Express
94/5 Roanoke Express
95/6 Roanoke Express
96/7 Roanoke Express 14
DUBNYK, DEVON
02/3 Kamloops Blazers
DUBOI, GUY
72 Semic Sticker 152
DUBOIS, ERIC
90/1 7th..Sketch LHJMQ 55
90 7th..Sketch Mem.Cup 68
DUBOIS, ÉRIC
93/4 Atlanta Knights
94/5 Atlanta Knights 13
95/6 Atlanta Knights
91/2 Greensboro Monarchs
01/2 UD DEL 230
DUBOIS, PIERRE
79/0 Montréal Juniors B&W
79/0 Montréal Jrs. Colour
DUBOIS, ROBERT
93/4 Slapshot / Oshawa 16
95/6 Slapshot 30
DUBROVSKI, DMITRI
98/9 Mir 87
99/0 Mir 235
DUCE, BRYAN
97/8 Bell
95/6 Slapshot 145
DUCHAÎNE, KEVIN
01/2 Drummondville
DUCHARME, BRUNO
90/1 7th..Sketch LHJMQ 202
91/2 7th...Sketch LHJMQ 250
DUCHARME, SYLVAIN
91/2 7th...Sketch LHJMQ 278
93/4 Slapshot / Drummondville 7
DUCHESNE, ALEXANDRE
91/2 7th...Sketch LHJMQ 290
93/4 Slapshot / Drummondville 24
DUCHESNE, ÉRIC
90/1 7th..Sketch LHJMQ 37
91/2 7th...Sketch LHJMQ 84
DUCHESNE, GAÉTAN
91/2 Bowman 120
92/3 Bowman 266
93/4 Donruss 301
92/3 Durivage 22
93/4 Durivage 40
92/3 Fleer Ultra 318
93/4 Leaf 339
94/5 Leaf 547
88/9 O-Pee-Chee 208
90/1 OPC/Topps 319
91/2 O-Pee-Chee 433
92/3 O-Pee-Chee 143
88/9 OPC Sticker 187-56
89/0 opcSticker 194-48
87/8 Panini Sticker 183
88/9 Panini Sticker 353
90/1 Panini Sticker 256
91/2 Panini Sticker 117
93/4 Panini Sticker 273
91/2 Parkhurst 305
93/4 Parkhurst 456
92/3 Pinnacle 198
93/4 Pinnacle 377
94/5 Pinnacle 219
94/5 POG 211
95/6 POG 119
82/3 Post [Wash.]
93/4 Power Play 433
94/5 Premier 232
90/1 Pro Set 137
91/2 Pro Set 110
87/8 QUÉB / Gene. Foods
88/9 QUÉB
88/9 QUÉB / Gene. Foods
80/1 Québec Remparts
92/3 SANJ / Pacific Bell
90/1 Score 375
91/2 Score CAN 440
92/3 Score 338
93/4 Score 226
93/4 Score 545
94/5 Score 196
92/3 Topps 406
91/2 To. Stadium 153
92/3 T. Stadium Club 307
90/1 Upper Deck 108
91/2 Upper Deck 207
92/3 Upper Deck 469
81/2 WASH
84/5 WASH / Pizza Hut
85/6 WASH / Pizza Hut
86/7 WASH / Kodak
86/7 WASH / Police
DUCHESNE, PAUL
52/3 Bas du Fleuve 46
51/2 Lac St-Jean 45
DUCHESNE, STEVE
98/9 Be A Player 215, ✍ Aut. 215
00/1 BAP Mem. 253
90/1 Bowman 146
91/2 Bowman 191
92/3 Bowman 31
93/4 Donruss 276
93/4 Donruss 484
94/5 Donruss 304
95/6 Donruss 278
96/7 Donruss 182
92/3 Durivage 38
93/4 EA Sports 109
94/5 Flair 152
94/5 Fleer 186
96/7 Fleer 75
95/6 Fleer Metal 105
92/3 Fleer Ultra 384
93/4 Fleer Ultra 7
94/5 Fleer Ultra 182
95/6 Fleer Ultra 138, 279
96/7 Fl. Ultra 117
93/4 Hockey Wit 8
89/0 Kraft 58
90/1 Kraft 65
93/4 Leaf 176
94/5 Leaf 3
95/6 Leaf 143
94/5 L. Limited 93
87/8 LOSA
88/9 LOSA / Smokey
89/0 LOSA / Smokey 14
90/1 LOSA / Smokey 15
93/4 McDonald's McD-14
96/7 Metal Univ. 106
88/9 OPC/Topps 182
89/0 OPC/Topps 123
90/1 OPC/Topps 86
91/2 O-Pee-Chee 31
92/3 O-Pee-Chee 296
89/0 Topps - Sticker 10
98/9 OPC Chrome 44
91/2 OPC Premier 13
92/3 OPC Premier 130
88/9 OPC Sticker 152-19
89/0 opcSticker 150-10, 162-27, / AS 32
97/8 Omega 192
95/6 OTTA
96/7 OTTA
98/9 Pacific 366
97/8 Pacific CC 302
97/8 Pa. Crown Roy. 115
97/8 Pa. Invincible 94
97/8 Pa. Revolution 119
88/9 Panini Sticker 70
89/0 Panini Sticker 93, 176
90/1 Panini Sticker 241
91/2 Panini Sticker 80
92/3 Panini Sticker 192
93/4 Panini Sticker 76
94/5 Panini Sticker 143
95/6 Panini Sticker 195
96/7 Panini Sticker 50
97/8 Panini Sticker 45
98/9 Panini Sticker 158
99/0 Panini Sticker 237
95 Panini Worlds 3
91/2 Parkhurst 125
92/3 Parkhurst 143
93/4 Parkhurst 168
94/5 Parkhurst 205, V26
95/6 Parkhurst 153
91/2 PHIL / J.C. Penney
91/2 Pinnacle 42
92/3 Pinnacle 320
93/4 Pinnacle 78
94/5 Pinnacle 108
97/8 Pinnacle 142
96/7 Pi. BAP 141, ✍ Aut. 141
97/8 Pi. Inside 136
95/6 Pi. Summit 145
95/6 Pi. Zenith 111
95/6 Playoff 88
96/7 Playoff 347
94/5 POG 210
95/6 POG 196
94/5 Post
93/4 Power Play 197
93/4 Premier 151
93/4 Prmr. - BG-Top. 2
94/5 Premier 401
90/1 Pro Set 115, 350
91/2 Pro Set 96
91/2 Pro Set 448
92/3 Pro Set 137
91/2 Pro Set Platinum 86
92/3 QUÉB / Petro-Canada
90/1 Score 26
90/1 Sco. Hot Cards 15
91/2 Score 205
91/2 Score 19T
91/2 Score CAN 205
91/2 Score CAN 569
92/3 Score 151
93/4 Score 190
93/4 Score 659
93/4 Score PiAS 16
94/5 Score 52
95/6 Score 99
96/7 Score 62
97/8 Score 230
97/8 Score SLou. 16
94/5 Select 145
91 Semic Sticker 61
93 Semic Sticker 194
95/6 SBx Emotion 124
95/6 SBx Impact 119
96/7 SBx Impact 89
97/8 SP Authentic 144
99/0 Stadium 166
95/6 Super Sticker 87, DC-15
96/7 Team Out✂
92/3 Topps 271
95/6 Topps 102, 337
98/9 Topps 44
95/6 To. Finest 17
96/7 Topps Picks 73
91/2 To. Stadium 58
92/3 T. Stadium Club 313
93/4 To. Stadium - All-Stars
94/5 T. Stadium Club 81
95/6 To. Stadium 126
98/9 UD Choice 182
90/1 Upper Deck 136
91/2 Upper Deck 570
92/3 Upper Deck 513
93/4 Upper Deck 217
94/5 Upper Deck 108, SP-158
95/6 Upper Deck 49, SE-147
96/7 Upper Deck 304
97/8 Upper Deck 114
98/9 Upper Deck 286
94/5 UD BAP R64, ✍ 137
95/6 UD CC 279
96/7 UD CC 182
97/8 UD Coll. Choice 179
98/9 UD G. Reserve 286
92/3 UD Locker 2
98/9 UD MVP 93
95/6 UD Post 3
96/7 UD Post
96 Wien 84
DUCHESNEAU, JONATHAN
99 Québec Pee Wee 271
DUCK, ALEXANDER
00/1 UD DEL 213
DUCK, IMA
00/1 Quad City Mallards
DÜCK, ALEXANDER
01/2 UD DEL 270
DUCOLON, TOBY
88/9 ProCards / Peoria
89/0 ProCards IHL 12
DUDA, JASON
93/4 Saskatoon Blades
98/9 Wichita Thunder
DUDA, RADEK
97/8 APS 16
99/0 Lethbridge Hurricanes
00/1 OFS 314
01/2 OFS 212
DUDAREV, DMITRI
00/1 Mir 239
DUDIK, DIMITRI
98/9 DEL 265
00/1 UD DEL 187
DUDIK, DMITRI
99/0 Eishockey 32
DUDLEY, GEORGE
83 HHOF Postcard E8
83&87 HHOF 68
DUDLEY, RHETT
98/9 Wichita Thunder
DUDLEY, RICK
73/4 BUFF
74/5 BUFF
80/1 BUFF / Wendt's 6
89/0 BUFF / Campbell's
90/1 BUFF / Campbell's
93/4 BUFF / Noco
75/6 Cincinnati Stingers
74/5 Loblaws
89/0 New Haven Nighthawks
74/5 O-Pee-Chee 268
79/0 O-Pee-Chee 37
80/1 O-Pee-Chee 355
81/2 O-Pee-Chee 362
75/6 OPC WHA 58
76/7 OPC WHA 17
93/4 Phoenix Roadrunners
90/1 Pro Set 662
88/9 ProCards / New Haven
92/3 San Diego Gulls
79/0 Topps 37
DUE-BOJE, CHRISTIAN
98/9 DEL 300
99/0 Eishockey 245
94/5 Leaf Elit Set 109, GC-4
95/6 Leaf Elit Set 28
94 Semic 55
89/0 Semic Elitserien 55
90/1 Semic Elitserien 278
91/2 Semic Elitserien 61
92/3 Semic Elitserien 77
95/6 UD Elitserien 39
97/8 UD Elitserien 169
00/1 UD Elitserien 139
DUERDEN, DAVE
97 Bowman 3
95/6 Classic 94
00/1 Hartford Wolf Pack
98/9 Kentucky Tho'blades
99/0 Louisville Panthers
00/1 Louisville Panthers
99/0 Omega 104
95/6 Slapshot 321
DUFALT, PASCAL
90/1 7th..Sketch LHJMQ 76
DUFF, DICK
45-64 BeeHive-2 [Toro.]
64-67 BeeHive-3 [Mont.]
63-65 Chex
64/5 Coke/Sprite [NYRa.]
65/6 Coca-Cola
70/1 Dad's Cookies
70/1 Eddie Sargent 65
71/2 Eddie Sargent 24
66/7 MONT / IGA Stamp
67/8 MONT
67/8 MONT / IGA Card
68/9 MONT / IGA Card
68/9 O-Pee-Chee 161
69/0 O-Pee-Chee 11
71/2 O-Pee-Chee 164
55/6 Parkhurst 18
57/8 Parkhurst [Toro.] 3
58/9 Parkhurst 29
59/0 Parkhurst 38
60/1 Parkhurst 12
61/2 Parkhurst 12
62/3 Parkhurst 2
63/4 Parkhurst 4
63/4 Parkhurst 64
92/3 Parkhurst PR-24
02/3 Parkie - Reprint 201, 219, 231, 248, 261, 271, 294
93/4 Parkie 56-57 126
93/4 Parkie 56-57 167
95/6 Parkie 66-67 78
94/5 Parkie Tall 106
67/8 Post Tips 6
60/1 Shirriff 2
61/2 Shirriff 53
62/3 Shirriff 12
68/9 Shirriff / Mont. 11
64/5 Topps 46
65/6 Topps 7
66/7 Topps 71
67/8 Topps 2
02/3 Topps - Reprint 12, ✍ Reprint 12
01/2 Topps Archives 48
64/5 TORO
80/1 TORO
57/8 Toronto Star Photo
58/9 Toronto Star Photo
63/4 Toronto Star Action
59/0 Toronto Star Weekend
71/2 Toronto Sun Photo
60/1 York Glass [Toro.]
60/1 York
61/2 York 2
62/3 York Transfer 7
63/4 York 9
67/8 York 26
DUFF, JOHN
91/2 Ferris State Bulldogs
DUFF, LESS
52/3 Anonymous 155
DUFFUS, PARRIS
91/2 Air Canada SJHL D49
02/3 Cardset 162
93/4 Cla. Prospects 68
98/9 DEL 119

96/7 Las Vegas Thunder
92/3 Peoria Rivermen
93/4 Peoria Rivermen
94/5 Peoria Rivermen
97/8 Pi. Inside 75
00/1 UD DEL 184

DUFFY, BEN
85/6 Minnesota-Duluth 31

DUFORT, JEAN-FRANÇOIS
01/2 Cape Breton Eagles 20
96 Québec Pee Wee 241
99/0 Shawinigan 20
00/1 Shawinigan 23
01/2 Shawinigan 23

DUFOUR, CLAUDE
53/4 La Patrie

DUFOUR, GUY
72/3 O-Pee-Chee 328
73/4 OPC WHA Poster 3
73/4 Québec Nordiques

DUFOUR, LUC
83/4 BOST
84/5 Chicoutimi Saguenéens
83/4 O-Pee-Chee 48
84/5 O-Pee-Chee 3
83/4 OPC/Topps Sticker 172
83/4 OPC/Topps Sticker 182
84/5 QUÉB
83/4 Souhaits Keychain [Bruins]

DUFOUR, MARCEL
51/2 Lac St-Jean 8

DUFOUR, MICHAEL
83/4 Fredericton Express

DUFRESNE, DAN
91/2 Air Canada SJHL A36

DUFRESNE, DONALD
92/3 Durivage 39
96/7 EDMO
93/4 Fleer Ultra 422
93/4 Leaf 355
89/0 MONT
90/1 MONT
91/2 MONT
92/3 MONT
90/1 Panini/MTL 10
93/4 Parkhurst 467
90/1 Pro Set 469
91/2 Pro Set 418
88/9 ProCards / Sherbrooke
90/1 Score 35T
91/2 Score CAN 392
90/1 Upper Deck 332
94/5 UD BAP ✍ 45

DUGGEN, BRAD
81/2 Saskatoon Blades

DUGRÉ, YVAN
51/2 Laval Dairy 49

DUGUAY, KEVIN
85/6 Kitchener Rangers

DUGUAY, RON
82/3 Dernière Heure
84/5 DETR / Little Caesars
85/6 DETR / Little Caesars
83/4 Funmate Puffy 13 [w/]
88/9 LOSA / Smokey
78/9 O-Pee-Chee 177
79/0 O-Pee-Chee 208
80/1 O-Pee-Chee 37
81/2 O-Pee-Chee 223
82/3 O-Pee-Chee 217
82/3 O-Pee-Chee 221
83/4 O-Pee-Chee 121
84/5 O-Pee-Chee 52
85/6 OPC/Topps 116
87/8 OPC/Topps 110
81/2 OPC Sticker 171
82/3 OPC/Topps Sticker 134
84/5 OPC Sticker 42
85/6 OPC Sticker 32-162
87/8 Panini Sticker 119
89/0 Panini Sticker 96
86/7 PITT / Kodak
82/3 Post [NYRa.]
91/2 ProCards 317
85/6 7-Eleven Superstars 5
83/4 Souhaits Keychain [Rangers]
78/9 Topps 177
79/0 Topps 208
80/1 Topps 37
81/2 Topps 96 [East]
84/5 Topps 40
02/3 UD Foundations 27, 41, 68, ✂ CH, ✂ CG

DUGUID, LORNE
33/4 Canadian Gum
33/4 O-Pee-Chee 58
33/4 WWGum 52

DUHAIME, TREVOR
92/3 Hampton Roads
90/1 7th..Sketch LHJMQ 210
91/2 7th...Sketch LHJMQ 165

DUHAMEL, BENOÎT
01/2 Drummondville

DUHAMEL, CÉDRICK
01/2 Sherbrooke Castors 8

DUHART, JIM
93/4 Flint Generals
94/5 Flint Generals
95/6 Flint Generals

DUKE, STEVE
00/1 Charlotte Checkers
99/0 Mississippi S'Wolves

DUKELOW, TYLER
99/0 Brampton Batallion 16

DUMA, PAVEL
99/0 Mir 130
00/1 Mir 287

DUMART, WOODY
34-43 BeeHive-1 [Bost.]
45-64 BeeHive-2 [Bost.]
91/2 BOST / SA Legends
98/9 BOST / Alumni 14
94/5 Legends 45
39/0 O-Pee-Chee 94
43-47 Parade Sportive
51/2 Parkhurst 28
52/3 Parkhurst 72
53/4 Parkhurst 96
01/2 Parkhurst PR6, PR23, PR99, ✍ PA9
93/4 Parkie 56-57 P-9

DUMAS, MARK
88/9 ProCards / Binghampton

DUMAS, MATHIEU
01/2 Cape Breton Eagles 19
02/3 Val d'Or Foreurs

DUMAS, ROGER
52/3 Bas du Fleuve 22

DUMNOV, VLADIMIR
99/0 Mir 34

DUMONSKI, STEVE
00/1 Rockford IceHogs
95/6 Slapshot 67

DUMONT, JEAN-PIERRE
01/2 Adrenaline 21, ✂ GWJ 3
01/2 Atomic 12
02/3 Atomic 10
99/0 Aurora 31
99/0 BAP Mem. 270, SL-21
00/1 BAP Mem. 428
01/2 BAP Memor. 71
95/6 Bowman P13
01/2 Bowman 52
97 Bowman 60
01/2 Crown Royale 17, ✂ TT 5
02/3 Crown Royale ✂ GWDP 2
99/0 Dynagon Ice 49
02/3 Exclusive 18
02/3 First Edition 76, ✂ Jers.
01/2 Heads Up 11, BTI 3
02/3 Heads Up 13, ✂ GWQ 4
99/0 HoloGrFX 13
99/0 Millenium 57, C-18, ✍ Aut. 57
99/0 NHL Power Play [x3]
01/2 O-Pee-Chee 21
02/3 O-Pee-Chee 30
99/0 Omega 58
99/0 Pacific 86
01/2 Pacific 47, 404
02/3 Pacific 41
02/3 Pacific Complete 122
99/0 Pa. Paramount 54
99/0 Panini Sticker 204
00/1 Parkhurst P-117
01/2 Parkhurst 228
02/3 Parkhurst ✂ TT12
02/3 Parkhurst Retro 131
97/8 Pi. BeeHive 68, ✍ Aut. 68
98/9 Portland Pirates
99/0 Prism 33
01/2 Pr. Stock 10, ✂ GUG 10
02/3 Pr. Stock Reserve 12
00/1 PS Titanium 8
01/2 PS Titanium 15, ✂ DSJ 4, ✂ DSJ 21
01/2 PS Titanium Draft ✂ 13
02/3 PS Titanium ✂ GWJ 7
99/0 Revolution 33, / CSC 33
00/1 Signature 123
01/2 Signature 4, ✍ Aut. 4
98/9 SP Authentic 94
01/2 SP Authentic 10
01/2 SP GU ✂ AF, ✂ AFD
02/3 SP Game-Used ✂ PC, ✂ PH
99/0 SPx 33
01/2 SPx ✂ DT (x2), ✂ TT
02/3 SPx ✂ WM
98/9 SPx Prospects 11
99/0 Stadium 190, Chrome 45, CA7
01/2 Stadium 69
02/3 Stadium 31
99/0 Topps 121
01/2 Topps 21
02/3 Topps 30, ✂ FRF
99/0 To. Chrome 121
01/2 To. Chrome 21
02/3 T. Chrome 30, ✂ FRF
01/2 To. Heritage 61
02/3 T. Limited 30
99/0 To. Prmr. Plus 131, PR9, / PP2
01/2 To. Reserve 66
02/3 T. Total 221
98/9 UD Choice 271
00/1 UD Heroes 15
99/0 Upper Deck 35, N20
01/2 Upper Deck 254
02/3 Upper Deck 17
99/0 UD G. Reserve 35
00/1 UD Ice 63
01/2 UD Mask ✂ GJ, ✂ JP, ✂ DP
99/0 UD MVP 44
01/2 UD MVP 22
02/3 UD MVP 20, SD, ST
99/0 UD Ovation 14
01/2 UD Vintage 29, 35
02/3 UD Vintage 33, ✂ HS
01/2 Vanguard 11, ✂ DGM 31
02/3 Vanguard ✂ GWJ 6
99/0 Victory 66
01/2 Victory 42
02/3 Victory 24
99/0 WGretzky 41

DUMONT, JUSTIN
00/1 Mississauga IceDogs

DUMONT, LOUIS
96/7 Louisiana Ice Gators
97/8 Louisiana Ice Gators
98/9 Louisiana Ice Gators
90/1 7th..Sketch WHL 168
91/2 7th...Sketch WHL 222

DUMOULIN, MARIO
90/1 7th..Sketch LHJMQ 120
91/2 7th...Sketch LHJMQ 260

DUNBAR, DALE
85/6 Fredericton Express

DUNCALFE, DARREN
97/8 Central Texas

DUNCAN, ART
19 Vancouver Millionaires
19 Vancouver Millionaires

DUNCAN, BOBBY
97/8 Portland Winter Hawks

DUNCAN, BRETT
94/5 Raleigh Icecaps
95/6 Saint John Flames
93/4 Seattle Thunderbirds

DUNCAN, GLEN
81/2 Indianapolis Checkers
82/3 Indianapolis Checkers

DUNCAN, IAIN
87/8 Moncton Hawks
89/0 Moncton Hawks
90/1 Moncton Hawks
88/9 O-Pee-Chee 209
89/0 O-Pee-Chee 293
88/9 OPC Sticker 132-268
88/9 OPC Sticker 140-11
88/9 OPC Sticker 108-238
89/0 opcSticker 136-257
88/9 Panini Sticker 154
89/0 Panini Sticker 170
90/1 ProCards 249
92/3 Toledo Storm WIOT
92/3 Toledo Storm
94/5 Toledo Storm
87/8 WINN
88/9 WINN / Safety Tips
89/0 WINN / Safeway
90/1 WINN / IGA

DUNCAN, TREVOR
89/0 Rayside-Balfour

DUNCAN, TROY
00/1 Sudbury Wolves 10

DUNCANSON, CRAIG
91/2 Baltimore Skipjacks
92/3 Binghampton Rangers
94/5 Binghampton Rangers
89/0 LOSA / Smokey 19
90/1 Moncton Hawks
90/1 ProCards 248
91/2 ProCards 566
85/6 Sudbury Wolves

DUNDAS, R.J.
83/4 Kelowna Wings
82/3 Regina Pats
83/4 Regina Pats

DUNDAS, ROCKY
83/4 Kelowna Wings
84/5 Kelowna Wings &...
88/9 ProCards / Sherbrooke

DUNDERDALE, TOMMY
91 C55 Reprint 6
83 HHOF Postcard I6
83&87 HHOF 127
10/1 Imperial
10/1 Imperial 14
11/2 Imperial 6
12/3 Imperial 5

DUNHAM, MIKE
01/2 Adrenaline 103, PP21
96/7 Albany River Rats
01/2 Atomic 54, ✂ GWJ 34
02/3 Atomic 59
98/9 Aurora 100
99/0 Aurora 78
00/1 Aurora 76
98/9 Be A Player 72, ✍ Aut. 72
99/0 BAP Mem. 299
00/1 BAP Mem. 249
01/2 BAP Memor. 136, ✂ Jers.
02/3 BAP Memorabilia 125, 391
01/2 BT Pipes 29, 91, -Mask, ✂ DM, ✂ Jers., ✂ S&J, ✂ GG, ✂ HSHSJers
02/3 Between the Pipes 12, M7, ✂ BM14, ✂ DM11, ✂ GUE15, ✂ GB8, ✂ GUJ15, ✂ GP13, ✂ GSJ15, ✂ ITN15, ✂ T11
98/9 Bicycle.. 3-S
01/2 Bowman 70
98/9 Bowman's Best 75
93/4 Classic 56
94/5 Classic ✍ Aut.
94/5 Classic 4 Sport 148
94/5 Cla. Images 61
93/4 Cla. Images 4 Sport 20
93/4 Cla. Prospects IA13
93/4 Cla. Prospects LP3
99/0 Crown Royale 74
00/1 Crown Royale 59
01/2 Crown Royale 80, ✂ TT 16
02/3 Crown Royale 54
97/8 Donruss 93
97/8 Do. Canadian 87
97/8 Do. Elite 59
97/8 Do. Preferred 40, CG-17
97/8 Do. Priority 86
97/8 Do. Studio 56
98/9 Dynagon Ice 101, -TC 14
99/0 Dynagon Ice 106
95/6 Edge Ice 6, TW-10, PR-3
02/3 Exclusive 97
02/3 First Edition 46, ✂ Jers.
93/4 Fleer Ultra 481
95/6 Future Legends 3, PC-1
01/2 Heads Up 53, ✂ JQ 13
02/3 In The Game-Used ✂ GP5
97/8 Leaf 104, PD-16
97/8 Limited 78, 194, FG-41
92/3 Maine Black Bears
92/3 Maine Black Bears
99/0 Millenium 142, ✍ Aut. 142
98/9 NASH / Wendy's 8
96/7 NJER / Sharp
98/9 NHL Power Play
01/2 O-Pee-Chee 84
02/3 O-Pee-Chee 195
98/9 Omega 128
99/0 Omega 126
98/9 Pacific 262
99/0 Pacific 222, TL-15
00/1 Pacific 220
01/2 Pacific 216
02/3 Pacific 207
02/3 Pacific Complete 474
98/9 Pa. Crown Roy. 73
97/8 Pa. Dynagon BKS-106
97/8 Pa. Invincible R-110
98/9 Pa. Paramount 122, -GS 9
99/0 Pa. Paramount 123
00/1 Pa. Paramount 134
98/9 Pa. Revolution 78
98/9 Panini Photocard
99/0 Panini Sticker 339
00/1 Parkhurst P-129
01/2 Parkhurst 110
02/3 Parkhurst 64, -CR16, ✂ CRM16, ✂ TT10
02/3 Parkhurst Retro 110
97/8 Pinnacle 79
96/7 Pi. Be A Player 212, ✍ Aut. 212
97/8 Pi. Be A Player 110, ✍ Aut. 110
93/4 Power Play 501
93/4 Premier - USA Hockey 1
99/0 Prism 75
00/1 Private Stock 54
01/2 Pr. Stock 52, ✂ GUG 56
02/3 Pr. Stock Reserve 57
01/2 PS Titanium 77
00/1 PS Titanium Draft ✂ 52
99/0 Revolution 78
00/1 Revolution 80
97/8 Score 45, 269
97/8 Score NJer. 13
94 Semic 108
01/2 Signature 93, ✍ Aut. 93
02/3 Signature 5, GS-57, ✍ 5
98/9 SP Authentic 44
99/0 SP Authentic 47
00/1 SP Authentic 50
01/2 SP Authentic 46
00/1 SP GU 34
01/2 SP GU 29
02/3 SP GU 27, ✂ PH
99/0 SPx 83
01/2 SPx 36
02/3 SPx 45, ✂ X
98/9 SPx Prospects 34
99/0 Stadium 125
00/1 Stadium 25
01/2 Stadium 67
02/3 Stadium 71
99/0 SLU 210
99/0 Topps 241
00/1 Topps 102
01/2 Topps 84
02/3 Topps 195
99/0 To. Chrome 241
00/1 To. Chrome 80
01/2 To. Chrome 84
02/3 T. Chrome 110
98/9 T. Gold Label 83
00/1 To. Heritage 189
01/2 To. Heritage 71
02/3 To. Heritage 48
02/3 T. Limited 195
01/2 To. Reserve 13
93/4 To. Stadium - Team U.S.A. 4
02/3 T. Total 400, TTC17
00/1 UD Heroes 69
01/2 UD PlayMakers Ltd 56, ✂ PCCJ
00/1 UD Reserve GG6
00/1 Ultimate Mem. ✂ G-17
91/2 Upper Deck 693
98/9 Upper Deck 210
99/0 Upper Deck 76
00/1 Upper Deck 100
01/2 Upper Deck 98, ✂ TendThr
02/3 Upper Deck 342, ✂ DM, ✂ GT, ✂ HS, ✂ SV, ✂ PW
02/3 UD Artistic ✂ AT
96/7 UD Black Diam. 3
98/9 UD Black Diam. 47
01/2 UD Challenge 48
02/3 UD Classic 56, ✂ CS, ✂ HR
91/2 Upper Deck WJC 80
98/9 UD G. Reserve 210
99/0 UD G. Reserve 76
02/3 UD Honor ✂ GA
01/2 UD Ice 26
00/1 UD Legends 75
01/2 UD Mask 117, 180, ✂ MM, ✂ MB, ✂ PM, ✂ SY, ✂ VC
02/3 UD Mask 54, 55, 57, ✂ CW, ✂ GG, ✂ MM, ✂ BM, ✂ NB, ✂ PW
98/9 UD MVP 110, ✍ PS
99/0 UD MVP 113
00/1 UD MVP 101
01/2 UD MVP 106
02/3 UD MVP 104, Souv.
99/0 UD MVP Cup 98
02/3 UD Piece 54, ✂ PH
01/2 UD Premier 31
02/3 UD Premier 38
00/1 UD Pros&Prosp. 48
99/0 UD Retro 44
02/3 UD Rookie 66, ✂ DJ
02/3 UD Top Shelf 48, ✂ HH, ✂ ST, ✂ SS, ✂ SW
00/1 UD Vintage 201, 208, 209
01/2 UD Vintage 141, 148, 269
02/3 UD Vintage 141, 277, GB 141, T37, ✂ EE
01/2 Vanguard 53
99/0 Victory 155
00/1 Victory 127
01/2 Victory 193, 199
02/3 Victory 119, -NP56
99/0 WGretzky 94

DUNK, BRETT
87/8 Brockville Braves

DUNLOP, BLAKE
83/4 Funmate Puffy 13 [w/]
74/5 Loblaws
74/5 O-Pee-Chee 308
75/6 O-Pee-Chee 16
76/7 O-Pee-Chee 263
79/0 O-Pee-Chee 174
80/1 O-Pee-Chee 370
81/2 O-Pee-Chee 293
82/3 O-Pee-Chee 301
83/4 O-Pee-Chee 314
81/2 OPC Sticker 131
82/3 OPC/Topps Sticker 199
83/4 OPC/Topps Sticker 131
82/3 Post [SLou.]
92/3 SLOU / McDon. 5
75/6 Topps 16
76/7 Topps 263
79/0 Topps 174
81/2 Topps 117 [West]

DUNMAR, JON
97/8 Pensacola Ice Pilots

DUNN, DAVE
74/5 Loblaws
74/5 Loblaws Update
74/5 O-Pee-Chee 152
75/6 O-Pee-Chee 187
74/5 Topps 152
75/6 Topps 187
74/5 TORO
75/6 TORO
73/4 VANC / Royal Bank

DUNN, JAMES
83 HHOF Postcard O7
83&87 HHOF 217

DUNN, JAMIE
92/3 MPS SJHL 161

DUNN, JAY
91/2 Air Canada SJHL 2
91/2 Air Canada SJHL A28

DUNN, PATRICK
95 Panini Worlds 110
92 Semic Sticker 233
93 Semic Sticker 263

DUNN, RICHIE
80/1 BUFF / Wendt's 6
81/2 BUFF / Wendt's 7
82/3 CALG
83/4 HART / Jr. Whalers
80/1 O-Pee-Chee 109
81/2 O-Pee-Chee 29
82/3 O-Pee-Chee 45
83/4 O-Pee-Chee 137
84/5 O-Pee-Chee 69
82/3 Post [Buff.]
88/9 ProCards / Rochester
89/0 ProCards AHL 259
83/4 Souhaits Keychain [Flames]
80/1 Topps 109

DUNNIGAN, DAVE
91/2 Avant Garde BCJHL 65
91/2 Avant Garde BCJHL 157

DUNPHY, SERGE
92/3 Oshawa Generals
95/6 Slapshot 404

DUNSTAN, GEORDIE
92/3 BCJHL 102

DUPAUL, COSMO
93/4 Cla. 4 Sport 215
97/8 Fort Worth Brahmas
98/9 Fort Worth Brahmas
99/0 Fort Worth Brahmas

DUPERE, DENIS
72/3 Eddie Sargent 210
71/2 O-Pee-Chee 200
72/3 O-Pee-Chee 167
73/4 O-Pee-Chee 210
74/5 O-Pee-Chee 105
74/5 O-Pee-Chee 219
75/6 O-Pee-Chee 159
75/6 O-Pee-Chee 382
76/7 O-Pee-Chee 334
77/8 O-Pee-Chee 388
78/9 O-Pee-Chee 283
74/5 Topps 105
74/5 Topps 219
75/6 Topps 159
71/2 TORO
72/3 TORO
73/4 TORO
71/2 Toronto Sun Photo
74/5 WASH

DUPERRON, CHRIS.
84/5 Chicoutimi Saguenéens

DUPLAIN, SAMUEL
01/2 Québec Remparts 12
00/1 Val d'Or Foreurs 15

DUPONT, ANDRÉ
79/0 Dernière Heure
81/2 Dernière Heure
72/3 Eddie Sargent 194
74/5 Loblaws
72/3 O-Pee-Chee 16
73/4 O-Pee-Chee 113
74/5 O-Pee-Chee 67
75/6 O-Pee-Chee 56
75/6 O-Pee-Chee 211
76/7 O-Pee-Chee 131
77/8 O-Pee-Chee 164
78/9 O-Pee-Chee 98
79/0 O-Pee-Chee 178
81/2 O-Pee-Chee 273
82/3 O-Pee-Chee 282
80/1 Pepsi Bottle Cap
82/3 Post [Québ.]
80/1 QUÉB
81/2 QUÉB
82/3 QUÉB
83/4 QUÉB
71/2 SLOU
72/3 Topps 19
73/4 Topps 183
74/5 Topps 67
75/6 Topps 56
75/6 Topps 211
76/7 Topps 131
77/8 Topps 164
78/9 Topps 98
79/0 Topps 178

DUPONT, ANDRÉ
02/3 Fleer Throwbacks 22

DUPONT, GEORGE
97/8 New Mexico Scorpions

DUPONT, JEROME (JERRY)
81/2 CHIC
86/7 TORO
86/7 TORO

DUPONT, MICKI
02/3 BAP All-Star 111
02/3 Choice Prospects 11
02/3 First Edition 201

DUPONT, MICKI
96/7 Kamloops Blazers
97/8 Kamloops Blazers
98/9 Kamloops Blazers

DUPONT, MICKI
99/0 Kamloops Blazers

DUPONT, MICKI
99/0 Kamloops Blazers
02/3 SP Authentic 138
02/3 SPx 167
02/3 T. Chrome 149
02/3 T. Total 431
02/3 Upper Deck 199
02/3 UD Classic 106
02/3 UD Foundations 125
02/3 UD Honor 148
02/3 UD Mask 116
02/3 UD MVP 197
02/3 UD Piece 124
02/3 UD Top Shelf 107
02/3 UD Vintage 324
02/3 Victory 35

DUPONT, NORM
83/4 HART / Jr. Whalers
79/0 MONT
77/8 Nova Scotia Voyageurs
81/2 O-Pee-Chee 363
82/3 O-Pee-Chee 378
81/2 OPC Sticker 139
80/1 Pepsi Bottle Cap
82/3 Post [Winn.]
83/4 Souhaits Keychain [Jets]
80/1 WINN
81/2 WINN
82/3 WINN

DUPONT, YANNICK
96/7 Rimouski Océanic

DUPRAS, JONATHAN
01/2 Baie-Comeau 16

DUPRÉ, YANICK
91/2 Classic 41
91/2 Classic Four Sport 41
94/5 Hershey Bears
91/2 OPC Premier 16
94/5 PHIL / Sheet
90/1 7th..Sketch LHJMQ 200
91/2 7th...Sketch LHJMQ 284
91 7th..Sketch Mem.Cup 59, 126
91/2 Star Pics 44
92/3 Topps 515
92/3 T. Stadium Club 137
91/2 Ultimate Draft Pick 36, 88, ✍ Aut.
92/3 Upper Deck 421

DUPUIS, BOB
88/9 EDMO / Action 118

DUPUIS, GUY
98/9 EBK IHL All-Star
92/3 Fort Wayne Komets 8
93/4 Fort Wayne Komets 5
94/5 Fort Wayne Komets 11
95/6 Fort Wayne Komets
97/8 Fort Wayne Komets
98/9 Fort Wayne Komets
87/8 Hull Olympiques
90/1 ProCards 478
91/2 ProCards 137
01/2 UD DEL 108

DUPUIS, LORI
97/8 UD Coll. Choice 291

DUPUIS, MARC
98/9 Indianapolis Ice
95/6 Slapshot 38

DUPUIS, PASCAL
01/2 Atomic 112
01/2 BAP Memor. 247
01/2 Bowman 132
02/3 Bowman 129
00/1 Cleveland Lumberjacks
01/2 Crown Royale 165
02/3 Exclusive 85
02/3 First Edition 272
01/2 Heads Up 109
01/2 O-Pee-Chee 341
02/3 O-Pee-Chee 56
02/3 Pacific 180
02/3 Pacific Complete 36
01/2 Parkhurst 267
01/2 Pr. Stock 125
01/2 PS Titanium 164
01/2 PS Titanium Draft 136
93 Québec Pee Wee 1045
02/3 Quest for the Cup 46
99/0 Shawinigan 6
01/2 Signature 236, ✍ Aut. 236
01/2 SP Authentic 153
01/2 SPx 142, -RT
01/2 Stadium 135
01/2 Topps 341
02/3 Topps 56
01/2 To. Chrome 159
02/3 T. Limited 56
02/3 T. Total 236
01/2 UD PlayMakers Ltd 122
01/2 Upper Deck 193
01/2 UD Challenge 110
01/2 UD Ice 140
01/2 UD MVP 204
01/2 UD Premier 65
02/3 UD Rookie 51
01/2 UD Top Shelf 56
01/2 Vanguard 116
01/2 Victory 375

DUPUIS, PHILIPPE
01/2 Hull Olympiques 8
02/3 Hull Olympiques

DUPUIS, YVON
77/8 Kalamazoo Wings

DURAK, MIROSLAV
99/0 Des Moines Buc's

DURAND, BRIAN
85/6 Minnesota-Duluth 25

DURAND, ERIC
93 Semic Sticker 253

DURBANO, STEVE
76/7 COLR / Hockey Talk
74/5 Loblaws
73/4 O-Pee-Chee 124
74/5 O-Pee-Chee 106
76/7 O-Pee-Chee 4
76/7 O-Pee-Chee 19
76/7 O-Pee-Chee 384
74/5 PITT
72/3 SLOU
73/4 SLOU
73/4 Topps 168
74/5 Topps 106
76/7 Topps 4
76/7 Topps 19

DURDLE, DARREN
96/7 DEL 27
98/9 DEL 172

DURIAU, VINCENT
01/2 Val d'Or Foreurs 7
02/3 Val d'Or Foreurs

DURIS, MARTIN
95/6 DEL 108

DURIS, VITEZSLAV
81/2 O-Pee-Chee 316
80/1 Pepsi Bottle Cap
80/1 TORO

DURNAN, BILL
45-64 BeeHive-2 [Mont.]
51 Berk Ross
51 Berk Ross
01/2 BT Pipes 126, 145, ✂ TW, ✂ VM
02/3 Between the Pipes ✂ GT2, ✂ VM5
02/3 Canada Post
93/4 High Liner 12
83 HHOF Postcard K4
83&87 HHOF 139
02/3 In The Game-Used ✂ VM17
91/2 Kraft 37
92/3 MONT / OPC 47
43-47 Parade Sportive
43-47 Parade Sportive
55/6 Parkhurst 63
94/5 Parkie Tall 6
45-54 Quaker Oats
02/3 Ultimate Mem. ✂ SU, ✂ SF
99/0 UD C. Legends 34

DUROCHER, ANDRÉ
90/1 7th..Sketch LHJMQ 257

DUROCHER, MARIO
00/1 Victoriaville Tigres 24

DUSABLON, BENOÎT
99 Bowman 73
96/7 Halifax Moosehead
96/7 Halifax Moosehead
99/0 Halifax Mooseheads
01/2 Hartford Wolf Pack

DUSANEK, JAN
98/9 Kelowna Rockets
99/0 OFS 89

DUSSAULT, NORM
45-64 BeeHive-2 [Mont.]
51/2 Laval Dairy 22
43-47 Parade Sportive
45-54 Quaker Oats
52/3 St. Lawrence 96

DUSTIN, BOBBY
92/3 Minnesota G'Gophers
93/4 Minnesota G'Gophers
94/5 Minnesota G'Gophers

DUTHIE, RYAN
95/6 Adirondack Red Wings
94/5 Saint John Flames
91/2 7th...Sketch WHL 17

DUTIAUME, MARK
98/9 BC Icemen 1
98/9 BC Icemen
95/6 Brandon Wheat Kings
95/6 Classic 37
97/8 Rochester Americans
94/5 Slapshot Memorial 41

DUTIAUME, TODD
92/3 Brandon Wheat Kings
91/2 7th...Sketch WHL 198

DUTIL, CHRISTIAN
91/2 Air Canada SJHL A33
92/3 MPS SJHL 158

DUTKOWSKI, DUKE
33/4 Canadian Gum
33-35 Diamond Match Silv.
23/4 Paulins Candy 26
33/4 WWGum 56

DUTTON, RED
33/4 Anonymous 23
34-43 BeeHive-1 [NYAm.]
33/4 Canadian Gum
33-35 Diamond Match Silv.
36-39 Diamond Match TT1
36-39 Diamond Match TT2
36-39 Diamond Match TT3
83 HHOF Postcard A6
83&87 HHOF 7
28/9 La Presse
23/4 Paulins Candy 62
60/1 Topps 16
02/3 Ultimate Mem. ✍ Cut
33/4 WWGum 25
37/8 World Wide Gum 14

DUUS, JESPER
96/7 DEL 185
98/9 DEL 301
94/5 Leaf Elit Set 122
95/6 Leaf Elit Set 217
89/0 Semic Elitserien 79
90/1 Semic Elitserien 254
91/2 Semic Elitserien 85
92/3 Semic Elitserien 105
95/6 UD Elitserien 57
99/0 UD Elitserien 172
00/1 UD Elitserien 156

DUVAL, JON
94/5 Birmingham Bulls
90/1 7th..Sketch WHL 39
91/2 7th...Sketch WHL 315

DUVAL, LUC
84/5 Chicoutimi Saguenéens

DUVAL, MURRAY
89/0 Kamloops Blazers
91/2 ProCards 312
90 7th..Sketch Mem.Cup 21
90/1 7th..Sketch WHL 302

DVORAK, ALES
98/9 BC Icemen 4
98/9 BC Icemen

DVORAK, FILIP
96/7 APS 283
96/7 DS Sticker 188

DVORAK, KAREL
97/8 APS 290
98/9 OFS 294

DVORAK, MAREK
99/0 Score 52

DVORAK, MICHAEL
99/0 Eishockey 360

DVORAK, MICHAL
96/7 APS 281
00/1 OFS 77
01/2 OFS 214

DVORAK, MIROSLAV
96/7 APS 373
79 Panini Sticker 78
83/4 PHIL / J.C. Penney
82 Semic Sticker 83
83/4 Souhaits Keychain [Flyers]

DVORAK, RADEK
01/2 Adrenaline 124
96/7 All-Sport PPF 99, 173
96/7 All-Sport PPF 173
99/0 BAP Mem. 298, 400
00/1 BAP Mem. 142
01/2 BAP Memor. 2
95/6 Bowman 130, BB22
95/6 Classic 10, BK9, ✍ Aut.
95/6 Cla. Assets 8
95/6 Cla. Clear Assets 59
95/6 Cla. 5 Sport 156, S-76, SFF-5
95/6 Cla. Vis. Signings 79, ✍ Aut.
95/6 Donruss 277, RR-10
96/7 Donruss 213
95/6 Do. Elite 19, R-10
96/7 Do. Elite 105
02/3 First Edition 67, ✂ Jers.
95/6 Fleer Metal 176
95/6 Fleer Ultra 338, EA-3
96/7 Fl. Ultra 64
96/7 FLOR / Winn-Dixie
97/8 FLOR / Winn-Dixie
96/7 Leaf 160
95/6 L. Limited 10, RP-7
96/7 Metal Univ. 57
99/0 Millenium 111, ✍ Aut. 111
01/2 O-Pee-Chee 161
02/3 O-Pee-Chee 178
00/1 OFS 387
99/0 Omega 148
98/9 Pacific 220
99/0 Pacific 172
00/1 Pacific 259
01/2 Pacific 255
02/3 Pacific 250
97/8 Pacific CC 50
00/1 Pa. Paramount 159
96/7 Panini Sticker 71
97/8 Panini Sticker 56
98/9 Panini Sticker 56
99/0 Panini Sticker 58
00/1 Panini Sticker 62
95/6 Parkhurst 260, 508, PP-45
00/1 Parkhurst P-58
01/2 Parkhurst 112
02/3 Parkhurst Retro 141
95/6 Pi. Summit 169
96/7 Pi. Summit 169
95/6 Pi. Zenith 147, RRC-2
00/1 PS Titanium ✂ GUG 32
96/7 Score 247
97/8 Score 221
99/0 Score JT21
95/6 Select CE 133
94/5 Sig. Rookies 39, ✍ 39
95/6 SR Tetrad 62
95/6 SR Tetrad Autobilia 42
00/1 Signature 198
01/2 Signature 118, ✍ Aut. 118
02/3 Signature GS-74
95/6 SBx Impact 200
96/7 SBx Impact 44
95/6 SP 59
01/2 SP GU ✂ AF, ✂ AFD
00/1 Stadion 111
95/6 Topps 319
00/1 Topps 141
01/2 Topps 161
02/3 Topps 178, ✂ FRF, ✂✍ FTF
02/3 T. Chrome ✂ FRF
95/6 To. Finest 125
02/3 T. Limited 178
95/6 To. Stadium ER200
95/6 T. Super Skills SR10
02/3 T. Total 344
95/6 Upper Deck 260, H-26
97/8 Upper Deck 71
98/9 Upper Deck 280
00/1 Upper Deck 345
01/2 Upper Deck 116
02/3 Upper Deck 117
95/6 UD BAP 163, ✍ S163
95/6 UD CC 398
97/8 UD Coll. Choice 103
98/9 UD G. Reserve 280
99/0 UD MVP Cup 122
02/3 UD Top Shelf ✂ GO
00/1 UD Vintage 242
01/2 UD Vintage 171
02/3 UD Vintage 166, ✂ OS
00/1 Victory 156
01/2 Victory 235

DWYER, GORDIE
97 Bowman 53
00/1 Pacific 383
92 Québec Pee Wee 185
94/5 Slapshot Memorial 61
01/2 SPx 192

DYAKIV, IGOR
98/9 Mir 124
00/1 Mir 181

DYCK, ED
72/3 VANC / Royal Bank

DYCK, JOEL
90/1 7th..Sketch WHL 57
91/2 7th...Sketch WHL 138

DYCK, LARRY
97/8 Central Texas
95/6 Kansas City Blades
96/7 Kansas City Blades
93/4 Milwaukee Admirals
88/9 ProCards / Kalamazoo
89/0 ProCards IHL 93
90/1 ProCards 104
91/2 ProCards 143

DYCK, MIKE
86/7 Regina Pats
87/8 Regina Pats
88/9 Regina Pats

DYCK, PAUL
92/3 Cleveland Lumberjacks
93/4 Cleveland Lumberjacks
99/0 Houston Aeros
95/6 Kansas City Blades
96/7 Kansas City Blades
91/2 ProCards 304
90/1 7th..Sketch WHL 160
01/2 UD DEL 115

DYE, CECIL (BABE)
24/5 Champ's Cigarettes
83 HHOF Postcard C4
83&87 HHOF 34
94/5 Legends 51
23/4 William Paterson 23
24/5 William Paterson 54

DYER, DEAN
89/0 Victoria Cougars

DYER, KELLY
94/5 Classic W22

DYHR, NICK
92/3 MPS SJHL 70

DYKEMAN, ROB
91/2 Cornwall Royals
91 7th..Sketch Mem.Cup 36
90/1 7th..Sketch OHL 33
91/2 7th...Sketch OHL 20

DYKHUIS, KARL
98/9 Aurora 173
98/9 Be A Player 255, ✍ Aut. 255
92 C.O.A. Winter Olympics 199
90/1 Canada Nationals 4
91/2 Canada Nationals
91/2 CHIC / Coke
92/3 Fleer Ultra 274
95/6 Fleer Ultra 283
93/4 Indianapolis Ice
94/5 Indianapolis Ice
95/6 Leaf 264
00/1 MONT
01/2 MONT
02/3 MONT
91/2 O-Pee-Chee 172
97/8 Omega 209
98/9 Pacific 399
01/2 Pacific 205
97/8 Pa. Invincible R-141
97/8 Pa. Paramount 172
98/9 Pa. Paramount 217
95/6 Panini Sticker 122
96/7 Panini Sticker 121
98/9 Panini Sticker 100
00/1 Panini Sticker 41
91/2 Parkhurst 262
94/5 Parkie SE34
94/5 PHIL / Sheet
96/7 PHIL / Ocean Spray
93/4 Power Play 48
90/1 Score 437
92/3 Score 462
90/1 7th..Sketch LHJMQ 229
95/6 Topps 118
98/9 To. Finest 122
90/1 Upper Deck 471
91/2 Upper Deck 688
92/3 Upper Deck 404
93/4 Upper Deck 106
96/7 Upper Deck 311
00/1 Upper Deck 323
95/6 UD BAP 75, ✍ S75
91/2 Upper Deck WJC 62
99/0 UD MVP Cup 94

DYKSTRA, STEVE
85/6 BUFF / Blue Shield
86/7 BUFF / Blue Shield
87/8 BUFF / Won. Bread
88/9 EDMO / Action 38
87/8 OPC Sticker 146-7
90/1 ProCards 317

DYLLA, ERIC
95/6 DEL 22
01/2 UD DEL 3

DYNES, BILL
83/4 Brantford Alexanders

DZIEDUSZYCKI, MATT
02/3 Syracuse Crunch

DZIEDZIC, JOE
94/5 Classic 37
97/8 Cleveland Lumberjacks
95/6 Donruss 235
95/6 Fleer Ultra 339
91/2 Minnesota G'Gophers
92/3 Minnesota G'Gophers
93/4 Minnesota G'Gophers
97/8 Pacific CC 305
96/7 Pi. Be A Player 149, ✍ Aut. 149
95/6 PITT / Foodland 13
94/5 Sig. Rookies 67, ✍ 67
95/6 Topps 336
95/6 Upper Deck 429
96/7 Upper Deck 136
96/7 UD CC 216
97/8 UD Coll. Choice 213

DZIKOWSKI, JOHN
83/4 Brandon Wheat Kings
84/5 Brandon Wheat Kings
85/6 Brandon Wheat Kings

DZURILLA, VLADIMIR
92/3 Future Trends C76 152
72 Hellas MM-Jenkki 80
70/1 Kuvajulkaisut 43
69/0 Mästär Serien 1
72/3 Williams Finnish 3

E

EADE, CHRIS
99/0 UD Prospects 9

EADY, TYLER
01/2 Mississauga IceDogs
02/3 Mississauga IceDogs

EAGLES, MIKE
83 Canada Juniors
88/9 CHIC / Coke
83/4 Fredericton Express
84/5 Fredericton Express
82/3 Kitchener Rangers
87/8 O-Pee-Chee 253
88/9 OPC Sticker 191-58
97/8 Pa. Dynagon BKS-101
87/8 Panini Sticker 170
88/9 Panini Sticker 354
91/2 Parkhurst 420
93/4 Parkhurst 229
97/8 Pi. Be A Player 149, ✍ Aut. 149
93/4 Premier 116
91/2 Pro Set 518
89/0 ProCards IHL 68
90/1 ProCards 395
85/6 QUÉB
85/6 QUÉB / Gene. Foods
85/6 QUÉB / McDonald's
85/6 QUÉB / Provigo
86/7 QUÉB
86/7 QUÉB / Gene. Foods
86/7 QUÉB / McDonald's
87/8 QUÉB / Gene. Foods
91/2 Score CAN 414
92/3 Score 345
93/4 Score 429
99/0 Topps 181
99/0 To. Chrome 181
93/4 To. Stadium 14
91/2 Upper Deck 523
94/5 UD BAP ✍ 157
95/6 WASH
91/2 WINN / IGA
93/4 WINN / Ruffles
93/4 WINN Readers

EAGLES, TRAVIS
99/0 Prince George Cougars
00/1 Prince George Cougars

EAKIN, BRUCE
94/5 DEL 91
95/6 DEL 93
96/7 DEL 234
84/5 Moncton G'Flames
85/6 Nova Scotia Oilers
81/2 Saskatoon Blades

EAKINS, DALLAS
99/0 Chicago Wolves
00/1 Chicago Wolves
01/2 Chicago Wolves
02/3 Chicago Wolves
93/4 Cincinnati Cyclones
94/5 Cincinnati Cyclones
97/8 FLOR / Winn-Dixie
90/1 Moncton Hawks
91/2 Moncton Hawks
96/7 PHOE / Coca-Cola
97/8 Pi. Be A Player 86, ✍ Aut. 86
88/9 ProCards / Baltimore
89/0 ProCards AHL 41
90/1 ProCards 253
91/2 ProCards 170

EARHART, BARRY
86/7 London Knights

EARL, TOMMY
72/3 New England Whalers

EARLE, DICK
98/9 Phoenix Mustangs 24

EASON, T.J.
01/2 Kitchener Rangers

EAST, JOHN
91/2 Hampton Roads
89/0 7th..Sketch OHL 62

EASTWOOD, MIKE
01/2 Crown Royale ✂ TT 18
95/6 Donruss 207
99/0 Kraft / PB
94/5 Leaf 378
95/6 Leaf 299
00/1 Pacific 342
02/3 Pacific Complete 334
97/8 Pa. Invincible R-125
95/6 Panini Sticker 213
92/3 Parkhurst 494
94/5 Parkie SE183
96/7 PHOE / Coca-Cola
95/6 Playoff 216
96/7 Playoff 399
94/5 POG 232
95/6 POG 290
01/2 Pr. Stock ✂ GUG 87
01/2 PS Titanium ✂ DSJ 37
01/2 PS Titanium Draft ✂ 83
91/2 ProCards 358
92/3 St. John's Maple Leafs
99/0 SLOU / Taco Bell 14
99/0 Topps 185
99/0 To. Chrome 185
94/5 T. Stadium Club 167
92/3 TORO / Kodak
93/4 TORO / Abalene
93/4 TORO / Black's 19
94/5 TORO / Coca-Cola
99/0 Ult. Victory 78
93/4 Upper Deck 57
95/6 Upper Deck 292
00/1 Upper Deck 385
01/2 Upper Deck 384
95/6 UD BAP 102, ✍ S102
01/2 Vanguard ✂ DGM 28
95/6 WINN
95/6 WINN Readers

EATON, J.D.
90/1 7th..Sketch OHL 382
91/2 7th...Sketch OHL 42
90/1 Sudbury Wolves

EATON, MARK
99/0 BAP Mem. 364
00/1 BAP Mem. 97
99/0 Dynagon Ice 146
99/0 Millenium C-47
00/1 Milwaukee Admirals
99/0 Omega 177
99/0 Stadium 153
00/1 Topps 276
99/0 To. Prmr. Plus 84
00/1 UD MVP 202
00/1 Victory 277

EATOUGH, JEFF
82/3 North Bay Centennials

EAVES, MIKE
80/1 MINS
81/2 MINS
82/3 MINS
80/1 O-Pee-Chee 206
81/2 O-Pee-Chee 171
83/4 O-Pee-Chee 79
84/5 O-Pee-Chee 221
85/6 O-Pee-Chee 213
84/5 OPC Sticker 244
79 Panini Sticker 222
89/0 PHIL
90/1 ProCards 26
91/2 ProCards 286
80/1 Topps 206
83/4 Vachon 4-124

EAVES, MURRAY
83/4 O-Pee-Chee 384
88/9 ProCards / Adirondack
89/0 ProCards AHL 324

EBERLE, DEREK
97/8 Fort Wayne Komets
00/1 Kudos 7
90/1 7th..Sketch WHL 184
91/2 7th...Sketch WHL 229

EBERLE, GREG
92/3 Peoria Rivermen
93/4 Peoria Rivermen
96/7 Peoria Rivermen

97/8 Peoria Rivermen
99/0 Peoria Rivermen
88/9 ProCards / Peoria

EBERLE, JÖRG
95 Globe 210
95 Panini Worlds 127
95 Semic 192
91 Semic Sticker 188
92 Semic Sticker 208
93 Semic Sticker 122
92/3 Upper Deck 384

EBERMANN, BOHUSLAV
96/7 APS 286
79 Panini Sticker 89

ECCLESTONE, TIM
74/5 ATLF
77/8 ATLF
68/9 Bauer Photo
71/2 Bazooka Panel
70/1 Colgate 58
70/1 Dad's Cookies
70/1 Eddie Sargent 188
71/2 Eddie Sargent 56
72/3 Eddie Sargent 78
70/1 Esso Power Player
72/3 Post 9
74/5 Loblaws
68/9 O-Pee-Chee 178
69/0 O-Pee-Chee 179
70/1 O-Pee-Chee 102
71/2 O-Pee-Chee 52
72/3 O-Pee-Chee 55
73/4 O-Pee-Chee 144
74/5 O-Pee-Chee 323
76/7 O-Pee-Chee 351
77/8 O-Pee-Chee 364
70/1 Topps 102
71/2 Topps 52
72/3 Topps 33
73/4 Topps 124
71/2 Toronto Sun Photo

ECKMAIER, BEPPI
98/9 DEL 313

ECKNAIR, JOSEF
95/6 DEL 382

EDBERG, ROLF
80/1 O-Pee-Chee 65
79 Panini Sticker 194
82 Semic Sticker 21
80/1 Topps 65
78/9 WASH
79/0 WASH
80/1 WASH

EDDOLLS, FRANK
45-64 BeeHive-2 [NYRa.]
43-47 Parade Sportive
51/2 Parkhurst 89
45-54 Quaker Oats

EDER, STEPHAN
94/5 DEL 332

EDESTRAND, DARRYL
72/3 Eddie Sargent 181
74/5 Loblaws
71/2 O-Pee-Chee 187
72/3 O-Pee-Chee 195
73/4 O-Pee-Chee 216
74/5 O-Pee-Chee 313
75/6 O-Pee-Chee 11
76/7 O-Pee-Chee 179
77/8 O-Pee-Chee 321
78/9 O-Pee-Chee 377
79/0 O-Pee-Chee 280
71/2 PITT / Sportcolor
75/6 Topps 11
76/7 Topps 179
71/2 Toronto Sun Photo

EDGAR, JAMES
01/2 Peterborough Petes

EDGAR, TREVOR
95/6 Slapshot 241

EDGERTON, DEVIN
93/4 Atlanta Knights
94/5 Atlanta Knights 10
99/0 Eishockey 83
95/6 Phoenix Roadrunners
00/1 UD DEL 7
01/2 UD DEL 168
92/3 Wheeling Thund'birds 7

EDGEWORTH, DAVID
02/3 Owen Sound Attack

#VALUE✂
91/2 Avant Garde BCJHL 161

#VALUE✂
94/5 Leaf Elit Set 106
95/6 Leaf Elit Set 142
90/1 Semic Elitserien 46
91/2 Semic Elitserien 297
92/3 Semic Elitserien 322
97/8 UD Elitserien 75

EDLUND, PÅR
95/6 UD Elitserien 216

EDLUND, PÅR
98/9 UD Elitserien 80
99/0 UD Elitserien 75

EDMOND, DOMINIC
84/5 Richelieu Riverains

EDMONDS, RANDY
94/5 Leaf Elit Set 305

EDMUNDSON, GARRY
45-64 BeeHive-2 [Toro.]
59/0 Parkhurst 48
60/1 Parkhurst 5
60/1 Shirriff 14

EDMUNDSON, MARK
92/3 Ottawa 67's

EDSTRÖM, LARS
94/5 Leaf Elit Set 176
95/6 Leaf Elit Set 202
89/0 Semic Elitserien 166
90/1 Semic Elitserien 244
91/2 Semic Elitserien 165
92/3 Semic Elitserien 192
95/6 UD Elitserien 214
98/9 UD Elitserien 147
99/0 UD Elitserien 149
00/1 UD Elitserien 133

EDUR, TOM
76/7 COLR / Hockey Talk
77/8 O-Pee-Chee 169
78/9 O-Pee-Chee 119
77/8 Topps 169
78/9 Topps 119

EDWARDS, DAN
89/0 Oshawa Generals
90/1 Oshawa Generals

EDWARDS, DON
79/0 BUFF / Bells Market
80/1 BUFF / Wendt's 3
81/2 BUFF / Wendt's 3
82/3 CALG
83/4 Funmate Puffy 2 [w/]
77/8 O-Pee-Chee 201
78/9 OPC 70
78/9 O-Pee-Chee 150
78/9 O-Pee-Chee 336
79/0 O-Pee-Chee 105
80/1 O-Pee-Chee 92
80/1 O-Pee-Chee 166
80/1 O-Pee-Chee 215
81/2 O-Pee-Chee 21
81/2 O-Pee-Chee 389
82/3 O-Pee-Chee 46
83/4 O-Pee-Chee 80
84/5 O-Pee-Chee 222
85/6 O-Pee-Chee 183
81/2 OPC Sticker 55
82/3 OPC/Topps Sticker 124
86/7 OPC Sticker 139-249
82/3 Post [Buff.]
83/4 Souhaits Keychain [Flames]
82/3 Stater Mint 2
77/8 Topps 201
78/9 Topps 70
78/9 Topps 150
79/0 Topps 105
80/1 Topps 92
80/1 Topps 166
80/1 Topps 215
81/2 Topps 75 [East]
85/6 TORO
83/4 Vachon 5-125

EDWARDS, GARY
88/9 EDMO / Action 78
72/3 Post 23
74/5 Loblaws
78/9 MINS / Cloverleaf 5
79/0 MINS
80/1 MINS
71/2 O-Pee-Chee 155
72/3 O-Pee-Chee 113
72/3 O-Pee-Chee Crest 9
73/4 O-Pee-Chee 199
75/6 O-Pee-Chee 105
76/7 O-Pee-Chee 365
77/8 O-Pee-Chee 345
78/9 O-Pee-Chee 6
80/1 O-Pee-Chee 335
72/3 Topps 151
75/6 Topps 105
78/9 Topps 6
71/2 Toronto Sun Photo

EDWARDS, MARV
52/3 Anonymous 17
72/3 Eddie Sargent 49
69/0 O-Pee-Chee 185
69/0 TORO

EDWARDS, PAUL
80/1 Oshawa Generals
81/2 Oshawa Generals

EDWARDS, RAY
92/3 Dayton Bombers
93/4 Dayton Bombers
94/5 Huntington Blizzard
98/9 Huntington Blizzard
99/0 Huntington Blizzard

EDWARDS, ROY
71/2 Bazooka Panel
70/1 Dad's Cookies
70/1 DETR / Marathon Oil
70/1 Eddie Sargent 62
71/2 Eddie Sargent 167
72/3 Eddie Sargent 174
70/1 Esso Power Player
68/9 O-Pee-Chee 144
69/0 O-Pee-Chee 56
70/1 O-Pee-Chee 21
71/2 O-Pee-Chee 99
73/4 O-Pee-Chee 82
71/2 PITT / Sportcolor
72 Semic Sticker 192
68/9 Shirriff / Detr. 7
67/8 Topps 106
69/0 Topps 56
70/1 Topps 21
71/2 Topps 99
73/4 Topps 82
71/2 Toronto Sun Photo
59/60 Whitby Dunlops

EDWARDS, TROY
91/2 Air Canada SJHL A44
92/3 MPS SJHL 1

EDWARDS, WALTER
95/6 Tallahasee Tiger Sharks

EGAN, PAT
34-43 BeeHive-1 [NYAm.]
45-64 BeeHive-2 [Bost.]
45-64 BeeHive-2 [NYRa.]

EGELAND, ALLAN
94/5 Atlanta Knights 15
95/6 Atlanta Knights
98/9 Orlando Solar Bears Geico
90/1 7th..Sketch WHL 126
91/2 7th...Sketch WHL 169
92/3 Tacoma Rockets
93/4 Tacoma Rockets

EGELAND, TRACY
99/0 Greensboro Generals
94/5 Hershey Bears
98/9 Huntington Blizzard
92/3 Indianapolis Ice
90/1 ProCards 404
91/2 ProCards 481

EGEN, ULRICH
82 Semic Sticker 109

EGENER, MIKE
00/1 Calgary Hitmen
01/2 Calgary Hitmen

EGERS, JACK
72/3 Eddie Sargent 196
70/1 Esso Power Player
74/5 Loblaws
72/3 O-Pee-Chee 107
73/4 O-Pee-Chee 79
74/5 O-Pee-Chee 93
75/6 O-Pee-Chee 134
71/2 SLOU
72/3 SLOU
72/3 Topps 147
73/4 Topps 79
74/5 Topps 93
75/6 Topps 134
71/2 Toronto Sun Photo
74/5 WASH

EGGEN,
92/3 Semic Nordisk 211 [Rookie]

EGGER, HEINZ
72 Semic Sticker 101

EGGER, KARL HEINE
72 Hellas MM-Jenkki 50

EGO, KLAUS
72 Semic Sticker 103

EGOROV, ALEXEI
00/1 Dynamo 26
98/9 Mir 144

EHLERS, HEINZ
98/9 DEL 125
99/0 Eishockey 283
89/0 Semic Elitserien 15
90/1 Semic Elitserien 88
92/3 Semic Elitserien 262
00/1 UD DEL 38
01/2 UD DEL 17

EHMAN, GERRY
45-64 BeeHive-2 [Toro.]
70/1 Dad's Cookies
70/1 Eddie Sargent 144
70/1 Esso Power Player
68/9 O-Pee-Chee 84
69/0 O-Pee-Chee 83
70/1 O-Pee-Chee 187
59/0 Parkhurst 19
60/1 Parkhurst 8
60/1 Shirriff 19
68/9 Shirriff / Oakl. 1
68/9 Topps 84
69/0 Topps 83

EHRHOFF, CHRISTIAN
00/1 UD DEL 145
01/2 UD DEL 257

EHRMAN, DAN
01/2 Calgary Hitmen

EHRMANTRAUT, LYLE
92/3 MPS SJHL 57

EHRMEN, DANNY
00/1 Calgary Hitmen

EIBL, MICHAEL
72 Hellas MM-Jenkki 58

EICHENMANN, ZDENEK
94/5 APS 14
95/6 APS 114
96/7 APS 84
97/8 APS 205
97/8 DS 93
98/9 DS 100
99/0 DS 163
96/7 DS Sticker 146
97/8 DS Sticker 236
98/9 OFS 400
99/0 OFS 163

EICHSTADT, SCOTT
91/2 ProCards 99

EIDE, ESKIL
92/3 Semic Nordisk 130

EIDE, PATRICK
92/3 Semic Nordisk 30

EIGNER, TRENT
94/5 Huntington Blizzard

EILERTSEN, LARS
92/3 Semic Nordisk 79

EIMANSBERGER, JOHAN
72 Hellas MM-Jenkki 56
72 Semic Sticker 100

EINHORN, ANDREW
97/8 Guildford Flames

EIRICKSON, SHANE
85/6 Brandon Wheat Kings

EISANHUT, NEIL
98/9 DEL 24

EISEBITT, TORSTEN
94/5 DEL 398
95/6 DEL 418

EISELT, VACLAV
94/5 APS 273
95/6 APS 144
96/7 APS 91
97/8 APS 209
98/9 DS 99
99/0 DS 154
97/8 DS Sticker 241
98/9 OFS 401, 462
99/0 OFS 103
00/1 OFS 75
01/2 OFS 216

EISENHUT, NEIL
93/4 Cla. Prospects 199
95/6 Edge Ice 172
99/0 Eishockey 128
96/7 Flint Generals
92/3 Hamilton Canucks
93/4 Power Play 459
91/2 ProCards 599
94/5 Saint John Flames
00/1 UD DEL 146
01/2 UD DEL 49

EISETT, VACLAV
96/7 DS Sticker 147

EISKONEN, MARKKU
66/7 Champion 89
65/6 Hellas 95

EISLER, GREG
99/0 Colorado Gold Kings

EISLER, MATT
99/0 Greensboro Generals

EJDEHOLM, DENNIS
99/0 UD Elitserien 131

EK, MARKO
92/3 Jyvas Hyva 165
93/4 Jyvas Hyva 149
93/4 Sisu 151
94/5 Sisu 131
96/7 Sisu 117

EKELUND, PETER
94/5 Leaf Elit Set 293
95/6 Leaf Elit Set 58
89/0 Semic Elitserien 119
90/1 Semic Elitserien 120
91/2 Semic Elitserien 125
92/3 Semic Elitserien 138
95/6 UD Elitserien 87
97/8 UD Elitserien 93
98/9 UD Elitserien 109
99/0 UD Elitserien 95, 218, H7
00/1 UD Elitserien 99, 215

EKLUND, PER
94/5 Leaf Elit Set 194, RR-5
95/6 Leaf Elit Set 34
95/6 UD Elitserien 50, 222, NA5
98/9 UD Elitserien 61
99/0 UD Elitserien 46, H4
96 Wien 69

EKLUND, PER-ERIK (PELLE)
90/1 Bowman 107
91/2 Bowman 241
92/3 Bowman 179
93/4 Donruss 250
92/3 Fleer Ultra 155
93/4 Fleer Ultra 386
95 Globe 53
93/4 Leaf 177
94/5 Leaf Elit Set 234
95/6 Leaf Elit Set 71, C-13, LM-11, SC
87/8 OPC/Topps 98
88/9 O-Pee-Chee 211
90/1 OPC/Topps 254
91/2 O-Pee-Chee 111
92/3 O-Pee-Chee 242
87/8 OPC Leaders 9
86/7 OPC Sticker 127-113
89/0 opcSticker 105-242
87/8 Panini Sticker 132
88/9 Panini Sticker 163
89/0 Panini Sticker 296
90/1 Panini Sticker 113
91/2 Panini Sticker 228
92/3 Panini Sticker 189
93/4 Panini Sticker 51
95 Panini Worlds 156
91/2 Parkhurst 128
93/4 Parkhurst 147
94/5 Parkhurst 56
86/7 PHIL
89/0 PHIL
90/1 PHIL
91/2 PHIL / J.C. Penney
92/3 PHIL / UD Sheet
92/3 PHIL / J.C. Penney
93/4 PHIL / Sheet
93/4 PHIL / J.C. Penney
91/2 Pinnacle 134
92/3 Pinnacle 149
93/4 Pinnacle 256
93/4 Power Play 180
93/4 Premier 449
90/1 Pro Set 215
91/2 Pro Set 179
91/2 Pro Set Platinum 89
90/1 Score 308
91/2 Score 91
91/2 Score CAN 91
92/3 Score 173
93/4 Score 181
91/2 Semic Elitserien 358
89 Semic Sticker 19
91 Semic Sticker 210
92 Semic Sticker 71
93 Semic Sticker 39
92/3 Topps 117
91/2 To. Stadium 182
92/3 T. Stadium Club 154
93/4 To. Stadium 289
90/1 Upper Deck 138
91/2 Upper Deck 103
93/4 Upper Deck 120
95/6 UD Elitserien 101, 228, 254
97/8 UD Elitserien 108, 213, S6
98/9 UD Elitserien 125
96 Wien 66, AS5

EKLUND, THOMAS
89/0 Semic Elitserien 226
90/1 Semic Elitserien 61
91/2 Semic Elitserien 238
89 Semic Sticker 13

EKMAN, KENNETH
72 Semic Sticker 64

EKMAN, NILS
99/0 BAP Mem. 324
98/9 Cardset 22
99/0 Detroit Vipers
97/8 Hockey-Box
99/0 Omega 220

EKROTH, PETER
89/0 Semic Elitserien 270
90/1 Semic Elitserien 55
91/2 Semic Elitserien 231

EKRT, MARTIN
96/7 DEL 329

EKSTRÖM, RIKARD
99/0 UD Elitserien 215
00/1 UD Elitserien 5

ELCOMBE, KELLY
82/3 Fredericton Express

ELDEBRINK, ANDERS
82/3 Fredericton Express
89/0 Semic Elitserien 219
89 Semic Sticker 9
93 Semic Sticker 20
95/6 UD Elitserien DS6
97/8 UD Elitserien 167, 208, C27
81/2 VANC
81/2 VANC / Silverwood

ELDER, BRIAN
99/0 Anchorage Aces
97 Bowman 102
95/6 Brandon Wheat Kings
94/5 Slapshot Memorial 27

ELDERS, JASON
92/3 BCJHL 241
98/9 EBK ECHL All-Star
99/0 Mobile Mysticks
02/3 Nottingham Panthers

ELDRED, MATT
00/1 Kudos 92
99/0 Milwaukee Admirals

ELIAS, PATRIK
01/2 Adrenaline 113, WB 10
96/7 Albany River Rats
94/5 APS 64
01/2 Atomic 58, TN 8
02/3 Atomic 61
98/9 Aurora 109, CF27
99/0 Aurora 85
00/1 Aurora 82
02/3 BAP All-Star 19, ✂ ASJ
98/9 Be A Player 81, ✍ Aut. 81
99/0 BAP Mem. 154
00/1 BAP Mem. 266
01/2 BAP Memor. 288
02/3 BAP Memorabilia 123, ✂ ASJ11, ✂ TM14
01/2 BAP Update ✂ HSHSJers 2
01/2 Bowman 11
02/3 Bowman 102
98/9 Bowman's Best 26, BP3
99/0 Crown Royale 79
00/1 Crown Royale 63
01/2 Crown Royale 86, ASH, JotC
02/3 Crown Royale 57, ✂ GWDP 14, ✂ GWJ 11
97/8 Do. Elite 65
97/8 Do. Priority 170, DD-24
99/0 DS 77
01/2 DS 46
98/9 Dynagon Ice 109
99/0 Dynagon Ice 115
01/2 eTopps 5
02/3 eTopps 20
02/3 Exclusive 103, -MO 12
02/3 First Edition 34, ✂ Jers., ✂ TSL 10
01/2 Heads Up 57
02/3 Heads Up 71, ✂ GWQ 17, ✂ GWQ 32
02/3 In The Game-Used 42, 142
96/7 NJER / Sharp
99/0 NHL Power Play
01/2 O-Pee-Chee 91, 319
02/3 O-Pee-Chee 261
98/9 OPC Chrome 62, SB9
99/0 OFS 90
00/1 OFS 385
97/8 Omega 128
98/9 Omega 137
99/0 Omega 134
98/9 Pacific 26, -GCDC 19
99/0 Pacific 237
00/1 Pacific 233, IO-13, ✍ Aut.
01/2 Pacific 229, 414, 433, 978PCC 355
02/3 Pacific 220
02/3 Pacific Complete 106
97/8 Pa. Crown Roy. 74
98/9 Pa. Crown Roy. 79
97/8 Pa. Invincible R-111
98/9 Pa. Paramount 133
99/0 Pa. Paramount 132
00/1 Pa. Paramount 143
97/8 Pa. Revolution 76
98/9 Pa. Revolution 84
98/9 Panini Sticker 70
00/1 Panini Sticker 51
00/1 Parkhurst P-25
01/2 Parkhurst 18, ✂ PJ34, ✂ T14
02/3 Parkhurst 91, ✂ TT5
02/3 Parkhurst Retro 37
97/8 Pi. Be A Player 228, OT-16, ✍ Aut. 228
97/8 Pi. BeeHive 53, BHT-20, ✍ Aut. 53
00/1 Premier Plus 61, MB6
99/0 Prism 80
00/1 Private Stock 58, PS-32, PSNW-13
01/2 Pr. Stock 56
02/3 Pr. Stock Reserve ✂ 130
00/1 PS Titanium 55
01/2 PS Titanium 84, TAS 13, ✂ DSJ 69
02/3 Quest for the Cup 57
99/0 Revolution 85
00/1 Revolution 86, HD-21
99/0 Score 160
00/1 Signature 186, ✍ Aut. 107
01/2 Signature 189, ✍ Aut. 189
02/3 Signature 157, ✍ 157, ✂ TW7
97/8 SP Authentic 185, I6
98/9 SP Authentic 50
00/1 SP Authentic ✍ SotT, ✍ SotTD, ✍ SotTT
01/2 SP Authentic 47
02/3 SP Authentic 54
01/2 SP GU 30
02/3 SP GU 29
02/3 Sports Vault 63
99/0 SPx 86
00/1 SPx 38
01/2 SPx 38
02/3 SPx 42
98/9 SPx Finite 49, 123
00/1 Stadion 96
99/0 Stadium 115
00/1 Stadium 152, BT26
01/2 Stadium 46, G4, NHLP10, ✍ LSS
02/3 Stadium 28, -W-16
98/9 Topps 62, SB9, ✍ CAI
99/0 Topps 234
00/1 Topps 147
01/2 Topps 91, 319, OTG3, SM13, SG5
02/3 Topps 261, CC10, PP6
99/0 To. Chrome 234
00/1 To. Chrome 107, RF8
01/2 To. Chrome 91
02/3 T. Chrome 143
98/9 To. Finest 59, C1
98/9 T. Gold Label 37
00/1 To. Gold Label 10
00/1 To. Heritage 38
01/2 To. Heritage 4, 114, 125
02/3 To. Heritage 50, ✍ Aut.
02/3 T. Limited 261
01/2 To. Reserve 2
00/1 To. Stars 36
02/3 T. Total 208, TT14
98/9 UD Choice 114, SQ12
00/1 UD Heroes 71
01/2 UD PlayMakers Ltd 59
00/1 UD Reserve 51
98/9 UD3 10, 70, 130
97/8 Upper Deck 189
98/9 Upper Deck 119, FF15
99/0 Upper Deck 78, N17
00/1 Upper Deck 331
01/2 Upper Deck 102, SS10, T5
02/3 Upper Deck 103, -SS10
02/3 UD Artistic 53, R53, / Art
97/8 UD Black Diam. 44,PC8
99/0 UD C. Legends 80
01/2 UD Challenge 53
02/3 UD Classic 58
98/9 UD G. Reserve 119
99/0 UD G. Reserve 78
01/2 UD Honor Roll SG5, -DPuck
02/3 UD Honor 40
97/8 UD Ice 60, L7A
01/2 UD Ice 28
01/2 UD Mask 57
02/3 UD Mask ✂ IO, ✂ PG
98/9 UD MVP 119
99/0 UD MVP 116
00/1 UD MVP 107
01/2 UD MVP 112, MT10
02/3 UD MVP 110
99/0 UD MVP Cup 108
02/3 UD Piece 50
02/3 UD Rookie ✂ 158c
01/2 UD SCup Champs 70
01/2 UD Top Shelf 26
02/3 UD Top Shelf 50
00/1 UD Vintage 213
01/2 UD Vintage 150, 156, 263, 265
02/3 UD Vintage 151, 278, GB 151, T40
00/1 Vanguard 58
01/2 Vanguard 57
02/3 Vanguard 61
99/0 Victory 169
00/1 Victory 138
01/2 Victory 207
02/3 Victory 128, -NP16
99/0 WGretzky 102
97/8 Zenith 81, RR-14, ZT-16, Z69

ELIASSON, MAGNUS
95/6 UD Elitserien 91

ELICH, MATT
00/1 Aurora 132
97 Bowman 124, ✍ Aut.
99/0 Detroit Vipers
00/1 Pacific 371
92 Québec Pee Wee 1852
95/6 Slapshot 418
00/1 SP GU 82
00/1 SPx 117
00/1 Topps 290
00/1 To. Chrome 185
00/1 Upper Deck 415
00/1 UD Pros&Prosp. 124
00/1 UD Vintage 392

ELICK, MICKEY
96/7 Charlotte Checkers
99/0 Eishockey 141
01/2 UD DEL 4

ELIGH, JARRETT
88/9 Brockville Braves

ELIK, TODD
90/1 Bowman 151
91/2 Bowman 185
92/3 Bowman 317
93/4 Donruss 489
94/5 Donruss 163
95/6 Donruss 388
93/4 EDMO / Sheet
92/3 EDMO
94/5 Flair 162
92/3 Fleer Ultra 93
94/5 Fleer Ultra 193
83/4 Kingston Canadians
84/5 Kingston Canadians
94/5 Leaf 226
95/6 Leaf 165
90/1 LOSA / Smokey 5
90/1 OPC/Topps 352
91/2 O-Pee-Chee 251
92/3 O-Pee-Chee 20
91/2 OPC Premier 74
91/2 Panini Sticker 85
93/4 Panini Sticker 238
94/5 Panini Sticker 218
91/2 Parkhurst 300
92/3 Parkhurst 77
92/3 Parkhurst 292
93/4 Parkhurst 71
94/5 Parkhurst 210
91/2 Pinnacle 264
92/3 Pinnacle 207
93/4 Pinnacle 202
94/5 Pinnacle 275
95/6 Playoff 118
94/5 POG 212
93/4 Power Play 434
93/4 Power Play 80
94/5 Premier 76
90/1 Pro Set 116
91/2 Pro Set 94
91/2 Pro Set 410
91/2 Pro Set Platinum 57
89/0 ProCards AHL 10
92/3 SANJ / Pacific Bell
90/1 Score 297
91/2 Score 83
91/2 Score 13T
91/2 Score CAN 83
91/2 Score CAN 563
92/3 Score 307
93/4 Score 185
93/4 Score 581
94/5 Score 125
95/6 Score 58
92/3 Topps 97
91/2 To. Stadium 310
92/3 T. Stadium Club 226
93/4 To. Stadium 363
90/1 Upper Deck 233
91/2 Upper Deck 544
92/3 Upper Deck 210
94/5 Upper Deck 363
95/6 Upper Deck 479
95/6 UD BAP 89, ✍ S89

ELIOT, DARREN
84/5 LOSA / Smokey 18
87/8 LOSA
87/8 Panini Sticker 272

ELLACOTT, KEN
82/3 VANC

ELLERMAN, BRYAN
00/1 Medicine Hat Tigers

ELLERY, JASON
02/3 London Knights

ELLETT, BOB
84/5 Ottawa 67's

ELLETT, DAVE
98/9 Aurora 12
90/1 Bowman 132
91/2 Bowman 163
92/3 Bowman 204
92/3 Bowman 291
93/4 Donruss 344
94/5 Donruss 230
95/6 Donruss 340
93/4 EA Sports 134
94/5 Flair 178
94/5 Fleer 213
92/3 Fleer Ultra 209
93/4 Fleer Ultra 38
94/5 Fleer Ultra 213
91/2 Gillette 17
92/3 Humpty Dumpty
91/2 Kellogg's / Score 23
89/0 Kraft 49
93/4 Leaf 86
94/5 Leaf 35
92/3 McDonald's McD-05
85/6 O-Pee-Chee 185
87/8 OPC/Topps 35
88/9 OPC/Topps 167
90/1 OPC/Topps 104
91/2 O-Pee-Chee 381
92/3 O-Pee-Chee 9
89/0 OPC/Topps 69
98/9 OPC Chrome 6
91/2 OPC Premier 180
87/8 OPC Sticker 251-142
88/9 OPC Sticker 150
89/0 opcSticker 139
98/9 Pacific 78
00/1 Pacific 343
97/8 Pa. Invincible R-112
97/8 Pa. Paramount 13
98/9 Pa. Paramount 14
87/8 Panini Sticker 358
88/9 Panini Sticker 150
89/0 Panini Sticker 167
90/1 Panini Sticker 310
90/1 Panini/WPG 9
91/2 Panini Sticker 94
92/3 Panini Sticker 83
93/4 Panini Sticker 231
94/5 Panini Sticker 197
95/6 Panini Sticker 205
91/2 Parkhurst 172
92/3 Parkhurst 181
93/4 Parkhurst 205
94/5 Parkhurst 227, V8
95/6 Parkhurst 475
91/2 Pinnacle 111
92/3 Pinnacle 273
93/4 Pinnacle 262
94/5 Pinnacle 209
96/7 Pi. Be A Player 177, ✍ Aut. 177
94/5 POG 238
95/6 POG 264
93/4 Power Play 243
93/4 Premier 297
90/1 Pro Set 326, 532
91/2 Pro Set 230
92/3 Pro Set 186
91/2 Pro Set Platinum 116
90/1 Score 65, 67T
90/1 Sco. Hot Cards 29
91/2 Score 275
91/2 Score CAN 495
92/3 Score 152
93/4 Score 119
94/5 Score 83
95/6 Score 129
97/8 Score Bost. 16
91 Semic Sticker 62
99/0 SLOU / Taco Bell 6
92/3 Topps 30
95/6 Topps 207
98/9 Topps 6
91/2 To. Stadium 274
92/3 T. Stadium Club 283
93/4 To. Stadium 469
94/5 T. Stadium Club 42
90/1 TORO
91/2 TORO / P.L.A.Y. 7
92/3 TORO / Kodak
93/4 TORO / Abalene
93/4 TORO / Black's 20
94/5 TORO / Coca-Cola
90/1 Upper Deck 71, 413
91/2 Upper Deck 96
91/2 Upper Deck 196
92/3 Upper Deck 214
93/4 Upper Deck 215, SP-157
94/5 Upper Deck 67
95/6 Upper Deck 144
96/7 Upper Deck 344
93/4 Upper Deck Be A Player 4
94/5 UD BAP R50, ✍ 65
95/6 UD CC 162
84/5 WINN / Safety Tips
85/6 WINN
85/6 WINN / Safety Tips
85/6 WINN / Silverwood
86/7 WINN
87/8 WINN
88/9 WINN / Safety Tips
89/0 WINN / Safeway

ELLFOLK, LARS
73/4 Williams Finnish 278

ELLINGSEN,
92/3 Semic Nordisk 199 [Draften Av NHL]

ELLINGSEN, ÅGE
92/3 Semic Nordisk 29
92 Semic Sticker 30

ELLIOTT, CHAUCER
83 HHOF Postcard M6
83&87 HHOF 171

ELLIOTT, JASON
02/3 BAP Memorabilia 317
02/3 Between the Pipes 109
02/3 Cardset 163
01/2 Cincinnati Mighty Ducks
99/0 Manitoba Moose

ELLIOTT, PAUL
00/1 Kamloops Blazers
99/0 Medicine Hat Tigers
01/2 Utah Grizzlies

ELLIOTT, W
70/1 PHIL

ELLIS, AARON
93/4 Donruss USA6
93/4 Pinnacle 479
93/4 Slapshot / Detroit 3
93/4 Upper Deck 554

ELLIS, JULIAN
02/3 Shawinigan Cataractes

ELLIS, MATT
00/1 Toronto St. Mike's

ELLIS, RON
71/2 Bazooka Panel
64-67 BeeHive-3 [Toro.]
64/5 Coke/Sprite [Toro.]
65/6 Coca-Cola
70/1 Colgate 54
70/1 Dad's Cookies
70/1 Eddie Sargent 200
71/2 Eddie Sargent 203
72/3 Eddie Sargent 201
70/1 Esso Power Player
71/2 Frito Lay
91/2 Future Trends C72 76, ✍ 76
71 Kellogg's Transfer
72/3 Post 22
74/5 Lipton Soup 6
74/5 Loblaws
73/4 Mac's Milk
68/9 O-Pee-Chee 126
69/0 O-Pee-Chee 46
70/1 O-Pee-Chee 221
70/1 O-Pee-Chee DE 46
71/2 O-Pee-Chee 113
72/3 O-Pee-Chee 36
72/3 O-Pee-Chee TC
73/4 O-Pee-Chee 55
74/5 O-Pee-Chee 12
75/6 O-Pee-Chee 59
77/8 O-Pee-Chee 311
78/9 O-Pee-Chee 92
79/0 O-Pee-Chee 373
80/1 O-Pee-Chee 329
95/6 Parkie 66-67 106
94/5 Parkie Tall 125, 162, 168
80/1 Pepsi Bottle Cap
68/9 Post Marble
67/8 Post Tips 8
70/1 Post Shooters
72 Semic Sticker 166
68/9 Shirriff / Toro. 7
65/6 Topps 82
66/7 Topps 81
67/8 Topps 14
68/9 Topps 126
69/0 Topps 46
71/2 Topps 113
72/3 Topps 152
73/4 Topps 55
74/5 Topps 12
75/6 Topps 59
78/9 Topps 92
64/5 TORO
68/9 TORO
69/0 TORO
70/1 TORO
71/2 TORO
72/3 TORO
73/4 TORO
74/5 TORO
77/8 TORO
78/9 TORO
79/0 TORO
64/5 Toronto Star Photo
71/2 Toronto Sun Photo
91/2 Ultimate Original Six 34, ✍ Aut. 34
67/8 York 16
67/8 York 17
67/8 York 22

ELLIS, STEVEN
99/0 Sudbury Wolves 15
00/1 Sudbury Wolves 17

ELLWOOD, JAMES
02/3 Peterborough Phantoms

ELM, MATTIAS
99/0 UD Elitserien 119, S9

ELMER, W.D.
23/4 Paulins Candy 34

ELO, HANNU
65/6 Hellas 158

ELOFSSON, JONAS
98/9 UD Elitserien 87
99/0 UD Elitserien 56, 205

ELOMO, MIIKA
98/9 Cardset 250
99/0 Cardset MW 8
02/3 Cardset 15
95/6 Classic 22
96/7 Portland Pirates Hershey
96/7 Portland Pirates
97/8 Portland Pirates
99/0 Portland Pirates
95/6 Sisu 336, DD-3
96/7 Sisu 148, RE-5
94/5 Topps Finest 143
95/6 Upper Deck 546
95/6 UD CC 333

ELOMO, TEEMU
98/9 Cardset 248
99/0 Cardset 141
00/1 Cardset 100
02/3 Cardset 164, -Nimik.
98/9 UD Choice 276
97/8 UD Black Diam. 15

ELORANTA, KARI
82/3 CALG
94/5 Leaf Elit Set 10
83/4 O-Pee-Chee 81
84/5 O-Pee-Chee 223
83/4 OPC/Topps Sticker 270
89 Pelimiehen Passi
92/3 Semic Elitserien 254
89 Semic Sticker 31
94/5 Sisu 362
83/4 Souhaits Keychain [Flames]
83/4 Vachon 6-126
82 Valio

ELORANTA, MIKKO
01/2 BAP Memor. 478
02/3 BAP Memorabilia 129
98/9 Cardset 239, Leij. 20
99/0 Cardset 189, PA 11, AH J-ruutu
02/3 Cardset 16
99/0 Crown Royale 13
97/8 Hockey-Box
99/0 Millenium 27, ✍ Aut. 27
00/1 Panini Sticker 15
95/6 Sisu 243
96/7 Sisu RE 2
99/0 To. Chrome 292
02/3 T. Total 2
99/0 Ult. Victory 93
00/1 UD Vintage 34
01/2 UD Vintage 21
01/2 Victory 29

ELSENER, DAN
93/4 Flint Generals

ELSNER, ALEXANDR
95/6 APS 206
99/0 Score 21

ELTERS, HELMUT
94/5 DEL 360

ELTNER, MARCO
95/6 DEL 177

ELVENES, ROGER
94/5 Leaf Elit Set 33, SS-10
95/6 Leaf Elit Set 121
92/3 Semic Elitserien 268
95/6 UD Elitserien 179

ELVENES, STEFAN
94/5 Leaf Elit Set 81, TG-4
95/6 Leaf Elit Set 264, FTF-9
94 Semic 76
92/3 Semic Elitserien 267
95/6 UD Elitserien 150

ELWING, SÉBASTIEN
99/0 Eishockey 67

ELYNUIK, PAT
90/1 Bowman 137
91/2 Bowman 198
92/3 Bowman 270
93/4 Donruss 368
94/5 Fleer 145
92/3 Fleer Ultra 434
93/4 Fleer Ultra 67
94/5 Fleer Ultra 338
95/6 Fort Wayne Komets
90/1 Kraft 12
93/4 Leaf 6
94/5 Leaf 535
96/7 Michigan K-Wings
90/1 OPC/Topps 71
91/2 O-Pee-Chee 326
92/3 O-Pee-Chee 201
89/0 OPC/Topps 94
90/1 OPC Premier 28
92/3 OPC Premier 119
89/0 opcSticker 142-263, 35-175, / FS 20
94/5 OTTA
89/0 Panini Sticker 165
90/1 Panini Sticker 312
90/1 Panini/WPG 10
91/2 Panini Sticker 66
92/3 Panini Sticker 54
93/4 Panini Sticker 29
91/2 Parkhurst 202
92/3 Parkhurst 205
93/4 Parkhurst 224
91/2 Pinnacle 117
91/2 Pinnacle 416
92/3 Pinnacle 53
93/4 Pinnacle 382
94/5 Pinnacle 381
93/4 Power Play 260
93/4 Power Play 442
93/4 Premier 51
94/5 Premier 107
84/5 Prince Albert Raiders
90/1 Pro Set 327
91/2 Pro Set 262
92/3 Pro Set 214
91/2 Pro Set Platinum 136
90/1 Score 205
90/1 Sco. Hot Cards 86
91/2 Score 295
91/2 Score 341
91/2 Score CAN 371
91/2 Score CAN 515
92/3 Score 233
92/3 Score SS 23
93/4 Score 223
93/4 Score 580
90/1 Sco. Young Stars 28
91/2 Score Young Stars 34
94/5 TAMP / Sky Box
92/3 Topps 56
91/2 To. Stadium 132
92/3 T. Stadium Club 410
93/4 To. Stadium 447
93/4 To. Stadium 49
90/1 Upper Deck 74
91/2 Upper Deck 109
92/3 Upper Deck 312
92/3 Upper Deck 537
93/4 Upper Deck 75
94/5 Upper Deck 421
94/5 UD BAP ✍ 164
95/6 UD CC 39
92/3 WASH / Kodak
87/8 WINN
88/9 WINN / Safety Tips
89/0 WINN / Safeway
90/1 WINN / IGA
91/2 WINN / IGA

ELZINGA, ADAM
01/2 Peterborough Petes

EMBERG, EDDIE
51/2 Laval Dairy 108

EMELEEV, IGOR
99/0 Mir 231
00/1 Mir 383

EMELYANOV, VALERI
00/1 Mir 205

EMERSIC, BLAZ
99/0 Peoria Rivermen

EMERSON, NELSON
98/9 Aurora 31
99/0 BAP Mem. 249
00/1 BAP Mem. 337
92/3 Bowman 40
97/8 CARO / Sprint
93/4 Donruss 383
94/5 Donruss 297
95/6 Donruss 7, 365
96/7 Donruss 73
97/8 Do. Priority 135
99/0 Dynagon Ice 15
94/5 Fleer 240
95/6 Fleer Metal 65
92/3 Fleer Ultra 393, -UR 5
93/4 Fleer Ultra 45
93/4 Fleer Ultra 453
94/5 Fleer Ultra 242
95/6 Fleer Ultra 179, 246
95/6 HART / Kids Club
96/7 HART / Kids Club
93/4 Leaf 75
94/5 Leaf 80
95/6 Leaf 163
96/7 Metal Univ. 68
99/0 Millenium 17, ✍ Aut. 17
92/3 O-Pee-Chee 181
98/9 OPC Chrome 218
91/2 OPC Premier 138
97/8 Omega 39
98/9 Omega 51
99/0 Omega 10
98/9 Pacific 131
00/1 Pacific 195
97/8 Pacific CC 349
97/8 Pa. Crown Roy. 23
97/8 Pa. Invincible R-35
97/8 Pa. Paramount 34
98/9 Pa. Paramount 35
92/3 Panini Sticker B
93/4 Panini Sticker 159
94/5 Panini Sticker 164
95/6 Panini Sticker 216
96/7 Panini Sticker 25
98/9 Panini Sticker 25
99/0 Panini Sticker 13
95 Panini Worlds 18
91/2 Parkhurst 151
92/3 Parkhurst 152
92/3 Parkhurst 232
93/4 Parkhurst 497
94/5 Parkhurst 267
95/6 Parkhurst 367
94/5 Parkie SE seV33
91/2 Pinnacle 314
92/3 Pinnacle 36
93/4 Pinnacle 245
94/5 Pinnacle 325
96/7 Pinnacle 60
95/6 Pi. Summit 132
95/6 Pi. Zenith 43
95/6 Playoff 217
96/7 Playoff 400
94/5 POG 252
93/4 Power Play 209
93/4 Power Play 472
93/4 Premier 35
94/5 Premier 352
00/1 PS Titanium ✂ GUG 21
91/2 Pro Set 557
92/3 Pro Set 161
92/3 Pro Set RGL 5
92/3 Pro Set TL 9
91/2 Pro Set Platinum 269
90/1 ProCards 88
90/1 Score 383
91/2 Score 89T
91/2 Score CAN 550
92/3 Score 376
92/3 Score 505
93/4 Score 28
93/4 Score 506
94/5 Score 41
95/6 Score 259
96/7 Score 37
92/3 Score Young Stars 13
92/3 Seasons 16
94/5 Select 125
95/6 SBx Emotion 192
95/6 SBx Impact 73
94/5 SP 135
95/6 SP 63
99/0 SPx 2
91/2 SLOU
92/3 Topps 11
92/3 Topps 480
95/6 Topps 311
98/9 Topps 218
00/1 Topps 130
95/6 To. Finest 102
96/7 Topps Picks 135
92/3 T. Stadium Club 306
93/4 To. Stadium 223
94/5 T. Stadium Club 240
95/6 To. Stadium 38
98/9 UD Choice 43
91/2 Upper Deck 445
92/3 Upper Deck 18
92/3 Upper Deck 166
93/4 Upper Deck 342, SP-175
94/5 Upper Deck 47, SP-179
95/6 Upper Deck 178, 311, SE-126
96/7 Upper Deck 269
97/8 Upper Deck 243
98/9 Upper Deck 60
99/0 Upper Deck 176
95/6 UD BAP 38, ✍ S38
95/6 UD CC 196
96/7 UD CC 116
97/8 UD Coll. Choice 115
98/9 UD G. Reserve 60
99/0 UD G. Reserve 176
97/8 UD Ice 1
00/1 UD Vintage 171
99/0 WGretzky 12
93/4 WINN / Ruffles
93/4 WINN Readers

EMERY, RAY
02/3 BAP Memorabilia 313
02/3 Calder 132
02/3 Choice Prospects 12
02/3 In The Game-Used 183
02/3 Pacific Complete 566
02/3 Parkhurst Retro 225
02/3 Quest for the Cup 132
02/3 SP Authentic 207
02/3 SPx 181
02/3 Ultimate Mem. 39
02/3 UD Artistic 134
02/3 UD Classic 138
02/3 UD Honor 120
02/3 UD Mask 153
02/3 UD Premier 91

EMILYANTSEV, DMITRI
98/9 Muskegon Fury

EMINGER, JOHN
00/1 London Knights
01/2 Mississauga IceDogs

EMINGER, STEVE
02/3 Atomic 125
02/3 BAP All-Star 144
02/3 BAP Draft Toronto 5
02/3 BAP Memorabilia 288
02/3 Bowman 128
02/3 Calder 149
02/3 Crown Royale 139
02/3 Exclusive 192
02/3 First Edition 440R
02/3 Heads Up 126
02/3 In The Game-Used 193
01/2 Kitchener Rangers
01/2 Kitchener Rangers
02/3 Pacific Complete 553
02/3 Parkhurst 218
02/3 Parkhurst Retro 218
02/3 Pr. Stock Reserve 184
02/3 PS Titanium 140
02/3 Quest for the Cup 150
02/3 Signature 200, ✍ 200
02/3 SP Authentic 160
02/3 SP GU 95
02/3 SPx 162
02/3 Stadium 139
02/3 T. Chrome 166
02/3 To. Heritage 152
02/3 T. Total 406
02/3 Ultimate Mem. 18
02/3 Upper Deck 246
02/3 UD Artistic 105
02/3 UD Classic 130
02/3 UD Foundations 163
02/3 UD Honor 166
02/3 UD Mask 180
02/3 UD Piece 150
02/3 UD Premier 70
02/3 UD Rookie ✂ 154
02/3 UD Top Shelf 104
02/3 Vanguard 136

EMMA, DAVID
93/4 Cla. Prospects 98
94/5 Flair 93
94/5 Fleer Ultra 319
00/1 Louisville Panthers
93/4 Power Play 377
93/4 Premier 448
96/7 Providence Bruins
91/2 Score 330
93/4 Score 468
92/3 Upper Deck 462
95/6 Upper Deck 155
01/2 UD DEL 201

EMMETT, RICK
97/8 Quad City Mallards
98/9 Quad City Mallards
99/0 Quad City Mallards
00/1 Quad City Mallards
93/4 Slapshot / Peterborough 14
94/5 Slapshot / Kitchener 13
94/5 Slapshot / Windsor 21

EMMONS, GARY
92/3 Kansas City Blades
93/4 Kansas City Blades
94/5 Kansas City Blades 10
95/6 Kansas City Blades
96/7 Kansas City Blades
98/9 Kansas City Blades 26
99/0 Kansas City Blades Moment
99/0 Kansas City Blades
89/0 ProCards IHL 83
91/2 ProCards 506

EMMONS, JOHN
99/0 BAP Mem. 363
96/7 Dayton Bombers
98/9 Detroit Vipers
93/4 Donruss USA7
99/0 Grand Rapids Griffins
93/4 Pinnacle 492
01/2 Providence Bruins
92/3 Upper Deck 608
93/4 Upper Deck 557

EMMS, HAP
34-43 BeeHive-1 [NYAm.]
33/4 Canadian Gum
36-39 Diamond Match TT2
36-39 Diamond Match TT3
33/4 O-Pee-Chee 40
33/4 WWGum 55
37/8 World Wide Gum 59

ÉMOND, PATRICK
84/5 Chicoutimi Saguenéens

ÉMOND, PIERRE-LUC
01/2 Cape Breton Eagles 12
02/3 Hershey Bears

EMPEY, LARRY
94/5 Erie Panthers
92/3 MPS SJHL 39

EMVALL, FREDRIK
99/0 UD Elitserien 129

ENANDER, MIKAEL
94/5 Leaf Elit Set 182
89/0 Semic Elitserien 36
91/2 Semic Elitserien 36
92/3 Semic Elitserien 57

ENCINAS, EZEQUIEL
79 Panini Sticker 374

ENDEAN, CRAIG
89/0 ProCards IHL 131
86/7 Regina Pats
87/8 Regina Pats

ENDICOTT, SHANE
01/2 BAP Memor. 360
02/3 Choice Prospects 13
02/3 O-Pee-Chee 311
01/2 Parkhurst 344
01/2 SPx 213
02/3 SPx 121
02/3 Topps 311
02/3 T. Limited 311
01/2 UD Ice 146
01/2 UD Mask 164
02/3 UD Piece 146
01/2 UD Premier 105
99/0 UD Prospects 40
02/3 UD Vintage 344
01/2 WBS Penguins
02/3 WBS Penguins

ENGA, R.J.
99/0 Colorado Gold Kings

ENGBERG, GARY
72 Panda MM-Toronto

ENGBLOM, BRIAN
86/7 CALG / Red Rooster
80/1 Dernière Heure
82/3 Dernière Heure
83/4 Funmate Puffy 20 [w/]
84/5 LOSA / Smokey 3
82/3 McDonald's Les Étoiles 29
77/8 MONT
78/9 MONT
79/0 MONT
80/1 MONT
81/2 MONT
79/0 O-Pee-Chee 361
80/1 O-Pee-Chee 304
81/2 O-Pee-Chee 175
82/3 O-Pee-Chee 362
83/4 O-Pee-Chee 368
84/5 O-Pee-Chee 83
85/6 OPC/Topps 5
86/7 OPC/Topps 40
81/2 OPC Sticker 33
83/4 OPC/Topps Sticker 203
84/5 OPC Sticker 271
85/6 OPC Sticker 233-101
86/7 OPC Sticker 46-187
80/1 Pepsi Bottle Cap
82/3 Post [Mont.]
81/2 Topps 10
84/5 Topps 65
82/3 WASH

ENGBLOM, DAVID
95/6 UD Elitserien 11
97/8 UD Elitserien 11

ENGEL, ALEXANDER
94/5 DEL 154
95/6 DEL 151
96/7 DEL 228

ENGELBRECHT, BERNHARD
94/5 DEL 337
79 Panini Sticker 97
82 Semic Sticker 102

ENGELLAND, DERYK
01/2 Moose Jaw Warriors 3
02/3 Moose Jaw Warriors

ENGEVIK, GLEN
89/0 Nashville Knights
92/3 Semic Nordisk 161

ENGFER, JON
95/6 Tallahasee Tiger Sharks

ENGLISH, JOHN
88/9 ProCards / New Haven
83/4 Soo Greyhounds

ENGLISH, SCOTT
01/2 Moncton Wildcats 23

ENGLUND, PATRIC
94/5 Leaf Elit Set 96
95/6 Leaf Elit Set 164
89/0 Semic Elitserien 21
90/1 Semic Elitserien 92
91/2 Semic Elitserien 22
92/3 Semic Elitserien 47
95/6 UD Elitserien 17
97/8 UD Elitserien 99

ENGMAN, PETRI
92/3 Jyvas Hyva 138
94/5 Sisu 333
95/6 Sisu 17

ENGQVIST, KNUT
92/3 BCJHL 25

ENGSTROM, MIKAEL
94/5 Leaf Elit Set 114
91/2 Semic Elitserien 174
92/3 Semic Elitserien 196

ENIO, JM
See Enio Sclisizzi.

ENNAFFATI, OMAR
00/1 Mississauga IceDogs

ENNIS, JIM
88/9 EDMO / Action 92
88/9 ProCards / Cape Breton
89/0 ProCards AHL 300

ENQVIST, OLLI
71/2 Williams Finnish 298

ENS, KELLY
88/9 Lethbridge Hurricanes
89/0 Lethbridge Hurricanes
90/1 ProCards 193
91/2 ProCards 113

ENSOM, JIM
93/4 Slapshot / North Bay 8
94/5 Slapshot / Kitchener 33
95/6 Slapshot 285

ENVOY, SEAN
84/5 Sudbury Wolves
85/6 Sudbury Wolves

EPANCHINSEV, VADIM
98/9 Mir 91

EPANCHINTSEV, VADIM
99/0 Mir 256

EPANTCHINSEV, VADIM
97/8 Cleveland Lumberjacks
00/1 Mir 374
94/5 Parkie SE231
94/5 Sig. Rookies 50, ✍ 50
94/5 SR Gold Standard 100
94/5 SP 164
94/5 Upper Deck 514

EPOCH, PAUL
86/7 Kitchener Rangers

EPP, KEVIN
98/9 Anchorage Aces

EPPERS, HENRIK
93/4 Slapshot / Peterborough 13

EQUALE, RYAN
98/9 Odessa Jackalopes
96/7 Roanoke Express 9

ERASMAS, RYAN
91/2 Avant Garde BCJHL 98

ERAT, MARTIN
01/2 Adrenaline 213
01/2 Atomic 113
01/2 BAP Memor. 310
02/3 BAP Memorabilia 91
01/2 Bowman 126
01/2 Crown Royale 167, CA 6, RR 12
02/3 First Edition 297
01/2 Heads Up 110
02/3 Heads Up ✂ GWQ 16, ✂ GWQ 36
01/2 O-Pee-Chee 336
02/3 O-Pee-Chee 236
02/3 Pacific 208, ✂ GWJ 28
02/3 Pacific Complete 257
01/2 PTC Calder 7
01/2 PTC High Voltage 6
01/2 Parkhurst 323
02/3 Parkhurst 189
01/2 Pr. Stock 128, -PS 98
01/2 PS Titanium 166
01/2 PS Titanium Draft 142
00/1 Saskatoon Blades
01/2 Signature 238, ✍ Aut. 238
02/3 Signature GS-52
01/2 SP Authentic 157
01/2 SP GU 83
02/3 SP Game-Used ✂ FF
01/2 SPx 109
01/2 SPx Rookie RR17
01/2 Topps 336
02/3 Topps 236
01/2 To. Chrome 154
02/3 T. Limited 236
02/3 T. Total 209
01/2 UD PlayMakers Ltd 125
01/2 Upper Deck 430
02/3 Upper Deck 99, ✂ BF, ✂ HS
02/3 UD Artistic ✂ RT
01/2 UD Challenge 115
01/2 UD Honor Roll 78
01/2 UD Ice 59
01/2 UD Mask 152
01/2 UD MVP 226
01/2 UD Premier 100
01/2 UD Top Shelf 131
02/3 UD Top Shelf ✂ ST
01/2 UD Vintage 283
02/3 UD Vintage 142, 277
01/2 Vanguard 118, PP 10
01/2 Victory 446

ERB, JAMIE
93/4 Raleigh Icecaps

ERDALL, RICK
89/0 Semic Elitserien 113
90/1 Semic Elitserien 144
91/2 Semic Elitserien 196

ERDMAN, JOSH
90/1 7th..Sketch WHL 330

ERDMANN, ALEXANDER
96/7 DEL 164

EREMEEV, OLEG
00/1 Mir 120

EREMEEV, VITALI
00/1 Dynamo 25
99/0 Mir 188

EREMENKO, RICK
91/2 Avant Garde BCJHL 17
91/2 Avant Garde BCJHL 155

EREVIK, JONE
79 Panini Sticker 296

ERHOLM, MIKKO
65/6 Hellas 32
70/1 Kuvajulkaisut 226
71/2 Williams Finnish 242
73/4 Williams Finnish 305

ERICKSON, AUT
60/1 Shirriff 112
61/2 Shirriff 18

ERICKSON, BRYAN
87/8 LOSA
85/6 OPC/Topps 80
86/7 OPC/Topps 101
87/8 OPC/Topps 130
86/7 OPC Sticker 93-224
87/8 Panini Sticker 282
93/4 Premier 294
91/2 Pro Set 516
91/2 Score CAN 657
91/2 WINN / IGA
93/4 WINN / Ruffles
93/4 WINN Readers

ERICKSON, CHAD
95/6 Birmingham Bulls
92/3 Cincinnati Cyclones
91/2 ProCards 421
93/4 Raleigh Icecaps

ERICKSON, GRANT
72/3 Clev. WHA / Linnett

ERICKSON, KYLE
93/4 Minnesota-Duluth

ERICKSON, PATRIK
95 Globe 54
94/5 Leaf Elit Set 98
95/6 Leaf Elit Set 36, FTF-13
89/0 Semic Elitserien 42
90/1 Semic Elitserien 186
92/3 Semic Elitserien 43
91 Semic Sticker 47
95/6 UD Elitserien 54
97/8 UD Elitserien 47
98/9 UD Elitserien 63

ERICKSSON, PATRIK
91/2 Semic Elitserien 15
91/2 Semic Elitserien 355

ERICSON, JAN
92/3 Semic Elitserien 264

ERICSSON, BO
82 Semic Sticker 11

ERICSSON, EDDY
89/0 Semic Elitserien 110
90/1 Semic Elitserien 115
91/2 Semic Elitserien 121

ERIKSEN,
92/3 Semic Nordisk 188 [Toppkeeper'n]
92/3 Semic Nordisk 202 [Draften Av NHL]

ERIKSEN, JARL
92/3 Semic Nordisk 2

ERIKSEN, PAL ANDRE
92/3 Semic Nordisk 76

ERIKSEN, PER ERIK
79 Panini Sticker 298

ERIKSEN, THOMMIE
95 Panini Worlds 242
90/1 ProCards 185

ERIKSEN, TOMMIE
92/3 Semic Nordisk 37

ERIKSSON, ANDERS
95/6 Adirondack Red Wings
99/0 BAP Mem. 91
00/1 BAP Mem. 293
01/2 BAP Memor. 154
93/4 Classic 129
93/4 Cla. 4 Sport 203
97/8 Donruss 174
96/7 Do. Canadian 145
96/7 Do. Elite 129
95/6 Edge Ice 2
96/7 Fl. Picks 180
96/7 Fl. Ultra 49, UR-6
95/6 Future Legends 4
95 Globe 58
96/7 Leaf 214
94/5 Leaf Elit Set 32
96/7 L. Preferred 125
97/8 Limited 54
96/7 Metal Univ. 177
99/0 Millenium 58, ✍ Aut. 58
00/1 Mir Fetisov 28
98/9 OPC Chrome 25
98/9 Pacific 189
99/0 Pacific 87
01/2 Pacific 170
97/8 Pa. Paramount 64
98/9 Pa. Paramount 73
99/0 Panini Sticker 199
93/4 Parkhurst 540
01/2 Parkhurst 240
94/5 Parkie SE233
96/7 Pinnacle 219
97/8 Pi. Be A Player 180, ✍ Aut. 180
96/7 Pi. Summit 190
96/7 Pi. Zenith 137
96/7 Select CE 92
91/2 Semic Elitserien 327
92/3 Semic Elitserien 230
94/5 SP 170
96/7 SP 176, SF-4
97/8 SP Authentic 56
00/1 SP Authentic ✍ SotT
98/9 SPx Finite 129
00/1 Stadium 164
98/9 Topps 25
99/0 Topps 36
99/0 To. Chrome 36
98/9 UD Choice RW16
98/9 UD3 28, 88, 148
94/5 Upper Deck 518
96/7 Upper Deck 183, X22
98/9 Upper Deck 88
99/0 Upper Deck 38
96/7 UD CC 356
98/9 UD G. Reserve 88
99/0 UD G. Reserve 38
96/7 UD Ice 83
99/0 Victory 69
01/2 Victory 152
96 Wien 55

ERIKSSON, BJORN
95/6 Leaf Elit Set 212

ERIKSSON, CLAS
94/5 Leaf Elit Set 87
95/6 Leaf Elit Set 45
90/1 Semic Elitserien 270
91/2 Semic Elitserien 100
92/3 Semic Elitserien 118
95/6 UD Elitserien 71
97/8 UD Elitserien 63
98/9 UD Elitserien 97
99/0 UD Elitserien 66
00/1 UD Elitserien 89

ERIKSSON, EDDY
92/3 Semic Elitserien 139

ERIKSSON, ESKO
70/1 Kuvajulkaisut 120
72 Panda MM-Toronto
71/2 Williams Finnish 170
72/3 Williams Finnish 121
73/4 Williams Finnish 175

ERIKSSON, FREDRIK
97/8 UD Elitserien 191

ERIKSSON, JAN
89/0 Semic Elitserien 242
90/1 Semic Elitserien 160
82 Semic Sticker 7

ERIKSSON, JOAKIM
97/8 UD Elitserien 175, C26

ERIKSSON, JONAS
96/7 DEL 227
94/5 Leaf Elit Set 113, CS-4
92/3 Semic Elitserien 102
95/6 UD Elitserien DS11

ERIKSSON, JORGEN
89/0 Semic Elitserien 178
90/1 Semic Elitserien 10
91/2 Semic Elitserien 206
92/3 Semic Elitserien 229

ERIKSSON, KRISTOFFER
99/0 Colorado Gold Kings

ERIKSSON, LARS
89/0 Semic Elitserien 27
90/1 Semic Elitserien 176
91/2 Semic Elitserien 29

ERIKSSON, LENNY
92/3 Semic Nordisk 108

ERIKSSON, MAGNUS
01/2 UD DEL 5, ✂ GJ
98/9 UD Elitserien 182
99/0 UD Elitserien 185, L11, ✍ Aut.
00/1 UD Elitserien 76, M3

ERIKSSON, MARKUS
94/5 Leaf Elit Set 289
95/6 Leaf Elit Set 66
92/3 Semic Elitserien 354
95/6 UD Elitserien 111

ERIKSSON, NIKLAS
94/5 Leaf Elit Set 41, GC-16
95/6 Leaf Elit Set 70, G-7
94 Semic 72
89/0 Semic Elitserien 135
90/1 Semic Elitserien 210
91/2 Semic Elitserien 147
92/3 Semic Elitserien 165
95/6 UD Elitserien 103
97/8 UD Elitserien 112
98/9 UD Elitserien 127
99/0 UD Elitserien 113
00/1 UD Elitserien 113

ERIKSSON, PETER
89/0 Semic Elitserien 45
90/1 Semic Elitserien 110, 193
91/2 Semic Elitserien 47
91/2 Semic Elitserien 115
92/3 Semic Elitserien 145
90/1 Upper Deck 145
95/6 UD Elitserien DS16

ERIKSSON, ROLAND
77/8 O-Pee-Chee 123
78/9 O-Pee-Chee 241
79/0 O-Pee-Chee 350
79 Panini Sticker 193
77/8 Topps 123
78/9 Topps 241
78/9 VANC / Royal Bank

ERIKSSON, THOMAS
94/5 Leaf Elit Set 262
84/5 O-Pee-Chee 158
83/4 PHIL / J.C. Penney
89/0 Semic Elitserien 52
90/1 Semic Elitserien 275
91/2 Semic Elitserien 57
91/2 Semic Elitserien 321
92/3 Semic Elitserien 83
82 Semic Sticker 5
89 Semic Sticker 12
91 Semic Sticker 30
92 Semic Sticker 53

ERIKSSON, TOMAZ
89/0 Semic Elitserien 236
90/1 Semic Elitserien 67
91/2 Semic Elitserien 237

ERIXON, JAN
91/2 Bowman 77
92/3 Bowman 253
89/0 NYRA / Marine
88/9 O-Pee-Chee 212
90/1 OPC/Topps 187
91/2 O-Pee-Chee 152
92/3 O-Pee-Chee 207
89/0 OPC/Topps 96
87/8 Panini Sticker 120
88/9 Panini Sticker 306
90/1 Panini Sticker 104
91/2 Panini Sticker 283
92/3 Panini Sticker 241
91/2 Pinnacle 187
92/3 Pinnacle 191
90/1 Pro Set 195
90/1 Score 272, 343
91/2 Score 264
91/2 Score CAN 484
92/3 Score 362
93/4 Score 287
82 Semic Sticker 24
93 Semic Sticker 35
92/3 Topps 153
91/2 To. Stadium 151
92/3 T. Stadium Club 161
90/1 Upper Deck 366
91/2 Upper Deck 178

ERKOVICH, SERGEI
00/1 Mir 359

ERLUND, PAR
00/1 UD Elitserien 65

ERMAKOV, ALEXANDER
99/0 Mir 181

ERNEST, DEREK
98/9 Hampton Roads
99/0 Hampton Roads

ERNST, BINGO
51/2 Laval Dairy 83
52/3 St. Lawrence 26

EROFEEV, DIMITRI
98/9 UD Elitserien 89

ERONEN, ANSSI
71/2 Williams Finnish 317

ERONEN, KIMMO
98/9 Cardset 229
99/0 Cardset 132
00/1 Cardset 96

ERREY, BOB
90/1 Bowman 212
91/2 Bowman 85
92/3 Bowman 304
92/3 Durivage 23
98/9 Hartford Wolf Pack
93/4 Leaf 377
94/5 Leaf 398
95/6 Leaf 315
90/1 OPC/Topps 230
91/2 O-Pee-Chee 94
92/3 O-Pee-Chee 323
89/0 OPC/Topps 50
89/0 opcSticker 233-96
97/8 Pa. Invincible R-177
87/8 Panini Sticker 152
89/0 Panini Sticker 315
90/1 Panini Sticker 133
91/2 Panini Sticker 279
91/2 Parkhurst 138
92/3 Parkhurst 374
93/4 Parkhurst 453
94/5 Parkie SE161
91/2 Pinnacle 257
92/3 Pinnacle 310
93/4 Pinnacle 410
93/4 Pinnacle CA21
94/5 Pinnacle 192
96/7 Pi. Be A Player 197, ✍ Aut. 197
83/4 PITT / Coke Is It!✂
84/5 PITT / Heinz
86/7 PITT / Kodak
87/8 PITT / Kodak
89/0 PITT / Foodland 8
92/3 PITT / Coke-Clark
92/3 PITT / Foodland 2
94/5 POG 361
93/4 Power Play 435
94/5 Premier 331
90/1 Pro Set 234
91/2 Pro Set 187
91/2 Pro Set Platinum 215
92/3 SANJ / Pacific Bell
90/1 Score 255
91/2 Score 169
91/2 Score CAN 169
92/3 Score 287
93/4 Score 208
93/4 Score 566
94/5 Score 87
95/6 Score 174
92/3 Topps 95
91/2 To. Stadium 191
92/3 T. Stadium Club 170
93/4 To. Stadium 404
94/5 T. Stadium Club 37
94/5 Upper Deck 401

ERSKINE, JOHN
01/2 BAP Memor. 382
01/2 Bowman 116
98 Bowman 134, ✍ A24
98 Bowman Chrome 134
01/2 DALL / Southwest
02/3 O-Pee-Chee 290
01/2 PS Titanium 154
01/2 PS Titanium Draft 123
02/3 Topps 290
02/3 T. Limited 290
01/2 UD PlayMakers Ltd 115
01/2 UD Ice 136
00/1 Utah Grizzlies
01/2 Utah Grizzlies

ERSKINE, WAYNE
84/5 Kingston Canadians
85/6 Kingston Canadians
86/7 Kingston Canadians

ERTEL, BOB
94/5 Slapshot / Kitchener 28

ERTEL, TYLER
87/8 Kitchener Rangers
89/0 7th..Sketch OHL 151
90/1 7th..Sketch OHL 180

ERUZIONE, MIKE
80 Olympic USA
94/5 SR Miracle 11,12, ✍ 10,11
94/5 SR Miracle 47
91/2 SI For Kids 10

ESAU, LEN
95/6 Cincinnati Cyclones
99/0 Cincinnati Cyclones
00/1 Cincinnati Cyclones
96/7 Detroit Vipers
90/1 ProCards 150
91/2 ProCards 352
94/5 Saint John Flames

ESBJÖRS, JOACIM
98/9 Cardset 253
94/5 Leaf Elit Set 195
95/6 Leaf Elit Set 144
94 Semic 61
89/0 Semic Elitserien 267
90/1 Semic Elitserien 32
91/2 Semic Elitserien 281
92/3 Semic Elitserien 303
95/6 UD Elitserien 205
97/8 UD Elitserien 70
99/0 UD Elitserien 88
00/1 UD Elitserien 93

ESBJÖRS, JONAS
98/9 Cardset 259
94/5 Leaf Elit Set 206
95/6 Leaf Elit Set 146
91/2 Semic Elitserien 299
92/3 Semic Elitserien 318
97/8 UD Elitserien 82
99/0 UD Elitserien 93
00/1 UD Elitserien 102, ✍ Sig.

ESCHE, ROBERT
99/0 BAP Mem. 332
00/1 BAP Mem. 389
01/2 BT Pipes 58, ✂ DM, ✂ GG, ✂ GT
02/3 Between the Pipes 49, ✂ GUJ34, ✂ T8
97 Bowman 41
98 Bowman 1
98 Bowman Chrome 1
00/1 Crown Royale 137
99/0 Omega 180
99/0 Pacific 332
00/1 Pacific 323
01/2 Pacific 302
02/3 Pacific 294
02/3 Pacific Complete 456
00/1 Pa. Paramount 188
00/1 Private Stock 137
00/1 PS Titanium 139
00/1 PS Titanium Draft 139
95/6 Slapshot 57
99/0 SPx 117
00/1 Topps 295
00/1 To. Chrome 190
99/0 Upper Deck 101
99/0 UD G. Reserve 101
02/3 UD Mask 60, 61
99/0 UD MVP 160
99/0 UD Retro 63
00/1 Vanguard 139
99/0 Victory 223

ESKELINEN, TUOMAS
99/0 Cardset 269

ESMANTOVICH, IGOR
90/1 O-Pee-Chee 479

ESPE, DAVID
89/0 Halifax Citadels
90/1 Halifax Citadels
89/0 ProCards AHL 161
90/1 ProCards 442
91/2 ProCards 531

ESPOSITO, PHIL
71/2 Bazooka Panel
01/2 BAP Memor. ✂ 500GS
02/3 BAP Memorabilia / Cup
64-67 BeeHive-3 [Chic.]
64-67 BeeHive-3 [Chic.]
70/1 BOST
71/2 BOST
91/2 BOST / SA Legends
02/3 Canada Post
63-65 Chex
64/5 Coke/Sprite [Chic.]
65/6 Coca-Cola
70/1 Dad's Cookies
70/1 Eddie Sargent 14
71/2 Eddie Sargent 7
72/3 Eddie Sargent 21
70/1 Esso Power Player
88/9 Esso All-Star
01/2 Fleer Greats 5, -RC 3, ✂ O6, ✍ Aut.
01/2 Fleer Legacy 4, 11, ✂ HK
91/2 Future Trends C72 12, 30, 40, 44, 70, 84, 86, ✍ 84
91/2 Future Trends C76 102
92/3 Future Trends C76 153
83&87 HHOF 244
71 Kellogg's Transfer
92/3 Legends 7
74/5 Loblaws
99/0 Millenium P-14, ✍ P-14
73/4 Nabisco s 11
74/5 Nabisco 11
95/6 Fanfest 1-5
68/9 O-Pee-Chee 7
68/9 O-Pee-Chee 208
68/9 O-Pee-Chee PS 5
69/0 O-Pee-Chee 30
69/0 O-Pee-Chee 205
69/0 O-Pee-Chee 214
69/0 O-Pee-Chee 4in1
69/0 O-Pee-Chee Stamp
70/1 O-Pee-Chee 11
70/1 O-Pee-Chee 233
70/1 O-Pee-Chee 237
70/1 O-Pee-Chee DE 6
71/2 OPC 20, 247, 253
71/2 O-Pee-Chee Book. 2
72/3 O-Pee-Chee 76
72/3 O-Pee-Chee 111
72/3 O-Pee-Chee 148
72/3 O-Pee-Chee 230
72/3 O-Pee-Chee 280
72/3 O-Pee-Chee 283
72/3 O-Pee-Chee Crest 2
72/3 O-Pee-Chee TC
73/4 O-Pee-Chee 120
73/4 O-Pee-Chee 133
73/4 O-Pee-Chee 134
73/4 O-Pee-Chee 135
73/4 O-Pee-Chee 138
74/5 O-Pee-Chee 1
74/5 O-Pee-Chee 3
74/5 O-Pee-Chee 28
74/5 O-Pee-Chee 129
74/5 O-Pee-Chee 200
74/5 O-Pee-Chee 244
74/5 O-Pee-Chee 246
75/6 O-Pee-Chee 200
75/6 O-Pee-Chee 200
75/6 O-Pee-Chee 208
75/6 O-Pee-Chee 210
75/6 O-Pee-Chee 212
75/6 O-Pee-Chee 292
75/6 O-Pee-Chee 314
76/7 O-Pee-Chee 5
76/7 O-Pee-Chee 245
76/7 OPC 390
77/8 O-Pee-Chee 5
77/8 O-Pee-Chee 55
78/9 O-Pee-Chee 2
78/9 O-Pee-Chee 67
78/9 O-Pee-Chee 100
79/0 O-Pee-Chee 220
80/1 O-Pee-Chee 100
80/1 O-Pee-Chee 149
92/3 O-Pee-Chee 283
92/3 OPC - Anniv. 10
98/9 OPC Chrome 10
71/2 O-Pee-Chee Poster 21
80/1 O-Pee-Chee Super 14
01/2 Parkhurst ✂ 500GS, ✂ H5, ✍ PA13
02/3 Parkhurst ✂ VT2
95/6 Parkie 66-67 33
94/5 Parkie Tall 29, ✍ A4
90/1 Pro Set 403
91/2 Pro Set 594
71/2 Pro Star Promotions
87/8 Soo Greyhounds 15
72 Semic Sticker 184
91 Semic Sticker 240
68/9 Shirriff / Bost. 8
01/2 Signature ✂ 500GS, ✂ VA2
01/2 SP Authentic ✍ SotTD
77-79 Sportscaster 03-19
77-79 Sportscaster 29-08 [The Power Play]
77-79 Sports. FIN 05-105
77-79 Sports. FIN 37-869
95/6 SLU Cdn. Legend
97/8 SLU Cdn. Leg.
92/3 TAMP / Sheraton Inn
94/5 TAMP / Sky Box
95/6 TAMP / Sky Box
65/6 Topps 116
66/7 Topps 63
67/8 Topps 32
68/9 Topps 7
69/0 Topps 30
70/1 Topps 11
71/2 Topps 1-3, 20
72/3 Topps 62
72/3 Topps 63
72/3 Topps 124
72/3 Topps 150
72/3 Topps 170
73/4 Topps 1
73/4 Topps 2
73/4 Topps 3
73/4 Topps 6
73/4 Topps 120
74/5 Topps 1
74/5 Topps 3
74/5 Topps 28
74/5 Topps 129
74/5 Topps 200
74/5 Topps 244
74/5 Topps 246
75/6 Topps 200
75/6 Topps 208
75/6 Topps 210
75/6 Topps 212
75/6 Topps 292
75/6 Topps 314
76/7 Topps 5
76/7 Topps 245
76/7 Topps NS 7
77/8 Topps 5
77/8 Topps 55
78/9 Topps 2
78/9 Topps 67
78/9 Topps 100
79/0 Topps 220
80/1 Topps 100
80/1 Topps 149
98/9 Topps -Reprint 10, ✍ Reprint
01/2 Topps -SCH, -Reprint, ✍ SCHA, ✍ Reprint
71/2 Toronto Sun Photo
01/2 Ultimate Mem. ✂ 500GS, ✂ BL, ✂ Corn., ✂ Emb., ✂ NP, ✍ Aut.
02/3 Ultimate Mem. ✂ Cor, ✂ EA, ✂ FS, ✂ SL (x5), ✂ Num, ✂ PS (x2), ✂ RAT, ✂ RT, ✂ VGJ
90/1 Upper Deck 510
00 ✂ UD APOH 500, ✂✍ 500
99/0 UD C. Legends 19, ✍ ES
02/3 UD Foundations 7, 67, 109, ✂ 1000Stick (x2)
00/1 UD Legends 7, ES12, PH12, SM13, ✍ ES
01/2 UD Legends 3, FC, ✂ PoH (x2), ✂ TT, ✍ ES
99/0 UD Retro 94, G9A, ✍ Ink., ✂ RM4
01/2 UD SCup Champs 1
01/2 UD Vintage ✂ SD
71/2 Williams Finnish 380

ESPOSITO, RAY
02/3 UD Foundations 118

ESPOSITO, TONY
01/2 ASG History
71/2 Bazooka Panel
99/0 BAP Mem. R-6, ✍ R-6
00/1 BAP Mem. ✂ G-12, ✂ G-16, ✂ G-25, ✂ G-30
01/2 BAP Memor. ✂ GT8, ✂ GT26, ✂ GT27, ✂ GT39
01/2 BT Pipes 119, 144, ✂ DM, ✂ S&J, ✂ GR, ✂ TW, ✂ VM
02/3 Between the Pipes ✂ HSHSJers 25, ✂ RB7, ✂ VM9, ✍ Aut.
79/0 CHIC
80/1 CHIC / Colour
80/1 CHIC / Brown
81/2 CHIC
82/3 CHIC
83/4 CHIC
98/9 CHIC / Pizza Hut
70/1 Dad's Cookies
70/1 Eddie Sargent 33
71/2 Eddie Sargent 44
72/3 Eddie Sargent 66
70/1 Esso Power Player
88/9 Esso All-Star
01/2 Fleer Greats 19, -RC 13, ✂ O6, ✍ Aut.
01/2 Fleer Legacy 17, ✂ HK, ✂ TM
83/4 Funmate Puffy 13 [w/]
91/2 Future Trends C72 30, 31, 96, ✍ 96
93/4 High Liner 8
94/5 Legends 39
72/3 Post 13
74/5 Lipton Soup 45
74/5 Loblaws
69/0 O-Pee-Chee 138
70/1 O-Pee-Chee 153
70/1 O-Pee-Chee 234
70/1 O-Pee-Chee 247
70/1 O-Pee-Chee 250
70/1 O-Pee-Chee DE 32
71/2 O-Pee-Chee 110
71/2 O-Pee-Chee Book. 13
72/3 O-Pee-Chee 137
72/3 O-Pee-Chee 155
72/3 O-Pee-Chee 196
72/3 O-Pee-Chee 226
72/3 O-Pee-Chee 272
72/3 O-Pee-Chee 286
72/3 O-Pee-Chee TC
73/4 O-Pee-Chee 90
73/4 O-Pee-Chee 136
74/5 O-Pee-Chee 170
75/6 O-Pee-Chee 240
76/7 O-Pee-Chee 100
77/8 O-Pee-Chee 170
78/9 OPC 70
78/9 O-Pee-Chee 250
79/0 OPC 8
79/0 O-Pee-Chee 80
80/1 O-Pee-Chee 86
80/1 O-Pee-Chee 150
80/1 O-Pee-Chee 168
81/2 O-Pee-Chee 54
81/2 O-Pee-Chee 67
82/3 O-Pee-Chee 64
83/4 O-Pee-Chee 99
92/3 O-Pee-Chee 194
92/3 OPC - Anniv. 2
71/2 O-Pee-Chee Poster 8
81/2 OPC Sticker 113
80/1 O-Pee-Chee Super 4
01/2 Parkhurst ✍ PA37
02/3 Parkhurst ✂ VT5
02/3 Parkhurst Retro ✂ NN19
91/2 Pinnacle 388
82/3 Post [Chic.]
90/1 Pro Set 659
72 Semic Sticker 231
94/5 SR Gold Standard HOF7
00/1 Signature ✂ GLS-3
01/2 Signature ✍ VA1
83/4 Souhaits Keychain [Blackhawks]
01/2 SP GU ✂ TotG, ✂ TotGC, ✂ TotGC (x2)
95/6 SLU Cdn. Legend
96/7 SLU Timeless
92/3 TAMP / Sheraton Inn
94/5 TAMP / Sky Box
95/6 TAMP / Sky Box
71/2 Topps 4
71/2 Topps 5
71/2 Topps 6
71/2 Topps 110
72/3 Topps 20
72/3 Topps 61
72/3 Topps 64
72/3 Topps 121
72/3 Topps 173
73/4 Topps 4
73/4 Topps 90
74/5 Topps 170
75/6 Topps 240
76/7 Topps 100
76/7 Topps NS 3
77/8 Topps 170
78/9 Topps 70
78/9 Topps 250
79/0 Topps 8
79/0 Topps 80
80/1 Topps 86
80/1 Topps 150
80/1 Topps 168
81/2 Topps 11
81/2 Topps 126 [West]
01/2 Topps Archives 3, -Seat, ✂ Stick, ✍ CAI
71/2 Toronto Sun Photo
00/1 UD Heroes 124
00/1 Ultimate Mem. ✂ UG-3, ✂ RE-3, ✂ RA-3, ✂ RA-4, ✂ GM-5, ✂ GM-8, ✂ GM-17
01/2 Ultimate Mem. ✂ ASGH, ✂ BL, ✂ CT, ✂ Deca., ✂ RN, ✂ RA
02/3 Ultimate Mem. ✂ EA, ✂ Num, ✂ VGJ
99/0 UD C. Legends ✍ ES
00/1 UD Legends 27, ES13, LC10, SM14, ✍ ES
01/2 UD Legends 14, 88, FC, ✂ PoH, ✍ ES
02/3 UD Mask / Mask, ✍ Mask
99/0 UD Retro 107, ✍ Ink.
00/1 UD Vintage ✂ O6-POH
96 Wien HL7
71/2 Williams Finnish 381

ESSELMONT, RYAN
92/3 BCJHL 49

ESSELMONT, SHEA
89/0 Kamloops Blazers
90 7th..Sketch Mem.Cup 4
90/1 7th..Sketch WHL 297
91/2 7th...Sketch WHL 62

ESSELMONT, TODD
89/0 Kamloops Blazers
90 7th..Sketch Mem.Cup 5
90/1 7th..Sketch WHL 65

ESSENSA, BOB
01/2 BT Pipes 70
98/9 Bicycle.. 6-D
90/1 Bowman 131
91/2 Bowman 193
92/3 Bowman 306
93/4 Donruss 382
98/9 Dynagon Ice 70
93/4 EA Sports 150
95/6 Edge Ice 126
96/7 EDMO
97/8 EDMO
92/3 Fleer Ultra 240
93/4 Fleer Ultra 89
95/6 Fort Wayne Komets
91/2 Gillette 8
92/3 Kraft / PB
93/4 Leaf 38
94/5 Leaf 93
87/8 Moncton Hawks
90/1 OPC/Topps 119
91/2 O-Pee-Chee 307
92/3 O-Pee-Chee 226
90/1 OPC Premier 29
89/0 opcSticker/FS 21
98/9 Pacific 206
01/2 Pacific 381
98/9 Pa. Crown Roy. 50
97/8 Pa. Invincible R-77
89/0 Panini Sticker 173
90/1 Panini Sticker 311
91/2 Panini Sticker 75
92/3 Panini Sticker 51
93/4 Panini Sticker 199
91/2 Parkhurst 199
92/3 Parkhurst 207
93/4 Parkhurst 234
94/5 Parkhurst 64
01/2 Parkhurst 243
91/2 Pinnacle 66
92/3 Pinnacle 190
93/4 Pinnacle 133
94/5 Pinnacle 428
97/8 Pi. Be A Player 185, ✍ Aut. 185
93/4 Power Play 270
93/4 Premier 161
90/1 Pro Set 328
91/2 Pro Set 266
91/2 Pro Set 602
91/2 Pro Set / Prototype
92/3 Pro Set 211
92/3 Pro Set 267
91/2 Pro Set Platinum 135
91/2 Pro Set Platinum 285
89/0 ProCards AHL 34
90/1 Score 112, 324
91/2 Score 251
91/2 Score CAN 471
92/3 Score 123
93/4 Score 26
94/5 Score 191
91/2 Score Young Stars 17
92/3 Topps 183
91/2 To. Stadium 152
92/3 T. Stadium Club 210
93/4 To. Stadium 254
90/1 Upper Deck 122, 337
91/2 Upper Deck 101
92/3 Upper Deck 217
93/4 Upper Deck 144
99/0 WGretzky 132
89/0 WINN / Safeway
90/1 WINN / IGA
91/2 WINN / IGA
93/4 WINN / Ruffles
93/4 WINN Readers

ESSEX, BRAD
99/0 Mississippi S'Wolves
99/0 Mississippi S'Wolves
96/7 Peoria Rivermen
97/8 Peoria Rivermen

ESTOLA, MATTI
72/3 Williams Finnish 300

ESTRADA, SERGIO
79 Panini Sticker 371

ETCHER, FRED
52/3 Anonymous 96
59/60 Whitby Dunlops

ETCHES, DEREK
90/1 7th..Sketch OHL 383
91/2 7th...Sketch OHL 43
89/0 Sudbury Wolves
90/1 Sudbury Wolves

ETHIER, MARTIN
97 Bowman 47

ETHIER, NEIL
89/0 Sudbury Wolves

ETHIER, TREVOR
93/4 Saskatoon Blades

ETTINGER, TREVOR
00/1 Shawinigan 22
02/3 Syracuse Crunch

EUSTACHE, EDDIE
52/3 Anonymous 167

EVANGELISTA, JOHN
99/0 Mississippi S'Wolves

EVANS, BLAKE
01/2 Peoria Rivermen
00/1 UD Prospects 74

EVANS, CHRIS
72/3 Eddie Sargent 192
74/5 Loblaws
74/5 Loblaws Update
72/3 O-Pee-Chee 236
73/4 O-Pee-Chee 208
74/5 O-Pee-Chee 59
76/7 OPC WHA 22
72/3 SLOU
73/4 SLOU
74/5 Topps 59

EVANS, CORY
99/0 Fort Worth Brahmas
91/2 7th...Sketch OHL 372
93/4 Slapshot / Windsor 16
94/5 Slapshot / Windsor 18

EVANS, DARYL
84/5 LOSA / Smokey 4
89/0 New Haven Nighthawks
83/4 O-Pee-Chee 153
83/4 OPC/Topps Sticker 144
88/9 ProCards / Newmarket
83/4 Souhaits Keychain [Kings]

EVANS, DOUG
91/2 Bowman 203
92/3 Dayton Bombers
95/6 Edge Ice 177
94/5 Greensboro Monarchs
90/1 O-Pee-Chee 413
91/2 O-Pee-Chee 438
92/3 OPC Premier 45
90/1 Panini/WPG 11
93/4 Peoria Rivermen
94/5 Peoria Rivermen
95/6 Peoria Rivermen
96/7 Peoria Rivermen
97/8 Peoria Rivermen
98/9 Peoria Rivermen
92/3 PHIL / UD Sheet
92/3 PHIL / J.C. Penney
93/4 Premier 203
90/1 Pro Set 561
91/2 Score CAN 399
87/8 SLOU
87/8 SLOU / Kodak
88/9 SLOU
88/9 SLOU / Kodak
91/2 To. Stadium 321
90/1 WINN / IGA
91/2 WINN / IGA

EVANS, FRANK
01/2 Cardiff Devils
00/1 Kudos 53
94/5 Las Vegas Thunder
01/2 Nottingham Panthers
92 7th...Sketch Awards 18
91 7th..Sketch Mem.Cup 76
90/1 7th..Sketch WHL 196
91/2 7th...Sketch WHL 8
89/0 Spokane Chiefs

EVANS, JACK
45-64 BeeHive-2 [NYRa.]
45-64 BeeHive-2 [Chic.]
62/3 Cowan Tile
51/2 Parkhurst 90
53/4 Parkhurst 54
54/5 Parkhurst 72
93/4 Parkie 56-57 101
60/1 Shirriff 76
61/2 Shirriff 39
54/5 Topps 14
57/8 Topps 55
58/9 Topps 31
59/0 Topps 30
59/0 Topps 48
60/1 Topps 30
61/2 Topps - Stamp
62/3 Topps 26

EVANS, JIMMY
28/9 Paulins Candy 60

EVANS, KEVIN
96/7 Mississippi S'Wolves
93/4 Peoria Rivermen
94/5 Peoria Rivermen
89/0 ProCards IHL 76
90/1 ProCards 100
91/2 ProCards 511
91/2 Score CAN 650

EVANS, MIKE
91/2 Air Canada SJHL C3
92/3 MPS SJHL 100

EVANS, SHAWN
95/6 Fort Wayne Komets
94/5 Milwaukee Admirals
88/9 ProCards / Springfield
89/0 ProCards AHL 244
91/2 ProCards 96

EVANS, STAN
23/4 Paulins Candy 60

EVANS, STEWART
34-43 BeeHive-1 [Maroons]
35-40 Canada Starch
35-40 Canada Starch
37/8 O-Pee-Chee 164
38/9 Quaker Oats
34/5 Sweet Caporal
37/8 World Wide Gum 67

EVANS-HARVEY, BLAKE
02/3 Worcester IceCats

EVANS-HARVEY, RONNIE
94/5 Guildford Flames 9
95/6 Guildford Flames 11

EVASON, DEAN
90/1 Bowman 262
91/2 Bowman 10
92/3 Bowman 133
94/5 DALL / Southwest
94/5 DALL / Cap
98/9 DEL 68
93/4 Donruss 86
92/3 Fleer Ultra 193
93/4 Fleer Ultra 298
94/5 Fleer Ultra 50
86/7 HART / Jr. Whalers
87/8 HART / Jr. Whalers
88/9 HART / Jr. Whalers
89/0 HART / Jr. Whalers
90/1 HART / Jr. Whalers
94/5 Leaf 45

87/8 OPC/Topps 166
90/1 OPC/Topps 376
91/2 O-Pee-Chee 325
92/3 O-Pee-Chee 381
91/2 OPC Premier 36
87/8 Panini Sticker 47
89/0 Panini Sticker 223
90/1 Panini Sticker 44
91/2 Panini Sticker 312
92/3 Panini Sticker 131
93/4 Panini Sticker 259
91/2 Parkhurst 388
92/3 Parkhurst 392
93/4 Parkhurst 319
95/6 Parkhurst 36
94/5 Parkie SE46
91/2 Pinnacle 153
92/3 Pinnacle 169
93/4 Pinnacle 384
94/5 Pinnacle 346
94/5 POG 78
93/4 Power Play 323
94/5 Premier 361
90/1 Pro Set 103
91/2 Pro Set 84
91/2 Pro Set Platinum 230
91/2 SANJ / Sports Action
90/1 Score 259
91/2 Score 17
91/2 Score 91T
91/2 Score CAN 17
91/2 Score CAN 641
92/3 Score 103
93/4 Score 353
93/4 Score 550
92/3 Topps 304
91/2 To. Stadium 145
92/3 T. Stadium Club 11
94/5 T. Stadium Club 82
90/1 Upper Deck 192
91/2 Upper Deck 127
91/2 Upper Deck 560
92/3 Upper Deck 281
94/5 Upper Deck 48
95/6 Upper Deck 22
94/5 UD BAP ✍ 138
95/6 UD CC 307

EVASON, HEAVY
88/9 Niagara Falls Thunder

EVDOKIMOV, VITALI
00/1 Mir 7

EVENSSON, CONNY
94/5 Leaf Elit Set 298
91/2 Semic Elitserien 359
92 Semic Sticker 50

EVERBERG, P.A.
97/8 UD Elitserien 198

EVSEEV, VLADISLAV
02/3 Russian Future Stars 3

EVSTAFIEV, ANDREI
98/9 Mir 90
99/0 Mir 249
00/1 Mir 335

EVSTIGNEEV, PAVEL
99/0 San Angelo Outlaws

EVTUSHEVSKI, GREG
94/5 DEL 229
95/6 DEL 165
96/7 DEL 240
98/9 DEL 44
99/0 Eishockey 182
84/5 Kamloops Blazers
01/2 UD DEL 79

EVTYUKHIN, GEORGI
99/0 Mir 221
00/1 Mir 260

EWACHA, ROD
90/1 Michigan Tech Huskies
91/2 Michigan Tech Huskies

EWEN, DEAN
99/0 Colorado Gold Kings
95/6 Kansas City Blades
96/7 Kansas City Blades
98/9 Las Vegas Thunder
89/0 ProCards AHL 242
91/2 ProCards 452

EWEN, TODD
94/5 ANAH / Carl's Jr. 6
93/4 Donruss 9
01/2 Fleer Legacy 40
93/4 Fleer Ultra 252
94/5 Fleer Ultra 2
93/4 Leaf 427
89/0 MONT / Kraft
90/1 MONT
91/2 MONT
92/3 MONT
97/8 Pa. Invincible R-178
90/1 Panini/MTL 11
94/5 Panini Sticker 123
93/4 Parkhurst 5
92/3 Pinnacle 250
93/4 Pinnacle 409
94/5 Pinnacle 503
93/4 Power Play 285
93/4 Premier 369
94/5 Premier 119
90/1 Pro Set 470
91/2 Pro Set 419
93/4 Score 565
87/8 SLOU
87/8 SLOU / Kodak
88/9 SLOU
88/9 SLOU / Kodak
91/2 To. Stadium 340
93/4 To. Stadium 309
92/3 Upper Deck 549
93/4 Upper Deck 449
94/5 Upper Deck 427
95/6 Upper Deck 340
95/6 UD BAP 155, ✍ S155
96/7 UD CC 11

EWEN, TODD
02/3 Fleer Throwbacks 23, ✂ 4SW, ✍ Aut.

EWING, STEVE
86/7 Kitchener Rangers

EXANTUS, PAUL-EMILE
90/1 7th..Sketch LHJMQ 265
91/2 7th...Sketch LHJMQ 296

EXELBY, GARNET
02/3 BAP Memorabilia 398
01/2 Chicago Wolves
02/3 Chicago Wolves
02/3 Choice Prospects 14
02/3 Ultimate Mem. 54

EXELBY, RANDY
90/1 Kansas City Blades
88/9 ProCards / Sherbrooke
89/0 ProCards IHL 115
90/1 ProCards 589

EXNER, KENRIC
99 Bowman 121
98/9 Kamloops Blazers
00/1 Peoria Rivermen

EYSSELT, JAN
95/6 DEL 287
96/7 DEL 315

EZINICKI, BILL
45-64 BeeHive-2 [Toro.]
45-54 Quaker Oats

F

FAASSEN, DANNY
90/1 7th..Sketch WHL 205
91/2 7th...Sketch WHL 19

FABIAN, PETR
94/5 APS 13
95/6 APS 313
96/7 APS 108, 424
96/7 DS Sticker 276

FABIAN, SEAN
91/2 Minnesota G'Gophers

FACKLER, AARON
99/0 Asheville Smoke
94/5 Knoxville Cherokees

FADEEV, SERGEI
00/1 Mir 101

FADEJEV, MICHAIL
95/6 APS 166
96/7 APS 333
96/7 DS Sticker 169

FADER, DUNCAN
93/4 Slapshot / Kingston 15
95/6 Slapshot 135

FADRNY, JAN
97/8 APS 168
98/9 Brandon Wheat Kings
99/0 Brandon Wheat Kings
00/1 Kelowna Rockets
01/2 WBS Penguins

FAFARD, DOMINIC
98/9 Oklahoma City Blazers

FAFARD, PERRY
84/5 Brandon Wheat Kings

FAGAN, ANDREW
95/6 Slapshot 165

FAGEMO, LINUS
98/9 UD Elitserien 74
99/0 UD Elitserien 80
00/1 UD Elitserien 174

FAGERHØI, KIM
92/3 Semic Nordisk 95

FAGERLI, JAN ROAR
95 Panini Worlds 238
92 Semic Sticker 32

FAGERLI, JAN_ROAR
92/3 Semic Nordisk 38

FAGERSTRÖM, KRISTIAN
94/5 Sisu 336
95/6 Sisu 7

FAGINKRANTZ, JOHN
92/3 Peoria Rivermen
93/4 Peoria Rivermen

FAGIOLI, LUCIANO
87/8 Sudbury Wolves

FAHEY, JIM
02/3 BAP Memorabilia 353
02/3 Calder 144
02/3 Choice Prospects 15
02/3 Pacific Complete 531
02/3 Parkhurst Retro 237
02/3 Quest for the Cup 145
02/3 SP Authentic 169
02/3 Ultimate Mem. 86
02/3 UD Artistic 112
02/3 UD Honor 141
02/3 UD Premier 51

FAHEY, REBECCA
97/8 UD Coll. Choice 292

FAHRUTDINOV, MISHAT
94/5 Leaf Elit Set 47
95/6 Leaf Elit Set 129
89/0 Semic Elitserien 262
90/1 Semic Elitserien 162
91/2 Semic Elitserien 264
92/3 Semic Elitserien 287
95/6 UD Elitserien 195

FAIR, KEITH
93 Semic Sticker 119

FAIR, QUINN
91/2 Air Canada SJHL C9
96/7 Mississippi S'Wolves
99/0 Mississippi S'Wolves

FAIRBAIRN, BILL
70/1 Eddie Sargent 123
71/2 Eddie Sargent 123
72/3 Eddie Sargent 150
70/1 Esso Power Player
74/5 Loblaws
71/2 O-Pee-Chee 215
72/3 O-Pee-Chee 87
73/4 O-Pee-Chee 41
74/5 O-Pee-Chee 231
75/6 O-Pee-Chee 109
76/7 O-Pee-Chee 57
77/8 O-Pee-Chee 303
78/9 O-Pee-Chee 267
73/4 Topps 41
74/5 Topps 231
75/6 Topps 109
76/7 Topps 57
77/8 Topps 255
71/2 Toronto Sun Photo

FAIRCHILD, KELLY
01/2 BAP Memor. 431
94/5 Classic 71
95/6 Future Legends 5
00/1 Hershey Bears
01/2 Hershey Bears
98/9 Michigan K-Wings
99/0 Michigan K-Wings
97/8 Milwaukee Admirals
94/5 Sig. Rookies 23, ✍ 23
01/2 SPx 202
94/5 St. John's Maple Leafs
95/6 St. John's Maple Leafs
02/3 Upper Deck 202
01/2 UD Honor Roll 68
02/3 UD Vintage 327

FALARDEAU, LEE
97 Québec Pee Wee 0801

FALESY, KEVIN
87/8 Kingston Canadians
89/0 Kitchener Rangers

FALK, LARS
91/2 Semic Elitserien 304
92/3 Semic Elitserien 326

FALK, NICHLAS
95/6 Leaf Elit Set 186, R-3
95/6 UD Elitserien 48
97/8 UD Elitserien 44, UDS3
98/9 UD Elitserien 57
99/0 UD Elitserien 42
00/1 UD Elitserien 53

FALK, STEFAN
94/5 Leaf Elit Set 52
95/6 Leaf Elit Set 54
89/0 Semic Elitserien 117
91/2 Semic Elitserien 126
92/3 Semic Elitserien 147
95/6 UD Elitserien 84
97/8 UD Elitserien 92

FALKENBERG, BOB
68/9 O-Pee-Chee 141
72/3 O-Pee-Chee 310

FALKMAN, CRAIG
72/3 Minn. Fight. Saints
72 Semic Sticker 127

FALLOON, CHRIS
99/0 Prince George Cougars
00/1 Prince George Cougars

FALLOON, PAT
91/2 Arena 1, -Hologram
91/2 Arena 32
98/9 Be A Player 205, ✍ Aut. 205
92/3 Bowman 361
91/2 Classic 2
91/2 Classic Four Sport 2
93/4 Donruss 308
93/4 Donruss T
94/5 Donruss 83
95/6 Donruss 213
96/7 Donruss 208
93/4 EA Sports 119
94/5 Flair 163
94/5 Fleer 195
96/7 Fl. Picks 102
92/3 Fleer Ultra 194, -UR 6
93/4 Fleer Ultra 56
94/5 Fleer Ultra 364
95/6 Fleer Ultra 284
91/2 Gillette 3
93/4 Hockey Wit 98
95/6 Hoyle / West. 3-Spade
92/3 Humpty Dumpty
91/2 Kraft 8
93/4 Kraft / KD
93/4 Leaf 49
93/4 Leaf SSS 2
94/5 Leaf 95
95/6 Leaf 241
96/7 Leaf 102
94/5 L. Limited 14
92/3 O-Pee-Chee 227
98/9 OPC Chrome 182
91/2 OPC Premier 56
92/3 OPC Premier SP12
99/0 Pacific 153
00/1 Pacific 326
97/8 Pacific CC 199
99/0 Pa. Paramount 90
92/3 Panini Sticker 273
92/3 Panini Sticker K
93/4 Panini Sticker W
94/5 Panini Sticker 219
91/2 Parkhurst 160
92/3 Parkhurst 161
92/3 Parkhurst 233
93/4 Parkhurst 183
94/5 Parkhurst V70
95/6 Parkhurst 424
94/5 Parkie SE165
96/7 PHIL / Ocean Spray
91/2 Pinnacle 329
92/3 Pinnacle 9
92/3 Pinnacle 238
92/3 Pinnacle T2K 26
93/4 Pinnacle 20
93/4 Pinnacle T2K1 26
94/5 Pinnacle 173
96/7 Pinnacle 115
95/6 Playoff 82
96/7 Playoff 361
94/5 POG 214
95/6 POG 227
93/4 Power Play 218
93/4 Premier 259
94/5 Premier 521
95/6 Pro Magnet 116
91/2 Pro Set 558
91/2 Pro Set CC3
92/3 Pro Set 166
92/3 Pro Set RGL 4
92/3 Pro Set TL 10
91/2 Pro Set Platinum 271
91/2 SANJ / Sports Action
92/3 SANJ / Pacific Bell
92/3 SANJ / Pacific Bell
91/2 Score 90T
91/2 Score CAN 640
92/3 Score 125
92/3 Score 436
93/4 Score 133
93/4 Score TF 19
94/5 Score 152
95/6 Score 184
96/7 Score 21
97/8 Score Phil. 16
92/3 Score Young Stars 14
92/3 Seasons 62
94/5 Select 116
92 7th...Sketch Awards 12
91 7th..Sketch Mem.Cup 87, 100
90/1 7th..Sketch WHL 189, 345
89/0 Spokane Chiefs
91/2 Star Pics 2
91/2 Star Pics 36
95/6 Super Sticker 107
92/3 Topps 7
92/3 Topps 418
95/6 Topps 147
98/9 Topps 182
94/5 Topps Finest 32
92/3 T. Stadium Club 56
92/3 T. Stadium Club 259
93/4 To. Stadium 224
94/5 T. Stadium Club 62
91/2 Ultimate Draft Pick 2, 56, 58, 78, 80, ✍ Aut.
90/1 Upper Deck 469
91/2 Upper Deck 593
92/3 Upper Deck 19
92/3 Upper Deck 286
92/3 Upper Deck 355
92/3 Upper Deck 386
92/3 Upper Deck WG13
93/4 Upper Deck 39, FH-29, SP-141
94/5 Upper Deck 307
95/6 Upper Deck 483
96/7 Upper Deck 122
95/6 UD BAP 95, ✍ S95
95/6 UD CC 188
96/7 UD CC 194
92/3 UD Locker 52

FALTA, PAVEL
94/5 APS 163

FANCY, JEFF
90/1 7th..Sketch WHL 106
91/2 7th...Sketch WHL 66

FANDUL, VIACHESLAV
98/9 Cardset 260
00/1 Cardset 296
97/8 Hockey-Box
92/3 Jyvas Hyva 197
93/4 Jyvas Hyva 353
93/4 Sisu 220
94/5 Sisu 327, FOI-12
95/6 Sisu 127, 370
01/2 UD DEL 28

FANDUL, VJATSHESLAV
02/3 Cardset 17

FANKHOUSER, SCOTT
00/1 Aurora 6
99/0 BAP Mem. 387
99/0 Crown Royale 6
99/0 Omega 15
00/1 Pacific 27
00/1 Pa. Paramount 12
00/1 PS Titanium 102
00/1 PS Titanium Draft 102
99/0 SP Authentic 93
00/1 Victory 273

FARDA, RICHARD
95/6 APS 123
97/8 APS 146, 375
72 Hellas MM-Jenkki 90
74 Hellas MM-Jenkki 68
70/1 Kuvajulkaisut 44
98/9 OFS 209
99/0 OFS 16, 236
72 Panda MM-Toronto
72 Semic Sticker 31
74 Semic Sticker 63
71/2 Williams Finnish 24
72/3 Williams Finnish 4
73/4 Williams Finnish 46

FARELLI, CARY
82 Semic Sticker 137

FARKAS, ANDRAS
79 Panini Sticker 267

FARKAS, JEFF
00/1 Aurora 138
00/1 BAP Mem. 223
02/3 Chicago Wolves
95/6 Do. Elite WJ 35
01/2 O-Pee-Chee 312
00/1 Pacific 389
00/1 Pa. Paramount 229
00/1 Parkhurst P-76
00/1 Premier Plus 99, PP6
00/1 Revolution 138
00/1 Signature 261, ✍ Aut. 8
00/1 St. John's Maple Leafs
01/2 St. John's Maple Leafs
01/2 St. John's / Clarenville
01/2 Topps 312
98/9 UD Choice 306
97/8 UD Black Diam. 125
00/1 UD Vintage 343
01/2 Victory 389

FARMER, SEAN
99/0 Peoria Rivermen
94/5 Slapshot Memorial 59

FARQUHARSON, STEVE
00/1 Toronto St. Mike's

FARR, ROCKY
74/5 BUFF

FARRELL, ARTHUR F.
83 HHOF Postcard L3
83&87 HHOF 153

FARRELL, BRIAN
94/5 Classic 33

FARRELL, MIKE
01/2 BAP Memor. 316
01/2 Parkhurst 349
00/1 Portland Pirates
01/2 To. Chrome 182
01/2 UD PlayMakers Ltd 143
01/2 UD Ice 151

FARRIS, KEVIN
84/5 Nova Scotia Oilers
85/6 Nova Scotia Oilers

FARRISH, DAVE
00/1 Louisiana Ice Gators
01/2 Louisiana Ice Gators
02/3 Louisiana Ice Gators
90/1 Moncton Hawks
91/2 Moncton Hawks
77/8 O-Pee-Chee 179
78/9 O-Pee-Chee 41
79/0 O-Pee-Chee 299
80/1 O-Pee-Chee 311
81/2 O-Pee-Chee 317
83/4 O-Pee-Chee 329
84/5 O-Pee-Chee 301
80/1 Pepsi Bottle Cap
88/9 ProCards / Baltimore
89/0 ProCards AHL 49
90/1 ProCards 263
91/2 ProCards 187
97/8 Springfield Falcons
77/8 Topps 179
78/9 Topps 41
80/1 TORO
83/4 TORO
83/4 Vachon 85-53

FATA, DREW
00/1 Toronto St. Mike's

FATA, RICO
96/7 All-Sport PPF 76
98/9 Be A Player 171, ✍ Aut. 171
99/0 BAP Mem. 149
00/1 BAP Mem. 366
01/2 BAP Memor. 220
99 Bowman 146, SC12
97 Bowman 24
98 Bowman 131, SC16, ✍ A40
98 Bowman Chrome 131
98/9 Bowman's Best 114
98/9 Collection Souvenir 24
00/1 Crown Royale ✂ GWJ 3
98/9 Dynagon Ice 24
01/2 Hartford Wolf Pack
01/2 Heads Up ✂ JQ 5
99/0 Millenium 46, ✍ Aut. 46
01/2 O-Pee-Chee 313
98/9 OPC Chrome 225
98/9 Omega 38
99/0 Pacific 66
98/9 Pa. Crown Roy. 17
99/0 Pa. Paramount 37
00/1 Premier Plus ✂ GP
01/2 Pr. Stock ✂ GUG 66
00/1 PS Titanium ✂ GUG 66
01/2 PS Titanium ✂ DSJ 26
94 Québec Pee Wee 573
95/6 Slapshot 369
98/9 SP Authentic 92
01/2 SP GU ✂ AF
99/0 SPx 25
99/0 Stadium 192
98/9 Topps 225
99/0 Topps 111
01/2 Topps 313
99/0 To. Chrome 111
98/9 To. Finest F6
98/9 T. Gold Label 46
99/0 To. Prmr. Plus 130
01/2 UD PlayMakers Ltd - PCPJ
97/8 Upper Deck 410
98/9 Upper Deck 413, GN20, P30
99/0 Upper Deck 29, 164, N16
01/2 Upper Deck ✂ GN
98/9 UD Black Diam. 11
98/9 UD G. Reserve 413
99/0 UD G. Reserve 29, 164
98/9 UD MVP 27, ✍ PS
99/0 UD MVP 34, DR7
01/2 UD MVP 26
99/0 Victory 47
01/2 Victory 365

FATIKOV, LEONID
00/1 Mir 165
01/2 UD DEL 124, ✂ GJ

FATKULLIN, ALFRED
99/0 Mir 259

FATROLA, RICHARD
96/7 Dayton Ice Bandits
95/6 Muskegon Fury
89/0 7th..Sketch OHL 73
90/1 7th..Sketch OHL 4

FATTEY, CHRIS
00/1 Rockford IceHogs

FAUBERT, MARIO
78/9 O-Pee-Chee 296
81/2 O-Pee-Chee 261
81/2 OPC Sticker 189

FAUCHER, FRÉDÉRIC
02/3 Québec Remparts
01/2 Victoriaville Tigres 14

FAULKNER, ALEX
45-64 BeeHive-2 [Detr.]
64-67 BeeHive-3 [Detr.]
62/3 Cowan Tile
63/4 Parkhurst 42
63/4 York 49

FAULKNER, ANDY
91/2 Avant Garde BCJHL 52
91/2 Avant Garde BCJHL 153
91/2 Nanaimo Clippers
97/8 Quad City Mallards

FAUSEL, SHANE
85/6 U. of Arizona Ice Cats

FAUSS, TED
83/4 Nova Scotia Voyageurs

FAUST, ANDRE
99/0 Eishockey 164

FAUST, ANDRÉ
92/3 Classic Prospects 47
96/7 DEL 20
98/9 DEL 275
94/5 Donruss 184
94/5 Hershey Bears
92/3 Parkhurst 365
93/4 Parkhurst 419
93/4 PHIL / Sheet
93/4 Pinnacle 209
93/4 To. Stadium 462
93/4 Upper Deck 63
00/1 UD DEL 137
01/2 UD DEL 137

FAUST, ELLIOTT
95/6 Slapshot 206

FAUTEUX, JONATHAN
99 Bowman 25, ✍ BA16
01/2 Peoria Rivermen
00/1 Victoriaville Tigres 13

FAVARO, RANDY
95/6 Spokane Chiefs 11

FAVELL, DOUG
77/8 Coke
70/1 Colgate 91
76/7 COLR / Hockey Talk
70/1 Dad's Cookies
70/1 Eddie Sargent 152
71/2 Eddie Sargent 156
72/3 Eddie Sargent 157
70/1 Esso Power Player
72/3 Post 11
72/3 Post 21
74/5 Loblaws
69/0 O-Pee-Chee 88
70/1 O-Pee-Chee 199
70/1 O-Pee-Chee DE 35
71/2 O-Pee-Chee 72
72/3 O-Pee-Chee 89
72/3 O-Pee-Chee Crest 16
73/4 O-Pee-Chee 158
74/5 O-Pee-Chee 4
74/5 O-Pee-Chee 46
75/6 O-Pee-Chee 381
76/7 O-Pee-Chee 292
77/8 O-Pee-Chee 370
78/9 O-Pee-Chee 54
79/0 O-Pee-Chee 274
70/1 PHIL
72/3 PHIL / Milk
68/9 Shirriff / Phil. 5
69/0 Topps 88
71/2 Topps 72
72/3 Topps 74
73/4 Topps 119
74/5 Topps 4
74/5 Topps 46
78/9 Topps 54
73/4 TORO
75/6 TORO
71/2 Toronto Sun Photo

FAVOT, TIM
89/0 7th..Sketch OHL 166
90/1 7th..Sketch OHL 307
91/2 7th...Sketch OHL 262
91/2 Sudbury Wolves

FAWCETT, LEN
86/7 Kitchener Rangers

FEAMSTER, DAVE
82/3 CHIC
83/4 CHIC
83/4 O-Pee-Chee 100

FEARNS, KENT
95/6 Classic 72, ✍ Aut.
95/6 Cla. 5 Sport 151, ✍ Aut.
99/0 Eishockey 325
96/7 Knoxville Cherokees
97/8 Manitoba Moose
98/9 Manitoba Moose
01/2 UD DEL 181

FEASBY, MIKE
98/9 Muskegon Fury
99/0 Muskegon Fury

FEASBY, SCOTT
93/4 Muskegon Fury
94/5 Muskegon Fury
95/6 Muskegon Fury
99/0 Muskegon Fury
89/0 7th..Sketch OHL 88

FEATHERSTONE, GLEN
91/2 BOST / Sports Action
91/2 Bowman 371
98/9 Chicago Wolves
99/0 Chicago Wolves
00/1 Chicago Wolves
95/6 HART / Kids Club
96/7 HART / Kids Club
97/8 Indianapolis Ice 6
90/1 OPC/Topps 387
91/2 O-Pee-Chee 436
91/2 OPC Premier 66
95/6 Parkhurst 363
93/4 Power Play 288
93/4 Premier 14
90/1 Pro Set 523
88/9 ProCards / Peoria
90/1 Score 25T
91/2 Score 37T
91/2 Score CAN 587
90/1 SLOU / Kodak
91/2 To. Stadium 319
93/4 To. Stadium 372
94/5 UD BAP ✍ 81

FEATHERSTONE, TONY
70/1 Esso Power Player
73/4 MINS
75/6 OPC WHA 122
71/2 Topps 106

FEDERENKO, BRAD
91/2 Air Canada SJHL 12
93/4 Minnesota-Duluth

FEDERENKO, GARVIN
94/5 Anchorage Aces 12

FEDERKO, BERNIE
90/1 Bowman 238
89/0 DETR / Little Caesars
01/2 Fleer Greats 63, ✍ Aut.
88/9 Frito Lay
83/4 Funmate Puffy 18 [w/]
93/4 Hockey Wit 47
84/5 Kellogg's 7
77/8 O-Pee-Chee 312
78/9 O-Pee-Chee 143
79/0 O-Pee-Chee 215
80/1 O-Pee-Chee 71
80/1 O-Pee-Chee 136
81/2 O-Pee-Chee 288
81/2 O-Pee-Chee 300
81/2 O-Pee-Chee 304
82/3 O-Pee-Chee 302
82/3 O-Pee-Chee 303
83/4 O-Pee-Chee 315
84/5 O-Pee-Chee 184
84/5 O-Pee-Chee 367
85/6 OPC/Topps 104
86/7 OPC/Topps 105
87/8 OPC/Topps 83
88/9 OPC/Topps 81
88/9 OPC/Topps Box E
90/1 OPC/Topps 191
89/0 OPC/Topps 107
81/2 OPC Sticker 128
82/3 OPC/Topps Sticker 197
83/4 OPC/Topps Sticker 125
84/5 OPC Sticker 54
84/5 OPC Sticker 55
85/6 OPC Sticker 53
86/7 OPC Sticker 174
87/8 OPC Sticker 24
88/9 OPC Sticker 21
89/0 opcSticker 247-108
80/1 O-Pee-Chee Super 18
87/8 Panini Sticker 312
88/9 Panini Sticker 104
90/1 Panini Sticker 209
82/3 Post [SLou.]
90/1 Pro Set 70
91/2 Pro Set 597
90/1 Score 252
84/5 7-Eleven
78/9 SLOU
87/8 SLOU
87/8 SLOU / Kodak
88/9 SLOU
88/9 SLOU / Kodak
92/3 SLOU / McDon. 14
78/9 Topps 143
79/0 Topps 215
80/1 Topps 71
80/1 Topps 136
81/2 Topps 12
81/2 Topps 62
81/2 Topps 127 [West]
84/5 Topps 131
01/2 To. Chrome -CA4, ✍ CA4
01/2 Topps Archives 60, -Seat
90/1 Upper Deck 58
02/3 UD Foundations 83, 116
00/1 UD Legends 114
01/2 UD Legends 57

FEDERKO, BERNIE
02/3 Fleer Throwbacks 7

FEDORCHUK, DEAN
94/5 Classic 52
94/5 Dayton Bombers 14

FEDORKO, MIKE
91/2 Prince Albert Raiders
91/2 7th...Sketch WHL 262

FEDOROV, ANTON
94/5 Raleigh Icecaps

FEDOROV, EVGENI
98/9 Mir 31
99/0 Mir 168

FEDOROV, FEDOR
02/3 Calder 97
02/3 Exclusive 191
01/2 Manitoba Moose
02/3 Manitoba Moose
02/3 Pacific Complete 586
02/3 PS Titanium -ROT 20
00/1 SP Authentic 129
00/1 SP GU 84
00/1 SPx ✂ 125
00/1 Sudbury Wolves 22
02/3 T. Total 436
00/1 UD Pros&Prosp. 126
00/1 UD Vintage 399

FEDOROV, SERGEI
94/5 Action Packed
01/2 Adrenaline 64
01/2 Atomic 35, PP12
02/3 Atomic 36
98/9 Aurora 62, -ALC 9, -CF 16, -Cube 8
99/0 Aurora 50, Stripe 50
00/1 Aurora 49, Pins. 49, CF-10, SR-9
02/3 BAP All-Star 20-21, ✂ ASJ, ✂ HSHSJers
98/9 Be A Player 45, H-17, P-8, ✍ Aut. 45, ✂ G-16, ✂ AS-15, ✂ S-14, ✂✍ G-16
99/0 BAP Mem. 87, ✂ J-15, ✂ D-20, ✂ TM-5, ✂ TM-37, ✂ TM-38
00/1 BAP Mem. 237, ✂ J-35, ✂ TM-16, ✂ TM-29
01/2 BAP Memor. 75, ✂ SCP
02/3 BAP Memorabilia 133, ✂ ASJ12, ✂ ASE3, ✂ ASN3, ✂ AS10, ✂ AST1, ✂ AST30, ✂ HSHSJers 28, ✂ SCC10, ✂ SC21, ✂ TM2
96/7 Bic.Sports Aces Q-H
95/6 Bicycle Sports Aces J-Heart
91/2 Bowman 50
92/3 Bowman 416
92/3 Bowman 205
95/6 Bowman 80, BB12
01/2 Bowman 74
02/3 Bowman 97
98/9 Bowman's Best 35, -F16, ✍ A4A, ✍ A4B
02/3 Calder 22
99/0 Crown Royale 49, -IG 9
00/1 Crown Royale 38
01/2 Crown Royale 51
02/3 Crown Royale 32, ✂ GWDP 9
90/1 DETR / Little Caesars
91/2 DETR / Little Caesars
99/0 DETR / News 2
93/4 Donruss 101
93/4 Donruss ES U2
94/5 Donruss 173, D-5, ES-4, IM-2
95/6 Donruss 285, D-5, E-4
96/7 Donruss 50, D-9, ES-8
97/8 Donruss 82, RA-3
96/7 Do. Canadian 55
97/8 Do. Canadian 72, SCS-26
95/6 Do. Elite 53, CE-9
96/7 Do. Elite 9, S-3
97/8 Do. Elite 96, BF-5, C-9, ✍ BF-5
97/8 Do. Preferred 122, 165, LT-1B
97/8 Do. Priority 12, 214, Post-15, Stamp-15
97/8 Do. Studio 21, HH-21, S-14, P-21
98/9 Dynagon Ice 62, -FT 9
99/0 Dynagon Ice 73
93/4 EA Sports 40
97/8 Esso 36
01/2 eTopps 28
02/3 eTopps 12
02/3 Exclusive 62, -MO 9, ✂ GWJ 7
02/3 First Edition 105, 304, 398, ✂ Jers., ✂ HSHSJers 20
94/5 Flair 48, 213-222, CIS-2, SP-3
96/7 Flair 26, CIS-2
94/5 Fleer 59, H-2
96/7 Fleer 30, 142, 143, ART-2, PA-2
95/6 Fleer Metal 45, HM-2, IS-3
96/7 Fl. Picks F50-10,DL-4, FF-9
92/3 Fleer Ultra 48, -UI 3
93/4 Fleer Ultra 121
93/4 Fleer Ultra SM 3
94/5 Fleer Ultra 60, AW3, GG1, PH1-12, PP-2, SK-2, SM-3, ✍ PH
95/6 Fleer Ultra 45, 381, EA-4, PP-1, UV1
96/7 Fl. Ultra 50, PL-1,UP-4
91/2 Gillette 12
95 Globe 175
96/7 Got-Um
01/2 Heads Up 34
02/3 Heads Up 41, ✂ GWQ 9, ✂ GWQ 30
93/4 Hockey Wit 69
99/0 HoloGrFX 23
95/6 Hoyle / West. A-Spade
92/3 Humpty Dumpty
02/3 In The Game-Used 29, 129, ✂ E34, ✂ GUJ36, ✂ SJ36, ✂ T20, ✂ TM11
91 Ivan Fiodorov 2
94 Koululainen
91/2 Kraft 51
94/5 Kraft / PB [x2]
95/6 Kraft / IP
96/7 Kraft / TT, KD
97/8 Kraft / JTP, KD
99/0 Kraft / KD
93/4 Leaf 129
94/5 Leaf 155, FOI-1, GLS-1, LL-7
95/6 Leaf 34, FOI-7
96/7 Leaf 1, LL-16, S-11
97/8 Leaf 135, BS-16
94/5 L. Limited 81, G-9
95/6 L. Limited 49, SG-11
96/7 L. Limited 61
96/7 L. Preferred 65, LS-1, SP-7
97/8 Limited 98, 126, 197, FG-6
96/7 Maggers 51
92/3 McDonald's McD-06
94/5 McDonald's McD-12
95/6 McDonald's McD-17
96/7 McDonald's McD-26
01/2 McDonald's 11
02/3 McDonald's -CC 3
96/7 Metal Univ. 45, IC-5, LW-3
99/0 Millenium 89, P-5, D-7, ✍ Aut. 89, ✍ P-5, ✍ D-7, ✂ J-19, ✂✍ J-19, ✂ JS-19
01/2 Nextel
95/6 Cool Trade 7
98/9 NHL Power Play
90/1 O-Pee-Chee 19R
91/2 O-Pee-Chee 8
91/2 O-Pee-Chee 401
92/3 O-Pee-Chee 195
01/2 O-Pee-Chee 53
02/3 O-Pee-Chee 46
98/9 OPC Chrome 67
90/1 OPC Premier 30
91/2 OPC Premier 68
91/2 OPC Premier 173
92/3 OPC Premier SP20
98/9 Omega 79, -EOP 9, -FTF 4, -Onl. 14, -PI 13, -Prism 8
99/0 Omega 81, -CC 8
98/9 Pacific 91, -DI 9, -GCDC 13, -TW 5
99/0 Pacific 138
00/1 Pacific 147, ES-4
01/2 Pacific 139, 429, GCDC 9, WAS 3
02/3 Pacific 127, ✂ GWJ 16
02/3 Pacific Complete 104
97/8 Pacific CC 91, CS-6, SS-3B
97/8 Pa. Crown Roy. 45, BOS-8
98/9 Pa. Crown Roy. 44, -MP 9, -PotG 12, -PP 8
97/8 Pa. Dynagon 41, DD-7A, T-8, BKS-32
97/8 Pa. Invincible 46, AZ-9, FP-12, OTG-7, R-69
97/8 Pa. Paramount 65, BN-8
98/9 Pa. Paramount 74, -SD 7
99/0 Pa. Paramount 80, PB-16
00/1 Pa. Paramount 85, FF-14
98/9 Pa. Revolution 47, -CTCL 8, -Show. 16
98/9 Panini Photocard
91/2 Panini Sticker 145
91/2 Panini Sticker 340
92/3 Panini Sticker 113
92/3 Panini Sticker 291
93/4 Panini Sticker 246
94/5 Panini Sticker 210, 236a, BB
95/6 Panini Sticker 178
96/7 Panini Sticker 178
97/8 Panini Sticker 148
98/9 Panini Sticker 129
99/0 Panini Sticker 232
00/1 Panini Sticker 151
95 Panini Worlds 282
91/2 Parkhurst 38
91/2 Parkhurst PHC5
92/3 Parkhurst 39
92/3 Parkhurst 219
93/4 Parkhurst 58
93/4 Parkhurst W10
94/5 Parkhurst 305, V39, YCTG-7
95/6 Parkhurst 238, 337, CCB-14, IAS-4, PP-3, PP-52
00/1 Parkhurst P-85
01/2 Parkhurst 96, ✂ PJ55, ✂ PS40, ✂ PSJ9, ✂ HSHSJers
02/3 Parkhurst 73, ✂ GJ28, ✂ SJ28, ✂ PP7, ✂ TT4
02/3 Parkhurst Retro 44, ✂ RJ28, ✂ RSJ28, ✂ HSHSJers, ✂ RM13
94/5 Parkie SE50, ES16
91/2 Pinnacle 157
92/3 Pinnacle 20
92/3 Pinnacle T2K 30
93/4 Pinnacle 54
93/4 Pinnacle T2K1 24
94/5 Pinnacle 150, GR3, TP8, WE5
95/6 Pinnacle 44, GG-7, CS-7, R20-6
96/7 Pinnacle 21, BTN-3, T-3
97/8 Pinnacle 77, P-21
96/7 Pi. Be A Player BB-7
97/8 Pi. Be A Player TN5
97/8 Pi. BeeHive 46
97/8 Pi. Certified 56
97/8 Pi. Epix E5
95/6 Pi. FANtasy 30
96/7 Pi. FANtasy 13
97/8 Pi. Inside 42, IT-13
96/7 Pi. Mint 8
97/8 Pi. Mint 14
95/6 Pl. Summit 31, GMC-15, MH-9
96/7 Pi. Summit 105, HV-13, U-10
97/8 Pi. Totally 56
95/6 Pi. Zenith 30, ZT-9
96/7 Pi. Zenith 80, ZT-5
95/6 Playoff 34,144, 253
96/7 Playoff 437
94/5 POG 87, 267, 360
95/6 POG 95
94/5 Post
97/8 Pi. Post 13
93/4 Power Play 72
93/4 Power Play Game. 1
93/4 Power Play GG 2
93/4 Power Play SA 3
93/4 Premier 318
93/4 Premier 441
94/5 Premier 40, 276, 520, TF-3, GTG-9
00/1 Premier Plus 20, MB9, TT10
99/0 Prism 50
00/1 Private Stock 35, PS-20, PSS-11, ✂ GUG-44
01/2 Pr. Stock 32
02/3 Pr. Stock Reserve ✂ 116
00/1 PS Titanium 31, 3SS-14, WAS-3
01/2 PS Titanium 48, TAS 8
02/3 PS Titanium 35, ✂ GWJ 23
95/6 Pro Magnet 102
90/1 Pro Set 604
91/2 Pro Set 53
92/3 Pro Set 40
91 Pro Set Awards AC10
91/2 Pro Set Platinum 30
91/2 Pro Set Platinum 277
91/2 Pro Set Platinum PC7
02/3 Quest for the Cup 32, -RTC 5
91/2 Red Ace
99/0 Revolution 51, SS-16, / CSC 51
00/1 Revolution 51, HD-14, ✂ GUG-4
90/1 Score 20T
91/2 Score 250
91/2 Score 352
91/2 Score 408
91/2 Score - Hot Card 4
91/2 Score CAN 298
91/2 Score CAN 382
91/2 Score CAN 470
92/3 Score 252
93/4 Score 250
93/4 Score DD9
93/4 Score IS 3
94/5 Score DT12, NP2, TF7
95/6 Score 100, BB-13, DT-2, L-5
96/7 Score 77, DT-11, SD-14, / Promo 77
97/8 Score 91, 264
97/8 Score Detr. 3
90/1 Sco. Young Stars 9
91/2 Score Young Stars 1
92/3 Score Young Stars 5
92/3 Seasons 5
94/5 Select 10
95/6 Select CE 29, DS14
96/7 Select CE 55, C-13
94 Semic 146
94 Semic 348
91 Semic Sticker 219
92 Semic Sticker 109
00/1 Signature 105, ✍ Aut. 49, ✂ J-19, ✂ HSHSJers
01/2 Signature C-38, ✂ GUE20, ✂ GJ21, ✂ GSJ21, ✂ HSHSJers, ✂ ITN20, ✂ IB10
02/3 Signature 148, ✍ 148, ✂ SGJ36, ✂ TQ13, ✂ TM8
95/6 SBx Emotion 53, Xce-3, Xci-4
95/6 SBx Impact 52, CTI-6, IQ-9
96/7 SBx Impact 34, CTI-2, VT-2
87/8 Soviet Stars
89/0 Soviet Stars
94/5 SP 33, P-24
95/6 SP 44, E12, FX5
96/7 SP 48,CW-4, HC-5
98/9 SP Authentic 28, SS29, SO22
99/0 SP Authentic 33, SS5, ✍ SotT
00/1 SP Authentic 34
01/2 SP Authentic 29
02/3 SP Authentic 35, ✂ SP
00/1 SP GU 23, ✂ TotG, ✂ C, ✂ P
01/2 SP GU ✂ AF, ✂ AFD, ✂ AFT, ✂ AFQ, ✂ Patch, ✂ PatchC, ✂ TotG, ✂ TotGC (x3), ✂ TotGT (x2)
02/3 SP Game-Used ✂ AF (x2), ✂ PH (x2), ✂ TG
02/3 Sports Vault 213
96/7 SPx 13
97/8 SPx 15, D-SPX11
99/0 SPx 54
00/1 SPx 22, X6, ✂ WM (x2)
01/2 SPx 24, 74, ✂ HT
02/3 SPx 27, 141, ✂ M, ✂ X
98/9 SPx Prospects 23, H15, L26
99/0 Stadium 38
00/1 Stadium 184
01/2 Stadium 32, G22, NHLP5, P12, ✂ SCS, ✂ SCSD
02/3 Stadium 19, -WS-1
91/2 Star Pics 30
94/5 Starting Lineup
95/6 SLU
96/7 SLU
00/1 SLU Classic Doubles 8
95/6 Super Sticker 36, 38
96/7 Team Out✂
92/3 Topps 252
95/6 Topps 185, 373, M5, 8PL, PF5
98/9 Topps 67, L13
99/0 Topps 120
00/1 Topps 125
01/2 Topps 53, SG9
02/3 Topps 46
99/0 To. Chrome 120
00/1 To. Chrome 96
01/2 To. Chrome 53
02/3 T. Chrome 38
94/5 Topps Finest 65, BBB-7, DF-13
95/6 To. Finest 95, 186
98/9 To. Finest 34, M32, M35, M38-39, F6
98/9 T. Gold Label 20
99/0 To. Gold Label 22
00/1 To. Gold Label 38, B3, GJ, GG11
00/1 To. Heritage 41, ✍ CAI
01/2 To. Heritage 44
02/3 To. Heritage 63
02/3 T. Limited 46
96/7 Topps Picks 17, FT17, TS11
99/0 To. Prmr. Plus 70
01/2 To. Reserve 28, ✂ TR
91/2 To. Stadium 316
92/3 T. Stadium Club 244
92/3 T. Stadium Club 300
93/4 To. Stadium 45
94/5 T. Stadium Club 250, 268, F-6
95/6 To. Stadium EC169, N7
93/4 TSC Members Only 15
94/5 TSC Members Only 36
95/6 TSC Members Only 15
95/6 T. Super Skills 34
02/3 T. Total 157, TP7
91/2 Tri Globe Mag. Five / Fedorov 1-5
98/9 UD Choice 75, RW2
00/1 UD Heroes 42
00/1 UD Reserve 31, GS4
98/9 UD3 42, 102, 162
00/1 Ultimate Mem. ✍ U-19, ✂ Jers. 17, ✂ D-16, ✂ H-7, ✂ J-19, ✂ S-19, ✂ TM-1, ✂ TM-6, ✂ TM-9
01/2 Ultimate Mem. ✂ DD, ✂ Emb., ✂ Jers., ✂ S&J, ✂ Gloves, ✂ ITN, ✂ NP, ✍ Aut.
02/3 Ultimate Mem. ✂ DD, ✂ Emb, ✂ FS, ✂ GUJ, ✂ GUSJ, ✂ GAO, ✂ HT, ✂ ITN, ✂ LA, ✂ PS, ✂ SCDE, ✂ SCDJ, ✂ SCDN, ✍ RAut
99/0 Ult. Victory sg-3
90/1 Upper Deck 521, 525
91/2 Upper Deck 6
91/2 Upper Deck 40
91/2 Upper Deck 82
91/2 Upper Deck 144
91/2 Upper Deck 631
91/2 Upper Deck E9
92/3 Upper Deck 157
92/3 Upper Deck 632
92/3 Upper Deck E1
92/3 Upper Deck WG16
93/4 Upper Deck 171, SP-44
94/5 Upper Deck 37, C21, H6, H18, R4, R23, R36, R52, SP-113
95/6 Upper Deck 215, 279, AS-15, F-8, H-6, R-24, R-34, R-44, SE-115
96/7 Upper Deck 206, 250, X10, LS14, SS8B
97/8 Upper Deck 266, SS3, S11, T7A, ✂ GJ5
98/9 Upper Deck 23, 262, LS9, P29
99/0 Upper Deck 224, ✂ GJ
00/1 Upper Deck 63, F5, SS9, TT7, ✂ GJ, ✂ DGJ
01/2 Upper Deck 294, ✂ CJers, ✂ JPatch, ✂ PatchL, ✂ PoaN, ✂ PoaND, ✂ PoaNT, ✂ SCFJers, ✂ SCFJersD, ✂ SCFJersT
02/3 Upper Deck 62, ✂ ASJ, ✂ PP, ✂ PA, ✂ R50, ✂ S, ✂ SD, ✂ PW, ✂ UDPL
95/6 UD ASG MVP2
02/3 UD Artistic 33, R33, CG16, UD8, ✂ AT, / Art
93/4 Upper Deck Be A Player 5
94/5 UD BAP R145, UC7, G6
95/6 UD BAP LL8
93/4 UD BAP Roots 12
96/7 UD Black Diam. 155, RC12
97/8 UD Black Diam. 82
98/9 UD Black Diam. 29, M26
99/0 UD Black Diam. 34, D7, DS5
00/1 UD Black Diam. IG3, ✂ GG
01/2 UD Challenge CM4
02/3 UD Classic 36, ✂ CS, ✂ HH, ✂ HR
95/6 UD CC 148, 365, C2
96/7 UD CC 80, 316, UD13, S23
97/8 UD Coll. Choice 79, SQ19
97/8 UD Diam. Vision 23
98/9 UD G. Reserve 23, 262
99/0 UD G. Reserve 224
01/2 UD Honor Roll 95, DF4, SS3, ✂ GAJ
02/3 UD Honor 25, -SG14, ✂ GA
96/7 UD Ice 84

97/8 UD Ice 69, L6C
00/1 UD Ice 70, ✂ IGJ
01/2 UD Ice 17, ✂ JC, ✂ GJ
00/1 UD Legends ✍ ES, ✂ LGJ
01/2 UD Mask 35, ✂ GG, ✂ GJ, ✂ JP, ✂ DP, ✂ PM
02/3 UD Mask ✂ PG
98/9 UD MVP 68, -Snip. S12, -Souv.
99/0 UD MVP 68, W30
00/1 UD MVP 69, M7, ✂ GS
01/2 UD MVP 68, MT5, MW5
02/3 UD MVP SO8
99/0 UD MVP Cup 64, PH5, SC7, GC
99/0 UD Ovation 22, ST2
02/3 UD Piece 33, 106, AC15, ✂ PH, ✂ TT
01/2 UD Premier 24, ✂ B, ✂ D
02/3 UD Premier ✂ Jers (x2), ✂ JD, ✂ Patch
00/1 UD Pros&Prosp. 31, PM4, ✂ GJ
99/0 UD Retro 28
02/3 UD Rookie 39
01/2 UD SCup Champs 56, ✂ S, ✂ G, ✂ T
01/2 UD Top Shelf 93, ✂ J, ✂ ✍ SJ, ✂ S
02/3 UD Top Shelf 30, ✂ AS, ✂ CP, ✂ GO, ✂ HH, ✂ R, ✂ SH, ✂ ST, ✂ SW
00/1 UD Vintage 127
01/2 UD Vintage 90
02/3 UD Vintage 89, 271, GB 89, T26
00/1 Vanguard 37, IF-8, VP-6, ✂ DGJ-6
01/2 Vanguard 34, EMW 7, ✂ DGM 14
02/3 Vanguard 35, EMW 4, ✂ GWJ 18
99/0 Victory 100
00/1 Victory 85, 301
01/2 Victory 122, 400
02/3 Victory 75, -NP34
99/0 WGretzky 65, EG4
96 Wien 141
97/8 Zenith 22, Z44

FEDOROV, YURI
80 Olympic USSR
79 Panini Sticker 146
79/0 Soviet Stars 9

FEDOROV , SERGEI
02/3 Slam Card

FEDORUK, TODD
00/1 BAP Mem. 469
02/3 Pacific Complete 472
01/2 PHIL
00/1 PS Titanium Draft 170
00/1 SP Authentic 157
00/1 UD Black Diam. 105

FEDOSOV, VLADIMIR
95/6 DEL 338
96/7 DEL 313
00/1 Mir 93
91 Semic Sticker 87

FEDOTENKO, RUSLAN
00/1 BAP Mem. 477
01/2 BAP Memor. 21
01/2 Pacific 286
02/3 Pacific Complete 154
01/2 PHIL
00/1 Premier Plus 109
00/1 PS Titanium 137
00/1 PS Titanium Draft 137
00/1 SP Authentic 120
00/1 SP GU 78
01/2 SP GU ✂ AF, ✂ D
00/1 SPx 167
01/2 SPx ✂ DT
01/2 Topps OTG16
02/3 T. Total 313
00/1 UD Reserve 108
01/2 Upper Deck ✂ GN
02/3 Upper Deck 402
00/1 UD Black Diam. 130
02/3 UD Classic ✂ HR
00/1 UD Ice 98
01/2 UD Mask ✂ GJ, ✂ JP, ✂ DP
02/3 UD MVP - SD
02/3 UD Top Shelf ✂ R, ✂ ST
02/3 UD Vintage ✂ HS
01/2 Victory 261

FEDOTOV, ANATOLI
93/4 Classic 130
93/4 Cla. 4 Sport 233
92/3 Classic Prospects 97
93/4 Cla. Prospects 62
93/4 Upper Deck 38
97/8 UD Elitserien 90

FEDOTOV, SERGEI
99/0 Mir 227

FEDOTOV, SERGEI*
98/9 Florida Everblades
00/1 Mir 143
96/7 UD Ice 140

FEDUIOV, IGOR
95 Semic 132

FEDYK, BRENT
91/2 Bowman 51
90/1 DETR / Little Caesars
97/8 Detroit Vipers
96/7 Donruss 163
92/3 Fleer Ultra 371
93/4 Fleer Ultra 387
93/4 Leaf 58
94/5 Leaf 517
95/6 Leaf 290
96/7 Leaf 82
96/7 Michigan K-Wings
98/9 NYRA
91/2 O-Pee-Chee 376
90/1 OPC Premier 31
92/3 OPC Premier 26
99/0 Pacific 268
91/2 Panini Sticker 140
93/4 Panini Sticker 48
94/5 Panini Sticker 42
91/2 Parkhurst 270
92/3 Parkhurst 131
93/4 Parkhurst 148
94/5 Parkhurst 170
95/6 Parkhurst 325
92/3 PHIL / UD Sheet
92/3 PHIL / J.C. Penney
93/4 PHIL / Sheet
93/4 PHIL / Sheet
93/4 PHIL / J.C. Penney
94/5 PHIL / Sheet
93/4 Pinnacle 119
94/5 Pinnacle 326
96/7 Pinnacle 116
94/5 POG 177
95/6 POG 204
93/4 Power Play 181
93/4 Premier 211
94/5 Premier 509
90/1 Pro Set 435
91/2 Pro Set 379
88/9 ProCards / Adirondack
91/2 Score CAN 412
92/3 Score 337
93/4 Score 14
96/7 Score 191
92/3 Topps 401
91/2 To. Stadium 238
92/3 T. Stadium Club 390
93/4 To. Stadium 181
94/5 T. Stadium Club 169
91/2 Upper Deck 373
92/3 Upper Deck 443
93/4 Upper Deck 373
94/5 Upper Deck 9
95/6 Upper Deck 116
96/7 Upper Deck 46
95/6 UD BAP 100, ✍ S100
95/6 UD CC 324
99/0 Victory 194

FEHER, ARTIE
84/5 Brandon Wheat Kings
85/6 Brandon Wheat Kings

FEHR, B.J.
98/9 Kelowna Rockets
00/1 Medicine Hat Tigers

FEICHEL, MARTIN
98/9 DEL 251

FEIFFER, JASON
91/2 Air Canada SJHL 31
91/2 Air Canada SJHL A21

FEIL, CHRIS
98/9 Barrie Colts

FEISSNER, B
85/6 Minnesota-Duluth 34

FELBER, HARALD
74 Hellas MM-Jenkki 110

FELICETTI, DINO
96/7 DEL 124

FELIX, CHRIS
88/9 ProCards / Baltimore
89/0 ProCards AHL 83
90/1 ProCards 213
81/2 Soo Greyhounds
82/3 Soo Greyhounds
83/4 Soo Greyhounds
84/5 Soo Greyhounds
87/8 Soo Greyhounds 11

FELLER, JENS
95/6 DEL 347

FELSKI, SVEN
94/5 DEL 39
95/6 DEL 37
96/7 DEL 36
98/9 DEL 158, 316
99/0 Eishockey 55, 372
00/1 UD DEL 63
01/2 UD DEL 33, GA3

FELSNER, BRIAN
00/1 Cincinnati Cyclones
98/9 Detroit Vipers
99/0 Houston Aeros
97/8 Indianapolis Ice 7
97/8 Omega 50

FELSNER, DENNY
92/3 Classic 63
92/3 Classic 64
92/3 Classic Four Sport 194
93/4 Cla. Prospects 189
96/7 Milwaukee Admirals
92/3 Parkhurst 493
93/4 Parkhurst 267
94/5 Parkie SE151
92/3 Peoria Rivermen
93/4 Peoria Rivermen
92/3 Pinnacle 413
94/5 Premier 436
92/3 Score 481
92/3 Topps 514
92/3 Upper Deck 413
94/5 Upper Deck 114

FENDT, TORSTEN
95/6 DEL 9
96/7 DEL 7
00/1 UD DEL 110
01/2 UD DEL 109

FENIAK, JEFF
98/9 Calgary Hitmen 3
99/0 Calgary Hitmen
01/2 Regina Pats

FENNIG, WADE
99/0 Colorado Gold Kings
89/0 Regina Pats

FENTON, ERIC
96/7 Charlotte Checkers
94/5 Classic ✍ Aut.
92/3 Maine Black Bears
96/7 Milwaukee Admirals
97/8 Milwaukee Admirals
98/9 Milwaukee Admirals
99/0 Milwaukee Admirals
95/6 Peoria Rivermen
93/4 Portland Pirates

FENTON, JEFF
83/4 Kelowna Wings

FENTON, PAUL
90/1 Bowman 139
91/2 Bowman 256
85/6 HART / Jr. Whalers
88/9 O-Pee-Chee 213
90/1 OPC/Topps 313
91/2 O-Pee-Chee 331
92/3 O-Pee-Chee 380
91/2 OPC Premier 187
90/1 Panini Sticker 313
90/1 Panini/WPG 12, G
90/1 Pro Set 329, 533
91/2 SANJ / Sports Action
90/1 Score 156, 57T
91/2 Score 14
91/2 Score CAN 14
91/2 Score CAN 593
92/3 Score 257
92/3 Topps 173
91/2 To. Stadium 327
92/3 T. Stadium Club 224
90/1 TORO
90/1 Upper Deck 92
89/0 WINN / Safeway

FENYVES, DAVID
85/6 BUFF / Blue Shield
86/7 BUFF / Blue Shield
88/9 ProCards / Hershey
89/0 ProCards AHL 335
90/1 ProCards 32
91/2 ProCards 283

FERA, RICK
84/5 Kingston Canadians
83/4 Soo Greyhounds
94 Semic 325

FERENCE, ANDREW
99/0 BAP Mem. 312
99 Bowman 115
01/2 Bowman 138, ✂ FFJ, ✂ FFS, ✂ FFDS, ✂ FFR, ✍ YSA
98 Bowman 48
98 Bowman Chrome 48
99/0 Millenium 196, ✍ Aut. 196
99/0 NHL Power Play [x3]
97/8 Portland Winter Hawks
99/0 Prism 113
02/3 Stadium ✂ YSS22
99/0 To. Prmr. Plus 95
02/3 T. Total 302
96/7 Upper Deck 374
99/0 Upper Deck 274
01/2 Upper Deck 142
02/3 Upper Deck 142
99/0 UD G. Reserve 274
01/2 UD Vintage 205
02/3 UD Vintage 205
00/1 WBS Penguins

FERENCE, BRAD
99/0 BAP Mem. 398
00/1 BAP Mem. 295
99 Bowman 116
97 Bowman 100, 133, BB9, ✍ Aut.
98 Bowman 43, SC6
98 Bowman Chrome 43
02/3 First Edition 375
99/0 Louisville Panthers
00/1 Louisville Panthers
00/1 Pacific 191
00/1 Pa. Paramount 103
00/1 Parkhurst P-61
00/1 Signature 275, ✍ Aut. 223
97/8 Spokane Chiefs
00/1 Topps 300
00/1 To. Chrome 195
02/3 T. Total 252
98/9 UD Choice 261
02/3 Upper Deck 79
02/3 UD Vintage 313

FERGUS, TOM
83/4 BOST
84/5 BOST
90/1 Bowman 157
92/3 Bowman 273
92/3 Fleer Ultra 426
86/7 Kraft Sports 55
82/3 O-Pee-Chee 11
83/4 O-Pee-Chee 49
84/5 O-Pee-Chee 4
85/6 OPC/Topps 113
86/7 OPC/Topps 84
87/8 OPC/Topps 120
88/9 O-Pee-Chee 214
90/1 OPC/Topps 63
92/3 O-Pee-Chee 356
89/0 OPC/Topps 103
82/3 OPC/Topps Sticker 88
83/4 OPC/Topps Sticker 55
84/5 OPC Sticker 189
85/6 OPC Sticker 164-34
86/7 OPC Sticker 143
87/8 OPC Sticker 159
88/9 OPC Sticker 170-39
89/0 opcSticker 173
87/8 Panini Sticker 332
89/0 Panini Sticker 135
90/1 Panini Sticker 282
91/2 Parkhurst 400
82/3 Post [Bost.]
90/1 Pro Set 279
91/2 Pro Set 234
91/2 Pro Set Platinum 238
90/1 Score 285
91/2 Score CAN 234
92/3 Score 190
83/4 Souhaits Keychain [Bruins]
84/5 Topps 3
92/3 Topps 311
92/3 T. Stadium Club 278
85/6 TORO
86/7 TORO
86/7 TORO
87/8 TORO / 5x8
87/8 TORO / P.L.A.Y. 7
88/9 TORO / P.L.A.Y. 3
90/1 TORO
91/2 TORO / P.L.A.Y. 15
90/1 Upper Deck 83
91/2 Upper Deck 384
92/3 VANC / Road Trip

FERGUSON, BOB
98/9 Florida Everblades
99/0 Florida Everblades
00/1 Florida Everblades
95/6 Indianapolis Ice
97/8 Indianapolis Ice 1

FERGUSON, CHRIS
99/0 Medicine Hat Tigers

FERGUSON, CRAIG
96/7 Carolina Monarchs
99/0 Choice 2
93/4 Cla. Prospects 45
92/3 Fredericton Canadiens
93/4 Fredericton Canadiens
94/5 Fredericton Canadiens
94/5 Leaf 525
99/0 Louisville Panthers
98/9 New Haven Beast 1

FERGUSON, DALLAS
98/9 Anchorage Aces
99/0 Anchorage Aces

FERGUSON, DAN
89/0 Soo Greyhounds
90/1 7th..Sketch OHL 358

FERGUSON, GEORGE
74/5 Loblaws Update
82/3 MINS
83/4 MINS
74/5 O-Pee-Chee 302
75/6 O-Pee-Chee 77
76/7 O-Pee-Chee 286
77/8 O-Pee-Chee 266
78/9 O-Pee-Chee 395
79/0 O-Pee-Chee 139
80/1 O-Pee-Chee 44
81/2 O-Pee-Chee 262
82/3 O-Pee-Chee 268
83/4 O-Pee-Chee 171
81/2 OPC Sticker 184
82/3 OPC/Topps Sticker 150
82/3 Post [Pitt.]
75/6 Topps 77
79/0 Topps 139
80/1 Topps 44
72/3 TORO
74/5 TORO
75/6 TORO
76/7 TORO
77/8 TORO

FERGUSON, IAN
83/4 Oshawa Generals

FERGUSON, JEFF
88/9 Lethbridge Hurricanes
89/0 Spokane Chiefs

FERGUSON, JOHN
99/0 BAP Mem. CH-9, ✍ CH-9
45-64 BeeHive-2 [Mont.]
64-67 BeeHive-3 [Mont.]
63-65 Chex
60/1 Cleveland Barons
64/5 Coke/Sprite [Mont.]
65/6 Coca-Cola
70/1 Dad's Cookies
70/1 Esso Power Player
66/7 MONT / IGA Stamp
67/8 MONT
67/8 MONT / IGA Card
68/9 MONT / IGA Card
69/0 MONT / Pro Star
70/1 MONT
68/9 O-Pee-Chee 20
69/0 O-Pee-Chee 7
70/1 O-Pee-Chee 264
63/4 Parkhurst 33
63/4 Parkhurst 92
02/3 Parkie - Reprint 289, 298
95/6 Parkie 66-67 59
94/5 Parkie Tall 66
68/9 Post Marble
89/0 ProCards AHL 198
90/1 ProCards 60
91/2 ProCards 74
68/9 Shirriff / Mont. 10
64/5 Topps 4
65/6 Topps 10
66/7 Topps 70
66/7 Topps / Test 65
67/8 Topps 69
69/0 Topps 7
02/3 Topps - SCH, ✍ SCH
01/2 Topps Archives 50
63/4 Toronto Star Weekend
02/3 Ultimate Mem. ✂ FS
91/2 Ultimate Original Six 9, ✍ Aut. 9
79/0 WINN
83/4 WINN
84/5 WINN / Safety Tips
85/6 WINN
85/6 WINN / Safety Tips
86/7 WINN
63/4 York 35
67/8 York 16
67/8 York 21

FERGUSON, JOHN
02/3 Fleer Throwbacks 48

FERGUSON, LORNE
45-64 BeeHive-2 [Bost.]
51/2 Parkhurst 35
93/4 Parkie 56-57 54
54/5 Topps 31
57/8 Topps 40
58/9 Topps 55
58/9 Toronto Star Photo

FERGUSON, NORM
70/1 Colgate 56
70/1 Dad's Cookies
70/1 Eddie Sargent 142
71/2 Eddie Sargent 136
69/0 O-Pee-Chee 146
71/2 O-Pee-Chee 179
75/6 OPC WHA 92
77/8 OPC WHA 52
90/1 ProCards 241
91/2 ProCards 236
76/7 San Diego Mariners
72 Semic Sticker 173
71/2 Toronto Sun Photo

FERGUSON, SCOTT
98/9 Cincinnati M'Ducks 28
99/0 Cincinnati M'Ducks
00/1 Hamilton Bulldogs
93/4 Kamloops Blazers
99/0 Pacific 3
91/2 7th...Sketch WHL 77

FERGUSON, SIMON
99/0 Lethbridge Hurricanes

FERGUSON, TIM
94/5 DEL 23
95/6 DEL 20
96/7 DEL 17
98/9 Florida Everblades
99/0 Florida Everblades

FERLAND, JEANNOT
91/2 7th...Sketch LHJMQ 187

FERLAND, JONATHAN
96 Québec Pee Wee 205

FERLARD, JEANNOT
90/1 7th..Sketch LHJMQ 259

FERMOYLE, ANDY
00/1 Quad City Mallards

FERNANDEZ, MANNY
01/2 Adrenaline 91, PP19
01/2 Atomic 49
02/3 Atomic 52
00/1 BAP Mem. 119
01/2 BAP Memor. 214
02/3 BAP Memorabilia 92, 255
01/2 BT Pipes 39, -Mask, ✂ Jers., ✂ S&J, ✂ HSHSJers
02/3 Between the Pipes 18, 135, M15, ✂ GUE9, ✂ GUJ9, ✂ GSJ9, ✂ ITN9
02/3 Bowman 56
94/5 Cla. Images 24, CE12, PR9
01/2 Crown Royale 73
02/3 Crown Royale 47, ✂ GWDP 13
93/4 Donruss CAN10
95/6 Donruss 10
96/7 Do. Canadian LG 8
95/6 Edge Ice 139, QM-1, TW-2
02/3 Exclusive 86, ✂ GWJ 13
02/3 First Edition 42, ✂ Jers.
01/2 Heads Up 48
02/3 Heads Up 60, ✂ GWQ 14
95/6 Leaf 169
96/7 Michigan K-Wings
01/2 MINW / Crime 23
01/2 O-Pee-Chee 175
02/3 O-Pee-Chee 74
97/8 Omega 68
99/0 Omega 71
98/9 Pacific 175
00/1 Pacific 129
01/2 Pacific 193
02/3 Pacific 181, ✂ GWJ 24
02/3 Pacific Complete 17
00/1 Pa. Paramount 118
00/1 Panini Sticker 177
95/6 Parkhurst 63
00/1 Parkhurst P-109
01/2 Parkhurst 45
02/3 Parkhurst 76
02/3 Parkhurst Retro 111
93/4 Pinnacle 457
95/6 Pinnacle 216
00/1 Private Stock 48, 124
01/2 Pr. Stock 47
02/3 Pr. Stock Reserve 49
00/1 PS Titanium 45
01/2 PS Titanium ✂ DSJ 67
01/2 PS Titanium Draft ✂ 44
02/3 PS Titanium 52
02/3 Quest for the Cup 47
00/1 Revolution 71
95/6 Score 299
91/2 7th...Sketch LHJMQ 242
00/1 Signature 57, ✍ Aut. 71
01/2 Signature 187, ✍ Aut. 187, ✂ TM15
95/6 SBx Impact Fox 14
00/1 SP Authentic 45
01/2 SP Authentic 41, 117, ✍ SotT, ✍ SotTD
02/3 SP Authentic 45, ✍ SotT
00/1 SP GU 31
02/3 SP Game-Used ✍ Sig
02/3 Sports Vault 250
00/1 SPx 34, 140
02/3 SPx 39
00/1 Stadium 204
01/2 Stadium 58, NR7, ✍ NR
00/1 Topps 283
01/2 Topps 175
02/3 Topps 74
00/1 To. Chrome 178
01/2 To. Chrome 120
02/3 T. Chrome 50
01/2 To. Heritage 67
02/3 T. Limited 74
01/2 To. Reserve 53
02/3 T. Total 229
00/1 UD Heroes 59
01/2 UD PlayMakers Ltd 49
00/1 Ultimate Mem. ✂ G-15
93/4 Upper Deck 536
00/1 Upper Deck 87, 314
01/2 Upper Deck 87
02/3 Upper Deck 333
02/3 UD Artistic 45, R45, / Art
01/2 UD Challenge 41
02/3 UD Classic 48
02/3 UD Honor 37, ✍ SC
01/2 UD Ice 24
01/2 UD Mask 115
02/3 UD Mask 42, 43, 44, 110
00/1 UD MVP 96
01/2 UD MVP 94
02/3 UD MVP 90, ✍ PSig
02/3 UD Piece 47
02/3 UD Premier ✍ Sig.
00/1 UD Pros&Prosp. 42
02/3 UD Top Shelf 42
00/1 UD Vintage 175, 184, 185
01/2 UD Vintage 124, 130
02/3 UD Vintage 129, 275
00/1 Vanguard 126
01/2 Vanguard 47
01/2 Victory 170, 175
02/3 Victory 107

FERNER, MARK
91/2 Baltimore Skipjacks
84/5 Kamloops Blazers
97/8 Long Beach Ice Dogs
98/9 Long Beach Ice Dogs
93/4 Parkhurst 275
93/4 Premier 478
88/9 ProCards / Rochester
89/0 ProCards AHL 89
90/1 ProCards 208
91/2 ProCards 568
93/4 To. Stadium 342

FERONE, PAUL
01/2 Belfast Giants
01/2 Manchester Storm

FERRANTI, STEVE
93/4 Michigan State

FERRARO, CHRIS
00/1 Albany River Rats
94/5 Atlanta Knights 11
95/6 Binghampton Rangers
96/7 Binghampton Rangers
94/5 Classic 39, ✍ Aut.
93/4 Cla. Prospects LP4
95/6 Edge Ice 18
93/4 Fleer Ultra 482
95/6 Future Legends 6
96/7 Leaf 229
92/3 Maine Black Bears
97/8 Pa. Dynagon BKS-60
96/7 Pinnacle 233
93/4 Power Play 502
93/4 Premier - USA Hockey 9
94 Semic 129
93/4 To. Stadium - Team U.S.A. 5
91/2 Upper Deck 648
91/2 Upper Deck WJC 74

FERRARO, PETER
94/5 Atlanta Knights 9
98/9 Be A Player 161, ✍ Aut. 161
95/6 Binghampton Rangers
96/7 Binghampton Rangers
95/6 Bowman 134
99/0 Choice 3
94/5 Classic 38, ✍ Aut.
93/4 Cla. Images 4 Sport 35
93/4 Cla. Prospects IA10
93/4 Cla. Prospects LP5
95/6 Edge Ice 17
96/7 Fleer 126, CC-3
96/7 Fl. Picks 140
93/4 Fleer Ultra 483
95/6 Future Legends 7
97/8 Hartford Wolf Pack
x96/7 Leaf GLR-4
92/3 Maine Black Bears
96/7 Metal Univ. 178
96/7 Panini Sticker 300
95 Panini Worlds 235
95/6 Parkhurst 532
96/7 Pinnacle 218
96/7 Pi. Summit 181
93/4 Power Play 503
93/4 Premier - USA Hockey 15
99/0 Providence Bruins
00/1 Providence Bruins
94 Semic 132
95/6 SBx Impact 211
96/7 SBx Impact 149, Win
93/4 To. Stadium - Team U.S.A. 6
91/2 Upper Deck 648
91/2 Upper Deck 696
91/2 Upper Deck WJC 83

FERRARO, RAY
01/2 Adrenaline 7
02/3 Atomic ✂ GWJ 21
99/0 BAP Mem. 255
00/1 BAP Mem. 297
01/2 BAP Memor. 272, 483
96/7 Bic.Sports Aces 3-C
90/1 Bowman 258
91/2 Bowman 212
92/3 Bowman 128
92/3 Bowman 229
01/2 Bowman 23
83/4 Brandon Wheat Kings
01/2 Crown Royale 5
93/4 Donruss 198
94/5 Donruss 162
95/6 Donruss 144, 297
96/7 Donruss 183
97/8 Do. Canadian 98
99/0 Dynagon Ice 16
94/5 Fleer 120
96/7 Fleer 49
95/6 Fleer Metal 94
92/3 Fleer Ultra 123
93/4 Fleer Ultra 16
94/5 Fleer Ultra 324
95/6 Fleer Ultra 93, 273
85/6 HART / Jr. Whalers
86/7 HART / Jr. Whalers
87/8 HART / Jr. Whalers
88/9 HART / Jr. Whalers
89/0 HART / Jr. Whalers
01/2 Heads Up 3
93/4 Hockey Wit 84
95/6 Hoyle / East. J-Heart
92/3 Humpty Dumpty
95/6 Kraft / KD
93/4 Leaf 121
94/5 Leaf 334
95/6 Leaf 284
96/7 L. Preferred 16
99/0 Millenium 14, ✍ Aut. 14
86/7 OPC/Topps 160
87/8 OPC/Topps 109
88/9 OPC/Topps 114
90/1 OPC/Topps 336
91/2 O-Pee-Chee 304
92/3 O-Pee-Chee 42
01/2 O-Pee-Chee 50
89/0 OPC/Topps 70
92/3 OPC Premier SP1
86/7 OPC Sticker 57-195
88/9 OPC Sticker 268-132
89/0 opcSticker 263-142
99/0 Omega 11
99/0 Pacific 189
00/1 Pacific 18
01/2 Pacific 16, 402
02/3 Pacific 322, ✂ GWJ 44
97/8 Pacific CC 53
97/8 Pa. Dynagon 59, T-40, BKS-45
97/8 Pa. Invincible 66
00/1 Pa. Paramount 13
87/8 Panini Sticker 46
88/9 Panini Sticker 241
89/0 Panini Sticker 222
90/1 Panini Sticker 45
91/2 Panini Sticker 250
92/3 Panini Sticker 198
94/5 Panini Sticker 46
95/6 Panini Sticker 103
96/7 Panini Sticker 269
97/8 Panini Sticker 224
99/0 Panini Sticker 12
00/1 Panini Sticker 8
91/2 Parkhurst 110
92/3 Parkhurst 98
92/3 Parkhurst 499
93/4 Parkhurst 123
94/5 Parkhurst 134, V86
95/6 Parkhurst 409
00/1 Parkhurst P-177
01/2 Parkhurst 102
91/2 Pinnacle 123
92/3 Pinnacle 154
93/4 Pinnacle 48
94/5 Pinnacle 314
96/7 Pinnacle 29
97/8 Pinnacle 146
96/7 Pi. Be A Player 139, ✍ Aut. 139
97/8 Pi. Certified 82
97/8 Pi. Inside 180
95/6 Pi. Summit 108
97/8 Pi. Totally 82
95/6 Playoff 173
96/7 Playoff 380
94/5 POG 154
95/6 POG 178
93/4 Power Play 382
93/4 Premier 349
94/5 Premier 335
00/1 Private Stock 4
01/2 Pr. Stock -PS 3
02/3 PS Titanium ✂ GWJ 57
90/1 Pro Set 104
91/2 Pro Set 156
92/3 Pro Set 105
91/2 Pro Set Platinum 76
99/0 Revolution 7
00/1 Revolution 6
90/1 Score 134, 15T
91/2 Score 48
91/2 Score CAN 48
92/3 Score 298
92/3 Score SS 3
93/4 Score 60
95/6 Score 66
96/7 Score 107
97/8 Score 169
94/5 Select 41
01/2 Signature 30, ✍ Aut. 30
95/6 SBx Emotion 111
95/6 SBx Impact 107
96/7 SBx Impact 57
94/5 SP 69
99/0 SP Authentic 4
99/0 SPx 3
00/1 SPx 131
99/0 Stadium 151
00/1 Stadium 49
01/2 Stadium 25
92/3 Topps 324
95/6 Topps 245
99/0 Topps 237
00/1 Topps 69
01/2 Topps 50
99/0 To. Chrome 237
00/1 To. Chrome 55
01/2 To. Chrome 50
95/6 To. Finest 36
00/1 To. Heritage 191
01/2 To. Heritage 23
96/7 Topps Picks 119
01/2 To. Reserve 50
91/2 To. Stadium 3
92/3 T. Stadium Club 123
93/4 To. Stadium 50
93/4 To. Stadium - Master Photo-1 6
94/5 T. Stadium Club 20
95/6 To. Stadium 120
95/6 T. Super Skills 23
01/2 UD PlayMakers Ltd 4
99/0 Ult. Victory 5
90/1 Upper Deck 289
91/2 Upper Deck 311
92/3 Upper Deck 12
92/3 Upper Deck 193
93/4 Upper Deck 153, SP-09
94/5 Upper Deck 14
95/6 Upper Deck 90, SE-143
96/7 Upper Deck 273
99/0 Upper Deck 178
00/1 Upper Deck 9
01/2 Upper Deck 7
94/5 UD BAP ✍ 92
96/7 UD Black Diam. 74
95/6 UD CC 33
96/7 UD CC 131, 320
99/0 UD G. Reserve 178
00/1 UD MVP 13
01/2 UD MVP 8
99/0 UD MVP Cup 8
00/1 UD Vintage 22
01/2 UD Vintage 14, 16, 17
00/1 Vanguard 4
99/0 Victory 19
00/1 Victory 16
01/2 Victory 21
99/0 WGretzky 11

FERRARO (ATL), RAY
01/2 PS Titanium Draft ✂ 84

FERRAS, JOE
88/9 ProCards / Adirondack

FERSCHWEILER, PAT
95/6 Kansas City Blades
98/9 Kansas City Blades 10
99/0 Kansas City Blades
00/1 Kudos 77
92/3 W. Michigan Broncos

FERSCHWELLER, PAT
93/4 Roanoke Express
94/5 Roanoke Express

FERSTER, RYLAN
96/7 Guildford Flames 11

FESER, COLLIN
84/5 Prince Albert Raiders

FESER, TILL
94/5 DEL 283
95/6 DEL 278
96/7 DEL 175

FESS, CHRIS
94/5 Knoxville Cherokees
96/7 Knoxville Cherokees

FETISOV, VIACHESLAV
90/1 Bowman 80
91/2 Bowman 273
92/3 Bowman 145
95/6 Donruss 272
96/7 Donruss 28
96/7 Do. Elite 99
93/4 EA Sports 74
96/7 Flair 27
96/7 Fleer 143
92/3 Fleer Ultra 337
95 Globe 236
91 Ivan Fiodorov 3
95/6 Leaf 280
96/7 Leaf 42
96/7 L. Limited 26
96/7 L. Preferred 34
00/1 Mir Fetisov 8
89/0 NJER
89/0 NJER / Caretta
90/1 NJER
90/1 OPC/Topps 27
91/2 O-Pee-Chee 175
92/3 O-Pee-Chee 162
97/8 Omega 78
98/9 Pacific 190
97/8 Pacific CC 111
97/8 Pa. Revolution 46
79 Panini Sticker 141
90/1 Panini Sticker 75, 339
96/7 Panini Sticker 187
91/2 Parkhurst 96
92/3 Parkhurst 334
95/6 Parkhurst 68, 249
91/2 Pinnacle 101
92/3 Pinnacle 247
92/3 Pinnacle 299
93/4 Pinnacle 397
96/7 Pi. Summit 128
95/6 POG 100
97/8 Pi. Post 24
93/4 Power Play 136
90/1 Pro Set 167
91/2 Pro Set 142
92/3 Pro Set 96
91/2 Pro Set Platinum 199
91/2 Red Ace
90/1 Score 62
91/2 Score 184
91/2 Score CAN 184
92/3 Score 97
93/4 Score 229
96/7 Score 73
97/8 Score Detr. 11
82 Semic Sticker 53
89 Semic Sticker 87
91 Semic Sticker 213
79/0 Soviet Stars 10
83/4 Soviet Stars
87/8 Soviet Stars
89/0 Soviet Stars
92/3 Topps 458
91/2 To. Stadium 24
92/3 T. Stadium Club 392
93/4 To. Stadium 265
98/9 UD Choice RW15
90/1 Upper Deck 176
91/2 Upper Deck 410
92/3 Upper Deck 278
94/5 Upper Deck 434
96/7 UD Black Diam. 2

FETTA, JOEY
98/9 Québec Remparts

FEUERSTEIN, H
95/6 Richmond Renegades

FEWSTER, NEIL
91/2 7th...Sketch OHL 208
93/4 Slapshot / Niagara Falls 15
94/5 Slapshot / Guelph 11

FIALA, JAN
99/0 OFS 377

FIALA, LUKAS
98/9 OFS 323

FIALA, PETR
99/0 OFS 322
00/1 OFS 108

FIANDER, CRAIG
93/4 Fredericton Canadiens

FIBIGER, JESSE
02/3 BAP Memorabilia 312
01/2 Cleveland Barons
02/3 UD Rookie 137

FICAL, PETR
97/8 APS 241

FICENEC, JAKUB
95/6 APS 129
98/9 EBK ECHL All-Star
99/0 Portland Pirates
00/1 Portland Pirates
01/2 UD DEL 6

FICHAUD, ÉRIC
94/5 Assets 62, 87, DC24
98/9 Be A Player 227, ✍ Aut. 227
01/2 BT Pipes 51
02/3 Between the Pipes 71
98/9 Bicycle.. 5-D
95/6 Bowman 155
94/5 Classic 14, C3, CP2, T68
94/5 Classic 4 Sport 130
94/5 Cla. Images 13
94/5 Cla. Images 4 Sport 107, CP20
96/7 Donruss RR 8
97/8 Donruss 183
96/7 Do. Canadian 120, LG-6
x97/8 Do. Canadian LG 8
95/6 Do. Elite R-6
96/7 Do. Elite 132, A-14
97/8 Do. Elite 87
97/8 Do. Preferred 49, CG-8
97/8 Do. Priority 40, PG-12
97/8 Do. Studio 91
95/6 Edge Ice 93, TW-11
94/5 Flair 179
96/7 Flair 115
96/7 Fleer 127, CC-4
94/5 Fleer Ultra 376
96/7 Fl. Ultra 100, UR-7
95/6 Future Legends 8, PC-2
02/3 Hamilton Bulldogs
94/5 Leaf 443, P-7
96/7 Leaf GLR-9
97/8 Leaf 20, PD-15
94/5 L. Limited 45
96/7 L. Limited 69
96/7 L. Preferred 119, LS-53
97/8 Limited 59, 124, 174, FG-56
96/7 Maggers 97
96/7 Metal Univ. 179
98/9 NASH / Wendy's 9
96/7 NYIS
97/8 Pacific CC 274
96/7 Panini Sticker 90, 303
95/6 Parkhurst 537
94/5 Parkie SE174
94/5 Pinnacle 493
96/7 Pinnacle 228
97/8 Pinnacle 66
96/7 Pi. Be A Player 214, ✍ Aut. 214
97/8 Pi. Inside 31, SU-5
96/7 Pi. Summit 178
96/7 Pi. Zenith 116
95/6 POG 177
94/5 Premier 533
99/0 Québec Citadelles 15
00/1 Québec Citadelles
96/7 Score 256
97/8 Score 26
94/5 Select 188
96/7 Select CE 103
94/5 SR Gold Standard 83
96/7 SBx Impact 150
95/6 SP 90
96/7 SP 92
94/5 Topps Finest 77
96/7 Topps Picks RS15
94/5 Upper Deck 338
96/7 Upper Deck 96, X27, SS12B
97/8 Upper Deck 102
96/7 UD Black Diam. 105
96/7 UD CC 155, 323
97/8 UD Coll. Choice 153

FICHUK, PETE
72 Semic Sticker 131

FICORELLI, TERRY
91/2 Cincinnati Cyclones
92/3 Cincinnati Cyclones
93/4 Cincinnati Cyclones
94/5 Cincinnati Cyclones
95/6 Muskegon Fury
98/9 Muskegon Fury
99/0 Muskegon Fury

FIDDLER, VERNON
02/3 BAP Memorabilia 314
02/3 Calder 128
98/9 Kelowna Rockets
00/1 Medicine Hat Tigers
02/3 Pacific Complete 510
02/3 PS Titanium 123
02/3 Quest for the Cup 128
02/3 SP Authentic 176
02/3 Ultimate Mem. 92
02/3 Upper Deck 456
02/3 UD Honor 119
02/3 UD Mask 127
02/3 UD Premier 59

FIDLER, MIKE
79/0 MINS
77/8 O-Pee-Chee 290
78/9 O-Pee-Chee 84
79/0 O-Pee-Chee 219
81/2 O-Pee-Chee 136
79 Panini Sticker 217
78/9 Topps 84
79/0 Topps 219

FIEBELKORN, JED
98/9 Grand Rapids Griffins
91/2 Minnesota G'Gophers
92/3 Minnesota G'Gophers
93/4 Minnesota G'Gophers
94/5 Minnesota G'Gophers

FIEDLER, JONAS
02/3 Plymouth Whalers

FIELD, WILF
34-43 BeeHive-1 [NYAm.]
39/0 O-Pee-Chee 64

FIELDER, GUYLE
57/8 Topps 36

FIFE, JEFF
89/0 7th..Sketch OHL 93, 197

FIGIOMENI, MIKE
00/1 Rockford IceHogs

FIGLIOMENI, MIKE
99/0 Rockford IceHogs

FIGLIUZZI, STEFANO
96/7 DEL 120
95 Globe 233
95 Panini Worlds 89
94 Semic 302
93 Semic Sticker 227
96 Wien 178

FILATOV, ANATOLI
00/1 Mir 95
93/4 Slapshot / Niagara Falls 22

FILCHEL, TODD
90/1 ProCards 247

FILEWICH, JONATHAN
00/1 Prince George Cougars

FILIATRAULT, JEAN-IAN
98/9 Oklahoma City Blazers

FILIATRAULT, JEAN-MICHEL
02/3 Québec Remparts

FILIMONOV, DMITRI
93/4 Donruss 239
94/5 Donruss 97
93/4 Fleer Ultra 381
95/6 Indianapolis Ice
93/4 Leaf 400
93/4 OTTA
93/4 Parkhurst 139
94/5 Parkhurst 162
93/4 Pinnacle 450
93/4 Power Play 398
93/4 Premier 496
92/3 Red Ace Blue 6
93/4 Score 598
92 Semic Sticker 106
93 Semic Sticker 132
91/2 Star Pics 19
93/4 To. Stadium 468
91/2 Upper Deck 3
93/4 Upper Deck 405, SP-109
94/5 Upper Deck 178

FILIMONOV, OLEG
98/9 Mir 72
99/0 Mir 88
00/1 Mir 1

FILINOV, EVGENI
99/0 Mir 238

FILION, MAURICE
72/3 Québec Nordiques

FILIP, JAN
94/5 APS 27

FILIP, MARTIN
96/7 APS 111
97/8 APS 182
99/0 DS 27
96/7 DS Sticker 279
97/8 DS Sticker 158
98/9 OFS 87
99/0 OFS 133, 360
00/1 OFS 49

FILIPEK, DARYL
91/2 Ferris State Bulldogs

FILIPENKO, MARK
92/3 BCJHL 132

FILIPENKO, WAYNE
91/2 Air Canada SJHL A20

FILIPI, MILAN
94/5 APS 39
98/9 OFS 207
99/0 OFS 179
00/1 OFS 24

FILIPOWICZ, JAYME
99/0 Milwaukee Admirals
00/1 Milwaukee Admirals
01/2 Québec Citadelles

FILIPPOV, ALEXANDER
98/9 Mir 64
99/0 Mir 121
00/1 Mir 180

FILLION, BOB
45-64 BeeHive-2 [Mont.]
48-52 Exhibits [Canadiens]
43-47 Parade Sportive
45-54 Quaker Oats

FILLION, CLAUDE
95/6 Hampton Roads

FILLION, DENIS
51/2 Bas du Fleuve 57
52/3 Bas du Fleuve 44

FILLION, JEAN-MARIE
51/2 Bas du Fleuve 48

FILLION, JIMMY
01/2 Shawinigan 4

FILLION, MARCEL
51/2 Bas du Fleuve 58
52/3 Bas du Fleuve 34

FILLION, MARTIN
98/9 Quad City Mallards

FILLION, PIERRE
90/1 7th..Sketch LHJMQ 169

FIMIN, YURI
98/9 Mir 70
99/0 Mir 117

FINDLAY, ANDY
02/3 Dundee Texol Stars

FINDLAY, TIM
94/5 Sig. Rookies 61, ✍ 61
94/5 Slapshot / Windsor 26
95/6 Slapshot 429

FINK, PATRIK
94/5 APS 178
95/6 APS 194
96/7 APS 328
99/0 OFS 463
00/1 OFS 203
01/2 OFS 262

FINKBEINER, LLOYD
51/2 Laval Dairy 90

FINLEY, BRIAN
98/9 Barrie Colts
99 Bowman 40, 141, SC5, ✍ BA1
98 Bowman 21, 161, SC17
98 Bowman Chrome 21, 161
98/9 OPC Chrome 240
99/0 UD Sobey's 12
98/9 SP Authentic 114, ✍ SotT
99/0 SPx 167
98/9 SPx Prospects 61
98/9 Topps 240
99/0 Topps 261
99/0 To. Chrome 261
98/9 Upper Deck 391
99/0 Upper Deck 316
98/9 UD Black Diam. 96
99/0 UD Black Diam. 97
98/9 UD G. Reserve 391
99/0 UD G. Reserve 316
99/0 UD MVP Cup 210, ✍ PS
99/0 UD Ovation 69
99/0 UD Prospects 14, C8, DS7, ✍ Sig.
00/1 UD Prospects 32, CC1, CS2

FINLEY, JEFF
00/1 BAP Mem. 100
98/9 Hartford Wolf Pack
94/5 Hershey Bears
97/8 Pa. Invincible R-151
93/4 PHIL / Sheet
93/4 PHIL / J.C. Penney
96/7 PHOE / Coca-Cola
96/7 Pi. Be A Player 156, ✍ Aut. 156
86/7 Portland Winter Hawks
93/4 Power Play 405
88/9 ProCards / Springfield
89/0 ProCards AHL 252
90/1 ProCards 503
91/2 ProCards 470
99/0 SLOU / Taco Bell 10
92/3 T. Stadium Club 426

FINN, MICHEL
00/1 Chicoutimi Saguenéens 4

FINN, RON
90/1 Pro Set 685

FINN, SEAN
89/0 Johnstown Chiefs

FINN, SHANNON
96/7 Milwaukee Admirals
97/8 Milwaukee Admirals
98/9 Milwaukee Admirals
95/6 Peoria Rivermen

FINN, STEVEN
91/2 Bowman 140
92/3 Bowman 185
92/3 Durivage 40
93/4 Durivage 20
86/7 Fredericton Express
93/4 Leaf 422
91/2 O-Pee-Chee 139
92/3 O-Pee-Chee 7
89/0 opcSticker 191-45
97/8 Pa. Invincible R-93
88/9 Panini Sticker 350
90/1 Panini/QUE 3
91/2 Panini Sticker 261
92/3 Panini Sticker 216
93/4 Panini Sticker 75
94/5 Panini Sticker 61
92/3 Parkhurst 379
91/2 Pinnacle 138
93/4 Pinnacle 307

94/5 Pinnacle 312
96/7 Pi. Be A Player 188, ✍ Aut. 188
93/4 Premier 326
94/5 Premier 398
90/1 Pro Set 514
91/2 Pro Set 204
85/6 QUÉB / Provigo
86/7 QUÉB
86/7 QUÉB / McDonald's
87/8 QUÉB / Gene. Foods
88/9 QUÉB
88/9 QUÉB / Gene. Foods
89/0 QUÉB
89/0 QUÉB / Gene. Foods
89/0 QUÉB / Police
90/1 QUÉB
90/1 QUÉB / Petro-Canada
91/2 QUÉB / Petro-Canada
92/3 QUÉB / Petro-Canada
94/5 QUÉB / Burger King
91/2 Score 278
91/2 Score CAN 498
92/3 Score 44
93/4 Score 322
92/3 Topps 449
91/2 To. Stadium 56
92/3 T. Stadium Club 384
93/4 To. Stadium 464
93/4 To. Stadium - Master Photo-2 9
94/5 T. Stadium Club 192
91/2 Upper Deck 340
96/7 UD CC 132

FINN-OLSSON, JONAS
99/0 UD Elitserien 198

FINNERTY, RYAN
01/2 Peoria Rivermen
02/3 Peoria Rivermen

FINNEY, MARK
96/7 Guildford Flames 10

FINNIE, JOHN
90 7th..Sketch Mem.Cup 28

FINNIGAN, FRANK
33/4 Anonymous 26
34-43 BeeHive-1 [Toro.]
33/4 Canadian Gum
24/5 Champ's Cigarettes
36-39 Diamond Match TT1
31/2 La Presse
32/3 Maple Leafs O'Keefe
33/4 O-Pee-Chee 25
24/5 William Paterson 9

FINNSTRÖM, JOHAN
94/5 Leaf Elit Set 202, ND-4
95/6 Leaf Elit Set 115
94/5 Sig. Rookies 6, ✍ 6
94/5 SR Gold Standard 84
95/6 UD Elitserien 173
97/8 UD Elitserien 118
98/9 UD Elitserien 136
99/0 UD Elitserien 138
00/1 UD Elitserien 125

FINSTAD, MORTEN
94 Semic 260
95 Semic 180
92/3 Semic Nordisk 64
93 Semic Sticker 248

FIORENTINO, PETER
92/3 Binghampton Rangers
94/5 Binghampton Rangers
96/7 Binghampton Rangers
95/6 Las Vegas Thunder
90/1 ProCards 5
91/2 ProCards 190
87/8 Soo Greyhounds 23

FIORETTI,
92/3 Semic Nordisk 189 [Backstoppen]

FIORETTI, MARK
83/4 Kelowna Wings
84/5 Kelowna Wings &...

FIORONI, PAUL
98/9 Odessa Jackalopes

FIRSOV, ANATOLI
70/1 Kuvajulkaisut 2
72 Panda MM-Toronto
72 Semic Sticker 11
74 Semic Sticker 42
91 Semic Sticker 243
69/0 Soviet Stars
70/1 Soviet Stars
71/2 Soviet Stars
96 Wien HL5
71/2 Williams Finnish 2

FIRTH, JASON
88/9 Kitchener Rangers
89/0 Kitchener Rangers
90/1 Kitchener Rangers
99/0 Rockford IceHogs
90 7th..Sketch Mem.Cup 33
89/0 7th..Sketch OHL 184
90/1 7th..Sketch OHL 232
91/2 7th...Sketch OHL 59
94/5 Thunder Bay Senators
95/6 Thunder Bay Senators

FISCHER, COLE
97/8 Spokane Chiefs

FISCHER, CRAIG
95/6 Future Legends 18

FISCHER, JIRI
99/0 BAP Mem. 396
00/1 BAP Mem. 298
02/3 BAP Memorabilia ✂ SCC1
99 Bowman 66, SC16
98 Bowman 155, ✍ A19
98 Bowman Chrome 155
99/0 Millenium 86, C-8, ✍ Aut. 86
99/0 NHL Power Play [x3]
98/9 OPC Chrome 242
99/0 Prism 51
01/2 Signature 59, ✍ Aut. 59
98/9 Topps 242
00/1 Topps 280
99/0 To. Chrome 296
00/1 To. Chrome 175
99/0 To. Prmr. Plus 127
02/3 T. Total 15
02/3 Ultimate Mem. ✂ SCDE, ✂ SCDGJ, ✂ SCDN
99/0 Upper Deck 225
99/0 UD G. Reserve 225
99/0 WGretzky 61

FISCHER, KAI
95/6 DEL 77
96/7 DEL 271
99/0 Eishockey 303

FISCHER, LUBOMIR
94/5 APS 277
95/6 APS 99

FISCHER, PATRICK
95 Panini Worlds 128

FISCHER, RON
94/5 DEL 379
95/6 DEL 366
95 Panini Worlds 58
89 Semic Sticker 112

FISCHER, WOLFGANG
74 Hellas MM-Jenkki 112

FISET, DOMINIC
01/2 Drummondville

FISET, MIKE
85/6 Kingston Canadians
86/7 Kingston Canadians
87/8 Kingston Canadians

FISET, STÉPHANE
98/9 Aurora 86
00/1 Aurora 66
98/9 Be A Player 214, ✍ Aut. 214
99/0 BAP Mem. 250
00/1 BAP Mem. 159
01/2 BAP Memor. 490
01/2 BT Pipes 74
02/3 Between the Pipes 20, ✂ GN5
98/9 Bicycle.. J-C
92/3 Bowman 398
99/0 Crown Royale 65
00/1 Crown Royale 48
93/4 Donruss 274
94/5 Donruss 225
95/6 Donruss 390
96/7 Donruss 186
97/8 Donruss 179
96/7 Do. Canadian 17, LG-5
97/8 Do. Canadian 30, LG-5
96/7 Do. Elite 13, PW-10
97/8 Do. Elite 54
97/8 Do. Preferred 136
97/8 Do. Priority 96
97/8 Do. Studio 52
92/3 Durivage 47
93/4 Durivage 21
98/9 Dynagon Ice 87
99/0 Dynagon Ice 96
94/5 Flair 145
94/5 Fleer 175
95/6 Fleer Metal 31
93/4 Fleer Ultra 55
94/5 Fleer Ultra 173
95/6 Fleer Ultra 131, 220, 369
96/7 Fl. Ultra 78
90/1 Halifax Citadels
95/6 Hoyle / East. Q-Heart
93/4 Kraft / JELL-O
94/5 Kraft / KD
95/6 Kraft / PS
93/4 Leaf 301
94/5 Leaf 329
96/7 Leaf 188
97/8 Leaf 93
96/7 L. Limited 72
96/7 L. Preferred 57, LS-15
97/8 Limited 150, 180
01/2 Manchester Monarchs
96/7 Metal Univ. 74
99/0 Millenium 119, ✍ Aut. 119
90/1 OPC/Topps 312
92/3 O-Pee-Chee 75
97/8 Omega 107
98/9 Omega 110
99/0 Omega 107
98/9 Pacific 234
99/0 Pacific 190
00/1 Pacific 196, ITC-5
02/3 Pacific 194
97/8 Pacific CC 245
97/8 Pa. Invincible 67
97/8 Pa. Paramount 88
98/9 Pa. Paramount 104
99/0 Pa. Paramount 109
00/1 Pa. Paramount 111
98/9 Pa. Revolution 66
98/9 Panini Photocard
91/2 Panini Sticker 258
92/3 Panini Sticker 207
94/5 Panini Sticker 63
98/9 Panini Sticker 200
99/0 Panini Sticker 256
95 Panini Worlds 2
91/2 Parkhurst 363
92/3 Parkhurst 378
93/4 Parkhurst 164
95/6 Parkhurst 317
00/1 Parkhurst P-148
93/4 Pinnacle 115
93/4 Pinnacle Mask 6
94/5 Pinnacle 102
96/7 Pinnacle M-8
97/8 Pinnacle 52
97/8 Pi. Certified 14
97/8 Pi. Inside 23
95/6 Pi. Summit 160, ITC-8
96/7 Pi. Summit 98
97/8 Pi. Totally 14
95/6 Pi. Zenith 119
96/7 Pi. Zenith 20
94/5 POG 292
95/6 POG 82
93/4 Power Play 198
93/4 Premier 165
94/5 Premier 333
99/0 Prism 66
00/1 Private Stock 45
95/6 Pro Magnet 80
92/3 Pro Set 152
90/1 ProCards 466
91/2 ProCards 530
89/0 QUÉB
89/0 QUÉB / Gene. Foods
89/0 QUÉB / Police
90/1 QUÉB
91/2 QUÉB / Petro-Canada
92/3 QUÉB / Petro-Canada
94/5 QUÉB / Burger King
99/0 Revolution 69
00/1 Revolution 67
90/1 Score 415
92/3 Score 354
93/4 Score 379
94/5 Score 126
95/6 Score 205
96/7 Score 17, NW-10
97/8 Score 35
90/1 Sco. Young Stars 22
96/7 Select CE 8
94/5 SP 99
95/6 SP 34
96/7 SP 77
97/8 SP Authentic 76
99/0 Stadium 78
00/1 Stadium 66
00/1 SLU 12
92/3 Topps 285
95/6 Topps 284
00/1 Topps 70
92/3 T. Stadium Club 196
93/4 To. Stadium 315
94/5 T. Stadium Club 246
95/6 To. Stadium 53
98/9 UD Choice 97
91/2 Upper Deck 452
93/4 Upper Deck 203
94/5 Upper Deck 450
95/6 Upper Deck 397, SE-23
96/7 Upper Deck 274
98/9 Upper Deck 288
99/0 Upper Deck 239
00/1 Upper Deck 81
95/6 UD BAP 121, ✍ S121
96/7 UD Black Diam. 85
99/0 UD Black Diam. 46
95/6 UD CC 150
96/7 UD CC 59
98/9 UD G. Reserve 288
99/0 UD G. Reserve 239
99/0 UD MVP 94
00/1 UD MVP 85
00/1 UD Vintage 164, 173
99/0 WGretzky 84

FISHBACK, BRUCE
85/6 Minnesota-Duluth 16

FISHER, (BUD)
26 Dominion Chocolates 29

FISHER, CRAIG
96/7 Carolina Monarchs
94/5 Cla. Images 22
95/6 Edge Ice 173
94/5 Indianapolis Ice
90/1 OPC/Topps 126
90/1 ProCards 30
91/2 ProCards 233
98/9 Rochester Americans
90/1 Score 412
90/1 Upper Deck 155

FISHER, DUNCAN
45-64 BeeHive-2 [NYRa.]

FISHER, MIKE
99/0 BAP Mem. 311
00/1 BAP Mem. 3
01/2 Bowman 112, ✂ FFJ, ✂ FFS, ✂ FFDS, ✂ FFR, ✍ YSA
99/0 Crown Royale 96
99/0 Dynagon Ice 3
02/3 First Edition 23, ✂ Jers.
99/0 Millenium C-20
99/0 NHL Power Play [x3]
99/0 Omega 166
99/0 OTTA
00/1 OTTA
01/2 OTTA
02/3 OTTA
00/1 Pacific 277
02/3 Pacific 265
02/3 Pacific Complete 341
02/3 Parkhurst 187
00/1 Signature 68, ✍ Aut. 184
02/3 Signature GS-58, ✂ YP1
99/0 SP Authentic 111
99/0 Stadium 182
02/3 Stadium ✂ YSS16
98/9 Sudbury Wolves 9
99/0 Sudbury Wolves 11
00/1 Topps 289
00/1 To. Chrome 184
99/0 To. Gold Label 96
99/0 To. Prmr. Plus 113
02/3 T. Total 148
00/1 Upper Deck 122
02/3 Upper Deck 125
99/0 UD Black Diam. 61
02/3 UD Vintage 177
00/1 Victory 276

FISHER, ROBERT
51/2 Parkhurst 24

FISHER, SHAUN
01/2 Florida Everblades

FITCHNER, BOB
78/9 Dernière Heure
76/7 Québec Nordiques
76/7 Québ. / Antoinette

FITZGERALD, B.
89/0 ProCards AHL 223

FITZGERALD, KEVIN
94/5 Anchorage Aces 1

FITZGERALD, ROB
95/6 Slapshot 48

FITZGERALD, RUSTY
96/7 Cleveland Lumberjacks
97/8 Cleveland Lumberjacks
95/6 Leaf 316
00/1 Manitoba Moose
93/4 Minnesota-Duluth
98/9 Quad City Mallards
99/0 Quad City Mallards
95/6 Topps 209
95/6 Upper Deck 142
01/2 UD DEL 110

FITZGERALD, TOM
01/2 Atomic ✂ GWJ 35
98/9 Aurora 101
98/9 Be A Player 73, ✍ Aut. 73
01/2 BAP Memor. 411
90/1 Bowman 116
92/3 Bowman 369
01/2 Crown Royale ✂ TT 10, ✂ TT16
93/4 Donruss 121
98/9 Dynagon Ice 102
92/3 Fleer Ultra 342
93/4 Fleer Ultra 324
93/4 FLOR
96/7 FLOR / Winn-Dixie
97/8 FLOR / Winn-Dixie
01/2 Heads Up ✂ JQ 13
93/4 Leaf 221
94/5 Leaf 516
98/9 NASH / Wendy's 10
89/0 NYIS
91/2 O-Pee-Chee 279
92/3 O-Pee-Chee 394
99/0 Pacific 223
00/1 Pacific 221
02/3 Pacific Complete 389
97/8 Pacific CC 113
98/9 Pa. Crown Roy. 74
98/9 Pa. Paramount 123, -TC 14
99/0 Pa. Paramount 124
98/9 Panini Sticker 140
99/0 Panini Sticker 271
93/4 Parkhurst 348
95/6 Parkhurst 352
94/5 Parkie SE64
93/4 Pinnacle 390
94/5 Pinnacle 207
96/7 Pinnacle 57
96/7 Pi. Be A Player 4, ✍ Aut. 4
93/4 Premier 338
94/5 Premier 53
01/2 Pr. Stock ✂ GUG 57
01/2 PS Titanium ✂ DSJ 22
01/2 PS Titanium Draft ✂ 22
00/1 PS Titanium Draft ✂ 53
91/2 Pro Set 431
88/9 ProCards / Springfield
89/0 ProCards AHL 239
93/4 Score 493
93/4 Score 554
94/5 Score 163
99/0 Stadium 73
92/3 Topps 31
95/6 Topps 294
99/0 Topps 127, PP6
00/1 Topps 202
99/0 To. Chrome 127
92/3 T. Stadium Club 102
93/4 To. Stadium 392
91/2 Upper Deck 389
92/3 Upper Deck 52
94/5 Upper Deck 320
95/6 Upper Deck 436
96/7 Upper Deck 69
97/8 Upper Deck 286
98/9 Upper Deck 300
98/9 UD G. Reserve 300
00/1 UD Vintage 203, 208
00/1 Vanguard ✂ DGJ 12
01/2 Victory 203

FITZPATRICK,
91/2 Avant Garde BCJHL 163

FITZPATRICK, BLAINE
98/9 Peoria Rivermen
99/0 Peoria Rivermen
00/1 Peoria Rivermen
95/6 Slapshot 377

FITZPATRICK, MARK
98/9 Be A Player 182, ✍ Aut. 182
98/9 Bicycle.. 5-H
90/1 Bowman 119
91/2 Bowman 213
92/3 Bowman 394
99/0 Cincinnati Cyclones
93/4 Donruss 133
94/5 Donruss 235
95/6 Donruss 301
92/3 Fleer Ultra 124, -AW 7
94/5 Fleer Ultra 296
96/7 FLOR / Winn-Dixie
92/3 Kraft / PB
93/4 Leaf 335
94/5 Leaf 308
95/6 Leaf 120
88/9 LOSA / Smokey
84/5 Medicine Hat Tigers
89/0 NYIS
90/1 OPC/Topps 395
91/2 O-Pee-Chee 47
92/3 O-Pee-Chee 204
98/9 OPC Chrome 194
99/0 Pacific 88
89/0 Panini Sticker 265
90/1 Panini Sticker 87
92/3 Panini Sticker 195
93/4 Panini Sticker 66
98/9 Panini Sticker 96
92/3 Parkhurst 99
93/4 Parkhurst 344
94/5 Parkhurst 87
95/6 Parkhurst 88
92/3 Pinnacle 24
93/4 Pinnacle 369
94/5 Pinnacle 236
95/6 Pinnacle 175, M-7
96/7 Pi. Be A Player 10, ✍ Aut. 10
93/4 Power Play 92
94/5 Premier 82
90/1 Pro Set 181
92/3 Pro Set 107
88/9 ProCards / New Haven
91/2 ProCards 472
90/1 Score 102
90/1 Sco. Hot Cards 50
91/2 Score 266
91/2 Score CAN 486
92/3 Score 210
92/3 Score 526
93/4 Score 171
93/4 Score 537
95/6 Score 173
97/8 Score 234
90/1 Sco. Young Stars 32
92/3 Topps 216
95/6 Topps 183
98/9 Topps 194
91/2 To. Stadium 345
92/3 T. Stadium Club 12
93/4 To. Stadium 307
90/1 Upper Deck 37
91/2 Upper Deck 602
92/3 Upper Deck 332
94/5 Upper Deck 457, SP-120
95/6 Upper Deck 423

FITZPATRICK, RORY
93/4 Cla. 4 Sport 209
95/6 Fredericton Canadiens
94/5 L. Limited USA 5
95/6 Parkhurst 535
02/3 Rochester Americans
93/4 Slapshot / Sudbury 5
94/5 Slapshot / Promo
94/5 Slapshot / Sudbury 3
94/5 SP 192
92/3 Sudbury Wolves
93/4 Sudbury Wolves
94/5 Topps Finest 115

FITZPATRICK, ROSS
89/0 ProCards AHL 340
90/1 ProCards 23
91/2 ProCards 207
83/4 Springfield Indians 15

FITZSIMMONS, JASON
90/1 7th..Sketch WHL 162
91/2 7th...Sketch WHL 280

FIXTER, P
91/2 Cornwall Royals

FIXTER, PAUL
01/2 Hershey Bears

FIZZELL, BERT
69 Columbus Checkers

FIZZELL, BRET
67/8 Columbus Checkers

FIZZELL, BRETT
93/4 Portland Winter Hawks

FIZZELL, KRIS
95/6 Prince Albert Raiders

FJELDSTAD, MORTEN
92/3 Semic Nordisk 179

FJELDSTAD, PER CHR.
92/3 Semic Nordisk 148

FJELDSTAD, RUNE
95 Panini Worlds 253
92/3 Semic Nordisk 218

FJELL, KENNETH
92/3 Semic Nordisk 157

FLACHE, PAUL
99/0 Brampton Batallion 7

FLACHE, PETER
99/0 Guelph Storm

FLAHERTY, JOE
88/9 ProCards / Maine

FLAHERTY, RAY
80/1 Oshawa Generals

FLAHERTY, WADE
01/2 Atomic ✂ GWJ 28
01/2 BT Pipes 154
02/3 Between the Pipes 53
95/6 Donruss 280
90/1 Kansas City Blades
92/3 Kansas City Blades
93/4 Kansas City Blades
99/0 Kansas City Blades Moment
98/9 Pacific 281
99/0 Pacific 254
02/3 Pacific ✂ GWJ 20
97/8 Pa. Invincible R-179
95/6 Parkhurst 189
95/6 Pinnacle 173
00/1 PS Titanium ✂ GUG 109
90/1 ProCards 601
91/2 ProCards 517
92/3 SANJ / Pacific Bell
95/6 Topps 249
95/6 Upper Deck 57
95/6 UD CC 97
01/2 Utah Grizzlies

FLAHIFF, ROB
99/0 Mississippi S'Wolves

FLAMAN, DALLAS
95/6 Prince Albert Raiders

FLAMAN, FERN
45-64 BeeHive-2 [Bost.]
45-64 BeeHive-2 [Bost.]
45-64 BeeHive-2 [Toro.]
57-58 BOST
91/2 BOST / SA Legends
91/2 BOST / SA Legends
98/9 BOST / Alumni 5
51/2 Parkhurst 80
52/3 Parkhurst 47
53/4 Parkhurst 14
54/5 Parkhurst 20
93/4 Parkhurst PR45
93/4 Parkie 56-57 2
45-54 Quaker Oats
90/1 Score 357
60/1 Shirriff 102
54/5 Topps 25
57/8 Topps 4
58/9 Topps 56
59/0 Topps 29
60/1 Topps 57
61/2 Topps 21
57/8 Toronto Star Photo
58/9 Toronto Star Photo
60/1 Toronto Star Photo
58/9 Toronto Star Weekend
91/2 Ultimate Original Six 48, 76, ✍ Aut. 48

FLANAGAN, DAVE
98/9 Hampton Roads
91/2 ProCards 128

FLANAGAN, JOE
93/4 Birmingham Bulls

FLASAR, ALES
94/5 APS 3
95/6 APS 338

FLATHA, JØRN A
92/3 Semic Nordisk 167

FLATLEY, PATRICK
90/1 Bowman 124
91/2 Bowman 218
92/3 Bowman 134
83 Canada Juniors
93/4 Donruss 199
95/6 Donruss 227
94/5 Flair 102
94/5 Fleer 121
92/3 Fleer Ultra 125
93/4 Fleer Ultra 34
94/5 Fleer Ultra 125
93/4 Kraft / PB
93/4 Leaf 43
94/5 Leaf 381
95/6 Leaf 151
84/5 NYIS / News 4
89/0 NYIS
84/5 O-Pee-Chee 124
85/6 OPC/Topps 83
86/7 OPC/Topps 162
87/8 OPC/Topps 136
88/9 OPC/Topps 191
90/1 OPC/Topps 350
91/2 O-Pee-Chee 343
92/3 O-Pee-Chee 342
89/0 O-Pee-Chee 250
85/6 OPC Sticker 73-200
86/7 OPC Sticker 207-81
87/8 OPC Sticker 245-136
97/8 Pa. Invincible R-126
87/8 Panini Sticker 101
88/9 Panini Sticker 286
89/0 Panini Sticker 268, 272
90/1 Panini Sticker 82
91/2 Panini Sticker 245
92/3 Panini Sticker 201
93/4 Panini Sticker 60
94/5 Panini Sticker 50
95/6 Panini Sticker 93
91/2 Parkhurst 111
92/3 Parkhurst 342
93/4 Parkhurst 391
95/6 Parkhurst 403
94/5 Parkie SE103
91/2 Pinnacle 67
91/2 Pinnacle 405
92/3 Pinnacle 44
93/4 Pinnacle 203, CA14
94/5 Pinnacle 176
95/6 Pinnacle 30
95/6 Playoff 62
94/5 POG 155
95/6 POG 173
93/4 Power Play 146
93/4 Premier 28
94/5 Premier 178
95/6 Pro Magnet 51
90/1 Pro Set 182
91/2 Pro Set 152
91/2 Pro Set 578
92/3 Pro Set 102
91/2 Pro Set Platinum 77
90/1 Score 174
91/2 Score 29
91/2 Score CAN 29
92/3 Score 99
93/4 Score 220
94/5 Score 116
95/6 Score 196
97/8 Score NYRa. 12
95/6 SBx Emotion 104
95/6 SBx Impact 100
92/3 Topps 135
95/6 Topps 139
91/2 To. Stadium 20
92/3 T. Stadium Club 477
93/4 To. Stadium 24
90/1 Upper Deck 118
91/2 Upper Deck 226
93/4 Upper Deck 210
94/5 Upper Deck 371
95/6 Upper Deck 106
95/6 UD BAP 13, ✍ S13
95/6 UD CC 202

FLEETWOOD, BRENT
88/9 Portland Winter Hawks
89/0 Portland Winter Hawks

FLEISCHMANN, TOMAS
02/3 Moose Jaw Warriors

FLEMING, ADAM
95/6 Slapshot 128

FLEMING, BOB
87/8 Flint Spirits

FLEMING, GERRY
92/3 Classic Prospects 37
01/2 Florida Everblades
92/3 Fredericton Canadiens
93/4 Fredericton Canadiens
96/7 Fredericton Canadiens
94/5 MONT

FLEMING, REGGIE
45-64 BeeHive-2 [Chic.]
64-67 BeeHive-3 [Bost.]
64-67 BeeHive-3 [NYRa.]
64/5 Coke/Sprite [Bost.]
65/6 Coca-Cola
70/1 Dad's Cookies
70/1 Eddie Sargent 21
70/1 Esso Power Player
62/3 Cowan Tile
73/4 Nabisco s 13
68/9 O-Pee-Chee 167
69/0 O-Pee-Chee 95
69/0 O-Pee-Chee 4in1
70/1 O-Pee-Chee 128
70/1 O-Pee-Chee DE 12
72/3 O-Pee-Chee 316
95/6 Parkie 66-67 83
94/5 Parkie Tall 8
73/4 Quaker Oats 45
60/1 Shirriff 78
61/2 Shirriff 24
68/9 Shirriff / NYRa. 4
61/2 Topps 26
62/3 Topps 42
62/3 Topps Dollar
63/4 Topps 31
64/5 Topps 35
65/6 Topps 104
66/7 Topps 93
66/7 Topps / Test 54
67/8 Topps 30
69/0 Topps 95
70/1 Topps 128

FLEMING, RYAN
93/4 Michigan State

FLEMING, SHAUN
97/8 Spokane Chiefs

FLEMING, WAYNE*
90/1 Canada Nationals 22
91/2 Canada Nationals
94/5 Leaf Elit Set 300
92/3 Semic Elitserien 329

FLEMMING, JONAS
96/7 Sisu 120

FLEMMING, MARKUS
94/5 DEL 288
95/6 DEL 265

FLEMMING, MICHAEL
94/5 DEL 412

FLEMMING, WAYNE**
87/8 Moncton Hawks
90/1 Moncton Hawks
91/2 Moncton Hawks
88/9 ProCards / Moncton

FLESCH, JOHN
74/5 Loblaws Update
81/2 Milwaukee Admirals
75/6 O-Pee-Chee 353

FLETCHER, CHUCK
99/0 Louisville Panthers

FLETCHER, CLIFF
91/2 TORO / P.L.A.Y. 4

FLETCHER, CRAIG
92/3 BCJHL 125
91/2 7th...Sketch WHL 57

FLETCHER, SCOTT
95/6 Spokane Chiefs 2

FLETCHER, STEVEN
92/3 Fort Wayne Komets 9
93/4 Fort Wayne Komets 6
94/5 Fort Wayne Komets 3
95/6 Fort Wayne Komets
88/9 ProCards / Moncton
89/0 ProCards AHL 347
90/1 ProCards 537
91/2 ProCards 256
86/7 Sherb. Canadiens 14

FLETT, BILL
68/9 Bauer Photo
70/1 Dad's Cookies
70/1 Eddie Sargent 75
71/2 Eddie Sargent 67
72/3 Eddie Sargent 164
79/0 EDMO
88/9 EDMO / Action 71
70/1 Esso Power Player
74/5 Loblaws
68/9 O-Pee-Chee 159
69/0 O-Pee-Chee 102
70/1 O-Pee-Chee 161
71/2 O-Pee-Chee 47
72/3 O-Pee-Chee 187
73/4 O-Pee-Chee 20
74/5 O-Pee-Chee 64
75/6 O-Pee-Chee 349
76/7 O-Pee-Chee 332
79/0 O-Pee-Chee 266
72 Semic Sticker 226
68/9 Shirriff / LosA. 8
69/0 Topps 102
71/2 Topps 47
72/3 Topps 139
73/4 Topps 20
74/5 Topps 64
74/5 TORO
71/2 Toronto Sun Photo

FLETT, JOSH
92/3 BCJHL 6

FLEURY, CARL
96/7 Johnstown Chiefs
94/5 Roanoke Express
91/2 7th...Sketch LHJMQ 104

FLEURY, CHRIS
95/6 Upper Deck 518

FLEURY, MARC-ANDRÉ
01/2 Cape Breton Eagles 21
98 Québec Pee Wee 1381

FLEURY, SYLVAIN
92/3 Oklahoma City Blazers

FLEURY, THEOREN
01/2 Adrenaline 125
92/3 American Licorice 1
01/2 Atomic 63, PP 22, TN 10
98/9 Aurora 24, -CF 8
99/0 Aurora 37, Stripe 37, CF-6, ST-4
00/1 Aurora 92, Pins. 92
02/3 BAP All-Star 22, ✂ ASJ
98/9 Be A Player 168, ✍ Aut. 168
99/0 BAP Mem. 226, ✂ J-14, ✂ TM-16, ✂ TM-27, ✂ TM-50
00/1 BAP Mem. 44, ✂ J-18, ✂ H-14, ✂ TM-19, ✂ TM-40
01/2 BAP Memor. 239, ✂ ASJ, ✂ ASE, ✂ ASN, ✂ ASD, ✂ ASS, ✂ AST, ✂ CoO
02/3 BAP Memorabilia ✂ ASJ13, ✂ AST8
01/2 BAP Update HSHS, ✂ HSHSJers 29, ✂ H16
96/7 Bic.Sports Aces J-D
97/8 Bicycle 7-Diamond
95/6 Bicycle Sports Aces K-Spade
90/1 Bowman 102
91/2 Bowman 249
91/2 Bowman 270
92/3 Bowman 206
92/3 Bowman 355
95/6 Bowman 52
01/2 Bowman 107
98/9 Bowman's Best 31
02/3 Calder 32
90/1 CALG / McGavin's
91/2 CALG / IGA
92/3 CALG / IGA 020
91 Canada Cup
99/0 Cardset AH 8-risti
02/3 Cardset 18
99/0 Crown Royale 89, IE-17, IG-16
00/1 Crown Royale 69, ✂ JR-6, NP-12
01/2 Crown Royale 94, ✂ TT 15
93/4 Donruss 46
93/4 Donruss D
94/5 Donruss 99
95/6 Donruss 289, M-6, PP-12
96/7 Donruss 159, HL-20
97/8 Donruss 160
96/7 Do. Canadian 78, OC-5
97/8 Do. Canadian 23, NP-19
95/6 Do. Elite 106
96/7 Do. Elite 54
97/8 Do. Elite 74
97/8 Do. Preferred 138
97/8 Do. Priority 141
97/8 Do. Studio 81
98/9 Dynagon Ice 25, -TC 4
99/0 Dynagon Ice 128, CM-6, LL-7
93/4 EA Sports 23
95/6 Edge Ice L9
97/8 Esso 12, ✍ Aut.
02/3 Exclusive 36, ✂ GWJ 4
02/3 First Edition 191
94/5 Flair 24
96/7 Flair 11
94/5 Fleer 29
96/7 Fleer 12, ART-3
95/6 Fleer Metal 18, HM-3, IW-3
96/7 Fl. Picks 24, F50-11, JE-2
92/3 Fleer Ultra 21
93/4 Fleer Ultra 41
94/5 Fleer Ultra 29
95/6 Fleer Ultra 24, 382, CC-3, RLS-2
96/7 Fl. Ultra 21
91/2 Gillette 4
95 Globe 83
96/7 Got-Um
01/2 Heads Up 63, SM 11, ✂ JQ 14
02/3 Heads Up 79, ✂ GWQ 18
93/4 Hockey Wit 94
99/0 HoloGrFX 38
95/6 Hoyle / West. 4-Spade
92/3 Humpty Dumpty
89/0 Kraft 2
91/2 Kraft 13
93/4 Kraft / KD
94/5 Kraft / HH
95/6 Kraft / KD, PB
96/7 Kraft / KD, PB
97/8 Kraft / KD, Casecard, PB
98/9 Kraft / Post 5
99/0 Kraft / KD, / PB
96/7 Kraft Magnet
93/4 Leaf 154
94/5 Leaf 55
95/6 Leaf 115, FOI-5, GLS-5
96/7 Leaf 61
97/8 Leaf 136
94/5 L. Limited 99
95/6 L. Limited 6
96/7 L. Limited 67
96/7 L. Preferred 67, LS-47
97/8 Limited 24, 157, 177
96/7 Maggers 19
91/2 McDonald's Mc-18
92/3 McDonald's McD-07
96/7 McDonald's McD-15
97/8 McDonald's McD-2, F9
98/9 McDonald's McD02
01/2 McDonald's -HP 6, ✂ JPatch 13
02/3 McDonald's -SLG 6
96/7 Metal Univ. 18
99/0 Millenium 160, ✍ Aut. 160, ✂ J-1, ✂✍ J-1, ✂ JS-1
98/9 NHL Power Play
00/1 Nortel Networks All-Star 9
90/1 OPC/Topps 386
91/2 O-Pee-Chee 282
91/2 O-Pee-Chee 322
91/2 Topps - Team Leader 14
92/3 O-Pee-Chee 99
01/2 O-Pee-Chee 37
02/3 O-Pee-Chee 202
89/0 O-Pee-Chee 232
98/9 OPC Chrome 27
91/2 OPC Premier 92
97/8 Omega 29, SHLC-3, TL-3
98/9 Omega 31, -Onl. 5
99/0 Omega 149, 5ST-16, CC-13
98/9 Pacific 117, -GCDC 6, -TC 4
99/0 Pacific 103, CI-5, GC-8, PAP-5
00/1 Pacific 260
01/2 Pacific 256, 416, 435
02/3 Pacific 251, ✂ GWJ 35
02/3 Pacific Complete 401
97/8 Pacific CC 45
97/8 Pa. Crown Roy. 18
98/9 Pa. Crown Roy. 18, -PotG 4
97/8 Pa. Dynagon 15, 137, DD-4A, T-23, T-35
97/8 Pa. Invincible 16
97/8 Pa. Paramount 28
98/9 Pa. Paramount 27, -TC 4
99/0 Pa. Paramount 148,PB-22
00/1 Pa. Paramount 160, ✂ GUS-14
97/8 Pa. Revolution 17, ASG-4, TC-4
98/9 Pa. Revolution 18, -ASG 6, -TPA 2, -CTLC 3, -Show. 6
98/9 Panini Photocard
90/1 Panini Sticker 176
91/2 Panini Sticker 51
92/3 Panini Sticker 46
93/4 Panini Sticker 179
94/5 Panini Sticker 159
95/6 Panini Sticker 237
96/7 Panini Sticker 234
97/8 Panini Sticker 199
98/9 Panini Sticker 176
99/0 Panini Sticker 99, 324
00/1 Panini Sticker 64
95 Panini Worlds 24
91/2 Parkhurst 22
92/3 Parkhurst 19
93/4 Parkhurst 28
94/5 Parkhurst V20
95/6 Parkhurst 29
00/1 Parkhurst P-96
01/2 Parkhurst 36, ✂ PJ43, ✂ M54, ✂ T3
02/3 Parkhurst 171
02/3 Parkhurst Retro 50
94/5 Parkie SE28
91/2 Pinnacle 190
91/2 Pinnacle 358
92/3 Pinnacle 125
93/4 Pinnacle 79
94/5 Pinnacle 38, NL15
95/6 Pinnacle 6, FS-15
96/7 Pinnacle 6
97/8 Pinnacle 103
96/7 Pi. Be A Player 159, BB-4, ✍ Aut. 159
97/8 Pi. BeeHive 18
97/8 Pi. Certified 42
95/6 Pi. FANtasy 9
97/8 Pi. Inside 40
95/6 Pi. Summit 8
96/7 Pi. Summit 91
97/8 Pi. Totally 42
95/6 Pi. Zenith 11
96/7 Pi. Zenith 55, A-11
95/6 Playoff 16
94/5 POG 54
94/5 POG / Western 14
95/6 POG 52, I-017
94/5 Post
93/4 Power Play 36
93/4 Premier 100
93/4 Prmr. - BG-OPC 13
94/5 Premier 295, TF-19, GTG-7
00/1 Premier Plus 53
99/0 Prism 89, CA-13, SGDC-14
00/1 Private Stock 64, PS-36
01/2 Pr. Stock 61
02/3 Pr. Stock Reserve ✂ 109
00/1 PS Titanium 60, 3SS-16, NAAS-8, ✂ GUG-33, ✂ GUG 111, ✂ GUG 112
01/2 PS Titanium 92, ✂ DSJ 25, ✂ DSJ 28
01/2 PS Titanium Draft ✂ 59
02/3 PS Titanium 22
00/1 PS Titanium Draft ✂ 65
95/6 Pro Magnet 41
90/1 Pro Set 33
91/2 Pro Set 28
91/2 Pro Set 274
92/3 Pro Set 23
91 Pro Set Awards AC20
91/2 Pro Set Platinum 16
91/2 Puck / Pro Set 4
02/3 Quest for the Cup 17
99/0 Revolution 95, IS-8, TL-27, / CSC 95
00/1 Revolution 94
88/9 Salt Lake G'Eagles
90/1 Score 226
91/2 Score 226
91/2 Score 407
91/2 Score - Hot Card 7
91/2 Score CAN 226
91/2 Score CAN 297
92/3 Score 280
93/4 Score 191
93/4 Score 441
94/5 Score 69, CI15, TF4
95/6 Score 121, GB-13, L-13
96/7 Score 12, CI-13
97/8 Score 97
90/1 Sco. Young Stars 6
91/2 Score Young Stars 4
94/5 Select 109
95/6 Select CE 5, DS-13
96/7 Select CE 75
94 Semic 96
94 Semic 357
95 Semic 96
92 Semic Sticker 90
96/7 SB 7-Eleven Phonecard
00/1 Signature 33, HSHS, ✍ Aut. 83, ✂ J-1
01/2 Signature C-46, ✂ GJ69, ✂ GSJ69, ✂ IG4
95/6 Sisu Limited 81, SAS-9
95/6 SBx Emotion 21, Xci-1
95/6 SBx Impact 21, IQ-13
96/7 SBx Impact 13
02/3 Slam Card
94/5 SP 17
95/6 SP 16, É6
96/7 SP 20, CW-14, GF-15
97/8 SP Authentic 18, I20
98/9 SP Authentic 12
99/0 SP Authentic 56, SS8, ✍ SotT
00/1 SP Authentic 56
01/2 SP GU ✂ AF, ✂ AFD
96/7 SPx 5
97/8 SPx 6, D-SPX14
99/0 SPx 96
00/1 SPx 45
01/2 SPx 43
98/9 SPx Finite 12, 107, 167
98/9 SPx Prospects 7, H6, L11, PS19
00/1 Stadion 118
99/0 Stadium 163, Chrome 42, Big 17
00/1 Stadium 69
95/6 SLU
98/9 SLU
95/6 Super Sticker 14, 15
96/7 Team Out✂
92/3 Topps 220
95/6 Topps 25, 382, 6CG, 1HG, HGC5
98/9 Topps 27
99/0 Topps 227, SC17
00/1 Topps 12
01/2 Topps 37
02/3 Topps 202
99/0 To. Chrome 227
00/1 To. Chrome 12
01/2 To. Chrome 37
94/5 Topps Finest 28, BBB-4, BBM-1
95/6 To. Finest 30, 181
98/9 To. Finest 2
98/9 T. Gold Label 8, GR7
99/0 To. Gold Label 14, PG3
00/1 To. Gold Label 60
00/1 To. Heritage 67, OSJ
02/3 T. Limited 202
96/7 Topps Picks TS14
99/0 To. Prmr. Plus 3, CR5
01/2 To. Reserve ✂ TR
91/2 To. Stadium 355
92/3 T. Stadium Club 2
93/4 To. Stadium 390
93/4 To. Stadium - Master Photo-2 5
94/5 T. Stadium Club 25
95/6 To. Stadium EC165, MP, EN5
94/5 TSC Members Only 33
95/6 TSC Members Only 7
00/1 To. Stars 50
95/6 T. Super Skills 35
98/9 UD Choice 34, BH25, SQ13
00/1 UD Heroes 80, ✂ GT, ✂ GC
01/2 UD PlayMakers Ltd 64
00/1 UD Reserve 56, GS7, PSJ
00/1 UD Reserve -PSJ
02/3 UD Superstars 53
98/9 UD3 40, 100, 160
00/1 Ultimate Mem. ✍ U-1, ✂ J-1, ✂ JJ-15, ✂ S-1, ✂ TM-37
01/2 Ultimate Mem. ✂ DD
02/3 Ultimate Mem. ✂ GD
99/0 Ult. Victory 57, sg7, S8, TV8
90/1 Upper Deck 47, 478
91/2 Upper Deck 80
91/2 Upper Deck 245
91/2 Upper Deck 506
91/2 Upper Deck 630
92/3 Upper Deck 285
93/4 Upper Deck 3, 229, 288, GG7, SP-21
94/5 Upper Deck 315, 566, R41, R58, SP-11
95/6 Upper Deck 179, 235, AS-11, F-12, R-8, SE-101
96/7 Upper Deck 22, 208, X30, LS9, P14, SS4A, ✂ GJ12
97/8 Upper Deck 232
98/9 Upper Deck 232, FF28, FT5, LS6, P27
99/0 Upper Deck 260
00/1 Upper Deck 114
01/2 Upper Deck 115, GA2, ✂ ASJ
02/3 Upper Deck 280, -NC2, ✂ GO
95/6 UD ASG MVP13
93/4 Upper Deck Be A Player 21
94/5 UD BAP R23, ✍ 123
93/4 UD BAP Roots 28
96/7 UD Black Diam. 70
97/8 UD Black Diam. 143
98/9 UD Black Diam. 13, WF19
99/0 UD Black Diam. 56, D11, DM10, DS9
00/1 UD Black Diam. 39
01/2 UD Challenge 58
95/6 UD CC 201, 384, C11
96/7 UD CC 35, 300, 312, UD11
97/8 UD Coll. Choice 40, SQ64, W11, C14, CR14, / 5x7 1
97/8 UD Diam. Vision 9
98/9 UD G. Reserve 232
99/0 UD G. Reserve 260
96/7 UD Ice 9
97/8 UD Ice 64
01/2 UD Ice 107
00/1 UD Legends 21, 91
01/2 UD Mask 63
98/9 UD MVP 57
99/0 UD MVP 53, ✍ PS
00/1 UD MVP 121, M11, VC7
01/2 UD MVP 126
02/3 UD MVP - SD, ST, Souv.
99/0 UD MVP Cup 117, -CP7, -GM7, -SC11
99/0 UD Ovation 36, 89, -LP2
96/7 UD Post, SU-2
99/0 UD PowerDeck 15
01/2 UD Premier ✂ B
02/3 UD Premier ✂ Jers
00/1 UD Pros&Prosp. 56
99/0 UD Retro 22, -G7B
02/3 UD Rookie ✂ 157c
01/2 UD SCup Champs 28, ✂ G
01/2 UD Top Shelf 106, ✂ S, ✂ ST
02/3 UD Top Shelf ✂ AS, ✂ HT, ✂ M, ✂ SH, ✂ ST
00/1 UD Vintage 235
01/2 UD Vintage 167, 172, 173
97/8 Valu-net, ✍ Aut.
00/1 Vanguard 64, HV-22, IF-13
01/2 Vanguard ✂ DGM 45
02/3 Vanguard 23, ✂ GWJ 11
99/0 Victory 190
00/1 Victory 150, 152, 312
01/2 Victory 232, 420
99/0 WGretzky 109, -CG7, -EG9
96 Wien 87
97/8 Zenith 12, Z46

FLICHEL, MARTY
96/7 Dayton Bombers
00/1 Kudos 101
98/9 Michigan K-Wings
92/3 Tacoma Rockets
93/4 Tacoma Rockets

FLICHEL, TODD
92/3 Cincinnati Cyclones
87/8 Moncton Hawks
90/1 Moncton Hawks
88/9 ProCards / Moncton
89/0 ProCards AHL 37
91/2 ProCards 246
93/4 Rochester Americans

FLIEGAUF, CHARLY
94/5 DEL 26

FLINCK, TAPIO
70/1 Kuvajulkaisut 189
80/1 Mallasjuoma 201
72 Panda MM-Toronto
78/9 SM-Liiga 222
71/2 Williams Finnish 81
72/3 Williams Finnish 244
73/4 Williams Finnish 241

FLINN, RYAN
01/2 BAP Memor. 399
99/0 Halifax Mooseheads
01/2 Manchester Monarchs
02/3 Pacific Complete 508
01/2 UD Ice 139

FLINN, TYSON
95/6 Slapshot 385
96/7 Sudbury Wolves

FLINT, CALVIN
89/0 Brandon Wheat Kings
90/1 Brandon Wheat Kings
90/1 7th..Sketch WHL 232

FLINTOFT, ROB
88/9 Portland Winter Hawks

FLINTON, ERIC
96/7 Binghampton Rangers
97/8 Charlotte Checkers
97/8 Charlotte Checkers
95/6 Classic 73, ✍ Aut.
95/6 Cla. 5 Sport 160

FLOCKHART, ROB*
84/5 Springfield Indians 13
77/8 VANC / Royal Bank

FLOCKHART, RON
84/5 Kelowna Wings &...
84/5 MONT
82/3 O-Pee-Chee 249
83/4 O-Pee-Chee 264
84/5 O-Pee-Chee 174
85/6 O-Pee-Chee 171
86/7 OPC/Topps 146
87/8 OPC/Topps 103
82/3 OPC/Topps Sticker 113
83/4 OPC/Topps Sticker 192
84/5 OPC Sticker 115
84/5 OPC Sticker 116
85/6 OPC Sticker 128-246
86/7 OPC Sticker 176-39
87/8 OPC Sticker 25-166
87/8 Panini Sticker 317
83/4 PITT / Coke Is It!
84/5 PITT / Heinz
83/4 Souhaits Keychain [Flyers]
87/8 SLOU / Kodak
84/5 Topps 124

FLODELL, JORDON
98/9 Kamloops Blazers
99/0 Lethbridge Hurricanes

FLOMENHOFT, STEVEN
93/4 Knoxville Cherokees
94/5 Knoxville Cherokees

FLOOD, MARK
01/2 Peterborough Petes

FLORA, PETER
79 Panini Sticker 269

FLORENTINO, PETER
89/0 ProCards IHL 46

FLORIAN, MILOTA
98/9 OFS 324
99/0 Score 137

FLORIO, PERRY
93/4 Johnstown Chiefs 18
94/5 Johnstown Chiefs 8
98/9 Roanoke Express

FLOYD, LARRY
83/4 NJER
88/9 ProCards / Cape Breton
89/0 ProCards IHL 113
90/1 ProCards 319
91/2 ProCards 314
92/3 San Diego Gulls
93/4 San Diego Gulls

FLUGGE, CHRISTIAN
94/5 DEL 327

FLYNN, BILLY
94/5 DEL 53
95/6 DEL 25

FLYNN, BRENDAN
91/2 Richmond Renegades
92/3 Richmond Renegades
93/4 Richmond Renegades
95/6 Richmond Renegades

FLYNN, DAN
93/4 Soo Greyhounds 30
89/0 7th..Sketch OHL 96
93/4 Slapshot / S.S.Marie 30

FLYNN, M
82/3 Fredericton Express
83/4 Fredericton Express
85/6 Fredericton Express
86/7 Fredericton Express

FLYNN, NORMAN
90/1 7th..Sketch LHJMQ 238

FLYNN, PADDY
93/4 Owen Sound Platers

FLYNN, ROBERT
97 Québec Pee Wee 1154

FLYNN, TERRY
98/9 Odessa Jackalopes

FOCHT, DAN
01/2 BAP Memor. 320
95/6 Bowman P20
02/3 Calder 90
02/3 Pacific Complete 585
97/8 Springfield Falcons
95/6 Tri-City Americans 22
01/2 UD Honor Roll 85

FOERSTER, DOUG
88/9 ProCards / Maine

FOGARTY, BRYAN
90/1 Bowman 173
91/2 Bowman 149
95/6 Edge Ice 165
89/0 Halifax Citadels
98/9 Indianapolis Ice
96/7 Kansas City Blades
85/6 Kingston Canadians
86/7 Kingston Canadians
87/8 Kingston Canadians
95/6 Minnesota Moose
94/5 MONT
94/5 MONT / Export
88/9 Niagara Falls Thunder
91/2 O-Pee-Chee 500
90/1 Panini Sticker 144
90/1 Panini/QUE 4
91/2 Panini Sticker 259
91/2 Parkhurst 146
91/2 Pinnacle 59
92/3 PITT / Coke-Clark
90/1 Pro Set 515
91/2 Pro Set 200
91/2 Pro Set Platinum 103
89/0 ProCards AHL 168
89/0 QUÉB
90/1 QUÉB
90/1 QUÉB / Petro-Canada
91/2 QUÉB / Petro-Canada
90/1 Score 54
91/2 Score 237
91/2 Score CAN 457
90/1 Upper Deck 548
91/2 Upper Deck 337

FOGLIETTA, BOB
86/7 Portland Winter Hawks

FOGLIETTA, GIUSEPPE
92 Semic Sticker 258

FOGLIETTA, JOE
94 Semic 301
93 Semic Sticker 220

FOGOLIN, LEE (JR.)
74/5 BUFF
79/0 EDMO
81/2 EDMO / Red Rooster
81/2 EDMO / West Mall
82/3 EDMO / Red Rooster
83/4 EDMO / Button
83/4 EDMO / McDonald's
83/4 EDMO / West Mall
83/4 EDMO
84/5 EDMO
84/5 EDMO / Red Rooster
85/6 EDMO / Red Rooster
86/7 EDMO
86/7 EDMO / Red Rooster
88/9 EDMO / Action 42
74/5 Loblaws
75/6 O-Pee-Chee 306
76/7 O-Pee-Chee 253
77/8 O-Pee-Chee 94
78/9 O-Pee-Chee 27
79/0 O-Pee-Chee 183
80/1 O-Pee-Chee 63
81/2 O-Pee-Chee 112
82/3 O-Pee-Chee 104
83/4 O-Pee-Chee 26
84/5 O-Pee-Chee 240
85/6 O-Pee-Chee 235
86/7 O-Pee-Chee 210
81/2 OPC Sticker 215
82/3 OPC/Topps Sticker 106
83/4 OPC/Topps Sticker 17
83/4 OPC/Topps Sticker 100
84/5 OPC Sticker 254
85/6 OPC Sticker 218-85
86/7 OPC Sticker 71
80/1 Pepsi Bottle Cap
82/3 Post [Edmo.]
83/4 Souhaits Keychain [Oilers]
83/4 Stater Mint H18
75/6 Topps 306
76/7 Topps 253
77/8 Topps 94
78/9 Topps 27
79/0 Topps 183
80/1 Topps 63
83/4 Vachon 23-103

FOGOLIN, LIDIO (SR.)
45-64 BeeHive-2 [Detr.]
45-64 BeeHive-2 [Chic.]
51/2 Parkhurst 46
52/3 Parkhurst 55
53/4 Parkhurst 72
54/5 Parkhurst 84

FOIS, JORDAN
87/8 Sudbury Wolves
88/9 Sudbury Wolves

FOKIN, SERGEI
94/5 Leaf Elit Set 185
95/6 Leaf Elit Set 40
92/3 Semic Elitserien 279
95/6 UD Elitserien 58
97/8 UD Elitserien 53
98/9 UD Elitserien 85
99/0 UD Elitserien 54
00/1 UD Elitserien 77

FOLEY, COLIN
93/4 Portland Winter Hawks
90/1 7th..Sketch WHL 319
91/2 7th...Sketch WHL 37

FOLEY, GERRY
93/4 Parkie 56-57 94
57/8 Topps 57

FOLEY, RICK
72/3 Eddie Sargent 165
72/3 O-Pee-Chee 80
72/3 Topps 98

FOLIGNO, MIKE
90/1 Bowman 247
91/2 Bowman 169
82/3 BUFF / Wendt's 12
84/5 BUFF / Blue Shield
85/6 BUFF / Blue Shield
86/7 BUFF / Blue Shield
87/8 BUFF / Blue Shield
87/8 BUFF / Won. Bread
88/9 BUFF / Blue Shield
88/9 BUFF / Won. Bread
89/0 BUFF / Blue Shield
89/0 BUFF / Campbell's
90/1 BUFF / Campbell's
93/4 BUFF / Noco
79/0 DETR
80/1 DETR
93/4 Donruss 433
92/3 Fleer Ultra 420
93/4 FLOR
88/9 Frito Lay
83/4 Funmate Puffy 7 [w/]
98/9 Hershey Bears
01/2 Hershey Bears
80/1 O-Pee-Chee 16
80/1 O-Pee-Chee 187
81/2 O-Pee-Chee 87
82/3 O-Pee-Chee 26
83/4 O-Pee-Chee 63
84/5 O-Pee-Chee 20
85/6 OPC/Topps 17
86/7 OPC/Topps 127
86/7 OPC/Topps Box D
87/8 OPC/Topps 40
88/9 OPC/Topps 184
90/1 OPC/Topps 123
91/2 O-Pee-Chee 18
89/0 OPC/Topps 78
81/2 OPC Sticker 122
82/3 OPC/Topps Sticker 120
83/4 OPC/Topps Sticker 237
84/5 OPC Sticker 212
85/6 OPC Sticker 174
86/7 OPC Sticker 42
87/8 OPC Sticker 150-12
88/9 OPC Sticker 257-125
89/0 opcSticker 260-141
87/8 Panini Sticker 29
88/9 Panini Sticker 226
89/0 Panini Sticker 210
90/1 Panini Sticker 25
92/3 Panini Sticker 84
93/4 Panini Sticker 228
92/3 Parkhurst 415
91/2 Pinnacle 292
82/3 Post [Buff.]
93/4 Power Play 346
93/4 Premier 262
90/1 Pro Set 20
90/1 Score 133
91/2 Score CAN 248
93/4 Score 387
93/4 Score 647
83/4 Souhaits Keychain [Sabres]
95/6 St. John's Maple Leafs
80/1 Topps 16
80/1 Topps 187
81/2 Topps 87 [West]
84/5 Topps 16
91/2 To. Stadium 29
01/2 Topps Archives 61
91/2 TORO / P.L.A.Y. 29
93/4 TORO / Black's 21
90/1 Upper Deck 378
91/2 Upper Deck 212
93/4 Upper Deck 155

FOLIGNO, MIKE
02/3 Fleer Throwbacks 4

FOLK, TREVOR
98/9 Wichita Thunder

FOLKETT, CURTIS
91/2 Air Canada SJHL C15
88/9 Brandon Wheat Kings

FOLTA, PETR
94/5 APS 134
95/6 APS 304
96/7 APS 61
97/8 APS 332
99/0 DS 110
00/1 DS 151
96/7 DS Sticker 242
97/8 DS Sticker 282
98/9 OFS 187
99/0 OFS 405
00/1 OFS 274
01/2 OFS 236

FOMIN, KAUKO
70/1 Kuvajulkaisut 293
71/2 Williams Finnish 224

FOMITCHEV, ALEXANDRE
00/1 Asheville Smoke
99 Bowman 101
98/9 Calgary Hitmen 21

FOMRADAS, BLAINE
91/2 Air Canada SJHL D34

FONE, JON
02/3 Peterborough Phantoms

FONSO, ANTONIO
94/5 DEL 408

FONTAINE, CHARLES
01/2 Hull Olympiques 3
02/3 Hull Olympiques

FONTAINE, LEN
72/3 O-Pee-Chee 244

FONTAS, JON
78/9 Saginaw Gears

FONTEYNE, VAL
45-64 BeeHive-2 [Detr.]
64-67 BeeHive-3 [Detr.]
64/5 Coke/Sprite [NYRa.]
65/6 Coca-Cola
70/1 Eddie Sargent 176
71/2 Eddie Sargent 163
62/3 Cowan Tile
68/9 O-Pee-Chee 109
69/0 O-Pee-Chee 119
70/1 O-Pee-Chee 208
71/2 O-Pee-Chee 189
72/3 O-Pee-Chee 319
60/1 Parkhurst 21
61/2 Parkhurst 21
62/3 Parkhurst 27
95/6 Parkie 66-67 57
94/5 Parkie Tall 95
71/2 PITT / Sportcolor
60/1 Shirriff 48
61/2 Shirriff 67
68/9 Shirriff / Pitt. 3
63/4 Topps 61
66/7 Topps 108
68/9 Topps 109
69/0 Topps 119

FONTINATO, LOU
45-64 BeeHive-2 [NYRa.]
45-64 BeeHive-2 [Mont.]
00 CSAS Signat. Series
62/3 Cowan Tile
92/3 MONT / OPC 52
62/3 Parkhurst 52
93/4 Parkhurst PR61
93/4 Parkie 56-57 93
60/1 Shirriff 97
61/2 Shirriff 111
62/3 Shirriff 23
81/2 TCMA 4
57/8 Topps 64
58/9 Topps 41
59/0 Topps 5
60/1 Topps 61
62/3 Toronto Star Photo
60/1 Toronto Star Weekend
91/2 Ultimate Original Six 19, ✍ Aut. 19
61/2 York 40

FOOTE, ADAM
98/9 Be A Player 33, ✍ Aut. 33
00/1 BAP All-Star AS-8
00/1 BAP Mem. 314
01/2 BAP Memor. 54, ✄ SCC
93/4 Donruss 272
97/8 Esso 21, ✍ Aut.
02/3 First Edition 115, ✄ Jers.
97/8 Kraft / PB
93/4 Leaf 229
94/5 Leaf 529
02/3 McDonald's -SLG 2
96/7 Metal Univ. 31
02/3 O-Pee-Chee 78
98/9 OPC Chrome 189
98/9 Pacific 52
99/0 Pacific 104
00/1 Pacific 112
01/2 Pacific 100
02/3 Pacific 89
02/3 Pacific Complete 256
97/8 Pacific CC 135
98/9 Pa. Paramount 54
00/1 Pa. Paramount 59
97/8 Panini Sticker 202
99/0 Panini Sticker 217
91/2 Parkhurst 371
01/2 Parkhurst 188, ✄ PJ49, ✄ PS44, ✄ T5
02/3 Parkhurst 85
02/3 Parkhurst Retro 175, ✄ NH3
91/2 Pinnacle 337
93/4 Pinnacle 26
94/5 Pinnacle 432
95/6 Pinnacle 195
96/7 Pi. Be A Player 196, ✍ Aut. 196
93/4 Power Play 418
00/1 Private Stock ✄ GUG 23
91/2 Pro Set Platinum 268
91/2 QUÉB / Petro-Canada
92/3 QUÉB / Petro-Canada
94/5 QUÉB / Burger King
89/0 Soo Greyhounds
92/3 Score 131
93/4 Score 149
94/5 Score 151
97/8 Score 257
97/8 Score Colo. 12
91 7th..Sketch Mem.Cup 5
90/1 7th..Sketch OHL 157
00/1 Signature ✄ DD-14
01/2 Signature 153, ✍ Aut. 153
02/3 Signature GS-1, ✄ DW1
02/3 Slam Card
96/7 SP 38
02/3 Sports Vault 188
01/2 Stadium 98
92/3 Topps Gold 528
98/9 Topps 189
99/0 Topps 52
00/1 Topps 140
02/3 Topps 78
99/0 To. Chrome 52
01/2 To. Heritage 96
02/3 T. Limited 78
92/3 T. Stadium Club 468
93/4 To. Stadium 496
02/3 T. Total 22
98/9 UD Choice 228
91/2 Upper Deck 529
95/6 Upper Deck 204
97/8 Upper Deck 255
99/0 Upper Deck 40
01/2 Upper Deck 273
02/3 Upper Deck 288
00/1 UD ASG CA2
94/5 UD BAP R42, ✍ 2
96/7 UD Black Diam. 52
97/8 UD Coll. Choice 64, W16
99/0 UD G. Reserve 40
01/2 UD SCup Champs 41
00/1 UD Vintage 96
02/3 UD Vintage 71
97/8 Valu-net, ✍ Aut.
99/0 Victory 82
00/1 Victory 68
01/2 Victory 95, 429

FORBES, COLIN
98/9 OPC Chrome 49
97/8 Omega 163
00/1 OTTA
98/9 Pacific 325
99/0 Pacific 388
98/9 Pa. Paramount 172
99/0 Pa. Paramount 216
99/0 Revolution 132
00/1 Signature 112, ✍ Aut. 121
98/9 Topps 49
99/0 Topps 95
99/0 To. Chrome 95
01/2 To. Reserve 80
97/8 Upper Deck 191
98/9 Upper Deck 335
98/9 UD G. Reserve 335
98/9 UD MVP 151

FORBES, DAVE
74/5 Loblaws
74/5 O-Pee-Chee 266
75/6 O-Pee-Chee 173
76/7 O-Pee-Chee 246
77/8 O-Pee-Chee 143
78/9 O-Pee-Chee 167
75/6 Topps 173
76/7 Topps 246
77/8 Topps 143
78/9 Topps 167

FORBES, IAN
99/0 Guelph Storm

FORBES, JAKE
25-27 Anonymous 77
25-27 Anonymous 77

FORBES, MIKE
81/2 EDMO / Red Rooster
88/9 EDMO / Action 72

FORBES, NICK
96/7 Flint Generals
98/9 Flint Generals

FORBES, VERNON
24/5 Champ's Cigarettes
25 Dominion Chocolates 82
24/5 Maple Crispette [V130] 25
23/4 William Paterson 29
24/5 William Paterson 11

FORCH, LIBOR
94/5 APS 241
95/6 APS 14

FORD, BRIAN
83/4 Fredericton Express
89/0 ProCards AHL 268
83/4 Vachon 64-44

FORD, CHAD
98/9 Quad City Mallards

FORD, COLIN
87/8 Soo Greyhounds 18

FORD, GEORGE
52/3 St. Lawrence 59

FORD, JOHN
52/3 Anonymous 114

FORD, MIKE
76/7 OPC WHA 75

FORD, PAT
93/4 N. Michigan Wildcats

FOREST, JONATHAN
00/1 Austin Ice Bats

FORESTELL, BRIAN
90/1 7th..Sketch OHL 181
89/0 Windsor Spitfires

FORGET, DOMINIC
99 Bowman 81
01/2 Louisiana Ice Gators
00/1 Shawinigan 21

FORSANDER, JOHAN
98/9 UD Choice 293
97/8 UD Black Diam. 99
97/8 UD Elitserien 85
98/9 UD Elitserien 218
99/0 UD Elitserien 94, 207
00/1 UD Elitserien 103

FORSBERG, JONAS
95 Globe 55
94/5 Leaf Elit Set 170
95/6 Leaf Elit Set 27, S-9
94/5 Parkie SE245
92/3 Semic Elitserien 349
98/9 UD Elitserien 1

FORSBERG, KENT
92/3 Semic Elitserien 332

FORSBERG, PASI
92/3 Jyvas Hyva 168
93/4 Jyvas Hyva 298
93/4 Sisu 74

FORSBERG, PETER
01/2 Adrenaline 47
01/2 ASG History
91/2 Arena 4
01/2 Atomic 24, AB 2, PP 8, Stat. 11, TN 4, ✄ GWJ 11
02/3 Atomic 24, -CF 8
98/9 Aurora 46, -ALC 5, -CF 11, -FL 2, -MCAF 5, -NC 3, -Cube 4
99/0 Aurora 38, -Stripe 38, -CC 4, -CF 7, -CP 4, -ST 5
00/1 Aurora 38, Pins. 38, CC-2, CF-5, SR-5, TPS-3A
02/3 BAP All-Star 23-25, ✄ ASJ, ✄ HSHSJers, Bobble
98/9 Be A Player 35, H-2, P-22, ✍ Aut. 35, ✄ G-7, ✄ AS-2, ✄ S-2
00/1 BAP All-Star AS-4
99/0 BAP Mem. 259, SL-1, ✄ J-2, ✄ D-3, ✄ TM-10, ✄ TM-23, ✄ TM-28, ✄ TM-42, ✄ TM-43
00/1 BAP Mem. 72, ✄ J-14, ✄ PP-4, ✄ TM-18, ✄ TM-34
01/2 BAP Memor. 91, ✄ ASJ, ✄ ASE, ✄ ASN, ✄ ASS, ✄ AST, ✄ CoO, HSHS, ✄ PP, ✄ SCC
02/3 BAP Memorabilia 128, 231, ✄ ASJ14, ✄ ASN4, ✄ ASTJ4, ✄ AST10, ✄ AST14, ✄ AST24, ✄ HSHSJers 10, ✄ SC12, ✄ TM4, /Cup
01/2 BAP Update HSHS, ✄ HSHSJers 21
02/3 Between the Pipes ✄ GN7
96/7 Bic.Sports Aces K-H
97/8 Bicycle Q-Spade
95/6 Bicycle Sports Aces 9-Heart
95/6 Bowman 85, BB1
01/2 Bowman 73
02/3 Bowman 14
98/9 Bowman's Best 12, F6, SB8
02/3 Calder 15, -CG 2, -HS 2, ✄ GWJ 7
99/0 Challenger 11
91/2 Classic 5
91/2 Classic Four Sport 5
99/0 COLO / Kid Smart
99/0 Crown Royale 37, IG-6, CS-6, C21-4, CCA-3
00/1 Crown Royale 28, ✄ GWJ-6, JotC-8, Land.-3, NP-5
01/2 Crown Royale 37, JotC 6
02/3 Crown Royale 23, LOR 6, ✄ GWDP 5
95/6 Donruss 65, D-1, RT-2
96/7 Donruss 139, GTS-10, HL-14
97/8 Donruss 1, ES-7, L2L-4
98/9 Donruss ES 14
96/7 Do. Canadian 6
97/8 Do. Canadian 6, SCS-18
95/6 Do. Elite 39, CE-4
96/7 Do. Elite 12, S-7
97/8 Do. Elite 1, BF-5, C-23, PN-1, ✍ BF-5
97/8 Do. Preferred 2, 173, LT-7B, PM-12, Tin-9, WideTin-4
97/8 Do. Priority 8, 185, DD-10, OD-8, Post-10, Stamp-10
97/8 Do. Studio 15, HH-16, S-13, P-15
96/7 Duracell JB8
98/9 Dynagon Ice 47, -AR 4, -FT 5, -PP 3
99/0 Dynagon Ice 56, CM-5, LotR-4
01/2 EASports
97/8 Esso 43
01/2 eTopps 15
02/3 eTopps 15
02/3 Exclusive 40, -MO 6
02/3 First Edition 144, 322, 406R, ✄ Jers., ✄ HSHSJers 1
94/5 Flair 146
96/7 Flair 18, CIS-3, NT-3
94/5 Fleer 176, RS-2
96/7 Fleer 20, 139, ART-4, PA-3
95/6 Fleer Metal 32, IS-4, MW-1
96/7 Fl. Picks F50-12, DL-3
94/5 Fleer Ultra 356, P-1
95/6 Fleer Ultra 132, 383, AR-3, EA-5, HS-8
96/7 Fl. Ultra 35, CTI-2
95 Globe 21, 255-258, 269
01/2 Heads Up 23, HD 2, SM 3, ✄ JQ 8
02/3 Heads Up 30, -EIT 6, -PSP 3, / Bobble
99/0 HoloGrFX 14, IZ6, PS2
95/6 Hoyle / East. K-Heart
02/3 In The Game-Used 16, 116, ✄ E3, ✄ IE7, ✄ GUJ3, ✄ SJ3, ✄ T2
95/6 Kraft / IP
96/7 Kraft / TT
97/8 Kraft / KD
99/0 Kraft / PB
94/5 Leaf 475, LL-28, P-3
95/6 Leaf 20, FOI-6, SR-2
96/7 Leaf 159, LL-6, TBO-8
97/8 Leaf 3, 170, BS-13, FOI-12
94/5 Leaf Elit Set 189, GC-19, GS-3
94/5 L. Limited 116
95/6 L. Limited 2, SG-4
96/7 L. Limited 29, BTB-8
96/7 L. Preferred 110, LS-60, SP-6
97/8 Limited 2, 48, 109, FG-72
96/7 Maggers 36
94/5 McDonald's McD-31
95/6 McDonald's McD-7
96/7 McDonald's McD-28
97/8 McDonald's McD-15
98/9 McDonald's McD07
99/0 McDonald's McD-10, ✄ GJ
00/1 McDonald's 8, GWJ-2
01/2 McDonald's 5, ✄ JPatch 2
02/3 McDonald's 8
96/7 Metal Univ. 32, CS-2, LW-4
99/0 Millenium 65, ✍ Aut. 65, ✄ J-1, ✄✍ J-1, ✄ JS-20
95/6 Cool Trade 12
98/9 NHL Power Play
00/1 Nortel Networks All-Star 2
01/2 O-Pee-Chee 87
02/3 O-Pee-Chee 71
98/9 OPC Chrome 1, SB21
97/8 Omega 56, GF-3, S-3, SHLC-5, TL-5
98/9 Omega 60, -EOP 4, -FTF 8, -Onl. 8, -PI 25, -Prism 4
99/0 Omega 62, -5ST 19, -CC 3, -EOP 5, -Gen. 3
98/9 Pacific 21, -CCA 3, -DI 5, -GCDC 8, -Time. 3
99/0 Pacific 105, CI-6, CCA-3, GC-9, HAA-4, HAA-14, PAP-6
00/1 Pacific 113, 434, IO-6, CCA-3, ES-3, GCDC-8, PR-5
01/2 Pacific 101, GCDC 5, WAS 2
02/3 Pacific 90, -CCA 4, -L 5
02/3 Pacific Complete 39
97/8 Pacific CC 21, CS-4, CCA-4, GCDC-7, SS-2A
97/8 Pa. Crown Roy. 33, BOS-5, CCA-4, HT-4, L-5
98/9 Pa. Crown Roy. 33, -CCA 4, -LL 4, -MP 4, -PP 4
97/8 Pa. Dynagon 29, 138, DD-5A, KN-2, T-5, T-25, BKS-24
97/8 Pa. Invincible 34, AZ-5, FP-7, OTG-5, R-51, R-216
97/8 Pa. Paramount 49, P-5, BN-5
98/9 Pa. Paramount 55, -HOFB 3, -SD 4, -IG 2
99/0 Pa. Paramount 63, HOFB-4, IAd-5, PB-9
00/1 Pa. Paramount 60, ES-5, FF-8, SZ-2
97/8 Pa. Revolution 32, ASG-6, I-3
98/9 Pa. Revolution 35, -ASG 7, -TPA 23, -CTLC 4, -Show. 10
01/2 PTC National 4
94 Panini Olympics 291
98/9 Panini Photocard [x2]
95/6 Panini Sticker 148, 244, 299
96/7 Panini Sticker 244
97/8 Panini Sticker 201
98/9 Panini Sticker 185
99/0 Panini Sticker 209, 320
00/1 Panini Sticker 130
95 Panini Worlds 287
95/6 Parkhurst 237, 316, CCB-13, CCP-6, IAS-4, PP-4, PP-13, TW-3
00/1 Parkhurst P-7
01/2 Parkhurst 8, HSHS, ✄ PJ13, ✄ PS13, ✄ PSJ14, ✄ T8, ✄ WCJ5, ✄ WCE5, ✄ WCN5
02/3 Parkhurst 99, -HHH8, HHP7, HHR7, ✄ GJ46, ✄ SJ46, ✄ HSHSJers, ✄ MS9, ✄ NH12, ✄ PP7, ✄ TT19
95/6 Parkhurst 24-karat Gold
02/3 Parkhurst Retro 171, ✄ RJ3, ✄ RSJ3, ✄ HSHSJers, ✄ RM17
94/5 Parkie SE149, ES1
94/5 Pinnacle 266, 479, RTP9
x95/6 Pinnacle CS 8, FS-11, R20-15
96/7 Pinnacle 78, 249, TP-2
97/8 Pinnacle 73, 191, TP-7, P-19
96/7 Pi. Be A Player LTH2B, BB-5, ✍ Aut. LTH2B
97/8 Pi. Be A Player OT 11
97/8 Pi. BeeHive 9, BHT-9
97/8 Pi. Certified 32, CT-10
97/8 Pi. Epix E14
95/6 Pi. FANtasy 25
96/7 Pi. FANtasy 15
97/8 Pi. Inside 8, IT-5, / Can 11
96/7 Pi. Mint 6
97/8 Pi. Mint 3, M-2
95/6 Pi. Summit 117
96/7 Pi. Summit 142, HV-6, U-5
97/8 Pi. Totally 32
95/6 Pi. Zenith 70, ZT-8
96/7 Pi. Zenith 76, CS-9
95/6 Playoff 25, 137, 239
96/7 Playoff 357
95/6 POG 4, 77, I-029
97/8 Pi. Post 20
94/5 Premier 385, 425
00/1 Premier Plus 57, MB8, PT2, WP16
99/0 Prism 38, CA-4, DAS-4, SGDC-5
00/1 Private Stock 23, AC-6, PS-10, PSS-6, ✄ GUG-24,25, Res. 5
01/2 Pr. Stock -PS 17, ✄ GUG 29
02/3 Pr. Stock Reserve 24, -RE 2
00/1 PS Titanium 20, WAS-2, ✄ GUG-7, ✄ GUG 74, ✄ GUG 153
02/3 PS Titanium 24
00/1 PS Titanium Draft ✄ 24
95/6 Pro Magnet 77
94/5 QUÉB / Burger King
02/3 Quest for the Cup 21, -RTC 1, ✄ GWJ 5
99/0 Revolution 39, NI-5, O-6, SS-9, TL-12, / CSC 39
00/1 Revolution 36, HD-8, II-5, NI-6, ✄ GUG-1
94/5 Score TR2
95/6 Score 31, CI-7, DT-5, GB-10
96/7 Score 99, CI-2, DT-4
97/8 Score 83
97/8 Score Colo. 4
94/5 Select 175, YE-7
95/6 Select CE 68, CF-1
96/7 Select CE C-15
94 Semic 355
94 Semic 75
95 Semic 64
91/2 Semic Elitserien 213
92/3 Semic Elitserien 242
92/3 Semic Elitserien 347
93 Semic Sticker 13
96/7 SB 7-Eleven Phonecard
00/1 Signature 139, HSHS, F-8, ✍ Aut. 110, ✄ J-20, ✄ HSHSJers
01/2 Signature C-58, ✍ Aut. LPF, ✄ GUE14, ✄ GU75, ✄ HSHSJers, ✄ ITN14
02/3 Signature 102, GS-72, ✍ 102, ✄ CJ7, ✄ SGJ3, ✄ TQ1
95/6 SBx Emotion 36, Xci-14
95/6 SBx Impact 35, 229, IQ-8
96/7 SBx Impact 22, BR-3, VT-3
02/3 Slam Card
94/5 SP 96, P-2
95/6 SP 29, E10, FX4
96/7 SP 33, GF-2, SF-1
97/8 SP Authentic 36, I12
98/9 SP Authentic 20, SS6, SO19
99/0 SP Authentic 26, SS3
00/1 SP Authentic 24, ST1
02/3 SP Authentic 23, 95, ✄ SP, ✄ DP
00/1 SP GU 15, ✄ TotG, ✄ C, ✄ P (x2)
01/2 SP GU ✄ AF, ✄ AFD, ✄ AFT, ✄ AFQ, ✄ Patch
02/3 SP GU 11, ✄ AF, ✄ CF, ✄ PC, ✄ PH (x2)
02/3 Sports Vault 183
96/7 SPx 8
97/8 SPx 11, D-SPX16
99/0 SPx 40, HH8, P13, X14, XT3
00/1 SPx 16, 71, S2, ✄ WM
01/2 SPx 14, 72, ✄ DT, ✄ TT
02/3 SPx 19, 85, ✄ WM, ✄ X
98/9 SPx Finite 95, 166, 178
98/9 SPx Prospects 13, H10, L28, PS23
00/1 Stadion 115
99/0 Stadium 8, Chrome 8, Big 6, CA12, EG2, OE2
00/1 Stadium 5, BT2, CA11, SF4
01/2 Stadium 2, G33, HS7, NHLP1, P5, ✄ SCS, ✄ SCSD, ✄ SCST
02/3 Stadium 46, -BT-10
91/2 Star Pics 35
97/8 SLU
99/0 SLU 69
00/1 SLU Classic Doubles 7
95/6 Super Sticker 26, 28
96/7 Team Out!
95/6 Topps 359, 380, 10NG, YS4
98/9 Topps 1, IA 18, L1, M8, SB21
99/0 Topps 12, 277, AT11, IM9, AM2, TW4, -SCH12
00/1 Topps 119, TC5, HM3
01/2 Topps 87, OTG9
02/3 Topps 71
99/0 To. Chrome 12, 277, AT11, IM9, AM2
00/1 To. Chrome 92, TC5, HM3
01/2 To. Chrome 87
02/3 T. Chrome 48
94/5 Topps Finest 1, BBM-2, BBR-12
95/6 To. Finest 26, 100
98/9 To. Finest 6, C7, M21, M25, M26, M27
96 Topps Finest Bronze 17
98/9 T. Gold Label 21
99/0 To. Gold Label 27, PG10
00/1 To. Gold Label 17, B4, ✄ GLJ
00/1 To. Heritage 42, HH8
01/2 To. Heritage 39, ✄ GWJ
02/3 To. Heritage 17, -Light 17, ✄ CC, ✄ CCB
00/1 To. Heritage ASG 3
02/3 T. Limited 71
96/7 Topps Picks 5, FT16, TS7
99/0 To. Prmr. Plus 5, CAC4, PT6
01/2 To. Reserve 37, ✄ TR
95/6 To. Stadium 105, GT4, N9
94/5 TSC Members Only 47
95/6 TSC Members Only 20
00/1 To. Stars 40, 128, P2, WF4, PP2
95/6 T. Super Skills 18
02/3 T. Total 122, TP4
98/9 UD Choice 56, 229, 241, BH14, SQ20
00/1 UD Heroes 31, 143, SS2
01/2 UD PlayMakers Ltd ✄ PCJ
00/1 UD Reserve 23, PSJ
02/3 UD Superstars 69
98/9 UD3 33, 93, 153
91/2 Ultimate Draft Pick 5, 61, 76, ✍ Aut.
00/1 Ultimate Mem. ✍ U-20, ✄ Jers. 18, ✄ J-20, ✄ S-20, ✄ TM-15, ✄ TM-16
01/2 Ultimate Mem. ✄ ASGH, ✄ CT, ✄ DD
02/3 Ultimate Mem. ✄ A8, ✄ DD, ✄ Emb, ✄ GUJ, ✄ GUSJ, ✄ GD, ✄ ITN, ✄ MO, ✄ NP, ✄ SL, ✄ Num, ✄ PS, ✄ RAT, ✄ RAut
99/0 Ult. Victory 26, sg5, S3, TV7, UV6
91/2 Upper Deck 64
92/3 Upper Deck 235
92/3 Upper Deck 369
92/3 Upper Deck 375
92/3 Upper Deck 595
94/5 Upper Deck 245, 528, 555, C1, H10, SP-156
95/6 Upper Deck 430, AS-17, F-1, H-8, R-25, R-37, R-54, SE-21
96/7 Upper Deck 239, X2, HH7, LS8, SS8A
97/8 Upper Deck 252, SS21, SG21, S21, T1C
98/9 Upper Deck 29, 69, FF17, FT2, GN25-27, LS12, P11
99/0 Upper Deck 39, 154, AS11, CT19, FF10, IG3, SB6, SS6, ✄ GJ
00/1 Upper Deck 46, FF3, F3, NC1, SS6, TT3, ✄ GJ, ✄ DGJ
01/2 Upper Deck 47, 229, FC4, GA9, SS9, ✄ CJers, ✄ JPatch, ✄ PatchL, ✄ PatchN, ✄ PoaN, ✄ PoaND, ✄ PoaNT, -SCGJers, ✄ SCFJersD, ✄ SupSwe
02/3 Upper Deck 48, 230, -GG5, ✄ FF, ✄ PP, ✄ PW, ✄ UDPL
95/6 UD ASG MVP11
00/1 UD ASG PP3, HH2
02/3 UD Artistic 23, R23, CG21, ✄ AT, / Art
94/5 UD BAP R152
96/7 UD Black Diam. 171, RC7
97/8 UD Black Diam. 106, PC11
98/9 UD Black Diam. 21, M28, WF7
99/0 UD Black Diam. 26, D18, DM1, ✄ APOH
00/1 UD Black Diam. 17, FP2, CC2
99/0 UD C. Legends 53
01/2 UD Challenge ✄ FP
02/3 UD Classic 26, GG2, ✄ HH, ✄ HR
95/6 UD CC 26, 371, 391, C20
96/7 UD CC 63, 298, 314, UD3, S3
97/8 UD Coll. Choice 54, SQ71, S21, C21, CR21
01/2 UD Collectors
97/8 UD Diam. Vision 14
95/6 UD Elitserien 234
97/8 UD Elitserien UDS1
98/9 UD G. Reserve 29, 69
99/0 UD G. Reserve 39, 154
02/3 UD Honor 17, -SG8, -TW4, ✄ GA (x2)
96/7 UD Ice 81
97/8 UD Ice 61, IC12, L4B
00/1 UD Ice 13, CC2, FP2, ✄ IGJ
01/2 UD Ice 9
00/1 UD Legends 34, 36, PH5, ✄ LGJ
01/2 UD Mask ✄ GJ, ✄ JP, ✄ DP
02/3 UD Mask ✄ IO
98/9 UD MVP 51, OT8, PG9, -Snip. S5, F14
99/0 UD MVP 52, 21st-4, S6, W24, H6, ✄ GU19
00/1 UD MVP 51, TD3, TP3, VC3, ✄ GS
01/2 UD MVP 44 , MT1, VC6, -J, ✄ S
02/3 UD MVP 46, SO6, SA, SD, ST
99/0 UD MVP Cup 54, GM3, SS3, GC, ✄ GU
99/0 UD Ovation 18, LP4
02/3 UD Piece 27, 107, AC8
99/0 UD PowerDeck 7
01/2 UD Premier 13, ✄ B, ✄ D
02/3 UD Premier 13, ✄ Jers, ✄ JD, ✄ Patch
00/1 UD Pros&Prosp. 24, PM3, ✄ GJ
99/0 UD Retro 19
02/3 UD Rookie 26
01/2 UD SCup Champs 30, ✄ S, ✄ G, ✄ T
01/2 UD Top Shelf 9, ✄ P, ✄ J, ✄ S, ✄ ST
02/3 UD Top Shelf 23, ✄ HH, ✄ SH
00/1 UD Vintage 92, UD8, NH9
01/2 UD Vintage 65, 70
02/3 UD Vintage 64, 268, GB 64, T16, ✄ SO
00/1 Vanguard 27, CF-3, HV-7, IF-5, VP-3, ✄ DGJ-2
01/2 Vanguard EMW 3, ✄ DGM 9, ✄ DGM 47
02/3 Vanguard 25, -EMW 7, -IF 3
99/0 Victory 75, 77, 314, 332, 339
00/1 Victory 58, 60, 291
01/2 Victory 84, 394
02/3 Victory 56
99/0 WGretzky 51, CG1, EG5, ✄ TG
96 Wien 57, 74, NS1
97/8 Zenith 2, CTC-12, ZT-5, Z19

FORSEY, JACK
34-43 BeeHive-1 [Toro.]

FORSLUND, TOMAS
92/3 Bowman 384
91/2 CALG / IGA
92/3 Classic Prospects 139
92/3 Classic Prospects BC15
96/7 DEL 357
98/9 DEL 88
99/0 Eishockey 115
95 Globe 46
94/5 Leaf Elit Set 65
95/6 Leaf Elit Set 242, FTF-7
92/3 O-Pee-Chee 70
91/2 OPC Premier 31
92/3 Panini Sticker D
95 Panini Worlds 157
91/2 Parkhurst 20
91/2 Pinnacle 333
91/2 Pro Set 527
92/3 Salt Lake G'Eagles
91/2 Score 79T
91/2 Score CAN 629
94 Semic 77
95 Semic 69
89/0 Semic Elitserien 134
90/1 Semic Elitserien 209
93 Semic Sticker 41
92/3 Topps 186
92/3 T. Stadium Club 280
91/2 Upper Deck 27
91/2 Upper Deck 586
92/3 Upper Deck 3
92/3 Upper Deck 429
92/3 Upper Deck ERT6
00/1 UD DEL 136
95/6 UD Elitserien 112
96 Wien 67

FORSMAN, JOHNNY
89/0 Semic Elitserien 207

FORSS, MATTI
92/3 Jyvas Hyva 133
80/1 Mallasjuoma 7
93/4 Sisu 200
93/4 Sisu 387
95/6 Sisu Limited 36
78/9 SM-Liiga 35
73/4 Williams Finnish 306

FORSS, RISTO
66/7 Champion 57
70/1 Kuvajulkaisut 294

FORSS, T.D.
95/6 Spokane Chiefs 27
97/8 Spokane Chiefs

FORSYTHE, TREVOR
91/2 Knoxville Cherokees

FORTH, MARK
97/8 Spokane Chiefs

FORTIER, DAVE
74/5 Loblaws Update
74/5 O-Pee-Chee 382
75/6 O-Pee-Chee 336
76/7 O-Pee-Chee 328
76/7 VANC / Royal Bank

FORTIER, ÉRIC
00/1 Val d'Or Foreurs 22
01/2 Val d'Or Foreurs 21

FORTIER, FRANÇOIS
00/1 Charlotte Checkers
99/0 Hartford Wolf Pack

FORTIER, FRANÇOIS*
99 Bowman 72
98 Bowman 90
98 Bowman Chrome 90

FORTIER, MARC
90/1 Bowman 167
84/5 Chicoutimi Saguenéens
98/9 DEL 164
99/0 Eishockey 63
90/1 OPC/Topps 176
89/0 O-Pee-Chee 262
89/0 opcSticker 189-43
89/0 Panini Sticker 335
90/1 Panini Sticker 153
90/1 Panini/QUE 5
93/4 Phoenix Roadrunners
90/1 Pro Set 245
92/3 Pro Set 128
88/9 ProCards / Halifax
88/9 QUÉB
88/9 QUÉB / Gene. Foods
89/0 QUÉB
89/0 QUÉB / Gene. Foods
89/0 QUÉB / Police
90/1 QUÉB
90/1 QUÉB / Petro-Canada
91/2 QUÉB / Petro-Canada
90/1 Score 78
92/3 Topps 226
92/3 T. Stadium Club 173
00/1 UD DEL 64, ✄ GJ
01/2 UD DEL 34

FORTIER, SÉBASTIEN
98/9 Phoenix Mustangs 12
90/1 7th..Sketch LHJMQ 81
91/2 7th...Sketch LHJMQ 39
93/4 Wheeling Thund'birds

FORTIN, DANY
91/2 7th...Sketch LHJMQ 18

FORTIN, EMILE
37/8 World Wide Gum 122

FORTIN, JEAN-FRANÇOIS
97 Bowman 46, 157, BB17, ✍ Aut.
02/3 O-Pee-Chee 266
02/3 Pacific Complete 292
99/0 Portland Pirates
00/1 Portland Pirates
93 Québec Pee Wee 1080
02/3 Topps 266
02/3 T. Limited 266
96/7 Upper Deck 375
02/3 Upper Deck 225
96/7 UD Black Diam. 4
02/3 UD Vintage 348

FORTIN, YVAN
51/2 Lac St-Jean 55

FORTUNAS, MAXIME
02/3 Baie-Comeau

FORTUNUS, MAXIME
00/1 Baie-Comeau 5
01/2 Baie-Comeau 4

FOSTER, AARON
99/0 Prince George Cougars
00/1 Prince George Cougars

FOSTER, ADRIAN
00/1 Saskatoon Blades

FOSTER, COREY
95/6 Cleveland Lumberjacks
96/7 Cleveland Lumberjacks
91/2 Parkhurst 344
91/2 PHIL / J.C. Penney
91/2 Pinnacle 332
91/2 Pro Set 551
91/2 Pro Set Platinum 265
89/0 ProCards AHL 146
90/1 ProCards 231
91/2 Upper Deck 591
92/3 Upper Deck 53

FOSTER, DARRYL
95/6 Classic 89
93/4 Slapshot / Niagara Falls 3
94/5 Slapshot / Detroit Jr. 2
94/5 Slapshot Memorial 76

FOSTER, DAVID
91/2 Air Canada SJHL D9
92/3 MPS SJHL 33

FOSTER, DWIGHT
81/2 COLR
84/5 DETR / Little Caesars
85/6 DETR / Little Caesars
78/9 O-Pee-Chee 271
81/2 O-Pee-Chee 3
82/3 O-Pee-Chee 138
83/4 O-Pee-Chee 122
84/5 O-Pee-Chee 53
85/6 OPC/Topps 14
81/2 OPC Sticker 52
83/4 OPC/Topps Sticker 133
87/8 Panini Sticker 17
82/3 Post [Colo.]
83/4 Souhaits Keychain [Red Wings]
81/2 Topps 67 [East]
84/5 Topps 41

FOSTER, JERRY
89/0 ProCards AHL 74

FOSTER, KURTIS
01/2 Chicago Wolves
02/3 Chicago Wolves
98/9 SP Authentic 116, ✍ SotT
98/9 Upper Deck 393
98/9 UD G. Reserve 393
99/0 UD Prospects 24

FOSTER, NORM
88/9 ProCards / Maine
89/0 ProCards AHL 60
90/1 ProCards 135
91/2 ProCards 225
91/2 Upper Deck 465

FOTHERINGHAM, SHAWN
92/3 Clarkson G'Knights

FOTIU, NICK
86/7 CALG / Red Rooster
01/2 Cleveland Barons
88/9 EDMO / Action 143
96/7 Johnstown Chiefs
00/1 Kentucky Tho'blades
77/8 O-Pee-Chee 11
78/9 O-Pee-Chee 367
79/0 O-Pee-Chee 286
80/1 O-Pee-Chee 184
82/3 O-Pee-Chee 222
83/4 O-Pee-Chee 243
85/6 OPC/Topps 22
75/6 OPC WHA 108
82/3 Post [NYRa.]
89/0 ProCards AHL 20
77/8 Topps 11
80/1 Topps 184
01/2 T/O Archives 26

FOTIU, NICK
01/2 Fleer Legacy 44

FOUNTAIN, MIKE
01/2 BT Pipes 48
92/3 Canada Nationals
94/5 Classic T70
94/5 Classic 4 Sport 158
92/3 Classic Prospects 106
93/4 Cla. Prospects 175
97/8 Donruss 218
97/8 Do. Canadian 136
99/0 Grand Rapids Griffins
00/1 Grand Rapids Griffins
92/3 Hamilton Canucks
98/9 New Haven Beast 14
90/1 Oshawa Generals
91/2 Oshawa Generals
91/2 Oshawa Generals
97/8 Pi. Inside 76
90/1 7th..Sketch OHL 336
91/2 7th...Sketch OHL 170
96/7 SP 162
96/7 Syracuse Crunch
91/2 Upper Deck WJC 52

FOURGET, DOMINIC
99/0 Shawinigan 18

FOURNEL, DAN
94/5 Huntington Blizzard
98/9 Oklahoma City Blazers

FOURNIER, GUILLAUME
00/1 Québec Remparts 12

FOURNIER, JACK
12/3 Imperial 36

FOURNIER, MARC
83/4 Soo Greyhounds
FOURNIER, MATHIEU
00/1 Rimouski Océanic 15
01/2 Rimouski Océanic 14
02/3 Shawinigan Cataractes
FOURNIER, ROB
88/9 Niagara Falls Thunder
89/0 7th..Sketch OHL 171
FOURNIER, WADE
95/6 Louisiana Ice Gators
95/6 Louisiana Ice Gators-2
FOUTAIN, MIKE
96/7 VANC / IGA
FOWLER, BOB
89/0 ProCards IHL 129
FOWLER, DAN
91/2 ProCards 32
FOWLER, HEC
24/5 Champ's Cigarettes
24/5 Maple Crispette [V130] 3
28/9 Paulins Candy 87
24/5 William Paterson 30
FOWLER, JIMMY
34-43 BeeHive-1 [Toro.]
36/7 O-Pee-Chee 103
37/8 O-Pee-Chee 135
39/0 O-Pee-Chee 55
28/9 Paulins Candy 74
38/9 Quaker Oats
FOWLER, ROB
87/8 Moncton Hawks
FOWLER, TEAL
00/1 UD DEL 105, ✂ GJ
FOX, GREG
78/9 ATLF / Colour
79/0 CHIC
80/1 CHIC / Colour
80/1 CHIC / Brown
81/2 CHIC
82/3 CHIC
77/8 Nova Scotia Voyageurs
79/0 O-Pee-Chee 116
80/1 O-Pee-Chee 268
81/2 O-Pee-Chee 69
82/3 O-Pee-Chee 65
83/4 O-Pee-Chee 101
84/5 O-Pee-Chee 175
84/5 PITT / Heinz
82/3 Post [Chic.]
83/4 Souhaits Keychain [Blackhawks]
79/0 Topps 116
FOX, HUGHIE J.
25 Dominion Chocolates 56
FOX, JIM
83/4 Funmate Puffy 7 [w/]
84/5 LOSA / Smokey 5
87/8 LOSA
88/9 LOSA / Smokey
81/2 O-Pee-Chee 153
82/3 O-Pee-Chee 154
83/4 O-Pee-Chee 154
84/5 O-Pee-Chee 84
85/6 OPC/Topps 61
86/7 O-Pee-Chee 215
87/8 OPC/Topps 75
88/9 OPC/Topps 139
82/3 OPC/Topps Sticker 235
83/4 OPC/Topps Sticker 293
84/5 OPC Sticker 268
85/6 OPC Sticker 236-103
86/7 OPC Sticker 89-219
87/8 OPC Sticker 216-84
88/9 OPC Sticker 154-25
87/8 Panini Sticker 281
88/9 Panini Sticker 76
82/3 Post [LosA.]
83/4 Souhaits Keychain [Kings]
84/5 Topps 66
FOY, CHRIS
93/4 Richmond Renegades
94/5 Richmond Renegades
FOYN, STEPHEN
92/3 Semic Nordisk 88
92 Semic Sticker 46
FOYSTON, FRANK
83 HHOF Postcard B4
83&87 HHOF 20
FRANCELLA, GIULIO
82 Semic Sticker 130
FRANCESCHETTI, LOU
90/1 Bowman 164
90/1 BUFF / Blue Shield
90/1 OPC/Topps 303
91/2 O-Pee-Chee 354
87/8 Panini Sticker 188
90/1 Panini Sticker 289
90/1 Panini/TOR 6
90/1 Pro Set 280
88/9 ProCards / Baltimore
91/2 ProCards 360
91/2 Rochester Americans GL
91/2 Rochester Americans WPC
90/1 Score 266
91/2 Score CAN 388
90/1 TORO
90/1 Upper Deck 396
91/2 Upper Deck 399
86/7 WASH / Kodak
86/7 WASH / Police
87/8 WASH
87/8 WASH / Kodak
88/9 WASH
88/9 WASH / Smokey
FRANCHE, DELPHIS
51/2 Laval Dairy 27
52/3 St. Lawrence 91
FRANCIS, BOB
89/0 ProCards IHL 200
90/1 ProCards 611
96/7 Providence Bruins
94/5 Saint John Flames
92/3 Salt Lake G'Eagles
FRANCIS, EMILE
83 HHOF Postcard I7
83&87 HHOF 231
92/3 Legends 120
74/5 O-Pee-Chee 9
66/7 Topps 21
74/5 Topps 9
FRANCIS, RON
01/2 Adrenaline 32
01/2 Atomic 16, TN 3
02/3 Atomic 16, -PC 5
99/0 Aurora 25
00/1 Aurora 28
98/9 Be A Player 174, M12, ✍ Aut. 174
99/0 BAP Mem. 10, H-8
00/1 BAP Mem. 206
01/2 BAP Memor. 256, ✂ 500GS
02/3 BAP Memorabilia 61, 206, ✂ FP6, ✂ HSHSJers 16, ✂ SC7, ✂ SC29
01/2 BAP Update HSHS, ✂ HSHSJers 24
96/7 Bic.Sports Aces 9-S
95/6 Bicycle Sports Aces 7-Club
90/1 Bowman 254
91/2 Bowman 90
92/3 Bowman 123
95/6 Bowman 31
01/2 Bowman 22
02/3 Bowman 6
98/9 Bowman's Best 50
98/9 CARO / Highwoods
99/0 Crown Royale 26
00/1 Crown Royale 20
01/2 Crown Royale 25
02/3 Crown Royale 17
93/4 Donruss 261
94/5 Donruss 122
95/6 Donruss 94, I-10
96/7 Donruss 149, D-4
97/8 Donruss 137
96/7 Do. Canadian 93
97/8 Do. Canadian 44, NP-20
95/6 Do. Elite 40
96/7 Do. Elite 40
97/8 Do. Elite 113
97/8 Do. Preferred 142
97/8 Do. Priority 77
97/8 Do. Studio 74
98/9 Dynagon Ice 31
99/0 Dynagon Ice 40
02/3 eTopps 33
02/3 Exclusive 28, -EIS 2
02/3 First Edition 22, 386, ✂ Jers., ✂ HSHSJers 12, ✂ TSL 5
94/5 Flair 134
96/7 Flair 75
94/5 Fleer 162
96/7 Fleer 85, 137, 139, ART-5
95/6 Fleer Metal 116, IW-4
96/7 Fl. Picks 16, F50-13, FF-7, JE-16
92/3 Fleer Ultra 163
93/4 Fleer Ultra 44
94/5 Fleer Ultra 163
95/6 Fleer Ultra 122, 384, EA-6, PP-2
96/7 Fl. Ultra 139, MM-3
88/9 Frito Lay
83/4 Funmate Puffy 18 [w/]
82/3 HART / Jr. Whalers
83/4 HART / Jr. Whalers
84/5 HART / Jr. Whalers
85/6 HART / Jr. Whalers
86/7 HART / Jr. Whalers
87/8 HART / Jr. Whalers
88/9 HART / Jr. Whalers
89/0 HART / Jr. Whalers
90/1 HART / Jr. Whalers
01/2 Heads Up 15
02/3 Heads Up 20, -EIT 5, -ITN 6, -PSP 2, -SM 6, ✂ GWQ 6
93/4 Hockey Wit 53
02/3 In The Game-Used 10, 110, ✂ GUJ40, ✂ SJ40
84/5 Kellogg's 8
90/1 Kraft 13, 83
96/7 Kraft / TT
97/8 Kraft / KD
93/4 Leaf 161
94/5 Leaf 235
95/6 Leaf 45
96/7 Leaf 11
97/8 Leaf 44
94/5 L. Limited 30
95/6 L. Limited 23
96/7 L. Limited 52
96/7 L. Preferred 62, LS-6
97/8 Limited 199
96/7 Maggers 126
02/3 McDonald's -A 2, ✂ JP 3
96/7 Metal Univ. 125, CS-3, LW-5
82/3 O-Pee-Chee 123
83/4 O-Pee-Chee 138
84/5 O-Pee-Chee 70
85/6 OPC/Topps 140
85/6 OPC/Topps Box F
86/7 OPC/Topps 43
87/8 OPC/Topps 187
87/8 OPC/Topps Box J
88/9 OPC/Topps 52
88/9 OPC/Topps Box A
90/1 OPC/Topps 311
90/1 Topps-TL 21
91/2 O-Pee-Chee 130
92/3 O-Pee-Chee 188
01/2 O-Pee-Chee 23
02/3 O-Pee-Chee 19, 315
89/0 OPC/Topps 175
98/9 OPC Chrome 4, SB22
87/8 OPC Leaders 10
90/1 OPC Premier 32
91/2 OPC Premier 120
82/3 OPC/Topps Sticker 129
83/4 OPC/Topps Sticker 255
84/5 OPC Sticker 196
85/6 OPC Sticker 172
86/7 OPC Sticker 51-190
87/8 OPC Sticker 206
88/9 OPC Sticker 264
89/0 opcSticker 269
97/8 Omega 184
98/9 Omega 40
99/0 Omega 43
98/9 Pacific 351
99/0 Pacific 70
00/1 Pacific 81
01/2 Pacific 71, 406, IZ 5
02/3 Pacific 65
02/3 Pacific Complete 210
97/8 Pacific CC 123, SS-8B
97/8 Pa. Crown Roy. 109
98/9 Pa. Crown Roy. 22
97/8 Pa. Dynagon 100, T-63
97/8 Pa. Invincible 111, AZ-19
97/8 Pa. Paramount 148
99/0 Pa. Paramount 44
00/1 Pa. Paramount 42, ✂ GUS-1
97/8 Pa. Revolution 112
98/9 Pa. Revolution 23
98/9 Panini Photocard [x2]
87/8 Panini Sticker 43
88/9 Panini Sticker 242
89/0 Panini Sticker 221
90/1 Panini Sticker 39
91/2 Panini Sticker 281
92/3 Panini Sticker 224
93/4 Panini Sticker 81
94/5 Panini Sticker 73
95/6 Panini Sticker 58, 152
96/7 Panini Sticker 57, 145
97/8 Panini Sticker 50
98/9 Panini Sticker 49, 227
99/0 Panini Sticker 44
00/1 Panini Sticker 30
91/2 Parkhurst 353
92/3 Parkhurst 141
93/4 Parkhurst 160
94/5 Parkhurst 176
95/6 Parkhurst 164, PP-47, TW-6
00/1 Parkhurst P-82
01/2 Parkhurst 153, ✂ 500GS, ✂ PJ14, ✂ PS14, ✂ M28, ✂ M48, ✂ T18
02/3 Parkhurst 128, ✂ GJ22, ✂ SJ22, ✂ MM6, ✂ MS7
02/3 Parkhurst Retro 14, ✂ RF6
91/2 Pinnacle 167
92/3 Pinnacle 303
93/4 Pinnacle 74
94/5 Pinnacle 72
95/6 Pinnacle 39
96/7 Pinnacle 143
97/8 Pinnacle 78
97/8 Pi. BeeHive 49
97/8 Pi. Certified 121
97/8 Pi. Inside 52
95/6 Pi. Summit 42
96/7 Pi. Summit 10, U-4
97/8 Pi. Totally 121
95/6 Pi. Zenith 35
96/7 Pi. Zenith 10, CS-7
91/2 PITT / Elby's
91/2 PITT / Foodland 3
91/2 PITT / Food. Stickers
92/3 PITT / Coke-Clark
92/3 PITT / Foodland 7
92/3 PITT / Food. Stickers
93/4 PITT / Foodland 14
94/5 PITT / Foodland 9
95/6 PITT / Foodland 9
96/7 PITT / Tribune
95/6 Playoff 77
96/7 Playoff 360
94/5 POG 183
95/6 POG 7, 12, 215
82/3 Post [Hart.]
93/4 Power Play 188
93/4 Premier 424
94/5 Premier 139
00/1 Premier Plus 49, TT12
99/0 Prism 28
00/1 Private Stock 16
01/2 Pr. Stock 14
02/3 Pr. Stock Reserve ✂ 108
00/1 PS Titanium 14
01/2 PS Titanium 24, ✂ DSJ 45, ✂ DSJ 61
02/3 PS Titanium 18
95/6 Pro Magnet 95
90/1 Pro Set 105, 367
91/2 Pro Set 188
92/3 Pro Set 144
91/2 Pro Set Platinum 214
02/3 Quest for the Cup 14
99/0 Revolution 27, / CSC 27
00/1 Revolution 26
80/1 Soo Greyhounds
81/2 Soo Greyhounds
87/8 Soo Greyhounds 8
89/0 Soo Greyhounds
90/1 Score 70
90/1 Sco. Hot Cards 37
91/2 Score 267
91/2 Score CAN 487
92/3 Score 267
92/3 Score 518
93/4 Score 151
94/5 Score 244, NP18
95/6 Score 187
96/7 Score 56
97/8 Score 132
97/8 Score Pitt. 5
94/5 Select 84
95/6 Select CE 52, DS-2
96/7 Select CE 12
84/5 7-Eleven
85/6 7-Eleven Superstars 7
00/1 Signature 216, ✍ Aut. 158
01/2 Signature C-36, ✍ Aut. LRF, ✂ 500GS, ✂ GUE10, ✂ GJ10, ✂ GSJ10, ✂ HSHSJers 4, ✂ ITN10, ✂ TM6
02/3 Signature 171, GS-80, ✍ 171, ✂ FJ6, ✂ SGJ40
95/6 SBx Emotion 136, Xce-7, Xci-11
95/6 SBx Impact 130
96/7 SBx Impact 100, BR-4
83/4 Souhaits Keychain [Whalers]
94/5 SP 92
95/6 SP 115
96/7 SP 127
97/8 SP Authentic 126
98/9 SP Authentic 14, SO21
99/0 SP Authentic 16
00/1 SP Authentic 16
01/2 SP Authentic 16
00/1 SP GU 9
02/3 SP GU 9, ✂ TG
02/3 Sports Vault 35
97/8 SPx 41
99/0 SPx 31
00/1 SPx 10
02/3 SPx 12, 82, 127
99/0 Stadium 25
00/1 Stadium 30, SF15
01/2 Stadium 22
02/3 Stadium 4, -BT-11
96/7 SLU
95/6 Super Sticker 95, 98
84/5 Topps 54
92/3 Topps 502
95/6 Topps 244, 5PL
98/9 Topps 4, SB22
99/0 Topps 23
00/1 Topps 5, PC-3
01/2 Topps 23, ✂ CC3, ✂ GWJ, ✍ CA
02/3 Topps 19, 315, HHU20, ✂ CC1, ✂ CC4, ✂ CC15
99/0 To. Chrome 23
00/1 To. Chrome 5, PC-3
01/2 To. Chrome 23
02/3 T. Chrome 19
94/5 Topps Finest RL-16
95/6 To. Finest 127
98/9 To. Finest 50
98/9 T. Gold Label 22
99/0 To. Gold Label 11
00/1 To. Gold Label 80
00/1 To. Heritage 32
01/2 To. Heritage 22
02/3 To. Heritage 4, 107
02/3 T. Limited 19, 315
99/0 To. Prmr. Plus 21, / PP6
01/2 To. Reserve ✂ TR
91/2 To. Stadium 73
92/3 T. Stadium Club 352
93/4 To. Stadium 185
94/5 T. Stadium Club 96
95/6 To. Stadium 22, PS3
94/5 TSC Members Only 22
95/6 TSC Members Only 45
02/3 T. Total 362, TTC5, AW6
98/9 UD Choice 169
00/1 UD Reserve 16
01/2 UD Reserve 16
00/1 Ultimate Mem. ✂ A8-2, ✂ D-10, ✂ MO-7
01/2 Ultimate Mem. ✂ 500GS, ✂ A8, ✂ UC
02/3 Ultimate Mem. ✂ A8, ✂ FS, ✂ LA, ✂ Num, ✂ RT
99/0 Ult. Victory 16
90/1 Upper Deck 67, 314
91/2 Upper Deck 299
92/3 Upper Deck 291
93/4 Upper Deck 351
94/5 Upper Deck 12, SP-150
95/6 Upper Deck 46, 255, AS-18, R-11, R59, SE-66
96/7 Upper Deck 133
97/8 Upper Deck 135, SS25
98/9 Upper Deck 241, LS8
99/0 Upper Deck 199
00/1 Upper Deck 31
01/2 Upper Deck 262
02/3 Upper Deck 276, -SS4
95/6 UD ASG MVP23
02/3 UD Artistic 15, R15, UD5, / Art
95/6 UD BAP 8, ✍ S8
96/7 UD Black Diam. 101
97/8 UD Black Diam. 11
98/9 UD Black Diam. 14
00/1 UD Black Diam. 10
02/3 UD Classic 17
95/6 UD CC 200, 393
96/7 UD CC 212, 328, UD2
97/8 UD Coll. Choice 204, SQ54
98/9 UD G. Reserve 241
99/0 UD G. Reserve 199
02/3 UD Honor 11, 76
96/7 UD Ice 55
97/8 UD Ice 65
00/1 UD Ice 8
00/1 UD Legends 22, 24
01/2 UD Mask 16
98/9 UD MVP 35
99/0 UD MVP 40
00/1 UD MVP 39
01/2 UD MVP 35
02/3 UD MVP 33
99/0 UD MVP Cup 36
99/0 UD Ovation 11
02/3 UD Piece 13
02/3 UD Premier 10
00/1 UD Pros&Prosp. 16
02/3 UD Rookie 21
00/1 UD Vintage 66, 73, 74
01/2 UD Vintage 50
02/3 UD Vintage 45, 266, GB 45, T12
00/1 Vanguard 19
01/2 Vanguard 15
02/3 Vanguard 18
99/0 Victory 59
00/1 Victory 42, 47, 289
01/2 Victory 61
02/3 Victory 39
99/0 WGretzky 37
97/8 Zenith 50, Z53
FRANCIS, TODD
83/4 Brantford Alexanders
94/5 Slapshot / Brantford 3
FRANCOEUR, JONATHAN
00/1 Chicoutimi Saguenéens 6
FRANCON, DEVIN
00/1 Red Deer Rebels
FRANCZ, ROBERT
95/6 DEL 19
FRANEK, KAREL
97/8 APS 100
FRANEK, PETR
94/5 APS 204
95/6 APS 151
00/1 DS 121
99/0 Eishockey 48
98/9 Las Vegas Thunder
00/1 OFS 160, -Star 21
01/2 OFS 189, -CL 1, -G2
FRANK, JEFF
82/3 Regina Pats
83/4 Regina Pats
FRANK, MARK
82/3 Medicine Hat Tigers
FRANKE, JOE
93/4 Fort Wayne Komets 26
94/5 Fort Wayne Komets 27
FRANKE, PETER
94/5 DEL 410
95/6 DEL 408
96/7 DEL 70
00/1 UD DEL 51
FRANKS, JIM
34-43 BeeHive-1 [NYRa.]
FRANKS, MARK
92/3 Brandon Wheat Kings
93/4 Huntington Blizzard
94/5 Huntington Blizzard
90/1 Saskatoon Blades
91/2 Saskatoon Blades
90/1 7th..Sketch WHL 74
91/2 7th..Sketch WHL 116
FRANTTI, GORD
94/5 Huntington Blizzard
91/2 ProCards 515
FRANZ, CHRISTIAN
01/2 UD DEL 251
FRANZ, GEORG
94/5 DEL 254
95/6 DEL 252
96/7 DEL 141
95 Panini Worlds 68
94 Semic 283
89 Semic Sticker 117
91 Semic Sticker 175
93 Semic Sticker 165
FRANZÉN, RIKARD
94/5 Leaf Elit Set 108, SS-1
95/6 Leaf Elit Set 165, LM-13
89/0 Semic Elitserien 8
90/1 Semic Elitserien 81
91/2 Semic Elitserien 7
92/3 Semic Elitserien 33
95/6 UD Elitserien 4, 219, 249
98/9 UD Elitserien 2, -DL1
99/0 UD Elitserien 2, L1, ✍ Aut.
00/1 UD Elitserien 4
96 Wien 51
FRAPPIER, SHAWN
96/7 Mississippi S'Wolves
93/4 Slapshot / Sudbury 7
94/5 Slapshot / Sudbury 6
95/6 Slapshot 12
92/3 Sudbury Wolves
93/4 Sudbury Wolves
FRASER, BARRY
88/9 EDMO / Action 158
FRASER, CHARLES
23/4 William Paterson 39
FRASER, CHRIS
89/0 Windsor Spitfires
FRASER, CRAIG
89/0 7th..Sketch OHL 74
90/1 7th..Sketch OHL 5
91/2 7th..Sketch OHL 34
FRASER, CURT
86/7 CHIC / Coke
87/8 CHIC / Coke
93/4 Milwaukee Admirals
88/9 MINS / ADA
79/0 O-Pee-Chee 117
80/1 O-Pee-Chee 287
81/2 O-Pee-Chee 334
82/3 O-Pee-Chee 343
83/4 O-Pee-Chee 102
84/5 O-Pee-Chee 34
85/6 OPC/Topps 3
86/7 OPC/Topps 31
82/3 OPC/Topps Sticker 9
82/3 OPC/Topps Sticker 244
85/6 OPC Sticker 24-153
98/9 Orlando Solar Bears
98/9 Orlando Solar Bears Geico
87/8 Panini Sticker 231
80/1 Pepsi Bottle Cap
82/3 Post [Vanc.]
90/1 ProCards 327
91/2 ProCards 619
79/0 Topps 117
84/5 Topps 29
78/9 VANC / Royal Bank
79/0 VANC / Royal Bank
80/1 VANC
80/1 VANC / Silverwood
81/2 VANC
81/2 VANC / Silverwood
82/3 VANC
82/3 Victoria Cougars
FRASER, GORD
25-27 Anonymous 136
29/0 La Presse
FRASER, IAIN
92/3 Classic Prospects 49
93/4 Cla. Prospects 15
93/4 Donruss 478
94/5 Donruss 270
99/0 Eishockey 214
93/4 Fleer Ultra 400
94/5 Fleer Ultra 73
93/4 Fleer Ultra Pros. 1
94/5 Fleer Ultra 174
96/7 Kentucky Tho'blades
94/5 Leaf 105
89/0 Oshawa Generals
94/5 Panini Sticker G
93/4 Parkhurst 434
93/4 Parkhurst C19
94/5 Parkhurst 187, 280
94/5 Pinnacle 513
93/4 Power Play 419
93/4 Power Play RooS 4
93/4 Premier 525
94/5 Premier 7, OF-6
91/2 ProCards 468
93/4 Score 625
90 7th..Sketch Mem.Cup 89
89/0 7th..Sketch OHL 19, 186, 198
93/4 To. Stadium 485
94/5 T. Stadium Club 32
93/4 Upper Deck 337
94/5 Upper Deck 162
00/1 UD DEL 43
01/2 UD DEL 85
FRASER, KERRY
90/1 Pro Set 686
FRASER, KRIS
00/1 Owen Sound Attack 12
FRASER, LEGS
51/2 Laval Dairy 104
FRASER, SCOTT*
94/5 Fredericton Canadiens
95/6 Fredericton Canadiens
96/7 Fredericton Canadiens
98/9 Pacific 207
96/7 Saint John Flames
FRASER, SCOTT**
80/1 Québec Remparts
FRASER, SCOTT***
23/4 Paulins Candy 53
FRASER, TREVER
98/9 Hampton Roads
91/2 7th..Sketch WHL 171
92/3 Tacoma Rockets
93/4 Tacoma Rockets
FRASER, WILLIAM
25 Dominion Chocolates 81
FRASZKOL, ADAM
89 Semic Sticker 146
FRAWLEY, DAN
87/8 Panini Sticker 153
88/9 Panini Sticker 338
86/7 PITT / Kodak
87/8 PITT / Kodak
89/0 ProCards IHL 160
90/1 ProCards 274
91/2 ProCards 3
91/2 Rochester Americans DD
91/2 Rochester Americans GL
91/2 Rochester Americans WPC
92/3 Rochester Americans DD
92/3 Rochester Americans WPC
95/6 Rochester Americans
96/7 Rochester Americans
97/8 Rochester Americans
83/4 Springfield Indians 9
FRAYN, ROBERT
89/0 7th..Sketch OHL 175
90/1 7th..Sketch OHL 6
91/2 7th..Sketch OHL 184
FRAZER, FRITZ
51/2 Laval Dairy 106
FREADRICH, KYLE
99/0 Detroit Vipers
00/1 Pacific 382
96/7 Regina Pats
97/8 Regina Pats
00/1 SPx 119
00/1 Upper Deck 192
00/1 UD MVP 205
00/1 Victory 267
FRÉCHETTE, YANNICK
90/1 7th..Sketch LHJMQ 60
91/2 7th..Sketch LHJMQ 237
FRED, FURIOUS
99/0 Muskegon Fury
FREDERICK, JOE
93/4 Classic 65
94/5 Classic 4 Sport 149
93/4 Cla. Prospects 131
99/0 Utah Grizzlies
FREDERICK, TROY
88/9 Brandon Wheat Kings
89/0 Brandon Wheat Kings
92/3 Kansas City Blades
90/1 ProCards 596
91/2 ProCards 512
98/9 Topeka Scarecrows
FREDERICKS, RAY
52/3 Laval Dairy Update 104
52/3 St. Lawrence 70
FREDERICKSON, FRANK
83 HHOF Postcard D3
83&87 HHOF 49
24/5 Holland Creameries 5
60/1 Topps 34
61/2 Topps - Stamp
FREDRICKSEN, JERRY
95/6 Tri-City Americans 30
FREDRIKSSON, DENNIS
91/2 Semic Elitserien 300
FREER, MARK
95/6 Edge Ice 132
02/3 Hershey Bears
95/6 Houston Aeros
92/3 OTTA
93/4 Panini Sticker 118
91/2 Parkhurst 343
92/3 Parkhurst 354
93/4 Premier 142
92/3 Pro Set 127
88/9 ProCards / Hershey
89/0 ProCards AHL 337
90/1 ProCards 47
91/2 ProCards 279
93/4 To. Stadium 29
92/3 Upper Deck 445
FREIBAUER, RADIM
99/0 OFS 73
FREITAG, WAYNE
63/4 Québec Aces
FRENCH, JOHN
72/3 New England Whalers
74/5 OPC WHA 33
76/7 OPC WHA 105
73/4 Quaker Oats 33
FRENETTE, DEREK
92/3 Peoria Rivermen
93/4 Peoria Rivermen
91/2 ProCards 27
FRENGLER, REINHARD
79 Panini Sticker 252
FRENZEL, DIETER
79 Panini Sticker 251
FRESTADIUS, ROBERT
89/0 Semic Elitserien 173
FREW, IRVIN
36-39 Diamond Match TT1
36-39 Diamond Match TT2
36-39 Diamond Match TT3
FRID, ROBERT
98/9 Quad City Mallards
FRIDAY, BILL
91/2 Ultimate Original Six 85
FRIDAY, BOB
51/2 Laval Dairy 87
FRIDAY, TIM
85/6 DETR / Little Caesars
FRIDFINSON, WALLY
24/5 Falcons Crescent 3
24/5 Holland Creameries 1
FRIDGEN, DAN
82/3 HART / Jr. Whalers
FRIEDMAN, DOUG
95/6 Donruss 350
97/8 EDMO
99/0 Kentucky Tho'blades
98/9 Milwaukee Admirals
00/1 Worcester IceCats
FRIESEN, CURTIS
90/1 7th..Sketch WHL 47
FRIESEN, JEFF
01/2 Adrenaline 1
02/3 Atomic ✂ GWJ 15
98/9 Aurora 166
99/0 Aurora 120
00/1 Aurora 127
98/9 Be A Player 267, ✍ Aut. 267
99/0 BAP Mem. 274
00/1 BAP Mem. 49
01/2 BAP Memor. 68
02/3 BAP Memorabilia 62
95/6 Bowman 84
01/2 Bowman 86
98/9 Bowman's Best 41
93/4 Classic 102, CL3
94/5 Classic 10, C4, R5, T61, ✍ Aut.
94/5 Classic 4 Sport 125
94/5 Cla. Images 2, CE2, ✍ Aut.
94/5 Cla. Images 4 Sport 103
93/4 Cla. Prospects 202, 209, ✍ Aut.
99/0 Crown Royale 123, -IG 24
01/2 Crown Royale 2
93/4 Donruss CAN11
95/6 Donruss 162, C3TWC-21, PP-21, PP-31, RT-7
96/7 Donruss 79
97/8 Donruss 55
97/8 Do. Canadian 81
96/7 Do. Elite 53
97/8 Do. Elite 93
97/8 Do. Preferred 14
97/8 Do. Priority 70
97/8 Do. Studio 98
98/9 Dynagon Ice 164
99/0 Dynagon Ice 172
02/3 Exclusive 104
02/3 First Edition 63, ✂ Jers.
94/5 Flair 164
94/5 Fleer 196, RS-3
95/6 Fleer Metal 129
94/5 Fleer Ultra 365
95/6 Fleer Ultra 145, AR-4
02/3 Heads Up ✂ GWQ 1
99/0 HoloGrFX 49
94/5 Leaf 482, P-9
95/6 Leaf 21, SR-7
96/7 Leaf 87
97/8 Leaf 102
94/5 L. Limited CAN 3
95/6 L. Limited 62
96/7 L. Limited 83
96/7 L. Preferred 97
97/8 Limited 72, 196
95/6 McDonald's McD-31
01/2 McDonald's -HP 1
99/0 Millenium 211, ✍ Aut. 211
98/9 NHL Power Play
99/0 NHL Power Play
01/2 O-Pee-Chee 57
02/3 O-Pee-Chee 73, Update 73
98/9 OPC Chrome 128
97/8 Omega 200
98/9 Omega 209
99/0 Omega 205
98/9 Pacific 379
99/0 Pacific 370
00/1 Pacific 357
01/2 Pacific 3
02/3 Pacific 2
02/3 Pacific Complete 439
97/8 Pacific CC 63
97/8 Pa. Crown Roy. 119
98/9 Pa. Crown Roy. 120
97/8 Pa. Dynagon 110, T-60
97/8 Pa. Invincible 124
97/8 Pa. Paramount 164
98/9 Pa. Paramount 209
99/0 Pa. Paramount 204
00/1 Pa. Paramount 213
97/8 Pa. Revolution 123
98/9 Pa. Revolution 126
98/9 Panini Photocard
95/6 Panini Sticker 278, 304
96/7 Panini Sticker 278
97/8 Panini Sticker 233
98/9 Panini Sticker 209
99/0 Panini Sticker 296
93/4 Parkhurst 505
95/6 Parkhurst 182
00/1 Parkhurst P-106
01/2 Parkhurst 156, ✂ PJ8, ✂ PS8
02/3 Parkhurst 133
02/3 Parkhurst Retro 153
94/5 Parkie SE166
93/4 Pinnacle 472
94/5 Pinnacle 252, 532, RTP7
95/6 Pinnacle 55
96/7 Pinnacle 18
97/8 Pinnacle 119
96/7 Pi. Be A Player 190, ✍ Aut. 190
97/8 Pi. Certified 81
97/8 Pi. Inside 121
96/7 Pi. Summit 144
97/8 Pi. Totally 81
95/6 Pi. Zenith 65
96/7 Pi. Zenith 69
95/6 Playoff 83
96/7 Playoff 362
95/6 POG 223, I-030
94/5 Premier 547
00/1 Premier Plus 13
99/0 Prism 124
00/1 Private Stock 88, PS-49, PSNW-21
01/2 Pr. Stock 1
02/3 Pr. Stock Reserve 61
01/2 PS Titanium 1, ✂ DSJ 2
01/2 PS Titanium Draft ✂ 1
95/6 Pro Magnet 120
02/3 Quest for the Cup 58
99/0 Revolution 127, TL-10
00/1 Revolution 128
94/5 Score 203, TR8
95/6 Score 91, CI-10, GB-11
96/7 Score 4
97/8 Score 170
94/5 Select 176, YE-9
95/6 Select CE 56
96/7 Select CE 61
00/1 Signature 172, ✂ J-28
01/2 Signature TM1
02/3 Signature 109, ✍ 109
95/6 SBx Emotion 155
95/6 SBx Impact 147, 235
96/7 SBx Impact 116
94/5 SP 145
95/6 SP 133
96/7 SP 143
97/8 SP Authentic 134
98/9 SP Authentic 76
99/0 SP Authentic 74
01/2 SP Authentic 1
02/3 SP Authentic 55
01/2 SP GU ✂ TotG, ✂ TotGC, ✂ TotGT
02/3 SP Game-Used ✂ AF, ✂ TG
02/3 Sports Vault 64
99/0 SPx 128
00/1 SPx 56, X11
01/2 SPx 152
99/0 Stadium 18, -Chrome 17
00/1 Stadium 106
01/2 Stadium 66
02/3 Stadium 108
95/6 Topps 360, 15CJ, 18NG, YS6
98/9 Topps 128
99/0 Topps 96, NS9
00/1 Topps 186
01/2 Topps 57
02/3 Topps 73, Update 73, / PP3
99/0 To. Chrome 96
00/1 To. Chrome 124
01/2 To. Chrome 57
02/3 T. Chrome 49
94/5 Topps Finest 11, 159, BBR-14
95/6 To. Finest 27
98/9 To. Finest 32
98/9 T. Gold Label 62
99/0 To. Gold Label 42
00/1 To. Gold Label 58, B8
00/1 To. Heritage 138
01/2 To. Heritage 73
02/3 To. Heritage 158
02/3 T. Limited 73
99/0 To. Prmr. Plus 53
01/2 To. Reserve 62
95/6 To. Stadium 106
00/1 To. Stars 56
95/6 T. Super Skills 69
02/3 T. Total 380
98/9 UD Choice 174
00/1 UD Heroes 156
01/2 UD PlayMakers Ltd 2
00/1 UD Reserve 72
99/0 Ult. Victory 75
93/4 Upper Deck 532, E8
94/5 Upper Deck 237, 526, SP-161
95/6 Upper Deck 134, SE-74
96/7 Upper Deck 332
97/8 Upper Deck 358
98/9 Upper Deck 351
99/0 Upper Deck 109
00/1 Upper Deck 145
01/2 Upper Deck 2
02/3 Upper Deck 348, ✂ CG
94/5 UD BAP R164
99/0 UD Black Diam. 76
00/1 UD Black Diam. 50
94/5 UD Canada Junior 13
01/2 UD Challenge 2
02/3 UD Classic ✂ CS, ✂ HH, ✂ HR
95/6 UD CC 309, 372
96/7 UD CC 238
97/8 UD Coll. Choice 215, SQ10
98/9 UD G. Reserve 351
99/0 UD G. Reserve 109, / Backup 166
96/7 UD Ice 58
00/1 UD Ice 61
00/1 UD Legends 112, 113
01/2 UD Mask 2, ✂ GJ, ✂ JP, ✂ DP
98/9 UD MVP 174
99/0 UD MVP 175, DR10, ✍ PS
00/1 UD MVP 148
01/2 UD MVP 3
99/0 UD MVP Cup 154, CC8
00/1 UD Pros&Prosp. 72
99/0 UD Retro 66
02/3 UD Top Shelf 2, ✂ ST, ✂ SW
00/1 UD Vintage 299, 307, 308
01/2 UD Vintage 2
00/1 Vanguard 87
01/2 Vanguard 1
99/0 Victory 246, 248
00/1 Victory 191, 193, 319
01/2 Victory 11
02/3 Victory 3
99/0 WGretzky 149
97/8 Zenith 33
FRIESEN, KARL
94/5 DEL 314
95/6 DEL 360
89 Semic Sticker 103
91 Semic Sticker 154
FRIESEN, ROB
94/5 Guildford Flames 12
FRIESEN, TERRY
98 Bowman 62
98 Bowman Chrome 62
95/6 Swift Current Broncos
FRIEST, RON
82/3 MINS
FRIG, LEN
74/5 Loblaws
74/5 O-Pee-Chee 242
75/6 O-Pee-Chee 174
76/7 O-Pee-Chee 352
77/8 O-Pee-Chee 384
74/5 Topps 242
75/6 Topps 174
FRIIS, JARLE
92/3 Semic Nordisk 50
FRIIS, MARTIN
92/3 Semic Nordisk 59
FRIMAN, JERRY
92/3 Semic Elitserien 96
FRIMAN, KARI-PEKKA
92/3 Jyvas Hyva 127
93/4 Jyvas Hyva 225
93/4 Sisu 190
94/5 Sisu 104
95/6 Sisu 175, 340
FRITZ, FABULOUS
94/5 Milwaukee Admirals
FRITZ, GEORGE
94/5 DEL 430
95/6 DEL 397
FRITZ, MITCH
98/9 Kelowna Rockets
FRITZ, TOMMY
89/0 Semic Elitserien 105
90/1 Semic Elitserien 108
91/2 Semic Elitserien 112
92/3 Semic Elitserien 129
FROESE, BOB
89/0 NYRA / Marine
83/4 O-Pee-Chee 265
84/5 O-Pee-Chee 159
86/7 OPC/Topps 55
86/7 O-Pee-Chee 263
86/7 O-Pee-Chee 264
87/8 OPC/Topps 195
83/4 OPC/Topps Sticker 183
84/5 OPC Sticker 113
86/7 OPC Sticker 236
86/7 OPC Sticker 182-122
86/7 OPC Sticker 186-45
86/7 OPC Sticker 193-55
88/9 Panini Sticker 299
89/0 Panini Sticker 284
83/4 PHIL / J.C. Penney
86/7 PHIL
78/9 Saginaw Gears
83/4 Souhaits Keychain [Flyers]
84/5 Topps 117
86/7 OPC/Topps - Stick. 7
FROESE, COLIN
92/3 MPS SJHL 37
FROGREN, JONAS
00/1 UD Elitserien 78
FROH, DAVID
93/4 Slapshot / Oshawa 5
95/6 Slapshot 192
FROIO, FRANK
99/0 San Angelo Outlaws
FROLIKOV, ALEXEI
90/1 O-Pee-Chee 502
FROLKIN, ANDREI
00/1 Mir 281
FROLOV, ALEXANDER
02/3 Atomic 112
02/3 BAP All-Star 148
02/3 BAP Memorabilia 287
02/3 Bowman 124, ✂ FFDS, ✂ FFJ, ✂ FFP, ✂ FFR, ✂ FFRP, ✂ FFS, ✂ FFTS, ✍ YSA, / ✍ Puck
02/3 Calder 122, -CR 14
02/3 Crown Royale 117, -RR 13
02/3 Exclusive 199, ✍ 199
02/3 First Edition 434H
02/3 Heads Up 126
02/3 In The Game-Used 192, ✂ C16
00/1 Mir 63
02/3 O-Pee-Chee 333
02/3 Pacific 126
02/3 Pacific Complete 579
02/3 PTC/ ASG 7
02/3 PTC/ Collections 6
02/3 Parkhurst 217
02/3 Parkhurst Retro 217, ✂ CH5
02/3 Pr. Stock Reserve 164, -MIT 5
02/3 PS Titanium 118, -ROT 12
02/3 Quest for the Cup 123
02/3 Signature 192, ✍ 192, ✂ SGJ63, ✂ TQ10
02/3 SP Authentic ✍ 188, ✍ SotT, ✍ ✂ Patch
02/3 SP GU 79, ✍ Sig
02/3 SPx 161
02/3 Stadium 123
02/3 Topps 333
02/3 T. Chrome 181
02/3 To. Heritage 133
02/3 T. Total 416
02/3 Ultimate Mem. 17, ✂ CC, ✍ RAut
02/3 Upper Deck 238
02/3 UD Artistic 121, R99, CG10, ✂ RT
02/3 UD Classic 117
02/3 UD Foundations 155
02/3 UD Honor 154
01/2 UD Mask 161
02/3 UD Piece 133
02/3 UD Premier ✍ 101
02/3 UD Rookie ✂ 159
02/3 UD Top Shelf 129
02/3 Vanguard 117, -PP 13
FROLOV, DMITRI
96/7 DEL 210
98/9 Mir 165
90/1 O-Pee-Chee 523
94 Semic 151
95 Semic 130
92/3 Upper Deck 348
FROLOV, KONSTANTIN
99/0 Mir 206
FROM, MARKO
98/9 Cardset 31
99/0 Cardset 22
FROSCH, FRANTISEK
94/5 DEL 428
95/6 DEL 391
96/7 DEL 76
98/9 DEL 35
FRUTEL, CHRISTIAN
94/5 DEL 315
FRY, CURTIS
92/3 BCJHL 51
99/0 Eishockey 247
FRY, RICK
89/0 Portland Winter Hawks
FRYCER, MIROSLAV
81/2 Dernière Heure
88/9 DETR / Little Caesars
88/9 EDMO
88/9 EDMO / Action 153
82/3 O-Pee-Chee 321
83/4 O-Pee-Chee 330
85/6 O-Pee-Chee 198
86/7 OPC/Topps 68
82/3 OPC/Topps Sticker 65
83/4 OPC/Topps Sticker 38
85/6 OPC Sticker 21
86/7 OPC Sticker 142
87/8 OPC Sticker 158-18
82/3 Post [Toro.]
81/2 QUEB
83/4 Souhaits Keychain [Maple Leafs]
82/3 TORO
83/4 TORO
84/5 TORO
85/6 TORO
86/7 TORO
86/7 TORO
87/8 TORO / 5x8
87/8 TORO / P.L.A.Y. 15
83/4 Vachon 86-56
FRYDL, KAREL
96/7 APS 104
FRYKBO, ANDERS
89/0 Semic Elitserien 233
90/1 Semic Elitserien 72
91/2 Semic Elitserien 245
FRYLÉN, EDVIN
94/5 Leaf Elit Set 105, ND-5
95/6 Leaf Elit Set 299
93/4 Parkhurst 536
92/3 Semic Elitserien 280
92/3 Semic Elitserien 351
94/5 Sig. Rookies 17, ✍ 17
94/5 SR Gold Standard 85
93/4 Upper Deck 572
95/6 UD Elitserien 188
97/8 UD Elitserien 184, UDS15
99/0 UD Elitserien 120
00/1 UD Elitserien 47
FRYZLEWICZ, STANISLAV
73/4 Williams Finnish 90
FTOREK, ROBBIE
81/2 Dernière Heure
92/3 Future Trends C76 189
89/0 Halifax Citadels
88/9 LOSA / Smokey
96/7 NJER / Sharp
79/0 O-Pee-Chee 267
80/1 O-Pee-Chee 35
81/2 O-Pee-Chee 274
82/3 O-Pee-Chee 223
83/4 O-Pee-Chee 244
81/2 OPC Sticker 72
75/6 OPC WHA 19
76/7 OPC WHA 13
77/8 OPC WHA 35
80/1 Pepsi Bottle Cap
75/6 Phoenix Roadrunners
76/7 Phoenix Roadrunners
81/2 Post 24
82/3 Post [NYRa.]
89/0 ProCards AHL 157
80/1 QUEB
90/1 QUEB / Petro-Canada
80/1 Topps 35
FUCHS, ANDREI
94/5 DEL 351
95/6 DEL 323
96/7 DEL 101
FUCHS, ANDREJ
99/0 Eishockey 298
FUCHS, BORIS
94/5 DEL 356
95/6 DEL 326
96/7 DEL 103
99/0 Eishockey 308
FUCHS, LOTHAR
70/1 Kuvajulkaisut 84
FUGÈRE, NICK
01/2 Hull Olympiques 11
02/3 Hull Olympiques
FUHR, GRANT
01/2 ASG History
98/9 Aurora 160, CF-41
99/0 Aurora 125, Stripe 125, GU-17
98/9 Be A Player 122, ✍ Aut. 122
99/0 BAP Mem. 179, H-24
00/1 BAP Mem. ✂ V-13
02/3 BAP Memorabilia / Cup
01/2 BT Pipes 113, HSHS, ✂ DM, ✂ S&J, ✂ GR, ✂ VM, ✂ -HSHSJers.
02/3 Between the Pipes ✂ CP11, ✂ GT18
96/7 Bic.Sports Aces 8-H
98/9 Bicycle.. 10-H
90/1 Bowman 189
91/2 Bowman 111
91/2 Bowman 407
92/3 Bowman 114
95/6 Bowman 25
98/9 Bowman's Best 22
93/4 BUFF / Noco
99/0 Challenger 14
99/0 Crown Royale 22
93/4 Donruss 34
94/5 Donruss 212
95/6 Donruss 310

96/7 Donruss 117
97/8 Donruss 153
96/7 Do. Canadian 109, 148
97/8 Do. Canadian 95
95/6 Do. Elite 42, PW-9
96/7 Do. Elite 29, P-12
97/8 Do. Elite 110
97/8 Do. Preferred 60
97/8 Do. Priority 82, PG-19
97/8 Do. Studio 102
98/9 Dynagon Ice 157, -IW 8, -TC 22
99/0 Dynagon Ice 35
93/4 EA Sports 18
81/2 EDMO / Red Rooster
81/2 EDMO / West Mall
82/3 EDMO / Red Rooster
83/4 EDMO / Button
83/4 EDMO / McDonald's
83/4 EDMO / West Mall
83/4 EDMO
84/5 EDMO
84/5 EDMO / Red Rooster
85/6 EDMO / Red Rooster
86/7 EDMO
86/7 EDMO / Red Rooster
87/8 EDMO
88/9 EDMO
88/9 EDMO / Action 65
88/9 EDMO / Action 130
88/9 Esso All-Star
96/7 Flair 80
96/7 Fleer 96
01/2 Fleer Greats 57, ✍ Aut.
01/2 Fleer Legacy 19
95/6 Fleer Metal 123
92/3 Fleer Ultra 210
93/4 Fleer Ultra 103
94/5 Fleer Ultra 262
95/6 Fleer Ultra 298
96/7 Fl. Ultra 145
00 Gatorade Sticker
91/2 Gillette 19
93/4 High Liner 3
93/4 Hockey Wit 40
92/3 Humpty Dumpty
89/0 Kraft 11
91/2 Kraft 9
92/3 Kraft / PB
95/6 Kraft / PS
86/7 Kraft Sports 13
93/4 Leaf 66
93/4 Leaf PW 5
94/5 Leaf 78
96/7 Leaf 64
97/8 Leaf 123
96/7 L. Limited 48
97/8 Limited 32, FG-45
96/7 Maggers 139
98/9 McD's T7
99/0 McDonald's ✄ GJ, ✍ SS
96/7 Metal Univ. 131
99/0 Millenium 38, ✍ Aut. 38, ✄ G-3
98/9 NHL Power Play
82/3 O-Pee-Chee 105
83/4 O-Pee-Chee 27
84/5 O-Pee-Chee 241
85/6 O-Pee-Chee 207
86/7 OPC/Topps 56
87/8 OPC/Topps 178
88/9 OPC/Topps 59
90/1 OPC/Topps 321
91/2 O-Pee-Chee 84
92/3 O-Pee-Chee 31
92/3 O-Pee-Chee 119
92/3 OPC - Anniv. 15
89/0 OPC/Topps 192
98/9 OPC Chrome 114, -Reprint 5
91/2 OPC Premier 100
91/2 OPC Premier 191
88/9 OPC Stars 9
82/3 OPC/Topps Sticker 95
82/3 OPC/Topps Sticker 161
84/5 OPC Sticker 259
85/6 OPC Sticker 221-88
86/7 OPC Sticker 121-135
86/7 OPC Sticker 67-198
87/8 OPC Sticker 85
88/9 OPC Sticker 223
88/9 OPC Sticker 122-252
88/9 OPC Sticker 212-83
89/0 opcSticker 228
97/8 Omega 193
98/9 Omega 202
99/0 Omega 36
98/9 Pacific 31
99/0 Pacific 356, ITCNF-17, TL-23
97/8 Pacific CC 228, ITC-18
97/8 Pa. Crown Roy. 116, FO-17
98/9 Pa. Crown Roy. 114
97/8 Pa. Dynagon 106, S-19, T-18
97/8 Pa. Invincible 119
97/8 Pa. Paramount 158, GSL-18
98/9 Pa. Paramount 203, -GS 17, -TC 22
99/0 Pa. Paramount 196, GS-18
97/8 Pa. Revolution 120, RTS-17
98/9 Pa. Revolution 122
98/9 Panini Photocard
87/8 Panini Sticker 254
88/9 Panini Sticker 52
88/9 Panini Sticker 180
88/9 Panini Sticker 188
88/9 Panini Sticker 403
90/1 Panini Sticker 230
92/3 Panini Sticker 75
93/4 Panini Sticker 108
96/7 Panini Sticker 203
97/8 Panini Sticker 172
98/9 Panini Sticker 155
99/0 Panini Sticker 186
91/2 Parkhurst 175
92/3 Parkhurst 182
92/3 Parkhurst 250
92/3 Parkhurst 497
93/4 Parkhurst 22
93/4 Parkhurst D7
95/6 Parkhurst 443, PP-9, PP-34
91/2 Pinnacle 168
92/3 Pinnacle 267
92/3 Pinnacle 301
93/4 Pinnacle 65
93/4 Pinnacle Mask 1
94/5 Pinnacle 421
96/7 Pinnacle 181
97/8 Pinnacle 81, M-10, / Tin 2
96/7 Pi. Be A Player SP-9
97/8 Pi. BeeHive 44
97/8 Pi. Certified 10
97/8 Pi. Inside 51, SU-6, S-20
96/7 Pi. Summit 14
97/8 Pi. Totally 10
95/6 Pi. Zenith 107
96/7 Pi. Zenith 82, CS-3
94/5 POG 273
95/6 POG 245, I-008
82/3 Post [Edmo.]
93/4 Power Play 27
93/4 Power Play Netm. 3
93/4 Premier 218
94/5 Premier 80
99/0 Prism 23
90/1 Pro Set 82
91/2 Pro Set 78
91/2 Pro Set 494
92/3 Pro Set 183
92/3 Pro Set PV5
91/2 Pro Set Platinum 117
91/2 Puck / Pro Set 27
90/1 Score 275
91/2 Score 114
91/2 Score 58T
91/2 Score CAN 114
91/2 Score CAN 608
92/3 Score 20
92/3 Score 437
93/4 Score 75
95/6 Score 228
96/7 Score 91
97/8 Score 5, NW-10
97/8 Score SLou. 11
92/3 Seasons 54
94/5 Select 93
96/7 Select CE 35
89 Semic Sticker 53
02/3 Signature GS-39
96/7 SBx Impact 112
95/6 SP 126
96/7 SP 133
97/8 SP Authentic 143, ✍ SotT
00/1 SP Authentic ✍ SotTT
01/2 SP GU ✄ TotG, ✄ TotGSig, ✄ TotGC, ✄ TotGCSig, ✄ TotGT
96/7 SPx HH10
98/9 SPx Finite 77
96/7 SLOU / Dispatch 3
93/4 SLU / Card-A
93/4 SLU / Card-B
93/4 Starting Lineup
94/5 Starting Lineup
98/9 SLU
96/7 Team Out✄
88/9 OPC/Topps - Stick. 6
92/3 Topps 350
95/6 Topps 242
98/9 Topps 114, -Reprint 5
99/0 Topps 24
00/1 Topps 252
99/0 To. Chrome 24
94/5 Topps Finest RL-4
95/6 To. Finest 113
98/9 To. Finest 27
98/9 T. Gold Label 95
96/7 Topps Picks ID15
91/2 To. Stadium 258
92/3 T. Stadium Club 412
93/4 To. Stadium 260
93/4 To. Stadium - Master Photo-2 3
95/6 To. Stadium 24
95/6 T. Super Skills 88
01/2 T/O Archives 33, -Jers., ✍ CAI
91/2 TORO / P.L.A.Y. 23
00/1 Ultimate Mem. ✄ D-3
01/2 Ultimate Mem. ✄ ASGH, ✄ SCW
02/3 Ultimate Mem. ✄ ASMVP, ✄ FS, ✄ Num, ✄ SCD (x3)
90/1 Upper Deck 264
91/2 Upper Deck 264
91/2 Upper Deck 553
92/3 Upper Deck 271
93/4 Upper Deck 163, GG10, SP-15
95/6 Upper Deck 484, SE-158
96/7 Upper Deck 140, X33
97/8 Upper Deck 145
98/9 Upper Deck 362
99/0 Upper Deck 194
94/5 UD BAP G7
95/6 UD BAP 196, ✍ S196
96/7 UD Black Diam. 128
97/8 UD Black Diam. 148
96/7 UD CC 224
97/8 UD Coll. Choice 225
02/3 UD Foundations 9, 31, 85, 91, 110, ✄ CH, ✄ CG, ✄ DF, ✄ MS, ✄ PP, ✍ SG
98/9 UD G. Reserve 362
99/0 UD G. Reserve 194
99/0 UD Gretzky Excl. 60
96/7 UD Ice 62
00/1 UD Legends 48, LC6, ✄ LGJ
01/2 UD Legends 24, 82
02/3 UD Mask / Mask (x2), ✍ Mask (x2)
99/0 UD MVP 185
01/2 UD SCup Champs 9
01/2 UD Vintage ✄ GG
83/4 Vachon 24-104
82/3 Victoria Cougars
99/0 Victory 264
99/0 WGretzky 31
97/8 Zenith 60, Z14

FUJITA, RYAN
91/2 Saskatoon Blades
90/1 7th..Sketch WHL 105
91/2 7th...Sketch WHL 110

FUKAMI, SCOTT
88/9 Lethbridge Hurricanes
90/1 7th..Sketch WHL 259
91/2 7th...Sketch WHL 68

FUKSA, ZDENEK
98/9 OFS 55
99/0 Score 40

FULLAN, LAWRENCE
74/5 Loblaws

FULLER, RON
89/0 Nashville Knights

FULLUM, RIVAL
91/2 Cornwall Royals
87/8 Kitchener Rangers
88/9 Kitchener Rangers
89/0 Kitchener Rangers
90 7th..Sketch Mem.Cup 46
90/1 7th..Sketch OHL 24, 182
91/2 7th...Sketch OHL 21
94/5 Thunder Bay Senators
95/6 Thunder Bay Senators

FUNK, FLORIAN
94/5 DEL 136
95/6 DEL 138
96/7 DEL 35
98/9 DEL 169

FUNK, FRANZ
72 Hellas MM-Jenkki 43

FUNK, LORENZ
94/5 DEL 81
95/6 DEL 87
96/7 DEL 34
98/9 DEL 168
99/0 Eishockey 54, 370
72 Hellas MM-Jenkki 51
79 Panini Sticker 105
72 Semic Sticker 102
92 Semic Sticker 187
00/1 UD DEL 56

FUREY, KIRK
93/4 Owen Sound Platers

FURNESS, RYAN
98/9 Dayton Bombers

FURRER, GASTON
72 Semic Sticker 140

FUSCO, MARK
84/5 HART / Jr. Whalers
85/6 OPC/Topps 74

FUSELLI, JOHN
89/0 Soo Greyhounds

FUSSEY, OWEN
99/0 Calgary Hitmen
00/1 Calgary Hitmen
01/2 Calgary Hitmen
02/3 Moose Jaw Warriors
00/1 UD Prospects 48

FUSTER, MARCO
91/2 Richmond Renegades

G

GABEL, MARTIN
95/6 DEL 240

GABLER, MICHAEL
94/5 DEL 293

GABORIK, MARIAN
01/2 Adrenaline 92, PM 6, WB 9
01/2 Atomic 50, CP 8, PP 18
02/3 Atomic 53
02/3 BAP All-Star 103
00/1 BAP Mem. 401
01/2 BAP Memor. 285
02/3 BAP Memorabilia 109, 215, ✄ FP15, ✄ FG8, ✄ HSHSJers 22
02/3 BAP Memorabilia 215 [Franchise]
01/2 BAP Update HSHS, ✄ HSHSJers 32
01/2 Bowman 136, ✄ FFJ, ✄ FFS, ✄ FFDS, ✄ FFR, ✍ YSA
02/3 Bowman 114
02/3 Calder 41
00/1 Crown Royale 127, 21CR-12
01/2 Crown Royale 74, JotC 16
02/3 Crown Royale 48, LOR 12, ✄ GWDP 13
00/1 Crown Royale CC
02/3 eTopps 49
02/3 Exclusive 87, -GE 10
02/3 First Edition 152, 320, 355, 422R, ✄ Jers., ✄ DGJ 11, ✄ HSHSJers 22
01/2 Heads Up 49, BTI 12, PP 3
02/3 Heads Up 61, -HF 6, ✄ GWQ 14, ✄ GWQ 34
02/3 In The Game-Used 38, 138, ✄ E19, ✄ F15, ✄ GUJ19, ✄ SJ19
01/2 McDonald's 20
02/3 McDonald's 19
01/2 MINW
01/2 MINW / Crime 18
01/2 O-Pee-Chee 18
02/3 O-Pee-Chee 26
01/2 Pacific 194, 447
02/3 Pacific 182
02/3 Pacific Complete 206
00/1 Parkhurst P-139
01/2 Parkhurst 15
02/3 Parkhurst 107, ✄ FP15, ✄ GJ12, ✄ SJ12
02/3 Parkhurst Retro 34, ✄ RF15, ✄ RJ36, ✄ RSJ24, ✄ HH6, ✄ HSHSJers, ✄ RR4
00/1 Premier Plus 130, PR1, ✍ PS
00/1 Private Stock 125, PSR-11
01/2 Pr. Stock 48, Res. 9, -PS 38
02/3 Pr. Stock Reserve ✄ 126
00/1 PS Titanium 126, 3SS-23
01/2 PS Titanium 70, SK 10, ✄ DSJ 67
01/2 PS Titanium Draft ✄ 45
02/3 PS Titanium 53, -S 6, ✄ GWJ 34
00/1 PS Titanium Draft 126
02/3 Quest for the Cup 48, -CTC 7
00/1 Signature 279, F-15, ✍ Aut. 241
01/2 Signature 84, ✍ Aut. 84, ✄ FP15, ✄ GJ15, ✄ GSJ15, ✄ TM15
02/3 Signature 13, ✍ 13, ✄ CJ6, ✄ FJ15, ✄ SGJ19
00/1 SP Authentic 110, ✍ SotT
01/2 SP Authentic 42, 123, ✍ SotT, ✍ SotTD, ✍ SotTT
02/3 SP Authentic 46, 119
00/1 SP GU 70
01/2 SP GU 27
02/3 SP GU 24
02/3 Sports Vault 244
00/1 SPx 163
01/2 SPx 33
02/3 SPx 38
00/1 Stadium 241
01/2 Stadium 27, G17, ✍ LSS
02/3 Stadium 42, -W-13, ✄ YSS6, ✄ YSD4
01/2 Topps 18, OTG15
02/3 Topps 26
00/1 To. Chrome 242
01/2 To. Chrome 18
02/3 T. Chrome 26
00/1 To. Gold Label 102, NG8, ✍ GLA
00/1 To. Heritage 85, NT10
01/2 To. Heritage 29, ✍ CAI
02/3 To. Heritage 16
02/3 T. Limited 26
01/2 To. Reserve 24
00/1 To. Stars 113, 150
02/3 T. Total 45, TTC15
00/1 UD Heroes 166
01/2 UD PlayMakers Ltd 50
00/1 UD Reserve 98, BT6
02/3 Ultimate Mem. ✄ DD, ✄ Emb, ✄ GUJ, ✄ GUSJ, ✄ ITN, ✄ NP, ✄ Num
00/1 Upper Deck 229
01/2 Upper Deck 85
02/3 Upper Deck 89, -SS9
02/3 UD Artistic 46, R46, GD11, / Art
00/1 UD Black Diam. 123
01/2 UD Challenge 42
02/3 UD Classic 50
02/3 UD Honor 36, -SG16
00/1 UD Ice 90
01/2 UD Ice 23, ✍ CCA
01/2 UD Mask 46
02/3 UD Mask 44
01/2 UD MVP 91
02/3 UD MVP 89
02/3 UD Piece 46
01/2 UD Premier 29, ✍ Sig
02/3 UD Premier 29
00/1 UD Pros&Prosp. 108, NA2
02/3 UD Rookie 49, 115
01/2 UD Top Shelf 22
02/3 UD Top Shelf 43
00/1 UD Vintage 184, 381
01/2 UD Vintage 123, 129, 130
02/3 UD Vintage 125, 275, T34
00/1 Vanguard 127, HV-18, IF-11
01/2 Vanguard 48, PP 9
02/3 Vanguard 52, -EMW 8, -IF 7
01/2 Victory 171
02/3 Victory 104

GABRIEL, JEFF
94/5 Greensboro Monarchs

GADOWSKY, GUY
91/2 Richmond Renegades
92/3 Richmond Renegades

GADSBY, BILL
01/2 ASG History
99/0 BAP Mem. R-8
01/2 BAP Update ✄ RR7
45-64 BeeHive-2 [Chic.]
45-64 BeeHive-2 [NYRa.]
45-64 BeeHive-2 [Detr.]
64-67 BeeHive-3 [Detr.]
63-65 Chex
64/5 Coke/Sprite [Detr.]
65/6 Coca-Cola
62/3 Cowan Tile
83 HHOF Postcard H4
83&87 HHOF 110
91/2 Kraft 74
95/6 Legends of Hockey 70
51/2 Parkhurst 37
52/3 Parkhurst 56
53/4 Parkhurst 76
54/5 Parkhurst 87
61/2 Parkhurst 27
62/3 Parkhurst 25
63/4 Parkhurst 59
92/3 Parkhurst PR-9
01/2 Parkhurst PR28, PR39, PR49, PR81, PR83, PR95, PR150, ✄ H16, ✄ PV9, ✍ PA18
02/3 Parkhurst ✄ VM20
93/4 Parkie 56-57 137
93/4 Parkie 56-57 89
94/5 Parkie Tall 54, 156
60/1 Shirriff 90
61/2 Shirriff 79
01/2 Signature ✍ VA26
54/5 Topps 20
57/8 Topps 65
58/9 Topps 34
59/0 Topps 62
60/1 Topps 22
64/5 Topps 96
65/6 Topps 44
00/1 To. Heritage OSA
01/2 T/O Archives 2
57/8 Toronto Star Photo
59/0 Toronto Star Photo
61/2 Toronto Star Photo
63/4 Toronto Star Action
55 Toronto Star Weekend
01/2 Ultimate Mem. ✄ ASGH, ✄ Gloves
02/3 Ultimate Mem. ✄ GAO
91/2 Ultimate Original Six 69, ✍ Aut. 69
62/3 York Transfer 31
63/4 York 39
76 DETR

GAETANO, PHIL
94 Semic 294

GAETZ, LINK
91/2 O-Pee-Chee 1S
90/1 OPC Premier 33
91/2 Pinnacle 339, 412
91/2 Pro Set 561
89/0 ProCards IHL 88
90/1 ProCards 110
90/1 Score 411
88/9 MINS / ADA
91/2 SANJ / Sports Action

GAETZ, LINK
02/3 Fleer Throwbacks 57

GAFFAR, SHAYNE
90/1 7th..Sketch OHL 34
91/2 7th...Sketch OHL 12
91/2 Cornwall Royals

GAFFNEY, MIKE
99/0 Cardset 225
00/1 Austin Ice Bats
98/9 Detroit Vipers

GAGE, JOAQUIN
01/2 BT Pipes 59
95/6 Bowman 154
95/6 Donruss 237
95/6 Leaf 255
95/6 Parkhurst 343
00/1 To. Heritage 203
00/1 Vanguard 118
94/5 Cape Breton Oilers
00/1 Hamilton Bulldogs
93/4 Prince Albert Raiders

GAGE, JODY
93/4 Cla. Prospects 82
95/6 Edge Ice 63
88/9 ProCards / Rochester
89/0 ProCards AHL 276
90/1 ProCards 285
91/2 ProCards 21
80/1 DETR
91/2 Rochester Americans DD
91/2 Rochester Americans WPC
92/3 Rochester Americans DD
92/3 Rochester Americans WPC
93/4 Rochester Americans
95/6 Rochester Americans
98/9 Rochester Americans

GAGGI, JASON
95/6 Slapshot 32
96/7 Sudbury Wolves

GAGNE, SIMON
02/3 UD Premier ✄ JD

GAGNÉ, ART
25-27 Anonymous 12
27/8 La Patrie
27/8 La Presse
23/4 Paulins Candy 31

GAGNÉ, KARL
01/2 Moncton Wildcats 7

GAGNÉ, LUC
94/5 Slapshot / Sudbury 13
95/6 Slapshot 398
96/7 Sudbury Wolves

GAGNÉ, MARTIN
90/1 7th..Sketch LHJMQ 39
91 7th..Sketch Mem.Cup 42

GAGNÉ, MAXIME
90/1 7th..Sketch LHJMQ 124

GAGNÉ, PAUL
81/2 O-Pee-Chee 75
82/3 O-Pee-Chee 139
85/6 OPC/Topps 163
81/2 OPC Sticker 233
85/6 OPC Sticker 60-186
88/9 ProCards / Newmarket
89/0 ProCards AHL 122
83/4 Souhaits Keychain [Devils]
81/2 Topps 80 [West]
81/2 COLR
83/4 NJER
84/5 NJER
85/6 NJER 4

GAGNÉ, RÉMI
83/4 Nova Scotia Voyageurs

GAGNÉ, SIMON
01/2 Adrenaline 139
02/3 Atomic 74, -CF 19
00/1 Aurora 106
02/3 BAP All-Star 26, ✄ ASJ
99/0 BAP Mem. 195
00/1 BAP Mem. 6
01/2 BAP Memor. 82, ✄ ASJ, ✄ ASE, ✄ ASN, ✄ AST
02/3 BAP Memorabilia 200, 222, ✄ ASJ15, ✄ FP22, ✄ FG9, ✄ TM10
99 Bowman 59, SC17
01/2 Bowman 76
02/3 Bowman 43
98 Bowman 107, 126, ✍ A36
98 Bowman Chrome 107, 126
98/9 Bowman's Best 140
98/9 Collection Souvenir 28
99/0 Crown Royale 101, IG-17
00/1 Crown Royale 79
01/2 Crown Royale 106
02/3 Crown Royale 70
99/0 Dynagon Ice 2
02/3 eTopps 34
02/3 Exclusive 126, -MO 15
02/3 First Edition 124, 362, 374, 420R, ✄ Jers.
02/3 Heads Up 90, -HF 12
99/0 HoloGrFX 42
02/3 In The Game-Used 58, 158, ✄ F22, ✄ T15, ✄ TM13
02/3 McDonald's 31, -SLG 10
99/0 Millenium 183, C-2, ✍ Aut. 183
01/2 O-Pee-Chee 65
02/3 O-Pee-Chee 97, 325
99/0 Omega 169, G-8
00/1 Pacific 296, ✍ Aut. 296
01/2 Pacific 287
02/3 Pacific 280, ✄ GWJ 39
02/3 Pacific Complete 18
00/1 Pa. Paramount 180
99/0 Panini Sticker 129
00/1 Parkhurst P-11
01/2 Parkhurst 82
02/3 Parkhurst 28, ✄ FP22, ✄ NH5, ✄ TT2
02/3 Parkhurst Retro 38
01/2 PHIL
00/1 Premier Plus 37
99/0 Prism 101, IP-6
00/1 Private Stock 72, PSNW-18
01/2 Pr. Stock 71
02/3 Pr. Stock Reserve ✄ 136
00/1 PS Titanium 69
01/2 PS Titanium 104, ✄ DSJ 51, ✄ DSJ 64
01/2 PS Titanium Draft ✄ 70
02/3 PS Titanium 75, ✄ GWJ 49
93 Québec Pee Wee 342
94 Québec Pee Wee 1077
02/3 Quest for the Cup 75
00/1 Revolution 108
00/1 Signature 119, ✍ Aut. 192
02/3 Signature 6, ✍ 6, ✄ YP2
02/3 Slam Card
99/0 SP Authentic SotT
00/1 SP Authentic 65
01/2 SP Authentic ✍ SotT
02/3 SP Authentic 67, ✍ SotT, ✍ SotTD (x2), ✄ SP, ✄ DP
01/2 SP GU ✄✍ IS, ✄✍ IS2, ✄✍ IDS (x3), ✄ Patch, ✄✍ PatchSig, ✄ PatchC (x2), ✄✍ PatchCSig
02/3 SP GU 36, ✄ PC, ✄ FF, ✄ PH, ✍ Sig
02/3 Sports Vault 103
00/1 SPx 48, X9
01/2 SPx 189, ✄ DT (x2), ✍ Sig
02/3 SPx 56, ✄ WM, ✄ SS, ✄ X
99/0 Stadium 188, Chrome 44
00/1 Stadium 81
01/2 Stadium 82
02/3 Stadium 24, ✄ NHLP6, ✍ LSS
99/0 Topps 251
00/1 Topps 236, OTG24
01/2 Topps 65, ✄ GWJ, ✍ Aut.
02/3 Topps 97, 325, /PP-1
99/0 To. Chrome 251
00/1 To. Chrome 146
01/2 To. Chrome 65
02/3 T. Chrome 61
99/0 To. Gold Label 92
00/1 To. Gold Label 59
00/1 To. Heritage 69
01/2 To. Heritage 72
02/3 To. Heritage 28, ✄ GS, ✄ GSB
02/3 T. Limited 97, 325
99/0 To. Prmr. Plus 139, PR10
01/2 To. Reserve 5, ✄ TR
02/3 T. Total 32
00/1 UD Heroes 86
01/2 UD PlayMakers Ltd - PCPJ, ✄ PCCJ, ✄ PCJ
01/2 Ultimate Mem. ✄ Gloves
02/3 Ultimate Mem. ✄ Cor, ✄ HT
97/8 Upper Deck 411
99/0 Upper Deck 270
00/1 Upper Deck 129, P8
01/2 Upper Deck 361, ✄ GN, ✄✍ SigJers
02/3 Upper Deck 377, -SS11, ✄ BF, ✄ PL, ✄ SD, ✄ GJ, ✄✍ SGJ, ✄ PW
02/3 UD Artistic 66, R66, ✄ AT
00/1 UD Black Diam. 44
01/2 UD Challenge ✄✍ UCS
02/3 UD Classic 74, ET12, ✄ CS, ✄ HH, ✄ HR (x2), ✄ SC
99/0 UD G. Reserve 270
01/2 UD Honor Roll SS6
02/3 UD Honor ✄ GA (x2)
01/2 UD Mask 70, ✄ GJ, ✄ JP, ✄ DP, ✄ PM
02/3 UD Mask ✄ IO, ✄ PG
00/1 UD MVP 132
01/2 UD MVP 137, -J, ✍ SJ
02/3 UD MVP 138, SO11, SD (x3), ST
99/0 UD MVP Cup 133, ✍ PS
99/0 UD Ovation 43
02/3 UD Piece 66, PH, ✄ TT, ✍ MD
01/2 UD Premier 39, ✄ B, ✍ SigS
02/3 UD Premier ✄ Jers., ✄ Patch, ✍ Sig
00/1 UD Pros&Prosp. 64
02/3 UD Rookie ✍ TD
02/3 UD Top Shelf 66, ✄ CP, ✄ GO, ✄ HT (x2), ✄ R, ✄ SH, ✄ ST (x2), ✄ TS, ✍ Sig
00/1 UD Vintage 263
02/3 UD Vintage 182, 282, 312, T48, ✄ HS
00/1 Vanguard 72
01/2 Vanguard QTH 18
02/3 Vanguard 73
99/0 Victory 362
00/1 Victory 174
01/2 Victory 258, 433
02/3 Victory 156, -NP10
99/0 WGretzky 125
98/9 Québec Remparts

GAGNÉ, SYLVAIN
79/0 Montréal Juniors B&W
79/0 Montréal Jrs. Colour

GAGNÉ, WAYNE
88/9 ProCards / Peoria

GAGNER, DAVE
98/9 Aurora 79
98/9 Be A Player 57, ✍ Aut. 57
90/1 Bowman 186
91/2 Bowman 131
92/3 Bowman 171
95/6 Bowman 33
93/4 Donruss 83
94/5 Donruss 164
95/6 Donruss 58
96/7 Donruss 170
97/8 Donruss 80
97/8 Do. Priority 103
98/9 Dynagon Ice 80
93/4 EA Sports 34
96/7 Flair 12
94/5 Fleer 49
95/6 Fleer Metal 38
92/3 Fleer Ultra 94
93/4 Fleer Ultra 92
94/5 Fleer Ultra 51
95/6 Fleer Ultra 229
96/7 Fl. Ultra 22
92/3 Humpty Dumpty
95/6 Kraft / KD
96/7 Kraft / Fav.
98/9 Kraft / Post 20
93/4 Leaf 128
94/5 Leaf 319
95/6 Leaf 222
96/7 Metal Univ. 19
88/9 O-Pee-Chee 215
90/1 OPC/Topps 168
91/2 O-Pee-Chee 74
91/2 Topps - Team Leader 7
92/3 O-Pee-Chee 80
89/0 OPC/Topps 109, Box N
91/2 OPC Premier 128
89/0 opcSticker 203
97/8 Omega 98
98/9 Pacific 221
99/0 Pacific 422
97/8 Pacific CC 159
97/8 Pa. Crown Roy. 56
97/8 Pa. Invincible 17
97/8 Pa. Paramount 79
98/9 Pa. Paramount 95
97/8 Pa. Revolution 59
89/0 Panini Sticker 103
90/1 Panini Sticker 248
91/2 Panini Sticker 112
92/3 Panini Sticker 90
93/4 Panini Sticker 269
94/5 Panini Sticker 227
95/6 Panini Sticker 167
96/7 Panini Sticker 219
97/8 Panini Sticker 191
98/9 Panini Sticker 59
95 Panini Worlds 25
91/2 Parkhurst 78
92/3 Parkhurst 311
93/4 Parkhurst 317
94/5 Parkhurst 58
95/6 Parkhurst 471
91/2 Pinnacle 71
92/3 Pinnacle 85
93/4 Pinnacle 77
94/5 Pinnacle 334
95/6 Pinnacle 125
96/7 Pinnacle 39
97/8 Pinnacle 156
97/8 Pi. Be A Player 174, ✍ Aut. 174
97/8 Pi. Certified 47
97/8 Pi. Inside 181
95/6 Pi. Summit 53
96/7 Pi. Summit 80
97/8 Pi. Totally 47
95/6 Pi. Zenith 56, GG-11
95/6 Playoff 30
96/7 Playoff 337
94/5 POG 79
95/6 POG 86
93/4 Power Play 60
93/4 Premier 183
94/5 Premier 298
90/1 Pro Set 138
91/2 Pro Set 108
91/2 Pro Set 288
92/3 Pro Set 77
91/2 Pro Set Platinum 60
90/1 Score 108
90/1 Sco. Hot Cards 52
91/2 Score 72
91/2 Score CAN 72
92/3 Score 227
93/4 Score 98
95/6 Score 93
96/7 Score 14
97/8 Score 79
94/5 Select 6
95/6 SBx Emotion 45
95/6 SBx Impact 44
94/5 SP 30
92/3 Topps 254
95/6 Topps 254
95/6 To. Finest 31
98/9 To. Finest 114
91/2 To. Stadium 117
92/3 T. Stadium Club 121
93/4 To. Stadium 436
94/5 T. Stadium Club 45
95/6 To. Stadium 31
98/9 UD Choice 92
90/1 Upper Deck 248
91/2 Upper Deck 180
91/2 Upper Deck 86
92/3 Upper Deck 174
93/4 Upper Deck 145
94/5 Upper Deck 382
95/6 Upper Deck 370, SE-24
94/5 UD BAP R5, ✍ 77
97/8 UD Black Diam. 58
95/6 UD CC 7
96/7 UD CC 260
97/8 UD Coll. Choice 38
97/8 Zenith 75, Z35
94/5 DALL / Southwest
94/5 DALL / Cap
97/8 FLOR / Winn-Dixie
87/8 MINS
88/9 MINS / ADA

GAGNER, KEN
83/4 Brantford Alexanders

GAGNER, ROGER
51/2 Bas du Fleuve 44
52/3 Bas du Fleuve 1

GAGNON, BUS
59/60 Whitby Dunlops

GAGNON, DAVID
90/1 ProCards 491
91/2 Score 387
91/2 Score CAN 277
92/3 Fort Wayne Komets 10
95/6 Minnesota Moose
94/5 Roanoke Express
96/7 Roanoke Express 1

GAGNON, FRANÇOIS
91/2 7th...Sketch LHJMQ 15
00/1 Shawinigan 15
01/2 Val d'Or Foreurs 12
02/3 Val d'Or Foreurs

GAGNON, GERMAIN
72/3 Eddie Sargent 133
74/5 Loblaws
72/3 O-Pee-Chee 200
73/4 O-Pee-Chee 161
74/5 O-Pee-Chee 344
75/6 O-Pee-Chee 101
73/4 Topps 178
75/6 Topps 101

GAGNON, GERRY
51/2 Lac St-Jean 11

GAGNON, HENRI-PAUL
52/3 Bas du Fleuve 27

GAGNON, JACQUES
52/3 Bas du Fleuve 40
51/2 Laval Dairy 21

GAGNON, JEAN-FRANÇOIS
90/1 7th..Sketch LHJMQ 263
91/2 7th...Sketch LHJMQ 169

GAGNON, JIM
01/2 Peterborough Petes

GAGNON, JIMMY
02/3 Plymouth Whalers

GAGNON, JOEL
93/4 Slapshot / Oshawa 2
94/5 Slapshot / North Bay 1
92/3 Oshawa Generals

GAGNON, JOHNNY
33/4 Anonymous 43
34-43 BeeHive-1 [Mont.]
35-40 Canada Starch
33-35 Diamond Match Silv.
36-39 Diamond Match TT2
36-39 Diamond Match TT3
30/1 La Presse
33/4 O-Pee-Chee 19
37/8 O-Pee-Chee 154
39/0 O-Pee-Chee 25
43-47 Parade Sportive
43-47 Parade Sportive
55/6 Parkhurst 65
38/9 Quaker Oats
33/4 WWGum 21
37/8 World Wide Gum 83

GAGNON, JONATHAN
00/1 Rouyn-Noranda 24

GAGNON, MARC
91/2 Avant Garde BCJHL 140
91/2 Avant Garde BCJHL 146
91/2 Avant Garde BCJHL 156

GAGNON, OVILA
52/3 Anonymous 162

GAGNON, PASCAL
91/2 7th...Sketch LHJMQ 46

GAGNON, PAUL
51/2 Bas du Fleuve 47
51/2 Lac St-Jean 6

GAGNON, PIERRE
90/1 7th..Sketch LHJMQ 3
91/2 7th...Sketch LHJMQ 292
91 7th..Sketch Mem.Cup 50
88/9 Kitchener Rangers
86/7 Sudbury Wolves
87/8 Sudbury Wolves

GAGNON, SEAN
99/0 Cardset 260
91/2 7th...Sketch OHL 264
93/4 Slapshot / S.S.Marie 7
94/5 Dayton Bombers 11
95/6 Dayton Bombers
95/6 Dayton Bombers
00/1 Grand Rapids Griffins
01/2 Hartford Wolf Pack
97/8 Springfield Falcons
93/4 Soo Greyhounds 7
91/2 Sudbury Wolves

GAGNON, YANNICK
93/4 Slapshot / Drummondville 3

GAHN, KRISTIAN
94/5 Leaf Elit Set 118
95/6 Leaf Elit Set 279
90/1 Semic Elitserien 95
91/2 Semic Elitserien 24
92/3 Semic Elitserien 48
92/3 Upper Deck 232
95/6 UD Elitserien 159
97/8 UD Elitserien 156
98/9 UD Elitserien 9
99/0 UD Elitserien 9
00/1 UD Elitserien 14, 180, ✍ Sig.

GAILBRAITH, WALTER
39/0 Bruins Magazine

GAILER, PETER
82 Semic Sticker 104

GAILLOUX, KRIS
92/3 BCJHL 224

GAINER, CLAYTON
93/4 Wheeling Thund'birds

GAINEY, BOB
99/0 BAP Mem. CH-7, ✍ CH-7
73/4 Dernière Heure
80/1 Dernière Heure
83/4 Esso Stars
92/3 Future Trends C76 140
91/2 Kraft 39
86/7 Kraft Sports 24
82/3 McDonald's Les Étoiles 12
74/5 O-Pee-Chee 388
75/6 O-Pee-Chee 278
76/7 O-Pee-Chee 217
76/7 O-Pee-Chee 44
77/8 O-Pee-Chee 129
78/9 O-Pee-Chee 76
79/0 O-Pee-Chee 170
80/1 O-Pee-Chee 58
81/2 O-Pee-Chee 176
81/2 O-Pee-Chee 194
82/3 O-Pee-Chee 181
83/4 O-Pee-Chee 187
84/5 O-Pee-Chee 261
85/6 O-Pee-Chee 169
86/7 OPC/Topps 96
87/8 O-Pee-Chee 228
88/9 O-Pee-Chee 216
81/2 OPC Sticker 269
81/2 OPC Sticker 30
81/2 OPC Sticker 43
82/3 OPC/Topps Sticker 36
83/4 OPC/Topps Sticker 66
84/5 OPC Sticker 153
85/6 OPC Sticker 138-10
86/7 OPC Sticker 12
87/8 OPC Sticker 12-150
88/9 OPC Sticker 42-173
89/0 opcSticker 58-200
80/1 O-Pee-Chee Super 9
87/8 Panini Sticker 53
87/8 Panini Sticker 69
88/9 Panini Sticker 164
80/1 Pepsi Bottle Cap
91/2 Pinnacle 395
82/3 Post [Mont.]
90/1 Pro Set 668
84/5 7-Eleven
83/4 Souhaits Keychain [Canadiens]
75/6 Topps 278
76/7 Topps 217
76/7 Topps 44
77/8 Topps 129
78/9 Topps 76
79/0 Topps 170
80/1 Topps 58
81/2 Topps 13
00/1 Topps SCH, ✍ SCHA
01/2 Ultimate Mem. ✄ LC, ✄ SCD, ✄ SCW
92/3 UD Locker 41
83/4 Vachon 44-64
94/5 DALL / Cap
96/7 DALL / Southwest
73/4 MONT / Pro Star
74/5 MONT
75/6 MONT
76/7 MONT
77/8 MONT
78/9 MONT
79/0 MONT
80/1 MONT
81/2 MONT
82/3 MONT
82/3 MONT / Steinberg
83/4 MONT
84/5 MONT
85/6 MONT
85/6 MONT / Provigo
86/7 MONT
87/8 MONT
87/8 MONT / Kodak Poster
87/8 MONT / Vachon 12
87/8 MONT / Vachon 13
87/8 MONT / Vachon 18
87/8 MONT / Vachon 53
87/8 MONT / Vachon 88
88/9 MONT
92/3 MONT / OPC 16

GAINEY, STEVE
00/1 BAP Mem. 509
02/3 O-Pee-Chee 275
01/2 Pacific 123
02/3 Topps 275
02/3 T. Limited 275
01/2 UD MVP 200
01/2 Victory 368
99/0 Michigan K-Wings
00/1 Utah Grizzlies
01/2 Utah Grizzlies
96/7 Kamloops Blazers
97/8 Kamloops Blazers
98/9 Kamloops Blazers

GAINOR, DUTCH
29/0 La Presse
34/5 Sweet Caporal
37/8 World Wide Gum 98

GAL, EVZEN
99/0 Score 66

GALANOV, MAXIM
98/9 Omega 200
93/4 Upper Deck 273
00/1 Victory 14
95/6 Binghampton Rangers
96/7 Binghampton Rangers
97/8 Hartford Wolf Pack

GALARNEAU, DANNY
91/2 Air Canada SJHL B39
92/3 MPS SJHL 160

GALARNEAU, MICHEL
82/3 HART / Jr. Whalers

GALATI, MIKE
95/6 Slapshot 300
95/6 Guelph Storm

GALBRAITH, LANCE
99/0 Ottawa 67's
00/1 Ottawa 67's 2

GALBRAITH, WALTER
33/4 O-Pee-Chee 7

GALCHENYUK, ALEXANDER
92/3 Classic Prospects 96
91/2 O-Pee-Chee 33R
92/3 Upper Deck 353
93/4 Milwaukee Admirals

GALIAY, GUY
79 Panini Sticker 383

GALIK, MARTIN
99/0 Greensboro Generals

GALKIN, ALEXANDER
00/1 Mir 209

GALKIN, ANDREI
94/5 APS 239
95/6 APS 15
96/7 APS 232
97/8 APS 35
96/7 DS Sticker 35
97/8 DS Sticker 182
00/1 Mir 55
98/9 OFS 74, 485

GALKIN, IGOR
96/7 Flint Generals

GALL, SANDOR
79 Panini Sticker 313

GALLACE, R.
91/2 7th...Sketch OHL 119

GALLACE, STEVE
95/6 Slapshot 295

GALLAGHER, JOHN
34-43 BeeHive-1 [NYAm.]
30/1 La Presse
36/7 O-Pee-Chee 108
37/8 World Wide Gum 41

GALLAGHER, MATT
89/0 Nashville Knights

GALLAGHER, RAY
94/5 Flint Generals
93/4 Huntington Blizzard
87/8 Brockville Braves
88/9 Brockville Braves

GALLANT, CHESTER
95/6 Slapshot 201

GALLANT, GERARD
90/1 Bowman 237
91/2 Bowman 56
92/3 Bowman 169
93/4 Donruss 320
92/3 Fleer Ultra 284
90/1 Kraft 14
91/2 Kraft 58
93/4 Leaf 310
87/8 OPC/Topps 67
88/9 OPC/Topps 12
90/1 OPC/Topps 133, 322
91/2 O-Pee-Chee 443
92/3 O-Pee-Chee 163
89/0 OPC/Topps 172
89/0 Topps - Sticker 2
87/8 OPC Sticker 106-240
88/9 OPC Sticker 254
89/0 opcSticker 253, 157-15, / AS 25
87/8 Panini Sticker 245
88/9 Panini Sticker 43
89/0 Panini Sticker 58, 61
90/1 Panini Sticker 205
91/2 Panini Sticker 142
92/3 Panini Sticker 116
91/2 Parkhurst 269
91/2 Pinnacle 205
92/3 Pinnacle 135
93/4 Pinnacle 404
93/4 Power Play 230
93/4 Premier 511
90/1 Pro Set 71
91/2 Pro Set 63
90/1 Score 180
90/1 Sco. Hot Cards 78
91/2 Score 34
91/2 Score CAN 34
92/3 Score 119
93/4 Score 402
93/4 Score 560
92/3 Topps 92
91/2 To. Stadium 165
92/3 T. Stadium Club 218
93/4 To. Stadium 16
93/4 To. Stadium 346
90/1 Upper Deck 134
92/3 Upper Deck 246
85/6 DETR / Little Caesars
86/7 DETR / Little Caesars
87/8 DETR / Little Caesars
88/9 DETR / Little Caesars
88/9 DETR / S.A.M.
89/0 DETR / Little Caesars
91/2 DETR / Little Caesars
94/5 TAMP / Sky Box
98/9 Fort Wayne Komets
99/0 Louisville Panthers

GALLANT, GORD
75/6 OPC WHA 96
76/7 O-Pee-Chee WHA 4
74/5 Minn. Fight. Saints

GALLANT, KEVIN
87/8 Regina Pats

GALLANT, SHAUN
95/6 Slapshot 282

GALLANT, TREVOR
00/1 Kudos 102
91/2 7th...Sketch OHL 80
93/4 Slapshot / Kitchener 10
93/4 Slapshot / Promo
94/5 Slapshot / Kitchener 11
94/5 Slapshot / North Bay 10
95/6 Slapshot 217
01/2 Manchester Storm

GALLATIN, RANDY
99/0 Missouri RiverOtters

GALLENTINE, BRIAN
95/6 Roanoke Express
92/3 W. Michigan Broncos
93/4 W. Michigan Broncos

GALLEY, GARRY
91/2 Bowman 360
92/3 Bowman 11
93/4 Donruss 251
94/5 Donruss 166
95/6 Donruss 116
96/7 Donruss 106
92/3 Durivage 41
93/4 Durivage 38
93/4 EA Sports 97
94/5 Fleer 153
92/3 Fleer Ultra 156
93/4 Fleer Ultra 124
94/5 Fleer Ultra 157
95/6 Fleer Ultra 17
93/4 Leaf 120
94/5 Leaf 264
95/6 Leaf 30
96/7 Leaf 8
94/5 L. Limited 5
90/1 OPC/Topps 331
91/2 O-Pee-Chee 86
92/3 O-Pee-Chee 317
97/8 Omega 108
98/9 Pacific 235
00/1 Pacific 197
01/2 Pacific 246
97/8 Pacific CC 288
97/8 Pa. Paramount 89
91/2 Panini Sticker 175
93/4 Panini Sticker 53
94/5 Panini Sticker 43
95/6 Panini Sticker 23
96/7 Panini Sticker 13
99/0 Panini Sticker 260
91/2 Parkhurst 350
91/2 Parkhurst 7
92/3 Parkhurst 364
93/4 Parkhurst 423
94/5 Parkhurst V87

95/6 Parkhurst 21
94/5 Parkie SE128
91/2 Pinnacle 171
92/3 Pinnacle 103
93/4 Pinnacle 72
94/5 Pinnacle 27
95/6 Pinnacle 4
96/7 Pinnacle 69
95/6 Playoff 124
94/5 POG 182
95/6 POG 46
93/4 Power Play 182
93/4 Premier 255
94/5 Premier 535
90/1 Pro Set 7
91/2 Pro Set 298
91/2 Pro Set 7
91/2 Pro Set Platinum 211
90/1 Score 253
91/2 Score 71
91/2 Score CAN 71
92/3 Score 19
93/4 Score 143
94/5 Score 26
95/6 Score 112
96/7 Score 131
94/5 Select 117
95/6 SBx Emotion 15
95/6 SBx Impact 15
97/8 SP Authentic 73
92/3 Topps 360
95/6 Topps 155
98/9 To. Finest 31
96/7 Topps Picks 95
91/2 To. Stadium 175
92/3 T. Stadium Club 424
93/4 To. Stadium 381
95/6 To. Stadium 3
93/4 TSC Members Only 29
95/6 T. Super Skills 37
90/1 Upper Deck 379
91/2 Upper Deck 439
91/2 Upper Deck 607
92/3 Upper Deck 319
93/4 Upper Deck 90
94/5 Upper Deck 19
95/6 Upper Deck 198
94/5 UD BAP ✍ 62
95/6 UD CC 73
97/8 UD Coll. Choice 30
99/0 UD MVP Cup 90
89/0 BOST / Sports Action
90/1 BOST / Sports Action
84/5 LOSA / Smokey 6
87/8 LOSA
92/3 PHIL / UD Sheet
92/3 PHIL / UD Sheet
92/3 PHIL / J.C. Penney
93/4 PHIL / Sheet
93/4 PHIL / J.C. Penney
94/5 PHIL / Sheet
87/8 WASH
87/8 WASH / Kodak

GALLINGER, DON
34-43 BeeHive-1 [Bost.]

GALLOWAY, KYLE
93/4 Roanoke Express

GALLSTEDT, NIKLAS
89/0 Semic Elitserien 32
90/1 Semic Elitserien 179
91/2 Semic Elitserien 33
92/3 Semic Elitserien 59

GALUPPO, SANDY
94/5 Birmingham Bulls
92/3 Dayton Bombers

GALVAS, DAVID
96/7 DS Sticker 268
97/8 DS Sticker 50

GALVAS, LUKAS
99/0 DS 172
98/9 OFS 351
99/0 OFS 222

GAMACHE, JEAN-GUY
52/3 Anonymous 35

GAMACHE, SIMON
02/3 BAP Memorabilia 366
02/3 SP Authentic 209
02/3 Ultimate Mem. 76
02/3 UD Rookie 141
02/3 Chicago Wolves
00/1 Val d'Or Foreurs 12

GAMBLE, BRUCE
45-64 BeeHive-2 [Bost.]
64-67 BeeHive-3 [Toro.]
70/1 Colgate 82
70/1 Dad's Cookies
70/1 Eddie Sargent 193
71/2 Eddie Sargent 160
70/1 Esso Power Player
68/9 O-Pee-Chee 197
69/0 O-Pee-Chee 44
69/0 O-Pee-Chee 4in1
70/1 O-Pee-Chee 105
70/1 O-Pee-Chee DE 44
71/2 O-Pee-Chee 201
71/2 O-Pee-Chee Poster 16
95/6 Parkie 66-67 118
68/9 Post Marble
60/1 Shirriff 119
68/9 Shirriff / Toro. 15
62/3 Topps 3
67/8 Topps 18
69/0 Topps 44
70/1 Topps 105
71/2 Topps 104
71/2 Toronto Sun Photo
68/9 TORO
69/0 TORO
70/1 TORO

GAMBLE, DICK
45-64 BeeHive-2 [Mont.]
48-52 Exhibits [Canadiens]
51/2 La Patrie
51/2 Parkhurst 16
52/3 Parkhurst 5
53/4 Parkhurst 18
45-54 Quaker Oats
54/5 Topps 1

GAMBLE, TROY
91/2 Bowman 315
92/3 Bowman 410
95/6 Edge Ice 133, TW-4
91/2 O-Pee-Chee 446
90/1 OPC Premier 34
90/1 Panini/VAN 8
91/2 Panini Sticker 37
91/2 Parkhurst 402
90/1 Pro Set 641
91/2 Pro Set 238
91/2 Pro Set Platinum 121
89/0 ProCards IHL 178
90/1 Score 32T
91/2 Score 282
91/2 Score CAN 502
91/2 Score Young Stars 29
92/3 Topps 412
91/2 To. Stadium 218
90/1 Upper Deck 434
91/2 Upper Deck 120
90/1 VANC / Mohawk
90/1 VANC / PotM
91/2 VANC
91/2 VANC / Photo
92/3 Hamilton Canucks
95/6 Houston Aeros
84/5 Medicine Hat Tigers

GAMBUCCI, GARY
69/0 Mästär Serien 19
72 Semic Sticker 123
74/5 Minn. Fight. Saints

GANCHAR, PERRY
89/0 ProCards IHL 148
90/1 ProCards 379
91/2 ProCards 292
92/3 Cleveland Lumberjacks
93/4 Cleveland Lumberjacks
95/6 Cleveland Lumberjacks
96/7 Cleveland Lumberjacks
97/8 Cleveland Lumberjacks
98/9 Cleveland Lumberjacks
86/7 Sherb. Canadiens 15
81/2 Saskatoon Blades

GANI, DARREN
83/4 Belleville Bulls
84/5 Belleville Bulls

GANS, DAVID
81/2 Oshawa Generals
82/3 Oshawa Generals
83/4 Oshawa Generals

GANSTER, FRIEDRICH
93 Semic Sticker 277

GANZ, BRYAN
93/4 N. Michigan Wildcats

GARANIN, EVGENY
92/3 Red Ace Violet 8

GARATTI, JASON
93/4 Minnesota-Duluth

GARBER, BRUCE
93/4 Birmingham Bulls

GARBOCZ, DARIUSZ
92 Semic Sticker 275

GARBUTT, MURRAY
91/2 ProCards 514
91 7th...Sketch Mem.Cup 90
90/1 7th..Sketch WHL 25
93/4 Huntington Blizzard

GARDEN, GRAHAM
00/1 Kudos 134
00/1 Nottingham Panthers

GARDINER, BERT
34-43 BeeHive-1 [Mont.]

GARDINER, BRUCE
98/9 Be A Player 97, ✍ Aut. 97
98/9 Pacific 309
99/0 Pacific 287
97/8 Pacific CC 172
97/8 Pi. Be A Player 51, ✍ Aut. 51
97/8 Upper Deck 115
01/2 Upper Deck 283
00/1 UD Vintage 108
96/7 OTTA
97/8 OTTA
98/9 OTTA
99/0 OTTA
01/2 Albany River Rats

GARDINER, CHARLIE
02/3 Between the Pipes ✂ VM15

GARDINER, CHUCK
01/2 BT Pipes 143, ✂ VM
33/4 Canadian Gum
33-35 Diamond Match Silv.
83 HHOF Postcard I8
83&87 HHOF 128
31/2 La Presse
28/9 Paulins Candy 89
23/4 Selkirks Crescent 9
60/1 Topps 32
61/2 Topps - Stamp

GARDINER, GEORGE
72/3 Post 16

GARDINER, HERB
83 HHOF Postcard L4
83&87 HHOF 154
27/8 La Patrie
27/8 La Presse
23/4 Paulins Candy 63
60/1 Topps 44
61/2 Topps - Stamp

GARDINER, JAMES
91 C55 Reprint 36
10/1 Imperial
11/2 Imperial 36
12/3 Imperial 24

GARDINER, JEFF
89/0 7th..Sketch OHL 159
90/1 7th..Sketch OHL 105
91/2 7th...Sketch OHL 44

GARDINER, SCOTT
83/4 Belleville Bulls

GARDNER, BILL
83/4 O-Pee-Chee 103
84/5 O-Pee-Chee 35
82/3 Post [Chic.]
88/9 ProCards / Saginaw
83/4 Souhaits Keychain [Blackhawks]
81/2 CHIC
82/3 CHIC
86/7 HART / Jr. Whalers
83/4 PITT / Heinz

GARDNER, CAL
45-64 BeeHive-2 [Toro.]
45-64 BeeHive-2 [Bost.]
60/1 Cleveland Barons
48-52 Exhibits [Maple Leafs]
51/2 Parkhurst 85
52/3 Parkhurst 30
53/4 Parkhurst 99
54/5 Parkhurst 53
93/4 Parkhurst PR57
93/4 Parkie 56-57 10
45-54 Quaker Oats
54/5 Topps 47

GARDNER, DAVE
91/2 Air Canada SJHL A23
74/5 Loblaws
74/5 Loblaws Update
74/5 O-Pee-Chee 47
75/6 O-Pee-Chee 119
76/7 O-Pee-Chee 274
77/8 O-Pee-Chee 258
78/9 O-Pee-Chee 278
74/5 Topps 47
75/6 Topps 119
77/8 Topps 258
73/4 MONT / Pro Star

GARDNER, GEORGE
70/1 Eddie Sargent 222
71/2 Eddie Sargent 213
70/1 O-Pee-Chee 224
71/2 O-Pee-Chee 235
71/2 Toronto Sun Photo
70/1 VANC / Royal Bank
71/2 VANC / Royal Bank 17
72/3 VANC / Nalley's
72/3 Los Angeles Sharks
73/4 Vancouver Blazers

GARDNER, JIMMY
83 HHOF Postcard M7
83&87 HHOF 172

GARDNER, JOEL
90/1 ProCards 381
91/2 Knoxville Cherokees
99/0 Muskegon Fury

GARDNER, PAUL
83/4 Funmate Puffy 10 [w/]
77/8 O-Pee-Chee 24
78/9 O-Pee-Chee 88
79/0 OPC 5
81/2 O-Pee-Chee 257
82/3 O-Pee-Chee 236
82/3 O-Pee-Chee 269
83/4 O-Pee-Chee 218 LL, w/ Second]
83/4 O-Pee-Chee 275
83/4 O-Pee-Chee 280
81/2 OPC Sticker 187
82/3 OPC/Topps Sticker 145
83/4 OPC/Topps Sticker 230
82/3 Post [Pitt.]
89/0 ProCards AHL 113
83/4 Souhaits Keychain [Penguins]
77/8 Topps 24
78/9 Topps 88
79/0 Topps 5
81/2 Topps 113 [East]
79/0 TORO
93/4 Portland Pirates
96/7 Portland Pirates

GARDNER, RYAN
95/6 Slapshot 166

GARDON, RADEK
00/1 DS 137, Star. 29
99/0 OFS 335
00/1 OFS 124
01/2 OFS 173

GARE, DANNY
83/4 Funmate Puffy 17 [w/]
84/5 Kelowna Wings &...
75/6 O-Pee-Chee 64
76/7 O-Pee-Chee 222
76/7 O-Pee-Chee 380
77/8 O-Pee-Chee 42
78/9 O-Pee-Chee 209
79/0 O-Pee-Chee 61
80/1 O-Pee-Chee 161
80/1 O-Pee-Chee 165
80/1 O-Pee-Chee 167
80/1 O-Pee-Chee 260
80/1 O-Pee-Chee 38
80/1 O-Pee-Chee 88
81/2 O-Pee-Chee 20
81/2 O-Pee-Chee 27
81/2 O-Pee-Chee 28
82/3 O-Pee-Chee 83
83/4 O-Pee-Chee 123
84/5 O-Pee-Chee 54
85/6 OPC/Topps 37
86/7 OPC/Topps 69
81/2 OPC Sticker 53
82/3 OPC/Topps Sticker 184
83/4 OPC/Topps Sticker 135
85/6 OPC Sticker 35-166
86/7 OPC Sticker 159-16
82/3 Post [Detr.]
83/4 Souhaits Keychain [Red Wings]
75/6 Topps 64
76/7 Topps 222
77/8 Topps 42
78/9 Topps 209
79/0 Topps 61
80/1 Topps 161
80/1 Topps 165
80/1 Topps 167
80/1 Topps 260
80/1 Topps 38
80/1 Topps 88
81/2 Topps 127 [East]
81/2 Topps 14
81/2 Topps 47
84/5 Topps 42
02/3 Topps - Reprint 6, ✍ Reprint 6
01/2 T/O Archives 46
74/5 BUFF
79/0 BUFF / Bells Market
80/1 BUFF / Wendt's 3
93/4 BUFF / Noco
84/5 DETR / Little Caesars
85/6 DETR / Little Caesars
86/7 EDMO / Red Rooster
88/9 EDMO / Action 20
94/5 TAMP / Sky Box
95/6 TAMP / Sky Box

GARE, DANNY
02/3 Fleer Throwbacks 5

GARE, MOREY
00/1 Hamilton Bulldogs
93/4 N. Michigan Wildcats

GAREAU, GUY
51/2 Lac St-Jean 2

GAREEV, ALIK
00/1 Mir 242

GARIEPY, RAY
30s A&BC Chewing Gum 39
45-64 BeeHive-2 [Bost.]

GARIÉPY, FRÉDÉRIC
02/3 Shawinigan Cataractes

GARIFULLIN, ALMAZ
98/9 Mir 105
99/0 Mir 73
00/1 Mir 38

GARLAND, SCOTT
76/7 O-Pee-Chee 243
77/8 O-Pee-Chee 302
78/9 O-Pee-Chee 274
76/7 TORO

GARNER, TYRONE
99/0 Pacific 66
95/6 Slapshot 232
99/0 Victory 51
99/0 UD MVP Cup 14

GARNETT, KEVIN
86/7 Kitchener Rangers

GARNETT, MICHAEL
02/3 BAP Memorabilia 322
02/3 Between the Pipes 110
02/3 Ultimate Mem. 59
01 UD Prospects GU 21, ✂ TPJ, ✂✍ TPJS, ✂ JC, ✍ SoT
00/1 Red Deer Rebels
00/1 Saskatoon Blades

GARON, MATHIEU
00/1 BAP Mem. 422
01/2 BAP Memor. 181
01/2 BT Pipes 12, ✂ FW, ✂ Jers.
02/3 Between the Pipes 81, ✂ FW6
95/6 Bowman P14
98 Bowman 81, SC21
98 Bowman Chrome 81
98/9 Bowman's Best 145
02/3 Calder 75
01/2 MONT
02/3 MONT
01/2 O-Pee-Chee 276
01/2 Pacific 206
02/3 Pacific 195
02/3 Pacific Complete 551
00/1 Parkhurst P-248
01/2 Parkhurst 270
97/8 Pi. BeeHive 71, ✍ Aut. 71
00/1 Premier Plus 101
00/1 PS Titanium 128
00/1 PS Titanium Draft 138
00/1 PS Titanium Draft 128
00/1 Signature 299
01/2 Signature 41, ✍ Aut. 41
01/2 Topps 276
01/2 To. Chrome 142
98/9 UD Choice 260
95/6 Upper Deck 525
02/3 Upper Deck 340
02/3 UD Mask 45, 46
00/1 Vanguard 129
97/8 Zenith 98, Z78
00/1 MONT
02/3 Hamilton Bulldogs
99/0 Québec Citadelles 17
00/1 Québec Citadelles
01/2 Québec Citadelles

GARPENLÖV, JOHAN
91/2 Bowman 45
92/3 Bowman 400
93/4 Donruss 309
94/5 Donruss 301
95/6 Donruss 322
93/4 EA Sports 118
94/5 Flair 165
92/3 Fleer Ultra 400
93/4 Fleer Ultra 83
94/5 Fleer Ultra 194
95 Globe 36
93/4 Leaf 133
94/5 Leaf 234
95/6 Leaf 282
99/0 Millenium 16, ✍ Aut. 16
91/2 O-Pee-Chee 278
90/1 OPC Premier 35
97/8 Pacific CC 348
91/2 Panini Sticker 144
93/4 Panini Sticker 257
96/7 Panini Sticker 75
97/8 Panini Sticker 62
99/0 Panini Sticker 11
00/1 Panini Sticker 4
91/2 Parkhurst 385
92/3 Parkhurst 397
94/5 Parkhurst 209
95/6 Parkhurst 90
92/3 Pinnacle 122
93/4 Pinnacle 63
94/5 Pinnacle 296
96/7 Pi. Be A Player 67, ✍ Aut. 67
94/5 POG 215
95/6 POG 120
93/4 Power Play 219
93/4 Premier 53
94/5 Premier 201
90/1 Pro Set 605
91/2 Pro Set 56
91/2 Pro Set Platinum 29
99/0 Revolution 9
90/1 Score 17T
91/2 Score 204
91/2 Score CAN 204
92/3 Score 406
93/4 Score 183
94/5 Score 176
89/0 Semic Elitserien 67
91/2 Semic Elitserien 353
91 Semic Sticker 212
93 Semic Sticker 38
94/5 SP 45
93/4 Topps 359
95/6 Topps 56
91/2 To. Stadium 268
92/3 T. Stadium Club 212
93/4 To. Stadium 44
95/6 To. Stadium 62
90/1 Upper Deck 521, 523
91/2 Upper Deck 167
91/2 Upper Deck 28
91/2 Upper Deck E15
92/3 Upper Deck 59
93/4 Upper Deck - SP 142
94/5 Upper Deck 64
95/6 Upper Deck 129
94/5 UD BAP R38, ✍ 61
95/6 UD CC 240
96/7 UD CC 106
95/6 UD Elitserien 242
00/1 UD Elitserien 56, 189, S1, ✍ Sig.
90/1 DETR / Little Caesars
91/2 DETR / Little Caesars
96/7 FLOR / Winn-Dixie
97/8 FLOR / Winn-Dixie
92/3 SANJ / Pacific Bell

GARRETT, GUNNAR
78/9 Saginaw Gears

GARRETT, JOHN
79/0 O-Pee-Chee 293
80/1 O-Pee-Chee 77
81/2 O-Pee-Chee 137
82/3 O-Pee-Chee 283
83/4 O-Pee-Chee 349
84/5 O-Pee-Chee 317
85/6 O-Pee-Chee 220
81/2 OPC Sticker 63
83/4 OPC/Topps Sticker 275
75/6 OPC WHA 12
76/7 OPC WHA 55
77/8 OPC WHA 23
97/8 Pi. CBC Sports 5
82/3 Post [Québ.]
80/1 Topps 77
83/4 Vachon 105-25
82/3 QUEB
83/4 QUEB
83/4 VANC
84/5 VANC
74/5 Minn. Fight. Saints

GARRETT, RED
34-43 BeeHive-1 [NYRa.]

GARRICK, JAMIE
99/0 San Angelo Outlaws

GARTHE, MARC
95/6 DEL 45

GARTNER, MIKE
01/2 BAP Memor. ✂ 500GS
96/7 BlC.Sports Aces 4-D
90/1 Bowman 220, -HT 8, -HT 17
91/2 Bowman 74
92/3 Bowman 146
93/4 Donruss 218
93/4 Donruss 494
94/5 Donruss 111
95/6 Donruss 293
96/7 Donruss 206
97/8 Donruss 110
96/7 Do. Canadian 18
97/8 Do. Canadian 54, 149
96/7 Do. Elite 123
97/8 Do. Elite 147
96/7 Do. Preferred 47
97/8 Do. Priority 93
97/8 Do. Studio 89
96/7 Duracell JB9
93/4 EA Sports 89
94/5 Flair 180
96/7 Flair N&T 1
94/5 Fleer 214
01/2 Fleer Greats 75, ✍ Aut.
01/2 Fleer Legacy 59, ✂ HK
95/6 Fleer Metal 142
96/7 Fl. Picks 170
92/3 Fleer Ultra 135
93/4 Fleer Ultra 25
93/4 Fleer Ultra RLS 3
93/4 Fleer Ultra SM 4
94/5 Fleer Ultra 214, RLS-3
95/6 Fleer Ultra 311
96/7 Fl. Ultra 130
88/9 Frito Lay
83/4 Funmate Puffy 21 [w/]
95 Globe 85
84/5 Kellogg's 10
90/1 Kraft 69
91/2 Kraft 27
93/4 Leaf 213
94/5 Leaf 135, FOI-11
95/6 Leaf 37
96/7 Leaf 91
95/6 L. Limited 109
97/8 Limited 40
93/4 McDonald's McD-15
96/7 Metal Univ. 116
80/1 O-Pee-Chee 195
80/1 O-Pee-Chee 49
81/2 O-Pee-Chee 347
82/3 O-Pee-Chee 363
83/4 O-Pee-Chee 364
83/4 O-Pee-Chee 369
84/5 O-Pee-Chee 197
84/5 O-Pee-Chee 370
85/6 OPC/Topps 46
86/7 OPC/Topps 59
87/8 OPC/Topps 168
88/9 OPC/Topps 50
88/9 OPC/Topps Box N
90/1 OPC/Topps 373
91/2 O-Pee-Chee 46
92/3 O-Pee-Chee 245
92/3 O-Pee-Chee 300
89/0 OPC/Topps 30
90/1 OPC Premier 36
91/2 OPC Premier 147
91/2 OPC Premier 164
81/2 OPC Sticker 190
82/3 OPC/Topps Sticker 153
83/4 OPC/Topps Sticker 207
84/5 OPC Sticker 131
85/6 OPC Sticker 111-244
86/7 OPC Sticker 251
87/8 OPC Sticker 239
88/9 OPC Sticker 67
89/0 opcSticker 196-52
97/8 Omega 173
98/9 Pacific 338
97/8 Pacific CC 22, SS-7C
97/8 Pa. Crown Roy. 102
97/8 Pa. Dynagon 95, T-65, BKS-74
97/8 Pa. Invincible 106, R-152
97/8 Pa. Paramount 139
97/8 Pa. Revolution 105
87/8 Panini Sticker 180
88/9 Panini Sticker 370
89/0 Panini Sticker 104
90/1 Panini Sticker 103
91/2 Panini Sticker 292
92/3 Panini Sticker 237
93/4 Panini Sticker 91
94/5 Panini Sticker 191
95/6 Panini Sticker 204
96/7 Panini Sticker 215
97/8 Panini Sticker 158
91/2 Parkhurst 122
91/2 Parkhurst 430
91/2 Parkhurst PHC8
92/3 Parkhurst 108
93/4 Parkhurst 400
94/5 Parkhurst 228
95/6 Parkhurst 206
01/2 Parkhurst ✂ 500GS, ✍ PA23
94/5 Parkie SE sеV29
91/2 Pinnacle 202
92/3 Pinnacle 94
93/4 Pinnacle 241
93/4 Pinnacle 27
94/5 Pinnacle 31
95/6 Pinnacle 75
96/7 Pinnacle 35
97/8 Pinnacle 137
96/7 Pi. Be A Player 25, ✍ Aut. 25
97/8 Pi. Certified 85
97/8 Pi. Inside 97
95/6 Pi. Summit 143
96/7 Pi. Summit 28
97/8 Pi. Totally 85
95/6 Pi. Zenith 62
95/6 Playoff 95
96/7 Playoff 349
94/5 POG 233
95/6 POG 261
82/3 Post [Wash.]
93/4 Power Play 157
93/4 Premier 375
93/4 Premier 384
94/5 Premier 253
90/1 Pro Set 196, 351
91/2 Pro Set 167
91/2 Pro Set 604
92/3 Pro Set 113
92/3 Pro Set 256
91/2 Pro Set Platinum 84
91/2 Pro Set Platinum PC11
90/1 Score 130, 333
90/1 Sco. Hot Cards 60
91/2 Score 135
91/2 Score CAN 135
92/3 Score 443
92/3 Score 445
92/3 Score 50
93/4 Score 2
93/4 Score 447
93/4 Score PIAS 46
93/4 Score PIAS 8
93/4 Score / Promo 2
94/5 Score 112, 242
95/6 Score 204
96/7 Score 154
97/8 Score 139
94/5 Select 95
95/6 Select CE 54
89 Semic Sticker 75
84/5 7-Eleven
85/6 7-Eleven Superstars 20
01/2 Signature ✂ 500GS, ✍ VA38
95/6 SBx Emotion 169
95/6 SBx Impact 159
96/7 SBx Impact BR 5
83/4 Souhaits Keychain [Capitals]
96/7 SP 123
97/8 SP Authentic 124
01/2 SP Authentic ✂ NN
96/7 Team Out!
80/1 Topps 195
80/1 Topps 49
81/2 Topps 117 [East]
84/5 Topps 143
92/3 Topps 264
92/3 Topps 404
95/6 Topps 98
02/3 Topps - Reprint 2, ✍ Reprint 2
94/5 Topps Finest 96
95/6 To. Finest 8
96/7 Topps Picks FC2
91/2 To. Stadium 51
92/3 T. Stadium Club 311
93/4 To. Stadium 110
93/4 To. Stadium - All-Stars
93/4 To. Stadium - Finest 6
95/6 To. Stadium 162
92 TSC Members Only
92 TSC Members Only
95/6 TSC Members Only 22
95/6 T. Super Skills 28
01/2 T/O Archives 81, ✂ Jers
01/2 Ultimate Mem. ✂ 500GS
02/3 Ultimate Mem. ✂ ASMVP
90/1 Upper Deck 277
91/2 Upper Deck 247
92/3 Upper Deck 126
93/4 Upper Deck 205, SP-98
94/5 Upper Deck 32, 230, SP-78
95/6 Upper Deck 110
96/7 Upper Deck 316
97/8 Upper Deck 128
00 ✂ UD APOH 500, ✂✍ 500
93/4 Upper Deck Be A Player 22
94/5 UD BAP R127
93/4 UD BAP Roots 26
96/7 UD Black Diam. 42
95/6 UD CC 149
97/8 UD Coll. Choice 196
02/3 UD Foundations ✂ 1000Stick, ✍ SG
96/7 UD Ice 52
00/1 UD Legends 129, 132, ✍ ES, ✂ LGJ
01/2 UD Legends 68, 98, ✂ M, ✂ PoH, ✂ TT (x2)
92/3 UD Locker 38
02/3 UD Piece ✂ HH, ✂ HS, ✍ MD
99/0 UD Retro 110
96/7 PHOE / Coca-Cola
96/7 PHOE / Coca-Cola
97/8 PHOE / Coca-Cola
94/5 TORO / Abalene
94/5 TORO / Coca-Cola
79/0 WASH
80/1 WASH
81/2 WASH
82/3 WASH
84/5 WASH / Pizza Hut
85/6 WASH / Pizza Hut
86/7 WASH / Kodak
86/7 WASH / Police
87/8 WASH
87/8 WASH / Kodak
88/9 WASH
88/9 WASH / Smokey

GARTSHORE, DAVID
91/2 L. Superior State Lakers

GARVEY, BRENDAN
92/3 Oklahoma City Blazers

GARVEY, LIAM
98/9 DEL 256
99/0 Eishockey 46
01/2 UD DEL 65
96/7 Peoria Rivermen

GARVIN, SCOTT
92/3 BCJHL 231

GARZONE, MATT
96/7 Richmond Renegades

GASSER, NORBERT
79 Panini Sticker 387

GASSOFF, BOB
74/5 Loblaws
75/6 O-Pee-Chee 58
76/7 O-Pee-Chee 301
76/7 O-Pee-Chee 393
77/8 O-Pee-Chee 4
75/6 Topps 58
77/8 Topps 4
92/3 SLOU / McDon. 13
01/2 Peoria Rivermen

GASSOFF, BOB
02/3 Fleer Throwbacks 64

GASSOFF, BRAD
78/9 O-Pee-Chee 388
79/0 O-Pee-Chee 353
76/7 VANC / Royal Bank
77/8 VANC / Royal Bank

GATENBY, DAN
87/8 Sudbury Wolves

GATHERCOLE, PHILIP
91/2 7th...Sketch LHJMQ 235

GATHERUM, DAVE
52/3 Laval Dairy Update 66
52/3 St. Lawrence 107

GATIYATULIN, ANVAR
00/1 Mir 132
99/0 Mir 183

GATTAMOUTSAS, HAKAN
98/9 DEL 128

GATTO, GREG
90/1 7th..Sketch WHL 315
91/2 7th...Sketch WHL 10
99/0 Colorado Gold Kings

GATZOS, STEVE
83/4 PITT / Coke Is It!
84/5 PITT / Heinz
80/1 Soo Greyhounds

GAUCHER, RYAN
01/2 Cincinnati Mighty Ducks
99/0 Mississippi S'Wolves

GAUCHER, YVES
84/5 Richelieu Riverains

GAUDET, DENIS
93/4 Slapshot / North Bay 17

GAUDET, KEVIN
96/7 DEL 203
98/9 DEL 202
99/0 Eishockey 241

GAUDET, MARC-ANDRÉ
97 Bowman 66
98 Bowman 91
98 Bowman Chrome 91

GAUDET, PIUS
51/2 Bas du Fleuve 32

GAUDETTE, ANDRÉ
74/5 OPC WHA 46
73/4 Quaker Oats 22
72/3 Québec Nordiques
73/4 Québec Nordiques

GAUDETTE, PETE
52/3 Bas du Fleuve 10

GAUDETTE, YAN
01/2 Sherbrooke Castors 9

GAUDREAU, ROB
92/3 Classic 82
92/3 Classic Four Sport 204
92/3 Classic Prospects 140
92/3 Classic Prospects 16
92/3 Classic Prospects LP3
93/4 Donruss 310
94/5 Fleer 146
93/4 Fleer Ultra 98
93/4 Fleer Ultra Pros. 2
94/5 Leaf 9
93/4 Leaf 39
93/4 Panini Sticker 258
93/4 Parkhurst 189
94/5 Parkhurst 207
93/4 Pinnacle 41
94/5 Pinnacle 349
93/4 Power Play 220
93/4 Power Play SYS 1
93/4 Premier 199
94/5 Premier 4
93/4 Score 247
95/6 Score 141
95/6 Topps 117
93/4 To. Stadium 174
93/4 Upper Deck 149, HT9, HB2, SP-143
94/5 Upper Deck 182, 277
95/6 Upper Deck 164
94/5 UD BAP ✍ 85
95/6 UD CC 158
94/5 OTTA
95/6 OTTA
92/3 SANJ / Pacific Bell

GAUDREAULT, ARMAND
51/2 Laval Dairy 14
43-47 Parade Sportive

GAUDREAULT, LEO
27/8 La Patrie
27/8 La Presse

GAUDREAULT, LÉON
51/2 Lac St-Jean 32

GAUL, HORACE
10/1 Imperial 31

GAUL, MICHAEL
99/0 Choice 4
91/2 7th...Sketch LHJMQ 236
94/5 Knoxville Cherokees
00/1 Syracuse Crunch

GAULIN, JEAN-MARC
84/5 QUEB
82/3 Fredericton Express
83/4 Fredericton Express
85/6 Fredericton Express
86/7 Fredericton Express

GAUME, DALLAS
88/9 ProCards / Binghamton
92/3 Semic Nordisk 112
92/3 Semic Nordisk 11
92/3 Semic Nordisk 186 [Toppscorer]
92/3 Semic Nordisk 194 [Årets Lag]

GAUMOND, ALEXANDRE
91/2 7th...Sketch LHJMQ 295

GAUS, THOMAS
94/5 DEL 417
95/6 DEL 388
96/7 DEL 296

GAUSTAD, PAUL
02/3 BAP Memorabilia 388
02/3 UD Rookie 174
02/3 Rochester Americans

GAUTHIER, ALAIN
26 Dominion Chocolates 24
91/2 7th...Sketch LHJMQ 251
91/2 7th...Sketch LHJMQ 249

GAUTHIER, CHARLES
02/3 Shawinigan Cataractes

GAUTHIER, DANIEL
92/3 Classic Prospects 23
91/2 ProCards 296
93/4 Cincinnati Cyclones
92/3 Cleveland Lumberjacks
94/5 Indianapolis Ice
95/6 Indianapolis Ice

GAUTHIER, DENIS
95/6 Classic 19, AS14
95/6 Do. Elite WJ 5
99/0 Millenium 44, ✍ Aut. 44
99/0 NHL Power Play
98/9 Pacific 118
02/3 Pacific 53
93/4 Slapshot / Drummondville 14
02/3 Sports Vault 168
95/6 Upper Deck 533
98/9 Upper Deck 50
98/9 UD G. Reserve 50
02/3 UD Vintage 41
96/7 Saint John Flames
97/8 Saint John Flames

GAUTHIER, DEREK
90/1 7th..Sketch OHL 233
91/2 7th...Sketch OHL 84
94/5 Slapshot / Brantford 8
98/9 Anchorage Aces
99/0 Anchorage Aces
90/1 Kitchener Rangers

GAUTHIER, DON
89/0 Rayside-Balfour

GAUTHIER, FERN
45-64 BeeHive-2 [Detr.]
45-64 BeeHive-2 [xJ.Couture's photo]
43-47 Parade Sportive

GAUTHIER, GERARD
90/1 Pro Set 687

GAUTHIER, JEAN
63-65 Chex
62/3 Cowan Tile
63/4 Parkhurst 28
63/4 Parkhurst 87
63/4 Québec Aces
61/2 Shirriff 120
61/2 York 42
63/4 York 29

GAUTHIER, JEAN-PHILIPPE
02/3 Baie-Comeau

GAUTHIER, JONATHAN
99/0 Rouyn-Noranda
00/1 Rouyn-Noranda 2
01/2 Val d'Or Foreurs 6

GAUTHIER, LUC
88/9 ProCards / Sherbrooke
89/0 ProCards AHL 197
90/1 ProCards 55
91/2 ProCards 76
92/3 Fredericton Canadiens
93/4 Fredericton Canadiens
94/5 Fredericton Canadiens
95/6 Fredericton Canadiens
96/7 Fredericton Canadiens
86/7 Sherb. Canadiens 16

GAUTHIER, SEAN
91/2 ProCards 180
90/1 7th..Sketch OHL 57
93/4 Fort Wayne Komets 7
98/9 Kentucky Tho'blades
99/0 Louisiana Ice Gators
99/0 Louisville Panthers
00/1 Louisville Panthers
91/2 Moncton Hawks
96/7 Pensacola Ice Pilots
97/8 Pensacola Ice Pilots

GAUTHIER, SÉBASTIEN
02/3 Shawinigan Cataractes

GAUTHIER, STEVE
84/5 Chicoutimi Saguenéens

GAUTIER, JONATHAN
00/1 Baie-Comeau 24

GAUVREAU, BRENT
98 Bowman 144, ✍ A37
98 Bowman Chrome 144

GAVALIER, MICHAL
01/2 Rimouski Océanic 4

GAVEY, AARON
00/1 BAP Mem. 390
95/6 Bowman 121
93/4 Classic 21
94/5 Classic 115, C5, R6, T64
93/4 Donruss CAN12
95/6 Donruss 369
96/7 Do. Elite 64
95/6 Edge Ice 101
94/5 Flair 172
94/5 Leaf 452
96/7 Leaf 167
94/5 L. Limited 118
97/8 Pa. Invincible R-27
96/7 Panini Sticker 129
95/6 Parkhurst 527
93/4 Pinnacle 473
94/5 Pinnacle 251
96/7 Pi. Summit 158
94/5 Premier 536
94/5 Score 207
96/7 Score 259
94/5 Select 180
91/2 7th...Sketch OHL 316
00/1 Signature 43, ✍ Aut. 185
95/6 SBx Impact 221
93/4 Slapshot / S.S.Marie 20
95/6 SP 138
00/1 To. Chrome 239
95/6 To. Finest 28
95/6 To. Stadium 138
93/4 Upper Deck 545
95/6 Upper Deck 276
97/8 Upper Deck 28
94/5 UD BAP R156
95/6 UD BAP 165, ✍ S165
96/7 UD CC 249
00/1 UD Vintage 179
01/2 Victory 177
94/5 Atlanta Knights 16
98/9 Michigan K-Wings
99/0 Michigan K-Wings
02/3 St. John's Maple Leafs
93/4 Soo Greyhounds 22

GAVEY, L
91/2 Michigan Tech Huskies

GAVIN, STEWART
83/4 O-Pee-Chee 331
84/5 O-Pee-Chee 302
87/8 OPC/Topps 61
88/9 O-Pee-Chee 217
90/1 O-Pee-Chee 402
89/0 O-Pee-Chee 214
85/6 OPC Sticker 17-148
87/8 Panini Sticker 49
89/0 Panini Sticker 113
90/1 Panini Sticker 260
80/1 Pepsi Bottle Cap
82/3 Post [Toro.]
90/1 Pro Set 139
91/2 Pro Set 404
90/1 Score 244
91/2 Score CAN 433
92/3 Score 117
90/1 Upper Deck 150
83/4 Vachon 87-57
86/7 HART / Jr. Whalers
87/8 HART / Jr. Whalers
88/9 MINS / ADA
80/1 TORO
81/2 TORO
82/3 TORO
83/4 TORO
84/5 TORO

GAVLAS, DAVID
96/7 APS 105
97/8 APS 105

GAVLAS, LUKAS
01/2 OFS 22

GAVRILIN, ANDREI
00/1 Mir 347

GAWLEY, SEAN
91/2 7th...Sketch OHL 298

GEBAUER, ANDREAS
95/6 DEL 350

GEBEL, MARTIN
94/5 DEL 237
96/7 DEL 73

GECSE, DEREK
91/2 Avant Garde BCJHL 101

GECSE, DOREL
91/2 Avant Garde BCJHL 72

GEDDES, PAUL
94/5 DEL 323
95/6 DEL 299
96/7 DEL 325

GEE, GEORGE
45-64 BeeHive-2 [Chic.]
45-64 BeeHive-2 [Detr.]
51/2 Parkhurst 43
52/3 Parkhurst 36
53/4 Parkhurst 83
54/5 Parkhurst 80
02/3 Parkie - Reprint 171

GEEKIE, CRAIG
91/2 7th...Sketch WHL 213
92/3 Brandon Wheat Kings

GEESINK, TONY
84/5 Ottawa 67's

GEFFERT, PAVEL
94/5 APS 87
95/6 APS 375
96/7 APS 131
97/8 APS 180
97/8 DS 53
98/9 DS 58
99/0 DS 96
96/7 DS Sticker 72
97/8 DS Sticker 156
98/9 OFS 40
99/0 OFS 121, 388
00/1 OFS 121
01/2 OFS 169

GEGENFURTH, CHRISTIAN
94/5 DEL 383
95/6 DEL 367
96/7 DEL 189

GEGENFURTNER, CHRISTIAN
98/9 DEL 310

GEHRIG, MARIO
94/5 DEL 276
95/6 DEL 273
96/7 DEL 168
98/9 DEL 122, 336

GEISEBRECHT, GUS
34-43 BeeHive-1 [Detr.]

GELACEK, LIBOR
99/0 OFS 431

GELDART, GREG
95/6 Tallahassee Tiger Sharks

GELECH, RANDALL
00/1 Kelowna Rockets

GELINAS, RYAN
95/6 Slapshot 406

GELINAS, JASMIN
98/9 Halifax Moosehead
99/0 Halifax Mooseheads

GELINAS, MARTIN
01/2 Adrenaline 33
98/9 Aurora 32
90/1 Bowman 190
91/2 Bowman 102
93/4 Donruss 271, 501
95/6 Donruss 223
96/7 Donruss 133
97/8 Donruss 41
97/8 Do. Canadian 61
97/8 Do. Preferred 83
93/4 Durivage 22
98/9 Dynagon Ice 32
93/4 Fleer Ultra 401
94/5 Fleer Ultra 383
93/4 Leaf 396
94/5 Leaf 138
96/7 Leaf 127
97/8 Leaf 37
97/8 Limited 185
90/1 OPC/Topps 64
91/2 O-Pee-Chee 244
92/3 O-Pee-Chee 19
97/8 Omega 40
98/9 Omega 41
98/9 Pacific 132
99/0 Pacific 71
01/2 Pacific 72
02/3 Pacific Complete 242
97/8 Pacific CC 67
97/8 Pa. Crown Roy. 134
97/8 Pa. Dynagon 126, T-60
97/8 Pa. Invincible 141
97/8 Pa. Paramount 187
98/9 Pa. Paramount 36
99/0 Pa. Paramount 45
97/8 Pa. Revolution 22
90/1 Panini/EDM 5
91/2 Panini Sticker 128
92/3 Panini Sticker 106
97/8 Panini Sticker 238
99/0 Panini Sticker 47
91/2 Parkhurst 283
93/4 Parkhurst 166
94/5 Parkhurst V36
95/6 Parkhurst 480
94/5 Parkie SE184
91/2 Pinnacle 93
92/3 Pinnacle 166
93/4 Pinnacle 366
94/5 Pinnacle 324
95/6 Pinnacle 161
96/7 Pinnacle 83
97/8 Pinnacle 168
97/8 Pi. Certified 113
97/8 Pi. Inside 103
96/7 Pi. Summit 79
97/8 Pi. Totally 113
94/5 POG 335
95/6 POG 273
94/5 Premier 101
00/1 PS Titanium ✂ GUG 2
90/1 Pro Set 83
91/2 Pro Set 66
91/2 Score 159
91/2 Score CAN 159
92/3 Score 281
93/4 Score 408
94/5 Score 534
96/7 Score 98
97/8 Score 133
97/8 Score Vanc. 5
90/1 Sco. Young Stars 21
91/2 Score Young Stars 14
02/3 Sports Vault 166
92/3 Topps 292
95/6 Topps 176
00/1 Topps 255
98/9 To. Finest 8
91/2 To. Stadium 11
92/3 T. Stadium Club 314
02/3 T. Total 171
90/1 Upper Deck 23
91/2 Upper Deck 266
92/3 Upper Deck 282
94/5 Upper Deck 322, SP-127
94/5 Upper Deck 54, SP-172
95/6 Upper Deck 359
96/7 Upper Deck 171
97/8 Upper Deck 167, 200
98/9 Upper Deck 238
99/0 Upper Deck 198
00/1 Upper Deck 261
01/2 Upper Deck 263
02/3 Upper Deck 270
95/6 UD BAP 149, ✍ S149
95/6 UD CC 176
97/8 UD Coll. Choice 257, SQ8
98/9 UD G. Reserve 238
99/0 UD G. Reserve 198
98/9 UD MVP 39
00/1 UD Vintage 68
99/0 Victory 61
97/8 CARO / Sprint
98/9 CARO / Highwoods
88/9 EDMO / Action 73
90/1 EDMO / IGA
91/2 EDMO / IGA
92/3 EDMO / IGA 007
94/5 VANC
95/6 VANC / Abalene 9
96/7 VANC / IGA
87/8 Hull Olympiques

GÉLINAS, PHILIPPE
99/0 Shawinigan 2

GELINAS, RYAN
97/8 Quad City Mallards

GÉLINEAU, JACK
45-64 BeeHive-2 [Bost.]
48-52 Exhibits [Bruins]
51/2 Laval Dairy 4
52/3 Laval Dairy Update 4
52/3 St. Lawrence 37

GELLARD, SAM
73/4 Vancouver Blazers

GENDRON, BRYAN
89/0 7th..Sketch OHL 120
90/1 7th..Sketch OHL 359
91/2 7th...Sketch OHL 141
91/2 Peterborough Petes

GENDRON, DENNIS
96/7 Albany River Rats
97/8 Albany River Rats

99/0 Albany River Rats
02/3 Albany River Rats

GENDRON, EDGAR
52/3 Bas du Fleuve 54
51/2 Lac St-Jean 50

GENDRON, JEAN-GUY
52/3 Anonymous 40
45-64 BeeHive-2 [NYRa.]
45-64 BeeHive-2 [Bost.]
64-67 BeeHive-3 [Bost.]
70/1 Dad's Cookies
70/1 Eddie Sargent 157
71/2 Eddie Sargent 153
70/1 Esso Power Player
62/3 Cowan Tile
53/4 La Patrie
68/9 O-Pee-Chee 185
69/0 O-Pee-Chee 169
69/0 O-Pee-Chee 4in1
70/1 O-Pee-Chee 86
71/2 O-Pee-Chee 204
72/3 O-Pee-Chee 302
93/4 Parkie 56-57 88
65/6 Québec Aces
60/1 Shirriff 109
61/2 Shirriff 93
57/8 Topps 52
58/9 Topps 51
59/0 Topps 24
60/1 Topps 31
61/2 Topps 57
62/3 Topps 16
63/4 Topps 16
69/0 Topps 96
70/1 Topps 86
63/4 Toronto Star Action
71/2 Toronto Sun Photo
60/1 York
72/3 PHIL / Milk
72/3 Québec Nordiques
73/4 Québec Nordiques

GENDRON, MARTIN
92/3 Classic 23
93/4 Classic 131
92/3 Classic Four Sport 172
93/4 Cla. 4 Sport 234
93/4 Cla. Prospects LP12
93/4 Donruss CAN13
95/6 Donruss 47
93/4 Fleer Ultra 460
95/6 Fleer Ultra 174
95/6 Parkhurst 489
93/4 Pinnacle 474
95/6 Pinnacle 201
93/4 Power Play 480
95/6 Score 315
90/1 7th..Sketch LHJMQ 234
91/2 7th...Sketch LHJMQ 27
95/6 SBx Impact 224
93/4 Upper Deck 259, 540
00/1 UD DEL 85
95/6 WASH
97/8 Indianapolis Ice 8
96/7 Las Vegas Thunder
97/8 Milwaukee Admirals
94/5 Portland Pirates
95/6 Portland Pirates

GENDRON, PIERRE
91/2 7th...Sketch LHJMQ 133
97/8 New Orleans Brass

GENDRON, RED
98/9 Albany River Rats

GENESSE, BENOÎT
00/1 Sherbrooke Castors 15
02/3 Val d'Or Foreurs

GENEST, PATRICK
90/1 7th..Sketch LHJMQ 106
91/2 7th...Sketch LHJMQ 188

GENIK, JASON
92/3 BCJHL 182

GENOVY, AL
77/8 Kalamazoo Wings

GENTILE, FLAVIO
85/6 U. of Arizona Ice Cats

GENZE, ALEXANDER
94/5 DEL 297
95/6 DEL 197, 428
96/7 DEL 340

GEOFFRION, BERNIE
01/2 BAP Memor. ✂ RM
45-64 BeeHive-2 [Mont.]
64-67 BeeHive-3 [Québec Aces]
64-67 BeeHive-3 [NYRa.]
63-65 Chex
77/8 Dernière Heure
48-52 Exhibits [Canadiens, action]
48-52 Exhibits [Canadiens]
01/2 Fleer Greats 37, ✍ Aut.
62/3 Cowan Tile
83 HHOF Postcard M8
83&87 HHOF 166
91/2 Kraft 84
51/2 La Patrie
92/3 Legends 5
74/5 O-Pee-Chee 147
51/2 Parkhurst 14
52/3 Parkhurst 3
53/4 Parkhurst 29
54/5 Parkhurst 100
54/5 Parkhurst 8
55/6 Parkhurst 43
57/8 Parkhurst [Mont.] 2
57/8 Parkhurst [Mont.] 24
58/9 Parkhurst 28
59/0 Parkhurst 33
60/1 Parkhurst 46
60/1 Parkhurst 59
61/2 Parkhurst 35
62/3 Parkhurst 48
62/3 Parkhurst 53
63/4 Parkhurst 29
63/4 Parkhurst 88
92/3 Parkhurst PR-32
93/4 Parkhurst PR46
01/2 Parkhurst PR3, PR18, PR32, PR40, PR51, PR57, PR62, PR69, PR79, PR98, PR112, ✍ PA14
02/3 Parkie - Reprint 217
93/4 Parkie 56-57 68, 164, ✍ A-3
02/3 Parkhurst Retro ✂ NN5
95/6 Parkie 66-67 89
45-54 Quaker Oats
65/6 Québec Aces
60/1 Shirriff 28
61/2 Shirriff 104
62/3 Shirriff 34
01/2 Signature ✍ VA22
92/3 Sport Flash 5
92/3 Sport Flash 5
66/7 Topps 85
66/7 Topps / Test 36
67/8 Topps 29
74/5 Topps 147
01/2 To. Heritage S9, ✍ CAI, ✂ Relic
57/8 Toronto Star Photo
63/4 Toronto Star Action
55 Toronto Star Weekend
60/1 Toronto Star Weekend
02/3 Ultimate Mem. ✂ FS, ✂ SL (x2), ✂ SF
91/2 Ultimate Original Six 10, 73, 83, ✍ Aut. 83
99/0 UD C. Legends 43
00/1 UD Legends 71, ✍ ES
01/2 UD Legends 39
99/0 UD Retro 104, ✍ Ink.
60/1 York Glass [Mont.]
60/1 York
61/2 York 28
62/3 York Transfer 12
63/4 York 20
72/3 ATLF
79/0 MONT
92/3 MONT / OPC 54

GEOFFRION, BERNIE
01/2 Fleer Legacy 50

GEOFFRION, DANNY
78/9 Dernière Heure
81/2 O-Pee-Chee 364
81/2 OPC Sticker 141
80/1 Pepsi Bottle Cap
79/0 MONT
80/1 WINN

GEORGE, CHRIS
94/5 Slapshot / Sarnia 10
95/6 Slapshot 7

GEORGE, DARCY
92/3 BCJHL 174

GEORGE, JUSTIN
93/4 N. Michigan Wildcats

GEORGE, ZAC
92/3 BCJHL 26

GERARD, DEAN
91/2 Air Canada SJHL 8
91/2 Air Canada SJHL A32
92/3 MPS SJHL 45

GERARD, EDDIE
83 HHOF Postcard N5
83&87 HHOF 200
12/3 Imperial 34
61/2 Topps - Stamp
23/4 William Paterson 1

GERBE, JOE
96/7 Guelph Storm
99/0 Guelph Storm

GERBER, MARTIN
02/3 Atomic 102
02/3 BAP All-Star 124
02/3 BAP Memorabilia 293
02/3 Between the Pipes 76, ✂ guj46, ✂ t13
02/3 Bowman 144
02/3 Crown Royale 102, -RR 2
02/3 Exclusive 176
02/3 Heads Up 126
02/3 In The Game-Used 186
02/3 Pacific Complete 600
02/3 Parkhurst 223
02/3 Parkhurst Retro 223
02/3 Pr. Stock Reserve 152
02/3 PS Titanium 102
02/3 Quest for the Cup 102
02/3 SP Authentic 136
02/3 SP GU 68
02/3 SPx 166
02/3 Stadium 130
02/3 T. Chrome 163
02/3 To. Heritage 132
02/3 T. Total 429
02/3 Ultimate Mem. 23
02/3 Upper Deck 427
02/3 UD Classic 103
02/3 UD Honor 102
02/3 UD Mask 1, 151
02/3 UD Premier 44
02/3 UD Top Shelf 121
02/3 Vanguard 102

GEREBI, NICK
91/2 Minnesota G'Gophers

GEREMIA, RYAN
98/9 Calgary Hitmen 12

GERHARDSSON, PETER
94/5 Leaf Elit Set 249
95/6 Leaf Elit Set 158

GERIS, DAVE
93/4 Slapshot / Windsor 20
94/5 Slapshot / Windsor 22
95/6 Slapshot 425

GERLITZ, H.
28/9 Paulins Candy 58

GERLITZ, J.
28/9 Paulins Candy 57

GERLITZ, P.
28/9 Paulins Candy 54

GERMAIN, CLAUDE
51/2 Lac St-Jean 57

GERMAIN, DANIEL
91/2 7th...Sketch LHJMQ 252

GERMAIN, ERIC
88/9 ProCards / New Haven
89/0 ProCards AHL 12
90/1 ProCards 19
93/4 Richmond Renegades

GERMYN, CARSEN
98/9 Kelowna Rockets
00/1 Kelowna Rockets

GERNANDER, KEN
91/2 ProCards 178
94/5 Binghampton Rangers
95/6 Binghampton Rangers
96/7 Binghampton Rangers
97/8 Hartford Wolf Pack
98/9 Hartford Wolf Pack
99/0 Hartford Wolf Pack
00/1 Hartford Wolf Pack
01/2 Hartford Wolf Pack
91/2 Moncton Hawks

GERNEMIA, RYAN
95/6 Swift Current Broncos

GEROW, ROD
85/6 London Knights

GERRITS, BRIAN
86/7 Portland Winter Hawks
89/0 Saskatoon Blades

GERSE, DAVE
88/9 Regina Pats

GERSTBERGER, HOLGER
99/0 Eishockey 402

GERUM, CHRISTIAN
94/5 DEL 322
95/6 DEL 291
96/7 DEL 318

GERVAIS, EDDY
91/2 7th...Sketch LHJMQ 79

GERVAIS, GASTON
52/3 Bas du Fleuve 23
51/2 Laval Dairy 84

GERVAIS, GEORGE
91/2 Air Canada SJHL B34

GERVAIS, GUY
52/3 Bas du Fleuve 20
51/2 Lac St-Jean 40

GERVAIS, HUGUES
99/0 Mobile Mysticks

GERVAIS, SHAWN
92/3 BCJHL 168
93/4 Seattle Thunderbirds

GERVAIS, VICTOR
98/9 DEL 140
99/0 Eishockey 94
90/1 ProCards 201
91/2 ProCards 558
00/1 UD DEL 83
01/2 UD DEL 80
95/6 Cleveland Lumberjacks
91/2 Hampton Roads
92/3 Hampton Roads
93/4 Hampton Roads
96/7 Hampton Roads
97/8 Hampton Roads
98/9 Hampton Roads

GESCE, DEREK
92/3 BCJHL 9

GETLIFFE, RAY
34-43 BeeHive-1 [Bost.]
34-43 BeeHive-1 [Mont.]
35-40 Canada Starch
39/0 O-Pee-Chee 29
40/1 O-Pee-Chee 147

GIACOMIN, ED
01/2 ASG History
68/9 Bauer Photo
99/0 BAP Mem. AH-10, ✍ AH-10
01/2 BAP Memor. ✂ GT
01/2 BAP Update ✂ PTT5
64-67 BeeHive-3 [NYRa.]
01/2 BT Pipes 142, -Mask, ✂ DM, ✂ VM
02/3 Between the Pipes ✂ HSHSJers 27, ✂ VM4, ✂ VM20, ✍ Aut.
65/6 Coca-Cola
70/1 Colgate 70
70/1 Dad's Cookies
70/1 Eddie Sargent 115
71/2 Eddie Sargent 128
72/3 Eddie Sargent 147
70/1 Esso Power Player
01/2 Fleer Greats 21, ✍ Aut.
83&87 HHOF 259
93/4 Legends of Hockey 31
72/3 Post 10
74/5 Lipton Soup 26
74/5 Loblaws
68/9 O-Pee-Chee 205
68/9 O-Pee-Chee 67
69/0 O-Pee-Chee 217
69/0 O-Pee-Chee 33
69/0 O-Pee-Chee 4in1
69/0 O-Pee-Chee Stamp
70/1 O-Pee-Chee 244
70/1 O-Pee-Chee 68
70/1 O-Pee-Chee DE 42
71/2 O-Pee-Chee 220
71/2 O-Pee-Chee 248, 250
71/2 O-Pee-Chee Book. 7
72/3 O-Pee-Chee 173
73/4 O-Pee-Chee 160
74/5 O-Pee-Chee 160
75/6 O-Pee-Chee 55
76/7 O-Pee-Chee 160
77/8 O-Pee-Chee 70
02/3 Parkhurst ✂ VT2
02/3 Parkhurst Retro ✂ NN3
95/6 Parkie 66-67 93, AS1
70/1 Post Shooters
71/2 Pro Star Promotions
71/2 Pro Star Promotions
71/2 Pro Star Promotions
72 Semic Sticker 213
68/9 Shirriff / NYRa. 3
77-79 Sportscaster 61-03
77-79 Sports. FIN 74-1758
65/6 Topps 21
66/7 Topps 23
67/8 Topps 123
67/8 Topps 85
68/9 Topps 67
69/0 Topps 33
70/1 Topps 68
71/2 Topps 4
71/2 Topps 5
71/2 Topps 6
71/2 Topps 90
72/3 Topps 165
73/4 Topps 140
74/5 Topps 160
75/6 Topps 55
76/7 Topps 160
77/8 Topps 70
65/6 Toronto Star Photo
66/7 Toronto Star Weekend
71/2 Toronto Sun Photo
01/2 Ultimate Mem. ✂ ASGH, ✂ Corn.
02/3 Ultimate Mem. ✂ Cor, ✂ EA, ✂ NO, ✂ RT, ✂ SCD, ✂ VGJ
91/2 Ultimate Original Six 20, ✍ Aut. 20
00/1 UD Legends 89
01/2 UD Legends 46, 85
95/6 Zellers

GIAMMARCO, FRANCO
86/7 Kingston Canadians
87/8 Kingston Canadians

GIANINI, TIZIANO
91/2 Upper Deck 670
91/2 Upper Deck WJC 31

GIANNETTI, MARK
93/4 Slapshot / Sudbury 13
93/4 Sudbury Wolves

GIARD, STÉPHANE
91/2 7th...Sketch LHJMQ 52

GIBB, MYLES
91/2 Air Canada SJHL B27

GIBBONS, BRIAN
72/3 Ottawa Nationals

GIBBONS, JEFF
92/3 Toledo Storm WIOT
92/3 Toledo Storm
93/4 Toledo Storm 5
94/5 Toledo Storm

GIBBONS, SAMUEL
00/1 Rimouski Océanic 18
01/2 Rimouski Océanic 16
01/2 Val d'Or Foreurs 16

GIBBS, BARRY
70/1 Eddie Sargent 91
71/2 Eddie Sargent 95
72/3 Eddie Sargent 108
70/1 Esso Power Player
74/5 Loblaws
74/5 Loblaws Update
72/3 O-Pee-Chee 101
73/4 O-Pee-Chee 166
74/5 O-Pee-Chee 203
75/6 O-Pee-Chee 214
76/7 O-Pee-Chee 341
77/8 O-Pee-Chee 319
78/9 O-Pee-Chee 390
79/0 O-Pee-Chee 304
80/1 O-Pee-Chee 334
72/3 Topps 169
73/4 Topps 30
74/5 Topps 203
75/6 Topps 214
71/2 Toronto Sun Photo
70/1 MINS / Colour
73/4 MINS
78/9 SLOU

GIBBS, RICHARD
92/3 MPS SJHL 135

GIBLIN, PAUL
99/0 Asheville Smoke
00/1 Charlotte Checkers

GIBSON, DON
90/1 ProCards 340
91/2 ProCards 610
91/2 Upper Deck 495
90/1 VANC / Mohawk
93/4 Milwaukee Admirals

GIBSON, DOUG
75/6 O-Pee-Chee 375

GIBSON, JACK
83 HHOF Postcard N6
83&87 HHOF 201
72/3 Ottawa Nationals

GIBSON, JASON
98/9 Anchorage Aces

GIBSON, JOHN
83/4 WINN

GIBSON, MIKE
86/7 Regina Pats

GIBSON, SCOTT
01/2 Hull Olympiques 9

GIBSON, STEVE
90/1 7th..Sketch OHL 183
91/2 7th...Sketch OHL 176
97/8 Quad City Mallards
98/9 Quad City Mallards
99/0 Quad City Mallards
00/1 Quad City Mallards
94/5 Wheeling Thund'birds
92/3 Windsor Spitfires

GIBSON, WADE
89/0 7th..Sketch OHL 66
90/1 7th..Sketch OHL 84
91/2 7th...Sketch OHL 73
93/4 Slapshot / S.S.Marie 21
93/4 Soo Greyhounds 23

GIES, JEFF
93/4 Slapshot / S.S.Marie 14
95/6 Slapshot 368

GIESEBRECHT, BERT
52/3 Laval Dairy Update 60

GIESEBRECHT, GUS
39/0 O-Pee-Chee 69

GIESEBRECHT, JACK
52/3 Laval Dairy Update 112
52/3 St. Lawrence 62

GIFFIN, BOB
83/4 Ottawa 67's
84/5 Ottawa 67's

GIFFIN, LEE
88/9 ProCards / Muskegon
89/0 ProCards IHL 37
90/1 ProCards 584
91/2 ProCards 464
90/1 Kansas City Blades
83/4 Oshawa Generals

GIFFIN, ROB
93/4 Slapshot / Peterborough 4
95/6 Slapshot 311
97/8 Peoria Rivermen

GIFFIN, S
95/6 Birmingham Bulls

GIGNAC, CHRIS
91/2 7th...Sketch OHL 307

GIGNAC, JEAN-GUY
52/3 Anonymous 74

GIGUÈRE, JEAN-SEBASTIEN
02/3 T. Total 51

GIGUÈRE, JEAN-SÉBASTIEN
01/2 Adrenaline 2, PP1
01/2 Atomic ✂ GWJ 1
02/3 Atomic 1, -D 1
99/0 Aurora 21
00/1 BAP Mem. 192
01/2 BAP Memor. 32
02/3 BAP Memorabilia 3
01/2 BT Pipes 2, ✂ GT
02/3 Between the Pipes 51, 121, M1, ✂ GUE11, ✂ GB5, ✂ GUJ11, ✂ GSJ11, ✂ ITN11, ✂ T13, ✍ Aut.
97 Bowman 62
95/6 Classic 13, AS13, BK12
01/2 Crown Royale 3, ✂ TT 4
02/3 Crown Royale 1
97/8 Donruss 200, RR-10
97/8 Do. Canadian 146, LG-4
97/8 Do. Preferred 160
97/8 Do. Studio 73
02/3 Exclusive 1, -EA 1
02/3 First Edition 57, 414H, ✂ Jers.
01/2 Heads Up ✂ JQ 1
02/3 Heads Up 1, -S 1
97/8 Limited 29, 102, FG-9
02/3 O-Pee-Chee 117
98/9 Omega 32
99/0 Pacific 55
00/1 Pacific 64
01/2 Pacific 4
02/3 Pacific 3
02/3 Pacific Complete 11
99/0 Pa. Paramount 38
98/9 Pa. Revolution 19
02/3 PTC/ Les Gardiens 1
01/2 Parkhurst 12
02/3 Parkhurst 172
02/3 Parkhurst Retro 180, ✂ VH5
94/5 Parkie SE270
97/8 Pi. Inside 63, S-13
01/2 Pr. Stock ✂ GUG 1
01/2 Pr. Stock Reserve 1, -ICS 1
01/2 PS Titanium 2
02/3 PS Titanium 1
00/1 PS Titanium Draft ✂ 1
02/3 Quest for the Cup 1
01/2 Signature 29, ✍ Aut. 29
02/3 Signature 76, GS46, ✍ 76, ✂ TQ19
01/2 SP Authentic 2
02/3 SP Authentic 1
02/3 SP Game-Used ✂ AF (x2), ✂ PC, ✂ FF
02/3 Sports Vault 160
99/0 SPx 26
01/2 SPx 153
02/3 SPx 2, ✂ WM, ✂ X
02/3 Stadium 92, -PSH-15
00/1 Topps 319
02/3 Topps 117
00/1 To. Chrome 214
02/3 T. Chrome 76
02/3 To. Heritage 94
02/3 T. Limited 117
98/9 Upper Deck 13, GN7
99/0 Upper Deck 30, CT7, N12
01/2 Upper Deck 5
02/3 Upper Deck 2, -LL1, ✂ BF, ✂ GT, ✂ SV, ✂ UDPL
02/3 UD Artistic 1, R1, / Art
02/3 UD Classic 1, ✂ HR
98/9 UD G. Reserve 13
99/0 UD G. Reserve 30, / Backup 170
02/3 UD Honor 2
96/7 UD Ice 25
01/2 UD Mask 101, ✂ GJ, ✂ JP, ✂ DP, ✂ SY
02/3 UD Mask 1, 2, 98, ✂ GG, ✂ MM, ✂ BM, ✂ PW, ✂ VC
98/9 UD MVP 32
99/0 UD MVP 35
01/2 UD MVP 1
02/3 UD MVP 2
02/3 UD Piece 2
02/3 UD Premier ✂ JD
99/0 UD Retro G10C
02/3 UD Rookie 3, ✂ DJ
02/3 UD Top Shelf 1, ✂ ST, ✂ SS
00/1 UD Vintage 5
01/2 UD Vintage 1
02/3 UD Vintage 7, 261, GB 7, T2
02/3 Vanguard 1
99/0 Victory 43, 45, 383
01/2 Victory 1, 6
02/3 Victory 4
97/8 Saint John Flames
95/6 Halifax Moosehead
96/7 Halifax Moosehead
96/7 Halifax Moosehead
96/7 Halifax Moosehead

GIGUÈRE, STÉPHANE
88/9 Flint Spirits

GILBERT, ED
74/5 Loblaws
75/6 O-Pee-Chee 370
76/7 O-Pee-Chee 329

GILBERT, GILLES
74/5 Loblaws
73/4 O-Pee-Chee 74
74/5 O-Pee-Chee 10
74/5 O-Pee-Chee 132
75/6 O-Pee-Chee 45
76/7 O-Pee-Chee 255
77/8 O-Pee-Chee 125
78/9 O-Pee-Chee 68
78/9 O-Pee-Chee 95
79/0 O-Pee-Chee 209
80/1 O-Pee-Chee 175
81/2 O-Pee-Chee 88
82/3 O-Pee-Chee 84
81/2 OPC Sticker 123
92/3 Sport Flash 6
92/3 Sport Flash 6
73/4 Topps 74
74/5 Topps 10
74/5 Topps 132
75/6 Topps 45
76/7 Topps 255
77/8 Topps 125
78/9 Topps 68
78/9 Topps 95
79/0 Topps 209
80/1 Topps 175
81/2 Topps 88 [West]
71/2 Toronto Sun Photo
02/3 Ultimate Mem. - RT, ✂ SCD
80/1 DETR

GILBERT, GREG
91/2 Bowman 401
92/3 Fleer Ultra 275
93/4 Leaf 348
94/5 Leaf 341
84/5 O-Pee-Chee 125
85/6 OPC/Topps 126
88/9 OPC/Topps 83
90/1 OPC/Topps 255
91/2 O-Pee-Chee 149
84/5 OPC Sticker 90
85/6 OPC Sticker 75-202
88/9 Panini Sticker 287
90/1 Panini Sticker 196
93/4 Parkhurst 404
94/5 Parkie SE111
93/4 Pinnacle 405
94/5 Pinnacle 415
93/4 Premier 216
94/5 Premier 169
90/1 Pro Set 429
91/2 Pro Set 372
90/1 Score 264
91/2 Score CAN 539
92/3 Score 134
93/4 Score 305
93/4 Score 561
84/5 Topps 93
92/3 Topps 218
95/6 Topps 96
91/2 To. Stadium 242
92/3 T. Stadium Club 323
93/4 To. Stadium 37
93/4 Upper Deck 404
89/0 CHIC / Coke
90/1 CHIC / Coke
91/2 CHIC / Coke
83/4 NYIS / News 5
84/5 NYIS / News 5
82/3 Indianapolis Checkers
74/5 Sioux City Musketeers

GILBERT, JEANNOT
73/4 Québec Nordiques

GILBERT, LUCIEN
51/2 Bas du Fleuve 25
52/3 Bas du Fleuve 64

GILBERT, PATRICK
99/0 Rouyn-Noranda
00/1 Rouyn-Noranda 15

GILBERT, ROD
71/2 Bazooka Panel
99/0 BAP Mem. AH-12, ✍ AH-12
01/2 BAP Update ✂ PTT5
45-64 BeeHive-2 [NYRa.]
64-67 BeeHive-3 [NYRa.]
64/5 Coke/Sprite [NYRa.]
65/6 Coca-Cola
77/8 Coke
70/1 Colgate 53
70/1 Dad's Cookies
70/1 Eddie Sargent 122
71/2 Eddie Sargent 113
72/3 Eddie Sargent 141
70/1 Esso Power Player
01/2 Fleer Greats 23, ✍ Aut.
91/2 Future Trends C72 74, ✍ 74
83 HHOF Postcard H5
83&87 HHOF 111
71 Kellogg's Transfer
91/2 Kraft 82
95/6 Legends of Hockey 61
72/3 Post 14
74/5 Lipton Soup 40
74/5 Loblaws
73/4 Mac's Milk
68/9 O-Pee-Chee 209
68/9 O-Pee-Chee 72
68/9 O-Pee-Chee PS 9
69/0 O-Pee-Chee 37
69/0 O-Pee-Chee 4in1
69/0 O-Pee-Chee Stamp
70/1 O-Pee-Chee 63
70/1 O-Pee-Chee DE 39
71/2 O-Pee-Chee 123
71/2 O-Pee-Chee Book. 18
72/3 O-Pee-Chee 153
72/3 O-Pee-Chee 229
72/3 O-Pee-Chee TC
73/4 O-Pee-Chee 156
74/5 O-Pee-Chee 141
74/5 O-Pee-Chee 201
75/6 O-Pee-Chee 225
75/6 O-Pee-Chee 324
76/7 O-Pee-Chee 90
76/7 OPC 390
77/8 O-Pee-Chee 25
71/2 O-Pee-Chee Poster 7
95/6 Parkie 66-67 79
94/5 Parkie Tall 104, 166, SL5, ✍ A1
91/2 Pro Set 593
91 Pro Set Awards AC23
71/2 Pro Star Promotions
68/9 Shirriff / NYRa. 10
77-79 Sportscaster 33-03
91/2 Star Pics 7
61/2 Topps 62
62/3 Topps 59
63/4 Topps 57
64/5 Topps 24
65/6 Topps 91
66/7 Topps 26
66/7 Topps / Test 26
67/8 Topps 90
68/9 Topps 72
69/0 Topps 37
70/1 Topps 63
71/2 Topps 123
72/3 Topps 125
72/3 Topps 80
73/4 Topps 88
74/5 Topps 141
74/5 Topps 201
75/6 Topps 225
75/6 Topps 324
76/7 Topps 90
76/7 Topps NS 18
77/8 Topps 25
62/3 Toronto Star Photo
64/5 Toronto Star Action
64/5 Toronto Star Photo
71/2 Toronto Sun Photo
02/3 Ultimate Mem. ✂ FS, ✂ Num, ✂ RT
90/1 Upper Deck 512
00/1 UD Legends 90
92/3 Zellers

GILBERT, ROD
01/2 Fleer Legacy 52

GILBERTSON, STAN
72/3 Eddie Sargent 52
72/3 Post 19
74/5 Loblaws
71/2 O-Pee-Chee 183
72/3 O-Pee-Chee 70
73/4 O-Pee-Chee 212
74/5 O-Pee-Chee 223
75/6 O-Pee-Chee 382
76/7 O-Pee-Chee 187
72/3 Topps 101
74/5 Topps 223
76/7 Topps 187
77/8 Topps 203
71/2 Toronto Sun Photo

GILBY, ANDREW
96/7 Halifax Moosehead
96/7 Halifax Moosehead
97/8 Halifax Moosehead

GILCHRIST, BRENT
91/2 Bowman 336
92/3 Bowman 322
94/5 Fleer 50
92/3 Fleer Ultra 293
84/5 Kelowna Wings &...
94/5 Leaf 340
90/1 O-Pee-Chee 422
91/2 O-Pee-Chee 90
92/3 O-Pee-Chee 221
98/9 OPC Chrome 95
92/3 OPC Premier 129
97/8 Omega 79
98/9 Pacific 191
02/3 Pacific Complete 189
97/8 Pacific CC 136
90/1 Panini/MTL 12
92/3 Panini Sticker 153
96/7 Panini Sticker 177
91/2 Parkhurst 315
93/4 Parkhurst 52
94/5 Parkhurst 55, V21
95/6 Parkhurst 326
91/2 Pinnacle 236
92/3 Pinnacle 357
93/4 Pinnacle 415
94/5 Pinnacle 185
97/8 Pi. Be A Player 85, ✍ Aut. 85
93/4 Power Play 324
90/1 Pro Set 421
91/2 Pro Set 414
92/3 Pro Set 90
91/2 Pro Set Platinum 192
90/1 Score 87T
91/2 Score CAN 259
92/3 Score 46
93/4 Score 206
95/6 Score 261
96/7 Score 49
97/8 Score Detr. 14
00/1 Signature 228, ✍ Aut. 24
92/3 Topps 386
98/9 Topps 95
91/2 To. Stadium 373
92/3 T. Stadium Club 449
94/5 T. Stadium Club 143
98/9 UD Choice RW17
92/3 Upper Deck 459
93/4 Upper Deck 329
94/5 Upper Deck 347
95/6 Upper Deck 326
00/1 Upper Deck 295
95/6 UD BAP 71, ✍ S71
94/5 DALL / Southwest
94/5 DALL / Cap
96/7 DALL / Southwest
92/3 EDMO / IGA 008
88/9 MONT
89/0 MONT
89/0 MONT / Kraft
90/1 MONT
91/2 MONT
83/4 Kelowna Wings

GILES, ANDY
93/4 Humberside Hawks 12

GILES, CURT
92 C.O.A. Winter Olympics 179
91/2 Canada Nationals
82/3 O-Pee-Chee 166
85/6 OPC/Topps 96
86/7 OPC/Topps 119
90/1 OPC/Topps 228
91/2 O-Pee-Chee 17
89/0 O-Pee-Chee 213
86/7 OPC Sticker 172-35
87/8 Panini Sticker 118
89/0 Panini Sticker 112
90/1 Panini Sticker 250
82/3 Post [Minn.]
90/1 Pro Set 140
91/2 Pro Set 114
90/1 Score 94
91/2 Score 137
91/2 Score CAN 137
83/4 Souhaits Keychain [North Stars]
92/3 Topps 202
92/3 T. Stadium Club 64
90/1 Upper Deck 9
80/1 MINS
82/3 MINS
83/4 MINS
84/5 MINS
85/6 MINS
85/6 MINS / 7-Eleven 3
87/8 MINS
88/9 MINS / ADA
79/0 NYIS

GILHEN, RANDY
91/2 Bowman 84
92/3 Bowman 327
90/1 OPC/Topps 250
91/2 O-Pee-Chee 418
92/3 O-Pee-Chee 26
91/2 OPC Premier 123
91/2 Parkhurst 335
91/2 Pinnacle 238
92/3 Pinnacle 126
93/4 Power Play 473
93/4 Power Play 93
90/1 Pro Set 510
91/2 Pro Set 403
91/2 Score 157
91/2 Score 16T
91/2 Score CAN 157
91/2 Score CAN 566
92/3 Score 268
92/3 Topps 27
91/2 To. Stadium 275
93/4 T. Stadium Club 318
91/2 Upper Deck 603
92/3 Upper Deck 82
93/4 Upper Deck 481
88/9 WINN / Safety Tips
95/6 WINN
97/8 Manitoba Moose
87/8 Moncton Hawks
86/7 Sherb. Canadiens 17

GILJE, MORTEN
92/3 Semic Nordisk 139

GILL, HAL
97/8 Omega 16
99/0 Pacific 23
00/1 Pacific 33
02/3 Pacific 26
02/3 Pacific Complete 498
01/2 Signature 3, ✍ Aut. 3
00/1 Topps 252
02/3 T. Total 59
01/2 UD PlayMakers Ltd 10
98/9 UD MVP 17
99/0 UD MVP 20
00/1 UD MVP 20
02/3 UD Vintage 26
99/0 Victory 29
00/1 Victory 24
97/8 Providence Bruins

GILL, TODD
98/9 Be A Player 127, ✍ 127
91/2 Bowman 171
92/3 Bowman 375
94/5 Cla. Images PL10
93/4 Donruss 335
95/6 Donruss 14
96/7 Donruss 15
96/7 Do. Elite 79
93/4 EA Sports 133
93/4 Fleer Ultra 77
94/5 Fleer Ultra 215
93/4 Leaf 22
94/5 Leaf 497
95/6 Leaf 278
91/2 O-Pee-Chee 361
87/8 OPC Sticker 163-22
98/9 Pacific 367
01/2 Pacific 140
97/8 Pacific CC 98
87/8 Panini Sticker 324
89/0 Panini Sticker 143
90/1 Panini/TOR 7
92/3 Panini Sticker 82
95/6 Panini Sticker 206
91/2 Parkhurst 393
94/5 Parkhurst 233
95/6 Parkhurst 202
91/2 Pinnacle 278
92/3 Pinnacle 290
93/4 Pinnacle 68
94/5 Pinnacle 181
95/6 Pinnacle 171
96/7 Pinnacle 176
96/7 Pi. Be A Player 1, ✍ Aut. 1
96/7 Pi. Summit 4
96/7 Pi. Zenith 14
94/5 POG 239
95/6 POG 265
93/4 Power Play 449
93/4 Premier 4
94/5 Premier 189
90/1 Pro Set 534
91/2 Pro Set 226
91/2 Score CAN 521
92/3 Score 196
93/4 Score 292
94/5 Score 55
95/6 Score 162
96/7 Score 208
95/6 SBx Emotion 170
95/6 SBx Impact 160
00/1 Stadium 140
92/3 Topps 374
95/6 Topps 124
91/2 To. Stadium 336
92/3 T. Stadium Club 261
93/4 To. Stadium 62
94/5 Upper Deck 440
95/6 Upper Deck 117
97/8 Upper Deck 151
94/5 UD BAP R24, G8, ✍ 104
95/6 UD CC 101
86/7 TORO
86/7 TORO
87/8 TORO / P.L.A.Y. 13
88/9 TORO / P.L.A.Y. 12
91/2 TORO / P.L.A.Y. 17
93/4 TORO / Abalene
93/4 TORO / Black's 22
94/5 TORO / Coca-Cola

GILLAM, SEAN
99/0 Mississippi S'Wolves
95/6 Spokane Chiefs 19

GILLARD, TONY
82/3 North Bay Centennials

GILLIES, CLARK
88/9 Esso All-Star
01/2 Fleer Greats 62, ✍ Aut.
01/2 Fleer Legacy 18
83/4 Funmate Puffy 20 [w/]
84/5 Kelowna Wings &...
74/5 Loblaws
82/3 McDonald's Les Étoiles 13
75/6 O-Pee-Chee 199
75/6 O-Pee-Chee 323
76/7 O-Pee-Chee 126
76/7 O-Pee-Chee 216
77/8 O-Pee-Chee 389
77/8 O-Pee-Chee 250
77/8 O-Pee-Chee NS 6
78/9 O-Pee-Chee 220
78/9 O-Pee-Chee 327
79/0 O-Pee-Chee 130
80/1 O-Pee-Chee 75
81/2 O-Pee-Chee 202
82/3 O-Pee-Chee 201
83/4 O-Pee-Chee 6
84/5 O-Pee-Chee 126
85/6 OPC/Topps 81
86/7 OPC/Topps 141
87/8 OPC/Topps 96
88/9 OPC/Topps 80
81/2 OPC Sticker 164
82/3 OPC/Topps Sticker 54
82/3 OPC/Topps Sticker 55
83/4 OPC/Topps Sticker 84
85/6 OPC Sticker 68-192
86/7 OPC Sticker 205-77
87/8 Panini Sticker 34
92/3 Pinnacle 250
82/3 Post [NYIs.]
83/4 Souhaits Keychain [Islanders]
75/6 Topps 199
75/6 Topps 323
76/7 Topps 126
76/7 Topps 216
77/8 Topps 250
77/8 ToppsNS 6
78/9 Topps 220
79/0 Topps 130
80/1 Topps 75
81/2 Topps 88 [East]
84/5 Topps 94
01/2 T/O Archives 35, ✍ CAI
91/2 Upper Deck 640
02/3 UD Foundations 8, 61, ✍ SG
00/1 UD Legends 86, ✂ LGJ
01/2 UD Legends 44, ✂ TT
00/1 UD Vintage ✂ D-POH
86/7 BUFF / Blue Shield
87/8 BUFF / Blue Shield
87/8 BUFF / Won. Bread
83/4 NYIS
83/4 NYIS / News 6
84/5 NYIS / News 6
93/4 NYIS / Bank
99/0 NYIS / UD NY5

GILLIES, CLARK
02/3 Fleer Throwbacks 6, ✍ 2SO, ✂ 5SC, ✂ 5SCTD, ✂ 2SO, ✍ Aut.

GILLIES, TREVOR
99/0 Mississippi S'Wolves
02/3 Peoria Rivermen

GILLIGAN, WILLIAM
79 Panini Sticker 223

GILLINGHAM, TODD
95/6 Edge Ice 151
91/2 ProCards 351
90/1 7th..Sketch LHJMQ 174
92/3 Salt Lake G'Eagles
93/4 St. John's Maple Leafs
97/8 St. John's Maple Leafs

GILLIS, BRUCE
00/1 Halifax Moosehead

GILLIS, ERROL
23/4 Paulins Candy 4
24/5 Selkirks Crescent 7

GILLIS, JERE
77/8 Dernière Heure
78/9 O-Pee-Chee 109
79/0 O-Pee-Chee 322
80/1 O-Pee-Chee 283
81/2 O-Pee-Chee 232
84/5 O-Pee-Chee 318
82/3 Post [Québ.]
78/9 Topps 109
83/4 Vachon 106-26
77/8 VANC / Royal Bank
78/9 VANC / Royal Bank
79/0 VANC / Royal Bank
83/4 VANC
84/5 Fredericton Express
85/6 Fredericton Express

GILLIS, MIKE
81/2 O-Pee-Chee 12
82/3 Post [Bost.]
84/5 BOST
79/0 COLR

GILLIS, PAUL
90/1 Bowman 165
89/0 Kraft 29
86/7 OPC/Topps 168
87/8 O-Pee-Chee 247
90/1 OPC/Topps 22, 122
91/2 O-Pee-Chee 469
89/0 O-Pee-Chee 265
85/6 OPC Sticker 150-19
86/7 OPC Sticker 24-164
87/8 OPC Sticker 221
89/0 opcSticker 183
87/8 Panini Sticker 167
89/0 Panini Sticker 330
90/1 Panini Sticker 143
90/1 Panini/QUE 6
90/1 Pro Set 246
91/2 ProCards 489
90/1 Score 141
91/2 Score 364
91/2 Score CAN 403
90/1 Upper Deck 49
91/2 HART / Jr. Whalers
92/3 HART / Dairymart
83/4 QUÉB
84/5 QUÉB
85/6 QUÉB
85/6 QUÉB / Gene. Foods
85/6 QUÉB / McDonald's
85/6 QUÉB / Provigo
86/7 QUÉB
86/7 QUÉB / Gene. Foods
86/7 QUÉB / McDonald's
86/7 QUÉB / Yum Yum
87/8 QUÉB / Gene. Foods
87/8 QUÉB / Yum Yum
88/9 QUÉB
88/9 QUÉB / Gene. Foods
89/0 QUÉB
89/0 QUÉB / Gene. Foods
89/0 QUÉB / Police
90/1 QUÉB
90/1 QUÉB / Petro-Canada
99/0 Guelph Storm
82/3 North Bay Centennials

GILLIS, RYAN
00/1 Kudos 128
93/4 Slapshot / North Bay 10
94/5 Slapshot / North Bay 12
95/6 Slapshot 218
96/7 Dayton Bombers
99/0 Hampton Roads
00/1 Nottingham Panthers

GILLOW, RUSS
72/3 Los Angeles Sharks

GILMORE, DAVE
95/6 Classic 88
91/2 7th...Sketch OHL 363

GILMORE, TOM
72/3 Los Angeles Sharks

GILMOUR, BILLY
83 HHOF Postcard D4
83&87 HHOF 50

GILMOUR, DARRYL
88/9 ProCards / Hershey
90/1 ProCards 427
91/2 ProCards 403
93/4 Fort Wayne Komets 8
94/5 Muskegon Fury
92/3 Phoenix Roadrunners
86/7 Portland Winter Hawks

GILMOUR, DOUG
94/5 Action Packed
02/3 Atomic 54
99/0 Aurora 32, Stripe 32
00/1 Aurora 18, Pins. 18, TPS-2A
98/9 Be A Player 178, M19, H-18, ✍ Aut. 178
99/0 BAP Mem. 82, 384, H-11
00/1 BAP Mem. 291
01/2 BAP Memor. 317, ✂ SCP
02/3 BAP Memorabilia 63, 333, /Cup
01/2 BAP Update ✂ H5
96/7 Bic.Sports Aces 3-H
96/7 Bicycle 3-Heart
95/6 Bicycle Sports Aces 3-Heart
90/1 Bowman 96
91/2 Bowman 255
92/3 Bowman 83
95/6 Bowman 18
98/9 Bowman's Best 13
93/4 Classic 119, ✍ Aut.
94/5 Classic ✍ Aut.
99/0 Crown Royale 33
00/1 Crown Royale 13
01/2 Crown Royale 75
93/4 Donruss 341
93/4 Donruss ES 7
94/5 Donruss 8, IM-3
95/6 Donruss D-5, I-3
96/7 Donruss 46, 239, D-6, HL-15
97/8 Donruss 10, L2L-7
96/7 Do. Canadian 112, OC-9
97/8 Do. Canadian 49, NP-9, SCS-13
95/6 Do. Elite 92
96/7 Do. Elite 44, P-6
97/8 Do. Elite 73
97/8 Do. Preferred 69
97/8 Do. Priority 52
97/8 Do. Studio 93
96/7 Duracell DC7,JB7
98/9 Dynagon Ice 41, -FT 4
99/0 Dynagon Ice 50
93/4 EA Sports 135
02/3 First Edition 188
94/5 Flair 181, CIS-3
96/7 Flair 90
94/5 Fleer 215, H-3
96/7 Fleer 107
95/6 Fleer Metal 143
96/7 Fl. Picks 68, CC-8
92/3 Fleer Ultra 211
93/4 Fleer Ultra 110
93/4 Fleer Ultra AS 16
93/4 Fleer Ultra AW 3
93/4 Fleer Ultra PP 1
94/5 Fleer Ultra 216, PP-3, SK-3
95/6 Fleer Ultra 160
96/7 Fl. Ultra 163
88/9 Frito Lay
95 Globe 93
96/7 Got-Um
02/3 Heads Up 63
93/4 Hockey Wit 61
95/6 Hoyle / West. 5-Spade
92/3 Humpty Dumpty
94/5 Incomnet Phonecard
94 Koululainen
89/0 Kraft 1
91/2 Kraft 78
93/4 Kraft / JELL-O
93/4 Kraft / KD
94/5 Kraft / SS
95/6 Kraft / IP
96/7 Kraft / PB
93/4 Leaf 440
93/4 Leaf 93
93/4 Leaf GLAS 6
93/4 Leaf SSS 1
94/5 Leaf 99, FOI-5, GLS-2, LL-23
95/6 Leaf 211
96/7 Leaf 74, FOI-10, LL-14
97/8 Leaf 80
94/5 L. Limited 8, G-3
95/6 L. Limited 72
96/7 L. Limited 70, BTB-4
96/7 L. Preferred 104, LS-10
97/8 Limited 66, 82, 155, FG-19
96/7 Maggers 149
93/4 McDonald's McD-05
94/5 McDonald's McD-28
95/6 McDonald's McD-9
96/7 McDonald's McD-14
02/3 McDonald's 20
96/7 Metal Univ. 149
01/2 MONT
02/3 MONT
95/6 Cool Trade 17
98/9 NHL Power Play
84/5 O-Pee-Chee 185
85/6 OPC/Topps 76
86/7 OPC/Topps 93
87/8 OPC/Topps 175
87/8 OPC/Topps Box E
88/9 OPC/Topps 56
90/1 OPC/Topps 136
91/2 O-Pee-Chee 208
92/3 O-Pee-Chee 177
02/3 O-Pee-Chee 161
89/0 OPC/Topps 74
87/8 OPC Leaders 11
92/3 OPC Premier SP8
84/5 OPC Sticker 60
85/6 OPC Sticker 48-178
86/7 OPC Sticker 177-40

87/8 OPC Sticker 27
88/9 OPC Sticker 20
89/0 opcSticker 103-240
97/8 Omega 129, SHLC-11
98/9 Omega 52, -Onl. 7
99/0 Omega 53
98/9 Pacific 93, GCDC 20, Time. 10
99/0 Pacific 89, TL-7
00/1 Pacific 80, PR-3
01/2 Pacific 48, IZ 3
02/3 Pacific 196
02/3 Pacific Complete 46
97/8 Pacific CC 93, CS-11
97/8 Pa. Crown Roy. 75
98/9 Pa. Crown Roy. 30, -PotG 6
97/8 Pa. Dynagon 69, T-41
97/8 Pa. Invincible 77, R-113
97/8 Pa. Paramount 102, BN-13
98/9 Pa. Paramount 47
99/0 Pa. Paramount 55
00/1 Pa. Paramount 28, FF-3
97/8 Pa. Revolution 77
98/9 Pa. Revolution 31, -Show. 9
98/9 Panini Photocard
87/8 Panini Sticker 311
88/9 Panini Sticker 105
89/0 Panini Sticker 15, 28, 31
90/1 Panini Sticker 172
90/1 Panini/CGY 2
91/2 Panini Sticker 59
92/3 Panini Sticker 77
93/4 Panini Sticker S
94/5 Panini Sticker 190, FF
95/6 Panini Sticker 200
96/7 Panini Sticker 214
97/8 Panini Sticker 66
98/9 Panini Sticker 69
99/0 Panini Sticker 201
91/2 Parkhurst 26
91/2 Parkhurst 396
91/2 Parkhurst / Promo
92/3 Parkhurst 183
92/3 Parkhurst 502
92/3 Parkhurst CP1
92/3 Parkhurst CP1993
93/4 Parkhurst 469
93/4 Parkhurst D9
93/4 Parkhurst G10
93/4 Parkhurst W4
94/5 Parkhurst 313, V80, YCTG-23
95/6 Parkhurst 199, CB-12
00/1 Parkhurst P-183
01/2 Parkhurst 382, ✂ M15
02/3 Parkhurst 68
95 Parkhurst Phonecard
02/3 Parkhurst Retro 122
94/5 Parkie SE176
91/2 Pinnacle 92
92/3 Pinnacle 233
92/3 Pinnacle 279
93/4 Pinnacle 100
93/4 Pinnacle 226
93/4 Pinnacle 135, GR11, NL8, TP10, WE2
95/6 Pinnacle 61, CS-6, FS-3
96/7 Pinnacle 127, BTN-7
97/8 Pinnacle 39, TP-9
96/7 Pi. Be A Player 22, ✍ Aut. 22
97/8 Pi. Be A Player TN7
97/8 Pi. BeeHive 47
97/8 Pi. Certified 51
97/8 Pi. Epix E24
97/8 Pi. Inside 73
95/6 Pi. Summit 62
96/7 Pi. Summit 118
97/8 Pi. Totally 51
95/6 Pi. Zenith 54
96/7 Pi. Zenith 47, CS-13
95/6 Playoff 96, 202, 315
96/7 Playoff 356
94/5 POG 45, 234
95/6 POG 257, I-022
94/5 Post
93/4 Power Play 244
93/4 Power Play Game. 2
93/4 Power Play PL 2
93/4 Premier 390
93/4 Prmr. - BG-OPC 11
94/5 Premier 225, 279, GTG-14
00/1 Premier Plus 79
99/0 Prism 34
00/1 Private Stock 11, PS-6
01/2 Pr. Stock -PS 39
00/1 PS Titanium 9
01/2 PS Titanium 72
95/6 Pro Magnet 73
90/1 Pro Set 34
91/2 Pro Set 34
92/3 Pro Set 184
92/3 Pro Set TL 11
91/2 Pro Set Platinum 234
99/0 Revolution 34, NI-4
00/1 Revolution 16, NI-3, SM-22
90/1 Score 155
90/1 Sco. Hot Cards 69
91/2 Score 218
91/2 Score CAN 218
92/3 Score 40
93/4 Score 66
93/4 Score/CAN DD1
93/4 Score PiAS 44
93/4 Score TF 21
94/5 Score 185, DT13, NP4, TF23
95/6 Score 73, BB-5, DT-6
96/7 Score 95, CI-9
97/8 Score 93, CI-6
97/8 Score NJer. 1
92/3 Seasons 55
93/4 Seasons 4
94/5 Select 69
95/6 Select CE 48, DS-1
96/7 Select CE 15
96/7 SB 7-Eleven Phonecard
00/1 Signature 1, ✍ Aut. 12
02/3 Signature 146, GS-34, ✍ 146, ✂ SGJ53, ✂ TQ6
95/6 SBx Emotion 171
95/6 SBx Impact 161, CTI-8
96/7 SBx Impact 126, BR-6
94/5 SP 115, P-21
95/6 SP 144
96/7 SP 152, GF-16, H-3
97/8 SP Authentic 88
98/9 SP Authentic 18, SS30, SO4
99/0 SP Authentic 21
00/1 SP Authentic 12
00/1 SP GU ✂ C
02/3 Sports Vault 55
96/7 SPx 45, HH-9
97/8 SPx 25, D-SPX5
99/0 SPx 37
98/9 SPx Finite 47
98/9 SPx Prospects 10, H7, L25
99/0 Stadium 90
00/1 Stadium 156
94/5 Starting Lineup
98/9 SLU
95/6 Super Sticker 116, 118
92/3 Topps 122
95/6 Topps 234,3HG, HGC24, PF17, 8RL
99/0 Topps 103
00/1 Topps 58, PC-6, NHLD11
02/3 Topps 161, HHC16
99/0 To. Chrome 103
00/1 To. Chrome 46, PC-6
02/3 T. Chrome 96
94/5 Topps Finest 100, BBR-19, BBM-2
95/6 To. Finest 55,170
98/9 To. Finest 54
94 Topps Finest Bronze 6
98/9 T. Gold Label 64
00/1 To. Gold Label 54
00/1 To. Heritage 53
02/3 T. Limited 161
91/2 To. Stadium 96
92/3 T. Stadium Club 359
93/4 To. Stadium 140
93/4 To. Stadium 149
93/4 To. Stadium - Master Photo-1 2
93/4 To. Stadium - All-Stars
95/6 To. Stadium EC184, MP, EN8, N7
93/4 TSC Members Only 21
94/5 TSC Members Only 44
95/6 T. Super Skills 14
02/3 T. Total 62
98/9 UD Choice 117
00/1 UD Heroes 14
00/1 UD Reserve 9
98/9 UD3 50, 110, 170
02/3 Ultimate Mem. ✂ LA, ✂ PS
99/0 Ult. Victory 21
90/1 Upper Deck 271
91/2 Upper Deck 188
91/2 Upper Deck 558
92/3 Upper Deck 21
92/3 Upper Deck 215
92/3 Upper Deck 639
93/4 Upper Deck 306, 382, AW6, NL5, R7, SP-158
94/5 Upper Deck 138, C18, H3, H21, R11, R27, R49, R56, SP-167
95/6 Upper Deck 240, 291, SE-80
96/7 Upper Deck 162, X10, LS11, P29, SS4B, ✂ GJ
97/8 Upper Deck 91, 198, SS16, SG33, T18B
98/9 Upper Deck 63, FT16, LS7, P15, ✂ GJ18
99/0 Upper Deck 206
00/1 Upper Deck 20, FT1
01/2 Upper Deck 322, ✂ PotL
95/6 UD ASG MVP10
02/3 UD Artistic 48, R48, / Art
93/4 Upper Deck Be A Player 41
93/4 Upper Deck Be A Player 42
93/4 Upper Deck Be A Player 43
93/4 Upper Deck Be A Player 44
93/4 Upper Deck Be A Player 45
94/5 UD BAP R1, R11, R180,UC10, ✍ 1
93/4 UD BAP Roots 11
93/4 UD BAP Roots 21
93/4 UD BAP Roots 5
96/7 UD Black Diam. 28
97/8 UD Black Diam. 70
98/9 UD Black Diam. 18, M25
99/0 UD Black Diam. 23
95/6 UD CC 5, 359, C21
96/7 UD CC 256, 332, UD45, C2, CR2
97/8 UD Coll. Choice 139, SQ70, S24, C13, CR13
02/3 UD Foundations 53
98/9 UD G. Reserve 63
99/0 UD G. Reserve 206
96/7 UD Ice 69
97/8 UD Ice 82
00/1 UD Legends 17, ✂ LGJ
02/3 UD Locker 24
98/9 UD MVP 43
99/0 UD MVP 48
00/1 UD MVP 24
01/2 UD MVP 19
99/0 UD MVP Cup 44
95/6 UD Post 18
96/7 UD Post, SU-1
00/1 UD Pros&Prosp. 11
99/0 UD Retro 18
02/3 UD Rookie 91
02/3 UD Top Shelf ✂ HH, ✂ SW
00/1 UD Vintage 42
00/1 Vanguard 12
01/2 Vanguard 49
99/0 Victory 67
00/1 Victory 29, 287
99/0 WGretzky 40
97/8 Zenith 46, Z12
91/2 CALG / McGavin's
91/2 CALG / IGA
87/8 SLOU / Kodak
92/3 SLOU / McDon. 2
92/3 TORO / Kodak
93/4 TORO / Abalene
93/4 TORO / Black's 2
94/5 TORO / Coca-Cola

GILMOUR, JAKE
01/2 Belleville Bulls

GILMOUR, LARRY
91 C55 Reprint 22
10/1 Imperial
11/2 Imperial 22

GIMAYEV, IREK
80 Olympic USSR
83/4 Soviet Stars

GIMBLETT, JESSE
01/2 Owen Sound Attack
02/3 Owen Sound Attack

GINGHER, ED
98/9 Dayton Bombers

GINGRAS, GASTON
80/1 Dernière Heure
82/3 Dernière Heure
86/7 Kraft Sports 25
80/1 O-Pee-Chee 322
81/2 O-Pee-Chee 182
82/3 O-Pee-Chee 182
83/4 O-Pee-Chee 332
84/5 O-Pee-Chee 303
87/8 O-Pee-Chee 229
88/9 OPC/Topps 35
89/0 O-Pee-Chee 270
83/4 OPC/Topps Sticker 40
87/8 OPC Sticker 8-147
89/0 opcSticker 21-161
80/1 Pepsi Bottle Cap
83/4 Souhaits Keychain [Maple Leafs]
83/4 Vachon 88-65
80/1 MONT
81/2 MONT
82/3 MONT
85/6 MONT
86/7 MONT
87/8 MONT
88/9 SLOU
87/8 SLOU / Kodak
88/9 SLOU
88/9 SLOU / Kodak
82/3 TORO
83/4 TORO
95/6 Fredericton Canadiens

GINGRAS, MAXIME
98/9 EBK ECHL All-Star
99/0 Houston Aeros
99/0 Providence Bruins

GINGRAS, MICHEL
90 7th..Sketch Mem.Cup 62

GINKO, YURI
99/0 Eishockey 221

GINNELL, ERIN
86/7 Regina Pats

GIONET, AARON
98/9 Kamloops Blazers
99/0 Kamloops Blazers
99/0 Kamloops Blazers
00/1 Kamloops Blazers
01/2 Kamloops Blazers
02/3 Kamloops Blazers

GIONTA, BRIAN
01/2 Bowman 151
01/2 Crown Royale 152
02/3 O-Pee-Chee 269
02/3 Pacific 221
02/3 Pacific Complete 52
01/2 PS Titanium 167
01/2 PS Titanium Draft 148
93 Québec Pee Wee 877
02/3 Signature 86, ✍ 86
02/3 SP Authentic 122
01/2 SPx 180
02/3 Stadium ✍ LSS
02/3 Topps 269
02/3 T. Chrome ✍ Graph
02/3 T. Limited 269
02/3 T. Total 141, ✍ Sig
98/9 UD Choice 298
02/3 Upper Deck 105
01/2 UD Top Shelf 100
02/3 Victory 125
01/2 Albany River Rats

GIORDANO, MARK
02/3 Owen Sound Attack

GIRARD, BOB
76/7 O-Pee-Chee 362
77/8 O-Pee-Chee 255
78/9 O-Pee-Chee 339

GIRARD, BRETT
98/9 Brandon Wheat Kings
99/0 Brandon Wheat Kings

GIRARD, DANY
90/1 7th..Sketch LHJMQ 21
91/2 7th...Sketch LHJMQ 78

GIRARD, FRÉDÉRIC
96/7 Rimouski Océanic

GIRARD, JONATHAN
99/0 BAP Mem. 156
00/1 BAP Mem. 177
01/2 BAP Memor. 191
99 Bowman 47
98 Bowman 97, 135, SC13, ✍ A30
98 Bowman Chrome 97, 135
98/9 Collection Souvenir 30
99/0 Millenium 28, C-46, ✍ Aut. 28
99/0 NHL Power Play [x3]
99/0 Pacific 32
02/3 Pacific Complete 417
99/0 Pa. Paramount 20
01/2 Parkhurst 135
93 Québec Pee Wee 903
94 Québec Pee Wee 617
99/0 SPx 14
00/1 Topps 325
00/1 To. Chrome 220
97/8 Upper Deck 403
98/9 Upper Deck 222
99/0 Upper Deck 19
01/2 Upper Deck 16
02/3 Upper Deck 259
98/9 UD G. Reserve 222
99/0 UD G. Reserve 19
99/0 UD MVP 19
01/2 UD MVP 16
99/0 Victory 26
00/1 Providence Bruins
01/2 Providence Bruins

GIRARD, KENNY
57/8 Parkhurst [Toro.] 18
93/4 Parkie 56-57 132

GIRARD, LUC
00/1 Val d'Or Foreurs 5

GIRARD, MANDA
99/0 Peoria Rivermen

GIRARD, RICK
94/5 Classic T71
98/9 DEL 274
93/4 Donruss CAN14
99/0 Eishockey 213
93/4 Pinnacle 475
91/2 7th...Sketch WHL 176
93/4 Upper Deck 539
00/1 UD DEL 172
01/2 UD DEL 81
96/7 Syracuse Crunch

GIRARD, ROLAND
51/2 Lac St-Jean 43

GIRGAN, KYLE
92/3 MPS SJHL 128

GIRHINY, RICK
90/1 7th..Sketch OHL 259
95/6 Muskegon Fury
98/9 Odessa Jackalopes
99/0 Odessa Jackalopes

GIROUARD, GILBERT
51/2 Bas du Fleuve 14

GIROUARD, GUY
92/3 Oklahoma City Blazers

GIROUARD, PIERRE-OLIVIER
01/2 Drummondville

GIROUX, ALEXANDRE
99 Bowman 12, ✍ BA32
95 Québec Pee Wee 1153
99/0 Topps 253
99/0 To. Chrome 253
01/2 Grand Rapids Griffins
99/0 Hull Olympiques BN
99/0 Hull Olympiques 7

GIROUX, LARRY
74/5 Loblaws
75/6 O-Pee-Chee 273
75/6 Topps 273
73/4 SLOU
78/9 SLOU

GIROUX, RAY
99/0 BAP Mem. 333
00/1 Cardset 134
00/1 Topps 306
00/1 To. Chrome 201
99/0 Lowell Lock Monsters

GIROUX, RAYMOND
02/3 Albany River Rats

GIROUX, REJEAN
72/3 Québec Nordiques

GIRVITCH, SANDIS
99/0 San Angelo Outlaws

GIUCO, SCOTT
93/4 Lethbridge Hurricanes

GIVEN, JASON
91/2 Avant Garde BCJHL 103
92/3 BCJHL 122

GIZATULLIN, IINUR
99/0 Mir 77

GIZATULLIN, ILNUR
98/9 Mir 106
00/1 Mir 40

GJERMUNDSEN, PÅL
92/3 Semic Nordisk 55

GJERTSEN, ØRJAN
92/3 Semic Nordisk 239

GLAD, JARKKO
98/9 Cardset 127
99/0 Cardset 68
00/1 Cardset 47
02/3 Cardset 165
93/4 Jyvas Hyva 48
93/4 Sisu 118
94/5 Sisu 231
95/6 Sisu 275

GLADNEY, BOB
78/9 Saginaw Gears

GLADNEY, JASON
91/2 7th...Sketch OHL 92
93/4 Slapshot / Kitchener 19
95/6 Toledo Storm
96/7 Toledo Storm
97/8 Toledo Storm 20

GLADU, FERNAND
52/3 Bas du Fleuve 3

GLADU, JEAN
43-47 Parade Sportive
43-47 Parade Sportive

GLADU, PATRICK
95/6 Toledo Storm

GLADU, PAUL
51/2 Cleveland Barons

GLADUE, GARY
00/1 Prince George Cougars

GLASS, FRANK
91 C55 Reprint 34
10/1 Imperial
10/1 Imperial 5
11/2 Imperial 34
12/3 Imperial 21

GLAUDE, ERIC
02/3 Val d'Or Foreurs

GLAUDE, GERARD
51/2 Laval Dairy 32

GLAUDE, JEAN-PHILIPPE
01/2 Victoriaville Tigres 4

GLAZACHEV, KONSTANTIN
02/3 Russian Future Stars 4

GLEASON, TIM
01/2 UD Prospects 29, 93

GLEASON, TIMOTHY
96 Québec Pee Wee 668

GLEASON, TODD
90/1 7th..Sketch OHL 208
91/2 7th...Sketch OHL 339

GLEASON, TRENT
90/1 7th..Sketch OHL 106
89/0 Windsor Spitfires

GLEASON, TROY
90/1 7th..Sketch OHL 107

GLEBOV, ANDREI
99/0 Mir 82

GLEBOV, OLEG
99/0 Mir 220
00/1 Mir 43

GLENNIE, BRIAN
77/8 Coke
70/1 Eddie Sargent 196
72/3 Eddie Sargent 205
70/1 Esso Power Player
91/2 Future Trends C72 88, ✍ 88
74/5 Loblaws
73/4 Mac's Milk
70/1 O-Pee-Chee 216
71/2 O-Pee-Chee 197
72/3 O-Pee-Chee 216
73/4 O-Pee-Chee 170
74/5 O-Pee-Chee 310
75/6 O-Pee-Chee 365
76/7 O-Pee-Chee 99
77/8 O-Pee-Chee 275
78/9 O-Pee-Chee 345
79/0 O-Pee-Chee 341
72/3 Topps 37
73/4 Topps 163
76/7 Topps 99
77/8 Topps 99
71/2 Toronto Sun Photo
69/0 TORO
71/2 TORO
72/3 TORO
73/4 TORO
74/5 TORO
75/6 TORO
76/7 TORO
77/8 TORO

GLENNON, MATT
91/2 ProCards 58
98/9 BOST / Alumni 23

GLICKMAN, JASON
87/8 Hull Olympiques
89/0 Regina Pats

GLODE, KEVIN
01/2 Moncton Wildcats 14

GLOVATSKI, VADIM
98/9 Mir 15
00/1 Mir 199
00/1 Metallurg 28

GLOVATSKIN, VADIM
99/0 Mir 5

GLOVER, CHRIS
83/4 Brantford Alexanders

GLOVER, FRED
45-64 BeeHive-2 [Detr.]
51/2 Cleveland Barons
51/2 Parkhurst 60
52/3 Parkhurst 40

GLOVER, HOWIE
45-64 BeeHive-2 [Detr.]
45-64 BeeHive-2 [NYRa.]
61/2 Parkhurst 19
62/3 Parkhurst 28
60/1 Shirriff 57
61/2 Shirriff 65

GLOVER, JASON
00/1 Kudos 103
96/7 Flint Generals
98/9 Flint Generals

GLOVER, MIKE
88/9 ProCards / Cape Breton
87/8 Soo Greyhounds 3

GLOVER, WILLY
00/1 Prince George Cougars

GLOWA, KELLY
82/3 Brandon Wheat Kings

GLYNN, BRIAN
91/2 Bowman 132
92/3 Bowman 379
93/4 Donruss 236
92/3 Fleer Ultra 58
91/2 O-Pee-Chee 506
91/2 Panini Sticker 114
92/3 Parkhurst 287
93/4 Parkhurst 141
92/3 Pinnacle 136
93/4 Power Play 399
91/2 Pro Set 406
89/0 ProCards IHL 191
91/2 Score CAN 446
92/3 Score 361
92/3 Topps 198
91/2 To. Stadium 388
92/3 T. Stadium Club 472
91/2 Upper Deck 158
92/3 Upper Deck 64
93/4 Upper Deck 458
87/8 CALG / Red Rooster
92/3 EDMO
92/3 EDMO / IGA 009
95/6 HART / Kids Club
93/4 OTTA
94/5 VANC
86/7 Saskatoon Blades

GOBEL, ERIC
84/5 Richelieu Riverains

GOBER, MIKE
88/9 ProCards / Adirondack
89/0 ProCards AHL 313
90/1 ProCards 312
91/2 Knoxville Cherokees

GOC, MARCEL
99/0 Eishockey 199
00/1 UD DEL 214
01/2 UD DEL 269

GOC, SASCHA
00/1 BAP Mem. 472
98/9 Collection Souvenir 15
96/7 DEL 294
01/2 Parkhurst 277
00/1 Premier Plus 138
00/1 PS Titanium Draft 166
92 Québec Pee Wee 1688
93 Québec Pee Wee 1775
01/2 Signature 225, ✍ Aut. 225
00/1 SP Authentic 150
00/1 To. Stars 110
98/9 Albany River Rats
99/0 Albany River Rats
00/1 Albany River Rats

GODARD, CHRIS
92/3 BCJHL 207

GODARD, ERIC
02/3 BAP Memorabilia 374
02/3 Calder 131
02/3 In The Game-Used 199
02/3 Pacific Complete 567
02/3 Parkhurst 249
02/3 Quest for the Cup 131
02/3 SP Authentic 152
02/3 T. Chrome 152
02/3 T. Total 433
02/3 Ultimate Mem. 42
02/3 Upper Deck 442
02/3 UD Artistic 111
02/3 UD Honor 121
02/3 UD Mask 137
02/3 UD Top Shelf 97
99/0 Lethbridge Hurricanes

GODBOUT, BRENT
93/4 Minnesota G'Gophers
94/5 Minnesota G'Gophers

GODBOUT, DANIEL
91/2 7th...Sketch OHL 102
94/5 Slapshot / Kitchener 4

GODBOUT, JASON
94/5 Minnesota G'Gophers

GODDEN, ERNIE
92/3 Windsor Spitfires

GODFREY, WARREN
45-64 BeeHive-2 [Bost.]
45-64 BeeHive-2 [Bost.]
45-64 BeeHive-2 [Bost.]
45-64 BeeHive-2 [Detr.]
64-67 BeeHive-3 [Bost.]
64-67 BeeHive-3 [Detr.]
65/6 Coca-Cola
62/3 Cowan Tile
52/3 Parkhurst 85
53/4 Parkhurst 93
54/5 Parkhurst 56
60/1 Parkhurst 30
61/2 Parkhurst 30
62/3 Parkhurst 36
93/4 Parkhurst PR54
93/4 Parkie 56-57 51
94/5 Parkie Tall 63
60/1 Shirriff 49
61/2 Shirriff 62
54/5 Topps 50
57/8 Topps 41
58/9 Topps 58
59/0 Topps 27
62/3 Topps 4
62/3 Topps Dollar
61/2 Toronto Star Weekend

GODIN, BERT
92/3 Cleveland Lumberjacks

GODRON, JACK
60/1 Cleveland Barons

GODYNYUK, ALEXANDER
93/4 Donruss 135
93/4 Donruss 438
94/5 Donruss 202
99/0 Eishockey 53
94/5 Flair 72
93/4 Fleer Ultra 325
94/5 Fleer Ultra 89
94/5 Leaf 29
91/2 O-Pee-Chee 471
92/3 O-Pee-Chee 10
97/8 Panini Sticker 26
91/2 Parkhurst 248
93/4 Parkhurst 74
94/5 Parkhurst 100
91/2 Pinnacle 318
94/5 Pinnacle 286
96/7 Pi. Be A Player 83, ✍ Aut. 83
93/4 Premier 289
91/2 Pro Set 563
91/2 Pro Set Platinum 251
91/2 Score 391
91/2 Score CAN 281
92/3 Topps 256
92/3 T. Stadium Club 88
93/4 To. Stadium 268
91/2 Upper Deck 466
92/3 Upper Deck 609
91/2 Upper Deck E16
93/4 Upper Deck 469
94/5 Upper Deck 168
94/5 UD BAP ✍ 67
00/1 UD DEL 61
92/3 CALG / IGA 018
93/4 HART / Coke
96/7 HART / Kids Club
91/2 TORO / P.L.A.Y. 30
98/9 Chicago Wolves Champs

GOEBEL, BRYCE
91/2 7th...Sketch WHL 104
91/2 Saskatoon Blades

GOEBEL, TOM
95/6 DEL 337

GOEGAN, GRANT
82 Semic Sticker 141

GOEGAN, PETER
45-64 BeeHive-2 [Detr.]
64-67 BeeHive-3 [Detr.]
60/1 Parkhurst 34
61/2 Parkhurst 23
63/4 Parkhurst 43
93/4 Parkie 66-67 54
94/5 Parkie Tall 61
60/1 Shirriff 50
61/2 Shirriff 75
58/9 Topps 47
59/0 Topps 4
63/4 York 53

GOEHRING, KARL
02/3 Syracuse Crunch

GOEPPERT, BOBBY
97 Québec Pee Wee 0835

GOERLITZ, MARCUS
95/6 DEL 303

GOERTZ, DAVE
88/9 ProCards / Muskegon
89/0 ProCards IHL 147
90/1 ProCards 377
84/5 Prince Albert Raiders
81/2 Regina Pats
82/3 Regina Pats
83/4 Regina Pats

GOETZINGER, JEREMY
00/1 Medicine Hat Tigers

GOGOLEV, DMITRI
99/0 Mir 237
00/1 Mir 263

GOGOLEV, DMITRIJ
99/0 OFS 223

GOHEEN, FRANCIS (MOOSE)
83 HHOF Postcard H6
83&87 HHOF 112
96/7 Legends 86
60/1 Tops 63
61/2 Topps - Stamp

GOICOECHEA, YANNICK
92 Semic Sticker 234

GOLDADE, AARON
98/9 Brandon Wheat Kings
99/0 Brandon Wheat Kings

GOLDEN, MATT
00/1 Peoria Rivermen
01/2 Peoria Rivermen

GOLDEN, MIKE
89/0 ProCards IHL 34
90/1 ProCards 11

GOLDHAM, BOB
34-43 BeeHive-1 [Toro.]
45-64 BeeHive-2 [Chic.]
45-64 BeeHive-2 [Detr.]
51/2 Parkhurst 67
52/3 Parkhurst 64
53/4 Parkhurst 49
54/5 Parkhurst 39
45-54 Quaker Oats
54/5 Topps 46

GOLDIE, DAN
93/4 Cla. Prospects 233

GOLDMANN, ERICH
94/5 DEL 289
95/6 DEL 272
96/7 DEL 117
00/1 Pacific 291
00/1 UD DEL 168
01/2 UD DEL 66
99/0 Grand Rapids Griffins

GOLDSTEIN, JORN
79 Panini Sticker 294

GOLDSWORTHY, BILL
70/1 Colgate 52
70/1 Dad's Cookies
70/1 Eddie Sargent 95
71/2 Eddie Sargent 86
72/3 Eddie Sargent 104
70/1 Esso Power Player
91/2 Future Trends C72 79, ✍ 79
74/5 Loblaws
68/9 O-Pee-Chee 148
69/0 O-Pee-Chee 195
70/1 O-Pee-Chee 46
71/2 O-Pee-Chee 55
72/3 O-Pee-Chee 159
72/3 O-Pee-Chee Crest 10
72/3 O-Pee-Chee TC
73/4 O-Pee-Chee 62
74/5 O-Pee-Chee 1
74/5 O-Pee-Chee 112
74/5 O-Pee-Chee 134
74/5 O-Pee-Chee 220
75/6 O-Pee-Chee 180
75/6 O-Pee-Chee 321
76/7 O-Pee-Chee 169
77/8 O-Pee-Chee 99
72 Semic Sticker 220
68/9 Shirriff / Minn. 4
70/1 Topps 46
71/2 Topps 55
72/3 Topps 115
73/4 Topps 62
74/5 Topps 1
74/5 Topps 112
74/5 Topps 134
74/5 Topps 220
75/6 Topps 180
75/6 Topps 321
76/7 Topps 169
77/8 Topps 99
71/2 Toronto Sun Photo
70/1 MINS / Colour
73/4 MINS

GOLDSWORTHY, LEROY
34-43 BeeHive-1 [Chic.]
36-39 Diamond Match TT1
36-39 Diamond Match TT2
36-39 Diamond Match TT3
35/6 O-Pee-Chee 96
37/8 World Wide Gum 73

GOLDUP, GLENN
74/5 O-Pee-Chee 275
75/6 O-Pee-Chee 391
78/9 O-Pee-Chee 337
79/0 O-Pee-Chee 376
80/1 O-Pee-Chee 382
80/1 LOSA 2
74/5 MONT

GOLDUP, HENRY (HANK)
34-43 BeeHive-1 [Toro.]
39/0 O-Pee-Chee 54

GOLEMBIEWSKI, LEO
85/6 U. of Arizona Ice Cats

GOLEMBROSKY, FRANK
72/3 Québec Nordiques

GOLIKOV, ALEXANDER
80 Olympic USSR
79 Panini Sticker 154
79/0 Soviet Stars 21

GOLIKOV, VLADIMIR
79 Panini Sticker 148
82 Semic Sticker 66
79/0 Soviet Stars 23

GOLOKHVASTOV, KONSTANTIN
98/9 Mir 69
99/0 Mir 149

GOLONKA, JOSEF
94/5 DEL 321
69/0 Mästär Serien 2
69/0 Mästär Serien 7
91 Semic Sticker 258

GOLOSJUMOV, SERGEI
89 Semic Sticker 80

GOLTZ, ALEXANDER
98/9 Mir 16
00/1 Mir 108
00/1 Metallurg 50

GOLTZ, FRED
90/1 7th..Sketch OHL 58
95/6 Louisiana Ice Gators

GOLTZ, JEREMY
85/6 U. of Arizona Ice Cats

GOLUBOVSKY, YAN
99/0 BAP Mem. 283
98/9 Bowman's Best 104, F8
94/5 Classic 19, T20
94/5 Classic 4 Sport 136
94/5 Cla. Images 30, ✍ Aut.
98/9 Upper Deck 11
98/9 UD G. Reserve 11
95/6 Adirondack Red Wings

GOMALYAKO, SERGEI
00/1 Mir 151

GOMAN, VESA
95/6 Sisu 361
96/7 Sisu 156

GOMBAR, JIRI
01/2 OFS 166
99/0 Score 30

GOMES, TOM
98/9 Oklahoma City Blazers

GOMEZ, JOHNNY
00/1 Louisiana Ice Gators

GOMEZ, ROBIN
99/0 Calgary Hitmen
00/1 Calgary Hitmen

GOMEZ, SCOTT
01/2 Adrenaline 114
00/1 Aurora 83, Pins. 83, CF-15, SR-14, TPS-7A
02/3 BAP All-Star 27, ✂ ASJ
99/0 BAP Mem. 301
00/1 BAP Mem. 146
01/2 BAP Memor. 60, ✂ ASJ, ✂ ASE, ✂ ASN, ✂ AST, ✂ SCP
02/3 BAP Memorabilia 152
99 Bowman 108, SC19
98 Bowman 145, SC19, ✍ A27
98 Bowman Chrome 145
02/3 Calder 5
99/0 Crown Royale 80, IG-15, CS-14, C21-6
00/1 Crown Royale 64
02/3 Crown Royale 58
99/0 Dynagon Ice 116
02/3 First Edition 114, ✂ Jers.
02/3 Heads Up ✂ GWQ 17
99/0 HoloGrFX 32
02/3 In The Game-Used 43, 143
00/1 McDonald's 21, GCDC-4
99/0 Millenium C-6
99/0 NHL Power Play [x3]
01/2 O-Pee-Chee 76
02/3 O-Pee-Chee 112
98/9 OPC Chrome 232
99/0 Omega 135, 5ST-4, EOP-12, G-6, NAAS-8
00/1 Pacific 234, IO-14, CCA-8, GCDC-19, NAS-8, PR-13, ✍ Aut. 234
01/2 Pacific 230
02/3 Pacific 222
02/3 Pacific Complete 87
00/1 Pa. Paramount 144, ES-14, FF-22
99/0 Panini Sticker 83, 354
00/1 Panini Sticker 50
00/1 Parkhurst P-54
01/2 Parkhurst 9, ✂ PJ9, ✂ PS9, ✂ H15, ✂ T15
02/3 Parkhurst 84
02/3 Parkhurst Retro 105
00/1 Premier Plus 1, CL, CTW1, PA1, PP1
99/0 Prism 81, IP-5
00/1 Private Stock 59, Res. 13,PS-33, PSNW-14
01/2 Pr. Stock 57
01/2 PS Titanium ✂ DSJ 69
01/2 PS Titanium Draft ✂ 52
02/3 PS Titanium 62, ✂ GWJ 39
00/1 Revolution 87, HD-22, II-14, SM-27
00/1 Signature 195, ✍ Aut. 199, ✂ HSHSJers
01/2 Signature C-39, ✂ GJ34, ✂ GSJ34
02/3 Signature ✂ YP3
99/0 SP Authentic 51, TH6, ✍ SotT
00/1 SP Authentic 52, PS4, ✍ SotT, ✍ SotTD, ✍ SotTT
00/1 SP GU 37
00/1 SPx 39
99/0 Stadium 198, Chrome 48
00/1 Stadium 57, BT9, CA3, ✍ CO2, ✍ LS3
01/2 Stadium 90
98/9 Topps 232
00/1 Topps 203, OTG21, ✍ CAI
01/2 Topps 76
02/3 Topps 112
99/0 To. Chrome 291
00/1 To. Chrome 134
02/3 T. Chrome 72
99/0 To. Gold Label 87, FG14
00/1 To. Gold Label 61, B1, NG1, ✍ GLA
00/1 To. Heritage 29, 229, 240, NT6
01/2 To. Heritage 85
02/3 To. Heritage ✂ CC
02/3 T. Limited 112
99/0 To. Prmr. Plus 136, PR4, ✍ SB, ✂ GP
01/2 To. Reserve 86
00/1 To. Stars 3, 129, P3
02/3 T. Total 110
00/1 UD Heroes 150, ✍ SG
00/1 Ultimate Mem. ✂ U-17, ✂ Jers. 36, ✂ J-44, ✂ S-44, ✂
01/2 Ultimate Mem. ✂ CT
99/0 Upper Deck 251
00/1 Upper Deck 102, L7, P5, RP4, TT1, UD4, ✂ GJ, ✂ DGJ
01/2 Upper Deck 105
99/0 UD Black Diam. 52
00/1 UD Black Diam. 34, IG5, CC4
01/2 UD Challenge 52
99/0 UD G. Reserve 251
00/1 UD Ice 25, CC4, IG5, ✍ CCA
00/1 UD Legends 77
00/1 UD MVP 108, TD6, TP7
01/2 UD MVP 116
99/0 UD MVP Cup 107, CC6
99/0 UD Ovation 34
00/1 UD Pros&Prosp. 50, NA4, ✂ ✍ GJS
02/3 UD Rookie 59
01/2 UD SCup Champs 75
00/1 UD Vintage 215, 221, 222, NH15, S4A
01/2 UD Vintage 154
00/1 Vanguard 59, HV-20
02/3 Vanguard ✂ GWJ 28
99/0 Victory 360
00/1 Victory 137, 252, 310
01/2 Victory 212
02/3 Victory 130

GOMOLYAKO, S.
98/9 Mir 1, 129
99/0 Mir 7
00/1 Mir 361
00/1 Metallurg 27

GONCHAR, SERGEI
01/2 Adrenaline 195
98/9 Aurora 195
99/0 Aurora 147
98/9 Be A Player 299, ✍ Aut. 299
99/0 BAP Mem. 78
00/1 BAP Mem. 126, ✂ TM-2
01/2 BAP Memor. 86
02/3 BAP Memorabilia 168
92/3 Classic 41
92/3 Classic 43
94/5 Classic 27
92/3 Classic Four Sport 184
94/5 Cla. Images 55
93/4 Cla. Prospects IA19
95/6 Donruss 173
95/6 Edge Ice 53
02/3 Exclusive 171
02/3 First Edition 2, 307, 382, ✂ Jers.
96/7 Fleer 117, RS-5
95/6 Fleer Metal 159
96/7 Fl. Picks F50-14
95/6 Fleer Ultra 322
96/7 Fl. Ultra 175
95/6 Leaf 26
96/7 Maggers 166
96/7 Metal Univ. 163
99/0 Millenium 249, ✍ Aut. 249
01/2 O-Pee-Chee 120
02/3 O-Pee-Chee 256, 321
98/9 Pacific 441
99/0 Pacific 439
00/1 Pacific 421
01/2 Pacific 392
02/3 Pacific 390
02/3 Pacific Complete 464
97/8 Pacific CC 103
98/9 Pa. Paramount 244
99/0 Pa. Paramount 244
00/1 Pa. Paramount 244
95/6 Panini Sticker 141
96/7 Panini Sticker 135
97/8 Panini Sticker 112
98/9 Panini Sticker 105
99/0 Panini Sticker 169, 344
00/1 Panini Sticker 103
95/6 Parkhurst 225
00/1 Parkhurst P-222
01/2 Parkhurst 134, ✂ PJ29, ✂ PS29, ✂ T6
02/3 Parkhurst 116, -HHN2
02/3 Parkhurst Retro 53
94/5 Parkie SE195
95/6 Pinnacle 71
96/7 Pinnacle 40
96/7 Pi. Be A Player 150, ✍ Aut. 150
95/6 POG 286
02/3 Pr. Stock Reserve 98
01/2 PS Titanium 141
92/3 Red Ace Violet 9
99/0 Revolution 148
00/1 Signature 248, ✂ DD-15, ✂ TM-11
01/2 Signature 200, ✍ Aut., ✂ DD8, ✂ GJ67, ✂ GSJ67, ✂ IB11
02/3 Signature 27, ✍ 27, ✂ DW9, ✂ TQ9
95/6 SBx Emotion 187
95/6 SBx Impact 176
96/7 SBx Impact 139, F-9
96/7 SP 165
97/8 SP Authentic 166
98/9 SP Authentic ✍ SotT
02/3 SP Game-Used ✂ PC, ✂ PH
02/3 Sports Vault 147
99/0 SPx 160
98/9 SPx Finite 90
00/1 Stadium 79
96/7 Team Out>
95/6 Topps 47
99/0 Topps 146
00/1 Topps 71
01/2 Topps 120
02/3 Topps 256, 321
99/0 To. Chrome 146
00/1 To. Chrome 56
02/3 T. Chrome 139
00/1 To. Heritage 214
02/3 To. Heritage 113, 126
02/3 T. Limited 256, 321
96/7 Topps Picks 91
00/1 To. Stars 71
02/3 T. Total 378
00/1 UD Heroes 118
00/1 Ultimate Mem. ✂ TM-11
93/4 Upper Deck 272
94/5 Upper Deck 264
95/6 Upper Deck 305
96/7 Upper Deck 175
97/8 Upper Deck 180
98/9 Upper Deck 201
00/1 Upper Deck 406
01/2 Upper Deck 175
02/3 Upper Deck 175
02/3 UD Classic ✂ HR
96/7 UD CC 286
97/8 UD Coll. Choice 273
98/9 UD G. Reserve 201
97/8 UD Ice 75
98/9 UD MVP 211
99/0 UD MVP 216, ✍ PS
00/1 UD MVP 183
01/2 UD MVP 185
02/3 UD MVP 183
02/3 UD Rookie ✂ 154b, ✂ 162c
02/3 UD Top Shelf ✂ CP, ✂ ST
00/1 UD Vintage 367
01/2 UD Vintage 253, 260
02/3 UD Vintage 254, 290, 310
99/0 Victory 308
00/1 Victory 238
01/2 Victory 351
02/3 Victory 212, -NP39
95/6 WASH
94/5 Portland Pirates

GONEAU, DANIEL
97/8 Donruss 190
96/7 Do. Canadian 126
96/7 Do. Elite 143, A-18
96/7 Flair 116
96/7 L. Preferred 145
97/8 Limited 148
96/7 Metal Univ. 180
97/8 Pacific CC 327
96/7 Pi. Be A Player 107, ✍ Aut. 107
96/7 Pi. Zenith 148
97/8 Score NYRa. 18
96/7 Select CE 107
96/7 SP 184
98/9 SPx Finite 55, 141
98/9 UD Choice 137
93/4 Upper Deck E5
96/7 Upper Deck 295
96/7 UD CC 353
96/7 UD Ice 42
97/8 Hartford Wolf Pack
98/9 Hartford Wolf Pack
99/0 Hartford Wolf Pack
02/3 Louisiana Ice Gators
00/1 Manitoba Moose

GONEAU, JASON
97 Bowman 63

GONZALEZ, FRANCISCO
79 Panini Sticker 372

GOODALL, GLEN
90/1 ProCards 482
91/2 ProCards 191

GOODALL, RON
85/6 Kitchener Rangers
86/7 Kitchener Rangers
87/8 Kitchener Rangers

GOODENOUGH, LARRY
75/6 O-Pee-Chee 373
76/7 O-Pee-Chee 96
77/8 O-Pee-Chee 359
79/0 O-Pee-Chee 383
76/7 Topps 96
77/8 VANC / Royal Bank

GOODFELLOW, EBBIE
33/4 Anonymous 20
34-43 BeeHive-1 [Detr.]
33/4 Canadian Gum
33/4 Hamilton Gum 42
83 HHOF Postcard C5
83&87 HHOF 35
30/1 La Presse
33/4 O-Pee-Chee 52
36/7 O-Pee-Chee 117
39/0 O-Pee-Chee 66
36/7 Sweet Caporal
02/3 Ultimate Mem. ✍ Cut
37/8 World Wide Gum 11

GOODMAN, PAUL
34-43 BeeHive-1 [Chic.]
40/1 O-Pee-Chee 150

GOODWIN, JOHN
83/4 Nova Scotia Voyageurs
80/1 Soo Greyhounds

GOODWIN, TODD
01/2 Belfast Giants

GOOLD, BILLY
51/2 Laval Dairy 89

GOOLEY, PAT
87/8 Brockville Braves
88/9 Brockville Braves

GORALCZYK, ROBERT
74 Hellas MM-Jenkki 96
73/4 Williams Finnish 91

GORBACHEV, EDUARD
96/7 APS 114
96/7 DS Sticker 272
98/9 Mir 27
00/1 Mir 60

GORBACHEV, SERGEI
94/5 Sig. Rookies FF4, ✍ FF4

GORBENKO, IGOR
98/9 Mir 58

GORBENKO, OLEG
99/0 Mir 95

GORBUSHIN, ILYA
00/1 Mir 230, 339

GORDIOUK, VIKTOR
92/3 Classic Prospects 88
96/7 DEL 277
95/6 Edge Ice 149
93/4 Fleer Ultra 120
93/4 Fleer Ultra ARS 2
94/5 Fleer Ultra 145
94/5 Leaf 468
91/2 O-Pee-Chee 15R
92/3 OPC Premier 60
92/3 Parkhurst 17
94/5 Parkie SE23
93/4 Power Play 28
94/5 Premier 456
91 Semic Sticker 97
92 Semic Sticker 119
92/3 Upper Deck 579
93/4 Upper Deck ER18
00/1 UD DEL 55
92/3 BUFF / Jubilee
93/4 Rochester Americans

GORDON, BOYD
00/1 Red Deer Rebels

GORDON, BRUCE
81/2 Saskatoon Blades
GORDON, CHRIS
95/6 Flint Generals
94/5 Huntington Blizzard
GORDON, IAN
94/5 SR Auto-Phonex 16, ✍ 16
00/1 UD DEL 224
01/2 UD DEL 231, ✂ GJ
97/8 Grand Rapids Griffins
98/9 Grand Rapids Griffins
95/6 Saint John Flames
96/7 Saint John Flames
99/0 Utah Grizzlies
GORDON, JACK
45-64 BeeHive-2 [NYRa.]
51/2 Cleveland Barons
74/5 O-Pee-Chee 238
74/5 Topps 238
GORDON, LARRY
92/3 Cleveland Lumberjacks
GORDON, RHETT
00/1 Kudos 17
98/9 Manitoba Moose
96/7 Springfield Falcons
97/8 Springfield Falcons
GORDON, ROBB
92/3 BCJHL 147
95/6 Do. Elite WJ 14
95/6 Upper Deck 538
96/7 Syracuse Crunch
GORDON, SCOTT
90/1 Bowman 171
90/1 Panini/QUE 7
90/1 Pro Set 634
88/9 ProCards / Halifax
89/0 ProCards AHL 153
90/1 ProCards 467
90/1 QUÉB / Petro-Canada
94/5 Atlanta Knights 26
95/6 Atlanta Knights
86/7 Fredericton Express
89/0 Halifax Citadels
90/1 Halifax Citadels
93/4 Knoxville Cherokees
98/9 Roanoke Express
GORDON, TODD
91/2 Greensboro Monarchs
92/3 Greensboro Monarchs 13
GORE, FORREST
99/0 Kansas City Blades
99/0 Missouri RiverOtters
01/2 Rockford IceHogs
GOREN, LEE
01/2 BAP Memor. 59
02/3 Calder 54
01/2 O-Pee-Chee 286
02/3 Pacific Complete 592
00/1 SP Authentic 95
00/1 SPx 152
01/2 Topps 286
00/1 UD Black Diam. 113
01/2 Victory 363
00/1 Providence Bruins
01/2 Providence Bruins
GORENCE, TOM
79/0 O-Pee-Chee 51
80/1 O-Pee-Chee 368
81/2 O-Pee-Chee 250
82/3 O-Pee-Chee 250
79/0 Topps 51
88/9 EDMO / Action 87
83/4 Moncton Alpines
GORENKO, DMITRI
98/9 Mir 59
99/0 Mir 120
GOREV, ROMAN
93/4 Cla. Prospects 141
GOREWICH, BEN
99/0 Missouri RiverOtters
GORGENLANDER, RUDI
94/5 DEL 120
95/6 DEL 109
96/7 DEL 54
GORGES, JOSH
00/1 Kelowna Rockets
GORGI, MARK
91/2 Air Canada SJHL C31
GORING, BUTCH
77/8 Coke
71/2 Eddie Sargent 73
72/3 Eddie Sargent 92
01/2 Fleer Greats 82, ✍ Aut.
01/2 Fleer Legacy 43
74/5 Loblaws
71/2 O-Pee-Chee 152
72/3 O-Pee-Chee 56
73/4 O-Pee-Chee 155
74/5 O-Pee-Chee 74
74/5 O-Pee-Chee 98
75/6 O-Pee-Chee 221
76/7 O-Pee-Chee 239
77/8 O-Pee-Chee 67
78/9 O-Pee-Chee 151
79/0 O-Pee-Chee 98
80/1 O-Pee-Chee 254
81/2 O-Pee-Chee 203
82/3 O-Pee-Chee 200
83/4 O-Pee-Chee 7
84/5 O-Pee-Chee 127
81/2 OPC Sticker 20
82/3 OPC/Topps Sticker 18
83/4 OPC/Topps Sticker 13
83/4 OPC/Topps Sticker 177
84/5 OPC Sticker 84
82/3 Post [NYIs.]
83/4 Souhaits Keychain [Islanders]
72/3 Topps 72
73/4 Topps 138
74/5 Topps 74
74/5 Topps 98
75/6 Topps 221
76/7 Topps 239
77/8 Topps 67
78/9 Topps 151
79/0 Topps 98
80/1 Topps 254
81/2 Topps 89 [East]
84/5 Topps 95
71/2 Toronto Sun Photo
02/3 UD Foundations 39, 60
00/1 UD Legends 83, ✂ LGJ
01/2 UD Legends 28
00/1 UD Vintage ✂ D-POH
83/4 NYIS / News 38
83/4 NYIS / News 7
99/0 NYIS / UD NY10
93/4 Las Vegas Thunder
GORMAN, DAVE
75/6 Phoenix Roadrunners
GORMAN, ED
25-27 Anonymous 25
GORMAN, JEFF
90/1 7th..Sketch WHL 274
91/2 7th...Sketch WHL 260
90/1 Prince Albert Raiders
91/2 Prince Albert Raiders
93/4 Prince Albert Raiders
GORMAN, MIKE
98 Bowman 12
98 Bowman Chrome 12
99/0 Sudbury Wolves 25
GORMAN, SEAN
93/4 Kansas City Blades
92/3 Oklahoma City Blazers
GORMAN, TOMMY
83 HHOF Postcard H7
83&87 HHOF 113
37/8 World Wide Gum 17
GOROKHOV, ILJA
95/6 SP 181
GOROVIKOV, KONSTANTIN
99/0 Grand Rapids Griffins
00/1 Grand Rapids Griffins
GORSKI, LEROY
81/2 Saskatoon Blades
GORSKI, SHELDON
99/0 Rockford IceHogs
GOSDECK, CARSTEN
98/9 DEL 18
00/1 UD DEL 201
01/2 UD DEL 267
GOSSELIN, CHRISTIAN
01/2 Hartford Wolf Pack
98/9 Kentucky Tho'blades
99/0 Kentucky Tho'blades
00/1 Kentucky Tho'blades
97/8 Pensacola Ice Pilots
GOSSELIN, DAVID
00/1 BAP Mem. 83
98 Bowman 109
98 Bowman Chrome 109
00/1 Pacific 230
00/1 Revolution 81
00/1 SP Authentic ✍ SotT
00/1 SPx 98
00/1 Topps 304
00/1 To. Chrome 199
00/1 UD Heroes 167
00/1 Upper Deck 186
00/1 UD Black Diam. 79
00/1 UD Ice 58
00/1 UD MVP 195
00/1 Victory 269
98/9 Milwaukee Admirals
99/0 Milwaukee Admirals
01/2 Milwaukee Admirals
GOSSELIN, DENIS
90/1 Rayside-Balfour
91/2 Rayside-Balfour
GOSSELIN, G.
59/60 Whitby Dunlops
GOSSELIN, GUY
88/9 ProCards / Moncton
89/0 ProCards AHL 36
85/6 Minnesota-Duluth 10
GOSSELIN, MARIO
83 Canada Juniors
86/7 Kraft Sports 44
85/6 OPC/Topps 18
85/6 O-Pee-Chee 235
87/8 O-Pee-Chee 250
88/9 OPC/Topps 173
90/1 O-Pee-Chee 442
89/0 O-Pee-Chee 258
85/6 OPC Sticker 146-16
86/7 OPC Sticker 21-162
87/8 OPC Sticker 231
88/9 OPC Sticker 193
87/8 Panini Sticker 157
88/9 Panini Sticker 347
90/1 ProCards 349
91/2 ProCards 115
90/1 Upper Deck 91
90/1 LOSA / Smokey 18
83/4 QUÉB
84/5 QUÉB
85/6 QUÉB
85/6 QUÉB / Gene. Foods
85/6 QUÉB / McDonald's
85/6 QUÉB / Provigo
86/7 QUÉB
86/7 QUÉB / Gene. Foods
86/7 QUÉB / Yum Yum
87/8 QUÉB / Gene. Foods
87/8 QUÉB / Yum Yum
87/8 QUÉB / Yum Yum
88/9 QUÉB
88/9 QUÉB / Gene. Foods
GOSSELIN, PATRICK
00/1 Sherbrooke Castors 5
GOSSELIN, STEVE
90/1 7th..Sketch LHJMQ 23
91/2 7th...Sketch LHJMQ 86
98/9 Chicago Wolves
GOSSMANN, CARSTEN
94/5 DEL 97
95/6 DEL 78
GOTAAS, STEVE
88/9 ProCards / Muskegon
90/1 ProCards 112
91/2 ProCards 157
93/4 Las Vegas Thunder
84/5 Prince Albert Raiders
GOTTSELIG, JOHNNY
34-43 BeeHive-1 [Chic.]
33/4 Canadian Gum
33-35 Diamond Match Silv.
36-39 Diamond Match TT1
36-39 Diamond Match TT2
36-39 Diamond Match TT3
36-39 Diamond Match BH TT
36-39 Diamond Match Chic.
36-39 Diamond Match BH BT
30/1 La Presse
35/6 O-Pee-Chee 80
39/0 O-Pee-Chee 50
37/8 World Wide Gum 55
GOTZIAMAN, CHRIS
95/6 Flint Generals
GOUDIE, BRIAN
91 7th..Sketch Mem.Cup 7
91/2 7th...Sketch OHL 336
93/4 Hampton Roads
94/5 Hampton Roads
95/6 Richmond Renegades
96/7 Richmond Renegades
GOUDREAU, MARCEL
69 Columbus Checkers
GOUGH, MICHAEL
02/3 Owen Sound Attack
00/1 Toronto St. Mike's
GOULD, BOB
84/5 O-Pee-Chee 196
87/8 OPC/Topps 55
90/1 O-Pee-Chee 398
89/0 O-Pee-Chee 289
87/8 OPC Sticker 237-104
82/3 Post [Wash.]
90/1 ProCards 144
83/4 Souhaits Keychain [Capitals]
89/0 BOST / Sports Action
81/2 WASH
82/3 WASH
84/5 WASH / Pizza Hut
85/6 WASH / Pizza Hut
86/7 WASH / Kodak
86/7 WASH / Police
87/8 WASH
87/8 WASH / Kodak
88/9 WASH
88/9 WASH / Smokey
GOULD, JOHN
74/5 Loblaws
74/5 O-Pee-Chee 381
75/6 O-Pee-Chee 266
76/7 O-Pee-Chee 85
77/8 O-Pee-Chee 382
78/9 O-Pee-Chee 309
79/0 O-Pee-Chee 282
75/6 Topps 266
76/7 Topps 85
77/8 ATLF
73/4 BUFF
74/5 VANC / Royal Bank
75/6 VANC / Royal Bank
76/7 VANC / Royal Bank
GOULD, JUSTIN
97/8 Charlotte Checkers
96/7 Providence Bruins
GOULET, BOB
89/0 Johnstown Chiefs
GOULET, BRAD
99/0 Mississippi S'Wolves
GOULET, JASON
99/0 Fort Wayne Komets
02/3 Manitoba Moose
01/2 Milwaukee Admirals
00/1 Saskatoon Blades
GOULET, MICHEL
01/2 BAP Memor. ✂ 500GS
01/2 BAP Update ✂ PTT2
91/2 Bowman 392
92/3 Bowman 310
81/2 Dernière Heure
93/4 Donruss 71
92/3 Durivage 24
93/4 Durivage 42
93/4 EA Sports 28
88/9 Esso All-Star
83/4 Esso Stars
01/2 Fleer Greats 59, ✍ Aut., ✂ O6
01/2 Fleer Legacy 37, ✂ TM
92/3 Fleer Ultra 35
93/4 Fleer Ultra 289
88/9 Frito Lay
83/4 Funmate Puffy 15 [w]
93/4 Hockey Wit 33
84/5 Kellogg's 15
89/0 Kraft 30
91/2 Kraft 87
86/7 Kraft Sports 45
93/4 Leaf 373
82/3 McDonald's Les Étoiles 14
82/3 McDonald's Les Étoiles 19
80/1 O-Pee-Chee 67
81/2 O-Pee-Chee 275
82/3 O-Pee-Chee 237
82/3 O-Pee-Chee 284
83/4 O-Pee-Chee 287
83/4 O-Pee-Chee 288
83/4 O-Pee-Chee 292
84/5 O-Pee-Chee 207
84/5 O-Pee-Chee 280
84/5 O-Pee-Chee 366
84/5 O-Pee-Chee 384
84/5 O-Pee-Chee 391
85/6 OPC/Topps 150
86/7 OPC/Topps 92
86/7 OPC/Topps Box E
87/8 OPC/Topps 77
87/8 OPC/Topps Box M
88/9 OPC/Topps 54
90/1 OPC/Topps 329
91/2 O-Pee-Chee 336
92/3 O-Pee-Chee 358
89/0 OPC/Topps 57
87/8 OPC Leaders 12
88/9 OPC Stars 10
81/2 OPC Sticker 75
82/3 OPC/Topps Sticker 25
83/4 OPC/Topps Sticker 166
83/4 OPC/Topps Sticker 249
83/4 OPC/Topps Sticker 250
84/5 OPC Sticker 140
84/5 OPC Sticker 168
84/5 OPC Sticker 169
84/5 OPC Sticker 64-63
85/6 OPC Sticker 141
86/7 OPC Sticker 113-127
86/7 OPC Sticker 22
87/8 OPC Sticker 113-125
87/8 OPC Sticker 225
88/9 OPC Sticker 188
89/0 opcSticker 186
87/8 Panini Sticker 163
88/9 Panini Sticker 355
89/0 Panini Sticker 326
91/2 Panini Sticker 11
92/3 Panini Sticker 6
93/4 Panini Sticker 148
94/5 Panini Sticker 131
91/2 Parkhurst 215
91/2 Parkhurst 36
91/2 Parkhurst 428
92/3 Parkhurst 272
93/4 Parkhurst 313
01/2 Parkhurst ✂ 500GS
80/1 Pepsi Bottle Cap
91/2 Pinnacle 109
92/3 Pinnacle 22
93/4 Pinnacle 399
82/3 Post [Québ.]
93/4 Power Play 49
93/4 Premier 386
90/1 Pro Set 430
91/2 Pro Set 50
92/3 Pro Set 32
91/2 Pro Set Platinum 166
91/2 Pro Set Platinum PC15
87/8 Pro Sport CW11
90/1 Score 221
91/2 Score 201
91/2 Score 375
91/2 Score CAN 201
91/2 Score CAN 265
92/3 Score 222
92/3 Score 444
93/4 Score 153
89 Semic Sticker 70
84/5 7-Eleven
85/6 7-Eleven Superstars 16
01/2 Signature ✂ 500GS, ✍ VA32
83/4 Souhaits Keychain [Nordiques]
80/1 Topps 67
84/5 Topps 129
84/5 Topps 153
86/7 OPC/Topps - Stick. 2
87/8 OPC/Topps - Stick. 6
88/9 OPC/Topps - Stick. 7
72 Semic Sticker 196
92/3 Topps 255
92/3 Topps 347
91/2 To. Stadium 66
92/3 T. Stadium Club 69
93/4 To. Stadium 12
92 TSC Members Only
00/1 UD Heroes 137, ✍ SG
01/2 Ultimate Mem. ✂ 500GS
02/3 Ultimate Mem. ✂ Cor
90/1 Upper Deck 133
91/2 Upper Deck 374
92/3 Upper Deck 113
00 ✂ UD APOH 500, ✂✍ 500
02/3 UD Foundations ✂ 1000Jers, ✂ CH, ✂ CG, ✂ PP, ✍ SG
00/1 UD Legends 110, ✍ ES
01/2 UD Legends 77
02/3 UD Piece ✂ HS, ✍ MD
83/4 Vachon 65-45
83/4 Vachon 65-88
80/1 CHIC / Coke
91/2 CHIC / Coke
93/4 CHIC / Coke
80/1 QUÉB
81/2 QUÉB
82/3 QUÉB
83/4 QUÉB
84/5 QUÉB
85/6 QUÉB
85/6 QUÉB / Gene. Foods
85/6 QUÉB / McDonald's
85/6 QUÉB / Provigo
86/7 QUÉB
86/7 QUÉB / McDonald's
86/7 QUÉB / Yum Yum
87/8 QUÉB / Gene. Foods
87/8 QUÉB / Yum Yum
88/9 QUÉB
88/9 QUÉB / Gene. Foods
89/0 QUÉB
89/0 QUÉB / Gene. Foods
89/0 QUÉB / Police
90/1 QUÉB
GOUPILLE, CLIFF (RED)
34-43 BeeHive-1 [Mont.]
35-40 Canada Starch
37/8 O-Pee-Chee 178
39/0 O-Pee-Chee 22
40/1 O-Pee-Chee 120
GOURLIE, BRYAN
90/1 7th..Sketch WHL 304
88/9 Portland Winter Hawks
89/0 Portland Winter Hawks
GOVEDARIS, CHRIS
90/1 Bowman 259
92/3 Classic Prospects 29
96/7 DEL 45
98/9 DEL 167
95/6 Edge Ice 166
99/0 Eishockey 72
94/5 Parkhurst 236
90/1 ProCards 97
91/2 ProCards 102
91/2 Score 325
91/2 Score CAN 355
00/1 UD DEL 73, A6
90/1 HART / Jr. Whalers
94/5 Milwaukee Admirals
95/6 Minnesota Moose
93/4 St. John's Maple Leafs
GOVERDE, DAVID
92/3 Classic Prospects 54
90/1 ProCards 352
91/2 ProCards 399
98/9 Phoenix Mustangs 2
92/3 Phoenix Roadrunners
93/4 Phoenix Roadrunners
95/6 Toledo Storm
96/7 Toledo Storm
88/9 Sudbury Wolves
89/0 Sudbury Wolves
GOWAN, MARK
92/3 Sudbury Wolves
GOWENS, MARK
93/4 Flint Generals
94/5 Flint Generals
GOYER, GERRY
67/8 Topps 54
GOYETTE, DANIELLE
94/5 Classic W7
97/8 UD Coll. Choice 285
GOYETTE, PHIL
52/3 Anonymous 141
45-64 BeeHive-2 [Mont.]
45-64 BeeHive-2 [NYRa.]
64-67 BeeHive-3 [NYRa.]
64/5 Coke/Sprite [NYRa.]
65/6 Coca-Cola
70/1 Colgate 10
70/1 Dad's Cookies
71/2 Eddie Sargent 30
70/1 Esso Power Player
62/3 Cowan Tile
68/9 O-Pee-Chee 73
69/0 O-Pee-Chee 21
69/0 O-Pee-Chee 4in1
70/1 O-Pee-Chee 127
70/1 O-Pee-Chee 251
71/2 O-Pee-Chee 88
57/8 Parkhurst [Mont.] 11
58/9 Parkhurst 47
59/0 Parkhurst 4
60/1 Parkhurst 50
60/1 Parkhurst 58
61/2 Parkhurst 46
62/3 Parkhurst 37
93/4 Parkhurst PR59
94/5 Parkie 56-57 74
95/6 Parkie 66-67 99, SL5
94/5 Parkie Tall 105, 173
72 Semic Sticker 196
60/1 Shirriff 27
61/2 Shirriff 116
62/3 Shirriff 28
68/9 Shirriff / NYRa. 5
63/4 Topps 58
64/5 Topps 87
65/6 Topps 92
66/7 Topps 28
66/7 Topps / Test 28
67/8 Topps 25
68/9 Topps 73
69/0 Topps 21
70/1 Topps 127
71/2 Topps 88
63/4 Toronto Star Weekend
71/2 Toronto Sun Photo
91/2 Ultimate Original Six 11, ✍ Aut. 11
60/1 York
61/2 York 30
GOZZI, ANDERS
94/5 Leaf Elit Set 223
95/6 Leaf Elit Set 11
89/0 Semic Elitserien 19
90/1 Semic Elitserien 190
91/2 Semic Elitserien 42
92/3 Semic Elitserien 67
95/6 UD Elitserien 10
97/8 UD Elitserien 9
98/9 UD Elitserien 12
00/1 UD Elitserien 8, ✍ Sig.
GRABESHKOV, DENIS
00/1 Mir 303
GRABINSKY, JEFF
92/3 BCJHL 38
GRABOSKI, TONY
34-43 BeeHive-1 [Mont.]
GRACHEV, IGOR
00/1 Mir 206
GRACHEV, OLEG
99/0 Mir 267
GRACHEV, VLADIMIR
92/3 Red Ace Blue 24
GRACIE, BOB
33/4 Anonymous 40
34-43 BeeHive-1 [Maroons]
35-40 Canada Starch
35-40 Canada Starch
33/4 Canadian Gum
33-35 Diamond Match Silv.
36-39 Diamond Match TT1
32/3 Maple Leafs O'Keefe
33/4 O-Pee-Chee 66
37/8 O-Pee-Chee 171
38/9 Quaker Oats
33/4 WWGum 63
37/8 World Wide Gum 38
GRADIN, HENRIK
92/3 Semic Elitserien 247
GRADIN, PETER
89/0 Semic Elitserien 12
90/1 Semic Elitserien 86
91/2 Semic Elitserien 13
GRADIN, THOMAS
83/4 Funmate Puffy 3 [w]
84/5 Kellogg's 36
79/0 O-Pee-Chee 53
80/1 O-Pee-Chee 241
81/2 O-Pee-Chee 327
81/2 O-Pee-Chee 338
81/2 O-Pee-Chee 346
82/3 O-Pee-Chee 337
82/3 O-Pee-Chee 344
82/3 O-Pee-Chee 345
83/4 O-Pee-Chee 350
84/5 O-Pee-Chee 319
85/6 OPC/Topps 16
81/2 OPC Sticker 243
82/3 OPC/Topps Sticker 240
83/4 OPC/Topps Sticker 273
84/5 OPC Sticker 282
85/6 OPC Sticker 240
79 Panini Sticker 201
80/1 Pepsi Bottle Cap
82/3 Post [Vanc.]
89/0 Semic Elitserien 13
82 Semic Sticker 148
83/4 Souhaits Keychain [Canucks]
79/0 Topps 53
80/1 Topps 241
81/2 Topps 15
81/2 Topps 64
83/4 Vachon 107-27
83/4 Vachon 107-92
78/9 VANC / Royal Bank
79/0 VANC / Royal Bank
80/1 VANC
80/1 VANC / Silverwood
81/2 VANC
81/2 VANC / Silverwood
82/3 VANC
83/4 VANC
84/5 VANC
85/6 VANC
GRAESEN, MATS
89/0 Semic Elitserien 284
GRAF, KRIS
95/6 Spokane Chiefs 8
97/8 Spokane Chiefs
GRAFF, DAVID
97/8 Fort Worth Brahmas
GRAHAM,
91/2 Avant Garde BCJHL 157
GRAHAM, DAVE
95/6 Guildford Flames 12
GRAHAM, DIRK
90/1 Bowman 8
91/2 Bowman 397
92/3 Bowman 68
91 Canada Cup
93/4 Donruss 63
94/5 Flair 33
94/5 Fleer 40
92/3 Fleer Ultra 36
93/4 Fleer Ultra 61
94/5 Fleer Ultra 41
93/4 Leaf 270
94/5 Leaf 335
86/7 OPC/Topps 143
87/8 OPC/Topps 184
88/9 OPC/Topps 135
90/1 OPC/Topps 179
91/2 O-Pee-Chee 217
91/2 O-Pee-Chee 521
92/3 O-Pee-Chee 210
89/0 OPC/Topps 52
91/2 OPC Premier 131
86/7 OPC Sticker 171-31
88/9 OPC Sticker 7-136
89/0 opcSticker 12-152
87/8 Panini Sticker 295
88/9 Panini Sticker 25
89/0 Panini Sticker 44
90/1 Panini Sticker 191
91/2 Panini Sticker 16
92/3 Panini Sticker 7
93/4 Panini Sticker 147
91/2 Parkhurst 33
92/3 Parkhurst 271
91/2 Pinnacle 261
92/3 Pinnacle 173
93/4 Pinnacle 24
93/4 Pinnacle CA5
94/5 Pinnacle 317
94/5 POG 66
93/4 Power Play 50
93/4 Premier 88
94/5 Premier 67
90/1 Pro Set 51
91/2 Pro Set 323
91/2 Pro Set 51
91/2 Pro Set 570
92/3 Pro Set 38
91 Pro Set Awards AC12
91/2 Pro Set Platinum 23
90/1 Score 17
91/2 Score 15
91/2 Score 432
91/2 Score CAN 15
91/2 Score CAN 322
92/3 Score 27
93/4 Score 12
94/5 Score 56
94 Semic 97
92/3 Topps 376
91/2 To. Stadium 181
92/3 T. Stadium Club 342
93/4 To. Stadium 90
90/1 Upper Deck 131
91/2 Upper Deck 271
91/2 Upper Deck 502
91/2 Upper Deck AW8
92/3 Upper Deck 272
93/4 Upper Deck 328
94/5 UD BAP ✍ 78
88/9 CHIC / Coke
89/0 CHIC / Coke
90/1 CHIC / Coke
91/2 CHIC / Coke
93/4 CHIC / Coke
85/6 MINS
85/6 MINS / 7-Eleven 12
87/8 MINS
84/5 Springfield Indians 21
GRAHAM, DIRK
02/3 Fleer Throwbacks 19
GRAHAM, JIM
69 Columbus Checkers
GRAHAM, JIMMY
28/9 Paulins Candy 42
GRAHAM, JOHN
91/2 Avant Garde BCJHL 77
GRAHAM, PAT
82/3 Post [Pitt.]
83/4 PITT / Heinz
83/4 TORO
GRAHAM, ROBB
87/8 Sudbury Wolves
GRAHAM, ROD
82/3 Kingston Canadians
GRAHAM, ROSS
52/3 Anonymous 7
GRAHAME, JOHN
00/1 Aurora 13
99/0 BAP Mem. 393
00/1 BAP Mem. 222
01/2 BT Pipes 11, ✂ DM, ✂ Jers., ✂ GT
02/3 Between the Pipes 43, ✂ GUJ42, ✂ T17
99/0 Dynagon Ice 24
99/0 Omega 23
00/1 Pacific 34
01/2 Pacific 30
02/3 Pacific 27
02/3 Pacific Complete 221
00/1 Pa. Paramount 19
00/1 Revolution 11
00/1 Signature 67, ✍ Aut. 174
99/0 SP Authentic 96
99/0 Stadium 179
99/0 To. Prmr. Plus 100
02/3 T. Total 57
99/0 Upper Deck 184
00/1 Upper Deck 15
99/0 UD G. Reserve 184
02/3 UD Vintage 22
99/0 WGretzky 15
97/8 Providence Bruins
98/9 Providence Bruins
99/0 Providence Bruins
GRAHAME, RON
78/9 O-Pee-Chee 219
75/6 OPC WHA 50
75/6 OPC WHA 61
76/7 OPC WHA 107
78/9 Topps 219
80/1 QUÉB
75/6 Houston Aeros
GRANATO, CAMMI
93/4 Classic 66
94/5 Classic W37
93/4 Cla. 4 Sport 254
93/4 Cla. Prospects 248
GRANATO, DON
99/0 Peoria Rivermen
00/1 Worcester IceCats
01/2 Worcester IceCats
02/3 Worcester IceCats
GRANATO, KEVIN
01/2 Peoria Rivermen
02/3 Peoria Rivermen
GRANATO, TONY
98/9 Aurora 167
98/9 Be A Player 272, ✍ Aut. 272
97/8 Bicycle K-Club
90/1 Bowman 140, -HT 18
91/2 Bowman 180
92/3 Bowman 50
94/5 Cla. Images PL2
93/4 Donruss 160
94/5 Donruss 145
95/6 Donruss 111
97/8 Donruss 121
98/9 Dynagon Ice 165
96/7 Flair 84
95/6 Fleer Metal 70
92/3 Fleer Ultra 82
93/4 Fleer Ultra 63
94/5 Fleer Ultra 305
95/6 Fleer Ultra 249
95/6 Globe 120
93/4 Hockey Wit 32
91/2 Kraft 35
93/4 Leaf 201
94/5 Leaf 229
95/6 Leaf 174
97/8 Limited 144
96/7 Maggers 80
90/1 OPC/Topps 62
91/2 O-Pee-Chee 88
92/3 O-Pee-Chee 65
89/0 OPC/Topps 160
98/9 OPC Chrome 147
89/0 opcSticker 241-104, 36-176, / FS 10
97/8 Omega 201
98/9 Pacific 380
99/0 Pacific 371
97/8 Pacific CC 203
97/8 Pa. Dynagon 111, T-67,BKS-109
97/8 Pa. Invincible 125
97/8 Pa. Paramount 165
98/9 Pa. Paramount 210
89/0 Panini Sticker 285
90/1 Panini Sticker 239
91/2 Panini Sticker 83
92/3 Panini Sticker 68
93/4 Panini Sticker 203
94/5 Panini Sticker 176
95/6 Panini Sticker 267
96/7 Panini Sticker 274
97/8 Panini Sticker 227
91/2 Parkhurst 66
92/3 Parkhurst 301
93/4 Parkhurst 93
94/5 Parkhurst V76
95/6 Parkhurst 376
94/5 Parkie SE83
91/2 Pinnacle 76
92/3 Pinnacle 262
92/3 Pinnacle 69
93/4 Pinnacle 137
94/5 Pinnacle 118
97/8 Pinnacle 187
96/7 Pi. Be A Player 142, ✍ Aut. 142
97/8 Pi. Inside 142
95/6 Pi. Summit 100
95/6 Playoff 49
96/7 Playoff 340
94/5 POG 125
95/6 POG 139
93/4 Power Play 115
93/4 Premier 144
93/4 Premier 504
94/5 Premier 183
90/1 Pro Set 117
91/2 Pro Set 98
92/3 Pro Set 74
91/2 Pro Set Platinum 49
90/1 Score 48
91/2 Score 57
91/2 Score CAN 57
92/3 Score 243
92/3 Score USAG 4
93/4 Score 444
93/4 Score 52
94/5 Score 71
95/6 Score 233
97/8 Score 77
90/1 Sco. Young Stars 33
92/3 Seasons 11
94 Semic 126
95 Semic 117
91 Semic Sticker 147
92 Semic Sticker 162
93 Semic Sticker 181
94/5 SP 56
96/7 SP 140
97/8 SP Authentic 135
92/3 Topps 242
95/6 Topps 58
98/9 Topps 147
91/2 To. Stadium 97
92/3 T. Stadium Club 281
93/4 To. Stadium 285
95/6 To. Stadium 116
90/1 Upper Deck 272
91/2 Upper Deck 272
91/2 Upper Deck 508
92/3 Upper Deck 185
93/4 Upper Deck 146, SP-69
94/5 Upper Deck 29, SP-126
95/6 Upper Deck 201
97/8 Upper Deck 360
98/9 Upper Deck 352
94/5 UD BAP R98, G9, ✍ 114
96/7 UD Black Diam. 121
95/6 UD CC 194
97/8 UD Coll. Choice 218
98/9 UD G. Reserve 352
90/1 LOSA / Smokey 11
GRAND-PIERRE, JEAN-LUC
99/0 BAP Mem. 80
00/1 BAP Mem. ✂ T-24
01/2 COLU
02/3 O-Pee-Chee 228
99/0 Omega 33
02/3 Topps 228
00/1 To. Chrome 223
02/3 T. Limited 228
02/3 T. Total 361
00/1 Upper Deck 281
02/3 Upper Deck 296
02/3 UD Vintage 77
01/2 Victory 106
97/8 Rochester Americans
98/9 Rochester Americans
GRANDBERG, GEOFF
91 7th..Sketch Mem.Cup 83
90/1 7th..Sketch WHL 208
91/2 7th...Sketch WHL 21
GRANDE, DUILIO
00/1 Baie-Comeau 13
01/2 Baie-Comeau 11
GRANDE, TRIO
77-79 Sports. FIN 54-1290
GRANDMAISON, DOMINIQUE
90/1 7th..Sketch LHJMQ 247
91/2 7th...Sketch LHJMQ 257
95/6 Flint Generals
GRANDMAITRE, SYL
81/2 Kingston Canadians
82/3 Kingston Canadians
GRANDMAÎTRE, PATRICK
99 Bowman 78
99/0 Québec Remparts 5
GRANHOLM, HENRIK
65/6 Hellas 134
70/1 Kuvajulkaisut 102
GRANKVIST, ERIK
95/6 Leaf Elit Set 247
91/2 Semic Elitserien 153
92/3 Semic Elitserien 176
GRANLUND, MIKAEL
93/4 Sisu 315
94/5 Sisu 84
GRANSTEDT, MICHAEL
89/0 Semic Elitserien 202
GRANT, BEN
32/3 Maple Leafs O'Keefe
GRANT, DANNY
70/1 Colgate 36
70/1 Dad's Cookies
70/1 Eddie Sargent 92
71/2 Eddie Sargent 88
72/3 Eddie Sargent 103
70/1 Esso Power Player
72/3 Post 11
74/5 Loblaws
68/9 O-Pee-Chee 52
69/0 O-Pee-Chee 125
69/0 O-Pee-Chee 208
69/0 O-Pee-Chee 4in1
69/0 O-Pee-Chee Stamp
70/1 O-Pee-Chee 47
71/2 O-Pee-Chee 79
71/2 O-Pee-Chee Book. 11
72/3 O-Pee-Chee 57
73/4 O-Pee-Chee 214
74/5 O-Pee-Chee 112
74/5 O-Pee-Chee 174
75/6 O-Pee-Chee 212
75/6 O-Pee-Chee 318
75/6 O-Pee-Chee 49
76/7 O-Pee-Chee 16
77/8 O-Pee-Chee 147
78/9 O-Pee-Chee 306
68/9 Topps 52
69/0 Topps 125
70/1 Topps 47
71/2 Topps 79
72/3 Topps 39
73/4 Topps 161
74/5 Topps 112
74/5 Topps 174
75/6 Topps 212
75/6 Topps 318
75/6 Topps 49
76/7 Topps 16
77/8 Topps 147
71/2 Toronto Sun Photo
70/1 MINS / Colour
73/4 MINS
67/8 MONT
67/8 MONT / IGA Card
97/8 Halifax Moosehead
97/8 Halifax Moosehead
GRANT, DEREK
93/4 Slapshot / Niagara Falls 14
GRANT, DOUG
74/5 Loblaws
74/5 O-Pee-Chee 347
77/8 O-Pee-Chee 294
78/9 O-Pee-Chee 373
GRANT, KEVIN
98/9 DEL 257
99/0 Eishockey 21
89/0 ProCards IHL 197
90/1 ProCards 606
91/2 ProCards 575
00/1 UD DEL 98
01/2 UD DEL 94
95/6 Houston Aeros
93/4 Phoenix Roadrunners
85/6 Kitchener Rangers
87/8 Kitchener Rangers
88/9 Sudbury Wolves
GRANT, LEE
92/3 BCJHL 48
GRANT, MIKE
83 HHOF Postcard O8
83&87 HHOF 218
GRANT, PETER
90/1 Michigan Tech Huskies
GRANT, VINCENT
99/0 Ottawa 67's
GRATTON, BENOÎT
99/0 Aurora 148
99/0 BAP Mem. 266
99/0 Pacific 440
99/0 Victory 311
02/3 Hamilton Bulldogs
96/7 Portland Pirates Hershey
96/7 Portland Pirates
97/8 Portland Pirates
98/9 Portland Pirates
01/2 Québec Citadelles
GRATTON, BRAD
87/8 Kingston Canadians
GRATTON, CHRIS
01/2 Adrenaline 22
98/9 Aurora 138
99/0 Aurora 129
98/9 Be A Player 101, ✍ Aut. 101
99/0 BAP Mem. 37, 361
00/1 BAP Mem. 153
01/2 BAP Memor. 145
97/8 Bicycle 5-Spade
93/4 Classic 3
93/4 Classic - Top Ten DP3
94/5 Classic ✍ Aut.
93/4 Cla. 4 Sport 187, DS60, LP24, PP20, ✍ Aut.
93/4 Cla. Images 4 Sport 138
93/4 Cla. Images 4 Sport 86
93/4 Cla. Prospects 16
99/0 Crown Royale 128
00/1 Crown Royale 14
02/3 Crown Royale 11
93/4 Donruss 330
93/4 Donruss 393
93/4 Donruss V
93/4 Donruss RR 2
94/5 Donruss 189
95/6 Donruss 122
96/7 Donruss 173
97/8 Donruss 56
96/7 Do. Canadian 62, OC-8
97/8 Do. Canadian 39
97/8 Do. Elite 91
97/8 Do. Preferred 130
97/8 Do. Priority 118
97/8 Do. Studio 90
98/9 Dynagon Ice 135
99/0 Dynagon Ice 180
02/3 First Edition 104, ✂ Jers.
94/5 Flair 173
94/5 Fleer 206
95/6 Fleer Metal 136
93/4 Fleer Ultra 423
93/4 Fleer Ultra WotF 5
94/5 Fleer Ultra 205, ARS-4, UP-3
95/6 Fleer Ultra 151
95/6 Hoyle / East. 2-Spade
93/4 Leaf 331
93/4 Leaf FP 3
94/5 Leaf 86, GLR-4, LL-22
95/6 Leaf 133
96/7 Leaf 120
97/8 Leaf 27
94/5 L. Limited 56
95/6 L. Limited 8
97/8 Limited 148
96/7 Metal Univ. 144
99/0 Millenium 222, ✍ Aut. 222
01/2 O-Pee-Chee 226
97/8 Omega 164
98/9 Omega 218
99/0 Omega 215
98/9 Pacific 55
99/0 Pacific 389
00/1 Pacific 51
01/2 Pacific 49
02/3 Pacific 42
02/3 Pacific Complete 284
97/8 Pacific CC 308
97/8 Pa. Crown Roy. 96
97/8 Pa. Dynagon 117, T-62
97/8 Pa. Invincible 131
97/8 Pa. Paramount 131
98/9 Pa. Paramount 173
99/0 Pa. Paramount 217
00/1 Pa. Paramount 29
97/8 Pa. Revolution 100
94/5 Panini Sticker U
95/6 Panini Sticker 126
96/7 Panini Sticker 124
97/8 Panini Sticker 103
99/0 Panini Sticker 143
93/4 Parkhurst 250
93/4 Parkhurst C3
93/4 Parkhurst D12
93/4 Parkhurst E6
94/5 Parkhurst 220, 282,YCTG-22
95/6 Parkhurst 462
00/1 Parkhurst P-80
01/2 Parkhurst 118
94/5 Parkie SE seV16
93/4 Pinnacle 443
93/4 Pinnacle SR3
94/5 Pinnacle 19, 468
95/6 Pinnacle 33
96/7 Pinnacle 141
97/8 Pinnacle 183
97/8 Pi. Be A Player 137, ✍ Aut. 137
97/8 Pi. Certified 84
97/8 Pi. Inside 110
95/6 Pi. Summit 45
97/8 Pi. Totally 84
95/6 Pi. Zenith 15
95/6 Playoff 92
94/5 POG 223
95/6 POG 247
93/4 Power Play 443
93/4 Power Play RooS 5
93/4 Premier 410
94/5 Premier 439, OF-20
99/0 Prism 131
02/3 PS Titanium 12
95/6 Pro Magnet 70
99/0 Revolution 131
93/4 Score 596
95/6 Score 39, CI-4
96/7 Score 148
97/8 Score 168
97/8 Score Phil. 6
94/5 Select 77
91/2 7th...Sketch OHL 225
00/1 Signature 99
01/2 Signature C-8, ✍ Aut. LCG
02/3 Signature GS-20, ✂ FS4
95/6 SBx Emotion 163
95/6 SBx Impact 154
96/7 SBx Impact 121
94/5 SP 111
96/7 SP 145, HC-12
97/8 SP Authentic 112
99/0 SP Authentic 80
02/3 Sports Vault 29
97/8 SPx 45
99/0 Stadium 43
95/6 Super Sticker 114
96/7 Team Out✂
95/6 Topps 70
99/0 Topps 170
00/1 Topps 84
01/2 Topps 226
99/0 To. Chrome 170
94/5 Topps Finest 58
98/9 To. Finest 139
93/4 To. Stadium 320
94/5 T. Stadium Club 112, 195
95/6 To. Stadium 134
02/3 T. Total 155
98/9 UD Choice 150
92/3 Upper Deck 590
93/4 Upper Deck 78, R4, SP-149
94/5 Upper Deck 345, SP-75
95/6 Upper Deck 407, SE-75
96/7 Upper Deck 337, X32, P1-
97/8 Upper Deck 155, 327
98/9 Upper Deck 149
00/1 Upper Deck 21
01/2 Upper Deck 24
02/3 Upper Deck 265
93/4 Upper Deck Be A Player 6
94/5 UD BAP R110, ✍ 116
96/7 UD Black Diam. 77
95/6 UD CC 140, 357
96/7 UD CC 245, 331
97/8 UD Coll. Choice 236, SQ61
98/9 UD G. Reserve 149
96/7 UD Ice 65
98/9 UD MVP 192
99/0 UD MVP 193
00/1 UD MVP 28
01/2 UD MVP 20
99/0 UD MVP Cup 169
00/1 UD Vintage 31
01/2 UD Vintage 30, 35
02/3 Vanguard 12
99/0 Victory 274
00/1 Victory 30
01/2 Victory 46
99/0 WGretzky 158
97/8 Zenith 56
97/8 PHIL / Comcast
93/4 TAMP / Kash N' Karry
94/5 TAMP / Health
94/5 TAMP / Sky Box
95/6 TAMP / Sky Box
GRATTON, DANNY
88/9 ProCards / New Haven
82/3 Oshawa Generals
83/4 Oshawa Generals
GRATTON, GILLES
01/2 BT Pipes -Mask
76/7 O-Pee-Chee 28
77/8 O-Pee-Chee 207
74/5 OPC WHA 65
76/7 Topps 28
77/8 Topps 207
72/3 Ottawa Nationals
GRATTON, JOSH
01/2 Kingston Frontenacs 4
GRATTON, KEN
94/5 Slapshot / Brantford 22
83/4 Brantford Alexanders
GRATTON, MIKE
90/1 Rayside-Balfour
GRATTON, NORM
74/5 Loblaws
74/5 Loblaws Update
74/5 O-Pee-Chee 288
75/6 O-Pee-Chee 34
75/6 Topps 34
74/5 BUFF
GRAUL, THOMAS
94/5 DEL 38
95/6 DEL 31
GRAVEL, FLORIAN
51/2 Lac St-Jean 53
GRAVEL, FRANÇOIS
98/9 DEL 192
99/0 Eishockey 310
88/9 ProCards / Sherbrooke
89/0 ProCards AHL 184
GRAVEL, GREG
80/1 Oshawa Generals
81/2 Oshawa Generals
GRAVEL, MATHIEU
01/2 Shawinigan 7
02/3 Shawinigan Cataractes
GRAVELLE, DAN
93/4 Cla. Prospects 234
93/4 Greensboro Monarchs
GRAVELLE, LÉO
45-64 BeeHive-2 [Mont.]
51/2 Laval Dairy 109
43-47 Parade Sportive
45-54 Quaker Oats
52/3 St. Lawrence 61
GRAVES, ADAM
98/9 Aurora 121
99/0 Aurora 93
00/1 Aurora 93
98/9 Be A Player 91, ✍ Aut. 91
99/0 BAP Mem. 15
00/1 BAP Mem. 181
02/3 BAP Memorabilia / Cup
91/2 Bowman 97
92/3 Bowman 373

95/6 Bowman 54
98/9 Bowman's Best 81
93/4 Classic - Team Canada TC7
93/4 Donruss 219
94/5 Donruss 43
95/6 Donruss 82
96/7 Donruss 66
97/8 Donruss 70
97/8 Do. Canadian 97
95/6 Do. Elite 10
96/7 Do. Elite 107
97/8 Do. Elite 47
97/8 Do. Preferred 133
97/8 Do. Priority 83
98/9 Dynagon Ice 120
99/0 Dynagon Ice 129
95/6 Edge Ice L-1
94/5 Flair 111
94/5 Fleer 132, FF-3
96/7 Fleer 67
96/7 Fl. Picks 90
92/3 Fleer Ultra 136
93/4 Fleer Ultra 43
94/5 Fleer Ultra 137, AW-4, RLS-4, UP-4
95/6 Fleer Ultra 274
95 Globe 96
01/2 Heads Up ✂ JQ 23
93/4 Hockey Wit 86
95/6 Hoyle / East. 3-Spade
93/4 Kraft / KD
94/5 Kraft / PB
96/7 Kraft / PB
93/4 Leaf 130
94/5 Leaf 255
95/6 Leaf 152
96/7 Leaf 20
97/8 Leaf 89
94/5 L. Limited 73
95/6 L. Limited 11
97/8 Limited 18
96/7 Maggers 106
94/5 McDonald's McD-2
99/0 Millenium 166, ✍ Aut. 166
90/1 O-Pee-Chee 480
90/1 OPC/Topps 251
91/2 O-Pee-Chee 167
92/3 O-Pee-Chee 158
01/2 O-Pee-Chee 122
98/9 OPC Chrome 89
91/2 OPC Premier 28
97/8 Omega 144
98/9 Omega 155
99/0 Omega 150
98/9 Pacific 293
99/0 Pacific 269
00/1 Pacific 261
01/2 Pacific 257
02/3 Pacific 333
02/3 Pacific Complete 160
97/8 Pacific CC 26
97/8 Pa. Crown Roy. 83
98/9 Pa. Crown Roy. 87
97/8 Pa. Dynagon 77, T-69, BKS-53
97/8 Pa. Invincible 85, R-127
97/8 Pa. Paramount 114
98/9 Pa. Paramount 151
99/0 Pa. Paramount 149
00/1 Pa. Paramount 161
97/8 Pa. Revolution 86
98/9 Panini Photocard
90/1 Panini/EDM 6
91/2 Panini Sticker 122
92/3 Panini Sticker 238
93/4 Panini Sticker 92
94/5 Panini Sticker 87, 238a
95/6 Panini Sticker 105
96/7 Panini Sticker 100
98/9 Panini Sticker 81
99/0 Panini Sticker 100
91/2 Parkhurst 339
92/3 Parkhurst 346
93/4 Parkhurst 134
94/5 Parkhurst 147, 307, YCTG-15
95/6 Parkhurst 137
00/1 Parkhurst P-209
01/2 Parkhurst 250
94/5 Parkie SE seV41
91/2 Pinnacle 16
92/3 Pinnacle 108
93/4 Pinnacle 99
94/5 Pinnacle 62, GR15, TP6
95/6 Pinnacle 45
96/7 Pinnacle 9
97/8 Pinnacle 174
97/8 Pi. Be A Player 58, ✍ Aut. 58
97/8 Pi. Certified 96
97/8 Pi. Inside 104
95/6 Pi. Summit 66
96/7 Pi. Summit 120
97/8 Pi. Totally 96
95/6 Pi. Zenith 33, GG-17
95/6 Playoff 66
94/5 POG 259, 352
95/6 POG 179
93/4 Power Play 158
93/4 Premier 106
94/5 Premier 128, 350, TF-7
00/1 Private Stock ✂ GUG 73
00/1 PS Titanium ✂ GUG 34, ✂ GUG 113
95/6 Pro Magnet 96
90/1 Pro Set 84
91/2 Pro Set 443
91/2 Pro Set 67
92/3 Pro Set 115
91/2 Pro Set Platinum 207
99/0 Revolution 96
00/1 Revolution 95
90/1 Score 163
91/2 Score 358
91/2 Score 44T
91/2 Score CAN 235
91/2 Score CAN 594
92/3 Score 71
93/4 Score 35
93/4 Score DD5
94/5 Score 164, CI9, DT9
95/6 Score 2
96/7 Score 81
97/8 Score 142
97/8 Score NYRa. 4
94/5 Select 48
95/6 Select CE 47
96/7 Select CE 51
00/1 Signature 37, ✍ Aut. 124
01/2 Signature 168, ✍ Aut. 168
02/3 Signature 90, ✍ 90
95/6 SBx Emotion 112
95/6 SBx Impact 108
96/7 SBx Impact 78
94/5 SP 77
95/6 SP 98
96/7 SP 103
97/8 SP Authentic 103
02/3 Sports Vault 284
99/0 SPx 100
00/1 Stadion 161
99/0 Stadium 149
00/1 Stadium 116, PP6
95/6 SLU
96/7 Team Out✂
92/3 Topps 329
95/6 Topps 295, HGC26, 3PL
98/9 Topps 89
99/0 Topps 148, PP1
00/1 Topps 174, ✂ GWS
01/2 Topps 122
99/0 To. Chrome 148
00/1 To. Chrome 117
94/5 Topps Finest 23, DF-2, RL-20
98/9 T. Gold Label 41
99/0 To. Gold Label 75
00/1 To. Heritage 134, Aut.
01/2 To. Heritage 171
99/0 To. Prmr. Plus 45
91/2 To. Stadium 332
92/3 T. Stadium Club 150
93/4 To. Stadium 270
93/4 To. Stadium - Master Photo-2 6
94/5 T. Stadium Club 9, 265
95/6 To. Stadium 57
93/4 TSC Members Only 35
00/1 To. Stars ✂ GG
02/3 T. Total 13
98/9 UD Choice 134
90/1 Upper Deck 344
91/2 Upper Deck 268
91/2 Upper Deck 574
92/3 Upper Deck 388
92/3 Upper Deck 453
93/4 Upper Deck 128, HT1, SP-99
94/5 Upper Deck 10, R5, IG7, R38, SP-140
95/6 Upper Deck 224, 239, 329, SE-57
96/7 Upper Deck 297, P5
97/8 Upper Deck 108
99/0 Upper Deck 88
00/1 Upper Deck 118
01/2 Upper Deck 377
02/3 Upper Deck 393
94/5 UD BAP R117
95/6 UD BAP 212, ✍ S212
96/7 UD Black Diam. 9
97/8 UD Black Diam. 2
95/6 UD CC 277, 358
96/7 UD CC 174, 325
97/8 UD Coll. Choice 163
99/0 UD G. Reserve 88
99/0 UD Gretzky Excl. 69
96/7 UD Ice 44
99/0 UD MVP 135
00/1 UD MVP 116
02/3 UD MVP 153
00/1 UD Vintage 238, 246
99/0 Victory 191
00/1 Victory 153
99/0 WGretzky 112
96 Wien 100
87/8 DETR / Little Caesars
88/9 DETR / Little Caesars
90/1 EDMO / IGA
98/9 NYRA
92/3 Windsor Spitfires

GRAVES, HILLIARD
73/4 O-Pee-Chee 110
74/5 O-Pee-Chee 306
75/6 O-Pee-Chee 62
76/7 O-Pee-Chee 273
77/8 O-Pee-Chee 286
78/9 O-Pee-Chee 357
79/0 O-Pee-Chee 294
73/4 Topps 110
75/6 Topps 62
74/5 ATLF
77/8 VANC / Royal Bank
78/9 VANC / Royal Bank
79/0 WINN

GRAVES, STEVE
90/1 ProCards 362
86/7 EDMO / Red Rooster
88/9 EDMO / Action 32
84/5 Nova Scotia Oilers
85/6 Nova Scotia Oilers
81/2 Soo Greyhounds
82/3 Soo Greyhounds
83/4 Soo Greyhounds

GRAY, ALEX
26 Dominion Chocolates 11
23/4 Paulins Candy 20

GRAY, BRANDON
93/4 Slapshot / Oshawa 6
96/7 Pensacola Ice Pilots

GRAY, JOHN
76/7 OPC WHA 25
75/6 Phoenix Roadrunners
78/9 Winnipeg Jets

GRAY, MIKE
91/2 7th...Sketch WHL 5
93/4 Saskatoon Blades

GRAY, ROY
95/6 Slapshot 261
99/0 Odessa Jackalopes

GRAY, TERRY
68/9 O-Pee-Chee 44
63/4 Québec Aces
65/6 Québec Aces
61/2 Topps 16
62/3 Topps 20
68/9 Topps 44

GRAYLING, TED
91/2 Air Canada SJHL D11
92/3 MPS SJHL 75

GREBESHKOV, DENIS
02/3 Russian Future Stars 6

GRECO, GUS
82/3 Soo Greyhounds
83/4 Soo Greyhounds

GRECO, PIERO
97/8 Sheffield Steelers

GREEDER, MIKE
82/3 Indianapolis Checkers

GREEN, CORY
92/3 BCJHL 106

GREEN, DARRYL
95/6 Slapshot 366

GREEN, DAVID*
93/4 Slapshot / Windsor 9
94/5 Slapshot / Windsor 11

GREEN, DAVID**
91/2 Avant Garde BCJHL 100
92/3 BCJHL 73
92/3 Clarkson G'Knights

GREEN, DUSTIN
91/2 Avant Garde BCJHL 26
92/3 BCJHL 55

GREEN, GARY
80/1 WASH

GREEN, GERALD
26 Dominion Chocolates 17

GREEN, JOSH
95/6 Bowman P15
98/9 Bowman's Best 119
95/6 Classic 60, ✍ Aut.
98/9 Dynagon Ice 88
95/6 Future Legends ✍ SSD-4
98/9 Omega 116
00/1 Pacific 249
98/9 SP Authentic 99
00/1 Topps 172
98/9 Upper Deck 418, GN13
98/9 UD G. Reserve 418
98/9 UD MVP 98
97/8 Portland Winter Hawks

GREEN, MORTEN
99/0 UD Elitserien 116

GREEN, REDVERS (RED)
24/5 Champ's Cigarettes
25 Dominion Chocolates 84
24/5 Maple Crispette [V130] 10
23/4 William Paterson 31
24/5 William Paterson 15

GREEN, RICK
86/7 Kraft Sports 26
01/2 MONT
02/3 MONT
77/8 O-Pee-Chee 245
78/9 O-Pee-Chee 363
79/0 O-Pee-Chee 309
80/1 O-Pee-Chee 33
81/2 O-Pee-Chee 348
82/3 O-Pee-Chee 183
83/4 O-Pee-Chee 188
84/5 O-Pee-Chee 262
87/8 O-Pee-Chee 234
90/1 OPC Premier 37
81/2 OPC Sticker 193
82/3 OPC/Topps Sticker 156
87/8 OPC Sticker 11-149
87/8 Panini Sticker 60
89/0 Panini Sticker 11
91/2 Panini Sticker 147
82/3 Post [Wash.]
90/1 Pro Set 436
90/1 Score 84T
83/4 Souhaits Keychain [Canadiens]
77/8 Topps 245
80/1 Topps 33
81/2 Topps 118 [East]
01/2 UD Legends 37
90/1 DETR / Little Caesars
91/2 DETR / Little Caesars
82/3 MONT
82/3 MONT / Steinberg
83/4 MONT
84/5 MONT
85/6 MONT
85/6 MONT / Provigo
86/7 MONT
87/8 MONT
87/8 MONT / Kodak Poster
87/8 MONT / Vachon 65
87/8 MONT / Vachon 66
87/8 MONT / Vachon 68
87/8 MONT / Vachon 70
88/9 MONT
00/1 MONT
78/9 WASH
79/0 WASH
80/1 WASH
81/2 WASH

GREEN, S.
88/9 ProCards / New Haven

GREEN, SCOTT
84/5 Soo Greyhounds

GREEN, SCOTT
93/4 N. Michigan Wildcats

GREEN, SHAWN*
82/3 Victoria Cougars

GREEN, SHAYNE
90/1 7th..Sketch WHL 256
91/2 7th...Sketch WHL 89
92/3 Dayton Bombers
89/0 Victoria Cougars

GREEN, TED
64-67 BeeHive-3 [Bost.]
64/5 Coke/Sprite [Bost.]
65/6 Coca-Cola
70/1 Dad's Cookies
70/1 Eddie Sargent 4
71/2 Eddie Sargent 6
70/1 Esso Power Player
62/3 Cowan Tile
68/9 O-Pee-Chee 4
69/0 O-Pee-Chee 218
69/0 O-Pee-Chee 23
69/0 O-Pee-Chee 4in1
70/1 O-Pee-Chee 134
71/2 O-Pee-Chee 173
75/6 OPC WHA 57
76/7 OPC WHA 112
95/6 Parkie 66-67 6
94/5 Parkie Tall 3, 167
61/2 Shirriff 16
68/9 Shirriff / Bost. 12
61/2 Topps 2
62/3 Topps 7
62/3 Topps Dollar
63/4 Topps 7
64/5 Topps 32
65/6 Topps 98
66/7 Topps 37
66/7 Topps / Test 37
67/8 Topps 94
68/9 Topps 4
69/0 Topps 23
64/5 Toronto Star Action
65/6 Toronto Star Photo
71/2 Toronto Sun Photo
71/2 BOST
81/2 EDMO / Red Rooster
82/3 EDMO / Red Rooster
83/4 EDMO / Button
83/4 EDMO / McDonald's
84/5 EDMO / Red Rooster
86/7 EDMO / Red Rooster
88/9 EDMO / Action 57
90/1 EDMO / IGA
91/2 EDMO / IGA
92/3 EDMO / IGA 027
72/3 New England Whalers
78/9 Winnipeg Jets

GREEN, TIM
98/9 Fort Worth Brahmas

GREEN, TRAVIS
98/9 Aurora 1
98/9 Be A Player 155, ✍ Aut. 155
00/1 BAP Mem. 327
96/7 Bic.Sports Aces 2-S
92/3 Classic Prospects 126
99/0 Crown Royale 107
93/4 Donruss 200
94/5 Donruss 75
95/6 Donruss 208
96/7 Donruss 175
97/8 Donruss 62
97/8 Do. Canadian 65
97/8 Do. Priority 102
98/9 Dynagon Ice 1
99/0 Dynagon Ice 151
96/7 Fleer 65
95/6 Fleer Metal 90
96/7 Fl. Picks 70
92/3 Fleer Ultra 343
93/4 Fleer Ultra 365
94/5 Fleer Ultra 126
95/6 Fleer Ultra 266, HS-12
96/7 Fl. Ultra 101
93/4 Leaf 127
94/5 Leaf 288
96/7 Leaf 131
95/6 L. Limited 100
96/7 L. Preferred 5
97/8 Limited 59, 110
96/7 Metal Univ. 92
01/2 O-Pee-Chee 142
98/9 OPC Chrome 162
97/8 Omega 137
98/9 Omega 1
99/0 Omega 181
98/9 Pacific 50
99/0 Pacific 4
00/1 Pacific 316
02/3 Pacific 360
02/3 Pacific Complete 58
97/8 Pacific CC 170
98/9 Pa. Crown Roy. 1
97/8 Pa. Dynagon 73, T-72
97/8 Pa. Invincible 81
97/8 Pa. Paramount 108
98/9 Pa. Paramount 1
00/1 Pa. Paramount 189
97/8 Pa. Revolution 81
96/7 Panini Sticker 92
97/8 Panini Sticker 79
99/0 Panini Sticker 277
00/1 Panini Sticker 188
92/3 Parkhurst 343
93/4 Parkhurst 126
94/5 Parkhurst 137
95/6 Parkhurst 400
01/2 Parkhurst 206
94/5 Pinnacle 216
96/7 Pinnacle 70
97/8 Pinnacle 167
97/8 Pi. Be A Player 63, ✍ Aut. 63
97/8 Pi. Certified 123
97/8 Pi. Inside 130
95/6 Pi. Summit 60
96/7 Pi. Summit 61
97/8 Pi. Totally 123
96/7 Pi. Zenith 26
95/6 Playoff 280
96/7 Playoff 418
94/5 POG 156
95/6 POG 170
93/4 Power Play 383
93/4 Premier 489
99/0 Prism 107
90/1 ProCards 510
91/2 ProCards 467
93/4 Score 661
96/7 Score 15
97/8 Score 173
00/1 Signature 66, ✍ Aut. 164
01/2 Signature 171, ✍ Aut. 171
96/7 SBx Impact 75
95/6 SP 87
96/7 SP 94
97/8 SP Authentic 94
98/9 SPx Finite 4
00/1 Stadium 148
95/6 Topps 89
98/9 Topps 162
00/1 Topps 204
01/2 Topps 142
95/6 To. Finest 79
93/4 To. Stadium 394
94/5 T. Stadium Club 236
02/3 T. Total 350
98/9 UD Choice 5
93/4 Upper Deck 59
94/5 Upper Deck 220
95/6 Upper Deck 473, SE-138
96/7 Upper Deck 290
97/8 Upper Deck 307
98/9 Upper Deck 215
00/1 Upper Deck 133
01/2 Upper Deck 395
02/3 Upper Deck 412
95/6 UD BAP 15, ✍ S15
96/7 UD CC 157
97/8 UD Coll. Choice 160, SQ39
98/9 UD G. Reserve 215
00/1 UD MVP 139
99/0 UD MVP Cup 141
00/1 UD Vintage 282
00/1 Victory 182
01/2 Victory 271
99/0 WGretzky 135
96/7 NYIS
89/0 Spokane Chiefs

GREEN, WILF (SHORTY)
24/5 Champ's Cigarettes
25 Dominion Chocolates 83
83 HHOF Postcard K5
83&87 HHOF 140
24/5 Maple Crispette [V130] 22
23/4 William Paterson 30
24/5 William Paterson 14

GREENAN, ROY
52/3 Anonymous 122

GREENE, MATT
93/4 W. Michigan Broncos

GREENE, MATTHEW
97 Québec Pee Wee 0975

GREENLAW, JEFF
88/9 ProCards / Baltimore
89/0 ProCards AHL 79
90/1 ProCards 210
91/2 ProCards 547
86/7 WASH / Kodak
91/2 WASH / Smokey
00/1 Austin Ice Bats
93/4 Cincinnati Cyclones
94/5 Cincinnati Cyclones
95/6 Cincinnati Cyclones
96/7 Cincinnati Cyclones
97/8 Cincinnati Cyclones

GREENLAY, MIKE
94/5 Classic 4 Sport 153
89/0 ProCards AHL 133
90/1 ProCards 225
93/4 Atlanta Knights
94/5 Atlanta Knights 2
91/2 Knoxville Cherokees
89/0 Saskatoon Blades

GREENOUGH, GLENN
84/5 Sudbury Wolves
85/6 Sudbury Wolves

GREENOUGH, NICK
02/3 Grand Rapids Griffins
00/1 Halifax Moosehead
99/0 Halifax Mooseheads

GREENWAY, DAVE
93/4 Red Deer Rebels

GREENWOOD, CHUCK
92/3 Wheeling Thund'birds 20

GREENWOOD, JEFF
91/2 Air Canada SJHL D20
92/3 MPS SJHL 119

GREER, BRIAN
00/1 Kudos 31
95/6 Muskegon Fury

GREER, SCOTT
89/0 Nashville Knights

GREGG, RANDY
83/4 O-Pee-Chee 28
84/5 O-Pee-Chee 242
85/6 O-Pee-Chee 199
90/1 OPC/Topps 275
89/0 O-Pee-Chee 229
83/4 OPC/Topps Sticker 145
84/5 OPC Sticker 257
85/6 OPC Sticker 225-92
87/8 OPC Sticker 94-227
90/1 Panini Sticker 231
91/2 Pinnacle 415
91/2 Score 48T
91/2 Score CAN 598
83/4 Vachon 25-105
82/3 EDMO / Red Rooster
83/4 EDMO / Button
83/4 EDMO / McDonald's
83/4 EDMO / West Mall
83/4 EDMO
84/5 EDMO
84/5 EDMO / Red Rooster
85/6 EDMO / Red Rooster
86/7 EDMO
86/7 EDMO / Red Rooster
88/9 EDMO
88/9 EDMO / Action 13
91/2 VANC
91/2 VANC / Photo

GREGG, VIC
52/3 St. Lawrence 64

GREGGA, SHAMUS
93/4 Hampton Roads

GREGGSON, TERRY
90/1 Pro Set 688

GREGOIR, BILL
84/5 Victoria Cougars

GRÉGOIRE, JEAN-FRANÇOIS
90/1 7th..Sketch LHJMQ 82
91/2 7th...Sketch LHJMQ 65

GREGOR, COLIN
90/1 7th..Sketch WHL 254
95/6 Birmingham Bulls
94/5 Hampton Roads
93/4 Richmond Renegades
88/9 Lethbridge Hurricanes

GREGOREK, PETR
97/8 APS 323
99/0 DS 102
00/1 DS 70
98/9 OFS 181
99/0 OFS 193, 474
00/1 OFS 217
01/2 OFS 48, -UHI 2

GREGORY, DAVE
98/9 Topeka Scarecrows
95/6 Guildford Flames 13

GREGORY, JIM
73/4 TORO

GREIG, JACK
96/7 Dayton Ice Bandits

GREIG, MARK
93/4 Donruss 137
93/4 Donruss 495
93/4 Fleer Ultra 334
93/4 Leaf 412
94/5 Leaf 522
92/3 O-Pee-Chee 186
92/3 OPC Premier 99
91/2 Pinnacle 352
93/4 Premier 301
91/2 Pro Set 537
90/1 ProCards 180
90/1 Score 431
91/2 Score 383
91/2 Score CAN 273
92/3 Topps 175
92/3 T. Stadium Club 421
93/4 To. Stadium 386
00/1 UD Heroes 89
91/2 Upper Deck 456
91/2 HART / Jr. Whalers
93/4 HART / Coke
95/6 Atlanta Knights
97/8 Grand Rapids Griffins
02/3 Philadelphia Phantoms
94/5 Saint John Flames
88/9 Lethbridge Hurricanes
89/0 Lethbridge Hurricanes

GREILINGER, THOMAS
00/1 UD DEL 223

GREIN, ANDRÉ
94/5 DEL 228
95/6 DEL 227
96/7 DEL 78

GRENIER, BLAKE
01/2 Moose Jaw Warriors 22
02/3 Moose Jaw Warriors

GRENIER, DAVE
02/3 Shawinigan Cataractes

GRENIER, DAVID
95/6 Fredericton Canadiens

GRENIER, LUCIEN
71/2 Eddie Sargent 76
72/3 Eddie Sargent 1
71/2 Toronto Sun Photo

GRENIER, MARTIN
99 Bowman 26, ✍ BA15
94 Québec Pee Wee 628
99/0 Topps 263
99/0 To. Chrome 263
98/9 Québec Remparts
99/0 Québec Remparts 16

GRENIER, MATT
01/2 Kitchener Rangers

GRENIER, RICHARD*
76/7 OPC WHA 59
76/7 Québec Nordiques
76/7 Québ. / Antoinette

GRENIER, TONY
84/5 Prince Albert Raiders

GRENKVIST, ERIK
94/5 Leaf Elit Set 27

GRENNIER, MATT
99/0 Brampton Batallion 18

GRENVILLE, CHRIS
91/2 7th...Sketch OHL 315
98/9 BC Icemen 9
98/9 BC Icemen
95/6 Birmingham Bulls

GRESCHNER, RON
75/6 O-Pee-Chee 146
76/7 O-Pee-Chee 154
77/8 O-Pee-Chee 256
78/9 O-Pee-Chee 154
79/0 O-Pee-Chee 78
80/1 O-Pee-Chee 248
81/2 O-Pee-Chee 224
82/3 O-Pee-Chee 224
84/5 O-Pee-Chee 141
85/6 O-Pee-Chee 182
86/7 OPC/Topps 18
87/8 OPC/Topps 159
90/1 O-Pee-Chee 447
81/2 OPC Sticker 167
86/7 OPC Sticker 222-91
87/8 Panini Sticker 104
87/8 Panini Sticker 108
82/3 Post [NYRa.]
90/1 Pro Set 197
75/6 Topps 146
76/7 Topps 154
77/8 Topps 256
78/9 Topps 154
79/0 Topps 78
80/1 Topps 248
81/2 Topps 97 [East]
89/0 NYRA / Marine

GRETZKY, BRENT
94/5 Classic 99, T65
94/5 Classic 4 Sport 159
94/5 Cla. Images 17
94/5 Cla. Images 4 Sport 116
93/4 Donruss 318
95/6 Edge Ice 82
93/4 Fleer Ultra 424
93/4 Parkhurst 248, C14
94/5 Parkhurst 218, 295, V62
93/4 Pinnacle 429
94/5 Premier 209
93/4 Score 606
89/0 7th..Sketch OHL 75
90/1 7th..Sketch OHL 7
91/2 7th...Sketch OHL 99
92/3 Upper Deck 37
93/4 Upper Deck 354, SP 150
94/5 Upper Deck 69
94/5 UD BAP R161, ✍ 154
95/6 UD CC 281
99/0 Asheville Smoke
92/3 Atlanta Knights
93/4 Atlanta Knights
94/5 Atlanta Knights 8
98/9 Chicago Wolves
96/7 Las Vegas Thunder
96/7 Pensacola Ice Pilots
95/6 St. John's Maple Leafs

GRETZKY, KEITH
92/3 Classic 118
92/3 Classic Prospects 99
89/0 ProCards IHL 101
91/2 ProCards 322
92/3 Upper Deck 37
99/0 Asheville Smoke
87/8 Flint Spirits
92/3 San Diego Gulls

GRETZKY, TY
99/0 UD Gretzky Excl. 93

GRETZKY, WALTER
98/9 McD's T1

GRETZKY, WAYNE
89/0 Action Packed 1
01/2 ASG History
98/9 Aurora 122, -ALC 13, -CF 30, -FL 9, -MACF 13, -NC 8, -Cube 12
98/9 Be A Player 90, M1, M7, H3, P24, ✍ Aut. 90, ✂ G-1, ✂ AS-25, ✂ S-23, ✂✍ G-1
99/0 BAP Mem. H-18, ✂ J-25, ✂ D-9, ✂ TM-2, ✂ TM-22
00/1 BAP Mem. ✂ PP-1, -GJ
01/2 BAP Memor. ✂ 500GS, ✂ ASJ, ✂ AST, ✂ PP
01/2 BAP Update ✂ H1
96/7 Bic.Sports Aces A-C
97/8 Bicycle J-Club
95/6 Bicycle Sports Aces A-Diamond
90/1 Bowman 143
91/2 Bowman 173, 176
92/3 Bowman 1, 207
95/6 Bowman 1, BB5
98/9 Bowman's Best 3, F15
91 Canada Cup
99/0 Canada Post
02/3 Canada Post
93/4 Coca-Cola 1 to 18
81/2 Dernière Heure
93/4 Donruss 152, 395, K, -ES 10, -IK 4
94/5 Donruss 127, DM-5, ES-5, IM-4
95/6 Donruss 13, D-5, E-7
96/7 Donruss 93, D-5, ES-2
97/8 Donruss 143, -ES 1, -L2L 1
98/9 Donruss ES 20
96/7 Do. Canadian 5, OC-7
97/8 Do. Canadian 5, -NP 1, -SCS 28
95/6 Do. Elite 58, -CE 3
96/7 Do. Elite 10, P-1
97/8 Do. Elite 9, 143, C-19
97/8 Do. Preferred 4, 172, LT-6A, PM-3, / Tin 3,23, WideTin 1,12
97/8 Do. Priority 10, 199, DD-8, OD-10, Post-7, Stamp-7
97/8 Do. Studio 1, 109, HH-1, S-1, P-1
98/9 Dynagon Ice 121, -AR 8, -FT 13, -PP 8, -TC 17
93/4 EA Sports 63, 192
88/9 Esso All-Star
93/4 Fax Pax 25
94/5 Flair 79, CIS-4, HN-2
96/7 Flair 59, HN-4, NT-1
94/5 Fleer 94, H-4
96/7 Fleer 68, ART-6, PA-4
95/6 Fleer Metal 71, -HM 4, -IS 5
96/7 Fl. Picks 8, F50-15, CC-4, -DL-1
92/3 Fleer Ultra 83, -AS 10, -AW 6
93/4 Fleer Ultra 114, -AS 15, -PP 2, -SK 2
94/5 Fleer Ultra 306, -ASG 10, -AW 5, -PP 4, -SK 4
95/6 Fleer Ultra 74, 385, -EA 7, -PP 3, -UV 2
96/7 Fl. Ultra 106, PL-2, UP-5
83/4 Funmate Puffy 1 [w/]
95 Globe 99, 265-67
96/7 Got-Um
92/3 High Five / Promo P3
93/4 Hockey Wit 99
99/0 HoloGrFX GG1-15, ✍ Aut.
95/6 Hoyle / West. A-Club
92/3 Humpty Dumpty
94 Koululainen
95 Koululainen
89/0 Kraft 59
90/1 Kraft 15, 67
91/2 Kraft 65
92/3 Kraft / Kraft Singles
93/4 Kraft / JELL-O
93/4 Kraft / PB
94/5 Kraft / HH, PB
95/6 Kraft / KD
97/8 Kraft / JTP, KD, PB, Spoon
98/9 Kraft / Post 1
99/0 Kraft / KD
86/7 Kraft Sports 14
89/0 Kraft Stickers 2
93/4 Leaf 304, -GLAS 6, -SSS 4
94/5 Leaf 345, -FOI 4, -GLS 1, -LL 11
95/6 Leaf 89, -FOI 10
96/7 Leaf 140, FOI-5, LL-8
97/8 Leaf 8, 175, BS-3, FOI-1
94/5 L. Limited 10, G-7
95/6 L. Limited 87, SG-3
96/7 L. Limited 7, S-3
96/7 L. Preferred 112, SP-5, VP-1
97/8 Limited 4, 97, 200, FG-1, FG-34
96/7 Maggers 135
82/3 McDonald's Les Étoiles 20
82/3 McDonald's Les Étoiles 22
91/2 McDonald's Mc-17, McH1
97/8 McDonald's McD-1, F1, 5x7, ✂ GJ
98/9 McDonald's McD01, -M1-9, -T1-13, -GJ
99/0 McDonald's Record
99/0 McDonald's GR81 1-5, ✂ GJ
96/7 Metal Univ. 96, LW-6
99/0 Millenium 99, P-9, D-1, ✍ Aut. 99, ✍ P-9, ✍ D-1, ✂ J-9, ✂ JS-9
82/3 Neilson's 1-50
95/6 Cool Trade 2
98/9 NHL Power Play
79/0 O-Pee-Chee 18
80/1 O-Pee-Chee 162
80/1 O-Pee-Chee 163
80/1 O-Pee-Chee 182
80/1 O-Pee-Chee 250
80/1 O-Pee-Chee 3
80/1 O-Pee-Chee 87
81/2 O-Pee-Chee 106
81/2 O-Pee-Chee 125
81/2 O-Pee-Chee 126
81/2 O-Pee-Chee 383
81/2 O-Pee-Chee 384
81/2 O-Pee-Chee 392
82/3 O-Pee-Chee 1
82/3 O-Pee-Chee 106
82/3 O-Pee-Chee 107
82/3 O-Pee-Chee 235
82/3 O-Pee-Chee 237
82/3 O-Pee-Chee 240
82/3 O-Pee-Chee 242
82/3 O-Pee-Chee 243
82/3 O-Pee-Chee 99
83/4 O-Pee-Chee 203
83/4 O-Pee-Chee 204
83/4 O-Pee-Chee 212
83/4 O-Pee-Chee 215
83/4 O-Pee-Chee 216
83/4 O-Pee-Chee 217
83/4 O-Pee-Chee 22
83/4 O-Pee-Chee 23
83/4 O-Pee-Chee 29
84/5 O-Pee-Chee 208
84/5 O-Pee-Chee 243
84/5 O-Pee-Chee 357
84/5 O-Pee-Chee 373
84/5 O-Pee-Chee 374
84/5 O-Pee-Chee 380
84/5 O-Pee-Chee 381
84/5 O-Pee-Chee 382
84/5 O-Pee-Chee 383
84/5 O-Pee-Chee 388
85/6 O-Pee-Chee 257
85/6 O-Pee-Chee 258
85/6 O-Pee-Chee 259
85/6 OPC/Topps 120
85/6 OPC/Topps Box G
86/7 O-Pee-Chee 259
86/7 O-Pee-Chee 260
86/7 OPC/Topps 3
86/7 OPC/Topps Box F
87/8 OPC/Topps 53
87/8 OPC/Topps Box A
88/9 OPC/Topps 120
88/9 OPC/Topps Box B
90/1 OPC/Topps 1-3, 120, 199, OPC 522, Topps-TL 12, Box D
91/2 O-Pee-Chee 201, 224, 257, 258, 321, 520, 522, 524, Topps-TL 10
92/3 O-Pee-Chee 15, 220, -Ann. 12
89/0 O-Pee-Chee 320, 325
89/0 OPC/Topps 156, / Box E
89/0 Topps - Sticker 11
98/9 OPC Chrome 219, SB20, -Reprint 1
87/8 OPC Leaders 13
90/1 OPC Premier 38
91/2 OPC Premier 3
88/9 OPC Stars 11
81/2 OPC Sticker 209
81/2 OPC Sticker 252
81/2 OPC Sticker 264
82/3 OPC/Topps Sticker 162
82/3 OPC/Topps Sticker 256
82/3 OPC/Topps Sticker 257
82/3 OPC/Topps Sticker 258
82/3 OPC/Topps Sticker 259
82/3 OPC/Topps Sticker 97
82/3 OPC/Topps Sticker 98
83/4 OPC/Topps Sticker 161
83/4 OPC/Topps Sticker 301
83/4 OPC/Topps Sticker 307
83/4 OPC/Topps Sticker 325
83/4 OPC/Topps Sticker 326
83/4 OPC/Topps Sticker 7
83/4 OPC/Topps Sticker 89
83/4 OPC/Topps Sticker 90
84/5 OPC Sticker 138
84/5 OPC Sticker 226-227
84/5 OPC Sticker 229-228
84/5 OPC Sticker 255
84/5 OPC Sticker 256
84/5 OPC Sticker 63-64
85/6 OPC Sticker 120
85/6 OPC Sticker 198-70
85/6 OPC Sticker 202-75
85/6 OPC Sticker 222
85/6 OPC Sticker 5
85/6 OPC Sticker 54-197
86/7 OPC Sticker 115-129
86/7 OPC Sticker 183-123
86/7 OPC Sticker 191-52
86/7 OPC Sticker 195-57
86/7 OPC Sticker 72
87/8 OPC Sticker 115-127
87/8 OPC Sticker 174-176
87/8 OPC Sticker 180-37
87/8 OPC Sticker 181-38
87/8 OPC Sticker 86
88/9 OPC Sticker 1
88/9 OPC Sticker 121-251
88/9 OPC Sticker 224
89/0 opcSticker 154, 166-28, 209-69, / AS 30
80/1 O-Pee-Chee Super 7
97/8 Omega 145, 250, GF-11, S-8, SHLC-13, TL-14
98/9 Omega 156, -CS 7, -EOP 14, -FTF 2, -Onl. 23, -PI 26, -Prism 13
98/9 Pacific 99, -CCA 7, -DI 13, -GCDC 23, -TC 17, -Time. 11
97/8 Pacific CC 99, CS-12, CCA-7, GCDC-15, SS-5A, TC-16
97/8 Pa. Crown Roy. 84, BOS-14, CCA-7, HT-11, L-11
98/9 Pa. Crown Roy. 88, -CCA 8, -LL 8, -MP 14, -PP 16
97/8 Pa. Dynagon 78, 140, DD-10A, KN-6, T-1, T-19, BKS-59
97/8 Pa. Invincible 86, AZ-14, FP-21, OTG-12, R-128, R-218
97/8 Pa. Paramount 115, BN-14, CG-10, P-13
98/9 Pa. Paramount 152, -HOFB 7, -IG 7, -SD 12, -TC 17
97/8 Pa. Revolution 87, ASG-14, I-7, TC-16
98/9 Pa. Revolution 92, -ASG 8, -TPA 27, -CTLC 11, -NI 8, -Show. 23
98/9 Panini Photocard [x2]
87/8 Panini Sticker 192
87/8 Panini Sticker 197
87/8 Panini Sticker 198
87/8 Panini Sticker 199
87/8 Panini Sticker 200
87/8 Panini Sticker 261
87/8 Panini Sticker 371
87/8 Panini Sticker 373
87/8 Panini Sticker 389
88/9 Panini Sticker 170
88/9 Panini Sticker 179
88/9 Panini Sticker 181
88/9 Panini Sticker 193
88/9 Panini Sticker 58
89/0 Panini Sticker 87, 179, 374
90/1 Panini Sticker 242, 332
91/2 Panini Sticker 78, 327
92/3 Panini Sticker 64, 287
93/4 Panini Sticker R
94/5 Panini Sticker 172, AA
95/6 Panini Sticker 266
96/7 Panini Sticker 200
97/8 Panini Sticker 82
98/9 Panini Sticker 3, 80
95 Panini Worlds 276
91/2 Parkhurst 73, 207, 222, 429, 433, 465
92/3 Parkhurst 65, 509
93/4 Parkhurst 99, D1, G1, W1
94/5 Parkhurst 103, 306, -YCTG 11,28
95/6 Parkhurst 100, 449, -AS 1, -CCB 6, -CCP 10
94/5 Parkie SE seV20
91/2 Pinnacle 100, 381, B-11
92/3 Pinnacle 200, 249, -TP 5
93/4 Pinnacle 237, 400, 512, CA11, -TP 5
94/5 Pinnacle 200, -TP 9
95/6 Pinnacle 101, CS-9, FS-2
96/7 Pinnacle 1, BTN-9, TP-1
97/8 Pinnacle 67, 192, TP-4, P-17
96/7 Pi. Be A Player BB-1
97/8 Pi. Be A Player OT 1, -TN 8
97/8 Pi. BeeHive 33, -BHT 7
97/8 Pi. Certified 100, -CT 7
97/8 Pi. Epix E1
95/6 Pi. FANtasy 13
96/7 Pi. FANtasy 5
97/8 Pi. Inside 3, -IT 1, -Can 9
97/8 Pi. Mint 18
95/6 Pi. Summit 24, GMC-18
96/7 Pi. Summit 67, HV-5, U-12
97/8 Pi. Totally 100
95/6 Pi. Zenith 13, ZT-4
96/7 Pi. Zenith 13, CS-2
95/6 Playoff 50, 159, 269
96/7 Playoff 430
94/5 POG 126, 268, 331
95/6 POG 132, I-001
82/3 Post [Edmo.]
94/5 Post
99/0 Post Moment
99/0 Post Great One
93/4 Power Play 116, -Game. 3, -PL 3
93/4 Premier 330, 380, -BG/OPC 1, -BG/Top. 7
94/5 Premier 130, 150, 154, 280, 375, -GTG 1
95/6 Pro Magnet 62, -MAG 1
90/1 Pro Set 118, 340, 394, 703, PotM P2
91/2 Pro Set 101, 285, 324, 574, CC5
92/3 Pro Set 246
92/3 Pro Set 66, -TL 6
91 Pro Set Awards AC4
91/2 Pro Set Platinum 52, PC4, PC14
91/2 Puck / Pro Set 11
90/1 Score 1, 321, 336, 338, 347, 352, 353, 361, 110T, Promo 1
90/1 Sco. Hot Cards 1
91/2 Score 100, 346, 405-06, 413, 422, 427, 434, -Hot 2, Promo 100, Shows 1
91/2 Score CAN 100, 295-96, 303, 312, 317, 324, 376
92/3 Score 1, 412, 426, 525
93/4 Score 300, 662, -DT 11, -DD7, -Pi.AS 45, -TF 9
94/5 Score 241, -DT 14, -NP 1, -TF 11
95/6 Score 250, BB-2, DT-1, L-1
96/7 Score 41, DT-8, SD-12
97/8 Score 99
97/8 Score NYRa. 1
92/3 Seasons 9
93/4 Seasons 5
94/5 Select 83, FL-11
95/6 Select CE 23, -GT 2
96/7 Select CE 4, C-4
94 Semic 99, 344
95 Semic 99
89 Semic Sticker 65
91 Semic Sticker 64
92 Semic Sticker 84
93 Semic Sticker 199
84/5 7-Eleven
84/5 7-Eleven Super
00/1 Signature 64, ✍ Aut. 143, ✂ HSHSJers
01/2 Signature C-60, ✍ Aut. XLWG
95/6 SBx Emotion 81, -Xcel 4, -Xcited 5
95/6 SBx Impact 79, -CTI 4, -IQ 6
96/7 SBx Impact 79, CTI-3, VT-4
83/4 Souhaits Keychain [Oilers]
94/5 SP 54, -SP 1, P-17
95/6 SP 127, Promo 66, É17, GC1, FX10
96/7 SP 99, Promo, CW-1, GF-1, HC-1, -Ins., -SF-1, ✍ Aut.
97/8 SP Authentic 99, I26, ✍ SotT, ✂ M6, ✍ T1
98/9 SP Authentic 56, -SS1, -Trade, -SO28-30, ✍ SotT
99/0 SP Authentic LH1, ✍ SotT
00/1 SP Authentic P4-P7, ✍ SotT, ✍ SotTD (x2), ✍ SotTT (x2)
01/2 SP Authentic 101, ✂ PP, ✍ SotT, ✍ SotTT
02/3 SP Authentic 99, ✍ SotT, ✍ SotTD (x2), ✍ SotTT, ✂ DP, ✂ TP
00/1 SP GU ✂ TotG, ✂ C (x3), ✂ P (x3), ✂✍ A
01/2 SP GU ✂ AF, ✂ AFD, ✂ AFQ, ✂✍ IS2, ✂✍ ISD, ✂ Patch, ✂✍ PatchSig, ✂✍ PatchCSig., ✂ PatchT, ✂ Tools
02/3 SP GU 53, 55, 62, ✂ AF (x2), ✂ CF (x2), ✂ PH, ✍ Sig
77-79 Sportscaster 77-01
77-79 Sports. FIN 89-2127
96/7 SPx 39, GT1, GF1, HH7, ✍ GT1
97/8 SPx 30, D-SPX1, DV1, ✍ DVS
99/0 SPx CH1-CH15, HH1, X1, XT20, ✂ WM
00/1 SPx ✂ WM (x2), ✂✍ WM
01/2 SPx ✍ Sig
02/3 SPx 95, ✂ SS
98/9 SPx Finite 53, 99, 151, 180
98/9 SPx Prospects 38, -H18, -L27, -PS1,PS16, -YotGO 1-30
00/1 Stadion 82, 159
97/8 SLU
98/9 SLU
99/0 SLU 135
83/4 Stater Mint H14
95/6 Super Sticker 57, -DC 21
96/7 Team Out✂
79/0 Topps 18
80/1 Topps 162
80/1 Topps 163
80/1 Topps 182
80/1 Topps 250
80/1 Topps 3
80/1 Topps 87
81/2 Topps 16
81/2 Topps 52
84/5 Topps 154
84/5 Topps 51
85/6 OPC/Topps-Stick. 2
86/7 OPC/Topps - Stick. 3
87/8 OPC/Topps - Stick. 5
88/9 OPC/Topps - Stick. 8
92/3 Topps 1, 123
95/6 Topps 85, 375, HGC20, M1, PF1, 10RL
98/9 Topps 219, L7, M4, SB20, -Reprint 1
94/5 Topps Finest 41, -DF18, -RL 5
95/6 To. Finest 5, 180
98/9 To. Finest 64, M1, M5, M8, M9, R9, Big 4
98/9 T. Gold Label 4
96/7 Topps Picks FT10, FC1, TS2
91/2 To. Stadium 1
92/3 T. Stadium Club 18, 256
93/4 To. Stadium 200, -Master, -AS, -Finest 1
94/5 T. Stadium Club 99, 270, F-4
95/6 To. Stadium EC173, M1, N2
91/2 TSC Charter [x2]
92 TSC Members Only
93/4 TSC Members Only 5
94/5 TSC Members Only 32
95/6 TSC Members Only 1
95/6 T. Super Skills 15
98/9 UD Choice 128, 225, 236, 308, -DYOTC, -BH1, -SQ1
00/1 UD Heroes 126, 180, PI4, SS6, ✂ GT, ✂ GC, ✍ SG
02/3 UD Superstars 84, B1, MM18, 02/3 UD14, 02/3 UD29, ✂ CAS, ✂ CAST, ✂ LLT (x2)
98/9 UD3 31, 91, 151
00/1 Ultimate Mem. ✍ U-9, ✂D-1, ✂H-12,H-14,H-15,H-16,H-17,H-18,H-19,H-20, ✂J-9, ✂Jers.7, ✂JJ-1, ✂MO-9, ✂RE-10, ✂RA-10, ✂S-9, ✂TM-36, ✂UC-9
01/2 Ultimate Mem. ✂ 500GS, ✂ ASG, ✂ CP, ✂ DD, ✂ EA, ✂ Gloves, ✂ GSL, ✂ JE, ✂ JJ, ✂ NP, ✂ RN, ✂ RT, ✂ RA, ✂ SCP, ✂ SCW, ✂ UC, ✍ Aut.
99/0 Ult. Victory 111-120, ,m> LF, ✂ UF
90/1 Upper Deck 54, 205, 307, 476, 545, Stickers, Promo 241
91/2 Upper Deck 13, 38, 45, 437, 501, 621, SP1, AW1, AW6
92/3 Upper Deck 25, 33, 37, 423, 435, 621, W1, G5, WG10, - Heroes
93/4 Upper Deck 99, NL1, HB9, R1, -Silver Skate, -SP 70
94/5 Upper Deck 1, 226, 228, 541, C16, H1, H16, R19, R21, R42, R59, -IG 15, -SP-36
95/6 Upper Deck 99, 222, 252, -AS 5, F2, Pred. H7, R13, R23, R31, R41, R51, -

SE128
96/7 Upper Deck 108, 361, X1, HH1, LS1, SS5A
97/8 Upper Deck 109, SS1, SG1, S1, T1B, ✄ GJ8, ✄✍ GJS
98/9 Upper Deck 135, 207, 388, 390, FF1, FT30, GN1-3, LS1, P9, YotGO1-30, ✄ GJ
99/0 Upper Deck 1-10, 86, 134-36, GP1-10, HOF1, -PD, ✄ GJ, ✄✍ GJS
00/1 Upper Deck ✄ DGJ, ✄ GJ, ✍ SG
01/2 Upper Deck 424, ✄ SupSwe
02/3 Upper Deck 188, 189, 426, -GG11, -SS9, ✄ ASJ, ✄ ASP, ✄ PL, ✄ PP, ✄ PN, ✄ R50, ✄ GJ, ✄✍ SGJ, ✄ UDPL
01/2 UD National
00 ✄ UD APOH 500, ✄✍ 500
01/2 UD Fantasy (x3)
95/6 UD ASG MVP1
96/7 UD All-Star YCTG AR20
02/3 UD Artistic 39, R39, CG3, GD1
94/5 UD BAP R99, R147, R176, UC-1, G1, ✍ 108
95/6 UD BAP 97, GM-1-10✍ S97
96/7 UD Black Diam. 180, RC1, Promo
97/8 UD Black Diam. 144, PC1
98/9 UD Black Diam. 55, M27, WF18, -YotGO 1-99
99/0 UD Bl. Diam. ✄ APOH
00/1 UD Black Diam. ✄ GG
99/0 UD C. Legends 1, 81-90, AC1, GM1-10, -Art., ✍ ES, ✄ JC6
01/2 UD Challenge AT2
02/3 UD Classic GG5, ✄ HR
95/6 UD CC 1, 361, C3
96/7 UD CC 170, 290, 329, 336, UD1, S1, C1, CR1
97/8 UD Coll. Choice 167, 312, MM1-5, SQ90, S1, W1, C1
01/2 UD Collectors
91/2 Upper Deck WJC - Sticker [x2]
97/8 UD Diam. Vision 1, DM1, RT1
02/3 UD Foundations 34, 44, 45, 70, 87, 101, 105, 106, 117, ✄ 1000Jers, ✄ 1000Stick, ✄ CH, ✄ CG, ✄ MS, ✄ PP, ✍ SG
98/9 UD G. Reserve 135, 207, 388, 390, ✍ Aut., ✄ Stick
99/0 UD G. Reserve 1-10, 86, 134-36, ✄ GR
99/0 UD Gretzky Excl. 1-99
98/9 UD Gretzky Retirement Set D1-16
01/2 UD Honor Roll 2, 32, OS5
02/3 UD Honor ✍ SC
96/7 UD Ice 112, S1
97/8 UD Ice 90, IC1, L1B
01/2 UD Ice ✍ CCA
00/1 UD Legends 49, 54, 61, 134, ES1, ES1, PH7, SM1, SM4, ✍ ES, ✄ LGJ
01/2 UD Legends 22, 92, 100, FC, ✄ M, ✄ PoH (x2), ✄ TT, ✍ ES
99/0 UD Living Legend
92/3 UD Locker 25
98/9 UD MVP 132, 218-220, D1-16, OT5, Snip. S2, F12, Souv.
99/0 UD MVP 1, 131, 219-20, S1, DR3, H1, MVP1, LO1-10, -Draw, GU6, ✄ GU20, ✍ PS
00/1 UD MVP ME10, ✄ GS, ✄ CG
01/2 UD MVP ✄ C
02/3 UD MVP ✍ PSig
99/0 UD MVP Cup -GC
99/0 UD Ovation -CS, APOH, ✍ SS
02/3 UD Piece 91, 92, 109, 110, 111, AC16, HB5, HB8, SB6, ✄ HS, ✄ PH, ✍ MD
95/6 UD Post 17
96/7 UD Post
99/0 UD PowerDeck 20, P1-4
01/2 UD Premier 25, ✄ B, ✄ G, ✄ D, ✍ SigS
02/3 UD Premier 56, ✄ Jers, ✄ JD, ✄ Patch, ✄ NHLP, ✍ Sig
00/1 UD Pros&Prosp. CR4, ✄✍ GJS
99/0 UD Prospects 1, -✍ Sig.
01 UD Prospects GU ✍ SoT
95/6 UD Record Collection
99/0 UD Retro 49, DR9, EG1-10, TC9, ✄ RM, ✍ Ink.
02/3 UD Rookie 102, 163, ✍ TD
01/2 UD SCup Champs 10, ✄ S, ✄ G
01/2 UD Top Shelf ✄ S
02/3 UD Top Shelf ✄ AS (x2), ✄ CP, ✄ HH (x3), ✄ HT, ✄ M (x2), ✄ ST, ✄ SW, ✍ Sig
00/1 UD Vintage ✄ D-POH
01/2 UD Vintage ✄ NL, ✄ SC
93 UD World Cup H4
94 UD World Cup of Soccer - Honourary Captain C6
99 UD YOTGO [x7]
83/4 Vachon 26-106
97/8 Valu-net, ✍ Aut.
99/0 Victory 391-440
00/1 Victory 260
99/0 WGretzky 99, 179, HOF1-30, V1-10, ✄ Mem., ✍ SG
96 Wien 99
97/8 Zenith 4, CTC-2, ZT-2, Z1
79/0 EDMO
80/1 EDMO / Zellers
81/2 EDMO / Red Rooster
81/2 EDMO / Red Rooster
81/2 EDMO / Red Rooster
81/2 EDMO / Red Rooster
81/2 EDMO / West Mall
82/3 EDMO / Red Rooster
82/3 EDMO / Red Rooster
82/3 EDMO / Red Rooster
82/3 EDMO / Red Rooster
83/4 EDMO / Button
83/4 EDMO / McDonald's
83/4 EDMO / West Mall
83/4 EDMO
84/5 EDMO
84/5 EDMO / Red Rooster
84/5 EDMO / Red Rooster
84/5 EDMO / Red Rooster
84/5 EDMO / Red Rooster
85/6 EDMO / Red Rooster
85/6 EDMO / Red Rooster
85/6 EDMO / Red Rooster
86/7 EDMO
86/7 EDMO / Red Rooster
86/7 EDMO / Red Rooster
87/8 EDMO
88/9 EDMO / Action 46
88/9 EDMO / Action 55
88/9 LOSA / Smokey
89/0 LOSA / Smokey 1
90/1 LOSA / Smokey 1
91/2 LOSA / GW Forum
98/9 NYRA
83/4 Belleville Bulls
87/8 Hull Olympiques
87/8 Soo Greyhounds 29

GREYEYES, MARK
88/9 Portland Winter Hawks

GRIBKO, EVGENY
00/1 Mir 323
95 Panini Worlds 33

GRIECO, SCOTT
95/6 Lethbridge Hurricanes

GRIER, MIKE
01/2 Adrenaline 75
98/9 Aurora 71
99/0 Aurora 57
00/1 Aurora 55, Pins. 55, ✍ Aut. 55
98/9 Be A Player 54, ✍ Aut. 54
99/0 BAP Mem. 222
00/1 BAP Mem. 79
01/2 BAP Memor. 116
97/8 Donruss 94
96/7 Do. Canadian 141
97/8 Do. Canadian 121
97/8 Do. Elite 62
97/8 Do. Preferred 44
97/8 Do. Priority 59
97/8 Do. Studio 51, HH-22
98/9 Dynagon Ice 71
99/0 Dynagon Ice 81
96/7 Flair 110
96/7 Fl. Ultra 58, UR-9
97/8 Leaf 81, BS-23
97/8 Limited 27, 50, 199, FG-22
96/7 Metal Univ. 181
99/0 Millenium 102, ✍ Aut. 102
01/2 O-Pee-Chee 131
98/9 OPC Chrome 31
97/8 Omega 90
98/9 Pacific 208
99/0 Pacific 154
00/1 Pacific 165
01/2 Pacific 157
02/3 Pacific 142
02/3 Pacific Complete 361
97/8 Pacific CC 164
97/8 Pa. Dynagon 48, T-10
97/8 Pa. Invincible 55, OTG-10
97/8 Pa. Paramount 74
98/9 Pa. Paramount 85
99/0 Pa. Paramount 91
00/1 Pa. Paramount 94
99/0 Panini Sticker 249
97/8 Pinnacle 177
96/7 Pi. Be A Player 220, ✍ Aut. 220
97/8 Pi. Certified 73
97/8 Pi. Inside 85, -IT 29
97/8 Pi. Totally 73
99/0 Revolution 57
97/8 Score 153, CI-10
96/7 Select CE 101
96/7 SP 177
97/8 SP Authentic 63, ✍ SotT
99/0 SPx 63
99/0 Stadium 61
00/1 SLU 15
98/9 Topps 31
99/0 Topps 246
00/1 Topps 132
01/2 Topps 131
99/0 To. Chrome 246
00/1 To. Chrome 99
02/3 T. Total 329
96/7 Upper Deck 259, P13
97/8 Upper Deck 67, 207, SG25, T16A
98/9 Upper Deck 94
99/0 Upper Deck 55
00/1 Upper Deck 300
01/2 Upper Deck 70
96/7 UD Black Diam. 15
97/8 UD Coll. Choice 88, SQ24
98/9 UD G. Reserve 94
99/0 UD G. Reserve 55
96/7 UD Ice 86
98/9 UD MVP 81
99/0 UD MVP 81
00/1 UD MVP 75
01/2 UD MVP 71
00/1 UD Vintage 141
01/2 UD Vintage 100
99/0 Victory 111
00/1 Victory 95
01/2 Victory 145
99/0 WGretzky 68
98/9 NHL Power Play
96/7 EDMO
97/8 EDMO

GRIEVE, BRENT
92/3 Classic 100
92/3 Classic Four Sport 213
93/4 Cla. Prospects 128
94/5 Fleer Ultra 274
94/5 Leaf 485
94/5 Parkhurst 79
94/5 Premier 99, 431
90/1 ProCards 506
91/2 ProCards 453
90 7th..Sketch Mem.Cup 92
89/0 7th..Sketch OHL 22
94/5 T. Stadium Club 257
94/5 Upper Deck 396
95/6 Upper Deck 307
94/5 UD BAP ✍ 42
93/4 EDMO / Sheet
90/1 Oshawa Generals

GRIEVE, BRIAN
90 7th..Sketch Mem.Cup 81
89/0 7th..Sketch OHL 12
90/1 7th..Sketch OHL 337
91/2 7th...Sketch OHL 165
89/0 Oshawa Generals
91/2 Oshawa Generals
91/2 Oshawa Generals
91/2 Oshawa Generals

GRIFFIN, SEAN
99/0 Kingston Frontenacs

GRIFFIS, SI
83 HHOF Postcard L5
83&87 HHOF 155

GRIFFITHS, FRANK
93/4 Action Packed 8

GRIFFITHS, TUFFY
37/8 World Wide Gum 132

GRIGG, KODY
94/5 Slapshot / North Bay 21

GRIGG, VIC
51/2 Laval Dairy 102

GRIGORENKO, IGOR
02/3 Russian Future Stars 2

GRILLO, DEAN
94/5 Classic 42
94/5 Kansas City Blades 16
95/6 Kansas City Blades
96/7 Kentucky Tho'blades

GRILLS, CHAD
91/2 7th...Sketch OHL 135
93/4 Slapshot / Peterborough 11
93/4 Slapshot / S.S.Marie 22
95/6 Flint Generals
96/7 Flint Generals
98/9 Flint Generals
91/2 Peterborough Petes

GRIMARD, RON
97/8 Spokane Chiefs

GRIMES, JAKE
93/4 Cla. Prospects 43
89/0 7th..Sketch OHL 76
90/1 7th..Sketch OHL 8
91/2 7th...Sketch OHL 111
94/5 Thunder Bay Senators

GRIMES, KEVIN
97 Bowman 136, ✍ Aut.

GRIMSON, STU
98/9 Be A Player 152, ✍ Aut. 152
00/1 BAP Mem. 343, ✄ T-3
01/2 BAP Update ✄ TC3, ✄ TC6
93/4 Donruss 15
93/4 Fleer Ultra 253
93/4 Kraft / KD
93/4 Leaf 330
99/0 Millenium 6, ✍ Aut. 6
98/9 OPC Chrome 96
98/9 Omega 2
98/9 Pacific 133
99/0 Pacific 5
01/2 Pacific 181, 413
02/3 Pacific 209
02/3 Pacific Complete 72
97/8 Pacific CC 296
93/4 Parkhurst 277
94/5 Parkhurst 3
93/4 Pinnacle 401
94/5 Pinnacle 512
94/5 POG 33
93/4 Power Play 1
93/4 Premier 357
89/0 ProCards IHL 199
93/4 Score 558
00/1 Signature 193, ✍ Aut. 179
98/9 Topps 96
91/2 Upper Deck 416
97/8 Upper Deck 33
95/6 UD BAP 224, ✍ S224
02/3 UD MVP 101
01/2 UD Vintage 266
02/3 UD Vintage 139, 277
93/4 ANAH / Cap 3
97/8 CARO / Sprint
90/1 CHIC / Coke
91/2 CHIC / Coke
96/7 HART / Kids Club
88/9 Salt Lake G'Eagles
82/3 Regina Pats
83/4 Regina Pats

GRIMWOOD, SCOTT
93/4 Red Deer Rebels

GRIS, PATRICK
90/1 7th..Sketch LHJMQ 62
91/2 7th...Sketch LHJMQ 30

GRISDALE, JOHN
75/6 O-Pee-Chee 339
77/8 O-Pee-Chee 277
78/9 O-Pee-Chee 318
72/3 TORO
74/5 VANC / Royal Bank
75/6 VANC / Royal Bank
76/7 VANC / Royal Bank
77/8 VANC / Royal Bank
78/9 VANC / Royal Bank

GRISE, PATRICK
88/9 Richelieu Riverains

GRISHIN, ALEXANDER
99/0 Mir 37
00/1 Mir 9

GRNAK, MARIANNE
94/5 Classic W16, W21

GROF, JAKUB
00/1 OFS 171
01/2 OFS 193

GROGER, THOMAS
94/5 DEL 12
95/6 DEL 322

GROKE, JAMIE
85/6 London Knights

GROLEAU, FRANÇOIS
91/2 Arena 29
91/2 Classic 35
91/2 Classic Four Sport 35
93/4 Cla. Prospects 47
98/9 DEL 281
90/1 7th..Sketch LHJMQ 225
91/2 7th...Sketch LHJMQ 55
91/2 Star Pics 63
91/2 Ultimate Draft Pick 30, ✍ Aut.
00/1 UD DEL 9
01/2 UD DEL 171
96/7 Fredericton Canadiens
99/0 Québec Citadelles 9
94/5 Saint John Flames

GROLEAU, JASON
94/5 Slapshot Memorial 54

GROLEAU, JOE
99/0 Halifax Mooseheads

GROLEAU, MARIUS
52/3 Laval Dairy Update 36

GROLEAU, SAMUEL
91/2 7th...Sketch LHJMQ 159

GRÖMLING, DIMITRI
98/9 DEL 286

GRON, STANISLAV
01/2 BAP Memor. 357
01/2 Parkhurst 328
01/2 SPx 115
01/2 Upper Deck 197
01/2 UD MVP 207
01/2 UD Premier 71
01/2 UD Top Shelf 59
99/0 Albany River Rats
00/1 Albany River Rats
01/2 Albany River Rats

GRONAU, MARK
94/5 DEL 72
95/6 DEL 51

GRONBORG, RIKAR
92/3 Semic Elitserien 257

GRONDIN, JIMMY
96/7 Rimouski Océanic
97/8 Rimouski Océanic

GRONDIN, PHILIPPE
96/7 Rimouski Océanic
97/8 Rimouski Océanic

GRÖNMAN, TUOMAS
99/0 Cardset 262, MW-11, AH 3-hertta
00/1 Cardset 302
02/3 Cardset 167
96/7 Do. Canadian 139
93/4 Jyvas Hyva 231
93/4 Parkhurst 523
96/7 Select CE 105
95 Semic 3, 225
91/2 7th...Sketch WHL 154
93/4 Sisu 188
94/5 Sisu 314, H-4
95/6 Sisu 126, DT-1
96/7 Sisu SH 4
95/6 Sisu Limited 4
91/2 Upper Deck 677
93/4 Upper Deck 270
96/7 Upper Deck 237
98/9 Upper Deck 163
91/2 Upper Deck WJC 40
98/9 UD G. Reserve 163
98/9 Kansas City Blades 6

GRÖNSTRAND, JARI
94/5 DEL 400
91/2 Semic Elitserien 158
93/4 Sisu 65
88/9 QUÉB
88/9 QUÉB / Gene. Foods
89/0 QUÉB
89/0 QUÉB / Gene. Foods

GRÖNVALL, JANNE
98/9 Cardset 211
99/0 Cardset 122
00/1 Cardset 87
02/3 Cardset 19
92/3 Classic 32
95/6 Edge Ice 80
92/3 Jyvas Hyva 162
93/4 Jyvas Hyva 291
93/4 Sisu 64
94/5 Sisu 159, 175
95/6 Sisu Limited 75
91/2 Upper Deck 672
91/2 Upper Deck WJC 35
94/5 St. John's Maple Leafs
95/6 St. John's Maple Leafs

GROSEK, MICHAL
98/9 Aurora 16
99/0 BAP Mem. 32, 342
00/1 BAP Mem. 281
93/4 Cla. Prospects 9
95/6 Donruss 125
98/9 Dynagon Ice 17
99/0 Dynagon Ice 30
95/6 Edge Ice 68
94/5 Fleer 241
94/5 Fleer Ultra 393
95/6 Leaf 53
98/9 OPC Chrome 152
97/8 Omega 21
98/9 Omega 22
98/9 Pacific 105
99/0 Pacific 36
00/1 Pacific 95
02/3 Pacific Complete 345
97/8 Pa. Crown Roy. 13
98/9 Pa. Crown Roy. 12
97/8 Pa. Invincible R-19
98/9 Pa. Paramount 18
99/0 Pa. Paramount 27
00/1 Pa. Paramount 49
98/9 Pa. Revolution 13
98/9 Panini Photocard
97/8 Panini Sticker 17
98/9 Panini Sticker 18
99/0 Panini Sticker 39
00/1 Panini Sticker 127
94/5 Parkhurst 266
95/6 Parkhurst 231
94/5 Pinnacle 482
97/8 Pi. Be A Player 187, ✍ Aut. 187
94/5 Premier 531
00/1 Revolution 30
97/8 Score 255
97/8 Score Buff. 8
98/9 SP Authentic 10
00/1 Stadion 160
00/1 Stadium 134
98/9 Topps 152
00/1 Topps 255
94/5 Topps Finest 64
94/5 Upper Deck 433
95/6 Upper Deck 111
00/1 Upper Deck 37
00/1 UD Black Diam. 13
98/9 UD MVP 25
99/0 UD MVP 28
00/1 Victory 53
00/1 Hartford Wolf Pack
01/2 Hartford Wolf Pack

GROSS, GABLE
97/8 Kamloops Blazers
98/9 Kamloops Blazers
99/0 Kamloops Blazers
99/0 Kamloops Blazers
00/1 Kamloops Blazers

GROSS, LLOYD
33-35 Diamond Match Silv.

GROSS, PAVEL
94/5 DEL 277
95/6 DEL 274
96/7 DEL 169
98/9 DEL 230
99/0 Eishockey 279
00/1 UD DEL 34, ✄ GJ

GROSSE, ERWIN
51/2 Laval Dairy 64
52/3 St. Lawrence 104

GROSSI, DINO
93/4 Cla. Prospects 137
93/4 Indianapolis Ice

GROSSMANN, VITALI
94/5 DEL 161
95/6 DEL 161

GROSSO, DON
34-43 BeeHive-1 [Detr.]
40/1 O-Pee-Chee 128

GROULX, DANNY
02/3 Grand Rapids Griffins
00/1 Victoriaville Tigres 23

GROULX, WAYNE
94 Semic 239
93 Semic Sticker 278
81/2 Soo Greyhounds
82/3 Soo Greyhounds
83/4 Soo Greyhounds
84/5 Soo Greyhounds

GROWDEN, DAN
01/2 Belleville Bulls

GRUBA, TONY
94/5 Dayton Bombers 15

GRUBAUER, EDGAR
79 Panini Sticker 258

GRUBER, GARRY
97/8 Peoria Rivermen

GRUDEN, JOHN
94/5 Classic 53, AA2
94/5 Donruss 179
94/5 Fleer 11
94/5 Fleer Ultra 254
94/5 Leaf 192
94/5 Premier 447
95/6 Topps 104
97/8 Detroit Vipers
98/9 Detroit Vipers
99/0 Grand Rapids Griffins
00/1 Grand Rapids Griffins
01/2 Grand Rapids Griffins
96/7 Providence Bruins
91/2 Ferris State Bulldogs

GRUDEN, LUKE
99/0 Peoria Rivermen
00/1 Peoria Rivermen

GRUEN, DANNY
75/6 OPC WHA 128

GRUHL, SCOTT
92/3 Classic Prospects 122
88/9 ProCards / Muskegon
89/0 ProCards IHL 150
90/1 ProCards 382
91/2 ProCards 254
92/3 Fort Wayne Komets 11
93/4 Milwaukee Admirals
94/5 Richmond Renegades
95/6 Richmond Renegades
96/7 Richmond Renegades

GRUNDMANN, OLAF
94/5 DEL 219
95/6 DEL 196
96/7 DEL 339

GRÜNN, CARLO
02/3 Cardset 166

GRUTH, HENRYK
79 Panini Sticker 121
89 Semic Sticker 133
92 Semic Sticker 269

GRYGIEL, ADRIAN
01/2 UD DEL 258

GRYP, BOB
74/5 Loblaws
75/6 O-Pee-Chee 348

GRYPIUK, SHANE
00/1 Red Deer Rebels

GSCHLIESSER, ALEX
95 Panini Worlds 94

GSCHWILL, TIMO
94/5 DEL 191
95/6 DEL 176

GUARD, STANDING
91/2 Future Trends C72 60

GUAY, FRANÇOIS
96/7 DEL 172
98/9 DEL 42
99/0 Eishockey 177
88/9 ProCards / Rochester
89/0 ProCards AHL 273
90/1 ProCards 291
00/1 UD DEL 119

GUAY, PAUL
84/5 O-Pee-Chee 160
88/9 ProCards / Maine
89/0 ProCards AHL 212
90/1 ProCards 513
91/2 ProCards 611
87/8 LOSA

GUAY, ROGER
51/2 Bas du Fleuve 21

GUBAREV, ALEXEI
99/0 Mir 87

GUBERNATOROV, SERGEI
00/1 Mir 117

GUDAS, LEO
95/6 APS 202, 408
98/9 DEL 279
99/0 Eishockey 150
95 Globe 148
91/2 Jyvas Hyva 30
99/0 OFS 19
94 Panini Olympics 318
99/0 Score JT24
94 Semic 166
89 Semic Sticker 186
92 Semic Sticker 125
96 Wien 112

GUENETTE, LUC
85/6 Fredericton Express

GUENETTE, STEVE
90/1 ProCards 627
91/2 ProCards 150
87/8 PITT / Kodak

GUENNELON, GERALD
95 Globe 206
95 Panini Worlds 100
94 Semic 219

GUERARD, DANIEL
93/4 Cla. 4 Sport 235

GUÉRARD, STÉPHANE
90/1 Panini/QUE 8
87/8 QUÉB / Gene. Foods
88/9 QUÉB
88/9 QUÉB / Gene. Foods
89/0 QUÉB
89/0 QUÉB / Gene. Foods
89/0 QUÉB / Police
90/1 QUÉB
90/1 Halifax Citadels

GUERASIMOV, KIRIL
79 Panini Sticker 352

GUERIN, BILL
01/2 Adrenaline 13
01/2 Atomic 7, TN 1
02/3 Atomic 32, -NPU 1, ✄ GWJ 4
98/9 Aurora 72
99/0 Aurora 56
00/1 Aurora 56
02/3 BAP All-Star 28, ✄ ASJ
98/9 Be A Player 53, ✍ Aut. 53
99/0 BAP Mem. 225
00/1 BAP Mem. 27
01/2 BAP Memor. 88, ✄ ASJ, ✄ ASE, ✄ ASN, ✄ AST, ✄ CoO
02/3 BAP Memorabilia 7, 247, 268, ✄ ASJ16, ✄ AST21
01/2 BAP Update HSHS, ✄ HSHSJers, ✄ H28
01/2 Bowman 53
02/3 Bowman 29
92/3 Classic 105
99/0 Crown Royale 54
00/1 Crown Royale 10
02/3 Crown Royale 29
02/3 DALL / Southwest
93/4 Donruss 186
94/5 Donruss 62
95/6 Donruss 35
96/7 Donruss 180
96/7 Do. Elite 69
98/9 Dynagon Ice 72
02/3 Exclusive 55
02/3 First Edition 132, 302, 372, 403H, ✄ Jers.
94/5 Flair 94
96/7 Flair 53
94/5 Fleer 112
92/3 Fleer Ultra 338
93/4 Fleer Ultra 359
94/5 Fleer Ultra 117
95/6 Fleer Ultra 191, 261
00 Gatorade Sticker
01/2 Heads Up 8, ASGUN 3
02/3 Heads Up 38, ✄ GWQ 29
99/0 HoloGrFX 25
02/3 In The Game-Used 22, 122, ✄ IE11
93/4 Leaf 7
94/5 Leaf 146
95/6 Leaf 201
96/7 L. Preferred 108
99/0 Millenium 97, ✍ Aut. 97
92/3 O-Pee-Chee 308
01/2 O-Pee-Chee 6
02/3 O-Pee-Chee 229, Update 229
92/3 OPC Premier 120
97/8 Omega 91
98/9 Omega 92
99/0 Omega 90
98/9 Pacific 209
99/0 Pacific 155, TL-11
00/1 Pacific 166
01/2 Pacific 31, NAAS 2
02/3 Pacific 28
02/3 Pacific Complete 307
97/8 Pacific CC 117
98/9 Pa. Crown Roy. 51
98/9 Pa. Paramount 86
99/0 Pa. Paramount 92, IAI-11
00/1 Pa. Paramount 95
97/8 Pa. Revolution 54
98/9 Pa. Revolution 54
95/6 Panini Sticker 81
96/7 Panini Sticker 83
99/0 Panini Sticker 247
91/2 Parkhurst 453
92/3 Parkhurst 97
93/4 Parkhurst 382
94/5 Parkhurst 127
95/6 Parkhurst 124
00/1 Parkhurst P-197
01/2 Parkhurst 33, ✄ T19
02/3 Parkhurst 108
02/3 Parkhurst Retro 40, ✄ RJ 33
93/4 Pinnacle 305
94/5 Pinnacle 23
95/6 Pinnacle 32
96/7 Pinnacle 170
97/8 Pinnacle 136
96/7 Pi. Be A Player 29, ✍ Aut. 29
97/8 Pi. Inside 131
95/6 Pi. Summit 111
96/7 Pi. Zenith 106
95/6 Playoff 58
94/5 POG 350
95/6 POG 166
93/4 Premier 421
94/5 Premier 231
99/0 Prism 55
00/1 Private Stock ✄ GUG 7
01/2 Pr. Stock 5
02/3 Pr. Stock Reserve ✄ 114
00/1 PS Titanium 6, NAAS-2
01/2 PS Titanium 8, ✄ DSJ 3, ✄ DSJ 74
01/2 PS Titanium Draft ✄ 9
02/3 PS Titanium 31
92/3 Pro Set 230
02/3 Quest for the Cup 27
99/0 Revolution 58, / CSC 58
00/1 Revolution 56
92/3 Score 470
93/4 Score 395
95/6 Score 106
96/7 Score 197
97/8 Score 199
97/8 Score NJer. 5
96/7 Select CE 26
00/1 Signature 95, ✍ Aut. 203
01/2 Signature C-4, ✄ LBG, ✄ C4, ✄ GUE4, ✄ GU84, ✄ HSHSJers 18, ✄ ITN4, ✄ IS7, ✄ TM3
02/3 Signature 125, ✍ 125, ✄ FS3, ✄ FS5, ✄ SGJ52, ✄ TQ16
96/7 SBx Impact 69
95/6 SP 82
96/7 SP 91
97/8 SP Authentic 86
98/9 SP Authentic 34
99/0 SP Authentic 35
00/1 SP Authentic 9
01/2 SP Authentic 5, ✍ SotT, ✍ SotTT
02/3 SP Authentic 28, ✄ SP, ✄ DP
01/2 SP GU 4, ✄ AF, ✄ AFD
02/3 SP GU 15, 64, ✄ AF (x2), ✄ PC, ✄ PH
02/3 Sports Vault 204
99/0 SPx 61
00/1 SPx 132
01/2 SPx 5
02/3 SPx 25, 86
98/9 SPx Finite 36
98/9 SPx Prospects 26
00/1 Stadion 195
99/0 Stadium 48
00/1 Stadium 26, PP1
01/2 Stadium 33, G30, NHLP14
02/3 Stadium 104
92/3 Topps 516
95/6 Topps 88
99/0 Topps 137
00/1 Topps 66
01/2 Topps 6, SM11
02/3 Topps 229, Update 229, HHU8, OTG8
99/0 To. Chrome 137
00/1 To. Chrome 53
01/2 To. Chrome 6
02/3 T. Chrome 125
95/6 To. Finest 82
98/9 To. Finest 12
98/9 T. Gold Label 75
00/1 To. Gold Label 22
00/1 To. Heritage 57
01/2 To. Heritage 70
02/3 To. Heritage 125, 163
02/3 T. Limited 229
96/7 Topps Picks 141
01/2 To. Reserve 7
92/3 T. Stadium Club 17
93/4 To. Stadium 467
95/6 To. Stadium 130
95/6 T. Super Skills 44
02/3 T. Total 168, TP5
98/9 UD Choice 84
01/2 Ultimate Mem. ✄ Emb., ✄ Jers., ✄ S&J, ✄ ITN, ✄ NP
02/3 Ultimate Mem. ✄ ASMVP, ✄ GUJ, ✄ JE, ✄ JGJ
92/3 Upper Deck 411
94/5 Upper Deck 359
95/6 Upper Deck 373, SE-48
96/7 Upper Deck 90, P11
97/8 Upper Deck T13C
98/9 Upper Deck 92
99/0 Upper Deck 54
00/1 Upper Deck 73
01/2 Upper Deck 244, SS2, ✄ PoaN, ✄ PoaND
02/3 Upper Deck 55, ✄ GO, ✄ PW
02/3 UD Artistic 29, R29, CG15, / Art
94/5 UD BAP ✍ 50
96/7 UD Black Diam. 112
97/8 UD Black Diam. 38
98/9 UD Black Diam. 35
99/0 UD Black Diam. 39
01/2 UD Challenge 6
02/3 UD Classic ✄ HR (x2), ✄ SC
95/6 UD CC 60
96/7 UD CC 146
97/8 UD Coll. Choice 147, SQ21
98/9 UD G. Reserve 92
99/0 UD G. Reserve 54
02/3 UD Honor 23, -SG11
96/7 UD Ice 35
00/1 UD Ice 62
01/2 UD Mask 9
02/3 UD Mask 29
98/9 UD MVP 80, PG14
99/0 UD MVP 78
00/1 UD MVP 73
01/2 UD MVP 13
01/2 UD Premier ✍ SigS
02/3 UD Premier 19
99/0 UD Retro 32
02/3 UD Rookie 32, ✄ 160c, ✄ DJ
01/2 UD Top Shelf 79
02/3 UD Top Shelf 8, ✄ CP, ✄ GO, ✄ HT, ✄ SH, ✄ ST (x2), ✄ SW, ✄ TS, ✍ Sig
00/1 UD Vintage 32, 147
01/2 UD Vintage 24, 26
02/3 UD Vintage 83
00/1 Vanguard 8
02/3 Vanguard 32
99/0 Victory 109
00/1 Victory 93
01/2 Victory 34, 421
02/3 Victory -NP51
98/9 NHL Power Play
96/7 NJER / Sharp

GUETENS, VERN
94/5 Erie Panthers

GUEVREMONT, JOCELYN
72/3 Eddie Sargent 222
91/2 Future Trends C72 35, ✍ 35
74/5 Lipton Soup 48
74/5 Loblaws
74/5 Loblaws Update
71/2 O-Pee-Chee 232
72/3 O-Pee-Chee 37
73/4 O-Pee-Chee 143
74/5 O-Pee-Chee 122
75/6 O-Pee-Chee 216
76/7 O-Pee-Chee 108
77/8 O-Pee-Chee 242
78/9 O-Pee-Chee 94
79/0 O-Pee-Chee 381
72/3 Topps 75
73/4 Topps 142
74/5 Topps 122
75/6 Topps 216
76/7 Topps 108
77/8 Topps 242
78/9 Topps 94
71/2 Toronto Sun Photo
74/5 BUFF
71/2 VANC / Royal Bank 4
72/3 VANC / Royal Bank
73/4 VANC / Royal Bank

GUGGEMOS, MARKUS
01/2 UD DEL 254

GUIDA, PETER
95/6 DEL 247
98/9 DEL 81
95 Panini Worlds 61

GUIDARELLI, TJ
01/2 Rockford IceHogs

GUIDOLIN, ALDO
45-64 BeeHive-2 [NYRa.]
60/1 Cleveland Barons
53/4 Parkhurst 66
52/3 St. Lawrence 17

GUIDOLIN, BEP
34-43 BeeHive-1 [Bost.]
45-64 BeeHive-2 [Chic.]
52/3 Laval Dairy Update 114
74/5 O-Pee-Chee 34
51/2 Parkhurst 42
52/3 St. Lawrence 65
74/5 Topps 34

GUIDOTTI, VINCE
92/3 Semic Nordisk 160

GUILLAUME, OLIVIER
91/2 7th...Sketch LHJMQ 248

GUILLET, ROBERT
98/9 DEL 111
99/0 Eishockey 280
90/1 7th..Sketch LHJMQ 241
91/2 7th...Sketch LHJMQ 129
00/1 UD DEL 35
01/2 UD DEL 7
92/3 Fredericton Canadiens
93/4 Fredericton Canadiens
95/6 Milwaukee Admirals
88/9 Richelieu Riverains

GUILMETTE, YVES
77/8 Kalamazoo Wings

GUINDON, BOB
74/5 OPC WHA 26
72/3 Québec Nordiques
73/4 Québec Nordiques
78/9 Winnipeg Jets

GUINN, ROB
95/6 Classic 96
94/5 Slapshot / Sarnia 20
95/6 Slapshot 47

GUIRESTANTE, JOHN
93/4 Slapshot / North Bay 19
94/5 Slapshot / North Bay 22

GUITARD, DEAN
87/8 Sudbury Wolves

GUITE, PIERRE
75/6 OPC WHA 17
76/7 OPC WHA 123
75/6 Cincinnati Stingers
72/3 Québec Nordiques
73/4 Québec Nordiques

GULA, LADISLAV
94/5 APS 94

GULASH, GARRY
92/3 BCJHL 10
98/9 Quad City Mallards
99/0 Quad City Mallards
00/1 Quad City Mallards
96/7 Richmond Renegades

GULDA, PETER
94/5 DEL 262
96/7 DEL 139
98/9 DEL 328
99/0 Eishockey 293
95 Semic 166
00/1 UD DEL 198
01/2 UD DEL 216

GULLIKSEN, RUNE
95 Panini Worlds 249
92/3 Semic Nordisk 24
92 Semic Sticker 42

GULUTZAN, GLEN
90/1 7th..Sketch WHL 222
91/2 7th...Sketch WHL 112
90/1 Brandon Wheat Kings
91/2 Saskatoon Blades

GUMMERUS, JARMO
71/2 Williams Finnish 278

GUNDERSEN, CARL_G
92/3 Semic Nordisk 4

GUNDERSEN, GORM
92/3 Semic Nordisk 91

GUNDERSEN, JARLE
92/3 Semic Nordisk 175

GUNDERSEN, JON
92/3 Semic Nordisk 83

GUNIKO, YURI
98/9 Mir 121

GUNLER, JOAKIM
92/3 Semic Elitserien 183

GUNN, JIM
83/4 Victoria Cougars

GUNN, ROYDON
84/5 Prince Albert Raiders

GÜNTER, MICHAEL
95 Panini Worlds 258
94 Semic 234
93 Semic Sticker 276

GUNVILLE, RON
89/0 Lethbridge Hurricanes

GUOLLA, STEPHEN
00/1 Pacific 19
01/2 Pacific 17
97/8 Pacific CC 281
97/8 Pa. Dynagon 112, T-66
97/8 Pa. Invincible 126
97/8 Upper Deck 148
99/0 Upper Deck 290
00/1 Upper Deck 239
01/2 Upper Deck 12
97/8 UD Coll. Choice 220
99/0 UD G. Reserve 290
00/1 UD Vintage 19
01/2 UD Vintage 15
01/2 Victory 19
01/2 Albany River Rats
96/7 Kentucky Tho'blades
97/8 Kentucky Tho'blades
98/9 Kentucky Tho'blades
93/4 Michigan State

GURARD, DANIEL
93/4 Classic 132

GUREN, MILOSLAV
94/5 APS 186
95/6 APS 35
99/0 BAP Mem. 151
01/2 OFS 50, -RE24D
99/0 Pacific 216
94/5 Sig. Rookies 56, ✍ 56
94/5 SP 154
98/9 Upper Deck 296
98/9 UD G. Reserve 296
96/7 Fredericton Canadiens
99/0 Québec Citadelles 19
00/1 Québec Citadelles

GURSKIS, JOHN
99/0 Fort Wayne Komets
99/0 Peoria Rivermen

GUSAKOV, EVGENY
00/1 Baie-Comeau 17

GUSAROV, ALEXEI
98/9 Be A Player 183, ✍ Aut. 183
91/2 Bowman 145
94/5 Donruss 216
92/3 Fleer Ultra 173
95 Globe 168
91 Ivan Fiodorov 4
94/5 Leaf 408
96/7 Maggers 42
91/2 O-Pee-Chee 355
92/3 O-Pee-Chee 389
00/1 Pacific 114
97/8 Pa. Invincible R-52
91/2 Panini Sticker 260
92/3 Panini Sticker 215
96/7 Panini Sticker 254
97/8 Panini Sticker 207
98/9 Panini Sticker 186
99/0 Panini Sticker 208
91/2 Parkhurst 364
93/4 Parkhurst 441
94/5 Parkie SE148
91/2 Pinnacle 230
92/3 Pinnacle 161
93/4 Pinnacle 261
94/5 Pinnacle 164
97/8 Pi. Be A Player 196, ✍ Aut. 196
93/4 Power Play 420
93/4 Premier 293
91/2 Pro Set 207
92/3 Pro Set 147
91/2 Pro Set Platinum 221
91/2 Red Ace
91/2 Score 326
91/2 Score CAN 356
92/3 Score 264
93/4 Score 260
94 Semic 159
89 Semic Sticker 82
92 Semic Sticker 105
87/8 Soviet Stars
89/0 Soviet Stars
91/2 To. Stadium 330
92/3 T. Stadium Club 451
93/4 To. Stadium 424
94/5 T. Stadium Club 67
91/2 Upper Deck 365
92/3 Upper Deck 127
93/4 Upper Deck 362
91/2 QUÉB / Petro-Canada
92/3 QUÉB / Petro-Canada
94/5 QUÉB / Burger King

GUSEV, ALEXANDER
91/2 Future Trends C72 19
72 Hellas MM-Jenkki 62
74 Hellas MM-Jenkki 44
74 Semic Sticker 30
73/4 Soviet Stars 4
74/5 Soviet Stars 4
72/3 Williams Finnish 23
73/4 Williams Finnish 3

GUSEV, SERGEY
98/9 Be A Player 192, ✍ Aut. 192
98/9 Dynagon Ice 54
98/9 Omega 78
96/7 Michigan K-Wings

GUSEV, VADIM
00/1 Mir 354

GUSEV, VLADIMIR
00/1 Mir 26

GUSKOV, ALEXANDER
99/0 Mir 109

GUSMANOV, RAVIL
94/5 Classic 73, T77
98/9 Mir 6
99/0 Mir 17
94/5 Parkie SE205
94/5 Premier 323
94/5 Topps Finest 107
94/5 Upper Deck 254
91/2 Upper Deck WJC 3
98/9 Chicago Wolves Champs
00/1 Metallurg 37

GUSTAFSON, DEREK
00/1 BAP Mem. 513
02/3 Between the Pipes 85
01/2 O-Pee-Chee 298
01/2 Pacific 195
01/2 Topps 298
01/2 Victory 376
00/1 Cleveland Lumberjacks

GUSTAFSON, JON
91/2 Richmond Renegades
92/3 Richmond Renegades
93/4 Richmond Renegades

GUSTAFSSON, BENGT-AKE*
00/1 Alfabilder
80/1 O-Pee-Chee 222
81/2 O-Pee-Chee 353
82/3 O-Pee-Chee 364
83/4 O-Pee-Chee 370
84/5 O-Pee-Chee 198
88/9 OPC/Topps 151
91/2 O-Pee-Chee 2S
82/3 OPC/Topps Sticker 157
84/5 OPC Sticker 130
88/9 Panini Sticker 371
82/3 Post [Wash.]
89/0 Semic Elitserien 89
90/1 Semic Elitserien 259
91/2 Semic Elitserien 348
91/2 Semic Elitserien 91
92/3 Semic Elitserien 116
82 Semic Sticker 146
89 Semic Sticker 20
91 Semic Sticker 45
92 Semic Sticker 65
93 Semic Sticker 15
83/4 Souhaits Keychain [Capitals]
80/1 Topps 222
84/5 Topps 144
79/0 WASH
80/1 WASH
82/3 WASH
84/5 WASH / Pizza Hut
85/6 WASH / Pizza Hut
87/8 WASH
87/8 WASH / Kodak
88/9 WASH
88/9 WASH / Smokey

GUSTAFSSON, JUHA
98/9 Cardset 15
99/0 Cardset 11
00/1 Cardset 126
02/3 Cardset 168

GUSTAFSSON, MAGNUS
90/1 Semic Elitserien 220

GUSTAFSSON, PER*
94/5 Leaf Elit Set 276
95/6 Leaf Elit Set 231, FTF-6, LM-15
96/7 Metal Univ. 58
97/8 Pacific CC 165
97/8 Panini Sticker 59
97/8 Pi. Be A Player 69, ✍ Aut. 69
89/0 Semic Elitserien 104
90/1 Semic Elitserien 106
91/2 Semic Elitserien 111
92/3 Semic Elitserien 131
96/7 SP 179
96/7 Upper Deck 267
96/7 UD Black Diam. 40
95/6 UD Elitserien 76, 226, 253, NA11
98/9 UD Elitserien 103
99/0 UD Elitserien 89, S7, ✍ Aut.
00/1 UD Elitserien 94, 196
96/7 FLOR / Winn-Dixie
97/8 St. John's Maple Leafs

GUSTAFSSON, PETER*
89/0 Semic Elitserien 46
90/1 Semic Elitserien 192
91/2 Semic Elitserien 45
92/3 Semic Elitserien 70

GUSTAVSON, BEN
95/6 Slapshot 268

GUSTAVSON, STEFAN
94/5 Leaf Elit Set 256
95/6 Leaf Elit Set 10
90/1 Semic Elitserien 291
95/6 UD Elitserien 9
97/8 UD Elitserien 8
98/9 UD Elitserien 8
99/0 UD Elitserien 11, ✍ Aut.
00/1 UD Elitserien 7

GUSTAVSSON, PATRIK
90/1 Semic Elitserien 139
91/2 Semic Elitserien 195

GUSTAVSSON, PER**
95/6 UD CC 343

GUSTAVSSON, PETER**
89/0 Semic Elitserien 282

GUSTAVSSON, THOMAS
95/6 Leaf Elit Set 225
95/6 UD Elitserien 82

GUT, KAREL
95/6 APS 398

GUTIERREZ, MOISES
02/3 Kamloops Blazers

GUTTLER, GEORG
94/5 DEL 165
95/6 DEL 155

GUY, KEVAN
90/1 Panini/VAN 9
90/1 Pro Set 545
89/0 ProCards IHL 177
91/2 ProCards 576
88/9 VANC / Mohawk
90/1 VANC / Mohawk
85/6 Moncton G'Flames
86/7 Moncton G'Flames
82/3 Medicine Hat Tigers
83/4 Medicine Hat Tigers

GUY, MARK
89/0 7th..Sketch OHL 27
90/1 7th..Sketch OHL 133

GUZDA, BRAD
96/7 Knoxville Cherokees
96/7 Knoxville Cherokees
98/9 Las Vegas Thunder

GUZE, RAY
92/3 BCJHL 120

GUZIOR, RUSS
99/0 Mobile Mysticks
97/8 New Orleans Brass

GYLYWOYCHUK, DWAYNE
90/1 7th..Sketch WHL 218
91/2 7th...Sketch WHL 210
97/8 Central Texas
95/6 Dayton Bombers
94/5 Greensboro Monarchs
89/0 Brandon Wheat Kings
90/1 Brandon Wheat Kings
92/3 Brandon Wheat Kings

GYNA, VLADIMIR
97/8 APS 86
00/1 DS 42
98/9 OFS 262
99/0 OFS 338
00/1 OFS 141
01/2 OFS 149

GYORI, ARPAD
94/5 APS 115
96/7 APS 254
97/8 APS 282

GYORI, DYLAN
99 Bowman 109
98 Bowman 51
98 Bowman Chrome 51
96/7 Upper Deck 381
00/1 WBS Penguins
95/6 Tri-City Americans 9

GYÖRI, ÁRPÁD
96/7 DS Sticker 93
97/8 DS Sticker 80

H

HAAKANA, KARI
02/3 Atomic 108
02/3 BAP All-Star 118
02/3 BAP Memorabilia 375
00/1 Cardset 160
02/3 Cardset 20
02/3 Crown Royale 112
98/9 DEL 309
99/0 Eishockey 259
02/3 In The Game-Used 182
02/3 Parkhurst 213
02/3 Pr. Stock Reserve 161
93/4 Sisu 264
94/5 Sisu 121
96/7 Sisu 84
02/3 SP Authentic 145
02/3 Ultimate Mem. 13
02/3 Upper Deck 437
02/3 UD Honor 113
02/3 UD Mask 147
02/3 UD Top Shelf 113

HAAKANA, LEO
65/6 Hellas 84
72/3 Williams Finnish 172

HAAKE, BERND
94/5 DEL 199
95/6 DEL 194
96/7 DEL 337

HAAKENSEN, MATTIS
92/3 Semic Nordisk 100

HAAKSTAD, JASON
92/3 BCJHL 47

HAALAND, JON ERIK
92/3 Semic Nordisk 136

HAANPÄÄ, ARI
91/2 Jyvas Hyva 27
92/3 Jyvas Hyva 80
93/4 Jyvas Hyva 287
91 Semic Sticker 13
93/4 Sisu 76
94/5 Sisu 22
95/6 Sisu 320
95/6 Sisu Limited 79

HAANPÄÄ, JUKKA
66/7 Champion 36

HAAPAKOSKI, MIKKO
98/9 Cardset 83
00/1 Cardset 55
97/8 Hockey-Box
92/3 Jyvas Hyva 173
95 Semic 48
92 Semic Sticker 9
93 Semic Sticker 49
93/4 Sisu 318

HAAPALA, JUKKA
66/7 Champion 1
70/1 Kuvajulkaisut 227

HAAPALA, MARTTI
71/2 Williams Finnish 259

HAAPALAINEN, HANNU
74 Hellas MM-Jenkki 5
70/1 Kuvajulkaisut 241
74 Semic Sticker 94
78/9 SM-Liiga 179
78/9 SM-Liiga 6
77-79 Sports. FIN 82-1949
71/2 Williams Finnish 207
72/3 Williams Finnish 155
73/4 Williams Finnish 151

HAAPALAINEN, OLAVI
66/7 Champion 182
72/3 Williams Finnish 156

HAAPAMÄKI, JARI
91/2 Jyvas Hyva 12
92/3 Jyvas Hyva 31
93/4 Jyvas Hyva 51
93/4 Sisu 240
94/5 Sisu 107
95/6 Sisu 19

HAAPANIEMI, HARRI
80/1 Mallasjuoma 80

HAAPANIEMI, MARKKU
80/1 Mallasjuoma 187
78/9 SM-Liiga 215

HAAPANIEMI, MIRO
93/4 Sisu 103
94/5 Sisu 96
95/6 Sisu 210

HAAPSAARI, TOMMI
92/3 Jyvas Hyva 156
93/4 Jyvas Hyva 296
93/4 Sisu 67
94/5 Sisu 60
95/6 Sisu 112

HAARMANN, MARK
83/4 Oshawa Generals

HAAS, DAVID
98/9 DEL 186
99/0 Eishockey 232
88/9 ProCards / Cape Breton
89/0 ProCards AHL 141
90/1 ProCards 220
91/2 ProCards 224
01/2 UD DEL 95
85/6 London Knights

HAAS, JULIUS
72 Hellas MM-Jenkki 93
74 Hellas MM-Jenkki 69
70/1 Kuvajulkaisut 45
72/3 Williams Finnish 5

HAAS, ROSTISLAV
96/7 APS 98
97/8 APS 102
97/8 DS 20
96/7 DS Sticker 265
97/8 DS Sticker 47

HABERT, SIEGFRIED
95 Panini Worlds 274

HABSCHEID, MARC
90/1 Bowman 228
95/6 DEL 15
90/1 OPC/Topps 342
91/2 O-Pee-Chee 250
89/0 OPC/Topps 151
89/0 opcSticker 198-54
90/1 Panini Sticker 204
91/2 Panini Sticker 138
90/1 Pro Set 437
91/2 Pro Set 365
90/1 Score 24T
91/2 Score 33T
91/2 Score CAN 583
92/3 Score 546
90/1 Upper Deck 374
91/2 CALG / IGA
89/0 DETR / Little Caesars
91/2 DETR / Little Caesars
82/3 EDMO / Red Rooster
84/5 EDMO / Red Rooster
88/9 EDMO / Action 59
88/9 MINS / ADA
93/4 Las Vegas Thunder
94/5 Las Vegas Thunder
83/4 Moncton Alpines
84/5 Nova Scotia Oilers
00/1 Kelowna Rockets
81/2 Saskatoon Blades

HACHBORN, LEN
90/1 ProCards 4
91/2 ProCards 318
83/4 Springfield Indians 4

HACKETT, JEFF
01/2 Atomic ✂ GWJ 32
98/9 Aurora 41
99/0 Aurora 74, GU-10
00/1 Aurora 71
98/9 Be A Player 27, ✍ Aut. 27
99/0 BAP Mem. 209
00/1 BAP Mem. 30
01/2 BAP Memor. 229, ✂ GoalJ
01/2 BAP Update ✂ H20
01/2 BT Pipes 73, 100, ✂ DM, ✂ Jers., ✂ S&J, ✂ GG, ✂ GT, ✂ HSHSJers
02/3 Between the Pipes 42, M29, ✂ GUJ50, ✂ T9
98/9 Bicycle.. 10-S
91/2 Bowman 219
92/3 Bowman 348
98/9 Bowman's Best 63
99/0 Crown Royale 69
01/2 Crown Royale 76
02/3 Crown Royale 50
93/4 Donruss 61
94/5 Donruss 35
96/7 Donruss 88
97/8 Donruss 116
97/8 Do. Canadian 101
97/8 Do. Preferred 139
97/8 Do. Priority 68
98/9 Dynagon Ice 42
99/0 Dynagon Ice 101
02/3 First Edition 119, ✂ Jers.
96/7 Fleer 147
92/3 Fleer Ultra 195
02/3 In The Game-Used ✂ GP18
92/3 Kraft / PB
93/4 Leaf 319
94/5 Leaf 128
96/7 Leaf 54
97/8 Leaf 32
97/8 Limited 160
00/1 McDonald's 18, CL-3
99/0 Millenium 134, ✍ Aut. 134, ✂ G-5
91/2 O-Pee-Chee 382
92/3 O-Pee-Chee 218
01/2 O-Pee-Chee 230
98/9 OPC Chrome 93, SB5
90/1 OPC Premier 39
91/2 OPC Premier 108
97/8 Omega 51
98/9 Omega 121
99/0 Omega 118
98/9 Pacific 144
99/0 Pacific 203, ITCNF-9
00/1 Pacific 208, TTC-6
01/2 Pacific 207
02/3 Pacific Complete 153
97/8 Pacific CC 160, ITC-4
97/8 Pa. Crown Roy. 30
98/9 Pa. Crown Roy. 69
97/8 Pa. Dynagon 27, S-5, T-39
97/8 Pa. Invincible 30
97/8 Pa. Paramount 44, GSL-4
98/9 Pa. Paramount 48, -GS 5
99/0 Pa. Paramount 116, GS-10, IAd-13, IAI-14
00/1 Pa. Paramount 125
97/8 Pa. Revolution 30, RTS-4
98/9 Pa. Revolution 73
89/0 Panini Sticker 276
91/2 Panini Sticker 240
92/3 Panini Sticker 123
98/9 Panini Sticker 115
99/0 Panini Sticker 72
92/3 Parkhurst 162
93/4 Parkhurst 312
95/6 Parkhurst 44
00/1 Parkhurst P-119
01/2 Parkhurst 157
02/3 Parkhurst 190
02/3 Parkhurst Retro 195
91/2 Pinnacle 119
92/3 Pinnacle 105
93/4 Pinnacle 373
96/7 Pinnacle 110
97/8 Pinnacle 72, M-7, / Tin 3
96/7 Pi. Be A Player 42, ✍ Aut. 42
97/8 Pi. Certified 30
97/8 Pi. Inside 41, SU-7, S-8
97/8 Pi. Totally 30
93/4 Power Play 312
00/1 Premier Plus 28
99/0 Prism 71
00/1 Private Stock ✂ GUG 56
01/2 Pr. Stock -PS 40
00/1 PS Titanium ✂ GUG 26
01/2 PS Titanium Draft ✂ 49
00/1 PS Titanium Draft ✂ 50
90/1 Pro Set 624
91/2 Pro Set 331
92/3 Pro Set 171
91/2 Pro Set Platinum 226
88/9 ProCards / Springfield
89/0 ProCards AHL 236
02/3 Quest for the Cup 6
99/0 Revolution 74
00/1 Revolution 75
90/1 Score 388
91/2 Score 367
91/2 Score 92T
91/2 Score CAN 326
91/2 Score CAN 642
92/3 Score 82
93/4 Score 38
93/4 Score 541
96/7 Score 85
97/8 Score 15
00/1 Signature 173
01/2 Signature 161, ✍ Aut. 161
99/0 SPx 79
98/9 SPx Finite 21
00/1 Stadium 19, CA7, ✂ SCS
01/2 Stadium ✂ SCS, ✂ SCSD
99/0 SLU
92/3 Topps 185
98/9 Topps 93, SB5
99/0 Topps 82
00/1 Topps 124
01/2 Topps 230
99/0 To. Chrome 82
00/1 To. Chrome 95
98/9 To. Finest 86
00/1 To. Gold Label 9
00/1 To. Heritage 126, ✂ OSS, ✂ OSS, ✍ CAI
01/2 To. Reserve ✂ TR
92/3 T. Stadium Club 108
93/4 To. Stadium 326
00/1 To. Stars 23
98/9 UD Choice 49
00/1 Ultimate Mem. ✂ G-16, ✂ PS-7, JJ-4
91/2 Upper Deck 58
92/3 Upper Deck 308
95/6 Upper Deck 387
96/7 Upper Deck 30
97/8 Upper Deck 38
99/0 Upper Deck 69
00/1 Upper Deck 321
01/2 UD Challenge 45
96/7 UD CC 54
97/8 UD Coll. Choice 47
99/0 UD G. Reserve 69
02/3 UD Mask 8, 9, 10
99/0 UD MVP 104, ✍ PS
02/3 UD Premier 6
02/3 UD Rookie 11
00/1 UD Vintage 191
00/1 Vanguard ✂ DGJ 18
02/3 Vanguard 54
99/0 Victory 145
99/0 WGretzky 88
93/4 CHIC / Coke
00/1 MONT
01/2 MONT
02/3 MONT
91/2 SANJ / Sports Action

HACQUOIL, FRANK
23/4 Paulins Candy 59

HADAMCZIK, ALOIS
94/5 APS 287
95/6 APS 219
96/7 APS 48
97/8 APS 313
98/9 OFS 383
99/0 OFS 191
00/1 OFS 236

HADDEN, GREG
00/1 Kudos 135
95/6 Richmond Renegades
00/1 Nottingham Panthers
01/2 Nottingham Panthers
02/3 Nottingham Panthers
93/4 N. Michigan Wildcats

HADELÖV, ANDREAS
99/0 UD Elitserien 151
00/1 UD Elitserien 135, M6, ✍ Sig.

HADFIELD, VIC
99/0 BAP Mem. AH-7, ✍ AH-7
45-64 BeeHive-2 [NYRa.]
64-67 BeeHive-3 [NYRa.]
64/5 Coke/Sprite [NYRa.]
65/6 Coca-Cola
70/1 Colgate 45
70/1 Dad's Cookies
70/1 Eddie Sargent 126
71/2 Eddie Sargent 121
72/3 Eddie Sargent 151
70/1 Esso Power Player
91/2 Future Trends C72 36, ✍ 36
62/3 Cowan Tile
72/3 Post 4
74/5 Loblaws
68/9 O-Pee-Chee 171
69/0 O-Pee-Chee 38
70/1 O-Pee-Chee 62
71/2 O-Pee-Chee 9
72/3 O-Pee-Chee 250
72/3 O-Pee-Chee 272
72/3 O-Pee-Chee 31
72/3 O-Pee-Chee TC
73/4 O-Pee-Chee 108
74/5 O-Pee-Chee 65
75/6 O-Pee-Chee 165
76/7 O-Pee-Chee 226
95/6 Parkie 66-67 98
94/5 Parkie Tall 90
61/2 Shirriff 97
68/9 Shirriff / NYRa. 13
62/3 Topps 60
63/4 Topps 54
64/5 Topps 62
65/6 Topps 27
66/7 Topps 86
66/7 Topps / Test 19
67/8 Topps 88
68/9 Topps 74
69/0 Topps 38
70/1 Topps 62
71/2 Topps 9
72/3 Topps 110
72/3 Topps 132
72/3 Topps 61
73/4 Topps 181
74/5 Topps 65
75/6 Topps 165
76/7 Topps 226
01/2 T/O Archives 41, ✍ CAI
63/4 Toronto Star Photo
64/5 Toronto Star Photo
71/2 Toronto Sun Photo
91/2 Ultimate Original Six 21, ✍ Aut. 21
74/5 PITT

HADLEY, JEFF
00/1 Québec Remparts 5
01/2 Québec Remparts 4

HADRASCHEK, CHRISTOPH
95/6 DEL 36

HAEGGLUND, ROGER
84/5 Fredericton Express

HAELZLE, JASON
92/3 Windsor Spitfires

HAFNER, EDVARD
79 Panini Sticker 398

HAFNER, PETER
96 Québec Pee Wee 547

HAFSMOE, CHRISTIAN
92/3 Semic Nordisk 149

HAGGERTY, RYAN
95/6 Edge Ice 32

HAGGERTY, SEAN
93/4 Classic 103
95/6 Classic 84
94/5 L. Limited USA 6
94/5 Sig. Rookies 51, ✍ 51
93/4 Slapshot / Detroit 21
94/5 Slapshot / Detroit Jr. 23
95/6 Slapshot 69, P
94/5 Slapshot Memorial 97
94/5 SP 191
94/5 Topps Finest 119
99/0 Kansas City Blades
96/7 Kentucky Tho'blades
97/8 Kentucky Tho'blades
00/1 Milwaukee Admirals
01/2 Providence Bruins

HÄGGROTH, LENNART
00/1 Alfabilder
96 Wien HL10

HAGLSPERGER, JOACHIM
95/6 DEL 355

HAGMAN, JOHAN
98/9 Odessa Jackalopes

HAGMAN, MATTI
92/3 Future Trends C76 148
92/3 Future Trends C76 187
81/2 O-Pee-Chee 113
82/3 O-Pee-Chee 108
81/2 OPC Sticker 10
81/2 OPC Sticker 213
82/3 OPC Sticker 8
82/3 OPC/Topps Sticker 103
79 Panini Sticker 172
80/1 Pepsi Bottle Cap
82/3 Post [Edmo.]
82 Semic Sticker 156
96/7 Sisu 199
78/9 SM-Liiga 39
77-79 Sports. FIN 32-747
73/4 Williams Finnish 127
80/1 EDMO / Zellers
81/2 EDMO / Red Rooster
88/9 EDMO / Action 58

HAGMAN, NIKLAS
01/2 Adrenaline 209
01/2 Atomic 109
01/2 BAP Memor. 398
02/3 BAP Memorabilia 37
01/2 Bowman 150
02/3 Bowman 106, ✂ FFDS, ✂ FFJ, ✂ FFP, ✂ FFR, ✂ FFRP, ✂ FFS, ✂ FFTS, ✍ YSA, / ✍ Puck
98/9 Cardset 43
00/1 Cardset 57
02/3 Cardset 21, -SGSP 4
01/2 Crown Royale 161
02/3 First Edition 218
01/2 O-Pee-Chee 347
02/3 O-Pee-Chee 42
02/3 Pacific 153
02/3 Pacific Complete 85
01/2 Parkhurst 274
02/3 Parkhurst 194
01/2 Pr. Stock 122
01/2 PS Titanium 160
01/2 PS Titanium Draft 131
01/2 Signature 234, ✍ Aut. 234
01/2 SP Authentic 150
01/2 SP GU 78
02/3 SPx 105
01/2 Stadium 128
01/2 Topps 347
02/3 Topps 42
01/2 To. Chrome 165
01/2 To. Heritage 155
02/3 T. Limited 42
01/2 To. Reserve 101
01/2 UD PlayMakers Ltd 119
01/2 Upper Deck 425
02/3 UD Challenge 107
01/2 UD Ice 76
01/2 UD Mask 146
01/2 UD Premier 97
01/2 UD Top Shelf 128
02/3 UD Vintage 113
01/2 Vanguard 113
02/3 Victory 94
01/2 FLOR

HAGRENIUS, JONATHAN
92/3 Semic Elitserien 309

HAGSTRÖM, ANDERS
70/1 Kuvajulkaisut 24

HAGSTRÖM, PETER
92/3 Semic Elitserien 122
95/6 UD Elitserien DS13
98/9 UD Elitserien 93
99/0 UD Elitserien 92

HAGUE, ALAN
93/4 Sheffield Steelers 2
94/5 Sheffield Steelers 20

HAHL, RIKU
01/2 BAP Memor. 356
02/3 Calder 64
98/9 Cardset 73
99/0 Cardset 242
00/1 Cardset 28
02/3 Cardset 22
02/3 O-Pee-Chee 285
02/3 Pacific Complete 541
01/2 Parkhurst 311
01/2 SPx 201
02/3 SPx 106
02/3 Topps 285
02/3 T. Limited 285
01/2 UD PlayMakers Ltd 111
01/2 UD Foundations 126
01/2 UD Ice 133
01/2 UD MVP 199
01/2 UD Premier 93
01/2 UD Top Shelf 126
02/3 UD Vintage 328
01/2 Hershey Bears
02/3 Hershey Bears

HAIB, JOSEPH
98/9 DEL 325

HAIDER, REINHARD
94/5 DEL 29

HAIDY, SAM
82/3 Soo Greyhounds
83/4 Soo Greyhounds

HAIGHT, STEVE
92/3 Oshawa Generals

HAINANEN, JOKKE
95/6 Sisu Pain. 1

HAINSEY, RON
02/3 Atomic 115
02/3 BAP All-Star 141
02/3 BAP Memor. 292
02/3 Bowman 132
02/3 Calder 126
02/3 Choice Prospects 16
02/3 Crown Royale 122
02/3 Exclusive 181
02/3 First Edition 433 [Retail]
02/3 Heads Up 126
02/3 In The GU 93, ✂ C8
02/3 Pacific Complete 581
02/3 PTC/ Collections 7
02/3 Parkhurst 222, HHC6, ✂ GJ54
02/3 Parkhurst Retro 222
02/3 Pr. Stock Reserve 168
02/3 PS Titanium 122
02/3 Quest for the Cup 126
02/3 Signature 186, ✍ 186, ✂ SGJ62
02/3 SP Authentic ✍ 189, ✍ ✂ Patch
02/3 SP GU 83
02/3 SPx ✍ 153
02/3 Stadium 131
02/3 T. Chrome 169
02/3 To. Heritage 144
02/3 T. Total 402
02/3 Ultimate Mem. 22, ✂ CC, ✍ RAut
02/3 Upper Deck 240
02/3 UD Artistic 100
02/3 UD Classic 119
02/3 UD Foundations 157
02/3 UD Honor 157
02/3 UD Mask 159
02/3 UD Piece 136
02/3 UD Premier ✍ 73, ✍ Sig
02/3 UD Rookie ✍ 165, ✍ TD
02/3 UD Top Shelf 94
02/3 Vanguard 121
02/3 MONT
02/3 Hamilton Bulldogs
01/2 Québec Citadelles

HAINSWORTH, GEORGE
25-27 Anonymous 1
33/4 Anonymous 13
34-43 BeeHive-1 [Toro.]
01/2 BT Pipes 130, 141
02/3 Between the Pipes 119, ✂ HSHSJers 24, ✂ I2, ✂ RB3, ✂ VM6
33/4 Canadian Gum
83 HHOF Postcard J7
83&87 HHOF 187
02/3 In The Game-Used ✂ VM16
27/8 La Patrie
27/8 La Presse
33/4 O-Pee-Chee 15
95/6 Parkhurst 59
01/2 Parkhurst PR25
93/4 Parkie 56-57 P-2
23/4 Paulins Candy 39
02/3 Ultimate Mem. ✂ EA, ✂ GMIH, ✂ SU, ✂ SCD, ✂ SF, ✂ VGJ

HAISZA, HERBERT
79 Panini Sticker 309

HAJDU, RICHARD
83/4 Victoria Cougars
84/5 Victoria Cougars

HAJDUSEK, STANISLAV
82 Semic Sticker 81

HAJEK, DAVID
00/1 OFS 116
01/2 OFS 178, 267
99/0 Score 31

HAJEK, MIROSLAV
99/0 OFS 43

HAJNOS, JANUSZ
92 Semic Sticker 283

HAJT, BILL
84/5 Kelowna Wings &...
75/6 O-Pee-Chee 233
76/7 O-Pee-Chee 128
77/8 O-Pee-Chee 27
78/9 O-Pee-Chee 108
79/0 O-Pee-Chee 221
80/1 O-Pee-Chee 337
83/4 O-Pee-Chee 64
84/5 O-Pee-Chee 21
85/6 OPC/Topps 119
86/7 OPC/Topps 52
84/5 OPC Sticker 214
85/6 OPC Sticker 176-45
87/8 Panini Sticker 26
82/3 Post [Buff.]
75/6 Topps 233
76/7 Topps 128
77/8 Topps 27
78/9 Topps 108
79/0 Topps 221
84/5 Topps 17
74/5 BUFF
80/1 BUFF / Wendt's 7
81/2 BUFF / Wendt's 9
84/5 BUFF / Blue Shield
85/6 BUFF / Blue Shield
86/7 BUFF / Blue Shield

HAJT, CHRIS
95/6 Bowman P16
97 Bowman 35
98 Bowman 2
98 Bowman Chrome 2
95/6 Classic 61, 85
95/6 Future Legends ✍ SSD-5
94/5 Slapshot / Guelph 7
95/6 Slapshot 87, 436
98/9 UD Choice 299
01/2 Victory 370
99/0 Hamilton Bulldogs
00/1 Hamilton Bulldogs
01/2 Hamilton Bulldogs
01/2 Hamilton Bulldogs/ Staz
95/6 Guelph Storm
96/7 Guelph Storm
96/7 Guelph Storm

HAJZER, JANOS
79 Panini Sticker 265

HAKALA, ANTERO
66/7 Champion 212

HAKALA, YRJO
66/7 Champion 86
65/6 Hellas 87

HAKAMAKI, PENTTI
72 Panda MM-Toronto

HAKANEN, MARKKU
66/7 Champion 193
65/6 Hellas 118
70/1 Kuvajulkaisut 121
72 Panda MM-Toronto
71/2 Williams Finnish 171
72/3 Williams Finnish 122
73/4 Williams Finnish 176

HAKANEN, MATTI
70/1 Kuvajulkaisut 122
72 Panda MM-Toronto
71/2 Williams Finnish 172
73/4 Williams Finnish 242

HAKANEN, REIJO
66/7 Champion 202
65/6 Hellas 128
70/1 Kuvajulkaisut 123
72 Panda MM-Toronto
71/2 Williams Finnish 173
73/4 Williams Finnish 177

HAKANEN, TIMO
98/9 Cardset 267
99/0 Cardset 156
02/3 Cardset 169
95/6 Sisu 366, DD-9
96/7 Sisu 159
95/6 UD CC 327

HÅKANSSON, JONAS
92/3 Semic Elitserien 216

HÅKANSSON, ANDERS
84/5 O-Pee-Chee 85
84/5 LOSA / Smokey 7
81/2 MINS
83/4 PITT / Heinz

HÅKANSSON, JONAS
91/2 Semic Elitserien 199

HÅKANSSON, MIKAEL
94/5 Leaf Elit Set 208
95/6 Leaf Elit Set 106
93/4 Parkhurst 539
91/2 Semic Elitserien 329
92/3 Semic Elitserien 94
95/6 UD Elitserien 164
98/9 UD Elitserien 58
99/0 UD Elitserien 43
00/1 St. John's Maple Leafs

HAKKARAINEN, ESA
80/1 Mallasjuoma 112
78/9 SM-Liiga 156
73/4 Williams Finnish 307

HAKKINEN, PASI
01/2 Nottingham Panthers

HÄKKINEN, PASI
98/9 Cardset 185
99/0 Cardset 303
00/1 Cardset 328

HAKSTOL, DAVE
92/3 Indianapolis Ice
93/4 Indianapolis Ice
94/5 Minnesota Moose
95/6 Minnesota Moose

HAKULINEN, MARKKU
82 Semic Sticker 47
78/9 SM-Liiga 126
77-79 Sports. FIN 82-1955

HAKULINEN, YRJO
80/1 Mallasjuoma 83
78/9 SM-Liiga 128
77-79 Sports. FIN 82-1955
71/2 Williams Finnish 260

HALA, JIRI
94/5 APS 96

HALAUCA, ALEXANDRU
79 Panini Sticker 315

HALE, LARRY
70/1 Eddie Sargent 155
71/2 Eddie Sargent 154
70/1 Esso Power Player
72/3 O-Pee-Chee 54
72/3 Topps 44
71/2 Toronto Sun Photo
75/6 Houston Aeros

HALE, ROB
88/9 Lethbridge Hurricanes
89/0 Lethbridge Hurricanes

HALEY, MIKE
95/6 Spokane Chiefs 17

HALFNIGHT, ASHLIN
93/4 Donruss USA8
93/4 Pinnacle 482
98/9 New Haven Beast 15

HALIFAX, SEAN
96/7 Knoxville Cherokees
93/4 Red Deer Rebels

HALKIDIS, BOB
92/3 Pro Set 190
89/0 ProCards AHL 270
85/6 BUFF / Blue Shield
86/7 BUFF / Blue Shield
87/8 BUFF / Blue Shield
88/9 BUFF / Blue Shield
88/9 BUFF / Won. Bread
95/6 TAMP / Sky Box
91/2 TORO / P.L.A.Y. 27
95/6 Atlanta Knights
96/7 Carolina Monarchs
85/6 London Knights

HALKO, STEVEN
99/0 Millenium 47, ✍ Aut. 47
01/2 O-Pee-Chee 251
01/2 Topps 251
00/1 Upper Deck 263
97/8 CARO / Sprint
98/9 CARO / Highwoods
98/9 New Haven Beast 6
96/7 Springfield Falcons
01/2 Worcester IceCats

HALL, ADAM
02/3 Atomic 116
02/3 BAP All-Star 143
02/3 BAP Memorabilia 294
02/3 Bowman 134, ✂ FFDS, ✂ FFJ, ✂ FFP, ✂ FFR, ✂ FFRP, ✂ FFS, ✂ FFTS, ✍ YSA, / ✍ Puck
02/3 Calder 129
02/3 Crown Royale 123
02/3 Exclusive 182
02/3 In The Game-Used 187
02/3 In The Game-Used ✂ C14
02/3 Pacific Complete 560
02/3 Parkhurst 224
02/3 Parkhurst Retro 224
02/3 Pr. Stock Reserve 169
02/3 PS Titanium 124
02/3 Quest for the Cup 129
02/3 Signature 181, ✍ 181
02/3 SP Authentic ✍ 190, ✍ ✂ Patch
02/3 SP GU 84
02/3 SPx ✍ 154
02/3 Stadium 136
02/3 T. Chrome 156
02/3 To. Heritage 137
02/3 T. Total 413
02/3 Ultimate Mem. 24, ✂ CC, ✍ RAut
02/3 Upper Deck 211
02/3 UD Classic 120
02/3 UD Foundations 134
02/3 UD Honor 117
02/3 UD Mask 149
02/3 UD Piece 137
02/3 UD Premier 68, ✍ Sig
02/3 UD Rookie ✂ 152
02/3 UD Top Shelf 131
02/3 UD Vintage 337
02/3 Vanguard 122

HALL, BILLY
91/2 7th...Sketch OHL 297
92/3 Ottawa 67's

HALL, CHRIS
93/4 Slapshot / Oshawa 23
94/5 Slapshot Memorial 53
92/3 Oshawa Generals

HALL, DEAN
89/0 Johnstown Chiefs

HALL, DEL
76/7 OPC WHA 78
75/6 Phoenix Roadrunners
76/7 Phoenix Roadrunners

HALL, GLENN
01/2 ASG History
01/2 BAP Memor. ✂ GT
01/2 BAP Update ✂ RR9
45-64 BeeHive-2 [Detr.]
45-64 BeeHive-2 [Chic.]
64-67 BeeHive-3 [Chic.]
01/2 BT Pipes 121, 140, HSHS, ✂ S&J, ✂ GR, ✂ TW, ✂ VM, ✂ HSHSJers
02/3 Between the Pipes 117, ✂ HSHSJers 30, ✂ RB6, ✂ VM12, ✍ Aut.
02/3 Canada Post, ✍ Aut.
63-65 Chex
64/5 Coke/Sprite [Chic.]
65/6 Coca-Cola
62 El Producto
70/1 Esso Power Player
01/2 Fleer Greats 2, ✍ Aut.
62/3 Cowan Tile
83 HHOF Postcard H8
83&87 HHOF 114
96/7 Legends 88
68/9 O-Pee-Chee 111
68/9 O-Pee-Chee 215
68/9 O-Pee-Chee PS 13
69/0 O-Pee-Chee 12
69/0 O-Pee-Chee 207
69/0 O-Pee-Chee 210
69/0 O-Pee-Chee Stamp
70/1 O-Pee-Chee 210
70/1 O-Pee-Chee DE 27
01/2 Parkhurst ✍ PA2
93/4 Parkie 56-57 141
93/4 Parkie 56-57 152
93/4 Parkie 56-57 158
93/4 Parkie 56-57 159
93/4 Parkie 56-57 176
93/4 Parkie 56-57 46
02/3 Parkhurst Retro ✂ NN10
95/6 Parkie 66-67 31, 121, TW6
94/5 Parkie Tall 32, 133, 165, 166, 175
66/7 Post Cereal Box
66/7 Post [Small]
72 Semic Sticker 187
60/1 Shirriff 61
61/2 Shirriff 29
62/3 Shirriff 49
68/9 Shirriff / SLou. 5
01/2 Signature ✍ VA13
91/2 Star Pics 52
97/8 SLU Cdn. Leg.
98/9 SLU -CL
57/8 Topps 20
58/9 Topps 13
59/0 Topps 28
59/0 Topps 32
60/1 Topps 25
61/2 Topps 22
61/2 Topps 32
61/2 Topps 44
61/2 Topps - Stamp
62/3 Topps 24
62/3 Topps Dollar
63/4 Topps 23
64/5 Topps 110
64/5 Topps 12
65/6 Topps 55
66/7 Topps 126
66/7 Topps 54
67/8 Topps 129
67/8 Topps 65
68/9 Topps 111
69/0 Topps 12
01/2 To. Heritage S3, ✍ CAI
01/2 T/O Archives 8, -Seat, ✍ CAI
59/0 Toronto Star Photo
61/2 Toronto Star Photo
63/4 Toronto Star Action
63/4 Toronto Star Photo
64/5 Toronto Star Action
64/5 Toronto Star Photo
58/9 Toronto Star Weekend
62/3 Toronto Star Weekend
65/6 Toronto Star Weekend
01/2 Ultimate Mem. ✂ ASGH, ✂ CT, ✂ Corn., ✂ EA, ✂ RN, ✂ RT, ✂ RA
02/3 Ultimate Mem. ✂ CSTW, ✂ EA, ✂ FS, ✂ GMIH, ✂ NO, ✂ Num, ✂ RA, ✂ RT, ✂ SU, ✂ SCD, ✂ VGJ
99/0 UD C. Legends 17
00/1 UD Legends 28
01/2 UD Legends 12, 80
99/0 UD Retro 93, G3A
01/2 UD SCup Champs 3
98/9 CHIC / Pizza Hut
92/3 SLOU / McDon. 1
85/6 U. of Arizona Ice Cats

HALL, JASON
90/1 Rayside-Balfour
91/2 Rayside-Balfour

HALL, JOE
91 C55 Reprint 2
83 HHOF Postcard G6
83&87 HHOF 97
10/1 Imperial
11/2 Imperial 2
12/3 Imperial 16

HALL, LEE
94/5 Peoria Rivermen

HALL, MAURICE
94/5 Anchorage Aces 19

HALL, MIKE
98/9 Indianapolis Ice

HALL, MURRAY
45-64 BeeHive-2 [Chic.]
64-67 BeeHive-3 [Chic.]
64-67 BeeHive-3 [Detr.]
70/1 Eddie Sargent 224
71/2 Eddie Sargent 211
72/3 Eddie Sargent 212
70/1 Esso Power Player
70/1 O-Pee-Chee 118
71/2 O-Pee-Chee 109
72/3 O-Pee-Chee 294
73/4 Quaker Oats 14
62/3 Topps 43
66/7 Topps 105
70/1 Topps 118
71/2 Topps 109
71/2 Toronto Sun Photo
70/1 VANC / Royal Bank
71/2 VANC / Royal Bank 3
75/6 Houston Aeros

HALL, RANDY
89/0 7th..Sketch OHL 132
90/1 7th..Sketch OHL 74
91/2 7th...Sketch OHL 210
93/4 Slapshot / Niagara Falls 26
89/0 Niagara Falls Thunder

HALL, SCOTT
92/3 BCJHL 219

HALL, TAYLOR
90/1 ProCards 303
84/5 VANC
85/6 VANC
86/7 VANC
86/7 Fredericton Express
81/2 Regina Pats
82/3 Regina Pats
83/4 Regina Pats

HALL, TODD
91/2 Upper Deck WJC 77
97/8 Hartford Wolf Pack
98/9 Hartford Wolf Pack
99/0 Hartford Wolf Pack
00/1 Hartford Wolf Pack

HALLA, HANS PETTER
92/3 Semic Nordisk 154

HÄLLBACK, MATHIAS
94/5 Leaf Elit Set 241
92/3 Semic Elitserien 98

HÄLLBERG, PER
98/9 UD Elitserien 168
99/0 UD Elitserien 170
00/1 UD Elitserien 155

HALLDORSON, DEREK
00/1 Saskatoon Blades

HALLÉ, YAN
00/1 Val d'Or Foreurs 2

HALLER, KEVIN
91/2 Bowman 28
92/3 Bowman 301
93/4 Donruss 168
92/3 Fleer Ultra 327
93/4 Fleer Ultra 352
93/4 Leaf 223
94/5 Leaf 371
91/2 O-Pee-Chee 473
92/3 O-Pee-Chee 290
99/0 Pacific 6
01/2 Pacific 247
97/8 Pa. Invincible R-36
93/4 Parkhurst 376
94/5 Parkhurst 120
95/6 Parkhurst 430
94/5 Parkie SE126
91/2 Pinnacle 307
92/3 Pinnacle 211
93/4 Pinnacle 193
94/5 Pinnacle 373
97/8 Pi. Be A Player 98, ✍ Aut. 98
95/6 Playoff 292
93/4 Power Play 370
93/4 Premier 339
94/5 Premier 351
91/2 Pro Set 525
91/2 Pro Set Platinum 250
90/1 ProCards 265
91/2 Score 386
91/2 Score CAN 276
92/3 Score 159
93/4 Score 268
92/3 Topps 445
95/6 Topps 178
91/2 To. Stadium 382
92/3 T. Stadium Club 38
93/4 To. Stadium 53
91/2 Upper Deck 192
92/3 Upper Deck 479
93/4 Upper Deck 333
94/5 Upper Deck 144
95/6 Upper Deck 357
97/8 Upper Deck 242
93/4 Upper Deck Be A Player 23
94/5 UD BAP R56, ✍ 56
95/6 UD CC 295
00/1 UD Vintage 224
91/2 BUFF / Blue Shield
91/2 BUFF / Campbell's
91/2 BUFF / Pepsi
97/8 CARO / Sprint
02/3 MONT
92/3 MONT / OPC 8
93/4 MONT
93/4 MONT / Export
94/5 PHIL / Sheet
91/2 Rochester Americans WPC
88/9 Regina Pats

HALLILA, JARI
72/3 Williams Finnish 342

HALLIN, MATS
83/4 O-Pee-Chee 8
83/4 OPC/Topps Sticker 184
90/1 Semic Elitserien 137
91/2 Semic Elitserien 187
00/1 UD Vintage ✂ D-POH
85/6 MINS
83/4 NYIS
83/4 NYIS / News 8
84/5 NYIS / News 7
81/2 Indianapolis Checkers
82/3 Indianapolis Checkers

HALLIN, PER
00/1 UD Elitserien 171

HALLOWAY, BRUCE
83/4 Fredericton Express
84/5 Fredericton Express

HALME, ILKKA
65/6 Hellas 119

HALME, JARI
91/2 Jyvas Hyva 55
94/5 Sisu 37

HALONEN, MARKO
93/4 Jyvas Hyva 205
93/4 Sisu 262

HALONEN, MIKKO
93/4 Jyvas Hyva 208
93/4 Sisu 275
94/5 Sisu 172, 334

HALPENNY, SCOTT
87/8 Brockville Braves

HALPERN, JEFF
01/2 Adrenaline 196
00/1 Aurora 147
99/0 BAP Mem. 378
00/1 BAP Mem. 365
01/2 BAP Memor. 7
02/3 BAP Memorabilia 64
99/0 Dynagon Ice 201
02/3 First Edition 267
99/0 NHL Power Play [x3]
01/2 O-Pee-Chee 158
99/0 Omega 246
00/1 Pacific 422
01/2 Pacific 393
02/3 Pacific 391
02/3 Pacific Complete 237
00/1 Pa. Paramount 245
01/2 Parkhurst 212
00/1 Private Stock 98
00/1 Revolution 147
00/1 Signature 194, ✍ Aut. 189
01/2 Signature 172, ✍ Aut. 172
99/0 SP Authentic 120
02/3 SP Game-Used ✂ FF (x2)
02/3 Sports Vault 146
00/1 Stadium 191
01/2 Stadium 63
00/1 Topps 222
01/2 Topps 158
00/1 To. Chrome 141
00/1 To. Heritage 112
01/2 To. Heritage 103
99/0 To. Prmr. Plus 96
02/3 T. Total 300
00/1 Upper Deck 178
01/2 Upper Deck 176
00/1 UD Black Diam. 60
02/3 UD Classic ✂ HR
00/1 UD MVP 180
01/2 UD MVP 186
99/0 UD MVP Cup 191
00/1 UD Vintage 361
02/3 UD Vintage 257, ✂ SO
00/1 Victory 237
01/2 Victory 356

HALTIA, PATRIK
94/5 Leaf Elit Set 215, ND-7, RR-8
95/6 Leaf Elit Set 39, S-5
90/1 Semic Elitserien 250
91/2 Semic Elitserien 81
92/3 Semic Elitserien 103
96/7 Saint John Flames

HALTTUNEN, NIKO
98/9 Cardset 172
94/5 Parkie SE220
95/6 Sisu 51
94/5 Topps Finest 132
00/1 UD Elitserien 27

HALVERSON, CHRIS
95/6 Halifax Moosehead

HALVERSON, DON
95/6 Prince Albert Raiders

HALVERSON, TREVOR
91/2 Arena 16
91/2 Classic 18
91/2 Classic Four Sport 18
91/2 ProCards 555
89/0 7th..Sketch OHL 157
90/1 7th..Sketch OHL 308
91/2 Star Pics 14
91/2 Ultimate Draft Pick 17, 73, ✍ Aut.
91/2 Baltimore Skipjacks
94/5 Hampton Roads
95/6 Hampton Roads
98/9 Hampton Roads
96/7 Portland Pirates
98/9 Portland Pirates
93/4 San Diego Gulls

HALWARD, DOUG
86/7 Kraft Sports 64
76/7 O-Pee-Chee 306
78/9 O-Pee-Chee 392
80/1 O-Pee-Chee 207
81/2 O-Pee-Chee 335
83/4 O-Pee-Chee 351
84/5 O-Pee-Chee 320
85/6 O-Pee-Chee 189
86/7 O-Pee-Chee 248
88/9 OPC/Topps 113
83/4 OPC/Topps Sticker 278
84/5 OPC Sticker 278
85/6 OPC Sticker 243-110
86/7 OPC Sticker 97-227
82/3 Post [Vanc.]
83/4 Souhaits Keychain [Canucks]
80/1 Topps 207
83/4 Vachon 108-28
86/7 DETR / Little Caesars
87/8 DETR / Little Caesars
88/9 DETR / Little Caesars
88/9 EDMO
88/9 EDMO / Action 157
80/1 LOSA 3
81/2 VANC
81/2 VANC / Silverwood
82/3 VANC
83/4 VANC
84/5 VANC
85/6 VANC

HAMAL, TOMI
00/1 UD Elitserien 17

HÄMÄLÄINEN, ERIK
98/9 Cardset 169
99/0 Cardset 83
00/1 Cardset 301
02/3 Cardset 178
95 Hartwall Karjala
91/2 Jyvas Hyva 36
92/3 Jyvas Hyva 60
93/4 Jyvas Hyva 106
94/5 Leaf Elit Set 163
94 Panini Olympics 304
95 Panini Worlds 164
95 Semic 4
93/4 Sisu 12
93/4 Sisu 362
93/4 Sisu 374
94/5 Sisu 98
95/6 Sisu 178, G-5
95 Suomen Beckett Card 4
95/6 UD Elitserien 2
97/8 UD Elitserien 3
96 Wien 4

HÄMÄLÄINEN, JARI
92/3 Jyvas Hyva 95

HÄMÄLÄINEN, JARI JANNU
71/2 Williams Finnish 319
HÄMÄLÄINEN, JARI PEKKA
71/2 Williams Finnish 320
HÄMÄLÄINEN, JARKKO
92/3 Jyvas Hyva 149
93/4 Jyvas Hyva 265
93/4 Sisu 287
HÄMÄLÄINEN, TERO
98/9 Cardset 17, Leij. 5
99/0 Cardset 115
95/6 Sisu 209
96/7 Sisu 14, RE-4
HÄMÄLÄINEN, TOMMI
93/4 Sisu 90
94/5 Sisu 241
95/6 Sisu 218
94/5 Topps Finest 140
HÄMÄLÄINEN, VILLE
99/0 Cardset 307
00/1 Cardset 81
97/8 Hockey-Box
HAMAN, RADEK
95/6 APS 215
99/0 DS 194
00/1 DS 107
99/0 OFS 74
00/1 OFS 206
01/2 OFS 103
HAMEL, DENIS
99/0 BAP Mem. 362
97 Bowman 70
00/1 PS Titanium 106
00/1 PS Titanium Draft 106
01/2 Signature 31, ✍ Aut. 31
01/2 Victory 47
97/8 Rochester Americans
98/9 Rochester Americans
02/3 Rochester Americans
HAMEL, GILLES
84/5 O-Pee-Chee 22
87/8 O-Pee-Chee 218
85/6 OPC Sticker 185-59
87/8 OPC Sticker 253-144
87/8 Panini Sticker 366
88/9 ProCards / Moncton
84/5 BUFF / Blue Shield
85/6 BUFF / Blue Shield
88/9 LOSA / Smokey
86/7 WINN
87/8 WINN
HAMEL, JEAN
74/5 Loblaws
74/5 O-Pee-Chee 383
75/6 O-Pee-Chee 257
76/7 O-Pee-Chee 340
77/8 O-Pee-Chee 348
78/9 O-Pee-Chee 281
79/0 O-Pee-Chee 262
81/2 O-Pee-Chee 97
84/5 O-Pee-Chee 263
84/5 OPC Sticker 158
88/9 ProCards / Sherbrooke
89/0 ProCards AHL 201
91/2 7th...Sketch LHJMQ 294
93/4 Slapshot / Drummondville 25
75/6 Topps 257
79/0 Topps 262
83/4 Vachon 45-65
79/0 DETR
80/1 DETR
83/4 MONT
84/5 MONT
82/3 QUÉB
83/4 QUÉB
72/3 SLOU
73/4 SLOU
HAMEL, JEAN-PHILIPPE
00/1 Rouyn-Noranda 22
HAMEL, PIERRE
80/1 O-Pee-Chee 205
81/2 O-Pee-Chee 365
81/2 OPC Sticker 143
80/1 Pepsi Bottle Cap
80/1 Topps 205
79/0 WINN
80/1 WINN
HAMELIN, CRAIG
97/8 New Mexico Scorpions
HAMELIN, HUGO
91/2 7th...Sketch LHJMQ 101
HAMELIN, RICHARD
90/1 7th..Sketch LHJMQ 187
91/2 7th...Sketch LHJMQ 56
HAMERLIK, PETER
00/1 Kingston Frontenacs 8
01/2 Kingston Frontenacs 5
HAMHUIS, DAN
01 UD Prospects GU 23, ✂ TPJ, ✂✍ TPJS, ✂ JC (x2), ✍ SoT
99/0 Prince George Cougars
00/1 Prince George Cougars
HAMILL, RED
34-43 BeeHive-1 [Bost.]
45-64 BeeHive-2 [Chic.]
HAMILTON, AL
70/1 Dad's Cookies
70/1 Eddie Sargent 22
71/2 Eddie Sargent 23
70/1 Esso Power Player
68/9 O-Pee-Chee 70
69/0 O-Pee-Chee 192
71/2 O-Pee-Chee 49
79/0 O-Pee-Chee 355
74/5 OPC WHA 29
75/6 OPC WHA 49
76/7 OPC WHA 97
77/8 OPC WHA 40
73/4 Quaker Oats 16
71/2 Topps 49
71/2 Toronto Sun Photo
79/0 EDMO
88/9 EDMO / Action 63
HAMILTON, DAVE
91/2 7th...Sketch WHL 51
HAMILTON, GORD
94/5 Slapshot / Sarnia 28
82/3 Ottawa 67's
83/4 Ottawa 67's
HAMILTON, GORD (JR.)
83/4 Ottawa 67's
HAMILTON, HUGH
97 Bowman 83
94/5 Parkie SE253
94/5 Sig. Rookies 16, ✍ 16
96/7 UD Ice 124
98/9 Florida Everblades
99/0 Florida Everblades
00/1 Florida Everblades
95/6 Spokane Chiefs 3
HAMILTON, JACK
52/3 Laval Dairy Update 65
52/3 St. Lawrence 101
HAMILTON, JIM
77/8 PITT / McDonald's
83/4 PITT / Coke Is It✂
HAMILTON, LEE
99/0 Charlotte Checkers
00/1 Charlotte Checkers
95/6 Lethbridge Hurricanes
HAMILTON, REG
34-43 BeeHive-1 [Toro.]
37/8 O-Pee-Chee 137
39/0 O-Pee-Chee 1
40/1 O-Pee-Chee 119
38/9 Quaker Oats
HAMILTON, STEVE
93/4 N. Michigan Wildcats
HAMM, TRENT
91/2 Air Canada SJHL 6
91/2 Air Canada SJHL C14
HAMMAR, JAN
98/9 UD Elitserien 156
99/0 UD Elitserien 159
00/1 UD Elitserien 149
HAMMARSTROM, PETER
99/0 Eishockey 71
HAMMARSTRÖM, INGE
72 Hellas MM-Jenkki 37
74/5 Loblaws
74/5 O-Pee-Chee 88
75/6 O-Pee-Chee 168
76/7 O-Pee-Chee 358
77/8 O-Pee-Chee 320
78/9 O-Pee-Chee 53
72 Panda MM-Toronto
72 Semic Sticker 61
74/5 Topps 88
75/6 Topps 168
78/9 Topps 53
71/2 Williams Finnish 44
72/3 Williams Finnish 44
73/4 Williams Finnish 26
78/9 SLOU
73/4 TORO
74/5 TORO
75/6 TORO
76/7 TORO
77/8 TORO
HAMMARSTRÖM, PETER
94/5 Leaf Elit Set 88
95/6 Leaf Elit Set 52
89/0 Semic Elitserien 18
90/1 Semic Elitserien 90
91/2 Semic Elitserien 14
92/3 Semic Elitserien 38
95/6 UD Elitserien 85
97/8 UD Elitserien 12
98/9 UD Elitserien 11
HAMMER, ROLF
94/5 DEL 189
95/6 DEL 189
96/7 DEL 128
HAMMILL, JESSIE
02/3 Peterborough Phantoms
HAMMOND, BRYAN
01/2 Peterborough Petes
HAMMOND, KEN
92/3 Parkhurst 358
91/2 Pro Set 484
92/3 Pro Set PV4
89/0 ProCards AHL 128
90/1 ProCards 141
91/2 Score 97T
91/2 Score CAN 647
88/9 EDMO / Action 52
91/2 SANJ / Sports Action
94/5 Kansas City Blades 2
95/6 Kansas City Blades
HAMMOND, RUSS
99/0 Guelph Storm
01/2 Guelph Storm
01/2 Guelph Storm M-Cup
HAMMOND, SCOTT
82/3 Ottawa 67's
83/4 Ottawa 67's
HAMPEIS, LADA
99/0 Anchorage Aces
93/4 Tacoma Rockets
HAMPSON, TED
45-64 BeeHive-2 [Toro.]
45-64 BeeHive-2 [NYRa.]
64-67 BeeHive-3 [Detr.]
70/1 Colgate 9
70/1 Dad's Cookies
70/1 Eddie Sargent 137
71/2 Eddie Sargent 94
70/1 Esso Power Player
62/3 Cowan Tile
68/9 O-Pee-Chee 85
69/0 O-Pee-Chee 86
69/0 O-Pee-Chee 4in1
69/0 O-Pee-Chee Stamp
70/1 O-Pee-Chee 190
71/2 O-Pee-Chee 101
59/0 Parkhurst 34
95/6 Parkie 66-67 47
73/4 Quaker Oats 4
72 Semic Sticker 176
60/1 Shirriff 98
61/2 Shirriff 92
68/9 Shirriff / Oakl. 3
61/2 Topps 59
62/3 Topps 55
67/8 Topps 108
68/9 Topps 85
69/0 Topps 86
71/2 Topps 101
71/2 Toronto Sun Photo
63/4 York 52
72/3 Minn. Fight. Saints
74/5 Minn. Fight. Saints
HAMPTON, RICK
74/5 Loblaws
74/5 O-Pee-Chee 329
75/6 O-Pee-Chee 65
76/7 O-Pee-Chee 113
76/7 OPC 383
77/8 O-Pee-Chee 63
78/9 O-Pee-Chee 174
79/0 O-Pee-Chee 330
79 Panini Sticker 54
75/6 Topps 65
76/7 Topps 113
77/8 Topps 63
78/9 Topps 174
HAMR, RADEK
95/6 APS 276
96/7 APS 128, 388
92/3 Classic Prospects 142
93/4 Cla. Prospects 87
96/7 DS Sticker 57
93/4 Leaf 265
01/2 OFS 17
93/4 Parkhurst 143
93/4 Score 476
93/4 Upper Deck 34
98/9 UD Elitserien 71
99/0 UD Elitserien 57
00/1 UD Elitserien 81, 192, 214
92/3 OTTA
94/5 Fort Wayne Komets 19
HAMRLA, ROBERT
97/8 APS 54
98/9 OFS 332
99/0 Score 144
HAMRLIK, MARTIN
91/2 Classic 27
91/2 Classic Four Sport 27
92/3 Classic Prospects 62
98/9 DS 109
99/0 DS 4
00/1 DS 53
97/8 DS Sticker 291
98/9 OFS 21
99/0 OFS 453, 513
00/1 OFS 354
01/2 OFS 83, -UHI 1
91/2 Star Pics 18
94/5 Peoria Rivermen
95/6 Peoria Rivermen
HAMRLIK, PAVEL
97/8 APS 59
HAMRLIK, PETER
00/1 UD Prospects 7
HAMRLIK, ROMAN
96/7 APS 360
98/9 Aurora 73
98/9 Be A Player 52, ✍ Aut. 52
99/0 BAP Mem. 254
00/1 BAP Mem. 117, 492
01/2 BAP Memor. 180
96/7 Bic.Sports Aces 3-S
97/8 Bicycle 6-Diamond
98 Bonaparte 8C
98 Bonaparte Pexeso 27
95/6 Bowman 82
92/3 CSC 5
92/3 Classic 1
92/3 Classic 60
92/3 Classic LP1
92/3 Classic / Promo
93/4 Classic 120
92/3 Classic Four Sport 151
92/3 Classic Four Sport BC7
92/3 Classic Four Sport LP22
92/3 Classic Four Sport / Promo PR3
92/3 Classic Prospects 50
92/3 Classic Prospects BC3
93/4 Donruss 327
94/5 Donruss 128
95/6 Donruss 256
96/7 Donruss 84, HL-16
97/8 Donruss 112
96/7 Do. Canadian 44
97/8 Do. Canadian 123
95/6 Do. Elite 36
96/7 Do. Elite 23
97/8 Do. Elite 94
97/8 Do. Preferred 141
97/8 Do. Priority 120
97/8 Do. Studio 75
99/0 DS 3, NS7
00/1 DS JT4
01/2 DS 44
98/9 Dynagon Ice 73
93/4 EA Sports 128
97/8 Esso 53
96/7 Flair 88
94/5 Fleer 207
96/7 Fleer 104
95/6 Fleer Metal 137, IS-6
96/7 Fl. Picks F50-16, DL-6
92/3 Fleer Ultra 201, -UI 4
93/4 Fleer Ultra 108
94/5 Fleer Ultra 206
95/6 Fleer Ultra 152, HS-9, RS-3
96/7 Fl. Ultra 157, PL-4, UP-6
95 Globe 149
93/4 Leaf 151
94/5 Leaf 132
95/6 Leaf 295
96/7 Leaf 118
97/8 Leaf 76
95/6 L. Limited 33
96/7 L. Limited 4
96/7 L. Preferred 90, LS-44
97/8 Limited 146
96/7 Metal Univ. 145
92/3 OPC Premier 46
92/3 OPC Premier TR2
98/9 OFS 232, OW 15
99/0 OFS 208
00/1 OFS 382
97/8 Omega 92
98/9 Omega 93
98/9 Pacific 219
99/0 Pacific 156
00/1 Pacific 167
01/2 Pacific 248
02/3 Pacific 236
02/3 Pacific Complete 336
97/8 Pacific CC 100
97/8 Pa. Crown Roy. 125
97/8 Pa. Dynagon 118, T-61
97/8 Pa. Invincible 132
97/8 Pa. Paramount 173
98/9 Pa. Paramount 87
97/8 Pa. Revolution 53
94/5 Panini Sticker 188
95/6 Panini Sticker 133
96/7 Panini Sticker 123
97/8 Panini Sticker 101
98/9 Panini Sticker 196
99/0 Panini Sticker 246
00/1 Panini Sticker 161
95 Panini Worlds 192
92/3 Parkhurst 173
92/3 Parkhurst 443
93/4 Parkhurst 190
93/4 Parkhurst F2
94/5 Parkhurst V53
95/6 Parkhurst 198, PP-25
00/1 Parkhurst P-90, P-214
01/2 Parkhurst 176
02/3 Parkhurst Retro 161
94/5 Parkie SE171
92/3 Pinnacle 408
93/4 Pinnacle 34
93/4 Pinnacle T2K1 18
94/5 Pinnacle 123
95/6 Pinnacle 59
96/7 Pinnacle 178
97/8 Pinnacle 175
97/8 Pi. Be A Player 147, ✍ Aut. 147
95/6 Pi. FANtasy 11
97/8 Pi. Inside 162
95/6 Pi. Summit 56
96/7 Pi. Summit 132
96/7 Pi. Zenith 92
95/6 Playoff 310
96/7 Playoff 416
95/6 POG 255
93/4 Power Play 231
93/4 Premier 281
93/4 Premier 323
93/4 Premier - Finest 2
94/5 Premier 54
95/6 Pro Magnet 67
93/4 Score 131
94/5 Score 48
95/6 Score 185
96/7 Score 127
97/8 Score 214
99/0 Score JT20
95/6 Select CE 20
96/7 Select CE 48
93 Semic Sticker 101
00/1 Signature 197
01/2 Signature 43, ✍ Aut. 43
02/3 Signature GS-78
95/6 SBx Emotion 164
95/6 SBx Impact 155
96/7 SBx Impact 122
94/5 SP 112
95/6 SP 135, É25
96/7 SP 144, HC-22
97/8 SP Authentic 149
02/3 Sports Vault 79
96/7 SPx 42
00/1 Stadium 221
95/6 Super Sticker 112, DC-20
96/7 Team Out✂
95/6 Topps 193, YS13
99/0 Topps 110
99/0 To. Chrome 110
95/6 To. Finest 93
00/1 To. Heritage 171
96/7 Topps Picks 35, FT9
93/4 To. Stadium 75
95/6 To. Stadium 89
94/5 TSC Members Only 11
95/6 TSC Members Only 37
02/3 T. Total 147
98/9 UD Choice 80
00/1 UD Reserve 54
02/3 Ultimate Mem. ✂ FO
92/3 Upper Deck 555
92/3 Upper Deck 631
92/3 Upper Deck CC8
92/3 Upper Deck ER11
93/4 Upper Deck 158, SP-151
94/5 Upper Deck 174, SP-164
95/6 Upper Deck 152, AS-8, H-39, SE-76
96/7 Upper Deck 153, 367, X8, SS13A
97/8 Upper Deck 157, 363, SG47
98/9 Upper Deck 96
00/1 Upper Deck 338
01/2 Upper Deck 339
02/3 Upper Deck 108
94/5 UD BAP R9
95/6 UD BAP 133, ✍ S133
96/7 UD Black Diam. 143
97/8 UD Black Diam. 142
95/6 UD CC 92
96/7 UD CC 244, 331, UD25, S18
97/8 UD Coll. Choice 240, SQ44
91/2 Upper Deck WJC 88
98/9 UD G. Reserve 96
96/7 UD Ice 102
98/9 UD MVP 83
01/2 UD MVP 119
00/1 UD Pros&Prosp. 55
00/1 UD Vintage 227
01/2 UD Vintage 161, 165
02/3 UD Vintage 155
99/0 Victory 116
01/2 Victory 221
92/3 TAMP / Sheraton Inn
94/5 TAMP / Sky Box
95/6 TAMP / Sky Box
HAMWAY, MARK
84/5 Springfield Indians 18
HANAS, TREVOR
91/2 7th...Sketch WHL 218
96/7 Peoria Rivermen
97/8 Peoria Rivermen
98/9 Topeka Scarecrows
99/0 Topeka Scarecrows
95/6 Lethbridge Hurricanes
93/4 Saskatoon Blades
HANCHUCK, TYLER
99/0 Brampton Batallion 5
HANCOCK, QUINN
98 Bowman 57
98 Bowman Chrome 57
02/3 Cardset 170
99/0 Muskegon Fury
98/9 Peoria Rivermen
HAND, TONY
00/1 Kudos 16
94 Semic 323
02/3 Dundee Texol Stars
01/2 Sheffield Steelers
95/6 Sheffield Steelers
97/8 Sheffield Steelers
HANDLEY, PETE
82/3 North Bay Centennials
HANDRICK, JORG
99/0 Eishockey 333
HANDRICK, JÖRG
95/6 DEL 259
96/7 DEL 147
98/9 DEL 72
95 Panini Worlds 69
00/1 UD DEL 181
HANDY, RON
88/9 ProCards / Indianapolis
89/0 ProCards IHL 140
90/1 ProCards 582
91/2 ProCards 513
90/1 Kansas City Blades
95/6 Louisiana Ice Gators
95/6 Louisiana Ice Gators-2
96/7 Louisiana Ice Gators
92/3 Peoria Rivermen
84/5 Springfield Indians 14
94/5 Sheffield Steelers 16
82/3 Kingston Canadians
80/1 Soo Greyhounds
HANDZUS, MICHAL
01/2 Adrenaline 148
00/1 Aurora 121
00/1 BAP Mem. 198
01/2 BAP Memor. 241
02/3 BAP Memorabilia 261 [w/ Boucher]
98/9 Bowman's Best 132
98/9 Dynagon Ice 158
02/3 Exclusive ✂ GWJ 19
02/3 Heads Up ✂ GWQ 21
99/0 NHL Power Play
01/2 O-Pee-Chee 188
02/3 O-Pee-Chee 69
99/0 Pacific 357
00/1 Pacific 344
01/2 Pacific 303
02/3 Pacific 295
02/3 Pacific Complete 234
00/1 Pa. Paramount 205
99/0 Panini Sticker 294
00/1 Panini Sticker 197
00/1 Parkhurst P-187
01/2 Parkhurst 152
01/2 PS Titanium ✂ DSJ 72
01/2 PS Titanium Draft ✂ 73
02/3 PS Titanium ✂ GWJ 50
00/1 Revolution 122
00/1 Signature 39, ✍ Aut. 144
02/3 Signature 88, ✍ 88
98/9 SP Authentic 108
01/2 SP Authentic 66
00/1 SP GU ✂ TotG
00/1 Stadium 73
99/0 Topps 191
00/1 Topps 164
01/2 Topps 188
02/3 Topps 69
99/0 To. Chrome 191
00/1 To. Heritage 180
02/3 T. Limited 69
02/3 T. Total 318
01/2 UD PlayMakers Ltd 75
98/9 Upper Deck 363
99/0 Upper Deck 286
00/1 Upper Deck 384
01/2 Upper Deck 135
02/3 Upper Deck 374
01/2 UD Challenge 64
98/9 UD G. Reserve 363
99/0 UD G. Reserve 286
00/1 UD Ice ✂ IGJ-MH
01/2 UD Mask 74
98/9 UD MVP 182
99/0 UD MVP 189
01/2 UD MVP 148
00/1 UD Vintage 313
01/2 UD Vintage 194, 199
99/0 Victory 265
00/1 Victory 206
01/2 Victory 268
99/0 SLOU / Taco Bell 9
HANEY, MERV
91/2 7th...Sketch WHL 251
91/2 Prince Albert Raiders
93/4 Prince Albert Raiders
HANFT, JÖRG
95/6 DEL 271, 436
89 Semic Sticker 111
HANGSLEBEN, AL
79/0 O-Pee-Chee 307
81/2 O-Pee-Chee 354
81/2 OPC Sticker 197
80/1 WASH
HANIG, GUSTAV
72 Hellas MM-Jenkki 53
72 Semic Sticker 108
HANISZ, ANDREI
94/5 DEL 361
89 Semic Sticker 129
92 Semic Sticker 267
HANKELA, TIMO
93/4 Jyvas Hyva 284
93/4 Sisu 59
HANKINSON, BEN
93/4 Pinnacle 210
91/2 ProCards 413
95/6 TAMP / Sky Box
95/6 Adirondack Red Wings
96/7 Grand Rapids Griffins
HANKINSON, CASEY
95/6 Do. Elite WJ 36
01/2 SP Authentic 140
01/2 SPx 100
01/2 SPx Rookie RR7
01/2 Upper Deck 184
01/2 UD Ice 49
01/2 UD MVP 194
01/2 UD Top Shelf 50
01/2 Victory 366
99/0 Cleveland Lumberjacks
01/2 Norfolk Admirals
98/9 Portland Pirates
94/5 Minnesota G'Gophers
HANKINSON, PETER
90/1 ProCards 254, 547
91/2 ProCards 239
92/3 Fort Wayne Komets 12
90/1 Moncton Hawks
92/3 San Diego Gulls
HANKKIO, GREG
85/6 Kitchener Rangers
86/7 London Knights
HANLEY, BILL
83&87 HHOF 251
HANLEY, TIM
89/0 ProCards AHL 238
95/6 Roanoke Express
91/2 L. Superior State Lakers
HANLON, GLEN
79/0 O-Pee-Chee 337
80/1 O-Pee-Chee 141
81/2 O-Pee-Chee 336
84/5 O-Pee-Chee 142
85/6 OPC/Topps 149
87/8 OPC/Topps 89
88/9 OPC/Topps 150
90/1 OPC/Topps 266
89/0 OPC/Topps 144
87/8 OPC Leaders 14
81/2 OPC Sticker 245
84/5 OPC Sticker 98
85/6 OPC Sticker 87-220
87/8 OPC Sticker 109-242
80/1 O-Pee-Chee Super 22
87/8 Panini Sticker 238
88/9 Panini Sticker 36
89/0 Panini Sticker 61, 65
90/1 Panini Sticker 203
90/1 Pro Set 72
90/1 ProCards 305
90/1 Score 228
83/4 Souhaits Keychain [NYR]
80/1 Topps 141
84/5 Topps 106
90/1 Upper Deck 395
86/7 DETR / Little Caesars
87/8 DETR / Little Caesars
88/9 DETR / Little Caesars
88/9 DETR / S.A.M.
89/0 DETR / Little Caesars
78/9 VANC / Royal Bank
79/0 VANC / Royal Bank
80/1 VANC
80/1 VANC / Silverwood
81/2 VANC
81/2 VANC / Silverwood
99/0 Portland Pirates
HANLON, JAMES
94/5 DEL 244
95/6 DEL 229
96/7 DEL 80
00/1 Kudos 60
HANNA, JOHN
63/4 Québec Aces
65/6 Québec Aces
HANNA, JOHN B.
88/9 ProCards / Cape Breton
83/4 Ottawa 67's
84/5 Ottawa 67's
HANNA, JOHN*
45-64 BeeHive-2 [Mont.]
64-67 BeeHive-3 [Mont.]
60/1 Shirriff 85
58/9 Topps 7
59/0 Topps 31
59/0 Topps 53
72/3 Cleveland Crusaders
HANNAH, ANDY
97/8 Guildford Flames
HANNAH, BILL
59/60 Whitby Dunlops
HANNAN, DAVE
91/2 Bowman 155
83/4 O-Pee-Chee 281
90/1 O-Pee-Chee 449
91/2 O-Pee-Chee 360
89/0 O-Pee-Chee 257
87/8 Panini Sticker 154
90/1 Panini/TOR 8
91/2 Pinnacle 413
94/5 Pinnacle 446
94/5 Premier 118
90/1 Pro Set 535
91/2 Score CAN 241
92/3 Score 538
83/4 Souhaits Keychain [Penguins]
91/2 To. Stadium 220
93/4 To. Stadium 47
91/2 Upper Deck 312
92/3 BUFF / Blue Shield
87/8 EDMO
88/9 EDMO / Action 83
96/7 OTTA
83/4 PITT / Coke Is It✂
83/4 PITT / Heinz
86/7 PITT / Kodak
91/2 TORO / P.L.A.Y. 8
HANNAN, SCOTT
99 Bowman 117
98/9 Dynagon Ice 166
99/0 Pacific 385
02/3 Pacific Complete 333
92 Québec Pee Wee 1015
00/1 Topps 278
00/1 To. Chrome 173
98/9 Upper Deck 353
99/0 Upper Deck 112
02/3 Upper Deck 395
98/9 UD G. Reserve 353
99/0 UD G. Reserve 112
99/0 UD MVP 180
99/0 Victory 249
00/1 Victory 278
99/0 Kentucky Tho'blades
98/9 Kelowna Rockets
HANNIGAN, GORD
45-64 BeeHive-2 [Toro.]
52/3 Parkhurst 54
53/4 Parkhurst 3
54/5 Parkhurst 27
45-54 Quaker Oats
HANNIGAN, PAT
61/2 Shirriff 83
68/9 Shirriff / Phil. 12
61/2 Topps 58
62/3 Topps 64
HANNON, BRIAN
94/5 DEL 170
95/6 DEL 120
89/0 ProCards IHL 136
HANSCH, RANDY
90/1 ProCards 490
85/6 Kamloops Blazers
83/4 Victoria Cougars
84/5 Victoria Cougars
HANSEN,
92/3 Semic Nordisk 213 [Rookie]
HANSEN, BENT
79 Panini Sticker 363
HANSEN, FRODE
92/3 Semic Nordisk 47
HANSEN, JUSTIN
99/0 Prince George Cougars
HANSEN, KEVIN
95/6 Slapshot 388
96/7 Sudbury Wolves
HANSEN, LARS
92/3 Semic Nordisk 232
HANSEN, RENE
92/3 Semic Nordisk 58
HANSEN, RONNY
89/0 Semic Elitserien 261
90/1 Semic Elitserien 169
HANSEN, RUNE
92/3 Semic Nordisk 168
92/3 Semic Nordisk 70
HANSEN, TAVIS
95/6 Edge Ice 69
95/6 Leaf 214
00/1 Topps 305
00/1 To. Chrome 200
96/7 Springfield Falcons
97/8 Springfield Falcons
93/4 Tacoma Rockets
HANSIS, RON
94/5 Erie Panthers
HANSON, DAVE
82/3 Indianapolis Checkers
HANSON, DEVON
93/4 Saskatoon Blades
HANSON, GREG
93/4 Minnesota-Duluth
HANSON, KEITH
84/5 Moncton G'Flames
HANSON, MATT
91/2 L. Superior State Lakers
HANSON, MICHAEL
95/6 Slapshot 342
HANSON, TOM
85/6 Minnesota-Duluth 13
HANSSEN, THOMAS
92/3 Semic Nordisk 230
HANSSON, JOHAN
97/8 UD Elitserien 21
98/9 UD Elitserien 36
HANSSON, MAGNUS
94/5 Leaf Elit Set 62
HANSSON, PATRIK
93/4 N. Michigan Wildcats
HANSSON, ROGER
96/7 DEL 236
98/9 DEL 50
99/0 Eishockey 176
95 Globe 32
94/5 Leaf Elit Set 207, GC-20
95/6 Leaf Elit Set 93
95 Panini Worlds 158
95 Semic 65
91/2 Semic Elitserien 194
92/3 Semic Elitserien 211
93 Semic Sticker 18
95/6 UD Elitserien 144
HANTSCHKE, RALF
94/5 DEL 263
98/9 DEL 151
99/0 Eishockey 89
91 Semic Sticker 169
HANUS, TIM
93/4 Johnstown Chiefs 8
HANUSCH, TORSTEN
94/5 DEL 129
95/6 DEL 127
HANWOOD, STEVE
02/3 Owen Sound Attack
HANZAL, MARCEL
99/0 OFS 306
HANZAWA, TSUTOMU
79 Panini Sticker 291
HANZLIK, JAN
00/1 OFS 301
01/2 OFS 97
HANZLIK, JIRI
95/6 APS 248
96/7 APS 295
97/8 APS 177
99/0 DS 90
00/1 DS 30
96/7 DS Sticker 213
97/8 DS Sticker 153
98/9 OFS 37
99/0 OFS 122, 475
00/1 OFS 62
01/2 OFS 204
HÄPPOLÄ, TONI
02/3 Cardset 179
HARALDSEN, HARRY
79 Panini Sticker 299
HARANT, TOMAS
00/1 OFS 222
HARAZIM, MAREK
96/7 APS 117
99/0 Score 105
HARBARUK, NICK
70/1 Eddie Sargent 172
71/2 Eddie Sargent 171
72/3 Eddie Sargent 171
70/1 Esso Power Player
71/2 O-Pee-Chee 191
72/3 O-Pee-Chee 106
75/6 OPC WHA 11
71/2 Toronto Sun Photo
71/2 PITT / Sportcolor
73/4 SLOU
HÅRD, VELI-PEKKA
98/9 Cardset 77
00/1 Cardset 346
92/3 Jyvas Hyva 82
93/4 Jyvas Hyva 141
93/4 Sisu 141
94/5 Sisu 36
95/6 Sisu 341
HARDER, GRAEME
91/2 Avant Garde BCJHL 21
92/3 BCJHL 67
HARDER, MIKE
91/2 Air Canada SJHL C35
92/3 MPS SJHL 145
99/0 Hartford Wolf Pack
97/8 Milwaukee Admirals
98/9 Rochester Americans
HARDILL, CHRIS
01/2 Kingston Frontenacs 6
HARDING, D.J.
98/9 Huntington Blizzard
HARDING, JEFF
88/9 ProCards / Hershey
HARDING, JOSH
02/3 BAP Memorabilia 369
02/3 UD Rookie 123
01/2 Regina Pats
HARDING, MIKE
00/1 Kudos 18
90/1 7th..Sketch OHL 360
91/2 7th...Sketch OHL 136
93/4 Slapshot / Detroit 12
93/4 Slapshot / Peterborough
93/4 Slapshot / Peterborough
96/7 Richmond Renegades
97/8 Guildford Flames
91/2 Peterborough Petes
93/4 N. Michigan Wildcats
HARDY, BRUCE
94/5 DEL 73
95/6 DEL 136
HARDY, DAMON
93/4 Slapshot / Oshawa 7
94/5 Slapshot / Sarnia 23
HARDY, JOE
70/1 Esso Power Player
72/3 Cleveland Crusaders
HARDY, MARK
92/3 Fleer Ultra 354
93/4 Fleer Ultra 343
82/3 O-Pee-Chee 155
83/4 O-Pee-Chee 155
84/5 O-Pee-Chee 86
91/2 O-Pee-Chee 406
89/0 O-Pee-Chee 252
84/5 OPC Sticker 272
85/6 OPC Sticker 234-102
87/8 Panini Sticker 275
91/2 Pinnacle 420
92/3 Pinnacle 220
82/3 Post [LosA.]
90/1 Pro Set 489
91/2 Pro Set 442
90/1 Score 104T
91/2 Score CAN 453
92/3 Score 247
93/4 Score 415
83/4 Souhaits Keychain [Kings]
93/4 To. Stadium 414
90/1 Upper Deck 416
84/5 LOSA / Smokey 8
87/8 LOSA
88/9 MINS / ADA
89/0 NYRA / Marine
93/4 Phoenix Roadrunners
HARE, RYAN
99/0 UD Prospects 72
HARFAOUI, NORDIN
98/9 DEL 284
HARGRAVES, JIM
72/3 VANC / Royal Bank
HARIKKALA, JAAKKO
98/9 Cardset 164
99/0 Cardset 81
02/3 Cardset 23
HARILA, KARI
99/0 Cardset 330
92/3 Jyvas Hyva 174
93/4 Jyvas Hyva 325
94 Semic 9
93 Semic Sticker 50
93/4 Sisu 36
95/6 Sisu 125
98/9 UD Elitserien 151
HARJU, ERKKI
65/6 Hellas 45
HARJU, MATTI
66/7 Champion 24
65/6 Hellas 70
70/1 Kuvajulkaisut 103
HARJU, PENTTI
66/7 Champion 116
HARJULA, TUOMO
00/1 Cardset 182
HARJUMÄKI, JARI
93/4 Sisu 62
94/5 Sisu 358
HARKANEN, TIMO
80/1 Mallasjuoma 72
HARKINS, BRETT
94/5 Classic ✍ Aut.
93/4 Cla. Prospects 221
95/6 Leaf 303
97/8 Pa. Invincible R-12
97/8 Cleveland Lumberjacks
98/9 Cleveland Lumberjacks
99/0 Cleveland Lumberjacks
96/7 Providence Bruins
01/2 Syracuse Crunch
87/8 Brockville Braves
HARKINS, TODD
92/3 Classic 113
98/9 DEL 208
99/0 Eishockey 209
90/1 ProCards 624
91/2 ProCards 589
93/4 Upper Deck 80
92/3 Salt Lake G'Eagles
HÄRKÖNEN, MARKO
94/5 Sisu 332
HÄRKÖNEN, TIMO
71/2 Williams Finnish 321
HARLOCK, DAVID
93/4 Canada Nationals
93/4 Cla. Prospects IA4
93/4 Cla. Prospects LP13
93/4 Donruss 496
93/4 Fleer Ultra 461
93/4 Power Play 481
94/5 Score CT15
94 Semic 102
00/1 Signature 114, ✍ Aut. 141
01/2 To. Reserve 89
99/0 Ult. Victory 4
90/1 Upper Deck 470
02/3 Philadelphia Phantoms
97/8 Portland Pirates
94/5 St. John's Maple Leafs
95/6 St. John's Maple Leafs
HARLOW, SCOTT
88/9 ProCards / Peoria
89/0 ProCards AHL 66
90/1 ProCards 421
86/7 Sherb. Canadiens 18
HARLTON, TYLER
99/0 St. John's Maple Leafs
00/1 St. John's Maple Leafs
HARMER, DUANE
98/9 EBK ECHL All-Star
91/2 7th...Sketch OHL 345
93/4 Slapshot / Detroit 18
93/4 Slapshot / Guelph 8
94/5 Slapshot / Detroit Jr. 21
94/5 Slapshot Memorial 95
01/2 Florida Everblades
95/6 Roanoke Express
96/7 Roanoke Express 6
HARMON, GLEN
45-64 BeeHive-2 [Mont.]
51/2 Laval Dairy 86
52/3 Laval Dairy Update 86
43-47 Parade Sportive
45-54 Quaker Oats
52/3 St. Lawrence 2
HARNEY, JOE
98/9 Providence Bruins
HARNEY, JUSTIN
00/1 Charlotte Checkers
HARPER, DERREK
91/2 Avant Garde BCJHL 76
92/3 BCJHL 87
92/3 BCJHL 90
HARPER, KELLY
94/5 Huntington Blizzard
98/9 Huntington Blizzard
99/0 Huntington Blizzard
93/4 Michigan State
HARPER, REGAN
97/8 New Mexico Scorpions
HARPER, STEVE
87/8 Brockville Braves
88/9 Brockville Braves
HARPER, TERRY
45-64 BeeHive-2 [Mont.]
64-67 BeeHive-3 [Mont.]
64-67 BeeHive-3 [Mont.]
63-65 Chex
64/5 Coke/Sprite [Mont.]
65/6 Coca-Cola
70/1 Dad's Cookies
70/1 Eddie Sargent 111
71/2 Eddie Sargent 107
72/3 Eddie Sargent 96
70/1 Esso Power Player
74/5 Loblaws
68/9 O-Pee-Chee 57
69/0 O-Pee-Chee 164
70/1 O-Pee-Chee 53
71/2 O-Pee-Chee 59
72/3 O-Pee-Chee 172
73/4 O-Pee-Chee 80
74/5 O-Pee-Chee 55
75/6 O-Pee-Chee 255
76/7 O-Pee-Chee 262
77/8 O-Pee-Chee 16
78/9 O-Pee-Chee 214
63/4 Parkhurst 32
63/4 Parkhurst 91
95/6 Parkie 66-67 66
94/5 Parkie Tall 83
68/9 Post Marble
68/9 Shirriff / Mont. 12
64/5 Topps 3
65/6 Topps 68
66/7 Topps 68
67/8 Topps 6
68/9 Topps 57
70/1 Topps 53
71/2 Topps 59
72/3 Topps 119
73/4 Topps 80
74/5 Topps 55
75/6 Topps 255
76/7 Topps 262
77/8 Topps 16
78/9 Topps 214
71/2 Toronto Sun Photo
63/4 York 31
67/8 York
67/8 York
66/7 MONT / IGA Stamp
67/8 MONT
67/8 MONT / IGA Card
68/9 MONT / IGA Card
69/0 MONT / Pro Star
70/1 MONT
71/2 MONT / Pro Star
HARPER, TRENT
92/3 MPS SJHL 74
HARPER, WARREN
88/9 ProCards / Hershey
HARPWOOD, MATT
01/2 Kitchener Rangers
02/3 Mississauga IceDogs
HARRELL, JOE
99/0 Odessa Jackalopes
HARRIGAN, JERRY
93/4 Owen Sound Platers
HARRINGTON, BILL
52/3 Anonymous 112
86/7 Kamloops Blazers
87/8 Kamloops Blazers
HARRINGTON, HUGO
25-27 Anonymous 36
HARRINGTON, JOHN
80 Olympic USA
94/5 SR Miracle 13,14, ✍ 11,12
HARRINGTON, NATHAN
00/1 Sudbury Wolves 14
HARRIS, BILLY
02/3 Parkie - Reprint 221, 224, 236, 249, 262, 270
HARRIS, BILLY E. (HINKY)
45-64 BeeHive-2 [Toro.]
64-67 BeeHive-3 [Toro.]
64-67 BeeHive-3 [Toro.]
64-67 BeeHive-3 [Detr.]
63-65 Chex
65/6 Coca-Cola
62/3 Cowan Tile
68/9 O-Pee-Chee 80
55/6 Parkhurst 20
57/8 Parkhurst [Toro.] 15
58/9 Parkhurst 4
59/0 Parkhurst 9
60/1 Parkhurst 15
61/2 Parkhurst 15
62/3 Parkhurst 1
63/4 Parkhurst 11
63/4 Parkhurst 71
93/4 Parkhurst PR39
93/4 Parkie 56-57 129
94/5 Parkie Tall 126
60/1 Shirriff 8
61/2 Shirriff 54
62/3 Shirriff 13
68/9 Shirriff / Oakl. 4
64/5 Topps 27
65/6 Topps 53
68/9 Topps 80
58/9 Toronto Star Photo
64/5 Toronto Star Action
59/0 Toronto Star Weekend
91/2 Ultimate Original Six 35, ✍ Aut. 35
60/1 York Glass [Toro.]
60/1 York
61/2 York 15
62/3 York Transfer 26
63/4 York 10
80/1 EDMO / Zellers
81/2 EDMO / Red Rooster
81/2 EDMO / West Mall
88/9 EDMO / Action 104
64/5 TORO
HARRIS, BILLY H.
72/3 Eddie Sargent 131
75/6 Hockey Heroes
74/5 Lipton Soup 35
74/5 Loblaws
73/4 O-Pee-Chee 130
74/5 O-Pee-Chee 228
74/5 O-Pee-Chee 233
75/6 O-Pee-Chee 242
76/7 O-Pee-Chee 216
76/7 O-Pee-Chee 252
77/8 O-Pee-Chee 126
78/9 O-Pee-Chee 182
79/0 O-Pee-Chee 115
80/1 O-Pee-Chee 46
81/2 O-Pee-Chee 144
82/3 O-Pee-Chee 322
83/4 O-Pee-Chee 333
81/2 OPC Sticker 242
83/4 OPC/Topps Sticker 27
73/4 Topps 130
74/5 Topps 228
74/5 Topps 233
75/6 Topps 242
76/7 Topps 216
76/7 Topps 252
77/8 Topps 126
78/9 Topps 182
79/0 Topps 115
80/1 Topps 46
81/2 Topps 96 [West]
83/4 Vachon 89-66
80/1 LOSA 4
79/0 NYIS
82/3 TORO
83/4 TORO
HARRIS, DARCY
99/0 Québec Citadelles 5
HARRIS, GORD
90/1 7th..Sketch OHL 59
91/2 7th...Sketch OHL 226
HARRIS, HUGH
75/6 OPC WHA 118
76/7 OPC WHA 39
HARRIS, JOE
93/4 Owen Sound Platers
HARRIS, KEITH
91/2 Air Canada SJHL B35
92/3 MPS SJHL 76
HARRIS, KELLY
90/1 7th..Sketch WHL 324
91/2 7th...Sketch WHL 41
HARRIS, KEVIN
99/0 Brandon Wheat Kings
HARRIS, RON
70/1 Eddie Sargent 52
71/2 Eddie Sargent 58
70/1 Esso Power Player
74/5 Loblaws
68/9 O-Pee-Chee 27
69/0 O-Pee-Chee 64
70/1 O-Pee-Chee 23
71/2 O-Pee-Chee 70
72/3 O-Pee-Chee 5
74/5 O-Pee-Chee 276
68/9 Topps 27
70/1 Topps 23
72/3 Topps 138
71/2 Toronto Sun Photo
85/6 QUÉB
85/6 QUÉB / Gene. Foods
HARRIS, ROSS
90/1 7th..Sketch WHL 244
91/2 7th...Sketch WHL 59
99/0 Fort Worth Brahmas
HARRIS, SMOKEY
24/5 Maple Crispette [V130] 7
28/9 Paulins Candy 71
19 Vancouver Millionaires
19 Vancouver Millionaires
24/5 William Paterson 22
HARRIS, TED
68/9 Bauer Photo
71/2 Bazooka Panel
64-67 BeeHive-3 [Mont.]
64/5 Coke/Sprite [Mont.]
65/6 Coca-Cola
70/1 Dad's Cookies
70/1 Eddie Sargent 82
71/2 Eddie Sargent 91
72/3 Eddie Sargent 109
70/1 Esso Power Player

72/3 Post 24
68/9 O-Pee-Chee 162
69/0 O-Pee-Chee 2
69/0 O-Pee-Chee 219
70/1 O-Pee-Chee 166
71/2 O-Pee-Chee 32
72/3 O-Pee-Chee 118
73/4 O-Pee-Chee 154
95/6 Parkie 66-67 63
94/5 Parkie Tall 78
68/9 Post Marble
68/9 Shirriff / Mont. 3
65/6 Topps 5
66/7 Topps 69
66/7 Topps / Test 41
67/8 Topps 10
69/0 Topps 2
71/2 Topps 32
72/3 Topps 23
73/4 Topps 14
71/2 Toronto Sun Photo
67/8 York
67/8 York 33
70/1 MINS / Colour
66/7 MONT / IGA Stamp
67/8 MONT
67/8 MONT / IGA Card
68/9 MONT / IGA Card
69/0 MONT / Pro Star

HARRIS, TIM
92/3 BCJHL 149
91/2 ProCards 587
92/3 Salt Lake G'Eagles

HARRIS, TODD
90 7th..Sketch Mem.Cup 15
90/1 7th..Sketch WHL 239
91/2 7th...Sketch WHL 307
94/5 Birmingham Bulls
89/0 Kamloops Blazers

HARRISON, BRAD
93/4 Cla. Prospects 236
90/1 7th..Sketch WHL 316
94/5 Erie Panthers
93/4 Huntington Blizzard
89/0 Portland Winter Hawks

HARRISON, BRUCE
98/9 Kelowna Rockets

HARRISON, DAN
96/7 Johnstown Chiefs

HARRISON, ED
45-64 BeeHive-2 [Bost.]

HARRISON, JAY
99/0 UD Prospects 82
00/1 UD Prospects 1, 97
01 UD Prospects GU 16, ✂ TPJ, ✂ TPJS, ✂ JC, ✍ SoT
99/0 Brampton Batallion 22

HARRISON, JIM
70/1 Eddie Sargent 194
71/2 Eddie Sargent 202
70/1 Esso Power Player
70/1 O-Pee-Chee 220
71/2 O-Pee-Chee 10
72/3 O-Pee-Chee 292
72/3 O-Pee-Chee Crest 20
76/7 O-Pee-Chee 183
77/8 O-Pee-Chee 243
75/6 OPC WHA 47
73/4 OPC WHA Poster 11
73/4 Quaker Oats 10
77/8 Topps 243
71/2 Toronto Sun Photo
88/9 EDMO / Action 119
69/0 TORO
70/1 TORO
71/2 TORO

HARRISON, PAUL
78/9 O-Pee-Chee 123
80/1 O-Pee-Chee 391
78/9 Topps 123
78/9 TORO
79/0 TORO
80/1 TORO

HARRISON, RYAN
90/1 7th..Sketch WHL 290
88/9 Kamloops Blazers
89/0 Victoria Cougars

HARRISON, STEVE
88/9 Flint Spirits
88/9 Flint Spirits

HARRISON, THOMAS
01/2 Kitchener Rangers

HARROLD, JOSH
99/0 Mobile Mysticks

HART, ANDRÉ
99/0 Québec Remparts 17
99/0 Rouyn-Noranda

HART, CECIL M.
27/8 La Patrie
27/8 La Presse
37/8 World Wide Gum 97

HART, DAN
84/5 Brandon Wheat Kings

HART, GERRY
72/3 Eddie Sargent 138
75/6 Hockey Heroes
74/5 Loblaws
72/3 O-Pee-Chee 139
73/4 O-Pee-Chee 34
74/5 O-Pee-Chee 199
75/6 O-Pee-Chee 18
76/7 O-Pee-Chee 77
77/8 O-Pee-Chee 162
78/9 O-Pee-Chee 77
79/0 O-Pee-Chee 365
80/1 O-Pee-Chee 349
72/3 Topps 92
73/4 Topps 34
74/5 Topps 199
75/6 Topps 18
76/7 Topps 77
77/8 Topps 162
78/9 Topps 77
71/2 Toronto Sun Photo
93/4 NYIS / Bank

HART, GIZZY
27/8 La Patrie
27/8 La Presse

HART, GREG
94/5 Slapshot Memorial 8
93/4 Kamloops Blazers

HARTIGAN, MARK
01/2 BAP Memor. 436
02/3 First Edition 299
01/2 Parkhurst 302
02/3 SPx 102
02/3 Upper Deck 196
02/3 UD Foundations 123
01/2 UD Mask 134
02/3 UD MVP 191
02/3 UD Vintage 322
02/3 Victory 13
02/3 Chicago Wolves

HARTIN, PENTTI
70/1 Kuvajulkaisut 124

HARTJE, TODD
91/2 ProCards 179
91/2 Upper Deck 568
91/2 Moncton Hawks

HARTLEY, JON
89/0 Windsor Spitfires

HARTMAN, MIKE
98/9 DEL 107
90/1 OPC/Topps 16
91/2 O-Pee-Chee 363
90/1 Panini Sticker 32
92/3 Parkhurst 407
90/1 Pro Set 414
91/2 Pro Set 519
91/2 Score CAN 454
92/3 Topps 518
91/2 To. Stadium 341
92/3 T. Stadium Club 497
87/8 BUFF / Blue Shield
88/9 BUFF / Blue Shield
88/9 BUFF / Won. Bread
89/0 BUFF / Blue Shield
89/0 BUFF / Campbell's
90/1 BUFF / Blue Shield
90/1 BUFF / Campbell's
91/2 WINN / IGA
97/8 Charlotte Checkers
84/5 Belleville Bulls

HARTMANN, EDUARD
94 Semic 191
91 Semic Sticker 104
96 Wien 219

HARTNELL, DEVIN
00/1 Florida Everblades

HARTNELL, ROB
90/1 7th..Sketch WHL 124
91/2 7th...Sketch WHL 340
94/5 Dayton Bombers 9

HARTNELL, SCOTT
01/2 Adrenaline 104
00/1 BAP Mem. 452
01/2 BAP Memor. 182
02/3 BAP Memorabilia 185, 217, ✂ FP17, ✂ FG13
01/2 Bowman 145, ✂ FFJ, ✂ FFS, ✂ FFDS, ✂ FFR, ✍ YSA
00/1 Crown Royale 130
02/3 Exclusive 98
02/3 First Edition 211, 357, 423R
02/3 Heads Up 68, -HF 7
02/3 In The Game-Used ✂ F17
01/2 O-Pee-Chee 140
02/3 O-Pee-Chee 206
01/2 Pacific 217
02/3 Pacific 210
02/3 Pacific Complete 125
00/1 Parkhurst P-160
01/2 Parkhurst 77
02/3 Parkhurst 86, ✂ FP17, ✂ TT10
02/3 Parkhurst Retro 165
00/1 Premier Plus 121, ✍ PS
00/1 Private Stock 129
02/3 Pr. Stock Reserve 58
00/1 PS Titanium 132
01/2 PS Titanium 78
00/1 PS Titanium Draft 132
00/1 Signature 300, ✍ Aut. 237
01/2 Signature 39, ✍ Aut. 39
02/3 Signature 66, GS-83, ✍ 66
00/1 SP Authentic 112, ✍ SotT
01/2 SP Authentic ✍ SotT
02/3 SP Authentic 52, 121
00/1 SP GU 71
02/3 SP Game-Used ✂ PC, ✂ FF, ✍ Sig
00/1 SPx 164
02/3 SPx 44
00/1 Stadium 250
02/3 Stadium 23, ✂ YSS15, ✂ YSD2
01/2 Topps 140
02/3 Topps 206
00/1 To. Chrome 247
01/2 To. Chrome 113
02/3 T. Chrome 116
00/1 To. Gold Label 104, ✍ GLA
00/1 To. Heritage 99
02/3 T. Limited 206
02/3 T. Total 255
00/1 UD Heroes 168
00/1 UD Reserve 100
00/1 Upper Deck 226
02/3 Upper Deck 101, -NC7, ✂ HS, ✂ GJ, ✂✍ SGJ
00/1 UD Black Diam. 124
02/3 UD Classic 55, ✂ HR
00/1 UD Ice 92
01/2 UD Mask 54
01/2 UD MVP ✂ S
02/3 UD MVP 103
02/3 UD Piece 53, ✂ TT
02/3 UD Premier ✍ Sig.
00/1 UD Pros&Prosp. 109, NA3
99/0 UD Prospects 28, 73
02/3 UD Rookie 56
02/3 UD Top Shelf ✂ R, ✂ SH, ✂ ST, ✍ Sig
00/1 UD Vintage 382
02/3 UD Vintage 140, 277, GB 140, T38
00/1 Vanguard 131
01/2 Victory 202
02/3 Victory 117

HARTNETT, TIM
90/1 Michigan Tech Huskies
91/2 Michigan Tech Huskies

HARTOGS, TOMMIE
98/9 DEL 34
99/0 Eishockey 136
00/1 UD DEL 234, ✂ GJ
01/2 UD DEL 125

HARTSBURG, CHRIS
02/3 Albany River Rats

HARTSBURG, CRAIG
83/4 Funmate Puffy 16 [w]
82/3 McDonald's Les Étoiles 30
80/1 O-Pee-Chee 317
81/2 O-Pee-Chee 162
82/3 O-Pee-Chee 167
83/4 O-Pee-Chee 172
84/5 O-Pee-Chee 98
85/6 O-Pee-Chee 242
86/7 OPC/Topps 12
87/8 OPC/Topps 165
88/9 OPC/Topps 159
81/2 OPC Sticker 91
82/3 OPC/Topps Sticker 192
83/4 OPC/Topps Sticker 117
86/7 OPC Sticker 173-36
87/8 OPC Sticker 54
88/9 OPC Sticker 199-70
87/8 Panini Sticker 290
88/9 Panini Sticker 86
82/3 Post [Minn.]
94/5 Slapshot / Guelph 27
83/4 Souhaits Keychain [North Stars]
81/2 Topps 106 [West]
79/0 MINS
80/1 MINS
81/2 MINS
82/3 MINS
83/4 MINS
84/5 MINS
84/5 MINS / 7-Eleven 3
85/6 MINS
85/6 MINS
85/6 MINS / 7-Eleven 8
86/7 MINS / 7-Eleven 7
87/8 MINS
88/9 MINS / ADA
87/8 Soo Greyhounds 21

HARTWICK, MIKE
90/1 7th..Sketch OHL 210
91/2 7th...Sketch OHL 354
92/3 Windsor Spitfires

HARVALA, HARRI
65/6 Hellas 153

HARVEY, ALAIN
94/5 Toledo Storm

HARVEY, DOUG
01/2 ASG History
01/2 BAP Memor. ✂ RM
45-64 BeeHive-2 [Mont.]
45-64 BeeHive-2 [NYRa.]
99/0 Canada Post
02/3 Canada Post
48-52 Exhibits [Canadiens]
62/3 Cowan Tile
83 HHOF Postcard O9
83&87 HHOF 219
02/3 In The Game-Used ✂ VM14
91/2 Kraft 71
51/2 La Patrie
68/9 O-Pee-Chee 1
68/9 O-Pee-Chee PS 14
43-47 Parade Sportive
51/2 Parkhurst 10
52/3 Parkhurst 14
53/4 Parkhurst 26
54/5 Parkhurst 14
54/5 Parkhurst 95
54/5 Parkhurst 98
55/6 Parkhurst 45
55/6 Parkhurst 77
57/8 Parkhurst [Mont.] 1
57/8 Parkhurst [Mont.] 23
58/9 Parkhurst 49
59/0 Parkhurst 8
60/1 Parkhurst 48
92/3 Parkhurst PR-14
93/4 Parkhurst PR40
01/2 Parkhurst HSHS, PR7, PR27, PR41, PR65, PR100, PR115, PR121, PR131, ✂ H7, ✂ PV10, ✂ PV11, ✂ PV12
02/3 Parkhurst ✂ VM8, ✂ VT8
93/4 Parkie 56-57 136
93/4 Parkie 56-57 148
93/4 Parkie 56-57 67
93/4 Parkie 56-57 / Promo 136
45-54 Quaker Oats
63/4 Québec Aces
60/1 Shirriff 26
61/2 Shirriff 81
62/3 Shirriff 45
62/3 Shirriff 60
01/2 SP GU ✍ Sig
61/2 Topps 45
61/2 Topps - Stamp
63/4 Topps 47
57/8 Toronto Star Photo
61/2 Toronto Star Photo
63/4 Toronto Star Action
58/9 Toronto Star Weekend
61/2 Toronto Star Weekend
01/2 Ultimate Mem. ✂ ASGH, ✂ Deca., ✂ Emb., ✂ Glove, ✂ LC, ✂ PP, ✂ RN, ✂ RT, ✂ RA, ✂ SCW
02/3 Ultimate Mem. ✂ BAPL, ✂ EA, ✂ FS, ✂ GAO, ✂ Num, ✂ SF, ✂ VGJ, ✍ Cut
91/2 Ultimate Original Six 12
01/2 Upper Deck ✍ Cut
99/0 UD C. Legends 7, AC5
00/1 UD Legends 65
60/1 York Glass [Mont.]
60/1 York
92/3 MONT / OPC 22

HARVEY, FRED (BUSTER)
70/1 Esso Power Player
74/5 Loblaws
72/3 O-Pee-Chee 246
73/4 O-Pee-Chee 190
74/5 O-Pee-Chee 319
75/6 O-Pee-Chee 298
76/7 O-Pee-Chee 212
77/8 O-Pee-Chee 122
73/4 Topps 78
75/6 Topps 298
76/7 Topps 212
77/8 Topps 122
71/2 Toronto Sun Photo
74/5 ATLF
73/4 MINS

HARVEY, GRAEME
89/0 Soo Greyhounds

HARVEY, GREG
93/4 Prince Albert Raiders

HARVEY, KURT
95/6 Atlanta Knights

HARVEY, LLOYD
23/4 Paulins Candy 11

HARVEY, LUKE
91/2 Ferris State Bulldogs

HARVEY, PAUL
99/0 Louisville Panthers

HARVEY, RENÉ
51/2 Lac St-Jean 15

HARVEY, TODD
99/0 BAP Mem. 176
95/6 Bowman 78
93/4 Classic 9
93/4 Classic - Top Ten DP9
94/5 Classic 40, R7, T16
93/4 Cla. 4 Sport 193
93/4 Donruss CAN15
95/6 Donruss 103, C3TWC-17, PP-20, RT-9
96/7 Donruss 94
97/8 Donruss 98
95/6 Do. Elite 34
97/8 Do. Preferred 144
97/8 Do. Priority 157
94/5 Flair 41
94/5 Fleer 51, RS-4
95/6 Fleer Metal 39
94/5 Fleer Ultra Pros. 2
95/6 Fleer Ultra 37, CC4, HS-10
95/6 Hoyle / West. 6-Spade
94/5 Leaf 467
95/6 Leaf 2, SR-9
96/7 Leaf 145
94/5 L. Limited CAN 4
95/6 L. Limited 26
96/7 L. Preferred 114
97/8 Limited 49
95/6 McDonald's McD-32
98/9 Omega 157
99/0 Omega 206
99/0 Pacific 270
00/1 Pacific 358
02/3 Pacific Complete 382
97/8 Pa. Invincible R-60
99/0 Pa. Paramount 150
98/9 Pa. Revolution 93
95/6 Panini Sticker 169
93/4 Parkhurst 513
95/6 Parkhurst 62
94/5 Parkie SE39, SE206
93/4 Pinnacle 476
94/5 Pinnacle 262, 533, RTP10
95/6 Pinnacle 48
96/7 Pinnacle 52
97/8 Pi. Be A Player 96, ✍ Aut. 96
95/6 Pi. Summit 148, MH-15
96/7 Pi. Summit 46
95/6 Pi. Zenith 75,GG-10
95/6 Playoff 247
94/5 Premier 473
95/6 Pro Magnet 123
94/5 Score 204, TR9
95/6 Score 38
96/7 Score 86
94/5 Select 182
95/6 Select CE 62, CF-7
91/2 7th...Sketch OHL 33
95/6 SBx Emotion 46
95/6 SBx Impact 45, 233
93/4 Slapshot / Detroit 1
94/5 SP 138, P-6
95/6 SP 39
96/7 SP 42
95/6 Topps 356, 10CJ, HGC17, 17NG
99/0 Topps 211
00/1 Topps 94
99/0 To. Chrome 211
94/5 Topps Finest 47, 160, BBR-4
95/6 To. Finest 97
95/6 To. Stadium 103
95/6 T. Super Skills 68
93/4 Upper Deck 535
94/5 Upper Deck 267, 500, 536, 546, SP-109
95/6 Upper Deck 199, SE-114
96/7 Upper Deck 45, P30
97/8 Upper Deck 55
98/9 Upper Deck 323
00/1 Upper Deck 149
01/2 Upper Deck 149
02/3 Upper Deck 149
94/5 UD BAP R162, ✍ 152
94/5 UD Canada Junior 14
95/6 UD CC 251
96/7 UD CC 67, 315
97/8 UD Coll. Choice 75
98/9 UD G. Reserve 323
98/9 UD MVP 138
99/0 UD MVP Cup 159
98/9 NHL Power Play
94/5 DALL / Southwest
96/7 DALL / Southwest
98/9 NYRA

HASANEN, PERTTI
92/3 Jyvas Hyva 154
78/9 SM-Liiga 175
72/3 Williams Finnish 226
73/4 Williams Finnish 259

HASCAK,
97/8 Hockey-Box

HASCAK, MAREK
02/3 Shawinigan Cataractes

HASCAK, OTO
96/7 APS 226

HASCAK, OTTO
94/5 DEL 179
95/6 DEL 181
96/7 DS Sticker 36
90/1 Semic Elitserien 62
91/2 Semic Elitserien 235
91 Semic Sticker 116
96 Wien 155

HASEK, DOMINIK
01/2 Adrenaline 65, BR 4, CL 6, PP 14
95/6 APS 392
97/8 APS 368
01/2 Atomic 36, Stat. 3, TN 6, ✂ GWJ 22
02/3 Atomic ✂ GWJ 6
98/9 Aurora 17, ALC-4, CF-6, FL-1, NC-2, / Cube 3
99/0 Aurora 16, Stripe 16, CC-3, CF-4, CP-3, GU-3, ST-3
00/1 Aurora 19, Pin. 19, CF-3, TPS-2B
98/9 Be A Player 162, ✍ Aut. 162, ✂ AS-20, ✂ S-18
99/0 BAP Mem. 134, SL-6, H-5, ✂ J-20, ✂ D-12, ✂ TM-13, ✂ TM-20
00/1 BAP Mem. 199, ✂ J-13, ✂ G-3, ✂ TM-6, ✂ V-2, ✂ V-3, ✂ V-4, ✂ V-6, ✂ V-7
01/2 BAP Memor. 198, 373, ✂ ASJ, ✂ ASE, ✂ ASN, ✂ ASD, ✂ ASS, ✂ AST, ✂ CoO, ✂ GoalJ, ✂ SCP
02/3 BAP Memorabilia 101, 240, 243, ✂ ASJ17, ✂ ASE5, ✂ ASN5, ✂ ASTJ5, ✂ AS7, ✂ AST9, ✂ AST11, ✂ AST14, ✂ AST23, ✂ HSHSJers 8, ✂ SCC4, ✂ SC27, ✂ SC30, ✂ TM1, /Cup
01/2 BAP Update HSHS, ✂ HSHSJers (x2), ✂ TP2
01/2 BT Pipes 56, 109, HSHS, ✂ ASJ, ✂ Jers., ✂ S&J, ✂ GG, ✂ GT, ✂ ITN, ✂ TW, ✂ -HSHSJers.
97/8 Bicycle A-Heart
98/9 Bicycle.. A-D
95/6 Bicycle Sports Aces K-Diamond
98 Bonaparte 2D, 8D
98 Bonaparte Pexeso 7, 28
92/3 Bowman 428
95/6 Bowman 56
01/2 Bowman 21
98/9 Bowman's Best 11, F9, SB1, ✍ A1A, ✍ A1B
99/0 Challenger 23
99/0 Crown Royale 18, IE-4, IG-3, CS-5, GC-2
00/1 Crown Royale 15, JotC-6, Land-2
01/2 Crown Royale 52, ASH 7, CA 14, JotC 10, LH 3
94/5 Donruss 94, D-3, MM-3
95/6 Donruss 33, BTP-2, D-4
96/7 Donruss 192
97/8 Donruss 9, BTP-4, ES-11
98/9 Donruss ES 10
96/7 Do. Canadian 60
97/8 Do. Canadian 10, SCS-22
95/6 Do. Elite 30
96/7 Do. Elite 37
97/8 Do. Elite 30, C-6
97/8 Do. Preferred 1, 169, CG-6
97/8 Do. Priority 80, OD-22, PG-13, Post-31, Stamp-31
97/8 Do. Studio 2, S-7, P-2
99/0 DS NS1, P1
00/1 DS BBH, ✍ BBH
01/2 DS 1, BB1, G1
98/9 Dynagon Ice 18, -AR 3, -IW 1, -PP 2, -TC 3
99/0 Dynagon Ice 31, ASP-4, LotR-3
97/8 Esso 54
01/2 eTopps 33
02/3 First Edition 136, 328, 380, 395, ✂ Jers.
94/5 Flair 17, HN-3
96/7 Flair 8, HG-4
94/5 Fleer 20, N-3
96/7 Fleer 10, 147, VT-4
95/6 Fleer Metal 15, IS-7
96/7 Fl. Picks DL-6
93/4 Fleer Ultra 274
94/5 Fleer Ultra 22, AW-6, GG-2, PPM-1
95/6 Fleer Ultra 18, 370, PPM-5, UV-3
96/7 Fl. Ultra 16, CTI-3
95 Globe 145
01/2 Heads Up 35, RI 4, SS 6, ✂ JQ 4, ✂ JQ 20, / Bobble
02/3 Heads Up 42, -EIT 9, -ITN 10, -PSP 6, -S 8, ✂ GWQ 12, ✂ GWQ 32
99/0 HoloGrFX 6, IZ1, PS3
95/6 Hoyle / East. 4-Spade
92/3 Kraft / PB
94/5 Kraft / KD, PB [x2]
95/6 Kraft / PS, PB
96/7 Kraft / KD
98/9 Kraft / OML
99/0 Kraft / JELL-O, / KD, / OML, / PB
00/1 Kraft 17
93/4 Leaf 256
94/5 Leaf 120, CP-6, GLS-8, LL-3
95/6 Leaf 56, GLS-1
96/7 Leaf 19
97/8 Leaf 2, 169, PD-1
94/5 L. Limited 102
95/6 L. Limited 76, SS-5
96/7 L. Limited 21
96/7 L. Preferred 91, LS-52, MM-7
97/8 Limited 76, 86, 147, FG-65
95/6 McDonald's McD-28
97/8 McDonald's McD-26
98/9 McDonald's McD16
99/0 McDonald's McD-3
00/1 McDonald's 5, GSNF-1
01/2 McDonald's 12, -HG 4, ✂ JPatch 9
02/3 McDonald's 11, -GSNF 2, ✂ JP 5
96/7 Metal Univ. 14, AP-4, CS-4
99/0 Millenium 29, P-2, D-4, ✍ Aut. 29, ✍ P-2, ✍ D-4, ✂ J-5, ✂✍ J-5, ✂ JS-5, ✂ G-7
01/2 Nextel
00/1 Nortel Networks All-Star 5
92/3 O-Pee-Chee 301
01/2 O-Pee-Chee 49, Update 49
02/3 O-Pee-Chee 143
98/9 OPC Chrome 163, SB1
92/3 OPC Premier 50
98/9 OFS 227, OW 2
97/8 Omega 22, NSZ-1
98/9 Omega 23, -CS 2, -EOP 3, -FTF 3, -Onl. 4, -PI 21, -Prism 3
99/0 Omega 28, -5ST 25, -CC 2, -EOP 4
98/9 Pacific 39, -CCA 2, -DI 4, -GCDC 4, -TC 3, -Time. 2, -TW 2
99/0 Pacific 37, CI-3, CCA-2, GC-5, HAA-3, HAA-13, ITCNF-3, PAP-4, TL-4
00/1 Pacific 52, ES-2, GCDC-4, ITC-1
01/2 Pacific 50, GCDC 3, IZ 4, SC 3, WAS 1
02/3 Pacific 128, -CCA 6, -MI 3, ✂ GWJ 17
97/8 Pacific CC 39, CCA-2, GCDC-3, ITC-2
97/8 Pa. Crown Roy. 14, FO-3
98/9 Pa. Crown Roy. 13, -CCA 3, -LL 3, -MP 3, -PP 2
97/8 Pa. Dynagon 10, 136, DD-3A, S-3, T-4, T-21, BKS-10, BKS-104
97/8 Pa. Invincible 12, FP-4, R-20
97/8 Pa. Paramount 19, P-4, GSL-2, BN-4
98/9 Pa. Paramount 19, -GS 3, -HOFB 2, -TC 3
99/0 Pa. Paramount 28, GS-3, HOFB-3, IAd-3, IAI-4, PB-5
00/1 Pa. Paramount 30, ES-3, FF-4, GS-3, HOF-2
97/8 Pa. Revolution 14, ASG-3, RTS-3
98/9 Pa. Revolution 14, -ASG 9, -TPA 11, -NI 2, -Show. 4
98/9 Panini Photocard [x2]
92/3 Panini Sticker 292
94/5 Panini Sticker 99
95/6 Panini Sticker 24, 149, 154
96/7 Panini Sticker 14
97/8 Panini Sticker 10, 118
98/9 Panini Sticker 19, 223
99/0 Panini Sticker 6, 32, 349
00/1 Panini Sticker 18
95 Panini Worlds 296
91/2 Parkhurst 263
91/2 Parkhurst 449
94/5 Parkhurst 24, V1
95/6 Parkhurst 236, 291, CCP-5, GP-4, IAS-1, PP-28, TW-5
00/1 Parkhurst P-41
01/2 Parkhurst 92, ✂ PS60, ✂ HSHSJers, ✂ M11, ✂ M42, ✂ T23, ✂ T27
94/5 Parkie SE ES-19
93/4 Pinnacle 403
94/5 Pinnacle 175, GT1, MVPU, WE6
95/6 Pinnacle 139, GG-19, CS-15, FS-14
96/7 Pinnacle 106
97/8 Pinnacle 28, TP-2, P-4
96/7 Pi. Be A Player SP-11
97/8 Pi. Be A Player STP 2
97/8 Pi. BeeHive 24
97/8 Pi. Certified 1, CT-4
97/8 Pi. Epix E22
95/6 Pi. FANtasy 17
97/8 Pi. Inside 2, IT-15, S-3
96/7 Pi. Mint 2
97/8 Pi. Mint 8, M-5
95/6 Pi. Summit 159, ITC-2
96/7 Pi. Summit 2, ITC-14
97/8 Pi. Totally 1
95/6 Pi. Zenith 109
96/7 Pi. Zenith 15
95/6 Playoff 12, 125
94/5 POG 274, 332, 333
95/6 POG 15, 48, I-014
97/8 Pi. Post 16
93/4 Power Play 297
93/4 Premier 320
93/4 Premier 463
94/5 Premier 35, 80, 152, 156, 312, 440
00/1 Premier Plus 17, MB15, TT1
99/0 Prism 19, CA-3, DAS-3, SGDC-4
00/1 Private Stock 12, AC-5, EA-3, PS-7, PSS-4, ✂ GUG-9, Res. 4
01/2 Pr. Stock 33, GR 4, -PS 26, ✂ GUG 42
02/3 Pr. Stock Reserve ✂ 117
00/1 PS Titanium 10, 3SS-1, WAS-1, ✂ GUG-59
01/2 PS Titanium 49, SK 5, TSS 4, TAS 7
01/2 PS Titanium Draft ✂ 37
02/3 PS Titanium ✂ GWJ 24
00/1 PS Titanium Draft ✂ 11
95/6 Pro Magnet 106
91/2 Pro Set 529
91/2 Pro Set Platinum 252
90/1 ProCards 409
91/2 ProCards 500
99/0 Revolution 18, IS-2, NI-3, O-4, SS-5, / CSC 18
00/1 Revolution 17, HD-5, II-3, NI-4, SM-12
91/2 Score 316
91/2 Score CAN 346
92/3 Score 373
93/4 Score 281
94/5 Score 78
95/6 Score 200, 325
96/7 Score 18, NW-4, SD-3
97/8 Score 39, 266, NW-17
97/8 Score Buff. 1
99/0 Score D1-7
94/5 Select 52
95/6 Select CE 89
96/7 Select CE 74, F-5
94 Semic 163
94 Semic 333
95 Semic 141, 214
89 Semic Sticker 178
91 Semic Sticker 103
92 Semic Sticker 124
00/1 Signature 50, HSHS, F-4, ✂ J-5, ✂ GJS-5, ✂ HSHSJers
01/2 Signature C-52, ✍ Aut. XLDH, ✂ GUE6, ✂ GJ6, ✂ GSJ6, ✂ ITN6, ✂ TM12
95/6 SBx Emotion 16
95/6 SBx Impact 16, D-1
96/7 SBx Impact 10, ZH-4
94/5 SP 14, P-19
95/6 SP 13
96/7 SP 17, HC-30, SF-3
97/8 SP Authentic 14, I34
98/9 SP Authentic 8, SS7, SO13
99/0 SP Authentic 10
00/1 SP Authentic 10, SS1
01/2 SP Authentic 27, 98
00/1 SP GU 6, ✂ C
01/2 SP GU 20, ✂ AF
02/3 SP Game-Used ✂ TG
97/8 SPx 4, DV
99/0 SPx 15, HH3, X6, XT14, S4, ✂ WM
00/1 SPx 6, 82, P1, ✂ WM
01/2 SPx 26, ✂ HT
02/3 SPx ✂ WM
98/9 SPx Finite 8, 103, 159, 173
98/9 SPx Prospects 6, H5, L6, PS4
00/1 Stadion 5, 190
99/0 Stadium 7, Chrome 7, Big 5, CA22, GC1, OE3
00/1 Stadium 12, BT14, CA5, GS8, SF18
01/2 Stadium 103
95/6 SLU
96/7 SLU
98/9 SLU
99/0 SLU 44
95/6 Super Sticker 10, 12
96/7 Team Out✂
92/3 Topps 136
95/6 Topps 2, 302, 4HG, M19, PF14
98/9 Topps 163, L5, M7, SB1, ✍ CAI
99/0 Topps 9, 279, AT1, IM2, PM1, TW16, ✍ TA2
00/1 Topps 21, TC4, HM4, NHLD12
01/2 Topps 49, OTG23, Update 49
02/3 Topps 143, OTG16
01/2 Topps All-Star Game 5
99/0 To. Chrome 9, 279, AT1, IM2, PM1
00/1 To. Chrome 20, TC4, HM4
01/2 To. Chrome 49
94/5 Topps Finest 43
95/6 To. Finest 72, 90
98/9 To. Finest 4, M2, M5, M6, M7, -Big 2
98/9 T. Gold Label 34
99/0 To. Gold Label 1, PG1
00/1 To. Gold Label 66, BTM3
00/1 To. Heritage 26, HH19
01/2 To. Heritage 116, 135, 159
02/3 T. Limited 143
96/7 Topps Picks ID10
99/0 To. Prmr. Plus 7, IG4, PT10
01/2 To. Reserve 92
92/3 T. Stadium Club 107
93/4 To. Stadium 178
94/5 T. Stadium Club 125, 179, 269
95/6 To. Stadium 60, M10, N6
94/5 TSC Members Only 12
95/6 TSC Members Only 42
00/1 To. Stars 6, 130, AS6, WF8
95/6 T. Super Skills 75
98/9 UD Choice 23, 221, 244, BH18, SQ4
00/1 UD Heroes 12, PI6, TM2, ✂ GT, ✂ GC
01/2 UD PlayMakers Ltd 35, / PM
00/1 UD Reserve 10, GG2, BT2
98/9 UD3 57, 117, 177
00/1 Ultimate Mem. ✂ A8-6, ✂ A8-7, ✂ A8-8, ✂ G-4, ✂ H-3, ✂ H-4, ✂ J-5, ✂ MO-8, ✂ S-5, ✂ TM-20, ✂ GM-12
01/2 Ultimate Mem. ✂ BAPL, ✂ Emb., ✂ Jers., ✂ S&J, ✂ ITN, ✂ JE, ✂ JJ, ✂ NP, ✂ PP, ✂ RA, ✂ WTF
99/0 Ult. Victory 10, NW1
91/2 Upper Deck 335
91/2 Upper Deck E14
92/3 Upper Deck 366
92/3 Upper Deck 506
92/3 Upper Deck 92
92/3 Upper Deck AR6
92/3 Upper Deck E3
92/3 Upper Deck ERT3
93/4 Upper Deck 387
94/5 Upper Deck 233, 285, 545, H31, SP-8
95/6 Upper Deck 104, AS-20, F-11, H-13, SE-98
96/7 Upper Deck 222, X28, SS26A
97/8 Upper Deck 225, SG39, S18, T2A, ✂ GJ3
98/9 Upper Deck 20, 44, FT10, LS27, P17, ✂ GJ17
99/0 Upper Deck 22, 145, AS1, CT23, HOF2, IG4, MA5, SS16, UD2, PD1, ✂ GJ
00/1 Upper Deck 248, F2, GA2, P1, SS3, TT10, ✂ DGJ, ✂ GJ
01/2 Upper Deck 66, 214, LL3, ✂ GoalJ, ✂ PoaN, ✂ PoaND, ✂ PoaNT, ✂ SCFJersD
02/3 Upper Deck -GG7, -SA6, ✂ GO, ✂ UDPL
95/6 UD BAP 192, ✍ S192
96/7 UD Black Diam. 156
97/8 UD Black Diam. 20
98/9 UD Black Diam. 10, M6, WF4
99/0 UD Black Diam. 11, ✂ APOH
00/1 UD Black Diam. 6, ✂ GG
99/0 UD C. Legends 51
01/2 UD Challenge 27, BB4, ✂ T200
02/3 UD Classic ✂ HH
95/6 UD CC 258, 367, 381, 394
96/7 UD CC 30, 311
97/8 UD Coll. Choice 22, SQ81
97/8 UD Coll. Choice S30
01/2 UD Collectors
97/8 UD Diam. Vision 24
98/9 UD G. Reserve 20, 44
99/0 UD G. Reserve 22, 145
01/2 UD Honor Roll 18, 48, ✂ HS, ✂ PPM
96/7 UD Ice 5
97/8 UD Ice 87, IC5
00/1 UD Ice 5
01/2 UD Ice 16
00/1 UD Legends 16, 18, LC3, ✂ LGJ
01/2 UD Mask 111, 177, ✂ CG, ✂ GP, ✂ StS
98/9 UD MVP 21, OT7, F4
99/0 UD MVP 21, S9, W4, W18, LL1, MVP3, ✂ GU17
00/1 UD MVP 23, MM1, TD2, TP2, ✂ GS
01/2 UD MVP 69, ✂ GS
02/3 UD MVP 63, MM2, VF8
99/0 UD MVP Cup 22, PH2, GC
99/0 UD Ovation 6, 83, LP16, ST5
02/3 UD Piece -AC13, / Giveaway
99/0 UD PowerDeck 6, T5
01/2 UD Premier 23, ✂ S, ✂ D
00/1 UD Pros&Prosp. 10, PM2
99/0 UD Retro 7, DR8, G10B, TC8
01/2 UD Top Shelf 17, -ASGN, ✂ GG-LP, ✂ S, ✂ ST
02/3 UD Top Shelf 31, ✂ HH, ✂ M, ✂ SS, ✂ TS
00/1 UD Vintage 39, 49, 50, GG3, NH5
01/2 UD Vintage 92, 267, 268, 270
02/3 UD Vintage 95, 316
00/1 Vanguard 13, CF-2, HV-5, VP-12
01/2 Vanguard 35, EMW 2, IF 3, SW 7, VT 4, ✂ DGM 50
99/0 Victory 32, 33, 319, 381
00/1 Victory 25, 26, 243, 286
01/2 Victory 36, 39, 398
02/3 Victory 74, -NP15
01/2 Waving the Flag 11
99/0 WGretzky 21, CG5, GH4, W4
96 Wien 103, SG1
97/8 Zenith 20, Z62
98/9 NHL Power Play
92/3 BUFF / Blue Shield
92/3 BUFF / Jubilee
93/4 BUFF / Noco

HASEK, JIRI
00/1 OFS 234
01/2 OFS 128

HASKETT, CHRIS
95/6 Slapshot 189

HASS, W.
52/3 Anonymous 27

HASSAN, SANA
95/6 DEL 405
96/7 DEL 301

HASSARD, BOB
45-64 BeeHive-2 [Toro.]
52/3 Parkhurst 105
53/4 Parkhurst 4
45-54 Quaker Oats

HASSELBLAD, PETER
94/5 Leaf Elit Set 31
95/6 Leaf Elit Set 267, FTF-14
89/0 Semic Elitserien 78
90/1 Semic Elitserien 253
92/3 Semic Elitserien 206
95/6 UD Elitserien 135

HASSINEN,
97/8 Hockey-Box

HASSINEN, JANI
98/9 Cardset 216
99/0 Cardset 127
00/1 Cardset 92
02/3 Cardset 24
93/4 Jyvas Hyva 57
93/4 Sisu 246
94/5 Sisu 42
95/6 Sisu 23
94/5 Topps Finest 136

HASSMAN, JEFF
91/2 Air Canada SJHL A14

HASTMAN, DARREN
90/1 7th..Sketch WHL 112
91/2 7th...Sketch WHL 294

HATCH, CHRIS
91/2 Air Canada SJHL B48
92/3 MPS SJHL 15

HATCHER, DARIAN
02/3 First Edition 381

HATCHER, DERIAN
01/2 Adrenaline ✂ GWJ 12
98/9 Aurora 54
98/9 Be A Player 194, ✍ Aut. 194
99/0 BAP Mem. 17
00/1 BAP Mem. 202
01/2 BAP Memor. 118
92/3 Bowman 365
01/2 Crown Royale ✂ TT 8
93/4 Donruss 77
94/5 Donruss 317
95/6 Donruss 326
97/8 Donruss 168
96/7 Do. Canadian 4
97/8 Do. Canadian 124
96/7 Do. Elite 28
97/8 Do. Elite 32
97/8 Do. Preferred 21
97/8 Do. Priority 30
97/8 Do. Studio 96
98/9 Dynagon Ice 55
99/0 Dynagon Ice 64, CM-9
97/8 Esso 32
02/3 First Edition 47, ✂ Jers.
96/7 Flair 22
94/5 Fleer 52
96/7 Fleer 26
95/6 Fleer Metal 40
92/3 Fleer Ultra 319
93/4 Fleer Ultra 139
94/5 Fleer Ultra 52
95/6 Fleer Ultra 38
96/7 Fl. Ultra 42
95 Globe 109
01/2 Heads Up ✂ JQ 10, ✂ JQ 22
99/0 Kraft / JELL-O
93/4 Leaf 212
94/5 Leaf 286
95/6 Leaf 279
97/8 Leaf 144
94/5 L. Limited 25
96/7 L. Preferred 80
97/8 Limited 21
96/7 Maggers 47
96/7 Metal Univ. 39
99/0 Millenium 77, ✍ Aut. 77
92/3 O-Pee-Chee 123
01/2 O-Pee-Chee 164
02/3 O-Pee-Chee 220
98/9 OPC Chrome 148, B13
91/2 OPC Premier 143
97/8 Omega 69
98/9 Omega 69
98/9 Pacific 176
99/0 Pacific 118
00/1 Pacific 130
01/2 Pacific 124, IZ 9, ✂ GWJ 10
02/3 Pacific 112
02/3 Pacific Complete 170
97/8 Pacific CC 214
97/8 Pa. Crown Roy. 40
97/8 Pa. Dynagon 35, T-38
97/8 Pa. Paramount 57
98/9 Pa. Paramount 63
99/0 Pa. Paramount 71
00/1 Pa. Paramount 74
92/3 Panini Sticker H
93/4 Panini Sticker 274
94/5 Panini Sticker 231
95/6 Panini Sticker 173
96/7 Panini Sticker 167
99/0 Panini Sticker 224
91/2 Parkhurst 75
92/3 Parkhurst 72
93/4 Parkhurst 46
94/5 Parkhurst V30
95/6 Parkhurst 58
00/1 Parkhurst P-123
01/2 Parkhurst 149
02/3 Parkhurst Retro ✂ NH8
94/5 Parkie SE45
91/2 Pinnacle 328
92/3 Pinnacle 34
93/4 Pinnacle 57
94/5 Pinnacle 55
95/6 Pinnacle 70
97/8 Pinnacle 182
97/8 Pi. Certified 54
97/8 Pi. Inside 138
95/6 Pi. Summit 72
97/8 Pi. Totally 54
96/7 Pi. Zenith 19
95/6 Playoff 140
94/5 POG 83
93/4 Power Play 61
93/4 Premier 520
94/5 Premier 332
00/1 Premier Plus 59
00/1 Private Stock ✂ GUG 35-36
01/2 Pr. Stock ✂ GUG 35
00/1 PS Titanium ✂ GUG 82
01/2 PS Titanium Draft ✂ 33
00/1 PS Titanium Draft ✂ 29
95/6 Pro Magnet 122
91/2 Pro Set 543
92/3 Pro Set 75
91/2 Pro Set Platinum 258
90/1 Score 430
91/2 Score 106T
91/2 Score CAN 656
92/3 Score 51
93/4 Score 168
94/5 Score 148
95/6 Score 225, CI-8
97/8 Score 198
94/5 Select 50
89/0 7th..Sketch OHL 154
90/1 7th..Sketch OHL 309
00/1 Signature 147
02/3 Signature ✂ DW5
95/6 SBx Emotion 47
95/6 SBx Impact 46
96/7 SBx Impact 29
95/6 SP 40
96/7 SP 45
97/8 SP Authentic 45
99/0 Stadium 54
00/1 Stadium 41, ✂ SCS
02/3 Stadium ✂ FC2, ✂ PC2
94 Starflics N4
00/1 SLU 21
96/7 Team Out✂
92/3 Topps 405
95/6 Topps 197
98/9 Topps 148, B13
99/0 Topps 105
00/1 Topps 87
01/2 Topps 164
02/3 Topps 220, ✂ CC3, ✂ CC16
99/0 To. Chrome 105
00/1 To. Chrome 69
98/9 To. Finest 39
99/0 To. Gold Label 70
00/1 To. Heritage 128
01/2 To. Heritage ✂ CC
02/3 T. Limited 220
99/0 To. Prmr. Plus 56
01/2 To. Reserve ✂ TR
92/3 T. Stadium Club 414
93/4 To. Stadium 494
94/5 T. Stadium Club 107
95/6 To. Stadium 78
00/1 To. Stars 39
02/3 T. Total 291
98/9 UD Choice 65
90/1 Upper Deck 359
91/2 Upper Deck 546
92/3 Upper Deck 287
93/4 Upper Deck 204, SP-37
94/5 Upper Deck 127, SP-20
95/6 Upper Deck 3, SE-112
96/7 Upper Deck 44, P27
97/8 Upper Deck 51, 397, T20A
98/9 Upper Deck 259, ✂ GJ9
99/0 Upper Deck 46
00/1 Upper Deck 61
02/3 Upper Deck 303
93/4 Upper Deck Be A Player 24
94/5 UD BAP R15, R136, ✍ 125
97/8 UD Black Diam. 94
95/6 UD CC 224
96/7 UD CC 70
97/8 UD Coll. Choice 70
98/9 UD G. Reserve 259
99/0 UD G. Reserve 46
02/3 UD Honor 80
97/8 UD Ice 2
98/9 UD MVP 66
99/0 UD MVP 65
00/1 UD MVP 58
02/3 UD MVP 60
01/2 UD SCup Champs 51
00/1 UD Vintage 122, 123
02/3 UD Vintage 86, 270
00/1 Vanguard ✂ DGJ 4
01/2 Vanguard ✂ DGM 11
99/0 Victory 89
00/1 Victory 78
01/2 Victory 115
02/3 Victory 72
94/5 DALL / Southwest
94/5 DALL / Cap
96/7 DALL / Southwest
97/8 DALL / Score 198
00/1 DALL / Southwest
01/2 DALL / Southwest
02/3 DALL / Southwest

HATCHER, KEVIN
98/9 Aurora 153
98/9 Be A Player 112, ✍ Aut. 112
99/0 BAP Mem. 68
00/1 BAP Mem. 466
90/1 Bowman 70
91/2 Bowman 296
92/3 Bowman 230
92/3 Bowman 271
95/6 Bowman 48
98/9 Bowman's Best 24
99/0 Challenger 28
93/4 Donruss 369
94/5 Donruss 199
95/6 Donruss 95
96/7 Donruss 29
97/8 Donruss 26
95/6 Do. Elite 17
96/7 Do. Elite 24
97/8 Do. Preferred 70
97/8 Do. Priority 100
98/9 Dynagon Ice 149
93/4 EA Sports 151
97/8 Esso 31
96/7 Flair 76
94/5 Fleer 53
95/6 Fleer Metal 41
96/7 Fl. Picks F50-17
92/3 Fleer Ultra 231
93/4 Fleer Ultra 118
94/5 Fleer Ultra 233
95/6 Fleer Ultra 230
96/7 Fl. Ultra 140
91/2 Gillette 36
95 Globe 105
93/4 Hockey Wit 17
95/6 Hoyle / West. 7-Spade
92/3 Humpty Dumpty
91/2 Kellogg's / Score 7
91/2 Kraft 20
93/4 Kraft / PB
93/4 Leaf 34
94/5 Leaf 369
95/6 Leaf 117
96/7 Leaf 48
97/8 Leaf 129
97/8 Limited 21
92/3 McDonald's McD-19
96/7 Metal Univ. 126
87/8 OPC/Topps 68
88/9 OPC/Topps 86
90/1 OPC/Topps 147
91/2 O-Pee-Chee 310
91/2 Topps - Team Leader 16
92/3 O-Pee-Chee 145
89/0 OPC/Topps 146
98/9 OPC Chrome 73, B14
91/2 OPC Premier 88
97/8 Omega 185
98/9 Pacific 352
99/0 Pacific 336
01/2 Pacific 73
97/8 Pacific CC 227
97/8 Pa. Dynagon 101, T-62
97/8 Pa. Invincible 112
97/8 Pa. Paramount 149
98/9 Pa. Paramount 191
98/9 Panini Photocard
87/8 Panini Sticker 179
88/9 Panini Sticker 165
88/9 Panini Sticker 365
89/0 Panini Sticker 347

90/1 Panini Sticker 167
91/2 Panini Sticker 198
92/3 Panini Sticker 167
93/4 Panini Sticker C
94/5 Panini Sticker 26
95/6 Panini Sticker 175
96/7 Panini Sticker 170
97/8 Panini Sticker 49
99/0 Panini Sticker 107
91/2 Parkhurst 191
92/3 Parkhurst 198
93/4 Parkhurst 221
94/5 Parkhurst 259, V54
95/6 Parkhurst 56
91/2 Pinnacle 131
92/3 Pinnacle 11
93/4 Pinnacle 90
93/4 Pinnacle CA25
94/5 Pinnacle 345
95/6 Pinnacle 10
96/7 Pinnacle 3
97/8 Pinnacle 171
96/7 Pi. Be A Player 14, ✍ Aut. 14
97/8 Pi. Certified 86
97/8 Pi. Inside 98, S-10
95/6 Pi. Summit 41
97/8 Pi. Totally 86
95/6 Pi. Zenith 44
95/6 Playoff 248
96/7 Playoff 408
94/5 POG 363
95/6 POG 89
93/4 Power Play 261
93/4 Premier 435
00/1 Pr. Stock ✂ GUG 13
90/1 Pro Set 311, 376
91/2 Pro Set 249
91/2 Pro Set 316
92/3 Pro Set 204
91/2 Pro Set Platinum 127
91/2 Puck / Pro Set 29
90/1 Score 90
90/1 Sco. Hot Cards 42
91/2 Score 20
91/2 Score 340
91/2 Score CAN 20
91/2 Score CAN 370
92/3 Score 273
92/3 Score 439
92/3 Score USAG 13
93/4 Score 136
93/4 Score 450
93/4 Score TF 23
95/6 Score 12
96/7 Score 117
97/8 Score 222
97/8 Score Pitt. 8
92/3 Seasons 48
94/5 Select 148
95/6 Select CE 41
94 Semic 114
94 Semic 342
95 Semic 106
91 Semic Sticker 136
92 Semic Sticker 151
93 Semic Sticker 175
95/6 SBx Emotion 48
95/6 SBx Impact 47
94/5 SP 31
95/6 SP 37
96/7 SP 130
97/8 SP Authentic 127
95/6 Super Sticker 34
92/3 Topps 149
95/6 Topps 273
98/9 Topps 73, B14
94/5 Topps Finest 17
95/6 To. Finest 148
96/7 Topps Picks 33
91/2 To. Stadium 140
92/3 T. Stadium Club 301
93/4 To. Stadium 153
94/5 T. Stadium Club 220
95/6 To. Stadium 42
94/5 TSC Members Only 28
95/6 TSC Members Only 11
95/6 T. Super Skills 53
98/9 UD Choice 172
90/1 Upper Deck 109, 486
91/2 Upper Deck 361
91/2 Upper Deck 511
91/2 Upper Deck 98
92/3 Upper Deck 198
93/4 Upper Deck 140, SP-169
94/5 Upper Deck 332, SP-86, SP-110
95/6 Upper Deck 256, 309, SE-25
96/7 Upper Deck 319, P21
97/8 Upper Deck 343
98/9 Upper Deck 159, 348
99/0 Upper Deck 261
94/5 UD BAP R131, ✍ 48
96/7 UD Black Diam. 54
95/6 UD CC 186
96/7 UD CC 71
97/8 UD Coll. Choice 207
98/9 UD G. Reserve 159, 348
99/0 UD G. Reserve 261
99/0 Victory 243
96 Wien 163
94/5 DALL / Southwest
86/7 WASH / Kodak
86/7 WASH / Police
87/8 WASH
87/8 WASH / Kodak
88/9 WASH
88/9 WASH / Smokey
89/0 WASH
89/0 WASH / Kodak
90/1 WASH / Kodak
90/1 WASH / Smokey
91/2 WASH / Kodak
91/2 WASH / Smokey
92/3 WASH / Kodak
83/4 North Bay Centennials

HATCHER, MARK
88/9 ProCards / Baltimore
82/3 North Bay Centennials
83/4 North Bay Centennials

HÄTINEN, MARKUS
99/0 Cardset 271
94/5 Sisu 253

HATOUM, ED
73/4 Vancouver Blazers

HATTELAND,
92/3 Semic Nordisk 207 [Rookie]

HATZIIOANNOU, FRED
01/2 Owen Sound Attack
02/3 Owen Sound Attack

HAUER, BRETT
93/4 Classic 67
94/5 Classic ✍ Aut.
98/9 EBK IHL All-Star
93/4 Fleer Ultra 484
94/5 Leaf Elit Set 268
95 Panini Worlds 221
93/4 Power Play 504
93/4 Premier - USA Hockey 20
93/4 To. Stadium - Team U.S.A. 7
93/4 Las Vegas Thunder
01/2 Manchester Monarchs
98/9 Manitoba Moose
99/0 Manitoba Moose
00/1 Manitoba Moose
01/2 Milwaukee Admirals

HAUGEN, GEIR
92/3 Semic Nordisk 113

HAUHTONEN, JANNE
00/1 Cardset 175

HAUKALI, TERJE
92/3 Semic Nordisk 227

HAUPT, KEVIN
97/8 Portland Winter Hawks

HAUSLER, OLIVER
94/5 DEL 382

HAUSWIRTH, MIKE
90/1 Michigan Tech Huskies
91/2 Michigan Tech Huskies

HAUTAMAA, JUHA
98/9 Cardset 86, OD4
99/0 Cardset 51
00/1 Cardset 36
97/8 Hockey-Box
93/4 Sisu 130
94/5 Sisu 120
95/6 Sisu 41, S-8
95/6 Sisu Limited 105

HAVANOV, ALEXANDER
93/4 Birmingham Bulls

HAVARD, JEFF
99/0 San Angelo Outlaws

HAVEL, JAN
01/2 DS L8
69/0 Mästär Serien 10
72 Semic Sticker 29
71/2 Williams Finnish 25

HAVEL, LUKAS
01/2 OFS 161
99/0 Brampton Batallion 14

HAVEL, MARIAN
01/2 Vancouver Giants

HAVEL, MICHAL
00/1 OFS 130
01/2 OFS 177
99/0 Score 94

HÄVELID, NICLAS
99/0 BAP Mem. 193
99/0 Dynagon Ice 8
94/5 Leaf Elit Set 36
95/6 Leaf Elit Set 5
99/0 Millenium 4, ✍ Aut. 4
02/3 Pacific Complete 418
99/0 Panini Sticker 179
91/2 Semic Elitserien 11
92/3 Semic Elitserien 35
99/0 Stadium 183
99/0 To. Prmr. Plus 110
01/2 To. Reserve 79
99/0 Upper Deck 172
95/6 UD Elitserien 5
97/8 UD Elitserien 6, 209
98/9 UD Elitserien 152
99/0 UD G. Reserve 172

HAVELKA, PETR
99/0 OFS 104
00/1 OFS 311
01/2 OFS 96

HAVELN, JAN
74 Semic Sticker 71

HAVENHAND, ANDY
93/4 Sheffield Steelers 1
93/4 Sheffield Steelers 19
94/5 Sheffield Steelers 10

HAVILAND, KYLE
95/6 Muskegon Fury
98/9 Topeka Scarecrows

HAVIR, DAVID
00/1 DS 104
99/0 OFS 75
00/1 OFS 195
01/2 OFS 109

HAVLAT, MARTIN
01/2 Adrenaline 133, PM, WB
01/2 Atomic 68
00/1 BAP Mem. 403
01/2 BAP Memor. 41, HSHS
02/3 BAP Memorabilia 115, ✂ FG12
01/2 BAP Update HSHS, ✂ HSHSJers
01/2 Bowman 142
02/3 Bowman 48
00/1 Crown Royale 134, 21CR-17
01/2 Crown Royale 100
02/3 Crown Royale ✂ GWJ 14
00/1 Crown Royale CC, G-4
99/0 DS 107
00/1 DS NT8, WCH7
01/2 eTopps 13
02/3 Exclusive 121
02/3 First Edition 98, 421H, ✂ Jers.
01/2 Heads Up 68, BTI 15, PP 5
02/3 Heads Up 86, -HF 11, ✂ GWQ 19
02/3 In The Game-Used 54, 154
01/2 McDonald's -FL 3
02/3 McDonald's -CA 5
01/2 O-Pee-Chee 93
02/3 O-Pee-Chee 49
98/9 OFS 393
99/0 OFS 194
01/2 Pacific 272, ✍ 448
02/3 Pacific 266, ✂ GWJ 37
02/3 Pacific Complete 444
00/1 Parkhurst P-240
01/2 Parkhurst 97
02/3 Parkhurst 59, ✂ TT11
02/3 Parkhurst Retro 85
00/1 Premier Plus 120
00/1 Private Stock 132, PSR-14
01/2 Pr. Stock 67, Res. 12, -PS 52
02/3 Pr. Stock Reserve 72
00/1 PS Titanium 134, 3SS-25
01/2 PS Titanium 99, SK 16, ✂ DSJ 47, ✂ DSJ 60
01/2 PS Titanium Draft ✂ 65
02/3 PS Titanium ✂ GWJ 47
00/1 PS Titanium Draft 134
02/3 Quest for the Cup 70
00/1 Signature 276, ✍ Aut. 238
01/2 Signature 140, ✍ Aut. 140, ✂ GJ4, ✂ GSJ4
02/3 Signature 67, ✍ 67, ✂ SGJ39, ✂ TQ20
00/1 SP Authentic 115, ✍ SotT
01/2 SP Authentic 118, ✍ SotT, ✍ SotTD, ✍ SotTT
02/3 SP Authentic ✍ SotT
00/1 SP GU 75
02/3 SP GU 34, ✍ Sig
02/3 Sports Vault 97
00/1 SPx 110
01/2 SPx 187
00/1 Stadion 116
00/1 Stadium 249
01/2 Stadium 79, G5, ✍ LSS
02/3 Stadium 27
01/2 Topps 93, OTG13, ✍ CA
02/3 Topps 49, ✍ SF
00/1 To. Chrome 248
01/2 To. Chrome 93
02/3 T. Chrome 40
00/1 To. Gold Label 109
00/1 To. Heritage 77
01/2 To. Heritage 43
02/3 To. Heritage 49
02/3 T. Limited 49
01/2 To. Reserve 12
00/1 To. Stars 101
02/3 T. Total 388
00/1 UD Heroes 173
01/2 UD PlayMakers Ltd 70
00/1 UD Reserve 107
01/2 Ultimate Mem. ✂ WTF
00/1 Upper Deck 414
01/2 Upper Deck 125
02/3 Upper Deck 366
02/3 UD Artistic 61, R61
00/1 UD Black Diam. 127
02/3 UD Classic 68
00/1 UD Ice 95
01/2 UD Ice 31
01/2 UD Mask 66
01/2 UD MVP 136
02/3 UD MVP 128
01/2 UD Premier ✍ Sig
02/3 UD Premier ✍ Sig.
00/1 UD Pros&Prosp. 116
02/3 UD Rookie ✍ TD
01/2 UD Top Shelf 110
02/3 UD Top Shelf 60, ✍ Sig
00/1 UD Vintage 388
01/2 UD Vintage 176
02/3 UD Vintage 178, 281, GB 178
00/1 Vanguard 135
01/2 Vanguard 68, PP 13
01/2 Victory 247
02/3 Victory 146, -NP19
01/2 Waving the Flag 12
00/1 OTTA
01/2 OTTA
02/3 OTTA

HAVRAN, PETER
79 Panini Sticker 271

HAVUKAINEN, ARI
71/2 Williams Finnish 360

HAWCO, JUSTIN
01/2 Cape Breton Eagles 11

HAWERCHUK, DALE
01/2 BAP Memor. ✂ 500GS
90/1 Bowman 129
91/2 Bowman 31
92/3 Bowman 308
91 Canada Cup
82/3 Dernière Heure
93/4 Donruss 35
94/5 Donruss 44
95/6 Donruss 384
96/7 Donruss 90
97/8 Donruss 36
95/6 Do. Elite 100
93/4 EA Sports 16
88/9 Esso All-Star
83/4 Esso Stars
94/5 Flair 18
96/7 Flair 67
94/5 Fleer 21
95/6 Fleer Metal 124
96/7 Fl. Picks 120
92/3 Fleer Ultra 15
93/4 Fleer Ultra 149
94/5 Fleer Ultra 23
95/6 Fleer Ultra 299
88/9 Frito Lay
83/4 Funmate Puffy 5 [w/]
93/4 Hockey Wit 22
84/5 Kellogg's 4
89/0 Kraft 50
90/1 Kraft 16
91/2 Kraft 36
86/7 Kraft Sports 75
93/4 Leaf 71
94/5 Leaf 313
95/6 Leaf 184
96/7 Leaf 124
94/5 L. Limited 94
96/7 Maggers 114
96/7 Metal Univ. 111
82/3 O-Pee-Chee 3
82/3 O-Pee-Chee 374
82/3 O-Pee-Chee 380
82/3 O-Pee-Chee 381
83/4 O-Pee-Chee 377
83/4 O-Pee-Chee 385
84/5 O-Pee-Chee 339
84/5 O-Pee-Chee 393
85/6 OPC/Topps 109
86/7 OPC/Topps 74
87/8 OPC/Topps 149
87/8 OPC/Topps Box I
88/9 OPC/Topps 65
88/9 OPC/Topps Box K
90/1 OPC/Topps 141
90/1 Topps-TL 11
91/2 O-Pee-Chee 65
91/2 Topps - Team Leader 2
92/3 O-Pee-Chee 212
89/0 OPC/Topps 122
90/1 OPC Premier 40
91/2 OPC Premier 1
88/9 OPC Stars 12
82/3 OPC/Topps Sticker 204
82/3 OPC/Topps Sticker 249
83/4 OPC/Topps Sticker 282
84/5 OPC Sticker 284
84/5 OPC Sticker 285
85/6 OPC Sticker 248
86/7 OPC Sticker 104
87/8 OPC Sticker 255
88/9 OPC Sticker 143
89/0 opcSticker 134
97/8 Pacific CC 225
87/8 Panini Sticker 363
88/9 Panini Sticker 155
89/0 Panini Sticker 162
90/1 Panini Sticker 317
91/2 Panini Sticker 296
92/3 Panini Sticker 247
93/4 Panini Sticker 102
94/5 Panini Sticker 91
95/6 Panini Sticker 189
96/7 Panini Sticker 116
91/2 Parkhurst 18
91/2 Parkhurst 216
92/3 Parkhurst 11
93/4 Parkhurst 23
94/5 Parkhurst 29, V82
95/6 Parkhurst 180
01/2 Parkhurst ✂ 500GS, ✍ PA22
91/2 Pinnacle 80
92/3 Pinnacle 316
93/4 Pinnacle 260
94/5 Pinnacle 43
96/7 Pinnacle 44
96/7 Pi. Be A Player 203, ✍ Aut. 203
95/6 Pi. Summit 95
95/6 Playoff 306
96/7 Playoff 409
94/5 POG 46
95/6 POG 238
82/3 Post [Winn.]
93/4 Power Play 29
93/4 Premier 7
93/4 Premier - Finest 11
94/5 Premier 320
90/1 Pro Set 330, 415
91/2 Pro Set 24
92/3 Pro Set 12
91/2 Pro Set Platinum 11
87/8 Pro Sport CW7
90/1 Score 50, 2T
90/1 Sco. Hot Cards 22
91/2 Score 259
91/2 Score 376
91/2 Score CAN 266
91/2 Score CAN 479
92/3 Score 272
93/4 Score 159
94/5 Score 192
95/6 Score 222
96/7 Score 51
92/3 Seasons 68
94/5 Select 42
95/6 Select CE 97
94 Semic 89
89 Semic Sticker 67
92 Semic Sticker 94
84/5 7-Eleven
85/6 7-Eleven Superstars 21
01/2 Signature ✂ 500GS, ✍ VA35
95/6 SBx Emotion 147
95/6 SBx Impact 140
96/7 SBx Impact 94
83/4 Souhaits Keychain [Jets]
94/5 SP 15
95/6 SP 123
83/4 Stater Mint H7
95/6 Super Sticker 103
84/5 Topps 152
85/6 OPC/Topps-Stick. 8
92/3 Topps 296
95/6 Topps 271
95/6 To. Finest 153
96/7 Topps Picks FC8
91/2 To. Stadium 312
92/3 T. Stadium Club 419
93/4 To. Stadium 220
94/5 T. Stadium Club 248
95/6 To. Stadium 46
01/2 T/O Archives ✂ Stick
01/2 Ultimate Mem. ✂ 500GS, ✂ CT
90/1 Upper Deck 53, 443
91/2 Upper Deck 12
91/2 Upper Deck 126
91/2 Upper Deck 79
92/3 Upper Deck 302
93/4 Upper Deck 411, SP-16
94/5 Upper Deck 102, SP-9
95/6 Upper Deck 38
96/7 Upper Deck 120
00 ✂ UD APOH 500, ✂✍ 500
94/5 UD BAP R7, ✍ 5
95/6 UD CC 245
96/7 UD CC 196
97/8 UD Coll. Choice 190
02/3 UD Foundations 10, 84, 100, ✂ 1000Stick, ✍ SG
96/7 UD Ice 50
00/1 UD Legends 133, ✍ ES
01/2 UD Legends 78
83/4 Vachon 126-6
83/4 Vachon 126-98
90/1 BUFF / Blue Shield
90/1 BUFF / Campbell's
91/2 BUFF / Blue Shield
91/2 BUFF / Campbell's
91/2 BUFF / Pepsi
92/3 BUFF / Blue Shield
92/3 BUFF / Jubilee
93/4 BUFF / Noco
96/7 PHIL / Ocean Spray
81/2 WINN
82/3 WINN
82/3 WINN
83/4 WINN
84/5 WINN / Safety Tips
85/6 WINN
85/6 WINN / Safety Tips
85/6 WINN / Silverwood
86/7 WINN
87/8 WINN
88/9 WINN / Safety Tips
89/0 WINN / Safeway

HAWES, CHRIS
91/2 7th...Sketch WHL 70

HAWGOOD, GREG
93/4 Donruss 245
98/9 EBK IHL All-Star
95/6 Edge Ice 152
93/4 Fleer Ultra 388
95/6 Future Legends 25
93/4 Leaf 266
94/5 Leaf 534
99/0 Millenium 240, ✍ Aut. 240
90/1 OPC/Topps 236
89/0 OPC/Topps 81
89/0 opcSticker/FS 1
89/0 Panini Sticker 189
90/1 Panini Sticker 10
92/3 Parkhurst 361
94/5 Parkhurst 181
93/4 Power Play 347
93/4 Premier 422
90/1 Pro Set 442
88/9 ProCards / Maine
91/2 ProCards 226
90/1 Score 79T
93/4 Score 396
93/4 Score 642
92/3 Topps 358
92/3 T. Stadium Club 495
00/1 UD Heroes 115
90/1 Upper Deck 391
89/0 BOST / Sports Action
92/3 EDMO / IGA 010
92/3 PHIL / UD Sheet
93/4 PHIL / Sheet
94/5 PITT / Foodland 2
95/6 Las Vegas Thunder
01/2 Utah Grizzlies
84/5 Kamloops Blazers
85/6 Kamloops Blazers
86/7 Kamloops Blazers
87/8 Kamloops Blazers

HAWKINS, RICHARD
85/6 Kitchener Rangers

HAWKINS, SHAWN
89/0 Rayside-Balfour

HAWKINS, TODD
89/0 ProCards IHL 183
90/1 ProCards 324
91/2 ProCards 342
01/2 UD DEL 67
95/6 Cincinnati Cyclones
96/7 Cincinnati Cyclones
97/8 Cincinnati Cyclones
98/9 Cincinnati Cyclones
99/0 Cincinnati Cyclones
93/4 Cleveland Lumberjacks
87/8 Flint Spirits
92/3 St. John's Maple Leafs
84/5 Belleville Bulls

HAWLEY, CHRIS
01/2 Mississauga IceDogs
02/3 Mississauga IceDogs

HAWLEY, JOE
91/2 ProCards 44
89/0 7th..Sketch OHL 105
90/1 7th..Sketch OHL 361
93/4 Muskegon Fury
92/3 Peoria Rivermen

HAWLEY, KENT
88/9 ProCards / Hershey
89/0 ProCards AHL 348
90/1 ProCards 40
98/9 Hampton Roads

HAWORTH, ALAN
84/5 O-Pee-Chee 199
85/6 OPC/Topps 117
86/7 OPC/Topps 107
88/9 OPC/Topps 131
85/6 OPC Sticker 108-241
86/7 OPC Sticker 255-147
88/9 OPC Sticker 195
87/8 Panini Sticker 187
83/4 Souhaits Keychain [Capitals]
81/2 BUFF / Wendt's 5
87/8 QUÉB / Gene. Foods
87/8 QUÉB / Yum Yum
82/3 WASH
84/5 WASH / Pizza Hut
85/6 WASH / Pizza Hut
86/7 WASH / Kodak
86/7 WASH / Police

HAWORTH, GORDIE
52/3 Laval Dairy Update 68
52/3 St. Lawrence 22

HAWRYLIW, NEIL
81/2 Indianapolis Checkers

HAWRYLUK, NEIL
89/0 Lethbridge Hurricanes

HAY, BILLY (RED)
45-64 BeeHive-2 [Chic.]
64-67 BeeHive-3 [Chic.]
63-65 Chex
64/5 Coke/Sprite [Chic.]
65/6 Coca-Cola
62/3 Cowan Tile
95/6 Parkie 66-67 30
94/5 Parkie Tall 42
60/1 Shirriff 77
61/2 Shirriff 34
60/1 Topps 6
61/2 Topps 35
61/2 Topps - Stamp
62/3 Topps 35
62/3 Topps Dollar
63/4 Topps 34
64/5 Topps 7
65/6 Topps 62
62/3 Toronto Star Photo
63/4 Toronto Star Action
64/5 Toronto Star Action
65/6 Toronto Star Photo
60/1 Toronto Star Weekend

HAY, CHARLES
83 HHOF Postcard C6
83&87 HHOF 36

HAY, DARRELL
99 Bowman 118
00/1 Florida Everblades
00/1 Kansas City Blades 10
01/2 Manitoba Moose
02/3 Manitoba Moose

HAY, DON
94/5 Slapshot Memorial 25
96/7 PHOE / Coca-Cola
01/2 Utah Grizzlies

HAY, DWAYNE
97 Bowman 25
95/6 Classic 38
94/5 Slapshot / Guelph 9
95/6 Slapshot 89
96/7 UD Ice 123
99/0 Louisville Panthers
98/9 New Haven Beast 10
97/8 Portland Pirates
95/6 Guelph Storm
96/7 Guelph Storm
96/7 Guelph Storm

HAY, GEORGE
83 HHOF Postcard G7
83&87 HHOF 98
23/4 Paulins Candy 28
60/1 Topps 15
61/2 Topps - Stamp

HAY, SCOTT
94/5 Slapshot / Sarnia 3

HAYDAR, DARREN
02/3 BAP Memorabilia 326
02/3 Choice Prospects 17
02/3 SP Authentic 175
02/3 Ultimate Mem. 49
02/3 UD Mask 140
02/3 UD Premier 60

HAYDEN, BRIAN
95/6 Slapshot 153

HAYDEN, CRAIG
97/8 Fort Worth Brahmas
98/9 Fort Worth Brahmas

HAYDEN, JAMIE
90/1 7th..Sketch WHL 171
93/4 Thunder Bay Senators

HAYES, ANDREW
02/3 Hull Olympiques

HAYES, HARLIN
95/6 Halifax Moosehead

HAYES, JAMES
52/3 Bas du Fleuve 29
51/2 Lac St-Jean 5

HAYES, PAUL
30/1 La Presse

HAYES, ROBERT
51/2 Laval Dairy 8

HAYFIELD, ROGER
51/2 Bas du Fleuve 39
52/3 Bas du Fleuve 12

HAYKO, RICK
85/6 Minnesota-Duluth 9

HAYNES, PAUL
34-43 BeeHive-1 [Mont.]
35-40 Canada Starch
36-39 Diamond Match TT2
36-39 Diamond Match TT3
35/6 O-Pee-Chee 95
37/8 O-Pee-Chee 155
39/0 O-Pee-Chee 31
40/1 O-Pee-Chee 112
38/9 Quaker Oats
34/5 Sweet Caporal
33/4 WWGum 6
37/8 World Wide Gum 33

HAYWARD, BRIAN
01/2 BT Pipes -Mask
91/2 Bowman 122
92/3 Bowman 60
86/7 Kraft Sports 27
85/6 O-Pee-Chee 226
86/7 O-Pee-Chee 255
87/8 O-Pee-Chee 230
88/9 OPC/Topps 195
90/1 OPC/Topps 23
91/2 O-Pee-Chee 178
89/0 O-Pee-Chee 237
87/8 OPC Leaders 15
88/9 OPC Stars 13
87/8 OPC Sticker 175-177
87/8 OPC Sticker 184-44
88/9 OPC Sticker 214
88/9 OPC Sticker 52
89/0 opcSticker 50, 211
87/8 Panini Sticker 376A
87/8 Panini Sticker 55
88/9 Panini Sticker 251
88/9 Panini Sticker 402
89/0 Panini Sticker 246, 376
90/1 Panini Sticker 61
91/2 Panini Sticker 106
93/4 Panini Sticker 265
91/2 Pinnacle 83
92/3 Pinnacle 266
90/1 Pro Set 150
91/2 Pro Set 327
90/1 Score 78T
91/2 Score 211
91/2 Score 4T
91/2 Score CAN 211
91/2 Score CAN 554
83/4 Stater Mint H12
92/3 Topps 436
91/2 To. Stadium 19
92/3 T. Stadium Club 364
90/1 Upper Deck 171, 449
91/2 Upper Deck 59
83/4 Vachon 127-7
86/7 MONT
87/8 MONT
87/8 MONT / Vachon 61
87/8 MONT / Vachon 64
87/8 MONT / Vachon 67
87/8 MONT / Vachon 84
88/9 MONT
89/0 MONT
89/0 MONT / Kraft
91/2 SANJ / Sports Action
83/4 WINN
84/5 WINN / Safety Tips
85/6 WINN
85/6 WINN / Safety Tips

HAYWARD, RICK
98/9 DEL 144
99/0 Eishockey 78
89/0 ProCards IHL 207
90/1 ProCards 345
91/2 ProCards 469
93/4 Cincinnati Cyclones
95/6 Cleveland Lumberjacks
96/7 Cleveland Lumberjacks
97/8 Cleveland Lumberjacks
86/7 Sherb. Canadiens 19

HAZLEHURST, MIKE
96/7 Guildford Flames 20

HEAD, BARRY
74/5 Sioux City Musketeers

HEAD, DON
45-64 BeeHive-2 [Bost.]
61/2 Shirriff 11
61/2 Topps 17

HEAD, GALEN
93/4 Fort Wayne Komets 27
94/5 Fort Wayne Komets 28
91/2 Knoxville Cherokees

HEADLEY, FERN (CURLY)
24/5 Champ's Cigarettes
24/5 Maple Crispette [V130] 4
23/4 Paulins Candy 37
24/5 William Paterson 23

HEALEY, ERIC
01/2 Manchester Monarchs
02/3 Manchester Monarchs

HEALEY, GRANT
90/1 Rayside-Balfour
91/2 Rayside-Balfour

HEALEY, PAUL
97/8 Donruss 205
95/6 Edge Ice 44
00/1 Hamilton Bulldogs
99/0 Milwaukee Admirals
01/2 St. John's Maple Leafs
01/2 St. John's / Clarenville
93/4 Prince Albert Raiders

HEALY, GLENN
98/9 Bicycle.. 2-S
91/2 Bowman 224
92/3 Bowman 434
93/4 Donruss 211
94/5 Donruss 283
95/6 Donruss 54
96/7 Donruss 212
93/4 EA Sports 84
92/3 Fleer Ultra 126
93/4 Fleer Ultra 106
93/4 Fleer Ultra 371
95/6 Fleer Ultra 101
01/2 Heads Up ✂ JQ 19
93/4 Leaf 327
94/5 Leaf 310
90/1 O-Pee-Chee 400
91/2 O-Pee-Chee 368
92/3 O-Pee-Chee 262
88/9 OPC Sticker 123-255
00/1 Pacific 390
01/2 Pacific 365
97/8 Pa. Dynagon BKS-61
97/8 Pa. Paramount 180
88/9 Panini Sticker 68
89/0 Panini Sticker 97
90/1 Panini Sticker 88
91/2 Panini Sticker 249
93/4 Panini Sticker 65
91/2 Parkhurst 107
92/3 Parkhurst 341
92/3 Parkhurst 505
93/4 Parkhurst 405
95/6 Parkhurst 406
94/5 Parkie SE117
91/2 Pinnacle 185
92/3 Pinnacle 121
93/4 Pinnacle 365
94/5 Pinnacle 430
95/6 Pinnacle 91
96/7 Pi. Be A Player 140, ✍ Aut. 140
94/5 POG 287
93/4 Power Play 390
93/4 Premier 486
94/5 Premier 388
00/1 PS Titanium ✂ GUG 146
01/2 PS Titanium ✂ DSJ 41
90/1 Pro Set 183
91/2 Pro Set 153
91/2 Pro Set Platinum 73
91/2 Puck / Pro Set 18
90/1 Score 294
91/2 Score 68
91/2 Score CAN 68
92/3 Score 188
93/4 Score 177
93/4 Score 533
95/6 Score 273
96/7 Score 34
97/8 Score 22
97/8 Score Toro. 2
92/3 Topps 305
95/6 Topps 292
91/2 To. Stadium 369
92/3 T. Stadium Club 356
93/4 To. Stadium 453
90/1 Upper Deck 18
91/2 Upper Deck 224
93/4 Upper Deck 321
94/5 Upper Deck 455
95/6 Upper Deck 30
96/7 Upper Deck 202
94/5 UD BAP R13, ✍ 128
95/6 UD CC 272
88/9 LOSA / Smokey
89/0 NYIS
99/0 TORO / Pizza Pizza 18

HEALY, JAMIE
99/0 Peoria Rivermen

HEANEY, GERALDINE
94/5 Classic W19, W21
97/8 Esso 57, ✍ Aut.
97/8 General Mills
97/8 UD Coll. Choice 282

HEANY, MIKE
95/6 Louisiana Ice Gators
95/6 Louisiana Ice Gators-2

HEAPHY, SHAWN
92/3 Classic Prospects 141
91/2 ProCards 588
93/4 Las Vegas Thunder
92/3 Salt Lake G'Eagles

HEARN, DON
91/2 Avant Garde BCJHL 36
92/3 BCJHL 58

HEARN, JAMIE
95/6 Flint Generals
95/6 Muskegon Fury
92/3 Oklahoma City Blazers

HEASLIP, MARK
76/7 O-Pee-Chee 376
79/0 O-Pee-Chee 320

HEASTY, JOHN
93/4 Flint Generals
96/7 Flint Generals

HEATHWOOD, STEVE
74/5 Sioux City Musketeers

HEATLEY, DANY
01/2 Adrenaline RR2
01/2 Atomic 103, RR
02/3 Atomic 4, -CF 2, -PC 1
02/3 BAP All-Star 101
01/2 BAP Memor. 385
02/3 BAP Memorabilia 5, ✂ FG5, ✂ HSHSJers 13
01/2 Bowman 134, ✂ FFJ, ✂ FFS, ✂ FFDS, ✂ FFR, ✍ YSA
02/3 Bowman 141
02/3 Calder 1, -HH 1, ✂ GWJ 1
01/2 Crown Royale 6, CA 1, RR 1
02/3 Crown Royale 4, LOR 2, ✂ GWDP 1, ✂ GWJ 1
02/3 eTopps 16
02/3 Exclusive 5, -DFG 2, -GE 1, -MO 2
02/3 First Edition 24, 383, 384, 422H, ✂ Jers., ✂ HSHSJers 17, ✂ TSL 2
02/3 Heads Up 4, -HF 1, -ITN 2, -SM 3, ✂ GWQ 35
02/3 In The Game-Used 4, 104, ✂ E30, ✂ GUJ30, ✂ SJ30, ✂ T7
02/3 McDonald's 2, -CA 1, ✂ JP 1
02/3 O-Pee-Chee 205
02/3 Pacific 13, -CCA 1, -L 1, -SM 1, ✂ GWJ 1
02/3 Pacific Complete 15
01/2 PTC Calder 1
01/2 PTC High Voltage 1
01/2 PTC Collectibles 1
01/2 PTC Rookie 1
01/2 Parkhurst 286
02/3 Parkhurst 125, -CR12, ✂ CRM12, ✂ GJ24, ✂ SJ24, ✂ HSHSJers, ✂ NH11, ✂ PP6, ✂ TT9
02/3 Parkhurst Retro 52, ✂ RF2, ✂ RJ23, ✂ RSJ16, ✂ HSHJers, ✂ RM10
01/2 Pr. Stock 101, MiT 1, RR 1, -PS 93
02/3 Pr. Stock Reserve ✂ 102
01/2 PS Titanium 4, TSS 21, TRT 1, ✂ DSJ 23
01/2 PS Titanium Draft 104, ✂ 4
02/3 PS Titanium 4, ✂ GWJ 2
02/3 Quest for the Cup 4, -CTC 2, ✂ GWJ 1
01/2 Signature 226, ✍ Aut. 226
02/3 Signature 1, ✍ 1, ✂ FJ2, ✂ SGJ30, ✂ TQ12
01/2 SP Authentic 3, 111, ✍ SotT
02/3 SP Authentic 4, 107, ✍ SotT, ✍ SotTD, ✍ SotTT
01/2 SP GU 2
02/3 SP GU 3, ✍ Sig
02/3 Sports Vault 3
01/2 SPx 94, 154
02/3 SPx 4
01/2 Stadium 111
02/3 Stadium 47, -BT-8, ✂ YSS5, ✂ YSD1, ✂ ✍ YSMVP
02/3 Topps 205, OTG11
01/2 To. Chrome 127
02/3 T. Chrome 115
02/3 To. Heritage 9, 103, 111, ✂ CC, ✂ CCB
02/3 T. Limited 205
02/3 T. Total 6, AW5
01/2 UD PlayMakers Ltd 6
02/3 UD Superstars 255
02/3 Ultimate Mem. ✂ ASMVP, ✂ DD, ✂ Emb, ✂ GUJ, ✂ GUSJ, ✂ ITN, ✂ RAT, ✍ RAut
00/1 Upper Deck 198
01/2 Upper Deck 239
02/3 Upper Deck 253
02/3 UD Artistic 3, R3, ✂ AT, ✂ RT, / ✍ Art
00/1 UD Black Diam. 63
01/2 UD Challenge 3
02/3 UD Classic 4
01/2 UD Honor Roll 25, 55
02/3 UD Honor 4, -SG2, ✍
00/1 UD Ice 43
01/2 UD Ice 85, ✍ CCA
01/2 UD Mask 4
02/3 UD Mask 5
00/1 UD MVP 211
02/3 UD MVP 8, ✍ PSig
02/3 UD Piece 4, ✍ MD
01/2 UD Premier 2, ✍ Sig
02/3 UD Premier 3, ✂ Jers, ✍ Sig (x2)
99/0 UD Prospects 71
02/3 UD Rookie 5, ✂ DJ, ✂ S, ✍ TD
01/2 UD Top Shelf 77
02/3 UD Top Shelf 5, ✍ Sig
02/3 UD Vintage 15, 262, 315, GB 15, T3
01/2 Vanguard 3, PP 1
02/3 Vanguard 5, ✂ GWJ 2
00/1 Victory 279
02/3 Victory 9

HEATLEY, MURRAY
75/6 OPC WHA 53
74/5 Minn. Fight. Saints

HEATON, SCOTT
94/5 Sheffield Steelers 3
95/6 Sheffield Steelers

HEAVEY, PAUL
00/1 Kudos 3

HEBENTON, ANDY
45-64 BeeHive-2 [NYRa.]
45-64 BeeHive-2 [Bost.]
64-67 BeeHive-3 [Bost.]
62/3 Cowan Tile
93/4 Parkie 56-57 97
60/1 Shirriff 91
61/2 Shirriff 90
57/8 Topps 58
58/9 Topps 46
59/0 Topps 16
60/1 Topps 42
61/2 Topps 55
61/2 Topps - Stamp
62/3 Topps 54
62/3 Topps Dollar
63/4 Topps 15
57/8 Toronto Star Photo
59/0 Toronto Star Weekend

HEBENTON, CLAY
76/7 Phoenix Roadrunners

HEBERT, GUY
01/2 Atomic ✂ GWJ 40
98/9 Aurora 2
99/0 Aurora 1, -GU 1
00/1 Aurora 1
98/9 Be A Player 4, ✍ Aut. 4
99/0 BAP Mem. 168
00/1 BAP Mem. 65, ✂ TM-23, ✂ TM-39
98/9 Bicycle.. 6-H
92/3 Bowman 32
99/0 Crown Royale 1
00/1 Crown Royale 1
93/4 Donruss 13
94/5 Donruss 81
95/6 Donruss 71
96/7 Donruss 164
97/8 Donruss 167
97/8 Do. Canadian 37
95/6 Do. Elite PW 5
97/8 Do. Elite 45
97/8 Do. Preferred 129
97/8 Do. Priority 124, PG-20
97/8 Do. Studio 37
98/9 Dynagon Ice 2
99/0 Dynagon Ice 9
93/4 EA Sports 6
94/5 Flair 3
96/7 Flair 1
96/7 Fleer 1, 147
95/6 Fleer Metal 1
92/3 Fleer Ultra 394
93/4 Fleer Ultra 254
94/5 Fleer Ultra 3
95/6 Fleer Ultra 1
96/7 Fl. Ultra 1
01/2 Heads Up ✂ JQ 1
95/6 Hoyle / West. 8-Spade
94/5 Kraft / KD
95/6 Kraft / PS
96/7 Kraft / KD
99/0 Kraft / JELL-O
94/5 Kraft Mask
93/4 Leaf 356
94/5 Leaf 142, LL-1
95/6 Leaf 271
96/7 Leaf 88
97/8 Leaf 72, PD-7
97/8 Limited 102
96/7 Maggers 5
96/7 Metal Univ. 1
99/0 Millenium 5, ✍ Aut. 5
98/9 NHL Power Play
92/3 O-Pee-Chee 116
98/9 OPC Chrome 48
92/3 OPC Premier 40
97/8 Omega 2
98/9 Omega 3
99/0 Omega 2
98/9 Pacific 54
99/0 Pacific 7, -ITCNF 1
00/1 Pacific 4
01/2 Pacific 258, ✂ GWJ 21
97/8 Pacific CC 260, ITC-1
97/8 Pa. Crown Roy. 1, FO-1
98/9 Pa. Crown Roy. 2
97/8 Pa. Dynagon 2, S-1, T-24
97/8 Pa. Invincible 2
97/8 Pa. Paramount 1, GSL-1
98/9 Pa. Paramount 2, -GS 1
99/0 Pa. Paramount 2, -GS 1
00/1 Pa. Paramount 4
97/8 Pa. Revolution 1, RTS-1
98/9 Pa. Revolution 1
94/5 Panini Sticker 126
95/6 Panini Sticker 232
96/7 Panini Sticker 223
98/9 Panini Sticker 168
99/0 Panini Sticker 181, 350
00/1 Panini Sticker 110
95 Panini Worlds 211
92/3 Parkhurst 386
93/4 Parkhurst 279
95/6 Parkhurst 4
00/1 Parkhurst P-136
94/5 Parkie SE1
93/4 Pinnacle 167
93/4 Pinnacle Expa. 1
94/5 Pinnacle 15, MA4
95/6 Pinnacle 143
96/7 Pinnacle 88
97/8 Pinnacle 90, M-6, / Tin 4
96/7 Pi. Be A Player 61, ✍ Aut. 61
97/8 Pi. Be A Player STP 1
97/8 Pi. Certified 19
97/8 Pi. Inside 70, SU-8, S-6, / Can 7, LargeCan
95/6 Pi. Summit 58
96/7 Pi. Summit 75
97/8 Pi. Totally 19
97/8 Pi. Uncut 3
95/6 Pi. Zenith 99
95/6 Playoff 1, 113
94/5 POG 269
95/6 POG 27
93/4 Power Play 2
93/4 Premier 519
94/5 Premier 338
00/1 Premier Plus 80
99/0 Prism 1
00/1 Private Stock 1, ✂ GUG-1
00/1 PS Titanium ✂ GUG 51, ✂ GUG 52
95/6 Pro Magnet 38
89/0 ProCards IHL 5
90/1 ProCards 89
91/2 ProCards 29
99/0 Revolution 1
00/1 Revolution 1
92/3 Score 460
93/4 Score 426
93/4 Score 489
93/4 Score 502
94/5 Score 42, TF1
95/6 Score 94
96/7 Score 13
97/8 Score 6, NW-1
97/8 Score Anah. 14
94/5 Select 79
95 Semic 210
00/1 Signature 48
95/6 SBx Emotion 2
95/6 SBx Impact 2
96/7 SBx Impact 1
94/5 SP 5
95/6 SP 3
96/7 SP 5
97/8 SP Authentic ✍ SotT
98/9 SP Authentic 3
99/0 SP Authentic 3
99/0 SPx 6
98/9 SPx Finite 2
99/0 Stadium 96
00/1 Stadium 118
00/1 SLU 7
96/7 Team Out✂
92/3 Topps 112
95/6 Topps 112
98/9 Topps 48
99/0 Topps 58
00/1 Topps 46, OTG
99/0 To. Chrome 58
00/1 To. Chrome 38
94/5 Topps Finest 20
95/6 To. Finest 122
98/9 To. Finest 58
98/9 T. Gold Label 57
99/0 To. Gold Label 38
00/1 To. Gold Label 62
00/1 To. Heritage 149
99/0 To. Prmr. Plus 74
92/3 T. Stadium Club 401
93/4 To. Stadium 295
94/5 T. Stadium Club 6
95/6 To. Stadium 82
98/9 UD Choice 1
00/1 UD Heroes 4
00/1 UD Reserve GG1
00/1 Ultimate Mem. ✂ A8-8, ✂ G-1, ✂ PJ-9, ✂ TM-22, ✂ TM-23
99/0 Ult. Victory NW9
92/3 Upper Deck 501
93/4 Upper Deck 1
94/5 Upper Deck 3
95/6 Upper Deck 467, SE-3
96/7 Upper Deck 2
97/8 Upper Deck 6
98/9 Upper Deck 212
99/0 Upper Deck 171
00/1 Upper Deck 6
94/5 UD BAP R47, ✍ 99
96/7 UD Black Diam. 53
97/8 UD Black Diam. 34
99/0 UD Black Diam. 3
95/6 UD CC 287
96/7 UD CC 5, 309
97/8 UD Coll. Choice 1, SQ42
98/9 UD G. Reserve 212
99/0 UD G. Reserve 171
98/9 UD MVP 6
99/0 UD MVP 6
99/0 UD MVP Cup 3
00/1 UD Pros&Prosp. 3
00/1 UD Vintage 6, 11, 12, GG1
00/1 Vanguard 1, ✂ DGJ-19
01/2 Vanguard ✂ DGM 2
99/0 Victory 7
00/1 Victory 6
01/2 Victory 240
99/0 WGretzky 2
97/8 Zenith 66, Z11
94/5 ANAH / Carl's Jr. 9
96/7 ANAH / Up Front 21

HEBERT, IAN
94/5 Birmingham Bulls

HEBERT, JAY
99/0 Missouri RiverOtters

HEBERT, ROLAND
51/2 Laval Dairy 19

HÉBERT, PATRICK*
90/1 7th..Sketch LHJMQ 195

HEBKY, DAVID
92/3 BCJHL 215
91/2 7th...Sketch WHL 56

HEBLING, TMO
01/2 Milwaukee Admirals

HEBST, MARCO
94/5 DEL 141

HECHT, JOCHEN
01/2 Adrenaline 76, ✂ GWJ 17
99/0 BAP Mem. 152
00/1 BAP Mem. 9
01/2 BAP Memor. 30
02/3 BAP Memorabilia 86
99/0 Crown Royale 116, -IG 23
01/2 Crown Royale ✂ TT 9, ✂ TT19
94/5 DEL 282
95/6 DEL 277
96/7 DEL 173
99/0 Millenium C-34
99/0 NHL Power Play [x3]
01/2 O-Pee-Chee 43
02/3 O-Pee-Chee 176
99/0 Omega 203
99/0 Pacific 367
00/1 Pacific 345
01/2 Pacific 323
02/3 Pacific 143
02/3 Pacific Complete 298
99/0 Pa. Paramount 197
99/0 Panini Sticker 290
00/1 Parkhurst P-91
01/2 Parkhurst 210

99/0 Prism 118
01/2 Pr. Stock ✂ GUG 47
01/2 PS Titanium ✂ DSJ 38
01/2 PS Titanium Draft ✂ 40
99/0 Revolution 122
94/5 SR Auto-Phonex 17, ✍ 17
00/1 Signature 155, ✍ Aut. 47
01/2 Signature 157, ✍ Aut. 157
99/0 SP Authentic 116, -TH8, ✍ SotT
01/2 SP Authentic ✍ SotT, ✍ SotTD
02/3 Sports Vault 26
99/0 SPx 136
99/0 Stadium 173
00/1 Stadium 186
00/1 Topps 149, OTG30
01/2 Topps 43
02/3 Topps 176
00/1 To. Chrome 108
99/0 To. Gold Label 99, FG19
00/1 To. Heritage 113
01/2 To. Heritage 176
02/3 To. Heritage 166
02/3 T. Limited 176
99/0 To. Prmr. Plus 116, PR6
02/3 T. Total 118
99/0 Ult. Victory 106
99/0 Upper Deck 116
00/1 Upper Deck 381, P10, ✂ GJ
01/2 Upper Deck 297
02/3 Upper Deck 267
99/0 UD Black Diam. 71
99/0 UD G. Reserve 116
01/2 UD Honor Roll ✂ GAJ
99/0 UD MVP 188
00/1 UD MVP 155
99/0 UD MVP Cup 164, ✍ PS
02/3 UD Top Shelf ✂ ST
00/1 UD Vintage 312
01/2 Vanguard ✂ DGM 29
02/3 Vanguard 13
99/0 Victory 262
00/1 Victory 203
01/2 Victory 309
02/3 Victory 85, -NP28
99/0 WGretzky 148
99/0 SLOU / Taco Bell 2

HECKER, BENJAMIN
99/0 Eishockey 289
01/2 UD DEL 265

HECL, RADOSLAV
02/3 BAP Memorabilia 370
02/3 Ultimate Mem. 78
02/3 UD Rookie 127
02/3 Rochester Americans

HEDBERG, ANDERS
00/1 Alfabilder
79/0 Dernière Heure
83/4 Funmate Puffy 19 [w/]
92/3 Future Trends C76 141
95 Globe 70
72 Hellas MM-Jenkki 38
74 Hellas MM-Jenkki 25
70/1 Kuvajulkaisut 25
78/9 O-Pee-Chee 25
79/0 O-Pee-Chee 240
80/1 O-Pee-Chee 73
81/2 O-Pee-Chee 225
81/2 O-Pee-Chee 237
82/3 O-Pee-Chee 225
83/4 O-Pee-Chee 245
84/5 O-Pee-Chee 143
81/2 OPC Sticker 166
83/4 OPC/Topps Sticker 215
84/5 OPC Sticker 102
85/6 OPC Sticker 200-73
80/1 O-Pee-Chee Super 15
74/5 OPC WHA 17
75/6 OPC WHA 40
75/6 OPC WHA 72
76/7 OPC WHA 125
76/7 OPC WHA 66
77/8 OPC WHA 3
72 Semic Sticker 69
74 Semic Sticker 12
91 Semic Sticker 235
83/4 Souhaits Keychain [Rangers]
77-79 Sportscaster 71-12
77-79 Sports. FIN 80-1911
78/9 Topps 25
79/0 Topps 240
80/1 Topps 73
81/2 Topps 58
81/2 Topps 98 [East]
84/5 Topps 107
71/2 Williams Finnish 45
72/3 Williams Finnish 45
73/4 Williams Finnish 27

HEDBERG, JOHAN
01/2 Adrenaline 151, CL 17, PP 28, RR 16
01/2 Atomic 77, RR 9, Stat 8, TN 11
02/3 Atomic 79
00/1 BAP Mem. 502
01/2 BAP Memor. 28, ✂ GoalJ, ✂ SCP
02/3 BAP Memorabilia 107
01/2 BT Pipes 42, 107, -Mask, ✂ DM, ✂ FW, ✂ Jers., ✂ Emb., ✂ S&J, ✂ GG, ✂ GT, ✂ ITN, ✂ HSHSJers
02/3 Between the Pipes 40, 144, M23, ✂ BM15, ✂ CP6, ✂ DM15, ✂ GUE17, ✂ FW7, ✂ GB9, ✂ GUJ17, ✂ GSJ17, ✂ GT5, ✂ I4, ✂ ITN17, ✂ T7, ✍ Aut.
01/2 Bowman 79
02/3 Bowman 63
01/2 Crown Royale 114, CA 10, RR 17
02/3 Crown Royale 76
01/2 eTopps 7
02/3 Exclusive 136
02/3 First Edition 189
95 Globe 6
01/2 Heads Up 76, BTI 16, PP 6, SS 17, / Bobble
02/3 Heads Up 98, ✂ GWQ 22, ✂ GWQ 31
02/3 In The Game-Used 61, 161, ✂ IE26
94/5 Leaf Elit Set 40, CS-7
95/6 Leaf Elit Set 61, S-7
01/2 McDonald's 30, -GSNF 5
01/2 O-Pee-Chee 294
02/3 O-Pee-Chee 106
01/2 Pacific 452
02/3 Pacific 307
02/3 Pacific Complete 188
01/2 Parkhurst 84
02/3 Parkhurst 69, ✂ TT14
02/3 Parkhurst Retro 112
01/2 Pr. Stock 108, MiT 10, -PS 102
02/3 Pr. Stock Reserve 79
01/2 PS Titanium 111
01/2 PS Titanium Draft ✂ 78
02/3 PS Titanium 80, ✂ GWJ 53
00/1 PS Titanium Draft 176
02/3 Quest for the Cup 79
92/3 Semic Elitserien 152
01/2 Signature 69, ✍ Aut. 69
02/3 Signature 22, GS-44, ✍ 22, ✂ TQ8
01/2 SP Authentic 70, ✍ SotT, ✍ SotTD
01/2 SP GU 44, ✂ TotG, ✂ TotGSig, ✂ TotGC, ✂ TotGCSig., ✂ TotGT
02/3 Sports Vault 120
01/2 SPx 53
01/2 Stadium 39, NR10, ✍ NR
02/3 Stadium 68
01/2 Topps 294
02/3 Topps 106
01/2 To. Chrome 146
02/3 T. Chrome 67
01/2 To. Heritage 37
02/3 To. Heritage 56
02/3 T. Limited 106
01/2 To. Reserve 35
02/3 T. Total 371
01/2 UD PlayMakers Ltd 80
01/2 Ultimate Mem. ✂ BAPL
02/3 Ultimate Mem. ✂ NO
01/2 Upper Deck 143, GL5, LL7
02/3 Upper Deck 143
02/3 UD Artistic 71, R71, / Art
01/2 UD Challenge 69
02/3 UD Classic 79
95/6 UD Elitserien 94
98/9 UD Elitserien 117, DL6
00/1 UD Ice 120
01/2 UD Ice 35
01/2 UD Mask 124, 186, ✂ GP, / Mask
02/3 UD Mask 68, 69, 70, 71, 101, ✂ MM, ✂ BM, ✂ PW, ✂ VC, / Mask
01/2 UD MVP 152, MM7
02/3 UD MVP 146
02/3 UD Piece 73
01/2 UD Premier ✍ Sig
01/2 UD Top Shelf 35, ✂ GG-B, ✂ GG-GG, ✂ GG-LP
02/3 UD Top Shelf 70, ✍ Sig
01/2 UD Vintage 202, 208
02/3 UD Vintage 203, 284, GB 203, T53
01/2 Vanguard 79, EMW 4, SW 16, VT 8
02/3 Vanguard 79, ✂ GWJ 36
01/2 Victory 277, 284, 385
02/3 Victory 170
97/8 Detroit Vipers
99/0 Kentucky Tho'blades
00/1 Manitoba Moose

HEDBERG, JON
99/0 Guelph Storm

HEDBERG, NICLAS
99/0 Cardset 207
00/1 Cardset 8

HEDE, NIKLAS
00/1 Cardset 230
96/7 DEL 43
98/9 DEL 161
99/0 Eishockey 271
94/5 Sisu 328
95/6 Sisu 223

HEDICAN, BRET
92/3 Classic 87
93/4 Donruss 291
93/4 Fleer Ultra 66
94/5 Fleer Ultra 224
95/6 Fleer Ultra 316
93/4 Leaf 286
94/5 Leaf 425
01/2 O-Pee-Chee 258
98/9 OPC Chrome 81
98/9 Omega 102
98/9 Pacific 426
02/3 Pacific 66
02/3 Pacific Complete 356
97/8 Pacific CC 284
92/3 Parkhurst 385
93/4 Parkhurst 177
94/5 Parkhurst 243
95/6 Parkhurst 216
92/3 Pinnacle 228
93/4 Pinnacle 315
94/5 Pinnacle 369
95/6 Playoff 317
93/4 Power Play 210
93/4 Premier 224
94/5 Premier 162
92/3 Pro Set 240
92/3 Score 471
97/8 SP Authentic 158
02/3 Sports Vault 38
92/3 Topps 517
95/6 Topps 72
98/9 Topps 81
01/2 Topps 258
92/3 T. Stadium Club 203
93/4 To. Stadium 81
94/5 T. Stadium Club 27
02/3 T. Total 136
92/3 Upper Deck 414
93/4 Upper Deck 185
94/5 Upper Deck 398
95/6 Upper Deck 95
96/7 Upper Deck 173
98/9 Upper Deck 196
02/3 Upper Deck 275
95/6 UD BAP 19, ✍ S19
95/6 UD CC 255
98/9 UD G. Reserve 196
00/1 UD MVP 78
01/2 UD Vintage 110
99/0 Victory 126
95/6 VANC / Abalene 3
96/7 VANC / IGA

HEDICAN, TOM
94/5 Slapshot / North Bay 25

HEDIN, PIERRE
98/9 UD Choice 291
97/8 UD Black Diam. 36
97/8 UD Elitserien 150
98/9 UD Elitserien 167, 216
99/0 UD Elitserien 169, 213
00/1 UD Elitserien 152

HEDINGTON, STEVE
83/4 Oshawa Generals
86/7 Sudbury Wolves

HEDLUND, MATTIAS
98/9 UD Elitserien 19
00/1 UD Elitserien 16

HEDLUND, TOMMY
95/6 Leaf Elit Set 160
89/0 Semic Elitserien 10
95/6 UD Elitserien 7

HEDMAN, GLENN
89/0 Semic Elitserien 200

HEDSTRÖM, JONATHAN
02/3 BAP Memorabilia 339
02/3 Choice Prospects 18
02/3 SP Authentic 170
02/3 Ultimate Mem. 99
02/3 UD Artistic 91
99/0 UD Elitserien 142, 211
00/1 UD Elits. 127, T8, ✍ Sig.
02/3 UD Honor 145
02/3 UD Mask 122
02/3 UD Premier 97

HEED, JONAS
89/0 Semic Elitserien 221
90/1 Semic Elitserien 30
91/2 Semic Elitserien 280
92/3 Semic Elitserien 305
97/8 UD Elitserien 170

HEED, KLAS
89/0 Semic Elitserien 102
90/1 Semic Elitserien 105
91/2 Semic Elitserien 109
92/3 Semic Elitserien 128

HEENEY, BOB
85/6 Brandon Wheat Kings

HEEREMA, JEFF
98 Bowman 146, ✍ A31
98 Bowman Chrome 146
98/9 Bowman's Best 147
02/3 Calder 61
02/3 Choice Prospects 19
98/9 OPC Chrome 233
02/3 Pacific Complete 536
98/9 Topps 233
98/9 To. Finest F9
99/0 Upper Deck 333
99/0 UD Black Diam. 110
99/0 UD G. Reserve 333
99/0 UD Ovation 65
00/1 Cincinnati Cyclones

HEFFERNAN, GERRY
34-43 BeeHive-1 [Mont.]
43-47 Parade Sportive

HEFFERNAN, JIMMY
37/8 World Wide Gum 130

HEFFLER, ERIC
99/0 Hamilton Bulldogs

HEFFORD, JAYNA
97/8 UD Coll. Choice 289

HEFFORD, WARREN
99/0 Sudbury Wolves 16

HEGBERG, JASON
99/0 Lethbridge Hurricanes

HEGEN, DIETER
94/5 DEL 311
95/6 DEL 94, 433
96/7 DEL 281
98/9 DEL 292
98/9 DEL 338
99/0 Eishockey 254
95 Globe 225
95 Panini Worlds 70
94 Semic 287
89 Semic Sticker 114
91 Semic Sticker 173
93 Semic Sticker 158
92/3 Upper Deck 370
96 Wien 198

HEGEN, GERHARD
94/5 DEL 169
95/6 DEL 148

HEHR, JASON
93/4 N. Michigan Wildcats

HEIB, JOSEPH
98/9 DEL 93

HEIDT, MICHAEL
94/5 DEL 275
95/6 DEL 246
96/7 DEL 138
89 Semic Sticker 113
91 Semic Sticker 159
92 Semic Sticker 174
93 Semic Sticker 151

HEIDT, ROBERT
94/5 DEL 24
95/6 DEL 21

HEIKKERI, ESKO
80/1 Mallasjuoma 147

HEIKKERI, PERTTI
80/1 Mallasjuoma 146

HEIKKILA, ANTTI
66/7 Champion 47
65/6 Hellas 36
70/1 Kuvajulkaisut 191
80/1 Mallasjuoma 200
80/1 Mallasjuoma 39
72 Panda MM-Toronto
78/9 SM-Liiga 221
78/9 SM-Liiga 63
71/2 Williams Finnish 82
72/3 Williams Finnish 245
73/4 Williams Finnish 243

HEIKKILA, KARI
80/1 Mallasjuoma 29
82 Semic Sticker 28
71/2 Williams Finnish 339

HEIKKILA, LASSE
65/6 Hellas 37

HEIKKILA, MATTI
80/1 Mallasjuoma 53
78/9 SM-Liiga 77

HEIKKINEN, KARI
91/2 Jyvas Hyva 56
92/3 Jyvas Hyva 164
93/4 Jyvas Hyva 292
93/4 Sisu 70
94/5 Sisu 11

HEIKKINEN, MARKKU
92/3 Jyvas Hyva 77
93/4 Jyvas Hyva 136
93/4 Sisu 139
94/5 Sisu 3

HEIKKINEN, PERTTI
66/7 Champion 120

HEIKKONEN, HANNU
66/7 Champion 163

HEIL, JEFF
97/8 Charlotte Checkers
98/9 Charlotte Checkers

HEINÄNEN, JOKKE
98/9 Cardset 262
99/0 Cardset 290
00/1 Cardset 68
97/8 Hockey-Box
92/3 Jyvas Hyva 198
93/4 Jyvas Hyva 352
95 Panini Worlds 181
93/4 Sisu 224
94/5 Sisu 116, J-2
95/6 Sisu 356
96/7 Sisu 154
95/6 Sisu Limited 24

HEINE, PETE
92/3 Wheeling Thund'birds 8

HEINISTÖ, PASI
92/3 Jyvas Hyva 115
93/4 Sisu 269
94/5 Sisu 288

HEINO, AKI
98/9 Cardset 53
99/0 Cardset 31

HEINO, HEIKKI
66/7 Champion 73
65/6 Hellas 15

HEINO, KIMMO
65/6 Hellas 130
70/1 Kuvajulkaisut 104
72 Panda MM-Toronto
71/2 Williams Finnish 112
72/3 Williams Finnish 82
73/4 Williams Finnish 128

HEINO, TIMO
80/1 Mallasjuoma 87
78/9 SM-Liiga 129

HEINOLD, PETER
94/5 DEL 434

HEINONEN, ISMO
71/2 Williams Finnish 361

HEINONEN, MARKKU
72/3 Williams Finnish 301

HEINONEN, MAURI
72/3 Williams Finnish 302

HEINONEN, RAINE
73/4 Williams Finnish 216

HEINONEN, RAUNO
66/7 Champion 72
65/6 Hellas 9
65/6 Hellas 99
70/1 Kuvajulkaisut 155

HEINONEN, REIJO
72 Panda MM-Toronto
71/2 Williams Finnish 83
72/3 Williams Finnish 246
73/4 Williams Finnish 244

HEINRICHS, MARCO
94/5 DEL 213

HEINS, SHAWN
99/0 BAP Mem. 227
99/0 Pacific 385
00/1 Premier Plus 91
91/2 7th...Sketch OHL 131
00/1 Stadium 237
99/0 Kentucky Tho'blades
91/2 Peterborough Petes
92/3 Windsor Spitfires

HEINTZ, DAVIN
00/1 Saskatoon Blades

HEINVIRTA, RISTO
66/7 Champion 94

HEINZE, DANA
96/7 Johnstown Chiefs

HEINZE, STEPHEN
98/9 Be A Player 157, ✍ Aut. 157
01/2 Crown Royale 68
92/3 Fleer Ultra 3
01/2 Heads Up 45
93/4 Leaf 116
94/5 Leaf 404
92/3 O-Pee-Chee 92
01/2 O-Pee-Chee 239
02/3 O-Pee-Chee 77
92/3 OPC Premier 24
98/9 Omega 15
98/9 Pacific 79
99/0 Pacific 24
00/1 Pacific 35
01/2 Pacific 51
02/3 Pacific 166
97/8 Pacific CC 261
99/0 Pa. Paramount 21
00/1 Pa. Paramount 70
91/2 Parkhurst 232
92/3 Parkhurst 247
01/2 Parkhurst 246
93/4 Pinnacle 53
94/5 Pinnacle 341
96/7 Pi. Be A Player 154, ✍ Aut. 154
95/6 Pi. Summit 87
94/5 POG 348
93/4 Power Play 289
93/4 Premier 378
94/5 Premier 387
01/2 PS Titanium 65
92/3 Pro Set 220
92/3 Score 476
93/4 Score 251
97/8 Score Bost. 10
92/3 Topps 519
95/6 Topps 278
99/0 Topps 56
01/2 Topps 239
02/3 Topps 77
99/0 To. Chrome 56
02/3 T. Limited 77
92/3 T. Stadium Club 166
93/4 To. Stadium 15
94/5 T. Stadium Club 137
00/1 UD Reserve 26
92/3 Upper Deck 400
92/3 Upper Deck AC3
94/5 Upper Deck 327
95/6 Upper Deck 293
98/9 Upper Deck 42
00/1 Upper Deck 280
01/2 Upper Deck 313
94/5 UD BAP ✍ 161
97/8 UD Coll. Choice 20
98/9 UD G. Reserve 42
99/0 UD MVP Cup 20
00/1 UD Vintage 106

HEINZE, STEVE
02/3 Manchester Monarchs

HEINZLE, KARL
94 Semic 248

HEISIG, BRANJO
94/5 DEL 394
95/6 DEL 164
96/7 DEL 238

HEISKALA, EARL
70/1 Esso Power Player
69/0 O-Pee-Chee 170
70/1 O-Pee-Chee 193
70/1 PHIL
72/3 Los Angeles Sharks

HEISKANEN, ARTO
92/3 Jyvas Hyva 194
93/4 Jyvas Hyva 347
93/4 Sisu 230
94/5 Sisu 30
95/6 Sisu 176
95/6 Sisu Limited 27

HEISKANEN, SANTERI
99/0 Cardset 20
00/1 Cardset 162

HEISS, JOSEF
94/5 DEL 200
95/6 DEL 195, 429
96/7 DEL 338
95 Globe 218
95 Panini Worlds 51
94 Semic 272
95 Semic 165
91 Semic Sticker 153
92 Semic Sticker 172
00/1 UD DEL 135

HEISS, JOSEPH
99/0 Eishockey 101

HEISTAD, JERAMIE
91/2 7th...Sketch WHL 324

HEISTEN, BARRETT
01/2 Parkhurst 265
01/2 Signature 218, ✍ Aut. 218
98/9 SPx Prospects 85
01/2 Stadium 114
01/2 Upper Deck 348
98/9 UD Black Diam. 116
01/2 UD Ice 108
00/1 UD Prospects 64, CS7
01/2 Hartford Wolf Pack

HEJDA, JAN
97/8 APS 157
97/8 DS Sticker 194
98/9 OFS 253
99/0 OFS 383
00/1 OFS 90
01/2 OFS 271

HEJDUK, MILAN
01/2 Adrenaline 48, PM 2
01/2 ASG History
94/5 APS 34
95/6 APS 330
96/7 APS 157, 400
97/8 APS 255
01/2 Atomic 25, PP 9
99/0 Aurora 39
00/1 Aurora 39, SR-6
02/3 BAP All-Star 29, ✂ ASJ
98/9 Be A Player 187, ✍ Aut. 187
00/1 BAP All-Star AS-6
99/0 BAP Mem. 130
00/1 BAP Mem. 239
01/2 BAP Memor. 73, ✂ ASJ, ✂ ASE, ✂ ASN, ✂ ASS, ✂ AST, ✂ CoO, HSHS, ✂ PP, ✂ SCC
02/3 BAP Memorabilia 149, ✂ ASJ18
98 Bonaparte 1D
98 Bonaparte Pexeso 4
01/2 Bowman 25
02/3 Bowman 46
98/9 Bowman's Best 110
02/3 Calder 33
99/0 Crown Royale 38, -IE 6
00/1 Crown Royale 29
01/2 Crown Royale 38
02/3 Crown Royale 24, ✂ GWDP 6
97/8 DS 70
00/1 DS JT11
01/2 DS 45
96/7 DS Sticker 259
97/8 DS Sticker 136
98/9 Dynagon Ice 48, -IR 2
99/0 Dynagon Ice 57
01/2 eTopps 25
02/3 Exclusive 41, ✂ GWJ 5
02/3 First Edition 16, ✂ Jers., ✂ HSHSJers 11
01/2 Heads Up 24
02/3 Heads Up 31, ✂ GWQ 8, ✂ GWQ 32
02/3 In The Game-Used 14, 114, ✂ E29, ✂ GUJ29, ✂ SJ29
99/0 McDonald's McD-19
99/0 Millenium 70, ✍ Aut. 70
99/0 NHL Power Play
01/2 O-Pee-Chee 51
02/3 O-Pee-Chee 99
98/9 OFS 249
00/1 OFS 386
98/9 Omega 67
99/0 Omega 63, G-2
99/0 Pacific 106, -GC 10
00/1 Pacific 115, IO-7, GCDC-9
01/2 Pacific 102
02/3 Pacific 91
02/3 Pacific Complete 110
98/9 Pa. Crown Roy. 34, -RC-2
99/0 Pa. Paramount 64
00/1 Pa. Paramount 61
98/9 Pa. Revolution 36
99/0 Panini Sticker 212
00/1 Panini Sticker 135
00/1 Parkhurst P-77
01/2 Parkhurst 38, ✂ PJ2, ✂ PS2, ✂ HSHSJers, ✂ T8
02/3 Parkhurst 122, ✂ GJ16, ✂ SJ16, ✂ HSHSJers
02/3 Parkhurst Retro 79, ✂ HSHSJers, ✂ RR8
00/1 Premier Plus 75, MB5, PA4
99/0 Prism 39
00/1 Private Stock 24, PS-11, PSNW-8
01/2 Pr. Stock 22
02/3 Pr. Stock Reserve 25
00/1 PS Titanium 21
01/2 PS Titanium 35, ✂ DSJ 11
02/3 PS Titanium 25, ✂ GWJ 17
02/3 Quest for the Cup 22
99/0 Revolution 40, TL-25
00/1 Revolution 37, HD-9, SM-3
94/5 Sig. Rookies 52, ✍ 52
00/1 Signature 60, ✍ Aut. 102, ✂ HSHSJers
01/2 Signature C-25, ✍ Aut. LMH, ✂ GJ24, ✂ GSJ24, ✂ HSHSJers, ✂ TM9
02/3 Signature GS-62, ✂ SGJ29
02/3 Slam Card
98/9 SP Authentic 95
99/0 SP Authentic 22, TH4
00/1 SP Authentic ✍ SotT
01/2 SP Authentic 17, ✍ SotT, ✍ SotTD, ✍ SotTT (x2)
01/2 SP GU ✂ ✍ ISD
02/3 SP Game-Used ✂ AF, ✂ PH
02/3 Sports Vault 184
99/0 SPx 46
00/1 SPx 14, HH5
01/2 SPx 16, ✂ DT
98/9 SPx Prospects 16
00/1 Stadion 71
99/0 Stadium 60, CA3
00/1 Stadium 114, BT24
01/2 Stadium 51, G27, NHLP11, ✍ LSS
02/3 Stadium 37, ✂ FC6, ✂ PC6
99/0 Topps 88, IF5, ✍ TA7
00/1 Topps 136
01/2 Topps 51, SM7, ✍ CA
02/3 Topps 99
99/0 To. Chrome 88, IF5
00/1 To. Chrome 102, RF6
01/2 To. Chrome 51
02/3 T. Chrome 63
98/9 T. Gold Label 90
99/0 To. Gold Label FG10
00/1 To. Gold Label 81
00/1 To. Heritage 62, NT3
01/2 To. Heritage 17
02/3 To. Heritage ✂ GS, ✂ GSB
00/1 To. Heritage ASG 5
02/3 T. Limited 99
99/0 To. Prmr. Plus 81, TNO8
01/2 To. Reserve 48
00/1 To. Stars 49
02/3 T. Total 219
00/1 UD Heroes 29
01/2 UD PlayMakers Ltd 24, ✂ PCCJ, -PCPJ
00/1 Ultimate Mem. ✍ U-12, ✂ Jers. 28, ✂ J-32, ✂ S-32
01/2 Ultimate Mem. ✂ ASGH, ✂ DD, ✂ WTF, ✍ Aut.
02/3 Ultimate Mem. ✂ GUJ, ✂ Num
99/0 Ult. Victory 22
98/9 Upper Deck 247
99/0 Upper Deck 42, NI4
00/1 Upper Deck 43, A3, TT1, UDF
01/2 Upper Deck 45, CT2, SS4, T2, ✂ SCFJers., ✂ SCFJersT
02/3 Upper Deck 46, ✂ PA, ✂ PW, ✂ UDPL
00/1 UD ASG PP5, HH2
99/0 UD Black Diam. 28
00/1 UD Black Diam. 16
99/0 UD C. Legends 75
01/2 UD Challenge 18, ✂ UC
02/3 UD Classic ✂ HR
98/9 UD G. Reserve 247
99/0 UD G. Reserve 42, / Backup 163
99/0 UD Gretzky Excl. 87
01/2 UD Honor Roll ✂ HS
00/1 UD Ice 12
01/2 UD Ice 92, ✍ CCA
00/1 UD Legends 35
01/2 UD Mask 21, ✂ GJ, ✂ JP, ✂ DP
98/9 UD MVP 55
99/0 UD MVP 58
00/1 UD MVP 49, ME4, ✍ ME
01/2 UD MVP 45, -J, ✍ SJ
02/3 UD MVP 45, SD (x2), ST (x2)
99/0 UD MVP Cup 50, CC3
01/2 UD Premier 15, ✂ B, ✂ D., ✍ SigS
02/3 UD Premier 16, ✂ Jers, ✂ JD, ✂ Patch
02/3 UD Rookie ✂ 158b, ✂ DJ
01/2 UD SCup Champs 32
01/2 UD Top Shelf 11 , ✂ J
02/3 UD Top Shelf ✂ CP, ✂ GO, ✂ HT (x2), ✂ SH, ✂ ST, ✍ Sig
00/1 UD Vintage 93
01/2 UD Vintage 67, 70
02/3 UD Vintage 66, GB 66, ✂ FS
00/1 Vanguard 28
01/2 Vanguard 25, ✂ DGM 49
02/3 Vanguard 26
99/0 Victory 80, 351
00/1 Victory 65, 295
01/2 Victory 86, 418
02/3 Victory 54, -NP14
01/2 Waving the Flag 10
99/0 WGretzky 48
98/9 COLO / Howler Says
99/0 COLO / Kid Smart

HEJI, PAVEL
99/0 Score 117

HEJNA, TONY
90/1 ProCards 90

HELANDER, HANNU
80/1 Mallasjuoma 157
82 Semic Sticker 34
78/9 SM-Liiga 45

HELANDER, PEKKA
71/2 Williams Finnish 340

HELANDER, PETER
82 Semic Sticker 9

HELANEN, MARKUS
02/3 Cardset 171

HELBER, MIKE
99/0 UD Elitserien 133, L7

HELD, DANIEL
94/5 DEL 46
95/6 DEL 16
89 Semic Sticker 125

HELD, RYAN
00/1 UD Prospects 40

HELENIUS, SAMI
99/0 BAP Mem. 354
93/4 Jyvas Hyva 266
99/0 Millenium C-32
99/0 Omega 69
01/2 Pacific 125
99/0 To. Prmr. Plus 86
00/1 DALL / Southwest
01/2 DALL / Southwest
98/9 Las Vegas Thunder
94/5 Saint John Flames
95/6 Saint John Flames
96/7 Saint John Flames
97/8 Saint John Flames

HELENIUS, TEUVO
66/7 Champion 37

HELIN, JIMI
92/3 Jyvas Hyva 111
93/4 Jyvas Hyva 206
93/4 Sisu 263

HELISTEN, MIKKO
94/5 Parkie SE219
95/6 Sisu 319
94/5 Topps Finest 131

HELJEMO, CLAES
89/0 Semic Elitserien 98

HELLE, JARI
72/3 Williams Finnish 343

HELLE, MARTTI
71/2 Williams Finnish 174
73/4 Williams Finnish 178

HELLENBERG, PAR
89/0 Semic Elitserien 241
90/1 Semic Elitserien 151
91/2 Semic Elitserien 253

HELLER, EBERHARDT
34-43 BeeHive-1 [NYRa.]

HELLER, OTT
33/4 Anonymous 34
33/4 Canadian Gum
33/4 O-Pee-Chee 16
39/0 O-Pee-Chee 33
40/1 O-Pee-Chee 142
37/8 World Wide Gum 87

HELLER, OTTO
33-35 Diamond Match Silv.
36-39 Diamond Match TT1
36-39 Diamond Match TT2
36-39 Diamond Match TT3

HELLGREN, ARI
80/1 Mallasjuoma 89
82 Skopbank
78/9 SM-Liiga 131

HELLGREN, JENS
89/0 Semic Elitserien 164
90/1 Semic Elitserien 243
91/2 Semic Elitserien 173

HELLKVIST, STEFAN
94/5 Leaf Elit Set 71
95/6 Leaf Elit Set 239, FTF-7
89/0 Semic Elitserien 253
90/1 Semic Elitserien 166
91/2 Semic Elitserien 271
92/3 Semic Elitserien 291
95/6 UD Elitserien 107
97/8 UD Elitserien 114
98/9 UD Elitserien 128
99/0 UD Elitserien 114, ✍ Aut.
00/1 UD Elitserien 9, 179

HELLWIG, WOLFGANG
99/0 Eishockey 408

HELMAN, HARRY
23/4 William Paterson 5

HELMER, BRYAN
98/9 Bowman's Best 131
00/1 To. Heritage 205
98/9 PHOE / Coca-Cola
96/7 Albany River Rats
97/8 Albany River Rats
00/1 Kansas City Blades 19
98/9 Las Vegas Thunder
01/2 Manitoba Moose
02/3 Manitoba Moose

HELMER, TIM
82/3 North Bay Centennials
83/4 North Bay Centennials
83/4 Ottawa 67's
84/5 Ottawa 67's

HELMINEN, DWIGHT
97 Québec Pee Wee 0774

HELMINEN, RAIMO
98/9 Cardset 87, -Leij. 21
99/0 Cardset 5, 52, 164, 190, -AH7-pata
00/1 Cardset 35, 235
02/3 Cardset 172
95 Globe 141
95 Hartwall Karjala
97/8 Hockey-Box
94/5 Leaf Elit Set 67, P-4
95/6 Leaf Elit Set 96, C-6, LM-10
95 Panini Worlds 179
94 Semic 31
95 Semic 14
90/1 Semic Elitserien 135
91/2 Semic Elitserien 186
92/3 Semic Elitserien 210
89 Semic Sticker 39
91 Semic Sticker 24
93 Semic Sticker 63
94/5 Sisu 363
95/6 Sisu Gold 12
95/6 UD Elitserien 141, 232
96 Wien 14

HELMUTH, ANDY
84/5 Ottawa 67's

HELPERL, JEFF
01/2 Norfolk Admirals

HELPPOLAINEN, RAIMO
66/7 Champion 97
65/6 Hellas 81

HELSINKI, JON
84/5 Kitchener Rangers

HEM, MORTEN
92/3 Semic Nordisk 158

HEMSKY, ALES
02/3 Atomic 109
02/3 BAP All-Star 128
02/3 BAP Draft Florida 13
02/3 BAP Memorabilia 281
02/3 Bowman 159
02/3 Calder 117, -CR 10
02/3 Crown Royale 113, -RR 10
02/3 eTopps 42
02/3 Exclusive 178
02/3 First Edition 437R
02/3 Heads Up 126
02/3 In The Game-Used 89, ✂ C6
02/3 O-Pee-Chee 337
99/0 OFS 350
02/3 Pacific 126
02/3 Pacific Complete 523
02/3 Parkhurst 211
02/3 Parkhurst Retro 211
02/3 Pr. Stock Reserve 162
02/3 PS Titanium 115, -ROT 8
02/3 Quest for the Cup 118, -CC 8
02/3 SP Authentic ✍ 197, ✍ SotT, ✍ ✂ Patch
02/3 SP GU 77
02/3 SPx 160
02/3 Stadium 129
02/3 Topps 337
02/3 T. Chrome 176
02/3 To. Heritage 139
02/3 T. Total 409
02/3 Ultimate Mem. 11, ✂ CC
02/3 Upper Deck 235
02/3 UD Artistic 104, CG2
02/3 UD Classic 113
02/3 UD Foundations 152
02/3 UD Honor 152
02/3 UD Mask 168
02/3 UD Piece 129
02/3 UD Premier ✍ 99
02/3 UD Rookie ✂ 158
02/3 UD Top Shelf 128
02/3 Vanguard 114, -PP 10
00/1 Hull Olympiques 9
01/2 Hull Olympiques 10

HEMSKY, PETR
94/5 APS 280
99/0 OFS 348
00/1 OFS 30
01/2 Kitchener Rangers
00/1 London Knights

HEMSTRÖM, JENS
94/5 Leaf Elit Set 219
90/1 Semic Elitserien 147
95/6 UD Elitserien 181

HENCHBERGER, LLOYD
51/2 Laval Dairy 66

HENCKLE, JAMES
87/8 Kingston Canadians

HENDERSON, ARCHIE
88/9 ProCards / Indianapolis
82/3 HART / Jr. Whalers
89/0 Nashville Knights
84/5 Nova Scotia Oilers

HENDERSON, BURT
92/3 BCJHL 70
97/8 Cincinnati Cyclones
98/9 Cincinnati Cyclones
93/4 Tacoma Rockets

HENDERSON, GARFIELD
92/3 MPS SJHL 55
91/2 7th...Sketch WHL

HENDERSON, JAY
99/0 BAP Mem. 358
98 Bowman 77
98 Bowman Chrome 77
99/0 Omega 23
99/0 UD MVP Cup 18
98/9 Providence Bruins
99/0 Providence Bruins
00/1 Providence Bruins
95/6 Red Deer Rebels

HENDERSON, JOHN
51/2 Parkhurst 23
59/60 Whitby Dunlops

HENDERSON, MATT
02/3 BAP Memorabilia 390
02/3 First Edition 215
02/3 SP Authentic 140
02/3 SPx 171
02/3 UD Honor 109
02/3 UD Mask 134
02/3 UD Top Shelf 109
98/9 Milwaukee Admirals
01/2 Norfolk Admirals

HENDERSON, MURRAY
45-64 BeeHive-2 [Bost.]

HENDERSON, PAUL
68/9 Bauer Photo
64-67 BeeHive-3 [Detr.]
63-65 Chex
64/5 Coke/Sprite [Detr.]
65/6 Coca-Cola
71/2 Colgate Head
70/1 Dad's Cookies
70/1 Eddie Sargent 195
71/2 Eddie Sargent 200
72/3 Eddie Sargent 203
70/1 Esso Power Player
01/2 Fleer Greats 42, ✍ Aut.
71/2 Frito Lay
91/2 Future Trends C72 63, 71, 81, 98, ✍ 98
72/3 Post 22
73/4 Mac's Milk
68/9 O-Pee-Chee 127
69/0 O-Pee-Chee 47
70/1 O-Pee-Chee 217
71/2 O-Pee-Chee 67
72/3 O-Pee-Chee 126
72/3 O-Pee-Chee Crest 19
72/3 O-Pee-Chee TC
73/4 O-Pee-Chee 7
74/5 O-Pee-Chee 219
74/5 OPC WHA 57
75/6 OPC WHA 42
76/7 OPC WHA 84
77/8 OPC WHA 31
95/6 Parkie 66-67 40
94/5 Parkie Tall 50
97/8 Pi. Certified -S72, ✍ S72
68/9 Post Marble
70/1 Post Shooters
72 Semic Sticker 167
68/9 Shirriff / Toro. 3
65/6 Topps 51
66/7 Topps 46
66/7 Topps / Test 46
67/8 Topps 103
68/9 Topps 127
69/0 Topps 47
71/2 Topps 67
72/3 Topps 73
73/4 Topps 7
74/5 Topps 219
64/5 Toronto Star Action
71/2 Toronto Sun Photo
68/9 TORO
70/1 TORO
71/2 TORO
72/3 TORO
73/4 TORO

HENDERSON, PAUL
01/2 Fleer Legacy 42

HENDRICK, JORG
94/5 DEL 266

HENDRICKSON,
91/2 Avant Garde BCJHL 156

HENDRICKSON, DAN
98/9 Dayton Bombers
98/9 Dayton Bombers
93/4 Minnesota G'Gophers
94/5 Minnesota G'Gophers

HENDRICKSON, DARBY
01/2 Adrenaline 93
00/1 BAP Mem. 121
95/6 Bowman 129
94/5 Classic 104
94/5 Classic 4 Sport 135
93/4 Cla. Prospects LP6
95/6 Donruss 184
95/6 Edge Ice 79
93/4 Fleer Ultra 485
95/6 Fleer Ultra 340
95/6 Leaf 76
02/3 Pacific 183
97/8 Pa. Invincible R-193
97/8 Pi. Be A Player 178, ✍ Aut. 178
95/6 Pi. Summit 178
93/4 Power Play 505
93/4 Premier - USA Hockey 4
97/8 Score Toro. 12
95/6 Select CE 142
95/6 SBx Impact 223
95/6 SP 145
00/1 SP Authentic 44
00/1 Stadium 205
99/0 Topps 151
99/0 To. Chrome 151
00/1 To. Chrome 234
93/4 To. Stadium - Team U.S.A. 8
95/6 Upper Deck 505
96/7 Upper Deck 100
97/8 Upper Deck 166
01/2 Upper Deck 88
02/3 Upper Deck 87
96/7 UD CC 158
97/8 UD Coll. Choice 250
01/2 Victory 176
01/2 MINW / Crime 19
94/5 St. John's Maple Leafs
91/2 Minnesota G'Gophers
92/3 Minnesota G'Gophers

HENDRIX, TREVOR
01/2 Peterborough Petes

HENDRY, GRANT
02/3 Peterborough Phantoms

HENDRY, JOHN
93/4 Toledo Storm 18
94/5 Toledo Storm
91/2 L. Superior State Lakers

HENDY, JAMES
83 HHOF Postcard B5
83&87 HHOF 19

HENKELMAN, JEFF
95/6 Swift Current Broncos

HENKELMAN, SCOTT
01/2 Kamloops Blazers

HENNESSEY, DEREK
99/0 Guelph Storm
01/2 Guelph Storm
01/2 Guelph Storm M-Cup

HENNESSEY, JOHN
99 Québec Pee Wee 153

HENNESSY, JOSH
01/2 Québec Remparts 5
02/3 Québec Remparts

HENNIGAR, STAN
83/4 Nova Scotia Voyageurs

HENNING, LORNE
77/8 Coke
72/3 Eddie Sargent 135
74/5 Loblaws
73/4 O-Pee-Chee 218
74/5 O-Pee-Chee 367
75/6 O-Pee-Chee 354
76/7 O-Pee-Chee 193
77/8 O-Pee-Chee 219
78/9 O-Pee-Chee 313
79/0 O-Pee-Chee 193
76/7 Topps 193
77/8 Topps 219
79/0 Topps 193
79/0 NYIS
83/4 NYIS / News 27
99/0 NYIS / UD NY6
84/5 Springfield Indians 24

HENRICH, ADAM
00/1 UD Prospects 3

HENRICH, ED
94/5 Toledo Storm
92/3 Clarkson G'Knights

HENRICH, MICHAEL
98 Bowman 30, 127, ✍ A6
98 Bowman Chrome 30, 127
98/9 OPC Chrome 223
94 Québec Pee Wee 656
99/0 UD Sobey's 3
98/9 Topps 223
99/0 UD Prospects 11
00/1 Hamilton Bulldogs
01/2 Hamilton Bulldogs
02/3 Hamilton Bulldogs
98/9 Barrie Colts

HENRIKSEN, KENNETH
79 Panini Sticker 365

HENRIKSON, GUNNAR
91/2 Avant Garde BCJHL 141

HENRIKSSON, HANNU
99/0 Cardset 246
91/2 Jyvas Hyva 11
93/4 Jyvas Hyva 76
91 Semic Sticker 11
93/4 Sisu 114
94/5 Sisu 128
95/6 Sisu 30, 177
96/7 Sisu SH 1
95/6 Sisu Limited 102

HENRIKSSON, LENNART
91/2 Semic Elitserien 219

HENRY, ALEX
02/3 Atomic 110
02/3 BAP All-Star 108
02/3 BAP Memorabilia 285
99 Bowman 155
98 Bowman 156, ✍ A17
98 Bowman Chrome 156
02/3 Calder 150
02/3 Crown Royale 140
02/3 Exclusive 179
02/3 Pacific Complete 571
02/3 Pr. Stock Reserve 185
02/3 SP Authentic 144
02/3 Ultimate Mem. 15
02/3 UD Mask 145
02/3 UD Top Shelf 105
99/0 Hamilton Bulldogs
99/0 Hamilton Bulldogs/ Staz
00/1 Hamilton Bulldogs
01/2 Hamilton Bulldogs

HENRY, BURKE
02/3 BAP Memorabilia 382
99 Bowman 96
98 Bowman 67
98 Bowman Chrome 67
02/3 Ultimate Mem. 94
02/3 UD Rookie 128
99/0 Hartford Wolf Pack
00/1 Hartford Wolf Pack
95/6 Brandon Wheat Kings
98/9 Brandon Wheat Kings

HENRY, CAMILLE
52/3 Anonymous 73
45-64 BeeHive-2 [NYRa.]
64-67 BeeHive-3 [Chic.]
64-67 BeeHive-3 [NYRa.]
64/5 Coke/Sprite [NYRa.]
52/3 La Patrie
68/9 O-Pee-Chee 116
69/0 O-Pee-Chee 17
54/5 Parkhurst 73
93/4 Parkhurst PR50
02/3 Parkie - Reprint 196
93/4 Parkie 56-57 100
94/5 Parkie Tall 107
60/1 Shirriff 83
61/2 Shirriff 87
54/5 Topps 32
57/8 Topps 63
58/9 Topps 54
59/0 Topps 28
59/0 Topps 46
60/1 Topps 53
61/2 Topps 56
61/2 Topps - Stamp
62/3 Topps 62
63/4 Topps 56
64/5 Topps 14
65/6 Topps 58
67/8 Topps 26
68/9 Topps 116
69/0 Topps 17
57/8 Toronto Star Photo
62/3 Toronto Star Photo
63/4 Toronto Star Action
58/9 Toronto Star Weekend
91/2 Ultimate Original Six 22, ✍ Aut. 22

HENRY, DALE
94/5 Classic E3
88/9 ProCards / Springfield
89/0 ProCards AHL 231
90/1 ProCards 529
93/4 Milwaukee Admirals
84/5 Springfield Indians 17
83/4 Saskatoon Blades

HENRY, DARYL
83/4 Medicine Hat Tigers

HENRY, FRÉDÉRIC
97 Bowman 43
98/9 Albany River Rats
99/0 Albany River Rats
00/1 Albany River Rats

HENRY, JIM
34-43 BeeHive-1 [NYRa.]
34-43 BeeHive-1 [NYRa.]
45-64 BeeHive-2 [Chic.]
45-64 BeeHive-2 [Bost.]
43-47 Parade Sportive
51/2 Parkhurst 19
52/3 Parkhurst 74
53/4 Parkhurst 86
54/5 Parkhurst 49
92/3 Parkhurst PR-7
02/3 Parkie - Reprint 153
54/5 Topps 37
02/3 Ultimate Mem. ✄ GMIH

HENRY, KYLE
99/0 San Angelo Outlaws

HENRY, SHANE
94/5 Richmond Renegades

HENTTONEN, JUHA
80/1 Mallasjuoma 154

HENTUNEN, JUKKA
01/2 BAP Memor. 381
01/2 Bowman 54
99/0 Cardset 39
00/1 Cardset 238, 283
02/3 Cardset 173
01/2 Crown Royale 149
02/3 Heads Up ✄ GWQ 16, ✄ GWQ 36
01/2 O-Pee-Chee 340
02/3 Pacific ✄ GWJ 29
01/2 Parkhurst 307
01/2 Pr. Stock 116
01/2 PS Titanium 151
01/2 PS Titanium Draft 143, ✄ 50
01/2 SP Authentic 138
01/2 Stadium 125
01/2 Topps 340
01/2 To. Chrome 158
01/2 To. Reserve 110
01/2 UD PlayMakers Ltd 107
01/2 Upper Deck 418
01/2 UD Challenge 98
01/2 UD Ice 75
01/2 Vanguard 105

HENZEN, CHARLY
72 Semic Sticker 150

HEON, COREY
92/3 MPS SJHL 42

HEON, DENIS
87/8 Hull Olympiques

HEPPLE, ALAN
88/9 ProCards / Newmarket
89/0 ProCards AHL 117
90/1 ProCards 157
91/2 ProCards 316
92/3 Cincinnati Cyclones
90/1 Newmarket Saints
81/2 Ottawa 67's
82/3 Ottawa 67's
82/3 Ottawa 67's

HEPPNER, KEN
81/2 Regina Pats

HERBERS, IAN
84/5 Kelowna Wings &...
93/4 Leaf 423
93/4 Parkhurst 70
93/4 EDMO / Sheet
94/5 Cape Breton Oilers
00/1 Cleveland Lumberjacks
96/7 Detroit Vipers
97/8 Detroit Vipers
98/9 Detroit Vipers

HERBERT, BJORN
71/2 Williams Finnish 279
73/4 Williams Finnish 195

HERBERT, IAN*
95/6 Birmingham Bulls

HERBERT, RICK
82/3 Regina Pats
83/4 Regina Pats

HERBERTS, JAMES
24/5 Champ's Cigarettes
24/5 Maple Crispette [V130] 8
24/5 William Paterson 25

HERBST, ABE
97/8 Upper Deck 404
98/9 Sudbury Wolves 22
99/0 Sudbury Wolves 6

HERBST, ALEXANDRE
95/6 DEL 179

HERBST, MARCO
95/6 DEL 125
96/7 DEL 205

HERCZEG, DON
83/4 Medicine Hat Tigers

HERGESHEIMER, P.
34-43 BeeHive-1 [Chic.]
40/1 O-Pee-Chee 143

HERGESHEIMER, WALLY
45-64 BeeHive-2 [NYRa.]
52/3 La Patrie
51/2 Parkhurst 100
52/3 Parkhurst 20
53/4 Parkhurst 67
54/5 Parkhurst 71
93/4 Parkie 56-57 26
54/5 Topps 22
57/8 Topps 33
54 Toronto Star Weekend

HERGOTT, ORRIN
91/2 Air Canada SJHL B51

HERLICK, DARCY
91/2 Air Canada SJHL D1
92/3 MPS SJHL 147

HERLOFSKY, DEREK
00/1 Kudos 52
95/6 Dayton Bombers
96/7 Dayton Bombers
01/2 Cardiff Devils

HERMANSSON, GÖRAN
99/0 UD Elitserien 27

HERMANSSON, JÖRGEN
98/9 UD Elitserien 20
00/1 UD Elitserien 18, 210, ✍ Sig.

HERMANSSON, LENNART
94/5 Leaf Elit Set 80
90/1 Semic Elitserien 142
92/3 Semic Elitserien 238

HERN, JAY
99/0 Indianapolis Ice

HERN, RILEY
91 C55 Reprint 32
83 HHOF Postcard K6
83&87 HHOF 232
10/1 Imperial
10/1 Imperial 22
11/2 Imperial 32

HERNEISEN, MATT
01/2 Peterborough Petes

HERNIMAN, SCOTT
88/9 Sudbury Wolves

HERNIMAN, STEVE
91/2 ProCards 146
93/4 Muskegon Fury
94/5 Muskegon Fury
95/6 Muskegon Fury
88/9 Kitchener Rangers
87/8 Soo Greyhounds 19

HERON, CHRIS
92 Québec Pee Wee 498
93 Québec Pee Wee 1405
96/7 Upper Deck 382

HERON, RED
34-43 BeeHive-1 [Toro.]
39/0 O-Pee-Chee 53
40/1 O-Pee-Chee 140

HEROUX, YVES
96/7 DEL 18
90/1 ProCards 96, 518
91/2 ProCards 34
94/5 Atlanta Knights 17
88/9 Flint Spirits
86/7 Fredericton Express
93/4 Indianapolis Ice
84/5 Chicoutimi Saguenéens

HERPERGER, CHRIS
99/0 BAP Mem. 367
95/6 Edge Ice 45
99/0 Omega 59
01/2 Pacific 86
01/2 Parkhurst 137
90/1 7th..Sketch WHL 67
91/2 7th...Sketch WHL 189
01/2 Signature 119, ✍ Aut. 119
00/1 UD MVP 189
01/2 Victory 81
01/2 OTTA
99/0 Cleveland Lumberjacks
98/9 Indianapolis Ice
93/4 Seattle Thunderbirds

HERR, CRAIG
95/6 Roanoke Express

HERR, MATT
95/6 Do. Elite WJ 37
98/9 Dynagon Ice 194
98/9 Omega 246
98/9 Pa. Crown Roy. 141
98/9 SP Authentic 113
98/9 Upper Deck 386
98/9 UD G. Reserve 386
98/9 UD MVP 214
99/0 Victory 312
01/2 Hershey Bears
98/9 Portland Pirates
99/0 Portland Pirates

HERRIMAN, DON
73/4 Quaker Oats 46

HERRINGTON, ROB
92/3 BCJHL 183

HERRON, DENIS
80/1 Dernière Heure
74/5 Loblaws
74/5 Loblaws Update
74/5 O-Pee-Chee 45
75/6 O-Pee-Chee 68
76/7 O-Pee-Chee 55
77/8 O-Pee-Chee 119
78/9 O-Pee-Chee 172
79/0 O-Pee-Chee 94
80/1 O-Pee-Chee 130
80/1 O-Pee-Chee 166
82/3 O-Pee-Chee 239
82/3 O-Pee-Chee 241
82/3 O-Pee-Chee 270
84/5 O-Pee-Chee 176
85/6 O-Pee-Chee 186
81/2 OPC Sticker 258
82/3 OPC/Topps Sticker 252
82/3 OPC/Topps Sticker 41
84/5 OPC Sticker 122
79 Panini Sticker 52
80/1 Pepsi Bottle Cap
74/5 Topps 45
75/6 Topps 68
76/7 Topps 55
77/8 Topps 119
78/9 Topps 172
79/0 Topps 94
80/1 Topps 130
80/1 Topps 166
79/0 MONT
80/1 MONT
81/2 MONT
77/8 PITT / McDonald's
83/4 PITT / Coke Is It✄
83/4 PITT / Heinz
84/5 PITT / Heinz

HERSH, HAROLD
91/2 7th...Sketch LHJMQ 219
91/2 7th...Sketch LHJMQ 219
95/6 Fredericton Canadiens
96/7 Fredericton Canadiens
98/9 Kentucky Tho'blades
01/2 Rockford IceHogs

HERSH, JAROLD
94/5 Slapshot Memorial 57

HERSKETH, BOB
59/60 Whitby Dunlops

HERTER, JASON
92/3 Classic Prospects 58
98/9 DEL 71
99/0 Eishockey 334
91/2 ProCards 600
90/1 Upper Deck 325
00/1 UD DEL 182
01/2 UD DEL 182
92/3 Hamilton Canucks
96/7 Kansas City Blades

HERVEY, MATT
88/9 ProCards / Moncton
89/0 ProCards AHL 40
90/1 ProCards 251
91/2 ProCards 63
92/3 Atlanta Knights
93/4 Milwaukee Admirals
87/8 Moncton Hawks
89/0 Moncton Hawks
90/1 Moncton Hawks
83/4 Victoria Cougars

HERZIG, FALK
94/5 DEL 402
95/6 DEL 421

HERZIG, ROLAND
79 Panini Sticker 249

HES, JIRI
94/5 APS 257
95/6 APS 130
96/7 APS 8
97/8 APS 151
99/0 DS 188
00/1 DS 100
96/7 DS Sticker 116
99/0 OFS 76
00/1 OFS 191
01/2 OFS 108

HESCHUK, BRAD
88/9 Kamloops Blazers

HESHKA, SCOTT
92/3 MPS SJHL 159

HESS, BOB
75/6 O-Pee-Chee 264
76/7 O-Pee-Chee 277
77/8 O-Pee-Chee 394
78/9 O-Pee-Chee 358
75/6 Topps 264

HESS, MANUEL
94/5 DEL 190
95/6 DEL 190
96/7 DEL 129

HETTLE, FRED
90/1 7th..Sketch WHL 300
91/2 7th...Sketch WHL 271

HEVONKORPI, RISTO
72/3 Williams Finnish 279

HEWARD, JAMIE
98/9 Bowman's Best 74
92/3 Classic Prospects 107
99/0 Pacific 224
91/2 ProCards 308
90/1 7th..Sketch WHL 167
99/0 Ult. Victory 53
01/2 UD Vintage 76
01/2 COLU
98/9 NASH / Wendy's 11
92/3 Cleveland Lumberjacks
93/4 Cleveland Lumberjacks
95/6 St. John's Maple Leafs
96/7 St. John's Maple Leafs
87/8 Regina Pats
89/0 Regina Pats

HEWER, OAK
01/2 Rockford IceHogs
96/7 Soo Greyhounds

HEWITSON, BOBBY
83 HHOF Postcard F6
83&87 HHOF 82

HEWITT, FOSTER
34-43 BeeHive-1 [Announcer]
34/5 CCM [Green]
83 HHOF Postcard A7
83&87 HHOF 8
92/3 Legends 13
38/9 Quaker Oats

HEWITT, JOHN
00/1 Asheville Smoke

HEWITT, WILLIAM A.
83 HHOF Postcard G8
83&87 HHOF 99

HEWSON, RUSSELL
01/2 Louisiana Ice Gators

HEXTALL, BRYAN
02/3 Ultimate Mem. ✍ Cut

HEXTALL, BRYAN (JR.)
70/1 Dad's Cookies
71/2 Eddie Sargent 173
72/3 Eddie Sargent 173
70/1 Esso Power Player
72/3 Post 13
69/0 O-Pee-Chee 154
70/1 O-Pee-Chee 94
71/2 O-Pee-Chee 16
72/3 O-Pee-Chee 174
73/4 O-Pee-Chee 43
75/6 O-Pee-Chee 26
76/7 O-Pee-Chee 13
70/1 Topps 94
71/2 Topps 16
72/3 Topps 157
73/4 Topps 43
75/6 Topps 26
76/7 Topps 13
71/2 Toronto Sun Photo
71/2 PITT / Sportcolor

HEXTALL, BRYAN (SR.)
34-43 BeeHive-1 [NYRa.]
83 HHOF Postcard K7
83&87 HHOF 141
93/4 Legends of Hockey 28
39/0 O-Pee-Chee 86

HEXTALL, DENNIS
70/1 Eddie Sargent 133
70/1 Esso Power Player
74/5 Loblaws
69/0 O-Pee-Chee 107
70/1 O-Pee-Chee 186
71/2 O-Pee-Chee 244
72/3 O-Pee-Chee 225
73/4 O-Pee-Chee 115
74/5 O-Pee-Chee 112
74/5 O-Pee-Chee 115
74/5 O-Pee-Chee 2
75/6 O-Pee-Chee 310
75/6 O-Pee-Chee 321
76/7 O-Pee-Chee 32
77/8 O-Pee-Chee 197
78/9 O-Pee-Chee 48
79/0 O-Pee-Chee 392
72 Semic Sticker 172
69/0 Topps 107
71/2 Topps 128
73/4 Topps 136
74/5 Topps 112
74/5 Topps 115
74/5 Topps 2
75/6 Topps 310
75/6 Topps 321
76/7 Topps 32
77/8 Topps 197
78/9 Topps 48
73/4 MINS
79/0 WASH

HEXTALL, DONEVAN
91/2 Arena 24
91/2 Classic 29
91/2 Classic Four Sport 29
92 7th...Sketch Awards 15
90/1 7th..Sketch WHL 277
91/2 7th...Sketch WHL 266
91/2 Star Pics 11
91/2 Ultimate Draft Pick 25, ✍ Aut.
93/4 Raleigh Icecaps
90/1 Prince Albert Raiders
91/2 Prince Albert Raiders

HEXTALL, RON
98/9 Aurora 139
98/9 Be A Player 99, ✍ Aut. 99
01/2 BT Pipes 114, ✄ DM, ✄ TW, ✄ VM, ✄ -HSHS Jers.
02/3 Between the Pipes ✄ I10
98/9 Bicycle.. 9-D
90/1 Bowman 105
91/2 Bowman 234
92/3 Bowman 195
95/6 Bowman 38
94/5 Cla. Images PL4
93/4 Donruss 196
94/5 Donruss 147
95/6 Donruss 147
96/7 Donruss 61
97/8 Donruss 114
96/7 Do. Canadian 51
97/8 Do. Canadian 48, NP-26
95/6 Do. Elite 108, PW-8
96/7 Do. Elite 2
97/8 Do. Elite 35
97/8 Do. Preferred 96, CG-14
97/8 Do. Priority 48, PG-9
97/8 Do. Studio 43
98/9 Dynagon Ice 136
93/4 EA Sports 114
88/9 Esso All-Star
94/5 Flair 127
96/7 Flair 68
94/5 Fleer 154
96/7 Fleer 80, 144, 145, VT-5
01/2 Fleer Legacy 61
95/6 Fleer Metal 110
96/7 Fl. Picks 80, F50-18, FF-3
92/3 Fleer Ultra 174, 385
93/4 Fleer Ultra 366
94/5 Fleer Ultra 127, 343
95/6 Fleer Ultra 117, 371
96/7 Fl. Ultra 124
88/9 Frito Lay
93/4 High Liner 4
95/6 Hoyle / East. 5-Spade
02/3 In The Game-Used ✄ GP19
90/1 Kraft 17
92/3 Kraft / PB
94/5 Kraft / KD
95/6 Kraft / PS
93/4 Leaf 341
94/5 Leaf 50, 495
95/6 Leaf 192
96/7 Leaf 194, SD-14
97/8 Leaf 52
95/6 L. Limited SS-7
96/7 L. Limited 35
96/7 L. Preferred 77, LS-9
97/8 Limited 89, FG-52
96/7 Maggers 113
96/7 Metal Univ. 112, AP-5
87/8 OPC/Topps 169
88/9 OPC/Topps 34
90/1 OPC/Topps 243
91/2 O-Pee-Chee 470
92/3 O-Pee-Chee 84
89/0 OPC/Topps 155
87/8 OPC Leaders 16
90/1 OPC Premier 41
91/2 OPC Premier 38
92/3 OPC Premier 57
88/9 OPC Stars 14
87/8 OPC Sticker 1
87/8 OPC Sticker 101-234
87/8 OPC Sticker 114-126
87/8 OPC Sticker 129-117
87/8 OPC Sticker 182-41
88/9 OPC Sticker 103
89/0 opcSticker 111
97/8 Omega 165, NSZ-9
98/9 Omega 174
98/9 Pacific 326
99/0 Pacific 302
97/8 Pacific CC 27, ITC-14
97/8 Pa. Crown Roy. 97, FO-13
98/9 Pa. Crown Roy. 98
97/8 Pa. Dynagon 89, S-15, T-55
97/8 Pa. Invincible 100
97/8 Pa. Paramount 132,GSL-14
98/9 Pa. Paramount 174, -GS 14
97/8 Pa. Revolution 101, RTS-14
98/9 Pa. Revolution 104
87/8 Panini Sticker 123
87/8 Panini Sticker 191
87/8 Panini Sticker 378
88/9 Panini Sticker 315
89/0 Panini Sticker 302
90/1 Panini Sticker 118
91/2 Panini Sticker 227
93/4 Panini Sticker 77
94/5 Panini Sticker 54
95/6 Panini Sticker 123
96/7 Panini Sticker 113, 146
97/8 Panini Sticker 91
91/2 Parkhurst 126
92/3 Parkhurst 144
92/3 Parkhurst CP20
93/4 Parkhurst 118
94/5 Parkhurst 136
95/6 Parkhurst 159, PP-33
01/2 Parkhurst ✍ PA50
94/5 Parkie SE130
91/2 Pinnacle 118
92/3 Pinnacle 340
93/4 Pinnacle 376
93/4 Pinnacle Mask 8
94/5 Pinnacle 274, MA6
95/6 Pinnacle 95, M-8
96/7 Pinnacle 101, M-6
97/8 Pinnacle 100
96/7 Pi. Be A Player SP-3
97/8 Pi. Inside 22, S-18
95/6 Pi. Summit 133, ITC-10
96/7 Pi. Summit 100, ITC-16, U-18
95/6 Pi. Zenith 97
96/7 Pi. Zenith 46
95/6 Playoff 181
94/5 POG 372
95/6 POG 210
93/4 Power Play 147
93/4 Premier 468
95/6 Pro Magnet 49, IC6
90/1 Pro Set 216
91/2 Pro Set 176
92/3 Pro Set 129
91/2 Pro Set Platinum 87
90/1 Score 25
90/1 Sco. Hot Cards 14
91/2 Score 239
91/2 Score CAN 459
92/3 Score 104
93/4 Score 152
93/4 Score 544
94/5 Score 140
95/6 Score 195
96/7 Score 80, NW-11, SD-14, S-9
97/8 Score 27
97/8 Score Phil. 1
94/5 Select 67
95/6 Select CE 78
96/7 Select CE 63, F-13
89 Semic Sticker 55
02/3 Signature ✄ FS8
95/6 SBx Emotion 131
95/6 SBx Impact 125
96/7 SBx Impact 95, ZH-5
94/5 SP 87
95/6 SP 109
96/7 SP 116
97/8 SP Authentic 116
97/8 SLU
96/7 Team Out✄
87/8 OPC/Topps - Stick. 2
92/3 Topps 40
95/6 Topps 167, 12HG
95/6 To. Finest 86
96/7 Topps Picks ID11
91/2 To. Stadium 173
92/3 T. Stadium Club 288
93/4 To. Stadium 433
94/5 T. Stadium Club 51, 182
95/6 To. Stadium 33
95/6 T. Super Skills 77
02/3 Ultimate Mem. ✄ CSTW, ✄ FS, ✄ RA, ✄ SCD
90/1 Upper Deck 227
91/2 Upper Deck 327
92/3 Upper Deck 532
93/4 Upper Deck 434
94/5 Upper Deck 170, SP-147
95/6 Upper Deck 428, SE-65
96/7 Upper Deck 119, 197, SS22B
95/6 UD BAP 198, ✍ S198
95/6 UD CC 203
96/7 UD CC 191, 326
97/8 UD Coll. Choice 188
02/3 UD Foundations 74, 79, ✍ SG
86/7 PHIL
89/0 PHIL
90/1 PHIL
91/2 PHIL / J.C. Penney
94/5 PHIL / Sheet [x2]
96/7 PHIL / Ocean Spray
01/2 PHIL
92/3 QUEB / Petro-Canada
82/3 Brandon Wheat Kings
83/4 Brandon Wheat Kings

HEXTALL, RON
02/3 Fleer Throwbacks 78, 9SO, ✄ 2DTG, ✄ 9SO

HEYLIGER, VIC
36-39 Diamond Match BH TT
36-39 Diamond Match BH BT

HIBBERT, JIMMY
00/1 Kudos 109
93/4 Slapshot / Niagara Falls 2
97/8 Sheffield Steelers

HICKE, BILL
45-64 BeeHive-2 [Mont.]
64-67 BeeHive-3 [Mont.]
64-67 BeeHive-3 [NYRa.]
63-65 Chex
64/5 Coke/Sprite [Mont.]
65/6 Coca-Cola
70/1 Dad's Cookies
70/1 Eddie Sargent 143
71/2 Eddie Sargent 175
70/1 Esso Power Player
62/3 Cowan Tile
68/9 O-Pee-Chee 86
69/0 O-Pee-Chee 145
69/0 O-Pee-Chee 4in1
70/1 O-Pee-Chee 76
70/1 O-Pee-Chee DE 38
71/2 O-Pee-Chee 142
72/3 O-Pee-Chee 327
59/0 Parkhurst 31
60/1 Parkhurst 40
60/1 Parkhurst 56
61/2 Parkhurst 38
62/3 Parkhurst 40
63/4 Parkhurst 25
63/4 Parkhurst 84
95/6 Parkie 66-67 91
94/5 Parkie Tall 86
60/1 Shirriff 38
61/2 Shirriff 108
62/3 Shirriff 38
68/9 Shirriff / Oakl. 9
64/5 Topps 98
65/6 Topps 30
68/9 Topps 86
69/0 Topps 84
70/1 Topps 76
71/2 Toronto Sun Photo
60/1 York
61/2 York 16
63/4 York 30

HICKE, ERNIE
71/2 Eddie Sargent 139
72/3 Eddie Sargent 3
70/1 Esso Power Player
74/5 Loblaws
74/5 Loblaws Update
71/2 O-Pee-Chee 61
72/3 O-Pee-Chee 72
73/4 O-Pee-Chee 18
74/5 O-Pee-Chee 387
75/6 O-Pee-Chee 71
76/7 O-Pee-Chee 87
77/8 O-Pee-Chee 132
71/2 Topps 61
72/3 Topps 154
73/4 Topps 18
75/6 Topps 71
76/7 Topps 87
77/8 Topps 132
71/2 Toronto Sun Photo

HICKEL, VERN
94/5 Anchorage Aces 14

HICKEY, PAT
75/6 O-Pee-Chee 345
76/7 O-Pee-Chee 107
77/8 O-Pee-Chee 221
78/9 O-Pee-Chee 112
79/0 O-Pee-Chee 86
80/1 O-Pee-Chee 28
81/2 O-Pee-Chee 318
82/3 O-Pee-Chee 304
81/2 OPC Sticker 104
74/5 OPC WHA 24
79 Panini Sticker 68
80/1 Pepsi Bottle Cap
88/9 ProCards / New Haven
76/7 Topps 107
77/8 Topps 221
78/9 Topps 112
79/0 Topps 86
80/1 Topps 28
79/0 TORO
80/1 TORO
92/3 Hamilton Canucks
92/3 Hamilton Canucks

HICKS, ALEX
98/9 Pacific 353
97/8 Pa. Invincible R-159
95/6 Parkhurst 271
97/8 Pi. Be A Player 177, ✍ Aut. 177
97/8 Score Pitt. 15
96/7 Upper Deck 6
96/7 UD CC 9
01/2 UD DEL 138
94/5 Las Vegas Thunder
92/3 Toledo Storm WIOT
92/3 Toledo Storm
93/4 Toledo Storm 23

HICKS, DOUG
77/8 O-Pee-Chee 361
78/9 O-Pee-Chee 228
79/0 O-Pee-Chee 379
80/1 O-Pee-Chee 221
81/2 O-Pee-Chee 114
82/3 O-Pee-Chee 365
82/3 Post [Wash.]
78/9 Topps 228
80/1 Topps 221
79/0 EDMO
80/1 EDMO / Zellers
81/2 EDMO / Red Rooster
88/9 EDMO / Action 95
81/2 WASH

HICKS, GLENN
81/2 O-Pee-Chee 98
79/0 DETR
80/1 DETR
78/9 Winnipeg Jets

HICKS, GREG
60/1 Cleveland Barons

HICKS, GRIEG
52/3 Anonymous 124

HICKS, JAMEY
98/9 EBK ECHL All-Star

HICKS, JASON
00/1 Sudbury Wolves 6

HICKS, WAYNE
62/3 Cowan Tile
70/1 O-Pee-Chee 95
63/4 Québec Aces
65/6 Québec Aces
70/1 Topps 95

HIDLEBAUGH, MIKE
91/2 Air Canada SJHL C50

HIEKKARANTA, AARNO
65/6 Hellas 55

HIEMER, MANUEL
96/7 DEL 186

HIEMER, ULI
94/5 DEL 94
95/6 DEL 84
86/7 O-Pee-Chee 226
95 Panini Worlds 54
94 Semic 277
89 Semic Sticker 108
91 Semic Sticker 155
93 Semic Sticker 153
84/5 NJER
86/7 NJER / S.O.B.E.R.

HIETALAL, TOMMI
93/4 Thunder Bay Senators

HIETANEN, JORMA
65/6 Hellas 89

HIETANEN, OLLI J.
73/4 Williams Finnish 106

HIETANEN, OLLI T.
73/4 Williams Finnish 107

HIETANEN, OLLI?
71/2 Williams Finnish 98
72/3 Williams Finnish 141

HIGDON, HENRY
98/9 Hampton Roads

HIGGINS, CHRIS
97 Québec Pee Wee 0831

HIGGINS, JACK
52/3 Anonymous 105

HIGGINS, MATT
99/0 BAP Mem. 36
95/6 Bowman P17
98/9 Bowman's Best 135
99/0 Millenium 131, ✍ Aut. 131
98/9 Omega 122
99/0 Pacific 204
98/9 SPx Finite 45
98/9 UD Choice 107
99/0 Québec Citadelles 24
00/1 Québec Citadelles

HIGGINS, PAUL
82/3 TORO

HIGGINS, TIM
81/2 O-Pee-Chee 57
82/3 O-Pee-Chee 66
83/4 O-Pee-Chee 104
84/5 O-Pee-Chee 111
86/7 O-Pee-Chee 227
82/3 OPC/Topps Sticker 177
87/8 Panini Sticker 250
82/3 Post [Chic.]
81/2 Topps 69 [West]
79/0 CHIC
80/1 CHIC / Colour
80/1 CHIC / Brown
81/2 CHIC
82/3 CHIC
86/7 DETR / Little Caesars
87/8 DETR / Little Caesars
88/9 DETR / Little Caesars
84/5 NJER

HIGGS, REG
98/9 Sudbury Wolves 7

HIIROS, PENTTI
70/1 Kuvajulkaisut 173
71/2 Williams Finnish 99
72/3 Williams Finnish 142
73/4 Williams Finnish 108

HIITELA, SEPPO
78/9 SM-Liiga 64

HILBERT, ANDY
01/2 Bowman 141
02/3 Choice Prospects 20
02/3 O-Pee-Chee 268
01/2 PS Titanium 150
01/2 PS Titanium Draft 110
95 Québec Pee Wee 762
01/2 SPx 156
02/3 SPx 103
98/9 SPx Prospects 87
02/3 Topps 268
02/3 T. Limited 268
02/3 Upper Deck 15
98/9 UD Black Diam. 118
02/3 UD MVP 194
01/2 Providence Bruins

HILDEBRAND, IKE
45-64 BeeHive-2 [NYRa.]
51/2 Cleveland Barons
54/5 Parkhurst 83

HILDEBRANDT, ROY
89/0 Rayside-Balfour

HILDEN, ANTTI
99/0 Cardset 256
00/1 Cardset 157

HILGER, RAIMOND
94/5 DEL 380
95/6 DEL 378
96/7 DEL 199
98/9 DEL 299
99/0 Eishockey 256
95 Panini Worlds 67
94 Semic 288
95 Semic 169
92 Semic Sticker 180
93 Semic Sticker 163
92/3 Upper Deck 373

HILKER, JERRY
95/6 Tallahasee Tiger Sharks

HILL, AL
79/0 O-Pee-Chee 166
80/1 O-Pee-Chee 348
88/9 ProCards / Hershey
89/0 ProCards AHL 359
90/1 ProCards 20
91/2 ProCards 213
79/0 Topps 166
95/6 Cincinnati Cyclones
96/7 Cincinnati Cyclones

HILL, EDWARD
99 Bowman 37, ✍ BA4
99/0 Topps 266
99/0 To. Chrome 266
98/9 Barrie Colts

HILL, JEFF
90/1 Michigan Tech Huskies
91/2 Michigan Tech Huskies

HILL, KILEY
91/2 7th...Sketch OHL 314
98/9 Dayton Bombers
99/0 Missouri RiverOtters
93/4 Soo Greyhounds 24

HILL, MEL (SUDDEN DEATH)
34-43 BeeHive-1 [Bost.]
34-43 BeeHive-1 [Toro.]
39/0 O-Pee-Chee 96
45-54 Quaker Oats
91/2 BOST / SA Legends

HILL, SEAN
98/9 Be A Player 173, ✍ Aut. 173
00/1 BAP Mem. 339, 445
01/2 BAP Memor. 487
92/3 Classic 101
92/3 Classic Four Sport 214
93/4 Donruss 7
94/5 Flair 121
94/5 Fleer 147
92/3 Fleer Ultra 328
93/4 Fleer Ultra 182
93/4 Fleer Ultra 255
94/5 Fleer Ultra 339
93/4 Leaf 353
94/5 Leaf 476
99/0 Omega 44
00/1 Pacific 82
02/3 Pacific Complete 270
97/8 Pa. Invincible R-133
94/5 Panini Sticker 125
95/6 Panini Sticker 56
95 Panini Worlds 214
92/3 Parkhurst 487
93/4 Parkhurst 2
94/5 Parkhurst 6
95/6 Parkhurst 416
94/5 Parkie SE124
93/4 Pinnacle 147
93/4 Pinnacle Expa. 3
94/5 Pinnacle 395
95/6 Pinnacle 93
95/6 Playoff 287
95/6 POG 198
93/4 Power Play 3
93/4 Premier 312
94/5 Premier 545
91/2 ProCards 84
93/4 Score 490
93/4 Score 500
02/3 Sports Vault 39
95/6 Topps 329
00/1 Topps 254
93/4 To. Stadium 387
94/5 T. Stadium Club 28
02/3 T. Total 104
92/3 Upper Deck 392
92/3 Upper Deck 523
93/4 Upper Deck 16, SP-1
94/5 Upper Deck 161
95/6 Upper Deck 323
96/7 Upper Deck 117
00/1 Upper Deck 382
95/6 UD BAP 74, ✍ S74
95/6 UD CC 65
99/0 UD MVP Cup 40
97/8 CARO / Sprint
98/9 CARO / Highwoods
92/3 MONT
92/3 MONT / OPC 19
94/5 OTTA
95/6 OTTA
96/7 OTTA

HILL, TIM
93/4 Slapshot / Peterborough

HILLBLOM, NIKLAS
90/1 Semic Elitserien 219

HILLEBRANDT, JON
93/4 Classic 68
94/5 Classic ✍ Aut.
93/4 Cla. Prospects 162
93/4 Premier - USA Hockey 10
93/4 To. Stadium - Team U.S.A. 9
98/9 BC Icemen 16
98/9 BC Icemen
95/6 Binghampton Rangers
96/7 Peoria Rivermen

HILLER, BERND
70/1 Kuvajulkaisut 85

HILLER, DUTCH
34-43 BeeHive-1 [NYRa.]
39/0 O-Pee-Chee 89
43-47 Parade Sportive
43-47 Parade Sportive
45-54 Quaker Oats

HILLER, GUIDO
94/5 DEL 45

HILLER, JIM
93/4 Cla. Prospects 117
96/7 DEL 195
98/9 DEL 294
99/0 Eishockey 276
92/3 Fleer Ultra 307
92/3 OPC Premier 34
92/3 Parkhurst 281
92/3 Parkhurst 70
92/3 Pinnacle 399
92/3 Upper Deck 560
00/1 UD DEL 33
94/5 Binghampton Rangers

HILLIER, CRAIG
95/6 Bowman P18
97/8 Pi. BeeHive 64, ✍ Aut. 64
95/6 Slapshot 257

HILLIER, RANDY
85/6 O-Pee-Chee 212
88/9 OPC/Topps 158
90/1 O-Pee-Chee 408
89/0 OPC/Topps 126
91/2 OPC Premier 122
87/8 Panini Sticker 145
90/1 Panini Sticker 137
91/2 Pinnacle 281
90/1 Pro Set 507
91/2 Pro Set 360
91/2 Pro Set Platinum 158
90/1 Score 76
91/2 Score 30T
91/2 Score CAN 580
83/4 Souhaits Keychain [Bruins]
83/4 BOST
91/2 BUFF / Blue Shield
91/2 BUFF / Campbell's
91/2 BUFF / Pepsi
86/7 PITT / Kodak
87/8 PITT / Kodak
89/0 PITT / Foodland 11
90/1 PITT / Foodland 3

HILLMAN, FLOYD
52/3 Anonymous 83

HILLMAN, JIM
92/3 Minnesota G'Gophers
93/4 Minnesota G'Gophers

HILLMAN, JOHN
93/4 Minnesota G'Gophers

HILLMAN, LARRY
52/3 Anonymous 3
45-64 BeeHive-2 [Detr.]
45-64 BeeHive-2 [Bost.]
45-64 BeeHive-2 [Toro.]
64-67 BeeHive-3 [Toro.]
70/1 Dad's Cookies
70/1 Eddie Sargent 158
71/2 Eddie Sargent 75
72/3 Eddie Sargent 39
70/1 Esso Power Player
68/9 O-Pee-Chee 48
69/0 O-Pee-Chee 90
69/0 O-Pee-Chee 4in1
70/1 O-Pee-Chee 81
71/2 O-Pee-Chee 168
72/3 O-Pee-Chee 176
61/2 Parkhurst 14
62/3 Parkhurst 17
93/4 Parkie 56-57 55
95/6 Parkie 66-67 104
94/5 Parkie Tall 118
67/8 Post Tips 12
72 Semic Sticker 178
61/2 Shirriff 59
62/3 Shirriff 17
68/9 Shirriff / Minn. 12
57/8 Topps 17
58/9 Topps 25
67/8 Topps 80
68/9 Topps 48
69/0 Topps 90
70/1 Topps 81
71/2 Toronto Sun Photo
91/2 Ultimate Original Six 36, ✍ Aut. 36
60/1 York
61/2 York 31
63/4 York 11
72/3 BUFF
70/1 PHIL
68/9 TORO
69/0 TORO
78/9 Winnipeg Jets

HILLMAN, WAYNE
71/2 Bazooka Panel
45-64 BeeHive-2 [Chic.]
64-67 BeeHive-3 [Chic.]
64-67 BeeHive-3 [NYRa.]
63-65 Chex
64/5 Coke/Sprite [Chic.]
65/6 Coca-Cola
70/1 Dad's Cookies
70/1 Eddie Sargent 160
71/2 Eddie Sargent 146
72/3 Eddie Sargent 156
70/1 Esso Power Player
62/3 Cowan Tile
68/9 O-Pee-Chee 47
69/0 O-Pee-Chee 91
70/1 O-Pee-Chee 198
71/2 O-Pee-Chee 62
72/3 O-Pee-Chee 255
95/6 Parkie 66-67 84
94/5 Parkie Tall 41
61/2 Shirriff 21
61/2 Topps 38
62/3 Topps 31
63/4 Topps 27
64/5 Topps 41
66/7 Topps 87
66/7 Topps / Test 34
67/8 Topps 22
68/9 Topps 47
69/0 Topps 91
71/2 Topps 62
64/5 Toronto Star Action
71/2 Toronto Sun Photo
67/8 York 29

HILLOCK, MIKE
91/2 Air Canada SJHL C12
92/3 MPS SJHL 67
93/4 N. Michigan Wildcats

HILLSTORM, ANDERS
00/1 Kudos 8

HILTNER, MIKE
90/1 ProCards 594

HILTON, KEVIN
93/4 Donruss USA9
93/4 Pinnacle 493
93/4 Upper Deck 567
99/0 Charlotte Checkers
00/1 Charlotte Checkers

HILTON, KEVIN
96/7 Mississippi S'Wolves

HILTON, KEVIN
99/0 Mississippi S'Wolves

HILTUNEN, HANNU
80/1 Mallasjuoma 93
71/2 Williams Finnish 299

HILTUNEN, HARRI
70/1 Kuvajulkaisut 328

HIMES, NORMIE
33/4 Anonymous 21
33/4 Canadian Gum
33-35 Diamond Match Silv.
36-39 Diamond Match TT1
31/2 La Presse
33/4 O-Pee-Chee 29
33/4 WWGum 44
37/8 World Wide Gum 92

HINDELANG, MARC
99/0 Eishockey 394

HINDMARCH, DAVE
83/4 O-Pee-Chee 82
84/5 O-Pee-Chee 224
83/4 Vachon 7-127
82/3 CALG

HINKS, ROD
90/1 7th..Sketch OHL 384
91/2 7th...Sketch OHL 252
94/5 Johnstown Chiefs 9
93/4 Owen Sound Platers
93/4 Owen Sound Platers
90/1 Sudbury Wolves
91/2 Sudbury Wolves
92/3 Sudbury Wolves

HINOTE, DAN
99/0 BAP Mem. 337
00/1 BAP Mem. 345
99/0 Dynagon Ice 58
01/2 Parkhurst 205
99/0 SP Authentic 100
02/3 SP Authentic ,m> SP
01/2 SPx ✄ HT
99/0 Stadium 177
99/0 To. Prmr. Plus 105
02/3 T. Total 246
99/0 Upper Deck 209
01/2 Upper Deck 278
02/3 Upper Deck 291
02/3 UD Classic ✄ HR
99/0 UD G. Reserve 209
02/3 UD MVP - SD, Souv.
01/2 UD SCup Champs 31
02/3 UD Top Shelf ✄ ST
00/1 Victory 261
98/9 Hershey Bears

HINSE, ANDRÉ
75/6 OPC WHA 35
75/6 Houston Aeros
76/7 Phoenix Roadrunners

HINTERSTOCKER, BENJAMIN
99/0 Eishockey 191
01/2 UD DEL 256

HINTERSTOCKER, HERMANN
79 Panini Sticker 109

HINTERSTOCKER, MARTIN
79 Panini Sticker 106

HINZ, CHAD
99 Bowman 86
98 Bowman 80
98 Bowman Chrome 80
96/7 Upper Deck 383
99/0 Hamilton Bulldogs
00/1 Hamilton Bulldogs
01/2 Hamilton Bulldogs
02/3 Hamilton Bulldogs

HIRADECKY, TOMAS
99/0 Score 126

HIRCHE, KLAUS
70/1 Kuvajulkaisut 86

HIRSCH, COREY
01/2 BT Pipes 76
02/3 Between the Pipes 70
95/6 Bowman 145
93/4 Canada Nationals
93/4 Classic 133
94/5 Classic 85, T43
93/4 Cla. 4 Sport 236
94/5 Cla. Images 62
92/3 Classic Prospects 65
92/3 Classic Prospects 74
92/3 Classic Prospects BC5
93/4 Cla. Prospects IA2
93/4 Cla. Prospects LP14
93/4 Donruss 216
96/7 Donruss 179
97/8 Donruss 162
96/7 Do. Canadian 73
97/8 Do. Canadian 109
96/7 Do. Elite 34
95/6 Edge Ice 19
96/7 Flair 94
93/4 Fleer Ultra 462
93/4 Fleer Ultra 64
93/4 Fleer Ultra ARS 3
94/5 Fleer Ultra 330
93/4 Leaf 313
96/7 Leaf 152, SD-12
97/8 Leaf 146
96/7 L. Limited 89
96/7 L. Preferred 33, LS-3
97/8 Limited 10
96/7 Maggers 155
98/9 Omega 235
97/8 Pacific CC 180
92/3 Parkhurst 344
94/5 Parkhurst 149
95/6 Parkhurst 483
93/4 Pinnacle 220
94/5 Pinnacle RTP1
96/7 Pinnacle 211
96/7 Pi. Be A Player 51, ✍ Aut. 51
97/8 Pi. Inside 29, SU-9
95/6 Pi. Summit 184
96/7 Pi. Summit 125, ITC-15
95/6 Pi. Zenith 134
96/7 Pi. Zenith 75
93/4 Power Play 482
93/4 Premier - Canada 18
93/4 Score 453
94/5 Score CT4
96/7 Score 149, NW-16, SD-13
97/8 Score 12
97/8 Score Vanc. 11
95/6 Select CE 143
96/7 Select CE 71
94 Semic 80
90 7th..Sketch Mem.Cup 25
90/1 7th..Sketch WHL 306
91/2 7th...Sketch WHL 76
95/6 SP 151
96/7 SP 159
96/7 Topps Picks RS16
92/3 Upper Deck 463
94/5 Upper Deck 218
95/6 Upper Deck 405
96/7 Upper Deck 168
97/8 Upper Deck 171
96/7 UD Black Diam. 131
96/7 UD CC 272
97/8 UD Coll. Choice 258
96/7 UD Ice 71
96/7 VANC / IGA
92/3 Binghampton Rangers
94/5 Binghampton Rangers
00/1 Cincinnati Cyclones
99/0 Milwaukee Admirals
00/1 Portland Pirates
88/9 Kamloops Blazers
89/0 Kamloops Blazers

HIRSCH, GREG
92/3 Maine Black Bears

HIRSCH, TOM
84/5 O-Pee-Chee 99
84/5 MINS
85/6 MINS
87/8 MINS

HIRSCHFELD, BERT
45-54 Quaker Oats

HIRSIMÄKI, JARI
94/5 Sisu 240
95/6 Sisu 143, S-7
95/6 Sisu Limited 99
71/2 Williams Finnish 341
72/3 Williams Finnish 344

HIRSIMÄKI, JUKKA
80/1 Mallasjuoma 173
78/9 SM-Liiga 182
72/3 Williams Finnish 303

HIRSIMÄKI, TIMO
66/7 Champion 188
70/1 Kuvajulkaisut 125
72 Panda MM-Toronto
71/2 Williams Finnish 175
72/3 Williams Finnish 123

HIRVONEN, PENTTI
71/2 Williams Finnish 261

HIRVONEN, RAIMO
80/1 Mallasjuoma 9
82 Semic Sticker 31
82 Skopbank
78/9 SM-Liiga 26

HIRVONEN, SEPPO
71/2 Williams Finnish 318

HIRVONEN, TIMO
98/9 Cardset 20
99/0 Cardset 14
00/1 Cardset 11
02/3 Cardset 25

93/4 Jyvas Hyva 207
93/4 Sisu 268
94/5 Sisu 106
95/6 Sisu 294
96/7 Sisu 94

HIRVONEN, TOMI
98/9 Cardset 88
99/0 Cardset 53
00/1 Cardset 288
95/6 Sisu 242, DD-11
96/7 Sisu 36
95/6 UD CC 338

HISLOP, JAMIE
79/0 O-Pee-Chee 380
80/1 O-Pee-Chee 327
81/2 O-Pee-Chee 40
82/3 O-Pee-Chee 47
83/4 O-Pee-Chee 83
80/1 Pepsi Bottle Cap
82/3 Post [Calg.]
89/0 ProCards IHL 200
90/1 ProCards 612
83/4 Souhaits Keychain [Flames]
83/4 Vachon 8-128
81/2 CALG
82/3 CALG
92/3 CALG / IGA 029
80/1 QUÉB

HITCHCOCK, KEN
96/7 DALL / Southwest
00/1 DALL / Southwest
01/2 DALL / Southwest
84/5 Kamloops Blazers
85/6 Kamloops Blazers

HITCHEN, ALLAN
95/6 Slapshot 306

HITCHINGS, TREVOR
98/9 Kelowna Rockets

HITCHINS, KELLY
85/6 Brandon Wheat Kings
88/9 Brandon Wheat Kings

HITCHMAN, LIONEL
39/0 Bruins Magazine
24/5 Champ's Cigarettes
33-35 Diamond Match Silv.
29/0 La Presse
33/4 O-Pee-Chee 5
23/4 William Paterson 8
24/5 William Paterson 4
33/4 WWGum 34
91/2 BOST / SA Legends

HITNER, MIKE
90/1 Kansas City Blades

HJALM, MICHAEL
95/6 Leaf Elit Set 123, FTF-11
89/0 Semic Elitserien 180
92/3 Semic Elitserien 263

HJÄLM, MICHAEL
94/5 Leaf Elit Set 83
90/1 Semic Elitserien 13
95/6 UD Elitserien 180

HJALMAR, HANS
89/0 Semic Elitserien 204
90/1 Semic Elitserien 242

HJALMARSSON, MATS
91/2 Semic Elitserien 301
92/3 Semic Elitserien 316

HJERPE, HAKAN
80/1 Mallasjuoma 193
82 Semic Sticker 36
78/9 SM-Liiga 218

HJERTAAS, TROY
90/1 7th..Sketch WHL 282
91/2 7th...Sketch WHL 252
90/1 Prince Albert Raiders
91/2 Prince Albert Raiders

HLADY, SCOTT
92/3 Brandon Wheat Kings

HLAVAC, JAN
94/5 APS 84
95/6 APS 288
96/7 APS 138
97/8 APS 18
00/1 Aurora 94
99/0 BAP Mem. 157
00/1 BAP Mem. 187
01/2 BAP Memor. 137, 466
95/6 Classic 25
95/6 Cla. 5 Sport 136, SFF-2
97/8 DS 86
98/9 DS 93
99/0 DS NS20
00/1 DS JT13
97/8 DS Sticker 219
99/0 Millenium 164, C-49, ✍ Aut. 164
01/2 O-Pee-Chee 220
98/9 OFS 140, 434, 457
99/0 Omega 155
00/1 Pacific 262, ✍ Aut. 262
01/2 Pacific 259
02/3 Pacific 377
02/3 Pacific Complete 432
00/1 Pa. Paramount 162
00/1 Panini Sticker 65
00/1 Parkhurst P-186
01/2 Parkhurst 211, 398
94/5 Parkie SE213
99/0 Prism 90
00/1 Signature 215, ✍ Aut. 147
01/2 Signature 82, ✍ Aut. 82
94/5 SP 158
01/2 SP GU ✂ AF
99/0 Stadium 193
01/2 Stadium ✂ SCS
00/1 Topps 221, OTG
01/2 Topps 220
99/0 To. Prmr. Plus 138
02/3 T. Total 285
94/5 Upper Deck 508
00/1 Upper Deck 117
01/2 Upper Deck 359
02/3 Upper Deck 172
01/2 UD Ice 123
01/2 UD MVP 125
99/0 UD MVP Cup 123
00/1 UD Vintage 244
01/2 Victory 236

HLAVKA, DAN
01/2 OFS 137

HLINKA, IVAN
95/6 APS 395
97/8 APS 340
98 Bonaparte 6B
98 Bonaparte Pexeso 20
01/2 DS L7
92/3 Future Trends C76 128
72 Hellas MM-Jenkki 99
74 Hellas MM-Jenkki 70
70/1 Kuvajulkaisut 46
82/3 O-Pee-Chee 348
98/9 OFS 225, 437, -Leg. 5, -OW 16
99/0 OFS 252
72 Panda MM-Toronto
79 Panini Sticker 83
82/3 Post [Vanc.]
72 Semic Sticker 40
74 Semic Sticker 66
91 Semic Sticker 250
92 Semic Sticker 122
83/4 Souhaits Keychain [Canucks]
77-79 Sports. FIN 103-2455
71/2 Williams Finnish 26
72/3 Williams Finnish 6
73/4 Williams Finnish 47
81/2 VANC / Silverwood
82/3 VANC

HLINKA, JAROSLAV
95/6 APS 287
96/7 APS 139
97/8 APS 13
99/0 DS 149
00/1 DS 8
01/2 DS 16
97/8 DS Sticker 221
98/9 OFS 142
99/0 OFS 396, 476
00/1 OFS 303
01/2 OFS 18, -UHI 32

HLINKA, JIRI
94/5 APS 262
95/6 APS 142
96/7 APS 17
97/8 APS 164
97/8 DS Sticker 201

HLINKA, MARTIN
00/1 Portland Pirates
99/0 Quad City Mallards
00/1 Quad City Mallards

HLINKA, MICHAL
94/5 APS 117
95/6 APS 221

HLINKA, MIROSLAV
94/5 APS 90
95/6 APS 286
96/7 APS 136
97/8 APS 19
97/8 DS Sticker 220
98/9 OFS 141

HLOUCH, ROMAN
99/0 Score 159

HLUSHKO, TODD
92/3 Canada Nationals
93/4 Canada Nationals
93/4 Donruss 469
99/0 Eishockey 117
93/4 Fleer Ultra 463
97/8 Pa. Invincible R-28
94/5 Parkie SE25
96/7 Pi. Summit 194
93/4 Power Play 483
93/4 Premier - Canada 12
90/1 ProCards 202
91/2 ProCards 567
94/5 Score CT9
89/0 7th..Sketch OHL 41
00/1 UD DEL 10
01/2 UD DEL 169
01/2 Baltimore Skipjacks
98/9 Grand Rapids Griffins
94/5 Saint John Flames
95/6 Saint John Flames

HLYNSKY, BILL
81/2 Saskatoon Blades

HNAT, DAVID
01/2 OFS 100

HNIDY, SHANE
00/1 BAP Mem. 414
00/1 PS Titanium Draft 168
91/2 7th...Sketch WHL 177
00/1 SP Authentic 156
00/1 Upper Deck 429
00/1 UD Ice 118
01/2 OTTA
02/3 OTTA
99/0 Cincinnati M'Ducks
97/8 Grand Rapids Griffins
93/4 Prince Albert Raiders
95/6 Prince Albert Raiders

HNILICKA, MILAN
01/2 Adrenaline 8, PP 3
95/6 APS 337
96/7 APS 74, 386
97/8 APS 3, 343
01/2 Atomic 3
99/0 BAP Mem. 370
02/3 BAP Memorabilia 124
01/2 BT Pipes 5
02/3 Between the Pipes 32, 122, M2, ✂ GUJ36, ✍ Aut.
98 Bonaparte 4D
98 Bonaparte Pexeso 15
99/0 Crown Royale 90
01/2 Crown Royale 7
97/8 DS 2
98/9 DS 21
99/0 DS NS2, P4
00/1 DS JT2
01/2 DS 27, G2
96/7 DS Sticker 132
97/8 DS Sticker 207
02/3 Exclusive 6
02/3 First Edition 229
01/2 Heads Up 4, BTI 1
02/3 Heads Up 5, ✂ GWQ 2
99/0 Millenium C-30
02/3 O-Pee-Chee 183
98/9 OFS 130, 229, 439, 446
99/0 OFS 20
00/1 OFS 379
01/2 Pacific 18
02/3 Pacific 14, ✂ GWJ 2
02/3 Parkhurst 4
01/2 Pr. Stock 3
02/3 Pr. Stock Reserve 4
01/2 PS Titanium 5
01/2 PS Titanium Draft ✂ 5
99/0 Score JT2
01/2 Signature 88, ✍ Aut. 88
02/3 Signature 49, ✍ 49
01/2 SP Authentic 4
00/1 Stadium 191
02/3 Topps 183
02/3 T. Chrome 106
02/3 T. Limited 183
02/3 T. Total 347
01/2 UD PlayMakers Ltd 5
01/2 Upper Deck 8
02/3 Upper Deck 9
01/2 UD Challenge 4
02/3 UD Classic 6
91/2 Upper Deck WJC 87
01/2 UD Mask 102
02/3 UD Mask 3, 4
01/2 UD MVP 6
01/2 UD Vintage 13, 17
02/3 UD Vintage 10, 262, GB 10
00/1 Vanguard 103
01/2 Vanguard 4, SW 1
01/2 Victory 12, 20
02/3 Chicago Wolves
99/0 Hartford Wolf Pack
93/4 Richmond Renegades

HOACK, RUEDIGER
74 Hellas MM-Jenkki 115

HOAD, JEFF
00/1 Kudos 28
90/1 7th..Sketch WHL 221
91/2 7th...Sketch WHL 215
01/2 Belfast Giants
02/3 London Knights
89/0 Brandon Wheat Kings
90/1 Brandon Wheat Kings
92/3 Brandon Wheat Kings

HOARD, BRIAN
88/9 ProCards / Newmarket
89/0 ProCards AHL 111

HOBERG, ANDERS
86/7 Sudbury Wolves

HOBIN, MIKE
76/7 Phoenix Roadrunners
77/8 Nova Scotia Voyageurs

HOBSON, CHRIS
93/4 Humberside Hawks 3
94/5 Humberside Hawks 11

HOBSON, DOUG
88/9 ProCards / Muskegon
84/5 Prince Albert Raiders

HOBSON, JONATHAN
96/7 Kamloops Blazers
97/8 Kamloops Blazers
98/9 Kamloops Blazers
99/0 Kamloops Blazers
00/1 Kamloops Blazers

HOCK, ROBERT
94/5 DEL 375
95/6 DEL 356
99/0 Eishockey 301
94 Semic 282
00/1 UD DEL 204
01/2 UD DEL 217, SS1

HOCKING, JUSTIN
92/3 Classic 16
92/3 Classic Four Sport 165
94/5 Leaf 479
91/2 7th...Sketch WHL 12
94/5 Upper Deck 210
98/9 Indianapolis Ice
94/5 Phoenix Roadrunners
95/6 St. John's Maple Leafs
01/2 Manchester Storm

HODEK, DANIEL
97/8 APS 312
98/9 OFS 302
99/0 Score 45

HODEK, PETR
94/5 APS 99

HODGE, CHARLIE
52/3 Anonymous 129
45-64 BeeHive-2 [Black script]
45-64 BeeHive-2 [Mont.]
64-67 BeeHive-3 [Mont.]
02/3 Between the Pipes ✂ GT6, ✂ VM11, ✍ Aut.
63-65 Chex
64/5 Coke/Sprite [Mont.]
65/6 Coca-Cola
70/1 Colgate 68
70/1 Dad's Cookies
70/1 Eddie Sargent 211
70/1 Esso Power Player
68/9 O-Pee-Chee 78
68/9 O-Pee-Chee PS 12
69/0 O-Pee-Chee 77
69/0 O-Pee-Chee 4in1
70/1 O-Pee-Chee 229
55/6 Parkhurst 69
57/8 Parkhurst [Mont.] 17
58/9 Parkhurst 17
59/0 Parkhurst 16
02/3 Parkie - Reprint 214, 228, 238
93/4 Parkie 56-57 FS-6
95/6 Parkie 66-67 70, 131
94/5 Parkie Tall 82, 139, 148
63/4 Québec Aces
63/4 Québec Aces
60/1 Shirriff 39
68/9 Shirriff / Oakl. 7
64/5 Topps 17
65/6 Topps 67
66/7 Topps 65
68/9 Topps 78
69/0 Topps 77
63/4 Toronto Star Photo
64/5 Toronto Star Action
64/5 Toronto Star Photo
02/3 Ultimate Mem. ✂ SF
60/1 York
67/8 MONT
70/1 VANC / Royal Bank

HODGE, DAN
96/7 Peoria Rivermen
98/9 Peoria Rivermen
99/0 Peoria Rivermen
00/1 Peoria Rivermen
01/2 Peoria Rivermen
02/3 Manchester Storm

HODGE, KEN (JR.)
91/2 Bowman 347
91/2 Bowman 362
96/7 DEL 110
92/3 Fleer Ultra 411
91/2 Kraft 17
91/2 O-Pee-Chee 440
91/2 O-Pee-Chee 5
91/2 OPC Premier 154
91/2 OPC Premier 41
91/2 Panini Sticker 178
91/2 Panini Sticker 341
91/2 Parkhurst 2
91/2 Parkhurst PHC3
91/2 Pinnacle 203
92/3 Pinnacle 390
90/1 Pro Set 587
91/2 Pro Set 3
92/3 Pro Set 260
91 Pro Set Awards AC11
91/2 Pro Set Platinum 6
91/2 Pro Set Platinum PC9
88/9 ProCards / Kalamazoo
89/0 ProCards IHL 89
90/1 ProCards 134
90/1 Score 85T
91/2 Score 113
91/2 Score 353
91/2 Score CAN 113
91/2 Score CAN 383
92/3 Score 274
91/2 Score Young Stars 9
92/3 Topps 306
91/2 To. Stadium 357
90/1 Upper Deck 529
91/2 Upper Deck 251
91/2 Upper Deck 41
92/3 Upper Deck 254
90/1 BOST / Sports Action
91/2 BOST / Sports Action
94/5 Kansas City Blades 7

HODGE, KEN R. (SR.)
68/9 Bauer Photo
99/0 BAP Mem. AH-1, ✍ AH-1
64-67 BeeHive-3 [Chic.]
65/6 Coca-Cola
70/1 Colgate 62
70/1 Dad's Cookies
70/1 Eddie Sargent 10
71/2 Eddie Sargent 8
72/3 Eddie Sargent 22
70/1 Esso Power Player
01/2 Fleer Greats 67, ✍ Aut.
74/5 Lipton Soup 28
74/5 Loblaws
68/9 O-Pee-Chee 8
69/0 O-Pee-Chee 27
69/0 O-Pee-Chee 4in1
69/0 O-Pee-Chee Stamp
70/1 O-Pee-Chee 233
70/1 O-Pee-Chee 8
71/2 O-Pee-Chee 115
71/2 O-Pee-Chee 254
72/3 O-Pee-Chee 169
72/3 O-Pee-Chee 49
73/4 O-Pee-Chee 26
74/5 O-Pee-Chee 128
74/5 O-Pee-Chee 230
75/6 O-Pee-Chee 215
76/7 O-Pee-Chee 25
77/8 O-Pee-Chee 192
95/6 Parkie 66-67 24
94/5 Parkie Tall FS-3
70/1 Post Shooters
68/9 Shirriff / Bost. 10
65/6 Topps 65
66/7 Topps 114
67/8 Topps 98
68/9 Topps 8
69/0 Topps 27
70/1 Topps 8
71/2 Topps 115
72/3 Topps 166
73/4 Topps 133
74/5 Topps 128
74/5 Topps 230
75/6 Topps 215
76/7 Topps 25
77/8 Topps 192
01/2 To. Chrome -CA10, ✍ CA10
01/2 T/O Archives 55, -Seat
71/2 Toronto Sun Photo
91/2 Ultimate Original Six 49, ✍ Aut. 49
70/1 BOST
71/2 BOST
98/9 BOST / Alumni 7

HODGE, KEN*
91/2 7th...Sketch WHL 44

HODGE, ROB1
93/4 W. Michigan Broncos

HODGES, BOB
90/1 Pro Set 669
77-79 Sportscaster 11-19 [Linseman]

HODGINS, JUSTIN
00/1 Owen Sound Attack 13

HODGSON, CHRIS
01/2 Shawinigan 13

HODGSON, DAN
84/5 Kelowna Wings &...
84/5 Prince Albert Raiders

HODGSON, TED
51/2 Laval Dairy 62
52/3 St. Lawrence 106
72/3 Cleveland Crusaders
72/3 Clev. WHA / Linnett

HODSON, JAMIE
02/3 BAP Memorabilia 361
02/3 Ultimate Mem. 79
02/3 UD Mask 152
02/3 UD Premier 71
98/9 Brandon Wheat Kings
99/0 Brandon Wheat Kings

HODSON, JASON
92/3 BCJHL 104

HODSON, KEVIN
99/0 Aurora 130
02/3 Between the Pipes 66
98/9 Bicycle.. 7-S
94/5 Classic T21
93/4 Cla. Prospects 218
96/7 Donruss 230
97/8 Donruss 199
96/7 Do. Canadian 136
97/8 Do. Priority 65
95/6 Edge Ice 13, TW-12
96/7 Flair 108
96/7 Leaf GLR-2
97/8 L. Preferred 137
97/8 Limited 17, 89
97/8 Omega 80
98/9 Pacific 192
99/0 Pacific 390
98/9 Pa. Paramount 75
95/6 Parkhurst 525
96/7 Pinnacle 238
97/8 Pinnacle 47
96/7 Pi. Be A Player 218, ✍ Aut. 218
96/7 Pi. Summit 183
96/7 Pi. Zenith 136
97/8 Score 24
97/8 Score Detr. 18
91 7th..Sketch Mem.Cup 2
90/1 7th..Sketch OHL 158
91/2 7th...Sketch OHL 320
97/8 SP Authentic 179
99/0 SPx 142
99/0 Topps 199
99/0 To. Chrome 199
98/9 UD Choice RW20
97/8 Upper Deck 253
97/8 Upper Deck 272
99/0 Upper Deck 119
99/0 UD G. Reserve 119
02/3 UD Ice 33
02/3 UD Mask 79, 80
99/0 UD MVP 195
99/0 Victory 272
95/6 Adirondack Red Wings
92/3 Indianapolis Ice
93/4 Soo Greyhounds 28

HOEKSTRA, CECIL
60/1 Shirriff 79

HOEKSTRA, ED
68/9 O-Pee-Chee 98
63/4 Québec Aces
65/6 Québec Aces
68/9 Shirriff / Phil. 3
68/9 Topps 98

HOELSCHER, HENRIK
95/6 DEL 305

HOFBAUER, PATRIK
95/6 Leaf Elit Set 184

HOFF, GEIR
95 Globe 193
95 Panini Worlds 244
94 Semic 263
93 Semic Nordisk 43
92 Semic Sticker 37
93 Semic Sticker 237

HOFFART, RANDY
85/6 Brandon Wheat Kings
84/5 Saskatoon Blades

HOFFER, ANTON
72 Hellas MM-Jenkki 60
72 Semic Sticker 104

HOFFMAN, AARON
91/2 Avant Garde BCJHL 66
92/3 BCJHL 80

HOFFMAN, KEVIN
00/1 Nottingham Panthers

HOFFMAN, LARS
95/6 DEL 73

HOFFMAN, MATT
90 7th..Sketch Mem.Cup 94
89/0 7th..Sketch OHL 15
90/1 7th..Sketch OHL 338
91/2 7th...Sketch OHL 154
93/4 Johnstown Chiefs 6
94/5 Johnstown Chiefs 10
89/0 Oshawa Generals
90/1 Oshawa Generals
91/2 Oshawa Generals
91/2 Oshawa Generals

HOFFMAN, MIKE
87/8 Flint Spirits
88/9 Flint Spirits
88/9 Flint Spirits

HOFFMAN, OLIVER
91 Semic Sticker 199

HOFFMANN, JIM
94/5 DEL 187
95/6 DEL 187
96/7 DEL 126

HOFFMEYER, BOB
89/0 ProCards AHL 208
91/2 ProCards 161
84/5 NJER
88/9 NJER / Caretta

HOFFORD, JIM
88/9 ProCards / Rochester
89/0 ProCards AHL 281
86/7 BUFF / Blue Shield

HOFFORD, LINDSAY
00/1 London Knights
01/2 London Knights

HOFFORT, BRUCE
90/1 OPC/Topps 80
90/1 OPC Premier 42
89/0 ProCards AHL 350
90/1 ProCards 36
91/2 ProCards 326
90/1 Score 413
90/1 Upper Deck 135

HOFHERR, FRANZ
72 Semic Sticker 112

HOFMANN, PETER
94/5 DEL 406

HÖFNER, ERNST
94/5 DEL 368
95/6 DEL 358
98/9 DEL 341
82 Semic Sticker 114

HOGABOAM, BILL
74/5 Loblaws
74/5 O-Pee-Chee 116
74/5 O-Pee-Chee 84
75/6 O-Pee-Chee 67
76/7 O-Pee-Chee 387
77/8 O-Pee-Chee 73
78/9 O-Pee-Chee 148
79/0 O-Pee-Chee 362
74/5 Topps 116
74/5 Topps 84
75/6 Topps 67
76/7 Topps 73
77/8 Topps 148
79/0 DETR
80/1 DETR

HOGAN, MATT
94/5 Slapshot / Sarnia 25

HOGAN, PETER
98 Bowman 26
98 Bowman Chrome 26
95/6 Slapshot 242
00/1 Florida Everblades

HOGANSON, DALE
72/3 Dernière Heure
78/9 Dernière Heure
81/2 Dernière Heure
70/1 Eddie Sargent 68
70/1 Esso Power Player
71/2 O-Pee-Chee 149
80/1 O-Pee-Chee 155
81/2 O-Pee-Chee 276
75/6 OPC WHA 2
80/1 Pepsi Bottle Cap
80/1 Topps 155
71/2 Toronto Sun Photo
71/2 MONT / Pro Star
80/1 QUÉB
73/4 Québec Nordiques
85/6 Minnesota-Duluth 34

HOGANSON, DAN
86/7 TORO
86/7 TORO

HOGARDH, PETER
95/6 Leaf Elit Set 200

HÖGARDH,
97/8 Hockey-Box

HÖGARDH, PETER
95/6 UD Elitserien 215
00/1 UD Elitserien 161

HOGDEN, JEFF
89/0 7th..Sketch OHL 46
91/2 Cincinnati Cyclones

HØGEMARK, SVERRE
92/3 Semic Nordisk 140

HOGG, JEFF
83/4 Kingston Canadians
82/3 Oshawa Generals

HOGG, KRIS
02/3 Kamloops Blazers

HOGG, MURRAY
93/4 Slapshot / Guelph 21
95/6 Slapshot 53
97/8 Fort Worth Brahmas
98/9 Fort Worth Brahmas
99/0 Fort Worth Brahmas

HOGG, STEVE
93/4 Slapshot / Peterborough 17
95/6 Slapshot 319
87/8 Brockville Braves

HOGGARTH, RON
90/1 Pro Set 690

HÖGLUND, JONAS
01/2 Adrenaline 180
00/1 BAP Mem. 313
97/8 Donruss 169
96/7 Do. Canadian 140
97/8 Do. Canadian 36
96/7 Do. Elite 146, A-12
99/0 Dynagon Ice 187
96/7 Fl. Ultra 23
94/5 Leaf Elit Set 292
95/6 Leaf Elit Set 213
96/7 L. Limited LR-10
96/7 L. Preferred 124
97/8 Limited 88
01/2 O-Pee-Chee 177
02/3 O-Pee-Chee 126
99/0 Omega 224
00/1 Pacific 391
01/2 Pacific 366
02/3 Pacific Complete 360
97/8 Pacific CC 185
97/8 Pa. Dynagon 16, T-36
97/8 Pa. Invincible 18
97/8 Pa. Paramount 29
97/8 Panini Sticker 198
98/9 Panini Sticker 38
99/0 Panini Sticker 156
00/1 Panini Sticker 98
00/1 Parkhurst P-196
96/7 Pi. Be A Player LTH8A, ✍ Aut. LTH8A
97/8 Pi. Inside 129
96/7 Pi. Zenith 117
97/8 Score 181
96/7 Select CE 102
90/1 Semic Elitserien 269
91/2 Semic Elitserien 99
92/3 Semic Elitserien 115
96/7 SP 172
99/0 SP Authentic 84
00/1 Stadium 126
00/1 Topps 37
01/2 Topps 177
02/3 Topps 126
00/1 To. Heritage 201
02/3 T. Limited 126
02/3 T. Total 197
92/3 Upper Deck 222
96/7 Upper Deck 232, X38
97/8 Upper Deck 27
98/9 Upper Deck 116
99/0 Upper Deck 292
01/2 Upper Deck 162
96/7 UD Black Diam. 44
96/7 UD CC 355
97/8 UD Coll. Choice 43
95/6 UD Elitserien 68, NA8
98/9 UD G. Reserve 116
99/0 UD G. Reserve 292
01/2 UD MVP 178
99/0 UD MVP Cup 175
00/1 UD Vintage 339
00/1 Victory 221
01/2 Victory 331
97/8 MONT
99/0 TORO / Pizza Pizza 2

HÖGLUND, PATRIK
94/5 Leaf Elit Set 266
91/2 Semic Elitserien 160
92/3 Semic Elitserien 178
95/6 UD Elitserien 115
97/8 UD Elitserien 187
98/9 UD Elitserien 185

HOGOSTA, GORAN
79 Panini Sticker 184

HÖGOSTA, GÖRAN
00/1 Alfabilder

HOGSTROM, JERK
91/2 Semic Elitserien 285

HOGUE, BENOIT
01/2 Atomic ✂ GWJ 17
01/2 BAP Memor. 457
91/2 Bowman 38
92/3 Bowman 28
94/5 Cla. Images PL7
93/4 Donruss 201
94/5 Donruss 188
95/6 Donruss 70
96/7 Donruss 135
92/3 Durivage 3
93/4 Durivage 29
93/4 EA Sports 83
96/7 Fl. Picks 136
92/3 Fleer Ultra 127
93/4 Fleer Ultra 157
94/5 Fleer Ultra 128
95/6 Fleer Ultra 312
01/2 Heads Up ✂ JQ 24
93/4 Leaf 155
94/5 Leaf 124
95/6 Leaf 134
96/7 Leaf 137
94/5 L. Limited 20
90/1 OPC/Topps 215
91/2 O-Pee-Chee 292
92/3 O-Pee-Chee 132
89/0 O-Pee-Chee 201
91/2 OPC Premier 179
89/0 opcSticker 37-177, / FS 4
98/9 Pacific 177
99/0 Pacific 119
97/8 Pacific CC 240
91/2 Panini Sticker 300
92/3 Panini Sticker 197
93/4 Panini Sticker 59
94/5 Panini Sticker 47
95/6 Panini Sticker 202
96/7 Panini Sticker 171
97/8 Panini Sticker 143
91/2 Parkhurst 332
92/3 Parkhurst 104
93/4 Parkhurst 396
95/6 Parkhurst 350
94/5 Parkie SE106
91/2 Pinnacle 146
92/3 Pinnacle 62
93/4 Pinnacle 18
94/5 Pinnacle 129
95/6 Pinnacle 186
96/7 Pinnacle 73
97/8 Pi. Be A Player 152, ✍ Aut. 152
96/7 Pi. Summit 56
94/5 POG 374
95/6 POG 258
93/4 Power Play 148
93/4 Premier 140
94/5 Premier 26
00/1 PS Titanium ✂ GUG 83
90/1 Pro Set 416
91/2 Pro Set 17
91/2 Pro Set 435
92/3 Pro Set 108
91/2 Pro Set Platinum 200
92/3 Score 134
92/3 Score 108T
91/2 Score CAN 134
92/3 Score 276
92/3 Score SS 21
93/4 Score 16
95/6 Score 262
96/7 Score 141
97/8 Score 277
91/2 Score Young Stars 31
94/5 Select 130
92/3 Topps 103
95/6 Topps 71
91/2 To. Stadium 157
92/3 T. Stadium Club 425
93/4 To. Stadium 76
90/1 Upper Deck 402
91/2 Upper Deck 159
92/3 Upper Deck 325
93/4 Upper Deck 456
94/5 Upper Deck 436
95/6 Upper Deck 351, SE-171
96/7 Upper Deck 247
95/6 UD BAP 126, ✍ S126
95/6 UD CC 72
96/7 UD CC 72
88/9 BUFF / Blue Shield
88/9 BUFF / Won. Bread
89/0 BUFF / Blue Shield
89/0 BUFF / Campbell's
90/1 BUFF / Blue Shield
90/1 BUFF / Campbell's
96/7 DALL / Southwest
97/8 DALL / Score 217
01/2 DALL / Southwest

HOGUE, RUSSELL
93/4 Prince Albert Raiders
95/6 Prince Albert Raiders

HOHENADL, FRANK
94/5 DEL 212
95/6 DEL 340
98/9 DEL 304
99/0 Eishockey 249

HOHENBERGER, HERBERT
94/5 DEL 216
95/6 DEL 204
96/7 DEL 345
95 Globe 186
95 Panini Worlds 262
90/1 ProCards 63
00/1 UD DEL 26
96 Wien 214
87/8 Hull Olympiques

HOHENBERGER, MARTIN
94/5 SR Auto-Phonex 18, ✍ 18
01/2 UD DEL 218

HOINESS, BRENT
91/2 Air Canada SJHL A43
92/3 MPS SJHL 91

HOKANSON, JEFF
91/2 Avant Garde BCJHL 139

HOLAN, MILOS
94/5 Donruss 10
95/6 Donruss 339
96/7 Donruss 20
99/0 DS 103
95/6 Fleer Ultra 2
94/5 Leaf 289
95/6 Leaf 324
98/9 OFS 359, 473
99/0 OFS 21
95/6 Panini Sticker 230
95 Panini Worlds 188
95/6 Parkhurst 2
96/7 Score 211
99/0 Score JT22
95/6 Topps 173
95/6 Upper Deck 77
95/6 UD CC 265
94/5 Hershey Bears

HOLÁN, MILOS
93/4 Classic 134
93/4 Cla. Prospects 70
93/4 Donruss 244
93/4 Fleer Ultra 389
93/4 Fleer Ultra WotF 6
93/4 Parkhurst 268
93/4 Pinnacle 427
93 Semic Sticker 91
93/4 Upper Deck 523, SP-115

HOLDEN, BARNEY
91 C55 Reprint 3
10/1 Imperial
10/1 Imperial 4
11/2 Imperial 3

HOLDEN, CORY
95/6 DEL 315
96/7 DEL 97

HOLDEN, JOSH
96/7 All-Sport PPF 78
95/6 Bowman P19
97 Bowman 114
98 Bowman 73
98 Bowman Chrome 73
95/6 Classic 62, ✍ Aut.
95/6 Future Legends ✍ SSD-6
01/2 O-Pee-Chee 265
99/0 Pacific 423
97/8 Pi. BeeHive 66, ✍ Aut. 66
00/1 Signature 239, ✍ Aut. 136
98/9 SP Authentic 112
99/0 SPx 155
99/0 Topps 44
01/2 Topps 265
99/0 To. Chrome 44
98/9 UD Choice 253
95/6 Upper Deck 513
99/0 Upper Deck 129
97/8 UD Black Diam. 45
99/0 UD G. Reserve 129
98/9 UD MVP 207
99/0 UD MVP 211
99/0 Victory 295
97/8 Zenith 100, Z80
00/1 Kansas City Blades 13
01/2 Manitoba Moose
02/3 St. John's Maple Leafs
96/7 Regina Pats
97/8 Regina Pats

HOLDEN, MARK
84/5 Nova Scotia Oilers
83/4 Nova Scotia Voyageurs

HOLDEN, MIKE
96/7 Roanoke Express 20

HOLDEN, PAUL
90/1 ProCards 431
91/2 ProCards 396
89/0 7th..Sketch OHL 24
92/3 Salt Lake G'Eagles
93/4 St. John's Maple Leafs

HOLECEK, JIRI
96/7 APS 374
01/2 DS L1
72 Hellas MM-Jenkki 81
74 Hellas MM-Jenkki 71
98/9 OFS Leg. 8
72 Panda MM-Toronto
79 Panini Sticker 74
72 Semic Sticker 22
74 Semic Sticker 51
91 Semic Sticker 246
77-79 Sports. FIN 83-1983
96 Wien HL16
71/2 Williams Finnish 27
72/3 Williams Finnish 7
73/4 Williams Finnish 48

HOLICK, MARK
84/5 Saskatoon Blades
86/7 Saskatoon Blades

HOLIK, BOBBY
98/9 Aurora 110
99/0 Aurora 86
99/0 BAP Mem. 142
00/1 BAP Mem. 12
02/3 BAP Memorabilia 263
91/2 Bowman 18
92/3 Bowman 407
98/9 Bowman's Best 53
99/0 Crown Royale 81
93/4 Donruss 183
94/5 Donruss 90
95/6 Donruss 220
97/8 Donruss 140
97/8 Do. Priority 110
98/9 Dynagon Ice 110
99/0 Dynagon Ice 117
02/3 Exclusive 114, ✂ GWJ 16
02/3 First Edition 110, ✂ Jers.
92/3 Fleer Ultra 339
93/4 Fleer Ultra 360
95/6 Fleer Ultra 262
01/2 Heads Up ✂ JQ 3
02/3 Heads Up 80
02/3 In The Game-Used ✂ E37, ✂ IE15
93/4 Leaf 227
94/5 Leaf 252
99/0 Millenium 150, ✍ Aut. 150
98/9 NHL Power Play
91/2 O-Pee-Chee 56
91/2 O-Pee-Chee 7
92/3 O-Pee-Chee 254
01/2 O-Pee-Chee 174
98/9 OPC Chrome 131
90/1 OPC Premier 43
92/3 OPC Premier 77
97/8 Omega 130
98/9 Omega 130
99/0 Omega 136
98/9 Pacific 263
99/0 Pacific 238
00/1 Pacific 235
01/2 Pacific 231, ✂ GWJ 18
02/3 Pacific 223
02/3 Pacific Complete 494
97/8 Pacific CC 55
97/8 Pa. Crown Roy. 76
98/9 Pa. Crown Roy. 80
97/8 Pa. Dynagon 70, T-45
97/8 Pa. Invincible 78
97/8 Pa. Paramount 103
98/9 Pa. Paramount 134
99/0 Pa. Paramount 134
97/8 Pa. Revolution 78
98/9 Pa. Revolution 85, -ASG 10
91/2 Panini Sticker 316
91/2 Panini Sticker 342
92/3 Panini Sticker 261
92/3 Panini Sticker 293
97/8 Panini Sticker 65
98/9 Panini Sticker 68
99/0 Panini Sticker 81
00/1 Panini Sticker 49
95 Panini Worlds 204
91/2 Parkhurst 290
92/3 Parkhurst 96
93/4 Parkhurst 385
94/5 Parkhurst 128
95/6 Parkhurst 125
00/1 Parkhurst P-245
01/2 Parkhurst 195, ✂ T15
02/3 Parkhurst 117
02/3 Parkhurst Retro 94
91/2 Pinnacle 65
92/3 Pinnacle 277
93/4 Pinnacle 71
94/5 Pinnacle 347
97/8 Pi. BAP 201, ✍ Aut. 201
94/5 POG 144
95/6 POG 159
93/4 Power Play 378
93/4 Premier 322
93/4 Premier 52
94/5 Premier 315
99/0 Prism 82
00/1 Private Stock ✂ GUG 63
01/2 Pr. Stock ✂ GUG 60
02/3 Pr. Stock Reserve 67
01/2 PS Titanium Draft ✂ 53
00/1 PS Titanium Draft ✂ 59
90/1 Pro Set 609
91/2 Pro Set 79
92/3 Pro Set 61
91/2 Pro Set Platinum 43
99/0 Revolution 86
90/1 Score 10T
91/2 Score 153
91/2 Score CAN 153
92/3 Score 128
93/4 Score 198
97/8 Score 183
97/8 Score NJer. 2
90/1 Sco. Young Stars 34
91/2 Score Young Stars 36
91 Semic Sticker 224
00/1 Signature 224
02/3 Signature 174, GS-11, ✍ 174
02/3 Slam Card
96/7 SP 87
97/8 SP Authentic 89
02/3 SP Authentic 60
02/3 Sports Vault 84
99/0 Stadium 108
00/1 Stadium 77
02/3 Stadium 102
92/3 Topps 330
95/6 Topps 303, 10PL
98/9 Topps 131
99/0 Topps 119
00/1 Topps 106, ✂ GWS
01/2 Topps 174
99/0 To. Chrome 119
98/9 To. Finest 95
99/0 To. Gold Label 39
00/1 To. Heritage 188
02/3 To. Heritage 156
99/0 To. Prmr. Plus 12
01/2 To. Stadium 299
92/3 T. Stadium Club 106
93/4 To. Stadium 159
94/5 T. Stadium Club 129
02/3 T. Total 316
98/9 UD Choice 115
00/1 UD Heroes 72
90/1 Upper Deck 354
91/2 Upper Deck 233
91/2 Upper Deck E3
92/3 Upper Deck 252
92/3 Upper Deck 500
93/4 Upper Deck 218
94/5 Upper Deck 314
95/6 Upper Deck 365
97/8 Upper Deck 304
98/9 Upper Deck 313
00/1 Upper Deck 332
01/2 Upper Deck 333
02/3 Upper Deck 360
95/6 UD BAP 202, ✍ S202
95/6 UD CC 185
97/8 UD Coll. Choice 143
98/9 UD G. Reserve 313
01/2 UD Mask 55
98/9 UD MVP 121
01/2 UD SCup Champs 77
00/1 UD Vintage 217
01/2 UD Vintage 157
00/1 Vanguard ✂ DGJ 8
01/2 Vanguard ✂ DGM 17
99/0 Victory 175
01/2 Victory 214
97/8 Zenith 68
90/1 HART / Jr. Whalers
91/2 HART / Jr. Whalers
96/7 NJER / Sharp

HOLIK, JAROSLAV
94/5 APS 291
96/7 APS 375
01/2 DS L10
72 Hellas MM-Jenkki 84
74 Hellas MM-Jenkki 72
70/1 Kuvajulkaisut 47
69/0 Mästär Serien 6
74 Semic Sticker 60
77-79 Sportscaster 55-14
77-79 Sports. FIN 51-1218
72/3 Williams Finnish 8
73/4 Williams Finnish 49

HOLIK, JIRI
95/6 APS 196, 393
96/7 APS 331
72 Hellas MM-Jenkki 98
74 Hellas MM-Jenkki 73
70/1 Kuvajulkaisut 48
69/0 Mästär Serien 3
72 Panda MM-Toronto
72 Semic Sticker 39
74 Semic Sticker 61
77-79 Sportscaster 55-14
77-79 Sports. FIN 51-1218
71/2 Williams Finnish 28
72/3 Williams Finnish 9
73/4 Williams Finnish 50

HOLIK, VLADIMIR
98/9 OFS 69
99/0 OFS 238
00/1 OFS 197
01/2 OFS 107

HOLK, BRIAN
90/1 7th..Sketch OHL 260

HOLLAND, BOB
81/2 Indianapolis Checkers
77/8 Nova Scotia Voyageurs

HOLLAND, DENNIS
89/0 ProCards AHL 322
90/1 ProCards 471
91/2 ProCards 593
92/3 Cincinnati Cyclones
99/0 Louisiana Ice Gators
97/8 Toledo Storm 14
86/7 Portland Winter Hawks
88/9 Portland Winter Hawks

HOLLAND, JASON
97/8 Donruss 214
97/8 Do. Canadian 144
95/6 Do. Elite WJ 6
94/5 Sig. Rookies 11, ✍ 11
94/5 Slapshot Memorial 3
95/6 Upper Deck 537
98/9 Upper Deck 224
98/9 UD G. Reserve 224
01/2 UD Vintage 119
96/7 Kentucky Tho'blades
97/8 Kentucky Tho'blades
01/2 Manchester Monarchs
98/9 Rochester Americans
00/1 Rochester Americans
93/4 Kamloops Blazers

HOLLAND, JERRY
75/6 O-Pee-Chee 392
76/7 O-Pee-Chee 315

HOLLAND, ROB
82/3 Indianapolis Checkers

HOLLENSTEIN, FELIX
95 Semic 191
91 Semic Sticker 194
92 Semic Sticker 209
93 Semic Sticker 127

HOLLETT, BILL
34-43 BeeHive-1 [Toro.]
35/6 O-Pee-Chee 83
39/0 O-Pee-Chee 41
37/8 World Wide Gum 62

HOLLETT, FLASH
02/3 Ultimate Mem. ✍ Cut

HOLLETT, STEVE
89/0 ProCards AHL 97
84/5 Soo Greyhounds

HOLLEY, PAT
87/8 Sudbury Wolves

HOLLINGER, TERRY
93/4 Cla. Prospects 171
94/5 Parkhurst 204
90/1 7th..Sketch WHL 165
91/2 7th...Sketch WHL 354
01/2 UD DEL 111
92/3 Peoria Rivermen
93/4 Peoria Rivermen
94/5 Peoria Rivermen
00/1 Providence Bruins
95/6 Rochester Americans
96/7 Rochester Americans
89/0 Regina Pats

HOLLINGER, TODD
91/2 Air Canada SJHL A27

HOLLINGSHEAD, KELLY
91/2 Air Canada SJHL B20
96/7 Knoxville Cherokees

HOLLINGWORTH, GORD (BUCKY)
52/3 Anonymous 131
93/4 Parkie 56-57 62
54/5 Topps 12

HOLLIS, SCOTT
90 7th..Sketch Mem.Cup 96
89/0 7th..Sketch OHL 11
90/1 7th..Sketch OHL 339
91/2 7th...Sketch OHL 155
95/6 Adirondack Red Wings
93/4 Las Vegas Thunder
98/9 Las Vegas Thunder
98/9 Orlando Solar Bears
00/1 Syracuse Crunch
89/0 Oshawa Generals
90/1 Oshawa Generals
91/2 Oshawa Generals
91/2 Oshawa Generals
92/3 Oshawa Generals

HOLLOWAY, BRUCE
81/2 Regina Pats

HOLLWEG, RYAN
00/1 UD Prospects 55
99/0 Medicine Hat Tigers
00/1 Medicine Hat Tigers

HOLMAN, JIM
92/3 W. Michigan Broncos
93/4 W. Michigan Broncos

HOLMBERG, ERIK
89/0 Semic Elitserien 237
90/1 Semic Elitserien 14
91/2 Semic Elitserien 212
92/3 Semic Elitserien 246

HOLMBERG, JORGEN
89/0 Semic Elitserien 260
90/1 Semic Elitserien 165
91/2 Semic Elitserien 270

HOLMBERG, MIKAEL
95/6 Leaf Elit Set 68
90/1 Semic Elitserien 92
90/1 Semic Elitserien 266
95/6 UD Elitserien 109

HOLMES, BILL
25-27 Anonymous 14

HOLMES, DARIL
84/5 Kingston Canadians
85/6 Kingston Canadians
86/7 Kingston Canadians

HOLMES, DARREN
91/2 Avant Garde BCJHL 153

91/2 Avant Garde BCJHL 46
91/2 Nanaimo Clippers

HOLMES, HARRY
25-27 Anonymous 121
83 HHOF Postcard L6
83&87 HHOF 156
94/5 Legends 49

HOLMES, JAMES
52/3 Anonymous 54

HOLMES, MARK
88/9 Salt Lake G'Eagles

HOLMES, TOM
96/7 Richmond Renegades

HOLMES, WARREN
95/6 Slapshot 243
78/9 Saginaw Gears

HOLMGREN, LEIF
79 Panini Sticker 192
91/2 Semic Elitserien 302
92/3 Semic Elitserien 324
82 Semic Sticker 23

HOLMGREN, PAUL
77/8 O-Pee-Chee 307
78/9 O-Pee-Chee 234
79/0 O-Pee-Chee 156
80/1 O-Pee-Chee 164
80/1 O-Pee-Chee 172
81/2 O-Pee-Chee 242
82/3 O-Pee-Chee 251
83/4 O-Pee-Chee 266
84/5 O-Pee-Chee 100
81/2 OPC Sticker 179
82/3 OPC/Topps Sticker 116
82/3 Post [Phil.]
90/1 Pro Set 673
83/4 Souhaits Keychain [Flyers]
78/9 Topps 234
79/0 Topps 156
80/1 Topps 164
80/1 Topps 172
81/2 Topps 105 [East]
84/5 Topps 74
01/2 T/O Archives 74
92/3 HART / Dairymart
84/5 MINS
84/5 MINS / 7-Eleven 7
86/7 PHIL
89/0 PHIL

HOLMGREN, PAUL
02/3 Fleer Throwbacks 73

HOLMKVIST, MICHAEL
02/3 Cardset 174

HOLMQVIST, JOHAN
00/1 BAP Mem. 493
01/2 BT Pipes 34, ✂ Jers.
02/3 Between the Pipes 80
00/1 SP Authentic 152
00/1 SPx 182
00/1 UD Heroes 171
98/9 UD Elitserien 33
99/0 UD Elitserien 18, S2, ✍ Aut.
00/1 UD Ice 117
00/1 Hartford Wolf Pack
01/2 Hartford Wolf Pack

HOLMQVIST, LEIF (HONKEN)
00/1 Alfabilder
95 Globe 64
72 Hellas MM-Jenkki 23
70/1 Kuvajulkaisut 26
69/0 Mästär Serien 38
69/0 Mästär Serien 44
72 Panda MM-Toronto
72 Semic Sticker 42
91 Semic Sticker 231
98/9 UD Elitserien 201, 212
71/2 Williams Finnish 46
72/3 Williams Finnish 84

HOLMQVIST, MIKAEL
99/0 Cardset 334
00/1 Cardset 221
98/9 UD Choice 289
98/9 UD Elitserien 96, 214

HOLMROOS, RAINER
73/4 Williams Finnish 260

HOLMSTRÖM, TOMAS
98/9 Be A Player 196, ✍ Aut. 196
99/0 BAP Mem. 132
00/1 BAP Mem. 381
02/3 BAP Memorabilia ✂ SCC14
96/7 Do. Canadian 129
96/7 Flair 107
95 Globe 50
94/5 Leaf Elit Set 218, ND-9, RR-3
95/6 Leaf Elit Set 84, FTF-8
96/7 L. Limited LR-9
98/9 Pacific 193
99/0 Pacific 139
00/1 Pacific 148
01/2 Pacific 141
02/3 Pacific Complete 438
97/8 Pacific CC 319
01/2 Parkhurst 181
97/8 Pi. Be A Player 188, ✍ Aut. 188
96/7 Pi. Zenith 118
97/8 Score Detr. 16
96/7 Select CE 97
94/5 SR Auto-Phonex 19, ✍ 19
01/2 Signature 37, ✍ Aut. 37
98/9 SP Authentic ✍ SotT
02/3 T. Total 167
98/9 UD Choice RW13
02/3 Ultimate Mem. ✂ SCDE, ✂ SCDGJ, ✂ SCDN
96/7 Upper Deck 255
98/9 Upper Deck 89
99/0 Upper Deck 222
00/1 Upper Deck 65
01/2 Upper Deck 292
02/3 Upper Deck 67
95/6 UD Elitserien 123, NA15
98/9 UD G. Reserve 89
99/0 UD G. Reserve 222
98/9 UD MVP 74
99/0 UD MVP 75
01/2 UD SCup Champs 65
00/1 UD Vintage 134
01/2 UD Vintage 96
99/0 Victory 104
00/1 Victory 89
01/2 Victory 133
02/3 Victory -NP45
96 Wien 70

HOLOIEN, DEAN
89/0 Saskatoon Blades

HOLOPAINEN, EERO
66/7 Champion 170
65/6 Hellas 106
70/1 Kuvajulkaisut 174
71/2 Williams Finnish 100
72/3 Williams Finnish 143
73/4 Williams Finnish 109

HOLOPAINEN, MIKKO
65/6 Hellas 159

HOLOPAINEN, PAAVO
71/2 Williams Finnish 300

HOLSAN, JIRI
97/8 APS 214
99/0 DS 167
00/1 DS 141
98/9 OFS 403
99/0 OFS 164
00/1 OFS 123

HOLSCHER, HENRIK
94/5 DEL 313
96/7 DEL 333

HOLT, BARTON
92/3 MPS SJHL 133

HOLT, RANDY
77/8 O-Pee-Chee 34
78/9 O-Pee-Chee 341
79/0 O-Pee-Chee 4
81/2 O-Pee-Chee 41
83/4 O-Pee-Chee 220
80/1 Pepsi Bottle Cap
82/3 Post [Wash.]
77/8 Topps 34
79/0 Topps 4
80/1 CALG
83/4 PHIL / J.C. Penney
78/9 VANC / Royal Bank
81/2 WASH
82/3 WASH

HOLT, TODD
90/1 7th...Sketch WHL 48
91/2 7th...Sketch WHL 192
94/5 Kansas City Blades 18

HOLTARI, JUKKA
80/1 Mallasjuoma 86

HOLTBY, GREG
83/4 Saskatoon Blades
84/5 Saskatoon Blades

HOLUM, DAVE
95/6 Roanoke Express

HOLUNGA, SHANE
91/2 Air Canada SJHL 20
91/2 Air Canada SJHL C45

HOLWAY, ALBERT
24/5 Champ's Cigarettes
24/5 William Paterson 56

HOLY, MARTIN
97/8 APS 9
99/0 OFS 105
00/1 OFS 299

HOLY, ROBERT
94/5 APS 23
99/0 Score 138

HOLZER, DAVID
89/0 Lethbridge Hurricanes

HOLZER, MARTIN
95/6 DEL 346

HOLZER, RENZO
79 Panini Sticker 262

HOLZINGER, BRIAN
01/2 Adrenaline 172
98/9 Aurora 18
98/9 Be A Player 15, ✍ Aut. 15
99/0 BAP Mem. 257, 381
00/1 BAP Mem. 347
01/2 BAP Memor. 294
95 Semic 190
95/6 Bowman 165
99/0 Challenger 22
95/6 Classic 74, BK18, ✍ Aut.
95/6 Cla. 5 Sport 159, S-77, Sprint, SFF-J
95/6 Donruss 298
96/7 Donruss 226
97/8 Donruss 74
97/8 Do. Preferred 93
97/8 Do. Priority 69
98/9 Dynagon Ice 19
95/6 Fleer Metal 177
95/6 Fleer Ultra 19, 341
95/6 Leaf 250, SR-14
96/7 Leaf 212
97/8 Leaf 120
97/8 Limited 58, 184
98/9 NHL Power Play
01/2 O-Pee-Chee 202
97/8 Omega 23
98/9 Omega 24
98/9 Pacific 106
99/0 Pacific 38
00/1 Pacific 372
01/2 Pacific 350
97/8 Pacific CC 158
97/8 Pa. Dynagon 11, T-32
97/8 Pa. Paramount 20
98/9 Pa. Paramount 20
00/1 Pa. Paramount 220
95/6 Panini Sticker 14
95/6 Parkhurst 27
95/6 Pinnacle 205
97/8 Pi. Be A Player 34, ✍ Aut. 34
97/8 Pi. Certified 118
97/8 Pi. Inside 163
95/6 Pi. Summit 168
97/8 Pi. Totally 118
95/6 Pi. Zenith 126, RRC-5
95/6 Playoff 126
95/6 POG 39
95/6 Score 310
96/7 Score 266
97/8 Score 172
97/8 Score Buff. 9
95/6 Select CE 110, CF-6
00/1 Signature 52, ✍ Aut. 21
95/6 SBx Emotion 17, gN-1
95/6 SBx Impact 190, F-15
95/6 SP 14
96/7 SP 18, HC-19
97/8 SP Authentic 16, ✍ SotT
95/6 Topps 24
99/0 Topps 193
01/2 Topps 202
99/0 To. Chrome 193
95/6 To. Finest 67
95/6 To. Stadium ER194
98/9 UD Choice 21
95/6 Upper Deck 88
96/7 Upper Deck 16
97/8 Upper Deck 15, SG49
98/9 Upper Deck 47
00/1 Upper Deck 387
01/2 Upper Deck 386
95/6 UD BAP 161, ✍ S161
96/7 UD Black Diam. 118
98/9 UD Black Diam. 9
96/7 UD CC 24, 342
97/8 UD Coll. Choice 25, SQ14
96/7 Upper Deck WJC 72
98/9 UD G. Reserve 47
97/8 UD Ice 19
98/9 UD MVP 20
99/0 Victory 40
01/2 Victory 317

HOLZMANN, GEORG
94/5 DEL 64
95/6 DEL 63
96/7 DEL 249
95 Panini Worlds 73
82 Semic Sticker 126
89 Semic Sticker 118
92 Semic Sticker 186
93 Semic Sticker 160

HOMBERG, MIKAEL
94/5 Leaf Elit Set 198

HOMER, JAN
99/0 OFS 458
00/1 OFS 357
01/2 OFS 82

HOMER, KENZIE
99/0 Peoria Rivermen

HOMNA, TEIJI
1936 Reemstma Olympia 54-39

HONGISTO, KALEVI
78/9 SM-Liiga 145

HONKANEN, ANTERO
71/2 Williams Finnish 262

HONKANEN, JAAKKO
66/7 Champion 40
65/6 Hellas 35
70/1 Kuvajulkaisut 190
72 Panda MM-Toronto
71/2 Williams Finnish 63
72/3 Williams Finnish 247
73/4 Williams Finnish 245

HONKANEN, JOUNI
70/1 Kuvajulkaisut 366

HONKAVAARA, AARNE
96/7 Sisu 187

HONKONEN, MIKKO
98/9 Cardset 156
95/6 Sisu 76
96/7 Sisu 76

HONMA, SADAKI
79 Panini Sticker 291

HONNEGER, DOUG
95 Semic 190

HONSSON, HANS
94/5 Leaf Elit Set 44

HOOD, BRUCE
91/2 Ultimate Original Six 86

HOOD, MURRAY
91/2 Hampton Roads
98/9 Hampton Roads

HOOEY, TODD
84/5 Moncton G'Flames
82/3 Oshawa Generals

HOOGE, CLINT
91/2 Air Canada SJHL D30
92/3 MPS SJHL 84

HOOGSTEEN, DAVID
01/2 Rockford IceHogs

HOOPER, DALE
96/7 Dayton Bombers

HOOPER, TOM
83 HHOF Postcard M9
83&87 HHOF 173

HOOPLE, RYAN
97 Bowman 101
99/0 Cincinnati M'Ducks
99/0 Huntington Blizzard
95/6 Lethbridge Hurricanes

HOOSON, BILL
91/2 7th...Sketch WHL 270

HOOVER, DAVID
84/5 Kingston Canadians

HOOVER, RON
89/0 ProCards AHL 65
90/1 ProCards 126
91/2 Upper Deck 287
92/3 Peoria Rivermen
93/4 Peoria Rivermen
94/5 Peoria Rivermen
95/6 Peoria Rivermen

HOOVER, TIM
82/3 Soo Greyhounds
83/4 Soo Greyhounds
84/5 Soo Greyhounds

HOPE, JARED
95/6 Spokane Chiefs 14

HOPE, JOEY
00/1 Prince George Cougars

HOPIAVOURI, RALPH
72/3 Cleveland Crusaders
72/3 Clev. WHA / Linnett

HOPKINS, DEAN
82/3 Post [LosA.]
88/9 ProCards / Halifax
89/0 ProCards AHL 164
90/1 ProCards 446
91/2 ProCards 545
88/9 EDMO / Action 135
89/0 Halifax Citadels
90/1 Halifax Citadels
84/5 Nova Scotia Oilers
85/6 Nova Scotia Oilers

HOPKINS, DOMINIC
02/3 Dundee Texol Stars
98/9 Guildford Flames

HOPKINS, LARRY
81/2 WINN
78/9 Saginaw Gears

HOPKINS, TOM
89/0 7th..Sketch OHL 115

HOPPE, MATTHIAS
94/5 DEL 435
95/6 DEL 386
96/7 DEL 293
98/9 DEL 224
89 Semic Sticker 105

HOPPER, RICK
90/1 7th...Sketch WHL 260
91/2 7th...Sketch WHL 50

HOPRAMON, RALPH
72/3 Clev. WHA / Linnett

HORACEK, JAN
01/2 DS 31
01/2 Hamilton Bulldogs
00/1 Worcester IceCats

HORACEK, JAROSLAV
96/7 APS 11
97/8 APS 297

HORACEK, TONY
90/1 Bowman 104
84/5 Kelowna Wings &...
90/1 Pro Set 499
91/2 Pro Set 455
88/9 ProCards / Hershey
90/1 PHIL
91/2 PHIL / J.C. Penney
96/7 Cincinnati Cyclones
92/3 Indianapolis Ice
93/4 Indianapolis Ice
94/5 Indianapolis Ice

HORACHEK, PETER
93/4 Flint Generals
94/5 Flint Generals
88/9 Flint Spirits
98/9 Orlando Solar Bears
99/0 Orlando Solar Bears Geico

HORAK, MICHAL
96/7 APS 260
97/8 APS 237
98/9 OFS 338
99/0 Score 59

HORAK, ROBERT
98/9 Rouyn-Noranda

HORAK, ROMAN
94/5 APS 113
95/6 APS 282, 373
96/7 APS 130
97/8 APS 371
98/9 DS 91
99/0 DS 49
00/1 DS 154
96/7 DS Sticker 68
98/9 OFS 368
99/0 OFS 307, 514
00/1 OFS 277
01/2 OFS 139
95 Panini Worlds 201
95 Semic 161
96 Wien 124

HORAK, ROMAN
93 Semic Sticker 96

HORAN, BRAD
99/0 Kingston Frontenacs
00/1 Kingston Frontenacs 9
01/2 Kingston Frontenacs 7

HORAN, BRIAN
91/2 ProCards 438

HORAVA, MILOSLAV
94/5 APS 253
95/6 APS 127, 430
96/7 APS 5
97/8 APS 338
99/0 DS 59
96/7 DS Sticker 4, 119
90/1 OPC/Topps 337
98/9 OFS 269, -Leg. 2
00/1 OFS 400
90/1 Pro Set 198
91/2 Semic Elitserien 203
92/3 Semic Elitserien 226
82 Semic Sticker 79
90/1 Upper Deck 13
89/0 NYRA / Marine

HORBUL, DOUG
74/5 Loblaws
74/5 O-Pee-Chee 317

HORCICKA, LUBOS
99/0 DS 156
00/1 DS 133
98/9 OFS 397
99/0 OFS 533
00/1 OFS 109, -Star 30

HORCICKA, PETR
99/0 Score 77

HORCOFF, SHAWN
00/1 BAP Mem. 511
02/3 Bowman 153, ✂ FFDS, ✂ FFJ, ✂ FFP, ✂ FFS, ✂ FFTS, ✍ YSA, / ✍ Puck
01/2 Pacific 158
02/3 Pacific Complete 453
00/1 PS Titanium 117
00/1 PS Titanium Draft 117
01/2 Signature 60, ✍ Aut. 60
00/1 SP Authentic 105
00/1 SPx 138
00/1 UD Reserve 95
00/1 UD Ice 87

HORDICHUK, DARCY
01/2 Parkhurst 258
01/2 PS Titanium Draft 159
00/1 SP Authentic 134
00/1 SPx 174
00/1 UD Ice 106
01/2 Chicago Wolves

HORDY, MIKE
81/2 Indianapolis Checkers

HORECK, PETE
45-64 BeeHive-2 [Detr.]
45-64 BeeHive-2 [Bost.]

HORESOVSKY, JOSEF
72 Hellas MM-Jenkki 82
74 Hellas MM-Jenkki 64
70/1 Kuvajulkaisut 49
72 Panda MM-Toronto
72 Semic Sticker 23
74 Semic Sticker 54
71/2 Williams Finnish 29
72/3 Williams Finnish 10
73/4 Williams Finnish 51

HORI, HIROSHI
79 Panini Sticker 287

HORISBERGER, MICHAEL
79 Panini Sticker 263

HORKKO, KARI
80/1 Mallasjuoma 188
78/9 SM-Liiga 216
72/3 Williams Finnish 208
73/4 Williams Finnish 279

HORN, ALEXANDER
94/5 DEL 424

HORN, BILL
92/3 Greensboro Monarchs 3
94/5 Greensboro Monarchs
93/4 Rochester Americans

HORNA, TOMAS
99/0 DS 161
00/1 DS 140
98/9 OFS 175
99/0 OFS 165
00/1 OFS 122
01/2 OFS 170

HORNE, BUDDY
52/3 Anonymous 119

HORNER, RED
33/4 Anonymous 1
34-43 BeeHive-1 [Toro.]
33/4 Canadian Gum
00 CSAS Signat. Series
33/4 Hamilton Gum 21
83 HHOF Postcard H9
83&87 HHOF 115
01/2 La Presse
95/6 Legends of Hockey 68
32/3 Maple Leafs O'Keefe
33/4 O-Pee-Chee 10
36/7 O-Pee-Chee 122
37/8 O-Pee-Chee 134
39/0 O-Pee-Chee 10
38/9 Quaker Oats
34/5 Sweet Caporal
33/4 WWGum 16
37/8 World Wide Gum 8

HORNUNG, BLAIRE
91/2 Air Canada SJHL A7

HORNUNG, BRAD
86/7 Regina Pats

HORNUNG, LARRY
72/3 O-Pee-Chee 317
73/4 Quaker Oats 26
71/2 SLOU

HORNUNG, TODD
97/8 Portland Winter Hawks

HORNY, KAREL
96/7 APS 112
97/8 APS 116
96/7 DS Sticker 278
97/8 DS Sticker 59

HORTON, BILL
72/3 Cleveland Crusaders
72/3 Clev. WHA / Linnett

HORTON, TIM
01/2 ASG History
02/3 BAP Memorabilia / Cup
01/2 BAP Update ✂ PTT6
45-64 BeeHive-2 [Toro.]
64-67 BeeHive-3 [Toro.]
64-67 BeeHive-3 [Toro.]
02/3 Canada Post
63-65 Chex
64/5 Coke/Sprite [Toro.]
65/6 Coca-Cola
70/1 Eddie Sargent 125
71/2 Eddie Sargent 169
72/3 Eddie Sargent 37
70/1 Esso Power Player
01/2 Fleer Greats 30
62/3 Cowan Tile
83 HHOF Postcard J8
83&87 HHOF 188
02/3 In The Game-Used ✂ VM13
91/2 Kraft 86
93/4 Legends of Hockey 24
68/9 O-Pee-Chee 123
68/9 O-Pee-Chee 201
68/9 O-Pee-Chee PS 18
69/0 O-Pee-Chee 182
69/0 O-Pee-Chee 213
69/0 O-Pee-Chee 4in1
70/1 O-Pee-Chee 59
71/2 O-Pee-Chee 186
72/3 O-Pee-Chee 197
73/4 O-Pee-Chee 189
71/2 O-Pee-Chee Poster 18
52/3 Parkhurst 58
53/4 Parkhurst 13
54/5 Parkhurst 31
54/5 Parkhurst 90
55/6 Parkhurst 3
57/8 Parkhurst [Toro.] 22
58/9 Parkhurst 42
59/0 Parkhurst 25
60/1 Parkhurst 1
61/2 Parkhurst 1
62/3 Parkhurst 7
63/4 Parkhurst 16, 76
92/3 Parkhurst PR-16
93/4 Parkhurst PR34
93/4 Parkhurst DPR-3
01/2 Parkhurst HSHS, PR24, PR67, PR75, PR89, PR97, PR103, PR113, PR119, PR127, PR137, ✂ H12, ✂ PV21
02/3 Parkhurst ✂ VM15, ✂ VT14
93/4 Parkie 56-57 127
95/6 Parkie 66-67 103
94/5 Parkie Tall 131, 135
66/7 Post Cereal Box
68/9 Post Marble
67/8 Post Tips 3
45-54 Quaker Oats
60/1 Shirriff 5
61/2 Shirriff 44
62/3 Shirriff 4
68/9 Shirriff / Toro. 14
01/2 SP GU ✍ Sig
90/1 Tim Horton
64/5 Topps 102
64/5 Topps 105
65/6 Topps 79
66/7 Topps 80
67/8 Topps 127
67/8 Topps 16
68/9 Topps 123
69/0 Topps 45
70/1 Topps 59
02/3 To. Heritage - Reprint TML, ✂ Reprint
01/2 T/O Archives 76
57/8 Toronto Star Photo
63/4 Toronto Star Action
63/4 Toronto Star Photo
64/5 Toronto Star Action
64/5 Toronto Star Photo
65/6 Toronto Star Photo
62/3 Toronto Star Weekend
71/2 Toronto Sun Photo
01/2 Ultimate Mem. ✂ ASGH, ✂ CP, ✂ RT
02/3 Ultimate Mem. ✂ BOS, ✂ CP, ✂ FS (x2), ✂ RT, ✂ VGJ, ✍ Cut
91/2 Ultimate Original Six 37
91/2 Ultimate Original Six 84
91/2 Ultimate Original Six 97
99/0 UD C. Legends 40
00/1 UD Legends 122
01/2 UD Legends 60
01/2 UD SCup Champs 25
60/1 York Glass [Toro.]
60/1 York
61/2 York 7
62/3 York Transfer 3
63/4 York 1
67/8 York
67/8 York 21
67/8 York 25
67/8 York 31
72/3 BUFF
73/4 BUFF
93/4 BUFF / Noco
64/5 TORO
68/9 TORO
69/0 TORO

HORVATH, BRONCO
45-64 BeeHive-2 [NYRa.]
45-64 BeeHive-2 [Bost.]
45-64 BeeHive-2 [Chic.]
45-64 BeeHive-2 [Toro.]
64-67 BeeHive-3 [Toro.]
62/3 Cowan Tile
93/4 Parkie 56-57 105
60/1 Shirriff 105
61/2 Shirriff 31
57/8 Topps 7
58/9 Topps 35
59/0 Topps 56
60/1 Topps 56
61/2 Topps 54
61/2 Topps 40
61/2 Topps - Stamp
62/3 Topps 63
59/0 Toronto Star Weekend
98/9 BOST / Alumni 33

HORVATH, JASON
91/2 7th...Sketch WHL 187

HORVATH, SCOTT
96 Québec Pee Wee 1422

HORYNA, ROBERT
96/7 APS 266
97/8 APS 221
99/0 DS 44
97/8 DS Sticker 28
99/0 OFS 7
90/1 ProCards 165
90/1 Newmarket Saints

HOSEK, MIROSLAV
94/5 APS 259

HOSHINO, YOSHIO
79 Panini Sticker 289

HOSPODAR, ED
80/1 O-Pee-Chee 366
81/2 O-Pee-Chee 233
87/8 BUFF / Blue Shield
87/8 BUFF / Won. Bread
82/3 HART / Jr. Whalers
83/4 HART / Jr. Whalers
86/7 PHIL

HOSSA, MARCEL
01/2 BAP Memor. 324
02/3 Bowman 110, ✂ FFDS, ✂ FFJ, ✂ FFP, ✂ FFR, ✂ FFRP, ✂ FFS, ✂ FFTS, ✍ YSA, / ✍ Puck
02/3 Calder 76, -CR 16
02/3 Exclusive 90, -GE 11
02/3 First Edition 288
02/3 O-Pee-Chee 296
02/3 Pacific Complete 556
01/2 PTC Draft 4
01/2 Parkhurst 320
02/3 Pr. Stock Reserve 52
01/2 PS Titanium Draft 139
02/3 Signature ✂ AR5, ✂ TQ6
01/2 SPx 206
02/3 SPx 114
02/3 Stadium 111
02/3 Topps 296
02/3 T. Limited 296
02/3 T. Total 114
01/2 UD PlayMakers Ltd 123
02/3 Upper Deck 210
02/3 UD Foundations 133
01/2 UD Honor Roll 76
01/2 UD Ice 142
01/2 UD Mask 151
01/2 UD MVP 225
02/3 UD MVP 207
01/2 UD Premier 99
99/0 UD Prospects 39, IN10
00/1 UD Prospects 58
02/3 UD Rookie 53
01/2 UD Top Shelf 130
02/3 UD Vintage 336
01/2 Victory 445
02/3 Victory 115
02/3 MONT
02/3 Hamilton Bulldogs
01/2 Québec Citadelles

HOSSA, MARIAN
01/2 Adrenaline 134
01/2 Atomic 69, CP 13, PP 25
02/3 Atomic 71
99/0 Aurora 99, Stripe 99
00/1 Aurora 101, Pins. 101, SR-15
98/9 Be A Player 249, ✍ Aut. 249
99/0 BAP Mem. 12, SL-15
00/1 BAP Mem. 94
01/2 BAP Memor. 98
02/3 BAP Memorabilia 83, 221, ✂ FP21
01/2 BAP Update HSHS, HSHSJers
01/2 Bowman 45
02/3 Bowman 20
98 Bowman 53, SC7
98 Bowman Chrome 53
98/9 Bowman's Best 107, F13
02/3 Calder 8, -CG 7, -HS 7
98/9 Collection Souvenir 16
99/0 Crown Royale 97, IE-18, C21-8
00/1 Crown Royale 75
01/2 Crown Royale 101, JotC 23
02/3 Crown Royale 67
97/8 Do. Elite 28
97/8 Do. Preferred 162
99/0 Dynagon Ice 139, CM-27
02/3 eTopps 52
02/3 Exclusive 122, ✂ GWJ 18
02/3 First Edition 75, 361, 418R, ✂ Jers.
01/2 Heads Up 69, SM 12
02/3 Heads Up 87, ✂ GWQ 19
99/0 HoloGrFX 41
02/3 In The Game-Used 53, 153, ✂ F21, ✂ GUJ48, ✂ SJ48
98/9 McDonald's McD23
99/0 McDonald's McD-20
00/1 McDonald's 23, CL-5
01/2 McDonald's 26
02/3 McDonald's 29
99/0 Millenium 170, ✍ Aut. 170
98/9 NHL Power Play
99/0 NHL Power Play
01/2 O-Pee-Chee 29
02/3 O-Pee-Chee 127
98/9 OPC Chrome 104
98/9 Omega 164
99/0 Omega 164, 5ST-17, G7
99/0 Pacific 288
00/1 Pacific 278, IO-16, GCDC-21, PR-14
01/2 Pacific 273, 417, 436, PCC 356, GCDC 15, IZ 13, WAS 6
02/3 Pacific 267
02/3 Pacific Complete 107
97/8 Pa. Dynagon Rookie
97/8 Pa. Paramount 125
99/0 Pa. Paramount 162, IAd-15
00/1 Pa. Paramount 172, FF-24
98/9 Pa. Revolution 99
99/0 Panini Sticker 114
00/1 Parkhurst P-98
01/2 Parkhurst 21, ✂ PJ57, ✂ PS52, ✂ PSJ10, ✂ T16
02/3 Parkhurst 37, ✂ FP21, ✂ TT11
02/3 Parkhurst Retro 48, ✂ RF21, ✂ RJ26, ✂ RSJ18, ✂ HH7, ✂ HSHSJers, ✂ RM4, ✂ RR2
97/8 Pinnacle 17
00/1 Premier Plus 23, PA6
99/0 Prism 96, CA-14
00/1 Private Stock 70, PS-40, PSNW-16
01/2 Pr. Stock 68
02/3 Pr. Stock Reserve ✂ 134
00/1 PS Titanium 65, WAS-7
01/2 PS Titanium 100, ✂ DSJ 47, ✂ DSJ 63
01/2 PS Titanium Draft ✂ 66
02/3 PS Titanium 72, -SK 6
02/3 Quest for the Cup 71, -CC 13, ✂ GWJ 13
99/0 Revolution 102, SS-24, TL-6, / CSC 102
00/1 Revolution 103, HD-23
00/1 Signature 237, F-21, ✍ Aut. 115
01/2 Signature 20, ✍ Aut. 20, ✂ GUE45, ✂ GJ46, ✂ GSJ46, ✂ ITN45
02/3 Signature 24, ✍ 24, ✂ FJ21, ✂ GSJ48, ✂ TQ20
98/9 SP Authentic ✍ SotT
99/0 SP Authentic 60, TH7, ✍ SotT
00/1 SP Authentic 62
01/2 SP Authentic 57, ✍ SotT, ✍ SotTD (x2), ✍ SotT
02/3 SP Authentic 63
01/2 SP GU 42
01/2 SP GU 36, ✂ IS, ✂ Patch, ✂ ✍ PatchSig, ✂ PatchC, ✂ ✍ PatchCSig
02/3 SP Game-Used ✂ AF (x2)
02/3 Sports Vault 95
99/0 SPx 107
00/1 SPx 46, HH9
01/2 SPx 44
02/3 SPx 53
98/9 SPx Finite 58, 140
00/1 Stadium 123
99/0 Stadium 82, Chrome 30, Big 14, CA5, ✍ CS2, ✍ CS3, ✍ LS13, ✂ SCS
00/1 Stadium 103
01/2 Stadium 15
02/3 Stadium 61, ✂ NHLP7
98/9 Topps 104
99/0 Topps 99, NS2, IF4, ✍ TA8
00/1 Topps 23
01/2 Topps 29
02/3 Topps 127
99/0 To. Chrome 99, IF4
00/1 To. Chrome 22
01/2 To. Chrome 29
02/3 T. Chrome 113
98/9 To. Finest F16
99/0 To. Gold Label 64, FG16
00/1 To. Gold Label 11, NG5
00/1 To. Heritage 68, NT1
01/2 To. Heritage 28
02/3 To. Heritage 73, ✂ GS, ✂ GSB
02/3 T. Limited 127
99/0 To. Prmr. Plus 44, TNO2, / PP3
01/2 To. Reserve 31
00/1 To. Stars 66
02/3 T. Total 10
98/9 UD Choice 142
00/1 UD Heroes 152
01/2 UD PlayMakers Ltd 69
00/1 UD Reserve 59
00/1 Ultimate Mem. ✂ Jers. 15, ✂ J-17, ✂ S-17
02/3 Ultimate Mem. ✂ GUJ, ✂ GUSJ, ✂ NP, ✂ Num
99/0 Ult. Victory 61, sg6
97/8 Upper Deck 326
98/9 Upper Deck 6, GN2
99/0 Upper Deck 92, N13
00/1 Upper Deck 120, A6, F7, RP5
01/2 Upper Deck 122, FF7, T6, ✂ NG
02/3 Upper Deck 122, ✂ UDPL
01/2 UD Artistic 62, R62, / Art
99/0 UD Black Diam. 59
00/1 UD Black Diam. 40
99/0 UD C. Legends 73
02/3 UD Classic 69
98/9 UD G. Reserve 6
99/0 UD G. Reserve 92, / Backup 161
99/0 UD Gretzky Excl. 84
01/2 UD Honor Roll SS5, -DPuck
02/3 UD Honor 50
00/1 UD Ice 28
01/2 UD Ice 32
00/1 UD Legends 93, 95
01/2 UD Mask 68
99/0 UD MVP 144, 21st-8, GU5
00/1 UD MVP 125
01/2 UD MVP 131
02/3 UD MVP 127, SO10
99/0 UD MVP Cup 124, CC7
99/0 UD Ovation 39
02/3 UD Piece 63
01/2 UD Premier 36, ✍ Sig
02/3 UD Premier 39
00/1 UD Pros&Prosp. 59
99/0 UD Retro 55
02/3 UD Rookie 70, ✂ DJ
01/2 UD Top Shelf 29, ✂ J, ✂ ✍ SJ
02/3 UD Top Shelf 62, ✂ HT
00/1 UD Vintage 249, 258, 259
01/2 UD Vintage 174, 182
02/3 UD Vintage 179, 281, GB 179, T46
00/1 Vanguard 69, HV-24
01/2 Vanguard 69, QTH 17, ✂ DGM 45
02/3 Vanguard 70, -EMW 8
99/0 Victory 200
00/1 Victory 158, 159, 313
01/2 Victory 242, 417
02/3 Victory 149, -NP42
99/0 WGretzky 116
98/9 OTTA
99/0 OTTA
00/1 OTTA
01/2 OTTA
02/3 OTTA
97/8 Portland Winter Hawks

HOSTAK, MARTIN
95/6 APS 367
96/7 APS 137
91/2 Bowman 233
96/7 DS Sticker 70
94/5 Leaf Elit Set 238
95/6 Leaf Elit Set 104, FTF-10
90/1 OPC Premier 44
95 Panini Worlds 208
90/1 Pro Set 629
91/2 ProCards 285
90/1 Score 36T
94 Semic 189
92/3 Semic Elitserien 236
91/2 To. Stadium 337
90/1 Upper Deck 542
91/2 Upper Deck 473
95/6 UD Elitserien 162
97/8 UD Elitserien 177
98/9 UD Elitserien 145
99/0 UD Elitserien 147
00/1 UD Elitserien 132, P6, ✍ Sig.
96 Wien 121
90/1 PHIL

HOTHAM, GREG
88/9 ProCards / Newmarket
89/0 ProCards AHL 118
83/4 PITT / Heinz
84/5 PITT / Heinz
79/0 TORO

HOTHAM, SCOTT
02/3 Mississauga IceDogs

HOUCK, PAUL
88/9 ProCards / Indianapolis

HOUCK, ROD
92/3 Dayton Bombers
88/9 Regina Pats

HOUDA, DOUG
94/5 Leaf 523
90/1 O-Pee-Chee 410
91/2 O-Pee-Chee 512
97/8 Pa. Dynagon BKS-55
97/8 Pi. Be A Player 193, ✍ Aut. 193
91/2 Pro Set 81
90/1 ProCards 479
90/1 Score 11
91/2 Score CAN 442
85/6 DETR / Little Caesars
88/9 DETR / Little Caesars
89/0 DETR / Little Caesars
91/2 HART / Jr. Whalers
92/3 HART / Dairymart
96/7 NYIS
00/1 Rochester Americans
02/3 Rochester Americans
84/5 Medicine Hat Tigers

HOUDE, ERIC
98/9 Pacific 251
00/1 Chicago Wolves
96/7 Fredericton Canadiens
99/0 Hamilton Bulldogs
95/6 Halifax Moosehead

HOUDE, MARCEL
51/2 Bas du Fleuve 41

HOUDEK, TOMAS
00/1 OFS 221

HOUGEN, JIM
82/3 Medicine Hat Tigers

HOUGH, MIKE
90/1 Bowman 174
91/2 Bowman 144
92/3 Bowman 178
93/4 Donruss 122
92/3 Durivage 25
93/4 Durivage 45
92/3 Fleer Ultra 175
94/5 Fleer Ultra 297
93/4 Leaf 247
94/5 Leaf 504
90/1 O-Pee-Chee 427
91/2 O-Pee-Chee 113
92/3 O-Pee-Chee 392
89/0 O-Pee-Chee 266
87/8 OPC Sticker 220-88
97/8 Pa. Dynagon BKS-40
90/1 Panini/QUE 9
91/2 Panini Sticker 254
92/3 Panini Sticker 211
94/5 Panini Sticker 70
91/2 Parkhurst 150
92/3 Parkhurst 380
91/2 Pinnacle 194
92/3 Pinnacle 113
93/4 Pinnacle 402
94/5 Pinnacle 333
96/7 Pinnacle 76
93/4 Power Play 94
93/4 Premier 482
94/5 Premier 116
90/1 Pro Set 247, 516
91/2 Pro Set 463
91/2 Pro Set 582
92/3 Pro Set 154
92/3 Pro Set 266
91/2 Pro Set Platinum 217
88/9 ProCards / Halifax
91/2 Score 112
91/2 Score CAN 112
92/3 Score 64
93/4 Score 393
93/4 Score 559
92/3 Topps 297
98/9 To. Finest 83
91/2 To. Stadium 80
92/3 T. Stadium Club 434
93/4 To. Stadium 466
91/2 Upper Deck 562
95/6 UD BAP 122, ✍ S122
96/7 FLOR / Winn-Dixie
86/7 QUÉB
86/7 QUÉB / Gene. Foods
86/7 QUÉB / McDonald's
87/8 QUÉB / Gene. Foods
88/9 QUÉB
89/0 QUÉB / Gene. Foods
89/0 QUÉB / Police
90/1 QUÉB
90/1 QUÉB / Petro-Canada
91/2 QUÉB / Petro-Canada
92/3 QUÉB / Petro-Canada
83/4 Fredericton Express
84/5 Fredericton Express
85/6 Fredericton Express
86/7 Fredericton Express
82/3 Kitchener Rangers

HOUGHTON, ART
92/3 MPS SJHL 68

HOUGHTON, DARREN
91/2 Air Canada SJHL D13
92/3 MPS SJHL 79

HOUK, ROD
87/8 Regina Pats

HOULDER, BILL
93/4 Donruss 8
93/4 Fleer Ultra 256
94/5 Fleer Ultra 4, 362
93/4 Leaf 315
90/1 O-Pee-Chee 399
89/0 OPC Chrome 46
98/9 Pacific 381
99/0 Pacific 372
93/4 Parkhurst 272
95/6 Parkhurst 464
94/5 Pinnacle 206
93/4 Power Play 4
93/4 Premier 403
94/5 Premier 92
90/1 Pro Set 417
88/9 ProCards / Baltimore
90/1 ProCards 273
91/2 ProCards 1
93/4 Score 639
98/9 Topps 46
93/4 To. Stadium 419
93/4 Upper Deck 429
94/5 Upper Deck 163
95/6 Upper Deck 475
96/7 Upper Deck 154
01/2 Upper Deck 384
94/5 UD BAP ✍ 43
95/6 UD CC 243
00/1 UD Vintage 207
87/8 WASH / Kodak
89/0 WASH
91/2 Rochester Americans GL
92/3 San Diego Gulls

HOULE, DANIEL
01/2 Québec Remparts 14

HOULE, GERARD
52/3 Anonymous 66

HOULE, KEVIN
86/7 Sherb. Canadiens 20

HOULE, RÉJEAN
01/2 AGF
72/3 Dernière Heure
80/1 Dernière Heure
72/3 Eddie Sargent 115
70/1 O-Pee-Chee 174
71/2 O-Pee-Chee 147
72/3 O-Pee-Chee 210
76/7 O-Pee-Chee 360
77/8 O-Pee-Chee 241
78/9 O-Pee-Chee 227
79/0 O-Pee-Chee 34
80/1 O-Pee-Chee 261
81/2 O-Pee-Chee 183
82/3 O-Pee-Chee 184
81/2 OPC Sticker 37
74/5 OPC WHA 41
75/6 OPC WHA 84
80/1 Pepsi Bottle Cap
92/3 Sport Flash 10
92/3 Sport Flash 10
77/8 Topps 241
78/9 Topps 227
79/0 Topps 34
80/1 Topps 261
71/2 Toronto Sun Photo
69/0 MONT / Pro Star
70/1 MONT
71/2 MONT / Pro Star
72/3 MONT / Pro Star
76/7 MONT
77/8 MONT
78/9 MONT
79/0 MONT
80/1 MONT
81/2 MONT
82/3 MONT
82/3 MONT / Steinberg
73/4 Québec Nordiques

HOULE, YVAN
52/3 Anonymous 46

HOUSE, BOBBY
93/4 Cla. Prospects 219
90/1 7th..Sketch WHL 190
91/2 7th...Sketch WHL 208
91/2 Star Pics 69
91/2 Ultimate Draft Pick 47, ✍ Aut.
96/7 Albany River Rats
97/8 Albany River Rats
93/4 Indianapolis Ice
94/5 Indianapolis Ice
99/0 St. John's Maple Leafs
00/1 St. John's Maple Leafs
01/2 St. John's Maple Leafs
01/2 St. John's / Clarenville
92/3 Brandon Wheat Kings
89/0 Spokane Chiefs

HOUSE, MATT
99/0 Guelph Storm

HOUSLEY, PHIL
01/2 Atomic ✂ GWJ 5
99/0 Aurora 22
02/3 BAP All-Star 30, ✂ ASJ
98/9 Be A Player 167, M-16, ✍ Aut. 167
99/0 BAP Mem. 218
00/1 BAP Mem. 203
01/2 BAP Memor. 171, 347
90/1 Bowman 239
91/2 Bowman 197
92/3 Bowman 20
92/3 Bowman 208
00/1 Crown Royale ✂ GWJ 4
93/4 Donruss 294
95/6 Donruss 74
96/7 Donruss 201
97/8 Donruss 150
98/9 Dynagon Ice 26
93/4 EA Sports 145
94/5 Fleer 30
96/7 Fleer 59, NT-5
95/6 Fleer Metal 19
96/7 Fl. Picks 22
92/3 Fleer Ultra 241
93/4 Fleer Ultra 100
93/4 Fleer Ultra 409
93/4 Fleer Ultra AS 18
94/5 Fleer Ultra 269
95/6 Fleer Ultra 25
96/7 Fl. Ultra 176
83/4 Funmate Puffy 12 [w/]
95 Globe 106
93/4 Hockey Wit 101
95/6 Hoyle / West. 9-Spade
92/3 Humpty Dumpty
90/1 Kraft 18, 65
91/2 Kraft 33
95/6 Kraft / IP
93/4 Leaf 61
94/5 Leaf 450
95/6 Leaf 141
96/7 Leaf 65
94/5 L. Limited 77
96/7 Maggers 93
92/3 McDonald's McD-08
93/4 McDonald's McD-06
96/7 Metal Univ. 164
83/4 O-Pee-Chee 65
84/5 O-Pee-Chee 23
85/6 OPC/Topps 63
86/7 OPC/Topps 154
87/8 OPC/Topps 33
88/9 OPC/Topps 119
90/1 OPC/Topps 89
91/2 O-Pee-Chee 395
91/2 Topps - Team Leader 11
92/3 O-Pee-Chee 298
02/3 O-Pee-Chee 262
89/0 OPC/Topps 59
87/8 OPC Leaders 17
90/1 OPC Premier 45
91/2 OPC Premier 50
92/3 OPC Premier SP16
83/4 OPC/Topps Sticker 238
84/5 OPC Sticker 203
84/5 OPC Sticker 204
85/6 OPC Sticker 173
86/7 OPC Sticker 47-188
87/8 OPC Sticker 151
88/9 OPC Sticker 255-123
89/0 opcSticker 261
97/8 Omega 238
99/0 Omega 37
98/9 Pacific 96
99/0 Pacific 56
00/1 Pacific 65
01/2 Pacific 60
02/3 Pacific 77
02/3 Pacific Complete 150
97/8 Pacific CC 259
99/0 Pa. Paramount 39
00/1 Pa. Paramount 35
97/8 Pa. Revolution 146
87/8 Panini Sticker 24
88/9 Panini Sticker 220
89/0 Panini Sticker 205
90/1 Panini Sticker 21
90/1 Panini/WPG 13, H
91/2 Panini Sticker 65
92/3 Panini Sticker 61

93/4 Panini Sticker 133
93/4 Panini Sticker 196
94/5 Panini Sticker 142
95/6 Panini Sticker 241
96/7 Panini Sticker 85
99/0 Panini Sticker 193, 345
00/1 Panini Sticker 120
91/2 Parkhurst 205
92/3 Parkhurst 208
93/4 Parkhurst 174
94/5 Parkhurst 197
95/6 Parkhurst 30
00/1 Parkhurst P-132
02/3 Parkhurst 135
94/5 Parkie SE30
91/2 Pinnacle 4
92/3 Pinnacle 70
93/4 Pinnacle 351
93/4 Pinnacle TP 9
94/5 Pinnacle 410
96/7 Pinnacle 19
95/6 Pi. Summit 40
96/7 Pi. Summit 121
95/6 Pi. Zenith 104
95/6 Playoff 17, 129
96/7 Playoff 429
95/6 POG 56
93/4 Power Play 271
93/4 Power Play 427
93/4 Premier 36
93/4 Premier 503
93/4 Prmr. - BG-OPC 4
93/4 Prmr. - BG-Top. 19
94/5 Premier 347, 353, 491
00/1 PS Titanium ✂ GUG 1, ✂ GUG 67
01/2 PS Titanium Draft ✂ 23
90/1 Pro Set 21, 364, 562
91/2 Pro Set 267
91/2 Pro Set 295
92/3 Pro Set 212
92/3 Pro Set TL 14
91/2 Pro Set Platinum 137
91/2 Puck / Pro Set 30
99/0 Revolution 24
00/1 Revolution 22
90/1 Score 145, 3T
90/1 Sco. Hot Cards 63
91/2 Score 271
91/2 Score CAN 491
92/3 Score 299
92/3 Score 440
93/4 Score 232
93/4 Score 482
93/4 Score 520
93/4 Score PiAS 25
95/6 Score 45
96/7 Score 153
92/3 Seasons 59
94/5 Select 146
95/6 Select CE 86
89 Semic Sticker 156
91 Semic Sticker 133
92 Semic Sticker 149
93 Semic Sticker 174
00/1 Signature 240, ✍ Aut. 146, ✂ DD-16
02/3 Signature 48, ✍ 48
95/6 SBx Emotion 22
95/6 SBx Impact 22
96/7 SBx Impact 140, BR-7, F-10
02/3 Slam Card
83/4 Souhaits Keychain [Sabres]
94/5 SP 19
95/6 SP 19
96/7 SP 167
97/8 SP Authentic 168
02/3 Sports Vault 177
99/0 SPx 23
00/1 Stadium 78
95/6 Super Sticker 16
84/5 Topps 18
92/3 Topps 268
92/3 Topps 456
95/6 Topps 166
00/1 Topps 120, PC-11
02/3 Topps 262
00/1 To. Chrome 93, PC-11
94/5 Topps Finest 91
95/6 To. Finest 7
02/3 T. Limited 262
91/2 To. Stadium 65
92/3 T. Stadium Club 14
93/4 To. Stadium 104
93/4 To. Stadium - All-Stars
95/6 To. Stadium 145
94/5 TSC Members Only 45
00/1 To. Stars ✂ GG
95/6 T. Super Skills 66
02/3 T. Total 166
98/9 UD Choice 220
90/1 Upper Deck 22, 435
91/2 Upper Deck 106
91/2 Upper Deck 624
92/3 Upper Deck 24
92/3 Upper Deck 276
92/3 Upper Deck 628
93/4 Upper Deck 525, SP-136
94/5 Upper Deck 169, SP-102
95/6 Upper Deck 294, SE-13
96/7 Upper Deck 357
98/9 Upper Deck 233
99/0 Upper Deck 195
00/1 Upper Deck 255
94/5 UD BAP R78
95/6 UD BAP 72, ✍ S72
96/7 UD Black Diam. 96
95/6 UD CC 212
96/7 UD CC 150
97/8 UD Coll. Choice 275
98/9 UD G. Reserve 233
99/0 UD G. Reserve 195
92/3 UD Locker 26
98/9 UD MVP 29
99/0 UD MVP 30
00/1 UD MVP 33
00/1 UD Vintage 55
99/0 Victory 50
00/1 Victory 38
02/3 Victory 47
99/0 WGretzky 30
96 Wien 161
82/3 BUFF / Wendt's 11
84/5 BUFF / Blue Shield
85/6 BUFF / Blue Shield
86/7 BUFF / Blue Shield
87/8 BUFF / Blue Shield
87/8 BUFF / Won. Bread
88/9 BUFF / Blue Shield
88/9 BUFF / Won. Bread
89/0 BUFF / Blue Shield
89/0 BUFF / Campbell's
90/1 WINN / IGA
91/2 WINN / IGA

HOUSTON, KEN
77/8 O-Pee-Chee 274
78/9 O-Pee-Chee 348
79/0 O-Pee-Chee 310
80/1 O-Pee-Chee 303
82/3 O-Pee-Chee 366
83/4 O-Pee-Chee 371
82/3 OPC/Topps Sticker 221
83/4 OPC/Topps Sticker 200
80/1 Pepsi Bottle Cap
82/3 Post [Calg.]
83/4 Souhaits Keychain [Capitals]
77/8 ATLF
78/9 ATLF / Colour
79/0 ATLF / B&W
79/0 ATLF / Colour
80/1 CALG
81/2 CALG
82/3 WASH

HOVI, SASU
00/1 Cardset 328
02/3 Cardset 26

HOVINHEIMO, JAAKKO
66/7 Champion 142

HOWALD, PATRICK
95 Globe 214
95 Panini Worlds 129
92 Semic Sticker 216
93 Semic Sticker 117

HOWARD, BRIAN
87/8 Soo Greyhounds 34

HOWARD, SIMON
98/9 Guildford Flames

HOWARTH, TODD
93/4 Thunder Bay Senators
94/5 Thunder Bay Senators
95/6 Thunder Bay Senators
98/9 Wichita Thunder

HOWATT, GARRY
74/5 Loblaws
74/5 O-Pee-Chee 375
75/6 O-Pee-Chee 54
76/7 O-Pee-Chee 206
76/7 O-Pee-Chee 389
77/8 O-Pee-Chee 194
78/9 O-Pee-Chee 29
79/0 O-Pee-Chee 205
80/1 O-Pee-Chee 386
82/3 O-Pee-Chee 140
83/4 O-Pee-Chee 229
82/3 OPC/Topps Sticker 133
82/3 Post [Hart.]
75/6 Topps 54
76/7 Topps 206
77/8 Topps 194
78/9 Topps 29
79/0 Topps 205
79/0 NYIS

HOWATT, GARRY
02/3 Fleer Throwbacks 84

HOWDEN, BRETT
02/3 Owen Sound Attack

HOWE, GORDIE
56 Adventure Gum 63
01/2 ASG History
98/9 Be A Player GH1, GH2
01/2 BAP Memor. ✂ 500GS
01/2 BAP Update ✂ PTT3, ✂ RR1, ✂ TC32
45-64 BeeHive-2 [Detr.]
45-64 BeeHive-2 [Detr.]
64-67 BeeHive-3 [Detr.]
64-67 BeeHive-3 [Detr.]
99/0 Canada Post
02/3 Canada Post
63-65 Chex
64/5 Coke/Sprite [Detr. #9]
65/6 Coca-Cola
70/1 Colgate 47
70/1 Dad's Cookies
97/8 Do. Elite BF-8, ✍ BF-8
64/5 Eaton's Sports Adviser [All-Star]
65/6 Eaton's Sports Adviser [Action]
66/7 Eaton's Sports Adviser [Standing]
70/1 Eddie Sargent 56
62/3 El Producto
70/1 Esso Power Player
88/9 Esso All-Star
48-52 Exhibits [Red Wings]
48-52 Exhibits [Red Wings]
01/2 Fleer Greats 1, -RC 1, ✍ Aut.
62/3 Cowan Tile
83 HHOF Postcard B6
83&87 HHOF 16
93/4 Hockey Wit 9
92/3 Legends 9
98/9 McD's T2
68/9 O-Pee-Chee 29
68/9 O-Pee-Chee 203
68/9 O-Pee-Chee 700
69/0 O-Pee-Chee 61
69/0 O-Pee-Chee 193
69/0 O-Pee-Chee 215
69/0 O-Pee-Chee 4in1
69/0 O-Pee-Chee Stamp
70/1 O-Pee-Chee 29, 238
70/1 O-Pee-Chee DE 18
71/2 O-Pee-Chee 262
71/2 O-Pee-Chee Book. 23
79/0 O-Pee-Chee 175
98/9 OPC Chrome 7
74/5 OPC WHA 1
75/6 OPC WHA 66, 100
76/7 OPC WHA 50, 72
77/8 OPC WHA 1
73/4 OPC WHA Poster 13
73/4 OPC WHA Poster 14
51/2 Parkhurst 66
52/3 Parkhurst 88
53/4 Parkhurst 50
54/5 Parkhurst 41
54/5 Parkhurst 92
60/1 Parkhurst 20
61/2 Parkhurst 20
62/3 Parkhurst 30
62/3 Parkhurst 31
63/4 Parkhurst 55
91/2 Parkhurst PHC1
93/4 Parkhurst D17
93/4 Parkhurst PR33
93/4 Parkhurst PR42
93/4 Parkhurst PR51
93/4 Parkhurst PR60
93/4 Parkhurst DPR-1
93/4 Parkhurst DPR-7
01/2 Parkhurst HSHS, PR1, PR12, PR30, PR58, PR71, PR76, PR140, ✂ 500GS, ✂ PV13, ✂ PV14, ✂ PV15, ✍ PA12, ✍ PA26, ✍ PA36
93/4 Parkie 56-57 43, 145, 160, 162, 171, 177, ✍ A-1
95/6 Parkie 66-67 42, 126, 142, MH1-5
94/5 Parkie Tall 46, 144, 154, 161, 171, 177, ✍ A5
66/7 Post Cereal Box
66/7 Post [Small]
67/8 Post Cereal Box
67/8 Post Cereal Box
90/1 Pro Set 654, 660
91/2 Pro Set 344
52 Royal Desserts 8
72 Semic Sticker 190
91 Semic Sticker 238
60/1 Shirriff 42
61/2 Shirriff 66
62/3 Shirriff 54
68/9 Shirriff / Detr. 11
01/2 Signature ✂ 500GS, ✍ VA3, ✍ VA4
97/8 SP Authentic ✍ M1, ✍ T1
99/0 SP Authentic LH3, ✍ SotT
00/1 SP Authentic ✍ SotT, P3
01/2 SP Authentic 99, ✍ SotT, ✍ SotTD (x2), ✍ SotTT
02/3 SP Authentic ✍ SotT, ✍ SotTD (x2), ✍ SotTT
00/1 SP GU ✂ TotG, ✂ C (x2), ✂ P
01/2 SP GU ✂ AF, ✂ AFQ, ✂✍ IS2, ✂✍ ISD
02/3 SP GU 51, ✍ Sig
77-79 Sportscaster 02-06
77-79 Sportscaster 63-09
77-79 Sports. FIN 07-168
77-79 Sports. FIN 70-1670
01/2 SPx ✍ Sig
02/3 SPx 89
95/6 SLU Cdn. Legend
95/6 SLU Timeless
54/5 Topps 8
57/8 Topps 42
58/9 Topps 8
59/0 Topps 48
59/0 Topps 63
64/5 Topps 89
65/6 Topps 108
65/6 Topps 122
66/7 Topps 109
66/7 Topps 121
66/7 Topps 125
66/7 Topps / Test 23
67/8 Topps 43
67/8 Topps 131
68/9 Topps 29
69/0 Topps 61
70/1 Topps 29
71/2 Topps 70
79/0 Topps 175
98/9 Topps -Reprint 7, ✍ Reprint
00/1 To. Heritage OSA, ✍ CAI, ✍ OSA
57/8 Toronto Star Photo
58/9 Toronto Star Photo
59/0 Toronto Star Photo
61/2 Toronto Star Photo
63/4 Toronto Star Action
63/4 Toronto Star Photo
64/5 Toronto Star Action
54 Toronto Star Weekend
60/1 Toronto Star Weekend
63/4 Toronto Star Weekend
65/6 Toronto Star Weekend
71/2 Toronto Sun Photo
00/1 UD Heroes 125, ✂ GT, ✂ GC, ✍ SG
02/3 UD Superstars 81, 02/3 UD13, 02/3 UD28
00/1 Ultimate Mem. ✂ #9-1,#9-2,#9-3, ✂ RE-9, ✂ RA-1,RA-6,RA-9, ✂ HL-1 to HL-7
01/2 Ultimate Mem. ✂ 500GS, ✂ ASGH, ✂ Corn., ✂ Emb., ✂ Glove, ✂ JE, ✂ JJ, ✂ NP, ✂ PL, ✂ PP, ✂ RN, ✂ RT, ✂ RA, ✂ SCW, ✍ Aut.
92/3 Upper Deck HH-19-27
02/3 Upper Deck 187, -GG9, -NC4, -SS6
01/2 UD National
00 ✂ UD APOH 500, ✂✍ 500
02/3 UD Artistic 36, R36, CG9, GD9, UD11, / ✍ Art
93/4 Upper Deck Be A Player 25
99/0 UD Black Diam. GH1-GH10, ✂ APOH
99/0 UD C. Legends 3, AC2, C7, E4, ✍ ES
01/2 UD Challenge AT3
01/2 UD Collectors
02/3 UD Foundations 23, 36, 38, 102, 104, ✂ 1000Stick, ✍ SG
01/2 UD Honor Roll 3, 33, OS3
02/3 UD Honor ✍ SC
00/1 UD Legends 41, 47, ES2, EG8, PH9, SM2, ✍ ES, ✂ LGJ
01/2 UD Legends 15, 26, 91, 99, FC, ✂ PoH, ✂ TT, ✍ ES
92/3 UD Locker 42, ✍ Aut.
02/3 UD MVP ✍ PSig
99/0 UD Ovation CS, ✍ SS
02/3 UD Piece 96, 112, 113, 114, HB5, SB5, ✍ MD
99/0 UD PowerDeck 19, T6
01/2 UD Premier 19, ✂ G., JersD, PrSigG
02/3 UD Premier 58, ✍ Sig
02/3 UD Rookie 50, 75, 101, 168, ✍ TD
01/2 UD SCup Champs 6, ✂ S
02/3 UD Top Shelf ✂ HH, ✂ M, ✍ Sig
01/2 UD Vintage ✂ NL, -SotTD
02/3 UD Vintage - Tall Boys T66-70
94 UD World Cup of Soccer - Honourary Captain C5
01/2 Victory 391-440
71/2 Williams Finnish 382
60/1 Wonder Bread
60/1 York Glass [Detr.]
62/3 York Transfer 19
63/4 York 45
95/6 Zellers
70/1 DETR / Marathon Oil
99/0 DETR / News 1
90/1 HART / Jr. Whalers
75/6 Houston Aeros

HOWE, MARK
82/3 Dernière Heure
88/9 Esso All-Star
92/3 Fleer Ultra 285
83/4 Funmate Puffy 8 [w/]
90/1 Kraft 19
93/4 Leaf 259
82/3 McDonald's Les Étoiles 31
79/0 O-Pee-Chee 216
80/1 O-Pee-Chee 91
80/1 O-Pee-Chee 160
81/2 O-Pee-Chee 128
82/3 O-Pee-Chee 252
83/4 O-Pee-Chee 267
84/5 O-Pee-Chee 161
85/6 OPC/Topps 35
86/7 OPC/Topps 123
87/8 OPC/Topps 54
88/9 OPC/Topps 6
90/1 OPC/Topps 185
91/2 O-Pee-Chee 466
89/0 OPC/Topps 191
87/8 OPC Leaders 18
81/2 OPC Sticker 62
81/2 OPC Sticker 145
82/3 OPC/Topps Sticker 131
83/4 OPC/Topps Sticker 171
83/4 OPC/Topps Sticker 195
83/4 OPC/Topps Sticker 196
84/5 OPC Sticker 109
85/6 OPC Sticker 93-226
86/7 OPC Sticker 246
86/7 OPC Sticker 116-130
86/7 OPC Sticker 184-124
87/8 OPC Sticker 100
87/8 OPC Sticker 112-124
87/8 OPC Sticker 176-174
88/9 OPC Sticker 104
88/9 OPC Sticker 124-256
89/0 opcSticker 109-248
74/5 OPC WHA 1
75/6 OPC WHA 7
76/7 OPC WHA 95
77/8 OPC WHA 25
73/4 OPC WHA Poster 14
87/8 Panini Sticker 124
88/9 Panini Sticker 316
89/0 Panini Sticker 300
90/1 Panini Sticker 122
92/3 Panini Sticker 191
91/2 Parkhurst 130
92/3 Parkhurst 279
91/2 Pinnacle 297
91/2 Pinnacle 418
92/3 Pinnacle 244
92/3 Pinnacle 322
93/4 Pinnacle 235
93/4 Pinnacle 254
94/5 Pinnacle 295
81/2 Post 11
82/3 Post [Hart.]
93/4 Power Play 329
93/4 Premier 157
90/1 Pro Set 217
91/2 Pro Set 182
90/1 Score 220
90/1 Sco. Hot Cards 92
91/2 Score 252
91/2 Score CAN 472
92/3 Score 217
93/4 Score 91
89 Semic Sticker 160
91 Semic Sticker 134
85/6 7-Eleven Superstars 14
83/4 Souhaits Keychain [Flyers]
77-79 Sportscaster 63-09
77-79 Sports. FIN 70-1670
79/0 Topps 216
80/1 Topps 91
80/1 Topps 160
81/2 Topps 82 [East]
84/5 Topps 118
86/7 OPC/Topps - Stick. 6
87/8 OPC/Topps - Stick. 3
93/4 To. Stadium 112
90/1 Upper Deck 261
92/3 Upper Deck 530
92/3 Upper Deck HH 25
93/4 Upper Deck Be A Player 25
02/3 UD Foundations 26, 37, 73, ✂ CH, ✂ CG, ✂ DF, ✂ PS
83/4 PHIL / J.C. Penney
86/7 PHIL
89/0 PHIL
90/1 PHIL
91/2 PHIL / J.C. Penney
75/6 Houston Aeros

HOWE, MARTY
79/0 O-Pee-Chee 46
83/4 O-Pee-Chee 139
84/5 O-Pee-Chee 71
83/4 OPC/Topps Sticker 54
74/5 OPC WHA 1
75/6 OPC WHA 75
76/7 OPC WHA 15
77/8 OPC WHA 65
73/4 OPC WHA Poster 14
77-79 Sportscaster 63-09
77-79 Sports. FIN 70-1670
79/0 Topps 46
84/5 Topps 55
92/3 Upper Deck HH 25
83/4 HART / Jr. Whalers
75/6 Houston Aeros
99/0 Chicago Wolves

HOWE, SYD
34-43 BeeHive-1 [Detr.]
36-39 Diamond Match TT1
83 HHOF Postcard M10
83&87 HHOF 174
94/5 Legends 44
33/4 O-Pee-Chee 24
39/0 O-Pee-Chee 72
33/4 WWGum 72
37/8 World Wide Gum 75

HOWELL, HARRY
68/9 Bauer Photo
45-64 BeeHive-2 [NYRa.]
64-67 BeeHive-3 [NYRa.]
64/5 Coke/Sprite [NYRa.]
65/6 Coca-Cola
70/1 Dad's Cookies
70/1 Eddie Sargent 134
71/2 Eddie Sargent 71
72/3 Eddie Sargent 90
70/1 Esso Power Player
01/2 Fleer Greats 58, ✍ Aut.
62/3 Cowan Tile
83 HHOF Postcard F7
83&87 HHOF 83
91/2 Kraft 73
95/6 Legends of Hockey 56
68/9 O-Pee-Chee 69
69/0 O-Pee-Chee 79
70/1 O-Pee-Chee 72
70/1 O-Pee-Chee DE 37
71/2 O-Pee-Chee 153
72/3 O-Pee-Chee 193
53/4 Parkhurst 57
54/5 Parkhurst 70
92/3 Parkhurst PR-15
93/4 Parkhurst DPR-6
02/3 Parkie - Reprint 183
93/4 Parkie 56-57 96
95/6 Parkie 66-67 80, AS3, TW4
94/5 Parkie Tall 92
66/7 Post Cereal Box
67/8 Post Cereal Box
67/8 Post Cereal Box
60/1 Shirriff 86
61/2 Shirriff 89
68/9 Shirriff / NYRa. 11
81/2 TCMA 6
54/5 Topps 3
57/8 Topps 51
58/9 Topps 60
59/0 Topps 20
60/1 Topps 49
61/2 Topps 51
61/2 Topps - Stamp
62/3 Topps 46
62/3 Topps Dollar
63/4 Topps 48
64/5 Topps 83
65/6 Topps 22
66/7 Topps 91
66/7 Topps / Test 18
67/8 Topps 84
67/8 Topps 119
67/8 Topps 121
68/9 Topps 69
69/0 Topps 79
70/1 Topps 72
02/3 Topps - Reprint 7, ✍ Reprint 7
01/2 To. Heritage S4, ✍ CAI
01/2 T/O Archives 4
64/5 Toronto Star Action
66/7 Toronto Star Weekend
66/7 Toronto Star Weekend
71/2 Toronto Sun Photo
91/2 Ultimate Original Six 23, ✍ Aut. 23
90/1 Upper Deck 511

HOWSE, DON
77/8 Nova Scotia Voyageurs

HOWSE, JASON
91/2 Avant Garde BCJHL 124

HOWSE, JON
01/2 Peterborough Petes

HOWSON, SCOTT
82/3 Indianapolis Checkers
84/5 Springfield Indians 9

HOYDA, DAVE
79/0 O-Pee-Chee 338
80/1 O-Pee-Chee 332
81/2 O-Pee-Chee 366
79/0 WINN

HOYDEN, RIKU
71/2 Williams Finnish 362

HØYEM, DAG
92/3 Semic Nordisk 159

HOYLE, JIMMY
28/9 Paulins Candy 88

HRACHOVINA, PETR
99/0 Score 131

HRADECKY, JIRI
99/0 OFS 77
99/0 Score 129

HRADECKY, TOMAS
99/0 OFS 464

HRANAC, JAN
97/8 APS 203
00/1 OFS 143
01/2 OFS 150
99/0 Score 90

HRAZDIRA, RICHARD
96/7 APS 168
97/8 APS 78
99/0 DS 1, G1
00/1 DS 50
97/8 DS Sticker 88
98/9 OFS 274
99/0 OFS 545
00/1 OFS 350, -Star 6

HRBACEK, MARCEL
99/0 Score 164

HRBATY, JAN
94/5 APS 292
95/6 APS 175
96/7 APS 310
70/1 Kuvajulkaisut 50
69/0 Mästär Serien 11

HRBEK, PETR
95/6 APS 281
96/7 APS 180
97/8 APS 90
92/3 Classic 39
92/3 Classic Prospects 67
94/5 DEL 381
97/8 DS 47
98/9 DS 45
99/0 DS 124
00/1 DS 118
96/7 DS Sticker 51
97/8 DS Sticker 97
95 Globe 160
98/9 OFS 257, 265
99/0 OFS 44
00/1 OFS 105, 313
95 Semic 163
92 Semic Sticker 132

HRDINA, JAN
01/2 Adrenaline 152
01/2 Atomic ✂ GWJ 44
00/1 Aurora 115
99/0 BAP Mem. 247
00/1 BAP Mem. 216
01/2 BAP Memor. 139
02/3 BAP Memorabilia 76
98/9 Dynagon Ice 150, -IR 6
02/3 First Edition 95, 388, ✂ Jers.
01/2 Heads Up ✂ JQ 17
99/0 Millenium 195, ✍ Aut. 195
99/0 NHL Power Play
01/2 O-Pee-Chee 201
02/3 O-Pee-Chee 246
99/0 OFS 22
00/1 OFS 394
98/9 Omega 200
99/0 Omega 187
99/0 Pacific 337
00/1 Pacific 327
01/2 Pacific 311, ✂ GWJ 26
02/3 Pacific 308
02/3 Pacific Complete 294
98/9 Pa. Crown Roy. 109
99/0 Pa. Paramount 188
00/1 Pa. Paramount 197
00/1 Parkhurst P-18
02/3 Parkhurst 142
02/3 Parkhurst Retro 76
00/1 Private Stock 79, PS-46
01/2 Pr. Stock ✂ GUG 76
00/1 PS Titanium ✂ GUG 132
01/2 PS Titanium ✂ DSJ 31, ✂ DSJ 35
00/1 PS Titanium Draft ✂ 81
99/0 Revolution 117
00/1 Revolution 117
99/0 Score JT16
00/1 Signature 25
01/2 Signature 23, ✍ Aut. 23
02/3 Signature 114, ✍ 114
98/9 SP Authentic 106
02/3 Sports Vault 113
99/0 SPx 122
99/0 Stadium 129, CA10
99/0 Topps 179
00/1 Topps 208
01/2 Topps 201
02/3 Topps 246
99/0 To. Chrome 179
00/1 To. Chrome 137
x99/0 To. Gold Label FG17
02/3 T. Limited 246
02/3 T. Total 351
98/9 Upper Deck 345
99/0 Upper Deck 106
00/1 Upper Deck 140
01/2 Upper Deck 369
02/3 Upper Deck 387
98/9 UD G. Reserve 345
99/0 UD G. Reserve 106
99/0 UD MVP 169, ✍ PS
00/1 UD MVP 142
01/2 UD MVP 151
02/3 UD MVP 147
00/1 UD Vintage 289
02/3 UD Vintage 204, 314
00/1 Vanguard 79
01/2 Vanguard ✂ DGM 24
99/0 Victory 238, 354
00/1 Victory 187
01/2 Victory 279
02/3 Victory 174
99/0 WGretzky 139
96/7 Cleveland Lumberjacks

HRDINA, JAROSLAV
82 Semic Sticker 97

HRDINA, JIRI
91/2 Bowman 82
90/1 OPC/Topps 234
91/2 O-Pee-Chee 213
89/0 opcSticker 97-234, / FS 5
98/9 OFS Leg. 13
00/1 OFS 416
90/1 Panini Sticker 182
90/1 Panini/CGY 3
90/1 Pro Set 421
91/2 Pro Set 461
91/2 Score CAN 418
92/3 Topps 272
91/2 To. Stadium 36
92/3 T. Stadium Club 158
90/1 Upper Deck 292
90/1 CALG / McGavin's

HREBEJK, STEPAN
01/2 OFS 138

HREBEN, VRATISLAV
99/0 Score 55

HRECHKOSY, DAVID
74/5 Loblaws
75/6 O-Pee-Chee 156
75/6 O-Pee-Chee 316
76/7 O-Pee-Chee 364
75/6 Topps 156
75/6 Topps 316

HREUS, MICHAEL
94/5 DEL 304
95/6 DEL 283
96/7 DEL 89

HRICZOV, NICK
97/8 New Mexico Scorpions

HRINA, SLAVOMIR
01/2 OFS 60

HRISTOV, KROUM
79 Panini Sticker 349

HRIVNAK, JIM
91/2 Bowman 305
92/3 Bowman 372
00/1 Cardset 102
92/3 Fleer Ultra 435
93/4 Fleer Ultra 410
93/4 Leaf 312
90/1 OPC/Topps 9
91/2 O-Pee-Chee 487
92/3 Parkhurst 430
93/4 Pinnacle 407
93/4 Power Play 428
90/1 Pro Set 646
91/2 Pro Set 509
89/0 ProCards AHL 93
90/1 ProCards 216
91/2 ProCards 549
90/1 Score 386
93/4 Score 201
93/4 Score 563
92/3 Topps 18
91/2 To. Stadium 264
92/3 T. Stadium Club 325
93/4 To. Stadium 421
91/2 Upper Deck 343
92/3 Upper Deck 151
90/1 WASH / Smokey
91/2 WASH / Kodak
92/3 WASH / Kodak
94/5 Milwaukee Admirals

HRKAC, TONY
90/1 Bowman 172
91/2 Bowman 141
93/4 Donruss 292
95/6 Edge Ice 161, PR-6
02/3 First Edition 283
93/4 Fleer Ultra 411
93/4 Leaf 329
88/9 OPC/Topps 129
91/2 O-Pee-Chee 241
89/0 OPC/Topps 64
91/2 OPC Premier 40
88/9 OPC Stars 15
88/9 OPC Sticker 129-265
88/9 OPC Sticker 19-152
88/9 OPC Sticker 36
89/0 opcSticker 25-163
98/9 Pacific 210
01/2 Pacific 5
02/3 Pacific 15
02/3 Pacific Complete 245
88/9 Panini Sticker 106
89/0 Panini Sticker 119
90/1 Panini Sticker 146
90/1 Panini/QUE 10
93/4 Parkhurst 448
01/2 Parkhurst 360
90/1 Pro Set 248
91/2 Pro Set 205
91/2 Pro Set Platinum 105
90/1 Score 256
91/2 Score 122
91/2 Score 5T
91/2 Score CAN 122
91/2 Score CAN 555
92/3 Score 407
00/1 Signature 218, ✍ Aut. 178
02/3 Sports Vault 8
92/3 Topps 524
91/2 To. Stadium 136
02/3 T. Total 43
90/1 Upper Deck 184
91/2 Upper Deck 56
01/2 UD Mask 6
99/0 UD MVP Cup 5
89/0 QUÉB
90/1 QUÉB
90/1 QUÉB / Petro-Canada
91/2 SANJ / Sports Action
87/8 SLOU
87/8 SLOU / Kodak
88/9 SLOU
88/9 SLOU / Kodak
92/3 Indianapolis Ice
94/5 Milwaukee Admirals
95/6 Milwaukee Admirals
96/7 Milwaukee Admirals

HRONEK, LUKAS
01/2 OFS 1, H1

HROOSHKIN, DALEN
00/1 Louisiana Ice Gators
99/0 Muskegon Fury

HRSTKA, IVO
94/5 APS 20

HRUBES, MILOS
96/7 APS 100
97/8 APS 106
97/8 DS 22
96/7 DS Sticker 271
97/8 DS Sticker 51

HRUBES, ROMAN
99/0 Score 2

HRUDEY, KELLY
98/9 Bicycle.. 6-C
90/1 Bowman 144
91/2 Bowman 183
92/3 Bowman 42
93/4 Donruss 161
94/5 Donruss 207
95/6 Donruss 215
96/7 Donruss 209
97/8 Donruss 92
96/7 Do. Canadian 36
96/7 Do. Elite 60
97/8 Do. Priority 85
93/4 EA Sports 66
94/5 Flair 80
94/5 Fleer 95
92/3 Fleer Ultra 84
93/4 Fleer Ultra 131
94/5 Fleer Ultra 99
95/6 Fleer Ultra 75
96/7 Fl. Ultra 150
93/4 Hockey Wit 93
92/3 Kraft / PB
93/4 Kraft / JELL-O
94/5 Kraft / KD
95/6 Kraft / PS
93/4 Leaf 39
94/5 Leaf 189
96/7 Leaf 109
96/7 L. Preferred 39
97/8 Limited FotG 27
96/7 Maggers 76
96/7 Metal Univ. 136
85/6 OPC/Topps 122
86/7 OPC/Topps 27
87/8 OPC/Topps 119
88/9 OPC/Topps 155
90/1 OPC/Topps 103
91/2 O-Pee-Chee 195
92/3 O-Pee-Chee 44
89/0 OPC/Topps 166
85/6 OPC Sticker 79-212
86/7 OPC Sticker 212-84
87/8 OPC Sticker 242-109
88/9 OPC Sticker 109-241
89/0 opcSticker 149-268
98/9 Pacific 382
97/8 Pacific CC 337
87/8 Panini Sticker 90
88/9 Panini Sticker 283
89/0 Panini Sticker 89, 91
90/1 Panini Sticker 246
91/2 Panini Sticker 81
92/3 Panini Sticker 63
93/4 Panini Sticker 210
94/5 Panini Sticker 180
95/6 Panini Sticker 276
91/2 Parkhurst 71
92/3 Parkhurst 66
93/4 Parkhurst 97
95/6 Parkhurst 103
94/5 Parkie SE81
91/2 Pinnacle 39
92/3 Pinnacle 19
93/4 Pinnacle 252
94/5 Pinnacle 292, MA3
95/6 Pinnacle 122
96/7 Pinnacle 120, M-10
96/7 Pi. Be A Player 45, ✍ Aut. 45
96/7 Pi. FANtasy - Mask
97/8 Pi. Inside SU-10A
95/6 Pi. Summit 55
96/7 Pi. Summit 126
95/6 Pi. Zenith 55
96/7 Pi. Zenith 57
95/6 Playoff 270
96/7 Playoff 367
94/5 POG 282
95/6 POG 143
93/4 Power Play 117
93/4 Premier 471
94/5 Premier 462
90/1 Pro Set 119
91/2 Pro Set 102
92/3 Pro Set 70
91/2 Pro Set Platinum 54
91/2 Pro Set Platinum PC6
90/1 Score 115
90/1 Sco. Hot Cards 55
91/2 Score 231
91/2 Score CAN 451
92/3 Score 155
93/4 Score 140
94/5 Score 145
95/6 Score 198
96/7 Score 68
97/8 Score 50
92/3 Seasons 12
94/5 Select 34
95/6 Select CE 65
96/7 Select CE 87
96/7 SP 141
95/6 Super Sticker 61
92/3 Topps 29
91/2 To. Stadium 120
92/3 T. Stadium Club 391
93/4 To. Stadium 54
94/5 T. Stadium Club 208
95/6 To. Stadium 8
95/6 T. Super Skills 87
90/1 Upper Deck 231
91/2 Upper Deck 262
92/3 Upper Deck 270
93/4 Upper Deck 216, SP-71
94/5 Upper Deck 432
95/6 Upper Deck 145
96/7 Upper Deck 330
94/5 UD BAP G13, ✍ 140
96/7 UD Black Diam. 62
95/6 UD CC 147
95/6 UD Post 19
89/0 LOSA / Smokey 16
90/1 LOSA / Smokey 17
83/4 NYIS
84/5 NYIS / News 26
81/2 Indianapolis Checkers
82/3 Indianapolis Checkers

HRUSKA, DAVID
96/7 APS 234
00/1 DS 130
99/0 OFS 314
00/1 OFS 175
01/2 OFS 158
95/6 Red Deer Rebels

HRYCUIK, JIM
74/5 Loblaws
74/5 WASH

HRYCUKK, TONY
92/3 BCJHL 144

HRYNEWICH, STEVE
83/4 Ottawa 67's
84/5 Ottawa 67's

HSI, LIU TE
79 Panini Sticker 359

HSIN, LI CHENG
79 Panini Sticker 359

HUARD, BILL
93/4 Parkhurst 414
97/8 Pi. Be A Player 31, ✍ Aut. 31
90/1 ProCards 566
91/2 ProCards 414
93/4 Upper Deck 485
96/7 DALL / Southwest
97/8 EDMO
93/4 OTTA
94/5 OTTA
89/0 Nashville Knights

HUARD, KELLY
96/7 Mississippi S'Wolves

HUARD, STÉPHANE
91/2 7th...Sketch LHJMQ 16

HUB, JAROSLAV
94/5 APS 191
95/6 APS 45
96/7 APS 324
97/8 APS 304
97/8 DS 39
99/0 DS 53
96/7 DS Sticker 162
97/8 DS Sticker 118
98/9 OFS 72
99/0 OFS 288

HUBACEK, JIRI
98/9 OFS 405
99/0 OFS 327

HUBACEK, PETR
00/1 BAP Mem. 454
01/2 BAP Memor. 185
99/0 DS 178
98/9 OFS 127
99/0 OFS 422
00/1 Premier Plus 133
00/1 Signature 257, ✍ Aut. 248
00/1 SP Authentic 117
00/1 SPx 168
00/1 Stadium 255
00/1 To. Chrome 246
00/1 To. Heritage 74
00/1 To. Stars 102
00/1 UD Reserve 110
00/1 Upper Deck 420
00/1 UD Pros&Prosp. 118
00/1 UD Vintage 390

HUBALEK, ROMAN
91/2 Knoxville Cherokees

HUBBAUER, MATT
00/1 UD Prospects 61
01/2 Regina Pats

HUBER, PHIL
98/9 DEL 7
99/0 Eishockey 322
91/2 ProCards 458
90 7th..Sketch Mem.Cup 6
94/5 Sig. Rookies 38, ✍ 38
92/3 Richmond Renegades
87/8 Kamloops Blazers
88/9 Kamloops Blazers
89/0 Kamloops Blazers

HUBER, WILLIE
83/4 Funmate Puffy 21 [w/]
79/0 O-Pee-Chee 17
80/1 O-Pee-Chee 173
81/2 O-Pee-Chee 89
82/3 O-Pee-Chee 85
83/4 O-Pee-Chee 246
87/8 OPC/Topps 93
81/2 OPC Sticker 126
82/3 OPC/Topps Sticker 185
83/4 OPC/Topps Sticker 139
87/8 OPC Sticker 31-172
87/8 Panini Sticker 109
82/3 Post [Detr.]
83/4 Souhaits Keychain [Red Wings]
79/0 Topps 17
80/1 Topps 173
81/2 Topps 89 [West]
79/0 DETR
80/1 DETR
87/8 VANC / Shell

HUBICK, GREG
75/6 TORO

HUBL, VIKTOR
00/1 DS 117
01/2 DS 17
98/9 OFS 267
99/0 OFS 148
00/1 OFS 95
01/2 OFS 7

HUCK, FRAN
70/1 Esso Power Player
69/0 Mästär Serien 25
69/0 Mästär Serien 34
74/5 OPC WHA 28
75/6 OPC WHA 121
73/4 Topps 63
72/3 SLOU
74/5 Minn. Fight. Saints

HUCKLE, JEFF
91/2 Air Canada SJHL C24

HUCKO, PATRIK
94/5 APS 189
96/7 APS 56
97/8 APS 322
00/1 Cardset 136
96/7 DS Sticker 233
97/8 DS Sticker 271
99/0 Eishockey 263
98/9 OFS 20
01/2 OFS 115

HUCUL, FRED
45-64 BeeHive-2 [Chic.]
51/2 Parkhurst 45
52/3 Parkhurst 26
53/4 Parkhurst 71

HUCZKOWSKI, HANS
95/6 UD Elitserien DS4
99/0 UD Elitserien 148
00/1 UD Elitserien 131

HUDACEK, VLADIMIR
94/5 APS 252
95/6 APS 294
96/7 APS 379
97/8 APS 220
97/8 DS 13
99/0 DS 2
00/1 DS 49, G5, VP1
01/2 DS 2
97/8 DS Sticker 27
98/9 OFS 286
99/0 OFS 8, 490, 551, -CL
00/1 OFS 349, -Star 4
01/2 OFS 85, -CL 6, -G6

HUDDY, CHARLIE
91/2 Bowman 103
92/3 Fleer Ultra 308
93/4 Fleer Ultra 344
89/0 Kraft 12
83/4 O-Pee-Chee 30
84/5 O-Pee-Chee 244
85/6 O-Pee-Chee 187
86/7 O-Pee-Chee 211
87/8 O-Pee-Chee 207
88/9 O-Pee-Chee 218
90/1 OPC/Topps 344
89/0 OPC/Topps 158
91/2 OPC Premier 125
83/4 OPC/Topps Sticker 96
84/5 OPC Sticker 258
85/6 OPC Sticker 216
86/7 OPC Sticker 69-199
87/8 OPC Sticker 87-219
88/9 OPC Sticker 221-97
89/0 opcSticker 220-79
87/8 Panini Sticker 260
88/9 Panini Sticker 53
89/0 Panini Sticker 82
90/1 Panini Sticker 221
90/1 Panini/EDM 7
91/2 Panini Sticker 129
91/2 Parkhurst 298
91/2 Pinnacle 225
92/3 Pinnacle 143
93/4 Pinnacle 296
94/5 Pinnacle 178
93/4 Power Play 361
93/4 Premier 219
90/1 Pro Set 85
91/2 Pro Set 400
90/1 Score 199
91/2 Score 20T
91/2 Score CAN 247
91/2 Score CAN 570
92/3 Score 92
93/4 Score 90
84/5 7-Eleven
83/4 Souhaits Keychain [Oilers]
92/3 Topps 279
91/2 To. Stadium 203
92/3 T. Stadium Club 372
93/4 To. Stadium 308
90/1 Upper Deck 341
91/2 Upper Deck 569
94/5 UD BAP G11
83/4 Vachon 27-107
81/2 EDMO / West Mall
82/3 EDMO / Red Rooster
83/4 EDMO / Button
83/4 EDMO / McDonald's
83/4 EDMO / West Mall
83/4 EDMO
84/5 EDMO
84/5 EDMO / Red Rooster
85/6 EDMO / Red Rooster
86/7 EDMO
86/7 EDMO / Red Rooster
87/8 EDMO
88/9 EDMO
88/9 EDMO / Action 45
90/1 EDMO / IGA
96/7 Rochester Americans

HUDEC, STANISLAV
00/1 Chicoutimi Saguenéens 10

HUDGIN, DANIEL
99/0 Hull Olympiques BN
99/0 Hull Olympiques 9
01/2 Moncton Wildcats 5

HUDLER, JIRI
00/1 DS 23
00/1 OFS 340
01/2 OFS 74, -RE21D

HUDON, GIL
83/4 Springfield Indians 1

HUDSON, DAVE
72/3 Eddie Sargent 134
74/5 Loblaws
72/3 O-Pee-Chee 211
73/4 O-Pee-Chee 234
74/5 O-Pee-Chee 335
75/6 O-Pee-Chee 122
76/7 O-Pee-Chee 299
77/8 O-Pee-Chee 343
78/9 O-Pee-Chee 299
75/6 Topps 122
76/7 COLR / Hockey Talk

HUDSON, GORDIE
52/3 Laval Dairy Update 117
52/3 St. Lawrence 46

HUDSON, MIKE
91/2 Bowman 399
92/3 Bowman 73
98/9 DEL 241
92/3 Fleer Ultra 37
90/1 O-Pee-Chee 424
91/2 O-Pee-Chee 495
92/3 O-Pee-Chee 331
91/2 Parkhurst 260
91/2 Pinnacle 38
92/3 Pinnacle 134
90/1 Pro Set 431
91/2 Pro Set 369
91/2 Score CAN 389
92/3 Score 156
92/3 Topps 172
91/2 To. Stadium 22
92/3 T. Stadium Club 182
94/5 UD BAP R31
88/9 CHIC / Coke
89/0 CHIC / Coke
90/1 CHIC / Coke
91/2 CHIC / Coke
92/3 EDMO
96/7 PHOE / Coca-Cola
94/5 PITT / Foodland 8
85/6 Sudbury Wolves
86/7 Sudbury Wolves

HUDSON, ROB
84/5 Ottawa 67's

HUEGUENIN, RENE
72 Semic Sticker 154

HUET, CRISTOBAL
02/3 BAP Memorabilia 324
02/3 Calder 123
02/3 Pacific Complete 593
02/3 Parkhurst Retro 248
02/3 SP Authentic 217
02/3 SPx 185
02/3 Ultimate Mem. 73
02/3 UD Premier 95
02/3 UD Rookie 122

HUFFMAN, KERRY
92/3 Fleer Ultra 386
93/4 Fleer Ultra 402
93/4 Leaf 291
90/1 O-Pee-Chee 516
92/3 OPC Premier 48
88/9 Panini Sticker 317
91/2 Parkhurst 349
92/3 Parkhurst 382
93/4 Premier 43
92/3 Pro Set 136
92/3 Score 239
93/4 Score 182
92/3 Topps 387
95/6 Topps 131
92/3 T. Stadium Club 381
93/4 To. Stadium 33

94/5 T. Stadium Club 127
92/3 Upper Deck 444
94/5 UD BAP ✍ 83
94/5 OTTA
95/6 OTTA
89/0 PHIL
90/1 PHIL
91/2 PHIL / J.C. Penney
92/3 QUEB / Petro-Canada
97/8 Grand Rapids Griffins
98/9 Grand Rapids Griffins
96/7 Las Vegas Thunder

HUGGINS, AL
30/1 La Presse

HUGHES, BRENT
00/1 Austin Ice Bats

HUGHES, BRENT*
94/5 Fleer Ultra 255
94/5 Leaf 218
97/8 Pa. Dynagon BKS-56
94/5 Panini Sticker 4
94/5 Pinnacle 510
88/9 ProCards / Moncton
89/0 ProCards AHL 31
90/1 ProCards 244
91/2 ProCards 561
94/5 T. Stadium Club 234
90/1 Upper Deck 333

HUGHES, BRENT**
70/1 Eddie Sargent 147
71/2 Eddie Sargent 147
72/3 Eddie Sargent 155
74/5 Loblaws
69/0 O-Pee-Chee 144
71/2 O-Pee-Chee 205
72/3 O-Pee-Chee 234
73/4 O-Pee-Chee 184
76/7 OPC WHA 34
74/5 Topps 73
71/2 Toronto Sun Photo

HUGHES, BRENT1
96/7 NYIS
89/0 WINN / Safeway
91/2 Baltimore Skipjacks
87/8 Moncton Hawks
90/1 Moncton Hawks

HUGHES, BRENT2
72/3 SLOU
76/7 San Diego Mariners

HUGHES, CHUCK E.
93/4 Birmingham Bulls

HUGHES, FRANK
76/7 OPC WHA 81
75/6 Houston Aeros
76/7 Phoenix Roadrunners

HUGHES, HOWIE
70/1 Eddie Sargent 80
68/9 O-Pee-Chee 158
69/0 O-Pee-Chee 142

HUGHES, JACK
25 Dominion Chocolates 92
23/4 Paulins Candy 3
28/9 Paulins Candy 66
24/5 Selkirks Crescent 2

HUGHES, JASON
91/2 7th...Sketch OHL 273
93/4 Slapshot / Kitchener 5
94/5 Slapshot / Kitchener 6

HUGHES, JOHN
75/6 OPC WHA 45
76/7 OPC WHA 106
80/1 Pepsi Bottle Cap
80/1 EDMO / Zellers
88/9 EDMO / Action 116
79/0 VANC / Royal Bank
75/6 Cincinnati Stingers

HUGHES, PAT
79/0 O-Pee-Chee 65
80/1 O-Pee-Chee 347
82/3 O-Pee-Chee 109
83/4 O-Pee-Chee 31
83/4 O-Pee-Chee 213
84/5 O-Pee-Chee 245
83/4 OPC/Topps Sticker 327
83/4 OPC/Topps Sticker 328
85/6 OPC Sticker 229-98
82/3 Post [Edmo.]
84/5 7-Eleven
83/4 Souhaits Keychain [Oilers]
79/0 Topps 65
83/4 Vachon 28-108
85/6 BUFF / Blue Shield
81/2 EDMO / Red Rooster
82/3 EDMO / Red Rooster
83/4 EDMO / Button
83/4 EDMO / McDonald's
83/4 EDMO / West Mall
83/4 EDMO
84/5 EDMO
84/5 EDMO / Red Rooster
88/9 EDMO / Action 24
78/9 MONT
77/8 Nova Scotia Voyageurs

HUGHES, PETER
86/7 Sudbury Wolves
87/8 Sudbury Wolves

HUGHES, RYAN
93/4 Classic 69
94/5 Classic ✍ Aut.
93/4 Cla. Prospects 74
91/2 Upper Deck WJC 47

HUHTALA, JARMO
78/9 SM-Liiga 59
72/3 Williams Finnish 304

HUHTALA, JORMA
80/1 Mallasjuoma 37

HUIKARI, JUHA
80/1 Mallasjuoma 100
82 Semic Sticker 33
71/2 Williams Finnish 301

HUIKURI, JUHA
78/9 SM-Liiga 142

HUKKANEN, VEIJO
72/3 Williams Finnish 280

HULBIG, JOE
00/1 Pacific 36
97/8 Pa. Dynagon BKS-38
97/8 EDMO
02/3 Albany River Rats
99/0 Providence Bruins
01/2 Providence Bruins

HULETT, DEAN
93/4 Cla. Prospects 142
95/6 Louisiana Ice Gators
95/6 Louisiana Ice Gators-2
93/4 Phoenix Roadrunners
91/2 L. Superior State Lakers

HULKKONEN, ANTTI
99/0 Cardset 59
02/3 Cardset 175

HULL, BOBBY
93/4 Action Packed / Promo BH1, BH2
01/2 ASG History
92/3 American Licorice P
71/2 Bazooka Panel
99/0 BAP Mem. R-1, ✍ R-1
01/2 BAP Memor. ✂ 500GS
01/2 BAP Update ✂ PTT2
45-64 BeeHive-2 [Chic.]
45-64 BeeHive-2 [Chic.]
64-67 BeeHive-3 [BeeHive]
64-67 BeeHive-3 [Chic.]
02/3 Canada Post, ✍ Aut.
63-65 Chex
64/5 Coke/Sprite [Chic.]
65/6 Coca-Cola
70/1 Dad's Cookies
79/0 Dernière Heure
97/8 Do. Elite BF-6, ✍ BF-6
70/1 Eddie Sargent 43
71/2 Eddie Sargent 34
70/1 Esso Power Player
88/9 Esso All-Star
01/2 Fleer Greats 7, -RC 4, ✂ O6, ✍ Aut.
01/2 Fleer Legacy 2, 12, ✂ HK
92/3 Future Trends C76 107, 142, 178, ✍ Aut.
62/3 Cowan Tile
83&87 HHOF 242
71 Kellogg's Transfer
96/7 Legends 89
68/9 O-Pee-Chee 16
68/9 O-Pee-Chee 204
68/9 O-Pee-Chee PS 3
69/0 O-Pee-Chee 70, 216
69/0 O-Pee-Chee 4in1
69/0 O-Pee-Chee Stamp
70/1 O-Pee-Chee 15, 235
70/1 O-Pee-Chee DE 30
71/2 O-Pee-Chee 50, 261
71/2 O-Pee-Chee Book. 1
72/3 OPC 228, 272, 336
72/3 OPC 272, 336
79/0 O-Pee-Chee 185
98/9 OPC Chrome 9
71/2 O-Pee-Chee Poster 9
74/5 OPC WHA 50
75/6 OPC WHA 1
75/6 OPC WHA 65
76/7 OPC WHA 3
76/7 O-Pee-Chee WHA 5
76/7 OPC WHA 65
76/7 OPC WHA 100
77/8 OPC WHA 50
73/4 OPC WHA Poster 16
01/2 Parkhurst HSHS, ✂ 500GS, ✂ HSHSJers, ✂ H13
02/3 Parkhurst ✂ VM3, ✂ VT1
02/3 Parkhurst Retro ✂ NN4
95/6 Parkie 66-67 21, 124, 129-30, 141, AS4
94/5 Parkie Tall 25, 136, 151, AS 5, TW-2, TW-6, ✍ A3
73/4 Quaker Oats 50
72 Semic Sticker 228
91 Semic Sticker 239
60/1 Shirriff 63
61/2 Shirriff 25
62/3 Shirriff 47
62/3 Shirriff 57
68/9 Shirriff / Chic. 1
94/5 SR Tetrad CXXII, ✍ Aut.
01/2 Signature ✂ 500GS, ✍ VA7, ✍ VA8
97/8 SP Authentic ✍ M5, ✍ T5
99/0 SP Authentic LH5, ✍ SotT
00/1 SP Authentic P2, ✍ SotT, ✍ SotTD, ✍ SotTT
77-79 Sportscaster 05-20
77-79 Sportscaster 50-03
77-79 Sportscaster 55-23
77-79 Sports. FIN 08-181
77-79 Sports. FIN 57-1358
77-79 Sports. FIN 58-1381
95/6 SLU Cdn. Legend
95/6 SLU Timeless
58/9 Topps 66
59/0 Topps 47
60/1 Topps 58
61/2 Topps 29
61/2 Topps - Stamp
62/3 Topps 33
62/3 Topps Dollar
63/4 Topps 33
64/5 Topps 20, 107
65/6 Topps 59
66/7 Topps 64
66/7 Topps 112
66/7 Topps 125
66/7 Topps / Test 40
67/8 Topps 113
67/8 Topps 124
68/9 Topps 16
69/0 Topps 70
70/1 Topps 15
71/2 Topps 1, 50
72/3 Topps 61, 126
79/0 Topps 185
98/9 Topps -Reprint 9, ✍ Reprint
01/2 T/O Archives 78, ✍ CAI
60/1 Toronto Star Photo
62/3 Toronto Star Photo
63/4 Toronto Star Action
63/4 Toronto Star Photo
64/5 Toronto Star Action
64/5 Toronto Star Photo
59/0 Toronto Star Weekend
63/4 Toronto Star Weekend
65/6 Toronto Star Weekend
66/7 Toronto Star Weekend
71/2 Toronto Sun Photo
00/1 UD Heroes 122, ✂ GT, ✂ GC, ✍ SG
01/2 Ultimate Mem. ✂ 500GS, ✂ ASGH, ✂ BL, ✂ Corn., ✂ Deca., ✂ Emb., ✂ PP, ✂ RN, ✂ RT, ✍ Aut.
02/3 Ultimate Mem. ✂ ASMVP (x2), ✂ Cor, ✂ EA, ✂ FS (x2), ✂ SL (x3), ✂ Num, ✂ PS, ✂ RAT (x2), ✂ RT, ✂ VGJ
91/2 Ultimate Original Six 57, 77, 82, 88-92, 96, -Hologram, Promo
98/9 Upper Deck ✂ GJ3, ✂✍ GJ3
00 ✂ UD APOH 500, ✂✍ 500
99/0 UD C. Legends 8, AC3, E7, ✍ ES
01/2 UD Challenge AT1
01/2 UD Honor Roll 1, 31, OS2
00/1 UD Legends 25, 30, ES4, PH10, SM3, ✍ ES
01/2 UD Legends 11, 90, FC, ✂ PoH, ✂ TT, ✂ TTC, ✍ ES
92/3 UD Locker 43
01/2 UD Premier ✂ G, ✍ SigS
99/0 UD Retro 86, ✍ Ink.
01/2 UD SCup Champs 4
71/2 Williams Finnish 383
60/1 Wonder Bread
93/4 Zellers, ✍ Aut.
70/1 CHIC
98/9 CHIC / Pizza Hut
79/0 WINN

HULL, BOBBY
02/3 Fleer Throwbacks 34, ✂ 10SW, ✍ Aut.

HULL, BRETT
94/5 Action Packed
01/2 Adrenaline 66, PM 4, WB 5, ✂ GWJ 15
01/2 ASG History
01/2 Atomic 37, Stat. 13
02/3 Atomic 37, -NPU 4, ✂ GWJ 7
98/9 Aurora 55
99/0 Aurora 44, -Stripe 44
00/1 Aurora 44, Pins. 44, CF-8, SR-7, TPS-5A
02/3 BAP All-Star 31, ✂ ASJ
98/9 Be A Player 189, M6, P1, ✍ Aut. 189, ✂ G-18, ✂ AS-12, ✂ S-11
99/0 BAP Mem. 45, H-12, ✂ J-12, ✂ D-16, ✂ TM-4, ✂ TM-46, ✂ TM-47
00/1 BAP Mem. 106, ✂ J-30, ✂ H-8, ✂ PP-5, ✂ TM-15
01/2 BAP Memor. 92, 378, ✂ 500GS, ✂ ASJ, ✂ ASE, ✂ ASN, ✂ AST
02/3 BAP Memorabilia 41, ✂ ASJ19, ✂ ASE6, ✂ ASN6, ✂ SCC15, ✂ TM3
01/2 BAP Update ✂ H13
96/7 Bic.Sports Aces 9-D
95/6 Bicycle Sports Aces J-Diamond
90/1 Bowman 24, -HT 1
91/2 Bowman 367, 375
92/3 Bowman 186, 209
95/6 Bowman 43
01/2 Bowman 2
02/3 Bowman 38
98/9 Bowman's Best 10
02/3 Calder 37, -HH 4
99/0 Crown Royale 44, -IE 10
00/1 Crown Royale 35, ✂ GWJ-8, JotC-11, NP-7
01/2 Crown Royale 53, ASH 8
02/3 Crown Royale 33
93/4 Donruss 286, U, -ES 5
94/5 Donruss Dom. 8
95/6 Donruss 68, D-6, M-7, PP-6
96/7 Donruss 197, ES-4, GTS-6
97/8 Donruss 71, -L2L 18, -RA 5
98/9 Donruss ES 2
96/7 Do. Canadian 65
97/8 Do. Canadian 17, -SCS 6
95/6 Do. Elite 7, -CE 12
96/7 Do. Elite 4, P-9
97/8 Do. Elite 12, BF-6, ✍ BF-6
97/8 Do. Preferred 15, 193, LT-3C, / Tin 18, -Wide Tin 2
97/8 Do. Priority 9, DD-23, OD-9, Post-28, Stamp-28
97/8 Do. Studio 11, HH-20, S-8, P-11
96/7 Duracell DC5, JB5
98/9 Dynagon Ice 56, -FT 7
99/0 Dynagon Ice 65, -CM 23
93/4 EA Sports 125
97/8 Esso 27
02/3 eTopps 32
02/3 Exclusive 63, -EIS 5
93/4 Fax Pax 26
02/3 First Edition 190, 335
94/5 Flair 153, HN-4
96/7 Flair 81, CIS-4
94/5 Fleer 187, -SA 2
96/7 Fleer 97, ART-7
95/6 Fleer Metal 125, -HM 5, -IS 8
96/7 Fl. Picks F50-19, DL-10, FF-6
92/3 Fleer Ultra 186, -AS 12
93/4 Fleer Ultra 117, -RLS 4, -SK 3
94/5 Fleer Ultra 183, -ASG 11, -RLS 5
95/6 Fleer Ultra 139, 386, -EA 8, -RLS 3
96/7 Fl. Ultra 146, MM-4
91/2 Gillette 14
95 Globe 115
96/7 Got-Um
01/2 Heads Up 30, RI 5, SM 5
02/3 Heads Up 43, -SM 8, ✂ GWQ 12, ✂ GWQ 29
92/3 High Five / Promo P2
93/4 Hockey Wit 97
99/0 HoloGrFX 18, PS7, ✍ Aut.
95/6 Hoyle / West. 10-Spade
92/3 Humpty Dumpty
02/3 In The Game-Used 19, 119, ✂ E32, ✂ T20, ✂ TM19
94/5 Incomnet Phonecard
91/2 Kellogg's / Score 21
95/6 Kellogg's / Donruss [x2]
90/1 Kraft 20, 66
91/2 Kraft 66
92/3 Kraft / Kraft Singles
93/4 Kraft / PB
94/5 Kraft / HH
95/6 Kraft / KD
96/7 Kraft / KD
97/8 Kraft / KD
99/0 Kraft / KD
93/4 Leaf 255, -GLAS 3, -SSS 8
94/5 Leaf 16, -GLS 4
95/6 Leaf 209, -FOI 9, -GLS 6
96/7 Leaf 45, LL-3, S-12
97/8 Leaf 11, 178, BS-11
94/5 L. Limited 2, G-2
95/6 L. Limited 28, SG-10
96/7 L. Limited 24, S-15
96/7 L. Preferred 106, SP-9, VP-5
97/8 Limited 20, 51, 185, FG-28, FG-38
96/7 Maggers 137
91/2 McDonald's Mc-13, McH4
92/3 McDonald's McH-02
93/4 McDonald's McD-07
94/5 McDonald's McD-13
95/6 McDonald's McD-6
96/7 McDonald's McD-24
97/8 McDonald's McD-16
98/9 McD's T5
99/0 McDonald's McD-7, ✍ SS
00/1 McDonald's 11
01/2 McDonald's 9, -HG 3, ✂ JPatch 6
02/3 McDonald's -A 3
96/7 Metal Univ. 132, LW-7
99/0 Millenium 82, P-7, D-8, ✍ Aut. 82, ✍ P-7, ✍ D-8, ✂ J-21, ✂✍ J-21, ✂ JS-21
95/6 Cool Trade 15
98/9 NHL Power Play
88/9 OPC/Topps 66
90/1 OPC/Topps 4, 77, 195, OPC 513, Topps-TL 2
91/2 O-Pee-Chee 190, 259, 303, 403, 516, Topps-TL 20
92/3 O-Pee-Chee 87, 124, -Ann. 21
01/2 O-Pee-Chee 86, Update 86
02/3 O-Pee-Chee 92
89/0 OPC/Topps 186, Box F
98/9 OPC Chrome 30, -Reprit 6
90/1 OPC Premier 47
91/2 OPC Premier 49
88/9 OPC Stars 16
88/9 OPC Sticker 127-259
88/9 OPC Sticker 16-145
88/9 OPC Sticker 81-210
89/0 opcSticker 22
97/8 Omega 194, GF-17
98/9 Omega 70, EOP 7, -Onl. 12, -PI 9
99/0 Omega 72, -CC 6
98/9 Pacific 16, -GCDC 30, -TC 22, -Time. 17
99/0 Pacific 120, -GC 14, -PAP 10
00/1 Pacific 131, GCDC-12, PR-7
01/2 Pacific 126, 428, NAAS 6
02/3 Pacific 129
02/3 Pacific Complete 311
97/8 Pacific CC 16, CS-18, GCDC-19, SS-9C, TC-21
97/8 Pa. Crown Roy. 117, BOS-18, HT-16, L-18
98/9 Pa. Crown Roy. 38, -MP 7, -PotG 10, -PP 6
97/8 Pa. Dynagon 107, 143, DD-14B, T-8, T-18, BKS-81
97/8 Pa. Invincible 120, AZ-21, FP-31, OTG-18, R-169
97/8 Pa. Paramount 159, BN-18, P-18
98/9 Pa. Paramount 64
99/0 Pa. Paramount 72, -PB 13
00/1 Pa. Paramount 75, ES-8, FF-12, HOFB-5
97/8 Pa. Revolution 121, TC-21
98/9 Pa. Revolution 41, -CTLC 6, -Show. 14
94 Panini Olympics 323, N
98/9 Panini Photocard
88/9 Panini Sticker 107
89/0 Panini Sticker 117
90/1 Panini Sticker 262, 333
91/2 Panini Sticker 25, 325
92/3 Panini Sticker 16, 289
94/5 Panini Sticker 140, 235b
95/6 Panini Sticker 194
96/7 Panini Sticker 202
97/8 Panini Sticker 168
98/9 Panini Sticker 152
99/0 Panini Sticker 225, 332
00/1 Panini Sticker 148
95 Panini Worlds 299
91/2 Parkhurst 157, 219, 432, 474, PHC6
92/3 Parkhurst 153, 459
93/4 Parkhurst 180, G4, W7
94/5 Parkhurst 309, V35, -YCTG 20
95/6 Parkhurst 172, -AS 2, -CCB 10, PP54
00/1 Parkhurst P-100
01/2 Parkhurst 67, ✂ 500GS, ✂ PS59, ✂ M24, ✂ M50, ✂ H13
02/3 Parkhurst 70, -CR8, ✂ CRM8, ✂ NH11, ✂ PP10
95 Parkhurst Phonecard [x2]
02/3 Parkhurst Retro 55, ✂ RJ5, ✂ RSJ5, ✂ NN23, ✂ RM30
94/5 Parkie SE154
91/2 Pinnacle 200, 356, 376, B-12
92/3 Pinnacle 100, 257, -TP 6
93/4 Pinnacle 200, CA20, -NF 10, -TP 6
94/5 Pinnacle 450, BR9, TP11
95/6 Pinnacle 15, CS-2, FS-12
96/7 Pinnacle 128, BTN-6, TP-6
97/8 Pinnacle 35, P-8
96/7 Pi. Be A Player BB-14
97/8 Pi. Be A Player 15, ✍ Aut. 15
97/8 Pi. BeeHive 6, -BHT 14
97/8 Pi. Certified 70, -CT 19
97/8 Pi. Epix E18
95/6 Pi. FANtasy 24
96/7 Pi. FANtasy 16
97/8 Pi. Inside 12, -IT 19, -Can
96/7 Pi. Mint 14
97/8 Pi. Mint 23, M-3
95/6 Pi. Summit 13, GMC-17, MH-2
96/7 Pi. Summit 35, 199, HV-16
97/8 Pi. Totally 70
95/6 Pi. Zenith 1, ZT-15
96/7 Pi. Zenith 67, ZT-7
95/6 Playoff 89, 195, 307
96/7 Playoff 427
94/5 POG 203
95/6 POG 236, I-007, I-023
97/8 Pi. Post 11
93/4 Power Play 211, -PL 4, -SA 4
93/4 Premier 425, -BG/OPC 22, -BG/Top. 21
94/5 Premier 417, 465, TF-2, GTG-3
00/1 Premier Plus 56, TT11, WP19
99/0 Prism 44, -CA 7
00/1 Private Stock 31, AC-9, EA-7, PS-17, PSS-9
01/2 Pr. Stock 34, -PS 27, ✂ GUG 43
02/3 Pr. Stock Reserve 36
00/1 PS Titanium 28, NAAS-6, ✂ GUG-15, ✂ GUG-84, ✂ GUG-154
01/2 PS Titanium 50
01/2 PS Titanium Draft ✂ 38
02/3 PS Titanium 36, ✂ GWJ 25
00/1 PS Titanium Draft ✂ 30
95/6 Pro Magnet 6
90/1 Pro Set 263, 342, 395, Promo 1, PotM P3
91/2 Pro Set 215, 290, 320, 326, CC6
92/3 Pro Set 156, 245, -TL 8
91 Pro Set Awards AC6, AC18
91/2 Pro Set Midwest
91/2 Pro Set Platinum 109, 282, PC5
91/2 Puck / Pro Set 24
02/3 Quest for the Cup 33, -RTC 6
99/0 Revolution 45, -NI 8, -Show. 13, -TotL 26, / CSC 45
00/1 Revolution 46, HD-13, II-8, NI-9, SM-4
90/1 Score 300, 317, 346, 351, 366
90/1 Sco. Hot Cards 100
91/2 Score 1, 337, 347, 371, 404, 412, 428, -Hot 3, Promo 1, Shows 2
91/2 Score CAN 1, 261, 294, 302, 318, 367, 377
92/3 Score 350, 411, 435, 442, 500
93/4 Score 335, -DT 18, DD4, -Pi.AS 34, -TF 18
94/5 Score 100, DT22, NP11, TF20
95/6 Score 235, BB-6, DT-9, L-11
96/7 Score 19, SD-4, S-11, / Promo 19
97/8 Score 81
97/8 Score SLou. 1
92/3 Seasons 13
93/4 Seasons 6
94/5 Select 97, FL-12
95/6 Select CE 4, -GT 6
96/7 Select CE 19, C-6
94 Semic 123, 347
95 Semic 113
89 Semic Sticker 167
91 Semic Sticker 144
92 Semic Sticker 156
93 Semic Sticker 185
00/1 Signature 71, HSHS, ✂ J-21, ✂ HSHSJers
01/2 Signature C-51, ✂ 500GS, ✂ IS12
02/3 Signature ✂ TQ13, ✂ TM7
95/6 SBx Emotion 148, Xci-8
95/6 SBx Impact 141, -IQ 2
96/7 SBx Impact 113, BR-8
02/3 Slam Card
94/5 SP 100, P-29
95/6 SP 121, E24
96/7 SP 136, GF-4, SF-2
97/8 SP Authentic 138, I2, ✍ SotT, ✍ T5
98/9 SP Authentic 24, SS4, SO2, ✍ SotT, -Trade
99/0 SP Authentic 28, SS4, ✍ SotT
00/1 SP Authentic 30, ST2, ✍ SotTD
01/2 SP Authentic 26, 100, ✂ PP
02/3 SP Authentic 32, 98
00/1 SP GU 19, ✂ TotG, ✂ C, ✂ P, ✂✍ A
01/2 SP GU 19
02/3 SP GU 57, ✂ AF (x2), ✂ CF, ✂ PH, ✂ TG
02/3 Sports Vault 214
96/7 SPx 40, HH8
97/8 SPx 43, D-SPX20
99/0 SPx 48, P3, X10, XT12, S1, ✂ WM
00/1 SPx 19, HH6, P3, ✂ WM, ✂✍ WM
01/2 SPx 172, ✂ HT
02/3 SPx 29, 132
98/9 SPx Finite 97
98/9 SPx Prospects 19, H12, L16, PS25
00/1 Stadion 94
99/0 Stadium 31, CA28, -Chrome 21
00/1 Stadium 94, BT7
01/2 Stadium 105
02/3 Stadium 100, -WS7
93/4 SLU [x2]
93/4 Starting Lineup
94/5 Starting Lineup
95/6 SLU
95/6 Super Sticker 101,-DC 11
96/7 Team Out✂
92/3 Topps 2, 260, 340
95/6 Topps 10, 372, 10HG, M7, PF19, 4RL
98/9 Topps 30, -Reprint
99/0 Topps 138
00/1 Topps 59, 330, PC-12, TC9, NHL13
01/2 Topps 86, Update 86, SM3, -Jers.
02/3 Topps 92, HHU7
99/0 To. Chrome 138
00/1 To. Chrome 47, PC-12, TC9
01/2 To. Chrome 86
02/3 T. Chrome 58
94/5 Topps Finest 42, -BBB 15, -DF 15
95/6 To. Finest 10, 184
98/9 To. Finest 19
95 Topps Finest Bronze 8
98/9 T. Gold Label 92
99/0 To. Gold Label 53, QC9
00/1 To. Gold Label 5, B2, GG6
00/1 To. Heritage 14, HH14
01/2 To. Heritage 162
02/3 To. Heritage 11, 130
02/3 T. Limited 92
96/7 Topps Picks 29, FT12, TS10
99/0 To. Prmr. Plus 9
01/2 To. Reserve 99
91/2 To. Stadium 67
92/3 T. Stadium Club 1, 258
93/4 To. Stadium 65, -Master, -AS, Finest 3
94/5 T. Stadium Club 100, DAD-3, F-2
95/6 To. Stadium EC183, PS9
91/2 TSC Charter [x2]
92 TSC Members Only
93/4 TSC Members Only 6
94/5 TSC Members Only 37
95/6 TSC Members Only 3
00/1 To. Stars 14, 131, AS2
95/6 T. Super Skills 48
02/3 T. Total 258, TT10
98/9 UD Choice 183, BH4, SQ22
00/1 UD Heroes 37, TM4
01/2 UD PlayMakers Ltd 34
00/1 UD Reserve 28, PP2
98/9 UD3 35, 95, 155
00/1 Ultimate Mem. ✂ A8-3, ✂H-10, ✂Jer. 19, ✂J-21, ✂JJ-9, ✂S-21, ✂TM-24, ✂TM-25, ✂TM-28, ✂TM-32
01/2 Ultimate Mem. ✂ 500GS, ✂ A8, ✂ ASGH, ✂ BL, ✂ DD, ✂ GSL, ✂ JE, ✂ JJ, ✂ PP, ✂ WTF
02/3 Ultimate Mem. ✂ A8, ✂ ASMVP, ✂ DD, ✂ Emb, ✂ FS, ✂ GUJ, ✂ GUSJ, ✂ GAO, ✂ HT, ✂ ITN, ✂ JE, ✂ JGJ, ✂ LA, ✂ PS (x3), ✂ RAT, ✂ SCDE, ✂ SCDGJ, ✂ SCDN
99/0 Ult. Victory 28, sg11, TV2
90/1 Upper Deck 154, 203, 312, 474, 546, Sticker
91/2 Upper Deck 7, 33, 45, 464, 622, SP1, AW3, -Heroes
92/3 Upper Deck 29, 423, 620, W2, G7
93/4 Upper Deck 160, 232, GG3, NL2, HB3, R5, SP 137
94/5 Upper Deck 229, 333, 569, C17, R2, R32, R57, SP-66
95/6 Upper Deck 233, 251, 486, AS3, F15, R5, SE157
96/7 Upper Deck 324, X6, HH13, SS15B, ✂ GJ3
97/8 Upper Deck 141, SS4, SG16, S16, T9C
98/9 Upper Deck 76, FF7, P2
99/0 Upper Deck 43, 144, CT8, FF1, HOF6, SB9, SS3, PD6, ✂ GJ, ✂✍ GJS
00/1 Upper Deck 284, D4, EC2, FF4, FT3, L3, TT4, ✂ DGJ, ✂ GJ
01/2 Upper Deck 62 , 213, CT5, SS5
02/3 Upper Deck 68, 192, ✂ GO, ✂ R50
00 ✂ UD APOH 500, ✂✍ 500
95/6 UD ASG MVP3
96/7 UD All-Star YCTG AR3
93/4 Upper Deck Be A Player 8
94/5 UD BAP R48, G10
95/6 UD BAP 1, LL-3, ✍ S1
96/7 UD Black Diam. 170
97/8 UD Black Diam. 19, PC18
98/9 UD Black Diam. 25, M16, WF26
99/0 UD Black Diam. 30, M5, ✂ APOH
00/1 UD Black Diam. 18
99/0 UD C. Legends 62, E7, ✍ ES
01/2 UD Challenge CM9, FF3
02/3 UD Classic ET7
95/6 UD CC 214, 364, C5
96/7 UD CC 223, 329, UD29, S2
97/8 UD Coll. Choice 224, SQ76, S26, C26, CR26
97/8 UD Diam. Vision 25
02/3 UD Foundations 82
98/9 UD G. Reserve 76
99/0 UD G. Reserve 43, 144, ✍ Aut., ✂ GR
99/0 UD Gretzky Excl. 59
01/2 UD Honor Roll ✂ GAJ, PPM
02/3 UD Honor 27
96/7 UD Ice 115
97/8 UD Ice 66, IC16, L8C
00/1 UD Ice 14, ✍ CCA, ✂ IGJ
01/2 UD Ice 14, 95, ✂ GJ
00/1 UD Legends 37, 117, PH8, SM6, ✍ ES, ✂ LGJ
92/3 UD Locker 27
01/2 UD Mask 34, ✂ GG
98/9 UD MVP 59, F1, Souv.
99/0 UD MVP 60, H2, GU3, ✍ PS
00/1 UD MVP 57, M6
01/2 UD MVP 66, MW4, ✂ S
02/3 UD MVP 66
99/0 UD MVP Cup 57, SC6, GC, ✂ GU, ✍ PS
99/0 UD Ovation 21, ST3, APOH, ✍ APOH
02/3 UD Piece 35, 99, AC11
99/0 UD PowerDeck 9, T8
01/2 UD Premier 22, ✂ D
00/1 UD Pros&Prosp. 28, NP2
99/0 UD Retro 25, ✍ Ink.
02/3 UD Rookie 36
01/2 UD SCup Champs 47, ✂ S, ✂ G
01/2 UD Top Shelf 21, ✂ J, ✂ S
02/3 UD Top Shelf ✂ HT, ✂ M, ✂ SH, ✂ SW
00/1 UD Vintage 114
02/3 UD Vintage 96, GB 96
00/1 Vanguard 34, HV-11, IF-7, VP-5
01/2 Vanguard 36, QTH 1, ✂ DGM 46
02/3 Vanguard 36, ✂ GWJ 19
99/0 Victory 86, 87, 322
00/1 Victory 72, 247, 297
01/2 Victory 110, 409
02/3 Victory 78
01/2 Waving the Flag 26
99/0 WGretzky 54, EG6, ✂ SG, ✂ TG
96 Wien 164
97/8 Zenith 25, CTC-7, Z48
87/8 CALG / Red Rooster
00/1 DALL / Southwest
87/8 SLOU
88/9 SLOU
88/9 SLOU / Kodak
89/0 SLOU / Kodak
90/1 SLOU / Kodak
91/2 SLOU
92/3 SLOU / McDon. 12
96/7 SLOU / Dispatch 1
86/7 Moncton G'Flames
85/6 Minnesota-Duluth 28

HULL, BRTT
02/3 Starz

HULL, DENNIS
99/0 BAP Mem. R-2, ✍ R-2
64-67 BeeHive-3 [Chic.]
65/6 Coca-Cola
70/1 Colgate 32
70/1 Dad's Cookies
70/1 Eddie Sargent 36
71/2 Eddie Sargent 46
72/3 Eddie Sargent 67
70/1 Esso Power Player
91/2 Future Trends C72 89, ✍ 89
72/3 Post 16
74/5 Lipton Soup 17
74/5 Loblaws
73/4 Nabisco s 12
68/9 O-Pee-Chee 153
69/0 O-Pee-Chee 71
70/1 O-Pee-Chee 14
71/2 O-Pee-Chee 85
72/3 O-Pee-Chee 52
72/3 O-Pee-Chee TC
73/4 O-Pee-Chee 171
74/5 O-Pee-Chee 150
75/6 O-Pee-Chee 254
76/7 O-Pee-Chee 195
77/8 O-Pee-Chee 225
01/2 Parkhurst ✍ PA55
02/3 Parkhurst ✂ VT1
95/6 Parkie 66-67 37
94/5 Parkie Tall 39
70/1 Post Shooters
68/9 Shirriff / Chic. 11
65/6 Topps 64
66/7 Topps 113
66/7 Topps / Test 1
67/8 Topps 56
69/0 Topps 71
70/1 Topps 14
71/2 Topps 85
72/3 Topps 164
73/4 Topps 60
74/5 Topps 150
75/6 Topps 254
76/7 Topps 195
76/7 Topps NS 16
77/8 Topps 225
01/2 T/O Archives 25, -Seat, ✍ CAI
71/2 Toronto Sun Photo
01/2 Ultimate Mem. ✂ BL
02/3 Ultimate Mem. ✂ FS, ✂ VGJ
68/9 CHIC
70/1 CHIC

HULL, JODY
95/6 Fleer Metal 59
95/6 Fleer Ultra 241
93/4 Leaf 157
90/1 OPC Premier 46
99/0 Pacific 303
00/1 Pacific 297
02/3 Pacific Complete 296
97/8 Pa. Dynagon BKS-41
89/0 Panini Sticker 230
93/4 Panini Sticker 115
94/5 Panini Sticker 66
95/6 Panini Sticker 74
92/3 Parkhurst 119
93/4 Parkhurst 76
94/5 Parkhurst 89
95/6 Parkhurst 353
93/4 Premier 212
94/5 Premier 427
95/6 Pro Magnet 87
90/1 Pro Set 490
91/2 ProCards 201
91/2 Score CAN 524
93/4 Score 320
95/6 SP 57
95/6 Topps 134
95/6 To. Finest 109
91/2 To. Stadium 100
93/4 To. Stadium 344
94/5 T. Stadium Club 199
90/1 Upper Deck 322
92/3 Upper Deck 539
93/4 Upper Deck 112, 510
94/5 Upper Deck 176
95/6 Upper Deck 50, SE-123
99/0 Upper Deck 16
00/1 Upper Deck 359
95/6 UD BAP 110, ✍ S110
96/7 UD CC 107
99/0 UD G. Reserve 16
99/0 UD MVP 2
99/0 Victory 12
96/7 FLOR / Winn-Dixie
89/0 HART / Jr. Whalers
92/3 OTTA
02/3 OTTA

HULLET, DEAN
93/4 Classic 70
94/5 Classic ✍ Aut.

HULSE, CALE
92/3 Classic 21
92/3 Classic Four Sport 170
93/4 Cla. Prospects 222
94/5 Leaf 481
01/2 O-Pee-Chee 115
98/9 OPC Chrome 32
98/9 Pacific 119
02/3 Pacific Complete 51
97/8 Pa. Dynagon BKS-12
96/7 Pinnacle 242
97/8 Pi. Be A Player 60, ✍ Aut. 60
94/5 Premier 407
91/2 7th...Sketch WHL 43
98/9 Topps 32
01/2 Topps 115
99/0 Ult. Victory 14
95/6 Upper Deck 437
02/3 Upper Deck 346
96/7 UD CC 36

HULST, KENT
89/0 ProCards AHL 109
90/1 ProCards 149
91/2 ProCards 380
90/1 Newmarket Saints
93/4 Portland Pirates
94/5 Portland Pirates
95/6 Portland Pirates
96/7 Portland Pirates Hershey
96/7 Portland Pirates
97/8 Portland Pirates
98/9 Portland Pirates
99/0 Portland Pirates
00/1 Portland Pirates

HULT, JOHAN
99/0 UD Elitserien 99
00/1 UD Elitserien 100

HULTBERG, JOHN
95/6 Slapshot 107

HULTGREN, KELLY
97/8 Pensacola Ice Pilots
99/0 Quad City Mallards

HULTON, JIM
01/2 Belleville Bulls

HUME, FRED
83 HHOF Postcard A8
83&87 HHOF 233

HUMENIUK, SCOTT
91/2 ProCards 97

HUMENNY, LAYNE
92/3 MPS SJHL 58

HUML, DUSAN
94/5 APS 152

HUML, IVAN
01/2 BAP Memor. 367
02/3 Bowman 142
02/3 Calder 55, -CR 2
02/3 Crown Royale -RR 4
02/3 Exclusive -DFG 4, -GE 3
02/3 In The Game-Used ✂ C19
02/3 O-Pee-Chee 286
02/3 Pacific Complete 587
01/2 Parkhurst 304
02/3 Pr. Stock Reserve -CA 3
02/3 PS Titanium -ROT 2
01/2 SP Authentic 136
02/3 SP Authentic 109
01/2 SPx 198
01/2 SPx Rookie RR3
02/3 Topps 286
02/3 T. Limited 286
01/2 UD PlayMakers Ltd 105
02/3 Ultimate Mem. ✂ CC
01/2 Upper Deck 416
01/2 UD Challenge 97
01/2 UD Honor Roll 65
01/2 UD Ice 128
01/2 UD Mask 136
01/2 UD Premier 90
01/2 UD Top Shelf 123
02/3 Vanguard - PP 3
00/1 Providence Bruins
01/2 Providence Bruins

HUMPHREY, TODD
93/4 Flint Generals
94/5 Flint Generals

HUMPHREYS, KIRK
98/9 Guildford Flames

HUMPHRIES, JOHN
83/4 Kingston Canadians

HUNGLE, CASEY
91/2 Avant Garde BCJHL 61
91/2 Avant Garde BCJHL 153
92/3 BCJHL 96
95/6 Tallahasee Tiger Sharks
91/2 Nanaimo Clippers

HUNT, BRIAN
89/0 ProCards AHL 38

HUNT, CURTIS
89/0 ProCards IHL 186
90/1 ProCards 516
91/2 ProCards 336
87/8 Flint Spirits
97/8 Grand Rapids Griffins
99/0 Grand Rapids Griffins
95/6 Houston Aeros
92/3 St. John's Maple Leafs
93/4 St. John's Maple Leafs
84/5 Prince Albert Raiders

HUNT, GORDY
97/8 Toledo Storm 5

HUNT, GREG
91/2 Avant Garde BCJHL 83
92/3 BCJHL 173

HUNT, JEFF
99/0 Ottawa 67's
00/1 Ottawa 67's 25
01/2 Ottawa 67's 25

HUNTER, ANDRIA
94/5 Classic W17

HUNTER, DALE
98/9 Be A Player M17
90/1 Bowman 71
91/2 Bowman 303
92/3 Bowman 303
81/2 Dernière Heure
93/4 Donruss 370
94/5 Donruss 149
95/6 Donruss 12
96/7 Donruss 199
97/8 Donruss 195
96/7 Duracell DC20
83/4 Esso Stars
94/5 Flair 199
96/7 Flair 99
94/5 Fleer 235
01/2 Fleer Greats 18, ✍ Aut.
92/3 Fleer Ultra 232
93/4 Fleer Ultra 135
94/5 Fleer Ultra 234
95/6 Fleer Ultra 175
84/5 Kellogg's 35
86/7 Kraft Sports 46
93/4 Leaf 118
94/5 Leaf 183
95/6 Leaf 215
96/7 Leaf 56
98/9 NHL Power Play
81/2 O-Pee-Chee 277
82/3 O-Pee-Chee 285
83/4 O-Pee-Chee 293
84/5 O-Pee-Chee 281
85/6 O-Pee-Chee 179
86/7 OPC/Topps 192
87/8 O-Pee-Chee 245
88/9 OPC/Topps 70
90/1 OPC/Topps 129
91/2 O-Pee-Chee 229
92/3 O-Pee-Chee 18
89/0 OPC/Topps 76
98/9 OPC Chrome 58
92/3 OPC Premier SP2
82/3 OPC/Topps Sticker 26
84/5 OPC Sticker 179
85/6 OPC Sticker 151-20
86/7 OPC Sticker 32
88/9 OPC Sticker 73-204
97/8 Omega 239
98/9 Pacific 442
99/0 Pacific 107
97/8 Pacific CC 129
97/8 Pa. Crown Roy. 139
97/8 Pa. Invincible 146
97/8 Pa. Paramount 194
97/8 Pa. Revolution 147
87/8 Panini Sticker 155
87/8 Panini Sticker 168
88/9 Panini Sticker 165
88/9 Panini Sticker 372
89/0 Panini Sticker 346
90/1 Panini Sticker 168
91/2 Panini Sticker 203
92/3 Panini Sticker 165
93/4 Panini Sticker 26
94/5 Panini Sticker 21
95/6 Panini Sticker 135
97/8 Panini Sticker 115
91/2 Parkhurst 195
92/3 Parkhurst CP7
93/4 Parkhurst D6
94/5 Parkhurst 254
95/6 Parkhurst 223
80/1 Pepsi Bottle Cap
91/2 Pinnacle 40
92/3 Pinnacle 104
92/3 Pinnacle 237
93/4 Pinnacle 13
94/5 Pinnacle 85
95/6 Pinnacle 21
95/6 Pi. Summit 5
95/6 Pi. Zenith GG-12
95/6 Playoff 322
94/5 POG 244
82/3 Post [Québ.]
93/4 Power Play 262
94/5 Premier 506
95/6 Pro Magnet 30
90/1 Pro Set 312
91/2 Pro Set 506
92/3 Pro Set 202
91/2 Pro Set Platinum 245
90/1 Score 44
91/2 Score 56
91/2 Score 306
91/2 Score CAN 56
91/2 Score CAN 336
92/3 Score 231
92/3 Score SS 4
93/4 Score 40
94/5 Score 143
95/6 Score 107
96/7 Score 110
97/8 Score 201
94/5 Select 33
95/6 SBx Emotion 188
95/6 SBx Impact 177
83/4 Souhaits Keychain [Nordiques]
94/5 SP 127
95/6 SP 159
92/3 Topps 464
95/6 Topps 177
98/9 Topps 58
91/2 To. Stadium 164
92/3 T. Stadium Club 40
94/5 T. Stadium Club 134
01/2 T/O Archives 9
90/1 Upper Deck 219
91/2 Upper Deck 209
92/3 Upper Deck 131
94/5 Upper Deck 68
95/6 Upper Deck 442
96/7 Upper Deck 178
97/8 Upper Deck 175
98/9 Upper Deck 383
95/6 UD BAP 213, ✍ S213
96/7 UD Black Diam. 82
95/6 UD CC 155
96/7 UD CC 288
97/8 UD Coll. Choice 271
02/3 UD Foundations 77, 97
98/9 UD G. Reserve 383
83/4 Vachon 66-46
83/4 Vachon 66-89
80/1 QUÉB
81/2 QUÉB
82/3 QUÉB
83/4 QUÉB
84/5 QUÉB
85/6 QUÉB
85/6 QUÉB / Gene. Foods
85/6 QUÉB / McDonald's
85/6 QUÉB / Provigo
86/7 QUÉB
86/7 QUÉB / Gene. Foods
86/7 QUÉB / McDonald's
86/7 QUÉB / Yum Yum
87/8 WASH
87/8 WASH / Kodak
88/9 WASH
88/9 WASH / Smokey
89/0 WASH
89/0 WASH / Kodak
90/1 WASH / Kodak
90/1 WASH / Smokey
91/2 WASH / Kodak
91/2 WASH / Smokey
92/3 WASH / Kodak
95/6 WASH
98/9 WASH / Kids 'n 4
00/1 London Knights
01/2 London Knights

HUNTER, DALE
01/2 Fleer Legacy 63
02/3 Fleer Throwbacks 8, 6SO, ✂ 8SC, ✂ 8SCTD, ✂ 6SO, ✂ 2SW, ✍ Aut.

HUNTER, DAVE
79/0 O-Pee-Chee 387
80/1 O-Pee-Chee 293
81/2 O-Pee-Chee 115
82/3 O-Pee-Chee 110
83/4 O-Pee-Chee 32
84/5 O-Pee-Chee 246
88/9 OPC/Topps 62
82/3 OPC/Topps Sticker 102
83/4 OPC/Topps Sticker 154
88/9 OPC Sticker 235-105
87/8 Panini Sticker 268
88/9 Panini Sticker 339
80/1 Pepsi Bottle Cap
82/3 Post [Edmo.]
83/4 Stater Mint H16
83/4 Vachon 29-109
79/0 EDMO
80/1 EDMO / Zellers
81/2 EDMO / Red Rooster
82/3 EDMO / Red Rooster
83/4 EDMO / Button
83/4 EDMO / McDonald's
83/4 EDMO / West Mall
83/4 EDMO
84/5 EDMO
84/5 EDMO / Red Rooster
85/6 EDMO / Red Rooster
86/7 EDMO
86/7 EDMO / Red Rooster
88/9 EDMO
88/9 EDMO / Action 40
87/8 PITT / Kodak
88/9 WINN / Safety Tips

HUNTER, DYLAN
01/2 London Knights

HUNTER, J.J.
98/9 Kelowna Rockets

HUNTER, JIM
83/4 North Bay Centennials

HUNTER, LOGAN
00/1 London Knights
00/1 London Knights
01/2 London Knights

HUNTER, MARK
91/2 Bowman 9
82/3 O-Pee-Chee 185
86/7 OPC/Topps 57
87/8 OPC/Topps 50
88/9 OPC/Topps 187
91/2 O-Pee-Chee 109
85/6 OPC Sticker 137-9
86/7 OPC Sticker 181
87/8 OPC Sticker 21-161
88/9 OPC Sticker 14-141
87/8 Panini Sticker 313
88/9 Panini Sticker 108
90/1 Panini/CGY 4
91/2 Pinnacle 253
82/3 Post [Mont.]
90/1 Pro Set 422
91/2 Pro Set 390
90/1 Score 77T
91/2 Score 156
91/2 Score 306
91/2 Score CAN 156
91/2 Score CAN 336
92/3 Score 194

95/6 Slapshot 355
92/3 Topps 36
91/2 To. Stadium 15
92/3 T. Stadium Club 396
91/2 Upper Deck 479
83/4 Vachon 46-66
90/1 CALG / McGavin's
91/2 HART / Jr. Whalers
81/2 MONT
82/3 MONT
82/3 MONT / Steinberg
83/4 MONT
84/5 MONT
87/8 SLOU / Kodak
96/7 St. John's Maple Leafs
00/1 London Knights

HUNTER, MARK & DALE
02/3 Kamloops Blazers

HUNTER, TIM
90/1 O-Pee-Chee 434
97/8 Pa. Dynagon BKS-85
87/8 Panini Sticker 216
89/0 Panini Sticker 343
90/1 Panini/CGY 5
91/2 Pinnacle 375
90/1 Pro Set 423
91/2 Pro Set 366
91/2 Score CAN 537
92/3 Score 403
91/2 Upper Deck 221
82/3 CALG
85/6 CALG / Red Rooster
86/7 CALG / Red Rooster
87/8 CALG / Red Rooster
90/1 CALG / McGavin's
91/2 CALG / IGA
92/3 QUÉB / Petro-Canada
94/5 VANC
95/6 VANC / Abalene 4

HUNTER, TIM
02/3 Fleer Throwbacks 53

HUNTER, TODD
90/1 7th..Sketch OHL 285
91/2 7th...Sketch OHL 182
94/5 Raleigh Icecaps

HUNTER, TRENT
01/2 BAP Memor. 369
02/3 BAP Memorabilia ✂ FG11
02/3 Choice Prospects 21
01/2 Parkhurst 340
02/3 SPx 117
02/3 Stadium 119
02/3 Upper Deck 213
02/3 UD Foundations 137
02/3 UD MVP 209
02/3 UD Piece 140
02/3 UD Vintage 341
99/0 Prince George Cougars

HUOKKO, JAN
94/5 Leaf Elit Set 6
95/6 Leaf Elit Set 65
92/3 Semic Elitserien 160
95/6 UD Elitserien 99, NA14
98/9 UD Elitserien 118
99/0 UD Elitserien 104
00/1 UD Elitserien 108

HUOTARI, HARRI
72/3 Williams Finnish 305

HUOTARI, JARI
71/2 Williams Finnish 342
72/3 Williams Finnish 323

HUPPE, CURTIS
99 Bowman 87

HURBANEK, JOACHIM
74 Hellas MM-Jenkki 111

HURD, KELLY
98/9 EBK ECHL All-Star
91/2 ProCards 253
92/3 Fort Wayne Komets 13
93/4 Fort Wayne Komets 9
94/5 Fort Wayne Komets 20
99/0 Fort Wayne Komets
99/0 Mississippi S'Wolves
90/1 Michigan Tech Huskies
90/1 Michigan Tech Huskies
90/1 Michigan Tech Huskies

HURLBUT, MIKE
92/3 Classic Prospects 138
95/6 Edge Ice 167
89/0 ProCards IHL 35
90/1 ProCards 12
91/2 ProCards 196
92/3 Upper Deck 448
92/3 Binghampton Rangers
95/6 Minnesota Moose
97/8 Rochester Americans
98/9 Rochester Americans
00/1 Rochester Americans

HURLEY, CRAIG
81/2 Saskatoon Blades

HURLEY, DARREN
00/1 Kudos 45
90/1 7th..Sketch OHL 9
91/2 7th...Sketch OHL 117

HURLEY, MARK
95/6 Tri-City Americans 7

HURLEY, MIKE
98 Bowman 54
98 Bowman Chrome 54
95/6 Tri-City Americans 12

HURME, HEIKKI
70/1 Kuvajulkaisut 138
71/2 Williams Finnish 225

HURME, JANI
00/1 BAP Mem. 179
01/2 BAP Memor. 144
02/3 BAP Memorabilia 52
01/2 BT Pipes 22, ✂ HSHSJers
02/3 Between the Pipes 10, GUE12, ✂ GB2, ✂ GUJ12, ✂ GSJ12, ✂ ITN12
99/0 Cardset -Aces/A-r
02/3 Cardset 176, -DD 8
00/1 Crown Royale 135, 21CR-18
02/3 First Edition 265
00/1 Pacific 279
01/2 Pacific 274
02/3 Pacific 268
02/3 Pacific Complete 424
00/1 Pa. Paramount 173
00/1 Parkhurst P-229
01/2 Parkhurst 166, ✂ T25
00/1 Premier Plus 124
00/1 Private Stock 133
00/1 PS Titanium 135
00/1 PS Titanium Draft 135
00/1 Signature 286, ✍ Aut. 227
01/2 Signature 109, ✍ Aut. 109
96/7 Sisu ATG-4, KIG-2, RE-1
00/1 SP Authentic 116, ✍ SotT
00/1 SP GU 76
01/2 SP GU ✂ Patch, ✂ PatchC
00/1 SPx 106
00/1 Stadium 258
01/2 Stadium NR9
00/1 To. Gold Label 111
00/1 To. Heritage 90
00/1 To. Stars 116
00/1 UD Heroes 172
00/1 UD Reserve 106
01/2 Ultimate Mem. ✂ WTF
00/1 Upper Deck 223
01/2 Upper Deck ✂ GoalJ, ✂ NG
00/1 UD Black Diam. 82
02/3 UD Mask 37, 38
00/1 UD Pros&Prosp. 117
00/1 UD Vintage 387
00/1 Vanguard 136
01/2 Victory 252
02/3 Victory -NP25
01/2 Waving the Flag 14
00/1 OTTA
01/2 OTTA
98/9 Cincinnati Cyclones
98/9 Detroit Vipers
99/0 Grand Rapids Griffins
97/8 Indianapolis Ice 9

HURME, MARKKU
98/9 Cardset 41
99/0 Cardset 27
00/1 Cardset 260
02/3 Cardset 27
97/8 Hockey-Box
94/5 Sisu 293
96/7 Sisu 9

HURST, RON
45-64 BeeHive-2 [Toro.]
52/3 Laval Dairy Update 119

HURTIG, LARS
96/7 DEL 153
94/5 Leaf Elit Set 90, TG-3
95/6 Leaf Elit Set 251
89/0 Semic Elitserien 158
90/1 Semic Elitserien 238
91/2 Semic Elitserien 168
92/3 Semic Elitserien 194
95/6 UD Elitserien 131

HURTUBISE, MARK
01/2 Québec Remparts 6
02/3 Québec Remparts
02/3 Val d'Or Foreurs

HUSBY, ROAR
92/3 Semic Nordisk 114

HUSCFO, DIETER
74 Hellas MM-Jenkki 114

HUSCROFT, JAMIE
99/0 Millenium 244, ✍ Aut. 244
97/8 Pa. Invincible R-185
96/7 Panini Sticker 241
97/8 Pi. Be A Player 88, ✍ Aut. 88
88/9 ProCards / Utica
89/0 ProCards AHL 217
90/1 ProCards 577
91/2 ProCards 424
95/6 UD CC 126
88/9 NJER / Caretta
99/0 Portland Pirates

HUSELIUS, KRISTIAN
01/2 Adrenaline 210, RR 9
01/2 Atomic 110
02/3 Atomic 45, -CF 14
01/2 BAP Memor. 393
02/3 BAP Memorabilia 27, ✂ FG14
01/2 Bowman 152, ✂ FFJ, ✂ FFS, ✂ FFDS, ✂ FFR, ✍ YSA
02/3 Bowman 143
01/2 Crown Royale 162, CA 5, RR 10
02/3 Crown Royale 42, ✂ GWDP 11
02/3 Exclusive 76, -DFG 7, -GE 8, ✂ GWJ 10
02/3 First Edition 32, 383, 384, ✂ Jers.
01/2 Heads Up 107
02/3 Heads Up 52, ✂ GWQ 36
02/3 In The Game-Used 33, 133
01/2 O-Pee-Chee 335
02/3 O-Pee-Chee 86
01/2 Pacific 456
02/3 Pacific 154, -SM 6
02/3 Pacific Complete 316
01/2 PTC Calder 5
01/2 PTC High Voltage 5
01/2 PTC Collectibles 5
01/2 PTC Rookie 7
01/2 Parkhurst 261
02/3 Parkhurst 75
02/3 Parkhurst Retro 144
01/2 Pr. Stock 123, -PS 97
02/3 Pr. Stock Reserve 42
01/2 PS Titanium 161, TSS 26, TRT 6
01/2 PS Titanium Draft 132
02/3 PS Titanium 45, ✂ GWJ 32
01/2 Signature 212, ✍ Aut. 212, ✂ GU95, ✂ HSHSJers
02/3 Signature 106, ✍ 106, ✂ TQ5
01/2 SP Authentic ✍ 177
02/3 SP Authentic 118
01/2 SP GU 79
02/3 SP Game-Used ✍ Sig
02/3 Sports Vault 47
01/2 SPx 106
02/3 SPx 35
01/2 SPx Rookie RR13
01/2 Stadium 132
02/3 Stadium 72, ✂ YSS7, ✂ YSD3
01/2 Topps 335
02/3 Topps 86, OTG13
01/2 To. Chrome 153
02/3 T. Chrome 54
01/2 To. Heritage 146
02/3 T. Limited 86
01/2 To. Reserve 113
02/3 T. Total 320
01/2 UD PlayMakers Ltd 120
01/2 Ultimate Mem. ✂ WTF
02/3 Ultimate Mem. ✂ Num
01/2 Upper Deck 426
02/3 Upper Deck 77
02/3 UD Artistic 41, R41, / Art
01/2 UD Challenge 108
02/3 UD Classic 44
01/2 UD Collectors
97/8 UD Elitserien 60, C22
98/9 UD Elitserien 98
99/0 UD Elitserien 77, H15, S15, ✍ Aut.
00/1 UD Elitserien 71, 193, S3, ✍ Sig.
01/2 UD Honor Roll 73
02/3 UD Honor 33
01/2 UD Ice 55, ✍ CCA
01/2 UD Mask 147
01/2 UD MVP 224
02/3 UD MVP 77, ✍ PSig
02/3 UD Piece 42
01/2 UD Premier 111, ✍ Sig
02/3 UD Rookie 44
01/2 UD Top Shelf 71
02/3 UD Top Shelf 37
01/2 UD Vintage 281
02/3 UD Vintage 114, 315, GB 114
01/2 Vanguard 114, PP 7
02/3 Vanguard 44, ✂ GWJ 22
01/2 Victory 444
02/3 Victory 88
01/2 Waving the Flag 20
01/2 FLOR

HUSGEN, JAMIE
88/9 ProCards / Moncton
87/8 Moncton Hawks

HUSKA, RYAN
94/5 Slapshot Memorial 10
95/6 Indianapolis Ice
97/8 Indianapolis Ice 10
93/4 Kamloops Blazers

HUSKINS, KENT
01/2 Norfolk Admirals

HUSS, ANDERS
91/2 Semic Elitserien 39
92/3 Semic Elitserien 69
95/6 UD Elitserien DS1
97/8 UD Elitserien 30, 205, S12, C18
98/9 UD Elitserien 47
00/1 UD Elitserien 177, T11

HUSSEY, MARC
92/3 Classic 18
92/3 Classic Four Sport 167
90/1 7th..Sketch WHL 146
91/2 7th...Sketch WHL 278
00/1 UD DEL 143
97/8 Indianapolis Ice 11
97/8 Milwaukee Admirals
95/6 Saint John Flames
96/7 Saint John Flames
94/5 St. John's Maple Leafs
02/3 Nottingham Panthers

HUSSEY, MATT
02/3 WBS Penguins

HUSTON, RON
74/5 Loblaws
76/7 OPC WHA 36
75/6 Phoenix Roadrunners
76/7 Phoenix Roadrunners

HUTAN, GHEORGHE
79 Panini Sticker 312

HUTANU, VASILE
79 Panini Sticker 315

HUTCHINGS, GREG
90/1 7th..Sketch WHL 228
88/9 Brandon Wheat Kings
89/0 Brandon Wheat Kings
90/1 Brandon Wheat Kings

HUTCHINGS, JOHN
81/2 Oshawa Generals
82/3 Oshawa Generals
83/4 Oshawa Generals

HUTCHINGS, STEVE
85/6 U. of Arizona Ice Cats

HUTCHINGS, TED
88/9 Lethbridge Hurricanes

HUTCHINSON, TROY
90/1 7th..Sketch OHL 286
91/2 7th...Sketch OHL 280

HUTCHISON, DAVE
74/5 Loblaws
75/6 O-Pee-Chee 390
76/7 O-Pee-Chee 346
76/7 O-Pee-Chee 386
77/8 O-Pee-Chee 380
78/9 O-Pee-Chee 289
79/0 O-Pee-Chee 302
80/1 O-Pee-Chee 78
82/3 Post [Chic.]
80/1 Topps 78
80/1 CHIC / Brown
81/2 CHIC
78/9 TORO
79/0 TORO
73/4 Vancouver Blazers

HUTSON, ROB
99/0 Muskegon Fury

HUTT, MALCOLM
01/2 Belleville Bulls

HUTTON, BOUSE
83 HHOF Postcard G9

HUTTON, DWAINE
84/5 Kelowna Wings &...
87/8 Flint Spirits
83/4 Saskatoon Blades

HUTTON, J.B.
83&87 HHOF 100

HUTTON, JIM
86/7 Kitchener Rangers

HUURA, ILKKA
71/2 Williams Finnish 343
72/3 Williams Finnish 324

HUURA, PASI
91/2 Jyvas Hyva 48
92/3 Jyvas Hyva 132
93/4 Jyvas Hyva 236
91 Semic Sticker 10
93 Semic Sticker 51
93/4 Sisu 191
94/5 Sisu 297
95/6 Sisu 34

HUUSKO, ANDERS
99/0 Eishockey 111
95 Globe 49
94/5 Leaf Elit Set 26
95/6 Leaf Elit Set 194, FTF-3
91/2 Semic Elitserien 77
92/3 Semic Elitserien 88
00/1 UD DEL 37
97/8 UD Elitserien 96, C24
98/9 UD Elitserien 112

HUUSKO, ERIK
95 Globe 45
94/5 Leaf Elit Set 14
95/6 Leaf Elit Set 32, FTF-3
95 Panini Worlds 150
91/2 Semic Elitserien 76
92/3 Semic Elitserien 87
95/6 UD Elitserien 44
98/9 UD Elitserien 113

HUUSS, ANDERS
94/5 Leaf Elit Set 61, SS-2
89/0 Semic Elitserien 37
90/1 Semic Elitserien 187

HUYBER, TODD
93/4 Huntington Blizzard

HVIID, JESPER
79 Panini Sticker 365

HWODEKY, RICK
98/9 Barrie Colts

HYACINTHE, SENEQUE
00/1 Val d'Or Foreurs 24

HYATT, BRAD
88/9 ProCards / New Haven

HYATT, TROY
90/1 7th..Sketch WHL 17
91/2 7th...Sketch WHL 130
93/4 Seattle Thunderbirds

HYDE, MATTHEW
00/1 Baie-Comeau 15
01/2 Baie-Comeau 13

HYDUKE, JOHN
85/6 Minnesota-Duluth 26

HYKA, TOMAS
94/5 APS 272

HYLAND, HARRY
91 C55 Reprint 30
83 HHOF Postcard L7
83&87 HHOF 157
10/1 Imperial
10/1 Imperial 10
11/2 Imperial 30
12/3 Imperial 19

HYMOVITZ, DAVID
98/9 EBK IHL All-Star
01/2 Grand Rapids Griffins
97/8 Indianapolis Ice 12
98/9 Indianapolis Ice
99/0 Lowell Lock Monsters
00/1 Lowell Lock Monsters

HYND, JASON
91/2 Air Canada SJHL B23

HYNEK, PAVEL
00/1 OFS 289

HYNES, CHRIS
99/0 Eishockey 93

HYNES, DAVE
98/9 BOST / Alumni 28

HYNES, GORD
90/1 Canada Nationals 5
91/2 Canada Nationals
95/6 DEL 387
96/7 DEL 295
98/9 DEL 233
99/0 Eishockey 2
92/3 O-Pee-Chee 8
91/2 Parkhurst 235
92/3 Score 483
92/3 Score COH 5
92/3 T. Stadium Club 49
00/1 UD DEL 1, S2
01/2 UD DEL 26
92/3 PHIL / UD Sheet
92/3 PHIL / J.C. Penney
93/4 Cincinnati Cyclones
86/7 Moncton G'Flames
83/4 Medicine Hat Tigers
84/5 Medicine Hat Tigers

HYNES, WAYNE
94/5 DEL 427
95/6 DEL 396
96/7 DEL 305
98/9 DEL 207
99/0 Eishockey 329
00/1 UD DEL 5
01/2 UD DEL 170
84/5 Medicine Hat Tigers

HYNNES, CHRIS
98/9 EBK ECHL All-Star
94/5 Sig. Rookies 41, ✍ 41
93/4 Thunder Bay Senators
95/6 Thunder Bay Senators

HYOKKI, KARI
73/4 Williams Finnish 271

HYRSKY, DAVE
87/8 Brockville Braves
88/9 Brockville Braves

HYRSKY, TIMO
70/1 Kuvajulkaisut 346

HYTÖNEN, JUHA-PEKKA
00/1 Cardset 174

HYTTI, JARI
80/1 Mallasjuoma 183
72/3 Williams Finnish 325

HYTTI, TIMO
72/3 Williams Finnish 281

HYTTINEN, KIMMO
93/4 Sisu 85
94/5 Sisu 115, 355

HYVARI, PAULI
65/6 Hellas 88

HYVARI, PENTTI
65/6 Hellas 93

HYVÄRINEN, JARI
98/9 Cardset 180
99/0 Cardset 287

HYVONEN, HANNES
02/3 UD MVP 215
01/2 Cleveland Barons

HYVONEN, SEPPO
72/3 Williams Finnish 173

HYVÖNEN, HANNES
01/2 BAP Memor. 426
98/9 Cardset 19
99/0 Cardset 13, 175
00/1 Cardset 19
02/3 Cardset 177
97/8 Hockey-Box
01/2 Parkhurst 343
95/6 Sisu 131
96/7 Sisu 141
01/2 UD Mask 165

HYYTAIENEN, PENTTI
66/7 Champion 164
79 Panini Sticker 304

I

IAFRATE, AL
90/1 Bowman 153
91/2 Bowman 300
92/3 Bowman 251
93/4 Donruss 371
93/4 Donruss 402
93/4 Donruss Y
94/5 Donruss 205
93/4 EA Sports 152
93/4 EA Sports 190
94/5 Flair 10
94/5 Fleer 12, SA-3
92/3 Fleer Ultra 233
93/4 Fleer Ultra 11
93/4 Fleer Ultra AS 8
93/4 Fleer Ultra SM 5
94/5 Fleer Ultra 256, SM-4
96/7 Fl. Ultra 151
93/4 Hockey Wit 74
90/1 Kraft 21
93/4 Kraft / KD
94/5 Kraft / HH
93/4 Leaf 141
94/5 Leaf 212
93/4 McDonald's McD-16
96/7 Metal Univ. 137
85/6 O-Pee-Chee 210
86/7 OPC/Topps 26
87/8 O-Pee-Chee 238
88/9 OPC/Topps 71
90/1 OPC/Topps 91
91/2 O-Pee-Chee 148
92/3 O-Pee-Chee 341
89/0 OPC/Topps 79
90/1 OPC Premier 48
85/6 OPC Sticker 13-143
86/7 OPC Sticker 148
87/8 OPC Sticker 160-20
88/9 OPC Sticker 180
89/0 opcSticker 178
97/8 Pacific CC 177
87/8 Panini Sticker 325
88/9 Panini Sticker 118
89/0 Panini Sticker 140
90/1 Panini Sticker 290
90/1 Panini/TOR 9, G
91/2 Panini Sticker 208
92/3 Panini Sticker 168
93/4 Panini Sticker 32
94/5 Panini Sticker 7
95/6 Panini Sticker 12
91/2 Parkhurst 194
92/3 Parkhurst 203
93/4 Parkhurst 217
94/5 Parkhurst 15
94/5 Parkie SE seV22
91/2 Pinnacle 207
92/3 Pinnacle 66
93/4 Pinnacle 189
93/4 Pinnacle TP 9
94/5 Pinnacle 39, BR1
96/7 Pi. Be A Player 19, ✍ Aut. 19
94/5 POG 36
93/4 Power Play 263
93/4 Power Play SA 5
93/4 Premier 174
93/4 Premier 45
94/5 Premier 20, 453
90/1 Pro Set 281, 354
91/2 Pro Set 250
92/3 Pro Set 205
91/2 Pro Set Platinum 130
90/1 Score 195, 334
90/1 Sco. Hot Cards 85
91/2 Score 209
91/2 Score CAN 209
92/3 Score 11
93/4 Score 188
93/4 Score 450
93/4 Score DT 9
93/4 Score PiAS 19
93/4 Score PiAS 47
94/5 Score 168
95/6 Score 237
92/3 Seasons 67
94/5 Select 80
89 Semic Sticker 162
91 Semic Sticker 135
93 Semic Sticker 173
95/6 SBx Emotion 7
95/6 SBx Impact 8
92/3 Topps 133
96/7 Topps Picks 117
91/2 To. Stadium 372
92/3 T. Stadium Club 302
93/4 To. Stadium 455
93/4 To. Stadium 80
93/4 To. Stadium - All-Stars
94/5 T. Stadium Club 202
93/4 TSC Members Only 31
90/1 Upper Deck 157, 539
91/2 Upper Deck 318
92/3 Upper Deck 54
93/4 Upper Deck 183, SP-170
94/5 Upper Deck 82, SP-94
96/7 Upper Deck 331
97/8 Upper Deck 357
93/4 Upper Deck Be A Player 26
95/6 UD CC 195
97/8 UD Coll. Choice 223
92/3 UD Locker 37
84/5 TORO
85/6 TORO
86/7 TORO
86/7 TORO
87/8 TORO / 5x8
87/8 TORO / P.L.A.Y. 19
88/9 TORO / P.L.A.Y. 19
90/1 TORO
90/1 WASH / Kodak
91/2 WASH / Kodak
91/2 WASH / Smokey
92/3 WASH / Kodak
83/4 Belleville Bulls

IAFRATE, AL
02/3 Fleer Throwbacks 75

IAKOVENKO, ANDREI
92/3 Greensboro Monarchs 9

IANDOLI, NICKY
94/5 Guildford Flames 15

IANIERO, ANDREW
99/0 Kingston Frontenacs
00/1 Kingston Frontenacs 10
01/2 Kingston Frontenacs 8

IANNETTA, MATT
01/2 London Knights

IAQUINTA, ALDO
97/8 New Mexico Scorpions

IGINLA, JAROME
01/2 Adrenaline 25, ✂ GWJ 5
96/7 All-Sport PPF 177
01/2 Atomic 13, PP 5, TN 2
02/3 Atomic 13, -CF 5, -NPC 2, -PC 4, -SC 3
98/9 Aurora 25
99/0 Aurora 23, -Stripe 23
00/1 Aurora 24
02/3 BAP All-Star 32, ✂ ASJ
98/9 Be A Player 18, ✍ Aut. 18
99/0 BAP Mem. 212
00/1 BAP Mem. 278
01/2 BAP Memor. 275
02/3 BAP Memorabilia 117, 205, 239, ✂ ASJ20, ✂ ASE7, ✂ ASN7, ✂ AST28, ✂ FP5, ✂ HSHSJers 25, ✂ TM20
01/2 BAP Update ✂ HSHSJers
02/3 Between the Pipes ✂ GN6
97/8 Bicycle 4-Spade
01/2 Bowman 7
02/3 Bowman 40
98/9 Bowman's Best 65
02/3 Calder 12
95/6 Classic 11, BK10
95/6 Cla. 5 Sport 132
99/0 Crown Royale 23
00/1 Crown Royale 18, ✂ JR-2
01/2 Crown Royale 20, CA 11, JotC 3, ✂ TT 9
02/3 Crown Royale 14, -LOR 5
97/8 Donruss 14, 226, L2L-17
96/7 Do. Canadian 124, OC-4
97/8 Do. Canadian 12, NP-13
95/6 Do. Elite WJ 15
96/7 Do. Elite 131, A-19
97/8 Do. Elite 13, 121, C-17
97/8 Do. Preferred 17, 166, LT-7A
97/8 Do. Priority 31, 191, DD-9, OD-19, Post-20, Stamp-20
97/8 Do. Studio 12, HH-12, S-24, P-12, ✍ Aut.
98/9 Dynagon Ice 27
99/0 Dynagon Ice 36
02/3 eTopps 1, -Intro
02/3 Exclusive 23, -MO 5
02/3 First Edition 142, 313, 345, 371, 372, 387, 413R, ✂ Jers., ✂ DGJ 4, ✂ HSHSJers 4, ✂ HSHSJers 26, ✂ TSL 4
96/7 Flair 103
96/7 Fl. Ultra 24, UR-10
00 Gatorade Sticker
96/7 Got-Um
01/2 Heads Up 12, ✂ JQ 5
02/3 Heads Up 16, -EIT 4, -ITN 5, -SM 5, / Bobble
02/3 In The Game-Used 9, 109, ✂ E5, ✂ F5, ✂ GUJ5, ✂ SJ5, ✂ TM4
96/7 Kraft / TT
97/8 Leaf 14, 180,BS-20
96/7 L. Limited LR-2
96/7 L. Preferred 118
97/8 Limited 43, 114, 177, FG-61
97/8 McDonald's McD-12
99/0 McDonald's McD-5
01/2 McDonald's 3, -HP 4, ✂ JPatch 1
02/3 McDonald's 5, -CA 3. -SLG 8
96/7 Metal Univ. 182
99/0 Millenium 39, ✍ Aut. 39
98/9 NHL Power Play
99/0 NHL Power Play
01/2 O-Pee-Chee 106
02/3 O-Pee-Chee 12, 328
98/9 OPC Chrome 52
97/8 Omega 30
98/9 Omega 33
99/0 Omega 38
98/9 Pacific 120
99/0 Pacific 57, -CI 4, -TL 5
00/1 Pacific 66, IO-4
01/2 Pacific 61, 405
02/3 Pacific 54, -IZ 4, -L 4, -MA 4, -MI 11
02/3 Pacific Complete 10
97/8 Pacific CC 12, CS-3, CCA-3, GCDC-5, TC-4
97/8 Pa. Crown Roy. 19
98/9 Pa. Crown Roy. 19
97/8 Pa. Dynagon 17, 137, DD-4B, T-3, T-23, BKS-13
97/8 Pa. Invincible 19, AZ-4, FP-5, OTG-4, R-29
97/8 Pa. Paramount 30,C-3
98/9 Pa. Paramount 28
99/0 Pa. Paramount 40, -IAd 4, -IAl 5
00/1 Pa. Paramount 36, ✂ J&P-1
97/8 Pa. Revolution 18
98/9 Pa. Revolution 20
97/8 Panini Sticker 194, 251, 252
98/9 Panini Sticker 181
99/0 Panini Sticker 190
00/1 Panini Sticker 117
00/1 Parkhurst P-62
01/2 Parkhurst 5, ✂ HSHSJers
02/3 Parkhurst 97, -HHH2, -HHP2, -HHR2, ✂ FP5, ✂ GJ44, ✂ SJ44, ✂ NH3
02/3 Parkhurst Retro 2, ✂ RF5, ✂ HSHSJers
94/5 Parkie SE260
97/8 Pinnacle 31, P-15
96/7 Pi. Be A Player LTH1A, ✍ Aut. LTH1A
97/8 Pi. Certified 55
96/7 Pi. FANtasy 7
97/8 Pi. Inside 17, IT-28
96/7 Pi. Mint 29
97/8 Pi. Mint 9
97/8 Pi. Totally 55
96/7 Pi. Zenith 119
00/1 Premier Plus 48, ✂ GP
99/0 Prism 24
00/1 Private Stock ✂ GUG 11
01/2 Pr. Stock 11, -PS 9, ✂ GUG 15
02/3 Pr. Stock Reserve ✂ 106
00/1 PS Titanium 11, ✂ GUG-68
01/2 PS Titanium 18, SK 3, TSS 12, TAS 2, ✂ DSJ 7
01/2 PS Titanium Draft ✂ 15
02/3 PS Titanium 15, -SK 1
02/3 Quest for the Cup 12
99/0 Revolution 25, -Orn. 5, -TotL 23, / CSC 25
00/1 Revolution 23, HD-6, ✂ GWJ-3
97/8 Score 123, CI-7
94/5 Select 165
96/7 Select CE 93
00/1 Signature 18, F-5, ✍ Aut. 186
01/2 Signature 5, ✍ Aut. 5, ✂ FP5, ✂ GUE11, ✂ GJ9, ✂ GSJ9, ✂ ITN11, ✂ IG11, ✂ TM5, ✂ HSHSJers
02/3 Signature 40, GS-42, ✍ 40, ✂ FS5, ✂ FJ5, ✂ SGJ5
94/5 Slapshot Memorial 9
94/5 SP 181
95/6 SP 170
96/7 SP 23, SF-4, SF-5, ✍ Aut.
97/8 SP Authentic 20, ✍ SotT
98/9 SP Authentic 13
00/1 SP Authentic 15
01/2 SP Authentic 11, ✍ SotT, ✍ SotTD
02/3 SP Authentic 12, 93, ✍ SotT, ✍ SotTD, ✍ SotTT, ✂ SP
01/2 SP GU ✂ AF, ✂ AFD, ✂✍ IS, ✂✍ISD, ✂ Patch, ✂✍ PatchSig, ✂ PatchC, ✂✍PatchCSig
02/3 SP GU 7, ✂ AF, ✂ PC, ✂ PH, ✍ Sig
02/3 Sports Vault 164
97/8 SPx 7, -DV, ✍ DVS
99/0 SPx 24
01/2 SPx 8, ✂ HT, ✂✍ HTSig
02/3 SPx 10, ✂ SS, ✂ X
99/0 Stadium 21
00/1 Stadium 52
01/2 Stadium 31, ✂ SCS
02/3 Stadium 2, -BT-4, ✍ LSS
98/9 Topps 52, -IA I3
99/0 Topps 74
00/1 Topps 15
01/2 Topps 106
02/3 Topps 12, 328, CC3, HHC1, OTG1, OTG6
99/0 To. Chrome 74
00/1 To. Chrome 15
01/2 To. Chrome 106
02/3 T. Chrome 12
98/9 To. Finest 111
98/9 T. Gold Label 35
99/0 To. Gold Label 74
00/1 To. Gold Label 31
00/1 To. Heritage 70
01/2 To. Heritage 40, ✂ GWJ
02/3 To. Heritage 2, 101, 108, 109, 119, -Light 2
02/3 T. Limited 12, 328
01/2 To. Reserve 38, ✂ TR
00/1 To. Stars 74
02/3 T. Total 130, TTC4, AW1, TP1, TT1
98/9 UD Choice 35
01/2 UD PlayMakers Ltd 16, -PCPJ, ✂ PCJ, ✂ PCCJ
00/1 UD Reserve 12
02/3 UD Superstars 41
01/2 Ultimate Mem. ✂ CP, ✂ DD, ✂ Gloves, ✂ NP, ✍ Aut.
02/3 Ultimate Mem. ✂ BOS, ✂ GUJ, ✂ GAO, ✂ HT, ✂ SL, ✂ Num, ✂ RA, ✍ Uaut
96/7 Upper Deck 181, X21, P19
97/8 Upper Deck 24, SG12, S24, ✂ GJ4
98/9 Upper Deck 55
99/0 Upper Deck 28
00/1 Upper Deck 254
01/2 Upper Deck 25, ✂ NG
02/3 Upper Deck 183, 269, -SS2, -SS3, ✂ DM, ✂ FF, ✂ LN, ✂ PA, ✂ R50, ✂ S
02/3 UD Artistic 13, R13, ✂ AT, / Art
96/7 UD Black Diam. 164, RC19
97/8 UD Black Diam. 132
98/9 UD Black Diam. 12
01/2 UD Challenge 9, ✂✍ FPS
02/3 UD Classic 14, PS2, ✂ CS, ✂ HR (x2)
96/7 UD CC 349
97/8 UD Coll. Choice 34, 315, SQ12, S12, C29, CR29
98/9 UD G. Reserve 55
99/0 UD G. Reserve 28
01/2 UD Honor Roll -DPuck
02/3 UD Honor 10, -SG4, -TW2
96/7 UD Ice 78
97/8 UD Ice 20, L5C
01/2 UD Ice 5, ✍ CCA
01/2 UD Mask 13, ✂ GJ, ✂ JP, ✂ DP
02/3 UD Mask 16, ✂ IO, ✂ PG
98/9 UD MVP 34, ✍ PS
99/0 UD MVP 32
00/1 UD MVP 31
01/2 UD MVP 25, -J (x2), ✍ SJ (x2)
02/3 UD MVP 29, HN3, SO3, VF4, SA
99/0 UD MVP Cup 33
02/3 UD Piece 17, AC4, ✍ MD
01/2 UD Premier 8, ✂ B, ✂ D., ✍ SigS
02/3 UD Premier 9, ✂ Jers, ✂ Patch, ✍ Sig
99/0 UD Retro 12
02/3 UD Rookie 17, 111, ✂ 152c, 167, ✂ DJ, ✍ TD
01/2 UD Top Shelf 5, ✂ J, ✂✍ SJ
02/3 UD Top Shelf 12, ✂ CP, ✂ HT (x2), ✂ R, ✂ ST, ✍ Sig
00/1 UD Vintage 60
01/2 UD Vintage 37, 42, 43
02/3 UD Vintage 39, 265, 306, 308, 309, T10, ✂ SO
00/1 Vanguard 16
01/2 Vanguard 12, EMW 9, VT 11, ✂ DGM 4
02/3 Vanguard 15, -EMW 2
99/0 Victory 46
00/1 Victory 37
01/2 Victory 49
02/3 Victory 31, -NP3
97/8 Zenith 1, Z20
93/4 Kamloops Blazers

IGNATIUS, OLLI
80/1 Mallasjuoma 8

IGNATJEVS, VIKTOR
99/0 Eishockey 33

IGNATJOV, NIKOLAI
00/1 Mir 327

IGNATJOV, VICTOR
92/3 Classic Prospects 128
92/3 Kansas City Blades
93/4 Kansas City Blades
97/8 Long Beach Ice Dogs

IGNATUSHKIN, IGOR
98 Québec Pee Wee 1290

IHALAINEN, VEIKKO
70/1 Kuvajulkaisut 228
71/2 Williams Finnish 243
73/4 Williams Finnish 308

IHNACAK, MIROSLAV
87/8 Panini Sticker 336
88/9 ProCards / Adirondack
89/0 ProCards AHL 155
90/1 ProCards 463
86/7 TORO
86/7 TORO
89/0 Halifax Citadels
90/1 Halifax Citadels

IHNACAK, PETER
94/5 DEL 240
95/6 DEL 234
96/7 DEL 85
98/9 DEL 268
99/0 Eishockey 49
83/4 Funmate Puffy 3 [w/]
83/4 O-Pee-Chee 334
83/4 OPC/Topps Sticker 32
85/6 OPC Sticker 19-150
87/8 Panini Sticker 334
89/0 ProCards AHL 120
82 Semic Sticker 96
83/4 Vachon 90-77
82/3 TORO
83/4 TORO
84/5 TORO
85/6 TORO
86/7 TORO
86/7 TORO
87/8 TORO / 5x8
87/8 TORO / P.L.A.Y. 24

IHRIG, J.C.
94/5 Huntington Blizzard

IIVONEN, SEPPO
66/7 Champion 139

IKOLA, SEPPO
65/6 Hellas 58

IKONEN, JOUKO
71/2 Williams Finnish 322

IKONEN, JUHA
98/9 Cardset 18, -Leij. 22, -OD 1
99/0 Cardset 169
02/3 Cardset 180
97/8 Hockey-Box
93/4 Jyvas Hyva 203
94/5 Sisu 16
95/6 Sisu 93
96/7 Sisu 89
99/0 UD Elitserien 79
00/1 UD Elitserien 69

IKONEN, MARKKU
93/4 Sisu 156
94/5 Sisu 110
95/6 Sisu 62

ILAVSKY, SLAVOMIR
94 Semic 206

ILIEV, ATANAS
79 Panini Sticker 347

ILIEV, GUEORGUI
79 Panini Sticker 348

ILITCH, MIKE
91 Pro Set Awards AC22

ILLIKAINEN, DARIN
85/6 Minnesota-Duluth 8

ILMIVALTA, PEKKA
93/4 Sisu 281

ILYIN, ROMAN
91/2 O-Pee-Chee 34R

IMBEAU, JEAN
91/2 7th...Sketch LHJMQ 67

IMBER, SHAUN
91 7th..Sketch Mem.Cup 19
90/1 7th..Sketch OHL 159
91/2 7th...Sketch OHL 323

IMBURGIA, CHUCK
95/6 Toledo Storm

IMDAHL, THOMAS
94/5 DEL 359
95/6 DEL 231

IMES, CHRIS
95/6 Edge Ice 168
93/4 Fleer Ultra 486
93/4 Power Play 506
93/4 Premier - USA Hockey 11
93/4 To. Stadium - Team U.S.A. 10
91/2 Upper Deck WJC 75
92/3 Maine Black Bears
92/3 Maine Black Bears

IMHAUSER, PETER
90/1 Semic Elitserien 133

IMLACH, GEORGE (PUNCH)
63-65 Chex
62/3 Cowan Tile
83&87 HHOF 243
51/2 Laval Dairy 37
93/4 Legends of Hockey 25
59/0 Parkhurst 15
63/4 Parkhurst 19
63/4 Parkhurst 79
60/1 Shirriff 20
61/2 Shirriff 57
62/3 Shirriff 15
52/3 St. Lawrence 54
64/5 Topps 45
65/6 Topps 11
66/7 Topps 11
66/7 Topps / Test 11
61/2 York 38
93/4 BUFF / Noco
64/5 TORO
79/0 TORO

IMLACH, PUNCH
02/3 Parkie - Reprint 237

IMMONEN, JARKKO
02/3 Cardset 181

IMMONEN, JORMA
80/1 Mallasjuoma 11
78/9 SM-Liiga 27
72/3 Williams Finnish 101
73/4 Williams Finnish 129

IMMONEN, MARTTI
80/1 Mallasjuoma 136
71/2 Williams Finnish 151
72/3 Williams Finnish 102

IMMONEN, SANTERI
98/9 Cardset 258
99/0 Cardset 148
00/1 Kudos 112
95/6 Sisu 44

IMMONEN, VILLE
98/9 Cardset 204
99/0 Cardset 117
00/1 Cardset 83
02/3 Cardset 28

IMMONEN, WALTTERI
98/9 Cardset 99
97/8 Hockey-Box
91/2 Jyvas Hyva 24
92/3 Jyvas Hyva 54
93/4 Jyvas Hyva 110
95 Panini Worlds 170
94 Semic 19
95 Semic 7
93 Semic Sticker 52
93/4 Sisu 8
94/5 Sisu 24
95/6 Sisu 46, DT-2
96/7 Sisu 45, ATG-3
95/6 Sisu Limited 11

IMOO, DUSTY
91/2 ProCards 258
90/1 7th..Sketch WHL 183
88/9 Lethbridge Hurricanes
89/0 Lethbridge Hurricanes

IMPOLA, KALLE
72/3 Williams Finnish 282

INFANGER, KARL
98/9 EBK ECHL All-Star
99/0 Mississippi S'Wolves

ING, PETER
91/2 Bowman 157
91/2 O-Pee-Chee 145
90/1 OPC Premier 49
91/2 OPC Premier 33
90/1 Panini/TOR 10
91/2 Panini Sticker 99
90/1 Pro Set 639
91/2 Pro Set 222
91/2 Pro Set 388
91/2 Pro Set Platinum 41
90/1 Score 414, 11T
91/2 Score 55
91/2 Score 62T
91/2 Score CAN 55
91/2 Score CAN 612
91/2 Score Young Stars 12
92/3 Topps 423
91/2 To. Stadium 352
92/3 T. Stadium Club 347
90/1 Upper Deck 432
91/2 Upper Deck 118
91/2 EDMO / IGA
90/1 TORO
94/5 Fort Wayne Komets 10
95/6 Fort Wayne Komets
93/4 Las Vegas Thunder

INGARFIELD, EARL
68/9 Bauer Photo
45-64 BeeHive-2 [NYRa.]
64-67 BeeHive-3 [NYRa.]
64/5 Coke/Sprite [NYRa.]
65/6 Coca-Cola
70/1 Dad's Cookies
70/1 Eddie Sargent 132
70/1 Esso Power Player
62/3 Cowan Tile
68/9 O-Pee-Chee 102
69/0 O-Pee-Chee 87
69/0 O-Pee-Chee 4in1
70/1 O-Pee-Chee 191
95/6 Parkie 66-67 87
94/5 Parkie Tall 91
72 Semic Sticker 177
60/1 Shirriff 92
61/2 Shirriff 82
68/9 Shirriff / Pitt. 2
58/9 Topps 18
59/0 Topps 10
61/2 Topps 49
62/3 Topps 51
62/3 Topps Dollar
63/4 Topps 55
64/5 Topps 65
66/7 Topps 30
68/9 Topps 102
69/0 Topps 87
62/3 Toronto Star Weekend

INGLIS, BILL
70/1 Eddie Sargent 27
70/1 O-Pee-Chee 130
70/1 Topps 130

INGMAN, JAN
89/0 Semic Elitserien 87
90/1 Semic Elitserien 264

INGRAHAM, CAL
95/6 Tallahasee Tiger Sharks
92/3 Maine Black Bears
92/3 Maine Black Bears
93/4 Maine Black Bears

INGRAM, GEOFF
89/0 7th..Sketch OHL 117

INGRAM, JIM
91/2 Avant Garde BCJHL 56
91/2 Nanaimo Clippers

INGRAM, RON
45-64 BeeHive-2 [Detr.]
64-67 BeeHive-3 [Detr.]
63/4 Parkhurst 54
93/4 Parkie 56-57 33
63/4 York 54

INKINEN, MIKKO
95/6 Sisu 270
96/7 Sisu 67
02/3 Dundee Texol Stars

INKPEN, DAVE
79/0 O-Pee-Chee 321
76/7 OPC WHA 83

INNANEN, DEREK
96/7 Mississippi S'Wolves
92/3 W. Michigan Broncos
93/4 W. Michigan Broncos

INNES, JUSON
89/0 Portland Winter Hawks

INNESS, GARY
75/6 O-Pee-Chee 227
76/7 O-Pee-Chee 331
79/0 O-Pee-Chee 358
77/8 OPC WHA 18
75/6 Topps 227
74/5 PITT
79/0 WASH

INSAM, ADOLF
79 Panini Sticker 390
82 Semic Sticker 132

INTRANUOVO, RALPH
92/3 Classic 27
92/3 Classic Four Sport 176
93/4 Cla. Prospects 186
96/7 Donruss 232
95/6 Edge Ice 33
99/0 Eishockey 10
95/6 Leaf 35
x96/7 Leaf GLR-5
96/7 Pinnacle 237
96/7 Pi. Summit 175
95/6 Score 294
96/7 Score 263
91 7th..Sketch Mem.Cup 20
90/1 7th..Sketch OHL 160
91/2 7th...Sketch OHL 332
93/4 Upper Deck 253
96/7 Upper Deck 182
00/1 UD DEL 158
01/2 UD DEL 68
94/5 Cape Breton Oilers
97/8 Manitoba Moose
98/9 Manitoba Moose
93/4 Soo Greyhounds 19

INTWERT, DEAN
90/1 7th..Sketch WHL 326
91/2 7th...Sketch WHL 333
89/0 Portland Winter Hawks

IOANNOU, YIANNY
95/6 Classic 82

IOB, TONY
91 7th..Sketch Mem.Cup 22
90/1 7th..Sketch OHL 60
91/2 7th...Sketch OHL 325
92/3 Rochester Americans WPC

ION, MICKEY
83 HHOF Postcard A9
83&87 HHOF 9

IONITA, ION
79 Panini Sticker 314

IORIANNI, MATT
01/2 London Knights

IOVIO, EMILIO
96/7 DEL 224
95 Panini Worlds 86
92 Semic Sticker 255

IRBE, ARTURS
01/2 Adrenaline 34, CL2, PP7
01/2 Atomic 17, TN 3
02/3 Atomic 17, -D 3
99/0 Aurora 26, -Stripe 26, -GU 4
00/1 Aurora 29
02/3 BAP All-Star 33, ✂ ASJ
98/9 Be A Player 172, ✍ Aut. 172
99/0 BAP Mem. 4
00/1 BAP Mem. 255

01/2 BAP Memor. 34, ✄ ASJ, ✄ ASE, ✄ ASN, ✄ AST, ✄ GoalJ, ✄ SCP
02/3 BAP Memorabilia 13, ✄ ASJ21, ✄ SC26
01/2 BT Pipes 16, 99, ✄ ASJ, ✄ Jers., ✄ S&J, ✄ GG, ✄ -HSHS Jers.
02/3 Between the Pipes 26, 126, ✄ ASJ15, ✄ BM9, ✄ GUE1, ✄ GUJ1, ✄ GSJ1, ✄ HSHSJers 17, ✄ ITN1, ✍ Aut.
98/9 Bicycle.. Q-C
92/3 Classic Prospects 117
99/0 Crown Royale 27, -IG 4
00/1 Crown Royale 21
01/2 Crown Royale 26
02/3 Crown Royale 18
93/4 Donruss 311
94/5 Donruss 7, D-7, MM-4
95/6 Donruss 239
98/9 Dynagon Ice 33
99/0 Dynagon Ice 41
93/4 EA Sports 120
02/3 Exclusive 29, -EA 3
02/3 First Edition 117, ✄ Jers.
94/5 Flair 166
94/5 Fleer 197, FF-4, N-4
95/6 Fleer Metal 130
92/3 Fleer Ultra 401, -UI 5
93/4 Fleer Ultra 145
94/5 Fleer Ultra 195, GG-3, PPM-2
95/6 Fleer Ultra 146
01/2 Heads Up 16
02/3 Heads Up 21, ✄ GWQ 6, -S 4
95/6 Hoyle / West. J-Spade
94/5 Kraft / KD
95/6 Kraft / PS
93/4 Leaf 199
94/5 Leaf 175, LL-21
95/6 Leaf 267
94/5 L. Limited 74
99/0 Millenium 50, ✍ Aut. 50
90/1 O-Pee-Chee 501, 7R
01/2 O-Pee-Chee 73
02/3 O-Pee-Chee 254
98/9 Omega 42
99/0 Omega 45
98/9 Pacific 427
99/0 Pacific 72, -ITC 4, -TL 6
00/1 Pacific 83
01/2 Pacific 74
02/3 Pacific 67, ✄ GWJ 6
02/3 Pacific Complete 549
97/8 Pacific CC 188
98/9 Pa. Crown Roy. 23
98/9 Pa. Paramount 235
99/0 Pa. Paramount 46, -GS 4
00/1 Pa. Paramount 43, GS-5
98/9 Pa. Revolution 24, -ASG 11
94/5 Panini Sticker 225
95/6 Panini Sticker 287
98/9 Panini Sticker 218
00/1 Panini Sticker 29
92/3 Parkhurst 396
93/4 Parkhurst 451
94/5 Parkhurst V79
95/6 Parkhurst 188, 251, GP-10, IAS-1
00/1 Parkhurst P-8
01/2 Parkhurst 136, ✄ PJ53, ✄ T18
02/3 Parkhurst 5
02/3 Parkhurst Retro 148
94/5 Parkie SE162, ES17
91/2 Pinnacle 323
93/4 Pinnacle 86
94/5 Pinnacle 121, GT9
97/8 Pinnacle 74
95/6 Pi. FANtasy 7
97/8 Pi. Inside 61
95/6 Pi. Summit 84
96/7 Pi. Summit 110
95/6 Pi. Zenith 81
96/7 Pi. Zenith 60
95/6 Playoff 84, 191, 302
96/7 Playoff 345
94/5 POG 294
95/6 POG 233
93/4 Power Play 221
93/4 Power Play RisS 1
93/4 Premier 110
93/4 Premier 442
94/5 Premier 260
00/1 Premier Plus 18
99/0 Prism 29
00/1 Private Stock 17
01/2 Pr. Stock 15
02/3 Pr. Stock Reserve 17, -ICS 3
00/1 PS Titanium 15
01/2 PS Titanium 25, ✄ DSJ 44, ✄ DSJ 61
02/3 PS Titanium ✄ GWJ 9
95/6 Pro Magnet 117, IC3
91/2 Pro Set Platinum 270
92/3 Red Ace Blue 13
99/0 Revolution 28, / CSC 28
00/1 Revolution 27
92/3 Score 457
93/4 Score 377
94/5 Score 10, TF21
95/6 Score 189
97/8 Score 7
97/8 Score Vanc. 12
94/5 Select 37
95/6 Select CE 91
91 Semic Sticker 77
00/1 Signature 238, ✍ Aut. 126, ✄ HSHSJers
01/2 Signature 129, ✍ Aut. 129
02/3 Signature 143, GS-14, ✍ 143
95/6 SBx Emotion 156
95/6 SBx Impact 148
89/0 Soviet Stars
94/5 SP 105
99/0 SP Authentic 17
01/2 SP Authentic ✍ SotT
02/3 SP Authentic 14
00/1 SP GU 10
99/0 SPx 28
00/1 SPx 11
01/2 SPx 10
02/3 SPx 13
00/1 Stadion 110
99/0 Stadium 67
00/1 Stadium 65
01/2 Stadium 73
02/3 Stadium 64
91/2 Star Pics 37
94/5 Starting Lineup
95/6 SLU
00/1 SLU 11
95/6 Super Sticker 108
92/3 Topps 25
95/6 Topps 296
99/0 Topps 107
00/1 Topps 82, OTG15
01/2 Topps 73, OTG25
02/3 Topps 254
99/0 To. Chrome 107
00/1 To. Chrome 65
01/2 To. Chrome 73
02/3 T. Chrome 137
94/5 Topps Finest 104, DF-16
99/0 To. Gold Label 46
00/1 To. Gold Label 20, BTM9
00/1 To. Heritage 63
01/2 To. Heritage 45, 127
02/3 T. Limited 254
99/0 To. Prmr. Plus 55
01/2 To. Reserve 83
92/3 T. Stadium Club 131
93/4 To. Stadium 4
94/5 T. Stadium Club 190, DAD-1
95/6 To. Stadium 58
93/4 TSC Members Only 17
00/1 To. Stars 88
02/3 T. Total 83
91/2 Tri Globe From... 23-24
91/2 Tri Globe Mag. Five 16-20
00/1 UD Heroes 21
01/2 UD PlayMakers Ltd 19
00/1 Ultimate Mem. ✄ Jers. 11, ✄G-6, ✄J-13, ✄S-13
02/3 Ultimate Mem. ✄ NO
91/2 Upper Deck 532
93/4 Upper Deck 125
94/5 Upper Deck 116, SP-71
95/6 Upper Deck 403, SE-162
96/7 Upper Deck 248
97/8 Upper Deck 377
99/0 Upper Deck 31
00/1 Upper Deck 34
01/2 Upper Deck 32
02/3 Upper Deck -SA3
02/3 UD Artistic 14, R14, / Art
95/6 UD BAP 23, ✍ S23
99/0 UD Black Diam. 19
01/2 UD Challenge 13, BB2
02/3 UD Classic 16
95/6 UD CC 64
99/0 UD G. Reserve 31
02/3 UD Honor 12
01/2 UD Ice 6, ✍ CCA
00/1 UD Legends 23, 24
01/2 UD Mask 106, 174
02/3 UD Mask 17, 18
99/0 UD MVP 37, -Draw. W7
00/1 UD MVP 35, ✄ GS
01/2 UD MVP 30, -MM12, ✄ GS
02/3 UD MVP 36
99/0 UD MVP Cup 38
02/3 UD Piece 14
01/2 UD Premier 9, ✍ Sig
00/1 UD Pros&Prosp. 18
01/2 UD Top Shelf 83
02/3 UD Top Shelf 16
00/1 UD Vintage 69, 73, 74, GG5
01/2 UD Vintage 45, 52
02/3 UD Vintage 52, 266, GB 52, T11
00/1 Vanguard 20
01/2 Vanguard 16
99/0 Victory 56, 379
00/1 Victory 44
01/2 Victory 59, 65
02/3 Victory 42
99/0 WGretzky 38, ✄ SG, ✄ TG
98/9 CARO / Highwoods
96/7 DALL / Southwest
92/3 SANJ / Pacific Bell

IRCANDIA, LEN
77/8 Kalamazoo Wings

IREDALE, JOHN
94 Semic 328

IRELAND, GREG
98/9 Dayton Bombers
98/9 Dayton Bombers

IRGL, ZBYNEK
99/0 DS 182
00/1 DS 164
98/9 OFS 128
99/0 OFS 224, 515

IRONSTONE, JOE
24/5 William Paterson 1

IRSAG, JAKE
95/6 Slapshot 44

IRVIN, ALEX
19 Vancouver Millionaires
19 Vancouver Millionaires

IRVIN, DICK (JR.)
97/8 Pi. CBC Sports 6

IRVIN, DICK (SR.)
25-27 Anonymous 138
83 HHOF Postcard G10
83&87 HHOF 101
95/6 Legends of Hockey 57
32/3 Maple Leafs O'Keefe
23/4 Paulins Candy 22
60/1 Topps 60
61/2 Topps - Stamp

IRVINE, JACK
51/2 Laval Dairy 78
52/3 St. Lawrence 31

IRVINE, KURT
02/3 Coventry Blaze

IRVINE, TED
70/1 Eddie Sargent 114
71/2 Eddie Sargent 126
72/3 Eddie Sargent 152
70/1 Esso Power Player
74/5 Loblaws
68/9 O-Pee-Chee 39
69/0 O-Pee-Chee 103
70/1 O-Pee-Chee 65
71/2 O-Pee-Chee 74
72/3 O-Pee-Chee 212
73/4 O-Pee-Chee 248
74/5 O-Pee-Chee 264
75/6 O-Pee-Chee 244
76/7 O-Pee-Chee 347
68/9 Shirriff / LosA. 2
68/9 Topps 39
69/0 Topps 103
70/1 Topps 65
74/5 Topps 264
75/6 Topps 244
71/2 Toronto Sun Photo

IRVING, BERG
28/9 Paulins Candy 62

IRVING, STU
78/9 Saginaw Gears

IRWIN, DOUG
94/5 DEL 326
95/6 DEL 312

IRWIN, GLEN
75/6 Houston Aeros

IRWIN, IVAN
93/4 Parkie 56-57 107
54/5 Topps 44

IRWIN, JOEL
92/3 BCJHL 62
99/0 Greensboro Generals

IRWIN, RICHARD
96/7 Guelph Storm

ISAKSSON, ESA
66/7 Champion 10
65/6 Hellas 25
70/1 Kuvajulkaisut 105
72 Panda MM-Toronto
72 Semic Sticker 78
71/2 Williams Finnish 61
71/2 Williams Finnish 113
73/4 Williams Finnish 309

ISAKSSON, ULF
82 Semic Sticker 14

ISBISTER, BRAD
01/2 Adrenaline 120
98/9 Aurora 144
00/1 Aurora 89
98/9 Be A Player 109, ✍ Aut. 109
00/1 BAP Mem. 102
01/2 BAP Memor. 250
02/3 BAP Memorabilia 397
97 Bowman 92
95/6 Classic 21
99/0 Crown Royale 86
00/1 Crown Royale 67
97/8 Do. Elite 46
97/8 Do. Preferred 154
97/8 Do. Priority 176
98/9 Dynagon Ice 142
02/3 Exclusive 107
97/8 Leaf 162
01/2 O-Pee-Chee 77
02/3 O-Pee-Chee 35
98/9 OPC Chrome 169
99/0 Omega 141
98/9 Pacific 339
00/1 Pacific 250
01/2 Pacific 249
02/3 Pacific 237
02/3 Pacific Complete 8
97/8 Pa. Crown Roy. 103
97/8 Pa. Paramount 140
98/9 Pa. Paramount 181
00/1 Pa. Paramount 154
99/0 Panini Sticker 96
00/1 Panini Sticker 53
00/1 Parkhurst P-200
01/2 Parkhurst 40
02/3 Parkhurst 193
97/8 Pinnacle 20
97/8 Pi. Be A Player 226, ✍ Aut. 226
97/8 Pi. Certified I
99/0 Prism 87
00/1 Revolution 92
97/8 Score 72
00/1 Signature 47
01/2 Signature 81, ✍ Aut. 81
02/3 Signature GS-12
97/8 SP Authentic 189
00/1 SP Authentic 59
02/3 Sports Vault 74
98/9 SPx Finite 65, 146
00/1 Stadium 20, PP5
01/2 Stadium 99
98/9 Topps 169
00/1 Topps 97
01/2 Topps 77
02/3 Topps 35
00/1 To. Chrome 77
00/1 To. Gold Label 83
00/1 To. Heritage 127
01/2 To. Heritage 98
02/3 T. Limited 35
02/3 T. Total 29
98/9 UD Choice 161
98/9 UD3 26, 86, 146
97/8 Upper Deck 340
98/9 Upper Deck 152, GN11
00/1 Upper Deck 337
01/2 Upper Deck 110
02/3 Upper Deck 356
97/8 UD Black Diam. 24
97/8 UD Coll. Choice 305
98/9 UD G. Reserve 152
96/7 UD Ice 125
98/9 UD MVP 159
00/1 UD Pros&Prosp. 54
00/1 UD Vintage 225
01/2 UD Vintage 163
99/0 Victory 182
00/1 Victory 148
01/2 Victory 225
97/8 Zenith RR-7
97/8 PHOE / Coca-Cola
98/9 PHOE / Coca-Cola
93/4 Portland Winter Hawks

ISEN, COREY
95/6 Slapshot 178
99/0 San Angelo Outlaws

ISERHOFF, NEIL
91/2 7th...Sketch OHL 156
91/2 Oshawa Generals
91/2 Oshawa Generals
92/3 Oshawa Generals

ISKRZYCKI, ANDRZEJ
79 Panini Sticker 123

ISO-ESKELI, JUHANI
66/7 Champion 84
65/6 Hellas 5

ISOMAKI, SAKARI
66/7 Champion 29

ISOSALO, SAMU
00/1 Cardset 309
99/0 UD Prospects 19

ISOTALO, JARKKO
94/5 Sisu 284

ISOTALUS, PETRI
00/1 Cardset 60

ISRAEL, AARON
94/5 Classic 119
94/5 Johnstown Chiefs 11

ISRAEL, JAMIE
90 7th..Sketch Mem.Cup 34
90/1 7th..Sketch OHL 234
89/0 Kitchener Rangers
90/1 Kitchener Rangers

ISRAELSON, LARRY
75/6 OPC WHA 46

ISSEL, JASON
93/4 Prince Albert Raiders
95/6 Prince Albert Raiders

ISSEL, KIM
88/9 ProCards / Cape Breton
89/0 ProCards AHL 145
90/1 Score 409
88/9 EDMO / Action 155
84/5 Prince Albert Raiders

ITÄMIES, IIRO
98/9 Cardset 206
95/6 Sisu 82
96/7 Sisu 82

ITO, NORIO
79 Panini Sticker 286

IULIANO, JERRY
83/4 Soo Greyhounds

IUSTINIAN, GHEORGHE
79 Panini Sticker 314

IVAN, MAREK
00/1 DS 165
99/0 OFS 454
00/1 OFS 255
01/2 OFS 21
98/9 Peoria Rivermen

IVAN, TOMMY
83 HHOF Postcard L8
83&87 HHOF 158
93/4 Legends of Hockey 35
93/4 Parkie 56-57 42
60/1 Shirriff 80
70/1 CHIC

IVANKOVIC, FRANK
95/6 Slapshot 156

IVANNIKOV, VALERI
99/0 Mir 65
95 Panini Worlds 26
95 Semic 122

IVANOV, DENIS
99/0 Mir 36
96/7 Guelph Storm

IVANOV, MIKHAIL
00/1 Dynamo 15

IVANY, RON
98/9 DEL 225

IVARSSON, LARS
94/5 Leaf Elit Set 23
95/6 Leaf Elit Set 128
89/0 Semic Elitserien 99
90/1 Semic Elitserien 104
92/3 Semic Elitserien 136
95/6 UD Elitserien 187

IVARSSON, PIERRE
90/1 Semic Elitserien 159
91/2 Semic Elitserien 263
92/3 Semic Elitserien 277

IVASHKIN, ALEXEI
99/0 Mir 64

IWAMOTO, TAKESHI
79 Panini Sticker 285

J

JAAKKOLA, JARMO
71/2 Williams Finnish 280

JAAKO, KARI
89/0 Semic Elitserien 162
90/1 Semic Elitserien 43
91/2 Semic Elitserien 291

JAAPAKOSKI, MIKKO
94 Semic 6

JÄÄSKELÄINEN, JOONAS
98/9 Cardset 23, Leij. 25
99/0 Cardset 17
00/1 Cardset 10
02/3 Cardset 186
97/8 Hockey-Box
94/5 Sisu 226
95/6 Sisu 290
96/7 Sisu 88

JÄÄSKELÄINEN, JUHA
91/2 Jyvas Hyva 37

JÄÄSKELÄINEN, TUOMO
00/1 Cardset 292

JABLONIC, DON
93/4 Minnesota-Duluth

JABLONSKI, JEFF
95/6 Roanoke Express
96/7 Roanoke Express 11
92/3 Toledo Storm WIOT
92/3 Toledo Storm

JABLONSKI, PAT
92/3 Bowman 66
98/9 EBK IHL All-Star
92/3 Fleer Ultra 202
93/4 Fleer Ultra 125
94/5 Leaf 446
91/2 O-Pee-Chee 246
92/3 O-Pee-Chee 311
91/2 OPC Premier 29
92/3 OPC Premier 95
92/3 Parkhurst 404
93/4 Parkhurst 192
95/6 Parkhurst 386
91/2 Pinnacle 331
93/4 Pinnacle Mask 5
96/7 Pi. Be A Player 99, ✍ Aut. 99
93/4 Power Play 444
93/4 Premier 186
92/3 Pro Set 178
88/9 ProCards / Peoria
89/0 ProCards IHL 3
90/1 ProCards 97
91/2 Score 329
91/2 Score CAN 359
93/4 Score 349
94/5 SR Tetrad CVI, ✍ Aut.
92/3 Topps 396
92/3 T. Stadium Club 231
91/2 Upper Deck 107
92/3 Upper Deck 458
96/7 MONT
89/0 SLOU / Kodak
91/2 SLOU
92/3 TAMP / Sheraton Inn
98/9 Chicago Wolves
97/8 Cleveland Lumberjacks

JACINA, GREG
00/1 UD Prospects 43
01/2 Mississauga IceDogs
02/3 Mississauga IceDogs
01/2 Owen Sound Attack

JACK, JUSTIN
98/9 Kelowna Rockets

JACKMAN, BARRET
99 Bowman 38, ✍ BA3
02/3 Bowman 127, ✄ FFDS, ✄ FFJ, ✄ FFP, ✄ FFR, ✄ FFRP, ✄ FFS, ✄ FFTS, ✍ YSA, / ✍ Puck
02/3 Calder 91, -CR 19
02/3 Exclusive 142, -GE 15
02/3 Pacific Complete 525
02/3 Parkhurst Retro ✄ CH7
02/3 Pr. Stock Reserve 83, -CA 10, -MIT 7
02/3 PS Titanium -ROT 18
02/3 Signature ✄ AR9
98/9 SP Authentic 117, ✍ SotT
99/0 SPx 179
02/3 Ultimate Mem. ✄ UC
98/9 Upper Deck 394
99/0 Upper Deck 312
99/0 UD Black Diam. 100
98/9 UD G. Reserve 394
99/0 UD G. Reserve 312
99/0 UD MVP Cup 209, ✄ GU, ✍ PS
02/3 Vanguard - PP 20
01/2 Worcester IceCats
97/8 Regina Pats

JACKMAN, JASON
94/5 Slapshot / Guelph 13
95/6 Slapshot 101
95/6 Guelph Storm
96/7 Guelph Storm

JACKMAN, RICHARD
96/7 All-Sport PPF 174
00/1 BAP Mem. 487
97/8 Bell
97 Bowman 36
98 Bowman 5
98 Bowman Chrome 5
95/6 Cla. Vis. Signings 65, ✍
95/6 Future Legends ✍ HP-3
99/0 Millenium C-50
99/0 Omega 79
02/3 Pacific Complete 461
01/2 Parkhurst 223
00/1 Private Stock 116
01/2 Signature 208, ✍ Aut. 208
95/6 Slapshot 374
00/1 Topps 310
00/1 To. Chrome 205
96/7 UD Ice 133
00/1 DALL / Southwest
98/9 Michigan K-Wings
99/0 Michigan K-Wings
96/7 Soo Greyhounds
96/7 Soo Greyhounds

JACKMAN, TIM
02/3 Syracuse Crunch

JACKSON, ART
34-43 BeeHive-1 [Toro.]
35/6 O-Pee-Chee 88
39/0 O-Pee-Chee 93

JACKSON, BUSHER
02/3 Ultimate Mem. ✍ Cut

JACKSON, DANE
93/4 Cla. Prospects 127
94/5 Score 216
92/3 Hamilton Canucks
01/2 Manchester Monarchs
02/3 Manchester Monarchs
95/6 Rochester Americans
96/7 Rochester Americans
97/8 Rochester Americans
00/1 Rochester Americans

JACKSON, DON
83/4 O-Pee-Chee 33
84/5 O-Pee-Chee 247
79 Panini Sticker 212
83/4 Vachon 30-110
82/3 EDMO / Red Rooster
83/4 EDMO / Button
83/4 EDMO / McDonald's
83/4 EDMO / West Mall
83/4 EDMO
84/5 EDMO
84/5 EDMO / Red Rooster
85/6 EDMO / Red Rooster
88/9 EDMO / Action 76
01/2 OTTA
02/3 OTTA
91/2 QUÉB / Petro-Canada
92/3 QUÉB / Petro-Canada
94/5 Cincinnati Cyclones
96/7 Kansas City Blades

JACKSON, HAROLD (HAL)
36-39 Diamond Match Chic.
36/7 O-Pee-Chee 112
76 DETR

JACKSON, HARVEY (BUSHER)
35/6 Amalgamated Press
33/4 Anonymous 6
34-43 BeeHive-1 [Toro.]
33/4 Canadian Gum
33/4 Hamilton Gum 29
83 HHOF Postcard M11
83&87 HHOF 175
30/1 La Presse
32/3 Maple Leafs O'Keefe
33/4 O-Pee-Chee 33
36/7 O-Pee-Chee 124
37/8 O-Pee-Chee 139
39/0 O-Pee-Chee 20
55/6 Parkhurst 22
02/3 Parkie - Reprint 203
91/2 Pro Set 338
38/9 Quaker Oats
34/5 Sweet Caporal
37/8 World Wide Gum 51

JACKSON, JEFF
88/9 O-Pee-Chee 219
90/1 OPC/Topps 249
91/2 O-Pee-Chee 159
88/9 OPC Sticker 190-57
89/0 opcSticker 184-40
90/1 Pro Set 249
90/1 ProCards 459
91/2 ProCards 365
90/1 Upper Deck 291
87/8 QUÉB / Gene. Foods
88/9 QUÉB
88/9 QUÉB / Gene. Foods
89/0 QUÉB
89/0 QUÉB / Gene. Foods
89/0 QUÉB / Police
90/1 QUÉB
84/5 TORO
85/6 TORO
90/1 Halifax Citadels
83/4 Brantford Alexanders
01/2 Guelph Storm
01/2 Guelph Storm M-Cup
91/2 L. Superior State Lakers

JACKSON, JEREMY
01/2 Vancouver Giants

JACKSON, JIM
83/4 O-Pee-Chee 84
84/5 O-Pee-Chee 225
83/4 OPC/Topps Sticker 146
88/9 ProCards / Rochester
89/0 ProCards AHL 279
82/3 Ottawa 67's
83/4 Ottawa 67's
84/5 Ottawa 67's

JACKSON, MIKE
90/1 ProCards 169
90/1 Newmarket Saints

JACKSON, PAUL
69 Columbus Checkers
94/5 Sheffield Steelers 14

JACKSON, STAN
24/5 Champ's Cigarettes
23/4 William Paterson 27
24/5 William Paterson 60

JACKSON, WALTER
33/4 Canadian Gum
33-35 Diamond Match Silv.

JACOB, GUY
88/9 Flint Spirits
79/0 Montréal Juniors B&W
79/0 Montréal Jrs. Colour
81/2 Oshawa Generals

JACOB, RICKY
97/8 Central Texas

JACOBS, IAN
99/0 Ottawa 67's

JACOBS, TIM
76/7 O-Pee-Chee 370

JACOBSEN, FREDRIK
92/3 Semic Nordisk 69

JACOBSEN, GRANT
02/3 Kamloops Blazers
01/2 Regina Pats

JACOBSEN, LARS
92/3 Semic Nordisk 71

JACOBSEN, MICHAEL
01/2 Owen Sound Attack

JACOBSEN, TOR_A
92/3 Semic Nordisk 103

JACOBSON, CHRIS
97/8 Portland Winter Hawks

JACOBSON, GARNET
95/6 Prince Albert Raiders

JACOBSSON, ÖRJAN
92/3 Semic Elitserien 251

JACOBSSON, PETER
94/5 Leaf Elit Set 117
89/0 Semic Elitserien 249
90/1 Semic Elitserien 158
91/2 Semic Elitserien 262
92/3 Semic Elitserien 283

JACQUES, ALEXANDRE
97 Bowman 80
00/1 Upper Deck 88
99/0 Cincinnati M'Ducks
97/8 Toledo Storm 4
97/8 Rimouski Océanic

JACQUES, JEAN-FRANÇOIS
99 Québec Pee Wee 245
01/2 Baie-Comeau 24
02/3 Baie-Comeau

JACQUES, RÉAL
52/3 Bas du Fleuve 7

JAEGER, BRETT
01/2 Vancouver Giants

JAFFES, IRVING
36-39 Diamond Match TT2

JAGER, JESPER
00/1 UD Elitserien 19

JAGR, JAROMIR
94/5 Action Packed
01/2 Adrenaline 197, BR 10, WB 20, ✄ GWJ 50
01/2 ASG History
94/5 APS 68
95/6 APS 384
96/7 APS 366
01/2 Atomic 98, AB 10, CP 20, PP 36, Stat 20, TN 15, ✄ GWJ 50
02/3 Atomic 99, -CF 24, ✄ GWJ 24
98/9 Aurora 154, -ALC 16, -CF 40, -FL 8, -MACF 16, -NC 10, -Cube 15
99/0 Aurora 116, Stripe 116, CC-10, CF-18, CP-10, ST-17
00/1 Aurora 116, Pins. 116, CC-9, CF-18, ✄ GWJ-14, TPS-9A
02/3 BAP All-Star 34-36, ✄ ASJ, ✄ HSHSJers, Bobble
98/9 Be A Player 261, H-5, P-7, ✍ Aut. 261, ✄ G-23, ✄ AS-18, ✄ S-17
99/0 BAP Mem. 147, SL-3, ✄ J-18, ✄ D-1, ✄ TM-8, ✄ TM-19, ✄ TM-32
00/1 BAP Mem. 1, ✄ J-9, ✄ PP-3, ✄ TM-3, ✄ TM-20
01/2 BAP Memor. 129, ✄ ASJ, ✄ ASE, ✄ ASN, ✄ ASD, ✄ AST, ✄ CoO, ✄ PP
02/3 BAP Memorabilia 34, 230, 237, ✄ ASJ22, ✄ ASE8, ✄ ASN8, ✄ ASTJ6, ✄ AS11, ✄ AST5, ✄ AST11, ✄ AST16, ✄ AST29, ✄ FP30, ✄ HSHSJers 4, ✄ TM11, /Cup
01/2 BAP Update ✄ TP16
02/3 Between the Pipes ✄ GN3
96/7 Bic.Sports Aces K-C
97/8 Bicycle 10-Club
95/6 Bicycle Sports Aces Q-Diamond
98 Bonaparte 2B, 3C, 5C, 6D
98 Bonaparte Pexeso 10, 18
92/3 Bowman 231
92/3 Bowman 302
95/6 Bowman 57, BB7
01/2 Bowman 4
02/3 Bowman 11
98/9 Bowman's Best 4, -F3, -SB 6, ✍ A2A, ✍ A2B
02/3 Calder 52, -HH 12, ✄ GWJ 25
99/0 Challenger 27
99/0 Crown Royale 112, IG-21, CS-18, C21-9, CCA-10, TC-7
00/1 Crown Royale 86
01/2 Crown Royale 142, CA 20, JotC 30, LH 10, ✄ TT 20
02/3 Crown Royale 99, -LOR 20, -RP 10, ✄ GWJ 25
93/4 Donruss 270
93/4 Donruss IK 3
94/5 Donruss 159, D-4
95/6 Donruss 142, D-2, E-10, M-5
96/7 Donruss 43, D-4, GTS-5
97/8 Donruss 188, ES-2, L2L-16
98/9 Donruss ES 17
96/7 Do. Canadian 1
97/8 Do. Canadian 8, SCS-9
95/6 Do. Elite 35, CE-6
96/7 Do. Elite 8, P-8
97/8 Do. Elite 11, 125, BF-4, C-25, PN-6, ✍ BF-4
97/8 Do. Preferred 125, 192, LT-1C, PM-10, / Tin 14,20, WideTin 7,11
97/8 Do. Priority 18, DD-4, OD-16, Post-4, Stamp-4
97/8 Do. Studio 5, HH-19, S-22, P-5
99/0 DS GC, NS3, P6
00/1 DS BBJ, JT12, ✍ BBJ
01/2 DS 36, -IH 2, -Gallery (x2)
98/9 Dynagon Ice 151, -AR 10, -FT 16, -PP 10, -TC 21
99/0 Dynagon Ice 159, ASP-16, CM-28, LL-10, LotR-10
93/4 EA Sports 107
97/8 Esso 52
01/2 eTopps 34
02/3 eTopps 5
02/3 Exclusive 172, -EIS 10, -MO 20
02/3 First Edition 131, 310, 370, 399, 404R, ✄ Jers., ✄ DGJ 12, ✄ HSHSJers 28, ✄ TSL 20
96/7 Flair 77, CIS-5
94/5 Fleer 163, SA-4
96/7 Fleer 86, 137, 138, 139, 141, 142, ART-8, PA-5
95/6 Fleer Metal 117, HM-6, IS-9
96/7 Fl. Picks F50-20,DL-6, FF-5
92/3 Fleer Ultra 164, -AS 6, -UI 6
93/4 Fleer Ultra 65
93/4 Fleer Ultra RLS 5
94/5 Fleer Ultra 164, GG-4
95/6 Fleer Ultra 123, 387, EA-9, RLS-4, UV-4
96/7 Fl. Ultra 141, CTI-4, MM-5
00 Gatorade Sticker
95 Globe 157
96/7 Got-Um
01/2 Heads Up 98, HD 10, RI 10, SM 20, ✄ JQ 17, / Bobble
02/3 Heads Up 124, -EIT 15, -ITN 24, -SM 15, ✄ GWQ 32
93/4 Hockey Wit 107
99/0 HoloGrFX 47, IZ2, PS9
95/6 Hoyle / East. 6-Spade
92/3 Humpty Dumpty
02/3 In The Game-Used 77, 177, ✄ E7, ✄ F30, ✄ IE20, ✄ GUJ7, ✄ SJ7, ✄ T18
92/3 Kraft / Kraft Singles
93/4 Kraft / KD
94/5 Kraft / HH
95/6 Kraft / KD, PB
96/7 Kraft / AS, TT
97/8 Kraft / JTP, KD
98/9 Kraft / KD
99/0 Kraft / KD (x2), / OML, / PB
00/1 Kraft 1
93/4 Leaf 346
94/5 Leaf 151, GLS-15
95/6 Leaf 71, FF-4, GLS-5, RTTC-3
96/7 Leaf 106, LL-5, TBO-1
97/8 Leaf 10, 177, BS-4, FOI-3
94/5 L. Limited 86, G-6
95/6 L. Limited 73,SG-8
96/7 L. Limited 11
96/7 L. Preferred 22, LS-LS-37, SP-8
97/8 Limited 8, 55, FG-14
96/7 Maggers 124
92/3 McDonald's McD-20
93/4 McDonald's McD-17
94/5 McDonald's McD-10
95/6 McDonald's McD-1
96/7 McDonald's McD-23
97/8 McDonald's McD-20
98/9 McDonald's McD11
99/0 McDonald's McD-6, ✄ GJ
00/1 McDonald's 27, DAS-5, GWJ-9
01/2 McDonald's 42, -CF 3, ✄ JPatch 20
02/3 McDonald's 42, -A6, ✄ JP 20
96/7 Metal Univ. 127, IC-6, LW-8
99/0 Millenium 194, P-1, D-5, ✍ Aut. 194, ✍ P-1, ✍ D-5, ✄ J-12, ✄ JS-12, ✄ JersSpecial
01/2 Nextel
95/6 Cool Trade 20
98/9 NHL Power Play
00/1 Nortel Networks All-Star 1
92/3 O-Pee-Chee 102
01/2 O-Pee-Chee 32, 320, 325, Update 32
02/3 O-Pee-Chee 5, 327
98/9 OPC Chrome 111, SB19
90/1 OPC Premier 50
98/9 OFS 247, 394, 469, -OW 3
99/0 OFS 23
00/1 OFS 384, 417
97/8 Omega 186, GF-16, S-10, SHLC-17
98/9 Omega 195, -CS 9, -EOP 18, -FTF 3, -Onl. 30, -PI 27, -Prism 18
99/0 Omega 188, 5ST-18, CC-17, EOP-16, G-10, WAS-6, ✄ GWJ 9
98/9 Pacific 68, -CCA 9, -DI 16, -GCDC 29, -TC 21, -Time. 16, -TW 3
99/0 Pacific 338, CI-7, CCA-9, GC-31, HAA-10, HAA-20, PAP-19, TL-22
00/1 Pacific 328, IO-18, CCA-9, ES-6, GCDC-28, PR-17, ✄ GWJ-13
01/2 Pacific 312, 439, CCA 8, GCDC 16, ✄ GWJ 27
02/3 Pacific 392, -L 14, -MA 20, ✄ GWJ 50
02/3 Pacific Complete 101
97/8 Pacific CC 68, CCA-10, GCDC-18, SS-8C, TC-20
97/8 Pa. Crown Roy. 110, BOS-17, CCA-9, HT-15, L-17
98/9 Pa. Crown Roy. 110, -CCA 10, -LL 10, -MP 17, -PotG 21
97/8 Pa. Dynagon 102, 142, DD-13A, KN-9, T-5, T-22, BKS-77
97/8 Pa. Invincible 113, AZ-20, FP-28, OTG-17, R-160, R-220
97/8 Pa. Paramount 150, P-17, BN-17
98/9 Pa. Paramount 192, -HOFB 9, -SD 16, -TC 21
99/0 Pa. Paramount 189, HOFB-9, , IAd-17, IAI-22, PB-31
00/1 Pa. Paramount 198, ES-17, FF-28, HOFB-10, SZ-8
97/8 Pa. Revolution 113, ASG-17, I-9, TC-20
98/9 Pa. Revolution 118, -ASG 12, -TPA 29, -CTLC 16, -NI 10, -Show. 31
98/9 Panini Photocard [x2]
92/3 Panini Sticker 282
92/3 Panini Sticker 294
92/3 Panini Sticker S
93/4 Panini Sticker 82
94/5 Panini Sticker 76, II
95/6 Panini Sticker 63, 150
96/7 Panini Sticker 58
97/8 Panini Sticker 47
98/9 Panini Sticker 4, 48
99/0 Panini Sticker 3, 131, 317
00/1 Panini Sticker 81
95 Panini Worlds 297
92/3 Parkhurst 135
92/3 Parkhurst 220
92/3 Parkhurst 465
93/4 Parkhurst 154
94/5 Parkhurst 174, 314
95/6 Parkhurst 165, 244, AS-2, CCP-1, IAS-5, PP-7, PP-14, TW-2
00/1 Parkhurst P-215
01/2 Parkhurst 34, ✄ PS58, ✄ HSHSJers, ✄ M3, ✄ M4, ✄ M8, ✄ M53, ✄ T27, ✄ WCJ7, ✄ WCE7, ✄ WCN7
02/3 Parkhurst 21, -HHH3, -HHP3, -HHR3, ✄ FP20, ✄ GJ4, ✄ SJ4, ✄ HSHSJers, ✄ MM3, ✄ MS5, ✄ PP3, ✄ TT17
95/6 Parkhurst 24-karat Gold
95 Parkhurst Phonecard
02/3 Parkhurst Retro 3, ✄ RF30, ✄ RJ14, ✄ RSJ27, ✄ HH8, ✄ HSHSJers, ✄ RM22, ✄ RR1
94/5 Parkie SE ES-20, seV42
92/3 Pinnacle 275
92/3 Pinnacle T2K 15
92/3 Pinnacle TP 6
93/4 Pinnacle 195
93/4 Pinnacle T2K1 12
93/4 Pinnacle TP 6
94/5 Pinnacle 98, GR5, TP11
95/6 Pinnacle 11, GG-2, CS-11, R20-13
96/7 Pinnacle 102, BTN-8, TP-6
97/8 Pinnacle 30, 193, TP-6, P-11
96/7 Pi. Be A Player BB-9
97/8 Pi. Be A Player OT 7, TN20
97/8 Pi. BeeHive 7, BHT-10
97/8 Pi. Certified 35, CT-14
97/8 Pi. Epix E20
97/8 Pi. Inside 6, IT-10, / Can 13
96/7 Pi. Mint 4
97/8 Pi. Mint 22
95/6 Pi. Summit 17, GMC-11, MH-10
96/7 Pi. Summit 85, HV-15
97/8 Pi. Totally 35
95/6 Pi. Zenith 3, ZT-11
96/7 Pi. Zenith 74, CS-6
95/6 Playoff 78, 185, 297
96/7 Playoff 433
94/5 POG 184
95/6 POG 2, 216, I-011
97/8 Pi. Post 21
93/4 Power Play 189
93/4 Power Play GG 3
93/4 Power Play PL 5
93/4 Premier 105
93/4 Premier 325
93/4 Prmr. - BG-OPC 19
94/5 Premier 460
00/1 Premier Plus 6, MB1, PT8, TT2, WP20
99/0 Prism 114, CA-18, DAS-10, SGDC-19
00/1 Private Stock 80, AC-18, EA-18, Res. 18, PS-47, PSS-22, ✄ GUG-89
01/2 Pr. Stock 98, Res. 20, -PS 75, ✄ GUG 100
02/3 Pr. Stock Reserve -RE 6, ✄ 149
00/1 PS Titanium 75, 3SS-17, ✄ GUG-133, ✄ GUG-152
01/2 PS Titanium 142, TSS 20, TAS 20, ✄ DSJ 43
01/2 PS Titanium Draft ✄ 100
02/3 PS Titanium 99, ✄ GWJ 74
00/1 PS Titanium Draft ✄ 82
95/6 Pro Magnet 93
90/1 Pro Set 632
92/3 Pro Set 141
02/3 Quest for the Cup 98, -RTC 12, ✄ GWJ 24
99/0 Revolution 118, IS-10, NI-17, O-16, TL-29, / CSC 118
00/1 Revolution 118, II-18, NI-17, SM-9, ✄ GUG-9
90/1 Score 428, 70T
92/3 Score 113
92/3 Score 494
93/4 Score 50
93/4 Score IS 9
93/4 Score PiAS 20
94/5 Score 135, NP9
95/6 Score 1, BB-14, DT-8, L-12
96/7 Score 29, DT-7, SD-9
97/8 Score 82, CI-13
97/8 Score Pitt. 4
99/0 Score JT1, JT27
92/3 Score Young Stars 4
92/3 Seasons 35
93/4 Seasons 7
94/5 Select 60
95/6 Select CE 38, GT-4
96/7 Select CE 43, C-3
94 Semic 183
94 Semic 351
95 Semic 158
91 Semic Sticker 225
94/5 SR Auto-Phonex JJ1-JJ5, ✍ JJ1-JJ5
95/6 SR Tetrad F8
00/1 Signature 22, HSHS, F-24, ✄ J-12, ✄ HSHSJers
01/2 Signature C-53, ✄ FP30, ✄ GUE43, ✄ GJ53, ✄ GSJ53, ✄ HSHSJers, ✄ ITN43, ✄ TM30
02/3 Signature ✄ CJ5, ✄ FJ30, ✄ SGJ7, ✄ TQ9
95/6 SBx Emotion 137, Xci-9
95/6 SBx Impact 131, CTI-2, IQ-1
96/7 SBx Impact 101, CTI-4, VT-5
94/5 SP 89, P-26
95/6 SP 114, E23, FX18
96/7 SP 126, SF-2, SF-5, ✍ Aut.
97/8 SP Authentic 125, I8
98/9 SP Authentic 70, SS5, SO7
99/0 SP Authentic 68, HR6, SF7, SS11
00/1 SP Authentic 70, ST6, SP7, SF7
01/2 SP Authentic 90, 110, ✄ PP
02/3 SP Authentic 88, ✄ SP, ✄ DP
00/1 SP GU 48, ✄ TotG, ✄ C, ✄ P (x2)
01/2 SP GU 58, ✄ AF, ✄ Patch, ✄ PatchC, ✄ TotG (x2), ✄ TotGC
02/3 SP GU 50, ✄ AF, ✄ CF (x2), ✄ PC, ✄ PH (x2), ✄ TG
02/3 Sports Vault 144
96/7 SPx 38
97/8 SPx 42, -DV, ✍ DVS
99/0 SPx 120, HH4, P2, X15, XT11, S2, ✄ WM
00/1 SPx 54, 90, HH12, P7, X10, S7, ✄ WM (x2)
01/2 SPx 68, ✄ DT
02/3 SPx 75, 100, 135, ✄ WM (x2), ✄ SS, ✄ X
98/9 SPx Finite 94, 165, 174
98/9 SPx Prospects 49, H25, L18, PS11, -WM
00/1 Stadion 57, 83, 146, 162
99/0 Stadium 1, CA26, EG1, OE1, -Chrome 1, -Big 1, ✍ CS4, ✍ CS5, ✍ CS6, ✍ LS1
00/1 Stadium 6, BT6, CA1, SF8
01/2 Stadium 74, 109, G16
02/3 Stadium 5, -WS10
93/4 SLU / Card-A
93/4 SLU / Card-B
93/4 Starting Lineup
94/5 Starting Lineup
97/8 SLU
98/9 SLU
99/0 SLU 161
00/1 SLU 16
00/1 SLU Classic Doubles 5
95/6 Super Sticker 96, DC-23
96/7 Team Out✄
92/3 Topps 24
95/6 Topps 200, 374, M8, 5PL, PF4, YS15
98/9 Topps 111, L4, M6, SB19, ✍ CAI
99/0 Topps 5, 280, AT13, IM4, AM1, FF2, SC11, TW17
00/1 Topps 1, TC10, HM5, OTG1, ✄ GWS
01/2 Topps 32, 320, 325, OTG1, SM5, Update 32, ✄ CC1, ✄ CC2
02/3 Topps 5, 327, OTG5
01/2 Topps All-Star Game 4
99/0 To. Chrome 5, 280, AT13, IM4, AM1, FF2
00/1 To. Chrome 1, TC10, HM5, RF4
01/2 To. Chrome 32
02/3 T. Chrome 5
94/5 Topps Finest 33, BBB-20, RL-15
95/6 To. Finest 70, 185
98/9 To. Finest 74, C13, M1-4, R1, -Big 6
94 Topps Finest Bronze 1
98/9 T. Gold Label 5, GR5
99/0 To. Gold Label 15, PG4
00/1 To. Gold Label 14, GG3
00/1 To. Heritage 3, 221, 235, 245, HH2
01/2 To. Heritage 113, 123, 137, 160
02/3 To. Heritage 6, -Light 6
02/3 T. Limited 5, 327
98/9 Topps Pearson Award
96/7 Topps Picks 1, FT14, TS6
99/0 To. Prmr. Plus 34, CR6, FP7, PT2, ✍ CS
01/2 To. Reserve 74
92/3 T. Stadium Club 498
93/4 To. Stadium 98
93/4 To. Stadium - All-Stars
94/5 T. Stadium Club 68
95/6 To. Stadium 70, GT3
93/4 TSC Members Only 44
94/5 TSC Members Only 5
95/6 TSC Members Only 25
00/1 To. Stars 21, 132, AS5, WF3
95/6 T. Super Skills 20
02/3 T. Total 101, TTC30, TP15, TT20
98/9 UD Choice 168, 226, BH5, SQ16
00/1 UD Heroes 155, L9, SS10, TM9, TS5, ✄ GT, ✄ GC
01/2 UD PlayMakers Ltd 100, / PM
00/1 UD Reserve 68, PP6, BT9, PSJ
02/3 UD Superstars 249, ✄ LLT
98/9 UD3 32, 92, 152
00/1 Ultimate Mem. ✄ A8-4, ✄D-8, ✄H-2, ✄J-12, ✄Jers. 10, ✄MO-2, ✄RA-9, ✄S-12, ✄TM-39, ✄UC-5
01/2 Ultimate Mem. ✄ A8, ✄ ASGH, ✄ DD, ✄ Emb., ✄ Jers., ✄ S&J, ✄ ITN, ✄ JE, ✄ JJ, ✄ NP, ✄ PP, ✄ RT, ✄ RA, ✄ UC, ✄ WTF
02/3 Ultimate Mem. ✄ 500GSE, ✄ 500GSJ, ✄ 500GSJS, ✄ DD, ✄ Emb, ✄ FS, ✄ GUJ, ✄ GUSJ, ✄ ITN, ✄ JE, ✄ JGJ, ✄ LA, ✄ MO, ✄ NP, ✄ SL (x5), ✄ RAT, ✄ RT
99/0 Ult. Victory 69, FF8, sg1, S11, TV4, UV1
90/1 Upper Deck 356
92/3 Upper Deck 16
92/3 Upper Deck 28
92/3 Upper Deck 622
92/3 Upper Deck W3
92/3 Upper Deck E14
92/3 Upper Deck WG6
93/4 Upper Deck 139, FH33, R8, SP-121
94/5 Upper Deck 93, 544, C24, H24, R18, R29, R39, SP-60
95/6 Upper Deck 465, AS-3, F-4, H-2, R3, R-22, R-38, R-46, SE-153
96/7 Upper Deck 320, X17, HH18, LS4, SS13B, ✄ GJ
97/8 Upper Deck 342, SS2, SG38, S3, T5B
98/9 Upper Deck 27, 161, FF4, FT29, GN22-24, LS3, P10, ✄ GJ15
99/0 Upper Deck 104, 138, AS3, CT9, FF4, HOF5, IG1, MA4, N1, SB4, SS9, PD3, ✄ GJ

00/1 Upper Deck 138, A9, D9, FF9, FT7, F8, GA10, L9, NC7, P8, SS17, TT9, ✂ GJ, ✂ DGJ
01/2 Upper Deck 178, 226, 404, CT14, SS19, ✂ ASJ, ✂ CJers, ✂ PatchL, ✂ PF, ✂ PoaN, ✂ PoaND, ✂ PoaNT
02/3 Upper Deck 193, 419, -GG14, -SS14, ✂ DM, ✂ FF, ✂ PL, ✂ PP, ✂ R50, ✂ FC, ✂ PW, ✂ UDPL
95/6 UD ASG MVP17
96/7 UD All-Star YCTG AR16
02/3 UD Artistic 88, R88, CG2, UD9, ✂ AT, ✂ SS, / ✍ Art
94/5 UD BAP R63
95/6 UD BAP LL12
96/7 UD Black Diam. 75, RC5
97/8 UD Black Diam. 72, PC20
98/9 UD Black Diam. 69, M18, WF25
99/0 UD Black Diam. 68, D14, DM5, DS7, M8, ✂ APOH
00/1 UD Black Diam. 47, 90, IG7, FP9, IC6, CC5, S-JA
99/0 UD C. Legends 37, 52, E3
01/2 UD Challenge 88, CM7, CR10
02/3 UD Classic 98, GG7, ✂ HH, ✂ HR (x2)
95/6 UD CC 127, 378, 389, C7
96/7 UD CC 211, 294, 328, UD43, S8, C6, CR6
96/7 UD Black Diam. 75, RC5
97/8 UD Black Diam. 72, PC20
98/9 UD Black Diam. 69, M18, WF25
99/0 UD Black Diam. 68, D14, DM5, DS7, M8, ✂ APOH
00/1 UD Black Diam. 47, 90, IG7, FP9, IC6, CC5, S-JA
99/0 UD C. Legends 37, 52, E3
01/2 UD Challenge 88, CM7, CR10
02/3 UD Classic 98, GG7, ✂ HH, ✂ HR (x2)
95/6 UD CC 127, 378, 389, C7
96/7 UD CC 211, 294, 328, UD43, S8, C6, CR6
97/8 UD Coll. Choice 205, 314, SQ89, S15, C28, CR28
01/2 UD Collectors
97/8 UD Diam. Vision 3, DM4
98/9 UD G. Reserve 27, 161
99/0 UD G. Reserve 104, 138
99/0 UD Gretzky Excl. 66, 73
01/2 UD Honor Roll 9, 39, 100
02/3 UD Honor 70, -SG30, ✂ GA (x2)
96/7 UD Ice 101, S7
97/8 UD Ice 68, IC18, L2C
00/1 UD Ice 32, CC5, IC6, IG7, FP9, ✂ IGJ
01/2 UD Ice 42, ✂ JC, ✂ FJ
00/1 UD Legends 107, 108, EG2, PH3, ✂ LGJ
92/3 UD Locker 3
01/2 UD Mask 100, ✂ GJ, ✂ JP, ✂ DP
02/3 UD Mask 87, ✂ IO, ✂ PG
98/9 UD MVP 163, OT3, PG10, F11
99/0 UD MVP 165, 21-6, S2, H9, MVP8, W14, GU12
00/1 UD MVP 143, M14, TD10, TP9, VC9, ✂ GS
01/2 UD MVP 188, MW3, -J, ✂ S
02/3 UD MVP 184, VF14, SD, ST, Souv.
99/0 UD MVP Cup 146, CP9, GM9, PH9, SS10, SC14, ✂ GU
99/0 UD Ovation 46, 81, LP8, ST7, APOH
00/1 UD Pearson
02/3 UD Piece 90, 102, AC27
99/0 UD PowerDeck 17, T1
01/2 UD Premier 50, ✂ B (x2), ✂ D (x2)
02/3 UD Premier 54, ✂ Jers, ✂ JD, ✂ Patch, ✂ NHLP
00/1 UD Pros&Prosp. 68, CR8, GS8, NP7, PM9, ✂ GJ
99/0 UD Retro 64, DR3, TC3
02/3 UD Rookie 98, 109, ✂ 158a, ✂ 159c, ✂ DJ, ✂ S
01/2 UD SCup Champs 85, ✂ S, ✂ G, ✂ T
01/2 UD Top Shelf 45, ✂ P, ✂ J, ✂ ST
02/3 UD Top Shelf 88, ✂ AS, ✂ CP, ✂ GO, ✂ HH (x2), ✂ HT, ✂ SH, ✂ ST (x2), ✂ SW, ✂ TS
00/1 UD Vintage 286, 295-96, UD9, NH19, ✂ D-POH
01/2 UD Vintage 256, 261, 262, 263
02/3 UD Vintage 258, 290, T64, ✂ FS, ✂ SO
00/1 Vanguard 80, CF-9, HV-29, IF-15, VP-18
01/2 Vanguard 99, EMW 1, IF 10, VT 20, ✂ DGM 33, ✂ DGM 42
02/3 Vanguard 99, -IF 10, -VT 12, ✂ GWJ 50
99/0 Victory 234-35, 315, 328, 331, 336
00/1 Victory 183, 184, 256, 318
01/2 Victory 278, 392
02/3 Victory 213, -NP21
01/2 Waving the Flag 9
99/0 WGretzky 136, CG4, EG11, GH1, W3
96 Wien 125
97/8 Zenith 31, CTC-3, Z8
90/1 PITT / Foodland 11
91/2 PITT / Elby's
91/2 PITT / Foodland 11
91/2 PITT / Food. Stickers
92/3 PITT / Coke-Clark
92/3 PITT / Foodland 3
92/3 PITT / Food. Stickers
93/4 PITT / Foodland 23
94/5 PITT / Foodland 23
95/6 PITT / Foodland 5
96/7 PITT / Tribune
91/2 Bowman 95
91/2 Gillette 34
91/2 Kraft 3
91/2 O-Pee-Chee 9
91/2 O-Pee-Chee 40
91/2 OPC Premier 24
91/2 Panini Sticker 275
91/2 Panini Sticker 344
91/2 Parkhurst 132
91/2 Pinnacle 53
91/2 Pro Set 183
91/2 Pro Set Platinum 92
91/2 Score 98
91/2 Score 351
91/2 Score - Hot Card 8
91/2 Score CAN 98
91/2 Score CAN 381
91/2 Score Young Stars 38
92 Semic Sticker 135
91/2 Star Pics 70
91/2 To. Stadium 343
91/2 Upper Deck 20
91/2 Upper Deck 42
91/2 Upper Deck 256
91/2 Upper Deck 617
91/2 Upper Deck E6

JAHMA, TAISTO
66/7 Champion 95

JAKES, JIRI
01 UD Prospects GU 17, ✂ TPJ

JAKES, TOMAS
95/6 APS 26
96/7 APS 221
97/8 APS 298
99/0 DS 186
00/1 DS 99
96/7 DS Sticker 20
97/8 DS Sticker 113
98/9 OFS 341
99/0 OFS 465, 516
00/1 OFS 190
01/2 OFS 106

JAKOBSEN,
92/3 Semic Nordisk 183 [Supporterprisen]

JAKOBSEN, TOMMY
96/7 DEL 11
98/9 DEL 288
99/0 Eishockey 166
95 Globe 194
95/6 Leaf Elit Set 193
94 Semic 256
95 Semic 179
92/3 Semic Nordisk 105
92 Semic Sticker 33
93 Semic Sticker 233
00/1 UD DEL 29
01/2 UD DEL 8
95/6 UD Elitserien 38
96 Wien 203

JAKOBSSON, PETER
01/2 UD DEL 96
97/8 UD Elitserien 51
98/9 UD Elitserien 88
99/0 UD Elitserien 155
00/1 UD Elitserien 137

JAKONEN, MATTI
70/1 Kuvajulkaisut 139
71/2 Williams Finnish 188

JAKOPIN, JOHN
99/0 BAP Mem. 60
99/0 Omega 105
01/2 Signature 16, ✍ Aut.
99/0 Louisville Panthers
98/9 New Haven Beast 16

JAKOVENKO, ANDREI
95/6 APS 131
96/7 APS 9
97/8 APS 152
98/9 DS 71
98/9 OFS 252
99/0 OFS 239
92/3 Rochester Americans DD
92/3 San Diego Gulls

JAKOVENKO, ANDREJ
97/8 DS Sticker 190

JAKS, PAULI
94/5 Classic 4 Sport 155
93/4 Cla. Prospects 80
91/2 Upper Deck 663
94/5 Upper Deck 387
91/2 Upper Deck WJC 24
93/4 Phoenix Roadrunners
94/5 Phoenix Roadrunners

JAKS, PETER
91 Semic Sticker 197
92 Semic Sticker 206

JALAVA, HARRI
95/6 Sisu 395

JALAVA, PEKKA
66/7 Champion 33

JALAVA, TUOMAS
95/6 Sisu 348

JALBERT, CRAIG
95/6 Slapshot 198

JALBERT, DEAN
86/7 Sudbury Wolves

JALO, RISTO
91/2 Jyvas Hyva 14
93/4 Jyvas Hyva 88
80/1 Mallasjuoma 31
93/4 Sisu 121
94/5 Sisu 213
95/6 Sisu 24, 170, S-6
96/7 Sisu 19
95/6 Sisu Limited 90
88/9 EDMO / Action 39

JALONEN, ARI
71/2 Williams Finnish 302

JALONEN, HANNU
80/1 Mallasjuoma 91
78/9 SM-Liiga 140

JALONEN, JUKKA
93/4 Jyvas Hyva 73
00/1 Kudos 108
93/4 Sisu 108

JALONEN, KARI
70/1 Kuvajulkaisut 367
80/1 Mallasjuoma 98
82 Semic Sticker 37
89 Semic Sticker 42
93/4 Sisu 386
78/9 SM-Liiga 152
71/2 Williams Finnish 303
82/3 CALG
88/9 EDMO / Action 148

JAMALAINEN, JARMO
72/3 Williams Finnish 326

JAMES, ANGELA
94/5 Classic W6
97/8 Game of Her Life
97/8 UD Coll. Choice 276

JAMES, BRAD
90/1 ProCards 137

JAMES, DAVID
83/4 Kingston Canadians

JAMES, GERRY
45-64 BeeHive-2 [Toro.]
57/8 Parkhurst [Toro.] 8
60/1 Parkhurst 7
93/4 Parkie 56-57 117
60/1 Shirriff 17

JAMES, GRAHAM
90/1 7th..Sketch WHL 66

JAMES, MIKE
92/3 Richmond Renegades
81/2 Ottawa 67's
82/3 Ottawa 67's
83/4 Ottawa 67's
99/0 Ottawa 67's

JAMIESON, DUSTY
99 Bowman 22, ✍ BA19
95 Québec Pee Wee 607
99/0 Topps 254
99/0 To. Chrome 254

JÄMSÄNEN, MIKAEL
99/0 Cardset 216
00/1 Cardset 248

JÄMSEN, LASSE
98/9 Cardset 140
99/0 Cardset 78
00/1 Cardset 316
02/3 Cardset 185
97/8 Hockey-Box
96/7 Sisu 64

JÄMSEN, LAURI
70/1 Kuvajulkaisut 156
71/2 Williams Finnish 227
72/3 Williams Finnish 210
73/4 Williams Finnish 282

JAN, IVO
99/0 Eishockey 309

JAN, MILAN
79 Panini Sticker 400

JANACEK, LUBOS
94/5 APS 244

JANASAK, STEVE
94/5 SR Miracle 15,16, ✍ 15,16

JANCARIK, PETR
94/5 APS 29
95/6 APS 318
96/7 APS 52
97/8 APS 319
99/0 DS 76
00/1 DS 89
96/7 DS Sticker 230
97/8 DS Sticker 272
98/9 OFS 151, 455
99/0 OFS 91
00/1 OFS 36
01/2 OFS 51

JANCEVSKI, DAN
01/2 Utah Grizzlies

JANCEVSKI, DANIEL
00/1 London Knights
00/1 London Knights

JANCINA, GREG
00/1 Owen Sound Attack 5

JANECEK, MARTIN
94/5 APS 22

JANECKY, OTAKAR
98/9 Cardset 116
99/0 Cardset 168, 217
02/3 Cardset 29
00/1 DS 90
97/8 Hockey-Box
92/3 Jyvas Hyva 57
93/4 Jyvas Hyva 108
00/1 OFS 42, -Star 12
01/2 OFS 245, -RE12D, -UHI 33
94 Panini Olympics 321
95 Panini Worlds 205
94 Semic 188
89 Semic Sticker 191
93/4 Sisu 26
93/4 Sisu 364
93/4 Sisu 315
94/5 Sisu 91, 373, FOI-13
95/6 Sisu 53, 171, 371, S-1
96/7 Sisu 185, MA-7
95/6 Sisu Limited 14

JANECYK, BOB
85/6 O-Pee-Chee 223
86/7 OPC/Topps 131
85/6 OPC Sticker 239-107
86/7 OPC Sticker 61
86/7 OPC Sticker 91-222
84/5 LOSA / Smokey 9
87/8 LOSA

JANELLE, DAN
51/2 Bas du Fleuve 42
52/3 Bas du Fleuve 9

JANELLEM, ROLAND
92 7th...Sketch Awards 29

JANES, BRANDON
99/0 UD Prospects 83
99/0 Lethbridge Hurricanes

JANICKI, TREVOR
93/4 N. Michigan Wildcats

JANIGA, MICHAL
99/0 Score 118

JANIK, DOUG
02/3 BAP Memorabilia 367
02/3 UD Rookie 148
02/3 Rochester Americans

JANIKOWSKI, JANUSZ
94/5 DEL 413
95/6 DEL 419

JANISZEWSKI, HENRYK
79 Panini Sticker 120

JANKA, MARKUS
00/1 UD DEL 240
01/2 UD DEL 232

JANKOVYCH, VITEZSLAV
99/0 Score 83

JANKOWSKI, LOU
45-64 BeeHive-2 [Chic.]
54/5 Parkhurst 79
54/5 Topps 28

JANKU, PAVEL
94/5 APS 193
95/6 APS 40, 380, 387
96/7 APS 43, 419
97/8 APS 64
97/8 DS 106
98/9 DS 28
99/0 DS 22
00/1 DS 72
96/7 DS Sticker 101
97/8 DS Sticker 295
98/9 OFS 89, 465
99/0 OFS 134, 412
00/1 OFS 227
01/2 OFS 54, -RE22D
96 Wien 118

JANNEY, CRAIG
95/6 Bicycle Sports Aces 2-Heart
90/1 Bowman 33
91/2 Bowman 355
92/3 Bowman 14
95/6 Bowman 3
98/9 Bowman's Best 94
93/4 Donruss 295
94/5 Donruss 28
95/6 Donruss 137
96/7 Donruss 154
97/8 Donruss 46
95/6 Do. Elite 33
96/7 Do. Elite 104
97/8 Do. Priority 154
93/4 EA Sports 123
94/5 Flair 154
95/6 Fleer Metal 131
96/7 Fl. Picks 60
92/3 Fleer Ultra 187
93/4 Fleer Ultra 134
94/5 Fleer Ultra 363
95/6 Fleer Ultra 147
96/7 Fl. Ultra 131
95 Globe 118
93/4 Hockey Wit 4
91/2 Kraft 31
94/5 Kraft / SS
93/4 Leaf 181
94/5 Leaf 52
95/6 Leaf 98
96/7 Leaf 36
94/5 L. Limited 91
95/6 L. Limited 13
96/7 L. Limited 51
96/7 L. Preferred 35
97/8 Limited 67
96/7 Metal Univ. 117
90/1 OPC/Topps 212
91/2 O-Pee-Chee 41
92/3 O-Pee-Chee 325
89/0 OPC/Topps 190
91/2 OPC Premier 93
88/9 OPC Sticker 90
89/0 opcSticker 29-167, 38-180, / FS 2
98/9 Pacific 340
97/8 Pacific CC 148
97/8 Pa. Revolution 106
89/0 Panini Sticker 198
90/1 Panini Sticker 14
91/2 Panini Sticker 170
92/3 Panini Sticker 22
93/4 Panini Sticker 157
94/5 Panini Sticker 136
95/6 Panini Sticker 277
96/7 Panini Sticker 198
97/8 Panini Sticker 161
98/9 Panini Sticker 145
95 Panini Worlds 228
91/2 Parkhurst 4
91/2 Parkhurst 378
92/3 Parkhurst 154
93/4 Parkhurst 443
94/5 Parkhurst 200
95/6 Parkhurst 455
91/2 Pinnacle 57
92/3 Pinnacle 196
93/4 Pinnacle 130
94/5 Pinnacle 84
95/6 Pinnacle 37
96/7 Pinnacle 48
95/6 Pi. Summit 49
96/7 Pi. Summit 64
96/7 Pi. Zenith 49
95/6 Playoff 192
96/7 Playoff 384
94/5 POG 204
95/6 POG 226
93/4 Power Play 212
93/4 Premier 120
94/5 Premier 60
95/6 Pro Magnet 119
90/1 Pro Set 8
91/2 Pro Set 2
92/3 Pro Set 157
91/2 Pro Set Platinum 3
90/1 Score 118
90/1 Sco. Hot Cards 58
91/2 Score 253
91/2 Score CAN 473
92/3 Score 285
92/3 Score USAG 11
93/4 Score 186
93/4 Score DD4
94/5 Score 127
95/6 Score 15
96/7 Score 57
97/8 Score 154
90/1 Sco. Young Stars 30
94/5 Select 139
95/6 Select CE 33
96/7 Select CE 60
94 Semic 119
95 Semic 107
89 Semic Sticker 173
91 Semic Sticker 143
92 Semic Sticker 160
93 Semic Sticker 186
95/6 SBx Emotion 157
95/6 SBx Impact 149
94/5 SP 109
97/8 SP Authentic 123
98/9 SP Authentic 80
95/6 Super Sticker 105, 106
92/3 Topps 134
95/6 Topps 95
95/6 To. Finest 4
91/2 To. Stadium 147
92/3 T. Stadium Club 41
93/4 To. Stadium 335
93/4 To. Stadium - Master Photo-2 10
95/6 To. Stadium EC179
95/6 T. Super Skills 13
98/9 UD Choice 156
90/1 Upper Deck 234
91/2 Upper Deck 128
91/2 Upper Deck 512
92/3 Upper Deck 125
93/4 Upper Deck 225, 303, 323, SP-138
94/5 Upper Deck 18, R16, SP-67
95/6 Upper Deck 315, SE-73
96/7 Upper Deck 127
97/8 Upper Deck 334
98/9 Upper Deck 366
94/5 UD BAP R52
95/6 UD BAP 47, ✍ S47
96/7 UD Black Diam. 45
98/9 UD Black Diam. 81
95/6 UD CC 264
96/7 UD CC 207
97/8 UD Coll. Choice 201
98/9 UD G. Reserve 366
96 Wien 170
88/9 BOST / Sports Action
88/9 BOST / Sports Action
89/0 BOST / Sports Action
90/1 BOST / Sports Action
96/7 PHOE / Coca-Cola
97/8 PHOE / Coca-Cola

JANOS, BRANISLAV
97/8 APS 72
97/8 DS 109
98/9 DS 124
99/0 DS 112
97/8 DS Sticker 300
98/9 OFS 391
99/0 OFS 195
00/1 OFS 229
01/2 OFS 55

JANOSTIN, PAT
85/6 Minnesota-Duluth 30

JANOSZ, BOB
99/0 Muskegon Fury

JANOV, MARTEM
94/5 DEL 363

JANSEN, ALEXANDER
98/9 DEL 305

JANSEN, ARVE
92/3 Semic Nordisk 238

JANSEN, LASSE
95/6 Sisu 268

JANSSEN, JAN
79 Panini Sticker 281

JANSSEN, LARS
99/0 Eishockey 219

JANSSENS, MARK
90/1 Bowman 226
91/2 Bowman 67
94/5 Leaf 361
90/1 OPC/Topps 391
91/2 O-Pee-Chee 186
92/3 OPC Premier 117
97/8 Pa. Invincible R-2
90/1 Panini Sticker 101
93/4 Panini Sticker 127
93/4 Parkhurst 355
94/5 Parkie SE70
96/7 Pi. Be A Player 199, ✍ Aut. 199
93/4 Premier 133
90/1 Pro Set 199
91/2 Pro Set 158
90/1 Score 33T
91/2 Score CAN 421
93/4 Score 339
99/0 Topps 55
99/0 To. Chrome 55
91/2 To. Stadium 113
93/4 To. Stadium 180
94/5 T. Stadium Club 212
90/1 Upper Deck 298
91/2 Upper Deck 228
93/4 Upper Deck 198
94/5 Upper Deck 35
95/6 Upper Deck 312
97/8 Upper Deck 5
99/0 UD Retro 16
92/3 HART / Dairymart
93/4 HART / Coke
95/6 HART / Kids Club
96/7 HART / Kids Club
89/0 NYRA / Marine
86/7 Regina Pats
87/8 Regina Pats

JANSSON, CONNY
89/0 Semic Elitserien 234
90/1 Semic Elitserien 60
91/2 Semic Elitserien 239

JANSSON, LARS
94/5 Leaf Elit Set 20
95/6 Leaf Elit Set 100
89/0 Semic Elitserien 174
90/1 Semic Elitserien 7
91/2 Semic Elitserien 205
92/3 Semic Elitserien 228
95/6 UD Elitserien 154
98/9 UD Elitserien 171
00/1 UD Elitserien 154

JANSSON, MAGNUS
95/6 Leaf Elit Set 185
90/1 Semic Elitserien 292
91/2 Semic Elitserien 70
95/6 UD Elitserien 47

JANSSON, MARTIN
99/0 UD Elitserien 111

JANSSON, MATTI
66/7 Champion 43
65/6 Hellas 43
70/1 Kuvajulkaisut 192

JANSSON, STEFAN
89/0 Semic Elitserien 11

JANTOVSKY, JIRI
95/6 APS 332
96/7 APS 159
97/8 APS 256
98/9 DS 54
99/0 DS 84
96/7 DS Sticker 258
97/8 DS Sticker 141
98/9 OFS 154
99/0 OFS 351, 389
00/1 OFS 342

JANTTI, JYRKI
71/2 Williams Finnish 365

JANTTI, KIMMO
71/2 Williams Finnish 366

JANTUNEN, MARKO
98/9 Cardset Leij. 23
91/2 Jyvas Hyva 50
92/3 Jyvas Hyva 100
93/4 Jyvas Hyva 324
94/5 Leaf Elit Set 214, FA-3
95/6 Leaf Elit Set 147, FTF-4, LM-3
95 Panini Worlds 173
94 Semic 32
93/4 Sisu 54
94/5 Sisu 154, 176, 364, 386, FOI-5
95/6 Sisu Limited 69
95/6 UD Elitserien 211
97/8 UD Elitserien 76, UDS4
98/9 UD Elitserien 75
99/0 UD Elitserien 67, ✍ Aut.
00/1 UD Elitserien 83
96/7 Saint John Flames

JAQUES, STEVE
90/1 ProCards 358
91/2 ProCards 385
95/6 Houston Aeros
93/4 Las Vegas Thunder

JARDEMYRE, DANIEL
90/1 Semic Elitserien 84
91/2 Semic Elitserien 9
92/3 Semic Elitserien 34

JARDINE, RYAN
01/2 BAP Memor. 402
99/0 SP Authentic 131
99/0 Upper Deck 310
99/0 UD Black Diam. 107
99/0 UD G. Reserve 310
99/0 UD MVP Cup 198
01/2 Utah Grizzlies

JARINA, KAMIL
99/0 Score 26

JARKKO, ERKKI
66/7 Champion 158

JARKKO, MARTTI
80/1 Mallasjuoma 189
79 Panini Sticker 171
78/9 SM-Liiga 15
78/9 SM-Liiga 193
72/3 Williams Finnish 261
73/4 Williams Finnish 152

JÄRN, HEIKKI
65/6 Hellas 136
70/1 Kuvajulkaisut 107
72 Panda MM-Toronto
72 Semic Sticker 77
71/2 Williams Finnish 62
71/2 Williams Finnish 115
72/3 Williams Finnish 103

JAROS, MIKE
99/0 Charlotte Checkers

JAROS, PETR
99/0 Score 51

JAROSLAV, WALTER
94/5 DEL 32

JARRAM, JOHN
00/1 Mississauga IceDogs

JARRETT, BLAIR
02/3 Mississauga IceDogs

JARRETT, COLE
00/1 UD Prospects 37
02/3 Plymouth Whalers
02/3 Plymouth Whalers

JARRETT, DOUG
64-67 BeeHive-3 [Chic.]
65/6 Coca-Cola
70/1 Dad's Cookies
70/1 Eddie Sargent 34
71/2 Eddie Sargent 41
72/3 Eddie Sargent 58
70/1 Esso Power Player
74/5 Loblaws
68/9 O-Pee-Chee 13
69/0 O-Pee-Chee 67
69/0 O-Pee-Chee 4in1
70/1 O-Pee-Chee 150
71/2 O-Pee-Chee 208
72/3 O-Pee-Chee 97
73/4 O-Pee-Chee 187
74/5 O-Pee-Chee 351
75/6 O-Pee-Chee 333
95/6 Parkie 66-67 27
94/5 Parkie Tall 38
68/9 Shirriff / Chic. 10
66/7 Topps 111
67/8 Topps 112
68/9 Topps 13
69/0 Topps 67
73/4 Topps 76
71/2 Toronto Sun Photo
68/9 CHIC
70/1 CHIC

JARRETT, GARY
70/1 Colgate 49
70/1 Dad's Cookies
70/1 Eddie Sargent 140
71/2 Eddie Sargent 138
70/1 Esso Power Player
68/9 O-Pee-Chee 87
69/0 O-Pee-Chee 85
70/1 O-Pee-Chee 75
71/2 O-Pee-Chee 93
74/5 OPC WHA 61
75/6 OPC WHA 87
73/4 Quaker Oats 27
68/9 Shirriff / Oakl. 11
67/8 Topps 44
68/9 Topps 87
69/0 Topps 85
70/1 Topps 75
71/2 Topps 93
71/2 Toronto Sun Photo
72/3 Cleveland Crusaders
72/3 Clev. WHA / Linnett

JARRETT, PATRICK
00/1 UD Prospects 13
00/1 Mississauga IceDogs
02/3 Owen Sound Attack

JARRY, PIERRE
72/3 Eddie Sargent 208
74/5 Loblaws
72/3 O-Pee-Chee 237
73/4 O-Pee-Chee 186
74/5 O-Pee-Chee 171
75/6 O-Pee-Chee 359
75/6 O-Pee-Chee 359
76/7 O-Pee-Chee 49
77/8 O-Pee-Chee 106
74/5 Topps 171
76/7 Topps 49
77/8 Topps 106

JARVELA, PEKKA
91/2 Jyvas Hyva 20
92/3 Jyvas Hyva 62
89/0 Semic Elitserien 203

JÄRVENPÄÄ, HANNU
92/3 Jyvas Hyva 66
89/0 O-Pee-Chee 292
89/0 opcSticker 145
91/2 Semic Elitserien 150
91 Semic Sticker 23
93/4 Sisu 273
94/5 Sisu 23, H-17
95/6 Sisu 181
86/7 WINN
87/8 WINN
88/9 WINN / Safety Tips

JÄRVENPÄÄ, JUHA
98/9 Cardset 96
97/8 Hockey-Box
92/3 Jyvas Hyva 41
93/4 Jyvas Hyva 77
93/4 Sisu 122
94/5 Sisu 87, 251
95/6 Sisu 25, 245
96/7 Sisu 39
95/6 Sisu Limited 107

JÄRVENPÄÄ, JUKKA-PEKKA
78/9 SM-Liiga 100
71/2 Williams Finnish 208
72/3 Williams Finnish 157
73/4 Williams Finnish 218

JÄRVENPÄÄ, PERTTI
80/1 Mallasjuoma 41
78/9 SM-Liiga 106
72/3 Williams Finnish 283
73/4 Williams Finnish 219

JÄRVENPÄÄ, TORSTI
72/3 Williams Finnish 262

JÄRVENTIE, MARTTI
98/9 Cardset 84
99/0 Cardset 47
00/1 Cardset 217
02/3 Cardset 31
01/2 Parkhurst 294
94/5 Sisu 235
95/6 Sisu 32
96/7 Sisu 98
01/2 SP Authentic 155
01/2 SPx Rookie RR16
94/5 Topps Finest 130
01/2 UD Challenge 114
01/2 UD Ice 58
01/2 Québec Citadelles

JÄRVI, IIRO
99/0 Cardset AH 6-risti
96/7 DEL 60
92/3 Jyvas Hyva 17
93/4 Jyvas Hyva 19
90/1 OPC/Topps 52
89/0 O-Pee-Chee 264
89/0 opcSticker 192, / FS 15
89/0 Panini Sticker 329
90/1 ProCards 451
92 Semic Sticker 13
93/4 Sisu 106
94/5 Sisu 31, 379
95/6 Sisu 213, S-4
96/7 Sisu SH 8
95/6 Sisu Limited 45
88/9 QUÉB
88/9 QUÉB / Gene. Foods
89/0 QUÉB
89/0 QUÉB / Gene. Foods
89/0 QUÉB / Police
90/1 QUÉB

JÄRVINEN, ERKKI
66/7 Champion 192
73/4 Williams Finnish 179

JÄRVINEN, JARI
92/3 Jyvas Hyva 88
93/4 Jyvas Hyva 171
80/1 Mallasjuoma 26
93/4 Sisu 164
93/4 Sisu 348
78/9 SM-Liiga 52
71/2 Williams Finnish 345
72/3 Williams Finnish 329

JÄRVINEN, JOUKO
66/7 Champion 122

JÄRVINEN, JUSSI-PEKKA
92/3 Jyvas Hyva 163

JÄRVINEN, KARI
80/1 Mallasjuoma 34
78/9 SM-Liiga 57
72/3 Williams Finnish 306
72/3 Williams Finnish 346

JÄRVINEN, KEIJO
70/1 Kuvajulkaisut 141
71/2 Williams Finnish 130
72/3 Williams Finnish 193
73/4 Williams Finnish 153

JÄRVINEN, PAULI
92/3 Jyvas Hyva 160
93/4 Jyvas Hyva 289
94 Semic 50
90/1 Semic Elitserien 237
91/2 Semic Elitserien 164
89 Semic Sticker 46
91 Semic Sticker 14
93 Semic Sticker 64
93/4 Sisu 73
94/5 Sisu 75, FOI-20
95/6 Sisu 318
95/6 Sisu Limited 78

JÄRVINEN, RAUNO
72/3 Williams Finnish 284

JÄRVINEN, TIMO
99/0 Cardset 313
70/1 Kuvajulkaisut 242
93/4 Sisu 209
71/2 Williams Finnish 209

JARVIS, DOUG
80/1 Dernière Heure
82/3 Dernière Heure
76/7 O-Pee-Chee 217
76/7 O-Pee-Chee 313
77/8 O-Pee-Chee 139
78/9 O-Pee-Chee 13
79/0 O-Pee-Chee 112
80/1 O-Pee-Chee 76
81/2 O-Pee-Chee 184
82/3 O-Pee-Chee 367
83/4 O-Pee-Chee 372
84/5 O-Pee-Chee 200
85/6 OPC/Topps 151
86/7 OPC/Topps 28
87/8 OPC/Topps 95
87/8 OPC Leaders 19
81/2 OPC Sticker 34
82/3 OPC/Topps Sticker 40
83/4 OPC/Topps Sticker 208
84/5 OPC Sticker 129
84/5 OPC Sticker 234-235
85/6 OPC Sticker 109-242
87/8 OPC Sticker 183-42
87/8 OPC Sticker 207-74
87/8 Panini Sticker 52
87/8 Panini Sticker 387
80/1 Pepsi Bottle Cap
82/3 Post [Mont.]
83/4 Souhaits Keychain [Capitals]
76/7 Topps 217
77/8 Topps 139
78/9 Topps 13
79/0 Topps 112
80/1 Topps 76
84/5 Topps 145
94/5 DALL / Cap
86/7 HART / Jr. Whalers
87/8 HART / Jr. Whalers
75/6 MONT
76/7 MONT
77/8 MONT
78/9 MONT
79/0 MONT
80/1 MONT
81/2 MONT
82/3 WASH
84/5 WASH / Pizza Hut
85/6 WASH / Pizza Hut

JARVIS, WES*
97 Bowman 158, ✍ Aut.

JARVIS, WES**
88/9 ProCards / Newmarket
89/0 ProCards AHL 106

JARVIS, WES1
80/1 WASH
81/2 WASH

JARVIS, WES2
99 Bowman 156
00/1 Charlotte Checkers
01/2 Hartford Wolf Pack

JARY, PIERRE
72/3 TORO

JAS, PETER
97/8 Central Texas
99/0 Indianapolis Ice

JASECKO, STANISLAV
00/1 DS 77
99/0 OFS 180
00/1 OFS 10
96/7 Grand Rapids Griffins

JASKARI, JAAKKO
66/7 Champion 48
65/6 Hellas 117

JASKIERSKI, MIECZYSLAW
74 Hellas MM-Jenkki 97
79 Panini Sticker 131
73/4 Williams Finnish 92

JASKIN, ALEXEI
94/5 APS 233
95/6 APS 5
96/7 APS 219, 426
97/8 APS 34
97/8 DS 59
98/9 DS 87
99/0 DS 139
96/7 DS Sticker 21
97/8 DS Sticker 171
98/9 OFS 103
99/0 OFS 439
00/1 OFS 328

JASMIN-RIEL, DERRICK
99 Québec Pee Wee 192

JASPERS, JASON
00/1 SP Authentic 130
00/1 SP GU 88
00/1 SPx ✂ 124
00/1 Upper Deck 211
00/1 UD Pros&Prosp. 130
00/1 UD Vintage 397
98/9 Sudbury Wolves 13
99/0 Sudbury Wolves 17
00/1 Sudbury Wolves 19

JAUFMANN, ANDREI
94/5 DEL 114

JAVANAINEN, ARTO
91/2 Jyvas Hyva 69
92/3 Jyvas Hyva 192
93/4 Jyvas Hyva 356
70/1 Kuvajulkaisut 329
80/1 Mallasjuoma 202
82 Semic Sticker 38
93/4 Sisu 218
93/4 Sisu 388
95/6 Sisu Limited 25
78/9 SM-Liiga 228

JAVEBLAD, TOMAS
89/0 Semic Elitserien 147
90/1 Semic Elitserien 225

JAVIN, MIROSLAV
94/5 APS 124
95/6 APS 32
96/7 APS 314
97/8 APS 294
99/0 DS 46
00/1 DS 148
96/7 DS Sticker 157
97/8 DS Sticker 110
98/9 OFS 317, 489
99/0 OFS 289
00/1 OFS 267
01/2 OFS 233

JAX, FREDRIK
93/4 Cla. Prospects 133
90/1 Semic Elitserien 221
91/2 Semic Elitserien 145
92/3 Upper Deck 230
94/5 Flint Generals

JAY, BOB
93/4 Parkhurst 361
90/1 ProCards 550
91/2 ProCards 252
93/4 Upper Deck 470
96/7 Detroit Vipers
97/8 Detroit Vipers
98/9 Detroit Vipers
92/3 Fort Wayne Komets 14
93/4 Phoenix Roadrunners

JEAN, ERIC
01/2 Victoriaville Tigres 6

JEAN, MAXIME
91/2 7th...Sketch LHJMQ 53

JEAN, YANICK
96/7 Mississippi S'Wolves

JEDAMZIK, RAFAEL
94/5 DEL 83
95/6 DEL 339

JEESIMAN, EARL
84/5 Fredericton Express

JEFFERSON, MIKE
See Mike Danton.

JEFFREY, LARRY
45-64 BeeHive-2 [Detr.]
64-67 BeeHive-3 [Detr.]
64-67 BeeHive-3 [Detr.]
64-67 BeeHive-3 [Toro.]
64/5 Coke/Sprite [Detr.]
68/9 O-Pee-Chee 74
70/1 O-Pee-Chee 28
63/4 Parkhurst 48
95/6 Parkie 66-67 115
94/5 Parkie Tall 59
68/9 Shirriff / NYRa. 14
64/5 Topps 49
65/6 Topps 83
67/8 Topps 21
70/1 Topps 28
64/5 Toronto Star Action
62/3 York Transfer 33
63/4 York 41
68/9 TORO

JEFFREY, MIKE
88/9 ProCards / Maine
89/0 Johnstown Chiefs
87/8 Moncton Hawks

JELEN, JIRI
97/8 APS 191
99/0 OFS 123
00/1 OFS 76

JELINEK, JIRI
98/9 OFS 167

JELINEK, MARIAN
99/0 OFS 17

JELINEK, PETR
02/3 Moose Jaw Warriors

JELINEK, TOMAS
94/5 APS 261
95/6 APS 138, 365, 441
96/7 APS 297, 405
97/8 APS 183
97/8 DS 54
98/9 DS 103
96/7 DS Sticker 221
97/8 DS Sticker 155
95 Globe 153
98/9 OFS 70
94 Semic 179
93/4 Upper Deck 165
92/3 OTTA

JELINEK, TOMAS
91 Semic Sticker 122
92 Semic Sticker 141
93 Semic Sticker 103
92/3 Upper Deck 497

JENACEK, LUBOS
94/5 APS 244
95/6 APS 16, 391

JENACEK, MARTIN
00/1 OFS 372
01/2 OFS 92
99/0 Score 128, 152

JENKINS, CRAIG
89/0 Nashville Knights

JENKINS, JON
94/5 Knoxville Cherokees
83/4 Oshawa Generals

JENKINS, ROGER
34-43 BeeHive-1 [Mont.]
35-40 Canada Starch
33-35 Diamond Match Silv.
36-39 Diamond Match TT1
35/6 O-Pee-Chee 92 [Error: Rogers]
34/5 Sweet Caporal

JENKINS, SCOTT
90/1 7th..Sketch OHL 211

JENKINS, TODD
89/0 Nashville Knights

JENNI, MARCEL
95 Panini Worlds 130
00/1 UD Elitserien 91

JENNINGS, BILL
83 HHOF Postcard K8

JENNINGS, GRANT
90/1 O-Pee-Chee 510
91/2 O-Pee-Chee 468
93/4 Parkhurst 427
90/1 Pro Set 106
90/1 Score 31T
91/2 Score CAN 531
92/3 Score 542
94/5 UD BAP ✍ 51
89/0 HART / Jr. Whalers
90/1 HART / Jr. Whalers
91/2 PITT / Elby's
92/3 PITT / Coke-Clark
93/4 PITT / Foodland 2
94/5 PITT / Foodland 1
83/4 Saskatoon Blades
84/5 Saskatoon Blades

JENNINGS, JASON
93/4 Cla. Prospects 238
93/4 Johnstown Chiefs 10
94/5 Johnstown Chiefs 12
92/3 W. Michigan Broncos

JENNINGS, JOHN
00/1 Florida Everblades
97/8 Louisiana Ice Gators
99/0 Louisiana Ice Gators

JENNINGS, WILLIAM
83&87 HHOF 142
01/2 UD Legends 49

JENNINGS, WILLIAMS
34-43 BeeHive-1 [Detr.]

JENSEN, AL
83/4 O-Pee-Chee 373
84/5 O-Pee-Chee 201
86/7 OPC/Topps 135
83/4 OPC/Topps Sticker 202
84/5 OPC Sticker 128
84/5 OPC Sticker 232-233
86/7 OPC Sticker 252-144
82/3 Post [Wash.]
83/4 Souhaits Keychain [Capitals]
84/5 Topps 146
80/1 DETR
81/2 WASH
84/5 WASH / Pizza Hut
85/6 WASH / Pizza Hut
86/7 WASH / Police

JENSEN, CHRIS
88/9 ProCards / Hershey
89/0 ProCards AHL 339
90/1 ProCards 38
91/2 ProCards 275
95/6 Minnesota Moose
93/4 Portland Pirates
94/5 Portland Pirates

JENSEN, CODY
99/0 Medicine Hat Tigers
96/7 Regina Pats
97/8 Regina Pats

JENSEN, DARREN
86/7 OPC Sticker 187-46

JENSEN, DAVID A.
92/3 Upper Deck 379
84/5 HART / Jr. Whalers
86/7 WASH / Kodak
86/7 WASH / Police
87/8 WASH

JENSEN, DAVID H.
84/5 Springfield Indians 5

JENSEN, JENS
79 Panini Sticker 368

JENSEN, JIM
98/9 Oklahoma City Blazers

JENSEN, STEVE
77/8 O-Pee-Chee 238
78/9 O-Pee-Chee 45
79/0 O-Pee-Chee 292
80/1 O-Pee-Chee 294
81/2 O-Pee-Chee 154
79 Panini Sticker 220
82/3 Post [LosA.]
77/8 Topps 238
78/9 Topps 45
80/1 LOSA 5

JENSON, WADE
81/2 Victoria Cougars

JERABEK, VLADIMIR
95/6 APS 173
96/7 APS 177, 367
97/8 APS 76
96/7 DS Sticker 13, 48
98/9 OFS 260
99/0 OFS 336

JERDING, SÖREN
79 Panini Sticker 368

JEROFEJEV, DMITRI
96/7 APS 199, 416
97/8 APS 129
97/8 DS 98
99/0 DS 171
00/1 DS 161
96/7 DS Sticker 193
97/8 DS Sticker 253
99/0 OFS 225, 413
00/1 OFS 243

JEROME, DARCY
90/1 7th..Sketch WHL 163

JERRARD, PAUL
89/0 ProCards IHL 96
91/2 ProCards 151
94/5 Hershey Bears

JERRETT, DARRELL
99/0 Halifax Mooseheads

JERWA, JOE
34-43 BeeHive-1 [NYAm.]
36-39 Diamond Match TT2
36-39 Diamond Match TT3

JESIOLOWSKI, DAVID
91/2 7th...Sketch WHL 274
93/4 Lethbridge Hurricanes

JESLINEK, MICHAL
98/9 OFS 290
99/0 OFS 124

JESMANTOVITI, IGOR
89 Semic Sticker 97

JESSEE, SCOTT
78/9 Saginaw Gears

JESSESEN,
92/3 Semic Nordisk 204 [Rookie]

JESSEY, IVAN
88/9 Lethbridge Hurricanes

JESSIMAN, BRENT
82/3 Brandon Wheat Kings
83/4 Brandon Wheat Kings

JESSIMAN, EARL
83/4 Fredericton Express

JESTADT, JEFF
93/4 Roanoke Express
94/5 Roanoke Express
95/6 Roanoke Express
91/2 Ferris State Bulldogs

JEZ, PETR
99/0 OFS 536

JICKLING, MIKE
91 7th..Sketch Mem.Cup 89
90/1 7th..Sketch WHL 191
91/2 7th...Sketch WHL 7
98/9 Florida Everblades
00/1 Florida Everblades
98/9 Long Beach Ice Dogs
89/0 Spokane Chiefs

JILLSON, JEFF
01/2 Adrenaline 223, RR 17
01/2 Atomic 123
01/2 BAP Memor. 306
01/2 Bowman 135
01/2 Cr. Royale 177, RR 19
02/3 First Edition 227
01/2 Heads Up 118
02/3 O-Pee-Chee 278
01/2 Pacific 461
02/3 Pacific 334
02/3 Pacific Complete 73
01/2 PTC Calder 10
01/2 PTC Draft 10
01/2 Parkhurst 272
02/3 Parkhurst 31
01/2 Pr. Stock 137, -PS 88
01/2 PS Titanium 180
01/2 PS Titanium Draft 165
01/2 Signature 245, ✍ Aut. 245
01/2 SP Authentic 170
02/3 SP Authentic 130
01/2 SP GU 95
01/2 SPx 124
01/2 SPx Rookie RR25
01/2 Stadium 124
02/3 Topps 278
01/2 To. Chrome 162
01/2 To. Heritage 141
02/3 T. Limited 278
01/2 To. Reserve 119
02/3 T. Total 394
01/2 UD PlayMakers Ltd 139
01/2 Upper Deck 225
01/2 UD Challenge 130
99/0 UD G. Reserve / Backup 168
01/2 UD Honor Roll 86
01/2 UD Ice 67
01/2 UD Mask 166
01/2 UD Premier 106
01/2 UD Top Shelf 135
01/2 UD Vintage 295
01/2 Vanguard 128, PP 17
01/2 Cleveland Barons

JILSSON, JEFF
01/2 O-Pee-Chee 344
01/2 Topps 344

JINDRA, JOSEF
99/0 OFS 181
00/1 OFS 14
01/2 OFS 123

JINDRICH, ROBERT
95/6 APS 251
96/7 APS 296
97/8 APS 176
97/8 DS 52
96/7 DS Sticker 214
97/8 DS Sticker 151
98/9 OFS 36
99/0 Kentucky Tho'blades
00/1 Kentucky Tho'blades

JINMAN, LEE
95/6 Classic 90
93/4 Slapshot / North Bay 14
94/5 Slapshot / North Bay 17
95/6 Slapshot 58, 223
99/0 Houston Aeros
96/7 Michigan K-Wings
01/2 Nottingham Panthers
02/3 Nottingham Panthers

JIRA, PETR
00/1 OFS 103
01/2 OFS 159

JIRANEK, MARTIN
92/3 Classic 69
93/4 Cla. Prospects 169
96/7 DEL 327
98/9 DEL 253
99/0 Eishockey 29
00/1 UD DEL 189, A1
01/2 UD DEL 202
93/4 Portland Pirates

JIRIK, JAROSLAV
77-79 Sportscaster 44-03
77-79 Sports. FIN 45-1069

JIRUS, VLADEMAR
01/2 OFS 112

JOANETTE, ROSARIO (KIT)
51/2 Laval Dairy 75
43-47 Parade Sportive
52/3 St. Lawrence 20

JOANISSE, ANDRÉ
01/2 Drummondville

JOBE, TREVOR
88/9 ProCards / Newmarket
90/1 ProCards 161
91/2 Richmond Renegades

JOBIN, FRÉDÉRICK
98/9 Long Beach Ice Dogs
00/1 Quad City Mallards

JOCHER, MARKUS
99/0 Eishockey 326

JODOIN, CLEMENT
90/1 ProCards 447

JODOIN, CLÉMENT
91/2 ProCards 544
02/3 MONT
90/1 Halifax Citadels
95/6 Halifax Moosehead
96/7 Halifax Moosehead
96/7 Halifax Moosehead

JODOIN, MARK
93/4 W. Michigan Broncos

JODOIN, ROGER
51/2 Bas du Fleuve 55
52/3 Bas du Fleuve 48

JODZIO, RICK
75/6 OPC WHA 99
76/7 OPC WHA 113

JOENVÄÄRÄ, JUHA
00/1 Cardset 183

JOFFE, AARON
85/6 U. of Arizona Ice Cats

JOH, BERNIE
91/2 7th...Sketch OHL 249

JOHANNESEN, GLEN
88/9 ProCards / Indianapolis

JOHANNESON, CONNIE
28/9 Paulins Candy 68
23/4 Selkirks Crescent 11

JOHANNSON, JIM
89/0 ProCards IHL 70
90/1 ProCards 396
93/4 Milwaukee Admirals
88/9 Salt Lake G'Eagles

JOHANSEN, PER R
92/3 Semic Nordisk 165

JOHANSEN, REINO
92/3 Semic Nordisk 80

JOHANSEN, ROY
94 Semic 264
92/3 Semic Nordisk 11
93 Semic Sticker 243

JOHANSEN, STIG
92/3 Semic Nordisk 17
92 Semic Sticker 47

JOHANSEN, TOM
92/3 Semic Nordisk 7

JOHANSEN, TREVOR
78/9 O-Pee-Chee 320
79/0 COLR
77/8 TORO
78/9 TORO

JOHANSEN, VIDAR
79 Panini Sticker 299

JOHANSSEN, TOM
94 Semic 269
92 Semic Sticker 45

JOHANSSON, ANDREAS
97/8 Do. Priority 134
95/6 Edge Ice 94
02/3 First Edition 90, ✂- Jers.
94/5 Leaf Elit Set 51
97/8 Limited 121, 159
98/9 Omega 165
99/0 Pacific 289
00/1 Pacific 67
02/3 Pacific Complete 434
97/8 Panini Sticker 53
96/7 Pi. Be A Player 103, ✍ Aut. 103
02/3 PS Titanium 59
94 Semic 70
91/2 Semic Elitserien 101
92/3 Semic Elitserien 113
02/3 Sports Vault 253
02/3 Vanguard 58
96 Wien 64
98/9 OTTA

JOHANSSON, BJÖRN
72 Hellas MM-Jenkki 29
74 Hellas MM-Jenkki 26
74 Semic Sticker 5
72/3 Williams Finnish 47
73/4 Williams Finnish 28

JOHANSSON, CALLE
98/9 Aurora 196
98/9 Be A Player 297, ✍ Aut. 297
99/0 BAP Mem. 173
00/1 BAP Mem. 166
01/2 BAP Memor. 204
90/1 Bowman 75
91/2 Bowman 294
92/3 Bowman 275
93/4 Donruss 372
94/5 Donruss 243
95/6 Donruss 309
98/9 Dynagon Ice 195
92/3 Fleer Ultra 234
94/5 Fleer Ultra 235
95/6 Fleer Ultra 176
95 Globe 8
93/4 Leaf 153
94/5 Leaf 242
95/6 Leaf 298
96/7 Metal Univ. 165
90/1 OPC/Topps 164
91/2 O-Pee-Chee 126
92/3 O-Pee-Chee 223
89/0 OPC/Topps 16
88/9 OPC Sticker 134-270
88/9 OPC Sticker 254
97/8 Omega 240
98/9 Pacific 6
99/0 Pacific 441
00/1 Pacific 423
02/3 Pacific 393
97/8 Pa. Invincible R-208
98/9 Pa. Paramount 245
88/9 Panini Sticker 221
91/2 Panini Sticker 205
93/4 Panini Sticker 31
95/6 Panini Sticker 143
96/7 Panini Sticker 142
97/8 Panini Sticker 113
98/9 Panini Sticker 107
99/0 Panini Sticker 170
00/1 Panini Sticker 107
91/2 Parkhurst 410
92/3 Parkhurst 201
95/6 Parkhurst 218
00/1 Parkhurst P-34
94/5 Parkie SE197
91/2 Pinnacle 232
92/3 Pinnacle 30
93/4 Pinnacle 107
94/5 Pinnacle 305
96/7 Pinnacle 85
95/6 POG 285
93/4 Power Play 465
93/4 Premier 278
94/5 Premier 59
90/1 Pro Set 313
91/2 Pro Set 248
92/3 Pro Set 203
91/2 Pro Set Platinum 243
90/1 Score 309
91/2 Score 155
91/2 Score CAN 155
92/3 Score 209
93/4 Score 76
91/2 Semic Elitserien 340
92/3 Semic Elitserien 341
91 Semic Sticker 207
92 Semic Sticker 57
93 Semic Sticker 25
00/1 Signature 94, ✍ Aut. 193
95/6 SBx Emotion 189
95/6 SBx Impact 178
97/8 SP Authentic 167
95/6 Super Sticker 132
92/3 Topps 498
95/6 Topps 274
00/1 Topps 185
96/7 Topps Picks 161
91/2 To. Stadium 188
92/3 T. Stadium Club 341
93/4 To. Stadium 451
02/3 T. Total 243
98/9 UD Choice 219
90/1 Upper Deck 149
91/2 Upper Deck 316
92/3 Upper Deck 139
97/8 Upper Deck 383
98/9 Upper Deck 382
00/1 Upper Deck 176
95/6 UD BAP 54, ✍ S54
95/6 UD CC 130
98/9 UD G. Reserve 382
01/2 UD Vintage 254
01/2 Victory 358
96 Wien 42
87/8 BUFF / Blue Shield
87/8 BUFF / Won. Bread
88/9 BUFF / Blue Shield
88/9 BUFF / Won. Bread
89/0 WASH
89/0 WASH / Kodak
90/1 WASH / Kodak
90/1 WASH / Smokey
91/2 WASH / Kodak
91/2 WASH / Smokey
92/3 WASH / Kodak
95/6 WASH
98/9 WASH / Kids 'n 5

JOHANSSON, DANIEL
99/0 Cardset 294
95 Globe 56
94/5 Leaf Elit Set 104
95/6 Leaf Elit Set 230
92/3 Semic Elitserien 252
92/3 Upper Deck 599
95/6 UD Elitserien 80
97/8 UD Elitserien 88
98/9 UD Elitserien 102

JOHANSSON, ERIC
99/0 UD Prospects 37
02/3 Albany River Rats

JOHANSSON, FREDRIK
94/5 Parkie SE241
90/1 Semic Elitserien 146
95/6 UD Elitserien 130
97/8 UD Elitserien 130

JOHANSSON, JAKOB
98/9 SPx Prospects 84
98/9 UD Black Diam. 114

JOHANSSON, JAN
89/0 Semic Elitserien 211

JOHANSSON, JONAS
02/3 Kamloops Blazers

JOHANSSON, KARI
66/7 Champion 59
70/1 Kuvajulkaisut 140
71/2 Williams Finnish 189
72/3 Williams Finnish 227
73/4 Williams Finnish 261

JOHANSSON, KENNETH
94/5 Leaf Elit Set 161
95/6 Leaf Elit Set 224
89/0 Semic Elitserien 66, 97
90/1 Semic Elitserien 101
92/3 Semic Elitserien 249

JOHANSSON, LEIF
89/0 Semic Elitserien 213

JOHANSSON, MAGNUS
97/8 UD Elitserien 73
98/9 UD Elitserien 69
99/0 UD Elitserien 71
00/1 UD Elitserien 61

JOHANSSON, MATTIAS
94/5 Leaf Elit Set 234
95/6 Leaf Elit Set 44, G-5
93/4 Parkhurst 537
91/2 Semic Elitserien 102
91/2 Semic Elitserien 330
92/3 Semic Elitserien 117
95/6 UD Elitserien 69
97/8 UD Elitserien 61
98/9 UD Elitserien 95
99/0 UD Elitserien 64, H6
00/1 UD Elitserien 86

JOHANSSON, MICHAEL
99/0 Cardset 100

JOHANSSON, MIKAEL
95 Globe 30
94/5 Leaf Elit Set 255
95/6 Leaf Elit Set 119
95 Semic 68
89/0 Semic Elitserien 61
90/1 Semic Elitserien 293
91/2 Semic Elitserien 65
91/2 Semic Elitserien 350
89 Semic Sticker 22
91 Semic Sticker 43
92 Semic Sticker 64
93 Semic Sticker 31
97/8 UD Elitserien 39, 42, C2
98/9 UD Elitserien 56
99/0 UD Elitserien 41
00/1 UD Elitserien 58, 187, P3, ✍ Sig.
96 Wien 65

JOHANSSON, NILS
70/1 Kuvajulkaisut 27

JOHANSSON, PER-JOHAN
94/5 Leaf Elit Set 251
95/6 Leaf Elit Set 174

JOHANSSON, PETER
89/0 Semic Elitserien 24
90/1 Semic Elitserien 94

JOHANSSON, ROGER
91/2 Bowman 257
92/3 Fleer Ultra 268
95 Globe 22
94/5 Leaf Elit Set 259, GC-21, GS-6
95/6 Leaf Elit Set 218, C-9, FTF-5
90/1 OPC/Topps 96
91/2 O-Pee-Chee 53
90/1 Panini/CGY 6, G
92/3 Parkhurst 263
93/4 Premier 253
90/1 Pro Set 424
90/1 Score 91T
94 Semic 62
95 Semic 58
91/2 Semic Elitserien 139
93 Semic Sticker 29
91/2 To. Stadium 375
93/4 To. Stadium 133
95/6 UD Elitserien 62
97/8 UD Elitserien 57, 206, 217, UDS7, C20
98/9 UD Elitserien 84
99/0 UD Elitserien 53,L4
00/1 UD Elitserien 82, T5
96 Wien 54
90/1 CALG / McGavin's
92/3 CALG / IGA 019

JOHANSSON, STIG-GÖRAN
72 Hellas MM-Jenkki 31
70/1 Kuvajulkaisut 28
69/0 Mästär Serien 37
72 Panda MM-Toronto
72 Semic Sticker 47
74 Semic Sticker 21
71/2 Williams Finnish 47
72/3 Williams Finnish 48

JOHANSSON, SVEN (TUMBA)
00/1 Alfabilder
95 Globe 68

JOHANSSON, THOMAS
00/1 Cardset 280
94/5 Leaf Elit Set 121
95/6 Leaf Elit Set 30
90/1 Semic Elitserien 282
91/2 Semic Elitserien 64
92/3 Semic Elitserien 81
95/6 UD Elitserien 40
98/9 UD Elitserien 52
99/0 UD Elitserien 38, H5

JOHANSSON, TORBJÖRN
95/6 Leaf Elit Set 243, R-5
95/6 UD Elitserien 96
97/8 UD Elitserien 102
98/9 UD Elitserien 119
99/0 UD Elitserien 105

JOHN, BERNIE
99/0 Indianapolis Ice
91/2 Sudbury Wolves
92/3 Sudbury Wolves

JOHNS, DON
64/5 Coke/Sprite [NYRa.]
94/5 Parkie Tall 98
65/6 Québec Aces
60/1 Shirriff 93
63/4 Topps 64

JOHNSON,
91/2 Avant Garde BCJHL 163

JOHNSON, AARON
02/3 Québec Remparts
99/0 Rimouski Océanic 21
00/1 Rimouski Océanic 22
01/2 Rimouski Océanic 21

JOHNSON, AL
45-64 BeeHive-2 [Detr.]
61/2 Parkhurst 22
61/2 Shirriff 72

JOHNSON, ANDERS
94/5 Leaf Elit Set 283
92/3 Semic Elitserien 42

JOHNSON, ANDY
95/6 Slapshot 323

JOHNSON, ANTHONY
94 Semic 322
93/4 Humberside Hawks 9
94/5 Humberside Hawks 8

JOHNSON, B.J.
74/5 PITT

JOHNSON, BEN
97/8 Spokane Chiefs

JOHNSON, BILL
52/3 St. Lawrence 60

JOHNSON, BOB*
74/5 Loblaws

JOHNSON, BOB**
90/1 Pro Set 674

JOHNSON, BOB1
72/3 SLOU

JOHNSON, BOB2
82/3 CALG
85/6 CALG / Red Rooster
86/7 CALG / Red Rooster
90/1 PITT / Foodland 7

JOHNSON, BRENT
01/2 Adrenaline 159, CL 18, PP 30
01/2 Atomic 81
02/3 Atomic 82, -D 17
00/1 BAP Mem. 439
02/3 BAP Memorabilia 42, ✂- SC16
01/2 BT Pipes 46, -Mask, ✂- GG
02/3 Between the Pipes 55, 145, M26, ✂- FW12, ✂- T15, ✍ Aut.
01/2 Bowman 87
02/3 Bowman 93
00/1 Crown Royale 139, 21CR-21
01/2 Crown Royale 119
02/3 Crown Royale 81
00/1 Crown Royale G-6
02/3 Exclusive 143, -EA 13
02/3 First Edition 205
02/3 Heads Up 103, -S 17
01/2 O-Pee-Chee 205
02/3 O-Pee-Chee 122
99/0 Pacific 367
01/2 Pacific 324, 440, ✍ 449
02/3 Pacific 323
02/3 Pacific Complete 372
00/1 Parkhurst P-190
01/2 Parkhurst 57
02/3 Parkhurst 29
02/3 Parkhurst Retro 189
00/1 Premier Plus 94
00/1 Private Stock 140, Roo. 19
01/2 Pr. Stock 80
02/3 Pr. Stock Reserve 84, -ICS 18
00/1 PS Titanium 141, 3SS-26
01/2 PS Titanium 116
02/3 PS Titanium 83
00/1 PS Titanium Draft 141
02/3 Quest for the Cup 82, ✂- GWJ 18
00/1 Signature 295
01/2 Signature 21, ✍ Aut. 21
02/3 Signature 139, ✍ 139, ✂- DW7, ✂- YP8
95/6 Slapshot 281
01/2 SP GU ✂- AF
02/3 SP Game-Used ✂- FF
02/3 Sports Vault 280
01/2 SPx 191
02/3 SPx 66
00/1 Stadium 236
01/2 Stadium 89, NR3, ✍ NR
02/3 Stadium 18, -PSH1
01/2 Topps 205
02/3 Topps 122, OTG20
02/3 T. Chrome 78
00/1 To. Gold Label 88
00/1 To. Heritage 58
01/2 To. Heritage 58
02/3 To. Heritage 75
02/3 T. Limited 122
01/2 To. Reserve 94
00/1 To. Stars 149
02/3 T. Total 161
01/2 Ultimate Mem. ✂- Blood
98/9 Upper Deck 358
01/2 Upper Deck 381
02/3 Upper Deck 153, -SA, ✂- SV
01/2 UD Challenge 75
98/9 UD G. Reserve 358
02/3 UD Honor 62
01/2 UD Mask 126, ✂- GJ, ✂- JP, ✂- DP, ✂- DM, ✂- SuS
02/3 UD Mask 75, 76, 77, 78, 114, ✂- BM, ✂- NB, ✂- PW
02/3 UD MVP 158
02/3 UD Piece 79
01/2 UD Top Shelf 116
02/3 UD Top Shelf 76, ✂- SS, ✂- TS
02/3 UD Vintage 224, 286, GB 224
00/1 Vanguard 143
01/2 Vanguard 81, PP 16
02/3 Victory 186
01/2 Worcester IceCats

JOHNSON, BRIAN
85/6 Minnesota-Duluth 18

JOHNSON, CHAZ
01/2 Rimouski Océanic 1
01/2 Val d'Or Foreurs 3
02/3 Val d'Or Foreurs

JOHNSON, CHING
02/3 Ultimate Mem. ✍ Cut

JOHNSON, CORY
91/2 7th...Sketch OHL 227
96/7 Grand Rapids Griffins
95/6 Muskegon Fury

JOHNSON, CRAIG
93/4 Cla. Prospects IA14
93/4 Cla. Prospects LP7
94/5 Flair 155
93/4 Fleer Ultra 487
95/6 Leaf 273
98/9 Pacific 236
99/0 Pacific 191
02/3 Pacific 167
02/3 Pacific Complete 380
97/8 Pa. Dynagon BKS-46
95/6 Pinnacle 208
97/8 Pi. Be A Player 100, ✍ Aut. 100
93/4 Power Play 507
93/4 Premier - USA Hockey 19
94/5 Premier 369
95/6 Score 292
95/6 SP 66
93/4 To. Stadium - Team U.S.A. 11
02/3 T. Total 42
94/5 Upper Deck 253
95/6 Upper Deck 139, 308
96/7 Upper Deck 80
00/1 Upper Deck 84
96/7 UD CC 129
00/1 UD Vintage 170
94/5 Birmingham Bulls
92/3 Oklahoma City Blazers
98/9 Oklahoma City Blazers
92/3 Windsor Spitfires
91/2 Minnesota G'Gophers
92/3 Minnesota G'Gophers

JOHNSON, DANNY
70/1 Eddie Sargent 214
71/2 Eddie Sargent 210
70/1 Esso Power Player
71/2 O-Pee-Chee 95
71/2 Toronto Sun Photo
70/1 VANC / Royal Bank

JOHNSON, DARREN
96/7 Knoxville Cherokees

JOHNSON, DION
91/2 Air Canada SJHL A11
92/3 MPS SJHL 121

JOHNSON, DOUG
98/9 BC Icemen 7
98/9 BC Icemen

JOHNSON, ERNEST (MOOSE)
91 C55 Reprint 28
83 HHOF Postcard A10
83&87 HHOF 10
10/1 Imperial
10/1 Imperial 30
11/2 Imperial 28
12/3 Imperial 25
60/1 Topps 4
61/2 Topps - Stamp

JOHNSON, G. A.
1935 J.A. Pattreiouex Sporting Events & Stars 89

JOHNSON, GARY
83/4 Medicine Hat Tigers

JOHNSON, GREG
98/9 Be A Player 225, ✍ Aut. 225
99/0 BAP Mem. 278
00/1 BAP Mem. 338
93/4 Classic - Team Canada TC1
93/4 Cla. Prospects 17
93/4 Donruss 94
94/5 Donruss 150
96/7 Donruss 111
99/0 Dynagon Ice 107
02/3 Exclusive 99
02/3 First Edition 174
96/7 Fl. Picks 100
93/4 Fleer Ultra 306
93/4 Fleer Ultra WotF 7
94/5 Fleer Ultra 283
95/6 Fleer Ultra 233
93/4 Leaf 370
94/5 Leaf 355
96/7 Leaf 33
99/0 Millenium 141, ✍ Aut. 141
02/3 O-Pee-Chee 185
98/9 Omega 129
98/9 Pacific 145
99/0 Pacific 225
00/1 Pacific 222
01/2 Pacific 218
02/3 Pacific 211
02/3 Pacific Complete 342
98/9 Pa. Crown Roy. 75
99/0 Pa. Paramount 125
00/1 Pa. Paramount 135
94 Panini Olympics 315
00/1 Panini Sticker 183
93/4 Parkhurst 270
95/6 Parkhurst 338
94/5 Parkie SE48
93/4 Pinnacle 453
94/5 Pinnacle 511
96/7 Pinnacle 140
96/7 Pi. Summit 49
93/4 Power Play 330
93/4 Premier 457
94/5 Premier 257
02/3 Pr. Stock Reserve 59
99/0 Revolution 79
93/4 Score 601
94/5 Score CT5
96/7 Score 132
97/8 Score Pitt. 11
01/2 Signature 17, ✍ Aut. 17
02/3 Sports Vault 254
99/0 Stadium 24
00/1 Topps 263
02/3 Topps 185
02/3 T. Limited 185
93/4 To. Stadium 367
02/3 T. Total 265
90/1 Upper Deck 460
93/4 Upper Deck 452
94/5 Upper Deck 212
95/6 Upper Deck 334
96/7 Upper Deck 254
97/8 Upper Deck 134
98/9 Upper Deck 306
00/1 Upper Deck 330
01/2 Upper Deck 99
95/6 UD BAP 73, ✍ S73
96/7 UD CC 78
97/8 UD Coll. Choice 206
98/9 UD G. Reserve 306
02/3 UD Honor 87
98/9 UD MVP 111
99/0 UD MVP Cup 102
00/1 UD Vintage 198
01/2 UD Vintage 145
00/1 Victory 129
01/2 Victory 200
02/3 Victory 121
98/9 NASH / Wendy's 12

JOHNSON, IVAN (CHING)
35/6 Amalgamated Press
33/4 Anonymous 33
34-43 BeeHive-1 [NYRa.]
36-39 Diamond Match TT1
36-39 Diamond Match TT2
36-39 Diamond Match TT3
33 Goudey Sport Kings 30
83 HHOF Postcard D5
83&87 HHOF 51
94/5 Legends 41
33/4 O-Pee-Chee 39
94/5 Parkie Tall 11
34/5 Sweet Caporal
37/8 World Wide Gum 21

JOHNSON, JASON
93/4 Slapshot / Kitchener 23

JOHNSON, JAY
91/2 Peterborough Petes

JOHNSON, JIM*
92/3 Bowman 177
92/3 Fleer Ultra 95
86/7 O-Pee-Chee 231
87/8 OPC/Topps 196
88/9 OPC/Topps 148
90/1 OPC/Topps 98
91/2 O-Pee-Chee 426
89/0 OPC/Topps 77
86/7 OPC Sticker 128-114
87/8 OPC Sticker 172-31
97/8 Pacific CC 174
87/8 Panini Sticker 143
88/9 Panini Sticker 334
89/0 Panini Sticker 320
92/3 Panini Sticker 94
91/2 Parkhurst 303
91/2 Pinnacle 235
92/3 Pinnacle 137
93/4 Pinnacle 192
94/5 Pinnacle 440
97/8 Pi. Be A Player 104, ✍ Aut. 104
93/4 Premier 98
90/1 Pro Set 235
91/2 Pro Set 116
92/3 Pro Set 83
90/1 Score 202
91/2 Score 52
91/2 Score CAN 52
92/3 Score 161
93/4 Score 144
94 Semic 110
92 Semic Sticker 155
92/3 Topps 54
92/3 T. Stadium Club 75
93/4 To. Stadium 298

JOHNSON, JIM1
94/5 DALL / Cap
96/7 PHOE / Coca-Cola
97/8 PHOE / Coca-Cola
86/7 PITT / Kodak
87/8 PITT / Kodak
89/0 PITT / Foodland 2
95/6 WASH

JOHNSON, JOHN
89/0 7th..Sketch OHL 144
90/1 7th..Sketch OHL 261
92/3 Toledo Storm
93/4 Wheeling Thund'birds
89/0 Niagara Falls Thunder

JOHNSON, KARL
92/3 MPS SJHL 17

JOHNSON, KENNY*
93/4 Humberside Hawks 1

JOHNSON, LANCE
90 7th..Sketch Mem.Cup 7
90/1 7th..Sketch WHL 288
91/2 7th...Sketch WHL 83
89/0 Kamloops Blazers

JOHNSON, MARK
83/4 Funmate Puffy 17 [w/]
80/1 O-Pee-Chee 69
83/4 O-Pee-Chee 140
84/5 O-Pee-Chee 72
85/6 OPC/Topps 44
86/7 OPC/Topps 112
87/8 OPC/Topps 101
88/9 OPC/Topps 45
90/1 OPC/Topps 178
89/0 O-Pee-Chee 244
83/4 OPC/Topps Sticker 254
84/5 OPC Sticker 193
85/6 OPC Sticker 50-181
86/7 OPC Sticker 200-70
87/8 OPC Sticker 64-205
80 Olympic USA
79 Panini Sticker 213
87/8 Panini Sticker 83
89/0 Panini Sticker 260
90/1 Panini Sticker 66
90/1 Pro Set 168
89 Semic Sticker 174
94/5 SR Miracle 17,18, ✍ 17,18
80/1 Topps 69
84/5 Topps 56
90/1 Upper Deck 180
82/3 HART / Jr. Whalers
83/4 HART / Jr. Whalers
84/5 HART / Jr. Whalers
85/6 NJER 1
86/7 NJER / S.O.B.E.R.
88/9 NJER / Caretta
89/0 NJER
89/0 NJER / Caretta

JOHNSON, MATT
00/1 BAP Mem. ✂- T-23
01/2 BAP Update ✂- TC7, ✂- TC22
94/5 Classic 65, T32
95/6 Donruss 217
95/6 Future Legends 28
95/6 Leaf 64
99/0 NHL Power Play
01/2 Pacific 196
97/8 Pacific CC 350
99/0 Pa. Paramount 12
94/5 Pinnacle 496
96/7 Pi. Be A Player 215, ✍ Aut. 215
94/5 Premier 339
02/3 Signature ✂- FS12
93/4 Slapshot / Peterborough 22
00/1 To. Heritage 177
94/5 Upper Deck 203
02/3 Upper Deck 334
98/9 UD MVP 100
01/2 MINW

JOHNSON, MICHAEL*
91/2 7th...Sketch OHL 300

JOHNSON, MICHAEL2
98/9 DEL 194
92/3 Ottawa 67's

JOHNSON, MIKE
98/9 Aurora 181
99/0 Aurora 135
00/1 Aurora 133
98/9 Be A Player 137, ✍ Aut. 137
00/1 BAP Mem. 380
01/2 BAP Memor. 264
98/9 Bowman's Best 71, BP1
98/9 Dynagon Ice 179
99/0 Dynagon Ice 188
98/9 Kraft / Post 12
98/9 NHL Power Play
98/9 OPC Chrome 42, SB7
97/8 Omega 221
98/9 Omega 227
98/9 Pacific 413
99/0 Pacific 406
00/1 Pacific 373
01/2 Pacific 304
02/3 Pacific 296
02/3 Pacific Complete 376
97/8 Pacific CC 335
98/9 Pa. Crown Roy. 130
98/9 Pa. Paramount 226
99/0 Pa. Paramount 224
00/1 Pa. Paramount 221
98/9 Pa. Revolution 137
98/9 Panini Photocard
00/1 Panini Sticker 91
97/8 Pi. Be A Player 218, OT-18, ✍ Aut. 218
97/8 Pi. BeeHive 54, ✍ Aut. 54
00/1 PS Titanium 88
99/0 Revolution 137, / CSC 137
00/1 Revolution 133
00/1 Signature 3, ✍ Aut. 33
01/2 Signature 166, ✍ Aut. 166
97/8 SP Authentic 194
98/9 SP Authentic 81
98/9 SPx Finite 81, 122
99/0 Stadium 95
00/1 Stadium 127
98/9 Topps 42, -IA I14, -SB7
99/0 Topps 172, NS11
00/1 Topps 239
99/0 To. Chrome 172
00/1 To. Chrome 149
98/9 To. Finest 37, C16
98/9 T. Gold Label 66
00/1 To. Heritage 151
98/9 UD Choice 199, SQ27
00/1 UD Reserve 79
98/9 UD3 23, 83, 143
98/9 Upper Deck 187, FF27, FT18
99/0 Upper Deck 294
00/1 Upper Deck 156
01/2 Upper Deck 137
97/8 UD Black Diam. 118, PC27
99/0 UD Black Diam. 81
98/9 UD G. Reserve 187
99/0 UD G. Reserve 294
97/8 UD Ice 48
98/9 UD MVP 199, ✍ PS
99/0 UD MVP 202
00/1 UD MVP 161, ✍ PS
00/1 UD Vintage 323
00/1 Vanguard 89
02/3 Vanguard 78
99/0 Victory 288
00/1 Victory 211
01/2 Victory 267
99/0 WGretzky 163
97/8 Zenith 82, RR-12, ZT-12, Z71

JOHNSON, N. JIM
70/1 Eddie Sargent 153
71/2 Eddie Sargent 145
70/1 Esso Power Player
68/9 O-Pee-Chee 186
69/0 O-Pee-Chee 97
71/2 O-Pee-Chee 48
69/0 Topps 97
71/2 Topps 48
71/2 Toronto Sun Photo
72/3 Minn. Fight. Saints
74/5 Minn. Fight. Saints

JOHNSON, NORM B.
58/9 Topps 17
59/0 Topps 54

JOHNSON, PAUL
99/0 Quad City Mallards
00/1 Quad City Mallards

JOHNSON, PERRY
98 Bowman 44
98 Bowman Chrome 44
00/1 Kudos 93
96/7 Regina Pats
97/8 Spokane Chiefs

JOHNSON, PETER
93/4 Humberside Hawks 18
94/5 Humberside Hawks 18

JOHNSON, RED
52/3 Laval Dairy Update 110

JOHNSON, RYAN
99/0 Millenium C-4
00/1 Pacific 374
98/9 UD3 2, 62, 122
98/9 Upper Deck 15, 283
01/2 Upper Deck 307
98/9 UD G. Reserve 15, 283
01/2 FLOR
96/7 Carolina Monarchs
98/9 New Haven Beast 13

JOHNSON, SCOTT
91/2 Hampton Roads

JOHNSON, SHANE
92/3 BCJHL 69
00/1 Kudos 29
91/2 7th...Sketch OHL 342
01/2 Belfast Giants

JOHNSON, SHAUN
93/4 Humberside Hawks 7
94/5 Humberside Hawks 5
02/3 Coventry Blaze

JOHNSON, STEPHEN
93/4 Humberside Hawks 10
94/5 Humberside Hawks 7

JOHNSON, TERRY
84/5 O-Pee-Chee 186
86/7 TORO
86/7 TORO
82/3 Fredericton Express

JOHNSON, TODD
90/1 7th..Sketch WHL 148
91/2 7th...Sketch WHL 79

JOHNSON, TOM
45-64 BeeHive-2 [Mont.]
45-64 BeeHive-2 [Bost.]
64-67 BeeHive-3 [Bost.]
64/5 Coke/Sprite [Bost.]
77/8 Dernière Heure
48-52 Exhibits [Canadiens]
62/3 Cowan Tile
83 HHOF Postcard D6
83&87 HHOF 52
51/2 La Patrie
51/2 Parkhurst 7
52/3 Parkhurst 9
54/5 Parkhurst 10
55/6 Parkhurst 49
55/6 Parkhurst 71
57/8 Parkhurst [Mont.] 6
58/9 Parkhurst 7
58/9 Parkhurst 10
59/0 Parkhurst 10
60/1 Parkhurst 44
61/2 Parkhurst 42
62/3 Parkhurst 50
93/4 Parkhurst PR55
93/4 Parkie 56-57 143
93/4 Parkie 56-57 79
94/5 Parkie Tall 12
45-54 Quaker Oats
60/1 Shirriff 25
61/2 Shirriff 106
62/3 Shirriff 36
94/5 Slapshot / Guelph 15
63/4 Topps 4
64/5 Topps 101
58/9 Toronto Star Photo
59/0 Toronto Star Photo
64/5 Toronto Star Action
59/0 Toronto Star Weekend
60/1 York Glass [Mont.]
60/1 York
61/2 York 11

JOHNSON, TREVOR
98/9 Hampton Roads
99/0 Hampton Roads

JOHNSON, TYLER
01/2 Moose Jaw Warriors 15
02/3 Moose Jaw Warriors

JOHNSSON, JONAS
94/5 Leaf Elit Set 13
95/6 Leaf Elit Set 177
95 Panini Worlds 148
91/2 Semic Elitserien 49
92/3 Semic Elitserien 71
95/6 UD Elitserien 26, 250
98/9 UD Elitserien 82
99/0 UD Elitserien 85, ✍ Aut.
00/1 UD Elitserien 74, P4

JOHNSSON, KIM
99/0 BAP Mem. 200
00/1 BAP Mem. 322
01/2 BAP Memor. 423
99/0 Dynagon Ice 130
95/6 Leaf Elit Set 266
99/0 Millenium 158, C-40, ✍ Aut. 158
99/0 NHL Power Play
02/3 O-Pee-Chee 140
99/0 Omega 155
00/1 Pacific 263
02/3 Pacific 281
02/3 Pacific Complete 395
99/0 Panini Sticker 102
01/2 Parkhurst 227, 368
99/0 SP Authentic 110
02/3 Sports Vault 109
00/1 Topps 227
02/3 Topps 140
02/3 T. Limited 140
99/0 To. Prmr. Plus 93
02/3 T. Total 35
02/3 Upper Deck 375
95/6 UD Elitserien 134
97/8 UD Elitserien 136
98/9 UD Elitserien 150
01/2 UD Vintage 170
02/3 UD Vintage 183
02/3 Victory - NP48
01/2 PHIL

JOHNSSON, PIERRE
94/5 Leaf Elit Set 128
95/6 Leaf Elit Set 117
95/6 UD Elitserien 172

JOHNSTON, ANDY
98/9 Guildford Flames

JOHNSTON, BERNHARD
94/5 DEL 247
95/6 DEL 241

JOHNSTON, BILLY-JAY
93/4 Slapshot / Oshawa 19
94/5 Slapshot / Sarnia 18
95/6 Slapshot 264
92/3 Oshawa Generals

JOHNSTON, CHRIS
91/2 7th...Sketch WHL 201
95/6 Dayton Bombers
98/9 Oklahoma City Blazers
92/3 Brandon Wheat Kings

JOHNSTON, DENNY
99/0 Medicine Hat Tigers
00/1 Medicine Hat Tigers

JOHNSTON, ED
45-64 BeeHive-2 [Bost.]
64-67 BeeHive-3 [Bost.]
64/5 Coke/Sprite [Bost.]
70/1 Dad's Cookies
70/1 Eddie Sargent 5
71/2 Eddie Sargent 15
72/3 Eddie Sargent 20
70/1 Esso Power Player
91/2 Future Trends C72 93, ✍ 93
93/4 Kraft / PB
72/3 Post 17
74/5 Loblaws
73/4 Mac's Milk
68/9 O-Pee-Chee 133
69/0 O-Pee-Chee 200
70/1 O-Pee-Chee 133
71/2 O-Pee-Chee 172
72/3 O-Pee-Chee 261
73/4 O-Pee-Chee 23
75/6 O-Pee-Chee 185
76/7 O-Pee-Chee 285
77/8 O-Pee-Chee 276
95/6 Parkie 66-67 18
94/5 Parkie Tall 15, 167, 168
63/4 Topps 2
64/5 Topps 21
65/6 Topps 97
66/7 Topps 99
66/7 Topps / Test 64
67/8 Topps 96
71/2 Topps 4
72/3 Topps 13
73/4 Topps 23
75/6 Topps 185
01/2 T/O Archives 34
71/2 Toronto Sun Photo
70/1 BOST
71/2 BOST
93/4 PITT / Foodland 19
94/5 PITT / Foodland 11
95/6 PITT / Foodland 22
73/4 TORO

JOHNSTON, GREG
94/5 DEL 155
95/6 DEL 156
96/7 DEL 229
98/9 DEL 43
99/0 Eishockey 285
87/8 OPC/Topps 102
90/1 ProCards 160
91/2 ProCards 353
92/3 Topps 413
00/1 UD DEL 39, A5
85/6 Moncton G'Flames
90/1 Newmarket Saints
87/8 Soo Greyhounds 35

JOHNSTON, JAY
90/1 7th..Sketch OHL 225

JOHNSTON, JOE**
97/8 Guildford Flames

JOHNSTON, JOEY*
71/2 Eddie Sargent 143
72/3 Eddie Sargent 45
74/5 Loblaws
71/2 O-Pee-Chee 182
72/3 O-Pee-Chee 96
73/4 O-Pee-Chee 172
74/5 O-Pee-Chee 56
74/5 O-Pee-Chee 185
75/6 O-Pee-Chee 193
76/7 O-Pee-Chee 325
72/3 Topps 48
73/4 Topps 143
74/5 Topps 56
74/5 Topps 185
75/6 Topps 193
71/2 Toronto Sun Photo

JOHNSTON, KARL
91/2 ProCards 95

JOHNSTON, KURT
95/6 Slapshot 125

JOHNSTON, LARRY
72/3 Eddie Sargent 82
73/4 O-Pee-Chee 251
75/6 O-Pee-Chee 352

JOHNSTON, MARK
90/1 Brandon Wheat Kings

JOHNSTON, MARSHALL
71/2 Eddie Sargent 141
72/3 Eddie Sargent 44
72/3 O-Pee-Chee 171
73/4 O-Pee-Chee 21
74/5 O-Pee-Chee 189
73/4 Topps 21
74/5 Topps 189
71/2 Toronto Sun Photo
81/2 COLR

JOHNSTON, MARTY
98 Bowman 86
98 Bowman Chrome 86

JOHNSTON, RANDY
81/2 Indianapolis Checkers
82/3 Indianapolis Checkers

JOHNSTON, ROBERT
98/9 Guildford Flames

JOHNSTON, RYAN
98/9 Brandon Wheat Kings

JOHNSTON, TYLER
92/3 BCJHL 15

JOHNSTON, WINGY
34-43 BeeHive-1 [Chic.]

JOHNSTONE, ALEX
96/7 Halifax Moosehead
96/7 Halifax Moosehead
97/8 Halifax Moosehead
97/8 Halifax Moosehead
98/9 Halifax Moosehead

JOHNSTONE, CHRIS
93/4 Slapshot / Niagara Falls 27
95/6 Slapshot 205

JOHNSTONE, DONALD
99/0 Hull Olympiques BN
99/0 Hull Olympiques 4

JOHNSTONE, EDDIE
79/0 O-Pee-Chee 179
80/1 O-Pee-Chee 277
81/2 O-Pee-Chee 226
82/3 O-Pee-Chee 226
83/4 O-Pee-Chee 124
84/5 O-Pee-Chee 55
81/2 OPC Sticker 169
82/3 OPC/Topps Sticker 139
82/3 Post [NYRa.]
83/4 Souhaits Keychain [Rangers]
79/0 Topps 179
81/2 Topps 99 [East]
84/5 Topps 43
98/9 Cincinnati M'Ducks 5
99/0 Cincinnati M'Ducks
93/4 Johnstown Chiefs 20
94/5 Johnstown Chiefs 22
89/0 New Haven Nighthawks

JOHNSTONE, JEFF
95/6 Classic 89
93/4 Slapshot / Niagara Falls 10
95/6 Slapshot 193

JOKELA, MIKKO
99/0 Cardset 306
00/1 Cardset 77
02/3 Cardset 182
98/9 SPx Prospects 72
98/9 UD Black Diam. 99
01/2 Albany River Rats
02/3 Albany River Rats

JOKIHARJU, JUHA
91/2 Jyvas Hyva 34
92/3 Jyvas Hyva 68
93/4 Jyvas Hyva 107
95/6 Leaf Elit Set 154
93/4 Sisu 13
94/5 Sisu 169, 320, 383

JOKILAHTI, JARMO
92/3 Jyvas Hyva 71
93/4 Jyvas Hyva 140
93/4 Sisu 140

JOKINEN, ARI
80/1 Mallasjuoma 28

JOKINEN, ARTO
80/1 Mallasjuoma 16
78/9 SM-Liiga 103

JOKINEN, JARI
71/2 Williams Finnish 363
72/3 Williams Finnish 327

JOKINEN, JORMA
70/1 Kuvajulkaisut 347

JOKINEN, JUHO
98/9 Cardset 241

JOKINEN, JUSSI
02/3 Cardset 183, -BFG 2, ✍ BFG

JOKINEN, JYRKI
93/4 Jyvas Hyva 143
93/4 Sisu 157
94/5 Sisu 130

JOKINEN, KARI
70/1 Kuvajulkaisut 310

JOKINEN, OLLI
99/0 BAP Mem. 115
00/1 BAP Mem. 11, 411
02/3 Bowman 64
98/9 Bowman's Best 101, F6
02/3 Calder ✂- GWJ 11
98/9 Cardset Leij. 24
99/0 Cardset 191, MW2, AH 7-ruutu
00/1 Cardset 116

02/3 Cardset 30, -DD 5, -SGSP 5
97/8 Do. Elite 72
97/8 Do. Preferred 147, 196
99/0 Dynagon Ice 124
02/3 eTopps 51
97/8 Leaf 155
99/0 Millenium 152, ✍ Aut. 152
99/0 NHL Power Play
02/3 O-Pee-Chee 168
98/9 Omega 117
99/0 Pacific 192
00/1 Pacific 441
02/3 Pacific Complete 476
97/8 Pa. Dynagon Rookie
97/8 Pa. Paramount 90
98/9 Pa. Revolution 67
99/0 Panini Sticker 88
00/1 Panini Sticker 58
02/3 Parkhurst 192
02/3 Parkhurst Retro 187
97/8 Pinnacle 4
97/8 Pi. Certified F
00/1 Private Stock ✂ GUG 51
00/1 PS Titanium ✂ GUG 18
02/3 PS Titanium 46
02/3 Quest for the Cup 41
97/8 Score 65
98/9 SP Authentic 100
02/3 SP Authentic 41
02/3 Sports Vault 44
99/0 SPx 95
99/0 Stadium 162
02/3 Topps 168
98/9 To. Finest F18
98/9 T. Gold Label 43
00/1 To. Heritage 172
02/3 T. Limited 168
02/3 T. Total 398
98/9 UD Choice 275
98/9 UD3 11, 71, 131
97/8 Upper Deck 288
98/9 Upper Deck 12, GN25
99/0 Upper Deck 254
00/1 Upper Deck 304
01/2 Upper Deck 305
02/3 Upper Deck 322
98/9 UD Black Diam. 42
98/9 UD G. Reserve 12
99/0 UD G. Reserve 254
97/8 UD Ice 58, L9A
98/9 UD MVP 95
99/0 UD Retro G8C
02/3 UD Rookie 43
02/3 UD Vintage 109, GB 109
02/3 Vanguard 45
99/0 Victory 183
00/1 Victory 149
01/2 FLOR

JOKINEN, PENTTI
65/6 Hellas 22

JOKINEN, PETRI
72/3 Williams Finnish 345

JOKINEN, SATU
99/0 Cardset AH Q-pata

JOLETTE, JONATHAN
00/1 Baie-Comeau 20

JOLIAT, AURÈLE
35/6 Amalgamated Press
25-27 Anonymous 8
34-43 BeeHive-1 [Mont.]
35-40 Canada Starch
33/4 Canadian Gum
24/5 Champ's Cigarettes
33-35 Diamond Match Silv.
36-39 Diamond Match TT1
36-39 Diamond Match TT2
36-39 Diamond Match TT3
25 Dominion Chocolates 119
33/4 Hamilton Gum 27
83 HHOF Postcard D7
83&87 HHOF 53
27/8 La Patrie
27/8 La Presse
95/6 Legends of Hockey 71
24/5 Maple Crispette [V130] 14
33/4 O-Pee-Chee 50
36/7 O-Pee-Chee 129
37/8 O-Pee-Chee 152
43-47 Parade Sportive
55/6 Parkhurst 58
34/5 Sweet Caporal
02/3 Ultimate Mem. ✂ BOS, ✂ Cor, ✂ EA, ✂ GAO, ✂ SF, ✂ VGJ, ✍ Cut
23/4 William Paterson 14
24/5 William Paterson 48
33/4 WWGum Premium 3
33/4 WWGum 3
37/8 World Wide Gum 65
92/3 MONT / OPC 21

JOLY, GREG
74/5 Loblaws
74/5 O-Pee-Chee 294
75/6 O-Pee-Chee 170
76/7 O-Pee-Chee 52
77/8 O-Pee-Chee 273
78/9 O-Pee-Chee 148
79/0 O-Pee-Chee 311
80/1 O-Pee-Chee 270
82/3 O-Pee-Chee 86
82/3 Post [Detr.]
75/6 Topps 170
76/7 Topps 52
78/9 Topps 148
79/0 DETR
80/1 DETR
74/5 WASH

JOLY, MARIO
99/0 Hull Olympiques BN
99/0 Hull Olympiques 13
00/1 Hull Olympiques 12
01/2 Québec Remparts 18

JOMPHE, DANIEL
84/5 Chicoutimi Saguenéens

JOMPHE, JEAN-FRANÇOIS
93/4 Cla. Prospects 123
99/0 Eishockey 143
97/8 Pa. Invincible R-3
90/1 7th..Sketch LHJMQ 108
96/7 Upper Deck 3
96/7 UD CC 8
00/1 UD DEL 13
96/7 ANAH / Up Front 19
93/4 San Diego Gulls

JONAK, JIRI
94/5 APS 144
96/7 APS 193
97/8 APS 127
97/8 DS 96
96/7 DS Sticker 190
97/8 DS Sticker 251

JONASSON, VINNIE
95/6 Brandon Wheat Kings

JONATHAN, STAN
77/8 O-Pee-Chee 270
78/9 O-Pee-Chee 181
79/0 O-Pee-Chee 263
80/1 O-Pee-Chee 113
81/2 O-Pee-Chee 13
82/3 Post [Bost.]
78/9 Topps 181
79/0 Topps 263
80/1 Topps 113
83/4 PITT / Heinz

JONES, BOB
90/1 ProCards 301
91/2 ProCards 251
93/4 Muskegon Fury
87/8 Soo Greyhounds 5
89/0 Soo Greyhounds
96/7 Soo Greyhounds
00/1 Toronto St. Mike's

JONES, BOBBY
99/0 Brampton Batallion 30

JONES, BRAD
91/2 Bowman 181
96/7 DEL 67
91/2 O-Pee-Chee 478
91/2 OPC Premier 115
91/2 Parkhurst 127
91/2 Pro Set 456
89/0 ProCards AHL 42
91/2 Score 53T
91/2 Score CAN 603
92/3 Topps 299
91/2 To. Stadium 368
92/3 T. Stadium Club 141
91/2 Upper Deck 304
90/1 LOSA / Smokey 21
91/2 PHIL / J.C. Penney
98/9 BC Icemen 18
98/9 BC Icemen
95/6 Binghampton Rangers
87/8 Soo Greyhounds 7

JONES, CHRIS
91/2 Avant Garde BCJHL 62
91/2 Avant Garde BCJHL 153
92/3 BCJHL 105
91/2 Nanaimo Clippers

JONES, COREY
90/1 7th..Sketch WHL 103
91/2 7th...Sketch WHL 26
89/0 Victoria Cougars

JONES, DARYL
92/3 MPS SJHL 153

JONES, DOUG
94/5 Flint Generals
85/6 Kitchener Rangers
86/7 Kitchener Rangers
87/8 Kitchener Rangers

JONES, HARALD
72 Semic Sticker 159

JONES, JIMMY*
78/9 O-Pee-Chee 288
79/0 O-Pee-Chee 288

JONES, JIMMY**
10/1 Imperial 19

JONES, JIMMY1
77/8 TORO
78/9 TORO
79/0 TORO

JONES, KEITH
99/0 BAP Mem. 223
00/1 BAP Mem. 340
92/3 Classic 96
92/3 Classic Prospects 43
95/6 Donruss 282
95/6 Fleer Metal 160
92/3 Fleer Ultra 436
93/4 Fleer Ultra 446
94/5 Leaf 506
95/6 Leaf 105
97/8 Limited 18
99/0 Millenium 187, ✍ Aut. 187
92/3 OPC Premier 14
98/9 Omega 175
99/0 Pacific 304
00/1 Pacific 298
97/8 Pacific CC 291
99/0 Pa. Paramount 170
95/6 Panini Sticker 140
92/3 Parkhurst 427
93/4 Parkhurst 495
95/6 Parkhurst 217
94/5 Pinnacle 378
95/6 Pinnacle 27
96/7 Pinnacle 93
96/7 Pi. Be A Player 194, ✍ Aut. 194
95/6 Playoff 323
96/7 Playoff 423
95/6 POG 282
93/4 Power Play 466
93/4 Premier 96
93/4 Score 417
95/6 Score 95
96/7 Score 225
97/8 Score 250
97/8 Score Colo. 9
95/6 Topps 73
93/4 To. Stadium 234
95/6 To. Stadium 88
92/3 Upper Deck 533
93/4 Upper Deck 377
94/5 Upper Deck 411
95/6 Upper Deck 451, SE-85
94/5 UD BAP ✍ 131
96/7 UD Black Diam. 39
95/6 UD CC 166
96/7 UD CC 285
97/8 UD Coll. Choice 59
98/9 UD MVP 150
99/0 UD MVP 151
00/1 UD Vintage 269
99/0 Victory 218
92/3 WASH / Kodak
95/6 WASH

JONES, NICK
95/6 Roanoke Express
99/0 Guelph Storm

JONES, ROB
95/6 Richmond Renegades

JONES, RON
75/6 O-Pee-Chee 247
75/6 Topps 247
89/0 Windsor Spitfires

JONES, STEVE
95/6 Slapshot 329

JONES, TY
99/0 BAP Mem. 172
97 Bowman 142, ✍ Aut.
98/9 Dynagon Ice 43
99/0 Pacific 99
99/0 SPx 34
98/9 UD Choice 303
98/9 Upper Deck 242, GN14
99/0 Upper Deck 36, N5
97/8 UD Black Diam. 52
98/9 UD G. Reserve 242
99/0 UD G. Reserve 36
99/0 UD MVP 45
99/0 Victory 68
99/0 Cleveland Lumberjacks
99/0 Florida Everblades
01/2 Norfolk Admirals
95/6 Spokane Chiefs 7
97/8 Spokane Chiefs

JONES, WINSTON
88/9 Brockville Braves

JONES-PARRY, SHON
97/8 Portland Winter Hawks
99/0 Prince George Cougars

JONSSON, HANS
95/6 Leaf Elit Set 102
99/0 Omega 189
91/2 Semic Elitserien 210
92/3 Semic Elitserien 231
99/0 To. Prmr. Plus 92
95/6 UD Elitserien 156
97/8 UD Elitserien 153
98/9 UD Elitserien 170
02/3 UD MVP 150

JONSSON, LARS
00/1 UD Elitserien 110, 216

JONSSON, MAGNUS
92/3 Semic Elitserien 92

JONSSON, PIERRE
96/7 DEL 94

JONSSON, TOMAS
95 Globe 14
94/5 Leaf Elit Set 100, GC-23
95/6 Leaf Elit Set 62, 303, C-1, FTF-15, LM-5
82/3 O-Pee-Chee 202
83/4 O-Pee-Chee 9
84/5 O-Pee-Chee 128
85/6 OPC/Topps 154
86/7 OPC/Topps 78
87/8 OPC/Topps 190
88/9 OPC/Topps 108
83/4 OPC/Topps Sticker 87
85/6 OPC Sticker 78-211
86/7 OPC Sticker 214-86
87/8 Panini Sticker 92
95 Panini Worlds 141
82/3 Post [NYIs.]
94 Semic 54
89/0 Semic Elitserien 124
90/1 Semic Elitserien 202
91/2 Semic Elitserien 131
91/2 Semic Elitserien 342
92/3 Semic Elitserien 153
89 Semic Sticker 5
91 Semic Sticker 32
93 Semic Sticker 5
83/4 Souhaits Keychain [Islanders]
95/6 UD Elitserien 95, 227, 255
97/8 UD Elitserien 101, 201, UDS11
96 Wien 47
88/9 EDMO
88/9 EDMO / Action 149
83/4 NYIS
83/4 NYIS / News 16
84/5 NYIS / News 20

JÖNSSON, ANDERS
89/0 Semic Elitserien 69
90/1 Semic Elitserien 289

JÖNSSON, FREDRIK
97/8 UD Elitserien 107

JÖNSSON, JONAS
96/7 DEL 150
90/1 Semic Elitserien 121
91/2 Semic Elitserien 124

JÖNSSON, JÖRGEN
00/1 BAP Mem. 225
99/0 Dynagon Ice 125
95 Globe 38
99/0 HoloGrFX 35
94/5 Leaf Elit Set 69, GC-10, TG-5
95/6 Leaf Elit Set 215
99/0 Omega 142
00/1 Pacific 431
99/0 Panini Sticker 87
95 Semic 66
92/3 Semic Elitserien 272
94/5 Sig. Rookies 46, ✍ 46
99/0 SP Authentic 109
99/0 SPx 93
99/0 Stadium 176
99/0 To. Prmr. Plus 112
99/0 Ult. Victory 102
99/0 UD Black Diam. 55
95/6 UD Elitserien 72, NA9
97/8 UD Elitserien 64, UDS6, S4, C21
98/9 UD Elitserien 99
00/1 UD Elitserien 90, 191, P5, S2
99/0 WGretzky 104

JÖNSSON, KENNY
99/0 Aurora 90
98/9 Be A Player 87, ✍ Aut. 87
99/0 BAP Mem. 232
00/1 BAP Mem. 150
01/2 BAP Memor. 183
95/6 Bowman 86
93/4 Classic 135
94/5 Classic 25, R8, T69
93/4 Cla. 4 Sport 195
94/5 Cla. Images 59, ✍ Aut.
99/0 Crown Royale 87
95/6 Donruss 115
96/7 Donruss 74
95/6 Do. Elite 4
96/7 Do. Elite 117
99/0 Dynagon Ice 126
95/6 Edge Ice C4
97/8 Esso 46
02/3 First Edition 97, ✂ Jers.
94/5 Flair 182
94/5 Fleer 216
96/7 Fleer 65
95/6 Fleer Metal 144
96/7 Fl. Picks 92
94/5 Fleer Ultra 377
95/6 Fleer Ultra 161
96/7 Fl. Ultra 102
95 Globe 15
01/2 Heads Up ✂ JQ 4
94/5 Leaf 472
95/6 Leaf 24
96/7 Leaf 60
94/5 Leaf Elit Set GC 11
94/5 L. Limited 115
95/6 L. Limited 88
96/7 L. Preferred 28
95/6 McDonald's McD-36
96/7 Metal Univ. 93
99/0 Millenium 156, ✍ Aut. 156
02/3 O-Pee-Chee 59
98/9 Omega 146
98/9 Pacific 282
99/0 Pacific 255
00/1 Pacific 442
01/2 Pacific 250
02/3 Pacific 238
02/3 Pacific Complete 161
97/8 Pa. Invincible R-116
98/9 Pa. Paramount 143
99/0 Pa. Paramount 142
98/9 Pa. Revolution 87
95/6 Panini Sticker 208, 306
96/7 Panini Sticker 93
97/8 Panini Sticker 76
98/9 Panini Sticker 77
99/0 Panini Sticker 92
00/1 Panini Sticker 57
93/4 Parkhurst 535
95/6 Parkhurst 203
00/1 Parkhurst P-149
01/2 Parkhurst 129, ✂ PS50
94/5 Parkie SE173
94/5 Pinnacle 264, 476, RTP4
95/6 Pinnacle 130
96/7 Pinnacle 91
95/6 Playoff 203
95/6 POG 267, I-031
94/5 Premier 329
01/2 Pr. Stock ✂ GUG 63
00/1 PS Titanium ✂ GUG 110
00/1 PS Titanium Draft ✂ 62
95/6 Pro Magnet 72
99/0 Revolution 91
94/5 Score TR6
95/6 Score 30
96/7 Score 168
94/5 Select 172, YE-4
95 Semic 59
92/3 Semic Elitserien 253
00/1 Signature 133, ✍ Aut. 79, ✂ DD-9, ✂ J-18
01/2 Signature ✂ GJ42, ✂ GSJ42, ✂ TM20
02/3 Signature GS-47
95/6 SBx Emotion 172
95/6 SBx Impact 162, F-13
96/7 SBx Impact 76
94/5 SP P-7
95/6 SP 147
96/7 SP 93
97/8 SP Authentic 95
99/0 SP Authentic 54
02/3 Sports Vault 78
99/0 SPx 94
00/1 SPx ✂ WM
99/0 Stadium 11
00/1 Stadium 39, CA14, ✂ SCS
95/6 Topps 211, 9NG
99/0 Topps 113, NS4
00/1 Topps 101
02/3 Topps 59
99/0 To. Chrome 113
00/1 To. Chrome 79
94/5 Topps Finest 5, BBR-18
95/6 To. Finest 29
98/9 T. Gold Label 27
99/0 To. Gold Label 50
02/3 T. Limited 59
99/0 To. Prmr. Plus 33
01/2 To. Reserve ✂ TR
95/6 To. Stadium 107
02/3 T. Total 74
98/9 UD Choice 125
00/1 UD Heroes ✍ SG
99/0 Ult. Victory 55
92/3 Upper Deck 596
94/5 Upper Deck 238, 530, 560, C11, SP-168
95/6 Upper Deck 463, SE-81
96/7 Upper Deck 101
97/8 Upper Deck 312
98/9 Upper Deck 318
99/0 Upper Deck 84
00/1 Upper Deck 112
01/2 Upper Deck 112
94/5 UD BAP R154
95/6 UD BAP 180, ✍ S180
96/7 UD Black Diam. 73
97/8 UD Black Diam. 10
95/6 UD CC 137, 373
96/7 UD CC 159
97/8 UD Coll. Choice 159
95/6 UD Elitserien 240
98/9 UD G. Reserve 318
99/0 UD G. Reserve 84
98/9 UD MVP 130
99/0 UD MVP 129
00/1 UD MVP 111
01/2 UD MVP 121
99/0 UD MVP Cup 114
00/1 UD Vintage 231, 233
99/0 Victory 179
00/1 Victory 145
01/2 Victory 227
99/0 WGretzky 107
96 Wien 53
96/7 NYIS
94/5 St. John's Maple Leafs

JÖNSSON, MIKAEL
83/4 Kelowna Wings

JÖNSSON, ROGER
97/8 UD Elitserien 194
99/0 UD Elitserien 191

JÖNSSON, STEFAN
94/5 Leaf Elit Set 162
95/6 Leaf Elit Set 79
89/0 Semic Elitserien 225
90/1 Semic Elitserien 54
91/2 Semic Elitserien 229
92/3 Semic Elitserien 185
95/6 UD Elitserien 121
97/8 UD Elitserien 123
98/9 UD Elitserien 134

JOORIS, MARK
95/6 DEL 357
96/7 DEL 217

JORDAN, RIC
72/3 New England Whalers

JORDAN, WILLIS
00/1 Kudos 126

JORDE, MANFRED
94/5 DEL 185

JORDE, RYAN
02/3 Rochester Americans
99/0 Lethbridge Hurricanes
01/2 Moose Jaw Warriors 1

JORGENSEN, REID
02/3 Kamloops Blazers

JORGENSON, KEN
82/3 Medicine Hat Tigers

JORGENSON, KEVIN
88/9 Portland Winter Hawks
89/0 Portland Winter Hawks

JORGENSON, LEN
88/9 Kamloops Blazers

JORGENSON, LYNN
78/9 Saginaw Gears

JORMAKKA, TUOMO
80/1 Mallasjuoma 153
78/9 SM-Liiga 161

JORTIKKA, ARI
78/9 SM-Liiga 99

JORTIKKA, HANNU
92/3 Jyvas Hyva 18
94/5 Leaf Elit Set 302
80/1 Mallasjuoma 177
78/9 SM-Liiga 200
73/4 Williams Finnish 280

JOSEFSSON, OLA
94/5 Leaf Elit Set 74
95/6 Leaf Elit Set 187
89/0 Semic Elitserien 71
90/1 Semic Elitserien 287
91/2 Semic Elitserien 68
92/3 Semic Elitserien 95
95/6 UD Elitserien 49

JOSEPH, CHRIS
00/1 BAP Mem. 173
91/2 Bowman 108
93/4 Donruss 492
94/5 Donruss 253
95/6 Donruss 64
94/5 Fleer Ultra 207
94/5 Leaf 158
91/2 O-Pee-Chee 432
92/3 O-Pee-Chee 203
88/9 OPC Sticker 218-88
89/0 opcSticker 225-84
97/8 Pa. Invincible R-202
90/1 Panini/EDM 8
95/6 Parkhurst 433
94/5 Parkie SE168
94/5 Pinnacle 156
94/5 POG 228
93/4 Power Play 445
93/4 Premier 87
94/5 Premier 374
90/1 Pro Set 443
89/0 ProCards AHL 131
91/2 Score CAN 415
93/4 Score 576
94/5 Score 98
95/6 Topps 93
91/2 To. Stadium 362
94/5 T. Stadium Club 224
90/1 Upper Deck 323
91/2 Upper Deck 436
94/5 Upper Deck 185
95/6 Upper Deck 449
95/6 UD BAP 98, ✍ S98
93/4 EDMO / Sheet
88/9 EDMO
88/9 EDMO / Action 2
90/1 EDMO / IGA
92/3 EDMO
92/3 EDMO / IGA 011
94/5 PITT / Foodland 17
95/6 PITT / Foodland 19
94/5 TAMP / Sky Box
96/7 VANC / IGA
98/9 Cincinnati Cyclones

JOSEPH, CURTIS
01/2 Adrenaline 181, CL 20, PP 34
91/2 Air Canada SJHL A49
01/2 Atomic 91, CP 19, Stat. 10, TN 13
02/3 Atomic 38, -D 7, -NPC 5, ✂ GWJ 8
98/9 Aurora 182
99/0 Aurora 136, Stripe 136, CF-19, GU-19, ST-18
00/1 Aurora 139, Pins. 139, CC-10, CF-19, SR-19, TPS-10A
02/3 BAP All-Star 37, ✂ ASJ, ✂ HSHSJers, Bobble
98/9 Be A Player 284, H-15, ✍ Aut. 284
99/0 BAP Mem. 202, H-13, ✂ J-11, ✂ TM-1, ✂ TM-41
00/1 BAP Mem. 114, ✂ J-40, ✂ G-5, ✂ G-13, ✂ G-17, ✂ G-18, ✂ G-20, ✂ G-27, ✂ G-29, ✂ H-5, ✂ TM-9, ✂ TM-24, ✂ TM-37
01/2 BAP Memor. 190, ✂ ASJ, ✂ ASE, ✂ ASN, ✂ ASD, ✂ AST, ✂ CoO, ✂ GoalJ, ✂ GT, HSHS, ✂ SCP
02/3 BAP Memorabilia 131, 265, ✂ ASJ23, ✂ ASE9, ✂ ASN9, ✂ AST2, ✂ AST18, ✂ SC25, ✂ TM8
01/2 BAP Update HSHS, ✂ HSHSJers, ✂ H2
01/2 BT Pipes 17, 97, HSHS, -Mask, ✂ ASJ, ✂ DM, ✂ Jers., ✂ Emb., ✂ S&J, ✂ GG, ✂ HSHSJers, ✂ ITN
02/3 Between the Pipes 17, 131, M11, ✂ ASJ2, ✂ CP2, ✂ GB1, ✂ GP4, ✂ GN8, ✂ I7, ✍ Aut.
98/9 Bicycle.. A-S
92/3 Bowman 368
01/2 Bowman 47
02/3 Bowman 83
98/9 Bowman's Best 20
02/3 Calder 38
99/0 Crown Royale 134, IE-24
00/1 Crown Royale 100, ✂ JR-10, JotC-24, Land. 10, NP-17
01/2 Crown Royale 131, ASH 19, JotC 28, LH 9
02/3 Crown Royale 34, -COA 3
93/4 Donruss 296
94/5 Donruss 287, MM-5
95/6 Donruss 135
96/7 Donruss 110, BTP-8
97/8 Donruss 43, BTP-8
96/7 Do. Canadian 116
97/8 Do. Canadian 20, NP-27, SCS-2
95/6 Do. Elite 59
96/7 Do. Elite 92
97/8 Do. Elite 19, C-29
97/8 Do. Preferred 84, CG-3
97/8 Do. Priority 123, PG-4
97/8 Do. Studio 29
96/7 Duracell DC4
98/9 Dynagon Ice 180, -IW 9
99/0 Dynagon Ice 189, ASP-18, GM-5, GM-10
93/4 EA Sports 126
95/6 Edge Ice L6
97/8 Esso 18, ✍ Aut.
01/2 eTopps 3
02/3 Exclusive 64, -EA 7
02/3 First Edition 145, ✂ Jers., ✂ DGJ 3
94/5 Flair 156
96/7 Flair 33, HG-5
94/5 Fleer 188, N-5
96/7 Fleer 37
92/3 Fleer Ultra 188
93/4 Fleer Ultra 172
94/5 Fleer Ultra 184, PPM-3
95/6 Fleer Ultra 140, PPM-6
96/7 Fl. Ultra 59
95/6 Future Legends 29
01/2 Heads Up 89, HD 20, SS 19, ✂ JQ 20, / Bobble
02/3 Heads Up 44, -S 9, ✂ GWQ 26, ✂ GWQ 28
93/4 Hockey Wit 35
99/0 HoloGrFX 57
95/6 Hoyle / West. Q-Spade
02/3 In The Game-Used 25, 125, ✂ IE9
96/7 Kellogg's
92/3 Kraft / PB
94/5 Kraft / KD
97/8 Kraft / PB
99/0 Kraft / JELL-O, / KD, / OML
94/5 Kraft Mask
93/4 Leaf 2
93/4 Leaf PW 2
94/5 Leaf 208, CP-3, GLS-7
95/6 Leaf 281
96/7 Leaf 28, SD-5
97/8 Leaf 16, PD-4
94/5 L. Limited 95
96/7 L. Limited 90
96/7 L. Preferred MM-10, VP-13
97/8 Limited 81, 103, 174, FG-23
96/7 McDonald's McD-40
97/8 McDonald's McD-27
98/9 McDonald's McD18
99/0 McDonald's McD-12, ✍ SS
00/1 McDonald's 32, CL-6, GSNF-6
01/2 McDonald's 38, -GSNF, ✂ JPatch 18
02/3 McDonald's 36, -SLG 1, ✂ JP 16
96/7 Metal Univ. 53
99/0 Millenium 227, ✍ Aut. 227, ✂ J-3, ✂✍ J-3, ✂ JS-4, ✂ G-1
98/9 NHL Power Play
90/1 OPC/Topps 171
91/2 O-Pee-Chee 417
92/3 O-Pee-Chee 339
01/2 O-Pee-Chee 62
02/3 O-Pee-Chee 212,Update 212
98/9 OPC Chrome 186, SB4
90/1 OPC Premier 51
91/2 OPC Premier 165
97/8 Omega 93
98/9 Omega 228, -CS 10, -Onl. 32, -PI 14
99/0 Omega 225, 5ST-30, CC-19, EOP-18, NAAS-9
98/9 Pacific 211
99/0 Pacific 407, CI-18, CCA-10, GC-34, ITCNF-19, PAP-20, TL-26
00/1 Pacific 392, GCDC-34, ITC-10, NAS-10
01/2 Pacific 367, 442, CCA 10, GCDC 20, IZ 18, SC 19
02/3 Pacific 361, -MI 8
02/3 Pacific Complete 379
97/8 Pacific CC 242, ITC-9, TC-10
97/8 Pa. Crown Roy. 53, FO-8
98/9 Pa. Crown Roy. 131, -PotG 22
97/8 Pa. Dynagon 49, S-9, T-11
97/8 Pa. Invincible 56
97/8 Pa. Paramount 75, GSL-8
98/9 Pa. Paramount 227, -GS 19, -IG 10
99/0 Pa. Paramount 225, GS-19, IAd-18, IAI-26, PB-34
00/1 Pa. Paramount 230, ES-20, FF-35, GS-18, SZ-9, ✂ GUS-17
97/8 Pa. Revolution 55, RTS-8
98/9 Pa. Revolution 138. -TPA 19, -Show. 33
98/9 Panini Photocard
90/1 Panini Sticker 272
91/2 Panini Sticker 22
92/3 Panini Sticker 15
93/4 Panini Sticker 166
94/5 Panini Sticker 144
95/6 Panini Sticker 265
96/7 Panini Sticker 255
98/9 Panini Sticker 195
99/0 Panini Sticker 157, 352
91/2 Parkhurst 152
92/3 Parkhurst 155
92/3 Parkhurst 503
93/4 Parkhurst 175
94/5 Parkhurst 199, V17
95/6 Parkhurst 350
00/1 Parkhurst P-14
01/2 Parkhurst 58, ✂ PJ33, ✂ HSHSJers, ✂ M10, ✂ M45, ✂ T7
02/3 Parkhurst 106, -CR14, -HHV1, ✂ CRM14
95 Parkhurst Phonecard
02/3 Parkhurst Retro 146
91/2 Pinnacle 105
92/3 Pinnacle 54
92/3 Pinnacle 264
93/4 Pinnacle 15
94/5 Pinnacle 6, GT13, MA10, TP2
96/7 Pinnacle 164
97/8 Pinnacle 93, M-4, TP-2, P-22, / Tin 5
96/7 Pi. Be A Player 206, SP-14, ✍ Aut. 206
97/8 Pi. Be A Player STP 7
97/8 Pi. BeeHive 12
97/8 Pi. Certified 18
97/8 Pi. Epix E17
97/8 Pi. Inside 25, IT-21, SU-10B, S-12, / Can 4, LargeCan
97/8 Pi. Mint 24
96/7 Pi. Summit 150, ITC-5
97/8 Pi. Totally 18
97/8 Pi. Uncut 4
96/7 Pi. Zenith 112
94/5 POG 293
93/4 Power Play 213
93/4 Power Play Game. 4
93/4 Power Play Netm. 4
93/4 Premier 222
93/4 Premier 272
93/4 Prmr. - BG-Top. 18
94/5 Premier 340
00/1 Premier Plus 15, MB14, PT7
99/0 Prism 137, SGDC-20
00/1 Private Stock 93, AC-20, EA-20, Res. 20, PS-55, PSS-24, ✂ GUG-96
01/2 Pr. Stock 90, GR 10, -PS 70, ✂ GUG 95
02/3 Pr. Stock Reserve -ICS 8, ✂ 118
00/1 PS Titanium 91, 3SS-8, ✂ GUG-147
01/2 PS Titanium 129, SK 19, TSS 10, ✂ DSJ 41
02/3 PS Titanium 37, -MM 3
00/1 PS Titanium Draft ✂ 96
90/1 Pro Set 638
91/2 Pro Set 473
92/3 Pro Set 164
91/2 Pro Set Platinum 225
89/0 ProCards IHL 7
02/3 Quest for the Cup 34, -CTC 6
99/0 Revolution 138,NI-18, O-18, SS-33, / CSC 138
00/1 Revolution 139, HD-35, II-19, NI-18, SM-19
90/1 Score 151
91/2 Score 296
91/2 Score CAN 516
92/3 Score 262
93/4 Score 116
94/5 Score 181
95/6 Score 251
96/7 Score 90, NW-7, SD-6
97/8 Score 31, NW-5
90/1 Sco. Young Stars 15
91/2 Score Young Stars 19
92/3 Score Young Stars 17
92/3 Seasons 14
94/5 Select 121
95/6 Select CE 84
96/7 Select CE 66, F-7
96/7 SB 7-Eleven Phonecard
00/1 Signature 104, HSHS, F-28, ✍ Aut. 39, ✂ J-3, ✂ HSHSJers
01/2 Signature C-9, ✂ GUE24, ✂ GJ61, ✂ GSJ61, ✂ ITN24, ✂ IG9, ✂ TM28
02/3 Signature 155, GS-24, ✍ 155
95/6 SBx Emotion 62
95/6 SBx Impact 60
96/7 SBx Impact 42
02/3 Slam Card
94/5 SP 102
95/6 SP 54
96/7 SP 54
97/8 SP Authentic 60
98/9 SP Authentic 82, ✍ SotT, SS27
99/0 SP Authentic 83, SF9, ✍ SotT, / Sample
00/1 SP Authentic 83, SS6, ✍ SotT
01/2 SP Authentic 82, 109, ✍ SotT, ✍ SotTT
02/3 SP Authentic 33, ✍ SotT
00/1 SP GU 55
01/2 SP GU 53, ✂✍ IS, ✂✍ IS2, ✂ Patch, ✂✍ PatchSig, ✂ PatchC (x2), ✂✍ PatchCSig, ✂ PatchT
02/3 SP GU 19, ✂ PH, ✍ Sig
02/3 Sports Vault 220
97/8 SPx 19, D-SPX9
99/0 SPx 144, XT16
00/1 SPx 65, HH14, ✂ WM, ✂✍ WM
01/2 SPx 64, ✂ HT, ✂✍ HTSig
02/3 SPx 30, 88, ✂ WM
98/9 SPx Prospects 54, H28, L12, PS14. -WM
00/1 Stadion 93
99/0 Stadium 118, Chrome 35, Big 15, ✍ CS11, ✍ CS12, ✍ LS9
00/1 Stadium 105, BT20, CA9, GS4, SF20
01/2 Stadium 6, G1,HS8,P13
02/3 Stadium 101
99/0 SLU 191
00/1 SLU 14
92/3 Topps 237
95/6 Topps 215
98/9 Topps 186, SB4
99/0 Topps 94, ✍ TA3
00/1 Topps 78, TC4, HM6, OTG14
01/2 Topps 62, OTG30, SG7
02/3 Topps 212, Update 212, HHC20
99/0 To. Chrome 94
00/1 To. Chrome 61, TC4, HM6
01/2 To. Chrome 62
02/3 T. Chrome 119, ✍ Graph
94/5 Topps Finest 29
98/9 To. Finest 36
98/9 T. Gold Label 39
99/0 To. Gold Label 71, PG15
00/1 To. Gold Label 42, BTM1, B6
00/1 To. Heritage 34, HH12, ✍ CAI
01/2 To. Heritage 42
02/3 To. Heritage 157
00/1 To. Heritage Expo 1
02/3 T. Limited 212
96/7 Topps Picks 83
99/0 To. Prmr. Plus 1, CL, IG5, ✍ CS3, ✍ CSC2, / PP1
01/2 To. Reserve 55
92/3 T. Stadium Club 327
93/4 To. Stadium 162
94/5 T. Stadium Club 142
93/4 TSC Members Only 22
94/5 TSC Members Only 29
00/1 To. Stars 42,133
02/3 T. Total 391, TT12
98/9 UD Choice 81, 251
00/1 UD Heroes 158, TM10, ✂ GT, ✂ GC
01/2 UD PlayMakers Ltd 94, / PM
00/1 UD Reserve 80, 120, GG10
02/3 UD Superstars 83
98/9 UD3 41, 101, 161
00/1 Ultimate Mem. ✍ U-3, ✂ G-28, ✂ PS-6, ✂ Jers. 2, ✂ J-3, ✂ JJ-6, ✂ S-3, ✂ TM-12, ✂ TM-13, ✂ TM-32, ✂ GM-4, ✂ GM-12
01/2 Ultimate Mem. ✂ BAPL, ✂ Emb., ✂ Jers., ✂ S&J, ✂ ITN, ✂ JE, ✂ JJ, ✂ NP, ✂ RA, ✂ WTF
02/3 Ultimate Mem. ✂ A8, ✂ CP, ✂ LA, ✂ NP, ✂ Num
99/0 Ult. Victory 84, NW8
90/1 Upper Deck 175
91/2 Upper Deck 139
92/3 Upper Deck 186
93/4 Upper Deck 157, SP-139
94/5 Upper Deck 91, H33, SP-68
95/6 Upper Deck 296
96/7 Upper Deck 256, X27
97/8 Upper Deck 273, SG31, S25, T10B
98/9 Upper Deck 191, LS29, P20, ✂ GJ4
99/0 Upper Deck 291, 305, CT3, HOF15, SB8, UD10, ✂ GJ, ✂✍ GJS, ✂ GO
00/1 Upper Deck 161, 180, A10, EC6, FT8, F9, GA11, ✂ GJ, ✍ SG
01/2 Upper Deck 163, GL1, LL9, ✂ GoalJ, ✂ PotL, ✂ TendThr, ✂✍ SigJers
02/3 Upper Deck 64, -LL4, ✂ GO, ✂ UDPL
02/3 UD Artistic 34, R34, ✂ AT, / ✍ Art
94/5 UD BAP R71, 107, 174, ✍ 109
96/7 UD Black Diam. 158, RC17
97/8 UD Black Diam. 126
98/9 UD Black Diam. 83, M12, WF13
99/0 UD Black Diam. 84, DS10
00/1 UD Black Diam. 55, IG9, ✂ GG
01/2 UD Challenge 82, BB9, ✂ T200, ✂ TN, ✂ UC, ✂✍ T200S, ✂✍ TNS
02/3 UD Classic 38
95/6 UD CC 291
96/7 UD CC 90, 317
97/8 UD Coll. Choice 89, SQ31, S6, W19, / 5x7 2
98/9 UD G. Reserve 191
99/0 UD G. Reserve 291, 305, ✍ Aut.
01/2 UD Honor Roll 24, 54, OS6
02/3 UD Honor 28, -SG12
96/7 UD Ice 21
97/8 UD Ice 81
00/1 UD Ice 37, CC6, IG9, ✍ CCA
01/2 UD Ice 40, ✍ CCA
00/1 UD Legends 124, 126, LC4, ✍ ES
01/2 UD Mask 128, 189, ✂ CG, ✂✍ SP, ✂ MB, ✂ PM, /Mask
02/3 UD Mask 30, 31, 32, 33, 93, ✂ CW, ✂ GG, ✂ BM, ✂ NB, ✂ PW, ✂ SS, ✂ VC, / Mask, ✍ Mask
98/9 UD MVP 194
99/0 UD MVP 198, LL6, GU14, ✂ GU27
00/1 UD MVP 165, MM9, ME1, VC10, ✂ CG, ✍ PS, ✍ ME
01/2 UD MVP 175, 220, MM11,✂ GS
02/3 UD MVP 65, ✍ PSig
99/0 UD MVP Cup 174, CP10, GM10, GC, ✂ GU, ✍ PS
99/0 UD Ovation 55, APOH, ✍ APOH
02/3 UD Piece 36
96/7 UD Post, SU-2
01/2 UD Premier 47, ✂ S, ✂ D (x2), ✍ SigG
02/3 UD Premier 22, ✂ Jers, ✂ JD, ✂ Patch
00/1 UD Pros&Prosp. 80, NP9
99/0 UD Retro 75
02/3 UD Rookie 37, ✍ TD
01/2 UD Top Shelf 41
02/3 UD Top Shelf 84, ✂ CP, ✂ M, ✂ SS, ✂ SW
00/1 UD Vintage 338, 345, 346, GG18, ✂ O6-POH
01/2 UD Vintage 235, 243
02/3 UD Vintage 94, GB 94, T27
97/8 Valu-net, ✍ Aut.
00/1 Vanguard 93, CF-10, HV-32, IF-17, VP-20
01/2 Vanguard 92, SW 19, VT 10, ✂ DGM 32
02/3 Vanguard 37, -SW 3, -VT 3, ✂ GWJ 20
99/0 Victory 284, 348, 389
00/1 Victory 220, 259, 327
01/2 Victory 325, 329, 415
02/3 Victory - NP13
01/2 Waving the Flag 5
99/0 WGretzky 166, 180, EG15, ✂ TG, ✍ SG
97/8 Zenith 17, Z38
96/7 EDMO
97/8 EDMO
97/8 EDMO / Ticket Card
89/0 SLOU / Kodak
90/1 SLOU / Kodak
91/2 SLOU
92/3 SLOU / McDon. 9
99/0 TORO / Pizza Pizza 5

JOSEPH, FABIAN
92 C.O.A. Winter Olympics 196
91/2 Canada Nationals
93/4 Canada Nationals
95/6 Edge Ice 162
93/4 Fleer Ultra 464
93/4 Power Play 484
93/4 Premier - Canada 7
88/9 ProCards / Cape Breton
89/0 ProCards AHL 137
92/3 Score COH 8
94/5 Score CT10
94/5 Milwaukee Admirals
95/6 Milwaukee Admirals
96/7 Milwaukee Admirals
97/8 Milwaukee Admirals
82/3 Victoria Cougars
83/4 Victoria Cougars

JOSEPH, TONY
89/0 ProCards AHL 48
90/1 ProCards 243
91/2 ProCards 155
90/1 Moncton Hawks

JOSEPH, CURTIS
01/2 SP GU ✂✍ ISD

JOSEPHSON, MIKE
91/2 Avant Garde BCJHL 75
91/2 Avant Garde BCJHL 166
93/4 Kamloops Blazers
95/6 Lethbridge Hurricanes

JOSS, EDDIE
52/3 Laval Dairy Update 120

JOSS, TERRY
95/6 Slapshot 407

JØSTNE, TOM
92/3 Semic Nordisk 236

JOTKUS, PETE
37/8 World Wide Gum 104

JOUBERT, JACQUES
96/7 Milwaukee Admirals
95/6 Peoria Rivermen

JOUTSENVUORI, TIMO
71/2 Williams Finnish 364

JOVANOVSKI, ED
96/7 All-Sport PPF 71, 198
94/5 Assets 8, 33, DC9
98/9 Aurora 80
02/3 BAP All-Star 38, ✂ ASJ
99/0 BAP Mem. 93
00/1 BAP Mem. 28
01/2 BAP Memor. 31
02/3 BAP Memorabilia 95, 238, ✂ ASJ24, ✂ TM19
01/2 BAP Update ✂ H17
96/7 Bic.Sports Aces Q-S
95/6 Bowman 100, BB19
94/5 Classic 1, C6, CP11, R9, T26
95/6 Classic 98, AS9, BK19, ✍ Aut.
95/6 Cla. Assets 17
95/6 Cla. Clear Assets 58
94/5 Classic Draft Day
95/6 Cla. 5 Sport 138, S-75, SFF-K
94/5 Classic 4 Sport 115, BC17, HV4, Sprint, 4in1
94/5 Cla. Images 15, CE17
94/5 Cla. Images 4 Sport 94, CP19
93/4 Cla. Prospects 203
95/6 Cla. Visions 92
95/6 Cla. Vis. Signings 75, ✍ Aut.
95/6 Donruss C3TWC 6
96/7 Donruss D-10, HL-3, RR-7
97/8 Donruss 144
96/7 Do. Canadian 35
97/8 Do. Canadian 14
95/6 Do. Elite 68, R-11
96/7 Do. Elite 82, A-6
97/8 Do. Elite 33
97/8 Do. Preferred 19
97/8 Do. Priority 27
97/8 Do. Studio 39
98/9 Dynagon Ice 81
02/3 Exclusive 167
02/3 First Edition 88, 411R, ✂ Jers.
96/7 Flair 37, HN-5
96/7 Fleer 39, RS-6
95/6 Fleer Metal 178
96/7 Fl. Picks 98, F50-21, JE-13
95/6 Fleer Ultra 342, EA-10
96/7 Fl. Ultra 65, PL-5, UP-7
96/7 Kraft / TT
96/7 Leaf 208, FOI-13, LL-19
97/8 Leaf 17
94/5 L. Limited CAN 5
96/7 L. Limited 14, BTB-7
96/7 L. Preferred 68, VP-8
97/8 Limited 5, 37
96/7 Maggers 71
96/7 McDonald's McD-6
02/3 McDonald's -SLG 3
96/7 Metal Univ. 59, CS-5
99/0 Millenium 234, ✍ Aut. 234
99/0 NHL Power Play
01/2 O-Pee-Chee 40
02/3 O-Pee-Chee 111
98/9 OPC Chrome 177
97/8 Omega 99
98/9 Pacific 222
99/0 Pacific 424
00/1 Pacific 408
01/2 Pacific 382
02/3 Pacific 378
02/3 Pacific Complete 216
97/8 Pa. Crown Roy. 57
98/9 Pa. Crown Roy. 58
97/8 Pa. Dynagon 53, T-49
97/8 Pa. Invincible 60, R-85
97/8 Pa. Paramount 80
98/9 Pa. Paramount 96
99/0 Pa. Paramount 234
00/1 Pa. Paramount 238
97/8 Pa. Revolution 60
96/7 Panini Sticker 68
98/9 Panini Sticker 61
99/0 Panini Sticker 315
95/6 Parkhurst 536, PP-42
00/1 Parkhurst P-141
01/2 Parkhurst 94
02/3 Parkhurst 46, -HHN 4
02/3 Parkhurst Retro 128, ✂ NH6
94/5 Parkie SE207
94/5 Pinnacle 524
96/7 Pinnacle 204, BTN-4, TP-7
97/8 Pinnacle 113
97/8 Pi. Be A Player 21, ✍ Aut. 21
97/8 Pi. Certified 48
97/8 Pi. Inside 86
95/6 Pi. Summit 171
96/7 Pi. Summit 163
97/8 Pi. Totally 48
95/6 Pi. Zenith 121,RRC-7
96/7 Pi. Zenith 45
96/7 Score 239, CI-12
97/8 Score 235
95/6 Select CE 137, CF-10
96/7 Select CE 30
00/1 Signature 122
01/2 Signature 199, ✍ Aut. 199
02/3 Signature 29, GS-36, ✍ 29, ✂ DW10
95/6 SBx Emotion gN 9
95/6 SBx Impact 201
96/7 SBx Impact 45, CTI-5, F-11
02/3 Slam Card
93/4 Slapshot / Windsor 1
94/5 Slapshot / Windsor 14
94/5 SP 140
95/6 SP 58
96/7 SP 60,GF-14
97/8 SP Authentic 65
98/9 SP Authentic 37, ✍ SotT
02/3 SP Authentic 86, ✂ SP
02/3 Sports Vault 298
97/8 SPx 21
99/0 SPx 153
98/9 SPx Finite 39
00/1 Stadium 14
96/7 Team Out!
95/6 Topps 354, 22CJ
98/9 Topps 177
99/0 Topps 35
00/1 Topps 206
01/2 Topps 40
02/3 Topps 111, HHC2
99/0 To. Chrome 35
01/2 To. Chrome 40
02/3 T. Chrome 71
94/5 Topps Finest 149
95/6 To. Finest 176
96 Topps Finest Bronze 21
02/3 T. Limited 111
96/7 Topps Picks FT8, ID5, RS11
95/6 To. Stadium ER196, GT19
95/6 TSC Members Only 47
95/6 T. Super Skills SR1
02/3 T. Total 125
98/9 UD Choice 91
02/3 Ultimate Mem. ✂ FO
94/5 Upper Deck 496
95/6 Upper Deck 501, H24
96/7 Upper Deck 66, 362, X11, P8, SS3B
97/8 Upper Deck 284, 389, SG15
98/9 Upper Deck 101
00/1 Upper Deck 171
01/2 Upper Deck 400
02/3 Upper Deck 416, -NC13, ✂ ASJ, ✂ ASP
95/6 UD BAP 178, ✍ S178
96/7 UD Black Diam. 18, RC15

97/8 UD Black Diam. 141
95/6 UD CC 399
96/7 UD CC 105, 318, 340, UD34
97/8 UD Coll. Choice 101
98/9 UD G. Reserve 101
96/7 UD Ice 88, S3
97/8 UD Ice 26
01/2 UD Mask 96
98/9 UD MVP 206
99/0 UD MVP 209
00/1 UD MVP 173
01/2 UD MVP 183
96/7 UD Post
02/3 UD Rookie ✂ 151b, 161c
02/3 UD Vintage 248
99/0 Victory 298
00/1 Victory 231
01/2 Victory 342, 428
02/3 Victory 210
96/7 FLOR / Winn-Dixie
97/8 FLOR / Winn-Dixie
01/2 VANC / Coke

JOYAL, EDDIE
64-67 BeeHive-3 [Detr.]
64-67 BeeHive-3 [Detr.]
64-67 BeeHive-3 [Toro.]
64/5 Coke/Sprite [Detr.]
70/1 Eddie Sargent 67
71/2 Eddie Sargent 74
70/1 Esso Power Player
68/9 O-Pee-Chee 40
69/0 O-Pee-Chee 108
69/0 O-Pee-Chee 4in1
69/0 O-Pee-Chee Stamp
70/1 O-Pee-Chee 39
70/1 O-Pee-Chee DE 3
71/2 O-Pee-Chee 23
75/6 OPC WHA 36
72 Semic Sticker 205
68/9 Shirriff / LosA. 6
65/6 Topps 85
68/9 Topps 40
69/0 Topps 108
70/1 Topps 39
71/2 Topps 23
71/2 Toronto Sun Photo
63/4 York 48

JOYAL, ERIC
90/1 7th..Sketch LHJMQ 192
91/2 7th...Sketch LHJMQ 64

JOYCE, BOB
98/9 DEL 82
99/0 Eishockey 332
88/9 OPC/Topps 2
89/0 OPC/Topps 73
89/0 opcSticker 126, 31-171, / FS 3
89/0 Panini Sticker 199
90/1 ProCards 206
91/2 ProCards 172
90/1 Score 291
88/9 BOST / Sports Action
88/9 BOST / Sports Action
89/0 BOST / Sports Action
89/0 WASH / Kodak
93/4 Las Vegas Thunder
94/5 Las Vegas Thunder
91/2 Moncton Hawks

JOYCE, DUANE
89/0 ProCards IHL 126
90/1 ProCards 105
91/2 ProCards 523
95/6 Cincinnati Cyclones
96/7 Cincinnati Cyclones
92/3 Kansas City Blades
93/4 Kansas City Blades
94/5 Kansas City Blades 1

JOYCE, GRAHAM
52/3 Anonymous 120

JOYCE, JOHN
94/5 Birmingham Bulls
95/6 Birmingham Bulls

JUBENVILLE, JEFF
90/1 7th..Sketch WHL 3
91/2 7th...Sketch WHL 123
93/4 Tacoma Rockets

JUCKES, BING
45-64 BeeHive-2 [NYRa.]

JUCKES, GORDON W.
83 HHOF Postcard K9
83&87 HHOF 143

JUDSON, RICK
92/3 Toledo Storm WIOT
92/3 Toledo Storm
93/4 Toledo Storm 22
94/5 Toledo Storm
95/6 Toledo Storm
96/7 Toledo Storm
97/8 Toledo Storm 16

JUHLIN, PATRIK
98/9 Cardset 117
99/0 Cardset 66, AH 8-ruutu
94/5 Classic 80, R10, T49
95/6 Donruss 60
94/5 Flair 128
94/5 Fleer 155
94/5 Fleer Ultra 344
95 Globe 31
97/8 Hockey-Box
95/6 Leaf 44
94/5 Leaf Elit Set 222, GC-18, GS-8
95/6 Parkhurst 160
94/5 Parkie SE133
94/5 Premier 378
94 Semic 68
95 Semic 76
89/0 Semic Elitserien 250
90/1 Semic Elitserien 171
91/2 Semic Elitserien 266
92/3 Semic Elitserien 286
93 Semic Sticker 11
94/5 Sig. Rookies FF3, ✍ FF3
94/5 SR Gold Standard 86
95/6 SR Tetrad Autobilia 43
94/5 Topps Finest 6
94/5 Upper Deck 246, 553, SP-148
95/6 UD BAP 119, ✍ S119
95/6 UD CC 236
95/6 UD Elitserien 244
96 Wien 62
94/5 PHIL / Sheet
94/5 PHIL / Sheet

JULIAN, JASON
91/2 7th...Sketch OHL 335
92/3 Oshawa Generals

JULIEN, CLAUDE
88/9 ProCards / Halifax
89/0 ProCards AHL 165
90/1 ProCards 587
91/2 ProCards 171
02/3 MONT
83/4 Fredericton Express
84/5 Fredericton Express
85/6 Fredericton Express
89/0 Halifax Citadels
00/1 Hamilton Bulldogs
01/2 Hamilton Bulldogs
01/2 Hamilton Bulldogs/ Staz
90/1 Kansas City Blades
91/2 Moncton Hawks

JULIEN, STÉPHANE
90/1 7th..Sketch LHJMQ 93
91/2 7th...Sketch LHJMQ 112
96/7 Pensacola Ice Pilots

JUNEAU, JOÉ
01/2 Adrenaline 96
98/9 Aurora 197
99/0 Aurora 17
00/1 Aurora 111
98/9 Be A Player 147, ✍ Aut. 147
96/7 Bic.Sports Aces 4-H
92/3 Bowman 292
95/6 Bowman 39
98/9 Bowman's Best 93
92 C.O.A. Winter Olympics 192
91/2 Canada Nationals
93/4 Cla. Prospects ✍ Aut.
98/9 Collection Souvenir 05
99/0 Crown Royale 98
93/4 Donruss 26
93/4 Donruss 394
93/4 Donruss 504
94/5 Donruss 258
95/6 Donruss 136
96/7 Donruss 151
97/8 Donruss 95
96/7 Do. Canadian 38
95/6 Do. Elite 104
96/7 Do. Elite 90
97/8 Do. Elite 41
97/8 Do. Preferred 13
97/8 Do. Priority 137
97/8 Do. Studio 68
93/4 Durivage 27
98/9 Dynagon Ice 196
93/4 EA Sports 19
94/5 Flair 200
94/5 Fleer 236, FF-5
96/7 Fleer 118
95/6 Fleer Metal 161
96/7 Fl. Picks 108
92/3 Fleer Ultra 4
93/4 Fleer Ultra 49
94/5 Fleer Ultra 388
95/6 Fleer Ultra 323
96/7 Fl. Ultra 177
95/6 Hoyle / East. 7-Spade
93/4 Kraft / KD
94/5 Kraft / SS
95/6 Kraft / IP
93/4 Leaf 218
93/4 Leaf GLR 2
94/5 Leaf 62, FOI-7, LL-25
95/6 Leaf 188
96/7 Leaf 21
97/8 Leaf 53
94/5 L. Limited 38
95/6 L. Limited 98
96/7 L. Preferred 49
97/8 Limited 61
96/7 Maggers 164
96/7 Metal Univ. 166
92/3 O-Pee-Chee 189
98/9 OPC Chrome 151
92/3 OPC Premier 101
97/8 Omega 241
98/9 Omega 247
98/9 Pacific 90
99/0 Pacific 39
00/1 Pacific 280
01/2 Pacific 305
02/3 Pacific 197
02/3 Pacific Complete 164
97/8 Pacific CC 155, SS-12A
97/8 Pa. Crown Roy. 140
98/9 Pa. Crown Roy. 142
97/8 Pa. Dynagon 131, T-57
97/8 Pa. Invincible 147
97/8 Pa. Paramount 195
98/9 Pa. Paramount 246
97/8 Pa. Revolution 148
98/9 Pa. Revolution 147
98/9 Panini Photocard
92/3 Panini Sticker L
93/4 Panini Sticker 143, A
94/5 Panini Sticker 19
95/6 Panini Sticker 138
96/7 Panini Sticker 138
91/2 Parkhurst 234
92/3 Parkhurst 2
93/4 Parkhurst 241
93/4 Parkhurst 280
94/5 Parkhurst YCTG 25
95/6 Parkhurst 221
01/2 Parkhurst 207
02/3 Parkhurst Retro 176
94/5 Parkie SE198, seV17
92/3 Pinnacle 221
92/3 Pinnacle T2K 19
93/4 Pinnacle 5
93/4 Pinnacle T2K1 4
94/5 Pinnacle 7
96/7 Pinnacle 160
97/8 Pinnacle 107
97/8 Pi. Be A Player 184, ✍ Aut. 184
97/8 Pi. Certified 63
97/8 Pi. Inside 151
95/6 Pi. Summit 139
96/7 Pi. Summit 7
97/8 Pi. Totally 63
95/6 Pi. Zenith 96
96/7 Pi. Zenith 27
95/6 Playoff 105
94/5 POG 245
95/6 POG 283
93/4 Power Play 19
93/4 Power Play SYS 2
93/4 Power Play PL 6
93/4 Premier 125
93/4 Premier 299
93/4 Prmr. - BG-Top. 12
94/5 Premier 100
01/2 Pr. Stock -PS 41
95/6 Pro Magnet 28
92/3 Pro Set 219
92/3 Score 453
92/3 Score COH 2
93/4 Score 330
93/4 Score DD3
94/5 Score 124, TF25
95/6 Score 256
96/7 Score 144
97/8 Score 140
92/3 Score Young Stars 22
92/3 Seasons 18
93/4 Seasons 8
94/5 Select 86
95/6 Select CE 80
95/6 SBx Emotion 190
95/6 SBx Impact 179
96/7 SBx Impact 141
94/5 SP 126
95/6 SP 158
96/7 SP 166, HC-17
97/8 SP Authentic 163
98/9 SP Authentic 89, ✍ SotT
97/8 SPx 49
00/1 Stadium 217
95/6 Super Sticker 129, DC-8
96/7 Team Out!
92/3 Topps 365
95/6 Topps 216, HGC25
98/9 Topps 151
00/1 Topps 33
94/5 Topps Finest 93
95/6 To. Finest 124
98/9 To. Finest 78
98/9 T. Gold Label 40
92/3 To. Stadium 297
93/4 To. Stadium 202
95/6 To. Stadium EC187
95/6 T. Super Skills 25
98/9 UD Choice 214
92/3 Upper Deck 354
92/3 Upper Deck 399
92/3 Upper Deck 455
92/3 Upper Deck AC1
92/3 Upper Deck CC9
92/3 Upper Deck G11
93/4 Upper Deck 282, 343, FH-35, HB-10, SP-9
94/5 Upper Deck 88, R15, SP-175
95/6 Upper Deck 25, R17, SE-86
96/7 Upper Deck 176, X40
97/8 Upper Deck 176, T18C
98/9 Upper Deck 203
00/1 Upper Deck 361
93/4 Upper Deck Be A Player 27
94/5 UD BAP R85, R100
95/6 UD BAP 58, ✍ S58
96/7 UD Black Diam. 90
95/6 UD CC 118
96/7 UD CC 277, 334
97/8 UD Coll. Choice 268
98/9 UD G. Reserve 203
92/3 UD Locker 53
98/9 UD MVP 216
99/0 UD MVP 22, W21
95/6 UD Post 7
00/1 UD Vintage 280
99/0 Victory 38
02/3 Victory 114
99/0 WGretzky 118
96 Wien 92
92/3 BOST / Postcard
01/2 MONT
02/3 MONT
99/0 OTTA
95/6 WASH

JUNG, ALEXANDER
00/1 UD DEL 60

JUNGWIRTH, THOMAS
94/5 DEL 130
95/6 DEL 128

JUNKER, STEVE
93/4 Cla. Prospects 193
98/9 DEL 76
93/4 Donruss 202
99/0 Eishockey 9
93/4 Fleer Ultra 367
93/4 Leaf 402
93/4 Parkhurst 394
91 7th..Sketch Mem.Cup 80
90/1 7th..Sketch WHL 193
91/2 7th...Sketch WHL 9
93/4 Upper Deck 241
91/2 Upper Deck WJC 57
00/1 UD DEL 4
01/2 UD DEL 179
89/0 Spokane Chiefs

JUNKIN, DALE
90/1 7th..Sketch OHL 62
91/2 7th...Sketch OHL 199
93/4 Slapshot / Detroit 9
93/4 Slapshot / Niagara Falls 12

JUNKINS, MATT
99/0 Kingston Frontenacs
00/1 London Knights
01/2 London Knights

JUNKKA, JONAS
97/8 UD Elitserien 154

JUNNO, JUHA
92/3 Jyvas Hyva 86

JUNTUNEN, EERO
71/2 Williams Finnish 226
72/3 Williams Finnish 209
73/4 Williams Finnish 281

JUOJARVI, TERO
71/2 Williams Finnish 344
72/3 Williams Finnish 328

JURAK, MILAN
96/7 APS 284

JURCINA, MILAN
00/1 Halifax Moosehead

JURECKA, PETR
97/8 APS 130
99/0 DS 174
97/8 DS Sticker 254
98/9 OFS 352
99/0 OFS 226
00/1 OFS 245
01/2 OFS 38, 282

JURIK, JURAJ
94/5 APS 197
95/6 APS 121
96/7 APS 107
97/8 APS 115
97/8 DS 26
96/7 DS Sticker 280
97/8 DS Sticker 57

JURME, MARKKU
95/6 Sisu 11

JURTRAS, CLAUDE
94/5 Cape Breton Oilers

JURY, FRANK
98/9 Anchorage Aces

JUSELIUS, HEIKKI
66/7 Champion 102
65/6 Hellas 92
72/3 Williams Finnish 174

JUSSILA, TIMO
65/6 Hellas 48
65/6 Hellas 156

JUTILA, TIMO
98/9 Cardset 210, Top 10, Leij. 6
99/0 Cardset AH 4-hertta
02/3 Cardset 184
95 Globe 130
95 Hartwall Karjala
97/8 Hockey-Box
92/3 Jyvas Hyva 161
93/4 Jyvas Hyva 285
80/1 Mallasjuoma 160
95 Panini Worlds 166
95/6 Radio City
94 Semic 5
95 Semic 5, 202
89/0 Semic Elitserien 152
90/1 Semic Elitserien 226
91/2 Semic Elitserien 154
91 Semic Sticker 5
93 Semic Sticker 53
93/4 Sisu 368
93/4 Sisu 63
93/4 Sisu 322
94/5 Sisu 59, 162, FOI-11
95/6 Sisu 180, 312, DT-8, G-6
96/7 Sisu 177
95/6 Sisu Limited 73
95 Suomen All-Star 8
96 Wien 5, AS2

JUTRAS, CLAUDE
00/1 Kudos 78
90/1 7th..Sketch LHJMQ 11
91/2 7th...Sketch LHJMQ 213
91 7th..Sketch Mem.Cup 65
98/9 Long Beach Ice Dogs

JUUTILAINEN, MIKKO
99/0 Cardset 298
00/1 Cardset 75

JUZDA, BILL
34-43 BeeHive-1 [NYRa.]
45-64 BeeHive-2 [Toro.]
48-52 Exhibits [Maple Leafs]
51/2 Parkhurst 77

45-54 Quaker Oats

JYLHA, JUHANI
65/6 Hellas 26
70/1 Kuvajulkaisut 106
71/2 Williams Finnish 114
73/4 Williams Finnish 310

JYLHASAARI, TAPIO
70/1 Kuvajulkaisut 330

JYRKKIO, JUHA
80/1 Mallasjuoma 206
78/9 SM-Liiga 75

K

KAARELA, JARI
72/3 Williams Finnish 307

KAARIO, MATTI
80/1 Mallasjuoma 69
78/9 SM-Liiga 112

KAARNA, ILKKA
80/1 Mallasjuoma 137

KAARTINEN, SAMI
98/9 Cardset 196
99/0 Cardset 312
00/1 Cardset 84

KABANOV, GEORGIE
00/1 Mir 80

KABANOV, VITALI
99/0 Mir 217

KABAT, KURT
92/3 Hampton Roads

KABAYAMA, MATT
82/3 Medicine Hat Tigers
83/4 Medicine Hat Tigers

KABERLE, FRANTIŠEK
02/3 BAP Mem. 59
02/3 Sports Vault 6
02/3 T. Total 50
02/3 Upper Deck 254
02/3 UD Vintage 14

KABERLE, FRANTIŠEK (SR.)
99/0 DS NS10

KABERLE, FRANTIŠEK*
94/5 APS 51
95/6 APS 361
96/7 APS 357
97/8 APS 345
95/6 Leaf Elit Set 272
95 Panini Worlds 190
93/4 Upper Deck 261
95/6 UD Elitserien 155, NA18
97/8 UD Elitserien 152

KABERLE, FRANTIŠEK**
96/7 APS 376
79 Panini Sticker 80

KABERLE, FRANTIŠEK1
00/1 BAP Mem. 35
99/0 Millenium C-33
99/0 NHL Power Play [x3]
98/9 OFS 420
99/0 OFS 24
00/1 OFS 381
99/0 Omega 115
02/3 Pacific 16
02/3 Pacific Complete 344
99/0 Panini Sticker 254, 357
99/0 Prism 67
99/0 Score JT6
00/1 Signature 107, ✍ Aut. 69
00/1 Upper Deck 240
98/9 UD Elitserien 172
02/3 UD MVP 7
01/2 Victory 22

KABERLE, TOMAS
01/2 Adrenaline 182
95/6 APS 80
96/7 APS 81
97/8 APS 199
02/3 BAP All-Star 39, ✂ ASJ
98/9 Be A Player 287, ✍ Aut. 287
00/1 BAP Mem. 254
01/2 BAP Mem. 105
01/2 DS 5, -BB 2
96/7 DS Sticker 136
97/8 DS Sticker 231
98/9 Dynagon Ice 181, -IR 9
02/3 First Edition 19, ✂ Jers.
99/0 Millenium 230, ✍ Aut. 230
99/0 NHL Power Play
01/2 O-Pee-Chee 119
99/0 OFS 25
00/1 OFS 380
01/2 OFS 167, -RE4D
98/9 Omega 233
99/0 Omega 226
99/0 Pacific 408
00/1 Pacific 393
02/3 Pacific 362
02/3 Pacific Complete 208
98/9 Pa. Crown Roy. RC 9
00/1 Pa. Paramount 231
98/9 Pa. Revolution 139
01/2 Parkhurst 88, ✂ T7, ✂ T27
02/3 Parkhurst Retro 134, ✂ NH7
01/2 Signature 50, ✍ Aut. 50, ✂ DD9
02/3 Signature ✂ DW2
98/9 SP Authentic 110
02/3 Sports Vault 138
99/0 SPx 147
98/9 SPx Prospects 56
99/0 Topps 209
00/1 Topps 179
01/2 Topps 119
99/0 To. Chrome 209
02/3 T. Total 140
98/9 Upper Deck 375
99/0 Upper Deck 125
00/1 Upper Deck 395
01/2 Upper Deck 393
02/3 Upper Deck 411
98/9 UD Black Diam. 82
98/9 UD G. Reserve 375
99/0 UD G. Reserve 125
98/9 UD MVP 197
99/0 UD MVP 203, ✍ PS
02/3 UD Vintage 234
99/0 Victory 285
01/2 Victory 330
02/3 Victory 199
99/0 TORO / Pizza Pizza 3

KABRT, PAVEL
96/7 APS 161
97/8 APS 259
97/8 DS Sticker 142
98/9 OFS 157
99/0 OFS 361
00/1 OFS 51

KACHOWSKI, MARK
89/0 ProCards IHL 159
90/1 ProCards 378
84/5 Kamloops Blazers
85/6 Kamloops Blazers

KACHOWSKI, MIKE
87/8 PITT / Kodak

KACHUR, EDDIE
93/4 Parkie 56-57 37

KACHUR, JOHN
98/9 Wichita Thunder

KACHUR, TRENT
86/7 Regina Pats
87/8 Regina Pats

KACIK, TADEUSZ
74 Hellas MM-Jenkki 98
73/4 Williams Finnish 93

KACIR, MARIAN
97/8 APS 335
98/9 DS 72
99/0 Eishockey 350
98/9 OFS 254, 268, 433
93/4 Owen Sound Platers
93/4 Owen Sound Platers

KACYANOV, RINAT
99/0 Mir 52

KADEIKIN, AIRAT
99/0 Mir 101

KADERA, ROMAN
94/5 APS 135
95/6 APS 234, 377, 410
96/7 APS 16
97/8 APS 334
97/8 DS 117
98/9 DS 120
99/0 DS 108
00/1 DS 163
96/7 DS Sticker 120
97/8 DS Sticker 277
98/9 OFS 189, 436
99/0 OFS 196, 421
00/1 OFS 254
01/2 OFS 37
93/4 Upper Deck 267

KADLEC, ARNOLD
82 Semic Sticker 82

KADLEC, DRAHOMIR
96/7 APS 344
97/8 APS 80
94/5 DEL 176
95/6 DEL 172
96/7 DEL 115
98/9 DS 68
92/3 Jyvas Hyva 9
98/9 OFS 315
95 Panini Worlds 189
94 Semic 170
95 Semic 144
89 Semic Sticker 187
93 Semic Sticker 92

KADLEC, PETR
95/6 APS 349
96/7 APS 6
97/8 APS 155
98/9 DS 69
00/1 DS 111
01/2 DS 6
96/7 DS Sticker 117
97/8 DS Sticker 193
98/9 OFS 214
99/0 OFS 45, 378
00/1 OFS 403
01/2 OFS 3, -UHI 34

KADLEK, PETR
00/1 OFS 85

KADOW, HARALD
72 Hellas MM-Jenkki 48

KADYEKIN, ARAT
98/9 Mir 79

KAEBEL, BUTCH
93/4 Birmingham Bulls
98/9 Huntington Blizzard
99/0 Huntington Blizzard
93/4 Peoria Rivermen
94/5 Peoria Rivermen
96/7 Peoria Rivermen
97/8 Peoria Rivermen

KAEBEL, KARSON
94/5 Dayton Bombers 7
98/9 Huntington Blizzard
99/0 Odessa Jackalopes
96/7 Peoria Rivermen
93/4 N. Michigan Wildcats

KAESE, TRENT
87/8 Flint Spirits

KAGAIKIN, SERGEI
99/0 Mir 182

KAHELIN, TIMO
92/3 Jyvas Hyva 139
93/4 Jyvas Hyva 255
93/4 Sisu 284

KAHILUOTO, TOMMI
96/7 Sisu 31

KAHL, EGON
79 Panini Sticker 367

KAHNBERG, MAGNUS
00/1 UD Elitserien 66

KAHONEN, JYRKI
70/1 Kuvajulkaisut 314

KAIKKONEN, ARI
70/1 Kuvajulkaisut 368
71/2 Williams Finnish 304

KAIPAINEN, MATTI
98/9 Cardset 89
99/0 Cardset 291
00/1 Cardset 65
02/3 Cardset 187
93/4 Sisu 124
94/5 Sisu 69
95/6 Sisu 236
96/7 Sisu 34

KAIPONEN, LASSE
71/2 Williams Finnish 323

KAISER, VERN
45-64 BeeHive-2 [Mont.]
45-54 Quaker Oats

KAISTAKARI, JARMO
80/1 Mallasjuoma 132

KAITALA, RISTO
66/7 Champion 8
65/6 Hellas 17

KAIVOLA, ANTTI
72/3 Williams Finnish 285

KAJER, MILOS
94/5 APS 69
95/6 APS 90

KAJKL, MILAN
79 Panini Sticker 77

KAJULA, TIMO
70/1 Kuvajulkaisut 369

KAKITALO, JAMO
94/5 Leaf Elit Set 77

KAKKO, ERIK
98/9 Cardset 54
02/3 Cardset 32
97/8 Hockey-Box
91/2 Jyvas Hyva 54
92/3 Jyvas Hyva 144
93/4 Jyvas Hyva 316
93/4 Sisu 33
94/5 Sisu 269
95/6 Sisu 21
96/7 Sisu 16

KALAWSKY, CRAIG
86/7 Regina Pats
87/8 Regina Pats

KALES, CRAIG
83/4 Kingston Canadians
82/3 North Bay Centennials

KALETA, ALEX
34-43 BeeHive-1 [Chic.]
45-64 BeeHive-2 [NYRa.]

KALININ, DIMITRI
99/0 BAP Mem. 321
00/1 BAP Mem. 323
01/2 BAP Mem. 111
00/1 Crown Royale 113
02/3 First Edition 203
99/0 Omega 29
02/3 Pacific Complete 387
01/2 Parkhurst 230
00/1 Premier Plus 89
00/1 Private Stock 105, PSR-3
00/1 Signature 259, ✍ Aut. 7
00/1 Stadium 240
00/1 Topps 318
00/1 To. Chrome 213
02/3 T. Total 81
00/1 Upper Deck 24
00/1 UD MVP 188
00/1 Vanguard 105
01/2 Victory 45

KALLA, JAROSLAV
98/9 OFS 370
99/0 OFS 135
00/1 OFS 179

KÄLLARSSON, TOMI
98/9 Cardset 57
99/0 Cardset 33

KALLIO, JORMA
66/7 Champion 194
70/1 Kuvajulkaisut 126
72 Panda MM-Toronto
78/9 SM-Liiga 177
71/2 Williams Finnish 176
72/3 Williams Finnish 124
73/4 Williams Finnish 180

KALLIO, MARKKU
94/5 Sisu 311

KALLIO, TAPIO
78/9 SM-Liiga 195
72/3 Williams Finnish 263

KALLIO, TOMI
01/2 Adrenaline 9
00/1 BAP Mem. 457
01/2 BAP Mem. 107
98/9 Cardset 242
99/0 Cardset 139, 192
00/1 Cardset 236, MB-8
02/3 Cardset 33, -DD 7
00/1 Crown Royale 110, 21CR-1
02/3 Exclusive 7, ✂ GWJ 1
02/3 Heads Up ✂ GWQ 2, ✂ GWQ 33
97/8 Hockey-Box
02/3 O-Pee-Chee 181
01/2 Pacific 19
02/3 Pacific 17
02/3 Pacific Complete 33
00/1 Parkhurst P-242
01/2 Parkhurst 220
00/1 PS Titanium 103
01/2 PS Titanium Draft ✂ 6
02/3 PS Titanium ✂ GWJ 51
00/1 PS Titanium Draft 103
00/1 Signature 291, ✍ Aut. 221
01/2 Signature 65, ✍ Aut. 65
95/6 Sisu 335, DD-5
96/7 Sisu 146
02/3 Topps 181
00/1 To. Heritage 148
01/2 To. Heritage 81
02/3 To. Limited 181
02/3 T. Total 298
02/3 Upper Deck 8
95/6 UD CC 334
01/2 UD Vintage 11, 17
02/3 Vanguard ✂ GWJ 14
01/2 Victory 17

KALLIOMÄKI, TUOMAS
93/4 Jyvas Hyva 172
93/4 Sisu 171
95/6 Sisu 350

KALLIONIEMI, RIKU
98/9 Cardset 188
99/0 Cardset 108
00/1 Cardset 202
97/8 Hockey-Box
95/6 Sisu 303
96/7 Sisu 97

KALLIONPAA, MARTTI
65/6 Hellas 64

KALLUR, ANDERS
00/1 Alfabilder
80/1 O-Pee-Chee 156
81/2 O-Pee-Chee 204
82/3 O-Pee-Chee 203
81/2 OPC Sticker 162
82/3 OPC/Topps Sticker 57
82/3 Post [NYIs.]
80/1 Topps 156
81/2 Topps 90 [East]
00/1 UD Vintage ✂ D-POH
79/0 NYIS
83/4 NYIS / News 9
84/5 NYIS / News 8
99/0 NYIS / UD NY9

KALMIKOV, KONSTANTIN
01/2 Louisiana Ice Gators
99/0 St. John's Maple Leafs
00/1 St. John's Maple Leafs
96/7 Sudbury Wolves

KALMOKOSKI, ARI
71/2 Williams Finnish 305

KALOUS, JIRI
99/0 OFS 380

KALT, DIETER
96/7 DEL 178
95 Panini Worlds 267
94 Semic 241
95 Semic 186
93 Semic Sticker 279
00/1 UD DEL 141
96 Wien 217

KALTEVA, PETRI
93/4 Jyvas Hyva 295
93/4 Sisu 61
94/5 Sisu 296
95/6 Sisu 316

KALTO, KARI
98/9 Cardset 38
99/0 Cardset 25
00/1 Cardset 249

KALTYGEN, SERGEI
00/1 Victoriaville Tigres 14

KALYUKHNY, ALEXEI
98/9 Mir 152
00/1 Mir 106

KAMALATDINOV, RUSTEM
99/0 Mir 154

KAMALETDINOV, RUSTEM
00/1 Mir 279

KAMARAINEN, JOUKO
80/1 Mallasjuoma 104
78/9 SM-Liiga 147

KAMBEITZ, JIM
83/4 Medicine Hat Tigers

KAMEL, NOEL
92/3 MPS SJHL 73

KAMENEV, VASILI
94/5 Sig. Rookies FF5, ✍ FF5

KAMENSKY, VALERI
98/9 Aurora 47
98/9 Be A Player 186, ✍ Aut. 186
01/2 BAP Mem. 496
92/3 Bowman 432
98/9 Bowman's Best 89
93/4 Donruss 277
94/5 Donruss 116
95/6 Donruss 236
96/7 Donruss 14
97/8 Donruss 132
96/7 Do. Canadian 32
97/8 Do. Canadian 82
95/6 Do. Elite 22
96/7 Do. Elite 118
97/8 Do. Elite 44
97/8 Do. Priority 87
98/9 Dynagon Ice 49
99/0 Dynagon Ice 131
94/5 Flair 147
94/5 Fleer 177
96/7 Fleer 21, ART-9
95/6 Fleer Metal 33
96/7 Fl. Picks F50-22, DL-9
93/4 Fleer Ultra 84
94/5 Fleer Ultra 357
95/6 Fleer Ultra 221
96/7 Fl. Ultra 36
91/2 Gillette 30
95 Globe 179
92/3 Humpty Dumpty
93/4 Leaf 207
94/5 Leaf 117
96/7 Leaf 170
96/7 L. Limited 81
96/7 L. Preferred 53, LS-59
97/8 Limited 47, 111
96/7 Maggers 43
96/7 Metal Univ. 33
99/0 Millenium 165, ✍ Aut. 165
00/1 Mir Fetisov 6
90/1 O-Pee-Chee 4R
91/2 O-Pee-Chee 513
92/3 O-Pee-Chee 266
98/9 OPC Chrome 39
97/8 Omega 57
98/9 Pacific 160
99/0 Pacific 108
00/1 Pacific 264
01/2 Pacific 260
97/8 Pacific CC 213
97/8 Pa. Crown Roy. 34
97/8 Pa. Dynagon 30, T-42
97/8 Pa. Invincible 35
97/8 Pa. Paramount 50
98/9 Pa. Paramount 56
99/0 Pa. Paramount 151
97/8 Pa. Revolution 33
92/3 Panini Sticker 295
92/3 Panini Sticker R
93/4 Panini Sticker 72
94/5 Panini Sticker 60
95/6 Panini Sticker 248
96/7 Panini Sticker 248
97/8 Panini Sticker 203
98/9 Panini Sticker 188
00/1 Panini Sticker 63
95 Panini Worlds 36
91/2 Parkhurst 362
92/3 Parkhurst 230
92/3 Parkhurst 377
93/4 Parkhurst 438
94/5 Parkhurst 190
95/6 Parkhurst 48
91/2 Pinnacle 340
92/3 Pinnacle 64
93/4 Pinnacle 244
94/5 Pinnacle 343
96/7 Pinnacle 47
97/8 Pinnacle 186
96/7 Pi. Be A Player 33, ✍ Aut. 33
97/8 Pi. Certified 67
97/8 Pi. Inside 114
95/6 Pi. Summit 6
96/7 Pi. Summit 59
97/8 Pi. Totally 67
96/7 Pi. Zenith 8
95/6 Playoff 243
96/7 Playoff 420
94/5 POG 195
95/6 POG 74
93/4 Power Play 199
93/4 Premier 85
94/5 Premier 32
00/1 Private Stock ✂ GUG 74
00/1 PS Titanium ✂ GUG 35
92/3 Pro Set 148
91/2 Red Ace
91/2 Score 76T
92/3 Score 360
93/4 Score 326
95/6 Score 268
96/7 Score 157
97/8 Score 186
97/8 Score Colo. 7
92/3 Score Young Stars 24
94/5 Select 144
95/6 Select CE 105
96/7 Select CE 67
94 Semic 157
95 Semic 131
89 Semic Sticker 91
91 Semic Sticker 88
92 Semic Sticker 112
95/6 SBx Emotion 37
95/6 SBx Impact 36
96/7 SBx Impact 23, BR-9
87/8 Soviet Stars
89/0 Soviet Stars
97/8 SP Authentic 39
98/9 SPx Finite 23
00/1 Stadion 112
99/0 Stadium 155
95/6 Super Sticker 31
92/3 Topps 53
98/9 Topps 39
95/6 To. Finest 164
98/9 To. Finest 43
96/7 To. Picks 39
92/3 To. Stadium 344
93/4 To. Stadium 237
95/6 To. Stadium 161
91/2 Tri Globe From... 11-12
91/2 Tri Globe Mag. Five 1-5
98/9 UD Choice 58
91/2 Upper Deck 273
91/2 Upper Deck SP1
92/3 Upper Deck 27
92/3 Upper Deck E20
93/4 Upper Deck 118
94/5 Upper Deck 355
95/6 Upper Deck 489
96/7 Upper Deck 241, X20
97/8 Upper Deck 254
98/9 Upper Deck 249
99/0 Upper Deck 257
00/1 Upper Deck 347
01/2 Upper Deck 289
94/5 UD BAP ✍ 158
95/6 UD CC 221
96/7 UD CC 62
97/8 UD Coll. Choice 58
98/9 UD G. Reserve 249
99/0 UD G. Reserve 257
99/0 Victory 196
99/0 WGretzky 111
96 Wien 149
01/2 DALL / Southwest
91/2 QUEB / Petro-Canada
92/3 QUEB / Petro-Canada
94/5 QUEB / Burger King

KAMENTSEV, PAVEL
98/9 Mir 41

KAMES, JAROSLAV
94/5 APS 181
95/6 APS 29, 356, 406
96/7 APS 27
97/8 APS 53
97/8 DS 102
98/9 DS 24
00/1 DS 13, G2
96/7 DS Sticker 94
97/8 DS Sticker 287
99/0 Eishockey 61
98/9 OFS 18
00/1 OFS 320, -Star 1

KAMES, JIRI
99/0 DS 166
98/9 OFS 404
99/0 OFS 328
00/1 OFS 119
01/2 OFS 269

KAMINSKI, BERNHARD
95/6 DEL 35

KAMINSKI, DARCY
91/2 Hampton Roads
89/0 Lethbridge Hurricanes

KAMINSKI, KEVIN
94/5 Classic E8
93/4 Donruss 505
93/4 Parkhurst 493
96/7 Pi. Be A Player 86, ✍ Aut. 86
89/0 ProCards AHL 170
90/1 ProCards 448, 544
89/0 QUEB
89/0 QUEB / Gene. Foods
90/1 QUEB
95/6 WASH
01/2 Cincinnati Mighty Ducks
89/0 Halifax Citadels
98/9 Las Vegas Thunder
93/4 Portland Pirates
94/5 Portland Pirates
97/8 Portland Pirates
86/7 Saskatoon Blades
89/0 Saskatoon Blades

KAMINSKI, KEVIN
02/3 Fleer Throwbacks 27, ✍ Aut.

KAMINSKY,
97/8 Hockey-Box

KAMINSKY, ANDREW
98/9 Brandon Wheat Kings

KAMINSKY, MAX
34-43 BeeHive-1 [Maroons]
36-39 Diamond Match TT1

KAMINSKY, YAN
93/4 Classic 88
93/4 Cla. Prospects 185
93/4 Donruss 456
94/5 Leaf 173
94/5 Panini Sticker F
94/5 Pinnacle 263
94/5 Premier 399
92/3 Red Ace Blue 33
94/5 Score 221
92/3 Upper Deck 344
93/4 WINN / Ruffles
93/4 WINN Readers

KAMMERER, AXEL
94/5 DEL 193
95/6 DEL 328
96/7 DEL 106
89 Semic Sticker 123
92 Semic Sticker 183

KAMP, CURT
93/4 Seattle Thunderbirds

KAMPERSAL, JEFFREY
92/3 Richmond Renegades

KAMPF, RADEK
96/7 APS 299
96/7 DS Sticker 226

KAMPMAN, BINGO
39/0 O-Pee-Chee 3
40/1 O-Pee-Chee 109
38/9 Quaker Oats

KAMPMAN, RUDOLPH
34-43 BeeHive-1 [Toro.]

KAMPPURI, HANNU
80/1 Mallasjuoma 168
82 Semic Sticker 26
82 Skopbank
78/9 SM-Liiga 1
78/9 SM-Liiga 65
84/5 NJER

KAMULA, PETE
52/3 Anonymous 19

KANAREKIN, LEONID
98/9 Mir 28
00/1 Mir 45

KANARSKI, PAVEL
00/1 Mir 50

KANE, BOYD
98/9 Charlotte Checkers
99/0 Charlotte Checkers
00/1 Charlotte Checkers
98/9 Hartford Wolf Pack
00/1 Hartford Wolf Pack
01/2 Hartford Wolf Pack
96/7 Regina Pats
97/8 Regina Pats

KANE, DAN
84/5 Moncton G'Flames

KANE, SHAUNE
93/4 Raleigh Icecaps

KANERVA, PETTERI
80/1 Mallasjuoma 71
78/9 SM-Liiga 109

KANERVO, KARI
92/3 Jyvas Hyva 175

KANGAS, ANTTI
00/1 Cardset 293

KANGAS, PASI
99/0 Cardset 276
95/6 Sisu 266

KANGAS, VESA
89/0 Semic Elitserien 161

KANGASALUSTA, PEKKA
98/9 Cardset 78
99/0 Cardset 46, 223
00/1 Cardset 295
95/6 Sisu 231
96/7 Sisu 30

KANGASNIEMI, MISKA
98/9 Cardset 208
99/0 Cardset 119
00/1 Cardset 86
97/8 Hockey-Box
95/6 Sisu 60
94/5 Topps Finest 134

KANIGAN, JUSTIN
00/1 Saskatoon Blades

KANKA, MICHAL
98/9 OFS 174
99/0 OFS 329

KANKAANPERÄ, ARI
78/9 SM-Liiga 50

KANKAANPERÄ, MARKUS
98/9 Cardset 126
99/0 Cardset 70
00/1 Cardset 46, NG-8

KANKAANPERÄ, RISTO
78/9 SM-Liiga 56

KANKO, PETR
00/1 OFS 316
01/2 Kitchener Rangers

KANKOVSKY, PETR
94/5 APS 192
95/6 APS 188, 414
96/7 APS 323, 423
99/0 DS 189
96/7 DS Sticker 165
99/0 OFS 466

KANKOVSKY, ROMAN
94/5 APS 190
95/6 APS 178, 412
96/7 APS 313
96/7 DS Sticker 154

KANNEGIESSER, SHELDON
74/5 Loblaws
71/2 O-Pee-Chee 190
74/5 O-Pee-Chee 338
75/6 O-Pee-Chee 69
76/7 O-Pee-Chee 335
78/9 O-Pee-Chee 310
75/6 Topps 69
71/2 Toronto Sun Photo
71/2 PITT / Sportcolor

KANNEWURF, FRANK
94/5 DEL 37
95/6 DEL 30

KANNISTO, MIKA
99/0 Cardset 341
94/5 Sisu 294
95/6 Sisu 221
96/7 Sisu 24

KANNISTO, MIKE
98/9 Cardset 61

KANTOR, ROBERT
95/6 APS 207
97/8 APS 336
02/3 Cardset 188
99/0 DS 56
97/8 DS Sticker 273
98/9 OFS 387, 475
99/0 OFS 352, 407
00/1 OFS 164

KAONPAA, ESKO
66/7 Champion 149
65/6 Hellas 129
72 Panda MM-Toronto
71/2 Williams Finnish 177
72/3 Williams Finnish 125

KAPANEN, HANNU
93/4 Jyvas Hyva 163
93/4 Sisu 160
94/5 Sisu 389
95/6 Sisu 389
78/9 SM-Liiga 34
71/2 Williams Finnish 281
73/4 Williams Finnish 196

KAPANEN, JARI
80/1 Mallasjuoma 14
78/9 SM-Liiga 80
73/4 Williams Finnish 283

KAPANEN, KIMMO
98/9 Cardset 141, -MM 7
99/0 Cardset 233, -Puck 6
00/1 Cardset 22
02/3 Cardset 34
97/8 Hockey-Box
93/4 Sisu 162
94/5 Sisu 229
95/6 Sisu 2
01/2 UD DEL 112, ✂ GJ

KAPANEN, NIKO
01/2 BAP Mem. 348
01/2 Bowman 143
02/3 Bowman 149, ✂ FFDS, ✂ FFJ, ✂ FFP, ✂ FFR, ✂ FFRP, ✂ FFS, ✂ FFTS, ✍ YSA, / ✍ Puck
02/3 Calder 66
98/9 Cardset 71
99/0 Cardset 41, 173
00/1 Cardset 120, 340
02/3 Cardset 35, -DD 9, -SGSP 6
01/2 Crown Royale 156
97/8 Hockey-Box

02/3 In The GU ✄ C15
01/2 O-Pee-Chee 354
02/3 Pacific Complete 503
01/2 Parkhurst 287
02/3 Parkhurst Retro 75, ✄ CH4
01/2 Pr. Stock 119
01/2 PS Titanium 155
01/2 PS Titanium Draft 124
01/2 Signature 232, ✍ Aut. 232
02/3 Signature ✄ SGJ60
01/2 SP Authentic 144
01/2 SP GU 74
01/2 SPx 103
01/2 SPx Rookie RR10
01/2 Stadium 140
01/2 Topps 354
01/2 To. Chrome 172
01/2 To. Heritage 139
01/2 To. Reserve 111
01/2 UD PlayMakers Ltd 114
02/3 Ultimate Mem. ✄ CC
01/2 Upper Deck 421
01/2 UD Challenge 104
01/2 UD Honor Roll 70
01/2 UD Ice 52
01/2 UD Premier 94
01/2 UD Top Shelf 70
01/2 UD Vintage 280
01/2 Vanguard 108
01/2 DALL / Southwest

KAPANEN, SAMI
01/2 Adrenaline 35
02/3 Atomic -PC 6
98/9 Aurora 33
99/0 Aurora 27
00/1 Aurora 30
02/3 BAP All-Star 40, ✄ ASJ
98/9 Be A Player 24, ✍ Aut. 24
99/0 BAP Mem. 55
00/1 BAP Mem. 176
01/2 BAP Mem. ✄ CoO
02/3 BAP Mem. 98
02/3 BAP Mem. 400
01/2 BAP Update ✄ HSHSJers
01/2 Bowman 62
98/9 Bowman's Best 97
98/9 Cardset Top. 7, Leij. 26
99/0 Cardset AH 10-ruutu
00/1 Cardset 358
02/3 Cardset 36, -DD 3, -SGSP 4
99/0 Crown Royale 28
00/1 Crown Royale 22
01/2 Crown Royale 27
97/8 Do. Priority 73
98/9 Dynagon Ice 34
99/0 Dynagon Ice 42
02/3 Exclusive 30
02/3 First Edition 30, ✄ Jers.
95 Hartwall Karjala
02/3 Heads Up 22
99/0 HoloGrFX 10
92/3 Jyvas Hyva 102
93/4 Jyvas Hyva 174
95/6 Kellogg's Pop-Ups 6
99/0 Millenium 49, ✍ Aut. 49
98/9 NHL Power Play
01/2 O-Pee-Chee 138
02/3 O-Pee-Chee 68
98/9 OPC Chrome 178
97/8 Omega 41
98/9 Omega 43
99/0 Omega 46
98/9 Pacific 134
99/0 Pacific 73
00/1 Pacific 84, 433
01/2 Pacific 75
02/3 Pacific 68
02/3 Pacific Complete 6
97/8 Pacific CC 192
98/9 Pa. Crown Roy. 24
98/9 Pa. Paramount 37
99/0 Pa. Paramount 47
00/1 Pa. Paramount 44
97/8 Pa. Revolution 23
97/8 Panini Sticker 25
98/9 Panini Sticker 29
99/0 Panini Sticker 43
00/1 Panini Sticker 25
95 Panini Worlds 183
95/6 Parkhurst 516
00/1 Parkhurst P-137
01/2 Parkhurst 184, ✄ T25
02/3 Parkhurst 131, ✄ GJ30, ✄ SJ30
02/3 Parkhurst Retro 29
96/7 Pi. Be A Player 145, ✍ Aut. 145
99/0 Prism 30
00/1 Private Stock 18, PSNW-4
01/2 Pr. Stock -PS 11
00/1 PS Titanium ✄ GUG 3
01/2 PS Titanium 26, TAS 3
02/3 Quest for the Cup 76
99/0 Revolution 29
00/1 Revolution 28
94 Semic 39
95 Semic 24, 231
00/1 Signature 225
01/2 Signature C-40, ✍ Aut. LSK, ✄ FP6, ✄ GU97, ✄ HSHSJers, ✄ TM6
02/3 Signature GS-82
93/4 Sisu 179
94/5 Sisu 163, 209, FOI-7, MN-5, SS-5
95/6 Sisu 12, DD-6, G-13
95/6 Sisu Limited 72, SAS-1
97/8 SP Authentic 27
98/9 SP Authentic 16
99/0 SP Authentic 18
02/3 Sports Vault 36
99/0 SPx 30
01/2 SPx 163
98/9 SPx Finite 16
99/0 Stadium 134
00/1 Stadium 200
95 Suomen Beckett Card 5
98/9 Topps 178
99/0 Topps 69
00/1 Topps 38, PP2
01/2 Topps 138
02/3 Topps 68
99/0 To. Chrome 69
00/1 To. Chrome 31
01/2 To. Chrome 112
02/3 To. Chrome 46
98/9 To. Finest 130
98/9 T. Gold Label 36
99/0 To. Gold Label 67
00/1 To. Heritage 144
02/3 To. Limited 68
02/3 T. Total 333
98/9 UD Choice 40
01/2 UD PlayMakers Ltd 18
00/1 UD Reserve 17
01/2 Ultimate Mem. ✄ WTF
99/0 Ult. Victory 18
91/2 Upper Deck 674
97/8 Upper Deck 239
98/9 Upper Deck 57
99/0 Upper Deck 32
00/1 Upper Deck 32
01/2 Upper Deck 36
02/3 Upper Deck 32, ✄ ASJ, ✄ ASP
97/8 UD Black Diam. 147
98/9 UD Black Diam. 17
99/0 UD Black Diam. 20
91/2 Upper Deck WJC 37
98/9 UD G. Reserve 57
99/0 UD G. Reserve 32
01/2 UD Mask 15, -GG
98/9 UD MVP 38
99/0 UD MVP 39, ✍ PS
00/1 UD MVP 40
01/2 UD MVP 34
02/3 UD MVP 31,SO4
99/0 UD MVP Cup 39
99/0 UD Retro 15
02/3 UD Top Shelf 17
00/1 UD Vintage 67
01/2 UD Vintage 49, 52
02/3 UD Vintage 44, GB 44
00/1 Vanguard 21
99/0 Victory 54
00/1 Victory 43
01/2 Victory 62
02/3 Victory 36, -NP22
01/2 Waving the Flag 16
99/0 WGretzky 34
96 Wien 19
97/8 Zenith 69
97/8 CARO / Sprint
98/9 CARO / Highwoods
96/7 HART / Kids Club

KAPKAIKIN, KONSTANTIN
91/2 O-Pee-Chee 51R

KAPOTOCNY, DANIEL
00/1 OFS 244

KAPUS, RICHARD
00/1 DS 71
00/1 OFS 226
93/4 Upper Deck 265

KAPUSTA, TOMAS
96/7 APS 227
97/8 APS 41
98/9 Cardset 25
97/8 DS 61
96/7 DS Sticker 33
97/8 DS Sticker 178
93/4 Jyvas Hyva 48
98/9 OFS 281
95 Panini Worlds 210
89/0 ProCards AHL 147
90/1 ProCards 235
91/2 ProCards 231
93 Semic Sticker 99
93/4 Sisu 250
93/4 Sisu 361
93/4 Sisu 356
94/5 Sisu 225, FOI-19
95/6 Sisu 357, 372
95/6 Sisu Limited 87
99/0 Muskegon Fury

KAPUSTIN, SERGEI
92/3 Future Trends C76 144
80 Olympic USSR
79 Panini Sticker 153
82 Semic Sticker 71
74/5 Soviet Stars 20
79/0 Soviet Stars 17
83/4 Soviet Stars

KAPYNEN, TERO
78/9 SM-Liiga 196

KARABIN, LADISLAV
93/4 Cla. Prospects 108
93/4 Donruss 472
93/4 Parkhurst 426
93/4 Upper Deck 467
00/1 UD DEL 208
01/2 UD DEL 219
93/4 Cleveland Lumberjacks
95/6 Rochester Americans

KARAKAS, KRAIG
93/4 Minnesota-Duluth

KARAKAS, MIKE
34-43 BeeHive-1 [Chic.]
36-39 Diamond Match TT3
36-39 Diamond Match BH TT
36-39 Diamond Match Chic.
36-39 Diamond Match BH BT
36/7 O-Pee-Chee 107
39/0 O-Pee-Chee 47
43-47 Parade Sportive
37/8 World Wide Gum 123

KARALAHTI, JERE
00/1 BAP Mem. 248
98/9 Cardset 36, Leij. 7
99/0 Cardset 182, 220, BP-2, PA-4
00/1 Cardset 232
02/3 Cardset 189
97/8 Hockey-Box
94/5 Parkie SE216
95 Semic 237
00/1 Signature 27, ✍ Aut. 22
93/4 Sisu 395
93/4 Sisu 86
94/5 Sisu 2, J-4
95/6 Sisu 206
96/7 Sisu 4
94/5 Topps Finest 126
00/1 Upper Deck 308
99/0 UD MVP Cup 88
00/1 Victory 110

KARALIS, TOM
89/0 ProCards IHL 117
90/1 ProCards 549
91/2 ProCards 176
87/8 Flint Spirits
85/6 Fredericton Express
86/7 Fredericton Express

KARAMNOV, VITALI
96/7 DEL 259
98/9 DEL 37
93/4 Donruss 287
93/4 Fleer Ultra 412
93/4 Leaf 408
94/5 Panini Sticker P
92/3 Parkhurst 387
93/4 Parkhurst 444
92/3 Pinnacle 398
93/4 Power Play 429
93/4 Premier 292
93/4 To. Stadium 478
92/3 Upper Deck 341
92/3 Upper Deck 510
93/4 Upper Deck 338

KARAPUU, MIKA
93/4 Sisu 44
96/7 Sisu 121

KARATCHUN, VIKTOR
99/0 Eishockey 312

KAREL, HELMUT
95 Panini Worlds 265

KARELIUS, PERTTI
66/7 Champion 80
65/6 Hellas 11

KARG, STEFFEN
98/9 DEL 220

KARGER, REINHARD
70/1 Kuvajulkaisut 87

KARHUNEN, PEKKA
70/1 Kuvajulkaisut 311

KARI, ESA
70/1 Kuvajulkaisut 193

KARI, HARRI
78/9 SM-Liiga 199

KARIYA, PAUL
01/2 Adrenaline 3, BR 1, WB 1
01/2 ASG History
01/2 Atomic 1, AB 1, CP 1, PP 1
02/3 Atomic 2, -CF 1, -NPC 1
98/9 Aurora 3, -ALC 1, -CF 1, -MACF 1, -Cube 1
99/0 Aurora 2, Stripe 2, CC-1, CF-1, CP-1, ST-1
00/1 Aurora 2, Pins. 2, CC-1, CF-1, SR-1, TPS-1A
91/2 Avant Garde BCJHL 84, 86, 91, 93, 168, ✍
02/3 BAP All-Star 41-43, ✄ ASJ, ✄ HSHSJers
98/9 Be A Player 2, P-18, ✍ Aut. 2, ✄ G-12, ✄ AS-7, ✄ S-7, ✄ ✍ G-12
94/5 Be A Player Magazine Postcard 3
99/0 BAP Mem. 117, SL-8, ✄ J-7, ✄ D-5, ✄ TM-10, ✄ TM-12, ✄ TM-26, ✄ TM-45
00/1 BAP Mem. 88, ✄ J-31, ✄ PP-2, ✄ TM-23, ✄ TM-26
01/2 BAP Mem. 196, ✄ ASJ, ✄ ASE, ✄ ASN, ✄ ASD, ✄ ASS, ✄ AST, ✄ CoO, HSHS, ✄ PP
02/3 BAP Mem. 179, 201, ✄ ASJ25, ✄ ASE10, ✄ ASN10, ✄ ASTJ7, ✄ AST6, ✄ AST25, ✄ FP1, ✄ HSHSJers 12
01/2 BAP Update ✄ HSHSJers
96/7 Bic.Sports Aces K-D
97/8 Bicycle A-Spade
95/6 Bicycle Sports Aces 7-Heart
95/6 Bowman 90, BB15
01/2 Bowman 20
02/3 Bowman 7
98/9 Bowman's Best 2, F2, SB9
02/3 Calder 30
93/4 Canada Nationals
99/0 Challenger 16
93/4 Classic 4
93/4 Classic 113
93/4 Classic N2
93/4 Classic - Team Canada TC2
93/4 Classic - Top Ten DP4
93/4 Cla. 4 Sport 188
93/4 Cla. 4 Sport LP25
93/4 Cla. Images 4 Sport 106
93/4 Cla. Prospects 18
93/4 Cla. Prospects IA3
93/4 Cla. Prospects LP15
99/0 Crown Royale 2, IE-1, CS-1, C21-1, CCA-1, TC-1
00/1 Crown Royale 2, JotC-1, Land.-1, NP-1
01/2 Crown Royale 4, ASH 1, JotC 1, LH 1, ✄ TT 1
02/3 Crown Royale 2, -LOR 1, -RP 1
95/6 Donruss 57, D-6, E-6, PP-19, RT-3
96/7 Donruss 142, D-8, GTS-8
97/8 Donruss 7, ES-4, L2L-20
98/9 Donruss ES 18
96/7 Do. Canadian 3, OC-2
97/8 Do. Canadian 2, NP-3, SCS-20
95/6 Do. Elite 31, CE-6
96/7 Do. Elite 1, S-5
97/8 Do. Elite 7, 136, C-22, PN-5
97/8 Do. Preferred 10, 183, LT-4C, PM-8, / Tin 2,22, WideTin 2,11
97/8 Do. Priority 13, 204, DD-14, OD-12, Post-13, Stamp-13
97/8 Do. Studio 4, HH-3, S-5, P-4
96/7 Duracell JB20
98/9 Dynagon Ice 3, -AR 1, -FT 1, -PP 1, -TC 1
99/0 Dynagon Ice 10, ASP-1, CM-16, LL-1, LotR-1
97/8 Esso 9, ✍ Aut.
01/2 eTopps 2
02/3 eTopps 25
02/3 Exclusive 2, -EIS 1, -MO 1
02/3 First Edition 155, 316, 341, 408R, ✄ Jers., ✄ DGJ 16, ✄ HSHSJers 8, ✄ TSL 1
94/5 Flair 4
96/7 Flair 2, CIS-6
94/5 Fleer 3, RS-5
96/7 Fleer 2, 141, ART-10, PA-6
95/6 Fleer Metal 2, HM-7
96/7 Fl. Picks 6, F50-23, DL-5, JE-6
93/4 Fleer Ultra 465
94/5 Fleer Ultra P-3
95/6 Fleer Ultra 3, 388, AR-5, EA-11, HS-11
96/7 Fl. Ultra 2, PL-3, UP-8
00 Gatorade Sticker
95 Globe 91
96/7 Got-Um
01/2 Heads Up 1, ASGUN 5, HD 1, RI 1, SM 1, / Bobble
02/3 Heads Up 2, -EIT 1, -SM 1
99/0 HoloGrFX 2, IZ5, PS1
95/6 Hoyle / West. K-Spade
02/3 In The GU 2, 102, ✄ E9, ✄ F1, ✄ GUJ9, ✄ SJ9
94/5 Incomnet Phonecard
95/6 Kraft / KD
96/7 Kraft / AS, TT,PB
97/8 Kraft / JTP, KD, PB, Casecard
98/9 Kraft / KD
99/0 Kraft / JELL-O, / KD (x2), / OML, / PB
00/1 Kraft 8
94/5 Leaf 455, LL-27, P-5
95/6 Leaf 304, FOI-11, SR-3
96/7 Leaf 176, FOI-4, S-5
97/8 Leaf 6, 173, BS-1, FOI-16
94/5 L. Limited 107, G-5
95/6 L. Limited 9,SG-5
96/7 L. Limited 17
96/7 L. Preferred 7, LS-34, SP-11
97/8 Limited 35, 56, 114, FG-10, FG-40
96/7 Maggers 1
94/5 McDonald's McD-32
95/6 McDonald's McD-11
96/7 McDonald's McD-29
97/8 McDonald's McD-9, F6
98/9 McDonald's McD08
99/0 McDonald's McD-1
00/1 McDonald's 1, DAS-1
01/2 McDonald's 1, -HP 2
02/3 McDonald's 1, -A 1, -SLG 7
96/7 Metal Univ. 2, IC-7, LW-9
99/0 Millenium 1, ✍ Aut. 1, ✄ J-16, ✄ JS-16
95/6 Cool Trade 8
98/9 NHL Power Play
00/1 Nortel Networks All-Star 7
01/2 O-Pee-Chee 28
02/3 O-Pee-Chee 8
98/9 OPC Chrome 53
97/8 Omega 3, GF-1, S-1, SHLC-1, TL-1
98/9 Omega 4, -CS 1, -EOP 1, -FTF 2, -Onl. 1, -PI 28, -Prism 1
99/0 Omega 3, 5ST-13, CC-1, EOP-1, G-1, NAAS-1
98/9 Pacific 9, -DI 1, -GCDC 1, -TC 1
99/0 Pacific 8, CI-1, CCA-1, GC-1, HAA-1, HAA-11, PAP-1, TL-1
00/1 Pacific 5, IO-1, CCA-1, GCDC-1, NAS-1, PR-1
01/2 Pacific 6, 401, CCA 1, GCDC 1, IZ 1, NAAS 1
02/3 Pacific 4, -IZ 1, -MI 1
02/3 Pacific Complete 108
97/8 Pacific CC 9, CS-1, CCA-1, GCDC-1, SS-1A
97/8 Pa. Crown Roy. 2, BOS-1, CCA-1, HT-1, L-1
98/9 Pa. Crown Roy. 3, -CCA 1, -LL 1, -MP 1, -PP 1
97/8 Pa. Dynagon 3, 135, DD-1A, KN-1, T-2, T-24, BKS-2, BKS-103
97/8 Pa. Invincible 3, AZ-1, FP-1, OTG-1, R-4, R-215
97/8 Pa. Paramount 2, P-1, CG-1, BN-1
98/9 Pa. Paramount 3, -IG 1, -SD 1
99/0 Pa. Paramount 3, HOFB-1, IAd-1, IAl-1, PB-1
00/1 Pa. Paramount 5, ES-1, FF-1, HOFB-1, SZ-1
97/8 Pa. Revolution 2, I-1, TC-1
98/9 Pa. Revolution 2, -ASG 13, -TPA 21, -CTLC 1, -NI 1, -Show. 1
98/9 Panini Photocard
95/6 Panini Sticker 227, 300
96/7 Panini Sticker 153, 222
97/8 Panini Sticker 121, 183
98/9 Panini Sticker 170
99/0 Panini Sticker 175, 321
00/1 Panini Sticker 109
95 Panini Worlds 23
95/6 Parkhurst 3, CCB-4, CCP-4, PP-15, PP-46
00/1 Parkhurst P-151
01/2 Parkhurst 1, HSHS, ✄ PJ24, ✄ PS24, ✄ PSJ4, ✄ HSHSJers, ✄ H6
02/3 Parkhurst 57, -CR9, ✄ CRM9, ✄ FP1, ✄ GJ36, ✄ SJ36, ✄ HSHSJers, ✄ MM9, ✄ PP4
95/6 Parkhurst 24-karat Gold
02/3 Parkhurst Retro 87, ✄ RF1, ✄ RJ18, ✄ RSJ12, ✄ HSHSJers, ✄ RM27
94/5 Parkie SE8, seV1
94/5 Pinnacle 265, 480, RTP9
95/6 Pinnacle 2, CS-3, R20-2
96/7 Pinnacle 184, TP-5, T-2
97/8 Pinnacle 53, TP-4, P-2
96/7 Pi. Be A Player LTH6B, BB-20, ✍ Aut. LTH6B
97/8 Pi. Be A Player OT 5
97/8 Pi. BeeHive 31, BHT-1
97/8 Pi. Certified 34, CT-9
97/8 Pi. Epix E19
95/6 Pi. FANtasy 26
97/8 Pi. Inside 10, IT-4, / Can 10
96/7 Pi. Mint 5
97/8 Pi. Mint 2
95/6 Pi. Summit 2, GMC-19
96/7 Pi. Summit 116, HV-3, U-7
97/8 Pi. Totally 34
95/6 Pi. Zenith 17, ZT-14
96/7 Pi. Zenith 90, ZT-2
95/6 Playoff 2, 114, 223
96/7 Playoff 353
95/6 POG 17, I-032
97/8 Pi. Post 7, F6
93/4 Power Play 485
93/4 Premier - Canada 17
94/5 Premier 405
00/1 Premier Plus 10, MB7, PT1, TT5, WP9
99/0 Prism 2, CA-1, DAS-1, SGDC-1
00/1 Private Stock 2, AC-1, EA-1, Res. 1, PS-1, PSS-1
01/2 Pr. Stock 2, Res. 1, -PS 1, ✄ GUG 2
02/3 Pr. Stock Reserve 2
00/1 PS Titanium 1, 3SS-11, NAAS-1
01/2 PS Titanium 3, SK 1, TSS 11, ✄ DSJ 1
01/2 PS Titanium Draft ✄ 2
02/3 PS Titanium 2
95/6 Pro Magnet 39
02/3 Quest for the Cup 2, -CTC 1
99/0 Revolution 2, IS-1, O-1, SS-1, TL-1, / CSC 2
00/1 Revolution 2, HD-1, II-1, NI-1, SM-21
94/5 Score CT1, TR1
95/6 Score 125, DT-7, GB-9
96/7 Score 8, DT-2, SD-13
97/8 Score 84, 260, 270
97/8 Score Anah. 1
94/5 Select 173,YE-5
95/6 Select CE 13, CF-3
96/7 Select CE 14, C-11
94 Semic 104
95 Semic 86, 206
96/7 SB 7-Eleven Phonecard
00/1 Signature 192, HSHS, F-1, ✍ Aut. 169, ✄ J-16, ✄ HSHSJers
01/2 Signature C-33, ✍ Aut. LPK, ✄ FP1, ✄ GUE1, ✄ GJ1, ✄ GSJ1, ✄ HSHSJers 7, ✄ ITN1, ✄ IG5, ✄ TM1
02/3 Signature 101, GS-70, ✍ 101, ✄ CJ4, ✄ FJ1, ✄ SGJ9, ✄ TQ19
95/6 SBx Emotion 3, Xci-15
95/6 SBx Impact 3, 230, CTI-7
96/7 SBx Impact 2, CTI-6, VT-6
94/5 SP 1, P-1
95/6 SP 1, E1, FX2
96/7 SP 1, CW-5, GF-9
97/8 SP Authentic 6, I11
98/9 SP Authentic 1, SS8, SO16
99/0 SP Authentic 1, HR1, SF1, SS1
00/1 SP Authentic 1, NPS1, SP1
01/2 SP Authentic 2, 91, ✄ NN
02/3 SP Authentic 2, 91, ✄ SP
00/1 SP GU 1, ✄ TotG, ✄ C, ✄ P (x2)
01/2 SP GU 1, ✄ AF (x2), ✄ AFD, ✄ Patch, ✄ PatchC (x3), ✄ PatchT
02/3 SP GU 1, ✄ AF (x2), ✄ CF, ✄ PC, ✄ PH (x2)
02/3 Sports Vault 153
96/7 SPx 1
97/8 SPx 1, D-SPX19
99/0 SPx 4, HH6, P1, X16, XT10, S6
00/1 SPx 1, 81,HH1, S1, ✄ WM
01/2 SPx 1, 71
02/3 SPx 1, 76, ✄ WM (x2), ✄ SS, ✄ X
98/9 SPx Finite 116, 153, 179
98/9 SPx Prospects 1, H1, L3, PS18
99/0 Stadium 4, Chrome 4, Big 3, CA11, EG3, OE5
00/1 Stadium 51, BT1, SF3
01/2 Stadium 4, G20, NHLP17, P7, ✄ SCS
02/3 Stadium 57, -BT15, ✄ NHLP8
96/7 SLU
98/9 SLU
99/0 SLU 31
00/1 SLU Classic Doubles 3
95/6 Super Sticker 2, DC-12
96/7 Team Out!
95/6 Topps 7, 217, HGC7, M13, 5NG, YS1
98/9 Topps 53, -IA 11
99/0 Topps 3, 281, AT8, IM13, AM3, TW13
00/1 Topps 3, TC2, HM7, OTG4
01/2 Topps 28, SM10, ✄ CC1, ✄ CC3, ✄ GWJ
02/3 Topps 8, CC8, HHU5, ✄ CC4, ✄ CC7, ✄ CC12
01/2 Topps All-Star Game 1
99/0 To. Chrome 3, 281, AT8, IM13, AM3
00/1 To. Chrome 3, TC2, HM7, RF2
01/2 To. Chrome 28
02/3 To. Chrome 8
94/5 Topps Finest 7, BBM-1, BBR-1
95/6 To. Finest 165, 189
98/9 To. Finest 100, C10, R3, M11-14
95 Topps Finest Bronze 9
98/9 T. Gold Label 51, GR4
99/0 To. Gold Label 13, PG2
00/1 To. Gold Label 39, GG2
00/1 To. Heritage 8, 218, 235, HH20
01/2 To. Heritage 54, ✄ CC
02/3 To. Heritage 37
02/3 To. Limited 8
96/7 To. Picks FT11, TS4
99/0 To. Prmr. Plus 40, FP5, PT1
01/2 To. Reserve 18, ✄ TR
95/6 To. Stadium EC174, GT1, N9
94/5 TSC Members Only 46
95/6 TSC Members Only 2
00/1 To. Stars 5, 134, WF2
95/6 T. Super Skills 16
02/3 T. Total 9, TTC14, TT13
98/9 UD Choice 4, 224, 240, BH11, SQ25
00/1 UD Heroes 139, L1, PI4, TS1, ✄ GT, ✄ GC
01/2 UD PlayMakers Ltd 3, ✄ PCCJ
00/1 UD Reserve 1, OS1, BT1
02/3 UD Superstars 6, ✄ CAS, ✄ CAST
98/9 UD3 34, 94, 154
00/1 Ultimate Mem. ✍ U-16, ✄ Jers. 14, ✄ J-16, ✄ S-16, ✄ TM-21, ✄ TM-23, ✄ UC-6
01/2 Ultimate Mem. ✄ A8, ✄ ASGH, ✄ BL, ✄ DD, ✄ Emb., ✄ Jers., ✄ S&J, ✄ NP, ✄ PP, ✄ RA, ✄ UC, ✄ WTF, ✍ Aut.
02/3 Ultimate Mem. ✄ DD, ✄ Emb, ✄ GUJ, ✄ GUSJ, ✄ ITN, ✄ MO, ✄ NP, ✄ Num, ✄ RAT, ✄ UC
99/0 Ult. Victory 1, FF2, sg2, S1, UV5
92/3 Upper Deck 586
93/4 Upper Deck E10
94/5 Upper Deck 235, 527, C2, H14, SP-91
95/6 Upper Deck 206, 245, AS-14, F-9, R-43, SE-1
96/7 Upper Deck 1, X1, HH9, LS12, SS1B
97/8 Upper Deck 211, SS9, SG9, S9, T13C
98/9 Upper Deck 17, 31, FF8, FT6, GN19-21, LS17, P21
99/0 Upper Deck 11, 139, AS4, CT29, FF13, MA2, IG2, SB6, PD2, ✄ GJ
00/1 Upper Deck 1, D1, FF1, F1, GA1, RP1, SS1, TT1, ✄ GJ, ✄ DGJ
01/2 Upper Deck 1, FC1, GA10, LP1, SS1, SS1, ✄ CJers, ✄ JPatch, ✄ PatchL, ✄ PatchNu, ✄ PF, ✄ PoaND, ✄ SupSwe
02/3 Upper Deck 4, 181, -GG1, -SS1, ✄ ASJ, ✄ ASP, ✄ DM, ✄ FF, ✄ LN, ✄ PP, ✄ PN, ✄ PA, ✄ R50, ✄ FC, ✄ PW, ✄ UDPL
95/6 UD ASG MVP6
96/7 UD All-Star YCTG AR2
02/3 UD Artistic 2, R2, ✄ AT, / Art
94/5 UD BAP R103, R126, R151, UC9, ✍ 151
95/6 UD BAP LL10
96/7 UD Black Diam. 175, RC8
97/8 UD Black Diam. 14, PC26
98/9 UD Black Diam. 1, M3, WF1
99/0 UD Black Diam. 1, D1, DS2, M10, ✄ APOH
00/1 UD Black Diam. 1, 85, IG1, CC1
94/5 UD Canada Junior 5
99/0 UD C. Legends 54, E1
01/2 UD Challenge 1, CR1
02/3 UD Classic 2, ET1, GG1, ✄ HH, ✄ HR (x2), ✄ SC
95/6 UD CC 159, 363, 370, C10
96/7 UD CC 1, 289, 309, UD10, S14, C24, CR24
97/8 UD Coll. Choice 9, 318, SQ85, S9, W5, C9, CR9
01/2 UD Collectors
91/2 Upper Deck WJC 50
97/8 UD Diam. Vision 6
98/9 UD G. Reserve 17, 31
99/0 UD G. Reserve 11, 139, ✄ GR
99/0 UD Gretzky Excl. 74
01/2 UD Honor Roll 13, 43, SS1, SG1, ✄ GAJ, ✄ HS
02/3 UD Honor 1, 71, -SG1, ✄ GA
96/7 UD Ice 76, S6
97/8 UD Ice 85,IC9, L1A
00/1 UD Ice 1, CC1, FP1, ✄ IGJ
01/2 UD Ice 1, ✄ JC, ✄ FJ
00/1 UD Legends 1, 3, EG1, ✄ LGJ
01/2 UD Mask 1, ✄ GJ, ✄ JP, ✄ DP
02/3 UD Mask 2, ✄ IO, ✄ PG
98/9 UD MVP 1, OT9, F6, -Snip. S6
99/0 UD MVP 4, 21st-3, W12, H8, MVP2, GU1, ✄ GU15
00/1 UD MVP 4, M1, TP1, VC1, ✄ GS
01/2 UD MVP 2, MT8
02/3 UD MVP 6, SO1, VF1, SA
99/0 UD MVP Cup 2, CP1, GM1, PH1, SC1, GC
99/0 UD Ovation 1, 84, LP3, ST1
02/3 UD Piece 1, AC1, ✄ PH, ✄ SS
95/6 UD Post 20
96/7 UD Post, SU-4
99/0 UD PowerDeck 1, T2
01/2 UD Premier 1, ✄ B, ✄ S, ✄ D (x4)
02/3 UD Premier 1, ✄ Jers, ✄ JD, ✄ Patch, ✄ NHLP
00/1 UD Pros&Prosp. 1, GS1, ✄ GJ
99/0 UD Retro 1, DR4, G7C, TC4
02/3 UD Rookie 1, 110, ✄ 157a, ✄ DJ
01/2 UD Top Shelf 1, ✄ J (x2), ✄ S, ✄ ST
02/3 UD Top Shelf 3, ✄ AS, ✄ CP, ✄ GO, ✄ HH, ✄ HT (x2), ✄ R, ✄ SH, ✄ ST, ✄ SW
00/1 UD Vintage 9, 11, 12, UD5, NH1, S1A
01/2 UD Vintage 3, 8, 9, ✄ NL
02/3 UD Vintage 2, 261, T1, ✄ SO
97/8 Valu-net, ✍ Aut.
00/1 Vanguard 2, CF-1, HV-1, IF-1, VP-1
01/2 Vanguard 2, EMW 6, ✄ DGM 1, ✄ DGM 2
02/3 Vanguard 2, -IF 1
99/0 Victory 1, 2, 316, 333, 338
00/1 Victory 1, 8, 242, 282
01/2 Victory 9
02/3 Victory 2, -NP 2
01/2 Waving the Flag 4
99/0 WGretzky 1, CG3, GH2, ✄ TG
96 Wien 94
97/8 Zenith 15, ZT-6, Z45
94/5 ANAH / Carl's Jr. 10
95/6 ANAH / Photo
96/7 ANAH / Up Front 22
92/3 Maine Black Bears
93/4 Maine Black Bears
x93/4 Maine Black Bears
x93/4 Maine Black Bears
x93/4 Maine Black Bears

KARIYA, STEVE
00/1 Aurora 143
99/0 BAP Mem. 211
00/1 BAP Mem. 86
99/0 Crown Royale 136, IE-25, CS-20
99/0 Dynagon Ice 1, CM-1
99/0 HoloGrFX 58
99/0 Millenium 241, C-15, ✍ Aut. 241
99/0 NHL Power Play [x3]
99/0 Omega 233, 5ST-6, G-1
00/1 Pacific 409
02/3 Pacific Complete 81
00/1 Pa. Paramount 239
99/0 Panini Sticker 313, 356
00/1 Parkhurst P-53
99/0 Prism 140, IP-9
00/1 Private Stock 95, PS-57, PSNW-25
00/1 Revolution 143
00/1 Signature 131, ✍ Aut. 58
99/0 SP Authentic 119, SF10, TH10
99/0 SPx 154, X11
99/0 Stadium 197, Chrome 47, Big 19
99/0 To. Chrome 290
99/0 To. Gold Label 100, FG18
99/0 To. Prmr. Plus 118, PR8, TNO5
01/2 Ultimate Mem. ✄ Blood
99/0 Ult. Victory 104, FF4, sg4
99/0 Upper Deck 297, AS13, IG9, SB14, SS11
99/0 UD Black Diam. 85, D16
99/0 UD G. Reserve 297
99/0 UD MVP Cup 181, CC10
99/0 UD Ovation 57, 82, LP10, APOH (x2)
99/0 Victory 363
00/1 Victory 242
99/0 WGretzky 171
01/2 Manitoba Moose
02/3 Manitoba Moose

KARJALA, PEKKA
78/9 SM-Liiga 135

KARJALAINEN, KYÖSTI
99/0 Eishockey 154
94/5 Leaf Elit Set 261
95/6 Leaf Elit Set 105
91/2 Parkhurst 295
90/1 ProCards 350
91/2 ProCards 398
89/0 Semic Elitserien 40
92/3 Semic Elitserien 193
91/2 Upper Deck 606
92/3 Upper Deck 111
92/3 Upper Deck E6
95/6 UD Elitserien 163
97/8 UD Elitserien 173, 219
00/1 UD Elitserien 52

KARJALAINEN, KYÖSTI
98/9 DEL 277

KARJALAINEN, PETRI
80/1 Mallasjuoma 169
78/9 SM-Liiga 176

KARJALAINEN, SAMI
99/0 Cardset 48
00/1 Cardset 37
95/6 Sisu 238

KARJALAINEN, VESA
00/1 DS 47
92/3 Jyvas Hyva 90
00/1 OFS 150
94/5 Sisu 291
95/6 Sisu 145
95/6 Sisu Limited 96

KARKKAINEN, PENTTI
66/7 Champion 133

KARLANDER, AL
70/1 Eddie Sargent 58
70/1 Esso Power Player
76/7 OPC WHA 104
71/2 Toronto Sun Photo

KARLANDER, KEVIN
00/1 Louisiana Ice Gators

KARLANDER, KORY
91/2 Air Canada SJHL 15
91/2 Air Canada SJHL D4
98/9 Detroit Vipers
98/9 Peoria Rivermen
01/2 Belfast Giants
93/4 N. Michigan Wildcats

KARLBERG, MICAEL
95/6 Leaf Elit Set 237

KARLBERG, MIKAEL
91/2 Semic Elitserien 274
92/3 Semic Elitserien 293
95/6 UD Elitserien 104
98/9 UD Elitserien 132
99/0 UD Elitserien 118
00/1 UD Elitserien 118

KARLIN, MATTIAS
98/9 UD Choice 290
98/9 UD Elitserien 215
99/0 UD Elitserien 184
00/1 Providence Bruins
01/2 Providence Bruins

KARLSSON, ANDREAS
99/0 BAP Mem. 308
00/1 BAP Mem. 447
99/0 Crown Royale 7
94/5 Leaf Elit Set 226, RR-9
95/6 Leaf Elit Set 67
00/1 Panini Sticker 7
00/1 Upper Deck 215
95/6 UD Elitserien 110
97/8 UD Elitserien 105
98/9 UD Elitserien 124
99/0 UD G. Reserve 337
00/1 UD MVP 185
00/1 Victory 273
02/3 Chicago Wolves

KARLSSON, BENGT-GÖRAN
72 Semic Sticker 65

KARLSSON, BERT-OLAV
90/1 Semic Elitserien 68
98/9 UD Elitserien 146

KARLSSON, GABRIEL
00/1 Cardset 227
99/0 UD Elitserien 98

KARLSSON, JACOB
99/0 Eishockey 237

KARLSSON, JAKOB
95/6 Leaf Elit Set 291
89/0 Semic Elitserien 84
90/1 Semic Elitserien 257
91/2 Semic Elitserien 88
92/3 Semic Elitserien 108
92/3 Upper Deck 229
97/8 UD Elitserien 185
98/9 UD Elitserien 184

KARLSSON, JAN
89/0 Semic Elitserien 248, 266
90/1 Semic Elitserien 155
91/2 Semic Elitserien 260

KARLSSON, LARS
94/5 Leaf Elit Set 231
95/6 Leaf Elit Set 168
89/0 Semic Elitserien 94
90/1 Semic Elitserien 265
91/2 Semic Elitserien 30
91/2 Semic Elitserien 93
92/3 Semic Elitserien 52
92/3 Semic Elitserien 121

KARLSSON, MARCUS
95/6 DEL 75
95/6 Leaf Elit Set 277, R-8
91/2 Semic Elitserien 326
95/6 UD Elitserien 158
97/8 UD Elitserien 155
00/1 UD Elitserien 169, 220

KARLSSON, MARTIN
96/7 DEL 269

KARLSSON, PENTTI
78/9 SM-Liiga 134
72/3 Williams Finnish 83
73/4 Williams Finnish 130

KARLSSON, PETER
92/3 Semic Elitserien 282

KARLSSON, RAGNAR
99/0 UD Elitserien 128

KARLSSON, RAUNO
70/1 Kuvajulkaisut 295

KARLSSON, ROBERT
98/9 UD Elitserien 23

KARLSSON, ROGER
92/3 Semic Elitserien 58

KARLSSON, ROLAND
94/5 Sisu 79

KARLSSON, RONNIE
92/3 Semic Elitserien 28

KARLSSON, STEFAN
72 Hellas MM-Jenkki 32
74 Hellas MM-Jenkki 27
70/1 Kuvajulkaisut 29
69/0 Mästär Serien 45
72 Panda MM-Toronto
72 Semic Sticker 51
74 Semic Sticker 14
71/2 Williams Finnish 48
72/3 Williams Finnish 49
73/4 Williams Finnish 29

KARLSTAD,
92/3 Semic Nordisk 182 [Gullpucken]

KARLSTAD, JON MAGNE
93 Semic Sticker 235

KARLSTAD, JON MAGNE
92/3 Semic Nordisk 14

KARMANOS, JASON
93/4 Donruss USA10
93/4 Pinnacle 494

KARPA, DAVE
92/3 Classic 68
93/4 Fleer Ultra 97
93/4 Fleer Ultra Pros. 3
98/9 Pacific 57
00/1 Pacific 85
01/2 Pacific 76
97/8 Pa. Dynagon BKS-3
92/3 Parkhurst 151
93/4 Parkhurst 165
95/6 Parkhurst 273
94/5 Parkie SE145
96/7 Pi. Be A Player 41, ✍ Aut. 41
93/4 Power Play 421
93/4 Premier 408
94/5 Premier 202
93/4 Score 611
97/8 Score Anah. 19
93/4 To. Stadium 296
92/3 Upper Deck 517
93/4 Upper Deck 375
94/5 Upper Deck 41
95/6 Upper Deck 119
97/8 Upper Deck 217
95/6 UD CC 192
96/7 ANAH / Up Front 17
98/9 CARO / Highwoods
92/3 QUÉB / Petro-Canada
99/0 Cincinnati Cyclones
91/2 Ferris State Bulldogs

KARPA, DAVID
95/6 ANAH / Photo

KÄRPÄT, OULUN
77-79 Sports. FIN 52-1235

KARPEN, MARK
90/1 Kansas City Blades
93/4 Muskegon Fury
98/9 Wichita Thunder

KARPENKO, IGOR
00/1 Mir 112, 113
96/7 Las Vegas Thunder

KARPOV, VALERI
93/4 Classic 90
94/5 Classic 43, R11, T1
93/4 Cla. Prospects IA20
95/6 Donruss 191
94/5 Fleer 4
94/5 Leaf 486, P-10
95/6 Leaf 80
94/5 L. Limited 51
98/9 Mir 8
99/0 Mir 1
00/1 Mir 159
95/6 Parkhurst 277
94/5 Parkie SE6, seV6
94/5 Pinnacle 486, RTP11
95/6 POG 19
94/5 Premier 284
95/6 Score 170
94/5 Select 183
94/5 SR Gold Standard 87, GS9
94/5 SR Tetrad CVII, ✍ Aut.
95/6 Topps 137
94/5 Upper Deck 256, 570, C6, SP-92
95/6 Upper Deck 378, SE-93
95/6 UD BAP 205, ✍ S205
95/6 UD CC 211
94/5 ANAH / Carl's Jr. 11
00/1 Metallurg 43

KARPOVTSEV, ALEXANDER
99/0 BAP Mem. 109
00/1 BAP Mem. 213, 449
93/4 Classic 89
94/5 Classic AR6
93/4 Cla. Prospects 19
93/4 Donruss 212
94/5 Donruss 327
93/4 Fleer Ultra 372
94/5 Leaf 118
00/1 Mir 321
91/2 O-Pee-Chee 35R
99/0 Pacific 409
00/1 Pacific 394
97/8 Pacific CC 223
94/5 Panini Sticker J
97/8 Panini Sticker 90
99/0 Panini Sticker 155, 329
93/4 Parkhurst 269
95/6 Parkhurst 142
94/5 Parkie SE114
93/4 Pinnacle 437
94/5 Pinnacle 364
96/7 Pi. Be A Player 118, ✍ Aut. 118
95/6 POG 188
93/4 Power Play 391
93/4 Premier 358
94/5 Premier 255, OF-4
92/3 Red Ace Violet 10
93/4 Score 591
97/8 Score NYRa. 8
94 Semic 138
93 Semic Sticker 133
99/0 Stadium 79
99/0 Topps PP1
99/0 To. Chrome PP1
93/4 To. Stadium 291
92/3 Upper Deck 351
93/4 Upper Deck 484, SP-100
94/5 Upper Deck 288
95/6 Upper Deck 288
96/7 Upper Deck 288
02/3 Upper Deck 283
97/8 UD Coll. Choice 169
99/0 UD MVP Cup 180
99/0 TORO / Pizza Pizza 9

KARPUK, KEN
94/5 DEL 174
95/6 DEL 222

KARRENBAUER, BERND
74 Hellas MM-Jenkki 105
70/1 Kuvajulkaisut 88

KARRER, GUILLAUME
00/1 Chicoutimi Saguenéens 20

KARTIO, DAVE
74/5 Sioux City Musketeers

KARTSALO, VESA
66/7 Champion 208

KARTSEV, DENIS
98/9 Mir 153
00/1 Dynamo 18

KARTTUNEN, JOHANNES
66/7 Champion 28
65/6 Hellas 66

KARVONEN, JORMA
72/3 Williams Finnish 286

KARVONEN, PEKKA
72/3 Williams Finnish 287

KASATONOV, ALEXEI
91/2 Bowman 276
92/3 Bowman 323
93/4 Donruss 5
93/4 EA Sports 1
92/3 Fleer Ultra 340
93/4 Fleer Ultra 257
94/5 Fleer Ultra 257
95 Globe 237
91 Ivan Fiodorov 5
93/4 Leaf 381
94/5 Leaf 473
90/1 OPC/Topps 358
91/2 O-Pee-Chee 439
92/3 O-Pee-Chee 353
90/1 Panini Sticker 335
91/2 Panini Sticker 216
92/3 Panini Sticker 180
91/2 Parkhurst 319
93/4 Parkhurst 276
94/5 Parkhurst 195
95/6 Parkhurst 15
94/5 Parkie SE9
91/2 Pinnacle 255
92/3 Pinnacle 289
93/4 Pinnacle 359
94/5 Pinnacle 398
95/6 Playoff 6
94/5 POG 37
95/6 POG 37
93/4 Power Play 5
93/4 Premier 492
94/5 Premier 159
90/1 Pro Set 169
92/3 Pro Set 101
91/2 Pro Set Platinum 198
91/2 Red Ace
90/1 Score 209
91/2 Score 194
91/2 Score CAN 194
92/3 Score 394
93/4 Score 528
93/4 Score 61
94/5 Score 183
94 Semic 143
82 Semic Sticker 57
89 Semic Sticker 81
91 Semic Sticker 214
92 Semic Sticker 101
83/4 Soviet Stars
87/8 Soviet Stars
89/0 Soviet Stars
92/3 Topps 152
91/2 To. Stadium 282
92/3 To. Stadium 406
93/4 To. Stadium 332
93/4 TSC Members Only 9
90/1 Upper Deck 286
91/2 Upper Deck 185
92/3 Upper Deck 96
93/4 Upper Deck 474
94/5 Upper Deck 208
95/6 Upper Deck 69
95/6 UD CC 115
90/1 NJER

KASIK, JAN
99/0 Score 100

KASIK, MARTIN
01/2 Cape Breton Eagles 8

KASIK, PETR
95/6 APS 81
96/7 APS 76
96/7 DS Sticker 138

KASKI, JARI
73/4 Williams Finnish 246

KASKI, MATTI
65/6 Hellas 145

KASKI, OLLI
99/0 Cardset 339
96/7 DEL 154
98/9 DEL 85
92/3 Jyvas Hyva 196
93/4 Jyvas Hyva 345
94/5 Leaf Elit Set 171, FA-8
95 Semic 32
93/4 Sisu 212
94/5 Sisu 365
95/6 Sisu 353, DT-3
95/6 Sisu Limited 20

KASKI, PEKKA
78/9 SM-Liiga 79

KASKINEN, AKI
99/0 Cardset 299

KASOWSKI, PETER
92/3 Dayton Bombers
97/8 Guildford Flames
98/9 Guildford Flames

KASPARAITIS, DARIUS
98/9 Aurora 155
98/9 Be A Player 113, ✍ Aut. 113
99/0 BAP Mem. 127
00/1 BAP Mem. 334
01/2 BAP Mem. 460
02/3 BAP Mem. 267
92/3 CSC 6
92/3 Classic 4
92/3 Classic LP4
92/3 Classic Four Sport 154
93/4 Donruss 203
94/5 Donruss 252
93/4 EA Sports 80
02/3 First Edition 245, 381
94/5 Fleer 122
92/3 Fleer Ultra 344
93/4 Fleer Ultra 160
94/5 Fleer Ultra 129
01/2 Heads Up ✄ JQ 17, ✄ JQ 29
02/3 In The GU ✄ IE23
93/4 Leaf 101
93/4 Leaf GLR 13
94/5 Leaf 27
95/6 Leaf 235
00/1 Mir Fetisov 29
01/2 O-Pee-Chee 221
92/3 OPC Premier 103
98/9 Pacific 354
99/0 Pacific 339
00/1 Pacific 329
01/2 Pacific 313
02/3 Pacific 92

02/3 Pacific Complete 390
97/8 Pacific CC 61
97/8 Pa. Paramount 151
98/9 Pa. Paramount 193
94/5 Panini Sticker 52
95/6 Panini Sticker 96
97/8 Panini Sticker 46
98/9 Panini Sticker 50
99/0 Panini Sticker 135
00/1 Panini Sticker 86
92/3 Parkhurst 102
92/3 Parkhurst 215
93/4 Parkhurst 122
94/5 Parkhurst 133
95/6 Parkhurst 402
01/2 Parkhurst 373
02/3 Parkhurst 105
02/3 Parkhurst Retro 192
94/5 Parkie SE seV27
92/3 Pinnacle 407
93/4 Pinnacle 84
94/5 Pinnacle 26
97/8 Pi. Be A Player 159, ✍ Aut. 159
94/5 POG 161
93/4 Power Play 149
93/4 Power Play SYS 3
93/4 Premier 112
93/4 Premier 443
94/5 Premier 211
00/1 PS Titanium ✂ GUG 134
00/1 PS Titanium Draft ✂ 83
92/3 Red Ace Blue 1
92/3 Red Ace Violet 11
93/4 Score 124
93/4 Score IS 17
94/5 Score 11, CI3
95/6 Score 40
97/8 Score 162
97/8 Score Pitt. 10
93 Semic Sticker 146
00/1 Signature 61, ✍ Aut. 112
01/2 Signature ✂ DD12, ✂ IB3
02/3 Signature GS-26, ✂ DW4
96/7 SP 129
02/3 Sports Vault 89
01/2 SPx 168
02/3 Stadium 109
96/7 Team Out!
99/0 Topps 98
00/1 Topps 104
01/2 Topps 221
99/0 To. Chrome 98
98/9 To. Finest 25
02/3 To. Heritage 161
93/4 To. Stadium 101
02/3 T. Total 169
01/2 Ultimate Mem. ✂ WTF
91/2 Upper Deck 650
92/3 Upper Deck 335
92/3 Upper Deck 554
92/3 Upper Deck 563
92/3 Upper Deck 623
92/3 Upper Deck CC13
92/3 Upper Deck ER7
93/4 Upper Deck 173, SP-91
94/5 Upper Deck 298, SP-46
95/6 Upper Deck 447
96/7 Upper Deck 293
97/8 Upper Deck 136, 391
98/9 Upper Deck 160, ✂ GJ22
00/1 Upper Deck 372
01/2 Upper Deck 371
02/3 Upper Deck 361
94/5 UD BAP R148, ✍ 142
96/7 UD Black Diam. 61
95/6 UD CC 2
96/7 UD CC 162
97/8 UD Coll. Choice 211
91/2 Upper Deck WJC 11
98/9 UD G. Reserve 160
99/0 UD MVP Cup 152
00/1 UD Vintage 295
01/2 Vanguard ✂ DGM 25
01/2 Victory 288
01/2 Waving the Flag 32

KASPAREK, MILAN
97/8 APS 218

KASPARIK, PAVEL
00/1 DS 132
99/0 OFS 106
00/1 OFS 177
01/2 OFS 20

KASPER, OLIVER
94/5 DEL 352

KASPER, PETER
95 Panini Worlds 260
99/0 Florida Everblades

KASPER, STEVE
90/1 Bowman 147
91/2 Bowman 187
92/3 Bowman 33
92/3 Durivage 4
81/2 O-Pee-Chee 4
82/3 O-Pee-Chee 12
83/4 O-Pee-Chee 50
85/6 OPC/Topps 79
86/7 OPC/Topps 97
87/8 OPC/Topps 162
88/9 OPC/Topps 176
90/1 OPC/Topps 153
91/2 O-Pee-Chee 302
89/0 OPC/Topps 194
91/2 OPC Premier 85
81/2 OPC Sticker 51
82/3 OPC/Topps Sticker 81
82/3 OPC/Topps Sticker 253
83/4 OPC/Topps Sticker 53
86/7 OPC Sticker 40-177
87/8 OPC Sticker 66B
88/9 OPC Sticker 30
88/9 OPC Sticker 27-156
89/0 opcSticker 152-12
87/8 Panini Sticker 15
88/9 Panini Sticker 210
89/0 Panini Sticker 92
90/1 Panini Sticker 238
91/2 Panini Sticker 88
92/3 Parkhurst 403
82/3 Post [Bost.]
93/4 Premier 73
90/1 Pro Set 120
91/2 Pro Set 449
90/1 Score 247
91/2 Score 256
91/2 Score 24T
91/2 Score CAN 574
92/3 Score 306
81/2 Topps 68 [East]
92/3 Topps 150
91/2 To. Stadium 139
92/3 To. Stadium 71
93/4 To. Stadium 122
90/1 Upper Deck 140
91/2 Upper Deck 576
83/4 BOST
84/5 BOST
88/9 BOST / Sports Action
89/0 LOSA / Smokey 5
90/1 LOSA / Smokey 7
91/2 PHIL / J.C. Penney
92/3 PHIL / UD Sheet
92/3 TAMP / Sheraton Inn

KASPERCZYK, JEDRZEJ
94/5 DEL 156
95/6 DEL 157
96/7 DEL 212
89 Semic Sticker 139
92 Semic Sticker 286

KASSLATTER, FABRIZIO
79 Panini Sticker 391

KASTAK, KAMIL
95/6 APS 283
96/7 APS 178
96/7 DS Sticker 55
95 Globe 162
95 Panini Worlds 199
94 Semic 175
92/3 Semic Elitserien 143
92 Semic Sticker 133
93 Semic Sticker 107
93/4 Sisu 193

KASTELIC, ED
90/1 O-Pee-Chee 404
90/1 Pro Set 450
89/0 HART / Jr. Whalers
90/1 HART / Jr. Whalers
91/2 HART / Jr. Whalers
87/8 WASH
87/8 WASH / Kodak
84/5 Moncton G'Flames
92/3 Phoenix Roadrunners

KASTELIC, JOE
52/3 Anonymous 31

KASTNER, MILAN
94/5 APS 91
95/6 APS 327
99/0 DS 190
96/7 DS Sticker 264
99/0 OFS 467

KASZAP, THIERRY
01/2 Victoriaville Tigres 5

KASZYCKI, MIKE
78/9 O-Pee-Chee 171
79/0 O-Pee-Chee 87
80/1 O-Pee-Chee 371
78/9 Topps 171
79/0 Topps 87
79/0 NYIS

KATAINEN, PENTTI
65/6 Hellas 60

KATAVISTO, ARI
99/0 Cardset 214

KATELNIKOFF, TRACEY
89/0 Saskatoon Blades

KATELNIKOFF, TRACY
86/7 Saskatoon Blades

KATHAN, KLAUS
98/9 DEL 298, 326
99/0 Eishockey 261,380
00/1 UD DEL 126
01/2 UD DEL 126

KATHAN, PETER
94/5 DEL 173

KAUFMANN, BEAT
72 Semic Sticker 156

KAUHANEN,
97/8 Hockey-Box

KAUHANEN, HEIKKI
71/2 Williams Finnish 244
73/4 Williams Finnish 311

KAUHANEN, ILPO
90/1 7th..Sketch OHL 35
91/2 7th...Sketch OHL 19
94/5 Sisu 278
95/6 Sisu 108, GG-10
96/7 Sisu 122,MA-3
01/2 UD DEL 127
91/2 Cornwall Royals

KAUKANEN, TIMO
95/6 Sisu 298

KAUKOKARI, MAURI
70/1 Kuvajulkaisut 108
72 Panda MM-Toronto
71/2 Williams Finnish 116
72/3 Williams Finnish 84
73/4 Williams Finnish 131

KAUKOKARI, MIKKO
99/0 Cardset 210
00/1 Cardset 12

KAULTANEN, JARNO
95/6 Sisu 73

KAUNONEN, ARTO
78/9 SM-Liiga 206
71/2 Williams Finnish 190
72/3 Williams Finnish 228
73/4 Williams Finnish 262

KAUPINSALO, KARI
80/1 Mallasjuoma 125
78/9 SM-Liiga 154

KAUPPILA,
97/8 Hockey-Box

KAUPPILA, JARI
98/9 Cardset 110
99/0 Cardset 63, 170
00/1 Cardset 137
02/3 Cardset 37
92/3 Jyvas Hyva 147
93/4 Jyvas Hyva 268
94/5 Sisu 230
95/6 Sisu 26
96/7 Sisu 21

KAUPPILA, KARI
80/1 Mallasjuoma 184
78/9 SM-Liiga 210
72/3 Williams Finnish 211
73/4 Williams Finnish 284

KAUPPILA, MATTI
73/4 Williams Finnish 285

KAUPPINEN, MARKO
98/9 Cardset 128
99/0 Cardset 261
00/1 Cardset 40
02/3 Cardset 190

KAUPPINEN, MIKA
98/9 Cardset 201
99/0 Cardset 311
00/1 Cardset 208
02/3 Cardset 191

KAUTONEN,
97/8 Hockey-Box

KAUTONEN, V-P
99/0 Cardset 293
00/1 Cardset 257
96/7 DEL 266
98/9 DEL 33
92/3 Jyvas Hyva 166
93/4 Jyvas Hyva 299
93/4 Sisu 68
93/4 Sisu 344
94/5 Sisu 265
95/6 Sisu 6, 198

KAUTTO, MATTI
65/6 Hellas 103

KAVANAGH, CHRIS
98/9 BC Icemen 14
98/9 BC Icemen

KAVANAGH, PAT
01/2 BAP Mem. 332
01/2 SPx 131
01/2 SPx Rookie RR29
01/2 Upper Deck 209
01/2 UD Ice 71
01/2 UD Top Shelf 66
00/1 Kansas City Blades 17
01/2 Manitoba Moose
02/3 Manitoba Moose

KAVEC, IGNAC
79 Panini Sticker 397

KAVULIC, ONDREJ
98/9 OFS 346
99/0 OFS 58

KAWAMURA, KATSUTOSHI
79 Panini Sticker 289

KAY, A.
28/9 Paulins Candy 55

KAYKHO, ARTTU
00/1 Kudos 113

KAYSER, STEVE
84/5 Ottawa 67's

KAZAK, DUSTIN
99/0 Lethbridge Hurricanes

KAZAKOV, ALEXANDER
98/9 Mir 60

KAZARIAN, BRYAN
99/0 Upper Deck 335
99/0 UD Black Diam. 113
99/0 UD G. Reserve 335
99/0 UD MVP Cup 208
00/1 Owen Sound Attack 7

KAZIONOV, DMITRI
98 Québec Pee Wee 1035

KAZUIK, GARNET
84/5 Brandon Wheat Kings

KE, YANG YUNG
79 Panini Sticker 355

KEA, ED
75/6 O-Pee-Chee 383
76/7 O-Pee-Chee 361
77/8 O-Pee-Chee 301
78/9 O-Pee-Chee 277
79/0 O-Pee-Chee 390
81/2 O-Pee-Chee 294
82/3 Post [SLou.]
81/2 Topps 118 [West]
77/8 ATLF
78/9 ATLF / Colour

KEALTY, JEFF
93/4 Classic 104
95/6 Do. Elite WJ 28
98/9 Milwaukee Admirals

KEAN, FRED
85/6 London Knights
86/7 London Knights

KEAN, MITCH
94/5 Huntington Blizzard

KEANE, MIKE
98/9 Be A Player 42, ✍ Aut. 42
01/2 BAP Mem. 476
91/2 Bowman 334
92/3 Bowman 290
93/4 Donruss 451
94/5 Donruss 134
92/3 Fleer Ultra 106
93/4 Fleer Ultra 196
94/5 Fleer Ultra 110
01/2 Heads Up ✂ JQ 24
93/4 Hockey Wit 63
92/3 Humpty Dumpty
93/4 Leaf 279
90/1 OPC/Topps 325
91/2 O-Pee-Chee 434
92/3 O-Pee-Chee 274
98/9 Pacific 178
99/0 Pacific 121
00/1 Pacific 132
02/3 Pacific Complete 194
97/8 Pacific CC 239
90/1 Panini/MTL 13
91/2 Panini Sticker 190
95/6 Panini Sticker 40
91/2 Parkhurst 311
92/3 Parkhurst 318
91/2 Pinnacle 265
92/3 Pinnacle 164
93/4 Pinnacle 339
94/5 Pinnacle 151
95/6 Pinnacle 83
97/8 Pi. Be A Player 101, ✍ Aut. 101
94/5 POG 135
95/6 POG 149
93/4 Power Play 129
93/4 Premier 139
94/5 Premier 497
00/1 PS Titanium ✂ GUG 85
90/1 Pro Set 151
91/2 Pro Set 121
91/2 Pro Set Platinum 191
90/1 Score 102T
91/2 Score 360
91/2 Score CAN 251
92/3 Score 179
93/4 Score 170
94/5 Score 187
95/6 Score 266
97/8 Score NYRa. 3
02/3 Signature GS-59
98/9 SPx Finite 27
92/3 Topps 478
95/6 Topps 281
00/1 Topps 256
00/1 To. Chrome 156
91/2 To. Stadium 236
92/3 To. Stadium 349
93/4 To. Stadium 92
94/5 To. Stadium 18
95/6 To. Stadium 43
90/1 Upper Deck 382
92/3 Upper Deck 164
95/6 Upper Deck 388
97/8 Upper Deck 315
98/9 Upper Deck 77
00/1 Upper Deck 57
95/6 UD BAP 103, ✍ S103
95/6 UD CC 153
97/8 UD Coll. Choice 63
98/9 UD G. Reserve 77
99/0 UD MVP Cup 62
01/2 UD SCup Champs 45
00/1 DALL / Southwest
88/9 MONT
89/0 MONT
89/0 MONT / Kraft
90/1 MONT
91/2 MONT
92/3 MONT
93/4 MONT
94/5 MONT / Export
94/5 MONT
95/6 MONT

KEANS, DOUG
84/5 O-Pee-Chee 5
85/6 OPC/Topps 133
86/7 OPC/Topps 22
87/8 OPC/Topps 147
87/8 OPC Sticker 139-249
87/8 Panini Sticker 4
88/9 ProCards / Baltimore
84/5 Topps 4
84/5 BOST
78/9 Saginaw Gears

KEARNS, DENNIS
72/3 Eddie Sargent 224
74/5 Loblaws
71/2 O-Pee-Chee 231
73/4 O-Pee-Chee 162
74/5 O-Pee-Chee 366
75/6 O-Pee-Chee 188
76/7 O-Pee-Chee 338
76/7 OPC 395
77/8 O-Pee-Chee 175
78/9 O-Pee-Chee 191
79/0 O-Pee-Chee 76
80/1 O-Pee-Chee 392
81/2 O-Pee-Chee 337
81/2 OPC Sticker 249
79 Panini Sticker 58
80/1 Pepsi Bottle Cap
73/4 Topps 173
75/6 Topps 188
77/8 Topps 175
78/9 Topps 191
79/0 Topps 76
71/2 Toronto Sun Photo
71/2 VANC / Royal Bank 12
72/3 VANC / Royal Bank
73/4 VANC / Royal Bank
74/5 VANC / Royal Bank
76/7 VANC / Royal Bank
77/8 VANC / Royal Bank
78/9 VANC / Royal Bank
79/0 VANC / Royal Bank
80/1 VANC
80/1 VANC / Silverwood

KEARNS, JUSTIN
98/9 BC Icemen 8
98/9 BC Icemen
00/1 Rockford IceHogs

KEARNS, RICHARD
99/0 Brampton Batallion 23

KEATING, JACK
34-43 BeeHive-1 [Detr.]
39/0 O-Pee-Chee 67

KEATS, DUKE
83 HHOF Postcard D8
83&87 HHOF 54
93/4 Legends of Hockey 20
23/4 Paulins Candy 45

KECZMER, DAN
93/4 Donruss 406
91/2 O-Pee-Chee 3S
99/0 Panini Sticker 267
93/4 Parkhurst 82
93/4 Pinnacle 218
93/4 Power Play 304
93/4 Premier 461
90/1 ProCards 114
94/5 To. Stadium 262
93/4 Upper Deck 249
95/6 Upper Deck 410
91/2 HART / Jr. Whalers
96/7 Michigan K-Wings
99/0 Milwaukee Admirals

KEECH, JEFF
99/0 Ottawa 67's

KEEFE, ADAM
01/2 Kitchener Rangers
00/1 Sudbury Wolves 18

KEEFE, JERRY
01/2 Belfast Giants

KEEFE, SHELDON
00/1 BAP Mem. 495
01/2 BAP Mem. 297
99 Bowman 14, 125, ✍ BA34
00/1 Crown Royale 141
01/2 O-Pee-Chee 274
02/3 O-Pee-Chee 264
02/3 Pacific Complete 413
94 Québec Pee Wee 1717
99/0 SP Authentic 123
00/1 SPx ✂ 130
99/0 Topps 264
01/2 Topps 274
02/3 Topps 264
99/0 To. Chrome 264
00/1 To. Heritage 135
02/3 To. Limited 264
02/3 T. Total 65
99/0 Ult. Victory 107
99/0 Upper Deck 309
99/0 UD Black Diam. 96
99/0 UD G. Reserve 309
01/2 UD Ice 120
99/0 UD MVP Cup 195
99/0 UD Ovation 64
99/0 UD Prospects 3
00/1 Vanguard 146
99/0 Victory 361
02/3 Victory 191
98/9 Barrie Colts

KEELING, BUTCH (MELVILLE)
36-39 Diamond Match TT1

KEELING, MELVILLE (BUTCH)
33/4 Anonymous 30
34-43 BeeHive-1 [NYRa.]
33-35 Diamond Match Silv.
36-39 Diamond Match TT2
36-39 Diamond Match TT3
33/4 O-Pee-Chee 36
33/4 WWGum 20
37/8 World Wide Gum 15

KEENAN, CORY
90 7th..Sketch Mem.Cup 40
89/0 7th..Sketch OHL 179
94/5 SR Auto-Phonex 20, ✍ 20
87/8 Kitchener Rangers
88/9 Kitchener Rangers
89/0 Kitchener Rangers

KEENAN, LARRY
71/2 Eddie Sargent 31
70/1 Esso Power Player
68/9 O-Pee-Chee 115
70/1 O-Pee-Chee 104
61/2 Parkhurst 13
61/2 Shirriff 55
68/9 Shirriff / SLou. 9
68/9 Topps 115
70/1 Topps 104
71/2 Toronto Sun Photo
61/2 York 32

KEENAN, MIKE
88/9 CHIC / Coke
89/0 CHIC / Coke
90/1 CHIC / Coke
91/2 CHIC / Coke
01/2 FLOR
86/7 PHIL

KEHLE, MARKUS
94/5 DEL 79
95/6 DEL 298

KEHLE, TONI
72 Semic Sticker 93

KEHLER, DREW
96/7 Kamloops Blazers
97/8 Regina Pats

KEHLER, J.D.
98/9 Brandon Wheat Kings
99/0 Brandon Wheat Kings

KEHOE, RICK
72/3 Eddie Sargent 209
01/2 Fleer Greats 87, ✍ Aut.
83/4 Funmate Puffy 8 [w/]
84/5 Kellogg's 5
74/5 Loblaws
73/4 Mac's Milk
73/4 O-Pee-Chee 60
74/5 O-Pee-Chee 81
75/6 O-Pee-Chee 39
76/7 O-Pee-Chee 124
77/8 O-Pee-Chee 33
78/9 O-Pee-Chee 213
79/0 O-Pee-Chee 109
80/1 O-Pee-Chee 18
80/1 O-Pee-Chee 117
81/2 O-Pee-Chee 254
81/2 O-Pee-Chee 260
81/2 O-Pee-Chee 267
82/3 O-Pee-Chee 271
83/4 O-Pee-Chee 274
83/4 O-Pee-Chee 282
84/5 O-Pee-Chee 177
81/2 OPC Sticker 182
81/2 OPC Sticker 261
82/3 OPC/Topps Sticker 143
83/4 OPC/Topps Sticker 11
83/4 OPC/Topps Sticker 231
83/4 OPC/Topps Sticker 232
84/5 OPC Sticker 117
82/3 Post [Pitt.]
84/5 7-Eleven
83/4 Souhaits Keychain [Penguins]
73/4 Topps 179
74/5 Topps 81
75/6 Topps 39
76/7 Topps 124
77/8 Topps 33
78/9 Topps 213
79/0 Topps 109
80/1 Topps 18
80/1 Topps 117
81/2 Topps 17
81/2 Topps 60
81/2 Topps 128 [East]
84/5 Topps 125
74/5 PITT
77/8 PITT / McDonald's
83/4 PITT / Heinz
84/5 PITT / Heinz
93/4 PITT / Foodland 6
95/6 PITT / Foodland 11
72/3 TORO
73/4 TORO

KEHRIG, RYAN
00/1 Saskatoon Blades

KEICHINGER, CLINT
98/9 Kelowna Rockets

KEILEY, DARREN
98/9 Barrie Colts

KEILLER, IAN
91/2 7th...Sketch OHL 104

KEILLER, JIMMY
37/8 World Wide Gum 120

KEILY, DARREN
99/0 Sudbury Wolves 3
00/1 Sudbury Wolves 3

KEINÄNEN, JANI
98/9 Cardset 63
99/0 Cardset 297
00/1 Cardset 73
02/3 Cardset 192

KEINASS, TORSTEN
94/5 DEL 84
95/6 DEL 79

KEINONEN, HEIKKI
66/7 Champion 176
70/1 Kuvajulkaisut 243
71/2 Williams Finnish 210

KEINONEN, HEIMO
70/1 Kuvajulkaisut 244
71/2 Williams Finnish 211
72/3 Williams Finnish 158
73/4 Williams Finnish 220

KEINONEN, MATTI
66/7 Champion 26
65/6 Hellas 23
92/3 Jyvas Hyva 120
70/1 Kuvajulkaisut 61
70/1 Kuvajulkaisut 229
72 Semic Sticker 91
77-79 Sports. FIN 40-937
71/2 Williams Finnish 152
72/3 Williams Finnish 62
72/3 Williams Finnish 104
73/4 Williams Finnish 64
73/4 Williams Finnish 197

KEKÄLÄINEN, JANNE
98/9 Cardset 154
93/4 Sisu 174
94/5 Sisu 21
95/6 Sisu 278
96/7 Sisu 79
95/6 Sisu Limited 71

KEKÄLÄINEN, JARMO
93/4 Cla. Prospects 198
91/2 Jyvas Hyva 33
92/3 Jyvas Hyva 158
94/5 Leaf Elit Set 229, FA-7
93/4 Parkhurst 410
94 Semic 26
92 Semic Sticker 22
93 Semic Sticker 65
94/5 Sisu 366
91/2 Upper Deck 108
91/2 Upper Deck E1
93/4 OTTA

KELFER, MIKE
89/0 ProCards AHL 246
90/1 ProCards 592
90/1 Kansas City Blades

KELHAM, A.J.
91/2 7th...Sketch WHL 237
02/3 London Knights

KELHAM, AJ
01/2 Nottingham Panthers

KELLAND, CHRIS
94 Semic 316
01/2 Sheffield Steelers
93/4 Sheffield Steelers 12
94/5 Sheffield Steelers 2
95/6 Sheffield Steelers
97/8 Sheffield Steelers

KELLEHER, CHRIS
01/2 BAP Mem. 440
93/4 Cla. 4 Sport 223
01/2 UD Mask 137
02/3 UD MVP 195
01/2 Providence Bruins
00/1 WBS Penguins

KELLER, AARON
94/5 Slapshot Memorial 7
93/4 Kamloops Blazers

KELLER, FLORIAN
94/5 DEL 386
95/6 DEL 374
96/7 DEL 174

KELLER, HENS
72 Semic Sticker 143

KELLER, JOHN
84/5 Kitchener Rangers

KELLER, RYAN
91/2 Avant Garde BCJHL 57
92/3 BCJHL 213
91/2 Nanaimo Clippers

KELLETT, KEVIN
95/6 Prince Albert Raiders

KELLN, TRAVIS
90/1 7th..Sketch WHL 21

KELLOG, ALLEN
52/3 Anonymous 24

KELLOGG, BOB
93/4 Cla. Prospects 63
93/4 Indianapolis Ice
94/5 Indianapolis Ice

KELLY, BOB (HOUNDOG)
71/2 Eddie Sargent 157
72/3 Eddie Sargent 163
70/1 Esso Power Player
74/5 Loblaws
71/2 O-Pee-Chee 203
73/4 O-Pee-Chee 253
74/5 O-Pee-Chee 380
75/6 O-Pee-Chee 184
76/7 O-Pee-Chee 219
77/8 O-Pee-Chee 178
78/9 O-Pee-Chee 71
79/0 O-Pee-Chee 14
81/2 O-Pee-Chee 349
81/2 OPC Sticker 195
92/3 Parkhurst 477
75/6 Topps 184
76/7 Topps 219
77/8 Topps 178
78/9 Topps 71
79/0 Topps 14
81/2 Topps 119 [East]
71/2 Toronto Sun Photo
80/1 WASH

KELLY, BRENT
99/0 Guelph Storm

KELLY, BROCK
89/0 Nashville Knights

KELLY, CHRIS
99 Bowman 8, ✍ BA28
94 Québec Pee Wee 658
99/0 Topps 270
99/0 To. Chrome 270
00/1 UD Prospects 35
01/2 Grand Rapids Griffins
00/1 London Knights
00/1 London Knights

KELLY, CHUCK
67/8 Columbus Checkers

KELLY, DIARMUID
00/1 Red Deer Rebels

KELLY, J. BOB (BATTLESHIP)
74/5 Loblaws
74/5 O-Pee-Chee 143
75/6 O-Pee-Chee 263
76/7 O-Pee-Chee 261
77/8 O-Pee-Chee 14
78/9 O-Pee-Chee 189
79/0 O-Pee-Chee 306
74/5 Topps 143
75/6 Topps 263
76/7 Topps 261
77/8 Topps 14
78/9 Topps 189
74/5 PITT
73/4 SLOU

KELLY, JASON
97/8 Charlotte Checkers

KELLY, JOHN PAUL
82/3 Post [LosA.]
84/5 LOSA / Smokey 10

KELLY, JUSTIN
00/1 Saskatoon Blades
97/8 Spokane Chiefs

KELLY, KENDEL
92/3 BCJHL 2

KELLY, LEONARD (RED)
99/0 BAP Mem. R-11, ✍ R-11
45-64 BeeHive-2 [Detr.]
45-64 BeeHive-2 [Toro.]
45-64 BeeHive-2 [Toro.]
64-67 BeeHive-3 [Toro.]
64/5 Coke/Sprite [Toro.]
65/6 Coca-Cola
00 CSAS Signat. Series
01/2 Fleer Greats 78, ✍ Aut.
01/2 Fleer Legacy 38
83 HHOF Postcard D9
83&87 HHOF 55
91/2 Kraft 81
94/5 Legends 53
74/5 O-Pee-Chee 76
51/2 Parkhurst 55
52/3 Parkhurst 67
53/4 Parkhurst 40
54/5 Parkhurst 42
54/5 Parkhurst 91
60/1 Parkhurst 9
61/2 Parkhurst 9
62/3 Parkhurst 5
63/4 Parkhurst 3
63/4 Parkhurst 63
92/3 Parkhurst PR-10
93/4 Parkhurst PR58
01/2 Parkhurst PR17, PR31, PR53, PR54, PR60, PR93, PR109, PR144, PR149, ✍ PA40
93/4 Parkie 56-57 142
93/4 Parkie 56-57 154
93/4 Parkie 56-57 52
95/6 Parkie 66-67 109
94/5 Parkie Tall 127
52 Royal Desserts 7
60/1 Shirriff 4
61/2 Shirriff 49
62/3 Shirriff 9
01/2 Signature ✍ VA12
54/5 Topps 5
57/8 Topps 48
58/9 Topps 61
59/0 Topps 65
64/5 Topps 44
65/6 Topps 15
66/7 Topps 79
66/7 Topps / Test 42
74/5 Topps 76
00/1 To. Heritage ✍ CAI
01/2 T/O Archives 72
63/4 Toronto Star Action
01/2 Ultimate Mem. ✂ SCW
91/2 Ultimate Original Six 38, 79, ✍ Aut.
90/1 Upper Deck 502
99/0 UD C. Legends 22
01/2 UD Legends 19
99/0 UD Retro 98
60/1 York
61/2 York 21
62/3 York Transfer 20
63/4 York 12
94/5 Zellers, ✍ Aut.
71/2 PITT / Sportcolor
64/5 TORO
68/9 TORO
73/4 TORO

KELLY, MARK
95/6 Toledo Storm
96/7 Toledo Storm
97/8 Toledo Storm 29

KELLY, MIKE
89/0 7th..Sketch OHL 47

KELLY, PAT
86/7 London Knights

KELLY, PAUL
88/9 ProCards / New Haven
89/0 ProCards AHL 3
93/4 Muskegon Fury
94/5 Muskegon Fury
95/6 Muskegon Fury
98/9 Topeka Scarecrows
99/0 Topeka Scarecrows

KELLY, PEP
35/6 Amalgamated Press

KELLY, PETE
35-40 Canada Starch

KELLY, PETE*
34-43 BeeHive-1 [Detr.]

KELLY, PETER**
87/8 Brockville Braves
88/9 Brockville Braves

KELLY, RED
02/3 Canada Post
63-65 Chex
62/3 Cowan Tile
02/3 In The GU ✂ VM8
02/3 Parkhurst ✂ VT14
02/3 Parkhurst Retro ✂ NN11
02/3 To. Heritage - Reprint TML, ✂ Reprint, ✍ Aut.
57/8 Toronto Star Photo
54 Toronto Star Weekend
60/1 Toronto Star Weekend
02/3 Ultimate Mem. ✂ EA, ✂ FS, ✂ Num, ✂ RT, ✂ VGJ
60/1 York Glass [Toro.]

KELLY, REG
38/9 Quaker Oats

KELLY, REG (REGIS)
34-43 BeeHive-1 [Toro.]
35/6 O-Pee-Chee 87
37/8 O-Pee-Chee 145
39/0 O-Pee-Chee 9
37/8 World Wide Gum 86

KELLY, STEVE
00/1 BAP Mem. 37
95/6 Classic 6, AS6, BK6
95/6 Cla. 5 Sport 128, SFF-4, ✍ Aut.
94/5 Cla. Images 39, PD3
97/8 Donruss 216, RR-8
97/8 Do. Canadian 130
97/8 Limited 107
96/7 Metal Univ. 183
97/8 Pi. Inside 117
97/8 Upper Deck 188
96/7 EDMO
97/8 EDMO
99/0 Albany River Rats
01/2 Manchester Monarchs
02/3 Manchester Monarchs
93/4 Prince Albert Raiders
95/6 Prince Albert Raiders

KELMAN, SCOTT
99 Bowman 9, SC2, ✍ BA29
98/9 SP Authentic 125, -SoT
98/9 Upper Deck 402
99/0 Upper Deck 325
98/9 UD G. Reserve 402
99/0 UD G. Reserve 325
99/0 UD MVP Cup ✂ GU, ✍ PS

KELMAN, TODD
92/3 BCJHL 198
00/1 Kudos 24
01/2 Belfast Giants

KELNER, ROMAN
98/9 OFS 360
99/0 OFS 423

KEMP, DYLAN
95/6 Prince Albert Raiders

KEMP, JOHN
82/3 Kingston Canadians

KEMPER, ANDREW
91/2 7th...Sketch WHL 128
93/4 Saskatoon Blades

KEMPF, MARKUS
94/5 DEL 116
95/6 DEL 117

KEMPFFER, MICK
96/7 Charlotte Checkers

KEMPPAINEN, HANNU
80/1 Mallasjuoma 120
78/9 SM-Liiga 166

KEMPPAINEN, PASI
94/5 Sisu 310
95/6 Sisu 282

KEMPPI, MIIKKA
94/5 Sisu 271
95/6 Sisu 118

KEMPPINEN, JYRI
71/2 Williams Finnish 324

KENADY, CHRIS
95/6 Classic 75, ✍ Aut.
95/6 Cla. 5 Sport 139
00/1 SPx 104
99/0 Hartford Wolf Pack
00/1 Hartford Wolf Pack

KENDALL, CARL
12/3 Imperial 35

KENDALL, WILLIAM
34-43 BeeHive-1 [Toro.]
33-35 Diamond Match Silv.
36-39 Diamond Match TT1
36-39 Diamond Match TT2

KENIG, MAX
02/3 Cardset 193

KENNEDY,
98/9 Las Vegas Thunder

KENNEDY, BOB
88/9 Flint Spirits
89/0 Johnstown Chiefs

KENNEDY, CRAIG
00/1 UD Prospects 30

KENNEDY, DEAN
90/1 Bowman 248
93/4 Kraft / PB
94/5 Leaf 500
91/2 O-Pee-Chee 388
87/8 Panini Sticker 276
92/3 Pinnacle 239
93/4 Pinnacle 178
90/1 Pro Set 22
90/1 Score 299
91/2 Score CAN 431
92/3 Score 211
93/4 Score 366
83/4 Souhaits Keychain [Kings]
90/1 Upper Deck 380
89/0 BUFF / Blue Shield
89/0 BUFF / Campbell's
90/1 BUFF / Blue Shield
90/1 BUFF / Campbell's
87/8 LOSA
91/2 WINN / IGA
93/4 WINN / Ruffles
82/3 Brandon Wheat Kings

KENNEDY, FORBES
45-64 BeeHive-2 [Chic.]
45-64 BeeHive-2 [Detr.]
64-67 BeeHive-3 [Bost.]
64/5 Coke/Sprite [Bost.]
65/6 Coca-Cola
68/9 O-Pee-Chee 97
93/4 Parkie 56-57 35
94/5 Parkie Tall 16
68/9 Shirriff / Phil. 10
57/8 Topps 50
58/9 Topps 11
59/0 Topps 52
63/4 Topps 19
68/9 Topps 97
64/5 Toronto Star Action

KENNEDY, JOEY
92/3 BCJHL 89

KENNEDY, MIKE
94/5 Cla. Images 73
93/4 Cla. Prospects 79
95/6 Donruss 192
95/6 Edge Ice 140, C-14
99/0 Eishockey 336
94/5 Fleer 54
95/6 Fleer Ultra 39
95/6 Leaf 7
95/6 Panini Sticker 171
91/2 7th...Sketch WHL 131
95/6 Topps 27, 7NG
94/5 Upper Deck 326
95/6 UD CC 205
00/1 UD DEL 237
01/2 UD DEL 183
94/5 DALL / Southwest
96/7 DALL / Southwest
97/8 St. John's Maple Leafs

KENNEDY, RON
95/6 DEL 123
96/7 DEL 22
77/8 Kalamazoo Wings

KENNEDY, SHELDON
97/8 Bicycle 10-Spade
93/4 Leaf 246
90/1 O-Pee-Chee 520
91/2 O-Pee-Chee 317
97/8 Pa. Invincible R-13
93/4 Premier 221
94/5 Premier 408
89/0 ProCards AHL 320
91/2 ProCards 134
93/4 Score 361
92/3 Topps 368
91/2 Upper Deck 408
94/5 Upper Deck 437
97/8 UD Coll. Choice 21
90/1 DETR / Little Caesars
91/2 DETR / Little Caesars

KENNEDY, TED
02/3 Parkie - Reprint 172, 176, 192, ✂ VM19
02/3 Ultimate Mem. ✂ Cor, ✂ GAO, ✂ GMIH

KENNEDY, TED (TEEDER)
01/2 ASG History
45-64 BeeHive-2 [Toro.]
64-67 BeeHive-3 [Toro.]
48-52 Exhibits [Maple Leafs]
83 HHOF Postcard E9
83&87 HHOF 69
95/6 Legends of Hockey 65
51/2 Parkhurst 86
52/3 Parkhurst 44
53/4 Parkhurst 7
54/5 Parkhurst 29
54/5 Parkhurst 96
54/5 Parkhurst 99
55/6 Parkhurst 29
93/4 Parkie 56-57 116
93/4 Parkie 56-57 166
45-54 Quaker Oats
00/1 To. Heritage OSA
54 Toronto Star Weekend
01/2 Ultimate Mem. ✂ ASGH, ✂ Glove, ✂ SWC

KENNEDY, TROY
95/6 Guildford Flames 14
88/9 Brandon Wheat Kings
85/6 Kamloops Blazers

KENNEY, JAY
96/7 Charlotte Checkers
97/8 Charlotte Checkers
98/9 Peoria Rivermen

KENNEY, NICK
94/5 Cincinnati Cyclones
95/6 Cincinnati Cyclones
96/7 Cincinnati Cyclones
97/8 Cincinnati Cyclones
98/9 Cincinnati Cyclones
99/0 Cincinnati Cyclones
00/1 Cincinnati Cyclones

KENNHOLT, KENNETH
94/5 Leaf Elit Set 5
95/6 Leaf Elit Set 50, C-14, FTF-6
89/0 Semic Elitserien 56
90/1 Semic Elitserien 277
91/2 Semic Elitserien 58
91/2 Semic Elitserien 344
92/3 Semic Elitserien 79
91 Semic Sticker 37
93 Semic Sticker 3
95/6 UD Elitserien 79
97/8 UD Elitserien 37

KENNY, BRENDAN
92/3 BCJHL 65
93/4 W. Michigan Broncos

KENNY, ROB
92/3 Binghampton Rangers
94/5 Binghampton Rangers
97/8 Long Beach Ice Dogs

KENNY, SHANE
95/6 Classic 42, 93
95/6 Cla. 5 Sport 158
94/5 SR Auto-Phonex 21, ✍ 21
95/6 Slapshot 283
98/9 Rochester Americans
93/4 Owen Sound Platers

KENOPKA, ZENON
00/1 Ottawa 67's 12
01/2 Ottawa 67's 14

KENT, BRIAN
92/3 Oshawa Generals

KENT, DERRICK
00/1 Halifax Moosehead

KEOGAN, MURRAY
74/5 OPC WHA 44
75/6 Phoenix Roadrunners

KEON, DAVE
71/2 Bazooka Panel
99/0 BAP Mem. CH-2, ✍ CH-2
45-64 BeeHive-2 [Toro.]
64-67 BeeHive-3 [Toro.]
63-65 Chex
64/5 Coke/Sprite [Toro.]
65/6 Coca-Cola
65/6 Coke How To... B, X
70/1 Dad's Cookies
70/1 Eddie Sargent 208
71/2 Eddie Sargent 206
72/3 Eddie Sargent 206
62/3 El Producto
70/1 Esso Power Player
62/3 Cowan Tile
83&87 HHOF 255
95/6 Legends of Hockey 58
72/3 Post 1
74/5 Lipton Soup 50
74/5 Loblaws
68/9 O-Pee-Chee 198
68/9 O-Pee-Chee PS 19
69/0 O-Pee-Chee 51
69/0 O-Pee-Chee 4in1
69/0 O-Pee-Chee Stamp
70/1 O-Pee-Chee 219
70/1 O-Pee-Chee DE 47
71/2 O-Pee-Chee 80, 259
71/2 O-Pee-Chee Book. 16
72/3 O-Pee-Chee 108, 209
73/4 O-Pee-Chee 150
74/5 O-Pee-Chee 151
79/0 O-Pee-Chee 279
80/1 O-Pee-Chee 272
81/2 O-Pee-Chee 129
71/2 O-Pee-Chee Poster 3
75/6 OPC WHA 97
76/7 OPC WHA 52
61/2 Parkhurst 5
62/3 Parkhurst 15
63/4 Parkhurst 75
92/3 Parkhurst PR-21
93/4 Parkhurst PR67
93/4 Parkie 56-57 FS-2
95/6 Parkie 66-67 100, SL6
94/5 Parkie Tall 111, ✍ A6
66/7 Post Cereal Box
66/7 Post [Small]
68/9 Post Marble
82/3 Post [Hart.]
67/8 Post Tips 6
61/2 Shirriff 58
62/3 Shirriff 16, 52, 55
68/9 Shirriff / Toro. 11
64/5 Topps 94
65/6 Topps 17
66/7 Topps 78
66/7 Topps / Test 30
67/8 Topps 11
68/9 Topps 128
69/0 Topps 51
71/2 Topps 80
72/3 Topps 88
73/4 Topps 85
74/5 Topps 151
81/2 Topps 83 [East]
61/2 Toronto Star Photo
63/4 Toronto Star Action
64/5 Toronto Star Action
65/6 Toronto Star Photo
61/2 Toronto Star Weekend
71/2 Toronto Sun Photo
91/2 Ultimate Original Six 39, ✍ Aut. 39
60/1 Wonder Bread
60/1 York Glass [Toro.]
60/1 York
61/2 York 27
62/3 York Transfer 9
63/4 York 6
67/8 York 13, 19
67/8 York
94/5 Zellers, ✍ Aut.
64/5 TORO
68/9 TORO
69/0 TORO
71/2 TORO
72/3 TORO
73/4 TORO
74/5 TORO

KERBER, CHRIS
94/5 Birmingham Bulls
95/6 Birmingham Bulls

KERCH, ALEKSANDRS
99/0 Eishockey 300

KERCH, ALEXANDER
93/4 Cla. Prospects 176
90/1 O-Pee-Chee 474
00/1 UD DEL 202
01/2 UD DEL 25, GA2
93/4 EDMO / Sheet

KERCH, KERRY
82/3 Kitchener Rangers

KERCS,
97/8 Hockey-Box

KERESZTES, OTTO
94/5 DEL 347

KERESZTY, ADAM
79 Panini Sticker 269

KERIN, PAT
98/9 Odessa Jackalopes

KERN, JOSH
02/3 Peoria Rivermen

KERR, ALAN
90/1 Bowman 118
88/9 OPC/Topps 63
90/1 OPC/Topps 50, 315
88/9 OPC Sticker 106-236
88/9 Panini Sticker 288
89/0 Panini Sticker 275
90/1 Panini Sticker 89
91/2 Parkhurst 273
90/1 Pro Set 184
91/2 Pro Set 376
90/1 Score 307
91/2 Score CAN 571
90/1 Upper Deck 388
84/5 NYIS / News 9
89/0 NYIS
84/5 Springfield Indians 8

KERR, ALBERT
91 C55 Reprint 10
10/1 Imperial
11/2 Imperial 10
12/3 Imperial 33

KERR, ALLEN*
90 7th..Sketch Mem.Cup 58
KERR, CHRIS
91/2 Avant Garde BCJHL 81
91/2 Avant Garde BCJHL 128
95/6 Slapshot 421
KERR, DAVID A.
34-43 BeeHive-1 [NYRa.]
35-40 Canada Starch
33/4 Canadian Gum
36-39 Diamond Match TT2
36-39 Diamond Match TT3
30/1 La Presse
33/4 O-Pee-Chee 59
39/0 O-Pee-Chee 37
40/1 O-Pee-Chee 139
34/5 Sweet Caporal
33/4 WWGum 19
37/8 World Wide Gum 53
KERR, KEVIN
88/9 ProCards / Rochester
90/1 ProCards 282
93/4 Birmingham Bulls
91/2 Cincinnati Cyclones
93/4 Flint Generals
94/5 Flint Generals
95/6 Flint Generals
96/7 Flint Generals
98/9 Quad City Mallards
99/0 Quad City Mallards
83/4 North Bay Centennials
KERR, RANDY
91/2 Air Canada SJHL C7
KERR, REG
79/0 O-Pee-Chee 67
80/1 O-Pee-Chee 377
81/2 O-Pee-Chee 58
82/3 O-Pee-Chee 67
81/2 OPC Sticker 118
82/3 OPC/Topps Sticker 176
82/3 Post [Chic.]
79/0 Topps 67
81/2 Topps 70 [West]
79/0 CHIC
80/1 CHIC / Brown
81/2 CHIC
88/9 EDMO / Action 75
83/4 Moncton Alpines
KERR, SCOTT
83/4 Kitchener Rangers
KERR, TIM
88/9 Esso All-Star
92/3 Fleer Ultra 74
81/2 O-Pee-Chee 251
82/3 O-Pee-Chee 253
84/5 O-Pee-Chee 162
84/5 O-Pee-Chee 364
85/6 OPC/Topps 91
85/6 O-Pee-Chee 260
85/6 OPC/Topps Box H
86/7 OPC/Topps 134
86/7 O-Pee-Chee 261
86/7 OPC/Topps Box G
87/8 OPC/Topps 144
87/8 OPC/Topps Box B
90/1 OPC/Topps 210
KERR, TIM
91/2 O-Pee-Chee 164
KERR, TIM
89/0 OPC/Topps 72, / Box G
87/8 OPC Leaders 20
91/2 OPC Premier 83
92/3 OPC Premier 127
84/5 OPC Sticker 105
84/5 OPC Sticker 106
85/6 OPC Sticker 96
86/7 OPC Sticker 240
87/8 OPC Sticker 103
89/0 opcSticker 110, 216-77
87/8 Panini Sticker 128
88/9 Panini Sticker 321
89/0 Panini Sticker 12, 294, 377
90/1 Panini Sticker 120
91/2 Panini Sticker 226
91/2 Pinnacle 52
92/3 Pinnacle 368
82/3 Post [Phil.]
90/1 Pro Set 218
91/2 Pro Set 180
91/2 Pro Set 446
91/2 Pro Set Platinum 80
90/1 Score 177
90/1 Sco. Hot Cards 77
91/2 Score 108
91/2 Score 15T
91/2 Score CAN 108
91/2 Score CAN 565
92/3 Score 93
84/5 7-Eleven
85/6 7-Eleven Superstars 14
84/5 Topps 119
87/8 OPC/Topps - Stick. 10
92/3 Topps 351
91/2 To. Stadium 130
01/2 T/O Archives 22
90/1 Upper Deck 247, 304
02/3 UD Foundations 75
92/3 HART / Dairymart
83/4 PHIL / J.C. Penney
86/7 PHIL
89/0 PHIL
90/1 PHIL
93/4 PHIL / Sheet
KERRIGAN, STEVE
92/3 Dayton Bombers
KERSEY, JADE
91/2 Avant Garde BCJHL 44
92/3 BCJHL 99
91/2 Nanaimo Clippers
KERSTROM, ROGER
97/8 UD Elitserien 122
KERTH, WERNER
95 Panini Worlds 266
94 Semic 243
93 Semic Sticker 280
96 Wien 218
KESA, DAN
93/4 Cla. Prospects 116
99/0 Pacific 340
93/4 Power Play 460
90/1 7th..Sketch WHL 271
91/2 7th...Sketch WHL 247
96/7 Detroit Vipers
97/8 Detroit Vipers
92/3 Hamilton Canucks
00/1 Manitoba Moose
91/2 Prince Albert Raiders
KESA, DON
90/1 Prince Albert Raiders
KESÄ, TEEMU
99/0 Cardset 247
KESALAINEN, ERKKI
73/4 Williams Finnish 181
KESKINEN, ESA
98/9 Cardset Leij. 27
99/0 Cardset 332
02/3 Cardset 194
95 Globe 144
95 Hartwall Karjala
91/2 Jyvas Hyva 62
92/3 Jyvas Hyva 176
93/4 Jyvas Hyva 318
94/5 Leaf Elit Set 177, FA-2
95/6 Leaf Elit Set 56, 306, C-7, LM-6
95 Panini Worlds 172
94 Semic 41
95 Semic 9
89 Semic Sticker 48
91 Semic Sticker 19
92 Semic Sticker 24
93/4 Sisu 360
93/4 Sisu 370
93/4 Sisu 372
93/4 Sisu 40
94/5 Sisu 156, 164, 367, FOI-2, SS-7
95/6 Sisu Gold 14
95/6 Sisu Limited 8
95/6 UD Elitserien 89, 225
97/8 UD Elitserien 94, 222, C25
98/9 UD Elitserien 108,-DL 5
96 Wien 9
KESKINEN, JERE
93/4 Sisu 18
#VALUE✂
93/4 Sisu 356
#VALUE✂
72/3 Eddie Sargent 177
KESSELRING, CASEY
98/9 EBK ECHL All-Star
92/3 MPS SJHL 111
KESSLER, DINO
95 Panini Worlds 121
92 Semic Sticker 204
KESTI, JARI
00/1 Cardset 146
KETOLA, JUHA-PEKKA (JR.)
01/2 Sherbrooke Castors 4
KETOLA, SIMO
80/1 Mallasjuoma 211
KETOLA, STEFAN
94/5 Leaf Elit Set 269
95/6 Leaf Elit Set 24
91/2 Semic Elitserien 75
92/3 Semic Elitserien 320
95/6 UD Elitserien 29
KETOLA, TONI
71/2 Williams Finnish 367
KETOLA, VELI-PEKKA
66/7 Champion 51
65/6 Hellas 38
72 Hellas MM-Jenkki 2
74 Hellas MM-Jenkki 6
93/4 Jyvas Hyva 343
70/1 Kuvajulkaisut 62
70/1 Kuvajulkaisut 175
80/1 Mallasjuoma 209
75/6 OPC WHA 15
76/7 OPC WHA 88
72 Panda MM-Toronto
72 Panda MM-Toronto
72 Semic Sticker 79
74 Semic Sticker 83
91 Semic Sticker 230
93/4 Sisu 207
94/5 Sisu 400
95/6 Sisu 387
96/7 Sisu 196
78/9 SM-Liiga 13
78/9 SM-Liiga 233
77-79 Sports. FIN 17-397
96 Wien HL13
71/2 Williams Finnish 63
71/2 Williams Finnish 85
72/3 Williams Finnish 63
72/3 Williams Finnish 248
73/4 Williams Finnish 65
73/4 Williams Finnish 247
81/2 COLR
KETTER, KERRY
72/3 ATLF
KETTERER, MARKUS
98/9 Cardset 97, Leij. 1, MM5
02/3 Cardset 38
93/4 Classic 39
93/4 Cla. Prospects 167
95 Globe 127
97/8 Hockey-Box
91/2 Jyvas Hyva 19
92/3 Jyvas Hyva 53
95/6 Leaf Elit Set 211
94 Panini Olympics 301
94 Semic 4
95 Semic 47
91 Semic Sticker 2
92 Semic Sticker 3
93 Semic Sticker 45
91/2 Upper Deck 23
95/6 UD Elitserien 56, 224
96 Wien 32, SG8
93/4 Rochester Americans
KETTLES, KYLE
02/3 Louisiana Ice Gators
99/0 Medicine Hat Tigers
00/1 Medicine Hat Tigers
01/2 Moose Jaw Warriors 21
KETTUNEN, PERTTI
70/1 Kuvajulkaisut 312
KETTUNEN, SEPPO
72/3 Williams Finnish 288
73/4 Williams Finnish 221
KEYES, RICHARD
99/0 Fort Wayne Komets
KEYES, TIM
95/6 Slapshot 256
KHABIBULIN, NIKOLAI
01/2 Adrenaline 173, PP 33, ✂ GWJ 44
01/2 Atomic 88
02/3 Atomic 89, -D 19
98/9 Aurora 145
99/0 Aurora 109, GU-16
02/3 BAP All-Star 44, ✂ ASJ, ✂ HSHSJers
98/9 Be A Player 108, ✍ Aut. 108
99/0 BAP Mem. 100, ✂ TM-20
00/1 BAP Mem. ✂ J-21, ✂ TM-33, ✂ TM-38
01/2 BAP Mem. 304, ✂ ASJ, ✂ ASE, ✂ ASN, ✂ AST
02/3 BAP Mem. 40, 227, ✂ ASJ26, ✂ FP27
01/2 BAP Update ✂ TP14
01/2 BT Pipes 63, HSHS, ✂ ASJ, ✂ Jers., ✂ S&J, ✂ HSHSJers
02/3 Between the Pipes 47, 147, M27, ✂ ASJ11, ✂ BM6, ✂ CP10, ✂ DM14, ✂ GUE22, ✂ GB15, ✂ GUJ22, ✂ GP10, ✂ GSJ22, ✂ GT7, ✂ I3, ✂ ITN22, ✍ Aut.
98/9 Bicycle.. 10-D
95/6 Bowman 89
01/2 Bowman 19
02/3 Bowman 74
98/9 Bowman's Best 23
94/5 Cla. Images 42
99/0 Crown Royale 108
01/2 Crown Royale 127
02/3 Crown Royale 87, -COA 9, ✂ GWDP 20
95/6 Donruss 185
96/7 Donruss 172, BTP-9, D-2
97/8 Donruss 120
96/7 Do. Canadian 95
97/8 Do. Canadian 75
96/7 Do. Elite 49, PW-9
97/8 Do. Preferred 101
97/8 Do. Priority 36
97/8 Do. Studio 63
98/9 Dynagon Ice 143
99/0 Dynagon Ice 152
95/6 Edge Ice 70, C-12
97/8 Esso 40
02/3 Exclusive 155
02/3 First Edition 80, 367, ✂ Jers.
96/7 Flair 71
94/5 Fleer 242
96/7 Fleer 90
95/6 Fleer Metal 162
96/7 Fl. Picks 86
95/6 Fleer Ultra 180, 372
96/7 Fl. Ultra 132
01/2 Heads Up 86
02/3 Heads Up 111, -ITN 20, -S 19, ✂ GWQ 25, ✂ GWQ 30
02/3 In The GU 59, 159, ✂ F27, ✂ IE28
95/6 Leaf 27
96/7 Leaf 63, SD-9, TBO-6
97/8 Leaf 62, PD-13
96/7 L. Limited 60
96/7 L. Preferred 10, LS-30, MM-9
97/8 Limited 124, FG-30
96/7 Metal Univ. 118
99/0 Millenium 191, ✍ Aut. 191
98/9 NHL Power Play
02/3 O-Pee-Chee 135
98/9 OPC Chrome 115
97/8 Omega 174
98/9 Omega 184, -Onl. 28
99/0 Omega 182
98/9 Pacific 341
99/0 Pacific 321, ITCNF-15
00/1 Pacific 317
01/2 Pacific 351
02/3 Pacific 348
02/3 Pacific Complete 447
97/8 Pacific CC 6, ITC-16
97/8 Pa. Crown Roy. 104, FO-15
98/9 Pa. Crown Roy. 103
97/8 Pa. Dynagon 96, S-17, T-64
97/8 Pa. Invincible 107, R-153
97/8 Pa. Paramount 141, GSL-16
98/9 Pa. Paramount 182, -GS 15
99/0 Pa. Paramount 179, GS-16
97/8 Pa. Revolution 107, RTS-15
98/9 Pa. Revolution 110, -ASG 14, -TPA 18, -Show. 28
98/9 Panini Photocard
95/6 Panini Sticker 221
96/7 Panini Sticker 189
97/8 Panini Sticker 155
98/9 Panini Sticker 147
95/6 Parkhurst 230
01/2 Parkhurst 241
02/3 Parkhurst 39, ✂ FP27
02/3 Parkhurst Retro 155, ✂ RM21, ✂ VH8
95/6 Pinnacle 118
96/7 Pinnacle 161, M-7
97/8 Pinnacle 94, M-9, / Tin 6
96/7 Pi. Be A Player SP-7
97/8 Pi. Be A Player 13, STP-13, ✍ Aut. 13
97/8 Pi. Certified 16
97/8 Pi. Inside 44, SU-9B, S-16
96/7 Pi. Summit 41, ITC-12
97/8 Pi. Totally 16
96/7 Pi. Zenith 40
99/0 Prism 108
00/1 Private Stock 75
01/2 Pr. Stock -PS 67
02/3 Pr. Stock Reserve ✂ 143
00/1 PS Titanium ✂ GUG 126
01/2 PS Titanium 125, TSS 9, TAS 18
02/3 PS Titanium 89, -MM 6, ✂ GWJ 64
02/3 Quest for the Cup 88
99/0 Revolution 111, / CSC 111
00/1 Revolution 113, ✂ GUG-8
95/6 Score 142
96/7 Score 105, NW-18, SD-15
97/8 Score 10, NW-9
96/7 Select CE 17, F-14
94 Semic 135
93 Semic Sticker 129
94/5 SR Gold Standard 88
94/5 SR Tetrad CVIII, ✍ Aut.
00/1 Signature 221, ✍ Aut. 209
01/2 Signature ✂ GU72, ✂ IB1, ✂ TM27
02/3 Signature 118, ✍ 118
95/6 SBx Emotion 193
95/6 SBx Impact 181
96/7 SBx Impact 105
96/7 SP 120
97/8 SP Authentic 120, ✍ SofT
98/9 SP Authentic 67
01/2 SP Authentic 81
02/3 SP Authentic 80, ✍ SofT, ✍ SofTD
02/3 SP Game-Used ✍ Sig
02/3 Sports Vault 130
99/0 SPx 118
01/2 SPx 193
02/3 SPx 67
98/9 SPx Finite 66
99/0 Stadium 120
02/3 Stadium 93, -PSH8
98/9 SLU
99/0 SLU 157
96/7 Team Out!
95/6 Topps 48
98/9 Topps 115, I15
99/0 Topps 47, PM3, TW8
02/3 Topps 135
99/0 To. Chrome 47, PM3
01/2 To. Chrome 136
02/3 To. Chrome 85
94/5 Topps Finest 27
95/6 To. Finest 63
98/9 To. Finest 15
98/9 T. Gold Label 70
02/3 To. Heritage 29
02/3 To. Limited 135
95/6 To. Stadium 157
02/3 T. Total 303, TTC27
98/9 UD Choice 162
01/2 UD PlayMakers Ltd 90
00/1 Ultimate Mem. ✍ U-31, ✂ G-23, ✂ TM-10
01/2 Ultimate Mem. ✂ BAPL, ✂ NP, ✂ WTF
91/2 Upper Deck 652
94/5 Upper Deck 420
95/6 Upper Deck 85
96/7 Upper Deck 126
97/8 Upper Deck 129
98/9 Upper Deck 157
99/0 Upper Deck 271, UD8
01/2 Upper Deck 157
02/3 Upper Deck 158, -LL12
02/3 UD Artistic 80, R80
95/6 UD BAP 176, ✍ S176
96/7 UD Black Diam. 36
97/8 UD Black Diam. 53
01/2 UD Challenge 81
02/3 UD Classic 89
95/6 UD CC 75
96/7 UD CC 204
97/8 UD Coll. Choice 193, SQ35
91/2 Upper Deck WJC 13
98/9 UD G. Reserve 157
99/0 UD G. Reserve 271
02/3 UD Honor 63, ✍ SC
01/2 UD Ice 121
01/2 UD Mask 127, 188
02/3 UD Mask 79, 80, 81, 106, / Mask, ✍ Mask
98/9 UD MVP 158
99/0 UD MVP 161, W26, LL10
01/2 UD MVP 171, ✂ GS
02/3 UD MVP 165
02/3 UD Piece 80
02/3 UD Premier 49, ✍ Sig
99/0 UD Retro 62
02/3 UD Rookie 90
01/2 UD Top Shelf 118
02/3 UD Top Shelf 81
01/2 UD Vintage 229, 234
02/3 UD Vintage 230, 287, 319, GB 230, T59
01/2 Vanguard SW 18
02/3 Vanguard 88, -SW 11, ✂ GWJ 42
99/0 Victory 225, 380
01/2 Victory 324
02/3 Victory 193, -NP38
01/2 Waving the Flag 31
99/0 W. Gretzky ✂ TG, ✍ SG
96 Wien 129
97/8 Zenith 76
96/7 PHOE / Coca-Cola
96/7 PHOE / Coca-Cola
97/8 PHOE / Coca-Cola
98/9 PHOE / Coca-Cola
x98/9 PHOE / Coca-Cola
95/6 WINN
95/6 WINN Readers
KHAIDAROV, RAVIL
91/2 O-Pee-Chee 36R
91/2 Red Ace
94 Semic 162
92 Semic Sticker 118
92/3 Upper Deck 347
KHAIDAROV, REMIR
98/9 Mir 84
99/0 Mir 80
00/1 Mir 32
KHAIRETDINOV, RENAT
00/1 Mir 16
KHALIZOV, SVIATOSLAV
89/0 Soviet Stars
KHARIN, SERGEI
90/1 ProCards 261
91/2 ProCards 540
91/2 Score 394
91/2 Score CAN 284
91/2 Upper Deck 381
90/1 WINN / IGA
92/3 Cincinnati Cyclones
94/5 Cincinnati Cyclones
93/4 Dayton Bombers
95/6 Dayton Bombers
95/6 Dayton Bombers
89/0 Moncton Hawks
90/1 Moncton Hawks
98/9 Muskegon Fury
99/0 Muskegon Fury
KHARITONOV, ALEXANDER
00/1 BAP Mem. 416
01/2 BAP Mem. 165
98/9 Mir 156
00/1 Mir Fetisov 21
01/2 Pacific 352
00/1 Premier Plus 114
00/1 Private Stock 145, Roo. 22
00/1 PS Titanium 144
00/1 PS Titanium Draft 144
00/1 Signature 272, ✍ Aut. 234
00/1 SP Authentic 123
00/1 SP GU 83
00/1 To. Gold Label 113
00/1 To. Heritage 95
00/1 UD Reserve 114
00/1 Upper Deck 437
00/1 UD Black Diam. 131
00/1 UD Pros&Prosp. 123
00/1 Dynamo 13
KHARLAMOV, ALEXANDER
93/4 Classic 105
94/5 Classic 13, T74
94/5 Classic 4 Sport 129
94/5 Cla. Images 4 Sport 106
95/6 Edge Ice 56
00/1 Mir 319
93/4 Parkhurst 529
93/4 Pinnacle 504
92/3 Red Ace Blue 17
92/3 Red Ace Violet 12
94/5 Score 213
97/8 Hampton Roads
98/9 Hampton Roads
95/6 Portland Pirates
96/7 Portland Pirates
KHARLAMOV, VALERI
91/2 Future Trends C72 58
91/2 Future Trends C72 100
92/3 Future Trends C76 108
95 Globe 241
72 Hellas MM-Jenkki 76
74 Hellas MM-Jenkki 45
70/1 Kuvajulkaisut 3
69/0 Mästär Serien 30
72 Panda MM-Toronto
79 Panini Sticker 151
02/3 Parkhurst 250, ✂ NH1, ✂ VT15
72 Semic Sticker 17
74 Semic Sticker 34
91 Semic Sticker 244
69/0 Soviet Stars
70/1 Soviet Stars
71/2 Soviet Stars
73/4 Soviet Stars 8
73/4 Soviet Stars 9
74/5 Soviet Stars 13
79/0 Soviet Stars 15
77-79 Sportscaster 102-14
77-79 Sports. FIN 26-673
02/3 Ultimate Mem. 100, ✂ Emb, ✂ GUJ, ✂ ITN, ✂ Num, ✂ VGJ
71/2 Williams Finnish 3
72/3 Williams Finnish 24
73/4 Williams Finnish 4
KHASANOV, RINAT
98/9 Mir 101
99/0 Mir 255
00/1 Mir 218
KHAVANOV, ALEXANDER
00/1 BAP Mem. 455
02/3 First Edition 292
02/3 Pacific Complete 287
00/1 SP Authentic 161
00/1 SPx 185
00/1 To. Stars 104
02/3 T. Total 133
00/1 UD Reserve 113
02/3 Upper Deck 401
00/1 UD Ice 122
00/1 Dynamo 7
KHLISTOV, DENIS
00/1 Mir 144
KHLOPOTNOV, DENIS
99/0 Mir 156
00/1 Mir 324
92 Québec Pee Wee 1787
96/7 UD Ice 141
98/9 Muskegon Fury
KHMYL, OLEG
00/1 Mir 166
KHMYLEV, YURI
93/4 Donruss 36
94/5 Donruss 324
95/6 Donruss 18
96/7 Donruss 185
94/5 Fleer 22
92/3 Fleer Ultra 260
93/4 Fleer Ultra 173
94/5 Fleer Ultra 264
93/4 Leaf 211
94/5 Leaf 297
91/2 O-Pee-Chee 16R
93/4 Panini Sticker 106
94/5 Panini Sticker 96
95/6 Panini Sticker 17
92/3 Parkhurst 255
94/5 Parkhurst 22
95/6 Parkhurst 23
93/4 Pinnacle 201
94/5 Pinnacle 69
95/6 Playoff 231
96/7 Playoff 414
94/5 POG 53
95/6 POG 45
93/4 Power Play 30
93/4 Premier 389
94/5 Premier 14
95/6 Pro Magnet 108
92/3 Red Ace Violet 13
93/4 Score 302
95/6 Score 61
96/7 Score 199
89 Semic Sticker 94
87/8 Soviet Stars
89/0 Soviet Stars
95/6 Topps 371
93/4 To. Stadium 241
92/3 Upper Deck 504
94/5 Upper Deck 368, SP-98
95/6 Upper Deck 27
95/6 UD BAP 4, ✍ S4
95/6 UD CC 23
92/3 BUFF / Blue Shield
92/3 BUFF / Jubilee
KHOLOMEYEV, ALEX
97/8 Fort Worth Brahmas
99/0 Fort Worth Brahmas
KHOMUTOV, ANDREI
95 Globe 178
90/1 O-Pee-Chee 3R
95 Panini Worlds 50
94 Semic 154
95 Semic 139
82 Semic Sticker 68
89 Semic Sticker 93
91 Semic Sticker 99
93 Semic Sticker 148
83/4 Soviet Stars
87/8 Soviet Stars
89/0 Soviet Stars
96 Wien 152
KHOMUTOV, DMITRI
99/0 Mir 110
KHRAMCHENKO, DMITRI
00/1 Mir 83
KHRISTICH, DMITRI
98/9 Aurora 13
98/9 Be A Player 11, ✍ Aut. 11
97/8 Bicycle 4-Heart
91/2 Bowman 307
92/3 Bowman 427
95/6 Bowman 61
93/4 Donruss 373
94/5 Donruss 264
95/6 Donruss 265
96/7 Donruss 56
97/8 Donruss 89
96/7 Do. Canadian 105
97/8 Do. Canadian 58
96/7 Do. Elite 70
97/8 Do. Preferred 92
97/8 Do. Priority 39
97/8 Do. Studio 80
98/9 Dynagon Ice 11
93/4 EA Sports 154
02/3 First Edition 213
94/5 Flair 201
96/7 Flair 46
94/5 Fleer 237
96/7 Fleer 50
95/6 Fleer Metal 72
96/7 Fl. Picks 134
92/3 Fleer Ultra 235, -UI 7
93/4 Fleer Ultra 59
94/5 Fleer Ultra 236
95/6 Fleer Ultra 250
96/7 Fl. Ultra 79
95/6 Hoyle / East. 8-Spade
93/4 Leaf 168
94/5 Leaf 190
95/6 Leaf 139
96/7 Leaf 168
97/8 Leaf 29
96/7 L. Preferred 79
97/8 Limited 73
96/7 Metal Univ. 75
90/1 O-Pee-Chee 16R
91/2 O-Pee-Chee 78
92/3 O-Pee-Chee 286
98/9 OPC Chrome 164
91/2 OPC Premier 176
97/8 Omega 17
98/9 Omega 16
99/0 Omega 227
98/9 Pacific 83
99/0 Pacific 25
00/1 Pacific 395
01/2 Pacific 394
02/3 Pacific 394
97/8 Pacific CC 219
98/9 Pa. Crown Roy. 9
97/8 Pa. Dynagon 60, T-36
97/8 Pa. Invincible 68
97/8 Pa. Paramount 14
98/9 Pa. Paramount 15
99/0 Pa. Paramount 22
97/8 Pa. Revolution 10
98/9 Pa. Revolution 10
92/3 Panini Sticker N
93/4 Panini Sticker 28
94/5 Panini Sticker 20
95/6 Panini Sticker 268
96/7 Panini Sticker 270
97/8 Panini Sticker 226
98/9 Panini Sticker 8
99/0 Panini Sticker 159, 330
91/2 Parkhurst 189
92/3 Parkhurst 428
93/4 Parkhurst 220
94/5 Parkhurst 252
95/6 Parkhurst 108
00/1 Parkhurst P-227
91/2 Pinnacle 162
92/3 Pinnacle 146
92/3 Pinnacle T2K 25
93/4 Pinnacle 44
93/4 Pinnacle T2K1 23
94/5 Pinnacle 59
96/7 Pinnacle 190
97/8 Pinnacle 179
97/8 Pi. Be A Player 61, ✍ Aut. 61
97/8 Pi. Certified 126
97/8 Pi. Inside 124
95/6 Pi. Summit 153
96/7 Pi. Summit 27
97/8 Pi. Totally 126
96/7 Pi. Zenith 88
94/5 POG 246
95/6 POG 133
93/4 Power Play 264
93/4 Premier 210
94/5 Premier 534
99/0 Prism 138
91/2 Pro Set 260
92/3 Pro Set 208
91/2 Pro Set Platinum 242
92/3 Red Ace Blue 3
91/2 Score 175
91/2 Score CAN 175
92/3 Score 33
92/3 Score SS 27
93/4 Score 80
93/4 Score IS 20
94/5 Score 118
95/6 Score 151
96/7 Score 122
97/8 Score 111
97/8 Score Bost. 5
91/2 Score Young Stars 6
92/3 Score Young Stars 15
94/5 Select 104
96/7 Select CE 46
00/1 Signature 53, ✍ Aut. 31
01/2 Signature 147, ✍ Aut. 147
95/6 SBx Emotion 82
95/6 SBx Impact 80
96/7 SBx Impact 58
94/5 SP 130
95/6 SP 67
97/8 SP Authentic 12
95/6 Super Sticker 60
92/3 Topps 470
95/6 Topps 248
98/9 Topps 164
99/0 Topps 68
99/0 To. Chrome 68
95/6 To. Finest 166
98/9 To. Finest 117
98/9 T. Gold Label 23
91/2 To. Stadium 359
92/3 To. Stadium 86
93/4 To. Stadium 277
94/5 To. Stadium 12
95/6 To. Stadium 68
98/9 UD Choice 12
90/1 Upper Deck 537
91/2 Upper Deck 157
92/3 Upper Deck 219
93/4 Upper Deck 135, SP-171
94/5 Upper Deck 76, SP-87
95/6 Upper Deck 287
96/7 Upper Deck 76
97/8 Upper Deck 80
01/2 Upper Deck 408
95/6 UD BAP 36, ✍ S36
96/7 UD Black Diam. 108
95/6 UD CC 183
96/7 UD CC 123, 320
97/8 UD Coll. Choice 119, SQ27, C17, CR17
98/9 UD MVP 16
99/0 WGretzky 164
99/0 TORO / Pizza Pizza 1
89/0 WASH
90/1 WASH / Kodak
91/2 WASH / Kodak
91/2 WASH / Smokey
92/3 WASH / Kodak
KIANG, CHEN HIS
79 Panini Sticker 358
KIANSTEN, JUSSI
72/3 Williams Finnish 264
KIBERMANIS, CHRIS
93/4 Red Deer Rebels
95/6 Red Deer Rebels
KIDD, IAN
89/0 ProCards IHL 182
90/1 ProCards 323
91/2 ProCards 601
93/4 Cincinnati Cyclones
KIDD, TREVOR
01/2 Adrenaline 81, PP16
98/9 Aurora 34
00/1 Aurora 61
98/9 Be A Player 22, ✍ Aut. 22
00/1 BAP Mem. 48
01/2 BAP Mem. GoalJ
01/2 BT Pipes 62, ✂ DM, ✂ Jers., ✂ S&J, ✂ GG, ✂ GT
02/3 Between the Pipes 46, ✂ DM16, ✂ GB17, ✂ GUJ39, ✂ T14
98/9 Bicycle.. 9-S
98/9 Bowman's Best 30
92 C.O.A. Winter Olympics 200
91/2 Canada Nationals
99/0 Crown Royale 60
02/3 Crown Royale 91
94/5 Donruss 4
95/6 Donruss 31, BTP-4, D-8, PP-16
96/7 Donruss 160
97/8 Donruss 59
96/7 Do. Canadian 37
97/8 Do. Canadian 60
96/7 Do. Elite 45
97/8 Do. Elite 107
97/8 Do. Preferred 73
97/8 Do. Priority 98
97/8 Do. Studio 61
98/9 Dynagon Ice 35
99/0 Dynagon Ice 89
95/6 Edge Ice C21
02/3 First Edition 130, ✂ Jers.
94/5 Flair 25
96/7 Flair 13
94/5 Fleer 31
96/7 Fleer 13
95/6 Fleer Metal 20
93/4 Fleer Ultra 281
94/5 Fleer Ultra 30
95/6 Fleer Ultra 26, RS-4
96/7 Fl. Ultra 25
94/5 Kraft / KD
95/6 Kraft / PS
93/4 Leaf 385
94/5 Leaf 322
95/6 Leaf 83
96/7 Leaf 67
97/8 Leaf 126
95/6 L. Limited 31
96/7 L. Limited 25
96/7 L. Preferred 116
97/8 Limited 10
96/7 Maggers 21
96/7 McDonald's McD-34
96/7 Metal Univ. 20
91/2 O-Pee-Chee 312
01/2 O-Pee-Chee 243
98/9 OPC Chrome 66
97/8 Omega 42
98/9 Omega 44
98/9 Pacific 135
99/0 Pacific 74
00/1 Pacific 178
01/2 Pacific 171
02/3 Pacific 155
02/3 Pacific Complete 263
97/8 Pacific CC 133, ITC-3
97/8 Pa. Crown Roy. 24
98/9 Pa. Crown Roy. 25
97/8 Pa. Dynagon 18, S-4, T-23
97/8 Pa. Invincible 20
97/8 Pa. Paramount 35, GSL-3
98/9 Pa. Paramount 38, -GS 4
00/1 Pa. Paramount 104
97/8 Pa. Revolution 24
98/9 Pa. Revolution 25
94/5 Panini Sticker R
95/6 Panini Sticker 243
96/7 Panini Sticker 233
98/9 Panini Sticker 24
94/5 Parkhurst 288
95/6 Parkhurst 35, GP-8
00/1 Parkhurst P-138
94/5 Parkie SE24
94/5 Pinnacle 365, MA7
95/6 Pinnacle 151
96/7 Pinnacle 174
97/8 Pinnacle 60
96/7 Pi. Be A Player 127, ✍ Aut. 127
97/8 Pi. Certified 21
97/8 Pi. Inside 87, SU-18
95/6 Pi. Summit 138
96/7 Pi. Summit 36
97/8 Pi. Totally 21
95/6 Pi. Zenith 67
96/7 Pi. Zenith 11
95/6 Playoff 233
94/5 POG 275
94/5 POG / Western 2
95/6 POG 60
93/4 Power Play 305
94/5 Premier 413, OF-5
99/0 Prism 61
00/1 Private Stock 43
00/1 PS Titanium 40
95/6 Pro Magnet 45
00/1 Revolution 62
90/1 Score 438
91/2 Score 381
91/2 Score CAN 271
92/3 Score COH 12
93/4 Score 660
94/5 Score 259
95/6 Score 19
96/7 Score 58
97/8 Score 37, NW-3
95/6 Select CE 40
96/7 Select CE 21
91 7th..Sketch Mem.Cup 74
90/1 7th..Sketch WHL 226, 334
00/1 Signature 23
01/2 Signature 185, ✍ Aut. 185
02/3 Signature GS-99
95/6 SBx Emotion 23
95/6 SBx Impact 23, D-10
96/7 SBx Impact 14
94/5 SP 21
95/6 SP 21
96/7 SP 21
99/0 SP Authentic 38
00/1 SP GU 28
99/0 SPx 72
00/1 SPx 29
98/9 SPx Finite 15
00/1 Stadium 166
98/9 SLU
95/6 Super Sticker 17
96/7 Team Out!
92/3 Topps 280
95/6 Topps 154, 4CG, HGC13
98/9 Topps 66
00/1 Topps 207
01/2 Topps 243
00/1 To. Chrome 136
98/9 To. Finest 85
94/5 To. Stadium 106
95/6 To. Stadium 72
95/6 T. Super Skills 82
98/9 UD Choice 42
00/1 UD Heroes 52
90/1 Upper Deck 463
91/2 Upper Deck 449
91/2 Upper Deck 684
92/3 Upper Deck 134
92/3 Upper Deck 385
93/4 Upper Deck 399
94/5 Upper Deck 395, SP-12
95/6 Upper Deck 143, 229, SE-15
96/7 Upper Deck 25
97/8 Upper Deck 23
98/9 Upper Deck 58
99/0 Upper Deck 230
00/1 Upper Deck 77
02/3 Upper Deck 407
94/5 UD BAP ✍ 167
99/0 UD Black Diam. 43
00/1 UD Black Diam. 27
94/5 UD Canada Junior 10
95/6 UD CC 69
96/7 UD CC 34, 312
97/8 UD Coll. Choice 37
91/2 Upper Deck WJC 58
98/9 UD G. Reserve 58
99/0 UD G. Reserve 230
02/3 UD Mask 83
98/9 UD MVP 36
00/1 UD MVP 82
00/1 UD Vintage 155, 161, GG10
99/0 Victory 127
00/1 Victory 107
99/0 WGretzky 75
97/8 CARO / Sprint
98/9 CARO / Highwoods
01/2 FLOR
92/3 Salt Lake G'Eagles
88/9 Brandon Wheat Kings
89/0 Brandon Wheat Kings
90/1 Brandon Wheat Kings
KIECA, MARIUSZ
92 Semic Sticker 268
KIENASS, TORSTEN
95/6 DEL 436
96/7 DEL 322
99/0 Eishockey 348, 368
95 Panini Worlds 55
94 Semic 274
92 Semic Sticker 179
00/1 UD DEL 45
01/2 UD DEL 51
KIENE, CHRIS
89/0 ProCards AHL 221
90/1 ProCards 575
91/2 ProCards 165
91/2 Moncton Hawks
KIERECK, MATT
92/3 Sudbury Wolves
KIESSLING, UDO
94/5 DEL 268
95/6 DEL 248
79 Panini Sticker 100
82 Semic Sticker 105
89 Semic Sticker 107
91 Semic Sticker 157
KIHLSTRÖM, MATS
89/0 Semic Elitserien 220
90/1 Semic Elitserien 53
89 Semic Sticker 7
KIILI, LASSE
66/7 Champion 74
65/6 Hellas 1
70/1 Kuvajulkaisut 157
71/2 Williams Finnish 228
72/3 Williams Finnish 212
73/4 Williams Finnish 198
KIIMALAINEN, MARKKU
80/1 Mallasjuoma 99
82 Semic Sticker 40
82 Skopbank
78/9 SM-Liiga 7
78/9 SM-Liiga 144
77-79 Sports. FIN 90-2150
KIISKI, TOMMI
92/3 Jyvas Hyva 39
KIISKINEN, VILLE
00/1 Cardset 323
KILBOURNE, B.J.
99/0 Mobile Mysticks
KILDUFF, DAVID
91/2 Avant Garde BCJHL 87
91/2 Avant Garde BCJHL 159
92/3 BCJHL 135
KILGER, CHAD
95/6 Bowman 137, BB25
94/5 Classic DP3
95/6 Classic 4, 86, AS10, BK4
95/6 Cla. 5 Sport 143, SFF-9
94/5 Cla. Images 84, PD7
95/6 Donruss 379, RR-7
96/7 Donruss 236
97/8 Donruss 175
95/6 Do. Elite 55, R-9
95/6 Fleer Metal 179
95/6 Fleer Ultra 343
96/7 Leaf 203
97/8 Leaf 137
95/6 L. Limited 34, RP-3
97/8 Limited 73
98/9 Pacific 146
99/0 Pacific 157
01/2 Pacific 208
02/3 Pacific Complete 195
96/7 Panini Sticker 190
95/6 Parkhurst 255, 500
95/6 Pi. Summit 179
96/7 Pi. Summit 155
95/6 Pi. Zenith 139, RRC-12
96/7 Score 255
95/6 Select CE 116
95/6 SBx Emotion gN 10
95/6 SBx Impact 188, F-18
93/4 Slapshot / Kingston 17
95/6 SP 163
95/6 Super Sticker 3
95/6 Topps 301
95/6 To. Finest 81
96/7 To. Picks 151
95/6 To. Stadium ER202
95/6 T. Super Skills SR5
95/6 Upper Deck 262
96/7 Upper Deck 130
97/8 Upper Deck 130
98/9 Upper Deck 244
01/2 Upper Deck 325
02/3 Upper Deck 338
95/6 UD BAP 167, ✍ S167
96/7 UD CC 200, 337
98/9 UD G. Reserve 244
01/2 Victory 190
00/1 MONT
01/2 MONT
02/3 MONT
96/7 PHOE / Coca-Cola
97/8 PHOE / Coca-Cola
99/0 Hamilton Bulldogs/ Staz
97/8 Springfield Falcons
KILLEN, FRANK
93/4 Humberside Hawks 15
KILPATRICK, JOHN
83 HHOF Postcard H10
83&87 HHOF 116
KILPIÖ, RAIMO
66/7 Champion 15
65/6 Hellas 79
70/1 Kuvajulkaisut 194
72 Panda MM-Toronto
96/7 Sisu 189
71/2 Williams Finnish 86
72/3 Williams Finnish 249
73/4 Williams Finnish 248
KILREA, BRIAN
90/1 7th..Sketch OHL 100
91/2 7th...Sketch OHL 309
84/5 NYIS / News 30
81/2 Ottawa 67's
82/3 Ottawa 67's
83/4 Ottawa 67's
92/3 Ottawa 67's
99/0 Ottawa 67's
00/1 Ottawa 67's 24
00/1 Ottawa 67's 27
01/2 Ottawa 67's 24
KILREA, HEC
25-27 Anonymous 19
25-27 Anonymous 20
33/4 Anonymous 17
34-43 BeeHive-1 [Detr.]
34-43 BeeHive-1 [Toro.]
29/0 La Presse
35/6 O-Pee-Chee 86
39/0 O-Pee-Chee 71
33/4 WWGum 64
37/8 World Wide Gum 24
KILREA, KEN
34-43 BeeHive-1 [Detr.]
KILREA, WALLY
34-43 BeeHive-1 [Detr.]
33/4 O-Pee-Chee 63
33/4 WWGum 53
KILSTROM, MATS
91/2 Semic Elitserien 228
KIM, ALEX
99/0 Des Moines Buc's
KIMBLE, DARIN
91/2 Bowman 381
90/1 O-Pee-Chee 437
91/2 O-Pee-Chee 156
90/1 Panini/QUE 11
91/2 Parkhurst 377
90/1 Pro Set 517
88/9 ProCards / Halifax
91/2 Score CAN 526
92/3 Topps 511
91/2 To. Stadium 278
92/3 To. Stadium 486
93/4 CHIC / Coke
89/0 QUÉB
89/0 QUÉB / Gene. Foods
89/0 QUÉB / Police
90/1 QUÉB
90/1 QUÉB / Petro-Canada
91/2 SLOU
99/0 Peoria Rivermen
KIMBLE, DARIN
02/3 Fleer Throwbacks 58
KIMURA, KEVIN
92/3 BCJHL 32
KINASCHUK, BRETT
91/2 Air Canada SJHL D5
92/3 MPS SJHL 30
KINASEWICH, RYAN
99/0 Medicine Hat Tigers
00/1 Medicine Hat Tigers
KINCAID, CAMERON
95/6 Slapshot 428
KINCH, MATT
01/2 Hartford Wolf Pack
98/9 Calgary Hitmen 1
99/0 Calgary Hitmen
00/1 Calgary Hitmen
KINCH, ROB
92/3 MPS SJHL 44
KINDER, SJUR
92/3 Semic Nordisk 178
KINDRACHUK, OREST
74/5 Loblaws
74/5 O-Pee-Chee 334
75/6 O-Pee-Chee 389
76/7 O-Pee-Chee 233
77/8 O-Pee-Chee 26
78/9 O-Pee-Chee 114
79/0 O-Pee-Chee 218
80/1 O-Pee-Chee 292
92/3 Parkhurst 476
76/7 Topps 233
77/8 Topps 26
78/9 Topps 114
79/0 Topps 218
KING, COLT
00/1 UD Prospects 41
01 UD Prospects GU 14, ✂ TPJ, ✂ TPJS, ✂ JC, ✍ SoT
99/0 Guelph Storm
KING, DAVE
90/1 Canada Nationals 21
91/2 Canada Nationals
93/4 Kraft / PB
89 Semic Sticker 52
92 Semic Sticker 74
92/3 CALG / IGA 026
KING, DEREK
98/9 Be A Player 135, ✍ Aut. 135
99/0 BAP Mem. 124
91/2 Bowman 220
92/3 Bowman 188
93/4 Donruss 204
94/5 Donruss 30
95/6 Donruss 300
97/8 Donruss 69
94/5 Flair 103
94/5 Fleer 123
92/3 Fleer Ultra 128
93/4 Fleer Ultra 176
94/5 Fleer Ultra 325
93/4 Hockey Wit 28
93/4 Leaf 119
94/5 Leaf 188
95/6 Leaf 261
90/1 OPC/Topps 128
91/2 O-Pee-Chee 455
92/3 O-Pee-Chee 79
89/0 OPC/Topps 6
98/9 OPC Chrome 84
89/0 opcSticker 116-255
98/9 Pacific 414
99/0 Pacific 410
97/8 Pa. Invincible 24, R-37
97/8 Pa. Paramount 181
98/9 Pa. Paramount 228
99/0 Pa. Paramount 226
88/9 Panini Sticker 289
89/0 Panini Sticker 271
91/2 Panini Sticker 247
92/3 Panini Sticker 199
93/4 Panini Sticker 58
95/6 Panini Sticker 92
97/8 Panini Sticker 23
91/2 Parkhurst 108
92/3 Parkhurst 100
93/4 Parkhurst 119
94/5 Parkhurst 132
95/6 Parkhurst 132
91/2 Pinnacle 107
92/3 Pinnacle 17
93/4 Pinnacle 128
94/5 Pinnacle 302
97/8 Pi. Be A Player 40, ✍ Aut. 40
94/5 POG 157

95/6 POG 172
93/4 Power Play 150
93/4 Premier 176
94/5 Premier 304
90/1 Pro Set 185
91/2 Pro Set 146
92/3 Pro Set 110
91/2 Pro Set Platinum 201
91/2 Pro Set Platinum 286
89/0 ProCards AHL 250
99/0 Revolution 139, / CSC 139
90/1 Score 86T
91/2 Score 167
91/2 Score CAN 167
92/3 Score 255
92/3 Score SS 15
93/4 Score 48
93/4 Score/CAN DD9
95/6 Score 238
97/8 Score Toro. 18
94/5 Select 9
96/7 SP 95
95/6 Super Sticker 76
92/3 Topps 431
95/6 Topps 202
98/9 Topps 84
91/2 To. Stadium 82
92/3 To. Stadium 82
93/4 To. Stadium 215
94/5 To. Stadium 108
95/6 To. Stadium 81
90/1 Upper Deck 407
91/2 Upper Deck 382
92/3 Upper Deck 191
93/4 Upper Deck 417
94/5 Upper Deck 59
98/9 Upper Deck 373
94/5 UD BAP ✍ 6
97/8 UD Coll. Choice 112
01/2 UD DEL 184
98/9 UD G. Reserve 373
96/7 UD Ice 40
99/0 Victory 291
96/7 NYIS
99/0 Grand Rapids Griffins
00/1 Grand Rapids Griffins
02/3 Grand Rapids Griffins
84/5 Soo Greyhounds

KING, ELDRED
90/1 Newmarket Saints

KING, FRANK
45-64 BeeHive-2 [Mont.]
51/2 Laval Dairy 10

KING, JASON
02/3 BAP Mem. 308
02/3 SP Authentic 218
02/3 Ultimate Mem. 55
02/3 UD Rookie 143
02/3 Manitoba Moose
00/1 Halifax Moosehead
99/0 Halifax Mooseheads

KING, KEVIN
90/1 7th..Sketch OHL 70, 161
91/2 7th...Sketch OHL 228
89/0 Soo Greyhounds

KING, KRIS
98/9 Be A Player 288, ✍ Aut. 288
91/2 Bowman 59
92/3 Bowman 380
93/4 Donruss 379
96/7 Kraft / PB
93/4 Leaf 253
94/5 Leaf 395
90/1 O-Pee-Chee 526
91/2 O-Pee-Chee 498
92/3 O-Pee-Chee 86
98/9 OPC Chrome 160
98/9 Pacific 415
97/8 Pacific CC 90
91/2 Parkhurst 337
92/3 Parkhurst 442
93/4 Parkhurst 478
94/5 Parkhurst 269
95/6 Parkhurst 502
91/2 Pinnacle 362
92/3 Pinnacle 168
92/3 Pinnacle 253
93/4 Pinnacle 316
96/7 Pinnacle T-7
97/8 Pi. Be A Player 108, ✍ Aut. 108
90/1 Pro Set 491
91/2 Pro Set 445
90/1 Score 76T
91/2 Score 363
91/2 Score CAN 402
92/3 Score 181
93/4 Score 362
92/3 Topps 509
98/9 Topps 160
91/2 To. Stadium 26
92/3 To. Stadium 187
94/5 To. Stadium 124
90/1 Upper Deck 440
91/2 Upper Deck 330
92/3 Upper Deck 78
93/4 Upper Deck 14
94/5 Upper Deck 308
95/6 Upper Deck 141
94/5 UD BAP ✍ 15
95/6 UD CC 215
88/9 DETR / Little Caesars
89/0 NYRA / Marine
96/7 PHOE / Coca-Cola
96/7 PHOE / Coca-Cola
93/4 WINN / Ruffles
93/4 WINN Readers
95/6 WINN
95/6 WINN Readers

KING, KRIS
02/3 Fleer Throwbacks 9

KING, MIKE
83/4 Kingston Canadians

KING, SCOTT
90/1 ProCards 492
93/4 Slapshot / S.S.Marie 5
92/3 To. Stadium 269
00/1 Charlotte Checkers
99/0 Mississippi S'Wolves
97/8 New Orleans Brass
92/3 Toledo Storm WIOT
92/3 Toledo Storm

KING, STEVE**
83/4 Kingston Canadians
82/3 Oshawa Generals

KING, STEVE***
72/3 Ottawa Nationals

KING, STEVEN*
93/4 Classic 136
93/4 Cla. 4 Sport 237
92/3 Classic Prospects 60
92/3 Classic Prospects 74
92/3 Classic Prospects / Promo PR1
93/4 Donruss 1
92/3 Fleer Ultra 355
93/4 Fleer Ultra 258
93/4 Leaf 410
92/3 Parkhurst 347
93/4 Parkhurst 1
93/4 Pinnacle 345
93/4 Pinnacle Expa. 6
93/4 Power Play 6
93/4 Premier 303
94/5 Premier 220
91/2 ProCards 199
93/4 Score 382
93/4 Score 514
93/4 To. Stadium 377
92/3 Upper Deck 575
93/4 Upper Deck 24
94/5 ANAH / Carl's Jr. 12
92/3 Binghampton Rangers
97/8 Cincinnati Cyclones

KING, WAYNE
74/5 Loblaws

KINGHAN, ROB
90/1 7th..Sketch OHL 36
91/2 7th...Sketch OHL 29

KINGHORN, RON
91/2 ProCards 433

KINGSTON, GEORGE
95/6 DEL 428

KINISKY, AL
92/3 BCJHL 178
90/1 7th..Sketch WHL 4
91/2 7th...Sketch WHL 339

KINKEL, BILL
01/2 Kitchener Rangers

KINNEAR, GEORDIE
90/1 7th..Sketch OHL 363
91/2 7th...Sketch OHL 132
96/7 Albany River Rats
97/8 Albany River Rats
98/9 Albany River Rats
01/2 Albany River Rats
02/3 Albany River Rats
91/2 Peterborough Petes

KINNEY, DONNIE
99 Bowman 110
97 Bowman 91
94/5 Slapshot Memorial 17
96/7 Kamloops Blazers
97/8 Kamloops Blazers
98/9 Kamloops Blazers

KINNIBURGH, TODD
89/0 Portland Winter Hawks

KINNUNEN, JORMA
70/1 Kuvajulkaisut 370

KINNUNEN, KARI
65/6 Hellas 63
70/1 Kuvajulkaisut 176
71/2 Williams Finnish 101
72/3 Williams Finnish 144
73/4 Williams Finnish 110

KINNUNEN, VELI-PEKKA
80/1 Mallasjuoma 52

KINOS, LAURI
00/1 Peoria Rivermen
02/3 Peoria Rivermen

KINSACHUK, KENT
92/3 MPS SJHL 36

KIPRUSOFF, JARMO
70/1 Kuvajulkaisut 296

KIPRUSOFF, MARKO
95/6 Bowman 109
98/9 Cardset 230, Leij. 8, OD 11
99/0 Cardset 3, 133, 183, AH 4-ruutu
02/3 Cardset 39
95/6 Donruss 351
95 Globe 131
95 Hartwall Karjala
93/4 Jyvas Hyva 321
95/6 Kellogg's Pop-Ups 2
96/7 Leaf 233
95 Panini Worlds 169
95/6 Parkhurst 268
01/2 Parkhurst 252
96/7 Pinnacle 234
94 Semic 18
95 Semic 2
93/4 Sisu 35
93/4 Sisu 338
94/5 Sisu 7, 161, ND-2
95/6 Sisu 163, 200, G-7
95/6 Sisu Limited 5
95 Suomen Beckett Card 6
95/6 To. Stadium 141
91/2 Upper Deck 671
96/7 Upper Deck 188
91/2 Upper Deck WJC 34
97/8 UD Elitserien 135, C13
96 Wien 2, AS3

KIPRUSOFF, MIIKKA
01/2 Adrenaline 165, PP 31, RR 18
00/1 BAP Mem. 506
01/2 BAP Mem. 201
01/2 BT Pipes 20, ✂ Jers., ✂ GT, ✂ HSHSJers
02/3 Between the Pipes 13, M25, ✂ GUE2, ✂ FW1, ✂ GUJ2, ✂ GSJ2, ✂ ITN2, ✂ T4
02/3 Calder 94
98/9 Cardset 228
99/0 Cardset 1, 178, BP-1, PA-8
02/3 Cardset 40
99/0 Choice 5
02/3 First Edition 239
02/3 Heads Up ✂ GWQ 24
01/2 O-Pee-Chee 275
01/2 Pacific 337
02/3 Pacific Complete 273
01/2 Parkhurst 293
02/3 Parkhurst 40
01/2 Pr. Stock 109, -PS 89
02/3 PS Titanium ✂ GWJ 61
01/2 Signature 221, ✍ Aut. 221
95/6 Sisu 122, DD-8
01/2 SPx 123
01/2 Stadium 115
01/2 Topps 275
01/2 To. Chrome 141
94/5 Topps Finest 125
01/2 Ultimate Mem. ✂ WTF
97/8 UD Elitserien 1, S1
02/3 UD Mask 72, 74
02/3 UD Vintage 320
01/2 Victory 386
01/2 Waving the Flag 15
99/0 Kentucky Tho'blades
00/1 Kentucky Tho'blades

KIRBY, TRAVIS
92/3 MPS SJHL 141

KIRCHHOFF, RYAN
99/0 Des Moines Buc's

KIRIAKOU, LOU
84/5 Moncton G'Flames

KIRIK, VLADIMIR
98/9 Mir 166

KIRILENKO, DMITRI
99/0 Mir 152

KIRK, BOBBY
34-43 BeeHive-1 [NYRa.]

KIRK, GAVIN
75/6 OPC WHA 103
76/7 OPC WHA 99
73/4 Quaker Oats 5
72/3 Ottawa Nationals

KIRKPATRICK, BOB
34-43 BeeHive-1 [NYRa.]

KIRKPATRICK, DAVE
92/3 BCJHL 5

KIRKWOOD, BRAD
96/7 Guildford Flames 18

KIRSCH, ROB
93/4 Slapshot / North Bay 24
95/6 Milwaukee Admirals

KIRTON, DOUG
99/0 Eishockey 87

KIRTON, DOUGLAS
98/9 DEL 149

KIRTON, MARK
81/2 O-Pee-Chee 90
82/3 O-Pee-Chee 87
83/4 O-Pee-Chee 352
82/3 Post [Detr.]
88/9 ProCards / Newmarket
81/2 Topps 90 [West]
83/4 Vachon 109-29
79/0 TORO
80/1 TORO
83/4 VANC
85/6 Fredericton Express
86/7 Fredericton Express

KIRTON, SCOTT
92/3 BCJHL 237
96/7 Charlotte Checkers
02/3 Dundee Texol Stars

KIRVESKOSKI, VEIKKO
73/4 Williams Finnish 222

KIRWAN, JEFF
95/6 Swift Current Broncos

KISELEV, ANDREI
00/1 Mir 10

KISELEV, SERGEI
00/1 Mir 111

KISER, NATE
02/3 Plymouth Whalers

KISH, LARRY
84/5 Nova Scotia Oilers
85/6 Nova Scotia Oilers
92/3 Wheeling Thund'birds 21
93/4 Wheeling Thund'birds

KISILIVICH, BRENT
82/3 Medicine Hat Tigers
83/4 Medicine Hat Tigers

KISIO, KELLY
91/2 Bowman 72
92/3 Bowman 166
93/4 Donruss 55
93/4 EA Sports 117
92/3 Fleer Ultra 196
93/4 Fleer Ultra 155
93/4 Fleer Ultra 282
93/4 Leaf 208
94/5 Leaf 493
84/5 O-Pee-Chee 56
85/6 OPC/Topps 101
86/7 OPC/Topps 116
87/8 OPC/Topps 76
88/9 OPC/Topps 143
90/1 OPC/Topps 239
91/2 O-Pee-Chee 335
92/3 O-Pee-Chee 232
89/0 OPC/Topps 171
91/2 OPC Premier 69
84/5 OPC Sticker 40
86/7 OPC Sticker 163-23
87/8 OPC Sticker 28-168
88/9 OPC Sticker 239
87/8 Panini Sticker 115
88/9 Panini Sticker 307
89/0 Panini Sticker 287
90/1 Panini Sticker 94
91/2 Panini Sticker 291
92/3 Panini Sticker 124
93/4 Panini Sticker 256
91/2 Parkhurst 165
92/3 Parkhurst 166
93/4 Parkhurst 33
91/2 Pinnacle 231
92/3 Pinnacle 362
93/4 Pinnacle 395
94/5 Pinnacle 306
94/5 POG 55
93/4 Power Play 37
93/4 Premier 455
90/1 Pro Set 200
91/2 Pro Set 168
91/2 Pro Set 479
92/3 Pro Set 167
91/2 Pro Set Platinum 104
91/2 Puck / Pro Set 26
90/1 Score 37
91/2 Score 288
91/2 Score 3T
91/2 Score CAN 553
92/3 Score 57
93/4 Score 27
93/4 Score 556
93/4 Score PiAS 30
92/3 Topps 331
91/2 To. Stadium 186
92/3 To. Stadium 454
93/4 To. Stadium 30
93/4 To. Stadium - All-Stars
90/1 Upper Deck 296
91/2 Upper Deck 515
93/4 Upper Deck 304
95/6 UD CC 193
92/3 UD Locker 28
84/5 DETR / Little Caesars
85/6 DETR / Little Caesars
89/0 NYRA / Marine
91/2 SANJ / Sports Action

KISTER, ED
86/7 Kitchener Rangers
85/6 London Knights

KITCHEN, BILL
83/4 Nova Scotia Voyageurs

KITCHEN, MIKE
77/8 O-Pee-Chee 267
78/9 O-Pee-Chee 338
81/2 O-Pee-Chee 83
82/3 Post [Colo.]
83/4 Souhaits Keychain [Devils]
79/0 COLR
81/2 COLR
83/4 NJER

KITCHENER, CRAIG
80/1 Oshawa Generals

KITCHING, GARY
91/2 Ferris State Bulldogs

KITTERINGHAM, CRAIG
88/9 ProCards / Hershey

KITTS, MARK
01/2 Moose Jaw Warriors 17
00/1 Prince George Cougars

KIURU, ESKO
66/7 Champion 141

KIURU, JUSSI
93/4 Sisu 201
94/5 Sisu 283
95/6 Sisu 105

KIVELÄ, ANTERO
80/1 Mallasjuoma 199
79 Panini Sticker 163
78/9 SM-Liiga 19
78/9 SM-Liiga 219
77-79 Sports. FIN 90-2148

KIVELÄ, KEIJO
78/9 SM-Liiga 54

KIVELÄ, KIMMO
65/6 Hellas 74

KIVELÄ, PASI
92/3 Jyvas Hyva 32

KIVELÄ, TEPPO
91/2 Jyvas Hyva 8
92/3 Jyvas Hyva 6
93/4 Jyvas Hyva 23
91 Semic Sticker 15
93/4 Sisu 95
93/4 Sisu 324
94/5 Sisu 210, 375, H-10
95/6 Sisu 155
96/7 Sisu 155
95/6 Sisu Limited 23
97/8 UD Elitserien 24
98/9 UD Elitserien 45

KIVELL, DREW
01/2 Kingston Frontenacs 9
99/0 Sudbury Wolves 19
00/1 Sudbury Wolves 20

KIVELL, ROB
84/5 Victoria Cougars

KIVELL, RON
85/6 Moncton G'Flames
83/4 Victoria Cougars

KIVENMÄKI, MARKO
98/9 Cardset 270
99/0 Cardset 152
00/1 Cardset 305

KIVI, KARRI
00/1 Cardset 54
93/4 Jyvas Hyva 346
95 Panini Worlds 165
93/4 Sisu 215
93/4 Sisu 345
94/5 Sisu 134
95/6 Sisu 352, DT-3
96/7 Sisu 153
97/8 UD Elitserien 2

KIVIAHO, TOMMY
98/9 Cardset 24
99/0 Cardset 15
93/4 Jyvas Hyva 257
93/4 Sisu 293
94/5 Sisu 338, H-16
95/6 Sisu 36
96/7 Sisu 8

KIVIHARJU, JANI
98/9 Cardset 244
99/0 Cardset 136
00/1 Cardset 99
02/3 Cardset 195

KIVILÄ, PASI
93/4 Jyvas Hyva 58
93/4 Sisu 248
94/5 Sisu 83

KIVINEN, TEEMU
93/4 Sisu 60

KJAER, LARS_ERIK
92/3 Semic Nordisk 163

KJELDSBERG, CHRISTIAN
92/3 Semic Nordisk 53

KJELLBERG, PATRIC
01/2 Adrenaline 105, ✂ GWJ 23
00/1 Aurora 77
00/1 BAP Mem. 301
92/3 Classic Prospects 21
00/1 Crown Royale ✂ GWJ 16
98/9 Dynagon Ice 103
94/5 Leaf Elit Set 16, GC-17,TG-9
95/6 Leaf Elit Set 190, C-2
01/2 O-Pee-Chee 148
92/3 OPC Premier 29
99/0 Omega 127
99/0 Pacific 226
00/1 Pacific 440
01/2 Pacific 219
02/3 Pacific Complete 200
99/0 Panini Sticker 264
00/1 Panini Sticker 180
01/2 Parkhurst 180
00/1 PS Titanium ✂ GUG 103
00/1 PS Titanium Draft ✂ 54
94 Semic 78
89/0 Semic Elitserien 25
90/1 Semic Elitserien 91
91/2 Semic Elitserien 20
93 Semic Sticker 42
00/1 Stadium 149
00/1 Topps 261
01/2 Topps 148
00/1 To. Chrome 157
92/3 Upper Deck 498
00/1 Upper Deck 326
01/2 Upper Deck 328
95/6 UD Elitserien 53
97/8 UD Elitserien 46, C1
00/1 UD MVP 102
01/2 UD MVP 109
99/0 UD MVP Cup 103
00/1 UD Vintage 204
01/2 UD Vintage 144
00/1 Victory 132
01/2 Victory 198
92/3 MONT
98/9 NASH / Wendy's 13
92/3 Fredericton Canadiens

KJENSTADT, OLAF
91/2 7th...Sketch WHL 313
00/1 Asheville Smoke
94/5 Birmingham Bulls
95/6 Birmingham Bulls
98/9 Cincinnati Cyclones
96/7 Knoxville Cherokees
93/4 Seattle Thunderbirds

KLAPAC, FILIP
96/7 APS 95

KLAPAC, JAN
72 Hellas MM-Jenkki 88
74 Hellas MM-Jenkki 74
72/3 Williams Finnish 11
73/4 Williams Finnish 52

KLAPAC, JIRI
74 Semic Sticker 62

KLAPSTEIN, TERRY
89/0 Victoria Cougars

KLASONS, GEORGE
77/8 Kalamazoo Wings

KLASSEN, JASON
91/2 7th...Sketch WHL 248
91/2 Prince Albert Raiders

KLASSEN, MIKE
79/0 Montréal Jrs. Colour

KLASSEN, RALPH
76/7 O-Pee-Chee 282
77/8 O-Pee-Chee 372
78/9 O-Pee-Chee 346

KLASSEN, TODD
90/1 7th..Sketch WHL 111
91/2 7th...Sketch WHL 295

KLATT, BILL
72/3 Minn. Fight. Saints

KLATT, DAVID
98/9 Kamloops Blazers

KLATT, TRENT
92/3 Classic 89
93/4 Donruss 82
94/5 Donruss 37
95/6 Donruss 330
93/4 Fleer Ultra 157
93/4 Fleer Ultra Pros. 4
94/5 Fleer Ultra 53
93/4 Leaf 14
94/5 Leaf 316
95/6 Leaf 57
97/8 Omega 166
98/9 Pacific 327
00/1 Pacific 410
02/3 Pacific Complete 355
97/8 Pacific CC 251
98/9 Pa. Paramount 175
95/6 Panini Sticker 172
91/2 Parkhurst 452
92/3 Parkhurst 317
93/4 Parkhurst 48
94/5 Parkie SE43
94/5 Pinnacle 442
95/6 Pinnacle 193
96/7 Pi. Be A Player 157, ✍ Aut. 157
94/5 POG 143
95/6 POG 88
93/4 Power Play 62
93/4 Premier 523
94/5 Premier 46
92/3 Pro Set 229
92/3 Score 482
97/8 Score Phil. 8
02/3 Signature GS-98
94/5 SP 29
95/6 Topps 106
92/3 Upper Deck 62
93/4 Upper Deck 152
94/5 Upper Deck 374
95/6 Upper Deck 162
97/8 Upper Deck 120
00/1 Upper Deck 172
01/2 Upper Deck 402
95/6 UD CC 36
97/8 UD Coll. Choice 191
94/5 DALL / Southwest
94/5 DALL / Cap
96/7 PHIL / Ocean Spray
91/2 Minnesota G'Gophers

KLAUDA, RADEK
96/7 APS 210

KLEARS, JOHN
92/3 Semic Nordisk 237

KLEE, KEN
98/9 Be A Player 149, ✍ Aut. 149
00/1 BAP Mem. 376
95/6 Bowman 163
92/3 Classic Prospects 82
01/2 O-Pee-Chee 250
99/0 Pacific 442
00/1 Pacific 424
97/8 Pa. Invincible R-209
97/8 Pi. Be A Player 91, ✍ Aut. 91
01/2 Topps 250
02/3 T. Total 20
95/6 Upper Deck 128
97/8 Upper Deck 386
02/3 Upper Deck 422
95/6 UD BAP 162, ✍ S162
95/6 WASH
93/4 Portland Pirates
94/5 Portland Pirates

KLEIN, DEDE
34-43 BeeHive-1 [NYAm.]

KLEIN, KEVIN
00/1 Toronto St. Mike's

KLEIN, LLOYD
33-35 Diamond Match Silv.
36-39 Diamond Match TT1
36-39 Diamond Match TT2
36-39 Diamond Match TT3

KLEINENDORST, KURT
93/4 Raleigh Icecaps

KLEINENDORST, SCOTT
85/6 HART / Jr. Whalers
86/7 HART / Jr. Whalers
87/8 HART / Jr. Whalers
88/9 HART / Jr. Whalers
89/0 WASH
89/0 WASH / Kodak

KLEISINGER, CURTIS
91/2 Air Canada SJHL B16

KLEMENC, PETAR-IGOR
79 Panini Sticker 400

KLEMM, JON
01/2 BAP Mem. ✂ SCC
01/2 Heads Up ✂ JQ 9
98/9 OPC Chrome 113
02/3 Pacific 78
02/3 Pacific Complete 331
97/8 Pa. Dynagon BKS-25
96/7 Pi. Be A Player 144, ✍ Aut. 144
00/1 PS Titanium ✂ GUG 75
91/2 ProCards 534
91 7th..Sketch Mem.Cup 77
90/1 7th..Sketch WHL 197
95/6 SBx Impact 194
00/1 Stadium 144
98/9 Topps 113
02/3 T. Total 47
95/6 Upper Deck 93, SE-20
01/2 Upper Deck 272
02/3 Upper Deck 37
01/2 UD SCup Champs 43
00/1 UD Vintage 89
89/0 Spokane Chiefs

KLENNER, SEBASTIAN
94/5 DEL 405
99/0 Eishockey 307

KLENNER, SEBASTIEN
00/1 UD DEL 22

KLESLA, ROSTISLAV
01/2 Adrenaline 53, RR 7
01/2 Atomic RR 4
00/1 BAP Mem. 420
01/2 BAP Mem. 210
02/3 BAP Mem. 106, 209, ✂ FP9, ✂ FG19
01/2 Bowman 139
02/3 Bowman 108, ✂ FFDS, ✂ FFJ, ✂ FFP, ✂ FFR, ✂ FFRP, ✂ FFS, ✂ FFTS, ✍ YSA, / ✍ Puck
01/2 Crown Royale 43, CA 4, RR 7
02/3 Crown Royale ✂ GWDP 7
02/3 Exclusive 51
02/3 First Edition 20, 332, 349, 423H, ✂ Jers.
02/3 Heads Up 35, ✂ GWQ 10
02/3 In The GU 18, 118, ✂ F9
01/2 O-Pee-Chee 271
02/3 O-Pee-Chee 21
01/2 Pacific 113
01/2 PTC Rookie 5
01/2 Parkhurst 260
02/3 Parkhurst 62, ✂ FP9, ✂ GJ2-, ✂ SJ20
02/3 Parkhurst Retro 115
00/1 Premier Plus 119, PR3
00/1 Private Stock 113
01/2 Pr. Stock 103, MiT 4, -PS 96
01/2 PS Titanium 40
01/2 PS Titanium Draft 120, ✂ 30
02/3 PS Titanium ✂ GWJ 19
00/1 PS Titanium Draft 157
00/1 Signature 285, ✍ Aut. 247
01/2 Signature 8, ✍ Aut. 8, ✂ DD12, ✂ FP9, ✂ GJ2, ✂ GSJ2
02/3 Signature 71, ✍ 71
00/1 SP Authentic 101, ✍ SotT
01/2 SP Authentic ✍ SotT
02/3 SP Authentic 27, 114
00/1 SP GU 66
02/3 SP Game-Used ✂ PC, ✂ FF
00/1 SPx 158
01/2 SPx 171, ✂ TT
02/3 SPx 21
00/1 Stadium 248
01/2 Stadium 112
02/3 Stadium 84, ✍ LSS
01/2 Topps 271
02/3 Topps 21
00/1 To. Chrome 245
01/2 To. Chrome 138
02/3 To. Chrome 21
00/1 To. Gold Label 110
00/1 To. Heritage 76
02/3 To. Heritage 41
02/3 To. Limited 21
00/1 To. Stars 108, P7
02/3 T. Total 8, ✍ Sig
00/1 UD Heroes 162
01/2 UD PlayMakers Ltd 30
00/1 UD Reserve 92
00/1 Upper Deck 228
01/2 Upper Deck 54
02/3 Upper Deck 49, ✂ BF, ✂ HS, ✂ OR
02/3 UD Artistic 27, R27, / Art
00/1 UD Black Diam. 116
02/3 UD Classic 30, ✂ CS, ✂ HR
01/2 UD Honor Roll 28, 58
00/1 UD Ice 86
01/2 UD Ice ✍ CCA
01/2 UD Mask 27, ✂ GJ, ✂ JP, ✂ DP
01/2 UD MVP 54
02/3 UD MVP 55, SA, ST, Souv.
02/3 UD Piece 22
01/2 UD Premier 16, ✍ Sig
00/1 UD Pros&Prosp. 101
99/0 UD Prospects 22
01 UD Prospects GU ✍ SoT
01/2 UD Top Shelf 13
02/3 UD Top Shelf ✂ R, ✂ ST, ✂ SW, ✍ Sig
00/1 UD Vintage 371
01/2 UD Vintage 75, 78
02/3 UD Vintage 73, 269, GB 73, T21, ✂ HS
00/1 Vanguard 114
01/2 Vanguard 29, PP 4
02/3 Vanguard ✂ GWJ 15
01/2 Victory 371
02/3 Victory 61
01/2 COLU
99/0 Brampton Batallion 9

KLESLA, ROSTISLAV
02/3 Pacific 100
02/3 Pacific Complete 40

KLETKE, DANIEL
00/1 Austin Ice Bats

KLETZEL, DEAN
94/5 Slapshot Memorial 39
95/6 Brandon Wheat Kings

KLETZEL, DEREK
90/1 7th..Sketch WHL 161
91/2 7th...Sketch WHL 283

KLEVAKIN, DMITRI
98/9 Mir 93
99/0 Mir 218
00/1 Mir 283
94/5 Parkie SE232
94/5 SP 166
94/5 Upper Deck 515

KLIEMANN, MATTHIAS
94/5 DEL 392
95/6 DEL 415

KLIMA, PETR
90/1 Bowman 197
91/2 Bowman 96
91/2 Bowman 104
92/3 Bowman 135
95/6 Bowman 22
93/4 Donruss 317
94/5 Donruss 249
95/6 Donruss 110
96/7 Donruss 196
93/4 EA Sports 47
94/5 Flair 174
94/5 Fleer 208
95/6 Fleer Metal 138
92/3 Fleer Ultra 59, -UI 8
93/4 Fleer Ultra 425
94/5 Fleer Ultra 208
95/6 Fleer Ultra 153
95/6 Hoyle / East. 9-Spade
91/2 Kellogg's / Score 17
93/4 Leaf 321
94/5 Leaf 171
95/6 Leaf 321
96/7 Leaf 39
96/7 Maggers 145
96/7 Metal Univ. 76
86/7 OPC/Topps 98
87/8 OPC/Topps 26
88/9 OPC/Topps 28
90/1 OPC/Topps 85
91/2 O-Pee-Chee 193
91/2 OPC Premier 61
86/7 OPC Sticker 129-115
86/7 OPC Sticker 162-21
87/8 OPC Sticker 104-237
88/9 OPC Sticker 251-121
01/2 OFS 165, -RE8D
97/8 Pacific CC 347
87/8 Panini Sticker 246
88/9 Panini Sticker 44
90/1 Panini Sticker 228
90/1 Panini/EDM 9
91/2 Panini Sticker 126
92/3 Panini Sticker 105
93/4 Panini Sticker 234
94/5 Panini Sticker 185
95/6 Panini Sticker 130
96/7 Panini Sticker 126
97/8 Panini Sticker 217
91/2 Parkhurst 280
92/3 Parkhurst 54
93/4 Parkhurst 195
94/5 Parkhurst 219
95/6 Parkhurst 197
91/2 Pinnacle 159
92/3 Pinnacle 344
93/4 Pinnacle 349
94/5 Pinnacle 311
96/7 Pinnacle 79
95/6 Pi. Summit 141
95/6 Playoff 311
96/7 Playoff 404
94/5 POG 224
95/6 POG 251
93/4 Power Play 232
94/5 Premier 318
90/1 Pro Set 86
91/2 Pro Set 72
91/2 Pro Set Platinum 37
90/1 Score 232
91/2 Score 136
91/2 Score CAN 136
92/3 Score 383
92/3 Score SS 24
93/4 Score 242
93/4 Score 518
95/6 Score 65
96/7 Score 202
91 Semic Sticker 220
93 Semic Sticker 104
95/6 SBx Emotion 165
95/6 SBx Impact 156
94/5 SP 110
95/6 SP 136
92/3 Topps 26
95/6 Topps 238
95/6 To. Finest 112
91/2 To. Stadium 61
92/3 To. Stadium 368
94/5 To. Stadium 136
95/6 To. Stadium EC185
90/1 Upper Deck 282
91/2 Upper Deck 111
92/3 Upper Deck 551
93/4 Upper Deck 291, 526, SP-152
94/5 Upper Deck 86
95/6 Upper Deck 118, SE-167
96/7 Upper Deck 156
94/5 UD BAP ✍ 155
95/6 UD CC 134
96/7 UD CC 246
85/6 DETR / Little Caesars
86/7 DETR / Little Caesars
87/8 DETR / Little Caesars
88/9 DETR / Little Caesars
90/1 EDMO / IGA
91/2 EDMO / IGA
92/3 EDMO / IGA 012
96/7 EDMO
94/5 TAMP / Sky Box
95/6 TAMP / Sky Box

KLIMENTIEV, SERGEI
95/6 Edge Ice 64
99/0 Mir 129
00/1 Mir 272
94/5 SR Tetrad CIX, ✍ Aut.
98/9 Milwaukee Admirals
95/6 Rochester Americans
96/7 Rochester Americans
97/8 Rochester Americans

KLIMES, MICHAL
98/9 OFS 412
99/0 OFS 182
01/2 OFS 122

KLIMES, TOMAS
01/2 OFS 265

KLIMOVICH, SERGEI
92/3 Classic 46
92/3 Classic Four Sport 187
95/6 Edge Ice 135
99/0 Eishockey 167
00/1 Mir 318
92/3 Red Ace Blue 30
92/3 Red Ace Violet 14
92/3 Upper Deck 339
93/4 Upper Deck 275
94/5 Indianapolis Ice
95/6 Indianapolis Ice
97/8 Las Vegas Thunder 18

KLIMT, TOMAS
95/6 APS 256
96/7 APS 304
97/8 APS 240
97/8 DS 18
96/7 DS Sticker 220
97/8 DS Sticker 37
98/9 OFS 335
00/1 OFS 127
01/2 OFS 175
99/0 Score 92
93/4 Upper Deck 263

KLISHIN, SERGEI
00/1 Mir 109

KLISIAK, WALDEMAR
95/6 APS 312

KLOBOUCEK, JAN
92/3 BCJHL 222
98/9 OFS 64
99/0 OFS 78
00/1 OFS 89
01/2 OFS 10

KLOBOUCEK, JIRI
97/8 APS 216

KLOCKARE, STEFAN
94/5 Leaf Elit Set 73
95/6 Leaf Elit Set 16
90/1 Semic Elitserien 183
91/2 Semic Elitserien 38
92/3 Semic Elitserien 56
92/3 Upper Deck 224
95/6 UD Elitserien 24
97/8 UD Elitserien 20
00/1 UD Elitserien 167

KLOEPZIG, STEVE
87/8 Kamloops Blazers
86/7 Portland Winter Hawks

KLOIBER, RALPH
74/5 Sioux City Musketeers

KLOUCEK, TOMAS
00/1 BAP Mem. 519
01/2 O-Pee-Chee 284
01/2 Signature 100, ✍ Aut.
00/1 SP Authentic 154
01/2 Stadium ✂ SCS, ✂ SCSD
01/2 Topps 284
00/1 To. Heritage 81
01/2 To. Reserve ✂ TR
01/2 Victory 239
99/0 Hartford Wolf Pack
00/1 Hartford Wolf Pack

KLUCZKOWSKI, STEVE
89/0 7th..Sketch OHL 54

KLUGE, RAINER
99/0 Eishockey 411

KLUKAY, JOE
45-64 BeeHive-2 [Toro.]
45-64 BeeHive-2 [Bost.]
48-52 Exhibits [Maple Leafs]
51/2 Parkhurst 74
52/3 Parkhurst 75
53/4 Parkhurst 94
54/5 Parkhurst 54
55/6 Parkhurst 6

45-54 Quaker Oats
76 DETR

KLUZAK, GORD
83/4 O-Pee-Chee 51
84/5 O-Pee-Chee 6
85/6 O-Pee-Chee 167
86/7 OPC/Topps 54
88/9 OPC/Topps 23
90/1 O-Pee-Chee 495
83/4 OPC/Topps Sticker 185
84/5 OPC Sticker 186
88/9 OPC Sticker 25-154
88/9 Panini Sticker 205
x90/1 Score 367
83/4 Souhaits Keychain [Bruins]
84/5 Topps 5
83/4 BOST
84/5 BOST
88/9 BOST / Sports Action
89/0 BOST / Sports Action

KLYAZMIN, SERGEI
00/1 Halifax Moosehead

KLYN, BRAD
91/2 Avant Garde BCJHL 161
92/3 BCJHL 161

KLYNCK, BERYL
52/3 Anonymous 123

KLYNE, LAWRENCE
92/3 BCJHL 91

KNAPP, JIM
85/6 Minnesota-Duluth 34

KNAUFT, LORNE
94/5 Slapshot / Brantford 5
93/4 Flint Generals
96/7 Flint Generals
98/9 Flint Generals

KNESAUREK, ROB
88/9 Sudbury Wolves
89/0 Sudbury Wolves

KNIBBS, KALVIN
90/1 7th..Sketch WHL 26

KNICKLE, RICK
92/3 Classic Prospects 121
92/3 Classic Prospects BC12
95/6 Edge Ice 122, TW-3
89/0 ProCards IHL 26
90/1 ProCards 515
91/2 ProCards 320
93/4 Score 466
96/7 Milwaukee Admirals
93/4 Phoenix Roadrunners
92/3 San Diego Gulls
86/7 Sherb. Canadiens 21

KNIGHT, BRAD
91/2 Avant Garde BCJHL 29

KNIGHT, CURTIS
91/2 Air Canada SJHL A17
92/3 MPS SJHL 40

KNIGHT, DARRYL
99/0 Kingston Frontenacs

KNIGHT, JASON
91/2 7th...Sketch WHL 337
91/2 Saskatoon Blades

KNIGHT, JEFF
91/2 Air Canada SJHL 38
91/2 Air Canada SJHL C39
90/1 7th..Sketch WHL 44

KNIGHT, KEITH
82/3 Kingston Canadians

KNIGHT, MICHAEL
01/2 Belleville Bulls

KNIGHT, TERRY
83/4 Medicine Hat Tigers

KNIPSCHEER, FRED
94/5 Classic T4, ✍ Aut.
93/4 Cla. Prospects 60
94/5 Leaf 331
93/4 Parkhurst 18
94/5 Pinnacle 249
95/6 Playoff 227
94/5 Score 220
94/5 To. Stadium 17
98/9 Cincinnati Cyclones

KNOBLOCH, THOMAS
94/5 DEL 401
95/6 DEL 420

KNOLD, MARTIN
99/0 UD Elitserien 121

KNOLD, PER CHRISTIAN
92 Semic Sticker 48

KNOLD, PER_CHR
92/3 Semic Nordisk 87

KNOPP, BEN
99/0 UD Sobey's 9
99/0 UD Prospects 29
00/1 UD Prospects 57
01/2 Kamloops Blazers

KNORR, DEREK
98/9 BC Icemen 13
98/9 BC Icemen
95/6 Flint Generals

KNOTTILA, MIKKO
98/9 Cardset 159

KNOX, BLAKE
00/1 Kudos 46
90/1 7th..Sketch WHL 49
91/2 7th...Sketch WHL 139

KNOX, CAMERON
92/3 BCJHL 145

KNOX, JASON
90/1 7th..Sketch WHL 248
91/2 7th...Sketch WHL 155
90/1 Saskatoon Blades
89/0 Victoria Cougars

KNOX, NORTHRUP
93/4 BUFF / Noco

KNOX, PAUL
52/3 Anonymous 143

KNOX, SEYMOUR
93/4 Action Packed 7
93/4 BUFF / Noco

KNUBLE, MIKE
97/8 Donruss 225
97/8 Limited 2, 17
98/9 Pacific 194
99/0 Pacific 271
00/1 Pacific 37
01/2 Pacific 32
02/3 Pacific Complete 184
97/8 Pi. Be A Player 43, ✍ Aut. 43
97/8 Pi. Inside 172
97/8 Score Detr. 20
97/8 SP Authentic 180
98/9 UD Choice RW19
97/8 Upper Deck 187
98/9 Upper Deck 325
98/9 UD G. Reserve 325
97/8 UD Ice 39
98/9 UD MVP 136
01/2 Victory 31
98/9 NYRA
95/6 Adirondack Red Wings

KNUTSEN, ESPEN
01/2 Adrenaline 54
02/3 Atomic 29
01/2 BAP Mem. 258
02/3 Exclusive 52
02/3 First Edition 225
01/2 O-Pee-Chee 70
02/3 O-Pee-Chee 175
01/2 Pacific 114
02/3 Pacific 101
02/3 Pacific Complete 126
00/1 Panini Sticker 142
00/1 Parkhurst P-198
01/2 Parkhurst 193
02/3 Parkhurst 173
02/3 Parkhurst Retro 149
01/2 Pr. Stock 26
02/3 Pr. Stock Reserve 31
92/3 Semic Nordisk 16
92/3 Semic Nordisk 181 [Årets Spiller]
92/3 Semic Nordisk 195 [Årets Lag]
92/3 Semic Nordisk 200 [Draften Av NHL]
01/2 Signature 181, ✍ Aut. 181
02/3 Signature 59, ✍ 59, ✂ YP12
02/3 SP Game-Used ✂ PH
01/2 Stadium 97
01/2 Topps 70
02/3 Topps 175
01/2 To. Chrome 70
02/3 To. Chrome 102
00/1 To. Heritage 159
01/2 To. Heritage 19
02/3 To. Limited 175
02/3 T. Total 349
00/1 Upper Deck 50
01/2 Upper Deck 53
02/3 Upper Deck 53
02/3 UD Artistic 26, R26
01/2 UD Challenge 21
02/3 UD Classic 29, ✂ HR
98/9 UD Elitserien 64
99/0 UD Elitserien 49, S5, ✍ Aut.
01/2 UD Mask ✂ GJ, ✂ JP, ✂ DP
01/2 UD MVP 52
02/3 UD MVP 56, SA
02/3 UD Piece 21
01/2 UD Top Shelf 89
02/3 UD Top Shelf 25, ✂ SH
01/2 UD Vintage 73, 78
02/3 UD Vintage 79, T20
01/2 Victory 101
02/3 Victory 59
01/2 COLU

KNUTSEN, ESPEN (SHAMPOO)
97/8 Do. Elite 106, 144
97/8 Do. Preferred 161
97/8 Do. Priority 172, DD-26
95 Globe 198, 251
94/5 Leaf Elit Set 264, FA-1
95/6 Leaf Elit Set 35, FTF-13
97/8 Pa. Dynagon Rookie
97/8 Pa. Paramount 3
95 Panini Worlds 248
97/8 Pinnacle 1
97/8 Pi. Certified K
97/8 Score 66
97/8 Score Anah. 20
94 Semic 261
92 Semic Sticker 40
93 Semic Sticker 241
97/8 SP Authentic 169
97/8 Upper Deck 216
97/8 UD Black Diam. 81
95/6 UD Elitserien 51, NA6
97/8 UD Ice 44
96 Wien 206

KNUUDE, MIKE
83/4 Belleville Bulls
84/5 Belleville Bulls

KNYAZEV, IGOR
99/0 Mir 140
00/1 Mir 274

KOBASEW, CHUCK
02/3 Atomic 104
02/3 BAP All-Star 135
02/3 BAP Draft Florida 14
02/3 BAP Mem. 278
02/3 Bowman 160
02/3 Calder 107
02/3 Crown Royale 106, -RR 5
02/3 eTopps 45
02/3 Exclusive 195, ✍ 195
02/3 First Edition 437 [Hobby]
02/3 Heads Up 126
02/3 In The GU 88, ✂ C5
02/3 O-Pee-Chee 339
02/3 Pacific 126
02/3 Pacific Complete 573
02/3 PTC/ ASG 2
02/3 Parkhurst 208, -HHC1, ✂ GJ56
02/3 Parkhurst Retro 208
02/3 Pr. Stock Reserve 155, -CA 4, -MIT 1
02/3 PS Titanium 108, -ROT 3
02/3 Quest for the Cup 108
02/3 Signature 185, ✍ 185, ✂ SGJ58
02/3 SP Authentic ✍ 183, ✍ ✂ Patch
02/3 SP GU 70
02/3 SPx ✍ 148
02/3 Stadium 125
02/3 Topps 339
02/3 To. Chrome 174
02/3 To. Heritage 141
02/3 T. Total 410
02/3 Ultimate Mem. 8, ✂ CC, ✍ RAut
02/3 Upper Deck 228
02/3 UD Artistic 116, CG15
02/3 UD Classic 105
02/3 UD Foundations 146
02/3 UD Honor 147
02/3 UD Mask 158
02/3 UD Piece 125
02/3 UD Premier ✍ ✂ 79, ✍ Sig

02/3 UD Rookie ✍ 167, ✍ TD
02/3 UD Top Shelf 125
02/3 Vanguard 106, -PP 5

KÖBERLE, WALTER
79 Panini Sticker 111
72 Semic Sticker 115

KOBEZDA, JAN
98/9 EBK ECHL All-Star
99/0 Missouri RiverOtters

KOBRC, ROMAN
92/3 BCJHL 233

KOCAR, JAROSLAV
99/0 Score 57

KOCH, PAUL
98/9 Chicago Wolves
98/9 Chicago Wolves Champs
95/6 Toledo Storm
96/7 Toledo Storm

KOCHAN, DIETER
92/3 BCJHL 64
00/1 BAP Mem. 234
01/2 BT Pipes 69
02/3 Between the Pipes 48
00/1 Pacific 375
02/3 Pacific 349
00/1 PS Titanium 145
00/1 PS Titanium Draft 145
00/1 Revolution 134
00/1 SPx 118
00/1 Upper Deck 227
00/1 UD Black Diam. 84
98/9 BC Icemen 17
98/9 BC Icemen
93/4 N. Michigan Wildcats

KOCHEGAROV, ALEXEI
99/0 Mir 162

KOCHIN, VLADIMIR
98/9 Mir 146
00/1 Mir 382

KOCHTA, JIRI
94/5 DEL 390
95/6 DEL 406
98/9 DEL 19
72 Hellas MM-Jenkki 87
74 Hellas MM-Jenkki 75
70/1 Kuvajulkaisut 51
72 Semic Sticker 28
74 Semic Sticker 58
71/2 Williams Finnish 30
72/3 Williams Finnish 12
73/4 Williams Finnish 53

KOCI, DAVID
01/2 WBS Penguins
00/1 Prince George Cougars

KOCUR, JOEY
91/2 Bowman 69
92/3 Bowman 80
01/2 Fleer Legacy 47
90/1 OPC/Topps 55
91/2 O-Pee-Chee 427
92/3 O-Pee-Chee 169
98/9 Omega 80
98/9 Pacific 195
97/8 Pa. Invincible R-70
87/8 Panini Sticker 251
89/0 Panini Sticker 67
90/1 Panini Sticker 211
93/4 Parkhurst 401
91/2 Pinnacle 240
92/3 Pinnacle 152
93/4 Pinnacle 184
94/5 Pinnacle 243
97/8 Pi. Be A Player 153, ✍ Aut. 153
93/4 Premier 512
90/1 Pro Set 73
90/1 Score 201
91/2 Score 92
91/2 Score CAN 92
92/3 Score 24
93/4 Score 270
92/3 Topps 128
91/2 To. Stadium 365
92/3 To. Stadium 417
94/5 To. Stadium 73
98/9 UD Choice RW18
90/1 Upper Deck 411
94/5 Upper Deck 479
95/6 Upper Deck 314
99/0 UD MVP W1
85/6 DETR / Little Caesars
86/7 DETR / Little Caesars
87/8 DETR / Little Caesars
88/9 DETR / Little Caesars
89/0 DETR / Little Caesars
83/4 Saskatoon Blades

KOCUR, JOEY
02/3 Fleer Throwbacks 65, 1SO, ✂ 4SC, ✂ 4SCTD, ✂ 1SO, ✍ Aut.

KOCUR, KORY
90/1 ProCards 483
91/2 ProCards 255
90/1 Score 384
92/3 Fort Wayne Komets 15
86/7 Saskatoon Blades
89/0 Saskatoon Blades

KOECK, MATT
93/4 Johnstown Chiefs 22

KOEHLER, GREG
02/3 Parkhurst 239
02/3 SP Authentic 149
02/3 SPx 165
02/3 Upper Deck 212
02/3 UD Honor 118
02/3 UD Mask 129
02/3 UD Top Shelf 116
99/0 Cincinnati Cyclones
00/1 Cincinnati Cyclones
98/9 Florida Everblades
98/9 New Haven Beast 19

KOENIG, TREVOR
98/9 Dayton Bombers
98/9 Dayton Bombers

KOFLER, MANUEL
00/1 UD DEL 112
01/2 UD DEL 252

KOHARSKI, DON
90/1 Pro Set 691

KOHL, PETER
99/0 Eishockey 395

KOHMANN, CHRISTIAN
94/5 DEL 345
95/6 DEL 320
99/0 Eishockey 346
00/1 UD DEL 199
01/2 UD DEL 220

KOHN, LADISLAV
95/6 Bowman 122
96/7 Fleer 128, CC-5
99/0 Millenium 8, C-13, ✍ Aut. 8
99/0 NHL Power Play [x3]
99/0 Omega 8
00/1 Pacific 6
94/5 Parkie SE211
96/7 SBx Impact 151
00/1 Topps 260
94/5 Upper Deck 509
00/1 Upper Deck 5
99/0 UD MVP Cup 7
00/1 Victory 2
01/2 Victory 23
95/6 Saint John Flames
96/7 Saint John Flames
97/8 Saint John Flames

KOHVAKKA, TEEMU
95 Semic 239
93/4 Sisu 153

KOIKKALAINEN, JAAKKO
66/7 Champion 143
70/1 Kuvajulkaisut 259

KOISTINEN, KEIJO
65/6 Hellas 39

KOIVENEN, TONI
96/7 Sisu 68

KOIVISTO, KEIJO
80/1 Mallasjuoma 73

KOIVISTO, RAMI
93/4 Jyvas Hyva 119
93/4 Sisu 15
94/5 Sisu 102

KOIVISTO, TOM
02/3 Atomic 131
02/3 BAP All-Star 130
02/3 BAP Mem. 290
02/3 Bowman 145
98/9 Cardset 55, OD 3
99/0 Cardset 263
00/1 Cardset 41
02/3 Cardset 41
02/3 Crown Royale 134
97/8 Hockey-Box
02/3 In The GU 86
02/3 Parkhurst 220
02/3 Pr. Stock Reserve 180
02/3 PS Titanium 134
93/4 Sisu 34
94/5 Sisu 292
95/6 Sisu 217
96/7 Sisu 17
02/3 SP Authentic 157
02/3 SP GU 91
02/3 To. Chrome 164
02/3 To. Heritage 148
02/3 T. Total 419
02/3 Ultimate Mem. 20
02/3 Upper Deck 451
02/3 UD Classic 127
02/3 UD Honor 125
02/3 UD Mask 135
02/3 Vanguard 131

KOIVISTO, TOMI
02/3 UD Top Shelf 118

KOIVISTO, TONI
00/1 Cardset 189
02/3 Cardset 196

KOIVU, JUKKA
73/4 Williams Finnish 287

KOIVU, MIKKO
00/1 Cardset 222, NG-1
02/3 Cardset 197, -BFG 3, -DD 1, ✍ BFG

KOIVU, SAKU
01/2 Adrenaline ✂ GWJ 22
01/2 Atomic 51, CP 9, PP 19, ✂ GWJ 33
02/3 Atomic 55, -CF 15
98/9 Aurora 94, CF-24
99/0 Aurora 75, Stripe 75
00/1 Aurora 72, ✂ GWJ-5, ✂ GWJ-11
02/3 BAP All-Star 45, ✂ ASJ
98/9 Be A Player 218, ✍ Aut. 218
99/0 BAP Mem. 185, ✂ J-26
00/1 BAP Mem. 151
01/2 BAP Mem. 286, HSHS
02/3 BAP Mem. 181, ✂ ASJ27, ✂ SC23, ✂ TM12
01/2 BAP Update ✂ PTT4
97/8 Bicycle 10-Diamond
95/6 Bowman 148, BB17
01/2 Bowman 95
02/3 Bowman 13
98/9 Bowman's Best 44
02/3 Calder 42
98/9 Cardset Top. 11, DT6
99/0 Cardset 193, BP-5, MW-6, AH K-hertta
00/1 Cardset 356
00/1 Cardset MT
02/3 Cardset 198, -DD 1, -SGSP 5
93/4 Classic 40
94/5 Classic 95, T35
93/4 Cla. 4 Sport 202
93/4 Cla. Prospects IA15
99/0 Crown Royale 70, IG-13
00/1 Crown Royale 55
01/2 Crown Royale JotC 17, ✂ TT 12
02/3 Crown Royale 51, LOR 13
95/6 Donruss 283, RR-1
96/7 Donruss D-10, HL-19, RR-6
97/8 Donruss 53
98/9 Donruss ES 3
96/7 Do. Canadian 40
97/8 Do. Canadian 19
95/6 Do. Elite 67, R-8
96/7 Do. Elite 80, A-5
97/8 Do. Elite 20
97/8 Do. Preferred 11
97/8 Do. Priority 14, 210, D-21, OD-27, Post-27, Stamp-27
97/8 Do. Studio 19, HH-15, P-19
96/7 Duracell JB10
98/9 Dynagon Ice 96, -FT 12, -TC 13
99/0 Dynagon Ice 102
97/8 Esso 48
02/3 eTopps 14
02/3 Exclusive 91, -MO 11
02/3 First Edition 92, ✂ Jers., ✂ HSHSJers 13
96/7 Flair 48, HN-6
96/7 Fleer 54, 136, RS-7
95/6 Fleer Metal 180, IS-10, MW-2
96/7 Fl. Picks 76, JE-7
95/6 Fleer Ultra 344, EA-12
96/7 Fl. Ultra 87
00 Gatorade Sticker
95 Globe 139
95 Hartwall Karjala
01/2 Heads Up 50
02/3 Heads Up 64, ✂ GWQ 15, / Bobble
02/3 In The GU 40, 140, ✂ E36, ✂ IE14, ✂ GUJ49, ✂ SJ49, ✂ T6
92/3 Jyvas Hyva 177
93/4 Jyvas Hyva 323
95/6 Kellogg's Pop-Ups 5
95 Koululainen
96/7 Kraft / KD
97/8 Kraft / JTP, KD, Casecard
99/0 Kraft / KD, / OML
96/7 Kraft Magnet
96/7 Leaf 204, LL-20, S-15
97/8 Leaf 19, BS-15
95/6 L. Limited 118, RP-9
96/7 L. Limited 10
96/7 L. Preferred 45, LS-5
97/8 Limited 9, 34, 165, FG-8
96/7 Maggers 86
95/6 McDonald's McD-39
96/7 McDonald's McD-5
97/8 McDonald's McD-4, F8
98/9 McDonald's McD04
99/0 McDonald's McD-14, ✍ SS
00/1 McDonald's 19, CL-4
01/2 McDonald's 21, ✂ JPatch 12
02/3 McDonald's 21, -CC 4
96/7 Metal Univ. 80
99/0 Millenium 128, ✍ Aut. 128, ✂ J-4, ✂ JS-4
95/6 Cool Trade 13
98/9 NHL Power Play
01/2 O-Pee-Chee 66
02/3 O-Pee-Chee 27
98/9 OPC Chrome 76
97/8 Omega 118, 247, GF-10, SHLC-10
98/9 Omega 123, -FTF 7, -Onl. 18
99/0 Omega 119
98/9 Pacific 252, -DI 11, -GCDC 17, -TC 13
99/0 Pacific 205, TL-14
00/1 Pacific 209, 439
01/2 Pacific 209
02/3 Pacific 198, -IZ 7
02/3 Pacific Complete 9
97/8 Pacific CC 272
97/8 Pa. Crown Roy. 69, BOS-12, L-10
98/9 Pa. Crown Roy. 70, -MP 12, -PotG 15, -PP 13
97/8 Pa. Dynagon 63, T-14
97/8 Pa. Invincible 71, FP-18, OTG-11
97/8 Pa. Paramount 95, P-12
98/9 Pa. Paramount 113, -SD 10, -TC 13
99/0 Pa. Paramount 117, PB-20
00/1 Pa. Paramount 126, FF-20, ✂ J&P-6
97/8 Pa. Revolution 71, ASG-12, TC-13
98/9 Pa. Revolution 74, -Show. 20
98/9 Panini Photocard [x2]
96/7 Panini Sticker 37
97/8 Panini Sticker 28
98/9 Panini Sticker 32
99/0 Panini Sticker 65
00/1 Panini Sticker 39
95 Panini Worlds 174
93/4 Parkhurst 521
95/6 Parkhurst 263, 505, CCB-15, PP-39, ✍ Aut.
00/1 Parkhurst P-124
01/2 Parkhurst 143, ✂ PJ37, ✂ HSHSJers
02/3 Parkhurst 48, ✂ GJ7, ✂ SJ7, ✂ TT7
02/3 Parkhurst Retro 181, ✂ RJ35, ✂ RM25
96/7 Pinnacle 202, TP-10
97/8 Pinnacle 26, TP-7, P-10
96/7 Pi. Be A Player BB-22
97/8 Pi. Be A Player 3, OT-14, ✍ Aut. 3
97/8 Pi. BeeHive 13, BHT-13
97/8 Pi. Certified 44, CT-18
97/8 Pi. Epix E10
97/8 Pi. Inside 13, IT-16, / Can 16
96/7 Pi. Mint 9
97/8 Pi. Mint 15
95/6 Pi. Summit 186
96/7 Pi. Summit 152, HV-14
97/8 Pi. Totally 44
95/6 Pi. Zenith 144, RRC-1
96/7 Pi. Zenith 58, A-5
95/6 Playoff 164
96/7 Playoff 388
97/8 Pi. Post 18
00/1 Premier Plus 83
99/0 Prism 72
00/1 Private Stock 51, ✂ GUG-57, Res. 12, PS-28, PSS-16
01/2 Pr. Stock ✂ GUG 54
02/3 Pr. Stock Reserve 53
00/1 PS Titanium 47
02/3 PS Titanium 55
02/3 Quest for the Cup 50
99/0 Revolution 75, / CSC 75
00/1 Revolution 76, HD-19, ✂ GWJ-6
96/7 Score 238, CI-11, / Promo 238
97/8 Score 94
97/8 Score Mont. 7
95/6 Select CE 117, CF-5
96/7 Select CE 64, C-8
94 Semic 27
95 Semic 11, 205, 219-224
00/1 Signature 91, F-16, ✍ Aut. 163, ✂ J-4
01/2 Signature C-41, ✂ GJ32, ✂ GSJ32, ✂ HSHSJers
02/3 Signature 130, ✍ 130, ✂ SGJ49, ✂ TQ6
93/4 Sisu 41
93/4 Sisu 310
93/4 Sisu 389
94/5 Sisu 211, FOI-1, J-1, SS-10, SC
95/6 Sisu 165, 199, 400, G-15, SS-3, GH, SB
95/6 Sisu Limited 6, PP
95/6 SBx Emotion gN 7
95/6 SBx Impact 206
96/7 SBx Impact 62, 169, F-13
95/6 SP 73
96/7 SP 79, CW-2, HC-15
97/8 SP Authentic 80, I31
98/9 SP Authentic 41
99/0 SP Authentic 43
02/3 SP Authentic 48, ✂ DP
01/2 SP GU ✂ AF
02/3 SP GU 26, ✂ AF, ✂ CF, ✂ PC, ✂ PH (x2)
02/3 Sports Vault 56
96/7 SPx 21,GF-1
97/8 SPx 24
99/0 SPx 78
00/1 SPx 35
01/2 SPx 34
02/3 SPx 41, ✂ X
98/9 SPx Finite 115
98/9 SPx Prospects 33, H16, L22
00/1 Stadion 84
99/0 Stadium 17, Chrome 16
00/1 Stadium 188
01/2 Stadium 12, G35, NHLP7, ✂ SCS, ✂ SCSD
02/3 Stadium 41, ✂ NHLP1
00/1 SLU 5
95 Suomen All-Star 3
95 Suomen Beckett Card 1
95/6 Super Sticker 65
96/7 Team Out!
95/6 Topps 306
98/9 Topps 76, IA 9, MI 8
99/0 Topps 90, TW2
00/1 Topps 89
01/2 Topps 66, ✂ CC2
02/3 Topps 27, HHC8, ✂ CC5, ✂ CC7, ✂ CC14
99/0 To. Chrome 90
00/1 To. Chrome 71
01/2 To. Chrome 66
02/3 To. Chrome 27
95/6 To. Finest 85
98/9 To. Finest 45, C4
98/9 T. Gold Label 17
99/0 To. Gold Label 7
00/1 To. Gold Label 48
00/1 To. Heritage 39, OSA, OSJ
01/2 To. Heritage 21, ✂ CC
02/3 To. Heritage 36
02/3 To. Limited 27
96/7 To. Picks RS5
99/0 To. Prmr. Plus 60, / PP4
01/2 To. Reserve 36, ✂ TR
95/6 To. Stadium ER203
95/6 TSC Members Only 46
00/1 To. Stars 69
95/6 T. Super Skills SR11
02/3 T. Total 395, AW9
98/9 UD Choice 105, BH28, SQ8
00/1 UD Heroes 62
00/1 UD Reserve 46
98/9 UD3 43, 103, 163
00/1 Ultimate Mem. ✍ U-4, ✂ J-48, ✂ S-48, ✂ UC-4
02/3 Ultimate Mem. ✂ Cor, ✂ DD, ✂ Emb, ✂ GUJ, ✂ GUSJ, ✂ ITN, ✂ RA, ✂ UC, ✍ UAut
99/0 Ult. Victory 44
92/3 Upper Deck 617
93/4 Upper Deck 569
95/6 Upper Deck 259, H22
96/7 Upper Deck 82, X16, HH6, LS20, SS14B
97/8 Upper Deck 293, SS15, SG18, T8B, ✂ GJ9
98/9 Upper Deck 28, 290, FT12, LS18, P19
99/0 Upper Deck 67, 157
00/1 Upper Deck 319
01/2 Upper Deck 90, ✂ PoaN, ✂ PoaND
02/3 Upper Deck 96, ✂ FF, ✂ LN, ✂ PL, ✂ PW, ✂ UDPL
02/3 UD Artistic 47, R47, CG8, / Art
95/6 UD BAP 174, LL5, ✍ S174
96/7 UD Black Diam. 178, RC2
97/8 UD Black Diam. 46
98/9 UD Black Diam. 46, M22
99/0 UD Black Diam. 48
00/1 UD Black Diam. 31
02/3 UD Classic 51, ✂ HH
95/6 UD CC 397
96/7 UD CC 134, 321, UD38, C15, CR15
97/8 UD Coll. Choice 129, SQ47, S5, C11, CR11
98/9 UD G. Reserve 28, 290
99/0 UD G. Reserve 67, 157
01/2 UD Honor Roll -DPuck
02/3 UD Honor 39, 86, -SG17, -TW8, ✂ GA
96/7 UD Ice 89, S4
97/8 UD Ice 78, IC4, L9B
00/1 UD Legends 63
01/2 UD Mask ✂ GJ, ✂ JP, ✂ DP
02/3 UD Mask 47, ✂ IO
98/9 UD MVP 104
99/0 UD MVP 100
00/1 UD MVP 94
01/2 UD MVP 97
02/3 UD MVP 99
99/0 UD MVP Cup 91
02/3 UD Piece 49
01/2 UD Premier ✂ B
02/3 UD Premier 30, ✂ Jers, ✂ JD, ✂ Patch
99/0 UD Retro 41
02/3 UD Rookie 52, ✂ DJ
01/2 UD Top Shelf 23
02/3 UD Top Shelf 46, ✂ SH, ✂ ST, ✂ SW
00/1 UD Vintage 186, 196, 197, NH13
01/2 UD Vintage 131, 138, 139
02/3 UD Vintage 132, 276, GB 132, T36
00/1 Vanguard 51
01/2 Vanguard ✂ DGM 15
02/3 Vanguard 55
99/0 Victory 142, 143
00/1 Victory 117, 118, 307
01/2 Victory 185
02/3 Victory 110
99/0 WGretzky 85
96 Wien 11, 37, 237-240, AS5, Super
97/8 Zenith 26, CTC-13, Z37
95/6 MONT
95/6 MONT / Export
96/7 MONT
96/7 MONT / Export
97/8 MONT
00/1 MONT
01/2 MONT
02/3 MONT

KOIVULA, VILLE
99/0 Cardset 292

KOIVULAHTI, PERTTI
70/1 Kuvajulkaisut 209
80/1 Mallasjuoma 166
79 Panini Sticker 174
82 Skopbank
78/9 SM-Liiga 17
78/9 SM-Liiga 190
77-79 Sports. FIN 76-1801
71/2 Williams Finnish 131
72/3 Williams Finnish 194
73/4 Williams Finnish 154

KOIVUNEN,
97/8 Hockey-Box

KOIVUNEN, HANNU
66/7 Champion 85
70/1 Kuvajulkaisut 158
71/2 Williams Finnish 229

KOIVUNEN, JARMO
70/1 Kuvajulkaisut 159
71/2 Williams Finnish 230
72/3 Williams Finnish 85
73/4 Williams Finnish 132

KOIVUNEN, KEIJO
72/3 Williams Finnish 145

KOIVUNEN, MATTI
65/6 Hellas 24
70/1 Kuvajulkaisut 297

KOIVUNEN, PETRO
98/9 Cardset 152
92/3 Jyvas Hyva 119
93/4 Jyvas Hyva 202
93/4 Sisu 277
94/5 Sisu 66, FOI-18
95/6 Sisu 89
95/6 Sisu Limited 60

KOIVUNEN, TONI
98/9 Cardset 132
99/0 Cardset 74
00/1 Cardset 127
02/3 Cardset 199
97/8 Hockey-Box
92/3 Jyvas Hyva 152
93/4 Jyvas Hyva 263
93/4 Sisu 300
95/6 Sisu 267

KOIVUNORO, MIKKO
00/1 Kudos 79
94/5 Sisu 266
95/6 Sisu 88
96/7 Sisu 92

KOJOLA, HEIKKI
72/3 Williams Finnish 86

KOKKO,
97/8 Hockey-Box

KOKKO, PETRI
00/1 Cardset 203
94/5 Sisu 19
95/6 Sisu 31
96/7 Sisu 29
94/5 Topps Finest 127

KOKKO, SAMI
92/3 Jyvas Hyva 112

KOKKOLA, JARI
70/1 Kuvajulkaisut 338

KOKKONEN, OLLI
72/3 Williams Finnish 213

KOKKONEN, TIMO
70/1 Kuvajulkaisut 298
71/2 Williams Finnish 191
72/3 Williams Finnish 229
73/4 Williams Finnish 263

KOKOREV, DMITRI
00/1 Dynamo 12

KOKRMENT, JINDRICH
82 Semic Sticker 90

KOLACEK, KAMIL
94/5 APS 226
99/0 Score 29

KOLACEK, RICHARD
99/0 Score 17

KOLANOS, KRYS
01/2 Adrenaline 221, RR 14
01/2 Atomic 120
01/2 BAP Mem. 365
01/2 Bowman 148
01/2 Crown Royale 174, CA 9, RR 15
02/3 Exclusive 134, -GE 14
02/3 First Edition 287
01/2 Heads Up 116
02/3 Heads Up 96, -HF 13, ✂ GWQ 21, ✂ GWQ 35
01/2 O-Pee-Chee 334
02/3 O-Pee-Chee 208
01/2 Pacific 460
02/3 Pacific 297, -SM 10
02/3 Pacific Complete 27
01/2 PTC Calder 9
01/2 PTC Draft 9
01/2 PTC High Voltage 8
01/2 PTC Collectibles 9
01/2 PTC Rookie 10
01/2 Parkhurst 266
02/3 Parkhurst 61
01/2 Pr. Stock 136, MiT 9, RR 8, -PS 101
01/2 PS Titanium 176, TSS 30, TRT 10, ✂ DSJ 71
01/2 PS Titanium Draft 160, ✂ 74
01/2 Signature 243, ✍ Aut. 243
02/3 Signature 97, ✍ 97
01/2 SP Authentic ✍ 179
01/2 SP GU 94
02/3 SP Game-Used ✂ PC
01/2 SPx 151, -RT
01/2 SPx Rookie RR23
02/3 Stadium 58
01/2 Topps 334
02/3 Topps 208, ✍ SF
01/2 To. Chrome 152
02/3 To. Chrome 117
01/2 To. Heritage 150
02/3 To. Heritage 92, ✍ Aut.
02/3 To. Limited 208
01/2 To. Reserve 109
02/3 T. Total 210, ✍ Sig
01/2 UD PlayMakers Ltd 136
01/2 Upper Deck 228
02/3 Upper Deck ✂ OR
01/2 UD Challenge 128
02/3 UD Classic ✂ CS, ✂ HH
01/2 UD Honor Roll 99
01/2 UD Ice 65, ✍ CCA
01/2 UD Mask 162
01/2 UD MVP 231
01/2 UD Premier 114
01/2 UD Top Shelf 73
02/3 UD Top Shelf ✂ R, ✂ SH, ✂ ST
01/2 UD Vintage 294
01/2 Vanguard 126, PP 15
02/3 Vanguard ✂ GWJ 35
01/2 Victory 451
02/3 Victory 162

KOLANOS, KRYS
02/3 BAP Mem. 78

KOLAR, JAN
99/0 OFS 362
00/1 OFS 54

KOLARIK, MICHAL
01/2 OFS 127

KOLARIK, PAVEL
97/8 APS 153
99/0 DS 117
01/2 DS 33
97/8 DS Sticker 191
98/9 OFS 212
99/0 OFS 384
00/1 SPx 153
00/1 UD Ice 108
01/2 Victory 363
00/1 Providence Bruins
01/2 Providence Bruins

KOLDA, LADISLAV
01/2 Owen Sound Attack
02/3 Owen Sound Attack

KOLEDAEEV, ALEXEI
99/0 Mir 219

KOLEDAEV, ALEXEI
98/9 Mir 94
00/1 Mir 189

KOLEHMAINEN, PASI
95/6 Sisu 273

KOLEHMAINEN, RAINER
65/6 Hellas 133

KOLEK, VLADIMIR
96/7 APS 2

KOLENDA, MIKE
95/6 Toledo Storm
96/7 Toledo Storm
97/8 Toledo Storm 18
91/2 Ferris State Bulldogs

KOLESAR, MARK
95/6 Bowman 142
95/6 Edge Ice 86
99/0 Eishockey 203
00/1 Kudos 80
91/2 7th...Sketch WHL 212
96/7 Upper Deck 190
94/5 St. John's Maple Leafs
95/6 St. John's Maple Leafs
96/7 St. John's Maple Leafs
02/3 London Knights
92/3 Brandon Wheat Kings

KOLEWASKI, TONY
00/1 Saskatoon Blades

KOLIJN, PATRICK
79 Panini Sticker 278

KOLKKA, VAINO
66/7 Champion 195
70/1 Kuvajulkaisut 63
70/1 Kuvajulkaisut 109
72 Panda MM-Toronto
71/2 Williams Finnish 117
72/3 Williams Finnish 87
73/4 Williams Finnish 133

KOLKUNOV, ALEXEI
95/6 SP 182

KOLLIKER, JAKOB
79 Panini Sticker 260

KOLNIK, JURAJ
00/1 BAP Mem. 518
01/2 BAP Mem. 160
99 Bowman 58
02/3 O-Pee-Chee 289
02/3 Topps 289
02/3 To. Limited 289
00/1 Upper Deck 207
00/1 UD Black Diam. 72
00/1 UD Ice 52
00/1 UD MVP 217
01/2 UD Top Shelf 105
01/2 Victory 380
00/1 Lowell Lock Monsters
99/0 Rimouski Océanic 22

KOLNIK, LUBOMIR
94 Semic 203
91 Semic Sticker 119
92 Semic Sticker 143
95/6 Sisu 291, 373
96 Wien 232

KOLSTAD, DEAN
91/2 O-Pee-Chee 4S
89/0 ProCards IHL 94
91/2 ProCards 518
97/8 Central Texas
92/3 Kansas City Blades
94/5 Minnesota Moose

KOLTSOV, KIRIL
02/3 Russian Future Stars 8

KOLTSOV, KIRILL
00/1 Mir 228

KOLTSOV, KONSTANTIN
02/3 BAP Mem. 354
98/9 Mir 136
99/0 Mir 269
02/3 SP Authentic 215
02/3 SPx 193
02/3 Ultimate Mem. 67
02/3 UD Premier 98
02/3 WBS Penguins

KOLU, TOMI-PEKKA
99/0 Cardset 101

KÖLZIG, OLAF
01/2 Adrenaline 198, PP 36
01/2 Atomic 99
02/3 Atomic 100
98/9 Aurora 198, CF-50, / Cube 20
99/0 Aurora 149, GU-20
00/1 Aurora 148, Pins. 148, ✍ Aut. 148
02/3 BAP All-Star 46, ✂ ASJ
99/0 BAP Mem. 54, ✂ TM-32
00/1 BAP Mem. 80, ✂ J-10, ✂ V-1
01/2 BAP Mem. 67, ✂ AST, ✂ GoalJ, ✂ SCP
02/3 BAP Mem. 94
01/2 BT Pipes 21, 105, 110, HSHS, -Mask, ✂ ASJ, ✂ DM, ✂ Jers., ✂ Emb., ✂ S&J, ✂ GG, ✂ HSHSJers, ✂ ITN, ✂ TW
02/3 Between the Pipes 3, 150, M30, ✂ ASJ7, ✂ BM16, ✂ DM6, ✂ GUE23, ✂ GB11, ✂ GUJ23, ✂ GSJ23, ✂ GT9, ✂ HSHSJers 3, ✂ ITN23, ✂ T20
98/9 Bicycle.. A-H
01/2 Bowman 57
02/3 Bowman 36
98/9 Bowman's Best 59
99/0 Crown Royale 143
00/1 Crown Royale 107
01/2 Crown Royale 143
02/3 Crown Royale 100, ✂ GWDP 23
95/6 Donruss 254
97/8 Do. Priority 35
98/9 Dynagon Ice 197, -IW 10
99/0 Dynagon Ice 202
02/3 Exclusive 173, ✂ GWJ 25
02/3 First Edition 94, 336, 403R, ✂ Jers.
93/4 Fleer Ultra 447
01/2 Heads Up 99, SS 20
02/3 Heads Up 125
99/0 HoloGrFX 60
02/3 In The GU 78, 178, ✂ IE9, ✂ T18
98/9 Kraft / OML
00/1 McDonald's 36
99/0 Millenium 246, ✍ Aut. 246
98/9 NHL Power Play
91/2 O-Pee-Chee 290
01/2 O-Pee-Chee 7
02/3 O-Pee-Chee 156
98/9 OPC Chrome 193
97/8 Omega 242
98/9 Omega 248
99/0 Omega 243, WAS-10
98/9 Pacific 37, -DI 20, -GCDC 36, -TC 27
99/0 Pacific 443, ITCNF-20
00/1 Pacific 425, ES-10, GCDC-36, ✂ GWJ-15
01/2 Pacific 395, SC 20
02/3 Pacific 395
02/3 Pacific Complete 486
97/8 Pa. Crown Roy. 141, FO-20
98/9 Pa. Crown Roy. 143, -PP 25
97/8 Pa. Invincible R-210
97/8 Pa. Paramount 196
98/9 Pa. Paramount 247, -GS 20
99/0 Pa. Paramount 245, GS-20
00/1 Pa. Paramount 246, FF-36, GS-20, ✂ J&P-10
97/8 Pa. Revolution 149, RTS-20
98/9 Pa. Revolution 148, -TPA 20
98/9 Panini Photocard
98/9 Panini Sticker 108
95/6 Parkhurst 220
00/1 Parkhurst P-93
01/2 Parkhurst 60, ✂ PJ60, ✂ PS39, ✂ PSJ11, ✂ T6, ✂ WCJ3, ✂ WCE3, ✂ WCN3
02/3 Parkhurst 50, -HHV9, ✂ TT17
02/3 Parkhurst Retro 127, ✂ NN27
95/6 Pinnacle 134
97/8 Pinnacle 89
96/7 Pi. Be A Player 78, ✍ Aut. 78
97/8 Pi. Inside SU-7B
96/7 Pi. Summit 48
93/4 Premier 291
00/1 Premier Plus 16, MB16
99/0 Prism 148
00/1 Private Stock 99, PS-60, ✂ GUG-104
01/2 Pr. Stock 99
02/3 Pr. Stock Reserve 99
00/1 PS Titanium 99, 3SS-10, ✂ GUG-150
01/2 PS Titanium 143
02/3 PS Titanium ✂ GWJ 75
91/2 ProCards 550
02/3 Quest for the Cup 99, ✂ GWJ 25
99/0 Revolution 149
00/1 Revolution 148, HD-36, II-20, NI-20, SM-20
90/1 Score 392
97/8 Score 25
00/1 Signature 12, F-30, ✍ Aut. 125, ✂ HSHSJers
01/2 Signature C-30, ✍ Aut. LDK, ✂ GUE31, ✂ GJ66, ✂ GSJ66, ✂ ITN31
02/3 Signature 120, GS-65, ✍ 120, ✂ DW9, ✂ TQ9
98/9 SP Authentic 87
99/0 SP Authentic 88
00/1 SP Authentic 89, SS7
01/2 SP Authentic 89, ✍ SotT
02/3 SP Authentic 89, ✂ SP, ✂ DP
00/1 SP GU 59
01/2 SP GU 59, ✂✍ IS, ✂✍ ISD, ✂ Patch, ✂✍ PatchSig, ✂ PatchC (x2), ✂✍ PatchCSig (x3), ✂ TotG, ✂ TotGC (x2), ✂ TotGT (x2)
02/3 SP GU 49, ✂ AF, ✂ PC, ✂ TG
02/3 Sports Vault 150
99/0 SPx 161
00/1 SPx 70
01/2 SPx 70
02/3 SPx 74, ✂ WM, ✂ X
98/9 SPx Finite 88
00/1 Stadion 66
99/0 Stadium 19, GC4
00/1 Stadium 129, CA6, GS7
01/2 Stadium 37, G10, ✍ LS
02/3 Stadium 36
98/9 SLU
99/0 SLU 205
00/1 SLU Classic Doubles 1
98/9 Topps 193, M2
99/0 Topps 132, TW19
00/1 Topps 8, OTG13
01/2 Topps 7, OTG24
02/3 Topps 156
99/0 To. Chrome 132
00/1 To. Chrome 8
01/2 To. Chrome 7
02/3 To. Chrome 95
98/9 To. Finest 126
98/9 T. Gold Label 63
00/1 To. Gold Label 4, BTM7
00/1 To. Heritage 5, 226, 244
01/2 To. Heritage 5, ✍ CAI
02/3 To. Heritage 70
02/3 To. Limited 156
99/0 To. Prmr. Plus 36
01/2 To. Reserve 93
93/4 To. Stadium 438
95/6 To. Stadium 217
00/1 To. Stars 20
02/3 T. Total 237
98/9 UD Choice 215
00/1 UD Heroes 117
01/2 UD PlayMakers Ltd 99
00/1 UD Reserve 88, GS10
00/1 Ultimate Mem. ✍ U-5, ✂ G-30, ✂ PJ-12, ✂ Jers. 35, ✂ J-43, ✂ S-43
01/2 Ultimate Mem. ✂ BAPL
02/3 Ultimate Mem. ✂ FS, ✂ SCD
99/0 Ult. Victory 88
93/4 Upper Deck 326
94/5 Upper Deck 486
95/6 Upper Deck 103
96/7 Upper Deck 354
98/9 Upper Deck 205
99/0 Upper Deck 301
00/1 Upper Deck 408, P10, SS20, TT10, UD8
01/2 Upper Deck 174, GL9, LL10
02/3 Upper Deck 173, -LL14, -SA14, ✂ GT, ✂ PN, ✂ SV, ✂ UDPL
02/3 UD Artistic 90, R90, ✂ AT, / Art
98/9 UD Black Diam. 89
99/0 UD Black Diam. 88
00/1 UD Black Diam. 59, ✂ GG
01/2 UD Challenge 89, BB10
02/3 UD Classic 100, PS10, ✂ HR
98/9 UD G. Reserve 205
99/0 UD G. Reserve 301
02/3 UD Honor 69, ✂ GA (x2)
00/1 UD Ice 40
01/2 UD Ice 126
00/1 UD Legends 131, 132
01/2 UD Mask 130, 190, ✂ GP, ✂ StS
02/3 UD Mask 87, 88, 89, 90, 107, ✂ CW, ✂ GG, ✂ MM, ✂ BM, ✂ PW, ✂ SS, ✂ VC
98/9 UD MVP 210
99/0 UD MVP 217
00/1 UD MVP 181, MM10
01/2 UD MVP 187, MM6, ✂ GS
02/3 UD MVP 186, MM7, SA, SD
99/0 UD MVP Cup 189
99/0 UD Ovation 60
02/3 UD Piece 88, AC28, / Giveaway
01/2 UD Premier ✂ B, ✍ SigS
02/3 UD Premier 55, ✂ Jers, ✂ JD, ✂ Patch
00/1 UD Pros&Prosp. 88
02/3 UD Rookie 99, ✂ DJ, ✂ S
01/2 UD Top Shelf 121
02/3 UD Top Shelf 90, ✂ HH, ✂ ST (x2), ✂ SS, ✂ SW, ✂ TS
00/1 UD Vintage 360, 369, 370, GG20
01/2 UD Vintage 257, 259, 260
02/3 UD Vintage 256, 290, GB 256, T65, ✂ EE
00/1 Vanguard 99
01/2 Vanguard 100, SW 20, ✂ DGM 35
02/3 Vanguard 100
99/0 Victory 309, 384
00/1 Victory 233, 239, 330
01/2 Victory 349, 355, 407
02/3 Victory 218, -NP30
99/0 WGretzky 176
97/8 Zenith 59, Z30
95/6 WASH
98/9 WASH / Kids 'n 1
91/2 Baltimore Skipjacks
91/2 Hampton Roads
98/9 Hampton Roads
93/4 Portland Pirates
92/3 Rochester Americans DD
92/3 Rochester Americans WPC

KOMADOSKI, NEIL
74/5 Loblaws
73/4 O-Pee-Chee 16
74/5 O-Pee-Chee 358
75/6 O-Pee-Chee 238
76/7 O-Pee-Chee 284
77/8 O-Pee-Chee 344
78/9 O-Pee-Chee 382
73/4 Topps 16
75/6 Topps 238

KOMARNISKI, ZENITH
97 Bowman 85
98 Bowman 46
98 Bowman Chrome 46
99/0 Omega 238
00/1 Topps 291
00/1 To. Chrome 186
98/9 UD Choice 263
95/6 Upper Deck 516
00/1 Kansas City Blades 4
01/2 Manitoba Moose
02/3 Manitoba Moose
97/8 Spokane Chiefs
95/6 Tri-City Americans 8

KOMAROV, ALEXEI
99/0 Mir 31

KOMAROV, PAVEL
99/0 Mir 257
00/1 Mir 141
95/6 Binghampton Rangers

KOMAROV, SERGEI
00/1 Mir 247

KOMISAREK, MIKE
02/3 BAP Mem. 304
02/3 Calder 127
02/3 Choice Prospects 22
02/3 Pacific Complete 570
02/3 Parkhurst Retro 239
02/3 Quest for the Cup 127
02/3 SP Authentic 204
02/3 SPx 186
02/3 Ultimate Mem. 34
02/3 UD Classic 136
02/3 UD Rookie 121
02/3 MONT
02/3 Hamilton Bulldogs

KOMISSAROV, OLEG
99/0 Mir 204
00/1 Mir 365

KOMMA, MICHAEL
94/5 DEL 61
95/6 DEL 61
99/0 Eishockey 291

KOMONOSKY, WARD
84/5 Prince Albert Raiders

KOMSI, ANTTI
66/7 Champion 209

KONDRASHKIN, SERGEI
93/4 Parkhurst 532
93/4 Pinnacle 511

KONECNY, KAMIL
96/7 APS 97
97/8 APS 314
98/9 OFS 177
99/0 OFS 403, 416
00/1 OFS 237

KONECNY, MICHAL
95/6 APS 210
99/0 Score 142

KONIG, RUDOLF
79 Panini Sticker 307

KONIGER, STEFAN
94/5 DEL 125

KONIK, BRAD
96/7 Providence Bruins

KONIK, GEORGE
72 Semic Sticker 132
72/3 Minn. Fight. Saints

KONOPASEK, STANISLAV
97/8 APS 380

KONOPKA, ZENON
99/0 Ottawa 67's

KONOVALENKO, VIKTOR
70/1 Kuvajulkaisut 5
72 Panda MM-Toronto
72 Semic Sticker 1
74 Semic Sticker 50
70/1 Soviet Stars
71/2 Soviet Stars
71/2 Williams Finnish 4

KONOWALCHUK, STEVE
01/2 Adrenaline 199
98/9 Be A Player 148, ✍ Aut. 148
99/0 BAP Mem. 283
00/1 BAP Mem. 315
01/2 BAP Mem. 189
91/2 Classic 46
91/2 Classic Four Sport 46
92/3 Classic Prospects 102
95/6 Donruss 296
92/3 Fleer Ultra 437
94/5 Fleer Ultra 389
95/6 Fleer Ultra 324
94/5 Leaf 423
95/6 Leaf 323
01/2 O-Pee-Chee 203
92/3 OPC Premier 15
99/0 Omega 244
98/9 Pacific 443
99/0 Pacific 444
00/1 Pacific 426
01/2 Pacific 396
02/3 Pacific 396
97/8 Pacific CC 69
97/8 Pa. Dynagon 132, T-58
97/8 Pa. Invincible 148
97/8 Pa. Paramount 197
98/9 Pa. Paramount 248
99/0 Pa. Paramount 246
00/1 Pa. Paramount 247
95/6 Panini Sticker 137
92/3 Parkhurst 202
93/4 Parkhurst 223
95/6 Parkhurst 493
94/5 Parkie SE192
94/5 Pinnacle 348
96/7 Pinnacle 131
96/7 Pi. Be A Player 173, ✍ Aut. 173
95/6 POG 279
94/5 Premier 273
00/1 PS Titanium ✂ GUG 50
93/4 Score 458
96/7 Score 135
97/8 Score 220
90/1 7th..Sketch WHL 312
91/2 7th...Sketch WHL 30
00/1 Signature 227, ✍ Aut. 13
02/3 Signature GS-88
95/6 SP 160
02/3 SP Game-Used ✂ PH
02/3 Sports Vault 149
99/0 Stadium 26, PP2
91/2 Star Pics 9
99/0 Topps 77
00/1 Topps 176
01/2 Topps 203
99/0 To. Chrome 77
93/4 To. Stadium 481
02/3 T. Total 188
91/2 Ultimate Draft Pick 41, ✍ Aut.
99/0 Ult. Victory 89
92/3 Upper Deck 418
93/4 Upper Deck 28
94/5 Upper Deck 214
96/7 Upper Deck 179
97/8 Upper Deck 174
00/1 Upper Deck 404
01/2 Upper Deck 406
02/3 Upper Deck 176
02/3 UD Classic ✂ HR
95/6 UD CC 318
96/7 UD CC 281
97/8 UD Coll. Choice 274
91/2 Upper Deck WJC 73
02/3 UD Honor 100
02/3 UD MVP 188
00/1 UD Vintage 363
01/2 UD Vintage 252, 260
02/3 UD Vintage 253, ✂ HS
01/2 Victory 352
02/3 Victory 215
92/3 WASH / Kodak
95/6 WASH
98/9 WASH / Kids 'n 6

KONROYD, STEVE
92/3 Bowman 18
92/3 Fleer Ultra 300
82/3 O-Pee-Chee 48
83/4 O-Pee-Chee 85
84/5 O-Pee-Chee 226
87/8 OPC/Topps 153
88/9 OPC/Topps 171
91/2 O-Pee-Chee 366
92/3 O-Pee-Chee 238
89/0 O-Pee-Chee 220
88/9 OPC Sticker 110-242
88/9 Panini Sticker 284
91/2 Parkhurst 287
92/3 Parkhurst 299
91/2 Pinnacle 180
92/3 Pinnacle 352
94/5 Pinnacle 339
94/5 Premier 394
90/1 Pro Set 52
92/3 Pro Set 62
91/2 Pro Set Platinum 177
90/1 Score 29
91/2 Score 189
91/2 Score CAN 189
92/3 Score 172
93/4 Score 219
92/3 Topps 411
92/3 To. Stadium 236
83/4 Vachon 9-129
81/2 CALG
82/3 CALG
85/6 CALG / Red Rooster
89/0 CHIC / Coke
90/1 CHIC / Coke
91/2 CHIC / Coke
91/2 HART / Jr. Whalers
92/3 HART / Dairymart
80/1 Oshawa Generals

KONSTANTINOV, EVGENY
01/2 BAP Mem. 391
01/2 Parkhurst 345
02/3 Upper Deck 221
02/3 UD Mask 81

KONSTANTINOV, VLADIMIR
97/8 Bicycle K-Diamond
92/3 Bowman 326
96/7 Donruss 83
97/8 Donruss 65
94/5 Flair 49
94/5 Fleer 60
96/7 Fleer 31, 143, NT-6
95/6 Fleer Metal 46
92/3 Fleer Ultra 49
93/4 Fleer Ultra 150
94/5 Fleer Ultra 61
95/6 Fleer Ultra 46
96/7 Fl. Ultra 51, PL-6, UP-9
91 Ivan Fiodorov 6
93/4 Leaf 237

94/5 Leaf 391
95/6 Leaf 283
96/7 Leaf 110
96/7 Metal Univ. 46,CS-6
90/1 O-Pee-Chee 21R
92/3 O-Pee-Chee 267
91/2 OPC Premier 118
91/2 OPC Premier 118
91/2 OPC Premier 155
97/8 Pacific CC 189, CS-7
97/8 Pa. Dynagon 42, DD-7B, T-26
97/8 Pa. Invincible 47, FP-13
96/7 Panini Sticker 147, 182
97/8 Panini Sticker 147
91/2 Parkhurst 46
92/3 Parkhurst 283
93/4 Parkhurst 325
95/6 Parkhurst 69
94/5 Parkie SE53
91/2 Pinnacle 311
92/3 Pinnacle 76
93/4 Pinnacle 264
94/5 Pinnacle 116
95/6 Pinnacle 129
96/7 Pinnacle 65
97/8 Pi. Inside 126
96/7 Pi. Summit 63
95/6 Playoff 145
94/5 POG 94
93/4 Power Play 73
93/4 Premier 108
94/5 Premier 448
91/2 Pro Set 533
92/3 Pro Set 44
91/2 Pro Set Platinum 254
91/2 Red Ace
91/2 Score 109T
91/2 Score CAN 659
92/3 Score 31
92/3 Score 503
93/4 Score 20
94/5 Score 96
95/6 Score 176
96/7 Score 84
97/8 Score 228
97/8 Score Detr. 9
92/3 Score Young Stars 23
89 Semic Sticker 86
91 Semic Sticker 81
92 Semic Sticker 108
95/6 SBx Emotion 54
95/6 SBx Impact 53
96/7 SBx Impact 35, F-12
87/8 Soviet Stars
89/0 Soviet Stars
96/7 SP 53
92/3 Topps 14
92/3 Topps 165
96/7 To. Picks 169
92/3 To. Stadium 418
93/4 To. Stadium 333
94/5 To. Stadium 159
91/2 Upper Deck 594
92/3 Upper Deck 267
92/3 Upper Deck 357
92/3 Upper Deck AR5
92/3 Upper Deck W5
92/3 Upper Deck E10
93/4 Upper Deck 366
94/5 Upper Deck 189
95/6 Upper Deck 190
96/7 Upper Deck 52, P12
97/8 Upper Deck 63, 203
95/6 UD BAP 216, ✍ S216
96/7 UD Black Diam. 16
96/7 UD CC 82, 302, 316
97/8 UD Coll. Choice 82, SQ33

KONTIO, ESA
70/1 Kuvajulkaisut 371

KONTNY, JOSEF
94/5 DEL 152
95/6 DEL 147

KONTOS, CHRIS
92 C.O.A. Winter Olympics 184
91/2 Canada Nationals
93/4 Canada Nationals
93/4 EA Sports 131
92/3 Fleer Ultra 412
93/4 Fleer Ultra 162
93/4 Leaf 160
92/3 OPC Premier 123
93/4 Panini Sticker 213
92/3 Parkhurst 176
93/4 Parkhurst 197
93/4 Pinnacle 8
93/4 Power Play 233
93/4 Premier 215
93/4 Premier - Canada 14
89/0 ProCards AHL 14
90/1 ProCards 359
93/4 Score 113
94/5 Score CT6
92/3 To. Stadium Members Only
92/3 Upper Deck 502
93/4 Upper Deck 54
87/8 PITT / Kodak
92/3 TAMP / Sheraton Inn
95/6 Cincinnati Cyclones

KONTSEK, ROMAN
96/7 APS 64
97/8 APS 337
97/8 DS 112
97/8 DS Sticker 280
99/0 OFS 290
00/1 OFS 281
94 Semic 204

KONTTILA, MIKKO
00/1 Cardset 350
97/8 Hockey-Box
93/4 Sisu 20
94/5 Sisu 111, 350

95/6 Sisu 280
99/0 UD Elitserien 51

KONTTO, PERTTI
65/6 Hellas 71

KOOPMAN, KEVIN
90/1 7th..Sketch WHL 257
91/2 7th...Sketch WHL 188

KOOPMANS, BRAD
91/2 Avant Garde BCJHL 70

KOOPMANS, LEO
79 Panini Sticker 282

KOPAT, VLADIMIR
98/9 Mir 145
99/0 Mir 191
00/1 Mir 381

KOPCZYNSKI, ADAM
74 Hellas MM-Jenkki 99
73/4 Williams Finnish 94

KOPEC, DAN
90/1 7th..Sketch WHL 227
91/2 7th...Sketch WHL 204
90/1 Brandon Wheat Kings

KOPECKY, JAN
99/0 DS 123
98/9 OFS 223
99/0 OFS 46, 471, 498
00/1 OFS 96
01/2 OFS 195

KOPECKY, TOMAS
02/3 Choice Prospects 23
00/1 UD Prospects 71
02/3 Grand Rapids Griffins

KÖPF, ERNST
94/5 DEL 98
96/7 DEL 283
95 Panini Worlds 71
94 Semic 284
95 Semic 168
92 Semic Sticker 181
93 Semic Sticker 161
92/3 Upper Deck 372

KOPINSKI, PHIL
99/0 Muskegon Fury

KOPITZ, LASSE
01/2 UD DEL 268

KOPOT, ARTIM
91/2 Upper Deck WJC 9

KOPRIVA, BRETISLAV
94/5 APS 300
95/6 APS 124

KOPTA, PETR
94/5 DEL 425
95/6 DEL 112
96/7 DEL 55

KOPTIN, NIKOLAI
00/1 Mir 345

KORAB, JERRY
74/5 Loblaws
73/4 Nabisco s 16
72/3 O-Pee-Chee 285
73/4 O-Pee-Chee 203
74/5 O-Pee-Chee 354
75/6 O-Pee-Chee 192
76/7 O-Pee-Chee 27
77/8 O-Pee-Chee 128
78/9 O-Pee-Chee 231
79/0 O-Pee-Chee 74
80/1 O-Pee-Chee 300
81/2 O-Pee-Chee 145
81/2 OPC Sticker 240
83/4 OPC/Topps Sticker 297
82/3 Post [LosA.]
83/4 Souhaits Keychain [Kings]
75/6 Topps 192
76/7 Topps 27
77/8 Topps 128
78/9 Topps 231
79/0 Topps 74
81/2 Topps 97 [West]
71/2 Toronto Sun Photo
74/5 BUFF
79/0 BUFF / Bells Market
80/1 LOSA 6
73/4 VANC / Royal Bank

KORBELA, JAROSLAV
82 Semic Sticker 95

KORBER, DANIEL
94/5 DEL 279
95/6 DEL 275
96/7 DEL 171

KÖRBER, DANIEL
98/9 DEL 17

KÖRBER, HANNES
99/0 Eishockey 30

KORCHINSKI, LARRY
83/4 Saskatoon Blades

KORDIC, DAN
97/8 Pa. Invincible R-142
91/2 Pinnacle 338
97/8 Pi. Be A Player 158, ✍ Aut. 158
91/2 Pro Set 553
90/1 7th..Sketch WHL 40
91/2 PHIL / J.C. Penney
96/7 PHIL / Ocean Spray
94/5 Hershey Bears

KORDIC, JOHN
90/1 O-Pee-Chee 401
90/1 Panini/TOR H
90/1 Pro Set 536
91/2 Pro Set 468
85/6 MONT
86/7 MONT
87/8 MONT
87/8 MONT / Vachon 57
87/8 MONT / Vachon 58
91/2 QUÉB / Petro-Canada

KORESHKOV, ALEXANDER
98/9 Mir 17

99/0 Mir 14
00/1 Metallurg 45

KORESHKOV, EVGENI
98/9 Mir 4, 128
99/0 Mir 13
00/1 Metallurg 44

KORHON, LUBOMIR
99/0 OFS 209
00/1 OFS 368
01/2 OFS 239

KORHONEN,
97/8 Hockey-Box

KORHONEN, AKI
98/9 Cardset 150
99/0 Cardset 209

KORHONEN, ERKKI
80/1 Mallasjuoma 60
78/9 SM-Liiga 84

KORHONEN, JUHA
71/2 Williams Finnish 368

KORHONEN, MARKUS
98/9 Cardset 75
00/1 Cardset 52, Mask. 6
02/3 Cardset 42
95/6 Sisu 136

KORHONEN, MATTI
66/7 Champion 106

KORINEK, PETR
96/7 APS 301
98/9 DS 59
99/0 DS 95
00/1 DS 32
96/7 DS Sticker 225
93/4 Jyvas Hyva 233
98/9 OFS 43, 464
99/0 OFS 125, 477
00/1 OFS 68, Star-17
01/2 OFS 218, -RE20D
93/4 Sisu 205
94/5 Sisu 244, FOI-17
95/6 Sisu 78, 374
95/6 Sisu Limited 68
97/8 UD Elitserien 181

KORJAKOFF, PEKKA
65/6 Hellas 51

KORKEAMAKI, JORMA
70/1 Kuvajulkaisut 331

KORMUNDA, PAVEL
99/0 Score 148

KORN, JIM
81/2 O-Pee-Chee 91
82/3 O-Pee-Chee 323
83/4 O-Pee-Chee 335
84/5 O-Pee-Chee 304
90/1 O-Pee-Chee 450
81/2 OPC Sticker 127
84/5 OPC Sticker 17
89/0 Panini Sticker 261
81/2 Topps 91 [West]
83/4 Vachon 91-67
86/7 BUFF / Blue Shield
79/0 DETR
80/1 DETR
88/9 NJER / Caretta
89/0 NJER
89/0 NJER / Caretta
82/3 TORO
83/4 TORO
84/5 TORO
85/6 TORO

KORNEEV, VLADIMIR
00/1 Mir 285

KORNEY, MIKE
75/6 O-Pee-Chee 342

KOROBKIN, SERGEI
98/9 Mir 51

KOROBOLIN, ALEXANDER
00/1 Mir 226
99/0 Hartford Wolf Pack

KOROL, DAVE
88/9 ProCards / Adirondack
89/0 ProCards IHL 121
90/1 ProCards 309
91/2 ProCards 328

KOROL, KEVIN
98/9 Kelowna Rockets
01/2 Regina Pats

KOROLEV, ANDREI
95/6 Leaf Elit Set 295
99/0 Mir 251
95/6 UD Elitserien 197

KOROLEV, EVGENY
99/0 Omega 146
95/6 Slapshot 325
99/0 Lowell Lock Monsters

KOROLEV, IGOR
98/9 Aurora 183
98/9 Be A Player 289, ✍ Aut. 289
99/0 BAP Mem. 207
95/6 Bowman 9
93/4 Donruss 297
94/5 Donruss 239
95/6 Donruss 352
98/9 Dynagon Ice 182
95/6 Fleer Metal 163
92/3 Fleer Ultra 395
93/4 Fleer Ultra 185
95/6 Fleer Ultra 327
93/4 Leaf 96
94/5 Leaf 90
95/6 Leaf 48
95/6 L. Limited 32
99/0 Millenium 231, ✍ Aut. 231
91/2 O-Pee-Chee 37R
92/3 OPC Premier 53
97/8 Omega 222
98/9 Omega 229
98/9 Pacific 416
99/0 Pacific 411

00/1 Pacific 396
02/3 Pacific Complete 369
98/9 Pa. Paramount 229
99/0 Pa. Paramount 227
97/8 Pa. Revolution 135
95/6 Panini Sticker 215
96/7 Panini Sticker 199
97/8 Panini Sticker 159
98/9 Panini Sticker 163
00/1 Panini Sticker 99
92/3 Parkhurst 158
93/4 Parkhurst 446
95/6 Parkhurst 227
94/5 Parkie SE156
92/3 Pinnacle 417
95/6 Pi. Summit 28
95/6 Pi. Zenith 63
95/6 Playoff 327
96/7 Playoff 407
95/6 POG 291
93/4 Power Play 214
93/4 Premier 409
92/3 Red Ace Blue 10
92/3 Red Ace Violet 15
93/4 Score 271
94 Semic 161
93 Semic Sticker 145
95/6 SP 168
00/1 Stadium 136
95/6 Topps 146
00/1 Topps 267
95/6 To. Finest 84
98/9 To. Finest 47
93/4 To. Stadium 119
94/5 To. Stadium 46
95/6 To. Stadium 131
02/3 T. Total 389
99/0 Ult. Victory 83
92/3 Upper Deck 338
92/3 Upper Deck 581
92/3 Upper Deck CC2
92/3 Upper Deck ER3
93/4 Upper Deck 353
94/5 Upper Deck 184, 344
95/6 Upper Deck 299, SE-90
00/1 Upper Deck 393
01/2 Upper Deck 268
95/6 UD BAP 135, ✍ S135
95/6 UD CC 257
96/7 UD CC 202
96 Wien 145
96/7 PHOE / Coca-Cola
99/0 TORO / Pizza Pizza 16
95/6 WINN
96/7 Michigan K-Wings

KOROLL, CLIFF
77/8 Coke
70/1 Eddie Sargent 37
71/2 Eddie Sargent 35
72/3 Eddie Sargent 59
70/1 Esso Power Player
74/5 Loblaws
70/1 O-Pee-Chee 147
71/2 O-Pee-Chee 209
72/3 O-Pee-Chee 222
73/4 O-Pee-Chee 28
74/5 O-Pee-Chee 35
75/6 O-Pee-Chee 139
76/7 O-Pee-Chee 242
76/7 OPC 382
77/8 O-Pee-Chee 146
78/9 O-Pee-Chee 239
79/0 O-Pee-Chee 102
73/4 Topps 28
74/5 Topps 35
75/6 Topps 139
76/7 Topps 242
77/8 Topps 146
78/9 Topps 239
79/0 Topps 102
71/2 Toronto Sun Photo
79/0 CHIC
80/1 CHIC / Brown

KOROLYUK, ALEXANDER
99/0 Millenium 215, ✍ Aut. 215
00/1 Mir Fetisov 1
99/0 Omega 207
98/9 Pacific 383
99/0 Pacific 373
00/1 Pacific 359
99/0 Pa. Paramount 205
00/1 Panini Sticker 205
94/5 Parkie SE228
94/5 SP 165
95/6 SP 179
00/1 Stadium 108
99/0 Topps 235
00/1 Topps 268
99/0 To. Chrome 235
99/0 To. Gold Label 82
94/5 Upper Deck 517
01/2 Upper Deck 148
99/0 UD MVP Cup 158
00/1 UD Vintage 303
01/2 Victory 301
97/8 Kentucky Tho'blades
98/9 Kentucky Tho'blades

KOROTKOV, KONSTANTIN
92/3 Classic 56
91/2 Upper Deck 654
91/2 Upper Deck WJC 15

KOROVKIN, NIKITA
00/1 Kamloops Blazers
01/2 Kamloops Blazers
02/3 Kamloops Blazers

KORPELA, KIMMO
72/3 Williams Finnish 265

KORPISALO, JARI
98/9 Cardset Leij. 28
00/1 Cardset 226
02/3 Cardset 43
98/9 DEL 80
99/0 Eishockey 324

92/3 Jyvas Hyva 202
93/4 Jyvas Hyva 357
95 Leaf Latkaliiga 3
94 Semic 42
95 Semic 18
93 Semic Sticker 66
93/4 Sisu 223
94/5 Sisu 217, 378, FOI-9, MN-8, SS-2
95/6 Sisu 154, S-2
96/7 Sisu 161, 184, MA-8
95/6 Sisu Limited 22

KORSUNOV, VLADIMIR
00/1 Mir 265

KORTALAINEN, MIKA
96/7 Sisu MA-4

KORTELAINEN, MIKA
98/9 Cardset 46
99/0 Cardset 229
00/1 Cardset 21
02/3 Cardset 44
97/8 Hockey-Box
92/3 Jyvas Hyva 10
93/4 Sisu 104
94/5 Sisu 105
95/6 Sisu 8
96/7 Sisu 13
95/6 Sisu Limited 43

KORTESOJA, JARKKO
95/6 Sisu 69

KORTKO, ROGER
88/9 ProCards / Binghampton
84/5 NYIS / News 10
84/5 Springfield Indians 22
81/2 Saskatoon Blades

KOS, KYLE
97 Bowman 156, ✍ Aut.
99/0 Detroit Vipers

KOSIR, SASO
79 Panini Sticker 399

KOSIR, TOMAZ
79 Panini Sticker 396

KOSKELA, ILPO
66/7 Champion 109
70/1 Kuvajulkaisut 64
70/1 Kuvajulkaisut 177
72 Panda MM-Toronto
72 Semic Sticker 72
74 Semic Sticker 100
91 Semic Sticker 227
96/7 Sisu 193
77-79 Sports. FIN 52-1243
71/2 Williams Finnish 64
71/2 Williams Finnish 102
72/3 Williams Finnish 146
73/4 Williams Finnish 66
73/4 Williams Finnish 111

KOSKELA, PEKKA
78/9 SM-Liiga 102

KOSKELA, PENTTI
72 Panda MM-Toronto
71/2 Williams Finnish 178
72/3 Williams Finnish 126

KOSKELA, TERHO
94/5 Leaf Elit Set 58, SS-12
89/0 Semic Elitserien 275
90/1 Semic Elitserien 42
91/2 Semic Elitserien 292
92/3 Semic Elitserien 313

KOSKELA, TIMO
00/1 Cardset 158

KOSKENKORVA, KIMMO
00/1 Cardset 181
02/3 Cardset 45

KOSKI, COREY
98/9 Kelowna Rockets

KOSKI, PETRI
92/3 Jyvas Hyva 150
93/4 Jyvas Hyva 261
93/4 Sisu 286

KOSKILAHTI, JUKKA
78/9 SM-Liiga 214
73/4 Williams Finnish 286

KOSKIMAKI, TAPANI
66/7 Champion 6
70/1 Kuvajulkaisut 230
78/9 SM-Liiga 160
71/2 Williams Finnish 245

KOSKIMIES, HEIKKI
65/6 Hellas 155

KOSKINEN, HANNU
80/1 Mallasjuoma 88
82 Semic Sticker 44
82 Skopbank
78/9 SM-Liiga 120
77-79 Sports. FIN 86-2064

KOSKINEN, KALLE
98/9 Cardset 124
99/0 Cardset 71
00/1 Cardset 312
97/8 Hockey-Box
93/4 Sisu 142
93/4 Sisu 6
94/5 Sisu 39, J-5
95/6 Sisu 58
96/7 Sisu 56

KOSKINEN, KARI
70/1 Kuvajulkaisut 332

KOSKINEN, MATTI
66/7 Champion 118
71/2 Williams Finnish 282
73/4 Williams Finnish 199

KOSKINEN, TAPIO
74 Hellas MM-Jenkki 7
70/1 Kuvajulkaisut 195
80/1 Mallasjuoma 205
72 Panda MM-Toronto
78/9 SM-Liiga 230
71/2 Williams Finnish 87

72/3 Williams Finnish 250
73/4 Williams Finnish 249

KOSLOWSKI, THORSTEN
94/5 DEL 218

KOSOBUD, JOHN
96/7 Mississippi S'Wolves
99/0 Mississippi S'Wolves
99/0 Mississippi S'Wolves

KOSONEN, LAURI
70/1 Kuvajulkaisut 313
72/3 Williams Finnish 330

KOSTADINE, JASON
00/1 Hull Olympiques 13
01/2 Hull Olympiques 14
02/3 Québec Remparts

KOSTAL, JAN
99/0 OFS 136
00/1 OFS 181
01/2 OFS 199

KOSTELNAK, DAVID
99/0 Score 104

KOSTI, RICK
85/6 Moncton G'Flames

KOSTIAINEN, JOUNI
71/2 Williams Finnish 325

KOSTICHKIN, PAVEL
92/3 Classic Prospects 137
90/1 O-Pee-Chee 20R
91/2 O-Pee-Chee 17R

KOSTKA, ROBERT
94/5 APS 30
95/6 APS 134
96/7 APS 12
97/8 APS 150
96/7 DS Sticker 115
97/8 DS Sticker 189
98/9 OFS 211

KOSTNER, ERWIN
79 Panini Sticker 388
82 Semic Sticker 125
92 Semic Sticker 245

KOSTOLNY, MILAN
94/5 Slapshot / Detroit Jr. 20
95/6 Slapshot 228
94/5 Slapshot Memorial 94

KOSTOPOULOS, TOM
01/2 BAP Mem. 331
01/2 Parkhurst 342
01/2 SPx 214
01/2 UD PlayMakers Ltd 138
01/2 UD Premier 79
00/1 WBS Penguins
01/2 WBS Penguins
02/3 WBS Penguins
98/9 Sudbury Wolves 10
99/0 Sudbury Wolves 20
00/1 Sudbury Wolves 21

KOSTUCH, JEFF
95/6 Classic 93
91/2 7th...Sketch OHL 41
95/6 Hampton Roads
99/0 Rockford IceHogs
93/4 Owen Sound Platers

KOSTUCHENKO, M.
91/2 Air Canada SJHL 10

KOSTURIK, MARK
94/5 DEL 65
95/6 DEL 64, 435
96/7 DEL 216
98/9 DEL 185
99/0 Eishockey 226
00/1 UD DEL 92

KOSTYNSKI, DOUG
85/6 Moncton G'Flames
86/7 Moncton G'Flames

KOSYL, VALERY
74 Hellas MM-Jenkki 100
73/4 Williams Finnish 95

KOTALA, LUMIR
94/5 APS 136

KOTALIK, ALES
97/8 APS 288
01/2 BAP Mem. 361
02/3 Calder 57, -CR 3
00/1 DS 83
01/2 DS 57
02/3 O-Pee-Chee 297
98/9 OFS 414
99/0 OFS 280
00/1 OFS 19
01/2 OFS -UHI 35
02/3 Pacific 43
02/3 Pacific Complete 546
01/2 Parkhurst 306
01/2 PS Titanium Draft 111
02/3 Quest for the Cup -CC 2
01/2 SPx 199
01/2 SPx Rookie RR4
02/3 Topps 297
02/3 To. Limited 297
01/2 UD Honor Roll 66
01/2 UD Ice 46
01/2 UD Premier 54
02/3 UD Vintage 349

KOTASEK, MARTIN
94/5 APS 200
95/6 APS 48
96/7 APS 46
97/8 APS 140
98/9 DS 107
99/0 DS 12
97/8 DS Sticker 260
98/9 OFS 123
99/0 OFS 210
00/1 OFS 367

KOTKANIEMI, MIKAEL
93/4 Jyvas Hyva 349
93/4 Sisu 231
94/5 Sisu 125
95/6 Sisu 159

KOTKAS, PENTTI
65/6 Hellas 141

KOTNAUER, FRANZ
79 Panini Sticker 306

KOTONSKI, ANDRZEJ
92 Semic Sticker 282

KOTRLA, JINDRICH
95/6 APS 163
96/7 APS 185
99/0 DS 67
98/9 OFS 11
99/0 OFS 339
00/1 OFS 149
01/2 OFS 157

KOTSCHNEW, DMITRI
01/2 UD DEL 113

KOTSOPOULOS, CHRIS
82/3 O-Pee-Chee 124
84/5 O-Pee-Chee 73
87/8 O-Pee-Chee 244
89/0 O-Pee-Chee 279
82/3 OPC/Topps Sticker 132
89/0 opcSticker 180-38
82/3 Post [Hart.]
89/0 ProCards AHL 309
83/4 Souhaits Keychain [Whalers]
82/3 HART / Jr. Whalers
83/4 HART / Jr. Whalers
84/5 HART / Jr. Whalers
85/6 TORO
86/7 TORO
86/7 TORO
87/8 TORO / 5x8
87/8 TORO / P.L.A.Y. 16
88/9 TORO / P.L.A.Y. 16

KOTSOPOULOS, EVAN
01/2 Guelph Storm

KOTYK, SEAMUS
99 Bowman 142
94 Québec Pee Wee 565
01/2 Cleveland Barons
99/0 Ottawa 67's
00/1 Ottawa 67's 20

KOUBA, LADISLAV
00/1 Red Deer Rebels

KOUDELKA, MARTIN
96/7 APS 160
97/8 DS Sticker 143
98/9 OFS 379
99/0 OFS 363
00/1 OFS 50

KOULIKOV, ALEXANDR
93/4 Humberside Hawks 17

KOULIKOV, VIACHESLAV
02/3 Dundee Texol Stars

KOUNOVSKY, PETR
99/0 OFS 330

KOURILIN, EVGENY
98/9 Anchorage Aces

KOURULA, AARRE
80/1 Mallasjuoma 48

KOUTUANIEMI, JOUNI
80/1 Mallasjuoma 102

KOVACEVIC, JURE
95/6 Slapshot 267

KOVACS, BILL
90/1 7th..Sketch OHL 385
91/2 7th...Sketch OHL 348
89/0 Sudbury Wolves
90/1 Sudbury Wolves

KOVACS, CSABA
79 Panini Sticker 268

KOVACS, FRANK
94/5 DEL 348
90/1 7th..Sketch WHL 179
91/2 7th...Sketch WHL 232
92/3 Dayton Bombers
90/1 Newmarket Saints
95/6 Saint John Flames
97/8 Sheffield Steelers
87/8 Regina Pats
88/9 Regina Pats
89/0 Regina Pats

KOVACS, JOHN
90/1 7th..Sketch LHJMQ 74
91/2 7th...Sketch LHJMQ 240

KOVALCHUK, ILYA
01/2 Adrenaline 203, ✍ 203, RR 3
01/2 Atomic 104, RR 2
02/3 Atomic 5, -CF 3, -PC 2, -SC 1
02/3 BAP All-Star 102
01/2 BAP Draft Florida 1
01/2 BAP Mem. 372
02/3 BAP Mem. 65, 202, ✂ FP2, ✂ FG3, ✂ HSHSJer 5
01/2 BAP Update ✂ HSHSJers
02/3 Between the Pipes ✂ GN1
01/2 Bowman 159, ✂ FFJ, ✂ FFS, ✂ FFDS, ✂ FFR, ✍ YSA
02/3 Bowman 165
02/3 Calder 2
01/2 Crown Royale 147, CA 2, RR 2
02/3 Crown Royale 5, -LOR 3, RP 2, ✂ GWDP 1, ✂ GWJ 2
01/2 eTopps 31
02/3 eTopps 10
02/3 Exclusive 8, -DFG 3, -GE 2, -MO 3
02/3 First Edition 134, 318, 342, 383, 384, 424H, ✂ Jers., ✂ DGJ 14, ✂ HSHSJers 16

02/3 First Edition 383
01/2 Heads Up 103
02/3 Heads Up 6, -EIT 2, -HF 2, -ITN 3, -SM 2, ✂ GWQ 2, ✂ GWQ 35, / Bobble
02/3 In The GU 5, 105, ✂ E10, ✂ F2, ✂ GUJ10, ✂ SJ10, ✂ T7
02/3 McDonald's 3, -CA 2, ✂ JP 2
99/0 Mir 141
00/1 Mir 127, 296
01/2 O-Pee-Chee 331
02/3 O-Pee-Chee 11
01/2 Pacific 454
02/3 Pacific 18, -CCA 2, -IZ 2, -L 2, -MA 2, -MI 9, -SM 2, ✂✍ StickJers
02/3 Pacific Complete 105
01/2 PTC Calder 2
01/2 PTC Draft 1
01/2 PTC High Voltage 2
01/2 PTC Collectibles 2
01/2 PTC National 1
01/2 PTC Rookie 2
01/2 Parkhurst 295, ✂ HSHSJers
02/3 Parkhurst 24, ✂ FP2, ✂ GJ19, ✂ SJ19, ✂ HSHSJers, ✂ NH1, ✂ PP9, ✂ TT9
02/3 Parkhurst Retro 54, ✂ RJ37, ✂ RSJ25, ✂ HSHSJers, ✂ RM11, ✂ RR6
01/2 Pr. Stock 113, MiT 2, RR 2, -PS 94, ✂ GUG 6
02/3 Pr. Stock Reserve -RE 1, ✂ 103
01/2 PS Titanium 147, TSS 22, TRT 2, ✂ DSJ 23, ✂ DSJ 39
01/2 PS Titanium Draft 105, ✂ 7
02/3 PS Titanium 5, -S 1, ✂ GWJ 3
02/3 Quest for the Cup 5, -CTC 3
01/2 Signature 207, ✍ Aut. 207, ✂ FP2, ✂ GUE2, ✂ GJ45, ✂ GSJ45, ✂ HSHSJers 5, ✂ ITN2, ✂ IB7, ✂ TM2
02/3 Signature 39, ✍ 39, ✂ FS7, ✂ SGJ10, ✂ TQ12
01/2 SP Authentic ✍ 175, ✍ SotT, ✍ SotTT
02/3 SP Authentic 5, 108, ✍ SotTD (x2)
01/2 SP GU 66
02/3 SP GU 2, ✂ AF (x2), ✂ PC, ✂ FF (x2), ✂ PH, ✍ Sig
02/3 Sports Vault 4
01/2 SPx 148, -RT
02/3 SPx 3, ✂ WM
01/2 SPx Rookie RR2
01/2 Stadium 121, ✍ LSS
02/3 Stadium 10, -WS-8, ✂ YSS1, ✂ YSD1, ✍ LSS
01/2 Topps 331
02/3 Topps 11, CC6, HHU17, OTG12, ✍ SF
01/2 Topps All-Star Game 6
01/2 To. Chrome 149
02/3 To. Chrome 11
01/2 To. Heritage 138, ✍ CAI
02/3 To. Heritage 79, -Light 79
02/3 To. Limited 11
01/2 To. Reserve 115
02/3 T. Total 335, TTC1, TT7
01/2 UD PlayMakers Ltd 104, / PM
02/3 UD Superstars 22, 253
01/2 Ultimate Mem. ✂ DD, ✂ Emb., ✂ Jers., ✂ S&J, ✂ ITN, ✂ NP
02/3 Ultimate Mem. ✂ DD, ✂ Emb, ✂ FO, ✂ GUJ, ✂ GUSJ, ✂ ITN, ✂ NP, ✂ Num
01/2 Upper Deck 211, 242
02/3 Upper Deck 7, -SS1, ✂ DM, ✂ HS, ✂ OR, ✂ PL, ✂ GJ, ✂✍ SGJ
02/3 UD Artistic 4, R4, GD5, ✂ AT, / ✍ Art
01/2 UD Challenge 95, CR2
02/3 UD Classic 5, PS1, ✂ HR
01/2 UD Collectors
01/2 UD Honor Roll 100
02/3 UD Honor 3
01/2 UD Ice 44, ✍ CCA
01/2 UD Mask 132
02/3 UD Mask 6, ✂ PG
01/2 UD MVP 221
02/3 UD MVP 10, HN1, SO2, VF2
02/3 UD Piece 3
01/2 UD Premier 109, ✂ B, ✍ SigG
02/3 UD Premier 2, ✂ Jers, ✂ Patch, ✍ Sig
02/3 UD Rookie 6, 114, ✂ DJ, ✂ S, ✍ TD
01/2 UD Top Shelf 68
02/3 UD Top Shelf 4, ✂ CP, ✂ GO, ✂ R
01/2 UD Vintage 275
02/3 UD Vintage 13, 262, 315, GB 13, T4
01/2 Vanguard 103, PP 2, ✂ DGM 42
02/3 Vanguard 6, -EMW 1, -IF 2, -VT 7, ✂ GWJ 3

01/2 Victory 441
02/3 Victory 10, -NP31

KOVALENKO, ANDREI
98/9 Be A Player 202, ✍ Aut. 202
93/4 Donruss 278
94/5 Donruss 6
95/6 Donruss 374
94/5 Fleer 178
92/3 Fleer Ultra 387, -UI 9
93/4 Fleer Ultra 144
94/5 Fleer Ultra 175
95 Globe 176
93/4 Leaf 122
93/4 Leaf GLR 6
94/5 Leaf 71
95/6 Leaf 130
96/7 Maggers 83
96/7 Metal Univ. 54
91/2 O-Pee-Chee 18R
92/3 OPC Premier 93
99/0 Pacific 75
00/1 Pacific 86
01/2 Pacific 33
97/8 Pacific CC 51
97/8 Pa. Paramount 76
98/9 Pa. Revolution 55
93/4 Panini Sticker 71
96/7 Panini Sticker 42
97/8 Panini Sticker 209
98/9 Panini Sticker 194
99/0 Panini Sticker 46
00/1 Panini Sticker 28
95 Panini Worlds 42
92/3 Parkhurst 150
92/3 Parkhurst 223
93/4 Parkhurst 167
95/6 Parkhurst 51, 382
92/3 Pinnacle 395
93/4 Pinnacle 171
94/5 Pinnacle 128
96/7 Pinnacle 152
97/8 Pi. Certified 106
97/8 Pi. Inside 177
97/8 Pi. Totally 106
95/6 Playoff 138
94/5 POG 196
95/6 POG 75
93/4 Power Play 200
93/4 Premier 124
93/4 Premier 198
93/4 Prmr. - BG-Top. 17
94/5 Premier 97
92/3 Red Ace Blue 34
92/3 Red Ace Violet 16
93/4 Score 174
94/5 Score 39
95/6 Score 253
96/7 Score 196
97/8 Score 178
95 Semic 133
92 Semic Sticker 117
96/7 SP 58
93/4 To. Stadium 77
99/0 Ult. Victory 17
92/3 Upper Deck 567
92/3 Upper Deck CC17
92/3 Upper Deck ER14
92/3 Upper Deck G19
93/4 Upper Deck 85
94/5 Upper Deck 272
95/6 Upper Deck 446
00/1 Upper Deck 246
95/6 UD BAP 118, ✍ S118
96/7 UD Black Diam. 51
95/6 UD CC 54
96/7 UD CC 137
97/8 UD Coll. Choice 90
00/1 UD Vintage 30
96 Wien 144
96/7 EDMO
97/8 EDMO
92/3 QUÉB / Petro-Canada
94/5 QUÉB / Burger King

KOVALEV, ALEX
01/2 Adrenaline 153, ✂ GWJ 35
01/2 Atomic 78, Stat 17, TN 11
98/9 Aurora 123
99/0 Aurora 117
00/1 Aurora 117
02/3 BAP All-Star 47, ✂ ASJ
98/9 Be A Player 92, ✍ Aut. 92
99/0 BAP Mem. 71
00/1 BAP Mem. 77
01/2 BAP Mem. 168, ✂ ASJ, ✂ ASE, ✂ ASN, ✂ AST, ✂ CoO
02/3 BAP Mem. 315
02/3 BAP Mem. 46, ✂ ASJ28, ✂ TM15
01/2 Bowman 56
02/3 Bowman 49
02/3 Calder 45
93/4 Classic 137
92/3 Classic Prospects 10
92/3 Classic Prospects 74
92/3 Classic Prospects BC1
92/3 Classic Prospects LP2
93/4 Cla. Prospects 52, ✍ Aut.
99/0 Crown Royale 113
01/2 Crown Royale 115, ✂ TT 17
02/3 Crown Royale 77
93/4 Donruss 220
94/5 Donruss 268
95/6 Donruss 216
96/7 Donruss 176
96/7 Do. Canadian 41
98/9 Dynagon Ice 122
99/0 Dynagon Ice 160
02/3 Exclusive 137, ✂ GWJ 20
02/3 First Edition 199, ✂ TSL

15
94/5 Flair 112, SP-4
94/5 Fleer 133
96/7 Fleer 69
95/6 Fleer Metal 95, MW-3
92/3 Fleer Ultra 137, -UI 10
93/4 Fleer Ultra 115
94/5 Fleer Ultra 331
95/6 Fleer Ultra 275
96/7 Fl. Ultra 107
95 Globe 177
01/2 Heads Up 77, ✂ JQ 18, ✂ JQ 29
02/3 Heads Up 99
02/3 In The GU ✂ T1
93/4 Leaf 147
94/5 Leaf 92
95/6 Leaf 203
96/7 Leaf 135
94/5 L. Limited 59
95/6 L. Limited 48
96/7 L. Preferred 96
94/5 McDonald's McD-38
96/7 Metal Univ. 97
99/0 Millenium 197, ✍ Aut. 197
01/2 O-Pee-Chee 95
02/3 O-Pee-Chee 147
92/3 OPC Premier 126
98/9 Omega 196
99/0 Omega 190
98/9 Pacific 294
99/0 Pacific 341
00/1 Pacific 330
01/2 Pacific 314, WAS 8
02/3 Pacific 309
02/3 Pacific Complete 3
97/8 Pacific CC 119
97/8 Pa. Dynagon 79, T-19, T-72
97/8 Pa. Invincible 87
97/8 Pa. Paramount 116
98/9 Pa. Paramount 153
99/0 Pa. Paramount 190
00/1 Pa. Paramount 199
98/9 Pa. Revolution 119
94/5 Panini Sticker 83
95/6 Panini Sticker 106
96/7 Panini Sticker 104
97/8 Panini Sticker 85
98/9 Panini Sticker 84
99/0 Panini Sticker 134
00/1 Panini Sticker 84
92/3 Parkhurst 109
92/3 Parkhurst 225
93/4 Parkhurst 130
93/4 Parkhurst 238
94/5 Parkhurst 142, V24
95/6 Parkhurst 139
00/1 Parkhurst P-84
01/2 Parkhurst 17
02/3 Parkhurst 2, ✂ TT41
02/3 Parkhurst Retro 4
94/5 Parkie SE ES-18
92/3 Pinnacle 403
93/4 Pinnacle 76
93/4 Pinnacle T2K1 7
94/5 Pinnacle 107, WE12
96/7 Pinnacle 45
97/8 Pinnacle 120
95/6 Pi. Summit 97
96/7 Pi. Summit 82
95/6 Playoff 67
94/5 POG 163
95/6 POG 184
93/4 Power Play 159
93/4 Premier 187
94/5 Premier 185
00/1 Premier Plus 46
99/0 Prism 115
01/2 Pr. Stock 77, ✂ GUG 77
02/3 Pr. Stock Reserve 80
00/1 PS Titanium 76, ✂ GUG-135, ✂ GUG-155
01/2 PS Titanium 112, ✂ DSJ 36
02/3 PS Titanium 81
00/1 PS Titanium Draft ✂ 84
02/3 Quest for the Cup 65
92/3 Red Ace Blue 8
92/3 Red Ace Violet 17
99/0 Revolution 119
00/1 Revolution 119
93/4 Score 203
93/4 Score IS 19
95/6 Score 79
96/7 Score 61
97/8 Score 156
97/8 Score NYRa. 7
94/5 Select 66
95/6 Select CE 88
00/1 Signature 24
01/2 Signature ✂ IB8
02/3 Signature 10, ✍ 10, ✂ SGJ69, ✂ TQ8
95/6 SBx Emotion 113
95/6 SBx Impact 109
96/7 SBx Impact 80
94/5 SP 76
95/6 SP 99
96/7 SP 104, HC-7
97/8 SP Authentic 102
99/0 SP Authentic 69
00/1 SP Authentic 71
01/2 SP Authentic 69, ✍ SotT, ✍ SotTT
02/3 SP Authentic 72
01/2 SP GU 45, ✂ AF, ✂ AFD, ✂ AFT, ✂✍ IS, ✂✍ ISD
02/3 SP Game-Used ✂ AF (x2), ✂ PC, ✂ TG
02/3 Sports Vault 114
99/0 SPx 124
01/2 SPx 51
02/3 SPx 60
99/0 Stadium 22

00/1 Stadium 46, PP2
01/2 Stadium 35, NHLP6
02/3 Stadium 35, -WS15
91/2 Star Pics 48
95/6 Super Sticker 81
95/6 Topps 90, YS9
99/0 Topps 66
00/1 Topps 31
01/2 Topps 95, OTG5, SM14, SG8
02/3 Topps 147
99/0 To. Chrome 66
00/1 To. Chrome 29
01/2 To. Chrome 95
02/3 To. Chrome 89
98/9 To. Finest 113
99/0 To. Gold Label 80
00/1 To. Gold Label 45
00/1 To. Heritage 123
01/2 To. Heritage 52
02/3 To. Heritage 95, ✂ GS, ✂ GSB
02/3 To. Limited 147
96/7 To. Picks 79
01/2 To. Reserve 42, ✂ TR
93/4 To. Stadium 129
95/6 To. Stadium 218
00/1 To. Stars 70
02/3 T. Total 162
00/1 UD Heroes 95
01/2 UD PlayMakers Ltd 78
02/3 UD Superstars ✂ CAST
91/2 Upper Deck 655
92/3 Upper Deck 573
92/3 Upper Deck 633
92/3 Upper Deck CC11
92/3 Upper Deck ER10
92/3 Upper Deck G13
92/3 Upper Deck WG9
93/4 Upper Deck 27, HT-7, HB-6, SP-101
94/5 Upper Deck 207, 567, SP-49
95/6 Upper Deck 132, SE-56
96/7 Upper Deck 103
97/8 Upper Deck 319
99/0 Upper Deck 275
00/1 Upper Deck 368
01/2 Upper Deck 139, GA6, SS13, ✂ PF, ✂ PoaNT
02/3 Upper Deck 140, ✂ PW, ✂ UDPL
02/3 UD Artistic 70, R70, / Art
95/6 UD BAP 182, LL15, ✍ S182
96/7 UD Black Diam. 27
99/0 UD Black Diam. 70
01/2 UD Challenge 67
02/3 UD Classic 78
95/6 UD CC 234
96/7 UD CC 176
91/2 Upper Deck WJC 16
99/0 UD G. Reserve 275
01/2 UD Honor Roll -DPuck
02/3 UD Honor 57
01/2 UD Ice 114
92/3 UD Locker 54
01/2 UD Mask 78
99/0 UD MVP 170
00/1 UD MVP 141
01/2 UD MVP 154
02/3 UD MVP 145, SO12, SD, ST, Souv.
99/0 UD MVP Cup 147
99/0 UD Ovation 47
02/3 UD Piece 71, ✂ EC
01/2 UD Premier ✍ Sig
02/3 UD Premier 35, ✂ Jers
00/1 UD Pros&Prosp. 70
02/3 UD Rookie 64
01/2 UD Top Shelf 33
02/3 UD Top Shelf 72, ✍ Sig
00/1 UD Vintage 291
01/2 UD Vintage 200, 207, 208
02/3 UD Vintage 206, 284, GB 206
01/2 Vanguard ✂ DGM 25, ✂ DGM 39
02/3 Vanguard 80
99/0 Victory 241
00/1 Victory 190
01/2 Victory 281, 416
02/3 Victory 173, -NP37
99/0 WGretzky 140

KOVALEV, ANDREI
94/5 DEL 423
96/7 DEL 81
98/9 DEL 22
99/0 Eishockey 130
91/2 O-Pee-Chee 38R
91 Semic Sticker 93
00/1 UD DEL 207, P9
01/2 UD DEL 221

KOVANEN, TOMMI
99/0 Cardset 295
96/7 Sisu 70

KOVAR, ROBIN
01/2 Vancouver Giants
01/2 Vancouver Giants

KOVARIK, MARTIN
94/5 APS 143
95/6 APS 247

KOVIN, V.
80 Olympic USSR

KOWALCHUCK, PETER
52/3 Anonymous 173

KOWALCHUK, KEVIN
83/4 Saskatoon Blades
83/4 Saskatoon Blades
84/5 Saskatoon Blades
84/5 Saskatoon Blades

KOWALCHUK, SHELDON
88/9 Brandon Wheat Kings
88/9 Brandon Wheat Kings
KOWALCZYK, PAVEL
94/5 APS 185
95/6 APS 34
96/7 APS 35
97/8 APS 55
97/8 DS 103
98/9 DS 105
99/0 DS 173
96/7 DS Sticker 96
97/8 DS Sticker 288
98/9 OFS 117
99/0 OFS 424
KOWALSKI, ED
99/0 San Angelo Outlaws
99/0 San Angelo Outlaws
KOWALSKI, SCOTT
91/2 Avant Garde BCJHL 53
91/2 Nanaimo Clippers
91/2 Nanaimo Clippers
KOWALSKY, RICK
93/4 Cla. Prospects 136
94/5 Hampton Roads
94/5 Hampton Roads
95/6 Hampton Roads
95/6 Hampton Roads
96/7 Hampton Roads
96/7 Hampton Roads
97/8 Hampton Roads
97/8 Hampton Roads
98/9 Hampton Roads
98/9 Hampton Roads
99/0 Hampton Roads
99/0 Hampton Roads
00/1 Kudos 61
98/9 Portland Pirates
98/9 Portland Pirates
89/0 Soo Greyhounds
89/0 Soo Greyhounds
93/4 Soo Greyhounds 13
93/4 Soo Greyhounds 13
91 7th..Sketch Mem.Cup 11
90/1 7th..Sketch OHL 162
91/2 7th...Sketch OHL 330
KOZACK, KELLY
83/4 Brandon Wheat Kings
83/4 Brandon Wheat Kings
KOZAK, DON
74/5 Loblaws
74/5 O-Pee-Chee 111
74/5 O-Pee-Chee 98
75/6 O-Pee-Chee 276
76/7 O-Pee-Chee 185
77/8 O-Pee-Chee 316
79/0 O-Pee-Chee 342
74/5 Topps 111
74/5 Topps 98
75/6 Topps 276
76/7 Topps 185
KOZAK, GEORGE
96/7 Pensacola Ice Pilots
96/7 Pensacola Ice Pilots
97/8 Pensacola Ice Pilots
97/8 Pensacola Ice Pilots
KOZAK, TODD
91/2 Air Canada SJHL C23
92/3 MPS SJHL 90
KOZAKOWSKI, JEFF
99/0 Mobile Mysticks
99/0 Mobile Mysticks
KOZITSYN, ARTEM
02/3 Val d'Or Foreurs
02/3 Val d'Or Foreurs
KOZJEVNIKOV, ALEXANDER
89/0 Semic Elitserien 17
82 Semic Sticker 73
KOZLOV, ANDREI
94/5 Erie Panthers
94/5 Erie Panthers
KOZLOV, VIKTOR
01/2 Adrenaline 82
98/9 Aurora 81
99/0 Aurora 63
00/1 Aurora 62
98/9 Be A Player 60, ✍ Aut. 60
99/0 BAP Mem. 5
00/1 BAP Mem. 171
01/2 BAP Mem. 259, ✂ ASJ, ✂ ASE, ✂ ASN, ✂ AST
95/6 Bowman 159
92/3 Classic 61
92/3 Classic 62
93/4 Classic 6
93/4 Classic - Top Ten DP6
94/5 Classic 113, R12, T62
92/3 Classic Four Sport 225
92/3 Classic Four Sport BC12
93/4 Cla. 4 Sport 190
92/3 Classic Prospects 93
92/3 Classic Prospects BC9
92/3 Classic Prospects LP4
93/4 Cla. Prospects IA17
01/2 Crown Royale 64
95/6 Donruss 171
98/9 Dynagon Ice 82
99/0 Dynagon Ice 90
95/6 Edge Ice 145, C-10, PR-4
02/3 First Edition 168
94/5 Fleer Ultra 366, P-4
97/8 FLOR / Winn-Dixie
97/8 FLOR / Winn-Dixie
01/2 FLOR
01/2 FLOR
95/6 Kansas City Blades
95/6 Kansas City Blades
94/5 Leaf 451,P-8
95/6 Leaf 73
94/5 L. Limited 21
95/6 L. Limited 77
94/5 McDonald's McD-33
99/0 Millenium 110, ✍ Aut. 110
00/1 Mir Fetisov 4
98/9 NHL Power Play
01/2 O-Pee-Chee 135
02/3 O-Pee-Chee 132
98/9 OPC Chrome 83
98/9 Omega 103
99/0 Omega 98, WAS-5
98/9 Pacific 223
99/0 Pacific 173
00/1 Pacific 179
01/2 Pacific 172
02/3 Pacific Complete 248
97/8 Pacific CC 125
97/8 Pa. Crown Roy. 58
98/9 Pa. Crown Roy. 59
97/8 Pa. Dynagon 113, T-64
97/8 Pa. Paramount 166
98/9 Pa. Paramount 97
99/0 Pa. Paramount 100
00/1 Pa. Paramount 105
98/9 Pa. Revolution 62
95/6 Panini Sticker 279
96/7 Panini Sticker 282
97/8 Panini Sticker 231
98/9 Panini Sticker 62
99/0 Panini Sticker 60
00/1 Panini Sticker 33
95/6 Parkhurst 187, 515
00/1 Parkhurst P-143
01/2 Parkhurst 171, ✂ PJ45, ✂ T10
94/5 Parkie SE159, seV43
94/5 Pinnacle 477, 481, RTP5
95/6 Pinnacle 99, GG-16
95/6 Pi. Summit 142
95/6 POG 229
99/0 Prism 62
00/1 Private Stock 44
01/2 PS Titanium 60
99/0 Revolution 64
00/1 Revolution 63
92/3 SANJ / Pacific Bell
92/3 SANJ / Pacific Bell
94/5 Score TR10
95/6 Score 114
97/8 Score 223
94/5 Select 174, YE-6
93 Semic Sticker 140
00/1 Signature 178, ✍ Aut. 26
94/5 SP P-3
97/8 SP Authentic 70
99/0 SP Authentic 39
99/0 SPx 71
00/1 SPx 30
00/1 Stadium 63
95/6 Topps 357
98/9 Topps 83
00/1 Topps 138
01/2 Topps 135
02/3 Topps 132
00/1 To. Chrome 103
94/5 Topps Finest 46
99/0 To. Gold Label 84
02/3 To. Limited 132
95/6 To. Stadium 137
02/3 T. Total 135
00/1 UD Heroes 53
99/0 Ult. Victory 40
92/3 Upper Deck 613
94/5 Upper Deck 265, C3, SP-162
95/6 Upper Deck 92
96/7 Upper Deck 152
97/8 Upper Deck 359
98/9 Upper Deck 98
99/0 Upper Deck 232
00/1 Upper Deck 305
01/2 Upper Deck 303, ✂ PoaN, ✂ PoaND, ✂ PoaNT
02/3 Upper Deck 320
94/5 UD BAP R158, ✍ 153
95/6 UD CC 252
96/7 UD CC 237
97/8 UD Coll. Choice 217
98/9 UD G. Reserve 98
99/0 UD G. Reserve 232
00/1 UD Legends 56
01/2 UD Mask 39
99/0 UD MVP 86
00/1 UD MVP 83
01/2 UD MVP 79
02/3 UD MVP 79
99/0 UD MVP Cup 78, GC
00/1 UD Pros&Prosp. 38
00/1 UD Vintage 152
01/2 UD Vintage 107, 113
02/3 UD Vintage 107, 273
00/1 Vanguard 46
99/0 Victory 123
00/1 Victory 104
01/2 Victory 148
99/0 WGretzky 76
96 Wien 147
KOZLOV, VYACHESLAV (SLAVA)
01/2 Adrenaline 23
98/9 Aurora 63
98/9 Be A Player 49, ✍ Aut. 49
99/0 BAP Mem. 290
00/1 BAP Mem. 4, ✂ TM-17, ✂ TM-35
02/3 BAP Mem. 243 [w/ Hasek]
92/3 Bowman 300
95/6 Bowman 77
92/3 Classic Prospects 135
93/4 Cla. Prospects 214
93/4 Donruss 91
94/5 Donruss 180
95/6 Donruss 134
96/7 Donruss 19
97/8 Donruss 119
96/7 Do. Canadian 71
97/8 Do. Cdn. Ice SCS 25
95/6 Do. Elite 87
96/7 Do. Elite 81
97/8 Do. Elite 25
97/8 Do. Preferred 134
97/8 Do. Priority 130
98/9 Dynagon Ice 63
99/0 Dynagon Ice 74
95/6 Edge Ice C17
94/5 Flair 50
94/5 Fleer 61
96/7 Fleer 32
95/6 Fleer Metal 47
92/3 Fleer Ultra 50
93/4 Fleer Ultra 174
94/5 Fleer Ultra 284
95/6 Fleer Ultra 47
96/7 Fl. Ultra 52
93/4 Leaf 303
94/5 Leaf 236
95/6 Leaf 210, RTTC-8
96/7 Leaf 196
97/8 Leaf 31
94/5 L. Limited 55
96/7 L. Limited 88
96/7 L. Preferred LS 38
97/8 Limited 91
96/7 Maggers 53
96/7 Metal Univ. 47
00/1 Mir Fetisov 27
92/3 O-Pee-Chee 235
01/2 O-Pee-Chee 228
92/3 OPC Premier 71
97/8 Omega 81
98/9 Pacific 196
99/0 Pacific 140
00/1 Pacific 149
01/2 Pacific 142
02/3 Pacific 44
02/3 Pacific Complete 127
97/8 Pacific CC 267
97/8 Pa. Crown Roy. 46
97/8 Pa. Invincible 48
97/8 Pa. Paramount 66
98/9 Pa. Paramount 76
99/0 Pa. Paramount 81
94/5 Panini Sticker 208
95/6 Panini Sticker 180
96/7 Panini Sticker 183
97/8 Panini Sticker 153
98/9 Panini Sticker 132
99/0 Panini Sticker 236
00/1 Panini Sticker 154
95 Panini Worlds 30
91/2 Parkhurst 266
92/3 Parkhurst 40
93/4 Parkhurst 57
94/5 Parkhurst 66, V48
95/6 Parkhurst 65
02/3 Parkhurst 226
92/3 Pinnacle 230
92/3 Pinnacle T2K 13
94/5 Pinnacle 92
95/6 Pinnacle 128
96/7 Pinnacle 129
97/8 Pinnacle 117
97/8 Pi. Be A Player 97, ✍ Aut. 97
97/8 Pi. Inside 116
95/6 Pi. Summit 83
96/7 Pi. Summit 84
96/7 Pi. Zenith 22
95/6 Playoff 254
94/5 POG 88
95/6 POG 97
93/4 Power Play 331
93/4 Power Play RisS 2
93/4 Premier 494
94/5 Premier 145
92/3 Pro Set 225
92/3 Red Ace Blue 18
99/0 Revolution 52
92/3 Score 473
93/4 Score 421
94/5 Score 70
95/6 Score 165
96/7 Score 158
97/8 Score 209
97/8 Score Detr. 7
92/3 Score Young Stars 32
94/5 Select 103
94 Semic 152
95 Semic 137
91 Semic Sticker 98
92 Semic Sticker 111
95/6 SBx Emotion 55
95/6 SBx Impact 54
96/7 SBx Impact 36
94/5 SP 35
95/6 SP 49
96/7 SP 49
97/8 SP Authentic 50
96/7 Team Out!
92/3 Topps 35
95/6 Topps 322, 8PL
99/0 Topps 213
00/1 Topps 231
01/2 Topps 228
99/0 To. Chrome 213
95/6 To. Finest 83
98/9 To. Finest 94
01/2 To. Heritage 187
96/7 To. Picks 67
92/3 To. Stadium 62
93/4 To. Stadium 388
94/5 To. Stadium 97
95/6 To. Stadium 84
02/3 T. Total 233
91/2 Tri Globe From... 13-14
98/9 UD Choice 78, RW4
00/1 Ultimate Mem. ✂ D-19, ✂ TM-2
02/3 Ultimate Mem. ✂ SCDE, ✂ SCDGJ, ✂ SCDN
91/2 Upper Deck 462
91/2 Upper Deck 5
92/3 Upper Deck 294
92/3 Upper Deck WG2
93/4 Upper Deck 294
94/5 Upper Deck 373, SP-23
95/6 Upper Deck 154, SE-117
96/7 Upper Deck 251
97/8 Upper Deck 271
98/9 Upper Deck 264
99/0 Upper Deck 53
00/1 Upper Deck 292
01/2 Upper Deck 252
02/3 Upper Deck 252
95/6 UD BAP 99, ✍ S99
96/7 UD Black Diam. 113
97/8 UD Black Diam. 129
95/6 UD CC 32
96/7 UD CC 81, C18, CR18
97/8 UD Coll. Choice 85, SQ13
98/9 UD G. Reserve 264
99/0 UD G. Reserve 53
01/2 UD Mask ✂ GJ, ✂ JP, ✂ DP
99/0 UD MVP 76
01/2 UD SCup Champs 60
00/1 UD Vintage 135
99/0 Victory 101
00/1 Victory 86
01/2 Victory 126
96 Wien 146
KOZNEV, ALEXEI
99/0 Mir 222
00/1 Mir 377
KOZORIZ, JOHN
01/2 Mississauga IceDogs
01/2 Mississauga IceDogs
00/1 UD Prospects 15
KOZREV, ANDREI
00/1 Mir 385
KOZUBACK, RICK
92/3 Phoenix Roadrunners
92/3 Phoenix Roadrunners
91/2 ProCards 406
90/1 7th...Sketch WHL 96
KOZYREV, ANDREI
98/9 Indianapolis Ice
98/9 Indianapolis Ice
KRAEMER, CHRIS
90/1 7th...Sketch OHL 163
91/2 7th...Sketch OHL 78
KRAEMER, GREG
93/4 Slapshot / Kingston 18
KRAEV, MAXIM
00/1 Mir 217
KRAFT,
92/3 Semic Nordisk 216 [Rookie]
KRAFT, BRIAN
94/5 Anchorage Aces 7
94/5 Anchorage Aces 7
KRAFT, MILAN
01/2 Adrenaline ✂ GWJ 36
97/8 APS 190
00/1 BAP Mem. 415
01/2 BAP Mem. 44
02/3 BAP Mem. 18
99 Bowman 88
00/1 Crown Royale 138, 21CR-20
02/3 First Edition 45, ✂ Jers.
01/2 Heads Up ✂ JQ 27
01/2 O-Pee-Chee 283
02/3 Pacific 310
02/3 Pacific Complete 479
00/1 Parkhurst P-170
01/2 Parkhurst 54, ✂ PJ52, ✂ T2
00/1 Premier Plus 98, ✍ PS
01/2 Pr. Stock ✂ GUG 78
00/1 PS Titanium 140
00/1 PS Titanium Draft 140, ✂ 85
00/1 Signature 282, ✍ Aut. 244
01/2 Signature 167, ✍ Aut. 167, ✂ TM24
99/0 SP Authentic 125
00/1 SP Authentic ✍ SotT, ✍ SotTD
01/2 SP Authentic ✍ SotT
02/3 SP Authentic ✍ SotT
02/3 SP Game-Used ✍ Sig
00/1 SPx 145
00/1 Stadium 228
01/2 Stadium 120
01/2 Topps 283
00/1 To. Gold Label ✍ GLA
00/1 To. Heritage 43
00/1 To. Stars 146
00/1 UD Heroes 94
00/1 UD Reserve 69
99/0 Ult. Victory 110
99/0 Upper Deck 326
00/1 Upper Deck 213, 371, TT9
99/0 UD Black Diam. 102
00/1 UD Black Diam. 106
99/0 UD G. Reserve 326
01/2 UD Ice ✍ CCA
99/0 UD MVP Cup 197, ✂ GU, ✂ SGU, ✍ PS
99/0 UD Ovation 72
99/0 UD Prospects 26, IN6
00/1 UD Vintage 290
00/1 Vanguard 142
02/3 WBS Penguins
02/3 WBS Penguins
KRAFT, RYAN
02/3 BAP Mem. 363
01/2 Cleveland Barons
01/2 Cleveland Barons
98/9 EBK ECHL All-Star
00/1 Kentucky Tho'blades
00/1 Kentucky Tho'blades
00/1 Kentucky Tho'blades
94/5 Minnesota G'Gophers
94/5 Minnesota G'Gophers
02/3 UD Rookie 140
KRAFT, STIAN
92/3 Semic Nordisk 169
KRAFT, THOMAS
92/3 BCJHL 34
KRAFTCHECK, STEVE
45-64 BeeHive-2 [NYRa.]
45-64 BeeHive-2 [Toro.]
51/2 Parkhurst 92
52/3 Parkhurst 23
58/9 Parkhurst 37
KRAHN, BRENT
99/0 Calgary Hitmen
99/0 Calgary Hitmen
00/1 Calgary Hitmen
00/1 Calgary Hitmen
99/0 UD Prospects 42
00/1 UD Prospects 49, ✂ GJ, ✍ Sig.
01 UD Prospects GU ✍ SoT
KRAIGER, YOGI
51/2 Laval Dairy 9
52/3 Laval Dairy Update 9
52/3 St. Lawrence 48
KRAINZ, MARTIN
95 Panini Worlds 264
94 Semic 235
93 Semic Sticker 274
KRAJCOVIC, LUBOS
99/0 Indianapolis Ice
99/0 Indianapolis Ice
98/9 Muskegon Fury
98/9 Muskegon Fury
KRAJICEK, JAN
94/5 APS 188
95/6 APS 37
96/7 APS 34
97/8 APS 95
99/0 DS 116
96/7 DS Sticker 98
97/8 DS Sticker 289
98/9 OFS 67
99/0 OFS 47
KRAJICEK, LUKAS
01/2 BAP Draft Florida 24
01/2 BAP Mem. 435
02/3 First Edition 257, 425R
02/3 O-Pee-Chee 284
01/2 OFS 121
01/2 Parkhurst 317
01/2 Peterborough Petes
01/2 Peterborough Petes
02/3 SPx 112
02/3 Topps 284
02/3 To. Limited 284
02/3 Upper Deck 206
02/3 UD Foundations 131
01/2 UD Mask 148
02/3 UD MVP 203
01/2 UD Premier 102
01 UD Prospects GU 18, ✂ TPJ, ✂ JC
02/3 UD Vintage 334
KRAKE, PAUL
92/3 Oklahoma City Blazers
92/3 Oklahoma City Blazers
KRAKE, SKIP
72/3 Cleveland Crusaders
72/3 Cleveland Crusaders
72/3 Clev. WHA / Linnett
72/3 Clev. WHA / Linnett
70/1 Dad's Cookies
70/1 Eddie Sargent 24
71/2 Esso Power Player
68/9 O-Pee-Chee 3
68/9 O-Pee-Chee 43
69/0 O-Pee-Chee 141
70/1 O-Pee-Chee 126
68/9 Shirriff / LosA. 11
67/8 Topps 37
67/8 Topps 93
68/9 Topps 43
70/1 Topps 126
KRAKIWSKY, SEAN
85/6 Minnesota-Duluth 32
85/6 Minnesota-Duluth 32
KRAL, RICHARD
94/5 APS 43
95/6 APS 236, 420
96/7 APS 60, 430
97/8 APS 327
97/8 DS 111
98/9 DS 118
99/0 DS 105
00/1 DS 67
96/7 DS Sticker 241
97/8 DS Sticker 274
98/9 OFS 389, 435
99/0 OFS 197
00/1 OFS 223, -Star 24
01/2 OFS 66, -RE23D
KRAL, VACLAV
97/8 APS 287
99/0 DS 35
00/1 DS 78
98/9 OFS 206, 460
99/0 OFS 261, 282, 499
00/1 OFS 15, -Star 13
KRALIC, JIRI
01/2 DS L2
98/9 OFS Leg. 12
82 Semic Sticker 76
KRALL, JUSTIN
98/9 Dayton Bombers
98/9 Dayton Bombers
98/9 Dayton Bombers
98/9 Dayton Bombers
96/7 Peoria Rivermen
96/7 Peoria Rivermen
97/8 Peoria Rivermen
97/8 Peoria Rivermen
KRAMER, TED
92/3 Phoenix Roadrunners
92/3 Phoenix Roadrunners
KRAMNY, TOMAS
94/5 APS 121
95/6 APS 297
96/7 APS 197
97/8 APS 108
97/8 DS Sticker 53
99/0 Score 141
KRAMSKOI, VLADIMIR
00/1 Mir 51
KRANWINKEL, MARKUS
94/5 DEL 236
KRASKE, WOLFGANG
79 Panini Sticker 249
KRASNY, TOMAS
95/6 APS 216
96/7 APS 182
97/8 APS 93
96/7 DS Sticker 53
KRASOTKIN, DMITRI
98/9 Mir 36
00/1 Mir 220
95 Panini Worlds 29
KRASSNER, MIKE
94/5 Birmingham Bulls
94/5 Birmingham Bulls
KRASTINOV, DIMO
79 Panini Sticker 348
KRATENA, ONDREJ
95/6 APS 119
96/7 APS 233, 368
97/8 APS 40, 366, 374
97/8 DS 63
98/9 DS 80
99/0 DS 150
00/1 DS 10
96/7 DS Sticker 31
97/8 DS Sticker 18, 179
98/9 OFS 109, 431, 490
99/0 OFS 107
00/1 OFS 305
01/2 OFS RE19D
95/6 Upper Deck 540
KRATKY, PETR
95/6 APS 157
96/7 APS 176
99/0 DS 61
98/9 OFS 219
99/0 OFS 149
KRATOCHVIL, JIRI
99/0 OFS 541
KRATOSKA, ALES
96/7 APS 208
97/8 APS 145
99/0 Cardset 342
00/1 Cardset 198
98/9 DS 108
96/7 DS Sticker 205
98/9 OFS 357
KRATZ, MICHAEL
94/5 DEL 353
KRAUS, JAKUB
98/9 OFS 339
01/2 OFS 187
99/0 Score 60
KRAUS, RICHARD
92/3 BCJHL 186
KRAUSE, SEAN
91/2 Avant Garde BCJHL 60
91/2 Nanaimo Clippers
91/2 Nanaimo Clippers
KRAUSS, DARYL
91/2 Air Canada SJHL B43
92/3 MPS SJHL 144
KRAUSS, ROB
93/4 Birmingham Bulls
93/4 Birmingham Bulls
KRAVCHUK, IGOR
98/9 Aurora 130
99/0 BAP Mem. 40
00/1 BAP Mem. 330
93/4 Bowman 408
93/4 Donruss 116
94/5 Donruss 259
98/9 Dynagon Ice 127
93/4 EA Sports 44
93/4 EDMO / Sheet
92/3 EDMO
92/3 EDMO
94/5 Flair 58
94/5 Fleer 70
92/3 Fleer Ultra 38
93/4 Fleer Ultra 80
94/5 Fleer Ultra 72
95/6 Fleer Ultra 54
95 Globe 167
93/4 Leaf 163
94/5 Leaf 244
91/2 O-Pee-Chee 19R
92/3 O-Pee-Chee 161
98/9 OPC Chrome 36
97/8 Omega 155
97/8 OTTA
97/8 OTTA
98/9 OTTA
98/9 OTTA
99/0 OTTA
99/0 OTTA
98/9 Pacific 310
99/0 Pacific 290
98/9 Pa. Crown Roy. 93
97/8 Pa. Invincible R-170
97/8 Pa. Paramount 126
98/9 Pa. Paramount 163
92/3 Panini Sticker 297
92/3 Panini Sticker A
94/5 Panini Sticker 205
95/6 Panini Sticker 264
97/8 Panini Sticker 165
98/9 Panini Sticker 46
99/0 Panini Sticker 99
00/1 Panini Sticker 68
91/2 Parkhurst 257
92/3 Parkhurst 291
92/3 Parkhurst 35
93/4 Parkhurst 65
95/6 Parkhurst 74
94/5 Parkie SE58
92/3 Pinnacle 225
93/4 Pinnacle 36
94/5 Pinnacle 96
96/7 Pi. Be A Player 3, ✍ Aut. 3
95/6 Playoff 148
96/7 Playoff 372
94/5 POG 367
95/6 POG 109
93/4 Power Play 81
93/4 Premier 495
94/5 Premier 172
92/3 Pro Set 35
91/2 Red Ace
92/3 Score 454
93/4 Score 309
94/5 Score 33
92/3 Seasons 69
91 Semic Sticker 82
92 Semic Sticker 103
95/6 SBx Emotion 63
95/6 SBx Impact 61
92/3 Topps 200
98/9 Topps 36
92/3 To. Stadium 7
93/4 To. Stadium 204
91/2 Tri Globe From... 17-18
92/3 Upper Deck 239
92/3 Upper Deck 367
92/3 Upper Deck E7
93/4 Upper Deck 174
94/5 Upper Deck 463
95/6 Upper Deck 146
98/9 Upper Deck 330
01/2 Upper Deck 257
98/9 UD G. Reserve 330
02/3 UD MVP 30
96 Wien 132
KRAVETS, MIKHAIL
92/3 Classic 106
92/3 Kansas City Blades
92/3 Kansas City Blades
93/4 Kansas City Blades
93/4 Kansas City Blades
96/7 Louisiana Ice Gators
96/7 Louisiana Ice Gators
97/8 Louisiana Ice Gators
97/8 Louisiana Ice Gators
99/0 Mississippi S'Wolves
99/0 Mississippi S'Wolves
99/0 Mississippi S'Wolves
99/0 Mississippi S'Wolves
91/2 ProCards 505
92/3 Upper Deck 542
KRAWINKEL, MARKUS
94/5 DEL 226
95/6 DEL 221
96/7 DEL 71
KRAYER, EDDIE
89/0 Nashville Knights
89/0 Nashville Knights
KRAYER, JIM
96/7 Johnstown Chiefs
96/7 Johnstown Chiefs
KRAYZEL, LUDEK
95/6 APS 311
96/7 APS 205
00/1 Cardset 207
99/0 DS 175
98/9 OFS 356
99/0 OFS 227, 478, 517
01/2 OFS 36
KRECHINE, VLADIMIR
93/4 Classic 41
93/4 Cla. 4 Sport 220
95/6 Slapshot 422
KREIS, HAROLD
95/6 DEL 266
96/7 DEL 160
82 Semic Sticker 106
89 Semic Sticker 109
KREISS, HAROLD
91 Semic Sticker 156
92 Semic Sticker 173
KREKULA, FREDRIK
97/8 UD Elitserien 14
98/9 UD Elitserien 13
99/0 UD Elitserien 13
KRELOVE, MICHAEL
01/2 Guelph Storm
01/2 Guelph Storm
01/2 Guelph Storm M-Cup
01/2 Guelph Storm M-Cup
KRENTZ, DALE
94/5 DEL 281
95/6 DEL 372
88/9 ProCards / Adirondack
89/0 ProCards AHL 319
KRENZELOK, LUKAS
01/2 OFS 283
KREPELKA, PAUL
91/2 Hampton Roads
91/2 Hampton Roads
92/3 Hampton Roads
92/3 Hampton Roads
KRESS, JAMIE
92/3 Oshawa Generals
92/3 Oshawa Generals
KRESS, JONATHAN
02/3 Moose Jaw Warriors
02/3 Moose Jaw Warriors
KRESTAN, RADEK
01/2 OFS 238, 270
KRESTANOVICH, DEREK
00/1 Kamloops Blazers
00/1 Kamloops Blazers
01/2 Moose Jaw Warriors 7
01/2 Moose Jaw Warriors 7
02/3 Moose Jaw Warriors
02/3 Moose Jaw Warriors
KRESTANOVICH, JORDAN
98/9 Calgary Hitmen 9
98/9 Calgary Hitmen 9
99/0 Calgary Hitmen
99/0 Calgary Hitmen
00/1 Calgary Hitmen
00/1 Calgary Hitmen
01/2 Hershey Bears
01/2 Hershey Bears
02/3 Hershey Bears
02/3 Hershey Bears
94 Québec Pee Wee 1169
00/1 SP Authentic 131
00/1 SP GU 89
00/1 SPx ✂ 126
02/3 SPx 107
00/1 UD Heroes 178
00/1 UD Reserve 117
00/1 Upper Deck 440
02/3 Upper Deck 201
00/1 UD Pros&Prosp. 131
00/1 UD Vintage 398
02/3 UD Vintage 326
KRETCHINE, VLADIMIR
93/4 Slapshot / Windsor 17
94/5 Slapshot / Windsor 19
KRETINSKY, ALES
99/0 Score 102
KRETSCHMER, HORST
79 Panini Sticker 102
KREUSER, JEFF
98/9 Kansas City Blades 28
98/9 Kansas City Blades 28
99/0 Kansas City Blades
99/0 Kansas City Blades
KREUTZER, CHRISTOPHER
94/5 DEL 85
95/6 DEL 80
KREUTZER, DANIEL
98/9 DEL 57
99/0 Eishockey 183
00/1 UD DEL 232, S4
01/2 UD DEL 253
KREUTZER, KEVIN
98/9 Charlotte Checkers
98/9 Charlotte Checkers
99/0 San Angelo Outlaws
99/0 San Angelo Outlaws
KREUZMANN, JAROSLAV
94/5 APS 160
95/6 APS 261
99/0 Score 68
KRIBOMAZOV, ROMAN
99/0 Mir 232
KRIES, HAROLD
94/5 DEL 274
KRIKKE, HENK
79 Panini Sticker 276
KRINNER, ANTON
94/5 DEL 16
95/6 DEL 144
96/7 DEL 244
91 Semic Sticker 171
KRISAK, PATRIK
93/4 Upper Deck 266
KRISKO, DAN
90/1 7th...Sketch OHL 262
91/2 7th...Sketch OHL 216
KRISS, AARON
98/9 Dayton Bombers
98/9 Dayton Bombers
98/9 Dayton Bombers
98/9 Dayton Bombers
95/6 Tallahassee Tiger Sharks
95/6 Tallahasee Tiger Sharks
KRISTEK, JAROSLAV
00/1 Rochester Americans
00/1 Rochester Americans
02/3 Rochester Americans
02/3 Rochester Americans
00/1 SP Authentic 127
99/0 Upper Deck 323
99/0 UD Black Diam. 111
99/0 UD G. Reserve 323
99/0 UD MVP Cup 201
99/0 UD Prospects 44, IN9
KRISTENSEN, TORE
92/3 Semic Nordisk 129
KRISTIANSEN, ERIK
94 Panini Olympics 312
94 Semic 262
92/3 Semic Nordisk 27
92 Semic Sticker 38
93 Semic Sticker 238
KRISTIANSEN, KENT INGE
92/3 Semic Nordisk 220
KRISTIANSEN, KETIL
92/3 Semic Nordisk 234
KRISTIANSEN, PÅL
94 Semic 257
92/3 Semic Nordisk 15
KRISTIANSEN, THOMAS
92/3 Semic Nordisk 152
KRISTOFFERSON, MARC
01/2 Utah Grizzlies
01/2 Utah Grizzlies
KRISTOFFERSSON, MARCUS
00/1 Cardset 225
98/9 UD Elitserien 111
KRIVCHENKOV, ALEXEI
97/8 Cleveland Lumberjacks
97/8 Cleveland Lumberjacks
95/6 Hampton Roads
95/6 Hampton Roads
96/7 Hampton Roads
96/7 Hampton Roads
00/1 Mir 375
KRIVOKHIJA, YURI
94/5 Cincinnati Cyclones
94/5 Cincinnati Cyclones
93/4 Milwaukee Admirals
93/4 Milwaukee Admirals
KRIVOKRASOV, SERGEI
98/9 Aurora 102
99/0 Aurora 79
98/9 Be A Player 223, ✍ Aut. 223
99/0 BAP Mem. 53, 372
00/1 BAP Mem. 271
01/2 BAP Mem. 260
92/3 Classic 42
93/4 Classic 138
92/3 Classic Four Sport 183
93/4 Cla. 4 Sport 238
92/3 Classic Prospects 38
93/4 Cla. Prospects 220
99/0 Crown Royale 75
93/4 Donruss 74
94/5 Donruss 91
95/6 Donruss 203
98/9 Dynagon Ice 104
99/0 Dynagon Ice 108
94/5 Fleer 41
92/3 Fleer Ultra 276
93/4 Fleer Ultra 112
95/6 Fleer Ultra 33
92/3 Indianapolis Ice
92/3 Indianapolis Ice
93/4 Indianapolis Ice
93/4 Indianapolis Ice
94/5 Indianapolis Ice
94/5 Indianapolis Ice
93/4 Leaf 434
94/5 Leaf 238
95/6 Leaf 32, SR-18
99/0 Millenium 140, ✍ Aut. 140
98/9 NASH / Wendy's 14
98/9 NASH / Wendy's 14
98/9 NHL Power Play
98/9 OPC Chrome 211
92/3 OPC Premier 9
98/9 Omega 130
98/9 Pacific 147
99/0 Pacific 227
00/1 Pacific 68
97/8 Pacific CC 134
98/9 Pa. Crown Roy. 76
97/8 Pa. Paramount 45
98/9 Pa. Paramount 124
99/0 Pa. Paramount 126
00/1 Pa. Paramount 119
98/9 Pa. Revolution 79, -ASG 15
95/6 Panini Sticker 161
97/8 Panini Sticker 135
98/9 Panini Sticker 138
99/0 Panini Sticker 270
00/1 Panini Sticker 173
92/3 Parkhurst 36
95/6 Parkhurst 314
94/5 Parkie SE37, seV19
92/3 Pinnacle 410
93/4 Pinnacle 419
94/5 Pinnacle RTP12
95/6 Pinnacle 154
95/6 POG 65
93/4 Power Play 51
94/5 Premier 513
00/1 Private Stock 49
99/0 Revolution 80
93/4 Score 464
95/6 Score 62
01/2 Signature 40, ✍ Aut. 40
95/6 SBx Emotion 29
95/6 SBx Impact 29, F-6
97/8 SP Authentic 34
98/9 SP Authentic 45
99/0 Stadium 46
00/1 Stadium 203
95/6 Topps 16NG
98/9 Topps 211
99/0 Topps 189
00/1 Topps 154
99/0 To. Chrome 189
00/1 To. Chrome 240
91/2 Tri Globe From... 9-10
99/0 Ult. Victory 48
91/2 Upper Deck 658
92/3 Upper Deck 582
92/3 Upper Deck ER5
94/5 Upper Deck 80
95/6 Upper Deck 11
97/8 Upper Deck 37
98/9 Upper Deck 302
99/0 Upper Deck 75
00/1 Upper Deck 315
95/6 UD BAP 187, ✍ S187
98/9 UD Black Diam. 48
95/6 UD CC 96
91/2 Upper Deck WJC 19
98/9 UD G. Reserve 302
99/0 UD G. Reserve 75
98/9 UD MVP 114
99/0 UD MVP 109
00/1 UD Vintage 180, 185
00/1 Vanguard 50
99/0 Victory 157
99/0 WGretzky 91
KRIVOMAZ, EVGENY
00/1 Rockford IceHogs
00/1 Rockford IceHogs
KRIVOMAZ, YEVGENY
99/0 Rockford IceHogs
99/0 Rockford IceHogs
KRIZ, DAVID
99/0 OFS 297
KRIZ, ONDREJ
93/4 Dayton Bombers
93/4 Dayton Bombers
99/0 DS 168
00/1 DS 142
98/9 OFS 38
99/0 OFS 166
00/1 OFS 114
01/2 OFS 174
KRIZ, PAVEL
96/7 APS 150
97/8 APS 250
98/9 DS 51
96/7 DS Sticker 250
98/9 OFS 150
94/5 SR Auto-Phonex 22, ✍ 22
KRIZEK, PAVEL
99/0 OFS 534
KROCAK, JIRI
95/6 APS 277
96/7 APS 126
97/8 APS 8
99/0 DS 159
98/9 OFS 398
99/0 OFS 167
KROG, JASON
99/0 BAP Mem. 346
00/1 BAP Mem. 392
98/9 Lowell Lock Monsters
98/9 Lowell Lock Monsters
00/1 Lowell Lock Monsters
00/1 Lowell Lock Monsters
00/1 Pacific 251, ✍ Aut. 251
02/3 Pacific Complete 415
00/1 Pa. Paramount 155
99/0 SP Authentic 108
00/1 Topps 294
00/1 To. Chrome 189
00/1 UD MVP 198
00/1 Victory 265
KROL, JOE
34-43 BeeHive-1 [NYAm.]
KROMM, RICHARD
85/6 CALG / Red Rooster
01/2 Calgary Hitmen
01/2 Calgary Hitmen
96/7 Carolina Monarchs
96/7 Carolina Monarchs
93/4 Cincinnati Cyclones
93/4 Cincinnati Cyclones
94/5 Cincinnati Cyclones
94/5 Cincinnati Cyclones
98/9 Muskegon Fury
98/9 Muskegon Fury
98/9 Muskegon Fury
98/9 Muskegon Fury
99/0 Muskegon Fury
99/0 Muskegon Fury
84/5 O-Pee-Chee 227
85/6 O-Pee-Chee 222
86/7 O-Pee-Chee 229
87/8 Panini Sticker 103
88/9 ProCards / Springfield
90/1 ProCards 498
91/2 ProCards 465
89/0 Semic Elitserien 136
KROMP, WOLFGANG
95 Panini Worlds 270
94 Semic 249
KRON, ROBERT
93/4 Aurora 35
98/9 Be A Player 25, ✍ Aut. 25
91/2 Bowman 320
92/3 Bowman 413
97/8 CARO / Sprint
97/8 CARO / Sprint
01/2 COLU
01/2 COLU
93/4 Donruss 143
94/5 Donruss 114
95/6 Donruss 231
98/9 Dynagon Ice 36
94/5 Fleer Ultra 90
93/4 HART / Coke
93/4 HART / Coke
95/6 HART / Kids Club
95/6 HART / Kids Club
96/7 HART / Kids Club
96/7 HART / Kids Club
93/4 Leaf 171
94/5 Leaf 101
95/6 Leaf 257
96/7 Leaf 57
91/2 O-Pee-Chee 52
92/3 O-Pee-Chee 2
90/1 OPC Premier 52
98/9 Pacific 136
99/0 Pacific 76
00/1 Pacific 87
97/8 Pacific CC 114
98/9 Pa. Paramount 39
00/1 Panini/VAN 10
91/2 Panini Sticker 47
92/3 Panini Sticker 33
96/7 Panini Sticker 31
97/8 Panini Sticker 19
98/9 Panini Sticker 27
99/0 Panini Sticker 45
91/2 Parkhurst PHC4
93/4 Parkhurst 90
95/6 Parkhurst 92
94/5 Parkie SE76
93/4 Pinnacle 421
94/5 Pinnacle 336
95/6 Pinnacle 85
96/7 Pinnacle 132
97/8 Pi. Be A Player 140, ✍ Aut. 140
94/5 POG 114
93/4 Power Play 351
94/5 Premier 296
90/1 Pro Set 642
91/2 Pro Set 239
91/2 Pro Set Platinum 122
90/1 Score 65T
91/2 Score CAN 257
93/4 Score 428
95/6 Score 154
96/7 Score 195
99/0 Score JT23
94 Semic 181
89 Semic Sticker 199
92 Semic Sticker 139
92/3 Topps 80
95/6 Topps 161
00/1 To. Chrome 225
98/9 To. Finest 97
91/2 To. Stadium 240
92/3 To. Stadium 155
94/5 To. Stadium 146
90/1 Upper Deck 528
91/2 Upper Deck 225
91/2 Upper Deck E8
92/3 Upper Deck 69
93/4 Upper Deck 359, SP-61
94/5 Upper Deck 408
95/6 Upper Deck 400
00/1 Upper Deck 282
94/5 UD BAP ✍ 66
95/6 UD CC 298
90/1 VANC / Mohawk
90/1 VANC / Mohawk
91/2 VANC
91/2 VANC
91/2 VANC / Photo
91/2 VANC / Photo
92/3 VANC / Road Trip
92/3 VANC / Road Trip
KRONWALL, NIKLAS
99/0 UD Elitserien 37
00/1 UD Elitserien 45, ✍ Sig.
KROOSHOOP, MIKE
93/4 Kamloops Blazers
93/4 Kamloops Blazers
KROPAC, RADOSLAV
00/1 Cardset 290
01/2 OFS 241, -RE14D
KROPF, BARRET
91/2 Air Canada SJHL A31
KROPF, MARTIN
95/6 DEL 380
KROUPA, VLASTIMIL
97/8 APS 353
93/4 Cla. Prospects 4
93/4 Donruss 315
94/5 Donruss 277
00/1 DS 4
99/0 Eishockey 343
93/4 Fleer Ultra 414
94/5 Fleer Ultra 196
93/4 Kansas City Blades
93/4 Kansas City Blades
94/5 Kansas City Blades 19
94/5 Kansas City Blades 19
98/9 Kansas City Blades 15
98/9 Kansas City Blades 15
93/4 Leaf 439
94/5 Leaf 265
94/5 L. Limited 64
00/1 OFS 294
01/2 OFS 156
93/4 Parkhurst 266
94/5 Parkie SE167
94/5 Pinnacle 242
94/5 Premier 113
92/3 SANJ / Pacific Bell
92/3 SANJ / Pacific Bell
93/4 Upper Deck 437, SP-144
94/5 Upper Deck 453
KROUSE, JOHN
98/9 Las Vegas Thunder
98/9 Las Vegas Thunder
97/8 Peoria Rivermen
97/8 Peoria Rivermen
KROVOPUSKOV, ALEXEI
99/0 Greensboro Generals
99/0 Greensboro Generals
00/1 Mir 195
KRSTEV, ANGEL
00/1 DS 113
99/0 Lethbridge Hurricanes
99/0 Lethbridge Hurricanes
99/0 OFS 48
00/1 OFS 87
KRUCHININ, ANDREI
00/1 Mir 169
KRUCHKOWSKI, COREY
92/3 BCJHL 191
KRUEGER, SHAWN
91/2 7th...Sketch OHL 276
KRUG, JASON
92/3 MPS SJHL 101
KRUGER, RAPHAEL
94/5 DEL 372
95/6 DEL 365
KRULIS, JAN
94/5 APS 74
95/6 APS 82
96/7 APS 77
97/8 APS 197
97/8 DS 90
99/0 DS 158
00/1 DS 135

96/7 DS Sticker 133
97/8 DS Sticker 229
99/0 OFS 331, 500
00/1 OFS 112
01/2 OFS 184, -UHI 36

KRULL, HARALD
82 Semic Sticker 108

KRUMPSCHMID, NORM
94/5 Muskegon Fury
94/5 Muskegon Fury

KRUPP, UWE
91/2 Bowman 26
92/3 Bowman 349
86/7 BUFF / Blue Shield
87/8 BUFF / Blue Shield
87/8 BUFF / Won. Bread
88/9 BUFF / Blue Shield
88/9 BUFF / Won. Bread
89/0 BUFF / Blue Shield
89/0 BUFF / Campbell's
90/1 BUFF / Blue Shield
90/1 BUFF / Blue Shield
90/1 BUFF / Campbell's
90/1 BUFF / Campbell's
95/6 DEL 444
93/4 Donruss 205
95/6 Donruss 49
96/7 Donruss 114
98/9 Dynagon Ice 64
94/5 Fleer 179
92/3 Fleer Ultra 129
94/5 Fleer Ultra 358
97/8 Kraft / KD
93/4 Leaf 57
94/5 Leaf 422
95/6 Leaf 266
96/7 Leaf 49
96/7 Metal Univ. 34
88/9 O-Pee-Chee 220
90/1 OPC/Topps 390
91/2 O-Pee-Chee 155
92/3 O-Pee-Chee 173
98/9 OPC Chrome 11
91/2 OPC Premier 140
97/8 Omega 58
98/9 Pacific 161
97/8 Pacific CC 265
97/8 Pa. Invincible R-53
89/0 Panini Sticker 216
90/1 Panini Sticker 22
91/2 Panini Sticker 305
92/3 Panini Sticker 202
95/6 Panini Sticker 252
96/7 Panini Sticker 249
97/8 Panini Sticker 200
98/9 Panini Sticker 187
91/2 Parkhurst 109
92/3 Parkhurst 101
92/3 Parkhurst 453
93/4 Parkhurst 388
95/6 Parkhurst 50
91/2 Pinnacle 19
92/3 Pinnacle 240
92/3 Pinnacle 86
93/4 Pinnacle 259
94/5 Pinnacle 382
95/6 Pinnacle 46, GG-8
96/7 Pinnacle 24
96/7 Pi. Be A Player 87, ✍ Aut. 87
96/7 Pi. Summit 38
94/5 POG 201
95/6 POG 79
93/4 Power Play 151
93/4 Premier 3
90/1 Pro Set 23
91/2 Pro Set 20
91/2 Pro Set 301
91/2 Pro Set 436
92/3 Pro Set 109
91/2 Pro Set Platinum 202
94/5 QUÉB / Burger King
94/5 QUÉB / Burger King
90/1 Score 169
91/2 Score 84
91/2 Score 104T
91/2 Score CAN 84
92/3 Score 77
93/4 Score 87
93/4 Score IS 11
95/6 Score 108
96/7 Score 175
97/8 Score Colo. 15
91 Semic Sticker 162
93 Semic Sticker 168
95/6 SBx Emotion 38
96/7 SBx Impact 24
92/3 Topps 158
98/9 Topps 11
96/7 To. Picks 163
91/2 To. Stadium 62
92/3 To. Stadium 177
93/4 To. Stadium 138
94/5 To. Stadium 172
90/1 Upper Deck 187
91/2 Upper Deck 102
91/2 Upper Deck 540
92/3 Upper Deck 187
94/5 Upper Deck 310
96/7 Upper Deck 39
98/9 Upper Deck 269
94/5 UD BAP ✍ 163
95/6 UD CC 80
96/7 UD CC 56
98/9 UD G. Reserve 269

KRUPPKE, GORD
95/6 Houston Aeros
95/6 Houston Aeros
89/0 ProCards AHL 312
90/1 ProCards 469
91/2 ProCards 138
93/4 Score 467

KRUSE, ERIC
93/4 Michigan State
93/4 Michigan State

KRUSE, PAUL
00/1 Chicago Wolves
00/1 Chicago Wolves
92/3 Classic 115
88/9 Kamloops Blazers
88/9 Kamloops Blazers
89/0 Kamloops Blazers
89/0 Kamloops Blazers
94/5 Leaf 352
95/6 Leaf 251
96/7 NYIS
96/7 NYIS
97/8 Pa. Invincible R-117
95/6 Panini Sticker 235
95/6 Pinnacle 66
97/8 Pi. Be A Player 42, ✍ Aut. 42
95/6 Playoff 130
95/6 POG 53
90/1 ProCards 621
91/2 ProCards 581
92/3 Salt Lake G'Eagles
92/3 Salt Lake G'Eagles
90 7th..Sketch Mem.Cup 8
95/6 Topps 51

KRUSHEL, ROD
91/2 Air Canada SJHL 33
91/2 Air Canada SJHL A12

KRUSHELNYSKI, MIKE
83/4 BOST
90/1 Bowman 145
91/2 Bowman 166
92/3 Bowman 2
92/3 Durivage 5
93/4 Durivage 31
84/5 EDMO
84/5 EDMO / Red Rooster
85/6 EDMO / Red Rooster
86/7 EDMO
86/7 EDMO / Red Rooster
87/8 EDMO
88/9 EDMO / Action 79
92/3 Fleer Ultra 421
86/7 Kraft Sports 15
94/5 Leaf 438
88/9 LOSA / Smokey
89/0 LOSA / Smokey 12
79/0 Montréal Juniors B&W
79/0 Montréal Juniors B&W
79/0 Montréal Jrs. Colour
79/0 Montréal Jrs. Colour
83/4 O-Pee-Chee 52
84/5 O-Pee-Chee 248
85/6 OPC/Topps 49
86/7 OPC/Topps 193
87/8 O-Pee-Chee 202
88/9 O-Pee-Chee 221
90/1 OPC/Topps 167
91/2 O-Pee-Chee 324
92/3 O-Pee-Chee 335
89/0 OPC/Topps 104
91/2 OPC Premier 189
83/4 OPC/Topps Sticker 43
84/5 OPC Sticker 188
85/6 OPC Sticker 223-90
86/7 OPC Sticker 74-201
87/8 OPC Sticker 90-223
88/9 OPC Sticker 226-100
89/0 opcSticker 153-13
87/8 Panini Sticker 266
89/0 Panini Sticker 94
90/1 Panini Sticker 245
91/2 Panini Sticker 97
92/3 Panini Sticker 78
93/4 Panini Sticker 229
92/3 Parkhurst 411
91/2 Pinnacle 269
93/4 Pinnacle 328
93/4 Premier 169
90/1 Pro Set 121, 537
91/2 Pro Set 233
91/2 Pro Set Platinum 119
90/1 Score 227, 47T
91/2 Score 33
91/2 Score CAN 33
92/3 Score 283
93/4 Score 367
83/4 Souhaits Keychain [Bruins]
84/5 Topps 6
92/3 Topps 450
91/2 To. Stadium 54
92/3 To. Stadium 487
93/4 To. Stadium 306
90/1 TORO
90/1 TORO
91/2 TORO / P.L.A.Y. 20
91/2 TORO / P.L.A.Y. 20
93/4 TORO / Abalene
93/4 TORO / Abalene
93/4 TORO / Black's 23
93/4 TORO / Black's 23
90/1 Upper Deck 394
91/2 Upper Deck 320
92/3 Upper Deck 87
94/5 UD BAP ✍ 177

KRUTOV, VLADIMIR
95 Globe 240
89/0 Kraft 40
00/1 Mir Fetisov 15
90/1 OPC/Topps 380
90/1 Panini Sticker 304, 337
90/1 Pro Set 296
90/1 Score 273
82 Semic Sticker 62
89 Semic Sticker 89
83/4 Soviet Stars
87/8 Soviet Stars
89/0 Soviet Stars
90/1 Upper Deck 77

KRUZICH, GARY
88/9 Flint Spirits
88/9 Flint Spirits

KRYAZHEV, OLEG
98/9 Mir 43
99/0 Mir 172

KRYGIER, TODD
94/5 ANAH / Carl's Jr. 13
94/5 ANAH / Carl's Jr. 13
90/1 Bowman 251
91/2 Bowman 2
95/6 Donruss 335
96/7 Donruss 202
95/6 Fleer Metal 3
92/3 Fleer Ultra 438
93/4 Fleer Ultra 448
95/6 Fleer Ultra 201
89/0 HART / Jr. Whalers
90/1 HART / Jr. Whalers
90/1 HART / Jr. Whalers
96/7 Leaf 70
90/1 OPC/Topps 260
91/2 O-Pee-Chee 449
98/9 Orlando Solar Bears Geico
98/9 Orlando Solar Bears Geico
97/8 Pacific CC 318
90/1 Panini Sticker 35
91/2 Panini Sticker 317
95/6 Panini Sticker 226
91/2 Parkhurst 408
94/5 Parkhurst 258
95/6 Parkhurst 276
91/2 Pinnacle 242
91/2 Pinnacle 394
92/3 Pinnacle 204
94/5 Pinnacle 455
95/6 Pinnacle 183
95/6 Playoff 224
96/7 Playoff 363
95/6 POG 20
93/4 Power Play 467
93/4 Premier 188
90/1 Pro Set 107
91/2 Pro Set 83
92/3 Pro Set 270
88/9 ProCards / Binghampton
89/0 ProCards AHL 294
90/1 Score 237
91/2 Score 97
91/2 Score 87T
91/2 Score CAN 637
91/2 Score CAN 97
92/3 Score 98
93/4 Score 357
96/7 Score 203
95/6 SBx Impact 4
92/3 Topps 502
95/6 Topps 163
95/6 To. Finest 114
91/2 To. Stadium 45
92/3 To. Stadium 474
93/4 To. Stadium 337
94/5 To. Stadium 256
95/6 To. Stadium 19
90/1 Upper Deck 417
91/2 Upper Deck 215
91/2 Upper Deck 582
93/4 Upper Deck 207
94/5 Upper Deck 477
95/6 Upper Deck 9
95/6 UD BAP 93, ✍ S93
95/6 UD CC 241
91/2 WASH / Kodak
91/2 WASH / Kodak
91/2 WASH / Smokey
91/2 WASH / Smokey
92/3 WASH / Kodak
92/3 WASH / Kodak

KRYKOV,
97/8 Hockey-Box

KRYKOV, VALERI
98/9 Cardset 217
99/0 Cardset 123
00/1 Cardset 129
02/3 Cardset 46
92/3 Jyvas Hyva 16
93/4 Jyvas Hyva 18
93/4 Sisu 99
94/5 Sisu 260, H-11
95/6 Sisu 115
96/7 Sisu 134

KRYS, MARK
98/9 DEL 77
93/4 Rochester Americans
93/4 Rochester Americans
96/7 Syracuse Crunch
96/7 Syracuse Crunch

KRYSKOW, DAVE
74/5 Loblaws
74/5 Loblaws Update
74/5 O-Pee-Chee 62
75/6 O-Pee-Chee 158
74/5 Topps 62
75/6 Topps 158
74/5 WASH

KRYWULAK, JASON
90/1 7th..Sketch WHL 27
91/2 7th...Sketch WHL 178

KRYZNOWSKI, ED
45-64 BeeHive-2 [Bost.]
51/2 Parkhurst 33
52/3 Parkhurst 29

KUBA, FILIP
95/6 APS 300
02/3 BAP Mem. 199
96/7 Carolina Monarchs
96/7 Carolina Monarchs
00/1 Crown Royale 128
02/3 Heads Up ✂ GWQ 14
98/9 Kentucky Tho'blades
98/9 Kentucky Tho'blades
99/0 Millenium 109, C-19, ✍ Aut. 109
02/3 O-Pee-Chee 118
99/0 Omega 105
01/2 Pacific 197
02/3 Pacific 184
02/3 Pacific Complete 75
00/1 Private Stock 126
00/1 PS Titanium 127
01/2 PS Titanium ✂ DSJ 70
01/2 PS Titanium Draft ✂ 46
00/1 PS Titanium Draft 127
02/3 Topps 118
00/1 To. Chrome 236
02/3 To. Limited 118
02/3 T. Total 198
01/2 Upper Deck 316
02/3 Upper Deck 90
99/0 UD MVP Cup 82
02/3 UD Vintage 128
00/1 Vanguard 128
02/3 Victory 106

KUBENA, PETR
96/7 APS 28
99/0 OFS 546
99/0 Score 14

KUBICEK, MICHAEL
94/5 APS 101
95/6 APS 62

KUBINA, PAVEL
95/6 APS 298
99/0 BAP Mem. 31
00/1 BAP Mem. 116
02/3 BAP Mem. 70
98/9 Bowman's Best 133
00/1 DS JT6
99/0 Millenium 221, ✍ Aut. 221
01/2 O-Pee-Chee 189
02/3 O-Pee-Chee 247
99/0 OFS 26
00/1 OFS 383
98/9 Omega 224
99/0 Pacific 391
00/1 Pacific 376
01/2 Pacific 353
02/3 Pacific 350
02/3 Pacific Complete 239
99/0 Pa. Paramount 218
99/0 Panini Sticker 146
00/1 Panini Sticker 92
00/1 Parkhurst P-48
01/2 Parkhurst 113
99/0 Score JT8
00/1 Signature 231, ✍ Aut. 54
02/3 Sports Vault 128
99/0 SPx 141
99/0 Stadium 131
00/1 Stadium 64
00/1 Topps 269
01/2 Topps 189
02/3 Topps 247
02/3 To. Limited 247
00/1 To. Stars 78
02/3 T. Total 249
98/9 Upper Deck 368
00/1 Upper Deck 388
02/3 Upper Deck 157
98/9 UD G. Reserve 368
99/0 UD MVP 194
01/2 UD Vintage 232
02/3 UD Vintage 229, 287
99/0 Victory 275
00/1 Victory 214
01/2 Victory 320
02/3 Victory 197

KUBINCAK, VOJTECH
00/1 DS 45
98/9 OFS 15
99/0 OFS 150
00/1 OFS 147
01/2 OFS 153

KUBIS, MILAN
97/8 DS Sticker 63
98/9 OFS 325

KUBOS, PETR
96/7 APS 222
99/0 OFS 59
00/1 OFS 329
01/2 OFS 59

KUCERA, FRANTISEK
94/5 APS 79
97/8 APS 6, 350
98 Bonaparte 5B
98 Bonaparte Pexeso 17
91/2 Bowman 404
92/3 Bowman 7
91/2 CHIC / Coke
91/2 CHIC / Coke
93/4 CHIC / Coke
93/4 CHIC / Coke
93/4 Donruss 439
97/8 DS 80
98/9 DS 10
99/0 DS 143, NS6
00/1 DS WCH5
97/8 DS Sticker 211
92/3 Fleer Ultra 277
95/6 Fleer Ultra 67
95/6 HART / Kids Club
95/6 HART / Kids Club
94/5 Leaf 392
95/6 Leaf 50
90/1 OPC Premier 53
98/9 OFS 134, 234, 448, OW 4
99/0 OFS 108, 262
00/1 OFS 401
01/2 OFS RE10D
94/5 Panini Sticker 116
95/6 Panini Sticker 34
92/3 Parkhurst 269
94/5 Pinnacle 210
95/6 Playoff 264
95/6 POG 129
90/1 Pro Set 599
90/1 ProCards 411
91/2 ProCards 495
91/2 Score CAN 390
92/3 Score 346
93/4 Score 372
94 Semic 169
95 Semic 146
89 Semic Sticker 184
92 Semic Sticker 128
95/6 SBx Emotion 75
92/3 Topps 520
95/6 Topps 84
92/3 To. Stadium 438
93/4 To. Stadium 442
94/5 To. Stadium 49
91/2 Upper Deck 468
95/6 UD BAP 33, ✍ S33
95/6 UD CC 304
96 Wien 106

KUCERA, FRANTISEK
00/1 DS VP2

KUCERA, FRANTISEK (JR.)
99/0 OFS 496

KUCERA, JIRI
94/5 APS 140
95/6 APS 78, 364
96/7 APS 302, 356, 390
96/7 DS Sticker 16, 219
95 Globe 161
91/2 Jyvas Hyva 57
94/5 Leaf Elit Set 187, FA-5
95/6 Leaf Elit Set 83
95 Panini Worlds 200
94 Semic 190
95 Semic 150
89 Semic Sticker 195
93 Semic Sticker 98
93/4 Sisu 72
94/5 Sisu 14
95/6 Sisu Limited 76
95/6 UD Elitserien 126
98/9 UD Elitserien 148
99/0 UD Elitserien 150, L8
00/1 UD Elitserien 126
96 Wien 117

KUCERA, JOSEF
01/2 OFS 126, -G8

KUCERA, MARCEL
01/2 OFS 192, H2
99/0 Score 61

KUCERA, RADEK
99/0 Score 146

KUCERA, ROBERT
97/8 APS 167
98/9 OFS 73

KUCHARCIK, TOMAS
94/5 APS 153
95/6 APS 253, 350, 381
96/7 APS 14
97/8 APS 162
00/1 Cardset 348
02/3 Cardset 200
97/8 DS 79
98/9 DS 76
99/0 DS 120
96/7 DS Sticker 124
97/8 DS Sticker 199
98/9 OFS 218, 463
99/0 OFS 263, 385

KUCHARCZYK, RADIM
99/0 OFS 60
01/2 OFS 73

KUCHERAN, BOB
80/1 Oshawa Generals
80/1 Oshawa Generals

KUCHLER, JIRI
97/8 APS 212
99/0 Score 5

KUCHMA, BILL
84/5 Ottawa 67's
84/5 Ottawa 67's

KUCHYNA, PETR
94/5 APS 170
95/6 APS 273, 359
96/7 APS 29
97/8 APS 57
99/0 Cardset 145
00/1 Cardset 271
97/8 DS 104
98/9 DS 67
96/7 DS Sticker 95
97/8 DS Sticker 290
98/9 OFS 314
96 Wien 110

KUCIREK, RICHARD
01/2 OFS 263

KUCIREK, ZDENEK
99/0 Score 154

KUCSULAIN, MIKE
99/0 Louisiana Ice Gators
99/0 Louisiana Ice Gators
00/1 Louisiana Ice Gators
00/1 Louisiana Ice Gators

KUDA, PETR
94/5 APS 50
95/6 APS 83

KUDASHOV, ALEXEI
93/4 Classic 42
93/4 Cla. Prospects 106
96/7 DEL 284
93/4 Donruss 345
94/5 Donruss 84
00/1 Dynamo 16
00/1 Dynamo 16
95/6 Edge Ice 23
97/8 Hockey-Box
94/5 Leaf 181
98/9 Mir 55
94/5 Panini Sticker V
93/4 Parkhurst 260
94/5 Parkie SE180
93/4 Pinnacle 445
94/5 Premier 78
93/4 Score 623
93/4 St. John's Maple Leafs
93/4 St. John's Maple Leafs
94/5 St. John's Maple Leafs
94/5 St. John's Maple Leafs
93/4 TORO / Abalene
93/4 TORO / Abalene
94/5 TORO / Coca-Cola
94/5 TORO / Coca-Cola
93/4 Upper Deck 427, SP-159

KUDELKA, DAVID
99/0 OFS 468

KUDELSKI, BOB
91/2 Bowman 189
92/3 Bowman 12
93/4 Donruss 232
93/4 Donruss 434
94/5 Donruss 227
93/4 EA Sports 95
94/5 Flair 64
94/5 Fleer 79
93/4 Fleer Ultra 85
94/5 Fleer Ultra 80
95/6 Hoyle / East. 10-Spade
93/4 Leaf 48
94/5 Leaf 314
89/0 LOSA / Smokey 20
90/1 LOSA / Smokey 20
90/1 LOSA / Smokey 20
90/1 OPC/Topps 46
91/2 O-Pee-Chee 61
92/3 O-Pee-Chee 326
91/2 OPC Premier 129
92/3 OTTA
92/3 OTTA
93/4 OTTA
93/4 OTTA
90/1 Panini Sticker 232
91/2 Panini Sticker 87
92/3 Panini Sticker 69
93/4 Panini Sticker 114
94/5 Panini Sticker 65
91/2 Parkhurst 299
92/3 Parkhurst 357
93/4 Parkhurst 408
94/5 Parkhurst 83
94/5 Parkie SE seV35
91/2 Pinnacle 113
92/3 Pinnacle 84
93/4 Pinnacle 38
94/5 Pinnacle 284
95/6 Playoff 260
94/5 POG 105
93/4 Power Play 170
93/4 Power Play 348
93/4 Premier 40
94/5 Premier 245, TF-23
95/6 Pro Magnet 88
90/1 Pro Set 122
91/2 Pro Set 99
91/2 Pro Set Platinum 181
88/9 ProCards / New Haven
90/1 Score 305
91/2 Score 154
91/2 Score CAN 154
92/3 Score 221
93/4 Score 257
93/4 Score 549
94/5 Score 28
94/5 Select 55
94/5 SP 46
92/3 Topps 145
91/2 To. Stadium 40
92/3 To. Stadium 149
93/4 To. Stadium 120
93/4 TSC Members Only 43
90/1 Upper Deck 433
91/2 Upper Deck 301
93/4 Upper Deck 17, SP-110
94/5 Upper Deck 376, SP-29
95/6 Upper Deck 138, SE-34
95/6 UD CC 226

KUDEMETOV, EDUARD
99/0 Mir 79

KUDERMETOV, EDUARD
98/9 Mir 122
00/1 Mir 33

KUDINOV, ANDREI
94/5 Binghampton Rangers
94/5 Binghampton Rangers
95/6 Binghampton Rangers
95/6 Binghampton Rangers
98/9 Mir 35
99/0 Mir 26
00/1 Mir 241

KUDMA, JIRI
99/0 Score 114

KUDRNA, JAROSLAV
95/6 APS 333
97/8 APS 260
97/8 DS 73
98/9 DS 56
99/0 DS 80
00/1 DS 93
97/8 DS Sticker 138
98/9 OFS 158
99/0 OFS 92
00/1 OFS 45
01/2 OFS 256

KUDRNA, LADISLAV
95/6 APS 147
96/7 APS 4
97/8 APS 339
99/0 DS 183
00/1 DS 98
99/0 OFS 9
00/1 OFS 188
01/2 OFS 111, H10

KUDRNA, PETER
98/9 Brandon Wheat Kings
98/9 Brandon Wheat Kings

KUDRNA, PETR
99/0 Lethbridge Hurricanes
99/0 Lethbridge Hurricanes

KUDROC, KRISTIAN
00/1 BAP Mem. 515
01/2 BAP Mem. 202
01/2 O-Pee-Chee 314
02/3 O-Pee-Chee 288
01/2 Pacific 354
99/0 Québec Remparts 21
99/0 Québec Remparts 21
01/2 Signature 85, ✍ Aut. 85
99/0 SP Authentic 126
01/2 Topps 314
02/3 Topps 288
02/3 To. Limited 288
99/0 Upper Deck 313
99/0 UD Black Diam. 108
99/0 UD G. Reserve 313
99/0 UD MVP Cup 199

KUENZI, WERNER
72 Semic Sticker 146

KUHL, MARCUS
94/5 DEL 272
95/6 DEL 263
79 Panini Sticker 113
82 Semic Sticker 110

KUHN, BERND
72 Hellas MM-Jenkki 55
72 Semic Sticker 110

KUHN, FLORIAN
96/7 DEL 116

KUHN, TYLER
91/2 Air Canada SJHL 17
91/2 Air Canada SJHL D45
92/3 MPS SJHL 19

KUHNHACKL, ERICH
98/9 DEL 340
79 Panini Sticker 103
82 Semic Sticker 112

KUHNHAUSER, BERND
99/0 Eishockey 250, 376

KÜHNHAUSER, BERND
94/5 DEL 87
95/6 DEL 92, 428
96/7 DEL 280
98/9 DEL 303
00/1 UD DEL 47
01/2 UD DEL 52

KUHNKE, HARALD
94/5 DEL 135
95/6 DEL 137

KUHTA, KIMMO
98/9 Cardset 39
99/0 Cardset 23
00/1 Cardset 139
02/3 Cardset 47

KUIRI, TAPIO
70/1 Kuvajulkaisut 372

KUISMA, ILPO
70/1 Kuvajulkaisut 210
71/2 Williams Finnish 132
72/3 Williams Finnish 195
73/4 Williams Finnish 155
73/4 Williams Finnish 67

KUISMA, JARMO
72/3 Williams Finnish 266

KUISMANEN, PERTTI
66/7 Champion 77
70/1 Kuvajulkaisut 160

KUIVALAINEN, PARI
96/7 Sisu 69

KUIVALAINEN, PASI
98/9 Cardset 251, MM12, OD12
99/0 Cardset 244, Puck 3
00/1 Cardset 193
02/3 Cardset 48
97/8 Hockey-Box
92/3 Jyvas Hyva 87
93/4 Jyvas Hyva 164
95 Leaf Latkaliiga 9
94 Semic 2
95 Semic 1
93/4 Sisu 161
94/5 Sisu 1, MN-1, N-8
95/6 Sisu 272, GG-9
96/7 Sisu ATG-5, MA-5
95/6 Sisu Limited 64

KUJALA, PETRI
93/4 Sisu 144
95/6 Sisu 269

KUK, DUSTIN
00/1 Peoria Rivermen
00/1 Peoria Rivermen
01/2 Peoria Rivermen
01/2 Peoria Rivermen

KUKACKA, ZBYNEK
94/5 APS 82
95/6 APS 285
97/8 APS 230
98/9 DEL 76
97/8 DS Sticker 39
91/2 7th...Sketch OHL 306

KUKHTINOV, ROMAN
98/9 Mir 97
99/0 Mir 211
00/1 Mir 185

KUKI, ARTO
99/0 Cardset 212
00/1 Cardset 215
02/3 Cardset 201
97/8 Hockey-Box
94/5 Sisu ND 4
95/6 Sisu 295
96/7 Sisu RE-7

KUKKO, JOUKO
80/1 Mallasjuoma 141

KUKKOLA, ILPO
78/9 SM-Liiga 133

KUKKONEN, LASSE
00/1 Cardset 180
02/3 Cardset 202, -Nimik.

KUKUK, PHILIP
94/5 DEL 20

KUKULIES, SVEN
99/0 Eishockey 396

KUKULOWICZ, ADOLPH
52/3 Anonymous 78

KULABUCHOV, VADIM
94/5 APS 270
95/6 DEL 426

KULAGIN, BORIS
73/4 Soviet Stars 23
74/5 Soviet Stars 23

KULAK, STU
86/7 EDMO
86/7 EDMO / Red Rooster
88/9 EDMO / Action 44
83/4 Fredericton Express
83/4 Fredericton Express
90/1 Kansas City Blades
90/1 Kansas City Blades
98/9 Phoenix Mustangs 7
98/9 Phoenix Mustangs 7
89/0 ProCards AHL 33
90/1 ProCards 586
87/8 QUÉB / Gene. Foods
86/7 VANC
81/2 Victoria Cougars
81/2 Victoria Cougars
82/3 Victoria Cougars
82/3 Victoria Cougars

KULAK, STUART
88/9 ProCards / Moncton

KULCHISKY, LYLE (SPARKY)
88/9 EDMO / Action 80
90/1 EDMO / IGA
90/1 EDMO / IGA

KULESHOV, MIKHAIL
01/2 Hershey Bears
01/2 Hershey Bears
02/3 Hershey Bears
02/3 Hershey Bears

KULHORANTA, KAI
71/2 Williams Finnish 326

KULIKOV, DMITRI
99/0 Mir 108

KULIKOV, VLADIMIR
99/0 Mir 143

KULLMAN, ARNIE
98/9 Hershey Bears
98/9 Hershey Bears

KULLMAN, ED
02/3 Parkie - Reprint 162

KULLMAN, EDDIE
45-64 BeeHive-2 [NYRa.]
51/2 Parkhurst 101
52/3 Parkhurst 18
53/4 Parkhurst 61

KULMALA, ARTO
98/9 Cardset 221, OD10
99/0 Cardset 124
94/5 Sisu 78
95/6 Sisu 114
96/7 Sisu 128

KULONEN, JOUNI
00/1 Cardset 176

KULONEN, TIMO
92/3 Jyvas Hyva 122
93/4 Jyvas Hyva 226
93/4 Sisu 189
94/5 Sisu 237
95/6 Sisu 139

KULTAKUUSI, MAURI
78/9 SM-Liiga 93

KULTANEN, JARNO
00/1 BAP Mem. 408
98/9 Cardset 33
99/0 Cardset 21
00/1 Cardset 15
02/3 Cardset 49
00/1 Signature 145, ✍ Aut. 201
94/5 Sisu 228
00/1 SP Authentic 136
00/1 SPx 176
00/1 Stadium 260
00/1 To. Stars 119
00/1 UD Ice 109
00/1 UD Pros&Prosp. 95

KULYK, G
85/6 Minnesota-Duluth 34
85/6 Minnesota-Duluth 34

KUMAR, BOJAN
79 Panini Sticker 396

KUMMER, WOLFGANG
94/5 DEL 96
95/6 DEL 97
96/7 DEL 131
98/9 DEL 312
99/0 Eishockey 258
93 Semic Sticker 164

KUMPEL, MARK
86/7 DETR / Little Caesars
84/5 Fredericton Express
84/5 Fredericton Express
91/2 Moncton Hawks
91/2 Moncton Hawks
90/1 O-Pee-Chee 444
90/1 Panini/WPG 14
98/9 Portland Pirates
98/9 Portland Pirates
99/0 Portland Pirates
99/0 Portland Pirates
91/2 ProCards 184
85/6 QUÉB
85/6 QUÉB / Gene. Foods
85/6 QUÉB / McDonald's
85/6 QUÉB / Provigo
86/7 QUÉB / Gene. Foods
86/7 QUÉB / McDonald's
89/0 WINN / Safeway
89/0 WINN / Safeway
90/1 WINN / IGA
90/1 WINN / IGA

KUMPULA, ARI
98/9 Cardset 98
99/0 Cardset 234

KUMSTAT, PAVEL
96/7 APS 200
97/8 APS 131
99/0 DS 185
00/1 DS 101
96/7 DS Sticker 191
97/8 DS Sticker 250
99/0 OFS 469
00/1 OFS 192
01/2 OFS 105

KUMSTAT, PETR
00/1 OFS 208

KUNA, MARTIN
01/2 Baie-Comeau 9
01/2 Baie-Comeau 9

KUNAST, CHRISTIAN
99/0 Eishockey 337

KÜNAST, CHRISTIAN
94/5 DEL 265
95/6 DEL 243
96/7 DEL 114
98/9 DEL 84
00/1 UD DEL 173
01/2 UD DEL 185, G8, ✂ GJ

KUNCE, DANIEL
94/5 DEL 183
95/6 DEL 175
96/7 DEL 133
98/9 DEL 266
99/0 Eishockey 41
00/1 UD DEL 196
01/2 UD DEL 159

KUNCE, GEORG
95/6 DEL 174, 433

KUNGLE, JEFF
91/2 Air Canada SJHL 1
91/2 Air Canada SJHL B41
00/1 Austin Ice Bats
00/1 Austin Ice Bats
96/7 Peoria Rivermen
96/7 Peoria Rivermen

KUNTAR, LES
92/3 Classic Prospects 72
95/6 Edge Ice TW9
92/3 Fredericton Canadiens
92/3 Fredericton Canadiens
93/4 Fredericton Canadiens
93/4 Fredericton Canadiens
94/5 Hershey Bears
94/5 Hershey Bears
94/5 Parkhurst 114

KUNTOS, JIRI
94/5 APS 7
95/6 APS 106
96/7 APS 54
97/8 APS 321
98/9 DS 116
99/0 DS 101
00/1 DS 66
96/7 DS Sticker 228
97/8 DS Sticker 269
98/9 OFS 180
99/0 OFS 198, 518
00/1 OFS 216

KUNTZ, AL
52/3 Laval Dairy Update 108
52/3 St. Lawrence 66

KUNTZ, DEAN
89/0 Saskatoon Blades
89/0 Saskatoon Blades

KUNTZ, MARK
88/9 Lethbridge Hurricanes
88/9 Lethbridge Hurricanes
84/5 Medicine Hat Tigers
84/5 Medicine Hat Tigers
91/2 Richmond Renegades
91/2 Richmond Renegades
92/3 Richmond Renegades
92/3 Richmond Renegades

KUOKKANEN, JUHA
00/1 Cardset 319
02/3 Cardset 203

KUOKKANEN, MARTTI
65/6 Hellas 57
71/2 Williams Finnish 283
73/4 Williams Finnish 200

KUOPPALA,
97/8 Hockey-Box

KUOPPALA, ISMO
98/9 Cardset 166
99/0 Cardset 82
00/1 Cardset 187
94/5 Sisu 354
95/6 Sisu 87
96/7 Sisu 52

KUOSMANEN, PENTTI
70/1 Kuvajulkaisut 349

KUPAKS, ARTURS
98/9 EBK ECHL All-Star
94/5 Greensboro Monarchs
94/5 Greensboro Monarchs
96/7 Toledo Storm
96/7 Toledo Storm

KUPARI, MARKO
93/4 Sisu 155

KUPARINEN, MIKKO
98/9 Cardset 60
99/0 Cardset PA 6
02/3 Cardset 50

KUPKA, TOMAS
94/5 APS 266
95/6 APS 143
96/7 APS 18
97/8 APS 165
99/0 DS 165
96/7 DS Sticker 128
97/8 DS Sticker 202
00/1 Kudos 119
98/9 OFS 172
99/0 OFS 168

KUPREENKOV, ALEXEI
99/0 Mir 210
00/1 Mir 140

KUPS, DEREK
99/0 Fort Worth Brahmas
99/0 Fort Worth Brahmas

KURASHOV, KONSTANTIN
90/1 O-Pee-Chee 469
91/2 O-Pee-Chee 52R

KURIS, MARCEL
97/8 Peoria Rivermen
97/8 Peoria Rivermen

KURJENIEMI, JANNE
95/6 Sisu 66

KURKA, TOMAS
02/3 BAP Mem. 368
02/3 Pacific Complete 548
02/3 SP Authentic 219
02/3 Ultimate Mem. 98
02/3 UD Rookie 130

KURKINEN, RISTO
92/3 Jyvas Hyva 85
93/4 Jyvas Hyva 139
90/1 Semic Elitserien 111
91/2 Semic Elitserien 116
91 Semic Sticker 16
93/4 Sisu 158
94/5 Sisu 325, FOI-16
95/6 Sisu Limited 51

KUROCHKIN, NIKOLAI
98/9 Mir 95
00/1 Mir 187

KUROCHKIN, VYACHESLAV
99/0 Mir 228

KURRI, JARI
96/7 ANAH / Up Front 23
96/7 ANAH / Up Front 23
01/2 BAP Mem. ✂ 500GS
02/3 BAP Mem. / Cup
90/1 Bowman 191, -HT 19
92/3 Bowman 94
98/9 Cardset 1, DT1
99/0 Cardset AH Joker
02/3 Cardset 51
93/4 Classic 121
93/4 Donruss 151
94/5 Donruss 93
95/6 Donruss 133
96/7 Do. Canadian 49
96/7 Do. Elite 85
80/1 EDMO / Zellers
81/2 EDMO / Red Rooster
82/3 EDMO / Red Rooster
83/4 EDMO / Button
83/4 EDMO / McDonald's
83/4 EDMO / West Mall
83/4 EDMO
84/5 EDMO
84/5 EDMO / Red Rooster
85/6 EDMO / Red Rooster
86/7 EDMO
86/7 EDMO / Red Rooster
87/8 EDMO
88/9 EDMO
88/9 EDMO / Action 41
88/9 Esso All-Star
94/5 Flair 81
94/5 Fleer 96
01/2 Fleer Greats 86, ✍ Aut.
01/2 Fleer Legacy 8, 57, ✂ ITC
92/3 Fleer Ultra 85, -UI 11
93/4 Fleer Ultra 165
94/5 Fleer Ultra 100, GG-5
95/6 Fleer Ultra 251
96/7 Fl. Ultra 3
83/4 Funmate Puffy 5 [w/]
95 Globe 137
93/4 Hockey Wit 89
95/6 Hoyle / West. 2-Diamond
84/5 Kellogg's 14
93 Koululainen
95 Koululainen
89/0 Kraft 13
90/1 Kraft 68
91/2 Kraft 67
86/7 Kraft Sports 16
89/0 Kraft Stickers 5
93/4 Leaf 240
94/5 Leaf 104
95/6 Leaf 122
94/5 L. Limited 105
93/4 McDonald's McD-08
98/9 McD's T9
96/7 Metal Univ. 3
00/1 Mir Fetisov 26
81/2 O-Pee-Chee 107
82/3 O-Pee-Chee 111
83/4 O-Pee-Chee 34
84/5 O-Pee-Chee 215
84/5 O-Pee-Chee 249
85/6 O-Pee-Chee 261
85/6 OPC/Topps 155
86/7 O-Pee-Chee 258
86/7 OPC/Topps 108
86/7 OPC/Topps Box H
87/8 OPC/Topps 148
88/9 OPC/Topps 147
90/1 OPC/Topps 5, 108
91/2 O-Pee-Chee 295
92/3 O-Pee-Chee 205
89/0 OPC/Topps 43
87/8 OPC Leaders 21
91/2 OPC Premier 111
81/2 OPC Sticker 11
81/2 OPC Sticker 211
82/3 OPC/Topps Sticker 108
82/3 OPC/Topps Sticker 109
83/4 OPC/Topps Sticker 104
83/4 OPC/Topps Sticker 19
83/4 OPC/Topps Sticker 21
84/5 OPC Sticker 249
84/5 OPC Sticker 250
85/6 OPC Sticker 121
85/6 OPC Sticker 201-74
85/6 OPC Sticker 231
86/7 OPC Sticker 118-132
86/7 OPC Sticker 185-125
86/7 OPC Sticker 73
87/8 OPC Sticker 117-129
87/8 OPC Sticker 82
88/9 OPC Sticker 227
89/0 opcSticker 221
97/8 Omega 59
98/9 Pacific 162
97/8 Pacific CC SS-1B
97/8 Pa. Crown Roy. 35
97/8 Pa. Paramount 51
97/8 Pa. Revolution 34
87/8 Panini Sticker 262
88/9 Panini Sticker 59
89/0 Panini Sticker 73, 181
90/1 Panini Sticker 222
92/3 Panini Sticker 66
93/4 Panini Sticker 202
94/5 Panini Sticker 173
95/6 Panini Sticker 270
96/7 Panini Sticker 109
97/8 Panini Sticker 189
95 Panini Worlds 293
91/2 Parkhurst 210
91/2 Parkhurst 223
91/2 Parkhurst 72
92/3 Parkhurst 445
92/3 Parkhurst 67
93/4 Parkhurst 365
94/5 Parkhurst 104
95/6 Parkhurst 102, 239
01/2 Parkhurst ✂ 500GS, ✂ PS66, ✍ PA32
02/3 Parkhurst ✂ VM6
94/5 Parkie SE ES-9, seV24
89 Pelimiehen Passi
80/1 Pepsi Bottle Cap
91/2 Pinnacle 48
92/3 Pinnacle 243
92/3 Pinnacle 60
93/4 Pinnacle 75
94/5 Pinnacle 35, WE7
95/6 Pinnacle 22, GG-4
97/8 Pi. Be A Player 7, ✍ Aut. 7
97/8 Pi. Inside 113
95/6 Pi. Summit 32
96/7 Pi. Summit 47
95/6 Pi. Zenith 50
95/6 Playoff 271
96/7 Playoff 412
94/5 POG 127
95/6 POG 134
82/3 Post [Edmo.]
94/5 Post
93/4 Power Play 118
93/4 Power Play GG 4
93/4 Premier 206
94/5 Premier 25
95/6 Pro Magnet 63
90/1 Pro Set 87, 348
91/2 Pro Set 93
92/3 Pro Set 68
91/2 Pro Set Platinum 48
90/1 Score 158, 348
91/2 Score 50T
91/2 Score CAN 600
92/3 Score 398
93/4 Score 100
93/4 Score 446
93/4 Score DD7
93/4 Score IS 7
93/4 Score PiAS 35
94/5 Score 114
95/6 Score 115
97/8 Score Colo. 5
94/5 Select 71
95/6 Select CE 35
96/7 Select CE 86
94 Semic 24
94 Semic 346
95 Semic 17, 204
91 Semic Sticker 18
92 Semic Sticker 17
93 Semic Sticker 67
84/5 7-Eleven
85/6 7-Eleven Superstars 6
01/2 Signature ✂ 500GS, ✍ VA29
94/5 Sisu 207, GS-2
95/6 Sisu SS 4
95/6 Sisu Limited 16, SAS-7
95/6 SBx Emotion 83
95/6 SBx Impact 81
78/9 SM-Liiga 76
83/4 Souhaits Keychain [Oilers]
94/5 SP 57
96/7 SP 3
97/8 SP Authentic 42
01/2 SP Authentic ✂ NN
77-79 Sports. FIN 77-1848
95 Suomen All-Star 2
81/2 Topps 18
84/5 Topps 161
84/5 Topps 52
85/6 OPC/Topps-Stick. 3
86/7 OPC/Topps - Stick. 10
87/8 OPC/Topps - Stick. 4
92/3 Topps 51
95/6 Topps 239
94/5 Topps Finest 81, RL-3
96/7 To. Picks FC3
92/3 To. Stadium 138
93/4 To. Stadium 400
93/4 To. Stadium - Master Photo-2 2
93/4 To. Stadium - All-Stars
95/6 To. Stadium 151
92/3 To. Stadium Members

Only
01/2 Ultimate Mem. ✂ 500GS, ✂ GSL, ✂ RN, ✂ RT, ✂ RA, ✂ SCP, ✂ SCW
02/3 Ultimate Mem. ✂ FS
90/1 Upper Deck 146
91/2 Upper Deck 24
91/2 Upper Deck 366
92/3 Upper Deck 218
92/3 Upper Deck WG4
93/4 Upper Deck 332
94/5 Upper Deck 293, 559
95/6 Upper Deck 372, SE-41
96/7 Upper Deck 212, X24
98/9 Upper Deck FT8
00 ✂ UD APOH 500, ✂✍ 500
94/5 UD BAP R25, G16
95/6 UD BAP 201, ✍ S201
99/0 UD C. Legends 48
95/6 UD CC 16
96/7 UD CC 173
97/8 UD Coll. Choice 10
02/3 UD Foundations ✂ 1000Stick (x2) ✍ SG
00/1 UD Legends 50, ✂ LGJ, ✍ ES
01/2 UD Legends 23, 97, ✂ PoH
92/3 UD Locker 29
02/3 UD Piece ✂ HH, ✍ MD, / Giveaway
99/0 UD Retro 108, G8A
01/2 UD SCup Champs 11
83/4 Vachon 31-111
83/4 Vachon 31-82
82 Valio
96 Wien 24, NS4

KURT, GARY
71/2 O-Pee-Chee 181
72/3 O-Pee-Chee 306
75/6 OPC WHA 126
76/7 OPC WHA 102
75/6 Phoenix Roadrunners
75/6 Phoenix Roadrunners
76/7 Phoenix Roadrunners
76/7 Phoenix Roadrunners

KURTENBACH, ORLAND
71/2 Bazooka Panel
45-64 BeeHive-2 [Bost.]
64-67 BeeHive-3 [Bost.]
64-67 BeeHive-3 [Toro.]
64-67 BeeHive-3 [NYRa.]
64/5 Coke/Sprite [Bost.]
65/6 Coca-Cola
70/1 Colgate 23
70/1 Dad's Cookies
70/1 Eddie Sargent 212
71/2 Eddie Sargent 216
72/3 Eddie Sargent 215
70/1 Esso Power Player
72/3 Post 7
73/4 Mac's Milk
68/9 O-Pee-Chee 170
69/0 O-Pee-Chee 188
70/1 O-Pee-Chee 117
70/1 O-Pee-Chee DE 45
71/2 O-Pee-Chee 42
71/2 O-Pee-Chee Book. 20
72/3 O-Pee-Chee 141
72/3 O-Pee-Chee 149
72/3 O-Pee-Chee Crest 22
73/4 O-Pee-Chee 4
71/2 O-Pee-Chee Poster 12
95/6 Parkie 66-67 90
94/5 Parkie Tall 7
70/1 Post Shooters
61/2 Shirriff 14
68/9 Shirriff / NYRa. 8
61/2 Topps 15
63/4 Topps 20
64/5 Topps 18
65/6 Topps 20
66/7 Topps 25
66/7 Topps / Test 25
67/8 Topps 87
70/1 Topps 117
71/2 Topps 42
72/3 Topps 46
73/4 Topps 157
68/9 TORO
64/5 Toronto Star Action
71/2 Toronto Sun Photo
91/2 Ultimate Original Six 24, ✍ Aut. 24
70/1 VANC / Royal Bank
71/2 VANC / Royal Bank 6
72/3 VANC / Royal Bank
73/4 VANC / Royal Bank

KURTENBACH, TERRY
94/5 Guildford Flames 6
94/5 Guildford Flames 6
95/6 Guildford Flames 15
95/6 Guildford Flames 15
95/6 Guildford Flames 27
95/6 Guildford Flames 27
96/7 Guildford Flames 5
96/7 Guildford Flames 5
97/8 Guildford Flames
97/8 Guildford Flames
98/9 Guildford Flames
98/9 Guildford Flames

KURTZ, JUSTIN
97 Bowman 111
95/6 Brandon Wheat Kings
95/6 Brandon Wheat Kings
97/8 Las Vegas Thunder 22
97/8 Las Vegas Thunder 22
99/0 Manitoba Moose
99/0 Manitoba Moose
00/1 Manitoba Moose
00/1 Manitoba Moose
01/2 Manitoba Moose
01/2 Manitoba Moose
02/3 Manitoba Moose
02/3 Manitoba Moose
94/5 Parkie SE262
94/5 SR Auto-Phonex 23, ✍ 23
01/2 Signature 205, ✍ Aut. 205
94/5 Slapshot Memorial 32
01/2 UD Honor Roll 89
01/2 UD Premier 85

KURVERS, TOM
94/5 ANAH / Carl's Jr. 14
94/5 ANAH / Carl's Jr. 14
91/2 Bowman 319
92/3 Bowman 259
86/7 BUFF / Blue Shield
94/5 Fleer 5
93/4 Fleer Ultra 368
94/5 Leaf 449
84/5 MONT
85/6 MONT
85/6 MONT / Provigo
88/9 NJER / Caretta
85/6 O-Pee-Chee 219
88/9 O-Pee-Chee 222
90/1 OPC/Topps 11
92/3 O-Pee-Chee 202
89/0 OPC/Topps 9
91/2 OPC Premier 98
85/6 OPC Sticker 129-249
86/7 OPC Sticker 10-155
89/0 opcSticker 84-225
89/0 Panini Sticker 252
90/1 Panini Sticker 287
90/1 Panini/TOR 11
91/2 Panini Sticker 43
91/2 Parkhurst 112
93/4 Parkhurst 392
94/5 Parkie SE4
91/2 Pinnacle 7
92/3 Pinnacle 324
94/5 Pinnacle 380
93/4 Power Play 384
93/4 Premier 279
90/1 Pro Set 282
91/2 Pro Set 244
91/2 Pro Set 428
90/1 Score 142
91/2 Score 174
91/2 Score 18T
91/2 Score CAN 174
91/2 Score CAN 568
92/3 Score 232
92/3 Topps 118
92/3 To. Stadium 409
93/4 To. Stadium 279
94/5 TSC Members Only 24
90/1 TORO
90/1 TORO
90/1 Upper Deck 160
92/3 Upper Deck 292
93/4 Upper Deck 381
94/5 Upper Deck 123
90/1 VANC / Mohawk
90/1 VANC / Mohawk

KURVINEN, MIKKO
00/1 Cardset 135

KURZAWSKI, MARK
88/9 ProCards / Saginaw
89/0 ProCards IHL 52

KUS, PETR
00/1 DS 26
00/1 OFS 58
99/0 Score 84

KUSHNER, DALE
91/2 Bowman 247
84/5 Medicine Hat Tigers
84/5 Medicine Hat Tigers
91/2 O-Pee-Chee 415
90/1 OPC Premier 54
90/1 PHIL
90/1 PHIL
89/0 ProCards AHL 243
90/1 ProCards 28
91/2 ProCards 268
94/5 Saint John Flames
94/5 Saint John Flames
91/2 Score CAN 512
91/2 To. Stadium 349
91/2 Upper Deck 429

KUSTER, HENRY
95/6 Bowman P21
95/6 Classic 63, AS3
95/6 Cla. Vis. Signings 73, ✍ Aut.

KUTLAK, ZDENEK
01/2 BAP Mem. 344
98/9 OFS 416
99/0 OFS 183
01/2 Parkhurst 305
00/1 Providence Bruins
00/1 Providence Bruins
01/2 Providence Bruins
01/2 Providence Bruins
01/2 SP GU 67
01/2 SPx 95
01/2 Upper Deck 182
01/2 UD Ice 45
01/2 UD MVP 191
01/2 UD Top Shelf 48
01/2 UD Vintage 277
01/2 Victory 363

KUTNY, VLADIMIR
02/3 Québec Remparts
02/3 Québec Remparts

KUTYAVIN, SERGEI
00/1 Mir 355

KUUKAUPPI, URPO
73/4 Williams Finnish 201

KUUSINEN, PENTTI
66/7 Champion 181

KUUSISAARI, JUHA
95/6 Sisu 346

KUUSISTO, JARMO
98/9 Cardset Top. 8
02/3 Cardset 52
97/8 Hockey-Box
91/2 Jyvas Hyva 47
92/3 Jyvas Hyva 128
93/4 Jyvas Hyva 230
80/1 Mallasjuoma 114
89 Semic Sticker 36
93/4 Sisu 186
93/4 Sisu 307
94/5 Sisu 5, MN-3
95/6 Sisu 169, 182, SS-5
95/6 Sisu Limited 30

KUUSISTO, OSMO
70/1 Kuvajulkaisut 178

KUUSISTO, PEKKA
66/7 Champion 20
65/6 Hellas 65
70/1 Kuvajulkaisut 127
72 Panda MM-Toronto
71/2 Williams Finnish 179
72/3 Williams Finnish 127
73/4 Williams Finnish 182
73/4 Williams Finnish 68

KUUSISTO, RIKU
92/3 Jyvas Hyva 113
93/4 Sisu 274

KUUSISTO, VEIKKO
66/7 Champion 113

KUUSKO, ANDERS
95/6 UD Elitserien 45

KUVALDIN, ALEXANDER
00/1 Dynamo 17
00/1 Dynamo 17
98/9 Mir 154

KUVEKO, EVGENI
98/9 Mir 61

KUWABARA, RYAN
92/3 Fredericton Canadiens
92/3 Fredericton Canadiens
93/4 Fredericton Canadiens
93/4 Fredericton Canadiens
89/0 7th..Sketch OHL 55
90/1 7th..Sketch OHL 85
91/2 7th...Sketch OHL 303

KUZELA, MILAN
72 Hellas MM-Jenkki 96
74 Hellas MM-Jenkki 76
72 Panda MM-Toronto
72/3 Williams Finnish 13
73/4 Williams Finnish 54

KUZKIN, VIKTOR
91/2 Future Trends C72 41
72 Hellas MM-Jenkki 64
72 Panda MM-Toronto
72 Semic Sticker 4
74 Semic Sticker 45
69/0 Soviet Stars
71/2 Soviet Stars
73/4 Soviet Stars 25
74/5 Soviet Stars 10
71/2 Williams Finnish 5
72/3 Williams Finnish 26

KUZMENKO, DENIS
99/0 Mir 192

KUZMIN, ANDREI
00/1 Mir 314
00/1 Mir 72

KUZMIN, BORIS
98/9 Mir 96
00/1 Mir 68

KUZMINSKI,
97/8 Hockey-Box

KUZMINSKI, ALEXANDER
99/0 Eishockey 272

KUZMINSKY, ALEXANDER
91/2 Upper Deck 656
91/2 Upper Deck WJC 17
00/1 UD DEL 106

KUZNETSOV, MAXIM
00/1 BAP Mem. 460
01/2 BAP Mem. 115
99/0 Cincinnati M'Ducks
99/0 Cincinnati M'Ducks
01/2 PS Titanium Draft 127
94/5 Select 157
94/5 Sig. Rookies FF7, ✍ FF7
95/6 SR Tetrad F9
01/2 Victory 369

KUZNETSOV, YURI
98/9 Cardset 187
99/0 Cardset 305
00/1 Cardset 322
02/3 Cardset 53
97/8 Hockey-Box
99/0 Mir 22
00/1 Mir 107, 273
90/1 O-Pee-Chee 489
94/5 Sisu 316
95/6 Sisu 3

KUZNIK, GREG
98 Bowman 47
98 Bowman Chrome 47
99/0 Cincinnati Cyclones
99/0 Cincinnati Cyclones
00/1 Cincinnati Cyclones
00/1 Cincinnati Cyclones
98/9 Florida Everblades
98/9 Florida Everblades
99/0 Florida Everblades
99/0 Florida Everblades
00/1 SPx 154

KVALEVOG, TOBY
93/4 Donruss USA11
93/4 Pinnacle 480
93/4 Upper Deck 555

KVARTALNOV, ANDREI
91/2 O-Pee-Chee 53R

KVARTALNOV, DMITRI
92/3 BOST / Postcard
92/3 BOST / Postcard
92/3 CSC 9
92/3 Classic 120
92/3 Classic 93
92/3 Classic LP6
92/3 Classic Four Sport 222
92/3 Classic Four Sport BC10
92/3 Classic Prospects 32, BC17, ✍ Aut.
93/4 Donruss 27
92/3 Fleer Ultra 252, -UI 12
93/4 Fleer Ultra 82
93/4 Leaf 143
92/3 OPC Premier 6
93/4 Panini Sticker 7
92/3 Parkhurst 222
92/3 Parkhurst 7
93/4 Parkhurst 287
92/3 Pinnacle 405
93/4 Pinnacle 161
93/4 Power Play 20
93/4 Power Play SYS 4
93/4 Premier 197
91/2 ProCards 313
92/3 Red Ace Blue 9
92/3 Red Ace Violet 18
93/4 Score 187
89/0 Soviet Stars
92/3 Upper Deck 455
92/3 Upper Deck 561
93/4 Upper Deck 19
92/3 UD Locker 55

KVASHA, OLEG
98/9 Be A Player 210, ✍ Aut. 210
99/0 BAP Mem. 11
00/1 BAP Mem. 402
98/9 Bowman's Best 126
98/9 Collection Souvenir 12
98/9 Dynagon Ice 83
99/0 Millenium 108, ✍ Aut. 108
99/0 NHL Power Play
98/9 Omega 108
99/0 Pacific 174
00/1 Pacific 180
02/3 Pacific Complete 326
98/9 Pa. Crown Roy. 60
99/0 Pa. Paramount 101
98/9 Panini Photocard
99/0 Panini Sticker 63
92 Québec Pee Wee 1778
98/9 SP Authentic 98
99/0 SPx 70
99/0 Topps 200
99/0 To. Chrome 200
98/9 T. Gold Label 25
02/3 T. Total 296
98/9 Upper Deck 416, GN24
99/0 Upper Deck 231
00/1 Upper Deck 341
02/3 Upper Deck 357
98/9 UD G. Reserve 416
99/0 UD G. Reserve 231
98/9 UD MVP 92
99/0 UD MVP 89
02/3 UD Vintage 159
99/0 Victory 124
00/1 Victory 105
01/2 Victory 228

KVERKA, JAROMIR
94/5 APS 89
95/6 APS 191
97/8 APS 10
98/9 DS 29
99/0 DS 23
00/1 DS 127
97/8 DS Sticker 218
98/9 OFS 88
99/0 OFS 137
00/1 OFS 172
01/2 OFS 190, -UHI 19

KVETAN, BRANISLAV
01/2 Louisiana Ice Gators
01/2 Louisiana Ice Gators
02/3 Louisiana Ice Gators
02/3 Louisiana Ice Gators

KWAS, CHRIS
97/8 Regina Pats
97/8 Regina Pats

KWASIGROCH, PETER
94/5 DEL 164
95/6 DEL 163
96/7 DEL 237

KWASIGROCH, PIOTR
89 Semic Sticker 148

KWIATKOWSKI, DARREN
87/8 Regina Pats
87/8 Regina Pats

KWIATKOWSKI, JASON
90/1 Prince Albert Raiders
90/1 Prince Albert Raiders
91/2 Prince Albert Raiders
91/2 Prince Albert Raiders
90/1 7th..Sketch WHL 276
91/2 7th...Sketch WHL 245
92/3 Tacoma Rockets
92/3 Tacoma Rockets

KWIATKOWSKI, JOEL
01/2 BAP Mem. 429
97 Bowman 84
98 Bowman 45
98 Bowman Chrome 45
02/3 Calder 99
98/9 Cincinnati M'Ducks 14
98/9 Cincinnati M'Ducks 14
99/0 Cincinnati M'Ducks
99/0 Cincinnati M'Ducks
00/1 Grand Rapids Griffins
00/1 Grand Rapids Griffins
01/2 Grand Rapids Griffins
01/2 Grand Rapids Griffins
02/3 OTTA
02/3 OTTA
02/3 Pacific Complete 529
01/2 SP Authentic 164
01/2 SPx 145, -RT
01/2 Upper Deck 200
01/2 UD MVP 209
01/2 UD Top Shelf 60
01/2 Victory 382

KWONG, LARRY
51/2 Laval Dairy 73
52/3 St. Lawrence 19

KYHÄ, TUOMO
99/0 Cardset 146
00/1 Cardset 106

KYHOS, VLADIMIR
95/6 APS 149
96/7 APS 166

KYKOPP, TIMO
95/6 Sisu 287

KYLE, DOUG
83/4 Saskatoon Blades
83/4 Saskatoon Blades

KYLE, WALTER (GUS)
45-64 BeeHive-2 [NYRa.]
99/0 Hamilton Bulldogs
99/0 Hamilton Bulldogs
51/2 Parkhurst 21
93/4 Seattle Thunderbirds
93/4 Seattle Thunderbirds

KYLE, WILLIAM
51/2 Laval Dairy 39

KYLLASTINEN, HANNU
65/6 Hellas 59

KYLLONEN, MARKKU
91/2 Jyvas Hyva 40

KYLLONEN, PEKKA
70/1 Kuvajulkaisut 373

KYNTOLA, JORMA
65/6 Hellas 53

KYNTOLA, TIMO
70/1 Kuvajulkaisut 179
71/2 Williams Finnish 103
72/3 Williams Finnish 147
73/4 Williams Finnish 112

KYOYA, YOSHIAKI
79 Panini Sticker 288

KYPREOS, NICK
90/1 Bowman 67
91/2 Bowman 301
93/4 Donruss 140
92/3 Fleer Ultra 301
92/3 HART / Dairymart
92/3 HART / Dairymart
93/4 Leaf 414
94/5 Leaf 406
83/4 North Bay Centennials
83/4 North Bay Centennials
90/1 O-Pee-Chee 440
91/2 O-Pee-Chee 511
91/2 Panini Sticker 204
91/2 Parkhurst 411
92/3 Parkhurst 297
93/4 Pinnacle 83
94/5 Pinnacle 408
97/8 Pi. Be A Player 128, ✍ Aut. 128
93/4 Power Play 105
90/1 Pro Set 551
91/2 Pro Set 513
91/2 Score CAN 432
93/4 Score 404
92/3 Topps 193
91/2 To. Stadium 307
94/5 To. Stadium 154
92/3 Upper Deck 447
93/4 Upper Deck 11
95/6 Upper Deck 493
94/5 UD BAP R21, ✍ 54
89/0 WASH
89/0 WASH
90/1 WASH / Kodak
90/1 WASH / Kodak
90/1 WASH / Smokey
90/1 WASH / Smokey
91/2 WASH / Kodak
91/2 WASH / Kodak
91/2 WASH / Smokey
91/2 WASH / Smokey

KYPREOS, NICK
02/3 Fleer Throwbacks 50

KYRES, TEDDY
01/2 Moncton Wildcats 13
01/2 Moncton Wildcats 13
00/1 Victoriaville Tigres 4
00/1 Victoriaville Tigres 4

KYRÖ, ROGER
95/6 Leaf Elit Set 173
92/3 Upper Deck 226
95/6 UD Elitserien 27
97/8 UD Elitserien 26
98/9 UD Elitserien 40
99/0 UD Elitserien 24
00/1 UD Elitserien 38

KYSELA, DANIEL
94/5 APS 118
96/7 APS 195
99/0 OFS 228

KYSELA, ROBERT
94/5 APS 220
95/6 APS 170
96/7 APS 179, 339
97/8 APS 88
97/8 DS 8
98/9 DS 48
99/0 DS 64
00/1 DS 48
96/7 DS Sticker 44
97/8 DS Sticker 94
98/9 OFS 264
99/0 OFS 151
00/1 OFS 151
01/2 OFS 172

KYTE, JIM
91/2 CALG / IGA
91/2 CALG / IGA
94/5 Classic E9
96/7 Kansas City Blades
96/7 Kansas City Blades
93/4 Las Vegas Thunder
93/4 Las Vegas Thunder
94/5 Las Vegas Thunder
94/5 Las Vegas Thunder
87/8 O-Pee-Chee 226
89/0 O-Pee-Chee 295
88/9 OPC Sticker 145-16
89/0 opcSticker 140-259
87/8 Panini Sticker 362
88/9 Panini Sticker 194
91/2 Pinnacle 398
91/2 Pro Set 612
90/1 ProCards 374
91/2 Score CAN 547
83/4 Vachon 128-8
82/3 WINN
83/4 WINN
84/5 WINN / Safety Tips
85/6 WINN
85/6 WINN / Safety Tips
86/7 WINN
87/8 WINN
88/9 WINN / Safety Tips

KYZIMIN, OLEG
00/1 Mir 75

L

L'HEUREUX, CONRAD
52/3 Bas du Fleuve 59
51/2 Lac St-Jean 28

L'HEUREUX, WILF
23/4 Paulins Candy 17

L'ITALIEN, ERIC
99/0 Rouyn-Noranda
99/0 Rouyn-Noranda

LAAKKIO, SEPPO
70/1 Kuvajulkaisut 280
71/2 Williams Finnish 153
72/3 Williams Finnish 105
73/4 Williams Finnish 202

LAAKKONEN, JANNE
02/3 Cardset 204

LAAKSO, AKI
72/3 Williams Finnish 331

LAAKSONEN, ANTTI
00/1 BAP Mem. 317
02/3 Cardset 205
98/9 Dynagon Ice 12
01/2 Pacific 198
02/3 Pacific 185
02/3 Pacific Complete 425
00/1 Panini Sticker 174
97/8 Providence Bruins
97/8 Providence Bruins
98/9 Providence Bruins
98/9 Providence Bruins
99/0 Providence Bruins
99/0 Providence Bruins
01/2 Signature 160, ✍ Aut. 160
02/3 Sports Vault 248
02/3 T. Total 393
98/9 Upper Deck 223
98/9 UD G. Reserve 223
02/3 UD MVP 93
01/2 UD Vintage 128
01/2 Victory 180

LAAKSONEN, ILKKA
73/4 Williams Finnish 288

LAAKSONEN, MIKA
98/9 Cardset 257
99/0 Cardset 282
00/1 Cardset 63
94/5 Sisu 137
95/6 Sisu 71
96/7 Sisu 73

LAAKSONEN, MIKKO
95/6 Sisu 347

LAAKSONEN, TOM
98/9 Cardset 42
99/0 Cardset 24
92/3 Jyvas Hyva 117
95/6 Sisu 208

LAAMANEN, J.P.
96/7 Sisu 57

LAAMANEN, JUKKA
95/6 Sisu 263

LAAMANEN, JUKKA-PEKKA
02/3 Cardset 206

LAAN, JOHN
94/5 Slapshot / Brantford 15

LAAPAS, JORMA
65/6 Hellas 3

LAAPAS, MANU
95/6 Sisu 327
96/7 Sisu 140

LAATIKAINEN, ARTO
99/0 Cardset 12
00/1 Cardset 124
02/3 Cardset 54
98/9 SPx Prospects 70
98/9 UD Black Diam. 102

LABADIE, MICHEL
52/3 Anonymous 70

LABARBERA, JASON
00/1 BAP Mem. 453
01/2 BT Pipes 55
02/3 Between the Pipes 86
98 Bowman 140, ✍ A2
98 Bowman Chrome 140
00/1 Charlotte Checkers
00/1 Charlotte Checkers
00/1 Hartford Wolf Pack
00/1 Hartford Wolf Pack
01/2 Hartford Wolf Pack
01/2 Hartford Wolf Pack
97/8 Portland Winter Hawks
97/8 Portland Winter Hawks
93 Québec Pee Wee 1227
00/1 SP GU 74
00/1 SPx 165
00/1 To. Stars 124
00/1 UD Reserve 105
00/1 Upper Deck 417

LABARBERA, JASON
02/3 UD Mask 56

LABARBERA, JASON
00/1 UD Pros&Prosp. 115

LABAYEN, PERICO
79 Panini Sticker 376

LABBE, KEVIN
99/0 Medicine Hat Tigers
99/0 Medicine Hat Tigers

LABBÉ, JEAN-FRANCOIS
00/1 Syracuse Crunch
00/1 Syracuse Crunch

LABBÉ, JEAN-FRANÇOIS
00/1 BAP Mem. 226
01/2 BT Pipes 159
02/3 Between the Pipes 64
99/0 Hartford Wolf Pack
99/0 Hartford Wolf Pack
02/3 Pacific Complete 404
90/1 7th..Sketch LHJMQ 88
91/2 7th...Sketch LHJMQ 122
01/2 Syracuse Crunch
01/2 Syracuse Crunch
02/3 UD Mask 24, 25

LABBÉ, JEAN-FRANÇOIS*
98/9 Hartford Wolf Pack
98/9 Hartford Wolf Pack
93/4 Thunder Bay Senators
93/4 Thunder Bay Senators

LABELLE, JONATHAN
00/1 Hull Olympiques 11
00/1 Hull Olympiques 11
01/2 Hull Olympiques 12
01/2 Hull Olympiques 12

LABELLE, MARC
93/4 Cincinnati Cyclones
93/4 Cincinnati Cyclones
94/5 Cincinnati Cyclones
94/5 Cincinnati Cyclones
95/6 Cincinnati Cyclones
95/6 Cincinnati Cyclones
97/8 Cincinnati Cyclones
97/8 Cincinnati Cyclones
91/2 ProCards 87

LABELLE, OLIVIER
02/3 Hull Olympiques
02/3 Hull Olympiques

LABELLE, SERGE
91/2 7th...Sketch LHJMQ 20

LABENSKI, GREG
99 Bowman 138
98 Bowman 6
98 Bowman Chrome 6
01/2 Louisiana Ice Gators
01/2 Louisiana Ice Gators
95/6 Slapshot 227

LABERGE, GILLES
84/5 Chicoutimi Saguenéens
84/5 Chicoutimi Saguenéens

LABINE, LEO
45-64 BeeHive-2 [Bost.]
45-64 BeeHive-2 [Detr.]
57-58 BOST
52/3 Parkhurst 81
53/4 Parkhurst 93
54/5 Parkhurst 61
61/2 Parkhurst 33
62/3 Parkhurst 26
93/4 Parkhurst DPR-10
93/4 Parkie 56-57 4
60/1 Shirriff 117
61/2 Shirriff 64
54/5 Topps 19
57/8 Topps 9
58/9 Topps 4
59/0 Topps 7
60/1 Topps 13
91/2 Ultimate Original Six 50, ✍ Aut. 50

LABONTÉ, CHARLINE
96 Québec Pee Wee 1288
99/0 UD Prospects 54, ✍ Sig., ✂ GJ

LABONTÉ, DORIS
00/1 Rimouski Océanic 25
00/1 Rimouski Océanic 25

LABOSSIÈRE, GASTON
51/2 Lac St-Jean 51

LABOSSIERE, GORD
45-64 BeeHive-2 [NYRa.]
64-67 BeeHive-3 [NYRa.]
70/1 Esso Power Player
75/6 Houston Aeros
75/6 Houston Aeros
68/9 O-Pee-Chee 38
69/0 O-Pee-Chee 109
70/1 O-Pee-Chee 38
72/3 O-Pee-Chee 303
75/6 OPC WHA 89
68/9 Shirriff / LosA. 5
68/9 Topps 38
69/0 Topps 109
70/1 Topps 38

LABOSSIÈRE, GORDON
65/6 Québec Aces

LABRAATEN, DAN
81/2 CALG
79/0 DETR
80/1 DETR
79/0 O-Pee-Chee 92
80/1 O-Pee-Chee 217
81/2 O-Pee-Chee 42
77/8 OPC WHA 57
72 Semic Sticker 67
74 Semic Sticker 23
79/0 Topps 92
80/1 Topps 217

LABRAATEN, JAN
94/5 SR Auto-Phonex 24, ✍ 24
95/6 SR Tetrad Autobilia 44
95/6 UD CC 353

LABRAATEN, ULF
94/5 Leaf Elit Set 306

LABRANCHE, EMMANUEL
93/4 Slapshot / Drummondville 9

LABRE, BRENT
00/1 Mississauga IceDogs
00/1 Mississauga IceDogs

LABRE, YVON
73/4 O-Pee-Chee 247
74/5 O-Pee-Chee 345
75/6 O-Pee-Chee 61
76/7 O-Pee-Chee 161
76/7 OPC 396
77/8 O-Pee-Chee 31
78/9 O-Pee-Chee 324
79/0 O-Pee-Chee 343
75/6 Topps 61
76/7 Topps 161
77/8 Topps 31
74/5 WASH
79/0 WASH
80/1 WASH

LABRECQUE, GUILLAUME
02/3 Hull Olympiques
02/3 Hull Olympiques

LABRECQUE, PATRICK
94/5 Fredericton Canadiens
94/5 Fredericton Canadiens
95/6 Fredericton Canadiens
95/6 Fredericton Canadiens
96/7 Leaf 224
96/7 Pinnacle 246
96/7 Pi. Summit 177
91/2 ProCards 532
90/1 7th..Sketch LHJMQ 215
95/6 Upper Deck 379

LABRIE, GUY
52/3 Bas du Fleuve 16
51/2 Laval Dairy 47
52/3 St. Lawrence 74

LABRIER, BOB
84/5 Kamloops Blazers
84/5 Kamloops Blazers

LABRIER, R.T.
85/6 Kamloops Blazers
85/6 Kamloops Blazers

LABROSSE, DWIGHT
01/2 Guelph Storm
01/2 Guelph Storm
01/2 Guelph Storm M-Cup
01/2 Guelph Storm M-Cup

LABZOV, LEONID
98/9 Mir 81
99/0 Mir 102

LACASSE, PHILIPPE
99/0 Hull Olympiques BN
99/0 Hull Olympiques BN
99/0 Hull Olympiques 16
99/0 Hull Olympiques 16
00/1 Hull Olympiques 15
00/1 Hull Olympiques 15
01/2 Hull Olympiques 16
01/2 Hull Olympiques 16

LACEDELLI, RENATO
79 Panini Sticker 389

LACH, ELMER
01/2 BAP Mem. ✂ RM
34-43 BeeHive-1 [Mont.]
45-64 BeeHive-2 [Mont.]
77/8 Dernière Heure
48-52 Exhibits [Canadiens]
48-52 Exhibits [Canadiens]
83 HHOF Postcard I9
83&87 HHOF 129
51/2 La Patrie
94/5 Legends 50
92/3 MONT / OPC 34
92/3 MONT / OPC 34
40/1 O-Pee-Chee 125
43-47 Parade Sportive
51/2 Parkhurst 1
52/3 Parkhurst 6
53/4 Parkhurst 30
53/4 Parkhurst 31
93/4 Parkhurst PR36
01/2 Parkhurst PR78, ✍ PA8
94/5 Parkie Tall 4
91/2 Pro Set 337
45-54 Quaker Oats
01/2 Signature ✍ VA15
54 Toronto Star Weekend

LACHAINE, DOMINIC
02/3 Val d'Or Foreurs
02/3 Val d'Or Foreurs

LACHAINE, MARTIN
96/7 Pensacola Ice Pilots
96/7 Pensacola Ice Pilots

LACHANCE, BOB
93/4 Donruss USA12
98/9 Indianapolis Ice
98/9 Indianapolis Ice
93/4 Pinnacle 495
93/4 Upper Deck 564

LACHANCE, GERARD
51/2 Bas du Fleuve 34
52/3 Bas du Fleuve 15

LACHANCE, JIMMY
88/9 Richelieu Riverains
88/9 Richelieu Riverains

LACHANCE, JONATHAN
01/2 Baie-Comeau 3
01/2 Baie-Comeau 3

LACHANCE, KEVIN
00/1 Québec Remparts 22
00/1 Québec Remparts 22
01/2 Québec Remparts 22
01/2 Québec Remparts 22
02/3 Québec Remparts
02/3 Québec Remparts

LACHANCE, SCOTT
91/2 Arena 3
91/2 Arena 32
98/9 Be A Player 84, ✍ Aut. 84
92/3 Bowman 438
91/2 Classic 4
91/2 Classic Four Sport 4
93/4 Donruss 206
94/5 Donruss 41
95/6 Donruss 353
97/8 Donruss 142
97/8 Do. Preferred 143
96/7 Flair 55
94/5 Fleer 124
92/3 Fleer Ultra 130
93/4 Fleer Ultra 369
94/5 Fleer Ultra 326
95/6 Fleer Ultra 94
95/6 Hoyle / East. J-Spade
93/4 Leaf 139
94/5 Leaf 372
95/6 Leaf 202
97/8 Leaf 95
97/8 Limited 166
96/7 NYIS
96/7 NYIS
92/3 O-Pee-Chee 390
01/2 O-Pee-Chee 254
92/3 OPC Premier 79
97/8 Pacific CC 85
92/3 Panini Sticker Q
93/4 Panini Sticker 63
95/6 Panini Sticker 97
96/7 Panini Sticker 99
99/0 Panini Sticker 69
91/2 Parkhurst 326
92/3 Parkhurst 105
93/4 Parkhurst 120
94/5 Parkhurst 140
92/3 Pinnacle 223
92/3 Pinnacle 244
92/3 Pinnacle T2K 6
93/4 Pinnacle 62
93/4 Pinnacle T2K1 21
94/5 Pinnacle 193
95/6 Pinnacle 167
96/7 Pi. Be A Player 27, ✍ Aut. 27
95/6 Playoff 281
93/4 Power Play 152
93/4 Premier 257
94/5 Premier 66
92/3 Pro Set 234
92/3 Score 449
93/4 Score 103
94/5 Score 195
95/6 Score 177
97/8 Score 259
92/3 Score Young Stars 12
92/3 Seasons 52
95/6 SBx Impact 101
02/3 Sports Vault 198
91/2 Star Pics 24
91/2 Star Pics 36
92/3 Topps 366
01/2 Topps 254
92/3 To. Stadium 201
93/4 To. Stadium 465
93/4 To. Stadium - Master Photo-2 4
91/2 Ultimate Draft Pick 4, 56, 60, 81, ✍ Aut.
91/2 Upper Deck 692
92/3 Upper Deck 360
92/3 Upper Deck 398
92/3 Upper Deck 409
92/3 Upper Deck 571
92/3 Upper Deck AC4
92/3 Upper Deck CC16
93/4 Upper Deck 320, SP-92
94/5 Upper Deck 412
95/6 Upper Deck 390
99/0 Upper Deck 241
94/5 UD BAP R44, ✍ 82
91/2 Upper Deck WJC 79
99/0 UD G. Reserve 241
99/0 Victory 152

LACHER, BLAINE
94/5 Classic 35, R13, T5
94/5 Cla. Images 9, CE9, ✍ Aut.
95/6 Donruss 123, BTP-1, RT-5
94/5 Fleer 13, RS-6
95/6 Fleer Metal 7
95/6 Fleer Ultra 10, AR-6, PPM-7
95/6 Kraft / PS
91/2 L. Superior State Lakers
91/2 L. Superior State Lakers
95/6 Leaf 3, SR-5
95/6 L. Limited 41
95/6 Panini Sticker 13, 302
95/6 Parkhurst 14
95/6 Pinnacle 147, M-1
95/6 Pi. Summit 127
95/6 Pi. Zenith 78
95/6 Playoff 7, 119
95/6 POG 38
95/6 Pro Magnet 12
95/6 Score 17
95/6 SBx Emotion 8
95/6 SBx Impact 9, 232, D-5, SM
94/5 SP 7, P-8
95/6 Topps 23, 15NG
94/5 Topps Finest 95, BBR-3
95/6 To. Stadium 104
94/5 TSC Members Only 50
94/5 Upper Deck 495, 539, SP-95
95/6 Upper Deck 385, H-15, SE-7
95/6 UD CC 22

LACKEY, CARL
69/0 Mästar Serien 17

LACKY, MIROSLAV
70/1 Kuvajulkaisut 52

LACOMBE, FRANÇOIS
72/3 Québec Nordiques
72/3 Québec Nordiques
73/4 Québec Nordiques
73/4 Québec Nordiques
76/7 Québec Nordiques
76/7 Québec Nordiques

LACOMBE, FRANÈOIS
78/9 Dernière Heure

LACOMBE, KEVIN
01/2 Drummondville
01/2 Drummondville

LACOMBE, MARTIN
90/1 7th..Sketch LHJMQ 27

LACOMBE, NORMAND
91/2 Bowman 248
85/6 BUFF / Blue Shield
86/7 BUFF / Blue Shield
87/8 EDMO
88/9 EDMO
88/9 EDMO / Action 81
91/2 O-Pee-Chee 357
89/0 Panini Sticker 84
90/1 PHIL
90/1 PHIL
90/1 Pro Set 500
90/1 Score 99T
91/2 Score CAN 394
91/2 To. Stadium 363

LACOMBE, PATRICK
91/2 7th...Sketch LHJMQ 87

LACOSTA, DAN
02/3 Owen Sound Attack
02/3 Owen Sound Attack

LACOSTE, YVON
65/6 Québec Aces

LACOUR, ROBIN
93/4 Slapshot / Detroit 5
94/5 Slapshot / Kitchener 32
95/6 Slapshot 36

LACOUR, ROBIN
96/7 Sudbury Wolves
96/7 Sudbury Wolves

LACOURSIÈRE, JOSEPH
52/3 Bas du Fleuve 4
51/2 Lac St-Jean 16

LACOUTURE, DAN
99/0 BAP Mem. 70
95/6 Classic 64
99/0 Hamilton Bulldogs
99/0 Hamilton Bulldogs
02/3 Pacific Complete 275
00/1 Private Stock 118
94/5 Select 154
01/2 UD MVP 214

LACOUTURE, DAVE
92/3 Maine Black Bears
92/3 Maine Black Bears
92/3 Maine Black Bears
92/3 Maine Black Bears

LACROIX, ALPHONSE
25-27 Anonymous 11
25-27 Anonymous 5

LACROIX, ANDRÉ
70/1 Colgate 29
70/1 Dad's Cookies
70/1 Eddie Sargent 154
71/2 Eddie Sargent 39
70/1 Esso Power Player
68/9 O-Pee-Chee 184
69/0 O-Pee-Chee 98
69/0 O-Pee-Chee 4in1
69/0 O-Pee-Chee Stamp
70/1 O-Pee-Chee 84
71/2 O-Pee-Chee 33
79/0 O-Pee-Chee 107
74/5 OPC WHA 60
75/6 OPC WHA 10
75/6 OPC WHA 64
76/7 OPC WHA 70
76/7 OPC WHA 80
77/8 OPC WHA 30
73/4 OPC WHA Poster 10
70/1 PHIL
73/4 Quaker Oats 6
68/9 Shirriff / Phil. 6
69/0 Topps 98
70/1 Topps 84
71/2 Topps 33
79/0 Topps 107
71/2 Toronto Sun Photo

LACROIX, DANIEL
92/3 Binghampton Rangers
95/6 Binghampton Rangers
99/0 Chicago Wolves
99/0 Chicago Wolves
94/5 Classic E2
93/4 Cla. Prospects 69
93/4 Leaf 351
97/8 Pa. Dynagon BKS-70
97/8 Pa. Invincible R-143
96/7 PHIL / Ocean Spray
96/7 PHIL / Ocean Spray
96/7 Pi. Be A Player 135, ✍ Aut. 135
89/0 ProCards IHL 31
90/1 ProCards 7
91/2 ProCards 194
97/8 Score Phil. 20
94/5 Upper Deck 283

LACROIX, ERIC
98/9 Be A Player 38, ✍ Aut. 38
92/3 Classic 58
92/3 Classic 77
93/4 Cla. Prospects 164
94/5 Fleer 97
95/6 Fleer Ultra 252
98/9 Pacific 163
97/8 Pacific CC 161
94/5 Parkhurst 234
95/6 Parkhurst 107
94/5 Phoenix Roadrunners
94/5 Phoenix Roadrunners
95/6 Pinnacle 82
95/6 POG 142
97/8 Score Colo. 13
92/3 St. John's Maple Leafs
92/3 St. John's Maple Leafs
93/4 St. John's Maple Leafs
93/4 St. John's Maple Leafs
00/1 Stadium 109
95/6 Topps 32
94/5 Upper Deck 352
95/6 Upper Deck 122
96/7 Upper Deck 244
98/9 Upper Deck 71
94/5 UD BAP ✍ 13
95/6 UD CC 276
98/9 UD G. Reserve 71

LACROIX, MARTIN
92/3 Classic 58
92/3 Classic 78
92/3 Classic Four Sport 200

LACROIX, PHILIP
02/3 Baie-Comeau
02/3 Baie-Comeau

LACROIX, PHILIPPE
99 Québec Pee Wee 100

LACROIX, PIERRE
81/2 Dernière Heure
83/4 HART / Jr. Whalers
81/2 O-Pee-Chee 278
82/3 O-Pee-Chee 286
83/4 OPC/Topps Sticker 261
80/1 Pepsi Bottle Cap
80/1 QUÉB
81/2 QUÉB
83/4 Souhaits Keychain [Whalers]

LACROIX, RÉNALD
52/3 Laval Dairy Update 116
52/3 St. Lawrence 29

LADOBRUK, KYLE
99/0 Kamloops Blazers
99/0 Kamloops Blazers
99/0 Kamloops Blazers
99/0 Kamloops Blazers
00/1 Kamloops Blazers
00/1 Kamloops Blazers
01/2 Regina Pats
01/2 Regina Pats

LADOUCEUR, RANDY
94/5 ANAH / Carl's Jr. 15
94/5 ANAH / Carl's Jr. 15
91/2 Bowman 5
92/3 Bowman 107
97/8 CARO / Sprint
97/8 CARO / Sprint
84/5 DETR / Little Caesars
85/6 DETR / Little Caesars
93/4 EA Sports 2
87/8 HART / Jr. Whalers
88/9 HART / Jr. Whalers
89/0 HART / Jr. Whalers
90/1 HART / Jr. Whalers
90/1 HART / Jr. Whalers
91/2 HART / Jr. Whalers
91/2 HART / Jr. Whalers
92/3 HART / Dairymart
92/3 HART / Dairymart
84/5 O-Pee-Chee 60
85/6 O-Pee-Chee 216
90/1 OPC/Topps 162
92/3 O-Pee-Chee 299
90/1 Panini Sticker 41
91/2 Parkhurst 289
95/6 Parkhurst 7
94/5 Parkie SE3
91/2 Pinnacle 224
92/3 Pinnacle 291
93/4 Pinnacle 389
93/4 Pinnacle Expa. 2
94/5 POG 365
93/4 Premier 469
90/1 Pro Set 108
91/2 Pro Set 396
91/2 Pro Set 573
91/2 Score 436
91/2 Score CAN 407
92/3 Score 61
93/4 Score 553
92/3 Topps 344
92/3 To. Stadium 156
93/4 To. Stadium 271
94/5 To. Stadium 69
90/1 Upper Deck 151
95/6 UD BAP 37, ✍ S37

LAFAYETTE, JUSTIN
91/2 ProCards 493

LAFAYETTE, NATHAN
93/4 Classic 22
94/5 Cla. Images 40
93/4 Cla. Prospects 195
91/2 Cornwall Royals
91/2 Cornwall Royals
94/5 Donruss 156
94/5 Flair 190
94/5 Fleer Ultra 225
94/5 Leaf 216
99/0 Lowell Lock Monsters
99/0 Lowell Lock Monsters
94/5 Panini Sticker Q
94/5 Parkhurst 247
94/5 Parkie SE seV44
93/4 Peoria Rivermen
93/4 Peoria Rivermen
94/5 Pinnacle 453
94/5 POG 340
94/5 Premier 18, OF-22
92 7th...Sketch Awards 3
91 7th..Sketch Mem.Cup 114
90/1 7th..Sketch OHL 25, 63
91/2 7th...Sketch OHL 14
91/2 Star Pics 56
91/2 Ultimate Draft Pick 46, ✍ Aut.
92/3 Upper Deck 588
94/5 Upper Deck 448
94/5 VANC
94/5 VANC
99/0 Victory 137

LAFERRIÈRE, RICK
81/2 COLR

LAFLAMME, CHRISTIAN
98/9 Be A Player 32, ✍ Aut. 32
95/6 Classic 40
95/6 Cla. 5 Sport 145
94/5 Cla. Images 87
00/1 MONT
00/1 MONT
97/8 Omega 52
98/9 Pacific 148
99/0 Ult. Victory 36
93/4 Upper Deck E6
97/8 Upper Deck 185
98/9 Upper Deck 64
98/9 UD G. Reserve 64
00/1 UD Vintage 194
01/2 Worcester IceCats
01/2 Worcester IceCats
02/3 Worcester IceCats
02/3 Worcester IceCats

LAFLAMME, DANIEL
90/1 7th..Sketch LHJMQ 103
91/2 7th...Sketch LHJMQ 183

LAFLEUR, BRIAN
93/4 Minnesota G'Gophers
93/4 Minnesota G'Gophers
94/5 Minnesota G'Gophers
94/5 Minnesota G'Gophers
97/8 Pensacola Ice Pilots
97/8 Pensacola Ice Pilots
98/9 Quad City Mallards
98/9 Quad City Mallards
99/0 Quad City Mallards
99/0 Quad City Mallards

LAFLEUR, GUY
01/2 ASG History
92/3 American Licorice 2
01/2 BAP Mem. ✄ 500GS
02/3 BAP Mem. 246, /Cup
01/2 BAP Update ✄ PTT4
02/3 Canada Post, ✍ Aut.
71/2 Colgate Head
72/3 Dernière Heure
73/4 Dernière Heure
80/1 Dernière Heure
83/4 Dernière Heure
88/9 Esso All-Star
01/2 Fleer Greats 8, =RC 5, -BC 1, BC, ✄ O6, ✍ Aut.
01/2 Fleer Legacy 3, 13, ✄ HK, ✄ ITC, ✄ TM
83/4 Funmate Puffy 4 [w/]
75/6 Hockey Heroes
84/5 Kellogg's 27
89/0 Kraft 31
90/1 Kraft 22
91/2 Kraft 66
74/5 Loblaws
82/3 McDonald's Les Étoiles 8
99/0 Millenium P-12, ✍ P-12
71/2 MONT / Pro Star
72/3 MONT / Pro Star
73/4 MONT / Pro Star
74/5 MONT
75/6 MONT
76/7 MONT
77/8 MONT
78/9 MONT
79/0 MONT
80/1 MONT
81/2 MONT
82/3 MONT
82/3 MONT / Steinberg
83/4 MONT
84/5 MONT
92/3 MONT / OPC 17
92/3 MONT / OPC 17
92/3 MONT / OPC 57
92/3 MONT / OPC 57
71/2 O-Pee-Chee 148
72/3 O-Pee-Chee 59
73/4 O-Pee-Chee 72
74/5 O-Pee-Chee 232
75/6 OPC 126,208,290,322
76/7 OPC 1-3,5,163,388
77/8 OPC 1-3,7,200
77/8 OPC 214,216,218
77/8 O-Pee-Chee NS 7
78/9 O-Pee-Chee 326
78/9 OPC 3,63-65,69,90
79/0 OPC 1-3,7,200
80/1 O-Pee-Chee 10
80/1 O-Pee-Chee 162
80/1 O-Pee-Chee 163
80/1 O-Pee-Chee 216
80/1 O-Pee-Chee 82
81/2 O-Pee-Chee 177
81/2 O-Pee-Chee 195
82/3 O-Pee-Chee 186
82/3 O-Pee-Chee 187
83/4 O-Pee-Chee 183
83/4 O-Pee-Chee 189
84/5 O-Pee-Chee 264
84/5 O-Pee-Chee 360
90/1 OPC/Topps 142
91/2 O-Pee-Chee 1
91/2 O-Pee-Chee 2
91/2 O-Pee-Chee 3
89/0 OPC/Topps 189
71/2 O-Pee-Chee Poster 13
90/1 OPC Premier 55
81/2 OPC Sticker 29
81/2 OPC Sticker 41
82/3 OPC/Topps Sticker 28
82/3 OPC/Topps Sticker 29
83/4 OPC/Topps Sticker 2
83/4 OPC/Topps Sticker 58
83/4 OPC/Topps Sticker 59
84/5 OPC Sticker 149
84/5 OPC Sticker 150
89/0 opcSticker 245-106
80/1 O-Pee-Chee Super 10
90/1 Panini Sticker 145
90/1 Panini/QUE 12, G
01/2 Parkhurst ✄ 500GS, ✄ PS64, ✄ H6, ✍ PA28
02/3 Parkhurst ✄ NH7, ✄ VM9, ✄ VT9
82/3 Post [Mont.]
93 Power Bar
90/1 Pro Set 250
91/2 Pro Set 317
89/0 QUÉB
89/0 QUÉB / Gene. Foods
89/0 QUÉB / Police
89/0 QUÉB / Police
90/1 QUÉB / Petro-Canada
90/1 QUÉB / Petro-Canada
92 Québec Pee Wee P1
90/1 Score 290
90/1 Sco. Hot Cards 96
91/2 Score 401
91/2 Score 402
91/2 Score 403
91/2 Score CAN 291
91/2 Score CAN 292
91/2 Score CAN 293
01/2 Signature ✄ 500GS, ✍ VA40
83/4 Souhaits Keychain [Canadiens]
77-79 Sportscaster 38-07
77-79 Sportscaster 51-18
77-79 Sports. FIN 38-895
77-79 Sports. FIN 57-1356
72/3 Topps 79
73/4 Topps 72
74/5 Topps 232
75/6 To. 126,208,290,322
76/7 Topps 1-3, 5, 163
76/7 Topps NS 11
77/8 Topps 1-3,7,200
77/8 Topps 214,216,218
77/8 ToppsNS 7
78/9 Topps 3,63-65,69,90
79/0 Topps 1-3,7,200
80/1 Topps 10
80/1 Topps 162
80/1 Topps 163
80/1 Topps 216
80/1 Topps 82
81/2 Topps 19
84/5 Topps 81
99/0 Topps SC3, ✍ SCH
01/2 T/O Archives 28, -Seat, ✍ CAI
71/2 Toronto Sun Photo
00/1 UD Heroes 129, ✍ SG
01/2 Ultimate Mem. ✄ 500GS, ✄ ASG, ✄ CP, ✄ Corn., ✄ EA, ✄ Glove, ✄ LC, ✄ RN, ✄ RT, ✄ RA, ✄ SCD, ✄ SCW, ✍ Aut.
02/3 Ultimate Mem. ✄ CP, ✄ CSTW, ✄ Cor, ✄ EA, ✄ FS, ✄ GAO, ✄ SL (x3), ✄ Num, ✄ RT, ✄ SU, ✄ SF, ✄ VGJ, ✄ VHT
90/1 Upper Deck 162
91/2 Upper Deck 219
91/2 Upper Deck 638
01/2 Upper Deck ✄ ASJ
00 ✄ UD APOH 500, ✄✍ 500
99/0 UD C. Legends 11
02/3 UD Foundations 51, 64, 78, 115, ✄ 1000Jers (x2), ✄ 1000Stick (x3), ✄ CH, ✄ CG, ✍ SG
00/1 UD Legends 67, 73, ES7, EG1, ✍ ES
01/2 UD Legends 34, 95, FC, ✄ M, ✄ PoH, ✄ TT (x4), ✄ TTC (x3)
02/3 UD Piece✄ HS, ✍ MD, / Giveaway
01/2 UD SCup Champs 15, ✄ S, ✄ G, ✄ T
01/2 UD Vintage ✄ NL, ✄ SD, ✄ SH
83/4 Vachon 47-67
83/4 Vachon 47-84
96 Wien HL2

LAFLEUR, PATRICK
95/6 Halifax Moosehead

LAFOLEY, GRAYSON
92/3 Ottawa 67's
92/3 Ottawa 67's

LAFONTAINE, PAT
96/7 Bic.Sports Aces 7-D
95/6 Bicycle Sports Aces 5-Spade
90/1 Bowman 123, -HT 9
91/2 Bowman 222
92/3 Bowman 142
95/6 Bowman 29
91/2 BUFF / Blue Shield
91/2 BUFF / Blue Shield
91/2 BUFF / Campbell's
91/2 BUFF / Campbell's
91/2 BUFF / Pepsi
91/2 BUFF / Pepsi
92/3 BUFF / Blue Shield
92/3 BUFF / Blue Shield
92/3 BUFF / Jubilee
92/3 BUFF / Jubilee
93/4 BUFF / Noco
93/4 BUFF / Noco
82/3 Dernière Heure
93/4 Donruss 37
93/4 Donruss IK 2
94/5 Donruss 300
95/6 Donruss 172, PP-2
96/7 Donruss 113
97/8 Donruss 133
96/7 Do. Canadian 11
97/8 Do. Canadian 69
95/6 Do. Elite 75
96/7 Do. Elite 101, P-10
97/8 Do. Elite 111, 146
97/8 Do. Preferred 58
97/8 Do. Priority 160
97/8 Do. Studio 50
93/4 EA Sports 15
94/5 Flair 19, CIS-5
96/7 Flair 9
94/5 Fleer 23
96/7 Fleer 11, ART-11
95/6 Fleer Metal 16, IS-11
96/7 Fl. Picks 38, DL-10
92/3 Fleer Ultra 16
93/4 Fleer Ultra 219
93/4 Fleer Ultra AS 4
93/4 Fleer Ultra PP 3
93/4 Fleer Ultra SK 1
93/4 Fleer Ultra SM 6
94/5 Fleer Ultra 24, PP-5, SM-5
95/6 Fleer Ultra 20, 389
96/7 Fl. Ultra 17, MM-6
88/9 Frito Lay
91/2 Gillette 23
95 Globe 116
93/4 Hockey Wit 105
95/6 Hoyle / East. Q-Spade
92/3 Humpty Dumpty
91/2 Kellogg's / Score 15
90/1 Kraft 23, 86
91/2 Kraft 25
93/4 Kraft / PB
94/5 Kraft / HH
96/7 Kraft / PB
93/4 Leaf 12
93/4 Leaf GLAS 1
93/4 Leaf SSS 3
94/5 Leaf 278, GLS-14
95/6 Leaf 140
96/7 Leaf 44
97/8 Leaf 34
94/5 L. Limited 63
95/6 L. Limited 113
96/7 L. Limited 59
96/7 L. Preferred 11, LS-22
97/8 Limited 111
91/2 McDonald's Mc-06
93/4 McDonald's McD-18
96/7 Metal Univ. 15, IC-8
84/5 NYIS / News 11
89/0 NYIS
84/5 O-Pee-Chee 129
84/5 O-Pee-Chee 392
85/6 OPC/Topps 137
86/7 OPC/Topps 2
87/8 OPC/Topps 173
88/9 OPC/Topps 123
88/9 OPC/Topps Box C
90/1 OPC/Topps 184, 315
90/1 Topps-TL 10
91/2 O-Pee-Chee 80
91/2 Topps - Team Leader 12
92/3 O-Pee-Chee 285
89/0 OPC/Topps 60
87/8 OPC Leaders 22
90/1 OPC Premier 56
91/2 OPC Premier 64
92/3 OPC Premier SP17
85/6 OPC Sticker 74-201
86/7 OPC Sticker 206
87/8 OPC Sticker 243-110
88/9 OPC Sticker 111
89/0 opcSticker 119
97/8 Omega 146, SHLC-14
98/9 Pacific 295, -Time. 12
97/8 Pa. Crown Roy. 85, L-12
97/8 Pa. Paramount 117
98/9 Pa. Paramount 154
97/8 Pa. Revolution 88
94 Panini Olympics 325
87/8 Panini Sticker 98
88/9 Panini Sticker 290
89/0 Panini Sticker 264
90/1 Panini Sticker 81
91/2 Panini Sticker 243
92/3 Panini Sticker 246
93/4 Panini Sticker 101
93/4 Panini Sticker 137
94/5 Panini Sticker 92
95/6 Panini Sticker 15
96/7 Panini Sticker 15
91/2 Parkhurst 16
92/3 Parkhurst 12
93/4 Parkhurst 289
93/4 Parkhurst E8
94/5 Parkhurst 310, V73, YCTG-3
95/6 Parkhurst 20, PP-49
94/5 Parkie SE18
91/2 Pinnacle 25
92/3 Pinnacle 254
92/3 Pinnacle 7
93/4 Pinnacle 300
93/4 Pinnacle CA3
93/4 Pinnacle NF 12
94/5 Pinnacle 350, GR2
95/6 Pinnacle 54
96/7 Pinnacle 27
97/8 Pinnacle 69
96/7 Pi. Be A Player LTH8B, ✍ Aut. LTH8B
97/8 Pi. Be A Player OT 15
97/8 Pi. BeeHive 43, BHT-18
97/8 Pi. Certified 80
97/8 Pi. Inside 39
95/6 Pi. Summit 34
96/7 Pi. Summit 127
97/8 Pi. Totally 80
95/6 Pi. Zenith 85
96/7 Pi. Zenith 83, A-9
95/6 Playoff 13, 127
94/5 POG 50
95/6 POG 3, 42
93/4 Power Play 31
93/4 Power Play PL 7
93/4 Premier 171
93/4 Premier 490
93/4 Prmr. - BG-OPC 14
93/4 Prmr. - BG-Top. 24
94/5 Premier 180, GTG-6
95/6 Pro Magnet 109
90/1 Pro Set 186, 372
91/2 Pro Set 149
91/2 Pro Set 308
91/2 Pro Set 358
92/3 Pro Set 13
91/2 Pro Set PotM P4
91/2 Pro Set Platinum 157
90/1 Score 250
90/1 Sco. Hot Cards 95
91/2 Score 260
91/2 Score 332
91/2 Score 100T
91/2 Score CAN 362
91/2 Score CAN 480
92/3 Score 420
92/3 Score 6
92/3 Score SS 8
92/3 Score USAG 1
93/4 Score 345
93/4 Score DT 13
93/4 Score DD2
93/4 Score PiAS 11
93/4 Score TF 2
94/5 Score 2, TF2
95/6 Score 201, BB-7, GB-8
96/7 Score 139
97/8 Score 104
97/8 Score NYRa. 10
92/3 Seasons 42
94/5 Select 57
95/6 Select CE 18
96/7 Select CE 9
94 Semic 120
94 Semic 359
95 Semic 114
89 Semic Sticker 164
91 Semic Sticker 138
92 Semic Sticker 159
93 Semic Sticker 183
95/6 SBx Emotion 18
95/6 SBx Impact 17
96/7 SBx Impact 11, BR-10
94/5 SP 12
95/6 SP 12, É5
96/7 SP 15, GF-18, HC-8
97/8 SP Authentic 98, I1
96/7 SPx 18
97/8 SPx 5
98/9 SPx Finite 56
93/4 SLU / Card-A
93/4 SLU / Card-B
93/4 Starting Lineup
94/5 Starting Lineup
96/7 SLU
95/6 Super Sticker 11, DC-3
84/5 Topps 96
92/3 Topps 345
95/6 Topps 13, 250, HGA-4, 6PL, 5RL
02/3 Topps - Reprint 1, ✍ Reprint 1
94/5 Topps Finest 70
95/6 To. Finest 40, 130
91/2 To. Stadium 123
92/3 To. Stadium 95
93/4 To. Stadium 20
93/4 To. Stadium 460
93/4 To. Stadium - Master Photo-1 1
93/4 To. Stadium - All-Stars
95/6 To. Stadium EC164
95/6 T. Super Skills 5
01/2 T/O Archives 79
98/9 UD Choice 130
90/1 Upper Deck 246, 306, 479
91/2 Upper Deck 253
91/2 Upper Deck 556
92/3 Upper Deck 165
92/3 Upper Deck 456
92/3 Upper Deck G3
93/4 Upper Deck 137, 221, 287, HT10, SP-17
94/5 Upper Deck 17, R17, R22, IG14, R47, R55, SP-99
95/6 Upper Deck 386, R19, R29, SE-10
96/7 Upper Deck 15, SS17B
97/8 Upper Deck 318
98/9 Upper Deck 133
93/4 Upper Deck Be A Player 28
94/5 UD BAP R79, R132, ✍ 63
97/8 UD Black Diam. 133, PC22
95/6 UD CC 157, C27
96/7 UD CC 23, 311, UD30, S21
97/8 UD Coll. Choice 31
98/9 UD G. Reserve 133
97/8 UD Ice 72
00/1 UD Legends 15, ✍ ES, ✄ LGJ
92/3 UD Locker 4
00/1 UD Vintage ✄ D-POH
96 Wien 165
97/8 Zenith 44, CTC-14, Z26

LAFORCE, ERNIE
43-47 Parade Sportive

LAFOREST, BOB
82/3 North Bay Centennials
82/3 North Bay Centennials

LAFOREST, MAGELLA
51/2 Bas du Fleuve 30

LAFOREST, MARK
95/6 Edge Ice 163
94/5 Milwaukee Admirals
94/5 Milwaukee Admirals
95/6 Milwaukee Admirals
95/6 Milwaukee Admirals
82/3 North Bay Centennials
82/3 North Bay Centennials
89/0 ProCards AHL 124
90/1 ProCards 13
91/2 ProCards 208
90/1 Upper Deck 81

LAFORGE, ALAIN
86/7 Kingston Canadians
86/7 Kingston Canadians
88/9 Niagara Falls Thunder
88/9 Niagara Falls Thunder
90/1 7th..Sketch OHL 386
89/0 Sudbury Wolves
89/0 Sudbury Wolves
90/1 Sudbury Wolves
90/1 Sudbury Wolves

LAFORGE, BILL
88/9 Niagara Falls Thunder
88/9 Niagara Falls Thunder
80/1 Oshawa Generals
80/1 Oshawa Generals

LAFORGE, CLAUDE
62/3 Parkhurst 24
68/9 Shirriff / Phil. 11
58/9 Topps 33
59/0 Topps 64

LAFORGE, MARC
94/5 Cape Breton Oilers
94/5 Cape Breton Oilers
84/5 Kingston Canadians
84/5 Kingston Canadians
85/6 Kingston Canadians
85/6 Kingston Canadians
86/7 Kingston Canadians
86/7 Kingston Canadians
88/9 ProCards / Binghampton
90/1 ProCards 233
91/2 ProCards 216

LAFOY, MIKE
82/3 Kingston Canadians
82/3 Kingston Canadians

LAFRAMBOISE, PETE
72/3 Eddie Sargent 53
72/3 O-Pee-Chee 263
73/4 O-Pee-Chee 244
74/5 O-Pee-Chee 166
75/6 O-Pee-Chee 364
74/5 Topps 166
74/5 WASH

LAFRAMBOISE, PETER
74/5 Loblaws

LAFRANCE, DARRYL
95/6 Classic 91
95/6 Flint Generals
95/6 Flint Generals
97/8 New Orleans Brass
97/8 New Orleans Brass
91/2 Oshawa Generals
91/2 Oshawa Generals
91/2 Oshawa Generals
91/2 Oshawa Generals
92/3 Oshawa Generals
92/3 Oshawa Generals
91/2 7th...Sketch OHL 157
93/4 Slapshot / Oshawa 14

LAFRANCE, ERIC
99/0 Hull Olympiques BN
99/0 Hull Olympiques BN
99/0 Hull Olympiques 22
99/0 Hull Olympiques 22
00/1 Hull Olympiques 21
00/1 Hull Olympiques 21
01/2 Hull Olympiques 21
01/2 Hull Olympiques 21
02/3 Hull Olympiques
02/3 Hull Olympiques
90/1 7th..Sketch LHJMQ 183
91/2 7th...Sketch LHJMQ 170

LAFRANCE, LEO
27/8 La Patrie

LAFRENIÈRE, CHRIS
91 7th..Sketch Mem.Cup 75
90/1 7th..Sketch WHL 195

LAFRENIÈRE, JASON
92/3 Atlanta Knights
83/4 Brantford Alexanders
90/1 Canada Nationals 14
98/9 DEL 182
96/7 Michigan K-Wings
93/4 Milwaukee Admirals
93/4 Milwaukee Admirals
88/9 O-Pee-Chee 223
87/8 OPC Sticker 130-118
87/8 OPC Sticker 219-87
88/9 OPC Sticker 185-54
87/8 Panini Sticker 171
93/4 Parkhurst 466
89/0 ProCards IHL 25
85/6 QUÉB
85/6 QUÉB / Gene. Foods
85/6 QUÉB / McDonald's
86/7 QUÉB
86/7 QUÉB / Gene. Foods
87/8 QUÉB / Gene. Foods
87/8 QUÉB / Yum Yum

LAFRENIÈRE, MARC
90/1 Rayside-Balfour
90/1 Rayside-Balfour
91/2 Rayside-Balfour
91/2 Rayside-Balfour

LAFRENIÈRE, PATRICK
99/0 Hull Olympiques BN
99/0 Hull Olympiques BN
99/0 Hull Olympiques 21
99/0 Hull Olympiques 21

LAFRENIÈRE, RÉAL
51/2 Bas du Fleuve 26
52/3 Bas du Fleuve 63

LAGACE, JEAN-GUY
74/5 Loblaws Update
74/5 O-Pee-Chee 299
75/6 O-Pee-Chee 141
74/5 PITT
75/6 Topps 141

LAGACÉ-DAIGLE, SIMON
99/0 UD Prospects 62

LAGANAS, CHRIS
91/2 Greensboro Monarchs
91/2 Greensboro Monarchs
92/3 Oklahoma City Blazers
92/3 Oklahoma City Blazers

LAGINSKI, AL
89/0 Rayside-Balfour
89/0 Rayside-Balfour

LAGRAND, SCOTT
92/3 Classic 79
92/3 Classic Four Sport 201

LAHAYE, LESTER
52/3 Anonymous 45

LAHDE, KYOSTI
72/3 Williams Finnish 176

LAHEY, MATT
96/7 Soo Greyhounds
96/7 Soo Greyhounds

LAHEY, MATTHEW
95/6 Slapshot 326

LAHEY, PAT
82/3 Soo Greyhounds
82/3 Soo Greyhounds
83/4 Soo Greyhounds
83/4 Soo Greyhounds

LAHN, STEFAN
95/6 DEL 290
96/7 DEL 317

LAHNALAMPI, DEREK
94/5 Slapshot / North Bay 3

LAHTEENMAKI, ARI
80/1 Mallasjuoma 20
78/9 SM-Liiga 42

LAHTELA, PEKKA
66/7 Champion 65
70/1 Kuvajulkaisut 161
71/2 Williams Finnish 231
72/3 Williams Finnish 214

LAHTI, PEKKA
66/7 Champion 27

LAHTINEN, JOUNI
95/6 Sisu 239
96/7 Sisu 37

LAHTINEN, JUHANI
66/7 Champion 201
65/6 Hellas 125
70/1 Kuvajulkaisut 128

LAHTINEN, TIMO
66/7 Champion 200
98/9 DEL 108
70/1 Kuvajulkaisut 129
91/2 Semic Elitserien 309
71/2 Williams Finnish 154
72/3 Williams Finnish 106
73/4 Williams Finnish 203

LAIDLAW, KEN
69 Columbus Checkers
69 Columbus Checkers

LAIDLAW, TOM
88/9 LOSA / Smokey
89/0 LOSA / Smokey 23
90/1 LOSA / Smokey 12
90/1 LOSA / Smokey 12
81/2 O-Pee-Chee 234
82/3 O-Pee-Chee 227
83/4 O-Pee-Chee 247
84/5 O-Pee-Chee 144
86/7 OPC/Topps 147
88/9 OPC/Topps 37
90/1 O-Pee-Chee 524
89/0 OPC/Topps 34
86/7 OPC Sticker 223-92
88/9 Panini Sticker 71
82/3 Post [NYRa.]
90/1 Pro Set 123
90/1 Score 69
90/1 Upper Deck 119

LAIHO, JARI
80/1 Mallasjuoma 130
78/9 SM-Liiga 172
73/4 Williams Finnish 312

LAINE, ANTTI
71/2 Williams Finnish 246

LAINE, ARI
71/2 Williams Finnish 369

LAINE, ARTO
70/1 Kuvajulkaisut 231
80/1 Mallasjuoma 50
71/2 Williams Finnish 247
72/3 Williams Finnish 347
73/4 Williams Finnish 313

LAINE, ERKKI
91/2 Jyvas Hyva 51
82 Semic Sticker 43
89 Semic Sticker 45
93/4 Sisu 291

LAINE, ISMO
72/3 Williams Finnish 332

LAINE, JUHANI
71/2 Williams Finnish 284
73/4 Williams Finnish 204

LAINE, MIKA
80/1 Mallasjuoma 77
71/2 Williams Finnish 346

LAINE, PEKKA
80/1 Mallasjuoma 79
78/9 SM-Liiga 125

LAINE, SAMI
98/9 Odessa Jackalopes
98/9 Odessa Jackalopes
99/0 Odessa Jackalopes
99/0 Odessa Jackalopes
95/6 Sisu 212
96/7 Sisu 7

LAING, JOEL
00/1 WBS Penguins
00/1 WBS Penguins

LAING, QUINTIN
98/9 Kelowna Rockets
98/9 Kelowna Rockets
01/2 Norfolk Admirals
01/2 Norfolk Admirals

LAINIO, KARI
71/2 Williams Finnish 370

LAIRD, ROB
94/5 Phoenix Roadrunners
94/5 Phoenix Roadrunners
95/6 Phoenix Roadrunners
95/6 Phoenix Roadrunners
90/1 ProCards 217
91/2 ProCards 571
89/0 WASH / Kodak
89/0 WASH / Kodak

LAITILA, JANNE
00/1 Cardset 107

LAITINEN, ILKKA
99/0 Cardset 252

LAITINEN, KARI
92/3 Jyvas Hyva 5
89 Semic Sticker 43

LAITINEN, MIRO
00/1 Cardset 331

LAITINEN, VELI-PEKKA
99/0 Cardset 95
00/1 Cardset 70
02/3 Cardset 55

LAITRE, MARTIN
99/0 Hamilton Bulldogs
99/0 Hamilton Bulldogs
99/0 Hamilton Bulldogs/ Staz
99/0 Hamilton Bulldogs/ Staz
00/1 Hamilton Bulldogs
00/1 Hamilton Bulldogs
90/1 7th..Sketch LHJMQ 254

LAITURI, TIMO
92/3 Semic Nordisk 98

LAJEUNESSE, BRUNO
90/1 7th..Sketch LHJMQ 132

LAJEUNESSE, MARTIN
90/1 7th..Sketch LHJMQ 242
91/2 7th...Sketch LHJMQ 126

LAJEUNESSE, SERGE
70/1 Esso Power Player
71/2 O-Pee-Chee 136

LAJEUNESSE, SIMON
01/2 BT Pipes 160
02/3 Between the Pipes 99, ✄ GUJ48
99 Bowman 39, ✍ BA2
02/3 Peoria Rivermen
02/3 Peoria Rivermen
93 Québec Pee Wee 272
99/0 Topps 258
99/0 To. Chrome 258
00/1 Val d'Or Foreurs 13
00/1 Val d'Or Foreurs 13

LAJOIE, CLAUDE
84/5 Chicoutimi Saguenéens
84/5 Chicoutimi Saguenéens

LAJOIE, ÉRICK
02/3 Val d'Or Foreurs
02/3 Val d'Or Foreurs

LAJOIE, SERGE
86/7 Kamloops Blazers
86/7 Kamloops Blazers

LAKE, ALLAN
86/7 Kitchener Rangers
86/7 Kitchener Rangers
87/8 Kitchener Rangers
87/8 Kitchener Rangers

LAKE, FRED
91 C55 Reprint 9
10/1 Imperial
10/1 Imperial 27
11/2 Imperial 9
12/3 Imperial 31

LAKERS, VERNON
91/2 Avant Garde BCJHL 7

LAKOS, ANDRE
99/0 Albany River Rats
99/0 Albany River Rats
00/1 Albany River Rats
00/1 Albany River Rats
01/2 Albany River Rats
01/2 Albany River Rats
98/9 Barrie Colts
98/9 Barrie Colts

LAKOSIL, VLASTIMIL
97/8 APS 316
99/0 DS 99, G8
00/1 DS 62, G6
98/9 OFS 384
99/0 OFS 10
00/1 OFS 213, -Star 23
01/2 OFS 47, G4

LAKOVIC, GREG
97/8 Toledo Storm 3
97/8 Toledo Storm 3

LAKOVIC, SASHA
97/8 Albany River Rats
97/8 Albany River Rats
99/0 Albany River Rats
99/0 Albany River Rats
95/6 Las Vegas Thunder
95/6 Las Vegas Thunder

LAKSO, BOB
92/3 Fort Wayne Komets 16
92/3 Fort Wayne Komets 16
88/9 ProCards / Indianapolis
89/0 ProCards IHL 125
91/2 ProCards 257

LAKSOLA, PEKKA
96/7 DEL 254
91/2 Jyvas Hyva 60
92/3 Jyvas Hyva 167
93/4 Jyvas Hyva 290
94 Semic 16
95 Semic 33
93/4 Sisu 66
94/5 Sisu 64, 377
95/6 Sisu 111, 183, DT-8
95/6 Sisu Limited 74

LAKSOLA, REIJO
80/1 Mallasjuoma 24
78/9 SM-Liiga 24
73/4 Williams Finnish 223

LALA, JIRI
94/5 DEL 113
95/6 DEL 115
01/2 DS L12
98/9 OFS Leg. 16
82 Semic Sticker 89
89 Semic Sticker 198
91 Semic Sticker 114

LALANCETTE, JACQUES
52/3 Bas du Fleuve 33
51/2 Lac St-Jean 24

LALANDE, HEC
57/8 Topps 31

LALIBERT, HUGUES
90/1 7th..Sketch LHJMQ 213
91/2 7th...Sketch LHJMQ 26

LALIBERTÉ, GAÉTAN
51/2 Bas du Fleuve 18

LALIBERTÉ, SPIKE
51/2 Laval Dairy 59

LALIME, PATRICK
01/2 Adrenaline 135, CL 14, PP 25
01/2 Atomic 70
02/3 Atomic 72, -D 14
00/1 BAP Mem. 273
01/2 BAP Mem. 27
02/3 BAP Mem. 155, ✄ SC2
01/2 BAP Update ✄ HSHSJers
01/2 BT Pipes 43, 104, -Mask, ✄ FW, ✄ S&J, ✄ GG, ✄ HSHSJers
02/3 Between the Pipes 7, 141, M20, ✄ BM8, ✄ GUE24, ✄ GB12, ✄ GUJ24, ✄ GSJ24, ✄ HSHSJers 10, ✄ ITN24, ✄ T5, ✍ Aut.
01/2 Bowman 71
02/3 Bowman 76
95/6 Cleveland Lumberjacks
95/6 Cleveland Lumberjacks
96/7 Cleveland Lumberjacks
96/7 Cleveland Lumberjacks
00/1 Crown Royale 76
01/2 Crown Royale 102
02/3 Crown Royale 68, -COA 8
97/8 Donruss 76
97/8 Do. Canadian LG 9
96/7 Do. Elite 133
99/0 Dynagon Ice 140
02/3 Exclusive 123
02/3 First Edition 121, ✄ Jers.
96/7 Flair 121, HG-6
96/7 Fl. Ultra 142
94/5 Hampton Roads
94/5 Hampton Roads
98/9 Hampton Roads
98/9 Hampton Roads
01/2 Heads Up 70, SS 15
02/3 Heads Up 88, -S 15, ✄ GWQ 19
98/9 Kansas City Blades 22
98/9 Kansas City Blades 22
97/8 Leaf 111
97/8 Limited 142, 159
01/2 McDonald's 27
02/3 McDonald's 30, -GSNF 5
01/2 O-Pee-Chee 133
02/3 O-Pee-Chee 61
99/0 Omega 160
99/0 OTTA
99/0 OTTA
00/1 OTTA
00/1 OTTA
01/2 OTTA
01/2 OTTA
02/3 OTTA
02/3 OTTA
00/1 Pacific 281
01/2 Pacific 275, IZ 14, SC 14
02/3 Pacific 269
02/3 Pacific Complete 473
97/8 Pacific CC 40, ITC-17
97/8 Pa. Dynagon 103, 142, DD-13B, S-18, T-9, T-22
97/8 Pa. Invincible 114, FP-29, R-161
00/1 Pa. Paramount 174
01/2 PTC Collectors 7
02/3 PTC/ Les Gardiens 7
97/8 Panini Sticker 246
00/1 Parkhurst P-43
01/2 Parkhurst 83
02/3 Parkhurst 8, -HHV 6
02/3 Parkhurst Retro 138, ✄ VH4
96/7 Pi. Be A Player LTH10A, SP-1, ✍ Aut. LTH10A
97/8 Pi. Certified 23
97/8 Pi. Inside 67, SU-6
97/8 Pi. Totally 23
01/2 Pr. Stock 69
02/3 Pr. Stock Reserve 73
00/1 PS Titanium 66
01/2 PS Titanium 101, ✄ DSJ 48, ✄ DSJ 64
01/2 PS Titanium Draft ✄ 67
02/3 PS Titanium 73, ✄ GWJ 48
02/3 Quest for the Cup 72
00/1 Revolution 104
97/8 Score 40
97/8 Score Pitt. 3
96/7 Select CE 108
91/2 7th...Sketch LHJMQ 71
00/1 Signature 78, ✍ Aut. 30
01/2 Signature 104, ✍ Aut. 104, ✄ GU76, ✄ TM21
02/3 Signature 35, ✍ 35, ✄ DW8, ✄ TQ20
99/0 SP Authentic 61
00/1 SP Authentic 63
02/3 SP Authentic 64
02/3 Sports Vault 100
01/2 SPx 186
02/3 SPx 52
00/1 Stadion 121
00/1 Stadium 125
01/2 Stadium 59
02/3 Stadium 70, ✍ LSS
97/8 SLU
00/1 Topps 265
01/2 Topps 133, OTG26
02/3 Topps 61, HHC11
00/1 To. Chrome 158
01/2 To. Chrome 133
02/3 To. Chrome 43
01/2 To. Heritage 83
02/3 To. Heritage 59, ✄ CP, ✄ CPB
02/3 To. Limited 61
01/2 To. Reserve 57
02/3 T. Total 358
00/1 UD Heroes 85
00/1 UD Reserve 60
00/1 Ultimate Mem. ✄ G-21
97/8 Upper Deck 133, SG40, T12A
00/1 Upper Deck 123
01/2 Upper Deck 124, GL8
02/3 Upper Deck 121, -SA10
96/7 UD Black Diam. 168
97/8 UD Coll. Choice 208, SQ40
96/7 UD Ice 54
01/2 UD Mask 121
02/3 UD Mask 58, 59, 113
00/1 UD MVP 123
01/2 UD MVP 133, MM9
02/3 UD MVP 126
02/3 UD Piece 62
02/3 UD Rookie 71
02/3 UD Top Shelf 61
00/1 UD Vintage 252, 258, 259
01/2 UD Vintage 179
02/3 UD Vintage 176, 281, GB 176
01/2 Vanguard 70, SW 14
02/3 Vanguard 71, -SW 9, ✄ GWJ 33
01/2 Victory 241, 248
02/3 Victory 147

LALONDE, BOBBY
78/9 ATLF / Colour
72/3 Eddie Sargent 221
74/5 Loblaws
72/3 O-Pee-Chee 217
73/4 O-Pee-Chee 179
74/5 O-Pee-Chee 392
75/6 O-Pee-Chee 246
76/7 O-Pee-Chee 278
77/8 O-Pee-Chee 313
78/9 O-Pee-Chee 285
79/0 O-Pee-Chee 326
80/1 O-Pee-Chee 265
73/4 Topps 189
75/6 Topps 246
71/2 Toronto Sun Photo
71/2 VANC / Royal Bank 1
72/3 VANC / Royal Bank
73/4 VANC / Royal Bank
74/5 VANC / Royal Bank
75/6 VANC / Royal Bank
76/7 VANC / Royal Bank

LALONDE, EDOUARD (NEWSY)
91 C55 Reprint 42
25 Dominion Chocolates 95
83 HHOF Postcard E10
83&87 HHOF 70
10/1 Imperial
10/1 Imperial 36
11/2 Imperial 42
12/3 Imperial 44
27/8 La Patrie
24/5 Maple Crispette [V130] 27
55/6 Parkhurst 55
23/4 Paulins Candy 38
60/1 Topps 48
61/2 Topps - Stamp
99/0 UD C. Legends 32

LALONDE, GREGG
95/6 Slapshot 384

LALONDE, GUY
51/2 Bas du Fleuve 16

LALONDE, HEC
52/3 Anonymous 170
93/4 Parkie 56-57 38

LALONDE, HERVE
52/3 Anonymous 38
53/4 La Patrie

LALONDE, NEWSY
02/3 In The GU ✄ VM1
02/3 Parkie - Reprint 208

LALONDE, PIERRE-FRANÇOIS
91/2 7th...Sketch LHJMQ 205

LALONDE, RON
74/5 Loblaws Update
75/6 O-Pee-Chee 152
76/7 O-Pee-Chee 339
77/8 O-Pee-Chee 378
78/9 O-Pee-Chee 371
74/5 PITT
75/6 Topps 152

LALONDE, TODD
94/5 Slapshot / Sudbury 24
95/6 Slapshot 405
85/6 Sudbury Wolves
85/6 Sudbury Wolves
86/7 Sudbury Wolves
86/7 Sudbury Wolves
87/8 Sudbury Wolves
87/8 Sudbury Wolves
88/9 Sudbury Wolves
88/9 Sudbury Wolves

LALOR, MIKE
92/3 Bowman 319
94/5 DALL / Southwest
94/5 DALL / Southwest
96/7 DALL / Southwest
96/7 DALL / Southwest
93/4 Donruss 306
93/4 Kraft / PB
86/7 Kraft Sports 28
93/4 Leaf 399
85/6 MONT
85/6 MONT / Provigo
86/7 MONT
87/8 MONT
87/8 MONT / Vachon 22
87/8 MONT / Vachon 59
87/8 MONT / Vachon 60
88/9 MONT
83/4 Nova Scotia Voyageurs
83/4 Nova Scotia Voyageurs
90/1 OPC/Topps 341
91/2 O-Pee-Chee 483
90/1 OPC Premier 57
87/8 OPC Sticker 73
90/1 Panini Sticker 267
91/2 Parkhurst 427
92/3 Pinnacle 123
90/1 Pro Set 264, 552
91/2 Pro Set 255
92/3 Pro Set 268
92/3 SANJ / Pacific Bell
92/3 SANJ / Pacific Bell
90/1 Score 67, 98T
91/2 Score 249
91/2 Score CAN 469
92/3 Score 363
88/9 SLOU / Kodak
89/0 SLOU / Kodak
89/0 SLOU / Kodak
92/3 Topps 140
92/3 To. Stadium 190
90/1 Upper Deck 40
90/1 WASH / Kodak
90/1 WASH / Kodak
90/1 WASH / Smokey
90/1 WASH / Smokey
91/2 WASH / Smokey
91/2 WASH / Smokey

LALUK, SCOTT
92/3 Brandon Wheat Kings
92/3 Brandon Wheat Kings
94/5 Slapshot Memorial 29

LAMARCHE, MARTIN
98/9 Fort Worth Brahmas
98/9 Fort Worth Brahmas
99/0 Fort Worth Brahmas
99/0 Fort Worth Brahmas
96/7 Saint John Flames
96/7 Saint John Flames
91/2 7th...Sketch LHJMQ 90

LAMARCHE-FROELICH, ALEXANDRE
02/3 Baie-Comeau

LAMB, GARTH
89/0 Nashville Knights

LAMB, JEFF
88/9 ProCards / Maine
89/0 ProCards IHL 110

LAMB, JOE
34-43 BeeHive-1 [NYAm.]
39/0 Bruins Magazine
33-35 Diamond Match Silv.
36-39 Diamond Match TT1
33/4 O-Pee-Chee 2
34/5 Sweet Caporal
33/4 WWGum 41
37/8 World Wide Gum 37

LAMB, MARK
93/4 Donruss 230
88/9 EDMO
88/9 EDMO / Action 61
90/1 EDMO / IGA
90/1 EDMO / IGA
91/2 EDMO / IGA
91/2 EDMO / IGA
95/6 Houston Aeros
95/6 Houston Aeros
99/0 Houston Aeros
99/0 Houston Aeros
93/4 Leaf 308
94/5 Leaf 337
82/3 Medicine Hat Tigers
82/3 Medicine Hat Tigers
83/4 Medicine Hat Tigers
83/4 Medicine Hat Tigers
84/5 Moncton G'Flames
84/5 Moncton G'Flames
85/6 Moncton G'Flames
85/6 Moncton G'Flames
90/1 OPC/Topps 25
92/3 O-Pee-Chee 322
92/3 OTTA
92/3 OTTA
93/4 OTTA
93/4 OTTA
93/4 Panini Sticker 117
92/3 Parkhurst 116
93/4 PHIL / Sheet
93/4 PHIL / Sheet
94/5 PHIL / Sheet
94/5 PHIL / Sheet
92/3 Pinnacle 374
93/4 Pinnacle 323
93/4 Pinnacle CA16
94/5 Pinnacle 163
94/5 POG 178
93/4 Power Play 171
93/4 Premier 271
90/1 Pro Set 88
88/9 ProCards / Cape Breton
91/2 Score CAN 652
92/3 Score 514
93/4 Score 407
92/3 Topps 230
93/4 To. Stadium 172
94/5 To. Stadium 206

LAMBERT, DAN
92/3 Bowman 356
99/0 Eishockey 110
93/4 Fort Wayne Komets 10
93/4 Fort Wayne Komets 10
95/6 Future Legends 30
93/4 Jyvas Hyva 26
97/8 Long Beach Ice Dogs
97/8 Long Beach Ice Dogs
98/9 Long Beach Ice Dogs
98/9 Long Beach Ice Dogs
92/3 O-Pee-Chee 357
91/2 Pinnacle 346
93/4 Sisu 87
92/3 Topps 364
91/2 Upper Deck 592
92/3 Upper Deck 251
00/1 UD DEL 149
01/2 UD DEL 160

LAMBERT, DENNY
98/9 Aurora 103
01/2 BAP Update ✄ TC23, ✄ TC33
95/6 Bowman 98
95/6 Fleer Ultra 4
98/9 NASH / Wendy's 15
98/9 NASH / Wendy's 15
98/9 Omega 131
96/7 OTTA
96/7 OTTA
97/8 OTTA
97/8 OTTA
98/9 Pacific 311
99/0 Pacific 228
00/1 Pacific 20
97/8 Pa. Invincible R-134
98/9 Pa. Paramount 125
96/7 Pi. Be A Player 68, ✍ Aut. 68
91/2 ProCards 324
92/3 San Diego Gulls
92/3 San Diego Gulls
93/4 San Diego Gulls
93/4 San Diego Gulls
89/0 Soo Greyhounds
89/0 Soo Greyhounds
91 7th..Sketch Mem.Cup 17
90/1 7th..Sketch OHL 164
95/6 Topps 286
00/1 UD Vintage 23

LAMBERT, JUDD
97/8 Albany River Rats
97/8 Albany River Rats
92/3 BCJHL 42

LAMBERT, LANE
96/7 Cleveland Lumberjacks
96/7 Cleveland Lumberjacks
97/8 Cleveland Lumberjacks
97/8 Cleveland Lumberjacks
98/9 Cleveland Lumberjacks
98/9 Cleveland Lumberjacks
84/5 DETR / Little Caesars
85/6 DETR / Little Caesars
99/0 Houston Aeros
99/0 Houston Aeros
84/5 O-Pee-Chee 57
88/9 O-Pee-Chee 224
88/9 OPC Sticker 183-48
88/9 Panini Sticker 356
87/8 QUÉB / Gene. Foods
88/9 QUÉB
88/9 QUÉB / Gene. Foods
81/2 Saskatoon Blades
81/2 Saskatoon Blades

LAMBERT, ROSS
83/4 Moncton Alpines
83/4 Moncton Alpines
84/5 Nova Scotia Oilers
84/5 Nova Scotia Oilers

LAMBERT, SYLVIO
51/2 Lac St-Jean 21

LAMBERT, YVES
91/2 7th...Sketch LHJMQ 272

LAMBERT, YVON
81/2 BUFF / Wendt's 16
73/4 Dernière Heure
80/1 Dernière Heure
74/5 Loblaws
73/4 MONT / Pro Star
74/5 MONT
74/5 MONT
75/6 MONT
76/7 MONT
77/8 MONT
78/9 MONT
79/0 MONT
80/1 MONT
74/5 O-Pee-Chee 342
75/6 O-Pee-Chee 17
76/7 O-Pee-Chee 232
77/8 O-Pee-Chee 151
78/9 O-Pee-Chee 147
79/0 O-Pee-Chee 24
80/1 O-Pee-Chee 246
81/2 O-Pee-Chee 185
82/3 O-Pee-Chee 27
81/2 OPC Sticker 35
82/3 OPC/Topps Sticker 125
80/1 Pepsi Bottle Cap
82/3 Post [Buff.]
75/6 Topps 17
76/7 Topps 232
77/8 Topps 151
78/9 Topps 147
79/0 Topps 24
80/1 Topps 246

LAMBY, DICK
79 Panini Sticker 208

LAMEY, ROB
96/7 Guildford Flames 3
96/7 Guildford Flames 3
97/8 Guildford Flames
97/8 Guildford Flames
98/9 Guildford Flames
98/9 Guildford Flames

LAMICH, MARTIN
97/8 APS 142
99/0 DS 177
98/9 OFS 125
99/0 OFS 425

LAMING, ANDREW
91/2 7th...Sketch WHL 65

LAMIRANDE, CHARLES
51/2 Lac St-Jean 31

LAMIRANDE, GASTON
51/2 Lac St-Jean 39

LAMIRANDE, JEAN PAUL
52/3 La Patrie
51/2 Laval Dairy 31
52/3 St. Lawrence 95
59/60 Whitby Dunlops

LAMIRANDE, MAURICE
51/2 Bas du Fleuve 38
52/3 Bas du Fleuve 5

LAMMENS, HANK
92/3 Canada Nationals
94 Panini Olympics 317
93/4 Parkhurst 409
88/9 ProCards / Springfield
89/0 ProCards AHL 233

LAMORIELLO, LOU
88/9 NJER / Caretta
89/0 NJER
89/0 NJER / Caretta
90/1 NJER
90/1 NJER
96/7 NJER / Sharp
96/7 NJER / Sharp

LAMOTHE, CARL
90/1 7th..Sketch LHJMQ 255
91/2 7th...Sketch LHJMQ 148

LAMOTHE, MARC
99/0 BAP Mem. 399
02/3 Between the Pipes 87
99/0 Cleveland Lumberjacks
99/0 Cleveland Lumberjacks
94/5 Fredericton Canadiens
94/5 Fredericton Canadiens
95/6 Fredericton Canadiens
95/6 Fredericton Canadiens
02/3 Grand Rapids Griffins
02/3 Grand Rapids Griffins
01/2 Hamilton Bulldogs
01/2 Hamilton Bulldogs
01/2 Hamilton Bulldogs/ Staz
01/2 Hamilton Bulldogs/ Staz
97/8 Indianapolis Ice 13
97/8 Indianapolis Ice 13
98/9 Indianapolis Ice
98/9 Indianapolis Ice
99/0 Omega 58
91/2 7th...Sketch OHL 240
93/4 Slapshot / Kingston 2
00/1 Syracuse Crunch
00/1 Syracuse Crunch

LAMOUREUX, DENIS
96/7 Johnstown Chiefs
96/7 Johnstown Chiefs

LAMOUREUX, LÉO
34-43 BeeHive-1 [Mont.]
43-47 Parade Sportive
43-47 Parade Sportive
45-54 Quaker Oats

LAMOUREUX, MITCH
94/5 Hershey Bears
94/5 Hershey Bears
98/9 Hershey Bears
98/9 Hershey Bears
98/9 Hershey Bears
98/9 Hershey Bears
80/1 Oshawa Generals
80/1 Oshawa Generals
81/2 Oshawa Generals
81/2 Oshawa Generals
96/7 Providence Bruins
96/7 Providence Bruins
92/3 San Diego Gulls
92/3 San Diego Gulls

LAMOUREUX, PATRICK
91/2 7th...Sketch LHJMQ 51

LAMOUREUX, ROBERT
72/3 Williams Finnish 215
73/4 Williams Finnish 289

LAMPAINEN, MATTI
65/6 Hellas 80

LAMPERT, REINHART
94 Semic 247
93 Semic Sticker 287

LAMPINEN, JUHA
96/7 DEL 95
92/3 Jyvas Hyva 42
93/4 Jyvas Hyva 85
93/4 Sisu 113
94/5 Sisu 54
95/6 Sisu 232

LAMPMAN, MIKE
76/7 O-Pee-Chee 375
77/8 O-Pee-Chee 396
72/3 SLOU
73/4 SLOU

LAMPRON, PATRICK
91/2 7th...Sketch LHJMQ 98

LANDGREN, REINE
89/0 Semic Elitserien 232
90/1 Semic Elitserien 64
91/2 Semic Elitserien 242

LANDMESSER, DEREK
99/0 Rockford IceHogs
99/0 Rockford IceHogs

LANDOLT, SHAUN
01/2 Moose Jaw Warriors 20
01/2 Moose Jaw Warriors 20

LANDON, BRUCE
72/3 New England Whalers
72/3 New England Whalers
76/7 OPC WHA 48

LANDON, LARRY
83/4 Nova Scotia Voyageurs
83/4 Nova Scotia Voyageurs

LANDRY, ANDRÉ
99/0 Shawinigan 21
99/0 Shawinigan 21

LANDRY, ÉRIC
00/1 Austin Ice Bats
00/1 Austin Ice Bats
99/0 Indianapolis Ice
99/0 Indianapolis Ice
99/0 Kentucky Tho'blades
99/0 Kentucky Tho'blades
00/1 MONT
00/1 MONT
00/1 PS Titanium 129
00/1 PS Titanium Draft 129
01/2 Québec Citadelles
01/2 Québec Citadelles
96/7 Roanoke Express 3
96/7 Roanoke Express 3
97/8 Saint John Flames
97/8 Saint John Flames
93/4 Slapshot / Guelph 10
95/6 Slapshot 318
00/1 SP Authentic 148
00/1 SPx 180
00/1 UD Ice 91

LANDRY, JOHN
82/3 Kingston Canadians
82/3 Kingston Canadians
84/5 Sudbury Wolves
84/5 Sudbury Wolves

LANDRY, ROGER
52/3 Anonymous 160

LANDRY, ROLAND
52/3 Bas du Fleuve 8

LANE, CHRIS
95/6 Spokane Chiefs 4
95/6 Spokane Chiefs 4

LANE, GORD
83/4 NYIS / News 17
84/5 NYIS / News 21
77/8 O-Pee-Chee 287
78/9 O-Pee-Chee 284
79/0 O-Pee-Chee 325
80/1 O-Pee-Chee 323
81/2 O-Pee-Chee 212
83/4 O-Pee-Chee 10
85/6 OPC Sticker 77-210
78/9 WASH

LANE, JESSE
99/0 Des Moines Buc's
99/0 Des Moines Buc's
01/2 Hull Olympiques 15
01/2 Hull Olympiques 15
96 Québec Pee Wee 28

LANG, BILL
90/1 7th..Sketch OHL 310
91/2 7th...Sketch OHL 60
93/4 Slapshot / North Bay 9

LANG, CHAD
95/6 Classic 94
93/4 Cla. 4 Sport 214
98/9 Huntington Blizzard
98/9 Huntington Blizzard
98/9 Peoria Rivermen
98/9 Peoria Rivermen
91/2 Peterborough Petes
91/2 Peterborough Petes
91/2 7th...Sketch OHL 129
93/4 Slapshot / Peterborough 15

LANG, KAREL
94/5 DEL 225
95/6 DEL 219
96/7 DEL 69
98/9 DEL 25
99/0 Eishockey 125
82 Semic Sticker 77
00/1 UD DEL 154

LANG, ROBERT
01/2 Adrenaline 154, ✂ GWJ 37
94/5 APS 222
96/7 APS 353, 383, 389
97/8 APS 355
02/3 Atomic ✂ GWJ 25
98/9 Be A Player 263, ✍ Aut. 263
00/1 BAP Mem. 382
01/2 BAP Mem. 103
02/3 BAP Mem. 172, 264
98 Bonaparte 1C
98 Bonaparte Pexeso 3
01/2 Bowman 99
92/3 Classic Prospects 46
99/0 Crown Royale 114
01/2 Crown Royale 116
96/7 DS Sticker 17, 73
97/8 DS Sticker 17
02/3 Exclusive 174
93/4 Fleer Ultra 188
94/5 Fleer Ultra 101
95 Globe 155
02/3 Heads Up ✂ GWQ 22
94/5 Leaf 429
01/2 O-Pee-Chee 78
02/3 O-Pee-Chee 182, Update 182
92/3 OPC Premier 47
98/9 OFS 238, OW 19
98/9 Omega 197
98/9 Pacific 355
99/0 Pacific 342
00/1 Pacific 331
01/2 Pacific 315
02/3 Pacific 311
02/3 Pacific Complete 306
00/1 Pa. Paramount 200
94/5 Panini Sticker T
99/0 Panini Sticker 133
00/1 Panini Sticker 85
92/3 Parkhurst 227
92/3 Parkhurst 64
94/5 Parkhurst 286
95/6 Parkhurst 101
00/1 Parkhurst P-201
02/3 Parkhurst 185
02/3 Parkhurst Retro 186
94/5 Parkie SE78
92/3 Phoenix Roadrunners
92/3 Phoenix Roadrunners
92/3 Pinnacle 411
94/5 Pinnacle 413
97/8 Pi. Be A Player 14, ✍ Aut. 14
94/5 Premier 218
01/2 Pr. Stock -PS 58
02/3 Pr. Stock Reserve ✂ 150
00/1 PS Titanium ✂ GUG 136
01/2 PS Titanium 113
01/2 PS Titanium Draft ✂ 79
93/4 Score 456
94 Semic 186
00/1 Signature 207, ✍ Aut. 65
02/3 Signature 30, GS-77, ✍ 30
01/2 SP GU ✂ AF, ✂ AFT
02/3 Sports Vault 145
01/2 SPx 54
00/1 Stadion 69
00/1 Stadium 104
95/6 Topps 186
00/1 Topps 224
01/2 Topps 78
02/3 Topps 182, Update 182
01/2 To. Chrome 78
02/3 To. Chrome 105
01/2 To. Heritage 89, ✂ GWJ
02/3 To. Heritage 175
02/3 To. Limited 182
01/2 To. Reserve ✂ TR
02/3 T. Total 216
92/3 Upper Deck 552
92/3 Upper Deck ER4
94/5 Upper Deck 175
95/6 Upper Deck 281
00/1 Upper Deck 139
01/2 Upper Deck 140, ✂ PoaNT
02/3 Upper Deck 420, ✂ S
94/5 UD BAP ✍ 174
02/3 UD Classic ✂ HR (x2)
95/6 UD CC 175
01/2 UD MVP 153
02/3 UD MVP 187
99/0 UD MVP Cup 150
02/3 UD Top Shelf ✂ GO, ✂ SH
00/1 UD Vintage 292
01/2 UD Vintage 203
02/3 UD Vintage 260, GB 260
01/2 Vanguard ✂ DGM 26
00/1 Victory 186
01/2 Victory 282
02/3 Victory -NP20

LANGAGER, SHANE
89/0 Saskatoon Blades
89/0 Saskatoon Blades

LÄNGBACKA, JAN
92/3 Jyvas Hyva 108
93/4 Jyvas Hyva 198
93/4 Sisu 266
94/5 Sisu 26

LANGDON, DARREN
00/1 BAP Mem. 360
01/2 BAP Update ✂ TC10, ✂ TC20
94/5 Binghampton Rangers
94/5 Binghampton Rangers
95/6 Bowman 92
92/3 Dayton Bombers
92/3 Dayton Bombers
95/6 Donruss 224
95/6 Fleer Metal 181
95/6 Fleer Ultra 102, 345
95/6 Leaf 262
98/9 NYRA
98/9 NYRA
98/9 OPC Chrome 172
98/9 Pacific 296
01/2 Pacific 406
95/6 Parkhurst 528
96/7 Pi. Be A Player 9, ✍ Aut. 9
95/6 SBx Impact 212
95/6 Topps 116
98/9 Topps 172
00/1 To. Heritage 165

LANGDON, SEAN
01/2 Kingston Frontenacs 10
01/2 Kingston Frontenacs 10

LANGE, PATRICK
94/5 DEL 195
95/6 DEL 309

LANGELLE, PETE
34-43 BeeHive-1 [Toro.]
39/0 O-Pee-Chee 7
40/1 O-Pee-Chee 117

LANGEN, MIKE
91/2 Air Canada SJHL A13
90/1 7th..Sketch WHL 270

LANGENBRUNNER, JAMIE
98/9 Aurora 56
99/0 Aurora 45
99/0 BAP Mem. 256
00/1 BAP Mem. 156
01/2 BAP Mem. 114, 465
02/3 BAP Mem. 28
94/5 Classic 24, T17
95/6 Classic 94
94/5 Cla. Images 48, ✍ Aut.
00/1 Crown Royale ✂ GWJ 9
96/7 DALL / Southwest
96/7 DALL / Southwest
97/8 DALL / Score 211
97/8 DALL / Score 211
00/1 DALL / Southwest
00/1 DALL / Southwest
01/2 DALL / Southwest
01/2 DALL / Southwest
93/4 Donruss USA13
96/7 Donruss 218
97/8 Donruss 97
96/7 Do. Canadian 137
97/8 Do. Canadian 103
96/7 Do. Elite 144, A-21
97/8 Do. Preferred 20
97/8 Do. Priority 79
98/9 Dynagon Ice 57
99/0 Dynagon Ice 66
95/6 Edge Ice 141
96/7 Flair 105
96/7 Fleer 129, CC-6
95/6 Fleer Ultra 346
96/7 Fl. Ultra 43, UR-11
95/6 Future Legends PC-6
96/7 Leaf 225
97/8 Leaf 46
94/5 L. Limited USA 7
96/7 L. Limited LR-8
96/7 L. Preferred 144
97/8 Limited 167
96/7 Metal Univ. 184
99/0 Millenium 75, ✍ Aut. 75
99/0 NHL Power Play
01/2 O-Pee-Chee 208
02/3 O-Pee-Chee 170
98/9 OPC Chrome 7
97/8 Omega 70
98/9 Omega 71
98/9 Pacific 15
99/0 Pacific 122
00/1 Pacific 133
01/2 Pacific 127, ✂ GWJ 11
02/3 Pacific 224, ✂ GWJ 30
02/3 Pacific Complete 450
97/8 Pacific CC 110
98/9 Pa. Crown Roy. 39
97/8 Pa. Dynagon 36, T-32
97/8 Pa. Invincible 40
97/8 Pa. Paramount 58
98/9 Pa. Paramount 65
99/0 Pa. Paramount 73
00/1 Pa. Paramount 76
97/8 Pa. Revolution 41
98/9 Pa. Revolution 42
99/0 Panini Sticker 228
00/1 Panini Sticker 149
95/6 Parkhurst 60
00/1 Parkhurst P-188
01/2 Parkhurst 385
94/5 Parkie SE248
93/4 Pinnacle 496
96/7 Pinnacle 247
96/7 Pi. Be A Player LTH6A, ✍ Aut. LTH6A
97/8 Pi. Inside 100
95/6 Pi. Summit 170
96/7 Pi. Summit 192
95/6 Pi. Zenith 129
96/7 Pi. Zenith 139
00/1 Private Stock ✂ GUG 37
01/2 Pr. Stock ✂ GUG 36
00/1 PS Titanium ✂ GUG 86
01/2 PS Titanium ✂ DSJ 16
01/2 PS Titanium Draft ✂ 54
00/1 PS Titanium Draft ✂ 31
02/3 Quest for the Cup 59
99/0 Revolution 46
00/1 Revolution ✂ GWJ 5
96/7 Score 254
97/8 Score 211
96/7 Select CE 115
96/7 SBx Impact 152
93/4 Slapshot / Peterborough 20
94/5 SP 194
96/7 SP 46
97/8 SP Authentic 47, ✍ SotT
02/3 Sports Vault 67
99/0 SPx 52
00/1 Stadium 130
95/6 Topps 182
98/9 Topps 7
99/0 Topps 60, NS10
00/1 Topps 118
01/2 Topps 208
02/3 Topps 170
99/0 To. Chrome 60
00/1 To. Chrome 91
94/5 Topps Finest 120
02/3 To. Limited 170
02/3 T. Total 75
98/9 UD Choice 61
93/4 Upper Deck 566
95/6 Upper Deck 503
96/7 Upper Deck 48
97/8 Upper Deck 260
98/9 Upper Deck 81
99/0 Upper Deck 45
00/1 Upper Deck 286
01/2 Upper Deck 58
02/3 Upper Deck 104
96/7 UD Black Diam. 126
96/7 UD CC 74
97/8 UD Coll. Choice 69
98/9 UD G. Reserve 81
99/0 UD G. Reserve 45
96/7 UD Ice 15
99/0 UD MVP 64
00/1 UD MVP 60
01/2 UD SCup Champs 52
00/1 UD Vintage 116
00/1 Vanguard ✂ DGJ 15
01/2 Vanguard ✂ DGM 12
02/3 Vanguard 62
99/0 Victory 90
00/1 Victory 75
01/2 Victory 116
99/0 WGretzky 56
97/8 Zenith 61, Z51

LANGER, CHRISTIAN
99/0 Eishockey 80, 374

LANGEVIN, CHRIS
85/6 BUFF / Blue Shield

LANGEVIN, DAVE
85/6 MINS
85/6 MINS / 7-Eleven 11
79/0 NYIS
83/4 NYIS
83/4 NYIS / News 18
84/5 NYIS / News 22
80/1 O-Pee-Chee 188
81/2 O-Pee-Chee 213
82/3 O-Pee-Chee 204
83/4 O-Pee-Chee 11
86/7 O-Pee-Chee 218
83/4 OPC/Topps Sticker 83
82/3 Post [NYIs.]
83/4 Souhaits Keychain [Islanders]
80/1 Topps 188
00/1 UD Vintage ✂ D-POH

LANGFELD, JOSH
01/2 BAP Mem. 430
01/2 Grand Rapids Griffins
01/2 Grand Rapids Griffins
01/2 Parkhurst 332
02/3 Upper Deck 217
01/2 UD Mask 158

LANGH, PIERRE
79 Panini Sticker 344

LANGILLE, DEREK
91/2 Moncton Hawks
91/2 Moncton Hawks
90/1 Newmarket Saints
90/1 Newmarket Saints
90/1 ProCards 153
91/2 ProCards 173

LANGKOW, DAYMOND
01/2 Adrenaline 149, ✂ GWJ 34
01/2 Atomic 76
02/3 Atomic ✂ GWJ 18
98/9 Be A Player 129, ✍ Aut. 129
00/1 BAP Mem. 324
02/3 BAP Mem. 48
94/5 Classic DP4
95/6 Classic 5, AS4, BK5
95/6 Cla. 5 Sport 147, SFF-8
94/5 Cla. Images 83, PD6
95/6 Donruss 324
97/8 Donruss 18
96/7 Do. Canadian 135
97/8 Do. Canadian 70, NP-21
95/6 Do. Elite WJ 16
96/7 Do. Elite 134, A-13
97/8 Do. Elite 36
97/8 Do. Preferred 23
97/8 Do. Priority 21
97/8 Do. Studio 48, HH-6
02/3 Exclusive 135
02/3 First Edition 274
96/7 Fleer 130, CC-7
95/6 Fleer Metal 182
96/7 Fl. Ultra 158
02/3 Heads Up 97, ✂ GWQ 21
96/7 Leaf 232
97/8 Leaf 103
95/6 L. Limited 45
96/7 L. Preferred 140
97/8 Limited 31, 133, 192, FG-48
96/7 Metal Univ. 185
02/3 O-Pee-Chee 244
98/9 OPC Chrome 72
97/8 Omega 210
99/0 Omega 170
98/9 Pacific 400
99/0 Pacific 305
00/1 Pacific 299, ✂ GWJ 11
01/2 Pacific 288
02/3 Pacific 298, ✂ GWJ 41
02/3 Pacific Complete 22
97/8 Pa. Dynagon 119, T-65
97/8 Pa. Invincible 133
97/8 Pa. Paramount 174
99/0 Pa. Paramount 171
00/1 Pa. Paramount 181
00/1 Panini Sticker 77
95/6 Parkhurst 270
00/1 Parkhurst P-175
02/3 Parkhurst 157
02/3 Parkhurst Retro 64
96/7 Pinnacle 240
97/8 Pinnacle 112
97/8 Pi. Be A Player 176, ✍ Aut. 176
97/8 Pi. Inside 99
96/7 Pi. Summit 186
95/6 Pi. Zenith 143
96/7 Pi. Zenith 141
00/1 Private Stock ✂ GUG 82
01/2 Pr. Stock 76
02/3 Pr. Stock Reserve ✂ 137
01/2 PS Titanium 109, ✂ DSJ 71
01/2 PS Titanium Draft ✂ 75
97/8 Score 167
95/6 Select CE 124
96/7 Select CE 117
94/5 Sig. Rookies 22, ✍ 22
94/5 SR Auto-Phonex P2, ✍ P2
95/6 SR Tetrad F4
95/6 SR Tetrad Autobilia 45
00/1 Signature 175
01/2 Signature 142, ✍ Aut. 142
02/3 Signature 96, ✍ 96
95/6 SBx Impact 222
96/7 SBx Impact 153
95/6 SP 139
96/7 SP 146
97/8 SP Authentic 145
02/3 Sports Vault 266
98/9 Topps 72
00/1 Topps 98
02/3 Topps 244
01/2 To. Heritage 183
02/3 To. Limited 244
02/3 T. Total 182
95/6 Tri-City Americans 31
95/6 Tri-City Americans 31
95/6 Tri-City Americans 5
95/6 Tri-City Americans 5
98/9 UD Choice 192
93/4 Upper Deck E7
95/6 Upper Deck 270, 526
96/7 Upper Deck 340, X30
97/8 Upper Deck 158, SG32, T15C
00/1 Upper Deck 355
01/2 Upper Deck 362
02/3 Upper Deck 381
96/7 UD Black Diam. 46
95/6 UD CC 402
96/7 UD CC 346
97/8 UD Coll. Choice 243
97/8 UD Ice 15
99/0 UD MVP Cup 136
00/1 UD Vintage 262
02/3 UD Vintage 196
01/2 Vanguard 77
00/1 Victory 173
01/2 Victory 255
02/3 Victory 167

LANGKOW, SCOTT
99/0 BAP Mem. 368
02/3 Cardset 207, 298
95/6 Edge Ice 71
99/0 Pacific 332
93/4 Portland Winter Hawks
93/4 Portland Winter Hawks
96/7 Springfield Falcons
96/7 Springfield Falcons
97/8 Springfield Falcons
97/8 Springfield Falcons
99/0 Victory 15

LANGLAIS, ALAIN
89/0 New Haven Nighthawks
89/0 New Haven Nighthawks

LANGLOIS, AL
45-64 BeeHive-2 [Mont.]
45-64 BeeHive-2 [NYRa.]
64-67 BeeHive-3 [Detr.]
64/5 Coke/Sprite [Detr.]
65/6 Coca-Cola
62/3 Cowan Tile
58/9 Parkhurst 5
59/0 Parkhurst 45
60/1 Parkhurst 39
61/2 Parkhurst 37
94/5 Parkie Tall 52
60/1 Shirriff 24
61/2 Shirriff 94
61/2 Topps 46
61/2 Topps - Stamp
62/3 Topps 47
62/3 Topps Dollar
63/4 Topps 49
64/5 Topps 13
65/6 Topps 33
60/1 York Glass [Mont.]
60/1 York

LANGLOIS, CHARLES
25-27 Anonymous 76
25-27 Anonymous 76
24/5 Champ's Cigarettes
27/8 La Patrie
27/8 La Presse
24/5 Maple Crispette [V130] 26
24/5 William Paterson 17

LANGLOIS, JOCELYN
00/1 Rockford IceHogs
00/1 Rockford IceHogs
90/1 7th..Sketch LHJMQ 79
91/2 7th...Sketch LHJMQ 40

LANGLOIS, PATRICK
92/3 Fredericton Canadiens
92/3 Fredericton Canadiens
93/4 Fredericton Canadiens
93/4 Fredericton Canadiens
94/5 Fredericton Canadiens
94/5 Fredericton Canadiens
95/6 Fredericton Canadiens
95/6 Fredericton Canadiens
96/7 Fredericton Canadiens
96/7 Fredericton Canadiens

LANGLOIS, PETER
84/5 Kitchener Rangers
84/5 Kitchener Rangers

LANGNER, PAUL
72 Hellas MM-Jenkki 47
72 Semic Sticker 111

LANGSTROM, JUHANI
71/2 Williams Finnish 286

LANGTRY, DOC
23/4 Paulins Candy 57

LANGTRY, JACK
25 Dominion Chocolates 86

LANGWAY, ROD
92/3 Bowman 279
80/1 Dernière Heure
82/3 Dernière Heure
88/9 Esso All-Star
83/4 Funmate Puffy 19 [w/]
93/4 Hockey Wit 26
90/1 Kraft 24
82/3 McDonald's Les Étoiles 32
78/9 MONT
79/0 MONT
80/1 MONT
81/2 MONT
80/1 O-Pee-Chee 344
81/2 O-Pee-Chee 186
82/3 O-Pee-Chee 368
83/4 O-Pee-Chee 207
83/4 O-Pee-Chee 365
83/4 O-Pee-Chee 374
84/5 O-Pee-Chee 202
84/5 O-Pee-Chee 210
84/5 O-Pee-Chee 377
85/6 OPC/Topps 8
86/7 OPC/Topps 164
87/8 OPC/Topps 108
88/9 OPC/Topps 192
90/1 OPC/Topps 353
91/2 O-Pee-Chee 105
92/3 O-Pee-Chee 347
89/0 OPC/Topps 55
81/2 OPC Sticker 39
82/3 OPC/Topps Sticker 34
83/4 OPC/Topps Sticker 201
83/4 OPC/Topps Sticker 313
84/5 OPC Sticker 125
84/5 OPC Sticker 126
84/5 OPC Sticker 230-231
85/6 OPC Sticker 105
85/6 OPC Sticker 113
86/7 OPC Sticker 249-139
87/8 OPC Sticker 236
88/9 OPC Sticker 69-198
89/0 opcSticker 77-216
87/8 Panini Sticker 178
88/9 Panini Sticker 163
88/9 Panini Sticker 366
89/0 Panini Sticker 350
91/2 Panini Sticker 209
92/3 Panini Sticker 169
91/2 Parkhurst 197
92/3 Parkhurst 433
80/1 Pepsi Bottle Cap
91/2 Pinnacle 195
92/3 Pinnacle 131
82/3 Post [Mont.]
90/1 Pro Set 314
91/2 Pro Set 259
91/2 Pro Set 587
97/8 Providence Bruins
97/8 Providence Bruins
96/7 Richmond Renegades
96/7 Richmond Renegades
90/1 Score 20
90/1 Sco. Hot Cards 11
91/2 Score 228
91/2 Score CAN 228
92/3 Score 143
93/4 Score 145
89 Semic Sticker 159
84/5 7-Eleven
85/6 7-Eleven Superstars 20
83/4 Souhaits Keychain [Capitals]
84/5 Topps 147
84/5 Topps 156
85/6 OPC/Topps-Stick. 10
92/3 Topps 46
91/2 To. Stadium 225
92/3 To. Stadium 215
90/1 Upper Deck 57, 309
91/2 Upper Deck 314
02/3 UD Foundations 55, 99
01/2 UD Legends 67
82/3 WASH
84/5 WASH / Pizza Hut
85/6 WASH / Pizza Hut
86/7 WASH / Kodak
86/7 WASH / Police
87/8 WASH
87/8 WASH / Kodak
88/9 WASH
88/9 WASH / Smokey
89/0 WASH
89/0 WASH
89/0 WASH / Kodak
89/0 WASH / Kodak
90/1 WASH / Kodak
90/1 WASH / Kodak
90/1 WASH / Smokey
90/1 WASH / Smokey
91/2 WASH / Kodak
91/2 WASH / Kodak
91/2 WASH / Smokey
91/2 WASH / Smokey
92/3 WASH / Kodak
92/3 WASH / Kodak
96 Wien HL8

LANGWAY, ROD
02/3 Fleer Throwbacks 16

LANICEK, MICHAL
99/0 Score 72

LANIEL, MARC
94/5 Cincinnati Cyclones
94/5 Cincinnati Cyclones
96/7 Cincinnati Cyclones
96/7 Cincinnati Cyclones
98/9 DEL 214
99/0 Eishockey 197
93/4 Fredericton Canadiens
93/4 Fredericton Canadiens
95/6 Houston Aeros
95/6 Houston Aeros
88/9 ProCards / Utica
89/0 ProCards AHL 227
90/1 ProCards 567
92/3 Semic Nordisk 125
00/1 UD DEL 169

LANIER, JONAS
01/2 UD DEL 243

LANIGAN, GERRY
94/5 Slapshot / Detroit Jr. 8
95/6 Slapshot 18
94/5 Slapshot Memorial 82

LANIGAN, SHANE
96/7 Regina Pats
96/7 Regina Pats
97/8 Regina Pats
97/8 Regina Pats

LANIUK, COREY
98/9 Phoenix Mustangs 13
98/9 Phoenix Mustangs 13

LANK, JEFF
91/2 Prince Albert Raiders
91/2 Prince Albert Raiders
93/4 Prince Albert Raiders
93/4 Prince Albert Raiders
91/2 7th...Sketch WHL 256

LANKSHEAR, MIKE
95/6 Guelph Storm
95/6 Guelph Storm
96/7 Guelph Storm
96/7 Guelph Storm
95/6 Slapshot 102

LANOIE, LAURENT
01/2 Drummondville
01/2 Drummondville

LANTEIGNE, ERIC
89/0 Rayside-Balfour
89/0 Rayside-Balfour

LANTHIER, JEAN-MARC
83/4 Fredericton Express
83/4 Fredericton Express
85/6 Fredericton Express
85/6 Fredericton Express
86/7 Fredericton Express
86/7 Fredericton Express
88/9 ProCards / Maine
89/0 ProCards AHL 220
80/1 Québec Remparts
80/1 Québec Remparts
85/6 VANC

LANTZ, KENT
89/0 Semic Elitserien 188
90/1 Semic Elitserien 16
91/2 Semic Elitserien 217

LANZ, RICK
92/3 Atlanta Knights
92/3 Atlanta Knights
81/2 O-Pee-Chee 338
82/3 O-Pee-Chee 348
83/4 O-Pee-Chee 353
84/5 O-Pee-Chee 321
85/6 O-Pee-Chee 197
86/7 OPC/Topps 179
87/8 O-Pee-Chee 239
88/9 O-Pee-Chee 225
83/4 OPC/Topps Sticker 280
84/5 OPC Sticker 276
87/8 OPC Sticker 157-17
88/9 OPC Sticker 176-43
80/1 Oshawa Generals
80/1 Oshawa Generals
80/1 Pepsi Bottle Cap
83/4 Souhaits Keychain [Canucks]
87/8 TORO / 5x8
87/8 TORO / P.L.A.Y. 11
88/9 TORO / P.L.A.Y. 9
83/4 Vachon 110-30
80/1 VANC
80/1 VANC / Silverwood
81/2 VANC
81/2 VANC / Silverwood
82/3 VANC
83/4 VANC
84/5 VANC
85/6 VANC
86/7 VANC

LANZINGER, GÜNTER
95 Panini Worlds 271

LAPACEK, STANISLAV
98/9 OFS 406

LAPENSEE, BRUNO
86/7 Kitchener Rangers
86/7 Kitchener Rangers

LAPERRIÈRE, DANIEL
92/3 Classic 57
92/3 Classic 75
92/3 Classic Four Sport 199
93/4 Cla. Prospects 184
98/9 DEL 206
93/4 Donruss 485
94/5 Donruss 187
99/0 Eishockey 198
94/5 Leaf 156
92/3 OPC Premier 39
92/3 Peoria Rivermen
92/3 Peoria Rivermen
93/4 Peoria Rivermen
93/4 Peoria Rivermen
94/5 Peoria Rivermen
94/5 Peoria Rivermen
96/7 Portland Pirates
96/7 Portland Pirates
93/4 Premier 526
94/5 Score 219
94/5 To. Stadium 243
92/3 Upper Deck 525
00/1 UD DEL 70
01/2 UD DEL 35

LAPERRIÈRE, GILLES
52/3 Anonymous 67

LAPERRIÈRE, IAN
98/9 Be A Player 65, ✍ Aut. 65
00/1 BAP Mem. ✂ T-26
01/2 BAP Update ✂ TC3, ✂ TC28
94/5 Classic 69, T59
94/5 Cla. Images 7, CE7, PR3
95/6 Donruss 5
95/6 Edge Ice C2
94/5 Fleer 189
95/6 Fleer Ultra 141, AR-7
94/5 Leaf 484
95/6 Leaf 99, SR-10
95/6 L. Limited 53
02/3 O-Pee-Chee 209
98/9 Pacific 237
02/3 Pacific 168
97/8 Pa. Dynagon BKS-47
95/6 Panini Sticker 155, 190, 305
95/6 Parkhurst 176, 408
94/5 Peoria Rivermen
94/5 Peoria Rivermen
95/6 Pinnacle 127
97/8 Pi. Be A Player 189, ✍ Aut. 189
95/6 Playoff 308
96/7 Playoff 403
95/6 POG 235, I-033
94/5 Premier 307
95/6 Score 72
90/1 7th..Sketch LHJMQ 14
91/2 7th...Sketch LHJMQ 281
91 7th..Sketch Mem.Cup 56
02/3 Signature ✂ FS3
95/6 SBx Emotion 149
95/6 SBx Impact 142, F-7
93/4 Slapshot / Drummondville 10
94/5 SP P-14
95/6 Topps 347, 20NG
02/3 Topps 209
00/1 To. Gold Label 93
02/3 To. Limited 209
02/3 T. Total 14
94/5 Upper Deck 306
95/6 Upper Deck 32, SE-69
97/8 Upper Deck 83
98/9 Upper Deck 108
00/1 Upper Deck 313
01/2 Upper Deck 81
02/3 Upper Deck 80
96/7 UD Black Diam. 10
95/6 UD CC 19
97/8 UD Coll. Choice 120
98/9 UD G. Reserve 108
96/7 UD Ice 30
01/2 Victory 169
99/0 WGretzky 79

LAPERRIÈRE, JACQUES
45-64 BeeHive-2 [Mont.]
64-67 BeeHive-3 [Mont.]
63-65 Chex
92/3 Classic 57
64/5 Coke/Sprite [Mont.]
65/6 Coca-Cola
65/6 Coke How To... C
65/6 Coke How To... Y
70/1 Dad's Cookies
72/3 Dernière Heure
73/4 Dernière Heure
70/1 Eddie Sargent 97
71/2 Eddie Sargent 108
72/3 Eddie Sargent 121
70/1 Esso Power Player
88/9 Esso All-Star
83&87 HHOF 260
72/3 Post 2
74/5 Loblaws
67/8 MONT
67/8 MONT / IGA Card
68/9 MONT / IGA Card
69/0 MONT / Pro Star
70/1 MONT
71/2 MONT / Pro Star
72/3 MONT / Pro Star
73/4 MONT / Pro Star
74/5 MONT
81/2 MONT
82/3 MONT
83/4 MONT
84/5 MONT
86/7 MONT
87/8 MONT
87/8 MONT / Vachon 11
87/8 MONT / Vachon 8
88/9 MONT
89/0 MONT
90/1 MONT
90/1 MONT
91/2 MONT
91/2 MONT
92/3 MONT / OPC 15
92/3 MONT / OPC 15
92/3 MONT / OPC 36
92/3 MONT / OPC 36
68/9 O-Pee-Chee 58
69/0 O-Pee-Chee 3
69/0 O-Pee-Chee 4in1
70/1 O-Pee-Chee 245
70/1 O-Pee-Chee 52
70/1 O-Pee-Chee DE 20
71/2 O-Pee-Chee 144
72/3 O-Pee-Chee 205
72/3 O-Pee-Chee Crest 11
73/4 O-Pee-Chee 40
74/5 O-Pee-Chee 202
63/4 Parkhurst 27
63/4 Parkhurst 86
01/2 Parkhurst ✍ PA46
02/3 Parkie - Reprint 287
95/6 Parkie 66-67 65, 122, 128
94/5 Parkie Tall 72, 140, 149, 161, AS3
66/7 Post Cereal Box
67/8 Post Cereal Box
67/8 Post Cereal Box
68/9 Post Marble
67/8 Post Tips 4
70/1 Post Shooters
68/9 Shirriff / Mont. 4
92/3 Sport Flash 1
64/5 Topps 53
65/6 Topps 3
66/7 Topps 122
66/7 Topps 67
67/8 Topps 7
68/9 Topps 58
69/0 Topps 3
70/1 Topps 52
73/4 Topps 137
74/5 Topps 202
64/5 Toronto Star Action
64/5 Toronto Star Photo
65/6 Toronto Star Photo
65/6 Toronto Star Weekend
71/2 Toronto Sun Photo
01/2 Ultimate Mem. ✂ SCW
02/3 Ultimate Mem. ✂ SF
63/4 York 34
67/8 York
67/8 York
67/8 York 18
95/6 Zellers

LAPEYRE, JODY
95/6 Tri-City Americans 18
95/6 Tri-City Americans 18

LAPIERRE, MAXIM
99 Québec Pee Wee 247

LAPIN, EVGENI
00/1 Mir 186

LAPIN, MISHA
92/3 W. Michigan Broncos
92/3 W. Michigan Broncos
93/4 W. Michigan Broncos
93/4 W. Michigan Broncos

LAPINKOSKI, MARKO
92/3 Jyvas Hyva 169

LAPLANTE, ALAIN
99/0 Muskegon Fury
99/0 Muskegon Fury

LAPLANTE, DARRYL
99/0 BAP Mem. 264
99/0 Cincinnati M'Ducks
99/0 Cincinnati M'Ducks
95/6 Classic 49
00/1 Cleveland Lumberjacks
00/1 Cleveland Lumberjacks
99/0 NHL Power Play
00/1 Pacific 150
00/1 Topps 316
00/1 To. Chrome 211
98/9 Upper Deck 9
00/1 Upper Deck 316
98/9 UD G. Reserve 9

LAPLANTE, ERIC
01/2 Cleveland Barons
01/2 Cleveland Barons

LAPLANTE, ÉRIC
96/7 Halifax Moosehead
96/7 Halifax Moosehead
96/7 Halifax Moosehead
96/7 Halifax Moosehead
97/8 Halifax Moosehead
97/8 Halifax Moosehead
00/1 Kentucky Tho'blades
00/1 Kentucky Tho'blades
98/9 Québec Remparts
98/9 Québec Remparts
99/0 Québec Remparts 6
99/0 Québec Remparts 6

LAPLANTE, SÉBASTIEN
01/2 Calgary Hitmen
01/2 Calgary Hitmen

LAPLANTE, SÉBASTIEN
93/4 Greensboro Monarchs
93/4 Greensboro Monarchs

LAPLANTE, STEVE
91/2 7th...Sketch LHJMQ 58

LAPOINTE, CLAUDE
92/3 Bowman 421
93/4 Donruss 285
92/3 Durivage 6
93/4 Durivage 24
92/3 Fleer Ultra 176
93/4 Fleer Ultra 403
89/0 Halifax Citadels
89/0 Halifax Citadels
90/1 Halifax Citadels
90/1 Halifax Citadels
93/4 Leaf 64
94/5 Leaf 304
96/7 NYIS
96/7 NYIS
91/2 O-Pee-Chee 431
92/3 O-Pee-Chee 320
01/2 O-Pee-Chee 150
98/9 OPC Chrome 167
99/0 Pacific 256
00/1 Pacific 252
01/2 Pacific 251
02/3 Pacific Complete 384
97/8 Pa. Invincible R-118
99/0 Pa. Paramount 143
00/1 Pa. Paramount 156
92/3 Panini Sticker 213
94/5 Panini Sticker 58
91/2 Parkhurst 370
93/4 Parkhurst 437
91/2 Pinnacle 313
92/3 Pinnacle 141
93/4 Pinnacle 294
94/5 Pinnacle 231
96/7 Pi. Be A Player 200, ✍ Aut. 200
93/4 Power Play 422
93/4 Premier 251
00/1 Private Stock ✂ GUG 70
00/1 PS Titanium Draft ✂ 63
91/2 Pro Set 556
92/3 Pro Set 151
92/3 Pro Set RGL 12
91/2 Pro Set Platinum 267
89/0 ProCards AHL 166
90/1 ProCards 445
91/2 QUÉB / Petro-Canada
91/2 QUÉB / Petro-Canada
92/3 QUÉB / Petro-Canada
92/3 QUÉB / Petro-Canada
94/5 QUÉB / Burger King
94/5 QUÉB / Burger King
92/3 Score 219
93/4 Score 352
94/5 Score 194
00/1 Stadium 198
92/3 Topps 94
98/9 Topps 167
99/0 Topps 210
00/1 Topps 91
01/2 Topps 150
99/0 To. Chrome 210
00/1 To. Chrome 73
00/1 To. Heritage 209
92/3 To. Stadium 93
02/3 T. Total 150
91/2 Upper Deck 488
92/3 Upper Deck 147
97/8 Upper Deck 311
00/1 Upper Deck 113
01/2 Upper Deck 342
99/0 UD MVP 128
00/1 UD MVP 115
00/1 UD Vintage 228
00/1 Vanguard ✂ DGJ 20
01/2 Vanguard ✂ DGM 36
99/0 Victory 186
00/1 Victory 146
99/0 WGretzky 106

LAPOINTE, GUY
93/4 Action Packed 2
51/2 Bas du Fleuve 11
02/3 BAP Mem. / Cup
77/8 Coke
72/3 Dernière Heure
73/4 Dernière Heure
80/1 Dernière Heure
70/1 Eddie Sargent 105
71/2 Eddie Sargent 98
72/3 Eddie Sargent 113
70/1 Esso Power Player
88/9 Esso All-Star
01/2 Fleer Greats 20, ✍ Aut.
91/2 Future Trends C72 92, ✍ 92
92/3 Future Trends C76 171
74/5 Lipton Soup 16
74/5 Loblaws
73/4 Mac's Milk
69/0 MONT / Pro Star
70/1 MONT
71/2 MONT / Pro Star
72/3 MONT / Pro Star
73/4 MONT / Pro Star
74/5 MONT
75/6 MONT
76/7 MONT
77/8 MONT
78/9 MONT
79/0 MONT
80/1 MONT
81/2 MONT
70/1 O-Pee-Chee 177
71/2 O-Pee-Chee 145
72/3 O-Pee-Chee 86
72/3 O-Pee-Chee TC
73/4 O-Pee-Chee 114
74/5 O-Pee-Chee 70
75/6 O-Pee-Chee 198
75/6 O-Pee-Chee 293
76/7 O-Pee-Chee 223
77/8 O-Pee-Chee 60
78/9 O-Pee-Chee 260
79/0 O-Pee-Chee 135
80/1 O-Pee-Chee 201
82/3 O-Pee-Chee 305
01/2 Parkhurst ✍ PA58
80/1 Pepsi Bottle Cap
82/3 Post [SLou.]

71/2 Pro Star Promotions
84/5 QUÉB
87/8 QUÉB / Gene. Foods
88/9 QUÉB
88/9 QUÉB / Gene. Foods
89/0 QUÉB
72/3 Topps 57
73/4 Topps 170
74/5 Topps 70
75/6 Topps 198
75/6 Topps 293
76/7 Topps 223
76/7 Topps NS 17
77/8 Topps 60
78/9 Topps 260
79/0 Topps 135
79/0 Topps 81
80/1 Topps 201
01/2 To. Chrome -CA7, ✍ CA7
01/2 T/O Archives 10, -Seat
71/2 Toronto Sun Photo
01/2 Ultimate Mem. ✂ LC, ✂ RT, ✂ SCD, ✂ SCW
02/3 Ultimate Mem. ✂ FS, ✂ SF
01/2 UD Legends 40
01/2 UD Vintage ✂ SH

LAPOINTE, HERV
90/1 7th..Sketch LHJMQ 107
91/2 7th...Sketch LHJMQ 179

LAPOINTE, MARTIN
01/2 Adrenaline 14
91/2 Arena 8
98/9 Be A Player 198, ✍ Aut. 198
99/0 BAP Mem. 235
00/1 BAP Mem. 361
01/2 BAP Mem. 319
91/2 Classic 9
91/2 Classic Four Sport 9
93/4 Cla. Prospects 173
91/2 DETR / Little Caesars
91/2 DETR / Little Caesars
93/4 Durivage 6
95/6 Edge Ice 4, QM-9
02/3 First Edition 230
94/5 Fleer Ultra 285
91/2 Gillette 20
93/4 Leaf 336
94/5 Leaf 201
00/1 Mir Fetisov 38
01/2 O-Pee-Chee 181
02/3 O-Pee-Chee 219
98/9 Omega 81
98/9 Pacific 197
99/0 Pacific 141
00/1 Pacific 151
01/2 Pacific 143
02/3 Pacific 29
02/3 Pacific Complete 135
97/8 Pacific CC 241
00/1 Pa. Paramount 86
91/2 Parkhurst 267
93/4 Parkhurst 63
94/5 Parkhurst 70
95/6 Parkhurst 340
00/1 Parkhurst P-153
01/2 Parkhurst 90
02/3 Parkhurst 34
02/3 Parkhurst Retro 133
91/2 Pinnacle 355
92/3 Pinnacle 365
94/5 Pinnacle 449
96/7 Pi. Be A Player 128, ✍ Aut. 128
93/4 Power Play 332
93/4 Premier - Gold 263
91/2 Pro Set 532
92/3 Pro Set 226
91/2 Score 105T
91/2 Score CAN 655
92/3 Score 409
97/8 Score Detr. 10
90/1 7th..Sketch LHJMQ 25
90 7th..Sketch Mem.Cup 61
91 7th..Sketch Mem.Cup 102
00/1 Signature 31, ✍ Aut. 62
01/2 Signature C-26, ✍ Aut. LML
02/3 Sports Vault 13
91/2 Star Pics 5
00/1 Topps 243
01/2 Topps 181
02/3 Topps 219
00/1 To. Heritage 122
01/2 To. Heritage 169
02/3 To. Limited 219
94/5 To. Stadium 151
00/1 To. Stars ✂ GG
02/3 T. Total 308
98/9 UD Choice RW9
00/1 UD Heroes 43
91/2 Ultimate Draft Pick 9, 65, ✍ Aut.
02/3 Ultimate Mem. ✂ SCDE, ✂ SCDGJ, ✂ SCDN
90/1 Upper Deck 467
91/2 Upper Deck 63
91/2 Upper Deck 66
91/2 Upper Deck 685
92/3 Upper Deck 405
92/3 Upper Deck 584
93/4 Upper Deck 257
94/5 Upper Deck 406
95/6 Upper Deck 200
97/8 Upper Deck 58
98/9 Upper Deck 86
00/1 Upper Deck 290
01/2 Upper Deck 245
02/3 Upper Deck 13
94/5 UD BAP ✍ 133
96/7 UD Black Diam. 13
94/5 UD Canada Junior 11
97/8 UD Coll. Choice 86
91/2 Upper Deck WJC 59
98/9 UD G. Reserve 86
01/2 UD Honor Roll TC1
02/3 UD MVP 16
99/0 UD MVP Cup 68
02/3 UD Vintage 20
00/1 Victory 91
02/3 Victory 21

LAPOINTE, NORMAND
75/6 OPC WHA 85

LAPOINTE, RICK
83/4 Fredericton Express
83/4 Fredericton Express
84/5 LOSA / Smokey 19
76/7 O-Pee-Chee 48
77/8 O-Pee-Chee 152
78/9 O-Pee-Chee 322
79/0 O-Pee-Chee 121
81/2 O-Pee-Chee 295
83/4 O-Pee-Chee 294
81/2 OPC Sticker 134
82/3 Post [SLou.]
82/3 QUÉB
83/4 QUÉB
76/7 Topps 48
77/8 Topps 152
79/0 Topps 121
81/2 Topps 119 [West]

LAPOINTE, RODNEY
87/8 Sudbury Wolves
87/8 Sudbury Wolves

LAPOINTE, RON
79/0 Montréal Juniors B&W
79/0 Montréal Juniors B&W
89/0 ProCards IHL 189
88/9 QUÉB
88/9 QUÉB / Gene. Foods

LAPOINTE, STEVE
90/1 7th..Sketch LHJMQ 208

LAPOINTE, SYLVAIN
91/2 7th...Sketch LHJMQ 216
93/4 Wheeling Thund'birds
93/4 Wheeling Thund'birds

LAPORTE, ALEXANDRE
95/6 Atlanta Knights
95/6 Atlanta Knights

LAPORTE, BENOÎT
95 Semic 198
92 Semic Sticker 235

LAPORTE, ROGER
88/9 Richelieu Riverains
88/9 Richelieu Riverains

LAPORTE, YVES
51/2 Lac St-Jean 56

LAPPALAINEN, HARRI
70/1 Kuvajulkaisut 211

LAPPÄNEN,
77-79 Sports. FIN 16-364

LAPPIN, CHRIS
92/3 Greensboro Monarchs 18
92/3 Greensboro Monarchs 18

LAPPIN, MIKE
92/3 Classic 76

LAPPIN, PETER
91/2 O-Pee-Chee 5S
89/0 ProCards IHL 84
90/1 ProCards 109
91/2 ProCards 522
88/9 Salt Lake G'Eagles
88/9 Salt Lake G'Eagles
90/1 Score 403
90/1 Upper Deck 235

LAPRADE, EDGAR
93/4 Action Packed 1
45-64 BeeHive-2 [NYRa.]
43-47 Parade Sportive
51/2 Parkhurst 96
52/3 Parkhurst 100
52 Royal Desserts 3
54/5 Topps 56

LAPRISE, PIERRE-LUC
01/2 Cape Breton Eagles 3
01/2 Cape Breton Eagles 3
02/3 Val d'Or Foreurs
02/3 Val d'Or Foreurs

LAPRISE, SÉBASTIEN
00/1 Chicoutimi Saguenéens 7
00/1 Chicoutimi Saguenéens 7
00/1 Chicoutimi Saguenéens 9
00/1 Chicoutimi Saguenéens 9
01/2 Drummondville
01/2 Drummondville
00/1 Halifax Moosehead
00/1 Halifax Moosehead

LARAQUE, GEORGES
01/2 BAP Update ✂ TC16, ✂ TC24, ✂ TC29
95/6 Classic 28
97/8 EDMO
97/8 EDMO
99/0 Millenium 100, ✍ Aut. 100
99/0 NHL Power Play
02/3 O-Pee-Chee 200
99/0 Pacific 158
00/1 Pacific 168
01/2 Pacific 159, 411
02/3 Pacific 144
02/3 Signature ✂ FS11, ✂ TQ17
02/3 Topps 200
00/1 To. Heritage 161
02/3 To. Limited 200
02/3 T. Total 337
00/1 Upper Deck 301
02/3 Upper Deck 317, -NC6
99/0 UD G. Reserve 341
00/1 UD Vintage 148
02/3 UD Vintage 103, 272
01/2 Victory 144

LARAQUE, JULES-EDY
00/1 Halifax Moosehead
00/1 Halifax Moosehead
99/0 Halifax Mooseheads
99/0 Halifax Mooseheads

LARCHE, ROGER
92/3 Greensboro Monarchs 10
92/3 Greensboro Monarchs 10
93/4 Roanoke Express
93/4 Roanoke Express
90/1 7th..Sketch LHJMQ 15
91/2 7th...Sketch LHJMQ 293
91 7th..Sketch Mem.Cup 67

LARIN, DANIEL
96/7 DEL 242
92/3 Oklahoma City Blazers
92/3 Oklahoma City Blazers
98/9 Oklahoma City Blazers
98/9 Oklahoma City Blazers

LARIONOV, IGOR
98/9 Aurora 64
98/9 Be A Player 199, ✍ Aut. 199
99/0 BAP Mem. 138
00/1 BAP Mem. 328, 490
90/1 Bowman 63
91/2 Bowman 326
92/3 Bowman 350
93/4 Donruss 305
94/5 Donruss 106
96/7 Donruss 167
96/7 Do. Canadian 117
97/8 Do. Elite 50
97/8 Do. Priority 90
96/7 Fl. Picks 110
93/4 Fleer Ultra 415
94/5 Fleer Ultra 197
95/6 Fleer Ultra 234
95 Globe 239
95/6 Hoyle / West. 3-Diamond
91 Ivan Fiodorov 7
89/0 Kraft 41
90/1 Kraft 25
93/4 Leaf 391
94/5 Leaf 311
95/6 Leaf 318
96/7 Leaf 104
94/5 L. Limited 47
96/7 L. Preferred 75
97/8 Limited 178
96/7 Maggers 61
00/1 Mir Fetisov 37
90/1 OPC/Topps 359
91/2 O-Pee-Chee 480
92/3 O-Pee-Chee 159
97/8 Omega 82
98/9 Omega 82
99/0 Omega 82
98/9 Pacific 198
99/0 Pacific 142
00/1 Pacific 152
01/2 Pacific 144
02/3 Pacific 130
02/3 Pacific Complete 339
97/8 Pacific CC 49
98/9 Pa. Paramount 77
99/0 Pa. Paramount 82
90/1 Panini Sticker 294, 336
90/1 Panini/VAN 11
91/2 Panini Sticker 42
92/3 Panini Sticker 32
94/5 Panini Sticker 217
96/7 Panini Sticker 188
97/8 Panini Sticker 152
98/9 Panini Sticker 131
99/0 Panini Sticker 230
00/1 Panini Sticker 155
95 Panini Worlds 283
91/2 Parkhurst 406
93/4 Parkhurst 185
94/5 Parkhurst V88
95/6 Parkhurst 184, 336
00/1 Parkhurst P-204
01/2 Parkhurst 150
02/3 Parkhurst 196
02/3 Parkhurst Retro 121
94/5 Parkie SE164
91/2 Pinnacle 293
93/4 Pinnacle 367
94/5 Pinnacle 74
95/6 Pinnacle 81
96/7 Pinnacle 74
97/8 Pinnacle 129
97/8 Pi. Inside 146
95/6 Pi. Summit 76
96/7 Pi. Summit 40
96/7 Pi. Zenith 96
95/6 Playoff 85
96/7 Playoff 346
94/5 POG 216
95/6 POG 222
93/4 Power Play 436
94/5 Premier 170
90/1 Pro Set 297
91/2 Pro Set 246
91/2 Pro Set Platinum 126
91/2 Red Ace
92/3 SANJ / Pacific Bell
93/4 SANJ / Pacific Bell
90/1 Score 123
91/2 Score 168
91/2 Score CAN 168
92/3 Score 58
92/3 Score SS 13
93/4 Score 535
93/4 Score DD8
94/5 Score 61
95/6 Score 254
96/7 Score 178
97/8 Score Detr. 5
94/5 Select 40
96/7 Select CE 62
94 Semic 156
89 Semic Sticker 90
91 Semic Sticker 217
00/1 Signature 146, ✍ Aut. 212
01/2 Signature 183, ✍ Aut. 183, ✂ IB9
02/3 Signature 169, ✍ 169
83/4 Soviet Stars
87/8 Soviet Stars
89/0 Soviet Stars
97/8 SP Authentic 54
99/0 SPx 59
00/1 SPx 137
00/1 Stadium 226
00/1 Topps 512
00/1 Topps 257
95/6 To. Finest 57
91/2 To. Stadium 150
92/3 To. Stadium 299
02/3 T. Total 278
91/2 Tri Globe From... 1-2
98/9 UD Choice 71, RW8
02/3 Ultimate Mem. ✂ GD, ✂ SCDE, ✂ SCDGJ, ✂ SCDN
90/1 Upper Deck 128, 342
91/2 Upper Deck 298
91/2 Upper Deck E18
94/5 Upper Deck 65, 85
95/6 Upper Deck 213, 349
96/7 Upper Deck 51
98/9 Upper Deck 261
99/0 Upper Deck 52
00/1 Upper Deck 302
01/2 Upper Deck 291
02/3 Upper Deck 65
95/6 UD BAP 206, ✍ S206
95/6 UD CC 239
96/7 UD CC 83
98/9 UD G. Reserve 261
99/0 UD G. Reserve 52
97/8 UD Ice L6B
99/0 UD MVP 74, ✍ PS
00/1 UD Vintage 153
89/0 VANC / Mohawk
89/0 VANC / Mohawk
89/0 VANC / Mohawk
90/1 VANC / Mohawk
90/1 VANC / Mohawk
91/2 VANC
91/2 VANC
91/2 VANC / Photo
91/2 VANC / Photo
91/2 VANC / PotM
91/2 VANC / PotM
99/0 Victory 102

LARIVÉE, CHRISTIAN
00/1 Chicoutimi Saguenéens 11
00/1 Chicoutimi Saguenéens 11

LARIVÉE, FRANCIS
95/6 Bowman P22
99/0 Greensboro Generals
99/0 Greensboro Generals
97/8 St. John's Maple Leafs
97/8 St. John's Maple Leafs

LARIVÉE, PAUL
51/2 Laval Dairy 79
52/3 St. Lawrence 33

LARIVIÈRE, CHRISTIAN
93/4 Fredericton Canadiens
93/4 Fredericton Canadiens
92 7th...Sketch Awards 28
90/1 7th..Sketch LHJMQ 221

LARIVIÈRE, GARRY
78/9 Dernière Heure
81/2 EDMO / Red Rooster
81/2 EDMO / West Mall
82/3 EDMO / Red Rooster
88/9 EDMO / Action 84
79/0 O-Pee-Chee 291
81/2 O-Pee-Chee 116
82/3 O-Pee-Chee 116
77/8 OPC WHA 26
80/1 Pepsi Bottle Cap
75/6 Phoenix Roadrunners
75/6 Phoenix Roadrunners
76/7 Phoenix Roadrunners
76/7 Phoenix Roadrunners
82/3 Post [Edmo.]
80/1 QUÉB

LARIVIÈRE, JACQUES
99/0 Rimouski Océanic 17
99/0 Rimouski Océanic 17
00/1 St. John's Maple Leafs
00/1 St. John's Maple Leafs
01/2 St. John's Maple Leafs
01/2 St. John's Maple Leafs

LARIVIÈRE, JEAN-PAUL
80/1 Québec Remparts
80/1 Québec Remparts

LARKIN, BRIAN
86/7 Saskatoon Blades
86/7 Saskatoon Blades

LARKIN, BRYAN
84/5 Saskatoon Blades
84/5 Saskatoon Blades

LARKIN, HUEY
80/1 Soo Greyhounds
80/1 Soo Greyhounds
81/2 Soo Greyhounds
81/2 Soo Greyhounds
82/3 Soo Greyhounds
82/3 Soo Greyhounds

LARKIN, JIM
93/4 Birmingham Bulls
93/4 Birmingham Bulls
94/5 Birmingham Bulls
94/5 Birmingham Bulls

LARKIN, MIKE
96/7 Hampton Roads
96/7 Hampton Roads
97/8 Hampton Roads
97/8 Hampton Roads

LARKIN, WAYNE
60/1 Cleveland Barons

LARMER, JEFF
93/4 Milwaukee Admirals
93/4 Milwaukee Admirals
83/4 NJER
85/6 Nova Scotia Oilers
85/6 Nova Scotia Oilers
83/4 O-Pee-Chee 230
84/5 O-Pee-Chee 36
83/4 OPC/Topps Sticker 186
91/2 ProCards 613
83/4 Souhaits Keychain [Devils]

LARMER, STEVE
90/1 Bowman 5
91/2 Bowman 395
92/3 Bowman 61
91 Canada Cup
82/3 CHIC
83/4 CHIC
86/7 CHIC / Coke
87/8 CHIC / Coke
88/9 CHIC / Coke
89/0 CHIC / Coke
90/1 CHIC / Coke
90/1 CHIC / Coke
91/2 CHIC / Coke
91/2 CHIC / Coke
98/9 CHIC / Pizza Hut
98/9 CHIC / Pizza Hut
93/4 Donruss 461
94/5 Donruss 231
95/6 Donruss 2
93/4 EA Sports 29
94/5 Flair 113
94/5 Fleer 134
01/2 Fleer Greats 24, ✍ Aut.
92/3 Fleer Ultra 39
93/4 Fleer Ultra 129
93/4 Fleer Ultra 373
94/5 Fleer Ultra 138
95/6 Fleer Ultra 103
83/4 Funmate Puffy 17 [w/]
93/4 Hockey Wit 43
90/1 Kraft 26
91/2 Kraft 69
94/5 Leaf 270
95/6 Leaf 178
91/2 McDonald's Mc-15
83/4 O-Pee-Chee 105
83/4 O-Pee-Chee 105
84/5 O-Pee-Chee 206
84/5 O-Pee-Chee 37
85/6 OPC/Topps 132
86/7 OPC/Topps 139
87/8 OPC/Topps 59
88/9 OPC/Topps 154
90/1 OPC/Topps 56
90/1 Topps-TL 1
91/2 O-Pee-Chee 75
91/2 Topps - Team Leader 21
92/3 O-Pee-Chee 32
89/0 OPC/Topps 179, / Box J
90/1 OPC Premier 58
91/2 OPC Premier 135
91/2 OPC Premier 60
88/9 OPC Stars 17
83/4 OPC/Topps Sticker 108
83/4 OPC/Topps Sticker 312
84/5 OPC Sticker 29
85/6 OPC Sticker 28-128
86/7 OPC Sticker 157-15
87/8 OPC Sticker 81
88/9 OPC Sticker 12
89/0 opcSticker 17
87/8 Panini Sticker 226
88/9 Panini Sticker 26
89/0 Panini Sticker 43
90/1 Panini Sticker 194
91/2 Panini Sticker 8
92/3 Panini Sticker 5
93/4 Panini Sticker 146
94/5 Panini Sticker 86
95/6 Panini Sticker 107
91/2 Parkhurst 34
92/3 Parkhurst 30
93/4 Parkhurst 404
94/5 Parkhurst 146
91/2 Pinnacle 29
91/2 Pinnacle 357
92/3 Pinnacle 74
93/4 Pinnacle 356
94/5 Pinnacle 88
94/5 POG 164
93/4 Power Play 392
93/4 Power Play 52
93/4 Premier 240
94/5 Premier 418, 532
90/1 Pro Set 53, 345
91/2 Pro Set 279
91/2 Pro Set 49
92/3 Pro Set 31
91 Pro Set Awards AC13
91/2 Pro Set Platinum 28
91/2 Pro Set Platinum 287
90/1 Score 135
90/1 Sco. Hot Cards 61
91/2 Score 140
91/2 Score CAN 140
92/3 Score 266
93/4 Score 3
93/4 Score 525
93/4 Score DT 22
93/4 Score / Promo 3
94/5 Score 400
95/6 Score 211
92/3 Seasons 2
94/5 Select 112
94 Semic 90
95 Semic 100
91 Semic Sticker 73
92 Semic Sticker 91
95/6 SBx Emotion 114
83/4 Souhaits Keychain [Chic]
84/5 Topps 30
92/3 Topps 497
95/6 Topps 7HG
94/5 Topps Finest 63
91/2 To. Stadium 270
92/3 To. Stadium 54
93/4 To. Stadium 236
93/4 To. Stadium 398
94/5 To. Stadium 242
90/1 Upper Deck 242, 499
91/2 Upper Deck 15
91/2 Upper Deck 257
92/3 Upper Deck 135
92/3 Upper Deck 4
92/3 Upper Deck G6
93/4 Upper Deck 172, 471, HT14
94/5 Upper Deck 40
94/5 UD BAP R169, G12, ✍ 146
93/4 UD BAP Roots 22
95/6 UD CC 154
02/3 UD Foundations 16, 69, ✍ SG

LARNER, DON
96/7 Las Vegas Thunder
96/7 Las Vegas Thunder
96/7 Toledo Storm
96/7 Toledo Storm

LAROCHE, GILLES
51/2 Bas du Fleuve 8

LAROCHE, JEAN-FRANÇOIS
91/2 7th...Sketch LHJMQ 62

LAROCHELLE, CLAUDE
78/9 Saginaw Gears
78/9 Saginaw Gears

LAROCHELLE, DANY
91/2 7th...Sketch LHJMQ 81

LAROCHELLE, ERIC
01/2 Guelph Storm M-Cup
01/2 Guelph Storm M-Cup

LAROCHELLE, MARTIN
91/2 7th...Sketch LHJMQ 137

LAROCHELLE, WILDOR
25-27 Anonymous 7 [Error: Victor]
25-27 Anonymous 7 [No Border]
33-35 Diamond Match Silv.
36-39 Diamond Match TT1
36-39 Diamond Match TT2
36-39 Diamond Match TT3
36-39 Diamond Match Chic.
33/4 Hamilton Gum 14
27/8 La Patrie
27/8 La Presse
33/4 O-Pee-Chee 21
34/5 Sweet Caporal
33/4 WWGum 28
37/8 World Wide Gum 34

LAROCQUE, ANDRÉ
80/1 Québec Remparts
80/1 Québec Remparts

LAROCQUE, DENIS
92/3 Dayton Bombers
92/3 Dayton Bombers
89/0 Moncton Hawks
89/0 Moncton Hawks
90/1 Moncton Hawks
90/1 Moncton Hawks
88/9 ProCards / New Haven
89/0 ProCards IHL 33
90/1 ProCards 257

LAROCQUE, MARIO
95/6 Bowman P23
98/9 Cleveland Lumberjacks
98/9 Cleveland Lumberjacks
99/0 Detroit Vipers
99/0 Detroit Vipers
99/0 Pacific 400
92 Québec Pee Wee 571

LAROCQUE, MICHEL
80/1 Dernière Heure

LAROCQUE, MICHEL (BUNNY)
73/4 Dernière Heure
74/5 Loblaws
73/4 MONT / Pro Star
74/5 MONT
75/6 MONT
76/7 MONT
77/8 MONT
78/9 MONT
79/0 MONT
80/1 MONT
74/5 O-Pee-Chee 297
75/6 O-Pee-Chee 362
76/7 O-Pee-Chee 6
76/7 O-Pee-Chee 79
77/8 O-Pee-Chee 177
77/8 O-Pee-Chee 6
78/9 O-Pee-Chee 158
79/0 O-Pee-Chee 296
80/1 O-Pee-Chee 319
81/2 O-Pee-Chee 324
82/3 O-Pee-Chee 326
81/2 OPC Sticker 105
81/2 OPC Sticker 259
82/3 OPC/Topps Sticker 77
82/3 Post [Toro.]
76/7 Topps 6
76/7 Topps 79
77/8 Topps 177
77/8 Topps 6
78/9 Topps 158
81/2 TORO
01/2 UD Vintage ✂ SH

LAROCQUE, MICHEL2
01/2 Pacific 87
01/2 SPx 125
01/2 Upper Deck 183
01/2 UD MVP 193
01/2 UD Top Shelf 49
01/2 Victory 366

LAROCQUE, STÉPHANE
97/8 Fort Worth Brahmas
97/8 Fort Worth Brahmas
98/9 Fort Worth Brahmas
98/9 Fort Worth Brahmas
99/0 Fort Worth Brahmas
99/0 Fort Worth Brahmas
91/2 7th...Sketch LHJMQ 259

LARORUK, CAM
84/5 Kelowna Wings &...

LAROSE, BENOÎT
92 7th...Sketch Awards 23
90/1 7th..Sketch LHJMQ 59
91/2 7th...Sketch LHJMQ 247

LAROSE, CHAD
02/3 Plymouth Whalers
02/3 Plymouth Whalers
02/3 Plymouth Whalers
02/3 Plymouth Whalers

LAROSE, CLAUDE
72/3 Dernière Heure
73/4 Dernière Heure

LAROSE, CLAUDE*
64-67 BeeHive-3 [Mont.]
64-67 BeeHive-3 [Mont.]
64/5 Coke/Sprite [Mont.]
65/6 Coca-Cola
70/1 Eddie Sargent 101
71/2 Eddie Sargent 106
72/3 Eddie Sargent 122
70/1 Esso Power Player
74/5 Loblaws
74/5 Loblaws Update
68/9 O-Pee-Chee 51
69/0 O-Pee-Chee 194
69/0 O-Pee-Chee 4in1
70/1 O-Pee-Chee 56
71/2 O-Pee-Chee 146
72/3 O-Pee-Chee 231
74/5 O-Pee-Chee 124
75/6 O-Pee-Chee 112
76/7 O-Pee-Chee 310
77/8 O-Pee-Chee 167
94/5 Parkie 66-67 69
94/5 Parkie Tall 71
88/9 ProCards / Binghampton
88/9 ProCards / Sherbrooke
68/9 Shirriff / Minn. 7
65/6 Topps 75
66/7 Topps 10
67/8 Topps 4
68/9 Topps 51
69/0 Topps 126
70/1 Topps 56
74/5 Topps 124
75/6 Topps 112
77/8 Topps 167
71/2 Toronto Sun Photo

LAROSE, CLAUDE**
77/8 OPC WHA 43

LAROSE, CLAUDE1
66/7 MONT / IGA Stamp
67/8 MONT
67/8 MONT / IGA Card
69/0 MONT / Pro Star
70/1 MONT
71/2 MONT / Pro Star
72/3 MONT / Pro Star

LAROSE, CLAUDE2
75/6 Cincinnati Stingers
75/6 Cincinnati Stingers

LAROSE, GUY
92/3 Bowman 281
98/9 Chicago Wolves
98/9 Chicago Wolves
99/0 Chicago Wolves
99/0 Chicago Wolves
00/1 Chicago Wolves
00/1 Chicago Wolves
87/8 Moncton Hawks
87/8 Moncton Hawks
90/1 Moncton Hawks
90/1 Moncton Hawks
92/3 O-Pee-Chee 269
92/3 OPC Premier 128
91/2 Parkhurst 399
94/5 Parkhurst 37
88/9 ProCards / Moncton
89/0 ProCards AHL 29
90/1 ProCards 259
91/2 ProCards 195
92/3 Topps 47
92/3 To. Stadium 237
92/3 Upper Deck 527
90/1 WINN / IGA
90/1 WINN / IGA

LAROSE, PAUL
72/3 Québec Nordiques
72/3 Québec Nordiques

LAROUCHE, MIKE
83/4 North Bay Centennials
83/4 North Bay Centennials
84/5 Ottawa 67's
84/5 Ottawa 67's

LAROUCHE, PIERRE
80/1 Dernière Heure
82/3 Dernière Heure
70s Dernière Heure
83/4 Funmate Puffy 13 [w/]
82/3 HART / Jr. Whalers
77/8 MONT
78/9 MONT
79/0 MONT
80/1 MONT
75/6 O-Pee-Chee 305
76/7 O-Pee-Chee 1
76/7 O-Pee-Chee 199
76/7 O-Pee-Chee 392
76/7 O-Pee-Chee 5
77/8 O-Pee-Chee 102
78/9 O-Pee-Chee 35
79/0 O-Pee-Chee 233
80/1 O-Pee-Chee 151
80/1 O-Pee-Chee 216
81/2 O-Pee-Chee 187
82/3 O-Pee-Chee 125
84/5 O-Pee-Chee 145
84/5 O-Pee-Chee 363
85/6 OPC/Topps 54
81/2 OPC Sticker 38
82/3 OPC/Topps Sticker 127
84/5 OPC Sticker 103
85/6 OPC Sticker 85-218
87/8 Panini Sticker 116
80/1 Pepsi Bottle Cap
74/5 PITT
77/8 PITT / McDonald's
82/3 Post [Hart.]
83/4 Souhaits Keychain [Whalers]
75/6 Topps 305
76/7 Topps 1
76/7 Topps 199
76/7 Topps 5
77/8 Topps 102
78/9 Topps 35
79/0 Topps 233
80/1 Topps 151
80/1 Topps 216
84/5 Topps 108
01/2 T/O Archives 40, -Seat

LAROUCHE, STEVE
93/4 Atlanta Knights
93/4 Atlanta Knights
95/6 Binghampton Rangers
95/6 Binghampton Rangers
98/9 Chicago Wolves
98/9 Chicago Wolves
98/9 Chicago Wolves Champs
98/9 Chicago Wolves Champs
99/0 Chicago Wolves
99/0 Chicago Wolves
00/1 Chicago Wolves
00/1 Chicago Wolves
94/5 Cla. Images 31
92/3 Classic Prospects 78
93/4 Cla. Prospects 160
95/6 Donruss 39
95/6 Fleer Ultra 112
92/3 Fredericton Canadiens
92/3 Fredericton Canadiens
95/6 Leaf 94
95/6 Panini Sticker 55
95/6 Pinnacle 209
95/6 Playoff 179
95/6 Pro Magnet 113
91/2 ProCards 83
95/6 Score 302
90/1 7th..Sketch LHJMQ 30
91 7th..Sketch Mem.Cup 29
95/6 SBx Emotion 125
95/6 Topps 38
95/6 Upper Deck 89
01/2 UD DEL 36

LAROUCHELLE, ALLAN
83/4 Saskatoon Blades
83/4 Saskatoon Blades

LARRANAGA, FELIPE
99/0 Des Moines Buc's
99/0 Des Moines Buc's

LARSEN, BRAD
97 Bowman 116
95/6 Classic 45
95/6 Do. Elite WJ 17
98/9 Hershey Bears
98/9 Hershey Bears
00/1 Hershey Bears
00/1 Hershey Bears
94/5 Parkie SE269
94/5 Select 164
94/5 SR Auto-Phonex 25, ✍ 25
01/2 Signature 210, ✍ Aut. 210
94/5 SP 187
95/6 Swift Current Broncos
95/6 Swift Current Broncos
95/6 Upper Deck 534
97/8 UD Coll. Choice 308
96/7 UD Ice 134
01/2 UD MVP 199

LARSEN, GREG
83/4 North Bay Centennials
83/4 North Bay Centennials

LARSEN, JONAS
92/3 Semic Nordisk 229

LARSEN, ROAR
92/3 Semic Nordisk 66

LARSEN, SJUR RAKSTAD
92/3 Semic Nordisk 221

LARSEN, TOMMY
92/3 Semic Nordisk 28

LARSON, BRETT
93/4 Minnesota-Duluth
93/4 Minnesota-Duluth

LARSON, DAVE
92/3 Minnesota G'Gophers
92/3 Minnesota G'Gophers
93/4 Minnesota G'Gophers
93/4 Minnesota G'Gophers
94/5 Minnesota G'Gophers
94/5 Minnesota G'Gophers

LARSON, DEAN
98/9 Anchorage Aces
98/9 Anchorage Aces
99/0 Anchorage Aces
99/0 Anchorage Aces

LARSON, JON
93/4 Knoxville Cherokees
93/4 Knoxville Cherokees
94/5 Roanoke Express
94/5 Roanoke Express
95/6 Roanoke Express
95/6 Roanoke Express

LARSON, NORM
34-43 BeeHive-1 [NYAm.]
34-43 BeeHive-1 [xR.Wycherly's card]
40/1 O-Pee-Chee 127

LARSON, REED
88/9 BOST / Sports Action
79/0 DETR
80/1 DETR
84/5 DETR / Little Caesars
84/5 DETR / Little Caesars
88/9 EDMO / Action 56
83/4 Funmate Puffy 18 [w/]
84/5 Kellogg's 24
78/9 O-Pee-Chee 226
79/0 O-Pee-Chee 213
80/1 O-Pee-Chee 43
81/2 O-Pee-Chee 92
82/3 O-Pee-Chee 88
82/3 O-Pee-Chee 89
83/4 O-Pee-Chee 125
84/5 O-Pee-Chee 58
85/6 OPC/Topps 55
86/7 OPC/Topps 110
87/8 OPC/Topps 131
88/9 OPC/Topps 145
81/2 OPC Sticker 124
82/3 OPC/Topps Sticker 180
83/4 OPC/Topps Sticker 134
84/5 OPC Sticker 36
85/6 OPC Sticker 33-163
86/7 OPC Sticker 39-176
87/8 OPC Sticker 142-251
87/8 Panini Sticker 7
82/3 Post [Detr.]
83/4 Souhaits Keychain [Red Wings]
78/9 Topps 226
79/0 Topps 213
80/1 Topps 43
81/2 Topps 92 [West]
84/5 Topps 44

LARSSON, CARL-ERIK
90/1 Semic Elitserien 143

LARSSON, CURT
74 Semic Sticker 24
73/4 Williams Finnish 30

LARSSON, JAN
95/6 Leaf Elit Set 274, C-8
95 Semic 73
89/0 Semic Elitserien 41
90/1 Semic Elitserien 188
91/2 Semic Elitserien 41
92/3 Semic Elitserien 66
93 Semic Sticker 16
95/6 UD Elitserien 165
97/8 UD Elitserien 32, C19
98/9 UD Elitserien 44
99/0 UD Elitserien 28, H3
00/1 UD Elitserien 43, P2, ✍ Sig.

LARSSON, KJELL
92 Semic Sticker 218

LARSSON, KURT
72 Hellas MM-Jenkki 39

LARSSON, PETER
98/9 Cardset 90
99/0 Cardset 162
02/3 Cardset 56
99/0 Eishockey 159
97/8 Hockey-Box
94/5 Leaf Elit Set 193, P-5
95/6 Leaf Elit Set 23
89/0 Semic Elitserien 235
90/1 Semic Elitserien 189
91/2 Semic Elitserien 43
92/3 Semic Elitserien 72
01/2 UD DEL 179
95/6 UD Elitserien 34

LARSSON, ROBERT
89/0 Semic Elitserien 195

LARSSON, STEFAN
95 Globe 25
94/5 Leaf Elit Set 34
95/6 Leaf Elit Set 139, FTF-4
95 Panini Worlds 142
89/0 Semic Elitserien 273
90/1 Semic Elitserien 34
91/2 Semic Elitserien 282
92/3 Semic Elitserien 308
93 Semic Sticker 7
95/6 UD Elitserien 208
97/8 UD Elitserien 74
98/9 UD Elitserien 72
99/0 UD Elitserien 73

LARSSON, STIG
72 Hellas MM-Jenkki 34
72/3 Williams Finnish 50

LARTAMA, MIKA
93/4 Jyvas Hyva 49
93/4 Sisu 249
95/6 Sisu Limited 85

LARTER, BRAD
01/2 Moncton Wildcats 12
01/2 Moncton Wildcats 12

LARTER, TYLER
89/0 Moncton Hawks
89/0 Moncton Hawks
90/1 Moncton Hawks
90/1 Moncton Hawks
91/2 Moncton Hawks
91/2 Moncton Hawks
88/9 ProCards / Baltimore
89/0 ProCards AHL 94
90/1 ProCards 207
91/2 ProCards 181
84/5 Soo Greyhounds
84/5 Soo Greyhounds
87/8 Soo Greyhounds 4
87/8 Soo Greyhounds 4

LARWAY, DON
75/6 Houston Aeros
75/6 Houston Aeros
77/8 OPC WHA 48

LASAK, JAN
02/3 BAP Mem. 60
02/3 Between the Pipes 92
02/3 Calder 77
99/0 Hampton Roads
99/0 Hampton Roads
00/1 Milwaukee Admirals
00/1 Milwaukee Admirals
01/2 Milwaukee Admirals
01/2 Milwaukee Admirals
02/3 Pacific Complete 530
01/2 Parkhurst 341
02/3 Signature ✂ AR7
02/3 SPx 115
02/3 UD Foundations 135
02/3 UD Mask 48, 49
02/3 UD MVP 208
02/3 UD Piece 138
02/3 UD Vintage 339

LASCALA, FRANK
96/7 DEL 220

LASKO, BOB
90/1 ProCards 542

LASKOSKI, GARY
83/4 O-Pee-Chee 156
83/4 OPC/Topps Sticker 296
83/4 Souhaits Keychain [Kings]

LASSILA, HANNU
82 Semic Sticker 27

LASXKLEWICZ, LESZEK
98/9 DEL 261

LATAL, JAROMIR
94/5 APS 5
95/6 APS 103, 418
96/7 APS 7
96/7 DS Sticker 114
92/3 Semic Nordisk 193 [Ärets Lag]
92/3 Semic Nordisk 6

LATAL, JIRI
95/6 APS 104, 407
96/7 APS 263
91/2 O-Pee-Chee 444
90/1 OPC Premier 59
98/9 OFS 326
90/1 PHIL
90/1 PHIL
91/2 PHIL / J.C. Penney
91/2 PHIL / J.C. Penney
90/1 Pro Set 501
91/2 Pro Set 454
89/0 ProCards AHL 344
91/2 Score CAN 540
90/1 Upper Deck 410
91/2 Upper Deck 404

LATENDRESSE, MIKE
95/6 Birmingham Bulls
95/6 Birmingham Bulls
92/3 Maine Black Bears
92/3 Maine Black Bears
93/4 Maine Black Bears
93/4 Maine Black Bears
94/5 Toledo Storm
94/5 Toledo Storm

LATENDRESSE, OLIVIER
02/3 Val d'Or Foreurs
02/3 Val d'Or Foreurs

LATERREUR, YVAN
91/2 7th...Sketch LHJMQ 261

LATOS, JIM
90/1 Kansas City Blades
90/1 Kansas City Blades
95/6 Louisiana Ice Gators
95/6 Louisiana Ice Gators
95/6 Louisiana Ice Gators-2
95/6 Louisiana Ice Gators-2
96/7 Louisiana Ice Gators
96/7 Louisiana Ice Gators
86/7 Portland Winter Hawks
86/7 Portland Winter Hawks
89/0 ProCards IHL 30
90/1 ProCards 585
84/5 Saskatoon Blades
84/5 Saskatoon Blades

LATOUR, YANNICK
99/0 Quad City Mallards
99/0 Quad City Mallards

LATTA, DAVID
92/3 Cincinnati Cyclones
92/3 Cincinnati Cyclones
90/1 Halifax Citadels
90/1 Halifax Citadels
83/4 Kitchener Rangers
83/4 Kitchener Rangers
84/5 Kitchener Rangers
84/5 Kitchener Rangers
85/6 Kitchener Rangers
85/6 Kitchener Rangers
86/7 Kitchener Rangers
86/7 Kitchener Rangers
90/1 ProCards 461
91/2 ProCards 376
87/8 QUÉB / Gene. Foods
88/9 QUÉB
88/9 QUÉB / Gene. Foods
89/0 QUÉB
89/0 QUÉB / Gene. Foods
89/0 QUÉB / Gene. Foods
89/0 QUÉB / Police
89/0 QUÉB / Police
90/1 QUÉB
90/1 QUÉB

LATTA, KEN
80/1 Soo Greyhounds
80/1 Soo Greyhounds
81/2 Soo Greyhounds
81/2 Soo Greyhounds

LÄTTI, PETRI
99/0 Cardset 89
00/1 Cardset 66
02/3 Cardset 65
97/8 Hockey-Box
93/4 Sisu 204
94/5 Sisu 356
95/6 Sisu 100
96/7 Sisu 14

LATULIPPE, MARTIN
93/4 Slapshot / Drummondville 5

LATVALA, JAN
98/9 Cardset 122
99/0 Cardset 97
00/1 Cardset 195
02/3 Cardset 208
97/8 Hockey-Box
93/4 Sisu 138
94/5 Sisu 29
95/6 Sisu 262
96/7 Sisu 60

LAUER, BRAD
91/2 CHIC / Coke
91/2 CHIC / Coke
95/6 Cleveland Lumberjacks
95/6 Cleveland Lumberjacks
96/7 Cleveland Lumberjacks
96/7 Cleveland Lumberjacks
97/8 Cleveland Lumberjacks
97/8 Cleveland Lumberjacks
92/3 Indianapolis Ice
92/3 Indianapolis Ice
88/9 O-Pee-Chee 226
90/1 OPC/Topps 217
91/2 Pro Set 375
90/1 ProCards 501
91/2 ProCards 490
91/2 To. Stadium 142
99/0 Utah Grizzlies
99/0 Utah Grizzlies
00/1 Utah Grizzlies
00/1 Utah Grizzlies

LAUFMAN, KEN
52/3 St. Lawrence 56

LAUGHLIN, CRAIG
81/2 MONT
83/4 O-Pee-Chee 375
84/5 O-Pee-Chee 203
85/6 O-Pee-Chee 190
86/7 OPC/Topps 35
87/8 OPC/Topps 161
89/0 O-Pee-Chee 275
86/7 OPC Sticker 253-145
89/0 opcSticker 171-31
87/8 Panini Sticker 182
82/3 Post [Mont.]
95/6 Richmond Renegades
95/6 Richmond Renegades
88/9 TORO / P.L.A.Y. 18
82/3 WASH
84/5 WASH / Pizza Hut
85/6 WASH / Pizza Hut
86/7 WASH / Kodak
86/7 WASH / Police
87/8 WASH
87/8 WASH / Kodak

LAUGHLIN, PATRICK
94/5 Erie Panthers
94/5 Erie Panthers

LAUGHTON, MIKE
70/1 Eddie Sargent 136
69/0 O-Pee-Chee 148
70/1 O-Pee-Chee 74
70/1 Topps 74

LAUKKANEN, JANNE
00/1 BAP Mem. 141
98/9 Cardset 3, Top 3, Leij. 9
99/0 Cardset AH 4-risti
00/1 Cardset 354
02/3 Cardset 209
93/4 Classic 43
94/5 Classic 102
93/4 Cla. 4 Sport 259
94/5 Cla. Images 63
95/6 Edge Ice 28
94/5 Flair 148
94/5 Fleer Ultra 359
95 Globe 134
92/3 Jyvas Hyva 21
93/4 Jyvas Hyva 46
94/5 Leaf 447
95/6 Leaf 46
98/9 OPC Chrome 153
96/7 OTTA
96/7 OTTA
97/8 OTTA
97/8 OTTA
98/9 OTTA
98/9 OTTA
99/0 OTTA
99/0 OTTA
98/9 Pacific 312
00/1 Pacific 332
97/8 Pa. Invincible R-135
97/8 Panini Sticker 40
98/9 Panini Sticker 45
99/0 Panini Sticker 109
95/6 Parkhurst 52
01/2 Parkhurst 163
94/5 Parkie SE142
94/5 Pinnacle 485, RTP3
97/8 Pi. Be A Player 90, ✍ Aut. 90
94/5 Premier 411
94/5 QUÉB / Burger King
94/5 QUÉB / Burger King
94/5 Select 181, YE-3
94 Semic 17
95 Semic 12

92 Semic Sticker 7
93 Semic Sticker 54
01/2 Signature 48, ✍ Aut. 48
93/4 Sisu 239
93/4 Sisu 367
95/6 Sisu Limited 83, LG-2
98/9 Topps 153
00/1 Topps 267
94/5 Topps Finest 8
02/3 T. Total 165
91/2 Upper Deck 22
94/5 Upper Deck 251, 565, SP-157
95/6 Upper Deck 123
96/7 Upper Deck 116
98/9 Upper Deck 141
96/7 UD CC 187
98/9 UD G. Reserve 141
00/1 UD Vintage 293
01/2 Victory 285
96 Wien 29

LAUKKANEN, JARI
00/1 Cardset 59
02/3 Cardset 210
92/3 Jyvas Hyva 97
93/4 Jyvas Hyva 17
93/4 Sisu 100
94/5 Sisu 84
95/6 Sisu 9
96/7 Sisu 10

LAUKKANEN, JARMO
70/1 Kuvajulkaisut 281

LAUKKANEN, PEKKA
70/1 Kuvajulkaisut 350

LAUKKANEN, TUOMO
80/1 Mallasjuoma 149

LAURENCE, DON (RED)
78/9 ATLF / Colour
81/2 Indianapolis Checkers
81/2 Indianapolis Checkers
82/3 Indianapolis Checkers
82/3 Indianapolis Checkers
79/0 O-Pee-Chee 369

LAURIE, ROB
98/9 Flint Generals
98/9 Flint Generals
97/8 Fort Worth Brahmas
97/8 Fort Worth Brahmas
93/4 Johnstown Chiefs 16
93/4 Johnstown Chiefs 16
94/5 Johnstown Chiefs 13
94/5 Johnstown Chiefs 13
95/6 Toledo Storm
95/6 Toledo Storm

LAURILA, HARRI
99/0 Cardset 237
91/2 Jyvas Hyva 29
92/3 Jyvas Hyva 72
93/4 Jyvas Hyva 135
94 Semic 13
95 Semic 36
93 Semic Sticker 55
93/4 Sisu 146
93/4 Sisu 351
94/5 Sisu 170, 326
95/6 Sisu 151, 184
96/7 Sisu 125
95/6 Sisu Limited 47

LAURILA, HENRI
00/1 Cardset 310

LAURIN, DON
88/9 Brandon Wheat Kings
88/9 Brandon Wheat Kings

LAURIN, STEVE
90/1 ProCards 555

LAURSEN, GORM
92/3 Semic Nordisk 164

LAUS, PAUL
98/9 Aurora 82
00/1 BAP Mem. 55, ✄ TM-8, ✄ T-5
01/2 BAP Update ✄ TC7, ✄ TC26, ✄ TC29
92/3 Cleveland Lumberjacks
92/3 Cleveland Lumberjacks
94/5 Donruss 201
98/9 Dynagon Ice 84
93/4 FLOR
93/4 FLOR
96/7 FLOR / Winn-Dixie
96/7 FLOR / Winn-Dixie
97/8 FLOR / Winn-Dixie
97/8 FLOR / Winn-Dixie
99/0 Millenium 117, ✍ Aut. 117
88/9 Niagara Falls Thunder
88/9 Niagara Falls Thunder
89/0 Niagara Falls Thunder
89/0 Niagara Falls Thunder
98/9 Omega 104
98/9 Pacific 224
99/0 Pacific 175
00/1 Pacific 181
97/8 Pa. Dynagon BKS-42
98/9 Pa. Paramount 98
97/8 Pa. Revolution 61
96/7 Panini Sticker 77
96/7 Pi. Be A Player 192, ✍ Aut. 192
95/6 Playoff 41
95/6 POG 121
93/4 Premier 402
90/1 ProCards 534
91/2 ProCards 293
89/0 7th..Sketch OHL 142
93/4 To. Stadium 292
02/3 T. Total 352
00/1 Ultimate Mem. ✄ TM-19
97/8 Upper Deck 75

LAUWERS, GUY
79 Panini Sticker 339

LAUZE, PHILIPPE
00/1 Rimouski Océanic 1
00/1 Rimouski Océanic 1
01/2 Rimouski Océanic 2
01/2 Rimouski Océanic 2

LAUZON, RYAN
99/0 Hull Olympiques BN
99/0 Hull Olympiques BN
99/0 Hull Olympiques 18
99/0 Hull Olympiques 18

LAUZON, SERGE
84/5 Chicoutimi Saguenéens
84/5 Chicoutimi Saguenéens

LAVALLÉE, GUILLAUME
01/2 Shawinigan 16
01/2 Shawinigan 16

LAVALLÉE, JORDAN
02/3 Québec Remparts
02/3 Québec Remparts

LAVALLÉE, KEVIN
80/1 CALG
81/2 CALG
82/3 CALG
94/5 DEL 100
95/6 DEL 142
81/2 O-Pee-Chee 43
82/3 O-Pee-Chee 49
83/4 O-Pee-Chee 157
84/5 O-Pee-Chee 183
82/3 OPC/Topps Sticker 220
80/1 Pepsi Bottle Cap
86/7 PITT / Kodak
82/3 Post [Calg.]

LAVALLÉE, MARTIN
90/1 7th..Sketch LHJMQ 24, 184
91/2 7th...Sketch LHJMQ 168
91 7th..Sketch Mem.Cup 27

LAVALLÉE, RICHARD
79/0 Montréal Juniors B&W
79/0 Montréal Juniors B&W
79/0 Montréal Jrs. Colour
79/0 Montréal Jrs. Colour

LAVALLIERE, SÉBASTIEN
90/1 7th..Sketch LHJMQ 185

LAVARRE, MARK
87/8 CHIC / Coke
83/4 North Bay Centennials
83/4 North Bay Centennials
85/6 Nova Scotia Oilers
85/6 Nova Scotia Oilers
88/9 ProCards / Binghampton

LAVE, ROB
93/4 Slapshot / North Bay 3

LAVELL, MIKE
95/6 Slapshot 274

LAVENDER, BRIAN
72/3 O-Pee-Chee 270
71/2 SLOU

LAVERGNE, DAN
98/9 Odessa Jackalopes
98/9 Odessa Jackalopes

LAVIGNE, ERIC
91/2 Arena 19
91/2 Classic 22
91/2 Classic Four Sport 22
93/4 Cla. Prospects 191
98/9 Cleveland Lumberjacks
98/9 Cleveland Lumberjacks
99/0 Cleveland Lumberjacks
99/0 Cleveland Lumberjacks
00/1 Kudos 129
00/1 Nottingham Panthers
00/1 Nottingham Panthers
93/4 Phoenix Roadrunners
93/4 Phoenix Roadrunners
94/5 Phoenix Roadrunners
94/5 Phoenix Roadrunners
96/7 Rochester Americans
96/7 Rochester Americans
97/8 Rochester Americans
97/8 Rochester Americans
90/1 7th..Sketch LHJMQ 150
91/2 7th...Sketch LHJMQ 214
00/1 Sherbrooke Castors 4
00/1 Sherbrooke Castors 4
91/2 Star Pics 42
91/2 Ultimate Draft Pick 21, ✍ Aut.

LAVIKAINEN, PEKKA
71/2 Williams Finnish 263

LAVIKAINEN, PENTTI
71/2 Williams Finnish 264

LAVINSH, RODRIGO
99/0 Cardset 251
94/5 Raleigh Icecaps
94/5 Raleigh Icecaps
95/6 Tallahasee Tiger Sharks
95/6 Tallahasee Tiger Sharks

LAVIOLETTE, JACK
91 C55 Reprint 45
83 HHOF Postcard L9
83&87 HHOF 159
10/1 Imperial
10/1 Imperial 21
11/2 Imperial 45
12/3 Imperial 46
27/8 La Patrie

LAVIOLETTE, KERRY
83/4 Saskatoon Blades
83/4 Saskatoon Blades

LAVIOLETTE, PETER
93/4 Fleer Ultra 488
93/4 Power Play 508
93/4 Premier - USA Hockey 2
89/0 ProCards IHL 43
90/1 ProCards 16
91/2 ProCards 197
96/7 Providence Bruins
98/9 Providence Bruins
93/4 To. Stadium - Team U.S.A. 12

LAVOIE, DANNY
99 Bowman 63

LAVOIE, DARYL
00/1 Kudos 130
00/1 Nottingham Panthers
00/1 Nottingham Panthers
93/4 Slapshot / Windsor 5
92/3 Windsor Spitfires
92/3 Windsor Spitfires

LAVOIE, DOMINIC
90/1 Bowman 26
99/0 Eishockey 228
92/3 Fleer Ultra 145
93/4 Leaf 415
93/4 Parkhurst 366
93/4 Phoenix Roadrunners
93/4 Phoenix Roadrunners
88/9 ProCards / Peoria
89/0 ProCards IHL 20
90/1 ProCards 95
90/1 Score 416
89/0 SLOU / Kodak
89/0 SLOU / Kodak
93/4 Upper Deck 444
00/1 UD DEL 94
01/2 UD DEL 97

LAVOIE, ÉTIENNE
90/1 7th..Sketch LHJMQ 230
91/2 7th...Sketch LHJMQ 127

LAVOIE, JULIEN
01/2 Moncton Wildcats 22
01/2 Moncton Wildcats 22

LAVOIE, PAUL
52/3 Bas du Fleuve 43

LAVOIE, ROBERTO
80/1 Québec Remparts
80/1 Québec Remparts

LAW, BRIAN
91/2 Avant Garde BCJHL 151

LAW, KIRBY
01/2 BAP Mem. 433
95/6 Lethbridge Hurricanes
95/6 Lethbridge Hurricanes
99/0 Louisville Panthers
99/0 Louisville Panthers
98/9 Orlando Solar Bears Geico
98/9 Orlando Solar Bears Geico
02/3 Philadelphia Phantoms
02/3 Philadelphia Phantoms
93/4 Saskatoon Blades
93/4 Saskatoon Blades
01/2 SPx 146, -RT
01/2 Upper Deck 202
01/2 UD MVP 210
01/2 UD Top Shelf 61

LAWLESS, PAUL
93/4 Cincinnati Cyclones
93/4 Cincinnati Cyclones
94/5 Cincinnati Cyclones
94/5 Cincinnati Cyclones
95/6 Cincinnati Cyclones
95/6 Cincinnati Cyclones
96/7 Cincinnati Cyclones
96/7 Cincinnati Cyclones
95/6 Edge Ice 112
85/6 HART / Jr. Whalers
86/7 HART / Jr. Whalers
87/8 HART / Jr. Whalers
83/4 O-Pee-Chee 141
87/8 Panini Sticker 48

LAWLEY, SHARON
95/6 Sheffield Steelers
95/6 Sheffield Steelers

LAWMASTER, JASON
99/0 Peoria Rivermen
99/0 Peoria Rivermen
00/1 Peoria Rivermen
00/1 Peoria Rivermen
01/2 Peoria Rivermen
01/2 Peoria Rivermen
02/3 Peoria Rivermen
02/3 Peoria Rivermen

LAWRENCE, BRETT
91/2 Knoxville Cherokees
91/2 Knoxville Cherokees

LAWRENCE, DEREK
92/3 BCJHL 220

LAWRENCE, MARK
00/1 Chicago Wolves
00/1 Chicago Wolves
93/4 Cla. Prospects 172
95/6 Leaf 59
96/7 Michigan K-Wings
96/7 Michigan K-Wings
88/9 Niagara Falls Thunder
88/9 Niagara Falls Thunder
89/0 Niagara Falls Thunder
89/0 Niagara Falls Thunder
99/0 Pacific 257
89/0 7th..Sketch OHL 131
90/1 7th..Sketch OHL 108
91/2 7th...Sketch OHL 40
94/5 Upper Deck 260
99/0 Upper Deck 252
99/0 UD G. Reserve 252

LAWSON, CHARLIE
99/0 Fort Wayne Komets
99/0 Fort Wayne Komets

LAWSON, DANNY
70/1 Esso Power Player
74/5 OPC WHA 25
75/6 OPC WHA 86
76/7 OPC WHA 8
73/4 Quaker Oats 48
71/2 Toronto Sun Photo
73/4 Vancouver Blazers
73/4 Vancouver Blazers

LAWSON, JEFF
92/3 MPS SJHL 124

LAWSON, KARL
96/7 Flint Generals

LAWSON, TOM
84/5 Ottawa 67's
84/5 Ottawa 67's

LAWTON, BRIAN
89/0 BOST / Sports Action
92/3 Bowman 254
92/3 Fleer Ultra 197
89/0 HART / Jr. Whalers
92/3 Kansas City Blades
92/3 Kansas City Blades
83/4 MINS
84/5 MINS
85/6 MINS
87/8 MINS
87/8 OPC/Topps 145
88/9 OPC/Topps 20
92/3 O-Pee-Chee 276
89/0 OPC/Topps 91
88/9 OPC Sticker 198-69
87/8 Panini Sticker 300
88/9 Panini Sticker 94
92/3 Panini Sticker 132
91/2 Parkhurst 167
92/3 Parkhurst 163
92/3 Pinnacle 71
91/2 Pro Set 482
92/3 Pro Set 173
90/1 ProCards 355
89/0 QUÉB
91/2 SANJ / Sports Action
91/2 SANJ / Sports Action
91/2 Score 98T
91/2 Score CAN 648
92/3 Score 343
89 Semic Sticker 172
92/3 Topps 435
92/3 To. Stadium 171
91/2 Upper Deck 572

LAXDAL, DEREK
83/4 Brandon Wheat Kings
83/4 Brandon Wheat Kings
84/5 Brandon Wheat Kings
84/5 Brandon Wheat Kings
85/6 Brandon Wheat Kings
85/6 Brandon Wheat Kings
92/3 Canada Nationals
89/0 OPC/Topps 169
89/0 opcSticker 181-39
89/0 ProCards AHL 108
90/1 ProCards 494
91/2 ProCards 466
94/5 Roanoke Express
94/5 Roanoke Express
88/9 TORO / P.L.A.Y. 21

LAXTON, DANIEL
79/0 Montréal Juniors B&W
79/0 Montréal Juniors B&W

LAXTON, DOUG
95/6 Birmingham Bulls
95/6 Birmingham Bulls

LAXTON, FRANÇOIS
79/0 Montréal Juniors B&W
79/0 Montréal Juniors B&W

LAY, MIKE
94/5 DEL 269
95/6 DEL 401
96/7 DEL 309
82/3 Medicine Hat Tigers
82/3 Medicine Hat Tigers
83/4 Medicine Hat Tigers
83/4 Medicine Hat Tigers

LAYCOCK, RICK
95/6 DEL 18

LAYCOCK, TRAVIS
90/1 Prince Albert Raiders
90/1 Prince Albert Raiders
91/2 Prince Albert Raiders
91/2 Prince Albert Raiders
90/1 7th..Sketch WHL 272
91/2 7th...Sketch WHL 255

LAYCOE, HAL
45-64 BeeHive-2 [Mont.]
45-64 BeeHive-2 [Bost.]
48-52 Exhibits [Canadiens]
43-47 Parade Sportive
51/2 Parkhurst 25
52/3 Parkhurst 71
53/4 Parkhurst 87
54/5 Parkhurst 52
45-54 Quaker Oats
54/5 Topps 38

LAYLIN, CORY
91/2 Minnesota G'Gophers
91/2 Minnesota G'Gophers
01/2 UD DEL 114

LAYTON, IAN
90/1 7th..Sketch WHL 154

LAYZELLE, BRAD
94/5 Fredericton Canadiens
94/5 Fredericton Canadiens
96/7 Milwaukee Admirals
96/7 Milwaukee Admirals

LAZARENKO, ALEXEI
99/0 Mir 29
00/1 Mir 2

LAZAREV, EVGENY
98/9 Hershey Bears
98/9 Hershey Bears
98/9 Hershey Bears
98/9 Hershey Bears
00/1 Hershey Bears
00/1 Hershey Bears
01/2 Hershey Bears
01/2 Hershey Bears

LAZARO, JEFF
91/2 BOST / Sports Action
91/2 BOST / Sports Action
91/2 Bowman 352
95/6 DEL 329
96/7 DEL 107
93/4 Fleer Ultra 489
97/8 New Orleans Brass
97/8 New Orleans Brass
91/2 O-Pee-Chee 380
92/3 OTTA
92/3 OTTA
92/3 Panini Sticker 139
95 Panini Worlds 230
93/4 Power Play 509
93/4 Premier - USA Hockey 21
91/2 Pro Set 13
90/1 ProCards 124
91/2 ProCards 65
91/2 Score CAN 445
94 Semic 131
95 Semic 119
92/3 Topps 224
91/2 To. Stadium 397
93/4 To. Stadium - Team U.S.A. 13
91/2 Upper Deck 364

LAZAROV, DIMITAR
79 Panini Sticker 347

LE BLOND, ?
79 Panini Sticker 381

LE BLOND, JEAN
79 Panini Sticker 383

LEACH, BRENN
82/3 Victoria Cougars
82/3 Victoria Cougars
83/4 Victoria Cougars
83/4 Victoria Cougars

LEACH, JAMIE
92/3 Bowman 320
93/4 Cincinnati Cyclones
93/4 Cincinnati Cyclones
00/1 Kudos 136
88/9 Niagara Falls Thunder
88/9 Niagara Falls Thunder
00/1 Nottingham Panthers
00/1 Nottingham Panthers
90/1 OPC/Topps 377
91/2 O-Pee-Chee 492
90/1 OPC Premier 60
91/2 PITT / Elby's
91/2 PITT / Elby's
93/4 Premier - Gold 528
89/0 ProCards IHL 143
95/6 Rochester Americans
95/6 Rochester Americans
90/1 Score 420
92/3 Topps 362
91/2 To. Stadium 296
92/3 To. Stadium 329
91/2 Upper Deck 447
92/3 Upper Deck 168

LEACH, JAY
94/5 Hershey Bears
94/5 Hershey Bears
91/2 ProCards 116

LEACH, MARK
90/1 Michigan Tech Huskies
90/1 Michigan Tech Huskies

LEACH, REGGIE
71/2 BOST
72/3 Eddie Sargent 54
01/2 Fleer Greats 35, ✍ Aut.
92/3 Future Trends C76 172
75/6 Hockey Heroes
74/5 Loblaws
71/2 O-Pee-Chee 175
72/3 O-Pee-Chee 51
73/4 O-Pee-Chee 84
74/5 O-Pee-Chee 95
75/6 O-Pee-Chee 166
75/6 O-Pee-Chee 325
76/7 O-Pee-Chee 1
76/7 O-Pee-Chee 110
76/7 O-Pee-Chee 215
76/7 O-Pee-Chee 65
76/7 OPC 391
77/8 O-Pee-Chee 185
77/8 O-Pee-Chee NS 8
78/9 O-Pee-Chee 165
79/0 O-Pee-Chee 95
80/1 O-Pee-Chee 249
80/1 O-Pee-Chee 70
81/2 O-Pee-Chee 243
82/3 O-Pee-Chee 90
81/2 OPC Sticker 181
83/4 OPC/Topps Sticker 9
92/3 Parkhurst 471
93/4 Parkhurst D19
01/2 Parkhurst ✍ PA54
82/3 Post [Phil.]
72/3 Topps 17
73/4 Topps 84
74/5 Topps 95
75/6 Topps 166
75/6 Topps 325
76/7 Topps 1
76/7 Topps 110
76/7 Topps 215
76/7 Topps 65
76/7 Topps NS 21
77/8 Topps 185
77/8 ToppsNS 8
78/9 Topps 165
79/0 Topps 95
80/1 Topps 249
80/1 Topps 70
81/2 Topps 106 [East]
02/3 Topps SCH, ✍ SCH
01/2 T/O Archives 43
71/2 Toronto Sun Photo
01/2 Ultimate Mem. ✄ SCD, ✄ SCP
01/2 Ultimate Mem. ✄ SCD, ✄ SCP
02/3 Ultimate Mem. ✄ ASMVP, ✄ CSTW
01/2 UD Legends 70

LEACH, STEPHEN
91/2 BOST / Sports Action
91/2 BOST / Sports Action
92/3 BOST / Postcard
92/3 BOST / Postcard
91/2 Bowman 306
92/3 Bowman 298
97/8 CARO / Sprint
97/8 CARO / Sprint
93/4 Donruss 28
92/3 Fleer Ultra 5
93/4 Fleer Ultra 268
93/4 Leaf 3
94/5 Leaf 420
90/1 OPC/Topps 235
91/2 O-Pee-Chee 100
92/3 O-Pee-Chee 112
89/0 OPC/Topps 67
98/9 OPC Chrome 28
91/2 OPC Premier 12
89/0 opcSticker 79-220
00/1 Pacific 333
97/8 Pa. Invincible R-171
97/8 Pa. Paramount 36
89/0 Panini Sticker 349
90/1 Panini Sticker 166
91/2 Panini Sticker 211
93/4 Panini Sticker 5
91/2 Parkhurst 6
92/3 Parkhurst 241
93/4 Parkhurst 285
95/6 Parkhurst 284
91/2 Pinnacle 46
92/3 Pinnacle 73
93/4 Pinnacle 73
94/5 Pinnacle 298
93/4 Power Play 21
93/4 Premier 507
94/5 Premier 268
90/1 Pro Set 315
91/2 Pro Set 253
91/2 Pro Set 346
92/3 Pro Set 6
91/2 Pro Set Platinum 151
90/1 Score 279
91/2 Score 26T
91/2 Score CAN 576
92/3 Score 54
93/4 Score 88
94/5 Score 79
92/3 Topps 16
98/9 Topps 28
91/2 To. Stadium 226
92/3 To. Stadium 68
93/4 To. Stadium 187
92/3 Upper Deck 61
94/5 Upper Deck 342
95/6 Upper Deck 453
96/7 Upper Deck 142
95/6 UD BAP 109, ✍ S109
86/7 WASH / Police
88/9 WASH
88/9 WASH / Smokey
89/0 WASH
89/0 WASH
89/0 WASH / Kodak
89/0 WASH / Kodak
90/1 WASH / Kodak
90/1 WASH / Kodak
90/1 WASH / Smokey
90/1 WASH / Smokey

LEADER, AL
83 HHOF Postcard M12
83&87 HHOF 176

LEAHY, GREG
88/9 Portland Winter Hawks
88/9 Portland Winter Hawks
89/0 Portland Winter Hawks
89/0 Portland Winter Hawks
90/1 Saskatoon Blades
90/1 Saskatoon Blades
90/1 7th..Sketch WHL 75

LEASK, ROB
96/7 DEL 31
98/9 DEL 177
93/4 Johnstown Chiefs 19
93/4 Johnstown Chiefs 19
94/5 Johnstown Chiefs 14
94/5 Johnstown Chiefs 14
91/2 Oshawa Generals
91/2 Oshawa Generals
90/1 7th..Sketch OHL 212
91/2 7th...Sketch OHL 166

LEASK, ROBERT
99/0 Eishockey 52

LEAVINS, JIM
90/1 Semic Elitserien 252

LEBEAU, PATRICK
93/4 Cincinnati Cyclones
93/4 Cincinnati Cyclones
92/3 Classic Prospects 28
90/1 ProCards 73
91/2 ProCards 72
92/3 Salt Lake G'Eagles
92/3 Salt Lake G'Eagles
91/2 Score 390
91/2 Score CAN 280
91/2 To. Stadium 373
91/2 Upper Deck 453
91/2 Upper Deck 644
93/4 Upper Deck 499

LEBEAU, STÉPHAN
94/5 ANAH / Carl's Jr. 16
94/5 ANAH / Carl's Jr. 16
90/1 Bowman 53
91/2 Bowman 333
92/3 Bowman 346
93/4 Donruss 175
94/5 Donruss 234
92/3 Durivage 7
93/4 Durivage 14
92/3 Fleer Ultra 329
93/4 Fleer Ultra 241
94/5 Fleer Ultra 5
95/6 Fleer Ultra 5
91/2 Kraft 26
93/4 Leaf 190
94/5 Leaf 162
89/0 MONT
89/0 MONT / Kraft
90/1 MONT
90/1 MONT
91/2 MONT
91/2 MONT
92/3 MONT
92/3 MONT
92/3 MONT / OPC 7
92/3 MONT / OPC 7
93/4 MONT
93/4 MONT
90/1 OPC/Topps 388
91/2 O-Pee-Chee 135
92/3 O-Pee-Chee 293
90/1 Panini/MTL 14
91/2 Panini Sticker 191
92/3 Panini Sticker 151
93/4 Panini Sticker 16
94/5 Panini Sticker 119
91/2 Parkhurst 87
92/3 Parkhurst 82
93/4 Parkhurst 374
94/5 Parkhurst 2, YCTG-1
94/5 Parkie SE seV11
91/2 Pinnacle 139
92/3 Pinnacle 341
93/4 Pinnacle 136
94/5 Pinnacle 67
94/5 POG 32
93/4 Power Play 130
93/4 Premier 462
94/5 Premier 63
90/1 Pro Set 152
91/2 Pro Set 120
91/2 Pro Set Platinum 190
88/9 ProCards / Sherbrooke
90/1 Score 262
91/2 Score 274
91/2 Score CAN 494
92/3 Score 246
93/4 Score 72
94/5 Score 128
91/2 Score Young Stars 7
94/5 Select 65
94/5 SP 3
92/3 Topps 69
91/2 To. Stadium 283
92/3 To. Stadium 431
93/4 To. Stadium 343
90/1 Upper Deck 51
91/2 Upper Deck 261
91/2 Upper Deck 644
92/3 Upper Deck 213
93/4 Upper Deck 402, SP-78
94/5 Upper Deck 53, SP-2

LEBEDEV, GENNADY
90/1 O-Pee-Chee 508

LEBEDEV, YURI
91/2 Future Trends C72 37
79 Panini Sticker 156
74 Semic Sticker 40
82 Semic Sticker 74
73/4 Soviet Stars 15
74/5 Soviet Stars 17
79/0 Soviet Stars 18
73/4 Williams Finnish 6

LEBEL, BOBBY
96/7 Rimouski Océanic
96/7 Rimouski Océanic

LEBEL, LAYNE
90/1 Michigan Tech Huskies
90/1 Michigan Tech Huskies
91/2 Michigan Tech Huskies
91/2 Michigan Tech Huskies

LEBEL, ROBERT
83 HHOF Postcard H11
83&87 HHOF 117

LEBLANC, BILL
51/2 Bas du Fleuve 31
52/3 Bas du Fleuve 13
51/2 Laval Dairy 7

LEBLANC, CARL
99/0 Colorado Gold Kings
99/0 Colorado Gold Kings
93/4 Knoxville Cherokees
93/4 Knoxville Cherokees
94/5 Knoxville Cherokees
94/5 Knoxville Cherokees
97/8 Quad City Mallards
97/8 Quad City Mallards
98/9 Quad City Mallards
98/9 Quad City Mallards
90/1 7th..Sketch LHJMQ 66
91/2 7th...Sketch LHJMQ 29

LEBLANC, DAN
89/0 7th..Sketch OHL 43

LEBLANC, DENIS
90/1 7th..Sketch LHJMQ 224

LEBLANC, FRANÇOIS
90/1 7th..Sketch LHJMQ 45

LEBLANC, JACQUES
90/1 7th..Sketch LHJMQ 211

LEBLANC, JEAN*
86/7 Fredericton Express
86/7 Fredericton Express

LEBLANC, JEAN-PAUL
72/3 Los Angeles Sharks
72/3 Los Angeles Sharks
76/7 O-Pee-Chee 326
77/8 O-Pee-Chee 133
74/5 OPC WHA 36
73/4 Quaker Oats 42
77/8 Topps 133

LEBLANC, JEFF
98/9 Québec Remparts
98/9 Québec Remparts

LEBLANC, JOHN
92/3 Bowman 419
88/9 EDMO
91/2 Moncton Hawks
91/2 Moncton Hawks
92/3 O-Pee-Chee 287
89/0 ProCards AHL 149
91/2 ProCards 169
92/3 Topps 88
92/3 To. Stadium 388

LEBLANC, MICHEL
95 Semic 197
92 Semic Sticker 222

LEBLANC, MIKE
89/0 Rayside-Balfour
89/0 Rayside-Balfour

LEBLANC, PIERRE-ANDRÉ
00/1 Baie-Comeau 3
00/1 Baie-Comeau 3

LEBLANC, RAY
98/9 Chicago Wolves Champs
98/9 Chicago Wolves Champs
93/4 Cincinnati Cyclones
93/4 Cincinnati Cyclones
95/6 Edge Ice TW1
87/8 Flint Spirits
87/8 Flint Spirits
92/3 Indianapolis Ice
92/3 Indianapolis Ice
83/4 Kitchener Rangers
83/4 Kitchener Rangers
91/2 Parkhurst 255
89/0 ProCards IHL 67
90/1 ProCards 553
91/2 ProCards 502
92/3 Score 486
92/3 Upper Deck 381

LEBLANC, ROBIN
00/1 Baie-Comeau 7
00/1 Baie-Comeau 7
01/2 Baie-Comeau 6
01/2 Baie-Comeau 6
02/3 Baie-Comeau
02/3 Baie-Comeau
00/1 UD Prospects 76
01 UD Prospects GU 15, ✄ TPJ

LEBNER, JOSEF
94/5 DEL 58

LEBODA, TED
67/8 Columbus Checkers
67/8 Columbus Checkers

LEBOLD, DAN
01/2 Kitchener Rangers
01/2 Kitchener Rangers
94/5 Slapshot / Sudbury 25

LEBOUTILIER, PETER
98/9 Cincinnati M'Ducks 25
98/9 Cincinnati M'Ducks 25
99/0 Cincinnati M'Ducks
99/0 Cincinnati M'Ducks
00/1 Lowell Lock Monsters
00/1 Lowell Lock Monsters
93/4 Red Deer Rebels
93/4 Red Deer Rebels
93/4 Red Deer Rebels
93/4 Red Deer Rebels
97/8 Score Anah. 17

LEBRASSEUR, PASCAL
90/1 7th..Sketch LHJMQ 17
91/2 7th...Sketch LHJMQ 76

LEBREAU, JEAN
90/1 7th..Sketch LHJMQ 267

LEBRETON, SHAYNE
98/9 Odessa Jackalopes
98/9 Odessa Jackalopes

LEBRUN, AL
61/2 Topps 61
62/3 Topps 50

LEBRUN, JEAN-CLAUDE
52/3 Laval Dairy Update 94

LEBRUN, SEAN
89/0 ProCards AHL 247
90/1 ProCards 495
91/2 ProCards 474
92/3 Richmond Renegades
92/3 Richmond Renegades

LEBSACK, GREG
83/4 Saskatoon Blades
83/4 Saskatoon Blades

LECACHEUR, ROB
90/1 Saskatoon Blades
90/1 Saskatoon Blades

LECAVALIER, VINCENT
01/2 Adrenaline 174, ✄ GWJ 45
01/2 Atomic 89, CP 18, PP 31
02/3 Atomic 90
99/0 Aurora 131, Stripe 131
00/1 Aurora 134, SR-18
98/9 Be A Player 279, ✍ Aut. 279
99/0 BAP Mem. 116, SL-20
00/1 BAP Mem. 209
01/2 BAP Mem. 85, HSHS
02/3 BAP Mem. 187
01/2 BAP Update ✄ HSHSJers
01/2 Bowman 68
02/3 Bowman 22
97 Bowman 69
98 Bowman 103, 128, SC12, ✍ A10
98 Bowman Chrome 103, 128
98/9 Bowman's Best 109, BP10, F5
02/3 Calder 49
98/9 Collection Souvenir 22
99/0 Crown Royale 129, IE-23, C21-10
00/1 Crown Royale 96, JotC-23, NP-16
01/2 Crown Royale 128
02/3 Crown Royale 88, -LOR 18
98/9 Dynagon Ice 173, -FT 17, -IR 8, -TC 24
99/0 Dynagon Ice 181
01/2 eTopps 29
02/3 Exclusive 156
02/3 First Edition 43, 419H, ✄ Jers.
01/2 Heads Up 87, SM 17, ✄ JQ 27
02/3 Heads Up 112, -HF 14
99/0 HoloGrFX 54
02/3 In The GU 70, 170
00/1 Kraft 18
00/1 McDonald's 30, GCDC-6
01/2 McDonald's 37, -HP 7, ✄ JPatch 17
99/0 Millenium 220, ✍ Aut. 220
98/9 NHL Power Play
99/0 NHL Power Play
01/2 O-Pee-Chee 44
02/3 O-Pee-Chee 14
98/9 OPC Chrome 224
98/9 Omega 219, -Onl. 31, -PI 3
99/0 Omega 216, 5ST-23, EOP-17,G-9
99/0 Pacific 392, GC-32, TL-25
00/1 Pacific 377, IO-19, GCDC-32, PR-18, ✍ Aut. 377
01/2 Pacific 355, 422, TDP 3
02/3 Pacific 351
02/3 Pacific Complete 16
98/9 Pa. Crown Roy. 124, -PP 21, -RC 8
99/0 Pa. Paramount 219, IAI-25, PB-33
00/1 Pa. Paramount 222, ES-18, FF-33
98/9 Pa. Revolution 133, -CTLC 17, -Show. 32
01/2 PTC Collectors 9
98/9 Panini Photocard
99/0 Panini Sticker 148
00/1 Panini Sticker 88
00/1 Parkhurst P-21
01/2 Parkhurst 87, ✄ PJ3, ✄ PS3, ✄ PSJ12, ✄ H1
02/3 Parkhurst 77
02/3 Parkhurst Retro 172, ✄ RF27, ✄ RJ39
00/1 Premier Plus 72, PA2, WP13
99/0 Prism 132, CA-19
00/1 Private Stock 91, AC-19, EA-19, Res. 19, PS-54, PSNW-23, ✄ GUG-93
01/2 Pr. Stock 88, Res. 18, -PS 68, ✄ GUG 93
02/3 Pr. Stock Reserve 91
00/1 PS Titanium 89, 3SS-19
01/2 PS Titanium 126, ✄ DSJ 40
01/2 PS Titanium Draft ✄ 88
02/3 PS Titanium 90
00/1 PS Titanium Draft ✄ 93
94 Québec Pee Wee 11
02/3 Quest for the Cup 89
99/0 Revolution 133, O-17, SS-32, / CSC 133
00/1 Revolution 135, HD-32
96/7 Rimouski Océanic
96/7 Rimouski Océanic
97/8 Rimouski Océanic
97/8 Rimouski Océanic
00/1 Signature 212, F-27, ✍ Aut. 116, ✄ HSHSJers
01/2 Signature C-49, ✍ Aut. LVL, ✄ FP27, ✄ GUE50, ✄ GJ59, ✄ GSJ59, ✄ ITN50, ✄ TM27
02/3 Signature 137, ✍ 137, ✄ FJ27, ✄ SGJ70
98/9 SP Authentic 109, SS18, SO27, ✍ SotT
99/0 SP Authentic 78, TH9
00/1 SP Authentic 80, PS7
01/2 SP Authentic 80, ✍ SotT, ✍ SotTD
02/3 SP Authentic 81
00/1 SP GU 54
01/2 SP GU 52, ✄✍ IS
02/3 SP GU 45, ✄ PC
02/3 Sports Vault 124
99/0 SPx 137, P8
00/1 SPx 63, X13
01/2 SPx 63, 79
02/3 SPx 68
98/9 SPx Prospects 53, H26, L1, PS12
99/0 Stadium 23,Chrome 19, CA9
00/1 Stadium 37, BT11, CA14
01/2 Stadium 14, G39
02/3 Stadium 26, ✄ NHLP9
00/1 SLU 13
98/9 Topps 224
99/0 Topps 147, NS13, ✍ TA9
00/1 Topps 26, TC7, NHLD1
01/2 Topps 44, ✄ CC1, ✄ CC3, ✄ GWJ, ✍ CA
02/3 Topps 14
99/0 To. Chrome 147
00/1 To. Chrome 25, TC7
01/2 To. Chrome 44
02/3 To. Chrome 14
98/9 To. Finest F3
98/9 T. Gold Label 61
99/0 To. Gold Label 66, FG20
00/1 To. Gold Label 69, NG2
00/1 To. Heritage 4, NT4
01/2 To. Heritage 55, ✄ CC, ✍ CAI
02/3 To. Heritage 69
02/3 To. Limited 14
99/0 To. Prmr. Plus 19, TNO1
01/2 To. Reserve 21, ✄ TR
00/1 To. Stars 1, 140, P1, PP6, ✍ CAI
02/3 T. Total 5
98/9 UD Choice 259
00/1 UD Heroes 157, PI5
01/2 UD PlayMakers Ltd 88
00/1 UD Reserve 77, BT10
00/1 Ultimate Mem. ✍ U-21, ✄ Jers. 12, ✄ J-14, ✄ S-14
02/3 Ultimate Mem. ✄ FO, ✄ CUJ, ✄ Num
99/0 Ult. Victory 79
97/8 Upper Deck 412
98/9 Upper Deck 414, GN3, P16, ✄ GJ2
99/0 Upper Deck 117, CT1, MA11, N9, SS18
00/1 Upper Deck 386, RP8, SS18
01/2 Upper Deck 387, FC5, SS18, T10, ✄ NG
02/3 Upper Deck 160, ✄ PP
02/3 UD Artistic 81, R81, / Art
97/8 UD Black Diam. 150
98/9 UD Black Diam. 80, M1, WF5
99/0 UD Black Diam. 78
00/1 UD Black Diam. 53, IG8
99/0 UD C. Legends 72
01/2 UD Challenge 79
02/3 UD Classic 90
98/9 UD G. Reserve 414
99/0 UD G. Reserve 117
99/0 UD Gretzky Excl. 82
01/2 UD Honor Roll -DPuck
02/3 UD Honor 64, 97, -SG28
00/1 UD Ice 36, IG8
01/2 UD Ice 39
00/1 UD Legends 118, 119
01/2 UD Mask 89
98/9 UD MVP 187, PG5, Snip. S1, F3, -Souv., ✍ PS
99/0 UD MVP 190, 21st-5
00/1 UD MVP 163
01/2 UD MVP 169, ✄ C
02/3 UD MVP 166
99/0 UD MVP Cup 167, CC9, GC
99/0 UD Ovation 53
02/3 UD Piece 81
02/3 UD Premier 48
00/1 UD Pros&Prosp. 79
99/0 UD Retro 72, G5C, TC1, ✍ Ink.
01/2 UD Top Shelf 40
01/2 UD Top Shelf ✄ J, ✄ J, ✄✍ SJ
02/3 UD Top Shelf 80
00/1 UD Vintage 322, 332, 333
01/2 UD Vintage 228, 234
02/3 UD Vintage 226, 287, GB 226, T58
00/1 Vanguard 90, HV-31, IF-16, VP-19
01/2 Vanguard 89, QTH 19, ✄ DGM 30
02/3 Vanguard 89, -EMW 7
99/0 Victory 269, 270
00/1 Victory 208, 209, 325
01/2 Victory 315, 440
02/3 Victory 195
99/0 WGretzky 156
97/8 Zenith 95, Z75

LECHL, JURGEN
94/5 DEL 329
95/6 DEL 302
96/7 DEL 330

LECHTALER, CHRISTIAN
91/2 Semic Elitserien 298
98/9 UD Elitserien 24
00/1 UD Elitserien 20

LECKLIN, KIMMO
99/0 Cardset 327
97/8 Hockey-Box
93/4 Sisu 30
94/5 Sisu 47
98/9 UD Elitserien 83

LECLAIR, ALAIN
90/1 Rayside-Balfour
90/1 Rayside-Balfour

LECLAIR, JACKIE
45-64 BeeHive-2 [Mont.]
51/2 Laval Dairy 12
52/3 Laval Dairy Update 98
55/6 Parkhurst 36
93/4 Parkie 56-57 83
52/3 St. Lawrence 57

LECLAIR, JOHN
01/2 Adrenaline 140, WB 14, ✄ GWJ 32
01/2 Atomic 72, CP 14, PP 26
02/3 Atomic ✄ GWJ 17
98/9 Aurora 140, ALC-14, CF-35, MACF-14, / Cube 13
99/0 Aurora 105, Stripe 105, CC-8, CF-16, CP-8, ST-14
00/1 Aurora 107, Pins. 107, CC-8, CF-17, CFA-17, SR-17, TPS-8A
02/3 BAP All-Star 48, ✄ ASJ, ✄ HSHSJers
98/9 Be A Player 250, P-13, ✍ Aut. 250, ✄ G-5, ✄ AS-22, ✄ S-20, ✄✍ G-5
99/0 BAP Mem. 73, H-2, ✄ J-22, ✄ D-14, ✄ TM-7, ✄ TM-15, ✄ TM-18, ✄ TM-49
00/1 BAP Mem. 111, ✄ J-32, ✄ PP-6
01/2 BAP Mem. 266, ✄ ASJ, ✄ AST
02/3 BAP Mem. 112, 250, ✄ ASJ29, ✄ ASTJ8, /Cup
97/8 Bicycle 4-Club
95/6 Bicycle Sports Aces Q-Spade
91/2 Bowman 344
92/3 Bowman 8
95/6 Bowman 63
01/2 Bowman 65
02/3 Bowman 9
98/9 Bowman's Best 7, F1
99/0 Challenger 29
93/4 Cla. Prospects 54
99/0 Crown Royale 102, IE-19, GC-6
00/1 Crown Royale 80, ✄ GWJ-20, JotC-19, NP-13
01/2 Crown Royale 107
02/3 Crown Royale 71
93/4 Donruss 176
94/5 Donruss 98
95/6 Donruss 114, D-2
96/7 Donruss 36, HL-13
97/8 Donruss 29, 229, RA-7
98/9 Donruss ES 1
96/7 Do. Canadian 100
97/8 Do. Canadian 93, SCS-29
95/6 Do. Elite 56
96/7 Do. Elite 57
97/8 Do. Elite 71
97/8 Do. Preferred 76, LT-3A
97/8 Do. Priority 132, 205, DD-28, OD-26, Post-21, Stamp-21
97/8 Do. Studio 22, S-15, P-25
98/9 Dynagon Ice 137, -FT 14
99/0 Dynagon Ice 147, ASP-14, CM-12, LL-8
97/8 Esso 25
01/2 eTopps 9
02/3 Exclusive 127
02/3 First Edition 51, ✄ Jers.
96/7 Flair 69
94/5 Fleer 156
96/7 Fleer 81, 142, ART-12
95/6 Fleer Metal 111, IW-5
96/7 Fl. Picks 30, F50-24, DL-7, FF-1
92/3 Fleer Ultra 330
93/4 Fleer Ultra 215
94/5 Fleer Ultra 111
95/6 Fleer Ultra 118, CC-5, RLS-5
96/7 Fl. Ultra 125, 179, 180, CTI-5
01/2 Heads Up 72, ✄ JQ 15
02/3 Heads Up 91
99/0 HoloGrFX 44
95/6 Hoyle / East. K-Spade
02/3 In The GU 56, 156, ✄ E26, ✄ GUJ26, ✄ SJ26, ✄ T15, ✄ TM6
95/6 Kraft / PB
96/7 Kraft / TT
97/8 Kraft / KD
98/9 Kraft / KD
00/1 Kraft 10
93/4 Leaf 98
94/5 Leaf 5
95/6 Leaf 95
96/7 Leaf 83
97/8 Leaf 100, BS-7
95/6 L. Limited 85
96/7 L. Limited 15
96/7 L. Preferred 105, LS-39
97/8 Limited 15, 90, 94, 168, FG-63
96/7 Maggers 117
95/6 McDonald's McD-20
96/7 McDonald's McD-4
99/0 McDonald's ✍ SS
00/1 McDonald's 25
01/2 McDonald's 29
96/7 Metal Univ. 113, LW-10
99/0 Millenium 179, ✍ Aut. 179, ✄ J-7, ✄✍ J-7, ✄ JS-7
91/2 MONT
91/2 MONT
92/3 MONT
92/3 MONT
93/4 MONT
93/4 MONT
94/5 MONT
94/5 MONT
98/9 NHL Power Play
91/2 O-Pee-Chee 209
92/3 O-Pee-Chee 386
01/2 O-Pee-Chee 42
02/3 O-Pee-Chee 7
98/9 OPC Chrome 60, SB16, SB28
91/2 OPC Premier 105
91/2 OPC Premier 186
97/8 Omega 167, GF-12, SHLC-15
98/9 Omega 176, -EOP 15, -FTF 9, -Onl. 25, -PI 15, -Prism 15
99/0 Omega 171, 5ST-8, CC-15, G-8, ✄ GWJ 6
98/9 Pacific 51, -DI 14, -GCDC 24, -Time. 13
99/0 Pacific 306,GC-25, HAA-8, HAA-18, PAP-16
00/1 Pacific 300, GCDC-23, NAS-9, PR-15, ✍ Aut. 300
01/2 Pacific 289
02/3 Pacific 282
02/3 Pacific Complete 129
97/8 Pacific CC 10, CS-14, SS-6C
97/8 Pa. Crown Roy. 98, HT-12, L-13
98/9 Pa. Crown Roy. 99, -MP 15, -PotG 17, -PP 18
97/8 Pa. Dynagon 90, 141, T-15, T-20, BKS-71

97/8 Pa. Invincible 101, AZ-17, FP-24, R-144
97/8 Pa. Paramount 133, P-14
98/9 Pa. Paramount 176, -SD 13
99/0 Pa. Paramount 172, PB-25
00/1 Pa. Paramount 182, ES-16, FF-26, HOFB-9
97/8 Pa. Revolution 102, ASG-15
98/9 Pa. Revolution 105, -ASG 16, -TPA 28, -CTLC 13, -Show. 25
98/9 Panini Photocard
95/6 Panini Sticker 116
96/7 Panini Sticker 112
97/8 Panini Sticker 96, 125
98/9 Panini Sticker 88
99/0 Panini Sticker 125, 325
00/1 Panini Sticker 74
91/2 Parkhurst 84
92/3 Parkhurst 326
93/4 Parkhurst 107
94/5 Parkhurst 111
95/6 Parkhurst 157
00/1 Parkhurst P-69
01/2 Parkhurst 95, ✂ PJ22, ✂ PS22, ✂ PSJ18, ✂ HSHSJers, ✂ T13
02/3 Parkhurst 66, ✂ GJ8, ✂ SJ8, ✂ HSHSJers, ✂ TT2
02/3 Parkhurst Retro 109, ✂ RJ25
94/5 PHIL / Sheet
94/5 PHIL / Sheet
94/5 PHIL / Sheet
94/5 PHIL / Sheet
94/5 PHIL / Sheet
94/5 PHIL / Sheet
94/5 PHIL / Sheet
96/7 PHIL / Ocean Spray
96/7 PHIL / Ocean Spray
97/8 PHIL / Comcast
97/8 PHIL / Comcast
01/2 PHIL
01/2 PHIL
91/2 Pinnacle 322
93/4 Pinnacle 112
94/5 Pinnacle 272
95/6 Pinnacle 51, R20-16
96/7 Pinnacle 49
97/8 Pinnacle 57, 196, TP-8, P-23
96/7 Pi. Be A Player BB-17
97/8 Pi. Be A Player 250, OT-9, ✍ Aut. 250
97/8 Pi. BeeHive 5, BHT-12
97/8 Pi. Certified 112, CT-20
97/8 Pi. Epix E23
97/8 Pi. Inside 58, IT-25, / Can 17
97/8 Pi. Mint 20
95/6 Pi. Summit 75, MH-3
96/7 Pi. Summit 6
97/8 Pi. Totally 119
95/6 Pi. Zenith 59, GG-7
96/7 Pi. Zenith 17, A-10
95/6 Playoff 293
94/5 POG 136
95/6 POG 206, I-010
93/4 Premier 181
94/5 Premier 117
00/1 Premier Plus 54, PT3, WP10, ✍ CS
99/0 Prism 102, CA-15, SGDC-15
00/1 Private Stock 73, AC-6, EA-15, Res. 16, PS-42, PSS-19, ✂ GUG-83
01/2 Pr. Stock 72, Res. 13, -PS 54, ✂ GUG 71
02/3 Pr. Stock Reserve 74
00/1 PS Titanium 70, ✂ GUG-42, ✂ GUG-122
01/2 PS Titanium 105, ✂ DSJ 50, ✂ DSJ 51
01/2 PS Titanium Draft ✂ 71
02/3 PS Titanium ✂ GWJ 52
00/1 PS Titanium Draft ✂ 73
95/6 Pro Magnet 48
91/2 Pro Set 545
91/2 Pro Set Platinum 259
99/0 Revolution 108,NI-13, O-14, SS-26, TL-7, / CSC 108
00/1 Revolution 109, HD-25, II-15, NI-16, SM-8
91/2 Score 313
91/2 Score CAN 343
93/4 Score 318
95/6 Score 9
96/7 Score 161
97/8 Score 108, CI-5
97/8 Score Phil. 4
95/6 Select CE 44
96/7 Select CE 33
96/7 SB 7-Eleven Phonecard
00/1 Signature 184, F-22, ✍ Aut. 87, ✂ J-7
01/2 Signature C-17, ✍ Aut. LJL, ✂ FP22, ✂ GUE48, ✂ GJ49, ✂ GSJ49, ✂ HSHSJers 14, ✂ ITN48, ✂ IS5, ✂ TM23
02/3 Signature 113, ✍ 113, ✂ SGJ26, ✂ TQ3
95/6 SBx Emotion 132
95/6 SBx Impact 126, 244
96/7 SBx Impact 96, BR-11
02/3 Slam Card
94/5 SP 85
95/6 SP 108
96/7 SP 112, GF-17
97/8 SP Authentic 114, I17
98/9 SP Authentic 63, SS1, SO9
99/0 SP Authentic 64, SS9, ✍ SotT
00/1 SP Authentic 64, PS6, SF5, ✍ SotT, ✂ SotTT
01/2 SP Authentic 61, 104, ✂ NN, ✍ SotT, ✂ SotTD
02/3 SP Authentic 68, ✍ SotT, ✂ SotTD (x2)
00/1 SP GU 45, ✂ TotG, ✂ C, ✂ P, ✂✍ A
01/2 SP GU 38, ✂ AF, ✂ AFD (x2), ✂ AFT, ✂✍ IS, ✂✍ IS2, ✂✍ ISD (x2), ✂ Patch, ✂✍ PatchSig, ✂ PatchC (x2), ✂✍ PatchCSig, ✂ PatchT, ✂ TotG, ✂✍ TotGSig (x2), ✂ TotGC, ✂✍ TotGCSig, ✂ TotGT
02/3 SP Game-Used ✂ AF, ✂ CF, ✂ PH, ✍ Sig, ✂ TG
02/3 Sports Vault 104
96/7 SPx 34
97/8 SPx 38
99/0 SPx 110, P12, X19, XT17
00/1 SPx 51, 75, 89, P6, S6, ✂ WM, ✂✍ WM
01/2 SPx 49, 88, ✂ HT (x2), ✂✍ HTSig (x2), ✍ Sig
02/3 SPx 96, ✂ WM, ✂ X
98/9 SPx Finite 60, 102, 164
98/9 SPx Prospects 44, H22, L24, PS9, ✂ WM
99/0 Stadium 65, Chrome 25, OE9, ✍ CS6, ✍ CS8, ✍ CS9, ✍ LS10, ✂ SCS
00/1 Stadium 36, CA4, CA8, SF9
01/2 Stadium 84, G18, NHLP15, P6
02/3 Stadium 77
96/7 SLU
95/6 Super Sticker 92
96/7 Team Out!
92/3 Topps 500
95/6 Topps 65, HGA-9, 1PL
98/9 Topps 60, M10, SB16, SB28, ✍ CAI
99/0 Topps 19, AT7, IM5, FF5, PP2, TW10
00/1 Topps 7, TC3, ✍ CAI
01/2 Topps 42, SM15
02/3 Topps 7, HHU11, ✂ CC2
99/0 To. Chrome 19, AT7, IM5, FF5, PP2
00/1 To. Chrome 7, TC3, RF3
01/2 To. Chrome 42
02/3 To. Chrome 7
95/6 To. Finest 60, 179
98/9 To. Finest 51, M41, M45, M46, M47, R16
98/9 T. Gold Label 86, GR2
99/0 To. Gold Label 25, PG8
00/1 To. Gold Label 56, GG4, ✂ GLJ
00/1 To. Heritage 30, HH13
01/2 To. Heritage 10, ✂ GWJ
02/3 To. Heritage 76
02/3 To. Limited 7
96/7 To. Picks TS1
99/0 To. Prmr. Plus 13
01/2 To. Reserve 32, ✂ TR
92/3 To. Stadium 181
93/4 To. Stadium 95
95/6 To. Stadium 77, PS6
95/6 TSC Members Only 43
00/1 To. Stars 9, AS11, WF9
95/6 T. Super Skills 42
02/3 T. Total 228, TTC22
98/9 UD Choice 153, 235, BH6, SQ15
00/1 UD Heroes 153, L7, SS9, TS4, ✂ GT, ✂ GC, ✍ SG
01/2 UD PlayMakers Ltd 71, -PCPJ, ✂ PCCJ
00/1 UD Reserve 62, BT8, PSJ, ✍ PSJ
02/3 UD Superstars ✂ CAS
98/9 UD3 56, 116, 176
00/1 Ultimate Mem. ✂ U-7, ✂ Jers. 5, ✂ J-7, ✂ S-7, ✂ TM-29
01/2 Ultimate Mem. ✂ DD, ✂ Emb., ✂ Jers., ✂ S&J, ✂ Glove, ✂ ITN, ✂ NP, ✂ WTF, ✍ Aut.
02/3 Ultimate Mem. ✂ Emb, ✂ GUJ, ✂ HT, ✂ ITN, ✂ SJ
99/0 Ult. Victory 65
99/0 Upper Deck 345
91/2 Upper Deck 55
93/4 Upper Deck 167, SP-79
94/5 Upper Deck 330
95/6 Upper Deck 7, 247, AS-14, SE-63
96/7 Upper Deck 118, 368, P3
97/8 Upper Deck 123, SG50, S20, T9B
98/9 Upper Deck 143, FF25, FT27, LS25, P25
99/0 Upper Deck 158
99/0 Upper Deck 269, AS8, CT22, FF2, SB13, ✂ GJ
00/1 Upper Deck 126, EC5, FF7, GA9, NC3, P7, SS15, TT4, UD6, ✂ GJ, ✂ DGJ
01/2 Upper Deck 220, 356, 410, FF5, FC14, GA4, SS12, SS19, T7, ✂ Jpatch, ✂ PatchN, ✂ PatchNu, ✂ PF, ✂ PoaND, ✂ SCFJers, ✂✍ JersSig, ✂✍ SigJers
02/3 Upper Deck 376, ✂ R50, ✂ GJ, ✂ PW, ✂ UDPL
95/6 UD ASG MVP24
96/7 UD All-Star YCTG AR15
02/3 UD Artistic 64, R64, ✂ SS, / ✍ Art
95/6 UD BAP 130, ✍ S130
96/7 UD Black Diam. 110
97/8 UD Black Diam. 65, PC6
98/9 UD Black Diam. 63, M24, WF22
99/0 UD Black Diam. 64, DM4, ✂ APOH
00/1 UD Black Diam. 43, IG6, FP8, IC5
99/0 UD C. Legends 67
01/2 UD Challenge 61, ✂ FP, ✂ UC, ✂✍ UCS
02/3 UD Classic 71, ✂ HR
95/6 UD CC 261, 376, C23
96/7 UD CC 190, 326, UD8, C12, CR12
97/8 UD Coll. Choice 182, SQ52
98/9 UD G. Reserve 143
99/0 UD G. Reserve 158, 269
01/2 UD Honor Roll 97, ✂ GAJ
02/3 UD Honor 53, -TW11, ✍ SC
96/7 UD Ice 98, S10
97/8 UD Ice 75, L8A
00/1 UD Ice 30, IC5, IG6, FP8, ✂ IGJ
01/2 UD Ice 112, ✂ JC, ✂ GJ
00/1 UD Legends 100, 101, ✍ ES, ✂ LGJ
01/2 UD Mask 71
02/3 UD Mask 63
98/9 UD MVP 148, OT14, PG6, -Souv.
99/0 UD MVP 148
00/1 UD MVP 124, M13, TD8, ✂ GS
01/2 UD MVP 140, MT12, -J (x2), ✍ S, ✂ S
02/3 UD MVP 133, SA, SD (x3), ST
99/0 UD MVP Cup 132, CP8, SS8, SC13, GC, ✂ GU
00/1 UD Ovation 42, LP6
01/2 UD Premier 38, ✂ B, ✍ SigS
02/3 UD Premier 41, ✍ Sig
00/1 UD Pros&Prosp. 62, PJS, GS7, NP5, PM8
99/0 UD Retro 58
02/3 UD Rookie 73, ✂ 149c, ✂ 150c, ✂ 152a, ✂ 159a, ✂ 160a, ✍ TD
01/2 UD SCup Champs 66
01/2 UD Top Shelf 112, ✂ J, ✂✍ SJ, ✂ S
02/3 UD Top Shelf 65, ✂ HT, ✂ M, ✂ TS, ✍ Sig
00/1 UD Vintage 260, 271, 272, UD6, NH17, S5A
01/2 UD Vintage 186, 191
02/3 UD Vintage 188, GB 188, ✂ SO
00/1 Vanguard 73, HV-25, IF-14
01/2 Vanguard 73
02/3 Vanguard 74, -EMW 5, ✂ GWJ 34
99/0 Victory 211, 330
00/1 Victory 166, 167, 253, 314
01/2 Victory 254, 399
02/3 Victory 158
01/2 Waving the Flag 27
99/0 WGretzky 123, W8
97/8 Zenith 8,CTC-8, ZT-7, Z47

LECLAIR, NELSON
67/8 Columbus Checkers
67/8 Columbus Checkers

LECLAIRE, COLIN
02/3 Québec Remparts
02/3 Québec Remparts

LECLAIRE, PASAL
02/3 Syracuse Crunch
02/3 Syracuse Crunch

LECLAIRE, PASCAL
02/3 BAP Draft Florida 8
02/3 BAP Mem. 350
02/3 Between the Pipes 108
02/3 Calder 111, -CR 7
02/3 Choice Prospects 24
02/3 First Edition 432 [Hobby]
98/9 Halifax Moosehead
98/9 Halifax Moosehead
00/1 Halifax Mooseheads
00/1 Halifax Moosehead
99/0 Halifax Mooseheads
00/1 Halifax Mooseheads
02/3 Pacific Complete 576
02/3 PTC/ Collections 2
02/3 Parkhurst 215
02/3 Parkhurst Retro 206
02/3 PS Titanium 110
96 Québec Pee Wee 328
02/3 Quest for the Cup 112, -CC 5
02/3 SP Authentic ✍ 185
02/3 SPx 176
02/3 Ultimate Mem. 43
02/3 UD Artistic 60, R96, CG1, CG22
02/3 UD Classic 132
02/3 UD Foundations 165
02/3 UD Honor 111
02/3 UD Mask 175
02/3 UD Premier ✍ 74, ✂ Jers, ✂ JD
99/0 UD Prospects 88
00/1 UD Prospects 79, 90, CC9, CS10, D6, GD6, ✍ Sig
01 UD Prospects GU ✍ SoT
02/3 UD Rookie ✍ 170
02/3 Vanguard 108

LECLERC, JEAN
52/3 Anonymous 43

LECLERC, MATHIEU
99/0 Rouyn-Noranda
99/0 Rouyn-Noranda
00/1 Rouyn-Noranda 12
00/1 Rouyn-Noranda 12

LECLERC, MIKE
99/0 BAP Mem. 170
02/3 BAP Mem. 82
98/9 Bowman's Best 117, F2
95/6 Brandon Wheat Kings
95/6 Brandon Wheat Kings
98/9 Cincinnati M'Ducks 8
98/9 Cincinnati M'Ducks 8
99/0 Cincinnati M'Ducks 8
99/0 Cincinnati M'Ducks
95/6 Classic 47
01/2 Heads Up ✂ JQ 1
99/0 NHL Power Play
01/2 O-Pee-Chee 199
02/3 O-Pee-Chee 62
02/3 Pacific 7, PCC 352
02/3 Pacific 5
02/3 Pacific Complete 93
99/0 Prism 3
01/2 Pr. Stock ✂ GUG 3
00/1 PS Titanium ✂ GUG 53
00/1 PS Titanium ✂ GWJ 1
00/1 PS Titanium Draft ✂ 2
01/2 Signature 73, ✍ Aut. 73
94/5 Slapshot Memorial 38
02/3 Sports Vault 156
02/3 Topps 199
02/3 Topps 62
02/3 To. Limited 62
02/3 T. Total 25
97/8 Upper Deck 181
98/9 Upper Deck 213
00/1 Upper Deck 4
01/2 Upper Deck 3
02/3 UD Classic 3
98/9 UD G. Reserve 213
01/2 UD MVP 5
02/3 UD MVP 1
99/0 UD MVP Cup 6
00/1 UD Vintage 7
01/2 UD Vintage 6, 9
02/3 UD Vintage 261

LECLERC, MIKE
02/3 UD Vintage 4

LECLERC, MIKE
01/2 Victory 7
02/3 Victory 7

LECLERC, PAUL
51/2 Laval Dairy 80
52/3 St. Lawrence 18

LECLERC, RENÉ
76/7 OPC WHA 28
73/4 Québec Nordiques
73/4 Québec Nordiques

LECLERC, ROLAND
52/3 Anonymous 79

LECOMPTE, ERIC
98/9 Cincinnati M'Ducks 10
98/9 Cincinnati M'Ducks 10
93/4 Classic 23
94/5 Classic 41, T13
93/4 Cla. 4 Sport 205
95/6 Edge Ice 136
95/6 Future Legends 31
95/6 Indianapolis Ice
95/6 Indianapolis Ice
97/8 Indianapolis Ice 14
97/8 Indianapolis Ice 14
91/2 7th...Sketch LHJMQ 217

LECOMPTE, FRANÇOIS
79/0 Montréal Juniors B&W
79/0 Montréal Juniors B&W
79/0 Montréal Jrs. Colour
79/0 Montréal Jrs. Colour

LECOURS, DANNY
81/2 Milwaukee Admirals
81/2 Milwaukee Admirals

LECUYER, DOUG
80/1 CHIC / Colour
80/1 CHIC / Brown
80/1 O-Pee-Chee 366
81/2 O-Pee-Chee 367

LEDIN, PER
98/9 UD Elitserien 30

LEDLIN, FREDERIK
94/5 DEL 291

LEDOCK, RENÉ
94/5 DEL 140

LEDUC, ALBERT
25-27 Anonymous 6 [Error]
33/4 Anonymous 27
27/8 La Patrie
27/8 La Presse
33/4 O-Pee-Chee 46
55/6 Parkhurst 61
02/3 Parkie - Reprint 209

LEDUC, BOB
72/3 O-Pee-Chee 322
73/4 OPC WHA Poster 9
72/3 Ottawa Nationals
72/3 Ottawa Nationals

LEDUC, MIKE
91/2 Avant Garde BCJHL 69

LEDUC, RAYMOND
51/2 Bas du Fleuve 5
52/3 Bas du Fleuve 60

LEDUC, RICH
79/0 O-Pee-Chee 283
80/1 O-Pee-Chee 122
75/6 OPC WHA 113
76/7 OPC WHA 41
77/8 OPC WHA 13
80/1 Pepsi Bottle Cap
80/1 QUEB
80/1 Topps 122

LEDYARD, GRANT
91/2 Bowman 40
92/3 Bowman 27
89/0 BUFF / Blue Shield
89/0 BUFF / Campbell's
90/1 BUFF / Blue Shield
90/1 BUFF / Blue Shield
90/1 BUFF / Campbell's
90/1 BUFF / Campbell's
91/2 BUFF / Blue Shield
91/2 BUFF / Blue Shield
91/2 BUFF / Campbell's
91/2 BUFF / Campbell's
91/2 BUFF / Pepsi
91/2 BUFF / Pepsi
92/3 BUFF / Blue Shield
92/3 BUFF / Blue Shield
94/5 DALL / Southwest
94/5 DALL / Southwest
94/5 DALL / Cap
94/5 DALL / Cap
96/7 DALL / Southwest
96/7 DALL / Southwest
93/4 Donruss 89
94/5 Donruss 312
94/5 Flair 42
93/4 Fleer Ultra 299
94/5 Fleer Ultra 54
95/6 Fleer Ultra 40
93/4 Leaf 394
94/5 Leaf 263
87/8 LOSA
90/1 O-Pee-Chee 406
91/2 O-Pee-Chee 386
92/3 O-Pee-Chee 393
98/9 Pacific 84
00/1 Pacific 282
97/8 Pacific CC 345
87/8 Panini Sticker 273
92/3 Panini Sticker 244
95/6 Panini Sticker 176
91/2 Parkhurst 241
93/4 Parkhurst 321
92/3 Pinnacle 205
93/4 Pinnacle 413
94/5 Pinnacle 204
95/6 Playoff 141
94/5 POG 84
95/6 POG 90
93/4 Power Play 325
94/5 Premier 98
90/1 Pro Set 24
90/1 Score 233
92/3 Score 362
91/2 Score CAN 401
92/3 Score 358
93/4 Score 568
97/8 Score Vanc. 15
92/3 Topps 321
95/6 Topps 157
91/2 To. Stadium 169
92/3 To. Stadium 78
95/6 UD BAP 104, ✍ S104
88/9 WASH
88/9 WASH / Smokey

LEE, BILL
52/3 Anonymous 144

LEE, CASEY
01/2 Kamloops Blazers
01/2 Kamloops Blazers
02/3 Kamloops Blazers
02/3 Kamloops Blazers

LEE, PETER
96/7 DEL 37
78/9 O-Pee-Chee 244
79/0 O-Pee-Chee 45
80/1 O-Pee-Chee 278
81/2 O-Pee-Chee 258
81/2 OPC Sticker 185
83/4 PITT / Heinz
82/3 Post [Pitt.]
83/4 Souhaits Keychain [Penguins]
78/9 Topps 244
79/0 Topps 45
81/2 Topps 114 [East]

LEE, PETER JOHN
98/9 DEL 180

LEE, PETER JOHN
99/0 Eishockey 74

LEE, STEVE
77/8 Kalamazoo Wings
77/8 Kalamazoo Wings

LEEB, BRAD
99 Bowman 89
00/1 Kansas City Blades 18
00/1 Kansas City Blades 18
01/2 Manitoba Moose
01/2 Manitoba Moose
99/0 Omega 240
01/2 PS Titanium 182
95/6 Red Deer Rebels
95/6 Red Deer Rebels

LEEB, GREG
97 Bowman 94
98 Bowman 55
98 Bowman Chrome 55
01/2 Hamilton Bulldogs
98/9 Michigan K-Wings
99/0 Michigan K-Wings
02/3 Pacific Complete 301
95/6 Spokane Chiefs 15
97/8 Spokane Chiefs
00/1 Utah Grizzlies

LEEMAN, GARY
90/1 Bowman 155, -HT 10
91/2 Bowman 161
92/3 Bowman 192
92/3 CALG / IGA 003
92/3 CALG / IGA 003
83 Canada Juniors
98/9 DEL 188
92/3 Fleer Ultra 22
93/4 Fleer Ultra 353
89/0 Kraft 36
90/1 Kraft 27
91/2 Kraft 10
86/7 Kraft Sports 56
93/4 MONT
93/4 MONT
84/5 O-Pee-Chee 305
87/8 O-Pee-Chee 240
88/9 OPC/Topps 11
90/1 OPC/Topps 135
90/1 Topps-TL 13
91/2 O-Pee-Chee 188
92/3 O-Pee-Chee 33
89/0 OPC/Topps 22
91/2 OPC Premier 106
91/2 OPC Premier 134
87/8 OPC Sticker 161-21
88/9 OPC Sticker 178
89/0 opcSticker 168
87/8 Panini Sticker 331
88/9 Panini Sticker 125
89/0 Panini Sticker 133
90/1 Panini Sticker 279
90/1 Panini/TOR 12, H
92/3 Panini Sticker 41
91/2 Parkhurst 173
91/2 Parkhurst 254
92/3 Parkhurst 323
91/2 Pinnacle 31
92/3 Pinnacle 184
93/4 Premier 397
90/1 Pro Set 283
91/2 Pro Set 231
91/2 Pro Set Platinum 115
91/2 Pro Set Platinum 162
81/2 Regina Pats
81/2 Regina Pats
82/3 Regina Pats
82/3 Regina Pats
83/4 Regina Pats
83/4 Regina Pats
90/1 Score 40, / Promo 40
90/1 Sco. Hot Cards 20
91/2 Score 77
91/2 Score CAN 77
92/3 Score 171
93/4 Score 147
92/3 Topps 85
91/2 To. Stadium 158
92/3 To. Stadium 272
93/4 To. Stadium 244
83/4 TORO
84/5 TORO
85/6 TORO
86/7 TORO
86/7 TORO
87/8 TORO / 5x8
87/8 TORO / P.L.A.Y. 10
88/9 TORO / P.L.A.Y. 8
90/1 TORO
90/1 TORO
91/2 TORO / P.L.A.Y. 10
91/2 TORO / P.L.A.Y. 12
90/1 Upper Deck 243, 310
91/2 Upper Deck 272
91/2 Upper Deck 528
92/3 Upper Deck 66
93/4 Upper Deck 96
95/6 UD BAP 73, ✍ S73

LEEMING, BOB
89/0 Windsor Spitfires
89/0 Windsor Spitfires

LEETCH, BRIAN
01/2 Adrenaline 126
01/2 ASG History
01/2 Atomic 64
02/3 Atomic -NPU 5
98/9 Aurora 124
99/0 Aurora 94, Stripe 94
00/1 Aurora 95
02/3 BAP All-Star 49-50, ✂ ASJ, ✂ HSHSJers
98/9 Be A Player 238, H-16, ✍ Aut. 238
99/0 BAP Mem. 18, SL-10, ✂ J-16, ✂ D-17, ✂ TM-6, ✂ TM-21, ✂ TM-50
00/1 BAP Mem. 89, ✂ J-38, ✂ TM-7, ✂ TM-40
01/2 BAP Mem. 290, ✂ ASJ, ✂ ASE, ✂ ASN, ✂ ASD, ✂ AST, ✂ CoO
02/3 BAP Mem. 24, ✂ ASJ30, ✂ ASE11, ✂ ASN11, ✂ ASTJ9, ✂ TM7, /Cup
01/2 BAP Update ✂ PTT5
96/7 Bic.Sports Aces 8-C
97/8 Bicycle K-Spade
95/6 Bicycle Sports Aces 6-Club
90/1 Bowman 215
91/2 Bowman 75
92/3 Bowman 149
92/3 Bowman 232
95/6 Bowman 32, BB14
01/2 Bowman 5
02/3 Bowman 42
98/9 Bowman's Best 25, F7
02/3 Calder 24
99/0 Crown Royale 90
00/1 Crown Royale 70
01/2 Crown Royale 95
02/3 Crown Royale ✂ GWJ 13
93/4 Donruss 221
94/5 Donruss 152, D-2
95/6 Donruss 181, D-3, PP-5
96/7 Donruss 13
97/8 Donruss 156, 230, L2L-3
96/7 Do. Canadian 108
97/8 Do. Canadian 88
95/6 Do. Elite 98
96/7 Do. Elite 125
97/8 Do. Elite 40, 116, C-30
97/8 Do. Preferred 22, 188
97/8 Do. Priority 74, Post-22, Stamp-22
97/8 Do. Studio 86, S-23, P-35
98/9 Dynagon Ice 123
99/0 Dynagon Ice 132
93/4 EA Sports 85
97/8 Esso 29
02/3 Exclusive 115
02/3 First Edition 3, 308, 427R, ✂ Jers.
94/5 Flair 114, SP-5
96/7 Flair 60
94/5 Fleer 135, H-5
96/7 Fleer 70, 140, NT-7
95/6 Fleer Metal 96, HM-8, IS-12
96/7 Fl. Picks 12, F50-25, JE-17
92/3 Fleer Ultra 138, -AW 2
93/4 Fleer Ultra 132
94/5 Fleer Ultra 139, ASG-2, AW-7, SM-6
95/6 Fleer Ultra 104, 390, UV-5
96/7 Fl. Ultra 108, PL-7, UP-10
95 Globe 103
01/2 Heads Up 64, ✂ JQ 14, ✂ JQ 22
02/3 Heads Up 81, ✂ GWQ 29
93/4 Hockey Wit 71
99/0 HoloGrFX 39
95/6 Hoyle / East. 2-Diamond
92/3 Humpty Dumpty
02/3 In The GU 47, 147, ✂ E28, ✂ IE22, ✂ GUJ28, ✂ SJ28, ✂ T11
91/2 Kellogg's / Score 8
90/1 Kraft 28
91/2 Kraft 73
94/5 Kraft / PB
96/7 Kraft / KD
98/9 Kraft / PB
93/4 Leaf 70
94/5 Leaf 403, GLS-6
95/6 Leaf 93, GLS-3
96/7 Leaf 165
97/8 Leaf 117, BS-17
94/5 L. Limited 33
95/6 L. Limited 90
96/7 L. Limited 82
96/7 L. Preferred 42, LS-23
97/8 Limited 70, 179, 182, FG-64
96/7 Maggers 102
91/2 McDonald's Mc-12
92/3 McDonald's McH-05
94/5 McDonald's McD-6
96/7 McDonald's McD-20
98/9 McD's T4
96/7 Metal Univ. 98, IC-9
99/0 Millenium 159, ✍ Aut. 159, ✂ J-26, ✂✍ J-26, ✂ JS-26
89/0 NYRA / Marine
92/3 NYRA
92/3 NYRA
98/9 NYRA
98/9 NYRA
98/9 NHL Power Play
90/1 OPC/Topps 221
91/2 O-Pee-Chee 108
91/2 O-Pee-Chee 269
91/2 Topps - Team Leader 4
92/3 O-Pee-Chee 378
92/3 O-Pee-Chee Box
01/2 O-Pee-Chee 4
02/3 O-Pee-Chee 57
89/0 O-Pee-Chee 321, 326
89/0 OPC/Topps 136
98/9 OPC Chrome 75, B3
90/1 OPC Premier 65
91/2 OPC Premier 183
91/2 OPC Premier 77
88/9 OPC Sticker 189
89/0 opcSticker 215-76, 240-103, 39-181, / FS 11
97/8 Omega 147
98/9 Omega 158
99/0 Omega 151
98/9 Pacific 297
99/0 Pacific 272
00/1 Pacific 265
01/2 Pacific 261, 435
02/3 Pacific 252
02/3 Pacific Complete 428
97/8 Pacific CC 2, SS-5C
97/8 Pa. Crown Roy. 86, BOS-15
98/9 Pa. Crown Roy. 89
97/8 Pa. Dynagon 80, DD-10B, T-19, BKS-62, BKS-108
97/8 Pa. Invincible 88, AZ-15, R-129
97/8 Pa. Paramount 118
98/9 Pa. Paramount 155
99/0 Pa. Paramount 152, IAI-18
00/1 Pa. Paramount 163
97/8 Pa. Revolution 89
98/9 Pa. Revolution 94
98/9 Panini Photocard
88/9 Panini Sticker 301
89/0 Panini Sticker 279, 378
90/1 Panini Sticker 95
91/2 Panini Sticker 284
92/3 Panini Sticker 239
93/4 Panini Sticker 96
94/5 Panini Sticker 88
95/6 Panini Sticker 110
96/7 Panini Sticker 102, 148
97/8 Panini Sticker 84, 120
98/9 Panini Sticker 83
99/0 Panini Sticker 98
00/1 Panini Sticker 60
95 Panini Worlds 300
91/2 Parkhurst 119
92/3 Parkhurst 438
91/2 Parkhurst 464
91/2 Parkhurst 471
91/2 Parkhurst PHC8
92/3 Parkhurst 110
92/3 Parkhurst 467
93/4 Parkhurst 131
94/5 Parkhurst 151, V15
95/6 Parkhurst 144, CCP-14, PP-21
00/1 Parkhurst P-29
01/2 Parkhurst 28, ✂ PJ27, ✂ PS27, ✂ M6, ✂ H7, ✂ T3, ✂ T24
02/3 Parkhurst 82, -HHN 9, ✂ GJ3, ✂ SJ3, ✂ HHSJers, ✂ TT1
95/6 Parkhurst 24-karat Gold
02/3 Parkhurst Retro 96
91/2 Pinnacle 136
91/2 Pinnacle B-3
92/3 Pinnacle 15
92/3 Pinnacle TP 3
93/4 Pinnacle 275
93/4 Pinnacle TP 2
94/5 Pinnacle 155, TP4, WE15
95/6 Pinnacle 133, FS-6
96/7 Pinnacle 193
97/8 Pinnacle 92, 195, TP-3
96/7 Pi. Be A Player 55, ✍ Aut. 55
97/8 Pi. BeeHive 28
97/8 Pi. Certified 36, CT-6
97/8 Pi. Inside 20
97/8 Pi. Mint 19
95/6 Pi. Summit 23, GMC-4
96/7 Pi. Summit 96
97/8 Pi. Totally 36
95/6 Pi. Zenith 32
96/7 Pi. Zenith 85
95/6 Playoff 68, 174, 283
94/5 POG 170, 260, 334
95/6 POG 186
97/8 Pi. Post 4
93/4 Power Play 160
93/4 Power Play SA 6
93/4 Premier 25
93/4 Premier 505
94/5 Premier 37, 450, 485, 500
00/1 Premier Plus TT15
99/0 Prism 91
00/1 Private Stock 65, PS-37, ✂ GUG-75-76
01/2 Pr. Stock 62
02/3 Pr. Stock Reserve 68
00/1 PS Titanium 61, ✂ GUG-36, ✂ GUG-114
01/2 PS Titanium 93, ✂ DSJ 26, ✂ DSJ 29
01/2 PS Titanium Draft ✂ 60
00/1 PS Titanium Draft ✂ 66
95/6 Pro Magnet 97
90/1 Pro Set 201, 373
91/2 Pro Set 159
91/2 Pro Set 309
92/3 Pro Set 112
92/3 Pro Set CC4
91/2 Pro Set Platinum 284
91/2 Pro Set Platinum 79
99/0 Revolution 97, / CSC 97
00/1 Revolution 96, ✂ GWJ-8
90/1 Score 225
90/1 Sco. Hot Cards 93
91/2 Score 333
91/2 Score 343
91/2 Score 5
91/2 Score CAN 363
91/2 Score CAN 373
91/2 Score CAN 5
92/3 Score 375
92/3 Score 416
92/3 Score 491
92/3 Score 522
92/3 Score USAG 8
93/4 Score 235
93/4 Score DT 6
93/4 Score TF 13
94/5 Score 184, DT4
95/6 Score 124
96/7 Score 179
97/8 Score 126
97/8 Score NYRa. 2
90/1 Sco. Young Stars 2
92/3 Seasons 28
94/5 Select 24, FL-3
95/6 Select CE 27
96/7 Select CE 76
94 Semic 113
94 Semic 339
95 Semic 105
89 Semic Sticker 161
91 Semic Sticker 131
92 Semic Sticker 150
93 Semic Sticker 171
96/7 SB 7-Eleven Phonecard
94/5 Sig. Rookies CF3, ✍ CF3
94/5 SR Gold Standard L1
00/1 Signature 219, F-20, ✍ Aut. 188, ✂ DD-1, ✂ J-26, ✂ HSHSJers
01/2 Signature C-5, ✍ Aut. LBL, ✂ DD2, ✂ GUE37, ✂ GJ39, ✂ GSJ39, ✂ ITN37, ✂ IS10
02/3 Signature 177, GS-9, ✍ 177, ✂ DW4, ✂ SGJ28, ✂ TQ4
95/6 SBx Emotion 115, Xci-6
95/6 SBx Impact 110
96/7 SBx Impact 81, F-14
02/3 Slam Card
94/5 SP 74
95/6 SP 94, E20
96/7 SP 101
97/8 SP Authentic 100, I39
98/9 SP Authentic 57, SS17
99/0 SP Authentic 58
00/1 SP Authentic 57
02/3 SP Authentic ✂ SP
00/1 SP GU ✂ TotG
02/3 SP Game-Used ✂ AF, ✂ PC, ✂ PH
02/3 Sports Vault 88
96/7 SPx 29
97/8 SPx 33
99/0 SPx 97
01/2 SPx ✂ DT
02/3 SPx ✂ WM, ✂ M
98/9 SPx Finite 111
98/9 SPx Prospects 39, PS6
00/1 Stadium 90
99/0 Stadium 12, Chrome 11
00/1 Stadium 194
01/2 Stadium 34
02/3 Stadium 87, ✂ FC8, ✂ PC8
94/5 Starting Lineup
96/7 SLU
98/9 SLU
95/6 Super Sticker 79, DC-7
96/7 Team Out!
92/3 Topps 261
92/3 Topps 293
95/6 Topps 75, HGA-1, M-16, PF-2
98/9 Topps 75, B3, ✍ CAI
99/0 Topps 30, AT6, IM10, SC15
00/1 Topps 153
01/2 Topps 4
02/3 Topps 57
99/0 To. Chrome 30, AT6, IM10
00/1 To. Chrome 109
01/2 To. Chrome 4
02/3 To. Chrome 57
94/5 Topps Finest 49, BBB-12, BBM-4
95/6 To. Finest 41, 115
98/9 To. Finest 137
95 Topps Finest Bronze 14
98/9 T. Gold Label 85
99/0 To. Gold Label 29
00/1 To. Gold Label 91, B9
00/1 To. Heritage 56
01/2 To. Heritage 33, 126, ✂ GWJ
02/3 To. Heritage 89, ✂ CC, ✂ GS
02/3 To. Limited 57
96/7 To. Picks FT5, ID1
99/0 To. Prmr. Plus 61, CAC10
01/2 To. Reserve 44, ✂ TR
91/2 To. Stadium 201
92/3 To. Stadium 248
92/3 To. Stadium 73
93/4 To. Stadium 88
94/5 To. Stadium 55, 150, F-7
95/6 To. Stadium 30, M8, N5
92 TSC Members Only
93/4 TSC Members Only 24
94/5 TSC Members Only 33
95/6 TSC Members Only 33
00/1 To. Stars 72
95/6 T. Super Skills 19
02/3 T. Total 64
98/9 UD Choice 129, 238, BH29, SQ7
00/1 UD Heroes 78
01/2 UD PlayMakers Ltd 65
00/1 UD Reserve 58
00/1 Ultimate Mem. ✂ U-26, ✂ J-26, ✂ N-4, ✂ N-9, ✂ S-26
01/2 Ultimate Mem. ✂ ASGH, ✂ CT, ✂ Corn., ✂ Emb., ✂ Jers., ✂ S&J, ✂ ITN, ✂ NP, ✂ RT, ✂ UC, ✂ WTF, ✍ Aut.
02/3 Ultimate Mem. ✂ A8, ✂ CSTW, ✂ Emb, ✂ ITN, ✂ LA, ✂ Num, ✂ PS, ✍ RAut
99/0 Ult. Victory 59
90/1 Upper Deck 253, 315, 485
91/2 Upper Deck 153
91/2 Upper Deck 35
91/2 Upper Deck 610
91/2 Upper Deck 612
92/3 Upper Deck 284
92/3 Upper Deck 434
92/3 Upper Deck 640
92/3 Upper Deck WG15
93/4 Upper Deck 348, NL4, SP-102
94/5 Upper Deck 231, 444, C28,H11, R13, R45, R51, SP-50
95/6 Upper Deck 236, 487, AS-7, F-18, H-33, R-18, SE-55
96/7 Upper Deck 300, X23, SS7B
97/8 Upper Deck 316, SS5, SG22, S28, T4B, ✂ GJ14
98/9 Upper Deck 322, LS13
99/0 Upper Deck 258, HOF9
00/1 Upper Deck 344, D8, ✂ DGJ
01/2 Upper Deck 117, ✂ PoaNT
02/3 Upper Deck 363, ✂ DM, ✂ FF, ✂ S, ✂ UDPL
95/6 UD ASG MVP25
96/7 UD All-Star YCTG AR19
02/3 UD Artistic 60, R60, UD4, / Art
93/4 Upper Deck Be A Player 9
94/5 UD BAP R46, R149, ✍ 46
96/7 UD Black Diam. 12
97/8 UD Black Diam. 33, PC10
98/9 UD Black Diam. 56
99/0 UD Black Diam. 57
01/2 UD Challenge - UC
02/3 UD Classic 66, ✂ HR
95/6 UD CC 247
96/7 UD CC 169, 303, 325, UD30, C27, CR27
97/8 UD Coll. Choice 162, SQ20
97/8 UD Diam. Vision 12
98/9 UD G. Reserve 322
99/0 UD G. Reserve 258, ✍ UDA
99/0 UD Gretzky Excl. 65
01/2 UD Honor Roll 17, 47, -DiPuck, ✂ GAJ
02/3 UD Honor 90
96/7 UD Ice 43
97/8 UD Ice 76, L10A
00/1 UD Ice ✍ CCA
00/1 UD Legends 92
02/3 UD Locker 5
98/9 UD MVP 133
99/0 UD MVP 132
00/1 UD MVP 117
01/2 UD MVP 124
02/3 UD MVP 120
99/0 UD MVP Cup 120, GC, ✍ PS
99/0 UD Ovation 38
02/3 UD Piece 61, AC19, ✂ PH
01/2 UD Premier ✂ D
99/0 UD Retro 51, G1B
02/3 UD Rookie 68, ✂ 154c, ✂ 155b, ✂ 162a
01/2 UD SCup Champs 82
01/2 UD Top Shelf 108
02/3 UD Top Shelf ✂ CP, ✂ HH, ✂ SH, ✂ ST
00/1 UD Vintage 236
01/2 UD Vintage 169, 173
02/3 UD Vintage 173, 300, GB 173
00/1 Vanguard 65
01/2 Vanguard 63
99/0 Victory 187, 192, 345
00/1 Victory 154
01/2 Victory 233, 410
02/3 Victory 141
01/2 Waving the Flag 24
99/0 WGretzky 114
96 Wien 160
97/8 Zenith 13, Z65

LEFEBVRE, FRÉDÉRIC
88/9 Richelieu Riverains
88/9 Richelieu Riverains
90/1 7th..Sketch LHJMQ 194

LEFEBVRE, GUILLAUME
01/2 BAP Mem. 425
02/3 Choice Prospects 25
02/3 O-Pee-Chee 309
01/2 Parkhurst 338
02/3 Philadelphia Phantoms
02/3 Philadelphia Phantoms
94 Québec Pee Wee 1329
00/1 Rouyn-Noranda 8
00/1 Rouyn-Noranda 8
02/3 Topps 309
02/3 To. Limited 309
01/2 UD Mask 161
02/3 UD MVP 214

LEFEBVRE, GUY
90/1 7th..Sketch LHJMQ 96

LEFEBVRE, JEAN-SEBASTIEN
91/2 7th...Sketch LHJMQ 144

LEFEBVRE, MARC
99/0 Ottawa 67's
99/0 Ottawa 67's
00/1 Ottawa 67's 9
00/1 Ottawa 67's 9

LEFEBVRE, MARTIN
90/1 7th..Sketch LHJMQ 186

LEFEBVRE, NICOLAS
90/1 7th..Sketch LHJMQ 84, 248
91/2 7th...Sketch LHJMQ 266

LEFEBVRE, PATRICE
98/9 EBK IHL All-Star
95/6 Edge Ice 153
99/0 Eishockey 8
93/4 Las Vegas Thunder
93/4 Las Vegas Thunder
94/5 Las Vegas Thunder
94/5 Las Vegas Thunder
95/6 Las Vegas Thunder
95/6 Las Vegas Thunder
96/7 Las Vegas Thunder
96/7 Las Vegas Thunder
97/8 Las Vegas Thunder 15
97/8 Las Vegas Thunder 15
98/9 Las Vegas Thunder
98/9 Las Vegas Thunder
90/1 ProCards 337
00/1 UD DEL 84, A2

LEFEBVRE, STÉPHANE
83/4 Nova Scotia Voyageurs
83/4 Nova Scotia Voyageurs
93/4 Slapshot / Guelph 19

LEFEBVRE, SYLVAIN
98/9 Be A Player 184, ✍ Aut. 184
90/1 Bowman 48
91/2 Bowman 332
92/3 Bowman 307
93/4 Donruss 331
95/6 Donruss 288
96/7 Donruss 81
94/5 Flair 149
94/5 Fleer 180
93/4 Fleer Ultra 430
94/5 Fleer Ultra 176, 360
95/6 Fleer Ultra 222
01/2 Heads Up ✂ JQ 25
94/5 Leaf 267
94/5 Leaf 507
95/6 Leaf 292
96/7 Leaf 98
89/0 MONT
89/0 MONT / Kraft
90/1 MONT
90/1 MONT
91/2 MONT
91/2 MONT
90/1 OPC/Topps 159
91/2 O-Pee-Chee 489
92/3 O-Pee-Chee 303
92/3 OPC Premier 108
99/0 Pacific 109
01/2 Pacific 262
97/8 Pa. Invincible R-54
00/1 Pa. Paramount 64
90/1 Panini Sticker 59
90/1 Panini/MTL 15
91/2 Panini Sticker 196
91/2 Parkhurst 307
92/3 Parkhurst 416
95/6 Parkhurst 321
93/4 Pinnacle 317
94/5 Pinnacle 379
95/6 Pinnacle 131
96/7 Pi. Be A Player 54, ✍ Aut. 54
96/7 Pi. Summit 149
95/6 Playoff 26
93/4 Power Play 450
93/4 Premier 331
94/5 Premier 364
00/1 PS Titanium ✂ GUG 115
90/1 Pro Set 472
88/9 ProCards / Sherbrooke
94/5 QUEB / Burger King
94/5 QUEB / Burger King
91/2 Score CAN 245
92/3 Score 405
93/4 Score 359
95/6 Score 192
96/7 Score 226
97/8 Score Colo. 16
92/3 Topps 341
95/6 Topps 279
91/2 To. Stadium 208
92/3 To. Stadium 367
93/4 To. Stadium 48
92/3 TORO / Kodak
92/3 TORO / Kodak
93/4 TORO / Abalene
93/4 TORO / Abalene
93/4 TORO / Black's 12
93/4 TORO / Black's 12
90/1 Upper Deck 421
91/2 Upper Deck 171
94/5 Upper Deck 335
95/6 Upper Deck 342
94/5 UD BAP R66, ✍ 41

LEFLEY, BRYAN
76/7 COLR / Hockey Talk
72/3 Eddie Sargent 139
74/5 Loblaws
72/3 O-Pee-Chee 252
76/7 O-Pee-Chee 159
77/8 O-Pee-Chee 297
78/9 O-Pee-Chee 274

LEFLEY, CHUCK
72/3 Dernière Heure
73/4 Dernière Heure
74/5 Loblaws
74/5 Loblaws Update
72/3 MONT / Pro Star
73/4 MONT / Pro Star
74/5 MONT
73/4 O-Pee-Chee 44
74/5 O-Pee-Chee 178
75/6 O-Pee-Chee 282
76/7 O-Pee-Chee 393
76/7 O-Pee-Chee 63
77/8 O-Pee-Chee 340
80/1 O-Pee-Chee 395
73/4 Topps 154
74/5 Topps 178
75/6 Topps 282
76/7 Topps 63

LEFRANÇOIS, GILBERT
99/0 Shawinigan 15
99/0 Shawinigan 15
00/1 Shawinigan 9
00/1 Shawinigan 9

LEGACÉ, MANNY
01/2 BAP Mem. 132
02/3 BAP Mem. ✂ SCC9
01/2 BT Pipes 28, -Mask, ✂ DM, ✂ Jers., ✂ S&J, ✂ GG, ✂ GT, ✂ HSHSJers
02/3 Between the Pipes 28, ✂ DM12
93/4 Canada Nationals
93/4 Classic 24
93/4 Cla. 4 Sport 227

93/4 Cla. Prospects IA5
93/4 Cla. Prospects LP16
02/3 First Edition 85, ✂ Jers.
95/6 Future Legends 9, PC-3
97/8 Las Vegas Thunder 2
97/8 Las Vegas Thunder 2
98/9 Long Beach Ice Dogs
98/9 Long Beach Ice Dogs
99/0 Manitoba Moose
99/0 Manitoba Moose
01/2 O-Pee-Chee 136
02/3 O-Pee-Chee 153
01/2 Pacific 145, SC 7
02/3 Pacific 131
02/3 Pacific Complete 109
98/9 Pa. Crown Roy. 63, -RC 4
00/1 Parkhurst P-208
01/2 Parkhurst 155
02/3 Parkhurst Retro 116
93/4 Premier - Canada 2
00/1 PS Titanium 32
94/5 Score CT20
90/1 7th..Sketch OHL 263
91/2 7th...Sketch OHL 217
01/2 Signature 10, ✍ Aut. 10
02/3 Signature 104, ✍ 104
93/4 Slapshot / Niagara Falls 25
96/7 Springfield Falcons
96/7 Springfield Falcons
01/2 Topps 136
02/3 Topps 153
02/3 To. Heritage ✂ CP, ✂ CPB
02/3 To. Limited 153
02/3 T. Total 129
02/3 Ultimate Mem. ✂ SCDE, ✂ SCDGJ, ✂ SCDN
92/3 Upper Deck 585
99/0 Upper Deck 66
02/3 Upper Deck 313
94/5 UD Canada Junior 2
99/0 UD G. Reserve 66
02/3 UD Mask 30, 31
99/0 UD MVP 99
01/2 UD Vintage 268
01/2 Victory 131

LEGAULT, ALEXANDRE
90/1 7th..Sketch LHJMQ 7
91/2 7th...Sketch LHJMQ 193
91 7th..Sketch Mem.Cup 51

LEGAULT, JAY
97 Bowman 148, ✍ Aut.
98 Bowman 20
98 Bowman Chrome 20
99/0 Cincinnati M'Ducks
99/0 Cincinnati M'Ducks
95/6 Slapshot 239

LEGAULT, JAYME
01/2 Milwaukee Admirals
01/2 Milwaukee Admirals

LEGAULT, MARC
91/2 7th...Sketch LHJMQ 211

LEGE, ROGER
45-54 Quaker Oats

LEGER, BOB
52/3 Bas du Fleuve 58
52/3 Laval Dairy Update 95
52/3 St. Lawrence 102

LEGER, GERMAIN
51/2 Laval Dairy 26

LEGER, JIM
00/1 WBS Penguins
00/1 WBS Penguins

LEGER, ROGER
45-64 BeeHive-2 [Mont.]
52/3 La Patrie
43-47 Parade Sportive
52/3 St. Lawrence 9

LEGGE, BARRY
80/1 Pepsi Bottle Cap
80/1 WINN

LEGGE, JOSH
00/1 Owen Sound Attack 4
00/1 Owen Sound Attack 4

LEGGE, RANDY
76/7 San Diego Mariners
76/7 San Diego Mariners

LEGGETT, ALAN
91/2 ProCards 315
93/4 Raleigh Icecaps
93/4 Raleigh Icecaps

LEGGETT, CASEY
99/0 Québec Remparts 22
99/0 Québec Remparts 22
97/8 Rimouski Océanic
97/8 Rimouski Océanic

LEGRIS, HECTOR
52/3 Bas du Fleuve 39

LEGWAND, DAVID
01/2 Adrenaline 106
01/2 Atomic 55
99/0 Aurora 80
00/1 Aurora 78, Pins. 78, ✍ Aut. 78
99/0 BAP Mem. 236
00/1 BAP Mem. 263
01/2 BAP Mem. 128
99 Bowman 147, SC13
01/2 Bowman 160, ✂ FFJ, ✂ FFS, ✂ FFDS, ✂ FFR, ✍ YSA
02/3 Bowman 96
98 Bowman 14, 147, ✍ A11
98 Bowman Chrome 14, 147
98/9 Bowman's Best 136
98/9 Collection Souvenir 23
99/0 Crown Royale 76, IE-15
00/1 Crown Royale 60, ✂ JR-4
01/2 Crown Royale 81
02/3 Crown Royale 55
99/0 Dynagon Ice 109
02/3 Exclusive 100, ✂ GWJ 15
02/3 First Edition 106, ✂ Jers.
01/2 Heads Up 54, BTI 13, ✂ JQ 13
02/3 Heads Up 69, ✂ GWQ 16
99/0 HoloGrFX 31, ✍ Aut.
99/0 McDonald's McD-17
00/1 McDonald's GCDC 3
99/0 Millenium 136, C-17, ✍ Aut. 136
99/0 NHL Power Play [x3]
01/2 O-Pee-Chee 244
02/3 O-Pee-Chee 25
98/9 OPC Chrome 234
99/0 Omega 130, 5ST-3, G-5
99/0 Pacific 229, GC-20
00/1 Pacific 223, ✍ Aut. 223
01/2 Pacific 220
02/3 Pacific 212
02/3 Pacific Complete 286
99/0 Pa. Paramount 127
00/1 Pa. Paramount 136
99/0 Panini Sticker 268
00/1 Parkhurst P-87
01/2 Parkhurst 47
02/3 Parkhurst 74, ✂ TT10
02/3 Parkhurst Retro 168, ✂ RF17
00/1 Premier Plus 4, PA9, PP5
99/0 Prism 76,IP-4
00/1 Private Stock 55, PS-30, PSNW-12
01/2 Pr. Stock 53, ✂ GUG 58
02/3 Pr. Stock Reserve ✂ 128
00/1 PS Titanium 51, ✂ GUG-104
01/2 PS Titanium 79
02/3 PS Titanium 60, ✂ GWJ 37
00/1 PS Titanium Draft ✂ 55
93 Québec Pee Wee 1760
94 Québec Pee Wee 888
02/3 Quest for the Cup 54
00/1 Revolution 82
00/1 Signature 101, F-17, ✍ Aut. 6
01/2 Signature 28, ✍ Aut. 28, ✂ FP17
02/3 Signature GS-30, ✂ YP4, ✂ FJ17
99/0 SP Authentic 46, TH5, ✍ SotT
00/1 SP Authentic 49, ✍ SotT
01/2 SP Authentic 45, 113
02/3 SP Authentic 51
00/1 SP GU 35, ✂ TotG
02/3 SP Game-Used ✂ PC, ✂ PH
02/3 Sports Vault 256
99/0 SPx 82, 177, P15, X5, XT19
00/1 SPx 36
01/2 SPx 35
02/3 SPx ✂ WM
98/9 SPx Prospects 88
99/0 Stadium 200, Chrome 50, Big 20
00/1 Stadium 32
01/2 Stadium 29
02/3 Stadium 52, ✂ YSS8, ✂ YSD2
98/9 Topps 234
99/0 Topps 248
00/1 Topps 24, ✂ GWS
01/2 Topps 244
02/3 Topps 25, ✍ SF
99/0 To. Chrome 248
00/1 To. Chrome 23
01/2 To. Chrome 20
02/3 To. Chrome 25
98/9 To. Finest F1
99/0 To. Gold Label 86, FG12
00/1 To. Gold Label 78, NG10
00/1 To. Heritage 47
01/2 To. Heritage 20
02/3 To. Heritage 60
02/3 To. Limited 25
99/0 To. Prmr. Plus 135, PR7, TNO6, ✍ SB1, ✂ GP
00/1 To. Stars 27, PP3, ✂ GG
02/3 T. Total 58
98/9 UD Choice 302
00/1 UD Heroes 68
01/2 UD PlayMakers Ltd 55
00/1 UD Reserve 47
99/0 Ult. Victory 47
99/0 Upper Deck 73, 160, CT17, N8, SS10
00/1 Upper Deck 97
01/2 Upper Deck 96
02/3 Upper Deck 343, ✂ BF, ✂ CG, ✂ HS
02/3 UD Artistic 50, R50, / Art
97/8 UD Black Diam. 35
98/9 UD Black Diam. 115
99/0 UD Black Diam. 49, D9
00/1 UD Black Diam. 32
99/0 UD C. Legends 77
02/3 UD Classic ✂ HR
99/0 UD G. Reserve 73, 160, ✍ UDA
99/0 UD Gretzky Excl. 83
01/2 UD Honor Roll ✂ GAJ
02/3 UD Honor 42
00/1 UD Ice 23, ✂ IGJ
00/1 UD Legends 74, 75
01/2 UD Mask 53
99/0 UD MVP 110, 21st-1, DR5
00/1 UD MVP 98, ✍ PS
01/2 UD MVP 104
99/0 UD MVP Cup 97, CC5, ✍ PS
99/0 UD Ovation 32
99/0 UD PowerDeck 13
02/3 UD Premier 32
00/1 UD Pros&Prosp. 47
99/0 UD Retro 43
02/3 UD Rookie 55
01/2 UD Top Shelf 24
02/3 UD Top Shelf 49, ✂ R, ✂ ST
00/1 UD Vintage 202, 208, 209
01/2 UD Vintage 140, 148
02/3 UD Vintage 145, GB 145
00/1 Vanguard 54
01/2 Vanguard 54
02/3 Vanguard 59
99/0 Victory 154, 156
00/1 Victory 126, 128, 308
01/2 Victory 201
02/3 Victory 118
99/0 WGretzky 90, ✍ SG

LEHIKOINEN, ARI
80/1 Mallasjuoma 139

LEHIKOINEN, TERO
92/3 Jyvas Hyva 79

LEHKONEN, ISMO
80/1 Mallasjuoma 55

LEHKONEN, TIMO
91/2 Jyvas Hyva 7
92/3 Jyvas Hyva 19
93/4 Sisu 358
93/4 Sisu 375
94/5 Sisu 219

LEHMAN, HUGHIE
83 HHOF Postcard N7
83&87 HHOF 202
60/1 Topps 38
61/2 Topps - Stamp
19 Vancouver Millionaires
19 Vancouver Millionaires

LEHMAN, JODY
02/3 Coventry Blaze
02/3 Coventry Blaze

LEHMANN, TOMMY
94/5 Leaf Elit Set 72
95/6 Leaf Elit Set 152, 159
90/1 Semic Elitserien 89
91/2 Semic Elitserien 18
92/3 Semic Elitserien 239
95/6 UD Elitserien 15

LEHNER, JOSEF
95/6 DEL 53
96/7 DEL 252
98/9 DEL 322
95 Panini Worlds 57

LEHOUX, GUY
98/9 DEL 215
99/0 Eishockey 200
91/2 ProCards 350
91 7th..Sketch Mem.Cup 55
92/3 St. John's Maple Leafs
92/3 St. John's Maple Leafs
93/4 St. John's Maple Leafs
93/4 St. John's Maple Leafs
94/5 St. John's Maple Leafs
94/5 St. John's Maple Leafs
95/6 St. John's Maple Leafs
95/6 St. John's Maple Leafs
96/7 St. John's Maple Leafs
96/7 St. John's Maple Leafs
01/2 UD DEL 204

LEHOUX, HUGO
00/1 Halifax Moosehead
00/1 Halifax Moosehead
99/0 Halifax Mooseheads
99/0 Halifax Mooseheads

LEHOUX, JASON
00/1 Albany River Rats
00/1 Albany River Rats
01/2 Albany River Rats
01/2 Albany River Rats
02/3 Albany River Rats
02/3 Albany River Rats
99/0 Hull Olympiques BN
99/0 Hull Olympiques BN
99/0 Hull Olympiques 14
99/0 Hull Olympiques 14
96/7 Rimouski Océanic
96/7 Rimouski Océanic
99/0 Rouyn-Noranda
99/0 Rouyn-Noranda
99/0 Rouyn-Noranda

LEHOUX, YANICK
00/1 Baie-Comeau 12
00/1 Baie-Comeau 12
01/2 Baie-Comeau 10
01/2 Baie-Comeau 10
02/3 Manchester Monarchs
02/3 Manchester Monarchs
99/0 UD Prospects 56
00/1 UD Prospects 77

LEHTERÄ, TERO
98/9 Cardset Leij. 29
99/0 Cardset 270
00/1 Cardset 214
02/3 Cardset 211
98/9 Fort Wayne Komets
98/9 Fort Wayne Komets
95 Hartwall Karjala
97/8 Hockey-Box
92/3 Jyvas Hyva 109
93/4 Jyvas Hyva 197
94/5 Leaf Elit Set 200, FA-10
95 Panini Worlds 176
95 Semic 27
93/4 Sisu 272
94/5 Sisu 9, FOI-10, ND-6
95/6 Sisu 257, G-16
96/7 Sisu 49
95/6 Sisu Limited 62
91/2 Upper Deck WJC 32
96 Wien 17

LEHTI, PERTTI
78/9 SM-Liiga 220

LEHTINEN, ARTO
71/2 Williams Finnish 306

LEHTINEN, JERE
98/9 Aurora 57
99/0 Aurora 46
98/9 Be A Player 44, ✍ Aut. 44
99/0 BAP Mem. 48
01/2 BAP Mem. 131
97/8 Bicycle 2-Club
95/6 Bowman 150
01/2 Bowman 91
02/3 Bowman 80
98/9 Bowman's Best 76
98/9 Cardset Top. 1, DT 5
99/0 Cardset TT, AH K-ruutu
00/1 Cardset 357
02/3 Cardset 212
99/0 Challenger 26
92/3 Classic 31
94/5 Classic 72, T18
93/4 Cla. Prospects IA16
99/0 Crown Royale 45
01/2 Crown Royale 47
96/7 DALL / Southwest
96/7 DALL / Southwest
97/8 DALL / Score 188
97/8 DALL / Score 188
00/1 DALL / Southwest
00/1 DALL / Southwest
01/2 DALL / Southwest
01/2 DALL / Southwest
02/3 DALL / Southwest
02/3 DALL / Southwest
95/6 Donruss 332
96/7 Donruss RR 4
97/8 Donruss 30
96/7 Do. Canadian 111
96/7 Do. Elite 77, A-10
97/8 Do. Elite 68
97/8 Do. Preferred 65
97/8 Do. Priority 63
98/9 Dynagon Ice 58
99/0 Dynagon Ice 67, ASP-10
01/2 EASports
02/3 Exclusive 56
95/6 Fleer Metal 183, IS-13
96/7 Fl. Picks 144
95/6 Fleer Ultra 347
95 Hartwall Karjala
01/2 Heads Up ✂ JQ 24
02/3 Heads Up ✂ GWQ 33
92/3 Jyvas Hyva 107
93/4 Jyvas Hyva 322
96/7 Leaf 201
97/8 Leaf 98
95 Leaf Latkaliiga 1
95/6 L. Limited 39
96/7 L. Limited 77
96/7 L. Preferred 47, LS-63
97/8 Limited 135
99/0 Millenium 81, ✍ Aut. 81
01/2 O-Pee-Chee 114
02/3 O-Pee-Chee 162
97/8 Omega 71
98/9 Omega 72
99/0 Omega 73
98/9 Pacific 179
99/0 Pacific 123
00/1 Pacific 134, 435
01/2 Pacific 128
02/3 Pacific 113
02/3 Pacific Complete 117
98/9 Pa. Crown Roy. 40
97/8 Pa. Invincible R-61
97/8 Pa. Paramount 59
98/9 Pa. Paramount 66
99/0 Pa. Paramount 74
00/1 Pa. Paramount 77
97/8 Pa. Revolution 42
98/9 Pa. Revolution 43
96/7 Panini Sticker 175
97/8 Panini Sticker 145
98/9 Panini Sticker 120, 226
99/0 Panini Sticker 7
95/6 Parkhurst 265, 518
00/1 Parkhurst P-184
02/3 Parkhurst 195
02/3 Parkhurst Retro 101
97/8 Pinnacle 118
97/8 Pi. Be A Player 123, ✍ Aut. 123
97/8 Pi. Inside 187
95/6 Pi. Summit 173
96/7 Pi. Summit 153
95/6 Pi. Zenith 145
96/7 Pi. Zenith 51
00/1 Private Stock ✂ GUG 38
00/1 PS Titanium ✂ GUG 87
01/2 PS Titanium 44
00/1 PS Titanium Draft ✂ 32
02/3 Quest for the Cup 28
99/0 Revolution 47
96/7 Score 246
97/8 Score 188
94 Semic 30
95 Semic 20, 232
00/1 Signature 62, ✍ Aut. 123
93/4 Sisu 47
94/5 Sisu 20, 155, 157, 387
95/6 Sisu 164, 397, G-17, SS-7
95/6 Sisu Limited 9, PP
95/6 SBx Impact 195
95/6 SP 41
97/8 SP Authentic 48
98/9 SP Authentic 27
99/0 SPx 51
98/9 SPx Finite 28
99/0 Stadium 148
95 Suomen Beckett Card 2
99/0 Topps 226, PP6, TW3
00/1 Topps 195
01/2 Topps 114
02/3 Topps 162
99/0 To. Chrome 226, PP6
00/1 To. Chrome 129
01/2 To. Chrome 114
02/3 To. Chrome 97
95/6 To. Finest 53
02/3 To. Limited 162
96/7 To. Picks RS2
99/0 To. Prmr. Plus 75
95/6 To. Stadium ER199
02/3 T. Total 138
98/9 UD Choice 68
00/1 UD Heroes 41
92/3 Upper Deck 615
95/6 Upper Deck 398
96/7 Upper Deck 49
97/8 Upper Deck 52, SG26, T8C
98/9 Upper Deck 258
99/0 Upper Deck 215
00/1 Upper Deck 60
01/2 Upper Deck 285
02/3 Upper Deck 60, ✂ S
95/6 UD BAP 175, ✍ S175
96/7 UD Black Diam. 87
97/8 UD Black Diam. 40
02/3 UD Classic ✂ HR (x2)
96/7 UD CC 75
97/8 UD Coll. Choice 74
98/9 UD G. Reserve 258
99/0 UD G. Reserve 215
01/2 UD Honor Roll DF2
01/2 UD Mask 29
98/9 UD MVP 67
99/0 UD MVP 63
01/2 UD MVP 58
02/3 UD MVP 58
01/2 UD SCup Champs 54
00/1 UD Vintage 113
01/2 UD Vintage 84
02/3 UD Vintage 84
00/1 Vanguard ✂ DGJ 15
01/2 Vanguard ✂ DGM 22
99/0 Victory 93
00/1 Victory 79
01/2 Victory 119
02/3 Victory 67, -NP24
99/0 WGretzky 59
96 Wien 20, 37, AS4

LEHTINEN, MIKA
98/9 Cardset 236
99/0 Cardset 329
00/1 Cardset 339
94/5 Sisu 321
95/6 Sisu 325
96/7 Sisu 136

LEHTINEN, SAMI
99/0 Cardset 92, Puck 4
00/1 Cardset 69, Mask. 3

LEHTIO, RAUNO
66/7 Champion 178
65/6 Hellas 100
70/1 Kuvajulkaisut 245
71/2 Williams Finnish 212

LEHTIO, RISTO
66/7 Champion 186
65/6 Hellas 101

LEHTO, ANTTI
80/1 Mallasjuoma 58

LEHTO, JONI
96/7 DEL 66
91/2 ProCards 455
91/2 Richmond Renegades
91/2 Richmond Renegades
89/0 7th..Sketch OHL 53
90/1 7th..Sketch OHL 86
94/5 Sisu 343
95/6 Sisu 162, 299, DT-4, P-3
96/7 Sisu 176, SH-9
95/6 Sisu Limited 31, SAS-5
96 Wien 33

LEHTO, KAI
72/3 Williams Finnish 308

LEHTO, MARKUS
80/1 Oshawa Generals
80/1 Oshawa Generals

LEHTO, MIKA
98/9 Cardset 252, Leij. 10
99/0 Cardset 336
00/1 Cardset 168
02/3 Cardset 213, 300

LEHTO, PETTERI
80/1 Mallasjuoma 197

LEHTOLAINEN, PEKKA
66/7 Champion 187
65/6 Hellas 104

LEHTONEN,
97/8 Hockey-Box

LEHTONEN, ANTERO
80/1 Mallasjuoma 176
78/9 SM-Liiga 14
78/9 SM-Liiga 188
77-79 Sports. FIN 54-1273
79/0 WASH
72/3 Williams Finnish 267
73/4 Williams Finnish 156

LEHTONEN, ERKKI
80/1 Mallasjuoma 164
78/9 SM-Liiga 187

LEHTONEN, KARI
00/1 Cardset 278
02/3 Cardset 147, 214, -BFG 4, -DD 2, -Lehtonen, -Trophy, ✍ BFG

LEHTONEN, LAURI
66/7 Champion 17
65/6 Hellas 69

LEHTONEN, MIKKO
00/1 Cardset 179
02/3 Cardset 57

LEHTONEN, PERTTI
98/9 Cardset Top. 2
02/3 Cardset 58
91/2 Jyvas Hyva 5
92/3 Jyvas Hyva 4
93/4 Jyvas Hyva 16
80/1 Mallasjuoma 17
93/4 Sisu 91
94/5 Sisu 223
95/6 Sisu 185, 204, DT-5
96/7 Sisu 5
95/6 Sisu Limited 38
78/9 SM-Liiga 29

LEHTONEN, RIKU-PETTERI
98/9 Cardset 12
99/0 Cardset 10
96/7 Sisu 138
01/2 UD DEL 70

LEHTONEN, SAMI
97/8 Hockey-Box
93/4 Sisu 115
94/5 Sisu 168, 342, H-19
95/6 Sisu 109
96/7 Sisu 126

LEHTONEN, TIMO
70/1 Kuvajulkaisut 299

LEHTONEN, TOPI
00/1 Cardset 188

LEHTONEN, VESA
94/5 Sisu 306

LEHTORANTA, VESA
71/2 Williams Finnish 133
72/3 Williams Finnish 196

LEHTORINNE, TIMO
71/2 Williams Finnish 248

LEHVONEN, HENRY
80/1 Mallasjuoma 43

LEIBEL, BRIAN
87/8 Regina Pats
87/8 Regina Pats
88/9 Regina Pats
88/9 Regina Pats

LEIBNITZ, JO_ESPEN
92/3 Semic Nordisk 225

LEIDBORG, GUNNAR
99/0 Eishockey 313

LEIDBORG, GÜNNAR
94/5 DEL 5
95/6 DEL 384

LEIDBORG, GÜNNAR
98/9 DEL 291

LEIER, DAN
83/4 Saskatoon Blades
83/4 Saskatoon Blades

LEIGHTON, MICHAEL
02/3 BAP Mem. 349
02/3 Choice Prospects 26
02/3 Parkhurst Retro 215
02/3 SP Authentic 171
02/3 Ultimate Mem. 63
02/3 UD Artistic 101
02/3 UD Honor 134
02/3 UD Mask 155
02/3 UD Premier 90

LEIGHTON, MIKE
01/2 Norfolk Admirals
01/2 Norfolk Admirals

LEIKKO, SAMU
66/7 Champion 30

LEIME, EIKKE
79/0 Montréal Juniors B&W
79/0 Montréal Juniors B&W
79/0 Montréal Jrs. Colour
79/0 Montréal Jrs. Colour

LEIMU, PEKKA
66/7 Champion 190
70/1 Kuvajulkaisut 130
70/1 Kuvajulkaisut 65
72 Panda MM-Toronto
71/2 Williams Finnish 180
72/3 Williams Finnish 128
73/4 Williams Finnish 183

LEINAUER, GERHARD
98/9 DEL
99/0 Eishockey 398

LEINONEN,
97/8 Hockey-Box

LEINONEN, ARI
72/3 Williams Finnish 348

LEINONEN, MARKO
98/9 Cardset 119, MM6, OD 6
93/4 Sisu 137
95/6 Sisu 261
96/7 Sisu 55

LEINONEN, MIKKO
80/1 Mallasjuoma 107
82/3 O-Pee-Chee 4
83/4 O-Pee-Chee 248
79 Panini Sticker 178
82 Skopbank
83/4 Souhaits Keychain [Rangers]
77-79 Sports. FIN 76-1821
72/3 Williams Finnish 268

LEINONEN, SAMI
94/5 Sisu 202
95/6 Sisu 141

LEINONEN, TERO
02/3 Cardset 215, 299

LEINONEN, TIMO
99/0 Cardset 202, 337

LEINONEN, TUOMAS
72/3 Williams Finnish 269

LEIRIVAARA, JUHANI
66/7 Champion 130

LEITER, BOBBY
72/3 ATLF
74/5 ATLF
64-67 BeeHive-3 [Bost.]
64/5 Coke/Sprite [Bost.]
72/3 Eddie Sargent 9
74/5 Loblaws
72/3 O-Pee-Chee 218
73/4 O-Pee-Chee 117
74/5 O-Pee-Chee 51
75/6 O-Pee-Chee 191
94/5 Parkie Tall 11
71/2 PITT / Sportcolor
63/4 Topps 14
64/5 Topps 63
73/4 Topps 117
74/5 Topps 51
75/6 Topps 191
71/2 Toronto Sun Photo

LEITER, KEN
87/8 OPC Sticker 131-119
87/8 Panini Sticker 93
84/5 Springfield Indians 6
84/5 Springfield Indians 6

LEITZA, BRIAN
98/9 Kansas City Blades 2
98/9 Kansas City Blades 2

LEJCZYK, LESZEK
89 Semic Sticker 127
92 Semic Sticker 266

LEJEUNE, JOZEF
79 Panini Sticker 344

LEKKERIMAKI, SAMI
92/3 Jyvas Hyva 151
93/4 Jyvas Hyva 267
93/4 Sisu 292

LEKNES, GEIR
92/3 Semic Nordisk 119

LEKUN, MIKE
80/1 Oshawa Generals
80/1 Oshawa Generals
81/2 Oshawa Generals
81/2 Oshawa Generals

LELACHEUR, ROB
89/0 Saskatoon Blades
89/0 Saskatoon Blades

LELACHEUR, ROBERT
90/1 7th..Sketch WHL 82

LEMAIRE, ED
85/6 Sudbury Wolves
85/6 Sudbury Wolves

LEMAIRE, JACQUES
70/1 Colgate 30
70/1 Dad's Cookies
72/3 Dernière Heure
73/4 Dernière Heure
70/1 Eddie Sargent 103
71/2 Eddie Sargent 105
72/3 Eddie Sargent 115
70/1 Esso Power Player
01/2 Fleer Greats 66, ✍ Aut.
83&87 HHOF 245
75/6 Hockey Heroes
94/5 Kraft / PB
72/3 Post 15
74/5 Lipton Soup 38
74/5 Loblaws
73/4 Mac's Milk
67/8 MONT
67/8 MONT / IGA Card
68/9 MONT / IGA Card
69/0 MONT / Pro Star
70/1 MONT
71/2 MONT / Pro Star
72/3 MONT / Pro Star
73/4 MONT / Pro Star
74/5 MONT
75/6 MONT
76/7 MONT
77/8 MONT
78/9 MONT
83/4 MONT
84/5 MONT
92/3 MONT / OPC 62
92/3 MONT / OPC 62
96/7 NJER / Sharp
96/7 NJER / Sharp
68/9 O-Pee-Chee 63
69/0 O-Pee-Chee 8
70/1 O-Pee-Chee 57
70/1 O-Pee-Chee DE 19
71/2 O-Pee-Chee 71
72/3 O-Pee-Chee 77
73/4 O-Pee-Chee 56
74/5 O-Pee-Chee 24
75/6 O-Pee-Chee 258
76/7 O-Pee-Chee 129
77/8 O-Pee-Chee 254
78/9 O-Pee-Chee 180
94/5 Parkie Tall FS-1
68/9 Post Marble
70/1 Post Shooters
72 Semic Sticker 208
68/9 Shirriff / Mont. 14
77-79 Sportscaster 81-19
77-79 Sports. FIN 85-2035
67/8 Topps 3
68/9 Topps 63
69/0 Topps 8
70/1 Topps 57
71/2 Topps 71
72/3 Topps 25
73/4 Topps 56
74/5 Topps 24
75/6 Topps 258
76/7 Topps 129
77/8 Topps 254
78/9 Topps 180
01/2 T/O Archives 65, -Seat, ✍ CAI
71/2 Toronto Sun Photo

LEMANDER, HANNU
66/7 Champion 90
65/6 Hellas 85
72/3 Williams Finnish 175

LEMANOWICZ, DAVID
91/2 Avant Garde BCJHL 18
96/7 Carolina Monarchs
96/7 Carolina Monarchs
95/6 Spokane Chiefs 1
95/6 Spokane Chiefs 1

LEMANSKI, CASEY
92/3 BCJHL 163

LEMARQUE, ERIC
91/2 Greensboro Monarchs
91/2 Greensboro Monarchs

LEMAY, DAVE
91/2 Cornwall Royals
91/2 Cornwall Royals
99/0 Fort Wayne Komets
99/0 Fort Wayne Komets
93/4 Owen Sound Platers
93/4 Owen Sound Platers
90/1 7th..Sketch OHL 37
91/2 7th...Sketch OHL 5

LEMAY, JEAN-SIMON
96/7 Halifax Moosehead
96/7 Halifax Moosehead
96/7 Halifax Moosehead
96/7 Halifax Moosehead

LEMAY, LOUIS-PHILIP
00/1 Sherbrooke Castors 12
00/1 Sherbrooke Castors 12
01/2 Sherbrooke Castors 14
01/2 Sherbrooke Castors 14

LEMAY, MARC
80/1 Québec Remparts
80/1 Québec Remparts

LEMAY, MAURICE
96/7 DEL 215

LEMAY, MOE
88/9 EDMO / Action 43
83/4 Fredericton Express
83/4 Fredericton Express
84/5 O-Pee-Chee 322
85/6 O-Pee-Chee 173
86/7 O-Pee-Chee 247
86/7 O-Pee-Chee 249
85/6 OPC Sticker 246-128
81/2 Ottawa 67's
81/2 Ottawa 67's
82/3 VANC
84/5 VANC
85/6 VANC
86/7 VANC

LEMAY, YANICK
90/1 7th..Sketch LHJMQ 223
91/2 7th...Sketch LHJMQ 17

LEMELIN, RÉJEAN
78/9 ATLF / Colour
88/9 BOST / Sports Action
89/0 BOST / Sports Action
89/0 BOST / Sports Action
90/1 BOST / Sports Action
90/1 BOST / Sports Action
90/1 BOST / Sports Action
90/1 BOST / Sports Action
98/9 BOST / Alumni 1
98/9 BOST / Alumni 1
90/1 Bowman 32
91/2 Bowman 354
80/1 CALG
81/2 CALG
82/3 CALG
85/6 CALG / Red Rooster
86/7 CALG / Red Rooster
76/7 COLR / Hockey Talk
92/3 Durivage 48
86/7 Kraft Sports 1
81/2 O-Pee-Chee 44
82/3 O-Pee-Chee 50
83/4 O-Pee-Chee 86
84/5 O-Pee-Chee 228
85/6 OPC/Topps 95
86/7 OPC/Topps 102
88/9 OPC/Topps 186
90/1 O-Pee-Chee 486
90/1 OPC/Topps 343
91/2 O-Pee-Chee 497
89/0 OPC/Topps 40
88/9 OPC Stars 18
83/4 OPC/Topps Sticker 266
84/5 OPC Sticker 240
85/6 OPC Sticker 210-77
86/7 OPC Sticker 83
88/9 OPC Sticker 24-153
87/8 Panini Sticker 204
88/9 Panini Sticker 164
88/9 Panini Sticker 203
89/0 Panini Sticker 195
90/1 Panini Sticker 13
91/2 Panini Sticker 172
90/1 Pro Set 9
90/1 Score 159, 365
91/2 Score 127
91/2 Score CAN 127
84/5 7-Eleven
84/5 Topps 25
91/2 To. Stadium 23
90/1 Upper Deck 209, 215
83/4 Vachon 10-130

LEMIEUX, ALAIN
85/6 Fredericton Express
85/6 Fredericton Express
86/7 QUÉB / McDonald's

LEMIEUX, BOB
77/8 Kalamazoo Wings
77/8 Kalamazoo Wings

LEMIEUX, CARL
84/5 Richelieu Riverains
84/5 Richelieu Riverains

LEMIEUX, CLAUDE
01/2 Adrenaline 150
98/9 Aurora 48
99/0 Aurora 40
99/0 BAP Mem. 208
00/1 BAP Mem. 373
95/6 Bicycle Sports Aces 4-Heart
91/2 Bowman 271
91/2 Bowman 277
92/3 Bowman 49
95/6 Bowman 13
01/2 Bowman 81
94/5 Cla. Images PL5
99/0 Crown Royale 82
01/2 Crown Royale 113
93/4 Donruss 187
94/5 Donruss 82
95/6 Donruss 343
96/7 Donruss 23, HL-18
97/8 Donruss 88
96/7 Do. Canadian 115
97/8 Do. Canadian NP 25
95/6 Do. Elite 44
96/7 Do. Elite 110
97/8 Do. Preferred 126
97/8 Do. Priority 127
97/8 Do. Studio 78
92/3 Durivage 14
93/4 Durivage 47
98/9 Dynagon Ice 50
93/4 EA Sports 77
94/5 Fleer 113
96/7 Fleer 22, 142
95/6 Fleer Metal 34, -IW 6
92/3 Fleer Ultra 114
93/4 Fleer Ultra 5
94/5 Fleer Ultra 118
95/6 Fleer Ultra 192, 223, -CC 6
96/7 Fl. Ultra 37
98/9 Kraft / KD
99/0 Kraft / KD, / PB
86/7 Kraft Sports 29
93/4 Leaf 125
94/5 Leaf 185
95/6 Leaf 311, -RTTC 10
96/7 Leaf 17
95/6 L. Limited 27
96/7 L. Limited 46, BTB-6
96/7 L. Preferred 24, LS-31
97/8 Limited 15
96/7 Maggers 40
96/7 Metal Univ. 35
85/6 MONT
86/7 MONT
87/8 MONT
87/8 MONT / Vachon 31
87/8 MONT / Vachon 33
88/9 MONT
89/0 MONT
89/0 MONT / Kraft
90/1 NJER
90/1 NJER
87/8 O-Pee-Chee 227
88/9 O-Pee-Chee 227
90/1 O-Pee-Chee 451
91/2 O-Pee-Chee 394
92/3 O-Pee-Chee 67
01/2 O-Pee-Chee 238
02/3 O-Pee-Chee 227
89/0 O-Pee-Chee 234
98/9 OPC Chrome 65
90/1 OPC Premier 62
87/8 OPC Sticker 19
88/9 OPC Sticker 43-176
89/0 opcSticker 52-196
97/8 Omega 60
98/9 Omega 61
99/0 Omega 137
98/9 Pacific 164
99/0 Pacific 110
00/1 Pacific 236
01/2 Pacific 306
02/3 Pacific 299
97/8 Pacific CC 3, SS-2C
97/8 Pa. Crown Roy. 36
97/8 Pa. Dynagon 31, DD-5B, T-25
97/8 Pa. Invincible 36, AZ-6, FP-8
97/8 Pa. Paramount 52
98/9 Pa. Paramount 57
99/0 Pa. Paramount 65
97/8 Pa. Revolution 35
98/9 Pa. Revolution 37
98/9 Panini Photocard
87/8 Panini Sticker 63
88/9 Panini Sticker 257
89/0 Panini Sticker 240
91/2 Panini Sticker 224
92/3 Panini Sticker 172
93/4 Panini Sticker 35
95/6 Panini Sticker 1-2, 82
96/7 Panini Sticker 246
99/0 Panini Sticker 80
91/2 Parkhurst 101
92/3 Parkhurst 89
93/4 Parkhurst 110
94/5 Parkhurst 129, V59
95/6 Parkhurst 319
00/1 Parkhurst P-181
91/2 Pinnacle 70
92/3 Pinnacle 259, 284
93/4 Pinnacle 251
94/5 Pinnacle 287
95/6 Pinnacle 119, -FS 10
96/7 Pinnacle 113
97/8 Pinnacle 163
97/8 Pi. Certified 129
97/8 Pi. Inside 156
95/6 Pi. Summit 129
96/7 Pi. Summit 113
97/8 Pi. Totally 129
95/6 Pi. Zenith 116, GG-4
96/7 Pi. Zenith 102, CS-10
95/6 Playoff 244
94/5 POG 145
95/6 POG 6
93/4 Power Play 137
93/4 Premier 134
94/5 Premier 204
99/0 Prism 83
01/2 PS Titanium 110
95/6 Pro Magnet 76
90/1 Pro Set 153, 478
91/2 Pro Set 135
92/3 Pro Set 98
91/2 Pro Set Platinum 196
99/0 Revolution 41
90/1 Score 111, 9T
91/2 Score 22
91/2 Score CAN 22
92/3 Score 8
93/4 Score 160
94/5 Score CI16
95/6 Score 269
96/7 Score 116
97/8 Score 158
97/8 Score Colo. 11
94/5 Select 73
95/6 Select CE 99, -DS 19
96/7 Select CE 53
01/2 Signature 121, ✍ Aut. 121
95/6 SBx Emotion 97
95/6 SBx Impact 37
96/7 SBx Impact 25, BR-12
95/6 SP 35
96/7 SP 39
97/8 SP Authentic 38
99/0 SP Authentic 50
02/3 SP Game-Used ✂ PH
00/1 SPx 143
01/2 Stadium 28
96/7 Team Out!
92/3 Topps 43
95/6 Topps 114
98/9 Topps 65
99/0 Topps SC13
00/1 Topps 54
01/2 Topps 238
02/3 Topps 227
01/2 To. Chrome 33
95/6 To. Finest 47
01/2 To. Heritage 68
02/3 To. Limited 227
96/7 To. Picks 89
91/2 To. Stadium 18
92/3 To. Stadium 50
93/4 To. Stadium 39
95/6 To. Stadium EC189, N3
02/3 T. Total 90
98/9 UD Choice 55
02/3 Ultimate Mem. ✂ CSTW
90/1 Upper Deck 447
91/2 Upper Deck 294
92/3 Upper Deck 163
93/4 Upper Deck 296, 391, SP 83
94/5 Upper Deck 303
95/6 Upper Deck 44, 258, 456, SE50, SE-108
96/7 Upper Deck 207, 243, P17
97/8 Upper Deck 47, 202
98/9 Upper Deck 73
01/2 Upper Deck ✂ SCFJers
02/3 Upper Deck 378, ✂ HS
94/5 UD BAP ✍ 27
01/2 UD Challenge 65
02/3 UD Classic ✂ HH, ✂
95/6 UD CC 262, 392, C28
96/7 UD CC 57, UD6
97/8 UD Coll. Choice 62
98/9 UD G. Reserve 73
01/2 UD Mask 75
00/1 UD MVP 104
99/0 UD MVP Cup 106, SS6
02/3 UD Piece -AC21, ✂ TT
01/2 UD SCup Champs 81
02/3 UD Top Shelf ✂ CP, ✂ ST, ✂ SW
02/3 UD Vintage 198, GB 198
99/0 Victory 84
96 Wien 91
97/8 Zenith 57, Z36

LEMIEUX, JEAN
74/5 Loblaws
75/6 O-Pee-Chee 367
76/7 O-Pee-Chee 272

LEMIEUX, JOCELYN
92/3 Bowman 72
90/1 CHIC / Coke
90/1 CHIC / Coke
91/2 CHIC / Coke
91/2 CHIC / Coke
93/4 CHIC / Coke
93/4 CHIC / Coke
93/4 Donruss 440
92/3 Durivage 15
93/4 Durivage 43
95/6 HART / Kids Club
95/6 HART / Kids Club
94/5 Leaf 502
98/9 Long Beach Ice Dogs
98/9 Long Beach Ice Dogs
89/0 MONT
90/1 OPC/Topps 237
91/2 O-Pee-Chee 453
92/3 O-Pee-Chee 153
87/8 Panini Sticker 319
90/1 Panini Sticker 190
91/2 Panini Sticker 20
92/3 Panini Sticker 8
93/4 Panini Sticker 152
94/5 Panini Sticker 114
91/2 Parkhurst 256
92/3 Parkhurst 275
93/4 Parkhurst 43
95/6 Parkhurst 393
97/8 PHOE / Coca-Cola
97/8 PHOE / Coca-Cola
98/9 PHOE / Coca-Cola
98/9 PHOE / Coca-Cola
93/4 Pinnacle 302
94/5 Pinnacle 89
95/6 Pinnacle 62
94/5 POG 115
93/4 Premier 295
94/5 Premier 122
90/1 Pro Set 432
88/9 ProCards / Sherbrooke
90/1 Score 66T
91/2 Score CAN 447
92/3 Score 309
93/4 Score 420
87/8 SLOU / Kodak
92/3 Topps 300
91/2 To. Stadium 356
92/3 To. Stadium 446
93/4 To. Stadium 255
90/1 Upper Deck 544
91/2 Upper Deck 438
94/5 Upper Deck 372
94/5 UD BAP ✍ 129
95/6 UD CC 138
96/7 UD CC 42

LEMIEUX, MARIO
94/5 Action Packed
89/0 Action Packed 2
01/2 Adrenaline 155, BR 9, WB 16, ✂ GWJ 38
01/2 ASG History
01/2 Atomic 79, AB 9, CP 15, PP 27, Stat 18, TN 11, ✂ GWJ 45
02/3 Atomic 80, -CF 20, -NPC 9, ✂ GWJ 19
02/3 BAP All-Star 51-53, ✂ ASJ, ✂ HSHSJers, Bobble
98/9 Be A Player L-1 to L-4
00/1 BAP Mem. 501, ✂ L1-10, ✂ PP-1, ✂ TM-3
01/2 BAP Mem. 66, ✂ 500GS, ✂ ASJ, ✂ ASE, ✂ ASN, ✂ ASE, ✂ AST, ✂ CoO, HSHS, ✂ PP, ✂ SCP
02/3 BAP Mem. 157, 224, ✂ ASJ31, ✂ ASE12, ✂ ASN12, ✂ ASTJ10, ✂ AST4, ✂ AST22, ✂ AST28, ✂ FP24, ✂ HSHSJers 2, ✂ Mag. 1-10, ✂ TM15, /Cup
02/3 Between the Pipes ✂ GN2
96/7 Bic.Sports Aces A-S
95/6 Bicycle Sports Aces Q-Heart
90/1 Bowman 204, -HT 2
91/2 Bowman 87, 425
92/3 Bowman 189, 233, 440
95/6 Bowman 40, -BB 10
01/2 Bowman 3
02/3 Bowman 26
02/3 Calder 27, -CG 8, -HH 10, ✂ GWJ 18
83 Canada Juniors
92/3 Classic 66, SP1, ✍ Aut., /Promo
00/1 Crown Royale 87, ✂ JR-11, JotC-22, Land. 9, NP-15
01/2 Crown Royale 117, ASH 17, CA 19, JotC 25, LH 8, ✂ TT 17
02/3 Crown Royale 78, -LOR 16, -RP 9, ✂ GWDP 17, ✂ GWJ 16
93/4 Donruss 262, EC, R, -ES 1, -IK 7
94/5 Donruss 5, D-1, ES-6, IM-5
95/6 Donruss 270, D-1, E-9, PP-14
96/7 Donruss 131, D-4, GTS-1
96/7 Do. Canadian 31, OC-13, ML, ✍ ML
95/6 Do. Elite 51, 66, -Cool, -CE 2, Lemieux 1-7, -Hart, ✍ Aut.
96/7 Do. Elite 109, P-4, HTH, ✍ HTH
92/3 Durivage 8
93/4 EA Sports 105, 189
01/2 EASports (x2)
88/9 Esso All-Star
01/2 eTopps 23
02/3 eTopps 18
02/3 Exclusive 138, -EIS 9, -MO 16
02/3 First Edition 1, 160, 323, 364, 426R, ✂ Jers., ✂ Jers., ✂ HSHSJers 2, ✂ Magnificent
94/5 Flair 135, CIS-6, HN-5
96/7 Flair 78, HN-7, NT-2
96/7 Fleer 87, 137-39, 141, ART-13, PA-7
01/2 Fleer All-Star Fantasy
01/2 Fleer Greats 81, -RC 12, -BC 5, ✍ Aut.
01/2 Fleer Legacy 1, 25, ✂ HK, ✂ ITC, ✂ TM
95/6 Fleer Metal 118, -HM 9, -IS 14
96/7 Fl. Picks F50-26, CC-3, DL-1
92/3 Fleer Ultra 165, -AS 4, -AW 5
93/4 Fleer Ultra 116, -AW 4, -PP 4, -RLS 6, -SK 4
94/5 Fleer Ultra 165, -SK 5
95/6 Fleer Ultra 288, 391, -EA 13, -UV 6
96/7 Fl. Ultra 143, PL-4, UP-11
88/9 Frito Lay
91/2 Gillette 33
95 Globe 87
96/7 Got-Um
01/2 Heads Up 78, HD 7, RI 9, SM 14, ✂ JQ 17, ✂ JQ 21, / Bobble
02/3 Heads Up 100, -EIT 13, -ITN 17, -SM 12, ✂ GWQ 28
92/3 High Five / Promo P5
93/4 Hockey Wit 66
92/3 Humpty Dumpty

02/3 In The GU 62, 162, ✂ E1, ✂ F24, ✂ IE1, ✂ GUJ1, ✂ MI1-10, ✂ SJ1, ✂ T1, ✂ TM2
92/3 Kellogg's
95/6 Kellogg's / Donruss [x4]
93 Koululainen
94 Koululainen
89/0 Kraft 55
90/1 Kraft 29, 87
91/2 Kraft 1
92/3 Kraft / Kraft Singles
93/4 Kraft / JELL-O
93/4 Kraft / KD
93/4 Kraft / PB
95/6 Kraft / IP
96/7 Kraft / AS, -TT, KD, -PB
96/7 Kraft Magnet
89/0 Kraft Stickers 5
93/4 Leaf 1, 210, -GLAS 1, -HTA 1,4, -Lemieux
94/5 Leaf 1, -FOI 9, -GLS 11, -LL 18
95/6 Leaf 1, -FF7, -Lem. 1-10
96/7 Leaf 84, FOI-1, S-1
94/5 L. Limited 1, G-1
95/6 L. Limited 1, -CL, SG-1
96/7 L. Limited 85, S-7
96/7 L. Preferred 113, SP-2, VP-6
96/7 Maggers 119
92/3 Mario Bun
92/3 McDonald's McD-21
93/4 McDonald's McH-01
95/6 McDonald's McD-15
96/7 McDonald's McD-21
98/9 McD's T12
01/2 McDonald's 31, -CF 4, ✂ JPatch 15
02/3 McDonald's 32, -SLG 10, ✂ JP 14
96/7 Metal Univ. 128, IC-10, LW-11
96 Metallic SM 1-5
99/0 Millenium P-3, ✍ P-3
85/6 O-Pee-Chee 262
85/6 OPC/Topps 9
85/6 OPC/Topps Box I
86/7 OPC/Topps 122
86/7 OPC/Topps Box I
87/8 OPC/Topps 15
88/9 OPC/Topps 1
90/1 OPC/Topps 175, Box G, Topps-TL 17
91/2 O-Pee-Chee 153, 523
92/3 O-Pee-Chee 138, 240, 292, -Ann. 18
01/2 O-Pee-Chee 1, 326-330
02/3 O-Pee-Chee 2
89/0 OPC/Topps 1, Box A, OPC 312, 319, 327, Topps-AS 3
87/8 OPC Leaders 23
90/1 OPC Premier 63
91/2 OPC Premier 114
92/3 OPC Premier SP22
88/9 OPC Stars 19
85/6 OPC Sticker 199-72
85/6 OPC Sticker 97
86/7 OPC Sticker 120-134
86/7 OPC Sticker 233
87/8 OPC Sticker 120-132
87/8 OPC Sticker 170
88/9 OPC Sticker 116-246
88/9 OPC Sticker 204-73
88/9 OPC Sticker 210-81
88/9 OPC Sticker 211-82
88/9 OPC Sticker 232
89/0 opcSticker 238, 158-18, 208-68, /AS 24
01/2 Pacific 316, 419, 439, PCC 66, CCA 9, GCDC 17, NAAS 10, TDP 10, ✂ GWJ 28
02/3 Pacific 312, -CCA 9, -IZ 9, -L 11, -MA 16, -MI 15, ✂ GWJ 42
02/3 Pacific Complete 303
01/2 PTC Collectors 8
87/8 Panini Sticker 146
88/9 Panini Sticker 340
88/9 Panini Sticker 400
88/9 Panini Sticker 401
89/0 Panini Sticker 184, 309, 375
90/1 Panini Sticker 136, 326
91/2 Panini Sticker 268
92/3 Panini Sticker 220, 280
93/4 Panini Sticker 136, H
94/5 Panini Sticker 74, 277
96/7 Panini Sticker 59, 144, 150
95 Panini Worlds 277
91/2 Parkhurst 137, 467, PHC7
92/3 Parkhurst 136, 462, 498
93/4 Parkhurst 425, D2, F10, G2, E2
94/5 Parkhurst 296, V6, -YCTG 18
00/1 Parkhurst P-166
01/2 Parkhurst 24, ✂ 500GS, ✂ PJ1, ✂ PS1, ✂ HSHSJers, ✂ M20, ✂ M25, ✂ M40, ✂ H14, ✂ T2, ✂ T28
02/3 Parkhurst 115, -HHH9, HHP8, -HHR8, ✂ FP24, ✂ GJ1, ✂ SJ1, ✂ HSHSJers, ✂ MI1-10, ✂ MM1-10, ✂ NH5, ✂ NH7, ✂ PP1, ✂ TT14
02/3 Parkhurst Retro 1, ✂ BIT1-15, ✂ RF24, ✂ RJ15, ✂ RSJ11, ✂ HH1, ✂ HSHSJers, ✂ MI1-10, ✂ NN30, ✂ RM1, ✂ RM8, ✂ RM29
91/2 Pinnacle 1, 380, B-5
92/3 Pinnacle 300
93/4 Pinnacle 221, 230, 310, CA18, -NF 4, -TP 5
94/5 Pinnacle 170, TP10, WE8
96/7 Pinnacle 86, TP-2, T-1
96/7 Pi. Be A Player BB-2, -DCS
96/7 Pi. FANtasy 4
96/7 Pi. Lemieux Moments 1-18
86/7 PITT / Kodak
87/8 PITT / Kodak
89/0 PITT / Elby's
89/0 PITT / Foodland 10
90/1 PITT / Foodland 13
90/1 PITT / Foodland 13
91/2 PITT / Elby's
91/2 PITT / Elby's
91/2 PITT / Foodland 4
91/2 PITT / Foodland 4
91/2 PITT / Food. Stickers
91/2 PITT / Food. Stickers
92/3 PITT / Coke-Clark
92/3 PITT / Coke-Clark
92/3 PITT / Foodland 1
92/3 PITT / Foodland 1
92/3 PITT / Food. Stickers
92/3 PITT / Food. Stickers
93/4 PITT / Foodland 1
93/4 PITT / Foodland 1
95/6 PITT / Foodland 23
95/6 PITT / Foodland 23
96/7 PITT / Tribune
96/7 PITT / Tribune
94/5 POG 185
93/4 Power Play 190, -Game. 5, -PL 8
93/4 Premier 37, 91, 185, 220, -BG/OPC 18, -BG-Top. 9, Finest 10
94/5 Premier 250
00/1 Premier Plus 66
00/1 Private Stock 152
01/2 Pr. Stock 78, Res. 15, -PS 59, ✂ GUG 79
02/3 Pr. Stock Reserve -RE 5, ✂ 138
00/1 PS Titanium 77, 3SS-18, NAAS-9, ✂ GUG-44, ✂ GUG-151, ✂ GUG-152
01/2 PS Titanium 114, SK 18, TSS 18, ✂ DSJ 32
01/2 PS Titanium Draft ✂ 80
02/3 PS Titanium 82, SK 7, ✂ GWJ 54
00/1 PS Titanium Draft ✂ 86
90/1 Pro Set 236, 362
91/2 Pro Set 194, 318, 581, PotM P3
92/3 Pro Set 1, 139
91/2 Pro Set Platinum 91
87/8 Pro Sport CW5
02/3 Quest for the Cup 80, -RTC 11, ✂ GWJ 17
90/1 Score 2, 337
90/1 Sco. Hot Cards 34
91/2 Score 200, 335, 425-26, -Hot 5
91/2 Score CAN 200, 315-16, 365
92/3 Score 390, 413, 433, 448, 519
93/4 Score 350, 479, 480, -DT 10, -DD8, -TF 16
94/5 Score DT15, TF18
92/3 Seasons 34
93/4 Seasons 9
95 Semic 93
89 Semic Sticker 64
92 Semic Sticker 86
93 Semic Sticker 198
85/6 7-Eleven Superstars 15
00/1 Signature 75, HSHS, R-1 to R-20, ✂ ML1-5, ✂✍ ML1-5, ✂ HSHSJers
01/2 Signature C-54, ✍ Aut. XLLM, ✂ 500GS, ✂ FP24, ✂ GUE13, ✂ GJ54, ✂ GSJ54, ✂ HSHSJers, ✂ ITN13, ✂ IG6, ✂ TM24
02/3 Signature 135, GS-49, ✍ 135, ✂ CJ1, ✂ FJ24, ✂ SGJ1, ✂ MI1-10, ✂ TQ8, ✂ TM1
00/1 SP Authentic 72, ST, SP6, ✍ SotT, ✍ SotTD, ✍ SotTT
01/2 SP Authentic 68, 106, ✂ NN, ✂ PP
02/3 SP Authentic 73, 102, ✂ SP, ✂ DP, ✂ TP
00/1 SP GU 49, ✂ TotG, ✂ C (x2), ✂ P (x2)
01/2 SP GU 43, ✂ AF, ✂ AFD (x2), ✂ AFT, ✂ AFQ (x2), ✂ Patch, ✂ PatchC, ✂ PatchT
02/3 SP GU 40, 52, 54, ✂ AF, ✂ CF, ✂ PC, ✂ PH
02/3 Sports Vault 115
00/1 SPx 144, ✂ WM, ✂✍ WM
01/2 SPx 52, 78, 89, ✂ HT, ✂ TT
02/3 SPx 61, 97, 129, ✂ WM, ✂ M, ✂ SS
00/1 Stadion 79, 147, 148, 162
01/2 Stadium 18, G21, HS4, ✂ NHLP18, P9
02/3 Stadium 6, -BT2
93/4 SLU [x2]
94/5 Starting Lineup
97/8 SLU
02/3 Starz
86/7 OPC/Topps - Stick. 9
87/8 OPC/Topps - Stick. 11
88/9 OPC/Topps - Stick. 2
92/3 Topps 212, 265, 504
99/0 Topps SC1, ✍ SCH
00/1 Topps TC10, CS 1-23, ✍ CS 1-23
01/2 Topps 1, 326-330, -CS1-10, SM1, SG1, ✍ MRA (x5)
02/3 Topps 2, CC1, HHU3, ✂ CC1, ✂ CC6, ✂ CC8
00/1 To. Chrome TC10, Comm. 1-23
01/2 To. Chrome 1, -CS1-10, -MR1-5
02/3 To. Chrome 2
00/1 To. Gold Label 37
00/1 To. Heritage 73
01/2 To. Heritage 1, 120
02/3 To. Heritage 7, -Light 7
02/3 To. Limited 2
99/0 To. Prmr. Plus ✍ CS6, ✍ CSC 3
01/2 To. Reserve 3, ✂ TR
91/2 To. Stadium 174
92/3 To. Stadium 94, 251
93/4 To. Stadium 143, 146, 148, 310, -AS, -Finest 10
94/5 To. Stadium 60, F-1
91/2 TSC Charter
92 TSC Members Only [x2]
00/1 To. Stars 100, P1, P2, P3, ✍ CAI
02/3 T. Total 96, TTC24, TT18
00/1 UD Heroes 136, PI5, ✂ GT, ✂ GC, ✍ SG
01/2 UD PlayMakers Ltd 79, ✂ PCJ
00/1 UD Reserve 70, GS8
02/3 UD Superstars 197, ✂ CAS, ✂ LLT (x2)
00/1 Ultimate Mem. ✍ U-11, ✂A8-1,A8-3,A8-4, ✂D-6, ✂H-5, ✂H-8, ✂H-13, ✂MO-1 to MO-10, ✂RE-7, ✂RA-3, ✂RA-6, ✂TM-39, ✂UC-10
01/2 Ultimate Mem. ✂ 500GS, ✂ A8, ✂ ASGH, ✂ CT, ✂ DD, ✂ Emb., ✂ Jers., ✂ S&J, ✂ Glove, ✂ GSL, ✂ ITN, ✂ NP, ✂ PP, ✂ RT, ✂ RA, ✂ SCP, ✂ UC, ✂ WTF, ✍ Aut.
02/3 Ultimate Mem. ✂ A8 (x3), ✂ ASMVP (x3), ✂ BOS, ✂ CP, ✂ CSTW (x2), ✂ DD, ✂ Emb, ✂ FS, ✂ GUJ, ✂ GUSJ, ✂ GD, ✂ GAO, ✂ GMIH, ✂ HT, ✂ ITN, ✂ LA, ✂ Mag (x10), ✂ MO (x10), ✂ NP, ✂ SL (x6), ✂ PS (x3), ✂ RAT (x4), ✂ RT, ✂ SU, ✂ UC, ✍ UAut
90/1 Upper Deck 59, 144, 305
91/2 Upper Deck 45, 47, 156, 611, AW9
92/3 Upper Deck 26, 433, 436, 454, G9, WG11
93/4 Upper Deck 301, 407, AW1, GG4, HB7, E13, H1, SP 122
94/5 Upper Deck 22, 200, SP-61
00/1 Upper Deck ✂ DGJ
01/2 Upper Deck 138, FF4, FC3, GA5, LP11, SS14, SS2, ✂ CJers, ✂ JPatch, ✂ PatchL, ✂ PatchN, ✂ PatchNu, ✂ PF, ✂ PoaN, ✂ PoaND, ✂ PoaNT
02/3 Upper Deck 141, 191, -GG13, -SS12, ✂ CG, ✂ DM, ✂ LN, ✂ PP, ✂ PN, ✂ PA, ✂ R50, ✂ FC, ✂ PW, ✂ UDPL
00 ✂ UD APOH 500, ✂✍ 500
02/3 UD Artistic 72, R72, CG6, GD6, UD3, ✂ AT, / Art
94/5 UD BAP R69
00/1 UD Black Diam. 107
99/0 UD C. Legends 4, AC7, E3, ✍ ES, ✂ JC5, ✂✍ JC5
01/2 UD Challenge 68, CM8, CR7, ✂ FP
02/3 UD Classic 80, ET13, PS8, ✂ HH, ✂ HR (x3)
01/2 UD Collectors
02/3 UD Foundations 159
01/2 UD Honor Roll 8, 38, ✂ GAJ, ✂ PPM
02/3 UD Honor 58, 94, -SG25, -TW12
00/1 UD Ice 75
01/2 UD Ice 36, ✂ JC
00/1 UD Legends 105, 108, ES3, SM11, ✍ ES, ✂ LGJ
92/3 UD Locker 6
01/2 UD Mask 79, ✂ GJ, ✂ JP, ✂ DP
02/3 UD Mask 70, ✂ IO
01/2 UD MVP 150, MT4, VC5, MW1, ✂ S
02/3 UD MVP 148, HN6, VF12
00/1 UD Pearson
02/3 UD Piece 72, 93, AC22, ✂ EC
01/2 UD Premier 41, ✂ G, ✂ D (x3)
02/3 UD Premier 43, ✂ Jers, ✂ JD, ✂ Patch, ✂ NHLP
00/1 UD Pros&Prosp. 69, GS2, NP8
99/0 UD Retro 83, DR12, G5B, TC13, ✍ Ink., ✂ RM
00/1 UD Return ML1-ML9
02/3 UD Rookie 79, 105, ✂ DJ
01/2 UD SCup Champs 86, ✂ S, ✂ G, ✂ T
01/2 UD Top Shelf 34, ✂ J, ✂ S
02/3 UD Top Shelf 71, ✂ CP, ✂ HH (x2), ✂ HT (x2), ✂ M, ✂ SH
00/1 UD Vintage ✂ D-POH
01/2 UD Vintage 201, 208
02/3 UD Vintage 202, 284, 303, T52
00/1 Vanguard 151
01/2 Vanguard 80, EMW 1, IF 8, QTH 2, VT 17, ✂ DGM 26, ✂ DGM 44
02/3 Vanguard 81, -EMW 3, -IF 9, VT 11, ✂ GWJ 37
01/2 Victory 280, 391
02/3 Victory 172, -NP11
01/2 Waving the Flag 1

LEMIEUX, REAL
70/1 Eddie Sargent 70
71/2 Eddie Sargent 72
72/3 Eddie Sargent 91
68/9 O-Pee-Chee 36
69/0 O-Pee-Chee 190
71/2 O-Pee-Chee 154
73/4 O-Pee-Chee 122
68/9 Shirriff / LosA. 1
68/9 Topps 36
73/4 Topps 122
71/2 Toronto Sun Photo

LEMIEUX, RICHARD
72/3 Eddie Sargent 218
74/5 Loblaws
72/3 O-Pee-Chee 202
73/4 O-Pee-Chee 53
74/5 O-Pee-Chee 114
75/6 O-Pee-Chee 274
76/7 OPC WHA 74
73/4 Topps 53
74/5 Topps 114
75/6 Topps 274
72/3 VANC / Royal Bank
73/4 VANC / Royal Bank

LEMIRE, BRUNO
99/0 Hull Olympiques BN
99/0 Hull Olympiques BN
99/0 Hull Olympiques 5
99/0 Hull Olympiques 5
00/1 Hull Olympiques 5
00/1 Hull Olympiques 5

LEMIRE, RENE
92/3 Semic Nordisk 151

LEMOIN, JEAN-PHILIPPE
94 Semic 213

LEMOINE, JEAN-PHILIPPE
95 Panini Worlds 101
92 Semic Sticker 223
93 Semic Sticker 254

LEMOLA, OLLI
71/2 Williams Finnish 327

LEMONDE, BERNIE
52/3 Bas du Fleuve 37
52/3 Laval Dairy Update 90

LEMPIÄINEN, MIKKO
93/4 Jyvas Hyva 204
93/4 Sisu 271

LEMPIO, JOACHIM
94/5 DEL 128
79 Panini Sticker 251

LENARDON, TIM
88/9 ProCards / Utica
91/2 ProCards 149

LENARDUZZI, MIKE
93/4 Fleer Ultra 72
93/4 Fleer Ultra Pros. 5
89/0 Oshawa Generals
89/0 Oshawa Generals
93/4 Parkhurst 87
93/4 Pinnacle 207
91 7th..Sketch Mem.Cup 1
90/1 7th..Sketch OHL 165
91/2 7th...Sketch OHL 310

LENDZYK, TARAS
91/2 Air Canada SJHL 37
91/2 Air Canada SJHL B13
99/0 Charlotte Checkers
99/0 Charlotte Checkers
93/4 Minnesota-Duluth
93/4 Minnesota-Duluth

LENER, SLAVOMIR
97/8 APS 1, 341
98 Bonaparte 6C
98 Bonaparte Pexeso 21
92/3 CALG / IGA 028
92/3 CALG / IGA 028
98/9 OFS 226

LEONARD, SEBASTIEN
02/3 Baie-Comeau
02/3 Baie-Comeau

LEONARD, SETH
00/1 Kelowna Rockets
00/1 Kelowna Rockets

LEONHARDT, BJORN
99/0 Eishockey 17

LEONHARDT, BJÖRN
98/9 DEL 193
01/2 UD DEL 250

LEONOV, DMITRI
00/1 Manitoba Moose
00/1 Manitoba Moose
95/6 Spokane Chiefs 5
95/6 Spokane Chiefs 5

LEONOV, YURI
91/2 O-Pee-Chee 39R

LEONTIEV, OLEG
00/1 Metallurg 48
00/1 Metallurg 48
98/9 Mir 33, 127
99/0 Mir 25

LEOPOLD, JORDAN
02/3 Atomic 126
02/3 BAP All-Star 132
02/3 BAP Mem. 283
02/3 Bowman 117, ✂ FFDS, ✂ FFJ, ✂ FFP, ✂ FFR, ✂ FFRP, ✂ FFS, ✂ FFTS, ✍ YSA, / ✍ Puck
02/3 Calder 108, -CR 5
02/3 Crown Royale 107, -RR 8
02/3 In The GU 97, ✂ C9
02/3 Pacific Complete 544
02/3 PTC/ ASG 3
02/3 Parkhurst 209, -HHC 5, ✂ GJ55
02/3 Parkhurst Retro 209
02/3 Pr. Stock Reserve 156
02/3 PS Titanium 109, -ROT 4
02/3 Quest for the Cup 109
02/3 Signature 195, ✍ 195, ✂ AR8, ✂ SGJ59
02/3 SP Authentic ✍ 196, ✍ ✂ Patch
02/3 SP GU 71
02/3 SPx 168
02/3 To. Chrome 160
02/3 T. Total 439
02/3 Ultimate Mem. 9, ✂ CC, ✍ RAut
02/3 Upper Deck 430
02/3 UD Artistic 129, CG14
02/3 UD Honor 105
02/3 UD Mask 173
02/3 UD Premier 47
02/3 UD Rookie ✂ 155
02/3 UD Top Shelf 124
02/3 Vanguard 107, -PP 6

LEOPOLD, MICHAEL
99/0 Eishockey 399

LEOPPKY, MARK
92/3 MPS SJHL 26

LEPAGE, ANDRÉ
93/4 Slapshot / Drummondville 27

LEPAGE, BERTRAND
52/3 Anonymous 69
52/3 Bas du Fleuve 42

LEPAGE, MARTIN
90/1 7th..Sketch LHJMQ 138
91/2 7th...Sketch LHJMQ 207

LEPAGE, PATRICK
02/3 Baie-Comeau
02/3 Baie-Comeau
01/2 Rimouski Océanic 19
01/2 Rimouski Océanic 19

LEPAUS, MARKO
70/1 Kuvajulkaisut 315
71/2 Williams Finnish 347

LEPHART, MIKE
02/3 Philadelphia Phantoms
02/3 Philadelphia Phantoms

LEPIN, HECTOR
25-27 Anonymous 10

LÉPINE, ALFRED (PIT)
25-27 Anonymous 13
33/4 Anonymous 42
34-43 BeeHive-1 [Mont.]
35-40 Canada Starch
33/4 Canadian Gum
33-35 Diamond Match Silv.
36-39 Diamond Match TT1
36-39 Diamond Match TT2
36-39 Diamond Match TT3
33/4 Hamilton Gum 23
27/8 La Patrie
27/8 La Presse
33/4 O-Pee-Chee 20
37/8 O-Pee-Chee 159
34/5 Sweet Caporal
33/4 WWGum 46
37/8 World Wide Gum 78

LÉPINE, JOSÉ
51/2 Laval Dairy 46

LEPISTO, JUSSI
80/1 Mallasjuoma 62
78/9 SM-Liiga 70

LEPLER, P.J.
96/7 Richmond Renegades
96/7 Richmond Renegades

LEPPA, HENRY
66/7 Champion 60
72 Hellas MM-Jenkki 3
74 Hellas MM-Jenkki 8
70/1 Kuvajulkaisut 180
80/1 Mallasjuoma 65
78/9 SM-Liiga 78
71/2 Williams Finnish 104
72/3 Williams Finnish 148
73/4 Williams Finnish 113
73/4 Williams Finnish 69

LEPPANEN, ANTTI
66/7 Champion 152
74 Hellas MM-Jenkki 9
71/2 Williams Finnish 134
72/3 Williams Finnish 197
73/4 Williams Finnish 157
73/4 Williams Finnish 70

LEPPANEN, JANNE
92/3 Jyvas Hyva 99

LEPPANEN, JARI
72/3 Williams Finnish 309

LEPPANEN, KALEVI
66/7 Champion 83
65/6 Hellas 10
70/1 Kuvajulkaisut 300

LEPPANEN, REIJO
74 Hellas MM-Jenkki 10
70/1 Kuvajulkaisut 142
80/1 Mallasjuoma 185
82 Skopbank
78/9 SM-Liiga 212
71/2 Williams Finnish 192
72/3 Williams Finnish 230
73/4 Williams Finnish 264

LEPPIK, HEIKKI
71/2 Williams Finnish 285
73/4 Williams Finnish 205

LEPPÖ, HENRY
74 Semic Sticker 84
77-79 Sports. FIN 108-2573

LEPPÖNEN, ANTTI
74 Semic Sticker 97

LEPPÖNEN, REIJO
77-79 Sports. FIN 83-1970

LEPSA, TOMAZ
79 Panini Sticker 398

LEROUX, DAVID
01/2 Shawinigan 17
01/2 Shawinigan 17
02/3 Shawinigan Cataractes
02/3 Shawinigan Cataractes

LEROUX, FRANCOIS
01/2 UD DEL 20

LEROUX, FRANÇOIS
99/0 Asheville Smoke
99/0 Asheville Smoke
88/9 EDMO / Action 147
92/3 EDMO
92/3 EDMO
97/8 Pa. Invincible R-162
93/4 Parkhurst 412
94/5 PITT / Foodland 13
94/5 PITT / Foodland 13
95/6 PITT / Foodland 6
95/6 PITT / Foodland 6
90/1 ProCards 239
91/2 ProCards 215
90/1 Score 393
92/3 W. Michigan Broncos
92/3 W. Michigan Broncos
02/3 WBS Penguins
02/3 WBS Penguins

LEROUX, JEAN-YVES
98/9 Aurora 42
97/8 Donruss 211
97/8 Do. Preferred 157
97/8 Leaf 161
01/2 Norfolk Admirals
01/2 Norfolk Admirals
98/9 Pacific 149
99/0 Pacific 90
98/9 Pa. Paramount 49
97/8 Pi. Be A Player 45, ✍ Aut. 45
97/8 Pi. Inside 186
98/9 UD Choice 52
97/8 Upper Deck 249
00/1 Upper Deck 270
00/1 UD Vintage 80

LEROUX, KELLY
96/7 Johnstown Chiefs
96/7 Johnstown Chiefs

LESCHYSHYN, CURTIS
91/2 Bowman 142
92/3 Bowman 335
97/8 CARO / Sprint
97/8 CARO / Sprint
98/9 CARO / Highwoods
98/9 CARO / Highwoods
93/4 Donruss 273
93/4 EA Sports 110
93/4 Fleer Ultra 404
96/7 HART / Kids Club
96/7 HART / Kids Club
93/4 Leaf 305
94/5 Leaf 548
90/1 OPC/Topps 216
91/2 O-Pee-Chee 39
92/3 O-Pee-Chee 306
99/0 Omega 47
01/2 OTTA
01/2 OTTA
02/3 OTTA
02/3 OTTA
97/8 Pa. Invincible R-38
89/0 Panini Sticker 334
90/1 Panini Sticker 150
90/1 Panini/QUE 13
91/2 Panini Sticker 256
92/3 Panini Sticker 217
98/9 Panini Sticker 26
00/1 Panini Sticker 172
91/2 Parkhurst 367
93/4 Parkhurst 436
91/2 Pinnacle 258
92/3 Pinnacle 46
93/4 Pinnacle 49
94/5 Pinnacle 24
94/5 POG 202
93/4 Power Play 423
93/4 Premier 487
94/5 Premier 62
00/1 Premier Plus 44
90/1 Pro Set 251
91/2 Pro Set 198
88/9 QUÉB
88/9 QUÉB / Gene. Foods
89/0 QUÉB
89/0 QUÉB / Gene. Foods
89/0 QUÉB / Gene. Foods
89/0 QUÉB / Police
89/0 QUÉB / Police
90/1 QUÉB
90/1 QUÉB
90/1 QUÉB / Petro-Canada
90/1 QUÉB / Petro-Canada
91/2 QUÉB / Petro-Canada
91/2 QUÉB / Petro-Canada
92/3 QUÉB / Petro-Canada
92/3 QUÉB / Petro-Canada
86/7 Saskatoon Blades
86/7 Saskatoon Blades
90/1 Score 92
90/1 Sco. Hot Cards 44
91/2 Score 58
91/2 Score CAN 58
92/3 Score 87
93/4 Score 42
94/5 Score 64
92/3 Topps 124
91/2 To. Stadium 156
92/3 To. Stadium 413
93/4 To. Stadium 336
02/3 T. Total 30
90/1 Upper Deck 295
91/2 Upper Deck 413
93/4 Upper Deck 133
97/8 Upper Deck 35
00/1 UD Vintage 177

LESHCHEV, ALBERT
00/1 Mir 251

LESIEUR, ART
35-40 Canada Starch
36-39 Diamond Match TT2
36-39 Diamond Match TT3

LESKA, PETR
97/8 APS 70
99/0 DS 10
00/1 DS 60
97/8 DS Sticker 303
94/5 Flint Generals
94/5 Flint Generals
98/9 OFS 31
99/0 OFS 211, 519
00/1 OFS 365
01/2 OFS 91, -RE17D, -UHI 25

LESLIE, ALEX
52/3 Anonymous 21

LESLIE, BOB
02/3 London Knights
02/3 London Knights

LESLIE, GLEN
85/6 London Knights
85/6 London Knights

LESLIE, LANCE
96/7 Kentucky Tho'blades
96/7 Kentucky Tho'blades
94/5 Thunder Bay Senators
94/5 Thunder Bay Senators
98/9 Wichita Thunder
98/9 Wichita Thunder

LESLIE, LAURA
94/5 Classic W11

LESLIE, LEE J.
92/3 Classic 26
92/3 Classic Four Sport 175
93/4 Kansas City Blades
93/4 Kansas City Blades
94/5 Kansas City Blades 12
94/5 Kansas City Blades 12
92/3 Peoria Rivermen
92/3 Peoria Rivermen
95/6 Peoria Rivermen
95/6 Peoria Rivermen
90/1 Prince Albert Raiders
90/1 Prince Albert Raiders
91/2 Prince Albert Raiders
91/2 Prince Albert Raiders
90/1 7th..Sketch WHL 275
91/2 7th...Sketch WHL 243

LESLIE, NATE
02/3 Dundee Texol Stars
02/3 Dundee Texol Stars

LESLIE, NATHAN
02/3 London Knights
02/3 London Knights

LESSARD, DAVID
97/8 New Mexico Scorpions
97/8 New Mexico Scorpions
91/2 7th...Sketch LHJMQ 288

LESSARD, FRANCIS
01/2 BAP Mem. 420
02/3 Chicago Wolves
02/3 Chicago Wolves
92 Québec Pee Wee 1024
93 Québec Pee Wee 1338
01/2 UD Mask 135

LESSARD, JIM
91/2 Avant Garde BCJHL 169
91/2 Avant Garde BCJHL 43
94/5 Dayton Bombers 6
94/5 Dayton Bombers 6
91/2 Nanaimo Clippers
91/2 Nanaimo Clippers

LESSARD, JONATHAN
99/0 Shawinigan 1
99/0 Shawinigan 1
00/1 Shawinigan 4
00/1 Shawinigan 4
01/2 Shawinigan 5
01/2 Shawinigan 5

LESSARD, LOUIS-PHILIPPE
01/2 Victoriaville Tigres 7
01/2 Victoriaville Tigres 7

LESSARD, MARIO*
80/1 LOSA 7
79/0 O-Pee-Chee 389
81/2 O-Pee-Chee 146
82/3 O-Pee-Chee 156
81/2 OPC Sticker 238
82/3 OPC/Topps Sticker 236
82/3 Post [LosA.]
81/2 Topps 98 [West]

LESSARD, MAXIME
01/2 Cape Breton Eagles 2
01/2 Cape Breton Eagles 2

LESSARD, OWEN
92/3 Indianapolis Ice
92/3 Indianapolis Ice
90/1 ProCards 405
91/2 ProCards 478

LESSARD, PAUL
51/2 Bas du Fleuve 24

LESSARD, RICK
84/5 Ottawa 67's
84/5 Ottawa 67's
91/2 Pro Set 560
89/0 ProCards IHL 196
90/1 ProCards 605
91/2 ProCards 519
88/9 Salt Lake G'Eagles
88/9 Salt Lake G'Eagles
91/2 Upper Deck 520

LESSARD, STÉPHANE
80/1 Québec Remparts
80/1 Québec Remparts

LESSOR, DOUGLAS
52/3 Anonymous 48

LESTER, DON
99/0 Colorado Gold Kings
99/0 Colorado Gold Kings
94/5 Richmond Renegades
94/5 Richmond Renegades

LESUEUR, PERCY
91 C55 Reprint 16
83 HHOF Postcard C7
83&87 HHOF 37
10/1 Imperial
10/1 Imperial 2
11/2 Imperial 16
12/3 Imperial 27

LESUK, BILL
72/3 O-Pee-Chee 245
73/4 O-Pee-Chee 205
79/0 O-Pee-Chee 312
76/7 OPC WHA 121
72/3 PHIL / Milk
71/2 Toronto Sun Photo
74/5 WASH
78/9 Winnipeg Jets
78/9 Winnipeg Jets
79/0 WINN

LESWICK, JACK
33-35 Diamond Match Silv.

LESWICK, TONY
45-64 BeeHive-2 [NYRa.]
45-64 BeeHive-2 [Detr.]
51/2 Parkhurst 59
52/3 Parkhurst 65
53/4 Parkhurst 43
54/5 Parkhurst 45
52 Royal Desserts 1
54/5 Topps 45

LETANG, ALAN
99/0 BAP Mem. 356
91/2 Cornwall Royals
91/2 Cornwall Royals
95/6 Fredericton Canadiens
95/6 Fredericton Canadiens
96/7 Fredericton Canadiens
96/7 Fredericton Canadiens
99/0 Omega 79
91/2 7th...Sketch OHL 26
94/5 Slapshot / Sarnia 24
99/0 To. Prmr. Plus 89
00/1 UD MVP 191
00/1 Utah Grizzlies
00/1 Utah Grizzlies

LETENDRE, LUCE
97/8 Game of Her Life
97/8 UD Coll. Choice 290

LETIZIA, MIKE
02/3 Plymouth Whalers
02/3 Plymouth Whalers

LETOURNEAU,
27/8 La Presse

LETOURNEAU, RAY
91/2 ProCards 263

LETOV, EVGENI
00/1 Mir 349

LETOWSKI, TREVOR
99/0 BAP Mem. 160
00/1 BAP Mem. 201
01/2 BAP Mem. 409
97 Bowman 26
99/0 Millenium 193, C-10, ✍ Aut. 193
99/0 NHL Power Play [x3]
01/2 O-Pee-Chee 191
99/0 Omega 186
00/1 Pacific 318
02/3 Pacific Complete 181
00/1 Pa. Paramount 190
01/2 Parkhurst 366
00/1 Signature 111, ✍ Aut. 140
94/5 Slapshot / Sarnia 13
99/0 SP Authentic 65
01/2 SP Authentic ✍ SotT
97/8 Springfield Falcons
97/8 Springfield Falcons
01/2 SPx ✍ Sig
00/1 Stadium 154
00/1 Topps 190, OTG26
01/2 Topps 191
00/1 To. Chrome 126
00/1 To. Heritage 137
01/2 To. Reserve ✂ TR
02/3 T. Total 396
99/0 Upper Deck 103
00/1 Upper Deck 134
01/2 Upper Deck 367
99/0 UD G. Reserve 103
99/0 UD MVP 164
00/1 UD MVP 140
00/1 UD Vintage 277
99/0 Victory 226
00/1 Victory 179
01/2 Victory 274

LEUENBERGER, MARC
91 Semic Sticker 187

LEUENBERGER, SVEN
95 Panini Worlds 122
91 Semic Sticker 180
92 Semic Sticker 201
93 Semic Sticker 115

LEURS, FRANK
70/1 PHIL

LEVAC, FRÉDÉRIC
96/7 Rimouski Océanic
96/7 Rimouski Océanic

LEVÄNEN, MARKO
98/9 Cardset 153

LEVASSEUR, CHRIS
87/8 Moncton Hawks
87/8 Moncton Hawks

LEVASSEUR, ROB
89/0 Nashville Knights
89/0 Nashville Knights

LEVEILLE, NORMAND
82/3 O-Pee-Chee 13

LEVEN, JONAS
89/0 Semic Elitserien 123
90/1 Semic Elitserien 201
91/2 Semic Elitserien 130
92/3 Semic Elitserien 151

LÉVÊQUE, GUY
91/2 Arena 30
91/2 Classic 36
91/2 Classic Four Sport 36
92/3 Classic Prospects 124
93/4 Cla. Prospects 163
91/2 Cornwall Royals
91/2 Cornwall Royals
92/3 Phoenix Roadrunners
92/3 Phoenix Roadrunners
93/4 Phoenix Roadrunners
93/4 Phoenix Roadrunners
91 7th..Sketch Mem.Cup 116
90/1 7th..Sketch OHL 38
91/2 7th...Sketch OHL 11
94/5 St. John's Maple Leafs
94/5 St. John's Maple Leafs
91/2 Star Pics 67
91/2 Ultimate Draft Pick 31, ✍ Aut.
92/3 Upper Deck 576
93/4 Upper Deck 236, 246

LEVER, DON
79/0 ATLF / Colour
87/8 BUFF / Won. Bread
88/9 BUFF / Won. Bread
89/0 BUFF / Campbell's
80/1 CALG
81/2 COLR
83/4 Funmate Puffy 7 [w/]
74/5 Loblaws
83/4 NJER
84/5 NJER
72/3 O-Pee-Chee 259
73/4 O-Pee-Chee 111
74/5 O-Pee-Chee 94
75/6 O-Pee-Chee 206
75/6 O-Pee-Chee 329
76/7 O-Pee-Chee 53
77/8 O-Pee-Chee 111
78/9 O-Pee-Chee 86
79/0 O-Pee-Chee 203
80/1 O-Pee-Chee 124
81/2 O-Pee-Chee 45
82/3 O-Pee-Chee 141
83/4 O-Pee-Chee 224
83/4 O-Pee-Chee 231
84/5 O-Pee-Chee 112
85/6 O-Pee-Chee 238
82/3 OPC/Topps Sticker 224
83/4 OPC/Topps Sticker 218
84/5 OPC Sticker 70
79 Panini Sticker 65
80/1 Pepsi Bottle Cap
82/3 Post [Colo.]
90/1 ProCards 293
91/2 ProCards 23
91/2 Rochester Americans GL
91/2 Rochester Americans GL
91/2 Rochester Americans WPC
91/2 Rochester Americans WPC
83/4 Souhaits Keychain [Devils]
73/4 Topps 111
74/5 Topps 94
75/6 Topps 206
75/6 Topps 329
76/7 Topps 53
77/8 Topps 111
78/9 Topps 86
79/0 Topps 203
80/1 Topps 124
84/5 Topps 86
72/3 VANC / Royal Bank
73/4 VANC / Royal Bank
74/5 VANC / Royal Bank
75/6 VANC / Royal Bank
76/7 VANC / Royal Bank
77/8 VANC / Royal Bank
78/9 VANC / Royal Bank
79/0 VANC / Royal Bank

LEVERS, ALAN
02/3 Coventry Blaze
02/3 Coventry Blaze

LEVERS, MARC
00/1 Nottingham Panthers
00/1 Nottingham Panthers

LÉVESQUE, BEN
82/3 Kingston Canadians
82/3 Kingston Canadians
83/4 Kingston Canadians
83/4 Kingston Canadians

LÉVESQUE, FRANÇOIS
96/7 Rimouski Océanic
96/7 Rimouski Océanic

LÉVESQUE, GUILDOR
52/3 Bas du Fleuve 38
51/2 Lac St-Jean 38
51/2 Laval Dairy 29

LÉVESQUE, HUGO
00/1 Val d'Or Foreurs 4
00/1 Val d'Or Foreurs 4
01/2 Val d'Or Foreurs 2
01/2 Val d'Or Foreurs 2

LÉVESQUE, JONATHAN
96/7 Rimouski Océanic
96/7 Rimouski Océanic

LÉVESQUE, LUC
00/1 Victoriaville Tigres 19
00/1 Victoriaville Tigres 19

LÉVESQUE, MICHEL
84/5 Richelieu Riverains
84/5 Richelieu Riverains

LÉVESQUE, PATRICK
01/2 Drummondville
01/2 Drummondville

LÉVESQUE, PATRIK
01/2 Sherbrooke Castors 5
01/2 Sherbrooke Castors 5

LÉVESQUE, PAUL
80/1 Québec Remparts
80/1 Québec Remparts

LEVIE, CRAIG
83/4 MINS
85/6 MINS
82/3 O-Pee-Chee 382
81/2 WINN
82/3 WINN

LEVINS, SCOTT
93/4 Donruss 130
93/4 Donruss 466
94/5 Donruss 119
93/4 Fleer Ultra 326
94/5 Fleer Ultra 148
90/1 Moncton Hawks
90/1 Moncton Hawks
91/2 Moncton Hawks
91/2 Moncton Hawks
98/9 New Haven Beast 9
98/9 New Haven Beast 9
94/5 OTTA
94/5 OTTA
95/6 OTTA
95/6 OTTA
93/4 Parkhurst 80
94/5 Parkhurst 155, 292
90/1 ProCards 258
91/2 ProCards 182
93/4 Score 617
96/7 Springfield Falcons
96/7 Springfield Falcons
97/8 Springfield Falcons
97/8 Springfield Falcons
93/4 Upper Deck 433, SP-56
94/5 Upper Deck 295
00/1 UD DEL 122
01/2 UD DEL 37

LEVINSKI, DMITRI
00/1 Mir 25

LEVINSKY, ALEX
33/4 Anonymous 9
34-43 BeeHive-1 [Chic.]
35-40 Canada Starch
36-39 Diamond Match TT2
36-39 Diamond Match TT2
36-39 Diamond Match TT3
36-39 Diamond Match BH TT
36-39 Diamond Match Chic.
36-39 Diamond Match BH BT
33/4 Hamilton Gum 36
32/3 Maple Leafs O'Keefe
33/4 O-Pee-Chee 11
94/5 Parkie Tall 2
33/4 WWGum 47
37/8 World Wide Gum 61

LEVO, TAPIO
81/2 COLR
83/4 Funmate Puffy 10 [w/]
91/2 Jyvas Hyva 71
80/1 Mallasjuoma 208
79 Panini Sticker 168
82 Skopbank
78/9 SM-Liiga 225
78/9 SM-Liiga 8
83/4 Souhaits Keychain [Devils]
77-79 Sports. FIN 78-1849
82 Valio

LEVOKARI, PAULI
99/0 Cardset 149
00/1 Cardset 105, 279
02/3 Cardset 216
02/3 Syracuse Crunch
02/3 Syracuse Crunch

LEVONEN, JARI
98/9 Cardset 263
02/3 Cardset 59
97/8 Hockey-Box
92/3 Jyvas Hyva 204
93/4 Jyvas Hyva 359
93/4 Sisu 221
94/5 Sisu 15, H-9

LEVONEN, JARKKO
72/3 Williams Finnish 251
73/4 Williams Finnish 250

LEVONEN, JARNO
93/4 Sisu 222
94/5 Sisu 258

LEVONEN, JYRKI
78/9 SM-Liiga 226

LEVONEN, RAULI
80/1 Mallasjuoma 212
78/9 SM-Liiga 235

LEVY, JEFF
92/3 Classic Prospects 52
93/4 Dayton Bombers
93/4 Dayton Bombers
94/5 Huntington Blizzard
94/5 Huntington Blizzard

LEWANDOWSKI, EDUARD
01/2 UD DEL 245

LEWICKI, DANNY
45-64 BeeHive-2 [Toro.]
45-64 BeeHive-2 [NYRa.]
51/2 Parkhurst 71
93/4 Parkie 56-57 98
45-54 Quaker Oats
54/5 Topps 23
57/8 Topps 61
58/9 Topps 6
58/9 Toronto Star Photo
55 Toronto Star Weekend

LEWIS, BOB
91/2 Avant Garde BCJHL 94

LEWIS, CARLYLE
99/0 Albany River Rats
99/0 Albany River Rats
00/1 Albany River Rats
00/1 Albany River Rats
98/9 Halifax Moosehead
98/9 Halifax Moosehead

LEWIS, DAVE
86/7 DETR / Little Caesars
89/0 DETR / Little Caesars
74/5 Loblaws
80/1 LOSA 8
83/4 NJER
84/5 NJER
79/0 NYIS
74/5 O-Pee-Chee 324
75/6 O-Pee-Chee 108
76/7 O-Pee-Chee 221
77/8 O-Pee-Chee 116
78/9 O-Pee-Chee 162
79/0 O-Pee-Chee 44
80/1 O-Pee-Chee 196
82/3 O-Pee-Chee 157
83/4 O-Pee-Chee 158
84/5 O-Pee-Chee 113
85/6 OPC/Topps 66
86/7 OPC/Topps 85
87/8 OPC/Topps 37
85/6 OPC Sticker 59-185
86/7 OPC Sticker 197-66
87/8 Panini Sticker 242
82/3 Post [LosA.]
83/4 Souhaits Keychain [Kings]
75/6 Topps 108
76/7 Topps 221
77/8 Topps 116
78/9 Topps 162
79/0 Topps 44
80/1 Topps 196
84/5 Topps 87

LEWIS, HERBIE
35/6 Amalgamated Press
34-43 BeeHive-1 [Detr.]
34/5 Sweet Caporal
37/8 World Wide Gum 64

LEWIS, RANDY
90/1 Michigan Tech Huskies
90/1 Michigan Tech Huskies
91/2 Michigan Tech Huskies
91/2 Michigan Tech Huskies
91/2 Michigan Tech Huskies
91/2 Michigan Tech Huskies

LEWIS, ROGER
00/1 Austin Ice Bats
00/1 Austin Ice Bats
93/4 N. Michigan Wildcats
93/4 N. Michigan Wildcats

LEWIS, SHAWN
99/0 Halifax Mooseheads
99/0 Halifax Mooseheads

LEY, RICK
70/1 Dad's Cookies
70/1 Eddie Sargent 198
71/2 Eddie Sargent 195
70/1 Esso Power Player
72/3 New England Whalers
72/3 New England Whalers
69/0 O-Pee-Chee 183
70/1 O-Pee-Chee 108
71/2 O-Pee-Chee 194
79/0 O-Pee-Chee 314
80/1 O-Pee-Chee 198
81/2 OPC Sticker 64
75/6 OPC WHA 14
76/7 OPC WHA 101
90/1 Pro Set 666
73/4 Quaker Oats 25
70/1 Topps 108
80/1 Topps 198
68/9 TORO
69/0 TORO
70/1 TORO
71/2 TORO
71/2 Toronto Sun Photo

LEYTE, ARTHUR
51/2 Bas du Fleuve 29
51/2 Laval Dairy 6

LEYTH, COOPER
52/3 St. Lawrence 52

LEZO, ANTON
01/2 OFS 154

LHENRY, FABRICE
98/9 DEL 138

LIAPKIN, YURI
91/2 Future Trends C72 83
74 Hellas MM-Jenkki 47
72 Panda MM-Toronto
72 Semic Sticker 14
74 Semic Sticker 32
71/2 Soviet Stars
73/4 Soviet Stars 22

74/5 Soviet Stars 7
71/2 Williams Finnish 6
73/4 Williams Finnish 7

LIBETT, NICK

70/1 Eddie Sargent 60
71/2 Eddie Sargent 53
72/3 Eddie Sargent 75
70/1 Esso Power Player
74/5 Loblaws
69/0 O-Pee-Chee 162
70/1 O-Pee-Chee 158
71/2 O-Pee-Chee 140
72/3 O-Pee-Chee 45
73/4 O-Pee-Chee 49
74/5 O-Pee-Chee 193
75/6 O-Pee-Chee 13
76/7 O-Pee-Chee 171
77/8 O-Pee-Chee 103
78/9 O-Pee-Chee 251
79/0 O-Pee-Chee 198
68/9 Shirriff / Detr. 16
72/3 Topps 67
73/4 Topps 49
74/5 Topps 193
75/6 Topps 13
76/7 Topps 171
77/8 Topps 103
78/9 Topps 251
79/0 Topps 198
71/2 Toronto Sun Photo

LICARI, TONY

30s A&BC Chewing Gum 76

LICHNOVSKY, MARCEL

94/5 DEL 399

LICHTNECKER, GERHARD

99/0 Eishockey 410

LIDDINGTON, BOB

75/6 OPC WHA 105
76/7 Phoenix Roadrunners
76/7 Phoenix Roadrunners
70/1 TORO

LIDGREN, JOAKIM

97/8 UD Elitserien 106
98/9 UD Elitserien 22

LIDSTER, DOUG

90/1 Bowman 56
91/2 Bowman 317
92/3 Bowman 267
93/4 EA Sports 140
92/3 Fleer Ultra 221
93/4 Fleer Ultra 374
86/7 Kraft Sports 65
93/4 Leaf 365
94/5 Leaf 353
85/6 O-Pee-Chee 241
86/7 OPC/Topps 32
87/8 O-Pee-Chee 256
88/9 O-Pee-Chee 228
90/1 OPC/Topps 207
91/2 O-Pee-Chee 179
92/3 O-Pee-Chee 51
89/0 O-Pee-Chee 284
86/7 OPC Sticker 102-231
87/8 OPC Sticker 191
88/9 OPC Sticker 63
89/0 opcSticker 69-209
97/8 Pa. Invincible R-130
87/8 Panini Sticker 341
88/9 Panini Sticker 135
90/1 Panini Sticker 295
90/1 Panini/VAN 12
91/2 Panini Sticker 40
92/3 Panini Sticker 37
93/4 Panini Sticker 176
91/2 Parkhurst 184
93/4 Parkhurst 403
91/2 Pinnacle 189
92/3 Pinnacle 147
93/4 Pinnacle 355
94/5 Pinnacle 409
97/8 Pi. Be A Player 208, ✍ Aut. 208
93/4 Premier 315
90/1 Pro Set 298
91/2 Pro Set 247
92/3 Pro Set 199
90/1 Score 73
91/2 Score 215
91/2 Score CAN 215
92/3 Score 124
93/4 Score 524
93/4 Score 65
92/3 Topps 403
91/2 To. Stadium 72
92/3 To. Stadium 404
93/4 To. Stadium 406
94/5 To. Stadium 122
90/1 Upper Deck 60
91/2 Upper Deck 290
94/5 Upper Deck 400
94/5 UD BAP ✍ 23
84/5 VANC
85/6 VANC
86/7 VANC
87/8 VANC / Shell
88/9 VANC / Mohawk
89/0 VANC / Mohawk
89/0 VANC / Mohawk
90/1 VANC / Mohawk
90/1 VANC / Mohawk
90/1 VANC / PotM
90/1 VANC / PotM
91/2 VANC
91/2 VANC
91/2 VANC / Photo
91/2 VANC / Photo
92/3 VANC / Road Trip
92/3 VANC / Road Trip

LIDSTRÖM, NICKLAS

01/2 Adrenaline 67
02/3 Atomic 39, -PC 7
98/9 Aurora 65, -CF 17
99/0 Aurora 51
00/1 Aurora 50
02/3 BAP All-Star 54-55, ✄ ASJ, ✄ HSHSJers
98/9 Be A Player 197, ✍ Aut. 197
99/0 BAP Mem. 3, SL-5, ✄ TM-25
00/1 BAP Mem. 217, ✄ J-17, ✄ TM-12, ✄ TM-17
01/2 BAP Mem. 93, ✄ ASJ, ✄ ASE, ✄ ASN, ✄ ASD, ✄ ASS, ✄ AST, ✄ CoO
02/3 BAP Mem. 194, ✄ ASJ32, ✄ ASE13, ✄ ASN13, ✄ ASTJ1, ✄ AS8, ✄ AST29, ✄ HSHSJers 29, ✄ SCC8, ✄ SC32, /Cup
01/2 BAP Update HSHS, ✄ HSHSJers
92/3 Bowman 305
01/2 Bowman 83
02/3 Bowman 1
98/9 Bowman's Best 47, F8, SB4
02/3 Calder 20, -HH 5
99/0 Crown Royale 50
01/2 Crown Royale 54
02/3 Crown Royale 35
91/2 DETR / Little Caesars
91/2 DETR / Little Caesars
93/4 Donruss 102
94/5 Donruss 194
97/8 Do. Priority 43
98/9 Dynagon Ice 65
99/0 Dynagon Ice 75, ASP-7
97/8 Esso 45
02/3 eTopps 8
02/3 Exclusive 65, ✄ GWJ 8
02/3 First Edition 158, 303, 382, 385, 396, ✄ Jers., ✄ DGJ 15
94/5 Fleer 62
92/3 Fleer Ultra 51, -UI 13, -UR 7
93/4 Fleer Ultra 220
94/5 Fleer Ultra 62
95 Globe 9
01/2 Heads Up ASGUN 6
02/3 Heads Up 45, ✄ GWQ 12
02/3 In The GU 27, 127, ✄ E25, ✄ IE5, ✄ GUJ25, ✄ SJ25, ✄ T9, ✄ TM5
98/9 Kraft / PB
99/0 Kraft / PB
93/4 Leaf 89
94/5 Leaf 141
94/5 Leaf Elit Set 285, GS-4
97/8 Limited 146
99/0 Millenium 87, ✍ Aut. 87
01/2 Nextel
98/9 NHL Power Play
00/1 Nortel Networks All-Star 4
92/3 O-Pee-Chee 369
01/2 O-Pee-Chee 22, 316
02/3 O-Pee-Chee 223, 324
98/9 OPC Chrome 203, B6
91/2 OPC Premier 117
91/2 OPC Premier 163
97/8 Omega 83, GF-6
98/9 Omega 83
99/0 Omega 83, -WAS 3
98/9 Pacific 5, -TW 6
99/0 Pacific 143
00/1 Pacific 153, 436
01/2 Pacific 146, 429
02/3 Pacific 132
02/3 Pacific Complete 1
97/8 Pacific CC 78
97/8 Pa. Crown Roy. 47
98/9 Pa. Crown Roy. 45
97/8 Pa. Invincible 49
97/8 Pa. Paramount 67
98/9 Pa. Paramount 78
99/0 Pa. Paramount 83
00/1 Pa. Paramount 87
97/8 Pa. Revolution 47
98/9 Pa. Revolution 48, -ASG 17
92/3 Panini Sticker 274
92/3 Panini Sticker 298
92/3 Panini Sticker J
93/4 Panini Sticker 253
94/5 Panini Sticker 216
97/8 Panini Sticker 146
98/9 Panini Sticker 134
99/0 Panini Sticker 233, 346
00/1 Panini Sticker 153
91/2 Parkhurst 37
91/2 Parkhurst 445
92/3 Parkhurst 239
92/3 Parkhurst 42
92/3 Parkhurst 451
93/4 Parkhurst 62
94/5 Parkhurst 61
00/1 Parkhurst P-49
01/2 Parkhurst 41, ✄ PJ11, ✄ PS11, ✄ T1
02/3 Parkhurst 113, -HHN 1, ✄ GJ39, ✄ SJ39, ✄ HSHSJers
02/3 Parkhurst Retro 61, ✄ RJ32, ✄ RSJ22, ✄ HH5, ✄ HSHSJers, ✄ NH1, ✄ RM5
94/5 Parkie SE ES-4
91/2 Pinnacle 320
92/3 Pinnacle 8
92/3 Pinnacle T2K 3
93/4 Pinnacle 98
93/4 Pinnacle T2K1 6
94/5 Pinnacle 66, WE16
97/8 Pi. Certified 75
97/8 Pi. Inside 91
97/8 Pi. Totally 75
94/5 POG 95
97/8 Pi. Post 14
93/4 Power Play 74
93/4 Premier 9
94/5 Premier 52
00/1 Premier Plus 70, WP7
99/0 Prism 52
00/1 Private Stock ✄ GUG 45
01/2 Pr. Stock 35
02/3 Pr. Stock Reserve ✄ 119
00/1 PS Titanium 33, WAS-4
01/2 PS Titanium 51, TAS 9
02/3 PS Titanium 38
00/1 PS Titanium Draft ✄ 38
91/2 Pro Set 531
91/2 Pro Set 610
92/3 Pro Set 42
92/3 Pro Set TL 4
91/2 Pro Set Platinum 253
02/3 Quest for the Cup 35, ✄ GWJ 9
99/0 Revolution 53
00/1 Revolution 52, ✄ GUG-5
91/2 Score 71T
91/2 Score CAN 621
92/3 Score 391
92/3 Score 502
93/4 Score 158
94/5 Score 119
97/8 Score 182
97/8 Score Detr. 4
92/3 Score Young Stars 11
94/5 Select 134
95 Semic 57
89/0 Semic Elitserien 247
90/1 Semic Elitserien 152
91/2 Semic Elitserien 255
91/2 Semic Elitserien 322
91/2 Semic Elitserien 341
91 Semic Sticker 31
92 Semic Sticker 56
93 Semic Sticker 23
00/1 Signature 30, ✍ Aut. 52, ✄ DD-4, ✄ J-37, ✄ HSHSJers
01/2 Signature 156, ✍ Aut. 156, ✄ DD3, ✄ GUE21, ✄ GJ22, ✄ GSJ22, ✄ ITN21
02/3 Signature 162, ✍ 162, ✄ SGJ25, ✄ TQ13, ✄ TM5
97/8 SP Authentic 53, ✍ SotT
98/9 SP Authentic 32, ✍ SotT
00/1 SP Authentic 33, ✍ SotT, ✍ SotTD
02/3 SP Authentic 34
00/1 SP GU 24, ✄ TotG, ✄ C
02/3 SP Game-Used ✄ PH (x2)
02/3 Sports Vault 218
99/0 SPx 58
00/1 SPx ✄ WM
01/2 SPx ✄ HT
02/3 SPx 28, ✄ X
98/9 SPx Finite 33, 112
98/9 SPx Prospects 25
99/0 Stadium 10, Chrome 10, CA20, OE7
00/1 Stadium 88, SF14
01/2 Stadium 81, G28, NHLP2
02/3 Stadium 3, -WS9
99/0 SLU 83
92/3 Topps 440
92/3 Topps 9
98/9 Topps 203, B6, M15
99/0 Topps 25, AT5, IM19, TW6
00/1 Topps 60
01/2 Topps 22, 316
02/3 Topps 223, 324
99/0 To. Chrome 25, AT5, IM19
00/1 To. Chrome 48
01/2 To. Chrome 22
02/3 To. Chrome 123
98/9 To. Finest 119
98/9 T. Gold Label 58
99/0 To. Gold Label 20, PG6
00/1 To. Gold Label 86
00/1 To. Heritage 61, 223, 236
01/2 To. Heritage 3, 112, 126, 134
02/3 To. Heritage 1, 104, 113, 121
02/3 To. Limited 223, 324
99/0 To. Prmr. Plus 47, ✄ GP
01/2 To. Reserve 39
92/3 To. Stadium 253
92/3 To. Stadium 43
93/4 To. Stadium 196
93/4 To. Stadium 429
94/5 To. Stadium 228
00/1 To. Stars 46
02/3 T. Total 1, AW3, TT3
98/9 UD Choice 77, 233, RW3
00/1 UD Heroes 46
00/1 Ultimate Mem. ✍ U-39, ✄ D-15, ✄ J-50, ✄ S-50, ✄ TM-6, ✄ TM-7, TM-8
01/2 Ultimate Mem. ✄ Emb., ✄ Jers., ✄ S&J, ✄ ITN, ✄ NP, ✄ PP, ✄ RA, ✄ WTF
02/3 Ultimate Mem. ✄ CSTW, ✄ Emb, ✄ FS, ✄ GUJ, ✄ GUSJ, ✄ ITN, ✄ LA, ✄ NP, ✄ Num, ✄ RAT (x2), ✄ SCDE, ✄ SCDGJ, ✄ SCDN
91/2 Upper Deck 26
91/2 Upper Deck 584
91/2 Upper Deck 587
92/3 Upper Deck 178
92/3 Upper Deck 363
92/3 Upper Deck AR4
92/3 Upper Deck W4
92/3 Upper Deck E9
92/3 Upper Deck ERT2
93/4 Upper Deck 150
94/5 Upper Deck 112, SP-114
97/8 Upper Deck 267, SG45, T14C
98/9 Upper Deck 83, FF29
99/0 Upper Deck 51, AS15
00/1 Upper Deck 67, ✄ GJ
01/2 Upper Deck 63, ✄ PoaNT, ✄ SCFJersD
02/3 Upper Deck 63, ✄ FF, ✄ PW, ✄ UDPL
02/3 UD Artistic 32, R32, CG4, CG18, / Art
94/5 UD BAP ✍ 162
97/8 UD Black Diam. 119, PC19
98/9 UD Black Diam. 31
99/0 UD Black Diam. 33
01/2 UD Challenge 30, ✄ FP
02/3 UD Classic 35, ✄ HH, ✄ HR (x2)
97/8 UD Coll. Choice 81, SQ5
01/2 UD Collectors
98/9 UD G. Reserve 83
99/0 UD G. Reserve 51
01/2 UD Honor Roll 16, 46, ✄ GAJ
02/3 UD Honor 26
97/8 UD Ice 5, L10C
01/2 UD Ice 98
01/2 UD Mask ✄ GJ, ✄ JP, ✄ DP
98/9 UD MVP 70
99/0 UD MVP 72
00/1 UD MVP 67
02/3 UD MVP 68
02/3 UD Piece 34, AC14
01/2 UD Premier ✄ D
02/3 UD Premier 24
02/3 UD Rookie 38
01/2 UD SCup Champs 58
01/2 UD Top Shelf 92, ✄ S, ✄ ST
02/3 UD Top Shelf ✄ CP, ✄ HH, ✄ R, ✄ SH, ✄ ST
00/1 UD Vintage 126
01/2 UD Vintage 93, 96, ✄ NL
02/3 UD Vintage 91, 271, 310, GB 91
00/1 Vanguard 38
01/2 Vanguard EMW 10, ✄ DGM 14
02/3 Vanguard 38
99/0 Victory 103, 324, 342
00/1 Victory 88
01/2 Victory 124, 401
02/3 Victory -NP 44
01/2 Waving the Flag 18
99/0 WGretzky 66
97/8 Zenith 58, Z55

LIDSTRÖM, NIKLAS

02/3 UD Rookie ✄ 154a, ✄ 162b

LIEBSCH, ULRICH

91 Semic Sticker 168

LIEN, PÅL RAAB

92/3 Semic Nordisk 84

LIEN, SVEN

79 Panini Sticker 297

LIEVERS, BRETT

00/1 Cardset 184
02/3 Cardset 60

LIFFITON, DAVID

02/3 Plymouth Whalers
02/3 Plymouth Whalers
02/3 Plymouth Whalers
02/3 Plymouth Whalers

LIGHTBODY, QUADE

94/5 Slapshot / Detroit Jr. 3
94/5 Slapshot Memorial 77

LIIKKANEN, JARI

94/5 Sisu 218

LIIMATAINEN, PETRI

94/5 Leaf Elit Set 19
89/0 Semic Elitserien 6
90/1 Semic Elitserien 80
91/2 Semic Elitserien 5
92/3 Semic Elitserien 32
00/1 UD DEL 40
01/2 UD DEL 139

LIIMTAINEN, PETRI

98/9 DEL 20

LIJVDAL, ÖRJAN

92 Semic Sticker 39

LILIUS, JARMO

80/1 Mallasjuoma 35
72/3 Williams Finnish 310

LILJA, ANDREAS

00/1 BAP Mem. 520
01/2 BAP Mem. 179
00/1 Lowell Lock Monsters
00/1 Lowell Lock Monsters
01/2 O-Pee-Chee 288
01/2 Pacific 182
01/2 Parkhurst 268
01/2 Signature 213, ✍ Aut. 213
01/2 Topps 288
99/0 UD Elitserien 154
01/2 Victory 374

LILJA, KARL-ERIK

89/0 Semic Elitserien 58

LILJA, TOBIAS

97/8 UD Elitserien 183

LILJA, TOMAS

94/5 Leaf Elit Set 227
89/0 Semic Elitserien 155
90/1 Semic Elitserien 230
91/2 Semic Elitserien 155
92/3 Semic Elitserien 184

LILLEY, CAM

02/3 Moose Jaw Warriors
02/3 Moose Jaw Warriors

LILLEY, JOHN

94/5 ANAH / Carl's Jr. 17
94/5 ANAH / Carl's Jr. 17
94/5 Classic ✍ Aut.
98/9 DEL 59
94/5 Donruss 260
99/0 Eishockey 205
94/5 Fleer 6
93/4 Fleer Ultra 490
94/5 Fleer Ultra 251
94/5 Leaf 178
95 Panini Worlds 225
94/5 Parkhurst 8
93/4 Power Play 510
93/4 Premier - USA Hockey 21
93/4 Premier - USA Hockey 8
94/5 Premier 499
94/5 Score 228
94/5 Select 191
94 Semic 130
95 Semic 111
93/4 To. Stadium - Team U.S.A. 14
94/5 To. Stadium 139
94/5 Upper Deck 165
91/2 Upper Deck WJC 70

LILLEY, LES

52/3 Anonymous 140

LILLIE, JEFF

93/4 Slapshot / Kitchener 25

LILLIE, SHAWN

91/2 Knoxville Cherokees
91/2 Knoxville Cherokees

LILLJEBJÖRN, ÅKE

94/5 Leaf Elit Set 102, CS-6
02/3 London Knights
02/3 London Knights
89/0 Semic Elitserien 2
90/1 Semic Elitserien 27
91/2 Semic Elitserien 277
92/3 Semic Elitserien 150
97/8 UD Elitserien 100

LILYHOLM, LEN

72/3 Minn. Fight. Saints
72/3 Minn. Fight. Saints
72 Semic Sticker 125

LIMOGES, RENALD

51/2 Bas du Fleuve 27
52/3 Bas du Fleuve 55

LIMPRIGHT, SHAWN

01/2 Moose Jaw Warriors 12
01/2 Moose Jaw Warriors 12

LINCOLN, BILL

97/8 Hampton Roads
97/8 Hampton Roads

LIND, JUHA

99/0 BAP Mem. 203
00/1 BAP Mem. 63
98/9 Cardset 118, Leij. 30
99/0 Cardset 194, PA 5, AH 8-hertta
00/1 Cardset 119
02/3 Cardset 61
97/8 Do. Preferred 164
97/8 Leaf 160
00/1 MONT
00/1 MONT
97/8 Omega 72
98/9 Pacific 180
98/9 Pa. Paramount 67
97/8 Pinnacle 2
97/8 Score 64
95 Semic 235
93/4 Sisu 24
94/5 Sisu 49, 150, H-1
98/9 UD Choice 64
97/8 Upper Deck 261

LIND, MATS

74 Hellas MM-Jenkki 28
72/3 Williams Finnish 51

LIND, MIKAEL

00/1 UD Elitserien 176

LINDBERG, ANDERS

98/9 Odessa Jackalopes
98/9 Odessa Jackalopes

LINDBERG, BOB

72 Semic Sticker 136

LINDBERG, CHRIS

92 C.O.A. Winter Olympics 190
92/3 CALG / IGA 021
92/3 CALG / IGA 021
90/1 Canada Nationals 15
91/2 Canada Nationals
94/5 DEL 235
92/3 Fleer Ultra 269
93/4 Fleer Ultra 405
93/4 Fleer Ultra 62
92/3 OPC Premier 4
91/2 Parkhurst 251
92/3 Parkhurst 27
93/4 Parkhurst 440
93/4 Premier 76
89/0 ProCards AHL 290
92/3 Score 485
92/3 Score COH 6
92/3 Topps 320
92/3 To. Stadium 407
93/4 To. Stadium 84
92/3 Upper Deck 97
93/4 Upper Deck 196

LINDBERG, HANNU

66/7 Champion 111
70/1 Kuvajulkaisut 282

LINDBERG, HANS

70/1 Kuvajulkaisut 30
72 Panda MM-Toronto
72 Semic Sticker 57
71/2 Williams Finnish 49

LINDBERG, JAN

73/4 Williams Finnish 114

LINDBERG, LASSE

80/1 Mallasjuoma 126

LINDBERG, MATS

94/5 Leaf Elit Set 60
89/0 Semic Elitserien 23
90/1 Semic Elitserien 93
91/2 Semic Elitserien 19
92/3 Semic Elitserien 40
97/8 UD Elitserien 13
98/9 UD Elitserien 16
99/0 UD Elitserien 16, H1
00/1 UD Elitserien 10, 209, ✍ Sig., P1

LINDBERG, TORBJÖRN

94/5 Leaf Elit Set 125
89/0 Semic Elitserien 151
90/1 Semic Elitserien 229
91/2 Semic Elitserien 159
92/3 Semic Elitserien 180
99/0 UD Elitserien 140
00/1 UD Elitserien 121

LINDBERGH, PELLE

01/2 BT Pipes 115
95 Globe 65
83/4 O-Pee-Chee 268
85/6 OPC/Topps 110
83/4 OPC/Topps Sticker 197
85/6 OPC Sticker 193-69
85/6 OPC Sticker 91-224
83/4 PHIL / J.C. Penney
85/6 OPC/Topps-Stick. 6

LINDBLOM, CLAES

94/5 Leaf Elit Set 83
89/0 Semic Elitserien 256
90/1 Semic Elitserien 164
91/2 Semic Elitserien 269
92/3 Semic Elitserien 295

LINDBOM, JOHAN

97/8 Hartford Wolf Pack
97/8 Hartford Wolf Pack
94/5 Leaf Elit Set 235
98/9 UD Elitserien 114
99/0 UD Elitserien 102, ✍ Aut.
00/1 UD Elitserien 101, 197

LINDEGREN, PENTTI

65/6 Hellas 140

LINDEN, JAMIE

93/4 Cincinnati Cyclones
93/4 Cincinnati Cyclones
94/5 Cincinnati Cyclones
94/5 Cincinnati Cyclones
93/4 Cla. Prospects 134
96/7 Grand Rapids Griffins
96/7 Grand Rapids Griffins
89/0 Portland Winter Hawks
89/0 Portland Winter Hawks
90/1 Prince Albert Raiders
90/1 Prince Albert Raiders
90/1 7th..Sketch WHL 283
91/2 7th...Sketch WHL 24
92/3 Upper Deck 38

LINDEN, TREVOR

94/5 Action Packed
98/9 Aurora 116, -CF 28
00/1 Aurora 73
98/9 Be A Player 234, ✍ Aut. 234
99/0 BAP Mem. 194
00/1 BAP Mem. 285, ✄ H-20, TLF, ✍ TLF
01/2 BAP Mem. 495
02/3 BAP Mem. 245
97/8 Bicycle 3-Club
90/1 Bowman 61
91/2 Bowman 327
92/3 Bowman 210
92/3 Bowman 261
98/9 Bowman's Best 100
99/0 Crown Royale 71, -IE 14
93/4 Donruss 354
94/5 Donruss 181
97/8 Donruss 86
97/8 Do. Canadian 32, NP-16, -TLF
97/8 Do. Elite 89
97/8 Do. Preferred 89
97/8 Do. Priority 111
97/8 Do. Studio 101
98/9 Dynagon Ice 115, -TC 16
99/0 Dynagon Ice 103
97/8 Esso 8, ✍ Aut.
02/3 First Edition 401 [Retail]
94/5 Flair 191
94/5 Fleer 225
92/3 Fleer Ultra 222
93/4 Fleer Ultra 109
94/5 Fleer Ultra 226
91/2 Gillette 5
93/4 Hockey Wit 106
92/3 Humpty Dumpty
91/2 Kellogg's / Score 20
89/0 Kraft 42
90/1 Kraft 30
91/2 Kraft 30
92/3 Kraft / Kraft Singles
93/4 Kraft / PB
94/5 Kraft / SS
97/8 Kraft / PB
00/1 Kraft 26
93/4 Leaf 193
94/5 Leaf 527
97/8 Leaf 39, 188-197
94/5 L. Limited 112
97/8 Limited 19
92/3 McDonald's McD-09
97/8 McDonald's McD-22
99/0 Millenium 129, ✍ Aut. 129
00/1 MONT
00/1 MONT
98/9 NHL Power Play
90/1 OPC/Topps 225
91/2 O-Pee-Chee 364
91/2 Topps - Team Leader 17
92/3 O-Pee-Chee 120
01/2 O-Pee-Chee 193
02/3 O-Pee-Chee 180
89/0 OPC/Topps 89
98/9 OPC Chrome 117
91/2 OPC Premier 77
89/0 opcSticker 61, 40-184, / FS 19
97/8 Omega 230
98/9 Omega 147
99/0 Omega 120
98/9 Pacific 32, -GCDC 21
99/0 Pacific 258, -CI 13
00/1 Pacific 210
01/2 Pacific 397
02/3 Pacific 379
02/3 Pacific Complete 53
97/8 Pacific CC 154, SS-11B
97/8 Pa. Crown Roy. 135
98/9 Pa. Crown Roy. 83, PP 15
97/8 Pa. Dynagon 127, T-59, BKS-110
97/8 Pa. Invincible 142
97/8 Pa. Paramount 188
98/9 Pa. Paramount 144
99/0 Pa. Paramount 118
00/1 Pa. Paramount 127
97/8 Pa. Revolution 141
98/9 Pa. Revolution 88
98/9 Panini Photocard
89/0 Panini Sticker 148
90/1 Panini Sticker 299
90/1 Panini/VAN 13,H
91/2 Panini Sticker 36
92/3 Panini Sticker 28
93/4 Panini Sticker 172
94/5 Panini Sticker 147
97/8 Panini Sticker 242
99/0 Panini Sticker 66
00/1 Panini Sticker 40
91/2 Parkhurst 179
92/3 Parkhurst 190
93/4 Parkhurst 215
94/5 Parkhurst 241
00/1 Parkhurst P-30
01/2 Parkhurst 161, 399
02/3 Parkhurst 183
95 Parkhurst Phonecard
94/5 Parkie SE seV5
91/2 Pinnacle 2
92/3 Pinnacle 47
92/3 Pinnacle T2K 24
93/4 Pinnacle 43
93/4 Pinnacle CA24
93/4 Pinnacle T2K1 16
94/5 Pinnacle 8, NL18
97/8 Pinnacle 106
97/8 Pi. Be A Player 9, ✍ Aut. 9
97/8 Pi. BeeHive 40
97/8 Pi. Certified 104
97/8 Pi. Inside 150
97/8 Pi. Totally 104
94/5 POG / Western 21
93/4 Power Play 251
93/4 Premier 225
94/5 Premier 75
99/0 Prism 73
00/1 Private Stock 52, EA-11, ✄ GUG-58
00/1 PS Titanium 48, ✄ GUG-27, ✄ GUG-28
90/1 Pro Set 299
91/2 Pro Set 236
91/2 Pro Set 294
91/2 Pro Set 586
92/3 Pro Set 197
92/3 Pro Set TL 12
91/2 Pro Set Platinum 124
00/1 Revolution 77
90/1 Score 32
90/1 Sco. Hot Cards 16
91/2 Score 339
91/2 Score 8
91/2 Score CAN 369
91/2 Score CAN 8
92/3 Score 305
92/3 Score 438
93/4 Score 117
97/8 Score 144
97/8 Score Vanc. 4
90/1 Sco. Young Stars 19
91/2 Score Young Stars 11
92/3 Score Young Stars 16
92/3 Seasons 30
94/5 Select 11
00/1 Signature 213, ✍ Aut. 127
01/2 Signature 125, ✍ Aut. 125
02/3 Signature 38, ✍ 38
02/3 Slam Card
94/5 SP 122
97/8 SP Authentic 160
98/9 SP Authentic 51
00/1 SP Authentic 48
00/1 SP GU 33
02/3 SP Game-Used ✄ PC
02/3 Sports Vault 294
99/0 SPx 80
01/2 SPx 196
98/9 SPx Finite 50
99/0 Stadium 159
00/1 Stadium 55
92/3 Topps 499
98/9 Topps 117
99/0 Topps 71
00/1 Topps 32
01/2 Topps 193
02/3 Topps 180
99/0 To. Chrome 71
98/9 To. Finest 110
98/9 T. Gold Label 42
99/0 To. Gold Label 63
02/3 To. Limited 180
91/2 To. Stadium 84
92/3 To. Stadium 80
93/4 To. Stadium 357
02/3 T. Total 105
98/9 UD Choice 122
01/2 UD PlayMakers Ltd 96
02/3 Ultimate Mem. ✄ Num
90/1 Upper Deck 256, 480
91/2 Upper Deck 174
91/2 Upper Deck 628
91/2 Upper Deck 97
92/3 Upper Deck 158
92/3 Upper Deck 38
92/3 Upper Deck WG14
93/4 Upper Deck 383, SP-164
94/5 Upper Deck 319, SP-83
97/8 Upper Deck 169, T17B
98/9 Upper Deck 124
99/0 Upper Deck 71
02/3 Upper Deck 418, ✄ CG
94/5 UD BAP R53, R139
93/4 UD BAP Roots 1
01/2 UD Challenge 85
97/8 UD Coll. Choice 259, W10
98/9 UD G. Reserve 124
99/0 UD G. Reserve 71
01/2 UD Ice 124
01/2 UD Mask ✄ GJ, ✄ JP, ✄ DP
98/9 UD MVP 131
99/0 UD MVP 106, ✍ PS
02/3 UD Top Shelf ✄ ST
00/1 UD Vintage 196
02/3 UD Vintage 244, 289
97/8 Valu-net, ✍ Aut.
88/9 VANC / Mohawk
89/0 VANC / Mohawk
89/0 VANC / Mohawk
90/1 VANC / Mohawk
90/1 VANC / Mohawk
90/1 VANC / PotM
90/1 VANC / PotM
91/2 VANC
91/2 VANC
91/2 VANC / Photo
91/2 VANC / Photo
91/2 VANC / PotM
91/2 VANC / PotM
92/3 VANC / Road Trip
92/3 VANC / Road Trip
94/5 VANC
94/5 VANC
95/6 VANC / Abalene 16
95/6 VANC / Abalene 16
96/7 VANC / IGA
96/7 VANC / IGA
00/1 Vanguard 52
99/0 Victory 146
01/2 Victory 357
02/3 Victory 207
99/0 WGretzky 87
97/8 Zenith 73

LINDER, ENGELBERT

95 Panini Worlds 261

LINDFORS, FREDDY

91/2 Semic Elitserien 309
92/3 Semic Elitserien 330

LINDFORS, SAKARI

00/1 Cardset 253
02/3 Cardset 62
97/8 Hockey-Box
91/2 Jyvas Hyva 1
92/3 Jyvas Hyva 2
93/4 Jyvas Hyva 14
89 Semic Sticker 29
91 Semic Sticker 3
92 Semic Sticker 4
93 Semic Sticker 46
93/4 Sisu 83
94/5 Sisu 35, N-9

LINDGREN, JARI

80/1 Mallasjuoma 171
78/9 SM-Liiga 194

LINDGREN, LARS

83/4 MINS
80/1 O-Pee-Chee 177
82/3 O-Pee-Chee 349
83/4 O-Pee-Chee 354
79 Panini Sticker 191
80/1 Pepsi Bottle Cap
82/3 Post [Vanc.]
80/1 Topps 177
78/9 VANC / Royal Bank
79/0 VANC / Royal Bank
80/1 VANC
80/1 VANC / Silverwood
81/2 VANC / Silverwood
82/3 VANC

LINDGREN, MATS

99/0 BAP Mem. 205
00/1 BAP Mem. 125
93/4 Classic 139
94/5 Classic 108, T23
93/4 Cla. 4 Sport 198
01/2 Crown Royale ✄ TT 14
96/7 EDMO
96/7 EDMO
97/8 EDMO
97/8 EDMO
95 Globe 63
94/5 Leaf Elit Set 63
98/9 Pacific 212
99/0 Pacific 259
97/8 Pacific CC 190
99/0 Pa. Paramount 144
97/8 Panini Sticker 213
98/9 Panini Sticker 193
99/0 Panini Sticker 90
00/1 Panini Sticker 55
95 Panini Worlds 153
93/4 Parkhurst 511
93/4 Parkhurst 534
97/8 Pi. Be A Player 154, ✍ Aut. 154
00/1 Private Stock ✄ GUG 71
01/2 PS Titanium Draft ✄ 56
99/0 Revolution 92
91/2 Semic Elitserien 328
99/0 Stadium 42
99/0 Topps 221
99/0 To. Chrome 221
93/4 Upper Deck 570
97/8 Upper Deck 68
01/2 Vanguard ✄ DGM 36

LINDGREN, TERRY

98/9 EBK ECHL All-Star
99/0 Florida Everblades
99/0 Florida Everblades
00/1 Florida Everblades
00/1 Florida Everblades
01/2 Florida Everblades
01/2 Florida Everblades
93/4 Red Deer Rebels
93/4 Red Deer Rebels
95/6 Red Deer Rebels
95/6 Red Deer Rebels

LINDGREN, TORE

89/0 Semic Elitserien 244
90/1 Semic Elitserien 157
91/2 Semic Elitserien 261

LINDH, FREDRIK

94/5 Leaf Elit Set 201
99/0 Odessa Jackalopes
99/0 Odessa Jackalopes
92/3 Semic Elitserien 355

LINDH, MATS

72 Hellas MM-Jenkki 35
74 Semic Sticker 25

LINDH, PATRIK

89/0 Semic Elitserien 238

LINDHOLM, MIKAEL

89/0 LOSA / Smokey 3
90/1 ProCards 351
91/2 Semic Elitserien 40
92/3 Semic Elitserien 73
98/9 UD Elitserien 160
99/0 UD Elitserien 163

LINDHOLM, ULF

65/6 Hellas 139

LINDMAN, MARTIN

99/0 Eishockey 146
00/1 UD DEL 72

LINDMAN, MIKAEL

94/5 Leaf Elit Set 37
89/0 Semic Elitserien 33
90/1 Semic Elitserien 180
91/2 Semic Elitserien 34
92/3 Semic Elitserien 54
98/9 UD Elitserien 106
99/0 UD Elitserien 91
00/1 UD Elitserien 96

LINDMARK, ORJAN

99/0 Eishockey 193

LINDMARK, ÖRJAN

98/9 DEL 52
94/5 Leaf Elit Set 124
89/0 Semic Elitserien 130
90/1 Semic Elitserien 208
91/2 Semic Elitserien 136
92/3 Semic Elitserien 159
01/2 UD DEL 128

LINDMARK, PETER

00/1 Alfabilder
94/5 Leaf Elit Set 75, CS-1
90/1 Semic Elitserien 125
91/2 Semic Elitserien 176
91/2 Semic Elitserien 337
92/3 Semic Elitserien 199
89 Semic Sticker 3
91 Semic Sticker 27

LINDQUIST, FREDRIK

98/9 Bowman's Best 122, F4
91/2 Classic 44
91/2 Classic Four Sport 44
94/5 Leaf Elit Set 86
91/2 Semic Elitserien 72
92/3 Semic Elitserien 97
91/2 Ultimate Draft Pick 39, ✍ Aut.
98/9 Upper Deck 270
97/8 UD Elitserien 45
00/1 UD Elitserien 146, 205, 218, ✍ Sig., T9
98/9 UD G. Reserve 270
99/0 UD MVP 83
99/0 Victory 115

LINDROOS, JARI

98/9 Cardset Top. 6
91/2 Jyvas Hyva 26
92/3 Jyvas Hyva 74
93/4 Jyvas Hyva 137
93/4 Sisu 154
94/5 Sisu 25, 374

LINDROS, BRETT

93/4 Canada Nationals
93/4 Cla. Prospects 204, LP17
94/5 Flair 104
94/5 Fleer 125, -RS 7
93/4 Fleer Ultra 466
94/5 Fleer Ultra 327, P-5
94/5 Leaf 445, P-2
94/5 L. Limited 50
94/5 McDonald's McD-34
94/5 Parkie SE109, seV36
93/4 Pinnacle Bros.
94/5 Pinnacle 257, 478, RTP11
93/4 Power Play 486
93/4 Premier - Canada 1
94/5 Premier 384, 514
94/5 Score CT24, TR3
94/5 Select 178, YE12
94 Semic 106
95 Semic 101
93/4 Slapshot / Kingston 23
94/5 SP 70, P-10
94/5 Topps Finest 9, -BBR 10
94/5 Upper Deck 240, 537, 551, C7, -SP-136
94/5 UD BAP R153

LINDROS, ERIC

01/2 Adrenaline 127, BR 8, WB 12, ✄ GWJ 28
01/2 ASG History
01/2 Atomic 65, AB 8, PP 23, TN 10
02/3 Atomic 68, -CF 17, -PC 14, -SC 10
98/9 Aurora 141, -ALC 15, -CF 36, -FL 7, -MACF 15, -NC 9, -Cube 14
99/0 Aurora 106, -Stripe 106, -CC 9, -CP 9, -ST 15
00/1 Aurora 108, ✄ GWJ-8
02/3 BAP All-Star 56, ✄ ASJ, ✄ HSHSJers
98/9 Be A Player 100, P-10, ✍ Aut. 100, ✄ G-4, ✄ AS-1, ✄ S-1, ✄✍ G-4
99/0 BAP Mem. 167, SL-7, ✄ J-1, ✄ D-2, ✄ TM-7, ✄ TM-18, ✄ TM-29, ✄ TM-49
00/1 BAP Mem. 224, ✄ J-16
01/2 BAP Mem. 315, ✄ ASJ, ✄ ASE, ✄ ASN, ✄ ASD, ✄ AST, ✄ CoO
02/3 BAP Mem. 85, 231, 236, ✄ ASJ33, ✄ ASE14, ✄ ASN14, ✄ ASTJ12, ✄ AST12, ✄ AST13, ✄ AST20, ✄ HSHSJers 6, ✄ TM6
01/2 BAP Update ✄ HSHSJers, ✄ TP10
02/3 Between the Pipes ✄ GN9
97/8 Bicycle 7-Heart
92/3 Bowman 442
01/2 Bowman 36
02/3 Bowman 8
98/9 Bowman's Best 42, F5, SB5
02/3 Calder 46, -HH 8
91 Canada Cup
91/2 Classic 1
91/2 Classic Four Sport 1
99/0 Crown Royale 103, -CS 16, -CCA 9, -IG 18, -TC 5
00/1 Crown Royale 81, JotC-20
01/2 Crown Royale 96, ASH 15, CA 18, JotC 21, LH 6, ✄ TT 11
02/3 Crown Royale 64, -LOR 15
93/4 Donruss 242, Q, -ES 4, -IK 9
94/5 Donruss 137, D-1, ES-7, IM-6
97/8 Donruss 3, -ES 3, -L2L 8
98/9 Donruss ES 19
97/8 Do. Canadian 3, NP-8, ✍ SCS 32
97/8 Do. Elite 10, 119, BF-1, C-2, PN-4, ✍ BF-1
97/8 Do. Preferred 5, 180, LT-2A, PM-7, / Tin 1,21, -Wide Tin 3,10
97/8 Do. Priority 2, 188, DD-16, OD-2, Post-8, Stamp-8
97/8 Do. Studio 3, 108, HH-2, S-2, P-3
98/9 Dynagon Ice 138, -AR 9, -FT 15, -PP 9, -TC 19
99/0 Dynagon Ice 148, -ASP 15, -CM 3, -LL 9, -LotR, 9
93/4 EA Sports 99
97/8 Esso 6, ✍ Aut.
01/2 eTopps 30
02/3 eTopps 19
02/3 Exclusive 116, EIS 8, ✄ GWJ 17
93/4 Fax Pax 27
02/3 First Edition 150, 325, 405R, ✄ Jers., ✄ DGJ 13, ✄ HSHSJers 18, ✄ TSL 12
94/5 Flair 129, CIS-7, SP-6
94/5 Fleer 157, -Head. 6
92/3 Fleer Ultra 157
93/4 Fleer Ultra 161, -PP 5
94/5 Fleer Ultra 345, -ASG 3, -PP 6, SK 6, UP-5
00 Gatorade Sticker
95 Globe 88, 262-64
02/3 Heads Up 82, -EIT 12, -ITN 15, -SM 11, ✄ GWQ 18, / Bobble
93/4 Hockey Wit 88
99/0 HoloGrFX 43, IZ3, PS8
02/3 In The GU 48, 148, ✄ E8, ✄ GUJ8, ✄ SJ8, ✄ T4, ✄ TM9
94/5 Incomnet Phonecard
94 Koululainen
93/4 Kraft / JELL-O
93/4 Kraft / KD
94/5 Kraft / SS
97/8 Kraft / JTP, KD, PB, Spoon
98/9 Kraft / Post 8
99/0 Kraft / KD, / OML, / PB
93/4 Leaf 233, -GLR 3, -HTA 7, -SSS 10
94/5 Leaf 415, -FOI 6, -GLS 11, -LL 17
97/8 Leaf 1, 168, BS-2, FOI-2, ✄ LC 1-5
94/5 L. Limited 58, G-4
97/8 Limited 30, 50, 183, FG-37, FG-55
94/5 McDonald's McD-9
97/8 McDonald's McD-8, F4
98/9 McDonald's McD10
99/0 McDonald's McD-2, ✄ GJ
00/1 McDonald's 26, DAS-4, GWJ-8
02/3 McDonald's 27, -SLG 6, ✄ JP 11
99/0 Millenium 178, P-4, D-6, ✍ Aut. 178, ✍ P-4, ✍ D-6, ✄ J-18, ✄✍ J-18, ✄ JS-18
92 National Game 21
98/9 NHL Power Play
02/3 O-Pee-Chee 17
98/9 OPC Chrome 18
92/3 OPC Premier 102, -TR 1
97/8 Omega 168, 248, GF-13, S-9, SHLC-16, TL-16
98/9 Omega 177, -CS 8, -EOP 16, -FTF 10, -Onl. 26, -PI 29, -Prism 16
99/0 Omega 172, -5ST 9, -EOP 13, -Gen. 9, ✄ GWJ 7
89/0 Oshawa Generals
89/0 Oshawa Generals
90/1 Oshawa Generals
90/1 Oshawa Generals
91/2 Oshawa Generals
91/2 Oshawa Generals
91/2 Oshawa Generals
91/2 Oshawa Generals
98/9 Pacific 88, -CCA 8, -DI 15, -GCDC 25, -TC 19, -Time. 14
99/0 Pacific 307, -CI 16, -CCA 8, -GC 26, -HAA 9,19, -PAP 17, -TL 20
00/1 Pacific 301, GCDC-24, PR-16
01/2 Pacific 290, TDP 5
02/3 Pacific 253, -IZ 8, -L 10, -MI 14
02/3 Pacific Complete 201
97/8 Pacific CC 88, CS-15, CCA-9, GCDC-17, SS-6B, TC-18
97/8 Pa. Crown Roy. 99, BOS-16, CCA-8, HT-13, L-14
98/9 Pa. Crown Roy. 100, -CCA 9, -LL 9, -MP 16, -PotG 18
97/8 Pa. Dynagon 91, 141, DD-11A, KN-8, T-1, T-20, BKS-72
97/8 Pa. Invincible 102, AZ-18, FP-25, OTG-14, R-145, R-219
97/8 Pa. Paramount 134, BN-15, CG-11, P-15
98/9 Pa. Paramount 177, -HOFB 8, -IG 9, -SD 14, -TC 19
99/0 Pa. Paramount 173, -HOFB 8, -IAd 16, -IAI 20, -PB 26
00/1 Pa. Paramount 183, ✄ GUS-15
97/8 Pa. Revolution 103, ASG-16, I-8, TC-18
98/9 Pa. Revolution 106, -ASG 18, -TPA 6, -CTLC 14, -NI 9, -Show. 26
01/2 PTC National 7
94 Panini Olympics 314
98/9 Panini Photocard [x2]
92/3 Panini Sticker P
93/4 Panini Sticker 144, E
94/5 Panini Sticker 38
97/8 Panini Sticker 92
98/9 Panini Sticker 94
99/0 Panini Sticker 121, 323
00/1 Panini Sticker 75
95 Panini Worlds 278
92/3 Parkhurst 128, CP6
93/4 Parkhurst 236, 416, D15, F3, G3, E1
94/5 Parkhurst 301, V69, -YCTG 17
01/2 Parkhurst 61, ✄ PS62, ✄ HSHSJers, ✄ T24
02/3 Parkhurst 58, -HHH1, -HHP1, -HHR 1, ✄ GJ15, ✄ SJ15, ✄ HSHSJers, ✄ MM5, ✄ NH6, ✄ PP8, ✄ TT1
95 Parkhurst Phonecard
02/3 Parkhurst Retro 9, ✄ RJ27, ✄ RSJ19, ✄ HSHSJers, ✄ NN29
94/5 Parkie SE131
92/3 PHIL / UD Sheet
92/3 PHIL / UD Sheet
92/3 PHIL / J.C. Penney
92/3 PHIL / J.C. Penney
93/4 PHIL / Sheet
93/4 PHIL / Sheet
93/4 PHIL / Sheet
93/4 PHIL / Sheet
93/4 PHIL / Sheet
93/4 PHIL / Sheet
93/4 PHIL / J.C. Penney
93/4 PHIL / J.C. Penney
94/5 PHIL / Sheet
94/5 PHIL / Sheet
94/5 PHIL / Sheet
94/5 PHIL / Sheet
94/5 PHIL / Sheet
94/5 PHIL / Sheet

94/5 PHIL / Sheet
94/5 PHIL / Sheet
94/5 PHIL / Sheet
94/5 PHIL / Sheet
96/7 PHIL / Ocean Spray
96/7 PHIL / Ocean Spray
91/2 Pinnacle 365
92/3 Pinnacle 88, 236, -T2K 1, -TP 5
93/4 Pinnacle 1, T2K-1 1, TP-11, Bros., ✍ Aut.
94/5 Pinnacle 1, BR16, GR16, TP8, WE14
97/8 Pinnacle 48, TP-5, P-1
97/8 Pi. Be A Player 1, OT3, TN-10, ✍ Aut. 1
97/8 Pi. BeeHive 1, -BHT 8
97/8 Pi. Certified 31, -CT 8
97/8 Pi. Epix E13
97/8 Pi. Inside 4, -IT 3, / Can 12
97/8 Pi. Mint 1, M-1
92/3 Pinnacle Road to the NHL 1-30
97/8 Pi. Totally 31
94/5 POG 358
94/5 Post
97/8 Pi. Post 1, F1, ✍ Aut.
93/4 Power Play 183, -SYS 5, -Game. 6
93/4 Premier 121, 310, -BG/OPC 12, -BG/Top. 13, -Finest 3
94/5 Premier 241, 400, TF-12, GTG-10
99/0 Prism 103, -CA 16, -DAS 9, SGDC-16
00/1 Private Stock 74, EA-16, Res. 17, PS-43, PSS-20, ✂ GUG-84, ✂ GUG-85
01/2 Pr. Stock 63, Res. 11, -PS 48, ✂ GUG 67
02/3 Pr. Stock Reserve ✂ 133
00/1 PS Titanium 71
01/2 PS Titanium 94, SK 14, TSS 16, ✂ DSJ 25, ✂ DSJ 27
01/2 PS Titanium Draft ✂ 61
02/3 PS Titanium 69, ✂ GWJ 44
92/3 Pro Set 236
02/3 Quest for the Cup 66, -CTC 11
99/0 Revolution 107, -IS 9, -NI 14, -Orn. 15, -TotL 18, / CSC 107
00/1 Revolution 110
90/1 Score 440, B1-B5, 88T
91/2 Score 354-56, 88T, -Hot 1, - Lindros, Young 30
91/2 Score CAN 329-30, 384-85
92/3 Score 432, 550, -Press, COH 1, Young 1
93/4 Score 1, -AS, -DT 12, -DD1, -TF 15, Promo
94/5 Score 1, CI1, DT19, NP12, TF17
97/8 Score 88, 265, CI-1
97/8 Score Phil. 3
90/1 Sco. Young Stars 40
92/3 Seasons 38
93/4 Seasons 10
94/5 Select 100, -FL 5
94 Semic 88, 360
95 Semic 94
92 Semic Sticker 88
93 Semic Sticker 201
92 7th...Sketch Awards 1, 8, 10
90 7th..Sketch Mem.Cup 88, 99
91 7th..Sketch Mem.Cup 96, 119
89/0 7th..Sketch OHL 1, 188, 195, 196
90/1 7th..Sketch OHL 1
00/1 Signature 246, ✍ Aut. 208
01/2 Signature C-14, ✂ FP19, ✂ GUE36, ✂ GJ38, ✂ GSJ38, ✂ HSHSJers 10, ✂ ITN36, ✂ IG7, ✂ TM19
02/3 Signature GS-38, ✂ SGJ8, ✂ TQ4
02/3 Slam Card
94/5 SP 84, P-30
97/8 SP Authentic 111, I7
98/9 SP Authentic 61, SS9, SO6
99/0 SP Authentic 63, HR5, SF8
01/2 SP Authentic 55, ✂ NN
02/3 SP Authentic 59, 100
00/1 SP GU ✂ TotG
01/2 SP GU 34
02/3 SP GU 32, ✂ PC, ✂ PH
02/3 Sports Vault 85
97/8 SPx 36, D-SPX4
99/0 SPx 108, HH9, X9, XT9, S5, ✂ WM
01/2 SPx 185
02/3 SPx 49, 145, ✂ WM
98/9 SPx Finite 100, 152, 172
98/9 SPx Prospects 43, H21, L14, PS8, ✂ WM
00/1 Stadion 68
99/0 Stadium 13, CA13, EG6, OE4, -Chrome 12, -Big 8
00/1 Stadium 97, BT29, CA2
01/2 Stadium 101
02/3 Stadium 17, ✂ NHLP3
93/4 SLU [x2]
94/5 Starting Lineup
97/8 SLU
98/9 SLU
99/0 SLU 333
92/3 Topps 529
98/9 Topps 18, I10, L9, M9
99/0 Topps 7, 282, AT10, IM3, AM6, PP3
00/1 Topps 197, NHLD2
02/3 Topps 17, ✂ FRF
99/0 To. Chrome 7, 282, AT10, IM3, AM6, PP3
00/1 To. Chrome 131
01/2 To. Chrome 134
02/3 To. Chrome 17, ✂ FRF
94/5 Topps Finest 38, -BBB 16, -DF 8
98/9 To. Finest 149, M3, M6, M8, M10, R11, Big 7
94 Topps Finest Bronze 2
98/9 T. Gold Label 13, GR1
99/0 To. Gold Label 12, QC3
01/2 To. Heritage 179
02/3 To. Heritage 74
02/3 To. Limited 17
99/0 To. Prmr. Plus 80, PT3
01/2 To. Reserve 63
92/3 To. Stadium 501
93/4 To. Stadium 10, -Master
94/5 To. Stadium 88, 203, -DAD 2
92/3 To. Stadium Members Only
93/4 TSC Members Only 28
94/5 TSC Members Only 15
00/1 To. Stars 41
02/3 T. Total 4, TT16
98/9 UD3 37, 97, 157
98/9 UD Choice 152, 237, BH8, SQ28
01/2 UD PlayMakers Ltd 67, / PM
02/3 UD Superstars ✂ CAS, ✂ CAST
98/9 UD3 37, 97, 157
00/1 Ultimate Mem. ✍ U-18, ✂ A8-4, ✂ H-6
01/2 Ultimate Mem. ✂ ASGH, ✂ CP, ✂ DD, ✂ Emb., ✂ Jers., ✂ S&J, ✂ Glove, ✂ ITN, ✂ NP, ✂ WTF
02/3 Ultimate Mem. ✂ CP, ✂ Cor, ✂ DD, ✂ Emb, ✂ FS, ✂ FO (x2), ✂ GUJ, ✂ GAO, ✂ HT, ✂ ITN, ✂ JE, ✂ JJ, ✂ LA, ✂ PS
99/0 Ult. Victory 64, FF1, sg10, S9, UV8
90/1 Upper Deck 473
91/2 Upper Deck 7, 9
92/3 Upper Deck 88, 470, CC6, G14, WG12
93/4 Upper Deck 30, 280, -FH 31, HB8, E12, H3, SP 116
94/5 Upper Deck 98, C23, H8, H23, R9, R28, -SP-149
97/8 Upper Deck 331, SS17, SG48, S6, T1A
98/9 Upper Deck 333, FF11, FT9, GN10-12, LS16, P4
99/0 Upper Deck 94, 137, AS12, CT18, FF3, HOF7, IG7, MA3, SB10, SS4, ✂ GJ
00/1 Upper Deck NC4, ✂ GJ
01/2 Upper Deck 118, 346
02/3 Upper Deck 115, -NC8, ✂ CG, ✂ UDPL
02/3 UD Artistic 58, R58, / Art
93/4 Upper Deck Be A Player 29
94/5 UD BAP R106, R178, UC-2
93/4 UD BAP Roots 23
97/8 UD Black Diam. 145, PC13
98/9 UD Black Diam. 62, M14, WF21
99/0 UD Black Diam. 62, D12, DM3, DS6, M9, ✂ APOH
00/1 UD Black Diam. ✂ GG
99/0 UD C. Legends 61, E4
01/2 UD Challenge 59, ✂ FP, ✂ UC
02/3 UD Classic 64, PS7, ✂ HR (x2)
97/8 UD Coll. Choice 186, SQ88, S10, W7, C20, CR20
97/8 UD Diam. Vision 22
98/9 UD G. Reserve 333
99/0 UD G. Reserve 94, 137, ✂ GR
99/0 UD Gretzky Excl. 62, 75
01/2 UD Honor Roll ✂ GAJ
02/3 UD Honor 47, -SG21, -TW10
97/8 UD Ice 88, IC3, L2B
01/2 UD Ice 106
00/1 UD Legends 98
92/3 UD Locker 56
01/2 UD Mask 65
02/3 UD Mask ✂ IO, ✂ PG
98/9 UD MVP 147, OT10, PG3, S7, F5, Souv.
99/0 UD MVP 146, S4, H7, MVP4, GU9, ✂ GU23
00/1 UD MVP 137, MI2, TD7, TP8, VC8, ✂ GS
01/2 UD MVP 127, -J
02/3 UD MVP 119, HN5, VF10, SA, SD (x3), ST
99/0 UD MVP Cup 131, GM8, PH8, SS7, SC12, GC, ✂ GU
99/0 UD Ovation 41, 85, LP15, ST6
02/3 UD Piece 58, 103, ✂ EC, ✂ PH
99/0 UD PowerDeck 16
01/2 UD Premier 34, ✂ B
02/3 UD Premier 36, ✂ Jers, ✂ JD, ✂ Patch
99/0 UD Retro 57
02/3 UD Rookie ✂ DJ, ✂ S
01/2 UD Top Shelf 28
02/3 UD Top Shelf 59, ✂ CP, ✂ M
02/3 UD Vintage 171, 280, GB 171, T43, ✂ SO
97/8 Valu-net, ✍ Aut.
00/1 Vanguard 74, CF-8, HV-26, VP-17, ✂ DGJ-3
01/2 Vanguard 64, EMW 5, QTH 10, VT 16, ✂ DGM 19, ✂ DGM 38
02/3 Vanguard 68
99/0 Victory 210, 212
00/1 Victory 168, 315
02/3 Victory 140, -NP9
01/2 Waving the Flag 7
99/0 WGretzky 122, CG2, EG7, GH7, ✂ TG
97/8 Zenith 6, CTC-4, ZT-4, Z2

LINDSAY, BERT
91 C55 Reprint 21
10/1 Imperial
11/2 Imperial 21
12/3 Imperial 13

LINDSAY, BILL
01/2 BAP Mem. 422
92/3 Bowman 404
92/3 Fleer Ultra 388
93/4 FLOR
93/4 FLOR
96/7 FLOR / Winn-Dixie
96/7 FLOR / Winn-Dixie
97/8 FLOR / Winn-Dixie
97/8 FLOR / Winn-Dixie
01/2 MONT
01/2 MONT
02/3 MONT
02/3 MONT
92/3 OPC Premier 5
99/0 Pacific 176
00/1 Pacific 69
97/8 Pa. Invincible R-86
92/3 Parkhurst 376
93/4 Parkhurst 350
93/4 Power Play 95
93/4 Premier 436
94/5 Premier 522
92/3 Pro Set 239
92/3 QUÉB / Petro-Canada
92/3 QUÉB / Petro-Canada
92/3 Score 463
90/1 7th..Sketch WHL 113
91/2 7th...Sketch WHL 304
92/3 Topps 373
93/4 To. Stadium 253
94/5 To. Stadium 222
92/3 Upper Deck 472
97/8 Upper Deck 74
98/9 Upper Deck 102
97/8 UD Coll. Choice 108
98/9 UD G. Reserve 102

LINDSAY, BOB
87/8 Brockville Braves
87/8 Brockville Braves
88/9 Brockville Braves
88/9 Brockville Braves

LINDSAY, EVAN
98 Bowman 61
98 Bowman Chrome 61

LINDSAY, RYAN
99/0 Quad City Mallards
99/0 Quad City Mallards
00/1 Quad City Mallards
00/1 Quad City Mallards
93/4 Slapshot / Oshawa 25

LINDSAY, SCOTT
91/2 7th...Sketch WHL 322

LINDSAY, TED
01/2 ASG History
99/0 BAP Mem. R-12, ✍ R-12
01/2 BAP Update ✂ RR2, ✂ TC31
45-64 BeeHive-2 [Detr.]
45-64 BeeHive-2 [Chic.]
64-67 BeeHive-3 [Detr.]
64/5 Coke/Sprite [Detr.]
76 DETR
80/1 DETR
99/0 DETR / News 5
99/0 DETR / News 5
48-52 Exhibits [Red Wings]
01/2 Fleer Greats 74, ✍ Aut.
01/2 Fleer Legacy 35
83 HHOF Postcard L10
83&87 HHOF 151
91/2 Kraft 70
93/4 Legends of Hockey 19
51/2 Parkhurst 56
52/3 Parkhurst 87
53/4 Parkhurst 52
54/5 Parkhurst 46
92/3 Parkhurst PR-31
93/4 Parkhurst PR49
01/2 Parkhurst HSHSPR90, PR96, PR126, ✂ HSHSJers, ✂ H10, ✂ PV28, ✂ PV29, ✍ PA39
93/4 Parkie 56-57 140
93/4 Parkie 56-57 155
93/4 Parkie 56-57 44
94/5 Parkie Tall 64
97/8 Pi. BeeHive 60, ✍ Aut. 60
52 Royal Desserts 5
01/2 Signature ✍ VA9
54/5 Topps 51
57/8 Topps 21
58/9 Topps 63
59/0 Topps 6
64/5 Topps 82
00/1 Topps SCH, ✍ SCHA
00/1 To. Heritage ✍ CAI
57/8 Toronto Star Photo
58/9 Toronto Star Photo
54 Toronto Star Weekend
01/2 Ultimate Mem. ✂ ASGH, ✂ Corn., ✂ EA, ✂ PL, ✂ RN, ✂ RT, ✂ SCW, ✍ Aut.
02/3 Ultimate Mem. ✂ Cor, ✂ EA, ✂ FS, ✂ SU, ✂ VGJ
91/2 Ultimate Original Six 70, 94, ✍ Aut. 70
92/3 Upper Deck HH 21
99/0 UD C. Legends 21, AC9, E8, ✍ ES
02/3 UD Foundations ✍ SG
00/1 UD Legends 42, ES15, ✍ ES
01/2 UD Legends 17, ✍ ES
99/0 UD Retro 97, ✍ Ink.
01/2 UD SCup Champs 7
92/3 Zellers

LINDSAY, TED
02/3 Fleer Throwbacks 10, ✍ Aut.

LINDSTÅHL, SAM
94/5 Leaf Elit Set 11
89/0 Semic Elitserien 192
90/1 Semic Elitserien 76
91/2 Semic Elitserien 3
92/3 Semic Elitserien 27

LINDSTEDT, JOHAN
90/1 Semic Elitserien 294
91/2 Semic Elitserien 74

LINDSTRÖM, CURT
95 Hartwall Karjala

LINDSTRÖM, JOHAN
99/0 UD Elitserien 33

LINDSTRÖM, KAJ
00/1 Cardset 71

LINDSTRÖM, SEPPO
70/1 Kuvajulkaisut 143
70/1 Kuvajulkaisut 66
69/0 Mästär Serien 20
72 Panda MM-Toronto
72 Semic Sticker 73
74 Semic Sticker 77
77-79 Sports. FIN 83-1982
71/2 Williams Finnish 193
71/2 Williams Finnish 65
72/3 Williams Finnish 231
73/4 Williams Finnish 265
73/4 Williams Finnish 71

LINDSTRÖM, WILLY
83/4 EDMO / Button
83/4 EDMO / McDonald's
83/4 EDMO / West Mall
83/4 EDMO
84/5 EDMO
84/5 EDMO / Red Rooster
88/9 EDMO / Action 23
79/0 O-Pee-Chee 368
80/1 O-Pee-Chee 142
81/2 O-Pee-Chee 368
82/3 O-Pee-Chee 384
83/4 O-Pee-Chee 35
84/5 O-Pee-Chee 250
85/6 O-Pee-Chee 217
86/7 O-Pee-Chee 232
82/3 OPC/Topps Sticker 209
83/4 OPC/Topps Sticker 91
84/5 OPC Sticker 260
85/6 OPC Sticker 226-93
86/7 OPC Sticker 228-98
77/8 OPC WHA 39
80/1 Pepsi Bottle Cap
86/7 PITT / Kodak
82/3 Post [Winn.]
89/0 Semic Elitserien 39
74 Semic Sticker 17
80/1 Topps 142
83/4 Vachon 32-112
78/9 Winnipeg Jets
78/9 Winnipeg Jets
79/0 WINN
80/1 WINN
81/2 WINN
82/3 WINN

LINDVIST, MAGNUS
97/8 UD Elitserien 166

LINFORD, DAVE
88/9 Kamloops Blazers
88/9 Kamloops Blazers

LING, DAVID
01/2 BAP Mem. 415
96/7 Fredericton Canadiens
96/7 Fredericton Canadiens
98/9 Kansas City Blades 12
98/9 Kansas City Blades 12
99/0 Kansas City Blades
99/0 Kansas City Blades
95/6 Saint John Flames
95/6 Saint John Flames
97/8 Score Mont. 16
93/4 Slapshot / Kingston 16
01/2 Syracuse Crunch
01/2 Syracuse Crunch
02/3 Syracuse Crunch
02/3 Syracuse Crunch
01/2 UD Ice 135

LING, JAMIE
91/2 Air Canada SJHL 25
91/2 Air Canada SJHL A29
98/9 Dayton Bombers
98/9 Dayton Bombers
98/9 Dayton Bombers
98/9 Dayton Bombers
98/9 EBK ECHL All-Star

LINGEMANN, BORIS
00/1 UD DEL 57

LINGLET, CHARLES
00/1 Baie-Comeau 23
00/1 Baie-Comeau 23
01/2 Baie-Comeau 21
01/2 Baie-Comeau 21
02/3 Baie-Comeau
02/3 Baie-Comeau

LINGREN, STEVE
94/5 Dayton Bombers 16
94/5 Dayton Bombers 16
95/6 Dayton Bombers
95/6 Dayton Bombers
95/6 Dayton Bombers
95/6 Dayton Bombers
96/7 Dayton Bombers
96/7 Dayton Bombers
99/0 Kansas City Blades
99/0 Kansas City Blades
00/1 Kansas City Blades 12
00/1 Kansas City Blades 12
98/9 Kentucky Tho'blades
98/9 Kentucky Tho'blades
91/2 7th...Sketch WHL 61

LINHART, TOMAS
02/3 Mississauga IceDogs
02/3 Mississauga IceDogs

LINK, BRAD
98/9 Wichita Thunder
98/9 Wichita Thunder

LINK, TONY
94/5 Anchorage Aces 2
94/5 Anchorage Aces 2

LINK, TRACY
94/5 Anchorage Aces 10
94/5 Anchorage Aces 10

LINNA, KAJ
98/9 Cardset Leij. 11

LINNELL, DEREK
93/4 Raleigh Icecaps
93/4 Raleigh Icecaps
94/5 Raleigh Icecaps
94/5 Raleigh Icecaps

LINNONMAA, HARRI
65/6 Hellas 61
72 Hellas MM-Jenkki 4
70/1 Kuvajulkaisut 110
70/1 Kuvajulkaisut 67
80/1 Mallasjuoma 10
72 Panda MM-Toronto
72 Panda MM-Toronto
74 Semic Sticker 85
78/9 SM-Liiga 36
71/2 Williams Finnish 118
71/2 Williams Finnish 66
72/3 Williams Finnish 64
72/3 Williams Finnish 88
73/4 Williams Finnish 134

LINNONMTAA, HARRI
72 Semic Sticker 80

LINQUIST, GARY
98/9 Cincinnati M'Ducks 3
98/9 Cincinnati M'Ducks 3

LINSEMAN, KEN
84/5 BOST
88/9 BOST / Sports Action
89/0 BOST / Sports Action
98/9 BOST / Alumni 13
98/9 BOST / Alumni 13
91/2 Bowman 105
82/3 EDMO / Red Rooster
83/4 EDMO / Button
83/4 EDMO / McDonald's
83/4 EDMO / West Mall
83/4 EDMO
88/9 EDMO / Action 47
90/1 EDMO / IGA
90/1 EDMO / IGA
83/4 Funmate Puffy 6 [w/]
79/0 O-Pee-Chee 241
80/1 O-Pee-Chee 24
81/2 O-Pee-Chee 244
82/3 O-Pee-Chee 115
83/4 O-Pee-Chee 36
84/5 O-Pee-Chee 7
88/9 OPC/Topps 118
90/1 OPC/Topps 345
91/2 O-Pee-Chee 146
89/0 OPC/Topps 62
81/2 OPC Sticker 176
82/3 OPC/Topps Sticker 112
83/4 OPC/Topps Sticker 102
89/0 opcSticker 26-164
87/8 Panini Sticker 16
88/9 Panini Sticker 164
88/9 Panini Sticker 175
88/9 Panini Sticker 211
89/0 Panini Sticker 190
90/1 Panini Sticker 111
90/1 Panini/EDM 11
82/3 Post [Phil.]
90/1 Pro Set 219, 444
90/1 Score 380, 95T
91/2 Score 359
91/2 Score CAN 239
91/2 Score CAN 622
83/4 Souhaits Keychain [Oilers]
83/4 Stater Mint H17
79/0 Topps 241
80/1 Topps 24
81/2 Topps 107 [East]
91/2 To. Stadium 295
01/2 T/O Archives 75, ✍ CAI
83/4 Vachon 33-113

LINSEMAN, KEN
02/3 Fleer Throwbacks 62

LINSEMAN, MIKE
81/2 Kingston Canadians
81/2 Kingston Canadians

LINSEMAN, STEVE
84/5 Belleville Bulls
84/5 Belleville Bulls
83/4 Brantford Alexanders
83/4 Brantford Alexanders

LINSEMAN, TED
83/4 Kingston Canadians
83/4 Kingston Canadians
84/5 Kingston Canadians
84/5 Kingston Canadians
85/6 Kingston Canadians
85/6 Kingston Canadians
86/7 Kingston Canadians
86/7 Kingston Canadians

LINTEAU, RICHARD
80/1 Québec Remparts
80/1 Québec Remparts

LINTNER, RICHARD
99/0 BAP Mem. 343
98/9 Milwaukee Admirals
98/9 Milwaukee Admirals
99/0 NHL Power Play
99/0 Omega 131
97/8 Springfield Falcons
97/8 Springfield Falcons
99/0 To. Prmr. Plus 94
00/1 Victory 269

LIPIANSKY, JAN
97/8 APS 238
00/1 DS 22
97/8 DS Sticker 43
00/1 OFS 339

LIPINA, PETR
00/1 OFS 207

LIPSETT,
91/2 Avant Garde BCJHL 161

LIPSETT, CHRIS
92/3 Clarkson G'Knights
92/3 Clarkson G'Knights
99/0 Kentucky Tho'blades
99/0 Kentucky Tho'blades
00/1 Kentucky Tho'blades
00/1 Kentucky Tho'blades
96/7 Roanoke Express 16
96/7 Roanoke Express 16
98/9 Roanoke Express
98/9 Roanoke Express

LIPSEY, DARYL
00/1 Kudos 88
01/2 Manchester Storm
01/2 Manchester Storm
02/3 Manchester Storm
02/3 Manchester Storm

LIPTROTT, PETER
86/7 Kingston Canadians
86/7 Kingston Canadians
87/8 Kingston Canadians
87/8 Kingston Canadians
94/5 Slapshot / Brantford 4

LIPUMA, CHRIS
92/3 Atlanta Knights
92/3 Atlanta Knights
93/4 Atlanta Knights
93/4 Atlanta Knights
94/5 Atlanta Knights 20
94/5 Atlanta Knights 20
95/6 Atlanta Knights
95/6 Atlanta Knights
98/9 Chicago Wolves
98/9 Chicago Wolves
99/0 Chicago Wolves
99/0 Chicago Wolves
00/1 Chicago Wolves
00/1 Chicago Wolves
92/3 Classic Prospects 118
93/4 Cla. Prospects 20
93/4 Donruss 493
93/4 Fleer Ultra 178
93/4 Fleer Ultra ARS 4
94/5 Fleer Ultra 372
96/7 Kentucky Tho'blades
96/7 Kentucky Tho'blades
88/9 Kitchener Rangers
88/9 Kitchener Rangers
89/0 Kitchener Rangers
89/0 Kitchener Rangers
90/1 Kitchener Rangers
90/1 Kitchener Rangers
93/4 Pinnacle 208
93/4 Power Play 446
90 7th..Sketch Mem.Cup 44
90/1 7th..Sketch OHL 235
91/2 7th...Sketch OHL 94
94/5 TAMP / Sky Box
94/5 TAMP / Sky Box

LIRETTE, NOEL
69 Columbus Checkers
69 Columbus Checkers

LISABETH, TRAVIS
99/0 Kingston Frontenacs
99/0 Kingston Frontenacs
00/1 Kingston Frontenacs 11
00/1 Kingston Frontenacs 11

LISCOMBE, CARL
34-43 BeeHive-1 [Detr.]
39/0 O-Pee-Chee 74

LISKA, JAN
99/0 OFS 344

LISKA, JAROSLAV
97/8 APS 265
98/9 OFS 409
99/0 OFS 176
00/1 OFS 2

LISKO, CRAIG
91/2 Ferris State Bulldogs
91/2 Ferris State Bulldogs

LISKO, MATTI
70/1 Kuvajulkaisut 316
72/3 Williams Finnish 333

LISMAN, TONY
99/0 Muskegon Fury
99/0 Muskegon Fury

LISY, PETER
85/6 Kitchener Rangers
85/6 Kitchener Rangers
86/7 London Knights
86/7 London Knights

LITKE, DANE
98/9 Florida Everblades
98/9 Florida Everblades
99/0 Florida Everblades
99/0 Florida Everblades

LITMA, LASSE
80/1 Mallasjuoma 159
79 Panini Sticker 169
78/9 SM-Liiga 181
78/9 SM-Liiga 9
77-79 Sports. FIN 84-2016
72/3 Williams Finnish 270
73/4 Williams Finnish 158

LITTLE, MIKE
93/4 Portland Winter Hawks
93/4 Portland Winter Hawks

LITTLE, NEIL
01/2 BAP Mem. 443
02/3 Between the Pipes 41
94/5 Classic 75
02/3 First Edition 300
98/9 Grand Rapids Griffins
98/9 Grand Rapids Griffins
94/5 Hershey Bears
94/5 Hershey Bears
02/3 Pacific 283
01/2 Parkhurst 335
02/3 Philadelphia Phantoms
02/3 Philadelphia Phantoms
01/2 UD Mask 160
02/3 UD MVP 213

LITTLE, RICHARD
92/3 Semic Nordisk 137

LITTMAN, DAVID
92/3 Atlanta Knights
92/3 Atlanta Knights
92/3 Classic 104
93/4 Fleer Ultra 237
93/4 Fleer Ultra ARS 5
98/9 Orlando Solar Bears
98/9 Orlando Solar Bears
98/9 Orlando Solar Bears Geico
98/9 Orlando Solar Bears Geico
89/0 ProCards IHL 103
90/1 ProCards 269
91/2 ProCards 19
91/2 Rochester Americans DD
91/2 Rochester Americans DD
91/2 Rochester Americans GL
91/2 Rochester Americans GL
91/2 Rochester Americans WPC
91/2 Rochester Americans WPC

LITVINENKO, ALEXEI
00/1 Dynamo 4
00/1 Dynamo 4

LITZENBERGER, ED
45-64 BeeHive-2 [Mont.]
45-64 BeeHive-2 [Chic.]
45-64 BeeHive-2 [Detr.]
45-64 BeeHive-2 [Toro.]
64-67 BeeHive-3 [Toro.]
63-65 Chex
00 CSAS Signat. Series
62/3 Cowan Tile
52/3 La Patrie
61/2 Parkhurst 28
62/3 Parkhurst 12
63/4 Parkhurst 6
63/4 Parkhurst 66
93/4 Parkhurst PR66
02/3 Parkie - Reprint 267, 276, 284
93/4 Parkie 56-57 24
60/1 Shirriff 62
61/2 Shirriff 71
62/3 Shirriff 18
52/3 St. Lawrence 7
57/8 Topps 26
58/9 Topps 16
59/0 Topps 61
60/1 Topps 21
58/9 Toronto Star Photo
58/9 Toronto Star Weekend
91/2 Ultimate Original Six 58

LIUS, JONI
98/9 Cardset 238, -Leij. 31
99/0 Cardset 140
00/1 Cardset 219
02/3 Cardset 217
92/3 Jyvas Hyva 84
93/4 Jyvas Hyva 142
93/4 Sisu 152
94/5 Sisu 17
97/8 UD Elitserien 77

LIUT, MIKE
90/1 Bowman 66
91/2 Bowman 290
83/4 Funmate Puffy 14 [w/]
90/1 Kraft 31
80/1 O-Pee-Chee 31
81/2 O-Pee-Chee 289
81/2 O-Pee-Chee 301
82/3 O-Pee-Chee 306
83/4 O-Pee-Chee 309
83/4 O-Pee-Chee 316
84/5 O-Pee-Chee 187
85/6 OPC/Topps 88
86/7 OPC/Topps 133
87/8 OPC/Topps 152
88/9 OPC/Topps 127
90/1 OPC/Topps 44
91/2 O-Pee-Chee 154
89/0 OPC/Topps 97
87/8 OPC Leaders 24
88/9 OPC Stars 20
81/2 OPC Sticker 129
81/2 OPC Sticker 153
82/3 OPC/Topps Sticker 196
83/4 OPC/Topps Sticker 129
84/5 OPC Sticker 57
85/6 OPC Sticker 169-40
86/7 OPC Sticker 52-191
87/8 OPC Sticker 121-133
87/8 OPC Sticker 209
88/9 OPC Sticker 263
89/0 opcSticker 267-148
87/8 Panini Sticker 38
88/9 Panini Sticker 235
90/1 Panini Sticker 165
91/2 Parkhurst 196
91/2 Pinnacle 169
81/2 Post 13
82/3 Post [SLou.]
90/1 Pro Set 316
91/2 Pro Set Platinum PC16
90/1 Score 68, 354
90/1 Sco. Hot Cards 32
91/2 Score 99
91/2 Score CAN 99
92/3 Score 368
85/6 7-Eleven Superstars 7
80/1 Topps 31
81/2 Topps 20
81/2 Topps 128 [West]
84/5 Topps 132
87/8 OPC/Topps - Stick. 8
92/3 Topps 307
91/2 To. Stadium 10
90/1 Upper Deck 127
91/2 Upper Deck 259

LIUT, MIKE
01/2 Fleer Greats 83, ✍ Aut.
01/2 Fleer Legacy 49
85/6 HART / Jr. Whalers
86/7 HART / Jr. Whalers
87/8 HART / Jr. Whalers
88/9 HART / Jr. Whalers
89/0 HART / Jr. Whalers
99/0 Millenium P-10, ✍ P-10
92/3 SLOU / McDon. 4
92/3 SLOU / McDon. 4
89/0 WASH / Kodak
89/0 WASH / Kodak
90/1 WASH / Kodak
90/1 WASH / Kodak
90/1 WASH / Smokey
90/1 WASH / Smokey
91/2 WASH / Kodak
91/2 WASH / Kodak
91/2 WASH / Smokey
91/2 WASH / Smokey

LIV, STEFAN
00/1 UD Elitserien 92

LIVERNOCHE, PATRICK
93/4 Slapshot / Drummondville 19

LIVIN, BRUCE
98/9 Louisiana Ice Gators
98/9 Louisiana Ice Gators

LIZARRAGA, JOSIAN
79 Panini Sticker 371

LJUNGBERG, CHRISTER
91/2 Semic Elitserien 248

LJUNGBERG, THOMAS
94/5 Leaf Elit Set 64
89/0 Semic Elitserien 230
90/1 Semic Elitserien 112
91/2 Semic Elitserien 119
92/3 Semic Elitserien 148

LJUSTERANG, PER
89/0 Semic Elitserien 154
90/1 Semic Elitserien 227
91/2 Semic Elitserien 157
92/3 Semic Elitserien 259

LLANO, KIRK
97/8 Quad City Mallards
97/8 Quad City Mallards
99/0 Topeka Scarecrows
99/0 Topeka Scarecrows

LLOYD, JASON
02/3 Kamloops Blazers
02/3 Kamloops Blazers

LOACH, LONNIE
92/3 Classic 95
92/3 Classic Four Sport 210
92/3 Fleer Ultra 146, 309
88/9 Flint Spirits
88/9 Flint Spirits
99/0 Missouri RiverOtters
99/0 Missouri RiverOtters
92/3 Parkhurst 305
93/4 Power Play 7
88/9 ProCards / Saginaw
89/0 ProCards IHL 60
90/1 ProCards 538
91/2 ProCards 120
93/4 San Diego Gulls
93/4 San Diego Gulls
92/3 Upper Deck 466

LOACH, MIKE
93/4 Slapshot / Windsor 11
97/8 Toledo Storm 25
97/8 Toledo Storm 25

LOANNOU, YIANNI
93/4 Slapshot / Niagara Falls 8

LOBB, AARON
01/2 Guelph Storm
01/2 Guelph Storm
01/2 Guelph Storm M-Cup
01/2 Guelph Storm M-Cup
00/1 London Knights
00/1 London Knights
01 UD Prospects GU 10, ✂ TPJ

LOCAS, JACQUES
75/6 Cincinnati Stingers
75/6 Cincinnati Stingers
48-52 Exhibits [Canadiens]
51/2 Laval Dairy 95
52/3 Laval Dairy Update 57
75/6 OPC WHA 129
43-47 Parade Sportive
45-54 Quaker Oats
52/3 St. Lawrence 81

LOCHEAD, BILL
94/5 DEL 343
74/5 Loblaws
74/5 O-Pee-Chee 318
75/6 O-Pee-Chee 103
76/7 O-Pee-Chee 122
77/8 O-Pee-Chee 212
78/9 O-Pee-Chee 122
79/0 O-Pee-Chee 301
75/6 Topps 103
76/7 Topps 122
77/8 Topps 212
78/9 Topps 122

LOCHER, JEAN-CLAUDE
79 Panini Sticker 260

LOCHI, PATRIC
02/3 Dundee Texol Stars
02/3 Dundee Texol Stars

LOCKE, COREY
01/2 Ottawa 67's 21
01/2 Ottawa 67's 21

LOCKE, STEVE
88/9 Niagara Falls Thunder
88/9 Niagara Falls Thunder

LOCKER, DEREK
93/4 Minnesota-Duluth
93/4 Minnesota-Duluth

LOCKETT, KEN
74/5 Loblaws
76/7 San Diego Mariners
76/7 San Diego Mariners
74/5 VANC / Royal Bank
75/6 VANC / Royal Bank

LOCKHART, TOMMY
83 HHOF Postcard C8
83&87 HHOF 38

LOCKING, NORMAN
36-39 Diamond Match TT1
36-39 Diamond Match TT2
36-39 Diamond Match TT3

LOCKRIDGE, TIM
81/2 Indianapolis Checkers
81/2 Indianapolis Checkers
82/3 Indianapolis Checkers
82/3 Indianapolis Checkers

LOCKWOOD, JOE
88/9 ProCards / Kalamazoo

LOCOCO, MIKE
81/2 Soo Greyhounds
81/2 Soo Greyhounds
82/3 Soo Greyhounds
82/3 Soo Greyhounds
83/4 Soo Greyhounds
83/4 Soo Greyhounds

LODER, GREG
94/5 Wheeling Thund'birds
94/5 Wheeling Thund'birds

LODER, JEFF
96/7 Roanoke Express 5
96/7 Roanoke Express 5

LODIN, HANS
99/0 Eishockey 316
94/5 Leaf Elit Set 112
89/0 Semic Elitserien 175
90/1 Semic Elitserien 8
91/2 Semic Elitserien 204
92/3 Semic Elitserien 227
00/1 UD DEL 171
01/2 UD DEL 186
97/8 UD Elitserien 103
98/9 UD Elitserien 120

LOEN, MATT
98/9 Cincinnati M'Ducks 16
98/9 Cincinnati M'Ducks 16

LOEWEN, DARCY
90/1 BUFF / Campbell's
90/1 BUFF / Campbell's
94/5 Las Vegas Thunder
94/5 Las Vegas Thunder
95/6 Las Vegas Thunder
95/6 Las Vegas Thunder
96/7 Las Vegas Thunder
96/7 Las Vegas Thunder
97/8 Las Vegas Thunder 5
97/8 Las Vegas Thunder 5
92/3 OPC Premier 7
92/3 OTTA
92/3 OTTA
93/4 OTTA
93/4 OTTA
92/3 Parkhurst 355
93/4 Parkhurst 407
93/4 Premier 184
89/0 ProCards AHL 269
90/1 ProCards 284
91/2 ProCards 4
91/2 Rochester Americans DD
91/2 Rochester Americans DD
91/2 Rochester Americans WPC
91/2 Rochester Americans WPC
93/4 To. Stadium 318
91/2 Upper Deck 421

LÖFQVIST, WILLIAM
74 Hellas MM-Jenkki 30
74 Semic Sticker 2
71/2 Williams Finnish 51
73/4 Williams Finnish 32

LÖFSTRÖM, PER
99/0 Cardset 315
97/8 UD Elitserien 22
98/9 UD Elitserien 38
00/1 UD Elitserien 111

LOFTHOUSE, MARK
89/0 New Haven Nighthawks
89/0 New Haven Nighthawks
80/1 O-Pee-Chee 331
88/9 ProCards / Hershey
78/9 WASH

LOFTHOUSE, MIKE
79/0 WASH

LOGAN, BOB
87/8 BUFF / Won. Bread
88/9 ProCards / New Haven

LOGAN, DAN
86/7 Regina Pats
86/7 Regina Pats
86/7 Saskatoon Blades
86/7 Saskatoon Blades

LOGAN, DAVE
78/9 O-Pee-Chee 343
80/1 Pepsi Bottle Cap
80/1 VANC
80/1 VANC / Silverwood

LOGAN, JIM1
52/3 Anonymous 151

LOGAN, JIM2
98/9 Dayton Bombers
98/9 Dayton Bombers
99/0 Fort Wayne Komets
99/0 Fort Wayne Komets

LOGAN, TIM
87/8 Regina Pats
87/8 Regina Pats

LOGHTBODY, QUADE
93/4 Slapshot / Peterborough 25

LOGINOV, ALBERT
98/9 Mir 46
99/0 Mir 157

LOGINOV, ANDREI
00/1 Mir 48

LOGINOV, VLADIMIR
00/1 Mir 71

LOHKO, RAIMO
66/7 Champion 88

LOI, BRAD
84/5 Richelieu Riverains
84/5 Richelieu Riverains

LOICQ, PAUL
83 HHOF Postcard F8
83&87 HHOF 234

LOIKALA, JANI-MATTI
99/0 Cardset 304

LOISELLE, CLAUDE
90/1 Bowman 175
85/6 DETR / Little Caesars
88/9 NJER / Caretta
87/8 Panini Sticker 85
88/9 Panini Sticker 273
90/1 Panini Sticker 151
90/1 Panini/QUE 14
91/2 Pinnacle 296
92/3 Pinnacle 219
93/4 Premier 328
90/1 Pro Set 252
91/2 Pro Set 493
89/0 QUÉB
89/0 QUÉB / Gene. Foods
89/0 QUÉB / Gene. Foods
89/0 QUÉB / Police
89/0 QUÉB / Police
90/1 QUÉB
90/1 QUÉB
90/1 QUÉB / Petro-Canada
90/1 QUÉB / Petro-Canada
90/1 Score 207
91/2 Score CAN 532
92/3 Score 328
92/3 Topps 338
91/2 TORO / P.L.A.Y. 12
91/2 TORO / P.L.A.Y. 12
90/1 Upper Deck 338

LOISELLE, PIERRE
98/9 Québec Remparts
98/9 Québec Remparts

LOJKIN, ALEXEI
95/6 Fredericton Canadiens
95/6 Fredericton Canadiens
96/7 Fredericton Canadiens
96/7 Fredericton Canadiens

LOMAKIN, ANDREI
92/3 Bowman 286
93/4 Donruss 128
94/5 Donruss 85
93/4 EA Sports 52
92/3 Fleer Ultra 372
93/4 Fleer Ultra 327
94/5 Fleer Ultra 81
93/4 FLOR
93/4 FLOR
93/4 Leaf 401
94/5 Leaf 302
90/1 O-Pee-Chee 472
91/2 O-Pee-Chee 40R
92/3 O-Pee-Chee 37
91/2 OPC Premier 178
92/3 Panini Sticker 193
93/4 Panini Sticker 52
91/2 Parkhurst 131
93/4 Parkhurst 349
94/5 Parkhurst 84
91/2 PHIL / J.C. Penney
91/2 PHIL / J.C. Penney
92/3 PHIL / UD Sheet
92/3 PHIL / UD Sheet
92/3 PHIL / J.C. Penney
92/3 PHIL / J.C. Penney
91/2 Pinnacle 305
92/3 Pinnacle 162
93/4 Pinnacle 360
94/5 Pinnacle 337
94/5 POG 106
93/4 Power Play 96
93/4 Premier 82
94/5 Premier 177
91/2 Pro Set Platinum 208
91/2 Red Ace
91/2 Score 110T
91/2 Score CAN 660
92/3 Score 129
93/4 Score 529
94 Semic 160
89 Semic Sticker 98
92 Semic Sticker 115
93 Semic Sticker 143
91/2 Star Pics 17
92/3 Topps 380
92/3 To. Stadium 115
93/4 To. Stadium 402
93/4 To. Stadium 57
91/2 Tri Globe From... 3-4
91/2 Upper Deck 518
92/3 Upper Deck 428
92/3 Upper Deck E17
93/4 Upper Deck 102
94/5 Upper Deck 471

LOMBARDI, MATTHEW
00/1 Victoriaville Tigres 3
00/1 Victoriaville Tigres 3

LOMBARDI, SAL
94/5 Las Vegas Thunder
94/5 Las Vegas Thunder
88/9 ProCards / New Haven

LOMBARDO, JOE
96/7 Sudbury Wolves
96/7 Sudbury Wolves

LOMONACO, ADRIAN
98/9 Guildford Flames
98/9 Guildford Flames

LOMOW, BOYD
83/4 Brandon Wheat Kings
83/4 Brandon Wheat Kings
84/5 Brandon Wheat Kings
84/5 Brandon Wheat Kings

LOMOW, BYRON
83/4 Brandon Wheat Kings
83/4 Brandon Wheat Kings
84/5 Brandon Wheat Kings
84/5 Brandon Wheat Kings
85/6 Brandon Wheat Kings
85/6 Brandon Wheat Kings
89/0 ProCards IHL 141
90/1 ProCards 526

LONEY,
97/8 Hockey-Box

LONEY, BRIAN
93/4 Cla. Prospects 217
99/0 Eishockey 160
96/7 Syracuse Crunch
96/7 Syracuse Crunch

LONEY, TROY
93/4 EA Sports 4
92/3 Fleer Ultra 378
93/4 Fleer Ultra 259
93/4 Kraft / PB
94/5 Leaf 435
90/1 OPC/Topps 347
88/9 Panini Sticker 341
89/0 Panini Sticker 319
90/1 Panini Sticker 138
94/5 Panini Sticker 124
91/2 Parkhurst 352
93/4 Parkhurst 9
94/5 Parkhurst 5
93/4 Pinnacle 379
93/4 Pinnacle CA1
93/4 Pinnacle Expa. 4
94/5 Pinnacle 396
83/4 PITT / Coke Is It✂
87/8 PITT / Kodak
89/0 PITT / Foodland 13
91/2 PITT / Elby's
91/2 PITT / Elby's
91/2 PITT / Foodland 7
91/2 PITT / Foodland 7
92/3 PITT / Coke-Clark
92/3 PITT / Coke-Clark
92/3 PITT / Foodland 8
92/3 PITT / Foodland 8
92/3 PITT / Food. Stickers
92/3 PITT / Food. Stickers
93/4 Power Play 8
93/4 Premier 340
94/5 Premier 363
90/1 Pro Set 237
90/1 Score 371
91/2 Score CAN 522
92/3 Score 348
93/4 Score 547
94/5 Score 67
92/3 Topps 397
92/3 To. Stadium 357
93/4 To. Stadium 395
90/1 Upper Deck 367
91/2 Upper Deck 489
92/3 Upper Deck 208
93/4 Upper Deck 438, SP-2
94/5 Upper Deck 385
94/5 UD BAP ✍ 84

LONG, ANDREW
98 Bowman 17
98 Bowman Chrome 17
01/2 Florida Everblades
01/2 Florida Everblades
95/6 Guelph Storm
95/6 Guelph Storm
96/7 Guelph Storm
96/7 Guelph Storm
99/0 Louisville Panthers
99/0 Louisville Panthers
98/9 New Haven Beast 19
98/9 New Haven Beast 19
94/5 Slapshot / Guelph 26

LONG, BARRY
79/0 DETR
72/3 O-Pee-Chee 288
80/1 O-Pee-Chee 258
81/2 O-Pee-Chee 369
81/2 OPC Sticker 142

75/6 OPC WHA 69
75/6 OPC WHA 90
76/7 OPC WHA 7
80/1 Pepsi Bottle Cap
80/1 Topps 258
78/9 Winnipeg Jets
78/9 Winnipeg Jets
80/1 WINN
83/4 WINN
84/5 WINN / Safety Tips
85/6 WINN
85/6 WINN / Safety Tips

LONG, BILL
86/7 London Knights
86/7 London Knights

LONG, ERIC
94/5 Raleigh Icecaps
94/5 Raleigh Icecaps

LONG, MARC
98/9 Sudbury Wolves 11
98/9 Sudbury Wolves 11

LONGAUER, MICHAL
90/1 7th..Sketch LHJMQ 139
91/2 7th...Sketch LHJMQ 202

LONGBROEK, DAVID
92/3 BCJHL 45

LONGE, BANNY
81/2 Ottawa 67's
81/2 Ottawa 67's

LONGMAN, GARY
69 Columbus Checkers
69 Columbus Checkers

LONGO, CHRIS
93/4 Cla. Prospects 89
97/8 Cleveland Lumberjacks
97/8 Cleveland Lumberjacks
98/9 Cleveland Lumberjacks
98/9 Cleveland Lumberjacks
99/0 Cleveland Lumberjacks
99/0 Cleveland Lumberjacks
00/1 Cleveland Lumberjacks
00/1 Cleveland Lumberjacks
91/2 Peterborough Petes
91/2 Peterborough Petes
93/4 Portland Pirates
93/4 Portland Pirates
94/5 Portland Pirates
94/5 Portland Pirates
89/0 7th..Sketch OHL 114, 178
90/1 7th..Sketch OHL 364
91/2 7th...Sketch OHL 128
96/7 Springfield Falcons
96/7 Springfield Falcons

LONGO, MIKE
90/1 Rayside-Balfour
90/1 Rayside-Balfour
91/2 Rayside-Balfour
91/2 Rayside-Balfour

LONGSTAFF, DAVID
00/1 Kudos 154
02/3 Manchester Storm
02/3 Manchester Storm
97/8 Sheffield Steelers
97/8 Sheffield Steelers
01/2 Sheffield Steelers
01/2 Sheffield Steelers
01/2 Sheffield Steelers GS
01/2 Sheffield Steelers GS

LONGSTAFF, SCOTT
91/2 Avant Garde BCJHL 155
91/2 Avant Garde BCJHL 2

LÖNN, ANDERS
97/8 UD Elitserien 116
98/9 UD Elitserien 130
99/0 UD Elitserien 97

LÖNNBERG, HARRI
98/9 Cardset 220
93/4 Sisu 225
94/5 Sisu 221

LONSBERRY, ROSS
70/1 Eddie Sargent 66
71/2 Eddie Sargent 69
72/3 Eddie Sargent 166
70/1 Esso Power Player
74/5 Loblaws
69/0 O-Pee-Chee 104
70/1 O-Pee-Chee 37
71/2 O-Pee-Chee 121
72/3 O-Pee-Chee 166
73/4 O-Pee-Chee 36
74/5 O-Pee-Chee 144
75/6 O-Pee-Chee 110
76/7 O-Pee-Chee 201
77/8 O-Pee-Chee 257
78/9 O-Pee-Chee 186
79/0 O-Pee-Chee 58
80/1 O-Pee-Chee 388
81/2 O-Pee-Chee 263
72 Semic Sticker 206
67/8 Topps 35
69/0 Topps 104
70/1 Topps 37
71/2 Topps 121
72/3 Topps 112
73/4 Topps 36
74/5 Topps 144
75/6 Topps 110
76/7 Topps 201
77/8 Topps 257
78/9 Topps 186
79/0 Topps 58
71/2 Toronto Sun Photo

LOOB, HÅKAN
00/1 Alfabilder
85/6 CALG / Red Rooster
86/7 CALG / Red Rooster
87/8 CALG / Red Rooster
87/8 CALG / Red Rooster
95 Globe 52
86/7 Kraft Sports 2
94/5 Leaf Elit Set 39, GC-8, P-6, TG-2
84/5 O-Pee-Chee 229
85/6 O-Pee-Chee 184
87/8 O-Pee-Chee 208
88/9 OPC/Topps 110
88/9 OPC/Topps Box O
88/9 OPC Stars 21
84/5 OPC Sticker 242
87/8 OPC Sticker 44-184
88/9 OPC Sticker 118-248
88/9 OPC Sticker 94
87/8 Panini Sticker 201
87/8 Panini Sticker 214
88/9 Panini Sticker 9
94 Semic 64
95 Semic 75
89/0 Semic Elitserien 91
90/1 Semic Elitserien 260
91/2 Semic Elitserien 315
91/2 Semic Elitserien 318
91/2 Semic Elitserien 325
91/2 Semic Elitserien 347
92/3 Semic Elitserien 92
92/3 Semic Elitserien 111
92/3 Semic Elitserien 337
92/3 Semic Elitserien 340
92/3 Semic Elitserien 346
91 Semic Sticker 38
92 Semic Sticker 61
93 Semic Sticker 9
88/9 OPC/Topps - Stick. 3
83/4 Vachon 11-131

LOOB, PETER
84/5 Fredericton Express
84/5 Fredericton Express

LÖÖF, MATTIAS
99/0 Eishockey 222
94/5 Leaf Elit Set 247
92/3 Semic Elitserien 171
00/1 UD DEL 90
01/2 UD DEL 98
97/8 UD Elitserien 188
98/9 UD Elitserien 188

LOONEY, SHELLEY
94/5 Classic W34

LÖÖV, MATS
94/5 Leaf Elit Set 93, TG-10
89/0 Semic Elitserien 108
90/1 Semic Elitserien 114
92/3 Semic Elitserien 266

LOPONEN, JOUNI
98/9 Cardset 231, -Leij. 12
99/0 Cardset 134
00/1 Cardset 94
02/3 Cardset 218
94/5 Sisu 286
97/8 UD Elitserien 86

LOPPONEN, JARI
71/2 Williams Finnish 328

LOPRESTI, PETE
88/9 EDMO / Action 122
76/7 O-Pee-Chee 184
77/8 O-Pee-Chee 13
78/9 O-Pee-Chee 230
79/0 O-Pee-Chee 364
79 Panini Sticker 206
76/7 Topps 184
77/8 Topps 13
78/9 Topps 230

LOPRESTI, SAM
34-43 BeeHive-1 [Chic.]

LORD, ADAM
92/3 BCJHL 160
99/0 San Angelo Outlaws
99/0 San Angelo Outlaws

LORD, LARS-ERIK
90/1 Semic Elitserien 200

LORD, PHILIPPE
96/7 Rimouski Océanic
96/7 Rimouski Océanic

LORENTZ, DAVID
90/1 7th..Sketch OHL 109

LORENTZ, JIM
72/3 BUFF
73/4 BUFF
73/4 BUFF / Bells Market
74/5 BUFF
75/6 BUFF / Linnett
70/1 Eddie Sargent 192
71/2 Eddie Sargent 192
72/3 Eddie Sargent 36
70/1 Esso Power Player
74/5 Loblaws
70/1 O-Pee-Chee 209
71/2 O-Pee-Chee 227
72/3 O-Pee-Chee 116
73/4 O-Pee-Chee 75
74/5 O-Pee-Chee 61
75/6 O-Pee-Chee 28
76/7 O-Pee-Chee 162
77/8 O-Pee-Chee 58
78/9 O-Pee-Chee 161
71/2 Topps 13
72/3 Topps 68
73/4 Topps 171
74/5 Topps 61
75/6 Topps 28
76/7 Topps 162
77/8 Topps 58
78/9 Topps 161
71/2 Toronto Sun Photo

LORENTZ, TOM
85/6 Minnesota-Duluth 20
85/6 Minnesota-Duluth 20

LORENZ, DANNY
94/5 Cincinnati Cyclones
94/5 Cincinnati Cyclones
95/6 Cincinnati Cyclones
95/6 Cincinnati Cyclones
92/3 Classic Prospects 132
98/9 DEL 244
92/3 Fleer Ultra 345
93/4 Leaf 343
96/7 Milwaukee Admirals
96/7 Milwaukee Admirals
97/8 Milwaukee Admirals
97/8 Milwaukee Admirals
01/2 Nottingham Panthers
01/2 Nottingham Panthers
01/2 Nottingham Panthers
01/2 Nottingham Panthers
91/2 ProCards 457

LORENZI, CARLO
95 Panini Worlds 84

LORENZO, JOHNNY
90/1 7th..Sketch LHJMQ 196
91/2 7th...Sketch LHJMQ 70

LORIMER, BOB
81/2 COLR
83/4 NJER
84/5 NJER
79/0 NYIS
79/0 O-Pee-Chee 181
80/1 O-Pee-Chee 138
81/2 O-Pee-Chee 214
82/3 O-Pee-Chee 142
83/4 O-Pee-Chee 232
84/5 O-Pee-Chee 114
82/3 OPC/Topps Sticker 228
82/3 Post [Colo.]
83/4 Souhaits Keychain [Devils]
79/0 Topps 181
80/1 Topps 138

LORING, AL
88/9 ProCards / New Haven

LORING, BRAD
91/2 Avant Garde BCJHL 145
92/3 BCJHL 36
90/1 7th..Sketch WHL 119

LORRAINE, ROD
34-43 BeeHive-1 [Mont.]
35-40 Canada Starch
37/8 O-Pee-Chee 176 [Error: Lorrain]
39/0 O-Pee-Chee 23
38/9 Quaker Oats

LOSCH, MIKE
94/5 DEL 49

LØSCHBRANDT, JAN P
92/3 Semic Nordisk 128

LOTH, ANDREAS
94/5 DEL 257
99/0 Eishockey 179, 389
00/1 UD DEL 120
01/2 UD DEL 129

LOTILA, PETTERI
99/0 Cardset 286

LOTILA, TENHO
66/7 Champion 5

LOTJONEN, OSMO
71/2 Williams Finnish 287
73/4 Williams Finnish 206

LOTVONEN, KIMMO
98/9 Cardset 167
99/0 Cardset 80
00/1 Cardset 303
02/3 Cardset 63

LOUBIER, YVES
91/2 7th...Sketch LHJMQ 274

LOUCKS, BOB
89/0 Lethbridge Hurricanes
89/0 Lethbridge Hurricanes
00/1 Medicine Hat Tigers
00/1 Medicine Hat Tigers
89/0 7th..Sketch WHL 137, 149
91/2 7th...Sketch WHL 359
95/6 Tri-City Americans 28
95/6 Tri-City Americans 28

LOUCKS, SCOTT
93/4 Kamloops Blazers
93/4 Kamloops Blazers
90/1 7th..Sketch WHL 296
91/2 7th...Sketch WHL 87

LOUGHLIN, CLEM
25-27 Anonymous 127
36-39 Diamond Match Chic.

LOUHI, JYRKI
98/9 Cardset 64
99/0 Cardset 37
00/1 Cardset 269

LOUIS, MARTIN
02/3 Signature 91, ✍ 91
02/3 Upper Deck 159
02/3 Victory 194

LOUSTEL, RON
82/3 Brandon Wheat Kings
82/3 Brandon Wheat Kings
81/2 Saskatoon Blades
81/2 Saskatoon Blades

LOUTTIT, EDDIE
52/3 Anonymous 11

LOUTTIT, PAUL
81/2 Ottawa 67's
81/2 Ottawa 67's
82/3 Ottawa 67's
82/3 Ottawa 67's

LOUZEK, MARTIN
99/0 OFS 432

LOVDAHL, ANDERS
99/0 Calgary Hitmen
99/0 Calgary Hitmen

LÖVDAL, ÖRJAN
95 Globe 191
95 Panini Worlds 247

LØVDAL, ØRJAN
92/3 Semic Nordisk 60

LOVE, BRAD
91/2 7th...Sketch OHL 198

LOVEDAY, LOWELL
83/4 Moncton Alpines
83/4 Moncton Alpines
84/5 Nova Scotia Oilers
84/5 Nova Scotia Oilers

LOVELL, GREG
93/4 Slapshot / Kingston 1

LOVELL, JOHN
91/2 Cornwall Royals
91/2 Cornwall Royals
91/2 7th...Sketch OHL 25
93/4 Slapshot / Guelph 28

LOVELL, TIM
93/4 Maine Black Bears
93/4 Maine Black Bears
99/0 Providence Bruins
99/0 Providence Bruins

LÖVGREN, MIKAEL
97/8 UD Elitserien 128
98/9 UD Elitserien 142
99/0 UD Elitserien 144

LOVSIN, DAVE
91/2 Air Canada SJHL D32

LOVSIN, KEN
91/2 Baltimore Skipjacks
91/2 Baltimore Skipjacks
93/4 Canada Nationals
93/4 Fleer Ultra 467
93/4 Power Play 487
93/4 Premier - Canada 4
90/1 ProCards 195
91/2 ProCards 557
94/5 Score CT16

LOW, JASON
91/2 Avant Garde BCJHL 158

LOW, KEN
90/1 EDMO / IGA
90/1 EDMO / IGA

LOW, REED
01/2 Pacific 325, 420
02/3 Pacific 324
02/3 Pacific Complete 491
00/1 PS Titanium 142
00/1 PS Titanium Draft 142
01/2 Signature 145, ✍ Aut. 145
00/1 SP Authentic 163
00/1 SPx 187
00/1 To. Heritage 89
02/3 Upper Deck 398
00/1 UD Ice 100

LOW, RON
93/4 EDMO / Sheet
80/1 EDMO / Zellers
81/2 EDMO / Red Rooster
82/3 EDMO / Red Rooster
88/9 EDMO / Action 36
90/1 EDMO / IGA
90/1 EDMO / IGA
91/2 EDMO / IGA
91/2 EDMO / IGA
92/3 EDMO / IGA 028
92/3 EDMO / IGA 028
99/0 Houston Aeros
99/0 Houston Aeros
74/5 Loblaws
83/4 NJER
84/5 NJER
85/6 Nova Scotia Oilers
85/6 Nova Scotia Oilers
72/3 O-Pee-Chee 258
74/5 O-Pee-Chee 39
75/6 O-Pee-Chee 25
76/7 O-Pee-Chee 69
77/8 O-Pee-Chee 305
78/9 O-Pee-Chee 237
79/0 O-Pee-Chee 348
80/1 O-Pee-Chee 333
82/3 O-Pee-Chee 112
83/4 O-Pee-Chee 233
84/5 O-Pee-Chee 115
82/3 OPC/Topps Sticker 107
80/1 Pepsi Bottle Cap
74/5 Topps 39
75/6 Topps 25
76/7 Topps 69
78/9 Topps 237
01/2 T/O Archives 64
72/3 TORO
74/5 WASH

LOW, STEVEN
98/9 Kansas City Blades 16
98/9 Kansas City Blades 16
97/8 Pensacola Ice Pilots
97/8 Pensacola Ice Pilots

LOWES, JOE
94/5 Slapshot / Brantford 25

LÖWGREN, TORGNY
92/3 Semic Elitserien 271

LOWE, DARREN
87/8 Flint Spirits
87/8 Flint Spirits
88/9 ProCards / Maine
89/0 ProCards IHL 45
90/1 ProCards 310

LOWE, JASON
91/2 Avant Garde BCJHL 28

LOWE, KEVIN
90/1 Bowman 198
91/2 Bowman 115
92/3 Bowman 99
92/3 Durivage 42
79/0 EDMO
81/2 EDMO / Red Rooster
82/3 EDMO / Red Rooster
83/4 EDMO / Button
83/4 EDMO / McDonald's
83/4 EDMO / West Mall
83/4 EDMO
84/5 EDMO
84/5 EDMO / Red Rooster
85/6 EDMO / Red Rooster
86/7 EDMO
86/7 EDMO / Red Rooster
87/8 EDMO
88/9 EDMO
88/9 EDMO / Action 5
90/1 EDMO / IGA
90/1 EDMO / IGA
91/2 EDMO / IGA
91/2 EDMO / IGA
96/7 EDMO
96/7 EDMO
97/8 EDMO
97/8 EDMO
92/3 Fleer Ultra 60, 356
93/4 Fleer Ultra 375
84/5 Kellogg's 26
89/0 Kraft 14
86/7 Kraft Sports 17
89/0 Kraft Stickers 6
81/2 O-Pee-Chee 117
82/3 O-Pee-Chee 113
83/4 O-Pee-Chee 37
84/5 O-Pee-Chee 251
85/6 O-Pee-Chee 239
86/7 OPC/Topps 197
87/8 O-Pee-Chee 200
88/9 O-Pee-Chee 229
90/1 OPC/Topps 307
91/2 O-Pee-Chee 160
92/3 O-Pee-Chee 302
89/0 O-Pee-Chee 227
87/8 OPC Leaders 25
82/3 OPC/Topps Sticker 96
83/4 OPC/Topps Sticker 101
84/5 OPC Sticker 253
85/6 OPC Sticker 219-86
86/7 OPC Sticker 70-200
87/8 OPC Sticker 84-216
88/9 OPC Sticker 219-91
89/0 opcSticker 224-83
97/8 Pa. Invincible R-78
87/8 Panini Sticker 257
88/9 Panini Sticker 54
89/0 Panini Sticker 79, 180
90/1 Panini Sticker 224, 330
90/1 Panini/EDM 12
91/2 Panini Sticker 131
92/3 Panini Sticker 107
93/4 Panini Sticker 97
91/2 Parkhurst 51
92/3 Parkhurst 348
94/5 Parkie SE112
80/1 Pepsi Bottle Cap
91/2 Pinnacle 188
91/2 Pinnacle 371
92/3 Pinnacle 338
93/4 Pinnacle 11
94/5 Pinnacle 338
94/5 POG 171
82/3 Post [Edmo.]
93/4 Power Play 393
93/4 Premier 464
90/1 Pro Set 89, 339
91/2 Pro Set 572
91/2 Pro Set 76
91/2 Pro Set Platinum 38
90/1 Score 170
90/1 Sco. Hot Cards 75
91/2 Score 109
91/2 Score CAN 109
92/3 Score 39
93/4 Score 112
93/4 Score PIAS 3
89 Semic Sticker 62
84/5 7-Eleven
83/4 Souhaits Keychain [Oilers]
92/3 Topps 290
94/5 Topps Finest RL-2
91/2 To. Stadium 179
92/3 To. Stadium 165
93/4 To. Stadium 165
93/4 To. Stadium - All-Stars
94/5 To. Stadium 173
02/3 Ultimate Mem. ✂ FS
90/1 Upper Deck 262
91/2 Upper Deck 186
94/5 Upper Deck 393
97/8 Upper Deck 279
02/3 UD Piece / Giveaway
83/4 Vachon 34-114

LOWE, ROSS ROBERT
45-64 BeeHive-2 [Mont.]
51/2 Parkhurst 18
45-54 Quaker Oats

LOWES, BOB
01/2 Regina Pats
01/2 Regina Pats
94/5 Slapshot Memorial 50

LOWREY, FRED
24/5 Champ's Cigarettes
24/5 Maple Crispette [V130] 28
24/5 William Paterson 36

LOWRY, DAVE
90/1 Bowman 15
91/2 Bowman 373
92/3 Bowman 370
93/4 Donruss 125
94/5 Donruss 20
94/5 Fleer Ultra 82
94/5 FLOR
94/5 FLOR
94/5 FLOR / Winn-Dixie
94/5 FLOR / Winn-Dixie
96/7 FLOR / Winn-Dixie
96/7 FLOR / Winn-Dixie
93/4 Leaf 238
94/5 Leaf 414
90/1 OPC/Topps 370
91/2 O-Pee-Chee 180
92/3 O-Pee-Chee 219
01/2 Pacific 62
97/8 Pa. Invincible R-87
87/8 Panini Sticker 353
91/2 Panini Sticker 32
92/3 Panini Sticker 21
94/5 Panini Sticker 69
91/2 Parkhurst 376
93/4 Parkhurst 79
91/2 Pinnacle 276
93/4 Pinnacle 408
93/4 Pinnacle Expa. 4
94/5 Pinnacle 184
97/8 Pi. Be A Player 183, ✍ Aut. 183
94/5 POG 107
93/4 Power Play 97
93/4 Premier 244
94/5 Premier 89
90/1 Pro Set 265
88/9 ProCards / Peoria
90/1 Score 38T
91/2 Score 149
91/2 Score CAN 149
92/3 Score 109
93/4 Score 564
94/5 Score 81
01/2 Signature 89, ✍ Aut. 89
89/0 SLOU / Kodak
89/0 SLOU / Kodak
90/1 SLOU / Kodak
90/1 SLOU / Kodak
91/2 SLOU
91/2 SLOU
92/3 Topps 42
99/0 Topps 190
99/0 To. Chrome 190
91/2 To. Stadium 303
92/3 To. Stadium 10
93/4 To. Stadium 121
93/4 To. Stadium 379
90/1 Upper Deck 349
93/4 Upper Deck 67
94/5 Upper Deck 291
01/2 Upper Deck 26
94/5 UD BAP ✍ 102
02/3 UD Vintage 42
85/6 VANC
86/7 VANC
87/8 VANC / Shell
01/2 Victory 53

LOXAM, RYAN
91/2 Avant Garde BCJHL 51
92/3 BCJHL 210
91/2 Nanaimo Clippers
91/2 Nanaimo Clippers

LOYER, PAT
83/4 Brandon Wheat Kings
83/4 Brandon Wheat Kings
84/5 Brandon Wheat Kings
84/5 Brandon Wheat Kings

LOYNS, LYNN
02/3 BAP All-Star 109
02/3 BAP Mem. 378
02/3 Calder 145
01/2 Cleveland Barons
01/2 Cleveland Barons
02/3 Crown Royale 136
02/3 In The GU 100
02/3 Pacific Complete 512
02/3 PS Titanium 136
02/3 Quest for the Cup 146
02/3 Signature 199, ✍ 199
02/3 SP Authentic 156
02/3 SP GU 101
97/8 Spokane Chiefs
97/8 Spokane Chiefs
02/3 SPx 170
02/3 T. Total 430
02/3 Upper Deck 449
02/3 UD Honor 163
02/3 UD Top Shelf 117
02/3 Vanguard 133

LOZINIK, TIM
99/0 Anchorage Aces
99/0 Anchorage Aces

LOZINSKI, LARRY
81/2 O-Pee-Chee 97

LOZORUK, CAM
83/4 Kelowna Wings
83/4 Kelowna Wings

LUBINA, LADISLAV
94/5 APS 45
95/6 APS 329
97/8 DS 114
98/9 DS 119
99/0 DS 82
00/1 DS 91
97/8 DS Sticker 275
98/9 OFS 185
99/0 OFS 353
00/1 OFS 43
01/2 OFS 255
91 Semic Sticker 121

LUBINIECKI, DARYL
81/2 Saskatoon Blades
81/2 Saskatoon Blades

LUCE, DON
72/3 BUFF
73/4 BUFF
74/5 BUFF
75/6 BUFF / Linnett
80/1 BUFF / Wendt's 5
93/4 BUFF / Noco
94/5 BUFF / Noco
71/2 Eddie Sargent 26
72/3 Eddie Sargent 33
70/1 Esso Power Player
74/5 Loblaws
71/2 O-Pee-Chee 166
72/3 O-Pee-Chee 95
73/4 O-Pee-Chee 38
74/5 O-Pee-Chee 79
75/6 O-Pee-Chee 113
76/7 O-Pee-Chee 94
77/8 O-Pee-Chee 231
78/9 O-Pee-Chee 58
79/0 O-Pee-Chee 194
80/1 O-Pee-Chee 302
81/2 O-Pee-Chee 147
72/3 Topps 106
73/4 Topps 38
74/5 Topps 79
75/6 Topps 113
76/7 Topps 94
77/8 Topps 231
78/9 Topps 58
79/0 Topps 194
81/2 Topps 99 [West]
81/2 TORO
71/2 Toronto Sun Photo

LUCE, SCOTT
87/8 Sudbury Wolves
87/8 Sudbury Wolves

LUCHINKIN, SERGEI
99/0 Mir 38
94/5 Sig. Rookies FF8, ✍ FF8

LUCHKIN, VLADISLAV
00/1 Mir 379

LUCIUK, ANDREW
99/0 Muskegon Fury
99/0 Muskegon Fury

LUCKNER, HARALD
91/2 Semic Elitserien 305
92/3 Semic Elitserien 327

LUCKY, JEFF
01 UD Prospects GU 29, ✂ TPJ

LUCYK, CAREY
92/3 Fort Wayne Komets 17
92/3 Fort Wayne Komets 17
93/4 Fort Wayne Komets 11
93/4 Fort Wayne Komets 11
94/5 Fort Wayne Komets 21
94/5 Fort Wayne Komets 21
89/0 ProCards IHL 133
90/1 ProCards 548
91/2 ProCards 242

LÜDEMANN, MIRCO
94/5 DEL 205
95 Panini Worlds 53
94 Semic 275

LÜDEMANN, MIRKO
98/9 DEL 96, 315
99/0 Eishockey 106
00/1 UD DEL 132, P7
01/2 UD DEL 140, SS8

LUDVIG, JAN
87/8 BUFF / Blue Shield
87/8 BUFF / Won. Bread
88/9 BUFF / Blue Shield
88/9 BUFF / Won. Bread
83/4 NJER
84/5 NJER
86/7 NJER / S.O.B.E.R.
84/5 O-Pee-Chee 116
84/5 OPC Sticker 76
84/5 Topps 88

LUDWAR, KANE
00/1 Saskatoon Blades
00/1 Saskatoon Blades

LUDWIG, CRAIG
91/2 Bowman 221
94/5 DALL / Southwest
94/5 DALL / Southwest
94/5 DALL / Cap
94/5 DALL / Cap
96/7 DALL / Southwest
96/7 DALL / Southwest
93/4 Fleer Ultra 320
94/5 Fleer Ultra 280
86/7 Kraft Sports 30
93/4 Leaf 432
94/5 Leaf 424
82/3 MONT
82/3 MONT / Steinberg
83/4 MONT
84/5 MONT
85/6 MONT
85/6 MONT / Provigo
86/7 MONT
87/8 MONT
87/8 MONT / Vachon 35
87/8 MONT / Vachon 80
87/8 MONT / Vachon 81
88/9 MONT
89/0 MONT
89/0 MONT / Kraft
83/4 O-Pee-Chee 190
84/5 O-Pee-Chee 265
85/6 O-Pee-Chee 192
86/7 O-Pee-Chee 220
88/9 OPC/Topps 230
90/1 O-Pee-Chee 412
91/2 O-Pee-Chee 150
89/0 O-Pee-Chee 236
90/1 OPC Premier 64
91/2 OPC Premier 80
84/5 OPC Sticker 154
85/6 OPC Sticker 130-250
86/7 OPC Sticker 14-154
88/9 OPC Sticker 48-183
98/9 Pacific 3
97/8 Pa. Invincible R-62
87/8 Panini Sticker 59
88/9 Panini Sticker 254
89/0 Panini Sticker 19
91/2 Panini Sticker 242
94/5 Panini Sticker 233
91/2 Pinnacle 248
91/2 Pinnacle 404
93/4 Pinnacle 303
94/5 Pinnacle 233
93/4 Premier 191
90/1 Pro Set 154, 484
91/2 Pro Set 155
91/2 Pro Set 411
92/3 Pro Set 79
90/1 Score 165, 87T
90/1 Sco. Hot Cards 74
91/2 Score 13
91/2 Score 11T
91/2 Score CAN 13
91/2 Score CAN 561
92/3 Score 94
93/4 Score 282
92/3 Topps 154
91/2 To. Stadium 38
92/3 To. Stadium 354
93/4 To. Stadium 173
94/5 To. Stadium 214
90/1 Upper Deck 186
00/1 Utah Grizzlies
00/1 Utah Grizzlies
83/4 Vachon 48-68

LUDZIK, STEVE
82/3 CHIC
83/4 CHIC
86/7 CHIC / Coke
87/8 CHIC / Coke
98/9 Detroit Vipers
98/9 Detroit Vipers
98/9 EBK IHL All-Star
93/4 Muskegon Fury
93/4 Muskegon Fury
83/4 O-Pee-Chee 105
83/4 O-Pee-Chee 106
84/5 O-Pee-Chee 38
88/9 ProCards / Saginaw
89/0 ProCards AHL 271
90/1 ProCards 276
91/2 ProCards 15
91/2 Rochester Americans WPC
91/2 Rochester Americans WPC

LUGER, MARK
94/5 Roanoke Express
94/5 Roanoke Express

LUHNING, WARREN
99/0 Pacific 260
97/8 Score 69
98/9 Upper Deck 125
98/9 UD G. Reserve 125

LUHRMANN, SCOTT
92/3 Toledo Storm WIOT
92/3 Toledo Storm WIOT
92/3 Toledo Storm
92/3 Toledo Storm
93/4 Toledo Storm 6
93/4 Toledo Storm 6
94/5 Toledo Storm
94/5 Toledo Storm
95/6 Toledo Storm
95/6 Toledo Storm
96/7 Toledo Storm
96/7 Toledo Storm

LUHTI, FREDY
91 Semic Sticker 189

LUIK, JAAN
91/2 Cincinnati Cyclones
91/2 Cincinnati Cyclones
91/2 ProCards 37

LUIK, SCOTT
91/2 Cincinnati Cyclones
91/2 Cincinnati Cyclones
89/0 Oshawa Generals
89/0 Oshawa Generals
90/1 Oshawa Generals
90/1 Oshawa Generals
90 7th..Sketch Mem.Cup 93
89/0 7th..Sketch OHL 21
90/1 7th..Sketch OHL 341

LUKAC, VINCENT
98/9 OFS Leg. 19

LUKACS, ROB
98/9 Odessa Jackalopes
98/9 Odessa Jackalopes

LUKES, CHRISTIAN
94/5 DEL 301
98/9 DEL 239
99/0 Eishockey 4, 384
01/2 UD DEL 9

LUKES, FRANTISEK
00/1 Toronto St. Mike's
00/1 Toronto St. Mike's

LUKES, RADEK
99/0 Score 143

LUKEY, CHRIS
87/8 Kingston Canadians
87/8 Kingston Canadians

LUKIN, JARRET
00/1 Kamloops Blazers
00/1 Kamloops Blazers
01/2 Kamloops Blazers
01/2 Kamloops Blazers
02/3 Kamloops Blazers
02/3 Kamloops Blazers

LUKNOWSKY, JAY
90/1 Michigan Tech Huskies
90/1 Michigan Tech Huskies

LUKOWICH, BRAD
99/0 BAP Mem. 51
00/1 DALL / Southwest
00/1 DALL / Southwest
01/2 DALL / Southwest
01/2 DALL / Southwest
98/9 EBK IHL All-Star
93/4 Kamloops Blazers
93/4 Kamloops Blazers
96/7 Michigan K-Wings
96/7 Michigan K-Wings
98/9 Michigan K-Wings
98/9 Michigan K-Wings
99/0 Millenium 80, C-39, ✍ Aut. 80
99/0 NHL Power Play
99/0 Pacific 124
01/2 Pacific 129
02/3 Pacific Complete 330
94/5 Slapshot Memorial 19
99/0 To. Prmr. Plus 97
99/0 UD MVP Cup 63

LUKOWICH, MORRIS
83/4 Esso Stars
83/4 Funmate Puffy 3 [w/]
87/8 LOSA
79/0 O-Pee-Chee 202
80/1 O-Pee-Chee 107
80/1 O-Pee-Chee 227
81/2 O-Pee-Chee 370
82/3 O-Pee-Chee 383
83/4 O-Pee-Chee 386
84/5 O-Pee-Chee 340
85/6 OPC/Topps 129
81/2 OPC Sticker 138
82/3 OPC/Topps Sticker 205
83/4 OPC/Topps Sticker 281
80/1 O-Pee-Chee Super 24
81/2 Post 19
82/3 Post [Winn.]
83/4 Souhaits Keychain [Jets]
83/4 Stater Mint H9
79/0 Topps 202
80/1 Topps 107
80/1 Topps 227
83/4 Vachon 129-9
78/9 Winnipeg Jets
78/9 Winnipeg Jets
79/0 WINN
80/1 WINN
81/2 WINN
82/3 WINN
83/4 WINN
84/5 WINN / Safety Tips

LUKSA, CHUCK
77/8 Nova Scotia Voyageurs
77/8 Nova Scotia Voyageurs
79/0 O-Pee-Chee 370

LULIN, ANDREI
98/9 UD Elitserien 183
99/0 UD Elitserien 186

LUMBARD, TODD
82/3 Regina Pats
82/3 Regina Pats
83/4 Regina Pats
83/4 Regina Pats
84/5 Springfield Indians 3
84/5 Springfield Indians 3

LUMBY, JEFF
92/3 Hamilton Canucks
92/3 Hamilton Canucks

LUMELA, PEKKA
80/1 Mallasjuoma 82

LUMLEY, DAVE
79/0 EDMO
80/1 EDMO / Zellers
81/2 EDMO / Red Rooster
81/2 EDMO / West Mall
82/3 EDMO / Red Rooster
83/4 EDMO / Button
83/4 EDMO / McDonald's
83/4 EDMO / West Mall
83/4 EDMO
84/5 EDMO
84/5 EDMO / Red Rooster
85/6 EDMO / Red Rooster
88/9 EDMO / Action 35
77/8 Nova Scotia Voyageurs
77/8 Nova Scotia Voyageurs
80/1 O-Pee-Chee 271
82/3 O-Pee-Chee 114
83/4 O-Pee-Chee 38
84/5 O-Pee-Chee 252
82/3 OPC/Topps Sticker 101
80/1 Pepsi Bottle Cap
82/3 Post [Edmo.]
83/4 Vachon 35-115

LUMLEY, HARRY
45-64 BeeHive-2 [Detr.]
45-64 BeeHive-2 [Chic.]
45-64 BeeHive-2 [Toro.]
45-64 BeeHive-2 [Bost.]
01/2 BT Pipes 125, 139
02/3 Between the Pipes ✂ GT10, ✂ HSHSJers 21, ✂ VM2
48-52 Exhibits [Red Wings]
83 HHOF Postcard B7
83&87 HHOF 21
02/3 In The GU ✂ VM9
92/3 Legends 1
43-47 Parade Sportive
51/2 Parkhurst 47
52/3 Parkhurst 59
53/4 Parkhurst 1
54/5 Parkhurst 16
54/5 Parkhurst 91
54/5 Parkhurst 92
54/5 Parkhurst 93
55/6 Parkhurst 1
55/6 Parkhurst 70
55/6 Parkhurst 70
55/6 Parkhurst 73
55/6 Parkhurst 74
55/6 Parkhurst 76
92/3 Parkhurst PR-5
01/2 Parkhurst PR15, PR22, PR58, PR104
02/3 Parkhurst ✂ VT16
45-54 Quaker Oats
59/0 Toronto Star Photo
55 Toronto Star Weekend
02/3 Ultimate Mem. ✂ EA, ✂ VGJ, ✍ Cut
91/2 Ultimate Original Six 51, ✍ Aut. 51

LUMME, JYRKI
01/2 Atomic ✂ GWJ 18
98/9 Be A Player 259, ✍ Aut. 259
99/0 BAP Mem. 260
00/1 BAP Mem. 280
91/2 Bowman 321
92/3 Bowman 170
98/9 Cardset DT 3
99/0 Cardset AH 5-hertta
00/1 Cardset 353
02/3 Cardset 64
00/1 Crown Royale ✂ GWJ 21
93/4 Donruss 347
94/5 Donruss 190
93/4 EA Sports 139
94/5 Flair 192
94/5 Fleer 226
92/3 Fleer Ultra 223
93/4 Fleer Ultra 126
94/5 Fleer Ultra 227
95 Globe 129
01/2 Heads Up ✂ JQ 26
02/3 Heads Up ✂ GWQ 33
93 Koululainen
93/4 Leaf 231
94/5 Leaf 287
89/0 MONT
91/2 O-Pee-Chee 419
92/3 O-Pee-Chee 265
98/9 Omega 185
98/9 Pacific 428
99/0 Pacific 322
00/1 Pacific 319
01/2 Pacific ✂ GWJ 25
02/3 Pacific Complete 283
97/8 Pacific CC 232
99/0 Pa. Paramount 180
90/1 Panini/VAN 14
92/3 Panini Sticker 36
93/4 Panini Sticker 175
94/5 Panini Sticker 151
97/8 Panini Sticker 244
98/9 Panini Sticker 222
99/0 Panini Sticker 279
00/1 Panini Sticker 187
91/2 Parkhurst 180
92/3 Parkhurst 191
93/4 Parkhurst 483
00/1 Parkhurst P-135
01/2 Parkhurst 218
94/5 Parkie SE190, ES8
98/9 PHOE / Coca-Cola
98/9 PHOE / Coca-Cola
91/2 Pinnacle 237
92/3 Pinnacle 65
93/4 Pinnacle 21
94/5 Pinnacle 86
94/5 POG 339
93/4 Power Play 252
93/4 Premier 475
94/5 Premier 442
00/1 PS Titanium ✂ GUG 127
00/1 PS Titanium Draft ✂ 77
90/1 Pro Set 300
91/2 Pro Set 240
92/3 Pro Set 196
91/2 Pro Set Platinum 237
88/9 ProCards / Sherbrooke
90/1 Score 132
91/2 Score 242
91/2 Score CAN 462
92/3 Score 318
93/4 Score 134
94/5 Score 35
97/8 Score Vanc. 8
92/3 Score Young Stars 34
94 Semic 8
95 Semic 38
91 Semic Sticker 202
92 Semic Sticker 6
93 Semic Sticker 56
00/1 Signature 10, ✍ Aut. 104
94/5 Sisu 360, GS-3
92/3 Topps 510
99/0 Topps 222
00/1 Topps 266
99/0 To. Chrome 222
91/2 To. Stadium 154
92/3 To. Stadium 321
93/4 To. Stadium 108
94/5 To. Stadium 132
98/9 UD Choice 205
90/1 Upper Deck 297
91/2 Upper Deck 114
92/3 Upper Deck 137
94/5 Upper Deck 148
97/8 Upper Deck 378
98/9 Upper Deck 65
98/9 Upper Deck 340
97/8 UD Coll. Choice 262
98/9 UD G. Reserve 340
99/0 UD MVP Cup 143
00/1 UD Vintage 279
90/1 VANC / Mohawk
90/1 VANC / Mohawk
91/2 VANC
91/2 VANC
91/2 VANC / Photo
91/2 VANC / Photo
92/3 VANC / Road Trip
92/3 VANC / Road Trip
94/5 VANC
94/5 VANC
95/6 VANC / Abalene 6
95/6 VANC / Abalene 6
96/7 VANC / IGA
96/7 VANC / IGA
01/2 Vanguard ✂ DGM 22

LUND, JAMIE
91/2 Avant Garde BCJHL 142

LUND, JOE
51/2 Cleveland Barons

LUND, LARRY
75/6 Houston Aeros
75/6 Houston Aeros
74/5 OPC WHA 22
77/8 OPC WHA 19
73/4 Quaker Oats 19

LUND, PENTTI
02/3 Parkie - Reprint 155

LUND, PENTTI (PENNY)
45-64 BeeHive-2 [NYRa.]
45-64 BeeHive-2 [Bost.]
51/2 Parkhurst 31
52/3 Parkhurst 83

LUND, TOM
70/1 Kuvajulkaisut 351

LUNDBACK, PATRIK
97/8 UD Elitserien 95

LUNDBERG, JOAKIM
94/5 Leaf Elit Set 213
92/3 Semic Elitserien 82
98/9 UD Elitserien 186
99/0 UD Elitserien 189
00/1 UD Elitserien 138

LUNDBERG, LARS GUNNAR
79 Panini Sticker 198

LUNDBERG, NICLAS
91/2 Semic Elitserien 275

LUNDBERG, PERTTI
71/2 Williams Finnish 348

LUNDBERGH, PER
89/0 Semic Elitserien 265

LUNDBOHM, ANDY
99/0 Kentucky Tho'blades
99/0 Kentucky Tho'blades
00/1 Kentucky Tho'blades
00/1 Kentucky Tho'blades

LUNDBOHM, BRYAN
01/2 Milwaukee Admirals
01/2 Milwaukee Admirals

LUNDE, DALE
72/3 Williams Finnish 334

LUNDE, LARS ERIK
92/3 Semic Nordisk 116

LUNDE, LEN
45-64 BeeHive-2 [Detr.]
45-64 BeeHive-2 [Chic.]
45-64 BeeHive-2 [Chic.]
64-67 BeeHive-3 [Chic.]
70/1 Esso Power Player
62/3 Cowan Tile
70/1 O-Pee-Chee 230
60/1 Parkhurst 35
61/2 Parkhurst 24
62/3 Parkhurst 35
60/1 Shirriff 54
58/9 Topps 15
59/0 Topps 22
72/3 Williams Finnish 129

LUNDE, RYAMOND
92/3 Semic Nordisk 150

LUNDELL, JAN
98/9 Cardset 28, MM 2
00/1 Cardset 264

LUNDELL, PER
98/9 DEL 264
94/5 Leaf Elit Set 4
89/0 Semic Elitserien 127
90/1 Semic Elitserien 204
91/2 Semic Elitserien 83
92/3 Semic Elitserien 107
99/0 UD Elitserien 106

LUNDEN, HANNU
70/1 Kuvajulkaisut 232
71/2 Williams Finnish 249
73/4 Williams Finnish 290

LUNDEN, MARTTI
70/1 Kuvajulkaisut 333

LUNDH, STAFFAN
89/0 Semic Elitserien 86
90/1 Semic Elitserien 267
91/2 Semic Elitserien 96
92/3 Semic Elitserien 114

LUNDHOLM, ANDY
01/2 Cleveland Barons
01/2 Cleveland Barons

LUNDHOLM, BENGT
82/3 O-Pee-Chee 385
83/4 O-Pee-Chee 387
84/5 O-Pee-Chee 341
79 Panini Sticker 197
82/3 Post [Winn.]
83/4 Vachon 130-10
81/2 WINN
82/3 WINN
83/4 WINN
84/5 WINN / Safety Tips

LUNDHOLM, JOAKIM
89/0 Semic Elitserien 259

LUNDIN, HENRIK
92/3 Semic Elitserien 317

LUNDMARK, CURT
91/2 Semic Elitserien 360

LUNDMARK, DAVID
83/4 Kingston Canadians
83/4 Kingston Canadians

LUNDMARK, ERIK
02/3 Plymouth Whalers
02/3 Plymouth Whalers

LUNDMARK, JAMIE
99 Bowman 32, 90, SC10, ✍ BA9
02/3 Bowman 152
02/3 Calder 84
02/3 Crown Royale -RR 16
02/3 Exclusive 185, -DFG 9
01/2 Hartford Wolf Pack
01/2 Hartford Wolf Pack
02/3 Pacific Complete 524
02/3 Pr. Stock Reserve -MIT 6
02/3 PS Titanium -ROT 16
95 Québec Pee Wee 1438
98/9 SP Authentic 126
99/0 SPx 169
02/3 Stadium 112
99/0 Topps 252
99/0 To. Chrome 252
02/3 To. Heritage 168
02/3 T. Total 425
98/9 Upper Deck 403
99/0 Upper Deck 321
02/3 Upper Deck ✂ BF
02/3 UD Artistic ✂ RT
99/0 UD Black Diam. 92
98/9 UD G. Reserve 403
99/0 UD G. Reserve 321
99/0 UD MVP Cup 211
99/0 UD Ovation 71
99/0 UD Prospects 27, C9, DS5, ✍ Sig.
00/1 UD Prospects 66, FL6, ✂ GJ, ✂ GJC (x3)
01 UD Prospects GU ✍ SoT
02/3 Vanguard - PP 17

LUNDMARK, PETER
94/5 Leaf Elit Set 221
89/0 Semic Elitserien 138
90/1 Semic Elitserien 211
92/3 Semic Elitserien 261

LUNDQVIST, HENRIK
00/1 UD Elitserien 60

LUNDQVIST, STEFAN
98/9 UD Elitserien 42
99/0 UD Elitserien 26

LUNDRIGAN, JOE
74/5 Loblaws
74/5 O-Pee-Chee 277
72/3 TORO
74/5 WASH

LUNDSTRÖM, LARS-ERIK
91/2 Semic Elitserien 306
92/3 Semic Elitserien 328

LUNDSTRÖM, MATS
89/0 Semic Elitserien 205
90/1 Semic Elitserien 38
91/2 Semic Elitserien 289
91/2 Semic Elitserien 312

LUNDSTRÖM, MIKAEL
92/3 Semic Elitserien 334

LUNDSTRÖM, PER-ANTON
98/9 UD Elitserien 18
99/0 UD Elitserien 8
00/1 UD Elitserien 2

LUNDSTRÖM, TOBIAS
99/0 UD Elitserien 168
00/1 UD Elitserien 150, ✍ Sig.

LUNDSTRÖM, TORD
00/1 Alfabilder
72 Hellas MM-Jenkki 30
74 Hellas MM-Jenkki 29
70/1 Kuvajulkaisut 31
69/0 Mästär Serien 40
69/0 Mästär Serien 47
69/0 Mästär Serien 49
72 Panda MM-Toronto
72 Semic Sticker 58
98/9 UD Elitserien 206, 211
71/2 Williams Finnish 50
72/3 Williams Finnish 52
73/4 Williams Finnish 31

LUNDY, PAT
45-64 BeeHive-2 [Chic.]

LUNE, KEVIN
88/9 Brockville Braves
88/9 Brockville Braves
96/7 Peoria Rivermen
96/7 Peoria Rivermen
98/9 Topeka Scarecrows
98/9 Topeka Scarecrows

LUOJOLA, HANNU
66/7 Champion 54
70/1 Kuvajulkaisut 144
72 Semic Sticker 74
78/9 SM-Liiga 159
71/2 Williams Finnish 194
71/2 Williams Finnish 67
72/3 Williams Finnish 232
73/4 Williams Finnish 266

LUOMA, JARI
89/0 Semic Elitserien 218
90/1 Semic Elitserien 52

LUOMA, MIKKO
98/9 Cardset 121
99/0 Cardset 273
00/1 Cardset 330
02/3 Cardset 219

LUOMALA, MARKO
99/0 Cardset 343

LUONGO, CHRIS
98/9 DEL 67
99/0 Eishockey 317
92/3 Fleer Ultra 362
93/4 Fleer Ultra 96
96/7 Milwaukee Admirals
96/7 Milwaukee Admirals
92/3 OPC Premier 35
92/3 OTTA
92/3 OTTA
89/0 ProCards IHL 107
90/1 ProCards 484
91/2 ProCards 125
92/3 Upper Deck 534
01/2 UD DEL 203

LUONGO, ROBERTO
01/2 Adrenaline 83, CL 8, PP 17
01/2 Atomic 46
02/3 Atomic 46, -D 8
00/1 Aurora 63, Pins. 63, ✄ GWJ-7, ✄ GWJ-12, SR-12
99/0 BAP Mem. 307
00/1 BAP Mem. 163, 463
01/2 BAP Mem. 77, ✄ GJ
02/3 BAP Mem. 88, 213, ✄ FP13, ✄ FG4, ✄ HSHSJers 21
01/2 BAP Update ✄ HSHSJers
01/2 BT Pipes 33, HSHS, -Mask, ✄ DM, ✄ FW, ✄ Jers., ✄ S&J, ✄ GG, ✄ GT, ✄ HSHSJers
02/3 Between the Pipes 4, 133, M13, ✄ BM4, ✄ GUE26, ✄ FW3, ✄ GB13, ✄ GUJ26, ✄ GSJ26, ✄ HSHSJers 2, ✄ ITN26, ✄ I4, ✍ Aut.
99 Bowman 43, SC21
01/2 Bowman 131, ✄ FFJ, ✄ FFS, ✄ FFDS, ✄ FFR, ✍ YSA
02/3 Bowman 25
97 Bowman 42, 159, BB18
99/0 Crown Royale 88, CS-15, C21-7
00/1 Crown Royale 123, 21CR-10
01/2 Crown Royale 65
02/3 Crown Royale 43, -COA 4
97/8 Do. Elite 51, BF-7, ✍ BF-7
01/2 eTopps 14
02/3 eTopps 36
02/3 Exclusive 77, -EA 8, -GWJ 11
02/3 First Edition 89, 337, 353, 417H, ✄ Jers.
01/2 FLOR
01/2 FLOR
01/2 Heads Up 44, BTI 11, PP 2, SS 9
02/3 Heads Up 53, -S 10, ✄ GWQ 25
02/3 In The GU 34, 134, ✄ F13
02/3 McDonald's 17
99/0 Millenium C-37
99/0 NHL Power Play [x3]
01/2 O-Pee-Chee 68
02/3 O-Pee-Chee 108
99/0 Omega 143, 5ST-5, G-4
00/1 Pacific 253, IO-5, GCDC-20
01/2 Pacific 173, 431, SC 9
02/3 Pacific 156
02/3 Pacific Complete 128
01/2 PTC Collectors 3
02/3 PTC/ Les Gardiens 4
00/1 Parkhurst P-72, P-244
01/2 Parkhurst 43, ✄ PJ35, ✄ T10, ✄ T20
02/3 Parkhurst 47, -HHV8, ✄ FP13
02/3 Parkhurst Retro 72, ✄ RF13, ✄ RJ19, ✄ HSHSJers
97/8 Pi. BeeHive 69, ✍ Aut. 69
99/0 Prism 88
00/1 Private Stock ✄ GUG 52
01/2 Pr. Stock 43, GR 6, -PS 34
02/3 Pr. Stock Reserve -ICS 10, ✄ 124
00/1 PS Titanium 120
01/2 PS Titanium 61
02/3 PS Titanium 47, ✄ GWJ 33
00/1 PS Titanium Draft 120
02/3 Quest for the Cup 42
00/1 Signature 278, ✍ Aut. 204, ✄ HSHSJers
01/2 Signature 12, ✍ Aut. 12, ✄ GUE27, ✄ GJ29, ✄ GSJ29, ✄ ITN27, ✄ TM13
02/3 Signature 127, ✍ 127, ✄ YP9, ✄ FJ13, ✄ TQ5
99/0 SP Authentic 53
01/2 SP Authentic 37, ✍ SotT, ✍ SotTD (x2)
02/3 SP Authentic 40
02/3 SP GU 21, ✄ PC, ✄ TG
02/3 Sports Vault 50
99/0 SPx 176
00/1 SPx ✄ WM
01/2 SPx 175
02/3 SPx 34
98/9 SPx Prospects 62
00/1 Stadium 220
01/2 Stadium 80, G11, NR6, ✍ NR
02/3 Stadium 29, -PSH9, ✄ YSS9, ✄ YSD3
99/0 Topps 250
00/1 Topps 271
01/2 Topps 68
02/3 Topps 108
99/0 To. Chrome 250
00/1 To. Chrome 166
01/2 To. Chrome 68
02/3 To. Chrome 69
99/0 To. Gold Label 94
00/1 To. Gold Label 63, NG9
00/1 To. Heritage 46
01/2 To. Heritage 32
02/3 To. Heritage 8
02/3 To. Limited 108
99/0 To. Prmr. Plus 121
01/2 To. Reserve 52
00/1 To. Stars P4
02/3 T. Total 54, TTC12
98/9 UD Choice 258
00/1 UD Heroes ✍ SG
01/2 UD PlayMakers Ltd 44
00/1 UD Reserve 38
00/1 Ultimate Mem. ✄ G-13, ✄ PS-10, ✄ J-41, ✄ Jers. 33, ✄ S-41
01/2 Ultimate Mem. ✄ BAPL
02/3 Ultimate Mem. ✄ GUSJ, ✄ NO, ✄ Num, ✄ CSTW
98/9 Upper Deck ✄ GJ5
99/0 Upper Deck 163
00/1 Upper Deck 303, ✄ GJ
01/2 Upper Deck 75, GL10
02/3 Upper Deck 76, -LL6, ✄ GT
02/3 UD Artistic 40, R40, / Art
97/8 UD Black Diam. 131
98/9 UD Black Diam. 92
00/1 UD Black Diam. ✄ GG
01/2 UD Challenge 35
02/3 UD Classic 42
99/0 UD G. Reserve 163
01/2 UD Honor Roll ✄ GAJ
02/3 UD Honor 32
01/2 UD Ice ✍ CCA
01/2 UD Mask 113, ✄ StS
02/3 UD Mask 37, 38, ✄ GG, ✄ MM, ✄ NB, ✄ PW, ✄ VC
00/1 UD MVP ME1, ✄ GS, ✍ PS, ✍ ME
01/2 UD MVP 82
02/3 UD MVP 76
99/0 UD MVP Cup 112
02/3 UD Piece 41
01/2 UD Premier 27
02/3 UD Premier 27
02/3 UD Rookie 45, ✄ DJ
01/2 UD Top Shelf 95, ✄ GG-LP
02/3 UD Top Shelf 36, ✄ ST
00/1 UD Vintage 158, 160
01/2 UD Vintage 111, 113
02/3 UD Vintage 111, 273, GB 111, T30
00/1 Vanguard 121
01/2 Vanguard 43, SW 9
02/3 Vanguard 46, -SW 4
99/0 Victory 359
01/2 Victory 146, 154
02/3 Victory 90
97/8 Zenith 97, Z77

LUOSTARINEN, ARI
98/9 Cardset 142

LUOSTARINEN, TIMO
66/7 Champion 138

LUOTO, HARRY
70/1 Kuvajulkaisut 162

LUOVI, MIKKO
92/3 Jyvas Hyva 40
93/4 Jyvas Hyva 82
93/4 Sisu 120
94/5 Sisu 267, H-14
93/4 Upper Deck 271
91/2 Upper Deck WJC 33
97/8 UD Elitserien 28
98/9 UD Elitserien 48
99/0 UD Elitserien 32
00/1 UD Elitserien 40

LUPANDIN, ANDREI
95/6 Brandon Wheat Kings
95/6 Brandon Wheat Kings
98/9 Brandon Wheat Kings
98/9 Brandon Wheat Kings

LUPASCHUK, ROSS
99 Bowman 18, ✍ BA38
00/1 Red Deer Rebels
00/1 Red Deer Rebels
98/9 SP Authentic 118, ✍ SotT
98/9 Upper Deck 395
98/9 UD G. Reserve 395
01/2 WBS Penguins
01/2 WBS Penguins
02/3 WBS Penguins
02/3 WBS Penguins

LUPIEN, CAMILLE
51/2 Lac St-Jean 26

LUPIEN, GILLES
77/8 MONT
78/9 MONT
79/0 MONT
80/1 O-Pee-Chee 298

LUPIEN, STEVE
90/1 7th..Sketch LHJMQ 2
91 7th..Sketch Mem.Cup 49

LUPUL, GARY
82/3 Fredericton Express
82/3 Fredericton Express
85/6 Fredericton Express
85/6 Fredericton Express
84/5 Kelowna Wings &...
82/3 O-Pee-Chee 354
83/4 O-Pee-Chee 355
84/5 O-Pee-Chee 323
82/3 Post [Vanc.]
84/5 7-Eleven
83/4 Vachon 111-31
80/1 VANC
80/1 VANC / Silverwood
81/2 VANC
81/2 VANC / Silverwood
83/4 VANC
84/5 VANC
85/6 VANC
82/3 Victoria Cougars
82/3 Victoria Cougars

LUPUL, JOFFREY
00/1 Medicine Hat Tigers
00/1 Medicine Hat Tigers

LUPZIG, ANDREAS
94/5 DEL 210
98/9 DEL 104, 320
99/0 Eishockey 113
95 Panini Worlds 64
92 Semic Sticker 189
00/1 UD DEL 133
01/2 UD DEL 211

LUSTH, MATS
94/5 Leaf Elit Set 236
90/1 Semic Elitserien 129
91/2 Semic Elitserien 181
92/3 Semic Elitserien 205
97/8 UD Elitserien 140
98/9 UD Elitserien 155
99/0 UD Elitserien 153

LUSTINEC, PETR
99/0 Score 145

LUTCHENKO, VLADIMIR
91/2 Future Trends C72 42
72 Hellas MM-Jenkki 63
74 Hellas MM-Jenkki 48
70/1 Kuvajulkaisut 6
72 Panda MM-Toronto
79 Panini Sticker 142
72 Semic Sticker 3
74 Semic Sticker 28
69/0 Soviet Stars
70/1 Soviet Stars
71/2 Soviet Stars
73/4 Soviet Stars 10
74/5 Soviet Stars 6
79/0 Soviet Stars 6
71/2 Williams Finnish 7
72/3 Williams Finnish 27
73/4 Williams Finnish 8

LUTES, CRAIG
94/5 Birmingham Bulls
94/5 Birmingham Bulls
95/6 Birmingham Bulls
95/6 Birmingham Bulls
90/1 Oshawa Generals
90/1 Oshawa Generals
91/2 Oshawa Generals
91/2 Oshawa Generals
90/1 7th..Sketch OHL 342
91/2 7th...Sketch OHL 353
93/4 Slapshot / Windsor 6
92/3 Windsor Spitfires
92/3 Windsor Spitfires

LUTHER, GARY
87/8 Soo Greyhounds 30
87/8 Soo Greyhounds 30

LUTHI, FREDY
95 Globe 211
92 Semic Sticker 210
93 Semic Sticker 121

LUTHI, PETER
72 Semic Sticker 144

LUTTER, PETER
94/5 DEL 362
98/9 DEL 15

LUTZ, RAINER
94/5 DEL 309

LUZA, PATRIK
99/0 OFS 212
00/1 OFS 355
91/2 Upper Deck WJC 90

LYASHENKO, ROMAN
99/0 BAP Mem. 375
02/3 Choice Prospects 27
00/1 DALL / Southwest
00/1 DALL / Southwest
01/2 DALL / Southwest
01/2 DALL / Southwest
99/0 Michigan K-Wings
99/0 Michigan K-Wings
99/0 Omega 78
00/1 Pa. Paramount 78
99/0 Prism 45
01/2 Signature 36, ✍ Aut. 36
00/1 Upper Deck 288
01/2 Utah Grizzlies
01/2 Utah Grizzlies
00/1 Victory 80

LYDMAN, TONI
00/1 BAP Mem. 488
01/2 BAP Mem. 146
01/2 Bowman 122
98/9 Cardset 34, -Leij. 13
99/0 Cardset 184, 222, PA 2
00/1 Cardset 233
02/3 Cardset 220, -SGSP 2
97/8 Hockey-Box
02/3 O-Pee-Chee 80
02/3 Pacific 55
02/3 Pacific Complete 179
00/1 Signature 255, ✍ Aut. 217
02/3 Topps 80
02/3 To. Limited 80
02/3 T. Total 392
01/2 Victory 58

LYLE, GEORGE
80/1 DETR
82/3 HART / Jr. Whalers
80/1 O-Pee-Chee 379
81/2 O-Pee-Chee 100
82/3 Post [Hart.]

LYLE, STEVIE
01/2 Cardiff Devils
01/2 Cardiff Devils
00/1 Kudos 51
01/2 Manchester Storm
01/2 Manchester Storm
01/2 Manchester Storm
01/2 Manchester Storm
02/3 Manchester Storm
02/3 Manchester Storm
02/3 Manchester Storm
02/3 Manchester Storm

LYLYK, DAVID
99/0 San Angelo Outlaws
99/0 San Angelo Outlaws
94/5 Slapshot / Guelph 21

LYNCH, BERNIE
88/9 Regina Pats
88/9 Regina Pats

LYNCH, DARREN
99/0 Lethbridge Hurricanes
99/0 Lethbridge Hurricanes
01/2 Vancouver Giants
01/2 Vancouver Giants

LYNCH, DOUG
00/1 Red Deer Rebels
00/1 Red Deer Rebels
01 UD Prospects GU 24, ✄ TPJ

LYNCH, JACK
74/5 Loblaws
74/5 Loblaws Update
72/3 O-Pee-Chee 160
73/4 O-Pee-Chee 232
74/5 O-Pee-Chee 331
75/6 O-Pee-Chee 116
76/7 O-Pee-Chee 288
77/8 O-Pee-Chee 369
75/6 Topps 116
78/9 WASH

LYNCH, JIM
00/1 Kudos 2

LYNCH, P.J.
97/8 Halifax Moosehead
97/8 Halifax Moosehead
98/9 Halifax Moosehead

LYNCH, SCOTT
00/1 Prince George Cougars

LYNESS, CHRIS
99 Bowman 44
99/0 Québec Remparts 8
99/0 Québec Remparts 8
00/1 Val d'Or Foreurs 3
00/1 Val d'Or Foreurs 3

LYNK, MARK
95/6 Halifax Moosehead
95/6 Halifax Moosehead
96/7 Halifax Moosehead
96/7 Halifax Moosehead
96/7 Halifax Moosehead
96/7 Halifax Moosehead
97/8 Halifax Moosehead
97/8 Halifax Moosehead

LYNN, VIC
45-54 Quaker Oats

LYNN, VICTOR IVAN
45-64 BeeHive-2 [Toro.]
51/2 Parkhurst 20

LYONS, COREY
99/0 Colorado Gold Kings
99/0 Colorado Gold Kings
88/9 Lethbridge Hurricanes
88/9 Lethbridge Hurricanes
89/0 Lethbridge Hurricanes
89/0 Lethbridge Hurricanes
90/1 ProCards 615
91/2 ProCards 583

LYONS, CRAIG
99/0 Colorado Gold Kings
99/0 Colorado Gold Kings
90/1 7th..Sketch WHL 301
91/2 7th...Sketch WHL 85

LYONS, DEREK
02/3 Mississauga IceDogs
02/3 Mississauga IceDogs

LYONS, LYNN
99/0 UD Prospects 49

LYONS, MARC
84/5 Kingston Canadians
84/5 Kingston Canadians
85/6 Kingston Canadians
85/6 Kingston Canadians
86/7 Kingston Canadians
86/7 Kingston Canadians
93/4 Toledo Storm 21
93/4 Toledo Storm 21

LYSAK, BRETT
99 Bowman 16, 91, ✍ BA36
96/7 Regina Pats
96/7 Regina Pats
97/8 Regina Pats
97/8 Regina Pats
99/0 SP Authentic 132
99/0 Topps 272
99/0 To. Chrome 272
99/0 UD Black Diam. 114
99/0 UD MVP Cup 204

LYSENKO, ALEXANDER
90/1 O-Pee-Chee 500

LYSENKO, ILYA
93/4 Slapshot / Sudbury 18
93/4 Sudbury Wolves
93/4 Sudbury Wolves

LYSIAK, TOM
74/5 ATLF
77/8 ATLF
78/9 ATLF / Colour
79/0 CHIC
80/1 CHIC / Brown
81/2 CHIC
82/3 CHIC
83/4 Funmate Puffy 15 [w/]
74/5 Loblaws
74/5 Nabisco 14
74/5 O-Pee-Chee 14
74/5 O-Pee-Chee 68
75/6 O-Pee-Chee 230
75/6 O-Pee-Chee 313
76/7 O-Pee-Chee 174
76/7 OPC 379
77/8 O-Pee-Chee 127
78/9 O-Pee-Chee 97
79/0 O-Pee-Chee 41
80/1 O-Pee-Chee 247
81/2 O-Pee-Chee 59
81/2 O-Pee-Chee 73
82/3 O-Pee-Chee 68
83/4 O-Pee-Chee 107
84/5 O-Pee-Chee 39
85/6 OPC/Topps 23
81/2 OPC Sticker 114
82/3 OPC/Topps Sticker 14
82/3 OPC/Topps Sticker 174
83/4 OPC/Topps Sticker 110
84/5 OPC Sticker 31
79 Panini Sticker 59
82/3 Post [Chic.]
83/4 Souhaits Keychain [Blackhawks]
74/5 Topps 14
74/5 Topps 68
75/6 Topps 230
75/6 Topps 313
76/7 Topps 174
77/8 Topps 127
78/9 Topps 97
79/0 Topps 41
80/1 Topps 247
81/2 Topps 49
81/2 Topps 71 [West]
84/5 Topps 31

LYUBIMOV, ALEXANDER
00/1 Mir 156

LYUTKEVICH, VITALI
99/0 Mir 173
00/1 Mir 391

LYUZENKOV, YAROSLAV
98/9 Mir 32

M

MÄÄTTÄ, EILERT
00/1 Alfabilder
98/9 UD Elitserien 204, 209

MÄÄTTÄ, TERO
02/3 Cardset 228
00/1 Cardset 125

MÄÄTTÄNEN,
97/8 Hockey-Box

MÄÄTTÄNEN, PASI
98/9 Cardset 194
99/0 Cardset 114
00/1 Cardset 270
92/3 Jyvas Hyva 50
93/4 Jyvas Hyva 84
93/4 Sisu 129
93/4 Sisu 306
94/5 Sisu 28
95/6 Sisu 240

MÄÄTTÄNEN, RAIMO
65/6 Hellas 75
70/1 Kuvajulkaisut 284

MABEY, SHANE
99/0 Guelph Storm
01/2 Guelph Storm
01/2 Guelph Storm M-Cup

MACADAM, AL
74/5 Loblaws
74/5 O-Pee-Chee 301
75/6 O-Pee-Chee 253
76/7 O-Pee-Chee 237
76/7 OPC 383
77/8 O-Pee-Chee 149
78/9 O-Pee-Chee 381
79/0 O-Pee-Chee 104
80/1 O-Pee-Chee 34
80/1 O-Pee-Chee 138
81/2 O-Pee-Chee 163
82/3 O-Pee-Chee 171
83/4 O-Pee-Chee 173
84/5 O-Pee-Chee 324
85/6 O-Pee-Chee 209
81/2 OPC Sticker 90
85/6 OPC Sticker 242-109
82/3 Post [Minn.]
75/6 Topps 253
76/7 Topps 237
77/8 Topps 149
79/0 Topps 104
80/1 Topps 34
80/1 Topps 138
81/2 Topps 107 [West]
84/5 Topps 75
78/9 MINS / Cloverleaf 4
79/0 MINS
80/1 MINS
81/2 MINS
82/3 MINS
83/4 MINS
84/5 VANC
85/6 Fredericton Express
97/8 St. John's Maple Leafs
99/0 St. John's Maple Leafs

MACADAM, DON
90/1 ProCards 240
91/2 ProCards 235
99/0 Charlotte Checkers
00/1 Charlotte Checkers
94/5 Milwaukee Admirals

MACANDREW, LARRY
83/4 Ottawa 67's

MACARTHUR, KEN
90/1 Canada Nationals 6

MACAULAY, ANTHONY
94/5 Hampton Roads

MACAULAY, JEFF
01/2 Québec Remparts 17

MACAUSLAND, LENNIE
90/1 7th..Sketch WHL 58
91/2 7th...Sketch WHL 185

MACCARTAN, JACK
72/3 Minn. Fight. Saints

MACDERMID, JEFF
01/2 Owen Sound Attack
02/3 Owen Sound Attack

MACDERMID, KEN
87/8 Hull Olympiques

MACDERMID, PAUL
91/2 Bowman 195
92/3 Bowman 282
92/3 Fleer Ultra 439
90/1 OPC/Topps 338
91/2 O-Pee-Chee 463
89/0 OPC/Topps 183
89/0 opcSticker 266-147
88/9 Panini Sticker 243
89/0 Panini Sticker 227
90/1 Panini/WPG 15
91/2 Panini Sticker 69
91/2 Pinnacle 279
90/1 Pro Set 331
91/2 Pro Set 269
90/1 Score 296
91/2 Score 219
91/2 Score CAN 219
92/3 Score 59
92/3 Topps 391
91/2 To. Stadium 254
92/3 To. Stadium 178
90/1 Upper Deck 218
85/6 HART / Jr. Whalers
86/7 HART / Jr. Whalers
87/8 HART / Jr. Whalers
88/9 HART / Jr. Whalers
89/0 HART / Jr. Whalers
94/5 QUÉB / Burger King
91/2 WASH / Kodak
92/3 WASH / Kodak
90/1 WINN / IGA
91/2 WINN / IGA
00/1 Owen Sound Attack 26

MACDONALD, AARON
95/6 Classic 32
95/6 Cla. 5 Sport 142, ✍ Aut.
95/6 Swift Current Broncos

MACDONALD, AB
72/3 Post 6

MACDONALD, B.J.
82/3 Fredericton Express

MACDONALD, BLAIR
80/1 O-Pee-Chee 32
81/2 O-Pee-Chee 340
82/3 O-Pee-Chee 350
76/7 OPC WHA 93
77/8 OPC WHA 16
80/1 Pepsi Bottle Cap
89/0 ProCards IHL 164
90/1 ProCards 390
80/1 Topps 32
79/0 EDMO
88/9 EDMO / Action 99
81/2 VANC
81/2 VANC / Silverwood
83/4 Medicine Hat Tigers

MACDONALD, BRETT
91/2 ProCards 430
95/6 Flint Generals
96/7 Flint Generals
98/9 Flint Generals
87/8 Flint Spirits
88/9 Flint Spirits
86/7 Fredericton Express
85/6 Kitchener Rangers
83/4 North Bay Centennials

MACDONALD, BRIAN
83/4 Brantford Alexanders

MACDONALD, BRUCE
92/3 Toledo Storm WIOT
92/3 Toledo Storm
93/4 Toledo Storm 20
97/8 Toledo Storm 21

MACDONALD, CHRIS
95/6 Slapshot 129

MACDONALD, CLINT
91/2 Avant Garde BCJHL 120
92/3 BCJHL 133

MACDONALD, CRAIG
99/0 BAP Mem. 175
99/0 Pacific 83
99/0 Cincinnati Cyclones
00/1 Cincinnati Cyclones
98/9 New Haven Beast 4

MACDONALD, DAVE
94/5 Slapshot / Sudbury 2
95/6 Slapshot 381
96/7 Guelph Storm
83/4 Kelowna Wings

MACDONALD, DOUG
92/3 Classic 92
93/4 Cla. Prospects 211
93/4 Upper Deck 97
95/6 Cincinnati Cyclones
96/7 Cincinnati Cyclones
97/8 Cincinnati Cyclones
98/9 Cincinnati Cyclones
92/3 Rochester Americans DD
92/3 Rochester Americans WPC
93/4 Rochester Americans

MACDONALD, GARRETT
94/5 Richmond Renegades
95/6 Richmond Renegades
93/4 N. Michigan Wildcats

MACDONALD, JASON
94/5 Classic 118
90/1 7th..Sketch OHL 311, 324
91/2 7th...Sketch OHL 277
95/6 Adirondack Red Wings
98/9 Manitoba Moose
99/0 Manitoba Moose
00/1 WBS Penguins
01/2 WBS Penguins
02/3 WBS Penguins
93/4 Owen Sound Platers
93/4 Owen Sound Platers

MACDONALD, JOEY
02/3 Grand Rapids Griffins
97/8 Halifax Moosehead
97/8 Halifax Moosehead

MACDONALD, JOHN
83/4 Belleville Bulls

MACDONALD, KEVIN
95/6 Edge Ice 106
88/9 ProCards / Muskegon
89/0 ProCards AHL 24
90/1 ProCards 366
91/2 ProCards 388
92/3 Fort Wayne Komets 18
93/4 Fort Wayne Komets 12
89/0 Rayside-Balfour

MACDONALD, KILBY
34-43 BeeHive-1 [NYRa.]
39/0 O-Pee-Chee 87

MACDONALD, LEONARD
90/1 7th..Sketch OHL 184
91/2 7th...Sketch OHL 185
89/0 Sudbury Wolves

MACDONALD, LOWELL
74/5 Loblaws
68/9 O-Pee-Chee 42
70/1 O-Pee-Chee 206
72/3 O-Pee-Chee 214
73/4 O-Pee-Chee 128
74/5 O-Pee-Chee 30
74/5 O-Pee-Chee 133
74/5 O-Pee-Chee 183
75/6 O-Pee-Chee 204
76/7 O-Pee-Chee 33
76/7 O-Pee-Chee 218
77/8 O-Pee-Chee 390
94/5 Parkie Tall 60
68/9 Shirriff / LosA. 7
68/9 Topps 42
73/4 Topps 128
74/5 Topps 30
74/5 Topps 133
74/5 Topps 183
75/6 Topps 204
76/7 Topps 33
76/7 Topps 218
74/5 PITT
77/8 PITT / McDonald's

MACDONALD, PARKER
45-64 BeeHive-2 [Toro.]
45-64 BeeHive-2 [Detr.]
64-67 BeeHive-3 [Detr.]
64-67 BeeHive-3 [Bost.]
63-65 Chex
64/5 Coke/Sprite [Detr.]
65/6 Coca-Cola
62/3 Cowan Tile
68/9 O-Pee-Chee 55
55/6 Parkhurst 9
55/6 Parkhurst 77
63/4 Parkhurst 44
93/4 Parkie 56-57 104
95/6 Parkie 66-67 55
94/5 Parkie Tall 44
60/1 Shirriff 59
61/2 Shirriff 69
68/9 Shirriff / Minn. 8
64/5 Topps 11
65/6 Topps 105
68/9 Topps 55
62/3 Toronto Star Photo
63/4 Toronto Star Action
64/5 Toronto Star Action
63/4 Toronto Star Weekend
62/3 York Transfer 27
63/4 York 40
73/4 MINS

MACDONALD, PARKER*
89/0 New Haven Nighthawks

MACDONALD, PAUL
91/2 7th...Sketch LHJMQ 200

MACDONALD, REID
90/1 Michigan Tech Huskies
91/2 Michigan Tech Huskies

MACDONALD, RYAN
94/5 Slapshot / Detroit Jr. 4
95/6 Slapshot 212
94/5 Slapshot Memorial 78

MACDONALD, TODD
95/6 Edge Ice 24
96/7 Cincinnati Cyclones
97/8 Cincinnati Cyclones
98/9 New Haven Beast 8
92/3 Tacoma Rockets
93/4 Tacoma Rockets

MACDONALD, TOM
91 7th..Sketch Mem.Cup 14
90/1 7th..Sketch OHL 166
91/2 7th...Sketch OHL 322
93/4 Slapshot / S.S.Marie 15
93/4 Soo Greyhounds 17

MACDONALD, WILLIE
87/8 Kamloops Blazers

MACEACHERN, ALI
97/8 Halifax Moosehead
97/8 Halifax Moosehead
98/9 Halifax Moosehead
99/0 Halifax Mooseheads

MACEACHERN, GREG
90/1 7th..Sketch LHJMQ 77
90 7th..Sketch Mem.Cup 57

MACEACHERN, LIAM
94/5 Slapshot / Sudbury 18
95/6 Slapshot 397

MACEACHERN, SHANE
88/9 ProCards / Peoria
94/5 Slapshot / Brantford 16

MACEK, PETR
94/5 APS 254
95/6 APS 132
99/0 OFS 138

MACERA, MARK
98/9 Wichita Thunder

MACFARLANE, EON
92/3 BCJHL 200

MACGILLIVRAY, BILL
93/4 N. Michigan Wildcats

MACGILLVRAY, JOHN
52/3 Anonymous 165

MACGREGOR, BRAD
88/9 ProCards / Cape Breton

MACGREGOR, BRUCE
45-64 BeeHive-2 [Detr.]
64-67 BeeHive-3 [Detr.]
64-67 BeeHive-3 [Detr.]
63-65 Chex
64/5 Coke/Sprite [Detr.]
65/6 Coca-Cola
70/1 Dad's Cookies
70/1 Eddie Sargent 51
71/2 Eddie Sargent 124
72/3 Eddie Sargent 153
70/1 Esso Power Player
62/3 Cowan Tile
68/9 O-Pee-Chee 30
69/0 O-Pee-Chee 63
70/1 O-Pee-Chee 27
71/2 O-Pee-Chee 216
72/3 O-Pee-Chee 103
73/4 O-Pee-Chee 201
74/5 OPC WHA 2
75/6 OPC WHA 22
62/3 Parkhurst 23
63/4 Parkhurst 41
95/6 Parkie 66-67 49
94/5 Parkie Tall 47
61/2 Shirriff 73
68/9 Shirriff / Detr. 8
64/5 Topps 76
65/6 Topps 110
66/7 Topps 104
66/7 Topps / Test 56
67/8 Topps 102
68/9 Topps 30
69/0 Topps 63
70/1 Topps 27
71/2 Toronto Sun Photo
62/3 York Transfer 36
63/4 York 51
70/1 DETR / Marathon Oil
88/9 EDMO / Action 154

MACGUIGAN, GARTH
81/2 Indianapolis Checkers
82/3 Indianapolis Checkers

MACH, ALES
96/7 APS 49
00/1 OFS 211

MACH, MIROSLAV
94/5 APS 63
95/6 APS 91
96/7 APS 300
96/7 DS Sticker 223

MACHAC, OLDRICH
72 Hellas MM-Jenkki 83
74 Hellas MM-Jenkki 77
70/1 Kuvajulkaisut 53
72 Panda MM-Toronto
72 Semic Sticker 24
74 Semic Sticker 55
71/2 Williams Finnish 31
72/3 Williams Finnish 14
73/4 Williams Finnish 55

MACHACEK, MARTIN
98/9 Fort Worth Brahmas

MACHALEK, ROBERT
95/6 APS 108

MACHOLDA, PETR
01/2 OFS 188

MACHULDA, VLADIMIR
02/3 Cardset 66
94/5 APS 225
95/6 APS 172
96/7 APS 69
97/8 APS 325
00/1 Cardset 80
98/9 DS 73
99/0 DS 126
96/7 DS Sticker 234
98/9 OFS 220
99/0 OFS 386

MACINNES, JOHN
91/2 Michigan Tech Huskies

MACINNIS, AL
02/3 BAP All-Star 57, ✄ ASJ, ✄ HSHSJers
02/3 BAP Mem. 12, ✄ ASJ34, ✄ ASTJ13, ✄ TM16
02/3 Bowman 67
02/3 Exclusive 144
02/3 First Edition 118, ✄ Jers.
02/3 In The GU 66, 166, ✄ E35, ✄ GUJ37, ✄ SJ37, ✄ TM10
02/3 McDonald's -SLG 3
02/3 O-Pee-Chee 199
02/3 Pacific 325
02/3 Pacific Complete 38
02/3 Parkhurst 6, ✄ GJ11, ✄ SJ11, ✄ NH9, ✄ TT16
02/3 Parkhurst Retro 104, ✄ NH4
02/3 Signature 159, ✍ 159, ✄ DW7, ✄ SGJ37, ✄ TQ15
02/3 Slam Card
02/3 Sports Vault 277
02/3 SPx 133
02/3 Topps 199, HHU14
02/3 To. Chrome 112
02/3 To. Heritage ✍ Aut.
02/3 To. Limited 199
02/3 T. Total 92

MACINNIS, AL
02/3 Ultimate Mem. ✄ CSTW, ✄ GD, ✄ GAP, ✄ HT

MACINNIS, AL
02/3 Upper Deck 152, ✄ GO
02/3 UD MVP 161
02/3 UD Piece -AC26
02/3 UD Rookie ✄ 155a
02/3 UD Top Shelf ✄ CP, ✄ HH
02/3 UD Vintage 225, GB 225
02/3 Victory 183
01/2 Adrenaline 160
98/9 Aurora 161
99/0 Aurora 126, Stripe 126
00/1 Aurora 122
98/9 Be A Player 274, M-22, ✍ Aut. 274
99/0 BAP Mem. 155, SL-11, H-9, ✄ J-13, ✄ D-15, ✄ TM-34
00/1 BAP Mem. 257, ✄ J-8, ✄ H-13
01/2 BAP Mem. 84, ✄ ASJ, ✄ ASE, ✄ ASN, ✄ ASD, ✄ AST, ✄ CoO, ✄ SCP
01/2 BAP Update ✄ H15
95/6 Bicycle Sports Aces 2-Diamond
90/1 Bowman 93
91/2 Bowman 262
92/3 Bowman 51
92/3 Bowman 211
95/6 Bowman 16
01/2 Bowman 103
98/9 Bowman's Best 57
91 Canada Cup
99/0 Challenger 15
99/0 Crown Royale 117
93/4 Donruss 47
94/5 Donruss D-6
95/6 Donruss 205, D-7
96/7 Donruss 12
97/8 Donruss 122
96/7 Do. Canadian 15
97/8 Do. Canadian 55
95/6 Do. Elite 15
96/7 Do. Elite 67
97/8 Do. Preferred 132
97/8 Do. Priority 144
98/9 Dynagon Ice 159
99/0 Dynagon Ice 166
93/4 EA Sports 20
94/5 Flair 157
96/7 Flair 82
94/5 Fleer 190, SA-5
96/7 Fleer 98
95/6 Fleer Metal 126
92/3 Fleer Ultra 23, -AS 8
93/4 Fleer Ultra 113
94/5 Fleer Ultra 185
95/6 Fleer Ultra 300
96/7 Fl. Ultra 147
88/9 Frito Lay
91/2 Gillette 7
95 Globe 79
93/4 Hockey Wit 90
99/0 HoloGrFX 52
92/3 Humpty Dumpty
91/2 Kellogg's / Score 16
89/0 Kraft 3
90/1 Kraft 33
91/2 Kraft 32
96/7 Kraft / PB
97/8 Kraft / PB
98/9 Kraft / PB
99/0 Kraft / OML, / PB
93/4 Leaf 180
94/5 Leaf 461
95/6 Leaf 312
96/7 Leaf 174
94/5 L. Limited 79
95/6 L. Limited 95
96/7 Maggers 142
91/2 McDonald's Mc-23
92/3 McDonald's McD-10
94/5 McDonald's McD-15
01/2 McDonald's -HP 9
96/7 Metal Univ. 133
99/0 Millenium 203, ✍ Aut. 203, ✄ J-6, ✄ ✍ J-6, ✄ JS-6
98/9 NHL Power Play
85/6 O-Pee-Chee 237
86/7 OPC/Topps 173
87/8 OPC/Topps 72
88/9 OPC/Topps 231
90/1 OPC/Topps 127, 197
91/2 O-Pee-Chee 262
91/2 O-Pee-Chee 491
92/3 O-Pee-Chee 330
01/2 O-Pee-Chee 96
89/0 OPC/Topps 49
89/0 Topps - Sticker 4
90/1 OPC/Topps H
98/9 OPC Chrome 100
87/8 OPC Leaders 26
90/1 OPC Premier 65
91/2 OPC Premier 81
88/9 OPC Stars 22
85/6 OPC Sticker 211-78
86/7 OPC Sticker 86-214
87/8 OPC Sticker 40
87/8 OPC Sticker 123-135
88/9 OPC Sticker 92-220
89/0 opcSticker 5, 95, 159-19, / AS 27
97/8 Omega 195
98/9 Omega 203
99/0 Omega 196, CC-18
98/9 Pacific 368
99/0 Pacific 358
00/1 Pacific 326
01/2 Pacific 326
97/8 Pacific CC 202
98/9 Pa. Crown Roy. 115
98/9 Pa. Paramount 204
99/0 Pa. Paramount 198
00/1 Pa. Paramount 206, ✄ GUS-16
98/9 Pa. Revolution 123, -ASG 19
98/9 Panini Photocard
87/8 Panini Sticker 205
88/9 Panini Sticker 5
89/0 Panini Sticker 20, 32
90/1 Panini Sticker 185, 328
91/2 Panini Sticker 50
91/2 Panini Sticker 330
92/3 Panini Sticker 49
92/3 Panini Sticker 285
93/4 Panini Sticker P
94/5 Panini Sticker 161
95/6 Panini Sticker 197
96/7 Panini Sticker 207
99/0 Panini Sticker 5, 287, 341
91/2 Parkhurst 28
92/3 Parkhurst 20
93/4 Parkhurst 36
93/4 Parkhurst D3
94/5 Parkhurst 35
95/6 Parkhurst 178
00/1 Parkhurst P-116
01/2 Parkhurst 37, ✄ PJ20, ✄ PS20, ✄ PSJ16, ✄ M52
94/5 Parkie SE152
91/2 Pinnacle 220
91/2 Pinnacle 399
91/2 Pinnacle B-8
92/3 Pinnacle 83
93/4 Pinnacle 155
93/4 Pinnacle TP 3
94/5 Pinnacle 387, BR3
95/6 Pinnacle 79
96/7 Pinnacle 153
97/8 Pinnacle 116
97/8 Pi. Be A Player 125, ✍ Aut. 125
97/8 Pi. Certified 120
97/8 Pi. Inside 161
95/6 Pi. Summit 90, GMC-14
97/8 Pi. Totally 120
95/6 Pi. Zenith 40
96/7 Pi. Zenith 18
95/6 Playoff 90
94/5 POG 264
95/6 POG 242
93/4 Power Play 38
93/4 Power Play SA 7
93/4 Premier 276
94/5 Premier 110, 127, 347, 488
00/1 Premier Plus 14
99/0 Prism 119
00/1 Private Stock 83
01/2 PS Titanium 117
95/6 Pro Magnet 9
90/1 Pro Set 35, 337
91/2 Pro Set 33
91/2 Pro Set 275
92/3 Pro Set 22
91 Pro Set Awards AC8
91/2 Pro Set Platinum 19
91/2 Pro Set Platinum 276
91/2 Puck / Pro Set 5
99/0 Revolution 123
00/1 Revolution 123
90/1 Score 5, 314, 335
90/1 Sco. Hot Cards 36
91/2 Score 2
91/2 Score 409
91/2 Score 417
91/2 Score / Promo 2
91/2 Score CAN 2
91/2 Score CAN 299
91/2 Score CAN 333
92/3 Score 302
92/3 Score 421
92/3 Score 496
93/4 Score 121
93/4 Score DT 4
93/4 Score TF 3
94/5 Score 120, DT7
95/6 Score 46
96/7 Score 114
97/8 Score 248
97/8 Score SLou. 6
91/2 Score Shows 4
92/3 Seasons 60
94/5 Select 28
95/6 Select CE 72
94 Semic 340
94 Semic 84
95 Semic 85
89 Semic Sticker 56
91 Semic Sticker 57
92 Semic Sticker 77
93 Semic Sticker 193
00/1 Signature 128, ✍ Aut. 28, ✄ DD-7, ✄ J-6, ✄ HSHSJers
01/2 Signature C-1, ✍ Aut. LAM, ✄ DD6, ✄ GUE28, ✄ GJ58, ✄ GSJ58, ✄ ITN28, ✄ IG3
95/6 SBx Emotion 150
95/6 SBx Impact 143
96/7 SBx Impact 114
94/5 SP 104
95/6 SP 125
97/8 SP Authentic 140
98/9 SP Authentic 72
01/2 SP Authentic 108, ✍ SotT, ✍ SotTD
00/1 SP GU ✄ TotG
01/2 SP GU ✄ ✍ ISD
99/0 SPx 133, XT1
98/9 SPx Prospects 51
00/1 Stadion 149
99/0 Stadium 14, Chrome 13, CA29, ✍ CS13, ✍ CS14, ✍ LS5, ✄ SCS
00/1 Stadium 172
96/7 SLU
95/6 Super Sticker 100, 102
96/7 Team Out!
87/8 OPC/Topps - Stick. 9
92/3 Topps 452
95/6 Topps 145, HGC22
98/9 Topps 100
99/0 Topps 13, AT4, IM12, PP5
00/1 Topps 62, PC-13
01/2 Topps 96
99/0 To. Chrome 13, AT4, IM12, PP5
00/1 To. Chrome 50, PC-13
01/2 To. Chrome 96
94/5 Topps Finest DF-12
95/6 To. Finest 48
98/9 To. Finest 88
98/9 T. Gold Label 15
99/0 To. Gold Label 2
01/2 To. Heritage 79
96/7 To. Picks 49
99/0 To. Prmr. Plus 25
91/2 To. Stadium 79
92/3 To. Stadium 128
93/4 To. Stadium 105

94/5 To. Stadium 56
95/6 To. Stadium 13
93/4 TSC Members Only 7
94/5 TSC Members Only 34
95/6 TSC Members Only 9
00/1 To. Stars 45
95/6 T. Super Skills 49
98/9 UD Choice 188
00/1 UD Heroes L10
00/1 Ultimate Mem. ✍ U-6, ✂-J-6, ✂-JJ-14, ✂-N-2, ✂-S-6, ✂-TM-37
01/2 Ultimate Mem. ✂ Glove, ✍ Aut.
90/1 Upper Deck 143, 319, 497
91/2 Upper Deck 8
91/2 Upper Deck 243
91/2 Upper Deck 632
92/3 Upper Deck 257
93/4 Upper Deck 412, SP-22
94/5 Upper Deck 150, 232, C33, R46, SP-159
95/6 Upper Deck 290, AS-9, SE-71
96/7 Upper Deck 141
97/8 Upper Deck 352
98/9 Upper Deck 176, ✂ GJ8
99/0 Upper Deck 114, AS18, CT15, ✂ GJ
00/1 Upper Deck 380
01/2 Upper Deck 152, ✂ ASJ, ✂ SupSwe
94/5 UD BAP G14
95/6 UD BAP 134, ✍ S134
93/4 UD BAP Roots 19
98/9 UD Black Diam. 77
01/2 UD Challenge ✂ TN, ✂✍ TNS
95/6 UD CC 313
96/7 UD CC 228, 329
97/8 UD Coll. Choice 234
98/9 UD G. Reserve 176
99/0 UD G. Reserve 114, / Backup 165
01/2 UD Honor Roll 22, 52, ✂ PPM
00/1 UD Legends ✂ LGJ
98/9 UD MVP 179
99/0 UD MVP 183
00/1 UD MVP 153, ✍ PS
01/2 UD MVP 167, ✂ C
99/0 UD MVP Cup ✍ PS
99/0 UD Ovation 49
96/7 UD Post
99/0 UD Retro 70
01/2 UD SCup Champs 29, ✂ S, ✂ G
00/1 UD Vintage 314
01/2 UD Vintage 223, 226
97/8 Valu-net, ✍ Aut.
00/1 Vanguard 82
99/0 Victory 258, 260, 318, 341
00/1 Victory 201, 321
01/2 Victory 308
99/0 WGretzky 146, CG8
96 Wien 81
82/3 CALG
85/6 CALG / Red Rooster
86/7 CALG / Red Rooster
87/8 CALG / Red Rooster
90/1 CALG / McGavin's
91/2 CALG / McGavin's
91/2 CALG / IGA
92/3 CALG / IGA 022
96/7 SLOU / Dispatch 2
99/0 SLOU / Taco Bell 20
82/3 Kitchener Rangers

MACINNIS, IAN
81/2 Kingston Canadians

MACINNIS, NEILL
01/2 Belleville Bulls

MACINNIS, ROB
88/9 ProCards / Cape Breton
90/1 ProCards 532
93/4 Richmond Renegades
83/4 Kitchener Rangers

MACINTOSH, ANDY
92/3 BCJHL 153

MACINTYRE, ANDY
90/1 7th..Sketch WHL 6
91/2 7th...Sketch WHL 98
99/0 Florida Everblades
00/1 Florida Everblades
94/5 Indianapolis Ice
95/6 Indianapolis Ice
98/9 Kentucky Tho'blades
93/4 Saskatoon Blades
93/4 Saskatoon Blades

MACINTYRE, COREY
98/9 Oklahoma City Blazers

MACINTYRE, DAVE
98/9 DEL 114
97/8 Milwaukee Admirals
94/5 Peoria Rivermen
95/6 Peoria Rivermen

MACINTYRE, DREW
00/1 Sherbrooke Castors 1
01/2 Sherbrooke Castors 1

MACINTYRE, DUNC
85/6 Fredericton Express
86/7 Fredericton Express
83/4 Belleville Bulls
84/5 Belleville Bulls

MACINTYRE, IAN
00/1 Kudos 63

MACINTYRE, JASON
94/5 Hampton Roads
95/6 Hampton Roads

MACISAAC, AL
91/2 Hampton Roads
92/3 Hampton Roads
93/4 Hampton Roads
95/6 Hampton Roads
96/7 Hampton Roads
97/8 Hampton Roads
98/9 Hampton Roads
98/9 Hampton Roads
99/0 Hampton Roads

MACISAAC, BOB
91/2 7th...Sketch OHL 263
00/1 Charlotte Checkers
91/2 Sudbury Wolves
92/3 Sudbury Wolves
93/4 Sudbury Wolves

MACISAAC, DAVE
01/2 Hartford Wolf Pack
01/2 Hershey Bears
00/1 Kentucky Tho'blades
98/9 Lowell Lock Monsters
95/6 Milwaukee Admirals
92/3 Maine Black Bears
93/4 Maine Black Bears

MACISAAC, TODD
91/2 7th...Sketch WHL 348
93/4 Lethbridge Hurricanes

MACISSAC, BOB
93/4 Slapshot / Sudbury 23

MACIVER, DOUG
99/0 Kingston Frontenacs
00/1 Kingston Frontenacs 12
01/2 Kingston Frontenacs 11

MACIVER, NORM
91/2 Bowman 99
92/3 Bowman 425
93/4 Donruss 233
94/5 Donruss 273
96/7 Donruss 69
93/4 EA Sports 91
94/5 Flair 122
96/7 Fl. Picks 112
92/3 Fleer Ultra 61, 363
93/4 Fleer Ultra 143
94/5 Fleer Ultra 149
95/6 Fleer Ultra 289
93/4 Leaf 189
94/5 Leaf 68
96/7 Leaf 35
91/2 O-Pee-Chee 103
92/3 O-Pee-Chee 344
92/3 OPC Premier 107
97/8 Pacific CC 60
88/9 Panini Sticker 302
93/4 Panini Sticker 112
91/2 Parkhurst 282
92/3 Parkhurst 117
93/4 Parkhurst 137
94/5 Parkhurst 154
95/6 Parkhurst 171, 499
92/3 Pinnacle 157
93/4 Pinnacle 120
94/5 Pinnacle 80
95/6 Pinnacle 170
96/7 Pi. Be A Player 133, ✍ Aut. 133
94/5 POG 175
93/4 Power Play 172
93/4 Premier 64
94/5 Premier 49
92/3 Pro Set 50
89/0 ProCards AHL 140
90/1 ProCards 224
91/2 Score CAN 434
92/3 Score 349
93/4 Score 123
94/5 Score 24
95/6 Score 276
96/7 Score 167
92/3 Topps 96
92/3 To. Stadium 46
93/4 To. Stadium 267
92/3 Upper Deck 511
93/4 Upper Deck 299, 335, SP-111
94/5 Upper Deck 466
94/5 UD BAP ✍ 127
95/6 UD CC 270
96/7 UD CC 208
91/2 EDMO / IGA
92/3 OTTA
93/4 OTTA
94/5 OTTA
96/7 PHOE / Coca-Cola
97/8 PHOE / Coca-Cola
95/6 PITT / Foodland 8
85/6 Minnesota-Duluth 5

MACKAY, BRIAN
52/3 Anonymous 133

MACKAY, CALUM (BALDY)
45-64 BeeHive-2 [Mont.]
53/4 La Patrie
51/2 Parkhurst 9
54/5 Parkhurst 11
55/6 Parkhurst 41
45-54 Quaker Oats

MACKAY, DAVE
34-43 BeeHive-1 [Chic.]

MACKAY, DUNCAN (MICKEY)
19 Vancouver Millionaires
19 Vancouver Millionaires

MACKAY, KEN
95/6 Red Deer Rebels

MACKAY, KEVIN*
90/1 7th..Sketch OHL 186
91/2 7th...Sketch OHL 190
89/0 Windsor Spitfires

MACKAY, MARK
95/6 DEL 404
96/7 DEL 312
98/9 DEL 203, 337
99/0 Eishockey 216, 391
00/1 UD DEL 216, ✂ GJ
01/2 UD DEL 233, GA4

MACKAY, MICKEY
83 HHOF Postcard N8
83&87 HHOF 203

MACKAY, MURDO
51/2 Laval Dairy 5
45-54 Quaker Oats
52/3 St. Lawrence 45

MACKAY, SCOTT
89/0 7th..Sketch OHL 35

MACKEIGAN, JACK
82/3 Victoria Cougars
83/4 Victoria Cougars

MACKELL, FLEMING
45-64 BeeHive-2 [Toro.]
45-64 BeeHive-2 [Bost.]
48-52 Exhibits [Maple Leafs]
51/2 Parkhurst 83
52/3 Parkhurst 82
53/4 Parkhurst 91
53/4 Parkhurst 91
54/5 Parkhurst 50
93/4 Parkie 56-57 3
45-54 Quaker Oats
54/5 Topps 36
57/8 Topps 16
58/9 Topps 29
59/0 Topps 19
59/0 Topps 60
55 Toronto Star Weekend
57-58 BOST
91/2 BOST / SA Legends

MACKELLAR, PETER
95/6 Slapshot 289

MACKELLER, PETER
93/4 Slapshot / S.S.Marie 9

MACKELLER, PETER
93/4 Soo Greyhounds 5

MACKENZIE, BILL
34-43 BeeHive-1 [Maroons]
35-40 Canada Starch
36/7 O-Pee-Chee 111
37/8 O-Pee-Chee 151
39/0 O-Pee-Chee 81
33/4 WWGum 61
37/8 World Wide Gum 41

MACKENZIE, BRIAN
91/2 7th...Sketch OHL 267

MACKENZIE, CHRIS
00/1 Cardset 169
99/0 Indianapolis Ice

MACKENZIE, DEREK
99 Bowman 10, ✍ BA30
98/9 SP Authentic 127, ✍ SotT
98/9 Upper Deck 404
98/9 UD G. Reserve 404
00/1 UD Prospects 39
01/2 Chicago Wolves
02/3 Chicago Wolves
98/9 Sudbury Wolves 6
99/0 Sudbury Wolves 14
00/1 Sudbury Wolves 15

MACKENZIE, JACK
59/60 Whitby Dunlops

MACKENZIE, JEAN-MARC
86/7 London Knights
83/4 Soo Greyhounds
84/5 Soo Greyhounds

MACKENZIE, KEN
90/1 7th..Sketch OHL 399
91/2 7th...Sketch OHL 265
98/9 Sudbury Wolves 2

MACKENZIE, ROBERT
91/2 7th...Sketch OHL 285

MACKENZIE, RODDIE
94/5 Slapshot Memorial 66

MACKENZIE, SHAWN
95/6 Halifax Moosehead
96/7 Halifax Moosehead
96/7 Halifax Moosehead
97/8 Halifax Moosehead
97/8 Halifax Moosehead

MACKEY, DAVID
94/5 Leaf 280
94/5 Parkhurst 202
94/5 Premier 48
88/9 ProCards / Saginaw
90/1 ProCards 328
91/2 ProCards 331
99/0 Chicago Wolves
94/5 Milwaukee Admirals
95/6 Milwaukee Admirals
96/7 Milwaukee Admirals
98/9 Orlando Solar Bears
98/9 Orlando Solar Bears Geico
92/3 Peoria Rivermen
93/4 Peoria Rivermen
84/5 Medicine Hat Tigers
82/3 Victoria Cougars
83/4 Victoria Cougars

MACKIE, DUB
23/4 Paulins Candy 14

MACKIE, KEVIN
97/8 Kamloops Blazers
98/9 Kamloops Blazers
99/0 Kamloops Blazers
99/0 Kamloops Blazers

MACKINNON, PAUL
78/9 Winnipeg Jets

MACKINNON, STEVE
98/9 Peoria Rivermen

MACLAREN, DONALD
81/2 Ottawa 67's
82/3 Ottawa 67's
83/4 Ottawa 67's

MACLEAN, A.J.
00/1 Halifax Moosehead

MACLEAN, CAIL
98/9 EBK ECHL All-Star
93/4 Slapshot / Kingston 12
95/6 Slapshot 117
02/3 Hershey Bears

MACLEAN, DAVE
83/4 Belleville Bulls
84/5 Belleville Bulls
81/2 Oshawa Generals

MACLEAN, DEREK
97/8 Portland Winter Hawks

MACLEAN, DONALD
95/6 Classic 30
95/6 Cla. 5 Sport 157
98/9 Pacific 238
01/2 Pacific 368
97/8 Pa. Crown Roy. 63
97/8 Pinnacle 14
97/8 Pi. Be A Player 241, ✍ Aut. 241
94/5 SR Auto-Phonex 26, ✍ 26
97/8 SP Authentic 184
98/9 UD Choice 102
97/8 Upper Deck 292
98/9 Upper Deck 106
97/8 UD Black Diam. 57
98/9 UD G. Reserve 106
97/8 UD Ice 53
99/0 Lowell Lock Monsters
00/1 St. John's Maple Leafs
01/2 St. John's Maple Leafs
01/2 St. John's / Clarenville

MACLEAN, DOUG
96/7 FLOR / Winn-Dixie

MACLEAN, JOHN
99/0 Aurora 95
99/0 BAP Mem. 295
90/1 Bowman 83
91/2 Bowman 272
91/2 Bowman 289
92/3 Bowman 130
95/6 Bowman 27
93/4 Donruss 184
94/5 Donruss 151
95/6 Donruss 88
96/7 Donruss 146
97/8 Donruss 155
95/6 Do. Elite 23
94/5 Flair 95
94/5 Fleer 114
95/6 Fleer Metal 83
92/3 Fleer Ultra 115
93/4 Fleer Ultra 53
94/5 Fleer Ultra 119
95/6 Fleer Ultra 89, 193
91/2 Kellogg's / Score 13
93/4 Leaf 264
94/5 Leaf 204
95/6 Leaf 176
96/7 Leaf 195
94/5 L. Limited 92
97/8 Limited 60
99/0 Millenium 162, ✍ Aut. 162
86/7 OPC/Topps 37
87/8 OPC/Topps 191
88/9 OPC/Topps 10
90/1 OPC/Topps 224
91/2 O-Pee-Chee 239
91/2 Topps - Team Leader 15
89/0 OPC/Topps 102
91/2 OPC Premier 4
88/9 OPC Sticker 78-207
89/0 opcSticker 87
97/8 Omega 202
98/9 Pacific 384
99/0 Pacific 273
00/1 Pacific 266
97/8 Pacific CC 169
97/8 Pa. Dynagon 71, T-48
97/8 Pa. Paramount 104
99/0 Pa. Paramount 153
97/8 Pa. Revolution 124
87/8 Panini Sticker 80
88/9 Panini Sticker 274
89/0 Panini Sticker 249
90/1 Panini Sticker 74
91/2 Panini Sticker 213
93/4 Panini Sticker 40
94/5 Panini Sticker 30
95/6 Panini Sticker 83
96/7 Panini Sticker 88
97/8 Panini Sticker 70
98/9 Panini Sticker 212
99/0 Panini Sticker 106
92/3 Parkhurst 90
93/4 Parkhurst 115
94/5 Parkhurst 125
95/6 Parkhurst 123
91/2 Pinnacle 115
92/3 Pinnacle 351
93/4 Pinnacle 183
94/5 Pinnacle 101
95/6 Pinnacle 26
96/7 Pinnacle 149
97/8 Pinnacle 184
97/8 Pi. Certified 91
97/8 Pi. Inside 145
95/6 Pi. Summit 106
96/7 Pi. Summit 143
97/8 Pi. Totally 91
95/6 Pi. Zenith 69
95/6 Playoff 278
94/5 POG 146
95/6 POG 160
93/4 Power Play 138
93/4 Premier 193
94/5 Premier 175
95/6 Pro Magnet 32
90/1 Pro Set 170
91/2 Pro Set 136
91/2 Pro Set 92
91/2 Pro Set Platinum 70
99/0 Revolution 98
90/1 Score 190
90/1 Sco. Hot Cards 83
91/2 Score 210
91/2 Score CAN 210
92/3 Score 30
93/4 Score 81
94/5 Score 172
95/6 Score 77
96/7 Score 143
97/8 Score 141
97/8 Score NJer. 4
94/5 Select 136
95/6 Select CE 92
95/6 SBx Emotion 98
95/6 SBx Impact 93
94/5 SP 65
95/6 SP 78
99/0 Stadium 127
92/3 Topps 273
95/6 Topps 140
99/0 Topps 81
99/0 To. Chrome 81
94/5 Topps Finest 90
95/6 To. Finest 38
91/2 To. Stadium 144
92/3 To. Stadium 28
93/4 To. Stadium 287
95/6 To. Stadium 26
95/6 T. Super Skills 62
98/9 UD Choice 176
90/1 Upper Deck 161
91/2 Upper Deck 88
91/2 Upper Deck 169
92/3 Upper Deck 521
93/4 Upper Deck 134
94/5 Upper Deck 8, SP-133
95/6 Upper Deck 74, SE-134
96/7 Upper Deck 95
97/8 Upper Deck 94
98/9 Upper Deck 320
94/5 UD BAP ✍ 134
97/8 UD Black Diam. 68
95/6 UD CC 34
97/8 UD Coll. Choice 146
98/9 UD G. Reserve 320
99/0 UD MVP 137
83/4 NJER
84/5 NJER
86/7 NJER / S.O.B.E.R.
88/9 NJER / Caretta
89/0 NJER
89/0 NJER / Caretta
90/1 NJER
96/7 NJER / Sharp
98/9 NYRA
00/1 Manitoba Moose
81/2 Oshawa Generals
82/3 Oshawa Generals

MACLEAN, MAC
87/8 Brockville Braves
88/9 Brockville Braves

MACLEAN, PAUL
90/1 Bowman 18
83/4 Funmate Puffy 6 [w/]
84/5 Kellogg's 21
86/7 Kraft Sports 76
82/3 O-Pee-Chee 386
83/4 O-Pee-Chee 388
84/5 O-Pee-Chee 342
84/5 O-Pee-Chee 371
85/6 OPC/Topps 145
86/7 OPC/Topps 114
87/8 OPC/Topps 91
88/9 OPC/Topps 38
90/1 OPC/Topps 110
89/0 OPC/Topps 129
88/9 OPC Stars 23
82/3 OPC/Topps Sticker 208
83/4 OPC/Topps Sticker 283
84/5 OPC Sticker 289
85/6 OPC Sticker 250-130
86/7 OPC Sticker 108-238
87/8 OPC Sticker 252
88/9 OPC Sticker 144
89/0 opcSticker 18-158
87/8 Panini Sticker 354
87/8 Panini Sticker 364
88/9 Panini Sticker 156
90/1 Panini Sticker 271
82/3 Post [Winn.]
90/1 Pro Set 266
90/1 Score 203
84/5 7-Eleven
85/6 7-Eleven Superstars 21
83/4 Souhaits Keychain [Jets]
90/1 Upper Deck 260
83/4 Vachon 131-11
88/9 DETR / Little Caesars
86/7 PHOE / Coca-Cola
89/0 SLOU / Kodak
90/1 SLOU / Kodak
81/2 WINN
82/3 WINN
83/4 WINN
84/5 WINN / Safety Tips
85/6 WINN
85/6 WINN / Safety Tips
85/6 WINN / Silverwood
86/7 WINN
87/8 WINN
98/9 Kansas City Blades 25
99/0 Kansas City Blades
93/4 Peoria Rivermen
00/1 Quad City Mallards
87/8 Brockville Braves
88/9 Brockville Braves

MACLEAN, RON
97/8 Pi. CBC Sports 7

MACLEAN, TERRY
88/9 ProCards / Peoria
89/0 ProCards IHL 10

MACLEISH, RICK
02/3 Topps SCH, ✍ SCH
72/3 Eddie Sargent 167
01/2 Fleer Greats 47, ✍ Aut.
75/6 Hockey Heroes
74/5 Lipton Soup 20
74/5 Loblaws
71/2 O-Pee-Chee 207
72/3 O-Pee-Chee 105
73/4 O-Pee-Chee 133
73/4 O-Pee-Chee 138
73/4 O-Pee-Chee 146
74/5 O-Pee-Chee 6
74/5 O-Pee-Chee 163
75/6 O-Pee-Chee 20
76/7 O-Pee-Chee 121
77/8 OPC 7
77/8 O-Pee-Chee 15
77/8 O-Pee-Chee NS 9
78/9 O-Pee-Chee 125
78/9 O-Pee-Chee 263
79/0 O-Pee-Chee 75
80/1 O-Pee-Chee 115
81/2 O-Pee-Chee 133
82/3 O-Pee-Chee 273
82/3 OPC/Topps Sticker 147
92/3 Parkhurst 472
73/4 Topps 1
73/4 Topps 6
73/4 Topps 135
74/5 Topps 6
74/5 Topps 163
75/6 Topps 20
76/7 Topps 121
77/8 Topps 7
77/8 Topps 15
77/8 ToppsNS 9
78/9 Topps 125
78/9 Topps 263
79/0 Topps 75
80/1 Topps 115
81/2 Topps 108 [East]
01/2 T/O Archives 36
71/2 Toronto Sun Photo

MACLELLAN, BRENT
00/1 UD Prospects 81
01 UD Prospects GU 33, ✂ TPJ
99/0 Rimouski Océanic 6
00/1 Rimouski Océanic 8
01/2 Rimouski Océanic 8

MACLELLAN, BRIAN
91/2 Bowman 269
84/5 O-Pee-Chee 87
85/6 O-Pee-Chee 204
86/7 OPC/Topps 33
87/8 OPC/Topps 31
88/9 OPC/Topps 193
90/1 OPC/Topps 286
91/2 O-Pee-Chee 50
89/0 O-Pee-Chee 208
88/9 OPC Sticker 162
88/9 OPC Sticker 197-62
87/8 Panini Sticker 294
88/9 Panini Sticker 95
89/0 Panini Sticker 18
90/1 Pro Set 36
90/1 Score 56T
91/2 Score 32T
91/2 Score CAN 582
91/2 To. Stadium 206
90/1 Upper Deck 372
90/1 CALG / McGavin's
84/5 LOSA / Smokey 11
86/7 MINS / 7-Eleven 2
87/8 MINS
88/9 MINS / ADA

MACLELLAN, SCOTT
81/2 Kingston Canadians
82/3 Kingston Canadians

MACLELLAN, SCOTT
91/2 Rayside-Balfour

MACLEOD, JEFF
99/0 Eishockey 175
01/2 UD DEL 130

MACLEOD, PAT
92/3 Bowman 433
92/3 O-Pee-Chee 273
92/3 OPC Premier 87
91/2 Parkhurst 161
91/2 Pro Set 559
89/0 ProCards IHL 90
90/1 ProCards 108
91/2 ProCards 525
91/2 Score 95T
91/2 Score CAN 645
92/3 Topps 317
92/3 To. Stadium 336
91/2 Upper Deck 578
92/3 Upper Deck 146
91/2 SANJ / Sports Action
97/8 Cincinnati Cyclones
98/9 Cincinnati Cyclones
99/0 Cincinnati Cyclones
93/4 Milwaukee Admirals
94/5 Milwaukee Admirals
87/8 Kamloops Blazers
88/9 Kamloops Blazers

MACMILLAN, BILLY
70/1 Eddie Sargent 205
71/2 Eddie Sargent 198
72/3 Eddie Sargent 5
70/1 Esso Power Player
74/5 Loblaws
70/1 O-Pee-Chee 98
74/5 O-Pee-Chee 349
76/7 O-Pee-Chee 312
72/3 Topps 77
71/2 Toronto Sun Photo
72/3 ATLF
81/2 COLR
71/2 TORO

MACMILLAN, BOB
83/4 Funmate Puffy 11 [w/]
76/7 O-Pee-Chee 38
77/8 O-Pee-Chee 141
78/9 O-Pee-Chee 82
79/0 OPC 2
79/0 O-Pee-Chee 210
80/1 O-Pee-Chee 267
81/2 O-Pee-Chee 46
82/3 O-Pee-Chee 143
83/4 O-Pee-Chee 234
84/5 O-Pee-Chee 40
85/6 O-Pee-Chee 193
82/3 OPC/Topps Sticker 225
83/4 OPC/Topps Sticker 220
84/5 OPC Sticker 72
79 Panini Sticker 66
80/1 Pepsi Bottle Cap
82/3 Post [Colo.]
83/4 Souhaits Keychain [Devils]
76/7 Topps 38
77/8 Topps 141
78/9 Topps 82
79/0 Topps 2
79/0 Topps 210
78/9 ATLF / Colour
79/0 ATLF / B&W
79/0 ATLF / Colour
80/1 CALG
81/2 COLR
83/4 NJER
72/3 Minn. Fight. Saints

MACMILLAN, GARRY
69 Columbus Checkers

MACMILLAN, JASON
95/6 Slapshot 315

MACMILLAN, JEFF
99/0 Michigan K-Wings
00/1 Utah Grizzlies
01/2 Utah Grizzlies

MACMILLAN, JOHN
45-64 BeeHive-2 [Toro.]
63-65 Chex
62/3 Cowan Tile
63/4 Parkhurst 15
61/2 Shirriff 56
62/3 Shirriff 14

MACMILLAN, MALCOLM
01/2 Guelph Storm
01/2 Guelph Storm M-Cup

MACMILLAN, TAVIS
94/5 SR Auto-Phonex 27, ✍ 27

MACNAIR, SCOTT
94/5 Raleigh Icecaps

MACNAMARA, JERRY
52/3 Anonymous 153

MACNEIL, AL
45-64 BeeHive-2 [Toro.]
45-64 BeeHive-2 [Mont.]
45-64 BeeHive-2 [Chic.]
45-64 BeeHive-2 [Chic.]
64-67 BeeHive-3 [Chic.]
64-67 BeeHive-3 [NYRa.]
64/5 Coke/Sprite [Chic.]
65/6 Coca-Cola
62/3 Cowan Tile
57/8 Parkhurst [Toro.] 19
93/4 Parkie 56-57 121
95/6 Parkie 66-67 94
94/5 Parkie Tall 40
61/2 Shirriff 119
62/3 Shirriff 40
62/3 Topps 32
63/4 Topps 28
64/5 Topps 26
65/6 Topps 57
66/7 Topps 89
64/5 Toronto Star Action
61/2 York 36
79/0 ATLF / B&W
71/2 MONT / Pro Star
77/8 Nova Scotia Voyageurs

MACNEIL, BERNIE
75/6 Cincinnati Stingers

MACNEIL, IAN
02/3 BAP Mem. 396
02/3 SP Authentic 179
02/3 Ultimate Mem. 85
02/3 UD Artistic 102
02/3 UD Honor 135
02/3 UD Mask 136
95/6 Slapshot 247
99/0 Cincinnati Cyclones
00/1 Cincinnati Cyclones
00/1 New Haven Beast 2
02/3 Philadelphia Phantoms

MACNEVIN, JOSH
00/1 Charlotte Checkers

MACNEVIN, TROY
84/5 Kingston Canadians
85/6 Kingston Canadians
86/7 Kingston Canadians

MACOUN, JAMIE
92/3 Bowman 9
92/3 Fleer Ultra 212
93/4 Fleer Ultra 431
94/5 Fleer Ultra 217
94/5 Leaf 418
84/5 O-Pee-Chee 230
85/6 O-Pee-Chee 201
86/7 O-Pee-Chee 203
87/8 O-Pee-Chee 214
90/1 OPC/Topps 265
91/2 O-Pee-Chee 168
92/3 O-Pee-Chee 371
89/0 O-Pee-Chee 207
85/6 OPC Sticker 212-79
86/7 OPC Sticker 85-213
87/8 OPC Sticker 48-187
97/8 Pacific CC 231
87/8 Panini Sticker 208
88/9 Panini Sticker 15, 38
90/1 Panini Sticker 178
90/1 Panini/CGY 9
91/2 Panini Sticker 61
93/4 Panini Sticker 230
94/5 Parkie SE179
91/2 Pinnacle 114
92/3 Pinnacle 293
93/4 Pinnacle 131
94/5 Pinnacle 297
94/5 POG 240
93/4 Power Play 451
93/4 Premier 517
94/5 Premier 102
90/1 Pro Set 37
91/2 Pro Set 38
92/3 Pro Set 188
91/2 Pro Set Platinum 235
90/1 Score 216
91/2 Score 284
91/2 Score CAN 504
92/3 Score 88
93/4 Score 224
94/5 Score 106
92/3 Topps 348
91/2 To. Stadium 160
92/3 To. Stadium 309
90/1 Upper Deck 101
91/2 Upper Deck 412
95/6 Upper Deck 331
96/7 Upper Deck 166
95/6 UD BAP 218, ✍ S218
83/4 Vachon 12-132
85/6 CALG / Red Rooster
86/7 CALG / Red Rooster
87/8 CALG / Red Rooster
90/1 CALG / McGavin's
91/2 CALG / IGA
92/3 TORO / Kodak
93/4 TORO / Abalene
93/4 TORO / Black's 11
94/5 TORO / Coca-Cola

MACOUX, HENRI
94/5 DEL 256
95/6 DEL 254

MACPHEE, WAYNE
94/5 Slapshot / Brantford 13
83/4 North Bay Centennials

MACPHERSON, B.J.
91/2 7th...Sketch OHL 158
93/4 Slapshot / North Bay 13
94/5 Toledo Storm
95/6 Toledo Storm
90/1 Oshawa Generals
91/2 Oshawa Generals
91/2 Oshawa Generals
92/3 Oshawa Generals

MACPHERSON, BLAIR
85/6 Kitchener Rangers

MACPHERSON, BUD
02/3 Parkie - Reprint 178
45-64 BeeHive-2 [Mont.]
48-52 Exhibits [Canadiens]
51/2 La Patrie
51/2 Parkhurst 6
52/3 Parkhurst 11
53/4 Parkhurst 22
55/6 Parkhurst 47
45-54 Quaker Oats

MACPHERSON, DONALD
90/1 7th..Sketch OHL 87

MACPHERSON, DUNCAN
88/9 ProCards / Springfield
83/4 Saskatoon Blades
84/5 Saskatoon Blades

MACPHERSON, RYAN
00/1 Halifax Moosehead

MACPHERSON, SCOTT
98/9 Cincinnati Cyclones

MACPHERSON, WILLIAM
90/1 7th..Sketch OHL 343

MACQUISTEN, DOUG
37/8 World Wide Gum 105

MACRAE, STUART
01/2 Cape Breton Eagles 5

MACSWAIN, STEVE
98/9 Anchorage Aces
99/0 Anchorage Aces

MACSWEYN, KURT
99/0 Brampton Battalion 19

MACSWEYN, RALPH
70/1 Eddie Sargent 145
69/0 O-Pee-Chee 96
72/3 Los Angeles Sharks
73/4 Vancouver Blazers

MACTAVISH, CRAIG
90/1 Bowman 193
91/2 Bowman 100
92/3 Bowman 118
93/4 Donruss 462
96/7 Donruss 103
92/3 Fleer Ultra 294
93/4 Fleer Ultra 316
93/4 Kraft / PB
94/5 Leaf 514
96/7 Leaf 192
86/7 OPC/Topps 178
87/8 O-Pee-Chee 203
88/9 OPC/Topps 232
90/1 OPC/Topps 189
91/2 O-Pee-Chee 68
92/3 O-Pee-Chee 118
89/0 O-Pee-Chee 230
86/7 OPC Sticker 76-204
87/8 OPC Sticker 91-224
88/9 OPC Sticker 217-87
89/0 opcSticker 226-85
87/8 Panini Sticker 267
88/9 Panini Sticker 60
88/9 Panini Sticker 175
89/0 Panini Sticker 78
90/1 Panini Sticker 220
90/1 Panini/EDM 13
91/2 Panini Sticker 132
92/3 Panini Sticker 101
93/4 Panini Sticker 240
91/2 Parkhurst 276
92/3 Parkhurst 48
93/4 Parkhurst 342
94/5 Parkhurst 145
94/5 Parkie SE132
91/2 Pinnacle 215
92/3 Pinnacle 78
93/4 Pinnacle 96
93/4 Pinnacle CA8
94/5 Pinnacle 392
95/6 Pinnacle 148
93/4 Power Play 82
93/4 Premier 23
94/5 Premier 103
90/1 Pro Set 90
91/2 Pro Set 77
90/1 Score 258
91/2 Score 202
91/2 Score CAN 202
92/3 Score 303
93/4 Score 8
94/5 Score 85
95/6 Score 249
96/7 Score 230
92/3 Topps 336
94/5 Topps Finest RL-8
91/2 To. Stadium 133
92/3 To. Stadium 125
93/4 To. Stadium 410
95/6 TSC Members Only 23
90/1 Upper Deck 169
91/2 Upper Deck 284
92/3 Upper Deck 425
93/4 Upper Deck 111
94/5 Upper Deck 225
94/5 UD BAP ✍ 72
96/7 UD CC 227
93/4 EDMO / Sheet
85/6 EDMO / Red Rooster
86/7 EDMO
86/7 EDMO / Red Rooster
87/8 EDMO
88/9 EDMO
88/9 EDMO / Action 21
90/1 EDMO / IGA
91/2 EDMO / IGA
92/3 EDMO
92/3 EDMO / IGA 013
94/5 PHIL / Sheet
94/5 PHIL / Sheet
94/5 STLO / Sheet

MACTAVISH, GORD
77/8 Nova Scotia Voyageurs

MACVICAR, ANDY
89/0 Sudbury Wolves

MACWILLIAM, MIKE
91/2 ProCards 348
88/9 Flint Spirits

MADACH, PETER
92/3 Semic Nordisk 23

MADDEN, CHRIS
99 Bowman 162
00/1 Hamilton Bulldogs
96/7 Guelph Storm
99/0 Guelph Storm

MADDEN, JOHN
02/3 Bowman 78
02/3 Pacific 225
02/3 Pacific Complete 416
02/3 PS Titanium 64
02/3 T. Total 339
02/3 Upper Deck 351
02/3 UD MVP 107
02/3 UD Rookie 58
02/3 UD Vintage 150
01/2 Adrenaline 115
00/1 Aurora 84
99/0 BAP Mem. 150
00/1 BAP Mem. 103
01/2 BAP Mem. 143
01/2 O-Pee-Chee 237, 321
99/0 Omega 139
99/0 Pacific 239
00/1 Pacific 237
01/2 Pacific 232
99/0 Pa. Paramount 134
00/1 Pa. Paramount 145
00/1 Parkhurst P-4
01/2 Parkhurst 23
00/1 Signature 243, ✍ Aut. 177
99/0 SP Authentic 107
00/1 Stadium 67, CA6
00/1 Topps 215
01/2 Topps 237, 321
99/0 To. Chrome 246
00/1 To. Chrome 138
01/2 To. Chrome 137
00/1 To. Heritage 234
01/2 To. Heritage 136
99/0 To. Prmr. Plus 104
99/0 Upper Deck 81
00/1 Upper Deck 105
01/2 Upper Deck 107
99/0 UD G. Reserve 81
01/2 UD Honor Roll DF5
99/0 UD MVP 122
00/1 UD MVP 105
99/0 UD Retro 47
01/2 UD SCup Champs 79
00/1 UD Vintage 216
99/0 Victory 167
00/1 Victory 136
01/2 Victory 216
97/8 Albany River Rats
98/9 Albany River Rats

MADDEN, MARTIN
00/1 MONT

MADELEY, DARRIN
92/3 Classic 65
92/3 Classic Four Sport 193
93/4 Cla. 4 Sport 239
92/3 Classic Prospects 17, 40
93/4 Donruss 229
93/4 Fleer Ultra 382
94/5 Fleer Ultra 340
93/4 Leaf 299
94/5 Leaf 300
93/4 Parkhurst 142
94/5 Parkie SE120
93/4 Pinnacle 211
94/5 Pinnacle 459
93/4 Power Play 400
93/4 Premier 283
94/5 Premier 109
93/4 Score 462
94/5 Score 51
93/4 To. Stadium 431
93/4 Upper Deck 61
95/6 Upper Deck 158
93/4 OTTA
94/5 OTTA
91/2 L. Superior State Lakers

MADER, BOB
52/3 Anonymous 87

MADER, MIKE
98/9 Roanoke Express
00/1 Rochester Americans

MADILL, JEFF
95/6 Edge Ice 191
91/2 O-Pee-Chee 6S
88/9 ProCards / Utica
89/0 ProCards AHL 204
90/1 ProCards 571
91/2 ProCards 521
93/4 Atlanta Knights
92/3 Cincinnati Cyclones
96/7 Kansas City Blades

MADL, MICHAL
99/0 DS 157
00/1 DS 136
98/9 OFS 166
99/0 OFS 169
00/1 OFS 113
01/2 OFS 191

MADORE, STÉPHANE
91/2 7th...Sketch LHJMQ 151
99/0 Colorado Gold Kings
98/9 Quad City Mallards

MAGARRELL, ADAM
94/5 Sig. Rookies 53, ✍ 53
95/6 Spokane Chiefs 22

MAGER, SAM
98/9 Guildford Flames

MAGERS, MARTY
02/3 Owen Sound Attack

MAGGS, DARYL
71/2 Toronto Sun Photo

MAGLIARDITI, MARC
95/6 Do. Elite WJ 24
00/1 Cincinnati Cyclones
98/9 Florida Everblades
99/0 Florida Everblades
00/1 Florida Everblades
01/2 Louisiana Ice Gators

MAGLIONE, KATHARINE
96 Québec Pee Wee 1316

MAGNASUN, KEITH
71/2 Eddie Sargent 48

MAGNERTÖFT, MARCUS
94/5 Leaf Elit Set 237
95/6 Leaf Elit Set 89
95/6 UD Elitserien 143
98/9 UD Elitserien 157
99/0 UD Elitserien 160

MAGNUSON, KEITH
02/3 Topps - Reprint 9, ✍ Reprint 9
70/1 Dad's Cookies
70/1 Eddie Sargent 35
72/3 Eddie Sargent 57
70/1 Esso Power Player
74/5 Loblaws
70/1 O-Pee-Chee 151
71/2 O-Pee-Chee 69
72/3 O-Pee-Chee 71
72/3 O-Pee-Chee 268
73/4 O-Pee-Chee 151
74/5 O-Pee-Chee 75
75/6 O-Pee-Chee 176
76/7 O-Pee-Chee 125
77/8 O-Pee-Chee 89
78/9 O-Pee-Chee 34
72 Semic Sticker 230
71/2 Topps 69
72/3 Topps 65
72/3 Topps 87
73/4 Topps 44
74/5 Topps 75
75/6 Topps 176
76/7 Topps 125
77/8 Topps 89
78/9 Topps 34
01/2 T/O Archives 54
71/2 Toronto Sun Photo
70/1 CHIC
79/0 CHIC
80/1 CHIC / Brown

MAGNUSON, KEITH
02/3 Fleer Throwbacks 26

MAGNUSSEN, TROND
95 Globe 196
95 Panini Worlds 246
94 Semic 265
92/3 Semic Elitserien 312
93 Semic Sticker 244
01/2 UD DEL 53
97/8 UD Elitserien 62
98/9 UD Elitserien 92
99/0 UD Elitserien 61
00/1 UD Elitserien 87
96 Wien 207

MAGNUSSON, MIKAEL
94/5 Leaf Elit Set 3
95/6 Leaf Elit Set 29
92/3 Semic Elitserien 85
95/6 UD Elitserien 43
98/9 UD Elitserien 55
99/0 UD Elitserien 40
00/1 UD Elitserien 48

MAGNUSSON, STEFAN
91/2 Semic Elitserien 106

MAGNUSSON, STEVE
91/2 Minnesota G'Gophers
92/3 Minnesota G'Gophers
93/4 Minnesota G'Gophers

MAGRUDER, DENNY
92/3 Wheeling Thund'birds 19
93/4 Wheeling Thund'birds

MAGUIRE, BILL
82/3 North Bay Centennials

MAGUIRE, DEREK
94/5 Classic 56
94/5 Fredericton Canadiens

MAGUIRE, E.J.
91/2 ProCards 67
88/9 CHIC / Coke
89/0 CHIC / Coke
90/1 CHIC / Coke
86/7 PHIL

MAGUIRE, KEVIN
91/2 Bowman 172
90/1 Panini/TOR 13
90/1 Pro Set 538
91/2 ProCards 347
87/8 BUFF / Blue Shield
87/8 BUFF / Won. Bread
88/9 BUFF / Blue Shield
88/9 BUFF / Won. Bread
89/0 BUFF / Blue Shield
89/0 BUFF / Campbell's
90/1 TORO

MAHAFFY, JOHN
51/2 Laval Dairy 55
37/8 World Wide Gum 133

MAHER, JEFF
98/9 Calgary Hitmen 25
99/0 Calgary Hitmen
00/1 Calgary Hitmen
01/2 Calgary Hitmen

MAHER, JIM
92/3 Phoenix Roadrunners
93/4 Phoenix Roadrunners
94/5 Toledo Storm

MAHEUX, NICOLAS
95/6 Halifax Moosehead

MAHON, BERNT
02/3 Plymouth Whalers

MAHON, DAN
82/3 Kingston Canadians

MAHON, MARK
96/7 DEL 219

MAHONEY, BILL
83/4 MINS
80/1 WASH

MAHONEY, SCOTT
89/0 Sudbury Wolves

MAHOVLICH, FRANK
02/3 BAP Mem. / Stanley Cup
02/3 Canada Post
02/3 Parkhurst ✂ VM10, ✂ VT7
02/3 Parkhurst Retro ✂ NN12
02/3 Ultimate Mem. ✂ ASMVP, ✂ EA, ✂ FS (x2), ✂ Num, ✂ SF, ✂ VGJ
02/3 UD Foundations ✍ SG
01/2 ASG History
71/2 Bazooka Panel
99/0 BAP Mem. CH-4, ✍ CH-4
01/2 BAP Mem. ✂ 500GS
45-64 BeeHive-2 [Toro.]
64-67 BeeHive-3 [Toro.]
64-67 BeeHive-3 [Toro.]
63-65 Chex
64/5 Coke/Sprite [Toro.]
65/6 Coca-Cola
71/2 Colgate Head
70/1 Dad's Cookies
72/3 Dernière Heure
73/4 Dernière Heure
70/1 Eddie Sargent 63
71/2 Eddie Sargent 104
72/3 Eddie Sargent 120
62/3 El Producto
70/1 Esso Power Player
88/9 Esso All-Star
01/2 Fleer Greats 55, ✍ Aut.
01/2 Fleer Legacy 21
71/2 Frito Lay
91/2 Future Trends C72 26, 30, ✍ 26
62/3 Cowan Tile
83 HHOF Postcard I10
83&87 HHOF 121
93/4 Hockey Wit 56
71 Kellogg's Transfer
91/2 Kraft 87
94/5 Legends 43
72/3 Post 8
73/4 Mac's Milk
68/9 O-Pee-Chee 31
68/9 O-Pee-Chee PS 2
69/0 O-Pee-Chee 62
69/0 O-Pee-Chee 222
69/0 O-Pee-Chee 4in1
69/0 O-Pee-Chee Stamp
70/1 O-Pee-Chee 22
70/1 O-Pee-Chee 242
70/1 O-Pee-Chee DE 17
71/2 O-Pee-Chee 105
72/3 O-Pee-Chee 102
72/3 O-Pee-Chee 128
72/3 O-Pee-Chee TC
73/4 O-Pee-Chee 145
74/5 O-Pee-Chee 124
74/5 OPC WHA 40
75/6 OPC WHA 110
76/7 OPC WHA 111
77/8 OPC WHA 61
57/8 Parkhurst [Toro.] 17
58/9 Parkhurst 33
59/0 Parkhurst 24
60/1 Parkhurst 2
61/2 Parkhurst 2
62/3 Parkhurst 4
62/3 Parkhurst 18

63/4 Parkhurst 17
63/4 Parkhurst 77
92/3 Parkhurst PR-29
93/4 Parkhurst PR44
01/2 Parkhurst PR8, PR38, PR48, PR64, PR86, PR101, PR124, PR134, PR146, ✄ 500GS, ✍ PA1, ✍ PA4
93/4 Parkie 56-57 FS-5, ✍ A-6
95/6 Parkie 66-67 102,124, 145
94/5 Parkie Tall 130, 143, SL6
66/7 Post Cereal Box
66/7 Post [Small]
67/8 Post Tips 5
70/1 Post Shooters
71/2 Pro Star Promotions
71/2 Pro Star Promotions
72 Semic Sticker 195
60/1 Shirriff 12
61/2 Shirriff 43
62/3 Shirriff 3
62/3 Shirriff 53
68/9 Shirriff / Detr. 12
01/2 Signature ✄ 500GS, ✍ VA27
91/2 Star Pics 27
81/2 TCMA 10
64/5 Topps 85
65/6 Topps 81
66/7 Topps 77
66/7 Topps 131
66/7 Topps / Test 51
67/8 Topps 79
68/9 Topps 31
69/0 Topps 62
70/1 Topps 22
71/2 Topps 105
72/3 Topps 140
73/4 Topps 40
74/5 Topps 124
99/0 Topps SC6, ✍ SCH
57/8 Toronto Star Photo
58/9 Toronto Star Photo
60/1 Toronto Star Photo
62/3 Toronto Star Photo
63/4 Toronto Star Action
64/5 Toronto Star Action
64/5 Toronto Star Photo
65/6 Toronto Star Photo
58/9 Toronto Star Weekend
62/3 Toronto Star Weekend
66/7 Toronto Star Weekend
71/2 Toronto Sun Photo
00/1 UD Heroes 138, ✍ SG
01/2 Ultimate Mem. ✄ 500GS, ✄ ASGH, ✄ Blood, ✄ EA, ✄ LC, ✄ RT, ✄ SCW, ✍ Aut.
91/2 Ultimate Original Six 40, ✍ Aut. 40
00 ✄ UD APOH 500, ✄✍ 500
99/0 UD C. Legends 27, ✍ ES
00/1 UD Legends 120, 126, ES10, ✍ ES
01/2 UD Legends 58, ✄ PoH, ✍ ES
92/3 UD Locker 44
01/2 UD SCup Champs 26
60/1 York Glass [Toro.]
60/1 York
61/2 York 3
62/3 York Transfer 11
63/4 York 5
67/8 York 18
67/8 York 20
67/8 York 28
67/8 York 35
92/3 Zellers
70/1 DETR / Marathon Oil
99/0 DETR / News 4
69/0 MONT / Pro Star
70/1 MONT
71/2 MONT / Pro Star
71/2 MONT / Pro Star
72/3 MONT / Pro Star
73/4 MONT / Pro Star
92/3 MONT / OPC 24
92/3 MONT / OPC 39
64/5 TORO
69/0 TORO

MAHOVLICH, PETER
02/3 Parkhurst ✄ VT7
02/3 Parkhurst Retro ✄ NN12
02/3 Topps - Reprint 3, ✍ Reprint 3
02/3 Ultimate Mem. ✄ ASMVP, ✄ VGJ
64-67 BeeHive-3 [Detr.]
72/3 Dernière Heure
73/4 Dernière Heure
70/1 Eddie Sargent 102
71/2 Eddie Sargent 99
72/3 Eddie Sargent 114
70/1 Esso Power Player
91/2 Future Trends C72 27, 30, ✍ 27
92/3 Future Trends C76 180
75/6 Hockey Heroes
74/5 Lipton Soup 39
74/5 Loblaws
73/4 Mac's Milk
68/9 O-Pee-Chee 143
70/1 O-Pee-Chee 58
71/2 O-Pee-Chee 84
72/3 O-Pee-Chee 124
72/3 O-Pee-Chee TC
73/4 O-Pee-Chee 164
74/5 O-Pee-Chee 97
75/6 O-Pee-Chee 50
75/6 O-Pee-Chee 209
75/6 O-Pee-Chee 322
76/7 O-Pee-Chee 2
76/7 O-Pee-Chee 15
76/7 OPC 388
77/8 O-Pee-Chee 205
77/8 O-Pee-Chee 262
78/9 O-Pee-Chee 51
79/0 O-Pee-Chee 187
80/1 O-Pee-Chee 72
80/1 O-Pee-Chee Super 6
01/2 Parkhurst ✍ PA47
95/6 Parkie 66-67 46
70/1 Post Shooters
71/2 Pro Star Promotions
68/9 Shirriff / Detr. 3
66/7 Topps 103
66/7 Topps / Test 21
70/1 Topps 58
71/2 Topps 84
72/3 Topps 42
73/4 Topps 186
74/5 Topps 97
75/6 Topps 50
75/6 Topps 209
75/6 Topps 322
76/7 Topps 2
76/7 Topps 15
77/8 Topps 205
77/8 Topps 262
78/9 Topps 51
79/0 Topps 187
80/1 Topps 72
01/2 T/O Archives 80, ✄ Jers
71/2 Toronto Sun Photo
01/2 Ultimate Mem. ✄ BL, ✄ LC
80/1 DETR
69/0 MONT / Pro Star
70/1 MONT
71/2 MONT / Pro Star
72/3 MONT / Pro Star
74/5 MONT
75/6 MONT
76/7 MONT

MAIA, PIERRICK
95 Globe 202
95 Panini Worlds 111
94 Semic 223

MAIDL, ANTON
94/5 DEL 138
95/6 DEL 131

MAIER, ARNO
94 Semic 245
93 Semic Sticker 281

MAIER, KIM
91/2 Air Canada SJHL 24
93/4 Knoxville Cherokees
92/3 Wheeling Thund'birds 9

MAILHOT, JACQUES
88/9 ProCards / Halifax
89/0 ProCards IHL 119
91/2 ProCards 431
97/8 Central Texas

MAILHOT, KEVIN
01/2 Drummondville

MAILLET, CHRIS
98/9 Muskegon Fury
99/0 Muskegon Fury
93/4 Red Deer Rebels

MAILLET, CLAUDE
92/3 Greensboro Monarchs 14

MAILLOUX, CHRIS
93/4 Slapshot / Detroit 4

MAILLOUX, ROBERT
98 Bowman 33
98 Bowman Chrome 33
95/6 Slapshot 114

MAINER, PETR
94/5 APS 100
95/6 APS 225
97/8 APS 223

MAIR, ADAM
02/3 Pacific Complete 454
99/0 BAP Mem. 199
00/1 BAP Mem. 247
01/2 BAP Mem. 231
99 Bowman 148
97 Bowman 144, ✍ Aut.
99/0 Omega 230
99/0 Pacific 412
00/1 PS Titanium 147
00/1 PS Titanium Draft 147
95/6 Slapshot 298
99/0 SP Authentic 117
00/1 Topps 296
00/1 To. Chrome 191
99/0 UD Black Diam. 80
99/0 St. John's Maple Leafs
00/1 St. John's Maple Leafs

MAIR, JIM
72/3 Eddie Sargent 140
72/3 O-Pee-Chee 232

MAIRER, KIM
91/2 Air Canada SJHL A42

MAISONNEUVE, ROGER
52/3 Anonymous 88

MAITLAND, SHANE
91 7th..Sketch Mem.Cup 93
90/1 7th..Sketch WHL 194
91/2 7th...Sketch WHL 15

MAJANIEMI, TAPIO
66/7 Champion 114
65/6 Hellas 97

MAJAPURO, RAIMO
73/4 Williams Finnish 224

MAJAURY, CRAIG
86/7 London Knights

MAJAVA, KYOSTI
78/9 SM-Liiga 22
73/4 Williams Finnish 207

MAJEAU, FERN
43-47 Parade Sportive

MAJESKE, BRIAN
94/5 Anchorage Aces 16

MAJESKY, BORIS
97/8 Halifax Moosehead

MAJESKY, IVAN
02/3 BAP All-Star 147
02/3 BAP Mem. 277
02/3 Cardset 67
02/3 Crown Royale 115
02/3 In The GU 87
02/3 Parkhurst 207
02/3 Signature 182, ✍ 182
02/3 SP Authentic 146
02/3 To. Chrome 150
02/3 T. Total 424
02/3 Ultimate Mem. 7
02/3 Upper Deck 438
02/3 UD Classic 115
02/3 UD Mask 132
02/3 UD Top Shelf 92
00/1 Cardset 151

MAJIC, RON
94/5 Hampton Roads
97/8 Hampton Roads
93/4 Huntington Blizzard

MAJIC, XAVIER
94/5 Classic 46
95/6 Fredericton Canadiens
94/5 Wheeling Thund'birds

MAJOR, BRUCE
90/1 ProCards 545

MAJOR, MARK
90/1 ProCards 380
91/2 ProCards 294
95/6 Adirondack Red Wings
92/3 Cleveland Lumberjacks
99/0 Houston Aeros
97/8 Portland Pirates
98/9 Portland Pirates

MAJOROV, BORIS
92/3 Jyvas Hyva 52
93/4 Jyvas Hyva 283
93/4 Sisu 57
94/5 Sisu 397

MAKAROV, SERGEI
99/0 Mir 153

MAKAROV, SERGEI B.
90/1 O-Pee-Chee 485

MAKAROV, SERGEI*
90/1 Bowman 92
91/2 Bowman 250
91/2 Bowman 264
92/3 Bowman 53
93/4 Donruss 304
94/5 Donruss 103
94/5 Flair 167
94/5 Fleer 198
92/3 Fleer Ultra 24
93/4 Fleer Ultra 416
94/5 Fleer Ultra 198
95/6 Fleer Ultra 148
95 Globe 238
91 Ivan Fiodorov 8
89/0 Kraft 4
93/4 Leaf 384
94/5 Leaf 282
95/6 Leaf 293
00/1 Mir 210
00/1 Mir Fetisov 5
90/1 OPC/Topps 60
90/1 O-Pee-Chee 503
91/2 O-Pee-Chee 482
92/3 O-Pee-Chee 90
90/1 OPC/Topps P
91/2 OPC Premier 45
79 Panini Sticker 157
90/1 Panini Sticker 184, 334
90/1 Panini/CGY 10
91/2 Panini Sticker 58
92/3 Panini Sticker 47
93/4 Panini Sticker 183
94/5 Panini Sticker 222
95/6 Panini Sticker 282
95 Panini Worlds 284
91/2 Parkhurst 247
92/3 Parkhurst 25
93/4 Parkhurst 188
94/5 Parkhurst 211
91/2 Pinnacle 271
92/3 Pinnacle 335
93/4 Pinnacle 362
94/5 Pinnacle 152
94/5 POG 217
93/4 Power Play 222
94/5 Premier 396
90/1 Pro Set 38, 396
91/2 Pro Set 39
92/3 Pro Set 24
91/2 Pro Set Platinum 15
91/2 Red Ace
90/1 Score 71, 329, 350, 362
90/1 Sco. Hot Cards 99
91/2 Score 51
91/2 Score CAN 51
92/3 Score 382
92/3 Score SS 2
93/4 Score 33
93/4 Score 531
93/4 Score DD8
95/6 Score 159
94/5 Select 8
94 Semic 155
89 Semic Sticker 96
91 Semic Sticker 216
95/6 SBx Emotion 158
79/0 Soviet Stars 22
83/4 Soviet Stars
87/8 Soviet Stars
89/0 Soviet Stars
94/5 SP 107
92/3 Topps 467
95/6 Topps 171
91/2 To. Stadium 31
92/3 To. Stadium 217
94/5 To. Stadium 123
90/1 Upper Deck 123, 202, 336
91/2 Upper Deck 321
92/3 Upper Deck 314
92/3 Upper Deck E16
93/4 Upper Deck 446, SP-145
94/5 Upper Deck 124, SP-72
95/6 Upper Deck 24
95/6 UD CC 207
90/1 CALG / McGavin's
90/1 CALG / McGavin's
91/2 CALG / IGA
92/3 CALG / IGA 015
92/3 SANJ / Pacific Bell

MAKAROV, SERGEI?
00/1 Mir 255

MAKAROV, VLADISLAV
98/9 Mir 83
99/0 Mir 59

MAKATSCH, RAINER
72 Hellas MM-Jenkki 57
72 Semic Sticker 116

MÄKELÄ, ERKKI
91/2 Jyvas Hyva 52
92/3 Jyvas Hyva 148
93/4 Jyvas Hyva 259
93/4 Sisu 297

MÄKELÄ, JAAKKO
99/0 Cardset 344

MÄKELÄ, JANNE
00/1 Cardset 108

MÄKELÄ, JARNO
93/4 Sisu 228
94/5 Sisu 247
95/6 Sisu 158

MÄKELÄ, MIKKO
91/2 Bowman 36
98/9 Cardset 226
95/6 DEL 98
96/7 DEL 286
94/5 Fleer Ultra 258
95 Globe 142
92/3 Jyvas Hyva 181
94/5 Leaf 515
88/9 OPC/Topps 44
90/1 OPC/Topps 229
91/2 O-Pee-Chee 503
89/0 O-Pee-Chee 247
90/1 OPC Premier 66
88/9 OPC Sticker 108-238
89/0 opcSticker 112-249
87/8 Panini Sticker 87
87/8 Panini Sticker 100
88/9 Panini Sticker 291
89/0 Panini Sticker 268, 270
90/1 Panini Sticker 237
91/2 Panini Sticker 302
90/1 Pro Set 418
90/1 Score 26T
91/2 Score CAN 549
94 Semic 29
95 Semic 42
89 Semic Sticker 41
92 Semic Sticker 20
93 Semic Sticker 68
94/5 Sisu 345, GS-5
95/6 Sisu Limited 106
91/2 To. Stadium 261
97/8 UD Elitserien 180, C28
90/1 BUFF / Blue Shield
90/1 BUFF / Campbell's
89/0 LOSA / Smokey 22
89/0 NYIS

MÄKELÄ, PEKKA
78/9 SM-Liiga 229

MÄKELÄ, PERTTI
66/7 Champion 34
70/1 Kuvajulkaisut 198
71/2 Williams Finnish 89
72/3 Williams Finnish 253
73/4 Williams Finnish 252

MÄKELÄ, SEPPO
93/4 Sisu 380

MÄKELÄ, TAUNO
80/1 Mallasjuoma 215
78/9 SM-Liiga 239

MÄKELÄ, TIMO
65/6 Hellas 72
91/2 Greensboro Monarchs

MÄKELÄ, TUUKKA
02/3 Cardset 77

MAKI, BRENT
83/4 Oshawa Generals

MAKI, CHICO
45-64 BeeHive-2 [Chic.]
45-64 BeeHive-2 [Chic.]
64-67 BeeHive-3 [Chic.]
64-67 BeeHive-3 [Chic.]
63-65 Chex
64/5 Coke/Sprite [Chic.]
65/6 Coca-Cola
70/1 Dad's Cookies
70/1 Eddie Sargent 46
71/2 Eddie Sargent 36
72/3 Eddie Sargent 60
70/1 Esso Power Player
62/3 Cowan Tile
72/3 Post 2
74/5 Loblaws
68/9 O-Pee-Chee 17
69/0 O-Pee-Chee 137
70/1 O-Pee-Chee 149
71/2 O-Pee-Chee 210
72/3 O-Pee-Chee 198
73/4 O-Pee-Chee 227
74/5 O-Pee-Chee 395
95/6 Parkie 66-67 32
94/5 Parkie Tall 24
61/2 Shirriff 28
68/9 Shirriff / Chic. 7
62/3 Topps 37
63/4 Topps 41
64/5 Topps 73
65/6 Topps 117
66/7 Topps 110
66/7 Topps / Test 53
67/8 Topps 111
68/9 Topps 17
64/5 Toronto Star Action
71/2 Toronto Sun Photo
68/9 CHIC

MAKI, WAYNE
70/1 Eddie Sargent 210
71/2 Eddie Sargent 217
72/3 Eddie Sargent 216
70/1 Esso Power Player
70/1 O-Pee-Chee 116
71/2 O-Pee-Chee 58
72/3 O-Pee-Chee 84
72 Semic Sticker 221
68/9 Shirriff / Chic. 3
67/8 Topps 55
70/1 Topps 116
71/2 Topps 58
72/3 Topps 32
71/2 Toronto Sun Photo
70/1 VANC / Royal Bank
71/2 VANC / Royal Bank 19
72/3 VANC / Nalley's
72/3 VANC / Royal Bank

MÄKI, TIMO
93/4 Jyvas Hyva 194
93/4 Sisu 257
94/5 Sisu 312

MÄKI-KOKKILA, KIMMO
93/4 Jyvas Hyva 209
93/4 Sisu 270
94/5 Sisu 323
95/6 Sisu 207

MAKIA, MARTTI
66/7 Champion 93
72/3 Williams Finnish 178

MAKIA, VEIKKO
66/7 Champion 96

MÄKIAHO, TONI
02/3 Cardset 226
98/9 Cardset 47, -Leij. 32
99/0 Cardset 28
00/1 Cardset 258
97/8 Hockey-Box
94/5 Sisu 272
95/6 Sisu 27
96/7 Sisu 23
94/5 Topps Finest 139

MAKILA, RAYNER
51/2 Lac St-Jean 41

MAKINEN, ARI
80/1 Mallasjuoma 66
78/9 SM-Liiga 73

MAKINEN, ESKO
70/1 Kuvajulkaisut 132
73/4 Williams Finnish 185

MAKINEN, JUHA
71/2 Williams Finnish 371

MAKINEN, KARI
66/7 Champion 153
65/6 Hellas 154
70/1 Kuvajulkaisut 214

MAKINEN, KEIJO
66/7 Champion 217

MAKINEN, MARKO
95/6 Sisu 333, DD-4

MAKINEN, PEKKA
70/1 Kuvajulkaisut 215
78/9 SM-Liiga 137
71/2 Williams Finnish 137
72/3 Williams Finnish 200
73/4 Williams Finnish 161

MAKINEN, SEPPO I.
73/4 Williams Finnish 162

MAKINEN, SEPPO S.
73/4 Williams Finnish 163

MAKINEN, SEPPO?
66/7 Champion 145
65/6 Hellas 151
70/1 Kuvajulkaisut 216
71/2 Williams Finnish 138
72/3 Williams Finnish 201

MAKINEN, SEPPO??
72/3 Williams Finnish 271

MÄKINEN, KARI
93/4 Jyvas Hyva 253
93/4 Sisu 279

MÄKINEN, MARKO
02/3 Cardset 78
00/1 Cardset 334

MÄKINEN, TAPIO
66/7 Champion 218

MÄKINEN, TIMO
96/7 Sisu 116

MÄKITALO, JARMO
89/0 Semic Elitserien 137
92/3 Semic Elitserien 173
82 Semic Sticker 41
94/5 Sisu 368
78/9 SM-Liiga 122

MÄKITALO, JOUNI
78/9 SM-Liiga 237

MÄKITALO, JUKKA
94/5 Sisu 340

MÄKITALO, KARI
78/9 SM-Liiga 123

MAKKONEN, KARI
80/1 Mallasjuoma 216
78/9 SM-Liiga 18
78/9 SM-Liiga 240
79/0 EDMO
88/9 EDMO / Action 144

MAKKONEN, PASI
71/2 Williams Finnish 329

MAKOMBO, ALEXANDRE
99/0 Rockford IceHogs

MAKRITZKY, ALEXANDER
99/0 Eishockey 311

MAKSIMENKO, ANDREI
00/1 Mir 66

MAKSIMOV, ALEXANDER
99/0 Mir 199

MAKSIMOV, DMITRI
98/9 Mir 21
99/0 Mir 107

MAKSYM, ANDREW
02/3 Owen Sound Attack

MALAC, PAVEL
94/5 APS 182
95/6 APS 30
01/2 OFS 237, G11
99/0 Score 25, 73

MALAKHOV, VLADIMIR
02/3 First Edition 172
02/3 Pacific 254
02/3 Pacific Complete 370
02/3 Slam Card
02/3 Upper Deck 362
98/9 Be A Player 222, ✍ Aut. 222
99/0 BAP Mem. 191, 395
00/1 BAP Mem. 99, 433
92/3 Classic Prospects 55
92/3 Classic Prospects BC4
93/4 Donruss 207
94/5 Donruss 307
95/6 Donruss 4
93/4 EA Sports 79
94/5 Flair 105
94/5 Fleer 126
96/7 Fl. Picks 118
92/3 Fleer Ultra 346, -UI 14
93/4 Fleer Ultra 235
94/5 Fleer Ultra 130
95/6 Fleer Ultra 81
95 Globe 166
98/9 Kraft / PB
93/4 Leaf 32
93/4 Leaf GLR 9
94/5 Leaf 194
95/6 Leaf 149
00/1 Mir Fetisov 10
90/1 O-Pee-Chee 2R
92/3 OPC Premier 89
97/8 Omega 119
98/9 Pacific 253
99/0 Pacific 206
00/1 Pacific 238
97/8 Pa. Invincible R-103
98/9 Pa. Paramount 114
99/0 Pa. Paramount 119
94/5 Panini Sticker 53
95/6 Panini Sticker 42
96/7 Panini Sticker 44
97/8 Panini Sticker 34
98/9 Panini Sticker 33
92/3 Parkhurst 339
93/4 Parkhurst 125
93/4 Parkhurst 239
94/5 Parkhurst V77
95/6 Parkhurst 115
94/5 Parkie SE108
92/3 Pinnacle 409
93/4 Pinnacle 104
94/5 Pinnacle 104, BR2
97/8 Pi. Be A Player 133, ✍ Aut. 133
95/6 Pi. Summit 157
95/6 Playoff 273
94/5 POG 162
95/6 POG 151
93/4 Power Play 153
93/4 Power Play SYS 6
93/4 Premier 129
93/4 Premier 445
93/4 Premier 515
94/5 Premier 546
92/3 Red Ace Blue 28
92/3 Red Ace Violet 19
99/0 Revolution 76
93/4 Score 157
94/5 Score 62
95/6 Score 117
97/8 Score 247
97/8 Score Mont. 11
94 Semic 137
94 Semic 341
91 Semic Sticker 80
92 Semic Sticker 104
93 Semic Sticker 142
01/2 Signature ✄ IB12
95/6 SBx Emotion 88
95/6 SBx Impact 85
94/5 SP 60
97/8 SP Authentic 83
00/1 Stadium 218
96/7 Team Out!
95/6 Topps 113
99/0 Topps 101
99/0 To. Chrome 101
98/9 To. Finest 57
93/4 To. Stadium 248
94/5 To. Stadium 144
91/2 Tri Globe From... 19-20
98/9 UD Choice 104
91/2 Upper Deck 1
92/3 Upper Deck 554
92/3 Upper Deck 577
92/3 Upper Deck CC12
92/3 Upper Deck ER15
92/3 Upper Deck G12
93/4 Upper Deck 29, 283, SP-93
94/5 Upper Deck 139, SP-47
95/6 Upper Deck 466, SE-45
96/7 Upper Deck 84
98/9 Upper Deck 112
99/0 Upper Deck 242
00/1 Upper Deck 346
94/5 UD BAP R125, ✍ 121
95/6 UD CC 143
96/7 UD CC 139
98/9 UD G. Reserve 112
99/0 UD G. Reserve 242
92/3 UD Locker 57
99/0 UD MVP 102
00/1 UD Vintage 240
99/0 Victory 148
96 Wien 135
95/6 MONT / Export
95/6 MONT
96/7 MONT / Export
96-98 MONT

MALANDRINO, SALVATORE
02/3 Mississauga IceDogs

MALARCHUK, CLINT
91/2 Bowman 23
92/3 Bowman 30
93/4 Cla. Prospects 85
86/7 Kraft Sports 47
86/7 OPC/Topps 47
87/8 O-Pee-Chee 246
88/9 OPC/Topps 25
90/1 OPC/Topps 371
91/2 O-Pee-Chee 97
89/0 OPC/Topps 170
86/7 OPC Sticker 33
88/9 OPC Sticker 72-201
87/8 Panini Sticker 158
88/9 Panini Sticker 363
90/1 Panini Sticker 26
91/2 Panini Sticker 301
91/2 Parkhurst 244
91/2 Pinnacle 103
91/2 Pinnacle 397
90/1 Pro Set 25
91/2 Pro Set Platinum 159
90/1 Score 289
91/2 Score 438
91/2 Score CAN 419
92/3 Score 138
92/3 Topps 363
91/2 To. Stadium 251
92/3 To. Stadium 186
90/1 Upper Deck 399
91/2 Upper Deck 368
89/0 BUFF / Blue Shield
89/0 BUFF / Campbell's
90/1 BUFF / Blue Shield
90/1 BUFF / Campbell's
91/2 BUFF / Blue Shield
91/2 BUFF / Campbell's
91/2 BUFF / Pepsi
82/3 QUÉB
83/4 QUÉB
85/6 QUÉB
85/6 QUÉB / Gene. Foods
85/6 QUÉB / McDonald's
85/6 QUÉB / Provigo
86/7 QUÉB
86/7 QUÉB / Gene. Foods
86/7 QUÉB / McDonald's
86/7 QUÉB / Yum Yum
87/8 WASH
87/8 WASH / Kodak
88/9 WASH
88/9 WASH / Smokey
82/3 Fredericton Express
84/5 Fredericton Express
93/4 Las Vegas Thunder
94/5 Las Vegas Thunder
95/6 Las Vegas Thunder
96/7 Las Vegas Thunder
97/8 Las Vegas Thunder 25
92/3 San Diego Gulls

MALCOLM, KEVIN
99/0 Ottawa 67's

MALEC, TOMAS
02/3 BAP Mem. 343
02/3 Choice Prospects 28
02/3 Pacific Complete 535
02/3 Parkhurst Retro 213
02/3 Quest for the Cup 111
02/3 SP Authentic 168
02/3 Ultimate Mem. 58
02/3 UD Artistic 127
02/3 UD Honor 144
02/3 UD Premier 64
00/1 Rimouski Océanic 7
01/2 Rimouski Océanic 7

MALECEK, PAVEL
99/0 Score 9

MALEK, ROMAN
99/0 DS 114
00/1 DS 110, G10
01/2 DS 3, - G5
98/9 OFS 210
99/0 OFS 538
00/1 OFS 84, -Star 36
01/2 OFS 4, -CL 10, -G1
99/0 Score 1

MALENA, ROSTISLAV
99/0 OFS 459
00/1 OFS 356
01/2 OFS 81
99/0 Score 165

MALENFANT, DAVE
96/7 Rimouski Océanic
97/8 Rimouski Océanic

MALENFANT, RAY
37/8 World Wide Gum 108

MALENKIKH, VLADIMIR
00/1 Mir 171

MALENOVSKY, MAREK
01/2 OFS 32

MALEY, BRENNAN
90/1 ProCards 562

MALEY, DAVID
90/1 O-Pee-Chee 438
91/2 O-Pee-Chee 476
91/2 Parkhurst 99
91/2 Pinnacle 272
90/1 Pro Set 171
91/2 Pro Set 421
90/1 Score 310
91/2 Score CAN 426
92/3 Score 370
93/4 To. Stadium 259
85/6 MONT
86/7 MONT
87/8 MONT
88/9 NJER / Caretta
89/0 NJER
89/0 NJER / Caretta
90/1 NJER
92/3 SANJ / Pacific Bell
99/0 Albany River Rats

MALEY, DAVID
02/3 Fleer Throwbacks 30

MALEYKO, JASON
99/0 Brampton Batallion 6
99/0 Brampton Batallion 31

MALGIN, ALBERT
99/0 Eishockey 302
91/2 O-Pee-Chee 54R

MALGUNAS, KEVIN
90/1 7th..Sketch WHL 5
91/2 7th...Sketch WHL 156
93/4 Hampton Roads
95/6 Houston Aeros
92/3 Richmond Renegades

MALGUNAS, STEWART
93/4 Donruss 470
93/4 Fleer Ultra 390
94/5 Leaf 170
93/4 Parkhurst 420
93/4 Premier 516
90/1 ProCards 487
91/2 ProCards 123
93/4 Score 612
93/4 To. Stadium 409
93/4 Upper Deck 425
01/2 UD DEL 82
93/4 PHIL / Sheet
93/4 PHIL / J.C. Penney
94/5 PHIL / Sheet
95/6 WINN
00/1 Hershey Bears
96/7 Portland Pirates
97/8 Portland Pirates
98/9 Portland Pirates
99/0 Utah Grizzlies

MALHOTRA, MANNY
02/3 SP Game-Used ✄ PC, ✄ FF
02/3 T. Total 112
02/3 Upper Deck ✄ BF
98/9 Be A Player 241, ✍ Aut. 241
99/0 BAP Mem. 240
00/1 BAP Mem. 160
01/2 BAP Mem. 473
97/8 Bell
98 Bowman 10, 148, SC2, ✍ A5
98 Bowman Chrome 10, 148
98/9 Bowman's Best 106, -BP6, ✍ A10A, ✍ A10B
01/2 Crown Royale ✄ TT 13
98/9 Dynagon Ice 124
01/2 Heads Up ✄ JQ 25
99/0 Millenium 163, ✍ Aut. 163
99/0 NHL Power Play
98/9 OPC Chrome 235
98/9 Omega 159
99/0 Pacific 274
98/9 Pa. Crown Roy. 90, -RC 6
99/0 Pa. Paramount 154
98/9 Pa. Revolution 95
00/1 PS Titanium ✄ GUG 116
94 Québec Pee Wee 1600
98/9 SP Authentic 101, ✍ SotT
99/0 SPx 101
98/9 SPx Prospects 40
99/0 Stadium 36, CA6
98/9 Topps 235
99/0 Topps 51
99/0 To. Chrome 51
98/9 To. Finest F2
98/9 T. Gold Label 93
98/9 UD Choice 255
97/8 Upper Deck 413
98/9 Upper Deck 420, GN6, P12, ✄ GJ11
99/0 Upper Deck 89
01/2 Upper Deck ✄ GN
97/8 UD Black Diam. 79
98/9 UD Black Diam. 57, M8, WF14
98/9 UD G. Reserve 420
99/0 UD G. Reserve 89
98/9 UD MVP 134, ✍ PS
99/0 UD MVP 136
00/1 UD MVP ME9, ✍ PS, ✍ ME
99/0 UD Retro 50
99/0 Victory 188
01/2 Victory 238
99/0 WGretzky 113
97/8 Zenith 96, Z76
98/9 NYRA
00/1 Hartford Wolf Pack
96/7 Guelph Storm
x96/7 Guelph Storm

MALIK, MAREK
02/3 Upper Deck 278
00/1 BAP Mem. 23
95/6 Donruss 150
96/7 Leaf 227
99/0 OFS 27
97/8 Pacific CC 322
97/8 Panini Sticker 22
00/1 Panini Sticker 27
95/6 Parkhurst 99
94/5 Parkie SE212
96/7 Pinnacle 225
96/7 Pi. Be A Player 110, ✍ Aut. 110
95/6 Score 298
99/0 Score JT5
95/6 Topps 57
94/5 Upper Deck 482, 506, 558
95/6 Upper Deck 58
96/7 UD CC 118
97/8 UD Elitserien 139
98/9 CARO / Highwoods
95/6 HART / Kids Club
96/7 HART / Kids Club
98/9 New Haven Beast 3

MALINOWSKI, MERLIN
81/2 O-Pee-Chee 76
82/3 O-Pee-Chee 128
83/4 O-Pee-Chee 142
81/2 OPC Sticker 228
82/3 OPC/Topps Sticker 229
82/3 Post [Colo.]
81/2 Topps 81 [West]
81/2 COLR

MALINSKY, JIRI
94/5 APS 26
96/7 APS 147
97/8 APS 247
99/0 DS 75
00/1 DS 88
96/7 DS Sticker 249
97/8 DS Sticker 135
98/9 OFS 147
99/0 OFS 321, 354
00/1 OFS 35
01/2 OFS 224

MALKIA, HEIKKI
80/1 Mallasjuoma 148

MALKOC, DEAN
97/8 Pi. Be A Player 23, ✍ Aut. 23
91/2 ProCards 409
90 7th..Sketch Mem.Cup 16
90/1 7th..Sketch WHL 69
95/6 To. Stadium 221
95/6 Upper Deck 330
99/0 Chicago Wolves
94/5 Indianapolis Ice
89/0 Kamloops Blazers

MALLARD, MO
00/1 Quad City Mallards

MALLEN, KEN
91 C55 Reprint 7
10/1 Imperial
11/2 Imperial 7

MALLETT, KURT
99/0 Charlotte Checkers
94/5 Richmond Renegades
95/6 Richmond Renegades

MALLETTE, CARL
99/0 UD Prospects 60
00/1 UD Prospects 84
00/1 Victoriaville Tigres 2

MALLETTE, JEAN
99/0 Québec Remparts 1
00/1 Québec Remparts 1

MALLETTE, TROY
90/1 Bowman 219
91/2 Bowman 65
93/4 Donruss 227
94/5 Donruss 329
94/5 Fleer Ultra 150
93/4 Leaf 228
94/5 Leaf 358
90/1 OPC/Topps 277
91/2 O-Pee-Chee 474
91/2 OPC Premier 39
97/8 Pa. Invincible R-14
90/1 Panini Sticker 100
91/2 Panini Sticker 295
93/4 Parkhurst 413
94/5 Parkhurst 160
96/7 Pi. BAP 72, ✍ Aut. 72
94/5 POG 354
93/4 Power Play 401
94/5 Premier 303
90/1 Pro Set 492
91/2 Pro Set 157
90/1 Score 288
91/2 Score 178
91/2 Score CAN 178
91/2 Score CAN 601
92/3 Topps 335
91/2 To. Stadium 134
92/3 To. Stadium 432
93/4 To. Stadium 444
94/5 To. Stadium 94
90/1 Upper Deck 11
91/2 Upper Deck 326
93/4 Upper Deck 418
94/5 Upper Deck 196
95/6 Upper Deck 461
91/2 EDMO / IGA
89/0 NYRA / Marine
93/4 OTTA
94/5 OTTA
95/6 OTTA
90/1 Rayside-Balfour
87/8 Soo Greyhounds 20

MALLETTE, VINCE
99/0 Ottawa 67's
00/1 Ottawa 67's 22
01/2 Ottawa 67's 22

MALLGRAVE, MATT
93/4 Cla. Prospects 109
94/5 Hampton Roads
93/4 St. John's Maple Leafs

MALLON, JASON
95/6 Richmond Renegades

MALLOY, MIKE
88/9 Brockville Braves

MALLY, MIROSLAV
84/5 Springfield Indians 20

MALMIO, JYRKI
65/6 Hellas 54

MALMIVAARA, OLLI
02/3 Cardset 68

MALMIVUORI, OLLI
65/6 Hellas 30

MALMSTRÖM, HENRIK
99/0 UD Elitserien 156
00/1 UD Elitserien 141

MALO, ANDRÉ
01/2 Sheffield Steelers
95/6 Sheffield Steelers
97/8 Sheffield Steelers

MALO, GAETAN
94/5 DEL 60
95/6 DEL 60
96/7 DEL 257

MALONE, CLIFF
51/2 Laval Dairy 91
52/3 St. Lawrence 15

MALONE, GREG
83/4 Funmate Puffy 7 [w/]
78/9 O-Pee-Chee 233
79/0 O-Pee-Chee 9
80/1 O-Pee-Chee 186
81/2 O-Pee-Chee 264
82/3 O-Pee-Chee 272
83/4 O-Pee-Chee 284
84/5 O-Pee-Chee 74
85/6 OPC/Topps 118
83/4 OPC/Topps Sticker 229
84/5 OPC Sticker 194
85/6 OPC Sticker 166-35
82/3 Post [Pitt.]
83/4 Souhaits Keychain [Penguins]
78/9 Topps 233
79/0 Topps 9
80/1 Topps 186
84/5 Topps 57
83/4 HART / Jr. Whalers
84/5 HART / Jr. Whalers
85/6 HART / Jr. Whalers
77/8 PITT / McDonald's
83/4 PITT / Heinz
86/7 Fredericton Express

MALONE, JOE
91 C55 Reprint 4
83 HHOF Postcard N9
83&87 HHOF 204
10/1 Imperial
11/2 Imperial 4
12/3 Imperial 48
95/6 Legends of Hockey 72
91/2 Pro Set 332
60/1 Topps 3
61/2 Topps - Stamp
99/0 UD C. Legends 41
23/4 William Paterson 13
92/3 MONT / OPC 55

MALONE, SCOTT
94/5 Classic 66, T45
94/5 Binghampton Rangers
95/6 Binghampton Rangers
97/8 Pensacola Ice Pilots

MALONEY, DAN
72/3 Eddie Sargent 70
74/5 Loblaws
72/3 O-Pee-Chee 264
73/4 O-Pee-Chee 32
74/5 O-Pee-Chee 172
75/6 O-Pee-Chee 177
76/7 O-Pee-Chee 101
77/8 O-Pee-Chee 172
78/9 O-Pee-Chee 21
79/0 O-Pee-Chee 271
80/1 O-Pee-Chee 118
81/2 O-Pee-Chee 320
82/3 O-Pee-Chee 326
81/2 OPC Sticker 102
82/3 OPC/Topps Sticker 72
80/1 Pepsi Bottle Cap
73/4 Topps 32
74/5 Topps 172
75/6 Topps 177
76/7 Topps 101
77/8 Topps 172
78/9 Topps 21
80/1 Topps 118
71/2 Toronto Sun Photo
78/9 TORO
79/0 TORO
81/2 TORO
82/3 TORO
83/4 TORO
84/5 TORO
86/7 WINN
88/9 WINN / Safety Tips

MALONEY, DAN
02/3 Fleer Throwbacks 35

MALONEY, DARREN
91/2 Air Canada SJHL 43
91/2 Air Canada SJHL B22
98/9 EBK ECHL All-Star
92/3 MPS SJHL 71
96/7 Peoria Rivermen
97/8 Peoria Rivermen
98/9 Peoria Rivermen
98/9 Peoria Rivermen
99/0 Peoria Rivermen
00/1 Peoria Rivermen
01/2 Nottingham Panthers
93/4 W. Michigan Broncos

MALONEY, DAVE
77/8 Coke
76/7 O-Pee-Chee 181
77/8 O-Pee-Chee 41, NS10
78/9 O-Pee-Chee 221
79/0 O-Pee-Chee 159
80/1 O-Pee-Chee 7
81/2 O-Pee-Chee 227
82/3 O-Pee-Chee 228
83/4 O-Pee-Chee 249
84/5 O-Pee-Chee 146
85/6 OPC/Topps 89
81/2 OPC Sticker 173
82/3 OPC/Topps Sticker 140
83/4 OPC/Topps Sticker 211
85/6 OPC Sticker 177-47
82/3 Post [NYRa.]
83/4 Souhaits Keychain [Rangers]
76/7 Topps 181
77/8 Topps 41
77/8 ToppsNS 10
78/9 Topps 221
79/0 Topps 159
80/1 Topps 7
81/2 Topps 100 [East]

MALONEY, DON
90/1 Bowman 117
83/4 Funmate Puffy 21 [w/]
79/0 O-Pee-Chee 42
79/0 O-Pee-Chee 162
80/1 O-Pee-Chee 231
81/2 O-Pee-Chee 228
82/3 O-Pee-Chee 229
83/4 O-Pee-Chee 250
84/5 O-Pee-Chee 147
85/6 OPC/Topps 94
86/7 OPC/Topps 81
87/8 OPC/Topps 49
90/1 OPC/Topps 31
81/2 OPC Sticker 170
82/3 OPC/Topps Sticker 137
83/4 OPC/Topps Sticker 212
84/5 OPC Sticker 95
84/5 OPC Sticker 96
87/8 OPC Sticker 29-169
87/8 Panini Sticker 117
88/9 Panini Sticker 308
89/0 Panini Sticker 231
90/1 Panini Sticker 84
82/3 Post [NYRa.]
90/1 Pro Set 187
90/1 Score 303
84/5 7-Eleven
83/4 Souhaits Keychain [Rangers]
79/0 Topps 42
79/0 Topps 162
80/1 Topps 231
81/2 Topps 101 [East]
84/5 Topps 109
90/1 Upper Deck 20
89/0 NYIS

MALONEY, PHIL
45-64 BeeHive-2 [Bost.]
45-64 BeeHive-2 [Toro.]
74/5 O-Pee-Chee 104
45-54 Quaker Oats
74/5 Topps 104

MALOV, ROMAN
00/1 Mir 90

MALTAIS, DOMINIC
90/1 7th..Sketch LHJMQ 85
91/2 7th...Sketch LHJMQ 108
00/1 Asheville Smoke
95/6 Hampton Roads
96/7 Hampton Roads
98/9 Hampton Roads
99/0 Hampton Roads

MALTAIS, FRÉDÉRIC
88/9 Richelieu Riverains

MALTAIS, STEVE
98/9 EBK IHL All-Star
95/6 Edge Ice 107
89/0 ProCards AHL 85
90/1 ProCards 205
91/2 ProCards 156
90/1 Score 417
92/3 TAMP / Sheraton Inn
89/0 WASH / Kodak
92/3 Atlanta Knights
98/9 Chicago Wolves
98/9 Chicago Wolves Champs
99/0 Chicago Wolves
00/1 Chicago Wolves
01/2 Chicago Wolves
02/3 Chicago Wolves

MALTBY, KIRK
02/3 BAP Mem. 150
02/3 Pacific Complete 277
02/3 T. Total 382
02/3 Ultimate Mem. ✄ SCDE, ✄ SCDGJ, ✄ SCDN
02/3 Upper Deck 312
92/3 Classic 20
92/3 Classic Four Sport 169
93/4 Cla. Prospects 21
93/4 Donruss 428
94/5 Donruss 53
94/5 Leaf 230
99/0 Millenium 93, ✍ Aut. 93
98/9 Pacific 199
00/1 Pacific 154
97/8 Pa. Dynagon BKS-33
97/8 Pa. Invincible R-71
94/5 Pinnacle 441
95/6 Pinnacle 126
95/6 Playoff 149
96/7 Playoff 373
94/5 POG / Western 16
93/4 Premier 290
94/5 Premier 72
93/4 Score 627
97/8 Score Detr. 15
90/1 7th..Sketch OHL 287
91/2 7th...Sketch OHL 278
95/6 Topps 133
93/4 To. Stadium 299
98/9 UD Choice RW11

93/4 Upper Deck 520
94/5 Upper Deck 472
95/6 Upper Deck 41
97/8 Upper Deck 61
94/5 UD BAP ✍ 38
95/6 UD CC 191
97/8 UD Coll. Choice 64
01/2 UD SCup Champs 64
01/2 Victory 129
93/4 EDMO / Sheet
93/4 Owen Sound Platers

MALTBY, SHAWN
97/8 Toledo Storm 24
02/3 Manchester Storm

MALTSEV, ALEXANDER
91/2 Future Trends C72 20
92/3 Future Trends C76 161
92/3 Future Trends C76 190
92/3 Future Trends C76 200
72 Hellas MM-Jenkki 70
74 Hellas MM-Jenkki 49
70/1 Kuvajulkaisut 7
72 Panda MM-Toronto
79 Panini Sticker 155
72 Semic Sticker 10
74 Semic Sticker 36
91 Semic Sticker 245
69/0 Soviet Stars
70/1 Soviet Stars
71/2 Soviet Stars
73/4 Soviet Stars 20
74/5 Soviet Stars 14
79/0 Soviet Stars 16
83/4 Soviet Stars
96 Wien HL6
71/2 Williams Finnish 8
72/3 Williams Finnish 28
73/4 Williams Finnish 9

MALY, MIROSLAV
94/5 DEL 331
95/6 DEL 293
96/7 DEL 321

MALYKHIN, IGOR
92/3 Classic Prospects 86
90/1 O-Pee-Chee 15R
91/2 O-Pee-Chee 20R
93/4 Fort Wayne Komets 13
94/5 Fort Wayne Komets 2
99/0 Fort Wayne Komets

MALYSIAK, ANDREI
79 Panini Sticker 128

MAMANE, SHAWN
00/1 Worcester IceCats

MANCARI, MARK
01/2 Ottawa 67's 18

MANCHAKOWSKI, CHRIS
00/1 Saskatoon Blades

MANCINI, RICK
93/4 Owen Sound Platers

MANCUSO, TONY
95/6 Tallahassee Tiger Sharks

MANDERVILLE, KENT
00/1 BAP Mem. 210
92 C.O.A. Winter Olympics 197
91/2 Canada Nationals
95/6 Edge Ice 83
94/5 Leaf 526
99/0 Millenium 52, ✍ Aut. 52
92/3 O-Pee-Chee 14
92/3 OPC Premier 23
99/0 Pacific 77
00/1 Pacific 302
97/8 Pacific CC 289
99/0 Panini Sticker 49
91/2 Parkhurst 392
92/3 Parkhurst 184
93/4 Parkhurst 204
94/5 Parkhurst 235
94/5 Pinnacle 454
97/8 Pi. Be A Player 165, ✍ Aut. 165
94/5 POG 235
94/5 Premier 474
92/3 Score 458
92/3 Score COH 10
92/3 Topps 148
92/3 To. Stadium 339
93/4 To. Stadium 417
94/5 To. Stadium 253
90/1 Upper Deck 465
92/3 Upper Deck 32
93/4 Upper Deck 420
94/5 Upper Deck 131
94/5 UD BAP ✍ 156
97/8 UD Coll. Choice 118
99/0 UD Retro 13
01/2 UD Vintage 187
97/8 CARO / Sprint
98/9 CARO / Highwoods
96/7 HART / Kids Club
01/2 PHIL
92/3 TORO / Kodak
93/4 TORO / Abalene
93/4 TORO / Black's 10
94/5 TORO / Coca-Cola
96/7 Springfield Falcons
92/3 St. John's Maple Leafs
95/6 St. John's Maple Leafs

MANDEVILLE, LOUIS
00/1 Halifax Moosehead
00/1 Rouyn-Noranda 17

MANDEVILLE, MARTIN
00/1 Baie-Comeau 21
01/2 Baie-Comeau 19
02/3 Baie-Comeau

MANDICH, DAN
82/3 MINS
83/4 MINS
84/5 MINS
85/6 MINS

MANDO, DEAN
95/6 Slapshot 420
99/0 Charlotte Checkers
99/0 Mississippi S'Wolves

MANELUK, GEORGE
88/9 ProCards / Springfield
89/0 ProCards AHL 241
90/1 ProCards 500
91/2 ProCards 370
95/6 Louisiana Ice Gators
95/6 Louisiana Ice Gators-2

MANELUK, MIKE
98/9 Bowman's Best 112
98/9 Dynagon Ice 139, -IR 5
95/6 Edge Ice 13
98/9 Omega 53
91/2 7th...Sketch WHL 199
98/9 SP Authentic 93
98/9 Upper Deck 332
98/9 UD G. Reserve 332
98/9 UD MVP 49
01/2 Victory 107
92/3 Brandon Wheat Kings

MANERY, KRIS
78/9 O-Pee-Chee 107
79/0 O-Pee-Chee 151
81/2 O-Pee-Chee 371
80/1 Pepsi Bottle Cap
78/9 Topps 107
79/0 Topps 151
78/9 MINS / Cloverleaf 8
79/0 MINS
80/1 WINN

MANERY, RANDY
72/3 Eddie Sargent 10
74/5 Loblaws
72/3 O-Pee-Chee 260
73/4 O-Pee-Chee 131
74/5 O-Pee-Chee 74
75/6 O-Pee-Chee 44
76/7 O-Pee-Chee 24
77/8 O-Pee-Chee 389
78/9 O-Pee-Chee 266
79/0 O-Pee-Chee 317
80/1 O-Pee-Chee 342
73/4 Topps 131
74/5 Topps 86
75/6 Topps 44
76/7 Topps 24
72/3 ATLF
74/5 ATLF

MANGANARO, SAL
96/7 Dayton Bombers
99/0 Greensboro Generals

MANGOLD, PAT
84/5 Kamloops Blazers

MANIAGO, CESARE
45-64 BeeHive-2 [Toro.]
45-64 BeeHive-2 [Mont.]
64-67 BeeHive-3 [NYRa.]
70/1 Colgate 63
70/1 Eddie Sargent 81
71/2 Eddie Sargent 92
72/3 Eddie Sargent 110
70/1 Esso Power Player
62/3 Cowan Tile
72/3 Post 24
74/5 Lipton Soup 27
74/5 Loblaws
68/9 O-Pee-Chee 45
69/0 O-Pee-Chee 121
69/0 O-Pee-Chee 4in1
70/1 O-Pee-Chee 173
71/2 O-Pee-Chee 117
72/3 O-Pee-Chee 138
73/4 O-Pee-Chee 127
74/5 O-Pee-Chee 26
75/6 O-Pee-Chee 261
76/7 O-Pee-Chee 240
77/8 O-Pee-Chee 23
63/4 Parkhurst 40
63/4 Parkhurst 99
95/6 Parkie 66-67 97
68/9 Shirriff / Minn. 5
68/9 Topps 45
69/0 Topps 121
71/2 Topps 5
71/2 Topps 117
72/3 Topps 104
73/4 Topps 146
74/5 Topps 26
75/6 Topps 261
76/7 Topps 240
77/8 Topps 23
72 Toronto Sun Photo
61/2 York 41
70/1 MINS / Colour
73/4 MINS
76/7 VANC / Royal Bank
77/8 VANC / Royal Bank

MANLEY, BILLY
95/6 Halifax Moosehead
96/7 Halifax Moosehead
96/7 Halifax Moosehead
97/8 Halifax Moosehead
97/8 Halifax Moosehead
98/9 Halifax Moosehead

MANLOW, ERIC
93/4 Cla. 4 Sport 210
95/6 Edge Ice 137
01/2 Pacific 34
91/2 7th...Sketch OHL 87
93/4 Slapshot / Kitchener 24
94/5 Slapshot / Detroit Jr. 11
94/5 Slapshot / Kitchener 26
94/5 Slapshot Memorial 85
00/1 UD Ice 110
95/6 Indianapolis Ice
97/8 Indianapolis Ice 15
00/1 Providence Bruins
01/2 Providence Bruins

MANN, ?
95/6 DEL 430

MANN, CAMERON
99/0 BAP Mem. 198
97 Bowman 4
98/9 Bowman's Best 127
98/9 McDonald's McD26
99/0 Millenium 26, ✍ Aut. 26
98/9 Pacific 85
99/0 Pacific 26
95/6 SR Tetrad Autobilia 47
93/4 Slapshot / Peterborough 16
95/6 Slapshot 313, P
98/9 SPx Finite 126
98/9 UD Choice 17
98/9 UD3 19, 79, 139
98/9 Upper Deck 2
97/8 UD Black Diam. 138
97/8 UD Coll. Choice 306
98/9 UD G. Reserve 2
96/7 UD Ice 130
98/9 UD MVP 11
01/2 Victory 27
97/8 Providence Bruins
98/9 Providence Bruins
99/0 Providence Bruins
00/1 Providence Bruins
01/2 Utah Grizzlies

MANN, DALLAS
98/9 BC Icemen 15
98/9 BC Icemen

MANN, JIMMY
80/1 O-Pee-Chee 164
80/1 O-Pee-Chee 353
81/2 O-Pee-Chee 372
80/1 Pepsi Bottle Cap
88/9 ProCards / Indianapolis
80/1 Topps 164
83/4 QUEB
84/5 QUEB
85/6 QUEB / Provigo
86/7 QUEB / McDonald's
79/0 WINN
80/1 WINN
81/2 WINN
82/3 WINN
83/4 WINN

MANN, JIMMY
02/3 Fleer Throwbacks 36

MANN, NORMIE
34-43 BeeHive-1 [Toro.]
34-43 BeeHive-1 [Toro.]

MANN, PAVEL
94/5 DEL 344
95/6 DEL 318

MANN, STEFAN
94/5 DEL 203
95/6 DEL 206
96/7 DEL 349
99/0 Eishockey 26

MANN, TROY
96/7 Mississippi S'Wolves
99/0 Mississippi S'Wolves

MANNBERG, NIKLAS
89/0 Semic Elitserien 209

MANNESS, ALAN
96/7 Kamloops Blazers
97/8 Kamloops Blazers
98/9 Kamloops Blazers

MÄNNIKKÖ, ERKKI
66/7 Champion 160

MÄNNIKKÖ, MIIKKA
99/0 Cardset 322

MANNINEN, K
90/1 Michigan Tech Huskies

MANNINEN, MIKA
95 Leaf Latkaliiga 11
93/4 Sisu 110
94/5 Sisu 108, J-7, N-1
95/6 Sisu 29

MANNING, BLAIR
98/9 Louisiana Ice Gators
99/0 Topeka Scarecrows

MANNING, PAUL
02/3 BAP Mem. 341
02/3 Parkhurst Retro 243
02/3 Ultimate Mem. 83
02/3 UD Artistic 135
02/3 UD Honor 129
01/2 Syracuse Crunch
02/3 Syracuse Crunch

MANNISTO, KEIJO
66/7 Champion 161
70/1 Kuvajulkaisut 217
78/9 SM-Liiga 191
71/2 Williams Finnish 139
73/4 Williams Finnish 164

MANNO, BOB
98/9 DEL 154
99/0 Eishockey 169
78/9 O-Pee-Chee 349
79/0 O-Pee-Chee 270
81/2 O-Pee-Chee 396
82/3 O-Pee-Chee 325
83/4 O-Pee-Chee 132
84/5 O-Pee-Chee 59
85/6 OPC/Topps 134
82/3 OPC/Topps Sticker 71
82/3 Post [Toro.]
84/5 DETR / Little Caesars
81/2 TORO
77/8 VANC / Royal Bank
78/9 VANC / Royal Bank
79/0 VANC / Royal Bank
80/1 VANC / Silverwood

MANSFIELD, GARY
95/6 Hampton Roads
96/7 Hampton Roads
97/8 Hampton Roads

MANSI, MAURIZIO
96/7 DEL 121
95 Panini Worlds 95
94 Semic 304
93 Semic Sticker 226
96 Wien 179

MANSI, MOE
88/9 Flint Spirits
02/3 London Knights

MANSIKKA, REIJO
78/9 SM-Liiga 91

MANSOFF, JASON
92/3 BCJHL 78
00/1 Kudos 35
97/8 Hampton Roads
99/0 Indianapolis Ice
98/9 Rochester Americans
93/4 Maine Black Bears

MANSON, DAVE
98/9 Be A Player 67, ✍ Aut. 67
00/1 BAP Mem. 436
91/2 Bowman 389
92/3 Bowman 339
93/4 Donruss 109
93/4 Donruss 509
94/5 Donruss 242
95/6 Donruss 317
93/4 EA Sports 43
94/5 Flair 207
94/5 Fleer 243
92/3 Fleer Ultra 62
93/4 Fleer Ultra 93
94/5 Fleer Ultra 243
95/6 Fleer Ultra 181
96/7 Fl. Ultra 133
93/4 Leaf 159
94/5 Leaf 239
95/6 Leaf 158
93/4 McDonald's McD-09
96/7 Metal Univ. 119
90/1 O-Pee-Chee 397
91/2 O-Pee-Chee 409
92/3 O-Pee-Chee 56
89/0 OPC/Topps 150
98/9 OPC Chrome 165
91/2 OPC Premier 137
89/0 opcSticker 13-153
98/9 Pacific 254
99/0 Pacific 91
00/1 Pacific 135
01/2 Pacific 369
97/8 Pa. Dynagon BKS-49
98/9 Pa. Paramount 115
89/0 Panini Sticker 47
90/1 Panini Sticker 199
91/2 Panini Sticker 15
92/3 Panini Sticker 108
93/4 Panini Sticker 242
96/7 Panini Sticker 197
91/2 Parkhurst 49
92/3 Parkhurst 47
92/3 Parkhurst CP15
93/4 Parkhurst 335
94/5 Parkhurst 262, V9
95/6 Parkhurst 233
91/2 Pinnacle 62
92/3 Pinnacle 334
93/4 Pinnacle 363
94/5 Pinnacle 51
95/6 Pinnacle 103
96/7 Pi. Be A Player 57, ✍ Aut. 57
95/6 Playoff 218
96/7 Playoff 401
94/5 POG 257
95/6 POG 295
93/4 Power Play 83
93/4 Premier 71
94/5 Premier 121
90/1 Pro Set 54
91/2 Pro Set 41
91/2 Pro Set 389
92/3 Pro Set 55
91/2 Pro Set Platinum 172
90/1 Score 193
91/2 Score 152
91/2 Score 74T
91/2 Score CAN 152
91/2 Score CAN 624
92/3 Score 214
93/4 Score 127
93/4 Score PIAS 38
95/6 Score 59
97/8 Score Mont. 17
92/3 Seasons 56
94/5 Select 13
95/6 SBx Emotion 194
95/6 SBx Impact 182
94/5 SP 134
92/3 Topps 389
95/6 Topps 120
98/9 Topps 165
91/2 To. Stadium 308
92/3 To. Stadium 436
93/4 To. Stadium 183
94/5 To. Stadium - AS
94/5 To. Stadium 61
98/9 UD Choice 108
90/1 Upper Deck 85
91/2 Upper Deck 280
91/2 Upper Deck 548
92/3 Upper Deck 84
93/4 Upper Deck 358, SP-50
94/5 Upper Deck 63, SP-180
95/6 Upper Deck 51
96/7 Upper Deck 317
98/9 Upper Deck 113
93/4 Upper Deck Be A Player 30
94/5 UD BAP R41, ✍ 95
95/6 UD CC 230
97/8 UD Coll. Choice 136
98/9 UD G. Reserve 113
92/3 UD Locker 30
99/0 Aurora 132
86/7 CHIC / Coke
87/8 CHIC / Coke
88/9 CHIC / Coke
89/0 CHIC / Coke
90/1 CHIC / Coke
01/2 DALL / Southwest
93/4 EDMO / Sheet
91/2 EDMO / IGA
92/3 EDMO
92/3 EDMO / IGA 014
96/7 MONT / Export
97/8 MONT
96/7 PHOE / Coca-Cola
95/6 WINN
95/6 WINN Readers
84/5 Prince Albert Raiders

MANSON, LANE
01/2 Moose Jaw Warriors 19
02/3 Moose Jaw Warriors

MANSSON, JOHAN
91/2 Semic Elitserien 178
92/3 Semic Elitserien 201

MANTERE, EERO
80/1 Mallasjuoma 74
78/9 SM-Liiga 114

MANTHA, BILLY
24/5 William Paterson 50

MANTHA, CARL
90/1 7th...Sketch LHJMQ 48
90 7th..Sketch Mem.Cup 51

MANTHA, GEORGES
34-43 BeeHive-1 [Mont.]
35-40 Canada Starch
33/4 Canadian Gum
33-35 Diamond Match Silv.
36-39 Diamond Match TT1
36-39 Diamond Match TT2
36-39 Diamond Match TT3
28/9 La Presse
33/4 O-Pee-Chee 22
37/8 O-Pee-Chee 153
39/0 O-Pee-Chee 26
43-47 Parade Sportive
38/9 Quaker Oats
34/5 Sweet Caporal
33/4 WWGum 26
37/8 World Wide Gum 45

MANTHA, MAURICE*
52/3 Anonymous 169

MANTHA, MOE
91/2 Bowman 205
60/1 Cleveland Barons
81/2 O-Pee-Chee 373
85/6 OPC/Topps 125
86/7 OPC/Topps 45
87/8 OPC/Topps 51
88/9 OPC/Topps 30
90/1 OPC/Topps 354
91/2 O-Pee-Chee 477
85/6 OPC Sticker 98-229
86/7 OPC Sticker 231-102
87/8 OPC Sticker 171-30
88/9 OPC Sticker 200-71
87/8 Panini Sticker 142
88/9 Panini Sticker 200
90/1 Panini/WPG 16
80/1 Pepsi Bottle Cap
90/1 Pro Set 330
91/2 Score CAN 506
91/2 To. Stadium 287
83/4 Vachon 132-12
88/9 EDMO / Action 34
88/9 MINS / ADA
86/7 PITT / Kodak
80/1 WINN
83/4 WINN
89/0 WINN / Safeway
90/1 WINN / IGA
91/2 WINN / IGA
98/9 Cincinnati M'Ducks 6
99/0 Cincinnati M'Ducks

MANTHA, SYLVIO
35/6 Amalgamated Press
25-27 Anonymous 3
25-27 Anonymous 4
34-43 BeeHive-1 [Mont.]
24/5 Champ's Cigarettes
33-35 Diamond Match Silv.
36-39 Diamond Match TT1
36-39 Diamond Match TT2
36-39 Diamond Match TT3
34/5 Hamilton Gum 18
83 HHOF Postcard F9
83&87 HHOF 84
27/8 La Patrie
27/8 La Presse
35/6 O-Pee-Chee 82
55/6 Parkhurst 60
34/5 Sweet Caporal
23/4 William Paterson 12
33/4 WWGum 42

MANTIONE, JOE
83/4 Kitchener Rangers

MANTUA, MIKE
99/0 Des Moines Buc's

MÄNTYLÄ, TUUKKA
02/3 Cardset 227, -DD 6
99/0 Cardset 318
00/1 Cardset 85, NG-2

MAPLETOFT, JUSTIN
02/3 Calder 82
02/3 Crown Royale -RR 15
02/3 Pacific Complete 589
02/3 Vanguard - PP 16
99 Bowman 33, ✍ BA8
99/0 Topps 265
99/0 To. Chrome 265
00/1 UD Prospects 60, CD6
00/1 Red Deer Rebels

MARA, PAUL
02/3 Pacific Complete 251
02/3 Stadium ✂ YSS19
02/3 Upper Deck 134
99/0 Aurora 132
99/0 BAP Mem. 65
00/1 BAP Mem. 71
99 Bowman 157
01/2 Bowman 158, ✂ FFJ, ✂ FFS, ✂ FFDS, ✂ FFR, ✍ YSA
97 Bowman 16, 137, BB3, ✍ Aut.
98/9 Collection Souvenir 17
99/0 HoloGrFX 53
99/0 Millenium 217, ✍ Aut. 217
99/0 NHL Power Play [x3]
99/0 Pacific 400
93 Québec Pee Wee 597
99/0 SP Authentic ✍ SotT
99/0 SPx 138
00/1 Stadium 176
99/0 Topps 133
00/1 Topps 187
99/0 To. Chrome 133
98/9 UD Choice 297
00/1 UD Heroes 108
99/0 Upper Deck 118, 150,CT16, N10
00/1 Upper Deck 158
01/2 Upper Deck 134
99/0 UD C. Legends 76
99/0 UD G. Reserve 118, 150
96/7 UD Ice 149
00/1 UD Legends 119
99/0 UD MVP 191, 21st-7
00/1 UD MVP 162
01/2 UD MVP 144
99/0 UD Ovation 54
99/0 UD Retro 71
00/1 UD Vintage 326
99/0 Victory 271
00/1 Victory 210
x99/0 W. Gretzky ✍ SG
96/7 Sudbury Wolves

MARACH, NICK
01/2 Vancouver Giants

MARACLE, IAN
02/3 Mississauga IceDogs

MARACLE, NORM
02/3 Between the Pipes 44
00/1 BAP Mem. 164
01/2 BT Pipes 64
99/0 Dynagon Ice 17
98/9 Omega 89
98/9 Pacific 200
01/2 Pacific 20
99/0 Pa. Paramount 13
98/9 Pa. Revolution 49
91/2 7th...Sketch WHL 117
98/9 SPx Finite 144
98/9 Upper Deck 3
99/0 Upper Deck 180
98/9 UD G. Reserve 3
99/0 UD G. Reserve 180
98/9 UD MVP 75
99/0 UD MVP Cup 10
99/0 Victory 16
95/6 Adirondack Red Wings
00/1 Chicago Wolves
02/3 Chicago Wolves
91/2 Saskatoon Blades
93/4 Saskatoon Blades

MARAK, ZBYNEK
94/5 APS 238
95/6 APS 19, 382, 421
96/7 APS 40
97/8 APS 112
97/8 DS 24
98/9 DS 84
99/0 DS 138
00/1 DS 105
96/7 DS Sticker 107
97/8 DS Sticker 55
98/9 OFS 344
99/0 OFS 440
00/1 OFS 201
01/2 OFS -UHI 24

MARAKHOVSKI, ROMAN
00/1 Louisiana Ice Gators

MARANDIUK, BILL
93/4 Slapshot / Kingston 13

MARBLE, EVAN
98/9 DEL 79
90/1 7th...Sketch WHL 59
91/2 7th...Sketch WHL 321

MARCEL, BERNARD
83&87 HHOF 246

MARCELLUS, TODD
97/8 New Mexico Scorpions

MARCETTA, MILAN
68/9 Shirriff / Minn. 6

MARCH, HAROLD (MUSH)
35/6 Amalgamated Press
34-43 BeeHive-1 [Chic.]
35-40 Canada Starch
33-35 Diamond Match Silv.
36-39 Diamond Match TT1
36-39 Diamond Match TT2
36-39 Diamond Match TT3
36-39 Diamond Match BH TT
36-39 Diamond Match Chic.
36-39 Diamond Match BH BT
39/0 O-Pee-Chee 45
34/5 Sweet Caporal
37/8 World Wide Gum 13

MARCHAND, HUGO
99/0 Louisiana Ice Gators

MARCHANT, EDDY
91/2 Air Canada SJHL C47
93/4 Red Deer Rebels

MARCHANT, TERRY
99/0 Houston Aeros

MARCHANT, TODD
02/3 Pacific 145
02/3 Pacific Complete 162
02/3 T. Total 115
02/3 Upper Deck 315, ✂ S, ✂ SD
00/1 UD MVP 75
98/9 Be A Player 55, ✍ Aut. 55
00/1 BAP Mem. 325
94/5 Classic 88
94/5 Classic 4 Sport 140
94/5 Cla. Images 8, CE8, PR5
93/4 Cla. Images 4 Sport 17
94/5 Cla. Images 4 Sport 115
93/4 Cla. Prospects IA8
93/4 Cla. Prospects LP8
95/6 Donruss 200, RT-8
96/7 Donruss 53
97/8 Donruss 184
95/6 Edge Ice 34, C-6, PR-1
94/5 Fleer 71
95/6 Fleer Metal 54
93/4 Fleer Ultra 491
95/6 Fleer Ultra 55, AR-8
94/5 Leaf 505
95/6 Leaf 61, SR-8
96/7 Leaf 153
97/8 Limited 144
01/2 O-Pee-Chee 169
98/9 OPC Chrome 64
98/9 Pacific 213
99/0 Pacific 159
00/1 Pacific 169, ✍ Aut. 169
01/2 Pacific 160
97/8 Pacific CC 320
98/9 Pa. Paramount 88
00/1 Pa. Paramount 96
95/6 Panini Sticker 257
99/0 Panini Sticker 248
95/6 Parkhurst 347
00/1 Parkhurst P-173
01/2 Parkhurst 186
94/5 Parkie SE61
95/6 Pinnacle 76
96/7 Pinnacle 117
97/8 Pinnacle 127
97/8 Pi. Be A Player 72, ✍ Aut. 72
95/6 POG 107
93/4 Power Play 511
93/4 Premier - USA Hockey 14
95/6 Pro Magnet 85
00/1 Revolution 57
94/5 Score 226
95/6 Score 34
96/7 Score 217
97/8 Score 243
00/1 Signature 208, ✍ Aut. 76
95/6 SBx Emotion 64
95/6 SBx Impact 62, 234, F-10
94/5 SP P-4
00/1 Stadium 93
95/6 Topps 29, 3NG
98/9 Topps 64
99/0 Topps 43
00/1 Topps 73
01/2 Topps 169
99/0 To. Chrome 43
00/1 To. Chrome 58
94/5 Topps Finest BBR-19
93/4 To. Stadium - Team U.S.A. 15
95/6 To. Stadium 102
94/5 TSC Members Only 49
92/3 Upper Deck 606
94/5 Upper Deck 159, 323
95/6 Upper Deck 71, SE-121
96/7 Upper Deck 59
97/8 Upper Deck 64
98/9 Upper Deck 275
00/1 Upper Deck 298
01/2 Upper Deck 69
95/6 UD BAP 190, ✍ S190
95/6 UD CC 210
96/7 UD CC 97
98/9 UD G. Reserve 275
01/2 UD MVP 77
00/1 UD Vintage 139
99/0 Victory 117
01/2 Victory 136
96/7 EDMO
97/8 EDMO
94/5 Cape Breton Oilers
92/3 Clarkson G'Knights

MARCHESSAULT, ALAIN
87/8 Brockville Braves

MARCHESSAULT, RICHARD
87/8 Brockville Braves

MARCHETTI, GIOVANNI
95 Panini Worlds 78
94 Semic 298
92 Semic Sticker 250

MARCHINKO, BRIAN
72/3 Eddie Sargent 136
72/3 O-Pee-Chee 179

MARCHMENT, BRYAN
02/3 Pacific 335
02/3 Pacific Complete 280
02/3 Signature GS-16
02/3 UD Rookie 24
00/1 BAP Mem. 378
91/2 Bowman 208
92/3 Bowman 418
93/4 Donruss 73
92/3 Fleer Ultra 278
93/4 Fleer Ultra 335
95/6 Fleer Ultra 238
93/4 Leaf 224
94/5 Leaf 127
96/7 O-Pee-Chee 116
91/2 OPC Premier 99
97/8 Omega 211
98/9 Omega 210
98/9 Pacific 385
99/0 Pacific 374
01/2 Pacific 338, 421
97/8 Pa. Invincible R-79
96/7 Panini Sticker 256
92/3 Parkhurst 267
93/4 Pinnacle 283
94/5 Pinnacle 407
93/4 Power Play 352
89/0 ProCards AHL 44
90/1 ProCards 250
91/2 Score 314
91/2 Score 56T
91/2 Score CAN 344
91/2 Score CAN 606
92/3 Score 288
93/4 Score 386
93/4 Score 577
94/5 Score 107
95/6 Score 270
92/3 Topps 501
99/0 Topps 54
99/0 To. Chrome 54
91/2 To. Stadium 384
92/3 To. Stadium 148
93/4 To. Stadium 161
94/5 To. Stadium 84
95/6 Upper Deck 371
97/8 Upper Deck 69, 392
98/9 Upper Deck 356
95/6 UD BAP 39, ✍ S39
97/8 UD Black Diam. 66
95/6 UD CC 67
96/7 UD CC 99
98/9 UD G. Reserve 356
91/2 CHIC / Coke
96/7 EDMO
97/8 EDMO
93/4 HART / Coke
90/1 WINN / IGA
90/1 Moncton Hawks

MARCINCZAK, MAREK
79 Panini Sticker 125

MARCINKO, MIROSLAV
94 Semic 196
96 Wien 226

MARCINYSHYN, DAVE
98/9 DEL 213
90/1 OPC Premier 67
90/1 Pro Set 623
88/9 ProCards / Utica
89/0 ProCards AHL 215
91/2 ProCards 543
92/3 Binghampton Rangers
95/6 Cincinnati Cyclones
96/7 Cincinnati Cyclones
93/4 Milwaukee Admirals
94/5 Milwaukee Admirals
85/6 Kamloops Blazers
86/7 Kamloops Blazers

MARCOLINI, STEVE
84/5 Kitchener Rangers
85/6 Kitchener Rangers
86/7 London Knights

MARCON, LOU
59/0 Topps 49

MARCOTTE, DON
72/3 Eddie Sargent 27
70/1 Esso Power Player
74/5 Loblaws
70/1 O-Pee-Chee 138
71/2 O-Pee-Chee 176
72/3 O-Pee-Chee 219
73/4 O-Pee-Chee 221
74/5 O-Pee-Chee 269
76/7 O-Pee-Chee 234
77/8 O-Pee-Chee 165
78/9 O-Pee-Chee 236
79/0 O-Pee-Chee 99
80/1 O-Pee-Chee 336
81/2 O-Pee-Chee 14
82/3 O-Pee-Chee 14
82/3 OPC/Topps Sticker 91
71/2 Pro Star Promotions
73/4 Topps 89
74/5 Topps 221
75/6 Topps 269
76/7 Topps 234
77/8 Topps 165
78/9 Topps 236
79/0 Topps 99
71/2 Toronto Sun Photo
70/1 BOST
71/2 BOST
91/2 BOST / SA Legends
98/9 BOST / Alumni 21

MARCOTTE, GASTON
52/3 Anonymous 14

MARCOTTE, JACQUES
52/3 Anonymous 82
53/4 La Patrie

MARCOTTE, RÉAL
51/2 Lac St-Jean 13

MARCOUX, CHRISTIAN
93/4 Slapshot / Drummondville 16

MARCOUX, ERIC
90/1 7th...Sketch LHJMQ 201
91/2 7th...Sketch LHJMQ 289

MARCOUX, HENRY
96/7 DEL 143

MARCOUX, MICHEL
99/0 Rouyn-Noranda

MAREČEK, PAVEL
94/5 APS 123
95/6 APS 95
97/8 APS 109
97/8 DS Sticker 54

MAREK, JAN
99/0 OFS 408
00/1 OFS 233
01/2 OFS 65

MAREK, PAVEL
99/0 OFS 86

MAREK, PETER
94/5 Wheeling Thund'birds

MARENGÈRE, STEVE
83/4 Nova Scotia Voyageurs

MARES, JAROSLAV
99/0 Score 53

MARHA, JOSEF
94/5 APS 171
95/6 Classic ✍ Aut.
98/9 Pacific 59
99/0 Pacific 92
98/9 Pa. Paramount 4
98/9 Panini Sticker 173
93/4 Parkhurst 516
97/8 Score Colo. 10
00/1 Signature 69, ✍ Aut. 194
94/5 SP 157
98/9 SPx Finite 3, 124
98/9 UD Choice 3
98/9 UD3 3, 63, 123
97/8 Upper Deck 256
98/9 Upper Deck 33, 216
99/0 Upper Deck 207
98/9 UD G. Reserve 33, 216
99/0 UD G. Reserve 207
00/1 UD Vintage 83

MARIC, DANIEL
79 Panini Sticker 379

MARIC, ROB
94/5 Slapshot / Kitchener 25
95/6 Slapshot 136

MARIETTI, BRETT
90/1 7th...Sketch OHL 134
91/2 7th...Sketch OHL 371

MÄRIJÄRVI, JUHA-MATTI
93/4 Jyvas Hyva 81
93/4 Sisu 117

MARIK, DUSAN
97/8 DS Sticker 147

MARIK, MICHAL
95/6 APS 245
96/7 APS 289
97/8 APS 172
99/0 DS 30
00/1 DS 73
97/8 DS Sticker 148
98/9 OFS 194
99/0 OFS 11
00/1 OFS 6, Star-15
01/2 OFS 125, -CL 4, -G9

MARIN, ALBERTO
79 Panini Sticker 373

MARINEK, RADEK
00/1 DS WCH3

MARINI, HECTOR
83/4 Funmate Puffy 8 [w/]
83/4 O-Pee-Chee 235
83/4 OPC/Topps Sticker 221
83/4 NJER

MARINIER, ROCH
84/5 Chicoutimi Saguenéens

MARINUCCI, CHRIS
94/5 Classic 100, AA3, T41
94/5 Cla. Images 95, CE19, PR7, ✍ Aut.
95/6 Donruss 6
95/6 Edge Ice 193
95/6 Leaf 92
95/6 Parkhurst 401
95/6 Pinnacle 206
95/6 Score 309
95/6 Topps 62
01/2 UD DEL 38
98/9 Chicago Wolves
98/9 Chicago Wolves Champs
99/0 Chicago Wolves
93/4 Minnesota-Duluth

MARIO, FRANK
52/3 Laval Dairy Update 14
52/3 St. Lawrence 51

MARIUCCI, JOHN
34-43 BeeHive-1 [Chic.]
83&87 HHOF 254

MARJAMÄKI, PEKKA
66/7 Champion 155
65/6 Hellas 146
72 Hellas MM-Jenkki 5
74 Hellas MM-Jenkki 11
70/1 Kuvajulkaisut 88
71/2 Kuvajulkaisut 212
72 Panda MM-Toronto
79 Panini Sticker 167
72 Semic Sticker 75
74 Semic Sticker 78
96/7 Sisu 195
78/9 SM-Liiga 178
71/2 Williams Finnish 68
71/2 Williams Finnish 135
72/3 Williams Finnish 65
72/3 Williams Finnish 198
73/4 Williams Finnish 159

MARJIN, ALEXEI
91 Semic Sticker 78

MARK, GORD
88/9 OPC Sticker 162
94/5 Parkhurst 80
93/4 EDMO / Sheet
84/5 Kamloops Blazers

MARK, LEN
84/5 Kamloops Blazers
85/6 Kamloops Blazers
86/7 Kamloops Blazers

MARKARIAN, RALPH
52/3 Anonymous 178

MARKER, GUS
34-43 BeeHive-1 [Maroons]
34-43 BeeHive-1 [Toro.]
35-40 Canada Starch
35/6 O-Pee-Chee 78
37/8 O-Pee-Chee 173
39/0 O-Pee-Chee 16
40/1 O-Pee-Chee 113
34/5 Sweet Caporal

MARKKANEN, ...
97/8 Hockey-Box

MARKKANEN, JUSSI
02/3 Between the Pipes 96, ✂ GUJ47, ✂ T18
02/3 Cardset 69, -SGSP 1
02/3 First Edition 296
02/3 Pacific 146
02/3 UD Mask 34, 35
01/2 BT Pipes 87
98/9 Cardset 184, -MM 9, -OD 9
99/0 Cardset 106
00/1 Cardset 209, Mask. 7
01/2 Crown Royale 160
94/5 Parkie SE215
01/2 PS Titanium 159
01/2 PS Titanium Draft 130
95/6 Sisu 311
01/2 To. Chrome 144
94/5 Topps Finest 124
01/2 Vanguard 112

MARKKANEN, MIKKO
95/6 Sisu 334, DD-12
95/6 UD CC 326

MARKLUND, LARS
89/0 Semic Elitserien 199

MARKOV, ANDREI
02/3 Pacific 199
02/3 Pacific Complete 249
02/3 T. Total 266
02/3 Upper Deck 91
02/3 UD Vintage 137
00/1 BAP Mem. 432
01/2 BAP Mem. 52
00/1 Crown Royale 129, 21CR-13
00/1 Parkhurst P-205
01/2 Parkhurst 109
00/1 Premier Plus 103, PR9
00/1 Private Stock 128, Roo. 12
00/1 PS Titanium 130
00/1 PS Titanium Draft 130
00/1 Signature 294, ✍ Aut. 236
00/1 SP Authentic 47
00/1 To. Heritage 105
00/1 UD Black Diam. 100
96/7 UD Ice 142
01/2 UD MVP 103
01/2 UD Vintage 136
00/1 Vanguard 130
01/2 Victory 192
00/1 MONT
02/3 MONT
01/2 Québec Citadelles
00/1 Dynamo 6

MARKOV, DANNY
02/3 O-Pee-Chee 93
02/3 Pacific 300
02/3 Pacific Complete 343
02/3 Parkhurst Retro 163
02/3 Sports Vault 269
02/3 Topps 93
02/3 To. Limited 93
02/3 T. Total 21
98/9 Be A Player 283, ✍ Aut. 283
00/1 BAP Mem. 396
01/2 BAP Mem. 424
98/9 Bowman's Best 123, F7
00/1 Mir Fetisov 20
99/0 NHL Power Play
98/9 Omega 233
98/9 Pacific 417
01/2 Parkhurst 396
99/0 SPx 148
99/0 Topps 63
99/0 To. Chrome 63
98/9 Upper Deck 372
99/0 Upper Deck 122
01/2 Upper Deck 364
98/9 UD G. Reserve 372
99/0 UD G. Reserve 122
99/0 UD MVP 197
99/0 Victory 286
99/0 TORO / Pizza Pizza 6
97/8 St. John's Maple Leafs

MARKOVICH, MIKE
93/4 Toledo Storm 11

MARKOVSKY, DMITRI
93/4 Portland Winter Hawks

MARKS, JACK*
12/3 Imperial 38

MARKS, JOHN
74/5 Loblaws
74/5 O-Pee-Chee 282
75/6 O-Pee-Chee 121
76/7 O-Pee-Chee 114
77/8 O-Pee-Chee 47
78/9 O-Pee-Chee 157
79/0 O-Pee-Chee 16
80/1 O-Pee-Chee 194
81/2 O-Pee-Chee 70
90/1 ProCards 121
91/2 ProCards 503
75/6 Topps 121
76/7 Topps 114
77/8 Topps 47
78/9 Topps 157
79/0 Topps 16
80/1 Topps 194
79/0 CHIC
80/1 CHIC / Colour
80/1 CHIC / Brown
81/2 CHIC
96/7 Charlotte Checkers
97/8 Charlotte Checkers
81/2 Indianapolis Checkers
92/3 Indianapolis Ice

MARKUS, TODD
91/2 Air Canada SJHL B31

MARKWART, KELLY
90/1 7th...Sketch WHL 175
88/9 Regina Pats
89/0 Regina Pats
90/1 Saskatoon Blades

MARKWART, NEVIN
84/5 O-Pee-Chee 8
91/2 O-Pee-Chee 238
90/1 Pro Set 408
84/5 Topps 7
84/5 BOST
89/0 BOST / Sports Action
90/1 BOST / Sports Action
82/3 Regina Pats
83/4 Regina Pats

MARLEAU, PATRICK
02/3 Atomic 85
02/3 BAP Mem. 105
02/3 Crown Royale ✂ GWDP 19
02/3 Exclusive 149, ✂ GWJ 22
02/3 First Edition 238
02/3 Heads Up 107, ✂ GWQ 24
02/3 O-Pee-Chee 63
02/3 Pacific 336
02/3 Pacific Complete 113
02/3 Parkhurst 147
02/3 Pr. Stock Reserve 87
02/3 PS Titanium 86, ✂ GWJ 62
02/3 Signature 69, GS-68, ✍ 69
02/3 SP Game-Used ✂ AF, ✂ PC, ✂ PH
02/3 Sports Vault 285
02/3 Topps 63, ✂ FRF
02/3 To. Chrome 44, ✂ FRF
02/3 To. Limited 63
02/3 T. Total 328
02/3 Upper Deck 144
02/3 UD Classic 81
02/3 UD MVP 156
02/3 UD Piece 74
02/3 UD Vintage 210, 285, GB 210
02/3 Vanguard ✂ GWJ40
02/3 Victory 178
01/2 Adrenaline 166
98/9 Aurora 168, -CF 43
99/0 Aurora 121
00/1 Aurora 128
98/9 Be A Player 120, ✍ Aut. 120
99/0 BAP Mem. 133
00/1 BAP Mem. 229
01/2 BAP Mem. 173
97 Bowman 88, 141, BB2
98/9 Bowman's Best 60, BP4
99/0 Crown Royale 124
00/1 Crown Royale 93
97/8 Do. Elite 99, 128, 145, BF-3, C-11, ✍ BF-3
97/8 Do. Preferred 150, 198, LT-5C
97/8 Do. Priority 175, 195, 216, DD-18, OD-29, Post-18, Stamp-18
98/9 Dynagon Ice 167
99/0 Dynagon Ice 173, CM-29
01/2 Heads Up 83
97/8 Leaf 154
97/8 Limited 200
97/8 McDonald's McD-34
99/0 Millenium 210, ✍ Aut. 210
98/9 NHL Power Play
99/0 NHL Power Play
01/2 O-Pee-Chee 9
98/9 OPC Chrome 170, SB10
97/8 Omega 203
98/9 Omega 211
99/0 Omega 208
98/9 Pacific 386, -TC 23
99/0 Pacific 375
00/1 Pacific 360
01/2 Pacific 339
97/8 Pa. Crown Roy. 120
98/9 Pa. Crown Roy. 119
97/8 Pa. Dynagon Rookie
97/8 Pa. Paramount 167
98/9 Pa. Paramount 211, -TC 23
99/0 Pa. Paramount 206
00/1 Pa. Paramount 214
97/8 Pa. Revolution 125
98/9 Pa. Revolution 127
99/0 Panini Sticker 301
00/1 Parkhurst P-71
01/2 Parkhurst 80
97/8 Pinnacle 12
97/8 Pi. Be A Player 221, ✍ Aut. 221
97/8 Pi. Certified C
99/0 Prism 125
01/2 Pr. Stock 84
00/1 PS Titanium 85
01/2 PS Titanium Draft ✂ 85
99/0 Revolution 128, SS-31, / CSC 128
00/1 Revolution 129
00/1 Signature 55, ✍ Aut. 51
01/2 Signature 144, ✍ Aut. 144
97/8 SP Authentic 191
98/9 SP Authentic 75
00/1 SP Authentic 74
00/1 SP GU ✂ TotG
01/2 SP GU ✂ AF
99/0 SPx 129
98/9 SPx Finite 73, 130
98/9 SPx Prospects 50
99/0 Stadium 72
01/2 Stadium 10, ✂ SCS
98/9 Topps 170, SB10
99/0 Topps 134
00/1 Topps 223
01/2 Topps 9

99/0 To. Chrome 134
00/1 To. Chrome 142
01/2 To. Chrome 9
98/9 To. Finest 18, C12
98/9 T. Gold Label 94
00/1 To. Gold Label 12, B8, ✂ GLJ
00/1 To. Heritage 153
01/2 To. Heritage 93, ✂ GWJ
01/2 To. Reserve ✂ TR
98/9 UD Choice 173
98/9 UD3 4, 64, 124
96/7 Upper Deck 384
97/8 Upper Deck 354, SG3
98/9 Upper Deck 26, 171, GN10
99/0 Upper Deck 110
00/1 Upper Deck 146
01/2 Upper Deck 147, ✂ GN
96/7 UD Black Diam. 103
97/8 UD Black Diam. 140
98/9 UD Black Diam. 72
99/0 UD Black Diam. 74
97/8 UD Coll. Choice 304
98/9 UD G. Reserve 26, 171
99/0 UD G. Reserve 110
97/8 UD Ice 41
98/9 UD MVP 170, PG13
99/0 UD MVP 176
00/1 UD Pros&Prosp. 73
00/1 UD Vintage 305
01/2 Vanguard 85
99/0 Victory 250
00/1 Victory 195
01/2 Victory 291
99/0 WGretzky 151
97/8 Zenith 84, RR-10

MAROIS, DANIEL
90/1 Bowman 160
91/2 Bowman 165
92/3 Bowman 245
99/0 Cardset 255
93/4 Donruss 17
92/3 Durivage 16
89/0 Kraft 37
90/1 OPC/Topps 267
91/2 O-Pee-Chee 212
92/3 O-Pee-Chee 58
89/0 O-Pee-Chee 273
89/0 opcSticker 176-36, / FS 18
89/0 Panini Sticker 137
90/1 Panini Sticker 284
90/1 Panini/TOR 14
91/2 Panini Sticker 95
91/2 Parkhurst 329
93/4 Parkhurst 282
94/5 Parkhurst 18
91/2 Pinnacle 27
92/3 Pinnacle 139
90/1 Pro Set 284
91/2 Pro Set 223
91/2 Pro Set Platinum 118
90/1 Score 122
91/2 Score 254
91/2 Score CAN 474
92/3 Score 63
90/1 Sco. Young Stars 3
92/3 Topps 49
91/2 To. Stadium 197
92/3 To. Stadium 63
90/1 Upper Deck 179
91/2 Upper Deck 331
92/3 Upper Deck 71
88/9 TORO / P.L.A.Y. 15
91/2 TORO / P.L.A.Y. 24

MAROIS, JEAN
52/3 La Patrie
51/2 Laval Dairy 2
43-47 Parade Sportive
52/3 St. Lawrence 36

MAROIS, JÉRÔME
98/9 Québec Remparts
00/1 Rouyn-Noranda 13

MAROIS, MARIO
91/2 Bowman 380
81/2 Dernière Heure
86/7 Kraft Sports 77
81/2 O-Pee-Chee 279
82/3 O-Pee-Chee 287
83/4 O-Pee-Chee 295
84/5 O-Pee-Chee 282
85/6 O-Pee-Chee 194
87/8 O-Pee-Chee 220
88/9 OPC/Topps 233 [Error: Marios]
90/1 OPC/Topps 158
91/2 O-Pee-Chee 82
89/0 O-Pee-Chee 260
84/5 OPC Sticker 166
84/5 OPC Sticker 167
85/6 OPC Sticker 144-14
87/8 OPC Sticker 250-141
88/9 OPC Sticker 142-15
89/0 opcSticker 185-41
87/8 Panini Sticker 359
88/9 Panini Sticker 151
89/0 Panini Sticker 328, 336
80/1 Pepsi Bottle Cap
82/3 Post [Québ.]
90/1 Pro Set 253, 524
91/2 Pro Set 477
90/1 Score 229, 94T
91/2 Score CAN 546
91/2 To. Stadium 12
90/1 Upper Deck 8
83/4 Vachon 67-47
83/4 Vachon 67-91
81/2 QUÉB
82/3 QUÉB
83/4 QUÉB
84/5 QUÉB
85/6 QUÉB / Provigo
89/0 QUÉB
89/0 QUÉB / Gene. Foods
89/0 QUÉB / Police
90/1 QUÉB
90/1 SLOU / Kodak
85/6 WINN / Safety Tips
86/7 WINN
87/8 WINN
88/9 WINN / Safety Tips
92/3 Hamilton Canucks
92/3 Hamilton Canucks

MARON, OLIVER
01/2 Belleville Bulls

MAROSTE, MARK
94/5 DEL 137
95/6 DEL 40

MAROTTE, GILLES
68/9 Bauer Photo
70/1 Colgate 65
70/1 Dad's Cookies
70/1 Eddie Sargent 78
71/2 Eddie Sargent 70
72/3 Eddie Sargent 89
70/1 Esso Power Player
72/3 Post 1
74/5 Loblaws
68/9 O-Pee-Chee 14
69/0 O-Pee-Chee 68
70/1 O-Pee-Chee 34
71/2 O-Pee-Chee 151
72/3 O-Pee-Chee 27
73/4 O-Pee-Chee 5
74/5 O-Pee-Chee 373
75/6 O-Pee-Chee 164
76/7 O-Pee-Chee 192
95/6 Parkie 66-67 17
72 Semic Sticker 202
68/9 Shirriff / Chic. 15
66/7 Topps 36
67/8 Topps 59
68/9 Topps 14
69/0 Topps 68
70/1 Topps 34
72/3 Topps 167
73/4 Topps 188
75/6 Topps 164
76/7 Topps 192
91/2 Ultimate Original Six 59, ✍ Aut. 59
68/9 CHIC

MAROUELLI, DAN
90/1 Pro Set 692

MARPLE, STAN
97/8 Guildford Flames
98/9 Guildford Flames

MARQUET, SEBASTIAN
93 Semic Sticker 256

MARQUETTE, DALE
88/9 ProCards / Saginaw
89/0 ProCards IHL 64

MARRIN, PETER
76/7 OPC WHA 96
77/8 OPC WHA 51

MARRIOTT, JAMIE
91/2 Avant Garde BCJHL 38

MARRJAMÖKI, PEKKA
77-79 Sports. FIN 19-436

MARSEILLE, FRANK
71/2 Bazooka Panel

MARSH,
91/2 Avant Garde BCJHL 160

MARSH, BLAIR
92/3 BCJHL 235
93/4 Maine Black Bears

MARSH, BRAD
90/1 Bowman 158
92/3 Fleer Ultra 364
80/1 O-Pee-Chee 338
81/2 O-Pee-Chee 47
82/3 O-Pee-Chee 254
83/4 O-Pee-Chee 269
84/5 O-Pee-Chee 163
85/6 OPC/Topps 72
86/7 OPC/Topps 175
87/8 OPC/Topps 128
88/9 OPC/Topps 64
90/1 OPC/Topps 155
91/2 O-Pee-Chee 19
89/0 O-Pee-Chee 276
81/2 OPC Sticker 225
86/7 OPC Sticker 235-106
88/9 OPC Sticker 101-233
89/0 opcSticker 175-35
87/8 Panini Sticker 127
89/0 Panini Sticker 141
90/1 Panini Sticker 277
90/1 Panini/TOR 15
92/3 Parkhurst 123
80/1 Pepsi Bottle Cap
91/2 Pinnacle 361
91/2 Pinnacle 401
92/3 Pinnacle 378
82/3 Post [Phil.]
90/1 Pro Set 285
91/2 Pro Set 378
92/3 Pro Set 126
92/3 Pro Set 264
90/1 Score 219
91/2 Score CAN 416
92/3 Score 293
92/3 Score 392
93/4 Score PiAS 10
92/3 Topps 215
92/3 To. Stadium 482
93/4 To. Stadium - AS
90/1 Upper Deck 199
78/9 ATLF / Colour
79/0 ATLF / B&W
79/0 ATLF / Colour
80/1 CALG
93/4 OTTA
94/5 OTTA
95/6 OTTA
83/4 PHIL / J.C. Penney
86/7 PHIL
88/9 TORO / P.L.A.Y. 25
90/1 TORO
01/2 Ottawa 67's 27

MARSH, PETER
79/0 O-Pee-Chee 147
80/1 O-Pee-Chee 314
81/2 O-Pee-Chee 71
79/0 Topps 147
81/2 CHIC
82/3 CHIC
79/0 WINN

MARSH, RYAN
01/2 Louisiana Ice Gators

MARSH, TYSON
01/2 Vancouver Giants

MARSHALL, BERT
71/2 Bazooka Panel
64-67 BeeHive-3 [Detr.]
65/6 Coca-Cola
70/1 Dad's Cookies
70/1 Eddie Sargent 131
71/2 Eddie Sargent 134
72/3 Eddie Sargent 47
74/5 Loblaws
68/9 O-Pee-Chee 79
69/0 O-Pee-Chee 80
69/0 O-Pee-Chee 4in1
70/1 O-Pee-Chee 188
71/2 O-Pee-Chee 73
72/3 O-Pee-Chee 130
73/4 O-Pee-Chee 51
74/5 O-Pee-Chee 177
75/6 O-Pee-Chee 72
76/7 O-Pee-Chee 62
77/8 O-Pee-Chee 206
78/9 O-Pee-Chee 49
68/9 Shirriff / Oakl. 8
66/7 Topps 51
67/8 Topps 45
68/9 Topps 79
69/0 Topps 80
71/2 Topps 73
72/3 Topps 162
73/4 Topps 51
74/5 Topps 177
75/6 Topps 72
76/7 Topps 62
77/8 Topps 206
78/9 Topps 49
71/2 Toronto Sun Photo
81/2 COLR

MARSHALL, BOB
98/9 DEL 14
99/0 Eishockey 295

MARSHALL, CHARLES
52/3 Anonymous 20

MARSHALL, CHRIS
93/4 Birmingham Bulls
91/2 Cincinnati Cyclones

MARSHALL, DON
45-64 BeeHive-2 [Mont.]
45-64 BeeHive-2 [NYRa.]
64-67 BeeHive-3 [NYRa.]
64/5 Coke/Sprite [NYRa.]
65/6 Coca-Cola
70/1 Colgate 27
70/1 Dad's Cookies
71/2 Eddie Sargent 208
70/1 Esso Power Player
62/3 Cowan Tile
68/9 O-Pee-Chee 75
69/0 O-Pee-Chee 39
70/1 O-Pee-Chee 129
71/2 O-Pee-Chee 199
55/6 Parkhurst 35
57/8 Parkhurst [Mont.] 8
58/9 Parkhurst 44
59/0 Parkhurst 37
60/1 Parkhurst 42
61/2 Parkhurst 57
60/1 Parkhurst 59
61/2 Parkhurst 40
62/3 Parkhurst 43
93/4 Parkie 56-57 76
95/6 Parkie 66-67 82
94/5 Parkie Tall 88
72 Semic Sticker 197
60/1 Shirriff 23
61/2 Shirriff 103
62/3 Shirriff 33
68/9 Shirriff / NYRa. 7
63/4 Topps 59
64/5 Topps 97
65/6 Topps 29
66/7 Topps 24
66/7 Topps / Test 24
67/8 Topps 23
67/8 Topps 130
68/9 Topps 75
69/0 Topps 39
70/1 Topps 129
60/1 Toronto Star Photo
60/1 Toronto Star Weekend
66/7 Toronto Star Weekend
71/2 Toronto Sun Photo
91/2 Ultimate Original Six 13, ✍ Aut. 13
60/1 York Glass [Mont.]
60/1 York
61/2 York 6
62/3 York Transfer 28
71/2 TORO

MARSHALL, GRANT
02/3 Pacific 102
02/3 Pacific Complete 448
02/3 Parkhurst 199
02/3 T. Total 160
02/3 Upper Deck 51
95/6 Bowman 162
92/3 Classic 13
93/4 Classic 140
92/3 Classic Four Sport 162
93/4 Cla. 4 Sport 240
93/4 Cla. Prospects 188
00/1 Crown Royale ✂ GWJ 10
96/7 Donruss 222
95/6 Leaf 327
96/7 Leaf 169
99/0 Pacific 125
01/2 Pacific 130, 409
96/7 Panini Sticker 172
95/6 Parkhurst 533
96/7 Pi. Be A Player 146, ✍ Aut. 146
01/2 Pr. Stock ✂ GUG 32
00/1 PS Titanium ✂ GUG 88
96/7 Score 261
90/1 7th..Sketch OHL 80, 88
91/2 7th..Sketch OHL 299
95/6 Upper Deck 362
96/7 Upper Deck 47
96/7 UD CC 77
98/9 UD MVP 64
01/2 UD SCup Champs 53
01/2 Victory 117
01/2 COLU
96/7 DALL / Southwest
00/1 DALL / Southwest
93/4 St. John's Maple Leafs
92/3 Ottawa 67's

MARSHALL, JACK
91 C55 Reprint 29
83 HHOF Postcard C9
83&87 HHOF 39
10/1 Imperial
10/1 Imperial 33
10/1 Imperial 35
11/2 Imperial 29

MARSHALL, JASON
98/9 Be A Player 1, ✍ Aut. 1
93/4 Canada Nationals
93/4 Fleer Ultra 468
95/6 Leaf 190
98/9 Pacific 60
97/8 Pa. Invincible R-5
97/8 Pi. Be A Player 54, ✍ Aut. 54
93/4 Power Play 488
91/2 ProCards 25
91/2 Score 388
91/2 Score CAN 278
94 Semic 105
90/1 7th..Sketch WHL 117
99/0 Ult. Victory 3
90/1 Upper Deck 453
92/3 Upper Deck 68
00/1 UD Vintage 8
96/7 ANAH / Up Front 15
92/3 Peoria Rivermen

MARSHALL, PAUL
90/1 ProCards 297
81/2 TORO
93/4 Birmingham Bulls

MARSHALL, RICK
90/1 7th..Sketch OHL 10
91/2 7th..Sketch OHL 105
92/3 Windsor Spitfires

MARSHALL, WILLIE
55/6 Parkhurst 17
58/9 Parkhurst 19

MARSON, L
91/2 Oshawa Generals

MARSON, MIKE
74/5 Loblaws
75/6 O-Pee-Chee 43
75/6 Topps 43
74/5 WASH

MARTAN, JOHN
52/3 Anonymous 109

MARTEL, JAKE
95/6 Slapshot 215

MARTEL, JOCELYN
90/1 7th..Sketch LHJMQ 258

MARTEL, KEN
90/1 Michigan Tech Huskies

MARTEL, RICHARD
00/1 Baie-Comeau 25
01/2 Baie-Comeau 25

MARTELL, STEVE
91/2 ProCards 559
89/0 7th..Sketch OHL 34
90/1 7th..Sketch OHL 135
92/3 Hampton Roads

MARTENSSON, TONY
00/1 UD Elitserien 36

MARTHINSEN,
92/3 Semic Nordisk 191 [Arets Lag]

MARTHINSEN, JIM
95 Globe 190
95 Panini Worlds 236
94 Semic 251
95 Semic 177
92/3 Semic Nordisk 1
92 Semic Sticker 27
93 Semic Sticker 229
96 Wien 202

MARTIKAINEN, KARI
02/3 Cardset 70
99/0 Cardset 185
92/3 Jyvas Hyva 59
93/4 Jyvas Hyva 105
93/4 Sisu 11
95/6 Sisu 95
95/6 Sisu 288

MARTIKAINEN, PERTTI
71/2 Williams Finnish 265

MARTIN, BENOÎT
99/0 Rimouski Océanic 9
00/1 Rimouski Océanic 10
01/2 Rimouski Océanic 10

MARTIN, BLAKE
90/1 7th..Sketch OHL 64

MARTIN, BRIAN
91/2 Hampton Roads
92/3 Hampton Roads
98/9 Hampton Roads
83/4 Belleville Bulls

MARTIN, CHRIS
82/3 Kitchener Rangers

MARTIN, CRAIG
94/5 Classic E6
93/4 Cla. Prospects 78
98/9 DEL 118
95/6 Leaf 189
95/6 Parkhurst 229
91/2 ProCards 241
90/1 7th..Sketch LHJMQ 228
95/6 Topps 94
96/7 Carolina Monarchs
87/8 Hull Olympiques

MARTIN, DERICK
99/0 Hull Olympiques BN
99/0 Hull Olympiques 6
00/1 Hull Olympiques 7
01/2 Hull Olympiques 7

MARTIN, DON
88/9 ProCards / Cape Breton
89/0 ProCards IHL 102
86/7 London Knights

MARTIN, FRANK
45-64 BeeHive-2 [Bost.]
53/4 Parkhurst 97
93/4 Parkie 56-57 34
63/4 Québec Aces
54/5 Topps 30

MARTIN, GEORGE CLARE
45-64 BeeHive-2 [Detr.]
51/2 Parkhurst 39

MARTIN, GRANT
94/5 DEL 436
95/6 DEL 399
96/7 DEL 308
82/3 Fredericton Express
83/4 Fredericton Express
84/5 Fredericton Express

MARTIN, HANS
70/1 Kuvajulkaisut 301

MARTIN, HUBERT
70/1 CHIC

MARTIN, JACQUES
88/9 CHIC / Coke
89/0 CHIC / Coke
96/7 OTTA
97/8 OTTA
98/9 OTTA
99/0 OTTA
00/1 OTTA
01/2 OTTA
02/3 OTTA
90/1 QUÉB / Petro-Canada
91/2 QUÉB / Petro-Canada
92/3 QUÉB / Petro-Canada

MARTIN, JASON
91/2 Air Canada SJHL D7

MARTIN, JEAN-MICHEL
00/1 Chicoutimi Saguenéens 22

MARTIN, JEFF
95/6 Slapshot 423

MARTIN, LOUIS-PHILIPPE
01/2 Baie-Comeau 2
02/3 Baie-Comeau

MARTIN, MATT
93/4 Classic 57
93/4 Cla. Images 4 Sport 28
93/4 Cla. Prospects 150
93/4 Cla. Prospects IA9
93/4 Cla. Prospects LP9
93/4 Donruss 497
94/5 Donruss 34
93/4 Fleer Ultra 432
94/5 Leaf 159
97/8 Pa. Invincible R-194
93/4 Parkhurst 471
93/4 Premier - USA Hockey 23
94/5 Premier SFX 550
93/4 Score 635
93/4 To. Stadium - Team U.S.A. 16
93/4 Upper Deck 447
98/9 Chicago Wolves Champs
98/9 Michigan K-Wings
99/0 Michigan K-Wings
94/5 St. John's Maple Leafs
92/3 Windsor Spitfires
92/3 Maine Black Bears

MARTIN, MIKE
95/6 Classic 9, 98
94/5 SR Auto-Phonex 28, ✍ 28
93/4 Slapshot / Windsor 4
94/5 Slapshot / Windsor 5
95/6 Slapshot 408, P
96/7 Binghampton Rangers
97/8 Fort Wayne Komets
97/8 Hartford Wolf Pack
98/9 Hartford Wolf Pack
99/0 Michigan K-Wings

MARTIN, NEAL
94/5 Slapshot / Sudbury 5
95/6 Slapshot 387
01/2 UD DEL 234
96/7 Hampton Roads
93/4 Soo Greyhounds 10

MARTIN, PETE
37/8 World Wide Gum 31

MARTIN, PETER
81/2 Victoria Cougars

MARTIN, PIERRE
79/0 Montréal Juniors B&W
79/0 Montréal Jrs. Colour

MARTIN, PIT
64-67 BeeHive-3 [Detr.]
63-65 Chex
64/5 Coke/Sprite [Detr.]
77/8 Coke
70/1 Colgate 31
70/1 Dad's Cookies
70/1 Eddie Sargent 39
71/2 Eddie Sargent 42
72/3 Eddie Sargent 68
70/1 Esso Power Player
74/5 Lipton Soup 37
74/5 Loblaws
68/9 O-Pee-Chee 18
69/0 O-Pee-Chee 75
70/1 O-Pee-Chee 18
70/1 O-Pee-Chee 253
71/2 O-Pee-Chee 39
72/3 O-Pee-Chee 24
73/4 O-Pee-Chee 73
74/5 O-Pee-Chee 58
75/6 O-Pee-Chee 48
76/7 O-Pee-Chee 76
76/7 OPC 382
77/8 O-Pee-Chee 135
78/9 O-Pee-Chee 286
95/6 Parkie 66-67 41
94/5 Parkie Tall 51
72 Semic Sticker 224
68/9 Shirriff / Chic. 6
64/5 Topps 1
65/6 Topps 52
66/7 Topps 41
67/8 Topps 116
68/9 Topps 18
69/0 Topps 75
70/1 Topps 18
71/2 Topps 39
72/3 Topps 99
73/4 Topps 164
74/5 Topps 58
75/6 Topps 48
76/7 Topps 76
77/8 Topps 135
66/7 Toronto Star Weekend
71/2 Toronto Sun Photo
90/1 Upper Deck 513
78/9 VANC / Royal Bank

MARTIN, RICHARD
71/2 Colgate Head
70s Dernière Heure

MARTIN, RICK
72/3 Eddie Sargent 35
01/2 Fleer Greats 49, ✍ Aut.
91/2 Future Trends C72 49, ✍ 49
92/3 Future Trends C76 125
74/5 Lipton Soup 33
74/5 Loblaws
73/4 Mac's Milk
71/2 O-Pee-Chee 161
72/3 O-Pee-Chee 157
72/3 O-Pee-Chee 182
72/3 O-Pee-Chee Crest 4
73/4 O-Pee-Chee 173
74/5 O-Pee-Chee 42
74/5 O-Pee-Chee 127
74/5 O-Pee-Chee 190
75/6 O-Pee-Chee 175
75/6 O-Pee-Chee 208
75/6 O-Pee-Chee 212
75/6 O-Pee-Chee 289
75/6 O-Pee-Chee 315
76/7 O-Pee-Chee 5
76/7 O-Pee-Chee 210
76/7 O-Pee-Chee 214
76/7 O-Pee-Chee 380
77/8 O-Pee-Chee 180
77/8 O-Pee-Chee NS 11
78/9 O-Pee-Chee 80
79/0 O-Pee-Chee 149
80/1 O-Pee-Chee 51
71/2 O-Pee-Chee Poster 6
72/3 Topps 145
73/4 Topps 155
74/5 Topps 42
74/5 Topps 127
74/5 Topps 190
75/6 Topps 175
75/6 Topps 208
75/6 Topps 212
75/6 Topps 289
75/6 Topps 315
76/7 Topps 5
76/7 Topps 210
76/7 Topps 214
76/7 Topps NS 19
77/8 Topps 180
77/8 ToppsNS 11
78/9 Topps 80
79/0 Topps 149
80/1 Topps 51
71/2 Toronto Sun Photo
72/3 BUFF
73/4 BUFF
73/4 BUFF / Bells Market
74/5 BUFF
75/6 BUFF / Linnett
79/0 BUFF / Bells Market
80/1 BUFF / Wendt's 8
83/4 BUFF / Noco

MARTIN, RON
33-35 Diamond Match Silv.
33/4 WWGum 7

MARTIN, RONNY
94/5 DEL 196
95/6 DEL 413

MARTIN, RYAN
01/2 Calgary Hitmen

MARTIN, STREIT
98/9 OFS 93

MARTIN, TERRY
77/8 O-Pee-Chee 318
78/9 O-Pee-Chee 118
81/2 O-Pee-Chee 321
82/3 O-Pee-Chee 329
83/4 O-Pee-Chee 336
84/5 O-Pee-Chee 306
82/3 OPC/Topps Sticker 66
80/1 Pepsi Bottle Cap
82/3 Post [Toro.]
89/0 ProCards AHL 261
90/1 ProCards 292
91/2 ProCards 22
83/4 Souhaits Keychain [Maple Leafs]
78/9 Topps 118
83/4 Vachon 92-107
88/9 EDMO / Action 146
79/0 TORO
80/1 TORO
81/2 TORO
82/3 TORO
83/4 TORO
84/5 Nova Scotia Oilers
91/2 Rochester Americans GL
91/2 Rochester Americans WPC
92/3 Rochester Americans WPC
93/4 Rochester Americans

MARTIN, TOM
90/1 ProCards 419
72/3 Ottawa Nationals
83/4 Victoria Cougars

MARTIN, TUOMO
80/1 Mallasjuoma 134
78/9 SM-Liiga 90

MARTINAK, TOMAS
98/9 OFS 282

MARTINEAU, ANDRÉ
01/2 Cape Breton Eagles 16
98/9 Québec Remparts
99/0 Québec Remparts 13

MARTINEAU, DON
74/5 Loblaws

MARTINEAU, PATRICE
90/1 7th..Sketch LHJMQ 28
91/2 7th..Sketch LHJMQ 88
91 7th..Sketch Mem.Cup 38

MARTINEC, PATRIK
94/5 APS 85
95/6 APS 284
96/7 APS 134
97/8 APS 22
97/8 DS 85
98/9 DS 95
99/0 DS 148
96/7 DS Sticker 69
97/8 DS Sticker 216
98/9 OFS 138
99/0 OFS 398
00/1 OFS 307
01/2 OFS -UHI 17

MARTINEC, TOMAS
94/5 APS 18
95/6 APS 117
96/7 APS 158
97/8 APS 229
94/5 DEL 181
95/6 DEL 184
97/8 DS 72
98/9 DS 53
96/7 DS Sticker 260
98/9 OFS 156
99/0 OFS 93, 317
00/1 OFS 153
00/1 UD DEL 104
01/2 UD DEL 116, SS6

MARTINEC, VLADIMIR
95/6 APS 396
01/2 DS L6
98/9 OFS Leg. 6
99/0 OFS 253

MARTINEC, VLADIMÍR
92/3 Future Trends C76 156
72 Hellas MM-Jenkki 89
74 Hellas MM-Jenkki 78
70/1 Kuvajulkaisut 54
72 Panda MM-Toronto
79 Panini Sticker 86
72 Semic Sticker 30
74 Semic Sticker 56
71/2 Williams Finnish 32
72/3 Williams Finnish 15
73/4 Williams Finnish 56

MARTINEK, PETR
00/1 OFS 91
01/2 OFS 2
99/0 Score 27

MARTINEK, RADEK
02/3 Pacific Complete 378
02/3 T. Total 72
01/2 Adrenaline 216
96/7 APS 248
97/8 APS 275
01/2 Atomic 115
01/2 BAP Mem. 384
01/2 Bowman 118
01/2 Crown Royale 169
97/8 DS 30
98/9 DS 32
99/0 DS 32
00/1 DS 75, TS2
01/2 DS 53
96/7 DS Sticker 79
97/8 DS Sticker 71
01/2 O-Pee-Chee 342
98/9 OFS 199
99/0 OFS 264, 283, 502
00/1 OFS 8
01/2 Parkhurst 264
01/2 Pr. Stock 130
01/2 PS Titanium 169
01/2 PS Titanium Draft 150
01/2 Signature 240, ✍ Aut. 240
01/2 SP Authentic 163
01/2 SP GU 87
01/2 SPx 116
01/2 Topps 342
01/2 To. Chrome 160
01/2 UD PlayMakers Ltd 129
01/2 Upper Deck 445
01/2 UD Challenge 123
01/2 UD Honor Roll 81
01/2 UD Premier 72
01/2 UD Vintage 287
01/2 Vanguard 120

MARTINI, DARCY
98/9 DEL 187
94/5 Cape Breton Oilers
90/1 Michigan Tech Huskies
91/2 Michigan Tech Huskies
91/2 Michigan Tech Huskies
91/2 Michigan Tech Huskies

MARTINI, MARIO
83/4 Belleville Bulls
84/5 Sudbury Wolves

MARTINIUK, ALEXANDER
91/2 Future Trends C72 50
74 Hellas MM-Jenkki 50
72 Panda MM-Toronto
72 Semic Sticker 15
74 Semic Sticker 39
71/2 Soviet Stars
73/4 Soviet Stars 17
71/2 Williams Finnish 9
73/4 Williams Finnish 10

MARTINO, TONY
97/8 New Mexico Scorpions

MARTINOV, SERGEI
00/1 Mir 61

MARTINS, STEVE
99/0 Omega 217
01/2 Signature 19, ✍ Aut. 19
95/6 HART / Kids Club
98/9 OTTA
98/9 Chicago Wolves Champs
01/2 Grand Rapids Griffins
96/7 Springfield Falcons

MARTINSEN, ANDERS
92/3 Semic Nordisk 166

MARTINSEN, JIM
94 Panini Olympics 311

MARTINSEN, KETIL
92/3 Semic Nordisk 56

MARTINSEN, PÅL
92/3 Semic Nordisk 33

MARTINSEN, PER
92/3 Semic Nordisk 146

MARTINSEN, REMO
92/3 Semic Nordisk 19

MARTINSON, JOEL
91/2 Air Canada SJHL C29

MARTINSON, STEVE
88/9 ProCards / Sherbrooke
90/1 ProCards 308
91/2 ProCards 319
88/9 MONT
89/0 MONT
92/3 San Diego Gulls

MARTINYUK, DENIS
99/0 Mir 40
00/1 Mir 27

MARTISEN, THOR
79 Panini Sticker 295

MARTONE, MIKE
97/8 Bell
95/6 Slapshot 308
99/0 Mississippi S'Wolves
99/0 Mississippi S'Wolves

MARTTILA, JUKKA
91/2 Jyvas Hyva 59
92/3 Jyvas Hyva 157
91 Semic Sticker 8

MARTTILA, NIKO
91/2 Jyvas Hyva 53
92/3 Jyvas Hyva 30
93/4 Jyvas Hyva 50
93/4 Sisu 241
94/5 Sisu 12
95/6 Sisu 18

MARTTINEN, JAAKKO
65/6 Hellas 138
70/1 Kuvajulkaisut 163
72 Panda MM-Toronto
78/9 SM-Liiga 30
71/2 Williams Finnish 119
72/3 Williams Finnish 89
73/4 Williams Finnish 135

MARTTINEN, JYRI
02/3 Cardset 221

MARTYNOWSKI, RAFA
01/2 Kitchener Rangers

MARUCA, DAVID
96/7 Regina Pats
97/8 Regina Pats

MARUK, DENNIS
01/2 Fleer Greats 6, ✍ Aut.
83/4 Funmate Puffy 18 [w/]
76/7 O-Pee-Chee 86
77/8 O-Pee-Chee 21
78/9 O-Pee-Chee 141
79/0 O-Pee-Chee 223
80/1 O-Pee-Chee 284
81/2 O-Pee-Chee 350
81/2 O-Pee-Chee 357
82/3 O-Pee-Chee 359
82/3 O-Pee-Chee 369
82/3 O-Pee-Chee 370
83/4 O-Pee-Chee 174
84/5 O-Pee-Chee 101
85/6 OPC/Topps 111
86/7 OPC/Topps 60
87/8 OPC/Topps 117
81/2 OPC Sticker 191
82/3 OPC/Topps Sticker 151
83/4 OPC/Topps Sticker 204
84/5 OPC/Topps Sticker 205
84/5 OPC Sticker 48
86/7 OPC Sticker 170-30
87/8 OPC Sticker 50-189
79 Panini Sticker 60
87/8 Panini Sticker 298
82/3 Post [Wash.]
83/4 Souhaits Keychain [Capitals]
76/7 Topps 86
77/8 Topps 21
78/9 Topps 141
79/0 Topps 223
81/2 Topps 65
81/2 Topps 120 [East]
84/5 Topps 76
01/2 UD Legends 71
83/4 MINS
84/5 MINS
84/5 MINS / 7-Eleven 9
85/6 MINS
86/7 MINS / 7-Eleven 8
87/8 MINS
78/9 WASH
79/0 WASH
80/1 WASH
81/2 WASH
82/3 WASH

MARUSAK, JIRI
95/6 APS 38
96/7 APS 30
97/8 APS 60
00/1 DS 5
00/1 DS 52
96/7 DS Sticker 100
97/8 DS Sticker 293
98/9 OFS 22
99/0 OFS 213, 520
00/1 OFS 353
01/2 OFS 80, -UHI 26

MARUSCHAK, DUANE
90/1 7th..Sketch WHL 133
89/0 Lethbridge Hurricanes

MARX, GORD
95/6 Las Vegas Thunder

MASA, MARTIN
92/3 BCJHL 60
96/7 Johnstown Chiefs

MASAK, MARTIN
95/6 APS 63
96/7 APS 247

MASCISAAC, AL
94/5 Hampton Roads

MASER, JOSH
00/1 Austin Ice Bats
99/0 Medicine Hat Tigers
97/8 Spokane Chiefs

MASKARINEC, MARTIN
94/5 APS 183
95/6 APS 128
96/7 APS 10
97/8 APS 104
97/8 DS 23
99/0 DS 19
96/7 DS Sticker 118
97/8 DS Sticker 49
98/9 OFS 96
99/0 OFS 139, 433
91 Semic Sticker 110

MASKARINEC, TOMAS
97/8 DS Sticker 139

MASLENNIKOV, IGOR
99/0 Eishockey 153
90/1 O-Pee-Chee 14R
91/2 O-Pee-Chee 21R
91 Semic Sticker 91
00/1 UD DEL 17
01/2 UD DEL 10

MASLOV, NIKOLAI
91/2 O-Pee-Chee 55R

MASLYUKOV, KONSTANTIN
98/9 Mir 39
99/0 Mir 150
00/1 Mir 373

MASNICK, PAUL
45-64 BeeHive-2 [Mont.]
48-52 Exhibits [Canadiens]
51/2 Parkhurst 8
54/5 Parkhurst 13
45-54 Quaker Oats
52/3 St. Lawrence 11

MASNY, RADEK
99/0 DS 86
00/1 DS 146
98/9 OFS 66
99/0 OFS 537, 549
00/1 OFS 265

MASON, BOB
87/8 OPC Sticker 238-105
89/0 opcSticker 188-42
87/8 Panini Sticker 175
88/9 Panini Sticker 161
89/0 Panini Sticker 344
89/0 ProCards AHL 88
91/2 ProCards 617
87/8 CHIC / Coke
88/9 QUÉB
88/9 QUÉB / Gene. Foods
86/7 WASH / Kodak
89/0 WASH
92/3 Hamilton Canucks
93/4 Milwaukee Admirals
94/5 Milwaukee Admirals

MASON, BRIAN
98/9 Guildford Flames

MASON, CHARLIE
36-39 Diamond Match TT1
36-39 Diamond Match TT2
36-39 Diamond Match TT3
36-39 Diamond Match TT3

MASON, CHRIS
02/3 Between the Pipes 106
01/2 BAP Mem. 234
01/2 BT Pipes 47
00/1 Pacific 230
01/2 Parkhurst 269
00/1 SP Authentic 113
00/1 UD Reserve 102
00/1 UD Ice 93
01/2 Victory 378
98/9 Milwaukee Admirals
99/0 Milwaukee Admirals
00/1 Milwaukee Admirals
01/2 Milwaukee Admirals

MASON, DALE
89/0 Kamloops Blazers

MASON, DOUG
98/9 DEL 41
99/0 Eishockey 147
91/2 7th..Sketch OHL 256

MASON, RON
93/4 Michigan State

MASON, WES
95/6 Bowman P24
94/5 Slapshot / Sarnia 19
95/6 Slapshot 349, 435

MASS, LOUIS
02/3 Louisiana Ice Gators

MASSA, ROB
94/5 Slapshot / Sarnia 15

MASSE, GERRARD
92/3 Windsor Spitfires

MASSE, MIKE
92/3 MPS SJHL 87

MASSÉ, DAVID
00/1 Québec Remparts 19
01/2 Québec Remparts 19
02/3 Québec Remparts
00/1 Victoriaville Tigres 18

MASSÉ, PATRICE
80/1 Québec Remparts

MASSINEN, VESA
71/2 Williams Finnish 330

MASSON, DALE
90 7th..Sketch Mem.Cup 24
90/1 7th..Sketch WHL 294
91/2 7th..Sketch WHL 86

MASSY, DIDIER
91 Semic Sticker 183
92 Semic Sticker 199

MASTAD, MILT
91/2 Avant Garde BCJHL 111
97/8 Charlotte Checkers
99/0 Fort Wayne Komets
98/9 Hampton Roads
96/7 Providence Bruins
93/4 Seattle Thunderbirds

MASTERS, CASSON
00/1 Nottingham Panthers

MASTERS, KEVIN
90/1 7th..Sketch WHL 147
91/2 7th..Sketch WHL 267

MASTERSON, MATT
95/6 Slapshot 413

MATALAMAKI, KAJ
66/7 Champion 46
65/6 Hellas 46
70/1 Kuvajulkaisut 196
72 Panda MM-Toronto
71/2 Williams Finnish 88
72/3 Williams Finnish 252
73/4 Williams Finnish 251

MATALIK, RADEK
99/0 Guelph Storm

MATATALL, BRUCE
91/2 Air Canada SJHL B47
92/3 MPS SJHL 64

MATATALL, CRAIG
91/2 Air Canada SJHL 29
91/2 Air Canada SJHL C1

MATCZAK, WOJCIECH
92 Semic Sticker 285

MATECHUK, ROD
84/5 Saskatoon Blades

MATEJNY, JAN
97/8 APS 138
99/0 OFS 426

MATEJOVSKY, RADEK
96/7 APS 24
97/8 APS 166
99/0 DS 125
97/8 DS Sticker 203
98/9 OFS 301
99/0 OFS 49, 364
00/1 OFS 100
01/2 OFS 9

MATEKA, EDDIE
52/3 Anonymous 30

MATERI, LEE
92/3 MPS SJHL 69

MATERI, LINDSEY
98/9 Kelowna Rockets

MATHERS, FRANK
45-64 BeeHive-2 [Toro.]
88/9 ProCards / Hershey
98/9 Hershey Bears

MATHERS, MIKE
90/1 7th..Sketch WHL 299
91/2 7th..Sketch WHL 81

MATHEWS, RONNIE
52/3 St. Lawrence 86

MATHIAS, TREVOR
91/2 Air Canada SJHL C42

MATHIASEN, DWIGHT
87/8 PITT / Kodak

MATHIES, JEREMY
91/2 Air Canada SJHL D33

MATHIESON, JIM
90/1 ProCards 197
91/2 ProCards 554
91/2 Baltimore Skipjacks
93/4 Portland Pirates
94/5 Portland Pirates
95/6 Portland Pirates
86/7 Regina Pats
87/8 Regina Pats
88/9 Regina Pats
89/0 Regina Pats

MATHIEU, ALEXANDRE
97 Bowman 123, ✍ Aut.
98 Bowman 115
98 Bowman Chrome 115
00/1 WBS Penguins
01/2 WBS Penguins
96/7 Halifax Moosehead
96/7 Halifax Moosehead
97/8 Halifax Moosehead
97/8 Halifax Moosehead
98/9 Halifax Moosehead

MATHIEU, GILBERT
72 Semic Sticker 160

MATHIEU, MARQUIS
99/0 BAP Mem. 369
90/1 7th..Sketch LHJMQ 114
91/2 7th..Sketch LHJMQ 162
98/9 Providence Bruins
99/0 Providence Bruins
00/1 Providence Bruins
94/5 Toledo Storm
93/4 Wheeling Thund'birds

MATHIEU, NANDO
72 Semic Sticker 138

MATHISRUD, BJØRN
92/3 Semic Nordisk 54

MATIER, MARK
00/1 Kudos 36
91 7th..Sketch Mem.Cup 18
90/1 7th..Sketch OHL 167
91/2 7th..Sketch OHL 326
93/4 Soo Greyhounds 3

MATIKAINEN, PENTII
89 Semic Sticker 27

MATIKAINEN, PENTTI
96/7 DEL 46
93/4 Jyvas Hyva 43
80/1 Mallasjuoma 143
92 Semic Sticker 2
93 Semic Sticker 88
93/4 Sisu 33
71/2 Williams Finnish 266

MATIKAINEN, PETRI
96/7 DEL 255
94/5 Sisu 233
95/6 Sisu 70

MATINEC, TOMAS
95/6 APS 117

MATOUSEK, JIRI
99/0 Score 82

MATSIJEVSKI, ALEXANDER
98/9 Cardset 194
97/8 Hockey-Box

MATSOS, DAVID
91 7th..Sketch Mem.Cup 10
90/1 7th..Sketch OHL 168
91/2 7th..Sketch OHL 329
01/2 Belfast Giants
89/0 Soo Greyhounds
93/4 Soo Greyhounds 12

MATSSON, JESPER
95/6 Leaf Elit Set 92

MATTE, CHRISTIAN
00/1 BAP Mem. 471
99/0 Choice 6
97/8 Donruss 207, RR-6
97/8 Do. Canadian 137
99/0 Topps 233
99/0 To. Chrome 233
97/8 Upper Deck 257
00/1 Cleveland Lumberjacks
98/9 Hershey Bears

MATTE, JOE
34-43 BeeHive-1 [Chic.]

MATTEAU, STÉPHANE
91/2 Bowman 258
92/3 Bowman 340
93/4 Donruss 463
94/5 Donruss 15
93/4 Durivage 44
92/3 Fleer Ultra 279
93/4 Fleer Ultra 290
94/5 Fleer Ultra 332
93/4 Leaf 114
94/5 Leaf 32
91/2 O-Pee-Chee 383
92/3 O-Pee-Chee 69
90/1 OPC Premier 68
98/9 Pacific 387
99/0 Pacific 376
00/1 Pacific 361
97/8 Pacific CC 280
97/8 Pa. Paramount 168
98/9 Pa. Paramount 212
90/1 Panini/CGY 11
91/2 Panini Sticker 62
93/4 Panini Sticker 150
00/1 Panini Sticker 202
91/2 Parkhurst 259
92/3 Parkhurst 268
93/4 Parkhurst 41
94/5 Parkhurst 150
95/6 Parkhurst 446
92/3 Pinnacle 180
93/4 Pinnacle 344
94/5 Pinnacle 329
96/7 Pi. Be A Player 169, ✍ Aut. 169
94/5 POG 165
93/4 Power Play 313
93/4 Premier 415
94/5 Premier 317
90/1 Pro Set 593
91/2 Pro Set 27
89/0 ProCards IHL 192

90/1 Score 381
91/2 Score CAN 242
92/3 Score 543
93/4 Score 398
95/6 Score 227
92/3 Topps 463
91/2 To. Stadium 391
92/3 To. Stadium 363
93/4 To. Stadium 127
94/5 To. Stadium 216
90/1 Upper Deck 535
91/2 Upper Deck 121
92/3 Upper Deck 540
93/4 Upper Deck 214
94/5 Upper Deck 136
95/6 Upper Deck 60
96/7 Upper Deck 326
98/9 Upper Deck 355
01/2 Upper Deck 379
95/6 UD BAP 5, ✍ S5
96/7 UD CC 230
98/9 UD G. Reserve 355
90/1 CALG / McGavin's
91/2 CALG / IGA
93/4 CHIC / Coke
87/8 Hull Olympiques

MATTER, TREVOR
99/0 Fort Wayne Komets

MATTERSDORFER, DARCY
91/2 7th...Sketch WHL 69

MATTEUCCI, MIKE
91/2 Air Canada SJHL 21
91/2 Air Canada SJHL D43
01/2 BAP Mem. 441
01/2 SP Authentic 152
01/2 SPx 141, -RT
01/2 Upper Deck 192
01/2 UD Challenge 111
01/2 UD MVP 203
01/2 Victory 376
02/3 Albany River Rats
00/1 Cleveland Lumberjacks
97/8 Long Beach Ice Dogs
98/9 Long Beach Ice Dogs
91/2 L. Superior State Lakers

MATTHEWS, JAMIE
91/2 Classic 37
91/2 Classic Four Sport 37
91 7th..Sketch Mem.Cup 124
90/1 7th..Sketch OHL 387
91/2 7th...Sketch OHL 261
93/4 Slapshot / Sudbury 16
91/2 Star Pics 6
91/2 Ultimate Draft Pick 32, ✍ Aut.
91/2 Upper Deck 76
89/0 Sudbury Wolves
90/1 Sudbury Wolves
91/2 Sudbury Wolves
92/3 Sudbury Wolves
93/4 Sudbury Wolves

MATTHEWS, RONNIE
52/3 Laval Dairy Update 40

MATTHIASON, MARCUS
97/8 UD Elitserien 34

MATTHIASSON, MARKUS
00/1 UD Elitserien 178

MATTHIES, JEREMY
92/3 MPS SJHL 155

MATTILA, HANNU
98/9 Cardset 94
92/3 Jyvas Hyva 49
93/4 Jyvas Hyva 78
93/4 Sisu 127
93/4 Sisu 318
93/4 Sisu 327
93/4 Sisu 335
94/5 Sisu 76
95/6 Sisu 38
96/7 Sisu 35

MATTILA, JUKKA
97/8 Hockey-Box
70/1 Kuvajulkaisut 131
71/2 Williams Finnish 181
72/3 Williams Finnish 130
73/4 Williams Finnish 184

MATTINGLY, J.P.
88/9 ProCards / Baltimore
89/0 ProCards AHL 103

MATTIS, MIKE
93/4 Michigan State

MATTIUSSI, DICK
70/1 Eddie Sargent 139
70/1 Esso Power Player
69/0 O-Pee-Chee 147
70/1 O-Pee-Chee 192

MATTLI, GEORG
79 Panini Sticker 261

MATTSSON, JESPER
93/4 Classic 141
93/4 Cla. 4 Sport 201
95/6 Edge Ice 76
95 Globe 61
94/5 Leaf Elit Set 280
94/5 Parkie SE244
91/2 Semic Elitserien 198
91/2 Semic Elitserien 332
92/3 Semic Elitserien 217
94/5 SP 171
94/5 Upper Deck 519
98/9 UD Elitserien 163
99/0 UD Elitserien 165
00/1 UD Elitserien 145
95/6 Saint John Flames
96/7 Saint John Flames
97/8 Saint John Flames

MATTSSON, MARKUS
80/1 O-Pee-Chee 394
81/2 O-Pee-Chee 374
80/1 Pepsi Bottle Cap
77-79 Sports. FIN 51-1201

82 Valio
72/3 Williams Finnish 311
80/1 WINN
78/9 Winnipeg Jets

MATTSSON, TEPPO
80/1 Mallasjuoma 111
78/9 SM-Liiga 155

MATTSSON, TORBJORN
90/1 Semic Elitserien 83

MATULIK, IVAN
00/1 Kudos 62
89/0 ProCards AHL 150
90/1 ProCards 527
91/2 ProCards 537
01/2 Cardiff Devils
01/2 Manchester Storm
02/3 Manchester Storm
93/4 Sheffield Steelers 9

MATUSHKIN, IGOR
98/9 UD Elitserien 138

MATUSOVICH, SCOTT
93/4 Birmingham Bulls

MATUSZEK, MIKE
89/0 7th..Sketch OHL 170

MATVICHUK, ALEX
94/5 Slapshot / North Bay 11
95/6 Slapshot 216
96/7 Toledo Storm
93/4 Seattle Thunderbirds

MATVICHUK, ALEXANDER
99/0 Mir 248

MATVICHUK, RICHARD
02/3 Pacific Complete 97
02/3 T. Total 324
02/3 Upper Deck 304
91/2 Arena 6
99/0 BAP Mem. 300
00/1 BAP Mem. 326
91/2 Classic 7
91/2 Classic Four Sport 7
93/4 Cla. Prospects 151
93/4 Donruss 418
94/5 Donruss 303
96/7 Donruss 97
97/8 Donruss 193
92/3 Fleer Ultra 321
93/4 Fleer Ultra 180
94/5 Leaf 269
98/9 OPC Chrome 210
92/3 OPC Premier 83
00/1 Pacific 136
97/8 Pa. Dynagon BKS-29
00/1 Panini Sticker 147
92/3 Parkhurst 74
94/5 Parkhurst 57
95/6 Parkhurst 328
92/3 Pinnacle 391
93/4 Pinnacle 182
96/7 Pi. Be A Player 195, ✍ Aut. 195
95/6 Playoff 249
94/5 Premier 187
93/4 Score 285
96/7 Score 229
91 7th..Sketch Mem.Cup 108
90/1 7th..Sketch WHL 83
91/2 7th...Sketch WHL 113
91/2 Star Pics 57
98/9 Topps 210
00/1 Topps 219
91/2 Ultimate Draft Pick 7, 63, ✍ Aut.
92/3 Upper Deck 505
93/4 Upper Deck 55
94/5 Upper Deck 157
95/6 Upper Deck 37
98/9 Upper Deck 255
91/2 Upper Deck WJC 48
98/9 UD G. Reserve 255
94/5 DALL / Southwest
96/7 DALL / Southwest
00/1 DALL / Southwest
01/2 DALL / Southwest
02/3 DALL / Southwest
90/1 Saskatoon Blades
91/2 Saskatoon Blades

MATWIJIW, STAN
91/2 7th...Sketch WHL 261
94/5 Flint Generals
93/4 Lethbridge Hurricanes
91/2 Prince Albert Raiders

MAUDIE, BOB
94/5 Slapshot Memorial 22
96/7 Binghamton Rangers
93/4 Kamloops Blazers

MAUND, JEFF
99/0 Florida Everblades
01/2 Providence Bruins

MAURER, ANDREAS
95/6 DEL 349

MAURICE, MIKE
93/4 Cla. Prospects 64
92/3 Hamilton Canucks
95/6 Houston Aeros
85/6 Kingston Canadians
86/7 Kingston Canadians

MAURICE, PAUL
93/4 Slapshot / Detroit 23
94/5 Slapshot / Detroit Jr. 25
94/5 Slapshot Memorial 99
97/8 CARO / Sprint
95/6 HART / Kids Club

MAVETY, LARRY
90/1 7th..Sketch OHL 23
91/2 7th...Sketch OHL 110
83/4 Belleville Bulls
84/5 Belleville Bulls
00/1 Kingston Frontenacs 3

MAXNER, WAYNE
89/0 7th..Sketch OHL 48
91/2 7th...Sketch OHL 192

86/7 London Knights
85/6 Sudbury Wolves

MAXWELL, BOBBY
94/5 Saint John Flames

MAXWELL, BRAD
78/9 O-Pee-Chee 83
79/0 O-Pee-Chee 231
80/1 O-Pee-Chee 152
81/2 O-Pee-Chee 102
82/3 O-Pee-Chee 168
83/4 O-Pee-Chee 175
84/5 O-Pee-Chee 102
85/6 O-Pee-Chee 224
86/7 O-Pee-Chee 242
84/5 OPC Sticker 50
85/6 OPC Sticker 154-26
86/7 OPC Sticker 145-253
79 Panini Sticker 56
82/3 Post [Minn.]
83/4 Souhaits Keychain [North Stars]
78/9 Topps 83
79/0 Topps 231
80/1 Topps 152
84/5 Topps 77
78/9 MINS / Cloverleaf 6
79/0 MINS
80/1 MINS
81/2 MINS
82/3 MINS
83/4 MINS
84/5 MINS
84/5 QUÉB
85/6 TORO
86/7 VANC

MAXWELL, BRYAN
78/9 O-Pee-Chee 216
82/3 O-Pee-Chee 387
76/7 OPC WHA 54
82/3 Post [Winn.]
91 7th..Sketch Mem.Cup 95
90/1 7th..Sketch WHL 209
91/2 7th...Sketch WHL 3
83/4 Souhaits Keychain [Jets]
78/9 Topps 216
88/9 LOSA / Smokey
83/4 PITT / Coke Is It✂
84/5 PITT / Heinz
81/2 WINN
82/3 WINN
95/6 Lethbridge Hurricanes
84/5 Medicine Hat Tigers

MAXWELL, DENNIS
95/6 Classic 96
91/2 7th...Sketch OHL 205
94/5 Slapshot / Sarnia 22
99/0 St. John's Maple Leafs
02/3 London Knights
92/3 Sudbury Wolves

MAXWELL, FRED
83&87 HHOF 177
95/6 Legends of Hockey 64

MAXWELL, KEVIN
83 HHOF Postcard M13
82/3 Post [Colo.]
81/2 COLR
81/2 MINS

MAXWELL, PETE
74/5 Sioux City Musketeers

MAXWELL, ROBERT
52/3 Anonymous 29

MAXWELL, ROGER
98/9 Louisiana Ice Gators
00/1 Louisiana Ice Gators
96/7 Mississippi S'Wolves

MAY, ALAN
90/1 Bowman 78
91/2 Bowman 295
93/4 Donruss 419
91/2 O-Pee-Chee 57
90/1 Panini Sticker 160
91/2 Parkhurst 417
93/4 Premier 518
90/1 Pro Set 317
91/2 Pro Set 508
91/2 Pro Set 614
88/9 ProCards / Cape Breton
91/2 Score CAN 545
92/3 Score 357
93/4 Score 430
91/2 To. Stadium 288
90/1 Upper Deck 240
88/9 EDMO / Action 159
89/0 WASH
89/0 WASH / Kodak
90/1 WASH / Kodak
90/1 WASH / Smokey
91/2 WASH / Kodak
91/2 WASH / Smokey
92/3 WASH / Kodak

MAY, ALAN
02/3 Fleer Throwbacks 42

MAY, BOB
93/4 Huntington Blizzard

MAY, BRAD
02/3 Pacific Complete 274
02/3 T. Total 200
02/3 Upper Deck 132
98/9 Be A Player 293, ✍ Aut. 293
00/1 BAP Mem. 474
92/3 Bowman 374
93/4 Donruss 38
94/5 Donruss 76
95/6 Donruss 93
96/7 Donruss 189
94/5 Fleer 24
92/3 Fleer Ultra 17
94/5 Fleer Ultra 25
93/4 Leaf 47
94/5 Leaf 215
95/6 Leaf 224
96/7 Leaf 4
99/0 Millenium 237, ✍ Aut. 237

92/3 O-Pee-Chee 256
98/9 Pacific 429
97/8 Pa. Dynagon BKS-11
92/3 Panini Sticker 252
94/5 Panini Sticker 97
96/7 Panini Sticker 18
91/2 Parkhurst 10
92/3 Parkhurst 240
92/3 Parkhurst 257
93/4 Parkhurst 27
94/5 Parkhurst 26
95/6 Parkhurst 289
91/2 Pinnacle 302
92/3 Pinnacle 197
93/4 Pinnacle 141
94/5 Pinnacle 194
96/7 Pi. Be A Player 52, ✍ Aut. 52
95/6 Pi. Summit 70
94/5 POG 362
95/6 POG 44
93/4 Power Play 298
93/4 Premier 192
94/5 Premier 409
91/2 Pro Set 523
90/1 Score 427
91/2 Score 78T
91/2 Score CAN 628
92/3 Score 96
93/4 Score 269
94/5 Score 104
95/6 Score 288
96/7 Score 48
97/8 Score Buff. 10
89/0 7th..Sketch OHL 125
90/1 7th..Sketch OHL 264
92/3 Topps 34
92/3 To. Stadium 51
93/4 To. Stadium 203
94/5 To. Stadium 2
95/6 To. Stadium 79
90/1 Upper Deck 455
91/2 Upper Deck 596
92/3 Upper Deck 74
93/4 Upper Deck 201
94/5 Upper Deck 391
95/6 Upper Deck 468
98/9 Upper Deck 380
94/5 UD BAP R26, ✍ 22
96/7 UD CC 29
98/9 UD G. Reserve 380
99/0 UD MVP Cup 187
00/1 UD Vintage 275
91/2 BUFF / Blue Shield
91/2 BUFF / Campbell's
91/2 BUFF / Pepsi
92/3 BUFF / Blue Shield
92/3 BUFF / Jubilee
93/4 BUFF / Noco
88/9 Niagara Falls Thunder
89/0 Niagara Falls Thunder

MAY, DARRELL
88/9 ProCards / Peoria

MAY, MIKE
91/2 Ferris State Bulldogs

MAYER, DEREK
92/3 Canada Nationals
93/4 Canada Nationals
96/7 DEL 30
98/9 DEL 160
93/4 Donruss 467
99/0 Eishockey 66
93/4 Fleer Ultra 469
94/5 Parkhurst 156, V60
93/4 Power Play 489
93/4 Premier - Canada 6
89/0 ProCards AHL 329
91/2 ProCards 135
94/5 Score 223, CT17
95/6 Sisu 315, 375
96/7 Sisu SH 5
94/5 To. Stadium 251
94/5 Upper Deck 107
00/1 UD DEL 62
94/5 Atlanta Knights 4

MAYER, GIL
60/1 Cleveland Barons

MAYER, HANS-JÖRG
94/5 DEL 184, 201
95/6 DEL 185
96/7 DEL 123
92 Semic Sticker 175
91/2 Upper Deck 682
91/2 Upper Deck WJC 45

MAYER, JORG
99/0 Eishockey 104

MAYER, PAT
88/9 ProCards / Muskegon

MAYER, STEFAN
94/5 DEL 28
95/6 DEL 8
96/7 DEL 9
98/9 DEL 16
99/0 Eishockey 44

MAYER, THIERRY
95/6 DEL 102
91/2 7th...Sketch LHJMQ 218

MAYERS, JAMAL
02/3 Pacific Complete 258
02/3 T. Total 286
02/3 Upper Deck 397
01/2 BAP Update ✂ TC5, ✂ TC35
97/8 Donruss 223
99/0 Millenium 206, ✍ Aut. 206
99/0 Pacific 359
00/1 Pa. Paramount 207
99/0 Stadium 74
00/1 UD Vintage 317
99/0 SLOU / Taco Bell 21
92/3 W. Michigan Broncos
93/4 W. Michigan Broncos

MAYES, JIM
94/5 Anchorage Aces 13

MAYHEW, MIKE
97/8 Pensacola Ice Pilots

MAYNARD, GEORDIE
90/1 7th..Sketch OHL 276, 288
91/2 7th...Sketch OHL 281

MAYNARD, NIALL
95/6 Slapshot 265

MAYNE, J
93/4 Soo Greyhounds 32

MAYNORT, BRUNO
95 Semic 196

MAYO, KEVIN
85/6 Brandon Wheat Kings

MAYO, MATTHEW
93/4 Slapshot / Niagara Falls 18

MAYR, JÖRG
95/6 DEL 199
96/7 DEL 341
98/9 DEL 100
99/0 DEL 318
01/2 UD DEL 141

MAYVILLE, DAVE
93/4 Slapshot / S.S.Marie 28
93/4 Soo Greyhounds 29

MAYVILLE, DAVID
96/7 Soo Greyhounds

MAZHUGIN, ANDREI
98/9 Mir 82

MAZUR, EDDIE
02/3 Parkie - Reprint 187
45-64 BeeHive-2 [Mont.]
60/1 Cleveland Barons
53/4 Parkhurst 20
54/5 Parkhurst 4

MAZUR, JAY
91/2 Bowman 322
91/2 O-Pee-Chee 28
89/0 ProCards IHL 176
91/2 ProCards 612
91/2 To. Stadium 272
91/2 Upper Deck 378
90/1 VANC / Mohawk
92/3 Hamilton Canucks
95/6 Rochester Americans

MAZUTINEC, SHANE
88/9 Lethbridge Hurricanes

MAZZOLI, PAT
91/2 Ferris State Bulldogs

MBARAGA, PATRICK
01/2 Sherbrooke Castors 17

MCADAM, GARY
77/8 O-Pee-Chee 253
78/9 O-Pee-Chee 42
79/0 O-Pee-Chee 72
80/1 O-Pee-Chee 288
81/2 O-Pee-Chee 93
84/5 O-Pee-Chee 117
82/3 Post [Calg.]
77/8 Topps 253
78/9 Topps 42
79/0 Topps 72
81/2 Topps 93 [West]
81/2 CALG

MCALENDIN, MARLIN
52/3 Anonymous 6

MCALLISTER, CHRIS
95/6 Classic 35
99/0 Millenium 228, ✍ Aut. 228
99/0 Stadium 114
01/2 To. Reserve 87
99/0 UD G. Reserve 349
01/2 PHIL
96/7 Syracuse Crunch

MCALLISTER, KYLE
00/1 Owen Sound Attack 15
01/2 Owen Sound Attack

MCALPINE, CHRIS
94/5 Classic 54, AA4
94/5 Cla. Images 80, ✍ Aut.
95/6 Donruss 113
95/6 Edge Ice 7
95/6 Leaf 14
99/0 Millenium 207, ✍ Aut. 207
01/2 O-Pee-Chee 263
95/6 Pinnacle 210
97/8 Pi. Be A Player 82, ✍ Aut. 82
95/6 Score 293
97/8 Score SLou. 14
99/0 Stadium 139
95/6 Topps 61
01/2 Topps 263
97/8 Upper Deck 348
96/7 Albany River Rats
01/2 Norfolk Admirals
91/2 Minnesota G'Gophers
92/3 Minnesota G'Gophers
93/4 Minnesota G'Gophers

MCALPINE, MIKE
92/3 Minnesota G'Gophers
93/4 Minnesota G'Gophers

MCAMMOND, DAVE
91/2 Air Canada SJHL B26

MCAMMOND, DEAN
02/3 BAP Mem. 53
02/3 Exclusive 42
02/3 Heads Up 17
02/3 O-Pee-Chee 89
02/3 Pacific 56
02/3 Pacific Complete 420
02/3 Parkhurst Retro 74
02/3 Pr. Stock Reserve 26
02/3 Topps 89
02/3 To. Limited 89
02/3 Upper Deck 25
02/3 Victory 32
91/2 Arena 17
00/1 BAP Mem. 379
01/2 BAP Mem. 461

98/9 Bowman's Best 90
91/2 Classic 19
91/2 Classic Four Sport 19
01/2 Crown Royale 21
93/4 Donruss 110
94/5 Donruss 123
94/5 Flair 59
92/3 Fleer Ultra 40
93/4 Fleer Ultra 317
94/5 Fleer Ultra 292
93/4 Leaf 436
94/5 Leaf 298
99/0 Millenium 60, ✍ Aut. 60
98/9 Pacific 214
99/0 Pacific 93
00/1 Pacific 96
97/8 Pa. Invincible R-80
98/9 Pa. Paramount 89
99/0 Pa. Paramount 56
00/1 Pa. Paramount 50
99/0 Panini Sticker 202
93/4 Parkhurst 64
93/4 Parkhurst C9
01/2 Parkhurst 371
94/5 Parkie SE62
94/5 Pinnacle 358
96/7 Pi. Be A Player 126, ✍ Aut. 126
95/6 Playoff 257
96/7 Playoff 419
93/4 Premier 366
01/2 PS Titanium 19
92/3 Pro Set 224
92/3 Score 469
91 7th..Sketch Mem.Cup 109
90/1 7th..Sketch WHL 267
91/2 7th...Sketch WHL 254
97/8 SP Authentic 62
91/2 Star Pics 66
94/5 To. Stadium 147
98/9 UD Choice 79
91/2 Ultimate Draft Pick 18, 74, ✍ Aut.
92/3 Upper Deck 403
93/4 Upper Deck 480, SP-51
94/5 Upper Deck 386
95/6 Upper Deck 363
96/7 Upper Deck 257
97/8 Upper Deck 275
98/9 Upper Deck 271
00/1 Upper Deck 269
01/2 Upper Deck 261
97/8 UD Coll. Choice 97
98/9 UD G. Reserve 271
99/0 UD MVP Cup 47
93/4 EDMO / Sheet
96/7 EDMO
97/8 EDMO
90/1 Prince Albert Raiders
91/2 Prince Albert Raiders

MCANDREW, HAZEN
34-43 BeeHive-1 [NYAm.]

MCANEELEY, TED
74/5 Loblaws
72/3 O-Pee-Chee 242
73/4 O-Pee-Chee 37
74/5 O-Pee-Chee 148
73/4 Topps 37
74/5 Topps 148

MCARTHUR, DARRYL
95/6 Slapshot 84
95/6 Guelph Storm
96/7 Guelph Storm

MCARTHUR, DEAN
82/3 Medicine Hat Tigers

MCARTHUR, DUSTIN
94/5 Slapshot / Sarnia 14
96/7 Peoria Rivermen

MCARTHUR, MARK
95/6 Edge Ice 194
95/6 Future Legends 33
94/5 Sig. Rookies 69, ✍ 69
93/4 Slapshot / Guelph 3
94/5 Slapshot / Guelph 2

MCASLAN, SEAN
98/9 Calgary Hitmen 8
99/0 Calgary Hitmen
00/1 Calgary Hitmen

MCAUSLAND, DARREN
00/1 Kudos 115
90/1 7th..Sketch WHL 7
91/2 7th...Sketch WHL 135
93/4 Portland Pirates
94/5 Portland Pirates
95/6 Portland Pirates
96/7 Portland Pirates
94/5 Wheeling Thund'birds

MCAVOY, KEEGAN
01/2 Kamloops Blazers

MCBAIN, ANDREW
95/6 Edge Ice 127
92/3 Fleer Ultra 147
88/9 Frito Lay
84/5 O-Pee-Chee 343
88/9 OPC/Topps 105
90/1 OPC/Topps 248
89/0 OPC/Topps 38
88/9 OPC Sticker 147
89/0 opcSticker 135
87/8 Panini Sticker 370
88/9 Panini Sticker 157
89/0 Panini Sticker 297
90/1 Panini/VAN 15
93/4 Premier 238
94/5 Premier 77
90/1 Pro Set 301
91/2 Pro Set 500
92/3 Pro Set 120
91/2 ProCards 605
90/1 Score 257
83/4 Vachon 133-13
92/3 OTTA
89/0 PITT / Foodland 13
90/1 VANC / Mohawk

83/4 WINN
84/5 WINN / Safety Tips
85/6 WINN
85/6 WINN / Safety Tips
86/7 WINN
87/8 WINN
88/9 WINN / Safety Tips
95/6 Fort Wayne Komets
94/5 Las Vegas Thunder
82/3 North Bay Centennials

MCBAIN, JASON
92/3 Classic 25
92/3 Classic Four Sport 174
93/4 Donruss USA14
95/6 Edge Ice 72
93/4 Pinnacle 483
90/1 7th..Sketch WHL 132
91/2 7th...Sketch WHL 48
93/4 Upper Deck 552
96/7 Upper Deck 189
00/1 UD DEL 157
01/2 UD DEL 222
97/8 Cleveland Lumberjacks
98/9 Las Vegas Thunder
96/7 Springfield Falcons
93/4 Portland Winter Hawks

MCBAIN, MIKE
97 Bowman 103
95/6 Classic 27
95/6 Do. Elite WJ 29
98/9 Pacific 401
94/5 Parkie SE252
94/5 Select 167
94/5 SP 176
95/6 Upper Deck 570
99/0 Québec Citadelles 1
00/1 Québec Citadelles
93/4 Red Deer Rebels
95/6 Red Deer Rebels

MCBEAN, WAYNE
91/2 Bowman 217
93/4 Leaf 413
91/2 O-Pee-Chee 62
92/3 O-Pee-Chee 50
91/2 Parkhurst 330
90/1 Pro Set 485
91/2 Pro Set 144
89/0 ProCards AHL 237
90/1 ProCards 502
91/2 Score CAN 530
92/3 Topps 443
91/2 To. Stadium 353
92/3 To. Stadium 397
93/4 To. Stadium 493
88/9 LOSA / Smokey
84/5 Medicine Hat Tigers

MCBETH, DON
59/60 Whitby Dunlops

MCBRIDE, BRANDON
01/2 Kingston Frontenacs 12

MCBRIDE, DARYN
90/1 ProCards 263
91/2 Cincinnati Cyclones

MCBURNEY, JIM
52/3 Anonymous 182

MCBURNIE, BOB
91/2 Avant Garde BCJHL 107

MCCABE, BRYAN
02/3 BAP Mem. 68
02/3 First Edition 126, ✂ Jers.
02/3 O-Pee-Chee 226, 322
02/3 Pacific 363
02/3 Pacific Complete 338
02/3 Parkhurst 170, -HHN 6
02/3 Parkhurst Retro 83
02/3 Signature 8, GS-17, ✍ 8, ✂ DW2
02/3 Sports Vault 139
02/3 Topps 226, 322
02/3 To. Chrome 124
02/3 To. Heritage ✍ Aut.
02/3 To. Limited 226, 322
02/3 T. Total 275
02/3 Upper Deck 161
02/3 UD Vintage 241
99/0 BAP Mem. 43
00/1 BAP Mem. 14, 446
95/6 Bowman 96
94/5 Cla. Images 91
93/4 Donruss CAN16
95/6 Donruss 333, 3TWC-8
96/7 Donruss 217
95/6 Fleer Ultra 348
96/7 Leaf 161
96/7 Metal Univ. 94
99/0 NHL Power Play
97/8 Omega 138
98/9 Pacific 430
99/0 Pacific 425
00/1 Pacific 97
97/8 Pacific CC 118
96/7 Panini Sticker 94
99/0 Panini Sticker 197
95/6 Parkhurst 256
94/5 Parkie SE209
93/4 Pinnacle 462
94/5 Pinnacle 523
96/7 Pi. Be A Player 162, ✍ Aut. 162
95/6 Pi. Summit 172
96/7 Pi. Summit 157
95/6 Pi. Zenith 138
95/6 POG 175
96/7 Score 253
95/6 Select CE 126
91/2 7th...Sketch WHL 331
01/2 Signature 146, ✍ Aut. 146
95/6 SBx Impact 209
94/5 Slapshot Memorial 34
94/5 SP 153
95/6 SP 91
99/0 SPx 38
99/0 Stadium 160

95/6 Topps 312, 7C
00/1 Topps 68
94/5 Topps Finest 150
95/6 To. Finest 54
96/7 To. Picks 175
95/6 To. Stadium 93
00/1 UD Heroes 112
93/4 Upper Deck 549
94/5 Upper Deck 502
95/6 Upper Deck 496
96/7 Upper Deck 99
97/8 Upper Deck 100
00/1 Upper Deck 40
95/6 UD CC 404
96/7 UD CC 161
97/8 UD Coll. Choice 157
01/2 UD Vintage 241
99/0 Victory 74
01/2 Victory 328
96/7 NYIS

MCCABE, JAMIE
02/3 Québec Remparts

MCCABE, JOHN
99/0 Mobile Mysticks

MCCABE, SCOTT
91/2 L. Superior State Lakers

MCCABE, TONY
90/1 7th..Sketch OHL 236
91/2 7th...Sketch OHL 77
90/1 Kitchener Rangers

MCCAFFREY, BERT
24/5 Champ's Cigarettes
25 Dominion Chocolates 60
29/0 La Presse
24/5 William Paterson 57

MCCAFFREY, CAM
01/2 Kamloops Blazers
02/3 Kamloops Blazers

MCCAFFREY, CHAD
01/2 Kitchener Rangers

MCCAFFREY, KEVIN
92/3 W. Michigan Broncos

MCCAGUE, MARK
90/1 7th..Sketch OHL 65

MCCAGUE, PETER
95/6 Slapshot 224

MCCAIG, DOUG
34-43 BeeHive-1 [Detr.]
45-64 BeeHive-2 [Chic.]

MCCAIG, ROB
99/0 Colorado Gold Kings
95/6 Louisiana Ice Gators
95/6 Louisiana Ice Gators-2
96/7 Louisiana Ice Gators

MCCALLION, PAUL
90/1 7th..Sketch OHL 237
91/2 7th...Sketch OHL 86
96/7 Guildford Flames 23
90/1 Kitchener Rangers

MCCALLUM, ANDY
52/3 St. Lawrence 93

MCCALLUM, DUNC
70/1 Esso Power Player
68/9 Shirriff / Pitt. 9
71/2 Topps 132

MCCALLUM, SCOTT
98/9 Brandon Wheat Kings
95/6 Tri-City Americans 14

MCCAMBRIDGE, KEITH
91/2 7th...Sketch WHL 186
94/5 Slapshot Memorial 5
99/0 Providence Bruins
00/1 Providence Bruins
01/2 Providence Bruins
95/6 Saint John Flames
96/7 Saint John Flames
97/8 Saint John Flames

MCCAMMON, BOB
90/1 Pro Set 678
85/6 EDMO / Red Rooster

MCCANN, DAVE
97/8 Las Vegas Thunder 27

MCCANN, GORDON
91/2 Air Canada SJHL C8
92/3 MPS SJHL 83

MCCANN, SEAN
94/5 Classic 55, AA5
94/5 Cincinnati Cyclones
96/7 Grand Rapids Griffins
98/9 Orlando Solar Bears
98/9 Orlando Solar Bears Geico

MCCARTAN, JACK
45-64 BeeHive-2 [NYRa.]
60/1 Shirriff 81
60/1 Topps 39

MCCARTHY, DOUG
00/1 Kudos 49
98/9 Phoenix Mustangs 14

MCCARTHY, JEREMIAH
95/6 Do. Elite WJ 30
00/1 Cincinnati Cyclones
99/0 Missouri RiverOtters

MCCARTHY, JOE
93/4 Raleigh Icecaps

MCCARTHY, KEVIN
83/4 Funmate Puffy 6 [w/]
79/0 O-Pee-Chee 287
80/1 O-Pee-Chee 21
81/2 O-Pee-Chee 341
82/3 O-Pee-Chee 351
83/4 O-Pee-Chee 356
84/5 O-Pee-Chee 178
81/2 OPC Sticker 248
82/3 OPC/Topps Sticker 246
83/4 OPC/Topps Sticker 279
84/5 OPC Sticker 119
80/1 Pepsi Bottle Cap
82/3 Post [Vanc.]
88/9 ProCards / Hershey

89/0 ProCards AHL 360
80/1 Topps 21
84/5 Topps 126
83/4 Vachon 112-32
79/0 VANC / Royal Bank
80/1 VANC
80/1 VANC / Silverwood
81/2 VANC
81/2 VANC / Silverwood
82/3 VANC
83/4 VANC

MCCARTHY, SANDY
02/3 O-Pee-Chee 79
02/3 Pacific 255
02/3 Pacific Complete 485
02/3 Signature ✂ FS12
02/3 Topps 79
02/3 To. Limited 79
02/3 T. Total 235
02/3 UD Vintage 165
98/9 Be A Player 282, ✍ Aut. 282
00/1 BAP Mem. 358, ✂ T-14
01/2 BAP Update ✂ TC15, ✂ TC39
91/2 Classic 42
93/4 Classic 142
91/2 Classic Four Sport 42
93/4 Cla. 4 Sport 241
93/4 Cla. Prospects 22
93/4 Donruss 59
94/5 Donruss 39
96/7 Donruss 42
93/4 Leaf 358
94/5 Leaf 411
99/0 Millenium 184, ✍ Aut. 184
98/9 OPC Chrome 82
98/9 Omega 220
98/9 Pacific 402
99/0 Pacific 308
01/2 Pacific 263, 416
98/9 Pa. Paramount 218
93/4 Parkhurst 30
94/5 POG / Western 5
93/4 Power Play 306
00/1 PS Titanium ✂ GUG 37
93/4 Score 633
96/7 Score 215
90/1 7th..Sketch LHJMQ 54
91/2 7th...Sketch LHJMQ 228
90 7th..Sketch Mem.Cup 53
97/8 SP Authentic 21
01/2 SP Authentic ✂ NN
98/9 Topps 82
98/9 To. Finest 124
00/1 To. Heritage 178
91/2 Upper Deck 77
93/4 Upper Deck 493
95/6 Upper Deck 361
96/7 Upper Deck 23
97/8 Upper Deck 25
98/9 Upper Deck 184
95/6 UD BAP 217, ✍ S217
96/7 UD CC 43
98/9 UD G. Reserve 184
92/3 Salt Lake G'Eagles

MCCARTHY, STEVE
02/3 First Edition 108, ✂ Jers.
02/3 Pacific Complete 236
99/0 BAP Mem. 319
00/1 BAP Mem. 26
01/2 BAP Mem. 269
99 Bowman 20, 97, ✍ BA40
00/1 Crown Royale 117, 21CR-6
99/0 Dynagon Ice 51
99/0 Millenium C-38
99/0 Omega 59
00/1 Pacific 98
00/1 Premier Plus 86
00/1 Private Stock 110
00/1 Signature 290, ✍ Aut. 220
98/9 SP Authentic 119, ✍ SotT
00/1 Stadium 229
00/1 Topps 293
00/1 To. Chrome 188
98/9 Upper Deck 396
98/9 UD G. Reserve 396
00/1 UD MVP SM
00/1 Vanguard 110
00/1 Victory 275
01/2 Victory 75
01/2 Norfolk Admirals

MCCARTHY, TOM J. (JUG)
80/1 O-Pee-Chee 93
81/2 O-Pee-Chee 164
82/3 O-Pee-Chee 169
83/4 O-Pee-Chee 176
84/5 O-Pee-Chee 103
87/8 OPC/Topps 38
81/2 OPC Sticker 95
83/4 OPC/Topps Sticker 115
84/5 OPC Sticker 52
87/8 OPC Sticker 141-250
87/8 Panini Sticker 13
82/3 Post [Minn.]
83/4 Souhaits Keychain [North Stars]
80/1 Topps 93
81/2 Topps 108 [West]
84/5 Topps 78
88/9 BOST / Sports Action
79/0 MINS
80/1 MINS
81/2 MINS
82/3 MINS
83/4 MINS
84/5 MINS
84/5 MINS / 7-Eleven 10
85/6 MINS
80/1 Oshawa Generals

MCCARTHY, TOM P.
57/8 Topps 37

MCCARTY, DARREN
02/3 BAP Mem. ✂ SCC11
02/3 First Edition 81, ✂ Jers.
02/3 Pacific Complete 42
02/3 Signature GS-27
02/3 T. Total 163
02/3 Ultimate Mem. ✂ SCDE, ✂ SCDGJ, ✂ SCDN
01/2 Atomic ✂ GWJ 23
98/9 Aurora 66
99/0 Aurora 52
98/9 Be A Player 50, ✍ Aut. 50
99/0 BAP Mem. 277
00/1 BAP Mem. 275, ✂ TM-13, ✂ T-11
98/9 Bowman's Best 79
92/3 Classic Prospects 147
93/4 Cla. Prospects 23
93/4 Donruss 103
94/5 Donruss 237
95/6 Donruss 313
97/8 Donruss 107
97/8 Do. Elite 84
97/8 Do. Preferred 114
97/8 Do. Priority 146
98/9 Dynagon Ice 66
99/0 Dynagon Ice 76
95/6 Edge Ice C19
93/4 Fleer Ultra 307
94/5 Fleer Ultra 63
95/6 Fleer Ultra 235, CC-9
93/4 Leaf 435
94/5 Leaf 197
95/6 Leaf 320
97/8 Leaf 88
97/8 Limited 72
01/2 O-Pee-Chee 100
98/9 OPC Chrome 105
97/8 Omega 84
98/9 Omega 84
98/9 Pacific 201, -TW 7
99/0 Pacific 144
00/1 Pacific 155
01/2 Pacific 147, 410
97/8 Pacific CC 163
97/8 Pa. Crown Roy. 48
98/9 Pa. Crown Roy. 46
97/8 Pa. Paramount 68
98/9 Pa. Paramount 79
99/0 Pa. Paramount 84
97/8 Pa. Revolution 48
98/9 Pa. Revolution 50, -TPA 4
93/4 Parkhurst 265
95/6 Parkhurst 341
01/2 Parkhurst ✂ PJ36, ✂ PS43
94/5 Pinnacle 180
95/6 Pinnacle 176
97/8 Pinnacle 176
96/7 Pi. Be A Player 175, ✍ Aut. 175
94/5 POG 89
95/6 POG 103
93/4 Power Play 333
93/4 Premier 412
94/5 Premier 203, OF-19
00/1 PS Titanium Draft ✂ 39
93/4 Score 631
94/5 Score 258
97/8 Score 190
97/8 Score Detr. 6
89/0 7th..Sketch OHL 77
90/1 7th..Sketch OHL 12
91/2 7th...Sketch OHL 113
00/1 Signature 59, ✍ Aut. 92
97/8 SP Authentic 57, ✍ SotT
00/1 Stadium ✂ SCS-7
01/2 Stadium 53, ✂ SCSD
95/6 Topps 28
98/9 Topps 105
99/0 Topps 188
00/1 Topps 214, ✂ GWS
01/2 Topps 100
99/0 To. Chrome 188
01/2 To. Chrome 100
01/2 To. Reserve ✂ TR
93/4 To. Stadium 441
00/1 To. Stars ✂ GG-DM
98/9 UD Choice 72, RW6
00/1 Ultimate Mem. ✂ D-18
93/4 Upper Deck 508
94/5 Upper Deck 365
95/6 Upper Deck 301
96/7 Upper Deck 55
97/8 Upper Deck 59, 390
98/9 Upper Deck 266
00/1 Upper Deck 64
01/2 Upper Deck 64
96/7 UD CC 89
97/8 UD Coll. Choice 83
98/9 UD G. Reserve 266
98/9 UD MVP 73
00/1 UD MVP 71
01/2 UD MVP 70
01/2 UD SCup Champs 62
00/1 UD Vintage 131
01/2 UD Vintage 94
00/1 Vanguard ✂ DGJ 13
99/0 Victory 107
01/2 Victory 128
99/0 DETR / News 5

MCCASKILL, TED
72/3 Los Angeles Sharks

MCCAUGHEY, BRAD
88/9 ProCards / Peoria
98/9 Phoenix Mustangs 23
92/3 Phoenix Roadrunners

MCCAULEY, ALEX
96/7 Sudbury Wolves
98/9 Sudbury Wolves 1

99/0 Sudbury Wolves 1
00/1 Sudbury Wolves 1

MCCAULEY, ALYN
02/3 BAP Mem. 38
02/3 Exclusive 160
02/3 First Edition 38, ✂ Jers.
02/3 Heads Up 115
02/3 Pacific 364
02/3 Pacific Complete 31
02/3 Parkhurst 140
02/3 Signature 36, GS-7, ✍ 36
02/3 To. Heritage 93
02/3 T. Total 56
02/3 Upper Deck 410
02/3 UD MVP 171
02/3 UD Vintage 242
98/9 Be A Player 138, ✍ Aut. 138
97 Bowman 5
94/5 Classic DP5
95/6 Classic 53, 92
95/6 Do. Elite WJ 18
97/8 Do. Elite 38, 117
97/8 Do. Preferred 153
97/8 Do. Priority 181, 206, 220, DD-20
98/9 Dynagon Ice 183
97/8 Leaf 152
98/9 OPC Chrome 79
98/9 Omega 230
98/9 Pacific 418
99/0 Pacific 413
97/8 Pa. Crown Roy. 130
97/8 Pa. Dynagon Rookie
97/8 Pa. Paramount 182
94/5 Parkie SE264
97/8 Pinnacle 18
97/8 Pi. Be A Player 222, ✍ Aut. 222
97/8 Pi. BeeHive 55, ✍ Aut. 55
97/8 Pi. Certified G
97/8 Pi. Mint 28
97/8 Score 52
97/8 Score Toro. 17
94/5 Select 162
94/5 Sig. Rookies 47, ✍ 47
01/2 Signature 124, ✍ Aut. 124
95/6 Slapshot 278
94/5 SP 183
95/6 SP 173
97/8 SP Authentic 195
98/9 SPx Finite 83, 132
98/9 Topps 79
98/9 T. Gold Label 79
98/9 UD Choice 200
98/9 UD3 8, 68, 128
97/8 Upper Deck 371
98/9 Upper Deck 185
96/7 UD Black Diam. 78
97/8 UD Black Diam. 128
97/8 UD Coll. Choice 299
98/9 UD G. Reserve 185
96/7 UD Ice 129
98/9 UD MVP 198, ✍ PS
99/0 UD MVP Cup 179
97/8 Zenith 88, RR-11, Z70
99/0 TORO / Pizza Pizza 11

MCCAULEY, BILL
93/4 Cla. 4 Sport 213
93/4 Slapshot / Detroit 10
94/5 Slapshot / Detroit Jr. 12
94/5 Slapshot Memorial 86
97/8 Charlotte Checkers
96/7 Providence Bruins

MCCAULEY, WES
93/4 Knoxville Cherokees
94/5 Muskegon Fury

MCCLANAHAN, ROB
83/4 Funmate Puffy 20 [w/]
80/1 O-Pee-Chee 232
83/4 O-Pee-Chee 251
84/5 O-Pee-Chee 325
80 Olympic USA
94/5 SR Miracle 19,20, ✍ 19,20
83/4 Souhaits Keychain [Rangers]
80/1 Topps 232

MCCLEARY, TRENT
95/6 Bowman 135
95/6 Fleer Ultra 280
95/6 Parkhurst 420
90/1 7th..Sketch WHL 50
91/2 7th...Sketch WHL 190
99/0 Topps 212
99/0 To. Chrome 212
95/6 OTTA
97/8 Detroit Vipers
93/4 Thunder Bay Senators

MCCLELLAND, DARWIN
88/9 Kamloops Blazers

MCCLELLAND, KEVIN
84/5 O-Pee-Chee 253
87/8 O-Pee-Chee 201
90/1 OPC/Topps 389
85/6 OPC Sticker 230-99
86/7 OPC Sticker 77-205
91/2 ProCards 344
90/1 Score 287
89/0 DETR / Little Caesars
90/1 DETR / Little Caesars
83/4 EDMO / Button
83/4 EDMO / McDonald's
83/4 EDMO / West Mall
83/4 EDMO
84/5 EDMO
84/5 EDMO / Red Rooster
85/6 EDMO / Red Rooster
86/7 EDMO
86/7 EDMO / Red Rooster
87/8 EDMO
88/9 EDMO

88/9 EDMO / Action 109
83/4 PITT / Heinz
92/3 St. John's Maple Leafs
00/1 St. John's Maple Leafs
01/2 St. John's Maple Leafs

MCCLELLAND, KEVIN
02/3 Fleer Throwbacks 44

MCCLEMENT, JAY
00/1 UD Prospects 2, 96
01 UD Prospects GU 8, ✂ TPJ, ✂✍ TPJS, ✂ JC, ✍ SoT
99/0 Brampton Batallion 17

MCCOLGAN, GARY
88/9 ProCards / Kalamazoo
83/4 Oshawa Generals

MCCONNELL, BRIAN
97 Québec Pee Wee 1158

MCCONNELL, DON
89/0 7th..Sketch OHL 146
90/1 7th..Sketch OHL 265
89/0 Niagara Falls Thunder
87/8 Soo Greyhounds 10

MCCONNELL, RYAN
92/3 MPS SJHL 113

MCCOOL, FRANK
45-54 Quaker Oats

MCCORD, BOB
52/3 Anonymous 130
64-67 BeeHive-3 [Bost.]
64/5 Coke/Sprite [Bost.]
68/9 O-Pee-Chee 146
69/0 O-Pee-Chee 123
70/1 O-Pee-Chee 41
95/6 Parkie 66-67 43
94/5 Parkie Tall 10
68/9 Shirriff / Minn. 11
63/4 Topps 6
64/5 Topps 10
65/6 Topps 46
69/0 Topps 123
70/1 Topps 41
72/3 SLOU

MCCORMACK, JOHN (GOOSE)
45-64 BeeHive-2 [Toro.]
45-64 BeeHive-2 [Mont.]
51/2 La Patrie
52/3 Parkhurst 15
53/4 Parkhurst 34
54/5 Parkhurst 9
45-54 Quaker Oats

MCCORMICK, CODY
01/2 Belleville Bulls

MCCORMICK, JOE
23/4 Paulins Candy 43

MCCORMICK, MIKE
97/8 Fort Worth Brahmas

MCCORMICK, MORGAN
99/0 Guelph Storm
01/2 Guelph Storm
01/2 Guelph Storm M-Cup

MCCOSH, SHAWN
92/3 Classic 111
92/3 Classic Four Sport 217
99/0 Eishockey 6
90/1 ProCards 436
91/2 ProCards 390
94/5 Binghampton Rangers
92/3 Phoenix Roadrunners
88/9 Niagara Falls Thunder

MCCOSH, SHAYNE
00/1 Kudos 145
90/1 7th..Sketch OHL 238, 370
91/2 7th...Sketch OHL 91
93/4 Slapshot / Detroit 20
93/4 Slapshot / Windsor 13
94/5 Slapshot / Detroit Jr. 22
94/5 Slapshot Memorial 96
01/2 Sheffield Steelers GS
90/1 Kitchener Rangers

MCCOURT, DALE
98/9 DEL 131
79/0 Dernière Heure
83/4 Funmate Puffy 11 [w/]
78/9 O-Pee-Chee 132
79/0 O-Pee-Chee 63
80/1 O-Pee-Chee 245
81/2 O-Pee-Chee 86
81/2 O-Pee-Chee 96
81/2 O-Pee-Chee 105
82/3 O-Pee-Chee 28
83/4 O-Pee-Chee 66
81/2 OPC Sticker 120
82/3 OPC/Topps Sticker 119
83/4 OPC/Topps Sticker 236
84/5 OPC Sticker 13
81/2 Post 4
82/3 Post [Buff.]
83/4 Souhaits Keychain [Sabres]
78/9 Topps 132
79/0 Topps 63
80/1 Topps 245
81/2 Topps 21
81/2 Topps 51
81/2 Topps 129 [West]
83/4 Vachon 93-119
81/2 BUFF / Wendt's 14
82/3 BUFF / Wendt's 14
79/0 DETR
80/1 DETR

MCCOURT, DAN
90/1 Pro Set 693

MCCOURT, MIKE
99/0 Muskegon Fury
94/5 Thunder Bay Senators

87/8 Brockville Braves
88/9 Brockville Braves

MCCOY, MARK
90/1 7th..Sketch WHL 68
91/2 7th...Sketch WHL 181

MCCRACKEN, JAKE
97/8 Upper Deck 400
96/7 Soo Greyhounds

MCCRADY, SCOTT
88/9 ProCards / Kalamazoo
90/1 ProCards 614
84/5 Medicine Hat Tigers

MCCREARY, BILL (SR.)
70/1 Esso Power Player
68/9 O-Pee-Chee 182
69/0 O-Pee-Chee 181

MCCREARY, BILL*
90/1 Pro Set 694

MCCREARY, BILL?
73/4 VANC / Royal Bank

MCCREARY, KEITH
70/1 Colgate 34
70/1 Dad's Cookies
70/1 Eddie Sargent 168
71/2 Eddie Sargent 174
72/3 Eddie Sargent 4
70/1 Esso Power Player
74/5 Loblaws
68/9 O-Pee-Chee 193
69/0 O-Pee-Chee 114
69/0 O-Pee-Chee 4in1
69/0 O-Pee-Chee Stamp
70/1 O-Pee-Chee 93
71/2 O-Pee-Chee 188
72/3 O-Pee-Chee 25
73/4 O-Pee-Chee 13
74/5 O-Pee-Chee 14
74/5 O-Pee-Chee 103
68/9 Shirriff / Pitt. 10
69/0 Topps 114
70/1 Topps 93
72/3 Topps 27
73/4 Topps 13
74/5 Topps 14
74/5 Topps 103
71/2 Toronto Sun Photo
91/2 Ultimate Original Six 98
72/3 ATLF
74/5 ATLF
71/2 PITT / Sportcolor

MCCREARY, MARK
93/4 Toledo Storm 15

MCCREARY, WILLIAM
52/3 Anonymous 59

MCCREEDY, JOHNNY
34-43 BeeHive-1 [Toro.]

MCCRIMMON, BRAD
91/2 Bowman 48
92/3 Bowman 67
92/3 Fleer Ultra 52
84/5 Kelowna Wings &...
93/4 Leaf 395
80/1 O-Pee-Chee 354
81/2 O-Pee-Chee 15
82/3 O-Pee-Chee 255
83/4 O-Pee-Chee 270
84/5 O-Pee-Chee 164
85/6 OPC/Topps 158
86/7 OPC/Topps 5
87/8 OPC/Topps 85
88/9 OPC/Topps 178
90/1 OPC/Topps 320
91/2 O-Pee-Chee 79
89/0 O-Pee-Chee 203
87/8 OPC Leaders 27
90/1 OPC Premier 69
88/9 OPC Stars 24
82/3 OPC/Topps Sticker 90
83/4 OPC/Topps Sticker 193
85/6 OPC Sticker 92-225
86/7 OPC Sticker 247
87/8 OPC Sticker 99-233
88/9 OPC Sticker 96
88/9 OPC Sticker 120-250
88/9 OPC Sticker 206-77
89/0 opcSticker 91
97/8 Pa. Dynagon BKS-75
87/8 Panini Sticker 121
87/8 Panini Sticker 126
88/9 Panini Sticker 6
88/9 Panini Sticker 408
89/0 Panini Sticker 31, 33
90/1 Panini Sticker 173
96/7 Panini Sticker 33
91/2 Parkhurst 271
93/4 Parkhurst 358
91/2 Pinnacle 214
92/3 Pinnacle 124
93/4 Pinnacle 358
94/5 Pinnacle 427
96/7 Pi. Be A Player 168, ✍ Aut. 168
82/3 Post [Bost.]
93/4 Premier 391
90/1 Pro Set 39, 438
91/2 Pro Set 377
91/2 Pro Set 609
91/2 Pro Set Platinum 170
90/1 Score 184, 37T
91/2 Score 16
91/2 Score CAN 16
92/3 Score 141
93/4 Score 527
93/4 Score 54
89 Semic Sticker 63
83/4 Souhaits Keychain [Flyers]
88/9 OPC/Topps - Stick. 10
92/3 Topps 301
91/2 To. Stadium 14
92/3 To. Stadium 21
90/1 Upper Deck 294, 430
95/6 UD BAP 51, ✍ S51
87/8 CALG / Red Rooster

90/1 DETR / Little Caesars
91/2 DETR / Little Caesars
93/4 HART / Coke
95/6 HART / Kids Club
83/4 PHIL / J.C. Penney
86/7 PHIL
96/7 PHOE / Coca-Cola

MCCRIMMON, KELLY
90/1 7th..Sketch WHL 214
91/2 7th...Sketch WHL 216
88/9 Brandon Wheat Kings
90/1 Brandon Wheat Kings

MCCRONE, JOHN
94 Semic 313

MCCRORY, SCOTT
98/9 DEL 209
99/0 Eishockey 204
88/9 ProCards / Baltimore
89/0 ProCards AHL 282
90/1 ProCards 275
95/6 Houston Aeros

MCCULLOUGH, SCOTT
87/8 Sudbury Wolves

MCCUNE, GRANT
99/0 Kamloops Blazers
99/0 Kamloops Blazers

MCCUSKER, DON
91/2 Avant Garde BCJHL 123
93/4 N. Michigan Wildcats

MCCUSKER, RED
23/4 Paulins Candy 24

MCCUTCHEON, DARWIN
88/9 ProCards / Indianapolis
86/7 Moncton G'Flames
98/9 Rochester Americans
88/9 Salt Lake G'Eagles

MCCUTCHEON, DAVID
98/9 Halifax Moosehead

MCCUTCHEON, JUSTIN
00/1 Kingston Frontenacs 13
01/2 Kingston Frontenacs 13

MCCUTCHEON, WARREN
99/0 Lethbridge Hurricanes

MCCUTHEON, JEFF
92/3 MPS SJHL 60

MCDADE, RORY
98/9 SP Authentic 128, ✍ SotT
98/9 Upper Deck 405
98/9 UD G. Reserve 405
98/9 Kelowna Rockets
00/1 Kelowna Rockets

MCDONAGH, BILL
45-64 BeeHive-2 [NYRa.]
51/2 Laval Dairy 52

MCDONALD, AB
45-64 BeeHive-2 [Mont.]
45-64 BeeHive-2 [Chic.]
64-67 BeeHive-3 [Bost.]
64-67 BeeHive-3 [Detr.]
64/5 Coke/Sprite [Bost.]
65/6 Coca-Cola
70/1 Dad's Cookies
70/1 Eddie Sargent 178
71/2 Eddie Sargent 59
70/1 Esso Power Player
62/3 Cowan Tile
68/9 O-Pee-Chee 107
68/9 O-Pee-Chee 180
69/0 O-Pee-Chee 18
70/1 O-Pee-Chee 215
71/2 O-Pee-Chee 134
72/3 O-Pee-Chee 321
58/9 Parkhurst 30
59/0 Parkhurst 20
60/1 Parkhurst 56
60/1 Parkhurst 60
95/6 Parkie 66-67 50
94/5 Parkie Tall 14
60/1 Shirriff 72
61/2 Shirriff 33
68/9 Shirriff / SLou. 12
60/1 Topps 33
61/2 Topps 27
62/3 Topps 38
62/3 Topps Dollar
63/4 Topps 37
64/5 Topps 16
65/6 Topps 50
68/9 Topps 107
69/0 Topps 18
58/9 Toronto Star Photo
62/3 Toronto Star Weekend
71/2 Toronto Sun Photo
91/2 Ultimate Original Six 60, ✍ Aut. 60
92/3 SLOU / McDon. 8

MCDONALD, ANDY
02/3 First Edition 207
02/3 O-Pee-Chee 91
02/3 Pacific 6
02/3 Pacific Complete 272
02/3 Signature 15, GS-8, ✍ 15
02/3 SP Authentic 106
02/3 Topps 91
02/3 To. Limited 91
02/3 T. Total 48
02/3 Upper Deck 5
02/3 UD MVP 4
02/3 UD Vintage 8
01/2 BAP Mem. 212, 397
01/2 Parkhurst 352
01/2 PS Titanium Draft 102
00/1 SP Authentic 92
00/1 SP GU 62
01/2 Upper Deck 4
00/1 UD Ice 103
00/1 UD Pros&Prosp. 92
01/2 Cincinnati Mighty Ducks

MCDONALD, BILL
97/8 Fort Worth Brahmas

MCDONALD, BRENT
00/1 Florida Everblades
01/2 Florida Everblades
95/6 Red Deer Rebels

MCDONALD, BRIAN
91/2 Avant Garde BCJHL 131

MCDONALD, BUCKO
34-43 BeeHive-1 [Toro.]
39/0 O-Pee-Chee 13
37/8 World Wide Gum 84

MCDONALD, DAVID
01/2 Regina Pats

MCDONALD, DEAN
91/2 Knoxville Cherokees

MCDONALD, JACK
91 C55 Reprint 8
10/1 Imperial
11/2 Imperial 8
12/3 Imperial 17

MCDONALD, KEVIN
98/9 Florida Everblades

MCDONALD, LANNY
02/3 Parkhurst ✂ VT20
02/3 Ultimate Mem. ✂ Cor, ✂ FS, ✂ RAT, ✂ VGJ
02/3 UD Foundations ✂ 1000Stick, ✍ SG
01/2 ASG History
99/0 BAP Mem. CH-6, ✍ CH-6
01/2 BAP Mem. ✂ 500GS
88/9 Esso All-Star
83/4 Esso Stars
01/2 Fleer Greats 53, ✍ Aut.
01/2 Fleer Legacy 58, ✂ ITC
83/4 Funmate Puffy 6 [w/]
92/3 Future Trends C76 174
75/6 Hockey Heroes
93/4 Hockey Wit 85
84/5 Kellogg's 12
86/7 Kraft Sports 3
93/4 Legends of Hockey 34
74/5 Loblaws
74/5 O-Pee-Chee 168
75/6 O-Pee-Chee 23
76/7 O-Pee-Chee 348
77/8 O-Pee-Chee 5
77/8 O-Pee-Chee 110
78/9 O-Pee-Chee 78
79/0 OPC 5
79/0 O-Pee-Chee 153
80/1 O-Pee-Chee 62
81/2 O-Pee-Chee 77
81/2 O-Pee-Chee 85
82/3 O-Pee-Chee 38
82/3 O-Pee-Chee 51
82/3 O-Pee-Chee 52
83/4 O-Pee-Chee 74
83/4 O-Pee-Chee 75
83/4 O-Pee-Chee 87
83/4 O-Pee-Chee 208
84/5 O-Pee-Chee 231
85/6 OPC/Topps 1
86/7 OPC/Topps 8
86/7 OPC/Topps Box J
87/8 OPC/Topps 20
88/9 OPC/Topps 234
89/0 OPC/Topps 7
81/2 OPC Sticker 227
82/3 OPC/Topps Sticker 214
83/4 OPC/Topps Sticker 8
83/4 OPC/Topps Sticker 162
83/4 OPC/Topps Sticker 263
83/4 OPC/Topps Sticker 303
84/5 OPC Sticker 237
84/5 OPC Sticker 238
85/6 OPC Sticker 215
86/7 OPC Sticker 80
87/8 OPC Sticker 43
88/9 OPC Sticker 85-215
89/0 opcSticker 92-231
80/1 O-Pee-Chee Super 5
87/8 Panini Sticker 215
88/9 Panini Sticker 10
89/0 Panini Sticker 39
01/2 Parkhurst ✂ 500GS, ✂ PS65, ✍ PA19
92/3 Pinnacle 242
82/3 Post [Calg.]
84/5 7-Eleven
85/6 7-Eleven Superstars 3
01/2 Signature ✂ 500GS, ✍ VA39
83/4 Souhaits Keychain [Flames]
82/3 Stater Mint 3
83/4 Stater Mint H1
74/5 Topps 168
75/6 Topps 23
77/8 Topps 5
77/8 Topps 110
78/9 Topps 78
79/0 Topps 5
79/0 Topps 153
80/1 Topps 62
81/2 Topps 50
81/2 Topps 82 [West]
84/5 Topps 26
99/0 Topps SC5, ✍ SCH
01/2 Ultimate Mem. ✂ 500GS, ✂ ASGH, ✂ Corn., ✂ RN, ✂ RA
90/1 Upper Deck 508
00/1 UD Legends 19, ✍ ES
01/2 UD Legends 9, ✂ M
92/3 UD Locker 45
99/0 UD Retro 95, DR13, ✍ Ink.
83/4 Vachon 13-133
83/4 Vachon 13-95
94/5 Zellers, ✍ Aut.
81/2 CALG
82/3 CALG

85/6 CALG / Red Rooster
85/6 CALG / Red Rooster
86/7 CALG / Red Rooster
86/7 CALG / Red Rooster
87/8 CALG / Red Rooster
79/0 COLR
73/4 TORO
74/5 TORO
75/6 TORO
76/7 TORO
77/8 TORO
78/9 TORO
79/0 TORO

MCDONALD, LANNY
02/3 Fleer Throwbacks 20

MCDONALD, NOLAN
97/8 Fort Worth Brahmas

MCDONALD, RANDY
74/5 Sioux City Musketeers

MCDONALD, RONALD
83/4 Oshawa Generals

MCDONALD, STEVE
92/3 Semic Nordisk 177

MCDONALD, T
85/6 Minnesota-Duluth 34

MCDONALD, WALKER
95/6 Slapshot 46
98/9 Wichita Thunder

MCDONALD, WILFRED
34-43 BeeHive-1 [Detr.]
34-43 BeeHive-1 [Detr.]

MCDONELL, KENT
99 Bowman 149
01/2 Syracuse Crunch
96/7 Guelph Storm

MCDONNELL, JOE
90 7th..Sketch Mem.Cup 26
90/1 7th..Sketch OHL 248
91/2 7th...Sketch OHL 97
93/4 Slapshot / Kitchener 27
83/4 Moncton Alpines
86/7 Kitchener Rangers
87/8 Kitchener Rangers
88/9 Kitchener Rangers
89/0 Kitchener Rangers
90/1 Kitchener Rangers

MCDONNELL, KENT
02/3 Syracuse Crunch
99/0 Guelph Storm

MCDONOUGH, AL
71/2 O-Pee-Chee 150
72/3 O-Pee-Chee 235
73/4 O-Pee-Chee 89
75/6 OPC WHA 33
76/7 OPC WHA 77
73/4 Topps 176
71/2 Toronto Sun Photo

MCDONOUGH, HUBIE
90/1 Bowman 120
91/2 Bowman 214
94/5 Cla. Images 29
95/6 Edge Ice QM 5
90/1 OPC/Topps 366
91/2 O-Pee-Chee 389
90/1 Panini Sticker 92
90/1 Pro Set 188
88/9 ProCards / New Haven
91/2 ProCards 473
90/1 Score 222
91/2 Score CAN 450
91/2 To. Stadium 260
92/3 To. Stadium 335
90/1 Upper Deck 226
91/2 Upper Deck 138
89/0 New Haven Nighthawks
98/9 Orlando Solar Bears
98/9 Orlando Solar Bears Geico
92/3 San Diego Gulls
93/4 San Diego Gulls

MCDONOUGH, KYLE
92/3 Semic Nordisk 142

MCDOUGALL, BILL
93/4 Cla. 4 Sport 242
93/4 Donruss 323
99/0 Eishockey 330
93/4 Fleer Ultra 426
93/4 Leaf 379
93/4 Parkhurst 463
90/1 ProCards 481
91/2 ProCards 133
93/4 Upper Deck 324
93/4 Atlanta Knights

MCDOUGALL, KEVIN
90/1 7th..Sketch OHL 289
89/0 Windsor Spitfires

MCDOUGALL, THOMAS
51/2 Bas du Fleuve 20
51/2 Laval Dairy 45
52/3 St. Lawrence 84

MCDOWALL, DAVE
90/1 ProCards 413
91/2 CHIC / Coke
82/3 Brandon Wheat Kings

MCDUFFE, PETER
74/5 Loblaws
71/2 O-Pee-Chee 225
74/5 O-Pee-Chee 173
75/6 O-Pee-Chee 256
74/5 Topps 173
75/6 Topps 256
71/2 Toronto Sun Photo

MCEACHERN, ALI
00/1 Halifax Moosehead

MCEACHERN, SHAWN
02/3 First Edition 125, ✂ Jers.
02/3 Pacific 270
02/3 Pacific Complete 324
02/3 Signature 79, ✍ 79
02/3 Sports Vault 9

02/3 To. Heritage 171
02/3 T. Total 71
02/3 Upper Deck 256
02/3 UD Honor 72
01/2 Adrenaline 136
98/9 Aurora 131
99/0 Aurora 100
00/1 Aurora 102
98/9 Be A Player 248, ✍ Aut. 248
99/0 BAP Mem. 108
00/1 BAP Mem. 148
01/2 BAP Mem. 81
92/3 Bowman 415
93/4 Donruss 154
93/4 Donruss 473
94/5 Donruss 95
95/6 Donruss 373
96/7 Donruss 190
98/9 Dynagon Ice 128
94/5 Flair 136
94/5 Fleer 164
95/6 Fleer Metal 8
92/3 Fleer Ultra 379
93/4 Fleer Ultra 133
93/4 Fleer Ultra 345
94/5 Fleer Ultra 166
95/6 Fleer Ultra 205
93/4 Leaf 217
93/4 Leaf GLR 7
94/5 Leaf 232
96/7 Leaf 9
99/0 Millenium 176, ✍ Aut. 176
92/3 O-Pee-Chee 359
01/2 O-Pee-Chee 206
92/3 OPC Premier 94
97/8 Omega 156
98/9 Omega 166
99/0 Omega 161
98/9 Pacific 313
99/0 Pacific 291
00/1 Pacific 283
01/2 Pacific 276
97/8 Pacific CC 224
97/8 Pa. Crown Roy. 91
98/9 Pa. Crown Roy. 94
98/9 Pa. Paramount 164
99/0 Pa. Paramount 163
00/1 Pa. Paramount 175
97/8 Pa. Revolution 93
98/9 Pa. Revolution 100
92/3 Panini Sticker 222
93/4 Panini Sticker 84
96/7 Panini Sticker 7
99/0 Panini Sticker 113
00/1 Panini Sticker 71
91/2 Parkhurst 355
92/3 Parkhurst 142
93/4 Parkhurst 242
93/4 Parkhurst 364
94/5 Parkhurst 173
95/6 Parkhurst 280
00/1 Parkhurst P-120
01/2 Parkhurst 120
92/3 Pinnacle 420
93/4 Pinnacle 105
93/4 Pinnacle T2K1 9
94/5 Pinnacle 127
96/7 Pi. Be A Player 119, ✍ Aut. 119
95/6 Pi. Summit 155
94/5 POG 186
95/6 POG 28
93/4 Power Play 119
93/4 Power Play SYS 7
93/4 Premier 123
93/4 Premier 353
93/4 Prmr. - BG-Top. 4
94/5 Premier 354
99/0 Prism 97
92/3 Pro Set 237
99/0 Revolution 103, / CSC 103
00/1 Revolution 105
92/3 Score 459
93/4 Score 497
93/4 Score 67
94/5 Score 108
95/6 Score 81
96/7 Score 151
93/4 Seasons 11
00/1 Signature 149
01/2 Signature 45, ✍ Aut. 45
94/5 Sisu 348, GS-4
95/6 SP 10
97/8 SP Authentic 110
00/1 Stadium 80
92/3 Topps 481
95/6 Topps 321
00/1 Topps 160
01/2 Topps 206
95/6 To. Finest 91
01/2 To. Reserve ✂ TR
92/3 To. Stadium 205
93/4 To. Stadium 189
94/5 To. Stadium 211
95/6 To. Stadium 83
98/9 UD Choice 138
92/3 Upper Deck 368
92/3 Upper Deck 412
92/3 Upper Deck 565
92/3 Upper Deck 634
92/3 Upper Deck CC14
92/3 Upper Deck G17
93/4 Upper Deck 454, SP-72
94/5 Upper Deck 163
95/6 Upper Deck 360, SE-95
98/9 Upper Deck 142
99/0 Upper Deck 93
00/1 Upper Deck 125
01/2 Upper Deck 350
94/5 UD BAP R75, ✍ 101
95/6 UD CC 145
96/7 UD CC 20
97/8 UD Coll. Choice 180
98/9 UD G. Reserve 142

99/0 UD G. Reserve 93
98/9 UD MVP 143
99/0 UD MVP 145
00/1 UD MVP 128
01/2 UD MVP 132
00/1 UD Vintage 254
01/2 UD Vintage 180
99/0 Victory 202
00/1 Victory 161
01/2 Victory 243
96/7 OTTA
97/8 OTTA
98/9 OTTA
99/0 OTTA
00/1 OTTA
01/2 OTTA
92/3 PITT / Coke-Clark
92/3 PITT / Foodland 9
92/3 PITT / Food. Stickers
94/5 PITT / Foodland 3

MCELMURY, JIM
75/6 O-Pee-Chee 14
77/8 O-Pee-Chee 352
72 Semic Sticker 119
75/6 Topps 14

MCELWEE, MATT
95/6 Dayton Bombers

MCENANEY, PETE
94/5 Anchorage Aces 20

MCEWEN, BRAD
91/2 Air Canada SJHL 23
92/3 MPS SJHL 95

MCEWEN, DENNIS
91/2 Hampton Roads
93/4 Hampton Roads
94/5 Hampton Roads
98/9 Hampton Roads
86/7 London Knights

MCEWEN, DOUG
94 Semic 326
02/3 Peterborough Phantoms

MCEWEN, HUGH
90/1 Michigan Tech Huskies
91/2 Michigan Tech Huskies

MCEWEN, MICHAEL
91/2 ProCards 374

MCEWEN, MIKE
77/8 O-Pee-Chee 232
78/9 O-Pee-Chee 187
79/0 O-Pee-Chee 66
80/1 O-Pee-Chee 185
81/2 O-Pee-Chee 215
82/3 O-Pee-Chee 207
82/3 Post [NYIs.]
77/8 Topps 232
78/9 Topps 187
79/0 Topps 66
80/1 Topps 185
79/0 COLR
86/7 HART / Jr. Whalers

MCFADDEN, JIM
45-64 BeeHive-2 [Detr.]
45-64 BeeHive-2 [Chic.]
51/2 Parkhurst 44
52/3 Parkhurst 38
53/4 Parkhurst 77

MCFARLANE, MARK
90/1 7th..Sketch WHL 51
97/8 Quad City Mallards
98/9 Quad City Mallards
99/0 Quad City Mallards
00/1 Quad City Mallards

MCFATRIDGE, SEAN
91/2 7th...Sketch WHL 108
92/3 Brandon Wheat Kings
91/2 Saskatoon Blades

MCFAYDEN, DONNIE
36-39 Diamond Match TT1
36-39 Diamond Match TT2
36-39 Diamond Match TT3

MCFEE, DALE
84/5 Prince Albert Raiders

MCGARVEY, WILLIE
89/0 7th..Sketch OHL 111

MCGEE, FRANK
83 HHOF Postcard D10
83&87 HHOF 56

MCGEOUGH, JIM
89/0 ProCards IHL 116
90/1 ProCards 315
92/3 Richmond Renegades
98/9 Wichita Thunder

MCGHAN, MIKE
93/4 Prince Albert Raiders
95/6 Prince Albert Raiders

MCGILL, BOB
92/3 Bowman 429
82/3 O-Pee-Chee 327
91/2 O-Pee-Chee 216
91/2 OPC Premier 8
85/6 OPC Sticker 15-145
91/2 Pinnacle 98
82/3 Post [Toro.]
90/1 Pro Set 55
91/2 Pro Set 47
91/2 Pro Set 480
90/1 Score 49T
91/2 Score 368
91/2 Score 10T
91/2 Score CAN 327
91/2 Score CAN 560
92/3 Score 386
92/3 Topps 209
92/3 To. Stadium 483
91/2 Upper Deck 62
87/8 CHIC / Coke
88/9 CHIC / Coke
89/0 CHIC / Coke
90/1 CHIC / Coke
91/2 SANJ / Sports Action
81/2 TORO
84/5 TORO
85/6 TORO

86/7 TORO
86/7 TORO

MCGILL, JACK
35-40 Canada Starch
36-39 Diamond Match TT1
36-39 Diamond Match TT2
36-39 Diamond Match TT3
35/6 O-Pee-Chee 74
34/5 Sweet Caporal
37/8 World Wide Gum 77

MCGILL, RYAN
92/3 Fleer Ultra 373
93/4 Fleer Ultra 177
94/5 Panini Sticker 44
92/3 Parkhurst 366
93/4 Parkhurst 415
89/0 ProCards IHL 56
90/1 ProCards 394
91/2 ProCards 498
93/4 Score 649
92/3 Upper Deck 494
94/5 Upper Deck 160
92/3 PHIL / UD Sheet
92/3 PHIL / J.C. Penney
93/4 PHIL / Sheet
93/4 PHIL / J.C. Penney

MCGILLIS, DAN
99/0 BAP Mem. 99
99/0 Millenium 186, ✍ Aut. 186
98/9 Pacific 328
99/0 Pacific 309
00/1 Pacific 303
01/2 Pacific 291
97/8 Pacific CC 294
97/8 Pi. Be A Player 131, ✍ Aut. 131
00/1 Upper Deck 357
01/2 Upper Deck 360
98/9 UD MVP 153
99/0 Victory 221
01/2 Victory 262
96/7 EDMO
97/8 EDMO
01/2 PHIL

MCGILLIS, DANIEL
02/3 T. Total 119
02/3 UD Rookie 8
00/1 BAP Mem. 383

MCGILLVARY, GLEN
92/3 MPS SJHL 85

MCGIMSIE, BILLY
83 HHOF Postcard E11
83&87 HHOF 71

MCGINN, MARK
92/3 Oklahoma City Blazers

MCGLYNN, DICK
72 Semic Sticker 133

MCGLYNN, PETE
89/0 7th..Sketch OHL 70
90/1 7th..Sketch OHL 89
91/2 7th...Sketch OHL 241

MCGOWAN, CAL
91/2 ProCards 152
90 7th..Sketch Mem.Cup 9
90/1 7th..Sketch WHL 293
95/6 Binghamton Rangers
88/9 Kamloops Blazers
89/0 Kamloops Blazers

MCGOWAN, EVERETT
28/9 Paulins Candy 81

MCGRATH, BRETT
00/1 Ottawa 67's 11
01/2 Ottawa 67's 13
02/3 Owen Sound Attack

MCGRATH, DON
97/8 Central Texas

MCGRATH, PETER
83/4 North Bay Centennials

MCGRATTAN, BRIAN
00/1 Mississauga IceDogs
98/9 Sudbury Wolves 20
99/0 Sudbury Wolves 18

MCGREGOR, PERCY
23/4 Paulins Candy 50

MCGUANE, DANA
93/4 Roanoke Express
94/5 Roanoke Express

MCGUFFIN, MATT
90/1 7th..Sketch OHL 39
91/2 7th...Sketch OHL 6

MCGUIGEN, BILL
94/5 Slapshot / Kitchener 18

MCGUIRE, CONNOR
00/1 Halifax Moosehead

MCGUIRE, CONOR
99/0 Shawinigan 19

MCGUIRE, E.J.
95/6 Slapshot 105
96/7 Guelph Storm

MCGUIRE, MICKEY
91/2 Avant Garde BCJHL 54
92/3 BCJHL 136
91/2 Nanaimo Clippers

MCGUIRE, PIERRE
93/4 HART / Coke

MCHUGH, JUSTIN
91/2 Minnesota G'Gophers
92/3 Minnesota G'Gophers
93/4 Minnesota G'Gophers
94/5 Minnesota G'Gophers

MCHUGH, MIKE
91/2 O-Pee-Chee 7S
88/9 ProCards / Kalamazoo
89/0 ProCards IHL 86
90/1 ProCards 113
91/2 Score CAN 651
94/5 Hershey Bears

MCIANTYRE, IAN
91/2 7th...Sketch LHJMQ 180

MCILHARGEY, JACK
78/9 O-Pee-Chee 294

79/0 O-Pee-Chee 367
82/3 Post [Hart.]
91/2 ProCards 618
77/8 VANC / Royal Bank
78/9 VANC / Royal Bank
79/0 VANC / Royal Bank
92/3 Hamilton Canucks
96/7 Syracuse Crunch

MCINENLY, BERT
33/4 O-Pee-Chee 41

MCINERNEY, EOIN
00/1 Kudos 125
95/6 Slapshot 157
00/1 Nottingham Panthers

MCINNES, DARIN
86/7 Regina Pats

MCINNES, PAUL
94/5 Slapshot / Sarnia 12
95/6 Slapshot 34

MCINNIS, MARTY
02/3 Pacific Complete 347
02/3 Upper Deck 262
01/2 Adrenaline 4
98/9 Aurora 26
99/0 Aurora 3
98/9 Be A Player 19, ✍ Aut. 19
99/0 BAP Mem. 144
00/1 BAP Mem. 386
01/2 BAP Mem. 419
92/3 Bowman 352
92/3 Classic Prospects 133
93/4 Donruss 457
94/5 Donruss 311
94/5 Flair 106
92/3 Fleer Ultra 347
93/4 Fleer Ultra 370
94/5 Fleer Ultra 131
94/5 Leaf 157
92/3 O-Pee-Chee 135
01/2 O-Pee-Chee 236
98/9 OPC Chrome 103
92/3 OPC Premier 12
98/9 Omega 5
99/0 Omega 4
98/9 Pacific 121
99/0 Pacific 9
00/1 Pacific 7
01/2 Pacific 8
98/9 Pa. Paramount 29
99/0 Pa. Paramount 4
97/8 Pa. Revolution 19
98/9 Pa. Revolution 3
93/4 Panini Sticker 62
96/7 Panini Sticker 95
97/8 Panini Sticker 193
99/0 Panini Sticker 180
91/2 Parkhurst 327
92/3 Parkhurst 106
93/4 Parkhurst 390
95/6 Parkhurst 134
01/2 Parkhurst 364
94/5 Parkie SE104
94/5 Pinnacle 153
96/7 Pinnacle 62
94/5 POG 158
93/4 Power Play 385
93/4 Premier 57
94/5 Premier 244
00/1 Private Stock ✂ GUG 2
92/3 Pro Set 233
99/0 Revolution 3
00/1 Revolution ✂ GWJ 1
92/3 Score 465
93/4 Score 405
94/5 Score 88
95/6 Score 217
97/8 Score 210
99/0 Stadium 147
92/3 Topps 302
95/6 Topps 323
98/9 Topps 103
99/0 Topps 48
00/1 Topps 181
01/2 Topps 236
99/0 To. Chrome 48
92/3 To. Stadium 213
93/4 To. Stadium 257
00/1 UD Heroes 2
92/3 Upper Deck 394
92/3 Upper Deck 410
93/4 Upper Deck 392, SP-94
94/5 Upper Deck 106
95/6 Upper Deck 52
96/7 Upper Deck 102
97/8 Upper Deck 26
00/1 Upper Deck 236
01/2 Upper Deck 237
94/5 UD BAP R4, ✍ 14
95/6 UD CC 59
96/7 UD CC 160
97/8 UD Coll. Choice 42
98/9 UD MVP 7
01/2 UD Vintage 9
00/1 Vanguard ✂ DGJ 16
99/0 Victory 10
96/7 NYIS

MCINTOSH, BOB
91/2 Air Canada SJHL D31

MCINTOSH, DON
52/3 Anonymous 90

MCINTOSH, MURRAY
94/5 DEL 162
95/6 DEL 154

MCINTOSH, PAUL
78/9 Saginaw Gears

MCINTYRE, ANDY
91/2 Saskatoon Blades

MCINTYRE, DAN
99/0 Asheville Smoke

MCINTYRE, IAN
96/7 Syracuse Crunch
01/2 Cardiff Devils
02/3 London Knights

MCINTYRE, JACK (J.A.)
45-64 BeeHive-2 [Bost.]
52/3 Parkhurst 77
54/5 Parkhurst 88
60/1 Parkhurst 24
93/4 Parkie 56-57 27
60/1 Shirriff 46
54/5 Topps 43
57/8 Topps 28

MCINTYRE, JASON
93/4 Hampton Roads

MCINTYRE, JOHN*
91/2 Bowman 180
92/3 Bowman 336
94/5 Leaf 365
90/1 OPC/Topps 382
91/2 O-Pee-Chee 37
90/1 Panini/TOR 16
91/2 Parkhurst 296
93/4 Parkhurst 482
92/3 Pinnacle 214
90/1 Pro Set 457
91/2 Pro Set 401
89/0 ProCards AHL 121
90/1 Score 46T
91/2 Score 182
91/2 Score CAN 182
92/3 Score 347
92/3 Topps 369
91/2 To. Stadium 324
92/3 To. Stadium 117
94/5 To. Stadium 244
91/2 Upper Deck 218
92/3 Upper Deck 118
93/4 Upper Deck 527
94/5 Upper Deck 478
90/1 LOSA / Smokey 22
95/6 VANC / Abalene 15

MCINTYRE, LARRY
72/3 TORO

MCINTYRE, LLOYD
28/9 Paulins Candy 48
37/8 World Wide Gum 121

MCINTYRE, MANY
51/2 Bas du Fleuve 54

MCINTYRE, ROBB
94/5 Knoxville Cherokees
94/5 St. John's Maple Leafs
91/2 Ferris State Bulldogs

MCIVOR, TREVOR
90 7th..Sketch Mem.Cup 95
89/0 7th..Sketch OHL 16
90/1 7th..Sketch OHL 109
89/0 Oshawa Generals

MCKAVE, TODD
92/3 BCJHL 229

MCKAY, BILL
92/3 MPS SJHL 14
97/8 New Orleans Brass

MCKAY, BRUCE
81/2 Milwaukee Admirals

MCKAY, DOUG
89/0 ProCards AHL 287
88/9 NJER / Caretta

MCKAY, KEN
99 Bowman 111

MCKAY, MARTIN
94 Semic 311
93/4 Sheffield Steelers 18
93/4 Sheffield Steelers 19
94/5 Sheffield Steelers 1
95/6 Sheffield Steelers

MCKAY, MICHAEL*
94/5 Slapshot Memorial 75

MCKAY, RANDY
02/3 Pacific Complete 253
02/3 Sports Vault 53
02/3 To. Heritage 167
02/3 T. Total 66
01/2 Adrenaline 116
98/9 Aurora 111
98/9 Be A Player 80, ✍ Aut. 80
00/1 BAP Mem. 342
01/2 BAP Mem. 482
90/1 Bowman 227
92/3 Bowman 296
93/4 Donruss 454
94/5 Leaf 400
95/6 Leaf 314
00/1 Mir Fetisov 35
01/2 O-Pee-Chee 192, 321
98/9 OPC Chrome 90, SB29
97/8 Omega 131
98/9 Pacific 264
99/0 Pacific 240
00/1 Pacific 239
01/2 Pacific 233
97/8 Pa. Invincible R-114
98/9 Pa. Paramount 135
99/0 Pa. Paramount 135
95/6 Panini Sticker 84
92/3 Parkhurst 331
93/4 Pinnacle 322
94/5 Pinnacle 222
95/6 Pinnacle 92
97/8 Pi. Be A Player 160, ✍ Aut. 160
95/6 POG 162
94/5 Premier 271
91/2 Pro Set 422
88/9 ProCards / Adirondack
89/0 ProCards AHL 318
91/2 Score 54T
91/2 Score CAN 604
92/3 Score 339
93/4 Score 319
97/8 Score NJer. 12
00/1 Signature 70, ✍ Aut. 205
95/6 SBx Emotion 99
95/6 SBx Impact 94
92/3 Topps 106

95/6 Topps 201, 10PL
98/9 Topps 90, SB29
01/2 Topps 192, 321
98/9 T. Gold Label 28
00/1 To. Heritage 150
92/3 To. Stadium 450
95/6 To. Stadium 153
91/2 Upper Deck 313
95/6 Upper Deck 444
00/1 Upper Deck 333
01/2 Upper Deck 337
95/6 UD BAP 52, ✍ S52
96/7 UD CC 154
99/0 UD MVP Cup 109
01/2 UD SCup Champs 71
00/1 UD Vintage 220
01/2 Victory 208
90/1 DETR / Little Caesars
02/3 MONT
96/7 NJER / Sharp

MCKAY, RAY
71/2 Toronto Sun Photo

MCKAY, ROSS
90/1 ProCards 177

MCKAY, SCOTT
93/4 Cla. Prospects 216
90/1 7th..Sketch OHL 136
91/2 7th...Sketch OHL 376
94/5 Greensboro Monarchs
97/8 Louisiana Ice Gators
93/4 San Diego Gulls

MCKECHNEY, GARNET
82/3 Kitchener Rangers
83/4 Kitchener Rangers
84/5 Kitchener Rangers

MCKECHNIE, CRAIG
91/2 Air Canada SJHL A8
92/3 MPS SJHL 149

MCKECHNIE, DARRIN
86/7 Regina Pats
87/8 Regina Pats

MCKECHNIE, WALT
71/2 Bazooka Panel
70/1 Colgate 1
70/1 Eddie Sargent 89
71/2 Eddie Sargent 129
72/3 Eddie Sargent 43
70/1 Esso Power Player
83/4 Funmate Puffy 14 [w/]
72/3 Post 5
74/5 Loblaws
74/5 Loblaws Update
70/1 O-Pee-Chee 172
71/2 O-Pee-Chee 124
72/3 O-Pee-Chee 192
73/4 O-Pee-Chee 152
74/5 O-Pee-Chee 56
75/6 O-Pee-Chee 194
76/7 O-Pee-Chee 196
76/7 O-Pee-Chee 385
77/8 O-Pee-Chee 32
78/9 O-Pee-Chee 344
79/0 O-Pee-Chee 68
80/1 O-Pee-Chee 378
82/3 O-Pee-Chee 91
71/2 O-Pee-Chee Poster 17
82/3 OPC/Topps Sticker 186
82/3 Post [Detr.]
83/4 Souhaits Keychain [Red Wings]
73/4 Topps 127
74/5 Topps 56
75/6 Topps 194
76/7 Topps 196
77/8 Topps 32
79/0 Topps 68
71/2 Toronto Sun Photo
78/9 TORO
79/0 TORO

MCKEE, BRIAN
90/1 ProCards 552
91/2 ProCards 40
93/4 Fort Wayne Komets 14
92/3 Peoria Rivermen

MCKEE, COREY
91/2 Air Canada SJHL A25

MCKEE, JAY
02/3 Heads Up ✂ GWQ 4
02/3 Pacific 45
02/3 Sports Vault 28
02/3 Upper Deck 22
02/3 UD Vintage 32
01/2 Adrenaline ✂ GWJ 4
95/6 Cla. 5 Sport 135
95/6 Cla. Vis. Signings 72, ✍ Aut.
96/7 Fleer 131
96/7 Fl. Ultra 18, UR-12
96/7 Metal Univ. 186
99/0 Pacific 40
01/2 Pacific ✂ GWJ 3
96/7 Pinnacle 222
97/8 Pi. Be A Player 122, ✍ Aut. 122
00/1 Private Stock ✂ GUG 10
01/2 Pr. Stock ✂ GUG 11
96/7 SBx Impact 154
93/4 Slapshot / Sudbury 3
95/6 Slapshot 183, P
97/8 Upper Deck 231
00/1 Upper Deck 252
01/2 Upper Deck 253
00/1 Victory 33
93/4 Sudbury Wolves

MCKEE, MIKE
93/4 Cla. Prospects 91
93/4 Donruss 479
93/4 Power Play 424
93/4 Score 630
97/8 Rochester Americans

MCKEGNEY, TONY
90/1 Bowman 168
91/2 Bowman 387

83/4 Funmate Puffy 17 [w/]
80/1 O-Pee-Chee 144
81/2 O-Pee-Chee 22
82/3 O-Pee-Chee 29
83/4 O-Pee-Chee 60
83/4 O-Pee-Chee 296
84/5 O-Pee-Chee 283
85/6 OPC/Topps 156
87/8 OPC/Topps 172
88/9 OPC/Topps 4
90/1 OPC/Topps 333
91/2 O-Pee-Chee 484
89/0 OPC/Topps 4
81/2 OPC Sticker 57
82/3 OPC/Topps Sticker 122
83/4 OPC/Topps Sticker 239
84/5 OPC Sticker 171
85/6 OPC Sticker 45-176
88/9 OPC Sticker 17-146
87/8 Panini Sticker 118
88/9 Panini Sticker 109
90/1 Panini Sticker 149
90/1 Panini/QUE 15
82/3 Post [Buff.]
90/1 Pro Set 254
91/2 Score 104
91/2 Score CAN 104
83/4 Souhaits Keychain [Sabres]
80/1 Topps 144
81/2 Topps 76 [East]
91/2 To. Stadium 281
90/1 Upper Deck 340
83/4 Vachon 68-48
79/0 BUFF / Bells Market
80/1 BUFF / Wendt's 7
81/2 BUFF / Wendt's 11
82/3 BUFF / Wendt's 13
85/6 MINS
85/6 MINS / 7-Eleven 5
89/0 QUÉB
90/1 QUÉB
90/1 QUÉB / Petro-Canada
87/8 SLOU
87/8 SLOU / Kodak
88/9 SLOU
88/9 SLOU / Kodak

MCKENNA, PAUL
92/3 BCJHL 7

MCKENNA, SEAN
87/8 Panini Sticker 284
88/9 ProCards / Newmarket
89/0 ProCards AHL 115
84/5 BUFF / Blue Shield
85/6 BUFF / Blue Shield
87/8 LOSA
88/9 TORO / P.L.A.Y. 27

MCKENNA, STEVE
92/3 MPS SJHL 108
01/2 O-Pee-Chee 252
97/8 Omega 109
98/9 Pacific 239
97/8 Pi. Be A Player 244, ✍ Aut. 244
00/1 Signature 203, ✍ Aut. 25
01/2 Topps 252

MCKENNEY, DON
52/3 Anonymous 111
45-64 BeeHive-2 [Bost.]
45-64 BeeHive-2 [NYRa.]
45-64 BeeHive-2 [Toro.]
64-67 BeeHive-3 [Toro.]
64-67 BeeHive-3 [Toro.]
64/5 Coke/Sprite [Toro.]
62/3 Cowan Tile
93/4 Parkie 56-57 6
94/5 Parkie Tall 112
60/1 Shirriff 108
61/2 Shirriff 6
54/5 Topps 35
57/8 Topps 13
58/9 Topps 62
59/0 Topps 9
60/1 Topps 40
61/2 Topps 12
61/2 Topps - Stamp
62/3 Topps 10
62/3 Topps Dollar
63/4 Topps 53
64/5 Topps 81
65/6 Topps 112
57/8 Toronto Star Photo
61/2 Toronto Star Photo
64/5 Toronto Star Action
61/2 Toronto Star Weekend
57-58 BOST
91/2 BOST / SA Legends
98/9 BOST / Alumni 31
64/5 TORO

MCKENNEY, SAM
96/7 Dayton Bombers

MCKENNY, JIM
70/1 Dad's Cookies
70/1 Eddie Sargent 201
71/2 Eddie Sargent 194
72/3 Eddie Sargent 198
70/1 Esso Power Player
74/5 Lipton Soup 23
74/5 Loblaws
73/4 Mac's Milk
71/2 O-Pee-Chee 43
72/3 O-Pee-Chee 83
73/4 O-Pee-Chee 39
74/5 O-Pee-Chee 198
75/6 O-Pee-Chee 311
76/7 O-Pee-Chee 302
77/8 O-Pee-Chee 374
71/2 Pro Star Promotions
72 Semic Sticker 189
68/9 Shirriff / Toro. 16
71/2 Topps 43
72/3 Topps 83
73/4 Topps 39
74/5 Topps 198
75/6 Topps 311
71/2 Toronto Sun Photo
69/0 TORO
70/1 TORO
71/2 TORO
72/3 TORO
73/4 TORO
74/5 TORO
75/6 TORO
76/7 TORO
77/8 TORO

MCKENZIE, BILL
76/7 O-Pee-Chee 267
78/9 O-Pee-Chee 275
79/0 COLR

MCKENZIE, GORDON
24/5 Falcons Crescent 12

MCKENZIE, JIM
91/2 Bowman 7
91/2 O-Pee-Chee 24
99/0 Pacific 10
01/2 Pacific 234
93/4 Parkhurst 357
94/5 Parkhurst 178
96/7 Pi. Be A Player 69, ✍ Aut. 69
91/2 Pro Set 391
89/0 ProCards AHL 302
90/1 ProCards 175
91/2 To. Stadium 354
91/2 Upper Deck 494
93/4 Upper Deck 23
97/8 Upper Deck 337
99/0 UD Retro 3
90/1 HART / Jr. Whalers
91/2 HART / Jr. Whalers
92/3 HART / Dairymart
96/7 PHOE / Coca-Cola
97/8 PHOE / Coca-Cola
97/8 PHOE / Coca-Cola
94/5 PITT / Foodland 20
95/6 WINN

MCKENZIE, JOHN
64-67 BeeHive-3 [Chic.]
64/5 Coke/Sprite [Chic.]
65/6 Coca-Cola
70/1 Colgate 59
70/1 Dad's Cookies
70/1 Eddie Sargent 9
71/2 Eddie Sargent 3
70/1 Esso Power Player
68/9 O-Pee-Chee 9
69/0 O-Pee-Chee 28
70/1 O-Pee-Chee 6
70/1 O-Pee-Chee 241
71/2 O-Pee-Chee 82
72/3 O-Pee-Chee 338
75/6 OPC WHA 77
76/7 OPC WHA 103
77/8 OPC WHA 41
80/1 Parkhurst 37
61/2 Parkhurst 34
95/6 Parkie 66-67 10
94/5 Parkie Tall 36
72 Semic Sticker 185
60/1 Shirriff 43
68/9 Shirriff / Bost. 11
63/4 Topps 42
64/5 Topps 30
65/6 Topps 94
66/7 Topps 97
66/7 Topps / Test 66
67/8 Topps 39
68/9 Topps 9
69/0 Topps 28
70/1 Topps 6
71/2 Topps 82
64/5 Toronto Star Action
71/2 Toronto Sun Photo
91/2 Ultimate Original Six 52, ✍ Aut. 52
70/1 BOST
71/2 BOST
98/9 BOST / Alumni 19

MCKERCHER, JEFF
99 Bowman 139
99/0 Fort Wayne Komets

MCKICHAN, STEVE
90/1 ProCards 341

MCKIE, RUSTY
98/9 Phoenix Mustangs 8

MCKIE, RYAN
95/6 Slapshot 177
98/9 Sudbury Wolves 15

MCKILLOP, BOB
90/1 7th..Sketch OHL 66

MCKIM, ANDREW
92/3 Classic Prospects 14
96/7 DEL 38
98/9 DEL 159
94/5 Parkhurst 16
90/1 ProCards 626
91/2 ProCards 343
96 Wien AS6

MCKINLAY, MIKE
91/2 Avant Garde BCJHL 125
92/3 BCJHL 164

MCKINLEY, BARRY
99/0 Rockford IceHogs
93/4 Thunder Bay Senators
94/5 Thunder Bay Senators
95/6 Thunder Bay Senators

MCKINLEY, ROB
84/5 Kamloops Blazers
85/6 Kamloops Blazers
86/7 Kamloops Blazers
87/8 Regina Pats
87/8 Regina Pats

MCKINNEY, BRYAN
94/5 Slapshot / Guelph 4
95/6 Slapshot 88
95/6 Guelph Storm

MCKINNON, ALEX
24/5 Champ's Cigarettes
24/5 William Paterson 16

MCKINNON, BRIAN
82/3 Ottawa 67's
83/4 Ottawa 67's

MCKINNON, KENNY
37/8 World Wide Gum 118

MCKINNON, KEVIN
99/0 Colorado Gold Kings
94/5 Erie Panthers
99/0 San Angelo Outlaws

MCKINNON, PAUL
79/0 WASH
80/1 WASH

MCKINNON, THOMAS
01/2 Guelph Storm

MCKNIGHT, WES
34-43 BeeHive-1

MCLANE, MARK
87/8 Hull Olympiques

MCLAREN, KYLE
02/3 First Edition 25, ✂ Jers.
02/3 Heads Up ✂ GWQ 3
02/3 Parkhurst ✂ TT8
02/3 Parkhurst Retro 157
02/3 UD Premier 46
02/3 UD Rookie 87
99/0 BAP Mem. 47, SL-22
00/1 BAP Mem. 85, ✂ TM-11
01/2 BAP Mem. 203
95/6 Bowman 151
95/6 Donruss 333
96/7 Donruss 219
95/6 Do. Elite R-15
97/8 Do. Preferred 107
96/7 Fleer 5
95/6 Fleer Metal 184
95/6 Fleer Ultra 349
96/7 Fl. Ultra 9
01/2 Heads Up ✂ JQ 2
96/7 Leaf 142
97/8 Limited 106
96/7 Metal Univ. 8
99/0 Millenium 25, ✍ Aut. 25
99/0 NHL Power Play
98/9 Pacific 86
99/0 Pacific 27
00/1 Pacific 38
01/2 Pacific CC 42
96/7 Panini Sticker 5
99/0 Panini Sticker 29
95/6 Parkhurst 262
00/1 Parkhurst P-52
95/6 Pi. Summit 194
96/7 Pi. Summit 159
95/6 Pi. Zenith 127, RRC-17
95/6 POG I-035
01/2 PS Titanium Draft ✂ 10
00/1 PS Titanium Draft ✂ 5
96/7 Score 258
97/8 Score Bost. 19
95/6 Select CE 139
00/1 Signature 97, ✂ DD-8, ✂ J-36
01/2 Signature C-22, ✂ LKM, ✂ DD7
95/6 SBx Impact 189
96/7 SBx Impact 6
95/6 SP 8
96/7 SP 8
97/8 SP Authentic 11
00/1 Stadium 139
95/6 Topps 309
99/0 Topps 218
00/1 Topps 126
99/0 To. Chrome 218
95/6 To. Finest 111
96/7 To. Picks RS13
95/6 To. Stadium 63
95/6 T. Super Skills SR9
98/9 UD Choice 16
00/1 Ultimate Mem. ✂ J-35, ✂ S-35
95/6 Upper Deck 421
96/7 Upper Deck 9, X37, SS25B
97/8 Upper Deck 13
98/9 Upper Deck 219
99/0 Upper Deck 186
00/1 Upper Deck 17
01/2 Upper Deck 15
95/6 UD BAP 173, ✍ S173
97/8 UD Black Diam. 54
96/7 UD CC 15, 341
97/8 UD Coll. Choice 15
98/9 UD G. Reserve 219
99/0 UD G. Reserve 186
98/9 UD MVP 15
99/0 UD MVP 16
00/1 UD MVP 18
01/2 UD MVP 15
00/1 UD Vintage 27, 36
01/2 UD Vintage 18
00/1 Vanguard ✂ DGJ 14
99/0 Victory 30
01/2 Victory 35
99/0 WGretzky 18
93/4 Tacoma Rockets

MCLAREN, STEVE
93/4 Slapshot / North Bay 4
94/5 Slapshot / North Bay 5
95/6 Indianapolis Ice
97/8 Indianapolis Ice 16
01/2 Worcester IceCats
02/3 Worcester IceCats

MCLARREN, RICK
92/3 BCJHL 141

MCLARTY, JIM
91/2 Air Canada SJHL 9
91/2 Air Canada SJHL C20

MCLAUGHIN, MIKE
92/3 Rochester Americans DD

MCLAUGHLIN, BLAIR
99/0 Brampton Batallion 25

MCLAUGHLIN, CAM
99/0 Brampton Batallion 8

MCLAUGHLIN, FREDERIC
83 HHOF Postcard J9
83&87 HHOF 189

MCLAUGHLIN, MIKE
94/5 Binghampton Rangers
92/3 Rochester Americans WPC

MCLAY, DAVE
83/4 Kelowna Wings
86/7 Portland Winter Hawks

MCLEAN, BRETT
99 Bowman 112
98/9 UD Choice 270
95/6 Upper Deck 506
00/1 Cleveland Lumberjacks
98/9 Kelowna Rockets

MCLEAN, CARL
01/2 Cape Breton Eagles 17

MCLEAN, DARREN
91/2 Air Canada SJHL C25
92/3 MPS SJHL 12

MCLEAN, GREG
93/4 Slapshot / Kitchener 4
94/5 Slapshot / Kitchener 5

MCLEAN, JACK
34-43 BeeHive-1 [Toro.]

MCLEAN, JEFF
92/3 Classic 85
92/3 Classic Four Sport 205
93/4 Cla. Prospects 130
92/3 Kansas City Blades
93/4 Kansas City Blades
95/6 Kansas City Blades
96/7 Kansas City Blades

MCLEAN, JIM
91/2 Air Canada SJHL B6

MCLEAN, KIRK
01/2 BT Pipes 77
98/9 Bicycle.. 3-D
90/1 Bowman 57
91/2 Bowman 310
92/3 Bowman 212
93/4 Donruss 355
94/5 Donruss 22, MM-6
95/6 Donruss 16
96/7 Donruss 3
97/8 Donruss 189
96/7 Do. Canadian 33
97/8 Do. Canadian 79
96/7 Do. Elite 121
97/8 Do. Priority 162
97/8 Do. Studio 88
93/4 EA Sports 144
94/5 Flair 193
94/5 Fleer 227, N-6
96/7 Fleer 113
95/6 Fleer Metal 152
92/3 Fleer Ultra 224
93/4 Fleer Ultra 29
94/5 Fleer Ultra 228
95/6 Fleer Ultra 170, 373
96/7 Fl. Ultra 169
92/3 Humpty Dumpty
89/0 Kraft 43
90/1 Kraft 70
92/3 Kraft / PB
93/4 Kraft / JELL-O
94/5 Kraft / KD
95/6 Kraft / PS
93/4 Leaf 55
93/4 Leaf PW 3
94/5 Leaf 109, CP-7
95/6 Leaf 162
96/7 Leaf 43
97/8 Leaf 74
94/5 L. Limited 23
95/6 L. Limited 67
97/8 Limited 3
95/6 McDonald's McD-30
96/7 Metal Univ. 158
90/1 OPC/Topps 257
91/2 O-Pee-Chee 221
92/3 O-Pee-Chee 349
89/0 OPC/Topps 61
90/1 OPC Premier 70
91/2 OPC Premier 158
88/9 OPC Sticker 136-7
89/0 OPC Sticker 55-186
90/1 OPC Sticker 11-140
89/0 opcSticker 64
97/8 Omega 43
98/9 Pacific 225
99/0 Pacific 177
00/1 Pacific 267
97/8 Pacific CC 258
97/8 Pa. Dynagon 128, T-56
97/8 Pa. Invincible 143
97/8 Pa. Paramount 189
88/9 Panini Sticker 133
89/0 Panini Sticker 4, 155
90/1 Panini Sticker 296
90/1 Panini/VAN G
91/2 Panini Sticker 45
92/3 Panini Sticker 27
93/4 Panini Sticker 177
94/5 Panini Sticker 153
95/6 Panini Sticker 298
96/7 Panini Sticker 291
91/2 Parkhurst 181
91/2 Parkhurst 440
92/3 Parkhurst 192
93/4 Parkhurst 213
94/5 Parkhurst 238
95/6 Parkhurst 213, GP-11
95 Parkhurst Phonecard
94/5 Parkie SE seV10
91/2 Pinnacle 158
92/3 Pinnacle 246
93/4 Pinnacle 330
93/4 Pinnacle 158
93/4 Pinnacle TP 7
94/5 Pinnacle 60, GT11
95/6 Pinnacle 132
96/7 Pinnacle 90
97/8 Pinnacle 88
97/8 Pi. Be A Player 118, ✍ Aut. 118
97/8 Pi. Certified 27
97/8 Pi. Inside 60
95/6 Pi. Summit 69, ITC-14
96/7 Pi. Summit 68
97/8 Pi. Totally 27
95/6 Pi. Zenith 57
95/6 Playoff 101
94/5 POG 270
94/5 POG / Western 19
95/6 POG 278
93/4 Power Play 253
93/4 Premier 113
94/5 Premier 85, 397
00/1 PS Titanium ✂ GUG 38, ✂ GUG-39
95/6 Pro Magnet 24
90/1 Pro Set 302, 355
91/2 Pro Set 501, 603, ✍ 501
91/2 Pro Set 193
92/3 Pro Set 250
91/2 Pro Set PotM P1
91/2 Pro Set Platinum 239
91/2 Puck / Pro Set 28
91/2 Puck / Pro Set Prototype
90/1 Score 93
90/1 Sco. Hot Cards 46
91/2 Score 261
91/2 Score CAN 481
92/3 Score 385
92/3 Score 417
93/4 Score 47
94/5 Score 60
95/6 Score 49
96/7 Score 155
97/8 Score 43
97/8 Score Vanc. 10
92/3 Seasons 71
94/5 Select 64
95/6 Select CE 63
96/7 Select CE 22
93 Semic Sticker 190
95/6 SBx Emotion 181
95/6 SBx Impact 170, D-12
96/7 SBx Impact 134
94/5 SP 124
95/6 SP 152
97/8 SP Authentic 159
98/9 SLU
95/6 Super Sticker 127
96/7 Team Out!
92/3 Topps 130
92/3 Topps 225
92/3 Topps 270
95/6 Topps 277, 13HG
94/5 Topps Finest 61
95/6 To. Finest 161
91/2 To. Stadium 105
92/3 To. Stadium 193
93/4 To. Stadium 163
94/5 To. Stadium 188, 223
95/6 To. Stadium 41, MP
95/6 T. Super Skills 89
90/1 Upper Deck 278
91/2 Upper Deck 191
92/3 Upper Deck 22
92/3 Upper Deck 299
93/4 Upper Deck 156, SP-165
94/5 Upper Deck 133, H34, SP-84
95/6 Upper Deck 136, SE-83
96/7 Upper Deck 348
97/8 Upper Deck 375
94/5 UD BAP R73, R107
95/6 UD BAP 200, ✍ S200
94/5 UD BAP Roots 7
97/8 UD Black Diam. 31
00/1 UD Black Diam. ✂ GG
95/6 UD CC 71
96/7 UD CC 271
99/0 Victory 197
87/8 VANC / Shell
88/9 VANC / Mohawk
89/0 VANC / Mohawk
90/1 VANC / Mohawk
90/1 VANC / PotM
90/1 VANC / PotM
91/2 VANC
91/2 VANC / Photo
91/2 VANC / PotM
92/3 VANC / Road Trip
94/5 VANC
95/6 VANC / Abalene 1
96/7 VANC / IGA
83/4 Oshawa Generals

MCLEARY, MARK
82/3 Victoria Cougars

MCLELLAN, CAM
89/0 Regina Pats

MCLELLAN, DUSTY
91/2 Avant Garde BCJHL 25
91/2 Avant Garde BCJHL 155
92/3 BCJHL 204
93/4 Johnstown Chiefs 11

MCLELLAN, TODD
88/9 ProCards / Springfield
00/1 Cleveland Lumberjacks
83/4 Saskatoon Blades
86/7 Saskatoon Blades
86/7 Saskatoon Blades

MCLENNAN, JAMIE
02/3 Between the Pipes 67
02/3 Heads Up ✂ GWQ 14
02/3 Pacific Complete 392
02/3 UD Mask 13, 14
02/3 Vanguard ✂ GWJ8
01/2 Adrenaline ✂ GWJ 21
98/9 Aurora 162
98/9 Be A Player 273, ✍ Aut. 273
01/2 BT Pipes 49
98/9 Bicycle.. 7-H
91/2 Classic 40
91/2 Classic Four Sport 40
93/4 Cla. Prospects 112
00/1 Crown Royale 53
01/2 Crown Royale ✂ TT 18
93/4 Donruss 458
94/5 Donruss 88
98/9 Dynagon Ice 160
94/5 Flair 107
94/5 Fleer 127
94/5 Fleer Ultra 328
94/5 Kraft / KD
94/5 Leaf 74
01/2 O-Pee-Chee 67
98/9 Omega 204
99/0 Omega 197
98/9 Pacific 369
99/0 Pacific 360
00/1 Pacific 347
01/2 Pacific 199
98/9 Pa. Paramount 205
00/1 Pa. Paramount 120
98/9 Panini Sticker 228
95/6 Parkhurst 404
94/5 Pinnacle 250
97/8 Pi. Be A Player 107, ✍ Aut. 107
94/5 POG 286
93/4 Power Play 386
94/5 Premier 143, OF-21
01/2 Pr. Stock ✂ GUG 53
01/2 PS Titanium ✂ DSJ 15, ✂ DSJ 70
01/2 PS Titanium Draft ✂ 47
00/1 Revolution 72
94/5 Score 224
97/8 Score SLou. 20
94/5 Select 189
92 7th...Sketch Awards 16
91 7th...Sketch Mem.Cup 79
90/1 7th..Sketch WHL 129
00/1 Stadium 206
91/2 Star Pics 32
01/2 Topps 67
00/1 To. Chrome 231
00/1 To. Heritage 104
98/9 UD Choice 187
00/1 UD Reserve 42
91/2 Ultimate Draft Pick 35, 57, ✍ Aut.
94/5 Upper Deck 252, SP-137
98/9 Upper Deck 361
98/9 UD G. Reserve 361
01/2 Vanguard ✂ DGM 29
01/2 Victory 179
99/0 SLOU / Taco Bell 3
91/2 Richmond Renegades
89/0 Lethbridge Hurricanes

MCLENNEN, BLONDIE
28/9 Paulins Candy 45

MCLEOD, AL
75/6 OPC WHA 88
76/7 OPC WHA 47
75/6 Phoenix Roadrunners

MCLEOD, DON
74/5 OPC WHA 82
75/6 OPC WHA 32
76/7 OPC WHA 129
77/8 OPC WHA 14

MCLEOD, GAVIN
98/9 Kelowna Rockets
00/1 Kelowna Rockets

MCLEOD, JACKIE
45-64 BeeHive-2 [NYRa.]
51/2 Parkhurst 98
52/3 Parkhurst 102

MCLEOD, JEFF
98/9 DEL 53

MCLEOD, JIM
73/4 Quaker Oats 17

MCLEOD, KIEL
99/0 UD Prospects 75
00/1 UD Prospects 52, 95
01 UD Prospects GU 40, ✂ TPJ, ✂ TPJS, ✂ JC, ✍ SoT
98/9 Kelowna Rockets
00/1 Kelowna Rockets

MCLEOD, PETE
85/6 London Knights

MCLLWAIN, DAVE
90/1 Bowman 136
91/2 Bowman 196
94/5 Donruss 315
94/5 Flair 123
94/5 Leaf 260
88/9 OPC/Topps 132
90/1 OPC/Topps 299
91/2 O-Pee-Chee 95
90/1 Panini Sticker 319
90/1 Panini/WPG 17
91/2 Panini Sticker 73
94/5 Panini Sticker 100
95/6 Panini Sticker 219
94/5 Parkhurst 157
94/5 Pinnacle 54
94/5 POG 355
93/4 Power Play 402
94/5 Premier 446
90/1 Pro Set 333
91/2 Pro Set 434
88/9 ProCards / Muskegon
90/1 Score 231
91/2 Score 102T
91/2 Score CAN 233
92/3 Score 122
93/4 Score 418
93/4 Score 583
92/3 Topps 393
91/2 To. Stadium 202
92/3 To. Stadium 491
94/5 To. Stadium 31
90/1 Upper Deck 216
91/2 Upper Deck 222
91/2 Upper Deck 527
92/3 Upper Deck 93
93/4 Upper Deck 524
94/5 Upper Deck 423
94/5 UD BAP ✍ 9
00/1 UD DEL 140
01/2 UD DEL 142
93/4 OTTA
94/5 OTTA
87/8 PITT / Kodak
92/3 TORO / Kodak
93/4 TORO / Black's 9
89/0 WINN / Safeway
90/1 WINN / IGA
95/6 Cleveland Lumberjacks
96/7 Cleveland Lumberjacks
84/5 Kitchener Rangers

MCMAHON, MARK
98 Bowman 3
98 Bowman Chrome 3
95/6 Slapshot 137

MCMAHON, MIKE C.
43-47 Parade Sportive
45-54 Quaker Oats

MCMAHON, MIKE W. (SR.)
68/9 Bauer Photo
65/6 Coca-Cola
70/1 Dad's Cookies
70/1 Eddie Sargent 28
68/9 O-Pee-Chee 46
70/1 O-Pee-Chee 143
72/3 O-Pee-Chee 305
68/9 Shirriff / Minn. 10
65/6 Topps 24
68/9 Topps 46
72/3 Minn. Fight. Saints
74/5 Minn. Fight. Saints

MCMANUS, SAMMY
37/8 World Wide Gum 79

MCMASTERS, JIM
72/3 Cleveland Crusaders
72/3 Clev. WHA / Linnett

MCMEEKIN, KEN
52/3 Anonymous 179

MCMICHAEL, SCOTT
83/4 Belleville Bulls

MCMILLAN, CASEY
86/7 Kamloops Blazers
87/8 Kamloops Blazers
88/9 Lethbridge Hurricanes

MCMILLAN, PAUL
91/2 Avant Garde BCJHL 108

MCMILLAN, TYLER
91/2 Air Canada SJHL A4
92/3 MPS SJHL 146
99/0 Peoria Rivermen

MCMILLEN, DAVE
90/1 7th..Sketch WHL 253
91/2 7th...Sketch WHL 157
92/3 Tacoma Rockets

MCMORRAN, LARRY
93/4 Lethbridge Hurricanes
93/4 Seattle Thunderbirds

MCMORRIS, DOYLE
95/6 Lethbridge Hurricanes

MCMORROW, SEAN
02/3 BAP Mem. 344
02/3 UD Rookie 146
02/3 Rochester Americans
00/1 Kingston Frontenacs 14
01/2 London Knights
00/1 Mississauga IceDogs

MCMULKIN, JOHN
91/2 7th...Sketch WHL 175

MCMULLEN, BRYAN
00/1 Austin Ice Bats
95/6 Guelph Storm

MCMULLEN, JOHN H.
96/7 NJER / Sharp

MCMULLIN, BEN
99/0 Medicine Hat Tigers
00/1 Medicine Hat Tigers

MCMULLIN, BENJAMIN
02/3 Québec Remparts

MCMUNN, HAROLD
24/5 Holland Creameries 2
28/9 Paulins Candy 70
23/4 Selkirks Crescent 13

MCMURCHY, TOM
88/9 EDMO / Action 31
85/6 Nova Scotia Oilers
83/4 Springfield Indians 10
82/3 Brandon Wheat Kings

MCMURRAY, ED
88/9 ProCards / Peoria

MCMURTRY, CHRIS
91/2 7th...Sketch OHL 340
93/4 Slapshot / Sudbury 4
93/4 Sudbury Wolves

MCNAB, MAX
45-64 BeeHive-2 [Detr.]

MCNAB, PETER
75/6 O-Pee-Chee 252
76/7 O-Pee-Chee 118
77/8 OPC 7
77/8 O-Pee-Chee 18
78/9 O-Pee-Chee 212
79/0 O-Pee-Chee 39
80/1 O-Pee-Chee 94
80/1 O-Pee-Chee 167
80/1 O-Pee-Chee 220
81/2 O-Pee-Chee 5
82/3 O-Pee-Chee 16
83/4 O-Pee-Chee 53
84/5 O-Pee-Chee 116
85/6 O-Pee-Chee 36
81/2 OPC Sticker 46
82/3 OPC/Topps Sticker 83
83/4 OPC/Topps Sticker 50
83/4 OPC/Topps Sticker 51
85/6 OPC Sticker 244-111
82/3 Post [Bost.]
75/6 Topps 252
76/7 Topps 118
77/8 Topps 7
77/8 Topps 18
78/9 Topps 212
79/0 Topps 39
80/1 Topps 94
80/1 Topps 167
80/1 Topps 220
81/2 Topps 69 [East]
01/2 T/O Archives 73, ✍ CAI
83/4 BOST
74/5 BUFF
75/6 BUFF / Linnett
86/7 NJER / S.O.B.E.R.
84/5 VANC

MCNALLY, IAN
01/2 Guelph Storm

MCNAMARA, GEORGE
83 HHOF Postcard O10
83&87 HHOF 203

MCNAMARA, GERRY
80/1 TORO

MCNAMARA, HAROLD
10/1 Imperial 32

MCNAMARA, LEN
90/1 7th..Sketch OHL 299

MCNAMEE, PETER
75/6 Phoenix Roadrunners

MCNEIL, DOUGLAS
51/2 Laval Dairy 99

MCNEIL, GERRY
45-64 BeeHive-2 [Mont.]
48-52 Exhibits [Canadiens]
51/2 La Patrie
43-47 Parade Sportive
51/2 Parkhurst 15
52/3 Parkhurst 12
53/4 Parkhurst 25
54/5 Parkhurst 1
55/6 Parkhurst 52
45-54 Quaker Oats

MCNEIL, SHAWN
97 Bowman 99
98 Bowman 71
98 Bowman Chrome 71
94/5 Slapshot Memorial 24
99/0 Louisiana Ice Gators
00/1 Louisiana Ice Gators
01/2 Louisiana Ice Gators
02/3 Louisiana Ice Gators
96/7 Kamloops Blazers

MCNEILL,
91/2 Avant Garde BCJHL 161

MCNEILL, BILLY
63/4 Parkhurst 56
93/4 Parkie 56-57 48
57/8 Topps 44
59/0 Topps 41

MCNEILL, JAY
96/7 Richmond Renegades

MCNEILL, MIKE
91/2 Bowman 143
92/3 Bowman 424
98/9 DEL 4
99/0 Eishockey 299
91/2 O-Pee-Chee 408
90/1 Pro Set 600
91/2 Pro Set 467
89/0 ProCards IHL 72
92/3 Topps 166
91/2 To. Stadium 241
92/3 To. Stadium 98
91/2 Upper Deck 524
90/1 CHIC / Coke
91/2 QUÉB / Petro-Canada
93/4 Milwaukee Admirals
94/5 Milwaukee Admirals
95/6 Milwaukee Admirals
96/7 Milwaukee Admirals
97/8 Milwaukee Admirals

MCNEILL, STEVE
94/5 DEL 264

MCNUTT, STEVE
90/1 7th..Sketch WHL 110

MCPHEE, GEORGE
85/6 O-Pee-Chee 84

MCPHEE, GEORGE
02/3 Fleer Throwbacks 24

MCPHEE, MIKE
90/1 Bowman 43
91/2 Bowman 339
92/3 Bowman 89
92/3 Fleer Ultra 322
93/4 Fleer Ultra 300
86/7 Kraft Sports 31
89/0 Kraft Stickers 1
94/5 Leaf 203
85/6 O-Pee-Chee 225
86/7 O-Pee-Chee 221
88/9 OPC/Topps 237
90/1 OPC/Topps 137
91/2 O-Pee-Chee 252
92/3 O-Pee-Chee 199
89/0 OPC/Topps 84
86/7 OPC Sticker 15-157
87/8 OPC Sticker 18
89/0 opcSticker 59-201
87/8 Panini Sticker 66
88/9 Panini Sticker 258
89/0 Panini Sticker 243
90/1 Panini Sticker 63
90/1 Panini/MTL 16
91/2 Panini Sticker 188
91/2 Parkhurst 310
92/3 Parkhurst 51
91/2 Pinnacle 147
92/3 Pinnacle 342
93/4 Pinnacle 163
94/5 Pinnacle 105
95/6 Pi. Summit GMC 21
94/5 POG 80
93/4 Power Play 326
93/4 Premier 214
94/5 Premier 163
90/1 Pro Set 155
91/2 Pro Set 129
91/2 Score 147
91/2 Score CAN 147
92/3 Score 91
93/4 Score 85
94/5 Score 17
92/3 Topps 45
91/2 To. Stadium 210
92/3 To. Stadium 210
93/4 To. Stadium 6
90/1 Upper Deck 384
91/2 Upper Deck 487
92/3 Upper Deck 538
93/4 Upper Deck 43
94/5 DALL / Cap
84/5 MONT
85/6 MONT
85/6 MONT / Provigo
86/7 MONT
87/8 MONT
87/8 MONT / Kodak Poster
87/8 MONT / Vachon 17
87/8 MONT / Vachon 29
87/8 MONT / Vachon 37
87/8 MONT / Vachon 38
88/9 MONT
89/0 MONT
89/0 MONT / Kraft
90/1 MONT
91/2 MONT
83/4 Nova Scotia Voyageurs

MCPHERSON, ALEX
71/2 SLOU

MCPHERSON, DARWIN
90/1 ProCards IHL 2
90/1 ProCards 94
92/3 Dayton Bombers
93/4 Dayton Bombers
84/5 Brandon Wheat Kings
89/0 Saskatoon Blades

MCPOLIN, JUSTIN
95/6 Slapshot 172

MCQUAID, CHRIS
89/0 ProCards AHL 158
89/0 Halifax Citadels
90/1 Halifax Citadels
95/6 Halifax Moosehead
96/7 Halifax Moosehead
97/8 Halifax Moosehead
97/8 Halifax Moosehead

MCQUAT, JASON
93/4 Slapshot / Oshawa 24
95/6 Louisiana Ice Gators
95/6 Louisiana Ice Gators-2
96/7 Louisiana Ice Gators
97/8 Louisiana Ice Gators
98/9 Louisiana Ice Gators
99/0 Louisiana Ice Gators
00/1 Louisiana Ice Gators
92/3 Oshawa Generals

MCQUAT, ROB
93/4 Slapshot / Oshawa 18
92/3 Oshawa Generals

MCQUEEN, DAVE
95/6 Slapshot 330

MCRAE, BASIL
90/1 Bowman 187
01/2 Fleer Legacy 27
90/1 OPC/Topps 151
89/0 OPC Sticker 216
87/8 OPC Sticker 227-94
89/0 Panini Sticker 109
90/1 Panini Sticker 249
91/2 Panini Sticker 119
92/3 Parkhurst 391
93/4 Power Play 430
90/1 Pro Set 141
91/2 Pro Set 409
92/3 Pro Set 576
90/1 Score 261
91/2 Score CAN 391
92/3 Score 356
92/3 Score 509
93/4 Score 436
93/4 To. Stadium 273
90/1 Upper Deck 30
91/2 Upper Deck 388
95/6 UD BAP 76, ✍ S6
86/7 DETR / Little Caesars
87/8 MINS
88/9 MINS / ADA
86/7 QUEB
83/4 TORO
82/3 Fredericton Express

MCRAE, BASIL
02/3 Fleer Throwbacks 46, ✂ 1SC, ✂ 1SCTD, ✍ Aut.

MCRAE, CHRIS
89/0 ProCards AHL 308
90/1 ProCards 472
91/2 ProCards 240

MCRAE, COLIN
99/0 Brandon Wheat Kings

MCRAE, GORD
75/6 O-Pee-Chee 203
76/7 O-Pee-Chee 337
75/6 Topps 203
74/5 TORO
75/6 TORO
76/7 TORO
77/8 TORO

MCRAE, JIM
82/3 Fredericton Express

MCRAE, KEN
90/1 O-Pee-Chee 411
90/1 Panini/QUE 16
90/1 Pro Set 255
88/9 ProCards / Halifax
91/2 ProCards 542
89/0 QUÉB
89/0 QUÉB / Gene. Foods
89/0 QUÉB / Police
90/1 QUÉB
91/2 QUÉB / Petro-Canada
00/1 Austin Ice Bats
95/6 Phoenix Roadrunners
92/3 St. John's Maple Leafs
93/4 St. John's Maple Leafs
85/6 Sudbury Wolves
86/7 Sudbury Wolves

MCREAVY, PAT
34-43 BeeHive-1 [Detr.]

MCREYNOLDS, BRIAN
98/9 DEL 103
95/6 Leaf Elit Set 260
89/0 ProCards AHL 47
90/1 ProCards 24
91/2 ProCards 209
91/2 Upper Deck 434
95/6 UD Elitserien 147
89/0 WINN / Safeway
92/3 Binghampton Rangers
93/4 Phoenix Roadrunners
94/5 Phoenix Roadrunners

MCSHEFFREY, BRYAN
74/5 Loblaws
74/5 Loblaws Update
73/4 O-Pee-Chee 219
72/3 VANC / Royal Bank
73/4 VANC / Royal Bank

MCSORLEY, CHRIS
00/1 Kudos 69
88/9 ProCards / Indianapolis
87/8 Flint Spirits
94/5 Las Vegas Thunder
95/6 Las Vegas Thunder
96/7 Las Vegas Thunder
97/8 Las Vegas Thunder 12
92/3 Toledo Storm WIOT
92/3 Toledo Storm
93/4 Toledo Storm 2

MCSORLEY, MARTY
02/3 UD Foundations 33, 43, ✂ CH, ✂ DF, ✂ PP, ✂ PS
98/9 Aurora 169
91/2 Bowman 180
92/3 Bowman 35
93/4 Donruss 256
94/5 Donruss 447
95/6 Donruss 168
95/6 Donruss 354
96/7 Duracell DC9
93/4 EA Sports 62
95/6 Edge Ice L2
94/5 Flair 82
94/5 Fleer 98
96/7 Fl. Picks 166
92/3 Fleer Ultra 310
93/4 Fleer Ultra 227
93/4 Fleer Ultra 394
94/5 Fleer Ultra 102
95/6 Fleer Ultra 76
95/6 Hoyle / West. 6-Diamond
96/7 Kraft / Fav.
93/4 Leaf 352
94/5 Leaf 174
95/6 Leaf 309
98/9 McD's T3
87/8 O-Pee-Chee 205
90/1 OPC/Topps 17, 392
91/2 O-Pee-Chee 225
91/2 O-Pee-Chee 322
92/3 O-Pee-Chee 261
98/9 OPC Chrome 155
97/8 Omega 204
98/9 Pacific 388
97/8 Pacific CC 333
98/9 Pa. Paramount 213
89/0 Panini Sticker 99
90/1 Panini Sticker 234
91/2 Panini Sticker 84
92/3 Panini Sticker 73
93/4 Panini Sticker 208
94/5 Panini Sticker 178
95/6 Panini Sticker 274
91/2 Parkhurst 69
92/3 Parkhurst 304
92/3 Parkhurst CP17
93/4 Parkhurst 161
94/5 Parkhurst 106
95/6 Parkhurst 105
91/2 Pinnacle 35
92/3 Pinnacle 156
93/4 Pinnacle 374
94/5 Pinnacle 61
95/6 Pinnacle 36
96/7 Pinnacle 67
95/6 Playoff 51
94/5 POG 130
95/6 POG 140
94/5 Post
93/4 Power Play 191
93/4 Premier 395
94/5 Premier 146
90/1 Pro Set 124
91/2 Pro Set 100
92/3 Pro Set 69
91 Pro Set AC21
91/2 Pro Set Platinum 184
90/1 Score 271
91/2 Score 217
91/2 Score 407
91/2 Score CAN 217
91/2 Score CAN 297
92/3 Score 26
93/4 Score 212
93/4 Score 542
94/5 Score 20
95/6 Score 92
94/5 Select 124
98/9 SP Authentic ✍ SotT
00/1 Stadion 64
92/3 Topps 171
95/6 Topps 162
98/9 Topps 155
94/5 Topps Finest RL-11
91/2 To. Stadium 267
92/3 To. Stadium 481
93/4 To. Stadium 155
93/4 To. Stadium - Finest 8
90/1 Upper Deck 212
91/2 Upper Deck 199
92/3 Upper Deck 322
93/4 Upper Deck 487, GG9
94/5 Upper Deck 33, SP-127
95/6 Upper Deck 193, SE-129
96/7 Upper Deck 106
94/5 UD BAP R10, R150, G15
95/6 UD BAP 225, ✍ S225
95/6 UD CC 44
96/7 UD CC 172
97/8 UD Coll. Choice 221
99/0 UD Gretzky Excl. 61
96/7 UD Ice 60
99/0 UD MVP Cup 21
85/6 EDMO / Red Rooster
86/7 EDMO
86/7 EDMO / Red Rooster
87/8 EDMO
87/8 EDMO / Action 37
88/9 LOSA / Smokey
89/0 LOSA / Smokey 17
90/1 LOSA / Smokey 18
83/4 PITT / Coke Is It!-
84/5 PITT / Heinz
93/4 PITT / Foodland 5
00/1 Grand Rapids Griffins

MCSORLEY, MARTY
02/3 Fleer Throwbacks 52, ✂ 7SO, ✂ 5DTG, ✂ 6SC, ✂ 6SCTD, ✂ 7SO, ✂ 9SW, ✍ Aut.

MCSWEEN, DON
95 Panini Worlds 215
94/5 POG 179
88/9 ProCards / Rochester
89/0 ProCards AHL 280
90/1 ProCards 290
91/2 ProCards 16
94/5 Upper Deck 301
94/5 ANAH / Carl's Jr. 18
96/7 Grand Rapids Griffins
97/8 Milwaukee Admirals
99/0 Muskegon Fury
91/2 Rochester Americans DD
91/2 Rochester Americans GL
91/2 Rochester Americans WPC
92/3 San Diego Gulls
93/4 San Diego Gulls

MCTAGGART, JIM
93/4 Seattle Thunderbirds

MCTAMNEY, JOEY
89/0 7th..Sketch OHL 63

MCTAVISH, DALE
02/3 Cardset 71
98/9 Cardset 193
99/0 Cardset 213, AH 9-ruutu
00/1 Cardset MB 5
97/8 Hockey-Box
89/0 7th...Sketch OHL 110
90/1 7th..Sketch OHL 365
91/2 7th...Sketch OHL 127
96/7 Saint John Flames
91/2 Peterborough Petes

MCTAVISH, GORD
79/0 WINN

MCVEIGH, CHARLEY
33-35 Diamond Match Silv.
36-39 Diamond Match TT1
33/4 O-Pee-Chee 44
23/4 Paulins Candy 27
33/4 WWGum 38
37/8 World Wide Gum 93

MCVEY, WARD
24/5 Falcons Crescent 7

MCVICAR, JACK
30/1 La Presse

MCVICAR, ROBERT
99/0 Brandon Wheat Kings

MCVIE, TOM
88/9 ProCards / Utica
89/0 ProCards AHL 214
90/1 ProCards 564
79/0 WINN
97/8 Providence Bruins

MEAD, SCOTT
92/3 MPS SJHL 123

MEADMORE, NEIL
88/9 ProCards / Moncton
89/0 ProCards AHL 39

MEAGHER, MAURICE
91/2 7th...Sketch WHL 345

MEAGHER, RICK
82/3 O-Pee-Chee 144
88/9 OPC/Topps 235
90/1 OPC/Topps 36
90/1 O-Pee-Chee 488
91/2 O-Pee-Chee 58
89/0 OPC/Topps 116
87/8 Panini Sticker 316
88/9 Panini Sticker 110
89/0 Panini Sticker 125
90/1 Panini Sticker 273
90/1 Pro Set 267
91/2 Pro Set Midwest
90/1 Score 267, 359
83/4 Souhaits Keychain [Devils]
91/2 To. Stadium 85
90/1 Upper Deck 208, 285
83/4 NJER
84/5 NJER
87/8 SLOU
87/8 SLOU / Kodak

88/9 SLOU
88/9 SLOU / Kodak
89/0 SLOU / Kodak
90/1 SLOU / Kodak
92/3 SLOU / McDon. 23
77/8 Nova Scotia Voyageurs
92/3 Peoria Rivermen

MEANS, ERIC
91/2 Minnesota G'Gophers
92/3 Minnesota G'Gophers
93/4 Minnesota G'Gophers

MEARNS, RICK
91/2 7th...Sketch WHL 33

MEARS, GLEN
94/5 Flint Generals
95/6 Toledo Storm

MEASURES, ALLAN
98/9 Cardset 80
99/0 Cardset 283
00/1 Cardset 62
97/8 Hockey-Box
92/3 Jyvas Hyva 123
93/4 Jyvas Hyva 86
93/4 Sisu 119
94/5 Sisu 61
95/6 Sisu 33, 376
95/6 Sisu Limited 103

MECHELLER, KLAUS
95/6 DEL 223

MECIAR, STANISLAV
95/6 APS 224
93/4 Jyvas Hyva 350
94/5 Leaf Elit Set 174
93/4 Sisu 216

MECKLING, BRENT
82/3 Medicine Hat Tigers
83/4 Medicine Hat Tigers

MEDE, ROGER
94/5 DEL 146

MEDEIROS, BRIAN
93/4 Owen Sound Platers

MEDICUS, DIETER
94/5 DEL 8
95/6 DEL 169

MEDRIK, STANISLAV
95/6 APS 33
96/7 APS 33
96/7 DS Sticker 97
94 Semic 197
91 Semic Sticker 112
96 Wien 225

MEDVEDEV, ANDREI
02/3 Russian Future Stars 15
00/1 Mir 266, 301

MEECH, DEREK
00/1 Red Deer Rebels

MEEHAN, GERRY
70/1 Colgate 20
70/1 Eddie Sargent 20
71/2 Eddie Sargent 17
72/3 Eddie Sargent 29
70/1 Esso Power Player
74/5 Loblaws
74/5 Loblaws Update
70/1 O-Pee-Chee 125
71/2 O-Pee-Chee 160
72/3 O-Pee-Chee 22
73/4 O-Pee-Chee 22
74/5 O-Pee-Chee 99
76/7 O-Pee-Chee 35
76/7 O-Pee-Chee 396
77/8 O-Pee-Chee 53
78/9 O-Pee-Chee 128
70/1 Topps 125
71/2 Topps 74
72/3 Topps 16
73/4 Topps 22
74/5 Topps 99
76/7 Topps 35
77/8 Topps 53
78/9 Topps 128
71/2 Toronto Sun Photo
72/3 BUFF
73/4 BUFF
75/6 BUFF / Linnett
74/5 VANC / Royal Bank

MEEHAN, JEREMY
93/4 Slapshot / Detroit 11

MEEHAN, PAT
91/2 Avant Garde BCJHL 68
92/3 BCJHL 84

MEEK,
91/2 Avant Garde BCJHL 163

MEEKER, HOWIE
45-64 BeeHive-2 [Toro.]
48-52 Exhibits [Maple Leafs]
51/2 Parkhurst 72
52/3 Parkhurst 42
93/4 Parkie 56-57 133
45-54 Quaker Oats

MEGER, PAUL
45-64 BeeHive-2 [Mont.]
48-52 Exhibits [Canadiens]
51/2 La Patrie
51/2 Parkhurst 2
52/3 Parkhurst 4
53/4 Parkhurst 21
54/5 Parkhurst 94
55/6 Parkhurst 51
45-54 Quaker Oats

MEHALKO, BRAD
94/5 Parkie SE265
94/5 SP 184
00/1 Charlotte Checkers
00/1 Hartford Wolf Pack
01/2 Hartford Wolf Pack
93/4 Lethbridge Hurricanes
95/6 Lethbridge Hurricanes

MEIGHAN, RON
83/4 PITT / Heinz
82/3 North Bay Centennials

MEIKLE, DEREK
91/2 Air Canada SJHL D48

MEINS, JERRY
99/0 Houston Aeros

MEISNER, KEVIN
88/9 Sudbury Wolves

MEISSNER, DICK
45-64 BeeHive-2 [Bost.]
60/1 Shirriff 111
61/2 Shirriff 15
61/2 Topps 6, 64
63/4 Topps 60

MEISTER, RUPERT
94/5 DEL 51
95/6 DEL 2
96/7 DEL 48

MEITINGER, HOLGER
82 Semic Sticker 113

MEJZLIK, ROMAN
94/5 APS 196
95/6 APS 212
97/8 APS 302
97/8 DS 37
98/9 DS 41
97/8 DS Sticker 116
98/9 OFS 300

MELAMETSA, ANSSI
80/1 Mallasjuoma 51
85/6 WINN
85/6 WINN / Safety Tips

MELANOVSKY, MAREK
95/6 Upper Deck 543

MELANSON, BRUCE
83/4 Oshawa Generals

MELANSON, DEAN
01/2 BAP Mem. 416
93/4 Classic 143
93/4 Cla. 4 Sport 243
93/4 Cla. Prospects 102
90/1 7th..Sketch LHJMQ 209
91/2 7th...Sketch LHJMQ 21
01/2 UD Ice 150
00/1 Chicago Wolves
93/4 Rochester Americans
95/6 Rochester Americans
97/8 Rochester Americans
98/9 Rochester Americans

MELANSON, JULES
01/2 Drummondville

MELANSON, ROB
90/1 7th..Sketch LHJMQ 153
92/3 Cleveland Lumberjacks
91/2 Knoxville Cherokees
93/4 Muskegon Fury
95/6 Muskegon Fury
98/9 Muskegon Fury
99/0 Muskegon Fury

MELANSON, ROLLIE
92/3 Bowman 187
83/4 O-Pee-Chee 12
84/5 O-Pee-Chee 130
84/5 O-Pee-Chee 387
85/6 O-Pee-Chee 230
87/8 OPC/Topps 19
88/9 OPC/Topps 160
90/1 OPC/Topps 173
91/2 OPC Premier 97
83/4 OPC/Topps Sticker 88
83/4 OPC/Topps Sticker 317
84/5 OPC Sticker 92
87/8 OPC Sticker 213-80
88/9 OPC Sticker 151-18
87/8 Panini Sticker 271
88/9 Panini Sticker 69
89/0 ProCards AHL 213
90/1 ProCards 579
92/3 Topps 298
92/3 To. Stadium 184
91/2 Upper Deck 575
87/8 LOSA
84/5 MINS
85/6 MINS
01/2 MONT
02/3 MONT
83/4 NYIS
83/4 NYIS / News 22

MELANSON, STAN
90/1 7th..Sketch LHJMQ 231
91/2 7th...Sketch LHJMQ 28
96/7 Louisiana Ice Gators
97/8 Louisiana Ice Gators
98/9 Louisiana Ice Gators
99/0 Louisiana Ice Gators
00/1 Louisiana Ice Gators

MELAS, MIKE
98/9 Quad City Mallards
99/0 Quad City Mallards

MELENFANT, KEN
91/2 Air Canada SJHL D27

MELENOVSKY, MAREK
95/6 APS 195
96/7 APS 329
97/8 APS 307
97/8 DS 40
98/9 DS 39
99/0 DS 52
97/8 DS Sticker 121
98/9 OFS 59
99/0 OFS 240
00/1 OFS 279

MELFI, PATRICK
91/2 7th...Sketch LHJMQ 72

MELICHAR, JOSEF
00/1 BAP Mem. 494
01/2 DS 28
01/2 PS Titanium 177
01/2 PS Titanium Draft 161
00/1 WBS Penguins

MELICHERCIK, JAN
95/6 Halifax Moosehead

MELICHERIK, MILOS
00/1 OFS 285

MELIN, BRAD
84/5 Victoria Cougars

MELKERSSON, TOMMY
94/5 Leaf Elit Set 119
95/6 Leaf Elit Set 180
89/0 Semic Elitserien 35
90/1 Semic Elitserien 184
91/2 Semic Elitserien 35
92/3 Semic Elitserien 55
95/6 UD Elitserien 23
97/8 UD Elitserien 19
98/9 UD Elitserien 34

MELLANBY, SCOTT
02/3 BAP Mem. 197
02/3 Pacific 326
02/3 Pacific Complete 134
02/3 Slam Card
02/3 T. Total 27
02/3 Upper Deck 400
98/9 Aurora 83
98/9 Be A Player 58, ✍ Aut. 58
99/0 BAP Mem. 14
00/1 BAP Mem. 2
91/2 Bowman 236
92/3 Bowman 163
95/6 Bowman 84
93/4 Donruss 126
94/5 Donruss 42
95/6 Donruss 37
96/7 Donruss 49
97/8 Donruss 171
96/7 Do. Canadian 107
95/6 Do. Elite 86
96/7 Do. Elite 32
97/8 Do. Elite 76
97/8 Do. Preferred 135
97/8 Do. Priority 129
97/8 Do. Studio 41
92/3 Durivage 17
93/4 Durivage 46
93/4 EA Sports 53
94/5 Flair 65
94/5 Fleer 80
96/7 Fleer 40
95/6 Fleer Metal 60
92/3 Fleer Ultra 295
93/4 Fleer Ultra 328
94/5 Fleer Ultra 298
95/6 Fleer Ultra 242, CC-10
96/7 Fl. Ultra 66
93/4 Leaf 262
94/5 Leaf 182
95/6 Leaf 87
96/7 Leaf 132
97/8 Leaf 110
94/5 L. Limited 103
95/6 L. Limited 114
96/7 L. Limited 50, S-17
96/7 L. Preferred 111, LS-8
97/8 Limited 110
96/7 Metal Univ. 60
98/9 NHL Power Play
88/9 OPC/Topps 21
90/1 OPC/Topps 21
91/2 O-Pee-Chee 200
92/3 O-Pee-Chee 140
89/0 O-Pee-Chee 253
90/1 OPC Premier 73
91/2 OPC Premier 30
97/8 Omega 100
98/9 Pacific 226
99/0 Pacific 178
00/1 Pacific 182
01/2 Pacific 327
97/8 Pacific CC 321
97/8 Pa. Crown Roy. 59
97/8 Pa. Dynagon 54, T-53
97/8 Pa. Invincible 61
97/8 Pa. Paramount 81
98/9 Pa. Paramount 99
99/0 Pa. Paramount 102
00/1 Pa. Paramount 106
88/9 Panini Sticker 322
91/2 Panini Sticker 238
93/4 Panini Sticker 243
94/5 Panini Sticker 67
95/6 Panini Sticker 75
96/7 Panini Sticker 67
97/8 Panini Sticker 63
99/0 Panini Sticker 62
00/1 Panini Sticker 32
91/2 Parkhurst 50
92/3 Parkhurst 52
93/4 Parkhurst 81
94/5 Parkhurst 85
95/6 Parkhurst 355
00/1 Parkhurst P-193
91/2 Pinnacle 45
92/3 Pinnacle 346
93/4 Pinnacle 168
93/4 Pinnacle Expa. 6
94/5 Pinnacle 73
95/6 Pinnacle 78
96/7 Pinnacle 126
96/7 Pi. Be A Player 171, ✍ Aut. 171
97/8 Pi. Certified 107
97/8 Pi. Inside 165
95/6 Pi. Summit 57
96/7 Pi. Summit 8
97/8 Pi. Totally 107
95/6 Pi. Zenith 25
96/7 Pi. Zenith 16
95/6 Playoff 154
96/7 Playoff 387
94/5 POG 108
95/6 POG 116
93/4 Power Play 98
93/4 Premier 249
94/5 Premier 144
00/1 Private Stock ✄ GUG 53
95/6 Pro Magnet 89
90/1 Pro Set 220
91/2 Pro Set 172
91/2 Pro Set 383
92/3 Pro Set 54
91/2 Pro Set Platinum 173
00/1 Revolution 64
90/1 Score 242
91/2 Score 279
92/3 Score 25T
91/2 Score CAN 575
92/3 Score 148
93/4 Score 503
93/4 Score 63
94/5 Score 102
95/6 Score 134
96/7 Score 31, S-13
97/8 Score 177
94/5 Select 85
95/6 Select CE 3
96/7 Select CE 84
00/1 Signature 202, ✍ Aut. 14
96/7 SBx Impact 46
94/5 SP 47
95/6 SP 55
96/7 SP 65
97/8 SP Authentic 68
96/7 SLU
95/6 Super Sticker 49
96/7 Team Out!
92/3 Topps 444
95/6 Topps 260
98/9 Topps 13
99/0 Topps 205
00/1 Topps 216
99/0 To. Chrome 75
95/6 To. Finest 136
96/7 To. Picks 101
91/2 To. Stadium 110
92/3 To. Stadium 462
93/4 To. Stadium 31
93/4 To. Stadium 369
95/6 To. Stadium EC170
95/6 TSC Members Only 32
98/9 UD Choice 90
91/2 Upper Deck 542
92/3 Upper Deck 119
93/4 Upper Deck 107, SP-57
94/5 Upper Deck 92, SP-121
95/6 Upper Deck 399
96/7 Upper Deck 200, 265, X25
97/8 Upper Deck 282
98/9 Upper Deck 279
99/0 Upper Deck 60
94/5 UD BAP ✍ 170
96/7 UD Black Diam. 127
97/8 UD Black Diam. 92
95/6 UD CC 171
96/7 UD CC 102
97/8 UD Coll. Choice 100, SQ37
98/9 UD G. Reserve 279
99/0 UD G. Reserve 60
99/0 UD MVP 90
00/1 UD MVP 81
00/1 UD Vintage 154
99/0 Victory 122
00/1 Victory 103
99/0 WGretzky 77
91/2 EDMO / IGA
92/3 EDMO / IGA 015
93/4 FLOR
94/5 FLOR / Health Plan
96/7 FLOR / Winn-Dixie
97/8 FLOR / Winn-Dixie
86/7 PHIL
89/0 PHIL
90/1 PHIL

MELLIOS, LOUI
91/2 Avant Garde BCJHL 117
92/3 BCJHL 180
92/3 BCJHL 184

MELLOR, TOM
72 Semic Sticker 121

MELNECHUK, JEFF
93/4 Slapshot / Sudbury 2
93/4 Sudbury Wolves

MELNYK, DOUG
91/2 Cincinnati Cyclones

MELNYK, GERRY
45-64 BeeHive-2 [Detr.]
45-64 BeeHive-2 [Chic.]
68/9 O-Pee-Chee 120
60/1 Parkhurst 28
60/1 Shirriff 51
61/2 Shirriff 38
68/9 Topps 120

MELNYK, LARRY
86/7 OPC/Topps 95
90/1 O-Pee-Chee 419
89/0 O-Pee-Chee 288
86/7 OPC Sticker 224-93
88/9 OPC Sticker 53-184
89/0 opcSticker 73-212
87/8 Panini Sticker 111
82/3 Post [Bost.]
84/5 EDMO
84/5 EDMO / Red Rooster
88/9 EDMO / Action 14
87/8 VANC / Shell
88/9 VANC / Mohawk
89/0 VANC / Mohawk
84/5 Nova Scotia Oilers

MELNYK, SCOTT
86/7 Portland Winter Hawks

MELOCH, JASON
91/2 7th...Sketch OHL 2

MELOCHE, DENIS
73/4 Vancouver Blazers

MELOCHE, ERIC
90/1 7th..Sketch LHJMQ 18
91/2 7th...Sketch LHJMQ 280
91 7th..Sketch Mem.Cup 69

MELOCHE, ERIC
01/2 BAP Mem. 396
01/2 UD PlayMakers Ltd 137
01/2 UD Ice 147
01/2 UD Premier 78
00/1 WBS Penguins
01/2 WBS Penguins
02/3 WBS Penguins

MELOCHE, GILLES
72/3 Eddie Sargent 50
72/3 Post 18
74/5 Loblaws
82/3 McDonald's Les Étoiles 3
72/3 O-Pee-Chee 112
73/4 O-Pee-Chee 2
74/5 O-Pee-Chee 205
75/6 O-Pee-Chee 190
76/7 O-Pee-Chee 36
77/8 O-Pee-Chee 109
78/9 O-Pee-Chee 28
79/0 O-Pee-Chee 136
80/1 O-Pee-Chee 47
81/2 O-Pee-Chee 165
82/3 O-Pee-Chee 170
83/4 O-Pee-Chee 177
84/5 O-Pee-Chee 104
87/8 OPC/Topps 107
88/9 OPC/Topps 8
81/2 OPC Sticker 93
82/3 OPC/Topps Sticker 195
84/5 OPC Sticker 51
86/7 OPC Sticker 59
87/8 OPC Sticker 168-28
88/9 OPC Sticker 238-108
87/8 Panini Sticker 140
82/3 Post [Minn.]
72/3 Topps 69
73/4 Topps 175
74/5 Topps 205
75/6 Topps 190
76/7 Topps 36
77/8 Topps 109
78/9 Topps 28
79/0 Topps 136
80/1 Topps 47
81/2 Topps 109 [West]
84/5 Topps 79
78/9 MINS / Cloverleaf 1
79/0 MINS
80/1 MINS
81/2 MINS
82/3 MINS
83/4 MINS
84/5 MINS
84/5 MINS / 7-Eleven 8
86/7 PITT / Kodak
87/8 PITT / Kodak

MELOCHE, JASON
91/2 Cornwall Royals

MELOFF, CHRIS
72/3 Ottawa Nationals

MELROSE, BARRY
93/4 Kraft / PB
79/0 O-Pee-Chee 386
82/3 O-Pee-Chee 328
80/1 Pepsi Bottle Cap
82/3 Post [Toro.]
89/0 ProCards AHL 321
90/1 ProCards 476
91/2 ProCards 140
01/2 To. Chrome -CA3, ✍ CA3
01/2 T/O Archives 45
81/2 TORO
79/0 WINN

MELROSE, KEVAN
90/1 ProCards 613
91/2 ProCards 574

MELSON, TAJ
98/9 Las Vegas Thunder

MELTON, KELLY
96/7 Dayton Ice Bandits

MELUZIN, ROMAN
94/5 APS 198
95/6 APS 41, 379, 404
96/7 APS 42, 350, 414
97/8 APS 62
99/0 Cardset 321
97/8 DS 9
98/9 DS 110
96/7 DS Sticker 15, 109
97/8 DS Sticker 294
98/9 OFS 25, 429, 483
01/2 OFS 64
91/2 Upper Deck WJC 94
00/1 UD DEL 161
96 Wien 119

MELYAKOV, IGOR
94/5 Classic DP6
00/1 Mir 110

MENARD, DERRY
98/9 Cardset 144

MENARD, HOWIE
69/0 O-Pee-Chee 73
70/1 O-Pee-Chee 124
70/1 Topps 124

MENARD, MARTIN
97 Bowman 54
94/5 Slapshot Memorial 68
97/8 Rochester Americans

MENARD, TERRY
97/8 Fort Worth Brahmas
98/9 Fort Worth Brahmas
99/0 Fort Worth Brahmas
93/4 Thunder Bay Senators
95/6 Thunder Bay Senators

MENARD, CARL
90/1 7th..Sketch LHJMQ 80
91/2 7th...Sketch LHJMQ 19

MENARD, STEPHANE
90/1 7th..Sketch LHJMQ 235
91/2 7th...Sketch LHJMQ 5
94/5 Knoxville Cherokees

MÉNARD BURROWS, ALEXANDRE
00/1 Shawinigan 19

MENDE, KARSTEN
94/5 DEL 211
95/6 DEL 203
96/7 DEL 344
94 Semic 278

MENDEL, ROB
95/6 DEL 6
96/7 DEL 5
90/1 ProCards 198
91/2 ProCards 335

MENGES, GREG
91/2 Greensboro Monarchs
92/3 Greensboro Monarchs 19

MENHART, MARIAN
98/9 OFS 8
99/0 OFS 152
95/6 Prince Albert Raiders

MENICCI, TOM
94/5 Hampton Roads
98/9 Phoenix Mustangs 15

MENSONEN, JARNO
98/9 BC Icemen 10
98/9 BC Icemen

MENTIS, JIM
84/5 Victoria Cougars

MENYHART, GASPAR
79 Panini Sticker 271

MENZ, R
85/6 Minnesota-Duluth 34

MERCALFE, SCOTT
93/4 Knoxville Cherokees

MERCIER, CHAD
96/7 Regina Pats
01/2 Regina Pats

MERCIER, DON
86/7 Moncton G'Flames

MERCIER, MARTIN
92/3 Maine Black Bears

MEREDITH, GREG
83/4 O-Pee-Chee 88

MERK, KLAUS
94/5 DEL 70
95/6 DEL 50, 440
96/7 DEL 247
98/9 DEL 273, 327
99/0 Eishockey 168
95 Globe 217
95 Panini Worlds 52
94 Semic 271
92 Semic Sticker 171
93 Semic Sticker 150
00/1 UD DEL 19
01/2 UD DEL 39, G2
96 Wien 192

MERKOSKY, GLENN
88/9 ProCards / Adirondack
89/0 ProCards AHL 323
90/1 ProCards 470
91/2 ProCards 141
94/5 Slapshot / Sudbury 24

MERRA, MARTTI
92/3 Jyvas Hyva 103
93/4 Jyvas Hyva 193
93/4 Sisu 255

MERRICK, WAYNE
74/5 Loblaws
74/5 O-Pee-Chee 66
75/6 O-Pee-Chee 228
76/7 O-Pee-Chee 18
76/7 OPC 383
77/8 O-Pee-Chee 176
78/9 O-Pee-Chee 258
79/0 O-Pee-Chee 169
80/1 O-Pee-Chee 345
81/2 O-Pee-Chee 216
82/3 O-Pee-Chee 205
82/3 Post [NYIs.]
74/5 Topps 66
75/6 Topps 228
76/7 Topps 18
77/8 Topps 176
78/9 Topps 258
79/0 Topps 169
79/0 NYIS
83/4 NYIS
83/4 NYIS / News 10
93/4 NYIS / Bank
72/3 SLOU
73/4 SLOU

MERRITT, RYAN
90/1 7th..Sketch OHL 187
91/2 7th...Sketch OHL 61
89/0 Windsor Spitfires

MERSCH, MIKE
89/0 ProCards IHL 161
90/1 ProCards 386
87/8 Flint Spirits
88/9 Flint Spirits
88/9 Flint Spirits

MERTZIG, JAN
95/6 Leaf Elit Set 253, R-6
95/6 UD Elitserien 117
97/8 UD Elitserien 120, C8

MERZ, SUZANNE
94/5 Classic W28

MESICEK, RADEK
94/5 APS 234
95/6 APS 321
97/8 APS 103
96/7 DS Sticker 270

MESIKAMMEN, ILKKA
66/7 Champion 75
65/6 Hellas 2
70/1 Kuvajulkaisut 197
78/9 SM-Liiga 203
71/2 Williams Finnish 232
72/3 Williams Finnish 216
73/4 Williams Finnish 291

MESSER, KEVIN
91/2 Air Canada SJHL D6
92/3 MPS SJHL 120

MESSIER, DOUG
83/4 Moncton Alpines

MESSIER, ERIC
02/3 Pacific Complete 329
02/3 T. Total 213
98/9 Aurora 49
01/2 BAP Mem. ✄ SCC
97/8 Limited 125
97/8 Omega 61
98/9 Pacific 165
00/1 Pacific 116, ✄ GWJ 2
97/8 Pa. Invincible R-55
98/9 Pa. Paramount 58
97/8 Pa. Revolution 36
97/8 Pi. Be A Player 204, ✍ Aut. 204
00/1 Private Stock ✄ GUG 26
91/2 7th...Sketch LHJMQ 111
97/8 SP Authentic 178
00/1 Stadium 122
98/9 UD Choice 53
97/8 Upper Deck 45
98/9 Upper Deck 70
97/8 UD Black Diam. 13
98/9 UD G. Reserve 70
01/2 Vanguard ✄ DGM 37

MESSIER, JOBY
92/3 Classic 72
92/3 Classic LP10
92/3 Classic Four Sport 196
92/3 Classic Prospects 76
92/3 Classic Prospects 127
92/3 Classic Prospects BC13
93/4 Fleer Ultra 170
93/4 Fleer Ultra ARS 6
93/4 Leaf 298
94/5 Leaf 375
93/4 Parkhurst 399
94/5 Pinnacle 497
93/4 Power Play 161
93/4 Premier 522
94/5 Premier 476
93/4 To. Stadium 339
93/4 Upper Deck 73
92/3 Binghampton Rangers
94/5 Binghampton Rangers
98/9 Long Beach Ice Dogs

MESSIER, MARK
02/3 Atomic ✄ GWJ 16
02/3 BAP All-Star 58-59, ✄ ASJ, ✄ HSHSJers
02/3 BAP Mem. 118, ✄ ASJ35, ✄ ASE15, ✄ ASN15, ✄ ASTJ14, ✄ AST3, ✄ AST4, ✄ AST20, ✄ HSHSJers 27, ✄ TM7, /Cup
02/3 Bowman 69
02/3 Calder 47, -HH 9
02/3 Crown Royale ✄ GWDP 16
02/3 Exclusive 117
02/3 First Edition 133, ✄ Jers., ✄ DGJ 18, ✄ HSHSJers 10
02/3 In The GU 49, 149, ✄ E17, ✄ GUJ17, ✄ SJ17, ✄ T11
02/3 O-Pee-Chee 242
02/3 Pacific 256, ✄ GWJ 36
02/3 Pacific Complete 24
02/3 Parkhurst 23, ✄ GJ21, ✄ SJ21, ✄ HSHSJers, ✄ NH3, ✄ NH6, ✄ PP9
02/3 Parkhurst Retro 145, ✄ RJ4, ✄ RSJ4
02/3 PS Titanium ✄ GWJ 45
02/3 Quest for the Cup 67, - RTC 10, ✄ GWJ 11
02/3 Signature ✄ SGJ17
02/3 Slam Card
02/3 Sports Vault 86
02/3 SPx 126
02/3 Starz
02/3 Topps 242
02/3 To. Chrome 133
02/3 To. Limited 242
02/3 T. Total 314
02/3 UD Superstars R1, ✄ LLT
02/3 Ultimate Mem. ✄ A8 (x3), ✄ CSTW, ✄ Emb, ✄ FS (x3), ✄ GUJ, ✄ GUSJ, ✄ ITN, ✄ LA, ✄ Num, ✄ PS (x2)
02/3 Ultimate Mem. ✄ Active 8 [Messier, Francis, Yzerman]
02/3 Upper Deck 364
02/3 UD Artistic ✄ SS
02/3 UD Foundations 32, 65
02/3 UD MVP -SD, ST, Souv.
02/3 UD Piece 108, ✄ EC (x2)
02/3 UD Rookie 67
02/3 UD Top Shelf ✄ M (x3), ✄ ST
02/3 UD Vintage 170, 280, GB 170
02/3 Vanguard ✄ GWJ31
02/3 Victory 139
94/5 Action Packed
01/2 Adrenaline 128
01/2 ASG History
01/2 Atomic 66, CP 12, PP 24, TN 10
98/9 Aurora 189, -ALC 19, -CF 48, -MACF 19, -Cube 18
99/0 Aurora 140, Stripe 140, ST-20
00/1 Aurora 96, Pins. 96, CF-20, ✄ GWJ-9
98/9 Be A Player 290, M-2, M-8, H-1, P-17, ✍ Aut. 290, ✄ G-20, ✄ AS-10, ✄ S-10
99/0 BAP Mem. 265, H-14, ✄ J-10, ✄ D-18, ✄ TM-3, ✄ TM-8, ✄ TM-36
00/1 BAP Mem. 133, 443, ✄ J-23, ✄ H-1, ✄ TM-7, ✄ TM-32
01/2 BAP Mem. 97, ✄ 500GS, ✄ ASJ, ✄ ASE, ✄ ASN, ✄ ASD, ✄ AST, HSHS
01/2 BAP Update ✄ H4
96/7 Bic.Sports Aces Q-D
97/8 Bicycle Q-Heart
95/6 Bicycle Sports Aces J-Club
90/1 Bowman 199, -HT 4
91/2 Bowman 114
92/3 Bowman 113
92/3 Bowman 234
95/6 Bowman 8, BB6
01/2 Bowman 82
98/9 Bowman's Best 5
91 Canada Cup
99/0 Crown Royale 137, TC-10
00/1 Crown Royale 71, JotC-18
01/2 Crown Royale 97, ASH 16, JotC 22, LH 7
93/4 Donruss 222
93/4 Donruss O
94/5 Donruss 9, D-1, IM-7
95/6 Donruss 271, I-5
96/7 Donruss 16, ES-5, HL-8
97/8 Donruss 14, L2L-23
98/9 Donruss ES 4
96/7 Do. Canadian 87, OC-3
97/8 Do. Canadian 50, NP-2, SCS-23
95/6 Do. Elite 46, CE-8
96/7 Do. Elite 22, P-2
97/8 Do. Elite 5, 127, 150, C-4, PN-3
97/8 Do. Preferred 17, 177, LT-7C, PM-4, / Tin 15, WideTin 8
97/8 Do. Priority 16, 189, DD-7, OD-14, Post-6, Stamp-6
97/8 Do. Studio 9, S-6, P-9
98/9 Dynagon Ice 189, -FT 19, -TC 26
99/0 Dynagon Ice 194
93/4 EA Sports 87
97/8 Esso 20
88/9 Esso All-Star
83/4 Esso Stars
01/2 eTopps 18
94/5 Flair 115, CIS-8
96/7 Flair 61, HN-9, NT-1
94/5 Fleer 136, H-7
96/7 Fleer 71, ART-15
95/6 Fleer Metal 97, IW-8
96/7 Fl. Picks F50-29, CC-5
92/3 Fleer Ultra 139, -AW 1, -AW 10
93/4 Fleer Ultra 183
93/4 Fleer Ultra PP 6
94/5 Fleer Ultra 140, ASG4, PP-7
95/6 Fleer Ultra 105, 393, CC-11, PP-5
96/7 Fl. Ultra 109, CTI-7, MM-8
88/9 Frito Lay
83/4 Funmate Puffy 4 [w/]
00 Gatorade Sticker
91/2 Gillette 31
95 Globe 84
96/7 Got-Um
01/2 Heads Up 65, / Bobble
92/3 High Five / Promo P4
93/4 Hockey Wit 102
95/6 Hoyle / East. A-Diamond
92/3 Humpty Dumpty
92/3 Kellogg's
94 Koululainen
89/0 Kraft 15
90/1 Kraft 32, 71
91/2 Kraft 16
92/3 Kraft / Kraft Singles
93/4 Kraft / PB
94/5 Kraft / SS
95/6 Kraft / KD
97/8 Kraft / JTP, KD, Casecard
98/9 Kraft / Post 15
99/0 Kraft / KD, / PB
00/1 Kraft 28
86/7 Kraft Sports 18
93/4 Leaf 158
94/5 Leaf 11, GLS-5, LL-15
95/6 Leaf 68
96/7 Leaf 180, FOI-15, S-8
97/8 Leaf 9, 176, FOI-11
94/5 L. Limited 89
95/6 L. Limited 75
96/7 L. Limited 65, BTB-2
96/7 L. Preferred 66, LS-42, SP-4
97/8 Limited 25, 84, 187, FG-44, FG-59
96/7 Maggers 99
82/3 McDonald's Les Étoiles 15
92/3 McDonald's McH-01
95/6 McDonald's McD-5
96/7 McDonald's McD-22
01/2 McDonald's -HG 6
96/7 Metal Univ. 99, CS-8, LW-13
99/0 Millenium 235, P-6, D-2, ✍ Aut. 235, ✍ P-6, ✍ D-2, ✄ J-11, ✄ JS-11
95/6 Cool Trade 5
98/9 NHL Power Play
80/1 O-Pee-Chee 289
81/2 O-Pee-Chee 118
82/3 O-Pee-Chee 117
83/4 O-Pee-Chee 23
83/4 O-Pee-Chee 39
84/5 O-Pee-Chee 213
84/5 O-Pee-Chee 254
85/6 O-Pee-Chee 177
86/7 OPC/Topps 186
87/8 OPC/Topps 112
88/9 OPC/Topps 93
90/1 OPC/Topps 130, 193
90/1 O-Pee-Chee 519
90/1 Topps-TL 16
91/2 O-Pee-Chee 346
92/3 O-Pee-Chee 208
92/3 O-Pee-Chee 258
92/3 OPC - Anniv. 13
92/3 O-Pee-Chee Box
01/2 O-Pee-Chee 55
89/0 OPC/Topps 65
98/9 OPC Chrome 138, -Reprint 2
90/1 OPC Leaders 28
90/1 OPC Premier 71
91/2 OPC Premier 51
92/3 OPC Premier SP15
88/9 OPC Stars 25
81/2 OPC Sticker 210
82/3 OPC/Topps Sticker 94
82/3 OPC/Topps Sticker 159
83/4 OPC/Topps Sticker 97
83/4 OPC/Topps Sticker 98
83/4 OPC/Topps Sticker 157
84/5 OPC Sticker 5
84/5 OPC Sticker 261
85/6 OPC Sticker 228-95
86/7 OPC Sticker 79
87/8 OPC Sticker 92
88/9 OPC Sticker 230
89/0 opcSticker 227
97/8 Omega 231, 250, GF-19, S-12, SHLC-20, TL 20
98/9 Omega 236, -EOP 20, -FTF 10, -Onl. 34, -PI 10, -Prism 20
99/0 Omega 234, 5ST-12, CC-20, EOP-20, NAAS-10
98/9 Pacific 11, -DI 18, -GCDC 34, -Time. 20
99/0 Pacific 426, CI-20, GC-36, TL-27
00/1 Pacific 411, ✄ GWJ-14, GCDC-35, PR-20
01/2 Pacific 264, GCDC 14
97/8 Pacific CC 11, CS-13, CM-1, CCA-8, GCDC-16, SS-5B
97/8 Pa. Crown Roy. 136, BOS-20, HT-19, L-20
98/9 Pa. Crown Roy. 135, -MP 19, -PotG 24, -PP 23
97/8 Pa. Dynagon 81, 140, KN-7, T-3, BKS-63
97/8 Pa. Invincible 89, AZ-16, FP-22, OTG-13, R-131
97/8 Pa. Paramount 190, P-20, CG-12, BN-20
98/9 Pa. Paramount 236, -HOFB 10, -SD 19, -TC 26
99/0 Pa. Paramount 235, HOFB-10, IAd-20, IAI-27, PB-36
00/1 Pa. Paramount 165
97/8 Pa. Revolution 142, ASG-19
98/9 Pa. Revolution 141, -CTLC 19, -Show. 35
98/9 Panini Photocard [x2]
87/8 Panini Sticker 194
87/8 Panini Sticker 195
87/8 Panini Sticker 196
87/8 Panini Sticker 252
87/8 Panini Sticker 263
88/9 Panini Sticker 61
89/0 Panini Sticker 74
90/1 Panini Sticker 219
90/1 Panini/EDM 14, G
91/2 Panini Sticker 124
92/3 Panini Sticker 233
93/4 Panini Sticker I
94/5 Panini Sticker 82
95/6 Panini Sticker 102
96/7 Panini Sticker 101
97/8 Panini Sticker 83
98/9 Panini Sticker 219
99/0 Panini Sticker 307, 331
00/1 Panini Sticker 209
95 Panini Worlds 279
91/2 Parkhurst 121
91/2 Parkhurst 213
91/2 Parkhurst 468
91/2 Parkhurst 475
91/2 Parkhurst PHC8
92/3 Parkhurst 111
92/3 Parkhurst CP4
93/4 Parkhurst 127
93/4 Parkhurst D4
94/5 Parkhurst V33, YCTG-27
95/6 Parkhurst 136, CCP-7, PP-6, PP-12
00/1 Parkhurst P-234
01/2 Parkhurst 50, ✄ 500GS, ✄ PJ6, ✄ PS6, ✄ HSHSJers, ✄ M12, ✄ M39, ✄ T3, ✄ T24
95 Parkhurst Phonecard
94/5 Parkie SE113
80/1 Pepsi Bottle Cap
91/2 Pinnacle 50
91/2 Pinnacle 390
92/3 Pinnacle 1
93/4 Pinnacle 125
93/4 Pinnacle 238
93/4 Pinnacle CA15
94/5 Pinnacle 300, GR9, TP9
95/6 Pinnacle 5, FS-1, FC-12
96/7 Pinnacle 2, BTN-12, TP-4
97/8 Pinnacle 27, 194, TP-5, P-9
96/7 Pi. Be A Player 111, BB-19, ✍ Aut. 111, ✍ DCS
97/8 Pi. Be A Player TN17
97/8 Pi. BeeHive 30, BHT-2
97/8 Pi. Certified 43, CT-12
97/8 Pi. Epix E12
95/6 Pi. FANtasy 18
96/7 Pi. FANtasy 6
97/8 Pi. Inside 50, IT-18, / Can 22
96/7 Pi. Mint 16
97/8 Pi. Mint 13
95/6 Pi. Summit 1, GMC-16
96/7 Pi. Summit 111, 198, HV-1
97/8 Pi. Totally 43
95/6 Pi. Zenith 18, ZT-5
96/7 Pi. Zenith 94, CS-1
95/6 Playoff 175, 284
96/7 Playoff 424
94/5 POG 166
95/6 POG 180, I-006, I-024
81/2 Post 15
82/3 Post [Edmo.]
97/8 Pi. Post 5, F3
93/4 Power Play 162
93/4 Power Play PL 9
93/4 Premier 430
94/5 Premier 1, 278, GTG-15
00/1 Premier Plus 11, TT7
99/0 Prism 141, DAS-8
00/1 Private Stock 66, AC-15, Res. 15, PS-38, PSS-18, ✄ GUG-77
01/2 Pr. Stock 64, -PS 49
00/1 PS Titanium 62
01/2 PS Titanium 95, ✄ DSJ 27
01/2 PS Titanium Draft ✄ 62
95/6 Pro Magnet 98
90/1 Pro Set 91, 349, 397, 704
91/2 Pro Set 74
91/2 Pro Set 282
91/2 Pro Set 439
91/2 Pro Set 579
92/3 Pro Set 111
92/3 Pro Set CC1
91/2 Pro Set Platinum 81
91/2 Pro Set Platinum PC20
87/8 Pro Sport CW13
91/2 Puck / Pro Set 19
99/0 Revolution 142, NI-20, O-20, SS-35, TL-20, / CSC 142
00/1 Revolution 97, ✄ GUG-7
90/1 Score 100, 315, 360, / Promo 100
90/1 Sco. Hot Cards 33
91/2 Score 285
91/2 Score 373
91/2 Score 420
92/3 Score 85T
91/2 Score CAN 263
91/2 Score CAN 310
91/2 Score CAN 505
91/2 Score CAN 635
92/3 Score 300
92/3 Score 431
92/3 Score 493
92/3 Score 521
93/4 Score 200
93/4 Score DD5
94/5 Score DT16, TF15
95/6 Score 50, DT-4, GB-15
96/7 Score 24, DT-5, SD-10
97/8 Score 85
97/8 Score Vanc. 3
92/3 Seasons 26
94/5 Select 1
95/6 Select CE 14, DS-15
96/7 Select CE 36, C-5
94 Semic 350
94 Semic 94
95 Semic 97
89 Semic Sticker 69
91 Semic Sticker 63
93 Semic Sticker 85
93 Semic Sticker 202
84/5 7-Eleven
00/1 Signature 98, HSHS, ✄ J-11, ✄ HSHSJers
01/2 Signature C-55, ✍ Aut., ✄ 500GS, ✄ GUE38, ✄ GJ40, ✄ HSHSJers, ✄ GSJ40, ✄ ITN38, ✄ TM19
95/6 SBx Emotion 116, NP-3
95/6 SBx Impact 111, CTI-5, IQ-5
96/7 SBx Impact 82, BR-14
83/4 Souhaits Keychain [Oilers]
94/5 SP 73, P-28
95/6 SP 92, E19, FX14
96/7 SP 98, CW-11, GF-10
97/8 SP Authentic 157, I16
98/9 SP Authentic 85, SO12
99/0 SP Authentic 85
00/1 SP Authentic 57, ST1, SP5, ✍ SotT, ✍ SotTD, ✍ SofTT
01/2 SP Authentic 54, 103, ✄ NN
00/1 SP GU 41, ✄ TotG, ✄ C, ✄ P (x2)
01/2 SP GU 35, ✄ TotG
91/2 SI For Kids 33
96/7 SPx 27, HH-5
97/8 SPx 32, D-SPX3
99/0 SPx 149
00/1 SPx 43, 74, P5, S5
01/2 SPx 42, ✍ Sig
98/9 SPx Finite 160
98/9 SPx Prospects 57, PS30
00/1 Stadion 67, 150
99/0 Stadium 3, Chrome 3, CA24
00/1 Stadium 213, BT19
01/2 Stadium 10, G40, HS1
93/4 SLU / Card 504085
93/4 SLU / Card 504107
93/4 Starting Lineup
94/5 Starting Lineup
96/7 SLU
97/8 SLU
98/9 SLU
83/4 Stater Mint H20
95/6 Super Sticker 78, 80
96/7 Team Out!
84/5 Topps 159
92/3 Topps 258
92/3 Topps 274
95/6 Topps 5, 240, HGC29, M3, 3PL, 1RL
98/9 Topps 138, L11, M19, -Reprint
99/0 Topps 92, 283, SCH8
00/1 Topps 20, PC-1
01/2 Topps 55
99/0 To. Chrome 92, 283
00/1 To. Chrome 19, PC-1
01/2 To. Chrome 55
94/5 Topps Finest 16, BBB-2, RL-1
95/6 To. Finest 50, 99
98/9 To. Finest 68, M41-44, R18
96 Topps Finest Bronze 15
98/9 T. Gold Label 6
99/0 To. Gold Label 36
00/1 To. Gold Label 47, B9
01/2 To. Heritage 7, HH7, OSA, ✄ OSS
01/2 To. Heritage 14
96/7 To. Picks 25, FC6, TS5
99/0 To. Prmr. Plus 24, FP2
01/2 To. Reserve 9
91/2 To. Stadium 111
92/3 To. Stadium 241
92/3 To. Stadium 443
93/4 To. Stadium 35
94/5 To. Stadium 1, DAD-2, F-3
95/6 To. Stadium EC178, M9,N8
92 TSC Members Only
93/4 TSC Members Only 27
94/5 TSC Members Only 19
95/6 TSC Members Only 40
00/1 To. Stars 92, AS3
95/6 T. Super Skills 60
98/9 UD Choice 211, BH9, SQ29
00/1 UD Heroes 151, 179, L5, PI1, SS8, ✄ GT, ✄ GC, ✍ SG
01/2 UD PlayMakers Ltd 66
00/1 UD Reserve 57, 119, OS6, PP5, PSJ, ✍ PSJ
98/9 UD3 53, 113, 173
00/1 Ultimate Mem. ✄ A8-1, ✄ A8-2, ✄ D-2, ✄ H-9, ✄ J-11, ✄ Jers. 9, ✄ JJ-2, ✄ MO-4, ✄ RA-10, ✄ S-11, ✄ TM-36, ✄ UC-7
01/2 Ultimate Mem. ✄ 500GS, ✄ A8, ✄ ASGH, ✄ DD, ✄ EA, ✄ Emb., ✄ Jers., ✄ S&J, ✄ ITN, ✄ JE, ✄ JJ, ✄ NP, ✄ RT, ✄ SCP, ✄ SCW, ✍ Aut.
99/0 Ult. Victory 85, TV1
90/1 Upper Deck 44, 206, 321, 494, -Sticker [x3]
91/2 Upper Deck 14
91/2 Upper Deck 246
91/2 Upper Deck 545
91/2 Upper Deck 610
91/2 Upper Deck 620
92/3 Upper Deck 242
92/3 Upper Deck 432
92/3 Upper Deck 437
92/3 Upper Deck 453
93/4 Upper Deck 51, 298, GG-5, SP-103
94/5 Upper Deck 62, 234, 563, C22, H4, R34, R54, SP-51
95/6 Upper Deck 169, 217, AS-16, F-7, H-9, R-39, R-56, SE-141
96/7 Upper Deck 299, HH2, LS2, SS9A, ✄ GJ1
97/8 Upper Deck 374, SS11, SG11, S5, T11B
98/9 Upper Deck 195, LS11
99/0 Upper Deck 126, HOF11
00/1 Upper Deck 119, 410, D10, EC8, FT5, L8, NC10, TT6, ✄ GJ
01/2 Upper Deck 114, 217, GA1, LP8, SS17

00 ✂ UD APOH 500, ✂✍ 500
95/6 UD ASG MVP19
96/7 UD All-Star YCTG AR14
96/7 UD Black Diam. 100, RC11
97/8 UD Black Diam. 7, PC23
98/9 UD Black Diam. 85, WF24
99/0 UD Black Diam. 86, DM9
00/1 UD Black Diam. 38, ✂ GG
99/0 UD C. Legends 12
01/2 UD Challenge 57,CM6, FF6
95/6 UD CC 220, C6
96/7 UD CC 166, 296, 336, S10, C30, CR30
97/8 UD Coll. Choice 168, SQ49, W2
98/9 UD G. Reserve 195
99/0 UD G. Reserve 126
99/0 UD Gretzky Excl. 58, 91
01/2 UD Honor Roll -DPuck
96/7 UD Ice 111, S1
97/8 UD Ice 71, IC11, L3B
00/1 UD Ice 39, 73
01/2 UD Ice 30
00/1 UD Legends 51, 92, PH6, SM8, ✍ ES
92/3 UD Locker 7
01/2 UD Mask ✂ GG
98/9 UD MVP 201, PG7
99/0 UD MVP 204
00/1 UD MVP ✂ GS
01/2 UD MVP 123, MW6, ✂ S
99/0 UD MVP Cup 182, PH10, SS12, SC19
99/0 UD Ovation 58
00/1 UD Pros&Prosp. 58, 89, CR7, NP4, ✂✍ GJS
99/0 UD Retro 77, DR6
01/2 UD SCup Champs 84, ✂ G
01/2 UD Top Shelf ✂ S
00/1 UD Vintage 237, 246, 247, ✂ D-POH
01/2 UD Vintage 166, 173
83/4 Vachon 36-116
83/4 Vachon 36-81
00/1 Vanguard 66, HV-23, VP-15
01/2 Vanguard 65, ✂ DGM 38
99/0 Victory 292, 293
00/1 Victory 225, 226, 328
01/2 Victory 230
99/0 WGretzky 167, W10
96 Wien 86
97/8 Zenith 16, Z64
79/0 EDMO
80/1 EDMO / Zellers
81/2 EDMO / Red Rooster
82/3 EDMO / Red Rooster
83/4 EDMO / Button
83/4 EDMO / McDonald's
83/4 EDMO / West Mall
83/4 EDMO
84/5 EDMO
84/5 EDMO / Red Rooster
85/6 EDMO / Red Rooster
86/7 EDMO
86/7 EDMO / Red Rooster
87/8 EDMO
88/9 EDMO
88/9 EDMO / Action 89
88/9 EDMO / Action 105
90/1 EDMO / IGA
90/1 EDMO / IGA
92/3 NYRA
97/8 VANC / Coke

MESSIER, MARKUS
01/2 UD Premier ✂ D

MESSIER, MITCH
92/3 Classic Prospects 76
88/9 ProCards / Kalamazoo
89/0 ProCards IHL 98
90/1 ProCards 102
91/2 ProCards 154
93/4 Fort Wayne Komets 15
95/6 Fort Wayne Komets

MESSURI, JOHN
91/2 ProCards 439
89/0 Johnstown Chiefs

MESZAROS, DAVE
84/5 Moncton G'Flames
85/6 Moncton G'Flames

MESZOLY, ANDRAS
79 Panini Sticker 270

METCALFE, JASON
95/6 Slapshot 244
00/1 Florida Everblades

METCALFE, SCOTT
98/9 DEL 190
99/0 Eishockey 231
00/1 Kudos 155
88/9 ProCards / Rochester
89/0 ProCards AHL 262
90/1 ProCards 267
88/9 EDMO / Action 127
95/6 Rochester Americans
96/7 Rochester Americans
97/8 Rochester Americans
01/2 Sheffield Steelers GS
83/4 Kingston Canadians
84/5 Kingston Canadians
85/6 Kingston Canadians
86/7 Kingston Canadians

METHOT, FRANÇOIS
95/6 Bowman P25
97 Bowman 57
98 Bowman 95
98 Bowman Chrome 95
92 Québec Pee Wee 562
95/6 Upper Deck 521
98/9 Rochester Americans
00/1 Rochester Americans
02/3 Rochester Americans
99/0 Rouyn-Noranda

METLICKA, PAVEL
95/6 APS 259
97/8 APS 232
98/9 OFS 92
99/0 OFS 315

METLYUK, DENIS
92/3 Classic 45
94/5 Classic 91, T50
92/3 Classic Four Sport 186
94/5 Classic 4 Sport 157
93/4 Cla. Prospects 215
99/0 Mir 44
00/1 Mir 154
91/2 Upper Deck 653
91/2 Upper Deck WJC 14

METRO, TERRY
91/2 Air Canada SJHL C22

METROPOLIT, GLEN
02/3 Pacific Complete 196
99/0 BAP Mem. 303
99/0 Millenium C-42
99/0 Omega 246
00/1 Pacific 427
99/0 Prism 149
00/1 Signature 85, ✍ Aut. 101
00/1 Topps 275
00/1 To. Chrome 170
99/0 To. Prmr. Plus 88
99/0 Ult. Victory 105
97/8 Grand Rapids Griffins
98/9 Grand Rapids Griffins
96/7 Pensacola Ice Pilots
99/0 Portland Pirates
00/1 Portland Pirates

METTAVAINIO, JAN-OVE
89/0 Semic Elitserien 149
90/1 Semic Elitserien 232

METTOVAARA, SAMI
02/3 Cardset 72
98/9 Cardset 107
93/4 Jyvas Hyva 177
93/4 Sisu 176
94/5 Sisu 44
95/6 Sisu 337
00/1 UD Elitserien 134

METZ, DON
34-43 BeeHive-1 [Toro.]
45-64 BeeHive-2 [Toro.]
39/0 O-Pee-Chee 8
40/1 O-Pee-Chee 111
45-54 Quaker Oats

METZ, NICK
35/6 Amalgamated Press
34-43 BeeHive-1 [Toro.]
45-64 BeeHive-2 [Toro.]
35/6 O-Pee-Chee 84
37/8 O-Pee-Chee 144
39/0 O-Pee-Chee 51
40/1 O-Pee-Chee 133
40/1 O-Pee-Chee 141
38/9 Quaker Oats
45-54 Quaker Oats
37/8 World Wide Gum 28

MEULENBROEKS, JOHN
85/6 Moncton G'Flames
83/4 Brantford Alexanders

MEUNIER, YVES
90/1 7th..Sketch LHJMQ 204
91/2 7th...Sketch LHJMQ 22
91/2 7th...Sketch LHJMQ 59

MEURER, PETER
24/5 Selkirks Crescent 13

MEWS, HARRY
91/2 ProCards 565
92/3 Hampton Roads
98/9 Hampton Roads

MEYER, ?
95/6 DEL 432

MEYER, ANDREAS
79 Panini Sticker 259

MEYER, DENNIS
95/6 DEL 72
99/0 Eishockey 274

MEYER, FRITZ
94/5 DEL 14
95/6 DEL 5

MEYER, JAYSON
95/6 DEL 202
96/7 DEL 343
98/9 DEL 30
95 Panini Worlds 56
94 Semic 276
95 Semic 167
96 Wien 195
81/2 Regina Pats
82/3 Regina Pats
83/4 Regina Pats

MEYER, SCOTT
01/2 Hartford Wolf Pack

MEYERS, BRET
98/9 EBK ECHL All-Star
99/0 Peoria Rivermen
00/1 Peoria Rivermen
01/2 Peoria Rivermen

MEYERS, DAN
91/2 Air Canada SJHL A2

MEYHOFF, CHAD
94/5 Anchorage Aces 17

MEZEI, BRANISLAV
00/1 BAP Mem. 504
01/2 BAP Mem. 199
99 Bowman 15, 136, ✍ BA35
01/2 O-Pee-Chee 282
01/2 Signature 94, ✍ Aut. 94
99/0 SP Authentic 124
99/0 Topps 269
01/2 Topps 282
99/0 To. Chrome 269
99/0 Ult. Victory 108
99/0 Upper Deck 314
99/0 UD Black Diam. 95
99/0 UD G. Reserve 314
99/0 UD MVP Cup 196
99/0 UD Ovation 67
x99/0 UD Prospects ✍ Sig. BM
99/0 Victory 366
00/1 Lowell Lock Monsters

MEZERA, VLADIMIR
99/0 Score 119

MEZIN, ANDREI
98/9 DEL 249
99/0 Eishockey 267
00/1 UD DEL 30, P2
01/2 UD DEL 21, G1, ✂ GJ
95/6 Flint Generals
96/7 Flint Generals

MIASKOWSKI, PHIL
98/9 Fort Worth Brahmas

MICALEF, CORRADO
83/4 O-Pee-Chee 116
83/4 O-Pee-Chee 126
85/6 O-Pee-Chee 200
83/4 OPC/Topps Sticker 147
83/4 Souhaits Keychain [Red Wings]
84/5 DETR / Little Caesars

MICHALCHUK, CHAD
91/2 7th...Sketch WHL 114
91/2 Saskatoon Blades

MICHALEK, MILAN
01/2 OFS 140

MICHALEK, VLADIMIR
95/6 APS 238

MICHALEK, ZBYNEK
01/2 Shawinigan 2

MICHAUD, ALFIE
99/0 BAP Mem. 366
99/0 Omega 240
00/1 Pacific 417
99/0 Prism 142
00/1 Upper Deck 230
00/1 UD MVP 207
00/1 Victory 271
00/1 Kansas City Blades 22
01/2 Manitoba Moose
02/3 Peoria Rivermen

MICHAUD, DANY
91/2 7th...Sketch LHJMQ 229

MICHAUD, MARK
94/5 Birmingham Bulls
93/4 Hampton Roads
98/9 Hampton Roads
87/8 Brockville Braves

MICHAUD, OLIVIER
02/3 Between the Pipes 101
02/3 First Edition 271
01/2 BAP Mem. 389
01/2 BT Pipes 85
01/2 Bowman 115
01/2 Parkhurst 321
01/2 SPx 207
01/2 UD PlayMakers Ltd 124
01/2 UD Honor Roll 77
01/2 UD Ice 141
01/2 UD Mask 150
01/2 UD MVP 233
01/2 UD Premier 98
01/2 UD Top Shelf 129
01/2 Victory 453
00/1 Shawinigan 16
01/2 Shawinigan 15

MICHAUD, SYLVAIN
99 Québec Pee Wee 249
01/2 Drummondville
01/2 Victoriaville Tigres 21

MICHAYLUK, DAVE
92/3 Classic Prospects 123
88/9 ProCards / Muskegon
89/0 ProCards IHL 153
90/1 ProCards 389
91/2 ProCards 288
92/3 Cleveland Lumberjacks
93/4 Cleveland Lumberjacks
95/6 Cleveland Lumberjacks
96/7 Cleveland Lumberjacks
83/4 Springfield Indians 11
81/2 Regina Pats

MICHEL, STEFFEN
94/5 DEL 278
95/6 DEL 269

MICHELETTI, JOE
82/3 Post [Colo.]
81/2 COLR

MICHELIN, LEON
52/3 Anonymous 36

MICHELLER, KLAUS
94/5 DEL 239
96/7 DEL 74

MICHON, MICHEL
90/1 7th..Sketch WHL 332

MICIAK, DARREN
91/2 ProCards 435

MICK, TROY
91/2 Knoxville Cherokees
86/7 Portland Winter Hawks
88/9 Portland Winter Hawks
89/0 Regina Pats

MICKEY, LARRY
70/1 Dad's Cookies
70/1 Eddie Sargent 74
71/2 Eddie Sargent 149
70/1 Esso Power Player
74/5 Loblaws
68/9 O-Pee-Chee 195
70/1 O-Pee-Chee 162
71/2 O-Pee-Chee 167
71/2 Toronto Sun Photo
72/3 BUFF
73/4 BUFF
74/5 BUFF
69/0 TORO

MICKOLAJAK, T
93/4 Minnesota-Duluth

MICKOSKI, NICK
45-64 BeeHive-2 [NYRa.]
51/2 Parkhurst 97
52/3 Parkhurst 101
53/4 Parkhurst 62
54/5 Parkhurst 75
93/4 Parkie 56-57 25
54/5 Topps 29
57/8 Topps 32
58/9 Topps 27
59/0 Topps 37
59/0 Topps 53

MICULINIC, JEREMY
95/6 Classic 82
94/5 Slapshot / Sarnia 7
95/6 Slapshot 28

MIDDENDORF, MAX
88/9 ProCards / Halifax
89/0 ProCards AHL 172
91/2 ProCards 217
87/8 QUÉB / Gene. Foods
93/4 Fort Wayne Komets 16
97/8 Fort Worth Brahmas
89/0 Halifax Citadels
84/5 Sudbury Wolves
85/6 Sudbury Wolves
86/7 Sudbury Wolves

MIDDERHOFF, MIC
96/7 Johnstown Chiefs

MIDDLEBROOK, LINDSAY
88/9 EDMO / Action 102

MIDDLETON, MARCUS
90/1 7th..Sketch OHL 40
89/0 Sudbury Wolves

MIDDLETON, RICK
01/2 Fleer Greats 70, ✍ Aut.
83/4 Funmate Puffy 10 [w/]
84/5 Kellogg's 28
74/5 Loblaws Update
82/3 McDonald's Les Étoiles 9
74/5 O-Pee-Chee 304
75/6 O-Pee-Chee 37
76/7 O-Pee-Chee 127
77/8 O-Pee-Chee 246
78/9 O-Pee-Chee 113
79/0 O-Pee-Chee 10
80/1 O-Pee-Chee 94
80/1 O-Pee-Chee 251
81/2 O-Pee-Chee 2
81/2 O-Pee-Chee 18
81/2 O-Pee-Chee 19
82/3 O-Pee-Chee 6
82/3 O-Pee-Chee 15
83/4 O-Pee-Chee 43
83/4 O-Pee-Chee 54
83/4 O-Pee-Chee 214
84/5 O-Pee-Chee 9
84/5 O-Pee-Chee 352
85/6 OPC/Topps 64
86/7 OPC/Topps 157
87/8 OPC/Topps 115
88/9 OPC/Topps 87
81/2 OPC Sticker 45
82/3 OPC/Topps Sticker 78
82/3 OPC/Topps Sticker 79
82/3 OPC/Topps Sticker 262
83/4 OPC/Topps Sticker 14
83/4 OPC/Topps Sticker 44
83/4 OPC/Topps Sticker 45
83/4 OPC/Topps Sticker 329
84/5 OPC Sticker 142
84/5 OPC Sticker 181
84/5 OPC Sticker 182
85/6 OPC Sticker 159-29
86/7 OPC Sticker 35-172
87/8 OPC Sticker 138-248
88/9 OPC Sticker 26-155
87/8 Panini Sticker 12
82/3 Post [Bost.]
84/5 7-Eleven
85/6 7-Eleven Superstars 1
83/4 Souhaits Keychain [Bruins]
75/6 Topps 37
76/7 Topps 127
77/8 Topps 246
78/9 Topps 113
79/0 Topps 10
79/0 Topps 81
80/1 Topps 94
80/1 Topps 251
81/2 Topps 22
81/2 Topps 46
81/2 Topps 129 [East]
84/5 Topps 8
01/2 T/O Archives 18, ✍ CAI
83/4 BOST
84/5 BOST
88/9 BOST / Sports Action
91/2 BOST / SA Legends

MIDGLEY, JIM
95/6 Slapshot 213

MIEHM, KEVIN
92/3 Classic Prospects 63
95/6 Edge Ice 128
93/4 Fleer Ultra 205
93/4 Fleer Ultra Pros. 6
93/4 Parkhurst 447
93/4 Premier - Gold 264
89/0 ProCards IHL 11
90/1 ProCards 93
91/2 ProCards 28
92/3 Upper Deck 543
00/1 UD DEL 194
94/5 Fort Wayne Komets 24
92/3 Peoria Rivermen

MIELCZAREK, TED
86/7 Sudbury Wolves
87/8 Sudbury Wolves
88/9 Sudbury Wolves

MIELKO, B.
91/2 7th...Sketch OHL 118

MIETTINEN, ANTTI
02/3 Cardset 73, -DD 9, -Nimik.
99/0 Cardset 240
00/1 Cardset 27, NG-7

MIETTINEN, TOMMI
98/9 Cardset 245
99/0 Cardset 253
00/1 Cardset 273
97/8 Hockey-Box
93/4 Jyvas Hyva 173
93/4 Parkhurst 522
94/5 Parkie SE221
95 Semic 236
94/5 Sisu 86, J-3, ND-7
95/6 Sisu 330
96/7 Sisu 144
94/5 Topps Finest 133

MIFEK, JIRI
99/0 Score 135

MIGAY, RUDY
45-64 BeeHive-2 [Toro.]
52/3 Parkhurst 96
53/4 Parkhurst 17
54/5 Parkhurst 21
55/6 Parkhurst 12
57/8 Parkhurst [Toro.] 6
93/4 Parkie 56-57 111
93/4 Parkie 56-57 159
45-54 Quaker Oats
60/1 Shirriff 18

MIGDAL, THOMAS
98/9 Wichita Thunder

MIGNACCA, SONNY
90/1 7th..Sketch WHL 23
91/2 7th...Sketch WHL 314

MIGNEAULT, JOHN
75/6 Phoenix Roadrunners
73/4 Vancouver Blazers

MIIKKULAINEN, JARNO
92/3 Jyvas Hyva 201
93/4 Jyvas Hyva 351
93/4 Sisu 213
94/5 Sisu 80
95/6 Sisu 152, 300

MIKA, DAVID
99/0 Score 113

MIKA, PETR
00/1 BAP Mem. 193
01/2 DS 34
98/9 OFS 221
00/1 Pacific 254
00/1 SPx 103
00/1 Upper Deck 190
00/1 UD Pros&Prosp. 113
00/1 Victory 265
99/0 Lowell Lock Monsters
00/1 Lowell Lock Monsters

MIKAELSSON, PAR
89/0 Semic Elitserien 214

MIKEL, JAN
00/1 Kudos 9
02/3 Dundee Texol Stars

MIKES, JOSEF
99/0 OFS 442

MIKESCH, PAT
00/1 UD DEL 117
01/2 UD DEL 131, SS7
98/9 Florida Everblades
96/7 Kentucky Tho'blades

MIKESKA, MICHAL
98/9 OFS 160
99/0 OFS 298, 365
00/1 OFS 46
01/2 OFS 254

MIKHAILOV, BORIS
91/2 Future Trends C72 43
95 Globe 243
72 Hellas MM-Jenkki 72
74 Hellas MM-Jenkki 51
70/1 Kuvajulkaisut 8
80 Olympic USSR
72 Panda MM-Toronto
79 Panini Sticker 150
72 Semic Sticker 13
74 Semic Sticker 33
69/0 Soviet Stars
70/1 Soviet Stars
71/2 Soviet Stars
73/4 Soviet Stars 6
73/4 Soviet Stars 9
73/4 Soviet Stars 24
74/5 Soviet Stars 11
74/5 Soviet Stars 24
79/0 Soviet Stars 13
77-79 Sportscaster 102-14
77-79 Sports. FIN 26-673
71/2 Williams Finnish 10
72/3 Williams Finnish 29
73/4 Williams Finnish 11

MIKHAILOV, DMITRI
99/0 Mir 253

MIKHAILOV, EGOR
99/0 Mir 66

MIKHAILOV, IGOR
98/9 Mir 65
00/1 Mir 259

MIKHAILOVSKI, MAXIM
99/0 Mir 155

MIKHAILOVSKY, MAXIM
00/1 Mir 329
90/1 O-Pee-Chee 9R
91/2 O-Pee-Chee 22R
91/2 O-Pee-Chee 29R
91/2 O-Pee-Chee 30R
92/3 Red Ace Violet 20

MIKHNOV, ALEXEI
02/3 Russian Future Stars 19

MIKITA, STAN
02/3 Canada Post
02/3 Parkhurst ✂ VM4, ✂ VT5
02/3 Parkhurst Retro ✂ NN16
02/3 Signature GS-86
02/3 Ultimate Mem. ✂ EA, ✂ FS, ✂ GMIH, ✂ SL (x4), ✂ Num, ✂ PS, ✂ RAT, ✂ RT, ✂ VGJ
02/3 UD Foundations ✂ 1000Stick, ✍ SG
01/2 ASG History
92/3 American Licorice 4
71/2 Bazooka Panel
99/0 BAP Mem. R-5,✍ R-5
01/2 BAP Mem. ✂ 500GS
01/2 BAP Update ✂ TC32
45-64 BeeHive-2 [Chic.]
64-67 BeeHive-3 [Chic.]
63-65 Chex
64/5 Coke/Sprite [Chic.]
65/6 Coca-Cola
70/1 Dad's Cookies
70/1 Eddie Sargent 48
71/2 Eddie Sargent 33
72/3 Eddie Sargent 63
70/1 Esso Power Player
88/9 Esso All-Star
01/2 Fleer Greats 31, ✍ Aut.
01/2 Fleer Legacy 34, ✂ HK
91/2 Future Trends C72 61, ✍ 61
62/3 Cowan Tile
83 HHOF Postcard O11
83&87 HHOF 226
93/4 Hockey Wit 39
71 Kellogg's Transfer
92/3 Legends 15
72/3 Post 10
74/5 Loblaws
68/9 O-Pee-Chee 155
68/9 O-Pee-Chee 202
68/9 O-Pee-Chee 211
68/9 O-Pee-Chee PS 1
69/0 O-Pee-Chee 76
69/0 O-Pee-Chee 4in1
69/0 O-Pee-Chee Stamp
70/1 O-Pee-Chee 20
70/1 O-Pee-Chee 240
71/2 O-Pee-Chee 125
72/3 O-Pee-Chee 156
72/3 O-Pee-Chee 177
72/3 O-Pee-Chee Crest 5
72/3 O-Pee-Chee TC
73/4 O-Pee-Chee 6
74/5 O-Pee-Chee 20
74/5 O-Pee-Chee 69
75/6 O-Pee-Chee 30
75/6 O-Pee-Chee 317
76/7 O-Pee-Chee 225
77/8 O-Pee-Chee 195
78/9 O-Pee-Chee 75
79/0 O-Pee-Chee 155
98/9 OPC Chrome 8
01/2 Parkhurst HSHS, ✂ 500GS, ✂ PS63, ✂ H8, ✍ PA35
93/4 Parkie 56-57 FS-3
95/6 Parkie 66-67 24, 125, AS5, SL2, TW1-3
94/5 Parkie Tall 26, 138, 147, 170, SL2, TW3
97/8 Pi. BeeHive 59, ✍ Aut. 59
66/7 Post Cereal Box
67/8 Post Cereal Box
67/8 Post Cereal Box
90/1 Pro Set 405, 655
72 Semic Sticker 227
60/1 Shirriff 71
61/2 Shirriff 22
62/3 Shirriff 46
68/9 Shirriff / Chic. 9
01/2 Signature ✂ 500GS, ✂ VA33
77-79 Sportscaster 12-22
77-79 Sports. FIN 51-1224
81/2 TCMA 13
60/1 Topps 14
61/2 Topps 36
61/2 Topps - Stamp
62/3 Topps 34
62/3 Topps Dollar
63/4 Topps 36
64/5 Topps 31
64/5 Topps 106
65/6 Topps 60
66/7 Topps 62
66/7 Topps 124
66/7 Topps / Test 62
67/8 Topps 64
67/8 Topps 114
67/8 Topps 126
68/9 Topps 20
69/0 Topps 76
70/1 Topps 20
71/2 Topps 125
72/3 Topps 56
73/4 Topps 145
74/5 Topps 20
74/5 Topps 69
75/6 Topps 30
75/6 Topps 317
76/7 Topps 225
77/8 Topps 195
78/9 Topps 75
79/0 Topps 155
98/9 Topps -Reprint 8, ✍ Reprint
01/2 T/O Archives 14, -Seat, ✂ Jers, ✍ CAI
63/4 Toronto Star Action
63/4 Toronto Star Photo
64/5 Toronto Star Action
64/5 Toronto Star Photo
61/2 Toronto Star Weekend
65/6 Toronto Star Weekend
66/7 Toronto Star Weekend
71/2 Toronto Sun Photo
00/1 UD Heroes 123, ✍ SG
01/2 Ultimate Mem. ✂ 500GS, ✂ ASGH, ✂ Corn., ✂ EA, ✂ RN, ✂ RT, ✍ Aut.
00 ✂ UD APOH 500, ✂✍ 500
99/0 UD C. Legends 18, ✍ ES
00/1 UD Legends 26, ES14, ✍ ES
01/2 UD Legends 13,FC, ✂ PoH, ✂ TT, ✂ TTC, ✍ ES
92/3 UD Locker 46
99/0 UD Retro 91, G7A, ✍ Ink.
92/3 Zellers
68/9 CHIC
70/1 CHIC
70/1 CHIC
79/0 CHIC

MIKKELSON, BILL
74/5 Loblaws
72/3 O-Pee-Chee 79
74/5 O-Pee-Chee 23
75/6 O-Pee-Chee 207
72/3 Topps 118
74/5 Topps 23
75/6 Topps 207
74/5 WASH

MIKKOLA, ARI
78/9 SM-Liiga 81
72/3 Williams Finnish 177

MIKKOLA, HEIKKI
66/7 Champion 104

MIKKOLA, ILKKA
02/3 Cardset 222
98/9 Cardset 232
99/0 Cardset 135
00/1 Cardset 338
98/9 SPx Prospects 71
98/9 UD Black Diam. 98

MIKKOLA, NIKO
02/3 Cardset 74
98/9 Cardset 264
99/0 Cardset 153
00/1 Cardset 166
97/8 Hockey-Box
95 Semic 240
93/4 Sisu 50
94/5 Sisu 88

MIKKOLAINEN, REIJO
92/3 Jyvas Hyva 180
89 Semic Sticker 38
93/4 Sisu 53
94/5 Sisu 206
95/6 Sisu 37, 187

MIKKONEN, VILLE
98/9 Cardset 175
99/0 Cardset 87

MIKLENDA, JAROSLAV
93/4 Parkhurst 519
93/4 Upper Deck 573

MIKLIK, MARTIN
99/0 OFS 241

MIKOL, JIM
45-64 BeeHive-2 [Toro.]
60/1 Cleveland Barons
64/5 Coke/Sprite [NYRa.]
94/5 Parkie Tall 99
64/5 Topps 36

MIKOLAS, JOSEF
97/8 APS 379

MIKOLASEK, TOMAS
94/5 APS 66
95/6 APS 92
96/7 APS 88
97/8 APS 217
96/7 DS Sticker 144
97/8 DS Sticker 239
98/9 OFS 168
99/0 Score 24

MIKULCHIK, OLEG
98/9 Mir 130
98/9 Mir 3
99/0 Mir 16
00/1 Mir 52
95/6 Upper Deck 471
00/1 Metallurg 35

MILANI, TOM
82 Semic Sticker 138
77/8 Kalamazoo Wings

MILBURY, MIKE
77/8 O-Pee-Chee 134
78/9 O-Pee-Chee 59
79/0 O-Pee-Chee 114
80/1 O-Pee-Chee 191
81/2 O-Pee-Chee 16
83/4 O-Pee-Chee 55
84/5 O-Pee-Chee 10
87/8 Panini Sticker 8
82/3 Post [Bost.]
90/1 Pro Set 661
83/4 Souhaits Keychain [Bruins]
77/8 Topps 134
78/9 Topps 59
79/0 Topps 114
80/1 Topps 191
01/2 T/O Archives 70
83/4 BOST
84/5 BOST
96/7 NYIS

MILD, HANS
98/9 UD Elitserien 202

MILESKA, MICHAL
00/1 DS 94

MILFORD, JAKE
83&87 HHOF 253

MILKS, HIB (HIBBERT)
25-27 Anonymous 48
25-27 Anonymous 52 [No Border]

MILL, JIM
93/4 Huntington Blizzard
93/4 Roanoke Express

MILLAR, COLIN
88/9 Niagara Falls Thunder

MILLAR, CRAIG
98/9 Omega 98
98/9 Pacific 215
00/1 Pacific 224
97/8 Pi. Be A Player 239, ✍ Aut. 239
97/8 SP Authentic 182
98/9 Upper Deck 95
98/9 UD G. Reserve 95
96/7 Rochester Americans
95/6 Swift Current Broncos

MILLAR, MIKE
94/5 DEL 159
95/6 DEL 159
96/7 DEL 235
88/9 ProCards / Baltimore
89/0 ProCards AHL 67
90/1 ProCards 168
89/0 BOST / Sports Action
90/1 Newmarket Saints
83/4 Brantford Alexanders

MILLAR, P
88/9 EDMO / Action 80

MILLEN, COREY
91/2 Bowman 60
92/3 Bowman 57
98/9 DEL 87
93/4 Donruss 181
94/5 Donruss 148
99/0 Eishockey 119
92/3 Fleer Ultra 86
93/4 Fleer Ultra 361
94/5 Fleer Ultra 120
93/4 Leaf 361
94/5 Leaf 187
91/2 O-Pee-Chee 461
92/3 O-Pee-Chee 334
97/8 Pacific CC 107
92/3 Panini Sticker 70
93/4 Panini Sticker 207
91/2 Parkhurst 292
92/3 Parkhurst 306
93/4 Parkhurst 381
94/5 Parkhurst 122
95/6 Parkhurst 304
92/3 Pinnacle 138
93/4 Pinnacle 350
94/5 Pinnacle 425
94/5 POG 147
95/6 POG 84
93/4 Power Play 379
93/4 Premier 493
91/2 Pro Set Platinum 185
89/0 ProCards IHL 44
91/2 Score 318
91/2 Score CAN 348
92/3 Score 111
92/3 Score SS 26
93/4 Score 519
93/4 Score 62
94/5 Score 99
95/6 Score 172
92/3 Topps 326
91/2 To. Stadium 71
92/3 To. Stadium 296
93/4 To. Stadium 437
91/2 Upper Deck 110
91/2 Upper Deck 604
92/3 Upper Deck 48
93/4 Upper Deck 483, SP-84
94/5 Upper Deck 25
95/6 Upper Deck 105
96/7 Upper Deck 231
95/6 UD CC 274
00/1 UD DEL 142, A8
01/2 UD DEL 143
94/5 DALL / Southwest
89/0 NYRA / Marine

MILLEN, GREG
90/1 Bowman 3
83/4 Funmate Puffy 16 [w/]
79/0 O-Pee-Chee 281
80/1 O-Pee-Chee 158
81/2 O-Pee-Chee 134
82/3 O-Pee-Chee 126
83/4 O-Pee-Chee 143
84/5 O-Pee-Chee 75
85/6 O-Pee-Chee 221
88/9 OPC/Topps 117
90/1 OPC/Topps 335
89/0 OPC/Topps 137
82/3 OPC/Topps Sticker 130
83/4 OPC/Topps Sticker 262
84/5 OPC Sticker 198
85/6 OPC Sticker 51-182
88/9 Panini Sticker 100
89/0 Panini Sticker 129
90/1 Panini Sticker 188
97/8 Pi. CBC Sports 8
82/3 Post [Hart.]
90/1 Pro Set 56
90/1 Score 42
83/4 Souhaits Keychain [Whalers]
80/1 Topps 158
81/2 Topps 115 [East]
84/5 Topps 58
90/1 Upper Deck 213
90/1 CHIC / Coke
82/3 HART / Jr. Whalers
83/4 HART / Jr. Whalers
84/5 HART / Jr. Whalers
89/0 QUÉB
87/8 SLOU
87/8 SLOU / Kodak
88/9 SLOU
88/9 SLOU / Kodak

MILLER, AARON
02/3 Pacific 169, ✂ GWJ 22
02/3 Pacific Complete 48
02/3 Upper Deck 325
02/3 UD Vintage 122
01/2 BAP Mem. 39
93/4 Cla. Prospects 105
95/6 Edge Ice 29
01/2 Heads Up ✂ JQ 8
99/0 Pacific 111
01/2 Pacific ✂ GWJ 18
97/8 Pacific CC 317
01/2 Parkhurst 141
97/8 Pi. Be A Player 75, ✍ Aut. 75
00/1 Pr. Stock ✂ GUG 27
01/2 Pr. Stock ✂ GUG 51
00/1 PS Titanium ✂ GUG 76
01/2 PS Titanium ✂ DSJ 19
01/2 Signat. 13, ✍ Aut. 13
97/8 Upper Deck 258
00/1 Upper Deck 49
00/1 UD ASG CA5
99/0 UD MVP Cup 49
01/2 Victory 164

MILLER, AL
51/2 Laval Dairy 57
52/3 Laval Dairy Update 7

MILLER, AREN
97/8 Pi. BeeHive 70, ✍ Aut. 70
99/0 Cincinnati M'Ducks
95/6 Spokane Chiefs 30
97/8 Spokane Chiefs

MILLER, BOB
79/0 O-Pee-Chee 196
80/1 O-Pee-Chee 236
82/3 Post [Colo.]
79/0 Topps 196
80/1 Topps 236
98/9 BOST / Alumni 11
81/2 COLR
84/5 LOSA / Smokey 20

MILLER, BRAD
91/2 Parkhurst 243
93/4 Parkhurst 306
90/1 Pro Set 591
91/2 Pro Set 354
89/0 ProCards AHL 264
90/1 ProCards 272
92/3 To. Stadium 475
88/9 BUFF / Won. Bread
90/1 BUFF / Campbell's
91/2 BUFF / Blue Shield
91/2 BUFF / Campbell's
91/2 BUFF / Pepsi
98/9 Las Vegas Thunder
94/5 Minnesota Moose
95/6 Minnesota Moose
91/2 Rochester Americans WPC
92/3 St. John's Maple Leafs
99/0 Utah Grizzlies
86/7 Regina Pats
87/8 Regina Pats
88/9 Regina Pats

MILLER, CHRIS
01/2 Manchester Storm

MILLER, COLIN
91 7th..Sketch Mem.Cup 23
90/1 7th..Sketch OHL 169
91/2 7th...Sketch OHL 321
92/3 Atlanta Knights
93/4 Atlanta Knights
94/5 Atlanta Knights 7
95/6 Dayton Bombers
96/7 Dayton Bombers
98/9 Dayton Bombers
98/9 Dayton Bombers
98/9 Dayton Bombers
89/0 Soo Greyhounds

MILLER, DENNIS
91/2 ProCards 434

MILLER, EARL
30/1 La Presse

MILLER, GARY
89/0 7th..Sketch OHL 160
90/1 7th..Sketch OHL 312
91/2 7th...Sketch OHL 89

MILLER, GUS
92/3 BCJHL 228

MILLER, JASON
92/3 Classic Prospects 13
98/9 DEL 254
99/0 Eishockey 37
91/2 O-Pee-Chee 163
91/2 ProCards 420
91/2 Score 312
91/2 Score CAN 342
90/1 7th..Sketch WHL 28
95/6 Sisu 222, 377
90/1 Upper Deck 335
00/1 UD DEL 192
01/2 UD DEL GA10
95/6 Peoria Rivermen

MILLER, JAY
91/2 Bowman 178
02/3 Fleer Throwbacks 70
91/2 O-Pee-Chee 467
87/8 Panini Sticker 18
88/9 Panini Sticker 212
91/2 Pro Set 402
91/2 Score CAN 543
91/2 To. Stadium 63
90/1 Upper Deck 414
88/9 BOST / Sports Action
89/0 LOSA / Smokey 15
90/1 LOSA / Smokey 16
85/6 Moncton G'Flames

MILLER, KEITH
88/9 ProCards / Halifax
89/0 ProCards IHL 137

MILLER, KELLY
90/1 Bowman 76
91/2 Bowman 292
92/3 Bowman 338
93/4 Donruss 365
94/5 Donruss 52
95/6 Donruss 159
92/3 Fleer Ultra 236
93/4 Fleer Ultra 88
94/5 Fleer Ultra 390
93/4 Leaf 254
94/5 Leaf 519
87/8 OPC/Topps 189
88/9 OPC/Topps 130
90/1 OPC/Topps 81
91/2 O-Pee-Chee 342
92/3 O-Pee-Chee 142
89/0 OPC/Topps 131
90/1 OPC Premier 72
89/0 opcSticker 74-213
98/9 Pacific 444
97/8 Pa. Invincible R-211
87/8 Panini Sticker 186
88/9 Panini Sticker 373
89/0 Panini Sticker 348
90/1 Panini Sticker 156
91/2 Panini Sticker 202
92/3 Panini Sticker 166
93/4 Panini Sticker 30
91/2 Parkhurst 414
93/4 Parkhurst 491
94/5 Parkhurst 256, V72
95/6 Parkhurst 219
91/2 Pinnacle 23
91/2 Pinnacle 372
92/3 Pinnacle 160
93/4 Pinnacle 284
94/5 Pinnacle 158
96/7 Pi. Be A Player 46, ✍ Aut. 46
95/6 Playoff 324
94/5 POG 247
95/6 POG 280
93/4 Power Play 468
93/4 Premier 474
94/5 Premier 222
90/1 Pro Set 318
91/2 Pro Set 256
91/2 Pro Set 611
91/2 Pro Set 615
90/1 Score 168
91/2 Score 81
91/2 Score 309
91/2 Score CAN 81
91/2 Score CAN 339
92/3 Score 55
92/3 Score USAG 14
93/4 Score 30
94/5 Score 63
95/6 Score 271
92/3 Topps 479
95/6 Topps 126
91/2 To. Stadium 106
92/3 To. Stadium 361
93/4 To. Stadium 17
90/1 Upper Deck 130
91/2 Upper Deck 133
92/3 Upper Deck 35
92/3 Upper Deck 179
93/4 Upper Deck 384
94/5 Upper Deck 151
95/6 Upper Deck 346
95/6 UD CC 82
86/7 WASH / Kodak
87/8 WASH
87/8 WASH / Kodak
88/9 WASH
88/9 WASH / Smokey
89/0 WASH
89/0 WASH / Kodak
90/1 WASH / Kodak
90/1 WASH / Smokey
91/2 WASH / Kodak
91/2 WASH / Smokey
92/3 WASH / Kodak
95/6 WASH

MILLER, KEVIN
91/2 Bowman 57
92/3 Bowman 391
93/4 Donruss 298
94/5 Donruss 11
92/3 Fleer Ultra 396
93/4 Fleer Ultra 218
94/5 Fleer Ultra 186
95 Globe 119
93/4 Leaf 192
94/5 Leaf 129
91/2 O-Pee-Chee 125
92/3 O-Pee-Chee 291
90/1 OPC Premier 73
97/8 Pacific CC 46
92/3 Panini Sticker 115
94/5 Panini Sticker 139
96/7 Panini Sticker 66
91/2 Parkhurst 40
93/4 Parkhurst 178
94/5 Parkie SE150
91/2 Pinnacle 133
92/3 Pinnacle 313
93/4 Pinnacle 126
94/5 Pinnacle 289
95/6 Pinnacle 146
96/7 Pinnacle 15
96/7 Pi. Be A Player 165, ✍ Aut. 165
94/5 POG 205
95/6 POG 224
93/4 Power Play 215
93/4 Premier 8
94/5 Premier 21
90/1 Pro Set 493
91/2 Pro Set 60
91/2 Pro Set Platinum 168
89/0 ProCards IHL 29
90/1 Score 18T
91/2 Score 126
91/2 Score 309
91/2 Score CAN 126
91/2 Score CAN 339
92/3 Score 229
93/4 Score 89
94/5 Score 25
91/2 Score Young Stars 40
94 Semic 116
92 Semic Sticker 166
92/3 Topps 129
91/2 To. Stadium 286
92/3 To. Stadium 229
93/4 To. Stadium 193
90/1 Upper Deck 444
91/2 Upper Deck 142
92/3 Upper Deck 35
92/3 Upper Deck 482
93/4 Upper Deck 408
94/5 Upper Deck 451
96/7 Upper Deck 236
95/6 UD CC 275
97/8 UD Coll. Choice 50
98/9 Chicago Wolves
99/0 Grand Rapids Griffins
97/8 Indianapolis Ice 17

MILLER, KIP
02/3 Pacific 239
02/3 Pacific Complete 232
00/1 BAP Mem. 303
91/2 Bowman 139
95/6 Edge Ice 138
01/2 Heads Up ✂ JQ 15
99/0 Millenium 199, ✍ Aut. 199
91/2 O-Pee-Chee 387
91/2 OPC Premier 42
99/0 Pacific 343
00/1 Pacific 8
01/2 Pacific ✂ GWJ 29
91/2 Parkhurst 142
91/2 Pinnacle 306
01/2 PS Titanium Draft ✂ 57
91/2 Pro Set 555
90/1 ProCards 452
90/1 Score 330
91/2 Score 384
91/2 Score CAN 274
99/0 Topps 40
99/0 To. Chrome 40
90/1 Upper Deck 522
91/2 Upper Deck 431
92/3 Upper Deck 35
92/3 Upper Deck 247
93/4 Upper Deck 421
01/2 Vanguard ✂ DGM 39
99/0 Victory 244
91/2 QUÉB / Petro-Canada
00/1 Grand Rapids Griffins
01/2 Grand Rapids Griffins
90/1 Halifax Citadels
95/6 Indianapolis Ice
93/4 Kansas City Blades

MILLER, KRIS
91/2 ProCards 394
94/5 Minnesota Moose
95/6 Minnesota Moose
92/3 Salt Lake G'Eagles

MILLER, KURT
95/6 Adirondack Red Wings
91/2 L. Superior State Lakers

MILLER, KURTIS
99/0 Eishockey 155

MILLER, LUCAS
94/5 Slapshot / Kitchener 23

MILLER, NATE
00/1 Lowell Lock Monsters
01/2 Manchester Monarchs

MILLER, PAUL
83/4 Moncton Alpines

MILLER, PERRY
78/9 O-Pee-Chee 16
79/0 O-Pee-Chee 157
81/2 O-Pee-Chee 101
75/6 OPC WHA 6
78/9 Topps 16
79/0 Topps 157
80/1 DETR

MILLER, ROD
93/4 Minnesota-Duluth

MILLER, RYAN
02/3 BAP All-Star 113
02/3 BAP Mem. 320
02/3 Between the Pipes 105
02/3 Bowman 118, ✂ FFDS, ✂ FFJ, ✂ FFP, ✂ FFR, ✂ FFRP, ✂ FFS, ✂ FFTS, ✍ YSA, / ✍ Puck
02/3 Calder 106, -CR 4
02/3 Choice Prospects 29
02/3 Crown Royale 105
02/3 eTopps 54
02/3 In The GU 92, ✂ C12
02/3 Pacific Complete 547
02/3 PTC/ Spring Expo 2
02/3 Parkhurst 210
02/3 Parkhurst Retro 249, ✂ CH3
02/3 PS Titanium 107
02/3 Quest for the Cup 107, -CC 3
02/3 Signature ✂ AR1
02/3 SP Authentic 166
02/3 SP GU 97
02/3 SPx 187
02/3 Ultimate Mem. 50, ✂ CC
02/3 Upper Deck 436
02/3 UD Artistic 126
02/3 UD Classic 137
02/3 UD Honor 131
02/3 UD Mask 165, ✂ MM, ✂ NB
02/3 UD Premier 46
02/3 UD Rookie 139
02/3 Vanguard 105, ✂ GWJ

PP 4
02/3 Rochester Americans
02/3 Rochester Americans

MILLER, SCOTT
92/3 Windsor Spitfires

MILLER, SHANNON
97/8 Game of Her Life

MILLER, TODD
95/6 Slapshot 343

MILLER, TOM
72/3 Eddie Sargent 137
72/3 O-Pee-Chee 32
73/4 O-Pee-Chee 249
72/3 Topps 76

MILLER, WARREN
81/2 O-Pee-Chee 130
82/3 O-Pee-Chee 127
82/3 Post [Hart.]
81/2 Topps 84 [East]
82/3 HART / Jr. Whalers

MILLER, ZDENEK
95/6 APS 76

MILLETTE, ANDRÉ
88/9 Richelieu Riverains

MILLEY, NORM
02/3 O-Pee-Chee 295
02/3 Topps 295
02/3 To. Limited 295
97/8 Bell
99 Bowman 126
98 Bowman 38, 129, ✍ A16
98 Bowman Chrome 38, 129
94 Québec Pee Wee 1025
97/8 Upper Deck 414
99/0 Upper Deck 320
99/0 UD Black Diam. 109
99/0 UD G. Reserve 320
99/0 UD Ovation 66
00/1 Rochester Americans
02/3 Rochester Americans
96/7 Sudbury Wolves
98/9 Sudbury Wolves 5
99/0 Sudbury Wolves 9

MILLHAM, MIKE
92/3 Wheeling Thund'birds 10

MILLIE, LES
93/4 Sheffield Steelers 14
94/5 Sheffield Steelers 22
95/6 Sheffield Steelers

MILLIER, PIERRE
84/5 Chicoutimi Saguenéens

MILLIKEN, ROB
92/3 BCJHL 232
99/0 Asheville Smoke

MILLS, CRAIG
95/6 Bowman 99
95/6 Donruss 292
95/6 Do. Elite WJ 19
95/6 Parkhurst 497
95/6 Slapshot 52
97/8 SP Authentic 176
95/6 Upper Deck 527
97/8 Upper Deck 251
97/8 Indianapolis Ice 18
98/9 Portland Pirates
01/2 St. John's Maple Leafs
01/2 St. John's / Clarenville
02/3 St. John's Maple Leafs

MILLS, LEE
93/4 Sheffield Steelers 13

MILLS, MARK
94/5 Cincinnati Cyclones
95/6 Cincinnati Cyclones
96/7 Cincinnati Cyclones
97/8 Cincinnati Cyclones
98/9 Cincinnati Cyclones
99/0 Cincinnati Cyclones
00/1 Cincinnati Cyclones

MILNIKOV, DMITRI
99/0 Mir 51

MILROY, DUNCAN
00/1 UD Prospects 67, 94
01 UD Prospects GU 37, ✂ TPJ, ✂ TPJS, ✂ JC (x4), ✍ SoT

MILTON, KJELL-RUNE
70/1 Kuvajulkaisut 32
69/0 Mästär Serien 43
72 Semic Sticker 62
74 Semic Sticker 16
71/2 Williams Finnish 52

MINARD, MIKE
00/1 BAP Mem. 21
95/6 Slapshot 56
00/1 SPx 96
00/1 Upper Deck 184
99/0 Hamilton Bulldogs
99/0 Hamilton Bulldogs/ Staz
97/8 New Orleans Brass
00/1 St. John's Maple Leafs
01/2 St. John's Maple Leafs
01/2 St. John's / Clarenville

MINDJIMBA, ANTOINE
93/4 San Diego Gulls

MINER, JOHN
98/9 DEL 97
99/0 Eishockey 121
00/1 UD DEL 139
01/2 UD DEL 144
88/9 EDMO / Action 30
85/6 Nova Scotia Oilers
82/3 Regina Pats
83/4 Regina Pats

MINETTI, TINO
71/2 Williams Finnish 349

MINGE, LESZEK
89 Semic Sticker 147

MINISTR, MILAN
97/8 APS 121
01/2 OFS 90
99/0 Score 125

MINKHORST, BILL
95/6 Slapshot 126

MINKKILA, TIMO
71/2 Williams Finnish 331

MINNIS, MIKE
92/3 BCJHL 83

MINOR, DOUG
90/1 7th..Sketch OHL 188
89/0 Soo Greyhounds

MINOR, GERRY
81/2 O-Pee-Chee 342
82/3 O-Pee-Chee 352
80/1 Pepsi Bottle Cap
80/1 VANC
80/1 VANC / Silverwood
81/2 VANC
81/2 VANC / Silverwood
82/3 VANC

MIO, ED
80/1 O-Pee-Chee 341
81/2 O-Pee-Chee 119
82/3 O-Pee-Chee 230
83/4 O-Pee-Chee 127
84/5 O-Pee-Chee 61
81/2 OPC Sticker 216
82/3 OPC/Topps Sticker 142
83/4 OPC/Topps Sticker 209
80/1 Pepsi Bottle Cap
84/5 Topps 45
91/2 Upper Deck 639
84/5 DETR / Little Caesars
79/0 EDMO
79/0 EDMO
80/1 EDMO / Zellers
88/9 EDMO / Action 51

MIRABELLO, JIM
93/4 Huntington Blizzard
95/6 Tallahasee Tiger Sharks

MIRABILE, STEVE
92/3 Hampton Roads

MIRAO, SILVERIO
91/2 Avant Garde BCJHL 39
92/3 BCJHL 46

MIREAU, BRENT
84/5 Brandon Wheat Kings
85/6 Brandon Wheat Kings

MIRNOV, IGOR
02/3 Russian Future Stars 11

MIRONOV, BORIS
02/3 Pacific 79
02/3 Pacific Complete 262
02/3 Parkhurst Retro 190
98/9 Aurora 74
98/9 Be A Player 51, ✍ Aut. 51
99/0 BAP Mem. 16
00/1 BAP Mem. 84
01/2 BAP Mem. 148
92/3 Classic 44
92/3 Classic Four Sport 185
93/4 Donruss 384
93/4 Donruss 429
93/4 Donruss RR 9
94/5 Donruss 218
96/7 Flair 34
93/4 Fleer Ultra 454
93/4 Fleer Ultra WotF 8
94/5 Fleer Ultra 73, ARS-5
95/6 Fleer Ultra 239
01/2 Heads Up ✂ JQ 7
98/9 Kraft / PB
93/4 Leaf 364
94/5 Leaf 179, GLR-8
97/8 Omega 94
98/9 Pacific 216
99/0 Pacific 94
00/1 Pacific 99
97/8 Pa. Invincible R-81
98/9 Pa. Paramount 90
99/0 Pa. Paramount 57
00/1 Pa. Paramount 51
96/7 Panini Sticker 265
97/8 Panini Sticker 216
98/9 Panini Sticker 192
00/1 Panini Sticker 124
93/4 Parkhurst 264
95/6 Parkhurst 75
00/1 Parkhurst P-35
94/5 Parkie SE57
94/5 Pinnacle 188
96/7 Pi. Be A Player 88, ✍ Aut. 88
95/6 Playoff 150
94/5 POG 102
93/4 Power Play 474
93/4 Power Play RooS 6
93/4 Premier 394
94/5 Premier 288, OF-17
01/2 Pr. Stock ✂ GUG 23
00/1 PS Titanium ✂ GUG 72
01/2 PS Titanium ✂ DSJ 8
00/1 PS Titanium Draft ✂ 18
92/3 Red Ace Blue 15
92/3 Red Ace Violet 21
93/4 Score 607
94/5 Score 255
00/1 Signature 187, ✍ Aut. 118
01/2 Signat. 179, ✍ Aut. 179
98/9 To. Finest 60
93/4 To. Stadium 338
94/5 To. Stadium 85
91/2 Tri Globe From... 21-22
98/9 UD Choice 83
00/1 Ultimate Mem. ✂ TM-18
91/2 Upper Deck 662
93/4 Upper Deck 492, SP-176
94/5 Upper Deck 172
97/8 Upper Deck 276
98/9 Upper Deck 273
00/1 Upper Deck 268
01/2 Upper Deck 42
91/2 Upper Deck WJC 23
98/9 UD G. Reserve 273
00/1 UD Vintage 78
01/2 Vanguard ✂ DGM 7
00/1 Victory 54
96/7 EDMO
97/8 EDMO
93/4 WINN / Ruffles
93/4 WINN Readers

MIRONOV, DMITRI
98/9 Be A Player 295, ✍ Aut. 295
99/0 BAP Mem. 27
94/5 Donruss 58
97/8 Donruss 130
94/5 Flair 183
94/5 Fleer 217
92/3 Fleer Ultra 422, -UI 15
93/4 Fleer Ultra 127
94/5 Fleer Ultra 218
95/6 Fleer Ultra 290
94/5 Leaf 254
95/6 Leaf 96
90/1 O-Pee-Chee 514
91/2 O-Pee-Chee 515
91/2 O-Pee-Chee 23R
92/3 O-Pee-Chee 71
97/8 Omega 4
98/9 Pacific 202
97/8 Pacific CC 234
97/8 Pa. Paramount 4
97/8 Pa. Revolution 3
95/6 Panini Sticker 67
96/7 Panini Sticker 65
97/8 Panini Sticker 182
99/0 Panini Sticker 165
91/2 Parkhurst 391
92/3 Parkhurst 417
93/4 Parkhurst 477
94/5 Parkhurst 232
95/6 Parkhurst 437
92/3 Pinnacle 247
92/3 Pinnacle 419
94/5 Pinnacle 229
97/8 Pinnacle 125
97/8 Pi. Be A Player 170, ✍ Aut. 170
95/6 Playoff 189
94/5 POG 241
95/6 POG 219
93/4 Power Play 245
93/4 Premier 419
94/5 Premier 165
92/3 Red Ace Blue 22
92/3 Red Ace Violet 22
92/3 Score 468
93/4 Score 209
95/6 Score 180
97/8 Score 240
97/8 Score Anah. 4
91 Semic Sticker 84
92 Semic Sticker 107
95/6 SBx Emotion 139
94/5 SP 120
98/9 SPx Finite 31
91/2 Star Pics 58
92/3 Topps 144
99/0 Topps 228
99/0 To. Chrome 228
96/7 To. Picks 167
92/3 To. Stadium 5
92/3 Upper Deck 83
93/4 Upper Deck 513
94/5 Upper Deck 222, SP-79
95/6 Upper Deck 322
96/7 Upper Deck 138
97/8 Upper Deck 213
98/9 Upper Deck 385
94/5 UD BAP ✍ 19
95/6 UD CC 125
96/7 UD CC 221
97/8 UD Coll. Choice 3
98/9 UD G. Reserve 385
99/0 UD MVP Cup 190
96 Wien 133
96/7 ANAH / Up Front 7
95/6 PITT / Foodland 25
92/3 TORO / Kodak
93/4 TORO / Abalene
93/4 TORO / Black's 8
94/5 TORO / Coca-Cola

MIROSHNIKOV, ALEXEI
99/0 Mir 159

MISAWA, MINORU
79 Panini Sticker 285

MISAWA, SATORU
79 Panini Sticker 290

MISCHLER, GRAIG
01/2 Cleveland Barons

MISEK, PETR
82 Semic Sticker 85

MISHAKOV, EVGENY
91/2 Future Trends C72 75
72 Hellas MM-Jenkki 71
70/1 Kuvajulkaisut 9
72 Semic Sticker 12
74 Semic Sticker 48
70/1 Soviet Stars
71/2 Soviet Stars
71/2 Williams Finnish 11
72/3 Williams Finnish 30

MISHKIN, VLADIMIR
82 Semic Sticker 52
89/0 Soviet Stars

MISHUKOV, IGOR
92/3 Semic Nordisk 81

MISITA, LORNE
00/1 Toronto St. Mike's

MISKOLCZI, TED
89/0 7th..Sketch OHL 78
90/1 7th..Sketch OHL 290
94/5 Slapshot / Brantford 18

MISZUK, JOHN
68/9 O-Pee-Chee 93
69/0 O-Pee-Chee 124
69/0 O-Pee-Chee 4in1
76/7 OPC WHA 57
68/9 Shirriff / Phil. 2
68/9 Topps 93
69/0 Topps 124

MITANI, DARCY
96/7 Charlotte Checkers

MITCHELL, BOBBY-CHAD
01/2 Moose Jaw Warriors 5

MITCHELL, DAN
95/6 Spokane Chiefs 29
97/8 Spokane Chiefs

MITCHELL, DAVE
92/3 W. Michigan Broncos
93/4 W. Michigan Broncos

MITCHELL, DAVID
92/3 Windsor Spitfires

MITCHELL, HERB
25-27 Anonymous 38
25-27 Anonymous 39 [No Border]
24/5 Champ's Cigarettes
24/5 William Paterson 29

MITCHELL, JEFF
95/6 Classic 84
94/5 L. Limited USA 8
93/4 Slapshot / Detroit 14
94/5 Slapshot / Detroit Jr. 15
94/5 Slapshot Memorial 89
94/5 SP 195
94/5 Topps Finest 121
96/7 Michigan K-Wings
98/9 Michigan K-Wings

MITCHELL, JOHN
02/3 Plymouth Whalers

MITCHELL, KEVIN
99 Bowman 158
01/2 Louisiana Ice Gators
02/3 Louisiana Ice Gators
99/0 Guelph Storm

MITCHELL, RED
34-43 BeeHive-1 [Chic.]

MITCHELL, ROY
89/0 ProCards AHL 192
90/1 ProCards 65
91/2 ProCards 144
86/7 Portland Winter Hawks
88/9 Portland Winter Hawks

MITCHELL, TOM
88/9 ProCards / Binghampton

MITCHELL, TOTE
24/5 Falcons Crescent 8

MITCHELL, WILLIE
02/3 Sports Vault 249
00/1 BAP Mem. 174
01/2 BAP Mem. 207
00/1 Pacific 246
01/2 Parkhurst 125
01/2 Signat. 62, ✍ Aut. 62
00/1 SPx 100
00/1 Topps 320
00/1 To. Chrome 215
00/1 UD Reserve 103
00/1 Upper Deck 188
00/1 UD MVP 197
00/1 UD Pros&Prosp. 111
00/1 UD Vintage 384
01/2 MINW / Crime 17
99/0 Albany River Rats
00/1 Albany River Rats

MITEW, THOMAS
95/6 DEL 47

MITHCELL, GREG
85/6 U. of Arizona Ice Cats

MITROSHKIN, KONSTANTIN
99/0 Mir 122
00/1 Mir 20

MITROVIC, SAVO
93/4 Greensboro Monarchs
99/0 Odessa Jackalopes
98/9 Phoenix Mustangs 16

MITSOU, PIERRE
00/1 Ottawa 67's 6
01/2 Ottawa 67's 7

MITTELSTEADT, JOEY
90 7th..Sketch Mem.Cup 17
90/1 7th..Sketch WHL 295
96/7 Louisiana Ice Gators
89/0 Kamloops Blazers
88/9 Portland Winter Hawks

MITTENFELLNER, VITUS
95/6 DEL 370

MITTON, PAUL
89/0 7th..Sketch OHL 107
90/1 7th..Sketch OHL 110
94/5 Slapshot / Brantford 12

MIX, HOLGER
94/5 DEL 42
95/6 DEL 39

MIX, TOM
92/3 BCJHL 74

MIZER, CHRIS
97/8 Indianapolis Ice 2

MLINCHENKO, EVGENI
98/9 Mir 80

MOBERG, DAN
82/3 Victoria Cougars

MOBERG, LARRY
96/7 Roanoke Express 18

MOBILE, R.A.
99/0 Sudbury Wolves 23

MOBORG, ANDREAS
02/3 Coventry Blaze

MODANO, MIKE
02/3 Atomic 33, -NPU 2
02/3 BAP All-Star 60-61, ✂ ASJ, ✂ HSHSJers
02/3 BAP Mem. 180, 210, ✂ ASJ36, ✂ ASE16, ✂ ASN16, ✂ ASTJ15, ✂ AST12, ✂ FP10, ✂ HSHSJers 20, /Cup
02/3 Bowman 16
02/3 Calder 23, -CG 4, -HS 4
02/3 Crown Royale 30, -LOR 8, ✂ GWDP 8
02/3 eTopps 11
02/3 Exclusive 57, -MO 8
02/3 First Edition 153, 326, 350, 401H, ✂ Jers., ✂ HSHSJers 9, ✂ TSL 8
02/3 Heads Up 39, -ITN 9, ✂ GWQ 11, ✂ GWQ 29
02/3 In The GU 21, 121, ✂ E11, ✂ F10, ✂ IE6, ✂ GUJ11, ✂ SJ11, ✂ T13
02/3 O-Pee-Chee 13
02/3 Pacific 114, -MA 6, ✂ GWJ 15
02/3 Pacific Complete 103
02/3 Parkhurst 22, ✂ FP10, ✂ GJ33, ✂ SJ33, ✂ HSHSJers, ✂ PP5
02/3 Parkhurst Retro 12, ✂ RF10, ✂ RJ2, ✂ RSJ2, ✂ HSHSJers, ✂ RM20
02/3 Pr. Stock Reserve ✂ 115
02/3 PS Titanium 32
02/3 Quest for the Cup 29, -RTC 4, ✂ GWJ 7
02/3 Signature ✂ FJ10, ✂ SGJ11, ✂ TQ16
02/3 SP Authentic 30, ✂ SP, ✂ DP
02/3 SP GU 16, ✂ AF (x2), ✂ CF, ✂ PC, ✂ PH (x2)
02/3 Sports Vault 205
02/3 SPx 23, 87, 139, ✂ WM, ✂ M, ✂ SS, ✂ X
02/3 Stadium 11, -WS-5
02/3 Topps 13, HHU6, ✂ CC3, ✂ FRF, ✂✍ FRF
02/3 T. Chrome 13, ✂ FRF
02/3 To. Heritage 33
02/3 To. Limited 13
02/3 To. Total 39, TTC9, TT9
02/3 UD Superstars 75, ✂ CAS, ✂ CAST, ✂ LLT
02/3 Ultimate Mem. ✂ DD, ✂ Emb, ✂ FS, ✂ FO, ✂ GUJ, ✂ GUSJ, ✂ ITN, ✂ MO, ✂ NP, ✂ Num
02/3 Upper Deck 56, -GG6, -SS5, -SS6, ✂ ASP, ✂ CG, ✂ DM, ✂ FF, ✂ LN, ✂ PN, ✂ PA, ✂ R50, ✂ S, ✂ PW, ✂ UDPL
02/3 UD Artistic 30, R30, CG20, UD2, ✂ AT, / Art
02/3 UD Classic 33, ET4, PS4, ✂ HR, ✂ SC
02/3 UD Foundations 48, 148
02/3 UD Honor 21, -SG10, -TW5, ✂ GA
02/3 UD Mask 28, ✂ IO, ✂ PG
02/3 UD MVP 59, SO7, VF7, SA, SD (x2), ST (x2), Souv.
02/3 UD Piece 29, ✂ PH, ✂ SS
02/3 UD Premier 18, ✂ Jers, ✂ Patch, ✂ NHLP
02/3 UD Rookie 31, 116, ✂ DJ
02/3 UD Top Shelf 26, ✂ CP, ✂ GO, ✂ M, ✂ R, ✂ SH, ✂ ST (x2), ✂ SW, ✂ TS
02/3 UD Vintage 81, 270, 293, T22
02/3 Vanguard 33, -EMW 5, ✂ GWJ 16
02/3 Victory 69, -NP54
94/5 Action Packed
01/2 Adrenaline 59, PM 3, WB 4
01/2 ASG History
01/2 Atomic 32, CP 4, PP 11, TN 5, ✂ GWJ 19
98/9 Aurora 58, ALC-8, CF-15, MACF-7, NC-5, / Cube 7
99/0 Aurora 47, Stripe 47, CF-11, CP-6, ST-8
00/1 Aurora 45, Pins. 45, CC-4, CF-9, TPS-5B
98/9 Be A Player 40, P-14, ✍ Aut. 40, ✂ G-17, ✂ AS-4, ✂ S-4
99/0 BAP Mem. 217, ✂ J-4, ✂ TM-22, ✂ TM-26, ✂ TM-46, ✂ TM-48
00/1 BAP Mem. 67, ✂ J-20, ✂ H-7, ✂ TM-15, ✂ TM-36
01/2 BAP Mem. 147, ✂ ASJ, ✂ ASE, ✂ ASN, ✂ ASD, ✂ AST, ✂ CoO, HSHS, ✂ PP, ✂ SCP
01/2 BAP Update ✂ H12
96/7 Bic.Sports Aces 6-D
97/8 Bicycle 7-Spade
95/6 Bicycle Sports Aces 3-Diamond
90/1 Bowman 188
91/2 Bowman 125
92/3 Bowman 151
95/6 Bowman 35
01/2 Bowman 6
98/9 Bowman's Best 48
99/0 Crown Royale 46, IG-8, CS-9, CCA-5
00/1 Crown Royale 36, ✂ GWJ-11, JotC-12
01/2 Crown Royale 48, ASH 6, JotC 9, ✂ TT 8
93/4 Donruss 76
93/4 Donruss F
94/5 Donruss 193, IM-8
95/6 Donruss 62, PP-8
96/7 Donruss 22, D-9, GTS-7
97/8 Donruss 104, L2L-14
96/7 Do. Canadian 25
97/8 Do. Canadian 13, SCS-1
95/6 Do. Elite 32
96/7 Do. Elite 116
97/8 Do. Elite 2, 129, C-18
97/8 Do. Preferred 8, 176, LT-5A, / Tin 7, WideTin 5
97/8 Do. Priority 11, 192, DD-13, OD-11, Post-12, Stamp-12
97/8 Do. Studio 13, S-19, P-13
98/9 Dynagon Ice 59, -FT 8, -PP 5, -TC 8
99/0 Dynagon Ice 68, ASP-11, CM-24
93/4 EA Sports 33
97/8 Esso 24
01/2 eTopps 12
94/5 Flair 43, CIS-9, SP-7
96/7 Flair 23
94/5 Fleer 55, SA-6
96/7 Fleer 27
95/6 Fleer Metal 42, HM-10
96/7 Fl. Picks F50-30, DL-7, JE-11
92/3 Fleer Ultra 96
93/4 Fleer Ultra 194
94/5 Fleer Ultra 55, PP-8, SM-7
95/6 Fleer Ultra 41, 394, EA-14
96/7 Fl. Ultra 44
00 Gatorade Sticker
91/2 Gillette 15
95 Globe 111
01/2 Heads Up 31, HD 4, SM 6, ✂ JQ 10, ✂ JQ 21
93/4 Hockey Wit 60
99/0 HoloGrFX 19
95/6 Hoyle / West. 7-Diamond
91/2 Kellogg's / Score 4
90/1 Kraft 34
91/2 Kraft 48
94/5 Kraft / SS
96/7 Kraft / PB
97/8 Kraft / KD
98/9 Kraft / KD
99/0 Kraft / KD, / PB
00/1 Kraft 5
93/4 Leaf 202
94/5 Leaf 9, GLS-10, LL-6
95/6 Leaf 227
96/7 Leaf 12, FOI-14, LL-15
97/8 Leaf 15, 181, BS-9, FOI-6
94/5 L. Limited 60
95/6 L. Limited 51
96/7 L. Limited 13, S-8
96/7 L. Preferred 44, 150, LS-28
97/8 Limited 19, 42, 193, FG-67
96/7 Maggers 49
93/4 McDonald's McD-10
99/0 McDonald's ✂ GJ
00/1 McDonald's 12, GWJ-4
01/2 McDonald's 10, ✂ JPatch 7
96/7 Metal Univ. 40
99/0 Millenium 76, ✍ Aut. 76, ✂ J-27, ✂✍ J-27, ✂ JS-27
98/9 NHL Power Play
90/1 OPC/Topps 348
91/2 O-Pee-Chee 367
92/3 O-Pee-Chee 313
01/2 O-Pee-Chee 52
90/1 OPC/Topps F
98/9 OPC Chrome 50
90/1 OPC Premier 74
97/8 Omega 73, 246, GF-5, SHLC-7
98/9 Omega 73, -EOP 8, -FTF 9, -Onl. 13, -PI 16, -Prism 7
99/0 Omega 74, 5ST-20, CC-7, EOP-7, G-5, NAAS-4, ✂ GWJ 2
98/9 Pacific 181, -CCA 5, -DI 8, -GCDC 12, -TC 8, -Time. 9
99/0 Pacific 126, CI-9, CCA-6, GC-15, HAA-6, HAA-16, PAP-11, TL-9
00/1 Pacific 137, GCDC-13, NAS-4, PR-8, ✍ Aut. 137, ✂ GWJ-5
01/2 Pacific 131, 409, 428, GCDC 8, IZ 10, TDP 8
97/8 Pacific CC 4, CS-5, TC-8
97/8 Pa. Crown Roy. 41, BOS-7, HT-6, L-7
98/9 Pa. Crown Roy. 41, -MP 8, -PotG 11, -PP 7
97/8 Pa. Dynagon 37, T-42, BKS-30
97/8 Pa. Invincible 41, AZ-8, FP-11, R-63
97/8 Pa. Paramount 60, P-8
98/9 Pa. Paramount 68, -SD 6, -TC 8
99/0 Pa. Paramount 75, IAI-9, PB-14
00/1 Pa. Paramount 79, ES-9, FF-13
97/8 Pa. Revolution 43, ASG-10, TC-8
98/9 Pa. Revolution 44, -ASG 20, -TPA 25, -CTLC 7, -NI 5, -Show. 15
01/2 PTC National 5
98/9 Panini Photocard
90/1 Panini Sticker 253, 340
91/2 Panini Sticker 116
92/3 Panini Sticker 91
93/4 Panini Sticker X
94/5 Panini Sticker 226, 239b
95/6 Panini Sticker 168
96/7 Panini Sticker 168
97/8 Panini Sticker 139
98/9 Panini Sticker 123
99/0 Panini Sticker 226
00/1 Panini Sticker 144
91/2 Parkhurst 81
92/3 Parkhurst 75
93/4 Parkhurst 49
93/4 Parkhurst F6
94/5 Parkhurst 308, V2, YCTG-6
95/6 Parkhurst 55
00/1 Parkhurst P-232
01/2 Parkhurst 10, ✂ PJ16, ✂ PS16, ✂ HSHSJers, ✂ M35, ✂ T12, ✂ T21, ✂ WCJ6, ✂ WCE6, ✂ WCN6
94/5 Parkie SE47
91/2 Pinnacle 5
92/3 Pinnacle 155
92/3 Pinnacle 260
92/3 Pinnacle T2K 2
93/4 Pinnacle 40
93/4 Pinnacle T2K1 17
94/5 Pinnacle 3, BR5, GR8, WE9
95/6 Pinnacle 108, R20-5
96/7 Pinnacle 154
97/8 Pinnacle 91
96/7 Pi. Be A Player BB-8
97/8 Pi. Be A Player OT 10
97/8 Pi. BeeHive 26, BHT-3
97/8 Pi. Certified 33
95/6 Pi. FANtasy 14
97/8 Pi. Inside 15
95/6 Pi. Summit 14
96/7 Pi. Summit 23
97/8 Pi. Totally 33
95/6 Pi. Zenith 24, ZT-10
96/7 Pi. Zenith 1, A-2
95/6 Playoff 31, 142, 250
96/7 Playoff 352
94/5 POG 81
95/6 POG 85
93/4 Power Play 63
93/4 Power Play SA 8
93/4 Premier 46
93/4 Premier - Finest 6
94/5 Premier 230, TF-9, GTG-4
00/1 Premier Plus 69, MB10, PT4, WP15
99/0 Prism 46, DAS-6, SGDC-9
00/1 Pr. Stock 32, AC-10, EA-8, Res. 8, PS-18, PSS-10, ✂ GUG-39
01/2 Pr. Stock 29, -PS 23, ✂ GUG 37
00/1 PS Titanium 29, 3SS-13, ✂ GUG-89, ✂ GUG-154
01/2 PS Titanium 45, ✂ DSJ 16, ✂ DSJ 52
01/2 PS Titanium Draft ✂ 34
00/1 PS Titanium Draft ✂ 33
95/6 Pro Magnet 124
90/1 Pro Set 142
91/2 Pro Set 105
92/3 Pro Set 76
92/3 Pro Set TL 7
91/2 Pro Set Platinum 55
99/0 Revolution 48, NI-9, O-9, SS-14, TL-15, / CSC 48
00/1 Revolution 47, II-9, NI-10, SM-25, ✂ GUG-3
90/1 Score 120, 327
90/1 Sco. Hot Cards 97
91/2 Score 247
91/2 Score 423
91/2 Score CAN 313
91/2 Score CAN 467
92/3 Score 139
92/3 Score 427
92/3 Score USAG 5
93/4 Score 142
93/4 Score PiAS 28
93/4 Score TF 5
94/5 Score 188, DT17, NP16, TF6
95/6 Score 120, BB-0, GB-3
96/7 Score 72, S-4
97/8 Score 92, 262
90/1 Sco. Young Stars 20
91/2 Score Young Stars 35
92/3 Score Young Stars 40
92/3 Seasons 65
94/5 Select 38
95/6 Select CE 17
96/7 Select CE 2
94 Semic 125
95 Semic 116
91 Semic Sticker 141
92 Semic Sticker 157
93 Semic Sticker 182
00/1 Signature 89, HSHS, F-10, ✍ Aut. 142, ✂ J-27, ✂ HSHSJers
01/2 Signat. C-27, ✂ FP10, ✂ GUE19, ✂ GJ20, ✂ GSJ20, ✂ HSHSJers 13, ✂ ITN19, ✂ IS6, ✂ TM10
95/6 SBx Emotion 49, Xci-3
95/6 SBx Impact 48
96/7 SBx Impact 30
94/5 SP 28
95/6 SP 36, E11
96/7 SP 40, HC-25
97/8 SP Authentic 43, I37
98/9 SP Authentic 25, SS12, SO14
99/0 SP Authentic 27, SF5
00/1 SP Authentic 29, PS3, SF2, ✍ SotT, ✍ SotTT
01/2 SP Authentic 23, 95, ✂ NN, ✍ SotT
00/1 SP GU 18, ✂ TotG, ✂ C, ✂ P
01/2 SP GU 14, ✂ AF, ✂ AFD, ✂ AFT, ✂✍ IS, ✂✍ ISD, ✂ Patch
96/7 SPx 11
97/8 SPx 13
99/0 SPx 47, P11, X18, XT8, ✂ WM
00/1 SPx 21, 85, X5, S3, ✂ WM
01/2 SPx 19, 73, 84, ✂ HT (x2)
98/9 SPx Finite 109, 169
98/9 SPx Prospects 18, H11, L5, PS24
00/1 Stadion 87
99/0 Stadium 20, Chrome 18, Big 10, CA19
00/1 Stadium 86, BT3, SF5
01/2 Stadium 5, G7, HS9, NHLP16
94 Starflics
95/6 SLU
96/7 SLU
99/0 SLU 256
95/6 Super Sticker 32, 33
96/7 Team Out!
92/3 Topps 441
95/6 Topps 80, HGA3
98/9 Topps 50, L12, M5
99/0 Topps 6, IM8, TW12
00/1 Topps 18, TC5, HM8, NHLD3, OTG8, ✍ CAI
01/2 Topps 52, SG6
99/0 To. Chrome 6, IM8
00/1 To. Chrome 18, 164, TC5, HM8
01/2 To. Chrome 52
94/5 Topps Finest 106, BBB-6
95/6 To. Finest 128
98/9 To. Finest 75, M31, M32, M33, M34, R2
98/9 T. Gold Label 2
99/0 To. Gold Label 85, PG13
00/1 To. Gold Label 64, D2, GG13
00/1 To. Heritage 45, 217, HH4
01/2 To. Heritage 8
96/7 To. Picks 51
99/0 To. Prmr. Plus 57, FP4, PT4
01/2 To. Reserve 47
91/2 To. Stadium 187
92/3 To. Stadium 4
93/4 To. Stadium 130
93/4 To. Stadium - AS
95/6 To. Stadium EC168
94/5 TSC Members Only 25
00/1 To. Stars 7, P1, WF5, ✂ GG, ✂✍ GGA, ✍ CAI
95/6 T. Super Skills 46
98/9 UD Choice 69, BH16, SQ24
00/1 UD Heroes 145, SS3
01/2 UD PlayMakers Ltd 33, / PM
00/1 UD Reserve 27, GS3, PSJ, ✍ PSJ
98/9 UD3 39, 99, 159
00/1 Ultimate Mem. ✍ U-27, ✂ J-27, ✂ Jers. 24, ✂ JJ-8, ✂ S-27, ✂ TM-24, ✂ TM-26
01/2 Ultimate Mem. ✂ ASGH, ✂ DD, ✂ Emb., ✂ Jers., ✂ S&J, ✂ ITN, ✂ JE, ✂ JJ, ✂ NP, ✂ WTF
99/0 Ult. Victory 27, FF5, S4
90/1 Upper Deck 46, 346
91/2 Upper Deck 32
91/2 Upper Deck 160
92/3 Upper Deck 9
92/3 Upper Deck 305
93/4 Upper Deck 294, 397, SP-38
94/5 Upper Deck 58, IG8, R37, SP-21
95/6 Upper Deck 220, 420, SE-26
96/7 Upper Deck 43, 363, X21, SS19A, ✂ GJ9
97/8 Upper Deck 56, SS29, SG29, S26, T16B
98/9 Upper Deck 30, 256, FF12, FT13, LS28, P18
99/0 Upper Deck 152, 216, CT14, MA13, SS20, ✂ GJ
00/1 Upper Deck 55, A4, F4, GA5, P3, SS8, TT5
01/2 Upper Deck 55, 218, CT4, FC11, GA14, LP4, SS8, ✂ ASJ, ✂ Cjers (x2), ✂ PatchL, ✂ PatchNu, ✂ PoaND, ✂ SCFJers, ✂ SCFJersD, ✂ SCFJersT, ✂ SupSwe, ✂✍ JersSig
95/6 UD ASG MVP14
93/4 Upper Deck Be A Player 31
94/5 UD BAP R8, R114
95/6 UD BAP 153, ✍ S153
93/4 UD BAP Roots 24
96/7 UD Black Diam. 99, RC16
97/8 UD Black Diam. 80, PC25
98/9 UD Black Diam. 27, M5, WF30
99/0 UD Black Diam. 29, D6, ✂ APOH
00/1 UD Black Diam. 20, FP4, IC2
99/0 UD C. Legends 60
01/2 UD Challenge 25, CR4, ✂ UC
95/6 UD CC 238, C16
96/7 UD CC 69, 315, UD17, S15
97/8 UD Coll. Choice 65, SQ82, S8, C2, CR2
98/9 UD G. Reserve 30, 256
99/0 UD G. Reserve 152, 216
01/2 UD Honor Roll 99, DF1, SS2, SG3, ✂ GAJ
96/7 UD Ice 82
97/8 UD Ice 62, L8B
00/1 UD Ice 15, IC2, FP4, ✂ IGJ
01/2 UD Ice 12, ✍ CCA, ✂ JC, ✂ FJ
00/1 UD Legends 39, 40, PH4, ✂ LGJ
92/3 UD Locker 31
01/2 UD Mask 30, ✂ GJ, ✂ JP, ✂ DP, ✂ PM
98/9 UD MVP 61, PG4, -Souv.
99/0 UD MVP 59, H11, MVP10
00/1 UD MVP 61, TP4, VC4
01/2 UD MVP 57, MT3, VC7, -J, ✍ SJ, ✂ C
99/0 UD MVP Cup 58, GM4, PH4, GC
99/0 UD Ovation 19, LP1
99/0 UD PowerDeck 10
01/2 UD Premier 17, ✂ S, ✂ D (x2)
00/1 UD Pros&Prosp. 27, PM5, ✂ GJ
99/0 UD Retro 24
01/2 UD SCup Champs 46, ✂ S, ✂ G
01/2 UD Top Shelf 14, ✂ P, ✂ J, ✂✍ SJ
00/1 UD Vintage 112, 123, 124, NH10
01/2 UD Vintage 79, 86, 87
00/1 Vanguard 35, HV-12, ✂ DGJ-4
01/2 Vanguard 32, QTH 5, ✂ DGM 11
99/0 Victory 88
00/1 Victory 70, 77, 298
01/2 Victory 109, 414
01/2 Waving the Flag 25
99/0 WGretzky 53
96 Wien 166
97/8 Zenith 37, CTC-5, Z58
94/5 DALL / Southwest
94/5 DALL / Cap
96/7 DALL / Southwest
97/8 DALL / Score 92
00/1 DALL / Southwest
01/2 DALL / Southwest
02/3 DALL / Southwest

MODDY, BILL
92/3 BCJHL 140

MODES, WERNER
72 Semic Sticker 99

MODIG, LARS
94/5 Leaf Elit Set 101
95/6 Leaf Elit Set 76
89/0 Semic Elitserien 148
90/1 Semic Elitserien 228
91/2 Semic Elitserien 156
92/3 Semic Elitserien 177
95/6 UD Elitserien 114

MODIN, FREDRIK
02/3 Crown Royale ✂ GWJ 21
02/3 First Edition 164
02/3 O-Pee-Chee 189
02/3 Pacific 352, ✂ GWJ 46
02/3 Pacific Complete 71
02/3 Parkhurst 127
02/3 Parkhurst Retro 114
02/3 PS Titanium ✂ GWJ 65
02/3 Topps 189
02/3 To. Limited 189
02/3 To. Total 256
02/3 Upper Deck 403
02/3 UD MVP 168
02/3 UD Vintage 232
02/3 Victory 196
01/2 Adrenaline 175
98/9 Be A Player 134, ✍ Aut. 134
00/1 BAP Mem. 191
01/2 BAP Mem. 65
00/1 Crown Royale 97
96/7 Do. Canadian 130
99/0 Dynagon Ice 182
95 Globe 59
94/5 Leaf Elit Set 273, ND-3, RR-1
95/6 Leaf Elit Set 19
99/0 Millenium 218, ✍ Aut. 218
01/2 O-Pee-Chee 246
99/0 Omega 218
98/9 Pacific 419
00/1 Pacific 378
01/2 Pacific 356
97/8 Pacific CC 127
00/1 Pa. Paramount 223
97/8 Panini Sticker 181
98/9 Panini Sticker 160
99/0 Panini Sticker 147
00/1 Panini Sticker 89
00/1 Parkhurst P-176
01/2 Parkhurst 167, ✂ PJ31
96/7 Pi. Be A Player 216, ✍ Aut. 216
97/8 Score Toro. 13
96/7 Select CE 112
94/5 Sig. Rookies 7, ✍ 7
01/2 Signat. 70, ✍ Aut. 70
00/1 SP Authentic 81
00/1 Stadium 138
00/1 Topps 92
01/2 Topps 246
01/2 To. Heritage 109
96/7 Upper Deck 345
97/8 Upper Deck 162
98/9 Upper Deck 192
00/1 Upper Deck 160
01/2 Upper Deck 159
97/8 UD Coll. Choice 249
95/6 UD Elitserien 35, 220, NA4
98/9 UD G. Reserve 192
01/2 UD Mask 87
98/9 UD MVP 193
00/1 UD MVP 160
01/2 UD MVP 172
00/1 UD Pros&Prosp. 78
00/1 UD Vintage 327
01/2 UD Vintage 230, 234
00/1 Victory 215
01/2 Victory 318
99/0 WGretzky 159
96 Wien 73

MODIN, JOHAN
97/8 UD Elitserien 190

MODRY, BOHUMIL
96/7 APS 372

MODRY, JAROSLAV
02/3 BAP Mem. 90
02/3 O-Pee-Chee 101
02/3 Pacific 170
02/3 Pacific Complete 265
02/3 Parkhurst Retro 151
02/3 Sports Vault 237
02/3 Topps 101
02/3 To. Limited 101
02/3 To. Total 170
94/5 APS 97
92/3 Classic Prospects 146
93/4 Cla. Prospects 24
93/4 Donruss 455
94/5 Donruss 197
93/4 Fleer Ultra 362
93/4 Fleer Ultra WotF 9
94/5 Leaf 496
99/0 Omega 108
94/5 Panini Sticker D
96/7 Panini Sticker 275
93/4 Parkhurst 386
94/5 Parkhurst 123, 290
95/6 Parkhurst 418
93/4 Power Play 380
93/4 Power Play RooS 7
93/4 Premier 307
94/5 Premier 512
93/4 Score 616
00/1 Signature 144, ✍ Aut. 191
00/1 Stadion 126
93/4 To. Stadium 411
93/4 Upper Deck 319
94/5 Upper Deck 473
01/2 Victory 166
95/6 OTTA

MOE, ASGAULT
92/3 Semic Nordisk 8

MOE, BILL
45-64 BeeHive-2 [NYRa.]

MOELLER, DARWEIN
83/4 Kelowna Wings

MOEN, JEFF
92/3 Minnesota G'Gophers
93/4 Minnesota G'Gophers
94/5 Minnesota G'Gophers

MOES, MIKE
90/1 ProCards 148
90/1 Newmarket Saints

MOESER, DUANE
99/0 Eishockey 151
00/1 UD DEL 24, ✂ GJ

MOESER, DUANNE
94/5 DEL 9
95/6 DEL 12
96/7 DEL 12
98/9 DEL 287
01/2 UD DEL 11

MOFFAT, CALEB
01/2 Baie-Comeau 17
02/3 Baie-Comeau

MOFFAT, CORRI
91/2 Air Canada SJHL 18
91/2 Air Canada SJHL A10
92/3 MPS SJHL 77

MOFFAT, LYLE
74/5 O-Pee-Chee 379
79/0 O-Pee-Chee 277
77/8 OPC WHA 64
74/5 TORO
79/0 WINN
78/9 Winnipeg Jets

MOFFAT, MIKE
81/2 Kingston Canadians

MOFFAT, RON
83/4 Brantford Alexanders

MOFFATT, STEVE
99/0 Florida Everblades

MOFFETT, GREG
83/4 Nova Scotia Voyageurs

MOGER, SANDY
98/9 Be A Player 64, ✍ Aut. 64
92/3 Classic 67
92/3 Classic Four Sport 192
93/4 Cla. Prospects 187
95/6 Donruss 245
95/6 Fleer Ultra 11
95/6 Leaf 272
98/9 OPC Chrome 59
98/9 Pacific 240
97/8 Pa. Invincible R-15
95/6 Panini Sticker 6
96/7 Pi. Be A Player 172, ✍ Aut. 172
95/6 Pi. Summit 185
96/7 Pi. Summit 53
95/6 Select CE 140
98/9 Topps 59
95/6 Upper Deck 332
92/3 Hamilton Canucks
99/0 Houston Aeros

MOGILNY, ALEXANDER
02/3 Atomic 92
02/3 BAP All-Star 62, ✂ ASJ
02/3 BAP Mem. 8, 248, ✂ ASJ37, ✂ AST6, ✂ SC19
02/3 Bowman 35
02/3 Crown Royale 92, ✂ GWDP 21, ✂ GWJ 22
02/3 Exclusive 161
02/3 First Edition 102, ✂ Jers.
02/3 Heads Up 116, ✂ GWQ 26
02/3 In The GU ✂ E33, ✂ IE12, ✂ GUJ41, ✂ SJ41, ✂ T12
02/3 McDonald's ✂ JP 17
02/3 O-Pee-Chee 187
02/3 Pacific 365, ✂ GWJ 47
02/3 Pacific Complete 28
02/3 Parkhurst 71, ✂ GJ14, ✂ SJ14, ✂ TT3
02/3 Parkhurst Retro 35
02/3 Pr. Stock Reserve 92
02/3 PS Titanium 93, ✂ GWJ 66
02/3 Quest for the Cup 92
02/3 Signature GS-5, ✂ SGJ41, ✂ TQ2
02/3 Slam Card
02/3 SP Authentic 82
02/3 SP Game-Used ✂ TG
02/3 Sports Vault 136
02/3 SPx 69
02/3 Stadium 44
02/3 Topps 187
02/3 T. Chrome 108
02/3 To. Heritage 82
02/3 To. Limited 187
02/3 To. Total 127, TP12
02/3 Ultimate Mem. ✂ GD, ✂ JE, ✂ JJ
02/3 Upper Deck 166
02/3 UD Artistic 84, R84, / Art
02/3 UD Classic 94
02/3 UD MVP 176
02/3 UD Piece 82
02/3 UD Top Shelf 82
02/3 UD Vintage 243, 288, GB 243, ✂ T61
02/3 Vanguard 92, ✂ GWJ 43
02/3 Victory 198
01/2 Adrenaline 183
01/2 Atomic 92, TN 13
98/9 Aurora 190
99/0 Aurora 142
98/9 Be A Player 141, P-2, ✍ Aut. 141, ✂ G-21, ✂ AS-14, ✂ S-13
99/0 BAP Mem. 286, 349, ✂ TM-36
00/1 BAP Mem. 219
01/2 BAP Mem. 96, 395
01/2 BAP Update ✂ HSHSJers, ✂ H25, ✂ TP7
96/7 Bic.Sports Aces J-C
90/1 Bowman 240
91/2 Bowman 30
92/3 Bowman 34
92/3 Bowman 235
95/6 Bowman 5, BB9
01/2 Bowman 78
98/9 Bowman's Best 40
99/0 Challenger 6
93/4 Classic 122, N7, ✍ Aut.
00/1 Crown Royale 65
01/2 Crown Royale 132
93/4 Donruss 39
93/4 Donruss C
93/4 Donruss ES 8
94/5 Donruss 92
95/6 Donruss 275
96/7 Donruss 181, D-7, GTS-4
97/8 Donruss 106
96/7 Do. Canadian 91
97/8 Do. Canadian 45
95/6 Do. Elite 18, CE-7
96/7 Do. Elite 56, S-9
97/8 Do. Elite 69
97/8 Do. Preferred 39, 170
97/8 Do. Priority 119
98/9 Dynagon Ice 190
99/0 Dynagon Ice 195
93/4 EA Sports 17
93/4 EA Sports 191
97/8 Esso 39
94/5 Flair 20, SP-8
96/7 Flair 96
94/5 Fleer 25
96/7 Fleer 114, 138, ART-16
95/6 Fleer Metal 153, IS-15, MW-5
96/7 Fl. Picks F50-31, DL-4, JE-3
92/3 Fleer Ultra 18, -UI 16
93/4 Fleer Ultra 238
93/4 Fleer Ultra AS 5
93/4 Fleer Ultra RLS 7
93/4 Fleer Ultra SM 7
94/5 Fleer Ultra 26, ASG-5, GG-6, SM-8
95/6 Fleer Ultra 21, 317, EA-15

96/7 Fl. Ultra 170, PL-5, UP-13
00 Gatorade Sticker
96/7 Got-Um
01/2 Heads Up 90
93/4 Hockey Wit 75
95/6 Hoyle / East. 3-Diamond
92/3 Humpty Dumpty
91 Ivan Fiodorov 9
94 Koululainen
91/2 Kraft 60
93/4 Kraft / KD
94/5 Kraft / SS
95/6 Kraft / KD
96/7 Kraft / KD
96/7 Kraft Magnet
93/4 Leaf 91
93/4 Leaf GLAS 8
93/4 Leaf HTA 2
94/5 Leaf 256, FOI-10
95/6 Leaf 187, FF-8
96/7 Leaf 162, FOI-2, LL-11
97/8 Leaf 25
94/5 L. Limited 36
95/6 L. Limited 83, SG-6
96/7 L. Limited 8, S-13
96/7 L. Preferred 2, LS-51
97/8 Limited 68, 104, 122, FG-51
96/7 Maggers 159
92/3 McDonald's McD-22
93/4 McDonald's McD-19
94/5 McDonald's McD-8
95/6 McDonald's McD-21
96/7 McDonald's McD-11
97/8 McDonald's F2
96/7 Metal Univ. 159, IC-11, LW-14
99/0 Millenium 243, ✍ Aut. 243, ✂ J-31, ✂ JS-31
95/6 Cool Trade 19
98/9 NHL Power Play
90/1 OPC/Topps 42
91/2 O-Pee-Chee 171
92/3 O-Pee-Chee 279
01/2 O-Pee-Chee 58, Update 58
90/1 OPC/Topps A
98/9 OPC Chrome 207
90/1 OPC Premier 75
97/8 Omega 232
98/9 Omega 235
99/0 Omega 235
98/9 Pacific 89
99/0 Pacific 427
00/1 Pacific 240
01/2 Pacific 235, 433
97/8 Pacific CC 89, SS-11C
97/8 Pa. Crown Roy. 137
98/9 Pa. Crown Roy. 136
97/8 Pa. Dynagon 129, DD-15B, T-55
97/8 Pa. Invincible 144, AZ-24, FP-35, R-203
98/9 Pa. Paramount 237
99/0 Pa. Paramount 236
00/1 Pa. Paramount 146, ✂ GUS-13
97/8 Pa. Revolution 143
98/9 Pa. Revolution 142
98/9 Panini Photocard
90/1 Panini Sticker 338
91/2 Panini Sticker 304
92/3 Panini Sticker 248
92/3 Panini Sticker 299
93/4 Panini Sticker J
94/5 Panini Sticker 94
95/6 Panini Sticker 294
96/7 Panini Sticker 288
97/8 Panini Sticker 237
98/9 Panini Sticker 217
99/0 Panini Sticker 309
00/1 Panini Sticker 46
95 Panini Worlds 285
91/2 Parkhurst 12
92/3 Parkhurst 13
92/3 Parkhurst 218
93/4 Parkhurst 21
94/5 Parkhurst 21
95/6 Parkhurst 212, 246, CCP-3, PP-18, PP-48
00/1 Parkhurst P-111
01/2 Parkhurst 56, ✂ PS70, ✂ HSHSJers, ✂ M31
94/5 Parkie SE ES-14, seV34
91/2 Pinnacle 163
92/3 Pinnacle 77
92/3 Pinnacle T2K 28
93/4 Pinnacle 10
93/4 Pinnacle NF 2
93/4 Pinnacle T2K1 2
93/4 Pinnacle TP 12
94/5 Pinnacle 125, BR17
96/7 Pinnacle 87
97/8 Pinnacle 58
96/7 Pi. Be A Player BB-24
97/8 Pi. Be A Player 247, TN-18, ✍ Aut. 247
97/8 Pi. Certified 60
97/8 Pi. Inside 34, IT-27
95/6 Pi. Summit 48
96/7 Pi. Summit 107, HV-11, U-9
97/8 Pi. Totally 60
95/6 Pi. Zenith 31
96/7 Pi. Zenith 34, ZT-9
95/6 Playoff 102, 209, 318
96/7 Playoff 422
94/5 POG 44
95/6 POG 272
94/5 Post
93/4 Power Play 32
93/4 Power Play GG 5
93/4 Power Play PL 10
93/4 Premier 148
93/4 Premier 172
93/4 Premier 245
93/4 Prmr. - BG-OPC 10
94/5 Premier 50, GTG-13
99/0 Prism 143
01/2 Pr. Stock 91
00/1 PS Titanium 56, ✂ GUG 30
01/2 PS Titanium 130
95/6 Pro Magnet 22
90/1 Pro Set 26
91/2 Pro Set 16
92/3 Pro Set 19
91/2 Pro Set Platinum 14
91/2 Pro Set Platinum 283
91/2 Red Ace
90/1 Score 43
91/2 Score 236
91/2 Score CAN 456
92/3 Score 248
93/4 Score 222
93/4 Score 477
93/4 Score DT 20
93/4 Score DD2
93/4 Score IS 8
93/4 Score PiAS 22
94/5 Score 200
95/6 Score 21, GB-3
96/7 Score 16, DT-9, SD-8, / Promo 16
97/8 Score 129
97/8 Score Vanc. 2
90/1 Sco. Young Stars 26
91/2 Score Young Stars 13
92/3 Score Young Stars 8
93/4 Seasons 12
94/5 Select 22
95/6 Select CE 43
96/7 Select CE 70
91 Semic Sticker 218
00/1 Signature 46
01/2 Signature ✂ GU71, ✂ HSHSJers
95/6 SBx Emotion 182
95/6 SBx Impact 171
96/7 SBx Impact 135, BR-15
94/5 SP 13
95/6 SP 148, E28
96/7 SP 158, GF-12
97/8 SP Authentic 155
98/9 SP Authentic ✍ SotT
99/0 SP Authentic 87
01/2 SP Authentic 84
01/2 SP GU 54
96/7 SPx 47
01/2 SPx 194
00/1 Stadium 157
01/2 Stadium 108
94/5 Starting Lineup
95/6 Super Sticker 122, 124
96/7 Team Out!
92/3 Topps 382
95/6 Topps 225, 376, 6PL
98/9 Topps 207
00/1 Topps 19
01/2 Topps 58, SM18, Update 58
01/2 To. Chrome 58
94/5 Topps Finest 99
95/6 To. Finest 140, 160
98/9 To. Finest 129
96 Topps Finest Bronze 19
98/9 T. Gold Label 62
99/0 To. Gold Label 77
00/1 To. Gold Label 55, GG7
00/1 To. Heritage 71
01/2 To. Heritage 165
96/7 To. Picks 9, FT19, TS9
01/2 To. Reserve 78
92/3 To. Stadium 195
92/3 To. Stadium 320
93/4 To. Stadium 91
93/4 To. Stadium - AS
95/6 To. Stadium 1, MP, EN9
93/4 TSC Members Only 26
94/5 TSC Members Only 6
95/6 TSC Members Only 10
95/6 T. Super Skills 36
98/9 UD Choice 210
00/1 UD Heroes 70
01/2 UD PlayMakers Ltd 92
01/2 Ultimate Mem. ✂ DD, ✂ GSL, ✂ JE, ✂ JJ
90/1 Upper Deck 24
91/2 Upper Deck 267
91/2 Upper Deck 618
91/2 Upper Deck E2
92/3 Upper Deck 167
92/3 Upper Deck 456
92/3 Upper Deck WG18
93/4 Upper Deck 234, 488, FH-34, HT-15, HB-1, H-10, SP-18
94/5 Upper Deck 334, 552, H9, SP-10
95/6 Upper Deck 188, 221, AS-10, R-6, R35, SE-173
96/7 Upper Deck 167, X29, HH12, SS10B
97/8 Upper Deck T19B
98/9 Upper Deck 376
99/0 Upper Deck 300
00/1 Upper Deck 104
01/2 Upper Deck 392, SS17
95/6 UD ASG MVP4
94/5 UD BAP R68
95/6 UD BAP 204, LL9, ✍ S204
96/7 UD Black Diam. 89
97/8 UD Black Diam. 97
99/0 UD Black Diam. 87
01/2 UD Challenge 83
95/6 UD CC 62
96/7 UD CC 267, 333, UD4, C3, CR3
97/8 UD Coll. Choice 256, SQ69
98/9 UD G. Reserve 376
99/0 UD G. Reserve 300
96/7 UD Ice 104
92/3 UD Locker 8
01/2 UD Mask 91, ✂ GG
98/9 UD MVP 204
99/0 UD MVP 210
00/1 UD MVP 103
01/2 UD MVP ✂ S
01/2 UD SCup Champs 73
00/1 UD Vintage 214
00/1 Vanguard 60
01/2 Vanguard 93
99/0 Victory 299
00/1 Victory 141
01/2 Victory 210, 427
99/0 WGretzky 168
97/8 Zenith 79
89/0 BUFF / Blue Shield
89/0 BUFF / Campbell's
90/1 BUFF / Blue Shield
90/1 BUFF / Campbell's
91/2 BUFF / Blue Shield
91/2 BUFF / Campbell's
91/2 BUFF / Pepsi
92/3 BUFF / Blue Shield
92/3 BUFF / Jubilee
92/3 BUFF / Noco
96/7 VANC / IGA

MOGILNYJ, ALEXANDER
00/1 Stadion 114

MOHAGEN, TONY
98/9 Cincinnati M'Ducks 23

MOHER, CHRIS
00/1 Hull Olympiques 1
01/2 Hull Olympiques 1

MOHNINGER, BRET
91/2 Air Canada SJHL C26

MOHNS, DOUG
52/3 Anonymous 107
68/9 Bauer Photo
45-64 BeeHive-2 [Bost.]
64-67 BeeHive-3 [Chic.]
64/5 Coke/Sprite [Chic.]
65/6 Coca-Cola
70/1 Dad's Cookies
70/1 Eddie Sargent 47
71/2 Eddie Sargent 84
72/3 Eddie Sargent 102
70/1 Esso Power Player
62/3 Cowan Tile
74/5 Loblaws
68/9 O-Pee-Chee 19
69/0 O-Pee-Chee 72
69/0 O-Pee-Chee 4in1
70/1 O-Pee-Chee 16
70/1 O-Pee-Chee DE 29
71/2 O-Pee-Chee 242
72/3 O-Pee-Chee 75
73/4 O-Pee-Chee 241
74/5 O-Pee-Chee 181
54/5 Parkhurst 57
93/4 Parkie 56-57 18
95/6 Parkie 66-67 35
94/5 Parkie Tall 27
60/1 Shirriff 106
61/2 Shirriff 10
68/9 Shirriff / Chic. 8
54/5 Topps 18
57/8 Topps 12
58/9 Topps 50
59/0 Topps 58
60/1 Topps 52
61/2 Topps 10
61/2 Topps - Stamp
62/3 Topps 6
62/3 Topps Dollar
63/4 Topps 3
64/5 Topps 25
65/6 Topps 118
66/7 Topps 61
66/7 Topps / Test 61
67/8 Topps 63
68/9 Topps 19
69/0 Topps 72
70/1 Topps 16
72/3 Topps 78
74/5 Topps 181
65/6 Toronto Star Photo
61/2 Toronto Star Weekend
66/7 Toronto Star Weekend
70/1 Toronto Sun Photo
91/2 Ultimate Original Six 53, ✍ Aut. 53
57-58 BOST
91/2 BOST / SA Legends
98/9 BOST / Alumni 34
74/5 WASH

MOHORIC, KLEMEN
96/7 Johnstown Chiefs

MOISE, MARTIN
99 Bowman 56
97 Bowman 72
98 Bowman 113
98 Bowman Chrome 113
99/0 Québec Remparts 15

MOÏSE, MARTIN
98/9 Québec Remparts

MOISIO, MARKKU
71/2 Williams Finnish 213
72/3 Williams Finnish 159
73/4 Williams Finnish 225

MOISIO, PEKKA
66/7 Champion 92

MOJZIS, PAVEL
98/9 OFS 23
99/0 OFS 214
00/1 OFS 11, 373
01/2 OFS 79

MOKHOV, STEPAN
99/0 Mir 236

MÖKITALO, JARMO
77-79 Sports. FIN 90-2152

MOKOSAK, CARL
88/9 ProCards / Maine
89/0 ProCards IHL 132
90/1 ProCards 304, 412
82/3 CALG

MOKOSAK, JOHN
88/9 ProCards / Adirondack
90/1 ProCards 127
91/2 ProCards 192
92/3 Phoenix Roadrunners
81/2 Victoria Cougars
82/3 Victoria Cougars

MOKREJS, PETR
98/9 OFS 61
99/0 Score 41

MOKROS, MILAN
94/5 DEL 153
95/6 DEL 149
96/7 DEL 245

MOLANDER, RUBAN
91/2 Semic Elitserien 37

MOLANDER, URBAN
90/1 Semic Elitserien 181

MOLBERG, RUNE
79 Panini Sticker 295

MOLE, MICHAEL
01/2 Belleville Bulls Update
00/1 Mississauga IceDogs

MOLER, MIKE
84/5 BUFF / Blue Shield

MOLIN, JOHAN
98/9 UD Elitserien 192
99/0 UD Elitserien 196
00/1 UD Elitserien 35

MOLIN, LARS
82/3 O-Pee-Chee 353
82/3 OPC/Topps Sticker 245
82/3 Post [Vanc.]
82 Semic Sticker 149
83/4 Souhaits Keychain [Canucks]
83/4 Vachon 113-33
81/2 VANC
81/2 VANC / Silverwood
82/3 VANC
83/4 VANC

MOLIN, OVE
94/5 Leaf Elit Set 85
95/6 Leaf Elit Set 20, G-2
91/2 Semic Elitserien 68
92/3 Semic Elitserien 68
95/6 UD Elitserien 33
97/8 UD Elitserien 27
98/9 UD Elitserien 41
99/0 UD Elitserien 25, S3
00/1 UD Elitserien 39, 185, T2, ✍ Sig.

MOLIN, SACHA
94/5 Leaf Elit Set 166
99/0 Fort Wayne Komets
98/9 Long Beach Ice Dogs

MOLINA, ALFIO
72 Semic Sticker 157

MOLLE, TIM
94/5 Anchorage Aces 23

MOLLEKEN, LORNE
91/2 7th...Sketch WHL 100
84/5 Springfield Indians 2
91/2 Saskatoon Blades

MOLLER, MIKE
89/0 ProCards AHL 305
88/9 EDMO / Action 136
85/6 Nova Scotia Oilers
93/4 Red Deer Rebels

MOLLER, PER HOLTEN
79 Panini Sticker 363

MOLLER, RANDY
91/2 Bowman 58
86/7 Kraft Sports 48
94/5 Leaf 344
83/4 O-Pee-Chee 297
84/5 O-Pee-Chee 284
85/6 O-Pee-Chee 240
87/8 O-Pee-Chee 251
90/1 O-Pee-Chee 515
91/2 O-Pee-Chee 371
89/0 O-Pee-Chee 259
83/4 OPC/Topps Sticker 248
84/5 OPC Sticker 174
85/6 OPC Sticker 145-15
87/8 OPC Sticker 229-96
89/0 opcSticker 195-49
87/8 Panini Sticker 162
88/9 Panini Sticker 351
89/0 Panini Sticker 331
91/2 Pinnacle 256
92/3 Pinnacle 176
94/5 Pinnacle 401
90/1 Pro Set 202
91/2 Pro Set 163
90/1 Score 45
91/2 Score 79
91/2 Score CAN 79
92/3 Score 289
93/4 Score 422
83/4 Souhaits Keychain [Nordiques]
92/3 Topps 407
91/2 To. Stadium 2
92/3 To. Stadium 484
93/4 To. Stadium 435
90/1 Upper Deck 418
83/4 Vachon 69-49
92/3 BUFF / Blue Shield
92/3 BUFF / Jubilee
89/0 NYRA / Marine
82/3 QUEB
83/4 QUEB
84/5 QUEB
85/6 QUEB
85/6 QUEB / Gene. Foods
85/6 QUEB / McDonald's
85/6 QUEB / Provigo
86/7 QUEB
86/7 QUEB / Gene. Foods
86/7 QUEB / McDonald's
87/8 QUEB / Gene. Foods
88/9 QUEB
88/9 QUEB / Gene. Foods
89/0 QUEB

MOLLING, JOCHEN
94/5 DEL 55
95/6 DEL 409
96/7 DEL 251
98/9 DEL 55
99/0 Eishockey 171, 373
01/2 UD DEL 132

MOLLOY, MITCH
88/9 ProCards / Maine
90/1 ProCards 283
89/0 Johnstown Chiefs
92/3 San Diego Gulls

MOLNAR, AARON
00/1 London Knights

MOLNAR, PETR
94/5 APS 207
95/6 APS 159
97/8 APS 83

MOLODTSOV, KONSTANTIN
00/1 Mir 280

MOLOTILOV, VADIM
98/9 Mir 149

MOLSON, SEN. H. DE M.
83 HHOF Postcard O12
83&87 HHOF 221

MOLYNEAUX, LARRY
34-43 BeeHive-1 [NYRa.]

MOMESSO, SERGIO
90/1 Bowman 17
91/2 Bowman 309
92/3 Bowman 316
98/9 DEL 248
93/4 Donruss 349
95/6 Donruss 380
92/3 Durivage 26
93/4 Durivage 33
99/0 Eishockey 122
92/3 Fleer Ultra 225
93/4 Fleer Ultra 47
94/5 Fleer Ultra 384
95/6 Fleer Ultra 313
86/7 Kraft Sports 32
94/5 Leaf 250
94/5 Leaf 499
95/6 Leaf 58
90/1 OPC/Topps 244
91/2 O-Pee-Chee 462
92/3 O-Pee-Chee 377
91/2 OPC Premier 55
97/8 Pa. Invincible 121
90/1 Panini Sticker 263
91/2 Panini Sticker 44
91/2 Parkhurst 185
92/3 Parkhurst 421
93/4 Parkhurst 212
94/5 Parkhurst 249
95/6 Parkhurst 473
91/2 Pinnacle 34
92/3 Pinnacle 163
93/4 Pinnacle 393
94/5 Pinnacle 307
95/6 Pi. Summit 163
94/5 POG 342
94/5 Premier 356
90/1 Pro Set 268
91/2 Pro Set 242
92/3 Pro Set 194
91/2 Pro Set Platinum 240
90/1 Score 224
91/2 Score 121
91/2 Score CAN 121
92/3 Score 79
93/4 Score 255
95/6 Score 161
92/3 Topps 214
91/2 To. Stadium 17
92/3 To. Stadium 42
93/4 To. Stadium 323
94/5 To. Stadium 65
95/6 To. Stadium 123
90/1 Upper Deck 19
91/2 Upper Deck 571
92/3 Upper Deck 85
93/4 Upper Deck 104
94/5 Upper Deck 65, 85
95/6 Upper Deck 125
94/5 UD BAP ✍ 178
95/6 UD CC 99
85/6 MONT
85/6 MONT / Provigo
86/7 MONT
87/8 MONT
87/8 MONT / Vachon 55
87/8 MONT / Vachon 56
87/8 SLOU
88/9 SLOU
88/9 SLOU / Kodak
89/0 SLOU / Kodak
90/1 SLOU / Kodak
91/2 VANC
91/2 VANC / Photo
92/3 VANC / Road Trip
95/6 VANC / Abalene 12

MONAHAN, GARRY
70/1 Colgate 13
70/1 Eddie Sargent 207
71/2 Eddie Sargent 199
72/3 Eddie Sargent 202
70/1 Esso Power Player
74/5 Loblaws Update
69/0 O-Pee-Chee 160
70/1 O-Pee-Chee 112
72/3 O-Pee-Chee 207
72/3 O-Pee-Chee 277
73/4 O-Pee-Chee 226
75/6 O-Pee-Chee 357
76/7 O-Pee-Chee 295
77/8 O-Pee-Chee 341
78/9 O-Pee-Chee 268
67/8 Topps 8
70/1 Topps 112
71/2 Toronto Sun Photo
67/8 MONT
67/8 MONT / IGA Card
68/9 MONT / IGA Card
70/1 TORO
71/2 TORO
72/3 TORO
73/4 TORO
78/9 TORO
74/5 VANC / Royal Bank
75/6 VANC / Royal Bank
76/7 VANC / Royal Bank
77/8 VANC / Royal Bank

MONAHAN, HARTLAND
76/7 O-Pee-Chee 203
77/8 O-Pee-Chee 96
78/9 O-Pee-Chee 393
76/7 Topps 203
77/8 Topps 96

MONDOU, ARMAND
33/4 Anonymous 44
34-43 BeeHive-1 [Mont.]
35-40 Canada Starch
36-39 Diamond Match TT1
36-39 Diamond Match TT2
36-39 Diamond Match TT3
28/9 La Presse
33/4 O-Pee-Chee 48
37/8 O-Pee-Chee 177
39/0 O-Pee-Chee 27
34/5 Sweet Caporal
33/4 WWGum 17

MONDOU, BENOIT
02/3 Baie-Comeau

MONDOU, BENOÎT
01/2 Baie-Comeau 23
02/3 Shawinigan Cataractes

MONDOU, PIERRE
80/1 Dernière Heure
83/4 Dernière Heure
78/9 O-Pee-Chee 102
79/0 O-Pee-Chee 211
80/1 O-Pee-Chee 42
81/2 O-Pee-Chee 188
82/3 O-Pee-Chee 188
83/4 O-Pee-Chee 191
84/5 O-Pee-Chee 266
85/6 O-Pee-Chee 211
82/3 OPC/Topps Sticker 35
83/4 OPC/Topps Sticker 68
84/5 OPC Sticker 162
85/6 OPC Sticker 133-253
80/1 Pepsi Bottle Cap
82/3 Post [Mont.]
Sport Flash 11
Sport Flash 11
78/9 Topps 102
79/0 Topps 211
80/1 Topps 42
83/4 Vachon 49-69
77/8 MONT
78/9 MONT
79/0 MONT
80/1 MONT
81/2 MONT
82/3 MONT
82/3 MONT / Steinberg
83/4 MONT
84/5 MONT

MONDT, NIKI
95/6 DEL 99
96/7 DEL 287
98/9 DEL 58
00/1 UD DEL 46
01/2 UD DEL 246

MONDT, NIKOLAUS
99/0 Eishockey 178, 375

MONETTE, JACQUES
51/2 Bas du Fleuve 45
52/3 Bas du Fleuve 35

MONGEAU, MICHEL
95/6 Edge Ice 178
92/3 Fleer Ultra 203
92/3 Pinnacle 388
89/0 ProCards IHL 107
90/1 ProCards 91
91/2 ProCards 26
90/1 Score 395
92/3 To. Stadium 415
90/1 Upper Deck 345
92/3 Upper Deck 213
91/2 SLOU
88/9 Flint Spirits
96/7 Milwaukee Admirals
93/4 Peoria Rivermen
94/5 Peoria Rivermen
95/6 Peoria Rivermen

MONGEON, HUGHES
90/1 7th...Sketch LHJMQ 189
91/2 7th...Sketch LHJMQ 32

MONGRAIN, STEVE
95/6 Halifax Moosehead
97/8 Halifax Moosehead

MONKMAN, BILL
99/0 Topeka Scarecrows

MONONEN, ERKKI
66/7 Champion 107
70/1 Kuvajulkaisut 181
72 Panda MM-Toronto
72 Semic Sticker 81
71/2 Williams Finnish 69
71/2 Williams Finnish 105
72/3 Williams Finnish 149

MONONEN, LAURI
72 Hellas MM-Jenkki 6
70/1 Kuvajulkaisut 69
70/1 Kuvajulkaisut 182
72 Panda MM-Toronto
72 Semic Sticker 82
74 Semic Sticker 99
78/9 SM-Liiga 32
71/2 Williams Finnish 70
71/2 Williams Finnish 288
72/3 Williams Finnish 73
73/4 Williams Finnish 72
73/4 Williams Finnish 115
75/6 Phoenix Roadrunners
76/7 Phoenix Roadrunners

MONRISSON, SANDY
52/3 Anonymous 164

MONTADOR, STEVE
02/3 O-Pee-Chee 303
02/3 Topps 303
02/3 To. Limited 303
01/2 BAP Mem. 340
01/2 UD Ice 130

MONTANARI, MARK
96/7 DEL 102
00/1 Kudos 19
95 Panini Worlds 91
89/0 ProCards AHL 57
90/1 ProCards 142
90 7th..Sketch Mem.Cup 30
86/7 Kitchener Rangers
87/8 Kitchener Rangers
88/9 Kitchener Rangers

MONTANDON, GIL
95 Globe 215
95 Panini Worlds 131
95 Semic 193
91 Semic Sticker 198
92 Semic Sticker 214
93 Semic Sticker 128

MONTEITH, DWAYNE
88/9 Regina Pats

MONTEMURRO, CARLO
52/3 Anonymous 92

MONTGOMERY, CHRIS
00/1 UD Prospects 80
02/3 Québec Remparts

MONTGOMERY, JIM
93/4 Classic 55, ✍ Aut.
93/4 Cla. Images 4 Sport 16
93/4 Cla. Prospects 25
96/7 DEL 348
93/4 Donruss 300
93/4 Donruss RR 13
95/6 Edge Ice 46
93/4 Fleer Ultra 413
94/5 Fleer Ultra 187, 312
95/6 Future Legends 11
94/5 Leaf 258, 348
93/4 Parkhurst 176
94/5 Parkhurst 198
94/5 Parkie SE93
93/4 Pinnacle 438
94/5 Pinnacle 159
93/4 Power Play 431
93/4 Premier 488
94/5 Premier 91
93/4 Score 621
93/4 Upper Deck 472
93/4 Upper Deck 132
94/5 MONT
00/1 Kentucky Tho'blades
99/0 Manitoba Moose
01/2 Utah Grizzlies
92/3 Maine Black Bears
92/3 Maine Black Bears
93/4 Maine Black Bears

MONTGOMERY, SCOTT
86/7 Kitchener Rangers
87/8 Kitchener Rangers

MONTREUIL, ERIC
96/7 Carolina Monarchs
97/8 New Orleans Brass

MOODIE, LANE
01/2 Ottawa 67's 11

MOOG, ANDY
02/3 BAP Mem. / Stanley Cup
02/3 Topps - Reprint 8, ✍ Reprint 8
02/3 Ultimate Mem. ✂ SCD (x2)
02/3 UD Foundations 1, 19, 29
02/3 UD Mask ✂ CW, ✂ BM, / Mask
90/1 Bowman 35
91/2 Bowman 361
92/3 Bowman 79
93/4 Donruss 87
94/5 Donruss 108
95/6 Donruss 290
96/7 Donruss 166
97/8 Donruss 40
96/7 Do. Canadian 90
97/8 Do. Canadian 85
96/7 Do. Elite 3
97/8 Do. Elite 66
97/8 Do. Preferred 113
97/8 Do. Priority 108
93/4 EA Sports 12
94/5 Flair 44
96/7 Flair 24
94/5 Fleer 56
95/6 Fleer Metal 43
92/3 Fleer Ultra 6
93/4 Fleer Ultra 2
93/4 Fleer Ultra 301
94/5 Fleer Ultra 56
95/6 Fleer Ultra 42, PPM-8
96/7 Fl. Ultra 45
91/2 Gillette 29
91/2 Kellogg's / Score 10
90/1 Kraft 35
91/2 Kraft 59
92/3 Kraft / PB
94/5 Kraft / KD
95/6 Kraft / PS
94/5 Kraft Mask
86/7 Kraft Sports 19
93/4 Leaf 369
94/5 Leaf 47
96/7 Leaf 99
97/8 Limited 28, FG-36
96/7 Maggers 50
91/2 McDonald's Mc-09
97/8 McDonald's McD-28
96/7 Metal Univ. 46
81/2 O-Pee-Chee 120
83/4 O-Pee-Chee 40
84/5 O-Pee-Chee 255
85/6 OPC/Topps 12
86/7 O-Pee-Chee 212
87/8 O-Pee-Chee 204
90/1 OPC/Topps 294
90/1 O-Pee-Chee 486
91/2 O-Pee-Chee 338
92/3 O-Pee-Chee 184
89/0 OPC/Topps 160
90/1 OPC Premier 76
91/2 OPC Premier 133
83/4 OPC/Topps Sticker 99
83/4 OPC/Topps Sticker 155
84/5 OPC Sticker 262
85/6 OPC Sticker 123
85/6 OPC Sticker 220-87
86/7 OPC Sticker 66-197
87/8 OPC Sticker 93-226
89/0 opcSticker 30-170
97/8 Omega 120, NSZ-6
98/9 Pacific 255
97/8 Pacific CC 35, ITC-6
97/8 Pa. Crown Roy. 70, FO-10
97/8 Pa. Dynagon BKS-31
97/8 Pa. Invincible 42, R-64
97/8 Pa. Paramount 96, GSL-10
97/8 Pa. Revolution 72, RTS-10
87/8 Panini Sticker 255
89/0 Panini Sticker 191
90/1 Panini Sticker 11
91/2 Panini Sticker 179
92/3 Panini Sticker 135
93/4 Panini Sticker 9
95/6 Panini Sticker 177
96/7 Panini Sticker 173
91/2 Parkhurst 8
92/3 Parkhurst 3
93/4 Parkhurst 47
94/5 Parkhurst 51
95/6 Parkhurst 59
95 Parkhurst Phonecard
91/2 Pinnacle 126
92/3 Pinnacle 379
92/3 Pinnacle 91
92/3 Pinnacle 263
93/4 Pinnacle 347
94/5 Pinnacle 315, GT14, MA8
95/6 Pinnacle 114, M-5
96/7 Pinnacle 166
97/8 Pinnacle 70
96/7 Pi. Be A Player 7, SP-12, ✍ Aut. 7
97/8 Pi. Certified 5
97/8 Pi. Inside 47
95/6 Pi. Summit 96, ITC-12
96/7 Pi. Summit 130
97/8 Pi. Totally 5
95/6 Pi. Zenith 105
96/7 Pi. Zenith 110
95/6 Playoff 32
96/7 Playoff 382
94/5 POG 277
95/6 POG 92
93/4 Power Play 64
93/4 Premier 476
94/5 Premier 81, 511
95/6 Pro Magnet 125
90/1 Pro Set 10
91/2 Pro Set 10
92/3 Pro Set 299
92/3 Pro Set 7
91/2 Pro Set PotM P5
91/2 Pro Set Platinum 4
91/2 Puck / Pro Set 2
91/2 Puck / Pro Set Prototype
90/1 Score 140, 365
90/1 Sco. Hot Cards 62
91/2 Score 90
91/2 Score CAN 90
92/3 Score 120
93/4 Score 11
93/4 Score 516
94/5 Score 173
95/6 Score 64
96/7 Score 104
97/8 Score 8
97/8 Score Mont. 1
92/3 Seasons 19
94/5 Select 94
95/6 Select CE 77
96/7 Select CE 25
95/6 SBx Emotion 50
95/6 SBx Impact 49
83/4 Souhaits Keychain [Oilers]
94/5 SP 32
96/7 SP 44
97/8 SP Authentic 81
98/9 SPx Finite 44
83/4 Stater Mint H15
95/6 Super Sticker 35
92/3 Topps 394
95/6 Topps 53, 14HG
91/2 To. Stadium 211
92/3 To. Stadium 430
93/4 To. Stadium 470
94/5 To. Stadium 231
95/6 T. Super Skills 83
01/2 T/O Archives 24, ✂ Jers
98/9 UD Choice 106
90/1 Upper Deck 209, 232
91/2 Upper Deck 147
92/3 Upper Deck 1
92/3 Upper Deck 329
93/4 Upper Deck 478, SP-39
94/5 Upper Deck 81, SP-111
95/6 Upper Deck 191
97/8 Upper Deck 294
94/5 UD BAP ✍ 30
97/8 UD Black Diam. 113
95/6 UD CC 62
97/8 UD Coll. Choice 67, SQ34
01/2 UD Vintage ✂ GG
83/4 Vachon 37-117
88/9 BOST / Sports Action
89/0 BOST / Sports Action
90/1 BOST / Sports Action
90/1 BOST / Sports Action
91/2 BOST / Sports Action
91/2 BOST / Sports Action
92/3 BOST / Postcard
94/5 DALL / Southwest
95/6 DALL / Cap
96/7 DALL / Southwest
81/2 EDMO / Red Rooster
82/3 EDMO / Red Rooster
83/4 EDMO / Button
83/4 EDMO / McDonald's
83/4 EDMO / West Mall
83/4 EDMO
84/5 EDMO
84/5 EDMO / Red Rooster
85/6 EDMO / Red Rooster
86/7 EDMO
86/7 EDMO / Red Rooster
86/7 EDMO / Red Rooster
88/9 EDMO / Action 91
97/8 MONT

MOON, CAM
90/1 7th..Sketch WHL 87
90/1 Saskatoon Blades

MOON, SCOTT
88/9 ProCards / Utica

MOONEY, MATT
90/1 Rayside-Balfour
91/2 Rayside-Balfour

MOONEY, MIKE
89/0 Rayside-Balfour

MOORE, BARRIE
95/6 Edge Ice 65
91/2 7th...Sketch OHL 259
93/4 Slapshot / Sudbury 15
94/5 Slapshot / Sudbury 14
98/9 Indianapolis Ice
99/0 Portland Pirates
95/6 Rochester Americans
96/7 Rochester Americans
91/2 Sudbury Wolves
92/3 Sudbury Wolves
93/4 Sudbury Wolves

MOORE, BLAINE
92/3 BCJHL 238
95/6 Las Vegas Thunder
96/7 Las Vegas Thunder
94/5 Richmond Renegades

MOORE, CHARLIE
83/4 Belleville Bulls
84/5 Belleville Bulls

MOORE, DAVID
91/2 Cincinnati Cyclones

MOORE, DEAN
91/2 Air Canada SJHL A15
92/3 MPS SJHL 106
97/8 Charlotte Checkers
96/7 Knoxville Cherokees

MOORE, DICKIE
02/3 Ultimate Mem. ✂ GAO, ✂ SL (x2)
99/0 BAP Mem. CH-8, ✍ CH-8
01/2 BAP Mem. ✂ RM
45-64 BeeHive-2 [Mont.]
64-67 BeeHive-3 [Toro.]
64/5 Coke/Sprite [Toro.]
97/8 Dernière Heure
51-53 Exhibits
62/3 Cowan Tile
83 HHOF Postcard J10
83&87 HHOF 190
51/2 La Patrie
52/3 Parkhurst 10
53/4 Parkhurst 28
54/5 Parkhurst 2
55/6 Parkhurst 38
57/8 Parkhurst [Mont.] 14
58/9 Parkhurst 8
59/0 Parkhurst 14
60/1 Parkhurst 38
60/1 Parkhurst 57
61/2 Parkhurst 36
62/3 Parkhurst 42
92/3 Parkhurst PR-26
93/4 Parkhurst DPR-12
01/2 Parkhurst PR19, PR29, PR61, PR77, PR94, PR102, PR120, PR145, ✂ M31, ✍ PA16
93/4 Parkie 56-57 70
94/5 Parkie Tall 116
45-54 Quaker Oats
60/1 Shirriff 22
61/2 Shirriff 107
62/3 Shirriff 37
01/2 Signature ✍ VA24
58/9 Toronto Star Photo
62/3 Toronto Star Photo
63/4 Toronto Star Action
58/9 Toronto Star Weekend
01/2 Ultimate Mem. ✂ Glove
99/0 UD C. Legends 31
60/1 York Glass [Mont.]
60/1 York
61/2 York 5
62/3 York Transfer 22
92/3 MONT / OPC 63
64/5 TORO

MOORE, GREG
92/3 MPS SJHL 98

MOORE, JAMES
02/3 Peterborough Phantoms

MOORE, JIMMY
51/2 Laval Dairy 36
52/3 St. Lawrence 3

MOORE, KEVIN
91/2 Ferris State Bulldogs

MOORE, MARK
00/1 Charlotte Checkers

MOORE, MIKE
88/9 Portland Winter Hawks

MOORE, SCOTT
90/1 Semic Elitserien 71
91/2 Semic Elitserien 241

MOORE, SKEETER
99/0 San Angelo Outlaws
65/6 Minnesota-Duluth 1

MOORE, STEVE
01/2 BAP Mem. 342
01/2 UD Premier 56
01/2 Hershey Bears
98/9 Oklahoma City Blazers
99/0 Topeka Scarecrows

MOORES, TOM
91/2 7th...Sketch OHL 214
93/4 Slapshot / Niagara Falls 17

MORABITO, JOHN
91/2 Avant Garde BCJHL 12
92/3 BCJHL 190
95/6 Birmingham Bulls

MORAN, AMBY
25-27 Anonymous 11
23/4 Paulins Candy 29

MORAN, BRAD
02/3 UD MVP 51
99 Bowman 92
98 Bowman 72
98 Bowman Chrome 72
99/0 SP Authentic 130
99/0 UD MVP Cup 203
99/0 UD Ovation 77
00/1 Syracuse Crunch
01/2 Syracuse Crunch
02/3 Syracuse Crunch
98/9 Calgary Hitmen 14
99/0 Calgary Hitmen

MORAN, GARY
00/1 Nottingham Panthers
01/2 Nottingham Panthers
02/3 Nottingham Panthers

MORAN, IAN
02/3 To. Total 222
94/5 Classic 101
93/4 Fleer Ultra 492
01/2 Pacific ✂ GWJ 30
97/8 Pa. Dynagon BKS-79
99/0 Pa. Paramount 191
97/8 Pi. Be A Player 93, ✍ Aut. 93
93/4 Power Play 512
01/2 Pr. Stock ✂ GUG 80
01/2 PS Titanium ✂ DSJ 35
95/6 SBx Impact 216
93/4 To. Stadium - Team U.S.A. 17
95/6 To. Stadium 219
95/6 PITT / Foodland 20
96/7 Cleveland Lumberjacks

MORAN, PADDY
91 C55 Reprint 1
83 HHOF Postcard K10
83&87 HHOF 144
10/1 Imperial
10/1 Imperial 28
11/2 Imperial 1
12/3 Imperial 18
60/1 Topps 2
61/2 Topps - Stamp

MORAN, PAUL
00/1 Nottingham Panthers
01/2 Nottingham Panthers
02/3 Nottingham Panthers

MORAVA, MARIAN
96/7 APS 318
97/8 APS 296
96/7 DS Sticker 152
97/8 DS Sticker 112
98/9 OFS 52
99/0 Score 39

MORAVEC, DAVID
95/6 APS 309
96/7 APS 206, 418
97/8 APS 134
98 Bonaparte 7D
98 Bonaparte Pexeso 25
97/8 DS 100
98/9 DS 6
99/0 DS NS19
00/1 DS 162
01/2 DS 18, 61, BB 5
96/7 DS Sticker 202
97/8 DS Sticker 257
98/9 OFS 243, 355, 482, OW 11
99/0 OFS 434, 479, 521
00/1 OFS 250
01/2 OFS 30, -RE7D, -UHI 23
99/0 Omega 33
99/0 Upper Deck 192
99/0 UD G. Reserve 192

MORCZINIETZ, ANDREAS
01/2 UD DEL 241

MORE, JAYSON
92/3 Bowman 388
94/5 Leaf 509
92/3 O-Pee-Chee 312
98/9 Pacific 98
98/9 Pa. Paramount 126
91/2 Parkhurst 387
92/3 Parkhurst 394
93/4 Parkhurst 452
91/2 Pinnacle 342
97/8 Pi. Be A Player 70, ✍ Aut. 70
95/6 Playoff 303
96/7 Playoff 417
93/4 Premier 227
92/3 Pro Set 169
90/1 ProCards 99
92/3 Score 147
92/3 Topps 245
92/3 To. Stadium 60
93/4 To. Stadium 208
94/5 To. Stadium 165
92/3 Upper Deck 488
98/9 NASH / Wendy's 16
97/8 PHOE / Coca-Cola
92/3 SANJ / Pacific Bell

MORE, PAUL
83/4 Brandon Wheat Kings
84/5 Brandon Wheat Kings

MOREAU, ERIC
91/2 7th...Sketch LHJMQ 191

MOREAU, ETHAN
02/3 Pacific Complete 44
02/3 UD Vintage 104
94/5 Classic 12, T14
95/6 Classic 97, AS12
94/5 Classic 4 Sport 128, BC20, CP25
94/5 Cla. Images 50
94/5 Cla. Images 4 Sport 105
96/7 Donruss 228
97/8 Donruss 50
96/7 Do. Canadian 127
97/8 Do. Canadian 83
96/7 Do. Elite 136, A-20
97/8 Do. Elite 52
97/8 Do. Preferred 35
97/8 Do. Priority 116
97/8 Do. Studio 83, HH-23
95/6 Edge Ice 134
96/7 Flair 104
96/7 Fl. Ultra 32, UR-13
95/6 Future Legends 34, PC-7
x96/7 Leaf GLR-1
97/8 Leaf 143
96/7 L. Limited LR-1
96/7 L. Preferred 139
97/8 Limited 60, 87, 94
96/7 Metal Univ. 187
99/0 Pacific 160
00/1 Pacific 170
97/8 Pa. Dynagon 28, T-40
97/8 Pa. Invincible 31
97/8 Pa. Paramount 46
95/6 Parkhurst 540
96/7 Pinnacle 239
97/8 Pinnacle 189
96/7 Pi. Be A Player LTH4A, ✍ Aut. LTH4A
97/8 Pi. Inside 184
96/7 Pi. Summit 184
96/7 Pi. Zenith 133
96/7 Score 268
97/8 Score 151
96/7 Select CE 116
91/2 7th...Sketch OHL 212
93/4 Slapshot / Niagara Falls 13
93/4 Slapshot / Niagara Falls 28
94/5 Slapshot / Sudbury 20
96/7 SP 31
00/1 Stadium 173
00/1 Topps 257
98/9 To. Finest 71
96/7 Upper Deck 187
97/8 Upper Deck 250
00/1 Upper Deck 71
96/7 UD Black Diam. 69
96/7 UD CC 354
97/8 UD Coll. Choice 51
99/0 UD MVP Cup 76
95/6 Indianapolis Ice

MOREAU, SÉBASTIEN
92/3 MPS SJHL 165
91/2 7th...Sketch LHJMQ 106

MOREL, ALEXANDRE
98/9 Québec Remparts
00/1 Rouyn-Noranda 9

MOREL, DENIS
90/1 Pro Set 695

MOREL, KELLY
97/8 New Mexico Scorpions

MOREN, DARREN
84/5 Saskatoon Blades
83/4 Victoria Cougars

MORENCY, PASCAL
01/2 Cape Breton Eagles 18

MORENCY, STEVE
00/1 Sherbrooke Castors 6

MORENZ, HOWIE
02/3 Canada Post
02/3 Ultimate Mem. ✂ RAT, ✂ SF
35-40 Canada Starch
33-35 Diamond Match Silv.
36-39 Diamond Match TT1
36-39 Diamond Match TT2
36-39 Diamond Match TT3
27/8 La Patrie
27/8 La Presse
43-47 Parade Sportive
34/5 Sweet Caporal

MORENZ, HOWIE (JR.)
37/8 World Wide Gum 100

MORENZ, HOWIE (SR.)
25-27 Anonymous 9
33/4 Anonymous 41
34-43 BeeHive-1 [Mont.]
33/4 Canadian Gum
24/5 Champ's Cigarettes
33 Goudey Sport Kings 24

33/4 Hamilton Gum 8
83 HHOF Postcard H12
83&87 HHOF 106
95/6 Legends of Hockey 69
24/5 Maple Crispette [V130] 12
33/4 O-Pee-Chee 23
36/7 O-Pee-Chee 121
55/6 Parkhurst 57
93/4 Parkie 56-57 P-1
91/2 Pro Set 336
60/1 Topps 59
61/2 Topps - Stamp
99/0 UD C. Legends 14
23/4 William Paterson 15
24/5 William Paterson 47
33/4 WWGum Premium 4
33/4 WWGum 36
37/8 World Wide Gum 18
92/3 MONT / OPC 13

MORET, LEO
28/9 Paulins Candy 44

MORGAN, BRAD
98/9 Sudbury Wolves 19
99/0 Sudbury Wolves 21

MORGAN, CHRIS
91/2 Air Canada SJHL A18

MORGAN, GAVIN
01/2 Utah Grizzlies

MORGAN, JASON
93/4 Slapshot / Kitchener 13
94/5 Slapshot / Kitchener 14
95/6 Slapshot 121
98/9 Upper Deck 109
98/9 UD G. Reserve 109
99/0 Florida Everblades
00/1 Florida Everblades
97/8 Springfield Falcons

MORI, AARON
96/7 Regina Pats
97/8 Regina Pats

MORIA, STEVE
00/1 Kudos 64
01/2 Cardiff Devils
01/2 Nottingham Panthers

MORIARITY, GERALD
95/6 Slapshot 333

MORIN, DEREK
89/0 7th..Sketch OHL 89
90/1 7th..Sketch OHL 13

MORIN, ERIC
79/0 Montréal Jrs. Colour

MORIN, GUILLAUME
91/2 7th...Sketch LHJMQ 173

MORIN, JEAN-JUNIOR
01/2 Baie-Comeau 14
01/2 Hull Olympiques 23

MORIN, JEAN-MARTIN
91/2 7th...Sketch LHJMQ 138

MORIN, JEAN-PIERRE
02/3 Louisiana Ice Gators

MORIN, JESPER
98/9 DEL 9

MORIN, JOEL
89/0 7th..Sketch OHL 165
87/8 Kingston Canadians

MORIN, KARL
99/0 Québec Remparts 12
02/3 Shawinigan Cataractes

MORIN, MARC
84/5 Chicoutimi Saguenéens

MORIN, MIKE
00/1 Kudos 104
95/6 Richmond Renegades
01/2 Manchester Storm
85/6 Brandon Wheat Kings
84/5 Saskatoon Blades
91/2 L. Superior State Lakers

MORIN, NATHAN
91/2 7th...Sketch LHJMQ 158

MORIN, OLIVIER
97 Bowman 74

MORIN, PETE
34-43 BeeHive-1 [Mont.]
43-47 Parade Sportive
52/3 St. Lawrence 16
37/8 World Wide Gum 129

MORIN, STÉPHANE
91/2 Bowman 148
98/9 DEL 109
92/3 Durivage 9
95/6 Edge Ice 169
91/2 O-Pee-Chee 159
91/2 Panini Sticker 263
92/3 Panini Sticker 214
91/2 Parkhurst 147
91/2 Pinnacle 245
91/2 Pro Set 201
91/2 Pro Set Platinum 100
89/0 ProCards AHL 167
90/1 ProCards 455
91/2 Score 361
91/2 Score CAN 254
91/2 Score Young Stars 39
92/3 Topps 316
91/2 To. Stadium 216
92/3 To. Stadium 469
90/1 Upper Deck 524
91/2 Upper Deck 433
91/2 QUEB / Petro-Canada
89/0 Halifax Citadels
90/1 Halifax Citadels
92/3 Hamilton Canucks
97/8 Long Beach Ice Dogs
94/5 Minnesota Moose
95/6 Minnesota Moose

MORIN, VIC
80/1 Soo Greyhounds

MORISSET, DAVID'
94 Québec Pee Wee 829
98/9 SP Authentic 129, ✍ SotT

98/9 Upper Deck 406
98/9 UD G. Reserve 406

MORISSETTE, ALAIN
91/2 ProCards 303

MORISSETTE, DAVE
90/1 7th..Sketch LHJMQ 199
98/9 UD MVP 106
91/2 Hampton Roads
92/3 Hampton Roads
95/6 Minnesota Moose
99/0 Québec Citadelles 18
93/4 Roanoke Express
93/4 Roanoke Express

MORISSETTE, SEBASTIEN
00/1 Québec Remparts 7
00/1 Victoriaville Tigres 21

MORK, GARY
69 Columbus Checkers

MORLEY, PETE
02/3 Peterborough Phantoms

MORLEY, PETER
94/5 Guildford Flames 3
97/8 Guildford Flames
98/9 Guildford Flames

MORMINA, BOB
83/4 Springfield Indians 12

MORNEAU, ADAM
01/2 Val d'Or Foreurs 23

MORO, MARC
00/1 BAP Mem. 50
97 Bowman 17
95/6 Classic 24
95/6 Cla. 5 Sport 140, ✍ Aut.
00/1 Pacific 229
01/2 Signat. 215, ✍ Aut. 215
93/4 Slapshot / Kingston 4
95/6 Slapshot 116
00/1 Upper Deck 418
98/9 Milwaukee Admirals
99/0 Milwaukee Admirals
00/1 Milwaukee Admirals
01/2 Milwaukee Admirals
96/7 Soo Greyhounds

MOROCCO, RICK
92 Semic Sticker 259
82/3 North Bay Centennials
80/1 Soo Greyhounds

MORODER, MIRKO
95 Panini Worlds 93

MOROZOV, ALEKSEY
02/3 Atomic 81
02/3 Crown Royale 79, ✂ GWDP 17, ✂ GWJ 17
02/3 Exclusive 139
02/3 First Edition 56, ✂ Jers.
02/3 Heads Up 101
02/3 O-Pee-Chee 172
02/3 Pacific 313
02/3 Pacific Complete 452
02/3 Parkhurst 188
02/3 Pr. Stock Reserve 81
02/3 Signature 95, ✍ 95
02/3 SP Authentic ✂ DP
02/3 Sports Vault 116
02/3 Topps 172
02/3 To. Limited 172
02/3 To. Total 123
02/3 Upper Deck 386, ✂ BF
02/3 UD Classic ✂ HH
02/3 UD Rookie 82
02/3 UD Vintage 207, 284
02/3 Victory 175
98/9 Aurora 156
98/9 Be A Player 111, ✍ Aut. 111
99/0 BAP Mem. 187
00/1 BAP Mem. 7
97/8 Do. Elite 108
97/8 Do. Preferred 155
97/8 Do. Priority 183
98/9 Dynagon Ice 152
99/0 Dynagon Ice 161
01/2 Heads Up ✂ JQ 28
97/8 Leaf 164
97/8 McDonald's McD-38
99/0 Millenium 201, ✍ Aut. 201
00/1 Mir Fetisov 3
99/0 NHL Power Play
98/9 OPC Chrome 70
97/8 Omega 187
98/9 Omega 198
98/9 Pacific 95
99/0 Pacific 344
00/1 Pacific 334
97/8 Pa. Crown Roy. 111
98/9 Pa. Crown Roy. 111
97/8 Pa. Paramount 152
98/9 Pa. Paramount 194
98/9 Panini Sticker 53
99/0 Panini Sticker 136
00/1 Panini Sticker 83
97/8 Pinnacle 6
97/8 Pi. Be A Player 212, ✍ Aut. 212
97/8 Pi. BeeHive BHT-24
97/8 Pi. Certified H
97/8 Pi. Mint 27
01/2 Pr. Stock ✂ GUG 81
00/1 PS Titanium ✂ GUG 137
01/2 PS Titanium ✂ DSJ 32
97/8 Score 74
97/8 Score Pitt. 18
94/5 Select 158
94/5 Sig. Rookies FF10, ✍ FF10
95/6 SR Draft / Promo
95/6 SR Tetrad 61
95/6 SR Tetrad Autobilia 48
97/8 SP Authentic 190, 115
98/9 SPx Finite 68, 149
98/9 Topps 70
98/9 UD Choice 166

98/9 UD3 22, 82, 142
95/6 Upper Deck 553
97/8 Upper Deck 341
98/9 Upper Deck 158, FT14
99/0 Upper Deck 277
00/1 Upper Deck 369
01/2 Upper Deck 370
97/8 UD Black Diam. 130, PC5
98/9 UD Black Diam. 71
98/9 UD G. Reserve 158
99/0 UD G. Reserve 277
96/7 UD Ice 139
97/8 UD Ice 56, L7B
98/9 UD MVP 165
00/1 UD Vintage 287
99/0 Victory 245
01/2 Victory 284
99/0 WGretzky 138
97/8 Zenith 94, RR-8, ZT-18, Z67

MOROZOV, VALENTIN
00/1 Mir 153
94/5 Sig. Rookies 68, ✍ 68

MOROZOV, VLADISLAV
98/9 Mir 104
99/0 Mir 212

MORQUE, CHRIS
94/5 Huntington Blizzard
98/9 Odessa Jackalopes
99/0 Odessa Jackalopes

MORRIS, BERNIE
23/4 Paulins Candy 64
28/9 Paulins Candy 73

MORRIS, DEREK
02/3 BAP Mem. 71
02/3 Exclusive 43
02/3 McDonald's 6
02/3 O-Pee-Chee 238
02/3 Pacific 57
02/3 Pacific Complete 226
02/3 Parkhurst Retro 139
02/3 Signature 124, GS-32, ✍ 124
02/3 Sports Vault 189
02/3 Topps 238
02/3 T. Chrome 131
02/3 To. Limited 238
02/3 To. Total 290
02/3 Upper Deck 27, 292
02/3 UD MVP 27
02/3 UD Vintage 40, 265
02/3 Victory 34
01/2 Adrenaline 26
98/9 Aurora 27
00/1 Aurora 25, Pins. 25
00/1 BAP Mem. 300
01/2 BAP Mem. 297
01/2 Bowman 72
97 Bowman 109
98/9 Bowman's Best 78
01/2 Crown Royale 22
97/8 Do. Elite 114, 132
97/8 Do. Priority 182
99/0 Dynagon Ice 37
98/9 NHL Power Play
99/0 NHL Power Play
01/2 O-Pee-Chee 171
98/9 OPC Chrome 69
97/8 Omega 31
98/9 Pacific 53
99/0 Pacific 58
00/1 Pacific 70
01/2 Pacific 63
98/9 Pa. Paramount 30
99/0 Pa. Paramount 41
99/0 Panini Sticker 192
00/1 Panini Sticker 121
97/8 Pi. Be A Player 245, ✍ Aut. 245
01/2 Pr. Stock -PS 10
01/2 PS Titanium 20
01/2 Signat. 177, ✍ Aut. 177
97/8 SP Authentic 175
98/9 SP Authentic 11
99/0 SPx 22
98/9 SPx Finite 13, 136
99/0 Stadium 84
98/9 Topps 69
99/0 Topps 197
00/1 Topps 74
01/2 Topps 171
99/0 To. Chrome 197
01/2 To. Chrome 118
98/9 To. Finest 136
98/9 UD Choice 29
98/9 UD3 5, 65, 125
97/8 Upper Deck 233
98/9 Upper Deck 51
99/0 Upper Deck 27
00/1 Upper Deck 27
01/2 Upper Deck 27
97/8 UD Black Diam. 104
98/9 UD G. Reserve 51
99/0 UD G. Reserve 27
97/8 UD Ice 51
98/9 UD MVP 28
99/0 UD MVP 31, ✍ PS
00/1 UD MVP 29
01/2 UD MVP 27
99/0 UD MVP Cup 30
00/1 UD Vintage 58
01/2 UD Vintage 38, 43
99/0 Victory 48
00/1 Victory 39
01/2 Victory 52
96/7 Regina Pats
97/8 Regina Pats

MORRIS, ELWYN
45-54 Quaker Oats

MORRIS, JAMIE
99/0 Indianapolis Ice

MORRIS, JON
90/1 Bowman 84
91/2 Bowman 286

90/1 O-Pee-Chee 457
91/2 O-Pee-Chee 332
90/1 Pro Set 621
91/2 Pro Set 424
89/0 ProCards AHL 207
91/2 ProCards 426
90/1 Score 401
91/2 Score CAN 548
91/2 To. Stadium 360
90/1 Upper Deck 65
91/2 Upper Deck 216
90/1 NJER
92/3 Cincinnati Cyclones

MORRIS, KEITH
92/3 Canada Nationals

MORRIS, MIKE
97 Québec Pee Wee 1159

MORRIS, RICK
75/6 OPC WHA 91

MORRISON, AARON
90/1 7th...Sketch OHL 267
91/2 7th...Sketch OHL 106

MORRISON, ADAM
83/4 Victoria Cougars
84/5 Victoria Cougars

MORRISON, ANDREW
95/6 Slapshot 29

MORRISON, BRENDAN
02/3 BAP Mem. 6
02/3 Bowman 86
02/3 Calder ✂ GWJ 23
02/3 Crown Royale 96
02/3 Exclusive 168
02/3 First Edition 214
02/3 Heads Up 120
02/3 McDonald's 40
02/3 O-Pee-Chee 149
02/3 Pacific 380
02/3 Pacific Complete 227
02/3 Parkhurst 186
02/3 Parkhurst Retro 58
02/3 Pr. Stock Reserve 96
02/3 PS Titanium 97, ✂ GWJ 70
02/3 Quest for the Cup 96, -CTC 19
02/3 Signature 56, GS-13, ✍ 56
02/3 Slam Card
02/3 Sports Vault 295
02/3 Stadium 89
02/3 Topps 149
02/3 T. Chrome 91
02/3 To. Heritage 57, ✂ GS, ✂ GSB
02/3 To. Limited 149
02/3 To. Total 283
02/3 Upper Deck 414
02/3 UD Classic 96
02/3 UD MVP 178
02/3 UD Top Shelf 86
02/3 UD Vintage 251
02/3 Vanguard 96, ✂ GWJ 47
02/3 Victory 205
01/2 Adrenaline 190
99/0 Aurora 87
92/3 BCJHL 117
99/0 BAP Mem. 146
00/1 BAP Mem. 91
01/2 BAP Mem. 58
01/2 Bowman 90
98/9 Bowman's Best 105, BP9, F15, ✍ A7A, ✍ A7B
01/2 Crown Royale 137
99/0 DS 78
98/9 Dynagon Ice 111, -IR 4
98/9 McDonald's McD24
01/2 McDonald's -HP 2
99/0 Millenium 149, ✍ Aut. 149
01/2 O-Pee-Chee 144
99/0 OFS 94
98/9 Omega 139, -Onl. 20
98/9 Pacific 265
99/0 Pacific 241
01/2 Pacific 383
97/8 Pa. Crown Roy. 81, -RC 5
99/0 Pa. Paramount 136
98/9 Pa. Revolution 86
98/9 Panini Photocard
00/1 Parkhurst P-23
01/2 Parkhurst 133
97/8 Pi. BeeHive 56, ✍ Aut. 56
01/2 Pr. Stock -PS 73
00/1 PS Titanium 95
01/2 PS Titanium ✂ DSJ 55, ✂ DSJ 57
01/2 PS Titanium Draft ✂ 95
99/0 Revolution 87
99/0 Score 157
00/1 Signature 126, ✍ Aut. 5
97/8 SP Authentic 193
98/9 SP Authentic 47
99/0 SPx 87
01/2 SPx 195
98/9 SPx Finite 48, 145
99/0 Stadium CS1, ✍ CS2, ✍ LS12
99/0 Topps 156, IF6
00/1 Topps 145
01/2 Topps 144
99/0 To. Chrome 156, IF6
00/1 To. Chrome 105
98/9 To. Finest F19
98/9 T. Gold Label 82
99/0 To. Gold Label FG13
00/1 To. Heritage 146
99/0 UD Choice 120
01/2 UD PlayMakers Ltd 95
98/9 UD3 30, 90, 150
98/9 Upper Deck 5, GN4, GN27

99/0 Upper Deck 248
00/1 Upper Deck 399
01/2 Upper Deck 170
98/9 UD Black Diam. 51
01/2 UD Challenge 87
98/9 UD G. Reserve 5
99/0 UD G. Reserve 248
01/2 UD Mask 93
98/9 UD MVP 118, ✍ PS
99/0 UD MVP 117
00/1 UD MVP 172
01/2 UD MVP 180
00/1 UD Vintage 348
01/2 UD Vintage 248
01/2 Vanguard 96
99/0 Victory 173, 352
00/1 Victory 228
01/2 Victory 343
99/0 WGretzky 95
97/8 Zenith 90, RR-4
01/2 VANC / Coke
97/8 Albany River Rats

MORRISON, BRENDAN
01/2 PS Titanium 136

MORRISON, CRAIG
83/4 Oshawa Generals

MORRISON, CRUTCHY
23/4 Paulins Candy 48

MORRISON, DAVE
94/5 DEL 157
95/6 DEL 158
96/7 DEL 233
84/5 Fredericton Express

MORRISON, DON
45-64 BeeHive-2 [Detr.]

MORRISON, GEORGE
71/2 Eddie Sargent 191
70/1 Esso Power Player
71/2 O-Pee-Chee 223
72/3 O-Pee-Chee 314
71/2 Toronto Sun Photo
72/3 Minn. Fight. Saints

MORRISON, IKEY
28/9 Paulins Candy 50

MORRISON, JIM
45-64 BeeHive-2 [Toro.]
00 CSAS Signat. Series
70/1 Eddie Sargent 169
70/1 Esso Power Player
69/0 O-Pee-Chee 156
70/1 O-Pee-Chee 90
52/3 Parkhurst 81
53/4 Parkhurst 15
54/5 Parkhurst 18
54/5 Parkhurst 94
55/6 Parkhurst 8
55/6 Parkhurst 76
57/8 Parkhurst [Toro.] 11
60/1 Parkhurst 61
93/4 Parkie 56-57 115
45-54 Quaker Oats
63/4 Québec Aces
60/1 Shirriff 95
59/0 Topps 36
60/1 Topps 9
70/1 Topps 90
57/8 Toronto Star Photo
58/9 Toronto Star Photo
81/2 Kingston Canadians
82/3 Kingston Canadians

MORRISON, JIMMY
65/6 Québec Aces

MORRISON, JUSTIN
90/1 7th...Sketch OHL 190
91/2 7th...Sketch OHL 229
91/2 Star Pics 45
91/2 Ultimate Draft Pick 52, ✍ Aut.
01/2 Manitoba Moose
93/4 Muskegon Fury
94/5 Muskegon Fury

MORRISON, KEN
85/6 Kamloops Blazers
84/5 Prince Albert Raiders

MORRISON, KEVIN
75/6 OPC WHA 63
75/6 OPC WHA 80
76/7 OPC WHA 10
76/7 OPC WHA 68
79/0 COLR
76/7 San Diego Mariners

MORRISON, LANCE
01/2 Calgary Hitmen

MORRISON, LEW
72/3 Eddie Sargent 13
70/1 Esso Power Player
74/5 Loblaws
74/5 Loblaws Update
70/1 O-Pee-Chee 197
71/2 O-Pee-Chee 89
72/3 O-Pee-Chee 143
74/5 O-Pee-Chee 125
76/7 O-Pee-Chee 307
77/8 O-Pee-Chee 300
72/3 Topps 58
74/5 Topps 125
72/3 ATLF
70/1 PHIL
72/3 PHIL / Milk

MORRISON, MARK
83 Canada Juniors
81/2 Victoria Cougars
82/3 Victoria Cougars
84/5 Victoria Cougars

MORRISON, MIKE
85/6 Kitchener Rangers

MORRISON, ROD
45-64 BeeHive-2 [Detr.]

MORRISON, SCOTT
94 Semic 321
94/5 Humberside Hawks 13

MORRISON, TAVIS
96/7 Dayton Bombers

MORRISONN, SHAONE
02/3 BAP All-Star 112
02/3 BAP Mem. 347
02/3 Calder 104
02/3 Choice Prospects 30
02/3 First Edition 432R
02/3 In The GU 181
02/3 Pacific Complete 580
02/3 Parkhurst 221
02/3 Parkhurst Retro 235
02/3 PS Titanium 105
02/3 Quest for the Cup 105
02/3 SP Authentic 161
02/3 SP GU 96
02/3 Ultimate Mem. 61
02/3 Upper Deck 441
02/3 UD Artistic 106
02/3 UD Honor 130
02/3 UD Mask 170
02/3 UD Premier 48
01 UD Prospects GU 25, ✂ TPJ
99/0 Kamloops Blazers
99/0 Kamloops Blazers
00/1 Kamloops Blazers
01/2 Kamloops Blazers

MORRISSEY, DAN
91/2 Avant Garde BCJHL 78
92/3 BCJHL 88

MORRISSEY, PAUL
99/0 Des Moines Buc's

MORRONE, MIKE
94/5 Slapshot / Detroit Jr. 9
95/6 Slapshot 65
94/5 Slapshot Memorial 83
93/4 Owen Sound Platers

MORROW, BRENDEN
02/3 BAP Mem. 43
02/3 Bowman 53
02/3 First Edition 234
02/3 O-Pee-Chee 152
02/3 Pacific 115
02/3 Pacific Complete 421
02/3 Parkhurst Retro 167
02/3 Signature 142, ✍ 142
02/3 SP Game-Used ✂ FF
02/3 Stadium ✂ YSS14
02/3 Topps 152
02/3 T. Chrome 93
02/3 To. Limited 152
02/3 To. Total 99
02/3 Upper Deck -NC3, ✂ OR
02/3 UD Classic 32, ✂ HR
02/3 UD MVP 61
02/3 UD Top Shelf ✂ SH, ✂ ST, ✂ TS
02/3 UD Vintage 87, ✂ FS
02/3 Victory 70
00/1 Aurora 46, Pins. 46, ✍ Aut. 46
99/0 BAP Mem. 322
00/1 BAP Mem. 196
01/2 BAP Mem. 14
99 Bowman 113
01/2 Bowman 144, ✂ FFJ, ✂ FFS, ✂ FFDS, ✂ FFR, ✍ YSA
97 Bowman 98, 147, BB16, ✍ Aut.
98 Bowman 60
98 Bowman Chrome 60
99/0 NHL Power Play [x3]
01/2 O-Pee-Chee 154
99/0 Omega 75
00/1 Pacific 138, ✍ Aut. 138
01/2 Pacific 132
00/1 Pa. Paramount 80
00/1 Parkhurst P-19
01/2 Parkhurst 138
00/1 Pr. Stock 33, PSNW-10
00/1 Revolution 48
00/1 Signature 58, ✍ Aut. 82
01/2 Signat. 9, ✍ Aut. 9
98/9 SPx Prospects 66
00/1 Stadium 171
00/1 Topps 246
01/2 Topps 154
00/1 To. Chrome 154
00/1 To. Heritage 116
01/2 To. Heritage 110
00/1 Upper Deck 59, P4
01/2 Upper Deck 59
98/9 UD Black Diam. 94
01/2 UD Ice 93
00/1 UD MVP 56, ✍ PS
01/2 UD MVP 60
99/0 UD MVP Cup 61
00/1 UD Vintage 119
00/1 Victory 74
01/2 Victory 111
00/1 DALL / Southwest
01/2 DALL / Southwest
99/0 Michigan K-Wings
97/8 Portland Winter Hawks

MORROW, JOSH
02/3 Kamloops Blazers
99/0 Medicine Hat Tigers
00/1 Medicine Hat Tigers

MORROW, KEN
80/1 O-Pee-Chee 9
81/2 O-Pee-Chee 205
82/3 O-Pee-Chee 206
83/4 O-Pee-Chee 13
84/5 O-Pee-Chee 131
85/6 OPC/Topps 93
86/7 OPC/Topps 65
87/8 OPC/Topps 66
88/9 OPC/Topps 53
81/2 OPC Sticker 23
81/2 OPC Sticker 25
81/2 OPC Sticker 165
82/3 OPC/Topps Sticker 58

83/4 OPC/Topps Sticker 73
84/5 OPC Sticker 93
86/7 OPC Sticker 215-87
87/8 OPC Sticker 246-137
87/8 Panini Sticker 94
88/9 Panini Sticker 285
82/3 Post [NYIs.]
94/5 SR Miracle 21,22, ✍ 21,22
80/1 Topps 9
81/2 Topps 91 [East]
84/5 Topps 97
91/2 Upper Deck 637
01/2 UD SCup Champs 21
83/4 NYIS
83/4 NYIS / News 19
84/5 NYIS / News 23
99/0 NYIS / UD NY8

MORROW, SCOTT
96/7 Cincinnati Cyclones
97/8 Cincinnati Cyclones
98/9 Cincinnati Cyclones
94/5 Saint John Flames

MORROW, STEVE
91/2 ProCards 284

MORSCHAUSER, GUS
87/8 Kitchener Rangers
88/9 Kitchener Rangers

MORTH, TOMMY
82 Semic Sticker 19

MORTIER, DARREN
94/5 Slapshot / Sarnia 8
95/6 Slapshot 337

MORTL, HERBERT
79 Panini Sticker 308

MORTON, DEAN
88/9 ProCards / Adirondack
89/0 ProCards AHL 328
90/1 ProCards 314
92/3 Cincinnati Cyclones

MORTON, RICK
90/1 7th..Sketch OHL 189
91/2 7th...Sketch OHL 272

MORTSON, CLEVELAND
63/4 Québec Aces
65/6 Québec Aces

MORTSON, GUS
45-64 BeeHive-2 [Toro.]
45-64 BeeHive-2 [Chic.]
48-52 Exhibits [Maple Leafs]
51/2 Parkhurst 73
52/3 Parkhurst 39
53/4 Parkhurst 81
54/5 Parkhurst 81
93/4 Parkie 56-57 30
45-54 Quaker Oats
54/5 Topps 17
57/8 Topps 25
58/9 Topps 38
57/8 Toronto Star Photo
54 Toronto Star Weekend

MORVAN, PIERRE
02/3 Québec Remparts
00/1 Val d'Or Foreurs 16
01/2 Val d'Or Foreurs 12

MÖRZ, JOHANN
82 Semic Sticker 117

MOSCALUK, GARY
88/9 ProCards / Saginaw
89/0 ProCards IHL 65

MOSDELL, KENNY
34-43 BeeHive-1 [NYAm.]
45-64 BeeHive-2 [Mont.]
48-52 Exhibits [Canadiens]
51/2 La Patrie
43-47 Parade Sportive
51/2 Parkhurst 11
52/3 Parkhurst 8
53/4 Parkhurst 33
54/5 Parkhurst 12
55/6 Parkhurst 39
93/4 Parkie 56-57 41
45-54 Quaker Oats
55 Toronto Star Weekend

MOSER, JAY
96/7 Providence Bruins
94/5 Minnesota G'Gophers

MOSEY, SCOTT
84/5 Soo Greyhounds

MOSHER, RALPH
85/6 Nova Scotia Oilers

MOSIENKO, BILL
02/3 In The GU ✂ VM12
02/3 Parkhurst ✂ VT16
02/3 Ultimate Mem. ✂ Cor, ✂ GMIH, ✂ SU, ✍ Cut
01/2 ASG History
01/2 BAP Update ✂ RR10
45-64 BeeHive-2 [Chic.]
83 HHOF Postcard A11
83&87 HHOF 11
93/4 Legends of Hockey 22
43-47 Parade Sportive
51/2 Parkhurst 49
52/3 Parkhurst 27
53/4 Parkhurst 80
92/3 Parkhurst PR-20
01/2 Parkhurst PR4, PR135, ✂ PV16
54/5 Topps 54
00/1 Ultimate Mem. ✂ RE-5, ✂ RA-7
01/2 Ultimate Mem. ✂ 01/2 ASG History
91/2 Ultimate Original Six 61, ✍ Aut. 61

MOSIENKO, TYLER
00/1 Kelowna Rockets

MOSKAL, PATRIK
98/9 OFS 191
00/1 OFS 231
01/2 OFS 219

MOSKALEV, SERGEI
98/9 Mir 98
99/0 Mir 214
00/1 Mir 179

MOSNAR, MIROSLAV
00/1 Hockey 114
99/0 OFS 355

MOSOVSKY, KAREL
02/3 Rochester Americans

MOSS, JIM
99/0 Huntington Blizzard

MOSS, JOEY
90/1 EDMO / IGA

MOSS, T.J.
93/4 Slapshot / Kingston 3

MOSS, TYLER
02/3 Between the Pipes 68
98/9 Be A Player 17, ✍ 17
01/2 BT Pipes 66
98/9 Bowman's Best F10
95/6 Classic 86, AS7
95/6 Cla. 5 Sport 144
97/8 Do. Priority 179
01/2 O-Pee-Chee 295
97/8 Omega 32
98/9 Omega 34
98/9 Pacific 122
01/2 Pacific 77
97/8 Pa. Crown Roy. 20, FO-4
98/9 Pa. Revolution 21
97/8 Pi. Be A Player 230, ✍ Aut. 230
97/8 SP Authentic 174
01/2 Topps 295
98/9 Upper Deck 56
97/8 UD Black Diam. 108
98/9 UD G. Reserve 56
97/8 UD Ice 32
95/6 Atlanta Knights
96/7 Grand Rapids Griffins
99/0 Kansas City Blades
02/3 Manitoba Moose
97/8 Saint John Flames

MOTA, KEVIN
98/9 Sudbury Wolves 23
99/0 Sudbury Wolves 8

MOTKOV, DMITRI
92/3 Classic Prospects 57
90/1 O-Pee-Chee 5R

MOTT, MORRIS
74/5 Loblaws Update
69/0 Mästär Serien 33
74/5 O-Pee-Chee 48
74/5 Topps 48

MOTTAU, MIKE
02/3 O-Pee-Chee 276
02/3 Topps 276
02/3 To. Limited 276
00/1 BAP Mem. 483
01/2 BAP Mem. 57
01/2 O-Pee-Chee 266
00/1 Premier Plus 102
01/2 Signat. 44, ✍ Aut. 44
01/2 Stadium ✂ SCSD
01/2 Topps 266
00/1 To. Heritage 117
01/2 To. Reserve ✂ TR
98/9 UD Choice 300
01/2 Upper Deck 119
00/1 UD Black Diam. 102
00/1 Hartford Wolf Pack
01/2 Hartford Wolf Pack

MOTTER, ALEX
34-43 BeeHive-1 [Bost.]
40/1 O-Pee-Chee 115

MOUGENEL, RYAN
97 Bowman 27
95/6 Slapshot 133
97/8 Cleveland Lumberjacks
93/4 Owen Sound Platers

MOULTON, TYSON
01/2 Regina Pats

MOUSER, TIM
92/3 Toledo Storm W/OT
92/3 Toledo Storm
93/4 Toledo Storm 4

MOUTON, CLAUDE
87/8 MONT

MOVSESSIAN, VICKI
94/5 Classic W23

MOWBRAY, MIKE
96/7 Guildford Flames 14

MOWERS, JOHNNY
34-43 BeeHive-1 [Detr.]
40/1 O-Pee-Chee 105

MOWERS, MARK
98/9 EBK IHL All-Star
99/0 Pacific 230
99/0 UD MVP 112
99/0 Victory 161
02/3 Grand Rapids Griffins
98/9 Milwaukee Admirals
99/0 Milwaukee Admirals
00/1 Milwaukee Admirals
01/2 Milwaukee Admirals

MOXAM, DARREN
84/5 Belleville Bulls
86/7 Kitchener Rangers

MOXAM, DARRYL
00/1 Kudos 137
93/4 Slapshot / Oshawa 15
93/4 Slapshot / Peterborough
95/6 Slapshot 390
00/1 Nottingham Panthers

MOXEY, JIM
76/7 O-Pee-Chee 349

MOXNESS, ROB
91/2 Rayside-Balfour

MOYER, RUSS
99/0 Ottawa 67's
00/1 Ottawa 67's
01/2 Ottawa 67's 6

MOYLAN, COREY
93/4 Slapshot / S.S.Marie 26

MOYLAN, DAVID
90/1 ProCards 439
91/2 ProCards 159
84/5 Sudbury Wolves
85/6 Sudbury Wolves
86/7 Sudbury Wolves

MOYON, CHRISTOPHE
95 Panini Worlds 99
94 Semic 214

MOZYAKIN, SERGEI
99/0 Mir 86
00/1 Mir 352

MRAZ, ZDENEK
98/9 OFS 176

MRAZEK, FRANK
00/1 St. John's Maple Leafs
01/2 St. John's Maple Leafs

MRAZEK, FRANTISEK
99 Bowman 93

MRAZEK, RADEK
94/5 APS 210
95/6 APS 160
96/7 APS 170
97/8 APS 82
99/0 DS 62
00/1 DS 41
96/7 DS Sticker 42
97/8 DS Sticker 93
98/9 OFS 4
99/0 OFS 153
00/1 OFS 139

MRENA, JOZEF
99/0 Prince George Cougars

MRHALEK, ROMAN
91/2 Air Canada SJHL C28

MROZIK, RICK
97/8 Portland Pirates
98/9 Portland Pirates
93/4 Minnesota-Duluth

MRUK, JERZY
89 Semic Sticker 128

MUCHA, JARO
94/5 DEL 158
95/6 DEL 153

MUCKALT, BILL
02/3 Crown Royale 49
02/3 Pacific Complete 351
99/0 Aurora 141
91/2 Avant Garde BCJHL 82
92/3 BCJHL 77
98/9 Be A Player 291, ✍ Aut. 291
99/0 BAP Mem. 238
00/1 BAP Mem. 341
98/9 Bowman's Best 124, F14, ✍ A6A, ✍ A6B
98/9 Dynagon Ice IR 10
99/0 Dynagon Ice 196
99/0 Millenium 236, ✍ Aut. 236
98/9 Omega 238, -Onl. 35
99/0 Omega 144
99/0 Pacific 428
98/9 Pa. Crown Roy. 137, -RC 10
99/0 Pa. Paramount 237
00/1 Pa. Paramount 157
98/9 Pa. Revolution 143
01/2 Parkhurst 214
99/0 Revolution 143
98/9 SP Authentic 111
99/0 SP Authentic ✂ SotT
99/0 SPx 150
98/9 SPx Prospects 59
99/0 Stadium 34, CA1
99/0 Topps 224, IF3
99/0 To. Chrome 224, IF3
98/9 T. Gold Label 73
01/2 To. Heritage 180
98/9 Upper Deck 377
99/0 Upper Deck 127
00/1 Upper Deck 352
98/9 UD Black Diam. 86
98/9 UD G. Reserve 377
99/0 UD G. Reserve 127, ✍ UDA
98/9 UD MVP 205
99/0 UD MVP 205, DR2, ✍ PS
99/0 UD Retro 78
00/1 UD Vintage 229
99/0 Victory 294
01/2 OTTA

MUCKLER, JOHN
52/3 Anonymous 175
93/4 Kraft / PB
90/1 Pro Set 665
99/0 UD Gretzky Excl. 90
92/3 BUFF / Blue Shield
82/3 EDMO / Red Rooster
83/4 EDMO / Button
83/4 EDMO / McDonald's
84/5 EDMO / Red Rooster
85/6 EDMO / Red Rooster
86/7 EDMO / Red Rooster
88/9 EDMO / Action 68
90/1 EDMO / IGA

MUDRA, RUDOLF
99/0 Score 64

MUDROCH, PETR
96/7 APS 152
97/8 APS 252
97/8 DS Sticker 133
98/9 OFS 152
99/0 OFS 366
00/1 OFS 41
01/2 OFS 223
99/0 Score 6

MUEGGLER, BRIAN
89/0 7th..Sketch OHL 127
89/0 Niagara Falls Thunder

MUEHKBAUER, THOMAS
95/6 DEL 327

MUELLER, BRAD
84/5 Brandon Wheat Kings

MUELLER, BRIAN
95/6 Classic 77, ✍ Aut.
95/6 Cla. 5 Sport 146
91/2 Upper Deck WJC 66
92/3 Clarkson G'Knights

MUELLER, REGAN
93/4 Seattle Thunderbirds

MUELLER, RICHARD
98/9 Brandon Wheat Kings
99/0 Brandon Wheat Kings

MUELLER-BOENIGK, BODO
99/0 Eishockey 342

MUFTIEV, RAIL
97/8 APS 98
99/0 Mir 187
95 Panini Worlds 39

MUFTIJEV, RAIL
97/8 DS Sticker 101

MUHLBAUER, THOMAS
94/5 DEL 115

MUHR, ALBERT
79 Panini Sticker 272

MÜHR, MANFRED
95 Panini Worlds 272
95 Semic 187

MUIKKU, JORMA
70/1 Kuvajulkaisut 260

MUIR, BRYAN
99/0 Millenium 59, ✍ Aut. 59
01/2 O-Pee-Chee 248
99/0 Panini Sticker 206
01/2 Topps 248
98/9 Upper Deck 314
98/9 UD G. Reserve 314
00/1 UD Vintage 328
97/8 EDMO
01/2 Hershey Bears
02/3 Hershey Bears

MUIR, JIMMY
37/8 World Wide Gum 128

MUIR, WAYNE
94/5 Slapshot / Brantford 17
92/3 Greensboro Monarchs 8
97/8 Quad City Mallards
87/8 Soo Greyhounds 28
89/0 Soo Greyhounds

MUISE, RANDY
91/2 Air Canada SJHL B33

MUJCIN, MIRSAD
91/2 7th...Sketch WHL 296

MUKHACHEV, ANDREI
99/0 Mir 84

MUKHOMETOV, ILDAR
99/0 Eishockey 233
98/9 Mir 143
00/1 Mir 388
91/2 Upper Deck WJC 10

MULCAHY, BILL
79/0 Montréal Juniors B&W
79/0 Montréal Jrs. Colour

MULHERN, RICHARD
76/7 O-Pee-Chee 265
77/8 O-Pee-Chee 373
78/9 O-Pee-Chee 256
79/0 O-Pee-Chee 133
80/1 O-Pee-Chee 350
78/9 Topps 256
79/0 Topps 133
77/8 ATLF
80/1 WINN

MULHERN, RYAN
96/7 Hampton Roads
98/9 Kansas City Blades 17
97/8 Portland Pirates
99/0 Portland Pirates

MULICK, ROBERT
95/6 Slapshot 378
01/2 Cleveland Barons
99/0 Kentucky Tho'blades
00/1 Kentucky Tho'blades
96/7 Soo Greyhounds

MULIN, MATT
94/5 Slapshot / Sudbury 21

MULLAHY, BRAD
94/5 Raleigh Icecaps

MULLEN, BRIAN
90/1 Bowman 217
91/2 Bowman 61
92/3 Bowman 139
92/3 Fleer Ultra 348
83/4 Funmate Puffy 4 [w/]
86/7 Kraft Sports 78
94/5 Leaf 419
83/4 O-Pee-Chee 389
84/5 O-Pee-Chee 344
85/6 O-Pee-Chee 195
86/7 OPC/Topps 38
88/9 OPC/Topps 91
90/1 OPC/Topps 292
91/2 O-Pee-Chee 129
92/3 O-Pee-Chee 260
89/0 OPC/Topps 24
91/2 OPC Premier 166
92/3 OPC Premier 111
83/4 OPC/Topps Sticker 148
86/7 OPC Sticker 109-242
89/0 opcSticker 245
89/0 Panini Sticker 286
90/1 Panini Sticker 96
91/2 Panini Sticker 289
92/3 Panini Sticker 125
93/4 Panini Sticker 61
91/2 Parkhurst 166
91/2 Pinnacle 135

92/3 Pinnacle 333
93/4 Pinnacle 324
93/4 Premier 154
90/1 Pro Set 203
91/2 Pro Set 165
91/2 Pro Set Platinum 106
90/1 Score 84
91/2 Score 59
92/3 Score 379
91/2 Score 2T
91/2 Score CAN 59
91/2 Score CAN 269
91/2 Score CAN 552
92/3 Score 278
92/3 Score USAG 12
93/4 Score 347
94 Semic 128
95 Semic 120
84/5 7-Eleven
83/4 Stater Mint H10
92/3 Topps 104
91/2 To. Stadium 222
92/3 To. Stadium 420
93/4 To. Stadium 227
94/5 To. Stadium 213
01/2 T/O Archives 30, ✂ Jers
90/1 Upper Deck 182
91/2 Upper Deck 57
92/3 Upper Deck 317
92/3 Upper Deck 468
83/4 Vachon 134-14
89/0 NYRA / Marine
91/2 SANJ / Sports Action
82/3 WINN
83/4 WINN
84/5 WINN / Safety Tips
85/6 WINN
85/6 WINN / Safety Tips
85/6 WINN / Silverwood
86/7 WINN

MULLEN, DENNIS
95/6 Lethbridge Hurricanes

MULLEN, JOE
01/2 BAP Mem. ✂ 500GS
90/1 Bowman 97
91/2 Bowman 79
92/3 Bowman 58
93/4 Donruss 257
95/6 Donruss 38, 251
96/7 Donruss 191
94/5 Fleer 165
01/2 Fleer Greats 79, ✍ Aut.
92/3 Fleer Ultra 166
93/4 Fleer Ultra 171
94/5 Fleer Ultra 167
95/6 Fleer Ultra 124, 206
95 Globe 112
93/4 Hockey Wit 78
89/0 Kraft 60
90/1 Kraft 36, 72
86/7 Kraft Sports 4
93/4 Leaf 300
94/5 Leaf 385
95/6 Leaf 155
96/7 Leaf 14
82/3 O-Pee-Chee 307
83/4 O-Pee-Chee 317
84/5 O-Pee-Chee 188
85/6 O-Pee-Chee 367
85/6 OPC/Topps 7
86/7 OPC/Topps 44
87/8 OPC/Topps 126
87/8 OPC/Topps Box G
88/9 OPC/Topps 76
90/1 OPC/Topps 218
91/2 O-Pee-Chee 69
92/3 O-Pee-Chee 23
89/0 OPC/Topps 196, / Box O
89/0 O-Pee-Chee 288
89/0 Topps - Sticker 5
87/8 OPC Leaders 29
90/1 OPC Premier 77
91/2 OPC Premier 153
82/3 OPC/Topps Sticker 200
84/5 OPC Sticker 61
85/6 OPC Sticker 47-177
86/7 OPC Sticker 82-208
87/8 OPC Sticker 36
87/8 OPC Sticker 186-47
88/9 OPC Sticker 95
89/0 opcSticker 90, 160-20, 214-75, / AS 23
87/8 Panini Sticker 210
87/8 Panini Sticker 384
88/9 Panini Sticker 11
89/0 Panini Sticker 27, 380, 384
90/1 Panini Sticker 183
91/2 Panini Sticker 278
92/3 Panini Sticker 223
93/4 Panini Sticker 83
95/6 Panini Sticker 64
91/2 Parkhurst 141
92/3 Parkhurst 368
93/4 Parkhurst 159
94/5 Parkhurst 180
01/2 Parkhurst ✂ 500GS
91/2 Pinnacle 176
92/3 Pinnacle 160
93/4 Pinnacle 122
93/4 Pinnacle 240
94/5 Pinnacle 149
96/7 Pinnacle 61
95/6 Pi. Summit 92
94/5 POG 187
95/6 POG 32
93/4 Power Play 192
93/4 Premier 498
94/5 Premier 517
90/1 Pro Set 40, 343, 508
91/2 Pro Set 191
92/3 Pro Set 142
92/3 Pro Set 262
87/8 Pro Sport CW8
90/1 Score 208, 7T
90/1 Sco. Hot Cards 88

91/2 Score 268
91/2 Score 379
91/2 Score CAN 269
91/2 Score CAN 488
92/3 Score 3
92/3 Score USAG 9
93/4 Score 7
94/5 Score 57
95/6 Score 252, BB-8
96/7 Score 201
94/5 Select 16
94 Semic 118
89 Semic Sticker 170
91 Semic Sticker 146
92 Semic Sticker 163
93 Semic Sticker 178
01/2 Signature ✂ 500GS
95/6 SBx Emotion 9
95/6 SBx Impact 10
96/7 SP 131
84/5 Topps 133
92/3 Topps 113
94/5 Topps Finest RL-10
91/2 To. Stadium 7
92/3 To. Stadium 20
93/4 To. Stadium 19
94/5 To. Stadium 50
95/6 To. Stadium M7
93/4 TSC Members Only 33
01/2 Ultimate Mem. ✂ 500GS
90/1 Upper Deck 252, 423
91/2 Upper Deck 201
92/3 Upper Deck 144
93/4 Upper Deck 186
94/5 Upper Deck 346
95/6 Upper Deck 16
00 ✂ UD APOH 500, ✂✍ 500
95/6 UD BAP 154, ✍ S154
95/6 UD CC 25
96/7 UD CC 22
00/1 UD Legends 106, ✍ ES
96 Wien 169
86/7 CALG / Red Rooster
86/7 CALG / Red Rooster
87/8 CALG / Red Rooster
90/1 PITT / Foodland 8
91/2 PITT / Elby's
91/2 PITT / Foodland 6
91/2 PITT / Food. Stickers
92/3 PITT / Coke-Clark
92/3 PITT / Foodland 6
92/3 PITT / Food. Stickers
93/4 PITT / Foodland 25
94/5 PITT / Foodland 6
96/7 PITT / Tribune
92/3 SLOU / McDon. 16

MULLEN, MARK
99/0 Des Moines Buc's

MULLER, CLAUS
99/0 Eishockey 397

MULLER, GERHARD
99/0 Eishockey 409

MULLER, GREG
94/5 DEL 298
95/6 DEL 319

MULLER, JAROSLAV
99/0 Score 65

MULLER, JOSEF
96/7 DEL 193

MULLER, KIRK
02/3 Pacific 116
02/3 Pacific Complete 278
02/3 Upper Deck 305
95/6 Bicycle Sports Aces 2-Spade
90/1 Bowman 82
91/2 Bowman 274
92/3 Bowman 138
92/3 Bowman 236
93/4 Donruss 177
94/5 Donruss 255
95/6 Donruss 129
96/7 Donruss 161
97/8 Donruss 38
96/7 Do. Canadian 47, OC-10
97/8 Do. Canadian 47
95/6 Do. Elite 54
97/8 Do. Preferred 120
96/7 Duracell DC10
93/4 EA Sports 69
94/5 Flair 89
96/7 Flair NT-2
94/5 Fleer 104
95/6 Fleer Metal 91
96/7 Fl. Picks 138
92/3 Fleer Ultra 107
93/4 Fleer Ultra 21
93/4 Fleer Ultra AS 9
94/5 Fleer Ultra 313
95/6 Fleer Ultra 96, 268
88/9 Frito Lay
91/2 Gillette 21
93/4 Hockey Wit 19
95/6 Hoyle / East. 4-Diamond
90/1 Kraft 37, 88
91/2 Kraft 12
93/4 Kraft / JELL-O
93/4 Kraft / KD
94/5 Kraft / HH
93/4 Leaf 182
94/5 Leaf 163
95/6 Leaf 41
96/7 Leaf 72
94/5 L. Limited 37
97/8 Limited 156
92/3 McDonald's McD-23
93/4 McDonald's McD-20
96/7 Metal Univ. 150
85/6 OPC/Topps 84
86/7 OPC/Topps 94
87/8 OPC/Topps 157
88/9 OPC/Topps 84
88/9 OPC/Topps Box F
90/1 OPC/Topps 245
90/1 Topps-TL 7
91/2 O-Pee-Chee 22
92/3 O-Pee-Chee 327
89/0 OPC/Topps 117
98/9 OPC Chrome 145
90/1 OPC Premier 78
91/2 OPC Premier 86
91/2 OPC Premier 145
85/6 OPC Sticker 64
86/7 OPC Sticker 61
86/7 OPC Sticker 201-74
87/8 OPC Sticker 65
88/9 OPC Sticker 75
89/0 opcSticker 83-224
98/9 Pacific 227
01/2 Pacific 133
97/8 Pacific CC 217
97/8 Pa. Invincible 62
97/8 Pa. Paramount 82
87/8 Panini Sticker 70
87/8 Panini Sticker 79
88/9 Panini Sticker 165
88/9 Panini Sticker 275
89/0 Panini Sticker 251
90/1 Panini Sticker 73
91/2 Panini Sticker 219
92/3 Panini Sticker 148
93/4 Panini Sticker 14
94/5 Panini Sticker 12
95/6 Panini Sticker 91
96/7 Panini Sticker 212
97/8 Panini Sticker 58
91/2 Parkhurst 89
92/3 Parkhurst 83
92/3 Parkhurst 504
92/3 Parkhurst CP5
93/4 Parkhurst 378
94/5 Parkhurst V4
95/6 Parkhurst 129, 474
94/5 Parkie SE88
91/2 Pinnacle 3
92/3 Pinnacle 111
93/4 Pinnacle 180
94/5 Pinnacle 82, GR7, NL2
96/7 Pinnacle 147
97/8 Pinnacle 190
97/8 Pi. Be A Player 121, ✍ Aut. 121
97/8 Pi. Certified 117
97/8 Pi. Inside 108
95/6 Pi. Summit 121
97/8 Pi. Totally 117
95/6 Pi. Zenith 45
95/6 Playoff 65
96/7 Playoff 344
94/5 POG 137
95/6 POG 168
94/5 Post
93/4 Power Play 131
93/4 Premier 509
93/4 Prmr. - BG-OPC 24
94/5 Premier 305, GTG-11
95/6 Pro Magnet 52
90/1 Pro Set 172, 371
91/2 Pro Set 134
91/2 Pro Set 412
92/3 Pro Set 87
91/2 Pro Set Platinum 66
90/1 Score 160
90/1 Sco. Hot Cards 71
91/2 Score 110
91/2 Score 331
91/2 Score 64T
91/2 Score CAN 110
91/2 Score CAN 361
91/2 Score CAN 614
92/3 Score 225
92/3 Score SS 29
93/4 Score 234
93/4 Score/CAN DD6
93/4 Score PiAS 7
94/5 Score 146, CI10
95/6 Score 96
96/7 Score 103
97/8 Score 105
92/3 Seasons 25
94/5 Select 107
95/6 Select CE 103
95/6 SBx Emotion 106
95/6 SBx Impact 103
96/7 SBx Impact 127
94/5 SP 68
95/6 SP 142
96/7 SP 156
95/6 SLU
95/6 Super Sticker 74
92/3 Topps 490
95/6 Topps 115
98/9 Topps 145
94/5 Topps Finest 44, BBB10
91/2 To. Stadium 193
92/3 To. Stadium 387
93/4 To. Stadium 67
93/4 To. Stadium - AS
94/5 To. Stadium 130
95/6 To. Stadium EC177
90/1 Upper Deck 267, 311
91/2 Upper Deck 149
91/2 Upper Deck 519
92/3 Upper Deck 180
93/4 Upper Deck 148, SP-80
94/5 Upper Deck 66, IG9, SP-40
x95/6 Upper Deck SE52
96/7 Upper Deck 165
97/8 Upper Deck 76
94/5 UD BAP R3, G17, ✍ 40
95/6 UD CC 142
96/7 UD CC 259
97/8 UD Coll. Choice 98
92/3 UD Locker 9
99/0 UD MVP W23
99/0 UD MVP Cup 60
00/1 DALL / Southwest
01/2 DALL / Southwest
02/3 DALL / Southwest
97/8 FLOR / Winn-Dixie
91/2 MONT
92/3 MONT
92/3 MONT / OPC 26
93/4 MONT / Export
93/4 MONT
94/5 MONT
84/5 NJER
85/6 NJER 9
86/7 NJER / S.O.B.E.R.
88/9 NJER / Caretta
89/0 NJER
89/0 NJER / Caretta
90/1 NJER
81/2 Kingston Canadians

MULLER, MIKE
93/4 Cla. Prospects 71
96/7 Mississippi S'Wolves
91/2 Minnesota G'Gophers

MULLER, ROBERT
99/0 Eishockey 264, 367

MÜLLER, ERNST
98/9 DEL

MÜLLER, ROBERT
98/9 DEL 297
00/1 UD DEL 226
01/2 UD DEL 260

MÜLLER, ZDENEK
94/5 APS 282
95/6 APS 76

MULLIN, KORY
91/2 7th...Sketch WHL 301
95/6 St. John's Maple Leafs
93/4 Tacoma Rockets

MULLIN, MATT
98/9 EBK ECHL All-Star
91/2 7th...Sketch OHL 181
97/8 Quad City Mallards
92/3 Windsor Spitfires

MULLINS, DWIGHT
97/8 Fort Worth Brahmas

MULOCK, T.J.
01/2 Vancouver Giants

MULOCK, TYSON
99/0 Medicine Hat Tigers
00/1 Medicine Hat Tigers

MULOIN, WAYNE
70/1 Dad's Cookies
70/1 Eddie Sargent 135
70/1 Esso Power Player
75/6 OPC WHA 102
72/3 Cleveland Crusaders
72/3 Clev. WHA / Linnett

MULROY, TERRY
74/5 Sioux City Musketeers

MULTANEN, JARI
93/4 Jyvas Hyva 258
93/4 Sisu 299

MULVENNA, GLENN
92/3 OPC Premier 97
88/9 ProCards / Muskegon
89/0 ProCards IHL 162
90/1 ProCards 387
91/2 ProCards 289
92/3 Upper Deck 490
94/5 Peoria Rivermen
95/6 Peoria Rivermen
87/8 Kamloops Blazers

MULVEY, GRANT
75/6 O-Pee-Chee 272
76/7 O-Pee-Chee 167
77/8 O-Pee-Chee 101
78/9 O-Pee-Chee 261
79/0 O-Pee-Chee 88
80/1 O-Pee-Chee 27
80/1 O-Pee-Chee 212
81/2 O-Pee-Chee 60
82/3 O-Pee-Chee 69
82/3 OPC/Topps Sticker 173
82/3 Post [Chic.]
92/3 Seasons 22
75/6 Topps 272
76/7 Topps 167
77/8 Topps 101
78/9 Topps 261
79/0 Topps 88
80/1 Topps 27
80/1 Topps 212
81/2 Topps 72 [West]
79/0 CHIC
80/1 CHIC / Colour
80/1 CHIC / Brown
81/2 CHIC
82/3 CHIC
83/4 NJER

MULVEY, PAUL
81/2 OPC Sticker 81
78/9 WASH
79/0 WASH
80/1 WASH

MULVIHILL, DANA
98/9 EBK ECHL All-Star

MUNCK, JARI
92/3 Jyvas Hyva 76
93/4 Jyvas Hyva 20
93/4 Sisu 92
94/5 Sisu 256

MUNDAY, TRAVIS
91/2 7th...Sketch WHL 355

MUNDY, BUSTER
37/8 World Wide Gum 101

MUNI, CRAIG
93/4 Donruss 405
94/5 Flair 21
92/3 Fleer Ultra 296
94/5 Fleer Ultra 265
94/5 Leaf 373
87/8 O-Pee-Chee 206
88/9 OPC/Topps 236
90/1 O-Pee-Chee 423
91/2 O-Pee-Chee 479
89/0 O-Pee-Chee 231
87/8 OPC Leaders 30
89/0 opcSticker 229-88
87/8 Panini Sticker 258
89/0 Panini Sticker 80
90/1 Panini Sticker 217
90/1 Panini/EDM 15
91/2 Panini Sticker 133
93/4 Parkhurst 291
91/2 Pinnacle 262
93/4 Pinnacle 298
94/5 Pinnacle 143
97/8 Pi. Be A Player 19, ✍ Aut. 19
93/4 Power Play 299
94/5 Premier 216
90/1 Pro Set 92
91/2 Pro Set 382
90/1 Score 38
91/2 Score 67
91/2 Score CAN 67
92/3 Score 81
93/4 Score 266
93/4 Score 579
94/5 Score 29
90/1 Upper Deck 21
91/2 Upper Deck 372
95/6 UD BAP 14, ✍ S14
86/7 EDMO
86/7 EDMO / Red Rooster
87/8 EDMO
88/9 EDMO
88/9 EDMO / Action 33
90/1 EDMO / IGA
91/2 EDMO / IGA
92/3 EDMO / IGA 016

MUNITIZ, RAMON
79 Panini Sticker 372

MUNRO, ADAM
01 UD Prospects GU 22, ✂ TPJ, ✂ TPJS, ✂ JC, ✍ SoT

MUNRO, BRYCE
92/3 BCJHL 30

MUNRO, DUNC
25-27 Anonymous 91
25-27 Anonymous 92 [No Border]
24/5 Champ's Cigarettes
25 Dominion Chocolates 57
26 Dominion Chocolates 12
24/5 Maple Crispette [V130] 1
23 Willards Chocolates 52
24/5 William Paterson 34

MUNRO, GERRY
25-27 Anonymous 62
24/5 Champ's Cigarettes
24/5 William Paterson 33

MUNRO, MIKE
99/0 Kamloops Blazers
99/0 Kamloops Blazers

MUNSTER, JAN
99/0 Eishockey 236

MÜNSTER, JAN
00/1 UD DEL 99
01/2 UD DEL 22

MURAKAMI, HIROYUKI
99/0 Score 86

MURANO, ERIC
98/9 DEL 296
90/1 ProCards 338
91/2 ProCards 606
91/2 Upper Deck 50
92/3 Hamilton Canucks
95/6 Peoria Rivermen

MURATOV, EVGENI
99/0 Mir 135
00/1 Mir 286

MURCHESON, BRENT
92/3 BCJHL 97

MURDOCH, BOB J.
94/5 DEL 296
95/6 DEL 193
96/7 DEL 336
72/3 Dernière Heure
74/5 Loblaws
74/5 O-Pee-Chee 194
75/6 O-Pee-Chee 33
76/7 O-Pee-Chee 74
77/8 O-Pee-Chee 371
78/9 O-Pee-Chee 91
79/0 O-Pee-Chee 276
81/2 O-Pee-Chee 48
82/3 O-Pee-Chee 53
80/1 Pepsi Bottle Cap
82/3 Post [Calg.]
90/1 Pro Set 680
74/5 Topps 194
75/6 Topps 33
76/7 Topps 74
78/9 Topps 91
78/9 ATLF / Colour
79/0 ATLF / B&W
79/0 ATLF / Colour
80/1 CALG
81/2 CALG
85/6 CALG / Red Rooster
86/7 CALG / Red Rooster
87/8 CHIC / Coke
72/3 MONT / Pro Star
89/0 WINN / Safeway
90/1 WINN / IGA

MURDOCH, BOB L.
76/7 O-Pee-Chee 54
76/7 O-Pee-Chee 384
77/8 O-Pee-Chee 39
79/0 O-Pee-Chee 351
76/7 Topps 54
77/8 Topps 39

MURDOCH, DON
77/8 O-Pee-Chee 244
77/8 O-Pee-Chee NS 12
78/9 O-Pee-Chee 11
79/0 O-Pee-Chee 168
80/1 O-Pee-Chee 203
80/1 Pepsi Bottle Cap
77/8 Topps 244
77/8 ToppsNS 12
78/9 Topps 11
79/0 Topps 168
80/1 Topps 203
80/1 EDMO / Zellers
88/9 EDMO / Action 120
99/0 Louisiana Ice Gators

MURDOCH, JOHN MURRAY
33/4 Anonymous 29
34-43 BeeHive-1 [NYRa.]
33/4 Canadian Gum
33-35 Diamond Match Silv.
36-39 Diamond Match TT1
36-39 Diamond Match TT2
36-39 Diamond Match TT3
24/5 Falcons Crescent 4
33/4 O-Pee-Chee 37
33/4 WWGum 68
37/8 World Wide Gum 88

MURDOCK, LORIN
92/3 BCJHL 181

MURLEY, MATT
02/3 WBS Penguins

MURNAGHAN, KEVIN
95/6 Slapshot 359

MURNAGHAN, KYLE
99 Québec Pee Wee 1031
01/2 Moncton Wildcats 4

MUROVIC, MIRKO
99 Bowman 19, ✍ BA39
95 Québec Pee Wee 107
98/9 SP Authentic 130, ✍ SotT
98/9 Upper Deck 407
98/9 UD G. Reserve 407

MURPHY, BURKE
98/9 DEL 1
99/0 Eishockey 304
96/7 Saint John Flames
97/8 Saint John Flames

MURPHY, CORY
02/3 Cardset 75
95/6 Slapshot 358
92/3 Ottawa 67's

MURPHY, CURTIS
02/3 BAP Mem. 325
02/3 SP Authentic 177
02/3 Ultimate Mem. 89
02/3 UD Artistic 128
02/3 UD Honor 137
98/9 EBK IHL All-Star
98/9 Orlando Solar Bears Geico

MURPHY, DAN
91/2 Avant Garde BCJHL 48
92/3 BCJHL 110
98/9 Peoria Rivermen
91/2 Nanaimo Clippers
92/3 Maine Black Bears
92/3 Maine Black Bears

MURPHY, GORD
90/1 Bowman 106
91/2 Bowman 235
92/3 Bowman 315
93/4 Donruss 131
94/5 Donruss 55
95/6 Donruss 161
93/4 EA Sports 50
94/5 Flair 66
94/5 Fleer 81
96/7 Fl. Picks 162
92/3 Fleer Ultra 253
93/4 Fleer Ultra 329
94/5 Fleer Ultra 83
95/6 Fleer Ultra 61, 243
93/4 Leaf 284
94/5 Leaf 250
95/6 Leaf 146
90/1 OPC/Topps 302
91/2 O-Pee-Chee 89
92/3 O-Pee-Chee 101
01/2 O-Pee-Chee 257
89/0 opcSticker/FS 12
97/8 Pa. Invincible R-88
89/0 Panini Sticker 303
90/1 Panini Sticker 115
91/2 Panini Sticker 230
94/5 Panini Sticker 71
95/6 Panini Sticker 77
91/2 Parkhurst 227
93/4 Parkhurst 345
95/6 Parkhurst 357
91/2 Pinnacle 140
92/3 Pinnacle 132
93/4 Pinnacle 380
93/4 Pinnacle Expa. 2
94/5 Pinnacle 141
95/6 Pinnacle 181
96/7 Pi. Be A Player 44, ✍ Aut. 44
95/6 Playoff 262
94/5 POG 112
95/6 POG 122
93/4 Power Play 99
93/4 Premier 465
94/5 Premier 19
90/1 Pro Set 221
91/2 Pro Set 171
91/2 Pro Set / Prototype
92/3 Pro Set 11
91/2 Pro Set Platinum 156
90/1 Score 117
90/1 Sco. Hot Cards 56
91/2 Score 43
91/2 Score CAN 43
92/3 Score 29
93/4 Score 548
93/4 Score 95
94/5 Score 117
95/6 Score 104
90/1 Sco. Young Stars 13
95/6 SBx Emotion 70
95/6 SBx Impact 68
99/0 Stadium 165
92/3 Topps 114
01/2 Topps 257
91/2 To. Stadium 248
92/3 To. Stadium 445
93/4 To. Stadium 439
94/5 To. Stadium 128
90/1 Upper Deck 86
91/2 Upper Deck 392
93/4 Upper Deck 521
94/5 Upper Deck 438
95/6 Upper Deck 21
96/7 Upper Deck 68
97/8 Upper Deck 285
95/6 UD CC 190
99/0 UD Retro 34
91/2 BOST / Sports Action
94/5 FLOR
94/5 FLOR / Winn-Dixie
96/7 FLOR / Winn-Dixie
97/8 FLOR / Winn-Dixie
89/0 PHIL
90/1 PHIL
91/2 PHIL / J.C. Penney

MURPHY, J.?
91/2 7th...Sketch WHL 291

MURPHY, JAY
97/8 Louisiana Ice Gators
98/9 Louisiana Ice Gators
99/0 Louisiana Ice Gators
00/1 Louisiana Ice Gators
01/2 Louisiana Ice Gators
94/5 Richmond Renegades
95/6 Richmond Renegades

MURPHY, JODI
93/4 Muskegon Fury
93/4 Soo Greyhounds 18

MURPHY, JOE
98/9 Be A Player 271, ✍ Aut. 271
90/1 Bowman 196
91/2 Bowman 109
92/3 Bowman 174
93/4 Donruss 66
94/5 Donruss 38
95/6 Donruss 146
96/7 Donruss 144
96/7 Do. Elite 102
94/5 Flair 34
94/5 Fleer 42
95/6 Fleer Metal 25
92/3 Fleer Ultra 63
93/4 Fleer Ultra 163
95/6 Fleer Ultra 217
93/4 Leaf 179
94/5 Leaf 284
95/6 Leaf 109
96/7 Leaf 185
96/7 Maggers 29
96/7 Metal Univ. 134
90/1 O-Pee-Chee 429
91/2 O-Pee-Chee 48
92/3 O-Pee-Chee 100
99/0 Pacific 377
97/8 Pacific CC 150
97/8 Pa. Paramount 160
92/3 Panini Sticker 100
94/5 Panini Sticker 129
95/6 Panini Sticker 162
97/8 Panini Sticker 171
91/2 Parkhurst 52
92/3 Parkhurst 273
93/4 Parkhurst 38
93/4 Parkhurst F8
94/5 Parkhurst 44
95/6 Parkhurst 309
91/2 Pinnacle 206
92/3 Pinnacle 23
93/4 Pinnacle 45
94/5 Pinnacle 68
95/6 Pinnacle 8
96/7 Pinnacle 200
96/7 Pi. Be A Player 28, ✍ Aut. 28
95/6 Pi. Summit 10
96/7 Pi. Summit 86
95/6 Pi. Zenith 4
94/5 POG 67
95/6 POG 66
93/4 Power Play 53
93/4 Premier 273
93/4 Premier - Finest 8
94/5 Premier 34
95/6 Pro Magnet 3
90/1 Pro Set 93
91/2 Pro Set 68
92/3 Pro Set 49
91/2 Pro Set Platinum 171
90/1 Score 293
91/2 Score 299
91/2 Score CAN 519
92/3 Score 321
93/4 Score 348
93/4 Score DD6
94/5 Score 170
95/6 Score 110
96/7 Score 100
97/8 Score 163
97/8 Score SLou. 3
94/5 Select 44
95/6 Select CE 50
95/6 SBx Emotion 30
95/6 SBx Impact 30
94/5 SP 27
96/7 SP 132
95/6 Super Sticker 24
92/3 Topps 38
95/6 Topps 280
95/6 To. Finest 58
96/7 To. Picks 143
91/2 To. Stadium 313
92/3 To. Stadium 34
95/6 To. Stadium 52
90/1 Upper Deck 190
91/2 Upper Deck 474
92/3 Upper Deck 152
93/4 Upper Deck 47, SP-29
94/5 Upper Deck 416
95/6 Upper Deck 278
96/7 Upper Deck 325
97/8 Upper Deck 349
00/1 Upper Deck 403, PC-8
94/5 UD BAP ✍ 87
95/6 UD CC 156
96/7 UD CC 48
97/8 UD Coll. Choice 231
93/4 CHIC / Coke
87/8 DETR / Little Caesars
88/9 DETR / Little Caesars
90/1 EDMO / IGA
91/2 EDMO / IGA
01/2 Grand Rapids Griffins
00/1 Rochester Americans

MURPHY, JONATHAN
93/4 Slapshot / Peterborough 2
95/6 Slapshot 309

MURPHY, KEITH
91/2 Air Canada SJHL 30
91/2 Air Canada SJHL B40

MURPHY, KEVIN
92/3 Clarkson G'Knights

MURPHY, LARRY
98/9 Be A Player 48, M20, ✍ Aut. 48
99/0 BAP Mem. 42
00/1 BAP Mem. 194
90/1 Bowman 177
91/2 Bowman 78
92/3 Bowman 153
95/6 Bowman 34
91 Canada Cup
93/4 Donruss 263
94/5 Donruss 27
95/6 Donruss 366
96/7 Donruss 39
96/7 Do. Canadian 86
95/6 Do. Elite 8
93/4 EA Sports 103
94/5 Flair 137
94/5 Fleer 166
96/7 Fleer 108, NT-9
95/6 Fleer Metal 145
96/7 Fl. Picks 52
92/3 Fleer Ultra 167
93/4 Fleer Ultra 184
94/5 Fleer Ultra 168
95/6 Fleer Ultra 125, 314
96/7 Fl. Ultra 164
83/4 Funmate Puffy 9 [w/]
93/4 Hockey Wit 48
91/2 Kraft 71
95/6 Kraft / PB
98/9 Kraft / PB
93/4 Leaf 16
93/4 Leaf GLAS 2
94/5 Leaf 249
95/6 Leaf 186
96/7 Leaf 100
94/5 L. Limited 12
95/6 L. Limited 97
96/7 Metal Univ. 151
81/2 O-Pee-Chee 148
81/2 O-Pee-Chee 393
82/3 O-Pee-Chee 158
83/4 O-Pee-Chee 159
84/5 O-Pee-Chee 204
85/6 O-Pee-Chee 236
86/7 OPC/Topps 185
87/8 OPC/Topps 133
87/8 OPC/Topps Box H
88/9 OPC/Topps 141
90/1 OPC/Topps 47
91/2 O-Pee-Chee 277
92/3 O-Pee-Chee 209
89/0 OPC/Topps 128
98/9 OPC Chrome 33, B9, SB26
87/8 OPC Leaders 31
81/2 OPC Sticker 239
82/3 OPC/Topps Sticker 232
83/4 OPC/Topps Sticker 298
84/5 OPC Sticker 127
87/8 OPC Sticker 119-131
87/8 OPC Sticker 232-98
88/9 OPC Sticker 71-200
89/0 opcSticker 199-55
97/8 Omega 85
98/9 Omega 85
98/9 Pacific 203
99/0 Pacific 145
00/1 Pacific 156
98/9 Pa. Paramount 80
99/0 Pa. Paramount 85
97/8 Pa. Revolution 49
87/8 Panini Sticker 176
88/9 Panini Sticker 367
89/0 Panini Sticker 108
90/1 Panini Sticker 251
91/2 Panini Sticker 270
92/3 Panini Sticker 228
93/4 Panini Sticker 135
93/4 Panini Sticker 86
94/5 Panini Sticker 80
95/6 Panini Sticker 209
96/7 Panini Sticker 216
99/0 Panini Sticker 235
91/2 Parkhurst 358
92/3 Parkhurst 137
93/4 Parkhurst 162
94/5 Parkhurst 179
95/6 Parkhurst 207, PP-23
91/2 Pinnacle 143
92/3 Pinnacle 292
93/4 Pinnacle 52
94/5 Pinnacle 215
96/7 Pinnacle 189
97/8 Pi. Be A Player 141, ✍ Aut. 141
95/6 Pi. Summit 126
96/7 Pi. Summit 11
95/6 Pi. Zenith 106
96/7 Pi. Zenith 111
95/6 Playoff 97
94/5 POG 191
95/6 POG 266, I-019
82/3 Post [LosA.]
93/4 Power Play 193
93/4 Premier 173
93/4 Premier 189
93/4 Prmr. - BG-Top. 23
94/5 Premier 10, 492
90/1 Pro Set 143
91/2 Pro Set 193
92/3 Pro Set 146
91/2 Pro Set Platinum 213
90/1 Score 206
91/2 Score 31
91/2 Score CAN 31
92/3 Score 45
93/4 Score 23
94/5 Score 5
95/6 Score 260
96/7 Score 75
97/8 Score Detr. 8
94/5 Select 143
95/6 Select CE 90
94 Semic 81
95 Semic 83
92 Semic Sticker 82
93 Semic Sticker 191
95/6 SBx Emotion 173
95/6 SBx Impact 163
96/7 SBx Impact 128, F-15
83/4 Souhaits Keychain [Kings]
95/6 SP 143
96/7 SP 154
99/0 Stadium CA30
95/6 Super Sticker 121
96/7 Team Out!
81/2 Topps 100 [West]
87/8 OPC/Topps - Stick. 7
92/3 Topps 447
95/6 Topps 255
98/9 Topps 33, B9, SB26
00/1 Topps PC8
00/1 To. Chrome PC-8
94/5 Topps Finest RL-18
95/6 To. Finest 42
91/2 To. Stadium 112
92/3 To. Stadium 375
93/4 To. Stadium 283
95/6 To. Stadium 144
93/4 TSC Members Only 32
95/6 TSC Members Only 16
98/9 UD Choice 70, RW14
00/1 Ultimate Mem. ✂ D-11
99/0 Ult. Victory 34
90/1 Upper Deck 229
91/2 Upper Deck 302
92/3 Upper Deck 241
93/4 Upper Deck 374
94/5 Upper Deck 99
95/6 Upper Deck 86, SE-170
96/7 Upper Deck 161, X39
98/9 Upper Deck 265
00/1 Upper Deck 294
94/5 UD BAP R170, ✍ 148
93/4 UD BAP Roots 8
95/6 UD CC 151, 386
96/7 UD CC 265
98/9 UD G. Reserve 265
95/6 UD Post 21
00/1 UD Vintage 130
96 Wien 82
91/2 PITT / Elby's
91/2 PITT / Foodland 10
91/2 PITT / Food. Stickers
92/3 PITT / Coke-Clark
92/3 PITT / Foodland 10
92/3 PITT / Food. Stickers
93/4 PITT / Foodland 13
94/5 PITT / Foodland 24
84/5 WASH / Pizza Hut
85/6 WASH / Pizza Hut
86/7 WASH / Kodak
86/7 WASH / Police
87/8 WASH
87/8 WASH / Kodak
88/9 WASH
88/9 WASH / Smokey

MURPHY, MARK
99/0 Des Moines Buc's
00/1 Portland Pirates

MURPHY, MIKE
72/3 Eddie Sargent 195
74/5 Loblaws
72/3 O-Pee-Chee 215
74/5 O-Pee-Chee 224
75/6 O-Pee-Chee 52
76/7 O-Pee-Chee 21
77/8 O-Pee-Chee 22
78/9 O-Pee-Chee 229
79/0 O-Pee-Chee 31
80/1 O-Pee-Chee 286
81/2 O-Pee-Chee 149
81/2 OPC Sticker 241
79 Panini Sticker 69
90/1 ProCards 335
83/4 Souhaits Keychain [Kings]
74/5 Topps 224
75/6 Topps 52
76/7 Topps 21
77/8 Topps 22
78/9 Topps 229
79/0 Topps 31
81/2 Topps 101 [West]
80/1 LOSA 9
71/2 SLOU
72/3 SLOU

MURPHY, ROB
98/9 DEL 73
99/0 Eishockey 62
90/1 OPC/Topps 37
90/1 Panini/VAN 16
90/1 Pro Set 546
92/3 Pro Set 121
89/0 ProCards IHL 172
91/2 ProCards 607
91/2 Score CAN 397
92/3 Upper Deck 108
00/1 UD DEL 95
01/2 UD DEL 99
90/1 VANC / Mohawk
91/2 VANC
91/2 VANC / Photo
95/6 Fort Wayne Komets
93/4 Phoenix Roadrunners

MURPHY, RON
52/3 Anonymous 61
45-64 BeeHive-2 [NYRa.]
45-64 BeeHive-2 [Chic.]
64-67 BeeHive-3 [Detr.]
64/5 Coke/Sprite [Detr.]
65/6 Coca-Cola
62/3 Cowan Tile
68/9 O-Pee-Chee 139
69/0 O-Pee-Chee 204
54/5 Parkhurst 76
93/4 Parkie 56-57 102
95/6 Parkie 66-67 15
94/5 Parkie Tall 48
60/1 Shirriff 75
61/2 Shirriff 36
57/8 Topps 29
58/9 Topps 59
59/0 Topps 66
60/1 Topps 41
61/2 Topps 34, -Stamp
62/3 Topps 40
63/4 Topps 40
64/5 Topps 56
65/6 Topps 111
66/7 Topps 96
66/7 Topps / Test 33
67/8 Topps 100

MURPHY, RYAN
01/2 Florida Everblades

MURPHY, RYAN**
96 Québoc Pee Wee 586

MURPHY, STEPHEN
02/3 Dundee Texol Stars

MURPHY, TODD
91/2 Air Canada SJHL D22
92/3 MPS SJHL 116

MURRAY, ADAM
91/2 7th...Sketch WHL 29

MURRAY, ADRIAN
93/4 Slapshot / Peterborough 26
95/6 Slapshot 310

MURRAY, ALLAN
34-43 BeeHive-1 [NYAm.]
36-39 Diamond Match TT1
36-39 Diamond Match TT2
36-39 Diamond Match TT3
36/7 O-Pee-Chee 104
37/8 World Wide Gum 54

MURRAY, ANDY
89/0 PHIL
93/4 WINN / Ruffles

MURRAY, BOB F.
76/7 O-Pee-Chee 309
77/8 O-Pee-Chee 12
78/9 O-Pee-Chee 89
79/0 O-Pee-Chee 55
80/1 O-Pee-Chee 181
81/2 O-Pee-Chee 61
82/3 O-Pee-Chee 70
83/4 O-Pee-Chee 108
84/5 O-Pee-Chee 41
85/6 OPC/Topps 114
86/7 OPC/Topps 64
87/8 OPC/Topps 156
90/1 OPC/Topps 138
81/2 OPC Sticker 119
83/4 OPC/Topps Sticker 109
84/5 OPC Sticker 26
90/1 Score 376
83/4 Souhaits Keychain [Blackhawks]
77/8 Topps 12
78/9 Topps 89
79/0 Topps 55
80/1 Topps 181
81/2 Topps 73 [West]
84/5 Topps 32
79/0 CHIC
80/1 CHIC / Brown
81/2 CHIC
82/3 CHIC
83/4 CHIC
86/7 CHIC / Coke
87/8 CHIC / Coke
89/0 CHIC / Coke

MURRAY, BOB J.
74/5 Loblaws
74/5 O-Pee-Chee 336
75/6 O-Pee-Chee 386
76/7 O-Pee-Chee 363
75/6 VANC / Royal Bank
76/7 VANC / Royal Bank

MURRAY, BRYAN
90/1 Pro Set 664
90/1 DETR / Little Caesars
91/2 DETR / Little Caesars
97/8 FLOR / Winn-Dixie
82/3 WASH
86/7 WASH / Kodak
86/7 WASH / Police
87/8 WASH / Kodak
88/9 WASH / Smokey

MURRAY, CHRIS
95/6 Future Legends 12
97/8 Pa. Invincible R-39
00/1 Stadium 216
96/7 MONT
98/9 OTTA
94/5 Fredericton Canadiens
95/6 Fredericton Canadiens
00/1 Worcester IceCats
93/4 Kamloops Blazers

MURRAY, DARWIN
01/2 Rockford IceHogs

MURRAY, GARTH
00/1 UD Prospects 62
01 UD Prospects GU 9, ✂ TPJ, ✂ JC
01/2 Regina Pats

MURRAY, GLEN
02/3 Atomic 6
02/3 BAP Mem. 67
02/3 Calder ✂ GWJ 3
02/3 Crown Royale 6
02/3 Exclusive 11
02/3 First Edition 208, 372, 374, 378
02/3 Heads Up 8
02/3 O-Pee-Chee 142
02/3 Pacific 30
02/3 Pacific Complete 299
02/3 Parkhurst 12
02/3 Parkhurst Retro 36
02/3 Pr. Stock Reserve 6
02/3 PS Titanium 7
02/3 Quest for the Cup 7, ✂ GWJ 2
02/3 Signature 53, ✍ 53, ✂ TQ11
02/3 Slam Card
02/3 SP Game-Used ✂ AF
02/3 Sports Vault 14
02/3 Topps 142, OTG9
02/3 T. Chrome 87
02/3 To. Heritage 85
02/3 To. Limited 142
02/3 To. Total 259
02/3 Upper Deck 16, ✂ CG
02/3 UD Classic ✂ HR
02/3 UD Honor ✂ GA
02/3 UD Mask ✂ PG
02/3 UD Piece 7
02/3 UD Premier ✂ Jers
02/3 UD Rookie 12
02/3 UD Top Shelf ✂ GO, ✂ SH
02/3 UD Vintage 24, 263, 306, GB 24, ✂ OS
02/3 Vanguard 7
91/2 Arena 14
99/0 BAP Mem. 2
00/1 BAP Mem. 122
01/2 BAP Mem. 134, ✂ 463
91/2 Classic 15
91/2 Classic Four Sport 15
92/3 Classic Prospects 89
01/2 Crown Royale 10
93/4 Donruss 22
94/5 Donruss 246
98/9 Kraft / Post 11
93/4 Leaf 317
94/5 Leaf 4
92/3 O-Pee-Chee 74
92/3 OPC Premier 52
97/8 Omega 110
98/9 Omega 111
99/0 Omega 109
98/9 Pacific 241
99/0 Pacific 193
00/1 Pacific 198
01/2 Pacific 183
98/9 Pa. Paramount 105
99/0 Pa. Paramount 110
00/1 Pa. Paramount 112
92/3 Panini Sticker 142
98/9 Panini Sticker 203
99/0 Panini Sticker 261
00/1 Panini Sticker 169
91/2 Parkhurst 229
92/3 Parkhurst 9
93/4 Parkhurst 16
95/6 Parkhurst 440
00/1 Parkhurst P-104
01/2 Parkhurst 126
94/5 Parkie SE11
92/3 Pinnacle 224
94/5 Pinnacle 169
95/6 Playoff 299
94/5 POG 41
93/4 Premier 477
94/5 Premier 173
92/3 Pro Set 222
92/3 Score 484
91 7th..Sketch Mem.Cup 111
90/1 7th..Sketch OHL 388
91/2 7th...Sketch OHL 245
00/1 Signature 79, ✍ Aut. 40
98/9 SP Authentic 40
01/2 SPx 158
00/1 Stadium 195
91/2 Star Pics 64
92/3 Topps 370
99/0 Topps 65
00/1 Topps 123
99/0 To. Chrome 65
00/1 To. Chrome 94
98/9 To. Finest 103
92/3 To. Stadium 393
93/4 To. Stadium 59
98/9 UD Choice 99
00/1 UD Heroes 58
91/2 Ultimate Draft Pick 15, 71, 84, ✍ Aut.
91/2 Upper Deck 69
92/3 Upper Deck 401
93/4 Upper Deck 189
94/5 Upper Deck 23
95/6 Upper Deck 394
97/8 Upper Deck 81
98/9 Upper Deck 284
00/1 Upper Deck 85
01/2 Upper Deck 249
95/6 UD BAP 144, ✍ S144
98/9 UD G. Reserve 284
01/2 UD Ice 86
99/0 UD MVP PS GM
00/1 UD Vintage 167
01/2 UD Vintage 117
01/2 Vanguard 6
99/0 Victory 138
00/1 Victory 113
01/2 Victory 163
95/6 PITT / Foodland 2
89/0 Sudbury Wolves
90/1 Sudbury Wolves
91/2 Sudbury Wolves

MURRAY, HERMAN
37/8 World Wide Gum 113

MURRAY, KEN
37/8 World Wide Gum 109

MURRAY, MARTY
02/3 Pacific Complete 267
00/1 BAP Mem. 468
95/6 Bowman 152
93/4 Donruss CAN17
95/6 Donruss 284, C3TWC-10, RR-11
97/8 Donruss 221
99/0 Eishockey 105
95/6 Fleer Metal 185
96/7 Fl. Picks 178
95/6 Fleer Ultra 350
95/6 Future Legends 35
97/8 Limited 39
95/6 Parkhurst 530
01/2 Parkhurst 394
93/4 Pinnacle 477
94/5 Pinnacle 536
97/8 Pi. Be A Player 199, ✍ Aut. 199
95/6 Pi. Summit 191
95/6 Pi. Zenith 142
95/6 Select CE 141
91/2 7th...Sketch WHL 206
95/6 SBx Impact 192
96/7 SBx Impact 155
94/5 Slapshot Memorial 48
94/5 SP 148
95/6 Topps 338, 6CJ
94/5 Topps Finest 161
00/1 To. Heritage 198
95/6 To. Stadium ER198
93/4 Upper Deck 550
95/6 Upper Deck 500
95/6 UD CC 405
01/2 Victory 365
01/2 PHIL
95/6 Saint John Flames
96/7 Saint John Flames
97/8 Saint John Flames
92/3 Brandon Wheat Kings

MURRAY, MICHAEL
94/5 Classic 114
95/6 Dayton Bombers
93/4 Knoxville Cherokees
94/5 Knoxville Cherokees
98/9 Louisiana Ice Gators
99/0 Louisiana Ice Gators
00/1 Louisiana Ice Gators
94/5 Saint John Flames
95/6 Saint John Flames

MURRAY, PAT
90/1 OPC Premier 79
90/1 Pro Set 630
91/2 ProCards 276
91/2 Score 321
91/2 Score CAN 351
91/2 Upper Deck 451
94/5 Knoxville Cherokees

MURRAY, REM
02/3 Pacific Complete 100
02/3 To. Total 33
99/0 BAP Mem. 63
01/2 BAP Mem. 484
97/8 Donruss 127
96/7 Do. Canadian 123
96/7 Do. Elite 145, A-22
97/8 Do. Preferred 56
96/7 Flair 111
96/7 Fl. Ultra 60, UR-14
95/6 Future Legends 14
96/7 Got-Um
97/8 Leaf 140
96/7 L. Preferred 136
97/8 Limited 141, 173
96/7 Metal Univ. 188
99/0 Millenium 104, ✍ Aut. 104
99/0 Pacific 161
01/2 Pacific 161
97/8 Pacific CC 112
97/8 Pa. Dynagon 50, T-50
97/8 Pa. Invincible 57
99/0 Pa. Paramount 93
97/8 Pinnacle 133
96/7 Pi. Be A Player LTH5A, ✍ Aut. LTH5A
97/8 Pi. Inside 94
96/7 Pi. Zenith 146
97/8 Score 227
96/7 Select CE 119
96/7 SP 178
99/0 Topps 183
99/0 To. Chrome 183
98/9 To. Finest 84
96/7 Upper Deck 261
97/8 Upper Deck 70
01/2 Upper Deck 300
96/7 UD Black Diam. 17
96/7 UD CC 352
97/8 UD Coll. Choice 91
96/7 UD Ice 19
01/2 Victory 141
96/7 EDMO
97/8 EDMO
93/4 Michigan State

MURRAY, ROB
90/1 Bowman 74
95/6 Future Legends 15
90/1 O-Pee-Chee 460
79 Panini Sticker 99
87/8 Panini Sticker 223
88/9 Panini Sticker 22
90/1 Pro Set 553
88/9 ProCards / Baltimore

91/2 ProCards 164
82 Semic Sticker 103
90/1 WASH / Smokey
91/2 WINN / IGA
99/0 Hamilton Bulldogs/ Staz
99/0 Hamilton Bulldogs/ Staz
91/2 Moncton Hawks
96/7 Springfield Falcons
97/8 Springfield Falcons

MURRAY, SCOTT
91/2 Air Canada SJHL B38

MURRAY, TERRY
73/4 O-Pee-Chee 259
74/5 O-Pee-Chee 126
90/1 Pro Set 679
88/9 ProCards / Baltimore
89/0 ProCards AHL 92
74/5 Topps 126
94/5 PHIL / Sheet
81/2 WASH
82/3 WASH
89/0 WASH / Kodak
90/1 WASH / Kodak

MURRAY, TIM
92/3 MPS SJHL 110
97/8 Detroit Vipers
98/9 Detroit Vipers

MURRAY, TROY
90/1 Bowman 13
91/2 Bowman 388
92/3 Bowman 93
92/3 Fleer Ultra 242, 443
88/9 Frito Lay
92/3 Humpty Dumpty
84/5 O-Pee-Chee 42
85/6 OPC/Topps 146
86/7 OPC/Topps 25
87/8 OPC/Topps 74
88/9 OPC/Topps 106
90/1 OPC/Topps 160
91/2 O-Pee-Chee 87
92/3 O-Pee-Chee 64
89/0 O-Pee-Chee 219
91/2 OPC Premier 75
85/6 OPC Sticker 29-159
86/7 OPC Sticker 154-9
86/7 OPC Sticker 189-48
87/8 OPC Sticker 79-212
88/9 OPC Sticker 10-139
89/0 opcSticker 11-151
87/8 Panini Sticker 227
88/9 Panini Sticker 27
89/0 Panini Sticker 48
90/1 Panini Sticker 200
91/2 Panini Sticker 17
92/3 Panini Sticker 57
94/5 Panini Sticker 104
91/2 Parkhurst 206
91/2 Pinnacle 33
92/3 Pinnacle 49
93/4 Pinnacle 318
94/5 Pinnacle 139
82/3 Post [Wash.]
93/4 Premier 182
94/5 Premier 188
90/1 Pro Set 57
91/2 Pro Set 46
91/2 Pro Set 514
91/2 Pro Set 588
92/3 Pro Set 215
91/2 Pro Set Platinum 247
90/1 Score 243
91/2 Score 53
91/2 Score 35T
91/2 Score CAN 53
91/2 Score CAN 585
92/3 Score 189
93/4 Score 272
92/3 Seasons 58
92/3 Topps 284
91/2 To. Stadium 167
92/3 To. Stadium 31
93/4 To. Stadium 230
90/1 Upper Deck 112
91/2 Upper Deck 565
92/3 Upper Deck 129
94/5 UD BAP ✍ 176
82/3 CHIC
83/4 CHIC
86/7 CHIC / Coke
87/8 CHIC / Coke
88/9 CHIC / Coke
89/0 CHIC / Coke
90/1 CHIC / Coke
93/4 CHIC / Coke
94/5 OTTA
91/2 WINN / IGA

MURTO, MATTI
72 Hellas MM-Jenkki 7
74 Hellas MM-Jenkki 12
70/1 Kuvajulkaisut 70
70/1 Kuvajulkaisut 111
80/1 Mallasjuoma 13
72 Panda MM-Toronto
72 Panda MM-Toronto
72 Semic Sticker 83
74 Semic Sticker 86
96/7 Sisu 197
78/9 SM-Liiga 37
77-79 Sports. FIN 41-961
71/2 Williams Finnish 71
71/2 Williams Finnish 120
72/3 Williams Finnish 67
72/3 Williams Finnish 90
73/4 Williams Finnish 136

MURTOVAARA, PETRI
95/6 Sisu 241

MURZIN, ALEXEI
98/9 Mir 113
99/0 Mir 203

MURZYN, DANA
92/3 Bowman 71
93/4 Donruss 348
93/4 Fleer Ultra 441
93/4 Leaf 292
86/7 OPC/Topps 58
87/8 OPC/Topps 138
90/1 OPC/Topps 304
92/3 O-Pee-Chee 241
97/8 Pa. Dynagon BKS-97
87/8 Panini Sticker 42
90/1 Panini/CGY 12
93/4 Parkhurst 486
91/2 Pinnacle 260
92/3 Pinnacle 172
93/4 Pinnacle 273
94/5 Pinnacle 198
96/7 Pi. Be A Player 160, ✍ Aut. 160
93/4 Premier 311
90/1 Pro Set 41
91/2 Pro Set 498
90/1 Score 274
91/2 Score 357
91/2 Score CAN 231
92/3 Score 168
93/4 Score 298
94/5 Score 134
92/3 Topps 194
92/3 To. Stadium 353
90/1 Upper Deck 348
87/8 CALG / Red Rooster
90/1 CALG / McGavin's
85/6 HART / Jr. Whalers
86/7 HART / Jr. Whalers
87/8 HART / Jr. Whalers
91/2 VANC
91/2 VANC / Photo
92/3 VANC / Road Trip
94/5 VANC
95/6 VANC / Abalene 5
96/7 VANC / IGA

MUSAKKA, JOAKIM
94/5 Leaf Elit Set 282
95/6 Leaf Elit Set 31

MUSATOV, VADIM
99/0 Mir 244

MUSIAL, DAVID
94/5 DEL 292
95/6 DEL 282
01/2 UD DEL 118

MUSIL, FRANTISEK
01/2 Signat. 99, ✍ Aut. 99

MUSIL, FRANTISEK (FRANK)
94/5 APS 75
91/2 Bowman 259
92/3 Bowman 157
92/3 Fleer Ultra 270
93/4 Fleer Ultra 283
94/5 Fleer Ultra 31
93/4 Leaf 236
94/5 Leaf 545
91/2 O-Pee-Chee 68
92/3 O-Pee-Chee 66
89/0 O-Pee-Chee 217
97/8 Pa. Invincible R-136
87/8 Panini Sticker 292
88/9 Panini Sticker 87
90/1 Panini Sticker 258
97/8 Panini Sticker 44
95 Panini Worlds 197
91/2 Pinnacle 282
92/3 Pinnacle 51
93/4 Pinnacle 101
94/5 Pinnacle 64
93/4 Power Play 307
93/4 Premier 229
94/5 Premier 258
90/1 Pro Set 425
91/2 Pro Set 368
90/1 Score 223, 19T
91/2 Score 142
91/2 Score CAN 142
92/3 Score 83
93/4 Score 303
94/5 Score 139
95 Semic 162
92 Semic Sticker 126
92/3 Topps 142
00/1 To. Heritage 210
91/2 To. Stadium 235
92/3 To. Stadium 67
93/4 To. Stadium 169
90/1 Upper Deck 383
99/0 Upper Deck 227
99/0 UD G. Reserve 227
96 Wien 111
90/1 CALG / McGavin's
91/2 CALG / IGA
92/3 CALG / IGA 016
87/8 MINS
88/9 MINS / ADA
95/6 OTTA
96/7 OTTA
97/8 Indianapolis Ice 19

MUSIL, MOJMIR
97/8 APS 189
97/8 DS Sticker 162
99/0 OFS 370

MUSTANIEMI, ARI
70/1 Kuvajulkaisut 374

MUSTONEN, JOUNI
91/2 Jyvas Hyva 39

MUSTONEN, PASI
80/1 Mallasjuoma 59

MUTCH, TOM
91/2 ProCards 441

MUTTON, JIM
87/8 Kitchener Rangers

MUUKKONEN, JARMO
92/3 Jyvas Hyva 118
93/4 Sisu 267
94/5 Sisu 81
95/6 Sisu 90
96/7 Sisu 85

MUZECHKA, MIKE
97/8 Portland Winter Hawks

MUZZATTI, JASON
02/3 Cardset 76
99/0 Cardset 314, Puck 5
92/3 Classic 114
92/3 Classic Four Sport 221
94/5 Cla. Images 52
96/7 Flair 42
93/4 Fleer Ultra 284
94/5 Leaf 470
97/8 Pa. Invincible R-40
95/6 Parkhurst 362
96/7 Pi. Be A Player 131, ✍ Aut. 131
94/5 Premier 373
91/2 ProCards 592
97/8 Score NYRa. 17
93/4 Upper Deck 482
95/6 Upper Deck 491
96/7 Upper Deck 71
96/7 UD CC 117
00/1 UD DEL 25
95/6 HART / Kids Club
96/7 HART / Kids Club
97/8 Hartford Wolf Pack
94/5 Saint John Flames
92/3 Salt Lake G'Eagles

MYAGKIKH, ALEXEI
99/0 Mir 263

MYDAN, SCOTT
90/1 7th..Sketch WHL 333
88/9 Portland Winter Hawks
89/0 Portland Winter Hawks

MYERS, ARAN
99/0 Guelph Storm

MYERS, MURRAY
73/4 Vancouver Blazers

MYERS, SCOTT
00/1 Quad City Mallards
99/0 Prince George Cougars

MYHRE, GEIR
92/3 Semic Nordisk 18

MYHRES, BRANTT
95/6 Donruss 45
95/6 Fleer Ultra 154
95/6 Leaf 75
97/8 Pacific CC 334
97/8 Pi. Be A Player 203, ✍ Aut. 203
90/1 7th..Sketch WHL 317
91/2 7th...Sketch WHL 360
00/1 To. Heritage 208
95/6 Upper Deck 23
95/6 TAMP / Sky Box
94/5 Atlanta Knights 24
95/6 Atlanta Knights

MYLANDER, KEVIN
93/4 Seattle Thunderbirds

MYLES, DAVID
90/1 7th..Sketch OHL 111
91/2 7th...Sketch OHL 191
89/0 Windsor Spitfires

MYLES, GORD
59/60 Whitby Dunlops

MYLES, MARK
89/0 7th..Sketch OHL 113
90/1 7th..Sketch OHL 366

MYLES, VIC
34-43 BeeHive-1 [NYRa.]

MYLLARI, RON
83/4 Ottawa 67's

MYLLYKOSKI, MIKKO
02/3 Cardset 223
98/9 Cardset 190
99/0 Cardset 110
97/8 Hockey-Box
93/4 Jyvas Hyva 45
93/4 Sisu 237
94/5 Sisu 317
95/6 Sisu 22
96/7 Sisu 110

MYLLYMAKI, ARI
66/7 Champion 117

MYLLYNIEMI, JERE
02/3 Cardset 224

MYLLYNIEMI, MIKKO
66/7 Champion 50
65/6 Hellas 40

MYLLYS, JARMO
02/3 Cardset 225
92/3 Bowman 125
98/9 Cardset 6, Leij. 2
99/0 Cardset AH A-ruutu
95 Globe 128
95 Hartwall Karjala
93/4 Jyvas Hyva 224
95/6 Kellogg's Pop-Ups 1
94/5 Leaf Elit Set 260, FA-4
95/6 Leaf Elit Set 74, 302, LM-12, S-8
91/2 O-Pee-Chee 8S
90/1 OPC Premier 80
91/2 OPC Premier 15
95 Panini Worlds 161
91/2 Parkhurst 162
88/9 ProCards / Kalamazoo
89/0 ProCards IHL 95
91/2 ProCards 509
95/6 Radio City
94 Semic 1
94 Semic 332
95 Semic 35, 207
93 Semic Sticker 47
93/4 Sisu 183
94/5 Sisu 160, SS-9
95/6 Sisu Gold 2
95/6 Sisu Limited 28
95 Suomen All-Star 1
92/3 Topps 251
92/3 To. Stadium 113
91/2 Upper Deck 537
92/3 Upper Deck E19
95/6 UD Elitserien 113, 230
97/8 UD Elitserien 117, S7
98/9 UD Elitserien 133, -DL 7
99/0 UD Elitserien 135, S10, ✍ Aut.
00/1 UD Elitserien 120, 202, M5, S4
96 Wien 1, SG3, AS1
91/2 SANJ / Sports Action

MYLNIKOV, DMITRI
98/9 Mir 22
99/0 Mir 60

MYLNIKOV, SERGEI
00/1 Mir 44
90/1 O-Pee-Chee 445
89 Semic Sticker 79
87/8 Soviet Stars
89/0 Soviet Stars
89/0 QUEB
89/0 QUEB / Gene. Foods
89/0 QUEB / Police

MYLNIKOV, SERGEI
99/0 Mir 47, 60

MYLYMOK, JEREMY
91/2 Air Canada SJHL C5
98/9 Chicago Wolves
98/9 Chicago Wolves Champs
96/7 Pensacola Ice Pilots
96/7 Toledo Storm

MYNTTINEN, MIKKO
70/1 Kuvajulkaisut 213
71/2 Williams Finnish 136
72/3 Williams Finnish 199
73/4 Williams Finnish 160

MYRE, PHIL
79/0 Dernière Heure
70/1 Eddie Sargent 112
71/2 Eddie Sargent 101
72/3 Eddie Sargent 2
70/1 Esso Power Player
74/5 Loblaws
72/3 O-Pee-Chee 43
73/4 O-Pee-Chee 77
74/5 O-Pee-Chee 270
75/6 O-Pee-Chee 308
76/7 O-Pee-Chee 17
77/8 O-Pee-Chee 193
78/9 O-Pee-Chee 87
79/0 O-Pee-Chee 189
80/1 O-Pee-Chee 8
72/3 Topps 109
73/4 Topps 77
75/6 Topps 308
76/7 Topps 17
77/8 Topps 193
78/9 Topps 87
79/0 Topps 189
80/1 Topps 8
71/2 Toronto Sun Photo
72/3 ATLF
74/5 ATLF
93/4 CHIC / Coke
81/2 COLR
89/0 DETR / Little Caesars
69/0 MONT / Pro Star
70/1 MONT
71/2 MONT / Pro Star
96/7 OTTA
02/3 OTTA
78/9 SLOU

MYRENG, KJELL ERIK
92/3 Semic Nordisk 78

MYRES, JOHNNY
24/5 Falcons Crescent 11

MYRRÄ, JOUKO
99/0 Cardset 105
00/1 Cardset 317
94/5 Sisu 344
95/6 Sisu 147

MYRVOLD, ANDERS
95/6 Donruss 228
96/7 Leaf 220
95/6 Parkhurst 517
96/7 Pi. Summit 197
94 Semic 254
98/9 UD Elitserien 54
99/0 UD Elitserien 6, S1
97/8 Providence Bruins

MYSHIKIN, V.
80 Olympic USSR

MYYRYLAINEN, REIJO
70/1 Kuvajulkaisut 283

N

NÄÄTÄNEN, MATTI
02/3 Cardset 238

NABOKOV, DIMITRI
99/0 BAP Mem. 263
00/1 BAP Mem. 363
97 Bowman 119
00/1 Mir 152
98/9 Pacific 150
97/8 Pa. Revolution 31
94/5 Select 159
94/5 SR Auto-Phonex 30, ✍ 30
95/6 SR Tetrad 70
95/6 SP 177
98/9 SPx Finite 19, 139
00/1 Topps 281
00/1 To. Chrome 176
98/9 UD Choice 50
95/6 Upper Deck 552
98/9 Upper Deck 319, GN29
99/0 Upper Deck 83
97/8 UD Black Diam. 85
98/9 UD G. Reserve 319
99/0 UD G. Reserve 83
98/9 UD MVP ✍ PS
99/0 UD MVP 127
99/0 Victory 180
97/8 Indianapolis Ice 20
99/0 Lowell Lock Monsters

NABOKOV, DMITRI
96/7 Regina Pats

NABOKOV, EVGENI
02/3 Atomic 86, -D 18
02/3 BAP All-Star 63, ✂ ASJ
02/3 BAP Mem. 14, ✂ ASJ38, ✂ AST23
02/3 Between the Pipes 9, 146, M24, ASJ6, ✂ GUE7, ✂ GB3, ✂ GUJ7, ✂ GSJ7, ✂ HSHSJers 12, ✂ ITN7, ✂ T4, ✍ Aut.
02/3 Bowman 84
02/3 Calder 3
02/3 Crown Royale 85, ✂ GWDP 19
02/3 eTopps 24
02/3 Exclusive 150, -EA 14
02/3 First Edition 72, 380, ✂ Jers.
02/3 Heads Up 108, -ITN 19, -S 18, ✂ GWQ 24, / Bobble
02/3 In The GU 63, 163
02/3 McDonald's 34, -GSNF 6
02/3 O-Pee-Chee 234
02/3 Pacific 337, -MI 7, ✂ GWJ 45
02/3 Pacific Complete 431
02/3 Parkhurst 11, -HHV 2, ✂ TT15
02/3 Parkhurst Retro 107
02/3 Pr. Stock Reserve -ICS 19, ✂ 141
02/3 PS Titanium 87
02/3 Quest for the Cup 86
02/3 Signature 7, ✍ 7, ✂ YP10, ✂ TQ18
02/3 SP Authentic 74, ✍ SotT, ✍ SotTD (x2)
02/3 SP GU 42
02/3 Sports Vault 290
02/3 SPx 63, 98
02/3 Stadium 51, -PSH3
02/3 Topps 234, OTG18
02/3 T. Chrome 128
02/3 To. Heritage 98
02/3 To. Limited 234
02/3 To. Total 19
02/3 Upper Deck 147, -LL11, -SA12
02/3 UD Artistic 74, R74, / Art
02/3 UD Classic 83
02/3 UD Honor 60
02/3 UD Mask 72, 73, 74, 104, / Mask, ✍ Mask
02/3 UD MVP 154
02/3 UD Piece 76, AC2
02/3 UD Premier 45
02/3 UD Rookie 88
02/3 UD Top Shelf 73
02/3 UD Vintage 215, 285, 316, T55
02/3 Vanguard 85, ✂ GWJ 41
02/3 Victory 179
01/2 Adrenaline 167, CL 19, PP 32
01/2 Atomic 85, Stat 9, TN 12
99/0 BAP Mem. 328
00/1 BAP Mem. 140
01/2 BAP Mem. 4, ✂ ASJ, ✂ ASE, ✂ ASN, ✂ AST, HSHS
01/2 BAP Update ✂ HSHSJers
01/2 BT Pipes 27, HSHS, -Mask, ✂ ASJ, ✂ DM, ✂ FW, ✂ GJ, ✂ JE, ✂ JS, ✂ GG, ✂ GT, ✂ ITN, ✂ TW, ✂ HSHSJers
01/2 Bowman 163
00/1 Crown Royale 140, 21CR-22
01/2 Crown Royale 124
00/1 Crown Royale CC, G-7
01/2 eTopps 6
01/2 Heads Up 84, ASGN 1, BTI 17, PP 7, SS 18
01/2 McDonald's 35, -FL 4
01/2 O-Pee-Chee 82
99/0 Omega 212
00/1 Pacific 362
01/2 Pacific 340, 441, 450, GCDC 19, SC 18, WAS 9
00/1 Parkhurst P-241
01/2 Parkhurst 93
00/1 Premier Plus ✍ PS
00/1 Pr. Stock 144, Roo. 21
01/2 Pr. Stock 85, GR 9, -PS 64
00/1 PS Titanium 143, 3SS-27, WAS-8
01/2 PS Titanium 122, TSS 8
01/2 PS Titanium Draft ✂ 86
00/1 PS Titanium Draft 143
00/1 Signature 292
01/2 Signat. 24, ✍ Aut. 24
00/1 SP Authentic 75
01/2 SP Authentic 73
01/2 SP GU 47
00/1 SPx 146
01/2 SPx 55
00/1 Stadion 125
01/2 Stadium 48,G31,NR4, ✍ NR
00/1 Topps 303
01/2 Topps 82, ✍ CA
00/1 To. Chrome 198
01/2 To. Chrome 82
00/1 To. Gold Label 92
00/1 To. Heritage 145
01/2 To. Heritage 2, 133
01/2 To. Reserve 10
01/2 UD PlayMakers Ltd 83
00/1 UD Reserve 73
01/2 Ultimate Mem. ✂ BAPL, ✂ CT, ✂ RA
01/2 Upper Deck 374, GL4, LL8
00/1 UD Black Diam. 108
01/2 UD Challenge 72, BB8
00/1 UD Ice 76
01/2 UD Ice 37
01/2 UD Mask 125, 187, / Mask
00/1 UD MVP 203
01/2 UD MVP 160, MM8
01/2 UD Premier 42
01/2 UD Top Shelf 36, -ASGN
01/2 UD Vintage 209, 216
00/1 Vanguard 145
01/2 Vanguard 86, SW 17, VT 9
00/1 Victory 278
01/2 Victory 289, 300, 437
99/0 Cleveland Lumberjacks
97/8 Kentucky Tho'blades
98/9 Kentucky Tho'blades
00/1 Kentucky Tho'blades

NACHBAUR, DON
81/2 O-Pee-Chee 138
82/3 Post [Hart.]
88/9 ProCards / Hershey
89/0 ProCards AHL 345
88/9 EDMO / Action 113

NACHTMANN, MARKUS
96/7 DEL 136

NADEAU, PATRICK
90/1 7th..Sketch LHJMQ 91
91/2 7th...Sketch LHJMQ 120
99/0 Quad City Mallards
00/1 Quad City Mallards

NADJIWAN, JAMIE
84/5 Sudbury Wolves

NADRACHAL, VLADIMIR
72 Panda MM-Toronto

NAGLER, MARCO
95/6 DEL 13

NAGURNY, SHAWN
82/3 Medicine Hat Tigers

NAGY, AARON
89/0 7th..Sketch OHL 32
90/1 7th..Sketch OHL 137
91/2 7th...Sketch OHL 365

NAGY, LADISLAV
02/3 First Edition 256
02/3 Pacific 301
02/3 Pacific Complete 138
02/3 Parkhurst Retro 142
02/3 Signature 92, ✍ 92
02/3 Sports Vault 267
02/3 To. Total 390
02/3 Upper Deck 382
02/3 UD MVP 142
02/3 UD Top Shelf 67
02/3 UD Vintage 195
02/3 Victory 166
99/0 BAP Mem. 385
00/1 BAP Mem. 286
99 Bowman 54, SC20
98/9 Collection Souvenir 21
99/0 Crown Royale 118
99/0 Omega 203
00/1 Pacific 355
00/1 Pr. Stock 141, PSR-20
93 Québec Pee Wee 1704
99/0 SP Authentic 115
01/2 SP Authentic 128
00/1 Topps 297
00/1 To. Chrome 192
99/0 To. Prmr. Plus 82
01/2 Upper Deck 136
00/1 UD MVP 204, ME8, ✍ PS, ✍ ME
01/2 UD MVP 149
01/2 UD Vintage 196
00/1 Vanguard 144
01/2 Victory 276
00/1 Worcester IceCats
98/9 Halifax Moosehead
98/9 Halifax Moosehead

NAGY, RICHARD
91/2 Air Canada SJHL 36
91/2 Air Canada SJHL A38

NAGY, ZOLTAN
79 Panini Sticker 317

NAIDA, ANATOLI
94/5 APS 271
95/6 APS 263
91/2 O-Pee-Chee 56R

NAKAYAMA, IWAO
79 Panini Sticker 287

NAMESTNIKOV, OLEG
00/1 Mir 86

NAMESTNIKOV, YEVGENY (JOHN)
93/4 Cla. Prospects 153
93/4 Donruss 502
94/5 Parkhurst 246
94/5 Score 218
95/6 Topps 46
00/1 Milwaukee Admirals
96/7 Syracuse Crunch

NANNE, LOU
77/8 Coke
71/2 Eddie Sargent 93
72/3 Eddie Sargent 111
70/1 Esso Power Player
74/5 Loblaws
69/0 O-Pee-Chee 198
71/2 O-Pee-Chee 240
72/3 O-Pee-Chee 10
73/4 O-Pee-Chee 246
74/5 O-Pee-Chee 325
75/6 O-Pee-Chee 143
76/7 O-Pee-Chee 173
77/8 O-Pee-Chee 36
72/3 Topps 93
75/6 Topps 143
76/7 Topps 173
77/8 Topps 36
71/2 Toronto Sun Photo
73/4 MINS
94/5 Minnesota G'Gophers

NANNE, MARTY
88/9 ProCards / Saginaw
89/0 ProCards IHL 54
90/1 ProCards 397

NANSEN, TOMAS
95/6 Leaf Elit Set 276

NANTAIS, RICHARD
76/7 O-Pee-Chee 357

NÄNZEN, TOMAS
94/5 Leaf Elit Set 56
90/1 Semic Elitserien 12
91/2 Semic Elitserien 209
95/6 UD Elitserien 157

NAPIER, MARK
80/1 Dernière Heure
86/7 Kraft Sports 20
79/0 O-Pee-Chee 222
80/1 O-Pee-Chee 111
81/2 O-Pee-Chee 178
82/3 O-Pee-Chee 178
82/3 O-Pee-Chee 189
83/4 O-Pee-Chee 182
83/4 O-Pee-Chee 192
84/5 O-Pee-Chee 105
85/6 O-Pee-Chee 253
86/7 OPC/Topps 183
81/2 OPC Sticker 36
82/3 OPC/Topps Sticker 38
82/3 OPC/Topps Sticker 39
83/4 OPC/Topps Sticker 64
83/4 OPC/Topps Sticker 65
86/7 OPC Sticker 75-202
75/6 OPC WHA 78
76/7 OPC WHA 108
77/8 OPC WHA 12
80/1 Pepsi Bottle Cap
82/3 Post [Mont.]
83/4 Souhaits Keychain [Canadiens]
79/0 Topps 222
80/1 Topps 111
81/2 Topps 23
87/8 BUFF / Blue Shield
87/8 BUFF / Won. Bread
88/9 BUFF / Blue Shield
88/9 BUFF / Won. Bread
84/5 EDMO
84/5 EDMO / Red Rooster
85/6 EDMO / Red Rooster
86/7 EDMO
86/7 EDMO / Red Rooster
88/9 EDMO / Action 28
83/4 MINS
84/5 MINS
78/9 MONT
79/0 MONT
80/1 MONT
81/2 MONT
82/3 MONT
82/3 MONT / Steinberg

NAPOLITANO, JOSEPH
90/1 7th..Sketch LHJMQ 249
91/2 7th...Sketch LHJMQ 268
88/9 Richelieu Riverains

NARDELLA, BOB
96/7 DEL 163
96 Wien 177
98/9 Chicago Wolves
98/9 Chicago Wolves Champs
99/0 Chicago Wolves
00/1 Chicago Wolves
01/2 Chicago Wolves

NARHI, MARKKU
71/2 Williams Finnish 307

NARINEN, MARTTI
72/3 Williams Finnish 179

NARVANEN, REIJO
72/3 Williams Finnish 273

NARVANMAA, JOUKO
91/2 Jyvas Hyva 65
92/3 Jyvas Hyva 178
93/4 Jyvas Hyva 320
89 Semic Sticker 35
93/4 Sisu 31

NASATO, LUCIO
94/5 Slapshot / Kitchener 15
95/6 Slapshot 13
98/9 Flint Generals

NASCHEIM, RICHARD
96 Wien 216

NASH, DON
52/3 Anonymous 28

NASH, RICK
02/3 Atomic 105
02/3 BAP All-Star 134
02/3 BAP Draft Toronto 1
02/3 BAP Mem. 272
02/3 Bowman 155, ✂ FFDS, ✂ FFJ, ✂ FFP, ✂ FFR, ✂ FFRP, ✂ FFS, ✂ FFTS, ✍ YSA, / ✍ Puck
02/3 Calder 112, -CR 8
02/3 Crown Royale 108, -RR 7, -RP 5
02/3 eTopps 39
02/3 Exclusive 196, -DFG 5, ✍ 196
02/3 First Edition 439H
02/3 Heads Up 126
02/3 In The GU 82, ✂ C2, ✂ E38
02/3 O-Pee-Chee 338
02/3 Pacific 126
02/3 Pacific Complete 557
02/3 PTC/ ASG 4
02/3 PTC/ Collections 3
02/3 PTC/ Spring Expo 3
02/3 Parkhurst 202, -HHC 7, ✂ GJ57, ✂ NH8
02/3 Parkhurst Retro 202, ✂ CH2, ✂ RF8, ✂ RJ10, ✂ HSHSJers, ✂ RM28
02/3 Pr. Stock Reserve 157, -CA 6, -MIT 2
02/3 PS Titanium 111, -ROT 6
02/3 Quest for the Cup 113, -CC 6
02/3 Signature 183, ✍ 183, ✂ AR12, ✂ FJ8, ✂ SGJ66
✍ 02/3 SP Authentic 184, ✍ SotT, ✍ ✂ Patch
02/3 SP GU 73
02/3 Sports Vault 193
02/3 SPx ✍ 149
02/3 Stadium 126
02/3 Topps 338
02/3 T. Chrome 175
02/3 To. Heritage 140
02/3 To. Total 414, TTC8
02/3 UD Superstars 261
02/3 Ultimate Mem. 2, ✂ CC, ✂ FO, ✂ GUJ, ✂ GUSJ, ✍ RAut
02/3 Upper Deck 232
02/3 UD Artistic 95, R92, CG6, CG9
02/3 UD Classic 109
02/3 UD Foundations 149
02/3 UD Honor 150, -SG9
02/3 UD Mask 178
02/3 UD Piece 127
02/3 UD Premier ✍ ✂ 80, ✂ Jers, ✂ JD, ✍ Sig
02/3 UD Rookie ✍ 172
02/3 UD Top Shelf 126
02/3 Vanguard 109, -IF 5, -PP 8
98 Québec Pee Wee 1367
00/1 UD Prospects 42
00/1 London Knights
00/1 London Knights
01/2 London Knights

NASH, SHANE
92 Québec Pee Wee 496
95/6 Slapshot 194

NASH, TOM
89/0 ProCards IHL 18

NASH, TYSON
02/3 UD MVP 164
02/3 UD Vintage 217, 286
99/0 BAP Mem. 344
00/1 BAP Mem. 344
99/0 NHL Power Play
01/2 O-Pee-Chee 213
99/0 Omega 198
99/0 Pacific 368
00/1 Pacific 348
00/1 Signature 54, ✍ Aut. 41
94/5 Slapshot Memorial 14
99/0 SP Authentic 114
01/2 Topps 213
00/1 To. Heritage 175
99/0 To. Prmr. Plus 98
01/2 Victory 311
99/0 SLOU / Taco Bell 23
96/7 Syracuse Crunch
01/2 Worcester IceCats
93/4 Kamloops Blazers

NASHEIM, RICHARD
94 Semic 244
93 Semic Sticker 282

NASIB, ERKAN
66/7 Champion 68
65/6 Hellas 122

NÄSLUND, MARKUS
02/3 Atomic 97, -CF 23, -PC 19
02/3 BAP All-Star 64, ✂ ASJ, ✂ HSHSJers
02/3 BAP Mem. 189, 229, ✂ ASJ39, ✂ FP29, ✂ TM19
02/3 Bowman 68
02/3 Calder 51, -CG 10, -HS 8, ✂ GWJ 24
02/3 Crown Royale 97, ✂ GWJ 23
02/3 eTopps 53
02/3 Exclusive 169, -MO 19
02/3 First Edition 148, 301, 369, 371, 407H, ✂ Jers., ✂ HSHSJers 30, ✂ TSL 19
02/3 Heads Up 122, -ITN 23
02/3 In The GU 75, 175, ✂ E31, ✂ F29, ✂ GUJ33, ✂ SJ33, ✂ T19
02/3 McDonald's 41, ✂ JP 19
02/3 O-Pee-Chee 32
02/3 Pacific 381, -MA 19
02/3 Pacific Complete 202
02/3 Parkhurst 103, -HHH 6, -HHP 5, -HHR 5, ✂ FP29, ✂ GJ5-, ✂ SJ50, ✂ TT18
02/3 Parkhurst Retro 8, ✂ RF29, ✂ RJ16, ✂ HH3, ✂ HSHSJers, ✂ RR5
02/3 Pr. Stock Reserve 97
02/3 PS Titanium 98
02/3 Quest for the Cup 97, -CTC 20, ✂ GWJ 23
02/3 Signature 31, ✍ 31, ✂ FJ29, ✂ SGJ33, ✂ TQ14
02/3 Slam Card
02/3 SP Authentic 85, ✍ SotT, ✂ SP
02/3 SP GU 48, ✂ AF (x2), ✂ PC, ✂ PH (x2)
02/3 Sports Vault 296
02/3 SPx 73, ✂ WM, ✂ SS, ✂ X
02/3 Stadium 15, ✂ NHLP11
02/3 Topps 32, HHC7, ✂ OTG2, ✂ OTG10, ✂ CC5, ✂ CC10
02/3 T. Chrome 32, ✂ FRF
02/3 To. Heritage 45
02/3 To. Heritage 120
02/3 To. Limited 32
02/3 To. Total 102, TP13
02/3 Ultimate Mem. ✂ Emb, ✂ GUJ, ✂ GUSJ, ✂ ITN, ✂ NP, ✂ UC
02/3 Upper Deck 171, ✂ ASJ, ✂ ASP, ✂ FF, ✂ LN, ✂ PL, ✂ PW, ✂ UDPL
02/3 UD Artistic 87, R87, / ✍ Art
02/3 UD Classic 97, ✂ HR, ✂ SC
02/3 UD Honor 68, 99
02/3 UD Mask ✂ IO, ✂ PG
02/3 UD MVP 179, HN7, SO13
02/3 UD Piece 87, ✂ PH, ✍ MD
02/3 UD Premier 53, ✍ Sig
02/3 UD Rookie 96, ✍ TD
02/3 UD Top Shelf 87, ✂ HT, ✂ ST, ✍ Sig
02/3 UD Vintage 246, 289, 308, GB 246, T62
02/3 Vanguard 97, -EMW 1, ✂ GWJ 48
02/3 Victory 211, -NP50
01/2 Adrenaline 191
91/2 Arena 12
01/2 Atomic 94, TN 14
99/0 Aurora 143
00/1 Aurora 144
98/9 Be A Player 140, ✍ Aut. 140
99/0 BAP Mem. 289
00/1 BAP Mem. 41
01/2 BAP Mem. 193, ✂ ASJ, ✂ ASE, ✂ ASN, ✂ AST, ✂ CoO
01/2 BAP Update ✂ HSHSJers
01/2 Bowman 18
91/2 Classic 13
91/2 Classic Four Sport 13
93/4 Cla. Prospects 26
99/0 Crown Royale 138
00/1 Crown Royale 104
01/2 Crown Royale 138
93/4 Donruss 269
93/4 Donruss RR 8
94/5 Donruss 51
99/0 Dynagon Ice 187
01/2 EASports
93/4 Fleer Ultra 395
93/4 Fleer Ultra WotF 10
94/5 Fleer Ultra 349
95/6 Fleer Ultra 291
95 Globe 43
01/2 Heads Up 94
00/1 Kraft 2
93/4 Leaf 289
93/4 Leaf FP 4
94/5 Leaf 211
99/0 Millenium 242, ✍ Aut. 242
98/9 NHL Power Play
01/2 O-Pee-Chee 15
97/8 Omega 233
98/9 Omega 239
99/0 Omega 236
98/9 Pacific 431
99/0 Pacific 429
00/1 Pacific 412, 449
01/2 Pacific 384, 424
97/8 Pacific CC 128
99/0 Pa. Paramount 238
00/1 Pa. Paramount 240
94 Panini Olympics 290
94/5 Panini Sticker I
96/7 Panini Sticker 296
97/8 Panini Sticker 239
98/9 Panini Sticker 220
99/0 Panini Sticker 310
00/1 Panini Sticker 212
93/4 Parkhurst 245
93/4 Parkhurst C5
94/5 Parkhurst 287
95/6 Parkhurst 163
00/1 Parkhurst P-216
01/2 Parkhurst 29, ✂ PS36, ✂ HSHSJers, ✂ T17, ✂ T26
94/5 Parkie SE136, seV4
93/4 Pinnacle 449
93/4 Pinnacle SR8
94/5 Pinnacle 370
96/7 Pi. Be A Player 123, ✍ Aut. 123
93/4 Power Play 412
94/5 Premier 44
00/1 Premier Plus 68
00/1 Pr. Stock 96, PS-58
01/2 Pr. Stock 94
00/1 PS Titanium 96
01/2 PS Titanium 137, ✂ DSJ 56, ✂ DSJ 58
01/2 PS Titanium Draft ✂ 96
99/0 Revolution 144
00/1 Revolution 144
93/4 Score 597
97/8 Score 150
97/8 Score Vanc. 7
95/6 Select CE 106
90/1 Semic Elitserien 23
91/2 Semic Elitserien 214
92/3 Semic Elitserien 240
92 Semic Sticker 67
93 Semic Sticker 14
00/1 Signature 247
01/2 Signat. 80, ✍ Aut. 80, ✂ FP29, ✂ GU70, ✂ GSJ70, ✂ HSHSJers 35, ✂ TM29
95/6 SP 116
00/1 SP Authentic 87
01/2 SP Authentic 85, ✍ SotT, ✍ SotTT
01/2 SP GU 56, ✂ AF, ✂ AFD
99/0 SPx 151
00/1 SPx 68
01/2 SPx 66, 80
99/0 Stadium 83
00/1 Stadium 153
01/2 Stadium 49
91/2 Star Pics 41
99/0 Topps 171
00/1 Topps 188
01/2 Topps 15
99/0 To. Chrome 171
00/1 To. Chrome 125
01/2 To. Chrome 15
95/6 To. Finest 154
98/9 To. Finest 90
99/0 To. Gold Label 58
00/1 To. Gold Label 13, B10
00/1 To. Heritage 136
01/2 To. Heritage 16
99/0 To. Prmr. Plus 42
01/2 To. Reserve 65
93/4 To. Stadium 393
00/1 To. Stars 79
01/2 UD PlayMakers Ltd 97
00/1 UD Reserve 83
91/2 Ultimate Draft Pick 13, 69, 76, 83, ✍ Aut.
92/3 Upper Deck 234
93/4 Upper Deck 500, SP-123
94/5 Upper Deck 190, SP-151
95/6 Upper Deck 73, SE-67
96/7 Upper Deck 170
97/8 Upper Deck 173
98/9 Upper Deck 379
99/0 Upper Deck 298
00/1 Upper Deck 167
01/2 Upper Deck 167, CT13, FF3, SS18, ✂ PF
94/5 UD BAP ✍ 68
00/1 UD Black Diam. 57
01/2 UD Challenge 86
96/7 UD CC 275
97/8 UD Coll. Choice 261
95/6 UD Elitserien 245
98/9 UD G. Reserve 379
99/0 UD G. Reserve 298
01/2 UD Honor Roll ✂ GAJ
01/2 UD Ice 41
00/1 UD Legends 128
01/2 UD Mask 95
99/0 UD MVP 206
00/1 UD MVP 177
01/2 UD MVP 179
99/0 UD MVP Cup 183
01/2 UD Premier 49, ✍ Sig
00/1 UD Pros&Prosp. 83
99/0 UD Retro 76
01/2 UD Top Shelf 43, ✂ J
00/1 UD Vintage 347, 357, 358
01/2 UD Vintage 244, 250, 251
00/1 Vanguard 96
01/2 Vanguard 97
99/0 Victory 296
00/1 Victory 229
01/2 Victory 338, 419
99/0 WGretzky 170
93/4 PITT / Foodland 20
94/5 PITT / Foodland 15
95/6 PITT / Foodland 4
96/7 VANC / IGA
01/2 VANC / Coke

NÄSLUND, MATS
02/3 UD Foundations 52, ✂ LI, ✍ SG
00/1 Alfabilder
83/4 Dernière Heure
95/6 Donruss 53
88/9 Esso All-Star
94/5 Fleer 14
88/9 Frito Lay
83/4 Funmate Puffy 1 [w/]
95 Globe 72
89/0 Kraft 23
86/7 Kraft Sports 33
94/5 Leaf Elit Set GC 14
83/4 O-Pee-Chee 193
84/5 O-Pee-Chee 267
85/6 OPC/Topps 102
86/7 OPC/Topps 161
87/8 OPC/Topps 16
87/8 OPC/Topps Box L
88/9 OPC/Topps 156
89/0 OPC/Topps 118, / Box H
88/9 OPC Stars 26
83/4 OPC/Topps Sticker 71
84/5 OPC Sticker 155
84/5 OPC Sticker 156
85/6 OPC Sticker 131
86/7 OPC Sticker 11
86/7 OPC Sticker 122-182
87/8 OPC Sticker 6
88/9 OPC Sticker 50
88/9 OPC Sticker 215-85
89/0 opcSticker 46
87/8 Panini Sticker 61
88/9 Panini Sticker 259
88/9 Panini Sticker 406
89/0 Panini Sticker 234
90/1 Panini Sticker 62
91/2 Pinnacle 389
87/8 Pro Sport CW17
91/2 Semic Elitserien 188
91/2 Semic Elitserien 349
92/3 Semic Elitserien 220
82 Semic Sticker 13
91 Semic Sticker 49
92 Semic Sticker 63
83/4 Souhaits Keychain [Canadiens]
86/7 OPC/Topps - Stick. 8
95/6 UD CC 321
83/4 Vachon 50-70
82/3 MONT
82/3 MONT / Steinberg
83/4 MONT
84/5 MONT
85/6 MONT
85/6 MONT / Provigo
86/7 MONT
87/8 MONT
87/8 MONT / Kodak Poster
87/8 MONT / Vachon 27
87/8 MONT / Vachon 45
87/8 MONT / Vachon 46
87/8 MONT / Vachon 47
87/8 MONT / Vachon 48
87/8 MONT / Vachon 87
88/9 MONT
89/0 MONT
89/0 MONT / Kraft

NÄSLUND, MAWRKUS
01/2 McDonald's 41

NASREDDINE, ALAIN
98/9 Bowman's Best 130
93/4 Cla. 4 Sport 225
91/2 7th...Sketch LHJMQ 277
00/1 Hamilton Bulldogs
01/2 Hamilton Bulldogs
01/2 Hamilton Bulldogs/ Staz
97/8 Indianapolis Ice 21

NASREDDINE, SAMY
97 Bowman 45
97/8 Peoria Rivermen

NASSTROM, ANDERS
92/3 Semic Elitserien 224

NASTER, MARIO
94/5 DEL 167

NASVALL, FREDRIK
00/1 UD Elitserien 28

NATTRASS, RALPH
45-64 BeeHive-2 [Chic.]

NATTRESS, RIC
91/2 Bowman 266
92/3 Bowman 63
92/3 Fleer Ultra 374
88/9 OPC/Topps 238
90/1 O-Pee-Chee 459
92/3 O-Pee-Chee 98
88/9 OPC Sticker 91-219
87/8 Panini Sticker 307
90/1 Panini/CGY 13
90/1 Pro Set 426
91/2 Pro Set 363
91/2 Score CAN 249
92/3 Score 344
93/4 Score 381
92/3 Topps 219
91/2 To. Stadium 217
92/3 To. Stadium 328
87/8 CALG / Red Rooster
90/1 CALG / McGavin's
91/2 CALG / IGA
82/3 MONT
82/3 MONT / Steinberg
83/4 MONT
84/5 MONT
92/3 PHIL / UD Sheet
92/3 PHIL / J.C. Penney

NATYSHAK, MIKE
88/9 ProCards / Halifax

NAUD, DANIEL
94/5 DEL 10

NAUD, ERIC
97/8 Providence Bruins
99/0 Rouyn-Noranda

NAUD, SYLVAIN
90/1 7th..Sketch LHJMQ 52
90 7th..Sketch Mem.Cup 63
97/8 New Mexico Scorpions

NAUKKARINEN, SEPPO
65/6 Hellas 132

NAULT, FRANCIS
98/9 Muskegon Fury
99/0 Muskegon Fury

NAUMANN, ANDREAS
95/6 DEL 44
91/2 Upper Deck 678
91/2 Upper Deck WJC 41

NAUMENKO, GREGG
00/1 BAP Mem. 516
01/2 BAP Mem. 205
01/2 BT Pipes 37, ✂ GJ
01/2 O-Pee-Chee 308
01/2 Topps 308
01/2 UD MVP 189
01/2 Victory 361
99/0 Cincinnati M'Ducks

NAUMENKO, NICK
00/1 Cleveland Lumberjacks
99/0 Kansas City Blades
98/9 Las Vegas Thunder

NAUMENKO, OLEG
00/1 Mir 14

NAUSS, RYAN
93/4 Slapshot / Peterborough 19

NAVRATIL, MILAN
94/5 APS 12
95/6 APS 115
96/7 APS 257
97/8 APS 188
98/9 DS 64
96/7 DS Sticker 88
97/8 DS Sticker 161
98/9 OFS 47
99/0 OFS 215
00/1 OFS 374

NAVROTSKIN, VADIM
00/1 Mir 350

NAYLOR, MIKE
95/6 Dayton Bombers

NAZAROV, ANDREI
02/3 Pacific 302
00/1 BAP Mem. 417
01/2 BAP Update ✂ TC9, ✂ TC28
92/3 Classic 7
94/5 Classic 87
92/3 Classic Four Sport 157
94/5 Cla. Images 93
93/4 Cla. Prospects 180
93/4 Donruss 490
95/6 Donruss 187
95/6 Edge Ice 146
94/5 Fleer 199
95/6 Fleer Metal 132
94/5 Fleer Ultra 367
95/6 Fleer Ultra 303
94/5 Leaf 328
95/6 Leaf 131
99/0 Pacific 59
00/1 Pacific 71
01/2 Pacific 35
97/8 Pacific CC 307
97/8 Panini Sticker 235
99/0 Panini Sticker 195
00/1 Panini Sticker 119
94/5 Parkhurst 216
95/6 Parkhurst 186
01/2 Parkhurst 363
95/6 Pinnacle 190
94/5 Premier 461
92/3 Red Ace Blue 26
92/3 Red Ace Violet 23
94/5 Score 239
95/6 Topps 121
00/1 Topps 249
94/5 Upper Deck 270
95/6 Upper Deck SE164
96/7 UD CC 242
99/0 UD MVP Cup 34
92/3 SANJ / Pacific Bell
93/4 Kansas City Blades
94/5 Kansas City Blades 17

NAZAROV, DMITRI
98/9 Mir 150
99/0 Mir 158

NAZEN, TOMAS
92/3 Semic Elitserien 232

NCWANA, LLEW
93/4 Thunder Bay Senators
94/5 Thunder Bay Senators
95/6 Thunder Bay Senators

NDUR, RUMUN
99/0 Pacific 275
01/2 Pacific 21
94/5 Sig. Rookies 37, ✍ 37
93/4 Slapshot / Guelph 25
94/5 Slapshot / Guelph 24
98/9 SP Authentic ✍ SotT
97/8 Upper Deck 184
98/9 Upper Deck 229
98/9 UD G. Reserve 229
01/2 Norfolk Admirals
95/6 Rochester Americans
96/7 Rochester Americans
97/8 Rochester Americans

NEAL, FRANK
80/1 Mallasjuoma 3
78/9 SM-Liiga 113

NEAL, JAY
00/1 Kudos 81
94/5 Toledo Storm

NEAL, MARTIN
00/1 Kudos 73

NEALE, HARRY
97/8 Pi. CBC Sports 9

NEALE, JOEY
00/1 Sherbrooke Castors 14

NEATON, PAT
94/5 Classic 107, T53
93/4 Cla. Prospects 10
98/9 EBK IHL All-Star
95/6 Edge Ice 174
94/5 Leaf 469
95 Panini Worlds 216
93/4 Power Play 413
94/5 Premier 483
93/4 Score 632
93/4 Cleveland Lumberjacks
98/9 Orlando Solar Bears
98/9 Orlando Solar Bears Geico

NEATON, PATRICK
99/0 Utah Grizzlies
00/1 Utah Grizzlies

NECAS, ANTONIN
94/5 APS 164

NECKAR, STANISLAV
02/3 Pacific Complete 149
96/7 APS 348
93/4 Classic 106
94/5 Classic ✍ Aut.
95/6 Donruss 131
95/6 Fleer Ultra 113
95/6 Leaf 43
99/0 NHL Power Play
00/1 Pa. Paramount 191
96/7 Panini Sticker 54
99/0 Panini Sticker 278
95/6 Parkhurst 148
95/6 Pinnacle 49
96/7 Pi. Be A Player 184, ✍ Aut. 184
95/6 POG 199
95/6 Topps 91
01/2 To. Reserve 73
95/6 To. Stadium 112
94/5 Upper Deck 377
95/6 Upper Deck 68
95/6 UD CC 170
96/7 UD CC 185
99/0 Victory 232
98/9 NYRA
94/5 OTTA
95/6 OTTA
96/7 OTTA
97/8 OTTA

NEDOMA, MILAN
94/5 APS 102
95/6 APS 56
96/7 APS 243, 404
97/8 APS 270
97/8 DS 4
98/9 DS 31
99/0 DS 31
00/1 DS 16
96/7 DS Sticker 78
97/8 DS Sticker 11, 70
98/9 OFS 196
99/0 OFS 184
00/1 OFS 324
01/2 OFS 131
91/2 Upper Deck WJC 89

NEDOMANSKY, VACLAV (BIG NED)
72 Hellas MM-Jenkki 92
74 Hellas MM-Jenkki 79
70/1 Kuvajulkaisut 55
69/0 Mästär Serien 4
69/0 Mästär Serien 5
69/0 Mästär Serien 8
79/0 O-Pee-Chee 132
80/1 O-Pee-Chee 202
81/2 O-Pee-Chee 94
81/2 OPC Sticker 125
74/5 OPC WHA 49
75/6 OPC WHA 27
76/7 O-Pee-Chee WHA 1
76/7 OPC WHA 64
76/7 OPC WHA 120
98/9 OFS Leg. 1
72 Panda MM-Toronto
82/3 Post [Detr.]
72 Semic Sticker 33
74 Semic Sticker 57
91 Semic Sticker 249
77-79 Sportscaster 74-24
77-79 Sports. FIN 20-469
79/0 Topps 132
80/1 Topps 202
81/2 Topps 94 [West]
96 Wien HL18
71/2 Williams Finnish 33
72/3 Williams Finnish 16
73/4 Williams Finnish 57
79/0 DETR
80/1 DETR

NEDOMANSKY, VACLAV (JR.)
98/9 Grand Rapids Griffins
94/5 Knoxville Cherokees
96/7 Knoxville Cherokees
95/6 Las Vegas Thunder
99/0 Louisiana Ice Gators
99/0 Mississippi S'Wolves

NEDOROST, ANDREJ
02/3 Pacific Complete 511
02/3 SPx 108
02/3 Upper Deck 203
02/3 UD Foundations 127
02/3 UD MVP 200
02/3 UD Piece 126
02/3 UD Vintage 329
01/2 BAP Mem. 403
99/0 Eishockey 362
00/1 OFS 74
01/2 Parkhurst 313
01/2 UD Mask 142
01/2 Syracuse Crunch
02/3 Syracuse Crunch

NEDOROST, DAVID
99/0 OFS 185

NEDOROST, VACLAV
02/3 Calder 65
02/3 First Edition 255
02/3 Heads Up ✂ GWQ 8
02/3 O-Pee-Chee 307
02/3 Pacific Complete 534
02/3 Topps 307
02/3 To. Limited 307
02/3 To. Total 151
02/3 UD Piece ✍ MD
01/2 Adrenaline 206, RR 6
01/2 Atomic 107, RR 3
01/2 BAP Mem. 308
01/2 Bowman 147
01/2 Crown Royale 151, RR 5
01/2 DS 56
01/2 Heads Up 105
01/2 O-Pee-Chee 333
98/9 OFS 417
99/0 OFS 284
01/2 Pacific 455
01/2 PTC Calder 4
01/2 PTC High Voltage 4
01/2 Parkhurst 284
01/2 Pr. Stock 118, MiT 3, RR 3, -PS 95
01/2 PS Titanium 153, ✂ DSJ 14
01/2 PS Titanium Draft 116, ✂ 26
01/2 Signat. 204, ✍ Aut. 204
01/2 SP Authentic ✍ 176
01/2 SP GU 71
01/2 SPx 101
01/2 SPx Rookie RR8
01/2 Stadium 126
01/2 Topps 333
01/2 To. Chrome 151
01/2 To. Heritage 145
01/2 To. Reserve 105
01/2 UD PlayMakers Ltd 112
01/2 Upper Deck 215
01/2 UD Challenge 102
01/2 UD Honor Roll 69
01/2 UD Ice 50
01/2 UD Mask 140
01/2 UD Premier 110
01/2 UD Top Shelf 69
01/2 UD Vintage 278
01/2 Vanguard 107, PP 3
01/2 Hershey Bears

NEDVED, JAROSLAV
94/5 APS 76
95/6 APS 278
96/7 APS 125
97/8 APS 7
98/9 Cardset 58
93/4 Cla. Prospects 6
97/8 DS 82
99/0 DS 146
96/7 DS Sticker 58
97/8 DS Sticker 212
99/0 OFS 109, 503
00/1 OFS 298
01/2 OFS 35
93/4 Cincinnati Cyclones

NEDVED, PETR
02/3 O-Pee-Chee 96
02/3 Pacific 257
02/3 Pacific Complete 90
02/3 Parkhurst Retro 129
02/3 Sports Vault 87
02/3 Topps 96
02/3 To. Limited 96
02/3 To. Total 205
02/3 Upper Deck 114
02/3 UD MVP 123
02/3 UD Vintage 167, GB 167
02/3 Victory 142
01/2 Adrenaline 129, ✂ GWJ 29
95/6 APS - Insert
96/7 APS 385
97/8 APS 25
99/0 Aurora 96
00/1 Aurora 97
98/9 Be A Player 243, ✍ Aut. 243
99/0 BAP Mem. 49
00/1 BAP Mem. 136
01/2 BAP Mem. 80
91/2 Bowman 324
92/3 Bowman 396
01/2 Crown Royale ✂ TT 15
93/4 Donruss 356
93/4 Donruss 486
95/6 Donruss 252
96/7 Donruss 76
97/8 Donruss 152
97/8 Do. Canadian 71
97/8 Do. Preferred 33
00/1 DS JT7
01/2 DS 40, IH 6
97/8 DS Sticker 223
99/0 Dynagon Ice 133
96/7 Flair 79
94/5 Fleer 137
96/7 Fleer 88, 143, ART-17
96/7 Fl. Picks F50-32, FF-10, JE-9
92/3 Fleer Ultra 226, -UI 17
93/4 Fleer Ultra 68
94/5 Fleer Ultra 141, 333, GG-7
95/6 Fleer Ultra 292
95 Globe 97
01/2 Heads Up ✂ JQ 14
90/1 Kraft 38
91/2 Kraft 11
93/4 Leaf 78
94/5 Leaf 360
95/6 Leaf 301
96/7 Leaf 71
97/8 Leaf 51
94/5 L. Limited 67
96/7 L. Limited 39, S-12
96/7 L. Preferred 82, LS-56
97/8 Limited 156
96/7 Maggers 123
96/7 Metal Univ. 129
99/0 Millenium 161, ✍ Aut. 161
91/2 O-Pee-Chee 141
92/3 O-Pee-Chee 89
01/2 O-Pee-Chee 83
90/1 OPC Premier 81
00/1 OFS 388
98/9 Omega 160
99/0 Omega 152
99/0 Pacific 276
00/1 Pacific 268
01/2 Pacific 265
97/8 Pacific CC 13, SS-8A
97/8 Pa. Dynagon 104, T-22, BKS-80
97/8 Pa. Invincible 115, R-163
97/8 Pa. Paramount 153
99/0 Pa. Paramount 155
00/1 Pa. Paramount 166
98/9 Pa. Revolution 96
90/1 Panini/VAN 17
91/2 Panini Sticker 49
92/3 Panini Sticker 31
92/3 Panini Sticker 300
93/4 Panini Sticker 171
94/5 Panini Sticker 137
95/6 Panini Sticker 104
96/7 Panini Sticker 56
97/8 Panini Sticker 52
00/1 Panini Sticker 61
91/2 Parkhurst 178
92/3 Parkhurst 418
92/3 Parkhurst 449
94/5 Parkhurst V44
95/6 Parkhurst 438
00/1 Parkhurst P-220
01/2 Parkhurst 101
94/5 Parkie SE116
91/2 Pinnacle 192
92/3 Pinnacle 127
92/3 Pinnacle 249
93/4 Pinnacle 106
94/5 Pinnacle 58, WE18
96/7 Pinnacle 108
97/8 Pinnacle 124
97/8 Pi. Certified 95
97/8 Pi. Inside 133
95/6 Pi. Summit 91
96/7 Pi. Summit 148
97/8 Pi. Totally 95
95/6 Pi. Zenith 103
96/7 Pi. Zenith 54, A-13
95/6 Playoff 300
94/5 POG 169
95/6 POG 212
93/4 Power Play 254
93/4 Power Play 490
93/4 Premier 6
93/4 Premier - Canada 15
94/5 Premier 286
01/2 Pr. Stock -PS 50, ✂ GUG 68
00/1 PS Titanium ✂ GUG 40, ✂ GUG-117
00/1 PS Titanium Draft ✂ 67
90/1 Pro Set 402, 643
91/2 Pro Set 235
99/0 Revolution 99
00/1 Revolution 98
90/1 Score 50T
91/2 Score 124
91/2 Score CAN 124
92/3 Score 101
93/4 Score 231
93/4 Score IS 22
94/5 Score CT2
95/6 Score 220
96/7 Score 38
97/8 Score 143
97/8 Score Pitt. 6
90/1 Sco. Young Stars 37
94/5 Select 120
00/1 Signature 154, ✍ Aut. 37
95/6 SBx Emotion 140
95/6 SBx Impact 133
96/7 SBx Impact 103, BR-16
96/7 SP 128
01/2 SP Authentic 56
99/0 SPx 99
98/9 SPx Prospects 41
00/1 Stadion 80
99/0 Stadium 58
00/1 Stadium 159
01/2 Stadium 88
92/3 Topps 422
95/6 Topps 304
99/0 Topps 182
00/1 Topps 80
01/2 Topps 83
99/0 To. Chrome 182
00/1 To. Chrome 63
01/2 To. Chrome 83
94/5 Topps Finest 101
99/0 To. Gold Label 61
01/2 To. Heritage 94
96/7 To. Picks 37
99/0 To. Prmr. Plus 51
91/2 To. Stadium 280
92/3 To. Stadium 457
93/4 To. Stadium 18
94/5 To. Stadium 205
95/6 To. Stadium 64
90/1 Upper Deck 351, 353
91/2 Upper Deck 227
91/2 Upper Deck E5
92/3 Upper Deck 263
94/5 Upper Deck 164, SP-141
95/6 Upper Deck 462, SE-154
96/7 Upper Deck 134, SS26B
97/8 Upper Deck 137
99/0 Upper Deck 259
00/1 Upper Deck 343
01/2 Upper Deck 347
95/6 UD BAP 156, ✍ S156
96/7 UD Black Diam. 95
95/6 UD CC 323
96/7 UD CC 219, 328
97/8 UD Coll. Choice 209, SQ3
99/0 UD G. Reserve 259
99/0 UD Gretzky Excl. 72
96/7 UD Ice 56
01/2 UD Mask 62
99/0 UD MVP 134
00/1 UD MVP 120
01/2 UD MVP 128
99/0 UD MVP Cup 121
00/1 UD Vintage 243
99/0 Victory 193
00/1 Victory 155
01/2 Victory 234
99/0 WGretzky 110
98/9 NYRA
95/6 PITT / Foodland 17
90/1 VANC / Mohawk
91/2 VANC
91/2 VANC / Photo
92/3 VANC / Road Trip
98/9 Las Vegas Thunder

NEDVED, ZDENEK
95/6 Bowman 91
99/0 Cardset 84
00/1 Cardset 306, MB-7
95/6 Classic 97
95/6 Donruss 157, RR-5
96/7 Leaf 230
93/4 Parkhurst 518
95/6 Parkhurst 254
96/7 Pinnacle 243
96/7 Pi. Summit 193
93/4 Slapshot / Sudbury 9
94/5 Slapshot / Promo
94/5 Slapshot / Sudbury 8
95/6 To. Stadium 139
95/6 Upper Deck 441
97/8 St. John's Maple Leafs
92/3 Sudbury Wolves
93/4 Sudbury Wolves

NEEDHAM, BILL
60/1 Cleveland Barons
72/3 Clev. WHA / Linnett

NEEDHAM, BOB
92/3 BCJHL 54

NEEDHAM, MIKE
92/3 Classic 108
92/3 Fleer Ultra 380
93/4 Leaf 214
92/3 OPC Premier 106
92/3 Parkhurst 370
93/4 Premier 472
90/1 ProCards 375
91/2 ProCards 297
90 7th..Sketch Mem.Cup 10
93/4 To. Stadium 452
92/3 Upper Deck 489
92/3 PITT / Coke-Clark
93/4 PITT / Foodland 15
95/6 Adirondack Red Wings
87/8 Kamloops Blazers
88/9 Kamloops Blazers
89/0 Kamloops Blazers

NEELY, BOB
74/5 Loblaws
74/5 O-Pee-Chee 272
75/6 O-Pee-Chee 245
76/7 O-Pee-Chee 194
77/8 O-Pee-Chee 347
75/6 Topps 245
76/7 Topps 194
73/4 TORO
74/5 TORO
75/6 TORO
76/7 TORO
77/8 TORO

NEELY, CAM
02/3 SP Authentic ✂ TP
02/3 Ultimate Mem. ✂ Cor, ✂ FS (x2)
02/3 UD Foundations 3, 107, ✂ CH, ✂ CH, ✂ LI, ✂ MS, ✂ PP, ✂ PS, ✍ SG
02/3 UD Piece ✂ EC, ✂ HS, ✍ MD
99/0 BAP Mem. AH-2, ✍ AH-2
01/2 BAP Update ✂ PTT1
95/6 Bicycle Sports Aces 10-Spade
90/1 Bowman 29
91/2 Bowman 348
91/2 Bowman 366
92/3 Bowman 62
95/6 Bowman 17
94/5 Classic ✍ Aut.
93/4 Donruss 29
93/4 Donruss ES U4
94/5 Donruss 269, D-4
95/6 Donruss 165
96/7 Donruss 205
95/6 Do. Elite 14
93/4 EA Sports 11
94/5 Flair 11
94/5 Fleer 15, H-8
01/2 Fleer Greats 56, -BC, ✂ OSS, ✍ Aut.
01/2 Fleer Legacy 5, 53, ✂ HK, ✂ ITC
95/6 Fleer Metal 9, IW-9
92/3 Fleer Ultra 7
93/4 Fleer Ultra 138
94/5 Fleer Ultra 13, AW-8, RLS-6, U-6
95/6 Fleer Ultra 12, CC-12, RLS-7
88/9 Frito Lay
93/4 Hockey Wit 36
95/6 Hoyle / East. 5-Diamond
92/3 Humpty Dumpty
84/5 Kelowna Wings &...
89/0 Kraft 56
90/1 Kraft 39, 84
94/5 Kraft / PB
95/6 Kraft / IP
96/7 Kraft / PB
93/4 Leaf 99
94/5 Leaf 267, GLS-9
95/6 Leaf 113
96/7 Leaf 86
94/5 L. Limited 49
95/6 L. Limited 81
96/7 Maggers 15
91/2 McDonald's Mc-01
91/2 McDonald's McH5
94/5 McDonald's McD-22
95/6 Cool Trade 1
84/5 O-Pee-Chee 327
85/6 O-Pee-Chee 228
86/7 O-Pee-Chee 250
87/8 OPC/Topps 69
88/9 OPC/Topps 58
90/1 OPC/Topps 69, 201
90/1 Topps-TL 3
91/2 O-Pee-Chee 170
91/2 O-Pee-Chee 192
91/2 O-Pee-Chee 266
92/3 O-Pee-Chee 174
89/0 OPC/Topps 15, / Box K
90/1 OPC Premier 82
91/2 OPC Premier 107
88/9 OPC Stars 27
87/8 OPC Sticker 143
88/9 OPC Sticker 22
88/9 OPC Sticker 167
89/0 opcSticker 33
87/8 Panini Sticker 10
88/9 Panini Sticker 191
88/9 Panini Sticker 213
89/0 Panini Sticker 182, 192
90/1 Panini Sticker 9, 327
91/2 Panini Sticker 176
91/2 Panini Sticker 332
92/3 Panini Sticker 143
93/4 Panini Sticker 3
94/5 Panini Sticker 3, 238b
95/6 Panini Sticker 8, 153
96/7 Panini Sticker 3
92/3 Parkhurst 248
92/3 Parkhurst CP14
93/4 Parkhurst 10
94/5 Parkhurst 11, V64
95/6 Parkhurst 12
01/2 Parkhurst ✍ PA49
91/2 Pinnacle 78
91/2 Pinnacle B-6
92/3 Pinnacle 25
92/3 Pinnacle 232
93/4 Pinnacle 30
94/5 Pinnacle 65, BR12, GR17, TP12
95/6 Pinnacle CS 5, FS-5, FC-1
96/7 Pinnacle 136
95/6 Pi. FANtasy 1
95/6 Pi. Summit 81, GMC-12, MH-4
96/7 Pi. Summit 29
95/6 Pi. Zenith 61
95/6 Playoff 8, 120, 228
94/5 POG 39, 328, 336
95/6 POG 31, I-003, I-025
93/4 Power Play 22
93/4 Premier 254
94/5 Premier 129, 419, 505, TF-8
95/6 Pro Magnet 13
90/1 Pro Set 11, 358
91/2 Pro Set 5
91/2 Pro Set 300
92/3 Pro Set 8
91/2 Pro Set Platinum 1
90/1 Score 4, 323, 340
90/1 Sco. Hot Cards 67
91/2 Score 6
91/2 Score 301
91/2 Score CAN 6
91/2 Score CAN 305
92/3 Score 10
93/4 Score 342
94/5 Score 4, CI-8, DT-23, TF-2
95/6 Score 209, BB-3, L-3
96/7 Score 111, CI-4
91/2 Score Shows 8
94/5 Select 39
95/6 Select CE 57, GT-7
89 Semic Sticker 71
91 Semic Sticker 68
95/6 SBx Emotion 10, NP1
95/6 SBx Impact 11, 238, IQ10
94/5 SP 9, P-23
95/6 SP 6, E4
97/8 SP Authentic ✍ M3, ✍ T3, ✍ T6
96/7 SPx 4
95/6 SLU
95/6 Super Sticker 7
88/9 OPC/Topps - Stick. 9
92/3 Topps 32
95/6 Topps 15, 221, HGC23, M11, 7PL, PF10
94/5 Topps Finest 22, BBB-3, BBM-5
95/6 To. Finest 9, 110
95 Topps Finest Bronze 10
96/7 To. Picks 137
99/0 To. Prmr. Plus ✍ CS2, ✍ CSC 1
91/2 To. Stadium 64
92/3 To. Stadium 316
93/4 To. Stadium 216
94/5 To. Stadium 8, 266
95/6 To. Stadium EC163, N3
94/5 TSC Members Only 4
95/6 TSC Members Only 36
95/6 T. Super Skills 63
00/1 UD Heroes 120, ✍ SG
01/2 Ultimate Mem. ✂ Corn., ✂ Deca.
90/1 Upper Deck 156, 493
91/2 Upper Deck 78
91/2 Upper Deck 234
92/3 Upper Deck 86
93/4 Upper Deck 356, SP-10
94/5 Upper Deck 364, R33, SP-6
95/6 Upper Deck 1, 237, AS-10, F-5, R-1, SE-94
96/7 Upper Deck 13
95/6 UD ASG MVP22
94/5 UD BAP R143
95/6 UD CC 102, 355, C14
96/7 UD CC 16, 310, UD41, S5
00/1 UD Legends 9, 13, EG6, ✍ ES
01/2 UD Legends 5, ✂ M, ✂ TT, ✍ ES
01/2 UD Premier ✍ SigS
88/9 BOST / Sports Action
88/9 BOST / Sports Action
89/0 BOST / Sports Action
89/0 BOST / Sports Action
90/1 BOST / Sports Action
91/2 BOST / Sports Action
91/2 BOST / Sports Action
98/9 BOST / Alumni 8
84/5 VANC
85/6 VANC

NEELY, CAM
02/3 Fleer Throwbacks 81, 3SO, ✂ 3SO, ✂ 11SW

NEHRLING, LUCAS
00/1 Albany River Rats
99/0 Muskegon Fury

NEIL, CHRIS
02/3 First Edition 375
02/3 Pacific Complete 259
02/3 Signature GS-21
02/3 To. Total 107
02/3 Upper Deck 370
02/3 UD Vintage 313
01/2 Adrenaline 218
01/2 Atomic 117
01/2 BAP Mem. 325
01/2 BAP Update ✂ TC8, ✂ TC38
01/2 Crown Royale 172
01/2 Heads Up 113
01/2 O-Pee-Chee 351
01/2 Parkhurst 259
01/2 Pr. Stock 133
01/2 PS Titanium 173
01/2 PS Titanium Draft 154
01/2 Signat. 219, ✍ Aut. 219
01/2 SP Authentic 166
01/2 SP GU 91
01/2 SPx 118
01/2 Topps 351
01/2 To. Chrome 169
01/2 To. Heritage 153
01/2 UD Ice 80
01/2 UD Vintage 291
01/2 Vanguard 123
01/2 OTTA
02/3 OTTA
99/0 Grand Rapids Griffins
00/1 Grand Rapids Griffins

NEIL, CONNIE
24/5 Holland Creameries 9
23/4 Selkirks Crescent 14

NEIL, HARRY
24/5 Falcons Crescent 13
24/5 Holland Creameries 7

NEIL, SCOTT
94 Semic 327
01/2 Sheffield Steelers
93/4 Sheffield Steelers 5
94/5 Sheffield Steelers 7
95/6 Sheffield Steelers

NEILL, MIKE
88/9 ProCards / Maine
82/3 Soo Greyhounds

NEILSON, COREY
93/4 Slapshot / North Bay 6
94/5 Slapshot / North Bay 7
95/6 Slapshot 59
99/0 Louisiana Ice Gators
00/1 Louisiana Ice Gators
01/2 Louisiana Ice Gators
97/8 Quad City Mallards

NEILSON, DAVID
90/1 7th..Sketch WHL 265
91/2 7th...Sketch WHL 250
94/5 Knoxville Cherokees
96/7 Knoxville Cherokees
94/5 Las Vegas Thunder
95/6 Saint John Flames

NEILSON, ÉRIC
01/2 Rimouski Océanic 18

NEILSON, JIM
64-67 BeeHive-3 [NYRa.]
64/5 Coke/Sprite [NYRa.]
65/6 Coca-Cola
70/1 Dad's Cookies
70/1 Eddie Sargent 121
71/2 Eddie Sargent 122
72/3 Eddie Sargent 154
70/1 Esso Power Player
74/5 Loblaws
68/9 O-Pee-Chee 172
68/9 O-Pee-Chee 207
69/0 O-Pee-Chee 35
69/0 O-Pee-Chee 4in1
70/1 O-Pee-Chee 185
71/2 O-Pee-Chee 112
72/3 O-Pee-Chee 60
73/4 O-Pee-Chee 123
74/5 O-Pee-Chee 109
75/6 O-Pee-Chee 270
76/7 O-Pee-Chee 344
77/8 O-Pee-Chee 317
95/6 Parkie 66-67 81
94/5 Parkie Tall 102
71/2 Pro Star Promotions
68/9 Shirriff / NYRa. 12
62/3 Topps 49
63/4 Topps 50
64/5 Topps 103
65/6 Topps 89
66/7 Topps 88
66/7 Topps / Test 55
67/8 Topps 91
68/9 Topps 70
69/0 Topps 35
71/2 Topps 112
72/3 Topps 66
73/4 Topps 123
74/5 Topps 109
75/6 Topps 270
64/5 Toronto Star Action
71/2 Toronto Sun Photo
91/2 Ultimate Original Six 25, ✍ Aut. 25

NEILSON, ROGER
90/1 Pro Set 672
89/0 NYRA / Marine
00/1 OTTA
01/2 OTTA
02/3 OTTA
78/9 TORO

NEININGER, TONY
72 Semic Sticker 147

NELIBA, JAN
94/5 APS 281
95/6 APS 75, 445
96/7 APS 212
97/8 APS 26
82 Semic Sticker 84

NELLIGAN, SAM
74/5 Sioux City Musketeers

NELLIS, JIM
91/2 Air Canada SJHL D39
92/3 MPS SJHL 89

NELSON, BRIAN
85/6 Minnesota-Duluth 27

NELSON, CHAD
95/6 Louisiana Ice Gators-2
96/7 Louisiana Ice Gators
97/8 Louisiana Ice Gators

NELSON, CHRIS
94/5 Atlanta Knights 3
92/3 Cincinnati Cyclones
93/4 Raleigh Icecaps

NELSON, CRAIG
95/6 Slapshot 152
02/3 Dundee Texol Stars

NELSON, DAVE
90/1 Prince Albert Raiders
91/2 Prince Albert Raiders

NELSON, FRANCIS
83 HHOF Postcard L11
83&87 HHOF 160

NELSON, JEFF
91/2 Arena 27
91/2 Classic 32
94/5 Classic 48
91/2 Classic Four Sport 32
94/5 Classic 4 Sport 146
94/5 Cla. Images 66, CE15, PR1
93/4 Cla. Prospects 155
95/6 Donruss 128
95/6 Edge Ice 54
95/6 Leaf 246
94/5 Parkie SE199
91 7th..Sketch Mem.Cup 104
90/1 7th..Sketch WHL 281
91/2 7th...Sketch WHL 265
91/2 Star Pics 43
91/2 Ultimate Draft Pick 28, 75, ✍ Aut.
91/2 Upper Deck 689
94/5 Upper Deck 250
94/5 UD Canada Junior 3
91/2 Upper Deck WJC 63
01/2 UD DEL 235
95/6 WASH
96/7 Grand Rapids Griffins
97/8 Milwaukee Admirals
98/9 Milwaukee Admirals
93/4 Portland Pirates
94/5 Portland Pirates
95/6 Portland Pirates
99/0 Portland Pirates
00/1 Portland Pirates

NELSON, KODIE
82/3 Medicine Hat Tigers
84/5 Victoria Cougars

NELSON, MIKE
99/0 Peoria Rivermen
02/3 Plymouth Whalers

NELSON, TODD
92/3 Classic Prospects 42
98/9 DEL 116
94/5 Donruss 238
94/5 Flair 202
94/5 Leaf 273
90/1 ProCards 383
91/2 ProCards 307
92/3 Topps 50
92/3 Cleveland Lumberjacks
96/7 Grand Rapids Griffins
97/8 Grand Rapids Griffins
99/0 Grand Rapids Griffins
02/3 Grand Rapids Griffins
93/4 Portland Pirates
94/5 Portland Pirates
00/1 Rochester Americans

NELSSON, HENRIK
94/5 Leaf Elit Set 59

NEMCHINOV, SERGEI
98/9 Be A Player 237, ✍ Aut. 237
92/3 Bowman 426
93/4 Donruss 214
94/5 Donruss 125
95/6 Donruss 378
94/5 Flair 116
94/5 Fleer 138
92/3 Fleer Ultra 140
93/4 Fleer Ultra 203
94/5 Fleer Ultra 142
93/4 Leaf 252
94/5 Leaf 153
95/6 Leaf 236
00/1 Mir Fetisov 19
90/1 O-Pee-Chee 493
91/2 O-Pee-Chee 514
91/2 O-Pee-Chee 24R
92/3 O-Pee-Chee 316
91/2 OPC Premier 25
97/8 Omega 139
98/9 Pacific 283
01/2 Pacific 236
97/8 Pacific CC 102
92/3 Panini Sticker 234
93/4 Panini Sticker 93
94/5 Panini Sticker 85
96/7 Panini Sticker 110
98/9 Panini Sticker 76
99/0 Panini Sticker 77
91/2 Parkhurst 334
92/3 Parkhurst 114
92/3 Parkhurst 236
92/3 Parkhurst 447
93/4 Parkhurst 128
95/6 Parkhurst 141
94/5 Parkie SE115
91/2 Pinnacle 317
92/3 Pinnacle 158
93/4 Pinnacle 51
94/5 Pinnacle 220
95/6 Pinnacle 152, GG-20
96/7 Pinnacle 11
95/6 Playoff 285
94/5 POG 167
95/6 POG 181
93/4 Power Play 163
93/4 Premier 42
94/5 Premier 443
91/2 Pro Set 441
92/3 Pro Set 117
91/2 Pro Set Platinum 205
91/2 Red Ace
91/2 Score 67T
91/2 Score CAN 617
92/3 Score 115
92/3 Score SS 5
93/4 Score 218
93/4 Score IS 16
94/5 Score 14
95/6 Score 41
89 Semic Sticker 95
91 Semic Sticker 96
89/0 Soviet Stars
92/3 Topps 287
95/6 Topps 141
98/9 To. Finest 16
92/3 To. Stadium 340
93/4 To. Stadium 245
94/5 To. Stadium 41
91/2 Upper Deck 355
92/3 Upper Deck 298
92/3 Upper Deck E13
93/4 Upper Deck 371
94/5 Upper Deck 156
95/6 Upper Deck 166
96/7 Upper Deck 298
99/0 Upper Deck 247
95/6 UD BAP 209, ✍ S209
95/6 UD CC 283
96/7 UD CC 175
99/0 UD G. Reserve 247

NEMCICKY, TOMAS
95/6 APS 47
96/7 APS 37
97/8 APS 65
97/8 DS 107
98/9 DS 112
96/7 DS Sticker 112
97/8 DS Sticker 299
99/0 Eishockey 361
98/9 OFS 28
00/1 OFS 230
01/2 OFS 217
93/4 Upper Deck 264

NEMEC, ONDREJ
01/2 OFS 58

NEMECEK, JAN
94/5 APS 275
99/0 BAP Mem. 326
00/1 Pacific 199
94/5 Slapshot Memorial 52
01/2 UD DEL 209
98/9 Long Beach Ice Dogs

NEMETH, STEVE
01/2 Sheffield Steelers
93/4 Sheffield Steelers 6
93/4 Sheffield Steelers 7
94/5 Sheffield Steelers
95/6 Sheffield Steelers

NEMETH, TOM
90/1 7th..Sketch OHL 41
91/2 7th...Sketch OHL 17
98/9 Cincinnati Cyclones
92/3 Dayton Bombers
93/4 Dayton Bombers
96/7 Dayton Bombers
98/9 Dayton Bombers
98/9 Dayton Bombers
98/9 Dayton Bombers
97/8 Fort Wayne Komets
91/2 Cornwall Royals

NEMIROVSKY, DAVID
02/3 Cardset 79
95/6 Bowman 119
96/7 Leaf 219
97/8 Pacific CC 191
95/6 Parkhurst 359
96/7 Pinnacle 236
97/8 Pi. Be A Player 167, ✍ Aut. 167
96/7 Pi. Summit 191
95/6 Slapshot 272, 346
95/6 To. Stadium 223
97/8 Upper Deck 77
97/8 UD Coll. Choice 106
96/7 FLOR / Winn-Dixie
96/7 Carolina Monarchs
98/9 Fort Wayne Komets
99/0 St. John's Maple Leafs

NEMIROVSKY, MIKHAIL
95/6 Flint Generals
98/9 Flint Generals
99/0 Muskegon Fury
97/8 New Orleans Brass

NENONEN, ESKO
65/6 Hellas 82

NENONEN, MARTTI
80/1 Mallasjuoma 219
78/9 SM-Liiga 236

NENOV, MILCHO
79 Panini Sticker 350

NEPRYAEV, IVAN
00/1 Mir 306

NERELL, ERIK
92/3 Semic Nordisk 39

NERUDA, STANISLAV
99/0 Score 155

NESICH, JIM
88/9 ProCards / Sherbrooke
89/0 ProCards AHL 182
90/1 ProCards 61
91/2 ProCards 148

NESS, JAY
91/2 L. Superior State Lakers

NESS, LARRY
99/0 Utah Grizzlies

NESSMAN, RYAN
91/2 Avant Garde BCJHL 22

NESTAK, PAVEL
95/6 APS 201
97/8 APS 103
97/8 DS Sticker 48

NESTER, KELLY
87/8 Hull Olympiques

NESTERENKO, ERIC
02/3 Parkie - Reprint 189
45-64 BeeHive-2 [Toro.]
45-64 BeeHive-2 [Chic.]
64-67 BeeHive-3 [Chic.]
64-67 BeeHive-3 [Chic.]
64/5 Coke/Sprite [Chic.]
65/6 Coca-Cola
70/1 Eddie Sargent 38
70/1 Esso Power Player
62/3 Cowan Tile
68/9 O-Pee-Chee 154
69/0 O-Pee-Chee 136
70/1 O-Pee-Chee 19
71/2 O-Pee-Chee 213
53/4 Parkhurst 10
54/5 Parkhurst 19
54/5 Parkhurst 95
55/6 Parkhurst 15
55/6 Parkhurst 75
93/4 Parkie 56-57 39
95/6 Parkie 66-67 26
94/5 Parkie Tall 33
45-54 Quaker Oats
60/1 Shirriff 69
61/2 Shirriff 23
68/9 Shirriff / Chic. 14
57/8 Topps 24
58/9 Topps 53
59/0 Topps 1
61/2 Topps 28
62/3 Topps 41
63/4 Topps 39
64/5 Topps 91
65/6 Topps 119
66/7 Topps 60
66/7 Topps / Test 60
67/8 Topps 60
70/1 Topps 19
57/8 Toronto Star Photo
63/4 Toronto Star Action
71/2 Toronto Sun Photo
90/1 Upper Deck 503
70/1 CHIC

NESTEROV, ALEXANDER
00/1 Mir 168

NETEDU, VALERIAN
79 Panini Sticker 312

NETHERY, LANCE
94/5 DEL 271
95/6 DEL 262
96/7 DEL 156
98/9 DEL 247
99/0 Eishockey 123
88/9 EDMO / Action 70

NETIK, TOMAS
01/2 OFS 117

NEUBAUER, R
95/6 DEL 288

NEUFELD, KYLE
01/2 Kingston Frontenacs 14
00/1 London Knights

NEUFELD, RAY
84/5 Kelowna Wings &...
83/4 O-Pee-Chee 144
84/5 O-Pee-Chee 76
85/6 OPC/Topps 58
86/7 OPC/Topps 177
88/9 OPC/Topps 239
83/4 OPC/Topps Sticker 260
84/5 OPC Sticker 199
85/6 OPC Sticker 171-43
86/7 OPC Sticker 106-235
88/9 OPC Sticker 141-14
87/8 Panini Sticker 369
89/0 ProCards AHL 69
83/4 Souhaits Keychain [Whalers]
84/5 Topps 59
82/3 HART / Jr. Whalers
83/4 HART / Jr. Whalers
84/5 HART / Jr. Whalers
85/6 HART / Jr. Whalers
85/6 WINN / Safety Tips
86/7 WINN
87/8 WINN
88/9 WINN / Safety Tips

NEUMEIER, TROY
00/1 Kudos 94
91/2 ProCards 602
90/1 7th..Sketch WHL 269
95/6 Adirondack Red Wings
92/3 Hamilton Canucks
90/1 Prince Albert Raiders

NEUVONEN, JARI
93/4 Sisu 128

NEVALAINEN, MATTI
96/7 Sisu 118

NEVALAINEN, SEPPO
71/2 Williams Finnish 267

NEVESELY, STANISLAV
98/9 OFS 65

NEVILLE, DAVE
37/8 World Wide Gum 111

NEVIN, BOB
02/3 Parkie - Reprint 226, 259, 275, 286
71/2 Bazooka Panel
45-64 BeeHive-2 [Toro.]
64-67 BeeHive-3 [NYRa.]
63-65 Chex
64/5 Coke/Sprite [NYRa.]
65/6 Coca-Cola
70/1 Colgate 38
70/1 Dad's Cookies
70/1 Eddie Sargent 127
71/2 Eddie Sargent 90
72/3 Eddie Sargent 112
70/1 Esso Power Player
62/3 Cowan Tile
74/5 Loblaws
68/9 O-Pee-Chee 76
69/0 O-Pee-Chee 40
69/0 O-Pee-Chee 4in1
70/1 O-Pee-Chee 60
71/2 O-Pee-Chee 44
72/3 O-Pee-Chee 267
74/5 O-Pee-Chee 378
75/6 O-Pee-Chee 123
75/6 O-Pee-Chee 320
76/7 OPC WHA 73
58/9 Parkhurst 13
61/2 Parkhurst 10
62/3 Parkhurst 10
63/4 Parkhurst 10
63/4 Parkhurst 70
95/6 Parkie 66-67 85, 144
94/5 Parkie Tall 103
66/7 Post Cereal Box
66/7 Post [Small]
61/2 Shirriff 47
62/3 Shirriff 7
68/9 Shirriff / NYRa. 9
64/5 Topps 77
65/6 Topps 93
66/7 Topps 27
66/7 Topps / Test 27
67/8 Topps 28
68/9 Topps 76
69/0 Topps 40
70/1 Topps 60
71/2 Topps 44
75/6 Topps 123
75/6 Topps 320
66/7 Toronto Star Weekend
71/2 Toronto Sun Photo
91/2 Ultimate Original Six 26, ✍ Aut. 26
60/1 York
61/2 York 26
63/4 York 8

NEWBERRY, JOHN
83/4 Nova Scotia Voyageurs

NEWBERRY, SCOT
92/3 MPS SJHL 125

NEWBURY, KRIS
99/0 UD Prospects 17, 76

NEWHOOK, RON
94/5 Slapshot / Sudbury 23
95/6 Slapshot 403
97/8 Toledo Storm 12

NEWMAN, DAN
77/8 O-Pee-Chee 362
78/9 O-Pee-Chee 270
88/9 EDMO / Action 129

NEWMAN, DARREL
93/4 Muskegon Fury

NEWMAN, DWAYNE
90/1 7th..Sketch WHL 237
91/2 7th...Sketch WHL 52
88/9 Brandon Wheat Kings
89/0 Brandon Wheat Kings

NEWMAN, JARED
99/0 UD Sobey's 14
99/0 UD Prospects 18

NEWMAN, MIKE*
91/2 Avant Garde BCJHL 89
92/3 BCJHL 124

NEWMAN, TOM
93/4 Greensboro Monarchs
91/2 Minnesota G'Gophers
92/3 Minnesota G'Gophers

NEWSON, MATT
92/3 Hamilton Canucks

NEWTON, CAM
75/6 OPC WHA 119

NEWTON, CRAIG
94/5 Slapshot / Brantford 24

NEZIOL, TOM
91/2 Cincinnati Cyclones
99/0 Mobile Mysticks

NICHOL, SCOTT
02/3 Pacific Complete 388
01/2 BAP Mem. 446
01/2 O-Pee-Chee 338
01/2 Signat. 209, ✍ Aut. 209
01/2 SP Authentic 137
01/2 SP GU 68
01/2 SPx 98
01/2 SPx Rookie RR5
01/2 Stadium 130
01/2 Topps 338
01/2 To. Chrome 156
01/2 To. Reserve 121
01/2 UD PlayMakers Ltd 108
01/2 Upper Deck 417
01/2 UD Challenge 99
01/2 UD Honor Roll 67
01/2 UD Ice 47
95/6 Rochester Americans
96/7 Rochester Americans
97/8 Rochester Americans
98/9 Rochester Americans
93/4 Portland Winter Hawks

NICHOLISHEN, MIKE
98/9 Orlando Solar Bears Geico

NICHOLLS, BERNIE
98/9 Be A Player M11
90/1 Bowman 221, -HT 20
91/2 Bowman 76
92/3 Bowman 161
93/4 Donruss 188
95/6 Donruss 24
96/7 Donruss 198
97/8 Donruss 34
96/7 Do. Canadian 106
96/7 Do. Elite 75
94/5 Flair 35
94/5 Fleer 43
95/6 Fleer Metal 26
92/3 Fleer Ultra 64
93/4 Fleer Ultra 86
94/5 Fleer Ultra 42, 275

95/6 Fleer Ultra 34
96/7 Fl. Ultra 152
88/9 Frito Lay
83/4 Funmate Puffy 10 [w/]
93/4 Hockey Wit 64
95/6 Hoyle / West. 8-Diamond
90/1 Kraft 40, 73
95/6 Kraft / KD
93/4 Leaf 169
94/5 Leaf 462
95/6 Leaf 84
96/7 Leaf 50
96/7 L. Preferred 60
97/8 Limited 36
96/7 Maggers 34
96/7 Metal Univ. 138
83/4 O-Pee-Chee 160
84/5 O-Pee-Chee 88
85/6 OPC/Topps 148
86/7 OPC/Topps 159
86/7 OPC/Topps Box K
87/8 OPC/Topps 183
88/9 OPC/Topps 169
90/1 OPC/Topps 13, 17
91/2 O-Pee-Chee 174
92/3 O-Pee-Chee 52
89/0 OPC/Topps 47
98/9 OPC Chrome 78
90/1 OPC Premier 83
88/9 OPC Stars 28
83/4 OPC/Topps Sticker 292
84/5 OPC Sticker 269
85/6 OPC Sticker 232
86/7 OPC Sticker 95
87/8 OPC Sticker 214
88/9 OPC Sticker 156-27
89/0 opcSticker 155
98/9 Pacific 389
97/8 Pacific CC 255
97/8 Pa. Invincible 127
87/8 Panini Sticker 278
88/9 Panini Sticker 77
89/0 Panini Sticker 88
90/1 Panini Sticker 106
91/2 Panini Sticker 288
92/3 Panini Sticker 109
93/4 Panini Sticker 39
94/5 Panini Sticker 28
95/6 Panini Sticker 156
96/7 Panini Sticker 161
97/8 Panini Sticker 228
91/2 Parkhurst 278
92/3 Parkhurst 49
92/3 Parkhurst 328
93/4 Parkhurst 117
95/6 Parkhurst 37
94/5 Parkie SE38
91/2 Pinnacle 300
92/3 Pinnacle 120
93/4 Pinnacle 165
94/5 Pinnacle 499
96/7 Pinnacle 41
97/8 Pinnacle 165
97/8 Pi. Certified 109
97/8 Pi. Inside 185
95/6 Pi. Summit 135, MH-1
96/7 Pi. Summit 115
97/8 Pi. Totally 109
95/6 Pi. Zenith 46
96/7 Pi. Zenith 32
95/6 Playoff 23
96/7 Playoff 355
94/5 POG 68
95/6 POG 64
93/4 Power Play 139
93/4 Premier 274
94/5 Premier 403
95/6 Pro Magnet 5
90/1 Pro Set 204, 352
91/2 Pro Set 166
91/2 Pro Set 286
92/3 Pro Set 52
91/2 Pro Set Platinum 174
90/1 Score 9
90/1 Sco. Hot Cards 5
91/2 Score 240
91/2 Score CAN 460
92/3 Score 340
93/4 Score 19
94/5 Score 74, 245
95/6 Score 29
96/7 Score 65
97/8 Score 180
94/5 Select 17
89 Semic Sticker 73
91 Semic Sticker 67
95/6 SBx Emotion 31
95/6 SBx Impact 31
83/4 Souhaits Keychain [Kings]
94/5 SP 25, P-25
95/6 SP 26
96/7 SP 139
97/8 SP Authentic 132
84/5 Topps 67
92/3 Topps 438
95/6 Topps 122
98/9 Topps 78
94/5 Topps Finest 87
96/7 To. Picks 131
91/2 To. Stadium 245
92/3 To. Stadium 448
93/4 To. Stadium 111
95/6 To. Stadium 28
95/6 T. Super Skills 72
90/1 Upper Deck 34
91/2 Upper Deck 356
91/2 Upper Deck 566
92/3 Upper Deck 290
92/3 Upper Deck 624
93/4 Upper Deck 58, SP-85
94/5 Upper Deck 83, SP-106
95/6 Upper Deck 97, SE-16
96/7 Upper Deck 334, X31
97/8 Upper Deck 150
96/7 UD Black Diam. 59
95/6 UD CC 169, C17
96/7 UD CC 50
96/7 UD Ice 57
92/3 EDMO / IGA 017
84/5 LOSA / Smokey 12
87/8 LOSA
88/9 LOSA / Smokey
89/0 NYRA / Marine

NICHOLLS, DAVE
94/5 Slapshot / Kitchener 29
82/3 Kitchener Rangers

NICHOLLS, JAMIE
92/3 Greensboro Monarchs 11

NICHOLS, JAMIE
88/9 ProCards / Cape Breton

NICHOLS, ROB
88/9 ProCards / Adirondack
89/0 ProCards IHL 111
90/1 ProCards 299
91/2 ProCards 329
95/6 Flint Generals
96/7 Flint Generals
98/9 Flint Generals
92/3 San Diego Gulls
83/4 North Bay Centennials

NICHOLSON, DAN
81/2 Oshawa Generals
82/3 Oshawa Generals

NICKEL, HARTMUT
94/5 DEL 127
74 Hellas MM-Jenkki 108
70/1 Kuvajulkaisut 89

NICKEL, STACEY
84/5 Kelowna Wings &...
86/7 Regina Pats

NICKULAS, ERIC
00/1 BAP Mem. 348
00/1 Pacific 39
00/1 Panini Sticker 14
00/1 SPx 92
00/1 Topps 292
00/1 To. Chrome 187
00/1 Upper Deck 181
00/1 UD Black Diam. 76
00/1 UD Ice 55
00/1 UD MVP 186
00/1 UD Pros&Prosp. 93
00/1 UD Vintage 373
00/1 Victory 268
98/9 Providence Bruins
99/0 Providence Bruins
00/1 Providence Bruins
01/2 Worcester IceCats
02/3 Worcester IceCats

NICOL, BRETT
90/1 7th..Sketch OHL 138

NICOL, CREGG
86/7 Regina Pats
87/8 Regina Pats

NICOLETTI, MARTIN
88/9 ProCards / Sherbrooke

NICOLLS, JAMIE
93/4 Greensboro Monarchs
86/7 Portland Winter Hawks

NICOLLS, PAUL
92/3 BCJHL 33

NICOLSON, DEREK
00/1 Austin Ice Bats
97/8 Central Texas
95/6 Thunder Bay Senators

NICOLSON, GRAEME
81/2 COLR

NIECKAR, BARRY
00/1 Kudos 138
93/4 Raleigh Icecaps
94/5 Saint John Flames
00/1 Nottingham Panthers
01/2 Nottingham Panthers
02/3 Nottingham Panthers

NIEDERBERGER, ANDREAS
94/5 DEL 88
95/6 DEL 82, 438
96/7 DEL 273
95 Globe 222
95 Panini Worlds 60
94 Semic 279
89 Semic Sticker 106
93 Semic Sticker 154

NIEDERMAYER, ROB
02/3 BAP Mem. 260
02/3 First Edition 116, ✂ Jers.
02/3 Pacific 58
02/3 Pacific Complete 88
02/3 To. Total 271
02/3 Ultimate Mem. ✂ FS
02/3 UD Vintage 37
01/2 Adrenaline 27
99/0 Aurora 64
98/9 Be A Player 208, ✍ Aut. 208
99/0 BAP Mem. 237
00/1 BAP Mem. 259
95/6 Bowman 76
99/0 Challenger 1
93/4 Classic 5, DP5, ✍ Aut.
94/5 Classic ✍ Aut.
93/4 Cla. 4 Sport 189, ✍ Aut.
93/4 Cla. Images 4 Sport 30
93/4 Cla. Images 4 Sport SI6
93/4 Cla. Prospects 27
00/1 Crown Royale 46
93/4 Donruss 134
93/4 Donruss I
93/4 Donruss RR 4
94/5 Donruss 113
95/6 Donruss 51
96/7 Donruss 24
97/8 Donruss 191
96/7 Do. Canadian 13
95/6 Do. Elite 65
96/7 Do. Elite 15
97/8 Do. Preferred 61
94/5 Flair 67
94/5 Fleer 82
96/7 Fleer 41
95/6 Fleer Metal 61
93/4 Fleer Ultra 330
93/4 Fleer Ultra SM 8
93/4 Fleer Ultra WotF 11
94/5 Fleer Ultra 84
95/6 Fleer Ultra 62
96/7 Fl. Ultra 67
95/6 Hoyle / East. 6-Diamond
93/4 Kraft / KD
96/7 Kraft / Fav.
93/4 Leaf 293
93/4 Leaf FP 6
94/5 Leaf 225, GLR-7
95/6 Leaf 197
96/7 Leaf 22
97/8 Leaf 58
94/5 L. Limited 11
95/6 L. Limited 35
96/7 L. Limited 78, S-19
96/7 L. Preferred 12, LS-61
97/8 Limited 79
96/7 Metal Univ. 61
99/0 Millenium 107, ✍ Aut. 107
98/9 NHL Power Play
01/2 O-Pee-Chee 184
98/9 OPC Chrome 37
98/9 Omega 105
99/0 Pacific 179
00/1 Pacific 183
01/2 Pacific 174
97/8 Pacific CC 269
97/8 Pa. Paramount 83
99/0 Pa. Paramount 103
98/9 Pa. Revolution 63
94/5 Panini Sticker H
95/6 Panini Sticker 71
96/7 Panini Sticker 72
99/0 Panini Sticker 59
93/4 Parkhurst 246
93/4 Parkhurst C4
93/4 Parkhurst G5
93/4 Parkhurst E5
94/5 Parkhurst 294, V22
95/6 Parkhurst 82
94/5 Parkie SE68
93/4 Pinnacle 439
93/4 Pinnacle SR4
94/5 Pinnacle 168, 469
95/6 Pinnacle 100
96/7 Pinnacle 32
97/8 Pinnacle 157
97/8 Pi. Inside 182
95/6 Pi. Summit 105
96/7 Pi. Summit 147
95/6 Pi. Zenith 110
96/7 Pi. Zenith 84
95/6 Playoff 42, 263
96/7 Playoff 435
94/5 POG 109
94/5 Post
93/4 Power Play 349
93/4 Power Play RooS 8
93/4 Premier 270
94/5 Premier 306, OF-9
95/6 Pro Magnet 86
93/4 Score 592
95/6 Score 48
96/7 Score 3
97/8 Score 253
94/5 Select 25
95/6 Select CE 96
96/7 Select CE 7
90/1 7th..Sketch WHL 29
91/2 7th...Sketch WHL 327
01/2 Signat. 151, ✍ Aut. 151
96/7 SBx Impact 47
95/6 SP 60
96/7 SP 62
97/8 SP Authentic 67, ✍ SotT
98/9 SP Authentic 36
99/0 Stadium 140
98/9 SLU
95/6 Super Sticker 50
95/6 Topps 31
98/9 Topps 37
99/0 Topps 45
00/1 Topps 198
01/2 Topps 184
99/0 To. Chrome 45
00/1 To. Chrome 132
95/6 To. Finest 98
98/9 To. Finest 41
00/1 To. Heritage 190
01/2 To. Heritage 178
96/7 To. Picks 99
93/4 To. Stadium 449
94/5 To. Stadium 22, 117
95/6 To. Stadium 94
95/6 T. Super Skills 22
98/9 UD Choice 94
01/2 Ultimate Mem. ✂ BL
92/3 Upper Deck 593
93/4 Upper Deck 98, E1, H4, SP-58
94/5 Upper Deck 287, SP-30
95/6 Upper Deck 310, SE-35
96/7 Upper Deck 262, X3, SS28A
97/8 Upper Deck 281, SG44
98/9 Upper Deck 277
99/0 Upper Deck 233
01/2 Upper Deck 260
93/4 Upper Deck Be A Player 10
94/5 UD BAP R55, R119
95/6 UD BAP 184, ✍ S184
96/7 UD Black Diam. 140
97/8 UD Black Diam. 22
98/9 UD Black Diam. 39
95/6 UD CC 40
96/7 UD CC 103, 318
97/8 UD Coll. Choice 105, SQ18
98/9 UD G. Reserve 277
99/0 UD G. Reserve 233
97/8 UD Ice 14
98/9 UD MVP 87, ✍ PS
99/0 UD MVP 88
00/1 UD Vintage 156
99/0 Victory 125
01/2 Victory 157
96/7 FLOR / Winn-Dixie
97/8 FLOR / Winn-Dixie

NIEDERMAYER, SCOTT
02/3 BAP All-Star 65, ✂ ASJ
02/3 BAP Mem. 136, ✂ ASJ40
02/3 First Edition 99, 406H, ✂ Jers.
02/3 In The GU ✂ T14, ✂ TM16
02/3 McDonald's -SLG 2
02/3 O-Pee-Chee 167
02/3 Pacific 226
02/3 Pacific Complete 152
02/3 Parkhurst 60
02/3 Parkhurst Retro 162
02/3 Signature ✂ DW6, ✂ TQ7
02/3 Slam Card
02/3 Sports Vault 69
02/3 Stadium ✂ FC7, ✂ PC7
02/3 Topps 167, ✂ FRF, ✂✍ FRF
02/3 T. Chrome ✂ FRF
02/3 To. Limited 167
02/3 To. Total 367
02/3 UD Classic 60
02/3 UD MVP 111
02/3 UD Rookie ✂ 155c
02/3 UD Top Shelf 53
02/3 UD Vintage 149, GB 149
02/3 Victory 126
91/2 Arena 2
01/2 Atomic ✂ GWJ 37
98/9 Aurora 112
98/9 Be A Player 232, ✍ Aut. 232
99/0 BAP Mem. 113
00/1 BAP Mem. 82, ✂ TM-10, ✂ TM-31
01/2 BAP Mem. 119, ✂ CoO
92/3 Bowman 313
95/6 Bowman 64
98/9 Bowman's Best 99
91/2 Classic 3
91/2 Classic Four Sport 3
00/1 Crown Royale ✂ JR 5
01/2 Crown Royale ✂ TT 13
93/4 Donruss 189
93/4 Donruss M
94/5 Donruss 161
95/6 Donruss 105
96/7 Donruss 188
97/8 Donruss 72
97/8 Do. Priority 37
99/0 Dynagon Ice 118
97/8 Esso 14, ✍ Aut.
94/5 Flair 96
96/7 Flair NT-3
94/5 Fleer 115
96/7 Fleer 60
95/6 Fleer Metal 84
96/7 Fl. Picks 116
92/3 Fleer Ultra 116
93/4 Fleer Ultra 95
94/5 Fleer Ultra 121
95/6 Fleer Ultra 90, 194, RS-5
96/7 Fl. Ultra 94
01/2 Heads Up ✂ JQ 3
93/4 Hockey Wit 54
95/6 Hoyle / East. 7-Diamond
98/9 Kraft / PB
93/4 Leaf 80
93/4 Leaf GLR 14
94/5 Leaf 237
95/6 Leaf 150, RTTC-9
96/7 Leaf 198
94/5 L. Limited 40
95/6 L. Limited 43
96/7 Metal Univ. 87
99/0 Millenium 144, ✍ Aut. 144
98/9 NHL Power Play
01/2 O-Pee-Chee 197
98/9 OPC Chrome 143, B8
91/2 OPC Premier 35
92/3 OPC Premier 113
97/8 Omega 132
98/9 Pacific 266
99/0 Pacific 242
00/1 Pacific 241
01/2 Pacific 237
97/8 Pacific CC 247
98/9 Pa. Paramount 136
99/0 Pa. Paramount 137
00/1 Pa. Paramount 147
97/8 Pa. Revolution 79
98/9 Panini Photocard
92/3 Panini Sticker 179
93/4 Panini Sticker 42
95/6 Panini Sticker 88
96/7 Panini Sticker 86
97/8 Panini Sticker 72
98/9 Panini Sticker 65
91/2 Parkhurst 94
92/3 Parkhurst 95
93/4 Parkhurst 111
93/4 Parkhurst 240
95/6 Parkhurst 388
00/1 Parkhurst P-169
01/2 Parkhurst 46
94/5 Parkie SE95, seV12
91/2 Pinnacle 349
92/3 Pinnacle 241
92/3 Pinnacle 304
92/3 Pinnacle T2K 12
93/4 Pinnacle 111
93/4 Pinnacle T2K1 14
94/5 Pinnacle 75
97/8 Pinnacle 115
96/7 Pi. Be A Player 59, ✍ Aut. 59
97/8 Pi. Inside 95
95/6 Pi. Summit 50
96/7 Pi. Summit 57
95/6 Pi. Zenith 27
95/6 Playoff 59
94/5 POG 351
95/6 POG 164
93/4 Power Play 140
93/4 Premier 470
94/5 Premier 240, 539
00/1 Pr. Stock ✂ GUG 64
00/1 PS Titanium ✂ GUG 106
00/1 PS Titanium Draft ✂ 60
95/6 Pro Magnet 33
91/2 Pro Set 547
91/2 Pro Set CC4
92/3 Pro Set 232
99/0 Revolution 88
91/2 Score 27T
91/2 Score CAN 577
92/3 Score 401
93/4 Score 217
94/5 Score 22
95/6 Score 52
96/7 Score 108
97/8 Score 229
97/8 Score NJer. 7
92/3 Score Young Stars 33
94/5 Select 101
95/6 Select CE 70
92 7th...Sketch Awards 11
92 7th...Sketch Awards 13
90 7th..Sketch Mem.Cup 18
91 7th..Sketch Mem.Cup 97
90/1 7th..Sketch WHL 289
00/1 Signature 148, ✂ DD-12, ✂ J-9
01/2 Signat. 162, ✍ Aut. 162, ✂ GJ37, ✂ GSJ37, ✂ TM18
95/6 SBx Emotion 100
95/6 SBx Impact 95
96/7 SBx Impact 70
94/5 SP 67
95/6 SP 84
96/7 SP 90
99/0 SPx 88
00/1 SPx 141
99/0 Stadium 45
00/1 Stadium 131
91/2 Star Pics 13
95/6 Super Sticker 71
96/7 Team Out!
92/3 Topps 223
95/6 Topps 164, YS14
98/9 Topps 143, B8
99/0 Topps 229
00/1 Topps 170
01/2 Topps 197
99/0 To. Chrome 229
95/6 To. Finest 103
98/9 To. Finest 120
99/0 To. Gold Label 33
99/0 To. Prmr. Plus 32
92/3 To. Stadium 209
93/4 To. Stadium 403
94/5 To. Stadium 93
95/6 To. Stadium 76, GT8
95/6 T. Super Skills 27
98/9 UD Choice 119
91/2 Ultimate Draft Pick 3, 56, 59, 75, 79, 80, ✍ Aut.
01/2 Ultimate Mem. ✂ BL, ✂ GAO
90/1 Upper Deck 461
92/3 Upper Deck 406
92/3 Upper Deck 562
92/3 Upper Deck AC5
92/3 Upper Deck CC5
92/3 Upper Deck WG1
93/4 Upper Deck 25, 284, SP-86
94/5 Upper Deck 324, C34, IG6, SP-134
95/6 Upper Deck 383, SE-137
96/7 Upper Deck 92, SS28B
97/8 Upper Deck 301
98/9 Upper Deck 308
99/0 Upper Deck 249
01/2 Upper Deck 104
93/4 Upper Deck Be A Player 32
94/5 UD BAP R37, R128, ✍ 88
96/7 UD Black Diam. 137
94/5 UD Canada Junior 12
01/2 UD Challenge 51
95/6 UD CC 3
96/7 UD CC 149
97/8 UD Coll. Choice 148, W12
91/2 Upper Deck WJC 53
98/9 UD G. Reserve 308
99/0 UD G. Reserve 249
96/7 UD Ice 36
98/9 UD MVP 120
99/0 UD MVP 118
01/2 UD MVP 113
01/2 UD SCup Champs 80
01/2 UD Vintage 152
00/1 Vanguard ✂ DGJ 20
01/2 Vanguard ✂ DGM 17
99/0 Victory 174
01/2 Victory 217
99/0 WGretzky 101
96/7 NJER / Sharp
89/0 Kamloops Blazers

NIEDERMEIER, BASTIAN
99/0 Eishockey 92

NIEKAMP, JIM
71/2 Toronto Sun Photo
72/3 Los Angeles Sharks
75/6 Phoenix Roadrunners
76/7 Phoenix Roadrunners

NIELIKAINEN, PASI
02/3 Manchester Storm

NIELIKÄINEN, PASI
99/0 Cardset 231
00/1 Cardset 18

NIELSEN, CARSTEN
79 Panini Sticker 367

NIELSEN, CHRIS
02/3 Victory 64
01/2 BAP Mem. 150
98 Bowman 130, ✍ A28
98 Bowman Chrome 130
01/2 O-Pee-Chee 279
01/2 Pacific 115
00/1 PS Titanium 114
00/1 PS Titanium Draft 114
00/1 SP Authentic 141
00/1 SPx 135
01/2 Topps 279
00/1 Upper Deck 197
00/1 UD Black Diam. 62
00/1 UD Ice 42
00/1 UD MVP 210
01/2 UD MVP 195
00/1 Victory 280
01/2 COLU
00/1 Syracuse Crunch
98/9 Calgary Hitmen 7
99/0 Calgary Hitmen

NIELSEN, FRITS
79 Panini Sticker 366

NIELSEN, JEFF
00/1 BAP Mem. 61
98/9 Pacific 61
00/1 Pa. Paramount 121
01/2 Signat. 91, ✍ Aut. 91
00/1 To. Chrome 232
00/1 UD Vintage 178
99/0 WGretzky 7
95/6 Binghampton Rangers
96/7 Binghampton Rangers
99/0 Cincinnati M'Ducks
91/2 Minnesota G'Gophers
92/3 Minnesota G'Gophers
93/4 Minnesota G'Gophers

NIELSEN, JENS
94/5 Leaf Elit Set 287
95/6 Leaf Elit Set 286
89/0 Semic Elitserien 141
90/1 Semic Elitserien 214
91/2 Semic Elitserien 142
92/3 Semic Elitserien 163
95/6 UD Elitserien 184
97/8 UD Elitserien 111
98/9 UD Elitserien 129
99/0 UD Elitserien 115
00/1 UD Elitserien 112, T7, ✍ Sig.

NIELSEN, KIRK
98/9 Cincinnati Cyclones
96/7 Providence Bruins
97/8 Providence Bruins

NIELSEN, LEN
86/7 Regina Pats

NIELSEN, ROBERT
92/3 Semic Nordisk 115

NIELSON, COREY
94/5 Sig. Rookies 48, ✍ 48

NIELSON, JEFF
94/5 Classic 89
94/5 Binghampton Rangers

NIELSON, JIM
72 Semic Sticker 211

NIELSON, LEN
88/9 ProCards / Moncton
87/8 Moncton Hawks

NIEMEGEERS, KYLE
91/2 Air Canada SJHL C10
92/3 MPS SJHL 11

NIEMELA, JOUNI
70/1 Kuvajulkaisut 352

NIEMELÄ, RIKU
99/0 Cardset 49

NIEMENRANTA, OLAVI
80/1 Mallasjuoma 78
78/9 SM-Liiga 124

NIEMI, ANTTI-JUSSI
02/3 Cardset 229
01/2 BAP Mem. 251
98/9 Cardset 100, Leij. 14
99/0 Cardset 58, 186
00/1 Cardset 113
01/2 O-Pee-Chee 301
95/6 Sisu 250
01/2 Topps 301
95/6 Upper Deck 549
01/2 Cincinnati Mighty Ducks

NIEMI, ESKO
96/7 Sisu 188

NIEMI, HEIKKI
72/3 Williams Finnish 272

NIEMI, JAAKKO
78/9 SM-Liiga 224
73/4 Williams Finnish 253

NIEMI, KARI
72/3 Williams Finnish 289

NIEMI, MARKO
70/1 Kuvajulkaisut 317

NIEMI, MIKKO
93/4 Sisu 116

NIEMI, TAUNO
65/6 Hellas 121

NIEMINEN,
97/8 Hockey-Box

NIEMINEN, KARI
94/5 Sisu 385

NIEMINEN, LASSE
97/8 Hockey-Box
92/3 Jyvas Hyva 78
93/4 Jyvas Hyva 138
93/4 Sisu 147
94/5 Sisu 57
95/6 Sisu 65

NIEMINEN, MIKA
02/3 Cardset 230
98/9 Cardset 48, Leij. 33
99/0 Cardset 29, 166
00/1 Cardset 20
95 Globe 135
95 Hartwall Karjala
91/2 Jyvas Hyva 44
94/5 Leaf Elit Set 22, P-3
95 Panini Worlds 185
94 Semic 36
95 Semic 40
92/3 Semic Elitserien 197
89 Semic Sticker 50
91 Semic Sticker 17
92 Semic Sticker 19
93 Semic Sticker 69
94/5 Sisu 369
95/6 Sisu Gold 18
95 Suomen All-Star 7
96 Wien 22

NIEMINEN, PEKKA
72/3 Williams Finnish 180

NIEMINEN, PERTTI
65/6 Hellas 6

NIEMINEN, VILLE
02/3 Cardset 80, -DD 6
02/3 Pacific Complete 352
02/3 SP Authentic 129
02/3 SP Game-Used ✂ FF
02/3 To. Total 263
02/3 Upper Deck 384, ✂ BF
02/3 UD Classic ✂ HR (x2)
02/3 UD MVP - Souv.
02/3 UD Top Shelf ✂ SW
02/3 UD Vintage 200, ✂ HS
02/3 Victory - NP23
01/2 BAP Mem. 56, 497
00/1 Pacific 125
01/2 Pacific 103
01/2 Parkhurst 248
01/2 Signat. 130, ✍ Aut. 130
95/6 Sisu 113
00/1 SP Authentic 99
01/2 SPx ✂ DT, ✂ TT
00/1 Topps 287
00/1 To. Chrome 182
01/2 Upper Deck 43
01/2 UD Mask ✂ GJ, ✂ JP, ✂ DP
01/2 UD Premier ✂ D
01/2 UD SCup Champs 39
01/2 Victory 93
98/9 Hershey Bears
00/1 Hershey Bears

NIENHUIS, KRAIG
96/7 DEL 42
86/7 Moncton G'Flames

NIEUWENDYK, JOE
02/3 Atomic 62
02/3 BAP Mem. 58, 239, 257
02/3 Calder 25
02/3 Crown Royale 59
02/3 Exclusive 105
02/3 First Edition 243
02/3 Heads Up 72
02/3 McDonald's -SLG 7
02/3 O-Pee-Chee 255
02/3 Pacific 227, ✂ GWJ 31
02/3 Pacific Complete 118
02/3 Parkhurst 89
02/3 Parkhurst Retro 73
02/3 Pr. Stock Reserve 62
02/3 Signature 131, ✍ 131
02/3 Slam Card
02/3 SP Game-Used ✂ CF, ✂ PH
02/3 Sports Vault 65
02/3 Topps 255
02/3 T. Chrome 138
02/3 To. Limited 255
02/3 To. Total 357
02/3 Ultimate Mem. ✂ CSTW, ✂ 500GSE, ✂ 500GSJ, ✂ 500GSGJ
02/3 Upper Deck 106, ✂ GO
02/3 UD Artistic 54, R54, / Art
02/3 UD Classic 59
02/3 UD MVP 112, SD (x2), ST, Souv.
02/3 UD Piece 52, AC17
02/3 UD Top Shelf 51, ✂ CP, ✂ HH, ✂ R, ✂ SH
02/3 UD Vintage 153, 297, GB 153
02/3 Victory 129
01/2 Adrenaline 60, ✂ GWJ 13
01/2 Atomic 33, TN 5
98/9 Aurora 59, MACF-8
99/0 Aurora 48
00/1 Aurora 47
98/9 Be A Player 193, ✍ Aut. 193
99/0 BAP Mem. 197, H-22
00/1 BAP Mem. 149
01/2 BAP Mem. 287, 468
95/6 Bicycle Sports Aces 10-Club
90/1 Bowman 91
91/2 Bowman 252
92/3 Bowman 59
01/2 Bowman 102
98/9 Bowman's Best 62
99/0 Crown Royale 47
00/1 Crown Royale 37, ✂ GWJ-12
01/2 Crown Royale 49
93/4 Donruss 48
94/5 Donruss 56
95/6 Donruss 40, I-9
96/7 Donruss 195
97/8 Donruss 186
96/7 Do. Canadian 63
97/8 Do. Canadian 51
95/6 Do. Elite 50
96/7 Do. Elite 62
97/8 Do. Elite 61
97/8 Do. Preferred 115
97/8 Do. Priority 140
97/8 Do. Studio 55
98/9 Dynagon Ice 60
99/0 Dynagon Ice 69
93/4 EA Sports 21
94/5 Fleer 32
95/6 Fleer Metal 21
96/7 Fl. Picks F50-33
92/3 Fleer Ultra 25
93/4 Fleer Ultra 130
96/7 Fl. Ultra 46
88/9 Frito Lay
00 Gatorade Sticker
01/2 Heads Up 32, ✂ JQ 10
93/4 Hockey Wit 82
95/6 Hoyle / West. 9-Diamond
89/0 Kraft 5
90/1 Kraft 41, 74
93/4 Kraft / JELL-O
93/4 Kraft / PB
96/7 Kraft / KD
97/8 Kraft / PB
98/9 Kraft / Post 3
99/0 Kraft / PB
93/4 Leaf 126
94/5 Leaf 228
95/6 Leaf 305
96/7 Leaf 34
97/8 Leaf 108
94/5 L. Limited 82
95/6 L. Limited 56
96/7 L. Limited 75
96/7 L. Preferred 27, LS-45
97/8 Limited 43
96/7 Maggers 45
94/5 McDonald's McD-21
95/6 McDonald's McD-12
01/2 McDonald's ✂ JPatch 8
96/7 Metal Univ. 42
99/0 Millenium 78, ✍ Aut. 78
98/9 NHL Power Play
88/9 OPC/Topps 16
90/1 OPC/Topps 87
90/1 Topps-TL 8
91/2 O-Pee-Chee 223
92/3 O-Pee-Chee 354
01/2 O-Pee-Chee 99
89/0 OPC/Topps 138
98/9 OPC Chrome 161
90/1 OPC Premier 84
91/2 OPC Premier 48
88/9 OPC Stars 29
88/9 OPC Sticker 90
88/9 OPC Sticker 125-257
88/9 OPC Sticker 205-74
88/9 OPC Sticker 216-86
88/9 OPC Sticker 134-270
89/0 opcSticker 101
97/8 Omega 74, TL-7
98/9 Omega 74
99/0 Omega 76
98/9 Pacific 25
99/0 Pacific 127
00/1 Pacific 139
01/2 Pacific 134
97/8 Pacific CC 266
97/8 Pa. Crown Roy. 42
98/9 Pa. Crown Roy. 42
97/8 Pa. Dynagon 38, T-43
97/8 Pa. Invincible 43
97/8 Pa. Paramount 61
98/9 Pa. Paramount 69
99/0 Pa. Paramount 76, IAd-8, PB-15
00/1 Pa. Paramount 81
97/8 Pa. Revolution 44
98/9 Pa. Revolution 45
98/9 Panini Photocard
88/9 Panini Sticker 12
88/9 Panini Sticker 404
89/0 Panini Sticker 4, 29
90/1 Panini Sticker 174
90/1 Panini/CGY 14
91/2 Panini Sticker 53
92/3 Panini Sticker 40
93/4 Panini Sticker 182
94/5 Panini Sticker 156
95/6 Panini Sticker 233
96/7 Panini Sticker 169
97/8 Panini Sticker 144
98/9 Panini Sticker 121
99/0 Panini Sticker 8, 222
00/1 Panini Sticker 145
91/2 Parkhurst 23
92/3 Parkhurst 21
93/4 Parkhurst 31
94/5 Parkhurst 33, YCTG-4
95/6 Parkhurst 33, 329
00/1 Parkhurst P-218
01/2 Parkhurst 122, 386, ✂ PJ58, ✂ PS69, ✂ M27
91/2 Pinnacle 54
92/3 Pinnacle 31
93/4 Pinnacle 198
93/4 Pinnacle CA4
94/5 Pinnacle 90
96/7 Pinnacle 183
97/8 Pinnacle 110
96/7 Pi. Be A Player 53, ✍ Aut. 53
97/8 Pi. BeeHive 20
97/8 Pi. Certified 76
97/8 Pi. Inside 115
95/6 Pi. Summit 162, MH-13
96/7 Pi. Summit 65
97/8 Pi. Totally 76
95/6 Pi. Zenith 112
96/7 Pi. Zenith 63
95/6 Playoff 18
96/7 Playoff 334
94/5 POG 56
94/5 POG / Western 4
95/6 POG 11, 49
93/4 Power Play 39
93/4 Premier 205
94/5 Premier 537
99/0 Prism 47
00/1 Pr. Stock 34
01/2 Pr. Stock 30, ✂ GUG 38
00/1 PS Titanium 30, ✂ GUG 90
01/2 PS Titanium 46
00/1 PS Titanium Draft ✂ 34
95/6 Pro Magnet 43
90/1 Pro Set 42, 344
91/2 Pro Set 29
91/2 Pro Set 569
92/3 Pro Set 26
91/2 Pro Set Platinum 18
99/0 Revolution 49, SS-15, TL-16, / CSC 49
00/1 Revolution 49
90/1 Score 30
90/1 Sco. Hot Cards 45
91/2 Score 170
91/2 Score CAN 170
92/3 Score 193
93/4 Score 199
93/4 Score/CAN DD4
94/5 Score 159
95/6 Score 229
96/7 Score 152
97/8 Score 135
94/5 Select 131
95/6 Select CE 32, DS-10
96/7 Select CE 88
89 Semic Sticker 74
91 Semic Sticker 69
00/1 Signature 205, ✍ Aut. 45
95/6 SBx Emotion 24
95/6 SBx Impact 24
96/7 SBx Impact 31
94/5 SP 20
95/6 SP 38
97/8 SP Authentic 49
00/1 SP GU ✂ TotG, ✂ C
01/2 SP GU ✂ AF, ✂ AFT
96/7 SPx 12
99/0 SPx 53
01/2 SPx ✂ HT
98/9 SPx Finite 26
99/0 Stadium 143, -Chrome 39
00/1 Stadium 145
01/2 Stadium 96
95/6 Super Sticker 18
92/3 Topps 105
95/6 Topps 233
98/9 Topps 161
99/0 Topps 215, 278, SCH20
00/1 Topps 183
01/2 Topps 99
99/0 To. Chrome 215, 278
00/1 To. Chrome 122
01/2 To. Chrome 99
95/6 To. Finest 168
98/9 To. Finest 112, R14
98/9 T. Gold Label 44
99/0 To. Gold Label 60
00/1 To. Gold Label 32
00/1 To. Heritage 147
01/2 To. Heritage 100
96/7 To. Picks 61
99/0 To. Prmr. Plus 28, CAC9
91/2 To. Stadium 60
92/3 To. Stadium 37
93/4 To. Stadium 96
94/5 To. Stadium 166
95/6 To. Stadium 18
93/4 TSC Members Only 18
00/1 To. Stars 67
98/9 UD Choice 62
00/1 UD Heroes 39
01/2 Ultimate Mem. ✂ A8, ✂ CT
90/1 Upper Deck 26
91/2 Upper Deck 263
92/3 Upper Deck 128
93/4 Upper Deck 396, SP-23
94/5 Upper Deck 276, SP-13
95/6 Upper Deck 285, SE-12
96/7 Upper Deck 245, P20
97/8 Upper Deck 50
98/9 Upper Deck 78, FF30, ✂ GJ24
99/0 Upper Deck 48
00/1 Upper Deck 56, ✂ DGJ, ✂ GJ
01/2 Upper Deck 286, ✂ CJers (x2), ✂ SCFJers, ✂ SCFJersD, ✂ SCFJersT
94/5 UD BAP ✍ 96
97/8 UD Black Diam. 16
95/6 UD CC 133
96/7 UD CC 68, 315
97/8 UD Coll. Choice 68
98/9 UD G. Reserve 78
99/0 UD G. Reserve 48
01/2 UD Honor Roll ✂ GAJ
00/1 UD Ice ✂ IGJ
00/1 UD Legends ✍ ES
01/2 UD Mask 56, ✂ GJ, ✂ JP, ✂ DP
98/9 UD MVP 63
99/0 UD MVP 67
00/1 UD MVP 63
01/2 UD MVP 62
01/2 UD Premier ✂ D
01/2 UD SCup Champs 48, ✂ S, ✂ G
01/2 UD Top Shelf 99
00/1 UD Vintage 121
01/2 UD Vintage 82, 87
97/8 Valu-net, ✍ Aut.
00/1 Vanguard 36
99/0 Victory 91
00/1 Victory 76
01/2 Victory 112
99/0 WGretzky 58
97/8 Zenith 63, Z15
87/8 CALG / Red Rooster
87/8 CALG / Red Rooster
90/1 CALG / McGavin's
91/2 CALG / IGA
92/3 CALG / IGA 017
96/7 DALL / Southwest
97/8 DALL / Score 135
00/1 DALL / Southwest
01/2 DALL / Southwest

NIGHBOR, FRANK
25-27 Anonymous 16
24/5 Champ's Cigarettes
83 HHOF Postcard E12
83&87 HHOF 72
60/1 Topps 35
61/2 Topps - Stamp
23/4 William Paterson 2
24/5 William Paterson 6

NIGRO, FRANK
83/4 O-Pee-Chee 337
83/4 OPC/Topps Sticker 149
92 Semic Sticker 256
82/3 TORO
83/4 TORO

NIINIMAA, JANNE
02/3 Cardset 231, -DD 4, -SGSP 2
02/3 O-Pee-Chee 125
02/3 Pacific 147
02/3 Pacific Complete 94
02/3 Parkhurst Retro 154
02/3 Sports Vault 229
02/3 Topps 125
02/3 To. Limited 125
02/3 To. Total 142
02/3 Upper Deck 74
02/3 UD Rookie 63
98/9 Aurora 75
99/0 BAP Mem. 76
00/1 BAP Mem. 282
01/2 BAP Mem. 76
98/9 Cardset DT 4
99/0 Cardset AH 3-pata
00/1 Cardset 114
93/4 Classic 44
94/5 Classic 105, T51
93/4 Cla. 4 Sport 207
97/8 Donruss 99
96/7 Do. Canadian 128
97/8 Do. Cdn. Ice SCS 21
96/7 Do. Elite A-16
97/8 Do. Elite 92
97/8 Do. Preferred 26
97/8 Do. Priority 84
97/8 Do. Studio 100
98/9 Dynagon Ice 74
96/7 Flair 120
96/7 Fl. Ultra 127, UR-15
95 Hartwall Karjala
97/8 Leaf 75
96/7 L. Preferred 127
97/8 Limited 16, 136, 168, FG-69
96/7 Metal Univ. 189
01/2 O-Pee-Chee 139
98/9 Omega 94
98/9 Pacific 24
99/0 Pacific 162
00/1 Pacific 437
01/2 Pacific 162
97/8 Pacific CC 173
98/9 Pa. Crown Roy. 52
97/8 Pa. Dynagon 92, T-16
97/8 Pa. Invincible 103, FP-26
97/8 Pa. Paramount 135
98/9 Pa. Paramount 91
97/8 Panini Sticker 94, 245
98/9 Panini Sticker 198
99/0 Panini Sticker 245
00/1 Panini Sticker 160
93/4 Parkhurst 520
00/1 Parkhurst P-31
01/2 Parkhurst 123
94/5 Parkie SE217
97/8 Pi. Be A Player 144, ✍ Aut. 144
97/8 Pi. Inside 179
96/7 Pi. Zenith 124
97/8 Score 165
97/8 Score Phil. 9
96/7 Select CE 104
95 Semic 227
00/1 Signature 28, ✍ Aut. 32
01/2 Signat. 132, ✍ Aut. 132
93/4 Sisu 390
94/5 Sisu 58
95/6 Sisu 251, G-8, Stud
95/6 Sisu Limited 13
94/5 SP 162
96/7 SP 186
97/8 SPx 37
98/9 SPx Finite 35
99/0 Topps 112
00/1 Topps 245
01/2 Topps 139
99/0 To. Chrome 112
94/5 Topps Finest 128
98/9 To. Finest 108
98/9 UD Choice 86
96/7 Upper Deck 310
97/8 Upper Deck 124, SG41, T8A
98/9 Upper Deck 91
99/0 Upper Deck 228
01/2 Upper Deck 299
96/7 UD Black Diam. 154
96/7 UD CC 361
97/8 UD Coll. Choice 183, SQ26
98/9 UD G. Reserve 91
99/0 UD G. Reserve 228
96/7 UD Ice 49
97/8 UD Ice 21
98/9 UD MVP 78
00/1 UD Vintage 145
01/2 UD Vintage 101
99/0 Victory 118
01/2 Victory 140
96 Wien 6
96/7 PHIL / Ocean Spray

NIINIMAKI, JARI
72/3 Williams Finnish 312

NIINIMÄKI, JESSE
02/3 Cardset 232, -BFG 5, ✍ BFG

NIINIVIRTA, TIMO
78/9 SM-Liiga 104
72/3 Williams Finnish 290

NIITTOAHO, HANNU
66/7 Champion 58
70/1 Kuvajulkaisut 145
80/1 Mallasjuoma 195
78/9 SM-Liiga 205
71/2 Williams Finnish 195
72/3 Williams Finnish 233
73/4 Williams Finnish 267

NIITTYMAKI, ANTERO
02/3 Philadelphia Phantoms

NIITTYMÄKI, ANTERO
02/3 Cardset 81
99/0 Cardset 326, Puck 1
00/1 Cardset 336, Mask-5, NG-9

NIITTYMÄKI, MIKA
94/5 Sisu 307
96/7 Sisu 133

NIKANDER, HARRY
91/2 Jyvas Hyva 72
92/3 Jyvas Hyva 200
80/1 Mallasjuoma 217
78/9 SM-Liiga 227

NIKANDER, JARKKO
98/9 Cardset 182
99/0 Cardset 254
00/1 Cardset 34
97/8 Hockey-Box
92/3 Jyvas Hyva 27
93/4 Jyvas Hyva 47
93/4 Sisu 247
94/5 Sisu 52
95/6 Sisu 317
96/7 Sisu 129

NIKITIN, IGOR
98/9 Mir 44
00/1 Mir 232

NIKITIN, VALERI
70/1 Kuvajulkaisut 10
70/1 Soviet Stars

NIKKILA, SEPPO
66/7 Champion 183
65/6 Hellas 112

NIKKO, JANI
98/9 Cardset 35
00/1 Cardset 272
97/8 Hockey-Box
92/3 Jyvas Hyva 37
93/4 Jyvas Hyva 75
93/4 Parkhurst 524
95 Semic 226
93/4 Sisu 111
94/5 Sisu 203
95/6 Sisu 220
96/7 Sisu 18
95/6 Sisu Limited 84
99/0 UD Elitserien 90

NIKOLAEV, ANDREI
98/9 Mir 114

NIKOLAEV, IGOR
98/9 Mir 62
99/0 Mir 89
00/1 Mir 15

NIKOLAEV, SERGEI
00/1 Mir 114

NIKOLIC, ALEX
95/6 Fort Wayne Komets
92/3 Salt Lake G'Eagles

NIKOLISHIN, ANDREI
02/3 Pacific 397
02/3 To. Total 363
02/3 UD Vintage 259
98/9 Be A Player 300, ✍ Aut. 300
99/0 BAP Mem. 106
00/1 BAP Mem. 391
92/3 Classic 48
94/5 Classic 70, R14, T28
92/3 Classic Four Sport 189
93/4 Cla. Prospects IA18
95/6 Donruss 124
94/5 Fleer 87
96/7 Fl. Picks 172
94/5 Fleer Ultra 301
95/6 Fleer Ultra 68
95/6 Leaf 11
99/0 Pacific 445
97/8 Pa. Dynagon BKS-102
99/0 Pa. Paramount 247
95/6 Panini Sticker 29
96/7 Panini Sticker 32
97/8 Panini Sticker 117
98/9 Panini Sticker 110
99/0 Panini Sticker 173
95/6 Parkhurst 94
94/5 Parkie SE72
94/5 Pinnacle 487
95/6 Pinnacle 98
96/7 Pinnacle 179
96/7 Pi. Be A Player 137, ✍ Aut. 137
94/5 Premier 421
95/6 Score 169
94/5 Select 184

95 Semic 123
95/6 SBx Emotion 76
95/6 SBx Impact 74
95/6 Topps 361, 22NG
94/5 Topps Finest 10
95/6 To. Stadium 149
92/3 Upper Deck 340
94/5 Upper Deck 241, C9, SP122
95/6 Upper Deck 55, SE-38
00/1 Upper Deck 177
01/2 Upper Deck 177
95/6 UD CC 21
96/7 UD CC 114
91/2 Upper Deck WJC 7
99/0 UD MVP Cup 192
00/1 UD Vintage 362
01/2 UD Vintage 258
01/2 Victory 360
95/6 HART / Kids Club

NIKOLOV, ANGEL
02/3 Cardset 82
94/5 APS 206
95/6 APS 153, 438
96/7 APS 172
97/8 APS 79
95/6 Classic ✍ Aut.
97/8 DS 42
98/9 DS 43
99/0 DS 60
00/1 DS 39
01/2 DS 7
96/7 DS Sticker 43
97/8 DS Sticker 90
98/9 OFS 3
99/0 OFS 154, 480
00/1 OFS 137

NIKULIN, IGOR
00/1 Mir 236
95 Panini Worlds 35
98/9 Cincinnati M'Ducks 21

NIKULIN, ILIA
00/1 Mir 312

NIKULIN, ILYA
02/3 Russian Future Stars 20

NIKULIN, VALERI
98/9 Mir 19
99/0 Mir 11
00/1 Metallurg 31

NILAN, CHRIS
91/2 Bowman 351
80/1 Dernière Heure
83/4 Dernière Heure
86/7 Kraft Sports 34
83/4 O-Pee-Chee 194
84/5 O-Pee-Chee 268
86/7 O-Pee-Chee 199
88/9 OPC/Topps 31
90/1 O-Pee-Chee 454
91/2 O-Pee-Chee 311
90/1 OPC Premier 85
85/6 OPC Sticker 127-245
87/8 OPC Sticker 15-154
88/9 OPC Sticker 245-115
87/8 Panini Sticker 68
91/2 Panini Sticker 183
80/1 Pepsi Bottle Cap
91/2 Pinnacle 289
90/1 Pro Set 205, 409
87/8 Pro Sport CW17
90/1 Score 311, 22T
91/2 Score 197
91/2 Score CAN 197
92/3 Score 76
89 Semic Sticker 175
91/2 To. Stadium 244
90/1 Upper Deck 368, 442
91/2 Upper Deck 237
83/4 Vachon 51-71
90/1 BOST / Sports Action
80/1 MONT
81/2 MONT
82/3 MONT
82/3 MONT / Steinberg
83/4 MONT
84/5 MONT
85/6 MONT
85/6 MONT / Provigo
86/7 MONT
87/8 MONT
87/8 MONT / Kodak Poster
87/8 MONT / Vachon 19
87/8 MONT / Vachon 20
89/0 NYRA / Marine

NILAN, CHRIS
02/3 Fleer Throwbacks 66

NILIMAA, MATTIAS
98/9 UD Elitserien 73
99/0 UD Elitserien 132

NILL, JIM
83/4 O-Pee-Chee 357
84/5 O-Pee-Chee 11
89/0 O-Pee-Chee 224
90/1 ProCards 475
83/4 Souhaits Keychain [Canucks]
83/4 Vachon 114-34
88/9 DETR / Little Caesars
82/3 VANC
83/4 VANC
85/6 WINN
85/6 WINN / Safety Tips
86/7 WINN

NILSEN,
92/3 Semic Nordisk 209 [Rookie]

NILSEN, ERIK S
92/3 Semic Nordisk 172

NILSEN, JOHNNY
92/3 Semic Nordisk 147

NILSEN, NILS
79 Panini Sticker 296

NILSEN, ODD
92/3 Semic Nordisk 145

NILSEN, SJUR ROBERT
95 Panini Worlds 251

NILSEN, SJUR ROBERT
92/3 Semic Nordisk 99

NILSEN, TOR
92/3 Semic Nordisk 96

NILSON, MARCUS
02/3 O-Pee-Chee 224
02/3 Pacific 157
02/3 Pacific Complete 141
02/3 SP Authentic 117
02/3 Sports Vault 45
02/3 Topps 224
02/3 To. Limited 224
02/3 To. Total 180
02/3 Upper Deck 323
02/3 UD MVP 78
02/3 Victory 93
01/2 Adrenaline 84
99/0 BAP Mem. 163
95/6 Future Legends ✍ HP-4
99/0 Millenium 115, ✍ Aut. 115
99/0 Pacific 185
01/2 Pacific 175
99/0 Pa. Paramount 104
01/2 PS Titanium 62
95/6 SP 185
99/0 Topps 125
99/0 To. Chrome 125
98/9 UD Choice 288, 296
95/6 Upper Deck 560
01/2 Upper Deck 74
97/8 UD Black Diam. 137
95/6 UD CC 345
97/8 UD Elitserien 43, 137, S2
98/9 UD Elitserien 221
01/2 UD Mask 40
01/2 UD MVP 80
01/2 UD Vintage 108, 113
01/2 Victory 149
99/0 Louisville Panthers
98/9 New Haven Beast 20

NILSSON, BILLY
92/3 Semic Elitserien 250

NILSSON, FREDRIK
98/9 Cardset 108
99/0 Cardset 62
94 Semic 59
89/0 Semic Elitserien 252
90/1 Semic Elitserien 170
91/2 Semic Elitserien 272
92/3 Semic Elitserien 290
93 Semic Sticker 17
97/8 UD Elitserien 132
95/6 Kansas City Blades

NILSSON, HARDY
95/6 DEL 74
96/7 DEL 268

NILSSON, HENRIK
95/6 Leaf Elit Set 205
90/1 Semic Elitserien 172
91/2 Semic Elitserien 267
92/3 Semic Elitserien 288
95/6 UD Elitserien 218
97/8 UD Elitserien 71
98/9 UD Elitserien 81
99/0 UD Elitserien 84
00/1 UD Elitserien 73

NILSSON, KENT
02/3 UD Foundations 11
00/1 Alfabilder
01/2 Fleer Greats 89, ✍ Aut.
83/4 Funmate Puffy 3 [w/]
95 Globe 71
80/1 O-Pee-Chee 106
80/1 O-Pee-Chee 197
81/2 O-Pee-Chee 34
81/2 O-Pee-Chee 52
81/2 O-Pee-Chee 53
82/3 O-Pee-Chee 54
83/4 O-Pee-Chee 89
84/5 O-Pee-Chee 232
81/2 OPC Sticker 218
82/3 OPC/Topps Sticker 217
83/4 OPC/Topps Sticker 267
83/4 OPC/Topps Sticker 268
84/5 OPC Sticker 245
85/6 OPC Sticker 208
87/8 OPC Sticker 88-220
80/1 O-Pee-Chee Super 3
80/1 Pepsi Bottle Cap
81/2 Post 28
82/3 Post [Calg.]
92/3 Semic Elitserien 93
82 Semic Sticker 147
89 Semic Sticker 24
91 Semic Sticker 50
83/4 Souhaits Keychain [Flames]
82/3 Stater Mint 4
80/1 Topps 106
80/1 Topps 197
81/2 Topps 24
81/2 Topps 48
01/2 UD Legends 69
83/4 Vachon 14-134
83/4 Vachon 14-96
79/0 ATLF / B&W
79/0 ATLF / Colour
80/1 CALG
81/2 CALG
82/3 CALG
88/9 EDMO / Action 27
78/9 Winnipeg Jets

NILSSON, LARS-GÖRAN
72 Hellas MM-Jenkki 33
70/1 Kuvajulkaisut 33
69/0 Mästär Serien 36
72 Panda MM-Toronto
72 Semic Sticker 54
74 Semic Sticker 19
71/2 Williams Finnish 53
72/3 Williams Finnish 53

NILSSON, MAGNUS
98/9 UD Elitserien 159, 213
99/0 UD Elitserien 162
00/1 Louisiana Ice Gators

NILSSON, MATS
89/0 Semic Elitserien 106
90/1 Semic Elitserien 109

NILSSON, MIKAEL
95/6 Leaf Elit Set 153

NILSSON, NISSE
00/1 Alfabilder

NILSSON, ÖRJAN
89/0 Semic Elitserien 22
91/2 Semic Elitserien 137
92/3 Semic Elitserien 157

NILSSON, PER
89/0 Semic Elitserien 186

NILSSON, PETER*
94/5 Leaf Elit Set 50
89/0 Semic Elitserien 64
90/1 Semic Elitserien 288
91/2 Semic Elitserien 71
92/3 Semic Elitserien 91

NILSSON, PETTER
96/7 DEL 347
94/5 Leaf Elit Set 7
95/6 Leaf Elit Set 254
91/2 Semic Elitserien 161
92/3 Semic Elitserien 182
95/6 UD Elitserien 118, DS8
98/9 UD Elitserien 68
99/0 UD Elitserien 70
00/1 UD Elitserien 122, 201, ✍ Sig.

NILSSON, RONNY
91/2 Semic Elitserien 127

NILSSON, STEFAN
94/5 Leaf Elit Set 18, 258, P-2, RR-10
95/6 Leaf Elit Set 42, 252
94 Semic 63
89/0 Semic Elitserien 114, 160
90/1 Semic Elitserien 240
91/2 Semic Elitserien 167
92/3 Semic Elitserien 186
92/3 Semic Elitserien 258
95/6 UD Elitserien 65, 122
97/8 UD Elitserien 58, 124, 200, 212, UDS12, C7

NILSSON, THOMAS
91/2 Semic Elitserien 10

NILSSON, ULF
01/2 Fleer Greats 26, ✍ Aut.
92/3 Future Trends C76 143
74 Hellas MM-Jenkki 31
78/9 O-Pee-Chee 255
79/0 O-Pee-Chee 30
80/1 O-Pee-Chee 116
81/2 O-Pee-Chee 229
81/2 OPC Sticker 172
74/5 OPC WHA 4
75/6 OPC WHA 83
76/7 OPC WHA 2
76/7 OPC WHA 3
76/7 O-Pee-Chee WHA 5
76/7 OPC WHA 9
77/8 OPC WHA 15
74 Semic Sticker 8
82 Semic Sticker 145
77-79 Sportscaster 71-12
77-79 Sports. FIN 80-1911
78/9 Topps 255
79/0 Topps 30
79/0 Topps 163
80/1 Topps 116
81/2 Topps 102 [East]
91/2 Upper Deck 643
96 Wien HL11
73/4 Williams Finnish 33

NIMIGON, STEVE
95/6 Cla. Vis. Signings 71, ✍ Aut.
93/4 Slapshot / Niagara Falls 9
95/6 Slapshot 188

NIRO, DOMINIC
93/4 Flint Generals

NISKALA, JANNE
02/3 Cardset 83, -Nimik.

NISKANEN, MIKA
99/0 Cardset 96
00/1 Cardset 72

NISKANEN, PETRI
70/1 Kuvajulkaisut 334

NISKAVAARA, JAAKKO
00/1 Cardset 56
95/6 UD CC 332

NISSINEN, PEKKA
78/9 SM-Liiga 127

NISSINEN, TERO
96/7 Sisu 86

NISSINEN, TUOMAS
02/3 Cardset 233

NISTICO, LOU
75/6 OPC WHA 13

NISTOR, CONSTANTIN
79 Panini Sticker 318

NITTEL, ADAM
95/6 Slapshot 203
01/2 Cleveland Barons
99/0 Kentucky Tho'blades
00/1 Kentucky Tho'blades
x00/1 Kentucky Tho'blades

NIUKKANEN, PETRI
80/1 Mallasjuoma 174

NIXON, DANNY
52/3 Laval Dairy Update 15
52/3 St. Lawrence 38

NIXON, JARET
95/6 Slapshot 324

NIXON, JULIAN
74/5 Sioux City Musketeers

NOACK, ERIK
00/1 Austin Ice Bats
99/0 San Angelo Outlaws

NOACK, RUDIGER
70/1 Kuvajulkaisut 90

NOBILI, JASON
00/1 Owen Sound Attack 27

NOBILI, MARIO
90/1 7th..Sketch LHJMQ 233
91/2 7th...Sketch LHJMQ 146
91/2 Star Pics 34
91/2 Ultimate Draft Pick 51, ✍ Aut.

NOBLE, JEFF
85/6 Kitchener Rangers
86/7 Kitchener Rangers
87/8 Kitchener Rangers

NOBLE, KIP
00/1 Kudos 54
01/2 Cardiff Devils

NOBLE, REG
25-27 Anonymous 96
24/5 Champ's Cigarettes
83 HHOF Postcard B8
83&87 HHOF 22
23/4 William Paterson 26
24/5 William Paterson 51

NOBLE, TOM
93/4 Cla. 4 Sport 229

NOCTOR, JOHN
94/5 Guildford Flames 18

NOEL, CLAUDE
99/0 Milwaukee Admirals

NOEL, DOMINIC
01/2 Cape Breton Eagles 6

NOEL, MIKE
74/5 Sioux City Musketeers

NOËL, CLAUDE
89/0 7th..Sketch OHL 176
92/3 Dayton Bombers
96/7 Michigan K-Wings
98/9 Milwaukee Admirals

NOGIER, PAT
85/6 Kamloops Blazers

NOGUES, JEAN-FRANÇOIS
00/1 Victoriaville Tigres 16

NOHEJL, MICHAL
99/0 Score 151

NOHEL, PAVEL
94/5 APS 15
95/6 APS 112
96/7 APS 275
97/8 DS 17
99/0 DS 50
96/7 DS Sticker 183
97/8 DS Sticker 35
98/9 OFS 71
99/0 OFS 242

NOISEAUX, YANNICK
99/0 Shawinigan 17
00/1 Shawinigan 11

NOKELAINEN, ESKO
92/3 Jyvas Hyva 137

NOKIKURU, KIMMO
66/7 Champion 39

NOKKOSMÄKI, NEMO
93/4 Sisu 217
94/5 Sisu 232

NOLAN, BILLY
91/2 Hampton Roads
98/9 Hampton Roads

NOLAN, JEFF
90/1 7th..Sketch OHL 112

NOLAN, OWEN
02/3 Atomic 87, -SC 14
02/3 BAP All-Star 66, ✂ ASJ, ✂ HSHSJers
02/3 BAP Mem. 74, 226, 254, 364, ✂ ASJ41, ✂ ASE17, ✂ ASN17, ✂ ASTJ16, ✂ AS5, ✂ AST7, ✂ AST27, ✂ FP26, ✂ HSHSJers 18, ✂ SC9, ✂ TM18
02/3 Bowman 21
02/3 Crown Royale ✂ GWJ 20
02/3 Exclusive 151
02/3 First Edition 156, 340, 366, 393, 404H, ✂ Jers., ✂ DGJ 8, ✂ HSHSJers 14, ✂ TSL 16
02/3 Heads Up 109, ✂ GWQ 24
02/3 In The GU 64, 164, ✂ E21, ✂ F26, ✂ GUJ21, ✂ SJ21, ✂ T16
02/3 McDonald's -SLG 8
02/3 O-Pee-Chee 28
02/3 Pacific 338
02/3 Pacific Complete 112
02/3 Parkhurst 111, ✂ FP26, ✂ GJ37, ✂ SJ37, ✂ HSHSJers, ✂ TT15
02/3 Parkhurst Retro 45
02/3 Pr. Stock Reserve ✂ 142
02/3 PS Titanium ✂ GWJ 63
02/3 Quest for the Cup -CTC 16
02/3 Signature GS-66, ✂ FS9, ✂ SGJ21, ✂ TQ18
02/3 SP Authentic 78
02/3 SP GU 41, ✂ PC
02/3 Sports Vault 286
02/3 SPx 62
02/3 Stadium 7, -BT12
02/3 Topps 28, HHU13
02/3 T. Chrome 28
02/3 To. Heritage 44
02/3 To. Limited 28
02/3 To. Total 261, TTC25, TT19
02/3 Ultimate Mem. ✂ FO
02/3 Upper Deck 145, 242, ✂ LN
02/3 UD Artistic 75, R75, / Art
02/3 UD Classic 84
02/3 UD Honor 59, 95, -TW13
02/3 UD MVP 152
02/3 UD Piece 75
02/3 UD Rookie 93
02/3 UD Top Shelf 74, ✂ M, ✂ ST
02/3 UD Vintage 211, 285, GB 211, T54
02/3 Vanguard 86
02/3 Victory 177
01/2 Adrenaline 168
01/2 Atomic 86, TN 12
98/9 Aurora 170
00/1 Aurora 129, Pins. 129
99/0 BAP Mem. 245, ✂ TM-16
00/1 BAP Mem. 227, ✂ J-26, ✂ H-18
01/2 BAP Mem. 63, ✂ ASJ, ✂ ASE, ✂ ASN, ✂ ASD, ✂ SCP
01/2 BAP Update ✂ H21
96/7 Bic.Sports Aces 4-C
97/8 Bicycle 5-Club
91/2 Bowman 134
92/3 Bowman 237
92/3 Bowman 328
95/6 Bowman 58
01/2 Bowman 46
98/9 Bowman's Best 70
99/0 Crown Royale 125, IE-22, TC-8
00/1 Crown Royale 94
01/2 Crown Royale 125
93/4 Donruss 279
94/5 Donruss 45
95/6 Donruss 153, 268, M-2
96/7 Donruss 6, HL-17
97/8 Donruss 84
96/7 Do. Canadian 54
97/8 Do. Canadian 108, NP-30
95/6 Do. Elite 26
96/7 Do. Elite 14, S-6
97/8 Do. Preferred 108
97/8 Do. Priority 46
96/7 Duracell DC19
98/9 Dynagon Ice 168
99/0 Dynagon Ice 174, CM-14
93/4 EA Sports 113
01/2 EASports
01/2 eTopps 21
96/7 Flair 85, HN-10
94/5 Fleer 181
96/7 Fleer 100
95/6 Fleer Metal 133
96/7 Fl. Picks F50-34
92/3 Fleer Ultra 177
93/4 Fleer Ultra 154
94/5 Fleer Ultra 177
95/6 Fleer Ultra 134, 304, CC-13, RLS-8
96/7 Fl. Ultra 153
91/2 Gillette 25
93/4 Hockey Wit 57
95/6 Hoyle / East. 8-Diamond
92/3 Humpty Dumpty
91/2 Kraft 55
96/7 Kraft / KD, PB
99/0 Kraft / JELL-O
00/1 Kraft 21
93/4 Leaf 42
94/5 Leaf 144
95/6 Leaf 240
96/7 Leaf 128
97/8 Leaf 23
94/5 L. Limited 41
95/6 L. Limited 93
96/7 L. Limited 20, BTB-3
96/7 L. Preferred 6, LS-62
97/8 Limited 117, 196
96/7 Maggers 131
92/3 McDonald's McD-24
95/6 McDonald's McD-24
96/7 Metal Univ. 139
01/2 Nextel
98/9 NHL Power Play
91/2 O-Pee-Chee 64
92/3 O-Pee-Chee 382
01/2 O-Pee-Chee 30
98/9 OPC Chrome 156
90/1 OPC Premier 86
92/3 OPC Premier 193
97/8 Omega 205
98/9 Omega 212
99/0 Omega 209, 5ST-11
98/9 Pacific 390
99/0 Pacific 378
00/1 Pacific 363, GCDC-31
01/2 Pacific 341, TDP 6
97/8 Pacific CC 151, TC-22
97/8 Pa. Crown Roy. 121
98/9 Pa. Crown Roy. 120
97/8 Pa. Dynagon 114, T-50
97/8 Pa. Invincible 128
97/8 Pa. Paramount 169
98/9 Pa. Paramount 214
99/0 Pa. Paramount 207
00/1 Pa. Paramount 215, FF-32
97/8 Pa. Revolution 126
98/9 Pa. Revolution 128
90/1 Panini/QUE 17
91/2 Panini Sticker 266
92/3 Panini Sticker 210
93/4 Panini Sticker 70
95/6 Panini Sticker 249
96/7 Panini Sticker 277
97/8 Panini Sticker 230
98/9 Panini Sticker 210
99/0 Panini Sticker 300
00/1 Panini Sticker 204
91/2 Parkhurst 143
92/3 Parkhurst 145
92/3 Parkhurst 455
92/3 Parkhurst CP13
93/4 Parkhurst 163
93/4 Parkhurst F4
94/5 Parkhurst V43
95/6 Parkhurst 49, 453
00/1 Parkhurst P-17
01/2 Parkhurst 55, ✂ PJ23, ✂ PS23, ✂ H10
94/5 Parkie SE143
91/2 Pinnacle 156
92/3 Pinnacle 6
92/3 Pinnacle T2K 10
93/4 Pinnacle 151
93/4 Pinnacle T2K1 28
94/5 Pinnacle 76
95/6 Pinnacle 12, FC-3
96/7 Pinnacle 186
97/8 Pinnacle 49
96/7 Pi. Be A Player BB-25
97/8 Pi. BeeHive 22
96/7 Pi. Certified 59
96/7 Pi. FANtasy 18
97/8 Pi. Inside 27
96/7 Pi. Summit 12, MH-1
96/7 Pi. Summit 45
97/8 Pi. Totally 59
95/6 Pi. Zenith 16, GG-9
96/7 Pi. Zenith 37, A-14
95/6 Playoff 27, 241
96/7 Playoff 335
94/5 POG 197
95/6 POG 76
93/4 Power Play 201
93/4 Premier 267
93/4 Premier - Finest 4
94/5 Premier 457
00/1 Premier Plus 7
99/0 Prism 126
00/1 Pr. Stock 89, PS-50
01/2 Pr. Stock 86, -PS 65
00/1 PS Titanium 86
01/2 PS Titanium 123, TAS 16
01/2 PS Titanium Draft ✂ 87
90/1 Pro Set 401, 635
91/2 Pro Set 196
92/3 Pro Set 153
91/2 Pro Set Platinum 101
00/1 Revolution 130, HD-31, SM-10
90/1 Score 435, 80T
91/2 Score 143
91/2 Score CAN 143
92/3 Score 286
92/3 Score SS 12
93/4 Score 32
95/6 Score 83, CI-2, L-4
96/7 Score 69, CI-8
97/8 Score 102, CI-17
90/1 Sco. Young Stars 36
92/3 Score Young Stars 37
92/3 Seasons 46
94/5 Select 4
95/6 Select CE 19
96/7 Select CE 56
93 Semic Sticker 207
89/0 7th..Sketch OHL 180
00/1 Signature 73, F-26
01/2 Signat. C57, ✍ Aut. XLON, ✂ FO25, ✂ GUE41, ✂ GJ55, ✂ GSJ55, ✂ HSHSJers, ✂ ITN41, ✂ IG14, ✂ TM25
95/6 SBx Emotion 40, NP-6
95/6 SBx Impact 150, 240, IQ-11
96/7 SBx Impact 117
94/5 SP 95
95/6 SP 129
96/7 SP 138
97/8 SP Authentic 131
98/9 SP Authentic 77, ✍ SotT
99/0 SP Authentic 73
00/1 SP Authentic 73
01/2 SP Authentic 73
00/1 SP GU 51
01/2 SP GU ✂ AF
96/7 SPx 41
97/8 SPx 44
99/0 SPx 127
00/1 SPx 79
01/2 SPx 57
98/9 SPx Finite 71
00/1 Stadion 74
99/0 Stadium 44
00/1 Stadium 43, SF11
01/2 Stadium 11
95/6 Super Sticker 110
96/7 Team Out!
92/3 Topps 349
95/6 Topps 305
98/9 Topps 156
99/0 Topps 206
00/1 Topps 11, NHLD4, OTG6
01/2 Topps 30
99/0 To. Chrome 206
00/1 To. Chrome 11
01/2 To. Chrome 30
95/6 To. Finest 142
98/9 To. Finest 23
98/9 T. Gold Label 14
99/0 T. Gold Label 49, QC8
00/1 T. Gold Label 26, B8
00/1 To. Heritage 17, 230, 232
01/2 To. Heritage 47
96/7 To. Picks 57
99/0 To. Prmr. Plus 15
01/2 To. Reserve 45
92/3 To. Stadium 259
92/3 To. Stadium 78
93/4 To. Stadium 397
94/5 To. Stadium 102
95/6 To. Stadium 65
95/6 TSC Members Only 8
00/1 To. Stars 11
98/9 UD Choice 175
00/1 UD Heroes 101
01/2 UD PlayMakers Ltd 81
00/1 UD Reserve 71
00/1 Ultimate Mem. ✂ Jers.-16, ✂ J-18, ✂ JJ-19, ✂ S-18, ✂ TM-34
01/2 Ultimate Mem. ✂ Emb., ✂ Jers., ✂ S&J, ✂ ITN, ✂ NP, ✍ Aut.
99/0 Ult. Victory 74
90/1 Upper Deck 351, 352
91/2 Upper Deck 367
92/3 Upper Deck 619
92/3 Upper Deck 17
92/3 Upper Deck 321
93/4 Upper Deck 175, HT-16, SP-128
94/5 Upper Deck 103, SP-63
95/6 Upper Deck 176, 225, 246, 495, AS-13, R-7, SE-163
96/7 Upper Deck 146, X19, P18
97/8 Upper Deck 147, SG24, T6A
98/9 Upper Deck 354, FF24, FT17
99/0 Upper Deck 282
00/1 Upper Deck 144, FF10, NC8
01/2 Upper Deck 144, LP12, SS15, SS5, T8
96/7 UD All-Star YCTG AR6
93/4 Upper Deck Be A Player 33
94/5 UD BAP R51, ✍ 59
96/7 UD Black Diam. 111
97/8 UD Black Diam. 9
98/9 UD Black Diam. 75
99/0 UD Black Diam. 75
01/2 UD Challenge 71
95/6 UD CC 259, C12
96/7 UD CC 233, 330, UD42, S25
97/8 UD Coll. Choice 214, SQ78, C30, CR30
97/8 UD Diam. Vision 13
98/9 UD G. Reserve 354
99/0 UD G. Reserve 282
01/2 UD Honor Roll TC5
96/7 UD Ice 59
97/8 UD Ice 10, L3C
01/2 UD Ice 116
00/1 UD Legends 113
01/2 UD Mask 81
98/9 UD MVP 173
99/0 UD MVP 174
00/1 UD MVP 150
01/2 UD MVP 156
99/0 UD MVP Cup 153
99/0 UD Ovation 50
00/1 UD Pros&Prosp. 71
01/2 UD Top Shelf 114
00/1 UD Vintage 298, 307
01/2 UD Vintage 211, 217
00/1 Vanguard 88
01/2 Vanguard 87
99/0 Victory 252
00/1 Victory 197, 320
01/2 Victory 292, 405
97/8 Zenith 27, Z60
90/1 QUÉB / Petro-Canada
91/2 QUÉB / Petro-Canada
92/3 QUÉB / Petro-Canada
94/5 QUÉB / Burger King

NOLAN, TED
91 7th..Sketch Mem.Cup 24
90/1 7th..Sketch OHL 176
91/2 7th...Sketch OHL 318
93/4 Slapshot / S.S.Marie 29
89/0 Soo Greyhounds
93/4 Soo Greyhounds 30

NOLAN, TOM
99/0 Mobile Mysticks

NOLET, DANNY
90/1 7th..Sketch LHJMQ 266

NOLET, SIMON
70/1 Colgate 51
70/1 Eddie Sargent 150
71/2 Eddie Sargent 148
72/3 Eddie Sargent 158
74/5 Loblaws
68/9 O-Pee-Chee 187
70/1 O-Pee-Chee 187
71/2 O-Pee-Chee 206
72/3 O-Pee-Chee 125
73/4 O-Pee-Chee 222
74/5 O-Pee-Chee 187
75/6 O-Pee-Chee 220
75/6 O-Pee-Chee 319
76/7 O-Pee-Chee 64
65/6 Québec Aces
72 Semic Sticker 174
72/3 Topps 26
74/5 Topps 187
75/6 Topps 220
75/6 Topps 319
76/7 Topps 64
71/2 Toronto Sun Photo
01/2 UD Legends 74
76/7 COLR / Hockey Talk
70/1 PHIL
84/5 QUÉB
85/6 QUÉB
85/6 QUÉB / Gene. Foods
86/7 QUÉB
86/7 QUÉB / Gene. Foods

NOONAN, BRIAN
92/3 Bowman 98
93/4 Donruss 464
94/5 Donruss 140
95/6 Donruss 242
98/9 EBK IHL All-Star
92/3 Fleer Ultra 280
93/4 Fleer Ultra 291
95/6 Fleer Ultra 301
93/4 Leaf 398
94/5 Leaf 217
88/9 OPC/Topps 165
92/3 O-Pee-Chee 234
90/1 OPC Premier 87
88/9 OPC Sticker 11-140
88/9 OPC Sticker 147
98/9 Pacific 432
97/8 Pacific CC 339
88/9 Panini Sticker 28
92/3 Panini Sticker 9
93/4 Panini Sticker 149
91/2 Parkhurst 264
94/5 Parkhurst 143
95/6 Parkhurst 445
92/3 Pinnacle 194
93/4 Pinnacle 162
94/5 Pinnacle 131
96/7 Pinnacle 30
96/7 Pi. Be A Player 201, ✍ Aut. 201
94/5 POG 168
95/6 POG 237
93/4 Power Play 314
93/4 Premier 13
94/5 Premier 28
90/1 Pro Set 433
91/2 Pro Set Platinum 165
88/9 ProCards / Saginaw
92/3 Score 89
93/4 Score 411
95/6 Score 156
97/8 Score Vanc. 18
92/3 Topps 159
92/3 To. Stadium 400
95/6 To. Stadium 121
91/2 Upper Deck 380
92/3 Upper Deck 117
94/5 Upper Deck 302
95/6 Upper Deck 272
98/9 Upper Deck 378
95/6 UD CC 116
96/7 UD CC 232
98/9 UD G. Reserve 378
87/8 CHIC / Coke
88/9 CHIC / Coke
91/2 CHIC / Coke
93/4 CHIC / Coke
99/0 Chicago Wolves
00/1 Chicago Wolves
98/9 Indianapolis Ice

NORBÄCK, ERIK
98/9 UD Elitserien 14
99/0 UD Elitserien 14

NORBERG, KENT
89/0 Semic Elitserien 189

NORBERG, ROBERT
94/5 Leaf Elit Set 42

NORD, BJÖRN
95 Globe 24
94/5 Leaf Elit Set 133
95/6 Leaf Elit Set 192
92/3 Semic Elitserien 84
92/3 Upper Deck 231
00/1 UD DEL 193
95/6 UD Elitserien 42
97/8 UD Elitserien 38
98/9 UD Elitserien 50
99/0 UD Elitserien 36

NORD, TOMAS
89/0 Semic Elitserien 128
90/1 Semic Elitserien 205

NORDBERG, ROBERT
98/9 Cardset 129
95/6 Leaf Elit Set 82
90/1 Semic Elitserien 245
91/2 Semic Elitserien 170
92/3 Semic Elitserien 188
95/6 UD Elitserien 128
97/8 UD Elitserien 127

NORDBLAD, CHRISTER
71/2 Williams Finnish 289

NORDFELDT, HENRIK
94/5 Leaf Elit Set 281
95/6 Leaf Elit Set 132
97/8 UD Elitserien 192
98/9 UD Elitserien 194
99/0 UD Elitserien 126
00/1 UD Elitserien 116

NORDGREN, JOHAN
97/8 UD Elitserien 168

NORDHUS, MORTEN
92/3 Semic Nordisk 132

NORDIN, ANDERS
70/1 Kuvajulkaisut 34

NORDIN, HAKAN
89/0 Semic Elitserien 272
90/1 Semic Elitserien 31
91/2 Semic Elitserien 279

NORDIN, URBAN
89/0 Semic Elitserien 181
90/1 Semic Elitserien 15

NORDLANDER, BERT-OLA
72 Panda MM-Toronto
72 Semic Sticker 48
98/9 UD Elitserien 203
71/2 Williams Finnish 54

NORDMARK, ROBERT
94/5 Leaf Elit Set 117
90/1 O-Pee-Chee 433
89/0 opcSticker 66-206
90/1 Panini/VAN 18
90/1 Pro Set 547
91/2 Semic Elitserien 256
92/3 Semic Elitserien 285
95/6 Sisu 302, 378, DT-4
96/7 Sisu SH 2
95/6 Sisu Limited 32
87/8 SLOU / Kodak
88/9 VANC / Mohawk
89/0 VANC / Mohawk
90/1 VANC / Mohawk
00/1 Nottingham Panthers

NORDNES, KÅRE
92/3 Semic Nordisk 117

NORDNES, MAGNE
92/3 Semic Nordisk 118

NORDQUIST, NICKLAS
94/5 Leaf Elit Set 277
95/6 Leaf Elit Set 244
98/9 UD Elitserien 121
99/0 UD Elitserien 123

NORDSTROM, CARLIN
91/2 Air Canada SJHL A46
87/8 Fort Wayne Komets

NORDSTRÖM, PETER
98/9 Dynagon Ice 13
94/5 Leaf Elit Set 180
95/6 Leaf Elit Set 214
98/9 Upper Deck 220
95/6 UD Elitserien 73
97/8 UD Elitserien 52
99/0 UD Elitserien 59, S6, ✍ Aut.
00/1 UD Elitserien 88
98/9 UD G. Reserve 220
98/9 Providence Bruins

NORDSTRÖM, ROGER
98/9 DEL 39
99/0 Eishockey 145
95 Globe 2
94/5 Leaf Elit Set 188, SS-8
95/6 Leaf Elit Set 258, LM-7, S-14
95 Panini Worlds 186
95 Semic 52, 209
90/1 Semic Elitserien 126
91/2 Semic Elitserien 177
92/3 Semic Elitserien 200
00/1 UD DEL 152
01/2 UD DEL 161, G6, ✂ GJ
95/6 UD Elitserien 133
97/8 UD Elitserien 133

NORDSTRØM, JON HROARD
92/3 Semic Nordisk 21

NOREN, DARRYL
90/1 ProCards 525
96/7 Charlotte Checkers
97/8 Charlotte Checkers
97/8 Charlotte Checkers
98/9 Charlotte Checkers
99/0 Charlotte Checkers
99/0 Charlotte Checkers
91/2 Greensboro Monarchs
92/3 Greensboro Monarchs 12

NORGREN, JOHAN
98/9 DEL 115
99/0 Eishockey 287
94/5 Leaf Elit Set 8
90/1 Semic Elitserien 134
91/2 Semic Elitserien 185
92/3 Semic Elitserien 204
92/3 Upper Deck 225
00/1 UD DEL 41

NORIS, JOE
76/7 OPC WHA 46
77/8 OPC WHA 5
71/2 Toronto Sun Photo
73/4 BUFF
71/2 PITT / Sportcolor
76/7 San Diego Mariners

NORMAN, TODD
97 Bowman 28
95/6 Classic 85
94/5 Parkie SE267
94/5 Select 168
94/5 SR Auto-Phonex 31, ✍ 31
93/4 Slapshot / Guelph 12
94/5 Slapshot / Promo
94/5 Slapshot / Guelph 19
95/6 Slapshot 99
94/5 SP 185
95/6 Guelph Storm
96/7 Guelph Storm
96/7 Guelph Storm

NORMAND, DEAN
91/2 Air Canada SJHL A1
92/3 MPS SJHL 29

NORMANDIN, ÉRIC
97 Bowman 77
96/7 Rimouski Océanic

NORMANDIN, MATHIEU
96/7 Rimouski Océanic

NORONEN, MIKA
02/3 Between the Pipes 73, ✂ GUE20, ✂ GUJ20, ✂ GSJ20, ✂ ITN20, ✂ T6
02/3 Calder 58
02/3 Cardset 234
02/3 Exclusive 19
02/3 First Edition 71, ✂ Jers.
02/3 O-Pee-Chee 299
02/3 Pacific 46
02/3 Pacific Complete 2
02/3 Parkhurst 174
02/3 Signature 82, ✍ 82
02/3 SP Game-Used ✂ PC
02/3 Topps 299
02/3 To. Limited 299
02/3 Upper Deck ✂ GT
02/3 UD Mask 11, 12, ✂ BM
02/3 UD Top Shelf ✂ ST, ✂ SS
00/1 BAP Mem. 448
01/2 BAP Mem. 24
01/2 BT Pipes 45
98/9 Cardset 205, MM10
99/0 Cardset MW 7, PA 9
97/8 Hockey-Box
01/2 O-Pee-Chee 272
00/1 Parkhurst P-122
01/2 Parkhurst 280
00/1 Premier Plus 92
00/1 Pr. Stock 106
01/2 PS Titanium Draft 112
00/1 Signature 252, ✍ Aut. 214
01/2 SP GU ✂ AF
01/2 SPx 97
00/1 Stadium 238
01/2 Topps 272
01/2 To. Chrome 139
00/1 To. Heritage 133
98/9 UD Choice 278
97/8 UD Black Diam. 26
01/2 UD Mask ✂ SY
00/1 Vanguard 106
01/2 Victory 364
00/1 Rochester Americans

NORPPA, TIMO
92/3 Jyvas Hyva 61
93/4 Jyvas Hyva 117
94 Semic 48
93 Semic Sticker 70
93 Semic Sticker 72
93/4 Sisu 14
94/5 Sisu 274
95/6 Sisu 296
96/7 Sisu 90

NORRENA,
97/8 Hockey-Box

NORRENA, FREDRIK
02/3 Cardset 84
98/9 Cardset 227, MM11
99/0 Cardset 131
00/1 Cardset 93
94/5 Sisu 97
95/6 Sisu 324, GG-5
96/7 Sisu 135, MA-7
95/6 Sisu Limited 1

NORRIE, JASON
98/9 Charlotte Checkers

NORRIE, SHAUN
99/0 Calgary Hitmen
00/1 Calgary Hitmen

NORRIS, BRUCE A.
83 HHOF Postcard N10
83&87 HHOF 205

NORRIS, CLAYTON
00/1 Kudos 55
90/1 7th..Sketch WHL 30
91/2 7th...Sketch WHL 318
94/5 Hershey Bears
98/9 Orlando Solar Bears
98/9 Orlando Solar Bears Geico
97/8 St. John's Maple Leafs
01/2 Cardiff Devils
01/2 Nottingham Panthers
02/3 Hershey Bears

NORRIS, DWAYNE
93/4 Canada Nationals
92/3 Classic 70
92/3 Classic Four Sport 195
94/5 Cla. Images 34
92/3 Classic Prospects 66
96/7 DEL 351
98/9 DEL 95
93/4 Donruss 480
99/0 Eishockey 107
93/4 Fleer Ultra 470
94/5 Leaf 494
93/4 Power Play 491
93/4 Premier - Canada 13
94/5 Score 238, CT-7
00/1 UD DEL 130
01/2 UD DEL 145

NORRIS, JACK
70/1 Esso Power Player
70/1 O-Pee-Chee 165
75/6 OPC WHA 114
75/6 Phoenix Roadrunners

NORRIS, JAMES (SR.)
83 HHOF Postcard K11
83&87 HHOF 145

NORRIS, JAMES D.
83 HHOF Postcard D11
83&87 HHOF 57

NORRIS, WARREN
00/1 Kudos 156
97/8 St. John's Maple Leafs
01/2 Sheffield Steelers GS

NORRISH, ROD
73/4 MINS

NÖRSTEBÖ, SVEIN ENOK
95 Globe 197
95 Panini Worlds 241
94 Semic 255
93 Semic Sticker 234
96 Wien 205

NØRSTEBØ, SVEIN_E
92/3 Semic Nordisk 102

NORSTRÖM, MATTIAS
02/3 First Edition 173
02/3 To. Total 322
02/3 Upper Deck 81
02/3 UD Honor 84
02/3 UD Vintage 116
94/5 Classic 96
93/4 Cla. Prospects 5
93/4 Donruss 465
95/6 Donruss 248
95/6 Edge Ice 20
93/4 Fleer Ultra 376
94/5 Fleer Ultra 334
95/6 Fleer Ultra 106
96/7 Fl. Ultra 80
93/4 Leaf 426
94/5 Leaf 57
95/6 Leaf 288
99/0 Millenium 127, ✍ Aut. 127
98/9 OPC Chrome 136
99/0 Pacific 194
97/8 Pa. Invincible R-94
96/7 Panini Sticker 276
97/8 Panini Sticker 219
98/9 Panini Sticker 206
99/0 Panini Sticker 253
00/1 Panini Sticker 170
93/4 Parkhurst 370
94/5 Parkhurst 152
95/6 Parkhurst 143
96/7 Pi. Be A Player 489, RTP2
97/8 Pi. Be A Player 38, ✍ Aut. 38
93/4 Premier 418
94/5 Select 194
91/2 Semic Elitserien 12
92/3 Semic Elitserien 30
96/7 SP 76
99/0 Stadium 133, PP5
98/9 Topps 136
00/1 Topps 259
96/7 To. Picks 171
93/4 To. Stadium 371
93/4 Upper Deck 522
94/5 Upper Deck 70
96/7 Upper Deck 277
97/8 Upper Deck 82
98/9 Upper Deck 289
00/1 Upper Deck 310
01/2 Upper Deck 312
96/7 UD CC 130
98/9 UD G. Reserve 289
00/1 UD Vintage 168
94/5 Binghampton Rangers

NORTHARD, JASON
91/2 Avant Garde BCJHL 80
92/3 BCJHL 114
91/2 Nanaimo Clippers

NORTHCOTT, BALDY
35/6 Amalgamated Press
33/4 Anonymous 49
34-43 BeeHive-1 [Maroons]
35-40 Canada Starch
33/4 Canadian Gum
33/4 O-Pee-Chee 60
36/7 O-Pee-Chee 130
37/8 O-Pee-Chee 166
34/5 Sweet Caporal
33/4 WWGum 48
37/8 World Wide Gum 22

NORTHEY, WILLIAM
83 HHOF Postcard L12
83&87 HHOF 161

NORTON, BRAD
01/2 BAP Mem. 407
01/2 SPx 205
01/2 UD Ice 137
99/0 Hamilton Bulldogs
99/0 Hamilton Bulldogs/ Staz
00/1 Hamilton Bulldogs
02/3 Hershey Bears

NORTON, CHRIS
88/9 ProCards / Moncton
89/0 ProCards AHL 43
90/1 ProCards 252
91/2 ProCards 386
89/0 Moncton Hawks
90/1 Moncton Hawks

NORTON, D'ARCY
88/9 ProCards / Kalamazoo
89/0 ProCards IHL 77
90/1 ProCards 320
91/2 ProCards 321
92/3 Cincinnati Cyclones
93/4 Cincinnati Cyclones
86/7 Kamloops Blazers
87/8 Kamloops Blazers

NORTON, JEFF
90/1 Bowman 122
91/2 Bowman 225
93/4 Donruss 303
94/5 Donruss 132
95/6 Donruss 117
94/5 Flair 168
92/3 Fleer Ultra 349
93/4 Fleer Ultra 417
94/5 Fleer Ultra 199
96/7 Fl. Ultra 61
93/4 Leaf 390
94/5 Leaf 98
95/6 Leaf 74
90/1 OPC/Topps 166
91/2 O-Pee-Chee 243
89/0 OPC/Topps 120
01/2 Pacific 342
89/0 Panini Sticker 273
90/1 Panini Sticker 93
91/2 Panini Sticker 248
92/3 Panini Sticker 205
93/4 Panini Sticker 64
94/5 Panini Sticker 224
96/7 Panini Sticker 264
91/2 Parkhurst 331
92/3 Parkhurst 337
93/4 Parkhurst 455
95/6 Parkhurst 349
91/2 Pinnacle 172
92/3 Pinnacle 102
93/4 Pinnacle 353
94/5 Pinnacle 99
95/6 Pinnacle 186
96/7 Pi. Be A Player 187, ✍ Aut. 187
94/5 POG 218
95/6 POG 220
93/4 Power Play 223
93/4 Premier 447
90/1 Pro Set 189
91/2 Pro Set 148

91/2 Pro Set Platinum 78
90/1 Score 157
90/1 Sco. Hot Cards 70
91/2 Score 222
91/2 Score CAN 222
92/3 Score 56
93/4 Score 522
93/4 Score 69
95/6 Score 178
91/2 Score Young Stars 16
92/3 Topps Gold 526
95/6 Topps 69
96/7 To. Picks 157
91/2 To. Stadium 98
92/3 To. Stadium 324
93/4 To. Stadium 495
94/5 To. Stadium 86
90/1 Upper Deck 386
91/2 Upper Deck 357
93/4 Upper Deck 512
95/6 Upper Deck 160
00/1 Upper Deck 378
94/5 UD BAP R57, ✍ 90
95/6 UD CC 112
99/0 Victory 255
96/7 EDMO
97/8 FLOR / Winn-Dixie
89/0 NYIS
92/3 SANJ / Pacific Bell

NORTON, STEVE
93/4 Michigan State

NORWICH, CRAIG
80/1 O-Pee-Chee 53
79 Panini Sticker 209
80/1 Topps 53
79/0 WINN

NORWOOD, LEE
88/9 OPC/Topps 240
90/1 OPC/Topps 285
89/0 OPC/Topps 75
89/0 opcSticker 251-114
87/8 Panini Sticker 235
89/0 Panini Sticker 68
90/1 Panini Sticker 202
91/2 Panini Sticker 214
91/2 Parkhurst 373
90/1 Pro Set 74
90/1 Score 74T
91/2 Score CAN 528
91/2 To. Stadium 317
90/1 Upper Deck 78
86/7 DETR / Little Caesars
87/8 DETR / Little Caesars
88/9 DETR / Little Caesars
88/9 DETR / S.A.M.
89/0 DETR / Little Caesars
90/1 NJER
80/1 QUEB
81/2 WASH
82/3 WASH

NOSE, VIRGIL
90/1 Rayside-Balfour
91/2 Rayside-Balfour

NOSEK, DAVID
99/0 OFS 199, 414
00/1 OFS 220
01/2 OFS 129

NOSEK, MARTIN
01/2 OFS 151
99/0 Score 70

NOSEWORTHY, DAVE
89/0 7th..Sketch OHL 44

NOTTINGHAM, MIKE
84/5 Kamloops Blazers
85/6 Kamloops Blazers

NOURISLAMOV, EVGENI
01/2 Drummondville

NOURISLAMOV, EVGUENI
01/2 Victoriaville Tigres 3

NOVAK, AARON
98/9 Wichita Thunder
93/4 Minnesota-Duluth

NOVAK, EDUARD
97/8 APS 51
99/0 OFS 323
00/1 OFS 107
72 Semic Sticker 37
74 Semic Sticker 75
71/2 Williams Finnish 34

NOVAK, FILIP
02/3 Choice Prospects 31
99/0 UD Prospects 52
01/2 Regina Pats

NOVAK, JACK
52/3 Anonymous 125

NOVAK, JAN
97/8 APS 156
00/1 DS 112
98/9 OFS 215
99/0 OFS 50
01/1 OFS 86
01/2 OFS 274

NOVAK, LUKAS
98/9 OFS 309

NOVAK, RICHARD
89/0 ProCards IHL 106

NOVAK, ROB
99/0 Des Moines Buc's

NOVAK, VACLAV
98/9 OFS 144
99/0 OFS 399
00/1 OFS 310
01/2 OFS 34

NOVAK, JIRI
79 Panini Sticker 82
74 Semic Sticker 65
73/4 Williams Finnish 58

NOVOPASHIN, VITALI
00/1 Mir 89

NOVOSELTSEV, IVAN
02/3 First Edition 96, ✂ Jers.
02/3 Pacific Complete 346
02/3 To. Total 212
02/3 Upper Deck 324
99/0 BAP Mem. 399
00/1 BAP Mem. 218
01/2 BAP Mem. 213
99 Bowman 150
99/0 Crown Royale 61
00/1 Crown Royale 124
99/0 Dynagon Ice 91
99/0 Millenium C-48
99/0 NHL Power Play [x3]
01/2 O-Pee-Chee 306
99/0 Omega 104
00/1 Pacific 184
00/1 Pa. Paramount 107
00/1 PS Titanium 121
00/1 PS Titanium Draft 121
99/0 SP Authentic 104
00/1 SP Authentic 40, ✍ SotT, ✍ SotTD
99/0 Stadium 172
00/1 Topps 282
01/2 Topps 306
00/1 To. Chrome 177
99/0 To. Prmr. Plus 109
99/0 Ult. Victory 99
00/1 Upper Deck 79
99/0 UD Black Diam. 42
00/1 UD MVP ME4, ✍ ME
99/0 UD MVP Cup 80
99/0 UD Ovation 28
00/1 Vanguard 122
99/0 Victory 371
99/0 WGretzky 74
99/0 Louisville Panthers

NOVOSJOLOV, WALDEMAR
94/5 DEL 358

NOVOTNY, ANDREJ
99/0 OFS 90
00/1 OFS 40
01/2 OFS 250

NOVOTNY, IVO
97/8 APS 15
98/9 OFS 310

NOVOTNY, JAN
96/7 APS 72
97/8 APS 193

NOVOTNY, JIRI
95/6 APS 241
96/7 APS 70, 307
00/1 OFS 26
02/3 Rochester Americans

NOVOTNY, JIRI?
99/0 Score 12
95/6 Lethbridge Hurricanes

NOVOTNY, MAREK
94/5 APS 162
95/6 APS 176
96/7 APS 312
97/8 APS 291
97/8 DS 34
98/9 DS 14
99/0 DS 100
00/1 DS 61
97/8 DS Sticker 107
98/9 OFS 295
99/0 OFS 542
00/1 OFS 212

NOVY, HELMUT
70/1 Kuvajulkaisut 91

NOVY, MILAN
96/7 APS 377
97/8 APS 215
01/2 DS L11
83/4 Funmate Puffy 19 [w/]
92/3 Future Trends C76 155
92/3 Future Trends C76 186
92/3 Future Trends C76 198
83/4 OPC/Topps Sticker 187
98/9 OFS Leg. 11
99/0 OFS 170
79 Panini Sticker 85
74 Semic Sticker 59
82 Semic Sticker 87
83/4 Souhaits Keychain [Capitals]
82/3 WASH

NOWAK, DANIEL
94/5 DEL 433
95/6 DEL 392, 431
96/7 DEL 299
98/9 DEL 211, 329
99/0 Eishockey 208

NOWAK, HANK
74/5 Loblaws
74/5 Loblaws Update
76/7 O-Pee-Chee 224
76/7 Topps 224

NOWICKI, ANDY
93/4 Red Deer Rebels

NUMMELA, TAPIO
70/1 Kuvajulkaisut 246

NUMMELIN, PETTERI
02/3 Cardset 85
00/1 BAP Mem. 476
98/9 Cardset Leij. 15
99/0 Cardset 187
00/1 Cardset 234
95 Hartwall Karjala
95/6 Leaf Elit Set 206
95 Panini Worlds 167
00/1 Premier Plus 112
00/1 PS Titanium Draft 158
95/6 Radio City
94 Semic 12
95 Semic 39
00/1 Signature 251, ✍ Aut. 240
93/4 Sisu 32
94/5 Sisu 62, 153, MN-2, SS-3
95/6 Sisu Gold 9
95/6 Sisu Limited 3
00/1 SP Authentic 142
00/1 SPx 136
00/1 To. Heritage 97
00/1 To. Stars 122
00/1 Upper Deck 423
95/6 UD Elitserien 209
96 Wien 3

NUMMELIN, TIMO
66/7 Champion 76
72 Hellas MM-Jenkki 8
70/1 Kuvajulkaisut 164
80/1 Mallasjuoma 178
82 Mallasjuoma
79 Panini Sticker 165
82 Semic Sticker 29
82 Skopbank
78/9 SM-Liiga 3
78/9 SM-Liiga 201
77-79 Sports. FIN 48-1152
71/2 Williams Finnish 233
72/3 Williams Finnish 68
72/3 Williams Finnish 217
73/4 Williams Finnish 73
73/4 Williams Finnish 292

NUMMINEN, KALEVI
66/7 Champion 148
65/6 Hellas 160
74 Semic Sticker 98
77-79 Sports. FIN 75-1800

NUMMINEN, REIMA
71/2 Williams Finnish 372

NUMMINEN, TEEMU
93/4 Jyvas Hyva 297
93/4 Sisu 71
94/5 Sisu 319
95/6 Sisu 329
98/9 Phoenix Mustangs 18

NUMMINEN, TEPPO
02/3 BAP All-Star 67, ✂ ASJ
02/3 Cardset 235
02/3 First Edition 40, ✂ Jers.
02/3 O-Pee-Chee 158
02/3 Pacific 303
02/3 Pacific Complete 321
02/3 Parkhurst ✂ TT20
02/3 Parkhurst Retro 117
02/3 Sports Vault 268
02/3 Topps 158
02/3 To. Limited 158
02/3 To. Total 55
02/3 Upper Deck 380
02/3 UD Honor 93
02/3 UD MVP 144
02/3 UD Vintage 192, 283
02/3 Victory 164, - NP26
99/0 Aurora 110
98/9 Be A Player 106, ✍ Aut. 106
99/0 BAP Mem. 186
00/1 BAP Mem. 155, ✂ TM-30, ✂ TM-33
01/2 BAP Mem. 43, ✂ ASJ, ✂ ASE, ✂ ASN, ✂ CoO
90/1 Bowman 138
91/2 Bowman 201
92/3 Bowman 299
99/0 Cardset AH 3-risti
93/4 Donruss 385
94/5 Donruss 267
95/6 Donruss 261
96/7 Donruss 126
93/4 EA Sports 146
94/5 Flair 208
96/7 Fleer 91, NT-8
95/6 Fleer Metal 164
96/7 Fl. Picks 72
92/3 Fleer Ultra 243
93/4 Fleer Ultra 455
94/5 Fleer Ultra 244
95/6 Fleer Ultra 182
96/7 Fl. Ultra 134
95 Globe 133
01/2 Heads Up ✂ JQ 26
93 Koululainen
98/9 Kraft / PB
99/0 Kraft / PB
93/4 Leaf 135
94/5 Leaf 233
95/6 Leaf 247
96/7 Leaf 113
96/7 Metal Univ. 120
99/0 Millenium 189, ✍ Aut. 189
90/1 OPC/Topps 385
91/2 O-Pee-Chee 274
92/3 O-Pee-Chee 4
01/2 O-Pee-Chee 123
98/9 OPC Chrome 57
97/8 Omega 175
98/9 Omega 186
99/0 Omega 183
98/9 Pacific 342
99/0 Pacific 323
00/1 Pacific 445
01/2 Pacific 307
97/8 Pacific CC 122
98/9 Pa. Paramount 183
99/0 Pa. Paramount 181
00/1 Pa. Paramount 192
89/0 Panini Sticker 172
90/1 Panini Sticker 307
90/1 Panini/WPG 18
91/2 Panini Sticker 71
92/3 Panini Sticker 52
93/4 Panini Sticker 197
94/5 Panini Sticker 169
95/6 Panini Sticker 220
96/7 Panini Sticker 194
97/8 Panini Sticker 156
98/9 Panini Sticker 148
99/0 Panini Sticker 280
00/1 Panini Sticker 189
91/2 Parkhurst 200
92/3 Parkhurst 438
93/4 Parkhurst 231
94/5 Parkhurst 270
95/6 Parkhurst 228
00/1 Parkhurst P-42
01/2 Parkhurst 53
94/5 Parkie SE ES-10
91/2 Pinnacle 166
92/3 Pinnacle 215
93/4 Pinnacle 92
94/5 Pinnacle 77
95/6 Pinnacle 67, GG-12
96/7 Pinnacle 8
95/6 Pi. Summit 113
96/7 Pi. Summit 55
95/6 Playoff 107, 328
96/7 Playoff 350
94/5 POG 346
95/6 POG 294
93/4 Power Play 272
93/4 Premier 269
94/5 Premier 376
00/1 PS Titanium ✂ GUG 43, ✂ GUG-128
01/2 PS Titanium Draft ✂ 76
90/1 Pro Set 334
91/2 Pro Set 261
92/3 Pro Set 210
91/2 Pro Set Platinum 248
99/0 Revolution 112
90/1 Score 176
91/2 Score 101
91/2 Score CAN 101
92/3 Score 102
93/4 Score 132
94/5 Score 91
95/6 Score 139
96/7 Score 5
94 Semic 10
94 Semic 335
95 Semic 37
91 Semic Sticker 201
92 Semic Sticker 5
93 Semic Sticker 57
00/1 Signature DD-10
01/2 Signat. 110, ✍ Aut. 110
94/5 Sisu 359, GS-6
95/6 Sisu Limited 93, SAS-6
95/6 SBx Emotion 195
95/6 SBx Impact 186
96/7 SBx Impact 106, F-16
96/7 SP 122
97/8 SP Authentic 122
99/0 SPx 119
99/0 Stadium 41
00/1 Stadium 76
92/3 Topps 339
95/6 Topps 67
98/9 Topps 57
99/0 Topps 80
00/1 Topps 79
01/2 Topps 123
99/0 To. Chrome 80
00/1 To. Chrome 62
01/2 To. Chrome 123
95/6 To. Finest 167
00/1 To. Gold Label B7
00/1 To. Heritage 186
91/2 To. Stadium 302
92/3 To. Stadium 77
93/4 To. Stadium 164
94/5 To. Stadium 152
00/1 To. Stars 64
98/9 UD Choice 157
00/1 UD Heroes 90
91/2 Upper Deck 240
92/3 Upper Deck 326
93/4 Upper Deck 53
94/5 Upper Deck 113
95/6 Upper Deck 275
96/7 Upper Deck 131
97/8 Upper Deck 336
98/9 Upper Deck 155
00/1 Upper Deck 135
01/2 Upper Deck 366
95/6 UD BAP 68, ✍ S68
95/6 UD CC 292
96/7 UD CC 209
97/8 UD Coll. Choice 200
98/9 UD G. Reserve 155
00/1 UD MVP 136
00/1 UD Vintage 274
01/2 UD Vintage 195, 199
99/0 Victory 233
01/2 Victory 275
96 Wien 27
96/7 PHOE / Coca-Cola
97/8 PHOE / Coca-Cola
98/9 PHOE / Coca-Cola
88/9 WINN / Safety Tips
89/0 WINN / Safeway
90/1 WINN / IGA
91/2 WINN / IGA
93/4 WINN / Ruffles
93/4 WINN Readers
95/6 WINN
95/6 WINN Readers

NUMMELIN, TIMO
94/5 Sisu 239
95/6 Sisu 116
96/7 Sisu 130

NURMI, HEIKKI
72/3 Williams Finnish 160
73/4 Williams Finnish 226

NURMI, JUHA
80/1 Mallasjuoma 167
89/0 Semic Elitserien 163

NURMI, PERTTI
70/1 Kuvajulkaisut 183
71/2 Williams Finnish 106
72/3 Williams Finnish 120
73/4 Williams Finnish 117

NURMI, SEPPO
66/7 Champion 166
70/1 Kuvajulkaisut 247
71/2 Williams Finnish 214
72/3 Williams Finnish 161
73/4 Williams Finnish 227

NURMINEN, AARO
65/6 Hellas 107

NURMINEN, JAAKKO
70/1 Kuvajulkaisut 199

NURMINEN, JARI
72/3 Williams Finnish 291

NURMINEN, JUHA
93/4 Sisu 290
94/5 Sisu 243, FOI-4
95/6 Sisu 10

NURMINEN, KAI
02/3 Cardset 86
99/0 Cardset 144, AH 6-pata
00/1 Cardset MB 1
93/4 Jyvas Hyva 329
95/6 Leaf Elit Set 228
97/8 Pa. Invincible R-95
97/8 Panini Sticker 221
96/7 Select CE 91
93/4 Sisu 48
94/5 Sisu 101, 305, FOI-8, H-13
95/6 Sisu 166, 197
95/6 Sisu Limited 86
96/7 SP 181
96/7 Upper Deck 275
95/6 UD Elitserien 90
97/8 UD Elitserien 81, 211, C6
96 Wien 36
00/1 Cleveland Lumberjacks

NURMINEN, PASI
97/8 Omega 33
02/3 Between the Pipes 94
02/3 Cardset 236, -DD 2, -SGSP 1
02/3 O-Pee-Chee 294
02/3 Pacific Complete 233
02/3 PS Titanium 6
02/3 Signature ✂ TQ12
02/3 SPx 101
02/3 Topps 294
02/3 To. Limited 294
02/3 Upper Deck 197, 255
02/3 UD Foundations 122
02/3 UD Mask 7
02/3 UD MVP 9
02/3 UD Vintage 321
02/3 Victory 8
01/2 BAP Mem. 358
01/2 BT Pipes 151
98/9 Cardset 51, MM3
99/0 Cardset 203, 258
00/1 Cardset 38, 351, MM
01/2 Parkhurst 303
01/2 PS Titanium Draft 106
01/2 SPx 197
01/2 UD Ice 127
01/2 UD Mask 133
01/2 UD Premier 89
01/2 UD Top Shelf 122
01/2 Chicago Wolves

NURMINEN, TIMO
70/1 Kuvajulkaisut 302
73/4 Williams Finnish 293

NURRO, KIMMO
94/5 Sisu 254

NURTDINOV, RUSLAN
00/1 Mir 243

NUTIKKA, VELI-PEKKA
98/9 Cardset 137
99/0 Cardset 75
00/1 Cardset 76
94/5 Parkie SE222
95/6 Sisu 279
96/7 Sisu 77
94/5 SP 159
94/5 Topps Finest 135

NUUTINEN, SAMI
98/9 Cardset 101
00/1 Cardset 142
99/0 Eishockey 262
97/8 Hockey-Box
92/3 Jyvas Hyva 106
93/4 Jyvas Hyva 195
93 Semic Sticker 58
93/4 Sisu 260
94/5 Sisu 122
95/6 Sisu 85, DT-6
95/6 Sisu Limited 56

NYBERG, PATRIK
91/2 Semic Elitserien 249

NYC, OLDRICH
99/0 Score 79

NYGARDS, PER
90/1 Semic Elitserien 280
91/2 Semic Elitserien 63

NYGREN, HÅKAN
69/0 Mästar Serien 39
72 Panda MM-Toronto
72 Semic Sticker 53
71/2 Williams Finnish 55

NYKOLUK, MIKE
45-64 BeeHive-2 [Toro.]
57/8 Parkhurst [Toro.] 16
93/4 Parkie 56-57 130
81/2 TORO
82/3 TORO
83/4 TORO
98/9 Hershey Bears

NYKOPP, TIMO
92/3 Jyvas Hyva 20
94/5 Sisu 341
95/6 Sisu 150

NYKVIST, HANNU
80/1 Mallasjuoma 63

NYKYFORUK, CURTIS
88/9 Regina Pats
89/0 Victoria Cougars

NYLANDER, MICHAEL
02/3 Cardset 237
02/3 First Edition 273
02/3 O-Pee-Chee 154
02/3 Pacific Complete 59
02/3 Parkhurst 175
02/3 PS Titanium 100
02/3 Quest for the Cup 100
02/3 Topps 154
02/3 To. Limited 154
02/3 To. Total 360
02/3 Upper Deck 35
02/3 UD MVP 39
02/3 UD Rookie 100
02/3 UD Vintage 55
01/2 Adrenaline 40
98/9 Aurora 28
00/1 BAP Mem. 335
01/2 BAP Mem. 117
99/0 Cardset AH 10-risti
91/2 Classic 47
91/2 Classic Four Sport 47
93/4 Donruss 144
93/4 Donruss 407
94/5 Donruss 74
95/6 Fleer Metal 22
93/4 Fleer Ultra 105
93/4 Fleer Ultra Pros. 7
94/5 Fleer Ultra 32
95/6 Fleer Ultra 213
95 Globe 35
01/2 Heads Up ✂ JQ 7
93/4 Leaf 94
94/5 Leaf 149
96/7 Leaf 115
01/2 O-Pee-Chee 127
92/3 OPC Premier 19
97/8 Omega 33
99/0 Omega 54
98/9 Pacific 123
99/0 Pacific 393
00/1 Pacific 100
01/2 Pacific 88
98/9 Pa. Paramount 31
00/1 Pa. Paramount 52
93/4 Panini Sticker 128
96/7 Panini Sticker 237
98/9 Panini Sticker 177
99/0 Panini Sticker 142
00/1 Panini Sticker 123
92/3 Parkhurst 294
93/4 Parkhurst 83
94/5 Parkhurst 32
95/6 Parkhurst 34
00/1 Parkhurst P-178
01/2 Parkhurst 224
92/3 Pinnacle 400
93/4 Pinnacle 166
94/5 Pinnacle 142
96/7 Pinnacle 151
94/5 POG 57
95/6 POG 54
93/4 Power Play 106
93/4 Premier 99
94/5 Premier 237
01/2 Pr. Stock ✂ GUG 24
01/2 PS Titanium ✂ DSJ 9
00/1 PS Titanium Draft ✂ 19
93/4 Score 383
94/5 Score 59
95/6 Score 289
96/7 Score 79
91/2 Semic Elitserien 21
92/3 Semic Elitserien 338
92/3 Semic Elitserien 339
93 Semic Sticker 40
01/2 Signat. 57, ✍ Aut. 57
94/5 Sisu 352, GS-7
95/6 Sisu SS 10
95/6 Sisu Limited 54, LG-3
95/6 SP 20
91/2 Star Pics 23
00/1 Topps 127
01/2 Topps 127
95/6 To. Finest 172
98/9 To. Finest 63
93/4 To. Stadium 186
95/6 To. Stadium 154
98/9 UD Choice 32
91/2 Ultimate Draft Pick 42, 76, 88, ✍ Aut.
92/3 Upper Deck 236
92/3 Upper Deck 378
92/3 Upper Deck 520
92/3 Upper Deck ER2
93/4 Upper Deck 70, HT-13, NL-1, SP-62
94/5 Upper Deck 79, 556, SP-103
95/6 Upper Deck 454, SE-102
96/7 Upper Deck 27
00/1 Upper Deck 41
01/2 Upper Deck 39
95/6 UD BAP 148, ✍ S148
95/6 UD CC 311
96/7 UD CC 38, 312
95/6 UD Elitserien 237
00/1 UD MVP 44
01/2 UD MVP 41
99/0 UD MVP Cup 48
00/1 UD Vintage 84
01/2 UD Vintage 56
01/2 Vanguard ✂ DGM 7
01/2 Victory 79
96 Wien 61
92/3 HART / Dairymart
93/4 HART / Coke

NYLANDER, PETER
92/3 Semic Elitserien 356
94/5 Sig. Rookies 21, ✍ 21
97/8 UD Elitserien 31
98/9 UD Elitserien 43
99/0 UD Elitserien 192

NYLUND, GARY
91/2 Bowman 228
84/5 O-Pee-Chee 307
85/6 O-Pee-Chee 172
86/7 O-Pee-Chee 243
87/8 OPC/Topps 82
88/9 OPC/Topps 15
90/1 OPC/Topps 233
91/2 O-Pee-Chee 101
89/0 OPC/Topps 105
84/5 OPC Sticker 15
84/5 OPC Sticker 16
85/6 OPC Sticker 14-144
86/7 OPC Sticker 137-245
87/8 OPC Sticker 80-213
89/0 opcSticker 114-251
87/8 Panini Sticker 224
88/9 Panini Sticker 23
90/1 Panini Sticker 80
91/2 Panini Sticker 251
91/2 Pinnacle 406
90/1 Pro Set 190
91/2 Pro Set 150
90/1 Score 86
91/2 Score 192
91/2 Score CAN 192
92/3 Score 381
84/5 7-Eleven
83/4 Souhaits Keychain [Maple Leafs]
91/2 To. Stadium 163
90/1 Upper Deck 139
91/2 Upper Deck 406
83/4 Vachon 94-101
86/7 CHIC / Coke
87/8 CHIC / Coke
89/0 NYIS
82/3 TORO
83/4 TORO
84/5 TORO
85/6 TORO

NYMAN, HARRI
80/1 Mallasjuoma 75
78/9 SM-Liiga 115

NYMAN, STEFAN
90/1 Semic Elitserien 59
91/2 Semic Elitserien 232

NYMAN, TERO
96/7 Sisu 11

NYMAN, TOMI
00/1 Cardset 254

NYROP, BILL
92/3 Future Trends C76 158
76/7 O-Pee-Chee 188
77/8 O-Pee-Chee 91
78/9 O-Pee-Chee 134
76/7 Topps 188
77/8 Topps 91
78/9 Topps 134
81/2 MINS
76/7 MONT
77/8 MONT
91/2 Knoxville Cherokees

NYSTROM, BOB
02/3 BAP Mem. / Cup
02/3 Parkhurst ✂ VT11
02/3 UD Foundations 59, 121, ✂ CG, ✂ LI, ✂ PP, ✂ PS
01/2 Fleer Greats 4, ✍ Aut.
01/2 Fleer Legacy 10
84/5 Kelowna Wings &...
74/5 Loblaws
73/4 O-Pee-Chee 202
74/5 O-Pee-Chee 123
75/6 O-Pee-Chee 259
75/6 O-Pee-Chee 323
76/7 O-Pee-Chee 153
77/8 O-Pee-Chee 62
78/9 O-Pee-Chee 153
79/0 O-Pee-Chee 217
80/1 O-Pee-Chee 102
81/2 O-Pee-Chee 217
82/3 O-Pee-Chee 208
83/4 O-Pee-Chee 14
84/5 O-Pee-Chee 132
85/6 OPC/Topps 11
86/7 OPC/Topps 104
82/3 OPC/Topps Sticker 59
83/4 OPC/Topps Sticker 85
85/6 OPC Sticker 85
85/6 OPC Sticker 69-193
86/7 OPC Sticker 204-76
01/2 Parkhurst ✂ PA57
82/3 Post [NYIs.]
74/5 Topps 123
75/6 Topps 259
75/6 Topps 323
76/7 Topps 153
77/8 Topps 62
78/9 Topps 153
79/0 Topps 217
80/1 Topps 102
84/5 Topps 98
01/2 Ultimate Mem. ✂ SCD
01/2 Ultimate Mem. ✂ SCD
91/2 Upper Deck 641
00/1 UD Legends 84, ✂ LGJ
01/2 UD SCup Champs 20
00/1 UD Vintage ✂ D-POH
79/0 NYIS
80/1 NYIS
83/4 NYIS / News 11
84/5 NYIS / News 12
93/4 NYIS / Bank
99/0 NYIS / UD NY4

NYSTROM, BOB
02/3 Fleer Throwbacks 59, ✍ Aut.

NYSTROM, BOBBY
02/3 Ultimate Mem. ✂ Num

NYSTROM, ERIC
97 Québec Pee Wee 0820

NYSTROM, JARI
80/1 Mallasjuoma 213

NYSTROM, KAREN
94/5 Classic W20
97/8 UD Coll. Choice 295

NYSTROM, MURRAY
85/6 London Knights
86/7 London Knights

NYSTROM, SEPPO
66/7 Champion 41
65/6 Hellas 47

NYYSSÄNEN, TOMMI
95/6 Sisu 83
96/7 Sisu 83

O

O'BRIEN, ANDY
82/3 Kitchener Rangers

O'BRIEN, BERT
89/0 Ottawa 67's

O'BRIEN, DAN
89/0 Nashville Knights

O'BRIEN, DAVID
88/9 ProCards / Binghampton
89/0 ProCards IHL 19
90/1 ProCards 92

O'BRIEN, DENNIS
74/5 Loblaws
73/4 O-Pee-Chee 88
74/5 O-Pee-Chee 96
75/6 O-Pee-Chee 53
76/7 O-Pee-Chee 34, 387
77/8 O-Pee-Chee 173
78/9 O-Pee-Chee 104
79/0 O-Pee-Chee 375
73/4 Topps 177
74/5 Topps 96
75/6 Topps 53
76/7 Topps 34
77/8 Topps 173
78/9 Topps 104
71/2 Toronto Sun Photo
73/4 MINS
92/3 Toledo Storm WIOT

O'BRIEN, DOUG
00/1 Hull Olympiques 4
01/2 Hull Olympiques 5
02/3 Hull Olympiques

O'BRIEN, J.A.
83 HHOF Postcard N11
83&87 HHOF 206

O'BRIEN, KEITH
00/1 Austin Ice Bats

O'BRIEN, MAURICE
90/1 7th..Sketch OHL 90

O'BRIEN, SEAN
94/5 Richmond Renegades
95/6 Tallahasee Tiger Sharks

O'BRIEN, SHANE
00/1 Kingston Frontenacs 15
01/2 Kingston Frontenacs 15

O'BRIEN, BERT
00/1 Ottawa 67's 23
01/2 Ottawa 67's 23

O'CALLAHAN, JACK
84/5 O-Pee-Chee 43
86/7 O-Pee-Chee 207
94/5 SR Miracle 23,24, ✍ 23,24
84/5 Topps 33
86/7 CHIC / Coke
88/9 NJER / Caretta

O'CALLAHAN, JACK
80 Olympic USA

O'CONNELL, JACK
37/8 World Wide Gum 107

O'CONNELL, JOHN
91/2 Minnesota G'Gophers

O'CONNELL, KEITH
99/0 Greensboro Generals
97/8 Pensacola Ice Pilots

O'CONNELL, MIKE
80/1 O-Pee-Chee 61
81/2 O-Pee-Chee 6
82/3 O-Pee-Chee 17
83/4 O-Pee-Chee 56
84/5 O-Pee-Chee 12
85/6 OPC/Topps 2
86/7 OPC/Topps 140
87/8 OPC/Topps 141
88/9 OPC/Topps 92
90/1 OPC/Topps 114
89/0 O-Pee-Chee 223
82/3 OPC/Topps Sticker 89
83/4 OPC/Topps Sticker 52
84/5 OPC Sticker 185
85/6 OPC Sticker 161-31
86/7 OPC Sticker 160-17
87/8 OPC Sticker 107-241
88/9 OPC Sticker 248-118
89/0 opcSticker 249-112
87/8 Panini Sticker 240
88/9 Panini Sticker 61, 69
90/1 Panini Sticker 215
82/3 Post [Bost.]
90/1 Pro Set 75
83/4 Souhaits Keychain [Bruins]
80/1 Topps 61
81/2 Topps 70 [East]
84/5 Topps 9
83/4 BOST
84/5 BOST
79/0 CHIC
80/1 CHIC / Brown
86/7 DETR / Little Caesars
87/8 DETR / Little Caesars
88/9 DETR / Little Caesars
88/9 DETR / S.A.M.
89/0 DETR / Little Caesars

O'CONNELL, MYLES
90/1 ProCards 296

O'CONNOR, BUDDY
34-43 BeeHive-1 [Mont.]
45-64 BeeHive-2 [NYRa.]
47-48 Parade Sportive
45-54 Quaker Oats
37/8 World Wide Gum 114

O'CONNOR, ERIC
91/2 7th...Sketch LHJMQ 166

O'CONNOR, MIKE
94 Semic 315
93/4 Humberside Hawks 13
01/2 Sheffield Steelers
94/5 Sheffield Steelers 9
95/6 Sheffield Steelers

O'CONNOR, MYLES
91/2 O-Pee-Chee 509
93/4 Parkhurst 274
93/4 Premier - Gold 527
89/0 ProCards AHL 206
90/1 ProCards 576
91/2 ProCards 425
91/2 Score 322
91/2 Score CAN 352
91/2 Upper Deck 485
90/1 NJER
96/7 Cincinnati Cyclones
95/6 Houston Aeros

O'CONNOR, PATRICK
94/5 Sheffield Steelers 13

O'CONNOR, SCOTT
94 Semic 312

O'CONNOR, SEAN
01/2 Moose Jaw Warriors 9

O'CONNOR, TED
59/60 Whitby Dunlops

O'CONNOR, TERRY
52/3 Anonymous 161

O'CONNOR, TOM
93/4 Classic 107
93/4 Classic - Class of '94 CL7
98/9 EBK ECHL All-Star
59/60 Whitby Dunlops

O'DETTE, MATT
93/4 Slapshot / Kitchener 21
95/6 Slapshot 154
02/3 Hamilton Bulldogs
00/1 Québec Citadelles
01/2 Québec Citadelles
96/7 Roanoke Express 15

O'DONNELL, FRED
73/4 O-Pee-Chee 223
85/6 Kingston Canadians
86/7 Kingston Canadians

O'DONNELL, MARK
91/2 7th...Sketch OHL 292
97/8 Fort Worth Brahmas

O'DONNELL, SEAN
02/3 Pacific Complete 66
02/3 To. Total 356
00/1 BAP Mem. 20
92/3 Classic Prospects 109
98/9 Pacific 242
99/0 Pacific 195
97/8 Pa. Invincible R-96
00/1 Pa. Paramount 122
00/1 Panini Sticker 176
01/2 Parkhurst 242
96/7 Pi. Be A Player 152, ✍ Aut. 152
91/2 ProCards 10
00/1 Revolution 73
90/1 7th..Sketch OHL 390
00/1 To. Chrome 238
00/1 Upper Deck 217
94/5 Phoenix Roadrunners
91/2 Rochester Americans GL
91/2 Rochester Americans WPC
92/3 Rochester Americans DD
92/3 Rochester Americans WPC
93/4 Rochester Americans
88/9 Sudbury Wolves
89/0 Sudbury Wolves
90/1 Sudbury Wolves

O'DONOGHUE, DON
71/2 Eddie Sargent 142
71/2 O-Pee-Chee 180
71/2 Toronto Sun Photo

O'DROWSKI, GERRY
63/4 Québec Aces

O'DWYER, BILLY
89/0 ProCards AHL 71
90/1 ProCards 420
98/9 BOST / Alumni 27

O'FLAHERTY, GERRY
74/5 Loblaws
72/3 O-Pee-Chee 278
73/4 O-Pee-Chee 250
74/5 O-Pee-Chee 71
75/6 O-Pee-Chee 307
76/7 O-Pee-Chee 287
77/8 O-Pee-Chee 377
78/9 O-Pee-Chee 365
74/5 Topps 71
75/6 Topps 307
72/3 VANC / Royal Bank
73/4 VANC / Royal Bank
74/5 VANC / Royal Bank
75/6 VANC / Royal Bank
76/7 VANC / Royal Bank
77/8 VANC / Royal Bank

O'FLAHERTY, JAMES
52/3 St. Lawrence 71

O'FLAHERTY, JOHNNY
34-43 BeeHive-1 [NYAm.]
52/3 Laval Dairy Update 111

O'FLAHERTY, PATRICK
91/2 Avant Garde BCJHL 114
92/3 BCJHL 179

O'GRADY, MIKE
95/6 Classic 51
95/6 Lethbridge Hurricanes

O'HAGAN, PAUL
90 7th..Sketch Mem.Cup 78
89/0 7th..Sketch OHL 14, 194
90/1 7th..Sketch OHL 344
89/0 Oshawa Generals
90/1 Oshawa Generals
91/2 Oshawa Generals

O'HAGAN, SEAN
90/1 7th..Sketch OHL 190
89/0 Windsor Spitfires

O'HANDLEY, P.K.
98/9 Florida Everblades
00/1 Florida Everblades
01/2 Florida Everblades

O'HANDLEY, P.K.
99/0 Florida Everblades

O'HARA, COLIN
95/6 Swift Current Broncos

O'HUNTER, PAT
28/9 Paulins Candy 43

O'KEEFE, RYAN
98/9 Barrie Colts

O'LEARY, B
91/2 Cornwall Royals

O'LEARY, BRIAN
00/1 Owen Sound Attack 25

O'LEARY, KELLY
94/5 Classic W39

O'LEARY, MICKEY
24/5 Champ's Cigarettes

O'MALLEY, TERRY
69/0 Mästar Serien 18

O'MEARA, CLIFF
23/4 Paulins Candy 9
28/9 Paulins Candy 78
23/4 Selkirks Crescent 1
24/5 Selkirks Crescent 10

O'NABIGON, NATHAN
01/2 Mississauga IceDogs

O'NEILL, DON
89/0 7th..Sketch OHL 112
90/1 7th..Sketch OHL 367
91/2 7th...Sketch OHL 138
91/2 Peterborough Petes

O'NEILL, JEFF
02/3 Atomic 18, -CF 6
02/3 BAP Mem. 148, ✂ SC24
02/3 Bowman 31
02/3 Exclusive 31
02/3 First Edition 9, 346, 412H, ✂ Jers.
02/3 Heads Up 23, ✂ GWQ 6
02/3 In The GU 6, 106, ✂ F6
02/3 O-Pee-Chee 258
02/3 Pacific 69
02/3 Pacific Complete 445
02/3 Parkhurst 120, ✂ FP6, ✂ GJ9, ✂ SJ9
02/3 Parkhurst Retro 41
02/3 Pr. Stock Reserve 18
02/3 PS Titanium 19, ✂ GWJ 10
02/3 Quest for the Cup 15
02/3 Signature 173, GS-41, ✍ 173
02/3 SP GU 8
02/3 Sports Vault 37
02/3 SPx 11, 81
02/3 Stadium 32
02/3 Topps 258
02/3 T. Chrome 141
02/3 To. Heritage 84
02/3 To. Limited 258
02/3 To. Total 241
02/3 Ultimate Mem. ✂ HT
02/3 Upper Deck 34
02/3 UD Artistic 16, R16, / Art
02/3 UD Classic 19
02/3 UD Honor -TW3
02/3 UD MVP 35
02/3 UD Piece 11
02/3 UD Top Shelf 15
02/3 UD Vintage 49, 266, GB 49
02/3 Vanguard 19
02/3 Victory 37
01/2 Adrenaline 36
94/5 Assets 57, 82
01/2 Atomic 18, PP 6, TN 3
98/9 Aurora 36
98/9 Be A Player 175, ✍ Aut. 175
00/1 BAP Mem. 110
01/2 BAP Mem. 276
95/6 Bowman 118, BB26
01/2 Bowman 77
93/4 Classic 108, 115, CL1, N3, ✍ Aut.
94/5 Classic 5, C7, R15, T29, ✍ Aut.
94/5 Classic Draft Day
94/5 Classic 4 Sport 119, BC19, T6, HV19, -Sprint
94/5 Cla. Images 44, CE16
94/5 Cla. Images 4 Sport 98
93/4 Cla. Prospects 205
93/4 Cla. Prospects 209
99/0 Crown Royale 29
01/2 Crown Royale 28, JotC 5
02/3 Crown Royale 19
95/6 Donruss 244, C3TWC-14, RR-4
96/7 Donruss RR-5
97/8 Donruss 16
96/7 Do. Canadian 82
95/6 Do. Elite 21, R-12
96/7 Do. Elite 39, A-9
97/8 Do. Preferred 30
97/8 Do. Priority 125
95/6 Fleer Metal 186
96/7 Fl. Picks 158
95/6 Fleer Ultra 351
01/2 Heads Up 17
96/7 Leaf 209
94/5 L. Limited CAN 6
95/6 L. Limited 63, RP-8
96/7 L. Limited 68
96/7 L. Preferred 9
97/8 Limited 61
96/7 Metal Univ. 69
99/0 Millenium 51, ✍ Aut. 51
99/0 NHL Power Play
01/2 O-Pee-Chee 107
99/0 Omega 48
98/9 Pacific 137
99/0 Pacific 78
00/1 Pacific 88
01/2 Pacific 78
97/8 Pacific CC 140
98/9 Pa. Paramount 40
99/0 Pa. Paramount 48
00/1 Pa. Paramount 45
96/7 Panini Sticker 30
95/6 Parkhurst 259
00/1 Parkhurst P-59
01/2 Parkhurst 6
94/5 Pinnacle 534
96/7 Pinnacle 210
97/8 Pinnacle 154
97/8 Pi. Be A Player 130, ✍ Aut. 130
97/8 Pi. Certified 128
97/8 Pi. Inside 149
95/6 Pi. Summit 183
96/7 Pi. Summit 168
97/8 Pi. Totally 128
95/6 Pi. Zenith 130, RRC-18
96/7 Pi. Zenith 29
01/2 Pr. Stock 16, -PS 12, ✂ GUG 19
01/2 PS Titanium 27, ✂ DSJ 45, ✂ DSJ 62
01/2 PS Titanium Draft ✂ 19
96/7 Score 250
97/8 Score 147
95/6 Select CE 118, CF-8
96/7 Select CE 90
00/1 Signature 229, F-6, ✍ Aut. 34
01/2 Signat. C18, ✍ Aut. LJO, ✂ GJ25, ✂ GSJ25
95/6 SBx Impact 202, F-11
93/4 Slapshot / Guelph 2
93/4 Slapshot / Guelph 26
94/5 Slapshot / Guelph 25
94/5 SP 152
95/6 SP 64
96/7 SP 67
97/8 SP Authentic 28
00/1 SP Authentic 17
01/2 SP Authentic ✍ SotT
01/2 SP GU 7
01/2 SPx 162
00/1 Stadium 142
95/6 Super Sticker 55
95/6 Topps 285, 20CJ
99/0 Topps 150
00/1 Topps 121
01/2 Topps 107
99/0 To. Chrome 150
01/2 To. Chrome 107
94/5 Topps Finest 162
95/6 To. Finest 96
01/2 To. Heritage 87
96/7 To. Picks RS17
01/2 To. Reserve 90
95/6 To. Stadium ER192
00/1 To. Stars 59
95/6 T. Super Skills SR3
98/9 UD Choice 37
00/1 UD Heroes 22
01/2 UD PlayMakers Ltd 17
93/4 Upper Deck E4
95/6 Upper Deck 264
96/7 Upper Deck 70
97/8 Upper Deck 34
98/9 Upper Deck 61
99/0 Upper Deck 200
00/1 Upper Deck 260
01/2 Upper Deck 31
95/6 UD BAP 166, ✍ S166
96/7 UD Black Diam. 92
00/1 UD Black Diam. 11
01/2 UD Challenge 12
95/6 UD CC 401
96/7 UD CC 121, 343
97/8 UD Coll. Choice 117
98/9 UD G. Reserve 61
99/0 UD G. Reserve 200
98/9 UD MVP 40
00/1 UD MVP 37
01/2 UD MVP 33
99/0 UD MVP Cup 37
00/1 UD Pros&Prosp. 17
01/2 UD Top Shelf 6
00/1 UD Vintage 65, 73
01/2 UD Vintage 44, 51, 52
01/2 Vanguard 17, QTH 14
99/0 Victory 62
00/1 Victory 49
01/2 Victory 63
97/8 CARO / Sprint
98/9 CARO / Highwoods
95/6 HART / Kids Club
96/7 HART / Kids Club

O'NEILL, MIKE
92/3 Classic Prospects 39
00/1 Kudos 143
92/3 Parkhurst 441
94/5 Parkhurst 268
90/1 ProCards 344
91/2 ProCards 259
90/1 Moncton Hawks
97/8 Portland Pirates
01/2 Sheffield Steelers GS

O'NEILL, PEGGY
34-43 BeeHive-1 [Bost.]
37/8 World Wide Gum 63

O'NEILL, RYAN
91/2 7th...Sketch OHL 180
92/3 Windsor Spitfires

O'REAGAN, TOM
94/5 DEL 59
O'REAR, HAYDEN
98/9 Anchorage Aces
99/0 Asheville Smoke
93/4 Knoxville Cherokees
94/5 Knoxville Cherokees
O'REE, WILLIE
45-64 BeeHive-2 [Bost.]
01/2 Fleer Greats ✂ OSS
97/8 Pi. BeeHive 75, ✍ Aut. 75
97/8 UD Promo 22
O'REGAN, TOM
95/6 DEL 54
96/7 DEL 250
84/5 PITT / Heinz
O'REILLY, SEAN
89/0 7th..Sketch OHL 90
90/1 7th..Sketch OHL 14
91/2 7th...Sketch OHL 382
98/9 Wichita Thunder
O'REILLY, TERRY
02/3 UD Foundations 5
01/2 Fleer Greats 80
01/2 Fleer Legacy 56
83/4 Funmate Puffy 12 [w/]
75/6 Hockey Heroes
74/5 Loblaws
73/4 O-Pee-Chee 254
74/5 O-Pee-Chee 295
75/6 O-Pee-Chee 301
76/7 O-Pee-Chee 130
76/7 O-Pee-Chee 381
77/8 O-Pee-Chee 220
78/9 O-Pee-Chee 40
78/9 O-Pee-Chee 332
79/0 O-Pee-Chee 238
80/1 O-Pee-Chee 56
81/2 O-Pee-Chee 7
82/3 O-Pee-Chee 18
84/5 O-Pee-Chee 13
81/2 OPC Sticker 50
82/3 OPC/Topps Sticker 85
85/6 OPC Sticker 162-32
82/3 Post [Bost.]
91/2 Pro Set Platinum 289
75/6 Topps 301
76/7 Topps 130
77/8 Topps 220
78/9 Topps 40
79/0 Topps 238
80/1 Topps 56
81/2 Topps 71 [East]
84/5 Topps 10
01/2 T/O Archives 71, -Seat, ✍ CAI
83/4 BOST
84/5 BOST
88/9 BOST / Sports Action
91/2 BOST / SA Legends
98/9 BOST / Alumni 24
O'REILLY, TERRY
02/3 Fleer Throwbacks 1, 4SO, ✂ 4SO, ✍ Aut.
O'ROURKE, CHRIS
93/4 Flint Generals
O'ROURKE, DAN
91/2 7th...Sketch WHL 311
95/6 Louisiana Ice Gators-2
96/7 Louisiana Ice Gators
O'ROURKE, STEVE
00/1 Kudos 37
O'SHEA, DAN
93/4 Dayton Bombers
O'SHEA, DANNY
70/1 Colgate 16
70/1 Dad's Cookies
70/1 Eddie Sargent 90
71/2 Eddie Sargent 37
72/3 Eddie Sargent 189
70/1 Esso Power Player
69/0 O-Pee-Chee 131
71/2 O-Pee-Chee 211
72/3 O-Pee-Chee 201
69/0 Topps 131
71/2 Toronto Sun Photo
71/2 SLOU
72/3 SLOU
O'SHEA, DARCY
95/6 Slapshot 251
O'SHEA, KEVIN
70/1 Eddie Sargent 25
71/2 Eddie Sargent 22
72/3 Eddie Sargent 190
72/3 O-Pee-Chee 257
71/2 Toronto Sun Photo
O'SULLIVAN, CHRIS
99/0 Choice 7
93/4 Donruss USA15
96/7 Do. Canadian 133
97/8 Leaf 141
96/7 L. Preferred 122
97/8 Limited 54
93/4 Pinnacle 484
96/7 Pi. Zenith 138
96/7 Select CE 111
93/4 Upper Deck 565
96/7 Upper Deck 230, X4
97/8 Upper Deck 235
96/7 UD Black Diam. 19
97/8 UD Coll. Choice 35
97/8 Saint John Flames
O'SULLIVAN, KEVIN
93/4 Classic 71
93/4 Fredericton Canadiens
94/5 Fredericton Canadiens
O'SULLIVAN, PATRICK
01/2 Mississauga IceDogs
02/3 Mississauga IceDogs
OAKE, SCOTT
97/8 Pi. CBC Sports 10
OAKLEY, ERNIE
51/2 Laval Dairy 60
OATES, ADAM
02/3 Atomic 3, ✂ GWJ 1
02/3 BAP Mem. 20, 242, 262
02/3 Crown Royale 3
02/3 Exclusive 3
02/3 First Edition 244, 373
02/3 Heads Up 3, -ITN 1, ✂ GWQ 20
02/3 In The GU 1, 101
02/3 McDonald's ✂ JP 13
02/3 O-Pee-Chee 173, Update 173
02/3 Pacific 284, ✂ GWJ 40
02/3 Pacific Complete 114
02/3 Parkhurst 110, -CR 6, ✂ CRM6
02/3 Parkhurst Retro 11
02/3 Pr. Stock Reserve ✂ 101
02/3 Signature GS-2, ✂ TQ19
02/3 SP Authentic 3
02/3 SPx 77
02/3 Stadium 107
02/3 Topps 173, Update 173
02/3 T. Chrome 100
02/3 To. Heritage 110
02/3 To. Heritage 164
02/3 To. Limited 173
02/3 To. Total 36
02/3 Ultimate Mem. ✂ A8 (x2), ✂ JE, ✂ JJ
02/3 Upper Deck 247
02/3 UD Rookie 2
02/3 UD Vintage 307
02/3 Vanguard ✂ GWJ 1
94/5 Action Packed
01/2 Adrenaline 200
01/2 Atomic 100, TN 15
98/9 Aurora 199
99/0 Aurora 150
00/1 Aurora 149
98/9 Be A Player 296, M15, ✍ Aut. 296
99/0 BAP Mem. 75, H-6
00/1 BAP Mem. 120, ✂ H-22, ✂ TM-2
01/2 BAP Mem. 300, 455
01/2 BAP Update ✂ H8
96/7 Bic.Sports Aces 4-S
97/8 Bicycle 5-Diamond
95/6 Bicycle Sports Aces 10-Heart
90/1 Bowman 16
91/2 Bowman 384
91/2 Bowman 406
92/3 Bowman 213
92/3 Bowman 258
95/6 Bowman 44
01/2 Bowman 32
98/9 Bowman's Best 72
92/3 Classic Prospects 35
92/3 Classic Prospects BC18
99/0 Crown Royale 144
00/1 Crown Royale 108
01/2 Crown Royale 144
93/4 Donruss 18
93/4 Donruss B
95/6 Donruss 386, I-1
96/7 Donruss 41
97/8 Donruss 25, 228
96/7 Do. Canadian 8
97/8 Do. Canadian 78, NP-7
95/6 Do. Elite 80
96/7 Do. Elite 31
97/8 Do. Preferred 100
97/8 Do. Priority 149
97/8 Do. Studio 32
98/9 Dynagon Ice 198
99/0 Dynagon Ice 203
93/4 EA Sports 188
93/4 EA Sports 8
95/6 Edge Ice L3
94/5 Flair 12, HN-6
96/7 Flair 5
94/5 Fleer 16
96/7 Fleer 6, ART-18
95/6 Fleer Metal 10, HM-11
96/7 Fl. Picks 28, F50-35, JE-15
92/3 Fleer Ultra 8
93/4 Fleer Ultra 156
93/4 Fleer Ultra AS 7
93/4 Fleer UltraCH to 10, Aut.
93/4 Fleer Ultra PP 7
94/5 Fleer Ultra 14, PP-9
95/6 Fleer Ultra 13, 395, EA-16, PP-6
96/7 Fl. Ultra 10, PL-6, UP-14
95 Globe 90
01/2 Heads Up 100
93/4 Hockey Wit 5
95/6 Hoyle / East. 9-Diamond
91/2 Kraft 5
94/5 Kraft / SS
95/6 Kraft / KD
96/7 Kraft / TT, KD
97/8 Kraft / KD
98/9 Kraft / Post 6
93/4 Leaf 235
93/4 Leaf HTA 8
94/5 Leaf 305, GLS-14, LL-2
95/6 Leaf 81
96/7 Leaf 112
97/8 Leaf 130
94/5 L. Limited 104
95/6 L. Limited 108
96/7 L. Limited 5
96/7 L. Preferred 40, LS-54
97/8 Limited 33, 112, 162
96/7 Maggers 13
92/3 McDonald's McD-11
93/4 McDonald's McD-21
96/7 Metal Univ. 9, LW-15
99/0 Millenium 248, ✍ Aut. 248
98/9 NHL Power Play
87/8 OPC/Topps 123
88/9 OPC/Topps 161
90/1 OPC/Topps 149
91/2 O-Pee-Chee 265
91/2 O-Pee-Chee 347
91/2 O-Pee-Chee 448
92/3 O-Pee-Chee 172
92/3 O-Pee-Chee 272
92/3 OPC - Anniv. 20
01/2 O-Pee-Chee 81
89/0 OPC/Topps 185
98/9 OPC Chrome 179, SB23
90/1 OPC Premier 88
91/2 OPC Premier 7
92/3 OPC Premier SP13
87/8 OPC Sticker 105-238
97/8 Omega 243
98/9 Omega 249
99/0 Omega 245
98/9 Pacific 445
99/0 Pacific 446
00/1 Pacific 428
01/2 Pacific 398, 443
97/8 Pacific CC 37, SS-12B
97/8 Pa. Crown Roy. 142
98/9 Pa. Crown Roy. 144
97/8 Pa. Dynagon 133, T-56
97/8 Pa. Invincible 149
97/8 Pa. Paramount 198
98/9 Pa. Paramount 249
99/0 Pa. Paramount 248
00/1 Pa. Paramount 248
97/8 Pa. Revolution 150
98/9 Pa. Revolution 149
98/9 Panini Photocard
87/8 Panini Sticker 248
88/9 Panini Sticker 45
90/1 Panini Sticker 275
91/2 Panini Sticker 31
92/3 Panini Sticker 136
93/4 Panini Sticker 138
93/4 Panini Sticker 2
94/5 Panini Sticker 1, CC
95/6 Panini Sticker 3
96/7 Panini Sticker 4
97/8 Panini Sticker 116
98/9 Panini Sticker 106
99/0 Panini Sticker 166
00/1 Panini Sticker 106
91/2 Parkhurst 155
91/2 Parkhurst 233
92/3 Parkhurst 4
93/4 Parkhurst 11
94/5 Parkhurst 311, V46
95/6 Parkhurst 16, PP-53
00/1 Parkhurst P-45
01/2 Parkhurst 85, ✂ PS42, ✂ M38, ✂ M49
94/5 Parkie SE13
91/2 Pinnacle 6
91/2 Pinnacle 378
92/3 Pinnacle 40
93/4 Pinnacle 185
94/5 Pinnacle 120
95/6 Pinnacle 3
96/7 Pinnacle 130
97/8 Pinnacle 62
97/8 Pi. Be A Player 5, ✍ Aut. 5
97/8 Pi. BeeHive 38
97/8 Pi. Certified 49
95/6 Pi. FANtasy 5
97/8 Pi. Inside 28
95/6 Pi. Summit 4
96/7 Pi. Summit 15
97/8 Pi. Totally 49
95/6 Pi. Zenith 10
96/7 Pi. Zenith 41
95/6 Playoff 9, 121, 229
94/5 POG 35
95/6 POG 29
93/4 Power Play 23
93/4 Power Play PL 11
93/4 Premier 50
93/4 Premier 74
93/4 Prmr. - BG-OPC 3
93/4 Prmr. - BG-Top. 5
94/5 Premier 135, 277
00/1 Premier Plus 63, ✂ GP
99/0 Prism 150
00/1 Pr. Stock 100, ✂ GUG 105
01/2 Pr. Stock 100
00/1 PS Titanium 100
01/2 PS Titanium 144
95/6 Pro Magnet 14
90/1 Pro Set 269
91/2 Pro Set 219
91/2 Pro Set 291
91/2 Pro Set CC7
92/3 Pro Set 3
91/2 Pro Set Midwest
91/2 Pro Set Platinum 113
91/2 Puck / Pro Set 25
99/0 Revolution 150, / CSC 150
00/1 Revolution 149, SM-30
90/1 Score 85
90/1 Sco. Hot Cards 41
91/2 Score 238
91/2 Score - Hot Card 6
91/2 Score CAN 458
92/3 Score 250
93/4 Score 125
93/4 Score 478
93/4 Score DT 17
93/4 Score DD3
93/4 Score PiAS 9
94/5 Score 141, NP-3
95/6 Score 119
96/7 Score 162
97/8 Score 117
92/3 Seasons 20
93/4 Seasons 13
94/5 Select 58
95/6 Select CE 11, DS-5
96/7 Select CE 68
00/1 Signature 179, ✍ Aut. 36, ✂ J-34
01/2 Signat. C-2, ✂ GUE33, ✂ GJ65, ✂ GSJ65, ✂ ITN33
95/6 SBx Emotion 11, Xce-1
95/6 SBx Impact 12
96/7 SBx Impact 7,BR-17
94/5 SP 8
95/6 SP 7
96/7 SP 11, HC-29
97/8 SP Authentic 162
98/9 SP Authentic 90
99/0 SP Authentic 89
00/1 SP Authentic 90
97/8 SPx 48, D-SPX12
99/0 SPx 158
00/1 SPx 69
99/0 Stadium 56
00/1 Stadium 168
01/2 Stadium 60, ✍ LSS
91/2 Star Pics 40
94/5 Starting Lineup
96/7 SLU
00/1 SLU 6
95/6 Super Sticker 5, 8
96/7 Team Out!
92/3 Topps 475
95/6 Topps 180, 381, 7PL
98/9 Topps 179, SB23
99/0 Topps 202
00/1 Topps 169, PC-7
01/2 Topps 81
99/0 To. Chrome 202
00/1 To. Chrome 116, PC-7
01/2 To. Chrome 81
94/5 Topps Finest 67, DF-3
95/6 To. Finest 43
98/9 To. Finest 98
98/9 T. Gold Label 80
00/1 To. Gold Label 25
00/1 To. Heritage 52
01/2 To. Heritage 92, ✂ CC
01/2 To. Reserve 34, ✂ TR
91/2 To. Stadium 108
92/3 To. Stadium 188
92/3 To. Stadium 245
93/4 To. Stadium 93
93/4 To. Stadium - Master Photo-1 11
93/4 To. Stadium - AS
95/6 To. Stadium 40
93/4 TSC Members Only 37
94/5 TSC Members Only 16
00/1 To. Stars 55
95/6 T. Super Skills 2
98/9 UD Choice 217
00/1 UD Heroes 116
00/1 Ultimate Mem. ✍ U-50, ✂ TM-11, ✂ TM-40
90/1 Upper Deck 173, 483
91/2 Upper Deck 94
91/2 Upper Deck 252
91/2 Upper Deck 627
92/3 Upper Deck 133
92/3 Upper Deck 455
92/3 Upper Deck 637
93/4 Upper Deck 226, 286, 327, HT5, H6, SP-11
94/5 Upper Deck 11, H20, R12, R26, R44, SP-7
95/6 Upper Deck 197, R16, SE5
96/7 Upper Deck 216, X40
97/8 Upper Deck 177, SS12, SG56, T18A
98/9 Upper Deck 199, FT20
99/0 Upper Deck 131, HOF8
00/1 Upper Deck 173
01/2 Upper Deck 407
95/6 UD ASG MVPR28
94/5 UD BAP R45
96/7 UD Black Diam. 152
97/8 UD Black Diam. 109
95/6 UD CC 197
96/7 UD CC 12, 310, UD15, C21, CR21
97/8 UD Coll. Choice 266, SQ23, S28
98/9 UD G. Reserve 199
99/0 UD G. Reserve 131
96/7 UD Ice 2
97/8 UD Ice 17
00/1 UD Legends 130
92/3 UD Locker 10
98/9 UD MVP 212
99/0 UD MVP 214
00/1 UD MVP 178
00/1 UD Pros&Prosp. 86
99/0 UD Retro 80
01/2 UD Top Shelf 111
00/1 UD Vintage 365, 370
01/2 UD Vintage 262
00/1 Vanguard 100
99/0 Victory 305
00/1 Victory 235
01/2 Victory 354
99/0 WGretzky 175
97/8 Zenith 32, Z41
91/2 BOST / Sports Action
92/3 BOST / Postcard
85/6 DETR / Little Caesars
86/7 DETR / Little Caesars
87/8 DETR / Little Caesars
88/9 DETR / Little Caesars
89/0 SLOU / Kodak
90/1 SLOU / Kodak
91/2 SLOU
92/3 SLOU / McDon. 17
98/9 WASH / Kids 'n 3
OATES, MATT
00/1 Kudos 120
94/5 Indianapolis Ice
OATMAN, ED
91 C55 Reprint 5
10/1 Imperial
11/2 Imperial 5
12/3 Imperial 47
23/4 Paulins Candy 61
ÖBERG, FREDRIK
95/6 Leaf Elit Set 301, FTF-12
92/3 Semic Elitserien 195
01/2 UD DEL 30
95/6 UD Elitserien 193
97/8 UD Elitserien 147
98/9 UD Elitserien 196
99/0 UD Elitserien 199
00/1 UD Elitserien 105
OBERLIN, RICH
88/9 ProCards / Indianapolis
OBERRAUCH, ROBERTO
95 Globe 228
95 Panini Worlds 81
92 Semic Sticker 246
93 Semic Sticker 211
96 Wien 176
OBLOJ, TADEUSZ
74 Hellas MM-Jenkki 101
79 Panini Sticker 133
73/4 Williams Finnish 96
OBRESA, PETER
94/5 DEL 104
95/6 DEL 101
99/0 Eishockey 99
89 Semic Sticker 119
OBSUT, JAROSLAV
01/2 BAP Mem. 313
98/9 EBK ECHL All-Star
01/2 Pacific 328
01/2 Parkhurst 310
01/2 SP Authentic 141
01/2 SP GU 70
01/2 SPx 102
01/2 Upper Deck 207
01/2 UD Challenge 101
01/2 UD MVP 215
01/2 UD Vintage 279
01/2 Victory 387
01/2 Hershey Bears
02/3 Manitoba Moose
00/1 Worcester IceCats
95/6 Swift Current Broncos
OCHOA, ALEX
92/3 Cincinnati Cyclones
ODDLEIFSON, CHRIS
74/5 Loblaws
74/5 O-Pee-Chee 108
75/6 O-Pee-Chee 169
76/7 O-Pee-Chee 112
76/7 OPC 395
77/8 O-Pee-Chee 209
78/9 O-Pee-Chee 183
79/0 O-Pee-Chee 305
80/1 O-Pee-Chee 295
81/2 OPC Sticker 246
74/5 Topps 108
75/6 Topps 169
76/7 Topps 112
77/8 Topps 209
78/9 Topps 183
74/5 VANC / Royal Bank
75/6 VANC / Royal Bank
76/7 VANC / Royal Bank
77/8 VANC / Royal Bank
78/9 VANC / Royal Bank
79/0 VANC / Royal Bank
ODELEIN, LEE
91/2 ProCards 447
ODELEIN, LYLE
02/3 Pacific Complete 386
02/3 Sports Vault 179
01/2 Atomic ✂ GWJ 15
93/4 Donruss 167
94/5 Donruss 272
95/6 Donruss 281
96/7 Duracell DC2,JB2
94/5 Fleer 105
92/3 Fleer Ultra 331
93/4 Fleer Ultra 354
94/5 Fleer Ultra 112
93/4 Leaf 283
94/5 Leaf 137
95/6 Leaf 195
91/2 O-Pee-Chee 350
98/9 Pacific 267
99/0 Pacific 243
97/8 Pacific CC 143
00/1 Pa. Paramount 71
92/3 Parkhurst 325
93/4 Parkhurst 370
95/6 Parkhurst 381
94/5 Parkie SE89
93/4 Pinnacle 301
94/5 Pinnacle 132
95/6 Pinnacle 196
96/7 Pi. Be A Player 148, ✍ Aut. 148
97/8 Pi. Be A Player 17, ✍ Aut. 17
95/6 Playoff 165
94/5 POG 140
93/4 Power Play 132
94/5 Premier 43
00/1 PS Titanium ✂ GUG 80
01/2 PS Titanium ✂ DSJ 15
00/1 PS Titanium Draft ✂ 27
90/1 Pro Set 617
88/9 ProCards / Peoria
89/0 ProCards AHL 185
93/4 Score 283
96/7 Score 224
97/8 Score NJer. 15
00/1 Signature 159, ✍ Aut. 88
00/1 Stadium 208
00/1 To. Chrome 222
94/5 To. Stadium 104
91/2 Upper Deck 482
93/4 Upper Deck 7
95/6 Upper Deck 153
96/7 Upper Deck 289
97/8 Upper Deck 306
95/6 UD BAP 111, ✍ S111
95/6 UD CC 6
00/1 UD Vintage 103
01/2 Vanguard ✂ DGM 40
01/2 Victory 103
01/2 COLU
90/1 MONT
91/2 MONT
92/3 MONT
93/4 MONT
94/5 MONT
94/5 MONT / Export
95/6 MONT
95/6 MONT / Export
96/7 NJER / Sharp
ODELEIN, SELMAR
88/9 ProCards / Cape Breton
87/8 EDMO
88/9 EDMO / Action 26
93/4 Sheffield Steelers 15
ODER, STEFFEN
99/0 Eishockey 201
ODGERS, JEFF
02/3 Pacific 19
02/3 Pacific Complete 435
00/1 BAP Mem. ✂ T-17
01/2 BAP Update ✂ TC13, ✂ TC17, ✂ TC24
92/3 Bowman 397
94/5 Fleer Ultra 368
94/5 Leaf 439
96/7 Maggers 133
92/3 O-Pee-Chee 190
97/8 Omega 62
98/9 Omega 62
98/9 Pacific 166
99/0 Pacific 112
01/2 Pacific 22, 402
97/8 Pacific CC 157
00/1 Pa. Paramount 123
92/3 Panini Sticker 130
93/4 Panini Sticker 260
97/8 Panini Sticker 2
91/2 Parkhurst 386
92/3 Parkhurst 398
96/7 Pi. Be A Player 193, ✍ Aut. 193
93/4 Power Play 224
93/4 Premier 497
90/1 ProCards 600
97/8 Score Bost. 18
92/3 Topps 483
92/3 To. Stadium 142
93/4 To. Stadium 114
94/5 To. Stadium 11
91/2 Upper Deck 597
01/2 Upper Deck 11
99/0 COLO / Kid Smart
92/3 SANJ / Pacific Bell
90/1 Kansas City Blades
88/9 Brandon Wheat Kings
89/0 Brandon Wheat Kings
ODJICK, GINO
02/3 Upper Deck 95
00/1 BAP Mem. 319, ✂ T-22
01/2 BAP Update ✂ TC27, ✂ TC40
91/2 Bowman 316
93/4 Donruss 346
94/5 Donruss 241
94/5 Fleer 228
92/3 Fleer Ultra 427
93/4 Fleer Ultra 442
94/5 Fleer Ultra 229
93/4 Leaf 418
94/5 Leaf 200
99/0 Millenium 154, ✍ Aut. 154
91/2 O-Pee-Chee 203
98/9 Omega 148
00/1 Pacific 304
97/8 Pa. Dynagon BKS-98
94/5 Panini Sticker 150
99/0 Panini Sticker 95
92/3 Parkhurst 422
93/4 Parkhurst 485
94/5 Parkie SE186
93/4 Pinnacle 308
94/5 Pinnacle 177
94/5 POG 151
94/5 POG / Western 15
93/4 Power Play 461
91/2 Pro Set 505
90/1 ProCards 334
91/2 Score CAN 237
92/3 Score 540
93/4 Score 385
94/5 Score 9
97/8 Score Vanc. 16
90 7th..Sketch Mem.Cup 54
01/2 Signat. 137, ✍ Aut. 137
91/2 To. Stadium 338
90/1 Upper Deck 518
91/2 Upper Deck 195
94/5 Upper Deck 465
95/6 Upper Deck 338
97/8 Upper Deck 206, 379
95/6 UD BAP 222, ✍ S222
95/6 UD CC 290
96/7 UD CC 274
97/8 UD Coll. Choice 263
00/1 MONT
01/2 MONT
01/2 MONT
90/1 VANC / Mohawk
91/2 VANC
91/2 VANC / Photo
92/3 VANC / Road Trip
94/5 VANC
95/6 VANC / Abalene 13
96/7 VANC / IGA
ODMARK, ULF
89/0 Semic Elitserien 184
90/1 Semic Elitserien 19
91/2 Semic Elitserien 221
92/3 Semic Elitserien 241
ODNOKON, MARK
91/2 7th...Sketch WHL 263
91/2 Prince Albert Raiders
85/6 Minnesota-Duluth 17
ODNOKON, PAT
90/1 Prince Albert Raiders
ODROWSKI, GERRY
45-64 BeeHive-2 [Detr.]
72/3 O-Pee-Chee 304
74/5 OPC WHA 14
62/3 Parkhurst 20
60/1 Shirriff 58
61/2 Shirriff 78
71/2 SLOU
72/3 Los Angeles Sharks
ODUYA, FREDRIK
95/6 Kansas City Blades
96/7 Kentucky Tho'blades
97/8 Kentucky Tho'blades
98/9 Orlando Solar Bears Geico
ODZHIK, DZHINO
00/1 Mir Fetisov 36
OGILVIE, BRIAN
74/5 Loblaws
OGRODNICK, JOHN
02/3 UD Foundations 24
90/1 Bowman 223
91/2 Bowman 71
01/2 Fleer Greats 46, ✍ Aut.
83/4 Funmate Puffy 16 [w/]
80/1 O-Pee-Chee 359
81/2 O-Pee-Chee 95
82/3 O-Pee-Chee 79
82/3 O-Pee-Chee 92
83/4 O-Pee-Chee 115
83/4 O-Pee-Chee 128
84/5 O-Pee-Chee 62
84/5 O-Pee-Chee 356
85/6 OPC/Topps 70
85/6 OPC/Topps Box J
86/7 OPC/Topps 87
87/8 OPC/Topps 134
88/9 OPC/Topps 153
90/1 OPC/Topps 174
90/1 Topps-TL 18
91/2 O-Pee-Chee 365
92/3 O-Pee-Chee 351
81/2 OPC Sticker 121
82/3 OPC/Topps Sticker 179
83/4 OPC/Topps Sticker 137
83/4 OPC/Topps Sticker 138
84/5 OPC Sticker 34
84/5 OPC Sticker 35
84/5 OPC Sticker 137
85/6 OPC Sticker 37
85/6 OPC Sticker 119
86/7 OPC Sticker 158
87/8 OPC Sticker 218
87/8 Panini Sticker 165
89/0 Panini Sticker 290
90/1 Panini Sticker 99
91/2 Panini Sticker 293
91/2 Parkhurst 115
91/2 Pinnacle 145
82/3 Post [Detr.]
90/1 Pro Set 206
91/2 Pro Set 169
91/2 Pro Set Platinum 204
90/1 Score 113
91/2 Score 36
91/2 Score CAN 36
92/3 Score 329
83/4 Souhaits Keychain [Red Wings]
81/2 Topps 95 [West]
84/5 Topps 46
85/6 OPC/Topps-Stick. 1
91/2 To. Stadium 273
92/3 To. Stadium 222
90/1 Upper Deck 258
91/2 Upper Deck 476
80/1 DETR
84/5 DETR / Little Caesars
85/6 DETR / Little Caesars
86/7 DETR / Little Caesars
89/0 NYRA / Marine
86/7 QUEB
ÖHLING, JENS
94/5 Leaf Elit Set 38, SS-3
95/6 Leaf Elit Set 33
89/0 Semic Elitserien 62
90/1 Semic Elitserien 286
91/2 Semic Elitserien 69
92/3 Semic Elitserien 90
95/6 UD Elitserien 52
97/8 UD Elitserien 176
OHLSSON, BENGT
92 Semic Sticker 26
ÖHLUND, MATTIAS
02/3 Calder 10
02/3 First Edition 44, ✂ Jers.
02/3 O-Pee-Chee 51
02/3 Pacific 382
02/3 Pacific Complete 57
02/3 Signature GS-56, ✂ DW10
02/3 Sports Vault 299
02/3 Topps 51
02/3 To. Limited 51
02/3 To. Total 60
02/3 Upper Deck 169, 417
98/9 Aurora 191
99/0 Aurora 144
98/9 Be A Player 142, ✍ Aut. 142
99/0 BAP Mem. 19
00/1 BAP Mem. 329
01/2 BAP Mem. 219
98/9 Bowman's Best 73, BP5
97/8 Do. Elite 98, 139
97/8 Do. Priority 171
98/9 Dynagon Ice 191
95 Globe 57
99/0 Kraft / KD
94/5 Leaf Elit Set 288, ND-1, RR-4
95/6 Leaf Elit Set 75, LM-8
98/9 McDonald's McD22
00/1 McDonald's 34, CI-8
99/0 Millenium 239, ✍ Aut. 239
98/9 NHL Power Play
99/0 NHL Power Play
01/2 O-Pee-Chee 147
98/9 OPC Chrome 54, B5, SB11
97/8 Omega 234
98/9 Omega 240
98/9 Pacific 2
99/0 Pacific 430
00/1 Pacific 413
01/2 Pacific 385, 419
98/9 Pa. Crown Roy. 138
97/8 Pa. Dynagon Rookie
97/8 Pa. Paramount 192
98/9 Pa. Paramount 238
99/0 Pa. Paramount 239
00/1 Pa. Paramount 241
97/8 Pa. Revolution 144
98/9 Pa. Revolution 144, -ASG 21
98/9 Panini Sticker 221
99/0 Panini Sticker 308
00/1 Panini Sticker 210
94/5 Parkie SE243
97/8 Pinnacle 8
97/8 Pi. Be A Player 215, ✍ Aut. 215
99/0 Revolution 145
97/8 Score 63
97/8 Score Vanc. 6
94/5 Sig. Rookies 14, ✍ 14
94/5 SR Gold Standard 89
94/5 SP 172
95/6 SP 184
97/8 SP Authentic 196
98/9 SP Authentic 84, ✍ SotT
99/0 SPx 152
98/9 SPx Finite 127
99/0 Stadium 124
00/1 Stadium 58
98/9 Topps 54,B5, IA 12, SB11, ✍ CAI
99/0 Topps 76, NS14
00/1 Topps 72
01/2 Topps 147
99/0 To. Chrome 76
00/1 To. Chrome 57
98/9 To. Finest 38, C14
98/9 T. Gold Label 87
00/1 To. Stars 37
98/9 UD Choice 206
98/9 UD3 14, 74, 134
94/5 Upper Deck 520
97/8 Upper Deck 380
98/9 Upper Deck 197, GN16
99/0 Upper Deck 299
97/8 UD Black Diam. 120
98/9 UD Black Diam. 87
95/6 UD Elitserien 119, 229, 256, NA16
98/9 UD G. Reserve 197
99/0 UD G. Reserve 299
97/8 UD Ice 42
98/9 UD MVP 203
99/0 UD MVP 207, W22
00/1 UD Vintage 356
99/0 Victory 300
96 Wien 52
97/8 Zenith 85, RR-13, ZT-11, Z73
01/2 VANC / Coke
ÖHMAN, JENS
89/0 Semic Elitserien 183
90/1 Semic Elitserien 18
91/2 Semic Elitserien 222
98/9 UD Elitserien 26
ÖHMAN, ROGER
96/7 DEL 232
94/5 Leaf Elit Set 272
95/6 Leaf Elit Set 88, G-9
89/0 Semic Elitserien 7
90/1 Semic Elitserien 131
91/2 Semic Elitserien 182
92/3 Semic Elitserien 209
95/6 UD Elitserien 139
87/8 Moncton Hawks
ÖHMAN, STEFAN
94/5 Leaf Elit Set 228
98/9 UD Elitserien 27
00/1 UD Elitserien 164
OHRLUND, TORBJÖRN
92/3 Semic Elitserien 44
OHRSTEDT, MARTIN
98/9 Odessa Jackalopes
OIJENNUS, MARKUS
93/4 Sisu 79
94/5 Sisu 114
95/6 Sisu 321
OIJENNUS, OIVA
80/1 Mallasjuoma 161
78/9 SM-Liiga 183
72/3 Williams Finnish 162
73/4 Williams Finnish 228
OJANEN, JANNE
02/3 Cardset 87
98/9 Cardset 222, Leij. 34
99/0 Cardset 128, 167, AH 7-hertta
00/1 Cardset 89
95 Globe 136
95 Hartwall Karjala
93 Koululainen
95 Leaf Latkaliiga 12
90/1 OPC/Topps 30
92/3 OPC Premier 17
90/1 Panini Sticker 78
95 Panini Worlds 171
93/4 Premier 16
90/1 Pro Set 173
88/9 ProCards / Utica
94 Semic 35
95 Semic 8
92 Semic Sticker 21
93 Semic Sticker 71
94/5 Sisu 208, FOI-6, MN-4, SS-4
95/6 Sisu 322, G-19, SS-6
96/7 Sisu MA-6
95/6 Sisu Limited 77, LG-4
93/4 To. Stadium 184
90/1 Upper Deck 290
91/2 Upper Deck 25
97/8 UD Elitserien 141, 214, UDS13, C12
96 Wien 8
89/0 NJER
89/0 NJER / Caretta
OJANEN, MARKO
02/3 Cardset 239
98/9 Cardset 131
99/0 Cardset 73
00/1 Cardset 333
97/8 Hockey-Box
93/4 Sisu 105
94/5 Sisu 132
95/6 Sisu 14
OJANEN, REIJO
65/6 Hellas 149
OJANSUU, JOUKO
66/7 Champion 49
ÖJRNSKOG, STEFAN
95 Semic 71
OKAL, MIROSLAV
94/5 APS 194
95/6 APS 42
96/7 APS 44
97/8 APS 67
98/9 DS 114
99/0 DS 8
00/1 DS 55
96/7 DS Sticker 110
97/8 DS Sticker 297
98/9 OFS 30
99/0 OFS 216
00/1 OFS 360
01/2 OFS 113
OKAL, ZDENEK
94/5 APS 195
95/6 APS 43
OKKONEN, ILKKA
71/2 Williams Finnish 308
OKSA, MIKA
02/3 Cardset 88
99/0 Cardset 205
00/1 Cardset 4
OKSALA, JORMA
66/7 Champion 154
70/1 Kuvajulkaisut 218
OKSALA, OSSI
70/1 Kuvajulkaisut 261
OKSANEN, HANNU
78/9 SM-Liiga 60
72/3 Williams Finnish 313
OKSANEN, JUKKA
72/3 Williams Finnish 349
OKSANEN, LASSE
66/7 Champion 203
65/6 Hellas 114
72 Hellas MM-Jenkki 9
70/1 Kuvajulkaisut 71
70/1 Kuvajulkaisut 133
80/1 Mallasjuoma 32
69/0 Mästär Serien 13
72 Panda MM-Toronto
72 Panda MM-Toronto
72 Semic Sticker 84
74 Semic Sticker 87
91 Semic Sticker 229
78/9 SM-Liiga 55
77-79 Sports. FIN 45-1057
96 Wien HL14
71/2 Williams Finnish 72
71/2 Williams Finnish 182
72/3 Williams Finnish 69
72/3 Williams Finnish 131
73/4 Williams Finnish 186
OKSIUTA, ROMAN
93/4 Cla. 4 Sport 244
94/5 Cla. Images 35
92/3 Classic Prospects 11
93/4 Donruss 111
93/4 Donruss RR 15
95/6 Donruss 66
96/7 Donruss 44
94/5 Fleer 72
95/6 Fleer Metal 154
95/6 Fleer Ultra 171, AR-9
96/7 Fl. Ultra 4
93/4 Leaf 411
95/6 Leaf 77, SR-16
96/7 Metal Univ. 4
00/1 Mir 357
91/2 O-Pee-Chee 57R
97/8 Pa. Invincible R-164
95/6 Panini Sticker 292
96/7 Panini Sticker 224
97/8 Panini Sticker 48
93/4 Parkhurst 258
95/6 Parkhurst 211
93/4 Pinnacle 451
95/6 Pinnacle 63
96/7 Pinnacle 139
95/6 Playoff 210
96/7 Playoff 397
92/3 Red Ace Blue 20
92/3 Red Ace Violet 24
95/6 Score 285
96/7 Score 76
97/8 Score Pitt. 13
93 Semic Sticker 141
95/6 SBx Emotion 183
95/6 SBx Impact 172, F-2
96/7 SBx Impact 3
95/6 Topps 317, 8NG
94/5 Topps Finest BBR-5
95/6 To. Finest 94
95/6 To. Stadium 132
93/4 Upper Deck 509
95/6 Upper Deck 476
96/7 UD CC 10
96/7 ANAH / Up Front 3
93/4 EDMO / Sheet
94/5 Cape Breton Oilers
OKTJABREV, ARTUR
00/1 Mir 380
92/3 Red Ace Blue 31
92/3 Red Ace Violet 25
OLASKI, MIKE
92/3 BCJHL 72
OLAUSSON, FREDRIK
02/3 Pacific Complete 350
02/3 Upper Deck 249
98/9 Be A Player 154, ✍ Aut. 154
99/0 BAP Mem. 165
90/1 Bowman 135
91/2 Bowman 210
92/3 Bowman 295
93/4 Donruss 386
93/4 Donruss 430
94/5 Fleer 73
92/3 Fleer Ultra 244, -UI 18
93/4 Fleer Ultra 147
94/5 Fleer Ultra 74
95 Globe 26
89/0 Kraft 51
93/4 Leaf 124
94/5 Leaf 327
87/8 O-Pee-Chee 225
90/1 OPC/Topps 242
91/2 O-Pee-Chee 45
92/3 O-Pee-Chee 121
98/9 OPC Chrome 150
98/9 Omega 6
98/9 Pacific 356
99/0 Pacific 11
97/8 Pacific CC 149
98/9 Pa. Paramount 195
99/0 Pa. Paramount 5
87/8 Panini Sticker 361
90/1 Panini Sticker 318
90/1 Panini/WPG 19
91/2 Panini Sticker 67
92/3 Panini Sticker 60
93/4 Panini Sticker 198
96/7 Panini Sticker 230
97/8 Panini Sticker 54
98/9 Panini Sticker 54
91/2 Parkhurst 203
92/3 Parkhurst 212
93/4 Parkhurst 227
91/2 Pinnacle 74
92/3 Pinnacle 202
93/4 Pinnacle 392
94/5 Pinnacle 303
96/7 Pi. Be A Player 134, ✍ Aut. 134
94/5 POG 103
93/4 Power Play 273
93/4 Power Play 342
93/4 Premier 63
94/5 Premier 319
90/1 Pro Set 335
91/2 Pro Set 264
91/2 Pro Set Platinum 133
90/1 Score 81
91/2 Score 18
91/2 Score CAN 18
92/3 Score 13
93/4 Score 645
93/4 Score 79
94/5 Score 147
89/0 Semic Elitserien 77
89 Semic Sticker 10
92 Semic Sticker 59
93 Semic Sticker 26
99/0 Stadium 117
92/3 Topps 120
98/9 Topps 150
99/0 Topps 175
99/0 To. Chrome 175
91/2 To. Stadium 185
92/3 To. Stadium 346
94/5 To. Stadium 198
90/1 Upper Deck 237
91/2 Upper Deck 383
92/3 Upper Deck 136
93/4 Upper Deck 209
94/5 Upper Deck 394
97/8 Upper Deck 139
99/0 Upper Deck 14
01/2 Upper Deck 295
94/5 UD BAP ✍ 8
95/6 UD CC 98
95/6 UD Elitserien 247
99/0 UD G. Reserve 14
99/0 Victory 8, 344
93/4 EDMO / Sheet
86/7 WINN
87/8 WINN
88/9 WINN / Safety Tips
89/0 WINN / Safeway
90/1 WINN / IGA
91/2 WINN / IGA
93/4 WINN / Ruffles
93/4 WINN Readers
OLBRICH, MICHAEL
94/5 DEL 175
95/6 DEL 170
OLCZYK, ED
90/1 Bowman 161
91/2 Bowman 204
92/3 Bowman 278
92/3 Fleer Ultra 245, 357
96/7 Fl. Ultra 81
88/9 Frito Lay
91/2 Kellogg's / Score 18
89/0 Kraft 38
91/2 Kraft 62
93/4 Leaf 90
96/7 Leaf 117
96/7 Metal Univ. 77
85/6 OPC/Topps 86
86/7 OPC/Topps 82
87/8 OPC/Topps 104
88/9 OPC/Topps 125
88/9 OPC/Topps Box G
90/1 OPC/Topps 206
91/2 O-Pee-Chee 182
92/3 O-Pee-Chee 375
89/0 OPC/Topps 133
91/2 OPC Premier 196
85/6 OPC Sticker 26-154
86/7 OPC Sticker 156-14
87/8 OPC Sticker 76-210
88/9 OPC Sticker 181
89/0 opcSticker 172
97/8 Omega 188
98/9 Pacific 357
99/0 Pacific 95
97/8 Pacific CC 92
97/8 Pa. Crown Roy. 112
97/8 Pa. Invincible 116
97/8 Pa. Paramount 154
87/8 Panini Sticker 230
88/9 Panini Sticker 126
89/0 Panini Sticker 132
90/1 Panini Sticker 283
90/1 Panini/TOR 17
91/2 Panini Sticker 64
92/3 Panini Sticker 55
96/7 Panini Sticker 193
91/2 Parkhurst 204
92/3 Parkhurst 213
92/3 Parkhurst 350
93/4 Parkhurst 402
91/2 Pinnacle 193
91/2 Pinnacle 386
92/3 Pinnacle 145
93/4 Pinnacle 154
94/5 Pinnacle 420
97/8 Pi. Inside 169
93/4 Power Play 394
93/4 Premier 398
90/1 Pro Set 286, 563
91/2 Pro Set 265
92/3 Pro Set 213
91/2 Pro Set Platinum 134
90/1 Score 210, 51T
90/1 Sco. Hot Cards 89
91/2 Score 60
91/2 Score CAN 60
92/3 Score 145
92/3 Score USAG 15
93/4 Score 37
95/6 Score 282
96/7 Score 198
97/8 Score 206
97/8 Score Pitt. 7
94 Semic 115
89 Semic Sticker 169
91 Semic Sticker 148
92 Semic Sticker 161
93 Semic Sticker 184
96/7 SP 75
92/3 Topps 17
91/2 To. Stadium 57
92/3 To. Stadium 157
93/4 To. Stadium 197
90/1 Upper Deck 222, 431
91/2 Upper Deck 99
91/2 Upper Deck 387
92/3 Upper Deck 211
93/4 Upper Deck 115
94/5 Upper Deck 274
95/6 UD BAP 141, ✍ S141
95/6 UD CC 106
86/7 CHIC / Coke
87/8 TORO / 5x8
87/8 TORO / P.L.A.Y. 9
88/9 TORO / P.L.A.Y. 6
90/1 WINN / IGA
91/2 WINN / IGA
95/6 WINN
OLDENBORGER, JEFF
94/5 Slapshot Memorial 2
OLEINIK, VALERI
99/0 Mir 268
00/1 Mir 341
OLENICI, ADRIAN
79 Panini Sticker 318
OLENIUK, DEVON
87/8 Kamloops Blazers
84/5 Saskatoon Blades
86/7 Saskatoon Blades
OLENYN, JERRY
94/5 Las Vegas Thunder
OLERS, DANIEL
99/0 Colorado Gold Kings
OLESCHUK, BILL
79/0 COLR
OLESEVICH, DAN
80/1 DETR
OLESON, CORY
85/6 U. of Arizona Ice Cats
OLIMB, LARRY
92/3 Classic 90
91/2 Minnesota G'Gophers
OLIVA, JIRI
99/0 Score 162
OLIVEIRA, MIKE
95/6 Slapshot 122
99/0 Louisiana Ice Gators
OLIVEIRA, SAM
91/2 7th...Sketch OHL 7
91/2 Cornwall Royals
OLIVER, DAVID
94/5 Classic 57, AA6, R16, T24

94/5 Cla. Images 79, ✍ Aut.
95/6 Donruss 8, RT-4
95/6 Edge Ice 35, C-7
94/5 Flair 60
94/5 Fleer 74
95/6 Fleer Metal 55
95/6 Fleer Ultra 56, AR-10
95/6 Hoyle / West. 10-Diamond
95/6 Leaf 9, SR-4
95/6 L. Limited 89
95/6 Panini Sticker 263
95/6 Parkhurst 76
94/5 Parkie SE60
94/5 Pinnacle 490
95/6 Pinnacle 42
96/7 Pinnacle 51
95/6 Pi. Summit 98
95/6 Playoff 38
96/7 Playoff 358
94/5 POG / Western 12
95/6 POG 108, I-034
95/6 Score 60
96/7 Score 193
95/6 SBx Emotion 65
95/6 SBx Impact 63, 231, F-3
94/5 SP P-13
95/6 Topps 366, 8HG, 14NG
94/5 Topps Finest BBR-6
95/6 To. Finest 62
95/6 To. Stadium 109
95/6 T. Super Skills 71
94/5 Upper Deck 269, SP-117
95/6 Upper Deck 217, SE-120
96/7 Upper Deck 60
95/6 UD BAP 64, ✍ S64
95/6 UD CC 13
96/7 UD CC 96
01/2 UD DEL 187
94/5 Cape Breton Oilers
00/1 Charlotte Checkers
00/1 Grand Rapids Griffins
99/0 Houston Aeros
99/0 Huntington Blizzard

OLIVER, HARRY
02/3 Ultimate Mem. ✍ Cut
33/4 Anonymous 39
39/0 Bruins Magazine
33-35 Diamond Match Silv.
36-39 Diamond Match TT1
36-39 Diamond Match TT2
36-39 Diamond Match TT3
83 HHOF Postcard K12
83&87 HHOF 146
94/5 Legends 38
33/4 O-Pee-Chee 9
23/4 Paulins Candy 69
33/4 WWGum 23

OLIVER, LAWRENCE
92/3 BCJHL 230

OLIVER, MATT
98/9 Phoenix Mustangs 17

OLIVER, MURRAY
45-64 BeeHive-2 [Detr.]
45-64 BeeHive-2 [Bost.]
64-67 BeeHive-3 [Bost.]
64/5 Coke/Sprite [Bost.]
65/6 Coca-Cola
70/1 Dad's Cookies
70/1 Eddie Sargent 86
71/2 Eddie Sargent 88
72/3 Eddie Sargent 107
70/1 Esso Power Player
62/3 Cowan Tile
74/5 Loblaws
68/9 O-Pee-Chee 194
69/0 O-Pee-Chee 52
70/1 O-Pee-Chee 167
71/2 O-Pee-Chee 139
74/5 O-Pee-Chee 291
75/6 O-Pee-Chee 335
60/1 Parkhurst 22
95/6 Parkie 66-67 9, 140
94/5 Parkie Tall 2, 169
66/7 Post Cereal Box
68/9 Post Marble
60/1 Shirriff 55
61/2 Shirriff 8
68/9 Shirriff / Toro. 9
61/2 Topps 14
61/2 Topps - Stamp
62/3 Topps 12
62/3 Topps Dollar
63/4 Topps 10
64/5 Topps 79
65/6 Topps 34
66/7 Topps 95
67/8 Topps 82
69/0 Topps 52
62/3 Toronto Star Weekend
71/2 Toronto Sun Photo
73/4 MINS
80/1 MINS
81/2 MINS
68/9 TORO
69/0 TORO

OLIVER, SIMON
96/7 Mississippi S'Wolves

OLIVERIO, MIKE
83/4 Soo Greyhounds
84/5 Soo Greyhounds
87/8 Soo Greyhounds 17

OLIVERIUS, MICHAL
01/2 OFS 160
99/0 Score 88

OLIVIER, SIMON
92/3 MPS SJHL 2
98/9 Oklahoma City Blazers

OLIWA, KRZYSZTOF
00/1 BAP Mem. 333, ✂ T-13
01/2 BAP Update ✂ TC12, ✂ TC30
93/4 Cla. Prospects 73
97/8 Omega 133
98/9 Omega 140
98/9 Pacific 268
99/0 Pacific 244
01/2 Pacific 419
98/9 Pa. Paramount 137
00/1 Panini Sticker 141
97/8 Pi. Be A Player 229, ✍ Aut. 229
00/1 Revolution 43
94/5 SR Tetrad CX, ✍ Aut.
00/1 Stadium 196
01/2 To. Reserve ✂ TR
99/0 Ult. Victory 52
97/8 Upper Deck 302
98/9 Upper Deck 117
98/9 UD G. Reserve 117
00/1 UD Vintage 104, 110
96/7 Albany River Rats

OLKKONEN, PEKKA
66/7 Champion 206
65/6 Hellas 12

OLLIKAINEN, JARKKO
99/0 Cardset 102
00/1 Cardset 313

OLLILA, JUKKA
92/3 Jyvas Hyva 38
93/4 Jyvas Hyva 80
93/4 Sisu 112
94/5 Sisu 330
95/6 Sisu 313
93/4 Upper Deck 269

OLLSON, JOHN
85/6 Nova Scotia Oilers
81/2 Ottawa 67's
82/3 Ottawa 67's

OLMSTEAD, BERT
45-64 BeeHive-2 [Chic.]
45-64 BeeHive-2 [Mont.]
45-64 BeeHive-2 [Toro.]
48-52 Exhibits [Canadiens]
83&87 HHOF 248
51/2 La Patrie
51/2 Parkhurst 5
52/3 Parkhurst 93
53/4 Parkhurst 19
54/5 Parkhurst 5
55/6 Parkhurst 42
57/8 Parkhurst [Mont.] 19
57/8 Parkhurst [Mont.] 25
58/9 Parkhurst 27
59/0 Parkhurst 40
60/1 Parkhurst 4
61/2 Parkhurst 4
93/4 Parkhurst PR56
93/4 Parkie 56-57 146
93/4 Parkie 56-57 164
93/4 Parkie 56-57 71
45-54 Quaker Oats
60/1 Shirriff 11
61/2 Shirriff 52
62/3 Shirriff 11
62/3 Topps 57
58/9 Toronto Star Photo
59/0 Toronto Star Photo
60/1 York Glass [Toro.]
60/1 York
61/2 York 19
92/3 MONT / OPC 58

OLOFSON, JON
98/9 Fort Worth Brahmas
99/0 Fort Worth Brahmas

OLOFSSON, TONY
89/0 Semic Elitserien 177
90/1 Semic Elitserien 11

OLSEN, ATLE
92/3 Semic Nordisk 10

OLSEN, DARRYL
89/0 ProCards IHL 195
90/1 ProCards 604
91/2 ProCards 577

OLSEN, EIVIND
92/3 Semic Nordisk 138

OLSEN, ERIC
95/6 Slapshot 108

OLSEN, ØSCAR
92/3 Semic Nordisk 9

OLSEN, ØYSTEIN
92 Semic Sticker 36
93 Semic Sticker 242

OLSEN, ROGER
92/3 Semic Nordisk 121

OLSEN, STIG
92/3 Semic Nordisk 231

OLSEN, SVEN ARILD
92/3 Semic Nordisk 208

OLSEN, TOM ERIK
95 Panini Worlds 243
93 Semic Sticker 247

OLSEN, TOM_ERIK
92/3 Semic Nordisk 22

OLSON, ATLE
97/8 UD Elitserien 65

OLSON, BOB
91/2 Michigan Tech Huskies

OLSON, BOYD
96/7 Fredericton Canadiens
99/0 Québec Citadelles 23
95/6 Tri-City Americans 20

OLSON, EDDIE
51/2 Cleveland Barons

OLSSON, ANDREAS
94/5 Leaf Elit Set 253

OLSSON, BJØRTE
92/3 Semic Nordisk 90

OLSSON, CHRISTER
94/5 Leaf Elit Set 97
95/6 Leaf Elit Set LM 14
97/8 Pa. Dynagon BKS-66
96/7 Panini Sticker 208
95 Panini Worlds 145
92/3 Semic Elitserien 60
97/8 UD Elitserien 69, 203, 223, S3, C4
98/9 UD Elitserien 67, DL10
00/1 UD Elitserien 33
96 Wien 50, AS2
96/7 OTTA

OLSSON, DANIEL
99/0 UD Elitserien 34

OLSSON, FREDRIK
90/1 Semic Elitserien 218

OLSSON, JOHN
83/4 Springfield Indians 5

OLSSON, JONAS
97/8 UD Elitserien 193
98/9 UD Elitserien 195

OLSSON, MATTIAS
94/5 Leaf Elit Set 225
95/6 Leaf Elit Set 296
89/0 Semic Elitserien 82
90/1 Semic Elitserien 255
91/2 Semic Elitserien 86
92/3 Semic Elitserien 110
95/6 UD Elitserien 191

OLSSON, NILS OLOV
79 Panini Sticker 199

OLSSON, OVE
82 Semic Sticker 20

OLSSON, PETER
95/6 UD Elitserien DS19

OLSSON, ROGER
70/1 Kuvajulkaisut 35

OLSSON, STEFAN
89/0 Semic Elitserien 231
90/1 Semic Elitserien 70
91/2 Semic Elitserien 244

OLUND, THOMAS
89/0 Semic Elitserien 47
90/1 Semic Elitserien 195

ÖLVESTAD, JIMMIE
02/3 O-Pee-Chee 277
02/3 Topps 277
02/3 To. Limited 277
02/3 To. Total 124
01/2 Signat. 222, ✍ Aut. 222
98/9 SPx Prospects 81
01/2 Upper Deck 391
98/9 UD Black Diam. 111
98/9 UD Elitserien 65
99/0 UD Elitserien 50, 204
00/1 UD Elitserien 55, 212

OLYMPIEV, SERGEI
93/4 Slapshot / Kitchener 26
94/5 Slapshot / Kitchener 24
98/9 Topeka Scarecrows

OLYNICK, CRAIG
99/0 UD Prospects 41, 84
01/2 Moose Jaw Warriors 18

OLYNYK, RYAN
00/1 Medicine Hat Tigers

OMICIOLI, MIKE
99/0 Hampton Roads

ONDREJKA, MARTIN
94/5 DEL 215
95/6 DEL 214

ONOFRYCHUK, DARRYL
91/2 7th...Sketch WHL 158

ONUFRECHUK, CHAD
99/0 Mobile Mysticks

OPP, DARREN
91/2 Air Canada SJHL 39
91/2 Air Canada SJHL D19

OPRANDI, ROBERT
79 Panini Sticker 380

OPULSKIS, JURIS
94/5 APS 127

ORAVEC, TOMAS
00/1 Kelowna Rockets

ORBAN, BILL
67/8 Topps 109

ORCT, ZDENEK
94/5 APS 203
95/6 APS 150
96/7 APS 167
97/8 APS 77
97/8 DS 41
98/9 DS 15
99/0 DS 57, G5
00/1 DS 47, G4
96/7 DS Sticker 37
97/8 DS Sticker 87
98/9 OFS 2
99/0 OFS 12, -CL
00/1 OFS 135, -Star 19
01/2 OFS 171, -CL 2, -H3

ORDMAN, ROB
83/4 Brandon Wheat Kings

OREKHOVSKY, OLEG
95/6 Classic 65, ✍ Aut.
00/1 Mir 338
94/5 Sig. Rookies FF6, ✍ FF6
95/6 SR Tetrad Autobilia 49
00/1 Dynamo 10

ORGAN, JAMEY
97/8 Guildford Flames
98/9 Guildford Flames

ORIMUS, PEKKA
78/9 SM-Liiga 58

ORLANDO, GAETANO (GATES)
95 Globe 232
95 Panini Worlds 87
94 Semic 299
95 Semic 174
92 Semic Sticker 253
93 Semic Sticker 218
96 Wien 180
85/6 BUFF / Blue Shield
86/7 BUFF / Blue Shield
92/3 Albany River Rats
79/0 Montréal Juniors B&W
79/0 Montréal Jrs. Colour

ORLANDO, JIM
76 DETR

ORLANDO, JIMMY
34-43 BeeHive-1 [Detr.]
39/0 O-Pee-Chee 65

ORLOV, MAXIM
00/1 Mir 253

ÖRNSKOG, STEFAN
98/9 Cardset 138
99/0 Cardset 76
95 Globe 39
94/5 Leaf Elit Set 28, GC-22
95/6 Leaf Elit Set 57, C-11, G-6
95 Panini Worlds 155
94 Semic 71
89/0 Semic Elitserien 115
90/1 Semic Elitserien 116
91/2 Semic Elitserien 118
92/3 Semic Elitserien 140
95/6 UD Elitserien 83
97/8 UD Elitserien 91, 207, 218, UDS8, C23

ORO, JANNE
71/2 Williams Finnish 316

ORPIK, BROOKS
02/3 BAP Mem. 377
02/3 Calder 139
02/3 First Edition 431R
02/3 Pacific Complete 584
02/3 Parkhurst 236
02/3 Parkhurst Retro 238
02/3 PS Titanium 132
02/3 Quest for the Cup 139
02/3 SP Authentic ✍ 200
02/3 SPx 178
02/3 Ultimate Mem. 70
02/3 UD Artistic 108, R97, CG11
02/3 UD Classic 134
02/3 UD Honor 140
02/3 UD Mask 167
02/3 UD Premier ✍ 102, ✂ Jers
02/3 UD Rookie ✂ 151
01/2 WBS Penguins
02/3 WBS Penguins

ORR, BOBBY
02/3 Canada Post
02/3 SP Authentic ✍ SotT, ✍ SotTD (x2), ✍ SotTT (x2)
02/3 SP Game-Used ✍ Sig
02/3 SPx 79
02/3 UD Superstars 36, MM17,02/3 UD12, 02/3 UD27
02/3 Upper Deck 182, -GG2
02/3 UD Artistic 7, R7, GD4, / ✍ Art
02/3 UD Classic PL1-10
02/3 UD Foundations 4, 103, ✂ LI, ✍ SG
02/3 UD Honor ✍ SC
02/3 UD MVP ✍ PSig
02/3 UD Piece 97, 115, 116, 117, -HB1, SB2, ✍ MD
02/3 UD Premier 57, ✍ Sig
02/3 UD Rookie 103, ✍ Sig
02/3 UD Top Shelf ✍ Sig
68/9 Bauer Photo
92/3 Baybank 1-3
71/2 Bazooka Panel
99/0 Canada Post
77/8 Coke
71/2 Colgate Head
70/1 Colgate 87
70/1 Dad's Cookies
70/1 Eddie Sargent 1
71/2 Eddie Sargent 10
72/3 Eddie Sargent 17
70/1 Esso Power Player
88/9 Esso All-Star
92/3 Future Trends C76 104, 126, 184, 196, ✍ Aut.
83 HHOF Postcard E13
83&87 HHOF 61
75/6 Hockey Heroes
92/3 Legends 4
72/3 Post 5
72/3 Post 17
74/5 Lipton Soup 8
74/5 Loblaws
73/4 Mac's Milk
99/0 Millenium P-13, ✍ P-13
68/9 O-Pee-Chee 2
x68/9 O-Pee-Chee 200
x68/9 O-Pee-Chee 214
x68/9 O-Pee-Chee PS 4
69/0 O-Pee-Chee 24
x69/0 O-Pee-Chee 209
x69/0 O-Pee-Chee 212
x69/0 O-Pee-Chee 4in1
x69/0 O-Pee-Chee Stamp
70/1 O-Pee-Chee 3
70/1 O-Pee-Chee 236
70/1 O-Pee-Chee 245
70/1 O-Pee-Chee 248
70/1 O-Pee-Chee 249
70/1 O-Pee-Chee 252
70/1 O-Pee-Chee DE 4
71/2 O-Pee-Chee 100
71/2 O-Pee-Chee 245
71/2 O-Pee-Chee 251
71/2 O-Pee-Chee Book. 24
72/3 O-Pee-Chee 58
72/3 O-Pee-Chee 127
72/3 O-Pee-Chee 129
72/3 O-Pee-Chee 142
72/3 O-Pee-Chee 227
72/3 O-Pee-Chee 280
72/3 O-Pee-Chee 283
72/3 O-Pee-Chee Crest 3
73/4 O-Pee-Chee 30
74/5 O-Pee-Chee 2
74/5 O-Pee-Chee 28
74/5 O-Pee-Chee 100
74/5 O-Pee-Chee 130
74/5 O-Pee-Chee 248
75/6 OPC 100,209-10
75/6 OPC 288,314
76/7 O-Pee-Chee 213
77/8 O-Pee-Chee 251
78/9 O-Pee-Chee 300
71/2 O-Pee-Chee Poster 1
95/6 Parkie 66-67 7, SR1-5, TW-5
91/2 Pinnacle 392
95/6 Pi. FANtasy 31
67/8 Post Cereal Box
67/8 Post Cereal Box
70/1 Post Shooters
71/2 Pro Star Promotions
71/2 Pro Star Promotions
71/2 Pro Star Promotions
71/2 Pro Star Promotions
91/2 Score - Orr
91/2 Score - Orr
91/2 Score - Orr
91/2 Score - Orr
91/2 Score - Orr
91/2 Score - Orr
72 Semic Sticker 223
91 Semic Sticker 237
68/9 Shirriff / Bost. 5
99/0 SP Authentic LH2, ✍ SotT
00/1 SP Authentic P1, ✍ SotT, ✍ SotTD, ✍ SotTT
01/2 SP Authentic ✍ SotT, ✍ SotTD, ✍ SotTT
00/1 SP GU ✍ P
77-79 Sportscaster 01-02
77-79 Sports. FIN 04-83
01/2 SPx ✍ Sig
81/2 TCMA 9
77-79 Sportscaster 01-02
66/7 Topps 35
66/7 Topps 130
66/7 Topps / Test 35
67/8 Topps 92
x67/8 Topps 118
x67/8 Topps 128
68/9 Topps 2
69/0 Topps 24
70/1 Topps 3
71/2 Topps 2
71/2 Topps 3
71/2 Topps 100
72/3 Topps 62
72/3 Topps 63
72/3 Topps 100
72/3 Topps 122
72/3 Topps 171
72/3 Topps 172
72/3 Topps 176
73/4 Topps 150
74/5 Topps 2
74/5 Topps 28
74/5 Topps 100
74/5 Topps 130
74/5 Topps 248
75/6 Topps 100,209-210
75/6 Topps 288, 314
76/7 Topps 213
76/7 Topps NS 20
77/8 Topps 251
71/2 Toronto Sun Photo
00/1 UD Heroes 119, ✂ GT, ✂ GC, ✍ SG
99/0 Ult. Victory UV4, ✂ LF, ✂ LF, ✂ UF
01/2 UD National
99/0 UD C. Legends 2, AC4, C6, E2, ✍ ES
01/2 UD Challenge AT4
01/2 UD Collectors
01/2 UD Honor Roll 4, 34, OS1
00/1 UD Legends 6, EG7, ✍ ES, ✂ LGJ
01/2 UD Legends 1, 89, FC, ✂ PoH, ✍ ES
99/0 UD PowerDeck 18, T4
01/2 UD Premier 5, ✍ SigS
00/1 UD Prospects ✍ Sig
01 UD Prospects GU ✍ SoT
99/0 UD Retro 81, DR10, G1A, G4B, TC15, ✍ Ink.
01/2 UD SCup Champs 2
71/2 Williams Finnish 384
70/1 BOST
71/2 BOST
91/2 BOST / SA Legends
98/9 BOST / Alumni 4, 35
80/1 Oshawa Generals

ORR, CLINT
96/7 Regina Pats

ORR, COLTON
00/1 Kamloops Blazers
01/2 Kamloops Blazers

ORRGREN, KENT
89/0 Semic Elitserien 285

ORSKAUG, TORBJØRN
92/3 Semic Nordisk 52

ORSOLINI, LIONEL
94 Semic 227

ORSZAGH, VLADIMIR
02/3 First Edition 281
02/3 O-Pee-Chee 159
02/3 Pacific 213
02/3 Pacific Complete 144
02/3 Sports Vault 257
02/3 Topps 159
02/3 To. Limited 159
02/3 To. Total 251
02/3 Upper Deck 344
99/0 Pa. Paramount 145
99/0 Topps 26
99/0 To. Chrome 26
00/1 UD Elitserien 59, 188, S1
99/0 UD MVP Cup 115
00/1 Victory 266
99/0 Lowell Lock Monsters
01/2 Utah Grizzlies

ORTIZ, SEAN
95/6 Dayton Bombers
97/8 Toledo Storm 9

OSADCHY, ALEXANDER
95/6 Kansas City Blades

OSAER, PHIL
01/2 Peoria Rivermen
02/3 Worcester IceCats

OSBORNE, BRAD
88/9 Brockville Braves

OSBORNE, CHRIS
00/1 Mississauga IceDogs

OSBORNE, DON
93/4 Thunder Bay Senators
94/5 Thunder Bay Senators
90/1 Michigan Tech Huskies
91/2 Michigan Tech Huskies

OSBORNE, JOHN
01/2 Kitchener Rangers

OSBORNE, KEITH
92/3 Classic Prospects 85
89/0 ProCards IHL 21
90/1 ProCards 76
91/2 ProCards 341
93/4 Upper Deck 76
92/3 Atlanta Knights
95/6 Peoria Rivermen
88/9 Niagara Falls Thunder

OSBORNE, MARK
90/1 Bowman 156
91/2 Bowman 200
93/4 Fleer Ultra 433
94/5 Fleer Ultra 335
94/5 Leaf 503
82/3 O-Pee-Chee 93
83/4 O-Pee-Chee 252
84/5 O-Pee-Chee 148
88/9 OPC/Topps 241 [Error: Osbourne]
90/1 OPC/Topps 227
91/2 O-Pee-Chee 345
89/0 O-Pee-Chee 274
82/3 OPC/Topps Sticker 182
88/9 OPC Sticker 168-28
89/0 opcSticker 174-34
88/9 Panini Sticker 127
89/0 Panini Sticker 136, 138
90/1 Panini Sticker 278
90/1 Panini/TOR 18
91/2 Panini Sticker 77
93/4 Parkhurst 476
91/2 Pinnacle 96
92/3 Pinnacle 305
94/5 Pinnacle 500
82/3 Post [Detr.]
93/4 Power Play 452
93/4 Premier 268
90/1 Pro Set 287, 564
91/2 Pro Set 270
90/1 Score 104, 28T
91/2 Score 39
91/2 Score CAN 39
92/3 Score 277
93/4 Score 316
83/4 Souhaits Keychain [Red Wings]
84/5 Topps 110
92/3 Topps 77
91/2 To. Stadium 21
92/3 To. Stadium 379
94/5 To. Stadium 76
90/1 Upper Deck 5
91/2 Upper Deck 296
92/3 Upper Deck 72
94/5 Upper Deck 316
94/5 UD BAP R113, ✍ 18
87/8 TORO / 5x8
87/8 TORO / P.L.A.Y. 23
88/9 TORO / P.L.A.Y. 23
92/3 TORO / Kodak
93/4 TORO / Abalene
93/4 TORO / Black's 7
94/5 TORO / Coca-Cola
90/1 WINN / IGA
91/2 WINN / IGA
95/6 Cleveland Lumberjacks
96/7 Cleveland Lumberjacks
97/8 Cleveland Lumberjacks

OSBORNE, MATT
95/6 Classic 93
95/6 Slapshot 299
95/6 Upper Deck 515

OSBURN, RANDY
72/3 TORO

OSGOOD, CHRIS
02/3 Atomic 63, -D 12
02/3 BAP All-Star 68, ✂ ASJ
02/3 BAP Mem. 87, 321
02/3 Between the Pipes 50, 139, ✂ ASJ16, ✂ DM4, ✂ GP9, ✂ T16, ✍ Aut.
02/3 Bowman 88
02/3 Crown Royale 60
02/3 Exclusive 108
02/3 First Edition 209
02/3 Heads Up 73, -S 14
02/3 In The GU 45, 145, ✂ GP10
02/3 O-Pee-Chee 174
02/3 Pacific 240
02/3 Pacific Complete 224
02/3 Parkhurst 13
02/3 Parkhurst Retro 95
02/3 Pr. Stock Reserve 63, -ICS 14
02/3 Signature 110, GS-22, ✍ 110, ✂ FS-10
02/3 SP Authentic 57
02/3 Sports Vault 80
02/3 SPx 47
02/3 Stadium 88, -PSH6
02/3 Topps 174
02/3 T. Chrome 101
02/3 To. Heritage 43
02/3 To. Limited 174
02/3 To. Total 199
02/3 Ultimate Mem. ✂ SCD, ✂ SCDE, ✂ SCDGJ, ✂ SCDN
02/3 Upper Deck 112, -LL9, -SA9
02/3 UD Artistic 57, R57, / Art
02/3 UD Classic 63
02/3 UD Honor 45
02/3 UD Mask 52, 53, ✂ CW, ✂ MM, ✂ NB, ✂ PW, ✂ SS
02/3 UD MVP 117, SD< Souv.
02/3 UD Piece 56
02/3 UD Rookie 85, ✂ DJ
02/3 UD Top Shelf 56
02/3 UD Vintage 162, 279, GB 162, T42
02/3 Victory 135
01/2 Adrenaline 121, ✂ GWJ 27
01/2 Atomic ✂ GWJ 24
98/9 Aurora 67, CF-18
99/0 Aurora 52, GU-8
00/1 Aurora 51
98/9 Be A Player 47, H13, ✍ Aut. 47
99/0 BAP Mem. 135
00/1 BAP Mem. 231, ✂ TM-22, ✂ TM-35
01/2 BAP Mem. 37, 339, ✂ GJ, ✂ GT
01/2 BT Pipes 72, ✂ DM, ✂ GJ, ✂ GG, ✂ GR
96/7 Bic.Sports Aces 10-S
98/9 Bicycle.. K-C
95/6 Bowman 66
01/2 Bowman 39
98/9 Bowman's Best 27, F20, SB3
99/0 Challenger 19
91/2 Classic 43
91/2 Classic Four Sport 43
94/5 Cla. Images 71, PR4
93/4 Cla. Images 4 Sport 56
92/3 Classic Prospects 26
93/4 Cla. Prospects 28
99/0 Crown Royale 51
00/1 Crown Royale 39, ✂ GWJ-14
01/2 Crown Royale 90
93/4 Donruss 424
94/5 Donruss 251
95/6 Donruss 23
96/7 Donruss 95,BTP-5, D-2
97/8 Donruss 13, BTP-5
96/7 Do. Canadian 10
97/8 Do. Canadian 28, NP-6,SCS-5
96/7 Do. Elite 21, 148
97/8 Do. Elite 53, C-7
97/8 Do. Preferred 81, CG-7
97/8 Do. Priority 81, 203, OD-23, PG-8, Post-30,Stamp-30
97/8 Do. Studio 87, P-36
98/9 Dynagon Ice 67, -IW 4
99/0 Dynagon Ice 77
95/6 Edge Ice C18
96/7 Flair 29,HG-7
94/5 Fleer 63
96/7 Fleer 33, 144, 145, 146, VT-6
95/6 Fleer Metal 49
96/7 Fl. Picks 10, F50-36, FF-2
93/4 Fleer Ultra 308
93/4 Fleer Ultra WotF 12
94/5 Fleer Ultra 64
95/6 Fleer Ultra 236, 374, HS-13
96/7 Fl. Ultra 54
01/2 Heads Up 36, HD 13, SS 7, ✂ JQ 11
96/7 Kraft / AS, TT
98/9 Kraft / OML
99/0 Kraft / JELL-O
94/5 Leaf 235, GLR-10
95/6 Leaf 254
96/7 Leaf 151, SD-13, TBO-4
97/8 Leaf 47, PD-14
94/5 L. Limited 96
95/6 L. Limited 61
96/7 L. Limited 6
96/7 L. Preferred 50, MM-6, VP-3
97/8 Limited 3, 115, 171, FG-25
96/7 Maggers 58
96/7 McDonald's McD-7
97/8 McDonald's McD-32
98/9 McDonald's McD20
99/0 McDonald's ✍ SS
00/1 McDonald's 13, GSNF-3
01/2 McDonald's 13
96/7 Metal Univ. 49, AP-6
99/0 Millenium ✂ G-6
01/2 O-Pee-Chee 85, Update 85
98/9 OPC Chrome 134
97/8 Omega 86, NSZ-4
98/9 Omega 86
99/0 Omega 84
98/9 Pacific 204, -GCDC 14, -TW 8
99/0 Pacific 146, ITCNF-7
00/1 Pacific 157
01/2 Pacific 148, IZ 11, ✂ GWJ 14
97/8 Pacific CC 137, ITC-7
97/8 Pa. Crown Roy. 48, PT-7
98/9 Pa. Crown Roy. 47, -PP 9
97/8 Pa. Dynagon 43, S-7, T-12
97/8 Pa. Invincible 50
97/8 Pa. Paramount 69, GSL-7
98/9 Pa. Paramount 81, -GS 8
99/0 Pa. Paramount 86, GS-8
00/1 Pa. Paramount 88, GS-9, ✂ GUS-10
97/8 Pa. Revolution 50, RTS-7
98/9 Pa. Revolution 51, -TPA 14
98/9 Panini Photocard
94/5 Panini Sticker X
95/6 Panini Sticker 187
96/7 Panini Sticker 180
98/9 Panini Sticker 128
99/0 Panini Sticker 239
93/4 Parkhurst 329
93/4 Parkhurst C17
94/5 Parkhurst 283
95/6 Parkhurst 67, PP-30
00/1 Parkhurst P-73
01/2 Parkhurst 204, ✂ M1
94/5 Parkie SE54
93/4 Pinnacle 431
94/5 Pinnacle 199, 471, GT16
95/6 Pinnacle 160
96/7 Pinnacle 99, TP-9, T-6
97/8 Pinnacle 34, TP-10
96/7 Pi. Be A Player SP-2
97/8 Pi. Be A Player 25, STP-6, ✍ Aut. 25
97/8 Pi. BeeHive 37
97/8 Pi. Certified 4
97/8 Pi. Inside 9
96/7 Pi. Mint 25
95/6 Pi. Summit 122, ITC-9
96/7 Pi. Summit 135, ITC-13, U-13
97/8 Pi. Totally 4
95/6 Pi. Zenith 80
96/7 Pi. Zenith 105, ZT-18
96/7 Playoff 378
93/4 Power Play 334
93/4 Power Play RooS 9
94/5 Premier 87, 199, OF-8
99/0 Prism 53
00/1 Pr. Stock 36, PS-21, ✂ GUG-46
01/2 Pr. Stock 58, ✂ GUG 64
00/1 PS Titanium ✂ GUG 96
01/2 PS Titanium 88, TSS 6
01/2 PS Titanium Draft ✂ 58
00/1 PS Titanium Draft ✂ 40
99/0 Revolution 54, / CSC 54
00/1 Revolution 53
93/4 Score 609
94/5 Score 256
95/6 Score 202
96/7 Score 129, NW-6, SD-5
97/8 Score 2,NW-4
97/8 Score Detr. 17
96/7 Select CE 20, F-10
91 7th..Sketch Mem.Cup 123
90/1 7th..Sketch WHL 24
91/2 7th...Sketch WHL 196
00/1 Signature 235, ✍ Aut. 95, ✂ J-14, ✂ HSHSJers
95/6 SBx Impact 56
96/7 SBx Impact 38, ZH-6
95/6 SP 48
96/7 SP 51, HC-21, SF-3
97/8 SP Authentic 51
98/9 SP Authentic 30
99/0 SP Authentic 31
01/2 SP Authentic 51
00/1 SP GU ✂ TotG, ✂ C
01/2 SP GU ✂ AF, ✂ AFD, ✂ AFQ, ✂ TotG
96/7 SPx 16
99/0 SPx 57
01/2 SPx 24, ✂ WM
02/3 SPx 182
98/9 SPx Prospects 24, ✂ WM
99/0 Stadium 89, Chrome 31, PP1, ✍ CS10,✍ CS11, ✍ LS7, ✂ SCS
00/1 Stadium 42, GS9
01/2 Stadium ✂ SCS
01/2 Star Pics 55
97/8 SLU
98/9 SLU
96/7 Team Out!
95/6 Topps 345, YS12
98/9 Topps 134
99/0 Topps 84, SC18
00/1 Topps 83, OTG18
01/2 Topps 85, Updat 85
99/0 To. Chrome 84
00/1 To. Chrome 66
01/2 To. Chrome 85
95/6 To. Finest 159
98/9 To. Finest 76, C3
98/9 T. Gold Label 76
99/0 T. Gold Label 45
00/1 To. Heritage 141, OSJ
96/7 To. Picks FT2, ID8
99/0 To. Prmr. Plus 10
93/4 To. Stadium 350
94/5 To. Stadium 138
95/6 To. Stadium 135
95/6 TSC Members Only 21
98/9 UD Choice 74, 248, RW5
00/1 UD Heroes 44
01/2 UD PlayMakers Ltd 62
00/1 UD Reserve -PSJ, ✍ PSJ
98/9 UD3 51, 111, 171
91/2 Ultimate Draft Pick 38, 57, ✍ Aut.
00/1 Ultimate Mem. ✂ A8-7, ✂ D-14, ✂ G-11, ✂ PJ-5, ✂ Jers. 34, ✂ S-42, ✂ TM-7, ✂ TM-9, ✂ GM-3
99/0 Ult. Victory 32, NW3
93/4 Upper Deck 519
94/5 Upper Deck 130
95/6 Upper Deck 445, AS-19, SE-116
96/7 Upper Deck 53, X7, SS30B
97/8 Upper Deck 269
98/9 Upper Deck 263, FT15, ✂ GJ16
99/0 Upper Deck 221, UD4
00/1 Upper Deck 66, EC9, ✂ GJ
01/2 Upper Deck 343, ✂ SCFJers, ✂ TendThr
95/6 UD BAP 193, ✍ S193
96/7 UD Black Diam. 132
97/8 UD Black Diam. 39
98/9 UD Black Diam. 32, WF12
99/0 UD Black Diam. 37
00/1 UD Black Diam. 22, ✂ GG
01/2 UD Challenge 55, ✂ T200
95/6 UD CC 136
96/7 UD CC 84
97/8 UD Coll. Choice 80
98/9 UD G. Reserve 263
99/0 UD G. Reserve 221
96/7 UD Ice 18
97/8 UD Ice 30
00/1 UD Ice 17, ✂ IGJ
01/2 UD Ice 103
00/1 UD Legends 45
01/2 UD Mask 119, 182, ✂ CG
98/9 UD MVP 71
99/0 UD MVP 71, LL9
00/1 UD MVP 66, MM4, ✂ CG
01/2 UD MVP ✂ GS
99/0 UD MVP Cup 66, GC
99/0 UD Ovation 23
01/2 UD SCup Champs 61
01/2 UD Top Shelf 103, ✂ GG-S
00/1 UD Vintage 128, 136, 137, ✂ D-POH
00/1 Vanguard 39, ✂ DGJ-6
01/2 Vanguard 59, SW 12, VT 6
99/0 Victory 105, 349, 378
00/1 Victory 90, 302
01/2 Victory 127, 137
99/0 WGretzky 63, ✍ SG
97/8 Zenith 35, Z17
99/0 DETR / News 3

OSIECKI, MARK
92/3 Pinnacle 376
91/2 Pro Set 528
90/1 ProCards 618
91/2 Upper Deck 533
91/2 CALG / IGA
94/5 Minnesota Moose

OSIECKI, MATT
95/6 Tallahasee Tiger Sharks

OSIPOV, MAXIM
99/0 Mir 85
00/1 Mir 70

OSIPOV, SERGEI
98/9 Mir 34
99/0 Mir 24
00/1 Metallurg 42

OSLIZLO, LUBOMIR
98/9 OFS 312

OSMAK, COREY
93/4 Minnesota-Duluth

OSSACHUK, JUSTIN
99/0 Lethbridge Hurricanes
97/8 Spokane Chiefs

OSSIPOV, SERGEI
92/3 Atlanta Knights

OSTLER, KARL
95/6 DEL 344

OSTLING, STIG
72 Hellas MM-Jenkki 26
74 Hellas MM-Jenkki 41
79 Panini Sticker 186
72/3 Williams Finnish 60

OSTLUND, TOMAS
95 Globe 5
94/5 Leaf Elit Set 66, CS-3
95/6 Leaf Elit Set 183, LM-4, S-3
95 Panini Worlds 137
89/0 Semic Elitserien 3
90/1 Semic Elitserien 75
91/2 Semic Elitserien 2
92/3 Semic Elitserien 75
95/6 UD Elitserien 37, 251
96 Wien 40

OSTROUSHKO, A.
98/9 Mir 134
99/0 Mir 254

ØSTVANG, BØRRE
92/3 Semic Nordisk 222

OSWALD, GÜNTER
94/5 DEL 243
95/6 DEL 351
96/7 DEL 260
98/9 DEL 47
95 Panini Worlds 72

OTEVREL, JAROSLAV
92/3 Classic Prospects 143
93/4 Cla. Prospects 126
92/3 Parkhurst 399
94/5 Sisu 268
95/6 Sisu 358, 379
93/4 To. Stadium 293
92/3 Kansas City Blades
93/4 Kansas City Blades

OTT, ANDREAS
94/5 DEL 411
95/6 DEL 225

OTT, STEVE
02/3 BAP Mem. 372
02/3 Bowman 125
02/3 Calder 114
02/3 Choice Prospects 32
02/3 First Edition 431H
02/3 Pacific Complete 518
02/3 Parkhurst 235
02/3 Parkhurst Retro 210
02/3 PS Titanium 112
02/3 Quest for the Cup 115
02/3 SP Authentic ✍ 201
02/3 SPx 177
02/3 Ultimate Mem. 10
02/3 UD Artistic 93, R98, CG19
02/3 UD Classic 133
02/3 UD Foundations 167
02/3 UD Honor 139
02/3 UD Premier ✍ 100, ✂ Jers
02/3 UD Rookie ✂ 157, ✍ TD
02/3 Vanguard 111
00/1 UD Prospects 31

OTTILA, RAULI
66/7 Champion 79
70/1 Kuvajulkaisut 165
71/2 Williams Finnish 234
72/3 Williams Finnish 218
73/4 Williams Finnish 294

OTTMANN, CHRIS
89/0 7th..Sketch OHL 169
90/1 7th..Sketch OHL 313

OTTO, JOEL
90/1 Bowman 99
91/2 Bowman 260
92/3 Bowman 69
93/4 Donruss 49
94/5 Donruss 102
95/6 Donruss 355
92/3 Fleer Ultra 26
93/4 Fleer Ultra 285
94/5 Fleer Ultra 275
95/6 Fleer Ultra 27, 285
95 Globe 113
89/0 Kraft 6
93/4 Leaf 28
94/5 Leaf 272
86/7 O-Pee-Chee 247
86/7 O-Pee-Chee 249
87/8 O-Pee-Chee 212
88/9 OPC/Topps 242
90/1 OPC/Topps 369
91/2 O-Pee-Chee 428
92/3 O-Pee-Chee 82
89/0 O-Pee-Chee 205
91/2 OPC Premier 102
86/7 OPC Sticker 130-116
87/8 OPC Sticker 42-183
88/9 OPC Sticker 83-212
89/0 opcSticker 96-233
97/8 Omega 169
98/9 Pacific 329
97/8 Pa. Invincible R-146
87/8 Panini Sticker 212
88/9 Panini Sticker 13
88/9 Panini Sticker 199
90/1 Panini/CGY 15, G
91/2 Panini Sticker 60
92/3 Panini Sticker 43
93/4 Panini Sticker 185
94/5 Panini Sticker 155
95/6 Panini Sticker 115
96/7 Panini Sticker 119
91/2 Parkhurst 253
92/3 Parkhurst 259
93/4 Parkhurst 34
94/5 Parkhurst V38
95/6 Parkhurst 162
94/5 Parkie SE31
91/2 Pinnacle 179
92/3 Pinnacle 328
93/4 Pinnacle 179
94/5 Pinnacle 217
96/7 Pi. Be A Player 76, ✍ Aut. 76
95/6 Playoff 295
94/5 POG 58
95/6 POG 205
93/4 Power Play 40
93/4 Premier 48
94/5 Premier 508
90/1 Pro Set 43
91/2 Pro Set 37
92/3 Pro Set 28
91/2 Pro Set Platinum 17
90/1 Score 128
91/2 Score 96
91/2 Score CAN 96
92/3 Score 332
93/4 Score 74
94/5 Score 18
95/6 Score 186
97/8 Score Phil. 14
94 Semic 124
95 Semic 115
92 Semic Sticker 167
95/6 SP 111
92/3 Topps 471
95/6 Topps 236
91/2 To. Stadium 170
92/3 To. Stadium 305
93/4 To. Stadium 128
94/5 To. Stadium 197
95/6 To. Stadium 14, N8
90/1 Upper Deck 141
91/2 Upper Deck 165
92/3 Upper Deck 220
93/4 Upper Deck 124, SP-24
94/5 Upper Deck 43
95/6 Upper Deck 366, SE-151
96/7 Upper Deck 124
97/8 Upper Deck 333
98/9 Upper Deck 146
93/4 Upper Deck Be A Player 34
94/5 UD BAP R2, R133, ✍ 69
96/7 UD Black Diam. 29
95/6 UD CC 88
96/7 UD CC 193
98/9 UD G. Reserve 146
96 Wien 171
85/6 CALG / Red Rooster
86/7 CALG / Red Rooster
87/8 CALG / Red Rooster
90/1 CALG / McGavin's
91/2 CALG / IGA
92/3 CALG / IGA 004
96/7 PHIL / Ocean Spray
84/5 Moncton G'Flames

OTTOSSON, KRISTOFER
95/6 Leaf Elit Set 195
95/6 UD Elitserien 46
99/0 UD Elitserien 47
00/1 UD Elitserien 51

OTTOSSON, PETER
98/9 DEL 311
99/0 Eishockey 255
94/5 Leaf Elit Set 99
95/6 Leaf Elit Set 46
94 Semic 65
89/0 Semic Elitserien 95
90/1 Semic Elitserien 268
91/2 Semic Elitserien 97
92/3 Semic Elitserien 119
92 Semic Sticker 66
95/6 UD Elitserien 74
00/1 UD Elitserien 97

OUELLET, GEORGES
51/2 Laval Dairy 53

OUELLET, MAXIME
02/3 Between the Pipes 91, ✂ GUJ31, ✂ T20
02/3 Choice Prospects 33
02/3 SP Authentic ✍ SotT2
02/3 UD MVP ✍ PSig
02/3 UD Top Shelf ✍ Sig
02/3 UD Vintage ✂ EE
00/1 BAP Mem. 434
01/2 BAP Mem. 20
01/2 BT Pipes 9
99 Bowman 2, 41, 163, SC4, ✍ BA22
01/2 O-Pee-Chee 268
00/1 Parkhurst P-250
01/2 Parkhurst 291
00/1 Premier Plus 90, PR8
00/1 Pr. Stock 135, PSR-15
00/1 Signature 277, ✍ Aut. 239
99/0 UD Sobey's 10
98/9 SP Authentic 115, ✍ SotT
01/2 SP GU ✂ ISD (x2)
99/0 SPx 180
00/1 Stadium 234
01/2 Topps 268
00/1 To. Heritage 49
00/1 To. Stars 142
01/2 UD PlayMakers Ltd - PCPJ
98/9 Upper Deck 392
99/0 Upper Deck 311
01/2 Upper Deck ✂ GN, ✂ GoalJ, ✂ ✍ SigJers
99/0 UD Black Diam. 101
98/9 UD G. Reserve 392
99/0 UD G. Reserve 311
02/3 UD Honor Roll ✂ GAJ
x99/0 UD MVP Cup ✂ GU, ✍ PS
99/0 UD Prospects 61, ✍ Sig.
00/1 UD Prospects 87, CC10
01/2 UD Vintage ✂ NL
01/2 Victory 383
98/9 Québec Remparts
99/0 Québec Remparts 18
00/1 Rouyn-Noranda 16

OUELLET, MAXIME*
94 Québec Pee Wee 1148
95 Québec Pee Wee 378

OUELLET, MICHEL
02/3 WBS Penguins
99/0 Rimouski Océanic 16
00/1 Rimouski Océanic 19
01/2 Rimouski Océanic 17

OUELLET, ROBERT
98/9 DEL 40
99/0 Eishockey 144

OUELLET, STEPHANE
90/1 7th..Sketch LHJMQ 125

OUELLETE, DENIS
93/4 Fredericton Canadiens

OUELLETTE, ADELARD
36-39 Diamond Match TT2
36-39 Diamond Match TT3

OUELLETTE, FRANCIS
91/2 ProCards 432
90/1 7th..Sketch LHJMQ 157
94/5 Erie Panthers

OUIMET, MARK
95/6 Adirondack Red Wings

OVASKA, NIKO
91/2 7th...Sketch WHL 240

OVCHINNIKOV, MAXIM
00/1 Mir 98

OVECHKIN, ALEXANDER
02/3 Russian Future Stars 1

OVIATT, STEVE
93/4 Tacoma Rockets

OVSTEDAL, ROAR
79 Panini Sticker 298

OWCHAR, DENNIS
75/6 O-Pee-Chee 380
76/7 O-Pee-Chee 314
77/8 O-Pee-Chee 391
78/9 O-Pee-Chee 19
78/9 Topps 19
74/5 PITT
77/8 PITT / McDonald's

OWEN, GARETH
02/3 Coventry Blaze

OWEN, GEORGE
31/2 La Presse

ÖYSTILÄ, JOUKO
72 Hellas MM-Jenkki 20
72 Panda MM-Toronto
72 Semic Sticker 76
74 Semic Sticker 82
71/2 Williams Finnish 80
71/2 Williams Finnish 110
72/3 Williams Finnish 80
72/3 Williams Finnish 154
73/4 Williams Finnish 84
73/4 Williams Finnish 125

OYSTRICK, TRENT
91/2 Rayside-Balfour

OYSTRICK, TREVOR
90/1 Rayside-Balfour

OZELLIS, FALK
94/5 DEL 166
95/6 DEL 166
96/7 DEL 241

OZOLIN, VLADISLAV
00/1 Mir 249

OZOLINSH, SANDIS
02/3 BAP All-Star 69, ✂ ASJ
02/3 BAP Mem. 96, 254, 319, ✂ ASJ43, ✂ AS9
02/3 First Edition 5, 312, 397, ✂ Jers.
02/3 O-Pee-Chee 215
02/3 Pacific 158
02/3 Pacific Complete 77
02/3 Parkhurst 118
02/3 Parkhurst Retro 108
02/3 Quest for the Cup 3
02/3 Signature 145, ✍ 145
02/3 Sports Vault 48
02/3 Topps 215
02/3 To. Limited 215
02/3 To. Total 18
02/3 Upper Deck 75, ✂ ASJ, ✂ ASP
02/3 UD MVP 80, SO9
02/3 UD Rookie 4
02/3 UD Top Shelf 38
02/3 UD Vintage 110, GB 110
02/3 Victory 91
98/9 Aurora 50
98/9 Be A Player 188, ✍ Aut. 188
99/0 BAP Mem. 181, SL-4, ✂ TM-23
00/1 BAP Mem. 118, 409, ✂ J-22
01/2 BAP Mem. 72, 390, ✂ ASJ, ✂ ASE, ✂ ASN, ✂ ASS, ✂ CoO
97/8 Bicycle J-Heart
99/0 Challenger 9
93/4 Donruss 312
94/5 Donruss 120
95/6 Donruss 34
96/7 Donruss 104
97/8 Donruss 60, L2L-24
97/8 Do. Canadian 119
95/6 Do. Elite 93
97/8 Do. Elite 83
97/8 Do. Preferred 103
97/8 Do. Priority 45
97/8 Do. Studio 82
94/5 Flair 169
96/7 Flair 19
94/5 Fleer 200, FF-6
96/7 Fleer 23, NT-10
95/6 Fleer Metal 35
96/7 Fl. Picks F50-37, DL-9, JE-8
92/3 Fleer Ultra 402, -UI 19
93/4 Fleer Ultra 169
94/5 Fleer Ultra 200
95/6 Fleer Ultra 149, 224
96/7 Fl. Ultra 38
95/6 Future Legends 46
00/1 Kraft 11
93/4 Leaf 73
94/5 Leaf 169
95/6 Leaf 183
96/7 Leaf 197
97/8 Leaf 118
94/5 L. Limited 43
95/6 L. Limited 52
97/8 Limited 106, 145
96/7 Maggers 44
94/5 McDonald's McD-11
96/7 Metal Univ. 36
99/0 Millenium 68, ✍ Aut. 68
01/2 Nextel
00/1 Nortel Networks All-Star 6
01/2 O-Pee-Chee 130
98/9 OPC Chrome 121, B10
92/3 OPC Premier 104
97/8 Omega 63
98/9 Omega 63
99/0 Omega 64
98/9 Pacific 167
99/0 Pacific 113
00/1 Pacific 117
01/2 Pacific 79
97/8 Pacific CC 75
97/8 Pa. Dynagon 32, T-41
97/8 Pa. Invincible 37
97/8 Pa. Paramount 53
98/9 Pa. Paramount 59
99/0 Pa. Paramount 66
97/8 Pa. Revolution 37
94/5 Panini Sticker 223
95/6 Panini Sticker 283
96/7 Panini Sticker 251
97/8 Panini Sticker 206
98/9 Panini Sticker 190
99/0 Panini Sticker 213
00/1 Panini Sticker 134
92/3 Parkhurst 164
93/4 Parkhurst 187
94/5 Parkhurst 208, V7, YCTG-21
95/6 Parkhurst 185, 320, IAS-2
00/1 Parkhurst P-66, P-158
01/2 Parkhurst 177, ✂ PS45, ✂ T18, ✂ T20
93/4 Pinnacle 142
94/5 Pinnacle 22, WE11
96/7 Pinnacle 159
97/8 Pinnacle 128
97/8 Pi. Be A Player 115, ✍ Aut. 115
97/8 Pi. Certified 89
97/8 Pi. Inside 137
95/6 Pi. Summit 137
96/7 Pi. Summit 12
97/8 Pi. Totally 89
95/6 Pi. Zenith 101
95/6 Playoff 193
96/7 Playoff 385
94/5 POG 219
95/6 POG 231
93/4 Power Play 225
93/4 Premier 168
94/5 Premier 239, 430
00/1 Pr. Stock ✂ GUG 14
00/1 PS Titanium ✂ GUG 4
92/3 Red Ace Blue 21
93/4 Score 261
93/4 Score IS 18
94/5 Score 36
95/6 Score 67
96/7 Score 43
97/8 Score 174
97/8 Score Colo. 6
94/5 Select 63
00/1 Signature 222, ✂ DD-5
01/2 Signat. 163, ✍ Aut., ✂ DD10
95/6 SBx Emotion 159
95/6 SBx Impact 39
96/7 SBx Impact 26, F-17
94/5 SP 108
95/6 SP 32
97/8 SP Authentic 41
00/1 SP Authentic 18
00/1 SP GU ✂ TotG
99/0 SPx 44
00/1 Stadium 222
95/6 SLU
97/8 SLU
95/6 Super Sticker 29
96/7 Team Out!
98/9 Topps 121, B10
99/0 Topps 164
00/1 Topps 247
01/2 Topps 130
99/0 To. Chrome 164
00/1 To. Chrome 155
94/5 Topps Finest 57, DF-17
95/6 To. Finest 141
98/9 To. Finest 116
00/1 To. Heritage 211
96/7 To. Picks 21
99/0 To. Prmr. Plus 78
93/4 To. Stadium 362
94/5 To. Stadium 177, 204
93/4 TSC Members Only 11
98/9 UD Choice 60
00/1 UD Heroes 23
00/1 UD Reserve 15
91/2 Upper Deck 661
92/3 Upper Deck 568
92/3 Upper Deck ER16
93/4 Upper Deck 72, SP-146
94/5 Upper Deck 490, C27, SP-73
95/6 Upper Deck 168, 470, SE-109
96/7 Upper Deck 37, X9, SS20B
97/8 Upper Deck 44, SG28, T20C
98/9 Upper Deck 250
99/0 Upper Deck 213, AS17
00/1 Upper Deck 264
01/2 Upper Deck 265
96/7 UD All-Star YCTG AR10
95/6 UD BAP 183, ✍ S183
96/7 UD Black Diam. 98
97/8 UD Black Diam. 27
95/6 UD CC 9
96/7 UD CC 60, UD35
97/8 UD Coll. Choice 60, SQ38
91/2 Upper Deck WJC 22
98/9 UD G. Reserve 250
99/0 UD G. Reserve 213
96/7 UD Ice 80
97/8 UD Ice 24
01/2 UD Ice 99
01/2 UD Mask 41
99/0 UD MVP 56
01/2 UD SCup Champs 44
01/2 UD Top Shelf ✂ S, ✂ ST
00/1 UD Vintage 64
99/0 Victory 83
00/1 Victory 66
01/2 Victory 64
99/0 COLO / Kid Smart
01/2 FLOR
92/3 SANJ / Pacific Bell

OZOLS, YURIS
00/1 Mir 208

P

PAAKKARINEN, JYRKI
80/1 Mallasjuoma 140

PAAKKONEN, KALEVI
72/3 Williams Finnish 274

PAANANEN, MIKA
00/1 Cardset 173
92/3 Jyvas Hyva 83
93/4 Jyvas Hyva 147
93/4 Sisu 148
94/5 Sisu 82
95/6 Sisu 61
96/7 Sisu 62

PAATERO, ORVO
66/7 Champion 129

PAAVOLA, JARI
80/1 Mallasjuoma 196

PACAL, TOMAS
94/5 APS 32
95/6 APS 319
96/7 APS 148
97/8 APS 249
99/0 DS 74
96/7 DS Sticker 248
98/9 OFS 149
99/0 OFS 96
00/1 OFS 38
01/2 OFS 249

PACK, RAY
95/6 Birmingham Bulls
94/5 Cincinnati Cyclones

PACKARD, DENNIS
96 Québec Pee Wee 1088

PACLIK, ROBERT
94/5 DEL 27

PACULA, GORDON
95/6 DEL 160

PACULA, IRENEUSZ
94/5 DEL 160
89 Semic Sticker 149

PADDOCK, GORDON
88/9 ProCards / Hershey
89/0 ProCards AHL 351
90/1 ProCards 524
83/4 Brandon Wheat Kings

PADDOCK, JOHN
80/1 Pepsi Bottle Cap
88/9 ProCards / Hershey
90/1 ProCards 15
80/1 QUÉB
91/2 WINN / IGA
93/4 WINN / Ruffles

PADELEK, ALES
98/9 OFS 303
00/1 OFS 260

PADELEK, IVAN
95/6 APS 13
96/7 APS 231
97/8 APS 37
00/1 DS 168
96/7 DS Sticker 25
98/9 OFS 304, 486
99/0 OFS 435
00/1 OFS 252
01/2 OFS 26

PADEN, KEVIN
93/4 Cla. 4 Sport 252
94/5 Slapshot / Windsor 15
98/9 Huntington Blizzard
95/6 Tallahassee Tiger Sharks

PAEK, JIM
92/3 Bowman 383
90/1 Canada Nationals 7
92/3 Fleer Ultra 168
00/1 Kudos 131
94/5 Leaf 512
91/2 O-Pee-Chee 437
92/3 O-Pee-Chee 328
91/2 Parkhurst 133
92/3 Parkhurst 375
91/2 Pinnacle 344
93/4 Pinnacle 278
94/5 Pinnacle 389
95/6 Playoff 288
93/4 Premier 243
94/5 Premier 422
91/2 Pro Set 554
91/2 Pro Set Platinum 266
88/9 ProCards / Muskegon
89/0 ProCards IHL 158
92/3 Score 537
93/4 Score 334
92/3 Topps 243
92/3 To. Stadium 437
93/4 To. Stadium 401
91/2 Upper Deck 308
93/4 Upper Deck 192
94/5 OTTA
91/2 PITT / Elby's
91/2 PITT / Foodland 1
92/3 PITT / Coke-Clark
92/3 PITT / Foodland 11
92/3 PITT / Food. Stickers
93/4 PITT / Foodland 9
96/7 Cleveland Lumberjacks
97/8 Cleveland Lumberjacks
98/9 Cleveland Lumberjacks
99/0 Cleveland Lumberjacks
95/6 Houston Aeros
00/1 Nottingham Panthers
01/2 Nottingham Panthers

PAEK, JIMMY
02/3 Nottingham Panthers

PAEPKE, CHRISTOPH
99/0 Eishockey 108
00/1 UD DEL 131

PAETSCH, NATHAN
01 UD Prospects GU 6, ✂ TPJ
01/2 Moose Jaw Warriors 4
02/3 Moose Jaw Warriors

PAGE, ANTHONY
97/8 Guildford Flames

PAGE, FRED
93/4 Action Packed 9

PAGE, MARGOT
94/5 Classic W10

PAGE, SCOTT
99 Bowman 127
96/7 Sudbury Wolves

PAGÉ, PIERRE
93/4 Kraft / PB
85/6 CALG / Red Rooster
86/7 CALG / Red Rooster
87/8 CALG / Red Rooster
91/2 QUÉB / Petro-Canada
92/3 QUÉB / Petro-Canada
84/5 Moncton G'Flames

PAGEAU, CORY
90/1 7th..Sketch OHL 268

PAGNUTTI, MATT
97/8 Louisiana Ice Gators
98/9 Louisiana Ice Gators
99/0 Louisiana Ice Gators
00/1 Louisiana Ice Gators

PÅHLSSON, SAMUEL
02/3 UD Vintage 3
00/1 BAP Mem. 399
00/1 Crown Royale 109
95/6 Leaf Elit Set 273
00/1 Pr. Stock 102, PSR-1
00/1 PS Titanium 101
00/1 PS Titanium Draft 101
00/1 Signature 263, ✍ Aut. 225
95/6 SP 183
00/1 Stadium 239
00/1 To. Stars 141
00/1 UD Black Diam. 91
95/6 UD CC 350
95/6 UD Elitserien 168
97/8 UD Elitserien 161
98/9 UD Elitserien 180, DL9
99/0 UD Elitserien 182, L10
00/1 Vanguard 101
01/2 Victory 10

PAICE, FRANK
62/3 Topps 61

PAIEMENT, ADAM
01/2 Belleville Bulls

PAIEMENT, JONATHAN
01/2 Sherbrooke Castors 7

PAIEMENT, REAL
81/2 Milwaukee Admirals

PAIEMENT, ROSAIRE
70/1 Colgate 39
70/1 Dad's Cookies
70/1 Eddie Sargent 220
71/2 Eddie Sargent 218
70/1 Esso Power Player
70/1 O-Pee-Chee 226
71/2 O-Pee-Chee 233
72/3 O-Pee-Chee 333
74/5 OPC WHA 7
75/6 OPC WHA 106
76/7 OPC WHA 37
77/8 OPC WHA 36
73/4 OPC WHA Poster 5
73/4 Quaker Oats 3
71/2 Topps 24
71/2 Toronto Sun Photo
70/1 VANC / Royal Bank
71/2 VANC / Royal Bank 9
72/3 VANC / Nalley's

PAIEMENT, STEVEN
90/1 7th..Sketch LHJMQ 126

PAIEMENT, WILF
02/3 UD Foundations 81, 93
79/0 Dernière Heure
82/3 Dernière Heure
74/5 O-Pee-Chee 292
75/6 O-Pee-Chee 195
75/6 O-Pee-Chee 319
76/7 O-Pee-Chee 37
77/8 O-Pee-Chee 130
78/9 O-Pee-Chee 145
79/0 O-Pee-Chee 190
80/1 O-Pee-Chee 225
81/2 O-Pee-Chee 306
81/2 O-Pee-Chee 311
81/2 O-Pee-Chee 326
82/3 O-Pee-Chee 288
83/4 O-Pee-Chee 298
84/5 O-Pee-Chee 285
87/8 OPC/Topps 180
81/2 OPC Sticker 96
81/2 OPC Sticker 110
82/3 OPC/Topps Sticker 22
84/5 OPC Sticker 175
85/6 OPC Sticker 152-23
79 Panini Sticker 67
87/8 Panini Sticker 32
80/1 Pepsi Bottle Cap
81/2 Post 22
82/3 Post [Québ.]
83/4 Souhaits Keychain [Nordiques]
75/6 Topps 195
75/6 Topps 319
76/7 Topps 37
77/8 Topps 130
78/9 Topps 145
79/0 Topps 190
80/1 Topps 225
81/2 Topps 25
81/2 Topps 63
01/2 UD Legends 72
83/4 Vachon 70-50
86/7 BUFF / Blue Shield
76/7 COLR / Hockey Talk
82/3 QUÉB
83/4 QUÉB
84/5 QUÉB
85/6 QUÉB / Provigo
86/7 QUÉB / McDonald's
79/0 TORO
80/1 TORO
81/2 TORO

PAILLE, DANIEL
01/2 Guelph Storm
01/2 Guelph Storm M-Cup

PAILLE, MARCEL
52/3 Anonymous 64
52/3 Bas du Fleuve 51
45-64 BeeHive-2 [NYRa.]
64-67 BeeHive-3 [NYRa.]
64/5 Coke/Sprite [NYRa.]
94/5 Parkie Tall 101
64/5 Topps 92

PAIN, JASON
98/9 Muskegon Fury

PAINE, GREG
91/2 Ferris State Bulldogs

PAISLEY, JEFF
00/1 Mississauga IceDogs

PAIVINEN, MATTI
66/7 Champion 23

PAJALA, JUKKA
70/1 Kuvajulkaisut 375

PAJERSKI, SEBASTIAN
99/0 Indianapolis Ice

PAJONKOWSKI, FRANCK
95 Globe 201
94 Semic 230
93 Semic Sticker 264
96 Wien 190

PAJOR, GREG
98/9 BC Icemen 12
98/9 BC Icemen

PAJULA, JARI-PEKKA
00/1 Cardset 154

PAKARINEN, STEN
72/3 Williams Finnish 350

PAKASLAHTI, PETRI
02/3 Cardset 89
98/9 Cardset 176
99/0 Cardset 289
00/1 Cardset 307

PAKOLA, SEPPO
80/1 Mallasjuoma 2
78/9 SM-Liiga 23

PAKRATZ, JOE
94/5 Minnesota G'Gophers

PAKSAL, REIJO
66/7 Champion 67
70/1 Kuvajulkaisut 146
71/2 Williams Finnish 196
72/3 Williams Finnish 234
73/4 Williams Finnish 268

PAL'OV, RASTISLAV
99/0 OFS 97

PALADIEV, EVGENY
91/2 Future Trends C72 38
74 Hellas MM-Jenkki 52
70/1 Kuvajulkaisut 12
74 Semic Sticker 31
69/0 Soviet Stars
70/1 Soviet Stars
73/4 Soviet Stars 21
73/4 Williams Finnish 12

PALAMAR, ED
52/3 Anonymous 9

PALANGIO, PETE
34-43 BeeHive-1 [Chic.]

PALAZZARI, DOUG
77/8 O-Pee-Chee 354

PALE, MARKO
95 Semic 13

PALECEK, JOSEF
95/6 APS 314
96/7 APS 142
97/8 APS 243
72 Hellas MM-Jenkki 94
74 Hellas MM-Jenkki 80
99/0 OFS 347
00/1 OFS 29
72/3 Williams Finnish 17
73/4 Williams Finnish 59

PALECEK, LUKAS
97/8 APS 263
99/0 Score 8

PALECZNY, LARRY
97/8 Bell
97 Bowman 29
95/6 Slapshot 303

PALFFY, ZIGMUND
02/3 Atomic 49, -PC 10
02/3 BAP All-Star 70, ✂ ASJ
02/3 BAP Mem. 165, 214, ✂ ASJ44, ✂ FP14, ✂ TM13
02/3 Bowman 91
02/3 Crown Royale 45, -LOR 11, ✂ GWJ 8
02/3 Exclusive 81
02/3 First Edition 17, 354, ✂ Jers.
02/3 Heads Up 57, ✂ GWQ 13, ✂ GWQ 14
02/3 In The GU 37, 137, ✂ F14, ✂ IE8, ✂ GUJ44, ✂ SJ44, ✂ T17
02/3 O-Pee-Chee 110
02/3 Pacific 171
02/3 Pacific Complete 203
02/3 Parkhurst 123, ✂ FP14, ✂ GJ17, ✂ SJ17, ✂ TT6
02/3 Parkhurst Retro 27
02/3 Pr. Stock Reserve 46
02/3 PS Titanium 50
02/3 Quest for the Cup 44
02/3 Signature 128, ✍ 128, ✂ SGJ-44
02/3 SP Authentic 43, ✂ SP
02/3 SP GU 23, ✂ AF, ✂ PH
02/3 Sports Vault 238
02/3 SPx 37, ✂ WM (x2)
02/3 Stadium 56, ✂ NHLP12, -WS 12
02/3 Topps 110
02/3 T. Chrome 70
02/3 To. Heritage 42
02/3 To. Limited 110
02/3 To. Total 77
02/3 UD Superstars 123, ✂ CAS, ✂ LL
02/3 Upper Deck 326, ✂ DM, ✂ SD, ✂ PW
02/3 UD Artistic 42, R42, ✂ AT, / Art
02/3 UD Classic 45, ✂ HR, ✂ SC
02/3 UD Honor 35
02/3 UD Mask 41, ✂ IO, ✂ PG
02/3 UD MVP 83, SD (x2), ST (x2), Souv.
02/3 UD Piece 45, ✂ PH
02/3 UD Premier 28
02/3 UD Rookie 47, ✂ DJ
02/3 UD Top Shelf 39, ✂ CP, ✂ GO, ✂ HT, ✂ R, ✂ SH, ✂ ST, ✂ SW, ✂ TS, ✍ Sig
02/3 UD Vintage 115, 274, GB 115, T33
02/3 Vanguard 49, ✂ GWJ 23
02/3 Victory 99, -NP 41
01/2 Adrenaline 87, WB 8
01/2 Atomic 47, CP 7, PP 17, Stat 15
98/9 Aurora 117, CF-29, MACF-12
99/0 Aurora 69, Stripe 69
00/1 Aurora 67
98/9 Be A Player 236, ✍ Aut. 236
99/0 BAP Mem. 98
00/1 BAP Mem. 184
01/2 BAP Mem. 284, ✂ ASJ, ✂ ASE, ✂ ASN, ✂ AST, ✂ CoO, ✂ SCP
01/2 BAP Update HSHS, ✂ HSHSJers
97/8 Bicycle 9-Diamond
01/2 Bowman 40
98/9 Bowman's Best 15
99/0 Challenger 7
99/0 Crown Royale 66 ,IG-12
00/1 Crown Royale 49
01/2 Crown Royale 69
95/6 Donruss 316
96/7 Donruss 45
97/8 Donruss 125, RA-8
96/7 Do. Canadian 58
97/8 Do. Canadian 33
95/6 Do. Elite 13
96/7 Do. Elite 52
97/8 Do. Elite 34, 130
97/8 Do. Preferred 106
97/8 Do. Priority 58, 212, DD-22, Post-32, Stamp-32
97/8 Do. Studio 46, HH-13, P-31
98/9 Dynagon Ice 116
99/0 Dynagon Ice 97, CM-26
95/6 Edge Ice 195, C-24
01/2 eTopps 32
96/7 Flair 56
94/5 Fleer 128
96/7 Fleer 66
95/6 Fleer Metal 92
96/7 Fl. Picks 50, F50-38, JE-20
94/5 Fleer Ultra 320
95/6 Fleer Ultra 97, 269, HS-14
96/7 Fl. Ultra 103
01/2 Heads Up 46, ASGN 4, SM 9
99/0 HoloGrFX 29
96/7 Kraft / KD, PB
97/8 Kraft / JTP, KD
94/5 Leaf 253
96/7 Leaf 23, FOI-7, LL-7
97/8 Leaf 55, BS-12
96/7 L. Limited 57
96/7 L. Preferred 103, LS-32
97/8 Limited 12, 163, 181, FG-24
96/7 Maggers 95
96/7 McDonald's McD-18
96/7 Metal Univ. 95
99/0 Millenium 120, ✍ Aut. 120
98/9 NHL Power Play
01/2 O-Pee-Chee 25
98/9 OPC Chrome 184, SB17
98/9 Omega 140, SHLC-12
98/9 Omega 149, -Onl. 21
99/0 Omega 110
98/9 Pacific 284, -GCDC 22, -TC 16
99/0 Pacific 261, TL-17
00/1 Pacific 200, PR-12
01/2 Pacific 184, 413, 432, WAS 5
97/8 Pacific CC 5, TC-15
97/8 Pa. Crown Roy. 79, HT-10
98/9 Pa. Crown Roy. 84
97/8 Pa. Dynagon 74, DD-9B, T-11, BKS-57
97/8 Pa. Invincible 82, AZ-13, FP-20, R-119
97/8 Pa. Paramount 109
98/9 Pa. Paramount 145, -SD 11, -TC 16
99/0 Pa. Paramount 111
00/1 Pa. Paramount 113
97/8 Pa. Revolution 82, TC-15
98/9 Pa. Revolution 89, -Show. 22
98/9 Panini Photocard
96/7 Panini Sticker 91
97/8 Panini Sticker 73
98/9 Panini Sticker 73
99/0 Panini Sticker 257
00/1 Panini Sticker 167
95/6 Parkhurst 131
00/1 Parkhurst P-75
01/2 Parkhurst 14, ✂ PJ26, ✂ PS26, ✂ WCJ4, ✂ WCE4, ✂ WCN4
94/5 Parkie SE107
94/5 Pinnacle 256, RTP5
95/6 Pinnacle 88, GG-14
96/7 Pinnacle 100
97/8 Pinnacle 56
96/7 Pi. Be A Player BB-15
97/8 Pi. Be A Player 135, ✍ Aut. 135
97/8 Pi. BeeHive 42
97/8 Pi. Certified 94
97/8 Pi. Inside 14, IT-22
95/6 Pi. Summit 144
96/7 Pi. Summit 20
97/8 Pi. Totally 94
96/7 Pi. Zenith 97, A-7
95/6 Playoff 172
96/7 Playoff 379
95/6 POG 169
94/5 Premier 459
00/1 Premier Plus 21, PP3
99/0 Prism 68, CA-11
00/1 Pr. Stock 46, PS-26, ✂ GUG-55
01/2 Pr. Stock 45, Res. 8, -PS 36
00/1 PS Titanium 42, 3SS-15, WAS-6, ✂ GUG-22, ✂ GUG-23
01/2 PS Titanium 66, TAS 11, ✂ DSJ 17, ✂ DSJ 75
99/0 Revolution 70, / CSC 70
00/1 Revolution 68, HD-17
94/5 Score 235
95/6 Score 267
96/7 Score 120
97/8 Score 106
94/5 Select 196
96/7 Select CE 23
00/1 Signature 191, HSHS, ✍ Aut. 159
01/2 Signat. C-50, ✍ Aut., ✂ FP14, ✂ GJ30, ✂ GSJ30, ✂ HSHSJers, ✂ TM14
96/7 SBx Impact 77, BR-18
95/6 SP 86
96/7 SP 97, HC-28
97/8 SP Authentic 91, I38
98/9 SP Authentic 52, SS24
99/0 SP Authentic 41, ✍ SotT
00/1 SP Authentic 42
01/2 SP Authentic 39, ✍ SotT, ✍ SotTD, ✍ SotTT
00/1 SP GU 30
01/2 SP GU 26, ✂ AF, ✂ AFD, ✂✍ IS, ✂✍ ISD (x2)
96/7 SPx 29
97/8 SPx 28, D-SPX13
99/0 SPx 76
00/1 SPx 32
01/2 SPx 30, 77, ✂ DT
98/9 SPx Finite 114
98/9 SPx Prospects 36, H19, L29
00/1 Stadion 124
99/0 Stadium 154, Chrome 41
00/1 Stadium 31, BT27
01/2 Stadium 20,G26, P14
97/8 SLU
96/7 Team Out!
95/6 Topps 348
98/9 Topps 184,L3, M11, SB17
99/0 Topps 8
00/1 Topps 13
01/2 Topps 25, OTG10, SM9
01/2 Topps All-Star Game 2
99/0 To. Chrome 8
00/1 To. Chrome 13
01/2 To. Chrome 25
95/6 To. Finest 117
98/9 To. Finest 40, C6, R20
99/0 To. Gold Label 17, PG5
00/1 To. Gold Label 16
00/1 To. Heritage 15
01/2 To. Heritage 13
99/0 To. Prmr. Plus 59, CR3
01/2 To. Reserve 27
95/6 To. Stadium 99
00/1 To. Stars 8, ✂ GG
98/9 UD Choice 121, BH13
00/1 UD Heroes 56
01/2 UD PlayMakers Ltd 48, ✂ PCJ
00/1 UD Reserve 40
98/9 UD3 44, 104, 164
99/0 Ult. Victory 42
94/5 Upper Deck 343, 529, SP-138
95/6 Upper Deck 140, SE-51
96/7 Upper Deck 97, X17, SS21A
97/8 Upper Deck 99, SS26, SG5, S22
98/9 Upper Deck 315, FF10
99/0 Upper Deck 238
00/1 Upper Deck 309, SS12
01/2 Upper Deck 79, 223, CT7, FF10, FC7, SS9, SS10, ✂ PF
95/6 UD BAP 24, ✍ S24
96/7 UD Black Diam. 16
97/8 UD Black Diam. 18
98/9 UD Black Diam. 53, WF17
99/0 UD Black Diam. 44, D20
01/2 UD Challenge 40, ✂ UC, ✂✍ UCS
95/6 UD CC 94
96/7 UD CC 156, 323, UD24
97/8 UD Coll. Choice 150, SQ66, S16, C16, CR16
97/8 UD Diam. Vision 21
98/9 UD G. Reserve 315
99/0 UD G. Reserve 238
01/2 UD Honor Roll 93
96/7 UD Ice 94
97/8 UD Ice 16
01/2 UD Ice 22
00/1 UD Legends 59
01/2 UD Mask 44, ✂ GJ, ✂ JP, ✂ DP
98/9 UD MVP 125
00/1 UD MVP 89, M9, ✂ GS
01/2 UD MVP 84, MT11, ✂ C
99/0 UD MVP Cup 84, SC9
99/0 UD Ovation 30, LP13
01/2 UD Premier ✂ B, ✂ D, ✍ SigS
00/1 UD Pros&Prosp. 41
01/2 UD Top Shelf 20, ✂ J, ✂ S
00/1 UD Vintage 162, 172
01/2 UD Vintage 114, 121, 122
00/1 Vanguard 48, HV-17, VP-8
01/2 Vanguard 45, ✂ DGM 48
99/0 Victory 139
00/1 Victory 114, 305
01/2 Victory 160, 424
99/0 WGretzky 80
96 Wien 234
97/8 Zenith 30, Z27
96/7 NYIS
01/2 Utah Grizzlies

PÁLFFY, ZIGMUND
91/2 Classic 23
91/2 Classic Four Sport 23
93/4 Cla. Prospects 50
93/4 Donruss 459
93/4 Parkhurst 397
94 Semic 207
92 Semic Sticker 140
91/2 Upper Deck 16
91/2 Upper Deck 71
91/2 Upper Deck WJC 97

PALICHUK, ED
82/3 Brandon Wheat Kings
83/4 Kelowna Wings

PALIN, BRETT
00/1 Kelowna Rockets

PALINEK, MARTIN
95/6 APS 231
99/0 Score 122

PALLA, ANTAL
79 Panini Sticker 270

PALLIN, ROB
85/6 Minnesota-Duluth 4

PALLO, SAIMAAN
77-79 Sports. FIN 108-2587

PALM, JORGEN
89/0 Semic Elitserien 271
90/1 Semic Elitserien 35

PALMATEER, MIKE
83/4 Funmate Puffy 5 [w]
77/8 O-Pee-Chee 211
78/9 OPC 70
78/9 O-Pee-Chee 160
79/0 OPC 8
79/0 O-Pee-Chee 197
80/1 O-Pee-Chee 95
81/2 O-Pee-Chee 351
81/2 O-Pee-Chee 394
83/4 O-Pee-Chee 338
84/5 O-Pee-Chee 308
81/2 OPC Sticker 194
83/4 OPC/Topps Sticker 39
84/5 OPC Sticker 22
80/1 O-Pee-Chee Super 23
81/2 Post 9
83/4 Souhaits Keychain [Maple Leafs]
77/8 Topps 211
78/9 Topps 70
78/9 Topps 160
79/0 Topps 8
79/0 Topps 197
80/1 Topps 95
81/2 Topps 121 [East]
83/4 Vachon 95-13
76/7 TORO
77/8 TORO
78/9 TORO
79/0 TORO
82/3 TORO
83/4 TORO
80/1 WASH
81/2 WASH

PALMER, BRAD
82/3 O-Pee-Chee 21
82/3 Post [Minn.]
83/4 BOST
81/2 MINS
82/3 Victoria Cougars

PALMER, CHRIS
90/1 ProCards 565

PALMER, DREW
93/4 Seattle Thunderbirds

PALMER, JAY
83/4 Brandon Wheat Kings

PALMER, ROB
78/9 O-Pee-Chee 298
79/0 O-Pee-Chee 352
80/1 O-Pee-Chee 104
80/1 Topps 104
80/1 LOSA 10

PALMER, SAMUEL
91 Semic Sticker 185
92 Semic Sticker 202
93 Semic Sticker 111

PALMER, STEVE
98/9 DEL 137
99/0 Eishockey 90
92/3 Clarkson G'Knights

PALMQVIST, BJÖRN
72 Hellas MM-Jenkki 36
74 Hellas MM-Jenkki 32
70/1 Kuvajulkaisut 36
72 Panda MM-Toronto
72 Semic Sticker 60
74 Semic Sticker 20
71/2 Williams Finnish 56
72/3 Williams Finnish 54

PALMU, HANNU
72/3 Williams Finnish 132

PALO,
97/8 Hockey-Box

PALO, MARKO
02/3 Cardset 240
98/9 Cardset 69, Leij. 35
99/0 Cardset 241
00/1 Cardset 29
95 Hartwall Karjala
92/3 Jyvas Hyva 22
93/4 Jyvas Hyva 54
94/5 Leaf Elit Set 197
95/6 Leaf Elit Set 268
99/0 OFS 61
95 Panini Worlds 175
94 Semic 37
93/4 Sisu 244
93/4 Sisu 379
94/5 Sisu 370
95/6 Sisu G-20
95/6 Sisu Limited 88
95 Suomen Beckett Card 8
95/6 UD Elitserien 140
96 Wien 13

PALOOJA, KARI
66/7 Champion 189
65/6 Hellas 127
70/1 Kuvajulkaisut 134
72 Panda MM-Toronto
71/2 Williams Finnish 183
72/3 Williams Finnish 133
73/4 Williams Finnish 187

PALSOLA, SAKARI
02/3 Cardset 241
00/1 Cardset 58
97/8 Hockey-Box
95/6 Sisu 106
96/7 Sisu 102

PALUCH, SCOTT
88/9 ProCards / Peoria
89/0 ProCards IHL 4

PANCHARTEK, FRANTISEK
72 Panda MM-Toronto
72 Semic Sticker 26
74 Semic Sticker 73
71/2 Williams Finnish 35

PANCOE, DON
89/0 7th..Sketch OHL 140
88/9 Niagara Falls Thunder
89/0 Niagara Falls Thunder

PANDOLFO, JAY
93/4 Donruss USA16
99/0 Pacific 245
97/8 Pa. Dynagon BKS-53
93/4 Pinnacle 497
00/1 Signature 92, ✍ Aut. 173
96/7 SP 180
93/4 Upper Deck 556
97/8 Upper Deck 93
96/7 UD Black Diam. 21
97/8 UD Coll. Choice 145
98/9 UD MVP 123
96/7 NJER / Sharp
96/7 Albany River Rats
97/8 Albany River Rats

PANDOLFO, MIKE
02/3 Syracuse Crunch

PANEK, CHRIS
95/6 DEL 49
88/9 ProCards / New Haven
89/0 ProCards AHL 19

PANG, DARREN
02/3 Topps - Reprint 14, ✍ Reprint 14
88/9 OPC/Topps 51
89/0 OPC/Topps 31
88/9 OPC Sticker 135-6
88/9 OPC Sticker 8-137
88/9 OPC Sticker 16-145
89/0 opcSticker 10-150
88/9 Panini Sticker 21
89/0 Panini Sticker 42
01/2 T/O Archives 47
87/8 CHIC / Coke
88/9 CHIC / Coke
82/3 Ottawa 67's
83/4 Ottawa 67's

PANIKAROVSKI, ALEXEI
00/1 Dynamo 3

PANIN, MIKHAIL
90/1 O-Pee-Chee 492

PANKEWICZ, GREG
93/4 Cla. Prospects 57
90/1 7th..Sketch WHL 180
99/0 Houston Aeros
91/2 Knoxville Cherokees
97/8 Manitoba Moose
89/0 Regina Pats

PANKOV, DMITRI
00/1 Mir 102
95/6 Richmond Renegades

PANKOV, VASILY
00/1 UD DEL 23
01/2 UD DEL 12

PANOV, KONSTANTIN
00/1 UD Prospects 69
01/2 Milwaukee Admirals
98/9 Kamloops Blazers
99/0 Kamloops Blazers
99/0 Kamloops Blazers
00/1 Kamloops Blazers

PANOV, YURI
98/9 Mir 24
99/0 Mir 179
00/1 Mir 222

PANTELEEV, GRIGORI
92/3 Classic Prospects 130
92/3 Fleer Ultra 254
93/4 Fleer Ultra 179
92/3 Parkhurst 243
93/4 Score 337
92/3 Upper Deck 492
98/9 Orlando Solar Bears
98/9 Orlando Solar Bears
98/9 Orlando Solar Bears Geico

PANTELEYEV, GRIGORI
99/0 Eishockey 225

PANZER, JEFF
01/2 Worcester IceCats
02/3 Worcester IceCats

PAOLO, DELLA
00/1 Mir 121

PAOLUCCI, DAN
90/1 7th..Sketch LHJMQ 144

PAONE, PAT
93/4 Slapshot / Peterborough 8

PAPAIOANNOU, RYAN
01/2 Calgary Hitmen

PAPIKE, JOE
34-43 BeeHive-1 [Chic.]

PAPINEAU, JUSTIN
02/3 Calder 92
02/3 Choice Prospects 34
02/3 Pacific Complete 501
02/3 SP Authentic 131
02/3 SPx 122
97/8 Bell
99 Bowman 128
98 Bowman 31, 149, ✍ A1
98 Bowman Chrome 31, 149
94 Québec Pee Wee 806
99/0 UD Sobey's 2
97/8 Upper Deck 415
99/0 Upper Deck 331
99/0 UD Black Diam. 117
99/0 UD G. Reserve 331
99/0 UD MVP Cup 216
99/0 UD Ovation 76
99/0 UD Prospects 5, C2
00/1 Worcester IceCats
01/2 Worcester IceCats
02/3 Worcester IceCats

PAPINEAU, ROB
90/1 7th..Sketch OHL 113

PAPISTA, COSTA
85/6 Sudbury Wolves
86/7 Sudbury Wolves

PAPPAS, PERRY
91 7th..Sketch Mem.Cup 13
90/1 7th..Sketch OHL 170
91/2 7th..Sketch OHL 319
93/4 Soo Greyhounds 11

PAPPIN, JIM
02/3 To. Heritage - Reprint TML, ✂ Reprint, ✍ Reprint
64-67 BeeHive-3 [Toro.]
70/1 Colgate 43
70/1 Eddie Sargent 41
71/2 Eddie Sargent 40
72/3 Eddie Sargent 64
70/1 Esso Power Player
72/3 Post 10
74/5 Lipton Soup 36
74/5 Loblaws
68/9 O-Pee-Chee 21
69/0 O-Pee-Chee 133
70/1 O-Pee-Chee 13
71/2 O-Pee-Chee 98
72/3 O-Pee-Chee 42
73/4 O-Pee-Chee 112
74/5 O-Pee-Chee 69
74/5 O-Pee-Chee 113
75/6 O-Pee-Chee 234
75/6 O-Pee-Chee 317
95/6 Parkie 66-67 107
94/5 Parkie Tall 123
67/8 Post Tips 7
68/9 Shirriff / Chic. 16
64/5 Topps 64
65/6 Topps 16
66/7 Topps 76
66/7 Topps / Test 49
67/8 Topps 78
68/9 Topps 21
69/0 Topps 73
70/1 Topps 13
71/2 Topps 98
72/3 Topps 148
73/4 Topps 112
74/5 Topps 69
74/5 Topps 113
75/6 Topps 234
75/6 Topps 317
64/5 Toronto Star Action
71/2 Toronto Sun Photo
91/2 Ultimate Original Six 62, ✍ Aut. 62
67/8 York 32
67/8 York
67/8 York
68/9 CHIC
70/1 CHIC
68/9 TORO
69/0 TORO

PAPPN, JIM
64/5 TORO

PAQUET, DAVE
90/1 7th..Sketch LHJMQ 16
91/2 7th..Sketch LHJMQ 113
91 7th..Sketch Mem.Cup 68

PAQUET, NORMAND
90/1 7th..Sketch LHJMQ 212
91/2 7th..Sketch LHJMQ 2
99/0 Rockford IceHogs

PAQUETTE, ANDY
85/6 Sudbury Wolves
88/9 Sudbury Wolves

PAQUETTE, CHARLES
91/2 7th...Sketch LHJMQ 103
96/7 Providence Bruins
97/8 Providence Bruins

PAQUETTE, DARRYL
95/6 Hampton Roads
96/7 Hampton Roads
95/6 Portland Pirates
90/1 Sudbury Wolves

PAQUETTE, FRANÇOIS
90/1 7th..Sketch LHJMQ 127
91/2 7th..Sketch LHJMQ 199

PAQUETTE, PHIL
86/7 Sudbury Wolves

PAQUETTE, R.
67/8 Columbus Checkers

PAQUIN, GERARD
52/3 Bas du Fleuve 18

PAQUIN, PATRICE
91/2 7th...Sketch LHJMQ 184

PARA, KELLY
86/7 Kamloops Blazers

PARADIS, CARL
97/8 New Mexico Scorpions
99/0 San Angelo Outlaws

PARADIS, DANIEL
90/1 7th..Sketch LHJMQ 42
91/2 7th..Sketch LHJMQ 95
91 7th..Sketch Mem.Cup 45

PARADIS, STÉPHANE
91/2 7th...Sketch LHJMQ 140

PARADISE, BOB
72/3 Eddie Sargent 11
74/5 Loblaws
74/5 O-Pee-Chee 343
75/6 O-Pee-Chee 21
76/7 O-Pee-Chee 368
77/8 O-Pee-Chee 203
78/9 O-Pee-Chee 375
75/6 Topps 21
72/3 ATLF
74/5 PITT

PARADISE, DAVE
99/0 Mississippi S'Wolves
97/8 Peoria Rivermen

PARADISE, DICK
73/4 Quaker Oats 49
72/3 Minn. Fight. Saints

PARADISE, JIM
95/6 Tallahasee Tiger Sharks

PARCO, JOHN
00/1 Kudos 65
99/0 Hampton Roads
01/2 Cardiff Devils

PARDAVY, JAN
02/3 Cardset 242
99/0 DS 136
00/1 DS 19
99/0 OFS 443, 552
00/1 OFS 333, -Star 3
01/2 OFS -UHI 22

PARE, PATRICE
79/0 Montréal Juniors B&W
79/0 Montréal Jrs. Colour

PARÉ, JEAN-PHILIPPE
98 Bowman 94
98 Bowman Chrome 94
99/0 Shawinigan Cataractes 10

PARÉ, MARTIN
99/0 Québec Remparts 19

PARENT, BERNIE
02/3 BAP Mem. / Cup
02/3 Between the Pipes ✂ CP9, ✂ GT11, ✂ HSHSJers 29, ✂ I5, ✂ RB10, ✂ VM8, ✂ VM19, ✍ Aut.
02/3 In The GU ✂ GP16
02/3 Parkhurst ✂ VM14, ✂ VT13
02/3 Ultimate Mem. ✂ CSTW (x2), ✂ Cor, ✂ EA, ✂ FS, ✂ Num, ✂ RT, ✂ SCD, ✂ VGJ
01/2 ASG History
00/1 BAP Mem. ✂ G-11, ✂ G-12, ✂ G-30
64-67 BeeHive-3 [Bost.]
01/2 BT Pipes 118, 138, ✂ DM, ✂ S&J, ✂ GR, ✂ TW, ✂ VM, ✂ HSHSJers
65/6 Coca-Cola
70/1 Colgate 93
70/1 Dad's Cookies
76/7 Dernière Heure
70/1 Eddie Sargent 146
71/2 Eddie Sargent 205
70/1 Esso Power Player
01/2 Fleer Greats 41, ✍ Aut.
01/2 Fleer Legacy 48
93/4 High Liner 7
75/6 Hockey Heroes
74/5 Lipton Soup 18
74/5 Loblaws
74/5 Nabisco 15

68/9 O-Pee-Chee 89
69/0 O-Pee-Chee 89
69/0 O-Pee-Chee 4in1
69/0 O-Pee-Chee Stamp
70/1 O-Pee-Chee 78
71/2 O-Pee-Chee 131
73/4 O-Pee-Chee 66
74/5 O-Pee-Chee 4
74/5 O-Pee-Chee 60
74/5 O-Pee-Chee 138
74/5 O-Pee-Chee 249
74/5 O-Pee-Chee 251
75/6 O-Pee-Chee 213
75/6 O-Pee-Chee 291
75/6 O-Pee-Chee 300
76/7 O-Pee-Chee 10
77/8 OPC 8
77/8 O-Pee-Chee 65
78/9 O-Pee-Chee 15
78/9 O-Pee-Chee 68
78/9 OPC 70
79/0 O-Pee-Chee 6
79/0 OPC 8
92/3 O-Pee-Chee 217
92/3 OPC - Anniv. 1
92/3 Parkhurst 470
01/2 Parkhurst ✍ PA56
95/6 Parkie 66-67 14
94/5 Parkie Tall FS-4
91/2 Pinnacle 384
92/3 Pinnacle 246
72 Semic Sticker 175
68/9 Shirriff / Phil. 1
00/1 Signature ✂ GLS-5
97/8 SLU Cdn. Leg.
68/9 Topps 89
69/0 Topps 89
70/1 Topps 78
71/2 Topps 131
73/4 Topps 66
74/5 Topps 4
74/5 Topps 60
74/5 Topps 138
74/5 Topps 249
74/5 Topps 251
75/6 Topps 213
75/6 Topps 291
75/6 Topps 300
76/7 Topps 10
77/8 Topps 8
77/8 Topps 65
78/9 Topps 15
78/9 Topps 68
78/9 Topps 70
79/0 Topps 6
79/0 Topps 8
00/1 Topps SCH, ✍ SCHA
01/2 To. Chrome -CA8, ✍ CA8
01/2 T/O Archives 16
71/2 Toronto Sun Photo
00/1 UD Heroes 135, ✍ SG
00/1 Ultimate Mem. ✂ UG-5, ✂RA-5, ✂GM-7, ✂GM-9, ✂GM-17
01/2 Ultimate Mem. ✂ ASGH, ✂ RN, ✂ RA, ✂ SCD
00/1 UD Legends 97, EG5
01/2 UD Legends 54, 83
01/2 UD SCup Champs 24
86/7 PHIL
71/2 TORO

PARENT, JACQUES
88/9 ProCards / Sherbrooke
89/0 ProCards AHL 196
90/1 7th..Sketch LHJMQ 98
92/3 Fredericton Canadiens
93/4 Fredericton Canadiens
94/5 Fredericton Canadiens
95/6 Fredericton Canadiens
96/7 Fredericton Canadiens
87/8 Hull Olympiques

PARENT, MICHAEL
00/1 Chicoutimi Saguenéens 16

PARENT, PHILIPPE
00/1 Québec Remparts 15

PARENT, RICH
01/2 BT Pipes 53
01/2 Heads Up ✂ JQ 18, ✂ JQ29
00/1 PS Titanium ✂ GUG 138
01/2 PS Titanium ✂ DSJ 36
01/2 PS Titanium Draft ✂ 81
00/1 SPx 115
00/1 Upper Deck 193
01/2 Vanguard ✂ DGM 27
96/7 Detroit Vipers
94/5 Muskegon Fury
95/6 Muskegon Fury
99/0 Utah Grizzlies
00/1 WBS Penguins

PARENT, SÉBASTIEN
90/1 7th..Sketch LHJMQ 36
91/2 7th...Sketch LHJMQ 91
91 7th..Sketch Mem.Cup 41

PARENT, TRAVIS
01/2 Mississauga IceDogs
02/3 Mississauga IceDogs

PARFET, GENE (VAN)
93/4 Indianapolis Ice
97/8 Las Vegas Thunder 26
98/9 Las Vegas Thunder

PARIKKA, PEKKA
70/1 Kuvajulkaisut 262

PARIKKA, SEPPO
66/7 Champion 55
70/1 Kuvajulkaisut 147
71/2 Williams Finnish 197
72/3 Williams Finnish 235
73/4 Williams Finnish 269

PARIS, BENOÎT
01/2 Victoriaville Tigres 15

PARIS, JOHN
94/5 Atlanta Knights 25
95/6 Atlanta Knights

PARIS, PHILIPPE
99/0 Québec Remparts 11
00/1 Québec Remparts 8

PARIS, TIM
88/9 ProCards / Adirondack

PARISE, JEAN-PAUL
70/1 Dad's Cookies
70/1 Eddie Sargent 94
71/2 Eddie Sargent 83
72/3 Eddie Sargent 101
70/1 Esso Power Player
91/2 Future Trends C72 99, ✍ 99
74/5 Lipton Soup 4
74/5 Loblaws
74/5 Loblaws Update
73/4 Mac's Milk
68/9 O-Pee-Chee 149
69/0 O-Pee-Chee 127
70/1 O-Pee-Chee 168
71/2 O-Pee-Chee 243
72/3 O-Pee-Chee 199
72/3 O-Pee-Chee TC
73/4 O-Pee-Chee 46
74/5 O-Pee-Chee 83
75/6 O-Pee-Chee 127
76/7 O-Pee-Chee 182
77/8 O-Pee-Chee 29
78/9 O-Pee-Chee 350
79/0 O-Pee-Chee 118
72 Semic Sticker 219
69/0 Topps 127
73/4 Topps 46
74/5 Topps 83
75/6 Topps 127
76/7 Topps 182
77/8 Topps 29
79/0 Topps 118
71/2 Toronto Sun Photo
70/1 MINS / Colour
73/4 MINS
78/9 MINS / Cloverleaf 3
80/1 MINS
81/2 MINS

PARISH, KEVIN
94/5 Guildford Flames 16

PARIZEAU, MICHEL
72/3 O-Pee-Chee 335
74/5 OPC WHA 52
73/4 Quaker Oats 43
71/2 Toronto Sun Photo
71/2 SLOU
72/3 Québec Nordiques
73/4 Québec Nordiques

PARIZEK, JAROSLAV
98/9 OFS 193
99/0 OFS 277
00/1 OFS 3

PARK, BRAD
99/0 BAP Mem. AH-9, ✍ AH-9
77/8 Coke
71/2 Colgate Head
98/9 Collection Souvenir 01
70/1 Dad's Cookies
79/0 Dernière Heure
70/1 Eddie Sargent 124
71/2 Eddie Sargent 116
72/3 Eddie Sargent 144
70/1 Esso Power Player
88/9 Esso All-Star
01/2 Fleer Greats 77, ✍ Aut., ✂ OSS
01/2 Fleer Legacy 20, ✂ HK
83/4 Funmate Puffy 15 [w/]
91/2 Future Trends C72 95, ✍ 95
75/6 Hockey Heroes
93/4 Hockey Wit 10
94/5 Legends 42
72/3 Post 20
74/5 Lipton Soup 10
74/5 Loblaws
73/4 Mac's Milk
74/5 Nabisco 13
70/1 O-Pee-Chee 67
70/1 O-Pee-Chee 239
70/1 O-Pee-Chee DE 43
71/2 O-Pee-Chee 40
71/2 O-Pee-Chee 257
72/3 O-Pee-Chee 85
72/3 O-Pee-Chee 85
72/3 O-Pee-Chee 114
72/3 O-Pee-Chee 227
72/3 O-Pee-Chee Crest 15
72/3 O-Pee-Chee TC
73/4 O-Pee-Chee 165
74/5 O-Pee-Chee 50
74/5 O-Pee-Chee 131
74/5 O-Pee-Chee 141
75/6 O-Pee-Chee 260
75/6 O-Pee-Chee 260
76/7 O-Pee-Chee 60
77/8 O-Pee-Chee 190
77/8 O-Pee-Chee NS 13
78/9 O-Pee-Chee 79
78/9 O-Pee-Chee 263
79/0 O-Pee-Chee 23
79/0 O-Pee-Chee 164
80/1 O-Pee-Chee 74
81/2 O-Pee-Chee 8
82/3 O-Pee-Chee 19
83/4 O-Pee-Chee 129
84/5 O-Pee-Chee 63
84/5 O-Pee-Chee 378
84/5 O-Pee-Chee 390
81/2 OPC Sticker 48
82/3 OPC/Topps Sticker 82
83/4 OPC/Topps Sticker 48
83/4 OPC/Topps Sticker 178
84/5 OPC Sticker 38
84/5 OPC Sticker 231-230
80/1 O-Pee-Chee Super 1
82/3 Post [Bost.]
72 Semic Sticker 194
94/5 Sig. Rookies CF2, ✍ CF2
77-79 Sportscaster 07-17
77-79 Sports. FIN 29-692
70/1 Topps 67
71/2 Topps 40
72/3 Topps 30
72/3 Topps 123
73/4 Topps 165
74/5 Topps 50
74/5 Topps 131
74/5 Topps 141
75/6 Topps 260
76/7 Topps 60
76/7 Topps NS 2
77/8 Topps 190
77/8 ToppsNS 13
78/9 Topps 79
78/9 Topps 263
79/0 Topps 23
79/0 Topps 164
80/1 Topps 74
81/2 Topps 72 [East]
84/5 Topps 47
71/2 Toronto Sun Photo
99/0 UD C. Legends ✍ ES
99/0 UD Retro 106, ✍ Ink.
93/4 Zellers, ✍ Aut.
91/2 BOST / SA Legends
98/9 BOST / Alumni 22
84/5 DETR / Little Caesars
85/6 DETR / Little Caesars

PARK, JIM
77/8 OPC WHA 56

PARK, RICHARD
02/3 Pacific Complete 247
02/3 To. Total 3
02/3 Upper Deck 332
02/3 UD Vintage 123, 275
95/6 Bowman 123
93/4 Donruss USA17
95/6 Donruss 331
95/6 Fleer Metal 187
95/6 Leaf 221
94/5 L. Limited USA 9
95/6 L. Limited 36
97/8 Pa. Invincible R-6
95/6 Parkhurst 169
94/5 Parkie SE249
93/4 Pinnacle 498
95/6 Pinnacle 220
94/5 Score 210
95/6 Score 295
94/5 Sig. Rookies 12, ✍ 12
95/6 SBx Impact 217
94/5 SP 175
95/6 SP 120
95/6 Topps 119
94/5 Topps Finest 112
95/6 To. Finest 89
95/6 To. Stadium 208
93/4 Upper Deck 553
94/5 Upper Deck 525
95/6 Upper Deck 419
97/8 Upper Deck 215
95/6 UD BAP 185, ✍ S185
96/7 UD CC 217
95/6 PITT / Foodland 7
96/7 Cleveland Lumberjacks
00/1 Cleveland Lumberjacks
99/0 Utah Grizzlies

PARKE, ANDRÉ
99/0 Rouyn-Noranda

PARKER, DEREK
99/0 Lethbridge Hurricanes

PARKER, JEFF
90/1 O-Pee-Chee 497
88/9 ProCards / Rochester
88/9 BUFF / Blue Shield
88/9 BUFF / Won. Bread
89/0 BUFF / Blue Shield
89/0 BUFF / Campbell's

PARKER, JONATHAN
99/0 Prince George Cougars

PARKER, SCOTT
02/3 Pacific 93
02/3 Upper Deck 293
01/2 BAP Update ✂ TC23, ✂ TC37
99/0 Millenium 64, ✍ Aut. 64
98/9 Omega 66
01/2 Pacific 408
00/1 To. Heritage 176
98/9 Hershey Bears

PARKER, SHANE
94/5 Slapshot / North Bay 25
95/6 Slapshot 230

PARKER, STAN
52/3 Anonymous 86

PARKHOMENKO, DMITRI
99/0 Mir 171

PARKIN, DANNY
94/5 Humberside Hawks 12

PARKS, GREG
95/6 Leaf Elit Set 175, FTF-2
90/1 OPC Premier 89
92/3 Parkhurst 491
91/2 ProCards 462
94/5 Score CT11
92/3 Semic Elitserien 170
95/6 UD Elitserien 32

PARLEY, DAVIS
99/0 Kamloops Blazers
00/1 Kamloops Blazers
01/2 Kamloops Blazers
02/3 Kamloops Blazers

PARLLEY, DAVIS
99/0 Kamloops Blazers

PARNELL, GREG
90/1 Michigan Tech Huskies
91/2 Michigan Tech Huskies

PAROSHY, ERICH
99/0 Hull Olympiques BN
99/0 Hull Olympiques 1

PAROULEK, MARTIN
00/1 OFS 338
01/2 Syracuse Crunch

PARR, MAURICE
51/2 Bas du Fleuve 53

PARRISH, DWIGHT
00/1 Kudos 56
96/7 Dayton Bombers
99/0 Hampton Roads
98/9 Portland Pirates
01/2 Cardiff Devils
01/2 Manchester Storm
02/3 Manchester Storm
91/2 Ferris State Bulldogs

PARRISH, MARK
02/3 BAP Mem. 121
02/3 Bowman 51
02/3 Exclusive 109
02/3 First Edition 221
02/3 Heads Up 74
02/3 O-Pee-Chee 163
02/3 Pacific 241
02/3 Pacific Complete 222
02/3 Parkhurst 19
02/3 Parkhurst Retro 49
02/3 Pr. Stock Reserve 64
02/3 Signature 54, GS-50, ✍ 54
02/3 Sports Vault 75
02/3 Stadium 63
02/3 Topps 163
02/3 To. Limited 163
02/3 To. Total 143
02/3 Upper Deck 113
02/3 UD MVP 113
02/3 UD Rookie 62
02/3 UD Vintage 158
02/3 Vanguard 63
02/3 Victory 132
99/0 Aurora 65, Stiped 65
00/1 Aurora 90
98/9 Be A Player 206, ✍ Aut. 206
99/0 BAP Mem. 180
00/1 BAP Mem. 482
01/2 Bowman 75
98/9 Bowman's Best 120, F3, ✍ A9A, ✍ A9B
01/2 Crown Royale 91
95/6 Do. Elite WJ 38
98/9 Dynagon Ice 85, -IR 3
99/0 Dynagon Ice 92
99/0 HoloGrFX 27
99/0 Millenium 113, ✍ Aut. 113
99/0 NHL Power Play
98/9 Omega 106, -PI 4
99/0 Omega 99
99/0 Pacific 180
00/1 Pacific 185
01/2 Pacific 252
98/9 Pa. Crown Roy. 61, -PP 12, -RC 3
99/0 Pa. Paramount 105
98/9 Pa. Revolution 64, -Show. 19
98/9 Panini Photocard
99/0 Panini Sticker 61
00/1 Parkhurst P-37
01/2 Parkhurst 187
99/0 Prism 63
01/2 PS Titanium 89
99/0 Revolution 65, -Show 20, / CSC 65
98/9 SP Authentic 97
01/2 SP Authentic 53
99/0 SPx 68
98/9 SPx Prospects 29
99/0 Stadium 29, CA4
99/0 Topps 141, IF1
00/1 Topps 117
99/0 To. Chrome 141, IF1
00/1 To. Chrome 27
01/2 To. Chrome 131
98/9 T. Gold Label 89
99/0 T. Gold Label FG11
99/0 T. Prmr. Plus 26
01/2 UD PlayMakers Ltd 63
98/9 Upper Deck 282
99/0 Upper Deck 58
00/1 Upper Deck 342
01/2 Upper Deck 109
98/9 UD Black Diam. 38, M20
98/9 UD G. Reserve 282
99/0 UD G. Reserve 58
01/2 UD Honor Roll 27, 57
01/2 UD Ice 105
01/2 UD Mask 59
98/9 UD MVP 91, PG12, ✍ PS
99/0 UD MVP 84, -DR8
01/2 UD MVP 118
99/0 UD Retro 36, G9C
01/2 UD Top Shelf 104
00/1 UD Vintage 232
01/2 UD Vintage 164
01/2 Vanguard 60
99/0 Victory 121, 355
00/1 Victory 102
01/2 Victory 226
99/0 WGretzky 73, ✍ SG

PARRO, DAVE
82/3 O-Pee-Chee 371
82/3 OPC/Topps Sticker 158
81/2 WASH
82/3 WASH

PARROTT, JEFF
96/7 Detroit Vipers
98/9 Manitoba Moose
99/0 Manitoba Moose

PARSON, MIKE
90/1 ProCards 129
94/5 Portland Pirates

PARSON, STEVE
90/1 7th..Sketch OHL 291
91/2 7th...Sketch OHL 283
93/4 Slapshot / Kingston 20
94/5 Thunder Bay Senators
95/6 Thunder Bay Senators

PARSONS, DARREN
86/7 Regina Pats
88/9 Regina Pats

PARSONS, DON
97/8 Louisiana Ice Gators
98/9 Louisiana Ice Gators

PARSONS, GEORGE
34-43 BeeHive-1 [Toro.]
38/9 Quaker Oats

PARSONS, STEVE
99/0 Fort Wayne Komets
01/2 WBS Penguins

PÄRSSINEN, TIMO
02/3 Cardset 101
02/3 Upper Deck ✂ BF
01/2 Adrenaline 202
01/2 Atomic 102
01/2 BAP Mem. 327
01/2 Bowman 129
98/9 Cardset 67
99/0 Cardset 40
00/1 Cardset 267, MB-9
01/2 Crown Royale 146
01/2 Heads Up 102
01/2 O-Pee-Chee 337
01/2 Pacific 453
01/2 Parkhurst 279
01/2 Pr. Stock 112, -PS 77
01/2 PS Titanium 146
01/2 PS Titanium Draft 103
01/2 Signature 224, ✍ Aut. 224
01/2 SP Authentic 132
01/2 SP GU 62
01/2 SPx 91
01/2 Stadium 127
01/2 Topps 337
01/2 To. Chrome 155
01/2 To. Heritage 144
01/2 To. Reserve 112
01/2 UD PlayMakers Ltd 101
01/2 Upper Deck 412
01/2 UD Challenge 92
01/2 UD Ice 73
01/2 UD Premier 51
01/2 UD Vintage 271
01/2 Vanguard 102
01/2 Cincinnati Mighty Ducks

PARTANEN, ERKKI
65/6 Hellas 135

PARTANEN, JARMO
71/2 Williams Finnish 350

PARTH, ELMAR
94 Semic 292

PARTINEN, LALLI
66/7 Champion 98
65/6 Hellas 83
70/1 Kuvajulkaisut 72
70/1 Kuvajulkaisut 112
72 Panda MM-Toronto
77-79 Sports. FIN 36-845
71/2 Williams Finnish 121
72/3 Williams Finnish 91
73/4 Williams Finnish 74
73/4 Williams Finnish 137

PARTINEN, TALLI
96/7 Sisu 191

PARVIAINEN, JARI
92/3 Jyvas Hyva 145
93/4 Jyvas Hyva 260
93/4 Sisu 283

PASANEN, JARI
96/7 DEL 221

PASCAL, BRENT
81/2 Regina Pats

PASCAL, TOMAS
97/8 DS Sticker 131

PASCALL, BRAD
92/3 Rochester Americans WPC
93/4 Rochester Americans

PASCHAL, KEVIN
92/3 BCJHL 214

PASCO, RON
98/9 DEL 240
99/0 Eishockey 180
00/1 UD DEL 8
94/5 Greensboro Monarchs
95/6 Tallahasee Tiger Sharks

PASCUCCI, RON
93/4 Hampton Roads
94/5 Hampton Roads
95/6 Hampton Roads
98/9 Hampton Roads
96/7 Portland Pirates

PASEK, DUSAN
92/3 Jyvas Hyva 101
98/9 OFS Leg. 20
89/0 ProCards IHL 82
82 Semic Sticker 93
91 Semic Sticker 113
88/9 MINS / ADA

PASHKOV, ALEXANDER
79/0 Soviet Stars 5

PASHULKA, STEVE
92/3 MPS SJHL 43

PASIN, DAVE
86/7 OPC/Topps 76
88/9 ProCards / New Haven
90/1 ProCards 425
86/7 Moncton G'Flames
84/5 Prince Albert Raiders

PASKA, JIRI
02/3 Owen Sound Attack

PASLAWSKI, GREG
92/3 Bowman 277
95/6 Edge Ice 179
92/3 Fleer Ultra 375
87/8 OPC/Topps 10
90/1 OPC/Topps 154
92/3 O-Pee-Chee 193
89/0 O-Pee-Chee 268
87/8 OPC Sticker 23-164
87/8 Panini Sticker 314
90/1 Panini Sticker 309
90/1 Panini/WPG 20
91/2 Parkhurst 365
92/3 Parkhurst 132
91/2 Pinnacle 286
92/3 Pinnacle 370
93/4 Pinnacle 337
90/1 Pro Set 336
91/2 Pro Set 469
92/3 Pro Set 155
91/2 Pro Set Platinum 220
90/1 Score 249
91/2 Score 29T
91/2 Score CAN 579
92/3 Score 175
92/3 Score SS 16
93/4 Score 290
92/3 Topps 33
92/3 To. Stadium 275
90/1 Upper Deck 239
92/3 Upper Deck 531
83/4 Vachon 52-72
92/3 PHIL / UD Sheet
92/3 PHIL / UD Sheet
92/3 PHIL / J.C. Penney
91/2 QUÉB / Petro-Canada
87/8 SLOU
87/8 SLOU / Kodak
88/9 SLOU
88/9 SLOU / Kodak
89/0 WINN / Safeway
90/1 WINN / IGA
94/5 Peoria Rivermen
95/6 Peoria Rivermen

PASMA, ROD
90/1 7th..Sketch OHL 42
91/2 7th...Sketch OHL 234
95/6 Louisiana Ice Gators
95/6 Louisiana Ice Gators-2

PASQUALOTTO,
79 Panini Sticker 388

PASSARELLI, VAL
97/8 Pensacola Ice Pilots
91/2 Ferris State Bulldogs

PASSERO, DAN
99 Bowman 159

PASSERO, DANIEL
96/7 Soo Greyhounds

PASSFIELD, MATT
02/3 Owen Sound Attack

PASSMORE, STEVE
02/3 Between the Pipes 16, ✂ T3
02/3 First Edition 123, ✂ Jers.
02/3 Pacific 80
02/3 Pacific Complete 244
02/3 Upper Deck 284
02/3 UD Mask 19, 20
01/2 BT Pipes 41, ✂ GT
99/0 Pacific 168
01/2 Pacific 89
90/1 7th..Sketch WHL 255
99/0 SP Authentic 20
99/0 UD G. Reserve 340
94/5 Cape Breton Oilers
00/1 Lowell Lock Monsters
93/4 Kamloops Blazers

PASTIKA, MICHAEL
94/5 DEL 421

PASTINSKY, OLIVER
93/4 Slapshot / S.S.Marie 4
93/4 Soo Greyhounds 4

PATAFIE, BRIAN
84/5 Moncton G'Flames
85/6 Moncton G'Flames
86/7 Moncton G'Flames
83/4 Nova Scotia Voyageurs
92/3 Salt Lake G'Eagles
81/2 Ottawa 67's

PATEMAN, JERRY
90/1 Pro Set 696

PATENAUDE, RUSTY
74/5 OPC WHA 51
75/6 OPC WHA 76
76/7 OPC WHA 19

PATERA, DAVID
01/2 OFS 183

PATERA, PAVEL
94/5 APS 58
95/6 APS 93, 371, 385, 428
96/7 APS 341
97/8 APS 356
99/0 BAP Mem. 190
01/2 BAP Mem. 263
98 Bonaparte 7C
98 Bonaparte Pexeso 24
98/9 DS 2
99/0 DS NS16, P9
00/1 DS JT14
01/2 DS 37, - IH3
99/0 Dynagon Ice 70
99/0 Millenium 84, ✍ Aut. 84
98/9 OFS 107, 239, 441, 480, -OW 5
99/0 OFS 28, 447, 481, 523
00/1 OFS 390
99/0 Panini Sticker 219
00/1 Panini Sticker 175
99/0 Score JT10
99/0 Stadium 170
99/0 T. Prmr. Plus 106
99/0 Upper Deck 219
97/8 UD Elitserien 10
99/0 UD G. Reserve 219
99/0 WGretzky 57
96 Wien 114
00/1 Cleveland Lumberjacks

PATERSON, CORY
92/3 Wheeling Thund'birds 11
93/4 Wheeling Thund'birds
88/9 Regina Pats
89/0 Regina Pats

PATERSON, CRAIG
96/7 Richmond Renegades

PATERSON, DUNCAN
00/1 Kudos 132
00/1 Nottingham Panthers

PATERSON, JOE
88/9 ProCards / New Haven
89/0 ProCards IHL 41
90/1 ProCards 8
91/2 ProCards 203
95/6 Slapshot 380
80/1 DETR
87/8 LOSA
99/0 Louisville Panthers
00/1 Louisville Panthers
96/7 Soo Greyhounds

PATERSON, MARK
88/9 ProCards / Saginaw
81/2 Ottawa 67's
82/3 Ottawa 67's
83/4 Ottawa 67's

PATERSON, RICK
83/4 O-Pee-Chee 109
84/5 O-Pee-Chee 44
82/3 Post [Chic.]
80/1 CHIC / Brown
81/2 CHIC
82/3 CHIC
86/7 CHIC / Coke
93/4 Cleveland Lumberjacks
95/6 Cleveland Lumberjacks
96/7 Cleveland Lumberjacks

PATEY, DOUG
79/0 O-Pee-Chee 298

PATEY, LARRY
74/5 Loblaws
75/6 O-Pee-Chee 137
75/6 O-Pee-Chee 316
76/7 O-Pee-Chee 320
77/8 O-Pee-Chee 199
78/9 O-Pee-Chee 8
79/0 O-Pee-Chee 57
80/1 O-Pee-Chee 310
81/2 O-Pee-Chee 303
82/3 O-Pee-Chee 308
84/5 O-Pee-Chee 149
82/3 Post [SLou.]
75/6 Topps 137
75/6 Topps 316
77/8 Topps 199
78/9 Topps 8
79/0 Topps 57
84/5 Topps 111
78/9 SLOU

PATOINE, RÉMY
88/9 Richelieu Riverains

PATRICK, CRAIG
72/3 Eddie Sargent 55
74/5 Lipton Soup 46
74/5 Loblaws
74/5 Loblaws Update
71/2 O-Pee-Chee 184
72/3 O-Pee-Chee 221
73/4 O-Pee-Chee 52
74/5 O-Pee-Chee 262
75/6 O-Pee-Chee 178
77/8 O-Pee-Chee 278
72 Semic Sticker 130
94/5 SR Miracle 43,44, ✍ 43,44
73/4 Topps 52
74/5 Topps 262
75/6 Topps 178

PATRICK, FRANK
83 HHOF Postcard B9
83&87 HHOF 23
10/1 Imperial 1
94/5 Legends 48

PATRICK, GLENN
79 Panini Sticker 210
00/1 WBS Penguins
01/2 WBS Penguins
02/3 WBS Penguins

PATRICK, JAMES
02/3 Upper Deck 268
90/1 Bowman 225
91/2 Bowman 66
92/3 Bowman 127
83 Canada Juniors
93/4 Donruss 213
93/4 Donruss 408
94/5 Donruss 185
96/7 Donruss 158
93/4 EA Sports 86
94/5 Flair 26
94/5 Fleer 33
92/3 Fleer Ultra 141
93/4 Fleer Ultra 336
94/5 Fleer Ultra 33
88/9 Frito Lay
93/4 Leaf 232
94/5 Leaf 271
96/7 Metal Univ. 21
84/5 O-Pee-Chee 150
85/6 OPC/Topps 15
86/7 OPC/Topps 113
87/8 OPC/Topps 18
88/9 OPC/Topps 69
90/1 OPC/Topps 131
91/2 O-Pee-Chee 253
92/3 O-Pee-Chee 215
89/0 OPC/Topps 90
91/2 OPC Premier 172
85/6 OPC Sticker 83-214
86/7 OPC Sticker 220-90
87/8 OPC Sticker 30-171
88/9 OPC Sticker 246-116
89/0 opcSticker 242-105
97/8 Pa. Dynagon BKS-14
87/8 Panini Sticker 107
88/9 Panini Sticker 303
89/0 Panini Sticker 289
90/1 Panini Sticker 97
91/2 Panini Sticker 287
92/3 Panini Sticker 240
96/7 Panini Sticker 236
91/2 Parkhurst 120
92/3 Parkhurst 113
93/4 Parkhurst 360
94/5 Parkhurst 40
95/6 Parkhurst 303
91/2 Pinnacle 26
92/3 Pinnacle 140
93/4 Pinnacle 246
94/5 Pinnacle 196
94/5 POG 59
93/4 Power Play 164
93/4 Power Play 353
93/4 Premier 149
94/5 Premier 30
90/1 Pro Set 207
91/2 Pro Set 164
92/3 Pro Set 119
91/2 Pro Set Platinum 82
90/1 Score 194
90/1 Sco. Hot Cards 84
91/2 Score 230
91/2 Score CAN 230
92/3 Score 203
93/4 Score 574
93/4 Score 73
94/5 Score 8
96/7 Score 189
89 Semic Sticker 61
84/5 Topps 112
92/3 Topps 71
99/0 Topps 123
99/0 To. Chrome 123
96/7 To. Picks 165
91/2 To. Stadium 277
92/3 To. Stadium 394
93/4 To. Stadium 302
90/1 Upper Deck 185
91/2 Upper Deck 275
92/3 Upper Deck 320
94/5 Upper Deck 424
95/6 Upper Deck 53
94/5 UD BAP ✍ 98
00/1 UD Vintage 44
93/4 HART / Coke
89/0 NYRA / Marine

PATRICK, LESTER
83 HHOF Postcard C10
83&87 HHOF 40
10/1 Imperial 26
12/3 Imperial 41
95/6 Legends of Hockey 60
93/4 Parkie 56-57 P-10
77-79 Sportscaster 62-17
77-79 Sports. FIN 72-1716
60/1 Topps 1
01/2 UD Legends 48
37/8 World Wide Gum 94

PATRICK, LYNN
34-43 BeeHive-1 [NYRa.]
36-39 Diamond Match TT2
36-39 Diamond Match TT2
36-39 Diamond Match TT3
83 HHOF Postcard N12
83&87 HHOF 207
35/6 O-Pee-Chee 79
36/7 O-Pee-Chee 128
39/0 O-Pee-Chee 36
40/1 O-Pee-Chee 136
37/8 World Wide Gum 57

PATRICK, MURRAY
34-43 BeeHive-1 [NYRa.]
39/0 O-Pee-Chee 38

PATRICK, MUZZ
62/3 Cowan Tile

PATRY, MARIO
79/0 Montréal Juniors B&W

PATSCHINSKI, RAINER
74 Hellas MM-Jenkki 107
70/1 Kuvajulkaisut 92
79 Panini Sticker 253

PATTERSEN, LARS
96/7 Regina Pats

PATTERSON, BRIAN
99/0 Lethbridge Hurricanes

PATTERSON, COLIN
89/0 Kraft 7
90/1 O-Pee-Chee 420
89/0 OPC/Topps 71
89/0 opcSticker 102-239
89/0 Panini Sticker 36
90/1 Panini/CGY 16
91/2 Pro Set 356
91/2 Score CAN 525
92/3 Score 312
92/3 Topps 91
83/4 Vachon 15-135
91/2 BUFF / Blue Shield
91/2 BUFF / Campbell's
91/2 BUFF / Pepsi
92/3 BUFF / Blue Shield
85/6 CALG / Red Rooster
86/7 CALG / Red Rooster
87/8 CALG / Red Rooster
90/1 CALG / McGavin's

PATTERSON, DENNIS
74/5 Loblaws
75/6 O-Pee-Chee 51
75/6 Topps 51

PATTERSON, ED
93/4 Cla. Prospects 159
93/4 Donruss 474
94/5 Donruss 265
94/5 Leaf 290
90/1 7th..Sketch WHL 52, 291
91/2 7th...Sketch WHL 94
94/5 To. Stadium 232
95/6 PITT / Foodland 14
98/9 Cincinnati Cyclones
92/3 Cleveland Lumberjacks
93/4 Cleveland Lumberjacks
96/7 Cleveland Lumberjacks
97/8 Grand Rapids Griffins
99/0 Grand Rapids Griffins
00/1 Grand Rapids Griffins
02/3 London Knights

PATTERSON, GEORGE
33-35 Diamond Match Silv.
27/8 La Patrie
27/8 La Presse
33/4 O-Pee-Chee 14
33/4 WWGum 35

PATTERSON, JOSH
01/2 Peterborough Petes

PATTERSON, PHIL
81/2 Ottawa 67's
82/3 Ottawa 67's
83/4 Ottawa 67's

PATTERSON, RON
91/2 Air Canada SJHL C30

PATTISON, ROB
98/9 Albany River Rats
97/8 Las Vegas Thunder 19

PÄTZOLD, DIMITRI
01/2 UD DEL 255

PAUKKUNEN, MARKKU
00/1 Cardset 172

PAUL, JEFF
02/3 BAP Mem. 297
02/3 SP Authentic 141
02/3 SP GU 72
02/3 SPx 174
02/3 T. Chrome 154
02/3 To. Total 412
02/3 Ultimate Mem. 27
02/3 Upper Deck 433
02/3 UD Classic 108
02/3 UD Honor 149
02/3 UD Mask 139
02/3 UD Top Shelf 110
95/6 Slapshot 185
99/0 Cleveland Lumberjacks
01/2 Hershey Bears
98/9 Indianapolis Ice

PAUL, KYLE
92/3 MPS SJHL 28

PAUL, MATHIEU
98/9 Halifax Moosehead

PAUL, RICHARD
00/1 Québec Remparts 3
00/1 Victoriaville Tigres 17

PAUL, TODD
01/2 Drummondville

PAULHUS, ROLAND
25-27 Anonymous 4
25-27 Anonymous 4

PAULIN, CHARLES
92/3 Fredericton Canadiens

PAULSEN, EIRIK
92/3 Semic Nordisk 141

PAULSEN, ERIK
95 Panini Worlds 250

PAUNA, MATTI
90/1 Semic Elitserien 138
91/2 Semic Elitserien 193

PAVELEC, STANISLAV
94/5 APS 236
95/6 APS 6
96/7 APS 55
97/8 APS 320
98/9 DS 117
96/7 DS Sticker 231
97/8 DS Sticker 270
98/9 OFS 179

PAVELEK, ZDENEK
96/7 APS 113
97/8 APS 119
99/0 DS 180
00/1 DS 159
96/7 DS Sticker 277
97/8 DS Sticker 62
98/9 OFS 124
99/0 OFS 229, 318
00/1 OFS 256
01/2 OFS 27, -UHI 31

PAVELICH, MARK
82/3 O-Pee-Chee 231
83/4 O-Pee-Chee 238
83/4 O-Pee-Chee 239
83/4 O-Pee-Chee 253
84/5 O-Pee-Chee 151
85/6 OPC/Topps 69
82/3 OPC/Topps Sticker 138
83/4 OPC/Topps Sticker 213
83/4 OPC/Topps Sticker 214
84/5 OPC Sticker 97
85/6 OPC Sticker 84
80 Olympic USA
82/3 Post [NYRa.]
94/5 SR Miracle 25,26, ✍ 25,26
83/4 Souhaits Keychain [Rangers]
84/5 Topps 113
81/2 NYRA

PAVELICH, MARTY
45-64 BeeHive-2 [Detr.]
51/2 Parkhurst 54
52/3 Parkhurst 66
53/4 Parkhurst 44
54/5 Parkhurst 43
93/4 Parkie 56-57 53
95/6 Parkie 66-67 22
54/5 Topps 34
76 DETR

PAVELICH, MATT
83&87 HHOF 261

PAVESE, JIM
87/8 Panini Sticker 310
82/3 Post [SLou.]
90/1 ProCards 423
88/9 DETR / Little Caesars
80/1 Soo Greyhounds
81/2 Soo Greyhounds

PAVLAS, PETR
95/6 APS 226
96/7 APS 267, 422
97/8 APS 222
97/8 DS 14
98/9 DS 26
99/0 DS 18
00/1 DS 149
96/7 DS Sticker 171
97/8 DS Sticker 29
98/9 OFS 83
99/0 OFS 140, 504
00/1 OFS 269
01/2 OFS 231
95 Semic 145
91 Semic Sticker 108
94/5 Sisu 205

PAVLIK, KAREL
95/6 APS 223
96/7 APS 58

PAVLIKOVSKY, RASTISLAV
98/9 Cincinnati Cyclones
99/0 Cincinnati M'Ducks

PAVLIKOVSKY, RICHARD
00/1 DS 156
00/1 OFS 268

PAVLIN, FABIAN
79/0 Montréal Juniors B&W

PAVLIS, LIBOR
96/7 APS 209
97/8 APS 137
97/8 DS Sticker 262
98/9 OFS 121, 327
99/0 OFS 427
01/2 OFS 215

PAVLOV, EVGENI
98/9 Mir 159

PAVLU, MARTIN
95 Semic 176
82 Semic Sticker 139
96 Wien 182

PAVONI, RETO
95 Globe 208
95 Panini Worlds 116
91 Semic Sticker 178
92 Semic Sticker 196

PAWLACZYK, DAN
93/4 Slapshot / Detroit 16
94/5 Slapshot / Detroit Jr. 19
95/6 Slapshot 63
94/5 Slapshot Memorial 93
96/7 Toledo Storm

PAWLUK, JEFF
91/2 7th...Sketch OHL 359

PAWLUK, MIKE
92/3 BCJHL 148
92/3 BCJHL 245

PAWLUK, RYAN
93/4 Slapshot / Kitchener 12
95/6 Slapshot 314, 426

PAWLYSHYN, WALTER
52/3 Laval Dairy Update 8
52/3 St. Lawrence 35

PAYAN, EUGENE
91 C55 Reprint 43
10/1 Imperial
11/2 Imperial 43
12/3 Imperial 9

PAYER, SERGE
00/1 PS Titanium 122
00/1 PS Titanium Draft 122
95/6 Slapshot 138
96/7 Upper Deck 385
01/2 Utah Grizzlies

PAYETTE, ANDRÉ
95/6 Classic 95
93/4 Slapshot / S.S.Marie 8
95/6 Slapshot 360
01/2 Manchester Monarchs

PAYETTE, DANIELLE
95/6 Halifax Moosehead

PAYETTE, GREG
99/0 Utah Grizzlies

PAYETTE, JEAN
72/3 O-Pee-Chee 311
72/3 Québec Nordiques

PAYETTE, MATHIEU
01/2 Shawinigan Cataractes 21

PAYNE, ANTHONY
93/4 Humberside Hawks 11

PAYNE, DAVIS
97/8 Pa. Dynagon BKS-7
92/3 Greensboro Monarchs 7
93/4 Greensboro Monarchs
94/5 Greensboro Monarchs
96/7 Providence Bruins
90/1 Michigan Tech Huskies
91/2 Michigan Tech Huskies
91/2 Michigan Tech Huskies

PAYNE, JASON
95/6 Slapshot 14
99/0 Cincinnati M'Ducks
96/7 Flint Generals
98/9 Flint Generals

PAYNE, STEVE
79/0 O-Pee-Chee 64
80/1 O-Pee-Chee 138
80/1 O-Pee-Chee 274
81/2 O-Pee-Chee 166
82/3 O-Pee-Chee 172
83/4 O-Pee-Chee 178
84/5 O-Pee-Chee 106
85/6 OPC/Topps 65
86/7 O-Pee-Chee 219
81/2 OPC Sticker 22
81/2 OPC Sticker 92
82/3 OPC/Topps Sticker 191
83/4 OPC/Topps Sticker 121
84/5 OPC Sticker 49
85/6 OPC Sticker 42-170
87/8 OPC Sticker 56-197
82/3 Post [Minn.]
83/4 Souhaits Keychain [North Stars]
79/0 Topps 64
80/1 Topps 138
81/2 Topps 110 [West]
84/5 Topps 80
78/9 MINS / Cloverleaf 7
79/0 MINS
80/1 MINS
81/2 MINS
82/3 MINS
83/4 MINS
84/5 MINS
84/5 MINS / 7-Eleven 11
85/6 MINS
87/8 MINS

PAYNTER, KENT
88/9 ProCards / Saginaw
89/0 ProCards AHL 101
90/1 ProCards 196
91/2 ProCards 168
91/2 WINN / IGA
94/5 Milwaukee Admirals
95/6 Milwaukee Admirals
96/7 Milwaukee Admirals
91/2 Moncton Hawks
85/6 Nova Scotia Oilers
82/3 Kitchener Rangers
83/4 Kitchener Rangers
84/5 Kitchener Rangers

PAZLER, LUBOS
94/5 APS 263

PAZOUREK, DAVID
00/1 DS 108
99/0 OFS 79
00/1 OFS 204
01/2 OFS 101

PAZOUREK, PAVEL
99/0 OFS 71
00/1 OFS 186

PAZOUREK, VACLAV
99/0 Asheville Smoke

PAZOUREK, ZBYNEK
01/2 OFS 102

PCHELYAKOV, ANDREI
99/0 Mir 139
00/1 Mir 367

PCHELYAKOV, OLEG
98/9 Mir 139

PEACOCK, RICHARD
98/9 Anchorage Aces

PEACOCK, SHANE
91/2 Classic 48
91/2 Classic Four Sport 48
98/9 DEL 45
99/0 Eishockey 338
90/1 7th..Sketch WHL 123
91/2 7th...Sketch WHL 343
91/2 Star Pics 33
91/2 Ultimate Draft Pick 43, ✍ Aut.
00/1 UD DEL 175, P5
01/2 UD DEL 188, SS10
96/7 Michigan K-Wings
89/0 Lethbridge Hurricanes
93/4 Lethbridge Hurricanes

PEACOSH, GENE
74/5 OPC WHA 27
75/6 OPC WHA 24
76/7 OPC WHA 60
76/7 OPC WHA 71
73/4 Quaker Oats 24

PEAKE, PAT
91/2 Arena 11
91/2 Classic 12
93/4 Classic 12, 33, ✍ Aut.
91/2 Classic Four Sport 12
93/4 Cla. Prospects 29
93/4 Donruss 361
94/5 Donruss 318
95/6 Donruss 230
94/5 Flair 203
94/5 Fleer 238
93/4 Fleer Ultra 449
94/5 Fleer Ultra 237
95/6 Fleer Ultra 325
94/5 Leaf 83, GLR-12
94/5 Panini Sticker C
93/4 Parkhurst 490
94/5 Parkhurst 281, V63
95/6 Parkhurst 488
94/5 Parkie SE196
93/4 Pinnacle 436
93/4 Pinnacle SR9
94/5 Pinnacle 136
97/8 Pi. Be A Player 171, ✍ Aut. 171
95/6 Playoff 214
93/4 Power Play 469
93/4 Power Play RooS 10
94/5 Premier 12
93/4 Score 590
95/6 Score 181
96/7 Score 67
91 7th..Sketch Mem.Cup 106
90/1 7th..Sketch OHL 114, 125
91/2 7th...Sketch OHL 35
91/2 Star Pics 39
95/6 To. Stadium 136
91/2 Ultimate Draft Pick 12,

68, ✍ Aut.
91/2 Upper Deck 697
93/4 Upper Deck 518, SP-172
94/5 Upper Deck 125, SP-176
95/6 Upper Deck 163, SE-175
96/7 Upper Deck 353
97/8 Upper Deck 179
96/7 UD CC 282
91/2 Upper Deck WJC 84
95/6 WASH
02/3 Plymouth Whalers

PEAL, ALLEN
52/3 Anonymous 113

PEARCE, BARCLAY
97/8 Guildford Flames
98/9 Guildford Flames

PEARCE, FRANK
51/2 Bas du Fleuve 9
52/3 Bas du Fleuve 25

PEARCE, GARRY
90/1 7th..Sketch WHL 176
91/2 7th...Sketch WHL 223
89/0 Regina Pats

PEARCE, RANDY
90 7th..Sketch Mem.Cup 29
91/2 Hampton Roads
96/7 Hampton Roads
98/9 Hampton Roads
93/4 Portland Pirates
87/8 Kitchener Rangers
88/9 Kitchener Rangers
89/0 Kitchener Rangers

PEARCE, ROBERT
00/1 Québec Remparts 13
01/2 Québec Remparts 8
02/3 Québec Remparts

PEARN, PERRY
96/7 OTTA
97/8 OTTA
00/1 OTTA
01/2 OTTA
02/3 OTTA
95/6 WINN

PEARSALL, ANDREW
99/0 Huntington Blizzard

PEARSON, ANDY
85/6 Kingston Canadians

PEARSON, MEL
72/3 Minn. Fight. Saints

PEARSON, ROB
92/3 Bowman 381
93/4 Donruss 339
92/3 Fleer Ultra 423
93/4 Fleer Ultra 434
93/4 Leaf 174
92/3 O-Pee-Chee 136
91/2 OPC Premier 65
92/3 Panini Sticker 80
91/2 Parkhurst 169
92/3 Parkhurst 414
93/4 Parkhurst 474
91/2 Pinnacle 304
92/3 Pinnacle 245
93/4 Pinnacle 287
92/3 Pinnacle T2K 23
93/4 Pinnacle 89
94/5 Pinnacle 375
93/4 Power Play 453
93/4 Premier 137
94/5 Premier 341
91/2 Pro Set 562
92/3 Pro Set 191
92/3 Pro Set RGL 9
91/2 Score 311
91/2 Score CAN 341
91/2 Score CAN 385
92/3 Score 333
93/4 Score 96
94/5 Score 137
92/3 Score Young Stars 18
89/0 7th..Sketch OHL 79
90/1 7th..Sketch OHL 15
92/3 Topps 168
92/3 To. Stadium 377
93/4 To. Stadium 498
91/2 Upper Deck 598
92/3 Upper Deck 318
93/4 Upper Deck 48
94/5 Upper Deck 180
95/6 Upper Deck 212
94/5 UD BAP ✍ 76
01/2 UD DEL 83
91/2 TORO / P.L.A.Y. 11
92/3 TORO / Kodak
93/4 TORO / Abalene
93/4 TORO / Black's 6
97/8 Cleveland Lumberjacks
95/6 Portland Pirates
90/1 Oshawa Generals

PEARSON, SCOTT
91/2 Bowman 150
93/4 Donruss 106
94/5 Donruss 196
94/5 Fleer Ultra 75
93/4 Leaf 297
94/5 Leaf 349
90/1 OPC/Topps 356
91/2 O-Pee-Chee 297
90/1 Panini/TOR 19
94/5 Panini Sticker 204
92/3 Parkhurst 381
94/5 Parkhurst 78
95/6 Parkhurst 22
93/4 Pinnacle 375
94/5 Pinnacle 213
94/5 POG 100
94/5 Premier 124
91/2 Pro Set 208
89/0 ProCards AHL 119
91/2 Score 138
91/2 Score CAN 138
93/4 Score 376
93/4 Score 543
91/2 To. Stadium 178
91/2 Upper Deck 336
93/4 Upper Deck 389
94/5 Upper Deck 97
95/6 Upper Deck 135
00/1 UD DEL 164
93/4 EDMO / Sheet
92/3 QUÉB / Petro-Canada
90/1 TORO
98/9 Chicago Wolves
98/9 Chicago Wolves Champs
99/0 Chicago Wolves
95/6 Rochester Americans
85/6 Kingston Canadians
86/7 Kingston Canadians
87/8 Kingston Canadians
88/9 Niagara Falls Thunder

PEARSON, TED
84/5 Moncton G'Flames

PEASE, JAMES
02/3 Coventry Blaze

PEAT, STEPHEN
02/3 Pacific 398
02/3 Signature GS-91
02/3 Upper Deck 423
98 Bowman 136, ✍ A4
98 Bowman Chrome 136
01/2 Parkhurst 276
01/2 PS Titanium Draft 170
01/2 Signature 249, ✍ Aut. 249
97/8 Upper Deck 405

PECA, DAVID
95/6 Slapshot 40

PECA, JUSTIN
94/5 Erie Panthers
91/2 Michigan Tech Huskies

PECA, MICHAEL
02/3 Atomic 64, -SC 9
02/3 BAP Mem. 153
02/3 Bowman 58
02/3 Crown Royale 61, ✄ GWDP 15, ✄ GWJ 12
02/3 eTopps 22
02/3 Exclusive 110
02/3 First Edition 194, 379
02/3 Heads Up 75, ✄ GWQ 18
02/3 McDonald's 24, -SLG 9
02/3 O-Pee-Chee 15
02/3 Pacific 242, ✄ GWJ 32
02/3 Pacific Complete 26
02/3 Parkhurst 79
02/3 Parkhurst Retro 62, ✄ RF19
02/3 Pr. Stock Reserve ✄ 131
02/3 PS Titanium 66, ✄ GWJ 41
02/3 Quest for the Cup 61
02/3 Signature 132, GS-60, ✍ 132, ✄ FJ19
02/3 SP Authentic 58
02/3 SP GU 30
02/3 Sports Vault 76
02/3 SPx 48
02/3 Stadium 40
02/3 Topps 15
02/3 T. Chrome 15
02/3 To. Heritage 64,106, ✍ J-32
02/3 To. Limited 15
02/3 To. Total 260, TTC19, AW10
02/3 UD Superstars 166
02/3 Ultimate Mem. ✄ FS, ✄ Num, ✄ RAT
02/3 Upper Deck 353
02/3 UD Artistic 56, R56, / Art
02/3 UD Classic 62
02/3 UD Honor 46, 89, -TW9
02/3 UD MVP 114
02/3 UD Piece 57
02/3 UD Premier 34
02/3 UD Rookie ✄ 156b
02/3 UD Top Shelf 55
02/3 UD Vintage 157, 279, 311, GB 157, T41
02/3 Vanguard 64, ✄ GWJ 29
02/3 Victory 136
01/2 Adrenaline 122
01/2 Atomic 61, TN 9
98/9 Aurora 19, -CF 7, -MACF 4
99/0 Aurora 18, Stripe 18, CF-5
00/1 Aurora 20
98/9 Be A Player 12, ✍ Aut. 12
99/0 BAP Mem. 131
99/0 BAP Mem. 36, ✄ TM-6
01/2 BAP Mem. 37
97/8 Bicycle A-Club
01/2 Bowman 28
98/9 Bowman's Best 32
99/0 Challenger 24
92/3 Classic 17
93/4 Classic 25
94/5 Classic 116, T72
92/3 Classic Four Sport 166
93/4 Cla. Prospects 154
99/0 Crown Royale 19
00/1 Crown Royale 16
01/2 Crown Royale 92
93/4 Donruss CAN18
94/5 Donruss 266
95/6 Donruss 266
97/8 Donruss 21
97/8 Do. Canadian 89
97/8 Do. Preferred 34
97/8 Do. Priority 145
97/8 Do. Studio 72
98/9 Dynagon Ice 20, -FT 3
99/0 Dynagon Ice 32, CM-8
94/5 Fleer 229, RS-8
94/5 Fleer Ultra P-6
95/6 Fleer Ultra 212
01/2 Heads Up 61
98/9 Kraft / Post 19
99/0 Kraft / KD
94/5 Leaf 193
95/6 Leaf 114
97/8 Leaf 107
97/8 Limited 39
99/0 McDonald's McD-13
99/0 Millenium 30, ✍ Aut. 30
98/9 NHL Power Play
98/9 OPC Chrome 94
97/8 Omega 24
98/9 Omega 25
99/0 Omega 30
98/9 Pacific 27, -GCDC 5
99/0 Pacific 41, GC-6
00/1 Pacific 53
97/8 Pacific CC 341, GCDC-4
97/8 Pa. Crown Roy. 15, L-4
98/9 Pa. Crown Roy. 14, -PotG 3, -PP 3
97/8 Pa. Dynagon 12, 136, DD-3B, T-21, T-33, BKS-105
97/8 Pa. Invincible 13, AZ-3, OTG-3
97/8 Pa. Paramount 21
98/9 Pa. Paramount 21
99/0 Pa. Paramount 29, PB-6
00/1 Pa. Paramount 31
97/8 Pa. Revolution 15, TC-3
98/9 Pa. Revolution 15, -Show. 5
98/9 Panini Photocard
97/8 Panini Sticker 13, 122
98/9 Panini Sticker 21
99/0 Panini Sticker 37
00/1 Panini Sticker 20
94/5 Parkhurst 245
95/6 Parkhurst 290
01/2 Parkhurst 32
93/4 Pinnacle 478
94/5 Pinnacle 260, RTP8
97/8 Pinnacle 110
97/8 Pi. Be A Player 44, ✍ Aut. 44
97/8 Pi. Certified 99
97/8 Pi. Inside 128
97/8 Pi. Totally 99
95/6 Playoff 128
95/6 POG 41
94/5 Premier SFX 275
00/1 Premier Plus 34
99/0 Prism 20
01/2 Pr. Stock 59, -PS 45
01/2 PS Titanium 90, SK 13
99/0 Revolution 19, SS-6, / CSC 19
00/1 Revolution 18
94/5 Score 237
95/6 Score 157
96/7 Score 209
97/8 Score 187, 268, CI-14
97/8 Score Buff. 11
94/5 Select 198
90/1 7th..Sketch OHL 391, 392
91/2 7th...Sketch OHL 247
00/1 Signature 9, ✍ Aut. 94, ✄ J-32
96/7 SBx Impact 12
98/9 SP Authentic 9
99/0 SP Authentic 9
00/1 SP GU ✄ TotG, ✄ C
99/0 SPx 17
01/2 SPx 40
98/9 SPx Finite 9
99/0 Stadium 141
00/1 Stadium 90
01/2 Stadium 104
95/6 Topps 350
98/9 Topps 94
99/0 Topps 162, NS3
00/1 Topps 241
99/0 To. Chrome 162
00/1 To. Chrome 151
01/2 To. Chrome 132
94/5 Topps Finest 59
98/9 To. Finest 92
98/9 T. Gold Label 91
99/0 T. Gold Label 5
01/2 To. Heritage 167
99/0 T. Prmr. Plus 77
01/2 To. Reserve 81
00/1 To. Stars 68
98/9 UD Choice 24
00/1 Ultimate Mem. ✍ U-41, ✄ TM-20
93/4 Upper Deck 542
94/5 Upper Deck 257, 533, 547, C10, SP-173
95/6 Upper Deck 225
96/7 Upper Deck 21
97/8 Upper Deck 227, T7C
98/9 Upper Deck 46
99/0 Upper Deck 23
01/2 Upper Deck 111, 340, LP9
94/5 UD BAP ✍ 165
99/0 UD Black Diam. 12
94/5 UD Canada Junior 7
01/2 UD Challenge 56
96/7 UD CC 32
97/8 UD Coll. Choice 26
98/9 UD G. Reserve 46
99/0 UD G. Reserve 23
01/2 UD Honor Roll DF6
00/1 UD Ice 6
01/2 UD Mask 60
98/9 UD MVP 25
99/0 UD MVP 23, ✍ PS
00/1 UD MVP 26
99/0 UD MVP Cup 27, GC
00/1 UD Ovation 7
99/0 UD Retro 9
01/2 UD Top Shelf 102
01/2 UD Vintage 158
01/2 Vanguard 61
99/0 Victory 34
00/1 Victory 27
99/0 WGretzky 27, EG2
95/6 VANC / Abalene 17
92/3 Ottawa 67's
90/1 Sudbury Wolves
91/2 Sudbury Wolves

PECA, MIKE
02/3 BAP Mem. 248, 253

PECK, JIM
74/5 Sioux City Musketeers

PEDDIGREW, JEFF
93/4 Seattle Thunderbirds

PEDERSEN, ALLEN
87/8 OPC/Topps 174
88/9 OPC/Topps 103
90/1 O-Pee-Chee 505
91/2 O-Pee-Chee 128
87/8 OPC Sticker 132-120
92/3 Parkhurst 300
93/4 Premier 439
90/1 Pro Set 12
90/1 Score 181
91/2 Score CAN 599
93/4 To. Stadium 366
88/9 BOST / Sports Action
89/0 BOST / Sports Action
90/1 BOST / Sports Action
92/3 HART / Dairymart
94/5 Atlanta Knights 6
85/6 Moncton G'Flames
96/7 Pensacola Ice Pilots
97/8 Pensacola Ice Pilots
82/3 Medicine Hat Tigers
83/4 Medicine Hat Tigers

PEDERSEN, KRISTIAN
91/2 Semic Elitserien 114
92/3 Semic Elitserien 130

PEDERSEN, TOMMY
79 Panini Sticker 364

PEDERSON, BARRY
92/3 Bowman 48
88/9 Frito Lay
83/4 Funmate Puffy 7 [w]
86/7 Kraft Sports 66
82/3 O-Pee-Chee 20
83/4 O-Pee-Chee 57
84/5 O-Pee-Chee 14
85/6 OPC/Topps 52
86/7 OPC/Topps 34
87/8 OPC/Topps 177
88/9 OPC/Topps 32
90/1 OPC/Topps 134
92/3 O-Pee-Chee 295
89/0 O-Pee-Chee 281
91/2 OPC Premier 124
82/3 OPC/Topps Sticker 92
82/3 OPC/Topps Sticker 93
83/4 OPC/Topps Sticker 49
83/4 OPC/Topps Sticker 50
84/5 OPC Sticker 187
86/7 OPC Sticker 38-175
87/8 OPC Sticker 188
88/9 OPC Sticker 65
89/0 opcSticker 60
87/8 Panini Sticker 346
88/9 Panini Sticker 138
89/0 Panini Sticker 153
90/1 Pro Set 238
91/2 Pro Set 351
91/2 Score CAN 639
83/4 Souhaits Keychain [Bruins]
84/5 Topps 11
92/3 Topps 241
90/1 Upper Deck 329
83/4 BOST
84/5 BOST
90/1 PITT / Foodland 4
86/7 VANC
87/8 VANC / Shell
88/9 VANC / Mohawk
89/0 VANC / Mohawk
82/3 Victoria Cougars

PEDERSON, DENIS
95/6 Bowman 138
93/4 Classic 26
94/5 Classic 112, T37
93/4 Cla. 4 Sport 196, ✍ Aut.
95/6 Donruss 257, C3TWC-20
95/6 Fleer Metal 195
95/6 Fleer Ultra 359
96/7 Leaf 226
97/8 Limited 154
99/0 Millenium 147, ✍ Aut. 147
98/9 OPC Chrome 214
98/9 Pacific 269
97/8 Pacific CC 221
97/8 Pa. Invincible 79
95/6 Parkhurst 395
94/5 Pinnacle 538
96/7 Pinnacle 221
96/7 Pi. Be A Player 217, ✍ Aut. 217
97/8 Score NJer. 11
95/6 SBx Impact 207
94/5 SP 144
95/6 Topps 12CJ
98/9 Topps 214, -IA I4
94/5 Topps Finest 163
98/9 To. Finest 144
95/6 Upper Deck 354
96/7 Upper Deck 288
97/8 Upper Deck 97
98/9 Upper Deck 312
97/8 UD Coll. Choice 149
98/9 UD G. Reserve 312
96/7 NJER / Sharp
97/8 Albany River Rats
93/4 Prince Albert Raiders

PEDERSON, MARK
91/2 Bowman 242
92/3 Bowman 390
98/9 DEL 32
99/0 Eishockey 131
90/1 OPC/Topps 82
91/2 O-Pee-Chee 399
92/3 O-Pee-Chee 157
90/1 Panini/MTL 17
92/3 Panini Sticker 188
91/2 Parkhurst 345
92/3 Pinnacle 213
90/1 Pro Set 618
88/9 ProCards / Sherbrooke
90/1 Score 387
91/2 Score CAN 435
92/3 Score 263
92/3 Topps 327
91/2 To. Stadium 291
92/3 To. Stadium 168
90/1 Upper Deck 532
91/2 Upper Deck 363
92/3 Upper Deck 209
01/2 UD DEL 100
90/1 MONT
91/2 PHIL / J.C. Penney
84/5 Medicine Hat Tigers

PEDERSON, TODD
82/3 Medicine Hat Tigers

PEDERSON, TOM
92/3 Classic Prospects 145
98/9 DEL 191
99/0 Eishockey 220
92/3 Fleer Ultra 403
92/3 OPC Premier 33
93/4 Parkhurst 184
94/5 Pinnacle 448
93/4 Power Play 226
94/5 Premier 142
93/4 Upper Deck 92
95/6 UD CC 38
92/3 SANJ / Pacific Bell
97/8 Fort Wayne Komets

PEER, BRIT
83/4 Soo Greyhounds
84/5 Soo Greyhounds

PEERLESS, BLAINE
81/2 Milwaukee Admirals

PEET, SHAUN
92/3 BCJHL 108
99/0 Kingston Frontenacs

PEETERS, PETE
91/2 Bowman 237
83/4 Funmate Puffy 9 [w]
80/1 O-Pee-Chee 279
81/2 O-Pee-Chee 245
82/3 O-Pee-Chee 22
83/4 O-Pee-Chee 44
83/4 O-Pee-Chee 58
83/4 O-Pee-Chee 209
84/5 O-Pee-Chee 221
86/7 O-Pee-Chee 222
84/5 O-Pee-Chee 6
85/6 OPC/Topps 75
86/7 OPC/Topps 6
87/8 OPC/Topps 44
88/9 OPC/Topps 180
89/0 OPC/Topps 109
91/2 O-Pee-Chee 29
89/0 OPC/Topps 195
88/9 OPC Stars 30
81/2 OPC Sticker 177
82/3 OPC/Topps Sticker 117
83/4 OPC/Topps Sticker 41
83/4 OPC/Topps Sticker 42
83/4 OPC/Topps Sticker 170
83/4 OPC/Topps Sticker 318
84/5 OPC Sticker 144
84/5 OPC Sticker 184
85/6 OPC Sticker 160
86/7 OPC Sticker 207-78
87/8 Panini Sticker 174
88/9 Panini Sticker 364
82/3 Post [Phil.]
90/1 Pro Set 502
91/2 Pro Set Platinum PC2
90/1 Pro Set PotM
91/2 Score CAN 544
83/4 Souhaits Keychain [Bruins]
81/2 Topps 109 [East]
84/5 Topps 12
91/2 To. Stadium 88
90/1 Upper Deck 424
91/2 Upper Deck 642
83/4 BOST
84/5 BOST
89/0 PHIL
90/1 PHIL
86/7 WASH / Kodak
86/7 WASH / Police
87/8 WASH
87/8 WASH / Kodak
88/9 WASH
88/9 WASH / Smokey

PEGG, JAMIE
89/0 7th..Sketch OHL 104
90/1 7th..Sketch OHL 368
99/0 Huntington Blizzard

PEHU, SAKARI
72/3 Williams Finnish 314

PEIETILÄ,
97/8 Hockey-Box

PEIPMANN, JASON
92/3 BCJHL 14

PEIRSON, JOHNNY
45-64 BeeHive-2 [Bost.]
45-64 BeeHive-2 [Bost.]
51/2 Parkhurst 34
52/3 Parkhurst 78
53/4 Parkhurst 88
54/5 Parkhurst 60
93/4 Parkie 56-57 5
57-58 BOST

PEITSOMA, JUKKA
80/1 Mallasjuoma 133

PEJCHAR, RUDOLF
94/5 APS 139
95/6 APS 244
96/7 APS 3
98/9 DS 12
99/0 DS 15, G2
96/7 DS Sticker 113
98/9 OFS 82
99/0 OFS 13, -CL

PEK, GYORGY
79 Panini Sticker 273

PEKAREK, DAVID
90/1 7th..Sketch LHJMQ 12
91 7th..Sketch Mem.Cup 66

PEKARIK, PAVOL
99/0 OFS 299

PEKKALA, JUSSI
98/9 Cardset 198
99/0 Cardset 109

PEKKARINEN, VELI-PEKKA
93/4 Jyvas Hyva 178
93/4 Sisu 170
94/5 Sisu 127
95/6 Sisu 79

PEKKI, SAMI
94/5 Sisu 70

PEKKI, SEMI
98/9 Cardset 66
97/8 Hockey-Box
95/6 Sisu 237
96/7 Sisu 40
95/6 Sisu Limited 108

PEKOREK, DAVID
91/2 7th...Sketch LHJMQ 239

PELCHAT, PATRICK
98 Bowman 88
98 Bowman Chrome 88
99/0 Rouyn-Noranda

PELCHAT, RODRIGUE
51/2 Lac St-Jean 27

PELENSKY, PERRY
83/4 Springfield Indians 13

PELHAM, LUKE
01/2 Moncton Wildcats 24

PELINO, MIKE
97/8 Spokane Chiefs

PELKTOLA, PEKKA
95/6 Sisu 362

PELL, GORDON
89/0 7th..Sketch OHL 80
90/1 7th..Sketch OHL 213
91/2 7th...Sketch OHL 23
91/2 Cornwall Royals

PELLA, DEAN
87/8 Kingston Canadians
88/9 Sudbury Wolves

PELLA, TYLER
87/8 Kingston Canadians
88/9 Sudbury Wolves

PELLAERS, RYAN
91/2 7th...Sketch WHL 67

PELLEGRIMS, MIKE
96/7 DEL 167
98/9 DEL 237
99/0 Eishockey 290
00/1 UD DEL 227, P10
01/2 UD DEL 54

PELLEGRINO, SANTINO
94 Semic 305
92 Semic Sticker 260
93 Semic Sticker 228

PELLERIN, BRIAN
91/2 ProCards 45
90/1 7th..Sketch WHL 266
92/3 Peoria Rivermen
93/4 Peoria Rivermen
90/1 Prince Albert Raiders

PELLERIN, JASON
99/0 Odessa Jackalopes

PELLERIN, SCOTT
02/3 Pacific 117
02/3 Pacific Complete 374
92/3 Classic 81
92/3 Classic Four Sport 202
92/3 Classic Prospects 18
92/3 Classic Prospects 93
00/1 Crown Royale 54
93/4 Fleer Ultra 142
00/1 Kraft 30
93/4 Leaf 167
01/2 McDonald's -HP 3
98/9 Pacific 370
99/0 Pacific 361
01/2 Pacific 80
97/8 Pacific CC 95
00/1 Pa. Paramount 124
99/0 Panini Sticker 333
93/4 Parkhurst 116
00/1 Parkhurst P-231
97/8 Pi. Be A Player 50, ✍ Aut. 50
00/1 PS Titanium 46
93/4 Score 373
97/8 Score SLou. 12
00/1 Stadium 201
00/1 To. Chrome 233
93/4 To. Stadium 13
00/1 To. Stars 93
00/1 UD Heroes 60
93/4 Upper Deck 52
99/0 Upper Deck 90, 318
01/2 Upper Deck 246
00/1 UD Pros&Prosp. 43
00/1 UD Vintage 183, 184
99/0 SLOU / Taco Bell 15
92/3 Maine Black Bears

PELLETIER, FRANÇOIS
90 7th..Sketch Mem.Cup 66

PELLETIER, GASTON
52/3 Anonymous 77
72 Semic Sticker 155

PELLETIER, JEAN-MARC
02/3 Between the Pipes 78
02/3 UD Mask 66
98/9 Collection Souvenir 11
92 Québec Pee Wee 612
99/0 Topps 118
99/0 To. Chrome 118
98/9 UD Choice 301
99/0 Upper Deck 95, CT4, N11
99/0 UD G. Reserve 95, / Backup 169
99/0 UD MVP 147
99/0 UD Retro G3C
99/0 Victory 216
00/1 Cincinnati Cyclones
97/8 Rimouski Océanic

PELLETIER, JON.
00/1 Rimouski Océanic 20
99/0 Rouyn-Noranda

PELLETIER, LLOYD
91/2 7th...Sketch WHL 235

PELLETIER, MARCEL
51/2 La Patrie
51/2 Laval Dairy 33
52/3 St. Lawrence 90

PELLETIER, NICOLAS
00/1 Val d'Or Foreurs 8
01/2 Val d'Or Foreurs 11

PELLETIER, PASCAL
00/1 Baie-Comeau 6
01/2 Baie-Comeau 5
02/3 Baie-Comeau

PELLETIER, STEVE
02/3 Québec Remparts
00/1 Val d'Or Foreurs 10
01/2 Val d'Or Foreurs 19

PELLINEN, PETRI
71/2 Williams Finnish 332

PELLITIER, LLOYD
90/1 7th..Sketch WHL 53

PELOFFY, ANDRÉ
74/5 WASH

PELTOLA, ARI
70/1 Kuvajulkaisut 336
80/1 Mallasjuoma 207
78/9 SM-Liiga 232

PELTOLA, JUHANI
66/7 Champion 159

PELTOLA, MIKKO
02/3 Cardset 90
98/9 Cardset 92
99/0 Cardset 50
00/1 Cardset 199
92/3 Jyvas Hyva 170
93/4 Jyvas Hyva 288
95 Semic 29
93/4 Sisu 69
94/5 Sisu 324
95/6 Sisu 102
96/7 Sisu 178
97/8 UD Elitserien 142

PELTOLA, PEKKA
91/2 Jyvas Hyva 10
92/3 Jyvas Hyva 131
93/4 Jyvas Hyva 22
93/4 Sisu 97
94/5 Sisu 68

PELTOLA, TEUVO
66/7 Champion 146

PELTOMAA, TIMO
02/3 Cardset 243
98/9 Cardset 93
99/0 Cardset 288
96/7 DEL 63
91/2 Jyvas Hyva 15
92/3 Jyvas Hyva 44
93/4 Jyvas Hyva 79
95 Semic 50
91 Semic Sticker 25
92 Semic Sticker 18
93/4 Sisu 125
93/4 Sisu 303
93/4 Sisu 30
94/5 Sisu 43, 158, H-8
95/6 Sisu 227
96/7 Sisu SH 7
95/6 Sisu Limited 104
00/1 UD Elitserien 173

PELTONEN, ESA
72 Hellas MM-Jenkki 10
74 Hellas MM-Jenkki 13
70/1 Kuvajulkaisut 73
70/1 Kuvajulkaisut 285
80/1 Mallasjuoma 5
72 Panda MM-Toronto
79 Panini Sticker 170
72 Semic Sticker 85
74 Semic Sticker 88
82 Semic Sticker 49
78/9 SM-Liiga 31
77-79 Sports. FIN 49-1175
71/2 Williams Finnish 73
71/2 Williams Finnish 155
72/3 Williams Finnish 70
72/3 Williams Finnish 107
73/4 Williams Finnish 75
73/4 Williams Finnish 138

PELTONEN, JARI
70/1 Kuvajulkaisut 337

PELTONEN, JARMO-SAKARI
96/7 DEL 267

PELTONEN, JARNO
00/1 Cardset 276
98/9 DEL 250
99/0 Eishockey 91
93/4 Jyvas Hyva 83
93/4 Sisu 123
94/5 Sisu 259
95/6 Sisu 235
96/7 Sisu 32

PELTONEN, JORMA
66/7 Champion 197
65/6 Hellas 126
70/1 Kuvajulkaisut 74
70/1 Kuvajulkaisut 135
72 Panda MM-Toronto
71/2 Williams Finnish 184
72/3 Williams Finnish 134
73/4 Williams Finnish 188

PELTONEN, JOUNI
80/1 Mallasjuoma 113
78/9 SM-Liiga 157
73/4 Williams Finnish 314

PELTONEN, KIMMO
02/3 Cardset 91
99/0 Cardset 235
00/1 Cardset 24

PELTONEN, MATTI
66/7 Champion 162
65/6 Hellas 148
70/1 Kuvajulkaisut 219

PELTONEN, PASI
02/3 Cardset 92
98/9 Cardset 255
99/0 Cardset 147
00/1 Cardset 103
93/4 Sisu 211
94/5 Sisu 103
95/6 Sisu 153
96/7 Sisu 152

PELTONEN, TIMO
80/1 Mallasjuoma 115
78/9 SM-Liiga 158

PELTONEN, VILLE
02/3 Cardset 244
99/0 BAP Mem. 275
95/6 Bowman 133
98/9 Cardset Leij. 36
99/0 Cardset 195, AH K-risti
00/1 Cardset 115
94/5 Classic 97, T63
96/7 Donruss 224
99/0 Dynagon Ice 110
95 Hartwall Karjala
92/3 Jyvas Hyva 15
93/4 Jyvas Hyva 28
95/6 Kellogg's Pop-Ups 4
96/7 Leaf 144
95 Leaf Latkaliiga 5
99/0 Millenium 138, ✍ Aut. 138
99/0 Panini Sticker 263
00/1 Panini Sticker 181
95 Panini Worlds 178
95/6 Parkhurst 456, 521
94 Semic 33
95 Semic 16, 230
93/4 Sisu 101
93/4 Sisu 365
93/4 Sisu 391
94/5 Sisu 166, 216, H-6
95/6 Sisu 172, G-21, P-5
95/6 Sisu Limited 41, PP
95 Suomen Beckett Card 3
92/3 Upper Deck 616
95/6 Upper Deck 384
96/7 Upper Deck 335
96/7 UD CC 241
97/8 UD Elitserien 79, UDS5, C5
96 Wien 16, 37, AS6
98/9 NASH / Wendy's 17
00/1 Milwaukee Admirals

PELTONIEMI, OSSI
66/7 Champion 219

PELTONIEMI, PEKKA
66/7 Champion 121

PELUCHA, PETR
97/8 APS 101

PELUSO, MIKE
92/3 Fleer Ultra 365
93/4 Leaf 407
94/5 Leaf 546
91/2 O-Pee-Chee 293
97/8 Pacific CC 306
93/4 Panini Sticker 116
92/3 Parkhurst 118
92/3 Pinnacle 379
93/4 Pinnacle 385
94/5 Pinnacle 43
96/7 Pi. Be A Player 136, ✍ Aut. 136
95/6 POG 161
90/1 Pro Set 601
92/3 Pro Set 122
89/0 ProCards IHL 57
91/2 ProCards 496
92/3 Score CAN 529
92/3 Score 536
93/4 Score 265
93/4 Score 551
95/6 Topps 10PL
93/4 To. Stadium 497
91/2 Upper Deck 414

PELUSO, MIKE
02/3 Fleer Throwbacks 28

PELUSO, MIKE1
90/1 CHIC / Coke
91/2 CHIC / Coke
92/3 OTTA
00/1 Worcester IceCats

PELUSO, MIKE2
01/2 BAP Mem. 322
01/2 SPx 200
01/2 UD PlayMakers Ltd 110
01/2 UD Ice 131
01/2 UD Mask 139
01/2 UD Premier 55
01/2 UD Top Shelf 125
01/2 Norfolk Admirals
98/9 Portland Pirates
99/0 Portland Pirates

PELYK, MIKE
70/1 Dad's Cookies
70/1 Eddie Sargent 203
71/2 Eddie Sargent 197
72/3 Eddie Sargent 200
70/1 Esso Power Player
70/1 O-Pee-Chee 107
71/2 O-Pee-Chee 92
72/3 O-Pee-Chee 17
73/4 O-Pee-Chee 71
76/7 O-Pee-Chee 342
74/5 OPC WHA 19
68/9 Post Marble
68/9 Shirriff / Toro. 8
70/1 Topps 107
71/2 Topps 92
72/3 Topps 107
73/4 Topps 71
71/2 Toronto Sun Photo
68/9 TORO
69/0 TORO
70/1 TORO
71/2 TORO
72/3 TORO
73/4 TORO
76/7 TORO
75/6 Cincinnati Stingers

PELZER, JAMES
91/2 Avant Garde BCJHL 96

PENCHTHALT, TONY
92/3 Tacoma Rockets

PENDERGAST, MIKE
91/2 Upper Deck WJC 69

PENELTON, PAUL
85/6 Kitchener Rangers

PENGELLY, DARCY
97/8 New Mexico Scorpions

PENICKA, LUBOMIR
82 Semic Sticker 94

PENK, JAN
94/5 APS 260
95/6 APS 133
97/8 APS 201
97/8 DS Sticker 233

PENKALA, CHIEF JOE
89/0 Saskatoon Blades

PENN, JOSH
98/9 Florida Everblades

PENN, SHAWN
97/8 Long Beach Ice Dogs
94/5 Toledo Storm
95/6 Toledo Storm
99/0 Utah Grizzlies

PENNANEN, OLLI
78/9 SM-Liiga 49

PENNANEN, PENTTI
66/7 Champion 136
70/1 Kuvajulkaisut 263

PENNELL, FRED
87/8 Sudbury Wolves
88/9 Sudbury Wolves

PENNER, ANDREW
01/2 Guelph Storm
01/2 Guelph Storm M-Cup

PENNER, JASON
00/1 UD Prospects 25
01/2 Peterborough Petes

PENNEY, CHAD
94/5 Classic 68, T48
94/5 Classic 4 Sport 145
93/4 Cla. Prospects 65
94/5 Leaf 241
94/5 Premier 267
90/1 7th..Sketch OHL 314
91/2 7th...Sketch OHL 58
93/4 Upper Deck 436
97/8 Kentucky Tho'blades
93/4 Soo Greyhounds 9

PENNEY, JACKSON
92/3 Canada Nationals
95/6 DEL 402
96/7 DEL 310
98/9 DEL 232
90/1 ProCards 115
01/2 UD DEL 236

PENNEY, RYAN
95/6 Slapshot 182

PENNEY, STEVE
86/7 Kraft Sports 79
84/5 O-Pee-Chee 269
85/6 OPC/Topps 4
86/7 O-Pee-Chee 222
85/6 OPC Sticker 126
83/4 MONT
84/5 MONT
85/6 MONT
85/6 MONT / Provigo
86/7 WINN
87/8 Moncton Hawks
83/4 Nova Scotia Voyageurs

PENNINGTON, CLIFF
45-64 BeeHive-2 [Bost.]
45-64 BeeHive-2 [Bost.]
64-67 BeeHive-3 [Bost.]
62/3 Cowan Tile
61/2 Shirriff 1
62/3 Topps 19
62/3 Topps 14

PENNISTON, DON
51/2 Laval Dairy 58

PENNOCK, BERKLEY
93/4 Red Deer Rebels

PENNOCK, TREVOR
91/2 Avant Garde BCJHL 126
90/1 7th..Sketch WHL 18

PENNOYER, ROB
92/3 BCJHL 128

PENSTOCK, BYRON
90/1 7th..Sketch WHL 247
91/2 7th...Sketch WHL 302
94/5 Slapshot Memorial 26
90/1 Brandon Wheat Kings
92/3 Brandon Wheat Kings

PENTON, SCOTT
93/4 Owen Sound Platers

PENTTILA, TIMO
80/1 Mallasjuoma 170

PENTTINEN, JUKKA
95/6 Sisu 258
96/7 Sisu 46
98/9 UD Elitserien 31

PEPEUNIG, GERHARD
79 Panini Sticker 308

PÉPIN, BOB
52/3 Laval Dairy Update 52
43-47 Parade Sportive
52/3 St. Lawrence 83

PEPIN, RENE
52/3 Bas du Fleuve 52
51/2 Laval Dairy 42
52/3 St. Lawrence 82

PEPLINSKI, JIM
83/4 Esso Stars
86/7 Kraft Sports 5
81/2 O-Pee-Chee 49
82/3 O-Pee-Chee 55
83/4 O-Pee-Chee 90
84/5 O-Pee-Chee 233
86/7 OPC/Topps 182
87/8 O-Pee-Chee 209
88/9 OPC/Topps 243
90/1 OPC/Topps 38
89/0 O-Pee-Chee 206
82/3 OPC/Topps Sticker 216
86/7 OPC Sticker 84-212
87/8 OPC Sticker 46
88/9 OPC Sticker 88-218
89/0 opcSticker 99-236
87/8 Panini Sticker 213
88/9 Panini Sticker 14
89/0 Panini Sticker 37
80/1 Pepsi Bottle Cap
82/3 Post [Calg.]
83/4 Souhaits Keychain [Flames]
82/3 Stater Mint 5
83/4 Vachon 16-136
80/1 CALG
81/2 CALG
82/3 CALG
85/6 CALG / Red Rooster
86/7 CALG / Red Rooster
87/8 CALG / Red Rooster

PEPPERALL, COLIN
97 Bowman 30
98 Bowman 19
98 Bowman Chrome 19
95/6 Slapshot 197
99/0 Hampton Roads
02/3 Manchester Storm

PEPPERALL, RYAN
95/6 Classic 46, 87
94/5 Slapshot / Kitchener 16
95/6 Slapshot 147, P
97/8 St. John's Maple Leafs
99/0 St. John's Maple Leafs

PERALA, OLLI-PEKKA
71/2 Williams Finnish 351

PERAOJA, SEPPO
70/1 Kuvajulkaisut 185

PERCIVAL, ROB
88/9 Brockville Braves

PERDIE, DENNIS
91 7th..Sketch Mem.Cup 120

PEREIRA, LENNY
94/5 Raleigh Icecaps

PEREYASLOV, MIKHAIL
98/9 Mir 63
99/0 Mir 112

PEREZ, DENIS
98/9 DEL 242
95 Panini Worlds 102
94 Semic 215
92 Semic Sticker 224
93 Semic Sticker 255
96 Wien 186

PEREZHOGIN, ALEXANDER
02/3 Russian Future Stars 7

PERHOMAA, PENTTI
70/1 Kuvajulkaisut 376
80/1 Mallasjuoma 95

PERHONMAA, MATTI
71/2 Williams Finnish 309

PERIARD, MICHEL
00/1 Rockford IceHogs

PÉRIARD, DOMINIC
00/1 Baie-Comeau 4

PÉRIARD, MICHEL
99 Bowman 70
99/0 Rimouski Océanic 23

PERILLAT, DUANE
00/1 Prince George Cougars

PERKINS, DARREN
90/1 7th..Sketch WHL 279
91/2 7th...Sketch WHL 244
93/4 Hampton Roads
94/5 Thunder Bay Senators
95/6 Thunder Bay Senators
93/4 Toledo Storm 12
94/5 Toledo Storm
90/1 Prince Albert Raiders
91/2 Prince Albert Raiders

PERKINS, ROSS
74/5 OPC WHA 39

PERKINS, TERRY
86/7 Fredericton Express
88/9 Salt Lake G'Eagles

PERKKIO, MARKKU
78/9 SM-Liiga 150

PERKOVIC, STEVEN
93/4 Hampton Roads

PERLINI, FRED
94/5 Guildford Flames 8
95/6 Guildford Flames 16
95/6 Guildford Flames 30
96/7 Guildford Flames 7

PERNA, DOMINIC
97 Bowman 49
98 Bowman 83, 163
98 Bowman Chrome 83, 163

PERNA, MIKE
93/4 Slapshot / Niagara Falls 24
95/6 Slapshot 202
98/9 Huntington Blizzard
99/0 Huntington Blizzard
02/3 Manchester Storm

PERONMOA, PETRI
96/7 Sisu 111

PERPICH, JOHN
90/1 WASH / Kodak

PERRAS, J.F.
01/2 Ottawa 67's 1

PERRAULT, JOCELYN
88/9 ProCards / Hershey

PERRAULT, JOËL
00/1 Baie-Comeau 2
01/2 Baie-Comeau 1
02/3 Baie-Comeau

PERRAULT, KELLY
00/1 Quad City Mallards

PERREAULT, ALBERT
37/8 World Wide Gum 115

PERREAULT, BOB (MICHE)
45-64 BeeHive-2 [Bost.]
45-64 BeeHive-2 [Bost.]
64-67 BeeHive-3 [Bost.]
62/3 Cowan Tile
62/3 Topps 2
62/3 Toronto Star Photo

PERREAULT, FERNAND
51/2 Cleveland Barons
51/2 Laval Dairy 98
52/3 Laval Dairy Update 38

PERREAULT, GERRY
51/2 Lac St-Jean 7

PERREAULT, GILBERT
02/3 Parkhurst ✄ VM2
02/3 Ultimate Mem. ✄ FS, ✄ Num, ✄ VGJ
02/3 UD Foundations ✍ SG
02/3 UD Piece ✄ HH, ✍ MD
01/2 ASG History
71/2 Bazooka Panel
01/2 BAP Mem. ✄ 500GS
70/1 Colgate 28
70/1 Dad's Cookies
82/3 Dernière Heure
70s Dernière Heure
70/1 Eddie Sargent 23
71/2 Eddie Sargent 19
72/3 Eddie Sargent 31
70/1 Esso Power Player
88/9 Esso All-Star
01/2 Fleer Greats 9, ✍ Aut.
01/2 Fleer Legacy 14, ✄ HK
83/4 Funmate Puffy 8 [w]
91/2 Future Trends C72 51, ✍ 51
92/3 Future Trends C76 162
84/5 Kellogg's 29
91/2 Kraft 80
74/5 Lipton Soup 2
74/5 Loblaws
70/1 O-Pee-Chee 131
71/2 O-Pee-Chee 60
71/2 O-Pee-Chee 246
71/2 O-Pee-Chee Book. 8
72/3 O-Pee-Chee 136
72/3 O-Pee-Chee TC
73/4 O-Pee-Chee 70
74/5 O-Pee-Chee 25
75/6 O-Pee-Chee 10
76/7 O-Pee-Chee 2
76/7 O-Pee-Chee 3
76/7 O-Pee-Chee 180
76/7 O-Pee-Chee 214
76/7 O-Pee-Chee 380
77/8 OPC 7
77/8 O-Pee-Chee 210
77/8 O-Pee-Chee NS 14
78/9 O-Pee-Chee 130
79/0 O-Pee-Chee 180
80/1 O-Pee-Chee 80
80/1 O-Pee-Chee 262
81/2 O-Pee-Chee 30
82/3 O-Pee-Chee 25
82/3 O-Pee-Chee 30
83/4 O-Pee-Chee 67
84/5 O-Pee-Chee 24
85/6 OPC/Topps 160
85/6 OPC/Topps Box K
86/7 OPC/Topps 79
71/2 O-Pee-Chee Poster 14
81/2 OPC Sticker 60
82/3 OPC/Topps Sticker 118
83/4 OPC/Topps Sticker 4
83/4 OPC/Topps Sticker 240
83/4 OPC/Topps Sticker 241
84/5 OPC Sticker 201
84/5 OPC Sticker 202
85/6 OPC Sticker 188
86/7 OPC Sticker 43-179
80/1 O-Pee-Chee Super 2
01/2 Parkhurst ✄ 500GS, ✄ H14, ✍ PA20
91/2 Pinnacle 394
81/2 Post 2
82/3 Post [Buff.]
91/2 Pro Set 596
90/1 Score 355
84/5 7-Eleven

85/6 7-Eleven Superstars 2
01/2 Signature ✂ 500GS, ✍ VA36
83/4 Souhaits Keychain [Sabres]
01/2 SP GU ✂ TotG, ✂ TotGSig
70/1 Topps 131
71/2 Topps 60
72/3 Topps 120
73/4 Topps 70
74/5 Topps 25
75/6 Topps 10
76/7 Topps 2
76/7 Topps 3
76/7 Topps 180
76/7 Topps 214
76/7 Topps NS 9
77/8 Topps 7
77/8 Topps 210
77/8 ToppsNS 14
78/9 Topps 130
79/0 Topps 180
80/1 Topps 80
80/1 Topps 262
84/5 Topps 19
71/2 Toronto Sun Photo
00/1 UD Heroes 121, ✂ GT, ✂ GC, ✍ SG
01/2 Ultimate Mem. ✂ 500GS, ✂ ASGH, ✂ CT, ✂ RN, ✂ UC, ✍ Aut.
00 ✂ UD APOH 500, ✂✍ 500
99/0 UD C. Legends 50
00/1 UD Legends 14, 18, ES11, ✍ ES
01/2 UD Legends 7, ✂ M, ✂ TT, ✍ ES
01/2 UD Vintage ✂ SD
95/6 Zellers
72/3 BUFF
73/4 BUFF
73/4 BUFF / Bells Market
74/5 BUFF
75/6 BUFF / Linnett
80/1 BUFF / Wendt's 4
81/2 BUFF / Wendt's 4
82/3 BUFF / Wendt's 7
84/5 BUFF / Blue Shield
85/6 BUFF / Blue Shield
86/7 BUFF / Blue Shield
93/4 BUFF / Noco

PERREAULT, KIRBY
90/1 Michigan Tech Huskies
91/2 Michigan Tech Huskies

PERREAULT, NICOLAS
94/5 Saint John Flames
95/6 Toledo Storm
93/4 Michigan State

PERREAULT, YANIC
02/3 Atomic 56
02/3 BAP Mem. 176
02/3 Calder ✂ GWJ 12
02/3 Exclusive 92
02/3 First Edition 276, 386
02/3 Heads Up 65, ✂ GWQ 15
02/3 McDonald's ✂ JP 7
02/3 O-Pee-Chee 133
02/3 Pacific 200, ✂ GWJ 26
02/3 Pacific Complete 414
02/3 Parkhurst 176
02/3 Parkhurst Retro 89
02/3 Pr. Stock Reserve 54
02/3 PS Titanium 56, ✂ GWJ 35
02/3 Quest for the Cup 51
02/3 Signature 42, ✍ 42
02/3 SP Authentic 49
02/3 Sports Vault 57
02/3 Topps 133, HHC17
02/3 To. Limited 133
02/3 To. Total 146
02/3 Upper Deck 339
02/3 UD Classic 52
02/3 UD MVP 94
02/3 UD Vintage 131, 276
02/3 Vanguard 56, ✂ GWJ 24
02/3 Victory 112
01/2 Adrenaline 97
91/2 Arena 31
01/2 Atomic 52
98/9 Aurora 87
99/0 Aurora 137
98/9 Be A Player 62, ✍ Aut. 62
99/0 BAP Mem. 121
00/1 BAP Mem. 292
01/2 BAP Mem. 141
01/2 Bowman 101
91/2 Classic 39
91/2 Classic Four Sport 39
93/4 Cla. Prospects 113
01/2 Crown Royale 77
95/6 Donruss 375
96/7 Donruss 21
96/7 Do. Canadian 76
96/7 Do. Elite 76
97/8 Do. Priority 142
98/9 Dynagon Ice 89
95/6 Edge Ice 184, C-8, QM-3
95/6 Fleer Metal 73
95/6 Fleer Ultra 253
96/7 Kraft / KD
99/0 Kraft / PB
95/6 Leaf 249
96/7 Leaf 7
96/7 L. Preferred 107
96/7 Maggers 81
98/9 NHL Power Play
01/2 O-Pee-Chee 224
97/8 Omega 111
98/9 Pacific 243
99/0 Pacific 414
00/1 Pacific 397
01/2 Pacific 370
97/8 Pa. Crown Roy. 64
98/9 Pa. Crown Roy. 64
97/8 Pa. Invincible R-97
98/9 Pa. Paramount 106
99/0 Pa. Paramount 228
00/1 Pa. Paramount 232
97/8 Pa. Revolution 65
98/9 Panini Photocard
96/7 Panini Sticker 272
99/0 Panini Sticker 158
00/1 Panini Sticker 100
94/5 Parkhurst 230
95/6 Parkhurst 372
01/2 Parkhurst 234
96/7 Pinnacle 42
97/8 Pi. BeeHive 35
95/6 Pi. Summit 166
95/6 Pi. Zenith 113
96/7 Pi. Zenith 86
00/1 Pr. Stock ✂ GUG 97
01/2 Pr. Stock 49
00/1 PS Titanium ✂ GUG 46
01/2 PS Titanium 73
91/2 ProCards 339
92/3 Score 487
96/7 Score 25
92 7th...Sketch Awards 22
92 7th...Sketch Awards 30
90/1 7th..Sketch LHJMQ 100
91 7th..Sketch Mem.Cup 115
97/8 SP Authentic 75, ✍ SotT
00/1 Stadium 178
91/2 Star Pics 22
95/6 Topps 223
00/1 Topps 268
01/2 Topps 224
99/0 T. Gold Label 81
98/9 UD Choice 96
01/2 UD PlayMakers Ltd 52
91/2 Ultimate Draft Pick 34, 54, 87, ✍ Aut.
92/3 Upper Deck 70
95/6 Upper Deck 28, SE-130
96/7 Upper Deck 79
98/9 Upper Deck 105
00/1 Upper Deck 164
01/2 Upper Deck 321
95/6 UD BAP 150, ✍ S150
97/8 UD Black Diam. 127
96/7 UD CC 126
98/9 UD G. Reserve 105
01/2 UD Mask 48
01/2 Vanguard 50
99/0 Victory 290
97/8 Zenith 64, Z29
01/2 MONT
02/3 MONT
99/0 TORO / Pizza Pizza 19
94/5 Phoenix Roadrunners
92/3 St. John's Maple Leafs
93/4 St. John's Maple Leafs
00/1 St. John's Maple Leafs

PERRETT, CRAIG
91/2 Air Canada SJHL C34

PERRICONE, ERIC
99/0 Odessa Jackalopes

PERRIER, BRYANT
89/0 ProCards IHL 100

PERRIN, ERIC
02/3 Cardset 245
00/1 Cardset 347
97/8 Cleveland Lumberjacks
97/8 Cleveland Lumberjacks
98/9 Kansas City Blades 7
99/0 Kansas City Blades

PERRON, JEAN
84/5 MONT
85/6 MONT
85/6 MONT / Provigo
86/7 MONT
87/8 MONT
87/8 MONT / Vachon 7
87/8 MONT / Vachon 10

PERROTT, NATHAN
01/2 BAP Mem. 442
95/6 Classic 39
01/2 Parkhurst 324
01/2 PS Titanium Draft 144
95/6 Slapshot 236
01/2 UD Premier 68
99/0 Cleveland Lumberjacks
98/9 Indianapolis Ice
01/2 Milwaukee Admirals
96/7 Soo Greyhounds

PERRY, ALAN
88/9 ProCards / Indianapolis
92/3 Oklahoma City Blazers

PERRY, BRIAN
69/0 O-Pee-Chee 84

PERRY, COREY
01/2 London Knights

PERRY, DON
78/9 Saginaw Gears

PERRY, JEFF
90/1 7th..Sketch OHL 292
94/5 Saint John Flames
95/6 Saint John Flames
96/7 Saint John Flames
97/8 Saint John Flames

PERRY, RANDY
97 Bowman 96
98/9 DEL 221
99/0 Eishockey 207
00/1 Kudos 74
01/2 Louisiana Ice Gators
93/4 Lethbridge Hurricanes
95/6 Lethbridge Hurricanes

PERRY, ROBERT
71/2 Toronto Sun Photo

PERRY, SEAN
96/7 Johnstown Chiefs

PERRY, TOM
91/2 Air Canada SJHL B10
92/3 MPS SJHL 35
99/0 Colorado Gold Kings
97/8 Quad City Mallards

PERRY, TYLER
00/1 Austin Ice Bats
97/8 Kamloops Blazers

PERSCHAU, DIRK
94/5 DEL 44
95/6 DEL 32
96/7 DEL 26

PERSHIN, EDUARD
98/9 Cleveland Lumberjacks

PERSIGEHL, DAVE
93/4 Huntington Blizzard

PERSSON, HAKAN
92/3 Semic Elitserien 256

PERSSON, JERRY
94/5 Leaf Elit Set 257
95/6 Leaf Elit Set 199
91/2 Semic Elitserien 294
92/3 Semic Elitserien 311
98/9 UD Elitserien 107

PERSSON, JOAKIM
96/7 DEL 92
94/5 Leaf Elit Set 192, RR-7
95/6 Leaf Elit Set 4, S-1
89/0 Semic Elitserien 43
90/1 Semic Elitserien 191, 274
91/2 Semic Elitserien 46
91/2 Semic Elitserien 55
95/6 UD Elitserien 1, NA1
97/8 UD Elitserien 182

PERSSON, MIKAEL
92/3 Semic Elitserien 315

PERSSON, NIKLAS
99/0 UD Elitserien 110, 209
00/1 UD Elitserien 115

PERSSON, RICARD
95/6 Donruss 304
94/5 Leaf Elit Set 55
97/8 Pa. Invincible R-172
99/0 Pa. Paramount 199
96/7 Pi. Be A Player 210, ✍ Aut. 210
89/0 Semic Elitserien 126
90/1 Semic Elitserien 203
91/2 Semic Elitserien 132
92/3 Semic Elitserien 156
95/6 To. Stadium 225
00/1 UD Heroes 83
00/1 OTTA
01/2 OTTA
99/0 SLOU / Taco Bell 11

PERSSON, STEFAN
00/1 Alfabilder
78/9 O-Pee-Chee 144
79/0 O-Pee-Chee 32
80/1 O-Pee-Chee 219
81/2 O-Pee-Chee 206
82/3 O-Pee-Chee 209
83/4 O-Pee-Chee 15
84/5 O-Pee-Chee 133
82/3 Post [NYIs.]
89/0 Semic Elitserien 112
90/1 Semic Elitserien 118
83/4 Souhaits Keychain [Islanders]
78/9 Topps 144
79/0 Topps 32
80/1 Topps 219
81/2 Topps 92 [East]
84/5 Topps 99
00/1 UD Vintage ✂ D-POH
79/0 NYIS
83/4 NYIS / News 20
84/5 NYIS / News 24

PERSSON, TORBJÖRN
94/5 Leaf Elit Set 132
90/1 Semic Elitserien 122
91/2 Semic Elitserien 123
92/3 Semic Elitserien 142

PERTHALER, CHRISTIAN
93 Semic Sticker 283

PERTTULA, ANTTI
70/1 Kuvajulkaisut 184
71/2 Williams Finnish 140
72/3 Williams Finnish 202
73/4 Williams Finnish 165

PERTTULA, PEKKA
65/6 Hellas 142

PERVUKHIN, VASILI
79 Panini Sticker 143
82 Semic Sticker 55
79/0 Soviet Stars 12
83/4 Soviet Stars
87/8 Soviet Stars

PESAN, FILIP
99/0 Score 80

PESAT, IVO
94/5 APS 229
95/6 APS 4
96/7 APS 215
97/8 APS 29
99/0 DS 128
00/1 DS 14
98/9 OFS 340
99/0 OFS 544
00/1 OFS 321
01/2 OFS 61, -H8

PESCHKE, FRANK
94/5 DEL 396
95/6 DEL 417

PESETTI, RON
87/8 Moncton Hawks

PESONEN, JUSSI
02/3 Cardset 246
99/0 Cardset 278
00/1 Cardset 50

PESOUT, MARTIN
99/0 OFS 131
00/1 OFS 159

PEST, TREVOR
91/2 Nanaimo Clippers

PESTUKA, IVO
99/0 OFS 287
00/1 OFS 262

PESUT, GEORGE
75/6 O-Pee-Chee 360

PETAJAAHO, SAKARI
80/1 Mallasjuoma 57

PETAWABANO, RODNEY
91/2 7th...Sketch LHJMQ 83

PETENDRA, KEVIN
82/3 Kitchener Rangers

PETEREK, JAN
94/5 APS 137
95/6 APS 305
97/8 APS 331
99/0 Cardset 157
00/1 DS 155
96/7 DS Sticker 201
97/8 DS Sticker 283
98/9 OFS 186
99/0 OFS 300, 524
00/1 OFS 278

PETERNOUSEK, GEORGE
79 Panini Sticker 277

PETERS, ANDREW
98 Bowman 150, ✍ A33
98 Bowman Chrome 150
00/1 Rochester Americans
02/3 Rochester Americans

PETERS, DAN
02/3 Philadelphia Phantoms

PETERS, DIETMAR
74 Hellas MM-Jenkki 104
70/1 Kuvajulkaisut 93
79 Panini Sticker 250

PETERS, FRANK
28/9 Paulins Candy 47

PETERS, GARRY
95/6 Classic 89
65/6 Coca-Cola
70/1 Eddie Sargent 151
70/1 Esso Power Player
68/9 O-Pee-Chee 99
69/0 O-Pee-Chee 171
70/1 O-Pee-Chee 196
65/6 Topps 28
68/9 Topps 99
71/2 BOST
70/1 PHIL

PETERS, GEOFF
95/6 Bowman P26
95/6 Cla. Vis. Signings 67, ✍ Aut.
95/6 Slapshot 190, 440
95/6 Upper Deck 522
99/0 Cleveland Lumberjacks
02/3 Manchester Storm

PETERS, JAMES M. (JIM)
45-64 BeeHive-2 [Bost.]
45-64 BeeHive-2 [Detr.]
45-64 BeeHive-2 [Chic.]
43-47 Parade Sportive
51/2 Parkhurst 41
52/3 Parkhurst 35
53/4 Parkhurst 69
45-54 Quaker Oats

PETERS, JAMES S. (JIM)
70/1 Eddie Sargent 77
69/0 O-Pee-Chee 143
72/3 O-Pee-Chee 224
73/4 O-Pee-Chee 231

PETERS, JASON
91/2 Avant Garde BCJHL 134
90/1 7th..Sketch WHL 251
90/1 Saskatoon Blades
89/0 Victoria Cougars

PETERS, JIM*
93/4 Birmingham Bulls
93/4 Dayton Bombers

PETERS, JON
99/0 Guelph Storm

PETERS, ROB
95/6 Dayton Bombers

PETERS, ROLAND
74 Hellas MM-Jenkki 103
79 Panini Sticker 254

PETERS, TONY
92/3 Dayton Bombers

PETERS, WARREN
99/0 UD Prospects 38
00/1 Saskatoon Blades

PETERSEN, TOBY
02/3 First Edition 113, ✂ Jers.
02/3 Heads Up ✂ GWQ 22
02/3 Pacific 314
02/3 PS Titanium ✂ GWJ 55
01/2 BAP Mem. 122
01/2 Crown Royale RR 18
01/2 PS Titanium Draft ✂ 82
01/2 Signature 244, ✍ Aut. 244
98/9 UD Choice 307
01/2 Upper Deck 372
97/8 UD Black Diam. 135
00/1 WBS Penguins
02/3 WBS Penguins

PETERSON, BRENT
01/2 UD DEL 133

PETERSON, BRENT*
86/7 Kraft Sports 67
83/4 O-Pee-Chee 68
84/5 O-Pee-Chee 25
85/6 OPC/Topps 47
86/7 O-Pee-Chee 251
87/8 O-Pee-Chee 263
85/6 OPC Sticker 178-48
86/7 OPC Sticker 100-229
87/8 OPC Sticker 199-58
91/2 7th...Sketch WHL 47
83/4 Souhaits Keychain [Sabres]
82/3 BUFF / Wendt's 17
84/5 BUFF / Blue Shield
80/1 DETR
88/9 HART / Jr. Whalers
85/6 VANC
86/7 VANC
93/4 Portland Winter Hawks
97/8 Portland Winter Hawks

PETERSON, BRENT**
95/6 Classic 78, ✍ Aut.
95/6 Cla. 5 Sport 148
95/6 Atlanta Knights
98/9 Cleveland Lumberjacks
97/8 Milwaukee Admirals
99/0 Milwaukee Admirals
91/2 Michigan Tech Huskies

PETERSON, CORY
94/5 SR Auto-Phonex 32, ✍ 32
99/0 Asheville Smoke
99/0 Asheville Smoke

PETERSON, KYLE
97/8 New Orleans Brass

PETERSON, MARK
86/7 Moncton G'Flames

PETHKE, MARC
94/5 DEL 192
95/6 DEL 171
96/7 DEL 113
98/9 DEL 10
00/1 UD DEL 239

PETIQUAY, DANIEL
00/1 Rimouski Océanic 12
01/2 Rimouski Océanic 11

PETIT, MICHEL
90/1 Bowman 170
91/2 Bowman 158
92/3 Bowman 101
92/3 Durivage 43
94/5 Leaf 444
87/8 O-Pee-Chee 262
90/1 OPC/Topps 271
91/2 O-Pee-Chee 166
92/3 O-Pee-Chee 185
89/0 O-Pee-Chee 251
87/8 OPC Sticker 196-55
87/8 Panini Sticker 342
88/9 Panini Sticker 304
89/0 Panini Sticker 283, 291
90/1 Panini Sticker 148
91/2 Panini Sticker 98
91/2 Parkhurst 252
93/4 Parkhurst 304
94/5 Parkhurst 39
91/2 Pinnacle 49
92/3 Pinnacle 206
93/4 Power Play 308
93/4 Premier 141
94/5 Premier 406
90/1 Pro Set 256, 539
91/2 Pro Set 492
90/1 Score 187, 54T
91/2 Score 103
91/2 Score CAN 103
92/3 Score 38
93/4 Score 275
92/3 Topps 337
91/2 To. Stadium 311
92/3 To. Stadium 195
93/4 To. Stadium 232
90/1 Upper Deck 181
91/2 Upper Deck 359
93/4 Upper Deck 66
92/3 CALG / IGA 013
98/9 PHOE / Coca-Cola
89/0 QUÉB
89/0 QUÉB / Gene. Foods
89/0 QUÉB / Police
90/1 QUÉB
90/1 QUÉB / Petro-Canada
90/1 TORO
91/2 TORO / P.L.A.Y. 18
83/4 VANC
84/5 VANC
86/7 VANC
85/6 Fredericton Express

PETITCLERC, MAXIME
91/2 7th...Sketch LHJMQ 291

PETLAK, DAVID
99/0 OFS 80
00/1 OFS 196

PETOVKA, VLADIMIR
91 Semic Sticker 124

PETRAKOV, ANDREI
98/9 Mir 131
99/0 Mir 12
00/1 Mir 271
98/9 Fort Wayne Komets
00/1 Metallurg 39

PETRASEK, DAVID
97/8 UD Elitserien 87
98/9 UD Elitserien 101
99/0 UD Elitserien 87
00/1 UD Elitserien 136

PETRASH, KEN
94/5 DEL 231
95/6 DEL 228
96/7 DEL 79

PETRÉ, HENRIK
98/9 UD Choice 292
97/8 UD Black Diam. 67
98/9 UD Elitserien 217
99/0 UD Elitserien 21
00/1 UD Elitserien 30

PETRENKO, SERGEI
93/4 Classic 91
93/4 Donruss 43
99/0 DS 179
93/4 Fleer Ultra 275
93/4 Leaf 425
99/0 Mir 201
99/0 OFS 230
93/4 Parkhurst 292
92/3 Red Ace Violet 26
93 Semic Sticker 139
93/4 To. Stadium 373
92/3 Upper Deck 346
93/4 Upper Deck 450
93/4 Rochester Americans

PETRIC, JEFF
95/6 Dayton Bombers

PETRILAINEN, PASI
02/3 Cardset 247
98/9 Cardset 214
99/0 Cardset 319
97/8 Hockey-Box
95/6 Sisu 110
96/7 Sisu 127
98/9 UD Choice 279
95/6 Upper Deck 550
97/8 UD Black Diam. 48
00/1 UD Elitserien 166

PETROCHININ, EVGENI
00/1 Mir 378

PETROCHININ, YEVGENY
99/0 Mir 193, 225

PETRONI, PIERRE
91/2 7th...Sketch LHJMQ 23

PETROV, ALEXEI
00/1 Mir 294

PETROV, NIKOLAY
79 Panini Sticker 349

PETROV, OLEG
02/3 Exclusive 93
02/3 First Edition 277
02/3 O-Pee-Chee 84
02/3 Pacific 201
02/3 Pacific Complete 323
02/3 Parkhurst Retro 143
02/3 Topps 84
02/3 To. Limited 84
02/3 To. Total 109
02/3 UD MVP 97
02/3 Victory 113
01/2 Adrenaline 98
94/5 Classic AR4
92/3 Classic Prospects 8
93/4 Cla. Prospects 177
93/4 Donruss 452
94/5 Donruss 61
94/5 Flair 90
94/5 Fleer Ultra 314
93/4 Leaf 260
94/5 Leaf 354
92/3 OPC Premier 96
00/1 Pacific 211
01/2 Pacific 210
94/5 Panini Sticker B
92/3 Parkhurst 486
94/5 Parkhurst 119, 291
94/5 Parkie SE seV40
93/4 Pinnacle 212
94/5 Pinnacle 203
94/5 POG 138
93/4 Power Play 371
94/5 Premier 377, OF-13
92/3 Red Ace Violet 27
93/4 Score 459
94/5 Score 260
01/2 Signature 63, ✍ Aut. 63
94/5 To. Stadium 241
93/4 Upper Deck 84
94/5 Upper Deck 137, SP-41
95/6 Upper Deck 343
01/2 Upper Deck 92
01/2 UD Challenge 46
01/2 UD MVP 98
01/2 UD Vintage 132
01/2 Victory 188
92/3 MONT
92/3 MONT / OPC 56
94/5 MONT
95/6 MONT
00/1 MONT
01/2 MONT
02/3 MONT
92/3 Fredericton Canadiens
93/4 Fredericton Canadiens

PETROV, SERGEI
01/2 Rockford IceHogs
93/4 Minnesota-Duluth

PETROV, VLADIMIR
91/2 Future Trends C72 52
95 Globe 242
72 Hellas MM-Jenkki 75
74 Hellas MM-Jenkki 53
70/1 Kuvajulkaisut 11
69/0 Mästär Serien 28
80 Olympic USSR
79 Panini Sticker 147
72 Semic Sticker 16
74 Semic Sticker 35
69/0 Soviet Stars
70/1 Soviet Stars
71/2 Soviet Stars
73/4 Soviet Stars 7
73/4 Soviet Stars 9
74/5 Soviet Stars 12
79/0 Soviet Stars 14
77-79 Sportscaster 102-14
77-79 Sports. FIN 26-673
71/2 Williams Finnish 12
72/3 Williams Finnish 31
73/4 Williams Finnish 13

PETROVICKY, ROB.
92/3 Classic 6
93/4 Classic 144
92/3 Classic Four Sport 156
93/4 Cla. 4 Sport 245
93/4 Donruss 145
98/9 EBK IHL All-Star
92/3 Fleer Ultra 302
93/4 Fleer Ultra 337
93/4 Leaf 187
94/5 Leaf 387
92/3 OPC Premier 36
97/8 Pa. Dynagon BKS-82
97/8 Panini Sticker 166
92/3 Parkhurst 61
93/4 Parkhurst 89
94/5 Parkhurst 94
92/3 Pinnacle 402
93/4 Power Play 107
93/4 Score 277
97/8 Score SLou. 9
94 Semic 210
93 Semic Sticker 106
92/3 Upper Deck 569
92/3 Upper Deck ER20
93/4 Upper Deck 37, SP-63
94/5 Upper Deck 361
97/8 Upper Deck 350
94/5 UD BAP R84
91/2 Upper Deck WJC 93
96 Wien 233
92/3 HART / Dairymart
00/1 Chicago Wolves
98/9 Grand Rapids Griffins

PETROVICKY, RONALD
00/1 BAP Mem. 478
01/2 BAP Mem. 235
98 Bowman 78
98 Bowman Chrome 78
00/1 Premier Plus 140
00/1 PS Titanium Draft 154
01/2 Signature 55, ✍ Aut. 55
00/1 SP Authentic 138
00/1 SPx 133
01/2 Victory 365
97/8 Regina Pats

PETROVKA, VLADIMIR
96/7 APS 381
97/8 APS 91
98/9 DS 47
97/8 DS Sticker 98
98/9 OFS 9

PETRUIC, JEFF
90/1 7th..Sketch WHL 151
91/2 7th...Sketch WHL 281

PETRUK, RANDY
95/6 Bowman P27
97 Bowman 82
98 Bowman 42, SC10
98 Bowman Chrome 42
94/5 Slapshot Memorial 23
95/6 Upper Deck 524
99/0 Cincinnati Cyclones
98/9 Florida Everblades
01/2 Florida Everblades
96/7 Kamloops Blazers
97/8 Kamloops Blazers

PETRUNIN, ANDREI
95/6 Classic 66, ✍ Aut.
00/1 Mir 170
92 Québec Pee Wee 1774
94/5 SP 190
95/6 SP 178
95/6 Upper Deck 556
96/7 UD Ice 143
99/0 Muskegon Fury

PETTERESSON, DANIEL
89/0 Semic Elitserien 208

PETTERLE, BRIAN
80/1 Soo Greyhounds

PETTERSEN, ERIK
92/3 Semic Nordisk 133

PETTERSSON, ANDERS
89/0 Semic Elitserien 132

PETTERSSON, HAKAN
72 Hellas MM-Jenkki 40
74 Hellas MM-Jenkki 33
72 Semic Sticker 66
71/2 Williams Finnish 57
72/3 Williams Finnish 55

PETTERSSON, HANS
89/0 Semic Elitserien 222
90/1 Semic Elitserien 58

PETTERSSON, HENRIK
92/3 Semic Elitserien 292

PETTERSSON, JÖRGEN
83/4 Funmate Puffy 15 [w/]
81/2 O-Pee-Chee 296
82/3 O-Pee-Chee 309
83/4 O-Pee-Chee 318
84/5 O-Pee-Chee 189
81/2 OPC Sticker 135
82/3 OPC/Topps Sticker 202
83/4 OPC/Topps Sticker 123
84/5 OPC Sticker 59
82/3 Post [SLou.]
89/0 Semic Elitserien 280
82 Semic Sticker 152
81/2 Topps 121 [West]
85/6 HART / Jr. Whalers
92/3 SLOU / McDon. 18
86/7 WASH / Police

PETTERSSON, LARS-GUNNAR
89/0 Semic Elitserien 157
90/1 Semic Elitserien 236
91/2 Semic Elitserien 166
92/3 Semic Elitserien 191
89 Semic Sticker 25

PETTERSSON, MARTIN
89/0 Semic Elitserien 206

PETTERSSON, MATTIAS
99/0 UD Elitserien 1

PETTERSSON, MIKAEL
94/5 Leaf Elit Set 239
95/6 Leaf Elit Set 134
92/3 Semic Elitserien 237
92/3 Semic Elitserien 289
95/6 UD Elitserien 196
97/8 UD Elitserien 189
98/9 UD Elitserien 175, 189
99/0 UD Elitserien 177, 193

PETTERSSON, OVE
89/0 Semic Elitserien 176
90/1 Semic Elitserien 9

PETTERSSON, PETER
95/6 UD Elitserien DS15

PETTERSSON, RONNIE
90/1 Semic Elitserien 283
97/8 UD Elitserien 36
98/9 UD Elitserien 205
98/9 UD Elitserien 51

PETTERSSON, TOMMY
90/1 Semic Elitserien 22
91/2 Semic Elitserien 223
99/0 UD Elitserien 181
00/1 UD Elitserien 159

PETTINEN, TOMI
02/3 BAP All-Star 110
02/3 BAP Mem. 376
02/3 Cardset 93
02/3 SP Authentic 151
02/3 SPx 169
02/3 T. Chrome 158
02/3 To. Total 408
02/3 UD Honor 159
02/3 UD Mask 121
02/3 UD Top Shelf 96
99/0 Cardset 249
00/1 Cardset 33

PETTINGER, GORD
34-43 BeeHive-1 [Detr.]
37/8 World Wide Gum 76

PETTINGER, MATT
02/3 SP Authentic 135
02/3 SP Game-Used ✂ FF
02/3 Upper Deck 421, ✂ BF
01/2 BAP Mem. 245
01/2 O-Pee-Chee 299
01/2 Parkhurst 202
01/2 PS Titanium Draft 171
94 Québec Pee Wee 1655
00/1 SP Authentic 125
01/2 Stadium ✂ SCS
01/2 Topps 299
01/2 To. Reserve ✂ TR
00/1 Upper Deck 196
00/1 UD Black Diam. 61
00/1 UD Ice 41, 80
00/1 UD MVP 209
99/0 UD Prospects 43
00/1 Victory 280
01/2 Victory 390
00/1 Portland Pirates

PETZ, RYAN
91/2 7th...Sketch WHL 323
96/7 Johnstown Chiefs

PEYTON, CHRIS
95/6 Halifax Moosehead

PHAIR, LYLE
88/9 ProCards / New Haven

PHELPS, CHRIS
90/1 7th..Sketch OHL 115
91/2 7th...Sketch OHL 27
94/5 Hampton Roads
95/6 Hampton Roads
96/7 Hampton Roads
97/8 Hampton Roads
98/9 Hampton Roads
98/9 Hampton Roads

PHILIP, JOCHEN
74 Hellas MM-Jenkki 118

PHILIPP, RADEK
98/9 OFS 118
99/0 OFS 301, 428
00/1 OFS 246
01/2 OFS 28

PHILIPP, RAINER
79 Panini Sticker 108
72 Semic Sticker 109

PHILIPS, CHRIS
95/6 Future Legends ✍ HP-1

PHILIPS, GUY
98/9 DEL 117

PHILLIP, MARSHALL
92/3 Dayton Bombers

PHILLIP, RADEK
01/2 DS 8

PHILLIPOFF, HAROLD
79/0 O-Pee-Chee 27
79/0 Topps 27
77/8 ATLF
78/9 ATLF / Colour

PHILLIPS, BILL
28/9 La Presse
33/4 O-Pee-Chee 43

PHILLIPS, CHRIS
02/3 First Edition 100, ✂ Jers.
02/3 Pacific 271
02/3 Pacific Complete 174
02/3 Signature ✂ DW8
02/3 Sports Vault 99
02/3 To. Total 76
02/3 Ultimate Mem. ✂ FO
96/7 All-Sport PPF 72
98/9 Aurora 132
00/1 BAP Mem. 372
95/6 Bowman P28
97 Bowman 105
95/6 Do. Elite WJ 7
97/8 Do. Elite 64
97/8 Do. Preferred 149, 197
97/8 Do. Priority 180
97/8 Do. Studio 103
97/8 Leaf 156, 198
97/8 Limited 80, FG-42
97/8 McDonald's McD-37
99/0 Millenium 169, ✍ Aut. 169
99/0 NHL Power Play
98/9 Pacific 314
00/1 Pacific 284
01/2 Pacific 277
97/8 Pa. Crown Roy. 92
97/8 Pa. Dynagon Rookie
97/8 Pa. Paramount 127
98/9 Pa. Paramount 165
97/8 Pinnacle 5
97/8 Pi. Be A Player 219, ✍ Aut. 219
97/8 Pi. Certified B
97/8 Score 71
01/2 Signature 7, ✍ Aut. 7
95/6 SP 176
97/8 SP Authentic 187, I22
98/9 UD Choice 143
98/9 UD3 13, 73, 133
95/6 Upper Deck 517
97/8 Upper Deck 325
98/9 Upper Deck 22, 140
99/0 Upper Deck 264
96/7 UD Black Diam. 57
97/8 UD Black Diam. 28
97/8 UD Coll. Choice 301
98/9 UD G. Reserve 22, 140
99/0 UD G. Reserve 264
96/7 UD Ice 137
97/8 UD Ice 47
98/9 UD MVP 144
99/0 UD Retro 56
99/0 Victory 208
97/8 Zenith 89
97/8 OTTA
98/9 OTTA
99/0 OTTA
00/1 OTTA
01/2 OTTA
02/3 OTTA
95/6 Prince Albert Raiders

PHILLIPS, GREG
99/0 Lowell Lock Monsters
00/1 Lowell Lock Monsters

PHILLIPS, GUY
88/9 ProCards / Saginaw
90/1 ProCards 42
93/4 Richmond Renegades
84/5 Medicine Hat Tigers

PHILLIPS, JASON
85/6 Brandon Wheat Kings

PHILLIPS, JONATHAN
01/2 Cardiff Devils

PHILLIPS, ROB
91/2 Air Canada SJHL B5
92/3 MPS SJHL 117
97/8 Peoria Rivermen

PHILLIPS, RYAN
98/9 Topeka Scarecrows
92/3 Tacoma Rockets
93/4 Tacoma Rockets

PHILLIPS, STEVE
02/3 Plymouth Whalers

PHILLIPS, TOMMY
83 HHOF Postcard N13
83&87 HHOF 208

PHILPOTT, DAVID
01/2 Moncton Wildcats 15

PICARD, ALEXANDRE
99 Québec Pee Wee 669

PICARD, JEAN-FRANÇOIS
90/1 7th..Sketch LHJMQ 121
99/0 Colorado Gold Kings

PICARD, MICHEL
92/3 Bowman 437
94/5 Cla. Images 67
95/6 Donruss 328
95/6 Edge Ice 49, QM-7
92/3 Fleer Ultra 404
95/6 Leaf 289
92/3 O-Pee-Chee 179
91/2 OPC Premier 20
91/2 Parkhurst 56
91/2 Pinnacle 327
91/2 Pro Set 538
89/0 ProCards AHL 297
90/1 ProCards 172
91/2 Score 317
91/2 Score CAN 347
92/3 Topps 439
92/3 To. Stadium 119
91/2 Upper Deck 48
01/2 UD DEL 172
91/2 HART / Jr. Whalers
96/7 Grand Rapids Griffins
97/8 Grand Rapids Griffins
99/0 Grand Rapids Griffins
02/3 Grand Rapids Griffins
93/4 Portland Pirates

PICARD, NATHALIE
94/5 Classic W14

PICARD, NOEL
70/1 Colgate 88
70/1 Dad's Cookies
70/1 Eddie Sargent 190
71/2 Eddie Sargent 180
72/3 Eddie Sargent 185
70/1 Esso Power Player
69/0 O-Pee-Chee 175
70/1 O-Pee-Chee 212
71/2 O-Pee-Chee 224
72/3 O-Pee-Chee 180
94/5 Parkie Tall 69
68/9 Shirriff / SLou. 7
71/2 Toronto Sun Photo
72/3 ATLF
71/2 SLOU
92/3 SLOU / McDon. 6

PICARD, ROBERT
77/8 Dernière Heure
79/0 Dernière Heure
78/9 O-Pee-Chee 39
79/0 O-Pee-Chee 91
80/1 O-Pee-Chee 255
81/2 O-Pee-Chee 189
82/3 O-Pee-Chee 190
84/5 O-Pee-Chee 345
85/6 O-Pee-Chee 215
87/8 O-Pee-Chee 248
89/0 O-Pee-Chee 261
85/6 OPC Sticker 252-132
86/7 OPC Sticker 30-170
87/8 OPC Sticker 230-97
89/0 opcSticker 190-44
79 Panini Sticker 55
87/8 Panini Sticker 160
89/0 Panini Sticker 333
80/1 Pepsi Bottle Cap
82/3 Post [Mont.]
78/9 Topps 39
79/0 Topps 91
80/1 Topps 255
83/4 Vachon 135-15
81/2 MONT
82/3 MONT
82/3 MONT / Steinberg
85/6 QUÉB
85/6 QUÉB / Gene. Foods
85/6 QUÉB / McDonald's
86/7 QUÉB
86/7 QUÉB / Gene. Foods
86/7 QUÉB / Yum Yum
87/8 QUÉB / Gene. Foods
87/8 QUÉB / Yum Yum
88/9 QUÉB
88/9 QUÉB / Gene. Foods
89/0 QUÉB
89/0 QUÉB / Gene. Foods
89/0 QUÉB / Police
80/1 TORO
78/9 WASH
79/0 WASH
83/4 WINN
84/5 WINN / Safety Tips

PICCARRETO, BRANDON
91/2 7th...Sketch LHJMQ 176

PICHAL, JAROMIR
99/0 Score 133

PICHETTE, DAVE
81/2 Dernière Heure
81/2 O-Pee-Chee 280
82/3 O-Pee-Chee 289
83/4 O-Pee-Chee 299
85/6 OPC/Topps 21
85/6 OPC Sticker 63-190
89/0 ProCards AHL 169
84/5 NJER
80/1 QUÉB
81/2 QUÉB
82/3 QUÉB
83/4 QUÉB
89/0 Halifax Citadels

PICHETTE, JEAN-JACQUES
52/3 Anonymous 7?
52/3 Bas du Fleuve 28

PICHETTE, JEAN-MARC
51/2 Lac St-Jean 10

PICKARD, ALLAN W.
83 HHOF Postcard N14
83&87 HHOF 209

PICKARD, JIM
83/4 NYIS / News 30
84/5 NYIS / News 31

PICKARD, PAUL
93/4 Huntington Blizzard
94/5 Huntington Blizzard

PICKELL, DOUG
89/0 ProCards IHL 201
88/9 Salt Lake G'Eagles
85/6 Kamloops Blazers
86/7 Kamloops Blazers
87/8 Kamloops Blazers

PICKETTS, HAL
33-35 Diamond Match Silv.

PICKFORD, WARREN
91/2 Air Canada SJHL C16
92/3 MPS SJHL 115

PICKLES, ANDY
98/9 Guildford Flames

PIECECHTEL, JAROMIR
94/5 APS 278

PIECKO, JAN
79 Panini Sticker 134

PIEN, CHENG KE
79 Panini Sticker 356

PIERCE, RANDY
79/0 O-Pee-Chee 137
80/1 O-Pee-Chee 340
79/0 Topps 137
79/0 COLR
84/5 HART / Jr. Whalers

PIERSOL, MIKE
91/2 7th...Sketch WHL 159
92/3 Tacoma Rockets
93/4 Tacoma Rockets

PIERSON, BOB
83/4 Brantford Alexanders

PIERSON, JOHN
91/2 BOST / SA Legends

PIETILA, MIKA
02/3 Nottingham Panthers

PIETILÄ, MIKA
00/1 Cardset 150, Mask. 1
95/6 Sisu 216
96/7 Sisu 15, KG-4, RE-6

PIETILÄ, SAKARI
95/6 Sisu 393
96/7 Sisu ATG-7

PIETRANGELO, FRANK
91/2 Bowman 89
92/3 Fleer Ultra 303
93/4 Fleer Ultra 338
00/1 Kudos 89
91/2 O-Pee-Chee 114
92/3 O-Pee-Chee 115
88/9 Panini Sticker 331
93/4 Panini Sticker 132
92/3 Parkhurst 296
93/4 Parkhurst 352
92/3 Pinnacle 309
93/4 Pinnacle 343
93/4 Premier 287
90/1 Pro Set 509
92/3 Pro Set 64
88/9 ProCards / Muskegon
90/1 Score 55T
91/2 Score 440
91/2 Score CAN 425
92/3 Score 535
93/4 Score 419
92/3 Topps 522
91/2 To. Stadium 364
92/3 To. Stadium 96
93/4 To. Stadium 272
90/1 Upper Deck 403
92/3 Upper Deck 273
93/4 Upper Deck 401
92/3 HART / Dairymart
93/4 HART / Coke
91/2 PITT / Elby's
91/2 PITT / Food. Stickers
94/5 Minnesota Moose

PIGOLITSYN, DENIS
99/0 Anchorage Aces

PIHL, ANDREAS
99/0 UD Elitserien 174
00/1 UD Elitserien 151

PIHLAPURO, PENTTI
66/7 Champion 135

PIHLMAN, TUOMAS
02/3 Cardset 94, -DD 7, -Nimik.
00/1 Cardset 49

PIIKKILÄ, MARKKU
92/3 Jyvas Hyva 34
93/4 Jyvas Hyva 59
93/4 Sisu 245

PIIKKIO, MARKKU
91/2 Jyvas Hyva 9

PIISINEN, JORMA
78/9 SM-Liiga 71

PIITULAINEN, OSSI
91/2 Jyvas Hyva 42

PIKE, ALF
34-43 BeeHive-1 [NYRa.]
39/0 O-Pee-Chee 84
60/1 Shirriff 100

PIKKARAINEN,
97/8 Hockey-Box

PIKKARAINEN, ILKKA
02/3 Cardset 95

PILAR, KAREL
02/3 Calder 96
02/3 First Edition 286
02/3 Pacific Complete 590
02/3 SPx 124
02/3 Upper Deck 222
02/3 UD Foundations 141
02/3 UD MVP 219
02/3 UD Piece 149
02/3 UD Vintage 346
01/2 BAP Mem. 312
00/1 DS 40
01/2 DS 30, 54
99/0 OFS 155
00/1 OFS 138
01/2 OFS -UHI 15
01/2 Parkhurst 347
01/2 SPx 216
01/2 UD Mask 169
01/2 UD Premier 83
01/2 St. John's Maple Leafs

PILAVKA, ROSTISLAV
99/0 OFS 291

PILLION, PIERRE
91/2 7th...Sketch LHJMQ 271

PILLONI, PATRICK
95 Panini Worlds 268

PILON, NEIL
84/5 Kamloops Blazers

PILON, RICH
00/1 Upper Deck 348

PILON, RICHARD
92/3 Bowman 264
91/2 O-Pee-Chee 379
98/9 OPC Chrome 91
98/9 Pacific 285
99/0 Pacific 262
01/2 Pacific 266
97/8 Pa. Invincible R-120
98/9 Pa. Paramount 146
92/3 Parkhurst 490
94/5 Parkie SE105
97/8 Pi. Be A Player 81, ✍ Aut. 81
93/4 Premier 417
90/1 Pro Set 486
90/1 Score 45T
91/2 Score CAN 417
92/3 Topps 492
98/9 Topps 91

92/3 To. Stadium 230
93/4 To. Stadium 113
97/8 Upper Deck 101
89/0 NYIS
96/7 NYIS
PILON, RONALD
52/3 Anonymous 132
PILOTE, NICOLAS
99/0 Rimouski Océanic 1
00/1 Rimouski Océanic 4
PILOTE, PIERRE
99/0 BAP Mem. R-4, ✍ R-4
45-64 BeeHive-2 [Chic.]
64-67 BeeHive-3 [Chic.]
64-67 BeeHive-3 [Chic.]
63-65 Chex
64/5 Coke/Sprite [Chic.]
65/6 Coca-Cola
62/3 Cowan Tile
83 HHOF Postcard J11
83&87 HHOF 191
68/9 O-Pee-Chee 124
93/4 Parkie 56-57 32
95/6 Parkie 66-67 34, 123, AS2
94/5 Parkie Tall 31, 134, 145, 159, AS-2, TW1
66/7 Post Cereal Box
68/9 Post Marble
60/1 Shirriff 66
61/2 Shirriff 27
62/3 Shirriff 50
68/9 Shirriff / Toro. 18
57/8 Topps 22
58/9 Topps 36
59/0 Topps 2
59/0 Topps 60
60/1 Topps 65
61/2 Topps 24
61/2 Topps - Stamp
62/3 Topps 28
62/3 Topps Dollar
63/4 Topps 25
64/5 Topps 59
64/5 Topps 109
65/6 Topps 56
66/7 Topps 59
66/7 Topps 123
66/7 Topps / Test 59
67/8 Topps 62
67/8 Topps 122
68/9 Topps 124
01/2 To. Heritage S5, ✍ CAI
01/2 T/O Archives 7, -Seat, ✍ CAI
64/5 Toronto Star Action
60/1 Toronto Star Weekend
65/6 Toronto Star Weekend
66/7 Toronto Star Weekend
91/2 Ultimate Original Six 63, ✍ Aut. 63
94/5 Zellers, ✍ Aut.
68/9 TORO
PILOUS, RUDY
83&87 HHOF 247
61/2 Shirriff 40
61/2 Topps 23
62/3 Topps 23
PILUT, LARRY
95/6 UD Elitserien DS18
PINC, MAREK
99/0 DS 58
00/1 DS 134, G12
98/9 OFS 261
99/0 OFS 535
00/1 OFS 110
01/2 OFS 148, H11
PINC, MICHAL
98/9 OFS 270
00/1 Rouyn-Noranda 10
PINCHES, JOHN
90/1 7th..Sketch OHL 116
91/2 7th...Sketch OHL 32
PINDER, ALLAN
70/1 CHIC
PINDER, GERRY
70/1 Eddie Sargent 42
71/2 Eddie Sargent 132
70/1 Esso Power Player
69/0 Mästär Serien 24
70/1 O-Pee-Chee 148
71/2 O-Pee-Chee 185
72/3 O-Pee-Chee 341
74/5 OPC WHA 9
76/7 OPC WHA 11
73/4 OPC WHA Poster 7
73/4 Quaker Oats 11
71/2 Toronto Sun Photo
72/3 Cleveland Crusaders
76/7 San Diego Mariners
PINDIAK, LUBOS
99/0 Score 111
PINEAU, MARCEL
93/4 Maine Black Bears
PINEO, GREGG
91/2 7th...Sketch LHJMQ 194
PINEVSKI, STANISLAV
00/1 Mir 182
PINFOLD, DENNIS
90/1 7th..Sketch WHL 108
99/0 Fort Wayne Komets
92/3 Tacoma Rockets
93/4 Tacoma Rockets
PINKAS, MICHAL
99/0 Score 108
PION, RICHARD
89/0 ProCards IHL 6
90/1 ProCards 77
91/2 ProCards 43
92/3 Peoria Rivermen
93/4 Peoria Rivermen
PIPA, LEOS
94/5 APS 172
95/6 APS 192

96/7 APS 326
97/8 APS 305
96/7 DS Sticker 168
97/8 DS Sticker 119
98/9 OFS 58
PIRILA, MIKA
71/2 Williams Finnish 373
PIRJETÄ, LASSE
02/3 BAP All-Star 119
02/3 BAP Mem. 385
02/3 Cardset 96
02/3 Crown Royale 109
02/3 In The GU 188
02/3 Parkhurst 225
02/3 Pr. Stock Reserve 158
02/3 Signature 189, ✍ 189
02/3 SP Authentic 142
02/3 SP GU 74
02/3 Stadium 135
02/3 T. Chrome 155
02/3 To. Heritage 146
02/3 To. Total 407
02/3 Ultimate Mem. 25
02/3 Upper Deck 434
02/3 UD Classic 110
02/3 UD Honor 110
02/3 UD Mask 119
02/3 UD Top Shelf 111
02/3 Vanguard 110
98/9 Cardset 223
99/0 Cardset 176, 232
00/1 Cardset 259
97/8 Hockey-Box
91/2 7th...Sketch WHL 160
93/4 Sisu 52
94/5 Sisu 123
95/6 Sisu 331
PIRKKALANIEMI, MARKKU
72/3 Williams Finnish 335
PIRNES, ESA
02/3 Cardset 97
99/0 Cardset 211
00/1 Cardset 250
PIROS, KAMIL
02/3 O-Pee-Chee 274
02/3 Topps 274
02/3 To. Limited 274
01/2 Adrenaline 204
96/7 APS 188
97/8 APS 96
01/2 Atomic 105
01/2 BAP Mem. 336
00/1 DS 46
97/8 DS Sticker 103
01/2 O-Pee-Chee 353
98/9 OFS 266
99/0 OFS 345, 482
00/1 OFS 148
01/2 Parkhurst 290
01/2 Pr. Stock 114
01/2 PS Titanium 148
01/2 PS Titanium Draft 107
01/2 Signature 247, ✍ Aut. 247
01/2 SP Authentic 135
01/2 SP GU 65
01/2 Topps 353
01/2 To. Chrome 171
01/2 Upper Deck 415
01/2 UD Challenge 96
01/2 UD Honor Roll 63
01/2 UD Ice 74
01/2 UD Vintage 274
01/2 Chicago Wolves
PIROS, KIMIL
02/3 Chicago Wolves
PIROUTEK, RADIM
94/5 APS 219
95/6 APS 161
PIROZHKOV, DMITRI
00/1 Mir 62
PIRRONG, JON
99/0 Asheville Smoke
96/7 Pensacola Ice Pilots
PIRSKAINEN, TUOMO
66/7 Champion 42
65/6 Hellas 42
PIRTTIAHO, RISTO
66/7 Champion 151
PIRUS, ALEX
77/8 O-Pee-Chee 204
77/8 Topps 204
PISA, ALES
02/3 Calder 85
02/3 Pacific Complete 528
02/3 UD Foundations 128
02/3 UD Vintage 331
94/5 APS 33
95/6 APS 335
96/7 APS 149
97/8 APS 248
98/9 DS 50
99/0 DS 73
00/1 DS 87
96/7 DS Sticker 252
97/8 DS Sticker 132
98/9 OFS 148, 452
99/0 OFS 265, 356, 505
00/1 OFS 34
01/2 OFS -UHI 12
95/6 Upper Deck 545
01/2 Hamilton Bulldogs
PISA, TOMAS
95/6 APS 334
99/0 Score 89
PISANI, FERNANDO
02/3 BAP Mem. 380
02/3 Calder 118
02/3 Pacific Complete 540
02/3 Quest for the Cup 119
02/3 SP Authentic 208
02/3 SPx 191
02/3 Ultimate Mem. 68

02/3 UD Mask 144
02/3 UD Premier 96
00/1 Hamilton Bulldogs
01/2 Hamilton Bulldogs
02/3 Hamilton Bulldogs
PISEK, DAVID
99/0 Score 120
PISIAK, RYAN
91/2 7th...Sketch WHL 259
97/8 Louisiana Ice Gators
91/2 Prince Albert Raiders
PISKOR, MICHAL
94/5 APS 133
95/6 APS 233
96/7 APS 67
97/8 APS 114
96/7 DS Sticker 243
97/8 DS Sticker 58
PISTEK, LUBOMIR
98/9 Kelowna Rockets
PISTO, JERMU
98/9 Cardset 145
99/0 Cardset 206
00/1 Cardset 6
97/8 Hockey-Box
93/4 Sisu 166
94/5 Sisu 287
96/7 Sisu 71
PITIRRI, RICHARD
97/8 Bell
95/6 Slapshot 169
99/0 Hampton Roads
PITKÄMÄKI, JUHA
02/3 Cardset 248
00/1 Cardset 30
PITKÄNEN, JONI
02/3 Cardset 249, -BFG 6, -DD 4, ✍ BFG
PITLICK, LANCE
99/0 Millenium 116, ✍ Aut. 116
97/8 Pa. Invincible R-137
97/8 Pi. Be A Player 109, ✍ Aut. 109
90/1 ProCards 27
00/1 Signature 134, ✍ Aut. 89
00/1 Upper Deck 76
96/7 OTTA
97/8 OTTA
98/9 OTTA
PITRE, DIDIER
91 C55 Reprint 41
83 HHOF Postcard I11
83&87 HHOF 130
10/1 Imperial
10/1 Imperial 23
11/2 Imperial 45
12/3 Imperial 45
27/8 La Patrie
PITTIS, DOMENIC
97/8 Donruss 212, RR-5
97/8 Do. Canadian 140
00/1 PS Titanium 119
00/1 PS Titanium Draft 119
97/8 Score Pitt. 20
91/2 7th...Sketch WHL 347
95/6 Cleveland Lumberjacks
98/9 Rochester Americans
PITTMAN, CHRIS
93/4 Slapshot / Kitchener 11
94/5 Slapshot / Kitchener 12
95/6 Slapshot 279
96/7 Richmond Renegades
PITTMAN, MIKE
93/4 Slapshot / Guelph 13
94/5 Slapshot / Guelph 17
95/6 Slapshot 97
95/6 Guelph Storm
PIUHOLA, JUSSI
66/7 Champion 134
70/1 Kuvajulkaisut 264
PIVETZ, MARK
92/3 MPS SJHL 140
PIVKO, LIBOR
99/0 DS 47
00/1 DS 152
98/9 OFS 211
99/0 OFS 243
00/1 OFS 275
01/2 OFS 89, -UHI 30
PIVONKA, MICHAL
98/9 Be A Player 150, ✍ Aut. 150
90/1 Bowman 68
91/2 Bowman 291
92/3 Bowman 294
93/4 Donruss 374
94/5 Donruss 292
95/6 Donruss 197
96/7 Donruss 60
96/7 Do. Canadian 50
97/8 Do. Elite 35
95/6 Edge Ice 124, C-23
92/3 Fleer 119
92/3 Fleer Ultra 237
93/4 Fleer Ultra 101
94/5 Fleer Ultra 238
95/6 Fleer Ultra 177
96/7 Fl. Ultra 178
95 Globe 156
95/6 Hoyle / East. 10-Diamond
96/7 Kraft / KD
93/4 Leaf 178
94/5 Leaf 114
95/6 Leaf 162
96/7 L. Limited 36
96/7 L. Preferred 100
96/7 Maggers 165
96/7 Metal Univ. 167
90/1 OPC/Topps 68
91/2 O-Pee-Chee 327
92/3 O-Pee-Chee 30
97/8 Pacific CC 285

90/1 Panini Sticker 154
91/2 Panini Sticker 206
92/3 Panini Sticker 161
93/4 Panini Sticker 27
95/6 Panini Sticker 136
96/7 Panini Sticker 139
97/8 Panini Sticker 111
91/2 Parkhurst 412
92/3 Parkhurst 432
93/4 Parkhurst 487
95/6 Parkhurst 487
91/2 Pinnacle 277
92/3 Pinnacle 151
93/4 Pinnacle 67
94/5 Pinnacle 323
96/7 Pinnacle 173
96/7 Pi. Be A Player 13, ✍ Aut. 13
95/6 Pi. Summit 147
96/7 Pi. Summit 25
96/7 Pi. Zenith 62
94/5 POG 248
93/4 Power Play 265
93/4 Premier 321
93/4 Premier 360
94/5 Premier 259
90/1 Pro Set 319
91/2 Pro Set 252
92/3 Pro Set 201
91/2 Pro Set Platinum 132
90/1 Score 268
91/2 Score 193
91/2 Score CAN 193
92/3 Score 253
93/4 Score 118
93/4 Score IS 15
95/6 Score 258
96/7 Score 33
96/7 Select CE 52
94 Semic 178
91 Semic Sticker 222
92 Semic Sticker 138
95/6 SBx Impact 172
96/7 SBx Impact 142
95/6 SP 157
92/3 Topps 107
95/6 Topps 330
95/6 To. Finest 147
96/7 To. Picks 55
91/2 To. Stadium 44
92/3 To. Stadium 382
93/4 To. Stadium 405
90/1 Upper Deck 60
92/3 Upper Deck 229
92/3 Upper Deck 261
93/4 Upper Deck 154
95/6 Upper Deck 392
96/7 Upper Deck 355
94/5 UD BAP ✍ 160
95/6 UD CC 260
96/7 UD CC 280
96 Wien 126
86/7 WASH / Kodak
86/7 WASH / Police
87/8 WASH
87/8 WASH / Kodak
88/9 WASH
88/9 WASH / Smokey
89/0 WASH
89/0 WASH / Kodak
90/1 WASH / Kodak
90/1 WASH / Smokey
91/2 WASH / Kodak
91/2 WASH / Smokey
92/3 WASH / Kodak
93/4 WASH
99/0 Kansas City Blades
PLACATKA, TOMAS
94/5 APS 274
PLACHTA, JACEK
94/5 DEL 253
95/6 DEL 251
96/7 DEL 140
98/9 DEL 11
99/0 Eishockey 297
00/1 UD DEL 218
01/2 UD DEL 205
PLAGER, BARCLAY
70/1 Dad's Cookies
70/1 Eddie Sargent 184
71/2 Eddie Sargent 182
72/3 Eddie Sargent 187
70/1 Esso Power Player
72/3 Post 12
74/5 Loblaws
68/9 O-Pee-Chee 177
69/0 O-Pee-Chee 176
70/1 O-Pee-Chee 99
71/2 O-Pee-Chee 66
72/3 O-Pee-Chee 35
73/4 O-Pee-Chee 47
74/5 O-Pee-Chee 87
75/6 O-Pee-Chee 205
72 Semic Sticker 186
68/9 Shirriff / SLou. 8
70/1 Topps 99
71/2 Topps 66
72/3 Topps 136
73/4 Topps 47
74/5 Topps 87
75/6 Topps 205
71/2 Toronto Sun Photo
71/2 SLOU
72/3 SLOU
73/4 SLOU
78/9 SLOU
92/3 SLOU / McDon. 24
PLAGER, BARCLAY
02/3 Fleer Throwbacks 76
PLAGER, BILL
70/1 Eddie Sargent 187
71/2 Eddie Sargent 190
72/3 Eddie Sargent 7
72/3 O-Pee-Chee 122
72/3 Topps 12
72/3 ATLF

71/2 SLOU
89/0 New Haven Nighthawks
PLAGER, BOB
70/1 Eddie Sargent 183
71/2 Eddie Sargent 189
72/3 Eddie Sargent 186
70/1 Esso Power Player
74/5 Loblaws
68/9 O-Pee-Chee 112
68/9 O-Pee-Chee 177
69/0 O-Pee-Chee 13
70/1 O-Pee-Chee 211
71/2 O-Pee-Chee 103
72/3 O-Pee-Chee 161
73/4 O-Pee-Chee 148
74/5 O-Pee-Chee 107
75/6 O-Pee-Chee 131
76/7 O-Pee-Chee 369
77/8 O-Pee-Chee 285
90/1 ProCards 98
68/9 Shirriff / SLou. 2
68/9 Topps 112
69/0 Topps 13
71/2 Topps 103
72/3 Topps 96
73/4 Topps 134
74/5 Topps 107
75/6 Topps 131
71/2 Toronto Sun Photo
71/2 SLOU
72/3 SLOU
73/4 SLOU
92/3 SLOU / McDon. 7
PLAMONDON, GERRY
52/3 Bas du Fleuve 50
45-64 BeeHive-2 [Mont.]
51/2 Laval Dairy 85
52/3 Laval Dairy Update 85
43-47 Parade Sportive
45-54 Quaker Oats
52/3 St. Lawrence 14
PLAMONDON, JEAN
88/9 Richelieu Riverains
PLAMONDON, JUSTIN
98/9 BC Icemen 8
98/9 BC Icemen
PLAMONDON, RAY
81/2 Regina Pats
PLAMONDON, SYLVAIN
98/9 Québec Remparts
99/0 Québec Remparts 14
PLANCHE, JAMES
51/2 Laval Dairy 50
PLANDOWSKI, DARRYL
93/4 Seattle Thunderbirds
PLANOVSKY, ANTONIN
94/5 APS 120
PLANT, RICKY
97/8 Guildford Flames
PLANT, RUSS
97/8 Guildford Flames
PLANTE, CAM
90/1 ProCards 583
90/1 Kansas City Blades
82/3 Brandon Wheat Kings
83/4 Brandon Wheat Kings
PLANTE, DAN
93/4 Classic 72
94/5 Classic 81, T42
93/4 Cla. Prospects 95
94/5 Donruss 48
94/5 Leaf 214
97/8 Pa. Invincible R-121
94/5 Pinnacle 488
94/5 Premier 266
95/6 SBx Impact 210
97/8 Upper Deck 309
96/7 NYIS
98/9 Chicago Wolves
99/0 Chicago Wolves
00/1 Chicago Wolves
01/2 Chicago Wolves
PLANTE, DEREK
93/4 Classic 73
94/5 Classic ✍ 37
93/4 Cla. Images 4 Sport 43
93/4 Cla. Images 4 Sport SI8
93/4 Cla. Prospects 30
93/4 Donruss 45
94/5 Donruss 78
95/6 Donruss 190
96/7 Donruss 107
97/8 Donruss 149
97/8 Do. Canadian 35
97/8 Do. Elite 82
97/8 Do. Preferred 72
97/8 Do. Priority 25
97/8 Do. Studio 36
94/5 Fleer 26
93/4 Fleer Ultra 276
93/4 Fleer Ultra WotF 13
94/5 Fleer Ultra 27, ARS-6
96/7 Fl. Ultra 19
95/6 Hoyle / East. J-Diamond
93/4 Leaf 258
94/5 Leaf 33, GLR-11
95/6 Leaf 166
97/8 Leaf 112
94/5 L. Limited 44
97/8 Limited 49, 184
96/7 Metal Univ. 16
97/8 Omega 25
98/9 Pacific 107
99/0 Pacific 128
97/8 Pacific CC 262
97/8 Pa. Dynagon 13, T-28
97/8 Pa. Invincible 14
97/8 Pa. Paramount 22
94/5 Panini Sticker K
95/6 Panini Sticker 18
96/7 Panini Sticker 22

97/8 Panini Sticker 12
93/4 Parkhurst 293
93/4 Parkhurst C18
94/5 Parkhurst 277
95/6 Parkhurst 294
93/4 Pinnacle 435
94/5 Pinnacle 95, 472
95/6 Pinnacle 149
96/7 Pinnacle 5
97/8 Pinnacle 169
97/8 Pi. Certified 110
97/8 Pi. Inside 148
97/8 Pi. Totally 110
94/5 POG 47
95/6 POG 40
93/4 Power Play 300
93/4 Power Play RooS 11
93/4 Premier 285
94/5 Premier 194, 501, OF-3
93/4 Score 589
94/5 Score 251
95/6 Score 213
96/7 Score 174
97/8 Score 109
97/8 Score Buff. 12
95/6 SBx Impact 18
96/7 SP 16
95/6 Topps 103
98/9 To. Finest 143
93/4 To. Stadium 491
94/5 To. Stadium 30
93/4 TSC Members Only 48
93/4 Upper Deck 475
94/5 Upper Deck 142, SP-100
95/6 Upper Deck 469
96/7 Upper Deck 223
95/6 UD BAP 16, ✍ S16
96/7 UD Black Diam. 83
95/6 UD CC 51
96/7 UD CC 27
97/8 UD Coll. Choice 24, SQ62
96/7 UD Ice 7
PLANTE, DOMINIC
02/3 Shawinigan Cataractes
PLANTE, ÉRIC
90/1 7th..Sketch LHJMQ 4
91/2 7th...Sketch LHJMQ 285
91 7th..Sketch Mem.Cup 60
93/4 Slapshot / Drummondville 15
PLANTE, JACQUES
02/3 BAP Mem. 234
02/3 Between the Pipes 113, ✄ CP4, ✄ DM18, ✄ GT8, ✄ I1, ✄ RB4, ✄ VM10
02/3 Canada Post
02/3 In The GU ✄ VM2
02/3 Parkie - Reprint 251
02/3 Parkhurst Retro ✄ NN21
02/3 Ultimate Mem. ✄ BAPL, ✄ BOS, ✄ CP, ✄ EA, ✄ GMIH, ✄ NO, ✄ RAT, ✄ RT, ✄ SCD (x2), ✄ SF, ✄ VGJ, ✍ Cut
02/3 UD Foundations ✄ LI
02/3 UD Mask / Mask (x2)
01/2 ASG History
00/1 BAP Mem. ✄ G-15, ✄ G-23
01/2 BAP Mem. ✄ GT, ✄ RM
45-64 BeeHive-2 [Mont.]
45-64 BeeHive-2 [NYRa.]
64-67 BeeHive-3 [NYRa.]
01/2 BT Pipes 122, 136, HSHS, -Mask, ✄ S&J, ✄ GR, ✄ TW, ✄ VM
99/0 Canada Post
64/5 Coke/Sprite [NYRa.]
71/2 Colgate Head
70/1 Dad's Cookies
77/8 Dernière Heure
70/1 Eddie Sargent 199
72/3 Eddie Sargent 207
70/1 Esso Power Player
71/2 Frito Lay
62/3 Cowan Tile
93/4 High Liner 10
83 HHOF Postcard F10
83&87 HHOF 76
91/2 Kraft 6
91/2 Kraft 76
51/2 Laval Dairy 92
52/3 Laval Dairy Update 92
92/3 Legends 11
72/3 Post 9
73/4 Mac's Milk
68/9 O-Pee-Chee 181
68/9 O-Pee-Chee PS 15
69/0 O-Pee-Chee 180
69/0 O-Pee-Chee 4in1
70/1 O-Pee-Chee 222
71/2 O-Pee-Chee 195
71/2 O-Pee-Chee 256
71/2 O-Pee-Chee Book 4
72/3 O-Pee-Chee 92
71/2 O-Pee-Chee Poster 15
74/5 OPC WHA 64
75/6 OPC WHA 34
54/5 Parkhurst 97
54/5 Parkhurst 98
54/5 Parkhurst 99
55/6 Parkhurst 50
55/6 Parkhurst 71
55/6 Parkhurst 75
57/8 Parkhurst [Mont.] 15
58/9 Parkhurst 21
58/9 Parkhurst 22
58/9 Parkhurst 26
58/9 Parkhurst 35
58/9 Parkhurst 39
59/0 Parkhurst 41
59/0 Parkhurst 50
60/1 Parkhurst 53
61/2 Parkhurst 49

62/3 Parkhurst 49
92/3 Parkhurst PR-1
93/4 Parkhurst PR43
01/2 Parkhurst HSHS, PR10, PR34, PR47, PR66, PR85, PR128, PR138, ✄ H9, ✄ PV4, ✄ PV5, ✄ PV6, ✄ PV7, ✄ PV8, ✄ HSHSJers
95/6 Parkhurst 24-karat Gold
93/4 Parkie 56-57 135
93/4 Parkie 56-57 151
93/4 Parkie 56-57 161
93/4 Parkie 56-57 163
93/4 Parkie 56-57 72
95 Parkhurst Phonecard
94/5 Parkie Tall 100
70/1 Post Shooters
91/2 Pro Set 341
72 Semic Sticker 169
60/1 Shirriff 21
61/2 Shirriff 113
62/3 Shirriff 25
62/3 Shirriff 43
62/3 Shirriff 58
62/3 Shirriff 59
52/3 St. Lawrence 1
81/2 TCMA 12
63/4 Topps 45
64/5 Topps 68
71/2 Topps 6
71/2 Topps 10
72/3 Topps 24
01/2 T/O Archives 6
57/8 Toronto Star Photo
59/0 Toronto Star Photo
61/2 Toronto Star Photo
64/5 Toronto Star Action
59/0 Toronto Star Weekend
63/4 Toronto Star Weekend
71/2 Toronto Sun Photo
00/1 Ultimate Mem. ✄ Plante 1-15, ✄ RE-4, ✄ RA-8, ✄ GM-1, ✄ GM-10, ✄ GM-14, ✄ GM-16
01/2 Ultimate Mem. ✄ ASGH, ✄ CP, ✄ EA, ✄ LC, ✄ PP, ✄ RN, ✄ RT, ✄ SCW
01/2 Upper Deck ✍ Cut
99/0 UD C. Legends 9, AC6, C9, E5
00/1 UD Legends 66, LC8
01/2 UD Legends 33, 84, FC, ✄ PoH
99/0 UD Retro 90
01/2 UD SCup Champs 16
60/1 York Glass [Mont.]
60/1 York
61/2 York 23
62/3 York Transfer 2
83/4 MONT
92/3 MONT / OPC 32
92/3 MONT / OPC 40
92/3 SLOU / McDon. 22
70/1 TORO
71/2 TORO
72/3 TORO
PLANTE, JEAN-MARC
94/5 Birmingham Bulls
PLANTE, JEAN-MARIE
52/3 Laval Dairy Update 67
PLANTE, MICHEL
73/4 Vancouver Blazers
PLANTE, PHILIPPE
99 Bowman 49
00/1 Austin Ice Bats
99/0 Grand Rapids Griffins
97/8 Rimouski Océanic
PLANTE, PIERRE
74/5 Loblaws
73/4 O-Pee-Chee 255
74/5 O-Pee-Chee 149
74/5 O-Pee-Chee 197
75/6 O-Pee-Chee 309
76/7 O-Pee-Chee 371
77/8 O-Pee-Chee 385
78/9 O-Pee-Chee 179
79/0 O-Pee-Chee 275
80/1 O-Pee-Chee 369
74/5 Topps 149
74/5 Topps 197
75/6 Topps 309
78/9 Topps 179
71/2 Toronto Sun Photo
72/3 SLOU
73/4 SLOU
PLANTÉ, DEREK
01/2 UD DEL 189
PLAQUIN, KEN
99/0 Asheville Smoke
91/2 Michigan Tech Huskies
91/2 Michigan Tech Huskies
PLAQUIN, KENT
90/1 Michigan Tech Huskies
PLASEK, KAREL
96/7 APS 164
97/8 APS 261
99/0 DS 105
98/9 OFS 159
99/0 OFS 81
00/1 OFS 200
PLASSE, MICHEL
72/3 Dernière Heure
73/4 Dernière Heure
81/2 Dernière Heure
74/5 Loblaws
74/5 Loblaws Update
73/4 O-Pee-Chee 252
74/5 O-Pee-Chee 257
75/6 O-Pee-Chee 249
76/7 O-Pee-Chee 172
77/8 O-Pee-Chee 92
78/9 O-Pee-Chee 36
79/0 O-Pee-Chee 69

81/2 O-Pee-Chee 281
80/1 Pepsi Bottle Cap
74/5 Topps 257
75/6 Topps 249
76/7 Topps 172
77/8 Topps 92
78/9 Topps 36
79/0 Topps 69
76/7 COLR / Hockey Talk
79/0 COLR
72/3 MONT / Pro Star
73/4 MONT / Pro Star
80/1 QUÉB
81/2 QUÉB
PLASSE, STEVE
88/9 Richelieu Riverains
PLATA, ED
52/3 Anonymous 148
PLATTNER, TONI
94/5 DEL 285
PLAVSIC, ADRIEN
90/1 Bowman 62
91/2 Bowman 312
92/3 Bowman 363
92 C.O.A. Winter Olympics 189
91/2 Canada Nationals
92/3 Fleer Ultra 428
91/2 O-Pee-Chee 162
92/3 O-Pee-Chee 156
90/1 OPC Premier 90
90/1 Panini/VAN 19
93/4 Premier 201
90/1 Pro Set 644
89/0 ProCards IHL 14
90/1 Score 394
92/3 Score 531
92/3 Score COH 11
93/4 Score 358
92/3 Topps 323
91/2 To. Stadium 196
92/3 To. Stadium 15
93/4 To. Stadium 201
91/2 Upper Deck 424
92/3 Upper Deck 519
94/5 Upper Deck 381
95/6 UD CC 233
89/0 SLOU / Kodak
95/6 TAMP / Sky Box
90/1 VANC / Mohawk
91/2 VANC
91/2 VANC / Photo
92/3 VANC / Road Trip
94/5 VANC
95/6 Atlanta Knights
PLAVUCHA, VLASTIMIL
94 Semic 208
PLAYFAIR, JIM
89/0 ProCards IHL 62
PLAYFAIR, JIM
90/1 ProCards 398
PLAYFAIR, JIM
91/2 ProCards 479
88/9 EDMO / Action 142
94/5 Dayton Bombers 20
95/6 Dayton Bombers
95/6 Dayton Bombers
92/3 Indianapolis Ice
96/7 Michigan K-Wings
84/5 Nova Scotia Oilers
85/6 Nova Scotia Oilers
PLAYFAIR, LARRY
84/5 Kelowna Wings &...
80/1 O-Pee-Chee 296
84/5 O-Pee-Chee 26
85/6 OPC/Topps 131
86/7 OPC/Topps 195
87/8 OPC/Topps 57
84/5 OPC Sticker 207
87/8 OPC Sticker 211-77
82/3 Post [Buff.]
84/5 Topps 20
81/2 BUFF / Wendt's 10
82/3 BUFF / Wendt's 11
84/5 BUFF / Blue Shield
85/6 BUFF / Blue Shield
88/9 BUFF / Blue Shield
88/9 BUFF / Won. Bread
89/0 BUFF / Blue Shield
89/0 BUFF / Campbell's
87/8 LOSA
PLAYFAIR, LARRY
02/3 Fleer Throwbacks 51, ✍ Aut.
PLAZA, ANTONIO
79 Panini Sticker 376
PLEAU, LARRY
70/1 Eddie Sargent 107
71/2 Eddie Sargent 100
75/6 OPC WHA 56
76/7 OPC WHA 26
73/4 Quaker Oats 18
72 Semic Sticker 229
71/2 Toronto Sun Photo
69/0 MONT / Pro Star
70/1 MONT
71/2 MONT / Pro Star
72/3 New England Whalers
PLEKANEC, TOMAS
00/1 OFS 129
01/2 OFS 181, -RE3D
02/3 Hamilton Bulldogs
PLEKHANOV, DMITRI
98/9 Mir 15
PLESH, MIKE
83/4 Kingston Canadians
84/5 Kingston Canadians
PLETKA, VACLAV
01/2 BAP Mem. 311
01/2 Bowman 121
98/9 OFS 190
99/0 OFS 200, 483
01/2 Parkhurst 337

01/2 SP Authentic 168
01/2 SP GU 92
01/2 To. Chrome 180
01/2 UD Challenge 127
01/2 UD Ice 81
01/2 UD Premier 77
PLETSCH, FRED
52/3 Anonymous 101
PLETT, TIM
01/2 Moose Jaw Warriors 11
PLETT, WILLI
02/3 UD Foundations 12, ✄ CTW, ✄ CH, ✄ PS
77/8 O-Pee-Chee 17
78/9 O-Pee-Chee 317
79/0 O-Pee-Chee 382
80/1 O-Pee-Chee 330
81/2 O-Pee-Chee 35
82/3 O-Pee-Chee 173
83/4 O-Pee-Chee 179
81/2 OPC Sticker 13
81/2 OPC Sticker 15
81/2 OPC Sticker 222
87/8 Panini Sticker 302
80/1 Pepsi Bottle Cap
81/2 Post 21
82/3 Post [Calg.]
83/4 Souhaits Keychain [North Stars]
77/8 Topps 17
81/2 Topps 26
77/8 ATLF
78/9 ATLF / Colour
79/0 ATLF / B&W
79/0 ATLF / Colour
88/9 BOST / Sports Action
80/1 CALG
81/2 CALG
82/3 MINS
83/4 MINS
84/5 MINS
84/5 MINS / 7-Eleven 2
85/6 MINS / 7-Eleven 7
86/7 MINS / 7-Eleven 3
PLETT, WILLI
02/3 Fleer Throwbacks 43
PLEVA, JAN
00/1 OFS 259
PLODEK, JAN
99/0 Score 78
PLODEK, MILAN
99/0 Score 81
PLOMMER, TOMMY
01/2 Sheffield Steelers
93/4 Sheffield Steelers 8
94/5 Sheffield Steelers 6
97/8 Sheffield Steelers
PLOTINKOV, ALEXEI
99/0 Mir 97
PLOTKA, WOLFGANG
70/1 Kuvajulkaisut 94
PLOTNIKOV, ALEXEI
00/1 Mir 21
PLOUFFE, BERTRAND-PIERRE
99/0 Rouyn-Noranda
00/1 Rouyn-Noranda 6
01/2 Sherbrooke Castors 15
PLOUFFE, STEVE
98/9 Fort Worth Brahmas
99/0 Fort Worth Brahmas
PLOURDE, JEAN-FRANÇOIS
00/1 Rimouski Océanic 9
01/2 Rimouski Océanic 9
PLSEK, LUKAS
00/1 OFS 322
PLUCK, DAVID
93/4 Slapshot / Windsor 7
94/5 Slapshot / Windsor 9
92/3 Windsor Spitfires
PLUFF, STEVE
99/0 Mir 124
00/1 Mir 4
PLUMB, ANDREW
92/3 BCJHL 152
96/7 Dayton Ice Bandits
PLUMB, RANDY
81/2 Kingston Canadians
PLUMB, RON
79/0 O-Pee-Chee 328
75/6 OPC WHA 98
76/7 OPC WHA 94
77/8 OPC WHA 24
75/6 Cincinnati Stingers
73/4 Vancouver Blazers
PLUMHOFF, CHRIS
00/1 Charlotte Checkers
98/9 Huntington Blizzard
PLUMMER, TOMMY
95/6 Sheffield Steelers
PLUNKETT, LINDSAY
99/0 Guelph Storm
00/1 Toronto St. Mike's
POAPST, STEVE
01/2 UD Ice 132
91/2 Hampton Roads
92/3 Hampton Roads
98/9 Hampton Roads
93/4 Portland Pirates
94/5 Portland Pirates
95/6 Portland Pirates
95/6 Portland Pirates Hershey
96/7 Portland Pirates
97/8 Portland Pirates
98/9 Portland Pirates
99/0 Portland Pirates
POCHIPINSKI, TREVOR
91/2 ProCards 378
92/3 Wheeling Thund'birds 12

POCHYLY, ROBERT
99/0 Fort Worth Brahmas
PODDUBNY, WALT
83/4 O-Pee-Chee 339
84/5 O-Pee-Chee 309
87/8 OPC/Topps 142
88/9 OPC/Topps Box K
88/9 OPC/Topps 170
90/1 O-Pee-Chee 426
89/0 OPC/Topps 184
83/4 OPC/Topps Sticker 150
87/8 OPC Sticker 32
88/9 OPC Sticker 240
89/0 opcSticker 85-226
87/8 Panini Sticker 112
88/9 Panini Sticker 309
82/3 Post [Toro.]
90/1 Pro Set 479
90/1 Score 278
91/2 Score CAN 400
83/4 Souhaits Keychain [Maple Leafs]
91/2 To. Stadium 177
83/4 Vachon 96
83/4 Vachon 96-14
88/9 EDMO / Action 141
89/0 NJER
89/0 NJER / Caretta
90/1 NJER
88/9 QUÉB
88/9 QUÉB / Gene. Foods
82/3 TORO
83/4 TORO
84/5 TORO
85/6 TORO
98/9 Anchorage Aces
99/0 Anchorage Aces
PODDYAKON, ANDREI
00/1 Mir 87
PODEIN, SHJON
02/3 Pacific Complete 297
02/3 UD Vintage 218
01/2 BAP Mem. 499, ✄ SCC
92/3 Classic Prospects 9
93/4 Fleer Ultra 140
94/5 Fleer Ultra 346
94/5 Leaf 531
99/0 Millenium 71, ✍ Aut. 71
98/9 Pacific 330
00/1 Pacific 118
01/2 Pacific 104
97/8 Pa. Invincible R-147
95 Panini Worlds 224
93/4 Parkhurst 66
94/5 Parkhurst 81
95/6 Parkhurst 426
01/2 Parkhurst 362
95/6 POG 203
93/4 Power Play 84
90/1 ProCards 229
91/2 ProCards 218
93/4 Score 424
97/8 Score Phil. 13
93/4 To. Stadium 474
93/4 Upper Deck 60
94/5 Upper Deck 356
95/6 Upper Deck 150
96/7 Upper Deck 308
97/8 Upper Deck 328
98/9 Upper Deck 337
00/1 Upper Deck 48
95/6 UD BAP 77, ✍ S77
98/9 UD G. Reserve 337
98/9 COLO / Howler Says
93/4 EDMO / Sheet
92/3 EDMO
94/5 PHIL / Sheet
96/7 PHIL / Ocean Spray
PODHRADSKY, PETER
01/2 Cincinnati Mighty Ducks
PODKONICKY, ANDREI
01/2 BAP Mem. 404
98 Bowman 56
01/2 Pacific 176
01/2 SP Authentic 149
01/2 SPx 107
01/2 Upper Deck 191
01/2 UD MVP 202
01/2 UD Top Shelf 55
01/2 Victory 373
PODKONICKY, ANDREJ
98 Bowman Chrome 56
97/8 Portland Winter Hawks
PODLAHA, JOSEF
94/5 APS 248
99/0 OFS 141
PODLESAK, MARTIN
01 UD Prospects GU 36, ✄ TPJ, ✄ JC
PODLOSKI, RAY
88/9 ProCards / Maine
86/7 Moncton GFlames
PODLUBNY, DAVID
90/1 7th...Sketch WHL 60
PODOLKA, MICHAL
00/1 DS 38
00/1 OFS 136
95/6 Slapshot 356
98/9 Topeka Scarecrows
98/9 Topeka Scarecrows
99/0 Topeka Scarecrows
96/7 Soo Greyhounds
PODOLLAN, JASON
91/2 Avant Garde BCJHL 104
94/5 Classic T27
95/6 Do. Elite WJ 20
94/5 Sig. Rookies 13, ✍ 13
94/5 SR Gold Standard 90
95/6 SP 172
96/7 SP 173
93/4 Upper Deck E2

97/8 Upper Deck 165
97/8 UD Coll. Choice 251
96/7 FLOR / Winn-Dixie
96/7 Carolina Monarchs
99/0 Lowell Lock Monsters
97/8 St. John's Maple Leafs
95/6 Spokane Chiefs 12
PODOLSKY, NELSON
52/3 Laval Dairy Update 59
PODOMATSKI, IGOR
00/1 Mir Fetisov 17
PODREZOV, VADIM
96/7 APS 32
99/0 Muskegon Fury
PODSIADLO, KRZYSZTOF
89 Semic Sticker 140
PODWYSOCKI, BOGDAN
74/5 Sioux City Musketeers
POESCHEK, RUDY
94/5 Leaf 75
97/8 Pa. Invincible R-186
94/5 Pinnacle 390
94/5 Premier SFX 274
90/1 ProCards 18
91/2 ProCards 167
93/4 Upper Deck 461
95/6 UD BAP 53, ✍ S53
89/0 NYRA / Marine
94/5 TAMP / Sky Box
95/6 TAMP / Sky Box
99/0 Houston Aeros
91/2 Moncton Hawks
92/3 St. John's Maple Leafs
84/5 Kamloops Blazers
85/6 Kamloops Blazers
86/7 Kamloops Blazers
POESCHEK, RUDY
02/3 Fleer Throwbacks 37, ✄ 6SW
POETA, TONY
52/3 Anonymous 110
POGONIN, ALEXEI
99/0 Mir 163
POHANKA, IGOR
00/1 UD Prospects 75
POHJA, HANNU
70/1 Kuvajulkaisut 318
POHJA, TOMMI
92/3 Jyvas Hyva 159
93/4 Jyvas Hyva 293
93/4 Sisu 77
93/4 Sisu 326
POHL, ANTON
72 Hellas MM-Jenkki 49
POHL, JOHN
02/3 Choice Prospects 35
02/3 Worcester IceCats
POHL, MICHAEL
94/5 DEL 388
95/6 DEL 379
98/9 DEL 302
99/0 Eishockey 251
92 Semic Sticker 191
POHL, TREVOR
86/7 Portland Winter Hawks
POHL, TROY
86/7 Portland Winter Hawks
POHLING, JORG
95/6 DEL 424
POHORELEC, DUSAN
01/2 OFS 242
94 Semic 209
POHTINEN, TAPIO
71/2 Williams Finnish 268
POIKILAINEN, PEKKA
95/6 Sisu 264
POIKOLAINEN, JUHA
71/2 Williams Finnish 290
POIKOLAINEN, JYRKI
93/4 Sisu 294
POIKOLAINEN, PEKKA
98/9 Cardset 149
99/0 Cardset 272
00/1 Cardset 170
97/8 Hockey-Box
94/5 Sisu 273
96/7 Sisu 59
POIKOVINKOV, OLEG
99/0 Mir 72
POILE, DAVID
82/3 WASH
86/7 WASH / Police
87/8 WASH / Kodak
88/9 WASH / Smokey
89/0 WASH / Kodak
90/1 WASH / Kodak
POILE, NORMAN (BUD)
34-43 BeeHive-1 [Toro.]
45-64 BeeHive-2 [Detr.]
45-64 BeeHive-2 [NYRa.]
45-54 Quaker Oats
POIRIER, JOEL
00/1 Kudos 121
POIRIER, CARL
91/2 7th...Sketch LHJMQ 258
POIRIER, CLAUDE
90/1 7th..Sketch LHJMQ 92
91/2 7th..Sketch LHJMQ 102
POIRIER, DAN
89/0 7th..Sketch OHL 64
95/6 Thunder Bay Senators
POIRIER, GAETAN
96/7 Carolina Monarchs
POIRIER, GORDON
51/2 Bas du Fleuve 1

POIRIER, JEAN-FRANÇOIS
88/9 Richelieu Riverains
POIRIER, JOEL
93/4 Slapshot / Sudbury 21
93/4 Slapshot / Windsor 15
94/5 Slapshot / Windsor 17
96/7 Hampton Roads
97/8 Hampton Roads
98/9 Hampton Roads
95/6 Portland Pirates
02/3 Coventry Blaze
01/2 Nottingham Panthers
92/3 Sudbury Wolves
93/4 Sudbury Wolves
POIRIER, NICOLAS
00/1 UD Prospects 85
99/0 Rimouski Océanic 4
00/1 Rimouski Océanic 5
01/2 Rimouski Océanic 5
POIRIER, PHILIPPE
95/6 Slapshot 226
POIRIER, S
90/1 EDMO / IGA
POITRAS, CONRAD
51/2 Bas du Fleuve 3
POITRAS, MARTIN
96/7 Rimouski Océanic
POITRAS, ROGER
79/0 Montréal Juniors B&W
POJAR, CHRIS
94/5 Raleigh Icecaps
POJKAR, DAVID
01/2 OFS 280
POJKAR, VLADIMIR
99/0 OFS 51
PÖK, HERBERT
79 Panini Sticker 306
POKOL, JOSH
01/2 Kamloops Blazers
02/3 Kamloops Blazers
POKORNY, ANDREAS
94/5 DEL 207
95/6 DEL 201
00/1 UD DEL 230
01/2 UD DEL 119
POKOTILO, VADIM
99/0 Mir 167
00/1 Mir 17
POKROVSKI, VALERI
99/0 Mir 226
00/1 Mir 116
POLACIK, RANDY
92/3 BCJHL 137
POLAK, JIRI
95/6 APS 109
96/7 APS 272
97/8 APS 226
00/1 DS 125
97/8 DS Sticker 32
98/9 OFS 224
99/0 OFS 319
00/1 OFS 165
01/2 OFS 57
99/0 Score 123
POLAK, MARK
97/8 Pensacola Ice Pilots
POLANO, MIKE
90/1 7th..Sketch OHL 191, 250
91/2 7th...Sketch OHL 76
89/0 Windsor Spitfires
POLANO, NICK
84/5 DETR / Little Caesars
POLANSKY, TOMAS
99/0 OFS 171
POLASEK, LIBOR
95/6 APS 340
96/7 APS 211
97/8 APS 139
99/0 DS 176
96/7 DS Sticker 204
97/8 DS Sticker 259
98/9 OFS 122, 320
99/0 OFS 429
92/3 Hamilton Canucks
POLÁSEK, LIBOR
92/3 Classic 34
92/3 Classic Four Sport 181
93/4 Cla. Prospects 161
POLCAR, ALES
95/6 APS 21
96/7 APS 41
97/8 APS 69, 311
94/5 DEL 19
98/9 DS 42
96/7 DS Sticker 105
97/8 DS Sticker 301
98/9 OFS 299
99/0 Score 46
POLERA, JASON
99/0 Kingston Frontenacs
POLICELLI, NICK
01/2 Kitchener Rangers
POLICH, MIKE
79/0 O-Pee-Chee 333
80/1 O-Pee-Chee 363
81/2 O-Pee-Chee 172
78/9 MINS / Cloverleaf 6
79/0 MINS
80/1 MINS
77/8 Nova Scotia Voyageurs
POLIKARKIN, VYACHESLAV
94/5 Erie Panthers
POLILLO, PAUL
94/5 Slapshot / Brantford 6
POLIS, GREG
71/2 Eddie Sargent 172
72/3 Eddie Sargent 178
74/5 Loblaws
71/2 O-Pee-Chee 41
71/2 O-Pee-Chee Book. 9
72/3 O-Pee-Chee 34
73/4 O-Pee-Chee 176
74/5 O-Pee-Chee 164
75/6 O-Pee-Chee 201
76/7 O-Pee-Chee 117
77/8 O-Pee-Chee 112
78/9 O-Pee-Chee 246
79/0 O-Pee-Chee 273
71/2 Topps 41
72/3 Topps 43
73/4 Topps 75
74/5 Topps 164
75/6 Topps 201
76/7 Topps 117
77/8 Topps 112
78/9 Topps 246
71/2 Toronto Sun Photo
71/2 PITT / Sportcolor
79/0 WASH
POLIZIANI, DANNY
52/3 Anonymous 23
POLJANSEK, SILVO
79 Panini Sticker 399
POLK, ROB
89/0 Nashville Knights
POLKOVNIKOV, OLEG
00/1 Mir 238
PÖLLÄ, STEFAN
94/5 Leaf Elit Set 205
95/6 Leaf Elit Set 170
95/6 UD Elitserien 31
POLLACK, CHRIS
95/6 Roanoke Express
POLLARD, RICK
90/1 7th..Sketch OHL 315
POLLOCK, JAME
00/1 Worcester IceCats
01/2 Worcester IceCats
02/3 Worcester IceCats
POLLOCK, SAM
83 HHOF Postcard K13
83&87 HHOF 147
96/7 Legends 90
POLLONI, FABIO
79 Panini Sticker 389
82 Semic Sticker 131
POLMAN TUIN, ROB
81/2 Milwaukee Admirals
POLONIC, TOM
69/0 O-Pee-Chee 199
POLONICH, DENNIS
77/8 O-Pee-Chee 4
77/8 O-Pee-Chee 228
78/9 O-Pee-Chee 66
78/9 O-Pee-Chee 106
79/0 O-Pee-Chee 224
80/1 O-Pee-Chee 54
77/8 Topps 4
77/8 Topps 228
78/9 Topps 66
78/9 Topps 106
79/0 Topps 224
80/1 Topps 54
79/0 DETR
80/1 DETR
POLORNY, ANDREAS
91 Semic Sticker 160
POLUPANOV, VIKTOR
70/1 Kuvajulkaisut 13
70/1 Soviet Stars
POLYAKOV, EDUARD
99/0 Mir 90
POLYCHRONOPOULOS, NICK
91/2 7th...Sketch WHL 249
91/2 Prince Albert Raiders
POMICHTER, MIKE
94/5 Classic 58, AA7, T15
94/5 Cla. Images 94, ✍ Aut.
92/3 Upper Deck 607
94/5 Indianapolis Ice
97/8 Springfield Falcons
POMINVILLE, JASON
01 UD Prospects GU 19, ✄ TPJ
02/3 Rochester Americans
99/0 Shawinigan Cataractes 23
00/1 Shawinigan Cataractes 20
01/2 Shawinigan Cataractes 22
PONER, JIM
84/5 Springfield Indians 15
PONIKAROVSKY, ALEXEI
00/1 BAP Mem. 521
01/2 O-Pee-Chee 290
01/2 Pacific 371
01/2 PS Titanium Draft 168
00/1 SP Authentic 124
01/2 Topps 290
00/1 UD Black Diam. 132
00/1 UD Ice 101
01/2 Victory 389
00/1 St. John's Maple Leafs
01/2 St. John's Maple Leafs
01/2 St. John's / Clarenville
PONTE, RANDY
98/9 Brandon Wheat Kings
99/0 Brandon Wheat Kings
PONTO, VESA
99/0 Cardset 274
93/4 Jyvas Hyva 145
93/4 Sisu 143
94/5 Sisu 8
95/6 Sisu 57
POOL, CLAYTON
96/7 Kamloops Blazers
97/8 Kamloops Blazers
POOLE, NICK
95/6 Dayton Bombers
POOLEY, PAUL
84/5 WINN / Safety Tips
POPE, BRENT
89/0 7th..Sketch OHL 101
90/1 7th..Sketch OHL 369
91/2 7th...Sketch OHL 352
00/1 Florida Everblades
93/4 Wheeling Thund'birds
01/2 Nottingham Panthers
POPEIN, LARRY
45-64 BeeHive-2 [NYRa.]
93/4 Parkie 56-57 95
60/1 Shirriff 84
54/5 Topps 55
57/8 Topps 54
58/9 Topps 28
59/0 Topps 21
58/9 Toronto Star Photo
POPIEL, JAN
73/4 Quaker Oats 21
POPIEL, POUL
70/1 Eddie Sargent 213
71/2 Eddie Sargent 212
70/1 Esso Power Player
69/0 O-Pee-Chee 158
70/1 O-Pee-Chee 122
71/2 O-Pee-Chee 1
72/3 O-Pee-Chee 67
74/5 OPC WHA 59
75/6 OPC WHA 68
75/6 OPC WHA 120
76/7 OPC WHA 27
77/8 OPC WHA 63
65/6 Topps 40
70/1 Topps 122
72/3 Topps 142
71/2 Toronto Sun Photo
88/9 EDMO / Action 86
70/1 VANC / Royal Bank
71/2 VANC / Royal Bank 7
75/6 Houston Aeros
POPIESCH, THOMAS
94/5 DEL 330
95/6 DEL 113
96/7 DEL 58
POPIKHIN, EVGENY
91/2 O-Pee-Chee 41R
POPOV, ALEXANDER
99/0 Mir 170
00/1 Mir 212
POPOV, DMITRI
98/9 Mir 7
99/0 Mir 10
00/1 Metallurg 46
POPOVIC, MARK
99/0 UD Prospects 85
00/1 UD Prospects 28
01 UD Prospects GU 7, ✄ TPJ, ✄ TPJS, ✄ JC, ✍ SoT
00/1 Toronto St. Mike's
POPOVIC, PETER
93/4 Donruss 180
94/5 Donruss 313
94/5 Fleer Ultra 315
95 Globe 19
93/4 Leaf 417
94/5 Leaf 176
94/5 Leaf Elit Set 203, GS-7
99/0 Pacific 277
97/8 Pa. Invincible R-104
96/7 Panini Sticker 43
97/8 Panini Sticker 35
98/9 Panini Sticker 36
93/4 Parkhurst 103
95/6 Parkhurst 111
94/5 Parkie SE86
94/5 Pinnacle 457
96/7 Pi. Be A Player 6, ✍ Aut. 6
94/5 POG 141
93/4 Power Play 372
93/4 Premier 361
94/5 Premier 158
93/4 Score 626
94 Semic 56
89/0 Semic Elitserien 243
90/1 Semic Elitserien 154
91/2 Semic Elitserien 259
92/3 Semic Elitserien 278
93 Semic Sticker 8
93/4 Upper Deck 445
94/5 Upper Deck 428
95/6 Upper Deck 192
00/1 Upper Deck 243
93/4 MONT
93/4 MONT / Export
94/5 MONT
95/6 MONT
95/6 MONT / Export
96/7 MONT / Export
96-98 MONT
98/9 NYRA
PORAK, MICHAL
97/8 APS 236
99/0 OFS 142
PORCO, JOHN
96/7 DEL 127
89/0 7th..Sketch OHL 81
90/1 7th..Sketch OHL 16
94/5 Hampton Roads
98/9 Hampton Roads
PORKKA, TONI
02/3 Cardset 250
96/7 DEL 51
98/9 DEL 147
99/0 Eishockey 84
91/2 ProCards 269
94/5 Sisu 289
95/6 Sisu 97
96/7 Sisu SH 6
00/1 UD DEL 77, ✄ GJ
01/2 UD DEL 146
PORT, ANDY
94/5 Humberside Hawks 16
PORTEOUS, F.
28/9 Paulins Candy 79
PORTEOUS, KEN
80/1 Soo Greyhounds
PORTER, AARON
99/0 Muskegon Fury
PORTER, J.C. (RED)
25 Dominion Chocolates 106
27/8 La Presse
PORTLAND, JACK
34-43 BeeHive-1 [Mont.]
39/0 O-Pee-Chee 40
PORVARI, JUHA-PEKKA
71/2 Williams Finnish 310
PORVARI, JUKKA
80/1 Mallasjuoma 163
82 Mallasjuoma
82 Semic Sticker 153
82 Skopbank
78/9 SM-Liiga 11
78/9 SM-Liiga 186
77-79 Sports. FIN 72-1705
82 Valio
81/2 COLR
PORVZNIK, JIRI
94/5 APS 46
POSA, VICTOR
87/8 Flint Spirits
POSMA, MIKE
90/1 ProCards 563
POSMYK, MAREK
95/6 APS 183
96/7 APS 320
00/1 BAP Mem. 24
98 Bowman 7
98 Bowman Chrome 7
96/7 DS Sticker 156
00/1 Pacific 383
95/6 Upper Deck 542
99/0 St. John's Maple Leafs
POSNOV, ANDREI
00/1 Mir 57
POSPISIL, DAVID
94/5 APS 40
95/6 APS 326, 439
96/7 APS 154
97/8 APS 181
97/8 DS 55
98/9 DS 62
99/0 DS 97
00/1 DS 35
96/7 DS Sticker 261
97/8 DS Sticker 157
98/9 OFS 41, 461
99/0 OFS 371
00/1 OFS 71
01/2 OFS 253
POSPISIL, FRANTISEK
95/6 APS 394
01/2 DS L9
98/9 OFS Leg. 15
POSPISIL, JAN
00/1 OFS 111
01/2 OFS 185, H5
POSPISIL, ROBERT
97/8 APS 253
98/9 OFS 377
99/0 Score 156
POSPISIL, FRANTISEK
72 Hellas MM-Jenkki 86
74 Hellas MM-Jenkki 81
70/1 Kuvajulkaisut 56
72 Panda MM-Toronto
72 Semic Sticker 27
74 Semic Sticker 52
71/2 Williams Finnish 36
72/3 Williams Finnish 18
73/4 Williams Finnish 60
POSS, GREG
89/0 ProCards AHL 61
90/1 ProCards 136
91/2 ProCards 30
POTAICHUK, ANDREI
94/5 APS 92
95/6 APS 289, 432
96/7 APS 380, 395
98/9 Cardset 265
99/0 Cardset 154
00/1 Cardset 299
97/8 Hockey-Box
92/3 Red Ace Violet 28
POTAITSHUK, ANDREI
02/3 Cardset 98
POTAJCUK, ANDREI
96/7 DS Sticker 74
POTAPOV, MIKHAIL
00/1 Mir 145
POTH, JANOS
79 Panini Sticker 272
POTHIER, BRIAN
01/2 BAP Mem. 408
01/2 Crown Royale 148
01/2 Parkhurst 225
01/2 Pr. Stock 115
01/2 PS Titanium 149
01/2 PS Titanium Draft 108
01/2 SP Authentic 134
01/2 SP GU 64
01/2 SPx 133, -RT
01/2 UD Challenge 94
01/2 UD Vintage 276
01/2 Vanguard 104
01/2 Victory 362
01/2 Chicago Wolves
POTI, TOM
02/3 BAP Mem. 195
02/3 O-Pee-Chee 64
02/3 Pacific Complete 230
02/3 PS Titanium 70
02/3 Signature GS-97
02/3 SP Authentic 125
02/3 Topps 64
02/3 To. Limited 64
02/3 To. Total 190
02/3 Upper Deck 118
02/3 UD MVP 121
02/3 UD Vintage 164
02/3 Victory 143
99/0 BAP Mem. 228
00/1 BAP Mem. 351
01/2 BAP Mem. 494
98/9 Bowman's Best 111, F18
95/6 Classic 67
95/6 Do. Elite WJ 31
98/9 Dynagon Ice 75
99/0 Dynagon Ice 82
99/0 Millenium 98, ✍ Aut. 98
99/0 NHL Power Play
01/2 O-Pee-Chee 215
98/9 Omega 98
99/0 Omega 91
99/0 Pacific 163
00/1 Pacific 171
98/9 Pa. Crown Roy. 53
99/0 Pa. Paramount 94
00/1 Pa. Paramount 97
99/0 Panini Sticker 242
01/2 Parkhurst 196, 391
00/1 Signature 26, ✍ Aut. 11
98/9 SP Authentic 35
99/0 SPx 66
01/2 SPx 184
98/9 SPx Prospects 28
99/0 Stadium 136
00/1 Stadium 54
99/0 Topps 70
00/1 Topps 196
01/2 Topps 215
99/0 To. Chrome 70
00/1 To. Chrome 130
95/6 Upper Deck 568
98/9 Upper Deck 274, GN17
99/0 Upper Deck 57
00/1 Upper Deck 299
01/2 Upper Deck 72
98/9 UD Black Diam. 36
98/9 UD G. Reserve 274
99/0 UD G. Reserve 57
98/9 UD MVP 79
99/0 UD MVP 82, DR9, ✍ PS
00/1 UD MVP 72
01/2 UD MVP 74
99/0 UD Ovation 26
99/0 UD Retro 33
00/1 UD Vintage 142
01/2 UD Vintage 99, 105
99/0 Victory 110
00/1 Victory 94
01/2 Victory 143
99/0 WGretzky 71
POTOK,
91/2 Avant Garde BCJHL 155
POTOMSKI, BARRY
96/7 Pi. Be A Player 24, ✍ Aut. 24
90/1 7th..Sketch OHL 139
91/2 7th...Sketch OHL 366
94/5 Phoenix Roadrunners
95/6 Phoenix Roadrunners
92/3 Toledo Storm
93/4 Toledo Storm 24
POTTER, CHRIS
93/4 Roanoke Express
94/5 Roanoke Express
95/6 Roanoke Express
POTTIE, CHRISTOPHER
02/3 Hull Olympiques
POTTINGER, MARKUS
99/0 Eishockey 270, 369
PÖTTINGER, MARKUS
95/6 DEL 364
96/7 DEL 187
00/1 UD DEL 31
01/2 UD DEL 23
POTVIN, DENIS
02/3 BAP Mem. / Cup
02/3 Canada Post
02/3 Parkhurst ✄ VT11
02/3 Ultimate Mem. ✄ Cor, ✄ FS, ✄ Num, ✄ PS
02/3 UD Foundations ✄ 1000Jers, ✄ 1000Stick, ✄ CG, ✄ DF, ✄ MS, ✍ SG
01/2 ASG History
76/7 Dernière Heure
88/9 Esso All-Star
01/2 Fleer Greats 51, ✍ Aut.
01/2 Fleer Legacy 41, ✄ ITC
83/4 Funmate Puffy 20 [w/]
92/3 Future Trends C76 181
75/6 Hockey Heroes
91/2 Kraft 61
91/2 Kraft 72
74/5 Loblaws
82/3 McDonald's Les Étoiles 18
82/3 McDonald's Les Étoiles 33
74/5 O-Pee-Chee 195
74/5 O-Pee-Chee 233
74/5 O-Pee-Chee 252
75/6 O-Pee-Chee 275
75/6 O-Pee-Chee 287
75/6 O-Pee-Chee 323
76/7 O-Pee-Chee 5
76/7 O-Pee-Chee 170
76/7 O-Pee-Chee 389
77/8 O-Pee-Chee 10
77/8 O-Pee-Chee NS 15
78/9 O-Pee-Chee 245
78/9 O-Pee-Chee 334
79/0 O-Pee-Chee 70
80/1 O-Pee-Chee 120
81/2 O-Pee-Chee 199
81/2 O-Pee-Chee 209
82/3 O-Pee-Chee 210
83/4 O-Pee-Chee 2
83/4 O-Pee-Chee 16
84/5 O-Pee-Chee 134
84/5 O-Pee-Chee 216
84/5 O-Pee-Chee 389
85/6 OPC/Topps 25
86/7 OPC/Topps 129
87/8 OPC/Topps 1
92/3 O-Pee-Chee 57
92/3 OPC - Anniv. 7
81/2 OPC Sticker 9
81/2 OPC Sticker 10
81/2 OPC Sticker 151
81/2 OPC Sticker 159
82/3 OPC/Topps Sticker 46
83/4 OPC/Topps Sticker 81
83/4 OPC/Topps Sticker 82
83/4 OPC/Topps Sticker 169
83/4 OPC/Topps Sticker 175
84/5 OPC Sticker 78
84/5 OPC Sticker 79
84/5 OPC Sticker 145
84/5 OPC Sticker 66-65
85/6 OPC Sticker 70-198
86/7 OPC Sticker 209
87/8 OPC Sticker 247
80/1 O-Pee-Chee Super 13
87/8 Panini Sticker 91
01/2 Parkhurst ✄ HSHS Jers, ✍ PA48
82/3 Post [NYIs.]
90/1 Pro Set 656
91/2 Pro Set HHOF 2
83/4 Souhaits Keychain [Islanders]
77-79 Sportscaster 17-09
77-79 Sports. FIN 56-1324
74/5 Topps 195
74/5 Topps 233
74/5 Topps 252
75/6 Topps 275
75/6 Topps 287
75/6 Topps 323
76/7 Topps 5
76/7 Topps 170
76/7 Topps NS 10
77/8 Topps 10
77/8 ToppsNS 15
78/9 Topps 245
79/0 Topps 70
80/1 Topps 120
81/2 Topps 27
81/2 Topps 130 [East]
84/5 Topps 100
84/5 Topps 162
01/2 Topps -SCH, -Reprint, ✍ SCHA, ✍ Reprint
01/2 T/O Archives 37 , ✍ CAI
00/1 UD Heroes 132, ✍ SG
01/2 Ultimate Mem. ✄ ASGH, ✄ CT, ✄ Deca., ✄ EA, ✄ RN, ✄ RT, ✄ SCD, ✄ SCW, ✄ UC
90/1 Upper Deck 515
99/0 UD C. Legends 15
00/1 UD Legends 80, ES6, ✍ ES, ✄ LGJ
01/2 UD Legends 41, ✄ M, ✄ PoH, ✄ TT
00/1 UD Vintage ✄ D-POH
79/0 NYIS
83/4 NYIS
83/4 NYIS / News 21
84/5 NYIS / News 25
84/5 NYIS / News 33
93/4 NYIS / Bank
99/0 NYIS / UD NY3
POTVIN, DENIS
02/3 Fleer Throwbacks 17, 5SO, ✄ 5SO, ✍ Aut.
POTVIN, FÉLIX
02/3 Atomic 50, -D 9
02/3 BAP All-Star 71, ✄ ASJ
02/3 BAP Mem. 35, 259, ✄ ASJ42, ✄ SC11, ✄ TM13
02/3 Between the Pipes 27, 134, M14, ✄ ASJ8, ✄ BM18, ✄ GUE8, ✄ GB4, ✄ GUJ8, ✄ GSJ8, ✄ GN4, ✄ HSHSJers 15, ✄ ITN8, ✄ T10, ✍ Aut.
02/3 Bowman 52
02/3 Crown Royale 46
02/3 Exclusive 82, -EA 9
02/3 First Edition 4, ✄ Jers.
02/3 Heads Up 58, -S 11, ✄ GWQ 13
02/3 In The GU 35, 135, ✄ T17
02/3 O-Pee-Chee 18
02/3 Pacific 172
02/3 Pacific Complete 368
02/3 Parkhurst 137, ✄ TT6
02/3 Parkhurst Retro 68, ✄ NN25
02/3 Pr. Stock Reserve -ICS 11, ✄ 125
02/3 PS Titanium 51
02/3 Quest for the Cup 45
02/3 Signature 63, ✍ 63, ✄ FS8, ✄ TQ10
02/3 SP Authentic 42
02/3 SP GU 22, ✄ AF, ✄ CF, ✄ PH
02/3 Sports Vault 240
02/3 SPx 36, ✄ WM
02/3 Stadium 97
02/3 Topps 18
02/3 T. Chrome 18
02/3 To. Heritage 83, ✄ CP, ✄ CPB
02/3 To. Limited 18
02/3 To. Total 154
02/3 UD Superstars ✄ CAS
02/3 Upper Deck 85, ✄ GT
02/3 UD Artistic 43, R43, ✄ AT, / Art
02/3 UD Classic 46, ✄ HR (x2), ✄ SC
02/3 UD Honor 34
02/3 UD Mask 39, 40, 41, 112, ✄ CW, ✄ GG, ✄ MM, ✄ BM, ✄ NB, ✄ PW, / Mask
02/3 UD MVP 85, SA, SD (x3)
02/3 UD Piece 44, ✄ PH
02/3 UD Rookie 48, ✄ DJ
02/3 UD Top Shelf 41, ✄ M, ✄ R, ✄ SS, ✄ SW, ✄ TS
02/3 UD Vintage 119, 274, GB 119, ✄ EE
02/3 Vanguard 50, -SW 5
02/3 Victory 96
94/5 Action Packed
01/2 Adrenaline 88, CL 9, PP 18, ✄ GWJ 20
01/2 Atomic 48
99/0 Aurora 91, Stripe 91, GU-12
00/1 Aurora 145, Pins. 145
94/5 Be A Player Magazine Postcard
99/0 BAP Mem. 139, 325
00/1 BAP Mem. 45, 503, ✄ G-9, ✄ G-20, ✄ H-19
01/2 BAP Mem. 78, ✄ GJ
01/2 BAP Update ✄ H3, ✄ TP13
01/2 BT Pipes 35, -Mask, ✄ DM, ✄ GJ, ✄ S&J, ✄ GG, ✄ HSHSJers
97/8 Bicycle 4-Diamond
98/9 Bicycle.. Q-H
95/6 Bicycle Sports Aces 4-Spade
92/3 Bowman 77
95/6 Bowman 79
01/2 Bowman 59
93/4 Classic 123
93/4 Classic N9
93/4 Cla. Images 4 Sport 121
92/3 Classic Prospects 80
92/3 Classic Prospects BC7
93/4 Cla. Prospects 51
00/1 Crown Royale 105, ✄ GWJ-25
01/2 Crown Royale 70
93/4 Donruss 343
93/4 Donruss W
93/4 Donruss ES U3
93/4 Donruss IK 6
94/5 Donruss 12, D-7, ES-8, MM-7
95/6 Donruss 9, BTP-9, D-8
96/7 Donruss 96, BTP-10
97/8 Donruss 154, BTP-9
96/7 Do. Canadian 67, LG-3
97/8 Do. Canadian 56, LG-2
95/6 Do. Elite 97, PW-2
96/7 Do. Elite 5, PW-6
97/8 Do. Elite 100, 131, C-13
97/8 Do. Preferred 99, CG-5
97/8 Do. Priority 101, 198, OD-25, PG-3, Post-29, Stamp-29
97/8 Do. Studio 66, S-20, P-34
96/7 Duracell JB12
93/4 Durivage 32
99/0 Dynagon Ice 127
93/4 EA Sports 138
95/6 Edge Ice L7
94/5 Flair 184
96/7 Flair 91, HG-8
94/5 Fleer 218, N-7
96/7 Fleer 109, VT-7
95/6 Fleer Metal 146
92/3 Fleer Ultra 213
93/4 Fleer Ultra 30
94/5 Fleer Ultra 219, ASG-12, PPM-4
95/6 Fleer Ultra 162, 375, PPM-9
96/7 Fl. Ultra 165
01/2 Heads Up 47, HD 15, SS 10
93/4 High Liner 13
93/4 Hockey Wit 34
95/6 Hoyle / West. J-Diamond
96/7 Kellogg's
93/4 Kraft / JELL-O
94/5 Kraft / KD
95/6 Kraft / PS
96/7 Kraft / Fav.
94/5 Kraft Mask
93/4 Leaf 409
93/4 Leaf GLAS 10
93/4 Leaf GLR 4
93/4 Leaf PW 1
94/5 Leaf 186, CP-4, GLS-13
95/6 Leaf 160
96/7 Leaf 156, SD-8
97/8 Leaf 24, PD-5
94/5 L. Limited 16
95/6 L. Limited 29, SS-3
96/7 L. Limited 80
96/7 L. Preferred 36, MM-5, VP-10
97/8 Limited 29, 57, 77, FG-15
96/7 Maggers 146
94/5 McDonald's McD-14
95/6 McDonald's McD-26
96/7 McDonald's McD-38
97/8 McDonald's McD-31
00/1 McDonald's 35, CL-9
01/2 McDonald's 19
96/7 Metal Univ. 152, AP-7
92/3 O-Pee-Chee 73
01/2 O-Pee-Chee 173
98/9 OPC Chrome 29
92/3 OPC Premier 114
92/3 OPC Premier TR4
97/8 Omega 223, NSZ-10, TL-18
98/9 Omega 150, -Onl. 22, -PI 5
99/0 Omega 237
98/9 Pacific 29, -GCDC 31
99/0 Pacific 263, GC-22, ITCNF-11
00/1 Pacific 414
01/2 Pacific 185
97/8 Pacific CC 29, CS-19, ITC-20, TC-24
97/8 Pa. Crown Roy. 131, FO-19
97/8 Pa. Dynagon 122, S-20, T-17, BKS-92
97/8 Pa. Invincible 137, FP-33, R-195
97/8 Pa. Paramount 183, GSL-20
99/0 Pa. Paramount 146, GS-12, IAI-17
00/1 Pa. Paramount 242, GS-19
97/8 Pa. Revolution 136, RTS-19
01/2 PTC Collectors 4
98/9 Panini Photocard
92/3 Panini Sticker G
93/4 Panini Sticker 139
93/4 Panini Sticker 232
94/5 Panini Sticker 198
95/6 Panini Sticker 210
96/7 Panini Sticker 211
98/9 Panini Sticker 165
99/0 Panini Sticker 91, 338
91/2 Parkhurst 398
92/3 Parkhurst 187
92/3 Parkhurst 507
93/4 Parkhurst 202
93/4 Parkhurst 237
93/4 Parkhurst D14
93/4 Parkhurst W9
94/5 Parkhurst 229
95/6 Parkhurst 204, CCB-2, GP-2
00/1 Parkhurst P-79
01/2 Parkhurst 59
95 Parkhurst Phonecard
95 Parkhurst Phonecard
94/5 Parkie SE seV32
91/2 Pinnacle 345
92/3 Pinnacle 364
92/3 Pinnacle T2K 5
93/4 Pinnacle 190
93/4 Pinnacle T2K1 5
94/5 Pinnacle 83, GT8, NL9, TP1
95/6 Pinnacle 142, M-4, R20-10
96/7 Pinnacle 96
97/8 Pinnacle 95
96/7 Pi. Be A Player SP-6
97/8 Pi. Be A Player 4, STP-3, ✍ Aut. 4
97/8 Pi. BeeHive 16
97/8 Pi. Certified 11
97/8 Pi. Epix E11
95/6 Pi. FANtasy 29
97/8 Pi. Inside 46, IT-20, S-21
96/7 Pi. Mint 24
95/6 Pi. Summit 80, ITC-5
96/7 Pi. Summit 72, ITC-9, U-17
97/8 Pi. Totally 11
95/6 Pi. Zenith 76, ZT-17
96/7 Pi. Zenith 31, ZT-16
95/6 Playoff 98, 204
96/7 Playoff 364
94/5 POG 296
95/6 POG 268
94/5 Post
93/4 Power Play 246
93/4 Power Play SYS 8
93/4 Power Play Game. 7
93/4 Power Play Netm. 5
93/4 Power Play RisS 3
93/4 Premier 111
93/4 Premier 126
93/4 Premier 30
93/4 Premier 385
93/4 Prmr. - BG-OPC 17
93/4 Prmr. - BG-Top. 3
94/5 Premier 238, 313, 355
00/1 Pr. Stock 97
01/2 Pr. Stock 46, -PS 37, ✄ GUG52
00/1 PS Titanium 97, 3SS-9, ✄ GUG-49, ✄ GUG-149
01/2 PS Titanium 67, ✄ DSJ 17, ✄ DSJ 20
01/2 PS Titanium Draft ✄ 43
00/1 PS Titanium Draft ✄ 48
95/6 Pro Magnet 74
92/3 Pro Set 242
91/2 ProCards 354
99/0 Revolution 93, SS-22, / CSC 93
00/1 Revolution 145
92/3 Score 472
92/3 Score 501
93/4 Score 484
93/4 Score 5
93/4 Score / Promo 5
94/5 Score 160, DT-2
95/6 Score 4, 316
96/7 Score 172, SD-12, S-5
97/8 Score 29, NW-16
97/8 Score Toro. 1
92/3 Score Young Stars 39
93/4 Seasons 14
94/5 Select 90
95/6 Select CE 69
96/7 Select CE 31, F-8
92 7th...Sketch Awards 26
90/1 7th..Sketch LHJMQ 35
91 7th..Sketch Mem.Cup 26, 72
00/1 Signature 90, ✍ Aut. 153
01/2 Signature ✄ GU87, ✄ TM14
95/6 SBx Emotion 174
95/6 SBx Impact 164, D-3
96/7 SBx Impact 129, ZH-7
94/5 SP 117
95/6 SP 146, E27
96/7 SP 153, GF-7, Ins.
97/8 SP Authentic 151
00/1 SP Authentic ✍ SotT
01/2 SP Authentic 40, ✍ SotT, ✍ SotTD, ✍ SotTT
01/2 SP GU ✄ AF, ✄ AFD (x2)
96/7 SPx 44
99/0 SPx 91
00/1 SPx 67, ✄ WM, ✄✍ WM
01/2 SPx 31, ✄ DT
98/9 SPx Prospects WM FP
99/0 Stadium 69
00/1 Stadium 75
01/2 Stadium 92
95/6 SLU
98/9 SLU
95/6 Super Sticker 120, DC-19
96/7 Team Out!
92/3 Topps 3
95/6 Topps 315, 8CG, HGC-18, M22
98/9 Topps 29
99/0 Topps 136
00/1 Topps 56
01/2 Topps 173
99/0 To. Chrome 136
00/1 To. Chrome 44
01/2 To. Chrome 119
94/5 Topps Finest 26
95/6 To. Finest 105, 135
98/9 To. Finest 70
96 Topps Finest Bronze 18
00/1 To. Heritage 124
01/2 To. Heritage 65
96/7 To. Picks ID14
01/2 To. Reserve 69
92/3 To. Stadium 338
93/4 To. Stadium 280
93/4 To. Stadium - Master Photo-2 12
93/4 To. Stadium - Finest 5
94/5 To. Stadium 15, 185
95/6 To. Stadium 80, MP, EN3
93/4 TSC Members Only 1
94/5 TSC Members Only 40
95/6 TSC Members Only 13
00/1 To. Stars 90, PP5
95/6 T. Super Skills 85
00/1 UD Heroes ✍ SG
01/2 UD PlayMakers Ltd 46
00/1 Ultimate Mem. ✄ G-29, ✄ PJ-14, ✄ J-37, ✄ JJ-20, ✄ S-37, ✄ TM-38, ✄ GM-4
01/2 Ultimate Mem. ✄ BAPL, ✄ JE, ✄ JJ
90/1 Upper Deck 458
91/2 Upper Deck 460
92/3 Upper Deck 79
92/3 Upper Deck CC3
93/4 Upper Deck 159, 285, FH-28, NL-6, SP-160
94/5 Upper Deck 367, H28, SP-80
95/6 Upper Deck 48, 228, AS-20, H-17, SE-168
96/7 Upper Deck 341, 360, X33, SS11A
97/8 Upper Deck 367
98/9 Upper Deck 371
99/0 Upper Deck 253
00/1 Upper Deck 170, ✄ DGJ
01/2 Upper Deck 308, LL4, ✄ PotL
93/4 Upper Deck Be A Player 11
94/5 UD BAP R81, R138, R173
95/6 UD BAP 195, ✍ S195
93/4 UD BAP Roots 3
96/7 UD Black Diam. 129
97/8 UD Black Diam. 5
98/9 UD Black Diam. 54
00/1 UD Black Diam. 58
01/2 UD Challenge 38, ✄ T200, ✄✍ T200S
95/6 UD CC 114
96/7 UD CC 257, 332, UD20, S11
97/8 UD Coll. Choice 252, SQ29
98/9 UD G. Reserve 371
99/0 UD G. Reserve 253
96/7 UD Ice 67
97/8 UD Ice 29
01/2 UD Ice 101
92/3 UD Locker 58
01/2 UD Mask 114, 179, ✄ GJ, ✄ JP, ✄ DP, ✄✍ SP, ✄ MB, ✄ StS, ✄ SuS, ✄ VC
98/9 UD MVP 126
99/0 UD MVP 124, W16
00/1 UD MVP 174, ✄ CG
01/2 UD MVP MM14
95/6 UD Post 22
96/7 UD Post
01/2 UD Premier 28, ✄ D (x2), ✍ SigS
01/2 UD Top Shelf 96
00/1 UD Vintage 357, 358, GG19
01/2 UD Vintage 115, 122
00/1 Vanguard 97
01/2 Vanguard 46, QTH 8
99/0 Victory 184
00/1 Victory 230
01/2 Victory 158, 167
99/0 WGretzky 108
97/8 Zenith 38, Z42
92/3 TORO / Kodak
93/4 TORO / Abalene
93/4 TORO / Black's 24
94/5 TORO / Coca-Cola
00/1 St. John's Maple Leafs
POTVIN, JEAN
74/5 Loblaws
74/5 O-Pee-Chee 101
75/6 O-Pee-Chee 36
76/7 O-Pee-Chee 93
77/8 O-Pee-Chee 144
78/9 O-Pee-Chee 287
79/0 O-Pee-Chee 334
74/5 Topps 101
75/6 Topps 36
76/7 Topps 93
77/8 Topps 144
71/2 Toronto Sun Photo
79/0 NYIS
POTVIN, MARC
94/5 Fleer Ultra 259
94/5 Leaf 541
90/1 ProCards 486
91/2 Upper Deck 405
93/4 HART / Coke
98/9 Chicago Wolves Champs
99/0 Mississippi S'Wolves
96/7 Portland Pirates
POTVIN, RICK
89/0 Rayside-Balfour
POTVIN, STEVE
95/6 Classic 89
93/4 Slapshot / Sudbury 20
00/1 UD DEL 114
92/3 Sudbury Wolves
93/4 Sudbury Wolves
POTVIN , FÉLIX
01/2 Atomic ✄ GWJ 29
POTYOK, SHAWN
91/2 Avant Garde BCJHL 11
POTZ, JERZV
89 Semic Sticker 135
POTZ, JERZY
74 Hellas MM-Jenkki 85
79 Panini Sticker 124
73/4 Williams Finnish 97
POUDRIER, DANIEL
94/5 DEL 75
95/6 DEL 34
87/8 QUÉB / Gene. Foods
85/6 Fredericton Express
86/7 Fredericton Express
POUDRIER, SERGE
96/7 DEL 6
95 Globe 204
95 Panini Worlds 103
94 Semic 220
92 Semic Sticker 227
93 Semic Sticker 252
96 Wien 185
POUDRIER, THIERY
01/2 Shawinigan Cataractes 14
02/3 Shawinigan Cataractes
POUGET, CHRISTIAN
96/7 DEL 177
98/9 DEL 231
95 Panini Worlds 113
92 Semic Sticker 236
96 Wien 189
POUIOT, MARTIN
96/7 Halifax Moosehead
POUKAR, JIRI
94/5 APS 173
95/6 APS 190, 415
96/7 APS 325
97/8 APS 161
97/8 DS 78
99/0 DS 191
96/7 DS Sticker 164
97/8 DS Sticker 198
98/9 OFS 321, 484
99/0 OFS 82
POULIN, CHARLES
92/3 Classic Prospects 27
90/1 7th..Sketch LHJMQ 220
91/2 7th...Sketch LHJMQ 12
93/4 Fredericton Canadiens
POULIN, DANIEL
77/8 Kalamazoo Wings
POULIN, DAVE
90/1 Bowman 36
91/2 Bowman 359
92/3 Bowman 19
93/4 Donruss 362
92/3 Fleer Ultra 9
93/4 Fleer Ultra 193
93/4 Fleer Ultra 450
93/4 Fleer Ultra AW 5
94/5 Fleer Ultra 391
88/9 Frito Lay
93/4 Leaf 332
84/5 O-Pee-Chee 165
85/6 OPC/Topps 128
86/7 OPC/Topps 71
87/8 OPC/Topps 39
88/9 OPC/Topps 100
90/1 OPC/Topps 362
91/2 O-Pee-Chee 507
92/3 O-Pee-Chee 367
89/0 OPC/Topps 115
87/8 OPC Leaders 32
84/5 OPC Sticker 110
85/6 OPC Sticker 89
86/7 OPC Sticker 241
87/8 OPC Sticker 179-34
87/8 OPC Sticker 98-232
87/8 Panini Sticker 130
87/8 Panini Sticker 386
88/9 Panini Sticker 323
89/0 Panini Sticker 305
90/1 Panini Sticker 4
92/3 Panini Sticker 137
93/4 Panini Sticker 4
92/3 Parkhurst 242
93/4 Parkhurst 488
94/5 Parkhurst 253
92/3 Pinnacle 116
93/4 Pinnacle 229
93/4 Pinnacle 387
94/5 Pinnacle 179
93/4 Power Play 470
93/4 Premier 228
94/5 Premier 236
90/1 Pro Set 13
91/2 Pro Set 12
92/3 Pro Set 9
91/2 Pro Set Platinum 5
90/1 Score 217
91/2 Score 232
91/2 Score CAN 452
92/3 Score 359
93/4 Score 228
93/4 Score 552
94/5 Score 38
84/5 Topps 120
92/3 Topps 155
91/2 To. Stadium 253
92/3 To. Stadium 13
93/4 To. Stadium 142
93/4 To. Stadium 301
90/1 Upper Deck 177
92/3 Upper Deck G16
93/4 Upper Deck 355, AW8
94/5 UD BAP ✍ 124
89/0 BOST / Sports Action
90/1 BOST / Sports Action
91/2 BOST / Sports Action
92/3 BOST / Postcard
83/4 PHIL / J.C. Penney
86/7 PHIL
89/0 PHIL
POULIN, DENE
00/1 Owen Sound Attack 3
POULIN, GEORGE
91 C55 Reprint 44
10/1 Imperial
10/1 Imperial 24
11/2 Imperial 44
12/3 Imperial 8
POULIN, PAT**
80/1 Oshawa Generals
POULIN, PATRICK
91/2 Arena 7
98/9 Be A Player 69, ✍ Aut. 69
91/2 Classic 8
91/2 Classic Four Sport 8
93/4 Donruss 146
94/5 Donruss 144
95/6 Donruss 269
93/4 Durivage 50
94/5 Fleer 44
95/6 Fleer Metal 27
92/3 Fleer Ultra 304
93/4 Fleer Ultra 122
93/4 Fleer Ultra 292
94/5 Fleer Ultra 43
93/4 Leaf 113
93/4 Leaf GLR 10
94/5 Leaf 390
95/6 Leaf 237
92/3 OPC Premier 85
99/0 Pacific 207
97/8 Pacific CC 230
00/1 Pa. Paramount 128
93/4 Panini Sticker 126
95/6 Panini Sticker 158
92/3 Parkhurst 60
93/4 Parkhurst 307
95/6 Parkhurst 42
94/5 Parkie SE32
92/3 Pinnacle 418
92/3 Pinnacle T2K 14
93/4 Pinnacle 61
93/4 Pinnacle T2K1 8
94/5 Pinnacle 283
95/6 Pinnacle 135
95/6 Pi. Summit 99
95/6 Playoff 133
96/7 Playoff 369
94/5 POG 69
95/6 POG 67
93/4 Power Play 108
93/4 Power Play 315
93/4 Power Play SYS 9
94/5 Premier 316
92/3 Pro Set 227
92/3 Score 478
93/4 Score 202
93/4 Score 571
94/5 Score 6
95/6 Score 158
92/3 Score Young Stars 31
90/1 7th..Sketch LHJMQ 1
91/2 7th...Sketch LHJMQ 10
91 7th..Sketch Mem.Cup 98
95/6 SBx Emotion 32
95/6 SBx Impact 32
91/2 Star Pics 36
91/2 Star Pics 68
95/6 Super Sticker 25
92/3 Topps 328
95/6 Topps 326, 4PL
92/3 To. Stadium 211
93/4 To. Stadium 157
94/5 To. Stadium 13
95/6 To. Stadium 212
91/2 Ultimate Draft Pick 8, 64,

✍ Aut.
99/0 Ult. Victory 45
91/2 Upper Deck 65
92/3 Upper Deck 416
92/3 Upper Deck 557
92/3 Upper Deck CC18
93/4 Upper Deck 138, NL2, SP-30
94/5 Upper Deck 36
95/6 Upper Deck 208, SE-106
97/8 Upper Deck 366
94/5 UD BAP ✍ 168
95/6 UD CC 187
97/8 UD Coll. Choice 242
91/2 Upper Deck WJC 51
00/1 UD Vintage 192
93/4 CHIC / Coke
92/3 HART / Dairymart
97/8 MONT
00/1 MONT
01/2 MONT

POULIN, RICK
89/0 Rayside-Balfour

POULIOT, MARC-ANTOINE
98 Québec Pee Wee 910
99 Québec Pee Wee 663
01/2 Rimouski Océanic 23

POULIOT, MARIO
91/2 7th...Sketch LHJMQ 24

POULSEN, MARCO
93/4 Jyvas Hyva 27
93/4 Sisu 98
94/5 Sisu 346
95/6 Sisu 345
95/6 Sisu Limited 94

POUND, IAN
84/5 Kitchener Rangers
85/6 Kitchener Rangers
86/7 London Knights

POUNDER, CHERYL
94/5 Classic W3

POUSAZ, JACQUES
72 Semic Sticker 148

POUSSE, PIERRE
95 Panini Worlds 109
92 Semic Sticker 240
93 Semic Sticker 265

POUSSU, PENTTI
72/3 Williams Finnish 292

POUZAR, JAROSLAV
95/6 APS 397
83/4 O-Pee-Chee 41
84/5 O-Pee-Chee 256
83/4 OPC/Topps Sticker 151
83/4 OPC/Topps Sticker 159
98/9 OFS Leg. 7
00/1 OFS 5
79 Panini Sticker 87
83/4 Vachon 38-118
82/3 EDMO / Red Rooster
83/4 EDMO / Button
83/4 EDMO / McDonald's
83/4 EDMO / West Mall
83/4 EDMO
84/5 EDMO
84/5 EDMO / Red Rooster
86/7 EDMO
88/9 EDMO / Action 18

POWELL, KEVIN
91/2 Air Canada SJHL D16
98/9 Wichita Thunder
92/3 Tacoma Rockets

POWER, ANDREW
93/4 Slapshot / Oshawa 12

POWER, CHAD
99/0 Anchorage Aces
00/1 Quad City Mallards

POWER, COLIN
01/2 Guelph Storm
01/2 Guelph Storm M-Cup

POWER, LARRY
81/2 Ottawa 67's
82/3 Ottawa 67's

POWER, RICHARD
00/1 Owen Sound Attack 21
01/2 Owen Sound Attack

POWER, ROCKET
91 C55 Reprint 40
10/1 Imperial
11/2 Imperial 40

POWER, RYAN
95/6 Slapshot 229
97/8 Halifax Moosehead
97/8 Halifax Moosehead

POWERS, JIMMY
93/4 Raleigh Icecaps
94/5 Raleigh Icecaps

POWIS, JEFF
67/8 Topps 110

POWIS, LYNN
74/5 Loblaws
73/4 O-Pee-Chee 209
74/5 O-Pee-Chee 227
76/7 OPC WHA 86
74/5 Topps 227

POYHIA, HARRI
80/1 Mallasjuoma 142

POZDNYAKOV, VLADIMIR
99/0 Mir 63
00/1 Mir 193

POZIVIL, LUKAS
01/2 OFS 152

POZNIK, LUKAS
98/9 OFS 407
99/0 OFS 172

POZZO, KEVIN
94/5 Slapshot Memorial 30
99/0 Charlotte Checkers
00/1 Charlotte Checkers
97/8 New Orleans Brass

POZZO, MICHAEL
98/9 Oklahoma City Blazers

PRACEY, RICK
88/9 Brockville Braves
89/0 Soo Greyhounds

PRACHAR, KAMIL
94/5 APS 208
95/6 APS 152
96/7 APS 169
94 Semic 167
92 Semic Sticker 127

PRAJSLER, PETR
90/1 O-Pee-Chee 481
88/9 ProCards / New Haven
90/1 ProCards 347
91/2 ProCards 57
89/0 LOSA / Smokey 11

PRATT, BABE
02/3 Ultimate Mem. ✍ Cut

PRATT, HARLAN
00/1 Cincinnati Cyclones
99/0 Florida Everblades
95/6 Red Deer Rebels

PRATT, JON
95/6 Peoria Rivermen
96/7 Peoria Rivermen
97/8 Peoria Rivermen

PRATT, KELLY
74/5 PITT

PRATT, NOLAN
99/0 Millenium 54, ✍ Aut. 54
98/9 Upper Deck 239
00/1 Upper Deck 272
98/9 UD G. Reserve 239
97/8 CARO / Sprint
98/9 CARO / Highwoods
96/7 HART / Kids Club
96/7 Springfield Falcons
93/4 Portland Winter Hawks

PRATT, STAN
37/8 World Wide Gum 126

PRATT, TOM
88/9 ProCards / New Haven

PRATT, TRACY
70/1 Dad's Cookies
70/1 Eddie Sargent 19
71/2 Eddie Sargent 25
72/3 Eddie Sargent 30
70/1 Esso Power Player
72/3 Post 3
74/5 Loblaws
69/0 O-Pee-Chee 111
70/1 O-Pee-Chee 146
71/2 O-Pee-Chee 107
72/3 O-Pee-Chee 69
73/4 O-Pee-Chee 54
74/5 O-Pee-Chee 41
75/6 O-Pee-Chee 133
76/7 O-Pee-Chee 275
68/9 Shirriff / Oakl. 10
69/0 Topps 111
71/2 Topps 107
72/3 Topps 84
73/4 Topps 54
74/5 Topps 41
75/6 Topps 133
71/2 Toronto Sun Photo
72/3 BUFF
73/4 BUFF
76/7 COLR / Hockey Talk
74/5 VANC / Royal Bank
75/6 VANC / Royal Bank

PRATT, WALTER (BABE)
34-43 BeeHive-1 [NYRa.]
34-43 BeeHive-1 [Toro.]
83 HHOF Postcard L13
83&87 HHOF 162
93/4 Legends of Hockey 29
39/0 O-Pee-Chee 85
55/6 Parkhurst 31
94/5 Parkie Tall 3
45-54 Quaker Oats

PRAWDZIK, WALTER
00/1 Sudbury Wolves 7

PRAZAK, KAREL
94/5 APS 285

PRAZMA, MARTY
86/7 Saskatoon Blades

PRAZNIK, JODY
89/0 Saskatoon Blades

PRECECHTEL, JAROMIR
94/5 APS 278
95/6 APS 100

PREFONTAINE, BRAD
91/2 Air Canada SJHL C2
95/6 Birmingham Bulls

PREMAK, GARTH
92/3 Canada Nationals
87/8 Kamloops Blazers

PRENTICE, DEAN
45-64 BeeHive-2 [NYRa.]
45-64 BeeHive-2 [NYRa.]
45-64 BeeHive-2 [Bost.]
64-67 BeeHive-3 [Bost.]
64-67 BeeHive-3 [Detr.]
64/5 Coke/Sprite [Bost.]
65/6 Coca-Cola
70/1 Dad's Cookies
70/1 Eddie Sargent 165
71/2 Eddie Sargent 89
70/1 Esso Power Player
62/3 Cowan Tile
68/9 O-Pee-Chee 32
69/0 O-Pee-Chee 115
70/1 O-Pee-Chee 201
72/3 O-Pee-Chee 289
54/5 Parkhurst 74
93/4 Parkhurst DPR-9
93/4 Parkie 56-57 91
95/6 Parkie 66-67 51
94/5 Parkie Tall 5
72 Semic Sticker 218
61/2 Shirriff 84
68/9 Shirriff / Detr. 5
57/8 Topps 62
58/9 Topps 32
59/0 Topps 17
60/1 Topps 37
61/2 Topps 54
61/2 Topps - Stamp
62/3 Topps 53
62/3 Topps Dollar
63/4 Topps 13
64/5 Topps 19
65/6 Topps 102
66/7 Topps 45
66/7 Topps / Test 45
67/8 Topps 46
68/9 Topps 32
69/0 Topps 115
58/9 Toronto Star Photo
62/3 Toronto Star Photo
64/5 Toronto Star Photo
60/1 Toronto Star Weekend
71/2 Toronto Sun Photo
91/2 Ultimate Original Six 27, ✍ Aut. 27
73/4 MINS

PRENTICE, RYAN
99/0 Asheville Smoke

PRESLEY, WAYNE
91/2 Bowman 402
92/3 Bowman 76
94/5 Leaf 521
87/8 OPC/Topps 179
88/9 OPC/Topps 185
90/1 O-Pee-Chee 456
91/2 O-Pee-Chee 385
89/0 OPC/Topps 98
91/2 OPC Premier 89
87/8 Panini Sticker 228
89/0 Panini Sticker 3, 52
91/2 Panini Sticker 19
93/4 Panini Sticker 107
91/2 Parkhurst 163
93/4 Parkhurst 294
94/5 Parkhurst 27
91/2 Pinnacle 68
93/4 Pinnacle 425
94/5 Pinnacle 321
93/4 Premier 162
90/1 Pro Set 434
91/2 Pro Set 44
91/2 Pro Set 488
91/2 Pro Set Platinum 228
90/1 Score 92T
91/2 Score 221
91/2 Score 9T
91/2 Score CAN 221
91/2 Score CAN 559
92/3 Score 213
93/4 Score 296
95/6 Score 223
92/3 Topps 424
91/2 To. Stadium 215
92/3 To. Stadium 24
93/4 To. Stadium 233
94/5 To. Stadium 196
90/1 Upper Deck 339
91/2 Upper Deck 371
95/6 UD BAP 45, ✍ S45
95/6 UD CC 179
92/3 BUFF / Blue Shield
92/3 BUFF / Jubilee
86/7 CHIC / Coke
87/8 CHIC / Coke
88/9 CHIC / Coke
89/0 CHIC / Coke
90/1 CHIC / Coke
91/2 SANJ / Sports Action
96/7 Detroit Vipers
85/6 Nova Scotia Oilers
82/3 Kitchener Rangers
83/4 Kitchener Rangers
84/5 Kitchener Rangers
84/5 Soo Greyhounds

PREST, TREVOR
91/2 Avant Garde BCJHL 42

PRESTBERG, PELLE
97/8 UD Elitserien 59
98/9 UD Elitserien 94, DL4
99/0 UD Elitserien 63
00/1 UD Elitserien 67

PRESTON, BRAD
98/9 Oklahoma City Blazers

PRESTON, BRIAN
92/3 BCJHL 23

PRESTON, DAN
91/2 7th...Sketch OHL 103
95/6 Slapshot 73
01/2 Manchester Storm
02/3 Manchester Storm

PRESTON, RICH
80/1 O-Pee-Chee 41
82/3 O-Pee-Chee 71
83/4 O-Pee-Chee 110
84/5 O-Pee-Chee 118
85/6 OPC/Topps 139
86/7 OPC/Topps 61
86/7 OPC Sticker 199-69
76/7 OPC WHA 115
82/3 Post [Chic.]
83/4 Souhaits Keychain [Blackhawks]
80/1 Topps 41
84/5 Topps 34
79/0 CHIC
80/1 CHIC / Colour
80/1 CHIC / Brown
81/2 CHIC
82/3 CHIC
83/4 CHIC
86/7 CHIC / Coke
91/2 CHIC / Coke
93/4 CHIC / Coke
84/5 NJER
75/6 Houston Aeros
78/9 Winnipeg Jets
96/7 Regina Pats

PRESTON, YVES
81/2 Milwaukee Admirals

PRETTY, DAVID
80/1 Québec Remparts

PREUCIL, PETR
00/1 Québec Remparts 14
01/2 Québec Remparts 13

PREUSS, GUNTHER
94/5 DEL 143
95/6 DEL 141

PREVOST, STACY
91/2 Air Canada SJHL B12
92/3 MPS SJHL 168

PRIAKIN, SERGEI
90/1 Bowman 103
97/8 Hockey-Box
89/0 Kraft 8
90/1 Panini/CGY 17
90/1 Pro Set 594
94/5 Sisu 214
95/6 Sisu 91, 380
96/7 Sisu 93
95/6 Sisu Limited 61
90/1 CALG / McGavin's

PRIBYLA, KAMIL
94/5 APS 125

PRICE, DAN
00/1 Austin Ice Bats

PRICE, GERRY
52/3 Anonymous 12

PRICE, MATT
95/6 Slapshot 119

PRICE, NOEL
52/3 Anonymous 149
72/3 Eddie Sargent 8
70/1 Esso Power Player
74/5 Loblaws
68/9 O-Pee-Chee 110
70/1 O-Pee-Chee 163
72/3 O-Pee-Chee 163
73/4 O-Pee-Chee 256
74/5 O-Pee-Chee 356
75/6 O-Pee-Chee 331
58/9 Parkhurst 6
59/0 Parkhurst 42
93/4 Parkie 56-57 131
65/6 Québec Aces
68/9 Shirriff / Pitt. 4
68/9 Topps 110
72/3 ATLF
74/5 ATLF

PRICE, PAT
86/7 Kraft Sports 49
76/7 O-Pee-Chee 318
77/8 O-Pee-Chee 308
78/9 O-Pee-Chee 368
79/0 O-Pee-Chee 347
80/1 O-Pee-Chee 299
81/2 O-Pee-Chee 265
82/3 O-Pee-Chee 274
84/5 O-Pee-Chee 286
80/1 Pepsi Bottle Cap
82/3 Post [Pitt.]
83/4 Vachon 71-51
79/0 EDMO
88/9 EDMO / Action 82
87/8 MINS
83/4 QUÉB
84/5 QUÉB
85/6 QUÉB
85/6 QUÉB / Gene. Foods
85/6 QUÉB / McDonald's
85/6 QUÉB / Provigo
86/7 QUÉB
86/7 QUÉB / McDonald's

PRIDDLE, PHIL
83/4 Brantford Alexanders

PRIEST, MERV
90/1 7th..Sketch WHL 220
91/2 7th...Sketch WHL 207
89/0 Brandon Wheat Kings
90/1 Brandon Wheat Kings

PRIESTLAY, KEN
90/1 Canada Nationals 16
91/2 Parkhurst 359
91/2 Pro Set 460
88/9 ProCards / Rochester
89/0 ProCards AHL 257
91/2 Score CAN 658
91/2 Upper Deck 525
87/8 BUFF / Blue Shield
89/0 BUFF / Blue Shield
91/2 PITT / Elby's
92/3 Cleveland Lumberjacks
01/2 Sheffield Steelers
95/6 Sheffield Steelers
97/8 Sheffield Steelers
84/5 Victoria Cougars

PRIKRYL, PETR
99/0 DS 142
00/1 DS 2
98/9 OFS 362
99/0 OFS 540
00/1 OFS 291
01/2 OFS 98, G3

PRIKRYL, STANISLAV
99/0 OFS 450

PRILLO, ERIC
90/1 7th..Sketch LHJMQ 90

PRIMEAU, ERIC
84/5 Richelieu Riverains

PRIMEAU, JOE
02/3 Parkie - Reprint 204
02/3 Ultimate Mem. ✍ Cut
33/4 Anonymous 7
34-43 BeeHive-1 [Toro.]
33/4 Hamilton Gum 2
83 HHOF Postcard I12
83&87 HHOF 131
29/0 La Presse
32/3 Maple Leafs O'Keefe
33/4 O-Pee-Chee 12
55/6 Parkhurst 24
91/2 Pro Set 338
34/5 Sweet Caporal
33/4 WWGum 40

PRIMEAU, KEITH
02/3 BAP Mem. 186, 249
02/3 Bowman 99
02/3 First Edition 86, ✂ Jers.
02/3 O-Pee-Chee 116
02/3 Pacific 285
02/3 Pacific Complete 213
02/3 Parkhurst 44
02/3 Parkhurst Retro 93
02/3 Signature 149, ✍ 149
02/3 Slam Card
02/3 SP Game-Used ✂ AF (x2), ✂ PC, ✂ PH, ✂ TG
02/3 Sports Vault 105
02/3 SPx ✂ WM, ✂ X
02/3 Topps 116, ✂ FRF, ✂✍ FRF, ✂ CC2, ✂ CC6, ✂ CC9
02/3 T. Chrome 75, ✂ FRF
02/3 To. Limited 116
02/3 To. Total 379
02/3 UD Superstars ✂ CAS
02/3 Upper Deck 126, -NC10, ✂ CG, ✂ FF, ✂ GO, ✂ PW, ✂ UDPL
02/3 UD Classic 73, ✂ HR
02/3 UD Honor 92, ✂ GA
02/3 UD MVP 132, SA, SD, ST
02/3 UD Piece ✂ PH
02/3 UD Rookie ✂ DJ
02/3 UD Top Shelf ✂ R, ✂ ST, ✂ SW
02/3 UD Vintage 186, GB 186, ✂ FS, ✂ SO
02/3 Victory 159
01/2 Adrenaline 141
98/9 Aurora 37, -CF 9
99/0 Aurora 28, Stripe 28
98/9 Be A Player 23, ✍ Aut. 23
99/0 BAP Mem. 261, 357
00/1 BAP Mem. 13, ✂ H-15
01/2 BAP Mem. 99
01/2 BAP Update ✂ H18
91/2 Bowman 46
01/2 Bowman 29
98/9 Bowman's Best 64
99/0 Crown Royale 104
93/4 Donruss 425
94/5 Donruss 46
95/6 Donruss 42
96/7 Donruss 138
97/8 Donruss 185
96/7 Do. Canadian 27
97/8 Do. Canadian 22
96/7 Do. Elite 73
97/8 Do. Elite 23
97/8 Do. Preferred 18
97/8 Do. Priority 38
97/8 Do. Studio 42
98/9 Dynagon Ice 37, -TC 5
99/0 Dynagon Ice 43
95/6 Edge Ice L4
97/8 Esso 19, ✍ Aut.
94/5 Flair 51
96/7 Flair 43
94/5 Fleer 64
96/7 Fleer 34
95/6 Fleer Metal 50, IW-10
92/3 Fleer Ultra 286
93/4 Fleer Ultra 239
94/5 Fleer Ultra 65
95/6 Fleer Ultra 48, CC-14, RS-6
96/7 Fl. Ultra 75
93/4 Hockey Wit 67
99/0 HoloGrFX 11
97/8 Kraft / PB
98/9 Kraft / Post 16
93/4 Leaf 276
94/5 Leaf 266
95/6 Leaf 170
96/7 Leaf 154
97/8 Leaf 119
94/5 L. Limited 110
95/6 L. Limited 92
96/7 L. Preferred 84
97/8 Limited 126
96/7 Maggers 54
96/7 Metal Univ. 70
99/0 Millenium 48, ✍ Aut. 48
98/9 NHL Power Play
91/2 O-Pee-Chee 309
01/2 O-Pee-Chee 13
98/9 OPC Chrome 124
90/1 OPC Premier 91
97/8 Omega 44
98/9 Omega 45
99/0 Omega 173
98/9 Pacific 138, -TC 5
99/0 Pacific 79
00/1 Pacific 305
01/2 Pacific 292, 437
97/8 Pacific CC 52, TC-5
97/8 Pa. Crown Roy. 25
98/9 Pa. Crown Roy. 26
97/8 Pa. Dynagon 22, T-30, BKS-17
97/8 Pa. Invincible 25
97/8 Pa. Paramount 37
98/9 Pa. Paramount 41, -TC 5
99/0 Pa. Paramount 49, IAI-6
00/1 Pa. Paramount 184
97/8 Pa. Revolution 25, TC-5
98/9 Pa. Revolution 26, -ASG 22
98/9 Panini Photocard
92/3 Panini Sticker 117
93/4 Panini Sticker 250
94/5 Panini Sticker 214
95/6 Panini Sticker 181
96/7 Panini Sticker 186
97/8 Panini Sticker 27
98/9 Panini Sticker 30
92/3 Parkhurst 277
93/4 Parkhurst 327
94/5 Parkhurst 67, V66
95/6 Parkhurst 72
00/1 Parkhurst P-125
01/2 Parkhurst 52, ✂ PJ59, ✂ PS38
93/4 Pinnacle 420
94/5 Pinnacle 40
95/6 Pinnacle 197
96/7 Pinnacle 168
97/8 Pinnacle 109
97/8 Pi. Be A Player TN15
97/8 Pi. Certified 57
97/8 Pi. Inside 189
95/6 Pi. Summit 140
96/7 Pi. Summit 16
97/8 Pi. Totally 57
95/6 Pi. Zenith 83
96/7 Pi. Zenith 101
95/6 Playoff 35
94/5 POG 90
95/6 POG 93
93/4 Power Play 75
93/4 Power Play RisS 4
93/4 Premier 256
94/5 Premier 330
00/1 Premier Plus 81
99/0 Prism 31
90/1 Pro Set 606
91/2 ProCards 126
99/0 Revolution 30
90/1 Score 436, 90T
91/2 Score 144
91/2 Score CAN 144
92/3 Score 316
93/4 Score 364
95/6 Score 264
96/7 Score 54
97/8 Score 98
90/1 Sco. Young Stars 38
94/5 Select 15
95/6 Select CE 71, DS-16
96/7 Select CE 40
89/0 7th..Sketch OHL 130, 189
00/1 Signature 132, ✍ Aut. 68, ✂ HSHSJers
01/2 Signature ✂ GJ51, ✂ GSJ51
95/6 SBx Emotion 57, NP-2, Xci-12
95/6 SBx Impact 57, 241
96/7 SBx Impact 39
94/5 SP 37
95/6 SP 47
96/7 SP 68
97/8 SP Authentic 24
98/9 SP Authentic 15
99/0 SP Authentic 62
01/2 SP Authentic 62, ✂ NN, ✍ SotT
01/2 SP GU ✂ AF, ✂ AFD, ✂ AFT, ✂ Patch, ✂✍ PatchSig, ✂ PatchC (x2), ✂✍ PatchCSig, ✂ PatchT, ✂✍ TotGSig, ✂✍ TotGCSig (x2)
99/0 SPx 29
00/1 SPx 76
01/2 SPx 48, ✂ HT, ✂✍ HTSig (x2)
98/9 SPx Prospects 8
99/0 Stadium 105
00/1 Stadium 17, PP3
01/2 Stadium 94
99/0 SLU 237
00/1 SLU 9
95/6 Super Sticker 40
92/3 Topps 99
95/6 Topps 54, HGC21
98/9 Topps 124
99/0 Topps 18, NS12, PP5
00/1 Topps 242
01/2 Topps 13
99/0 To. Chrome 18
00/1 To. Chrome 152
01/2 To. Chrome 13
98/9 To. Finest 42
98/9 T. Gold Label 56
00/1 T. Gold Label 23
00/1 To. Heritage 111
01/2 To. Heritage 36
96/7 To. Picks 109
91/2 To. Stadium 305
92/3 To. Stadium 485
93/4 To. Stadium 217
94/5 To. Stadium 16
95/6 To. Stadium 66, F3
95/6 T. Super Skills 47
98/9 UD Choice 39
00/1 UD Heroes 88
00/1 UD Reserve 64
00/1 Ultimate Mem. ✍ U-33
01/2 Ultimate Mem. ✂ JE, ✂ JJ
90/1 Upper Deck 351, 354
91/2 Upper Deck 258
93/4 Upper Deck 413, SP-45
94/5 Upper Deck 337, SP-24
95/6 Upper Deck 159, 223, SE-7
96/7 Upper Deck 203, 271, X34, P4, SS29A
97/8 Upper Deck 29, SG55
98/9 Upper Deck 237
99/0 Upper Deck 201
00/1 Upper Deck 356
01/2 Upper Deck 127, ✂ CJers, ✂ PF
95/6 UD BAP 115, ✍ S115
96/7 UD Black Diam. 5
97/8 UD Black Diam. 3
98/9 UD Black Diam. 16
99/0 UD Black Diam. 63
01/2 UD Challenge 63, ✂ TN, ✂✍ TNS
95/6 UD CC 161
96/7 UD CC 87
97/8 UD Coll. Choice 110, SQ55, W9, C6, CR6
98/9 UD G. Reserve 237
99/0 UD G. Reserve 201
96/7 UD Ice 27
97/8 UD Ice 25
01/2 UD Mask ✂ GJ, ✂ JP, ✂ DP
98/9 UD MVP 37, PG11
99/0 UD MVP 38
00/1 UD MVP 126
01/2 UD MVP -J, ✍ SJ
99/0 UD MVP Cup 135
99/0 UD Retro 14, ✍ Ink.
01/2 UD Top Shelf 113
00/1 UD Vintage 264
01/2 UD Vintage 185, 191
97/8 Valu-net, ✍ Aut.
99/0 Victory 53, 57
00/1 Victory 170
01/2 Victory 256, 438
99/0 WGretzky 39
97/8 Zenith 54, Z13
97/8 CARO / Sprint
98/9 CARO / Highwoods
90/1 DETR / Little Caesars
91/2 DETR / Little Caesars
96/7 HART / Kids Club
01/2 PHIL
88/9 Niagara Falls Thunder
89/0 Niagara Falls Thunder

PRIMEAU, KEVIN
93/4 EDMO / Sheet
91/2 EDMO / IGA
92/3 EDMO / IGA 029
80/1 VANC / Silverwood

PRIMEAU, WAYNE
02/3 Pacific 315
02/3 Pacific Complete 400
02/3 Sports Vault 117
00/1 BAP Mem. 311
95/6 Bowman 157
94/5 Classic 15, CP1, T8
95/6 Classic 93
94/5 Classic 4 Sport 131
94/5 Cla. Images 47
94/5 Cla. Images 4 Sport 108
97/8 Donruss 67
97/8 Do. Priority 72
96/7 Fleer 132
96/7 Fl. Ultra 20, UR-16
95/6 Future Legends 36
01/2 Heads Up ✂ JQ 27
96/7 Leaf 231
96/7 L. Preferred 131
97/8 Limited 101
96/7 Metal Univ. 17
98/9 OPC Chrome 146
00/1 Pacific 379
97/8 Pacific CC 43
95/6 Parkhurst 26
96/7 Pinnacle 220
01/2 Pr. Stock ✂ GUG 82
00/1 PS Titanium ✂ GUG 139
97/8 Score Buff. 13
01/2 Signature 14, ✍ Aut. 14
95/6 SBx Impact 191
96/7 SBx Impact 156
95/6 Slapshot 240, 301
95/6 Topps 222
98/9 Topps 146
00/1 Topps 266
93/4 Upper Deck E9
95/6 Upper Deck 433
96/7 Upper Deck 20
97/8 Upper Deck 17
00/1 Upper Deck 390
96/7 UD Black Diam. 76
96/7 UD CC 25
99/0 UD MVP Cup 28
00/1 Victory 213
96/7 Rochester Americans
93/4 Owen Sound Platers
93/4 Owen Sound Platers

PRINCE, WALTER (GUY)
91/2 Avant Garde BCJHL 71
92/3 BCJHL 75
93/4 Dayton Bombers

PRIONDOLO, CONSTANT
79/0 Montréal Juniors B&W
79/0 Montréal Jrs. Colour

PRIOR, CHRIS
88/9 ProCards / Springfield

PRIOR, CRAIG
90/1 7th..Sketch LHJMQ 214

PRIOR, DAVE
91/2 ProCards 188
91/2 WINN / IGA
91/2 Moncton Hawks

PRIOR, GARY
94/5 DEL 6
95/6 DEL 1
96/7 DEL 1

PRIOR, STEVE
89/0 Rayside-Balfour

PRITCHARD, BRUCE
84/5 Victoria Cougars

PRITCHETT, GRANT
91/2 7th...Sketch OHL 343
93/4 Slapshot / Guelph 24

PROBERT, BOB
02/3 Fleer Throwbacks 92, 1SO, ✂ 1DTG, ✂ 1SO, ✂ 13SW, ✍ Aut.
02/3 Pacific 81
02/3 Pacific Complete 91
02/3 Signature ✂ FS2, ✂ FS9
02/3 Upper Deck 285
02/3 UD Foundations 15
02/3 Victory 49
98/9 Be A Player 181, ✍ Aut. 181
00/1 BAP Mem. ✂ TM-4, ✂ T-1
01/2 BAP Update ✂ TC2, ✂ TC6, ✂ TC19, ✂ TC34
91/2 Bowman 55
92/3 Bowman 85
93/4 Donruss 104
95/6 Donruss 247
96/7 Donruss 8
98/9 Dynagon Ice 44
92/3 Fleer Ultra 53
93/4 Fleer Ultra 309
95/6 Fleer Ultra 218
88/9 Frito Lay
93/4 Leaf 186
98/9 NHL Power Play
88/9 OPC/Topps 181
91/2 O-Pee-Chee 198
92/3 O-Pee-Chee 252
01/2 O-Pee-Chee 113
98/9 OPC Chrome 97
88/9 OPC Sticker 247-117
98/9 Omega 54
99/0 Pacific 96
00/1 Pacific 101
01/2 Pacific 90, 407
97/8 Pacific CC 290
88/9 Panini Sticker 46
91/2 Panini Sticker 146
93/4 Panini Sticker 249
94/5 Panini Sticker 213
91/2 Parkhurst 272
92/3 Parkhurst 41
92/3 Parkhurst CP9
93/4 Parkhurst 333
94/5 Parkhurst 71
95/6 Parkhurst 312
91/2 Pinnacle 183
92/3 Pinnacle 56
93/4 Pinnacle 7
94/5 Pinnacle 404
96/7 Pinnacle 84
95/6 Playoff 134
95/6 POG 68
93/4 Power Play 335
93/4 Premier 177
90/1 Pro Set 76
91/2 Pro Set 61
92/3 Pro Set 46
91/2 Pro Set Platinum 34
90/1 Score 143
91/2 Score 73
91/2 Score CAN 73
92/3 Score 52
92/3 Score SS 17
93/4 Score 59
96/7 Score 156
92/3 Seasons 8
01/2 SP Authentic ✂ NN
92/3 Topps 63
95/6 Topps 299
98/9 Topps 97
00/1 Topps 194
01/2 Topps 113
00/1 To. Heritage 196, ✂ OSS
91/2 To. Stadium 59
92/3 To. Stadium 355
93/4 To. Stadium 137
95/6 To. Stadium 152
90/1 Upper Deck 448
91/2 Upper Deck 239
92/3 Upper Deck 248
93/4 Upper Deck 200, SP-46
95/6 Upper Deck 469, SE-105
96/7 Upper Deck 33, SS29B
97/8 Upper Deck 39, 197
95/6 UD BAP 221, ✍ S221
97/8 UD Coll. Choice 49
98/9 UD MVP 46
99/0 UD MVP ✂ PS
00/1 UD Vintage 85
85/6 DETR / Little Caesars
86/7 DETR / Little Caesars
87/8 DETR / Little Caesars
88/9 DETR / Little Caesars
90/1 DETR / Little Caesars
91/2 DETR / Little Caesars
83/4 Brantford Alexanders
84/5 Soo Greyhounds

PROBERT, ROB
00/1 Stadion 197

PROBST, PAUL
72 Semic Sticker 151

PROBST, SKIP
88/9 ProCards / Peoria
91/2 ProCards 450

PROCEVIAT, DICK
67/8 Columbus Checkers

PROCEVIAT, STEVE
90/1 Rayside-Balfour

PROCHAZKA, FRANTISEK
97/8 APS 81
95/6 DEL 410
97/8 DS 43
97/8 DS Sticker 89
00/1 OFS 405

PROCHAZKA, LIBOR
94/5 APS 52
95/6 APS 84, 363, 425
96/7 APS 78, 398
97/8 APS 351
98 Bonaparte 8B
98 Bonaparte Pexeso 26
98/9 DS 7
99/0 DS NS11
00/1 DS 123
01/2 DS 9
96/7 DS Sticker 135
98/9 OFS 235, 386, 440, 471
00/1 OFS 163, -Star 22
01/2 OFS 52, -UHI 11
99/0 Score JT25
97/8 UD Elitserien 4
96 Wien 109

PROCHAZKA, MARTIN
94/5 APS 57
95/6 APS 94, 370, 386, 427
96/7 APS 352
97/8 APS 357
98 Bonaparte 1A
98 Bonaparte Pexeso 1
98/9 DS 3
99/0 DS NS15, P5
00/1 DS 166, JT8, TS6
01/2 DS 19, -BB 6
98/9 OFS 106, 240, 442, 479, -OW 14
99/0 OFS 29, 448, 525
00/1 OFS 251, -Star 27
01/2 OFS 46, -RE6D
98/9 Pacific 420
97/8 Pa. Paramount 184
97/8 Score 62
97/8 Score Toro. 20
99/0 Score JT15
95 Semic 155
96 Wien 116

PROCHAZKA, MICHAEL
01/2 OFS 232, 284

PROCHAZKA, MILAN
96/7 APS 163
99/0 DS 196
00/1 DS 106
96/7 DS Sticker 263
99/0 OFS 83
00/1 OFS 202
01/2 OFS 261

PROCHAZKA, PETR
00/1 Saskatoon Blades

PROCHAZKA, RADEK
96/7 APS 279
97/8 APS 234
97/8 DS 19
99/0 DS 28
00/1 DS 129
96/7 DS Sticker 184
97/8 DS Sticker 41
98/9 OFS 336
99/0 OFS 316
00/1 OFS 174

PROCHAZKA, ROBERT
98/9 OFS 183
00/1 OFS 218
99/0 Score 98

PROCHAZKA, STANISLAV
94/5 APS 36
95/6 APS 328
96/7 APS 155
97/8 APS 257
97/8 DS 71
98/9 DS 55
99/0 DS 83
00/1 DS 95
96/7 DS Sticker 262
97/8 DS Sticker 140
98/9 OFS 155
99/0 OFS 357
00/1 OFS 47
01/2 OFS 252

PROCHÁZKA, FRANTISEK
94 Semic 172
93 Semic Sticker 94

PROCHÁZKA, MARTIN
91/2 Upper Deck WJC 96

PROCYSHYN, JEREMY
92/3 MPS SJHL 88

PRODGERS, GOLDIE
24/5 Champ's Cigarettes
12/3 Imperial 37
23/4 William Paterson 32

PROFT, PARIS
96/7 DEL 202

PROHASKA, ?
79 Panini Sticker 303

PROKEPETZ, JASON
98/9 Florida Everblades

PROKHOROV, VITALI
92/3 Classic 51
93/4 Cla. Prospects 92
93/4 Donruss 290
94/5 Donruss 126
92/3 Fleer Ultra 397
94/5 Fleer Ultra 188
93/4 Leaf 326
94/5 Leaf 295
95/6 Leaf Elit Set 221
92/3 OPC Premier 64
92/3 Parkhurst 157
93/4 Parkhurst 450
94/5 Parkhurst 206
92/3 Pinnacle 404
94/5 Pinnacle 367
94/5 POG 206
93/4 Power Play 432
93/4 Premier 452
92/3 Red Ace Blue 5
92/3 Red Ace Violet 29
92 Semic Sticker 120
94/5 To. Stadium 19
92/3 Upper Deck 486
93/4 Upper Deck 363
94/5 Upper Deck 173
95/6 UD Elitserien 66
93/4 Peoria Rivermen
00/1 Metallurg 51

PROKHOV, VILTAI
99/0 Mir 18

PROKOPEC, MIKE
98/9 EBK IHL All-Star
95/6 Future Legends 50
95/6 Parkhurst 308
96/7 Pi. Zenith 149
91/2 7th...Sketch OHL 13
93/4 Slapshot / Guelph 16
98/9 Detroit Vipers
94/5 Indianapolis Ice
95/6 Indianapolis Ice
99/0 Manitoba Moose
91/2 Cornwall Royals

PROKOPETZ, JASON
92/3 MPS SJHL 82
99/0 Florida Everblades

PROKOPIEV, ALEXANDER
00/1 Mir 137
00/1 Dynamo 14

PROKOPJEV, ALEXANDER
96/7 APS 207
97/8 APS 135
97/8 DS 101
96/7 DS Sticker 200
97/8 DS Sticker 258
91/2 O-Pee-Chee 25R

PROKUPEK, LADISLAV
94/5 APS 176
95/6 APS 193
96/7 APS 327
97/8 APS 306
96/7 DS Sticker 166
97/8 DS Sticker 120
98/9 OFS 94
99/0 OFS 309
93/4 Parkhurst 514

PRONGER, CHRIS
02/3 Atomic 83, -NPC 10, -SC 12
02/3 BAP All-Star 72, ✂ ASJ, ✂ HSHSJers
02/3 BAP Mem. 72, 225, 235, ✂ ASJ45, ✂ AS2, ✂ AST19, ✂ FP25, ✂ HSHSJers 17, ✂ TM16
02/3 Crown Royale ✂ GWJ 18
02/3 eTopps 27
02/3 Exclusive 145
02/3 First Edition 103, 365, 385, 390, 408H, ✂ Jers.
02/3 Heads Up 104, ✂ GWQ 23, ✂ GWQ 28
02/3 In The GU 67, 167, ✂ F25, ✂ GUJ42, ✂ SJ42, ✂ T8
02/3 McDonald's 33, -SLG 3, ✂ JP 15
02/3 O-Pee-Chee 6
02/3 Pacific 327
02/3 Pacific Complete 499
02/3 Parkhurst 72, ✂ FP25, ✂ GJ23, ✂ SJ23, ✂ NH9, ✂ TT16
02/3 Parkhurst Retro 113, ✂ RF26, ✂ RJ34, ✂ RSJ23
02/3 Pr. Stock Reserve ✂ 139
02/3 PS Titanium ✂ GWJ 58
02/3 Signature 167, ✍ 167, ✂ DW7, ✂ FJ26, ✂ SGJ42, ✂ TQ15
02/3 Slam Card
02/3 SP GU 43, ✂ PC
02/3 Sports Vault 278
02/3 SPx 65
02/3 Stadium 69, -BT7, ✍ LSS
02/3 Topps 6, HHU15, ✂ CC4, ✂ CC17
02/3 T. Chrome 6
02/3 To. Heritage 58
02/3 To. Limited 6
02/3 To. Total 49
02/3 Upper Deck 243, 399, ✂ LN
02/3 UD Artistic 76, R76, / Art
02/3 UD Classic 85
02/3 UD Honor 96
02/3 UD MVP 162
02/3 UD Piece 78, AC25
02/3 UD Top Shelf 78, ✂ HH, ✂ R, ✂ TS
02/3 UD Vintage 223, 286, GB 223, T57
02/3 Victory 185, -NP 12
01/2 Adrenaline 161
01/2 Atomic 82, CP 16, PP 28
98/9 Aurora 163
99/0 Aurora 127
00/1 Aurora 123
98/9 Be A Player 123, ✍ Aut. 123
99/0 BAP Mem. 89, ✂ TM-34
00/1 BAP Mem. 220, ✂ J-7
01/2 BAP Mem. 64, ✂ ASJ, ✂ ASE, ✂ ASN, ✂ ASD, ✂ AST, HSHS, ✂ PP, ✂ SCP
95/6 Bowman 62
01/2 Bowman 10
98/9 Bowman's Best 18, F18
93/4 Classic 2
93/4 Classic - Top Ten DP2
94/5 Classic AR5
93/4 Cla. 4 Sport 186
93/4 Cla. 4 Sport - Acetate 12
93/4 Cla. 4 Sport DS59
93/4 Cla. 4 Sport LP23
93/4 Cla. 4 Sport PP19
93/4 Cla. 4 Sport TC4
93/4 Cla. Images 4 Sport 135
93/4 Cla. Images 4 Sport 8
93/4 Cla. Prospects 31, ✍ Aut.
99/0 Crown Royale 119
00/1 Crown Royale 89
01/2 Crown Royale 120
93/4 Donruss 150
93/4 Donruss 393
93/4 Donruss J
93/4 Donruss RR 3
94/5 Donruss 215
95/6 Donruss 63, 319, PP-17
96/7 Donruss 63
97/8 Donruss 100
97/8 Do. Canadian 90
97/8 Do. Preferred 109
97/8 Do. Priority 91
98/9 Dynagon Ice 161
99/0 Dynagon Ice 167, CM-4
01/2 EASports
97/8 Esso 15, ✍ Aut.
94/5 Flair 73
94/5 Fleer 88
96/7 Fleer 99
95/6 Fleer Metal 127
96/7 Fl. Picks 114
93/4 Fleer Ultra 339
93/4 Fleer Ultra WotF 14
94/5 Fleer Ultra 91, ARS-7
95/6 Fleer Ultra 69, 302
00 Gatorade Sticker
01/2 Heads Up 80, ASGN 27
95/6 Hoyle / East. Q-Diamond
93/4 Kraft / KD
97/8 Kraft / PB
98/9 Kraft / Post 18
99/0 Kraft / KD
00/1 Kraft 20
93/4 Leaf 257
93/4 Leaf FP 2
94/5 Leaf 268, GLR-9, LL-10
95/6 Leaf 242
96/7 Leaf 5
97/8 Leaf 90
94/5 L. Limited 22
95/6 L. Limited 107
97/8 Limited 85
96/7 Maggers 141
99/0 McDonald's ✂ GJ
00/1 McDonald's 28
01/2 McDonald's 33
96/7 Metal Univ. 135
99/0 Millenium 202, ✍ Aut. 202
01/2 Nextel
98/9 NHL Power Play
00/1 Nortel Networks All-Star 12
01/2 O-Pee-Chee 16
98/9 OPC Chrome 181, B1, SB25
97/8 Omega 196, TL-17
98/9 Omega 205
99/0 Omega 199
98/9 Pacific 44
99/0 Pacific 362
00/1 Pacific 349, GCDC-29
01/2 Pacific 329, IZ 16
97/8 Pacific CC 124
98/9 Pa. Crown Roy. 116
98/9 Pa. Paramount 206
99/0 Pa. Paramount 200
00/1 Pa. Paramount 208, FF-30
98/9 Pa. Revolution 124, -ASG 23
01/2 PTC National 8
98/9 Panini Photocard
94/5 Panini Sticker M
95/6 Panini Sticker 198
96/7 Panini Sticker 201
97/8 Panini Sticker 170
98/9 Panini Sticker 5, 153
99/0 Panini Sticker 286
00/1 Panini Sticker 193
93/4 Parkhurst 249
93/4 Parkhurst C2
93/4 Parkhurst D13
94/5 Parkhurst 274, V40
95/6 Parkhurst 175
00/1 Parkhurst P-3
01/2 Parkhurst 86, HSHS, ✂ PJ40, ✂ PS46, ✂ PSJ6, ✂ H16
94/5 Parkie SE73
93/4 Pinnacle 456
93/4 Pinnacle SR2
94/5 Pinnacle 11, 466
96/7 Pinnacle 58
97/8 Pi. Inside 175
95/6 Pi. Summit 30
95/6 Pi. Zenith 28
95/6 Playoff 309
94/5 POG 121
95/6 POG 243
93/4 Power Play 354
93/4 Power Play RooS 12
93/4 Premier 485
94/5 Premier 198, 381, 484, OF-11
00/1 Premier Plus 65, PT9, TT4, WP3, ✍ PS
99/0 Prism 120
00/1 Pr. Stock 84, PS-52
01/2 Pr. Stock 81, -PS 61
00/1 PS Titanium 81
01/2 PS Titanium 118, TAS 15
95/6 Pro Magnet 8
99/0 Revolution 124
00/1 Revolution 124, HD-29
93/4 Score 586
94/5 Score 252
95/6 Score 6, CI-5
96/7 Score 166
97/8 Score SLou. 7
94/5 Select 111
91/2 7th...Sketch OHL 134
00/1 Signature 108, F-25, ✍

Aut. 80, ✂ DD-19, ✂ J-13, ✂ HSHSJers
01/2 Signature C-10, ✍ Aut., ✂ DD5, ✂ GUE23, ✂ GJ57, ✂ GSJ57, ✂ ITN23, ✂ IG10
95/6 SBx Emotion 151
95/6 SBx Impact 144
96/7 SBx Impact 115
93/4 Slapshot / Peterborough 29
94/5 SP 48
95/6 SP 124
96/7 SP 135, HC-10
97/8 SP Authentic 139
98/9 SP Authentic 71
00/1 SP Authentic 77
01/2 SP Authentic 78
01/2 SP GU 49
99/0 SPx 135
00/1 SPx 59, 80, HH13
01/2 SPx 58, 90
98/9 SPx Finite 75
98/9 SPx Prospects 52
00/1 Stadion 151
99/0 Stadium 146
00/1 Stadium 3, BT30, CA10, SF2
01/2 Stadium 3, G36, HS5
99/0 SLU 174
95/6 Super Sticker 104
95/6 Topps 308, HGC15
98/9 Topps 181, B1, I7, SB25
99/0 Topps 79
00/1 Topps 9, TC6, ✍ CAI
01/2 Topps 16, ✂ CC2
99/0 To. Chrome 79
00/1 To. Chrome 9, TC6
01/2 To. Chrome 16
94/5 Topps Finest 62
98/9 To. Finest 22
98/9 T. Gold Label 49
99/0 T. Gold Label 34, QC6
00/1 T. Gold Label 85, B5
00/1 To. Heritage 31, 222, 228, 246
01/2 To. Heritage 34
99/0 T. Prmr. Plus 41
01/2 To. Reserve 4
93/4 To. Stadium 290
94/5 To. Stadium 111, 235, DAD 5
95/6 To. Stadium 69
00/1 To. Stars 15, 135, P9, ✂ GG, ✂✍ GGA, ✍ CAI
95/6 T. Super Skills 54
98/9 UD Choice 185
00/1 UD Heroes 102
01/2 UD PlayMakers Ltd 84
00/1 UD Reserve 74
00/1 Ultimate Mem. ✍ U-42, ✂ H-1, ✂ Jers. 31, ✂ J-38, ✂ N-1, ✂ RA-1, ✂ S-38
01/2 Ultimate Mem. ✂ Emb., ✂ S&J, ✂ ITN, ✂ NP, ✂ PP, ✂ UC, ✂ WTF
92/3 Upper Deck 591
93/4 Upper Deck 190, H5, SP-46
94/5 Upper Deck 52, SP-33
95/6 Upper Deck 174, SE-160
96/7 Upper Deck 144, X36, P24, SS27B
97/8 Upper Deck 142, 398
98/9 Upper Deck 174, LS20
99/0 Upper Deck 284
00/1 Upper Deck 151, NC9, TT8, ✂ GJ
01/2 Upper Deck 380, GA15, LP14, SS3
93/4 Upper Deck Be A Player 35
94/5 UD BAP R43
95/6 UD BAP 18, ✍ S18
96/7 UD Black Diam. 150
97/8 UD Black Diam. 83
98/9 UD Black Diam. 78
99/0 UD Black Diam. 73
00/1 UD Black Diam. 51
01/2 UD Challenge 77, CR8
95/6 UD CC 232
96/7 UD CC 226
97/8 UD Coll. Choice 233, W14
01/2 UD Collectors
98/9 UD G. Reserve 174
99/0 UD G. Reserve 284
01/2 UD Honor Roll 10, 40, TC6
96/7 UD Ice 63
00/1 UD Ice 34
01/2 UD Ice 118
00/1 UD Legends 115
01/2 UD Mask 84
98/9 UD MVP 180
99/0 UD MVP 186
00/1 UD MVP 154
01/2 UD MVP 162, MT13, MW7
99/0 UD MVP Cup 163
01/2 UD Premier 45, ✂ D
00/1 UD Pros&Prosp. 74, ✂ GJ
99/0 UD Retro 68
01/2 UD Top Shelf 38, ✂ S, ✂ ST
00/1 UD Vintage 309, 320, 321, UD3
01/2 UD Vintage 218, 226
97/8 Valu-net, ✍ Aut.
00/1 Vanguard 83
01/2 Vanguard 82, EMW 10
99/0 Victory 263, 323
00/1 Victory 199, 204, 257, 323
01/2 Victory 305, 393
01/2 Waving the Flag 8
99/0 WGretzky 147
93/4 HART / Coke
96/7 SLOU / Dispatch 5
99/0 SLOU / Taco Bell 16
91/2 Peterborough Petes

PRONGER, SEAN
02/3 Pacific Complete 478
95/6 Bowman 153
94/5 Classic 93
97/8 Donruss 98
97/8 Do. Preferred 123
97/8 Do. Priority 109
97/8 Limited 101
97/8 Pacific CC 156
96/7 Pinnacle 223
97/8 Pi. Be A Player 132, ✍ Aut. 132
97/8 Score Anah. 18
97/8 SP Authentic 2
97/8 Upper Deck 7
97/8 UD Coll. Choice 2
96/7 ANAH / Up Front 20
98/9 NYRA
94/5 Knoxville Cherokees
00/1 Manitoba Moose
01/2 Syracuse Crunch

PRONIN, NIKOLAI
99/0 Mir 81
00/1 Mir 29
98/9 Charlotte Checkers

PRONOVOST, ANDRÉ
45-64 BeeHive-2 [Mont.]
45-64 BeeHive-2 [Bost.]
45-64 BeeHive-2 [Detr.]
64-67 BeeHive-3 [Detr.]
62/3 Cowan Tile
57/8 Parkhurst [Mont.] 7
58/9 Parkhurst 3
59/0 Parkhurst 35
60/1 Parkhurst 55
60/1 Parkhurst 58
61/2 Parkhurst 51
63/4 Parkhurst 45
93/4 Parkie 56-57 75
94/5 Parkie Tall 62
60/1 Shirriff 32
61/2 Shirriff 3
61/2 Topps 5
61/2 Topps - Stamp
62/3 Topps 19
62/3 York Transfer 30
63/4 York 43

PRONOVOST, CLAUDE
53/4 La Patrie
93/4 Parkie 56-57 15

PRONOVOST, JEAN
70/1 Colgate 50
70/1 Dad's Cookies
70s Dernière Heure
70/1 Eddie Sargent 162
71/2 Eddie Sargent 168
72/3 Eddie Sargent 176
70/1 Esso Power Player
72/3 Post 23
74/5 Loblaws
69/0 O-Pee-Chee 155
70/1 O-Pee-Chee 202
71/2 O-Pee-Chee 118
72/3 O-Pee-Chee 64
73/4 O-Pee-Chee 11
74/5 O-Pee-Chee 110
75/6 O-Pee-Chee 280
75/6 O-Pee-Chee 326
76/7 O-Pee-Chee 14
76/7 O-Pee-Chee 218
77/8 O-Pee-Chee 261
78/9 O-Pee-Chee 184
79/0 OPC 7
79/0 O-Pee-Chee 77
81/2 O-Pee-Chee 355
81/2 OPC Sticker 196
79 Panini Sticker 64
72 Semic Sticker 216
71/2 Topps 118
72/3 Topps 143
73/4 Topps 11
74/5 Topps 110
75/6 Topps 280
75/6 Topps 326
76/7 Topps 14
76/7 Topps 218
77/8 Topps 261
78/9 Topps 184
79/0 Topps 7
79/0 Topps 77
71/2 Toronto Sun Photo
78/9 ATLF / Colour
79/0 ATLF / B&W
79/0 ATLF / Colour
71/2 PITT / Sportcolor
74/5 PITT
77/8 PITT / McDonald's
80/1 WASH
99/0 Rouyn-Noranda
00/1 Rouyn-Noranda 26
01/2 Sherbrooke Castors 22

PRONOVOST, MARCEL
02/3 Parkie - Reprint 174, 179, 254, 268, 279, 291
45-64 BeeHive-2 [Detr.]
64-67 BeeHive-3 [Toro.]
64-67 BeeHive-3 [Toro.]
63-65 Chex
64/5 Coke/Sprite [Detr.]
65/6 Coca-Cola
01/2 Fleer Greats 84, ✍ Aut.
62/3 Cowan Tile
83 HHOF Postcard K14
83&87 HHOF 148
96/7 Legends 77
68/9 O-Pee-Chee 125
51/2 Parkhurst 68
52/3 Parkhurst 61
53/4 Parkhurst 41
54/5 Parkhurst 34
60/1 Parkhurst 29
61/2 Parkhurst 29
62/3 Parkhurst 33
63/4 Parkhurst 46
93/4 Parkhurst PR65
93/4 Parkie 56-57 58
95/6 Parkie 66-67 108
94/5 Parkie Tall 55
68/9 Post Marble
67/8 Post Tips 4
60/1 Shirriff 56
61/2 Shirriff 68
68/9 Shirriff / Toro. 13
54/5 Topps 27
57/8 Topps 43
58/9 Topps 24
59/0 Topps 44
64/5 Topps 39
65/6 Topps 80
66/7 Topps 20
66/7 Topps / Test 20
67/8 Topps 81
68/9 Topps 125
60/1 Toronto Star Photo
63/4 Toronto Star Action
63/4 Toronto Star Photo
64/5 Toronto Star Action
65/6 Toronto Star Photo
58/9 Toronto Star Weekend
62/3 Toronto Star Weekend
91/2 Ultimate Original Six 71, ✍ Aut. 71
62/3 York Transfer 23
63/4 York 38
67/8 York 33
67/8 York 34
76 DETR
80/1 DETR
68/9 TORO
69/0 TORO

PRONOVOST, RENÉ
52/3 Bas du Fleuve 47
51/2 Lac St-Jean 35

PROPP, BRIAN
02/3 UD Foundations 71, ✍ SG
90/1 Bowman 37
91/2 Bowman 123
92/3 Bowman 272
93/4 Donruss 441
93/4 Fleer Ultra 340
94/5 Fleer Ultra 92
83/4 Funmate Puffy 11 [w]
84/5 Kelowna Wings &...
80/1 O-Pee-Chee 1
80/1 O-Pee-Chee 39
81/2 O-Pee-Chee 246
82/3 O-Pee-Chee 256
83/4 O-Pee-Chee 218
83/4 O-Pee-Chee 271
84/5 O-Pee-Chee 166
85/6 OPC/Topps 141
86/7 OPC/Topps 86
87/8 OPC/Topps 158
88/9 OPC/Topps 168
89/0 OPC/Topps Box J
90/1 OPC/Topps 8
91/2 O-Pee-Chee 227
92/3 O-Pee-Chee 350
89/0 OPC/Topps 139
87/8 OPC Leaders 33
90/1 OPC Premier 92
81/2 OPC Sticker 180
82/3 OPC/Topps Sticker 111
83/4 OPC/Topps Sticker 199
84/5 OPC Sticker 112
85/6 OPC Sticker 90-223
86/7 OPC Sticker 239
87/8 OPC Sticker 67
87/8 OPC Sticker 97-230
88/9 OPC Sticker 97-221
89/0 opcSticker 106-245
87/8 Panini Sticker 131
87/8 Panini Sticker 193
88/9 Panini Sticker 324
89/0 Panini Sticker 306
90/1 Panini Sticker 5, 325
91/2 Panini Sticker 115
92/3 Panini Sticker 93
93/4 Panini Sticker 267
94/5 Panini Sticker 115
91/2 Parkhurst 82
93/4 Parkhurst 85
91/2 Pinnacle 184
92/3 Pinnacle 178
93/4 Pinnacle 342
82/3 Post [Phil.]
90/1 Pro Set 14, 360, 460
91/2 Pro Set 413
92/3 Pro Set 257
91/2 Pro Set Platinum 187
91/2 Pro Set Platinum PC17
90/1 Score 269, 34T
91/2 Score 223
91/2 Score CAN 223
92/3 Score 72
93/4 Score 513
94/5 Score 247
83/4 Souhaits Keychain [Flyers]
80/1 Topps 1
80/1 Topps 39
81/2 Topps 110 [East]
92/3 Topps 65
91/2 To. Stadium 237
92/3 To. Stadium 374
01/2 T/O Archives 44
90/1 Upper Deck 2, 409
91/2 Upper Deck 260
92/3 Upper Deck 177
93/4 Upper Deck 368
89/0 BOST / Sports Action
93/4 HART / Coke
83/4 PHIL / J.C. Penney
86/7 PHIL
89/0 PHIL

PROROK, IVO
94/5 APS 423
95/6 APS 137
96/7 APS 15
97/8 APS 92
97/8 DS 48
98/9 DS 46
99/0 DS 65
96/7 DS Sticker 131
97/8 DS Sticker 99
98/9 OFS 10, 467
99/0 OFS 156, 501
00/1 OFS 414

PROSEK, ROMAN
99/0 OFS 310
00/1 OFS 167
01/2 OFS 198

PROSFSKY, TYLER
93/4 Tacoma Rockets

PROSHKIN, VITALI
00/1 Mir 126
00/1 Dynamo 8

PROSKYNICKI, ANDREW
95/6 Slapshot 348

PROSOFSKY, G.
97/8 Upper Deck 416

PROSOFSKY, JASON
91/2 ProCards 325
90/1 7th..Sketch WHL 31
91/2 Upper Deck 432

PROSOFSKY, TYLER
00/1 Asheville Smoke
92/3 Tacoma Rockets

PROSPAL, VACLAV
02/3 First Edition 269
02/3 O-Pee-Chee 109
02/3 Pacific 353
02/3 Pacific Complete 69
02/3 Parkhurst Retro 200
02/3 Sports Vault 125
02/3 Topps 109
02/3 To. Limited 109
02/3 To. Total 63
02/3 UD Vintage 227
00/1 Aurora 103
01/1 BAP Mem. 308
93/4 Cla. Prospects 174
94/5 Classic 29
97/8 Donruss 219, RR-3
97/8 Do. Canadian 135
97/8 Do. Elite 80
97/8 Do. Preferred 105
97/8 Do. Priority 165, 190
00/1 DS JT9
01/2 DS 47
98/9 Dynagon Ice 129
97/8 Leaf 132, 165
97/8 Limited 38, 91, 100
97/8 McDonald's McD-39
99/0 Millenium 173, ✍ Aut. 173
99/0 OFS 30
00/1 OFS 389
99/0 Pacific 292
00/1 Pacific 285
97/8 Pa. Crown Roy. 100
97/8 Pa. Paramount 136
00/1 Pa. Paramount 176
00/1 Panini Sticker 69
97/8 Pinnacle 19
97/8 Pi. Be A Player 213, ✍ Aut. 213
97/8 Pi. BeeHive 52, BHT-21, ✍ Aut. 52
97/8 Pi. Inside 143
97/8 Pi. Mint 30
97/8 Score 51
97/8 Score Phil. 18
97/8 SP Authentic 188
00/1 Stadium 179
00/1 Topps 210
98/9 To. Finest 49
98/9 UD Choice 145
97/8 Upper Deck 125, SG27
98/9 Upper Deck 328
00/1 Upper Deck 350
01/2 Upper Deck 389
x97/8 UD Black Diam. PC21
97/8 UD Coll. Choice 185
98/9 UD G. Reserve 328
97/8 UD Ice 45, L7C
98/9 UD MVP 145
00/1 UD Vintage 257
99/0 Victory 209
00/1 Victory 162
01/2 Victory 153
97/8 Zenith 91, RR-6, ZT-13
98/9 OTTA
99/0 OTTA
00/1 OTTA
94/5 Hershey Bears

PROSPISIL, DAVID
95/6 APS 439

PROTSENKO, BORIS
95/6 Bowman P29

PROULX, CHRISTIAN
93/4 Cla. Prospects 8
94/5 Parkhurst 121
90/1 7th..Sketch LHJMQ 218
91/2 7th...Sketch LHJMQ 167
93/4 Fredericton Canadiens
94/5 Fredericton Canadiens
96/7 Milwaukee Admirals
97/8 Milwaukee Admirals

PROULX, HUGO
91/2 7th...Sketch LHJMQ 282
91 7th...Sketch Mem.Cup 57
94/5 Greensboro Monarchs
97/8 Quad City Mallards
98/9 Quad City Mallards
99/0 Quad City Mallards
00/1 Quad City Mallards

PROULX, OLIVIER
01/2 Victoriaville Tigres 10

PROULX, STEVE
01/2 Victoriaville Tigres 9

PROVARI, JUKKO
79 Panini Sticker 177

PROVAZNIK, JIRI
94/5 APS 46

PROVENCAL, JACQUES
88/9 Richelieu Riverains

PROVENCHER, JIMMY
00/1 Cardset 191

PROVENZANO, MARK
95/6 Slapshot 220

PROVOST, CLAUDE
02/3 Parkie - Reprint 212, 233, 257, 281
52/3 Anonymous 138
68/9 Bauer Photo
45-64 BeeHive-2 [Mont.]
64-67 BeeHive-3 [Mont.]
63-65 Chex
64/5 Coke/Sprite [Mont.]
65/6 Coca-Cola
77/8 Dernière Heure
62/3 Cowan Tile
53/4 La Patrie
68/9 O-Pee-Chee 163
68/9 O-Pee-Chee 216
69/0 O-Pee-Chee 167
57/8 Parkhurst [Mont.] 12
58/9 Parkhurst 43
59/0 Parkhurst 18
60/1 Parkhurst 54
60/1 Parkhurst 58
61/2 Parkhurst 50
62/3 Parkhurst 41
63/4 Parkhurst 36
63/4 Parkhurst 95
93/4 Parkie 56-57 73
95/6 Parkie 66-67 61
94/5 Parkie Tall 70, AS6, SL4
60/1 Shirriff 33
61/2 Shirriff 105
62/3 Shirriff 35
68/9 Shirriff / Mont. 16
64/5 Topps 23
65/6 Topps 8
66/7 Topps 9
66/7 Topps / Test 9
67/8 Topps 71
61/2 Toronto Star Photo
63/4 Toronto Star Action
64/5 Toronto Star Action
65/6 Toronto Star Photo
62/3 Toronto Star Weekend
60/1 York
61/2 York 17
62/3 York Transfer 14
63/4 York 28
67/8 York 20
67/8 York 36
67/8 York
67/8 York
67/8 MONT
67/8 MONT / IGA Card
68/9 MONT / IGA Card
69/0 MONT / Pro Star
92/3 MONT / OPC 43

PROVOST, PAUL
51/2 Bas du Fleuve 37

PRPIC, JOEL
99/0 BAP Mem. 316
99/0 UD G. Reserve 330
00/1 Victory 268
01/2 Cleveland Barons
00/1 Hershey Bears
97/8 Providence Bruins
98/9 Providence Bruins
99/0 Providence Bruins

PRPIC, TONY
93/4 Fredericton Canadiens
96/7 Fredericton Canadiens
96/7 Pensacola Ice Pilots
97/8 Toledo Storm 10

PRPICH, DAVE
91/2 7th...Sketch OHL 193

PRTT, STACY
83/4 Brandon Wheat Kings

PRUD'HOMME, CARL
94/5 Slapshot Memorial 58

PRUNEAU, MARTIAL
52/3 Bas du Fleuve 2
51/2 Laval Dairy 13
52/3 Laval Dairy Update 56
52/3 St. Lawrence 79

PRUSA, PETER
74 Hellas MM-Jenkki 106
70/1 Kuvajulkaisut 95

PRUSA, SVEN
94/5 DEL 346

PRUSEK, MARTIN
02/3 Between the Pipes 82, ✂ GUJ41, ✂ T5
02/3 First Edition 289
02/3 Pacific Complete 156
02/3 Signature 111, ✍ 111
02/3 SPx 118
02/3 Stadium 116
02/3 Upper Deck 215
02/3 UD Foundations 138
02/3 UD Mask 58, 59
02/3 UD MVP 211
02/3 UD Piece 141
02/3 UD Vintage 342
95/6 APS 293
96/7 APS 191, 409
97/8 APS 125, 344
01/2 BAP Mem. 437
01/2 BT Pipes 162
97/8 DS 95
98/9 DS 23
99/0 DS 169, G13
00/1 DS 157, G14
01/2 DS 52
96/7 DS Sticker 189
97/8 DS Sticker 247
98/9 OFS 350, 419
99/0 OFS 14, 255, -CL
00/1 OFS 239, -Star 26
01/2 OFS -UHI 29
01/2 Parkhurst 333
01/2 UD Mask 156
02/3 OTTA
01/2 Grand Rapids Griffins

PRYL, STANISLAV
70/1 Kuvajulkaisut 57

PRYOR, CHRIS
89/0 ProCards AHL 254
90/1 ProCards 499
91/2 ProCards 475
87/8 MINS
84/5 Springfield Indians 16

PRYSTAI, METRO
45-64 BeeHive-2 [Chic.]
45-64 BeeHive-2 [Detr.]
51/2 Parkhurst 65
52/3 Parkhurst 60
53/4 Parkhurst 42
54/5 Parkhurst 35
93/4 Parkie 56-57 57
54/5 Topps 24

PSENKA, TOMAS
00/1 Val d'Or Foreurs 7

PTACEK, FRANTISEK
94/5 APS 77
95/6 APS 275
96/7 APS 129
97/8 APS 5
98/9 DS 90
00/1 DS 5
96/7 DS Sticker 62
97/8 DS Sticker 213
98/9 OFS 131
99/0 OFS 110
00/1 OFS 295
01/2 OFS 33

PUCHER, PETER
99/0 DS 192
00/1 DS 103
99/0 OFS 84
00/1 OFS 198
01/2 OFS 120

PUCHER, RENE
94 Semic 205

PUCHNIAK, ROB
90/1 7th..Sketch WHL 231
91/2 7th...Sketch WHL 197
89/0 Brandon Wheat Kings
90/1 Brandon Wheat Kings

PUDAS, ALBERT
23/4 Paulins Candy 21

PUDLICK, MIKE
00/1 Lowell Lock Monsters
01/2 Manchester Monarchs
02/3 Manchester Monarchs

PUGA, DUANE
92/3 BCJHL 79

PUGLIESE, MARIO
79 Panini Sticker 392

PUHAKKA, KEIJO
70/1 Kuvajulkaisut 286
71/2 Williams Finnish 156
72/3 Williams Finnish 108
73/4 Williams Finnish 208

PUHAKKA, MIKA
94/5 Sisu 282
95/6 Sisu 226
96/7 Sisu 25

PUHALSKI, GREG
92/3 Toledo Storm WIOT
92/3 Toledo Storm
93/4 Toledo Storm 19
94/5 Toledo Storm
95/6 Toledo Storm
96/7 Toledo Storm
97/8 Toledo Storm 26
82/3 Kitchener Rangers
83/4 Kitchener Rangers
84/5 Kitchener Rangers
85/6 London Knights

PUISTOLA, PASI
02/3 Cardset 99
98/9 Cardset 81
99/0 Cardset 58
00/1 Cardset 344

PULENTE, GINO
91/2 L. Superior State Lakers

PULFORD, BOB
02/3 To. Heritage - Reprint TML, ✂ Reprint, ✍ Reprint
45-64 BeeHive-2 [Toro.]
64-67 BeeHive-3 [Toro.]
64-67 BeeHive-3 [Toro.]
63-65 Chex
64/5 Coke/Sprite [Toro.]
65/6 Coca-Cola
70/1 Colgate 2
70/1 Dad's Cookies
70/1 Eddie Sargent 72
71/2 Eddie Sargent 66
70/1 Esso Power Player
62/3 Cowan Tile
68/9 O-Pee-Chee 129
69/0 O-Pee-Chee 53
69/0 O-Pee-Chee 4in1
70/1 O-Pee-Chee 36
71/2 O-Pee-Chee 94
74/5 O-Pee-Chee 229
71/2 O-Pee-Chee Poster 2
57/8 Parkhurst [Toro.] 4
58/9 Parkhurst 1
58/9 Parkhurst 45
59/0 Parkhurst 28
60/1 Parkhurst 9
61/2 Parkhurst 8
62/3 Parkhurst 11
63/4 Parkhurst 12
63/4 Parkhurst 72
93/4 Parkie 56-57 113
95/6 Parkie 66-67 114, 145
94/5 Parkie Tall 110
66/7 Post Cereal Box
66/7 Post [Small]
68/9 Post Marble
67/8 Post Tips 11
91/2 Pro Set HHOF 3
72 Semic Sticker 203
60/1 Shirriff 13
61/2 Shirriff 46
62/3 Shirriff 6
68/9 Shirriff / Toro. 4
64/5 Topps 60
65/6 Topps 18
66/7 Topps 19
67/8 Topps 19
68/9 Topps 129
69/0 Topps 53
70/1 Topps 36
71/2 Topps 94
74/5 Topps 229
57/8 Toronto Star Photo
63/4 Toronto Star Action
63/4 Toronto Star Photo
64/5 Toronto Star Action
64/5 Toronto Star Photo
58/9 Toronto Star Weekend
63/4 Toronto Star Weekend
71/2 Toronto Sun Photo
60/1 York
61/2 York 14
62/3 York Transfer 15
63/4 York 18
67/8 York 15
67/8 York 24
67/8 York 32
67/8 York
67/8 York
67/8 York
67/8 York
79/0 CHIC
81/2 CHIC
93/4 CHIC / Coke
64/5 TORO
69/0 TORO

PULFORD, HARVEY
83 HHOF Postcard B10
83&87 HHOF 24

PULKKINEN, HANNU
78/9 SM-Liiga 48
72/3 Williams Finnish 254
73/4 Williams Finnish 254

PULKKINEN, PETRI
92/3 Jyvas Hyva 116
93/4 Jyvas Hyva 200
93/4 Sisu 258

PULKKINEN, REINO
78/9 SM-Liiga 92
72/3 Williams Finnish 163

PULLI, HEINO
66/7 Champion 185
65/6 Hellas 111

PULLI, KAI
71/2 Williams Finnish 374

PULLI, KALEVI
65/6 Hellas 108

PULLI, MARKKU
66/7 Champion 174
65/6 Hellas 105
70/1 Kuvajulkaisut 248

PULLIAINEN, JARI
91/2 Jyvas Hyva 64
94/5 Sisu 322

PULLINEN, REIMA
80/1 Mallasjuoma 192
78/9 SM-Liiga 107

PULLISHY, GLEN
91/2 Avant Garde BCJHL 33

PULLOLA, TOMMI
91/2 Jyvas Hyva 46
92/3 Jyvas Hyva 135
93/4 Jyvas Hyva 237
93/4 Sisu 196
94/5 Sisu 244
95/6 Sisu 349

PUMPLE, RICH
72/3 Cleveland Crusaders
72/3 Clev. WHA / Linnett

PUNCOCHAR, IVAN
98/9 OFS 328
99/0 OFS 292
00/1 OFS 169

PUNCOCHAR, PETR
00/1 OFS 170

PUNSCHNIK, GERHARD
93 Semic Sticker 285

PUNTURERI, MATT
01/2 Guelph Storm
01/2 Guelph Storm M-Cup

PUOLANNE, LAURI
95/6 Sisu 203
96/7 Sisu 6

PUPILLO, DANIEL
82 Semic Sticker 129

PUPKOV, EVGENI
98/9 Mir 99
99/0 Mir 196
00/1 Mir 178

PUPPA, DAREN
98/9 Be A Player 281, ✍ Aut. 281
99/0 BAP Mem. 220
96/7 Bic.Sports Aces 6-S
98/9 Bicycle.. 10-C
90/1 Bowman 242
91/2 Bowman 37
92/3 Bowman 16
93/4 Donruss 316
94/5 Donruss 100
95/6 Donruss 84
96/7 Donruss 34
97/8 Donruss 123
96/7 Do. Canadian 102
97/8 Do. Canadian 110
96/7 Do. Elite 114
97/8 Do. Elite 79
97/8 Do. Preferred 110
97/8 Do. Priority 136
97/8 Do. Studio 44
94/5 Flair 175
94/5 Fleer 209
96/7 Fleer 105, 146, 147, VT-8
95/6 Fleer Metal 139
92/3 Fleer Ultra 261
93/4 Fleer Ultra 427
94/5 Fleer Ultra 429
95/6 Fleer Ultra 155, 376
96/7 Fl. Ultra 159
90/1 Kraft 43
94/5 Kraft / KD
95/6 Kraft / PS
96/7 Kraft / KD
93/4 Leaf 403
94/5 Leaf 224
95/6 Leaf 243
96/7 Leaf 73, SD-15
97/8 Leaf 50
94/5 L. Limited 109
95/6 L. Limited 58
96/7 L. Limited 58
96/7 L. Preferred 69, LS-17
97/8 Limited 170, 192
96/7 Maggers 144
96/7 Metal Univ. 146, AP-8
90/1 OPC/Topps 204, 238
91/2 O-Pee-Chee 333
92/3 O-Pee-Chee 53
89/0 O-Pee-Chee 200
97/8 Omega 212
98/9 Pacific 403
97/8 Pa. Crown Roy. 126
97/8 Pa. Invincible R-187
97/8 Pa. Revolution 129
98/9 Pa. Revolution 132
98/9 Panini Photocard
87/8 Panini Sticker 23
89/0 Panini Sticker 214
90/1 Panini Sticker 31
91/2 Panini Sticker 298
94/5 Panini Sticker 189
95/6 Panini Sticker 134
96/7 Panini Sticker 125
91/2 Parkhurst 14
92/3 Parkhurst 412
93/4 Parkhurst 468
94/5 Parkhurst 225
95/6 Parkhurst 195
91/2 Pinnacle 137
92/3 Pinnacle 327
93/4 Pinnacle 361
94/5 Pinnacle 71, GT15
95/6 Pinnacle 105
96/7 Pinnacle 97
97/8 Pinnacle 84
97/8 Pi. Be A Player 76, TN-16, ✍ Aut. 76
97/8 Pi. Certified 22
97/8 Pi. Inside 45
95/6 Pi. Summit 85
96/7 Pi. Summit 77, ITC-4
97/8 Pi. Totally 22
95/6 Pi. Zenith 120
96/7 Pi. Zenith 43
95/6 Playoff 198
94/5 POG 295
95/6 POG 256
93/4 Power Play 234
93/4 Premier 364
94/5 Premier 410
90/1 Pro Set 27, 365
91/2 Pro Set 21
91/2 Pro Set Platinum 9
90/1 Score 60, 318
90/1 Sco. Hot Cards 26
91/2 Score 106
91/2 Score CAN 106
92/3 Score 47
93/4 Score 273
93/4 Score 530
94/5 Score 72, TF-22
95/6 Score 210
96/7 Score 118, NW-13, SD-11
97/8 Score 18
94/5 Select 45
95/6 Select CE 58
96/7 Select CE 69, F-9
95/6 SBx Emotion 166
95/6 SBx Impact 157
96/7 SBx Impact 123, ZH-8
95/6 SP 137
97/8 SP Authentic 147
97/8 SLU
98/9 SLU
92/3 Topps 457
95/6 Topps 226
94/5 Topps Finest 53
95/6 To. Finest 11
91/2 To. Stadium 231
92/3 To. Stadium 370
93/4 To. Stadium 275
94/5 To. Stadium 162, 183
95/6 To. Stadium 6
98/9 UD Choice 191
90/1 Upper Deck 166
91/2 Upper Deck 248
93/4 Upper Deck 473
94/5 Upper Deck 200
95/6 Upper Deck 205, SE-78
96/7 Upper Deck 338
97/8 Upper Deck 362
98/9 Upper Deck 367
95/6 UD BAP 85, ✍ S85
97/8 UD Black Diam. 74
95/6 UD CC 117
96/7 UD CC 247, 331
97/8 UD Coll. Choice 235
98/9 UD G. Reserve 367
98/9 UD MVP 186
85/6 BUFF / Blue Shield
86/7 BUFF / Blue Shield
87/8 BUFF / Blue Shield
87/8 BUFF / Won. Bread
88/9 BUFF / Blue Shield
88/9 BUFF / Won. Bread
89/0 BUFF / Blue Shield
89/0 BUFF / Campbell's
90/1 BUFF / Blue Shield
90/1 BUFF / Campbell's
91/2 BUFF / Blue Shield
91/2 BUFF / Campbell's
91/2 BUFF / Pepsi
92/3 BUFF / Blue Shield
92/3 BUFF / Jubilee
94/5 TAMP / Health
94/5 TAMP / Sky Box
95/6 TAMP / Sky Box

PURCELL, BILL
90/1 Newmarket Saints

PURCELL, TOM
89/0 7th..Sketch OHL 164

PURDIE, BRAD
91/2 Air Canada SJHL D36
00/1 UD DEL 150
01/2 UD DEL 162, SS3
88/9 Fort Wayne Komets
97/8 Manitoba Moose
96/7 Peoria Rivermen
92/3 Maine Black Bears
93/4 Maine Black Bears

PURDIE, DENNIS
89/0 7th..Sketch OHL 36
90/1 7th..Sketch OHL 140
91/2 7th...Sketch OHL 362
93/4 Johnstown Chiefs 12
94/5 Johnstown Chiefs 15
95/6 Toledo Storm
96/7 Toledo Storm
92/3 Windsor Spitfires

PURDON, NEAL
94/5 Thunder Bay Senators
95/6 Thunder Bay Senators

PURDY, BRIAN
90/1 7th..Sketch WHL 216
91/2 7th...Sketch WHL 202
89/0 Brandon Wheat Kings
90/1 Brandon Wheat Kings

PURINTON, DALE
00/1 BAP Mem. 473
00/1 Premier Plus 129
01/2 Signature 95, ✍ Aut. 95
00/1 SP Authentic 155
00/1 Stadium 244
00/1 To. Stars 118
97/8 Charlotte Checkers
97/8 Hartford Wolf Pack
98/9 Hartford Wolf Pack
99/0 Hartford Wolf Pack
00/1 Hartford Wolf Pack

PUROLA, LAVI
52/3 Anonymous 62

PURPUR, FIDO
34-43 BeeHive-1 [Chic.]

PURSCHEL, DIETER
70/1 Kuvajulkaisut 96

PURSIAINEN, JUHA
00/1 Cardset 204

PURVES, JOHN
98/9 EBK IHL All-Star
95/6 Edge Ice 190
95/6 Future Legends 37
89/0 ProCards AHL 78
90/1 ProCards 212
91/2 ProCards 551
91/2 Baltimore Skipjacks
93/4 Fort Wayne Komets 17
94/5 Fort Wayne Komets 6
96/7 Kansas City Blades
99/0 Utah Grizzlies
00/1 Utah Grizzlies
01/2 Utah Grizzlies
02/3 Nottingham Panthers
84/5 Belleville Bulls

PUSCHACHER, MICHAEL
95 Globe 182
95 Panini Worlds 256
95 Semic 183
96 Wien 211

PUSCHNIG, ANDREAS
95 Globe 185
94 Semic 240
95 Semic 188
93 Semic Sticker 284

PUSCHNIK, GERHARD
94 Semic 242

PUSEY, CHRIS
83/4 Brantford Alexanders

PUSHKOV, SERGEI
94/5 Leaf Elit Set 291
94 Semic 153

PUSHKOV, VICTOR
69/0 Mästar Serien 22
69/0 Soviet Stars

PUSHOR, JAMIE
91/2 Arena 23
95/6 Bowman 103
91/2 Classic 28
91/2 Classic Four Sport 28
95/6 Donruss 337
97/8 Donruss 52
96/7 Do. Canadian 118
94/5 Leaf 459
97/8 Limited 136
98/9 OPC Chrome 51
97/8 Pacific CC 215
96/7 Pi. Be A Player 102, ✍ Aut. 102
96/7 Pi. Summit 196
96/7 Pi. Zenith 147
94/5 Premier 478
97/8 Score Detr. 19
91 7th..Sketch Mem.Cup 122
90/1 7th..Sketch WHL 128
91/2 7th...Sketch WHL 342
96/7 SBx Impact 157
91/2 Star Pics 3
98/9 Topps 51
00/1 To. Chrome 229
95/6 To. Stadium 224
91/2 Ultimate Draft Pick 24, ✍ Aut.
91/2 Upper Deck 63
91/2 Upper Deck 73
96/7 Upper Deck 54
99/0 Upper Deck 220
00/1 Upper Deck 51
99/0 UD G. Reserve 220
01/2 UD Mask 77
00/1 UD Vintage 107
01/2 COLU
95/6 Adirondack Red Wings

PUSIE, JEAN
36-39 Diamond Match TT1
35/6 O-Pee-Chee 91

PUSKAS, CHRIS
90/1 Rayside-Balfour

PUSNIK, ANDREAS
96 Wien 215

PUSTOVALOV, VLADISLAV
00/1 Mir 346

PUTILIN, ALEXEI
98/9 Mir 147

PUTNIK, WALTER
93 Semic Sticker 286

PUURULA, JONI
02/3 Cardset 100

PUUSTINEN, KARI
71/2 Williams Finnish 269

PYATT, NELSON
74/5 Loblaws
76/7 O-Pee-Chee 98
76/7 OPC 396
77/8 O-Pee-Chee 252
78/9 O-Pee-Chee 354
76/7 Topps 98
77/8 Topps 252
76/7 COLR / Hockey Talk

PYATT, TAYLOR
02/3 Bowman 105, ✂ FFDS, ✂ FFJ, ✂ FFP, ✂ FFR, ✂ FFRP, ✂ FFS, ✂ FFTS, ✍ YSA, / ✍ Puck
02/3 First Edition 231
02/3 O-Pee-Chee 280
02/3 Pacific Complete 353
02/3 SP Game-Used ✂ PC, ✂ FF
02/3 Topps 280
02/3 To. Limited 280
02/3 To. Total 37
02/3 Upper Deck 21, ✂ BF
02/3 Victory 28
01/1 BAP Mem. 423
99 Bowman 35, SC8, ✍ BA6
00/1 Crown Royale 133, 21CR-16
01/2 O-Pee-Chee 231
00/1 Parkhurst P-167
01/2 Parkhurst 222
00/1 Premier Plus 93, ✂ GP
00/1 Pr. Stock 131
00/1 Signature 254, ✍ Aut. 216
98/9 SP Authentic 131, ✍ SotT
00/1 SP Authentic 60
99/0 SPx 168
00/1 Stadium 235
01/2 Topps 231
00/1 To. Heritage 65
01/2 To. Heritage 182
98/9 Upper Deck 408
99/0 Upper Deck 319
99/0 UD Black Diam. 98
00/1 UD Black Diam. 103
98/9 UD G. Reserve 408
99/0 UD G. Reserve 319
00/1 UD MVP Cup 213, ✂ GU, ✂ PS
99/0 UD Ovation 70
x99/0 UD Prospects DS6, ✍ Sig.
00/1 Vanguard 134
01/2 Victory 220
98/9 Sudbury Wolves 21
99/0 Sudbury Wolves 10

PYCHA, PAVEL
94/5 APS 114
95/6 APS 66
96/7 APS 251
97/8 APS 278
97/8 DS 33
96/7 DS Sticker 82
97/8 DS Sticker 76
91 Semic Sticker 118

PYE, BILL
98/9 Odessa Jackalopes
99/0 Odessa Jackalopes
92/3 Rochester Americans DD
92/3 Rochester Americans WPC

PYKA, NICO
98/9 DEL 166
99/0 Eishockey 51, 371
00/1 UD DEL 59
01/2 UD DEL 40

PYKA, REEMT
94/5 DEL 233
95/6 DEL 230, 432
96/7 DEL 82
98/9 DEL 31, 317
99/0 Eishockey 133
94 Semic 285
00/1 UD DEL 18
01/2 UD DEL 13

PYKE, DERRICK
95/6 Halifax Moosehead

PYLE, JEFF
99/0 Mobile Mysticks

PYLYPOW, KEVIN
82/3 Brandon Wheat Kings
81/2 Regina Pats

PYLYPUIK, PAT
90/1 7th..Sketch WHL 139
92/3 Toledo Storm WIOT
92/3 Toledo Storm
93/4 Toledo Storm 9
88/9 Lethbridge Hurricanes
89/0 Lethbridge Hurricanes

PYNNONEN, PENTTI
66/7 Champion 198
65/6 Hellas 113

PYÖRÄLÄ, MIKA
02/3 Cardset 251

PYSZ, PATRIK
94/5 DEL 17
95/6 DEL 280

PYTEL, HENRYK
79 Panini Sticker 130

PYYHTIA, JUHANI
65/6 Hellas 90

PYYKKO, PAULI
78/9 SM-Liiga 98

Q

QUACKENBUSH, BILL
02/3 Parkie - Reprint 186, 300
45-64 BeeHive-2 [Detr.]
45-64 BeeHive-2 [Bost.]
51 Berk Ross
51 Berk Ross
83 HHOF Postcard C11
83&87 HHOF 235
96/7 Legends 78
51/2 Parkhurst 26
52/3 Parkhurst 68
53/4 Parkhurst 100
54/5 Parkhurst 51
55/6 Topps 49
55 Toronto Star Weekend
91/2 BOST / SA Legends
91/2 BOST / SA Legends

QUAPP, VLADIMIR
94/5 DEL 105

QUENNEVILLE, CHAD
95/6 Classic 79, ✍ Aut.
95/6 Cla. 5 Sport 149, ✍ Aut.
96/7 Pensacola Ice Pilots
97/8 Pensacola Ice Pilots

QUENNEVILLE, JOEL
79/0 O-Pee-Chee 336
80/1 O-Pee-Chee 19
81/2 O-Pee-Chee 78
83/4 O-Pee-Chee 145
84/5 O-Pee-Chee 77
85/6 OPC/Topps 103
86/7 OPC/Topps 118
88/9 OPC/Topps 3
90/1 O-Pee-Chee 418
89/0 O-Pee-Chee 211
01/2 OPC Sticker 234
83/4 OPC/Topps Sticker 225
85/6 OPC Sticker 170-42
86/7 OPC Sticker 55-193
91/2 ProCards 356
83/4 Souhaits Keychain [Devils]
80/1 Topps 19
81/2 Topps 83 [West]
84/5 Topps 60
01/2 T/O Archives 49
79/0 COLR
81/2 COLR
83/4 HART / Jr. Whalers
84/5 HART / Jr. Whalers
85/6 HART / Jr. Whalers
86/7 HART / Jr. Whalers
87/8 HART / Jr. Whalers
88/9 HART / Jr. Whalers
89/0 HART / Jr. Whalers
79/0 TORO
92/3 St. John's Maple Leafs

QUENNEVILLE, YVON
90/1 Rayside-Balfour

QUESSY, ANTHONY
99/0 Shawinigan Cataractes 4
00/1 Shawinigan Cataractes 7

QUIGLEY, DAVE
87/8 Moncton Hawks

QUILTY, JOHN
34-43 BeeHive-1 [Mont.]
40/1 O-Pee-Chee 106
43-47 Parade Sportive
45-54 Quaker Oats

QUINN, DAN
90/1 Bowman 65
91/2 Bowman 376
92/3 Bowman 289
95/6 Donruss 240
96/7 Donruss 92
95/6 Fleer Metal 106
94/5 Fleer Ultra 376
95/6 Fleer Ultra 281
94/5 Leaf 61, 413
95/6 Leaf 258
84/5 O-Pee-Chee 185
85/6 O-Pee-Chee 176
86/7 O-Pee-Chee 204
87/8 OPC/Topps 171

88/9 OPC/Topps 41
90/1 OPC/Topps 272
91/2 O-Pee-Chee 393
92/3 O-Pee-Chee 264
89/0 OPC/Topps 152
90/1 OPC Premier 93
91/2 OPC Premier 27
86/7 OPC Sticker 87-215
87/8 OPC Sticker 173
88/9 OPC Sticker 236-106
89/0 opcSticker 234-97
87/8 Panini Sticker 147
88/9 Panini Sticker 342
89/0 Panini Sticker 314
90/1 Panini Sticker 305
90/1 Panini/VAN 20
91/2 Panini Sticker 27
95/6 Panini Sticker 49
91/2 Parkhurst 351
91/2 Pinnacle 8
91/2 Pinnacle 408
94/5 Pinnacle 504
95/6 Pi. Summit 116
95/6 POG 192
90/1 Pro Set 303
91/2 Pro Set 209
91/2 Pro Set Platinum 209
90/1 Score 55
90/1 Sco. Hot Cards 24
91/2 Score 62
91/2 Score 65T
91/2 Score CAN 62
91/2 Score CAN 615
92/3 Score 43
95/6 Score 175
96/7 Score 228
97/8 Score Pitt. 14
95/6 SBx Emotion 126
95/6 SBx Impact 120
95/6 Super Sticker 85
92/3 Topps 143
95/6 Topps 261
91/2 To. Stadium 243
92/3 To. Stadium 22
95/6 To. Stadium 142
90/1 Upper Deck 260
91/2 Upper Deck 358
91/2 Upper Deck 563
94/5 UD BAP ✍ 89
95/6 UD CC 70
96/7 UD CC 198
85/6 CALG / Red Rooster
95/6 OTTA
91/2 PHIL / J.C. Penney
86/7 PITT / Kodak
87/8 PITT / Kodak
89/0 PITT / Foodland 6
90/1 VANC / Mohawk
83/4 Belleville Bulls

QUINN, DAVID
92/3 Cleveland Lumberjacks

QUINN, JIM
82/3 Kitchener Rangers
83/4 Kitchener Rangers

QUINN, KEVIN
94/5 Johnstown Chiefs 16

QUINN, MATTHEW
99/0 Rouyn-Noranda
00/1 Rouyn-Noranda 3

QUINN, PAT
70/1 Colgate 72
70/1 Dad's Cookies
70/1 Eddie Sargent 209
71/2 Eddie Sargent 219
72/3 Eddie Sargent 6
70/1 Esso Power Player
74/5 Loblaws
69/0 O-Pee-Chee 186
69/0 O-Pee-Chee 4in1
70/1 O-Pee-Chee 120
70/1 O-Pee-Chee DE 1
71/2 O-Pee-Chee 122
72/3 O-Pee-Chee 183
72/3 O-Pee-Chee Crest 1
73/4 O-Pee-Chee 61
74/5 O-Pee-Chee 286
75/6 O-Pee-Chee 172
76/7 O-Pee-Chee 289
76/7 OPC 379
70/1 Topps 120
71/2 Topps 122
73/4 Topps 61
75/6 Topps 172
71/2 Toronto Sun Photo
72/3 ATLF
74/5 ATLF
84/5 LOSA / Smokey 23
69/0 TORO
70/1 VANC / Royal Bank
71/2 VANC / Royal Bank 5
72/3 VANC / Nalley's

QUINNELL, BOB
91/2 Avant Garde BCJHL 132
92/3 BCJHL 101

QUINNEY, KEN
98/9 DEL 152
99/0 Eishockey 95
88/9 ProCards / Halifax
89/0 ProCards AHL 162
90/1 ProCards 458
91/2 ProCards 127
91/2 Upper Deck 419
00/1 UD DEL 86
85/6 QUEB
85/6 QUEB / Gene. Foods
86/7 QUEB / Gene. Foods
87/8 QUEB / Gene. Foods
85/6 Fredericton Express
89/0 Halifax Citadels
90/1 Halifax Citadels
93/4 Las Vegas Thunder
94/5 Las Vegas Thunder
95/6 Las Vegas Thunder
96/7 Las Vegas Thunder
97/8 Las Vegas Thunder 1

QUINT, DERON
02/3 Pacific 103
95/6 Bowman 107
93/4 Classic 109
93/4 Classic - Class of '94 CL5
94/5 Classic T78
94/5 Cla. Images 74, ✍ Aut.
93/4 Cla. Prospects 206
93/4 Donruss USA18
95/6 Donruss 364
96/7 Donruss 225
95/6 Do. Elite 89
95/6 Fleer Metal 188
95/6 Fleer Ultra 352
96/7 Leaf 143
94/5 L. Limited USA 10
99/0 Millenium 192, ✍ Aut. 192
01/2 O-Pee-Chee 264
97/8 Pacific CC 304
95/6 Parkhurst 269
01/2 Parkhurst 217
94/5 Parkie SE247
93/4 Pinnacle 485
95/6 Pi. Summit 181
94/5 Score 208
95/6 Select CE 129
94/5 Sig. Rookies 26, ✍ 26
95/6 SBx Impact 227
94/5 SP 193
95/6 SP 165
99/0 Stadium 150
95/6 Topps 258
01/2 Topps 264
94/5 Topps Finest 116
95/6 To. Finest 101
95/6 To. Stadium ER197
93/4 Upper Deck 561
94/5 Upper Deck 524
95/6 Upper Deck 498
96/7 Upper Deck 128
96/7 UD CC 206
97/8 UD Coll. Choice 202
01/2 COLU
96/7 PHOE / Coca-Cola
97/8 PHOE / Coca-Cola
98/9 PHOE / Coca-Cola
95/6 WINN
96/7 Springfield Falcons
93/4 Seattle Thunderbirds

QUINTAL, STÉPHANE
02/3 First Edition 177
02/3 Pacific Complete 197
99/0 BAP Mem. 188
92/3 Bowman 337
92/3 Durivage 50
95/6 Donruss 314
94/5 Fleer 244
93/4 Fleer Ultra 456
94/5 Fleer Ultra 245
95/6 Fleer Ultra 257
94/5 Leaf 293
99/0 Pacific 208
01/2 Pacific 91
97/8 Pacific CC 324
94/5 Panini Sticker 170
95/6 Panini Sticker 45
99/0 Panini Sticker 105
92/3 Parkhurst 384
93/4 Parkhurst 500
95/6 Parkhurst 117
93/4 Pinnacle 326
94/5 Pinnacle 501
97/8 Pi. Be A Player 94, ✍ Aut. 94
94/5 POG 258
93/4 Power Play 475
94/5 Premier 6
90/1 Pro Set 410
91/2 Pro Set 350
88/9 ProCards / Maine
91/2 Score CAN 437
92/3 Score 242
93/4 Score 412
93/4 Score 509
95/6 SBx Emotion 89
96/7 Team Out!
92/3 Topps 484
92/3 To. Stadium 350
93/4 To. Stadium 242
93/4 Upper Deck 529
95/6 UD CC 280
99/0 UD Retro 40
89/0 BOST / Sports Action
90/1 BOST / Sports Action
95/6 MONT / Export
95/6 MONT
96/7 MONT / Export
96/7 MONT
97/8 MONT
01/2 MONT
02/3 MONT
93/4 WINN / Ruffles
93/4 WINN Readers
84/5 Richelieu Riverains

QUINTIN, JEAN-FRANCOIS
01/2 UD DEL 55

QUINTIN, JEAN-FRANÇOIS
92/3 Classic 107
99/0 Eishockey 253
93/4 Fleer Ultra 192
93/4 Fleer Ultra Pros. 8
92/3 OPC Premier 37
94/5 Parkhurst 212
89/0 ProCards IHL 97
90/1 ProCards 117
92/3 Score 488
92/3 Upper Deck 483
93/4 Upper Deck 21
00/1 UD DEL 163
92/3 Kansas City Blades
93/4 Kansas City Blades
94/5 Kansas City Blades 14
95/6 Kansas City Blades

96/7 Kansas City Blades

QUIRING, TYLER
91/2 Avant Garde BCJHL 116
93/4 Red Deer Rebels

QUIRK, STEPHEN
97/8 Halifax Moosehead

RAATESALMI, REIJO
70/1 Kuvajulkaisut 377

RABBITT, PAT
81/2 Milwaukee Admirals

RABY, MATHIEU
00/1 Québec Citadelles

RACCOON, ROCKY
96/7 Binghampton Rangers

RACETTE, JULES
51/2 Lac St-Jean 12

RACHUNEK, IVAN
98/9 OFS 283
00/1 OFS 369
01/2 OFS 89

RACHUNEK, KAREL
02/3 Stadium ✂ YSS23
97/8 APS 61
01/2 BAP Mem. 162
01/2 Bowman 124, ✂ FFJ, ✂ FFS, ✂ FFDS, ✂ FFR, ✍ YSA
98/9 OFS 275
00/1 Pr. Stock 134
01/2 Signature 101, ✍ Aut. 101
01/2 Topps OTG19
99/0 UD G. Reserve 345
01/2 Victory 250
00/1 OTTA
01/2 OTTA
02/3 OTTA
99/0 Grand Rapids Griffins

R

RACICOT, ANDRÉ
91/2 Bowman 337
92/3 Durivage 49
93/4 Durivage 15
92/3 Fleer Ultra 332
93/4 Fleer Ultra 355
93/4 Leaf 294
91/2 O-Pee-Chee 450
92/3 OPC Premier 11
92/3 Parkhurst 321
93/4 Pinnacle 332
93/4 Premier 313
89/0 ProCards AHL 180
90/1 ProCards 67
91/2 ProCards 78
91/2 Score 395
93/4 Score CAN 285
93/4 Score 437
91/2 To. Stadium 377
93/4 To. Stadium 26
91/2 Upper Deck 377
92/3 Upper Deck 430
91/2 MONT
92/3 MONT
93/4 MONT
95/6 Indianapolis Ice
94/5 Phoenix Roadrunners
94/5 Portland Pirates

RACICOT, PAOLO
91/2 7th...Sketch LHJMQ 105

RACINE, BRUCE
02/3 Cardset 102
00/1 Cardset 186, Mask. 2
88/9 ProCards / Muskegon
89/0 ProCards IHL 152
90/1 ProCards 517
91/2 ProCards 295
92/3 Cleveland Lumberjacks
97/8 Fort Wayne Komets
98/9 Fort Wayne Komets
99/0 Kansas City Blades
93/4 St. John's Maple Leafs
94/5 St. John's Maple Leafs

RACINE, JEAN-FRANÇOIS
00/1 UD Prospects 78
01/2 Victoriaville Tigres 1

RACINE, YVES
90/1 Bowman 230
91/2 Bowman 44
92/3 Bowman 331
98/9 Cardset 102
94/5 Donruss 246
93/4 Durivage 34
99/0 Eishockey 14
92/3 Fleer Ultra 287
94/5 Fleer Ultra 316
93/4 Leaf 115
94/5 Leaf 388
90/1 OPC/Topps 361
91/2 O-Pee-Chee 228
92/3 O-Pee-Chee 297
97/8 Pa. Invincible R-30
91/2 Panini Sticker 141
92/3 Panini Sticker 119
95 Panini Worlds 7
91/2 Parkhurst 265
93/4 Parkhurst 422
94/5 Parkhurst 168
91/2 Pinnacle 233
92/3 Pinnacle 332
93/4 Pinnacle 372
94/5 Pinnacle 391
95/6 Pinnacle 178
97/8 Pi. Be A Player 27, ✍ Aut. 27
95/6 POG 154
93/4 Power Play 406
94/5 Premier 176, 426
91/2 Pro Set 54
89/0 ProCards AHL 317

90/1 ProCards 474
91/2 Score 158
91/2 Score CAN 158
92/3 Score 74
93/4 Score 264
93/4 Score 540
94/5 Score 162
95/6 Score 221
91/2 Score Young Stars 37
95 Semic 80
92/3 Topps 277
95/6 Topps 138
91/2 To. Stadium 198
92/3 To. Stadium 6
93/4 To. Stadium 304
94/5 To. Stadium 239
91/2 Upper Deck 498
92/3 Upper Deck 142
93/4 Upper Deck 194
94/5 Upper Deck 171
01/2 UD DEL 173
94/5 MONT
94/5 MONT / Export
95/6 MONT
93/4 PHIL / Sheet
93/4 PHIL / J.C. Penney

RADEMAKER, AXEL
99/0 Eishockey 262

RADEVIC, RADIM
94/5 APS 17
96/7 APS 109
96/7 DS Sticker 281

RADIVOJEVIC, BRANKO
02/3 Bowman 154, ✂ FFDS, ✂ FFJ, ✂ FFP, ✂ FFR, ✂ FFRP, ✂ FFS, ✂ FFTS, ✍ YSA, / ✍ Puck
02/3 O-Pee-Chee 273
02/3 SPx 120
02/3 Topps 273
02/3 To. Limited 273
02/3 Upper Deck 219
02/3 UD Foundations 139
02/3 UD Piece 145
02/3 UD Vintage 343
01/2 BAP Mem. 343
01/2 Parkhurst 339
01/2 SPx 212
01/2 UD Mask 163
01/2 UD Premier 104
00/1 UD Prospects 44
01/2 UD Top Shelf 134

RADKE, AL
91/2 Avant Garde BCJHL 152

RADLEIN, PETER
87/8 Brockville Braves

RADMALL, ADAM
02/3 Coventry Blaze

RADULOV, IGOR
02/3 BAP Mem. 342
02/3 Calder 110
02/3 Pacific Complete 595
02/3 SP Authentic 202
02/3 Ultimate Mem. 82
02/3 UD Rookie 173
01/2 Mississauga IceDogs

RAEDAR, CAP
88/9 LOSA / Smokey

RAFALSKI, BRIAN
02/3 Cardset 103
02/3 First Edition 220
02/3 O-Pee-Chee 160
02/3 Pacific 228
02/3 Pacific Complete 204
02/3 Parkhurst 159, -HHN 5
02/3 Signature 57, ✍ 57
02/3 Slam Card
02/3 Topps 160
02/3 To. Limited 160
02/3 To. Total 359
02/3 Upper Deck 349
02/3 UD MVP 106
02/3 UD Vintage 154, 278
99/0 BAP Mem. 67
00/1 BAP Mem. 312
01/2 BAP Mem. 19
98/9 Cardset 32
99/0 Cardset 2, 161, AH 4-pata, PA 3
99/0 Dynagon Ice 119
97/8 Hockey-Box
95/6 Leaf Elit Set 172
99/0 Millenium 151, C-31, ✍ Aut. 151
99/0 Omega 139
00/1 Pacific 242
00/1 Pa. Paramount 148
99/0 Panini Sticker 82, 358
00/1 Parkhurst P-67
01/2 Parkhurst 78
00/1 Signature 42, ✍ Aut. 175
99/0 SP Authentic 106
99/0 Stadium 189
00/1 Stadium 185
00/1 Topps 116
00/1 To. Chrome 90
99/0 T. Prmr. Plus 111
99/0 Ult. Victory 101
00/1 Upper Deck 334
01/2 Upper Deck 335
99/0 UD Black Diam. 53
91/2 Upper Deck WJC 78
01/2 UD MVP 113

RAGLAN, CLARE
45-64 BeeHive-2 [Chic.]
51/2 Parkhurst 36
53/4 Parkhurst 79

RAGLAN, HERB
90/1 Pro Set 525
91/2 Pro Set 470
91/2 Score CAN 536
91/2 QUEB / Petro-Canada
92/3 QUEB / Petro-Canada

87/8 SLOU
87/8 SLOU / Kodak
88/9 SLOU
88/9 SLOU / Kodak
89/0 SLOU / Kodak
84/5 Kingston Canadians

RAGNARSSON, MARCUS
02/3 First Edition 193
02/3 Pacific Complete 191
02/3 To. Total 294
02/3 UD Vintage 213
98/9 Be A Player 117, ✍ Aut. 117
99/0 BAP Mem. 206
00/1 BAP Mem. 305
95/6 Bowman 111, BB29
95/6 Donruss 264, RR-13
96/7 Donruss 234
96/7 Do. Canadian 83
95/6 Do. Elite 38, R-7
96/7 Fleer 101, RS-8
95/6 Fleer Metal 189
96/7 Fl. Picks 126
95/6 Fleer Ultra 353, HS-15
95 Globe 18
96/7 Leaf 183
94/5 Leaf Elit Set 224
95/6 L. Limited 78, RP-1
96/7 L. Limited 42
96/7 L. Preferred 52, LS-13
96/7 Metal Univ. 140
00/1 Pacific 446
97/8 Pa. Dynagon BKS-86
96/7 Panini Sticker 279
97/8 Panini Sticker 234
98/9 Panini Sticker 208
00/1 Panini Sticker 203
95 Panini Worlds 144
95/6 Parkhurst 519, 531, PP-41
00/1 Parkhurst P-156
01/2 Parkhurst 197
96/7 Pinnacle 207
95/6 Pi. Summit 195
96/7 Pi. Summit 165
95/6 Pi. Zenith 141, RRC-8
96/7 Pi. Zenith 79
96/7 Score 242
95/6 Select CE 138
89/0 Semic Elitserien 59
90/1 Semic Elitserien 281
91/2 Semic Elitserien 62
92/3 Semic Elitserien 80
95/6 SBx Impact 220
96/7 SBx Impact 118, F-18
95/6 SP 132
96/7 Team Out!
95/6 Topps 287
95/6 To. Finest 76
96/7 To. Picks RS7
95/6 To. Stadium 148
98/9 UD Choice 178
99/0 Ult. Victory 79
95/6 Upper Deck 439
96/7 Upper Deck 148
97/8 Upper Deck 149
98/9 Upper Deck 166
95/6 UD BAP 164, ✍ S164
96/7 UD CC 236
97/8 UD Coll. Choice 222
98/9 UD G. Reserve 166
01/2 Victory 293
96 Wien 49

RAGOT, MIKE
85/6 Kamloops Blazers

RAGULIN, ALEXANDER
91/2 Future Trends C72 65
72 Hellas MM-Jenkki 65
74 Hellas MM-Jenkki 54
70/1 Kuvajulkaisut 14
69/0 Mästär Serien 23
69/0 Mästär Serien 31
72 Panda MM-Toronto
72 Semic Sticker 5
74 Semic Sticker 27
91 Semic Sticker 242
69/0 Soviet Stars
70/1 Soviet Stars
71/2 Soviet Stars
71/2 Williams Finnish 13
72/3 Williams Finnish 32
73/4 Williams Finnish 14

RAHKONEN, ANTTI
95/6 Sisu 314
96/7 Sisu 124

RAHM, NIKLAS
95/6 Leaf Elit Set 232
92/3 Semic Elitserien 133
95/6 UD Elitserien 77
98/9 UD Elitserien 105
00/1 UD Elitserien 63

RAIKKONEN, MIKKO
66/7 Champion 168
70/1 Kuvajulkaisut 251
71/2 Williams Finnish 217
72/3 Williams Finnish 166
73/4 Williams Finnish 232

RAILIO, SEPPO
72/3 Williams Finnish 109

RAINVILLE, KEVIN
01/2 Victoriaville Tigres 20

RAISANEN, PERTTI
71/2 Williams Finnish 314

RAISKI, ANDREI
99/0 Mir 270

RAITANEN, RAULI
98/9 Cardset 266
92/3 Jyvas Hyva 203
93/4 Jyvas Hyva 358
94 Semic 38
95 Semic 51
93 Semic Sticker 73
93/4 Sisu 229

94/5 Sisu 48, 381
95/6 Sisu 363
95/6 Sisu Limited 21

RAITER, MARK
90/1 7th...Sketch WHL 84
91/2 7th...Sketch WHL 103
95/6 Birmingham Bulls
90/1 Saskatoon Blades
91/2 Saskatoon Blades

RAJALA, KARI
98/9 Cardset 37
99/0 Cardset 224
00/1 Cardset 255
65/6 Hellas 76

RAJALA, MIKA
78/9 SM-Liiga 162
72/3 Williams Finnish 315
73/4 Williams Finnish 116

RAJALA, OLLI-PEKKA
80/1 Mallasjuoma 127

RAJAMÄKI, ERKKI
02/3 Cardset 252
00/1 Cardset 261

RAJAMÄKI, TOMMI
98/9 Cardset 234
99/0 Cardset 328
00/1 Cardset 95
94/5 Parkie SE226
94/5 Sisu 315, ND-5
95/6 Sisu 355
96/7 Sisu 151
94/5 Topps Finest 123
94/5 Upper Deck 512

RAJANIEMI, VESA
78/9 SM-Liiga 82

RAJNOHA, PAVEL
94/5 APS 184
95/6 APS 184
97/8 APS 58
97/8 DS Sticker 292
98/9 OFS 305

RAKOVSKY, KAREL
99/0 Score 96

RALEIGH, DON
45-64 BeeHive-2 [NYRa.]
52/3 La Patrie
51/2 Parkhurst 93
52/3 Parkhurst 99
53/4 Parkhurst 68
54/5 Parkhurst 68
54/5 Topps 53

RALPH, BRAD
99 Bowman 29, ✍ BA12
99/0 SP Authentic 135
99/0 Topps 275
99/0 To. Chrome 275
99/0 UD Black Diam. 103
99/0 UD MVP Cup 207

RALPH, JAMIE
88/9 ProCards / Newmarket

RALPH, JASON
96/7 Flint Generals

RALPH, JIM
85/6 Nova Scotia Oilers
83/4 Springfield Indians 2
81/2 Ottawa 67's

RAM, JAMIE
02/3 Cardset 104
94/5 Classic 59, AA8
95/6 Edge Ice 21
96/7 Leaf 235
94/5 Binghampton Rangers
95/6 Binghampton Rangers
98/9 Cincinnati M'Ducks 12
96/7 Kentucky Tho'blades
97/8 Kentucky Tho'blades
90/1 Michigan Tech Huskies
91/2 Michigan Tech Huskies
91/2 Michigan Tech Huskies

RAMAGE, ROB
90/1 Bowman 162
91/2 Bowman 154
92/3 Fleer Ultra 413
83/4 Funmate Puffy 16 [w/]
89/0 Kraft 39
90/1 Kraft 44
80/1 O-Pee-Chee 213
81/2 O-Pee-Chee 79
82/3 O-Pee-Chee 310
83/4 O-Pee-Chee 319
84/5 O-Pee-Chee 190
85/6 O-Pee-Chee 196
86/7 OPC/Topps 17
87/8 OPC/Topps 160
88/9 OPC/Topps 244
90/1 OPC/Topps 317
91/2 O-Pee-Chee 55
91/2 OPC Premier 76
81/2 OPC Sticker 154
81/2 OPC Sticker 229
82/3 OPC/Topps Sticker 223
83/4 OPC/Topps Sticker 130
84/5 OPC Sticker 62
84/5 OPC Sticker 136
86/7 OPC Sticker 180-44
87/8 OPC Sticker 20-160
88/9 OPC Sticker 84-213
87/8 Panini Sticker 306
89/0 Panini Sticker 31
90/1 Panini Sticker 280
90/1 Panini/TOR 20
91/2 Panini Sticker 96
91/2 Parkhurst 175
92/3 Parkhurst 175
91/2 Pinnacle 228
92/3 Pinnacle 389
81/2 Post 21
82/3 Post [Colo.]
93/4 Power Play 407
93/4 Premier - Finest 12
90/1 Pro Set 288
91/2 Pro Set 232
91/2 Pro Set 407
92/3 Pro Set 177
90/1 Score 36

91/2 Score 233
91/2 Score 23T
91/2 Score CAN 573
92/3 Score 351
93/4 Score 36
93/4 Score 653
84/5 7-Eleven
85/6 7-Eleven Superstars 17
80/1 Topps 213
81/2 Topps 84 [West]
84/5 Topps 134
91/2 To. Stadium 239
90/1 Upper Deck 62
92/3 Upper Deck 105
79/0 COLR
81/2 COLR
93/4 MONT
93/4 PHIL / Sheet
93/4 PHIL / J.C. Penney
87/8 SLOU / Kodak
92/3 SLOU / McDon. 21
90/1 TORO

RAMAGE, ROB
02/3 Fleer Throwbacks 12

RAMBO, DEAN
90/1 7th..Sketch WHL 76
90/1 Saskatoon Blades

RAMN, MARCUS
94/5 Leaf Elit Set 167

RAMO, MIKKO
02/3 Cardset 257

RAMOSER, ROLAND
91/2 Avant Garde BCJHL 24
91/2 Avant Garde BCJHL 155
96/7 DEL 326
98/9 DEL 60
99/0 Eishockey 28

RAMPA, PEKKA
73/4 Williams Finnish 189

RAMPF, SVEN
98/9 DEL 243
99/0 Eishockey 162
00/1 UD DEL 15

RAMPTON, JOEY
83/4 Soo Greyhounds

RAMSAY, BEATTIE
25 Dominion Chocolates 59

RAMSAY, BRUCE
99/0 Fort Wayne Komets
96/7 Grand Rapids Griffins
97/8 Grand Rapids Griffins
98/9 Grand Rapids Griffins
93/4 Thunder Bay Senators
94/5 Thunder Bay Senators
95/6 Thunder Bay Senators

RAMSAY, CRAIG
77/8 Coke
72/3 Eddie Sargent 38
74/5 Loblaws
72/3 O-Pee-Chee 262
73/4 O-Pee-Chee 213
74/5 O-Pee-Chee 305
75/6 O-Pee-Chee 271
76/7 O-Pee-Chee 78
77/8 O-Pee-Chee 191
78/9 O-Pee-Chee 9
79/0 O-Pee-Chee 207
80/1 O-Pee-Chee 13
81/2 O-Pee-Chee 31
83/4 O-Pee-Chee 69
84/5 O-Pee-Chee 27
85/6 OPC/Topps 32
84/5 OPC Sticker 215
85/6 OPC Sticker 175-44
85/6 OPC Sticker 192-68
82/3 Post [Buff.]
83/4 Souhaits Keychain [Sabres]
75/6 Topps 271
76/7 Topps 78
77/8 Topps 191
78/9 Topps 9
79/0 Topps 207
80/1 Topps 13
84/5 Topps 21
72/3 BUFF
73/4 BUFF
74/5 BUFF
79/0 BUFF / Bells Market
80/1 BUFF / Wendt's 1
81/2 BUFF / Wendt's 1
82/3 BUFF / Wendt's 3
84/5 BUFF / Blue Shield
85/6 BUFF / Blue Shield
93/4 BUFF / Noco
96/7 OTTA
97/8 OTTA

RAMSAY, RYAN
00/1 UD Prospects 19
01/2 Kitchener Rangers
02/3 Plymouth Whalers

RAMSEY, MIKE
91/2 Bowman 32
92/3 Fleer Ultra 19
93/4 Fleer Ultra 396
94/5 Leaf 536
80/1 O-Pee-Chee 127
82/3 O-Pee-Chee 32
83/4 O-Pee-Chee 70
84/5 O-Pee-Chee 28
85/6 OPC/Topps 77
86/7 OPC/Topps 115
87/8 OPC/Topps 63
88/9 OPC/Topps 133
90/1 OPC/Topps 102
91/2 O-Pee-Chee 236
89/0 OPC/Topps 140
83/4 OPC/Topps Sticker 243
84/5 OPC Sticker 211
85/6 OPC Sticker 180-49
86/7 OPC Sticker 44-180
87/8 OPC Sticker 149-11
88/9 OPC Sticker 260-128
80 Olympic USA
87/8 Panini Sticker 25

88/9 Panini Sticker 222
90/1 Panini Sticker 24
91/2 Panini Sticker 299
92/3 Panini Sticker 253
91/2 Parkhurst 19
92/3 Parkhurst 256
91/2 Pinnacle 64
92/3 Pinnacle 21
93/4 Pinnacle 394
94/5 Pinnacle 412
82/3 Post [Buff.]
90/1 Pro Set 28
91/2 Pro Set 25
91/2 Pro Set 568
91/2 Pro Set Platinum 13
90/1 Score 23
90/1 Sco. Hot Cards 13
91/2 Score 61
91/2 Score CAN 61
92/3 Score 28
93/4 Score 179
89 Semic Sticker 158
94/5 SR Miracle 27,28, ✍ 27,28
83/4 Souhaits Keychain [Sabres]
80/1 Topps 127
84/5 Topps 22
92/3 Topps 473
91/2 To. Stadium 135
92/3 To. Stadium 386
90/1 Upper Deck 168
81/2 BUFF / Wendt's 12
82/3 BUFF / Wendt's 15
84/5 BUFF / Blue Shield
85/6 BUFF / Blue Shield
86/7 BUFF / Blue Shield
87/8 BUFF / Blue Shield
87/8 BUFF / Won. Bread
88/9 BUFF / Blue Shield
88/9 BUFF / Won. Bread
89/0 BUFF / Blue Shield
89/0 BUFF / Campbell's
90/1 BUFF / Blue Shield
90/1 BUFF / Campbell's
91/2 BUFF / Blue Shield
91/2 BUFF / Campbell's
91/2 BUFF / Pepsi
92/3 BUFF / Blue Shield
92/3 BUFF / Jubilee
93/4 BUFF / Noco
93/4 PITT / Foodland 16

RAMSTEDT, JOHAN
94/5 SR Auto-Phonex 33, ✍ 33
95/6 SR Tetrad Autobilia 50
95/6 UD CC 341
95/6 UD Elitserien DS5
98/9 UD Elitserien 29
00/1 UD Elitserien 22

RANCOURT, ALAIN
88/9 Richelieu Riverains

RANCOURT, FERNAND
52/3 Bas du Fleuve 30

RANCOURT, MARC
01/2 Belleville Bulls

RANDALL, BRUCE
88/9 ProCards / Hershey

RANDALL, BRYAN
96/7 Regina Pats
97/8 Regina Pats

RANDALL, GREG
98/9 Guildford Flames

RANDALL, KEN
24/5 Champ's Cigarettes
24/5 Maple Crispette [V130] 24
23/4 William Paterson 34
24/5 William Paterson 12

RANDALL, SHAWN
98/9 Topeka Scarecrows

RANFORD, BILL
02/3 Ultimate Mem. ✂ CSTW, ✂ SCD
02/3 UD Foundations 2, 30, ✂ CG, ✂ LI
98/9 Bicycle.. 3-C
95/6 Bicycle Sports Aces 3-Club
91/2 Bowman 101
92/3 Bowman 106
95/6 Bowman 24
98/9 Bowman's Best 87
91 Canada Cup
93/4 Classic - Team Canada TC4
93/4 Donruss 117
94/5 Donruss 171
95/6 Donruss 323
96/7 Donruss 87
97/8 Donruss 172
96/7 Do. Canadian 75
97/8 Do. Canadian 46
95/6 Do. Elite 12
96/7 Do. Elite 12
97/8 Do. Preferred 52
97/8 Do. Priority 55
99/0 Dynagon Ice 83
93/4 EA Sports 48
95/6 Edge Ice L5
94/5 Flair 61
96/7 Flair 6
94/5 Fleer 75
96/7 Fleer 7
95/6 Fleer Metal 56
92/3 Fleer Ultra 65
93/4 Fleer Ultra 158
94/5 Fleer Ultra 76
95/6 Fleer Ultra 57
96/7 Fl. Ultra 11
91/2 Gillette 9
95 Globe 75
93/4 Hockey Wit 76
95/6 Hoyle / West. Q-

Diamond
92/3 Humpty Dumpty
90/1 Kraft 45
91/2 Kraft 44
92/3 Kraft / PB
93/4 Kraft / KD
94/5 Kraft / KD
95/6 Kraft / PS
99/0 Kraft / KD
93/4 Leaf 68
93/4 Leaf PW 10
94/5 Leaf 60, CP-10
95/6 Leaf 86
96/7 Leaf 2
97/8 Leaf 33
94/5 L. Limited 9
95/6 L. Limited 103
96/7 L. Limited 22
96/7 L. Preferred 3, LS-40
97/8 Limited 14
96/7 Maggers 12
91/2 McDonald's Mc-21
96/7 Metal Univ. 10
87/8 OPC/Topps 13
90/1 OPC/Topps 226
90/1 O-Pee-Chee 467
91/2 O-Pee-Chee 356
92/3 O-Pee-Chee 137
89/0 O-Pee-Chee 233
90/1 OPC Premier 94
91/2 OPC Premier 60
92/3 OPC Premier SP19
89/0 opcSticker 230-89
98/9 Pacific 446
99/0 Pacific 147
97/8 Pacific CC 233
98/9 Pa. Crown Roy. 125
97/8 Pa. Dynagon 134, T-51
97/8 Pa. Invincible 150
97/8 Pa. Paramount 199
87/8 Panini Sticker 5
89/0 Panini Sticker 81
90/1 Panini Sticker 218
90/1 Panini/EDM 17
91/2 Panini Sticker 125
92/3 Panini Sticker 105
93/4 Panini Sticker U
94/5 Panini Sticker 207
96/7 Panini Sticker 2
97/8 Panini Sticker 110
99/0 Panini Sticker 250
95 Panini Worlds 1
91/2 Parkhurst 53
92/3 Parkhurst 50
93/4 Parkhurst 67
94/5 Parkhurst 72, V75
95/6 Parkhurst 78, 282, GP-9
91/2 Pinnacle 170
91/2 Pinnacle B-7
92/3 Pinnacle 14
93/4 Pinnacle 81
94/5 Pinnacle 185, GT6, NL13
96/7 Pinnacle 89
97/8 Pinnacle 46
96/7 Pi. Be A Player 16, ✍ Aut. 16
97/8 Pi. Certified 12
97/8 Pi. Inside 35, S-23
95/6 Pi. Summit 71
97/8 Pi. Totally 12
95/6 Pi. Zenith 47
96/7 Pi. Zenith 72
95/6 Playoff 151, 258
96/7 Playoff 374
94/5 POG 279
94/5 POG / Western 8
95/6 POG 113
93/4 Power Play 85
93/4 Power Play Netm. 6
93/4 Premier 258
94/5 Premier 435
95/6 Pro Magnet 84
90/1 Pro Set 94
91/2 Pro Set 70
91/2 Pro Set 283
92/3 Pro Set 51
91/2 Pro Set Platinum 36
90/1 Score 79, 331, 345, 358
90/1 Sco. Hot Cards 39
91/2 Score 30
91/2 Score CAN 30
92/3 Score 236
93/4 Score 424
92/3 Score 495
93/4 Score 155
93/4 Score TF 7
95/6 Score 239
96/7 Score 40, NW-15
97/8 Score 13
92/3 Seasons 57
94/5 Select 5
95/6 Select CE 55
94 Semic 331
94 Semic 79
95 Semic 77, 201, 208
92 Semic Sticker 75
95/6 SBx Emotion 66
95/6 SBx Impact 64
96/7 SBx Impact 8
94/5 SP 41
95/6 SP 9
96/7 SP 9
97/8 SP Authentic 165
98/9 SP Authentic 78
01/2 SP GU ✂ TotG, ✂ TotGC, ✂ TotGCSig, ✂ TotGT
99/0 SPx 65
99/0 Stadium 157
95/6 Super Sticker 42, 45
92/3 Topps 126
95/6 Topps 241, HGC-8
94/5 Topps Finest RL-17
95/6 To. Finest 51
97/8 To. Picks 85
91/2 To. Stadium 249
92/3 To. Stadium 66

93/4 To. Stadium 131
94/5 To. Stadium 29
95/6 To. Stadium 2, EN6
95/6 T. Super Skills 86
00/1 Ultimate Mem. ✂ D-5
90/1 Upper Deck 42, 201
91/2 Upper Deck 10
91/2 Upper Deck 117
92/3 Upper Deck 262
93/4 Upper Deck 180, SP-52
94/5 Upper Deck 21, SP-27
x95/6 Upper Deck SE32
96/7 Upper Deck 8, SS30A
97/8 Upper Deck 178
98/9 Upper Deck 364
94/5 UD BAP R28, ✍ 16
96/7 UD Black Diam. 80
95/6 UD CC 246
96/7 UD CC 17
97/8 UD Coll. Choice 267
98/9 UD G. Reserve 364
96/7 UD Ice 3
01/2 UD Legends 25, 86, ✂ TT
98/9 UD MVP 188
01/2 UD SCup Champs 12
96 Wien 76
93/4 EDMO / Sheet
88/9 EDMO
88/9 EDMO / Action 60
90/1 EDMO / IGA
91/2 EDMO / IGA
92/3 EDMO
92/3 EDMO / IGA 018
86/7 Moncton G'Flames

RANGER, JOE
87/8 Kitchener Rangers
85/6 London Knights

RANHEIM, PAUL
98/9 Be A Player 176, ✍ Aut. 176
90/1 Bowman 100
91/2 Bowman 251
92/3 Bowman 96
93/4 Donruss 442
94/5 Donruss 50
92/3 Fleer Ultra 27
93/4 Fleer Ultra 286
89/0 Kraft 9
93/4 Leaf 170
94/5 Leaf 370
90/1 OPC/Topps 20
91/2 O-Pee-Chee 15
92/3 O-Pee-Chee 36
98/9 OPC Chrome 102
98/9 Pacific 139
01/2 Pacific 293
90/1 Panini Sticker 181, 342
90/1 Panini/CGY 18
91/2 Panini Sticker 54
92/3 Panini Sticker 44
93/4 Panini Sticker 184
91/2 Parkhurst 249
92/3 Parkhurst 260
93/4 Parkhurst 32
95/6 Parkhurst 361
91/2 Pinnacle 252
92/3 Pinnacle 67
93/4 Pinnacle 265
94/5 Pinnacle 138
95/6 Playoff 265
94/5 POG 116
95/6 POG 127
93/4 Power Play 309
93/4 Premier 481
94/5 Premier 96
90/1 Pro Set 44
91/2 Pro Set 31
92/3 Pro Set 29
90/1 Score 248
91/2 Score 21
91/2 Score CAN 21
92/3 Score 149
93/4 Score 165
92/3 Topps 486
95/6 Topps 232
98/9 Topps 102
91/2 To. Stadium 50
92/3 To. Stadium 144
93/4 To. Stadium 151
90/1 Upper Deck 104
91/2 Upper Deck 472
92/3 Upper Deck 328
93/4 Upper Deck 131
94/5 Upper Deck 430
95/6 Upper Deck 13
99/0 Upper Deck 202
95/6 UD BAP 87, ✍ S87
95/6 UD CC 78
99/0 UD G. Reserve 202
90/1 CALG / McGavin's
91/2 CALG / IGA
92/3 CALG / IGA 014
97/8 CARO / Sprint
98/9 CARO / Highwoods
95/6 HART / Kids Club
96/7 HART / Kids Club
01/2 PHIL

RANKIN, FRANK
83 HHOF Postcard I13
83887 HHOF 132

RANNARD, FRED
98/9 Anchorage Aces
99/0 Anchorage Aces

RANTALA, MIKKO
98/9 Cardset 133

RANTALA, TIMO
66/7 Champion 103

RANTANEN,
97/8 Hockey-Box

RANTANEN, ASKO
99/0 Cardset 317
00/1 Cardset 246

RANTANEN, ESKO
66/7 Champion 169

70/1 Kuvajulkaisut 249
71/2 Williams Finnish 215
72/3 Williams Finnish 164
73/4 Williams Finnish 229

RANTANEN, JARMO
66/7 Champion 61
65/6 Hellas 14
92/3 Jyvas Hyva 81
93/4 Jyvas Hyva 146
70/1 Kuvajulkaisut 148
93/4 Sisu 145
71/2 Williams Finnish 198
72/3 Williams Finnish 236
73/4 Williams Finnish 270

RANTANEN, KALEVI
78/9 SM-Liiga 110

RANTANEN, KARI
70/1 Kuvajulkaisut 353

RANTANEN, KIMMO
71/2 Williams Finnish 291

RANTANEN, MARKO
93/4 Sisu 4
94/5 Sisu 295
95/6 Sisu 247

RANTASILA, JUHA
66/7 Champion 35
65/6 Hellas 34
70/1 Kuvajulkaisut 75
70/1 Kuvajulkaisut 113
72 Panda MM-Toronto
72 Semic Sticker 92
71/2 Williams Finnish 122
72/3 Williams Finnish 71
72/3 Williams Finnish 93
73/4 Williams Finnish 139

RAPOZA, BOBBY
00/1 Asheville Smoke
96/7 Dayton Ice Bandits
98/9 Phoenix Mustangs 19

RAPPANA, KEVIN
96/7 Charlotte Checkers

RASANEN, ERKKI
66/7 Champion 125
70/1 Kuvajulkaisut 266

RASANEN, JUHA
71/2 Williams Finnish 333

RASANEN, PEKKA
80/1 Mallasjuoma 47

RASANEN, TEIJO
72/3 Williams Finnish 181

RASK, JEFF
97/8 Central Texas

RASMUSSEN, ERIK
02/3 Pacific Complete 366
02/3 To. Heritage 174
02/3 Upper Deck 330
01/2 Atomic ✂ GWJ 4
94/5 Classic DP7
95/6 Do. Elite WJ 39
01/2 Heads Up ✂ JQ 23
97/8 Leaf 153
99/0 Millenium 31, ✍ Aut. 31
99/0 NHL Power Play
99/0 Pacific 42
00/1 Pacific 54
01/2 Pacific 52
97/8 Pa. Dynagon Rookie
97/8 Pa. Paramount 23
97/8 Pinnacle 3
97/8 Pi. Be A Player 217, ✍ Aut. 217
00/1 PS Titanium ✂ GUG 60
01/2 PS Titanium Draft ✂ 14
00/1 PS Titanium Draft ✂ 12
97/8 Score 58
97/8 Score Buff. 16
94/5 Select 152
97/8 SP Authentic 173
98/9 SPx Finite 10, 142
99/0 Topps 64
99/0 To. Chrome 64
98/9 To. Finest F20
98/9 UD Choice 25
97/8 Upper Deck 226
98/9 Upper Deck 43
98/9 UD G. Reserve 43
96/7 UD Ice 146
97/8 UD Ice 57
98/9 UD MVP 23, ✍ PS
97/8 Zenith RR-3
97/8 Rochester Americans
98/9 Rochester Americans

RASOLKO, ANDREI
98/9 Mir 148
99/0 Mir 164
00/1 Mir 371

RASTIO, JARI
80/1 Mallasjuoma 124
78/9 SM-Liiga 170

RASTIO, TEPPO
66/7 Champion 13
65/6 Hellas 20
77-79 Sports. FIN 50-1199
71/2 Williams Finnish 250

RASZKA, TAYLOR
02/3 Plymouth Whalers

RATCHFORD, MIKE
52/3 Anonymous 150

RATCHUK, PETER
98 Bowman 99, SC14
98 Bowman Chrome 99
95/6 Classic 68
00/1 Upper Deck 434
99/0 Louisville Panthers
00/1 Louisville Panthers
98/9 New Haven Beast 17
02/3 Rochester Americans
01/2 WBS Penguins

RATELLE, JEAN
45-64 BeeHive-2 [NYRa.]
45-64 BeeHive-2 [NYRa.]
64-67 BeeHive-3 [NYRa.]
65/6 Coca-Cola

71/2 Colgate Head
70/1 Colgate 25
70/1 Dad's Cookies
79/0 Dernière Heure
70/1 Eddie Sargent 118
71/2 Eddie Sargent 114
72/3 Eddie Sargent 142
70/1 Esso Power Player
01/2 Fleer Greats 27, ✍ Aut.
91/2 Future Trends C72 66, ✍ 66
62/3 Cowan Tile
83&87 HHOF 249
75/6 Hockey Heroes
72/3 Post 14
74/5 Loblaws
73/4 Mac's Milk
99/0 Millenium P-16, ✍ P-16
68/9 O-Pee-Chee 77
69/0 O-Pee-Chee 42
69/0 O-Pee-Chee 4in1
69/0 O-Pee-Chee Stamp
70/1 O-Pee-Chee 181
70/1 O-Pee-Chee DE 40
71/2 O-Pee-Chee 97
72/3 O-Pee-Chee 12
72/3 O-Pee-Chee 48
72/3 O-Pee-Chee 48
72/3 O-Pee-Chee 168
72/3 O-Pee-Chee 250
72/3 O-Pee-Chee 280
72/3 O-Pee-Chee 283
72/3 O-Pee-Chee TC
73/4 O-Pee-Chee 141
74/5 O-Pee-Chee 145
75/6 O-Pee-Chee 243
75/6 O-Pee-Chee 324
76/7 O-Pee-Chee 2
76/7 O-Pee-Chee 80
76/7 O-Pee-Chee 381
77/8 O-Pee-Chee 40
77/8 O-Pee-Chee NS 16
78/9 O-Pee-Chee 155
79/0 O-Pee-Chee 225
80/1 O-Pee-Chee 6
71/2 O-Pee-Chee Poster 19
95/6 Parkie 66-67 88
94/5 Parkie Tall 89, 152
70/1 Post Shooters
72 Semic Sticker 214
61/2 Shirriff 98
68/9 Shirriff / NYRa. 2
61/2 Topps 60
62/3 Topps 58
63/4 Topps 63
65/6 Topps 25
66/7 Topps 29
66/7 Topps / Test 29
67/8 Topps 31
68/9 Topps 77
69/0 Topps 42
71/2 Topps 97
72/3 Topps 50
72/3 Topps 62
72/3 Topps 63
72/3 Topps 130
72/3 Topps 175
73/4 Topps 73
74/5 Topps 145
75/6 Topps 243
75/6 Topps 324
76/7 Topps 2
76/7 Topps 80
76/7 Topps NS 22
77/8 Topps 40
77/0 ToppsNS 16
78/9 Topps 155
79/0 Topps 225
80/1 Topps 6
71/2 Toronto Sun Photo
01/2 UD Legends 47, ✂ PoH
93/4 Zellers, ✍ Aut.
91/2 BOST / SA Legends
98/9 BOST / Alumni 10

RATH, MARIUS
95 Globe 195
94 Semic 266
95 Semic 182
92/3 Semic Nordisk 12
92 Semic Sticker 43
93 Semic Sticker 246
96 Wien 209

RATHBONE, JASON
92/3 Hampton Roads

RATHJE, MIKE
02/3 O-Pee-Chee 50
02/3 Pacific Complete 354
02/3 Topps 50
02/3 To. Limited 50
02/3 To. Total 73
02/3 Upper Deck 146
00/1 BAP Mem. 346
92/3 CSC 8
92/3 Classic 3
92/3 Classic 60
92/3 Classic LP3
93/4 Classic 145
92/3 Classic Four Sport 153
92/3 Classic Four Sport LP23
93/4 Cla. 4 Sport 246
93/4 Cla. Images 4 Sport 92
93/4 Cla. Prospects 32
93/4 Donruss 314
94/5 Donruss 170
95/6 Donruss 305
93/4 Fleer Ultra 418
93/4 Fleer Ultra WotF 15
94/5 Fleer Ultra 201
93/4 Leaf 419
94/5 Leaf 139
99/0 Millenium 209, ✍ Aut. 209
99/0 Pacific 379
97/8 Pa. Invincible R-180
94/5 Panini Sticker Y
95/6 Panini Sticker 285
93/4 Parkhurst 458
94/5 Parkie SE160
93/4 Pinnacle 442
94/5 Pinnacle 363
95/6 Pinnacle 155
93/4 Power Play 437
93/4 Premier 427
93/4 Score 595
94/5 Score 261
90/1 7th..Sketch WHL 41
91/2 7th...Sketch WHL 330
95/6 SBx Emotion 160
95/6 SBx Impact 151
95/6 Topps 191
93/4 To. Stadium 322
94/5 To. Stadium 215
92/3 Upper Deck 589
93/4 Upper Deck 460, SP-147
94/5 Upper Deck 168
99/0 UD MVP Cup 157
01/2 Victory 298
92/3 SANJ / Pacific Bell

RATTRAY, DONOVAN
00/1 Red Deer Rebels

RATUSHNY, DAN
92 C.O.A. Winter Olympics 195
91/2 Canada Nationals
00/1 Cardset 265
98/9 EBK IHL All-Star
93/4 Upper Deck 245
92/3 Fort Wayne Komets 19
94/5 Fort Wayne Komets 7
98/9 Kansas City Blades 3
95/6 Peoria Rivermen

RÄTY, TERO
72/3 Williams Finnish 151

RÄTY, TUOMO
94/5 Sisu 299

RAU, THORSTEN
94/5 DEL 180

RAUBAL, ANDREAS
95/6 DEL 341

RAUBAL, ANTON
95/6 DEL 110

RAUBAL, MICHAEL
94/5 DEL 119

RAUBAL, TONI
94/5 DEL 124

RAUCH, MARTIN
91 Semic Sticker 186
92 Semic Sticker 203

RAUHALA, REINE
91/2 Semic Elitserien 146
92/3 Semic Elitserien 161
92/3 Upper Deck 598

RAUNIO, MATTI
98/9 Cardset 174
95/6 Sisu 304

RAUNIO, TAPIO
65/6 Hellas 50

RAUSSE, ERROL
79/0 WASH

RAUTAKALLIO, PEKKA
72 Hellas MM-Jenkki 11
74 Hellas MM-Jenkki 14
70/1 Kuvajulkaisut 200
80/1 O-Pee-Chee 356
81/2 O-Pee-Chee 50
81/2 OPC Sticker 223
82/3 OPC/Topps Sticker 218
76/7 OPC WHA 116
72 Panda MM-Toronto
79 Panini Sticker 164
80/1 Pepsi Bottle Cap
82/3 Post [Calg.]
74 Semic Sticker 79
82 Semic Sticker 161
91 Semic Sticker 228
78/9 SM-Liiga 2
78/9 SM-Liiga 223
77-79 Sports. FIN 47-1106
82 Valio
96 Wien HL15
71/2 Williams Finnish 90
72/3 Williams Finnish 72
72/3 Williams Finnish 255
73/4 Williams Finnish 76
73/4 Williams Finnish 255
79/0 ATLF / B&W
80/1 CALG
81/2 CALG
75/6 Phoenix Roadrunners
76/7 Phoenix Roadrunners

RAUTAKALLIO, PENTTI
80/1 Mallasjuoma 218

RAUTAKILLO, PEKKA
79/0 ATLF / Colour

RAUTAKORPI, JUKKA
95/6 Sisu 394

RAUTALAMMI, TAPIO
66/7 Champion 21
65/6 Hellas 73
70/1 Kuvajulkaisut 201

RAUTALIN, PENTTI
66/7 Champion 11
65/6 Hellas 27
70/1 Kuvajulkaisut 233
71/2 Williams Finnish 251

RAUTEE, MATTI
70/1 Kuvajulkaisut 166
71/2 Williams Finnish 235
72/3 Williams Finnish 219
73/4 Williams Finnish 295

RAUTEE, MIKKO
98/9 Cardset 243
99/0 Cardset 335
00/1 Cardset 101

RAUTEE, PEKKA
70/1 Kuvajulkaisut 167
78/9 SM-Liiga 207
71/2 Williams Finnish 236
72/3 Williams Finnish 220
73/4 Williams Finnish 296

RAUTIAINEN, MATTI
80/1 Mallasjuoma 40
79 Panini Sticker 179
78/9 SM-Liiga 12
78/9 SM-Liiga 105
72/3 Williams Finnish 293
73/4 Williams Finnish 230

RAUTIAINEN, TUOMO
70/1 Kuvajulkaisut 220
71/2 Williams Finnish 141
72/3 Williams Finnish 203
73/4 Williams Finnish 166

RAUTIO, JANI
93/4 Jyvas Hyva 167
93/4 Sisu 173

RAUTIO, KAI
98/9 Cardset 59
96/7 DEL 53
97/8 Hockey-Box
92/3 Jyvas Hyva 8
94/5 Sisu 261
95/6 Sisu 72, 219

RAUTIO, MIKA
91/2 Jyvas Hyva 31
95 Leaf Latkaliiga 6
94/5 Sisu 118, N-10
95/6 Sisu 284
95/6 Sisu Limited 55

RAUTIO, SAMULI
93/4 Jyvas Hyva 286
93/4 Sisu 78
94/5 Sisu 126

RAVENTOS, TONI
79 Panini Sticker 374

RAVI, ANTTI
66/7 Champion 100
65/6 Hellas 94
70/1 Kuvajulkaisut 287
71/2 Williams Finnish 157
72/3 Williams Finnish 110
73/4 Williams Finnish 209

RAVLICH, MATT
64-67 BeeHive-3 [Chic.]
65/6 Coca-Cola
70/1 Colgate 69
70/1 Dad's Cookies
70/1 Eddie Sargent 71
70/1 Esso Power Player
68/9 O-Pee-Chee 152
69/0 O-Pee-Chee 161
70/1 O-Pee-Chee 32
94/5 Parkie Tall 35
68/9 Shirriff / Chic. 12
65/6 Topps 115
66/7 Topps 58
66/7 Topps / Test 58
70/1 Topps 32

RAWLES, BILL
94/5 Guildford Flames 13

RAWSON, GEOFF
89/0 7th..Sketch OHL 129
90/1 7th..Sketch OHL 269
91/2 7th...Sketch OHL 215
89/0 Niagara Falls Thunder

RAY, DEREK
92/3 Fort Wayne Komets 29
93/4 Fort Wayne Komets 25
94/5 Fort Wayne Komets 26
95/6 Fort Wayne Komets

RAY, JEAN-MICHEL
84/5 Richelieu Riverains

RAY, ROB
02/3 O-Pee-Chee 136
02/3 Pacific 47
02/3 Pacific Complete 84
02/3 Signature ✂ FS6
02/3 Topps 136
02/3 To. Limited 136
98/9 Be A Player 165, ✍ Aut. 165
00/1 BAP Mem. ✂ T-7
01/2 BAP Update ✂ TC8, ✂ TC11
01/2 Heads Up ✂ JQ 23
98/9 Omega 26
98/9 Pacific 108
99/0 Pacific 43
00/1 Pacific 55
01/2 Pacific 53, 404
97/8 Pa. Invincible R-21
92/3 Parkhurst 252
94/5 Parkhurst 30
94/5 Pinnacle 514
01/2 Pr. Stock ✂ GUG 12
00/1 PS Titanium ✂ GUG 61
90/1 Pro Set 419
91/2 Pro Set 355
88/9 ProCards / Rochester
89/0 ProCards AHL 256
90/1 ProCards 277
91/2 Score CAN 610
93/4 Score 433
96/7 Score 200
97/8 Score 242
97/8 Score Buff. 14
00/1 To. Heritage 166
90/1 Upper Deck 516
91/2 Upper Deck 349
97/8 Upper Deck 228
95/6 UD BAP 56, ✍ S56
96/7 UD Black Diam. 32
95/6 UD CC 198
97/8 UD Coll. Choice 23
00/1 UD Vintage 49
89/0 BUFF / Campbell's
90/1 BUFF / Blue Shield
90/1 BUFF / Campbell's
91/2 BUFF / Blue Shield
91/2 BUFF / Campbell's
91/2 BUFF / Pepsi
92/3 BUFF / Blue Shield
92/3 BUFF / Jubilee

RAY, VERN
93/4 Thunder Bay Senators

RAYCROFT, ANDREW
02/3 Between the Pipes 84
02/3 Calder 56
02/3 O-Pee-Chee 281
02/3 Pacific Complete 583
02/3 Topps 281
02/3 To. Limited 281
00/1 BAP Mem. 485
01/2 BAP Mem. 125
01/2 BT Pipes 32
00/1 Crown Royale 111, 21CR-2
01/2 O-Pee-Chee 304
01/2 Parkhurst 271
00/1 Premier Plus 115
00/1 Pr. Stock 103, PSR-2
00/1 PS Titanium 105
00/1 PS Titanium Draft 105
00/1 Signature 253, ✍ Aut. 215
00/1 SP Authentic 94
00/1 SP GU 63
00/1 SPx ✂ 121
00/1 Stadium 251
01/2 Topps 304
00/1 To. Chrome 250
01/2 To. Chrome 147
00/1 T. Gold Label 101
00/1 To. Heritage 93
00/1 To. Stars 111
00/1 UD Reserve 89
00/1 Upper Deck 206
00/1 UD Black Diam. 71
00/1 UD Ice 51
00/1 UD MVP 218
00/1 UD Pros&Prosp. 94
00/1 UD Vintage 374
00/1 Vanguard 104
01/2 Providence Bruins
99/0 Kingston Frontenacs
98/9 Sudbury Wolves 25

RAYMOND, ALAIN
90/1 ProCards 78
91/2 ProCards 38
82/3 North Bay Centennials

RAYMOND, ERIC
90/1 7th..Sketch LHJMQ 73
91/2 7th...Sketch LHJMQ 241
90 7th..Sketch Mem.Cup 55
93/4 Wheeling Thund'birds

RAYMOND, JACQUES
92/3 MONT / OPC 18

RAYMOND, PAUL
36-39 Diamond Match TT1
43-47 Parade Sportive
34/5 Sweet Caporal
33/4 WWGum 18

RAYMOND, RICHARD
90/1 7th..Sketch OHL 43
91/2 7th...Sketch OHL 4
91/2 Cornwall Royals

RAYMOND, SEN. DONAT
83 HHOF Postcard E14
83&87 HHOF 73

RAYNER, CHUCK
02/3 Between the Pipes 116
02/3 Ultimate Mem. ✂ Cor
56 Adventure Gum 63
01/2 ASG History
01/2 BAP Mem. GT
01/2 BAP Update ✂ RR8
34-43 BeeHive-1 [NYAm.]
45-64 BeeHive-2 [NYRa.]
01/2 BT Pipes 137
48-52 Exhibits [Rangers]
48-52 Exhibits [Rangers]
83 HHOF Postcard L14
83&87 HHOF 163
96/7 Legends 80
51/2 Parkhurst 104
52/3 Parkhurst 22
53/4 Parkhurst 59
01/2 Parkhurst PR36, PR59, PR141, ✂ PV24, ✍ PA10
52 Royal Desserts 2
01/2 Signature ✍ VA14
Sport Flash 3
Sport Flash 3
01/2 Ultimate Mem. ✂ ASGH, ✂ Corn.

RAZIN, ANDREI
98/9 Mir 5
99/0 Mir 9
00/1 Mir 336
00/1 Metallurg 36

RAZIN, GENNADY
99/0 Québec Citadelles 2
00/1 Québec Citadelles
01/2 Québec Citadelles
96/7 Kamloops Blazers
97/8 Kamloops Blazers

RAZINGER, TOMAZ
99/0 Peoria Rivermen
00/1 Peoria Rivermen

READ, CLAYTON
99/0 Anchorage Aces

READ, MEL
51/2 Laval Dairy 65

READE, MARK
81/2 Kingston Canadians
82/3 Kingston Canadians

READER, ALAN
98/9 DEL 283

READY, RYAN
99 Bowman 129
95/6 Slapshot 45
00/1 Kansas City Blades 6
01/2 Manitoba Moose
02/3 Manitoba Moose

REARDON, KEN
34-43 BeeHive-1 [Mont.]
45-64 BeeHive-2 [Mont.]
48-52 Exhibits [Canadiens]
83 HHOF Postcard B11
83&87 HHOF 25
40/1 O-Pee-Chee 116
43-47 Parade Sportive
55/6 Parkhurst 64
59/0 Parkhurst 22
45-54 Quaker Oats
92/3 MONT / OPC 42

REARDON, TERRY
34-43 BeeHive-1 [Mont.]

REASONER, MARTY
02/3 Upper Deck 70
99/0 BAP Mem. 253
00/1 BAP Mem. 241
98/9 Bowman's Best 113, F16
94/5 Classic DP8
95/6 Do. Elite WJ 40
98/9 Dynagon Ice 162, -IR 7
98/9 Omega 208
99/0 Pacific 368
00/1 Pacific 350
01/2 Parkhurst 229
94/5 Select 150
00/1 Signature 56, ✍ Aut. 61
98/9 SP Authentic 107
99/0 Topps 49
00/1 Topps 262
99/0 To. Chrome 49
98/9 T. Gold Label 72
95/6 Upper Deck 566
98/9 Upper Deck 419, GN5, P1
00/1 Upper Deck 155
98/9 UD Black Diam. 76
98/9 UD G. Reserve 419
96/7 UD Ice 150
98/9 UD MVP 178
00/1 UD Vintage 311
00/1 Worcester IceCats

REAUGH, DARYL
91/2 Bowman 19
91/2 O-Pee-Chee 391
88/9 ProCards / Cape Breton
89/0 ProCards AHL 291
90/1 ProCards 184
91/2 ProCards 93
91/2 To. Stadium 326
90/1 Upper Deck 541
87/8 EDMO
88/9 EDMO / Action 62
90/1 HART / Jr. Whalers
85/6 Nova Scotia Oilers
84/5 Kamloops Blazers

REAUME, MARC
52/3 Anonymous 146
45-64 BeeHive-2 [Toro.]
63-65 Chex
70/1 Esso Power Player
70/1 O-Pee-Chee 119
55/6 Parkhurst 7
57/8 Parkhurst [Toro.] 12
58/9 Parkhurst 20
59/0 Parkhurst 11
60/1 Parkhurst 25
63/4 Parkhurst 37
63/4 Parkhurst 96
93/4 Parkie 56-57 114
60/1 Shirriff 52
70/1 Topps 119
63/4 York 32
76 DETR
70/1 VANC / Royal Bank

REAY, BILLY
02/3 Parkie - Reprint 152, 163, 230
45-64 BeeHive-2 [Mont.]
48-52 Exhibits [Canadiens]
51/2 La Patrie
74/5 O-Pee-Chee 204
43-47 Parade Sportive
51/2 Parkhurst 13
52/3 Parkhurst 2
55/6 Parkhurst 66
57/8 Parkhurst [Toro.] 25
58/9 Parkhurst 25
94/5 Parkie Tall 43
45-54 Quaker Oats
63/4 Topps 22
64/5 Topps 38
65/6 Topps 54
66/7 Topps 53
74/5 Topps 204
70/1 CHIC

REBEK, JEREMY
95/6 Slapshot 297
99/0 Missouri RiverOtters
97/8 Toledo Storm 8
93/4 Owen Sound Platers

REBOLJ, MIHA
99/0 OFS 111
00/1 OFS 300

RECCHI, MARK
02/3 BAP All-Star 73, ✂ ASJ, ✂ HSHSJers
02/3 BAP Mem. 182, 250, ✂ ASJ 46, ✂ TM10
02/3 Bowman 34
02/3 Exclusive 128
02/3 First Edition 83, 311, ✂ Jers.
02/3 Heads Up 92
02/3 In The GU 57, 157, ✂ GUJ47, ✂ SJ47
02/3 O-Pee-Chee 40
02/3 Pacific 286
02/3 Pacific Complete 20
02/3 Parkhurst 42, ✂ GJ25, ✂ SJ25, ✂ TT2
02/3 Parkhurst Retro 63
02/3 Signature 158, ✍ 158, ✂ TQ3
02/3 SP GU 60, ✂ AF, ✂ PH
02/3 Sports Vault 106
02/3 SPx 136, ✂ M
02/3 Stadium 96
02/3 Topps 40, ✂ CC2
02/3 T. Chrome 36
02/3 To. Heritage 67, ✂ GS, ✂ GSB
02/3 To. Limited 40
02/3 To. Total 270
02/3 Ultimate Mem. ✂ ASMVP
02/3 Upper Deck 130, ✂ CG, ✂ PA, ✂ S
02/3 UD Classic ✂ HR
02/3 UD MVP 134, SD (x2), ST, Souv.
02/3 UD Top Shelf ✂ HT, ✂ M, ✂ ST
02/3 UD Vintage 185, 302, GB 185, ✂ SO
02/3 Victory 155
01/2 Adrenaline 142
01/2 Atomic 73
98/9 Aurora 95, -CF 25
99/0 Aurora 107, Stripe 107
00/1 Aurora 109, Pins. 109
98/9 Be A Player 68, ✍ Aut. 68
99/0 BAP Mem. 13
00/1 BAP Mem. 267, ✂ J-36
01/2 BAP Mem. 292
01/2 BAP Update ✂ H23
97/8 Bicycle 5-Heart
90/1 Bowman 206
91/2 Bowman 83
92/3 Bowman 314
95/6 Bowman 51
01/2 Bowman 108
98/9 Bowman's Best 96
93/4 Classic TC5, ✍ Aut.
94/5 Cla. Images PL6
92/3 Classic Prospects 34
92/3 Classic Prospects BC20
93/4 Cla. Prospects LP24
99/0 Crown Royale 105, IE-20
01/2 Crown Royale 108
93/4 Donruss 252
94/5 Donruss 121
95/6 Donruss 48
96/7 Donruss 27
97/8 Donruss 136
96/7 Do. Canadian 23
97/8 Do. Canadian 53, NP-18
95/6 Do. Elite 103
96/7 Do. Elite 26
97/8 Do. Preferred 46
97/8 Do. Priority 61
97/8 Do. Studio 57
98/9 Dynagon Ice 97
99/0 Dynagon Ice 149
93/4 EA Sports 101
94/5 Flair 130
96/7 Flair 49
94/5 Fleer 106, H-9
96/7 Fleer 55
95/6 Fleer Metal 77
92/3 Fleer Ultra 158
93/4 Fleer Ultra 236
93/4 Fleer Ultra RLS 8
94/5 Fleer Ultra 158
95/6 Fleer Ultra 82
96/7 Fl. Ultra 88
00 Gatorade Sticker
95 Globe 98
01/2 Heads Up 73
93/4 Hockey Wit 104
95/6 Hoyle / East. K-Diamond
01/2 Kellogg's / Score 9
91/2 Kraft 2
94/5 Kraft / HH
95/6 Kraft / KD
98/9 Kraft / Post 7
93/4 Leaf 205
94/5 Leaf 89, GLS-15
95/6 Leaf 65
96/7 Leaf 37
97/8 Leaf 127
94/5 L. Limited 71
95/6 L. Limited 54
96/7 L. Preferred 115
97/8 Limited 52, 152
91/2 McDonald's Mc-04
93/4 McDonald's McD-22
95/6 McDonald's McD-24
96/7 Metal Univ. 81
99/0 Millenium 182, ✍ Aut. 182
98/9 NHL Power Play
90/1 OPC/Topps 280
91/2 O-Pee-Chee 196
91/2 Topps - Team Leader 5
92/3 O-Pee-Chee 373
01/2 O-Pee-Chee 101, 322
97/8 Omega 121, TL-12
98/9 Omega 124
99/0 Omega 174, 5ST-22
98/9 Pacific 256
99/0 Pacific 310, GC-27
00/1 Pacific 306, GCDC-25
01/2 Pacific 294
97/8 Pacific CC 298, SS-4A
97/8 Pa. Crown Roy. 71
98/9 Pa. Crown Roy. 71
97/8 Pa. Dynagon 64, T-47
97/8 Pa. Invincible 72
97/8 Pa. Paramount 97
98/9 Pa. Paramount 116
99/0 Pa. Paramount 174, PB-27
00/1 Pa. Paramount 185, FF-27
97/8 Pa. Revolution 73
98/9 Pa. Revolution 75, -ASG 24
98/9 Panini Photocard
90/1 Panini Sticker 130, 341
91/2 Panini Sticker 280
92/3 Panini Sticker 185
93/4 Panini Sticker 46
94/5 Panini Sticker 39, DD
95/6 Panini Sticker 41
96/7 Panini Sticker 38
97/8 Panini Sticker 32
98/9 Panini Sticker 34
99/0 Panini Sticker 126
00/1 Panini Sticker 76
91/2 Parkhurst 134
91/2 Parkhurst 347
92/3 Parkhurst 130
93/4 Parkhurst 149
94/5 Parkhurst 165, 315
95/6 Parkhurst 383
00/1 Parkhurst P-50
01/2 Parkhurst 22, ✂ PJ5, ✂ PS5, ✂ PSJ15, ✂ M9, ✂ M34, ✂ T13
94/5 Parkie SE seV28
91/2 Pinnacle 151
91/2 Pinnacle 360
92/3 Pinnacle 80
93/4 Pinnacle 50
93/4 Pinnacle NF 13
93/4 Pinnacle T2K1 30
94/5 Pinnacle 53
95/6 Pinnacle 24
96/7 Pinnacle 64
97/8 Pinnacle 104
96/7 Pi. Be A Player 20, ✍ Aut. 20
97/8 Pi. BeeHive 23
97/8 Pi. Certified 58
97/8 Pi. Inside 112
95/6 Pi. Summit 26
96/7 Pi. Summit 17
97/8 Pi. Totally 58
95/6 Pi. Zenith 8, GG-14
95/6 Playoff 54
94/5 POG 180
95/6 POG 150
93/4 Power Play 184
93/4 Power Play PL 12
93/4 Premier 230
94/5 Premier 90, TF-21
00/1 Premier Plus 31
99/0 Prism 104, CA-17
01/2 Pr. Stock 73
01/2 PS Titanium 106
95/6 Pro Magnet 17
90/1 Pro Set 239
91/2 Pro Set 184
91/2 Pro Set 313
91/2 Pro Set CC8
92/3 Pro Set 131
91/2 Pro Set Platinum 97
88/9 ProCards / Muskegon
99/0 Revolution 109, TL-28, / CSC 109
00/1 Revolution 111, HD-26, II-16, SM-28
90/1 Score 186
90/1 Sco. Hot Cards 81
91/2 Score 145
91/2 Score CAN 145
92/3 Score 180
92/3 Score SS 18
93/4 Score 150
93/4 Score 442
93/4 Score DD1
93/4 Score PiAS 6
94/5 Score 50, NP-7
95/6 Score 10, GB-18
96/7 Score 26
97/8 Score 130, CI-2
97/8 Score Mont. 5
90/1 Sco. Young Stars 35
91/2 Score Young Stars 22
92/3 Score Young Stars 7
92/3 Seasons 41
94/5 Select 30
95/6 Select CE 10
94 Semic 101
91 Semic Sticker 74
93 Semic Sticker 205
00/1 Signature 88, ✍ Aut. 132, ✂ HSHSJers
01/2 Signature C-28, ✍ Aut., ✂ GUE47, ✂ GJ48, ✂ GSJ48, ✂ HSHSJers, ✂ ITN47, ✂ TM22
95/6 SBx Emotion 90
95/6 SBx Impact 86
96/7 SBx Impact 63
94/5 SP 62
95/6 SP 72
96/7 SP 85
97/8 SP Authentic 79, I25
98/9 SP Authentic 42
00/1 SP Authentic 66
01/2 SP Authentic 63, ✂ NN, ✍ SotTD
01/2 SP GU ✂ AF, ✂ AFD, ✂ AFT
99/0 SPx 112
98/9 SPx Finite 43
99/0 Stadium 109
00/1 Stadium 48, BT25
01/2 Stadium 56, ✂ SCS
97/8 SLU
95/6 Super Sticker 64
92/3 Topps 267
92/3 Topps 410
95/6 Topps 165, HGC27, 9PL
99/0 Topps 130
00/1 Topps 42, OTG3, ✍ CAI
01/2 Topps 101, 322
99/0 To. Chrome 130
00/1 To. Chrome 34
01/2 To. Chrome 101
94/5 Topps Finest 109, DF-5
95/6 To. Finest 119
98/9 To. Finest 81
98/9 T. Gold Label 47
99/0 T. Gold Label 30
00/1 T. Gold Label 3
00/1 To. Heritage 37
01/2 To. Heritage 49
96/7 To. Picks 63
99/0 T. Prmr. Plus 52
01/2 To. Reserve 54, ✂ TR
91/2 To. Stadium 256
92/3 To. Stadium 183
93/4 To. Stadium 136
93/4 To. Stadium - AS
95/6 To. Stadium 48
93/4 TSC Members Only 34
94/5 TSC Members Only 9
00/1 To. Stars 29, ✂ GG
95/6 T. Super Skills 58
98/9 UD Choice 109, 231
01/2 UD PlayMakers Ltd 72, ✂ PCJ, ✂ PCCJ
00/1 UD Reserve 63, PSJ, ✍ PSJ
01/2 Ultimate Mem. ✂ DD, ✂ LC, ✂ NP, ✍ Aut.
90/1 Upper Deck 178, 487
91/2 Upper Deck 92
91/2 Upper Deck 346
92/3 Upper Deck 327
93/4 Upper Deck 222, 300, 350, SP-117
94/5 Upper Deck 94, 441, SP-58
95/6 Upper Deck 490, SE-43
96/7 Upper Deck 87
97/8 Upper Deck 84
98/9 Upper Deck 111, FF19
99/0 Upper Deck 97
00/1 Upper Deck 127
01/2 Upper Deck 128, CT10
94/5 UD BAP R18, ✍ 7
96/7 UD Black Diam. 149
97/8 UD Black Diam. 23
98/9 UD Black Diam. 44
95/6 UD CC 108
96/7 UD CC 135
97/8 UD Coll. Choice 133, SQ75
98/9 UD G. Reserve 111
99/0 UD G. Reserve 97
97/8 UD Ice 23
92/3 UD Locker 11
01/2 UD Mask 73
98/9 UD MVP 152
99/0 UD MVP 150
00/1 UD MVP 131
01/2 UD MVP 141, -J, ✍ SJ, ✂ S
99/0 UD MVP Cup 134
95/6 UD Post 9
96/7 UD Post
00/1 UD Pros&Prosp. 63
99/0 UD Retro 59
00/1 UD Vintage 268
01/2 UD Vintage 188, 190, 191
99/0 Victory 213
00/1 Victory 169
01/2 Victory 260, 431
99/0 WGretzky 126
96 Wien 96
97/8 Zenith 36, Z24
95/6 MONT
95/6 MONT / Export
96/7 MONT / Export
96-98 MONT
92/3 PHIL / UD Sheet
92/3 PHIL / UD Sheet
92/3 PHIL / UD Sheet
92/3 PHIL / J.C. Penney
93/4 PHIL / Sheet
93/4 PHIL / Sheet
93/4 PHIL / J.C. Penney
01/2 PHIL
90/1 PITT / Foodland 6
91/2 PITT / Elby's
91/2 PITT / Food. Stickers
86/7 Kamloops Blazers
87/8 Kamloops Blazers

RECCHI, MARKUS
02/3 Slam Card

REDDEN, WADE
02/3 First Edition 236
02/3 O-Pee-Chee 166
02/3 Pacific 272
02/3 Pacific Complete 362
02/3 Parkhurst 146
02/3 Signature GS-100, ✂ DW8
02/3 Sports Vault 98
02/3 Topps 166, /PP4
02/3 T. Chrome 99
02/3 To. Limited 166
02/3 To. Total 217
02/3 Upper Deck 124
02/3 UD MVP 131
02/3 UD Vintage 174
02/3 Victory 151
01/2 Adrenaline 137
98/9 Be A Player 95, ✍ Aut. 95
99/0 BAP Mem. 105
00/1 BAP Mem. 283
01/2 BAP Mem. 138
98/9 Bowman's Best 85
94/5 Classic CP3
95/6 Classic 2, 100, AS2, BK2
95/6 Cla. Clear Assets - Phone
95/6 Cla. 5 Sport 124, S-71, SFF-A, Sprint
x95/6 Cla. 5 Sport SFF A
94/5 Cla. Images 5, CE5, PD2
95/6 Donruss C3TWC 5
97/8 Donruss 48, L2L-19
96/7 Do. Canadian 121
97/8 Do. Canadian 31
95/6 Do. Elite WJ 8
96/7 Do. Elite 140, A-24
97/8 Do. Elite 86
97/8 Do. Preferred 97
97/8 Do. Priority 131
97/8 Do. Studio 97
96/7 Flair 118
96/7 Fl. Ultra 118, UR-17
98/9 Kraft / Post 10
97/8 Leaf 113
94/5 L. Limited CAN 7
96/7 L. Limited LR-5
96/7 L. Preferred 130
97/8 Limited 176, 189
97/8 McDonald's McD-6
01/2 McDonald's -HP 1
96/7 Metal Univ. 190
98/9 NHL Power Play
99/0 NHL Power Play
01/2 O-Pee-Chee 117
98/9 OPC Chrome 61
98/9 Omega 167
98/9 Pacific 315
99/0 Pacific 293
00/1 Pacific 286
01/2 Pacific 278
97/8 Pacific CC 276
97/8 Pa. Dynagon 85, T-68
97/8 Pa. Invincible 95
99/0 Pa. Paramount 164
01/2 Parkhurst 148
94/5 Parkie SE256
94/5 Pinnacle 527
96/7 Pi. Be A Player LTH9A, ✍ Aut. LTH9A
96/7 Pi. Zenith 128
00/1 Premier Plus 30
94/5 Select 160
96/7 Select CE 100
94/5 SR Auto-Phonex 34, P5, Sprint, ✍ 34, ✍ P5
95/6 SR Tetrad F5
95/6 SR Tetrad Autobilia 51
01/2 Signature 27, ✍ Aut. 27
94/5 Slapshot Memorial 31
94/5 SP 139
95/6 SP 169
96/7 SP 185
97/8 SP Authentic 108
98/9 SP Authentic 58
98/9 SPx Finite 59
99/0 Stadium 119, ✍ CS14, ✍ CS15, ✍ LS6
00/1 Stadium 101, ✂ SCS
95/6 Topps 1CJ
98/9 Topps 61, B15, -IA I5
99/0 Topps 61, NS8
00/1 Topps 225
01/2 Topps 117
99/0 To. Chrome 61
00/1 To. Chrome 143
94/5 Topps Finest 151
98/9 To. Finest 109, C9
98/9 T. Gold Label 88
99/0 T. Gold Label 44,FG3
00/1 To. Heritage 184
99/0 T. Prmr. Plus 16
01/2 To. Reserve ✂ TR
00/1 To. Stars 77
98/9 UD Choice 140
94/5 Upper Deck 504
96/7 Upper Deck 305, X35
97/8 Upper Deck 118, SG36, T20B
98/9 Upper Deck 329
99/0 Upper Deck 267
00/1 Upper Deck 124
01/2 Upper Deck 351
96/7 UD Black Diam. 179
97/8 UD Black Diam. 50
98/9 UD Black Diam. 60
96/7 UD CC 362
97/8 UD Coll. Choice 176, SQ6, / 5x7 4
98/9 UD G. Reserve 329
99/0 UD G. Reserve 267
96/7 UD Ice 97
97/8 UD Ice 50
98/9 UD MVP 146, ✍ PS
99/0 UD MVP 141
01/2 UD MVP 134
00/1 UD Vintage 251
99/0 Victory 206
00/1 Victory 165
01/2 Victory 244
99/0 WGretzky 119
96/7 OTTA
97/8 OTTA
98/9 OTTA
99/0 OTTA
00/1 OTTA
01/2 OTTA
02/3 OTTA
95/6 Brandon Wheat Kings

REDDICK, ELDON
01/2 UD DEL 84, ✂ GJ

REDDICK, ELDON (POKEY)
93/4 Cla. 4 Sport 247
95/6 Edge Ice 154, QM-2, TW-5
90/1 O-Pee-Chee 452
88/9 OPC Sticker 146-17
89/0 opcSticker 137-258
87/8 Panini Sticker 357
88/9 Panini Sticker 194
90/1 Panini/EDM 18
90/1 Pro Set 445
89/0 ProCards AHL 143
91/2 ProCards 222
00/1 UD DEL 88
86/7 WINN
87/8 WINN
88/9 WINN / Safety Tips
93/4 Cincinnati Cyclones
92/3 Fort Wayne Komets 20
98/9 Fort Wayne Komets
96/7 Grand Rapids Griffins
97/8 Grand Rapids Griffins
94/5 Las Vegas Thunder
95/6 Las Vegas Thunder
84/5 Brandon Wheat Kings

REDDICK, POKEY
99/0 Eishockey 98

REDDICK, STAN
93/4 Raleigh Icecaps

REDDING, GEORGE
24/5 Champ's Cigarettes
24/5 William Paterson 28

REDDO, RONNY
95/6 DEL 416

REDDO, TONY
94/5 DEL 204

REDDON, LESLIE
94/5 Classic W15
97/8 UD Coll. Choice 278

REDLICK, JACK
01/2 Vancouver Giants

REDLIHS, KRISJANIS
02/3 Albany River Rats

REDMOND, CRAIG
85/6 OPC/Topps 121
88/9 EDMO
88/9 EDMO / Action 161
84/5 LOSA / Smokey 13

REDMOND, DAN
89/0 ProCards AHL 82

REDMOND, DICK
71/2 Eddie Sargent 144
72/3 Eddie Sargent 46
72/3 Post 18
74/5 Loblaws
71/2 O-Pee-Chee 106
72/3 O-Pee-Chee 151
73/4 O-Pee-Chee 12
74/5 O-Pee-Chee 186
75/6 O-Pee-Chee 218
76/7 O-Pee-Chee 12
77/8 O-Pee-Chee 213
78/9 O-Pee-Chee 23
79/0 O-Pee-Chee 129
80/1 O-Pee-Chee 36
81/2 O-Pee-Chee 9
72/3 Topps 113
73/4 Topps 12
74/5 Topps 186
75/6 Topps 218
76/7 Topps 12
77/8 Topps 213
78/9 Topps 23
79/0 Topps 129
80/1 Topps 36
81/2 Topps 73 [East]
71/2 Toronto Sun Photo

REDMOND, ED
59/60 Whitby Dunlops

REDMOND, EDDIE
51/2 Laval Dairy 72

REDMOND, KEITH
92/3 Classic Prospects 144
93/4 Cla. Prospects 76
93/4 Donruss 448
94/5 Leaf 15
94/5 Parkhurst 110
91/2 7th...Sketch OHL 122
92/3 Phoenix Roadrunners
93/4 Phoenix Roadrunners

REDMOND, MICKEY
99/0 BAP Mem. R-9, ✍ R-9
70/1 Colgate 44
70/1 Dad's Cookies
70/1 Eddie Sargent 106
71/2 Eddie Sargent 52
72/3 Eddie Sargent 74
70/1 Esso Power Player
91/2 Future Trends C72 18, ✍ 18
74/5 Loblaws
73/4 Mac's Milk
73/4 Nabisco s 22
74/5 Nabisco 16
68/9 O-Pee-Chee 64
70/1 O-Pee-Chee 175
71/2 O-Pee-Chee 102
72/3 O-Pee-Chee 99
72/3 O-Pee-Chee TC
73/4 O-Pee-Chee 180
74/5 O-Pee-Chee 6
74/5 O-Pee-Chee 84
74/5 O-Pee-Chee 120
75/6 O-Pee-Chee 120
72 Semic Sticker 233
68/9 Shirriff / Mont. 18
71/2 Topps 102
72/3 Topps 155
73/4 Topps 190
74/5 Topps 6
74/5 Topps 84
74/5 Topps 120
75/6 Topps 120
76/7 Topps 243
71/2 Toronto Sun Photo
90/1 DETR / Little Caesars
67/8 MONT
67/8 MONT / IGA Card
68/9 MONT / IGA Card
69/0 MONT / Pro Star
70/1 MONT

REDNICEK, JOSEF
94/5 DEL 393

REDPATH, OLIVER
24/5 Falcons Crescent 5

REED, KELLY
90/1 7th..Sketch OHL 141
91/2 7th...Sketch OHL 368

REEDS, MARK
88/9 ProCards / Binghampton
99/0 Missouri RiverOtters
92/3 Peoria Rivermen
93/4 Peoria Rivermen
94/5 Peoria Rivermen
96/7 Peoria Rivermen
97/8 Peoria Rivermen
98/9 Peoria Rivermen

REEKIE, JOE
90/1 Bowman 125
91/2 Bowman 215
92/3 Bowman 137
93/4 Donruss 321
93/4 Leaf 234
94/5 Leaf 437
91/2 O-Pee-Chee 144
92/3 O-Pee-Chee 224
92/3 OPC Premier 70
97/8 Pa. Invincible R-212
91/2 Panini Sticker 252
91/2 Parkhurst 328
93/4 Parkhurst 460
91/2 Pinnacle 285
92/3 Pinnacle 382
93/4 Pinnacle 288
94/5 Pinnacle 351
97/8 Pi. Be A Player 136, ✍ Aut. 136
93/4 Premier 433
94/5 Premier 167
90/1 Pro Set 487
91/2 Pro Set 429
92/3 Pro Set 179
91/2 Score 123
91/2 Score CAN 123
92/3 Score 397
92/3 Score 510
93/4 Score 167
95/6 SBx Emotion 191
99/0 Stadium 59
92/3 Topps 184
91/2 To. Stadium 304
92/3 To. Stadium 264
93/4 To. Stadium 486
91/2 Upper Deck 483
92/3 Upper Deck 106
00/1 Upper Deck 405
95/6 UD BAP 66, ✍ S66
87/8 BUFF / Blue Shield
87/8 BUFF / Won. Bread
88/9 BUFF / Blue Shield
88/9 BUFF / Won. Bread
92/3 TAMP / Sheraton Inn
95/6 WASH
82/3 North Bay Centennials

REESE, JEFF
92/3 Bowman 412
93/4 Donruss 443
96/7 Donruss 31
94/5 Leaf 59
90/1 OPC/Topps 349
91/2 O-Pee-Chee 81
92/3 O-Pee-Chee 77
90/1 Panini Sticker 281
90/1 Panini/TOR 21
93/4 Panini Sticker 187
91/2 Parkhurst 250
92/3 Parkhurst 264
95/6 Parkhurst 460
94/5 Parkie SE74
93/4 Power Play 355
93/4 Premier 302
94/5 Premier 27
90/1 Pro Set 540
88/9 ProCards / Newmarket
91/2 Score CAN 410
93/4 Score 394
93/4 Score 650
96/7 Score 213
92/3 Topps 385
92/3 To. Stadium 322
93/4 To. Stadium 22
92/3 Upper Deck 442
94/5 Upper Deck 476
92/3 CALG / IGA 009
93/4 HART / Coke
91/2 TORO / P.L.A.Y. 26
96/7 Detroit Vipers
97/8 Detroit Vipers
85/6 London Knights

REESOR, JASON
93/4 Slapshot / Niagara Falls 16

REEVE, JAMIE
82/3 Regina Pats
83/4 Regina Pats
93/4 Tacoma Rockets

REEVES, KYLE
91/2 ProCards 39
90/1 7th..Sketch WHL 109
94/5 Flint Generals
92/3 Peoria Rivermen
93/4 Toledo Storm 26

REEVES, SHERYL
88/9 ProCards / Peoria

REGAN, BRIAN
98/9 Dayton Bombers
98/9 Dayton Bombers
99/0 Missouri RiverOtters

REGAN, LARRY
45-64 BeeHive-2 [Bost.]
45-64 BeeHive-2 [Toro.]
59/0 Parkhurst 17
60/1 Parkhurst 13
93/4 Parkie 56-57 16
60/1 Shirriff 16
52/3 St. Lawrence 103
57/8 Topps 6
58/9 Topps 10
60/1 York
57-58 BOST

REGEHR, RICHIE
00/1 Kelowna Rockets

REGEHR, ROBYN
02/3 First Edition 182
02/3 O-Pee-Chee 44
02/3 Stadium ✂ YSS21
02/3 Topps 44
02/3 To. Limited 44
02/3 To. Total 192
99/0 BAP Mem. 304
00/1 BAP Mem. 214
99 Bowman 119

01/2 Bowman 125, ✂ FFJ, ✂ FFS, ✂ FFDS, ✂ FFR, ✍ YSA
98 Bowman 137, ✍ A14
98 Bowman Chrome 137
99/0 Crown Royale 24
99/0 Millenium C-44
99/0 NHL Power Play [x3]
99/0 Omega 42
00/1 Parkhurst P-88
00/1 Signature 65, ✍ Aut. 154
00/1 Stadium 92
00/1 Topps 213
98/9 To. Finest F15
97/8 Upper Deck 406
99/0 Upper Deck 197
01/2 Upper Deck 259
99/0 UD Black Diam. 17
99/0 UD G. Reserve 197
00/1 UD Vintage 59
96/7 Kamloops Blazers
97/8 Kamloops Blazers
98/9 Kamloops Blazers

REGIER, DARCY
81/2 Indianapolis Checkers
82/3 Indianapolis Checkers

REGNIER, CURT
90/1 7th..Sketch WHL 264
91/2 7th...Sketch WHL 253
90/1 Prince Albert Raiders
91/2 Prince Albert Raiders

REGNIER, RICHARD
80/1 Mallasjuoma 85

REGNIER, TOM
80/1 Mallasjuoma 84

REGULIN, ALEXANDER
73/4 Soviet Stars 12

REHNBERG, HENRIK
95/6 UD CC 347
95/6 UD Elitserien 61
99/0 UD Elitserien 58
98/9 Albany River Rats
00/1 Albany River Rats

REHOR, JAN
01/2 OFS 146

REIBEL, EARL
45-64 BeeHive-2 [Detr.]
45-64 BeeHive-2 [Bost.]
53/4 Parkhurst 36
54/5 Parkhurst 37
54/5 Parkhurst 97
93/4 Parkie 56-57 147
93/4 Parkie 56-57 49
54/5 Topps 52
57/8 Topps 45
58/9 Topps 57
55 Toronto Star Weekend

REICH, JEREMY
97 Bowman 143, ✍ Aut.
96/7 Upper Deck 386
00/1 Syracuse Crunch
01/2 Syracuse Crunch
02/3 Syracuse Crunch

REICHEL, MARTIN
92/3 Classic 28
92/3 Classic Four Sport 177
94/5 DEL 378
95/6 DEL 376, 439
96/7 DEL 198
98/9 DEL 332
99/0 Eishockey 35
00/1 UD DEL 190
01/2 UD DEL 206
96 Wien 199

REICHEL, ROBERT
02/3 Pacific 366
02/3 Pacific Complete 78
02/3 To. Total 79
02/3 Upper Deck 408
96/7 APS 349
97/8 APS 354
98/9 Aurora 118
98/9 Be A Player 86, ✍ Aut. 86
98 Bonaparte 1B
98 Bonaparte Pexeso 2
91/2 Bowman 267
92/3 Bowman 401
98/9 Bowman's Best 95
95/6 DEL 116, 445
93/4 Donruss 51
94/5 Donruss 169
99/0 DS 63, NS12, P11
00/1 DS 43, NT5, TS5, VP4, WCH8
01/2 DS 42, 59, -BB 8, -IH 8
98/9 Dynagon Ice 117
94/5 Flair 27
94/5 Fleer 34
92/3 Fleer Ultra 28
93/4 Fleer Ultra 164
94/5 Fleer Ultra 34
96/7 Fl. Ultra 26
95 Globe 159
94/5 Kraft / SS
93/4 Leaf 59
94/5 Leaf 243, LL-4
94/5 L. Limited 39
96/7 Metal Univ. 22
91/2 O-Pee-Chee 411
92/3 O-Pee-Chee 93
90/1 OPC Premier 95
98/9 OFS 237, -OW 6
99/0 OFS 31, 157, 266, 507
00/1 OFS 145, 409, -Star 20
01/2 OFS -UHI 13
97/8 Omega 141
98/9 Omega 151
98/9 Pacific 286
99/0 Pacific 324
97/8 Pacific CC 326
97/8 Pa. Crown Roy. 80
98/9 Pa. Crown Roy. 85
97/8 Pa. Paramount 110
98/9 Pa. Paramount 147
97/8 Pa. Revolution 83
91/2 Panini Sticker 63
91/2 Panini Sticker 343
92/3 Panini Sticker 42
92/3 Panini Sticker 301
93/4 Panini Sticker 180
94/5 Panini Sticker 154
97/8 Panini Sticker 77
98/9 Panini Sticker 75
95 Panini Worlds 298
91/2 Parkhurst 21
91/2 Parkhurst / Promo
92/3 Parkhurst 26
93/4 Parkhurst 300
94/5 Parkhurst 34, V47
01/2 Parkhurst 239
91/2 Pinnacle 56
92/3 Pinnacle 101
93/4 Pinnacle 35
94/5 Pinnacle 12, WE13
96/7 Pi. Be A Player 81, ✍ Aut. 81
94/5 POG 60
93/4 Power Play 41
93/4 Power Play RisS 5
93/4 Premier 404
94/5 Premier 213, TF-20
01/2 Pr. Stock ✂ GUG 96
90/1 Pro Set 595
91/2 Pro Set 361
91/2 Pro Set Platinum 163
90/1 Score 30T
91/2 Score 263
91/2 Score CAN 483
92/3 Score 106
93/4 Score 204
93/4 Score IS 6
94/5 Score NP17
97/8 Score 218
99/0 Score JT12
90/1 Sco. Young Stars 29
91/2 Score Young Stars 24
94/5 Select 138
94 Semic 184
91 Semic Sticker 223
92 Semic Sticker 142
01/2 Signature 112, ✍ Aut. 112
97/8 SP Authentic 97
98/9 SP Authentic 54
92/3 Topps 157
98/9 T. Gold Label 19
91/2 To. Stadium 393
92/3 To. Stadium 180
93/4 To. Stadium 198
98/9 UD Choice 126
90/1 Upper Deck 533
91/2 Upper Deck 223
92/3 Upper Deck 42
93/4 Upper Deck 313, HT-4
94/5 Upper Deck 357, SP-104
96/7 Upper Deck 228
97/8 Upper Deck 104
99/0 Upper Deck 99
01/2 Upper Deck 396
97/8 UD Black Diam. 49
97/8 UD Coll. Choice 151
99/0 UD G. Reserve 99
98/9 UD MVP 127
99/0 UD MVP 157
99/0 Victory 227
96 Wien 128
97/8 Zenith 70
90/1 CALG / McGavin's
91/2 CALG / IGA
92/3 CALG / IGA 005

REICHENBERG, RONNY
89/0 Semic Elitserien 139
90/1 Semic Elitserien 217

REICHERT, CRAIG
91/2 7th...Sketch WHL 18
00/1 UD DEL 48
98/9 Cincinnati M'Ducks 13
01/2 Hamilton Bulldogs
99/0 Louisville Panthers
93/4 Red Deer Rebels

REID, BILL
92/3 MPS SJHL 126

REID, BRANDON
02/3 BAP Mem. 394
02/3 Choice Prospects 36
02/3 SP Authentic 211
02/3 SPx 180
02/3 Ultimate Mem. 51
02/3 UD Rookie 133
00/1 UD Prospects 88, FL10, GD5
01/2 Manitoba Moose
02/3 Manitoba Moose
97/8 Halifax Moosehead
97/8 Halifax Moosehead
98/9 Halifax Moosehead
99/0 Halifax Mooseheads
00/1 Val d'Or Foreurs 17

REID, CHARLIE
23/4 Paulins Candy 68

REID, DAVE
01/2 Atomic ✂ GWJ 12
00/1 BAP Mem. 367
01/2 BAP Mem. ✂ SCC
91/2 Bowman 153
93/4 Donruss 403
96/7 Fl. Picks 176
93/4 Fleer Ultra 269
01/2 Heads Up ✂ JQ 8
94/5 Leaf 501
90/1 OPC/Topps 290
91/2 O-Pee-Chee 423
89/0 opcSticker 170-30
00/1 Pacific 119
97/8 Pa. Invincible R-65
90/1 Panini/TOR 22
91/2 Panini Sticker 104
96/7 Panini Sticker 11
97/8 Panini Sticker 141
92/3 Parkhurst 249
95/6 Parkhurst 281
94/5 Parkie SE12
93/4 Pinnacle 191
94/5 Pinnacle 234
96/7 Pinnacle 182
96/7 Pi. Be A Player 121, ✍ Aut. 121
96/7 Pi. Summit 146
95/6 Playoff 122
96/7 Playoff 386
93/4 Power Play 290
93/4 Premier 67
94/5 Premier 51
00/1 PS Titanium ✂ GUG 77
90/1 Pro Set 541
91/2 Pro Set 229
91/2 Pro Set 348
91/2 Pro Set / Prototype
91/2 ProCards 66
90/1 Score 109T
91/2 Score 173
91/2 Score CAN 173
92/3 Score 380
93/4 Score 371
94/5 Score 80
96/7 Score 220
92/3 Topps 521
95/6 Topps 76
99/0 Topps 34
99/0 To. Chrome 34
91/2 To. Stadium 78
93/4 To. Stadium 100
90/1 Upper Deck 364
91/2 Upper Deck 217
91/2 Upper Deck 531
97/8 Upper Deck 264
94/5 UD BAP R88, ✍ 103
97/8 UD Coll. Choice 73
00/1 UD Vintage 97
91/2 BOST / Sports Action
96/7 DALL / Southwest
88/9 TORO / P.L.A.Y. 24
90/1 TORO
85/6 Moncton G'Flames
86/7 Moncton G'Flames

REID, DAVID*
45-64 BeeHive-2 [Toro.]

REID, EDWARD
52/3 Anonymous 4

REID, GRAYDEN
90/1 7th..Sketch OHL 293
91/2 7th...Sketch OHL 294
91/2 Ultimate Draft Pick 53, ✍ Aut.

REID, JARRET
91 7th..Sketch Mem.Cup 12
90/1 7th..Sketch OHL 150, 171
91/2 7th...Sketch OHL 324
93/4 Soo Greyhounds 15

REID, JAY
82/3 Medicine Hat Tigers

REID, JEFF
90/1 7th..Sketch OHL 44
91/2 7th...Sketch OHL 18
93/4 Knoxville Cherokees
94/5 Las Vegas Thunder
91/2 Cornwall Royals

REID, JERRY
51/2 Cleveland Barons

REID, JOHN
88/9 ProCards / Saginaw
91/2 ProCards 449
89/0 Nashville Knights
89/0 Nashville Knights
84/5 Belleville Bulls

REID, KEVIN
90/1 7th..Sketch OHL 172
91/2 7th...Sketch OHL 355

REID, REG
24/5 William Paterson 55

REID, SHAWN
94/5 Classic 60, AA9
95/6 Binghampton Rangers
94/5 Fort Wayne Komets 4

REID, TOM
70/1 Eddie Sargent 85
71/2 Eddie Sargent 81
72/3 Eddie Sargent 99
70/1 Esso Power Player
74/5 Loblaws
70/1 O-Pee-Chee 43
71/2 O-Pee-Chee 21
73/4 O-Pee-Chee 109
74/5 O-Pee-Chee 52
75/6 O-Pee-Chee 277
76/7 O-Pee-Chee 123
77/8 O-Pee-Chee 306
70/1 Topps 43
73/4 Topps 109
74/5 Topps 52
75/6 Topps 277
76/7 Topps 123
71/2 Toronto Sun Photo
70/1 MINS / Colour
73/4 MINS

REID, TYLER
98/9 Halifax Moosehead
02/3 Hull Olympiques

REIER, MIKE
90/1 7th..Sketch OHL 214
92/3 Dayton Bombers

REIERSON, DAVID
94/5 DEL 131
95/6 DEL 129
88/9 Salt Lake G'Eagles

REIGLE, ED
51/2 Cleveland Barons

REIGSTAD, JARED
01/2 Rockford IceHogs

REIJONEN, ESKO
66/7 Champion 124
65/6 Hellas 4

REIJONEN, TUOMAS
99/0 Cardset 129
00/1 Cardset 325
95/6 UD CC 336

REIJONES, TUOMAS
96/7 Sisu 131

REIL, JOACHIM
94/5 DEL 376
82 Semic Sticker 107

REILLY, GARY
89/0 Lethbridge Hurricanes

REILLY, GENE
01/2 Grand Rapids Griffins

REIMANN, DAN
98/9 Florida Everblades
96/7 Johnstown Chiefs

REIMARI, ANTTI-JUSSI
99/0 Cardset 93
00/1 Cardset 194

REIMER, ANDREW
91/2 7th...Sketch WHL 142

REIMER, MARK*
88/9 ProCards / Adirondack
89/0 ProCards AHL 325
90/1 ProCards 311
91/2 ProCards 121
86/7 Saskatoon Blades

REIMER, ROB
90/1 7th..Sketch WHL 150

REIMOLA, PEKKA
70/1 Kuvajulkaisut 354

REINDL, FRANZ
79 Panini Sticker 110
82 Semic Sticker 118

REINER, PHILIP
72 Hellas MM-Jenkki 54

REINHARD, FRANCIS
72 Semic Sticker 139

REINHART, PAUL
90/1 Bowman 60
83/4 Esso Stars
83/4 Funmate Puffy 5 [w/]
84/5 Kellogg's 13
89/0 Kraft 44
86/7 Kraft Sports 6
89/0 Kraft Stickers 1
80/1 O-Pee-Chee 157
81/2 O-Pee-Chee 36
82/3 O-Pee-Chee 56
83/4 O-Pee-Chee 91
84/5 O-Pee-Chee 235
85/6 OPC/Topps 48
86/7 O-Pee-Chee 205
87/8 OPC/Topps 143
90/1 OPC/Topps 293
90/1 Topps-TL 5
89/0 OPC/Topps 148
87/8 OPC Leaders 34
81/2 OPC Sticker 224
82/3 OPC/Topps Sticker 219
83/4 OPC/Topps Sticker 264
85/6 OPC Sticker 209-76
87/8 OPC Sticker 39
89/0 opcSticker 65
87/8 Panini Sticker 206
90/1 Panini Sticker 293
80/1 Pepsi Bottle Cap
82/3 Post [Calg.]
90/1 Pro Set 304
90/1 Score 173
84/5 7-Eleven
85/6 7-Eleven Superstars 3
83/4 Souhaits Keychain [Flames]
82/3 Stater Mint 6
80/1 Topps 157
81/2 Topps 28
90/1 Upper Deck 110
83/4 Vachon 17-137
83/4 Vachon 17-97
79/0 ATLF / B&W
80/1 CALG
81/2 CALG
82/3 CALG
85/6 CALG / Red Rooster
86/7 CALG / Red Rooster
86/7 CALG / Red Rooster
87/8 CALG / Red Rooster
88/9 VANC / Mohawk
89/0 VANC / Mohawk

REINHOLZ, JERRID
99/0 Des Moines Buc's

REINPRECHT, STEVE
02/3 UD Rookie ✂ 156a

REINPRECHT, STEVEN
02/3 Atomic 25
02/3 BAP Mem. 2
02/3 Exclusive 44
02/3 First Edition 6, ✂ Jers.
02/3 Pacific 94
02/3 Pacific Complete 116
02/3 Parkhurst 119, -CR13, ✂ CRM13
02/3 Parkhurst Retro 51
02/3 Pr. Stock Reserve 27
02/3 Signature 47, GS-92, ✍ 47
02/3 SP Game-Used ✂ FF
02/3 To. Total 173
02/3 Upper Deck 287, ✂ OR
02/3 UD Artistic ✂ RT
02/3 UD Classic ✂ CS, ✂ HR
02/3 UD MVP 50, SD
02/3 UD Premier ✂ Jers
02/3 UD Top Shelf ✂ GO, ✂ R, ✂ SH, ✂ ST, ✂ SW
02/3 UD Vintage 61, GB 61
00/1 BAP Mem. 461
01/2 BAP Mem. 174
00/1 Crown Royale 126, 21CR-11
01/2 Pacific 105, 445
00/1 Parkhurst P-165
01/2 Parkhurst 168
00/1 Premier Plus 118
00/1 Pr. Stock 122, PSR-10
00/1 PS Titanium 124, 3SS-22
00/1 PS Titanium Draft 124
00/1 Signature 293, ✍ Aut. 224
01/2 Signature 114, ✍ Aut. 114
00/1 SP Authentic 108, ✍ SotT
01/2 SP Authentic 122
00/1 SP GU 69
00/1 SPx 97
00/1 Stadium 253
01/2 Topps OTG17
00/1 To. Chrome 249
00/1 T. Gold Label 107
00/1 To. Heritage 82
00/1 To. Stars 115
00/1 UD Heroes 165
00/1 UD Reserve 97
00/1 Upper Deck 185
01/2 Upper Deck 48
00/1 UD Black Diam. 78
00/1 UD Ice 57, 67
00/1 UD MVP 193
00/1 UD Pros&Prosp. 107
01/2 UD SCup Champs 40
00/1 Vanguard 124
00/1 Victory 264
01/2 Victory 94

REIRDEN, TODD
99/0 BAP Mem. 313
99/0 Omega 200
00/1 Signature 2, ✍ Aut. 23
00/1 Upper Deck 153
99/0 UD MVP Cup 165
99/0 SLOU / Taco Bell 17
94/5 Raleigh Icecaps

REIS, SHAWN
91/2 Air Canada SJHL B14

REISE, LEO (JR.)
45-64 BeeHive-2 [Detr.]
45-64 BeeHive-2 [NYRa.]
51/2 Parkhurst 69
52/3 Parkhurst 49
53/4 Parkhurst 65
54/5 Parkhurst 67
52 Royal Desserts 6
91/2 Ultimate Original Six 28, ✍ Aut. 28
76 DETR

REISE, LEO (SR.)
23/4 Paulins Candy 36
23/4 William Paterson 33

REISINGER, RALF
94/5 DEL 312
95/6 DEL 211
01/2 UD DEL 56

REITER, JODY
91/2 Air Canada SJHL C4
92/3 MPS SJHL 97

REJA, DAN
95/6 Slapshot 50

REJTHAR, MARTIN
97/8 APS 228
99/0 Score 95

REKIS, ARVID
00/1 Peoria Rivermen
01/2 Peoria Rivermen
02/3 Peoria Rivermen

REKOMAA, ESKO
65/6 Hellas 143

RELAS, TIMO
70/1 Kuvajulkaisut 186
71/2 Williams Finnish 107

REMACKEL, CHAD
96/7 Grand Rapids Griffins

REMENDA, DREW
95/6 Kansas City Blades

REMPEL, NATHAN
01/2 Louisiana Ice Gators
02/3 Louisiana Ice Gators

REMSTAM, MATTIAS
99/0 UD Elitserien 100
00/1 UD Elitserien 104, ✍ Sig.

REN, PATRICE
90/1 7th..Sketch LHJMQ 94

RENARD, JASON
91/2 7th...Sketch WHL 246
94/5 Fort Wayne Komets 18
91/2 Prince Albert Raiders

RENARD, JOHN
93/4 Richmond Renegades

RENAUD, IANNIQUE
98/9 Phoenix Mustangs 4
99/0 Quad City Mallards

RENAUD, MARK
83/4 Souhaits Keychain [Whalers]
82/3 HART / Jr. Whalers

RENAUD, PHIL
51/2 Laval Dairy 18
52/3 St. Lawrence 40

RENBERG, MIKAEL
02/3 First Edition 268
02/3 O-Pee-Chee 192
02/3 Pacific 367
02/3 Pacific Complete 269
02/3 Topps 192
02/3 To. Limited 192
02/3 To. Total 152
02/3 Victory 202
98/9 Aurora 174
98/9 Be A Player 131, ✍ Aut. 131
99/0 BAP Mem. 201
00/1 BAP Mem. 289
95/6 Bicycle Sports Aces Q-Club
95/6 Bowman 83
93/4 Cla. Prospects 33
93/4 Donruss 255
93/4 Donruss ES U1
93/4 Donruss RR 5
94/5 Donruss 236, D-4
95/6 Donruss 80, D-2, E-3
96/7 Donruss 125
97/8 Donruss 151
96/7 Do. Canadian 77
97/8 Do. Canadian 96
95/6 Do. Elite 94
96/7 Do. Elite 33
97/8 Do. Preferred 68
97/8 Do. Priority 75
97/8 Do. Studio 49
94/5 Flair 131
94/5 Fleer 158, FF-7
96/7 Fleer 83
95/6 Fleer Metal 113, IS-16
96/7 Fl. Picks 46
93/4 Fleer Ultra 391
93/4 Fleer Ultra WotF 16
94/5 Fleer Ultra 159,ARS-8, GG-8, UP-7
95/6 Fleer Ultra 120, HS-16, RS-7
96/7 Fl. Ultra 128
95 Globe 29
95 Globe 259-261,268
95/6 Hoyle / East. 2-Club
97/8 Kraft / KD
93/4 Leaf 323
93/4 Leaf FP 5
94/5 Leaf 54, GLR-6, GLS-9
95/6 Leaf 128, FOI-12, FF-3, GLS-6
96/7 Leaf 108
97/8 Leaf 38
94/5 Leaf Elit Set 199, GS-5
94/5 L. Limited 48
95/6 L. Limited 119
96/7 L. Limited 79
96/7 L. Preferred 58, LS-58
97/8 Limited 64
96/7 Maggers 115
94/5 McDonald's McD-39
95/6 McDonald's McD-22
96/7 Metal Univ. 115
98/9 OPC Chrome 16
97/8 Omega 213
98/9 Omega 178
99/0 Omega 175
98/9 Pacific 404
99/0 Pacific 311
00/1 Pacific 320
97/8 Pacific CC 59
97/8 Pa. Invincible 104
97/8 Pa. Paramount 175
98/9 Pa. Paramount 219
99/0 Pa. Paramount 175
97/8 Pa. Revolution 130
94 Panini Olympics 293
94/5 Panini Sticker E
95/6 Panini Sticker 117
96/7 Panini Sticker 118
97/8 Panini Sticker 99
98/9 Panini Sticker 98
99/0 Panini Sticker 122
95 Panini Worlds 288
93/4 Parkhurst 251
93/4 Parkhurst C12
94/5 Parkhurst 272, V78, 458
95/6 Parkhurst 161, 243, CCB-7, IAS-6, ✍ Aut.
01/2 Parkhurst 208
94/5 Parkie SE129, ES3
93/4 Pinnacle 454
93/4 Pinnacle SR6
94/5 Pinnacle 79, 464, WE10
95/6 Pinnacle 41, GG-5, R20-12
96/7 Pinnacle 55
97/8 Pinnacle 144
96/7 Pi. Be A Player 91, ✍ Aut. 91
97/8 Pi. Inside 119
95/6 Pi. Summit 44
96/7 Pi. Summit 73
95/6 Pi. Zenith 42, GG-8
96/7 Pi. Zenith 109, A-4
95/6 Playoff 183
94/5 POG 181
93/4 Power Play 408
93/4 Power Play GG 6
93/4 Power Play RooS 13
94/5 Premier 191, 294, 383, OF-16
95/6 Pro Magnet 50
93/4 Score 602
94/5 Score 249
95/6 Score 35, L-8
96/7 Score 177
97/8 Score 138
94/5 Select 61
95/6 Select CE 31, DS-12
94 Semic 67
90/1 Semic Elitserien 241
91/2 Semic Elitserien 171
92/3 Semic Elitserien 190
93 Semic Sticker 12
01/2 Signature 136, ✍ Aut. 136
95/6 SBx Emotion 134, NP-5
95/6 SBx Impact 128, 245
96/7 SBx Impact 98
94/5 SP 83
95/6 SP 107
96/7 SP 115
96/7 SLU
95/6 Super Sticker 91, DC-18
96/7 Team Out!
95/6 Topps 18, 353, M12, 1PL, YS3
98/9 Topps 16
99/0 Topps 184
99/0 To. Chrome 184
95/6 To. Finest 120
98/9 To. Finest 87
96 Topps Finest Bronze 22
93/4 To. Stadium 269
94/5 To. Stadium 145, DAD 4
95/6 To. Stadium 110, GT7, PS5
93/4 TSC Members Only 47
95/6 T. Super Skills 8
98/9 UD Choice 197
92/3 Upper Deck 233
93/4 Upper Deck 486, SP-118
94/5 Upper Deck 271, 561, SP-59
95/6 Upper Deck 194, SE-149
96/7 Upper Deck 307, P2, SS23B
97/8 Upper Deck 119, 361
98/9 Upper Deck 179
01/2 Upper Deck 394
94/5 UD BAP R74, ✍ 24
96/7 UD Black Diam. 49
95/6 UD CC 222
96/7 UD CC 189, 326, C25
97/8 UD Coll. Choice 184, SQ9
95/6 UD Elitserien 235
00/1 UD Elitserien 129, 176, 200, 217, ✍ Sig., ✂ GJ
98/9 UD G. Reserve 179
96/7 UD Ice 46
00/1 Victory 176
96 Wien 58, 237-40, Super
97/8 Zenith 45, Z31
93/4 PHIL / Sheet
93/4 PHIL / J.C. Penney
94/5 PHIL / Sheet
94/5 PHIL / Sheet
94/5 PHIL / Sheet
96/7 PHIL / Ocean Spray

RENDEN, WARREN
95/6 Tri-City Americans 29

RENFREW, BRIAN
95/6 Dayton Bombers
96/7 Dayton Ice Bandits
92/3 W. Michigan Broncos
93/4 W. Michigan Broncos

RENNER, JUSTIN
01/2 Owen Sound Attack
02/3 Owen Sound Attack

RENNETTE, TYLER
97/8 Bell
97 Bowman 6, 131, ✍ Aut.
01/2 Peoria Rivermen
02/3 Peoria Rivermen
00/1 Worcester IceCats

RENNEY, TOM
92/3 Canada Nationals
93/4 Canada Nationals
92 7th...Sketch Awards 17
90/1 7th..Sketch WHL 287
91/2 7th...Sketch WHL 75

RENTZSCH, MARCO
94/5 DEL 63
95/6 DEL 56
96/7 DEL 253
92 Semic Sticker 176

RENZ, ANDREAS
94/5 DEL 438
95/6 DEL 393
96/7 DEL 300
98/9 DEL 223
99/0 Eishockey 211
00/1 UD DEL 222
01/2 UD DEL 147

RENZI, MICHAEL
01/2 Belleville Bulls

REPNEV, VLADIMIR
00/1 Mir 276
74/5 Soviet Stars 21

REPO, SEPPO
72 Hellas MM-Jenkki 12
70/1 Kuvajulkaisut 265
72 Panda MM-Toronto
79 Panini Sticker 173
72 Semic Sticker 86
74 Semic Sticker 89
77-79 Sports. FIN 74-1760
71/2 Williams Finnish 74
71/2 Williams Finnish 292
72/3 Williams Finnish 73
73/4 Williams Finnish 77
73/4 Williams Finnish 210
76/7 Phoenix Roadrunners

REPP, CARL
89/0 ProCards AHL 8

RESCH, CHICO
02/3 UD Mask / Mask

RESCH, GLENN
02/3 Topps - Reprint 15, ✍ Reprint 15

RESCH, GLENN (CHICO)
01/2 Fleer Greats 64, ✍ Aut.
83/4 Funmate Puffy 12 [w/]
75/6 Hockey Heroes
84/5 Kellogg's 32
74/5 Loblaws
74/5 O-Pee-Chee 353
75/6 O-Pee-Chee 145
76/7 O-Pee-Chee 6
76/7 O-Pee-Chee 250
77/8 O-Pee-Chee 6
77/8 O-Pee-Chee 50
77/8 O-Pee-Chee NS 17
78/9 O-Pee-Chee 105
79/0 O-Pee-Chee 6
79/0 O-Pee-Chee 20
80/1 O-Pee-Chee 235
81/2 O-Pee-Chee 80
81/2 O-Pee-Chee 389
82/3 O-Pee-Chee 145
82/3 O-Pee-Chee 146
83/4 O-Pee-Chee 236
84/5 O-Pee-Chee 119
85/6 OPC/Topps 36
85/6 OPC/Topps Box L
86/7 OPC/Topps 158
81/2 OPC Sticker 230
82/3 OPC/Topps Sticker 222
83/4 OPC/Topps Sticker 222
83/4 OPC/Topps Sticker 223
84/5 OPC Sticker 68
84/5 OPC Sticker 69
85/6 OPC Sticker 61-187
86/7 OPC Sticker 234-105
91/2 Pinnacle 393
82/3 Post [Colo.]
84/5 7-Eleven
85/6 7-Eleven Superstars 11
83/4 Souhaits Keychain [Devils]
75/6 Topps 145
76/7 Topps 6
76/7 Topps 250
76/7 Topps NS 6
77/8 Topps 6
77/8 Topps 50
77/8 ToppsNS 17
78/9 Topps 105
79/0 Topps 6
79/0 Topps 20
80/1 Topps 235
81/2 Topps 85 [West]
84/5 Topps 89
01/2 T/O Archives 58
90/1 Upper Deck 507
00/1 UD Legends 85, ✂ LGJ
00/1 UD Vintage ✂ D-POH
81/2 COLR
83/4 NJER
84/5 NJER
85/6 NJER 6
79/0 NYIS
86/7 PHIL

RESHETNIKOV, SERGEI
99/0 Mir 39

RESSMANN, GERALD
95 Panini Worlds 273

RETTER, CHARLIE
98/9 Hampton Roads

RETTEW, SCOTT
84/5 Chicoutimi Saguenéens

RETTSCHLAG, ADAM
91/2 7th...Sketch WHL 299

RETTSCHLAG, GUS
92/3 BCJHL 3

RETZER, STEPHAN
94/5 DEL 255
95/6 DEL 253
96/7 DEL 142

REUBEN, ALEXANDRE
00/1 Québec Remparts 18

REUNAMAKI, MATTI
66/7 Champion 167
65/6 Hellas 98

REUSSE, WES
92/3 BCJHL 13

REUTA, VIKTOR
93/4 Slapshot / Guelph 15

REUTER, RENE
94/5 DEL 139
95/6 DEL 139

REVELL, DAN
82/3 Indianapolis Checkers
80/1 Oshawa Generals
81/2 Oshawa Generals

REVELLE, DANY
02/3 Mississauga IceDogs

REVENBERG, JIM
89/0 ProCards IHL 180
90/1 ProCards 339

REY, PHILIPPE
79 Panini Sticker 382

REYNOLDS, BOBBY
95/6 DEL 331
89/0 ProCards AHL 126
90/1 ProCards 152
91/2 ProCards 552
91/2 Baltimore Skipjacks
98/9 Flint Generals
90/1 Newmarket Saints

REYNOLDS, MATT
99/0 Brampton Batallion 12

REYNOLDS, PETER
99 Bowman 17, ✍ BA37
98/9 SP Authentic 120, ✍ SotT
98/9 Upper Deck 397
98/9 UD G. Reserve 397
01/2 Florida Everblades

REYNOLDS, ROBERT
96/7 DEL 105

REYNOLDS, T.J.
01/2 Mississauga IceDogs

REYNOLDS, TJ
00/1 Toronto St. Mike's

REYNOLDS, TODD
88/9 Brockville Braves

REZANSOFF, JESSE
96/7 Fredericton Canadiens
99/0 Louisiana Ice Gators
95/6 Swift Current Broncos

REZNAR, JIRI
00/1 OFS 263

REZNICEK, JOSEF
96/7 APS 291
97/8 APS 174
95/6 DEL 411
97/8 DS 50
98/9 DS 57
99/0 DS 87
00/1 DS 27
96/7 DS Sticker 210
97/8 DS Sticker 149
98/9 OFS 35, 450
99/0 OFS 126
00/1 OFS 59
01/2 OFS 205, -UHI 14

REZNICEK, LADISLAV
00/1 Sudbury Wolves 11

REZNÍCEK, JOSEF
91 Semic Sticker 107

RHÉAUME, DOMINIC
90/1 7th..Sketch LHJMQ 232
91/2 7th...Sketch LHJMQ 128

RHÉAUME, HERB
25-27 Anonymous 12 [No Border]

RHÉAUME, MANON
94/5 Assets 21, 46, 72, 97, DC10, Phone
92/3 Classic 59
93/4 Classic 112, 146, 149, 150, MR1, N8, ✍ Aut.
94/5 Classic 120, CP15, W1, W21, ✍ Aut.
95/6 Classic ✍ Aut.
95/6 Cla. Clear Assets - Phone
92/3 Classic Four Sport 224
92/3 Classic Four Sport BC11
93/4 Cla. 4 Sport 253, ✍ Aut.
94/5 Cla. Images 72, CE20, ✍ Phone
93/4 Cla. Images 4 Sport 111
93/4 Cla. Images 4 Sport 147
93/4 Cla. Images 4 Sport CC15
94/5 Cla. Images 4 Sport 118, E5
92/3 Classic Prospects 1-7, 100, BC10, LP1, PR2, ✍ Aut.
93/4 Cla. Prospects 129, 239, 250, ✍ Aut.
95/6 Cla. Visions 94
95/6 Cla. Vis. Signings 78, ✍ Aut.
98/9 Collection Souvenir 03
95/6 Edge Ice 155, Promo
95/6 Future Legends 38
97/8 Game of Her Life
95 Globe 250
96/7 Visions 94
96/7 Visions Signings 78
92/3 Atlanta Knights
93/4 Atlanta Knights
93/4 Knoxville Cherokees
94/5 Las Vegas Thunder

RHÉAUME, PASCAL
02/3 To. Total 86
02/3 UD MVP 12
02/3 Victory 11
01/2 BAP Mem. 479
93/4 Cla. Prospects 129
93/4 Cla. Prospects 145
97/8 Donruss 215
97/8 Limited 53, 66
97/8 Omega 197
98/9 Pacific 371
99/0 Pacific 363
97/8 Pi. Be A Player 227, ✍ Aut. 227
91/2 7th...Sketch LHJMQ 115
01/2 SPx 155
98/9 Upper Deck 175
98/9 UD G. Reserve 175
99/0 SLOU / Taco Bell 22
96/7 Albany River Rats
00/1 Worcester IceCats

RHINEHART, DWAYNE
91/2 Air Canada SJHL 40
91/2 Air Canada SJHL C46

RHINES, BRAD
76/7 San Diego Mariners

RHODES, DAMIAN
02/3 Between the Pipes 65
02/3 First Edition 176
02/3 Pacific 20
01/2 Adrenaline 10
98/9 Aurora 133, -CF 33
99/0 Aurora 8
00/1 Aurora 7
98/9 Be A Player 96, ✍ Aut. 96
99/0 BAP Mem. 234
00/1 BAP Mem. 33
01/2 BAP Mem. 206
01/2 BT Pipes 24, -Mask, ✂ DM, ✂ GJ, ✂ S&J, ✂ GG, ✂ HSHSJers
98/9 Bicycle.. K-H
98/9 Bowman's Best 54
92/3 Classic Prospects 111
93/4 Cla. Prospects 34
99/0 Crown Royale 8
00/1 Crown Royale 6
95/6 Donruss 274
96/7 Donruss 156
97/8 Donruss 166
96/7 Do. Canadian 16
97/8 Do. Canadian 125
96/7 Do. Elite 113
97/8 Do. Elite 42
97/8 Do. Preferred 37, CG-18
97/8 Do. Priority 57
97/8 Do. Studio 71
98/9 Dynagon Ice 130
99/0 Dynagon Ice 18
96/7 Flair 64
96/7 Fleer 76
93/4 Fleer Ultra 435
96/7 Fl. Ultra 119
98/9 Kraft / OML
93/4 Leaf 367
96/7 Leaf 47, SD-7
97/8 Leaf 45, PD-11
96/7 L. Limited 55
96/7 L. Preferred 109, LS-50
97/8 Limited 57, 186, FG-60
96/7 McDonald's McD-39
97/8 McDonald's McD-30
96/7 Metal Univ. 107, AP-9
99/0 Millenium 13, ✍ Aut. 13
01/2 O-Pee-Chee 112
98/9 OPC Chrome 74
97/8 Omega 157
98/9 Omega 168
99/0 Omega 12
98/9 Pacific 1
99/0 Pacific 294
00/1 Pacific 21
01/2 Pacific 23
97/8 Pacific CC 146
98/9 Pa. Crown Roy. 95
97/8 Pa. Dynagon 86, T-69
97/8 Pa. Paramount 128
98/9 Pa. Paramount 166, -GS 13
99/0 Pa. Paramount 14, IAI-2
00/1 Pa. Paramount 14
97/8 Pa. Revolution 94
98/9 Pa. Revolution 101
96/7 Panini Sticker 47
98/9 Panini Sticker 40
99/0 Panini Sticker 17
93/4 Parkhurst 470
95/6 Parkhurst 200, 417
00/1 Parkhurst P-127
01/2 Parkhurst 231
96/7 Pinnacle 150
97/8 Pinnacle 44
96/7 Pi. Be A Player 202, ✍ Aut. 202
97/8 Pi. Certified 20
97/8 Pi. Inside 65
96/7 Pi. Summit 21, ITC-7
97/8 Pi. Totally 20
96/7 Pi. Zenith 53
93/4 Power Play 454
94/5 Premier 269, OF-18
99/0 Prism 8
00/1 Pr. Stock 5
90/1 ProCards 167
91/2 ProCards 355
99/0 Revolution 8, / CSC 8
00/1 Revolution 7
93/4 Score 604
96/7 Score 136, NW-17
97/8 Score 16, NW-7
96/7 Select CE 28, F-15
01/2 Signature 53, ✍ Aut. 53
96/7 SBx Impact 90
95/6 SP 104
96/7 SP 110
00/1 SP Authentic 6
99/0 SPx 1
99/0 Stadium 169
00/1 Stadium 15
00/1 SLU 22
98/9 Topps 74
99/0 Topps 143
00/1 Topps 76
01/2 Topps 112
99/0 To. Chrome 143
00/1 To. Chrome 59
98/9 To. Finest 146
98/9 T. Gold Label 97
99/0 T. Prmr. Plus 43
98/9 UD Choice 139
00/1 UD Reserve 4
00/1 Ultimate Mem. ✂ G-2
93/4 Upper Deck 364
94/5 Upper Deck 154
95/6 Upper Deck 337
96/7 Upper Deck 112
97/8 Upper Deck 322
98/9 Upper Deck 137
99/0 Upper Deck 15, 175
00/1 Upper Deck 11
01/2 Upper Deck 241
96/7 UD Black Diam. 71
99/0 UD Black Diam. 4
96/7 UD CC 186, 324
97/8 UD Coll. Choice 178
98/9 UD G. Reserve 137
99/0 UD G. Reserve 15, 175
96/7 UD Ice 45
00/1 UD Legends 5
98/9 UD MVP 140
99/0 UD MVP 2, DR1
00/1 UD MVP 9
x99/0 UD MVP Cup GC
00/1 UD Vintage 14, 23, 24
00/1 Vanguard 5
99/0 Victory 11, 13, 388
00/1 Victory 13
99/0 WGretzky 13
96/7 OTTA
97/8 OTTA
98/9 OTTA
93/4 TORO / Abalene
94/5 TORO / Coca-Cola
90/1 Newmarket Saints
92/3 St. John's Maple Leafs
93/4 St. John's Maple Leafs
90/1 Michigan Tech Huskies

RHODIN, THOMAS
98/9 DEL 165
99/0 Eishockey 70
94/5 Leaf Elit Set 15
95/6 Leaf Elit Set 41
90/1 Semic Elitserien 258
91/2 Semic Elitserien 87
92/3 Semic Elitserien 109
95/6 UD Elitserien 60
00/1 UD Elitserien 79

RIAZANTSEV, ALEX
99 Bowman 67
00/1 Hershey Bears
01/2 Hershey Bears
02/3 Hershey Bears

RIBBLE, JERRY
90/1 7th..Sketch OHL 45

RIBBLE, PAT
79/0 O-Pee-Chee 199
80/1 O-Pee-Chee 393
81/2 O-Pee-Chee 339
79/0 Topps 199
77/8 ATLF
78/9 ATLF / Colour
82/3 CALG
80/1 WASH

RIBEIRO, MIKE
02/3 O-Pee-Chee 76
02/3 Pacific 202, -SM 8
02/3 Pacific Complete 171
02/3 SP Authentic 120
02/3 SP Game-Used ✂ FF (x2)
02/3 Stadium ✂ YSS20
02/3 Topps 76
02/3 To. Limited 76
02/3 Upper Deck 93, ✂ BF
02/3 Victory 111
99/0 BAP Mem. 348
00/1 BAP Mem. 258
01/2 BAP Mem. 209
99 Bowman 71
01/2 Bowman 120, ✂ FFJ, ✂ FFS, ✂ FFDS, ✂ FFR, ✍ YSA
98 Bowman 85, 132, ✍ A32
98 Bowman Chrome 85, 132
98/9 Bowman's Best 143
98/9 Collection Souvenir 29
99/0 Dynagon Ice 4
99/0 HoloGrFX 30
99/0 Millenium C-12
99/0 Omega 125
00/1 Pa. Paramount 129
01/2 PTC Draft 5
01/2 PTC Collectibles 6
99/0 Panini Sticker 71
01/2 Parkhurst 257
01/2 PS Titanium 74, TSS 27, TRT 7
01/2 PS Titanium Draft 140
93 Québec Pee Wee 1391
94 Québec Pee Wee 1701
01/2 Signature 237, ✍ Aut. 237
99/0 SP Authentic 44, ✍ SotT
00/1 SP Authentic ✍ SotT
01/2 SP Authentic ✍ SotT
99/0 Stadium 174
00/1 Topps 315
00/1 To. Chrome 210
99/0 T. Prmr. Plus 134
97/8 Upper Deck 417
99/0 Upper Deck 243
99/0 UD Black Diam. 47
99/0 UD G. Reserve 243
00/1 UD MVP ✍ PS
99/0 UD Ovation 31, APOH
99/0 Victory 370
01/2 MONT
02/3 MONT
00/1 Québec Citadelles
01/2 Québec Citadelles
99/0 Québec Remparts 24
99/0 Rouyn-Noranda
x99/0 Rouyn-Noranda

RICARD, ERIC
89/0 ProCards AHL 16
90/1 ProCards 434
91/2 ProCards 371
98/9 Florida Everblades
97/8 New Mexico Scorpions

RICCI, MIKE
02/3 BAP Mem. 44
02/3 O-Pee-Chee 107
02/3 Pacific 339
02/3 Pacific Complete 70
02/3 Parkhurst Retro 92
02/3 Signature GS-61
02/3 Sports Vault 289
02/3 Topps 107
02/3 T. Chrome 68
02/3 To. Limited 107
02/3 To. Total 34
02/3 Upper Deck 390
02/3 UD MVP 155
02/3 UD Vintage 212, 285
02/3 Victory 181
01/2 Adrenaline 169
98/9 Be A Player 270, ✍ Aut. 270
99/0 BAP Mem. 296
00/1 BAP Mem. 318
91/2 Bowman 246
92/3 Bowman 406
93/4 Donruss 280
94/5 Donruss 104
95/6 Donruss 120
96/7 Donruss 177
97/8 Donruss 180
96/7 Do. Canadian 99
97/8 Do. Priority 107
94/5 Flair 150
94/5 Fleer 182
92/3 Fleer Ultra 178, 389
93/4 Fleer Ultra 168
94/5 Fleer Ultra 178
95/6 Fleer Ultra 135
91/2 Gillette 32
93/4 Hockey Wit 79
91/2 Kraft 52
93/4 Kraft / KD
93/4 Leaf 23
94/5 Leaf 240
95/6 Leaf 156
96/7 Leaf 141
97/8 Leaf 65
96/7 L. Preferred 78
97/8 Limited 58

96/7 Maggers 39
99/0 Millenium 216, ✍ Aut. 216
91/2 O-Pee-Chee 13
91/2 O-Pee-Chee 194
92/3 O-Pee-Chee 329
01/2 O-Pee-Chee 160
90/1 OPC Premier 96
91/2 OPC Premier 23
92/3 OPC Premier 91
98/9 Omega 213
98/9 Pacific 391
99/0 Pacific 380
00/1 Pacific 364
01/2 Pacific 343
97/8 Pacific CC 109
99/0 Pa. Paramount 208
00/1 Pa. Paramount 216
91/2 Panini Sticker 231
91/2 Panini Sticker 338
92/3 Panini Sticker 184
93/4 Panini Sticker 69
95/6 Panini Sticker 245
99/0 Panini Sticker 298
95 Panini Worlds 14
91/2 Parkhurst 123
92/3 Parkhurst 146
93/4 Parkhurst 439
94/5 Parkhurst 186, V52
95/6 Parkhurst 318
01/2 Parkhurst 190
91/2 Pinnacle 32
92/3 Pinnacle 314
93/4 Pinnacle 110
93/4 Pinnacle T2K1 22
94/5 Pinnacle 280
96/7 Pi. Be A Player 116, ✍ Aut. 116
95/6 Pi. Summit 109
96/7 Pi. Summit 70
95/6 Pi. Zenith 91
94/5 POG 198
95/6 POG 73
93/4 Power Play 202
93/4 Premier 62
94/5 Premier 548
95/6 Pro Magnet 78
90/1 Pro Set 631
91/2 Pro Set 170
92/3 Pro Set 133
91/2 Pro Set Platinum 85
90/1 Score 433, 60T
91/2 Score 28
91/2 Score CAN 28
92/3 Score 84
93/4 Score 120
95/6 Score 234, CI-12
96/7 Score 106
97/8 Score Colo. 17
90/1 Sco. Young Stars 39
91/2 Score Young Stars 10
94/5 Select 114
95/6 Select CE DS 6
95 Semic 92
89/0 7th..Sketch OHL 100, 183, 190
01/2 Signature 122, ✍ Aut. 122
95/6 SBx Emotion 41
95/6 SBx Impact 40
94/5 SP 98
96/7 SP 37
97/8 SP Authentic 136
00/1 Stadion 61
99/0 Stadium 111
00/1 Stadium 10
91/2 Star Pics 60
95/6 Super Sticker 30
92/3 Topps 86
99/0 Topps 37
00/1 Topps 27
01/2 Topps 160
99/0 To. Chrome 37
98/9 To. Finest 145
00/1 To. Heritage 204
91/2 To. Stadium 386
92/3 To. Stadium 408
93/4 To. Stadium 176
94/5 To. Stadium 3
95/6 To. Stadium 71
00/1 To. Stars 44
98/9 UD Choice 180
90/1 Upper Deck 351, 355
91/2 Upper Deck 143
92/3 Upper Deck 477
92/3 Upper Deck 627
93/4 Upper Deck 352, SP-129
94/5 Upper Deck 284, SP-64
95/6 Upper Deck 457
96/7 Upper Deck 36, P25
97/8 Upper Deck 48
98/9 Upper Deck 170
99/0 Upper Deck 111
00/1 Upper Deck 374
01/2 Upper Deck 375
94/5 UD BAP R49, R108, ✍ 37
93/4 UD BAP Roots 10
96/7 UD Black Diam. 109
97/8 UD Black Diam. 64
95/6 UD CC 282
97/8 UD Coll. Choice 61
98/9 UD G. Reserve 170
99/0 UD G. Reserve 111
98/9 UD MVP 177
99/0 UD MVP 178
00/1 UD MVP 149
01/2 UD MVP 161
00/1 UD Vintage 304
01/2 UD Vintage 212
99/0 Victory 251
00/1 Victory 196
01/2 Victory 295
90/1 PHIL
91/2 PHIL / J.C. Penney
92/3 QUÉB / Petro-Canada
94/5 QUÉB / Burger King

RICCI, SCOTT
98/9 BC Icemen 6
98/9 BC Icemen

RICCIARDI, JEFF
98/9 DEL 106
89/0 7th..Sketch OHL 61
90/1 7th..Sketch OHL 91
91/2 7th...Sketch OHL 304
93/4 Indianapolis Ice
94/5 Indianapolis Ice

RICE, (STEVE)
26 Dominion Chocolates 27

RICE, MIKE
99/0 Brampton Batallion 15

RICE, MURRAY
84/5 Brandon Wheat Kings
85/6 Brandon Wheat Kings

RICE, STEVEN
92/3 Classic Prospects 150
93/4 Donruss 107
95/6 Donruss 81
95/6 Edge Ice C13
93/4 Fleer Ultra 181
94/5 Fleer Ultra 302
94/5 Leaf 324, 477
95/6 Leaf 198
90/1 OPC Premier 97
97/8 Pa. Dynagon BKS-18
97/8 Pa. Paramount 38
95/6 Panini Sticker 33
93/4 Parkhurst 72
95/6 Parkhurst 95
91/2 Pinnacle 334
94/5 Pinnacle 154
95/6 Pinnacle 166
96/7 Pi. Be A Player 8, ✍ Aut. 8
95/6 Playoff 156
95/6 POG 128
93/4 Power Play 86
90/1 Pro Set 626
91/2 ProCards 227
90/1 Score 390
91/2 Score CAN 420
92/3 Score 545
95/6 Score 167
97/8 Score 76
90 7th..Sketch Mem.Cup 38
89/0 7th..Sketch OHL 181, 187
90/1 7th..Sketch OHL 249
94/5 Slapshot / Promo
95/6 Topps 109
93/4 To. Stadium 446
94/5 To. Stadium 54
90/1 Upper Deck 462, 473
91/2 Upper Deck 440
91/2 Upper Deck 441
92/3 Upper Deck 98
93/4 Upper Deck 367
94/5 Upper Deck 294
95/6 Upper Deck 210
97/8 Upper Deck 32
94/5 UD BAP ✍ 49
95/6 UD CC 218
97/8 CARO / Sprint
93/4 EDMO / Sheet
91/2 EDMO / IGA
92/3 EDMO
95/6 HART / Kids Club
96/7 HART / Kids Club
87/8 Kitchener Rangers
88/9 Kitchener Rangers
89/0 Kitchener Rangers
90/1 Kitchener Rangers

RICE, TYLER
91/2 Air Canada SJHL 34

RICH, CURTIS
98/9 Calgary Hitmen 16

RICH, DAVE
95/6 DEL 325

RICHARD, CHAD
99/0 Anchorage Aces

RICHARD, HENRI
02/3 BAP Mem. / Cup
02/3 Parkhurst ✂ VM11, ✂ VT9
02/3 Parkhurst Retro ✂ NN2
02/3 Ultimate Mem. ✂ ASMVP, ✂ EA, ✂ FS, ✂ RAT, ✂ SF (x2), ✂ VGJ
01/2 AGF
01/2 ASG History
52/3 Anonymous 139
71/2 Bazooka Panel
01/2 BAP Mem. ✂ RM4
45-64 BeeHive-2 [Mont.]
64-67 BeeHive-3 [Mont.]
63-65 Chex
64/5 Coke/Sprite [Mont.]
65/6 Coca-Cola
65/6 Coke How To... D
65/6 Coke How To... Z
70/1 Colgate 14
70/1 Dad's Cookies
72/3 Dernière Heure
73/4 Dernière Heure
77/8 Dernière Heure
70/1 Eddie Sargent 98
71/2 Eddie Sargent 103
72/3 Eddie Sargent 119
62/3 El Producto
70/1 Esso Power Player
01/2 Fleer Greats 13, -RC 7, ✂ OSS, ✍ Aut.
01/2 Fleer Legacy 15, ✂ HK
71/2 Frito Lay
62/3 Cowan Tile
83 HHOF Postcard G11
83&87 HHOF 91
93/4 Hockey Wit 52
91/2 Kraft 88
52/3 La Patrie
72/3 Post 15
74/5 Loblaws
68/9 O-Pee-Chee 165
68/9 O-Pee-Chee PS 21
69/0 O-Pee-Chee 163
69/0 O-Pee-Chee 4in1
70/1 O-Pee-Chee 176
70/1 O-Pee-Chee DE 24
71/2 O-Pee-Chee 120
71/2 O-Pee-Chee Book. 6
72/3 O-Pee-Chee 251
73/4 O-Pee-Chee 87
74/5 O-Pee-Chee 243
74/5 O-Pee-Chee 321
57/8 Parkhurst [Mont.] 4
58/9 Parkhurst 2
59/0 Parkhurst 39
60/1 Parkhurst 47
60/1 Parkhurst 57
61/2 Parkhurst 43
62/3 Parkhurst 38
63/4 Parkhurst 23
63/4 Parkhurst 82
92/3 Parkhurst PR-28
93/4 Parkhurst D18
01/2 Parkhurst PR35, PR37, PR56, PR74, PR84, PR122, PR142, PR147, ✂ H15, ✂ PV22, ✂ PV23, ✍ PA5, ✍ PA11
93/4 Parkie 56-57 153
93/4 Parkie 56-57 66
95/6 Parkie 66-67 58
94/5 Parkie Tall 67, 155
66/7 Post Cereal Box
67/8 Post Cereal Box
67/8 Post Cereal Box
68/9 Post Marble
67/8 Post Tips 5
71/2 Pro Star Promotions
72 Semic Sticker 198
60/1 Shirriff 34
61/2 Shirriff 110
62/3 Shirriff 41
68/9 Shirriff / Mont. 15
94/5 Sig. Rookies CF5, ✍ CF5
01/2 Signature ✍ VA20, ✍ VA21
Sport Flash 13
Sport Flash 13
81/2 TCMA 7
64/5 Topps 48
65/6 Topps 71
66/7 Topps 8
66/7 Topps / Test 8
67/8 Topps 72
68/9 Topps 64
69/0 Topps 11
71/2 Topps 120
73/4 Topps 87
74/5 Topps 243
01/2 To. Heritage S8, ✍ CAI, ✂ Relic
57/8 Toronto Star Photo
58/9 Toronto Star Photo
59/0 Toronto Star Photo
62/3 Toronto Star Photo
63/4 Toronto Star Action
63/4 Toronto Star Photo
64/5 Toronto Star Action
65/6 Toronto Star Photo
58/9 Toronto Star Weekend
62/3 Toronto Star Weekend
71/2 Toronto Sun Photo
01/2 Ultimate Mem. ✂ ASGH, ✂ BL, ✂ EA, ✂ LC, ✂ RN, ✂ TM, ✂ SCW, ✂ UC
91/2 Ultimate Original Six 14, 81, 95, ✍ Aut. 14
99/0 UD C. Legends 28
01/2 UD Legends 38
92/3 UD Locker 47
99/0 UD Retro 109
01/2 UD SCup Champs 18
60/1 York Glass [Mont.]
60/1 York
61/2 York 18
62/3 York Transfer 10
63/4 York 19
94/5 Zellers, ✍ Aut.
67/8 MONT
67/8 MONT / IGA Card
68/9 MONT / IGA Card
69/0 MONT / Pro Star
70/1 MONT
71/2 MONT / Pro Star
72/3 MONT / Pro Star
73/4 MONT / Pro Star
74/5 MONT
82/3 MONT
92/3 MONT / OPC 3
92/3 MONT / OPC 61

RICHARD, JACQUES
81/2 Dernière Heure
74/5 Loblaws
72/3 O-Pee-Chee 279
73/4 O-Pee-Chee 169
74/5 O-Pee-Chee 14
74/5 O-Pee-Chee 139
75/6 O-Pee-Chee 117
76/7 O-Pee-Chee 8
77/8 O-Pee-Chee 366
81/2 O-Pee-Chee 268
81/2 O-Pee-Chee 285
82/3 O-Pee-Chee 290
81/2 OPC Sticker 71
80/1 Pepsi Bottle Cap
82/3 Post [Québ.]
73/4 Topps 169
74/5 Topps 14
74/5 Topps 139
75/6 Topps 117
76/7 Topps 8
81/2 Topps 29
72/3 ATLF
80/1 QUÉB
81/2 QUÉB
82/3 QUÉB
83/4 QUÉB

RICHARD, JASON
94/5 Johnstown Chiefs 17

RICHARD, JEAN-MARC
98/9 DEL 148
99/0 Eishockey 85
88/9 ProCards / Halifax
89/0 ProCards AHL 173
90/1 ProCards 457
91/2 ProCards 243
00/1 UD DEL 79
92/3 Fort Wayne Komets 21
89/0 Halifax Citadels
90/1 Halifax Citadels
93/4 Las Vegas Thunder
94/5 Las Vegas Thunder
95/6 Las Vegas Thunder
84/5 Chicoutimi Saguenéens

RICHARD, MAURICE
02/3 Canada Post
02/3 Canadian Museum
02/3 In The GU ✂ VM7
02/3 Parkie - Reprint 264, 273, 285, 295, ✂ VM12
02/3 Parkhurst Retro ✂ NN17
02/3 Ultimate Mem. -BAP (x10), ✂ BOS, ✂ CP, ✂ EA, ✂ FS, ✂ GAO, ✂ GMIH (x3), ✂ Num, ✂ PS, ✂ RAT, ✂ RT, ✂ SF, ✂ VGJ, ✂ VHT
01/2 ASG History
92/3 American Licorice 5
01/2 BAP Mem. ✂ 500GS, ✂ RM1-10
01/2 BAP Update ✂ PTT4, ✂ TC31
34-43 BeeHive-1 [Mont.]
45-64 BeeHive-2 [Mont.]
64-67 BeeHive-3 [Mont.]
99/0 Canada Post
77/8 Dernière Heure
80/1 Dernière Heure
48-52 Exhibits
83 HHOF Postcard A12
83&87 HHOF 1
93/4 Hockey Wit 16
91/2 Kraft 6
91/2 Kraft 65
51/2 La Patrie
45/6 La Presse
92/3 Legends 3
48(c.) M.Richard Playing Cards
43-47 Parade Sportive
51/2 Parkhurst 4
52/3 Parkhurst 1
53/4 Parkhurst 24,30
54/5 Parkhurst 7
55/6 Parkhurst 37,72,73
57/8 Parkhurst [Mont.] 5
58/9 Parkhurst 38
59/0 Parkhurst 2
60/1 Parkhurst 45
93/4 Parkhurst D16
93/4 Parkhurst PR36
93/4 Parkhurst PR48
93/4 Parkhurst PR63
93/4 Parkhurst DPR-5
01/2 Parkhurst HSHS, PR2, PR14, PR88, PR92, PR108, ✂ 500GS, ✂ H4, ✂ PV1, ✂ PV2, ✂ PV3
93/4 Parkie 56-57 65, 139, 162, ✍ A-2
94/5 Parkie Tall 5
97/8 Pi. BeeHive 61, ✍ Aut. 61
91/2 Pro Set 337
45-54 Quaker Oats
92/3 Score 548
92/3 Score 549
92/3 Score MR, MR
94/5 Sig. Rookies CF4, ✍ CF4
01/2 Signature ✂ 500GS
99/0 SP Authentic LH4, ✍ SotT
Sport Flash 9
Sport Flash 9
95/6 SLU Cdn. Legend
96/7 SLU Timeless
99/0 Topps SC4
00/1 To. Heritage OSA
57/8 Toronto Star Photo
58/9 Toronto Star Photo
54 Toronto Star Weekend
00/1 UD Heroes 128
00/1 Ultimate Mem. ✍ RR-1 to RR-5
01/2 Ultimate Mem. ✂ 500GS, ✂ ASGH, ✂ BL, ✂ Corn., ✂ EA, ✂ GAO, ✂ LC, ✂ RN, ✂ RT, ✂ SCP, ✂ SCW
00 ✂ UD APOH 500, ✂✍ 500
99/0 UD C. Legends 5, AC8, E6, ✍ ES
01/2 UD Legends 30, 94, FC, ✂ PoH
99/0 UD Retro 84, DR14, G6A, TC14, ✍ Ink.
01/2 UD SCup Champs 17
60/1 Wonder Bread
92/3 Zellers
92/3 MONT / OPC 6, 29

RICHARD, MIKE
88/9 ProCards / Baltimore
89/0 ProCards AHL 86

RICHARD, RODNEY
98 Bowman 13
98 Bowman Chrome 13

RICHARD, SERGE
84/5 Richelieu Riverains

RICHARDS, BRAD
02/3 BAP Mem. 10, ✂ FG18
02/3 Bowman 62
02/3 Calder 4
02/3 Crown Royale ✂ GWDP 20
02/3 Exclusive 157, ✂ GWJ 23
02/3 First Edition 37, ✂ Jers., ✂ TSL 17
02/3 Heads Up 113, ✂ GWQ 25
02/3 O-Pee-Chee 144
02/3 Pacific 354
02/3 Pacific Complete 308
02/3 Parkhurst 3
02/3 Parkhurst Retro 57
02/3 Pr. Stock Reserve ✂ 144
02/3 Signature 16, ✍ 16
02/3 SP Authentic 132
02/3 Sports Vault 126
02/3 Stadium 43, ✂ YSS10, ✂ YSD6, ✍ LSS
02/3 Topps 144
02/3 T. Chrome 88, ✍ Graph
02/3 To. Heritage 87
02/3 To. Limited 144
02/3 To. Total 386
02/3 Upper Deck 156
02/3 UD Artistic 79, R79, / Art
02/3 UD Classic 88
02/3 UD MVP 169
02/3 UD Top Shelf 79
02/3 UD Vintage 233, 287, GB 233
02/3 Victory 192
01/2 Adrenaline 176
01/2 Atomic 90
00/1 BAP Mem. 464
01/2 BAP Mem. 17
99 Bowman 57
01/2 Bowman 162, ✂ FFJ, ✂ FFS, ✂ FFDS, ✂ FFR, ✍ YSA
98 Bowman 116
98 Bowman Chrome 116
00/1 Crown Royale 142, 21CR-23
01/2 Crown Royale 129
00/1 Crown Royale CC, G-8
01/2 Heads Up 88, BTI 18, PP 8, SM 18
01/2 McDonald's -HP 5
01/2 O-Pee-Chee 64
01/2 Pacific 357, 451
00/1 Parkhurst P-162
01/2 Parkhurst 27, ✂ PS41
00/1 Premier Plus 104, PR4, ✍ PS
00/1 Pr. Stock 146, PSR-23
01/2 Pr. Stock 89, -PS 69
00/1 PS Titanium 146, 3SS-28
01/2 PS Titanium 127
00/1 PS Titanium Draft 146
00/1 Signature 289, ✍ Aut. 219
01/2 Signature 26, ✍ Aut. 26, ✂ GJ60, ✂ GSJ60
00/1 SP Authentic 79
01/2 SP Authentic 79, 130
01/2 SPx 62
01/2 Stadium 75
01/2 Topps 64, OTG11
01/2 To. Chrome 64
00/1 T. Gold Label 87, ✍ GLA
00/1 To. Heritage 25
01/2 To. Heritage 26
01/2 To. Reserve 96
00/1 UD Heroes 107
01/2 UD PlayMakers Ltd 89
00/1 UD Reserve 78
97/8 Upper Deck 418
01/2 Upper Deck 156, T10
00/1 UD Black Diam. 109
01/2 UD Challenge 80
00/1 UD Ice 77
01/2 UD Mask 88
01/2 UD MVP 170
01/2 UD Premier 46
01/2 UD Top Shelf 119
00/1 UD Vintage 324
01/2 UD Vintage 227, 233, 234
00/1 Vanguard 147
01/2 Vanguard 90
01/2 Victory 316
97/8 Rimouski Océanic
99/0 Rimouski Océanic 20

RICHARDS, MARK
95/6 Tallahasee Tiger Sharks
95/6 Tallahasee Tiger Sharks
92/3 Toledo Storm

RICHARDS, MIKE
01/2 Kitchener Rangers

RICHARDS, STEVE
95/6 Hampton Roads
01/2 Val d'Or Foreurs 5

RICHARDS, TODD
98/9 EBK IHL All-Star
95/6 Edge Ice 175
89/0 ProCards AHL 183
92/3 Topps 79
91/2 Upper Deck 430
93/4 Las Vegas Thunder
94/5 Las Vegas Thunder
98/9 Orlando Solar Bears
98/9 Orlando Solar Bears Geico

RICHARDS, TRAVIS
93/4 Classic 74
94/5 Classic ✍ Aut.
94/5 Cla. Images 92
93/4 Fleer Ultra 493
93/4 Power Play 513
93/4 Premier - USA Hockey 7
93/4 To. Stadium - Team U.S.A. 18
96/7 Grand Rapids Griffins
97/8 Grand Rapids Griffins
98/9 Grand Rapids Griffins
99/0 Grand Rapids Griffins
00/1 Grand Rapids Griffins
01/2 Grand Rapids Griffins
02/3 Grand Rapids Griffins
91/2 Minnesota G'Gophers
92/3 Minnesota G'Gophers

RICHARDSON, BILL
52/3 Laval Dairy Update 113
52/3 St. Lawrence 68

RICHARDSON, BRAD
01/2 Owen Sound Attack
02/3 Owen Sound Attack

RICHARDSON, BRUCE
01/2 Cincinnati Mighty Ducks
98/9 Hershey Bears
00/1 Louisiana Ice Gators
02/3 Louisiana Ice Gators
00/1 Manitoba Moose
98/9 Quad City Mallards

RICHARDSON, BRYAN
96/7 Dayton Bombers

RICHARDSON, DAVE
94/5 Parkie Tall 94

RICHARDSON, GEORGE
83 HHOF Postcard F11
83&87 HHOF 85

RICHARDSON, KEN
91/2 7th...Sketch WHL 230
93/4 Red Deer Rebels

RICHARDSON, LEE
02/3 Coventry Blaze

RICHARDSON, LUKE
02/3 First Edition 41, ✂ Jers.
02/3 Pacific Complete 489
02/3 Sports Vault 197
02/3 To. Total 111
02/3 Upper Deck 297
98/9 Be A Player 103, ✍ Aut. 103
00/1 BAP Mem. ✂ T-16
01/2 BAP Update ✂ TC13, ✂ TC25
91/2 Bowman 167
92/3 Bowman 255
93/4 Donruss 115
92/3 Fleer Ultra 297
93/4 Fleer Ultra 318
88/9 OPC/Topps 245
90/1 O-Pee-Chee 428
91/2 O-Pee-Chee 123
91/2 O-Pee-Chee 351
92/3 O-Pee-Chee 171
98/9 OPC Chrome 159
91/2 OPC Premier 46
88/9 OPC Sticker 173-42
97/8 Pa. Invincible R-82
88/9 Panini Sticker 119
89/0 Panini Sticker 142
90/1 Panini/TOR 23
94/5 Panini Sticker 206
95 Panini Worlds 5
91/2 Parkhurst 274
91/2 Pinnacle 212
92/3 Pinnacle 41
92/3 Pinnacle 235
93/4 Pinnacle 139
94/5 Pinnacle 431
94/5 POG 338
94/5 POG / Western 10
94/5 Premier 466
90/1 Pro Set 289
91/2 Pro Set 387
90/1 Score 236
91/2 Score 139
91/2 Score 70T
91/2 Score CAN 139
91/2 Score CAN 620
92/3 Score 62
93/4 Score 252
97/8 Score Phil. 10
92/3 Topps 409
95/6 Topps 108
98/9 Topps 159
91/2 To. Stadium 172
92/3 To. Stadium 456
90/1 Upper Deck 362
91/2 Upper Deck 418
91/2 Upper Deck 522
94/5 Upper Deck 215
96/7 Upper Deck 61
97/8 Upper Deck 330
00/1 Upper Deck 360
95/6 UD BAP 70, ✍ S70
97/8 UD Coll. Choice 96
01/2 UD Ice 111
99/0 UD MVP Cup 138
93/4 EDMO / Sheet
91/2 EDMO / IGA
92/3 EDMO
92/3 EDMO / IGA 019
96/7 EDMO
01/2 PHIL
87/8 TORO / 5x8
87/8 TORO / P.L.A.Y. 27
90/1 TORO

RICHARDSON, RUSS
01/2 Manchester Storm

RICHARDSON, RYAN
00/1 Kudos 82

RICHARDSON, TERRY
79/0 O-Pee-Chee 377

RICHER, ANTOINE
95 Globe 207
95 Panini Worlds 114
94 Semic 224
95 Semic 200
92 Semic Sticker 237
93 Semic Sticker 266
96 Wien 187

RICHER, STÉPHANE J.G.
95/6 DEL 270
96/7 DEL 165
98/9 DEL 228
93/4 Premier 327
88/9 ProCards / Sherbrooke
89/0 ProCards AHL 195
90/1 ProCards 354
91/2 ProCards 86
93/4 To. Stadium 347
00/1 UD DEL 3, ✂ GJ
01/2 UD DEL 174, SS9
93/4 Cincinnati Cyclones
94/5 Cincinnati Cyclones

RICHER, STÉPHANE J.J.
98/9 Aurora 175
98/9 Be A Player 133, ✍ Aut. 133
99/0 BAP Mem. 85
01/2 BAP Mem. 491
90/1 Bowman 45, -HT 11
91/2 Bowman 330
92/3 Bowman 46
95/6 Bowman 14
93/4 Donruss 190
94/5 Donruss 79
95/6 Donruss 178
96/7 Donruss 108
96/7 Do. Canadian 98
97/8 Do. Canadian 104
96/7 Do. Elite 36
92/3 Durivage 18
93/4 Durivage 48
98/9 Dynagon Ice 174
93/4 EA Sports 76
94/5 Flair 97
94/5 Fleer 116, SA-7
95/6 Fleer Metal 86
96/7 Fl. Picks 128
92/3 Fleer Ultra 117
93/4 Fleer Ultra 152
94/5 Fleer Ultra 122
95/6 Fleer Ultra 92, 195
96/7 Fl. Ultra 89
88/9 Frito Lay
95/6 Hoyle / East. 3-Club
89/0 Kraft 24
90/1 Kraft 46, 89
91/2 Kraft 21
95/6 Kraft / KD
86/7 Kraft Sports 35
93/4 Leaf 138
94/5 Leaf 24
95/6 Leaf 91
96/7 Leaf 18
95/6 L. Limited 68
96/7 L. Preferred 76
96/7 Metal Univ. 82
87/8 O-Pee-Chee 233
88/9 OPC/Topps 5
90/1 OPC/Topps 186
90/1 Topps-TL 4
91/2 O-Pee-Chee 369
92/3 O-Pee-Chee 76
89/0 OPC/Topps 153
90/1 OPC Premier 98
91/2 OPC Premier 113
92/3 OPC Premier SP18
88/9 OPC Stars 31
88/9 OPC Sticker 49
89/0 opcSticker 51
98/9 Omega 221
98/9 Pacific 405
99/0 Pacific 394
00/1 Pacific 351
97/8 Pacific CC 44, SS-4C, TC-13
97/8 Pa. Crown Roy. 72
98/9 Pa. Crown Roy. 126
97/8 Pa. Dynagon 65, T-48, BKS-50
97/8 Pa. Invincible 73, R-105
97/8 Pa. Paramount 98
98/9 Pa. Paramount 220
98/9 Pa. Revolution 134
87/8 Panini Sticker 65
88/9 Panini Sticker 260
89/0 Panini Sticker 239
90/1 Panini Sticker 53
90/1 Panini/MTL 18
91/2 Panini Sticker 193
92/3 Panini Sticker 173
93/4 Panini Sticker 37
94/5 Panini Sticker 32
95/6 Panini Sticker 85
99/0 Panini Sticker 145
00/1 Panini Sticker 198
91/2 Parkhurst 100
92/3 Parkhurst 91
93/4 Parkhurst 113
94/5 Parkhurst V50
95/6 Parkhurst 118
01/2 Parkhurst 356
94/5 Parkie SE100
91/2 Pinnacle 14
92/3 Pinnacle 361
93/4 Pinnacle 143
94/5 Pinnacle 166, BR14
95/6 Pinnacle 35
96/7 Pinnacle 33
97/8 Pinnacle 160
96/7 Pi. Be A Player 50, ✍ Aut. 50
95/6 Pi. Summit 52
96/7 Pi. Summit 99
95/6 Pi. Zenith 39
96/7 Pi. Zenith 42
95/6 Playoff 60
96/7 Playoff 342
94/5 POG 148
95/6 POG 163
93/4 Power Play 141
93/4 Premier 158
94/5 Premier 105
95/6 Pro Magnet 34
90/1 Pro Set 156, 370
91/2 Pro Set 122
91/2 Pro Set 420
92/3 Pro Set 93
91/2 Pro Set Platinum 67
90/1 Score 75
90/1 Sco. Hot Cards 38
91/2 Score 234
91/2 Score 31T
91/2 Score CAN 581
92/3 Score 140
93/4 Score 34
95/6 Score 130, GB-14
96/7 Score 232
97/8 Score 213
97/8 Score Mont. 8
94/5 Select 108
95/6 Select CE 39
95/6 SBx Emotion 101
95/6 SBx Impact 96
94/5 SP 64
95/6 SP 85
96/7 SP 83
98/9 SPx Finite 78
96/7 SLU
95/6 Super Sticker 69
96/7 Team Out!
92/3 Topps 160
95/6 Topps 231, HGC28
00/1 Topps 226
94/5 Topps Finest 94, DF-10
91/2 To. Stadium 86
92/3 To. Stadium 9
93/4 To. Stadium 61
95/6 To. Stadium EC176, PS10
95/6 T. Super Skills 41
98/9 UD Choice 193
90/1 Upper Deck 276
91/2 Upper Deck 244
91/2 Upper Deck 536
92/3 Upper Deck 56
93/4 Upper Deck 403, SP-87
94/5 Upper Deck 388, SP-44
95/6 Upper Deck 426, SE-47
96/7 Upper Deck 94
98/9 Upper Deck 183
95/6 UD CC 250
97/8 UD Coll. Choice 138
98/9 UD G. Reserve 183
99/0 Victory 278
85/6 MONT
85/6 MONT / Provigo
86/7 MONT
87/8 MONT
87/8 MONT
87/8 MONT / Vachon 51
87/8 MONT / Vachon 52
87/8 MONT / Vachon 54
88/9 MONT
89/0 MONT
89/0 MONT / Kraft
90/1 MONT
96/7 MONT
99/0 SLOU / Taco Bell 24
84/5 Chicoutimi Saguenéens

RICHER, STÉPHANE JG
99/0 Eishockey 12

RICHEY, STEVE
81/2 Kingston Canadians
82/3 Kingston Canadians

RICHISON, GRANT
89/0 ProCards AHL 46
90/1 ProCards 255
91/2 ProCards 244
92/3 Fort Wayne Komets 22
93/4 Fort Wayne Komets 18
94/5 Fort Wayne Komets 17
95/6 Fort Wayne Komets
98/9 Kansas City Blades 19
99/0 Kansas City Blades
90/1 Moncton Hawks

RICHMOND, STEVE
86/7 O-Pee-Chee 208
88/9 ProCards / New Haven

RICHTER, BARRY
93/4 Classic 75
94/5 Classic ✍ Aut.
93/4 Cla. Images 4 Sport 24
93/4 Fleer Ultra 494
95/6 Future Legends 39
99/0 Pacific 264
95 Panini Worlds 217
93/4 Power Play 514
93/4 Premier - USA Hockey 18
96/7 To. Picks 177
93/4 To. Stadium - Team U.S.A. 19
96/7 Upper Deck 219
99/0 Victory 195
94/5 Binghampton Rangers
95/6 Binghampton Rangers
97/8 Providence Bruins
00/1 Québec Citadelles

RICHTER, DAVE
87/8 O-Pee-Chee 261
87/8 OPC Sticker 190-51
87/8 Panini Sticker 344
90/1 ProCards 522
83/4 MINS
84/5 MINS
87/8 SLOU
88/9 SLOU
88/9 SLOU / Kodak
86/7 VANC
87/8 VANC / Shell

RICHTER, MARTIN
02/3 Cardset 105
97/8 APS 227
00/1 Cardset 78
99/0 DS 17
97/8 DS Sticker 33
98/9 OFS 85, 451
99/0 OFS 143, 267
99/0 Score N 9

RICHTER, MIKE
02/3 Atomic 69, -D 13, -NPU 6
02/3 BAP All-Star 74, ✂ ASJ
02/3 BAP Mem. 154, ✂ ASJ47
02/3 Between the Pipes 29, 140, M18, ✂ ASJ5, ✂ GUE21, ✂ GUJ21, ✂ GSJ21, ✂ GN2, ✂ GN6, ✂ HSHSJers 5, ✂ ITN21, ✂ I9, ✂ T1
02/3 Crown Royale 65, -COA 7, ✂ GWDP 16
02/3 Exclusive 118, -EA 12
02/3 First Edition 128, ✂ Jers.
02/3 Heads Up 83
02/3 In The GU 50, 150
02/3 O-Pee-Chee 128
02/3 Pacific 258
02/3 Pacific Complete 21
02/3 Parkhurst 33, -CR17, -HHV 5, ✂ CRM17, ✂ MS4
02/3 Parkhurst Retro 177
02/3 Pr. Stock Reserve 69, -ICS 15
02/3 SP GU 58
02/3 Sports Vault 90
02/3 SPx 50
02/3 Stadium - PSH-13
02/3 Topps 128
02/3 T. Chrome 80
02/3 To. Heritage 54
02/3 To. Limited 128
02/3 To. Total 193
02/3 Ultimate Mem. ✂ ASMVP
02/3 Upper Deck 365
02/3 UD Honor 48
02/3 UD Mask ✂ CW, ✂ GG, ✂ MM, ✂ NB, ✂ PW, ✂ VC
02/3 UD MVP -MM5
02/3 UD Piece 59, 105, ✍ MD
02/3 UD Top Shelf 57, ✂ CP, ✂ M, ✂ ST, ✂ SS
02/3 UD Vintage 280
02/3 Vanguard - Stonewallers 8
02/3 Victory 145, -NP57
01/2 Adrenaline 130, CL 1, PP 24, ✂ GWJ 30
01/2 Atomic -Stat 6
98/9 Aurora 125, -CF 31
99/0 Aurora 97, Stripe 97, GU-13
00/1 Aurora 98
98/9 Be A Player 89, H-6, ✍ Aut. 89
99/0 BAP Mem. 21, ✂ TM-33
00/1 BAP Mem. 52, ✂ J-5, ✂ G-1, ✂ TM-19, ✂ TM-32
01/2 BAP Mem. 222, ✂ GJ, ✂ GT
01/2 BT Pipes 50, 92, -Mask, ✂ ASH, ✂ GJ, ✂ S&J, ✂ HSHSJers
98/9 Bicycle.. J-D
90/1 Bowman 218
91/2 Bowman 70
92/3 Bowman 238
92/3 Bowman 354
01/2 Bowman 9
98/9 Bowman's Best 43
99/0 Crown Royale 92
00/1 Crown Royale 72, ✂ GWJ-17
01/2 Crown Royale 98, ✂ TT 15
93/4 Donruss 223
94/5 Donruss 165, MM-8
95/6 Donruss 59
96/7 Donruss 184
97/8 Donruss 124
96/7 Do. Canadian 26
97/8 Do. Canadian 107, SCS-15
96/7 Do. Elite 96, PW-2
97/8 Do. Elite 56
97/8 Do. Preferred 124, CG-15
97/8 Do. Priority 143, PG-5
97/8 Do. Studio 59, P-33
98/9 Dynagon Ice 125, -IW 6
99/0 Dynagon Ice 134, GM-3, GM-8
93/4 EA Sports 90
97/8 Esso 33
94/5 Flair 117
96/7 Flair 62, HG-9
94/5 Fleer 139, N-8
95/6 Fleer Metal 98
96/7 Fl. Picks 84, DL-2
92/3 Fleer Ultra 142
93/4 Fleer Ultra 228
94/5 Fleer Ultra 143, PPM-5
95/6 Fleer Ultra 276
96/7 Fl. Ultra 110
91/2 Gillette 39
95 Globe 100
01/2 Heads Up 66, HD 18, SS 14, ✂ JQ 14, ✂ JQ 20
93/4 Hockey Wit 1
99/0 HoloGrFX 40
95/6 Hoyle / East. 4-Club
91/2 Kraft 88
94/5 Kraft / KD
95/6 Kraft / PS
96/7 Kraft / TT
98/9 Kraft / OML
93/4 Leaf 185
94/5 Leaf 18, CP-8, GLS-3
95/6 Leaf 42
96/7 Leaf 178, SD-11
97/8 Leaf 70, PD-8
94/5 L. Limited 17
96/7 L. Limited 41
96/7 L. Preferred 55, LS-46, MM-11
97/8 Limited 32, 134, FG-11
96/7 Maggers 101
92/3 McDonald's McD-25
94/5 McDonald's
97/8 McDonald's McD-29
98/9 McD's T8
96/7 Metal Univ. 100, AP-10
99/0 Millenium 168, ✍ Aut. 168
98/9 NHL Power Play
90/1 OPC/Topps 330
91/2 O-Pee-Chee 11
91/2 O-Pee-Chee 91
92/3 O-Pee-Chee 259
01/2 O-Pee-Chee 187
98/9 OPC Chrome 200
91/2 OPC Premier 78
97/8 Omega 148, NSZ-8
98/9 Omega 161
99/0 Omega 153, CC-14, ✂ GWJ 5
98/9 Pacific 298
99/0 Pacific 278, GC-23, ITCNF-12, TL-18
00/1 Pacific 269, ITC-8
01/2 Pacific 267, SC 13, ✂ GWJ 22
97/8 Pacific CC 197, ITC-13
97/8 Pa. Crown Roy. 87, FO-12
98/9 Pa. Crown Roy. 91
97/8 Pa. Dynagon 82, S-14, T-70
97/8 Pa. Invincible 90
97/8 Pa. Paramount 119, GSL-13
98/9 Pa. Paramount 156, -GS 12
99/0 Pa. Paramount 156, GS-13, PB-23
00/1 Pa. Paramount 167, GS-13
97/8 Pa. Revolution 90, RTS-13
98/9 Pa. Revolution 97, -TPA 16
94 Panini Olympics 322
98/9 Panini Photocard
90/1 Panini Sticker 98, 345
91/2 Panini Sticker 290
92/3 Panini Sticker 231
93/4 Panini Sticker 99
94/5 Panini Sticker 90
95/6 Panini Sticker 112
96/7 Panini Sticker 103
98/9 Panini Sticker 82
99/0 Panini Sticker 101
95 Panini Worlds 212
91/2 Parkhurst 117
92/3 Parkhurst 112
93/4 Parkhurst 129
94/5 Parkhurst V5
95/6 Parkhurst 138, GP-12, PP-31
00/1 Parkhurst P-110
01/2 Parkhurst 178, ✂ PJ56, ✂ M46
94/5 Parkie SE110
91/2 Pinnacle 164
91/2 Pinnacle 384
92/3 Pinnacle 75
92/3 Pinnacle 270
92/3 Pinnacle TP 1
93/4 Pinnacle 242
94/5 Pinnacle 10, GT2, TP2
95/6 Pinnacle 47
96/7 Pinnacle 112, M-9
97/8 Pinnacle 55, M-2, / Tin 7
96/7 Pi. Be A Player SP-10
97/8 Pi. Be A Player 37, STP-10, ✍ Aut. 37
97/8 Pi. BeeHive 41
97/8 Pi. Certified 13
96/7 Pi. FANtasy 10
97/8 Pi. Inside 81, IT-26, S-5, / Can 5, LargeCan
95/6 Pi. Summit 115, ITC-11
96/7 Pi. Summit 145, ITC-2
97/8 Pi. Totally 13
97/8 Pi. Uncut 2
95/6 Pi. Zenith 53
96/7 Pi. Zenith 66, CS-14
95/6 Playoff 69
94/5 POG 288, 337
95/6 POG 189
93/4 Power Play 165
93/4 Premier 135
94/5 Premier 70, 155, 314
00/1 Premier Plus 43, MB19
99/0 Prism 92
00/1 Pr. Stock 67, PS-39, ✂ GUG-78, ✂ GUG-79
01/2 Pr. Stock 65, ✂ GUG 69
00/1 PS Titanium 63, 3SS-5, ✂ GUG-118
01/2 PS Titanium 96, TSS 7, ✂ DSJ 29
01/2 PS Titanium Draft ✂ 63
00/1 PS Titanium Draft ✂ 68
95/6 Pro Magnet 99, IC4
90/1 Pro Set 398, 627
91/2 Pro Set 161
92/3 Pro Set 116
91 Pro Set Awards AC2
91/2 Pro Set Platinum 83
91/2 Pro Set Platinum 279
89/0 ProCards IHL 48
99/0 Revolution 100, SS-23, / CSC 100
00/1 Revolution 99
90/1 Score 74
91/2 Score 120
91/2 Score CAN 120
92/3 Score 5
92/3 Score USAG 6
93/4 Score 99
94/5 Score 130
95/6 Score 140, 321
96/7 Score 150, SD-9, S-12
97/8 Score 11, NW-6
97/8 Score NYRa. 16
90/1 Sco. Young Stars 27
91/2 Score Young Stars 2
92/3 Score Young Stars 9
92/3 Seasons 29
94/5 Select 133, FL-7
95/6 Select CE 73
96/7 Select CE 39, F-11
94 Semic 107
95 Semic 218
91 Semic Sticker 128
92 Semic Sticker 148
93 Semic Sticker 170
96/7 SB 7-Eleven Phonecard
00/1 Signature 165, ✍ Aut. 149, ✂ J-39
01/2 Signature ✂ GUE39, ✂ GJ41, ✂ GSJ41, ✂ ITN39, ✂ IS1
95/6 SBx Emotion 117
95/6 SBx Impact 112
96/7 SBx Impact 83
94/5 SP 75
95/6 SP 95
96/7 SP 100, HC-27, SF-3
97/8 SP Authentic 101
98/9 SP Authentic 55
99/0 SP Authentic 55
00/1 SP Authentic ✍ SotT
00/1 SP GU 40, ✂ TotG, ✂ C
96/7 SPx 28
97/8 SPx 31
99/0 SPx 98
98/9 SPx Prospects PS7, -WM
00/1 Stadion 152
99/0 Stadium 85, GC5
00/1 Stadium 9, CA15
94/5 Starting Lineup
95/6 Super Sticker 83
96/7 Team Out!
92/3 Topps 367
95/6 Topps 212, HGA10
98/9 Topps 200
99/0 Topps 59, SC16
00/1 Topps 45
01/2 Topps 187
99/0 To. Chrome 59
00/1 To. Chrome 37
01/2 To. Chrome 124
94/5 Topps Finest 86, BBR-13,DF-6
95/6 To. Finest 169
98/9 To. Finest 89
98/9 T. Gold Label 54
99/0 T. Gold Label 54
00/1 T. Gold Label 27, BTM10, B9
00/1 To. Heritage 102
96/7 To. Picks ID13
99/0 T. Prmr. Plus 76, IG7, ✂ GP
91/2 To. Stadium 92
92/3 To. Stadium 242
92/3 To. Stadium 266
93/4 To. Stadium 64
94/5 To. Stadium 181
95/6 To. Stadium 49, N4
93/4 TSC Members Only 45
00/1 To. Stars 86, ✂ GG
95/6 T. Super Skills 74
98/9 UD Choice 135, 246
00/1 UD Heroes 81
00/1 Ultimate Mem. ✍ U-34, ✂ G-20, ✂ PJ-8, ✂ J-33, ✂ Jers. 29, ✂ S-33, ✂ GM-15
01/2 Ultimate Mem. ✂ BAPL
99/0 Ult. Victory 56,NW5
90/1 Upper Deck 32
91/2 Upper Deck 34
91/2 Upper Deck 175
91/2 Upper Deck 610
91/2 Upper Deck 634
92/3 Upper Deck 145
93/4 Upper Deck 42
94/5 Upper Deck 78, H30, SP-52
95/6 Upper Deck 438, H12, SE-58
96/7 Upper Deck 109
97/8 Upper Deck 107, SG53, T10C, ✂ GJ11
98/9 Upper Deck 324
99/0 Upper Deck 87, UD7
00/1 Upper Deck 115, EC10, ✂ GJ
01/2 Upper Deck 344, ✂ TendThr
95/6 UD BAP 191, ✍ S191
96/7 UD Black Diam. 35
97/8 UD Black Diam. 4
98/9 UD Black Diam. 58
99/0 UD Black Diam. 58
01/2 UD Challenge ✂ T200, ✂✍ T200S
95/6 UD CC 306
96/7 UD CC 167, 325
97/8 UD Coll. Choice 161, SQ30
98/9 UD G. Reserve 324
99/0 UD G. Reserve 87

99/0 UD Gretzky Excl. 68
01/2 UD Honor Roll 96
96/7 UD Ice 41
97/8 UD Ice 3
00/1 UD Legends LC7
01/2 UD Mask 120, 183, ✂ CG, ✂ GJ, ✂ JP, ✂ DP, ✂✍ SP, ✂ MB
98/9 UD MVP 135
99/0 UD MVP 133, W2
00/1 UD MVP 119, ✂ GS
01/2 UD MVP ✂ GS
99/0 UD MVP Cup 118, GC
99/0 UD Ovation 37
01/2 UD Premier ✂ B, ✂ D (x2), ✍ SigG
00/1 UD Pros&Prosp. 57
99/0 UD Retro 52
01/2 UD SCup Champs 83, ✂ G
01/2 UD Top Shelf 107, ✂ J
00/1 UD Vintage 239, 246-47, GG12
01/2 UD Vintage 168, 173
00/1 Vanguard 67, ✂ DGJ-9
01/2 Vanguard 66, SW 13, ✂ DGM 20
99/0 Victory 189, 390
00/1 Victory 151
01/2 Victory 229, 237
99/0 WGretzky 115, ✂ TG
96 Wien 158
97/8 Zenith 18, Z63
89/0 NYRA / Marine
98/9 NYRA

RICHTER, PAVEL
94/5 APS 299
98/9 OFS 371, 444
99/0 OFS 101
79 Panini Sticker 88

RICHTER, RICHARD
98/9 OFS 95
99/0 Score 63

RIDDELL, BRYAN
01/2 Hull Olympiques 2

RIDDERWALL, ROLF
94 Semic 53
89/0 Semic Elitserien 50
91/2 Semic Elitserien 320
91/2 Semic Elitserien 336
92/3 Semic Elitserien 26
89 Semic Sticker 4
91 Semic Sticker 28

RIDDLE, TROY
99/0 Des Moines Buc's

RIDEOUT, SCOTT
93/4 Portland Winter Hawks

RIDLER, GLENN
01/2 Belleville Bulls Update
00/1 Kingston Frontenacs 16

RIDLEY, CURT
76/7 O-Pee-Chee 197
77/8 O-Pee-Chee 395
78/9 O-Pee-Chee 302
76/7 Topps 197
80/1 TORO
76/7 VANC / Royal Bank
77/8 VANC / Royal Bank
79/0 VANC / Royal Bank

RIDLEY, MIKE
90/1 Bowman 77
91/2 Bowman 308
92/3 Bowman 360
93/4 Donruss 375
95/6 Donruss 250
96/7 Donruss 141
93/4 EA Sports 153
94/5 Flair 185
94/5 Fleer 219
95/6 Fleer Metal 155
92/3 Fleer Ultra 238
93/4 Fleer Ultra 148
94/5 Fleer Ultra 378
95/6 Fleer Ultra 163, 318
93/4 Leaf 102
94/5 Leaf 374
95/6 Leaf 212
86/7 OPC/Topps 66
86/7 OPC/Topps Box L
87/8 OPC/Topps 8
88/9 OPC/Topps 104
90/1 OPC/Topps 327
91/2 O-Pee-Chee 245
92/3 O-Pee-Chee 305
89/0 OPC/Topps 165, / Box B
86/7 OPC Sticker 221
86/7 OPC Sticker 131-117
87/8 OPC Sticker 234-101
88/9 OPC Sticker 74-205
89/0 opcSticker 81
97/8 Pacific CC 206
87/8 Panini Sticker 181
88/9 Panini Sticker 374
89/0 Panini Sticker 339
90/1 Panini Sticker 163
91/2 Panini Sticker 199
92/3 Panini Sticker 162
93/4 Panini Sticker 25
94/5 Panini Sticker 23
95/6 Panini Sticker 289
97/8 Panini Sticker 243
91/2 Parkhurst 192
92/3 Parkhurst 200
93/4 Parkhurst 218
94/5 Parkhurst 250
95/6 Parkhurst 214
94/5 Parkie SE178
91/2 Pinnacle 94
92/3 Pinnacle 170
93/4 Pinnacle 135
94/5 Pinnacle 384
96/7 Pinnacle 172
95/6 Playoff 319
94/5 POG 236
95/6 POG 270
93/4 Power Play 266
93/4 Premier 78
94/5 Premier 301
90/1 Pro Set 320
91/2 Pro Set 254
91/2 Pro Set Platinum 128
90/1 Score 33
91/2 Score 283
91/2 Score CAN 503
92/3 Score 187
92/3 Score SS 6
93/4 Score 197
94/5 Score 199
95/6 Score 236
96/7 Score 184
94/5 Select 19
95/6 SBx Emotion 184
95/6 SBx Impact 173
94/5 SP 118
92/3 Topps 236
91/2 To. Stadium 68
92/3 To. Stadium 200
93/4 To. Stadium 123
94/5 To. Stadium 105
95/6 To. Stadium 51
90/1 Upper Deck 97
91/2 Upper Deck 112
92/3 Upper Deck 173
93/4 Upper Deck 341, SP-173
94/5 Upper Deck 177, SP-169
95/6 Upper Deck 75
95/6 UD BAP 63, ✍ S63
96/7 UD Black Diam. 125
95/6 UD CC 48
97/8 UD Coll. Choice 264
01/2 UD Legends 66
96/7 VANC / IGA
86/7 WASH / Kodak
87/8 WASH
87/8 WASH / Kodak
88/9 WASH
88/9 WASH / Smokey
89/0 WASH
89/0 WASH / Kodak
90/1 WASH / Kodak
90/1 WASH / Smokey
91/2 WASH / Kodak
91/2 WASH / Smokey
92/3 WASH / Kodak

RIDOLFI, BRIAN
96/7 Dayton Bombers
98/9 Dayton Bombers
98/9 Dayton Bombers

RIDPATH, BRUCE
91 C55 Reprint 14
10/1 Imperial
10/1 Imperial 34
11/2 Imperial 14
12/3 Imperial 28

RIECICIAR, PAVOL
01/2 OFS 164

RIEDEL, BEAU
96/7 Johnstown Chiefs

RIEDER, DANA
90/1 7th..Sketch WHL 32
91/2 7th...Sketch WHL 317

RIEDMEIER, ERWIN
72 Semic Sticker 98

RIEHL, JEREMY
91/2 7th...Sketch WHL 179

RIEHL, KEVIN
00/1 Kudos 25
90/1 7th..Sketch WHL 33
91/2 7th...Sketch WHL 329
94/5 SR Auto-Phonex 35, ✍ 35
93/4 Raleigh Icecaps
94/5 Raleigh Icecaps
01/2 Belfast Giants

RIEKKINEN, ANNTTI
98/9 Cardset 155

RIEKKINEN, PAAVO
70/1 Kuvajulkaisut 234

RIEL, GUY
80/1 Québec Remparts

RIENDEAU, VINCENT
90/1 Bowman 20
91/2 Bowman 372
92/3 Bowman 262
95/6 DEL 335
94/5 Flair 13
92/3 Fleer Ultra 288
94/5 Fleer Ultra 15
94/5 Kraft / KD
94/5 Kraft Mask
90/1 OPC/Topps 177
91/2 O-Pee-Chee 370
89/0 opcSticker/FS 17
89/0 Panini Sticker 120
90/1 Panini Sticker 268
92/3 Parkhurst 278
94/5 Parkhurst 14
92/3 Pinnacle 177
93/4 Pinnacle 312
94/5 Pinnacle 212
94/5 POG 272
93/4 Premier 411
94/5 Premier 324
90/1 Pro Set 270
91/2 Pro Set 213
91/2 Pro Set Platinum 112
90/1 Score 107
91/2 Score 23
91/2 Score 43T
91/2 Score CAN 23
92/3 Score 396
93/4 Score 276
92/3 Topps 466
91/2 To. Stadium 128
92/3 To. Stadium 172
94/5 To. Stadium 43
90/1 Upper Deck 152
91/2 Upper Deck 220
87/8 SLOU
88/9 SLOU
88/9 SLOU / Kodak
89/0 SLOU / Kodak
90/1 SLOU / Kodak
86/7 Sherb. Canadiens 22

RIENDEAU, YANICK
01/2 Victoriaville Tigres 12

RIENDEAU, YANNICK
01/2 Drummondville

RIESEN, MICHEL
00/1 BAP Mem. 480
01/2 BAP Mem. 177
00/1 Premier Plus 111
00/1 PS Titanium Draft 160
00/1 SP Authentic 144, ✍ SotT
00/1 To. Heritage 100
00/1 To. Stars 123
00/1 UD Heroes 164
00/1 Upper Deck 412
00/1 UD Black Diam. 119
00/1 UD Pros&Prosp. 105
00/1 UD Vintage 379
00/1 Vanguard 119
99/0 Hamilton Bulldogs
00/1 Hamilton Bulldogs

RIFFEL, KEVIN
91/2 Air Canada SJHL B9

RIGGIN, DENNIS
52/3 Anonymous 1
62/3 Cowan Tile

RIGGIN, PAT
83/4 Funmate Puffy 21 [w/]
81/2 O-Pee-Chee 37
82/3 O-Pee-Chee 372
84/5 O-Pee-Chee 205
84/5 O-Pee-Chee 218
84/5 O-Pee-Chee 386
85/6 OPC/Topps 136
81/2 OPC Sticker 12
81/2 OPC Sticker 221
84/5 OPC Sticker 233-232
84/5 OPC Sticker 65-66
85/6 OPC Sticker 106-238
86/7 OPC Sticker 41-178
80/1 Pepsi Bottle Cap
82/3 Post [Calg.]
81/2 Topps 30
84/5 Topps 148
84/5 Topps 164
79/0 ATLF / Colour
80/1 CALG
81/2 CALG
87/8 PITT / Kodak
82/3 WASH
84/5 WASH / Pizza Hut
85/6 WASH / Pizza Hut

RIGGIN, TRAVIS
93/4 Slapshot / Kitchener 29
93/4 Slapshot / Kitchener 7
94/5 Slapshot / Kitchener 9
95/6 Slapshot 173

RIGOLET, GERALD
72 Semic Sticker 158

RIHA, MILOS
96/7 APS 141
97/8 APS 242
98/9 OFS 374
99/0 OFS 308
00/1 OFS 287

RIIHIJÄRVI, HEIKKI
92/3 Jyvas Hyva 64
93/4 Jyvas Hyva 116
93/4 Sisu 10

RIIHIJÄRVI, JUHA
02/3 Cardset 106
98/9 Cardset Leij. 37
93/4 Classic 45
93/4 Cla. Prospects 48
92/3 Jyvas Hyva 73
95 Leaf Latkaliiga 7
94 Semic 40
95 Semic 46
93 Semic Sticker 74
93/4 Sisu 369
93/4 Sisu 384
94/5 Sisu 301, 382, H-12
95/6 Sisu 99, S-3
96/7 Sisu 179, ATG-2, GH
95/6 Sisu Limited 35
97/8 UD Elitserien 146, C14
98/9 UD Elitserien 162
99/0 UD Elitserien 164, L9
00/1 UD Elitserien 144, P7
96 Wien 34

RIIHIJÄRVI, TEEMU
02/3 Cardset 107
98/9 Cardset 27
99/0 Cardset 18, 302, MW 4
00/1 Cardset 315
95/6 Classic 12, BK11
95/6 Sisu 92, DD-2
96/7 Sisu 91
95/6 Upper Deck 548
95/6 UD CC 331

RIIHIMAKI, HANNU
80/1 Mallasjuoma 21

RIIHIMAKI, MARKKU
70/1 Kuvajulkaisut 202
71/2 Williams Finnish 91
72/3 Williams Finnish 256
73/4 Williams Finnish 256

RIIHINEN, JANI
98/9 Cardset 8
95/6 UD CC 330

RIIHIRANTA, HEIKKI
72 Hellas MM-Jenkki 13
70/1 Kuvajulkaisut 76
70/1 Kuvajulkaisut 114
80/1 Mallasjuoma 4
74/5 OPC WHA 31
75/6 OPC WHA 125
76/7 OPC WHA 58
72 Panda MM-Toronto
74 Semic Sticker 80
78/9 SM-Liiga 25
71/2 Williams Finnish 123
72/3 Williams Finnish 74
72/3 Williams Finnish 93
73/4 Williams Finnish 78
73/4 Williams Finnish 140

RIITAHAARA, PENTTI
66/7 Champion 19
65/6 Hellas 68

RIKALA, JORMA
65/6 Hellas 49
70/1 Kuvajulkaisut 115
72 Panda MM-Toronto
71/2 Williams Finnish 124
72/3 Williams Finnish 94
73/4 Williams Finnish 141

RILAY, BILL
83/4 Nova Scotia Voyageurs

RILCOF, KEVAN
91/2 Avant Garde BCJHL 5
92/3 BCJHL 22

RILEY, BILL
77/8 O-Pee-Chee 360
78/9 O-Pee-Chee 292
79/0 O-Pee-Chee 303
78/9 WASH

RILEY, JACK
36-39 Diamond Match TT1
34/5 Sweet Caporal

RILEY, RON
72/3 Ottawa Nationals

RIMMEL, PATRIK
94/5 APS 10
95/6 APS 107
00/1 OFS 270
01/2 OFS 230

RIMSKY, DALIBOR
96/7 APS 116

RINDELL, HARRI
92/3 Jyvas Hyva 1
93/4 Jyvas Hyva 13
93/4 Sisu 82
94/5 Sisu 395
95/6 Sisu 391

RING, TOMAS
91/2 Semic Elitserien 138

RINGLER, TIM
81/2 Milwaukee Admirals

RINKINEN, JUHA-PEKKA
96/7 Sisu 115

RINNE, JOUNI
78/9 SM-Liiga 169
77-79 Sports. FIN 87-2072
73/4 Williams Finnish 315

RINTANEN, KIMMO
02/3 Cardset 108
98/9 Cardset 109, -Leij. 38, -OD 5
99/0 Cardset 196, 333
00/1 Cardset 97, 355
97/8 Hockey-Box
93/4 Jyvas Hyva 229
95 Semic 19, 229
93/4 Sisu 203
94/5 Sisu 257
95/6 Sisu 130
96/7 Sisu 145,MA-1
92/3 Upper Deck 618

RIOPELLE, HOWARD (RIP)
45-64 BeeHive-2 [Mont.]
51/2 Laval Dairy 101
43-47 Parade Sportive
45-54 Quaker Oats
52/3 St. Lawrence 55

RIOUX, DANIEL
80/1 Québec Remparts

RIOUX, PIERRE
94/5 DEL 92
98/9 DEL 271
84/5 Moncton G'Flames

RIPLEY, VIC
33-35 Diamond Match Silv.
36-39 Diamond Match TT1
33/4 O-Pee-Chee 67
33/4 WWGum 54

RIPLINGER, BRENT
93/4 N. Michigan Wildcats

RISDALE, MIKE
90/1 7th..Sketch WHL 166
91/2 7th...Sketch WHL 238
89/0 Regina Pats

RISEBROUGH, DOUG
80/1 Dernière Heure
82/3 Dernière Heure
83/4 Funmate Puffy 1 [w/]
75/6 Hockey Heroes
84/5 Kellogg's 20
86/7 Kraft Sports 7
75/6 O-Pee-Chee 107
76/7 O-Pee-Chee 109
76/7 O-Pee-Chee 388
77/8 O-Pee-Chee 189
78/9 O-Pee-Chee 249
79/0 O-Pee-Chee 13
80/1 O-Pee-Chee 275
81/2 O-Pee-Chee 190
82/3 O-Pee-Chee 57
83/4 O-Pee-Chee 92
84/5 O-Pee-Chee 236
85/6 O-Pee-Chee 243
86/7 OPC/Topps 196
83/4 OPC/Topps Sticker 269
84/5 OPC Sticker 241
80/1 Pepsi Bottle Cap
82/3 Post [Mont.]
90/1 Pro Set 663
84/5 7-Eleven
83/4 Souhaits Keychain [Flames]
75/6 Topps 107
76/7 Topps 109
77/8 Topps 189
78/9 Topps 249
79/0 Topps 13
83/4 Vachon 18-138
82/3 CALG
85/6 CALG / Red Rooster
85/6 CALG / Red Rooster
86/7 CALG / Red Rooster
87/8 CALG / Red Rooster
90/1 CALG / McGavin's
91/2 CALG / IGA
74/5 MONT
75/6 MONT
76/7 MONT
77/8 MONT
78/9 MONT
79/0 MONT
80/1 MONT
81/2 MONT

RISIDORE, RYAN
94/5 SR Tetrad CXII, ✍ Aut.
93/4 Slapshot / Guelph 5
94/5 Slapshot / Guelph 5
95/6 Slapshot 85
99/0 Hamilton Bulldogs
99/0 Hamilton Bulldogs/ Staz
00/1 Hamilton Bulldogs
00/1 Hamilton Bulldogs/ Staz
98/9 Hartford Wolf Pack
97/8 Indianapolis Ice 22
96/7 Springfield Falcons
95/6 Guelph Storm

RISK, DAVE
99/0 Charlotte Checkers

RISKU, RAINER
80/1 Mallasjuoma 19
78/9 SM-Liiga 85

RISSLING, GARY
84/5 PITT / Heinz

RISSLING, GARY
02/3 Fleer Throwbacks 85

RITA, JANI
02/3 Calder 69
02/3 Cardset 253
02/3 Choice Prospects 37
02/3 O-Pee-Chee 287
02/3 Pacific Complete 542
02/3 SPx 110
02/3 Stadium 117
02/3 Topps 287
02/3 T. Chrome 146
02/3 To. Limited 287
02/3 Upper Deck 314
02/3 UD Foundations 129
02/3 UD Piece 130
02/3 UD Vintage 332
98/9 Cardset 106
99/0 Cardset 60, MW 5
00/1 Cardset 45, NG-4
99/0 SPx 171
01/2 SPx 173
98/9 SPx Prospects 67
98/9 UD Black Diam. 97
01/2 Hamilton Bulldogs
01/2 Hamilton Bulldogs/ Staz
02/3 Hamilton Bulldogs

RITCHIE, BYRON
99/0 BAP Mem. 7
01/2 BAP Mem. 309
97 Bowman 108
99/0 NHL Power Play
99/0 Pacific 83
01/2 Parkhurst 357
99/0 SP Authentic 95
99/0 UD MVP Cup 41
00/1 Victory 274
98/9 CARO / Highwoods
00/1 Cincinnati Cyclones
98/9 New Haven Beast 5
93/4 Lethbridge Hurricanes
95/6 Lethbridge Hurricanes

RITCHIE, DARREN
94/5 Slapshot Memorial 40
95/6 Saint John Flames
92/3 Brandon Wheat Kings

RITCHIE, JIM
89/0 Soo Greyhounds

RITTIS, DOMENIC
93/4 Lethbridge Hurricanes

RIUTTA, BRUCE
72 Semic Sticker 120

RIUTTA, TOPI
99/0 Cardset 277

RIVA, DAN
01/2 Manchester Monarchs
99/0 Milwaukee Admirals
00/1 Milwaukee Admirals

RIVARD, FERN
74/5 Loblaws

RIVARD, FRANÇOIS*
91/2 7th...Sketch LHJMQ 130

RIVARD, JEAN-FRANÇOIS
90/1 7th..Sketch LHJMQ 102
91/2 7th...Sketch LHJMQ 181
99/0 Rockford IceHogs
00/1 Rockford IceHogs
01/2 Rockford IceHogs

RIVARD, STEFAN
93/4 Slapshot / North Bay 12
94/5 Slapshot / North Bay 14

RIVERS, A.J.
97/8 Halifax Moosehead

RIVERS, ANDY
84/5 Kingston Canadians
86/7 Kingston Canadians

RIVERS, DARYL
95/6 Slapshot 280

RIVERS, GUS
29/0 La Presse

RIVERS, JAMIE
00/1 BAP Mem. 384
95/6 Bowman 132
95/6 Classic 97
95/6 Donruss 342, C3TWC-7
95/6 Edge Ice 95
95/6 Future Legends 40
96/7 Leaf 236
94/5 L. Limited CAN 8
01/2 O-Pee-Chee 255
97/8 Omega 198
98/9 Pacific 372
94/5 Pinnacle 526
96/7 Pinnacle 216
97/8 Pi. Be A Player 231, ✍ Aut. 231
97/8 Score SLou. 13
91/2 7th...Sketch OHL 257
94/5 Sig. Rookies 36, ✍ 36
94/5 SR Auto-Phonex B1, ✍ B1
95/6 SBx Impact 218
96/7 SBx Impact 158
93/4 Slapshot / Sudbury 8
94/5 Slapshot / Promo
94/5 Slapshot / Sudbury 7
94/5 SP 141
95/6 Topps 21CJ
01/2 Topps 255
94/5 Topps Finest 152
94/5 Upper Deck 501
95/6 Upper Deck 477
96/7 Upper Deck 145
98/9 Upper Deck 359
98/9 UD G. Reserve 359
00/1 OTTA
91/2 Sudbury Wolves
92/3 Sudbury Wolves
93/4 Sudbury Wolves

RIVERS, SHAWN
93/4 Cla. Prospects 107
96/7 DEL 8
95/6 Edge Ice 108
93/4 Score 470
90/1 7th..Sketch OHL 393
91/2 7th...Sketch OHL 260
94/5 SR Tetrad CXIII, ✍ Aut.
92/3 Atlanta Knights
93/4 Atlanta Knights
90/1 Sudbury Wolves
91/2 Sudbury Wolves

RIVERS, WAYNE
72/3 O-Pee-Chee 315
74/5 OPC WHA 13
75/6 OPC WHA 38
73/4 Quaker Oats 44
63/4 Topps 17
64/5 Toronto Star Action
76/7 San Diego Mariners

RIVET, ADAM
99/0 Hull Olympiques BN
99/0 Hull Olympiques 20
00/1 Hull Olympiques 20

RIVET, CRAIG
02/3 First Edition 179
02/3 Pacific Complete 314
02/3 Parkhurst ✂ TT7
02/3 Sports Vault 58
02/3 To. Total 326
02/3 Upper Deck 341
02/3 UD Vintage 136
95/6 Leaf 310
97/8 Pa. Dynagon BKS-51
97/8 Pi. Be A Player 102, ✍ Aut. 102
91/2 7th...Sketch OHL 235
93/4 Slapshot / Kingston 21
99/0 Stadium 76
97/8 MONT
00/1 MONT
01/2 MONT
02/3 MONT
94/5 Fredericton Canadiens
95/6 Fredericton Canadiens
96/7 Fredericton Canadiens

ROACH, ANDY
98/9 EBK IHL All-Star
99/0 Eishockey 126
01/2 UD DEL 175
98/9 Long Beach Ice Dogs

ROACH, BRENT
02/3 Hull Olympiques

ROACH, BRENT G.
00/1 Hull Olympiques 18
01/2 Hull Olympiques 17

ROACH, DAVE
88/9 ProCards / Cape Breton

ROACH, GARY
91/2 7th...Sketch OHL 337
93/4 Slapshot / S.S.Marie 13
94/5 Slapshot / North Bay 23
98/9 Louisiana Ice Gators
93/4 Soo Greyhounds 14

ROACH, HAYLEY
95/6 Sheffield Steelers

ROACH, JOHN
33/4 Anonymous 18
33/4 Canadian Gum
24/5 Champ's Cigarettes
29/0 La Presse
33/4 O-Pee-Chee 53
23/4 William Paterson 28
24/5 William Paterson 52
33/4 WWGum 67

ROACH, MICKEY
24/5 Champ's Cigarettes
24/5 Maple Crispette [V130] 23
23/4 William Paterson 38
24/5 William Paterson 18

ROB, LUBOS
94/5 APS 106
95/6 APS 67
96/7 APS 252
97/8 APS 277
98/9 Cardset 161
97/8 DS 32
99/0 DS 39
00/1 DS 80
96/7 DS Sticker 87
97/8 DS Sticker 75
98/9 OFS 418
99/0 OFS 186
00/1 OFS 17
01/2 OFS 145
93 Semic Sticker 97

ROBAZZA, RINO
63/4 Québec Aces
65/6 Québec Aces
61/2 Topps 39

ROBB, DOUG
81/2 Milwaukee Admirals

ROBBINS, ADAM
95/6 Slapshot 41
97/8 Fort Worth Brahmas

ROBBINS, MATT
93/4 Cla. Prospects 230
96/7 Charlotte Checkers

ROBERGE, JEAN
90/1 7th..Sketch LHJMQ 53
91/2 7th...Sketch LHJMQ 234

ROBERGE, MARIO
92/3 Durivage 27
93/4 Durivage 16
92/3 Parkhurst 322
91/2 Pro Set 415
88/9 ProCards / Sherbrooke
89/0 ProCards AHL 187
90/1 ProCards 57
91/2 MONT
92/3 MONT
93/4 MONT
93/4 MONT / Export
95/6 Fredericton Canadiens

ROBERGE, MARIO
02/3 Fleer Throwbacks 90

ROBERGE, ROGER
52/3 Laval Dairy Update 44
52/3 St. Lawrence 73

ROBERGE, SERGE
88/9 ProCards / Sherbrooke
89/0 ProCards AHL 200
90/1 ProCards 454
91/2 ProCards 538
90/1 Halifax Citadels
95/6 Rochester Americans

ROBERGE, SERGE
02/3 Fleer Throwbacks 91

ROBERT, CLAUDE
51/2 Laval Dairy 17
52/3 St. Lawrence 47

ROBERT, JONATHAN
00/1 Sherbrooke Castors 9
01/2 Sherbrooke Castors 12

ROBERT, RENÉ
79/0 Dernière Heure
72/3 Eddie Sargent 42
74/5 Lipton Soup 24
74/5 Loblaws
72/3 O-Pee-Chee 2
73/4 O-Pee-Chee 139
74/5 O-Pee-Chee 42
74/5 O-Pee-Chee 142
75/6 O-Pee-Chee 46
75/6 O-Pee-Chee 296
75/6 O-Pee-Chee 315
76/7 O-Pee-Chee 42
76/7 O-Pee-Chee 214
77/8 O-Pee-Chee 222
78/9 O-Pee-Chee 188
79/0 O-Pee-Chee 12
80/1 O-Pee-Chee 239
80/1 O-Pee-Chee 259
81/2 O-Pee-Chee 322
82/3 O-Pee-Chee 330
72/3 Topps 161
73/4 Topps 139
74/5 Topps 42
74/5 Topps 142
75/6 Topps 46
75/6 Topps 296
75/6 Topps 315
76/7 Topps 42
76/7 Topps 214
77/8 Topps 222
78/9 Topps 188
79/0 Topps 12
80/1 Topps 239
80/1 Topps 259
71/2 Toronto Sun Photo
01/2 UD Legends 8
72/3 BUFF
73/4 BUFF
74/5 BUFF
75/6 BUFF / Linnett
93/4 BUFF / Noco
79/0 COLR
71/2 PITT / Sportcolor
81/2 TORO

ROBERT, RYAN
00/1 Toronto St. Mike's

ROBERTO, PHIL
71/2 Eddie Sargent 109
74/5 Loblaws
74/5 Loblaws Update
71/2 O-Pee-Chee 228
72/3 O-Pee-Chee 82
73/4 O-Pee-Chee 3
74/5 O-Pee-Chee 208
75/6 O-Pee-Chee 80
76/7 O-Pee-Chee 345
72/3 Topps 52
73/4 Topps 151
74/5 Topps 208
75/6 Topps 80
71/2 Toronto Sun Photo
76/7 COLR / Hockey Talk
69/0 MONT / Pro Star
71/2 MONT / Pro Star
71/2 MONT / Pro Star
71/2 SLOU
72/3 SLOU
73/4 SLOU
93/4 Birmingham Bulls
94/5 Birmingham Bulls
95/6 Birmingham Bulls

ROBERTS, ALEX
90/1 ProCards 408
92/3 Toledo Storm WIOT
92/3 Toledo Storm

ROBERTS, BOBBY
51/2 Laval Dairy 103

ROBERTS, CORY
00/1 Owen Sound Attack 1
01/2 Owen Sound Attack

ROBERTS, DAVID
93/4 Classic 76
94/5 Classic 106, T58, ✍ Aut.
94/5 Classic 4 Sport 141
95/6 Edge Ice C1
93/4 Fleer Ultra 495
94/5 Leaf 478
95/6 Leaf 13
97/8 Limited 31
97/8 Pa. Invincible R-204
95/6 Panini Sticker 191
97/8 Panini Sticker 240
94/5 Parkhurst 201
95/6 Parkhurst 179
95/6 Pinnacle 157
96/7 Pi. Be A Player 93, ✍ Aut. 93
93/4 Power Play 515
93/4 Premier - USA Hockey 16
94/5 Score 222
95/6 Score 286
97/8 Score Vanc. 19
94 Semic 134
94/5 SR Auto-Phonex 36, ✍ 36
95/6 SBx Emotion 152
95/6 Topps 43
93/4 To. Stadium - Team U.S.A. 20
97/8 UD Coll. Choice 265
01/2 UD DEL 41
96/7 VANC / IGA
00/1 Grand Rapids Griffins
98/9 Michigan K-Wings
94/5 Peoria Rivermen

ROBERTS, DOUG
70/1 Eddie Sargent 138
72/3 Eddie Sargent 26
70/1 Esso Power Player
74/5 Loblaws
68/9 O-Pee-Chee 88
69/0 O-Pee-Chee 81
70/1 O-Pee-Chee 71
73/4 O-Pee-Chee 207
74/5 O-Pee-Chee 312
67/8 Topps 50
68/9 Topps 88
69/0 Topps 81
70/1 Topps 71
71/2 Topps 83

ROBERTS, GARY
02/3 Atomic 93, -SC 15
02/3 BAP Mem. 191, ✂ SC3
02/3 Exclusive 162
02/3 First Edition 200, 427H
02/3 Heads Up 117, ✂ GWQ 26
02/3 McDonald's 37, ✂ JP 18
02/3 O-Pee-Chee 88
02/3 Pacific 368
02/3 Pacific Complete 468
02/3 Parkhurst 32, ✂ GJ10, ✂ SJ10, ✂ TT3
02/3 Parkhurst Retro 84
02/3 Pr. Stock Reserve 93
02/3 PS Titanium ✂ GWJ 67
02/3 Quest for the Cup ✂ GWJ 22
02/3 Slam Card
02/3 Sports Vault 137
02/3 Stadium 80
02/3 Topps 88
02/3 T. Chrome 56
02/3 To. Limited 88
02/3 To. Total 184
02/3 Ultimate Mem. ✂ Numerology [Robinson & Yzerman]
02/3 Upper Deck 162
02/3 UD Classic 92
02/3 UD MVP 172
02/3 UD Vintage 238
02/3 Vanguard ✂ GWJ 44
02/3 Victory 201
01/2 Adrenaline 184
99/0 BAP Mem. 153
00/1 BAP Mem. 115, 400
01/2 BAP Mem. 175
01/2 BAP Update ✂ H30
96/7 Bic.Sports Aces 2-C
90/1 Bowman 95
91/2 Bowman 263
92/3 Bowman 109
92/3 Bowman 214
01/2 Bowman 94
00/1 Crown Royale 101
01/2 Crown Royale 133
93/4 Donruss 52
94/5 Donruss 143
95/6 Donruss 372
97/8 Do. Preferred 63
97/8 Do. Priority 106
93/4 EA Sports 22
94/5 Flair 28
94/5 Fleer 35
92/3 Fleer Ultra 29
93/4 Fleer Ultra 187
94/5 Fleer Ultra 35, RLS-7
95/6 Fleer Ultra 28
01/2 Heads Up 91
95/6 Hoyle / West. K-Diamond
94/5 Kraft / HH
93/4 Leaf 36
94/5 Leaf 326
95/6 Leaf 277
94/5 L. Limited 114
96/7 Maggers 25
93/4 McDonald's McD-11
01/2 McDonald's -HP 10
99/0 Millenium 53, ✍ Aut. 53
98/9 NHL Power Play
90/1 OPC/Topps 161
91/2 O-Pee-Chee 320
92/3 O-Pee-Chee 72
01/2 O-Pee-Chee 80
89/0 O-Pee-Chee 202
91/2 OPC Premier 126
92/3 OPC Premier SP14
89/0 opcSticker 98-235
97/8 Omega 45
98/9 Omega 46
99/0 Omega 49
98/9 Pacific 140
99/0 Pacific 80
00/1 Pacific 89
01/2 Pacific 372
97/8 Pa. Paramount 39
98/9 Pa. Paramount 42
99/0 Pa. Paramount 50
97/8 Pa. Revolution 26
87/8 Panini Sticker 217
88/9 Panini Sticker 15
89/0 Panini Sticker 35
90/1 Panini Sticker 179
90/1 Panini/CGY 19
91/2 Panini Sticker 52
92/3 Panini Sticker 45
93/4 Panini Sticker 181
94/5 Panini Sticker 160
95/6 Panini Sticker 236
96/7 Panini Sticker 149, 240
98/9 Panini Sticker 28
99/0 Panini Sticker 50
91/2 Parkhurst 24
91/2 Parkhurst 436
92/3 Parkhurst 22
92/3 Parkhurst CP8
93/4 Parkhurst 302
94/5 Parkhurst V29
95/6 Parkhurst 301
01/2 Parkhurst 114, ✂ PS51
94/5 Parkie SE27
91/2 Pinnacle 37
92/3 Pinnacle 3
92/3 Pinnacle 242
93/4 Pinnacle 55
94/5 Pinnacle 115, NL16
95/6 Pinnacle 137
97/8 Pinnacle 170
97/8 Pi. Be A Player 73, ✍ Aut. 73
95/6 Pi. Summit 150
95/6 Playoff 19
94/5 POG 61
94/5 POG / Western 18
95/6 POG 55
93/4 Power Play 42
93/4 Premier 382
93/4 Premier 510
94/5 Premier 445, TF-16
00/1 Pr. Stock ✂ GUG 98
00/1 PS Titanium 92, ✂ GUG-47
01/2 PS Titanium 131
95/6 Pro Magnet 44
90/1 Pro Set 45
91/2 Pro Set 30
92/3 Pro Set 21
92/3 Pro Set TL 1
91/2 Pro Set Platinum 161
99/0 Revolution 31
90/1 Score 106
91/2 Score 199
91/2 Score CAN 199
92/3 Score 322
92/3 Score SS 1
93/4 Score 241
93/4 Score/CAN DD4
93/4 Score PiAS 29
94/5 Score 186, CI-12
95/6 Score 97
94/5 Select 147
93 Semic Sticker 208
00/1 Signature 249
95/6 SBx Emotion 25
97/8 SP Authentic 26
00/1 SP Authentic 84
00/1 SPx 148
99/0 Stadium 102
00/1 Stadium 223
01/2 Stadium 85
92/3 Topps 116
95/6 Topps 78
99/0 Topps 50
00/1 Topps 199
01/2 Topps 80, ✍ CA
99/0 To. Chrome 50
00/1 To. Chrome 133
01/2 To. Chrome 80
94/5 Topps Finest 82, DF-19
00/1 To. Heritage 109
01/2 To. Heritage 106
91/2 To. Stadium 126
92/3 To. Stadium 48
93/4 To. Stadium 235
93/4 To. Stadium - AS
93/4 To. Stadium - Finest 9
94/5 To. Stadium 230
98/9 UD Choice 36
00/1 UD Heroes 109
90/1 Upper Deck 29
91/2 Upper Deck 190
92/3 Upper Deck 289
93/4 Upper Deck 151, HT-3, SP-25
94/5 Upper Deck 20, SP-14
95/6 Upper Deck 19
97/8 Upper Deck 240
98/9 Upper Deck 236
99/0 Upper Deck 33
00/1 Upper Deck 392
01/2 Upper Deck 161
94/5 UD BAP ✍ 17
97/8 UD Black Diam. 86
98/9 UD Black Diam. 15
95/6 UD CC 174
98/9 UD G. Reserve 236
99/0 UD G. Reserve 33
92/3 UD Locker 32
98/9 UD MVP 41
99/0 UD MVP 42
01/2 UD MVP 174
00/1 UD Pros&Prosp. 82
00/1 UD Vintage 342
01/2 UD Vintage 240, 243
99/0 Victory 58
00/1 Victory 46
01/2 Victory 327
86/7 CALG / Red Rooster
87/8 CALG / Red Rooster
90/1 CALG / McGavin's
91/2 CALG / IGA
92/3 CALG / IGA 006
97/8 CARO / Sprint
98/9 CARO / Highwoods
86/7 Moncton G'Flames
82/3 Ottawa 67's
83/4 Ottawa 67's
84/5 Ottawa 67's

ROBERTS, GORD*
10/1 Imperial
10/1 Imperial 3
11/2 Imperial 33
12/3 Imperial 23

ROBERTS, GORD**
92/3 Bowman 197
91 C55 Reprint 33
92/3 Fleer Ultra 255
83 HHOF Postcard O13
83&87 HHOF 222
79/0 O-Pee-Chee 265
80/1 O-Pee-Chee 112
81/2 O-Pee-Chee 167
82/3 O-Pee-Chee 174
83/4 O-Pee-Chee 180
84/5 O-Pee-Chee 107
85/6 OPC/Topps 28
86/7 OPC/Topps 42
87/8 OPC/Topps 41
90/1 OPC/Topps 256
91/2 O-Pee-Chee 494
92/3 O-Pee-Chee 233
92/3 OPC Premier 86
83/4 OPC/Topps Sticker 114
85/6 OPC Sticker 43-171
87/8 OPC Sticker 55-196
88/9 Panini Sticker 102
90/1 Panini Sticker 269
91/2 Pinnacle 274
92/3 Pinnacle 312
93/4 Pinnacle 319
82/3 Post [Minn.]
93/4 Premier 275
90/1 Pro Set 271, 510
91/2 Pro Set 458
90/1 Score 245, 83T
91/2 Score 439
91/2 Score CAN 422
92/3 Score 201
93/4 Score 274
80/1 Topps 112
81/2 Topps 111 [West]
92/3 Topps 176
92/3 To. Stadium 185
93/4 To. Stadium 41

ROBERTS, GORD2
92/3 BOST / Postcard
81/2 MINS
82/3 MINS
83/4 MINS
84/5 MINS
84/5 MINS / 7-Eleven 5
85/6 MINS
86/7 MINS / 7-Eleven 10
87/8 MINS
97/8 PHOE / Coca-Cola
91/2 PITT / Elby's
87/8 SLOU
88/9 SLOU
88/9 SLOU / Kodak
89/0 SLOU / Kodak
83/4 Victoria Cougars

ROBERTS, JAMES D. (JIM)
77/8 O-Pee-Chee 392
78/9 O-Pee-Chee 342

ROBERTS, JAMES W. (JIM)
64-67 BeeHive-3 [Mont.]
64/5 Coke/Sprite [Mont.]
65/6 Coca-Cola
70/1 Dad's Cookies
70/1 Eddie Sargent 179
71/2 Eddie Sargent 181
72/3 Eddie Sargent 126
70/1 Esso Power Player
74/5 Loblaws
68/9 O-Pee-Chee 113
69/0 O-Pee-Chee 174
69/0 O-Pee-Chee 4in1
70/1 O-Pee-Chee 213
71/2 O-Pee-Chee 116
72/3 O-Pee-Chee 269
73/4 O-Pee-Chee 181
74/5 O-Pee-Chee 78
75/6 O-Pee-Chee 378
76/7 O-Pee-Chee 119, 217
77/8 O-Pee-Chee 281
95/6 Parkie 66-67 72
94/5 Parkie Tall 79
88/9 ProCards / Springfield
89/0 ProCards AHL 253
90/1 ProCards 182
72 Semic Sticker 182
68/9 Shirriff / SLou. 6
65/6 Topps 74
66/7 Topps 6
68/9 Topps 113
69/0 Topps 14
71/2 Topps 116
74/5 Topps 78
76/7 Topps 119
76/7 Topps 217
71/2 Toronto Sun Photo
67/8 MONT
69/0 MONT / Pro Star
71/2 MONT / Pro Star
72/3 MONT / Pro Star
73/4 MONT / Pro Star
74/5 MONT
75/6 MONT
76/7 MONT
86/7 PITT / Kodak

ROBERTS, JIM
72/3 Dernière Heure
73/4 Dernière Heure
72/3 Post 14
71/2 Pro Star Promotions

ROBERTS, MINPY
52/3 Anonymous 22

ROBERTS, SAM
02/3 Hull Olympiques

ROBERTS, SCOTT
93/4 Huntington Blizzard

ROBERTS, STEVE
91/2 Avant Garde BCJHL 27
92/3 BCJHL 50
00/1 Kudos 157
95/6 Dayton Bombers
96/7 Dayton Bombers
01/2 Belfast Giants
01/2 Sheffield Steelers GS

ROBERTS, TIM
92/3 Wheeling Thund'birds 13
93/4 Wheeling Thund'birds
94/5 Wheeling Thund'birds

ROBERTS, W.
23/4 Paulins Candy 6
24/5 Selkirks Crescent 5

ROBERTSON, BOB
52/3 Laval Dairy Update 103
52/3 St. Lawrence 69

ROBERTSON, CHRIS
88/9 Brandon Wheat Kings

ROBERTSON, EARL
34-43 BeeHive-1 [NYAm.]
39/0 O-Pee-Chee 63

ROBERTSON, FRED
33/4 Anonymous 15
32/3 Maple Leafs O'Keefe

ROBERTSON, GEORGE
45-64 BeeHive-2 [Mont.]
45-54 Quaker Oats

ROBERTSON, GRANT
83/4 Belleville Bulls
84/5 Belleville Bulls

ROBERTSON, JAMES
52/3 Anonymous 103

ROBERTSON, JOHN ROSS
83 HHOF Postcard G12
83&87 HHOF 102

ROBERTSON, KENNETH
52/3 Anonymous 99

ROBERTSON, KEVIN
91/2 Avant Garde BCJHL 110
92/3 BCJHL 170
90/1 7th..Sketch WHL 215
89/0 Brandon Wheat Kings
90/1 Brandon Wheat Kings

ROBERTSON, LAIN
94 Semic 329

ROBERTSON, ROGER
84/5 Belleville Bulls

ROBERTSON, TORRIE
85/6 O-Pee-Chee 218
86/7 O-Pee-Chee 214
90/1 Pro Set 77
90/1 ProCards 520
83/4 HART / Jr. Whalers
84/5 HART / Jr. Whalers
85/6 HART / Jr. Whalers
86/7 HART / Jr. Whalers
87/8 HART / Jr. Whalers
88/9 HART / Jr. Whalers
81/2 WASH
84/5 Victoria Cougars

ROBERTSSON, BERT
99/0 BAP Mem. 386
99/0 Omega 92
01/2 Cincinnati Mighty Ducks
00/1 Hartford Wolf Pack
96/7 Syracuse Crunch

ROBICHAUD, ANDRÉ
92/3 BCJHL 85

ROBICHAUD, RYAN
95/6 Slapshot 91
95/6 Guelph Storm
96/7 Guelph Storm

ROBIDAS, STÉPHANE
99/0 BAP Mem. 377
01/2 BAP Mem. 112
97 Bowman 65
99/0 Omega 124
02/3 DALL / Southwest
00/1 MONT
01/2 MONT
99/0 Québec Citadelles 7

ROBIDOUX, FLORENT
83/4 Springfield Indians 16

ROBILLARD, MARC
91/2 7th...Sketch OHL 83

ROBINS, TREVOR
00/1 Kudos 70
90/1 7th..Sketch WHL 88

91/2 7th...Sketch WHL 101
93/4 Kansas City Blades
94/5 Kansas City Blades 20
92/3 Brandon Wheat Kings
90/1 Saskatoon Blades
91/2 Saskatoon Blades

ROBINSON, BILL
51/2 Laval Dairy 107
90/1 7th..Sketch OHL 68
52/3 St. Lawrence 58

ROBINSON, BRANDON
00/1 Mississauga IceDogs

ROBINSON, CLAUDE
83 HHOF Postcard J12
83&87 HHOF 192

ROBINSON, DARCY
01/2 WBS Penguins
02/3 WBS Penguins

ROBINSON, DEREK
92/3 BCJHL 165

ROBINSON, DOUG
64/5 Coke/Sprite [Chic.]
65/6 Coca-Cola
70/1 Esso Power Player
68/9 O-Pee-Chee 160
95/6 Parkie 66-67 96
94/5 Parkie Tall 34
68/9 Shirriff / LosA. 12
64/5 Topps 84
65/6 Topps 26

ROBINSON, EARLE
34-43 BeeHive-1 [Maroons]
34-43 BeeHive-1 [Mont.]
35-40 Canada Starch
35-40 Canada Starch
33/4 O-Pee-Chee 55
36/7 O-Pee-Chee 115
37/8 O-Pee-Chee 165
34/5 Sweet Caporal
33/4 WWGum 5
37/8 World Wide Gum 85

ROBINSON, JANE
94/5 Classic W8

ROBINSON, JASON
95/6 Slapshot 195

ROBINSON, JUSTIN
94/5 Slapshot / North Bay 20
95/6 Slapshot 11

ROBINSON, LARRY
02/3 BAP Mem. / Stanley Cup
02/3 Parkhurst ✄ VT4
02/3 Ultimate Mem. ✄ CSTW, ✄ FS, ✄ Num, ✄ RAT, ✄ SF, ✄ VGJ
02/3 UD Piece / Giveaway (x2)
99/0 BAP Mem. CH-10, ✍ CH-10
90/1 Bowman 150
91/2 Bowman 177
92/3 Bowman 215
93/4 Cla. Prospects 53
77/8 Coke
72/3 Dernière Heure
73/4 Dernière Heure
80/1 Dernière Heure
83/4 Dernière Heure
88/9 Esso All-Star
83/4 Esso Stars
01/2 Fleer Greats 44, ✍ Aut., ✄ OSS
01/2 Fleer Legacy 46, ✄ ITC, ✄ TM
83/4 Funmate Puffy 2 [w/]
92/3 Future Trends C76 182
75/6 Hockey Heroes
93/4 Hockey Wit 92
84/5 Kellogg's 19
90/1 Kraft 47
91/2 Kraft 80
86/7 Kraft Sports 36
74/5 Loblaws
82/3 McDonald's Les Étoiles 17
82/3 McDonald's Les Étoiles 34
00/1 Mir Fetisov 39
73/4 O-Pee-Chee 237
74/5 O-Pee-Chee 280
75/6 O-Pee-Chee 241
76/7 O-Pee-Chee 151
77/8 OPC 2
77/8 O-Pee-Chee 30
77/8 O-Pee-Chee NS 18
78/9 O-Pee-Chee 210
78/9 O-Pee-Chee 264
78/9 O-Pee-Chee 329
79/0 O-Pee-Chee 50
80/1 O-Pee-Chee 84
80/1 O-Pee-Chee 230
81/2 O-Pee-Chee 179
81/2 O-Pee-Chee 196
82/3 O-Pee-Chee 191
83/4 O-Pee-Chee 195
84/5 O-Pee-Chee 270
85/6 OPC/Topps 147
86/7 OPC/Topps 62
86/7 OPC/Topps Box M
87/8 OPC/Topps 192
88/9 OPC/Topps 246
90/1 OPC/Topps 261
91/2 O-Pee-Chee 458
92/3 O-Pee-Chee 167
92/3 OPC - Anniv. 6
89/0 O-Pee-Chee 235
81/2 OPC Sticker 31
81/2 OPC Sticker 42
81/2 OPC Sticker 148
82/3 OPC/Topps Sticker 31
82/3 OPC/Topps Sticker 169
83/4 OPC/Topps Sticker 60
83/4 OPC/Topps Sticker 61
84/5 OPC Sticker 147
84/5 OPC Sticker 148
85/6 OPC Sticker 140
86/7 OPC Sticker 8
86/7 OPC Sticker 123-183
87/8 OPC Sticker 16
88/9 OPC Sticker 39-170
89/0 opcSticker 55-199
80/1 O-Pee-Chee Super 11
87/8 Panini Sticker 57
88/9 Panini Sticker 195
89/0 Panini Sticker 245
90/1 Panini Sticker 244
91/2 Panini Sticker 82
91/2 Parkhurst 74
01/2 Parkhurst ✍ PA59
80/1 Pepsi Bottle Cap
91/2 Pinnacle 208
91/2 Pinnacle 382
91/2 Pinnacle 403
81/2 Post 16
82/3 Post [Mont.]
90/1 Pro Set 125
91/2 Pro Set 104
87/8 Pro Sport CW1
90/1 Score 260
91/2 Score 291
91/2 Score CAN 511
84/5 7-Eleven
85/6 7-Eleven Superstars 10
83/4 Souhaits Keychain [Canadiens]
75/6 Topps 241
76/7 Topps 151
77/8 Topps 2
77/8 Topps 30
77/8 ToppsNS 18
78/9 Topps 210
78/9 Topps 264
79/0 Topps 50
80/1 Topps 84
80/1 Topps 230
81/2 Topps 31
84/5 Topps 82
86/7 OPC/Topps - Stick. 12
00/1 Topps SCH, ✍ SCHA
01/2 To. Chrome -CA9, ✍ CA9
91/2 To. Stadium 252
00/1 To. Stars 98, P7, P8, P9, ✍ CAI
01/2 T/O Archives 5, -Seat, ✄ Jers
01/2 Ultimate Mem. ✄ EA, ✄ LC, ✄ SCD, ✄ SCP, ✄ SCW
90/1 Upper Deck 52
91/2 Upper Deck 499
99/0 UD C. Legends 25, ✍ ES, ✄ JC3
00/1 UD Legends 69, ✍ ES, ✄ LGJ
92/3 UD Locker 48
99/0 UD Retro 100, TC11
83/4 Vachon 53-73
83/4 Vachon 53-85
89/0 LOSA / Smokey 7
90/1 LOSA / Smokey 9
73/4 MONT / Pro Star
74/5 MONT
75/6 MONT
76/7 MONT
77/8 MONT
78/9 MONT
79/0 MONT
80/1 MONT
81/2 MONT
82/3 MONT
82/3 MONT / Steinberg
83/4 MONT
84/5 MONT
85/6 MONT
85/6 MONT / Provigo
86/7 MONT
87/8 MONT
87/8 MONT / Kodak Poster
87/8 MONT / Vachon 72
87/8 MONT / Vachon 73
88/9 MONT

ROBINSON, MOE
77/8 Nova Scotia Voyageurs

ROBINSON, NATHAN
02/3 Grand Rapids Griffins
01/2 Belleville Bulls

ROBINSON, NICK
96/7 Soo Greyhounds

ROBINSON, ROB
00/1 Kudos 95
89/0 ProCards IHL 22
90/1 ProCards 79
92/3 Topps Gold 527
91/2 SLOU
92/3 Peoria Rivermen

ROBINSON, SCOTT
89/0 ProCards IHL 78
90/1 ProCards 118
91/2 ProCards 153
91/2 Milwaukee Admirals

ROBINSON, STEPHANE
84/5 Richelieu Riverains

ROBINSON, TODD
97 Bowman 93
98 Bowman 52
98 Bowman Chrome 52
95/6 Upper Deck 508
97/8 Portland Winter Hawks

ROBISON, JEFF
93/4 Raleigh Icecaps

ROBITAILLE, LUC
02/3 Atomic -PC 8, ✄ GWJ 9
02/3 BAP All-Star 75, ✄ ASJ
02/3 BAP Mem. 170, ✄ ASJ48, ✄ ASE18, ✄ ASN18, ✄ SCC7, ✄ TM3
02/3 Calder 26, ✄ GWJ 10
02/3 Crown Royale ✄ GWDP 9
02/3 Exclusive 66
02/3 First Edition 18, 324, ✄ Jers.
02/3 Heads Up 46, ✄ GWQ 9
02/3 In The GU 26, 126, ✄ GUJ38, ✄ SJ38
02/3 O-Pee-Chee 232, 318
02/3 Pacific 133
02/3 Pacific Complete 240
02/3 Parkhurst 124, ✄ GJ18, ✄ SJ18, ✄ HSHSJers
02/3 Parkhurst Retro 120
02/3 Pr. Stock Reserve ✄ 120
02/3 PS Titanium ✄ GWJ 26
02/3 Signature 153, GS-48, ✍ 153, ✄ SGJ38
02/3 Slam Card
02/3 SP Game-Used ✄ CF
02/3 SPx 130
02/3 Topps 232, 318
02/3 T. Chrome 126
02/3 To. Limited 232, 318
02/3 To. Total 52
02/3 Ultimate Mem. ✄ Emb, ✄ FS, ✄ ITN, ✄ LA, ✄ SCDE, ✄ SCDJ, ✄ SCDN
02/3 Upper Deck 66
02/3 UD Piece -AC10
02/3 UD Top Shelf ✄ CP, ✄ HH, ✄ HT, ✄ M (x2)
02/3 UD Vintage 92
02/3 Victory 80
94/5 Action Packed
01/2 Adrenaline 68
01/2 ASG History
01/2 Atomic 38
98/9 Aurora 89
99/0 Aurora 70, Stripe 70
00/1 Aurora 68, Pins. 68
98/9 Be A Player 61, M18, ✍ Aut. 61
99/0 BAP Mem. 162
00/1 BAP Mem. 51
01/2 BAP Mem. 95, 376, ✄ 500GS, ✄ SCP
01/2 BAP Update HSHS, ✄ HSHSJers (x2), H27, ✄ TP8
90/1 Bowman 152, -HT 12
91/2 Bowman 188
92/3 Bowman 70
92/3 Bowman 216
95/6 Bowman 23
01/2 Bowman 61
91 Canada Cup
99/0 Crown Royale 67, IE-13
00/1 Crown Royale 51
01/2 Crown Royale 55
93/4 Donruss 162
93/4 Donruss 395, WC
94/5 Donruss IM-9
95/6 Donruss 104, 348
96/7 Donruss 7
97/8 Donruss 90
96/7 Do. Canadian 64
97/8 Do. Canadian 68
95/6 Do. Elite 105
96/7 Do. Elite 78
97/8 Do. Elite 85
97/8 Do. Preferred 121
97/8 Do. Priority 32
97/8 Do. Studio 53
92/3 Durivage 28
93/4 Durivage 41
98/9 Dynagon Ice 90
99/0 Dynagon Ice 98
93/4 EA Sports 64
88/9 Esso All-Star
94/5 Flair 138, HN-7
94/5 Fleer 167
95/6 Fleer Metal 99
92/3 Fleer Ultra 87, -AS 11
93/4 Fleer Ultra 208
93/4 Fleer Ultra AS 13
93/4 Fleer Ultra RLS 9
94/5 Fleer Ultra 103, 350
95/6 Fleer Ultra 277
96/7 Fl. Ultra 111
88/9 Frito Lay
00 Gatorade Sticker
91/2 Gillette 13
95 Globe 94
01/2 Heads Up 37
93/4 Hockey Wit 96
99/0 HoloGrFX 28
95/6 Hoyle / East. 5-Club
92/3 Humpty Dumpty
94/5 Incomnet Phonecard
92/3 Kellogg's
90/1 Kraft 48, 75
91/2 Kraft 70
93/4 Kraft / KD
00/1 Kraft 3
93/4 Leaf 20
93/4 Leaf GLAS 9
94/5 Leaf 20, 463
95/6 Leaf 129
96/7 Leaf 134
97/8 Leaf 121
94/5 L. Limited 88
95/6 L. Limited 91
96/7 L. Limited 27
96/7 L. Preferred 13
97/8 Limited 75
96/7 Maggers 104
91/2 McDonald's Mc-14
92/3 McDonald's McD-12
93/4 McDonald's McH-03
98/9 McD's T13
99/0 McDonald's ✍ SS
01/2 McDonald's -HP 7
96/7 Metal Univ. 101
99/0 Millenium 122, ✍ Aut. 122
98/9 NHL Power Play
87/8 OPC/Topps 42
87/8 OPC/Topps Box D
88/9 OPC/Topps 124
88/9 OPC/Topps Box P
90/1 OPC/Topps 194, 209
91/2 O-Pee-Chee 260
91/2 O-Pee-Chee 405
92/3 O-Pee-Chee 6
01/2 O-Pee-Chee 54
89/0 OPC/Topps 88
98/9 OPC Chrome 174
98/9 OPC Leaders 35
90/1 OPC Premier 99
91/2 OPC Premier 34
88/9 OPC Stars 32
87/8 OPC Sticker 217
x87/8 OPC Sticker 122-134
x87/8 OPC Sticker 133-121
x87/8 OPC Sticker 177-175
x87/8 OPC Sticker 1x87-48
88/9 OPC Sticker 157
x88/9 OPC Sticker 114-244
89/0 opcSticker 148-267
97/8 Omega 112
98/9 Omega 112
99/0 Omega 111
98/9 Pacific 244
99/0 Pacific 196, TL-13
00/1 Pacific 201, GCDC-17
01/2 Pacific 186, 432, NAAS 8
97/8 Pacific CC 145
97/8 Pa. Crown Roy. 65
98/9 Pa. Crown Roy. 65
97/8 Pa. Invincible 91
97/8 Pa. Paramount 91
98/9 Pa. Paramount 107
99/0 Pa. Paramount -IAI-13
00/1 Pa. Paramount 114, FF-19, ✄ GUS-12
97/8 Pa. Revolution 66
98/9 Pa. Revolution 68
98/9 Panini Photocard
87/8 Panini Sticker 277
x87/8 Panini Sticker 379
88/9 Panini Sticker 78
89/0 Panini Sticker 95, 177
90/1 Panini Sticker 233, 331
91/2 Panini Sticker 91
91/2 Panini Sticker 324
92/3 Panini Sticker 65
92/3 Panini Sticker 288
93/4 Panini Sticker 201
94/5 Panini Sticker 174
95/6 Panini Sticker 61
96/7 Panini Sticker 105
99/0 Panini Sticker 258
00/1 Panini Sticker 166
95 Panini Worlds 21
91/2 Parkhurst 68
91/2 Parkhurst 224
92/3 Parkhurst 68
92/3 Parkhurst 501
93/4 Parkhurst 91
94/5 Parkhurst V67
95/6 Parkhurst 140
00/1 Parkhurst P-213
01/2 Parkhurst 215, ✄ 500GS, ✄ PS61, ✄ M7, ✄ M23
94/5 Parkie SE137
91/2 Pinnacle 17
91/2 Pinnacle 385
91/2 Pinnacle B-10
92/3 Pinnacle 175
92/3 Pinnacle 251
93/4 Pinnacle 145
93/4 Pinnacle NF 5
93/4 Pinnacle TP 4
94/5 Pinnacle 400, TP7
97/8 Pinnacle 149
96/7 Pi. Be A Player 12, ✍ Aut. 12
97/8 Pi. BeeHive 36
97/8 Pi. Certified 92
97/8 Pi. Inside 168
95/6 Pi. Summit 89, MH-14
96/7 Pi. Summit 13
97/8 Pi. Totally 92
95/6 Pi. Zenith 48
96/7 Pi. Zenith 36
95/6 Playoff 71, 286
96/7 POG 183
94/5 Post
93/4 Power Play 120
93/4 Power Play PL 13
93/4 Premier 90
93/4 Premier 180
94/5 Premier 346, 526, 540, TF-13
00/1 Premier Plus 73, ✍ CS
99/0 Prism 69
00/1 Pr. Stock 47, EA-10, PS-27, PSS-15
01/2 Pr. Stock 36
00/1 PS Titanium 43
01/2 PS Titanium 52
95/6 Pro Magnet 100
90/1 Pro Set 126, 341
91/2 Pro Set 95
91/2 Pro Set 286
92/3 Pro Set 72
91 Pro Set Awards AC9
91/2 Pro Set PotM P6
91/2 Pro Set Platinum 50
91/2 Puck / Pro Set 12
99/0 Revolution 71, TL-5, / CSC 71
00/1 Revolution 69, HD-18, NI-14, SM-7
90/1 Score 159, 360
90/1 Sco. Hot Cards 66
91/2 Score 3
91/2 Score 345
91/2 Score / Promo 3
91/2 Score CAN 3
91/2 Score CAN 375
92/3 Score 290
92/3 Score 498
93/4 Score 245
93/4 Score 451
93/4 Score DT 24
93/4 Score PIAS 37
94/5 Score DT10
95/6 Score 54, L-9
96/7 Score 113
97/8 Score 149
91/2 Score Shows 5
92/3 Seasons 10
94/5 Select 32, FL-10
95/6 Select CE 53
96/7 Select CE 13
94 Semic 92
93 Semic 353
95 Semic 89
89 Semic Sticker 68
91 Semic Sticker 70
92 Semic Sticker 89
93 Semic Sticker 204
00/1 Signature 204, HSHS, ✍ Aut. 35, ✄ J-33, ✄ HSHSJers
01/2 Signature C-23, ✍ Aut., ✄ 500GS, ✄ GUE30, ✄ GJ26, ✄ GSJ26, ✄ HSHSJers, ✄ ITN30, ✄ TM12
95/6 SBx Emotion 118
95/6 SBx Impact 113, IQ-14
94/5 SP 93
95/6 SP 97
97/8 SP 102
97/8 SP Authentic 77, I18
98/9 SP Authentic 38
99/0 SP Authentic 40, ✍ SotT
00/1 SP Authentic 43, ✍ SotT
01/2 SP Authentic 30, ✄ PP
00/1 SP GU 29
01/2 SP GU 21, ✄ AF
99/0 SPx 75
00/1 SPx 33
01/2 SPx 25
99/0 Stadium 27, Chrome 20
00/1 Stadium 146
94/5 Starting Lineup
95/6 SLU
95/6 Super Sticker 82
96/7 Team Out!
87/8 OPC/Topps - Stick. 12
88/9 OPC/Topps - Stick. 1
92/3 Topps 101
92/3 Topps 266
95/6 Topps 40, 362, 379, 2HG, HGC19
98/9 Topps 174
99/0 Topps 53
00/1 Topps 111, PC-10, NHL14, PP6
01/2 Topps 54
99/0 To. Chrome 53
00/1 To. Chrome 87, PC-10, RF5
01/2 To. Chrome 54
94/5 Topps Finest 89, DF-4
95/6 To. Finest 24
98/9 To. Finest 128
99/0 To. Gold Label 3
00/1 To. Gold Label 28, GG12
00/1 To. Heritage 40
01/2 To. Heritage 122, 166
96/7 To. Picks 87
99/0 To. Prmr. Plus 11
91/2 To. Stadium 159
92/3 To. Stadium 44
92/3 To. Stadium 247
93/4 To. Stadium 87
93/4 To. Stadium - AS
93/4 To. Stadium - Finest 7
94/5 To. Stadium 57, DAD 4
95/6 To. Stadium 100
00/1 To. Stars 58
95/6 T. Super Skills 56
98/9 UD Choice 98, BH12
00/1 UD Heroes 57
01/2 UD PlayMakers Ltd 37
00/1 UD Reserve 39, OS5
00/1 Ultimate Mem. ✍ U-44, ✄ J-40, ✄ Jers. 32, ✄ S-40
01/2 Ultimate Mem. ✄ 500GS, ✄ A8, ✄ ASGH, ✄ CT, ✄ DD, ✄ Emb., ✄ J, ✄ S&J, ✄ ITN, ✄ JE, ✄ JJ, ✄ NP, ✄ PP, ✄ RT, ✍ Aut.
99/0 Ult. Victory 41
90/1 Upper Deck 73
91/2 Upper Deck 145
91/2 Upper Deck 507
91/2 Upper Deck 623
92/3 Upper Deck 8
92/3 Upper Deck 216
92/3 Upper Deck G2
92/3 Upper Deck WG20
93/4 Upper Deck 231, 293, 414, GG8, HT17, SP-73
94/5 Upper Deck 194, SP-152
95/6 Upper Deck 8, 244, SE-144
97/8 Upper Deck 290
98/9 Upper Deck 104
99/0 Upper Deck 234, HOF12
00/1 Upper Deck 80, D7
01/2 Upper Deck 65 , SS7
00 ✄ UD APOH 500, ✍ 500
93/4 Upper Deck Be A Player 12
94/5 UD BAP R95, ✍ 113
97/8 UD Black Diam. 76
99/0 UD Black Diam. 45
00/1 UD Black Diam. 29
01/2 UD Challenge 31, CM5, FF4
95/6 UD CC 164
96/7 UD CC 171
97/8 UD Coll. Choice 170
98/9 UD G. Reserve 104
99/0 UD G. Reserve 234
99/0 UD Gretzky Excl. 64
01/2 UD Honor Roll 7, 37, ✄ GAJ, ✄ PPM
00/1 UD Ice 21
01/2 UD Ice 96
00/1 UD Legends 60, 61, SM10
92/3 UD Locker 33
98/9 UD MVP 97
99/0 UD MVP 96, ✍ PS
00/1 UD MVP 87
01/2 UD MVP 67, ✄ S
99/0 UD MVP Cup 85,CP5
99/0 UD Ovation 29
95/6 UD Post 8
96/7 UD Post
00/1 UD Pros&Prosp. 39
99/0 UD Retro 39
01/2 UD Top Shelf 16
00/1 UD Vintage 163, 173
01/2 UD Vintage 91
00/1 Vanguard 49
99/0 Victory 134
00/1 Victory 111
01/2 Victory 159, 423
99/0 WGretzky 81, ✄ TG
96 Wien 93
97/8 Zenith 41, Z56
87/8 LOSA
88/9 LOSA / Smokey
89/0 LOSA / Smokey 8
90/1 LOSA / Smokey 10
94/5 PITT / Foodland 14
99/0 Hull Olympiques BN

ROBITAILLE, MARC
99/0 St. John's Maple Leafs

ROBITAILLE, MIKE
71/2 Eddie Sargent 29
74/5 Loblaws
74/5 Loblaws Update
71/2 O-Pee-Chee 8
73/4 O-Pee-Chee 121
74/5 O-Pee-Chee 159
75/6 O-Pee-Chee 24
76/7 O-Pee-Chee 359
71/2 Topps 8
73/4 Topps 121
74/5 Topps 159
75/6 Topps 24
71/2 Toronto Sun Photo
72/3 BUFF
73/4 BUFF
74/5 VANC / Royal Bank
75/6 VANC / Royal Bank
76/7 VANC / Royal Bank

ROBITAILLE, PATRICE
98/9 BC Icemen 3
98/9 BC Icemen
96/7 Milwaukee Admirals
95/6 Peoria Rivermen
92/3 Clarkson G'Knights

ROBITAILLE, RANDY
02/3 Pacific 316
02/3 Upper Deck 385
00/1 BAP Mem. 175
01/2 BAP Mem. 351
00/1 Millenium C-36
99/0 NHL Power Play
99/0 Omega 130
01/2 Parkhurst 367
97/8 Score Bost. 12
00/1 Signature 135, ✍ 99
00/1 Topps 155
00/1 UD Heroes 67
97/8 Upper Deck 182
99/0 Upper Deck 246
00/1 Upper Deck 69
99/0 UD G. Reserve 246
00/1 Vanguard 55
99/0 Victory 18
99/0 WGretzky 92
01/2 Manchester Monarchs
97/8 Providence Bruins
98/9 Providence Bruins

ROBITAILLE, STEPHANE
98/9 DEL 51
99/0 Eishockey 174
00/1 UD DEL 118

ROBSON, B.
91/2 Air Canada SJHL 50

ROBSON, BLAKE
99/0 UD Sobey's 8
99/0 UD Prospects 34, 77

ROBSON, RYAN
94/5 Slapshot Memorial 42
95/6 Brandon Wheat Kings
98/9 Brandon Wheat Kings

ROCCA, TONY
84/5 Kingston Canadians

ROCCOARDO, JEFF
95/6 Las Vegas Thunder

ROCHE, DAVE
95/6 Bowman 144
93/4 Cla. 4 Sport 211
95/6 Donruss 287
97/8 Pacific CC 253
97/8 Score Pitt. 17
91/2 7th...Sketch OHL 139
93/4 Slapshot / Peterborough 3
93/4 Slapshot / Windsor 18
94/5 Slapshot / Windsor 20
95/6 PITT / Foodland 16
02/3 Albany River Rats
91/2 Peterborough Petes

ROCHE, DAVID
01/2 Cincinnati Mighty Ducks

ROCHE, DESSE
36-39 Diamond Match TT1
30/1 La Presse
33/4 WWGum 70

ROCHE, EARL
36-39 Diamond Match TT1
30/1 La Presse
33/4 WWGum 62

ROCHE, SCOTT
94/5 Classic DP9
95/6 Classic 54, 90
94/5 Sig. Rookies FF9, ✍ FF9
93/4 Slapshot / North Bay 21
94/5 Slapshot / North Bay 2
95/6 Slapshot 207, P
96/7 Peoria Rivermen
98/9 Peoria Rivermen

ROCHE, TRAVIS
01/2 BAP Mem. 349
01/2 SP GU 82
01/2 Upper Deck 429
01/2 UD Challenge 113
01/2 UD Ice 77
01/2 UD Premier 67

ROCHEFORT, DANNY
84/5 Richelieu Riverains

ROCHEFORT, LEON
71/2 Eddie Sargent 63
72/3 Eddie Sargent 81
68/9 O-Pee-Chee 95
69/0 O-Pee-Chee 105
69/0 O-Pee-Chee 4in1
71/2 O-Pee-Chee 135
72/3 O-Pee-Chee 204
75/6 O-Pee-Chee 374
63/4 Québec Aces
68/9 Shirriff / Phil. 9
Sport Flash 8
Sport Flash 8
68/9 Topps 95
69/0 Topps 105
71/2 Toronto Sun Photo
67/8 York
72/3 ATLF
67/8 MONT
71/2 MONT / Pro Star
74/5 VANC / Royal Bank

ROCHEFORT, NORMAND
91/2 Bowman 73
81/2 Dernière Heure
92/3 Durivage 44
82/3 McDonald's Les Étoiles 35
82/3 O-Pee-Chee 291
83/4 O-Pee-Chee 300
84/5 O-Pee-Chee 287
84/5 OPC Sticker 176
85/6 OPC Sticker 148-17
88/9 OPC Sticker 182-47
87/8 Panini Sticker 161
91/2 Pinnacle 273
82/3 Post [Québ.]
90/1 Pro Set 494
90/1 Score 149
91/2 Score 171
91/2 Score CAN 171
92/3 Score 377
83/4 Souhaits Keychain [Nordiques]
90/1 Upper Deck 437
83/4 Vachon 72-52
89/0 NYRA / Marine
80/1 QUÉB
81/2 QUÉB
82/3 QUÉB
83/4 QUÉB
84/5 QUÉB
85/6 QUÉB
85/6 QUÉB / Gene. Foods
85/6 QUÉB / McDonald's
86/7 QUÉB
86/7 QUÉB / Gene. Foods
86/7 QUÉB / McDonald's
86/7 QUÉB / Yum Yum
87/8 QUÉB / Gene. Foods
87/8 QUÉB / Yum Yum
93/4 Atlanta Knights
96/7 Kansas City Blades

ROCHEFORT, RICHARD
97 Bowman 21
94/5 Slapshot / Sudbury 15
95/6 Slapshot 399
97/8 Albany River Rats
98/9 Albany River Rats
99/0 Albany River Rats
00/1 Albany River Rats
01/2 Albany River Rats
96/7 Sudbury Wolves

ROCHETTE, ERIC
90/1 7th..Sketch LHJMQ 22
91 7th..Sketch Mem.Cup 35

ROCHETTE, GAETON
77/8 Nova Scotia Voyageurs

ROCHON, CARLE
00/1 Hull Olympiques 14

ROCHON, FRANK
75/6 OPC WHA 51

ROCHON, PATRICK
98/9 EBK ECHL All-Star
96/7 Mississippi S'Wolves
98/9 Mississippi S'Wolves
99/0 Mississippi S'Wolves

ROCK, MATT
99/0 Guelph Storm

ROCKMAN, GREG
02/3 Coventry Blaze

RODDEN, MIKE
83 HHOF Postcard L15
83&87 HHOF 164

RODEK, STAN
52/3 Anonymous 168

RODERICK, JOHN
93/4 Peoria Rivermen

RODGERS, ANDREW
97/8 Pensacola Ice Pilots

RODGERS, MARC
91/2 7th...Sketch LHJMQ 45
99/0 SP Authentic 102
99/0 To. Prmr. Plus 91
99/0 Ult. Victory 97
98/9 Chicago Wolves Champs
93/4 Las Vegas Thunder
94/5 Las Vegas Thunder
95/6 Las Vegas Thunder
99/0 Manitoba Moose
92/3 Wheeling Thund'birds 14

RODGERS, MARC"?
93/4 Knoxville Cherokees

RODIGUE, SYLVAIN
91 7th..Sketch Mem.Cup 25

RODINE, DMITRI
01/2 OFS 196
96/7 Flint Generals

RODMAN, ANDY
87/8 Brockville Braves

RODMAN, DAVID
01/2 Val d'Or Foreurs 24
02/3 Val d'Or Foreurs

RODMAN, MARCEL
00/1 UD Prospects 20

RODNEY, BRYAN
00/1 Ottawa 67's 18
01/2 Ottawa 67's 20

RODRIGUE, ALEX
94/5 Slapshot Memorial 55

RODRIGUE, GUILLAUME
96/7 Rimouski Océanic

RODRIGUE, JACQUE
96/7 Dayton Ice Bandits
98/9 Odessa Jackalopes
99/0 Odessa Jackalopes

RODRIGUE, SYLVAIN
90/1 7th...Sketch LHJMQ 20
91/2 7th...Sketch LHJMQ 96

ROE, ZACK
01/2 Regina Pats

ROED, PETER
00/1 UD DEL 109
97/8 Kentucky Tho'blades
99/0 Kentucky Tho'blades

ROEDGER, ROY
82 Semic Sticker 121
89 Semic Sticker 122

ROENICK, JEREMY
02/3 Atomic 75, -NPU 7, -SC 11
02/3 BAP All-Star 76, ✄ ASJ
02/3 BAP Mem. 80, 252, ✄ ASJ49, ✄ AST2, ✄ AST17, ✄ HSHSJers 19, ✄ TM9
02/3 Bowman 77
02/3 Crown Royale 72, ✄ GWJ 15
02/3 eTopps 50
02/3 Exclusive 129
02/3 First Edition 149, 309, 374, 402H, ✄ Jers., ✄ HSHSJers 27, ✄ TSL 14
02/3 Heads Up 93, ✄ GWQ 20
02/3 In The GU 55, 155, ✄ E14, ✄ GUJ43, ✄ SJ14
02/3 O-Pee-Chee 87, 314
02/3 Pacific 287, -MA 15
02/3 Pacific Complete 252
02/3 Parkhurst 104, ✄ GJ32, ✄ SJ32, ✄ HSHSJers, ✄ MS1, ✄ PP4
02/3 Parkhurst Retro 26, ✄ RF22, ✄ RJ31, ✄ RSJ29
02/3 Pr. Stock Reserve 75
02/3 PS Titanium 76
02/3 Quest for the Cup 77, -CTC 14, ✄ GWJ 16
02/3 Signature 134, ✍ 134, ✄ FJ22, ✄ SGJ14, ✄ TQ3
02/3 Slam Card
02/3 SP Authentic 65, ✄ SP, ✄ DP
02/3 SP GU 37, ✄ AF (x2), ✄ PC, ✄ PH (x2), ✄ TG
02/3 Sports Vault 107
02/3 SPx 55, 138, ✄ WM, ✄ M
02/3 Stadium 16, -W-6
02/3 Topps 87, 314, HHU10
02/3 T. Chrome 55
02/3 To. Heritage 20, 112
02/3 To. Limited 87, 314
02/3 To. Total 239, TP9
02/3 UD Superstars 190, ✄ LLT
02/3 Ultimate Mem. ✄ Emb, ✄ FS, ✄ GUJ, ✄ ITN, ✄ JE, ✄ JJ
02/3 Upper Deck 127, -NC11, -SS12, ✄ PP, ✄ UDPL
02/3 UD Artistic 65, R65, CG17, UD10, ✄ AT, / Art
02/3 UD Classic 72, ✄ HH, ✄ HR, ✄ SC
02/3 UD Foundations 72
02/3 UD Honor 52, -SG23, ✄ GA
02/3 UD Mask 62, ✄ IO
02/3 UD MVP 136, VF11
02/3 UD Piece 65
02/3 UD Premier 40, ✄ Jers (x2), ✄ JD, ✄ Patch
02/3 UD Rookie 72, ✄ 153c, ✄ 156c, ✄ DJ
02/3 UD Top Shelf 63, ✄ CP, ✄ HT, ✄ M (x2)
02/3 UD Vintage 189, 282, 301, 312, GB 189, T47
02/3 Vanguard 75
02/3 Victory 157, -NP58
94/5 Action Packed
01/2 Adrenaline 143
01/2 ASG History
01/2 Atomic 74
98/9 Aurora 146
99/0 Aurora 111, Stripe 111
00/1 Aurora 112, Pins. 112
98/9 Be A Player 107, P-12, ✍ Aut. 107, ✄ AS-17, ✄ S-16
99/0 BAP Mem. 9, H-3, ✄ TM-1, ✄ TM-31
00/1 BAP Mem. 235, ✄ J-1, ✄ TM-5, ✄ TM-38
01/2 BAP Mem. 186, 355, ✄ ASD, ✄ AST, ✄ CoO
01/2 BAP Update ✄ HSHSJers, ✄ H22, ✄ TP11
96/7 Bic.Sports Aces 5-D
97/8 Bicycle 6-Spade
95/6 Bicycle Sports Aces 5-Diamond
90/1 Bowman 1
91/2 Bowman 386
91/2 Bowman 403
92/3 Bowman 78
92/3 Bowman 217
95/6 Bowman 20
01/2 Bowman 49
98/9 Bowman's Best 55
99/0 Crown Royale 109, IE-21
00/1 Crown Royale 84, ✄ JR-8
01/2 Crown Royale 109, JotC 24
95/6 DEL 446
93/4 Donruss 67
93/4 Donruss E
93/4 Donruss ES 6
94/5 Donruss 222, D-5, ES-9
95/6 Donruss 27, I-7, PP-1
96/7 Donruss 2, D-9, HL-4
97/8 Donruss 6
96/7 Do. Canadian 57
97/8 Do. Canadian 100, SCS-7
95/6 Do. Elite 47, CE-14
96/7 Do. Elite 27, S-12
97/8 Do. Elite 77
97/8 Do. Preferred 88
97/8 Do. Priority 133, Post-33, Stamp-33
97/8 Do. Studio 40, P-30
98/9 Dynagon Ice 144
99/0 Dynagon Ice 153
93/4 EA Sports 27
97/8 Esso 28
94/5 Flair 36, CIS-10, SP-9
96/7 Flair 72
94/5 Fleer 45, SA-8
96/7 Fleer 18, ART-19
95/6 Fleer Metal 28, IS-17
96/7 Fl. Picks F50-39, DL-2, JE-10
92/3 Fleer Ultra 41, -PH 1-12, ✍ Aut.
93/4 Fleer Ultra 186
93/4 Fleer Ultra PP 8
94/5 Fleer Ultra 44, SM-9, UP-8
95/6 Fleer Ultra 35, 396, CC-15, PP-7, UV-8
96/7 Fl. Ultra 135
91/2 Gillette 13
95 Globe 117
96/7 Got-Um
01/2 Heads Up 74, SM 13, ✄ JQ 16
93/4 Hockey Wit 103
99/0 HoloGrFX 46
95/6 Hoyle / West. A-Heart
92/3 Humpty Dumpty
94/5 Incomnet Phonecard
91/2 Kellogg's / Score 5
91/2 Kraft 56
92/3 Kraft / Kraft Singles
93/4 Kraft / PB
94/5 Kraft / SS
00/1 Kraft 23
93/4 Leaf 27
93/4 Leaf SSS 7
94/5 Leaf 63, FOI-2, GLS-2, LL-5
95/6 Leaf 116
96/7 Leaf 191, FOI-11, LL-13
97/8 Leaf 22
94/5 L. Limited 61, G-8
95/6 L. Limited 80, SG-12
96/7 L. Limited 86
96/7 L. Preferred 4
97/8 Limited 105, 120, 140, FG-35
96/7 Maggers 30
92/3 McDonald's McD-13
93/4 McDonald's McD-12
94/5 McDonald's McD-20
95/6 McDonald's McD-16
96/7 McDonald's McD-12
96/7 Metal Univ. 121
99/0 Millenium 190, ✍ Aut. 190, ✄ J-29, ✄ JS-29
95/6 Cool Trade 3
98/9 NHL Power Play
90/1 OPC/Topps 7
91/2 O-Pee-Chee 106
91/2 O-Pee-Chee 345
92/3 O-Pee-Chee 383
92/3 OPC - Anniv. 23
01/2 O-Pee-Chee 94, Update 94
98/9 OPC Chrome 171
90/1 OPC Premier 100
91/2 OPC Premier 52
91/2 OPC Premier 174
92/3 OPC Premier SP5
97/8 Omega 176
98/9 Omega 187
99/0 Omega 184, CC-16
98/9 Pacific 97
99/0 Pacific 325, GC-29
00/1 Pacific 321, GCDC-27
01/2 Pacific 308, 418, 438
97/8 Pacific CC 97, CS-16, SS-7B, TC-19
97/8 Pa. Crown Roy. 105
98/9 Pa. Crown Roy. 104
97/8 Pa. Dynagon 97, DD-12A, T-63
97/8 Pa. Invincible 108, FP-27
97/8 Pa. Paramount 142
98/9 Pa. Paramount 184
99/0 Pa. Paramount 182, PB-29
00/1 Pa. Paramount 193, FF-29
97/8 Pa. Revolution 108
98/9 Pa. Revolution 111, -ASG 25, -Show. 29
98/9 Panini Photocard
90/1 Panini Sticker 201
91/2 Panini Sticker 12
92/3 Panini Sticker 4
93/4 Panini Sticker M
94/5 Panini Sticker 127, HH
95/6 Panini Sticker 157
96/7 Panini Sticker 158
97/8 Panini Sticker 157
98/9 Panini Sticker 150
99/0 Panini Sticker 281
00/1 Panini Sticker 186
91/2 Parkhurst 29
91/2 Parkhurst 439
92/3 Parkhurst 31
92/3 Parkhurst CP2
93/4 Parkhurst 309
93/4 Parkhurst W6
94/5 Parkhurst 302, V65, YCTG-5
95/6 Parkhurst 307
00/1 Parkhurst P-95
01/2 Parkhurst 3, ✄ PS67, ✄ HSHSJers, ✄ M22, ✄ M56
94/5 Parkie SE35
91/2 Pinnacle 120
91/2 Pinnacle 359
92/3 Pinnacle 10
92/3 Pinnacle 256
92/3 Pinnacle T2K 27
93/4 Pinnacle 110
93/4 Pinnacle NF 15
93/4 Pinnacle T2K1 20
93/4 Pinnacle TP 11
94/5 Pinnacle 165, GR14, WE3
95/6 Pinnacle 106, FC-4, R20-4
96/7 Pinnacle 98, TP-3
97/8 Pinnacle 33, 197
96/7 Pi. Be A Player 5, ✍ Aut. 5
97/8 Pi. Be A Player TN12
97/8 Pi. Certified 65
95/6 Pi. FANtasy 23
97/8 Pi. Inside 59
96/7 Pi. Mint 15
95/6 Pi. Summit 82
96/7 Pi. Summit 138, HV-10
97/8 Pi. Totally 65
95/6 Pi. Zenith 72, ZT-6
96/7 Pi. Zenith 30, ZT-10
95/6 Playoff 24, 135, 236
94/5 POG 70
95/6 POG 61, I-026
93/4 Power Play 54
93/4 Power Play Game. 8
93/4 Power Play PL 14
93/4 Premier 450
93/4 Premier 500
94/5 Premier 200, TF-11, GTG-8
00/1 Premier Plus 12
99/0 Prism 109
00/1 Pr. Stock 76, AC-17, EA-17, PS-44, PS-21
01/2 Pr. Stock 74, Res. 14, -PS 55, ✄ GUG 72
00/1 PS Titanium 73, ✄ GUG-129
01/2 PS Titanium 107, SK 17, ✄ DSJ 50, ✄ DSJ 59
01/2 PS Titanium Draft ✄ 72
00/1 PS Titanium Draft ✄ 78
95/6 Pro Magnet 4
90/1 Pro Set 58
91/2 Pro Set 40
91/2 Pro Set 280
91/2 Pro Set 605
92/3 Pro Set 30
92/3 Pro Set 252
91/2 Pro Set TL 2
91/2 Pro Set Platinum 24
91/2 Puck / Pro Set 6
99/0 Revolution 113, SS-28, / CSC 113
00/1 Revolution 114, HD-27, II-17
90/1 Score 179, / Promo 179
90/1 Sco. Hot Cards 31
91/2 Score 220
91/2 Score 305
91/2 Score 418
91/2 Score - Hot Card 10
91/2 Score CAN 220
91/2 Score CAN 309
91/2 Score CAN 334
92/3 Score 200
92/3 Score 422
92/3 Score 499
92/3 Score SS 10
92/3 Score USAG 3
93/4 Score 240
93/4 Score DD6
93/4 Score PIAS 39
93/4 Score TF 4
94/5 Score Cl6, DT-16, NP-6, TF-5
95/6 Score 55, BB-10, GB-19
96/7 Score 137, CI-5, SD-5
97/8 Score 107
90/1 Sco. Young Stars 24
91/2 Score Young Stars 21
92/3 Score Young Stars 10
92/3 Seasons 1
93/4 Seasons 15
94/5 Select 29
95/6 Select CE 60, DS-7
96/7 Select CE 77
94 Semic 122
94 Semic 352
95 Semic 118
91 Semic Sticker 149
92 Semic Sticker 158
93 Semic Sticker 180
00/1 Signature 106, ✍ Aut. 59, ✄ J-29, ✄ HSHSJers
01/2 Signature C-19, ✍ Aut., ✄ GUE29, ✄ GJ52, ✄ GSJ52, ✄ HSHSJers, ✄ ITN29, ✄ IS13, ✄ TM22
95/6 SBx Emotion 33, Xce-2, Xci-2, SM
95/6 SBx Impact 33, 243
96/7 SBx Impact 108, BR-19
94/5 SP 22, P-18
95/6 SP 24, E7
96/7 SP 119, CW-7
97/8 SP Authentic 118
98/9 SP Authentic 65, SS22
99/0 SP Authentic 67, ✍ SotT
00/1 SP Authentic 67
01/2 SP Authentic 60, 105
00/1 SP GU 46, ✄ TotG, ✄ C, ✄ P
01/2 SP GU 39
96/7 SPx 7
97/8 SPx 39, D-SPX2
99/0 SPx 114, P10
00/1 SPx 52, 78, HH11, ✄ WM (x2)
01/2 SPx 46
98/9 SPx Prospects 47, H24, L20
99/0 Stadium 55, Chrome 24, PP3
00/1 Stadium 21, BT28
01/2 Stadium 110
93/4 SLU / Card-A
93/4 SLU / Card-B
93/4 Starting Lineup
94/5 Starting Lineup
96/7 SLU
98/9 SLU
95/6 Super Sticker 21, DC-9
92/3 Topps 400
95/6 Topps 3, 235, HGA2, 4PL, PF8
98/9 Topps 171
99/0 Topps 42
00/1 Topps 10
01/2 Topps 94, Update 94
99/0 To. Chrome 42
00/1 To. Chrome 10
01/2 To. Chrome 94
94/5 Topps Finest 73, BBB-5
95/6 To. Finest 25, 175
98/9 To. Finest 30
95 Topps Finest Bronze 13
98/9 T. Gold Label 84
99/0 To. Gold Label 40, PG12
00/1 To. Gold Label 70, B7, GG15
00/1 To. Heritage 36
01/2 To. Heritage 164
96/7 To. Picks 47,FT18
99/0 To. Prmr. Plus 14
01/2 To. Reserve 95
91/2 To. Stadium 46
92/3 To. Stadium 167
92/3 To. Stadium 255
93/4 To. Stadium 190
93/4 To. Stadium - AS
94/5 To. Stadium 59
95/6 To. Stadium EC166
93/4 TSC Members Only 20
94/5 TSC Members Only 27
00/1 To. Stars 16
95/6 T. Super Skills 65
98/9 UD Choice 158
00/1 UD Heroes 154, ✍ SG
01/2 UD PlayMakers Ltd 74
00/1 UD Reserve 65
00/1 Ultimate Mem. ✍ U-29, ✄ J-29, ✄ JJ-17, ✄ S-29, ✄ TM-5, ✄ TM-10
01/2 Ultimate Mem. ✄ ASGH, ✄ DD, ✄ Emb., ✄ GJ, ✄ S&J, ✄ ITN, ✄ JE, ✄ JJ, ✄ NP, ✄ RT, ✍ Aut.
99/0 Ult. Victory 68
90/1 Upper Deck 63, 316, 481
91/2 Upper Deck 36
91/2 Upper Deck 166
91/2 Upper Deck 629
92/3 Upper Deck 274
92/3 Upper Deck G8
92/3 Upper Deck WG19
93/4 Upper Deck 235, 289, 314, HT18, R10, SP-31
94/5 Upper Deck 322, C19, H13, R8, IG3, SP-17
95/6 Upper Deck 227, 241, 422, F6, R47, SE-104
96/7 Upper Deck 35, 205, 312, X12, HH17, SS15A
97/8 Upper Deck 127, SG57, S17, T16C
98/9 Upper Deck 339, FF22

99/0 Upper Deck 273, ✂ GJ
00/1 Upper Deck 132, EC12, FT6, NC6, SS16, TT4, ✂ GJ
01/2 Upper Deck 131, CT9, T7
95/6 UD ASG MVP12
93/4 Upper Deck Be A Player 13
94/5 UD BAP R12, R144, UC6, ✍ 12
93/4 UD BAP Roots 30
96/7 UD Black Diam. 167
97/8 UD Black Diam. 59
98/9 UD Black Diam. 68
99/0 UD Black Diam. 65
00/1 UD Black Diam. 45
01/2 UD Challenge 62, CM1
95/6 UD CC 85
96/7 UD CC 46, 297, 313, UD18, S6
97/8 UD Coll. Choice 195, SQ79, S13
98/9 UD G. Reserve 339
99/0 UD G. Reserve 273
01/2 UD Honor Roll TC4
96/7 UD Ice 51, S8
97/8 UD Ice 27
00/1 UD Ice 31
01/2 UD Ice 33, ✂ FJ, ✂ CJ
00/1 UD Legends 102, 104
92/3 UD Locker 34
01/2 UD Mask 72, ✂ GG
98/9 UD MVP 160, PG15
99/0 UD MVP 156, W28, ✂ GU25, ✍ PS
00/1 UD MVP 134, M15, TP10
01/2 UD MVP 143, ✂ C
99/0 UD MVP Cup 140, GC, SC15
99/0 UD Ovation 45
96/7 UD Post
01/2 UD Premier 37
00/1 UD Pros&Prosp. 65, NP6, ✂✍ GJS
99/0 UD Retro 60
01/2 UD Top Shelf 30, ✂ S
00/1 UD Vintage 273, 283, NH18
01/2 UD Vintage 183
00/1 Vanguard 76, HV-27, VP-9
01/2 Vanguard 74, QTH 6, ✂ DGM 16
99/0 Victory 228
00/1 Victory 175, 181, 255, 317
01/2 Victory 270, 425
01/2 Waving the Flag 21
99/0 WGretzky 130
x99/0 WGretzky W6
96 Wien 167
97/8 Zenith 19, Z22
89/0 CHIC / Coke
90/1 CHIC / Coke
91/2 CHIC / Coke
93/4 CHIC / Coke
01/2 PHIL
96/7 PHOE / Coca-Cola
96/7 PHOE / Coca-Cola
96/7 PHOE / Coca-Cola
97/8 PHOE / Coca-Cola
97/8 PHOE / Coca-Cola
97/8 PHOE / Coca-Cola
98/9 PHOE / Coca-Cola
98/9 PHOE / Coca-Cola
98/9 PHOE / Coca-Cola

ROENICK, TREVOR
97/8 Las Vegas Thunder 6
98/9 Las Vegas Thunder
93/4 Maine Black Bears

ROEST, STACY
02/3 Pacific 186
98/9 Omega 89
00/1 Pr. Stock 50
00/1 Revolution 74
91/2 7th...Sketch WHL 326
01/2 Signature 135, ✍ Aut. 135
00/1 To. Chrome 237
00/1 Upper Deck 88
01/2 Upper Deck 319
01/2 UD MVP 96
99/0 UD MVP Cup 70
00/1 UD Vintage 174
01/2 Victory 172
95/6 Adirondack Red Wings
02/3 Grand Rapids Griffins

ROFF, PAUL
85/6 Minnesota-Duluth 11

ROGANO, BENNY
88/9 Niagara Falls Thunder

ROGER, SÉBASTIEN
99 Bowman 53
98 Bowman 106
98 Bowman Chrome 106
98/9 Bowman's Best 148

ROGERS, BART
99/0 Peoria Rivermen

ROGERS, DAN
01/2 Owen Sound Attack
02/3 Owen Sound Attack

ROGERS, KENT
91/2 Air Canada SJHL 7
91/2 Air Canada SJHL B17
92/3 MPS SJHL 134

ROGERS, MIKE
82/3 Dernière Heure
79/0 O-Pee-Chee 43
80/1 O-Pee-Chee 143
81/2 O-Pee-Chee 127
81/2 O-Pee-Chee 135
81/2 O-Pee-Chee 140
82/3 O-Pee-Chee 232
83/4 O-Pee-Chee 254
84/5 O-Pee-Chee 152
85/6 OPC/Topps 39
81/2 OPC Sticker 61
82/3 OPC/Topps Sticker 136
83/4 OPC/Topps Sticker 217
84/5 OPC Sticker 99
85/6 OPC Sticker 86-219
75/6 OPC WHA 8
77/8 OPC WHA 17
82/3 Post [NYRa.]
83/4 Souhaits Keychain [Rangers]
79/0 Topps 43
80/1 Topps 143
81/2 Topps 32
81/2 Topps 53
81/2 Topps 131 [East]
84/5 Topps 114
85/6 EDMO / Red Rooster
88/9 EDMO / Action 128

ROGERS, SCOTT
91/2 Air Canada SJHL C44
93/4 Cla. Prospects 241

ROGGER, BRIAN
90/1 7th..Sketch LHJMQ 154

ROGLES, CHRIS
93/4 Classic 77
94/5 Classic ✍ Aut.
93/4 Cla. Prospects 213
98/9 DEL 46
99/0 Eishockey 188
00/1 UD DEL 124
01/2 UD DEL 148, G5, ✂ GJ
93/4 Indianapolis Ice
94/5 Indianapolis Ice
92/3 Clarkson G'Knights

ROHDE, CHRISTIAN
01/2 UD DEL 242

ROHL, DIETER
70/1 Kuvajulkaisut 98

ROHLICEK, JEFF
84/5 Kelowna Wings &...
89/0 ProCards IHL 175
90/1 ProCards 357
91/2 ProCards 397
94/5 Fort Wayne Komets 16
95/6 Fort Wayne Komets
86/7 Fredericton Express
96/7 Mississippi S'Wolves
92/3 Toledo Storm
93/4 Toledo Storm 16

ROHLIK, PAVEL
94/5 APS 249

ROHLIN, LEIF
95/6 Donruss 344
95 Globe 23
94/5 Leaf Elit Set 175, GC-12, SS-11
95 Panini Worlds 143
89/0 Semic Elitserien 245
90/1 Semic Elitserien 153
91/2 Semic Elitserien 257
92/3 Semic Elitserien 281
96/7 VANC / IGA

ROHLOFF, JON
93/4 Classic 78
94/5 Classic ✍ Aut.
93/4 Cla. Prospects 224
95/6 Donruss 86
94/5 Fleer Ultra 260
95/6 Leaf 322
97/8 Pa. Invincible R-16
96/7 Pi. Be A Player 207, ✍ Aut. 207
94/5 Premier 516
95/6 Topps 196
94/5 Upper Deck 378
95/6 Upper Deck 127
96/7 Upper Deck 11
96/7 UD CC 21
00/1 Cincinnati Cyclones
99/0 Kansas City Blades
97/8 Providence Bruins

ROHLOFF, TODD
01/2 BAP Mem. 451
01/2 UD PlayMakers Ltd 144
99/0 Cleveland Lumberjacks
98/9 Portland Pirates
00/1 Portland Pirates

ROHRBACH, DIRK
94/5 DEL 134
95/6 DEL 135

ROHRBACH, WILFRIED
70/1 Kuvajulkaisut 97

ROKAMA, JOUNI
91/2 Jyvas Hyva 61
92/3 Jyvas Hyva 172
93/4 Jyvas Hyva 314
94/5 Sisu 201, N-4

ROKAMA, JUONI
93/4 Sisu 29

ROLAND, LAYNE
90/1 7th..Sketch WHL 331
91/2 7th...Sketch WHL 42
97/8 Central Texas
93/4 Portland Winter Hawks

ROLES, SCOTT
97/8 Regina Pats

ROLFE, DALE
70/1 Dad's Cookies
70/1 Eddie Sargent 55
71/2 Eddie Sargent 118
72/3 Eddie Sargent 146
70/1 Esso Power Player
74/5 Loblaws
68/9 O-Pee-Chee 41
69/0 O-Pee-Chee 100
69/0 O-Pee-Chee 4in1
70/1 O-Pee-Chee 156
71/2 O-Pee-Chee 219
72/3 O-Pee-Chee 271
73/4 O-Pee-Chee 177
74/5 O-Pee-Chee 341
68/9 Topps 41
69/0 Topps 100
71/2 Toronto Sun Photo
70/1 DETR / Marathon Oil

ROLINEK, TOMAS
00/1 OFS 53
01/2 OFS 251

ROLLINS, AL
02/3 Parkie - Reprint 169, 197
45-64 BeeHive-2 [Toro.]
45-64 BeeHive-2 [Chic.]
45-64 BeeHive-2 [Chic.]
48-52 Exhibits [Maple Leafs]
51/2 Parkhurst 76
52/3 Parkhurst 31
53/4 Parkhurst 82
54/5 Parkhurst 77
92/3 Parkhurst PR-8
93/4 Parkhurst DPR-4
93/4 Parkie 56-57 166
93/4 Parkie 56-57 28
45-54 Quaker Oats
54/5 Topps 26

ROLLINS, JERRY
76/7 OPC WHA 43
76/7 Phoenix Roadrunners

ROLOSON, DWAYNE
02/3 Between the Pipes 38, ✍ Aut.
02/3 First Edition 261
02/3 O-Pee-Chee 34
02/3 Pacific 187
02/3 Pacific Complete 136
02/3 Parkhurst Retro 19
02/3 Signature 4, ✍ 4
02/3 Topps 34
02/3 To. Limited 34
02/3 To. Total 281
02/3 Upper Deck 88
02/3 UD Mask 42, 43
02/3 Vanguard 53
01/2 BT Pipes 83
98/9 Bicyclo.. 4-H
94/5 Classic 61, AA10
94/5 Cla. Images 41, ✍ Aut.
97/8 Donruss 148
95/6 Edge Ice 73, TW-8, PR-5
95/6 Future Legends 19
97/8 Omega 34
98/9 Pacific 124
97/8 Pa. Invincible R-31
97/8 Pinnacle 87
96/7 Pi. Be A Player 211, ✍ Aut. 211
01/2 PS Titanium 71
97/8 Score 38
97/8 UD Coll. Choice 41
94/5 Saint John Flames
95/6 Saint John Flames
00/1 Worcester IceCats

ROLSTON, BRIAN
02/3 BAP Mem. 258
02/3 Bowman 45
02/3 Exclusive 12
02/3 First Edition 109, 379, ✂ Jers.
02/3 Heads Up 9
02/3 O-Pee-Chee 250
02/3 Pacific 31
02/3 Pacific Complete 120
02/3 Parkhurst 81
02/3 Parkhurst Retro 69
02/3 Pr. Stock Reserve 7
02/3 PS Titanium 8
02/3 Signature 78, ✍ 78
02/3 Slam Card
02/3 Sports Vault 15
02/3 Stadium 65, ✂ NHLP14
02/3 Topps 250
02/3 To. Limited 250
02/3 To. Total 376
02/3 Upper Deck 12
02/3 UD Classic 8
02/3 UD MVP 15
02/3 UD Vintage 25, 311, GB 25
02/3 Vanguard 8
02/3 Victory 20
98/9 Be A Player 230, ✍ Aut. 230
99/0 BAP Mem. 88, 320
00/1 BAP Mem. 132
01/2 BAP Mem. 170
01/2 Bowman 33
93/4 Classic 79
94/5 Classic 76, T38, ✍ Aut.
94/5 Classic 4 Sport 142
94/5 Cla. Images 97
93/4 Cla. Prospects 90
93/4 Cla. Prospects IA11
93/4 Cla. Prospects LP10
01/2 Crown Royale 11
95/6 Donruss 286, PP-9
95/6 Edge Ice 8
94/5 Flair 98
94/5 Fleer 117
93/4 Fleer Ultra 496
94/5 Fleer Ultra 320, P-7
94/5 Leaf 441
95/6 Leaf 294
94/5 L. Limited 4
01/2 O-Pee-Chee 129
98/9 Omega 141
98/9 Pacific 270
99/0 Pacific 246
00/1 Pacific 40
01/2 Pacific 36
97/8 Pa. Dynagon BKS-54
97/8 Pa. Paramount 105
99/0 Pa. Paramount 138
00/1 Pa. Paramount 20
99/0 Panini Sticker 334
95/6 Parkhurst 394
00/1 Parkhurst P-112
94/5 Parkie SE99
94/5 Pinnacle 255, 473, RTP8
95/6 Pinnacle 172
96/7 Pinnacle 7
93/4 Power Play 516
93/4 Premier - USA Hockey 5
94/5 Premier 438
01/2 PS Titanium 9
94/5 Score TR7
95/6 Score 80
97/8 Score 205
97/8 Score NJer. 6
94/5 Select 177, YE-10
94 Semic 133
00/1 Signature 136, ✍ 109
01/2 Signature ✂ IS8
94/5 SP P-12
00/1 Stadium 151
95/6 Topps 362, 13NG
99/0 Topps 128
00/1 Topps 75
01/2 Topps 129
99/0 To. Chrome 128
01/2 To. Chrome 129
94/5 Topps Finest 4, BBR-9
93/4 To. Stadium - Team U.S.A. 21
91/2 Upper Deck 699
94/5 Upper Deck 258, C13, SP-135
95/6 Upper Deck 14
96/7 Upper Deck 285
97/8 Upper Deck 92, SG17
98/9 Upper Deck 123
00/1 Upper Deck 14
01/2 Upper Deck 17
94/5 UD BAP ✍ 33
95/6 UD CC 273, 366
96/7 UD CC 151
97/8 UD Coll. Choice 144
91/2 Upper Deck WJC 86
98/9 UD G. Reserve 123
00/1 UD MVP 14
00/1 UD Vintage 26
01/2 UD Vintage 19
00/1 Victory 18
01/2 Victory 28
96/7 NJER / Sharp
91/2 L. Superior State Lakers

ROMAINE, MARK
90/1 ProCards 578
93/4 Birmingham Bulls
91/2 Cincinnati Cyclones

ROMAN, TOM
87/8 Brockville Braves

ROMANCHUK, TYLER
90/1 7th..Sketch WHL 34
91/2 7th...Sketch WHL 23

ROMANCHYCH, LARRY
72/3 Eddie Sargent 12
74/5 Loblaws
73/4 O-Pee-Chee 185
74/5 O-Pee-Chee 157
75/6 O-Pee-Chee 153
76/7 O-Pee-Chee 281
73/4 Topps 185
74/5 Topps 157
75/6 Topps 153
72/3 ATLF
74/5 ATLF

ROMANIUK, RUSS
92/3 Bowman 276
93/4 Canada Nationals
99/0 Eishockey 36
93/4 Fleer Ultra 471
94/5 Fleer Ultra 394
92/3 O-Pee-Chee 263
91/2 OPC Premier 162
92/3 Panini Sticker 59
91/2 Parkhurst 198
94/5 Parkhurst 265
91/2 Pinnacle 324
93/4 Power Play 492
91/2 Pro Set 565
91/2 Pro Set Platinum 274
91/2 Score 77T
91/2 Score CAN 627
92/3 Topps 390
92/3 To. Stadium 164
94/5 To. Stadium 260
91/2 Upper Deck 46
91/2 WINN / IGA
98/9 Las Vegas Thunder
97/8 Long Beach Ice Dogs
97/8 Manitoba Moose
01/2 Manchester Storm

ROMANO, ROBERTO
86/7 OPC/Topps 152
86/7 OPC Sticker 229-100
84/5 PITT / Heinz
86/7 PITT / Kodak
80/1 Québec Remparts

ROMANOV, OLEG
00/1 Cardset 201
99/0 Mir 71
98/9 OFS 7

ROMANOV, STANISLAV
95 Panini Worlds 48
96 Wien 150
00/1 Dynamo 19

ROMASHKO, OLEG
00/1 Mir 343

ROMBOUGH, DOUG
74/5 Loblaws
74/5 Loblaws Update
74/5 O-Pee-Chee 279
75/6 O-Pee-Chee 161
75/6 Topps 161
73/4 BUFF

ROME, ASHTON
02/3 Moose Jaw Warriors

ROME, BRIAN
82/3 Ottawa 67's
84/5 Soo Greyhounds

ROMER, ANDY
94/5 DEL 11

ROMER, HEINRICH
94/5 DEL 18
95/6 DEL 17

ROMFO, JEFF
93/4 Minnesota-Duluth

ROMINSKI, DALE
00/1 SPx 108
99/0 Detroit Vipers

ROMISHEVSKI, IGOR
72 Hellas MM-Jenkki 66
70/1 Kuvajulkaisut 15
69/0 Mästär Serien 29
72 Panda MM-Toronto
72 Semic Sticker 6
74 Semic Sticker 46
69/0 Soviet Stars
70/1 Soviet Stars
71/2 Soviet Stars
71/2 Williams Finnish 14
72/3 Williams Finnish 33

ROMMEL, WES
91/2 Air Canada SJHL B3

ROMNES, DOC
34-43 BeeHive-1 [Chic.]
34-43 BeeHive-1 [Toro.]
33-35 Diamond Match Silv.
36-39 Diamond Match TT1

RONAN, DAN
99/0 Fort Wayne Komets

RONAN, ED
92/3 Classic Prospects 134
92/3 Fleer Ultra 333
92/3 OPC Premier 41
92/3 Parkhurst 88
91/2 ProCards 90
93/4 To. Stadium 262
92/3 Upper Deck 491
92/3 MONT
92/3 MONT / OPC 45
93/4 MONT
94/5 MONT
95/6 WINN
96/7 Rochester Americans

RONAN, SKENE
91 C55 Reprint 26
10/1 Imperial
11/2 Imperial 26
12/3 Imperial 14

RONDEAU, JEREMY
95/6 Swift Current Broncos

RONKAINEN, JARMO
70/1 Kuvajulkaisut 319

RONKAINEN, VESA
72/3 Williams Finnish 294

RONKOSKE, JEFF
99/0 Des Moines Buc's

RONNING, CLIFF
02/3 Exclusive 88
02/3 First Edition 235
02/3 Pacific 173, ✂ GWJ 23
02/3 Pacific Complete 402
02/3 Parkhurst 145
02/3 Pr. Stock Reserve 50
02/3 PS Titanium 54
02/3 Quest for the Cup 49
02/3 Signature 85, ✍ 85
02/3 Sports Vault 245
02/3 Victory 100
01/2 Adrenaline 107
98/9 Aurora 147
99/0 Aurora 81
00/1 Aurora 79
98/9 Be A Player 226, ✍ Aut. 226
99/0 BAP Mem. 25
00/1 BAP Mem. 207
01/2 BAP Mem. 249, 459
91/2 Bowman 313
92/3 Bowman 411
98/9 Bowman's Best 61
99/0 Crown Royale 77
01/2 Crown Royale 82, ✂ TT 10
93/4 Donruss 357
94/5 Donruss 278
95/6 Donruss 79
96/7 Donruss 47
99/0 Dynagon Ice 111
93/4 EA Sports 141
94/5 Flair 194
94/5 Fleer 230
92/3 Fleer Ultra 227
93/4 Fleer Ultra 119
94/5 Fleer Ultra 230
00/1 Kraft 16
93/4 Leaf 183
94/5 Leaf 66
96/7 Leaf 173
99/0 Millenium 137, ✍ Aut. 137
91/2 O-Pee-Chee 59
92/3 O-Pee-Chee 94
01/2 O-Pee-Chee 180
89/0 OPC/Topps 45
89/0 opcSticker 20-160
98/9 Omega 132
99/0 Omega 128
98/9 Pacific 343
99/0 Pacific 231
00/1 Pacific 225
01/2 Pacific 221, ✂ GWJ 17
97/8 Pacific CC 200
97/8 Pa. Crown Roy. 106
97/8 Pa. Paramount 143
98/9 Pa. Paramount 185
99/0 Pa. Paramount 128, IAI-15
00/1 Pa. Paramount 137
98/9 Pa. Revolution 80
89/0 Panini Sticker 122
91/2 Panini Sticker 46
92/3 Panini Sticker 30
93/4 Panini Sticker 168
94/5 Panini Sticker 145
95/6 Panini Sticker 290
96/7 Panini Sticker 295
98/9 Panini Sticker 149
99/0 Panini Sticker 269
00/1 Panini Sticker 182
91/2 Parkhurst 182
92/3 Parkhurst 193
93/4 Parkhurst 210
95/6 Parkhurst 479
00/1 Parkhurst P-57
01/2 Parkhurst 172, 359
94/5 Parkie SE188
91/2 Pinnacle 106
92/3 Pinnacle 12
93/4 Pinnacle 69, 234
94/5 Pinnacle 113
95/6 Pinnacle 184
96/7 Pinnacle 163
97/8 Pi. Inside 173
95/6 Playoff 211
96/7 Playoff 398
94/5 POG 27
94/5 POG / Western 23
95/6 POG 269
93/4 Power Play 255
93/4 Premier 81
94/5 Premier 291
99/0 Prism 77
00/1 Pr. Stock ✂ GUG 62
01/2 Pr. Stock -PS 42, ✂ GUG 59
00/1 PS Titanium 52
01/2 PS Titanium 80, ✂ DSJ22
00/1 PS Titanium Draft ✂ 56
95/6 Pro Magnet 25
90/1 Pro Set 526
91/2 Pro Set 241
92/3 Pro Set 195
91/2 Pro Set Platinum 236
88/9 ProCards / Peoria
99/0 Revolution 81
00/1 Revolution 83
90/1 Score 81T
91/2 Score 212
91/2 Score CAN 212
92/3 Score 254
93/4 Score 17
93/4 Score 443
94/5 Score 86
95/6 Score 75
96/7 Score 163
97/8 Score 244
92/3 Seasons 32
94/5 Select 122
00/1 Signature 242, ✍ Aut. 167
95/6 SP 154
96/7 SP 124
00/1 SP Authentic 51
99/0 SPx 81
99/0 Stadium 103
00/1 Stadium 61
92/3 Topps 81
95/6 Topps 99
99/0 Topps 155
00/1 Topps 90
01/2 Topps 180
99/0 To. Chrome 155
00/1 To. Chrome 72
98/9 To. Finest 44
98/9 T. Gold Label 55
99/0 To. Gold Label 78
00/1 To. Heritage 157
96/7 To. Picks 105
01/2 To. Reserve 46
91/2 To. Stadium 298
92/3 To. Stadium 373
93/4 To. Stadium 125
94/5 To. Stadium 200
95/6 To. Stadium 128
00/1 To. Stars 85
00/1 UD Heroes 66
01/2 UD PlayMakers Ltd 57
00/1 UD Reserve 48
91/2 Upper Deck 208
92/3 Upper Deck 160
93/4 Upper Deck 211
94/5 Upper Deck 358
95/6 Upper Deck 102, SE-174
96/7 Upper Deck 315
97/8 Upper Deck 132
98/9 Upper Deck 156
99/0 Upper Deck 72
00/1 Upper Deck 325
01/2 Upper Deck 97
95/6 UD BAP 91, ✍ S91
01/2 UD Challenge 47
95/6 UD CC 17
96/7 UD CC 270
97/8 UD Coll. Choice 199
98/9 UD G. Reserve 156
99/0 UD G. Reserve 72
96/7 UD Ice 53
98/9 UD MVP 112
99/0 UD MVP 108
00/1 UD MVP 97
01/2 UD MVP 105
99/0 UD MVP Cup 100
00/1 UD Pros&Prosp. 49
00/1 UD Vintage 199
01/2 UD Vintage 143, 147, 148
00/1 Vanguard ✂ DGJ 11
01/2 Vanguard ✂ DGM 16
99/0 Victory 158
00/1 Victory 130
01/2 Victory 194
98/9 NASH / Wendy's 18
96/7 PHOE / Coca-Cola
97/8 PHOE / Coca-Cola
87/8 SLOU / Kodak
88/9 SLOU / Kodak
90/1 SLOU / Kodak
91/2 VANC
91/2 VANC / Photo
91/2 VANC / PotM
92/3 VANC / Road Trip
94/5 VANC
95/6 VANC / Abalene 7

RØNNINGEN, JAN TORE
92/3 Semic Nordisk 20

RÖNNQVIST, JONAS
00/1 BAP Mem. 427
01/2 BAP Mem. 142
00/1 Pr. Stock 101
00/1 PS Titanium Draft 152
01/2 Signature 52, ✍ Aut. 52
00/1 SP GU 61
00/1 To. Stars 107
00/1 UD Heroes 159
00/1 Upper Deck 416
97/8 UD Elitserien 125
98/9 UD Elitserien 139
99/0 UD Elitserien 141, H10
00/1 UD Pros&Prosp. 91
00/1 UD Vintage 372
00/1 Vanguard 102
01/2 Cincinnati Mighty Ducks

RÖNNQVIST, PETTER
94/5 Leaf Elit Set 271
95/6 Leaf Elit Set 99, S-10
91/2 Semic Elitserien 56
92/3 Semic Elitserien 76
95/6 UD Elitserien 152
97/8 UD Elitserien 149
98/9 UD Elitserien 166

RONTY, PAUL
02/3 Parkie - Reprint 167,195
45-64 BeeHive-2 [Bost.]
45-64 BeeHive-2 [NYRa.]
48-52 Exhibits [Bruins]
51/2 Parkhurst 95
52/3 Parkhurst 24
53/4 Parkhurst 63
54/5 Parkhurst 66
54/5 Topps 15

ROODBOL, KEES
91/2 Avant Garde BCJHL 112
92/3 BCJHL 166
92/3 BCJHL 212

ROONEEM, MARK
99/0 Kamloops Blazers
99/0 Kamloops Blazers
00/1 Kamloops Blazers
01/2 Kamloops Blazers

ROONEY, AL
99/0 Fort Worth Brahmas

ROONEY, LARRY
91/2 Richmond Renegades

ROONEY, STEVE
87/8 O-Pee-Chee 223
89/0 ProCards AHL 210
90/1 ProCards 364
85/6 MONT
85/6 MONT / Provigo
86/7 MONT
87/8 MONT
88/9 NJER / Caretta
87/8 WINN

ROOT, BILL
83/4 Dernière Heure
83/4 O-Pee-Chee 196
84/5 O-Pee-Chee 271
88/9 ProCards / Newmarket
89/0 ProCards AHL 112
90/1 ProCards 162
82/3 MONT
82/3 MONT / Steinberg
83/4 MONT
84/5 TORO
86/7 TORO
86/7 TORO
90/1 Newmarket Saints

ROPE, RICKY
85/6 U. of Arizona Ice Cats

ROSA, MARCO
96 Québec Pee Wee 1193

ROSA, PAVEL
02/3 Cardset 109
99/0 BAP Mem. 213
97 Bowman 51
00/1 Cardset 148
99/0 Millenium 125, ✍ Aut. 125
98/9 Omega 117
99/0 Pacific 197
98/9 Pa. Revolution 69
99/0 SPx 74
98/9 SPx Prospects 31
99/0 Topps 207
99/0 To. Chrome 207
99/0 Upper Deck 63
98/9 UD Black Diam. 40
99/0 UD C. Legends 79
99/0 UD G. Reserve 63
99/0 UD MVP 83
99/0 UD Retro 38
99/0 Victory 122
98/9 Long Beach Ice Dogs

ROSA, STANISLAV
94/5 APS 215

ROSANDER, OLA
89/0 Semic Elitserien 227
90/1 Semic Elitserien 69
91/2 Semic Elitserien 243

ROSATI, MIKE
96/7 DEL 159
99/0 Eishockey 18
95 Globe 226
95 Panini Worlds 77
95 Semic 171
93 Semic Sticker 210
00/1 UD DEL 11
01/2 UD DEL 176, G7, ✂ GJ
96 Wien 174
98/9 Portland Pirates
88/9 Niagara Falls Thunder

ROSBERG, JARI
70/1 Kuvajulkaisut 303
71/2 Williams Finnish 237
72/3 Williams Finnish 221
73/4 Williams Finnish 297

ROSE, ARTHUR
51/2 Laval Dairy 94

ROSE, BRANDON
98/9 Oklahoma City Blazers

ROSE, JARRETT
95/6 Slapshot 132

ROSE, JASON
99/0 Muskegon Fury
98/9 Phoenix Mustangs 20

ROSE, JAY
91/2 Cincinnati Cyclones

ROSEN, JOHAN
99/0 Eishockey 335

ROSÉN, JOHAN
98/9 DEL 83
94/5 Leaf Elit Set 12
95/6 Leaf Elit Set 80, G-8
01/2 UD DEL 190
95/6 UD Elitserien 132, NA17

ROSÉN, ROGER
95/6 Leaf Elit Set 297, R-9
95/6 UD Elitserien 201
97/8 UD Elitserien 195, 220, C30
98/9 UD Elitserien 197
99/0 UD Elitserien 200

ROSENBERG, KARI
98/9 Cardset 52
93/4 Jyvas Hyva 44
95 Leaf Latkaliiga 10
93/4 Sisu 234
94/5 Sisu 34, J-6, N-5
95/6 Sisu 16, GG-6
95/6 Sisu Limited 82

ROSENBLATT, HOWIE
92/3 Classic Prospects 44
91/2 ProCards 60
92/3 Cincinnati Cyclones
94/5 Greensboro Monarchs
97/8 Quad City Mallards
98/9 Quad City Mallards

ROSENHECK, JERRY
92/3 Clarkson G'Knights

ROSENQVIST, PER
92/3 Semic Elitserien 212

ROSOL, PETR
00/1 DS 44
99/0 OFS 346
00/1 OFS 146, 408
94 Panini Olympics 320
94 Semic 187
89 Semic Sticker 200

ROSS, ART
39/0 Bruins Magazine
91 C55 Reprint 31
83 HHOF Postcard E15
83&87 HHOF 74
10/1 Imperial
10/1 Imperial 8
10/1 Imperial 12
11/2 Imperial 31
12/3 Imperial 20
96/7 Legends 82
60/1 Topps 27
61/2 Topps - Stamp
37/8 World Wide Gum 96
91/2 BOST / SA Legends

ROSS, BRIAN
83/4 Kitchener Rangers

ROSS, DON
72 Semic Sticker 122

ROSS, GORDON
91/2 7th...Sketch OHL 361

ROSS, KHARIS
00/1 Mir 28

ROSS, MIKE
98/9 Odessa Jackalopes

ROSS, PATRIK
89/0 Semic Elitserien 116
90/1 Semic Elitserien 117
91/2 Semic Elitserien 120
92/3 Semic Elitserien 141

ROSS, PHILIP
83 HHOF Postcard D12
83&87 HHOF 58

ROSS, TOM
93/4 Michigan State

ROSSETTI, LUCA
79 Panini Sticker 263

ROSSETTI, MIKE
91/2 ProCards 56
89/0 Johnstown Chiefs

ROSSI, REIJO
72/3 Williams Finnish 275

ROSSIGNOL, ROLAND
51/2 Bas du Fleuve 43

ROSSINI, FREDERICO
96 Québec Pee Wee 889

ROSSITER, KYLE
02/3 Upper Deck 207
02/3 UD MVP 204
02/3 UD Vintage 350
01/2 BAP Mem. 434
98 Bowman 157, ✍ A7
98 Bowman Chrome 157
01/2 Parkhurst 316
00/1 Louisville Panthers
01/2 Utah Grizzlies
97/8 Spokane Chiefs

ROST, SONNY
30s A&BC Chewing Gum 37

ROSVALL, KAI
70/1 Kuvajulkaisut 235
71/2 Williams Finnish 252
73/4 Williams Finnish 316

ROTA, BLAIR
96/7 Kamloops Blazers

ROTA, DARCY
83/4 Funmate Puffy 5 [w/]
74/5 Loblaws
74/5 O-Pee-Chee 269
75/6 O-Pee-Chee 66
76/7 O-Pee-Chee 47
77/8 O-Pee-Chee 117
78/9 O-Pee-Chee 47
79/0 O-Pee-Chee 360
80/1 O-Pee-Chee 301
81/2 O-Pee-Chee 343
82/3 O-Pee-Chee 355
83/4 O-Pee-Chee 344
83/4 O-Pee-Chee 345
83/4 O-Pee-Chee 358
84/5 O-Pee-Chee 328
83/4 OPC/Topps Sticker 272
84/5 OPC Sticker 280
80/1 Pepsi Bottle Cap
82/3 Post [Vanc.]
84/5 7-Eleven
83/4 Souhaits Keychain [Canucks]
75/6 Topps 66
76/7 Topps 47
77/8 Topps 117
78/9 Topps 47
84/5 Topps 139
83/4 Vachon 115-35
79/0 ATLF / B&W
80/1 VANC
80/1 VANC / Silverwood
81/2 VANC
81/2 VANC / Silverwood
82/3 VANC
83/4 VANC
84/5 VANC

ROTA, RANDY
74/5 Loblaws
74/5 O-Pee-Chee 362
75/6 O-Pee-Chee 237
76/7 O-Pee-Chee 353
75/6 Topps 237

RÖTHELI, ANDRE
91 Semic Sticker 195
92 Semic Sticker 213

ROTHSCHILD, SAM
25-27 Anonymous 100 [Error: Rotchild]
24/5 Champ's Cigarettes
24/5 Maple Crispette [V130] 19
24/5 William Paterson 37

ROTHWELL, NICK
95/6 Guildford Flames 19
97/8 Guildford Flames

ROTKIRCH, JOHANN
72 Semic Sticker 114

ROUBIK, JAROSLAV
98/9 OFS 372
99/0 Score 4

ROUHIAINEN, MARKKU
71/2 Williams Finnish 270

ROULEAU, ALEXANDRE
02/3 Québec Remparts
00/1 Val d'Or Foreurs 14
01/2 Val d'Or Foreurs 13

ROULEAU, GUY
86/7 Sherb. Canadiens 23

ROULEAU, MICHEL
72/3 Québec Nordiques

ROULETTE, ALLAN
99/0 Missouri RiverOtters

ROULSTON, TOM
82/3 O-Pee-Chee 118
83/4 O-Pee-Chee 42
84/5 O-Pee-Chee 179
83/4 OPC/Topps Sticker 103
84/5 OPC Sticker 123
83/4 Vachon 39-119
82/3 EDMO / Red Rooster
88/9 EDMO / Action 15
84/5 PITT / Heinz

ROUPE, CLAES
89/0 Semic Elitserien 118

ROUPÉ, MAGNUS
89/0 Semic Elitserien 90
90/1 Semic Elitserien 263
91/2 Semic Elitserien 94
95/6 UD Elitserien DS14

ROURKE, ALLAN
00/1 St. John's Maple Leafs
01/2 St. John's Maple Leafs
01/2 St. John's / Clarenville

ROUSE, BOB
93/4 Donruss 333
92/3 Fleer Ultra 214
93/4 Leaf 230
89/0 OPC/Topps 26
91/2 OPC Premier 151
97/8 Pa. Invincible R-72
89/0 Panini Sticker 351
90/1 Panini Sticker 164
91/2 Panini Sticker 101
91/2 Parkhurst 176
94/5 Parkie SE51
92/3 Pinnacle 358
93/4 Pinnacle 289
94/5 Pinnacle 374
95/6 Pinnacle 163
94/5 POG 359
93/4 Premier 207
94/5 Premier 393
90/1 Pro Set 554
91/2 Pro Set 228
90/1 Score 147
91/2 Score CAN 246
92/3 Score 130
93/4 Score 304
96/7 Score 125
95/6 Topps 206
93/4 To. Stadium 353
94/5 To. Stadium 238
90/1 Upper Deck 389
94/5 Upper Deck 55
95/6 UD BAP 88, ✍ S88
98/9 UD MVP 175
84/5 MINS
85/6 MINS
86/7 MINS / 7-Eleven 9
87/8 MINS
88/9 MINS / ADA
91/2 TORO / P.L.A.Y. 6
92/3 TORO / Kodak
93/4 TORO / Abalene
93/4 TORO / Black's 5
89/0 WASH
89/0 WASH / Kodak

ROUSEK, MARTIN
94/5 APS 217
95/6 APS 168
96/7 APS 181, 402
97/8 APS 89
97/8 DS 46
98/9 DS 30
99/0 DS 24
96/7 DS Sticker 49
97/8 DS Sticker 96
98/9 OFS 90
99/0 OFS 311
00/1 OFS 178
01/2 OFS 8

ROUSSEAU, BOBBY
45-64 BeeHive-2 [Mont.]
64-67 BeeHive-3 [Mont.]
63-65 Chex
63-65 Chex
64/5 Coke/Sprite [Mont.]
65/6 Coca-Cola
70/1 Colgate 35
70/1 Dad's Cookies
70/1 Eddie Sargent 96
71/2 Eddie Sargent 117
72/3 Eddie Sargent 145
70/1 Esso Power Player
62/3 Cowan Tile
74/5 Loblaws
68/9 O-Pee-Chee 65
69/0 O-Pee-Chee 9
70/1 O-Pee-Chee 170
70/1 O-Pee-Chee DE 14
71/2 O-Pee-Chee 218
72/3 O-Pee-Chee 233
73/4 O-Pee-Chee 233
74/5 O-Pee-Chee 326
62/3 Parkhurst 47
63/4 Parkhurst 35
63/4 Parkhurst 94
95/6 Parkie 66-67 77, 126, 143, SL4
94/5 Parkie Tall 84
66/7 Post Cereal Box
66/7 Post [Small]
68/9 Post Marble
67/8 Post Tips 12
71/2 Pro Star Promotions
72 Semic Sticker 200
61/2 Shirriff 117
62/3 Shirriff 29
62/3 Shirriff 56
68/9 Shirriff / Mont. 9
64/5 Topps 80
65/6 Topps 70
66/7 Topps 7
66/7 Topps 132
66/7 Topps / Test 7
67/8 Topps 68
68/9 Topps 65
69/0 Topps 9
63/4 Toronto Star Photo
63/4 Toronto Star Weekend
66/7 Toronto Star Weekend
71/2 Toronto Sun Photo
61/2 York 35
62/3 York Transfer 18
63/4 York 25
67/8 York 33
70/1 MINS / Colour
66/7 MONT / IGA Stamp
67/8 MONT
67/8 MONT / IGA Card
68/9 MONT / IGA Card
69/0 MONT / Pro Star

ROUSSEAU, GHYSLAIN
00/1 Baie-Comeau 18
01/2 Baie-Comeau 15

ROUSSEAU, GUY
52/3 Anonymous 142
52/3 La Patrie
53/4 La Patrie

ROUSSEAU, ROLLIE
51/2 Laval Dairy 88
52/3 St. Lawrence 8

ROUSSEL, DOMINIC
01/2 BT Pipes 75
92/3 Bowman 92
93/4 Cla. Prospects 55
93/4 Donruss 243
94/5 Donruss 263
95/6 Donruss 267
96/7 Do. Canadian LG-7
93/4 Durivage 39
92/3 Fleer Ultra 159
93/4 Fleer Ultra 392
92/3 Kraft / PB
93/4 Kraft / JELL-O
93/4 Leaf 244
94/5 Leaf 223
99/0 Millenium 11, ✍ Aut. 11
92/3 O-Pee-Chee 198
92/3 OPC Premier 51
92/3 OPC Premier TR3
99/0 Pacific 12
00/1 Pacific 9
01/2 Pacific 163
92/3 Panini Sticker 183
94/5 Panini Sticker 45
99/0 Panini Sticker 340
91/2 Parkhurst 450
92/3 Parkhurst 129
93/4 Parkhurst 417
94/5 Parkhurst 169
91/2 Pinnacle 343
92/3 Pinnacle 96
92/3 Pinnacle T2K 11
93/4 Pinnacle 97
93/4 Pinnacle Mask 4
94/5 Pinnacle 208
96/7 Pi. Summit 50
94/5 POG 290
93/4 Power Play 409
93/4 Premier 335
94/5 Premier 56
91/2 Pro Set 552
92/3 Pro Set 235
90/1 ProCards 31
91/2 ProCards 265
92/3 Score 464
93/4 Score 82
94/5 Score 105
95/6 Score 182
92/3 Score Young Stars 36
92/3 Seasons 40
92/3 Topps 10
92/3 Topps 213
92/3 To. Stadium 315
93/4 To. Stadium 109
91/2 Upper Deck 583
92/3 Upper Deck 31
92/3 Upper Deck AC6
93/4 Upper Deck 336
94/5 Upper Deck 397
95/6 UD BAP 157, ✍ S157
92/3 PHIL / UD Sheet
92/3 PHIL / UD Sheet
92/3 PHIL / J.C. Penney
93/4 PHIL / Sheet
93/4 PHIL / Sheet
93/4 PHIL / J.C. Penney
94/5 PHIL / Sheet

ROUSSIN, DANY
98 Québec Pee Wee 899
99 Québec Pee Wee 660
01/2 Sherbrooke Castors 3

ROUSSON, BORIS
02/3 Cardset 110
99/0 Cardset AH A-hertta
93/4 Cla. Prospects 183
98/9 DEL 98
99/0 Eishockey 315
91/2 ProCards 200
90/1 7th..Sketch LHJMQ 64
94/5 Sisu 329
95/6 Sisu 95, 161, 381, GG-2, SS-2
96/7 Sisu 95, 181, KG-3, MA-2
95/6 Sisu Limited 29
00/1 UD DEL 236, P8
01/2 UD DEL 191
97/8 UD Elitserien 50
92/3 Binghampton Rangers

ROUSU, MIIKKA
00/1 Cardset 185
96/7 Sisu RE-9

ROUSU, MIKKA
96/7 Sisu 142

ROUSU, MIUIKA
95/6 Sisu 332

ROUTANEN, ARTO
89/0 Semic Elitserien 100

ROUTHIER, JEAN-MARC
88/9 ProCards / Halifax
89/0 ProCards AHL 160
89/0 QUÉB / Police
89/0 Halifax Citadels

ROUTHIER, STÉPHANE
93/4 Slapshot / Drummondville 2

ROUVALI, SIMO
98/9 Cardset 246
95/6 Sisu 132
96/7 Sisu 143

ROW, TODD
96/7 Halifax Moosehead
96/7 Halifax Moosehead
97/8 Halifax Moosehead

ROWAN, CHRIS
99/0 Brampton Batallion 13

ROWBOTHAM, DAVE
88/9 ProCards / Binghampton

ROWBOTHAM, KEN
89/0 7th..Sketch OHL 82
90/1 7th..Sketch OHL 17

ROWE, BOBBY
91 C55 Reprint 23
10/1 Imperial
11/2 Imperial 23
12/3 Imperial 11

ROWE, JON
92/3 MPS SJHL 99

ROWE, RANDY
01/2 Peoria Rivermen
02/3 Peoria Rivermen

ROWE, SEAN
98/9 Anchorage Aces
99/0 Anchorage Aces
95/6 Louisiana Ice Gators

ROWE, TOM
79/0 O-Pee-Chee 113
80/1 O-Pee-Chee 214
81/2 O-Pee-Chee 139
79/0 Topps 113
80/1 Topps 214
78/9 WASH
79/0 WASH

99/0 Lowell Lock Monsters
00/1 Lowell Lock Monsters
83/4 Moncton Alpines

ROWELL, RYAN
96/7 Halifax Moosehead
96/7 Halifax Moosehead

ROWLAND, CHRIS
90/1 7th..Sketch WHL 310
91/2 7th...Sketch WHL 34
94/5 Fort Wayne Komets 9
94/5 Thunder Bay Senators
89/0 Spokane Chiefs

ROWLAND, DEAN
91/2 Avant Garde BCJHL 85

ROWORTH, KIRK
89/0 Saskatoon Blades

ROY, A
93/4 Minnesota-Duluth

ROY, ALLAIN
92/3 Canada Nationals
94 Panini Olympics 316
94/5 Score CT23
94/5 Sisu Nolla 7

ROY, ANDRÉ
02/3 Pacific Complete 74
01/2 BAP Mem. 439
01/2 BAP Update ✂ TC17, ✂ TC18, ✂ TC33
95/6 Edge Ice 60
99/0 Omega 166
01/2 Pacific 279, 417
01/2 Parkhurst 361
00/1 Signature 210, ✍ Aut. 96
01/2 Upper Deck 353
99/0 OTTA
00/1 OTTA
01/2 OTTA
97/8 Charlotte Checkers
98/9 Fort Wayne Komets
96/7 Providence Bruins
97/8 Providence Bruins

ROY, CLAUDE
52/3 Anonymous 34

ROY, DARCY
81/2 Ottawa 67's
82/3 Ottawa 67's
83/4 Ottawa 67's

ROY, DEREK
00/1 UD Prospects 9
01 UD Prospects GU 11, ✂ TPJ, ✂ JC
01/2 Kitchener Rangers
01/2 Kitchener Rangers

ROY, GEORGES
51/2 Laval Dairy 30
52/3 St. Lawrence 92

ROY, JEAN-YVES
92/3 Classic 80
92/3 Classic Four Sport 203
94/5 Cla. Images 96
93/4 Cla. Prospects 182
99/0 Eishockey 114
97/8 Pacific CC 313
94/5 Score CT12
97/8 Score Bost. 11
94/5 Upper Deck 407
97/8 Upper Deck 12
97/8 UD Coll. Choice 19
92/3 Binghampton Rangers
94/5 Binghampton Rangers
96/7 Providence Bruins
97/8 Providence Bruins
92/3 Maine Black Bears

ROY, JIMMY
98/9 Manitoba Moose
99/0 Manitoba Moose
00/1 Manitoba Moose
01/2 Manitoba Moose
02/3 Manitoba Moose

ROY, LUCIEN
51/2 Lac St-Jean 22

ROY, MARC OLIVIER
97 Bowman 44

ROY, MARC-ANDRÉ
97 Québec Pee Wee 0013
01/2 Baie-Comeau 18
02/3 Baie-Comeau

ROY, MARTIN
90/1 7th..Sketch LHJMQ 118
91/2 7th...Sketch LHJMQ 186
95/6 Richmond Renegades

ROY, MATHIEU
00/1 Val d'Or Foreurs 1
01/2 Val d'Or Foreurs 15
02/3 Val d'Or Foreurs

ROY, PATRICK
02/3 Atomic 26, -D 5
02/3 BAP All-Star 77-79, ✂ ASJ, ✂ HSHSJers, Bobble
02/3 BAP Mem. 164, 208, 232, ✂ ASJ50, ✂ ASE19, ✂ ASN19, ✂ ASTJ17, ✂ AS1, ✂ AST3, ✂ AST22, ✂ AST26, ✂ FP8, ✂ HSHSJers 3, ✂ SC28, ✂ TM5, /Cup
02/3 Between the Pipes 1, 128, M8, ✂ ASJ4, ✂ BM3, ✂ CP1, ✂ DM7, ✂ GUE25, ✂ GUJ25, ✂ GP2, ✂ GSJ25, ✂ GT12, ✂ HSHSJers 1, ✂ ITN25, ✂ I1, ✂ I3, ✂ I4, ✂ I8, ✂ RB12, ✂ RB2, ✂ RB5, ✂ RB12, ✂ RB15, ✂ T2
02/3 Bowman 55
02/3 Calder 34, -CG 3, -HH 2, -HS 3, ✂ GWJ 8
02/3 Crown Royale 25, -COA 1, -RP 3, ✂ GWDP 5
02/3 eTopps 3
02/3 Exclusive 45, -EIS 3, -EA 4
02/3 First Edition 147, 327, 348, 376, 377, 389, ✂ Jers., ✂ DGJ 2, HSHSJers 23
02/3 Heads Up 32, -EIT 7, -ITN 7, -PSP 4, -S 6
02/3 In The GU 15, 115, ✂ E4, ✂ F8, ✂ GP2, ✂ GUJ4, ✂ SJ4, ✂ T2
02/3 McDonald's 9, -CC 2, -GSNF 1
02/3 O-Pee-Chee 1, 317, 320
02/3 Pacific 95, -CCA 5, -MA 5, -MI 2
02/3 Pacific Complete 165
02/3 PTC/ Les Gardiens 3
02/3 Parkhurst 102, -HHV 7, ✂ FP8, ✂ GJ49, ✂ SJ49, ✂ HSHSJers, ✂ MM1, ✂ MS11, ✂ TT19
02/3 Parkhurst Retro 18, ✂ RJ1, ✂ RSJ1, ✂ HSHSJers, ✂ NN24, ✂ RM6, ✂ VH7
02/3 Pr. Stock Reserve -ICS 5, -RE 3, ✂ 110
02/3 PS Titanium 26, -MM 1, -SK 2, -S 3, ✂ GWJ 18
02/3 Quest for the Cup 23, -RTC 2, ✂ GWJ 6
02/3 Signature 160, GS-69, ✍ 160, ✂ CJ2, ✂ DW1, ✂ FS10, ✂ SGJ4, ✂ TQ1, ✂ TM6
02/3 Slam Card
02/3 SP Authentic 22, ✍ SotT, ✍ SotTD, ✂ SP, ✂ DP, ✂ TP
02/3 SP GU 13, ✂ AF (x2), ✂ PH (x2), ✂ TG, ✍ Sig
02/3 Sports Vault 190
02/3 SPx 16, 84, ✂ WM, ✂ M, ✂ X
02/3 Stadium 73, -BT3, -PSH-14, ✂ StP
02/3 Starz
02/3 Topps 1, 317, 320, HHU19, CS1-14, ✍ CS1-14
02/3 T. Chrome 1, -CS1-25, ✍ Reprint, ✂ Reprint, ✂ Reprint Patch
02/3 To. Heritage 27, 102, 116, 117, 123, -Light 27
02/3 To. Limited 1, 317, 320, -CS1-14
02/3 To. Total 11, TTC7, AW2, TT2
02/3 UD Superstars 67, K6, MM19, ✂ LLT
02/3 Ultimate Mem. ✂ A8 (x2), ✂ CP, ✂ CSTW (x3), ✂ Emb, ✂ FS (x4), ✂ GUJ, ✂ GUSJ, ✂ GMIH, ✂ ITN, ✂ JE, ✂ JJ, ✂ LA, ✂ MO, ✂ NP, ✂ RAT, ✂ SCD (x4), ✂ SF, UAut
02/3 Upper Deck 43, 179, 185, -GG4, -LL3, -SA4, ✂ ASP, ✂ DM, ✂ PL, ✂ SV, ✂ FC, ✂ GJ, ✂✍ SGJ, ✂ PW, ✂ UDPL
02/3 UD Artistic 21, R21, CG1, GD2, ✂ AT, ✂ SS, / Art
02/3 UD Classic 24, ET3, GG3, ✂ HH, ✂ HR
02/3 UD Foundations 17, 54, 112, 120, 147, ✂ CH (x2), ✂ MS, ✂ PP (x2)
02/3 UD Honor 15, -SG7, ✂ GA (x2), ✍ SC
02/3 UD Mask 21, 22, 23, 92, ✂ CW (x2), ✂ GG, ✂ MM, ✂ BM, ✂ NB, ✂ PW, ✂ SS, ✂ VC, / Mask, ✍ Mask
02/3 UD MVP 44, 190, MM1, VF5, SA, SD, ST, ✍ PSig
02/3 UD Piece 24, 94, AC9,HB6, SB3, ✂ EC, ✂ PH, ✍ MD
02/3 UD Premier 15, ✂ Jers, ✂ JD, ✂ Patch, ✂ NHLP, ✍ Sig (x2)
02/3 UD Rookie 27, 104, 170, ✂ DJ, ✂ S, ✍ TD
02/3 UD Top Shelf 21, ✂ CP, ✂ HH (x4), ✂ M, ✂ R, ✂ SS, ✂ TS, ✍ Sig
02/3 UD Vintage 65, 268, 292, 317, 318, 319, T15
02/3 Vanguard 27, -EMW 9, -SW 1, -VT 1
02/3 Victory 50, 219
94/5 Action Packed
01/2 Adrenaline 49, BR 2, CL 4, PP 9, ✂ GWJ 9
01/2 ASG History
01/2 Atomic 26, CP 3, Stat 1, TN 4, ✂ GWJ 13
98/9 Aurora 51, -ALC 6, -CF 12, -FL 3, -NC 4, -Cube 4
99/0 Aurora 41, -Stripe 41, -CC 5, -CF 8, -CP 5, -ST 6, -GU 6
00/1 Aurora 40, Pins. 40, CC-3, CF-6, ✂ GWJ-2, ✂ GWJ-12, TPS-3B
98/9 Be A Player 34, H-8, P-16, ✍ Aut. 34, ✂ G-8, ✂ AS-6, ✂ S-6, ✂ G-8
00/1 BAP All-Star AS-1
99/0 BAP Mem. 262, H-10, ✂ J-6, ✂ D-4, ✂ TM-3, ✂ TM-21, ✂ TM-42, ✂ TM-44
00/1 BAP Mem. 104, ✂ J-34, ✂ G-2, ✂ G-15, ✂ G-21, ✂ G-28, ✂ H-11, ✂ RB-1, ✂ TM-18, ✂ TM-28, ✂ V-9, ✂ V-11, ✂ V-12
01/2 BAP Mem. 133, ✂ ASJ, ✂ ASE, ✂ ASN, ✂ ASD, ✂ ASS, ✂ AST, ✂ CoO, ✂ GJ, ✂ GT, HSHS, ✂ SCC, ✂ SCP
01/2 BAP Update HSHS, ✂ HSHSJers, ✂ H19
01/2 BT Pipes 1, 94, 111, HSHS, -Mask, ✂ ASJ, ✂ GJ, ✂ JE, ✂ S&J, ✂ GG, ✂ GR, ✂ ITN, ✂ TW, ✂ HSHSJers
96/7 Bic.Sports Aces A-H
97/8 Bicycle K-Heart
98/9 Bicycle.. A-C
95/6 Bicycle Sports Aces A-Spade
90/1 Bowman 50
91/2 Bowman 335
92/3 Bowman 74, 239
95/6 Bowman 15
01/2 Bowman 1
98/9 Bowman's Best 28, F10
92/3 Classic Prospects 33
98/9 Collection Souvenir 04
99/0 Crown Royale 39, -CS 7, -CCA 4, -GC 3, -IE 7
00/1 Crown Royale 30, JotC-9, Land. 4, NP-6
01/2 Crown Royale 39, ASH 4, CA 12, JotC 7, LH 2, ✂ TT 4, ✂ TT 7
93/4 Donruss 178, L, -ES 9, -IK 1
94/5 Donruss 328, D-3, ES-10, MM-9
95/6 Donruss 338, -BTP 7
96/7 Donruss 112, BTP-1, ES-10
97/8 Donruss 5, BTP 1, -ES 5
98/9 Donruss ES 16
96/7 Do. Canadian 19, LG-1
97/8 Do. Canadian 1, LG-1, SCS-27
95/6 Do. Elite 64, -PW 1
96/7 Do. Elite 66, PW-1
97/8 Do. Elite 14, 142, C-14, PN-2
97/8 Do. Preferred 86, 168, CG-1, PM-6, / Tin 5,24, -Wide Tin 9,12
97/8 Do. Priority 1, 197, OD-1, PG-1, Post-1, Stamp-1
97/8 Do. Studio 7, 110, S-3, P-7
96/7 Duracell DC17, JB17
92/3 Durivage 50, ✍ Aut.
93/4 Durivage 17, ✍ Aut.
98/9 Dynagon Ice 51, -AR 5, -IW 2, -PP 4, -TC 7
99/0 Dynagon Ice 59, -ASP 5, -Mask 1,6, -LotR 5
93/4 EA Sports 72
97/8 Esso 17, ✍ Aut.
01/2 eTopps 8
94/5 Flair 91, HN-8
96/7 Flair 20, HG-10, NT-2
94/5 Fleer 107, N-9
96/7 Fleer 24, PA-9, VT-9
95/6 Fleer Metal 78
96/7 Fl. Picks F50-40, DL-8
92/3 Fleer Ultra 108, -AS 3, -AW 4
93/4 Fleer Ultra 39, -AS 1
94/5 Fleer Ultra 113, -ASG 6, -PPM 6
95/6 Fleer Ultra 83, 225, 377, PPM-10
96/7 Fl. Ultra 39, CTI-8
00 Gatorade Sticker
91/2 Gillette 28
95 Globe 73
96/7 Got-Um
01/2 Heads Up 25, RI 2, SS 4, ✂ JQ 9, ✂ JQ 20, / Bobble
92/3 High Liner 1
93/4 Hockey Wit 3
99/0 HoloGrFX 17, IZ4, PS6
95/6 Hoyle / East. A-Spade
92/3 Humpty Dumpty
94/5 Incomnet Phonecard
91/2 Kellogg's / Score 1
92/3 Kellogg's
94 Koululainen
89/0 Kraft 25
90/1 Kraft 49, 90
91/2 Kraft 76
92/3 Kraft / Kraft Singles
92/3 Kraft / PB
93/4 Kraft / JELL-O
93/4 Kraft / KD
94/5 Kraft / KD
95/6 Kraft / PS
96/7 Kraft / KD
97/8 Kraft / JTP, PB, Spoon
98/9 Kraft / OML
99/0 Kraft / JELL-O
94/5 Kraft Mask
86/7 Kraft Sports 37
93/4 Leaf 33, 102, 100, -GLAS 5, -PW 4, -SSS 6
94/5 Leaf 41, -CP 1, -GLS 3, -LL 12
95/6 Leaf 200
96/7 Leaf 38, SD-1, S-2
97/8 Leaf 128, 187, PD-3
94/5 L. Limited 28
95/6 L. Limited 66, SS-4
96/7 L. Limited 9, S-1
96/7 L. Preferred 1, LS-36, MM-4
97/8 Limited 44, 151, 198, FG-20
96/7 Maggers 35
91/2 McDonald's Mc-08, McH6
92/3 McDonald's McH-06
93/4 McDonald's McD-23
94/5 McDonald's McD-4
95/6 McDonald's McD-25
96/7 McDonald's McD-30
97/8 McDonald's McD-23, F5
98/9 McDonald's McD15
99/0 McDonald's McD-15
00/1 McDonald's 9, GWJ-3, GSNF-2
01/2 McDonald's 6, -GSNF 1, ✂ JPatch 3
96/7 Metal Univ. 37, AP-11, CS-9
99/0 Millenium 66, D-3, ✍ Aut. 66, ✍ D-3, ✂ J-23, ✂✍ J-23, ✂ JS-23, ✂ G-2
01/2 Nextel
95/6 Cool Trade 16
98/9 NHL Power Play
00/1 Nortel Networks All-Star 11
86/7 OPC/Topps 53
87/8 OPC/Topps 163
88/9 OPC/Topps 116
90/1 OPC/Topps 198, 219
90/1 O-Pee-Chee 512
91/2 O-Pee-Chee 270, 413
92/3 O-Pee-Chee 111, 164, -Ann. 19, Box
01/2 O-Pee-Chee 47, 324
89/0 OPC/Topps 17
89/0 O-Pee-Chee 322
89/0 Topps - Sticker 6
90/1 OPC/Topps E
98/9 OPC Chrome 190, -Reprint 4
87/8 OPC Leaders 36
90/1 OPC Premier 101
91/2 OPC Premier 14, 170
88/9 OPC Stars 33
86/7 OPC Sticker 1
x86/7 OPC Sticker 2
x86/7 OPC Sticker 3
x86/7 OPC Sticker 4
x86/7 OPC Sticker 5
x86/7 OPC Sticker 19
x86/7 OPC Sticker 132-118
87/8 OPC Sticker 13
87/8 OPC Sticker 73
87/8 OPC Sticker 185-45
88/9 OPC Sticker 31
x88/9 OPC Sticker 32
x88/9 OPC Sticker 45
x88/9 OPC Sticker 159
x88/9 OPC Sticker 167
x88/9 OPC Sticker 214
x88/9 OPC Sticker 115-245
89/0 opcSticker 57, 128, 211, 161-21, 210-72, / AS 28
97/8 Omega 64, 249, NSZ-2, S-4, TL-4
98/9 Omega 64, -CS 3, -EOP 5, -FTF 1, -Onl. 9, -PI 30, -Prism 5
99/0 Omega 65, -5ST 26, -CC 4, -EOP 6, -Gen. 4
98/9 Pacific 33, -CCA 4, -DI 5, -GCDC 9, -TC 7, -Time. 4
99/0 Pacific 114, - CI 7, -CCA 4, -GC 11, -HAA 5,15, -ITC 5, -PAP 7, -TL 8
00/1 Pacific 120, IO-8, CCA-4, GCDC-11, ITC-3, NAS-3, ✂ GWJ-3
01/2 Pacific 106, 427, CCA 3, GCDC 6, IZ 7, NAAS 4, SC 5
97/8 Pacific CC 33, CCA-5, GCDC-8, ITC-5, TC-7
97/8 Pa. Crown Roy. 37, BOS-6, CCA-5, FO-5
98/9 Pa. Crown Roy. 35, -CCA 5, -LL 5, -MP 5, -PotG 7
97/8 Pa. Dynagon 33, 138, DD-6A, KN-3, S-6, T-4, T-25, BKS-26
97/8 Pa. Invincible 38, FP-9, R-56, R-217
97/8 Pa. Paramount 54, BN-6, CG-4, GSL-5, P-6
98/9 Pa. Paramount 60, -GS 6, -HOFB 4, -IG 3, -TC 7
99/0 Pa. Paramount 67, -GS 6, -HOFB 5, -IAdv. 6, -IAI. 6, -PB 10
00/1 Pa. Paramount 62, ES-6, FF-10, GS-7, HOFB-4, SZ-3
97/8 Pa. Revolution 38, ASG-7, I-4, RTS-5, TC-7
98/9 Pa. Revolution 38, -TPA 12, -NI 4, -Show. 11
01/2 PTC Collectors 2
98/9 Panini Photocard [x2]
87/8 Panini Sticker 56
87/8 Panini Sticker 376B
88/9 Panini Sticker 252
x88/9 Panini Sticker 402
89/0 Panini Sticker 9, 13, 16, 18, 19, 235, 376, 383
90/1 Panini Sticker 51, 323
90/1 Panini/MTL 19, G
91/2 Panini Sticker 184, 333
92/3 Panini Sticker 147, 277
93/4 Panini Sticker B
94/5 Panini Sticker 18
95/6 Panini Sticker 46
96/7 Panini Sticker 247
97/8 Panini Sticker 127, 208
98/9 Panini Sticker 184
99/0 Panini Sticker 211, 336
00/1 Panini Sticker 131
91/2 Parkhurst 90, 220, 442, 463, 470
92/3 Parkhurst 84, 463, 510
93/4 Parkhurst 100, D10, G9, E4
94/5 Parkhurst 113, 312, -YCTG 12
95/6 Parkhurst 113, 323, -CCP 2, -GP 3, -PP 35
00/1 Parkhurst P-97
01/2 Parkhurst 4, ✂ PJ38, ✂ PS54, ✂ PSJ5, ✂ HSHSJers, ✂ M18, ✂ M41, ✂ M43, ✂ H3, ✂ T8, ✂ T22
95/6 Parkhurst 24-karat Gold
95 Parkhurst Phonecard
94/5 Parkie SE seV3
91/2 Pinnacle 175, 387, B-1
92/3 Pinnacle 130
93/4 Pinnacle 150, 228, -TP 1
94/5 Pinnacle 30, -GT5, -MA1, -NL1, -TP1
95/6 Pinnacle 169, CS-10, FS-4
96/7 Pinnacle 138, M-1, TP-8
97/8 Pinnacle 29, M-5, TP-1, P-5, / Tin 8
96/7 Pi. Be A Player SP-13
97/8 Pi. Be A Player STP 4, -TN 4
97/8 Pi. BeeHive 19, -BHT 15
97/8 Pi. Certified 2, -CT 2
97/8 Pi. Epix E7
95/6 Pi. FANtasy 10
96/7 Pi. FANtasy 19
97/8 Pi. Inside 37, IT-2, SU-5, S-1, / Can 1, -Large Can
96/7 Pi. Mint 21
97/8 Pi. Mint 11
95/6 Pi. Summit 149, GMC-1, ITC-3
96/7 Pi. Summit 87, ITC-1, U-15
97/8 Pi. Totally 2
97/8 Pi. Uncut 5
95/6 Pi. Zenith 117, ZT-1
96/7 Pi. Zenith 35, CS-11
95/6 Playoff 55, 166, 274
96/7 Playoff 431
94/5 POG 283
95/6 POG 155, I-005, I-027
97/8 Pi. Post 2, F2
93/4 Power Play 133, -Game. 9, -Netm. 7
93/4 Premier 1, -BG/OPC 8, -BG/Top. 22
94/5 Premier 125, 310, 455
00/1 Premier Plus 8, MB12, TT3, WP1
99/0 Prism 40, -CA 5, -DAS 5, -SGDC 6
00/1 Pr. Stock 25, AC-7, EA-4, Res. 6, PS-12, PSS-7, ✂ GUG-28
01/2 Pr. Stock 23, GR 2, -PS 18, ✂ GUG 30
00/1 PS Titanium 22, 3SS-2, NAAS-4, ✂ GUG-8, ✂ GUG-78
01/2 PS Titanium 36, TSS 3, TA3 0, ✂ DSJ 10
00/1 PS Titanium Draft ✂ 25
95/6 Pro Magnet 19
90/1 Pro Set 157, 359, 399
91/2 Pro Set 125, 304, 599, 613, CC2, Gazette, ✍ 125, ✍ 599
92/3 Pro Set 2, 85, CC2
91 Pro Set Awards AC3
91/2 Pro Set Platinum 61
91/2 Puck / Pro Set 14
99/0 Revolution 42, -IS 3, -NI 6, -Orn. 7, -Show. 10, / CSC 42
00/1 Revolution 38, HD-11, II-6, NI-7, SM-13
90/1 Score 10, 312, 344, 354, 364, Promo 10
90/1 Sco. Hot Cards 25
91/2 Score 75, 342, 424, Promo, Shows 10
91/2 Score CAN 75, 314, 372
92/3 Score 295, 418, 428, 489, 527
93/4 Score 315, -DT 2, -PLAS 18, -TF 10
94/5 Score DT1, -TF12
95/6 Score 145, 324, DT-11
96/7 Score 1, DT-12, NW-1, / Promo 1
97/8 Score 33, NW-13
97/8 Score Colo. 1
92/3 Seasons 21
93/4 Seasons 16
94/5 Select 96, -FL1
95/6 Select CE 81, -GT 10
96/7 Select CE 81, F-2
89 Semic Sticker 54
91 Semic Sticker 52
93 Semic Sticker 189
00/1 Signature 211, HSHS, ✍ Aut. 106, ✂ J-23, ✂ HSHSJers
01/2 Signature C-59, ✂ GUE16, ✂ GJ17, ✂ GSJ17, ✂ ITN16, ✂ TM8
95/6 SBx Emotion 91
95/6 SBx Impact 87, D-8
96/7 SBx Impact 27, CTI-9, ZH-9
94/5 SP 59
95/6 SP 30, -É9
96/7 SP 35, CW-6, GF-3
97/8 SP Authentic 37, I24, ✍ SotT, ✍ T2
98/9 SP Authentic 21, SS2, SO15, ✍ SotT, -Trade
99/0 SP Authentic 24, HR2, SF3
00/1 SP Authentic 23, SP2, SS2
01/2 SP Authentic 18, 93, ✂ PP, ✍ SotT
00/1 SP GU 13, ✂ TotG, ✂ C, ✂ P (x2)
01/2 SP GU 12, ✂ AF, ✂ AFD, ✂ AFT, ✂ AFQ, ✂ Patch, ✂ PatchC (x2), ✂ TotG, ✂ TotGC (x3), ✂ TotGT (x3)
96/7 SPx 10, HH2
97/8 SPx 10, -DV, ✍ DVS
99/0 SPx 43, HH5, X2, XT5, S9, ✂ WM
00/1 SPx 15, 83, ✂ WM (x2)
01/2 SPx 17, 83, ✂ HT
98/9 SPx Finite 24, 119, 154, 171
98/9 SPx Prospects 14, H9, L23, PS21, ✂ WM
00/1 Stadion 75, 120
99/0 Stadium 66, CA23, -Chrome 26, -Big 13
00/1 Stadium 40, BT12, GS3, SF16
01/2 Stadium 87, G29, HS2,P4, ✂ SCSD, ✂ SCST
93/4 SLU [x2]
96/7 SLU
98/9 SLU
00/1 SLU Classic Doubles 2
95/6 Super Sticker 66, -DC 2
96/7 Team Out!
x88/9 OPC/Topps - Stick. 12
92/3 Topps 110, 263, 491, 508
95/6 Topps 60, 377, 1CG, HGC1, M20, PF3
98/9 Topps 190, L8, M16, -Reprint
99/0 Topps 16, 284, IM18, PM5, SC9
00/1 Topps 2, TC8, HM9, OTG16
01/2 Topps 47, 324, OTG22
99/0 To. Chrome 16, 284, IM18, PM5
00/1 To. Chrome 2, TC8, HM9
01/2 To. Chrome 47
94/5 Topps Finest 30, -DF 1, -RL 14
95/6 To. Finest 13, 145
98/9 To. Finest 140, M22, M25, M28, M29
94 Topps Finest Bronze 3
98/9 T. Gold Label 77
99/0 To. Gold Label 16, QC4
00/1 To. Gold Label 51, BTM8, B4
00/1 To. Heritage 24, HH5
01/2 To. Heritage 76, 128, 131
00/1 To. Heritage ASG 2
96/7 To. Picks 11, FT-1, ID-7
99/0 To. Prmr. Plus 23, IG2, PT8
01/2 To. Reserve 19, ✂ TR
91/2 To. Stadium 107
92/3 To. Stadium 133, 149, 438, 440, W6
93/4 To. Stadium 231, -Master, -AS, -Finest 11
94/5 To. Stadium 33, 178, F-9
95/6 To. Stadium 15, EN4, M3
92 TSC Members Only
93/4 TSC Members Only 23
94/5 TSC Members Only 1
00/1 To. Stars 2, 136, AS4, P4, WF6, ✂ GG
95/6 T. Super Skills 81
98/9 UD Choice 54, 232, 243, 309, BH21, SQ3
00/1 UD Heroes 141, PI2, SS1, TM3, ✂ GT, ✂ GC
01/2 UD PlayMakers Ltd 26, ✂ PCCJ, / PM
00/1 UD Reserve 22, GG3, PP1
98/9 UD3 46, 106, 166
00/1 Ultimate Mem. ✍ U-23, ✂ A8-5, ✂ A8-6, ✂ G-8, ✂ PJ-1, ✂ J-23, ✂ Jers. 21, ✂ JJ-12, ✂ MO-5, ✂ RE-2, ✂ RA-2, ✂ RA-8, ✂ S-23, ✂ TM-15, ✂ TM-17, ✂ GM-1, ✂ GM-2, ✂ GM-11, ✂ GM-20
01/2 Ultimate Mem. ✂ A8, ✂ BAPL, ✂ CP, ✂ Corn., ✂ Emb., ✂ Jers., ✂ S&J, ✂ ITN, ✂ JE, ✂ JJ, ✂ LC, ✂ NP, ✂ PP, ✂ RA, ✂ SCP
99/0 Ult. Victory 24, NW2, TV5, UV2
90/1 Upper Deck 153, 207, 317, 496, Promo 241
91/2 Upper Deck 137, 614
93/4 Upper Deck 49, AW 4, NL6, SP 81
94/5 Upper Deck 121, H5, H26, -SP-42
95/6 Upper Deck 39, 297, H14, R55, -SE110
96/7 Upper Deck 38, 199, 365, X5, HH11, LS6, SS2A
97/8 Upper Deck 43, SS30, SG2, S2, T2B, ✂ GJ1, ✂ GJ2, ✂✍ GJS
98/9 Upper Deck 74, 208, FT11, GN7-9, LS10, P24
99/0 Upper Deck 141, 210, AS2, CT27, HOF10, IG5, MA6, SB1, SS2, UD3, PD5, ✂ GJ
00/1 Upper Deck 45,D3, GA4, L1, SS5, TT2, ✂ GJ
01/2 Upper Deck 219, 276, FC9, GL6, LL1, SS12, ✂ CJers, ✂ GoalJ, ✂ PatchL, ✂ PatchN, ✂ PatchNu, ✂ PoaN, ✂ PoaND, ✂ PoaNT, ✂ SCFJers, ✂ SCFJersD, ✂ SCFJersT, ✂ SupSwe, ✂ TendThr
00/1 UD ASG PP1, HH1
94/5 UD BAP R121, R179, UC-8
95/6 UD BAP 197, ✍ S197
93/4 UD BAP Roots 9
96/7 UD Black Diam. 174, RC4
97/8 UD Black Diam. 41, PC2
98/9 UD Black Diam. 22, M23, WF6
99/0 UD Black Diam. 24, D5, DS3, ✂ APOH
00/1 UD Black Diam. 14, 86, IG2, IC1
99/0 UD C. Legends 35, 55, E5
01/2 UD Challenge 20, AT6, BB3, FF2, ✂ T200, ✂✍ T200S, ✂ TN
95/6 UD CC 95
96/7 UD CC 65, 307, 314, UD19, S4
97/8 UD Coll. Choice 56, 316, MM6-10, SQ86, S23, W18
01/2 UD Collectors
97/8 UD Diam. Vision 2, DM2
98/9 UD G. Reserve 74, 208
99/0 UD G. Reserve 141, 210, ✂ GR
01/2 UD Honor Roll 6, 36, OS4, ✂ HS, ✂ PPM
96/7 UD Ice 107, S5
97/8 UD Ice 83, IC2, L10B
00/1 UD Ice 10, IC1, IG2, ✂ IGJ
01/2 UD Ice 8, ✂ JC, ✂ GJ
00/1 UD Legends 31, 36, 73, EG4, LC1, PH1, SM9, ✂ LGJ
92/3 UD Locker 12
01/2 UD Mask 108, 175, ✂ CG, ✂ GP, ✂ GJ, ✂ JP, ✂ DP, ✂✍ SP, ✂ MB, ✂ PM, ✂ SY, ✂ VC, / Mask
98/9 UD MVP 52, OT2, F13, -Souv.
99/0 UD MVP 55, S3, LL3, MVP7, W10, W19
00/1 UD MVP 50, MM2, M5, VC2, ✂ GS
01/2 UD MVP 49 , MM3, ✂ GS
99/0 UD MVP Cup 51, GM2, PH3, SC5, GC
99/0 UD Ovation 15, 86, LP20, ST4, APOH
95/6 UD Post 10
96/7 UD Post
99/0 UD PowerDeck 8, T3
01/2 UD Premier 12, ✂ B, ✂ G, ✂ D (x2), ✍ SigG
00/1 UD Pros&Prosp. 23, CR1, GS3, ✂ GJ
99/0 UD Retro 20, DR7, G3B, TC7
01/2 UD SCup Champs 38, 67, ✂ S (x2), ✂ G (x2), ✂ T (x2)
01/2 UD Top Shelf 12, -ASGN, ✂ P, ✂ J, ✂ S, ✂ ST (x2)
00/1 UD Vintage 87, 98, 99, UD1, GG6, NH8, S2B
01/2 UD Vintage 68, 70, 267
97/8 Valu-net, ✍ Aut.
00/1 Vanguard 29, CF-4, HV-8, IF-6, VP-4
01/2 Vanguard 26, EMW 2, IF 1, QTH 3, SW 5, VT 2, ✂ DGM 10, ✂ DGM 43
99/0 Victory 78, 325, 350, 376
00/1 Victory 61, 244, 292
01/2 Victory 83, 92, 396
99/0 WGretzky 50, CG10, GH5, W5, ✂ TG
96 Wien SG7
97/8 Zenith 10, CTC-1, ZT-3, Z3
97/8 COLO / Denver Post
99/0 COLO / Kid Smart
85/6 MONT
85/6 MONT / Provigo
86/7 MONT
87/8 MONT
87/8 MONT / Vachon 42
87/8 MONT / Vachon 43
87/8 MONT / Vachon 69
87/8 MONT / Vachon 71
87/8 MONT / Vachon 74
87/8 MONT / Vachon 76
88/9 MONT
89/0 MONT
89/0 MONT / Kraft
90/1 MONT
91/2 MONT
92/3 MONT
92/3 MONT / OPC 30
93/4 MONT
94/5 MONT
95/6 MONT

ROY, PIERRE
75/6 OPC WHA 25
72/3 Québec Nordiques
76/7 Québec Nordiques
77/8 Nova Scotia Voyageurs

ROY, SÉBASTIEN
97/8 Rimouski Océanic

ROY, SERGE
90/1 ProCards 426

ROY, SIMON
91/2 7th...Sketch LHJMQ 61

ROY, STEPHANE
00/1 Kudos 47

ROY, STÉPHANE
92 C.O.A. Winter Olympics 175
90/1 Canada Nationals 17
91/2 Canada Nationals
92/3 Canada Nationals
88/9 ProCards / Kalamazoo
94/5 Sig. Rookies 8, ✍ 8
99/0 Québec Citadelles 11

ROY, TRAVIS
95/6 Pi. FANtasy 31

ROYER, GAETAN
98/9 Grand Rapids Griffins
99/0 Michigan K-Wings

ROYER, GAÉTAN
02/3 UD MVP 216
01/2 UD Mask 168

ROYER, REMI
99/0 Cleveland Lumberjacks

ROYER, RÉMI
99/0 BAP Mem. 145
95/6 Bowman P30
98 Bowman 87
98 Bowman Chrome 87
99/0 Pacific 99
98/9 Upper Deck 246
98/9 UD G. Reserve 246
98/9 UD MVP 50
99/0 UD MVP 49
99/0 Victory 70
98/9 Indianapolis Ice
00/1 Portland Pirates
99/0 Rouyn-Noranda

ROYMARK, TOM
79 Panini Sticker 297

ROZAKOV, RAIL
00/1 Mir 192, 290

ROZENDAL, SCOTT
01/2 Guelph Storm M-Cup

ROZINAK, VACLAV
01/2 DS L4

ROZON, MARTI
91/2 7th...Sketch LHJMQ 175

ROZSIVAL, MICHAL
02/3 First Edition 169
02/3 Pacific 317
02/3 Pacific Complete 241
02/3 Sports Vault 118
02/3 To. Total 387
02/3 Upper Deck 388
99/0 BAP Mem. 371
98 Bowman 64, SC20
98 Bowman Chrome 64
00/1 Crown Royale ✂ GWJ 22
01/2 DS 29
99/0 Dynagon Ice 162
99/0 NHL Power Play
00/1 OFS 397
99/0 Omega 194
00/1 Pacific 335
01/2 Pr. Stock ✂ GUG 83
00/1 PS Titanium ✂ GUG 140
01/2 PS Titanium ✂ DSJ 34
00/1 Signature 84, ✍ Aut. 91
99/0 SP Authentic 112
99/0 Stadium 185
00/1 Stadium 35
99/0 To. Prmr. Plus 115

ROZSIVAL, MICHEL
01/2 Heads Up ✂ JQ 29

ROZSIVAL, PATRIK
98/9 APS 246
98/9 OFS 380
99/0 OFS 98

ROZUM, PETR
99/0 Score 107

RUARK, MIKE
91/2 ProCards 393
90/1 7th..Sketch WHL 203, 311
97/8 Manitoba Moose
98/9 Manitoba Moose
99/0 Manitoba Moose
00/1 Manitoba Moose
92/3 Phoenix Roadrunners
89/0 Portland Winter Hawks

RUBACHUK, BRAD
91/2 ProCards 11
90/1 7th..Sketch WHL 127
94/5 Binghampton Rangers
91/2 Rochester Americans DD
91/2 Rochester Americans WPC
92/3 Rochester Americans DD
92/3 Rochester Americans WPC
93/4 Rochester Americans
88/9 Lethbridge Hurricanes
89/0 Lethbridge Hurricanes

RUBIC, ROBIN
84/5 Kitchener Rangers
85/6 Sudbury Wolves

RUBOV, ALEXEI
99/0 Mir 223

RUCCHIN, LARRY
99/0 Eishockey 284

RUCCHIN, LAWRENCE
98/9 DEL 124

RUCCHIN, STEVE
02/3 BAP Mem. 132
02/3 Bowman 79
02/3 Pacific 7
02/3 Parkhurst Retro 126
02/3 Signature GS-89
02/3 Sports Vault 155
02/3 To. Total 330
02/3 Upper Deck 3
02/3 Vanguard 3
01/2 Atomic ✂ GWJ 2
98/9 Aurora 4
99/0 Aurora 4
00/1 Aurora 3
98/9 Be A Player 151, ✍ Aut. 151
99/0 BAP Mem. 107
00/1 BAP Mem. 154
94/5 Cla. Images 56
99/0 Crown Royale 3
01/2 Crown Royale ✂ TT 1
95/6 Donruss 140
97/8 Donruss 49
97/8 Do. Preferred 45
98/9 Dynagon Ice 4
99/0 Dynagon Ice 11
95/6 Fleer Metal 4
95/6 Fleer Ultra 202
95/6 Leaf 54
97/8 Leaf 101
97/8 Limited 117
96/7 Metal Univ. 5
99/0 Millenium 10, ✍ Aut. 10
98/9 NHL Power Play
01/2 O-Pee-Chee 185
97/8 Omega 5
98/9 Omega 7
99/0 Omega 5
98/9 Pacific 62
99/0 Pacific 13
00/1 Pacific 10
01/2 Pacific 9
97/8 Pacific CC 104
97/8 Pa. Crown Roy. 3
97/8 Pa. Dynagon 4, T-30
97/8 Pa. Paramount 5
98/9 Pa. Paramount 5
99/0 Pa. Paramount 6
00/1 Pa. Paramount 6
98/9 Pa. Revolution 4
95/6 Panini Sticker 222
96/7 Panini Sticker 226
97/8 Panini Sticker 184
98/9 Panini Sticker 171
99/0 Panini Sticker 182
95/6 Parkhurst 272
95/6 Pinnacle 58
96/7 Pinnacle 137
97/8 Pinnacle 151
96/7 Pi. Be A Player 186, ✍ Aut. 186
97/8 Pi. Certified 64
97/8 Pi. Inside 188
97/8 Pi. Totally 64
95/6 POG 26
99/0 Prism 4
01/2 Pr. Stock ✂ GUG 4
01/2 PS Titanium ✂ DSJ 1
99/0 Revolution 5
00/1 Revolution 3
96/7 Score 186
97/8 Score 176
97/8 Score Anah. 3
00/1 Signature 185, ✍ Aut. 97
95/6 SP 4
96/7 SP 6
97/8 SP Authentic 5
99/0 SPx 5
00/1 Stadium 162
95/6 Topps 33
99/0 Topps 198
00/1 Topps 129
01/2 Topps 185
99/0 To. Chrome 198
95/6 To. Finest 64
98/9 To. Finest 26
00/1 To. Heritage 173
95/6 To. Stadium 214
98/9 UD Choice 6
00/1 UD Heroes 1
00/1 UD Reserve 2
94/5 Upper Deck 480
95/6 Upper Deck 425, SE-92
96/7 Upper Deck 214
97/8 Upper Deck 2
98/9 Upper Deck 214
99/0 Upper Deck 13
00/1 Upper Deck 2
01/2 Upper Deck 6
01/2 UD Black Diam. 20
96/7 UD CC 3
97/8 UD Coll. Choice 7
98/9 UD G. Reserve 214
99/0 UD G. Reserve 13
98/9 UD MVP 8
99/0 UD MVP 5
00/1 UD MVP 5
00/1 UD Vintage 10
01/2 UD Vintage 5
99/0 Victory 5
00/1 Victory 4
01/2 Victory 2
99/0 WGretzky 3
94/5 ANAH / Carl's Jr. 19
95/6 ANAH / Photo
96/7 ANAH / Up Front 11

RUCHAR, MILAN
94/5 APS 67

RUCHTY, MATT
91/2 ProCards 410
96/7 Grand Rapids Griffins
97/8 Grand Rapids Griffins

RUCINSKI, MIKE
98/9 Pacific 46
88/9 ProCards / Saginaw
89/0 ProCards IHL 61
93/4 Slapshot / Detroit 6
94/5 Slapshot / Detroit Jr. 5
95/6 Slapshot 61
94/5 Slapshot Memorial 79
00/1 To. Heritage 207
98/9 Upper Deck 235
98/9 UD G. Reserve 235
98/9 CARO / Highwoods
99/0 Charlotte Checkers
99/0 Charlotte Checkers
99/0 Cincinnati Cyclones
00/1 Cincinnati Cyclones
86/7 Moncton G'Flames
96/7 Richmond Renegades

RUCINSKY, MARTIN
02/3 Pacific 259
02/3 Victory - NP18
01/2 Adrenaline 99
94/5 APS 221
98/9 Aurora 96
99/0 Aurora 76
00/1 Aurora 74
98/9 Be A Player 221, ✍ Aut. 221
99/0 BAP Mem. 119
00/1 BAP Mem. 197
01/2 BAP Mem. 248, 474
98 Bonaparte 2A
98 Bonaparte Pexeso 5
99/0 Challenger 12
91/2 Classic 17
91/2 Classic Four Sport 17
00/1 Crown Royale 56
93/4 Donruss 281
96/7 Donruss 123
96/7 Do. Canadian 81
98/9 DS 4
99/0 DS NS13, P12
00/1 DS NT7
01/2 DS 25, 41, -BB 7, -IH 7
99/0 Dynagon Ice 104
01/2 EASports
96/7 Flair 50
92/3 Fleer Ultra 390
93/4 Fleer Ultra 191
94/5 Fleer Ultra 179
93/4 Leaf 152
96/7 Leaf 96
99/0 Millenium 132, ✍ Aut. 132
98/9 NHL Power Play
01/2 O-Pee-Chee 124
98/9 OPC Chrome 15
92/3 OPC Premier 124
98/9 OFS 245, OW 7
99/0 OFS 32
00/1 OFS 410
97/8 Omega 122
98/9 Omega 125
99/0 Omega 121
98/9 Pacific 257
99/0 Pacific 209
00/1 Pacific 212
01/2 Pacific 211
97/8 Pacific CC 220
98/9 Pa. Paramount 117
99/0 Pa. Paramount 120
00/1 Pa. Paramount 130
93/4 Panini Sticker 74
96/7 Panini Sticker 39
97/8 Panini Sticker 36
98/9 Panini Sticker 37
99/0 Panini Sticker 68
00/1 Panini Sticker 43
95 Panini Worlds 202
91/2 Parkhurst 366
92/3 Parkhurst 149
93/4 Parkhurst 170
94/5 Parkhurst 191
95/6 Parkhurst 379
00/1 Parkhurst P-239
01/2 Parkhurst 199, ✂ 384
93/4 Pinnacle 196
94/5 Pinnacle 416
96/7 Pinnacle 63
97/8 Pinnacle 172
96/7 Pi. Be A Player 124, ✍ Aut. 124
97/8 Pi. Inside 96
93/4 Power Play 203
93/4 Premier 367
00/1 PS Titanium 49
92/3 Pro Set 238
91/2 ProCards 230
99/0 Revolution 77
00/1 Revolution 78
92/3 Score 474
93/4 Score 254
96/7 Score 134
97/8 Score 152
97/8 Score Mont. 9
99/0 Score JT13
94 Semic 177
95 Semic 152
92 Semic Sticker 136
00/1 Signature 200
01/2 Signature 117, ✍ Aut. 117
96/7 SBx Impact 64
99/0 Stadium 113
00/1 Stadium 165
92/3 Topps 523
98/9 Topps 15
99/0 Topps 166
00/1 Topps 95
01/2 Topps 124
99/0 To. Chrome 166
00/1 To. Chrome 75
96/7 To. Picks 59
93/4 To. Stadium 11
94/5 To. Stadium 126
00/1 To. Stars 81
00/1 UD Heroes 64
91/2 Upper Deck 19
91/2 Upper Deck 70
92/3 Upper Deck 556
93/4 Upper Deck 6
94/5 Upper Deck 201
95/6 Upper Deck 485
96/7 Upper Deck 280
97/8 Upper Deck 89
00/1 Upper Deck 94
01/2 Upper Deck 324
96/7 UD CC 143
99/0 UD MVP 101
00/1 UD MVP 93
01/2 UD MVP 102
00/1 UD Pros&Prosp. 46
00/1 UD Vintage 195
01/2 UD Vintage 133, 139
99/0 Victory 149
00/1 Victory 122
01/2 Victory 184
01/2 DALL / Southwest
96-98 MONT
00/1 MONT
01/2 MONT
92/3 QUÉB / Petro-Canada
94/5 QUÉB / Burger King

RUCK, COLIN
90/1 7th..Sketch WHL 181
89/0 Regina Pats

RUCK, DERRICK
99/0 Lethbridge Hurricanes

RUD, ERIC
98/9 Florida Everblades
99/0 Florida Everblades
98/9 Kansas City Blades 5

RUDBERG, JONAS
91/2 7th...Sketch OHL 333

RUDDICK, KEN
89/0 7th..Sketch OHL 134
90/1 7th..Sketch OHL 18
96/7 Louisiana Ice Gators
89/0 Niagara Falls Thunder

RUDDOCK, KEN
92/3 MPS SJHL 51

RUDENKO, BOGDAN
95/6 Slapshot 140
00/1 Asheville Smoke
99/0 Colorado Gold Kings
97/8 Quad City Mallards

RUDISUELA, DAN
01/2 Mississauga IceDogs
02/3 Mississauga IceDogs

RUDKOWSKY, CODY
02/3 BAP All-Star 106
02/3 BAP Mem. 355
02/3 Between the Pipes 89
02/3 Parkhurst 248
02/3 SP Authentic 159
02/3 SP GU 90
02/3 Ultimate Mem. 48
02/3 Upper Deck 453
02/3 UD Artistic 120
02/3 UD Honor 127
02/3 UD Mask 117
02/3 UD Premier 66
02/3 UD Top Shelf 120
99 Bowman 122
99/0 Peoria Rivermen
00/1 Worcester IceCats
01/2 Worcester IceCats

RUDSLÄTT, DANIEL
99/0 UD Elitserien 29
00/1 UD Elitserien 41

RUDY, WES
92/3 BCJHL 20

RUEL, CLAUDE
80/1 Dernière Heure
69/0 MONT / Pro Star
76/7 MONT
77/8 MONT
78/9 MONT
79/0 MONT
80/1 MONT

RUETER, DIRK
80/1 Soo Greyhounds
81/2 Soo Greyhounds

RUFF, JASON
92/3 Classic 109
92/3 Classic Four Sport 216
92/3 Classic Prospects 45
99/0 Eishockey 91
91/2 ProCards 46
90/1 7th..Sketch WHL 138, 347
92/3 Upper Deck 522
00/1 UD DEL 80
93/4 Atlanta Knights
94/5 Atlanta Knights 12
95/6 Atlanta Knights
98/9 Cleveland Lumberjacks
92/3 Peoria Rivermen
01/2 Belfast Giants
88/9 Lethbridge Hurricanes
89/0 Lethbridge Hurricanes

RUFF, LINDY
80/1 O-Pee-Chee 319
82/3 O-Pee-Chee 31
84/5 O-Pee-Chee 24
86/7 OPC/Topps 4
88/9 OPC/Topps 40
90/1 OPC/Topps 143
84/5 OPC Sticker 213
87/8 Panini Sticker 35
82/3 Post [Buff.]
91/2 ProCards 6
84/5 Topps 23
01/2 T/O Archives 57
82/3 BUFF / Wendt's 5
84/5 BUFF / Blue Shield
85/6 BUFF / Blue Shield

86/7 BUFF / Blue Shield
87/8 BUFF / Blue Shield
87/8 BUFF / Won. Bread
88/9 BUFF / Blue Shield
88/9 BUFF / Won. Bread
96/7 FLOR / Winn-Dixie
89/0 NYRA / Marine
91/2 Rochester Americans DD
91/2 Rochester Americans GL
91/2 Rochester Americans WPC
92/3 San Diego Gulls

RUGG, STEWART
02/3 Dundee Texol Stars

RUGGIERO, BILL
01/2 Moncton Wildcats 1

RUGGLES, HILTON
02/3 Coventry Blaze

RUID, J.C.
00/1 Asheville Smoke

RUISMA, MATTI
80/1 Mallasjuoma 214

RUISMA, VELI-MATTI
78/9 SM-Liiga 20
78/9 SM-Liiga 238

RULIK, RADIM
96/7 APS 287
97/8 APS 171
98/9 OFS 33
99/0 OFS 368
00/1 OFS 158

RULLIER, JOÉ
00/1 Lowell Lock Monsters
01/2 Manchester Monarchs
02/3 Manchester Monarchs
96/7 Rimouski Océanic
97/8 Rimouski Océanic
99/0 Rimouski Océanic 2

RUMBLE, DARREN
92/3 Fleer Ultra 148
93/4 Fleer Ultra 153
01/2 Pacific 330
94/5 Panini Sticker 107
92/3 Parkhurst 356
93/4 Parkhurst 411
93/4 Power Play 173
93/4 Premier 356
89/0 ProCards AHL 342
90/1 ProCards 34
91/2 ProCards 271
93/4 To. Stadium 418
92/3 Upper Deck 110
93/4 OTTA
98/9 Grand Rapids Griffins
00/1 Worcester IceCats
01/2 Worcester IceCats
86/7 Kitchener Rangers
87/8 Kitchener Rangers
88/9 Kitchener Rangers

RUMMO, ALEX
97/8 Central Texas

RUMRICH, JURGEN
99/0 Eishockey 181

RUMRICH, JÜRGEN
94/5 DEL 66
95/6 DEL 66
96/7 DEL 262
98/9 DEL 49, 321
99/0 Eishockey 377
95 Panini Worlds 74
94 Semic 286
92 Semic Sticker 185
00/1 UD DEL 186, ✂ GJ
01/2 UD DEL 207

RUMRICH, MICHAEL
94/5 DEL 214
95/6 DEL 213, 434
95 Globe 220
95 Panini Worlds 65
92 Semic Sticker 184
93 Semic Sticker 167

RUNDQVIST, THOMAS
94 Semic 69
89/0 Semic Elitserien 85
90/1 Semic Elitserien 261
91/2 Semic Elitserien 90
91/2 Semic Elitserien 314
91/2 Semic Elitserien 324
91/2 Semic Elitserien 346
92/3 Semic Elitserien 112
82 Semic Sticker 17
89 Semic Sticker 18
91 Semic Sticker 39
92 Semic Sticker 62
93 Semic Sticker 10

RUNGE, DAVID
00/1 Rockford IceHogs

RUNGE, PAUL
34-43 BeeHive-1 [Maroons]
36-39 Diamond Match TT2
36-39 Diamond Match TT3
36/7 O-Pee-Chee 106
37/8 O-Pee-Chee 167
28/9 Paulins Candy 56
37/8 World Wide Gum 81

RUOHONEN, JUHANI
66/7 Champion 171
70/1 Kuvajulkaisut 250
78/9 SM-Liiga 89
71/2 Williams Finnish 216
72/3 Williams Finnish 165
73/4 Williams Finnish 231

RUOKONEN, MIIKKA
93/4 Jyvas Hyva 56
94/5 Sisu 298
95/6 Sisu 74
96/7 Sisu 74

RUOKOSALMI, ILPO
71/2 Williams Finnish 293

RUONTIMO, KARI
66/7 Champion 87

RUOTANEN, ARTO
94/5 Leaf Elit Set 190
95/6 Leaf Elit Set 114
80/1 Mallasjuoma 90
90/1 Semic Elitserien 102
91/2 Semic Elitserien 110
91 Semic Sticker 12
95/6 UD Elitserien 174
71/2 Williams Finnish 311

RUOTSALAINEN, MARKKU
70/1 Kuvajulkaisut 378

RUOTSALAINEN, REIJO
99/0 Cardset AH 2-pata
83/4 Funmate Puffy 19 [w]
70/1 Kuvajulkaisut 379
80/1 Mallasjuoma 96
82 Mallasjuoma
82/3 O-Pee-Chee 233
83/4 O-Pee-Chee 255
84/5 O-Pee-Chee 153
85/6 OPC/Topps 112
85/6 OPC/Topps Box M
86/7 OPC/Topps 128
83/4 OPC/Topps Sticker 216
84/5 OPC Sticker 101
85/6 OPC Sticker 81
86/7 OPC Sticker 60
86/7 OPC Sticker 225-94
89 Pelimiehen Passi
82/3 Post [NYRa.]
82 Semic Sticker 155
89 Semic Sticker 30
85/6 7-Eleven Superstars 13
95/6 Sisu 274, DT-7
95/6 Sisu Limited 66
82 Skopbank
78/9 SM-Liiga 10
78/9 SM-Liiga 138
83/4 Souhaits Keychain [Rangers]
77-79 Sports. FIN 86-2041
84/5 Topps 115
71/2 Williams Finnish 312
88/9 EDMO / Action 22
89/0 NJER
89/0 NJER / Caretta

RUOTSALAINEN, VESA
98/9 Cardset 191
99/0 Cardset 111
92/3 Jyvas Hyva 93
93/4 Jyvas Hyva 175
93/4 Sisu 168
96/7 Sisu 112

RUPNOW, MARK
96/7 Mississippi S'Wolves
99/0 Mississippi S'Wolves
99/0 Mississippi S'Wolves

RUPONEN, PASI
92/3 Jyvas Hyva 140
93/4 Jyvas Hyva 256
93/4 Sisu 288

RUPP, DUANE
70/1 Eddie Sargent 166
72/3 Eddie Sargent 180
70/1 Esso Power Player
69/0 O-Pee-Chee 153
69/0 O-Pee-Chee 4in1
70/1 O-Pee-Chee 89
72/3 O-Pee-Chee 154
75/6 OPC WHA 18
67/8 Topps 20
70/1 Topps 89
72/3 Topps 28
71/2 Toronto Sun Photo

RUPP, MICHAEL
02/3 Calder 80
98 Bowman 151, ✍ A3
98 Bowman Chrome 151
98/9 OPC Chrome 236
98/9 Topps 236
98/9 To. Finest F8
00/1 Albany River Rats
01/2 Albany River Rats
02/3 Albany River Rats

RUPRECHT, TOMAS
95/6 APS 264

RUPRECHT, VACLAV
94/5 APS 146
95/6 APS 252
96/7 APS 293

RUSHFORTH, PAUL
00/1 Kudos 83
91/2 7th...Sketch OHL 67
97/8 Louisiana Ice Gators
96/7 Rochester Americans
02/3 London Knights

RUSHMER, BART
98/9 SP Authentic 121
98/9 Upper Deck 398
98/9 UD G. Reserve 398
99/0 Brandon Wheat Kings
00/1 Kelowna Rockets

RUSHTON, JASON
92/3 BCJHL 195

RUSK, MIKE
93/4 Slapshot / Guelph 6
94/5 Slapshot / Guelph 20
98/9 Topeka Scarecrows
99/0 Topeka Scarecrows

RUSKOWSKI, TERRY
79/0 O-Pee-Chee 141
80/1 O-Pee-Chee 119
81/2 O-Pee-Chee 62
82/3 O-Pee-Chee 72
83/4 O-Pee-Chee 161
84/5 O-Pee-Chee 89
85/6 OPC/Topps 33
86/7 OPC/Topps 111
87/8 OPC/Topps 73
81/2 OPC Sticker 117
82/3 OPC/Topps Sticker 178
83/4 OPC/Topps Sticker 291
84/5 OPC Sticker 270
85/6 OPC Sticker 237-104
86/7 OPC Sticker 226
87/8 OPC Sticker 167-26
76/7 OPC WHA 38
77/8 OPC WHA 37
87/8 Panini Sticker 138
87/8 Panini Sticker 150
82/3 Post [Chic.]
90/1 7th...Sketch WHL 92
79/0 Topps 141
80/1 Topps 119
81/2 Topps 74 [West]
84/5 Topps 68
79/0 CHIC
80/1 CHIC / Colour
80/1 CHIC / Brown
81/2 CHIC
84/5 LOSA / Smokey 14
87/8 MINS
88/9 MINS / ADA
86/7 PITT / Kodak
75/6 Houston Aeros
78/9 Winnipeg Jets
95/6 Houston Aeros
90/1 Saskatoon Blades

RUSNAK, CHAD
92/3 MPS SJHL 47
91/2 7th...Sketch WHL 107
91/2 Saskatoon Blades

RUSNAK, DARIUS
92/3 Jyvas Hyva 91
82 Semic Sticker 92
91 Semic Sticker 115

RUSS, OTHMAR
79 Panini Sticker 304

RUSSELL, BLAINE
98/9 Huntington Blizzard
99/0 Huntington Blizzard
95/6 Prince Albert Raiders

RUSSELL, BLAIR
83 HHOF Postcard M14
83&87 HHOF 178

RUSSELL, BOBBY
98/9 Hampton Roads
99/0 Hampton Roads
98/9 Milwaukee Admirals
01/2 Norfolk Admirals
97/8 Portland Winter Hawks

RUSSELL, CAM
94/5 Leaf 382
97/8 Pa. Invincible R-45
89/0 ProCards IHL 71
90/1 ProCards 400
91/2 ProCards 486
90/1 Score 408
93/4 To. Stadium 286
91/2 Upper Deck 352
95/6 UD BAP 84, ✍ S84
93/4 CHIC / Coke

RUSSELL, DUSTIN
99/0 Hull Olympiques BN
99/0 Hull Olympiques 8

RUSSELL, ERNIE
91 C55 Reprint 35
83 HHOF Postcard I14
83&87 HHOF 133
10/1 Imperial
10/1 Imperial 20
11/2 Imperial 35
12/3 Imperial 26

RUSSELL, KERRY
91/2 ProCards 105

RUSSELL, PHIL
83/4 Funmate Puffy 9 [w]
84/5 Kelowna Wings &...
74/5 Loblaws
73/4 O-Pee-Chee 243
74/5 O-Pee-Chee 226
75/6 O-Pee-Chee 102
75/6 O-Pee-Chee 211
76/7 O-Pee-Chee 31
76/7 OPC 382
77/8 O-Pee-Chee 235
78/9 O-Pee-Chee 12
79/0 O-Pee-Chee 143
80/1 O-Pee-Chee 226
81/2 O-Pee-Chee 51
82/3 O-Pee-Chee 58
83/4 O-Pee-Chee 237
84/5 O-Pee-Chee 120
85/6 OPC/Topps 30
86/7 OPC/Topps 142
81/2 OPC Sticker 226
83/4 OPC/Topps Sticker 271
84/5 OPC Sticker 75
85/6 OPC Sticker 58-184
80/1 Pepsi Bottle Cap
82/3 Post [Calg.]
89/0 ProCards IHL 163
90/1 ProCards 391
91/2 ProCards 309
83/4 Souhaits Keychain [Flames]
74/5 Topps 226
75/6 Topps 102
75/6 Topps 211
76/7 Topps 31
77/8 Topps 235
78/9 Topps 12
79/0 Topps 143
80/1 Topps 226
79/0 ATLF / B&W
79/0 ATLF / Colour
80/1 ATLF / Colour
80/1 CALG
81/2 CALG
82/3 CALG
83/4 NJER
84/5 NJER
92/3 Cleveland Lumberjacks

RUSSELL, PHIL
02/3 Fleer Throwbacks 71

RUSSELL, SCOTT
97/8 Pi. CBC Sports 11

RUSSELL, TED
95/6 Dayton Bombers
96/7 Johnstown Chiefs

RUSSELL-SAMWAYS, DEAN
94/5 Guildford Flames 19
95/6 Guildford Flames 20

RUSSO, MATT
92/3 MPS SJHL 63

RUSTY, INFLATABLE
99/0 San Angelo Outlaws

RUTHERFORD, JIM
77/8 Coke
71/2 Eddie Sargent 176
72/3 Eddie Sargent 175
70/1 Esso Power Player
72/3 Post 7
74/5 Loblaws
72/3 O-Pee-Chee 15
73/4 O-Pee-Chee 59
74/5 O-Pee-Chee 225
75/6 O-Pee-Chee 219
76/7 O-Pee-Chee 88
77/8 O-Pee-Chee 239
78/9 O-Pee-Chee 74
79/0 O-Pee-Chee 122
80/1 O-Pee-Chee 125
80/1 Pepsi Bottle Cap
91/2 7th...Sketch OHL 47
72/3 Topps 97
73/4 Topps 59
74/5 Topps 225
75/6 Topps 219
76/7 Topps 88
77/8 Topps 239
78/9 Topps 74
79/0 Topps 122
80/1 Topps 125
70/1 DETR / Marathon Oil
79/0 DETR
80/1 DETR
71/2 PITT / Sportcolor

RUTHERFORD, M.
25 Dominion Chocolates 58

RUTHERFORD, PAUL
91/2 Richmond Renegades

RUTLAND, ART
82/3 Fredericton Express

RUTLEDGE, CHRIS
84/5 Belleville Bulls

RUTLEDGE, WAYNE
72/3 O-Pee-Chee 329
76/7 O-Pee-Chee WHA 5
77/8 OPC WHA 11
68/9 Shirriff / LoSA. 9
75/6 Houston Aeros

RUTTAN, JACK
83 HHOF Postcard K15
83&87 HHOF 149

RUUSKA, ARI
71/2 Williams Finnish 352

RUUTTI, MATTI
71/2 Williams Finnish 313

RUUTTU, CHRISTIAN
02/3 Cardset 111
90/1 Bowman 244
91/2 Bowman 25
92/3 Bowman 341
98/9 Cardset 16, Leij. 39
99/0 Cardset AH 10-pata
93/4 Donruss 72
92/3 Fleer Ultra 281
95 Globe 143
97/8 Hockey-Box
93 Koululainen
93/4 Leaf 334
95/6 Leaf Elit Set 207, 307
00/1 Mir Fetisov 34
87/8 OPC/Topps 121
88/9 OPC/Topps 18
90/1 OPC/Topps 182
91/2 O-Pee-Chee 115
89/0 OPC/Topps 68
87/8 OPC Leaders 37
92/3 OPC Premier 2
87/8 OPC Sticker 134-122
87/8 OPC Sticker 144-253
88/9 OPC Sticker 256-124
89/0 opcSticker 255-116
87/8 Panini Sticker 28
88/9 Panini Sticker 227
89/0 Panini Sticker 207
90/1 Panini Sticker 20
91/2 Panini Sticker 306
92/3 Panini Sticker 250
91/2 Parkhurst 242
92/3 Parkhurst 34
93/4 Parkhurst 39
94/5 Parkhurst 42
94/5 Parkie SE ES-12
89 Pelimiehen Passi
91/2 Pinnacle 60
92/3 Pinnacle 317
93/4 Pinnacle 116
94/5 Pinnacle 434
95/6 Playoff 103
94/5 POG 71
93/4 Premier 355
90/1 Pro Set 29
91/2 Pro Set 22
95/6 Radio City
90/1 Score 77
91/2 Score 45
91/2 Score CAN 45
92/3 Score 334
93/4 Score 84
94 Semic 43
95 Semic 22
91 Semic Sticker 205
92 Semic Sticker 15
93 Semic Sticker 75
94/5 Sisu 234, GS-8
95/6 Sisu Limited 42, SAS-2
95 Suomen All-Star 6
92/3 Topps 485
91/2 To. Stadium 33
92/3 To. Stadium 330
93/4 To. Stadium 293
94/5 To. Stadium 131
90/1 Upper Deck 170
91/2 Upper Deck 104
91/2 Upper Deck E11
92/3 Upper Deck 446
93/4 Upper Deck 141
94/5 Upper Deck 56
95/6 UD CC 278
95/6 UD Elitserien 210, 233, 258
96 Wien 25
86/7 BUFF / Blue Shield
87/8 BUFF / Blue Shield
87/8 BUFF / Won. Bread
88/9 BUFF / Blue Shield
88/9 BUFF / Won. Bread
89/0 BUFF / Blue Shield
89/0 BUFF / Campbell's
90/1 BUFF / Blue Shield
90/1 BUFF / Campbell's
91/2 BUFF / Blue Shield
91/2 BUFF / Campbell's
91/2 BUFF / Pepsi
93/4 CHIC / Coke

RUUTU, JARKKO
02/3 Cardset 254
02/3 Pacific Complete 462
99/0 BAP Mem. 347
01/2 BAP Mem. 123
98/9 Cardset 49, Leij. 40
99/0 Cardset PA 12
97/8 Hockey-Box
00/1 Pacific 417
99/0 Prism 144
01/2 Signature 97, ✍ Aut. 97
00/1 Topps 323
00/1 To. Chrome 218
00/1 Michigan City Blades 16

RUUTU, MIKKO
02/3 Cardset 255
00/1 Cardset 284

RUUTU, TUOMO
02/3 Cardset 256, -BFG 7, -DD 3, ✍ BFG
00/1 Cardset 165, NG-3

RUZICKA, VLADIMIR
94/5 APS 265
95/6 APS 135, 434
96/7 APS 20, 369, 397
97/8 APS 158
98 Bonaparte 4A, 8A
98 Bonaparte Pexeso 12
93/4 Donruss 228
97/8 DS 76
98/9 DS 9
99/0 DS 119, NS17
96/7 DS Sticker 130
97/8 DS Sticker 195
93/4 Fleer Ultra 383
93/4 Leaf 438
98/9 OFS 216, 248, OW 8
99/0 OFS 33, 52
00/1 OFS 407
93/4 Pinnacle 406
93/4 Power Play 174
93/4 Score 154
93/4 Score 562
99/0 Score JT19
91/2 BOST / Sports Action
92/3 BOST / Postcard
93/4 OTTA

RUZICKA, VLADIMÍR
92/3 Bowman 431
92/3 Fleer Ultra 10
90/1 OPC/Topps 393
92/3 O-Pee-Chee 228
91/2 OPC Premier 144
92/3 Panini Sticker 138
91/2 Parkhurst 3
92/3 Parkhurst 5
91/2 Pinnacle 181
92/3 Pinnacle 59
90/1 Pro Set 588
91/2 Pro Set 353
92/3 Pro Set 5
91/2 Pro Set Platinum 152
90/1 Score 44T
91/2 Score 83T
91/2 Score CAN 411
92/3 Score 208
89 Semic Sticker 190
92/3 Topps 333
91/2 To. Stadium 383
92/3 To. Stadium 358
90/1 Upper Deck 538
91/2 Upper Deck 288
92/3 Upper Deck 258
92/3 Upper Deck E4

RUZICKA, VLADIMIR (JR.)
00/1 OFS 417

RYABCHIKOV, EVGENY
94/5 Classic 18, T6
94/5 Classic 4 Sport 123
94/5 Cla. Images 70
95/6 Edge Ice 61
93/4 Parkhurst 533
93/4 Pinnacle 508
94/5 Sig. Rookies 9, ✍ 9
96/7 Charlotte Checkers
96/7 Dayton Bombers

RYABKIN, DMITRI
99/0 Mir 177

RYABYKIN, DMITRI
98/9 Mir 54
00/1 Mir 128, 332
94/5 SR Tetrad CXI, ✍ Aut.
95/6 Upper Deck 557

RYAN, GREG
89/0 7th...Sketch OHL 33
90/1 7th...Sketch OHL 142
91/2 7th...Sketch OHL 377
92/3 Ottawa 67's

RYAN, TERRY
92/3 BCJHL 201
95/6 Classic 8, BK8
95/6 Cla. 5 Sport 130
94/5 Cla. Images 18, PD8
97/8 Donruss 24
96/7 Do. Canadian 142, OC-16
97/8 Do. Canadian 128
96/7 Do. Elite A-11
96/7 L. Preferred 141
97/8 Limited 123
98/9 McDonald's McD28
99/0 Pacific 216
97/8 Pinnacle 11
97/8 Pi. Inside 167
96/7 Pi. Zenith 144
97/8 Score Mont. 15
94/5 SR Auto-Phonex 37, B2, Sprint, ✍ 37, ✍ B2
95/6 SR Tetrad 66, F10
95/6 SR Tetrad Autobilia 98
98/9 Upper Deck 294
98/9 UD Black Diam. 45
98/9 UD G. Reserve 294
98/9 UD MVP 103
77/8 Kalamazoo Wings
99/0 St. John's Maple Leafs
95/6 Tri-City Americans 3
95/6 Tri-City Americans 31

RYAN, TERRY*
72/3 Minn. Fight. Saints

RYBAR, JOE
98/9 Peoria Rivermen
99/0 Peoria Rivermen
00/1 Peoria Rivermen
01/2 Peoria Rivermen

RYBAR, JOSEF
94/5 APS 159
95/6 APS 260
96/7 APS 305

RYBAR, PAVOL
99/0 DS 184, G14
99/0 OFS 547

RYBAR, JOSEF
92/3 BCJHL 76

RYBIN, MAXIM
00/1 UD Prospects 38

RYBOVIC, LUBOMIR
94 Semic 195

RYCHEL, WARREN
93/4 Donruss 156
94/5 Donruss 240
93/4 Fleer Ultra 346
93/4 Leaf 263
94/5 Leaf 323
98/9 Pacific 168
97/8 Pacific CC 130
92/3 Parkhurst 309
93/4 Parkhurst 98
94/5 Parkie SE84
94/5 Pinnacle 509
97/8 Pi. Be A Player 32, ✍ Aut. 32
94/5 POG 128
93/4 Power Play 352
93/4 Premier 266
88/9 ProCards / Saginaw
89/0 ProCards IHL 69
90/1 ProCards 399
91/2 ProCards 175
97/8 Score Anah. 13
93/4 To. Stadium 258
92/3 Upper Deck 547
93/4 Upper Deck 93
96/7 ANAH / Up Front 8
98/9 COLO / Howler Says
91/2 Moncton Hawks
84/5 Sudbury Wolves

RYCROFT, MARK
01/2 Adrenaline 222
01/2 Atomic 122
01/2 BAP Mem. 326
01/2 Bowman 119
01/2 Crown Royale 176
01/2 Heads Up 117
01/2 O-Pee-Chee 352
01/2 Pr. Stock 138, -PS 87
01/2 PS Titanium 179
01/2 PS Titanium Draft 162
01/2 Signature 246, ✍ Aut. 246
01/2 SP Authentic 171
01/2 SP GU 96
01/2 SPx 126
01/2 SPx Rookie RR26
01/2 Topps 352
01/2 To. Chrome 170
01/2 UD PlayMakers Ltd 140
01/2 Upper Deck 439
01/2 UD Challenge 131
01/2 UD Honor Roll 87
01/2 UD Ice 68
01/2 UD Premier 80
01/2 UD Vintage 296
01/2 Vanguard 127
00/1 Worcester IceCats
01/2 Worcester IceCats
02/3 Worcester IceCats

RYDEN, JORGEN
89/0 Semic Elitserien 75
90/1 Semic Elitserien 249
91/2 Semic Elitserien 80

RYDER, COLIN
92/3 BCJHL 134
00/1 Kudos 5

RYDER, DAN
90/1 7th...Sketch OHL 394
91/2 7th...Sketch OHL 255

93/4 Roanoke Express
94/5 Roanoke Express
90/1 Sudbury Wolves
91/2 Sudbury Wolves

RYDER, MICHAEL
93 Québec Pee Wee 1417
00/1 Upper Deck 210
00/1 UD Black Diam. 75
00/1 UD Vintage 396
02/3 Hamilton Bulldogs
00/1 Québec Citadelles
01/2 Québec Citadelles
99/0 Hull Olympiques BN
99/0 Hull Olympiques 19

RYDING, STEVE
91/2 Knoxville Cherokees

RYDMAN, BLAINE
72/3 Minn. Fight. Saints

RYDMARK, DANIEL
95 Globe 33
94/5 Leaf Elit Set 91, GC-5, TG-7
95 Panini Worlds 151
94 Semic 66
89/0 Semic Elitserien 93
90/1 Semic Elitserien 141
91/2 Semic Elitserien 192
92/3 Semic Elitserien 214
92 Semic Sticker 68
97/8 UD Elitserien 144, S8
98/9 UD Elitserien 191
99/0 UD Elitserien 195, H14
00/1 UD Elitserien 143, ✍ Sig.
95/6 Phoenix Roadrunners

RYHANEN, LEEVI
65/6 Hellas 86

RYMSHA, ANDY
99/0 Eishockey 134
96/7 DEL 130
98/9 DEL 210
90/1 ProCards 80

RYPIEN, WES
01/2 Calgary Hitmen
02/3 Mississauga IceDogs

RYSANEK, ROMAN
94/5 APS 138
95/6 APS 302, 416
96/7 APS 201
97/8 APS 133
97/8 DS 99
96/7 DS Sticker 206
97/8 DS Sticker 256
99/0 OFS 293
93 Semic Sticker 100

RYZHEINKOV, NIKOLAI
00/1 Mir 69

S

SAADETIN, ALI
66/7 Champion 197
70/1 Kuvajulkaisut 136

SAAL, JASON
95/6 Classic 84
93/4 Cla. 4 Sport 221
95/6 Edge Ice 81
93/4 Slapshot / Detroit 2
94/5 Slapshot / Detroit Jr. 16
94/5 Slapshot Memorial 90
97/8 Hampton Roads
98/9 Hampton Roads
00/1 Louisiana Ice Gators
96/7 Peoria Rivermen
95/6 St. John's Maple Leafs
96/7 St. John's Maple Leafs

SAARELA, JARI
78/9 SM-Liiga 117

SAARELA, PASI
98/9 Cardset 111
99/0 Cardset 159
00/1 Cardset 192
02/3 Cardset 112
97/8 Hockey-Box
93/4 Jyvas Hyva 227
93/4 Sisu 199
94/5 Sisu 277
95/6 Sisu 253
96/7 Sisu 54, MA-2
99/0 UD Elitserien 78

SAARELAINEN, JUHANI
71/2 Williams Finnish 142

SAARI, TIMO
66/7 Champion 196
72 Hellas MM-Jenkki 21
70/1 Kuvajulkaisut 137
80/1 Mallasjuoma 49
71/2 Williams Finnish 158
72/3 Williams Finnish 111
73/4 Williams Finnish 211

SAARIKKO, ILKKA
71/2 Williams Finnish 253

SAARIKKO, KARI
80/1 Mallasjuoma 152
78/9 SM-Liiga 94

SAARIKORPI, JORMA
66/7 Champion 177
70/1 Kuvajulkaisut 252
71/2 Williams Finnish 143
72/3 Williams Finnish 204
73/4 Williams Finnish 167

SAARIKOSKI, TIMO
98/9 Cardset 112
99/0 Cardset 309
00/1 Cardset 285
02/3 Cardset 258
97/8 Hockey-Box
92/3 Jyvas Hyva 125
93/4 Jyvas Hyva 113

95 Panini Worlds 182
94 Semic 47
93 Semic Sticker 76
93/4 Sisu 25
94/5 Sisu 135, 380, H-7
95/6 Sisu 54

SAARINEN, ARI
98/9 Cardset 197
97/8 Hockey-Box
93/4 Jyvas Hyva 354
93/4 Sisu 226
94/5 Sisu 94
95/6 Sisu 160

SAARINEN, OLLI
80/1 Mallasjuoma 68
78/9 SM-Liiga 116

SAARINEN, PASI
98/9 Cardset 82
99/0 Cardset 45
00/1 Cardset 161
02/3 Cardset 259
95/6 Sisu 233

SAARINEN, ROD
90/1 7th...Sketch OHL 239
90/1 Kitchener Rangers

SAARINEN, SAMI
92/3 Jyvas Hyva 190

SAARINEN, SIMO
91/2 Jyvas Hyva 6
92/3 Jyvas Hyva 3
93/4 Jyvas Hyva 15
89 Semic Sticker 33
91 Semic Sticker 7
92 Semic Sticker 10
93/4 Sisu 88
94/5 Sisu 99
95/6 Sisu 4
95/6 Sisu Limited 39

SAARINEN, TONI
99/0 Cardset 103
00/1 Cardset 314
95/6 Sisu 228
96/7 Sisu 26

SAARINEN, VEIJO
66/7 Champion 64
70/1 Kuvajulkaisut 304
71/2 Williams Finnish 199

SAARIO, KAI
71/2 Williams Finnish 353

SAARNI, TARMO
73/4 Williams Finnish 298

SAARNIO, RAUNO
72/3 Williams Finnish 336

SABLIK, LUKAS
95/6 APS 177
97/8 APS 292
97/8 DS Sticker 108
98/9 OFS 296
99/0 Score 38

SABO, ED
92/3 Richmond Renegades

SABO, STEVE
92/3 MPS SJHL 163

SABOL, SHAUN
88/9 ProCards / Hershey
89/0 ProCards AHL 333
90/1 ProCards 46
91/2 ProCards 202

SABOURIN, COREY
00/1 Kingston Frontenacs 17
98/9 Sudbury Wolves 16
99/0 Sudbury Wolves 4

SABOURIN, DANY
02/3 BAP All-Star 115
02/3 BAP Mem. 345
02/3 Between the Pipes 104
02/3 Parkhurst Retro 245
02/3 SP Authentic 172
02/3 Ultimate Mem. 87
02/3 UD Honor 106
02/3 UD Mask 130

SABOURIN, GARY
68/9 Bauer Photo
70/1 Colgate 57
70/1 Dad's Cookies
70/1 Eddie Sargent 186
71/2 Eddie Sargent 177
72/3 Eddie Sargent 183
70/1 Esso Power Player
72/3 Post 6
74/5 Loblaws
68/9 O-Pee-Chee 117
69/0 O-Pee-Chee 19
69/0 O-Pee-Chee 4in1
70/1 O-Pee-Chee 96
70/1 O-Pee-Chee DE 28
71/2 O-Pee-Chee 13
72/3 O-Pee-Chee 91
73/4 O-Pee-Chee 168
74/5 O-Pee-Chee 368
75/6 O-Pee-Chee 299
76/7 O-Pee-Chee 266
68/9 Shirriff / SLou. 11
68/9 Topps 117
69/0 Topps 19
70/1 Topps 96
72/3 Topps 163
73/4 Topps 184
75/6 Topps 299
71/2 Toronto Sun Photo
71/2 SLOU
72/3 SLOU
73/4 SLOU
92/3 SLOU / McDon. 15
74/5 TORO

SABOURIN, KEN
91/2 O-Pee-Chee 43
90/1 Panini/CGY 20
90/1 Pro Set 596
89/0 ProCards IHL 204
90/1 ProCards 603
91/2 Score CAN 398
91/2 To. Stadium 396

91/2 Upper Deck 417
90/1 WASH / Kodak
91/2 WASH / Smokey
93/4 Milwaukee Admirals
94/5 Milwaukee Admirals
95/6 Milwaukee Admirals
96/7 Milwaukee Admirals
97/8 Milwaukee Admirals
86/7 Moncton G'Flames
98/9 Orlando Solar Bears Geico
88/9 Salt Lake G'Eagles
92/3 Salt Lake G'Eagles
82/3 Soo Greyhounds
83/4 Soo Greyhounds
84/5 Soo Greyhounds

SACCO, DAVID
93/4 Classic 80
94/5 Classic ✍ Aut.
94/5 Donruss 309
95/6 Edge Ice 14
93/4 Fleer Ultra 497
94/5 Leaf 58
96/7 Leaf 218
96/7 Pinnacle 213
93/4 Power Play 517
93/4 Premier - USA Hockey 13
94/5 Score 240
93/4 Topps Stadium - Team U.S.A. 22
94/5 Upper Deck 328
94/5 ANAH / Carl's Jr. 20

SACCO, JOE
92/3 Bowman 417
93/4 Donruss 2
94/5 Donruss 64
95/6 Donruss 302
92/3 Fleer Ultra 215
93/4 Fleer Ultra 260
94/5 Fleer Ultra 6
95/6 Hoyle / West. 2-Club
94/5 Leaf 274
95/6 Leaf 164
92/3 O-Pee-Chee 355
98/9 Pacific 287
97/8 Pacific CC 208
94/5 Panini Sticker 122
96/7 Panini Sticker 232
97/8 Panini Sticker 186
99/0 Panini Sticker 168
00/1 Panini Sticker 104
95 Panini Worlds 229
91/2 Parkhurst 395
92/3 Parkhurst 185
93/4 Parkhurst 273
94/5 Parkie SE5
94/5 Pinnacle 252
97/8 Pi. Be A Player 39, ✍ Aut. 39
94/5 POG 29
95/6 POG 21
93/4 Power Play 9
93/4 Premier 329
94/5 Premier 309
90/1 ProCards 156
91/2 Score 319
91/2 Score CAN 349
92/3 Score 532
95/6 Score 68
97/8 Score Anah. 7
95 Semic 112
97/8 SP Authentic 3
95/6 Topps
92/3 To. Stadium 398
93/4 To. Stadium 256
94/5 To. Stadium 161
92/3 Upper Deck 266
92/3 Upper Deck 382
93/4 Upper Deck 36, SP-3
94/5 Upper Deck 166
95/6 Upper Deck 43
96/7 Upper Deck 4
97/8 Upper Deck 214
01/2 Upper Deck 405
94/5 UD BAP R87, ✍ 79
95/6 UD CC 68
97/8 UD Coll. Choice 5
00/1 WGretzky 174
94/5 ANAH / Carl's Jr. 21
96/7 ANAH / Up Front 6
90/1 TORO
90/1 Newmarket Saints
92/3 St. John's Maple Leafs

SACHARUK, LARRY
74/5 Loblaws
75/6 O-Pee-Chee 76
75/6 O-Pee-Chee 327
75/6 Topps 76
75/6 Topps 327

SACHL, PETR
97/8 APS 285
97/8 DS Sticker 83
99/0 Fort Wayne Komets
00/1 Milwaukee Admirals
01/2 Milwaukee Admirals

SACILOTTO, ENIO
00/1 Kudos 30

SACRATINI, VEZIO
00/1 Kudos 66
01/2 Cardiff Devils
02/3 London Knights

SADJINA, ALEXANDER
79 Panini Sticker 307

SAFARIK, MICHAL
97/8 APS 46
98/9 OFS 342
00/1 OFS 331, 375
01/2 OFS 71
99/0 Score 22

SAFARIK, RICHARD
94/5 Slapshot Memorial 62

SAFFER, ADAM
01/2 OFS 279

SAFIN, VENER
00/1 Mir 246

SAFONOV, IGOR
00/1 Mir 96

SAFRONOV, KIRILL
01/2 BAP Mem. 472
02/3 Pacific Complete 596
98/9 SPx Prospects 73
98/9 UD Black Diam. 103
02/3 Chicago Wolves
99/0 Québec Remparts 3

SAGANIUK, ROCKY
80/1 O-Pee-Chee 64
81/2 O-Pee-Chee 323
82/3 O-Pee-Chee 331
82/3 OPC/Topps Sticker 69
80/1 Pepsi Bottle Cap
82/3 Post [Toro.]
80/1 Topps 64
84/5 PITT / Heinz
79/0 TORO
80/1 TORO
81/2 TORO

SAGISSOR, TOM
90/1 ProCards 58
91/2 ProCards 81

SAGLO, ROSTISLAV
96/7 Pensacola Ice Pilots

SAHARCHUK, DENNIS
90/1 7th...Sketch WHL 199, 327
91/2 7th...Sketch WHL 38
89/0 Spokane Chiefs

SAHLMAN, JARMO
71/2 Williams Finnish 271

SAHLSTEDT, KALLE
98/9 Cardset 247
99/0 Cardset 138
00/1 Cardset 342, MB6
02/3 Cardset 260
97/8 Hockey-Box
92/3 Jyvas Hyva 134
93/4 Jyvas Hyva 228
95 Semic 21
93/4 Sisu 195
94/5 Sisu 55, J-10
95/6 Sisu 103
96/7 Sisu 101

SAHLSTEN, PETTER
94 Panini Olympics 313
91/2 Semic Elitserien 8

SAIFULLIN, RAMIL
98/9 Mir 125
99/0 Mir 148
00/1 Mir 233

SAIKKONEN, MATTI
78/9 SM-Liiga 132

SAILER, PETR
95/6 APS 72
96/7 APS 259
97/8 APS 283
99/0 DS 41
97/8 DS Sticker 82
98/9 OFS 203
99/0 OFS 187
00/1 OFS 23
01/2 OFS 144

SAILYNOJA, KEIJO
98/9 Cardset 202
99/0 Cardset 118
91/2 Jyvas Hyva 22
92/3 Jyvas Hyva 56
93/4 Jyvas Hyva 112
93/4 Sisu 17
94/5 Sisu 124
95/6 Sisu 52
96/7 Sisu 48

SAIMO, SIMO
66/7 Champion 2

SAINDON, PAUL
51/2 Laval Dairy 70

SAINE, ERKKI
65/6 Hellas 44

SAINIO, SIMO
65/6 Hellas 28

SAINOMAA, TEEMU
00/1 Cardset 286
02/3 Cardset 261

SAINT GERMAIN, RALPH
30/1 La Presse

SAKAC, MARCEL
92/3 BCJHL 118
72 Panda MM-Toronto
72 Semic Sticker 21
74 Semic Sticker 72
71/2 Williams Finnish 37

SAKAROV, PETR
99/0 Score 147

SAKIC, BRIAN
90/1 7th...Sketch WHL 114, 344
91/2 7th...Sketch WHL 292
91/2 Upper Deck 461
92/3 Upper Deck 36
93/4 Flint Generals
94/5 Flint Generals
95/6 Flint Generals
98/9 Flint Generals

SAKIC, JOE
01/2 Adrenaline 50, BR 3, WB 3, ✂ GWJ 10
01/2 ASG History
01/2 Atomic 27, AB 3, PP 10, Stat 12, TN 4, ✂ GWJ 14
02/3 Atomic 27, -CF 9, -NPC 4
98/9 Aurora 52, ALC-7, CF-13, FL-4, MACF-6, / Cube 6
99/0 Aurora 42, Stripe 42, CF-9
00/1 Aurora 41, Pins. 41,

TPS-4A
02/3 BAP All-Star 80-81, ✂ ASJ, ✂ HSHSJers, Bobble
98/9 Be A Player 37, P-15, H-10, ✍ Aut. 37, ✂ G-6, ✂ AS-13, ✂ S-12, ✂ G-6
00/1 BAP All-Star AS-2
94/5 Be A Player Magazine Postcard 4
99/0 BAP Mem. 103, ✂ Tm-43, ✂ TM-44
00/1 BAP Mem. 233, ✂ J-24, ✂ TM-28, ✂ TM-34
01/2 BAP Mem. 149, ✂ ASJ, ✂ ASE, ✂ ASN, ✂ ASD, ✂ ASS, ✂ AST, ✂ CoO, HSHS, ✂ PP, ✂ SCC, ✂ SCP
02/3 BAP Mem. 108, ✂ ASJ51, ✂ ASE20, ✂ ASN20, ✂ AST21, ✂ HSHSJers 9, ✂ TM4
02/3 Between the Pipes ✂ GN8
96/7 Bic.Sports Aces A-D
95/6 Bicycle Sports Aces K-Club
90/1 Bowman 169
91/2 Bowman 133
92/3 Bowman 240
92/3 Bowman 244
95/6 Bowman 42, BB11
01/2 Bowman 15
02/3 Bowman 41
98/9 Bowman's Best 49
02/3 Calder 35, -HH 3
99/0 Crown Royale 40, IE-8, TC-3
00/1 Crown Royale 31, ✂ JR-3, JotC-10
01/2 Crown Royale 40, ASH 5, CA 13, JotC 8, ✂ TT 7, ✂ TT 11
02/3 Crown Royale 26, -LOR 7, -RP 4, ✂ GWDP 6, ✂ GWJ 3
93/4 Donruss 282
94/5 Donruss 141
95/6 Donruss 167, E-2
96/7 Donruss 1, ES-7, GTS-3
97/8 Donruss 117, L2L-12
98/9 Donruss ES 12
96/7 Do. Canadian 74, OC-1
97/8 Do. Canadian 102, NP-17, SCS-3
95/6 Do. Elite 16
96/7 Do. Elite 120, S-11
97/8 Do. Elite 49, 115, C-3, PN-11
97/8 Do. Preferred 128, 175, LT-8A, PM-11, / Tin 8, WideTin 3
97/8 Do. Priority 17, 208, DD-11, OD15, Post-9, Stamp-9
97/8 Do. Studio 23, HH-17, S-12, P-23
96/7 Duracell DC3,JB3
98/9 Dynagon Ice 52, -AR 6, -FT 6
99/0 Dynagon Ice 60, ASP-6, CM-21, LL-4, LotR-6
93/4 EA Sports 112
97/8 Esso 7, ✍ Aut.
01/2 eTopps
02/3 eTopps 9
02/3 Exclusive 46, -EIS 4, -MO 7
02/3 First Edition 154, 321, 373, 429H, ✂ Jers., ✂ DGJ 20, ✂ HSHSJers 6, ✂ TSL 7
94/5 Flair 151
96/7 Flair 21, CIS-7
94/5 Fleer 183
96/7 Fleer 25, 137, ART-20, PA-10
95/6 Fleer Metal 36, HM-12, IS-18
96/7 Fl. Picks 2, F50-41, CC-6, DL-9
92/3 Fleer Ultra 179
93/4 Fleer Ultra 242
94/5 Fleer Ultra 180
95/6 Fleer Ultra 136, 397, EA-17, PP-8, UV-9
96/7 Fl. Ultra 40, PL-7, UP-15
00 Gatorade Sticker
91/2 Gillette 22
96/7 Got-Um
01/2 Heads Up 26, HD 3, RI 3, SM 4, ✂ JQ 8, ✂ JQ 21, / Bobble
02/3 Heads Up 33, -EIT 8, -ITN 8, -PSP 5, -SM 7, ✂ GWQ 9
93/4 Hockey Wit 100
99/0 HoloGrFX 15
95/6 Hoyle / East. A-Club
92/3 Humpty Dumpty
02/3 In The GU 13, 113, ✂ E22, ✂ IE17, ✂ GUJ22, ✂ SJ22, ✂ T10, ✂ TM8
91/2 Kellogg's / Score 12
89/0 Kraft 32
90/1 Kraft 50, 79
91/2 Kraft 41
93/4 Kraft / JELL-O
94/5 Kraft / PB
94/5 Kraft / SS
95/6 Kraft / KD
96/7 Kraft / TT, PB
97/8 Kraft / JTP, PB
98/9 Kraft / Post 14
99/0 Kraft / JELL-O, / KD (x2)
01/2 Kraft 22
93/4 Leaf 87
94/5 Leaf 165, LL-19

95/6 Leaf 182
96/7 Leaf 139, FOI-3, LL-1
97/8 Leaf 35, BS-24, FOI-7
94/5 L. Limited 106
95/6 L. Limited 64
96/7 L. Limited 56, S-16
96/7 L. Preferred 37, LS-11, SP-1
97/8 Limited 36, 132, 190, FG-4, FG-5
96/7 Maggers 37
91/2 McDonald's Mc-05
92/3 McDonald's McD-26
93/4 McDonald's McD-24
94/5 McDonald's McD-1
95/6 McDonald's
96/7 McDonald's McD-10
97/8 McDonald's McD-5
98/9 McDonald's McD03
00/1 McDonald's 10
01/2 McDonald's 7, -HG 2, ✄ JPatch 4
02/3 McDonald's 10, -SLG 9, ✄ JP 4
96/7 Metal Univ. 38, IC-12, LW-16
99/0 Millenium 67, ✍ Aut. 67, ✄ J-28, ✄✍ J-28, ✄ JS-28
98/9 NHL Power Play
00/1 Nortel Networks All-Star 8
90/1 OPC/Topps 384
90/1 Topps-TL 14
91/2 O-Pee-Chee 16
91/2 Topps - Team Leader 8
92/3 O-Pee-Chee 54
92/3 O-Pee-Chee 55
92/3 OPC - Anniv. 22
01/2 O-Pee-Chee 27, 318
02/3 O-Pee-Chee 196, 330
89/0 OPC/Topps 113
89/0 O-Pee-Chee 313
98/9 OPC Chrome 68
90/1 OPC Premier 102
91/2 OPC Premier 70
92/3 OPC Premier SP11
89/0 opcSticker 187, 41-185, / FS 16
97/8 Omega 65, GF-4, S-5, SHLC-6
98/9 Omega 65, -EOP 6, -FTF 6, -Onl. 10, -PI 22, -Prism 6
99/0 Omega 66, CC-5,NAAS-3
98/9 Pacific 169, -DI 7, -GCDC 10, -Time. 5
99/0 Pacific 115, CI-8, CCA-5, GC-12, PAP-8
00/1 Pacific 121, GCDC-10, NAS-2, PR-6, ✄ GWJ-4
01/2 Pacific 107, 408, 427, CCA 4, GCDC 7, NAAS 5, ✄ GWJ 9
02/3 Pacific 96, -IZ 5, -L 6, -MI 12, ✄ GWJ 11
02/3 Pacific Complete 13
97/8 Pacific CC 38, GCDC-9, SS-2B
97/8 Pa. Crown Roy. 38, HT-5, L-6
98/9 Pa. Crown Roy. 36, -MP 6, -PotG 8, -PP 5
97/8 Pa. Dynagon 34, DD-6B, KN-4, T-2, BKS-27
97/8 Pa. Invincible 39, AZ-7, FP-10, OTG-6, R-57
97/8 Pa. Paramount 55, P-7, CG-5, BN-7
98/9 Pa. Paramount 61, -IG 4, -SD 5
99/0 Pa. Paramount 68, IAd-7, PB-11
00/1 Pa. Paramount 63, ES-7, FF-9, ✄ GUS-5, ✄ J&P-4
97/8 Pa. Revolution 39, ASG-8
98/9 Pa. Revolution 39, -TPA 24, -CTLC 5, -Show. 12
98/9 Panini Photocard
89/0 Panini Sticker 327
90/1 Panini Sticker 139
90/1 Panini/QUE 18
91/2 Panini Sticker 257
91/2 Panini Sticker 334
92/3 Panini Sticker 209
93/4 Panini Sticker G
94/5 Panini Sticker 56
95/6 Panini Sticker 246
96/7 Panini Sticker 155, 245
97/8 Panini Sticker 204
98/9 Panini Sticker 189
99/0 Panini Sticker 210, 327
00/1 Panini Sticker 132
95 Panini Worlds 20
91/2 Parkhurst 148
92/3 Parkhurst 147
93/4 Parkhurst 169
93/4 Parkhurst E9
94/5 Parkhurst V34, YCTG-19
95/6 Parkhurst 46, PP-8, PP-16
00/1 Parkhurst P-13
01/2 Parkhurst 26, ✄ PJ15, ✄ PS15, ✄ PSJ13, ✄ HSHSJers, ✄ M51, ✄ H8, ✄ T5, ✄ T22
02/3 Parkhurst 109, -HHH4, -HHP4, -HHR4, ✄ GJ34, ✄ SJ34, ✄ HSHSJers, ✄ MM8, ✄ PP5, ✄ TT19
02/3 Parkhurst Retro 15, ✄ RF9, ✄ RJ20, ✄ RSJ13, ✄ HSHSJers, ✄ RM2, ✄ RM23
94/5 Parkie SE147
91/2 Pinnacle 150
91/2 Pinnacle 381
92/3 Pinnacle 150
92/3 Pinnacle T2K 21
93/4 Pinnacle 290
93/4 Pinnacle CA19
93/4 Pinnacle T2K1 25
94/5 Pinnacle 50, NL4
95/6 Pinnacle R20-17
96/7 Pinnacle 201, TP-1, T-9
97/8 Pinnacle 32, P-12
96/7 Pi. Be A Player BB-16
97/8 Pi. Be A Player 83, TN-19, ✍ Aut. 83
97/8 Pi. BeeHive 4, BHT-19
97/8 Pi. Certified 50
97/8 Pi. Epix E3
96/7 Pi. FANtasy 17
97/8 Pi. Inside 54, IT-8, / Can 15
96/7 Pi. Mint 11
97/8 Pi. Mint 12
95/6 Pi. Summit 61
96/7 Pi. Summit 1, HV-2, U-3
97/8 Pi. Totally 50
95/6 Pi. Zenith 64, ZT-13
96/7 Pi. Zenith 44, CS-8
95/6 Playoff 28, 139, 242
96/7 Playoff 432
94/5 POG 199
95/6 POG 72
94/5 Post
97/8 Pi. Post 3, F5
93/4 Power Play 204
93/4 Power Play PL 15
93/4 Premier 10
93/4 Prmr. - BG-OPC 15
94/5 Premier 480, GTG-2
00/1 Premier Plus 19, PP2
99/0 Prism 41, SGDC-7
00/1 Pr. Stock 26, AC-8, EA-5, Res. 7, PS-13, PSS-8, ✄ GUG-29, ✄ GUG-30
01/2 Pr. Stock 24, Res. 3, -PS 19, ✄ GUG 31
02/3 Pr. Stock Reserve ✄ 111
00/1 PS Titanium 23, 3SS-12, NAAS-5, ✄ GUG-9, ✄ GUG-79, ✄ GUG-153
01/2 PS Titanium 37, TSS 13, ✄ DSJ 12, ✄ DSJ 42
01/2 PS Titanium Draft ✄ 27
02/3 PS Titanium 27, -SK 3, -S 4
00/1 PS Titanium Draft ✄ 26
95/6 Pro Magnet 79
90/1 Pro Set 257, 375
91/2 Pro Set 199
91/2 Pro Set 315
92/3 Pro Set 150
91 Pro Set Awards AC5
91/2 Pro Set Platinum 102
91/2 Puck / Pro Set 23
02/3 Quest for the Cup 24, -RTC 3
99/0 Revolution 43, IS-4, NI-7, SS-11, TL-13, / CSC 43
00/1 Revolution 39, HD-10, NI-8, SM-24, ✄ GUG-2
90/1 Score 8
90/1 Sco. Hot Cards 7
91/2 Score 25
91/2 Score 336
91/2 Score CAN 25
91/2 Score CAN 366
92/3 Score 240
92/3 Score 434
93/4 Score 135
93/4 Score DT 14
93/4 Score/CAN DD5
93/4 Score PiAS 13
93/4 Score TF 17
94/5 Score NP19, TF-19
95/6 Score 5, BB-4, GB-1
96/7 Score 9, DT-3, SD-11
97/8 Score 125
97/8 Score Colo. 18
90/1 Sco. Young Stars 10
91/2 Score Young Stars 20
92/3 Score Young Stars 20
92/3 Seasons 47
93/4 Seasons 17
94/5 Select 62
95/6 Select CE 45, GT-8
96/7 Select CE 16, C-9
95 Semic 87
91 Semic Sticker 75
93 Semic Sticker 206
96/7 SB 7-Eleven Phonecard
00/1 Signature 167, HSHS, ✍ Aut. 170, ✄ J-31, ✄ HSHSJers
01/2 Signature C-20, ✍ Aut., ✄ FP8, ✄ GUE15, ✄ GJ16, ✄ GSJ16, ✄ HSHSJers 2, ✄ ITN15, ✄ IG12, ✄ TM8
02/3 Signature 141, GS-43, ✍ 141, ✄ CJ9, ✄ FJ9, ✄ SGJ22, ✄ TQ1, ✄ TM10
95/6 SBx Emotion 42, Xce-9, Xci-13
95/6 SBx Impact 41
96/7 SBx Impact 28, CTI-10, VT-9
95/6 SkyBox SkyMint
02/3 Slam Card
94/5 SP 94, P-27
95/6 SP 31, E8
96/7 SP 34, CW-19, Ins.
97/8 SP Authentic 35, I4
98/9 SP Authentic 22, SS19, SO18
99/0 SP Authentic 23, SF2
00/1 SP Authentic 25
01/2 SP Authentic 16, 94, ✄ NN, ✄ PP
01/2 SP Authentic 94
02/3 SP Authentic 21, 94, ✄ SP, ✄ DP
00/1 SP GU 14, ✄ TotG, ✄ C, ✄ P
01/2 SP GU 10, ✄ AF (x2), ✄ AFD, ✄ AFT, ✄ AFQ (x2), ✄ Patch, ✄ PatchC, ✄ PatchT
02/3 SP GU 12, ✄ AF (x2), ✄ CF, ✄ PC, ✄ PH (x2)
02/3 Sports Vault 185
96/7 SPx 9
97/8 SPx 12, -DV
99/0 SPx 39, P4
00/1 SPx 13, X4, ✄ WM
01/2 SPx 13, 81, ✄ TT
02/3 SPx 18, 83, 131, ✄ M, ✄ SS
98/9 SPx Finite 22, 92, 163
98/9 SPx Prospects 15, H8, L13, PS22, ✄ WM
00/1 Stadion 192
99/0 Stadium 47, Chrome 23, Big 12, EG5, OE6
00/1 Stadium 182, BT8, ✄ SCS
01/2 Stadium 61, G6,NHLP19, P2, ✄ SCSD (x2), ✄ SCST
02/3 Stadium 9, -WS-4
96/7 SLU
98/9 SLU
00/1 SLU 2
02/3 Starz
95/6 Super Sticker 27, DC-4
96/7 Team Out!
92/3 Topps 495
95/6 Topps 266, M6, PF20
98/9 Topps 68, L10, M20
99/0 Topps 1, 285, IM1, AM5, FF6, TW14, SC10, ✍ SCH, ✍ TA1
00/1 Topps 109, PC-15, OTG9
01/2 Topps 27, 318, OTG2, SM4, SG4, ✄ CC1
02/3 Topps 196, 330, CC9, HHU2, ✄ CC1, ✄ CC7, ✄ CC13
01/2 Topps All-Star Game 3
99/0 To. Chrome 1, 285, IM1, AM5, FF6
00/1 To. Chrome 85, PC-15
01/2 To. Chrome 27
02/3 T. Chrome 111
94/5 Topps Finest 69, BBB-18, BBM-3
95/6 To. Finest 15, 80
98/9 To. Finest 91, M23, M26, M28, M30, R15
98/9 T. Gold Label 65, GR10
99/0 To. Gold Label 35, PG11
00/1 To. Gold Label 65, GG8
00/1 To. Heritage 54
01/2 To. Heritage 74, 115, 123, 124, 125, 130
02/3 To. Heritage 34, 118
00/1 To. Heritage ASG 4
02/3 To. Limited 196, 330
96/7 To. Picks FT20, TS-12
99/0 To. Prmr. Plus 68, FP1
01/2 To. Reserve 1, ✄ TR
91/2 To. Stadium 389
92/3 To. Stadium 3
93/4 To. Stadium 32
93/4 To. Stadium - AS
95/6 To. Stadium EC167
93/4 TSC Members Only 39
94/5 TSC Members Only 13
95/6 TSC Members Only 17
00/1 To. Stars 25, 137, AS9
95/6 T. Super Skills 17
02/3 To. Total 319, TP2, TT5
98/9 UD Choice 59, 230, BH19, SQ11
00/1 UD Heroes 142, L3
01/2 UD PlayMakers Ltd 23, / PM
00/1 UD Reserve 24, GS2, OS3
02/3 UD Superstars 68, ✄ CAS
98/9 UD3 59, 119, 179
00/1 Ultimate Mem. ✍ U-28, ✄ J-28, ✄ Jers. 25, ✄ S-28, ✄ TM-16, ✄ TM-17, ✄ UC-8
01/2 Ultimate Mem. ✄ A8, ✄ ASGH, ✄ DD, ✄ GUE, ✄ GUJ, ✄ GUSJ, ✄ GAO, ✄ ITN, ✄ NP, ✄ PP, ✄ RA (x3), ✄ SCPR, ✄ WTF, ✍ Aut.
02/3 Ultimate Mem. ✄ 500GSJ, ✄ 500GSSJ, ✄ A8, ✄ CSTW, ✄ DD, ✄ Emb, ✄ FS, ✄ GUSJ, ✄ GUSJ, ✄ GD, ✄ GAO, ✄ HT, ✄ ITN, ✄ LA, ✄ MO, ✄ NP, ✄ Num, ✄ PS (x2), ✄ RAT, ✄ UC, ✍ UAut
99/0 Ult. Victory 23, FF9, S2
90/1 Upper Deck 164, 301, 490
91/2 Upper Deck 333
91/2 Upper Deck 616
92/3 Upper Deck 36
92/3 Upper Deck 255
92/3 Upper Deck WG8
93/4 Upper Deck 69, 223, NL3, H9, SP-130
94/5 Upper Deck 404, H17, SP-65
95/6 Upper Deck 54, 242, R14, R27, R36, R45, SE-111
96/7 Upper Deck 204, 240, X3, HH20, LS7, SS16A
97/8 Upper Deck 253, SS19, SG35, S4, T3A, ✄ GJ7
98/9 Upper Deck 248, FF6, FT23, LS2
99/0 Upper Deck 159, 211, CT6, FF15, HOF13, ✄ GJ
00/1 Upper Deck 273, L2, P2, TT5, ✄ GJ, ✄ DGJ
01/2 Upper Deck 274, CT1, FF9, FC6, GA8, LP3, SS3, SS13, T2, ✄ ASJ, ✄ CJers, ✄ PatchN, ✄ PatchNu, ✄ PF, ✄ PoaN, ✄ PoaND, ✄ SCFJers, ✄ SCFJersD, ✄ SCFJersT
02/3 Upper Deck 47, 184, -GG3, -SS4, -SS5, ✄ ASJ, ✄ CG, ✄ GO, ✄ LN, ✄ PN, ✄ R50, ✄ FC, ✄ GJ, ✄ PW, ✄ UDPL
95/6 UD ASG MVP5
00/1 UD ASG PP2, HH3
02/3 UD Artistic 22, R22, UD1, ✄ AT, / Art
93/4 Upper Deck Be A Player 14
94/5 UD BAP R96
93/4 UD BAP Roots 16
96/7 UD Black Diam. 169, RC10
97/8 UD Black Diam. 96, PC29
98/9 UD Black Diam. 23,M13, WF8
99/0 UD Black Diam. 25, M4, ✄ APOH
00/1 UD Black Diam. ✄ GG
99/0 UD C. Legends 65
01/2 UD Challenge 17, CM2, CR3, FF1, ✄ TN, ✄ UC
02/3 UD Classic 25, ET2, PS3, ✄ HH, ✄ HR (x3)
95/6 UD CC 288, 362, C9
96/7 UD CC 64, 299, 314, 336, UD5, C7, CR7
97/8 UD Coll. Choice 55, SQ63, S19, W6, C18, CR18
01/2 UD Collectors
97/8 UD Diam. Vision 20, DM5
98/9 UD G. Reserve 248
99/0 UD G. Reserve 159, 211
01/2 UD Honor Roll 14, 44, SG2, ✄ GAJ, ✄ PPM
02/3 UD Honor 16, 78, -SG6, ✄ GA
96/7 UD Ice 108, S5
97/8 UD Ice 79, IC10
00/1 UD Ice ✄ IGJ
01/2 UD Ice 90, ✄ JC, ✄ FJ
00/1 UD Legends SM7, ✄ LGJ
92/3 UD Locker 13
01/2 UD Mask 22, ✄ PM
02/3 UD Mask 23, ✄ IO, ✄ PG
98/9 UD MVP 53, OT15, -Snip. S10, F15
99/0 UD MVP 51, ✄ GU22
00/1 UD MVP 48, M4
01/2 UD MVP 43 , MT2, VC3, MW2, -J, ✄ C
02/3 UD MVP 49, VF6, SA, SD, ST
99/0 UD MVP Cup 52, CP3, SC4, ✄ GU
99/0 UD Ovation 17
00/1 UD Pearson
02/3 UD Piece 26, 104, AC6, ✄ PH, ✄ SS
96/7 UD Post, SU-4
01/2 UD Premier 11, ✄ B, ✄ S, ✄ D (x2)
02/3 UD Premier 14, ✄ Jers, ✄ JD, ✄ Patch, ✄ NHLP
99/0 UD Retro 21
02/3 UD Rookie 25, 112, ✄ DJ, ✄ S
01/2 UD SCup Champs 37, ✄ S, ✄ G, ✄ T
01/2 UD Top Shelf 8, ✄ J, ✄ S, ✄ ST (x2)
02/3 UD Top Shelf 22, ✄ AS, ✄ CP, ✄ GO, ✄ HH (x3), ✄ HT, ✄ ST, ✄ SW, ✄ TS
00/1 UD Vintage 88, 98, 99, S2A
01/2 UD Vintage 64, 69, 70, 261, 263, 264, 265, ✄ NL
02/3 UD Vintage 67, 268, 291, 307, T17
97/8 Valu-net, ✍ Aut.
00/1 Vanguard 30, HV-9, ✄ DGJ-3
01/2 Vanguard 27, EMW 3, IF 2, VT 12
02/3 Vanguard 28, -EMW 7, -IF 4, VT 9, ✄ GWJ 13
99/0 Victory 79, 335, 340
00/1 Victory 62, 245, 293
01/2 Victory 91, 397
02/3 Victory 53, -NP4
01/2 Waving the Flag 2
99/0 WGretzky 46, EG14, GH3
96 Wien 95
97/8 Zenith 29, Z7
99/0 COLO / Kid Smart
88/9 QUÉB
88/9 QUÉB / Gene. Foods
89/0 QUÉB
89/0 QUÉB / Gene. Foods
89/0 QUÉB / Police
90/1 QUÉB
90/1 QUÉB / Petro-Canada
91/2 QUÉB / Petro-Canada
92/3 QUÉB / Petro-Canada
94/5 QUÉB / Burger King

SAKURAI, TERUO
79 Panini Sticker 290

SALAJKO, JEFF
95/6 Slapshot 331
92/3 Ottawa 67's

SALASHCHENKO, ALEXEI
98/9 Sudbury Wolves 3
99/0 Sudbury Wolves 13

SALEI, RUSLAN
02/3 First Edition 196
96/7 Fl. Ultra 5
96/7 Metal Univ. 191
98/9 OPC Chrome 99
99/0 Pacific 14
01/2 Pacific 10
02/3 Pacific Complete 455
99/0 Pa. Paramount 7
97/8 Pa. Revolution 4
98/9 Panini Sticker 174
00/1 Panini Sticker 112
97/8 Pi. Be A Player 124, ✍ Aut. 124
96/7 Select CE 109
96/7 SP 169
98/9 Topps 99
99/0 Topps 140
99/0 To. Chrome 140
02/3 To. Total 85
96/7 Upper Deck 215
02/3 Upper Deck 251
02/3 UD Vintage 6
02/3 Victory - NP1
99/0 Cincinnati M'Ducks
95/6 Las Vegas Thunder

SALESKI, DON
77/8 Coke
74/5 Loblaws
72/3 O-Pee-Chee 213
74/5 O-Pee-Chee 283
75/6 O-Pee-Chee 262
76/7 O-Pee-Chee 81
77/8 O-Pee-Chee 233
78/9 O-Pee-Chee 257
75/6 Topps 262
76/7 Topps 81
77/8 Topps 233
78/9 Topps 257
79/0 COLR

SALEVA, HENRY
80/1 Mallasjuoma 182
78/9 SM-Liiga 86
72/3 Williams Finnish 95
73/4 Williams Finnish 143

SALFI, KENT
92/3 Maine Black Bears

SALFICKY, DUSAN
94/5 APS 25
95/6 APS 317
96/7 APS 144
97/8 APS 173
97/8 DS 49
98/9 DS 17
99/0 DS 85, G7
00/1 DS 25, G3, NT1, WCH2
01/2 DS 50
96/7 DS Sticker 246
98/9 OFS 34, 447
99/0 OFS 15, 488, 552, -CI
00/1 OFS 57, Star. 16
01/2 OFS -UHI 16

SALITKOV, OLEG
99/0 Mir 266

SALLAMAA, ASKO
66/7 Champion 210

SÄLLE, JOHAN
94/5 Leaf Elit Set 244
95/6 Leaf Elit Set 265
90/1 Semic Elitserien 130
91/2 Semic Elitserien 183
92/3 Semic Elitserien 208
95/6 UD Elitserien 137

SALLINEN, PASI
71/2 Williams Finnish 334

SALMELAINEN, TOMMI
72 Hellas MM-Jenkki 14
80/1 Mallasjuoma 6
72 Panda MM-Toronto
72 Panda MM-Toronto
72 Semic Sticker 87
78/9 SM-Liiga 33
71/2 Williams Finnish 75
71/2 Williams Finnish 125
72/3 Williams Finnish 96
73/4 Williams Finnish 142

SALMELAINEN, TONY
00/1 Cardset 138, 277
02/3 Cardset 262
02/3 Hamilton Bulldogs

SALMI, MATTI
66/7 Champion 52
65/6 Hellas 41
70/1 Kuvajulkaisut 203
72 Panda MM-Toronto
71/2 Williams Finnish 92
72/3 Williams Finnish 257

SALMINEN, ASKO
73/4 Williams Finnish 299

SALMINEN, HEIKKI
73/4 Williams Finnish 190

SALMINEN, JUSSI
00/1 Cardset 311
95/6 UD CC 339

SALMINEN, KIMMO
98/9 Cardset 261
00/1 Cardset 297
94/5 Sisu 73, MN-9
95/6 Sisu 63
96/7 Sisu 63

SALMINEN, MAURI
72/3 Williams Finnish 295

SALMINEN, PETRI
70/1 Kuvajulkaisut 338

SALMINEN, TEIJO
70/1 Kuvajulkaisut 355

SALMING, BÖRJE
00/1 Alfabilder
99/0 BAP Mem. CH-1, ✍ CH-1
79/0 Dernière Heure
88/9 Esso All-Star
01/2 Fleer Greats 73, ✍ Aut., ✄ OSS
01/2 Fleer Legacy 33, ✄ ITC, ✄ TM
83/4 Funmate Puffy 6 [w/]
92/3 Future Trends C76 145
92/3 Future Trends C76 188
92/3 Future Trends C76 197
95 Globe 67
72 Hellas MM-Jenkki 42
75/6 Hockey Heroes
93/4 Hockey Wit 37
84/5 Kellogg's 25
86/7 Kraft Sports 57
74/5 Lipton Soup 41
74/5 Loblaws
74/5 O-Pee-Chee 180
75/6 O-Pee-Chee 283
75/6 O-Pee-Chee 294
76/7 O-Pee-Chee 22
77/8 OPC 2
77/8 O-Pee-Chee 140
78/9 O-Pee-Chee 240
78/9 O-Pee-Chee 328
79/0 O-Pee-Chee 40
80/1 O-Pee-Chee 85
80/1 O-Pee-Chee 210
81/2 O-Pee-Chee 307
82/3 O-Pee-Chee 332
83/4 O-Pee-Chee 341
84/5 O-Pee-Chee 311
85/6 O-Pee-Chee 248
86/7 OPC/Topps 169
87/8 O-Pee-Chee 237
88/9 OPC/Topps 247
89/0 O-Pee-Chee 278
81/2 OPC Sticker 98
81/2 OPC Sticker 111
82/3 OPC/Topps Sticker 75
82/3 OPC/Topps Sticker 76
83/4 OPC/Topps Sticker 33
83/4 OPC/Topps Sticker 34
84/5 OPC Sticker 7
84/5 OPC Sticker 8
85/6 OPC Sticker 12
86/7 OPC Sticker 136-244
87/8 OPC Sticker 165
88/9 OPC Sticker 174
80/1 O-Pee-Chee Super 19
87/8 Panini Sticker 326
88/9 Panini Sticker 120
80/1 Pepsi Bottle Cap
81/2 Post 18
82/3 Post [Toro.]
87/8 Pro Sport CW16
90/1 Semic Elitserien 77
91/2 Semic Elitserien 4
92/3 Semic Elitserien 36
82 Semic Sticker 143
92 Semic Sticker 60
85/6 7-Eleven Superstars 18
83/4 Souhaits Keychain [Maple Leafs]
77-79 Sports. FIN 70-1663
74/5 Topps 180
75/6 Topps 283
75/6 Topps 294
76/7 Topps 22
77/8 Topps 2, 140
78/9 Topps 240
79/0 Topps 40
80/1 Topps 85
80/1 Topps 210
81/2 Topps 33
01/2 Upper Deck ✄ PotL
02/3 UD Foundations 21, 88, ✄ CG, ✄ DF, ✄ PP
02/3 UD Piece ✄ HH, ✄ HS
83/4 Vachon 97-17
72/3 Williams Finnish 56
73/4 Williams Finnish 34
89/0 DETR / Little Caesars
73/4 TORO
74/5 TORO
75/6 TORO
76/7 TORO
77/8 TORO
78/9 TORO
79/0 TORO
80/1 TORO
81/2 TORO
82/3 TORO
83/4 TORO
84/5 TORO
85/6 TORO
86/7 TORO
86/7 TORO
87/8 TORO / 5x8
87/8 TORO / P.L.A.Y. 8
88/9 TORO / P.L.A.Y. 5

SALMING, STIG
79 Panini Sticker 189

SALMON, TIM
83/4 Kingston Canadians

SALMOND, SCOTT
91/2 Avant Garde BCJHL 73

SALNIKOV, ROMAN
98/9 Mir 116
00/1 Mir 59

SALO, ARI
92/3 Jyvas Hyva 65
93/4 Jyvas Hyva 115
90/1 Semic Elitserien 5
93/4 Sisu 5
94/5 Sisu 119

SALO, JUHA
92/3 Jyvas Hyva 63
70/1 Kuvajulkaisut 339

SALO, KALEVI
65/6 Hellas 56

SALO, ROBERT
98/9 Cardset 14
92/3 Jyvas Hyva 110
93/4 Jyvas Hyva 201
93/4 Sisu 259
93/4 Sisu 341
94/5 Sisu 93
95/6 Sisu 84

SALO, SAMI
99/0 BAP Mem. 56, SL-17
00/1 BAP Mem. 387
99/0 Cardset AH 3-ruutu
02/3 Cardset 263, -SGSP 3
98/9 Dynagon Ice 131
02/3 First Edition 178
99/0 Millenium 174, ✍ Aut. 174
98/9 Omega 171
99/0 Pacific 295
00/1 Pacific 287
02/3 Pacific 273
02/3 Pacific Complete 482
99/0 Pa. Paramount 165
94/5 Sisu 236
95/6 Sisu 124
96/7 Sisu 137, RE-3
99/0 SPx 106
99/0 Topps 168
99/0 To. Chrome 168
99/0 Upper Deck 91
01/2 Upper Deck 354
99/0 UD G. Reserve 91
99/0 UD MVP 143
00/1 UD Vintage 255
99/0 Victory 203
98/9 OTTA
99/0 OTTA
00/1 OTTA
01/2 OTTA

SALO, TAPANI
66/7 Champion 207

SALO, TOMMY
01/2 Adrenaline 77, CL 7, PP 15
01/2 Atomic 42, TN 7
02/3 Atomic 43
98/9 Aurora 119
99/0 Aurora 58, -GU 9
00/1 Aurora 57
02/3 BAP All-Star 82, ✄ ASJ
98/9 Be A Player 83, ✍ Aut. 83
99/0 BAP Mem. 39
00/1 BAP Mem. 68
01/2 BAP Mem. 50, ✄ ASJ, ✄ ASE, ✄ ASN, ✄ AST, ✄ CoO, ✄ SCP
02/3 BAP Mem. 160
01/2 BT Pipes 30, HSHS, -Mask, ✄ ASJ, ✄ GJ, ✄ GE, ✄ S&J, ✄ ITN, ✄ -HSHS Jers.
02/3 Between the Pipes 5, 132, M12, ✄ ASJ9, ✄ BM5, ✄ DM8, ✄ GUE30, ✄ GB16, ✄ GUJ30, ✄ GSJ30, ✄ GN3, ✄ GN7, ✄ HSHSJers 7, ✄ ITN30, ✄ T18
98/9 Bicycle.. Q-D
01/2 Bowman 12
02/3 Bowman 89
94/5 Cla. Images 3, CE3, PR8
99/0 Crown Royale 55
00/1 Crown Royale 42
01/2 Crown Royale 61
02/3 Crown Royale 40, ✄ GWDP 10
95/6 Donruss 196
97/8 Donruss 33
97/8 Do. Canadian 106
97/8 Do. Elite 101
97/8 Do. Preferred 32
97/8 Do. Priority 121, PG-15
98/9 Dynagon Ice 118
99/0 Dynagon Ice 84
95/6 Edge Ice 196, C-22, PR-2
02/3 Exclusive 71, ✄ GWJ 9
02/3 First Edition 52, ✄ Jers.
96/7 Flair 57
95/6 Fleer Metal 191, MW-6
95/6 Fleer Ultra 98, 354
95/6 Future Legends 41
95 Globe 3
01/2 Heads Up 41, HD 14, SS 8
02/3 Heads Up 50, ✄ GWQ 31
02/3 In The GU ✄ IE24
99/0 Kraft / JELL-O
95/6 Leaf 177
96/7 Leaf 221
94/5 Leaf Elit Set GC 24
97/8 Limited 130
01/2 McDonald's 16, -GSNF 2
02/3 McDonald's -GSNF 3
99/0 Millenium 103, ✍ Aut. 103
01/2 O-Pee-Chee 108
02/3 O-Pee-Chee 218
98/9 OPC Chrome 88
97/8 Omega 142
98/9 Omega 152
99/0 Omega 93
98/9 Pacific 288
99/0 Pacific 164, -ITCNF 8
00/1 Pacific 172, 438, ✍ Aut. 172
01/2 Pacific 164, SC 8
02/3 Pacific 148, ✄ GWJ 19
02/3 Pacific Complete 254
97/8 Pacific CC 56
97/8 Pa. Crown Roy. 81
98/9 Pa. Crown Roy. 86
97/8 Pa. Dynagon 75, S-13, T-67
97/8 Pa. Invincible 83
97/8 Pa. Paramount 111, GSL-12
98/9 Pa. Paramount 148, -GS 11
99/0 Pa. Paramount 95, -GS 9
00/1 Pa. Paramount 98, GS-10
97/8 Pa. Revolution 84, RTS-12
98/9 Pa. Revolution 90
98/9 Panini Photocard
95/6 Panini Sticker 101
97/8 Panini Sticker 74
98/9 Panini Sticker 72
99/0 Panini Sticker 241
95/6 Parkhurst 128
00/1 Parkhurst P-224
01/2 Parkhurst 72, ✄ HSHJers, ✄ T26
02/3 Parkhurst 67
02/3 Parkhurst Retro 33
95/6 Pinnacle 202
96/7 Pinnacle 244
97/8 Pinnacle 59
96/7 Pi. Be A Player 77, ✍ Aut. 77
97/8 Pi. Be A Player STP 14
97/8 Pi. Certified 24
97/8 Pi. Inside 49
96/7 Pi. Summit 189
97/8 Pi. Totally 24
95/6 Playoff 282
00/1 Premier Plus 77, MB20
99/0 Prism 56
00/1 Pr. Stock 39, ✄ GUG-49
01/2 Pr. Stock 40, GR 5, -PS 31
02/3 Pr. Stock Reserve -ICS 9, ✄ 123
00/1 PS Titanium 36
01/2 PS Titanium 57
02/3 PS Titanium 43, ✄ GWJ 29
02/3 Quest for the Cup 39
99/0 Revolution 59, / CSC 59
00/1 Revolution 58
95/6 Score 314
97/8 Score 9, NW-12
95/6 Select CE 112
95 Semic 53
91/2 Semic Elitserien 254
92/3 Semic Elitserien 275
00/1 Signature 157, ✍ Aut. 67
01/2 Signature C-48, ✍ Aut., ✄ GP12, ✄ GU88
02/3 Signature 105, ✍ 105, ✄ TQ17
95/6 SBx Emotion 107, GN-5
95/6 SBx Impact 104
97/8 SP Authentic 93
00/1 SP Authentic 37, ✍ SotT
01/2 SP Authentic 32, ✍ SotT, ✍ SotTD, ✍ SotTT
02/3 SP Authentic 38
00/1 SP GU 26
02/3 Sports Vault 230
99/0 SPx 64
00/1 SPx 27
01/2 SPx 27
02/3 SPx 33
00/1 Stadium 74
01/2 Stadium 26
02/3 Stadium 81, -PSH12
98/9 Topps 88
00/1 Topps 107, PP3
01/2 Topps 108, OTG27, SG10
02/3 Topps 218, HHC14
00/1 To. Chrome 83
01/2 To. Chrome 108
02/3 T. Chrome 121
00/1 To. Gold Label 49
00/1 To. Heritage 66
01/2 To. Heritage 51, 127
02/3 To. Heritage 65
02/3 To. Limited 218
01/2 To. Reserve 72
95/6 To. Stadium 211
00/1 To. Stars 52
02/3 To. Total 341, TTC11
00/1 UD Heroes 48, ✍ SG
01/2 UD PlayMakers Ltd 40
00/1 UD Reserve 34, GG4
00/1 Ultimate Mem. ✄ G-12
01/2 Ultimate Mem. ✄ BAPL, ✄ WTF
95/6 Upper Deck 413
98/9 Upper Deck 317
99/0 Upper Deck 56
00/1 Upper Deck 70
01/2 Upper Deck 68, GL7
02/3 Upper Deck 71, -LL5
02/3 UD Artistic 38, R38, / Art
96/7 UD Black Diam. 31
00/1 UD Black Diam. 25, ✄ GG
01/2 UD Challenge 34, BB5
02/3 UD Classic 40
95/6 UD CC 235
97/8 UD Coll. Choice 158
95/6 UD Elitserien 246
98/9 UD G. Reserve 317
99/0 UD G. Reserve 56
02/3 UD Honor 31
01/2 UD Ice 18
01/2 UD Mask 112, 178, -StS
02/3 UD Mask 34, 35, 36, ✄ CW, ✄ PW, ✄ VC
98/9 UD MVP 129
99/0 UD MVP 80
00/1 UD MVP 77
01/2 UD MVP 75, MM5, ✄ GS
02/3 UD MVP 73, ✍ PSig
99/0 UD MVP Cup 71
02/3 UD Piece 39
01/2 UD Premier 26, -PrSig
00/1 UD Pros&Prosp. 34
02/3 UD Rookie 42, ✄ DJ
01/2 UD Top Shelf 18
02/3 UD Top Shelf 34, ✍ Sig
00/1 UD Vintage 144, 148, 149, GG9
01/2 UD Vintage 97, 105
02/3 UD Vintage 99, 272, GB 99, T29
00/1 Vanguard 43
01/2 Vanguard 40, SW 8
02/3 Vanguard 43
99/0 Victory 112
00/1 Victory 96
01/2 Victory 134, 138
02/3 Victory 84, - NP46
01/2 Waving the Flag 19
96 Wien 39, SG9
96/7 NYIS
01/2 Utah Grizzlies

SALO, VESA
98/9 Cardset 256
99/0 Cardset 150
00/1 Cardset 345
96/7 DEL 151
97/8 Hockey-Box
92/3 Jyvas Hyva 89
93/4 Jyvas Hyva 166
95/6 Leaf Elit Set 227
93/4 Sisu 169
94/5 Sisu 242, 384
95/6 Sisu 96
95/6 Sisu Limited 67
95/6 UD Elitserien 81

SALOMAA, LAURI
66/7 Champion 150
70/1 Kuvajulkaisut 221
71/2 Williams Finnish 218
72/3 Williams Finnish 167
73/4 Williams Finnish 233

SALOMAA, SAMI-VILLE
98/9 Cardset 212
95/6 SR Tetrad Autobilia 52
96/7 Sisu 123

SALOMATIN, ALEXEI
94/5 Leaf Elit Set 35
95/6 Leaf Elit Set 133, FTF-12
95/6 UD Elitserien 194
97/8 UD Elitserien 98

SALOMONSSON, ANDREAS
01/2 Adrenaline 215
01/2 BAP Mem. 364
01/2 Crown Royale 168
96/7 DEL 104
94/5 Leaf Elit Set 265
95/6 Leaf Elit Set 108
01/2 O-Pee-Chee 356
01/2 Parkhurst 256
01/2 PS Titanium 168
01/2 PS Titanium Draft 149
91/2 Semic Elitserien 224
92/3 Semic Elitserien 243
01/2 Signature 203, ✍ Aut. 203
01/2 SP Authentic 158
01/2 SPx 113
01/2 SPx Rookie RR18
01/2 Stadium 129
01/2 Topps 356
01/2 To. Chrome 174
01/2 To. Heritage 143
01/2 To. Reserve 114
01/2 UD PlayMakers Ltd 127
01/2 Upper Deck 431
01/2 UD Challenge 118
95/6 UD Elitserien 167
97/8 UD Elitserien 163
98/9 UD Elitserien 173
99/0 UD Elitserien 175
00/1 UD Elitserien 57
01/2 UD Honor Roll 80
01/2 UD Ice 60
01/2 UD Premier 70
01/2 UD Vintage 286
01/2 Vanguard 119

SALOMONSSON, STIG
93/4 Greensboro Monarchs

SALON, IVAN
93/4 Saskatoon Blades
93/4 Saskatoon Blades

SALONEN, JOEL
98/9 Cardset 198
99/0 Cardset 308
00/1 Cardset 326
97/8 Hockey-Box

SALONEN, KARI
72/3 Williams Finnish 237
73/4 Williams Finnish 272

SALONEN, MARTTI
66/7 Champion 56
70/1 Kuvajulkaisut 149
71/2 Williams Finnish 200

SALONEN, SAMI
98/9 Cardset 224
99/0 Cardset 130
00/1 Cardset 228
95/6 UD CC 328

SALONEN, TIMO
99/0 Cardset 151
02/3 Cardset 264
97/8 Hockey-Box
00/1 Kudos 122
94/5 Parkie SE223
94/5 Sisu 255
95/6 Sisu 359
96/7 Sisu 162
94/5 Topps Finest 137
95/6 Upper Deck 547

SALOSENSAARI, ESA
70/1 Kuvajulkaisut 340

SALOVAARA, BARRY
78/9 SM-Liiga 96

SALSTEN, FETTER
92 Semic Sticker 29

SALSTEN, JØRGEN
92/3 Semic Nordisk 104

SALSTEN, PETTER
95 Panini Worlds 239
94 Semic 258
95 Semic 178
90/1 Semic Elitserien 79
92/3 Semic Nordisk 48
93 Semic Sticker 231
96 Wien 204

SALVADOR, BRYCE
00/1 BAP Mem. 465
00/1 Premier Plus 123
00/1 Pr. Stock 143
00/1 PS Titanium Draft 172
00/1 SP Authentic 162
00/1 SPx 186
00/1 To. Stars 106
02/3 To. Total 304
00/1 Upper Deck 431
00/1 UD Ice 123
01/2 UD Vintage 224
93/4 Lethbridge Hurricanes
95/6 Lethbridge Hurricanes

SALVAIL, ERIC
99/0 Rimouski Océanic 18
00/1 Rimouski Océanic 21
01/2 Rimouski Océanic 20

SALVIS, RYAN
01/2 Moncton Wildcats 16

SALVO, LINO
91/2 7th...Sketch LHJMQ 156

SALZBRUNN, JEFF
89/0 Nashville Knights

SAMEC, JIM
83/4 Soo Greyhounds

SAMIS, PHIL
51/2 Cleveland Barons
52/3 St. Lawrence 10

SAMMALKANGAS, TAPIO
99/0 Cardset 250
00/1 Cardset 32

SAMOILOV, IGOR
00/1 Mir 118

SAMOKHVALOV, ANDREI
98/9 Mir 47
99/0 Mir 180
00/1 Mir 231

SAMOLENKO, G.
59/60 Whitby Dunlops

SAMPSON, GARY
86/7 WASH / Kodak

SAMSONOV, SERGEI
01/2 Adrenaline 15, ✄ GWJ 2
96/7 All-Sport PPF 176
01/2 Atomic 8, PP 3, TN 1
02/3 Atomic 7
98/9 Aurora 14, ALC-3, CF-5
99/0 Aurora 13
00/1 Aurora 14
96/7 Auto. Coll. ✍ Aut.
98/9 Be A Player 10, ✍ Aut. 10
99/0 BAP Mem. 280, SL-14
00/1 BAP Mem. 95
01/2 BAP Mem. 70
02/3 BAP Mem. 169
01/2 Bowman 106
02/3 Bowman 71
98/9 Bowman's Best 66, BP2, F11
02/3 Calder 9
98/9 Collection Souvenir 06
99/0 Crown Royale 14
00/1 Crown Royale 11
01/2 Crown Royale 12, ✄ TT 13
02/3 Crown Royale 7
98/9 Donruss ES 7
97/8 Do. Elite 16, 134, C-12
97/8 Do. Preferred 148, 195, LT-4B, PM-15, / Tin 11, WideTin 6
97/8 Do. Priority 178, 200, 218, DD-6, OD-30, Post-17, Stamp-17
98/9 Dynagon Ice 14
99/0 Dynagon Ice 25
02/3 Exclusive 13
02/3 First Edition 31, 418H, ✄ Jers., ✄ TSL 3
01/2 Heads Up 9, ✄ JQ 2
02/3 Heads Up 10, -HF 3, ✄ GWQ 3
99/0 HoloGrFX 4, PS4
02/3 In The GU 8, 108, ✄ GUJ31, ✄ SJ31, ✄ T3, ✄ TM12
97/8 Leaf 151, 199, FOI-15
97/8 Limited 131, FG-21
97/8 McDonald's McD-40
98/9 McDonald's McD13
99/0 Millenium 22, ✍ Aut. 22
98/9 NHL Power Play
99/0 NHL Power Play
01/2 O-Pee-Chee 104
02/3 O-Pee-Chee 134
98/9 OPC Chrome 108, SB8
97/8 Omega 18
98/9 Omega 17
99/0 Omega 21
98/9 Pacific 87, -CCA 1, -DI 3, -GCDC 3, -TC 2, -TW 4
99/0 Pacific 28
00/1 Pacific 41
01/2 Pacific 37, PCC 353
02/3 Pacific 32
02/3 Pacific Complete 403
98/9 Pa. Crown Roy. 10
97/8 Pa. Dynagon Rookie
97/8 Pa. Paramount 15
98/9 Pa. Paramount 16, -SD 3, -TC 2
99/0 Pa. Paramount 23, PB-4
00/1 Pa. Paramount 21
98/9 Pa. Revolution 11
98/9 Panini Photocard [x2]
98/9 Panini Sticker 13, 225
99/0 Panini Sticker 25
00/1 Panini Sticker 11
00/1 Parkhurst P-107
01/2 Parkhurst 7, ✄ PS49, ✄ T19
02/3 Parkhurst 132, ✄ GJ31, ✄ SJ31, ✄ TT8
02/3 Parkhurst Retro 21, ✄ RJ30, ✄ RSJ21
97/8 Pinnacle 9
97/8 Pi. Be A Player 220, ✍ Aut. 220
97/8 Pi. BeeHive BHT 23
97/8 Pi. Certified D
97/8 Pi. Mint 26
99/0 Prism 14
00/1 Pr. Stock 8, PS-3, PSS-3, ✄ GUG-8
01/2 Pr. Stock 6
02/3 Pr. Stock Reserve 8
01/2 PS Titanium 10, ✄ DSJ 3
00/1 PS Titanium Draft ✄ 6
92 Québec Pee Wee 1776
99/0 Revolution 14, O-3, TL-2, / CSC 14
00/1 Revolution 12
97/8 Score 59
97/8 Score Bost. 14
00/1 Signature 236, ✍ Aut. 105
01/2 Signature C-42, ✍ Aut., ✄ GU93, ✄ HSHSJers, ✄ IB2
02/3 Signature 140, ✍ 140, ✄ SGJ31, ✄ TQ11
02/3 Slam Card
94/5 SP 189
95/6 SP 180, GC2
97/8 SP Authentic 172, ✍ SotT
98/9 SP Authentic 4, SS26
99/0 SP Authentic 8, ✍ SotT
00/1 SP Authentic ✍ SotT
01/2 SP Authentic 7
02/3 SP Authentic 7, ✍ SotT, ✍ SotTD, ✍ SotTT, ✄ SP, ✄ DP
00/1 SP GU ✄ TotG
01/2 SP GU ✄✍ ISD, ✄ Patch, ✄✍ PatchSig, ✄ PatchC, ✄ PatchT, ✄ TotG (x2), ✄ TotGSig (x2), ✄ TotGC (x2), ✄✍ TotGCSig (x2), ✄ TotGT
02/3 SP GU 5, ✄ AF (x2), ✄ CF, ✄ PC, ✄ PH (x2), ✄ TG, ✍ Sig
02/3 Sports Vault 16
99/0 SPx 10, HH2, P5, X7, XT6
00/1 SPx 5, X2
01/2 SPx 3, ✄ HT
02/3 SPx 6, 78, ✄ WM, ✄ SS, ✄ X
98/9 SPx Finite 5, 101, 121, 155
98/9 SPx Prospects 4, H4, L30, PS2
99/0 Stadium 135, Chrome 37
00/1 Stadium 50, ✄ SCS
01/2 Stadium ✄ SCSD, ✄ SCST
02/3 Stadium 20, ✄ NHLP16
99/0 SLU 39
98/9 Topps 108, IA 11, SB8, ✍ CAI
99/0 Topps 152
00/1 Topps 108
01/2 Topps 104
02/3 Topps 134
99/0 To. Chrome 152
00/1 To. Chrome 84
01/2 To. Chrome 104
02/3 T. Chrome 84
98/9 To. Finest 48, C20, M13, M16, M18, M20
98/9 T. Gold Label 45
99/0 To. Gold Label 19, FG1
00/1 To. Heritage 130
01/2 To. Heritage 88
02/3 To. Heritage 35, ✄ CC, ✄ CCB
02/3 To. Limited 134
99/0 To. Prmr. Plus 22, CAC2
01/2 To. Reserve ✄ TR
02/3 To. Total 207
98/9 UD Choice 13, BH22, SQ6
00/1 UD Heroes 9
01/2 UD PlayMakers Ltd 7
02/3 UD Superstars ✄ CAS
98/9 UD3 1, 61, 121
01/2 Ultimate Mem. ✄ CT,

✂ GAO
02/3 Ultimate Mem. ✂ DD, ✂ GUJ, ✂ HT
99/0 Ult. Victory 7
95/6 Upper Deck 554
97/8 Upper Deck 219, SG30
98/9 Upper Deck 24, 39, FF3, FT3, GN1, GN30, LS15, P13
99/0 Upper Deck 143, 183, CT11, FF5, N3, SS5, ✂ GJ
00/1 Upper Deck 245, EC1, TT7, ✂ GJ, ✂ DGJ, ✍ SG
01/2 Upper Deck 14, T1
02/3 Upper Deck 257, ✂ DM, ✂ FF, ✂ PP, ✂ S, ✂ GJ, ✂✍ SGJ, ✂ PW, ✂ UDPL
02/3 UD Artistic 8, R8, CG13, / Art
97/8 UD Black Diam. 37, PC28
98/9 UD Black Diam. 5, M30, WF3
99/0 UD Black Diam. 7, D3, M3
00/1 UD Black Diam. 5
99/0 UD C. Legends 71, ✍ ES
01/2 UD Challenge ✂✍ UCS
02/3 UD Classic 9, ✂ CS, ✂ HH
98/9 UD G. Reserve 24, 39
99/0 UD G. Reserve 143, 183, ✍ UDA
99/0 UD Gretzky Excl. 79
01/2 UD Honor Roll ✂ GAJ
02/3 UD Honor 6, ✂ GA
96/7 UD Ice 138
97/8 UD Ice 43, IC20, L6A
00/1 UD Ice ✂ IGJ
01/2 UD Ice 3
00/1 UD Legends 12, ✍ ES
01/2 UD Mask 7
02/3 UD Mask ✂ IO
98/9 UD MVP 10, F2, OT6, Snip. S3, Souv.
99/0 UD MVP 12, 21st-2, GU8, W27, H5
00/1 UD MVP 15, ME3, ✍ PS, ✍ ME
01/2 UD MVP 14, ✂ C
02/3 UD MVP 13
99/0 UD MVP Cup 17, CC2, GC, ✍ PS
99/0 UD Ovation 4, APOH
02/3 UD Piece 6, AC3, ✂ PH, ✍ MD
99/0 UD PowerDeck 5
01/2 UD Premier 6, ✂ B, ✂ D, ✍ SigG
02/3 UD Premier 7, ✂ Jers, ✂ JD, ✂ Patch, ✍ Sig
00/1 UD Pros&Prosp. 9, ✂✍ GJS
99/0 UD Retro 5, G6C, ✍ Ink.
02/3 UD Rookie 10, ✂ 157b, 164, ✂ DJ, ✂ S, ✍ TD
01/2 UD Top Shelf 78
02/3 UD Top Shelf 7, ✂ CP, ✂ GO, ✂ HH, ✂ R, ✂ ST, ✂ SW, ✍ Sig
00/1 UD Vintage 28, NH4, ✂ O6-POH
01/2 UD Vintage 22, 26
02/3 UD Vintage 17, 263, GB 17, T6
00/1 Vanguard 9, ✂ DGJ-1
01/2 Vanguard 7, QTH 15, ✂ DGM 3
99/0 Victory 22
00/1 Victory 19, 284
01/2 Victory 25
02/3 Victory 16, - NP32
97/8 Visions Signings 43, ✍ 43
99/0 WGretzky 14, CG6, EG3, ✂ TG, ✍ SG
97/8 Zenith 86, RR-1, ZT-14, Z66
96/7 Detroit Vipers

SAMUELSSON, KJELL
90/1 Bowman 111
91/2 Bowman 240
92/3 Bowman 165
93/4 Donruss 259
95/6 Donruss 368
92/3 Fleer Ultra 169
94/5 Fleer Ultra 351
95/6 Fleer Ultra 286
95 Globe 27
93/4 Leaf 274
90/1 OPC/Topps 61
91/2 O-Pee-Chee 211
92/3 O-Pee-Chee 230
89/0 OPC/Topps 100
98/9 OPC Chrome 205
97/8 Pacific CC 329
88/9 Panini Sticker 318
90/1 Panini Sticker 110
91/2 Panini Sticker 239
91/2 Parkhurst 356
92/3 Parkhurst 373
93/4 Parkhurst 432
95/6 Parkhurst 155
94/5 Parkie SE138, ES7
91/2 Pinnacle 149
91/2 Pinnacle 407
92/3 Pinnacle 306
93/4 Pinnacle 293
96/7 Pi. Be A Player 189, ✍ Aut. 189
95/6 Playoff 184
94/5 POG 192
93/4 Power Play 414
93/4 Premier 34
94/5 Premier 73
90/1 Pro Set 222
91/2 Pro Set 181
90/1 Score 197
91/2 Score 207
91/2 Score CAN 207
92/3 Score 195
93/4 Score 184
91/2 Semic Elitserien 339
93 Semic Sticker 22
92/3 Topps 352
95/6 Topps 259
98/9 Topps 205
91/2 To. Stadium 70
92/3 To. Stadium 466
93/4 To. Stadium 251
93/4 To. Stadium 426
90/1 Upper Deck 116
91/2 Upper Deck 396
94/5 Upper Deck 128
95/6 Upper Deck 350
89/0 PHIL
90/1 PHIL
91/2 PHIL / J.C. Penney
96/7 PHIL / Ocean Spray
92/3 PITT / Coke-Clark
92/3 PITT / Foodland 14
93/4 PITT / Foodland 18
94/5 PITT / Foodland 21

SAMUELSSON, MARTIN
02/3 BAP Mem. 389
02/3 Parkhurst Retro 234
02/3 Ultimate Mem. 56

SAMUELSSON, MIKAEL
01/2 BAP Mem. 295
01/2 Bowman 117
01/2 O-Pee-Chee 291
02/3 Pacific Complete 377
01/2 Parkhurst 330
01/2 PS Titanium 172
01/2 PS Titanium Draft 153
01/2 SP Authentic 162
01/2 SPx 144, RT
01/2 Topps 291
01/2 To. Chrome 181
02/3 To. Total 67
01/2 UD PlayMakers Ltd 130
01/2 Upper Deck 198
01/2 UD Challenge 120
98/9 UD Elitserien 78
01/2 UD Honor Roll 95
01/2 UD Ice 144
01/2 UD Premier 73
01/2 UD Top Shelf 46
01/2 UD Vintage 288
01/2 Victory 386
00/1 Kentucky Tho'blades

SAMUELSSON, MORGAN
94/5 Leaf Elit Set 172
95/6 Leaf Elit Set 12, FTF-1, G-1
95 Panini Worlds 146
89/0 Semic Elitserien 159
90/1 Semic Elitserien 63
91/2 Semic Elitserien 236
92/3 Semic Elitserien 49
95/6 UD Elitserien 18

SAMUELSSON, TOMMY
94/5 Leaf Elit Set 110, SS-4
89/0 Semic Elitserien 76
90/1 Semic Elitserien 251
91/2 Semic Elitserien 82
92/3 Semic Elitserien 104
92/3 Semic Sticker 10
89 Semic Sticker 8
91 Semic Sticker 33

SAMUELSSON, ULF
98/9 Aurora 126
98/9 Be A Player 93, ✍ Aut. 93
91/2 Bowman 88
92/3 Bowman 351
93/4 Donruss 264
94/5 Donruss 296
95/6 Donruss 89, 243
93/4 EA Sports 104
94/5 Flair 139
94/5 Fleer 168
95/6 Fleer Metal 100
92/3 Fleer Ultra 170, -UI 20
93/4 Fleer Ultra 204
94/5 Fleer Ultra 169
95/6 Fleer Ultra 126, 278
95 Globe 7
93/4 Leaf 92
94/5 Leaf 205
95/6 Leaf 206
87/8 OPC/Topps 23
88/9 OPC/Topps 136
90/1 O-Pee-Chee 511
91/2 O-Pee-Chee 323
92/3 O-Pee-Chee 270
89/0 O-Pee-Chee 210
98/9 OPC Chrome 127
87/8 OPC Sticker 205-64
88/9 OPC Sticker 265-129
98/9 Pacific 299
99/0 Pacific 148
97/8 Pacific CC 171
98/9 Pa. Paramount 157
87/8 Panini Sticker 41
88/9 Panini Sticker 238
89/0 Panini Sticker 228
91/2 Panini Sticker 277
92/3 Panini Sticker 229
93/4 Panini Sticker 87
94/5 Panini Sticker 79
95/6 Panini Sticker 66
96/7 Panini Sticker 107
97/8 Panini Sticker 88
98/9 Panini Sticker 85
99/0 Panini Sticker 120
00/1 Panini Sticker 78
95 Panini Worlds 289
91/2 Parkhurst 361
92/3 Parkhurst 369
92/3 Parkhurst 446
93/4 Parkhurst 155
94/5 Parkhurst 183
95/6 Parkhurst 411
91/2 Pinnacle 267
92/3 Pinnacle 296
93/4 Pinnacle 29
94/5 Pinnacle 46, 277
97/8 Pi. Be A Player 126, ✍ Aut. 126
95/6 Pi. Summit 78
95/6 Playoff 176
94/5 POG 193
95/6 POG 187
93/4 Power Play 194
93/4 Premier 132
94/5 Premier 391
90/1 Pro Set 109
91/2 Pro Set 459
92/3 Pro Set 143
91/2 Pro Set Platinum 95
90/1 Score 152
90/1 Sco. Hot Cards 64
91/2 Score 82
91/2 Score 304
91/2 Score CAN 82
91/2 Score CAN 308
92/3 Score 90
93/4 Score 161
94/5 Score 156, CI-7
95/6 Score 203
97/8 Score 239
97/8 Score NYRa. 15
92 Semic Sticker 58
93 Semic Sticker 21
95/6 SBx Emotion 119
95/6 SBx Impact 114
96/7 SBx Impact 84
92/3 Topps 127
95/6 Topps 144
98/9 Topps 127
91/2 To. Stadium 328
92/3 To. Stadium 440
93/4 To. Stadium 356
95/6 To. Stadium 11, F7
94/5 TSC Members Only 17
00/1 Ultimate Mem. ✂ D-12
90/1 Upper Deck 287
91/2 Upper Deck 230
91/2 Upper Deck E17
92/3 Upper Deck 189
93/4 Upper Deck 142
94/5 Upper Deck 209
95/6 Upper Deck 448, SE-142
96/7 Upper Deck 104
97/8 Upper Deck 204, 313, 395
95/6 UD BAP 223, ✍ S223
95/6 UD CC 79
97/8 UD Coll. Choice 171
96 Wien 44
84/5 HART / Jr. Whalers
85/6 HART / Jr. Whalers
86/7 HART / Jr. Whalers
87/8 HART / Jr. Whalers
88/9 HART / Jr. Whalers
89/0 HART / Jr. Whalers
90/1 HART / Jr. Whalers
98/9 NYRA
91/2 PITT / Elby's
91/2 PITT / Foodland 2
91/2 PITT / Food. Stickers
92/3 PITT / Coke-Clark
92/3 PITT / Foodland 12
92/3 PITT / Food. Stickers
93/4 PITT / Foodland 3
94/5 PITT / Foodland 5
96/7 PITT / Tribune

SAMUELSSON, ULF
01/2 Fleer Legacy 24
02/3 Fleer Throwbacks 82, 3SO, ✂ 3SO

SAMULI, JOUNI
70/1 Kuvajulkaisut 168
71/2 Williams Finnish 238
72/3 Williams Finnish 222
73/4 Williams Finnish 300

SANBERG, MIKAEL
95/6 Leaf Elit Set 198

SANDA, DALIBOR
95/6 APS 265
96/7 APS 306
97/8 APS 187
99/0 Score 11

SANDALAX, ALEX
51/2 Laval Dairy 38

SANDBACK, DARRELL
93/4 Seattle Thunderbirds

SANDBERG, MIKAEL
94/5 Leaf Elit Set 290
95/6 Leaf Elit Set S-13
92/3 Semic Elitserien 301
95/6 UD Elitserien 204
97/8 UD Elitserien 68
98/9 UD Elitserien 66

SANDELIN, SCOTT
88/9 ProCards / Sherbrooke
89/0 ProCards AHL 332
90/1 ProCards 41
87/8 MONT
86/7 Sherb. Canadiens 24

SANDERS, FRANK
72/3 Minn. Fight. Saints

SANDERS, GRANT
84/5 Kitchener Rangers

SANDERS, REGGIE
95/6 Edge Ice 102

SANDERSON, DEREK
71/2 Bazooka Panel
99/0 BAP Mem. AH-3, ✍ AH-3
71/2 Colgate Head
70/1 Colgate 6
70/1 Dad's Cookies
70/1 Eddie Sargent 3
71/2 Eddie Sargent 4
70/1 Esso Power Player
74/5 Loblaws
73/4 Nabisco s 15
68/9 O-Pee-Chee 6
68/9 O-Pee-Chee 213
69/0 O-Pee-Chee 201
69/0 O-Pee-Chee 4in1
70/1 O-Pee-Chee 136
70/1 O-Pee-Chee DE 5
71/2 O-Pee-Chee 65
73/4 O-Pee-Chee 183
74/5 O-Pee-Chee 290
75/6 O-Pee-Chee 73
76/7 O-Pee-Chee 20
77/8 O-Pee-Chee 46
95/6 Parkie 66-67 19
94/5 Parkie Tall FS-6
68/9 Shirriff / Bost. 7
67/8 Topps 33
68/9 Topps 6
69/0 Topps 31
71/2 Topps 65
73/4 Topps 182
75/6 Topps 73
76/7 Topps 20
77/8 Topps 46
02/3 Topps - SCH, ✍ SCH
01/2 T/O Archives 42, -Seat
71/2 Toronto Sun Photo
70/1 BOST
71/2 BOST
98/9 BOST / Alumni 16

SANDERSON, GEOFF
01/2 Adrenaline 55
01/2 Atomic 30
98/9 Be A Player 163, ✍ Aut. 163
00/1 BAP Mem. 38
01/2 BAP Mem. 279
97/8 Bicycle 2-Diamond
95/6 Bicycle Sports Aces 6-Heart
92/3 Bowman 136
95/6 Bowman 67
93/4 Classic TC6, ✍ Aut.
93/4 Cla. Prospects 56
00/1 Crown Royale 32
01/2 Crown Royale 44
02/3 Crown Royale ✂ GWJ 4
93/4 Donruss 147
94/5 Donruss 77
95/6 Donruss 201
96/7 Donruss 40
97/8 Donruss 79
96/7 Do. Canadian 114, OC-15
97/8 Do. Canadian 41, NP-14
96/7 Do. Elite 127
97/8 Do. Elite 67
96/7 Do. Preferred 85
97/8 Do. Priority 50
97/8 Do. Studio 84
93/4 EA Sports 58
02/3 First Edition 263
94/5 Flair 74
96/7 Flair 44
94/5 Fleer 89, SA-9
96/7 Fleer 47
95/6 Fleer Metal 66
92/3 Fleer Ultra 75
93/4 Fleer Ultra 151
93/4 Fleer Ultra SM 9
94/5 Fleer Ultra 93, SM-10
95/6 Fleer Ultra 70
96/7 Fl. Ultra 76
01/2 Heads Up 28
02/3 Heads Up ✂ GWQ 10
93/4 Hockey Wit 16
95/6 Hoyle / East. 6-Club
93/4 Kraft / KD
96/7 Kraft / KD
93/4 Leaf 77
94/5 Leaf 219
95/6 Leaf 88
96/7 Leaf 105
97/8 Leaf 28
94/5 L. Limited 54
96/7 L. Preferred 86
97/8 Limited 119, 135
01/2 McDonald's -HP 5
96/7 Metal Univ. 71
92/3 O-Pee-Chee 122
01/2 O-Pee-Chee 242
98/9 Omega 27
98/9 Pacific 80
99/0 Pacific 44
00/1 Pacific 56
01/2 Pacific 116
02/3 Pacific 104
02/3 Pacific Complete 427
97/8 Pacific CC 270
97/8 Pa. Crown Roy. 26
97/8 Pa. Dynagon 23, T-38
97/8 Pa. Invincible 26
99/0 Pa. Paramount 30
98/9 Panini Photocard
92/3 Panini Sticker V
93/4 Panini Sticker L
94/5 Panini Sticker 109
95/6 Panini Sticker 28
96/7 Panini Sticker 23
97/8 Panini Sticker 20
98/9 Panini Sticker 33
00/1 Panini Sticker 137
95 Panini Worlds 12
91/2 Parkhurst 57
92/3 Parkhurst 62
93/4 Parkhurst 86
94/5 Parkhurst 95, V49, YCTG-10
95/6 Parkhurst 91
00/1 Parkhurst P-212
01/2 Parkhurst 128
95/6 Pinnacle 309
92/3 Pinnacle 307
93/4 Pinnacle 9
94/5 Pinnacle 48, BR8
95/6 Pinnacle 38
96/7 Pinnacle 187
97/8 Pinnacle 45
97/8 Pi. Be A Player 112, ✍ Aut. 112
95/6 Pi. BeeHive 50
97/8 Pi. Certified 125
97/8 Pi. Inside 78
95/6 Pi. Summit 38
96/7 Pi. Summit 24
97/8 Pi. Totally 125
95/6 Pi. Zenith 14
95/6 Playoff 266
94/5 POG 117
95/6 POG 125
93/4 Power Play 109
93/4 Power Play RisS 6
93/4 Premier 156
94/5 Premier 205, 527, TF-15
00/1 Pr. Stock 29
01/2 Pr. Stock -PS 21
00/1 PS Titanium 25
02/3 PS Titanium 30, ✂ GWJ 20
95/6 Pro Magnet 129
91/2 Pro Set 536
92/3 Pro Set 63
92/3 Pro Set RGL 11
91/2 Pro Set Platinum 256
00/1 Revolution 44
91/2 Score 324
91/2 Score CAN 354
92/3 Score 108
93/4 Score 213
94/5 Score 144, TF-10
95/6 Score 111
96/7 Score 119
97/8 Score 110
94/5 Select 68
95/6 Select CE 26
90/1 7th..Sketch WHL 54, 336
01/2 Signature 154, ✍ Aut. 154
95/6 SBx Emotion 77
95/6 SBx Impact 75
96/7 SBx Impact 54
94/5 SP 52
96/7 SP 69
97/8 SP Authentic 25
00/1 SP Authentic 27
01/2 SP Authentic 22
02/3 Sports Vault 194
97/8 SPx 22
00/1 Stadium 212
95/6 Super Sticker 51, 53
92/3 Topps 402
95/6 Topps 14, 318
01/2 Topps 242
00/1 To. Chrome 224
94/5 Topps Finest 108
95/6 To. Finest 173
00/1 To. Heritage 195
96/7 To. Picks 65
01/2 To. Reserve 51
92/3 To. Stadium 111
93/4 To. Stadium 408
95/6 To. Stadium EC172
93/4 TSC Members Only 35
94/5 TSC Members Only 8
95/6 T. Super Skills 21
02/3 To. Total 145
98/9 UD Choice 27
99/0 Ult. Victory 12
91/2 Upper Deck 588
92/3 Upper Deck 293
93/4 Upper Deck 292, 316, HT2, SP-65
94/5 Upper Deck 6, SP-34
95/6 Upper Deck 20, SE-127
96/7 Upper Deck 75
97/8 Upper Deck 30, SS22
98/9 Upper Deck 45
00/1 Upper Deck 279
01/2 Upper Deck 51
02/3 Upper Deck 294, ✂ PA
95/6 UD BAP 62, ✍ S62
96/7 UD Black Diam. 128
95/6 UD CC 293, C22
96/7 UD CC 113, 319
97/8 UD Coll. Choice 116, SQ73
98/9 UD G. Reserve 45
96/7 UD Ice 28
97/8 UD Ice 8
01/2 UD Mask ✂ GJ, ✂ JP, ✂ DP
98/9 UD MVP 24
01/2 UD MVP 51
02/3 UD Rookie 29
00/1 UD Vintage 101, 111
01/2 UD Vintage 72, 77, 78
02/3 UD Vintage 78, 269
00/1 Vanguard 31
02/3 Vanguard 31
01/2 Victory 97
97/8 CARO / Sprint
01/2 COLU
02/3 COLU
91/2 HART / Jr. Whalers
92/3 HART / Dairymart
93/4 HART / Coke
95/6 HART / Kids Club
96/7 HART / Kids Club

SANDERSON, GUY
02/3 Clarkson G'Knights

SANDERSON, MIKE
99/0 Fort Worth Brahmas
97/8 New Mexico Scorpions

SANDFORD, ED
45-64 BeeHive-2 [Bost.]
51/2 Parkhurst 22
52/3 Parkhurst 69
53/4 Parkhurst 90
54/5 Parkhurst 64
02/3 Parkie - Reprint 154, 185
54/5 Topps 48
54 Toronto Star Weekend
91/2 BOST / SA Legends
98/9 BOST / Alumni 12

SANDHOLM, RYAN
91/2 Air Canada SJHL A24
92/3 MPS SJHL 103

SANDIE, JOEL
90/1 7th..Sketch OHL 69
91/2 7th...Sketch OHL 244
91/2 Sudbury Wolves
92/3 Sudbury Wolves

SANDILANDS, NEIL
83/4 Kitchener Rangers

SANDIS, MIKE
84/5 Springfield Indians 1

SANDKE, PETER
91/2 7th...Sketch LHJMQ 275

SANDKE, PIERRE
90/1 7th..Sketch LHJMQ 58

SANDLAK, JIM
90/1 Bowman 55
93/4 Donruss 138
92/3 Fleer Ultra 228
87/8 O-Pee-Chee 264
90/1 OPC/Topps 18
92/3 O-Pee-Chee 168
86/7 O-Pee-Chee 267
87/8 OPC Sticker 135-123
87/8 OPC Sticker 194-53
87/8 OPC Sticker 66A
87/8 Panini Sticker 352
88/9 Panini Sticker 139
89/0 Panini Sticker 156
90/1 Panini Sticker 306
90/1 Panini/VAN 21
92/3 Panini Sticker 34
94/5 Panini Sticker 113
91/2 Parkhurst 405
93/4 Parkhurst 84
94/5 Parkhurst 91
91/2 Pinnacle 294
92/3 Pinnacle 210
93/4 Pinnacle 364
94/5 POG 118
90/1 Pro Set 305
91/2 Pro Set 497
91/2 Score CAN 260
92/3 Score 379
93/4 Score 397
93/4 Score 532
92/3 Topps 41
92/3 To. Stadium 175
91/2 Upper Deck 577
92/3 Upper Deck 120
93/4 Upper Deck 393
93/4 HART / Coke
85/6 VANC
86/7 VANC
87/8 VANC / Shell
88/9 VANC / Mohawk
89/0 VANC / Mohawk
90/1 VANC / Mohawk
91/2 VANC
91/2 VANC / Photo
92/3 VANC / Road Trip

SANDLES, DALE
85/6 Kingston Canadians
86/7 Kingston Canadians

SANDLIN, TOMMY
94/5 Leaf Elit Set 296
91/2 Semic Elitserien 303
92/3 Semic Elitserien 325
92/3 Semic Elitserien 342
89 Semic Sticker 2

SANDNER, CHRISTOPHER
94/5 DEL 317
95/6 DEL 354

SANDROCK, ROBBY
99/0 San Angelo Outlaws
98/9 Kelowna Rockets

SANDS, CHARLIE
33/4 Anonymous 16
34-43 BeeHive-1 [Bost.]
34-43 BeeHive-1 [Mont.]
35-40 Canada Starch
39/0 O-Pee-Chee 56
40/1 O-Pee-Chee 102
33/4 WWGum 58
37/8 World Wide Gum 27

SANDS, JASON
95/6 Slapshot 118

SANDS, MIKE
83 Canada Juniors

SANDSTRÖM, JAN
98/9 UD Elitserien 5
99/0 UD Elitserien 5
00/1 UD Elitserien 6

SANDSTRÖM, PETTER
00/1 UD Elitserien 15
02/3 Nottingham Panthers

SANDSTRÖM, TOMAS
98/9 Aurora 5
98/9 Be A Player 153, ✍ Aut. 153
90/1 Bowman 141, -HT 21
91/2 Bowman 174
91/2 Bowman 179
92/3 Bowman 22
95/6 Bowman 10
93/4 Donruss 163
93/4 Donruss 475
94/5 Donruss 271
95/6 Donruss 118
96/7 Donruss 70
95/6 Do. Elite 74
97/8 Do. Priority 117
98/9 Dynagon Ice 5
93/4 EA Sports 65
94/5 Fleer 169
95/6 Fleer Metal 119
96/7 Fl. Picks 66
92/3 Fleer Ultra 88
93/4 Fleer Ultra 246
94/5 Fleer Ultra 352
95/6 Fleer Ultra 293, CC-16
95 Globe 28
93/4 Hockey Wit 87
91/2 Kraft 63
93/4 Leaf 106
94/5 Leaf 207
95/6 Leaf 265
96/7 Leaf 81
94/5 Leaf Elit Set 286, GS-2
95/6 L. Limited 60
96/7 Maggers 127
85/6 OPC/Topps 123
86/7 O-Pee-Chee 230
87/8 OPC/Topps 28
88/9 OPC/Topps 121
90/1 OPC/Topps 301
91/2 O-Pee-Chee 173
92/3 O-Pee-Chee 91
89/0 OPC/Topps 54, / Box C
98/9 OPC Chrome 12
87/8 OPC Leaders 38
91/2 OPC Premier 82
87/8 OPC Sticker 35
88/9 OPC Sticker 242-110
89/0 opcSticker 244
97/8 Omega 6
98/9 Pacific 63
99/0 Pacific 15
97/8 Pacific CC 293
97/8 Pa. Crown Roy. 4
98/9 Pa. Crown Roy. 4
97/8 Pa. Paramount 5
98/9 Pa. Paramount 6
87/8 Panini Sticker 114
88/9 Panini Sticker 310
89/0 Panini Sticker 281
90/1 Panini Sticker 243
91/2 Panini Sticker 79
92/3 Panini Sticker 67
93/4 Panini Sticker 205
95/6 Panini Sticker 62
96/7 Panini Sticker 61
97/8 Panini Sticker 150
98/9 Panini Sticker 172
95 Panini Worlds 290
91/2 Parkhurst 70
93/4 Parkhurst 362
94/5 Parkhurst 175
95/6 Parkhurst 166
91/2 Pinnacle 178
92/3 Pinnacle 345
93/4 Pinnacle 263
94/5 Pinnacle 313
96/7 Pinnacle 156
97/8 Pinnacle 180
95/6 Pi. Summit 94
96/7 Pi. Summit 81
95/6 Pi. Zenith 79
94/5 POG 188
95/6 POG 214
93/4 Power Play 121
93/4 Premier 434
94/5 Premier 108
90/1 Pro Set 127
91/2 Pro Set 97
92/3 Pro Set 287
91/2 Pro Set Platinum 53
90/1 Score 183
90/1 Sco. Hot Cards 79
91/2 Score 270
91/2 Score CAN 490
92/3 Score 199
93/4 Score 129
93/4 Score IS 21
95/6 Score 279
96/7 Score 126
97/8 Score 258
97/8 Score Anah. 12
95/6 Select CE 107
94 Semic 354
91/2 Semic Elitserien 319
91 Semic Sticker 208
92 Semic Sticker 69
93 Semic Sticker 32
95/6 SBx Emotion 141
95/6 SBx Impact 134
94/5 SP 90
95/6 SP 118
97/8 SP Authentic 4
92/3 Topps 421
95/6 Topps 228
98/9 Topps 12
95/6 To. Finest 12
91/2 To. Stadium 209
92/3 To. Stadium 220
93/4 To. Stadium 25
95/6 To. Stadium 118
90/1 Upper Deck 251
91/2 Upper Deck 30
91/2 Upper Deck 85
91/2 Upper Deck 141
91/2 Upper Deck E7
92/3 Upper Deck 424
93/4 Upper Deck 188
94/5 Upper Deck 461
95/6 Upper Deck 185, SE-156
96/7 Upper Deck 137
95/6 UD BAP 160, ✍ S160
95/6 UD CC 139
96/7 UD CC 215
99/0 UD Elitserien 157, S11, ✍ Aut.
00/1 UD Elitserien 147, 203
98/9 UD MVP 6
96 Wien 59
90/1 LOSA / Smokey 6
94/5 PITT / Foodland 10
95/6 PITT / Foodland 15

SANDSTROM, ULF
89/0 Semic Elitserien 179
90/1 Semic Elitserien 235
91/2 Semic Elitserien 172
89 Semic Sticker 16
95/6 UD Elitserien DS3

SANDWITH, TERRAN
92/3 Classic Prospects 114
91/2 7th...Sketch WHL 214
98/9 Cincinnati M'Ducks 11
99/0 Hamilton Bulldogs/ Staz
00/1 Hamilton Bulldogs
00/1 Hamilton Bulldogs/ Staz
00/1 Hamilton Bulldogs/ Staz
94/5 Hershey Bears
99/0 St. John's Maple Leafs
01/2 Belfast Giants

SANFORD, CURTIS
02/3 BAP All-Star 121
02/3 BAP Mem. 362
02/3 Between the Pipes 75, ✂ GUJ35
02/3 Calder 141
02/3 Crown Royale 135
02/3 In The GU 197
02/3 Pacific Complete 515
02/3 Parkhurst 241
02/3 Parkhurst Retro 241
02/3 Pr. Stock Reserve 181
02/3 PS Titanium 135
02/3 Quest for the Cup 142
02/3 Signature 178, ✍ 178
02/3 SP Authentic 158
02/3 SP GU 92
02/3 To. Total 438
02/3 Ultimate Mem. 41
02/3 Upper Deck 452
02/3 UD Artistic 109
02/3 UD Honor 126
02/3 UD Mask 125
02/3 UD Premier 67
02/3 UD Top Shelf 119
02/3 Vanguard 132
00/1 Peoria Rivermen
01/2 Peoria Rivermen
02/3 Worcester IceCats

SANFORD, JAMES
01/2 Moncton Wildcats 3
00/1 Victoriaville Tigres 1

SANFORD, JASON
91/2 Avant Garde BCJHL 138
92/3 BCJHL 95

SANGSTER, DARRYL
92/3 MPS SJHL 104

SANGSTER, JACK
83/4 Brandon Wheat Kings
84/5 Brandon Wheat Kings
85/6 Brandon Wheat Kings

SANGSTER, ROB
89/0 7th..Sketch OHL 58
87/8 Kitchener Rangers
88/9 Kitchener Rangers
89/0 Kitchener Rangers

SANIPASS, EVERETT
91/2 Bowman 135
91/2 O-Pee-Chee 315
90/1 Panini/QUE 19
91/2 Panini Sticker 262
88/9 ProCards / Saginaw
89/0 ProCards IHL 63
90/1 Score 28
91/2 To. Stadium 284
87/8 CHIC / Coke
88/9 CHIC / Coke
89/0 CHIC / Coke
90/1 QUEB / Petro-Canada

SANKO, RON
82/3 Kingston Canadians
85/6 Kitchener Rangers
83/4 North Bay Centennials

SANSCARTIER, ALAIN
90/1 7th..Sketch LHJMQ 113
91/2 7th...Sketch LHJMQ 75

SANTA, NICK
82 Semic Sticker 123

SANTALA, SEPPO
73/4 Williams Finnish 317

SANTALA, TOMMI
99/0 Cardset 267
00/1 Cardset 147
02/3 Cardset 265
98/9 SPx Prospects 68
98/9 UD Black Diam. 100

SANTANEN, ARI
98/9 Cardset 199, Top 9
99/0 Cardset 113
97/8 Hockey-Box
96/7 Sisu 119

SANTANEN, PEKKA
78/9 SM-Liiga 163

SANTURIAN, OLEG
93/4 Richmond Renegades

SAPERGIA, BRENT
88/9 ProCards / Indianapolis
89/0 ProCards IHL 114
90/1 ProCards 318
91/2 ProCards 331
92/3 Toledo Storm WIOT

SAPOSHNIKOV, ANDREI
93/4 Classic 92
96/7 DEL 211
93 Semic Sticker 135

SAPOZHNIKOV, ANDREI
99/0 Mir 15
00/1 Mir 240
00/1 Metallurg 32

SAPOZNIKOV, ANDREI
98/9 Mir 20

SAPRYKIN, OLEG
99/0 BAP Mem. 215
00/1 BAP Mem. 228
01/2 BAP Mem. 10
99 Bowman 13, ✍ BA33
99/0 Crown Royale 25
00/1 Crown Royale 114, 21CR-4
99/0 Prism Ice 5
02/3 First Edition 180
99/0 HoloGrFX 9
99/0 Millenium 41, C-23, ✍ Aut. 41
01/2 O-Pee-Chee 137
99/0 Omega 39
00/1 Pacific 72
01/2 Pacific 64
02/3 Pacific Complete 441
00/1 Pa. Paramount 37
00/1 Parkhurst P-237
01/2 Parkhurst 65
00/1 Premier Plus 95, PA7, PR10, ✂ GP
99/0 Prism 25
00/1 Pr. Stock 107, NW-6, Roo. 4
00/1 PS Titanium 108
00/1 PS Titanium Draft 108
00/1 Revolution 24
00/1 Signature 287, ✍ Aut. 232
01/2 Signature 128, ✍ Aut. 128
99/0 SP Authentic 98, ✍ SotT
99/0 SPx 172
99/0 Stadium 186
00/1 Stadium 233
99/0 Topps 268
00/1 Topps 274
01/2 Topps 137
99/0 To. Chrome 268
00/1 To. Chrome 169
00/1 To. Gold Label 89
00/1 To. Heritage 50
99/0 To. Prmr. Plus 99
01/2 To. Reserve ✂ TR
00/1 To. Stars 148
00/1 UD Reserve 13
99/0 Ult. Victory 94
99/0 Upper Deck 169, 193
00/1 Upper Deck 25
01/2 Upper Deck 29
99/0 UD Black Diam. 15
99/0 UD G. Reserve 169, 193
00/1 UD Ice 64
00/1 UD MVP ME3, ✍ PS, ✍ ME
01/2 UD MVP 29
99/0 UD Ovation 9
00/1 UD Pros&Prosp. 13
99/0 UD Prospects 36, IN8
01/2 UD Vintage 39, 43
00/1 Vanguard 107
99/0 Victory 356
01/2 Victory 56
99/0 WGretzky 33

SARAMAA, ERKKI
99/0 UD Elitserien 122

SARAULT, YVES
91/2 Classic 49
91/2 Classic Four Sport 49
97/8 Score Colo. 20
90/1 7th..Sketch LHJMQ 175
91/2 7th...Sketch LHJMQ 163
91 7th..Sketch Mem.Cup 125
91/2 Ultimate Draft Pick 44, ✍ Aut.
92/3 Fredericton Canadiens
93/4 Fredericton Canadiens
94/5 Fredericton Canadiens
99/0 Grand Rapids Griffins
01/2 Milwaukee Admirals

SARAVO, PEKKA
00/1 Cardset 211

SARAZIBAR, JOSE
79 Panini Sticker 375

SARAZIN, PIERRE
79 Panini Sticker 341

SARDA, ROGER
51/2 Lac St-Jean 49

SARGANT, SHANE
87/8 Soo Greyhounds 27

SARGENT, GARY
77/8 O-Pee-Chee 113
78/9 O-Pee-Chee 37
79/0 O-Pee-Chee 52
80/1 O-Pee-Chee 237
82/3 Post [Minn.]
77/8 Topps 113
78/9 Topps 37
79/0 Topps 52
80/1 Topps 237
78/9 MINS / Cloverleaf 1
79/0 MINS
80/1 MINS
81/2 MINS
82/3 MINS

SARICH, CORY
99/0 BAP Mem. 66
95/6 Bowman P31
97 Bowman 115
98 Bowman 68
98 Bowman Chrome 68
99/0 Millenium 37, ✍ Aut. 37
99/0 NHL Power Play
00/1 Pacific 380
02/3 Pacific Complete 487
01/2 Signature 96, ✍ Aut. 96
99/0 SPx 18
99/0 Topps 46
99/0 To. Chrome 46
95/6 Upper Deck 519
96/7 UD Ice 132
99/0 UD MVP 24
99/0 Victory 39
00/1 Victory 267
98/9 Rochester Americans

SARICH, ROD
02/3 Louisiana Ice Gators
98/9 Calgary Hitmen 5
99/0 Calgary Hitmen
00/1 Calgary Hitmen
01/2 Calgary Hitmen

SARJEANT, GEOFF
94/5 Classic 4 Sport 154
92/3 Classic Prospects 71
95/6 Edge Ice 147
96/7 Leaf 228
94/5 Upper Deck 375
00/1 UD DEL 166
96/7 Cincinnati Cyclones
97/8 Cincinnati Cyclones
95/6 Kansas City Blades
92/3 Peoria Rivermen
93/4 Peoria Rivermen
94/5 Peoria Rivermen
90/1 Michigan Tech Huskies
91/2 Michigan Tech Huskies
91/2 Michigan Tech Huskies
91/2 Michigan Tech Huskies

SARKILAHTI, OLLI
72/3 Williams Finnish 353

SARMATIN, MIKHAIL
98/9 Mir 110

SARNO, PETER
97/8 Bell
99 Bowman 151
98 Bowman 16
98 Bowman Chrome 16
02/3 Cardset 266
99/0 Hamilton Bulldogs
00/1 Hamilton Bulldogs
00/1 Hamilton Bulldogs/ Staz
01/2 Hamilton Bulldogs
01/2 Hamilton Bulldogs
01/2 Hamilton Bulldogs/ Staz

SAROS, SEPPO
71/2 Williams Finnish 272

SARRONLAHTI, JARI
71/2 Williams Finnish 254
73/4 Williams Finnish 318

SARTIALA, TIMO
72/3 Williams Finnish 182

SARTJARVI, PEKKA
72/3 Williams Finnish 183

SASKAMOOSE, FRED
54/5 Parkhurst 82

SASS, PAUL
91/2 L. Superior State Lakers

SASSEVILLE, FRANÇOIS
93/4 Slapshot / Drummondville 21
00/1 Rockford IceHogs
96/7 Halifax Moosehead
96/7 Halifax Moosehead

SASSO, TOM
91/2 ProCards 436

SATAN, MIROSLAV
01/2 Adrenaline 24
02/3 Atomic 11, -PC 3
98/9 Aurora 20
99/0 Aurora 19
00/1 Aurora 21
98/9 Be A Player 164, ✍ Aut. 164
99/0 BAP Mem. 110
00/1 BAP Mem. 246
01/2 BAP Mem. 89
02/3 BAP Mem. 69, 204, ✂ FP4
95/6 Bowman 112
01/2 Bowman 24
02/3 Bowman 65
02/3 Calder ✂ GWJ 5
95/6 Classic ✍ Aut.
94/5 Cla. Images 58
99/0 Crown Royale 20
01/2 Crown Royale 18
02/3 Crown Royale 12
96/7 Donruss 215
98/9 Dynagon Ice 21
99/0 Dynagon Ice 33
02/3 Exclusive 20, ✂ GWJ 3
02/3 First Edition 53, 344, 379, ✂ Jers.
95/6 Fleer Metal 190
95/6 Fleer Ultra 355
96/7 Fl. Ultra 62
02/3 Heads Up 14, ✂ GWQ 4
02/3 In The GU ✂ F4
96/7 Leaf 189
96/7 Metal Univ. 55
99/0 Millenium 33, ✍ Aut. 33
98/9 NHL Power Play
01/2 O-Pee-Chee 103
02/3 O-Pee-Chee 26
97/8 Omega 26
98/9 Omega 28
99/0 Omega 31
98/9 Pacific 81
99/0 Pacific 45
00/1 Pacific 57, ✍ Aut. 57
01/2 Pacific 54
02/3 Pacific 48, ✂ GWJ 4
02/3 Pacific Complete 205
97/8 Pacific CC 132
97/8 Pa. Crown Roy. 16
98/9 Pa. Crown Roy. 15
97/8 Pa. Dynagon 14, T-21
97/8 Pa. Invincible 15
97/8 Pa. Paramount 24
98/9 Pa. Paramount 22
99/0 Pa. Paramount 31
00/1 Pa. Paramount 32
97/8 Pa. Revolution 16
98/9 Pa. Revolution 16
96/7 Panini Sticker 260
97/8 Panini Sticker 18, 126
98/9 Panini Sticker 16
99/0 Panini Sticker 38, 335
00/1 Panini Sticker 23
95/6 Parkhurst 348, 509
00/1 Parkhurst P-56
01/2 Parkhurst 103, ✂ T11
02/3 Parkhurst 141, ✂ FP4, ✂ TT12
02/3 Parkhurst Retro 42, ✂ RF4
97/8 Pinnacle 135
96/7 Pi. Be A Player 39, ✍ Aut. 39
96/7 Pi. Summit 166
95/6 Pi. Zenith 150
00/1 Premier Plus 52
99/0 Prism 21
00/1 Pr. Stock 13
01/2 Pr. Stock -PS 8
02/3 Pr. Stock Reserve ✂ 105
01/2 PS Titanium 16, ✂ DSJ 66
02/3 PS Titanium 13
02/3 Quest for the Cup 10
99/0 Revolution 20, -TotL 22
00/1 Revolution 19
96/7 Score 249
97/8 Score 232
97/8 Score Buff. 15
95/6 Select CE 125
00/1 Signature 234, ✍ Aut. 85
01/2 Signature ✂ FP4, ✂ GUE7, ✂ GJ7, ✂ GSJ7, ✂ ITN7, ✂ TM4
02/3 Signature 52, GS-63, ✍ 52, ✂ FJ4
95/6 SBx Impact 197
96/7 SBx Impact 170
95/6 SP 52
97/8 SP Authentic 15
99/0 SP Authentic 11
00/1 SP Authentic ✍ SotT
01/2 SP Authentic 8
02/3 SP Authentic 10
01/2 SP GU 5, ✂ AF, ✂ AFD, ✂ Patch, ✂ PatchC
02/3 SP Game-Used ✂ AF, ✂ CF
02/3 Sports Vault 25
99/0 SPx 20
00/1 SPx 7, ✂ WM
01/2 SPx 7, ✂ DT
02/3 SPx 7, ✂ SS
99/0 Stadium 80
00/1 Stadium 141
01/2 Stadium 12, ✂ SCS
02/3 Stadium 78, ✂ NHLP10
00/1 SLU Classic Doubles 4
95/6 Topps 283
99/0 Topps 244
00/1 Topps 41
01/2 Topps 103
02/3 Topps 20
99/0 To. Chrome 244
00/1 To. Chrome 33, RF9
01/2 To. Chrome 103
02/3 T. Chrome 20
98/9 To. Finest 65
99/0 To. Gold Label 57
00/1 To. Gold Label 75
00/1 To. Heritage 152
01/2 To. Heritage 31, ✍ CAI
02/3 To. Heritage 18
02/3 To. Limited 20
96/7 To. Picks RS12
99/0 To. Prmr. Plus 49
01/2 To. Reserve 26, ✂ TR
95/6 To. Stadium 122
00/1 To. Stars 84
02/3 To. Total 354, TTC3
98/9 UD Choice 22
00/1 UD Heroes 13, ✍ SG
01/2 UD PlayMakers Ltd 11, -PCPJ
00/1 UD Reserve 11
99/0 Ult. Victory 11
95/6 Upper Deck 302
96/7 Upper Deck 260
98/9 Upper Deck 225
99/0 Upper Deck 24
00/1 Upper Deck 22
01/2 Upper Deck 19, ✂ SCFJers., ✂ SCFJersD
02/3 Upper Deck 19, ✂ DM, ✂ S
02/3 UD Artistic 11, R11, / Art
97/8 UD Black Diam. 62
98/9 UD Black Diam. 8
99/0 UD Black Diam. 13
01/2 UD Challenge 7
02/3 UD Classic 10, ✂ HR, ✂ SC
96/7 UD CC 98
98/9 UD G. Reserve 225
99/0 UD G. Reserve 24
01/2 UD Honor Roll ✂ GAJ
02/3 UD Honor 7, ✂ GA
00/1 UD Ice ✂ IGJ
01/2 UD Mask ✂ GJ, ✂ JP, ✂ DP
02/3 UD Mask ✂ IO
98/9 UD MVP 19
99/0 UD MVP 26
00/1 UD MVP 27
01/2 UD MVP 23
02/3 UD MVP 21, ST (x2), Souv.
99/0 UD MVP Cup 23
99/0 UD Ovation 8
02/3 UD Piece 8
02/3 UD Premier 8
99/0 UD Retro 8
02/3 UD Rookie 13
01/2 UD Top Shelf 4, ✂ J
02/3 UD Top Shelf 10, ✂ GO, ✂ HT, ✂ R, ✂ SH, ✂ ST, ✂ SW, ✂ TS
00/1 UD Vintage 38, 49, 50

01/2 UD Vintage 32, 34, 35
02/3 UD Vintage 29, 264, 311, GB 29, T7
00/1 Vanguard 14
99/0 Victory 35
00/1 Victory 28
01/2 Victory 38
02/3 Victory 27, - NP40
99/0 WGretzky 22
96 Wien 231
97/8 Zenith 51
96/7 EDMO

SATERDALEN, JEFF
92/3 Richmond Renegades

SATERI, ESA
93/4 Sisu 242
94/5 Sisu 65

SATHER, GLEN
70/1 Dad's Cookies
70/1 Eddie Sargent 167
70/1 Esso Power Player
01/2 Fleer Greats ✄ OSS
68/9 O-Pee-Chee 134
69/0 O-Pee-Chee 116
70/1 O-Pee-Chee 205
71/2 O-Pee-Chee 221
75/6 O-Pee-Chee 222
76/7 OPC WHA 56
68/9 Shirriff / Bost. 15
67/8 Topps 38
69/0 Topps 116
75/6 Topps 222
02/3 Topps - Reprint 11, ✍ Reprint 11
01/2 T/O Archives 67
71/2 Toronto Sun Photo
99/0 UD Gretzky Excl. 89
92/3 UD Locker 49
93/4 EDMO / Sheet
81/2 EDMO / Red Rooster
82/3 EDMO / Red Rooster
83/4 EDMO / Button
83/4 EDMO / McDonald's
84/5 EDMO / Red Rooster
85/6 EDMO / Red Rooster
86/7 EDMO / Red Rooster
88/9 EDMO / Action 49
88/9 EDMO / Action 117
92/3 EDMO / IGA 026
74/5 MONT
73/4 SLOU

SATOR, TED
87/8 BUFF / Won. Bread
88/9 BUFF / Won. Bread
97/8 New Orleans Brass

SATOSAARI, TOMMI
98/9 Cardset 120
99/0 Cardset 67, 204
02/3 Cardset 267
00/1 Kudos 110

SAUER, E.J.
91/2 ProCards 440

SAUER, KURT
02/3 BAP All-Star 117
02/3 BAP Mem. 276
02/3 Bowman 119
02/3 Calder 102
02/3 Pacific Complete 564
02/3 PS Titanium 103
02/3 Quest for the Cup 103
02/3 SP Authentic ✍ 193
02/3 SP GU 69
02/3 SPx ✍ 147
02/3 Stadium 134
02/3 T. Chrome 170
02/3 To. Heritage 145
02/3 To. Total 415
02/3 Ultimate Mem. 6
02/3 Upper Deck 428
02/3 UD Classic 104
02/3 UD Honor 103
02/3 UD Mask 126
02/3 UD Top Shelf 106

SAUERS, MICHAEL
99/0 Peoria Rivermen

SAULNIER, JULES
00/1 Halifax Moosehead

SAUMIER, MARC
88/9 ProCards / Sherbrooke
89/0 ProCards AHL 188
91/2 ProCards 392
94/5 Muskegon Fury
87/8 Hull Olympiques

SAUMIER, RAYMOND
89/0 ProCards AHL 284

SAUNDERCOOK, PAUL
90/1 ProCards 415

SAUNDERS, DAVID
88/9 OPC/Topps 248
88/9 OPC Sticker 61-196
87/8 VANC / Shell

SAUNDERS, LEE
96/7 Guildford Flames 21
92/3 Maine Black Bears
93/4 Maine Black Bears

SAUNDERS, NATHAN
01/2 Moncton Wildcats 11

SAUNIER, BRUNO
94 Semic 216
92 Semic Sticker 225

SAURDIFF, CORWIN
94/5 Hampton Roads
95/6 Hampton Roads

SAURETTE, KEVIN
97/8 Regina Pats

SAURIO, MATTI
66/7 Champion 7
65/6 Hellas 31
70/1 Kuvajulkaisut 236
71/2 Williams Finnish 255
73/4 Williams Finnish 319

SAURIOL, CLAUDE-CHARLES
90/1 7th..Sketch LHJMQ 134
87/8 Hull Olympiques

SAUTER, DOUG
98/9 Oklahoma City Blazers
83/4 Springfield Indians 25
92/3 Wheeling Thund'birds 22
93/4 Wheeling Thund'birds
88/9 Brandon Wheat Kings
89/0 Brandon Wheat Kings
84/5 Medicine Hat Tigers
86/7 Regina Pats
87/8 Regina Pats

SAUTER, HARDY
90/1 7th..Sketch WHL 217
91/2 7th...Sketch WHL 2
98/9 Oklahoma City Blazers
89/0 Brandon Wheat Kings
90/1 Brandon Wheat Kings

SAUVE, BOB
76/7 O-Pee-Chee 308
78/9 O-Pee-Chee 265
79/0 O-Pee-Chee 49
80/1 O-Pee-Chee 166
80/1 O-Pee-Chee 168
80/1 O-Pee-Chee 266
81/2 O-Pee-Chee 23
82/3 O-Pee-Chee 34
83/4 O-Pee-Chee 61
83/4 O-Pee-Chee 71
84/5 O-Pee-Chee 30
85/6 O-Pee-Chee 174
86/7 OPC/Topps 124
87/8 OPC/Topps 140
81/2 OPC Sticker 56
82/3 OPC/Topps Sticker 181
83/4 OPC/Topps Sticker 242
84/5 OPC Sticker 208
85/6 OPC Sticker 181-50
85/6 OPC Sticker 190-63
86/7 OPC Sticker 152-7
87/8 OPC Sticker 75-208
87/8 Panini Sticker 220
82/3 Post [Detr.]
79/0 Topps 49
80/1 Topps 166
80/1 Topps 168
81/2 Topps 77 [East]
79/0 BUFF / Bells Market
80/1 BUFF / Wendt's 8
81/2 BUFF / Wendt's 8
82/3 BUFF / Wendt's 6
84/5 BUFF / Blue Shield
86/7 CHIC / Coke
87/8 NJER
88/9 NJER / Caretta

SAUVÉ, JEAN-FRANÇOIS
82/3 O-Pee-Chee 33
85/6 OPC Sticker 155-27
86/7 OPC Sticker 23-163
82/3 Post [Buff.]
83/4 QUEB
84/5 QUEB
85/6 QUEB / Provigo
86/7 QUEB / McDonald's

SAUVÉ, PHILIPPE
02/3 Between the Pipes 103
98 Bowman 101, 160, ✍ A23
98 Bowman Chrome 101, 160
02/3 Choice Prospects 38
98/9 Collection Souvenir 19
98/9 OPC Chrome 241
93 Québec Pee Wee 1053
94 Québec Pee Wee 512
98/9 Topps 241
99/0 UD Prospects 65
00/1 Hershey Bears
01/2 Hershey Bears
02/3 Hershey Bears
99/0 Hull Olympiques BN
99/0 Hull Olympiques 23
96/7 Rimouski Océanic
97/8 Rimouski Océanic

SAUVÉ, SIMON-PIERRE
02/3 Shawinigan Cataractes

SAVAGE, ALAIN
91/2 7th...Sketch LHJMQ 69
96/7 Hampton Roads

SAVAGE, ANDRE
99/0 Providence Bruins

SAVAGE, ANDRÉ
99/0 BAP Mem. 341
00/1 BAP Mem. 377
99/0 Pacific 32
00/1 Pacific 42
01/2 Pacific ✄ GWJ 1
00/1 PS Titanium ✄ GUG 57
00/1 Signature 230, ✍ Aut. 44
99/0 SP Authentic 97
00/1 Topps 230
00/1 Upper Deck 18
01/2 Vanguard ✄ DGM 40
00/1 Victory 262
01/2 Manitoba Moose
02/3 Philadelphia Phantoms
98/9 Providence Bruins

SAVAGE, BRIAN
01/2 Adrenaline 100
98/9 Aurora 97
99/0 Aurora 77
00/1 BAP Mem. 170
01/2 BAP Mem. 157, 458
95/6 Bowman 87
93/4 Canada Nationals
93/4 Classic 81
93/4 Classic - Team Canada TC3
94/5 Classic 34, T36, ✍ Aut.
93/4 Cla. Prospects LP18
99/0 Crown Royale 72
00/1 Crown Royale 57
01/2 Crown Royale 78
94/5 Donruss 276
95/6 Donruss 20
96/7 Donruss 168
97/8 Donruss 109
95/6 Do. Elite 28
97/8 Do. Preferred 62
97/8 Do. Priority 128
99/0 Dynagon Ice 105
94/5 Fleer 108
95/6 Fleer Metal 79, MW-7
93/4 Fleer Ultra 472
95/6 Fleer Ultra 84, HS-17
01/2 Heads Up 51
94/5 Leaf 292
95/6 Leaf 175, SR-15
96/7 Leaf 111
97/8 Leaf 68
95/6 L. Limited 82
97/8 Limited 71
99/0 Millenium 133, ✍ Aut. 133
01/2 O-Pee-Chee 162
02/3 O-Pee-Chee 120
97/8 Omega 123
98/9 Omega 126
99/0 Omega 122
98/9 Pacific 49
99/0 Pacific 210
00/1 Pacific 213
01/2 Pacific 212
02/3 Pacific 304
02/3 Pacific Complete 43
97/8 Pacific CC 142
97/8 Pa. Paramount 99
98/9 Pa. Paramount 118
00/1 Pa. Paramount 131
98/9 Pa. Revolution 76
95/6 Panini Sticker 36
96/7 Panini Sticker 30
99/0 Panini Sticker 67
95/6 Parkhurst 112
00/1 Parkhurst P-154
01/2 Parkhurst 147, 395
02/3 Parkhurst Retro 159
94/5 Parkie SE90
94/5 Pinnacle 248, RTP10
95/6 Pinnacle 94
96/7 Pinnacle 134
97/8 Pinnacle 152
97/8 Pi. Inside 135
95/6 Pi. Summit 167
95/6 Pi. Zenith 20
95/6 POG 144
94/5 Power Play 493
93/4 Premier - Canada 16
94/5 Premier 16
99/0 Prism 74
00/1 Pr. Stock ✄ GUG 59
01/2 Pr. Stock 50
01/2 PS Titanium 75
94/5 Score 230, CT-8
95/6 Score 76
96/7 Score 147
97/8 Score 191
97/8 Score Mont. 6
94/5 Select 192
00/1 Signature 76, ✍ Aut. 9
01/2 Signature 15, ✍ Aut. 15, ✄ GJ31, ✄ GSJ31, ✄ TM16
02/3 Signature GS-15
95/6 SBx Emotion 92
95/6 SBx Impact 88, F-9
01/2 SP Authentic 44
01/2 SPx 190
00/1 Stadium 153
00/1 Stadium 199
95/6 Topps 349, 21NG
00/1 Topps 261
01/2 Topps 162
02/3 Topps 120
94/5 Topps Finest BBR-8
95/6 To. Finest 23
99/0 To. Gold Label 69
02/3 To. Limited 120
95/6 To. Stadium 37
98/9 UD Choice 111
01/2 UD PlayMakers Ltd 54
00/1 UD Reserve 44
99/0 Ult. Victory 46
94/5 Upper Deck 244
95/6 Upper Deck 36, SE-132
97/8 Upper Deck 299
98/9 Upper Deck 115
99/0 Upper Deck 244
00/1 Upper Deck 93
01/2 Upper Deck 94
02/3 Upper Deck 383
95/6 UD BAP 138, ✍ S138
01/2 UD Challenge 44
96/7 UD CC 140
97/8 UD Coll. Choice 131
98/9 UD G. Reserve 115
99/0 UD G. Reserve 244
96/7 UD Ice 34
98/9 UD MVP 108
99/0 UD MVP 107
00/1 UD MVP 90
00/1 UD Pros&Prosp. 45
00/1 UD Vintage 190
01/2 UD Vintage 135, 139
02/3 Vanguard 51
99/0 Victory 150
00/1 Victory 123
01/2 Victory 187
99/0 WGretzky 86
94/5 MONT
95/6 MONT / Export
95/6 MONT
96-98 MONT
00/1 MONT
01/2 MONT

SAVAGE, JEAN-FRANÇOIS
01/2 Baie-Comeau 22

SAVAGE, JOEL
95/6 DEL 381
96/7 DEL 192
98/9 DEL 150
99/0 Eishockey 11
89/0 ProCards AHL 263
90/1 ProCards 266
91/2 ProCards 13
91/2 Upper Deck 423
92/3 Fort Wayne Komets 23
91/2 Rochester Americans DD
91/2 Rochester Americans GL
91/2 Rochester Americans WPC
92/3 Rochester Americans WPC

SAVAGE, MIKE
83/4 Belleville Bulls

SAVAGE, NICOLAS
93/4 Slapshot / Drummondville 6

SAVAGE, REGGIE
93/4 Durivage 23
89/0 Panini Sticker 49
92/3 OPC Premier 121
92/3 Parkhurst 426
94/5 Parkhurst 194
90/1 ProCards 199
91/2 ProCards 570
91/2 Score 320
91/2 Score CAN 350
92/3 To. Stadium Members Only
92/3 Upper Deck 474
92/3 WASH / Kodak
95/6 Atlanta Knights
91/2 Baltimore Skipjacks
96/7 Springfield Falcons
00/1 Syracuse Crunch

SAVAGE, SÉBASTIEN
00/1 Ottawa 67's 19

SAVARD, ANDRÉ
75/6 Hockey Heroes
74/5 Loblaws
74/5 O-Pee-Chee 285
75/6 O-Pee-Chee 155
76/7 O-Pee-Chee 43
77/8 O-Pee-Chee 118
78/9 O-Pee-Chee 253
79/0 O-Pee-Chee 25
80/1 O-Pee-Chee 375
81/2 O-Pee-Chee 24
84/5 O-Pee-Chee 288
81/2 OPC Sticker 54
84/5 OPC Sticker 170
82/3 Post [Buff.]
83/4 Souhaits Keychain [Sabres]
75/6 Topps 155
76/7 Topps 43
77/8 Topps 118
78/9 Topps 253
79/0 Topps 25
81/2 Topps 78 [East]
83/4 Vachon 73-53
80/1 BUFF / Wendt's 5
81/2 BUFF / Wendt's 13
00/1 MONT
83/4 QUEB
84/5 QUEB
87/8 QUEB / Gene. Foods
92/3 QUEB / Petro-Canada
85/6 Fredericton Express
86/7 Fredericton Express

SAVARD, DENIS
99/0 BAP Mem. R-3, ✍ R-3
02/3 BAP Mem. 241
90/1 Bowman 6
91/2 Bowman 342
92/3 Bowman 64
82/3 Dernière Heure
93/4 Donruss 319
94/5 Donruss 284
95/6 Donruss 233
96/7 Donruss 51
92/3 Durivage 10
93/4 Durivage 25
88/9 Esso All-Star
01/2 Fleer Greats 22, ✍ Aut., ✄ OSS
92/3 Fleer Ultra 109
93/4 Fleer Ultra 428
94/5 Fleer Ultra 373
95/6 Fleer Ultra 219
88/9 Frito Lay
83/4 Funmate Puffy 18 [w]
93/4 Hockey Wit 35
95/6 Hoyle / West. 3-Club
90/1 Kraft 51
91/2 Kraft 77
93/4 Kraft / PB
93/4 Leaf 372
94/5 Leaf 166
95/6 Leaf 127
96/7 Maggers 28
82/3 McDonald's Les Étoiles 23
81/2 O-Pee-Chee 63
82/3 O-Pee-Chee 73
83/4 O-Pee-Chee 96
83/4 O-Pee-Chee 111
84/5 O-Pee-Chee 45
84/5 O-Pee-Chee 355
85/6 OPC/Topps 73
86/7 OPC/Topps 7
86/7 OPC/Topps Box N
87/8 OPC/Topps 127
87/8 OPC/Topps Box N
88/9 OPC/Topps 26
88/9 OPC/Topps Box H
90/1 OPC/Topps 28
91/2 O-Pee-Chee 330
92/3 O-Pee-Chee 35
89/0 OPC/Topps 5
87/8 OPC Leaders 39
90/1 OPC Premier 103
91/2 OPC Premier 71
92/3 OPC Premier SP6
88/9 OPC Stars 34
81/2 OPC Sticker 112
82/3 OPC/Topps Sticker 171
83/4 OPC/Topps Sticker 106
83/4 OPC/Topps Sticker 107
83/4 OPC/Topps Sticker 153
84/5 OPC Sticker 24
84/5 OPC Sticker 25
85/6 OPC Sticker 22
86/7 OPC Sticker 150
87/8 OPC Sticker 78
88/9 OPC Sticker 13
89/0 opcSticker 16
97/8 Pacific CC 343
87/8 Panini Sticker 225
88/9 Panini Sticker 29
89/0 Panini Sticker 49
90/1 Panini Sticker 198
90/1 Panini/MTL 20
91/2 Panini Sticker 187
92/3 Panini Sticker 152
93/4 Panini Sticker 17
94/5 Panini Sticker 181
96/7 Panini Sticker 164
91/2 Parkhurst 93
91/2 Parkhurst 211
92/3 Parkhurst 85
93/4 Parkhurst 193
94/5 Parkhurst 217
95/6 Parkhurst 40
91/2 Pinnacle 28
92/3 Pinnacle 61
93/4 Pinnacle 391
93/4 Pinnacle CA22
94/5 Pinnacle 340
95/6 Playoff 237
94/5 POG 225
95/6 POG 62
81/2 Post 3
82/3 Post [Chic.]
93/4 Power Play 447
93/4 Premier 305
94/5 Premier 69
90/1 Pro Set 59, 473
91/2 Pro Set 128
91/2 Pro Set 305
92/3 Pro Set 84
92/3 Pro Set 260
91/2 Pro Set Platinum 64
91/2 Pro Set Platinum PC18
90/1 Score 125, 1T
90/1 Sco. Hot Cards 59
91/2 Score 165
91/2 Score CAN 165
92/3 Score 202
93/4 Score 105
93/4 Score 555
95/6 Score 281
96/7 Score 121
92/3 Seasons 23
89 Semic Sticker 66
84/5 7-Eleven
85/6 7-Eleven Superstars 4
83/4 Souhaits Keychain [Blackhawks]
81/2 Topps 75 [West]
84/5 Topps 35
92/3 Topps 414
91/2 To. Stadium 213
92/3 To. Stadium 467
93/4 To. Stadium 397
95/6 TSC Members Only 23
90/1 Upper Deck 244, 426
91/2 Upper Deck 242
92/3 Upper Deck 10
92/3 Upper Deck 162
93/4 Upper Deck 638
94/5 Upper Deck 502, GG1, SP153
94/5 Upper Deck 415, SP-76
96/7 Upper Deck 434
94/5 UD BAP ✍ 94
96/7 UD Black Diam. 58
95/6 UD CC 132
02/3 UD Foundations 14, 50, 111, ✄ 1000Jers, ✄ 1000Stick, ✄ CH, ✄ CG, ✍ SG
80/1 CHIC / Colour
80/1 CHIC / Brown
81/2 CHIC
82/3 CHIC
83/4 CHIC
86/7 CHIC / Coke
87/8 CHIC / Coke
88/9 CHIC / Coke
89/0 CHIC / Coke
98/9 CHIC / Pizza Hut
90/1 MONT
91/2 MONT
92/3 MONT
92/3 MONT / OPC 50
94/5 TAMP / Sky Box
79/0 Montréal Juniors B&W
79/0 Montréal Jrs. Colour

SAVARD, DENIS
01/2 Fleer Legacy 45, ✄ TM

SAVARD, FRÉDÉRIC
88/9 Richelieu Riverains

SAVARD, JEAN
77/8 Dernière Heure

SAVARD, MARC
02/3 Pacific 59
02/3 Pacific Complete 407
02/3 Parkhurst Retro 124
02/3 SP Game-Used ✄ PH
01/2 SPx 9
01/2 To. Heritage 97
02/3 To. Total 164
01/2 Upper Deck 28
02/3 Upper Deck 23
02/3 UD Classic ✄ HR
01/2 UD DEL 72
01/2 UD Ice ✄ GJ
01/2 UD MVP 28
02/3 UD Piece 16
02/3 UD Top Shelf ✄ ST
01/2 UD Vintage 36, 43
02/3 UD Vintage 38, GB 38
02/3 Victory 33

SAVARD, MARC*
01/2 Adrenaline 28
01/2 Atomic 14, TN 2, ✄ GWJ 6
00/1 Aurora 26
99/0 BAP Mem. 224
00/1 BAP Mem. 183
01/2 BAP Mem. 90
97 Bowman 7
95/6 Classic 91
00/1 Crown Royale 19, ✄ GWJ-5
01/2 Crown Royale 23, ✄ TT 2
99/0 Dynagon Ice 38
02/3 First Edition 61, ✄ Jers.
01/2 Heads Up 13, ✄ JQ 5
02/3 Heads Up ✄ GWQ 5
99/0 HoloGrFX 8
01/2 O-Pee-Chee 128
02/3 O-Pee-Chee 72
99/0 Omega 40
98/9 Pacific 300
99/0 Pacific 279
00/1 Pacific 73
01/2 Pacific 65, ✄ GWJ 5
00/1 Pa. Paramount 38
99/0 Panini Sticker 194
00/1 Panini Sticker 118
00/1 Parkhurst P-6
01/2 Parkhurst 119
94/5 Parkie SE263
97/8 Pinnacle 15
97/8 Pi. Certified L
01/2 Pr. Stock 12, ✄ GUG 16
00/1 PS Titanium 12, ✄ GUG-69
01/2 PS Titanium 21, ✄ DSJ 5, ✄ DSJ 7
01/2 PS Titanium Draft ✄ 16
00/1 PS Titanium Draft ✄ 15
97/8 Score 67
97/8 Score NYRa. 19
00/1 Signature 17, ✍ Aut. 176
01/2 Signature 32, ✍ Aut. 32
93/4 Slapshot / Oshawa 22
95/6 Slapshot 250
94/5 SP 182
99/0 SP Authentic 14
00/1 SP Authentic 14
01/2 SP GU ✄ AF, ✄ AFD
99/0 SPx 27
98/9 SPx Finite 54
00/1 Stadium 167
00/1 Stadium 80
01/2 Stadium 83, ✄ SCS
00/1 Topps 135
01/2 Topps 128
02/3 Topps 72
01/2 To. Chrome 128
00/1 To. Heritage 129
02/3 To. Limited 72
01/2 To. Reserve ✄ TR
98/9 UD Choice 133
00/1 UD Heroes 18
01/2 UD PlayMakers Ltd 14
98/9 UD3 21, 81, 141
98/9 Upper Deck 132
99/0 Upper Deck 196
00/1 Upper Deck 28
00/1 UD Black Diam. 9
98/9 UD G. Reserve 132
99/0 UD G. Reserve 196
01/2 UD Mask ✄ GJ, ✄ JP, ✄ DP
00/1 UD MVP 32
02/3 UD MVP 28
00/1 UD Vintage 53
02/3 UD Vintage 265
00/1 Vanguard 17
01/2 Vanguard 13, ✄ DGM 4, ✄ DGM 41
99/0 Victory 52
00/1 Victory 41
01/2 Victory 50
99/0 WGretzky 28
98/9 NYRA
97/8 Hartford Wolf Pack
98/9 Hartford Wolf Pack

SAVARD, MARC**
98/9 DEL 130
99/0 Eishockey 358
90/1 7th..Sketch LHJMQ 250
91/2 7th...Sketch LHJMQ 74
91 7th..Sketch Mem.Cup 64, 130
00/1 UD DEL 160, ✄ GJ
93/4 Dayton Bombers

SAVARD, MIKE
91/2 Air Canada SJHL B21
92/3 MPS SJHL 154

SAVARD, RAY
86/7 Regina Pats

SAVARD, SERGE
99/0 BAP Mem. CH-12, ✍ CH-12
02/3 BAP Mem. / Cup
02/3 Canada Post
70/1 Colgate 74
70/1 Dad's Cookies
72/3 Dernière Heure
73/4 Dernière Heure
80/1 Dernière Heure
82/3 Dernière Heure
70/1 Eddie Sargent 110
71/2 Eddie Sargent 110
72/3 Eddie Sargent 123
70/1 Esso Power Player
88/9 Esso All-Star
01/2 Fleer Greats 85, ✍ Aut.
91/2 Future Trends C72 53, ✍ 53
92/3 Future Trends C76 117
83&87 HHOF 256
93/4 Hockey Wit 42
91/2 Kraft 77
74/5 Lipton Soup 11
74/5 Loblaws
73/4 Mac's Milk
69/0 O-Pee-Chee 4
69/0 O-Pee-Chee 210
69/0 O-Pee-Chee 4in1
70/1 O-Pee-Chee 51
71/2 O-Pee-Chee 143
72/3 O-Pee-Chee 185
72/3 O-Pee-Chee TC
73/4 O-Pee-Chee 24
74/5 O-Pee-Chee 53
75/6 O-Pee-Chee 144
76/7 O-Pee-Chee 205
77/8 O-Pee-Chee 45
78/9 O-Pee-Chee 190
78/9 O-Pee-Chee 335
79/0 O-Pee-Chee 101
80/1 O-Pee-Chee 26
80/1 O-Pee-Chee 275
82/3 O-Pee-Chee 390
01/2 Parkhurst ✍ PA45
02/3 Parkhurst ✄ VT4
95/6 Parkie 66-67 74
80/1 Pepsi Bottle Cap
68/9 Post Marble
82/3 Post [Winn.]
71/2 Pro Star Promotions
68/9 Shirriff / Mont. 17
83/4 Souhaits Keychain [Jets]
69/0 Topps 4
70/1 Topps 51
73/4 Topps 24
74/5 Topps 53
75/6 Topps 144
76/7 Topps 205
77/8 Topps 45
78/9 Topps 190
79/0 Topps 101
80/1 Topps 26
01/2 T/O Archives 53, -Seat, ✍
71/2 Toronto Sun Photo
01/2 Ultimate Mem. ✄ LC, ✄ SCD, ✄ SCW
02/3 Ultimate Mem. ✄ CSTW, ✄ Num, ✄ RT, ✄ SF
90/1 Upper Deck 506
99/0 UD C. Legends 47
00/1 UD Legends 68
01/2 UD Legends 32
95/6 Zellers
67/8 MONT / IGA Card
68/9 MONT / IGA Card
69/0 MONT / Pro Star
70/1 MONT
71/2 MONT / Pro Star
72/3 MONT / Pro Star
73/4 MONT / Pro Star
74/5 MONT
75/6 MONT
76/7 MONT
77/8 MONT
78/9 MONT
79/0 MONT
80/1 MONT
87/8 MONT
88/9 MONT
89/0 MONT
90/1 MONT
91/2 MONT
92/3 MONT / OPC 4
92/3 MONT / OPC 11
81/2 WINN
82/3 WINN

SAVARIA, MARTIN
84/5 Richelieu Riverains

SAVARY, NEIL
94/5 Slapshot Memorial 74

SAVCHENKO, ANDREI
99/0 Mir 83

SAVCHENKOV, ALEXANDER
98/9 Mir 29
95/6 Tallahassee Tiger Sharks
00/1 Dynamo 20

SAVENKO, BOGDAN
99/0 DS 55
98/9 OFS 79
99/0 OFS 244
93/4 Slapshot / Niagara Falls 19
94/5 Indianapolis Ice
96/7 Syracuse Crunch

SAVICKIJ, ALEXANDER
94/5 APS 145

SAVIELS, AGRIS
99/0 UD Prospects 16
02/3 Hershey Bears
00/1 Owen Sound Attack 2
01/2 Owen Sound Attack

SAVIJOKI, JARKKO
98/9 Cardset 68
99/0 Cardset 38
96/7 Sisu 22
00/1 UD DEL 159

SAVILLE, JOHN
74/5 Sioux City Musketeers

SAVILOV, GENNADI
00/1 Mir 257

SAVITSKI, ALEXANDER
98/9 Mir 109

SAVOIA, RYAN
95/6 Edge Ice 117
00/1 UD DEL 27
95/6 Cleveland Lumberjacks
96/7 Johnstown Chiefs

SAVOIE, CLAUDE
93/4 Classic 147
93/4 Cla. Prospects 121
90/1 7th..Sketch LHJMQ 260
91/2 7th...Sketch LHJMQ 262
01/2 Nottingham Panthers

SAVOIE, MICHEL
91/2 7th...Sketch LHJMQ 49

SAVOLAINEN, HANNU
94/5 Sisu 390
78/9 SM-Liiga 130

SAVOLAINEN, KARI
93/4 Jyvas Hyva 133
93/4 Sisu 135
94/5 Sisu 393
95/6 Sisu 390

SAVOLAINEN, MATIAS
66/7 Champion 215

SAVOLAINEN, PERTTI
78/9 SM-Liiga 69

SAVOLAINEN, RAIMO
66/7 Champion 214

SAVOLAINEN, RISTO
66/7 Champion 216

SAVOLAINEN, VEIKKO
66/7 Champion 172
70/1 Kuvajulkaisut 253
71/2 Williams Finnish 219
73/4 Williams Finnish 234

SAVOSIN, MAXIM
00/1 Mir 202

SAVUNEN, JUKKA
66/7 Champion 4
70/1 Kuvajulkaisut 237

SAWCHUK, TERRY
01/2 ASG History
00/1 BAP Mem. ✄ G-6, ✄ G-17, ✄ G-23, ✄ G-24, ✄ G-28, ✄ G-29, ✄ RB-1
01/2 BAP Mem. ✄ GT
02/3 BAP Mem. 233, / Cup
01/2 BAP Update ✄ RR4
45-64 BeeHive-2 [Detr.]
45-64 BeeHive-2 [Detr.]
45-64 BeeHive-2 [Bost.]
64-67 BeeHive-3 [Toro.]
01/2 BT Pipes 124, 135, HSHS, ✄ DM, ✄ S&J, ✄ GR, ✄ TW, ✄ VM
02/3 Between the Pipes 114, ✄ CP3, ✄ DM19, ✄ GT13, ✄ HSHSJers 28, ✄ I2, ✄ RB1, ✄ RB11, ✄ RB16, ✄ VM16
02/3 Canada Post
64/5 Coke/Sprite [Toro.]
65/6 Coca-Cola
48-52 Exhibits [Red Wings]
01/2 Fleer Greats 36, -RC 11, ✄ OSS
62/3 Cowan Tile
93/4 High Liner 11
83 HHOF Postcard D13
83&87 HHOF 46
93/4 Hockey Wit 83
02/3 In The GU ✄ GP20, ✄ VM18
91/2 Kraft 75
96/7 Legends 73
68/9 O-Pee-Chee 34
68/9 O-Pee-Chee PS 20
69/0 O-Pee-Chee 189
70/1 O-Pee-Chee 231
51/2 Parkhurst 61
52/3 Parkhurst 86
53/4 Parkhurst 46
54/5 Parkhurst 33
54/5 Parkhurst 96
54/5 Parkhurst 100
60/1 Parkhurst 31
61/2 Parkhurst 31
63/4 Parkhurst 53
91/2 Parkhurst PHC9
92/3 Parkhurst PR-2
93/4 Parkhurst PR37
93/4 Parkhurst PR53
01/2 Parkhurst HSHS, PR5, PR13, PR21, PR45, PR46, PR67, PR112, PR133, ✄ HSHSJers, ✄ H5, ✄ PV25, ✄ PV26, ✄ PV27
02/3 Parkhurst ✄ VM16, ✄ VT6
93/4 Parkie 56-57 153
93/4 Parkie 56-57 167
93/4 Parkie 56-57 168
93/4 Parkie 56-57 17
95/6 Parkie 66-67 120
94/5 Parkie Tall 119, 154, 163, TW4
91/2 Pro Set 343
60/1 Shirriff 41
61/2 Shirriff 77
54/5 Topps 58
57/8 Topps 35
58/9 Topps 2
59/0 Topps 42
64/5 Topps 6
65/6 Topps 12
66/7 Topps 13
68/9 Topps 34
02/3 To. Heritage - Reprint TML, ✄ Reprint
01/2 T/O Archives 69
57/8 Toronto Star Photo
60/1 Toronto Star Photo
62/3 Toronto Star Photo
63/4 Toronto Star Action
64/5 Toronto Star Photo
59/0 Toronto Star Weekend
63/4 Toronto Star Weekend
66/7 Toronto Star Weekend
00/1 Ultimate Mem. ✄ RE-1, ✄ RA-2, ✄ GM-2, ✄ GM-19, ✄ GM-20
01/2 Ultimate Mem. ✄ ASGH, ✄ BAPL, ✄ CT, ✄ CP, ✄ Corn., ✄ EA, ✄ RN, ✄ RT, ✄ RA, ✄ SCW
02/3 Ultimate Mem. ✄ CP, ✄ Cor, ✄ EA, ✄ Cor, ✄ EA, ✄ FS (x2), ✄ GMIH, ✄ NO, ✄ Num, ✄ RAT, ✄ RT, ✄ SCD (x3), ✄ VGJ, ✍ Cut
01/2 Upper Deck ✍ Cut
99/0 UD C. Legends 13, AC12, C10
00/1 UD Legends 43, EG4, LC9
01/2 UD Legends 16, 81, FC
02/3 UD Mask Replica Mask TS
99/0 UD Retro 87, G10A
01/2 UD SCup Champs 8
60/1 York Glass [Detr.]
62/3 York Transfer 25
63/4 York 37
91/2 BOST / SA Legends
92/3 BOST / SA Legends
99/0 DETR / News 3
64/5 TORO

SAWCHUK, TERRY
01/2 Fleer Legacy 30, ✄ HK

SAWTELL, DREW
89/0 Saskatoon Blades

SAWYER, DAN
94/5 Johnstown Chiefs 18

SAWYER, KEVIN
01/2 BAP Mem. 432
01/2 SP Authentic 133
01/2 SP GU 63
01/2 SPx 93
02/3 To. Heritage 114
01/2 Upper Deck 414
01/2 UD Challenge 93
01/2 UD Vintage 273
96/7 Providence Bruins

SAXBY, TONY
94/5 Humberside Hawks 9

SAYDE, CARLOS
99/0 Halifax Mooseheads

SAYLER, CURTIS
99/0 Missouri RiverOtters

SBROCCA, CHRISTIAN
96/7 Pensacola Ice Pilots

SBROCCA, SANDROS
00/1 Victoriaville Tigres 12

SCAMURRA, PETER
79/0 WASH

SCANDELLA, GIULIO
00/1 Halifax Moosehead

SCANLAN, DEREK
94/5 Thunder Bay Senators

SCANLAN, FRED
83 HHOF Postcard H13
83&87 HHOF 98

SCANTLEBURY, STU
90/1 7th..Sketch WHL 233
91/2 7th...Sketch WHL 211
90/1 Brandon Wheat Kings
92/3 Tacoma Rockets

SCANTLEBURY, THOMAS
96/7 Kamloops Blazers
99/0 Lethbridge Hurricanes

SCANZANO, JASON
92/3 MPS SJHL 142

SCANZANO, SHAWN
99/0 Rimouski Océanic 15
99/0 Rouyn-Noranda
00/1 Rouyn-Noranda 23

SCANZANO, WESLEY
99 Bowman 51
98/9 Québec Remparts
99/0 Québec Remparts 7
00/1 Rouyn-Noranda 18

SCAP, IVAN
79 Panini Sticker 395

SCAPINELLO, MARCO
92 Semic Sticker 257

SCAPINELLO, RAY
90/1 Pro Set 697

SCARDOCCHIO, ENRICO
91/2 7th...Sketch LHJMQ 171

SCARLATA, CHRIS
92/3 Hampton Roads

SCATCHARD, DAVE
01/2 O-Pee-Chee 200
97/8 Omega 235
98/9 Pacific 433
99/0 Pacific 431
00/1 Pacific 255
01/2 Pacific 253
02/3 Pacific Complete 89
98/9 Pa. Paramount 239
97/8 Pi. Be A Player 234, ✍ Aut. 234
94/5 Sig. Rookies 54, ✍ 54
97/8 SP Authentic 161
00/1 Topps 150
01/2 Topps 200
02/3 To. Total 373
98/9 UD Choice 209
00/1 Upper Deck 340
01/2 Upper Deck 341
02/3 Upper Deck 355
00/1 UD MVP 110
01/2 UD MVP 122
99/0 UD MVP Cup 113
01/2 UD Vintage 162, 165
02/3 UD Vintage 161
00/1 Victory 143
01/2 Victory 224
96/7 Syracuse Crunch
93/4 Portland Winter Hawks

SCERBAN, BEDRICH
95/6 APS 358
96/7 APS 217
96/7 DS Sticker 7, 24
99/0 Eishockey 364
94/5 Leaf Elit Set 25
95/6 Leaf Elit Set 17, FTF-2
95 Panini Worlds 191
94 Semic 174
92/3 Semic Elitserien 53
89 Semic Sticker 182
91 Semic Sticker 105
93 Semic Sticker 93
95/6 UD Elitserien 20

SCEVIOUR, DARIN
85/6 Nova Scotia Oilers

SCHAAL, JURGEN
94/5 DEL 121
95/6 DEL 121
96/7 DEL 01

SCHACHLE, TRENT
96/7 Dayton Bombers

SCHADEN, MARIO
95 Panini Worlds 269
94 Semic 246
93 Semic Sticker 268
93 Semic Sticker 288

SCHADLER, THOMAS
94/5 DEL 422

SCHAEFER, PETER
99/0 BAP Mem. 355
00/1 BAP Mem. 395
97 Bowman 118
02/3 Cardset 113
95/6 Classic 14
99/0 Crown Royale 139
99/0 Millenium C-28
99/0 NHL Power Play
01/2 O-Pee-Chee 157
98/9 Omega 242
99/0 Omega 239
99/0 Pacific 432
00/1 Pacific 415
01/2 Pacific 386
99/0 Panini Sticker 314, 353
01/2 Parkhurst 189
99/0 Prism 145, IP-10
01/2 Signature 86, ✍ Aut. 86
94/5 Slapshot Memorial 47
99/0 SP Authentic 86
00/1 Stadium 128
00/1 Topps 168
01/2 Topps 157
99/0 To. Gold Label 90
99/0 To. Prmr. Plus 128, PR3, ✍ SB3
99/0 Ult. Victory 87
00/1 Upper Deck 397
01/2 Upper Deck 171
96/7 UD Black Diam. 68
97/8 UD Coll. Choice 297
96/7 UD Ice 135
98/9 UD MVP 208
01/2 UD Vintage 246
99/0 Victory 302
01/2 Victory 347
99/0 WGretzky 172
02/3 OTTA
95/6 Brandon Wheat Kings

SCHAEFFER, JEFF
95/6 Swift Current Broncos

SCHAEFFLER, JAMES
91/2 Air Canada SJHL B2

SCHAFER, MIKE
92/3 W. Michigan Broncos
93/4 W. Michigan Broncos

SCHAFER, PAXTON
95/6 Classic 41
97/8 Donruss 201, RR-2
97/8 Do. Canadian 133
97/8 Limited 142
97/8 Pa. Dynagon BKS-8
97/8 Upper Deck 183
97/8 Charlotte Checkers

SCHAFFER, JERRY
79 Panini Sticker 280

SCHAFFER, RYAN
92/3 BCJHL 169

SCHALLER, PASCAL
95 Panini Worlds 132

SCHAMEHORN, KEVIN
89/0 ProCards IHL 75
87/8 Flint Spirits

SCHARF, CHRIS
91/2 7th...Sketch OHL 231

SCHASTLIVY, PETR
99/0 BAP Mem. 340
00/1 BAP Mem. 238
01/2 BAP Mem. 120
01/2 O-Pee-Chee 285
02/3 O-Pee-Chee 301
99/0 Omega 162
00/1 Pacific 291
00/1 PS Titanium 136
00/1 PS Titanium Draft 136
00/1 Signature 267, ✍ 229
02/3 Signature 133, ✍ 133
02/3 SP Authentic 126
00/1 Topps 311
01/2 Topps 285
02/3 Topps 301
00/1 To. Chrome 206
02/3 To. Limited 301
02/3 Upper Deck 368
00/1 UD MVP 200
00/1 UD Vintage 256
00/1 Victory 276
02/3 OTTA
99/0 Grand Rapids Griffins
00/1 Grand Rapids Griffins
01/2 Grand Rapids Griffins

SCHEFFELMAIER, BRETT
02/3 Worcester IceCats
99/0 Medicine Hat Tigers
00/1 Medicine Hat Tigers

SCHEIDT, TYLER
91/2 Air Canada SJHL A34

SCHEIFELE, STEVE
90/1 ProCards 44
91/2 Richmond Renegades

SCHELLA, JOHN
75/6 OPC WHA 21
76/7 OPC WHA 128
73/4 Quaker Oats 7
71/2 Toronto Sun Photo
71/2 VANC / Royal Bank 18
75/0 Houston Aeros

SCHENDELEV, SERGEI
94/5 DEL 306
95/6 DEL 107
96/7 DEL 52

SCHERBAN, JOEL
00/1 London Knights

SCHERTZ, JAN
94/5 DEL 48
95/6 DEL 42
96/7 DEL 41
01/2 UD DEL 42

SCHEUER, TYSON
92/3 BCJHL 225

SCHEV, ALEXANDER
99/0 Mir 134
00/1 Mir 270

SCHICHTL, HANS
72 Hellas MM-Jenkki 59
72 Semic Sticker 97

SCHIEBEL, BRIAN
91/2 Avant Garde BCJHL 58
92/3 BCJHL 43
91/2 Nanaimo Clippers

SCHIFFL, HEINRICH
94/5 DEL 387
95/6 DEL 168
96/7 DEL 190
99/0 Eishockey 282
92 Semic Sticker 177

SCHIFFT, HEINRICH
98/9 DEL 126

SCHILCHER, WERNER
79 Panini Sticker 303
79 Panini Sticker 309

SCHILL, DAVE
89/0 Kitchener Rangers

SCHILL, JONATHAN
01/2 Syracuse Crunch
02/3 Syracuse Crunch
99/0 Kingston Frontenacs

SCHILL, LEE
91/2 Avant Garde BCJHL 137
SCHILLER, PETER
82 Semic Sticker 111
SCHILLGARD, JOHAN
91/2 Semic Elitserien 50
SCHILLING, PAUL
72 Semic Sticker 135
SCHIMM, WILLI
99/0 Eishockey 414
SCHINKEL, CHRIS
91/2 Air Canada SJHL C43
92/3 MPS SJHL 32
SCHINKEL, KEN
52/3 Anonymous 26
71/2 Bazooka Panel
45-64 BeeHive-2 [NYRa.]
70/1 Colgate 61
70/1 Dad's Cookies
70/1 Eddie Sargent 174
71/2 Eddie Sargent 162
72/3 Eddie Sargent 170
70/1 Esso Power Player
68/9 O-Pee-Chee 106
69/0 O-Pee-Chee 117
69/0 O-Pee-Chee 4in1
70/1 O-Pee-Chee 92
71/2 O-Pee-Chee 64
72/3 O-Pee-Chee 256
60/1 Shirriff 96
61/2 Shirriff 99
68/9 Shirriff / Pitt. 1
60/1 Topps 50
63/4 Topps 62
68/9 Topps 106
69/0 Topps 117
70/1 Topps 92
71/2 Topps 64
71/2 Toronto Sun Photo
71/2 PITT / Sportcolor
SCHINKO, MARCO
94/5 DEL 62
SCHINKO, THOMAS
95/6 DEL 62
96/7 DEL 258
98/9 DEL 121
99/0 Eishockey 68
94 Semic 289
91 Semic Sticker 170
92 Semic Sticker 188
SCHISTAD, ROBERT
96/7 APS 121
98/9 DEL 222
96/7 DS Sticker 56
99/0 Eishockey 210
95 Panini Worlds 237
94 Semic 252
92/3 Semic Nordisk 127
93 Semic Sticker 230
96 Wien 201
SCHLEGEL, BRAD
92 COA Winter Olympics 198
90/1 Canada Nationals 8
91/2 Canada Nationals
95/6 DEL 133
92/3 OPC Premier 28
95 Panini Worlds 4
91/2 Parkhurst 413
92/3 Parkhurst 199
92/3 Score 477
92/3 Score COH 9
94/5 Score CT18
92/3 Topps 377
92/3 To. Stadium 29
92/3 Upper Deck 101
00/1 UD DEL 221
91/2 WASH / Kodak
85/6 London Knights
86/7 London Knights
SCHLENKER, CHRIS
01/2 Regina Pats
SCHLICKENRIEDER, JOSEF
94/5 DEL 148
95/6 DEL 126
89 Semic Sticker 104
SCHLIEBENER, ANDY
84/5 O-Pee-Chee 329
82/3 Fredericton Express
83/4 Fredericton Express
84/5 Fredericton Express
85/6 Fredericton Express
SCHLODER, ALOIS
72 Hellas MM-Jenkki 52
79 Panini Sticker 107
72 Semic Sticker 107
SCHMALZ, KEVIN
90/1 7th..Sketch WHL 236
89/0 Brandon Wheat Kings
SCHMAUTZ, BOBBY
72/3 Eddie Sargent 219
74/5 Loblaws
72/3 O-Pee-Chee 181
73/4 O-Pee-Chee 35
74/5 O-Pee-Chee 27
74/5 OPC 117
75/6 O-Pee-Chee 251
76/7 O-Pee-Chee 189
77/8 O-Pee-Chee 59
78/9 O-Pee-Chee 248
79/0 O-Pee-Chee 144
80/1 Pepsi Bottle Cap
73/4 Topps 35
74/5 Topps 27
74/5 Topps 117
75/6 Topps 251
76/7 Topps 189
77/8 Topps 59
78/9 Topps 248
79/0 Topps 144
71/2 Toronto Sun Photo
79/0 EDMO
88/9 EDMO / Action 160
71/2 VANC / Royal Bank 11
72/3 VANC / Royal Bank
73/4 VANC / Royal Bank
80/1 VANC
80/1 VANC / Silverwood
SCHMAUTZ, CLIFF
70/1 Esso Power Player
70/1 O-Pee-Chee 142
SCHMID, LORENZ
79 Panini Sticker 264
SCHMID, UDO
94/5 DEL 365
SCHMIDT, CHRIS
02/3 BAP Mem. 351
90/1 7th..Sketch WHL 152
91/2 7th...Sketch WHL 268
02/3 Ultimate Mem. 35
02/3 UD Rookie 124
00/1 Lowell Lock Monsters
01/2 Manchester Monarchs
99/0 Mississippi S'Wolves
93/4 Seattle Thunderbirds
SCHMIDT, DARREN
92/3 MPS SJHL 31
93/4 Slapshot / Kitchener 22
82/3 Brandon Wheat Kings
SCHMIDT, DON
85/6 Kamloops Blazers
86/7 Kamloops Blazers
87/8 Kamloops Blazers
88/9 Kamloops Blazers
84/5 Prince Albert Raiders
SCHMIDT, GREG
95/6 Red Deer Rebels
SCHMIDT, JACK
34-43 BeeHive-1 [Bost.]
51/2 Laval Dairy 69
52/3 Laval Dairy Update 69
52/3 St. Lawrence 17
SCHMIDT, JEFF
02/3 Kamloops Blazers
SCHMIDT, JOE
51/2 Bas du Fleuve 7
SCHMIDT, MICHAEL
94/5 DEL 299
95/6 DEL 336
91 Semic Sticker 158
93 Semic Sticker 152
SCHMIDT, MILT
34-43 BeeHive-1 [Bost.]
83 HHOF Postcard L16
83&87 HHOF 165
94/5 Legends 40
40/1 O-Pee-Chee 132
43-47 Parade Sportive
51/2 Parkhurst 29
52/3 Parkhurst 70
53/4 Parkhurst 92
54/5 Parkhurst 59
92/3 Parkhurst PR-23
93/4 Parkhurst DPR-2
01/2 Parkhurst PR72, PR117, PR123, ✍ PA7
93/4 Parkie 56-57 21
94/5 Parkie Tall 22
60/1 Shirriff 120
01/2 Signature ✍ VA11
54/5 Topps 60
63/4 Topps 1
64/5 Topps 70
65/6 Topps 96
02/3 Topps - Reprint 10, ✍ Reprint 10
00/1 To. Heritage OSA
01/2 T/O Archives 62
54 Toronto Star Weekend
99/0 UD C. Legends 26
57-58 BOST
91/2 BOST / SA Legends
91/2 BOST / SA Legends
91/2 BOST / SA Legends
98/9 BOST / Alumni 15
74/5 WASH
SCHMIDT, MORITZ
94/5 DEL 40
SCHMIDT, NORM
83/4 PITT / Coke Is It!✄
86/7 PITT / Kodak
80/1 Oshawa Generals
81/2 Oshawa Generals
82/3 Oshawa Generals
SCHMIDT, RYAN
95/6 Slapshot 327
SCHMIESS, TREVOR
91/2 Air Canada SJHL A26
SCHMITZ, CHRISTIAN
94/5 DEL 81
95/6 DEL 313
96/7 DEL 96
SCHNABEL, ROBERT
01/2 BAP Mem. 337
02/3 DS 32
01/2 Parkhurst 326
01/2 SPx 208
01/2 Milwaukee Admirals
SCHNARR, WERNER
24/5 Champ's Cigarettes
24/5 William Paterson 26
SCHNEIDAWIND, MICHAEL
96/7 DEL 200
SCHNEIDER,
95/6 DEL 437
SCHNEIDER, ANDY
93/4 Cla. Prospects 170
94/5 DEL 371
95/6 DEL 369
98/9 DEL 212
93/4 Donruss 468
99/0 Eishockey 215
94/5 Leaf Elit Set 255
90/1 7th..Sketch WHL 55
91/2 7th...Sketch WHL 174
91/2 Upper Deck WJC 56
00/1 UD DEL 183
01/2 UD DEL 192
SCHNEIDER, BUZZ
94/5 SR Miracle 29,30, ✍ 29,30
SCHNEIDER, ERIC
95/6 Tri-City Americans 6
SCHNEIDER, GEOFF
87/8 Kingston Canadians
SCHNEIDER, JEAN-ALAIN
90/1 7th..Sketch OHL 46
91/2 7th...Sketch OHL 10
93/4 Birmingham Bulls
91/2 Cornwall Royals
SCHNEIDER, MATHIEU
01/2 Adrenaline 89
98/9 Aurora 84
98/9 Be A Player 239, ✍ 239
99/0 BAP Mem. 101
00/1 BAP Mem. 431
01/2 BAP Mem. 270
02/3 BAP Mem. 327
90/1 Bowman 52
91/2 Bowman 343
92/3 Bowman 190
95/6 Bowman 81
93/4 Donruss 179
94/5 Donruss 233
95/6 Donruss 55
96/7 Donruss 18
97/8 Do. Canadian 97
97/8 Do. Canadian 116
96/7 Do. Elite 88
97/8 Do. Priority 34
93/4 EA Sports 68
02/3 First Ed. 170
94/5 Fleer 109
95/6 Fleer Metal 93
92/3 Fleer Ultra 110
93/4 Fleer Ultra 78
94/5 Fleer Ultra 114
95/6 Fleer Ultra 99, 270
98/9 Kraft / PB
93/4 Leaf 53
94/5 Leaf 195
95/6 Leaf 67
96/7 Leaf 190
94/5 L. Limited 101
96/7 Metal Univ. 153
90/1 OPC/Topps 372
91/2 O-Pee-Chee 392
92/3 O-Pee-Chee 166
91/2 OPC Premier 181
97/8 Omega 224
98/9 Pacific 72
99/0 Pacific 280
00/1 Pacific 270
01/2 Pacific 187
02/3 Pacific 174
02/3 Pacific Complete 139
97/8 Pacific CC 179
98/9 Pa. Paramount 230
90/1 Panini Sticker 60
90/1 Panini/MTL 21
91/2 Panini Sticker 195
92/3 Panini Sticker 157
93/4 Panini Sticker 22
94/5 Panini Sticker 16
95/6 Panini Sticker 99
96/7 Panini Sticker 220
99/0 Panini Sticker 104
91/2 Parkhurst 88
92/3 Parkhurst 319
93/4 Parkhurst 373
94/5 Parkhurst V32
95/6 Parkhurst 130
94/5 Parkie SE92
91/2 Pinnacle 209
92/3 Pinnacle 79
93/4 Pinnacle 37
93/4 Pinnacle T2K1 27
94/5 Pinnacle 56
95/6 Pinnacle 28
96/7 Pinnacle 124
97/8 Pinnacle 150
97/8 Pi. BAP 206, ✍ Aut. 206
95/6 Pi. Summit 25
96/7 Pi. Summit 30
95/6 Pi. Zenith 21
95/6 Playoff 64
96/7 Playoff 343
94/5 POG 142
95/6 POG 176
93/4 Power Play 134
93/4 Premier 163
94/5 Premier 181
95/6 Pro Magnet 53
90/1 Pro Set 58
91/2 Pro Set 119
92/3 Pro Set 91
89/0 ProCards AHL 199
90/1 Score 127
91/2 Score 105
91/2 Score CAN 105
92/3 Score 69
93/4 Score 18
94/5 Score 103
95/6 Score 206
96/7 Score 115
97/8 Score 160
97/8 Score Toro. 10
90/1 Sco. Young Stars 18
94/5 Select 23
95/6 Select CE 8
91 Semic Sticker 137
93 Semic Sticker 177
01/2 Signature 159, ✍ 159
95/6 SBx Emotion 108
95/6 SBx Impact 105
95/6 SP 89
96/7 SP 155
02/3 Sports Vault 236
00/1 Stadium CA15
95/6 Super Sticker 73, 75
96/7 Team Out!
92/3 Topps 253
95/6 Topps 36
00/1 Topps 264
95/6 To. Finest 56
96/7 To. Picks 53
91/2 To. Stadium 262
92/3 To. Stadium 70
93/4 To. Stadium 391, MP
95/6 To. Stadium 59
95/6 TSC Members Only 44
95/6 To. Super Skills 6
02/3 To. Total 139
98/9 UD Choice 198
90/1 Upper Deck 334
91/2 Upper Deck 328
92/3 Upper Deck 545
93/4 Upper Deck 31
94/5 Upper Deck 101
95/6 Upper Deck 161
96/7 Upper Deck 343
97/8 Upper Deck 372
01/2 Upper Deck 310
02/3 Upper Deck 329
95/6 UD BAP 20, ✍ S20
95/6 UD CC 322
96/7 UD CC 262
01/2 UD MVP 87
02/3 UD MVP 86
96/7 UD Post
02/3 UD Rookie 40
02/3 UD Vintage 117
02/3 Victory 101
89/0 MONT / Kraft
90/1 MONT
91/2 MONT
92/3 MONT
93/4 MONT
93/4 MONT / Export
94/5 MONT
98/9 NYRA
74/5 O-Pee-Chee 121
75/6 O-Pee-Chee 138
76/7 O-Pee-Chee 241
77/8 O-Pee-Chee 108
78/9 O-Pee-Chee 178
79/0 O-Pee-Chee 171
80/1 O-Pee-Chee 96
82/3 O-Pee-Chee 94
83/4 O-Pee-Chee 59
82/3 OPC/Topps Sticker 183
83/4 OPC/Topps Sticker 136
82/3 Post [Detr.]
83/4 Souhaits Keychain [Red Wings]
73/4 Topps 5
73/4 Topps 86
74/5 Topps 121
75/6 Topps 138
76/7 Topps 241
77/8 Topps 108
78/9 Topps 178
79/0 Topps 171
80/1 Topps 96
90/1 Upper Deck 505
72/3 BUFF
73/4 BUFF
74/5 BUFF
75/6 BUFF / Linnett
79/0 BUFF / Bells Market
80/1 BUFF / Wendt's 1
81/2 BUFF / Wendt's 6
85/6 BUFF / Blue Shield
93/4 BUFF / Noco
88/9 NJER / Caretta
97/8 PHOE / Coca-Cola
98/9 PHOE / Coca-Cola
95/6 WASH
SCHOFIELD, DAVE
88/9 ProCards / Kalamazoo
SCHOFIELD, DWIGHT
84/5 O-Pee-Chee 191
SCHNEIDER, ROCHUS
94/5 DEL 123
95/6 DEL 24
96/7 DEL 21
SCHNEIDER, SCOTT
88/9 ProCards / Moncton
89/0 ProCards AHL 52
90/1 ProCards 260
91/2 ProCards 362
87/8 Moncton Hawks
90/1 Moncton Hawks
SCHNEIDER, WALTER
79 Panini Sticker 305
SCHNEITBERGER, OTTO
72 Hellas MM-Jenkki 44
72 Semic Sticker 105
SCHNELLE, TIM
00/1 UD DEL 231
SCHNOBRICH, TIM
94/5 DEL 22
95/6 DEL 182
SCHOCK, RON
64-67 BeeHive-3 [Bost.]
64/5 Coke/Sprite [Bost.]
70/1 Colgate 42
70/1 Eddie Sargent 170
71/2 Eddie Sargent 170
72/3 Eddie Sargent 179
70/1 Esso Power Player
72/3 Post 23
74/5 Lipton Soup 43
74/5 Loblaws
68/9 O-Pee-Chee 118
69/0 O-Pee-Chee 120
69/0 O-Pee-Chee 4in1
70/1 O-Pee-Chee 91
70/1 O-Pee-Chee DE 9
71/2 O-Pee-Chee 56
72/3 O-Pee-Chee 81
73/4 O-Pee-Chee 200
74/5 O-Pee-Chee 167
75/6 O-Pee-Chee 75
75/6 O-Pee-Chee 326
76/7 O-Pee-Chee 248
76/7 O-Pee-Chee 392
77/8 O-Pee-Chee 51
78/9 O-Pee-Chee 384
95/6 Parkie 66-67 13
94/5 Parkie Tall 24
68/9 Shirriff / SLou. 1
65/6 Topps 36
66/7 Topps 100
68/9 Topps 118
69/0 Topps 120
70/1 Topps 91
71/2 Topps 56
72/3 Topps 59
73/4 Topps 113
74/5 Topps 167
75/6 Topps 75
75/6 Topps 326
76/7 Topps 248
77/8 Topps 51
71/2 Toronto Sun Photo
71/2 PITT / Sportcolor
74/5 PITT
SCHOCKENMAIER, CHAD
99/0 Kamloops Blazers
99/0 Kamloops Blazers
00/1 Kamloops Blazers
SCHOEN, BRIAN
95/6 Louisiana Ice Gators
93/4 Toledo Storm 28
SCHOENFELD, JIM
72/3 Eddie Sargent 41
02/3 Fleer Throwbacks 13, 4SO, ✍ 4SO, ✄ 4SO
83/4 Funmate Puffy 8 [w/]
74/5 Loblaws
72/3 O-Pee-Chee 220
73/4 O-Pee-Chee 86
73/4 O-Pee-Chee 137
74/5 O-Pee-Chee 115
75/6 O-Pee-Chee 52
76/7 O-Pee-Chee 18
77/8 O-Pee-Chee 32
78/9 O-Pee-Chee 114
79/0 O-Pee-Chee 42
80/1 O-Pee-Chee 271
81/2 O-Pee-Chee 31
82/3 O-Pee-Chee 33
83/4 O-Pee-Chee 72
84/5 O-Pee-Chee 27
84/5 OPC Sticker 218
80/1 Pepsi Bottle Cap
82/3 Post [Buff.]
72/3 Topps 131
73/4 Topps 137
74/5 Topps 115
75/6 Topps 52
76/7 Topps 18
77/8 Topps 32
78/9 Topps 114
79/0 Topps 42
80/1 Topps 32
81/2 Topps 12
82/3 Topps 72
83/4 Topps 27
84/5 Topps 218
90/1 Upper Deck 505
72/3 BUFF
73/4 BUFF
SCHUCASK, C.
91/2 7th...Sketch OHL 000
SCHUHMACHER, PHILIP
01/2 UD DEL 249
SCHULER, ALAN
00/1 Kudos 57
92/3 Richmond Renegades
93/4 Richmond Renegades
01/2 Cardiff Devils
SCHULER, LAURA
97/8 UD Coll. Choice 294
SCHULTE, PAXTON
93/4 Cla. Prospects 124
00/1 Kudos 26
91/2 7th...Sketch WHL 13
96/7 Saint John Flames
97/8 Saint John Flames
01/2 Belfast Giants
SCHULTZ, ANDREAS
94/5 Leaf Elit Set 165
SCHULTZ, DAVE
01/2 BAP Update ✄ TC1
01/2 Fleer Greats 45, ✍ Aut.
01/2 Fleer Legacy 55
02/3 Fleer Throwbacks 67, 2SO, 8SO, ✍ 2SO, ✄ 8SO, ✍ ...
75/6 Hockey Heroes
74/5 Lipton Soup 30
74/5 Loblaws
73/4 O-Pee-Chee 137
73/4 O-Pee-Chee 166
74/5 O-Pee-Chee 5
74/5 O-Pee-Chee 154
74/5 O-Pee-Chee 196
75/6 O-Pee-Chee 147
75/6 O-Pee-Chee 211
76/7 O-Pee-Chee 4
76/7 O-Pee-Chee 150
76/7 OPC 391
77/8 O-Pee-Chee 353
78/9 O-Pee-Chee 66
78/9 O-Pee-Chee 225
79/0 O-Pee-Chee 4
79/0 O-Pee-Chee 134
92/3 Parkhurst 473
01/2 Parkhurst ✄ PA43
01/2 Parkhurst ✄ VT13
02/3 Signature ✄ FS1
73/4 Topps 5
73/4 Topps 149
74/5 Topps 5
74/5 Topps 154
74/5 Topps 196
75/6 Topps 147
75/6 Topps 211
76/7 Topps 4
76/7 Topps 150
78/9 Topps 66
78/9 Topps 225
79/0 Topps 4
79/0 Topps 134
01/2 T/O Archives 66, ✍ CAI
01/2 Ultimate Mem. ✄ RT, ✄ SCD
02/3 Ultimate Mem. ✄ FS, ✄ RT
SCHULTZ, DEREK
97/8 Spokane Chiefs
SCHULTZ, IGOR
94/5 DEL 117
95/6 DEL 161
96/7 DEL 64
SCHULTZ, KEN
51/2 Cleveland Barons
SCHULTZ, LASSE
80/1 Mallasjuoma 155
SCHULTZ, MARTIN
94/5 DEL 118
95/6 DEL 119
SCHULTZ, MICHAEL
98/9 Huntington Blizzard
98/9 Peoria Rivermen
SCHULTZ, NICK
01/2 Adrenaline 212
01/2 BAP Mem. 383
01/2 Bowman 128
02/3 Bowman 136, ✄ FFDS, ✄ FFJ, ✄ FFP, ✄ FFR, ✄ FFRP, ✄ FFS, ✄ FFTS, ✍ YSA, / ✍ Puck
01/2 Crown Royale 166
01/2 O-Pee-Chee 339
02/3 O-Pee-Chee 293
02/3 Pacific Complete 49
01/2 Parkhurst 296
01/2 Pr. Stock 126
01/2 PS Titanium 165
01/2 PS Titanium Draft 137
01/2 Signature 214, ✍ Aut. 214
01/2 SP GU 81
01/2 SPx Rookie RR15
01/2 Topps 339
02/3 Topps 293
01/2 To. Chrome 157
01/2 To. Limited 293
01/2 To. Reserve 107
02/3 To. Total 16
01/2 Upper Deck 428
01/2 UD Challenge 112
01/2 UD Honor Roll 75
01/2 UD Ice 57
01/2 UD Premier 66
99/0 UD Prospects 51, 86
02/3 UD Vintage 124
01/2 Vanguard 117
01/2 MINW
01/2 MINW / Crime 24
SCHULTZ, RAY
02/3 Atomic 119
02/3 BAP Mem. 328
02/3 Crown Royale 125
02/3 Heads Up 126
02/3 Pr. Stock Reserve 171
02/3 SP Authentic 150
02/3 Upper Deck 214
02/3 UD Foundations 136
02/3 UD Mask 133
02/3 UD MVP 210
02/3 UD Piece 139
02/3 UD Top Shelf 95
02/3 UD Vintage 340
02/3 Victory 131
00/1 Cleveland Lumberjacks
99/0 Kansas City Blades
SCHULZ, KARSTEN
94/5 DEL 439
95/6 DEL 400
SCHUMACHER, PHILIP
99/0 Eishockey 19
SCHUMPERLI, BERNHARD
91/2 Upper Deck 667
91/2 Upper Deck WJC 28
SCHUR, HARTWIG
74 Hellas MM-Jenkki 117
SCHURE, PETER
91/2 Cincinnati Cyclones
SCHUST, BEN
95/6 Slapshot 364
96/7 Soo Greyhounds
SCHUSTER, ALEXANDER
94/5 DEL 286
SCHUSTER, MANFRED
89 Semic Sticker 110
SCHUTT, ROD
79/0 O-Pee-Chee 234
80/1 O-Pee-Chee 307
81/2 O-Pee-Chee 259
81/2 OPC Sticker 186
79/0 Topps 234
81/2 Topps 116 [East]
77/8 Nova Scotia Voyageurs
SCHUTTE, KYLE
01/2 Val d'Or Foreurs 18
SCHUTZ, DEREK
97 Bowman 97, 127, ✍ Aut.
95/6 Spokane Chiefs 20
SCHÜTZ, RICHARD
99/0 Eishockey 413
SCHWAB, COREY
02/3 BAP Mem. 97
01/2 BT Pipes 81
02/3 Between the Pipes 62
98/9 Bicycle.. 3-H
95/6 Bowman 164
94/5 Classic E5
97/8 Donruss 77
96/7 Do. Elite 128
95/6 Edge Ice 9, QM-12
02/3 First Ed. 241
97/8 Leaf 96
96/7 L. Preferred 126
97/8 Limited 130
99/0 Pacific 395
02/3 Pacific 369
02/3 Pacific Complete 426
97/8 Pacific CC 126
95/6 Parkhurst 389
96/7 Pi. Be A Player 104, ✍ Aut. 104
91/2 ProCards 416
90/1 7th..Sketch WHL 19
97/8 Upper Deck 157
97/8 UD Coll. Choice 244
00/1 UD Mask 50, 51
98/9 Cleveland Lumberjacks
00/1 Kansas City Blades 21
SCHWABE, JENS
94/5 DEL 395
90/1 Upper Deck 680
91/2 Upper Deck WJC 43
SCHWALB, MIKE
89/0 Nashville Knights
SCHWARK, BOB
91/2 Air Canada SJHL D10
SCHWARTZ, DARREN
93/4 Cla. Prospects 247
89/0 Johnstown Chiefs
95/6 Tallahasee Tiger Sharks
92/3 Wheeling Thund'birds 15
93/4 Wheeling Thund'birds
SCHWARTZ, OLIVER
94/5 DEL 355
SCHWEITZER, AARON
99/0 Colorado Gold Kings
SCHWELE, SEBASTIEN
95/6 DEL 192
SCHWEYER, ROB
93/4 Owen Sound Platers
SCISSONS, JEFF
00/1 Kansas City Blades 15
SCISSONS, SCOTT
91/2 Canada Nationals
93/4 Donruss 210
93/4 Leaf 243
93/4 Parkhurst 121
90/1 Score 432
90/1 7th..Sketch WHL 77
90/1 Upper Deck 357
91/2 Upper Deck 298
93/4 Upper Deck 511
89/0 Saskatoon Blades
90/1 Saskatoon Blades
SCLISIZZI, ENIO
45-64 BeeHive-2 [Detr.]
52/3 Parkhurst 32
SCMITZ, CHRISTIAN
98/9 DEL 13
SCOLLAN, MARK
91/2 Air Canada SJHL 11
SCORSUNE, MATT
00/1 Hershey Bears
01/2 Hershey Bears
SCOTT, BLAIR
93/4 Cla. Prospects 148
00/1 Kudos 96
91/2 7th...Sketch OHL 101
89/0 Victoria Cougars
SCOTT, BRAD
90/1 7th..Sketch WHL 173
SCOTT, BRIAN
94/5 Parkie SE268
94/5 SR Auto-Phonex 38, ✍ 38
93/4 Slapshot / Kingston 8
94/5 Slapshot / Kitchener 31
95/6 Slapshot 396
94/5 SP 186
96/7 Sudbury Wolves
SCOTT, CHUBBY
23/4 Paulins Candy 52
SCOTT, CLAUDE
92/3 Toledo Storm
SCOTT, DENNIS
89/0 7th..Sketch OHL 137
89/0 Niagara Falls Thunder
SCOTT, FRED
96/7 Dayton Ice Bandits
SCOTT, GANTON
24/5 Champ's Cigarettes
24/5 Maple Crispette [V130] 29
24/5 William Paterson 38
SCOTT, GARY
98/9 Barrie Colts
SCOTT, GREG
91/2 7th...Sketch OHL 206
93/4 Huntington Blizzard
SCOTT, IRVIN
52/3 Anonymous 49
SCOTT, JERRY
84/5 Ottawa 67's
SCOTT, KEVIN
91/2 Cincinnati Cyclones
SCOTT, LAURIE
23/4 Paulins Candy 40
SCOTT, MARK
97/8 Kamloops Blazers
SCOTT, RICHARD
01/2 BAP Mem. 370
01/2 O-Pee-Chee 360
01/2 To. Chrome 178
01/2 UD Challenge 122
01/2 UD Honor Roll 82
99/0 Charlotte Checkers
00/1 Charlotte Checkers
00/1 Hartford Wolf Pack
SCOTT, RON
89/0 ProCards AHL 5
90/1 ProCards 424
89/0 New Haven Nighthawks
SCOTT, TRAVIS
01/2 BT Pipes 38
02/3 Between the Pipes 37
93/4 Slapshot / Windsor 3
94/5 Slapshot / Windsor 3
95/6 Slapshot 231
00/1 SP Authentic 146
00/1 UD Black Diam. 121
01/2 Victory 374
99/0 Lowell Lock Monsters
00/1 Lowell Lock Monsters
01/2 Manchester Monarchs
02/3 Manchester Monarchs
99/0 Mississippi S'Wolves
SCOVILLE, DARREL
99/0 BAP Mem. 338
01/2 Syracuse Crunch
02/3 Syracuse Crunch
SCREMIN, CLAUDIO
98/9 DEL 195
90/1 ProCards 597
91/2 ProCards 508
90/1 Kansas City Blades
92/3 Kansas City Blades
94/5 Kansas City Blades 15
95/6 Kansas City Blades
96/7 Kansas City Blades
99/0 Kansas City Blades Moment
SCRUTON, HOWIE
81/2 Kingston Canadians
SCUDERI, ROB
01/2 WBS Penguins
02/3 WBS Penguins
SCULLION, BERT
51/2 Bas du Fleuve 49
SCULLY, SEAN
00/1 Ottawa 67's 10
01/2 Ottawa 67's 12
SEABROOKE, GLEN
88/9 ProCards / Hershey
89/0 ProCards AHL 336
SEALE, T
91/2 Michigan Tech Huskies
SEARLE, DOUG
89/0 7th..Sketch OHL 119
90/1 7th..Sketch OHL 371
91/2 7th...Sketch OHL 140
93/4 Knoxville Cherokees
94/5 Knoxville Cherokees
96/7 Roanoke Express 10
98/9 Roanoke Express
91/2 Peterborough Petes
SEARLES, STEVE
90/1 7th..Sketch LHJMQ 173
91/2 7th...Sketch LHJMQ 119
SEARLES, YANNICK
00/1 Québec Remparts 10
01/2 Québec Remparts 9
SEARS, SVERRE
95/6 Flint Generals
93/4 Greensboro Monarchs
94/5 Greensboro Monarchs
SEATON, BRYANT
81/2 Victoria Cougars
SEATON, MIKE
90/1 7th..Sketch WHL 8
89/0 Victoria Cougars
SEBASTIAN, JEFF
98/9 DEL 6
99/0 Eishockey 305
00/1 Kudos 146
90/1 7th..Sketch WHL 313
91/2 7th...Sketch WHL 136
01/2 Sheffield Steelers GS
89/0 Portland Winter Hawks
88/9 Regina Pats
SEBEK, VENCI
94/5 DEL 385
95/6 DEL 150
SEBESTA, PAVEL
95/6 APS 308
97/8 APS 107
97/8 DS Sticker 60
99/0 Score 103
SEBESTU, RICHARD
95/6 APS 211
SEBOR, JAN
98/9 OFS 258
SECA, DYLAN
94/5 Slapshot / Kitchener 34
SECEMSKI, KRYSTOF
94/5 Slapshot / Sudbury 16
SECORD, AL
90/1 Bowman 12
94/5 Cla. Images 89
83/4 Funmate Puffy 16 [w/]
80/1 O-Pee-Chee 129
81/2 O-Pee-Chee 72
82/3 O-Pee-Chee 60
82/3 O-Pee-Chee 74
83/4 O-Pee-Chee 95
83/4 O-Pee-Chee 112
83/4 O-Pee-Chee 218
84/5 O-Pee-Chee 46
86/7 OPC/Topps 100
87/8 OPC/Topps 111
88/9 OPC/Topps 249
82/3 OPC/Topps Sticker 175
83/4 OPC/Topps Sticker 111
83/4 OPC/Topps Sticker 156
83/4 OPC/Topps Sticker 160
86/7 OPC Sticker 155-10
87/8 OPC Sticker 74-207
88/9 OPC Sticker 179
87/8 Panini Sticker 229
82/3 Post [Chic.]
90/1 Pro Set 60
84/5 7-Eleven
83/4 Souhaits Keychain [Blackhawks]
80/1 Topps 129
91/2 Upper Deck 635
02/3 UD Foundations 13, ✍ SG
01/2 UD Legends 10
81/2 CHIC
82/3 CHIC
83/4 CHIC
86/7 CHIC / Coke
89/0 CHIC / Coke
87/8 TORO / 5x8
87/8 TORO / P.L.A.Y. 14
88/9 TORO / P.L.A.Y. 14
SECORD, BRIAN
95/6 Classic 83
95/6 Slapshot 370
98/9 Dayton Bombers
98/9 Dayton Bombers
96/7 Pensacola Ice Pilots
96/7 Richmond Renegades
SEDER, CONLAN
00/1 Kamloops Blazers
01/2 Kamloops Blazers
02/3 Kamloops Blazers
SEDIN, DANIEL
01/2 Adrenaline 192, PM 9
01/2 Atomic 95, PP 33, TN 14
00/1 BAP Mem. 397
01/2 BAP Mem. 6, ✄ SCP
02/3 BAP Mem. 66
00/1 Crown Royale 143, 21CR-24, NP-19
01/2 Crown Royale 139
02/3 Crown Royale ✄ GWDP 22
00/1 Crown Royale CC
02/3 First Ed. 39, 430R, ✄ Jers.
01/2 Heads Up 95, BTI 19, PP 9
02/3 Heads Up -HF15, ✄ GWQ 27
02/3 In The G-U 73, 173
01/2 McDonald's - FL 5
01/2 O-Pee-Chee 63
02/3 O-Pee-Chee 58
01/2 Pacific 387
02/3 Pacific 383
02/3 Pacific Complete 130
00/1 Pa. Paramount 251
00/1 Parkhurst P-101
01/2 Parkhurst 89, ✄ PJ12, ✄ PS12, ✄ T17
02/3 Parkhurst 167
00/1 Premier Plus 97, PR7
00/1 Pr. Stock 148, PSR-24
01/2 Pr. Stock 96
00/1 PS Titanium 148, 3SS-29
01/2 PS Titanium 138, ✄ DSJ 54
01/2 PS Titanium Draft ✄ 97
02/3 PS Titanium ✄ GWJ 71
00/1 PS Titanium Draft 148
00/1 Signature 280, F-29, ✍ Aut. 242
01/2 Signature 51, ✍ Aut. 51, ✄ GJ63, ✄ GSJ63, ✄ TM29
02/3 Signature 55, GS25, ✍ 55, ✄ TQ14
00/1 SP Authentic 85, ✍ SotT, ✍ SotTD
01/2 SP Authentic 86, ✍ SotT, ✍ SotTD, ✍ SotTT
00/1 SP GU 57
01/2 SP GU 57
99/0 SPx 164
00/1 SPx 149
01/2 SPx 67
98/9 SPx Prospects 79
00/1 Stadium 232
01/2 Stadium 17, G38
01/2 Topps 63 , OTG18
02/3 Topps 58
00/1 To. Chrome 171
01/2 To. Chrome 63
00/1 To. Gold Label 68, B10, NG11
00/1 To. Heritage 33, NT2
01/2 To. Heritage 48
02/3 To. Limited 58
01/2 To. Reserve 67
00/1 To. Stars 145
02/3 To. Total 309
98/9 UD Choice 294
00/1 UD Heroes 114
00/1 UD Reserve 84
00/1 Ultimate Mem. ✍ U-47
99/0 Upper Deck 165, 307
00/1 Upper Deck 400, TT3
01/2 Upper Deck 168, ✄ CJers, ✄ NG, ✄✍ JersSig
02/3 Upper Deck 167
97/8 UD Black Diam. 114
98/9 UD Black Diam. 109
99/0 UD Black Diam. 119
00/1 UD Black Diam. 110
97/8 UD Elitserien 159, UDS2, S11, C15
98/9 UD Elitserien 177, 219, ✄ GJ, ✄✍ GJA1
99/0 UD Elitserien 179, 217, H12, PD2, ✍ Aut.
00/1 UD Elitserien ✄ GJ
99/0 UD G. Reserve 165, 307
00/1 UD Ice 79
01/2 UD Ice ✍ CCA
00/1 UD MVP ME7, ✍ ME
01/2 UD MVP 182
02/3 UD MVP 181, ✍ PSig
99/0 UD MVP Cup 217
99/0 UD Ovation 62
02/3 UD Piece ✍ MD
00/1 UD Pros&Prosp. 84, NA7
99/0 UD Prospects 66, DS4, IN1, ✄ GJ, ✍ Sig.
01/2 UD Top Shelf 44, ✄ J, ✄✍ SJ
02/3 UD Top Shelf ✄ Sig
00/1 UD Vintage 353
01/2 UD Vintage 245, 251
02/3 UD Vintage 249, GB 249
00/1 Vanguard 149, HV-34, IF-19
01/2 Vanguard PP 19
99/0 Victory 368
01/2 Victory 344
01/2 VANC / Coke
SEDIN, HENRIK
01/2 Adrenaline 193, PM 10
01/2 Atomic 96, PP 34, TN 14
00/1 BAP Mem. 496
01/2 BAP Mem. 46
02/3 BAP Mem. 173
00/1 Crown Royale 144, 21CR-25, NP-20
01/2 Crown Royale 140
02/3 Crown Royale ✄ GWDP 22
00/1 Crown Royale CC
02/3 First Ed. 27, 430R, ✄ Jers.
01/2 Heads Up 96, BTI 20, PP 10
02/3 Heads Up -HF16, ✄ GWQ 27
02/3 In The G-U 74, 174
01/2 McDonald's - FL 6
01/2 O-Pee-Chee 45
02/3 O-Pee-Chee 213
01/2 Pacific 388
02/3 Pacific 384
02/3 Pacific Complete 235
00/1 Pa. Paramount 252
00/1 Parkhurst P-207
01/2 Parkhurst 75
02/3 Parkhurst 165
02/3 Parkhurst Retro 169
00/1 Premier Plus 87, PR2
00/1 Pr. Stock 149, PSR-25
01/2 Pr. Stock 96
00/1 PS Titanium 149, 3SS-30
01/2 PS Titanium 139, ✄ DSJ 54
01/2 PS Titanium Draft ✄ 98
02/3 PS Titanium ✄ GWJ 72
00/1 PS Titanium Draft 149
00/1 Signature 281, ✍ Aut. 243
01/2 Signature 72, ✍ Aut. 72, ✄ GJ13, ✄ GSJ13, ✄ HSHSJers
02/3 Signature 17, ✍ 17, ✄ TQ14
00/1 SP Authentic 86, ✍ SotT, ✍ SotTD
01/2 SP Authentic 87, ✍ SotT, ✍ SotTD, ✍ SotTT
00/1 SP GU 58
01/2 SP GU ✄✍ IS
02/3 Sports Vault 297
99/0 SPx 165
00/1 SPx 150
98/9 SPx Prospects 80
00/1 Stadium 231
01/2 Stadium 43, G15
01/2 Topps 45
02/3 Topps 213
00/1 To. Chrome 209
01/2 To. Chrome 45
00/1 To. Gold Label 77, B10, NG7
00/1 To. Heritage 19, NT9
01/2 To. Heritage 27
02/3 To. Limited 213
01/2 To. Reserve 22
00/1 To. Stars 144
02/3 To. Total 12
98/9 UD Choice 295
00/1 UD Heroes 113
00/1 UD Reserve 85
99/0 Upper Deck 166, 308
00/1 Upper Deck 401
01/2 Upper Deck 169, ✄ CJers, ✄ NG, ✄✍ JersSig
02/3 Upper Deck 413
97/8 UD Black Diam. 136
98/9 UD Black Diam. 110
99/0 UD Black Diam. 120
00/1 UD Black Diam. 111
97/8 UD Elitserien 178, 220, UDS9, S10, C16
98/9 UD Elitserien 178, 220, ✄ GJ, ✄✍ GJA1
99/0 UD Elitserien 180, 220, H13, PD2, ✍ Aut.
00/1 UD Elitserien ✄ GJ
99/0 UD G. Reserve 166, 308
00/1 UD Ice 78
01/2 UD Ice ✍ CCA
00/1 UD MVP ME7, ✍ ME
02/3 UD MVP 182, ✍ PSig
99/0 UD MVP Cup 218
99/0 UD Ovation 63
02/3 UD Piece ✍ MD
00/1 UD Pros&Prosp. 85, NA8
99/0 UD Prospects 67, DS3, IN2, ✄ GJ, ✍ Sig.
01/2 UD Top Shelf ✄ J, ✄✍ SJ
02/3 UD Top Shelf ✄ Sig
00/1 UD Vintage 355
01/2 UD Vintage 251
02/3 UD Vintage 247, GB 247
00/1 Vanguard 150, HV-35, IF-20
01/2 Vanguard PP 20
99/0 Victory 369
01/2 Victory 345
01/2 VANC / Coke
SEDLACEK, MIROSLAV
99/0 Score 62
SEDLAK, PREMYSL
98/9 OFS 402
00/1 OFS 128
01/2 OFS 265
99/0 Score 69
SEDLAK, ZDENEK
94/5 APS 201
95/6 APS 49
96/7 APS 38
97/8 APS 68
00/1 Cardset 291
00/1 DS 93
97/8 DS Sticker 302
98/9 OFS 80
99/0 OFS 376
01/2 OFS 220
SEDLBAUER, RON
76/7 O-Pee-Chee 271
77/8 O-Pee-Chee 368
78/9 O-Pee-Chee 139
79/0 O-Pee-Chee 19
80/1 O-Pee-Chee 134
81/2 O-Pee-Chee 324
78/9 Topps 139
79/0 Topps 19
80/1 Topps 134
80/1 CHIC / Brown
75/6 VANC / Royal Bank
76/7 VANC / Royal Bank
77/8 VANC / Royal Bank
78/9 VANC / Royal Bank
79/0 VANC / Royal Bank
SEDY, PETR
94/5 APS 98
95/6 APS 59
96/7 APS 245
SEEBERGER, CHRISTIAN
94/5 DEL 177
95/6 DEL 173
SEELEY, RICHARD
99 Bowman 98
99/0 Lowell Lock Monsters
00/1 Lowell Lock Monsters
01/2 Manchester Monarchs
02/3 Manchester Monarchs
SEESVUORI, RISTO
70/1 Kuvajulkaisut 222
71/2 Williams Finnish 144
SEFCIK, KAREL
98/9 OFS 284
99/0 Score 163
SEFTEL, STEVE
88/9 ProCards / Baltimore

89/0 ProCards AHL 90
90/1 ProCards 203
91/2 ProCards 556
91/2 Baltimore Skipjacks
85/6 Kingston Canadians
86/7 Kingston Canadians
87/8 Kingston Canadians

SEGAL, BRANDON
97 Québec Pee Wee 1218
99/0 Calgary Hitmen
00/1 Calgary Hitmen
01/2 Calgary Hitmen

SÉGUALDO, RENE
72 Semic Sticker 153

SEGUIN, BRETT
89/0 7th..Sketch OHL 49
90/1 7th..Sketch OHL 92
91/2 7th...Sketch OHL 301
00/1 Austin Ice Bats
93/4 Muskegon Fury
94/5 Muskegon Fury
95/6 Muskegon Fury
98/9 Topeka Scarecrows
99/0 Topeka Scarecrows

SEGUIN, JEAN-FRANÇOIS
99/0 Kingston Frontenacs
00/1 Kingston Frontenacs 18

SEGUIN, SAMUEL
98/9 Halifax Moosehead

SEGUIN, STEVE
84/5 LOSA / Smokey 21
81/2 Kingston Canadians
82/3 Kingston Canadians

SÉGUIN, IAN
01/2 Moncton Wildcats 8

SÉGUIN, JOFFRE
38/9 Brighton Tigers

SÉGUIN, PHILIPPE
01/2 Val d'Or Foreurs 1

SEHER, KURT
90/1 7th..Sketch WHL 61
91/2 7th...Sketch WHL 133
96/7 Charlotte Checkers
97/8 Charlotte Checkers
97/8 Charlotte Checkers
98/9 Charlotte Checkers
98/9 Charlotte Checkers
99/0 Charlotte Checkers
00/1 Charlotte Checkers

SEIBEL, CHAD
90/1 7th..Sketch WHL 280
91/2 7th...Sketch WHL 40
94/5 Greensboro Monarchs
88/9 Lethbridge Hurricanes
90/1 Prince Albert Raiders

SEIBEL, KEVIN
99/0 Prince George Cougars

SEIBERT, EARL
34-43 BeeHive-1 [Chic.]
36-39 Diamond Match TT1
36-39 Diamond Match BH TT
36-39 Diamond Match Chic.
36-39 Diamond Match BH BT
83 HHOF Postcard K16
83&87 HHOF 150
93/4 Legends of Hockey 27
39/0 O-Pee-Chee 76
93/4 Parkie 56-57 P-12

SEIBERT, OLIVER
83 HHOF Postcard J14
83&87 HHOF 193

SEIDENBERG, DENNIS
02/3 Atomic 121
02/3 BAP All-Star 125
02/3 BAP Mem. 273
02/3 Bowman 147, ✂ FFDS, ✂ FFJ, ✂ FFP, ✂ FFR, ✂ FFRP, ✂ FFS, ✂ FFTS, ✍ YSA, / ✍ Puck
02/3 Calder 135
02/3 Crown Royale 129
99/0 Eishockey 23
02/3 Exclusive 187
02/3 Heads Up 126
02/3 In The G-U 83, ✂ C13
02/3 Pacific Complete 538
02/3 Parkhurst 203
02/3 Parkhurst Retro 203
02/3 Pr. Stock Reserve 175
02/3 PS Titanium 128
02/3 Quest for the Cup 135
02/3 Signature 180, ✍ 180, ✂ AR3, ✂ DW3, ✂ SGJ65
02/3 SP Authentic 153
02/3 SP GU 87
02/3 Stadium 137
02/3 T. Chrome 172
02/3 To. Heritage 143
02/3 To. Total 427
02/3 Ultimate Mem. 3, ✂ CC
02/3 Upper Deck 445
02/3 UD Classic 123
01/2 UD DEL 261
02/3 UD Honor 122
02/3 UD Mask 142
02/3 UD Piece 144
02/3 UD Premier 63
02/3 UD Top Shelf 99
02/3 Vanguard 126

SEIF, BRAD
01/2 Peterborough Petes

SEIKER, SHANE
90/1 7th..Sketch WHL 328

SEIKKULA, TIMO
98/9 Cardset 157

SEIKOLA, MARKUS
00/1 Cardset 337
02/3 Cardset 114

SEILING, RIC
78/9 O-Pee-Chee 242
79/0 O-Pee-Chee 119
80/1 O-Pee-Chee 159
81/2 O-Pee-Chee 32
82/3 O-Pee-Chee 35
83/4 O-Pee-Chee 72
84/5 O-Pee-Chee 31
86/7 O-Pee-Chee 201
82/3 OPC/Topps Sticker 123
84/5 OPC Sticker 216
85/6 OPC Sticker 182-51
82/3 Post [Buff.]
83/4 Souhaits Keychain [Sabres]
78/9 Topps 242
79/0 Topps 119
80/1 Topps 159
80/1 BUFF / Wendt's 4
81/2 BUFF / Wendt's 15
82/3 BUFF / Wendt's 8
84/5 BUFF / Blue Shield
85/6 BUFF / Blue Shield
86/7 DETR / Little Caesars

SEILING, ROD
64-67 BeeHive-3 [NYRa.]
64/5 Coke/Sprite [NYRa.]
70/1 Dad's Cookies
70/1 Eddie Sargent 128
71/2 Eddie Sargent 119
72/3 Eddie Sargent 148
70/1 Esso Power Player
91/2 Future Trends C72 21, ✍ 21
74/5 Loblaws
74/5 Loblaws Update
68/9 O-Pee-Chee 71
69/0 O-Pee-Chee 36
69/0 O-Pee-Chee 4in1
70/1 O-Pee-Chee 184
71/2 O-Pee-Chee 53
72/3 O-Pee-Chee 194
72/3 O-Pee-Chee TC
73/4 O-Pee-Chee 9
74/5 O-Pee-Chee 102
75/6 O-Pee-Chee 229
76/7 O-Pee-Chee 280
77/8 O-Pee-Chee 226
78/9 O-Pee-Chee 394
95/6 Parkie 66-67 95
94/5 Parkie Tall 93
71/2 Pro Star Promotions
71/2 Pro Star Promotions
71/2 Pro Star Promotions
68/9 Shirriff / NYRa. 1
64/5 Topps 67
65/6 Topps 23
66/7 Topps 22
66/7 Topps / Test 22
67/8 Topps 27
68/9 Topps 71
69/0 Topps 36
71/2 Topps 53
72/3 Topps 149
73/4 Topps 9
74/5 Topps 102
75/6 Topps 229
77/8 Topps 226
71/2 Toronto Sun Photo
78/9 ATLF / Colour
74/5 TORO
75/6 TORO

SEILING, SCOTT
95/6 Slapshot 254, 296

SEILS, JASON
94/5 Minnesota G'Gophers

SEISTAMO, JOUNI
66/7 Champion 156
65/6 Hellas 152

SEITZ, DAVID
98/9 EBK ECHL All-Star
92/3 Clarkson G'Knights

SEIVO, JYRKI
73/4 Williams Finnish 118

SEJBA, JIRI
94/5 APS 37
99/0 Eishockey 356
92/3 Jyvas Hyva 58
98/9 OFS Leg. 4
90/1 ProCards 286
91/2 ProCards 5
89 Semic Sticker 196
91/2 Upper Deck 362
90/1 BUFF / Blue Shield
90/1 BUFF / Campbell's
91/2 Rochester Americans DD
91/2 Rochester Americans GL
91/2 Rochester Americans WPC

SEJEJS, NORMUNDS
95/6 APS 156, 437
96/7 APS 175, 394
00/1 DS 124
96/7 DS Sticker 39
98/9 OFS 334
00/1 OFS 166

SEJNA, PETER
99/0 Des Moines Buc's

SEKERA, MARTIN
94/5 APS 44
97/8 APS 122

SEKERAS, LUBOMIR
01/2 Adrenaline 94
95/6 APS 227
96/7 APS 53
97/8 APS 317
00/1 BAP Mem. 491
96/7 DS Sticker 229
97/8 DS Sticker 268
97/8 DS 5
98/9 DS 115
99/0 DS 104
98/9 OFS 385
99/0 OFS 409
00/1 OFS 402
01/2 Pacific 200
02/3 Pacific Complete 359
00/1 Parkhurst P-219
00/1 Premier Plus 108
94 Semic 192
00/1 Signature 271, ✍ 233
00/1 SP Authentic 147
00/1 SPx 179
00/1 Stadium 256
02/3 To. Total 348
00/1 Upper Deck 432
01/2 Upper Deck 86
01/2 UD MVP 92
01/2 UD Vintage 126, 130
00/1 UD Ice 113
01/2 Victory 174
96 Wien 222

SELÄNNE, TEEMU
94/5 Action Packed
01/2 Adrenaline 170, PM 8, WB 18, ✂ GWJ 43
01/2 Atomic 87, CP 17, PP 30, TN 21, ✂ GWJ 47
02/3 Atomic 88, -CF 21
98/9 Aurora 6, ALC-2, CF-2, MACF-2, NC-1, / Cube 2
99/0 Aurora 5, Stripe 5, CC-2, CF-2, CP-2, ST-2
00/1 Aurora 4, Pins. 4, CF-2, ✂ GWJ-11, SR-2, TPS-1B
02/3 BAP All-Star 83, ✂ ASJ, ✂ HSHSJers
98/9 Be A Player 3, P-9, ✍ Aut. 3, ✂ G-11, ✂ AS-3, ✂ S-3, ✂✍ G-11
94/5 Be A Player Magazine Postcard
99/0 BAP Mem. 171, H-7, ✂ J-3, ✂ D-10, ✂ TM-4, ✂ TM-12, ✂ TM-28, ✂ TM-45
00/1 BAP Mem. 272, 498, ✂ J-15, ✂ H-9, ✂ PP-5, ✂ TM-26, ✂ TM-39
01/2 BAP Mem. 265, ✂ ASJ, ✂ ASE, ✂ ASN, ✂ ASD, ✂ AST, ✂ CoO, HSHS
02/3 BAP Mem. 162, ✂ AS52, ✂ ASE21, ✂ ASN21, ✂ ASTJ18, ✂ AS12, ✂ AST1, ✂ AST15, ✂ AST30, ✂ HSHSJers 30, ✂ SC17, ✂ TM18
01/2 BAP Update ✂ H7, ✂ TP4
96/7 Bic.Sports Aces J-H
97/8 Bicycle J-Diamond
95/6 Bicycle Aces 8-Club
95/6 Bowman 75, BB2
01/2 Bowman 17
02/3 Bowman 101
98/9 Bowman's Best 45, F4
02/3 Calder 18
98/9 Cardset Top. 5, DT 7
99/0 Cardset 197, GG, AH-Joker, BP 4, MW 3
00/1 Cardset 117
02/3 Cardset 115, -DD 10, -SGSP 6
99/0 Challenger 17
93/4 Classic 124
93/4 Classic N5
93/4 Cla. Prospects LP23
99/0 Crown Royale 4, IE-2, IG-1, CS-2, CCA-2, GC-1
00/1 Crown Royale 3, JotC-2, NP-2
01/2 Crown Royale 126, JotC 27
02/3 Crown Royale 86, -LOR 17
93/4 Donruss 387
93/4 Donruss 394
93/4 Donruss Z
93/4 Donruss ES 3
93/4 Donruss IK 10
94/5 Donruss 210, D-8
95/6 Donruss 100
96/7 Donr. 157, D-8, GTS-2
97/8 Donruss 159, ES-12, L2L-2
98/9 Donruss ES 6
96/7 Do. Canadian 85
97/8 Do. Canadian 74, SCS-8
95/6 Do. Elite 73, CE-15
96/7 Do. Elite 59, S-10
97/8 Do. Elite 17, 120, 149, BF-3, C-15, PN-7, ✍ BF-3
97/8 Do. Preferred 95, 178, LT-5B, PM-9, / Tin 4, WideTin 4
97/8 Do. Priority 6, 187, DD-15, OD-6, Post-14, Stamp-14
97/8 Do. Studio 18, 107, HH-11, S-17, P-18
98/9 Dynagon Ice 6, -AR 2, -FT 2
99/0 Dynagon Ice 12, ASP-2, CM-17, LL-2, LotR-2
93/4 EA Sports 149
97/8 Esso 50
01/2 eTopps 11
02/3 eTopps 30
02/3 Exclusive 152, -MO 17
02/3 First Ed. 135, 306, 400, 429R, ✂ Jers., ✂ DGJ 6, ✂ HSHSJers 19
94/5 Flair 209
96/7 Flair 3, CIS-8
94/5 Fleer 245
96/7 Fleer 3, ART-21
95/6 Fleer Metal 165, IS-19
96/7 Fl. Picks F50-42, DL-5
92/3 Fleer Ultra 444, -UI 21
93/4 Fleer Ultra 48
93/4 Fleer Ultra AS 11
93/4 Fleer Ultra AW 6
93/4 Fleer Ultra RLS 10
93/4 Fleer Ultra SM 10
94/5 Fleer Ultra 246, GG-9, RLS-8
95/6 Fleer Ultra 183
96/7 Fl. Ultra 6, PL-8, UP-16
00 Gatorade Sticker
95 Globe 140
01/2 Heads Up 85, HD 8, SM 16, ✂ JQ 1
02/3 Heads Up 110, ✂ GWQ 33
93/4 Hockey Wit 55
99/0 HoloGrFX 1, PS5
95/6 Hoyle / West. 4-Club
02/3 In The G-U 65, 165, ✂ E24, ✂ IE10, ✂ GUJ24, ✂ SJ24, ✂ T16
91/2 Jyvas Hyva 21
93 Koululainen
93/4 Kraft / KD
95/6 Kraft / IP
96/7 Kraft / Fav.
97/8 Kraft / KD
99/0 Kraft / PB
93/4 Leaf 110
93/4 Leaf 13
93/4 Leaf GLAS 3
93/4 Leaf GLR 1
93/4 Leaf HTA 3
94/5 Leaf 362, FOI-12, LL-26
95/6 Leaf 137
96/7 Leaf 52, 238, FOI-9
97/8 Leaf 18, 182, BS-8, FOI-10
94/5 L. Limited 68
95/6 L. Limited 44, SG-7
96/7 L. Limited 64
96/7 L. Preferred 56, SP-10, VP-11
97/8 Limited 11, 56, 143, FG-43
96/7 Maggers 2
93/4 McDonald's McH-02
94/5 McDonald's McD-25
95/6 McDonald's McD-19
96/7 McDonald's McD-2
97/8 McDonald's McD-11
00/1 McDonald's 2, GWJ-1
01/2 McDonald's 36, -CF 5, ✂ JPatch 16
02/3 McDonald's 35
96/7 Metal Univ. 6, LW-17
99/0 Millenium 2, ✍ Aut. 2, ✂ J-8, ✂✍ J-8, ✂ JS-8
01/2 Nextel
98/9 NHL Power Play
01/2 O-Pee-Chee 11
02/3 O-Pee-Chee 105
98/9 OPC Chrome 109, SB13
92/3 OPC Premier 68
97/8 Omega 7, 247, GF-2, S-2, SHLC-2
98/9 Omega 8, -EOP 2, -FTF 7, -Onl. 2, -PI 23, -Prism 2
99/0 Omega 6, 5ST-14, EOP-2, G-2, WAS-1, ✂ GWJ 1
98/9 Pacific 8, -DI 2, -GCDC 2, -Time. 1
99/0 Pacific 16, CI-2, GC-2, HAA-2, HAA-12, PAP-2
00/1 Pacific 11, 432, IO-2, CCA-2, ES-1, GCDC-2, PR-2
01/2 Pacific 344, 421, 441, ✂ GWJ 34
02/3 Pacific 340, -IZ 10
02/3 Pacific Complete 436
97/8 Pacific CC 8, CS-2, GCDC-2, SS-1C, TC-1
97/8 Pa. Crown Roy. 5, BOS-2, CCA-2, HT-2, L-2
98/9 Pa. Crown Roy. 5, -CCA 2, -LL 2, -MP 2, -PotG 1
97/8 Pa. Dynagon 5, 135, DD-1B, T-7, T-24, BKS-4
97/8 Pa. Invincible 4, AZ-2, FP-2, OTG-2, R-7
97/8 Pa. Paramount 7, P-2, BN-2
98/9 Pa. Paramount 7, -HOFB 1, -SD 2, -TC 1
99/0 Pa. Paramount 8, IAd-2, PB-2
00/1 Pa. Paramount 7, ES-2, FF-2
97/8 Pa. Revolution 5, ASG-1, I-2
98/9 Pa. Revolution 5, -ASG 26, -TPA 22, -CTLC 2, -Show. 2
98/9 Panini Photocard [x2]
93/4 Panini Sticker 142
93/4 Panini Sticker Q
94/5 Panini Sticker 166
95/6 Panini Sticker 217
96/7 Panini Sticker 225
97/8 Panini Sticker 188
98/9 Panini Sticker 1, 169
99/0 Panini Sticker 176, 318
00/1 Panini Sticker 111
95 Panini Worlds 294
92/3 Parkhurst 209
92/3 Parkhurst 217
92/3 Parkhurst 500
93/4 Parkhurst 233
93/4 Parkhurst 235
93/4 Parkhurst G8
93/4 Parkhurst W3
94/5 Parkhurst 300, V81, YCTG-26
95/6 Parkhurst 232, 250, 275, CCB-9, IAS-5, PP-17, PP-51, ✍ Aut.
00/1 Parkhurst P-33
01/2 Parkhurst 25, ✂ HHSJers, ✂ PS34, ✂ M36, ✂ PS34, ✂ T25, ✂ WCJ2, ✂ WCE2, ✂ WCN2
02/3 Parkhurst 25, ✂ GJ13, ✂ SJ13, ✂ HSHSJers, ✂ PP3, ✂ TT15
95/6 Parkhurst 24-karat Gold
02/3 Parkhurst Retro 97, ✂ RF25, ✂ RJ40, ✂ HSHSJers, ✂ NN26
94/5 Parkie SE201, ES13
92/3 Pinnacle 406
93/4 Pinnacle 222
93/4 Pinnacle 4
93/4 Pinnacle NF 3
93/4 Pinnacle T2K1 10
93/4 Pinnacle TP 12
94/5 Pinnacle 25, BR15, GR1, NL11, WE1
x95/6 Pinnacle R20s 19
96/7 Pinnacle 155, 250, BTN-1
97/8 Pinnacle 86, P-24
96/7 Pi. Be A Player LTH1B, BB-11, ✍ Aut. LTH1B
97/8 Pi. Be A Player OT 8
97/8 Pi. BeeHive 2, BHT-11
97/8 Pi. Certified 39, CT-16
97/8 Pi. Epix E15
95/6 Pi. FANtasy 15
97/8 Pi. Inside 38, IT-11, / Can 19
96/7 Pi. Mint 13
97/8 Pi. Mint 7, M-4
95/6 Pi. Summit 54
96/7 Pi. Summit 133, HV-12, U-8
97/8 Pi. Totally 39
95/6 Pi. Zenith 102
96/7 Pi. Zenith 28, ZT-3
95/6 Playoff 108, 219, 329
96/7 Playoff 428
94/5 POG 253
95/6 POG 292
94/5 Post
97/8 Pi. Post 19
93/4 Power Play 274
93/4 Power Play SYS 10
93/4 Power Play GG 7
93/4 Power Play PL 16
93/4 Power Play SA 9
93/4 Premier 130
93/4 Premier 148
93/4 Premier 483
93/4 Premier 92
93/4 Prmr. - BG-OPC 20
93/4 Prmr. - BG-Top. 1
94/5 Premier 95, 243, 416
00/1 Premier Plus 35, MB2, PT10, TT14, WP18, ✂ GP
99/0 Prism 5, CA-2, DAS-2, SGDC-2
00/1 Pr. Stock 3, AC-2, EA-2, Res. 2, PS-2, PSS-2, ✂ GUG-3
01/2 Pr. Stock 87, Res. 17, -PS 66, ✂ GUG 92
02/3 Pr. Stock Reserve 88
00/1 PS Titanium 2, ✂ GUG-54
01/2 PS Titanium 124, TAS 17, ✂ DSJ 39
02/3 PS Titanium 88
00/1 PS Titanium Draft ✂ 92
95/6 Pro Magnet 58
02/3 Quest for the Cup 87, -CTC 15
99/0 Revolution 4, NI-1, O-2, SS-2, TL-21, / CSC 4
00/1 Revolution 4, HD-2, II-2, NI-2, SM-1
93/4 Score 331
93/4 Score 477
93/4 Score DT 21
93/4 Score/CAN DD2
93/4 Score IS 2
93/4 Score PiAS 32
93/4 Score PiAS 50
93/4 Score TF 24
94/5 Score 178, TF-26
95/6 Score 7, GB-2, L-14
96/7 Score 145, SD-15, S-1
97/8 Score 113
97/8 Score Anah. 2
93/4 Seasons 18
94/5 Select 74
95/6 Select CE 76
96/7 Select CE 32, C-12
94 Semic 20
94 Semic 345
95 Semic 41
91 Semic Sticker 21
92 Semic Sticker 11
93 Semic Sticker 77
00/1 Signature 41, ✍ Aut. 165, ✂ J-8
01/2 Signature C-47, ✂ GUE8, ✂ GJ8, ✂ GSJ8, ✂ ITN8, ✂ TM25, ✂ HSHSJers
02/3 Signature 116, GS-93, ✍ 116, ✂ CJ10, ✂ FJ25, ✂ SGJ24, ✂ TQ18
94/5 Sisu 263, GS-9
95/6 Sisu Limited 15, SAS-3
95/6 SBx Emotion 196
95/6 SBx Impact 184, IQ-15
96/7 SBx Impact 4, BR-20, VT-10
94/5 SP 131, P-22
95/6 SP 2, E2
96/7 SP 2, Ins., SF-2
97/8 SP Authentic 1, I19
98/9 SP Authentic 2, SS10, SO26
99/0 SP Authentic 2, SS2
00/1 SP Authentic SF1
01/2 SP Authentic 71, 107, ✂ PP, ✍ SotT
02/3 SP Authentic 76, ✍ SotT, ✍ SotTD
00/1 SP GU 2, ✂ TotG, ✂ C, ✂ P
01/2 SP GU 46, ✂ AF, ✂✍ PatchSig, ✂ TotGSig
02/3 SP GU 61, ✂ PC, ✂ PH, ✂ TG, ✍ Sig
02/3 Sports Vault 287
96/7 SPx 2
97/8 SPx 2, D-SPX18
x99/0 SPx HH10, X20, XT4, S8
00/1 SPx 2, X1, ✂ WM (x2)
01/2 SPx 56, ✂ TT
02/3 SPx 142, ✂ M
98/9 SPx Finite 1, 104, 157
98/9 SPx Prospects 2, H2, L7, PS17
99/0 Stadium 40, Chrome 22, Big 11, CA15, EG4, OE8
00/1 Stadium 13, BT10, CA12
01/2 Stadium 40, G14, NHLP8
02/3 Stadium 91, -WS-14
94/5 Starting Lineup
97/8 SLU
95 Suomen All-Star 4
95/6 Super Sticker 133, 134
96/7 Team Out!
95/6 Topps 195, 9CG, M9, 2PL, PF18, YS11
98/9 Topps 109, L15, M1, SB13
99/0 Topps 17, AT14, IM20, AM4, FF1, TW1
00/1 Topps 64, TC2, OTG5
01/2 Topps 11 , SM17
02/3 Topps 105
99/0 To. Chrome 17, AT14, IM20, AM4, FF1
00/1 To. Chrome 52, TC2, RF10
01/2 To. Chrome 11
02/3 T. Chrome 66
94/5 Topps Finest 76, BBB-14
95/6 To. Finest 35, 155
98/9 To. Finest 1, C15, M11, M15, M16, M17, R8, -Big 1
94 Topps Finest Bronze 5
98/9 T. Gold Label 7, GR3
99/0 To. Gold Label 23, PG7
00/1 To. Gold Label 82, GG10
00/1 To. Heritage 28, HH10
01/2 To. Heritage 18
02/3 To. Heritage 21
02/3 To. Limited 105
96/7 To. Picks 7, FT-21, TS-8
99/0 To. Prmr. Plus 17, CAC6, CR2
01/2 To. Reserve 77
93/4 To. Stadium 141
93/4 To. Stadium 210
93/4 To. Stadium - Master Photo-1 4
93/4 To. Stadium - AS
95/6 To. Stadium EC188, EN2, GT2
93/4 TSC Members Only 10
94/5 TSC Members Only 43
95/6 TSC Members Only 14
00/1 To. Stars 35, 138, AS7, ✂ GG
95/6 To. Super Skills 31
02/3 To. Total 260, TP11
98/9 UD Choice 8, 242, BH15, SQ5
00/1 UD Heroes 140, TM1, ✂ GT, ✂ GC
01/2 UD PlayMakers Ltd 82, ✂ PCJ
00/1 UD Reserve 3, GS1, PSJ
02/3 UD Superstars 216
98/9 UD3 58, 118, 178
00/1 Ultimate Mem. ✍ U-8, ✂ J-8, ✂ Jers. 6, ✂ JJ-10, ✂ RE-6, ✂ S-8, ✂ TM-21, ✂ TM-22, ✂ TM-33
01/2 Ultimate Mem. ✂ A8, ✂ CT, ✂ DD, ✂ Emb., ✂ Jers., ✂ S&J, ✂ GSL, ✂ ITN, ✂ JE, ✂ JJ, ✂ NP, ✂ WTF
02/3 Ultimate Mem. ✂ ASMVP, ✂ DD, ✂ GUJ, ✂ GUSJ, ✂ GMIH
99/0 Ult. Victory 2, sg12
91/2 Upper Deck 21
92/3 Upper Deck 574
92/3 Upper Deck CC10
92/3 Upper Deck ER6
92/3 Upper Deck G15
93/4 Upper Deck 281, 309, 448, SP4, AW2, FH32, R2, SP-177
94/5 Upper Deck 90, 557, R3, IG13, SP-88
95/6 Upper Deck 171, 253, AS-12, R49, SE-89
96/7 Upper Deck 211, X16, HH15, LS16, SS10A
97/8 Upper Deck 1, SS8, SG8, S8, T5A
98/9 Upper Deck 16, 34, FF23, FT28, LS30, P8
99/0 Upper Deck 153, 174, AS5, CT21, FF6, IG6, MA12, N6, SB11, ✂ GJ
00/1 Upper Deck 231, A1, FF2, SS2, TT9, UD1, ✂ CGJ, ✂ GJ
01/2 Upper Deck 145, CT11, FF8, FC13, FA11, SS16, SS4, T8, ✂ ASJ, ✂ CJers, ✂ PoaN, ✂ PoaND
02/3 Upper Deck 195, 392, -SS13, ✂ ASJ, ✂ ASP, ✂ GO, ✂ UDPL
95/6 UD ASG MVP7
96/7 UD All-Star YCTG AR4
02/3 UD Artistic 73, R73, / Art
93/4 Upper Deck Be A Player 15
94/5 UD BAP R11, UC-4, ✍ 11
93/4 UD BAP Roots 17
96/7 UD Black Diam. 146, RC18
97/8 UD Black Diam. 95, PC15
98/9 UD Black Diam. 2, M7, WF2
99/0 UD Black Diam. 2, D4, DM7, DS1, M2, ✂ APOH
00/1 UD Black Diam. 2, FP1, ✂ GG
99/0 UD C. Legends 59
01/2 UD Challenge 73
02/3 UD Classic 82, ET14, PS9, ✂ HR
95/6 UD CC 244
96/7 UD CC 2, 309, 336, UD7, S13, C19, CR19
97/8 UD Coll. Choice 8, SQ80, S18, C8, CR8
01/2 UD Collectors
97/8 UD Diam. Vision 16
98/9 UD G. Reserve 16, 34
99/0 UD G. Reserve 153, 174
99/0 UD Gretzky Excl. 77
01/2 UD Honor Roll 21, 51
02/3 UD Honor ✍ SC, -SG26
96/7 UD Ice 77, S6
97/8 UD Ice 80, IC8, L9C
00/1 UD Ice 2, IG1, ✂ IGJ
01/2 UD Ice 115
00/1 UD Legends 2, 3, ✂ LGJ
92/3 UD Locker 35
01/2 UD Mask 82, ✂ GJ, ✂ JP, ✂ DP
98/9 UD MVP 2, F10, Snip. S4
99/0 UD MVP 5, H4, S8, GU2, ✂ GU16
00/1 UD MVP 6, M2, TD1, ✂ GS
01/2 UD MVP 159, MT9, ✂ S
02/3 UD MVP 157, VF13, SD, ST (x2), Souv., ✍ PSig
99/0 UD MVP Cup 1, SS1, SC2, GC, ✂ GU
99/0 UD Ovation 2, LP12, ST10
02/3 UD Piece 100, AC24, ✂ PH, ✍ MD
99/0 UD PowerDeck 2
01/2 UD Premier 43, ✂ B, ✂ D, ✍ SigG
02/3 UD Premier ✂ Patch
00/1 UD Pros&Prosp. 2, PM1, ✂ GJ
99/0 UD Retro 2, G8B
02/3 UD Rookie 86
01/2 UD Top Shelf 37, ✂ J, ✂✍ SJ
02/3 UD Top Shelf 75, ✂ AS, ✂ CP, ✂ GO, ✂ HH, ✂ HT, ✂ M, ✂ SH, ✂ ST, ✂ SW
00/1 UD Vintage 2, 11, NH2, S1B
01/2 UD Vintage 210, 217
02/3 UD Vintage 304
00/1 Vanguard 3, HV-2, IF-2, VP-2
01/2 Vanguard 88, EMW 6, VT 18, ✂ DGM 15
02/3 Vanguard 87
99/0 Victory 3, 321, 326, 334, 337
00/1 Victory 7, 281
01/2 Victory 290
02/3 Victory - NP27
01/2 Waving the Flag 13
99/0 WGretzky 4, EG1, GH9, ✂ TG
96 Wien 31, NS2
97/8 Zenith 24, ZT-1, Z6
96/7 ANAH / Up Front 24
93/4 WINN / Ruffles
93/4 WINN Readers
95/6 WINN
95/6 WINN Readers

SELBY, BRIT
64-67 BeeHive-3 [Toro.]
65/6 Coca-Cola
70/1 Colgate 37
70/1 Dad's Cookies
70/1 Eddie Sargent 202
71/2 Eddie Sargent 183
70/1 Esso Power Player
68/9 O-Pee-Chee 96
69/0 O-Pee-Chee 48
70/1 O-Pee-Chee 111
71/2 O-Pee-Chee 226
95/6 Parkie 66-67 111, 132
94/5 Parkie Tall 121
73/4 Quaker Oats 39
68/9 Shirriff / Phil. 7
66/7 Topps 18
68/9 Topps 96
69/0 Topps 48
70/1 Topps 111
69/0 TORO

SELIGER, MARC
94/5 DEL 384
95/6 DEL 103
98/9 DEL 2
99/0 Eishockey 40
94/5 Sig. Rookies 30, ✍ 30
91/2 Upper Deck 683
91/2 Upper Deck WJC 46
00/1 UD DEL 195
01/2 UD DEL G9
96 Wien 193
96/7 Hampton Roads

SELINGR, PAVEL
98/9 OFS 75
99/0 OFS 201
00/1 OFS 258
01/2 OFS 45

SELIVANOV, ALEXANDER
98/9 Aurora 176
98/9 Be A Player 130, ✍ Aut. 130
00/1 BAP Mem. 310
95/6 Bowman 73
94/5 Cla. Images 16
99/0 Crown Royale 56
95/6 Donruss 90
96/7 Donruss 32
95/6 Do. Elite 84
96/7 Do. Elite 95
94/5 Fleer 210
96/7 Fleer 106
95/6 Fleer Metal 140
95/6 Fleer Ultra 310
96/7 Fl. Ultra 160
95/6 Leaf 49
96/7 Leaf 62
96/7 L. Limited 45
96/7 L. Preferred 43
96/7 Metal Univ. 147
98/9 OPC Chrome 85
97/8 Omega 214
99/0 Omega 94
98/9 Pacific 406
99/0 Pacific 165
00/1 Pacific 173
97/8 Pa. Dynagon BKS-89
97/8 Pa. Paramount 176
98/9 Pa. Paramount 221
00/1 Pa. Paramount 99
95/6 Panini Sticker 132
97/8 Panini Sticker 102
98/9 Panini Sticker 97
00/1 Panini Sticker 163
95/6 Parkhurst 194
95/6 Pinnacle 116, GG-17
96/7 Pinnacle 77
96/7 Pi. Summit 58
96/7 Pi. Zenith 21
95/6 Playoff 199
96/7 Playoff 390
95/6 POG 252
99/0 Prism 57
96/7 Score 27, S-10
97/8 Score 245
94/5 SR Auto-Phonex 39, ✍ 39
96/7 SBx Impact 124
94/5 SP 113
95/6 SP 140
96/7 SP 148
97/8 SP Authentic 146
98/9 SP Authentic ✍ SotT
99/0 SP Authentic 36
98/9 SPx Finite 80
99/0 Stadium 116
95/6 Topps 367, 11NG
98/9 Topps 85
00/1 Topps 233
94/5 Topps Finest 79, BBR-17
95/6 To. Finest 32
99/0 To. Gold Label 76
96/7 To. Picks 123
95/6 To. Stadium 111
98/9 UD Choice 195
99/0 Ult. Victory 37
94/5 Upper Deck 425, 532, SP-165
95/6 Upper Deck 316, SE-77
96/7 Upper Deck 339
97/8 Upper Deck 156
98/9 Upper Deck 182
95/6 UD BAP 145, ✍ S145
97/8 UD Black Diam. 121
95/6 UD CC 165
96/7 UD CC 253
97/8 UD Coll. Choice 241
01/2 UD DEL 86, GA5
98/9 UD G. Reserve 182
99/0 UD MVP Cup 73
00/1 Victory 99
95/6 TAMP / Sky Box

SELKE, FRANK
83 HHOF Postcard C12
83&87 HHOF 41
55/6 Parkhurst 68
59/0 Parkhurst 47
02/3 Parkie - Reprint 244
93/4 Parkie 56-57 85
01/2 UD Legends 62
81/2 TORO

SELKIRK, JASON
91/2 Air Canada SJHL A5

SELLAN, MIKE
00/1 Toronto St. Mike's

SELLARS, LUKE
99 Bowman 28, ✍ BA13
95 Québec Pee Wee 834
99/0 SP Authentic 134
99/0 Topps 274
99/0 To. Chrome 274
99/0 UD Black Diam. 112
99/0 UD MVP Cup 206
01/2 Chicago Wolves
02/3 Chicago Wolves
99/0 Ottawa 67's
00/1 Ottawa 67's 14

SELMSER, SEAN
01/2 SP Authentic 147
01/2 SPx 139, -RT
01/2 Upper Deck 189
01/2 Hamilton Bulldogs
95/6 Hampton Roads
00/1 Syracuse Crunch
93/4 Red Deer Rebels
98/9 Fort Wayne Komets
99/0 Hamilton Bulldogs

SELTHUN, DAVE
01/2 Vancouver Giants

SELTHUN, DAVID
98/9 Kelowna Rockets
00/1 Kelowna Rockets

SELTZER, DANA G.
98/9 Phoenix Mustangs 3

SELUYANOV, ALEXANDER
00/1 Mir 305

SELWOOD, BRAD
71/2 Eddie Sargent 207
75/6 OPC WHA 82
71/2 Toronto Sun Photo
70/1 TORO
71/2 TORO
72/3 New England Whalers

SELYANIN, SERGEI
91/2 O-Pee-Chee 58R
94 Semic 141

SELYUTIN, SERGEI
99/0 Mir 209
00/1 Mir 211

SEMAK, ALEXANDER
92/3 Bowman 164
93/4 Donruss 191
96/7 Donruss 26
93/4 EA Sports 75
94/5 Flair 99
94/5 Fleer 118
92/3 Fleer Ultra 341
93/4 Fleer Ultra 166
94/5 Fleer Ultra 321
95/6 Fleer Ultra 271
93/4 Leaf 35
94/5 Leaf 543
00/1 Mir 146
91/2 O-Pee-Chee 42R
92/3 Panini Sticker 176
92/3 Panini Sticker 296
93/4 Panini Sticker 36
94/5 Panini Sticker 29
95/6 Panini Sticker 127
96/7 Panini Sticker 97, 127
91/2 Parkhurst 323
92/3 Parkhurst 329
93/4 Parkhurst 109
95/6 Parkhurst 135
93/4 Pinnacle 47
94/5 Pinnacle 362
96/7 Pinnacle 188
93/4 Power Play 142
93/4 Premier 102
92/3 Red Ace Violet 30
92/3 Score 451
93/4 Score 284
93/4 Score IS 14
96/7 Score 212
94 Semic 158
91 Semic Sticker 94
92 Semic Sticker 113
95/6 SBx Emotion 109
92/3 Topps 419
95/6 Topps 97
92/3 To. Stadium 444
93/4 To. Stadium 365
94/5 To. Stadium 245
91/2 Upper Deck 4
92/3 Upper Deck 45
92/3 Upper Deck ERT5
93/4 Upper Deck 178, SP-68
94/5 Upper Deck 210
95/6 Upper Deck 40
96/7 Upper Deck 98
94/5 UD BAP ✍ 4
95/6 UD CC 56
96/7 UD CC 163
95/6 TAMP / Sky Box
96/7 VANC / IGA
98/9 Albany River Rats
98/9 Chicago Wolves Champs

SEMAN, DANIEL
99/0 OFS 231
00/1 OFS 248

SEMANDEL, KURT
90/1 ProCards 598
90/1 Kansas City Blades

SEMCHUK, BRANDY
90/1 ProCards 430
92/3 Phoenix Roadrunners

SEMENIUK, DARRIN
94/5 Anchorage Aces 6

SEMENIUK, TREVOR
83/4 Medicine Hat Tigers
84/5 Victoria Cougars

SEMENKO, DAVE
01/2 Fleer Legacy 28
79/0 O-Pee-Chee 371
80/1 O-Pee-Chee 360
81/2 O-Pee-Chee 121
82/3 O-Pee-Chee 119
80/1 Pepsi Bottle Cap
82/3 Post [Edmo.]
83/4 Souhaits Keychain [Oilers]
83/4 Stater Mint H19
83/4 Vachon 40-120
79/0 EDMO
80/1 EDMO / Zellers
81/2 EDMO / Red Rooster
82/3 EDMO / Red Rooster
83/4 EDMO / Button
83/4 EDMO / McDonald's
83/4 EDMO / West Mall
83/4 EDMO
84/5 EDMO
84/5 EDMO / Red Rooster
85/6 EDMO / Red Rooster
88/9 EDMO / Action 6
87/8 TORO / 5x8
87/8 TORO / P.L.A.Y. 26
02/3 Fleer Throwbacks 29

SEMENOV, ALEXEI
02/3 BAP Mem. 381
02/3 Parkhurst Retro 221
02/3 SP Authentic 203
02/3 SPx 192
02/3 Ultimate Mem. 88
02/3 UD Artistic 131
02/3 UD Honor 133
02/3 UD Premier 60, ✂ Jers
00/1 UD Prospects 27
01/2 Hamilton Bulldogs
99/0 Sudbury Wolves 12
00/1 Sudbury Wolves 12

SEMENOV, ANATOLI
91/2 Bowman 113
92/3 Bowman 423
93/4 Donruss 3
94/5 Donruss 326
95/6 Donruss 312
93/4 EA Sports 5
94/5 Flair 5
92/3 Fleer Ultra 429
93/4 Fleer Ultra 261
94/5 Fleer Ultra 7
93/4 Leaf 338
94/5 Leaf 303
95/6 Leaf 238
90/1 O-Pee-Chee 468
91/2 O-Pee-Chee 390
92/3 O-Pee-Chee 83
90/1 OPC Premier 104
97/8 Pacific CC 106
90/1 Panini/EDM 19
91/2 Panini Sticker 127
93/4 Panini Sticker 174
94/5 Panini Sticker 118
91/2 Parkhurst 279
92/3 Parkhurst 420
93/4 Parkhurst 3
94/5 Parkhurst 1
95/6 Parkhurst 429
92/3 Pinnacle 386
93/4 Pinnacle 368
94/5 Pinnacle 322
94/5 POG 347
93/4 Power Play 10
93/4 Premier 506
94/5 Premier 524
90/1 Pro Set 608
91/2 Red Ace
90/1 Score 39T
91/2 Score CAN 258
92/3 Score 336
92/3 Score SS 28
93/4 Score 536
93/4 Score 93
94/5 Score 16
89 Semic Sticker 99
92/3 Topps 68
91/2 To. Stadium 366
92/3 To. Stadium 143
93/4 To. Stadium 368
91/2 Tri Globe Mag. Five 11-15
90/1 Upper Deck 405
91/2 Upper Deck 269
91/2 Upper Deck E4
92/3 Upper Deck 20
92/3 Upper Deck 535
93/4 Upper Deck 46, SP-4
94/5 Upper Deck 105
96/7 UD CC 7
90/1 EDMO / IGA
91/2 EDMO / IGA
94/5 PHIL / Sheet

SEMIN, DMITRI
02/3 Russian Future Stars 14

SEMIN, NIKOLAI
99/0 Mir 42
92/3 Upper Deck 610

SEMIN, SERGEI
00/1 Mir 330

SEMJONOVS, ALEKSANDRS
98/9 UD Elitserien 32
00/1 UD Elitserien 25

SENDT, THORSTEN
94/5 DEL 217

SENECAL, MARIO
51/2 Bas du Fleuve 56
52/3 Bas du Fleuve 49

SENECAL, SYLVAIN
84/5 Richelieu Riverains

SENGER, PATRICK
98/9 DEL 200
99/0 Eishockey 278
01/2 UD DEL 24

SENN, TREVOR
95/6 Richmond Renegades
96/7 Richmond Renegades
92/3 Wheeling Thund'birds 16

SENTES, DICK
72/3 Ottawa Nationals

SENTNER, PETER
90/1 ProCards 361
91/2 Greensboro Monarchs

SEPKOWSKI, TODD
84/5 Sudbury Wolves

SEPOVALOV, VLADIMIR
72 Hellas MM-Jenkki 61
74 Hellas MM-Jenkki 63

SEPPA, JYRKI
80/1 Mallasjuoma 36
72/3 Williams Finnish 351

SEPPANEN, LEO
72 Hellas MM-Jenkki 15
74 Hellas MM-Jenkki 15
70/1 Kuvajulkaisut 254
74 Semic Sticker 93
78/9 SM-Liiga 87
71/2 Williams Finnish 220
72/3 Williams Finnish 168
73/4 Williams Finnish 235

SEPPANEN, VEIKKO
73/4 Williams Finnish 236

SEPPO, JUKKA
98/9 Cardset Leij. 41
99/0 Cardset MW 9
96/7 DEL 239
98/9 DEL 48
99/0 Eishockey 357
91/2 Jyvas Hyva 2
92/3 Jyvas Hyva 11
95 Leaf Latkaliiga 8
99/0 OFS 62
93 Semic Sticker 78
93/4 Sisu 253
94/5 Sisu 246, H-2
95/6 Sisu 343, SS-9
95/6 Sisu Limited 95

SERAFINI, RON
75/6 Phoenix Roadrunners

SERGAEV, DENIS
01/2 Calgary Hitmen

SERGOTT, KEITH
91/2 Ferris State Bulldogs

SERIKOV, ALEXANDER
95/6 DEL 279
96/7 DEL 176
98/9 DEL 235, 333
99/0 Eishockey 331, 379
00/1 UD DEL 178

SEROSKI, JOE
95/6 Slapshot 362
97/8 New Orleans Brass
96/7 Soo Greyhounds

SEROV, VLAD
99/0 Manitoba Moose
00/1 Quad City Mallards

SEROWIK, JEFF
90/1 ProCards 154
91/2 ProCards 337
93/4 Cincinnati Cyclones
95/6 Indianapolis Ice
96/7 Las Vegas Thunder
92/3 St. John's Maple Leafs

SERRATORE, FRANK
94/5 Minnesota Moose
95/6 Minnesota Moose

SERTICH, MIKE
85/6 Minnesota-Duluth 33
93/4 Minnesota-Duluth

SERVATIUS, DARREN
89/0 Johnstown Chiefs

SERVATIUS, RON
89/0 Nashville Knights

SERVISS, TOM
72/3 Los Angeles Sharks

SESSA, JASON
99/0 Louisiana Ice Gators

SESTITO, TIM
02/3 Plymouth Whalers

SETHERENG, MORTEN
79 Panini Sticker 300

SETIKOVSKY, JINDRICH
94/5 APS 290
95/6 APS 243

SETZINGER, OLIVER
00/1 Cardset 275
02/3 Cardset 116, BFG 8, ✍ BFG

SEVA, JANNE
98/9 Cardset 177
99/0 Cardset 88
92/3 Jyvas Hyva 43
93/4 Jyvas Hyva 87
93/4 Sisu 131
93/4 Sisu 343
94/5 Sisu 347
95/6 Sisu 35

SEVASTYANOV, SERGEI
00/1 Mir 196

SEVCIK, FRANTISEK
94/5 APS 111
95/6 APS 209
96/7 APS 258
96/7 DS Sticker 92
70/1 Kuvajulkaisut 58

SEVCIK, JAROSLAV
95/6 DEL 332
88/9 ProCards / Halifax
89/0 ProCards AHL 176
90/1 ProCards 460
89/0 Halifax Citadels
90/1 Halifax Citadels

SEVCIK, JIRI
99/0 Score 158

SEVECEK, RENÉ
95/6 APS 299
96/7 APS 198
98/9 DS 104
96/7 DS Sticker 194
97/8 DS Sticker 252
98/9 OFS 115

SEVERSON, CAM
02/3 BAP Mem. 310
02/3 Ultimate Mem. 93
02/3 UD Rookie 176
01/2 Hartford Wolf Pack
00/1 Quad City Mallards

SEVERYN, BRENT
02/3 Fleer Throwbacks 77
93/4 Fleer Ultra 331
94/5 Leaf 342
97/8 Pa. Invincible R-58
93/4 Parkhurst 77
94/5 Parkhurst 90
96/7 Pi. Be A Player 185, ✍ Aut. 185

93/4 Premier 392
94/5 Premier 334
88/9 ProCards / Halifax
89/0 ProCards AHL 171
90/1 ProCards 456
91/2 ProCards 408
93/4 Score 652
95/6 Topps 243
93/4 Upper Deck 453
00/1 UD DEL 144, S10
93/4 FLOR
89/0 Halifax Citadels
90/1 Halifax Citadels
84/5 Brandon Wheat Kings

SÉVIGNY, LOUIS-PHILIPPE
94/5 Parkie SE259
94/5 SP 180

SÉVIGNY, PIERRE
92/3 Classic Prospects 51
93/4 Donruss 169
94/5 Donruss 195
93/4 Durivage 2
93/4 Leaf 392
94/5 Leaf 309
94/5 Panini Sticker 11
93/4 Parkhurst 106
93/4 Parkhurst C7
94/5 Parkhurst 117
91/2 ProCards 88
93/4 Score 634
90/1 7th..Sketch LHJMQ 226
94/5 To. Stadium 193
90/1 Upper Deck 456
93/4 Upper Deck 455, SP-82
94/5 Upper Deck 402
93/4 MONT
94/5 MONT
94/5 MONT / Export
92/3 Fredericton Canadiens
95/6 Fredericton Canadiens
96/7 Fredericton Canadiens
97/8 Hartford Wolf Pack
98/9 Orlando Solar Bears Geico
99/0 Québec Citadelles 13
00/1 Québec Citadelles
01/2 Québec Citadelles
84/5 Chicoutimi Saguenéens

SÉVIGNY, RICHARD
80/1 Dernière Heure
80/1 O-Pee-Chee 385
81/2 O-Pee-Chee 191
81/2 O-Pee-Chee 387
83/4 O-Pee-Chee 197
84/5 O-Pee-Chee 289
81/2 OPC Sticker 40
81/2 OPC Sticker 256
82/3 Post [Mont.]
83/4 Souhaits Keychain [Canadiens]
83/4 Vachon 54-74
79/0 MONT
80/1 MONT
81/2 MONT
82/3 MONT
82/3 MONT / Steinberg
83/4 MONT
84/5 QUÉB
85/6 QUÉB
85/6 QUÉB / Gene. Foods
85/6 QUÉB / McDonald's
85/6 QUÉB / Provigo
86/7 QUÉB
86/7 QUÉB / Gene. Foods
86/7 QUÉB / McDonald's
87/8 QUÉB / Gene. Foods

SEVON, JORMA
82 Semic Sticker 42
78/9 SM-Liiga 192

SEVON, SEPPO
80/1 Mallasjuoma 42
78/9 SM-Liiga 101
72/3 Williams Finnish 276

SEXSMITH, DEAN
84/5 Brandon Wheat Kings
85/6 Brandon Wheat Kings

SEXTON, DAN
87/8 Regina Pats
83/4 Victoria Cougars
84/5 Victoria Cougars

SEXTON, WILLIAM
52/3 Anonymous 108

SEYMOUR, DEAN
91/2 Air Canada SJHL 26
91/2 Air Canada SJHL A47
96/7 Louisiana Ice Gators
93/4 N. Michigan Wildcats

SEYMOUR, GLEN
86/7 Portland Winter Hawks

SGROI, MIKE
01/2 Rockford IceHogs

SHABANOV, SERGEI
00/1 Mir 172

SHACK, EDDIE
45-64 BeeHive-2 [NYRa.]
45-64 BeeHive-2 [Toro.]
45-64 BeeHive-2 [Toro.]
64-67 BeeHive-3 [Toro.]
63-65 Chex
64/5 Coke/Sprite [Toro.]
65/6 Coca-Cola
70/1 Colgate 41
70/1 Dad's Cookies
70/1 Eddie Sargent 69
71/2 Eddie Sargent 20
70/1 Esso Power Player
62/3 Cowan Tile
68/9 O-Pee-Chee 137
69/0 O-Pee-Chee 139
69/0 O-Pee-Chee 4in1
70/1 O-Pee-Chee 35
70/1 O-Pee-Chee DE 2
71/2 O-Pee-Chee 96
72/3 O-Pee-Chee 186
72/3 O-Pee-Chee 274
72/3 O-Pee-Chee Crest 17
73/4 O-Pee-Chee 242
61/2 Parkhurst 7
62/3 Parkhurst 14
63/4 Parkhurst 9
63/4 Parkhurst 69
93/4 Parkie 56-57 FS-4
95/6 Parkie 66-67 113
94/5 Parkie Tall 117, 164
60/1 Shirriff 87
61/2 Shirriff 48
62/3 Shirriff 8
68/9 Shirriff / Bost. 1
58/9 Topps 30
59/0 Topps 57
60/1 Topps 7
64/5 Topps 71
66/7 Topps 17
67/8 Topps 34
69/0 Topps 106
70/1 Topps 35
71/2 Topps 96
02/3 To. Heritage - Reprint TML, ✄ Reprint, ✍ Reprint
61/2 Toronto Star Photo
63/4 Toronto Star Action
65/6 Toronto Star Photo
71/2 Toronto Sun Photo
91/2 Ultimate Original Six 41, ✍ Aut. 41
00/1 UD Legends 123
60/1 York
61/2 York 25
62/3 York Transfer 32
63/4 York 4
64/5 TORO
68/9 TORO
73/4 TORO
74/5 TORO

SHADILOV, IGOR
00/1 Dynamo 2

SHADRIN, VLADIMIR
91/2 Future Trends C72 54
72 Hellas MM-Jenkki 78
74 Hellas MM-Jenkki 55
70/1 Kuvajulkaisut 16
72 Panda MM-Toronto
72 Semic Sticker 19
74 Semic Sticker 37
70/1 Soviet Stars
71/2 Soviet Stars
73/4 Soviet Stars 18
74/5 Soviet Stars 15
71/2 Williams Finnish 35
72/3 Williams Finnish 34
73/4 Williams Finnish 15

SHAFIKOV, RUSLAN
99/0 Mir 246

SHAFRANOV, KONSTANTIN
98/9 Mir 11
00/1 Metallurg 53
95/6 Fort Wayne Komets
97/8 Fort Wayne Komets
99/0 Fort Wayne Komets

SHAIDULLIN, VADIM
94/5 Sisu 300

SHAKHRAICHUK, VADIM
98/9 DEL 260
99/0 Eishockey 27
00/1 Mir 224

SHAKOTKO, DARREN
95/6 Lethbridge Hurricanes

SHALAMAI, SERGEI
98/9 Mir 102
99/0 Mir 241
00/1 Mir 175

SHALDYBIN, YEVGENY
96/7 Providence Bruins
97/8 Providence Bruins

SHALIMOV, VIKTOR
82 Semic Sticker 65

SHALNOV, STANISLAV
00/1 Mir 252

SHANAHAN, BRENDAN
94/5 Action Packed
01/2 Adrenaline 69
01/2 Atomic 39, PP 13, TN 6, ✄ GWJ 25
02/3 Atomic 40, -CF 11, -NPC 6, -SC 6
98/9 Aurora 68, -ALC 10, -CF 19, -MACF 9, -Cube 9
99/0 Aurora 54, Stripe 54, CF-12, ST-9
00/1 Aurora 52, Pins. 52, CF-11, ✄ GWJ-3, ✄ GWJ-13, SR-10, TPS-6A
02/3 BAP All-Star 84-86, ✄ ASJ, ✄ HSHSJers
98/9 Be A Player 195, P-21, ✍ Aut. 195, ✄ G-14, ✄ AS-23, ✄ S-21, ✄✍ G-14
99/0 BAP Mem. 231, H-1, ✄ J-23, ✄ D-11, ✄ H-1, ✄ TM-5, ✄ TM-9, ✄ TM-35, ✄ TM-38, ✄ TM-40
00/1 BAP Mem. 165, ✄ J-6, ✄ H-17, ✄ PP-6, ✄ TM-16, ✄ TM-22
01/2 BAP Mem. 161, ✄ ASD, ✄ AST
02/3 BAP Mem. 23, 235, 249, ✄ ASJ53, ✄ ASE22, ✄ ASN22, ✄ ASTJ19, ✄ AS6, ✄ AST5, ✄ AST27, ✄ HSHSJers 14, ✄ SCC6, ✄ TM2
01/2 BAP Update ✄ H14
96/7 Bic.Sports Aces 6-C
97/8 Bicycle 10-Heart
90/1 Bowman 85
91/2 Bowman 288
92/3 Bowman 183
95/6 Bowman 28
01/2 Bowman 50
02/3 Bowman 104
98/9 Bowman's Best 52
02/3 Calder 39
91 Canada Cup
99/0 Challenger 20
99/0 Crown Royale 52, IE-11, IG-10, CS-10
00/1 Crown Royale 40, ✄ GWJ-15, JotC-13
01/2 Crown Royale 56, ASH 9, JotC 11
02/3 Crown Royale 36, -LOR 9
95/6 DEL 447
93/4 Donruss 299
94/5 Donruss 174
95/6 Donruss 180, 377, M-8
96/7 Donruss 178, ES-6, HL-7
97/8 Donruss 181, ES-9, L2L-10
98/9 Donruss ES 9
96/7 Do. Canadian 101, OC-12
97/8 Do. Canadian 67, NP-5, ✍ SCS-33
95/6 Do. Elite 3
96/7 Do. Elite 126, P-7
97/8 Do. Elite 18, 133, C-27, PN-9
97/8 Do. Preferred 3, 184, LT-2C, PM-1, / Tin 12,19, WideTin 7,10
97/8 Do. Priority 19, 186, DD-1, OD-17, Post-2, Stamp-2
97/8 Do. Studio 6, 105, HH-9, S-11, P-6
96/7 Duracell DC12
98/9 Dynagon Ice 68, -FT 10
99/0 Dynagon Ice 78, CM-2
93/4 EA Sports 124
97/8 Esso 10, ✍ Aut.
01/2 eTopps 4
02/3 eTopps 31
02/3 Exclusive 67
02/3 First Ed. 139, 319, 394, 428H, ✄ Jers., ✄ HSHSJers 21, ✄ TSL 9
94/5 Flair 158, HN-9
96/7 Flair 30
94/5 Fleer 191, H-10
96/7 Fleer 48
95/6 Fleer Metal 67, IW-13
96/7 Fl. Picks 40, F50-43, CC-10, DL-7
92/3 Fleer Ultra 189
93/4 Fleer Ultra 245
94/5 Fleer Ultra 189, RLS-9, UP-9
95/6 Fleer Ultra 142, 247, CC-17
96/7 Fl. Ultra 55, CTI-9
97/8 General Mills
95 Globe 86
01/2 Heads Up 38, ✄ JQ 11
02/3 Heads Up 47, -ITN 11, -PSP 7, / Bobble
93/4 Hockey Wit 29
99/0 HoloGrFX 22
95/6 Hoyle / West. 5-Club
92/3 Humpty Dumpty
02/3 In The G-U 23, 123, ✄ E20, ✄ GUJ2-, ✄ SJ20, ✄ T9
91/2 Kraft 7
93/4 Kraft / KD
94/5 Kraft / PB
96/7 Kraft / TT
97/8 Kraft / PB
98/9 Kraft / KD
99/0 Kraft / KD, / PB
93/4 Leaf 30
93/4 Leaf GLAS 9
94/5 Leaf 113, LL-20
95/6 Leaf 121
96/7 Leaf 146, LL-17, S-10
97/8 Leaf 12, 179, BS-6, FOI-5
94/5 L. Limited 97
95/6 L. Limited 94
96/7 L. Limited 2, BTB-9
96/7 L. Preferred 31, LS-29
97/8 Limited 1, 38, 169, FG-13, FG-53
96/7 Maggers 74
94/5 McDonald's McD-30
97/8 McDonald's McD-14
98/9 McDonald's McD05
00/1 McDonald's 14
01/2 McDonald's 14, ✄ JPatch 10
02/3 McDonald's 12, -SLG 5
96/7 Metal Univ. 50, CS-10, LW-18
99/0 Millenium 90, ✍ Aut. 90, ✄ J-2, ✄✍ J-2, ✄ JS-2
01/2 Nextel
98/9 NHL Power Play
88/9 OPC/Topps 122
90/1 OPC/Topps 259
91/2 O-Pee-Chee 140
92/3 O-Pee-Chee 244
01/2 O-Pee-Chee 69
02/3 O-Pee-Chee 263, 316, 326
89/0 OPC/Topps 147
98/9 OPC Chrome 216
90/1 OPC Premier 105
91/2 OPC Premier 130
89/0 opcSticker 89-230
97/8 Omega 87, GF-7, SHLC-8, TL-8
98/9 Omega 87, -EOP 10, -FTF 5, -Onl. 5, -PI 17, -Prism 9
99/0 Omega 85, 5ST-7, CC-9, EOP-8, NAAS-5
98/9 Pacific 14, -GCDC 15, -Time. 7, -TW 9
99/0 Pacific 149, CI-10, GC-17, PAP-12
00/1 Pacific 158, GCDC-14, NAS-5, PR-9, ✄ GWJ-7
01/2 Pacific 149
02/3 Pacific 134, -IZ 6
02/3 Pacific Complete 483
97/8 Pacific CC 14, GCDC-10, SS-3A
97/8 Pa. Crown Roy. 50, BOS-9, HT-7, L-8
98/9 Pa. Crown Roy. 48, -MP 10, -PotG 13, -PP 10
97/8 Pa. Dynagon 44, 139, DD-8A, T-6, T-26, BKS-34
97/8 Pa. Invincible 51, AZ-10, FP-14, OTG-8, R 73
97/8 Pa. Paramount 70, P-9, CG-6, BN-9
98/9 Pa. Paramount 82, -SD 8
99/0 Pa. Paramount 87, IAd-9, PB-17
00/1 Pa. Paramount 89, ES-10, FF-15, SZ-4
97/8 Pa. Revolution 51, ASG-11
98/9 Pa. Revolution 52, -ASG 27, -TPA 5, -CTLC 9, -Show. 17
98/9 Panini Photocard
88/9 Panini Sticker 276
89/0 Panini Sticker 255
90/1 Panini Sticker 64
91/2 Panini Sticker 222
92/3 Panini Sticker 17
93/4 Panini Sticker 158
94/5 Panini Sticker 141, 237a, EE
95/6 Panini Sticker 31
96/7 Panini Sticker 26
97/8 Panini Sticker 154
98/9 Panini Sticker 133
99/0 Panini Sticker 234
00/1 Panini Sticker 152
95 Panini Worlds 16
91/2 Parkhurst 153
92/3 Parkhurst 156
92/3 Parkhurst CP10
93/4 Parkhurst 172
94/5 Parkhurst 196, 298
95/6 Parkhurst 97, AS-3
00/1 Parkhurst P-10
01/2 Parkhurst 11, ✄ 500GS, ✄ PJ39, ✄ PS53, ✄ HSHSJers, ✄ M29, ✄ M55, ✄ T1, ✄ T23
02/3 Parkhurst 94, ✄ GJ41, ✄ SJ41, ✄ HSHSJers, ✄ PP1, ✄ TT4
95 Parkhurst Phonecard
02/3 Parkhurst Retro 16, ✄ RJ17, ✄ RSJ26, ✄ HSHSJers, ✄ RM18
91/2 Pinnacle 41
92/3 Pinnacle 114
92/3 Pinnacle 248
93/4 Pinnacle 205
93/4 Pinnacle NF 14
93/4 Pinnacle T2K1 29
94/5 Pinnacle 32, BR6, GR10, TP6
x95/6 Pinnacle FC 5, R20-18
96/7 Pinnacle 56, BTN-2, TP-5
97/8 Pinnacle 80, TP-8, P-20
96/7 Pi. Be A Player LTH3B, BB-10, ✍ Aut. LTH3B
97/8 Pi. Be A Player OT 4
97/8 Pi. BeeHive 3, BHT-4
97/8 Pi. Certified 61, CT-17
97/8 Pi. Epix E16
95/6 Pi. FANtasy 6
96/7 Pi. FANtasy 8
97/8 Pi. Inside 1, IT-14, / Can 21
96/7 Pi. Mint 18
97/8 Pi. Mint 6
95/6 Pi. Summit 124, GMC-20
96/7 Pi. Summit 139
97/8 Pi. Totally 61
95/6 Pi. Zenith 86, ZT-16
96/7 Pi. Zenith 77, ZT-4
95/6 Playoff 47, 157
94/5 POG 207, 265
95/6 POG 126
93/4 Power Play 216
93/4 Power Play SA 10
93/4 Premier 247
94/5 Premier 215, 529, TF-5
00/1 Premier Plus 50, WP12
99/0 Prism 48, CA-8, SGDC-10
00/1 Pr. Stock 37, AC-11, Res. 9, PS-22, PSS-12, ✄ GUG-47
01/2 Pr. Stock 37, Res. 4, -PS 28, ✄ GUG 44
02/3 Pr. Stock Reserve 37
00/1 PS Titanium 34, ✄ GUG-97
01/2 PS Titanium 53, SK 6, TSS 14, TAS 10
02/3 PS Titanium 39
00/1 PS Titanium Draft ✄ 41
95/6 Pro Magnet 130
90/1 Pro Set 174
91/2 Pro Set 131
91/2 Pro Set 475
92/3 Pro Set 163
91/2 Pro Set Platinum 111
02/3 Quest for the Cup 36, -RTC 7
99/0 Revolution 55, NI-10, O-10, SS-17, TL-3, / CSC 55
00/1 Revolution 54, HD-15, II-10, NI-11, SM-5
90/1 Score 146
91/2 Score 286
91/2 Score 38T
91/2 Score CAN 588
92/3 Score 392
93/4 Score 238
94/5 Score 155, CI-5,NP-8
95/6 Score 20, GB-17
96/7 Score 2, CI-6, SD-3
97/8 Score 80, CI-3
97/8 Score Detr. 1
90/1 Sco. Young Stars 23
92/3 Seasons 15
94/5 Select 129, FL-4
95/6 Select CE 64, DS-9
96/7 Select CE 72
94 Semic 100
95 Semic 88
96/7 SB 7-Eleven Phonecard
00/1 Signature 206, HSHS, ✍ Aut. 55, ✄ J-2, ✄ HSHSJers
01/2 Signature C-6, ✍ Aut., ✄ 500GS, ✄ GUE18, ✄ GJ27, ✄ GSJ27, ✄ HSHSJers, ✄ ITN18, ✄ IG13, ✄ TM11
02/3 Signature 126, ✍ 126, ✄ SGJ20
95/6 SBx Emotion 78,NP-7
95/6 SBx Impact 76
96/7 SBx Impact 55, BR-21
94/5 SP 101
95/6 SP 62, E16
96/7 SP 50, CW-8, Ins.
97/8 SP Authentic 55, I10
98/9 SP Authentic 29, SS14, SO1
99/0 SP Authentic 32
00/1 SP Authentic 32, SF3
01/2 SP Authentic 31, ✄ NN
02/3 SP Authentic 31, 97, ✄ SP, ✄ DP
00/1 SP GU 22, ✄ C
01/2 SP GU 17, ✄ AF, ✄ AFD, ✄ AFT, ✄ AFQ, ✄ Patch, ✄ PatchC (x2), ✄ PatchT
02/3 SP GU 18, ✄ AF (x2), ✄ CF, ✄ PC, ✄ PH (x2)
02/3 Sports Vault 215
96/7 SPx 19
97/8 SPx 16, D-SPX7
99/0 SPx 56, P7, X17, XT7
00/1 SPx 23, 72, HH7, ✄ WM
01/2 SPx 23, ✄ TT
02/3 SPx 31, 137, ✄ M (x2), ✄ X
98/9 SPx Finite 32, 96
98/9 SPx Prospects 22, H13, L9, PS27
99/0 Stadium 106, Chrome 34
00/1 Stadium 2, SF12
01/2 Stadium 8, G2, HS10
02/3 Stadium 95, -BT-6
95/6 SLU
96/7 SLU
98/9 SLU
95/6 Super Sticker 52, DC-22
92/3 Topps 295
95/6 Topps 16, 370, HGC10, M10
98/9 Topps 216
99/0 Topps 196
00/1 Topps 115
01/2 Topps 69
02/3 Topps 263, 316, 326, HHU12
99/0 To. Chrome 196
00/1 To. Chrome 89
01/2 To. Chrome 69
02/3 T. Chrome 144
94/5 Topps Finest 92, DF-14
95/6 To. Finest 39, 65
98/9 To. Finest 123, M38, R10
98/9 T. Gold Label 1, GR8
99/0 To. Gold Label 55
00/1 To. Gold Label 2, B3, GG14
00/1 To. Heritage 27, 219, HH18
01/2 To. Heritage 24
02/3 To. Heritage 80, 126
02/3 To. Limited 263, 316, 326
99/0 To. Prmr. Plus 58
01/2 To. Reserve 75
91/2 To. Stadium 199
92/3 To. Stadium 371
93/4 To. Stadium 389
95/6 To. Stadium 25, F1
93/4 TSC Members Only 16
95/6 TSC Members Only 26
00/1 To. Stars 26
95/6 To. Super Skills 55
02/3 To. Total 369, TP6
98/9 UD Choice 76, BH24, RW7, SQ9
00/1 UD Heroes 147, PI1, TS2
01/2 UD PlayMakers Ltd 36
00/1 UD Reserve 30
98/9 UD3 47, 107, 167
00/1 Ultimate Mem. ✄ U-2, ✄ J-2, ✄ Jers. 1, ✄ JJ-18, ✄ S-2, ✄ TM-2, ✄ TM-4, ✄ TM-8
01/2 Ultimate Mem. ✄ 500GS, ✄ DD, ✄ Emb., ✄ Jers., ✄ S&J, ✄ ITN, ✄ JE, ✄ JJ, ✄ PP, ✍ Aut.
02/3 Ultimate Mem. ✄ DD, ✄ Emb, ✄ GUJ, ✄ GUSJ, ✄ GD, ✄ ITN, ✄ LA, ✄ MO, ✄ SCDE, ✄ SCDJ, ✄ SCDN
99/0 Ult. Victory 33, S5
90/1 Upper Deck 269
91/2 Upper Deck 561
92/3 Upper Deck 122
93/4 Upper Deck - SP 140
94/5 Upper Deck 292, R7, IG4, SP-69
95/6 Upper Deck 184, AS-4, R-4, SE-125
96/7 Upper Deck 252, X14, P1, SS6B
97/8 Upper Deck 268, SS14, SG14, T6B, ✄ GJ13
98/9 Upper Deck 87, FF5, FT22, GN13-15, LS4, P14, ✄ GJ14
99/0 Upper Deck 50, 155, CT5, FF11, SB12, SS14
00/1 Upper Deck 62, L5, NC2, P4, SS10, TT6, ✄ DGJ, ✄ GJ
01/2 Upper Deck 290, GA13, SS6, T3, ✄ CJers, ✄ JPatch, ✄ PatchN, ✄ PatchNu, ✄ PF, ✄ PoaND, ✄ SCFJers, ✄ SCFJersD, ✄ SCFJersT
02/3 Upper Deck 233, 306, -NC5, -SS7, ✄ DM, ✄ GO, ✄ PL, ✄ PA, ✄ PW, ✄ UDPL
95/6 UD ASG MVP20
96/7 UD All-Star YCTG AR9
02/3 UD Artistic 35, R35, ✄ AT, / Art
93/4 Upper Deck Be A Player 16
94/5 UD BAP R86, R104, R137, ✍ 86
95/6 UD BAP LL13
96/7 UD Black Diam. 114
97/8 UD Black Diam. 149, PC3
98/9 UD Black Diam. 33, M9, WF10
99/0 UD Black Diam. 35, DM2
00/1 UD Black Diam. 21, FP5
99/0 UD C. Legends 70
01/2 UD Challenge 29, ✄ TN, ✄ UC
02/3 UD Classic 37, ET6, PS5, ✄ HR, ✄ SC
95/6 UD CC 4
96/7 UD CC 112, 319, UD26, S12, C14, CR14
97/8 UD Coll. Choice 76, SQ74, S14, W4, C4, CR4
97/8 UD Diam. Vision 11, DM6
98/9 UD G. Reserve 87
99/0 UD G. Reserve 50, 155
01/2 UD Honor Roll 19, 49,94, ✄ GAJ
02/3 UD Honor 29, ✄ GA, ✄ TW6
96/7 UD Ice 85, S2
97/8 UD Ice 84, IC14, L2A
00/1 UD Ice 16, IG3, ✄ IGJ
01/2 UD Ice 97
00/1 UD Legends 44, EG6
01/2 UD Mask 32, ✄ GG, ✄ GJ, ✄ JP, ✄ DP
02/3 UD Mask 33, ✄ IO, ✄ PG
98/9 UD MVP 72, OT13, PG1, F8, Souv.
99/0 UD MVP 70, S5, GU7, ✄ GU21
00/1 UD MVP 64, TD4, ✄ GS
01/2 UD MVP 65, ✄ S
02/3 UD MVP 64, HN4
99/0 UD MVP Cup 67, GC, SS4
x99/0 UD Ovation LP18
02/3 UD Piece 37, ✄ PH, / Giveaway
95/6 UD Post 11
96/7 UD Post, SU-3
01/2 UD Premier 20, ✄ B, ✄ D
02/3 UD Premier 23, ✄ Jers, ✄ JD, ✄ Patch
00/1 UD Pros&Prosp. 30, CR2, GS4, ✄ GJ
99/0 UD Retro 29, G9B
02/3 UD Rookie 35, ✄ 149a, ✄ DJ, ✄ S
01/2 UD SCup Champs 64, ✄ G, ✄ S, ✄ T
01/2 UD Top Shelf 91, ✄ J (x2), ✄ S
02/3 UD Top Shelf 32, ✄ CP, ✄ HT, ✄ M (x2), ✄ R, ✄ SH, ✄ ST, ✄ TS
00/1 UD Vintage 129, 136, S3B
01/2 UD Vintage 89, 95, 96
02/3 UD Vintage 97, 271, 294, GB 97, T25
97/8 Valu-net, ✍ Aut.
00/1 Vanguard 40, HV-13, ✄ DGJ-5
01/2 Vanguard 37, EMW 8, IF 4, QTH 7, VT 13
02/3 Vanguard 39
99/0 Victory 97
00/1 Victory 82, 248, 299
01/2 Victory 132, 439
02/3 Victory 73, -NP7
99/0 WGretzky 62, ✄ TG
96 Wien 90
97/8 Zenith 3, CTC-6, ZT-9, Z9
99/0 DETR / News 4
95/6 HART / Kids Club
88/9 NJER / Caretta
89/0 NJER
89/0 NJER / Caretta
90/1 NJER
91/2 SLOU
85/6 London Knights
86/7 London Knights

SHANAHAN, CHRIS
96/7 Sudbury Wolves

SHANAHAN, RYAN
93/4 Slapshot / Sudbury 10
94/5 Slapshot / Sudbury 9
95/6 Slapshot 392
96/7 Louisiana Ice Gators
98/9 Louisiana Ice Gators
99/0 Louisiana Ice Gators
00/1 Louisiana Ice Gators
01/2 Louisiana Ice Gators
92/3 Sudbury Wolves
93/4 Sudbury Wolves

SHANAHAN, SEAN
76/7 COLR / Hockey Talk

SHAND, DAVE
79/0 ATLF / B&W

SHAND, DAVID
77/8 O-Pee-Chee 355
78/9 O-Pee-Chee 356
79/0 O-Pee-Chee 394
80/1 O-Pee-Chee 282
79 Panini Sticker 57
80/1 Pepsi Bottle Cap
77/8 ATLF
78/9 ATLF / Colour
79/0 ATLF / Colour
80/1 TORO

SHANDUROV, DMITRI
99/0 Mir 62, 99

SHANK, DANIEL
90/1 Bowman 235
90/1 OPC/Topps 34
90/1 Pro Set 78
88/9 ProCards / Adirondack
90/1 ProCards 489
91/2 ProCards 119
90/1 Score 377
90/1 Upper Deck 99
95/6 Las Vegas Thunder
94/5 Minnesota Moose
98/9 Phoenix Mustangs 6
92/3 San Diego Gulls
93/4 San Diego Gulls

SHANNON, DARRIN
91/2 Bowman 24
92/3 Bowman 385
93/4 Donruss 388
94/5 Donruss 139
94/5 Flair 210
92/3 Fleer Ultra 246
94/5 Fleer Ultra 395
93/4 Leaf 194
94/5 Leaf 251
90/1 OPC/Topps 310
91/2 O-Pee-Chee 214
92/3 O-Pee-Chee 332
91/2 OPC Premier 146
97/8 Pa. Invincible R-154
92/3 Panini Sticker 58
93/4 Panini Sticker 192
91/2 Parkhurst 201
92/3 Parkhurst 436
93/4 Parkhurst 499
94/5 Parkie SE204
91/2 Pinnacle 243
92/3 Pinnacle 106
93/4 Pinnacle 266
94/5 Pinnacle 279
95/6 Pinnacle 69
96/7 Pi. Be A Player 183, ✍ Aut. 183
94/5 POG 254
93/4 Premier 261
94/5 Premier 254
90/1 Pro Set 592
91/2 Pro Set 14
91/2 Pro Set 515
92/3 Pro Set 218
91/2 Pro Set Platinum 246
89/0 ProCards AHL 275
90/1 ProCards 278
90/1 Score 410
91/2 Score 107T
91/2 Score CAN 438
92/3 Score 36
93/4 Score 280
95/6 Score 103
92/3 Topps 167
91/2 To. Stadium 361
92/3 To. Stadium 55
93/4 To. Stadium 191
91/2 Upper Deck 322
91/2 Upper Deck 581
92/3 Upper Deck 132
90/1 BUFF / Campbell's
96/7 PHOE / Coca-Cola
97/8 PHOE / Coca-Cola
91/2 WINN / IGA
93/4 WINN / Ruffles
93/4 WINN Readers
95/6 WINN
95/6 WINN Readers
99/0 St. John's Maple Leafs

SHANNON, DARRYL
98/9 Pacific 109
99/0 Pacific 46
97/8 Pacific CC 72
96/7 Panini Sticker 21
97/8 Panini Sticker 14
91/2 Parkhurst 390
96/7 Pi. Be A Player 90, ✍ Aut. 90
91/2 Pro Set 490
88/9 ProCards / Newmarket
90/1 ProCards 151
97/8 Score Buff. 19
00/1 UD Heroes 65
91/2 Upper Deck 493
94/5 Upper Deck 483
95/6 Upper Deck 282
91/2 TORO / P.L.A.Y. 22
95/6 WINN
90/1 Newmarket Saints

SHANNON, GERRY
34-43 BeeHive-1 [Maroons]
35-40 Canada Starch
36-39 Diamond Match TT1
37/8 O-Pee-Chee 179 [Error: Jerry]

SHANNON, JOHN
97/8 Pi. CBC Sports 12

SHANNON, RYAN
98 Bowman 63
98 Bowman Chrome 63
98/9 Calgary Hitmen 2

SHANTZ, BRIAN
90 7th..Sketch Mem.Cup 11
88/9 Kamloops Blazers
89/0 Kamloops Blazers

SHANTZ, JEFF
01/2 Atomic ✄ GWJ 7
98/9 Aurora 43
98/9 Be A Player 31, ✍ Aut. 31
92/3 Classic 15
93/4 Classic 27
92/3 Classic Four Sport 164
93/4 Donruss 75
94/5 Donruss 247
95/6 Donruss 209
93/4 Leaf 405
94/5 Leaf 196
95/6 Leaf 252
98/9 Pacific 151
99/0 Pacific 60
00/1 Pacific 74
97/8 Pa. Invincible R-46
94/5 Panini Sticker O
93/4 Parkhurst 314
94/5 Parkhurst 46, 289
93/4 Pinnacle 428
94/5 Pinnacle 458
97/8 Pi. Be A Player 173, ✍ Aut. 173
93/4 Power Play 316
94/5 Premier 342, OF-23
00/1 PS Titanium ✄ GUG 70
93/4 Score 605
90/1 7th..Sketch WHL 174
91/2 7th...Sketch WHL 219
00/1 Signature 169, ✍ Aut. 190
95/6 Topps 179
93/4 To. Stadium 348
94/5 To. Stadium 92
93/4 Upper Deck 258, 451, SP-32
94/5 Upper Deck 379
95/6 Upper Deck 182
97/8 Upper Deck 248
00/1 Upper Deck 258
95/6 UD CC 124
96/7 UD CC 53
98/9 UD MVP 33
99/0 UD MVP Cup 35
01/2 UD Vintage 40
93/4 CHIC / Coke
94/5 Indianapolis Ice

SHAPLEY, LARRY
99/0 Manitoba Moose

SHARAPOV, ANDREI
00/1 Mir 84

SHARAPOV, VADIM
99/0 Fort Wayne Komets

SHARGORODSKY, OLEG
99/0 Mir 208
00/1 Mir 138
98/9 Fort Wayne Komets

SHARIFIJANOV, VADIM
99/0 BAP Mem. 123
93/4 Classic 110
93/4 Classic - Class of '94 CL6
94/5 Classic 21, T39
94/5 Classic 4 Sport 138
94/5 Cla. Images 4 Sport 112
93/4 Cla. Prospects 207
97/8 Donruss 204
97/8 Do. Canadian 134
99/0 HoloGrFX 34
97/8 Leaf 163
97/8 Limited 78
99/0 Millenium 146, ✍ Aut. 146
98/9 Omega 142
99/0 Pacific 247
93/4 Parkhurst 527
93/4 Pinnacle 503
97/8 Pi. Inside 183
94/5 Score 212
97/8 Score 56
97/8 Score NJer. 17
94/5 SR Gold Standard 91
94/5 SR Tetrad CXIV, ✍ Aut.
99/0 SPx 89
99/0 Topps 160
99/0 To. Chrome 160
92/3 Upper Deck 612
93/4 Upper Deck 574
98/9 Upper Deck 309, GN28
99/0 Upper Deck 80, N4
98/9 UD G. Reserve 309
99/0 UD G. Reserve 80
99/0 UD MVP 121
99/0 UD Retro 48
99/0 Victory 168
99/0 W. Gretzky ✍ SG
96/7 Albany River Rats
97/8 Albany River Rats
00/1 Kansas City Blades 11

SHARIPOV, AZAT
00/1 Mir 148

SHARNIN, ALEXEI
00/1 Mir 142

SHARP, PATRICK
02/3 Atomic 122
02/3 BAP All-Star 150
02/3 BAP Mem. 282
02/3 Bowman 163
02/3 Crown Royale 130
02/3 Exclusive 188
02/3 Parkhurst 212
02/3 Pr. Stock Reserve 176
02/3 SP Authentic 155
02/3 SP GU 88
02/3 SPx 173
02/3 Stadium 138
02/3 T. Chrome 165
02/3 To. Heritage 150
02/3 To. Total 417
02/3 Ultimate Mem. 12
02/3 Upper Deck 447
02/3 UD Artistic 125
02/3 UD Classic 124
02/3 UD Mask 128
02/3 UD Piece 143
02/3 UD Premier 62
02/3 UD Rookie ✄ 156
02/3 UD Top Shelf 101
02/3 Vanguard 127
02/3 Philadelphia Phantoms

SHARP, RYAN
00/1 Owen Sound Attack 11
01/2 Owen Sound Attack

SHARPLES, JEFF
95/6 Edge Ice 156
84/5 Kelowna Wings &...
88/9 OPC/Topps 48
89/0 OPC/Topps 42
88/9 OPC Sticker 249-119
88/9 OPC Sticker 74-205
88/9 Panini Sticker 38
89/0 Panini Sticker 66
90/1 ProCards 559
87/8 DETR / Little Caesars
88/9 DETR / Little Caesars
88/9 DETR / S.A.M.
92/3 Kansas City Blades
93/4 Las Vegas Thunder
94/5 Las Vegas Thunder
95/6 Las Vegas Thunder
99/0 Utah Grizzlies
83/4 Kelowna Wings
86/7 Portland Winter Hawks

SHARPLES, SCOTT
92/3 St. John's Maple Leafs

SHARPLES, WARREN
90/1 ProCards 625
91/2 ProCards 591

SHARPLEY, GLEN
77/8 O-Pee-Chee 158
78/9 O-Pee-Chee 175
79/0 O-Pee-Chee 93
80/1 O-Pee-Chee 218
81/2 O-Pee-Chee 64
82/3 O-Pee-Chee 75
81/2 OPC Sticker 116
79 Panini Sticker 63
77/8 Topps 158
78/9 Topps 175
79/0 Topps 93
80/1 Topps 218
81/2 Topps 76 [West]
81/2 CHIC
78/9 MINS / Cloverleaf 7
80/1 MINS

SHARRERS, MATT
92/3 BCJHL 155

SHASHOV, VLADIMIR
90/1 O-Pee-Chee 506

SHASTIN, EVGENY
90/1 O-Pee-Chee 6R

SHASTIN, IGOR
00/1 Mir 130, 288

SHATALOV, YURI
91/2 Future Trends C72 29
74/5 Soviet Stars 9

SHAUNESSY, SCOTT
88/9 ProCards / Halifax
89/0 ProCards IHL 124
90/1 ProCards 385
91/2 ProCards 247
92/3 Cincinnati Cyclones
93/4 Cincinnati Cyclones
98/9 Fort Worth Brahmas

SHAUNESSY, STEVE
91/2 Cincinnati Cyclones

SHAVER, AL
93/4 Action Packed 6

SHAVER, RYAN
95/6 Slapshot 427

SHAVTSOV, IGOR
00/1 Mir 100

SHAW, BOB
83/4 Kelowna Wings

SHAW, BRAD
90/1 Bowman 260
91/2 Bowman 8
92/3 Bowman 111
93/4 Donruss 234
93/4 EA Sports 92
98/9 EBK IHL All-Star
92/3 Fleer Ultra 366
93/4 Fleer Ultra 167
94/5 Fleer Ultra 151
93/4 Kraft / PB
93/4 Leaf 11
90/1 OPC/Topps 279
91/2 O-Pee-Chee 442
90/1 Panini Sticker 48, 344
91/2 Panini Sticker 311
92/3 Panini Sticker 265
93/4 Panini Sticker 120
91/2 Parkhurst 62
92/3 Parkhurst 352
94/5 Parkie SE122
91/2 Pinnacle 88
92/3 Pinnacle 372
93/4 Pinnacle 271
94/5 Pinnacle 162
94/5 POG 176
93/4 Power Play 175
94/5 Premier 161
90/1 Pro Set 110
91/2 Pro Set 87
92/3 Pro Set 124
91/2 Pro Set Platinum 45
90/1 Score 99, 325
91/2 Score 289
91/2 Score CAN 509
92/3 Score 85
93/4 Score 15
94/5 Score 76
92/3 Topps 89
91/2 To. Stadium 83
92/3 To. Stadium 65
90/1 Upper Deck 90, 327
91/2 Upper Deck 297
92/3 Upper Deck 109
89/0 HART / Jr. Whalers
90/1 HART / Jr. Whalers
91/2 HART / Jr. Whalers
92/3 OTTA
93/4 OTTA
96/7 Detroit Vipers
97/8 Detroit Vipers
98/9 Detroit Vipers
81/2 Ottawa 67's
82/3 Ottawa 67's
83/4 Ottawa 67's

SHAW, DAVID
91/2 Bowman 64
92/3 Bowman 141
92/3 Fleer Ultra 256
93/4 Leaf 249
86/7 O-Pee-Chee 236
87/8 O-Pee-Chee 252
88/9 OPC/Topps 57
90/1 O-Pee-Chee 403
91/2 O-Pee-Chee 306
89/0 OPC/Topps 39
89/0 O-Pee-Chee 326
86/7 OPC Sticker 133-119
86/7 OPC Sticker 31-171
87/8 OPC Sticker 223-90
88/9 OPC Sticker 243-113
97/8 Pa. Invincible R-188
91/2 Panini Sticker 294
91/2 Pinnacle 251
92/3 Pinnacle 343
93/4 Pinnacle 124
94/5 Pinnacle 435
93/4 Premier 179
94/5 Premier 358
90/1 Pro Set 495
90/1 Score 98
90/1 Score 161
91/2 Score CAN 161
92/3 Score 183
93/4 Score 205
92/3 Topps 420
91/2 To. Stadium 306
92/3 To. Stadium 162
93/4 To. Stadium 229
90/1 Upper Deck 15
91/2 Upper Deck 409
94/5 UD BAP ✍ 136
91/2 EDMO / IGA
89/0 NYRA / Marine
85/6 QUÉB
85/6 QUÉB / Gene. Foods
85/6 QUÉB / McDonald's
85/6 QUÉB / Provigo
86/7 QUÉB
86/7 QUÉB / Gene. Foods
86/7 QUÉB / McDonald's
84/5 Fredericton Express
82/3 Kitchener Rangers
83/4 Kitchener Rangers

SHAW, DEAN
84/5 Brandon Wheat Kings

SHAW, EVAN
02/3 Québec Remparts

SHAW, JIM
75/6 OPC WHA 55

SHAW, LLOYD
98/9 Cincinnati M'Ducks 20
99/0 Cincinnati M'Ducks
00/1 Hamilton Bulldogs
93/4 Seattle Thunderbirds

SHAWARA, MITCH
93/4 Prince Albert Raiders
95/6 Prince Albert Raiders

SHAYAKHMETOV, N.
00/1 Mir 248

SHEA, JAMIE
90/1 7th...Sketch OHL 117
91/2 7th...Sketch OHL 45

SHEA, MICHAEL
95 Globe 189
94 Semic 236
95 Semic 185
93 Semic Sticker 271

SHEARER, ROB
93/4 Slapshot / Windsor 14
94/5 Slapshot / Windsor 16
95/6 Slapshot 419
00/1 UD Black Diam. 94
01/2 Victory 367
98/9 Hershey Bears
00/1 Hershey Bears

SHEDDEN, DARRYL
96/7 Hampton Roads
95/6 Louisiana Ice Gators
95/6 Louisiana Ice Gators-2
96/7 Louisiana Ice Gators

SHEDDEN, DOUG
83/4 O-Pee-Chee 285
85/6 O-Pee-Chee 247
86/7 OPC/Topps 153
87/8 O-Pee-Chee 249
83/4 OPC/Topps Sticker 228
84/5 OPC Sticker 120
85/6 OPC Sticker 102-234
86/7 OPC Sticker 164-24
87/8 OPC Sticker 226-93
82/3 Post [Pitt.]
90/1 Pro Set 542
88/9 ProCards / Newmarket
89/0 ProCards AHL 125
90/1 ProCards 158
83/4 Souhaits Keychain [Penguins]
86/7 DETR / Little Caesars
83/4 PITT / Heinz
84/5 PITT / Heinz
86/7 QUÉB
90/1 TORO
95/6 Louisiana Ice Gators
95/6 Louisiana Ice Gators-2
96/7 Louisiana Ice Gators
97/8 Louisiana Ice Gators
98/9 Louisiana Ice Gators
90/1 Newmarket Saints
80/1 Soo Greyhounds

SHEEHAN, BOBBY
71/2 O-Pee-Chee 177
72/3 O-Pee-Chee 297
78/9 O-Pee-Chee 311
77/8 OPC WHA 47
73/4 Quaker Oats 20
76/7 Topps 183
71/2 Toronto Sun Photo
71/2 MONT / Pro Star
98/9 Charlotte Checkers
98/9 Charlotte Checkers
89/0 New Haven Nighthawks

SHEEHAN, JAMES
90/1 7th..Sketch OHL 118
91/2 7th...Sketch OHL 65

SHEEHAN, MIKE
95/6 Slapshot 68

SHEEHAN, MURRAY
94/5 Slapshot / Detroit Jr. 6
94/5 Slapshot Memorial 80

SHEEHY, NEIL
87/8 O-Pee-Chee 213
90/1 OPC/Topps 188
91/2 O-Pee-Chee 407
87/8 OPC Sticker 38-181
87/8 Panini Sticker 209
91/2 Score 86T
91/2 Score CAN 636
85/6 CALG / Red Rooster
86/7 CALG / Red Rooster
91/2 CALG / IGA
88/9 WASH
88/9 WASH / Smokey
89/0 WASH
89/0 WASH / Kodak
90/1 WASH / Smokey
84/5 Moncton G'Flames

SHEEHY, TIM
76/7 OPC WHA 33
72 Semic Sticker 128
72/3 New England Whalers

SHEFER, ANDREI
00/1 Mir 304
99/0 UD Sobey's 6
99/0 SP Authentic 129
99/0 Upper Deck 329
99/0 UD Black Diam. 115
99/0 UD G. Reserve 329
99/0 UD MVP Cup 202
99/0 UD Prospects 63
99/0 Halifax Mooseheads

SHELFO, ALEC
87/8 Kamloops Blazers

SHELKUNOV, ALEX
01/2 Kamloops Blazers

SHELLEY, JODY
01/2 BAP Mem. 428
97 Bowman 76
01/2 Crown Royale 154
02/3 Pacific 105
01/2 PS Titanium Draft 121
01/2 SP Authentic 142
01/2 SPx 135, -RT
02/3 To. Total 385
01/2 Upper Deck 185
02/3 Upper Deck 299
02/3 UD Vintage 76, 269
00/1 Syracuse Crunch
01/2 Syracuse Crunch
95/6 Halifax Moosehead
96/7 Halifax Moosehead
96/7 Halifax Moosehead
96/7 Halifax Moosehead

SHELTON, DOUG
67/8 Topps 53

SHEMKO, MIKE
90/1 7th..Sketch WHL 240

SHENDELEV, SERGEI
94 Semic 142
95 Semic 127

SHENG, CHANG YUNG
79 Panini Sticker 357

SHEPARD, BRADLEY
90/1 7th..Sketch OHL 316
91/2 7th...Sketch OHL 55

SHEPARD, KEN
93/4 Slapshot / Oshawa 3
96/7 Binghampton Rangers

SHEPELEV, SERGEI
82 Semic Sticker 61
83/4 Soviet Stars

SHEPOVALOV, VLADIMIR
72/3 Williams Finnish 35

SHEPPARD, BRENT
91/2 Air Canada SJHL D40

SHEPPARD, GREGG
75/6 Hockey Heroes
74/5 Lipton Soup 29
74/5 Loblaws
72/3 O-Pee-Chee 240
73/4 O-Pee-Chee 8
74/5 O-Pee-Chee 184
75/6 O-Pee-Chee 235
76/7 O-Pee-Chee 155
77/8 O-Pee-Chee 95
78/9 O-Pee-Chee 18
79/0 O-Pee-Chee 172
80/1 O-Pee-Chee 325
82/3 Post [Pitt.]
73/4 Topps 8
74/5 Topps 184
75/6 Topps 235
76/7 Topps 155
77/8 Topps 95
78/9 Topps 18
79/0 Topps 172

SHEPPARD, JOHN**
84/5 Ottawa 67's

SHEPPARD, JOHNNY*
25-27 Anonymous 129
33/4 Canadian Gum
33-35 Diamond Match Silv.
33/4 O-Pee-Chee 30
23/4 Paulins Candy 47

SHEPPARD, KEN
91/2 Oshawa Generals

SHEPPARD, RAY
99/0 Aurora 29
91/2 Bowman 63
92/3 Bowman 25
93/4 Donruss 105
94/5 Donruss 293
95/6 Donruss 198, 276, M-4
96/7 Donruss 210
97/8 Donruss 101
97/8 Do. Canadian 29
95/6 Do. Elite 102
97/8 Do. Preferred 36
97/8 Do. Priority 114
94/5 Flair 52
96/7 Flair 38
94/5 Fleer 65
96/7 Fleer 42
95/6 Fleer Metal 134
92/3 Fleer Ultra 289
93/4 Fleer Ultra 310
94/5 Fleer Ultra 66
95/6 Fleer Ultra 49, 305, RLS-9
96/7 Fl. Ultra 68
95/6 Hoyle / West. 6-Club
93/4 Leaf 44
94/5 Leaf 107
95/6 Leaf 118
96/7 Leaf 114
97/8 Leaf 115
94/5 L. Limited 26
95/6 L. Limited 106
96/7 L. Preferred 92
97/8 Limited 141
96/7 Metal Univ. 62
88/9 OPC/Topps 55
90/1 O-Pee-Chee 446
91/2 O-Pee-Chee 289
92/3 O-Pee-Chee 154
89/0 OPC/Topps 119
90/1 OPC Premier 106
91/2 OPC Premier 2
88/9 OPC Stars 35
88/9 OPC Sticker 262
88/9 OPC Sticker 126-258
88/9 OPC Sticker 161
89/0 opcSticker 259-140
98/9 Omega 47
99/0 Pacific 81
97/8 Pacific CC 80
97/8 Pa. Dynagon 55, T-52
97/8 Pa. Invincible 63
97/8 Pa. Paramount 84
98/9 Pa. Revolution 27
88/9 Panini Sticker 228
89/0 Panini Sticker 211
91/2 Panini Sticker 286
92/3 Panini Sticker 121
93/4 Panini Sticker 247
94/5 Panini Sticker 211, 237b
95/6 Panini Sticker 183
96/7 Panini Sticker 69
97/8 Panini Sticker 61
91/2 Parkhurst 41
92/3 Parkhurst 280
93/4 Parkhurst 330
95/6 Parkhurst 457
94/5 Parkie SE49
91/2 Pinnacle 155
92/3 Pinnacle 119
93/4 Pinnacle 153
94/5 Pinnacle 14
97/8 Pinnacle 164
97/8 Pi. Be A Player 46, ✍ Aut. 46
97/8 Pi. Certified 90
97/8 Pi. Inside 139
95/6 Pi. Summit 77
96/7 Pi. Summit 88
97/8 Pi. Totally 90
95/6 Pi. Zenith 92
95/6 Playoff 36
96/7 Playoff 338
94/5 POG 91
95/6 POG 98
93/4 Power Play 76
94/5 Premier 429, TF-6
95/6 Pro Magnet 104
90/1 Pro Set 496
91/2 Pro Set 162
91/2 Pro Set 380
92/3 Pro Set 47
91/2 Pro Set Platinum 169
90/1 Score 97T
91/2 Score 213
91/2 Score 36T
91/2 Score CAN 213
91/2 Score CAN 586
92/3 Score 163
92/3 Score SS 20
93/4 Score 83
94/5 Score 175, NP-15
95/6 Score 127
96/7 Score 112
97/8 Score 121
94/5 Select 56
95/6 SBx Emotion 58
95/6 SBx Impact 152
96/7 SBx Impact 48
94/5 SP 38
95/6 SP 130
96/7 SP 66
92/3 Topps 257
99/0 Topps 243
99/0 To. Chrome 243
94/5 Topps Finest 50
95/6 To. Finest 16
96/7 To. Picks 129
91/2 To. Stadium 381
92/3 To. Stadium 85
94/5 To. Stadium 40
95/6 To. Stadium 215
90/1 Upper Deck 420
91/2 Upper Deck 390, 573
92/3 Upper Deck 296
93/4 Upper Deck 398
94/5 Upper Deck 152
95/6 Upper Deck 254, 348, SE-161
96/7 Upper Deck 263
97/8 Upper Deck 280
98/9 Upper Deck 240
94/5 UD BAP R54
95/6 UD BAP 60, ✍ S60
96/7 UD Black Diam. 66
95/6 UD CC 177
96/7 UD CC 111
97/8 UD Coll. Choice 99, SQ60, C5, CR5
98/9 UD G. Reserve 240
96/7 UD Ice 23
99/0 UD MVP Cup 83
87/8 BUFF / Blue Shield
87/8 BUFF / Won. Bread
88/9 BUFF / Blue Shield
88/9 BUFF / Won. Bread
89/0 BUFF / Blue Shield
89/0 BUFF / Campbell's
98/9 CARO / Highwoods
96/7 FLOR / Winn-Dixie
97/8 FLOR / Winn-Dixie

SHEPPARD, SCOTT
01/2 Kingston Frontenacs 16

SHEPTAK, CURTIS
00/1 Cardset 224

SHERBAN, TREVOR
90/1 7th..Sketch WHL 85
91/2 7th...Sketch WHL 297
98/9 Kansas City Blades 4
99/0 Missouri RiverOtters
90/1 Saskatoon Blades

SHERBLANOV, ALEXEI
99/0 Mir 69

SHERF, JOHNNY
34-43 BeeHive-1 [Detr.]

SHERIDAN, JOHN
75/6 OPC WHA 107

SHERIDAN, RHONDA
87/8 Kingston Canadians

SHERMERHORN, DANNY
92/3 BCJHL 193
92/3 BCJHL 206
97/8 Las Vegas Thunder 20
93/4 Maine Black Bears

SHERO, FRED
45-64 BeeHive-2 [NYRa.]
51/2 Cleveland Barons
74/5 O-Pee-Chee 21
92/3 Parkhurst 480
74/5 Topps 21

SHERRID, DAVE
88/9 ProCards / Baltimore

SHERRY, SIMON
93/4 Slapshot / Sudbury 19
94/5 Slapshot / Sudbury 19
95/6 Slapshot 401
93/4 Sudbury Wolves

SHERSTENKA, DAN
90/1 7th..Sketch WHL 115
91/2 7th...Sketch WHL 183

SHERVEN, GORD
83 Canada Juniors
94/5 DEL 302
95/6 DEL 89
96/7 DEL 278
98/9 DEL 295
99/0 Eishockey 248
85/6 EDMO / Red Rooster
88/9 EDMO / Action 12
85/6 MINS

SHETCHYK, MARK
01/2 Calgary Hitmen

SHEVALIER, JEFF
97/8 Pa. Invincible R-98
91/2 7th...Sketch OHL 68
93/4 Slapshot / North Bay 20
97/8 UD Coll. Choice 127
98/9 Cincinnati Cyclones
99/0 Detroit Vipers
94/5 Phoenix Roadrunners
95/6 Phoenix Roadrunners
99/0 Québec Citadelles 21
97/8 Springfield Falcons

SHEVTSOV, OLEG
00/1 Mir 322

SHEWCHUK, JACK
34-43 BeeHive-1 [Bost.]
40/1 O-Pee-Chee 126

SHIBICKY, ALEX
34-43 BeeHive-1 [NYRa.]
36/7 O-Pee-Chee 109
39/0 O-Pee-Chee 88
37/8 World Wide Gum 90
74/5 Sioux City Musketeers

SHICK, ROB
90/1 Pro Set 698

SHIEFFERS, STEVE
00/1 Cardset 294

SHIELDS, AL
34-43 BeeHive-1 [NYAm.]
35-40 Canada Starch
35/6 O-Pee-Chee 89
37/8 O-Pee-Chee 162
33/4 WWGum Premium 5
37/8 World Wide Gum 60

SHIELDS, JORDAN
96/7 Dayton Bombers
97/8 New Mexico Scorpions

SHIELDS, STEVE
01/2 Adrenaline 5, PP 2
01/2 Atomic 2
99/0 Aurora 122, GU-18
00/1 Aurora 130
98/9 Be A Player 269, ✍ 269
99/0 BAP Mem. 288
00/1 BAP Mem. 182
02/3 BAP Mem. 57
01/2 BT Pipes 52, -Mask, ✂ GJ, ✂ S&J, ✂ GT, ✂ HSHSJers
02/3 Between the Pipes 52, 123, M3, ✂ BM20, ✂ GUJ37, ✂ GP12, ✂ T17, ✍ Aut.
98/9 Bicycle.. 5-S
94/5 Classic 62, T9
99/0 Crown Royale 126
00/1 Crown Royale 95
02/3 Crown Royale 8
97/8 Donruss 51
97/8 Do. Canadian 132, SCS-12
97/8 Do. Preferred 80
97/8 Do. Priority 115
97/8 Do. Studio 79
99/0 Dynagon Ice 175
02/3 Exclusive 14
02/3 First Ed. 91, ✂ Jers.
01/2 Heads Up 2, SS 1
97/8 Leaf 86
97/8 Limited 23, 63
99/0 Millenium 213, ✍ 213
97/8 Omega 27
98/9 Omega 214
99/0 Omega 210
98/9 Pacific 110
99/0 Pacific 381
00/1 Pacific 365
01/2 Pacific 11, PCC 357, SC 1
02/3 Pacific 8
02/3 Pacific Complete 481
97/8 Pa. Invincible R-22
99/0 Pa. Paramount 209
00/1 Pa. Paramount 217, GS-17
00/1 Parkhurst P-150
02/3 Parkhurst 144
97/8 Pinnacle 97
97/8 Pi. Be A Player 233, ✍ Aut. 233
97/8 Pi. Certified 7
97/8 Pi. Inside 77, S-19
97/8 Pi. Totally 7
99/0 Prism 127
01/2 Pr. Stock -PS 2
02/3 Pr. Stock Reserve 9
00/1 PS Titanium 87
02/3 PS Titanium 9
99/0 Revolution 129
00/1 Revolution 131
97/8 Score 44
97/8 Score Buff. 2
00/1 Signature 250
01/2 Signature 173, ✍ Aut. 173
02/3 Signature 73, ✍ 73, ✂ SGJ51, ✂ TQ11
99/0 SP Authentic 72
00/1 SP Authentic ✍ SotT
02/3 SP Authentic 8
00/1 SP GU 50
02/3 SP Game-Used ✂ AF, ✂ TG
02/3 Sports Vault 20
00/1 SPx 57
99/0 Stadium 137
00/1 Stadium 68
00/1 Topps 161, OTG20
00/1 To. Chrome 112
02/3 To. Heritage 176
02/3 To. Total 292
00/1 UD Heroes 99
01/2 UD PlayMakers Ltd 1
00/1 Ultimate Mem. ✂ G-26
99/0 Ult. Victory 73, NW7
97/8 Upper Deck 18
99/0 Upper Deck 278
00/1 Upper Deck 148
01/2 Upper Deck 233
02/3 Upper Deck 258, ✂ GT
99/0 UD Black Diam. 77
00/1 UD Black Diam. 49, ✂ GG
99/0 UD G. Reserve 278
00/1 UD Ice 33
00/1 UD Legends 111
02/3 UD Mask 8, 9, 100
00/1 UD MVP 151, MM7
99/0 UD MVP Cup 155, SC17
99/0 UD Ovation 52
01/2 UD Top Shelf ✂ GG-LP
02/3 UD Top Shelf ✂ ST, ✂ SS
00/1 UD Vintage 306, 307, 308, GG15
02/3 Vanguard 9
99/0 Victory 256
00/1 Victory 198
99/0 WGretzky 150
95/6 Rochester Americans
96/7 Rochester Americans

SHIER, ANDREW
94/5 Classic 44
95/6 Milwaukee Admirals
94/5 Richmond Renegades
96/7 Richmond Renegades

SHIKHANOV, SERGEI
00/1 Mir 150

SHILL, JACK
34-43 BeeHive-1 [Toro.]
36/7 O-Pee-Chee 99
37/8 World Wide Gum 39

SHILOV, SERGEI
99/0 Mir 58

SHIMKOVSKI, SERGEI
98/9 Mir 138

SHINKARI, ALEXANDER
00/1 Mir 79

SHINSKE, RICK
78/9 SLOU

SHIPLEY, BLAKE
92/3 MPS SJHL 41

SHIPULIN, ROMAN
98/9 Mir 66

SHIRES, JIM
71/2 Toronto Sun Photo

SHIRREFFS, STEVE
02/3 Cardset 268
99/0 Portland Pirates

SHIRYAEV, DENNIS
99/0 Fort Worth Brahmas
01/2 Louisiana Ice Gators
02/3 Louisiana Ice Gators

SHIRYEV, VALERI
00/1 Mir Fetisov 32
90/1 O-Pee-Chee 13R
91/2 O-Pee-Chee 59R
89 Semic Sticker 84
89/0 Soviet Stars

SHISHKANOV, TIMOFEI
99/0 Mir 242
02/3 Québec Remparts

SHITIKOV, DMITRI
02/3 Russian Future Stars 13

SHITKOVSKI, SERGEI
99/0 Mir 146
00/1 Mir 384

SHMAUTZ, CLIFF
70/1 Eddie Sargent 29

SHMYR, DEAN
91/2 Avant Garde BCJHL 127
99/0 Greensboro Generals

SHMYR, JASON
02/3 Manitoba Moose
99/0 Portland Pirates
00/1 Portland Pirates

SHMYR, PAUL
71/2 Eddie Sargent 140
71/2 O-Pee-Chee 6
80/1 O-Pee-Chee 66
75/6 OPC WHA 5
76/7 OPC WHA 69
77/8 OPC WHA 59
82/3 Post [Hart.]
80/1 Topps 66
71/2 Toronto Sun Photo
70/1 CHIC
79/0 MINS
80/1 MINS
72/3 Cleveland Crusaders
72/3 Clev. WHA / Linnett
76/7 San Diego Mariners

SHMYRKO, GORD
82/3 Medicine Hat Tigers
83/4 Medicine Hat Tigers

SHOCK, BECKY
92/3 Toledo Storm WIOT

SHOCKEY, JOHN
95/6 Spokane Chiefs 24

SHOCKEY, JONATHON
00/1 Cleveland Lumberjacks

SHOCKEY, PARRY
95/6 Spokane Chiefs 26

SHOEBOTTOM, BRUCE
90/1 Pro Set 411
88/9 ProCards / Maine
89/0 ProCards AHL 63
90/1 ProCards 130
91/2 ProCards 36
92/3 Rochester Americans DD
92/3 Rochester Americans WPC

SHOLD, TERRY
85/6 Minnesota-Duluth 2

SHORE, EDDIE
35/6 Amalgamated Press
33/4 Anonymous 37
34-43 BeeHive-1 [Bost.]
39/0 Bruins Magazine
02/3 Canada Post
33-35 Diamond Match Silv.
33 Goudey Sport Kings 19
83 HHOF Postcard O14
83&87 HHOF 223
02/3 In The G-U ✂ VM10
27/8 La Presse
95/6 Legends of Hockey 63
33/4 O-Pee-Chee 3
36/7 O-Pee-Chee 118
39/0 O-Pee-Chee 100
02/3 Parkhurst ✂ VT19
93/4 Parkie 56-57 P-7
34/5 Sweet Caporal
60/1 Topps 20
02/3 Ultimate Mem. ✂ GAO, ✂ GMIH, ✂ VHT
01/2 Upper Deck ✍ Cut
99/0 UD C. Legends 10, AC10
00/1 UD Legends 10
01/2 UD Legends 2
99/0 UD Retro 88, G4A
37/8 World Wide Gum 5
91/2 BOST / SA Legends

SHORE, HAMBY
91 C55 Reprint 12
10/1 Imperial
11/2 Imperial 12
12/3 Imperial 30

SHORT, KAYLE
00/1 Kudos 147
90/1 7th..Sketch OHL 215
91/2 7th...Sketch OHL 349
93/4 Slapshot / Guelph 4
97/8 Hampton Roads
97/8 Portland Pirates
01/2 Manchester Storm
01/2 Sheffield Steelers
01/2 Sheffield Steelers GS
92/3 Sudbury Wolves

SHORT, STEVE
83/4 Brantford Alexanders

SHPAKOVSKI, DMITRI
98/9 Mir 67

SHRUM, STEVE
96/7 Kamloops Blazers
97/8 Kamloops Blazers
98/9 Kamloops Blazers
99/0 Kamloops Blazers
99/0 Kamloops Blazers

SHTALENKOV, MIKHAIL
98/9 Aurora 104
98/9 Be A Player 204, ✍ Aut. 204
98/9 Bicycle.. 9-C
93/4 Classic 148
93/4 Cla. 4 Sport 219
92/3 Classic Prospects 94
93/4 Cla. Prospects 49
94/5 Donruss 314
99/0 Dynagon Ice 154
94/5 Fleer 7
94/5 Fleer Ultra 252
95 Globe 164
94/5 Leaf 209
00/1 Mir 317
91/2 O-Pee-Chee 43R
97/8 Omega 8
98/9 Omega 95
99/0 Omega 100
98/9 Pacific 65
99/0 Pacific 326
00/1 Pacific 186
97/8 Pa. Invincible R-8
98/9 Pa. Paramount 127
98/9 Pa. Revolution 56
95 Panini Worlds 27
94/5 Parkhurst 4
95/6 Parkhurst 6
94/5 Pinnacle 331
95/6 Pinnacle 145
97/8 Pi. Be A Player 66, ✍ Aut. 66
94/5 Premier 3
92/3 Red Ace Blue 19
97/8 Score 21
97/8 Score Anah. 16
95 Semic 121, 211
91 Semic Sticker 79
92 Semic Sticker 100
95/6 Topps 344
98/9 UD Choice 2
94/5 Upper Deck 462
95/6 Upper Deck 91
96/7 Upper Deck 7
95/6 UD BAP 69, ✍ S69
95/6 UD CC 227
96/7 UD CC 4
94/5 ANAH / Carl's Jr. 22
95/6 ANAH / Photo
96/7 ANAH / Up Front 1

SHUCHUK, GARY
93/4 Donruss 157
93/4 Fleer Ultra 12
93/4 Fleer Ultra Pros. 9
93/4 Leaf 222
92/3 Parkhurst 484
93/4 Parkhurst 95
94/5 Parkie SE85
93/4 Premier 499
91/2 ProCards 132
91/2 Score 315
91/2 Score CAN 345
93/4 To. Stadium 351
94/5 To. Stadium 47
91/2 Upper Deck 376
93/4 Upper Deck 13
94/5 UD BAP ✍ 36
00/1 UD DEL 44
01/2 UD DEL 163
95/6 Phoenix Roadrunners

SHUDRA, RON
88/9 ProCards / Cape Breton
89/0 ProCards IHL 128
88/9 EDMO / Action 11
02/3 Coventry Blaze
01/2 Sheffield Steelers
01/2 Sheffield Steelers
93/4 Sheffield Steelers 16
93/4 Sheffield Steelers 17
94/5 Sheffield Steelers 8
95/6 Sheffield Steelers
97/8 Sheffield Steelers
85/6 Kamloops Blazers
86/7 Kamloops Blazers

SHUKAEV, MIKHAIL
00/1 Mir 131

SHULAKOV, DMITRI
98/9 Mir 68
99/0 Mir 115
00/1 Mir 23

SHULGA, DMITRI
00/1 Mir 215

SHULMISTRA, RICHARD
94/5 Classic 31
98/9 EBK IHL All-Star
01/2 UD DEL 43, ✂ GJ
96/7 Albany River Rats
99/0 Louisville Panthers
98/9 Manitoba Moose

SHUMAN, CLINT
00/1 Austin Ice Bats

SHUMAN, MIKE
90/1 Halifax Citadels

SHUMIKHIN, SERGEI
00/1 Mir 342

SHUN, WEI CHANG
79 Panini Sticker 358

SHUPE, JACK
81/2 Victoria Cougars

SHURUPOV, ANDREI
95/6 Slapshot 54

SHUTE, DAVID
90/1 7th..Sketch WHL 35
91/2 Knoxville Cherokees
93/4 Raleigh Icecaps

SHUTT, STEVE
93/4 Action Packed 4
01/2 AGF
02/3 BAP Mem. / Cup
77/8 Coke
72/3 Dernière Heure
73/4 Dernière Heure
80/1 Dernière Heure
83/4 Dernière Heure
88/9 Esso All-Star
01/2 Fleer Greats 12, ✍ Aut.
83/4 Funmate Puffy 6 [w/]
92/3 Future Trends C76 183
74/5 Loblaws
74/5 O-Pee-Chee 316
75/6 O-Pee-Chee 181
76/7 O-Pee-Chee 59
77/8 O-Pee-Chee 1
77/8 O-Pee-Chee 3
77/8 OPC 7
77/8 O-Pee-Chee 120
77/8 O-Pee-Chee 217
77/8 O-Pee-Chee NS 19
78/9 O-Pee-Chee 63
78/9 O-Pee-Chee 67
78/9 O-Pee-Chee 170
78/9 O-Pee-Chee 333
79/0 O-Pee-Chee 90
80/1 O-Pee-Chee 89
80/1 O-Pee-Chee 165
80/1 O-Pee-Chee 180
81/2 O-Pee-Chee 180
81/2 O-Pee-Chee 197
82/3 O-Pee-Chee 192
83/4 O-Pee-Chee 198
84/5 O-Pee-Chee 272
81/2 OPC Sticker 32
81/2 OPC Sticker 44
82/3 OPC/Topps Sticker 32
82/3 OPC/Topps Sticker 33
83/4 OPC/Topps Sticker 6
83/4 OPC/Topps Sticker 57
01/2 Parkhurst ✍ PA51
80/1 Pepsi Bottle Cap
82/3 Post [Mont.]
83/4 Souhaits Keychain [Canadiens]
77-79 Sportscaster 45-13
77-79 Sports. FIN 50-1178
75/6 Topps 181
76/7 Topps 59
77/8 Topps 1
77/8 Topps 3
77/8 Topps 7
77/8 Topps 120
77/8 Topps 217
77/8 ToppsNS 19
78/9 Topps 63
78/9 Topps 67
78/9 Topps 170
79/0 Topps 90
80/1 Topps 89
80/1 Topps 165
80/1 Topps 180
81/2 Topps 34
81/2 Topps 56
02/3 Topps - SCH, ✍ SCH
01/2 T/O Archives 32, -Seat
01/2 Ultimate Mem. ✂ LC, ✂ SCD, ✂ SCW
02/3 Ultimate Mem. ✂ FS, ✂ SF
01/2 UD Legends 36, ✂ M, ✂ TT, ✂ TTC
01/2 UD Vintage ✂ SH
83/4 Vachon 55-75
95/6 Zellers
72/3 MONT / Pro Star
73/4 MONT / Pro Star
74/5 MONT
75/6 MONT
76/7 MONT
77/8 MONT
78/9 MONT
79/0 MONT
80/1 MONT
81/2 MONT
82/3 MONT
82/3 MONT / Steinberg
83/4 MONT

SHUTTER, WALTER
86/7 Saskatoon Blades

SHVIDKI, DENIS
00/1 BAP Mem. 421
01/2 BAP Mem. 109
99 Bowman 24, 130, SC6, ✍ BA17
00/1 Crown Royale 125
02/3 O-Pee-Chee 304
00/1 Premier Plus 100
00/1 Pr. Stock 120
00/1 PS Titanium 123
00/1 PS Titanium Draft 123
00/1 Signature 283, ✍ Aut. 245
99/0 SPx 170
98/9 SPx Prospects 74
02/3 Topps 304
00/1 To. Heritage 158
02/3 To. Limited 304
98/9 UD Choice 286
00/1 UD Heroes 54
99/0 Upper Deck 170, 315
01/2 Upper Deck 304
97/8 UD Black Diam. 116
98/9 UD Black Diam. 107
99/0 UD Black Diam. 99
99/0 UD G. Reserve 170, 315
01/2 UD MVP 83
99/0 UD MVP Cup 212, ✂ GU, ✂ SGU, ✍ PS
99/0 UD Ovation 68
99/0 UD Prospects 6, C6, DS9, IN5, ✍ Sig.
01/2 UD Vintage 109
01/2 Victory 155
00/1 Louisville Panthers
98/9 Barrie Colts

SHYBUNKA, DEREK
97/8 New Mexico Scorpions

SIBR, DREW
85/6 U. of Arizona Ice Cats

SICAK, VLADIMIR
02/3 Cardset 117
98/9 OFS 200
99/0 Medicine Hat Tigers

SICARD, M
93/4 Soo Greyhounds 32

SICILIANO, PETE
91/2 Hampton Roads

SICINSKI, BOB
73/4 Quaker Oats 12

SIDELNIKOV, ALEXANDER
91/2 Future Trends C72 28
74 Hellas MM-Jenkki 56
73/4 Soviet Stars 3
74/5 Soviet Stars 3
73/4 Williams Finnish 16

SIDEROFF, DEAN
91/2 Air Canada SJHL A35

SIDORKIEWICZ, PETER
90/1 Bowman 255
91/2 Bowman 13
92/3 Bowman 162
93/4 EA Sports 96
92/3 Fleer Ultra 150, 367
92/3 Kraft / PB
90/1 OPC/Topps 14
91/2 O-Pee-Chee 296
92/3 O-Pee-Chee 175
89/0 OPC/Topps 11
92/3 OPC Premier 112
89/0 opcSticker 42-188, / FS 6
89/0 Panini Sticker 220
90/1 Panini Sticker 38
91/2 Panini Sticker 310
93/4 Panini Sticker 121
91/2 Parkhurst 286
92/3 Parkhurst 120
92/3 Parkhurst 450
91/2 Pinnacle 234
92/3 Pinnacle 371
93/4 Pinnacle 381
93/4 Pinnacle Mask 10
90/1 Pro Set 451
91/2 Pro Set 90
92/3 Pro Set 125
90/1 Score 46
91/2 Score 203
91/2 Score CAN 203
92/3 Score 41
92/3 Score 515
93/4 Score 102
93/4 Score PiAS 17
93/4 Score TF 14
90/1 Sco. Young Stars 4
92/3 Topps 332
91/2 To. Stadium 125
92/3 To. Stadium 27
93/4 To. Stadium - AS
90/1 Upper Deck 69
91/2 Upper Deck 325
92/3 Upper Deck 14
92/3 Upper Deck 480
89/0 HART / Jr. Whalers
90/1 HART / Jr. Whalers
91/2 HART / Jr. Whalers
96/7 Albany River Rats
97/8 Albany River Rats
94/5 Fort Wayne Komets 13
80/1 Oshawa Generals
81/2 Oshawa Generals
82/3 Oshawa Generals
83/4 Oshawa Generals

SIDOROVSKI, ALEXANDER
00/1 Mir 237

SIDYAKIN, ANDREI
00/1 Mir 149

SIEBERT, BABE
33/4 Anonymous 28
34-43 BeeHive-1 [Mont.]
35-40 Canada Starch
33/4 Canadian Gum
83 HHOF Postcard D14
83&87 HHOF 59
28/9 La Presse
33/4 O-Pee-Chee 49
37/8 O-Pee-Chee 150
55/6 Parkhurst 62
02/3 Parkie - Reprint 210
38/9 Quaker Oats
34/5 Sweet Caporal
33/4 WWGum 8 [Error: Seibert]
37/8 World Wide Gum 3

SIEG, GREG
00/1 Louisiana Ice Gators
01/2 Louisiana Ice Gators
02/3 Louisiana Ice Gators

SIEGEL, MARC
96/7 Johnstown Chiefs
97/8 New Mexico Scorpions

SIEKKINEN, ARI-PEKKA
98/9 Cardset 7, MM 1
99/0 Cardset 7, Puck. 2
00/1 Cardset 287
02/3 Cardset 118
97/8 Hockey-Box
91/2 Jyvas Hyva 25
92/3 Jyvas Hyva 70
93/4 Jyvas Hyva 134
95 Leaf Latkaliiga 4
93/4 Sisu 136
94/5 Sisu 50, N-6
95/6 Sisu 56, GG-7
96/7 Sisu MA-9
95/6 Sisu Limited 46

SIGNORETTI, ANDRE
00/1 Charlotte Checkers

SIGOUIN, MICHAEL
92/3 BCJHL 21

SIHVONEN, PERTTI
70/1 Kuvajulkaisut 255

SIHVONEN, PETTERI
92/3 Jyvas Hyva 141

SIHVONEN, TONI
98/9 Cardset 45, OD 2
99/0 Cardset 198, 230
00/1 Cardset 16, 237
02/3 Cardset 119
92/3 Jyvas Hyva 142
93/4 Jyvas Hyva 327
93/4 Sisu 45
94/5 Sisu 136
95/6 Sisu 211
96/7 Sisu 12

SIILANPÄÄ, TEEMU
98/9 DEL 306

SIIMES, RAULI
70/1 Kuvajulkaisut 341

SIISSALA, ARTO
71/2 Williams Finnish 294
73/4 Williams Finnish 212

SIITARINEN, JORMA
70/1 Kuvajulkaisut 223
71/2 Williams Finnish 145
72/3 Williams Finnish 205
73/4 Williams Finnish 119

SIIVONEN, HANNU
70/1 Kuvajulkaisut 238
78/9 SM-Liiga 153
71/2 Williams Finnish 256

SIIVONEN, JANNE
00/1 Cardset 304

SIKELA, LUBO
92/3 Semic Nordisk 217

SIKL, ZDENEK
96/7 Flint Generals

SIKLENKA, MIKE
02/3 BAP Mem. 384
02/3 Ultimate Mem. 81
02/3 UD Rookie 147
99/0 Hampton Roads
02/3 Philadelphia Phantoms

SILANDER, JUKKA
72/3 Williams Finnish 337

SILFWERPLATZ, JOHAN
00/1 Kudos 10
98/9 UD Elitserien 6

SILIUS, KARI
72/3 Williams Finnish 296

SILK, DAVE
84/5 O-Pee-Chee 16
80 Olympic USA
94/5 SR Miracle 31,32, ✍ 31,32
85/6 WINN
85/6 WINN / Safety Tips

SILLANPÄÄ, KARI
66/7 Champion 25
65/6 Hellas 13

SILLANPÄÄ, TEEMU
99/0 Eishockey 246
97/8 Hockey-Box
92/3 Jyvas Hyva 105
93/4 Jyvas Hyva 196
93/4 Sisu 261
94/5 Sisu 56
95/6 Sisu 285

SILLGREN, HARRI
98/9 Cardset 178
99/0 Cardset 90
00/1 Cardset 308
02/3 Cardset 269
93/4 Jyvas Hyva 328
93/4 Sisu 49
94/5 Sisu 112
95/6 Sisu 133, P-6
97/8 UD Elitserien 197

SILLINGER, MIKE
00/1 BAP Mem. 250
99/0 Crown Royale 130
93/4 Donruss 92
95/6 Donruss 219
02/3 First Ed. 275
92/3 Fleer Ultra 290
93/4 Fleer Ultra 311
95/6 Fleer Ultra 203
93/4 Leaf 306
94/5 Leaf 394
99/0 Millenium 223, ✍ Aut. 223
91/2 O-Pee-Chee 337
01/2 O-Pee-Chee 194
02/3 O-Pee-Chee 193
90/1 OPC Premier 107
99/0 Omega 219
98/9 Pacific 331
99/0 Pacific 396
01/2 Pacific 280
02/3 Pacific 106
02/3 Pacific Complete 228
97/8 Pacific CC 336
92/3 Parkhurst 38
93/4 Parkhurst 331
95/6 Parkhurst 274
01/2 Parkhurst 374
97/8 Pi. Be A Player 16, ✍ Aut. 16
95/6 Playoff 3, 225
96/7 Playoff 331
95/6 POG 22
93/4 Power Play 336
94/5 Premier 171
91/2 ProCards 130
91/2 Score 327
91/2 Score CAN 357
93/4 Score 651
90/1 7th..Sketch WHL 186
02/3 Signature 32, ✍ 32
02/3 Sports Vault 199
00/1 Stadium 82
00/1 Topps 173
01/2 Topps 194
02/3 Topps 193
98/9 To. Finest 28
02/3 To. Limited 193
91/2 To. Stadium 171
02/3 To. Total 158
90/1 Upper Deck 452
91/2 Upper Deck 457
92/3 Upper Deck 524
94/5 Upper Deck 22, 200
95/6 Upper Deck 72, SE-91
96/7 Upper Deck 349
97/8 Upper Deck 170
98/9 Upper Deck 147
00/1 Upper Deck 307
01/2 Upper Deck 282
02/3 Upper Deck 54
94/5 UD BAP ✍ 171
97/8 UD Coll. Choice 260
98/9 UD G. Reserve 147
01/2 UD Mask 25
99/0 UD MVP Cup 171
00/1 UD Vintage 159
02/3 Victory 63
01/2 COLU
96/7 VANC / IGA
87/8 Regina Pats
88/9 Regina Pats
89/0 Regina Pats

SILLMAN, TUOMO
71/2 Williams Finnish 185
72/3 Williams Finnish 135
73/4 Williams Finnish 191

SILLS, FRANÇOIS
94/5 DEL 238
95/6 DEL 114
96/7 DEL 59

SILTALA, MIKE
81/2 Kingston Canadians
82/3 Kingston Canadians

SILTANEN, RISTO
99/0 Cardset AH 5-risti
83/4 Funmate Puffy 14 [w/]
91/2 Jyvas Hyva 18
80/1 O-Pee-Chee 315
81/2 O-Pee-Chee 122
82/3 O-Pee-Chee 129
83/4 O-Pee-Chee 146
84/5 O-Pee-Chee 78
86/7 OPC/Topps 187
81/2 OPC Sticker 214
83/4 OPC/Topps Sticker 257
86/7 OPC Sticker 29-168
79 Panini Sticker 166
87/8 Panini Sticker 159
80/1 Pepsi Bottle Cap
82/3 Post [Edmo.]
82 Semic Sticker 157
94/5 Sisu 250
95/6 Sisu 140
95/6 Sisu Limited 92
78/9 SM-Liiga 5
78/9 SM-Liiga 51
83/4 Souhaits Keychain [Whalers]
77-79 Sports. FIN 75-1796
84/5 Topps 61
72/3 Williams Finnish 316
79/0 EDMO
80/1 EDMO / Zellers
81/2 EDMO / Red Rooster
81/2 EDMO / West Mall
88/9 EDMO / Action 48
82/3 HART / Jr. Whalers
83/4 HART / Jr. Whalers
84/5 HART / Jr. Whalers
85/6 HART / Jr. Whalers
85/6 QUÉB
85/6 QUÉB / Gene. Foods
85/6 QUÉB / McDonald's
86/7 QUÉB
86/7 QUÉB / Gene. Foods

SILVASTI, MIKKO
70/1 Kuvajulkaisut 320

SILVCHENKO, VADIM
93/4 Wheeling Thund'birds
94/5 Wheeling Thund'birds

SILVENNOINEN, JUHA
74 Hellas MM-Jenkki 16
80/1 Mallasjuoma 81
78/9 SM-Liiga 189
71/2 Williams Finnish 273
73/4 Williams Finnish 168

SILVER, CHAD
88/9 Regina Pats

SILVER, HARRI
71/2 Williams Finnish 239
72/3 Williams Finnish 223

SILVER, SHAWN
00/1 Kudos 71
93/4 Slapshot / Sudbury 1
93/4 Slapshot / Windsor 2
93/4 Sudbury Wolves

SILVERMAN, ANDY
95/6 Binghampton Rangers
96/7 Binghampton Rangers
92/3 Maine Black Bears
93/4 Maine Black Bears

SILVERSTONE, DAVID
01/2 Belleville Bulls

SIM, JONATHAN
99/0 BAP Mem. 65
97 Bowman 31
98 Bowman 15
98 Bowman Chrome 15
98/9 EBK IHL All-Star
99/0 NHL Power Play
99/0 Pacific 133
95/6 Slapshot 340
99/0 SP Authentic 101
00/1 Topps 324
00/1 To. Chrome 219
99/0 Ult. Victory 96
99/0 Upper Deck 47
99/0 UD Black Diam. 32
99/0 UD G. Reserve 47
99/0 UD MVP 66
99/0 Victory 92
00/1 DALL / Southwest
98/9 Michigan K-Wings
99/0 Michigan K-Wings
01/2 Utah Grizzlies

SIM, MIKE
95/6 Slapshot 263
00/1 Quad City Mallards

SIM, TREVOR
92/3 Canada Nationals
93/4 Canada Nationals
93/4 Fleer Ultra 473
93/4 Power Play 494
93/4 Premier - Canada 11
90/1 ProCards 230
90 7th..Sketch Mem.Cup 20
94/5 Milwaukee Admirals
89/0 Kamloops Blazers

SIMAKOV, ALEXEI
00/1 Mir 353

SIMANEK, JIRI
00/1 DS 82
99/0 OFS 188
00/1 OFS 21
01/2 OFS 143

SIMARD, MARTIN
91/2 Pro Set 526
90/1 ProCards 616
91/2 CALG / IGA
94/5 Milwaukee Admirals
96/7 Providence Bruins
88/9 Salt Lake G'Eagles
97/8 Springfield Falcons

SIMARD, MATHIEU
00/1 Rimouski Océanic 17
01/2 Val d'Or Foreurs 22

SIMARD, SÉBASTIEN
96/7 Rimouski Océanic

SIMCHUK, KONSTANTIN
98/9 Las Vegas Thunder

SIMCIK, JAN*
91/2 7th...Sketch LHJMQ 141

SIMEK, MARTIN
94/5 APS 81

SIMICEK, RADEK
01/2 OFS 23

SIMICEK, ROMAN
94/5 APS 130
95/6 APS 306
96/7 APS 202, 429
97/8 APS 132, 363
00/1 BAP Mem. 404
98/9 Cardset 65
99/0 Cardset 34, 163
02/3 Cardset 270
97/8 DS 10
96/7 DS Sticker 196
97/8 DS Sticker 255
01/2 O-Pee-Chee 219
99/0 OFS 268
00/1 Premier Plus 110
00/1 PS Titanium Draft 162
00/1 Signature 268, ✍ Aut. 230
00/1 SP Authentic 121
00/1 SP GU 80
00/1 SPx 170
00/1 Stadium 246
01/2 Topps 219
00/1 UD Heroes 176
00/1 Upper Deck 426
01/2 Upper Deck 89
00/1 UD Black Diam. 99
01/2 UD MVP 95
00/1 UD Pros&Prosp. 121
00/1 UD Vintage 391
01/2 Victory 178

SIMIONI, MARIO
92 Semic Sticker 262
84/5 Moncton G'Flames

SIMMER, CHARLIE
83/4 Funmate Puffy 8 [w/]
79/0 O-Pee-Chee 191
80/1 O-Pee-Chee 4
80/1 O-Pee-Chee 83
80/1 O-Pee-Chee 161
80/1 O-Pee-Chee 165
80/1 O-Pee-Chee 171
80/1 O-Pee-Chee 240
81/2 O-Pee-Chee 142
81/2 O-Pee-Chee 151
81/2 O-Pee-Chee 391
82/3 O-Pee-Chee 159
83/4 O-Pee-Chee 162
84/5 O-Pee-Chee 90
84/5 O-Pee-Chee 358
85/6 OPC/Topps 87
86/7 OPC/Topps 145
87/8 OPC/Topps 52
88/9 OPC/Topps 250
81/2 OPC Sticker 144
81/2 OPC Sticker 236
81/2 OPC Sticker 266
82/3 OPC/Topps Sticker 237
83/4 OPC/Topps Sticker 290
84/5 OPC Sticker 266
85/6 OPC Sticker 158-28
86/7 OPC Sticker 36-173
87/8 OPC Sticker 137-246
87/8 Panini Sticker 2
87/8 Panini Sticker 11
82/3 Post [LosA.]
90/1 ProCards 300
91/2 ProCards 333
83/4 Souhaits Keychain [Kings]
79/0 Topps 191
80/1 Topps 4
80/1 Topps 83
80/1 Topps 161
80/1 Topps 165
80/1 Topps 171
80/1 Topps 240
81/2 Topps 35
81/2 Topps 130 [West]
84/5 Topps 69
02/3 UD Foundations 40, ✍ SG
84/5 BOST
80/1 LOSA 11
87/8 PITT / Kodak

SIMMONS, DON
45-64 BeeHive-2 [Bost.]
45-64 BeeHive-2 [Bost.]
45-64 BeeHive-2 [Toro.]
64-67 BeeHive-3 [Toro.]
63-65 Chex
65/6 Coca-Cola
63/4 Parkhurst 2
63/4 Parkhurst 62
60/1 Shirriff 101
62/3 Shirriff 22
57/8 Topps 14
58/9 Topps 44
59/0 Topps 11
60/1 Topps 43
65/6 Topps 88
57/8 Toronto Star Photo
58/9 Toronto Star Photo
63/4 York 15
64/5 TORO

SIMMONS, GARY
74/5 Loblaws Update
74/5 O-Pee-Chee 371
75/6 O-Pee-Chee 29
76/7 O-Pee-Chee 176
78/9 O-Pee-Chee 385
75/6 Topps 29
76/7 Topps 176

SIMMS, BRAD
95/6 Slapshot 345

SIMMS, DAVID
01/2 Sheffield Steelers GS

SIMOES, STEFAN
90/1 7th..Sketch LHJMQ 148
91/2 7th...Sketch LHJMQ 197
94/5 Flint Generals

SIMOLA, JARI
72/3 Williams Finnish 352

SIMON, BEN
01/2 BAP Mem. 321
01/2 Upper Deck 420
01/2 UD Honor Roll 64
01/2 UD Premier 52
01/2 Chicago Wolves
02/3 Chicago Wolves

SIMON, CHRIS
00/1 Aurora 150
00/1 BAP Mem. 172
02/3 BAP Mem. 4
01/2 BAP Update ✂ TC21, ✂ TC27
93/4 Cla. 4 Sport 217
99/0 Dynagon Ice 204
96/7 Flair 100
93/4 Fleer Ultra 224
93/4 Fleer Ultra ARS 7
93/4 Leaf 416
94/5 Leaf 339
01/2 O-Pee-Chee 225
02/3 O-Pee-Chee 198
00/1 Pacific 429
01/2 Pacific 399, 425
02/3 Pacific 399
02/3 Pacific Complete 495
97/8 Pa. Invincible R-213

00/1 Pa. Paramount 249
99/0 Panini Sticker 171
93/4 Parkhurst 171
93/4 Parkhurst C13
00/1 Parkhurst P-63
93/4 Pinnacle 219
94/5 Pinnacle 506
97/8 Pi. Be A Player 65, ✍ Aut. 65
00/1 Premier Plus 38
00/1 Revolution 150
93/4 Score 473
96/7 Score 190
89/0 7th..Sketch OHL 56
91/2 7th...Sketch OHL 313
00/1 Signature 49
02/3 Signature GS-23
00/1 SP GU 60
00/1 Stadium 70
00/1 Topps 93
01/2 Topps 225
02/3 Topps 198
00/1 To. Chrome 74
98/9 To. Finest 99
00/1 To. Heritage 168
02/3 To. Limited 198
02/3 To. Total 82
00/1 UD Reserve 86
93/4 Upper Deck 243, SP-131
94/5 Upper Deck 299
97/8 Upper Deck 205, 387
00/1 Upper Deck 174
02/3 Upper Deck 177
94/5 UD BAP ✍ 58
96/7 UD Black Diam. 67
96/7 UD CC 66
97/8 UD Coll. Choice 269
96/7 UD Ice 73
00/1 UD MVP 179
00/1 UD Vintage 359, 369
00/1 Victory 240
01/2 Victory 353
92/3 QUEB / Petro-Canada
94/5 QUEB / Burger King

SIMON, DARCY
91/2 ProCards 71
92/3 Fredericton Canadiens
96/7 Grand Rapids Griffins
97/8 Grand Rapids Griffins

SIMON, DIETER
74 Hellas MM-Jenkki 116
79 Panini Sticker 250

SIMON, JASON
89/0 ProCards AHL 203
90/1 ProCards 569
91/2 ProCards 442
96/7 Las Vegas Thunder
89/0 Nashville Knights
86/7 London Knights

SIMON, JOEY
94/5 Slapshot / Brantford 9
93/4 Muskegon Fury
87/8 Sudbury Wolves

SIMON, JURGEN
94/5 DEL 194
95/6 DEL 178, 437
96/7 DEL 118

SIMON, TODD
93/4 Cla. Prospects 228
94/5 Donruss 16
95/6 Edge Ice 157
94/5 Pinnacle 491
94/5 Premier 469
94/5 Score 234
94/5 Select 195
90/1 7th..Sketch OHL 270
91/2 7th...Sketch OHL 211
94/5 To. Stadium 221
94/5 Upper Deck 456
00/1 UD DEL 162
01/2 UD DEL 73, SS4
97/8 Cincinnati Cyclones
98/9 Cincinnati Cyclones
99/0 Cincinnati Cyclones
96/7 Detroit Vipers
95/6 Las Vegas Thunder
92/3 Rochester Americans DD
92/3 Rochester Americans WPC
93/4 Rochester Americans

SIMONEN, SAMI
98/9 Cardset 158, OD 7
97/8 Hockey-Box
93/4 Sisu 177
94/5 Sisu 33
95/6 Sisu 77
96/7 Sisu 75

SIMONETTI, FRANK
98/9 BOST / Alumni 32

SIMONI, STEVE
92/3 Oklahoma City Blazers
83/4 Ottawa 67's
84/5 Ottawa 67's

SIMONOVIC, MIROSLAV
01/2 OFS 203, -CL 5, -G10

SIMONSON, DEREK
92/3 MPS SJHL 50

SIMONTON,
97/8 Hockey-Box

SIMONTON, REID
98/9 DEL 238
00/1 Kudos 38
01/2 UD DEL 14
99/0 UD Elitserien 76

SIMPSON, BOBBY
77/8 O-Pee-Chee 310
78/9 O-Pee-Chee 372

SIMPSON, BRIAN
97/8 Bell

SIMPSON, CRAIG
90/1 Bowman 201
91/2 Bowman 107
92/3 Bowman 150
93/4 Donruss 31
94/5 Donruss 112
92/3 Fleer Ultra 66
93/4 Fleer Ultra 277
94/5 Fleer Ultra 266
89/0 Kraft 16
90/1 Kraft 52
91/2 Kraft 81
93/4 Leaf 344
94/5 Leaf 198
87/8 OPC/Topps 80
88/9 OPC/Topps 27
90/1 OPC/Topps 240
91/2 O-Pee-Chee 460
92/3 O-Pee-Chee 225
89/0 OPC/Topps 99
88/9 OPC Stars 36
87/8 OPC Sticker 166-25
88/9 OPC Sticker 228
88/9 OPC Sticker 123-255
89/0 opcSticker 217
87/8 Panini Sticker 149
88/9 Panini Sticker 62
89/0 Panini Sticker 75
90/1 Panini Sticker 229
90/1 Panini/EDM 20
91/2 Panini Sticker 130
92/3 Panini Sticker 102
93/4 Panini Sticker 237
91/2 Parkhurst 54
92/3 Parkhurst 51
93/4 Parkhurst 19
94/5 Parkhurst V11
94/5 Parkie SE22
91/2 Pinnacle 196
92/3 Pinnacle 321
93/4 Pinnacle 396
94/5 Pinnacle 294
93/4 Power Play 301
93/4 Premier 231
93/4 Premier 333
94/5 Premier 349
90/1 Pro Set 95
91/2 Pro Set 69
92/3 Pro Set 56
91/2 Pro Set Platinum 40
91/2 Puck / Pro Set 9
90/1 Score 58
90/1 Sco. Hot Cards 2
91/2 Score 255
91/2 Score CAN 475
92/3 Score 260
92/3 Score SS 30
93/4 Score 139
93/4 Score 557
94/5 Score 54
92/3 Topps 356
94/5 Topps Finest RL-7
91/2 To. Stadium 137
92/3 To. Stadium 473
93/4 To. Stadium 305
90/1 Upper Deck 129
91/2 Upper Deck 286
92/3 Upper Deck 309
93/4 Upper Deck 430, SP-19
94/5 Upper Deck 50
94/5 UD BAP R77, R120, ✍ 122
95/6 UD CC 231
87/8 EDMO
88/9 EDMO
88/9 EDMO / Action 93
90/1 EDMO / IGA
91/2 EDMO / IGA
92/3 EDMO
92/3 EDMO / IGA 020
86/7 PITT / Kodak

SIMPSON, DAVE
82/3 Indianapolis Checkers

SIMPSON, GEOFF
93/4 Huntington Blizzard

SIMPSON, JOE
25-27 Anonymous 82
25-27 Anonymous 82
83 HHOF Postcard B12
83&87 HHOF 26
23/4 Paulins Candy 41

SIMPSON, KENT
00/1 Kudos 158
01/2 UD DEL 237
01/2 Sheffield Steelers GS

SIMPSON, PAUL
93/4 Humberside Hawks 5
94/5 Humberside Hawks 4

SIMPSON, REGAN
92/3 MPS SJHL 86

SIMPSON, REID
01/2 O-Pee-Chee 262
97/8 Pi. Be A Player 47, ✍ Aut. 47
89/0 ProCards AHL 354
90/1 ProCards 29
91/2 ProCards 272
99/0 Topps 87
01/2 Topps 262
99/0 To. Chrome 87
01/2 MONT
96/7 NJER / Sharp
99/0 Cleveland Lumberjacks

SIMPSON, SEAN
99/0 Eishockey 339

SIMPSON, SHAWN
88/9 ProCards / Baltimore
89/0 ProCards AHL 98
90/1 ProCards 215
87/8 Soo Greyhounds 13

SIMPSON, TERRY
90/1 WINN / IGA
91/2 WINN / IGA
95/6 WINN

SIMPSON, TODD
00/1 BAP Mem. 375, ✂ T-12
01/2 O-Pee-Chee 261
99/0 Pacific 61
97/8 Pacific CC 73
96/7 Pi. Be A Player 105, ✍ Aut. 105
00/1 Signature 93, ✍ Aut. 183
99/0 Topps 174
01/2 Topps 261
99/0 To. Chrome 174
97/8 Upper Deck 238
97/8 UD Coll. Choice 36
99/0 UD Retro 10
94/5 Saint John Flames
95/6 Saint John Flames
93/4 Saskatoon Blades

SIMPSON, TOM
74/5 OPC WHA 16
75/6 OPC WHA 81
72/3 Ottawa Nationals

SIMPSON, WADE
90 7th..Sketch Mem.Cup 83
89/0 7th..Sketch OHL 8
90/1 7th..Sketch OHL 345
91/2 7th...Sketch OHL 167
89/0 Oshawa Generals
90/1 Oshawa Generals
91/2 Oshawa Generals
91/2 Oshawa Generals
92/3 Oshawa Generals

SIMS, AL
74/5 Loblaws
74/5 O-Pee-Chee 333
75/6 O-Pee-Chee 136
79/0 O-Pee-Chee 272
80/1 O-Pee-Chee 233
81/2 O-Pee-Chee 131
81/2 OPC Sticker 66
89/0 ProCards IHL 138
90/1 ProCards 539
91/2 ProCards 261
75/6 Topps 136
80/1 Topps 233
81/2 Topps 85 [East]
92/3 Fort Wayne Komets 28
97/8 Milwaukee Admirals
98/9 Milwaukee Admirals
99/0 Milwaukee Admirals

SIMURDA, DAVE
82/3 Kingston Canadians
83/4 Kingston Canadians

SINAGL, PETR
00/1 OFS 183

SINASAC, TIM
00/1 Rimouski Océanic 2

SINCLAIR, DARREN
96/7 Syracuse Crunch
95/6 Spokane Chiefs 6

SINCLAIR, REG
45-64 BeeHive-2 [NYRa.]
51/2 Parkhurst 103
52/3 Parkhurst 104

SINDEL, JAROMIR
94/5 APS 70
91/2 Jyvas Hyva 49
92/3 Jyvas Hyva 155
98/9 OFS Leg. 18
00/1 OFS 81
82 Semic Sticker 78
89 Semic Sticker 179
93/4 Sisu 58, 329

SINDEL, ROMAN
95/6 APS 228

SINDELAR, FILIP
99/0 Score 50

SINDELAR, ROMAN
85/6 Minnesota-Duluth 21

SINDEN, HARRY
52/3 Anonymous 85
91/2 Future Trends C72 94, ✍ 94
83&87 HHOF 241
93/4 Legends of Hockey 33
66/7 Topps 31
59/60 Whitby Dunlops
91/2 BOST / SA Legends
98/9 BOST / Alumni 2

SINDLER, ZDENEK
98/9 OFS 161

SINGBUSH, ALEX
34-43 BeeHive-1 [Mont.]
40/1 O-Pee-Chee 114

SINGH, HARKIE
95/6 Slapshot 35

SINISALO, ILKKA
90/1 Bowman 112
99/0 Cardset AH 9-risti
80/1 Mallasjuoma 15
82 Mallasjuoma
00/1 Mir Fetisov 31
84/5 O-Pee-Chee 167
85/6 O-Pee-Chee 188
86/7 OPC/Topps 36
88/9 OPC/Topps 111
90/1 OPC/Topps 152
91/2 O-Pee-Chee 510
90/1 OPC Premier 108
86/7 OPC Sticker 238-108
87/8 Panini Sticker 136
88/9 Panini Sticker 325
90/1 Panini Sticker 123
82/3 Post [Phil.]
90/1 Pro Set 223, 461
90/1 Score 286, 93T
82 Semic Sticker 158
91 Semic Sticker 206
94/5 Sisu 90
95/6 Sisu 293
95/6 Sisu Limited 59
78/9 SM-Liiga 40
83/4 Souhaits Keychain [Flyers]
90/1 Upper Deck 120
83/4 PHIL / J.C. Penney
86/7 PHIL
89/0 PHIL

SINK, EDDIE
92/3 Fort Wayne Komets 32

SINKKONEN, JANNE
00/1 Cardset 197

SINKKONEN, KEIJO
66/7 Champion 99
72/3 Williams Finnish 184

SINKKONEN, MARTTI
66/7 Champion 101
65/6 Hellas 96
72/3 Williams Finnish 185

SINNER, STEPHAN
94/5 DEL 71
95/6 DEL 57
96/7 DEL 207

SIP, RADEK
94/5 APS 216
95/6 APS 167
96/7 APS 276
96/7 DS Sticker 187
99/0 Score 35
90/1 7th..Sketch WHL 141
91/2 7th...Sketch WHL 341

SIPCHENKO, IGOR
00/1 Mir 115

SIPILÄINEN, OLLI
00/1 Cardset 324

SIREN, ESA
71/2 Williams Finnish 159
72/3 Williams Finnish 112

SIREN, JAAKKO
66/7 Champion 105
65/6 Hellas 131
71/2 Williams Finnish 186

SIREN, JORMA
72/3 Williams Finnish 277
73/4 Williams Finnish 169

SIREN, NIKI
00/1 Cardset 212

SIREN, TEEMU
99/0 Cardset 215
00/1 Cardset 9

SIREN, VILLE
98/9 Cardset 30
99/0 Cardset MW 12
91/2 Jyvas Hyva 17
94/5 Leaf Elit Set 246
90/1 OPC/Topps 383
88/9 Panini Sticker 335
90/1 Pro Set 144
94 Semic 15
92/3 Semic Elitserien 181
91 Semic Sticker 9
92 Semic Sticker 8
93 Semic Sticker 59
94/5 Sisu 371
86/7 PITT / Kodak
87/8 PITT / Kodak

SIRKKA, JEFF
89/0 ProCards AHL 59
90/1 ProCards 406
91/2 ProCards 477
97/8 Cincinnati Cyclones
93/4 Portland Pirates
92/3 Rochester Americans DD
92/3 Rochester Americans WPC
85/6 Kingston Canadians
86/7 Kingston Canadians
87/8 Kingston Canadians

SIRKKOLA, RISTO
72/3 Williams Finnish 278

SIRO, JARMO
72/3 Williams Finnish 317

SIRO, JUKKA
72/3 Williams Finnish 318

SIROIS, ALLAN
98/9 EBK ECHL All-Star

SIROIS, BOB
76/7 O-Pee-Chee 323
77/8 O-Pee-Chee 351
78/9 O-Pee-Chee 96
79/0 O-Pee-Chee 29
80/1 O-Pee-Chee 313
78/9 Topps 96
79/0 Topps 29
78/9 WASH
79/0 WASH

SIROTA, JASON
91/2 Avant Garde BCJHL 64

SIRVIÖ, ARTO
92/3 Jyvas Hyva 92
93/4 Jyvas Hyva 179
80/1 Mallasjuoma 12
89/0 Semic Elitserien 278
90/1 Semic Elitserien 41
93/4 Sisu 175
94/5 Sisu 92
95/6 Sisu 292
96/7 Sisu 78

SISCA, DANIEL
01/2 Mississauga IceDogs
02/3 Mississauga IceDogs
00/1 Owen Sound Attack 14
01/2 Owen Sound Attack

SISKA, RANDY
84/5 Medicine Hat Tigers
83/4 Victoria Cougars
84/5 Victoria Cougars

SISTONEN, TEEMU
70/1 Kuvajulkaisut 224

SITTLER, DARRYL
99/0 BAP Mem. CH-3, ✍ CH-3
77/8 Coke
82/3 Dernière Heure
71/2 Eddie Sargent 204
72/3 Eddie Sargent 204
70/1 Esso Power Player
88/9 Esso All-Star
01/2 Fleer Legacy 62, ✂ HK, ✂ ITC
01/2 Fleer Greats 52, ✍ Aut., ✂ OSS
83/4 Funmate Puffy 10 [w/]
92/3 Future Trends C76 173, 175, 199, ✍ Aut.
75/6 Hockey Heroes
93/4 Hockey Wit 73
84/5 Kellogg's 33
91/2 Kraft 40
95/6 Legends of Hockey 67
74/5 Lipton Soup 3
74/5 Loblaws
73/4 Mac's Milk
99/0 NHL FANtasy (x3)
70/1 O-Pee-Chee 218
71/2 O-Pee-Chee 193
72/3 O-Pee-Chee 188
73/4 O-Pee-Chee 132
74/5 O-Pee-Chee 40
74/5 O-Pee-Chee 219
75/6 O-Pee-Chee 150
75/6 O-Pee-Chee 328
76/7 O-Pee-Chee 66
76/7 O-Pee-Chee 207
76/7 OPC 394
77/8 O-Pee-Chee 30
77/8 O-Pee-Chee NS 20
78/9 O-Pee-Chee 4
78/9 O-Pee-Chee 30
78/9 O-Pee-Chee 64
78/9 O-Pee-Chee 65
78/9 OPC 69
79/0 O-Pee-Chee 331
79/0 O-Pee-Chee 120
80/1 O-Pee-Chee 50
80/1 O-Pee-Chee 165
80/1 O-Pee-Chee 193
81/2 O-Pee-Chee 308
81/2 O-Pee-Chee 312
82/3 O-Pee-Chee 257
83/4 O-Pee-Chee 257, 258
83/4 O-Pee-Chee 272
84/5 O-Pee-Chee 168
92/3 O-Pee-Chee 191
92/3 OPC - Anniv. 8
81/2 OPC Sticker 97
81/2 OPC Sticker 109
82/3 OPC/Topps Sticker 114
83/4 OPC/Topps Sticker 3
83/4 OPC/Topps Sticker 191
84/5 OPC Sticker 108
85/6 OPC Sticker 36-167
80/1 O-Pee-Chee Super 20
92/3 Pinnacle 248
82/3 Post [Phil.]
90/1 Pro Set 404
84/5 7-Eleven
02/3 Signature GS-28
83/4 Souhaits Keychain [Flyers]
77-79 Sportscaster 47-18
77-79 Sports. FIN 53-1265
73/4 Topps 132
74/5 Topps 40
74/5 Topps 219
75/6 Topps 150
75/6 Topps 328
76/7 Topps 66
76/7 Topps 207
76/7 Topps NS 8
77/8 Topps 38
77/8 ToppsNS 20
78/9 Topps 4
78/9 Topps 30
78/9 Topps 64
78/9 Topps 65
78/9 Topps 69
79/0 Topps 120
80/1 Topps 50
80/1 Topps 165
80/1 Topps 193
81/2 Topps 36
84/5 Topps 121
01/2 To Archives 39, -Seat, ✍ CAI
71/2 Toronto Sun Photo
02/3 Ultimate Mem. ✂ GMIH, ✂ RT
90/1 Upper Deck 504
01/2 UD Legends 59, ✂ PoH
95/6 Zellers
84/5 DETR / Little Caesars
83/4 PHIL / J.C. Penney
70/1 TORO
71/2 TORO
72/3 TORO
73/4 TORO
74/5 TORO
75/6 TORO
76/7 TORO
77/8 TORO
78/9 TORO
79/0 TORO
80/1 TORO
81/2 TORO

SITTLER, RYAN
94/5 Cla. Images 65
93/4 Donruss USA19
93/4 Pinnacle 499
91/2 Upper Deck 695
93/4 Upper Deck 551
91/2 Upper Deck WJC 82
98/9 Charlotte Checkers
98/9 Charlotte Checkers
94/5 Hershey Bears

SITTLOW, CHRIS
93/4 Minnesota-Duluth

SIVEK, MICHAL
97/8 APS 17
98/9 OFS 369
00/1 OFS 312
99/0 SP Authentic 133
99/0 UD Black Diam. 116
99/0 UD MVP Cup 205
99/0 UD Prospects 59
02/3 WBS Penguins

SIVERTSON, DARYN
84/5 Kelowna Wings &...
85/6 U. of Arizona Ice Cats

SIVES, DEAN
85/6 U. of Arizona Ice Cats

SIVONEN, HEIKKI
66/7 Champion 173

SIVOV, ALEXANDER
99/0 Mir 243

SJERVIN, GRANT
94/5 Richmond Renegades
95/6 Richmond Renegades
96/7 Richmond Renegades

SJÖBERG, GORAN
89/0 Semic Elitserien 251
90/1 Semic Elitserien 161

SJÖBERG, LARS-ERIK
72 Hellas MM-Jenkki 27
74 Hellas MM-Jenkki 34
70/1 Kuvajulkaisut 37
69/0 Mästär Serien 42
79/0 O-Pee-Chee 396
74/5 OPC WHA 66
75/6 OPC WHA 109
76/7 OPC WHA 30
76/7 OPC WHA 63
77/8 OPC WHA 21
72 Semic Sticker 45
74 Semic Sticker 4
72/3 Williams Finnish 57
73/4 Williams Finnish 35
79/0 WINN
78/9 Winnipeg Jets

SJÖDIN, TOMMY
93/4 EA Sports 12
92/3 Fleer Ultra 323
93/4 Fleer Ultra 233
95 Globe 16
92/3 OPC Premier 109
95 Panini Worlds 139
92/3 Parkhurst 79
92/3 Parkhurst 224
92/3 Pinnacle 401
93/4 Power Play 65
93/4 Score 248
95 Semic 61
89/0 Semic Elitserien 30
90/1 Semic Elitserien 177
91/2 Semic Elitserien 336
92/3 Semic Elitserien 344
93 Semic Sticker 24
93/4 To. Stadium 106
92/3 Upper Deck 528
99/0 UD Elitserien 19, ✍ Aut.
00/1 UD Elitserien 32, 184
96 Wien 48, AS3

SJÖGREN, CHRISTIAN
01/2 Nottingham Panthers

SJÖGREN, THOMAS
99/0 Eishockey 273
94/5 Leaf Elit Set 46
90/1 ProCards 204
89/0 Semic Elitserien 229
91/2 Semic Elitserien 296
92/3 Semic Elitserien 323
95/6 Sisu 265, 382, S-5
96/7 Sisu 65, MA-5
95/6 Sisu Limited 52
00/1 UD DEL 32
98/9 UD Elitserien 140

SJOKIN, TOMMY
91/2 Semic Elitserien 31

SJÖKVIST, NIKLAS
97/8 UD Elitserien 54
98/9 UD Elitserien 91
99/0 UD Elitserien 60

SJOLUND, ANDREAS
95/6 UD CC 340

SJOMAN, ARI
73/4 Williams Finnish 320

SJOO, HASSE
89/0 Semic Elitserien 107

SJOROOS, RAUNO
80/1 Mallasjuoma 194

SJOSTEDT, BO
71/2 Williams Finnish 295

SJÖSTROM, FREDRIK
01/2 Calgary Hitmen

SKAARBERG, TOMMY
92/3 Semic Nordisk 86

SKAARE,
92/3 Semic Nordisk 197 [Draften Av NHL]

SKABELKA, ANDREI
98/9 Mir 74
00/1 Mir 164

SKALDE, JARROD
93/4 Cla. Prospects 192
95/6 Edge Ice 15
93/4 Leaf 333
97/8 Pi. Be A Player 198, ✍ Aut. 198
93/4 Power Play 11
92/3 Pro Set 231
91/2 ProCards 411
92/3 Score 392
91/2 Score CAN 282
90 7th..Sketch Mem.Cup 91
89/0 7th..Sketch OHL 2, 193
90/1 7th..Sketch OHL 346
92/3 Topps 84
00/1 To. Heritage 213
92/3 To. Stadium 189
91/2 Upper Deck 446
92/3 Upper Deck 91
93/4 Upper Deck 12
01/2 Chicago Wolves
98/9 Kentucky Tho'blades
94/5 Las Vegas Thunder
95/6 Saint John Flames
96/7 Saint John Flames
93/4 San Diego Gulls
99/0 Utah Grizzlies
89/0 Oshawa Generals

SKARDA, RANDY
90/1 ProCards 81

SKARPERUD, TIM
02/3 Grand Rapids Griffins

SKELLETT, JASON
89/0 7th..Sketch OHL 91
90/1 7th..Sketch OHL 216

SKENE, DAN
92/3 BCJHL 234

SKIEHAR, SHAWN
02/3 Louisiana Ice Gators

SKILLGARD, JOHAN
90/1 7th..Sketch WHL 223
90/1 Brandon Wheat Kings

SKILLITER, WILLIE
91/2 7th...Sketch OHL 275
93/4 Owen Sound Platers

SKILNICK, JASON
95/6 Brandon Wheat Kings

SKINNARI, VILLE
93/4 Sisu 285

SKINNER, ALF
24/5 Champ's Cigarettes
24/5 Maple Crispette [V130] 5
24/5 William Paterson 27

SKINNER, JIM
93/4 Parkie 56-57 63
80/1 DETR

SKINNER, KURT
92/3 Fort Wayne Komets 31

SKINNER, LARRY
76/7 COLR / Hockey Talk

SKJODT, CHARLIE
81/2 Indianapolis Checkers

SKOGLUND, EMIL
92/3 Semic Elitserien 162

SKOKAN, ALES
99/0 Score 58

SKOLD, JOAKIM
91/2 Semic Elitserien 250

SKOLNEY, WADE
02/3 Philadelphia Phantoms
98/9 Brandon Wheat Kings
99/0 Brandon Wheat Kings

SKOOG, ROBERT
89/0 Semic Elitserien 146
90/1 Semic Elitserien 224
91/2 Semic Elitserien 152
92/3 Semic Elitserien 175

SKOPAC, TONY
94/5 Leaf Elit Set 230
92/3 Semic Elitserien 89
95/6 UD Elitserien DS10

SKOPINTSEV, ANDREI
00/1 BAP Mem. 251
95/6 DEL 10
95 Panini Worlds 31
96 Wien 140
98/9 Cleveland Lumberjacks

SKOPTSOV, ALEX.
00/1 Mir 328

SKOREPA, ZDENEK
94/5 APS 214
99/0 DS 68
00/1 DS 120
98/9 OFS 271
99/0 OFS 158, 309
00/1 OFS 98
01/2 OFS 63
95/6 Slapshot 120
96/7 Albany River Rats
97/8 Albany River Rats

SKORODENSKI, WARREN
85/6 O-Pee-Chee 255
85/6 O-Pee-Chee 264
87/8 EDMO
88/9 EDMO / Action 131
85/6 Nova Scotia Oilers

SKOROHOD, ALEXANDER
01/2 Mississauga IceDogs

SKORYNA, CHRIS
91/2 7th...Sketch OHL 36
93/4 Slapshot / Guelph 18

SKOSYREV, SERGEI
90/1 O-Pee-Chee 496

SKOULA, MARTIN
99/0 BAP Mem. 314
00/1 BAP Mem. 29
01/2 BAP Mem. 283, ✂ SCC
99 Bowman 140
98 Bowman 22, 158, ✍ A39
98 Bowman Chrome 22, 158
99/0 Dynagon Ice 61
02/3 First Ed. 50, ✂ Jers.
99/0 Millenium C-14
01/2 O-Pee-Chee 151
99/0 Omega 68
00/1 Pacific 122
02/3 Pacific Complete 76
00/1 Pa. Paramount 64, ✂ GUS-6
00/1 Pr. Stock ✂ GUG 31
00/1 Signature 109, ✍ Aut. 90
01/2 Signature 106, ✍ Aut. 106
02/3 Signature GS-53
99/0 Stadium 187
00/1 Topps 48
01/2 Topps 151
00/1 To. Chrome 39
98/9 To. Finest F14
99/0 To. Prmr. Plus 132
00/1 To. Stars P9
02/3 To. Total 299
00/1 Upper Deck 47
98/9 Barrie Colts

SKOV, ELMER
52/3 Anonymous 10

SKOV, GLEN
45-64 BeeHive-2 [Detr.]
51/2 Parkhurst 57
52/3 Parkhurst 63
53/4 Parkhurst 48
54/5 Parkhurst 40
93/4 Parkie 56-57 23
54/5 Topps 16
57/8 Topps 30
58/9 Topps 3
59/0 Topps 12
76 DETR

SKOVIRA, MIROSLAV
95/6 APS 237

SKRASTINS, KARLIS
99/0 BAP Mem. 379
99/0 Omega 131
95/6 Sisu 326, 383
00/1 Topps 212
99/0 UD G. Reserve 344
01/2 UD Mask 52
98/9 Milwaukee Admirals

SKRBEK, PAVEL
95/6 APS 348
96/7 APS 82
97/8 APS 200
01/2 BAP Mem. 354
97/8 DS 91
97/8 DS Sticker 232
99/0 OFS 34
01/2 Parkhurst 325
99/0 Score JT9
01/2 SP Authentic 156
01/2 UD Challenge 116
01/2 UD Ice 78
01/2 Victory 378
00/1 Milwaukee Admirals

SKRIKO, PETRI
90/1 Bowman 54
91/2 Bowman 364
86/7 Kraft Sports 68
86/7 O-Pee-Chee 252
87/8 O-Pee-Chee 255
88/9 OPC/Topps 137
90/1 OPC/Topps 316
91/2 O-Pee-Chee 30
92/3 O-Pee-Chee 346
89/0 OPC/Topps 33, / Box D
87/8 OPC Leaders 40
86/7 OPC Sticker 103-232
87/8 OPC Sticker 192
88/9 OPC Sticker 64
89/0 opcSticker 70
87/8 Panini Sticker 347
88/9 Panini Sticker 140
89/0 Panini Sticker 147
90/1 Panini Sticker 298
90/1 Panini/VAN 22
90/1 Pro Set 306
91/2 Pro Set 8
91/2 Pro Set 517
90/1 Score 154
91/2 Score 188
92/3 Score 72T
91/2 Score CAN 188
89 Semic Sticker 44
91 Semic Sticker 204
92 Semic Sticker 12
93 Semic Sticker 79
91/2 To. Stadium 315
90/1 Upper Deck 147, 302
91/2 Upper Deck 334
84/5 VANC
85/6 VANC
86/7 VANC
87/8 VANC / Shell
88/9 VANC / Mohawk
89/0 VANC / Mohawk

SKRLAC, ROB
97/8 Albany River Rats
98/9 Albany River Rats
99/0 Albany River Rats
00/1 Albany River Rats
02/3 Albany River Rats
96/7 Kamloops Blazers

SKRUDLAND, BRIAN
90/1 Bowman 49
91/2 Bowman 331
93/4 Donruss 124
94/5 Donruss 130
96/7 Donruss 118
93/4 EA Sports 51
94/5 Flair 68
92/3 Fleer Ultra 111
93/4 Fleer Ultra 332
94/5 Fleer Ultra 85
95/6 Fleer Ultra 63
93/4 Kraft / PB
96/7 Kraft / PB
86/7 Kraft Sports 38
93/4 Leaf 325
94/5 Leaf 177
96/7 Leaf 69
87/8 O-Pee-Chee 235
90/1 OPC/Topps 270
91/2 O-Pee-Chee 349
92/3 O-Pee-Chee 45
89/0 OPC Sticker 38
88/9 OPC Sticker 54
98/9 Pacific 182
97/8 Pacific CC 295
97/8 Pa. Paramount 120
87/8 Panini Sticker 67
90/1 Panini Sticker 55
90/1 Panini/MTL 22
91/2 Panini Sticker 194
94/5 Panini Sticker 64
95/6 Panini Sticker 72
91/2 Parkhurst 314
92/3 Parkhurst 266
93/4 Parkhurst 75
95/6 Parkhurst 358
94/5 Parkie SE63
91/2 Pinnacle 160
92/3 Pinnacle 347
93/4 Pinnacle 188
93/4 Pinnacle CA9
93/4 Pinnacle Expa. 5
94/5 Pinnacle 21
96/7 Pi. Be A Player 205, ✍ Aut. 205
95/6 Pi. Summit 136
96/7 Pi. Summit 39
95/6 Playoff 43
94/5 POG 110
93/4 Power Play 100
93/4 Premier 26
93/4 Premier 508
94/5 Premier 265
90/1 Pro Set 159
91/2 Pro Set 127
91/2 Pro Set 306
90/1 Score 238
91/2 Score 294
91/2 Score CAN 514
92/3 Score 136
93/4 Score 258
93/4 Score 505
94/5 Score 53
95/6 Score 74
96/7 Score 133
94/5 Select 126
96/7 SP 64
92/3 Topps 408
91/2 To. Stadium 129
92/3 To. Stadium 114
93/4 To. Stadium 177
93/4 To. Stadium 349
94/5 To. Stadium 36
90/1 Upper Deck 93
91/2 Upper Deck 422
93/4 Upper Deck 96, SP-59
94/5 Upper Deck 331
95/6 Upper Deck 276
96/7 UD Black Diam. 64
94/5 FLOR / Health Plan
96/7 FLOR / Winn-Dixie
85/6 MONT
85/6 MONT / Provigo
86/7 MONT
87/8 MONT
87/8 MONT / Vachon 34
87/8 MONT / Vachon 36
88/9 MONT
89/0 MONT
89/0 MONT / Kraft
90/1 MONT
91/2 MONT
92/3 MONT
83/4 Nova Scotia Voyageurs
81/2 Saskatoon Blades

SKRYPEC, GERRY
90/1 7th..Sketch OHL 94
91/2 7th...Sketch OHL 296
93/4 Slapshot / Detroit 19
93/4 Slapshot / Niagara Falls 4
92/3 Ottawa 67's

SKUDRA, PETER
98/9 Be A Player 110, ✍ Aut. 110
01/2 BT Pipes 89
02/3 Between the Pipes 54
98/9 Bicycle.. 4-D
98/9 Pacific 358
99/0 Pacific 345
01/2 Pacific 38
02/3 Pacific 385
02/3 Pacific Complete 335
97/8 Pa. Revolution 114
97/8 SP Authentic 130
98/9 UD Choice 170
98/9 UD3 12, 72, 132
98/9 Upper Deck 165
98/9 UD G. Reserve 165
02/3 UD Mask 85, 86
99/0 WGretzky 141
94/5 Greensboro Monarchs

SKUGAREV, ALEXANDER
99/0 Mir 111

SKUHRAVY, VACLAV
00/1 OFS 131
01/2 OFS 179

SKUHROVEC, RADIM
99/0 OFS 332
01/2 OFS 180

SKUTA, VITEZSLAV
94/5 APS 122
95/6 APS 341
96/7 APS 196, 410
97/8 APS 128
97/8 DS 97
98/9 DS 65
99/0 DS 115
00/1 DS 160
96/7 DS Sticker 192
97/8 DS Sticker 15, 249
98/9 OFS 116, 319
99/0 OFS 391
00/1 OFS 242
01/2 OFS 40

SKVARIDLO, TOMAS
99/0 Kingston Frontenacs
00/1 Kingston Frontenacs 19

SKVORTSOV, ALEXANDER
83/4 Soviet Stars

SKYTTÄ, MIKA
98/9 Cardset 200
99/0 Cardset 116
00/1 Cardset 82

SLABY, LUKAS
99/0 OFS 63

SLABY, VACLAV
95/6 APS 229
97/8 APS 110

SLADOVNIK, JEREMY
98/9 Flint Generals

SLAMA, BOREK
01/2 OFS 272

SLANEC, JOSEF
99/0 OFS 400
00/1 OFS 315
01/2 OFS 213

SLANEY, JOHN
94/5 Donruss 298
96/7 Fl. Picks 154
94/5 Leaf 96
00/1 Pa. Paramount 201
93/4 Parkhurst 494
94/5 Parkhurst 257
95/6 Parkhurst 47
94/5 Pinnacle 214
96/7 Pi. Be A Player 100, ✍ Aut. 100
94/5 Premier 402
93/4 Score 636
94/5 Score 262
89/0 7th..Sketch OHL 185
90/1 7th..Sketch OHL 47
91/2 7th...Sketch OHL 1
94/5 To. Stadium 39, 113
90/1 Upper Deck 360, 457
94/5 Upper Deck 39
96/7 Upper Deck 301
91/2 Upper Deck WJC 54
99/0 WGretzky 142
98/9 NASH / Wendy's 19
97/8 PHOE / Coca-Cola
97/8 Las Vegas Thunder 9
02/3 Philadelphia Phantoms
93/4 Portland Pirates
00/1 WBS Penguins
91/2 Cornwall Royals

SLANINA, PETER
89 Semic Sticker 183
91 Semic Sticker 109

SLANINAN, PETER
82 Semic Sticker 99

SLANSKY, VACLAV
93/4 Red Deer Rebels

SLAPKE, PETER
99/0 Eishockey 415
74 Hellas MM-Jenkki 120
70/1 Kuvajulkaisut 99
79 Panini Sticker 252

SLATER, CHRIS
02/3 London Knights
93/4 Michigan State

SLATER, KEN
83/4 Kingston Canadians
84/5 Kingston Canadians

SLATER, PETER
72/3 Los Angeles Sharks

SLAVIK, JAN
99/0 OFS 53
00/1 OFS 92
01/2 OFS 53
98/9 Huntington Blizzard
96/7 Peoria Rivermen

SLAVIK, MICHAL
94/5 APS 11
95/6 APS 111
96/7 APS 274
96/7 DS Sticker 186
98/9 OFS 259
99/0 Score 140

SLAVIK, ROBERT
94/5 APS 95
95/6 APS 54
96/7 APS 240
97/8 APS 267
99/0 Score 109

SLAWSON, RANDY
82/3 Brandon Wheat Kings

SLEAVER, JOHN
52/3 Anonymous 177

SLEGR, JIRI
94/5 APS 209
97/8 APS 346
99/0 BAP Mem. 62
00/1 BAP Mem. 123
01/2 BAP Mem. 169, 447
98 Bonaparte 3D, 7A
98 Bonaparte Pexeso 13, 22
93/4 Cla. 4 Sport 249
93/4 Donruss 358
94/5 Donruss 294
99/0 DS NS4, P7
98/9 Dynagon Ice 153
92/3 Fleer Ultra 430
93/4 Fleer Ultra 136
94/5 Fleer Ultra 385
95 Globe 151
93/4 Leaf 31
94/5 Leaf 520
92/3 OPC Premier 54
98/9 OFS 233, -OW 9
99/0 OFS 35
98/9 Pacific 71
99/0 Pacific 346
00/1 Pacific 336
01/2 Pacific 24
02/3 Pacific 135
98/9 Pa. Paramount 196
96/7 Panini Sticker 263
99/0 Panini Sticker 132
92/3 Parkhurst 196
93/4 Parkhurst 214
94/5 Parkhurst V27
95/6 Parkhurst 344
01/2 Parkhurst P-145
94/5 Parkie SE189
93/4 Pinnacle 417
95/6 POG 110
93/4 Power Play 256
93/4 Premier 164
94/5 Premier 543
93/4 Score 378
99/0 Score JT7
94 Semic 182
94 Semic 343
91 Semic Sticker 106
92 Semic Sticker 131
00/1 Signature 110, ✍ Aut. 100
00/1 Stadium 113
91/2 Star Pics 29
98/9 To. Finest 46
93/4 To. Stadium 42
91/2 Upper Deck 18
92/3 Upper Deck 515
92/3 Upper Deck ER9
93/4 Upper Deck 18, SP-166
94/5 Upper Deck 95
95/6 Upper Deck 42
00/1 Upper Deck 143
01/2 Upper Deck 10
94/5 UD Be A Player R123, ✍ 119
95/6 UD CC 144
01/2 UD MVP 9
92/3 VANC / Road Trip
94/5 VANC
95/6 VANC / Abalene 11
01/2 Victory 16
96 Wien 113

SLEIGHER, LOUIS
83/4 O-Pee-Chee 301
84/5 O-Pee-Chee 290
83/4 Vachon 74-54
84/5 BOST
82/3 QUEB
83/4 QUEB

SLEIGHER, PIERRE-LUC
00/1 Victoriaville Tigres 11

SLEMKO, RYAN
90/1 7th..Sketch WHL 322

SLETNER, FRODE
92/3 Semic Nordisk 173

SLIVCHENKO, VADIM
00/1 UD DEL 217
01/2 UD DEL 87
95/6 Houston Aeros

SLIZ, GREG
84/5 Ottawa 67's

SLIZEK, LADISLAV
94/5 APS 268
96/7 APS 21
97/8 APS 147
96/7 DS Sticker 127
98/9 OFS 250, 393
99/0 Score 3

SLOAN, BLAKE
99/0 BAP Mem. 166
01/2 BAP Mem. 452
93/4 Donruss USA20
01/2 Heads Up ✂ JQ 24
99/0 Millenium 74, ✍ Aut. 74
99/0 Pacific 133
00/1 Pacific 140
02/3 Pacific Complete 408
93/4 Pinnacle 484
01/2 Pr. Stock ✂ GUG 33
00/1 PS Titanium ✂ GUG 91
99/0 Topps 124
99/0 To. Chrome 124
99/0 Ult. Victory 30
01/2 Victory 105
01/2 COLU
00/1 DALL / Southwest

SLOAN, TOD
45-64 BeeHive-2 [Toro.]
45-64 BeeHive-2 [Chic.]
48-52 Exhibits [Maple Leafs]
51/2 Parkhurst 87
52/3 Parkhurst 48
53/4 Parkhurst 5
54/5 Parkhurst 30
54/5 Parkhurst 98
55/6 Parkhurst 10
55/6 Parkhurst 77
57/8 Parkhurst [Toro.] 5
01/2 Parkhurst PR85
93/4 Parkie 56-57 112
93/4 Parkie 56-57 144
93/4 Parkie 56-57 168
93/4 Parkie 56-57 174
45-54 Quaker Oats
60/1 Shirriff 64
58/9 Topps 42
59/0 Topps 13
60/1 Topps 51
58/9 Toronto Star Photo
59/0 Toronto Star Photo
59/0 Toronto Star Weekend
91/2 Ultimate Original Six 42, ✍ Aut. 42

SLOAN, TYLER
02/3 Syracuse Crunch
00/1 Kamloops Blazers
01/2 Kamloops Blazers

SLOBODA, KAROL
01/2 Ottawa 67's 3

SLOBODIAN, PETE
34-43 BeeHive-1 [NYAm.]

SLOTA, KEVIN
95/6 Slapshot 176
99/0 Fort Wayne Komets

SLOTTE, ULF
66/7 Champion 213

SLOVAK, JURAJ
99/0 Greensboro Generals

SLOWAKIEWICZ, ANDRZEJ
74 Hellas MM-Jenkki 86
79 Panini Sticker 122
73/4 Williams Finnish 98

SLOWAKIEWICZ, JOSEF
74 Hellas MM-Jenkki 87
73/4 Williams Finnish 99

SLOWAKIEWICZ, TADEUSZ
79 Panini Sticker 119

SLOWINSKI, EDDIE
45-64 BeeHive-2 [NYRa.]
51/2 Parkhurst 102
52/3 Parkhurst 19

SLUKYNSKY, TIM
91/2 Air Canada SJHL C27
92/3 MPS SJHL 166

SLUPINA, ROMAN
96/7 APS 99

SLY, DARRYL
70/1 Eddie Sargent 221
70/1 Esso Power Player
70/1 O-Pee-Chee 115
70/1 Topps 115
68/9 TORO
70/1 VANC / Royal Bank

SLY, RYAN
95/6 Slapshot 386
96/7 Sudbury Wolves

SMAGIN, ALEXANDER
00/1 Mir 386

SMAIL, DOUG
90/1 Bowman 134
91/2 Bowman 118
92/3 Bowman 362
82/3 O-Pee-Chee 388
83/4 O-Pee-Chee 390
84/5 O-Pee-Chee 346
85/6 O-Pee-Chee 175
86/7 O-Pee-Chee 256
87/8 OPC/Topps 181
88/9 OPC/Topps 251
90/1 OPC/Topps 268
91/2 O-Pee-Chee 334
92/3 O-Pee-Chee 196
89/0 O-Pee-Chee 294
83/4 OPC/Topps Sticker 287
85/6 OPC Sticker 255-135
87/8 OPC Sticker 254-145
88/9 OPC Sticker 137-8
89/0 opcSticker 141-260
87/8 Panini Sticker 367
88/9 Panini Sticker 158
89/0 Panini Sticker 171
90/1 Panini Sticker 308
90/1 Panini/WPG 21
91/2 Panini Sticker 111
80/1 Pepsi Bottle Cap
92/3 Pinnacle 377
90/1 Pro Set 356, 462
91/2 Pro Set 117
91/2 Pro Set 466
90/1 Score 196, 69T
91/2 Score 12
91/2 Score CAN 12
91/2 Score CAN 592
92/3 Score 197
92/3 Topps 459
91/2 To. Stadium 255
92/3 To. Stadium 334
90/1 Upper Deck 105
92/3 Upper Deck 124
83/4 Vachon 136-16
92/3 OTTA
91/2 QUÉB / Petro-Canada
80/1 WINN
81/2 WINN
82/3 WINN
83/4 WINN
84/5 WINN / Safety Tips
85/6 WINN
85/6 WINN / Safety Tips
86/7 WINN
87/8 WINN
88/9 WINN / Safety Tips
89/0 WINN / Safeway

SMAILL, WALTER
91 C55 Reprint 27
10/1 Imperial
11/2 Imperial 27
11/2 Imperial 27
12/3 Imperial 22

SMALE, ANDREW
01/2 Mississauga IceDogs

SMALL, BRIAN
83/4 Belleville Bulls
81/2 Ottawa 67's

SMALL, JIM
99/0 Peoria Rivermen

SMALL, TODD
91/2 Air Canada SJHL A30

SMANIOTTO, LOUIS
79 Panini Sticker 384

SMARDA, JAN
98/9 OFS 311

SMART, CADRIN
91/2 7th...Sketch WHL 344

SMART, JASON
91/2 ProCards 305
92/3 Cleveland Lumberjacks
95/6 Toledo Storm
89/0 Saskatoon Blades

SMART, KELLY
97 Bowman 106
94/5 Slapshot Memorial 35
00/1 Austin Ice Bats
95/6 Brandon Wheat Kings

SMAZAL, HEIKO
95/6 DEL 292
96/7 DEL 319
98/9 DEL 259
99/0 Eishockey 319, 385
01/2 UD DEL 194

SMAZAL, MIKE
94/5 DEL 252

SMEATON, COOPER
83 HHOF Postcard C13
83&87 HHOF 42

SMEDSO, DALE
75/6 Cincinnati Stingers

SMEETS, PIERRE
79 Panini Sticker 339

SMEHLIK, RICHARD
94/5 APS 128
98 Bonaparte 2C
98 Bonaparte Pexeso 6
92/3 Classic 40
01/2 Crown Royale ✄ TT 5
93/4 Donruss 40
94/5 Donruss 136
95/6 Donruss 76
94/5 Flair 22
94/5 Fleer 27
92/3 Fleer Ultra 262, -UI 22
93/4 Fleer Ultra 200
94/5 Fleer Ultra 28
95 Globe 147
01/2 Heads Up ✄ JQ 23
93/4 Leaf 188
94/5 Leaf 306
95/6 Leaf 276
92/3 OPC Premier 90
98/9 OFS 230, -OW 12
98/9 Pacific 42
97/8 Pa. Invincible R-23
93/4 Panini Sticker 110
94/5 Panini Sticker 98
95/6 Panini Sticker 22
98/9 Panini Sticker 20
99/0 Panini Sticker 34
92/3 Parkhurst 14
93/4 Parkhurst 20
94/5 Parkhurst 28
92/3 Pinnacle 393
93/4 Pinnacle 152
94/5 Pinnacle 17
95/6 Pinnacle 187
97/8 Pi. Be A Player 74, ✍ Aut. 74
94/5 POG 52
93/4 Power Play 33
93/4 Premier 521
94/5 Premier 93
01/2 Pr. Stock ✄ GUG 13
00/1 PS Titanium ✄ GUG 62
93/4 Score 249
94/5 Score 129
94 Semic 168
92 Semic Sticker 129
00/1 Stadium 29
95/6 Topps 168
93/4 To. Stadium 107
92/3 Upper Deck 564
92/3 Upper Deck ER1
93/4 Upper Deck 169
94/5 Upper Deck 181
96/7 UD Ice 6
92/3 BUFF / Blue Shield
92/3 BUFF / Jubilee

SMELLE, CARL
52/3 Laval Dairy Update 81
52/3 St. Lawrence 34

SMELLE, TOM
52/3 Laval Dairy Update 84
52/3 St. Lawrence 21

SMERCIAK, MARIAN
94 Semic 193
96 Wien 223

SMETAK, MARTIN
94/5 APS 9
95/6 APS 339
96/7 APS 203
96/7 DS Sticker 207

SMICEK, JIRI
94/5 DEL 349

SMID, KAREL
94/5 APS 142
95/6 APS 246
96/7 APS 292
97/8 DS 21
96/7 DS Sticker 209
97/8 DS Sticker 52

SMID, ZDENEK
99/0 DS 16
00/1 DS 122, G11
99/0 OFS 532
00/1 OFS 161

SMILLIE, ROB
92/3 BCJHL 176

SMILLIE, STEVE
91/2 7th...Sketch OHL 367

SMIRNOV, ALEXANDER
95 Globe 170
92/3 Jyvas Hyva 179
93/4 Jyvas Hyva 326
90/1 O-Pee-Chee 499
91/2 O-Pee-Chee 60R
94 Panini Olympics 283
94 Semic 139
95 Semic 125
93/4 Sisu 39
93/4 Sisu 316
94/5 Sisu 77
96 Wien 139

SMIRNOV, ALEXEI
02/3 Atomic 103
02/3 BAP All-Star 127
02/3 BAP Mem. 300
02/3 Bowman 151
02/3 Calder 103
02/3 Cr. Royale 103, -RR 3
02/3 eTopps 44
02/3 Exclusive 194, ✍ 194
02/3 First Ed. 433 [Hobby]
02/3 Heads Up 126
02/3 In The G-U 196, ✄ C11
00/1 Mir 315
02/3 Pacific 126
02/3 Pacific Complete 582
02/3 Parkhurst 230
02/3 Parkhurst Retro 230
02/3 Pr. Stock Reserve 153, -CA 2
02/3 PS Titanium 104
02/3 Quest for the Cup 104
02/3 Signature 184, ✍ 184, ✄ SGJ56
02/3 SP Authentic ✍ 181, ✍ ✄ Patch
02/3 SP GU 66
02/3 SPx ✍ 146
02/3 Stadium 124
02/3 T. Chrome 178
02/3 To. Heritage 134
02/3 To. Total 418
02/3 Ultimate Mem. 30, ✄ CC, ✍ RAut
02/3 Upper Deck 227
02/3 UD Artistic 99
02/3 UD Classic 101
02/3 UD Foundations 144
02/3 UD Honor 101
02/3 UD Mask 177
02/3 UD Piece 122
02/3 UD Premier ✍ 71, ✍ Sig
02/3 UD Rookie ✄ 150
02/3 UD Top Shelf 122
02/3 Vanguard 103, -PP 2
02/3 Hamilton Bulldogs

SMIRNOV, ANDREI
89 Semic Sticker 83

SMIRNOV, OLEG
99/0 Mir 35

SMIRNOV, SERGEI
99/0 Mir 56

SMIRNOV, VASILI
00/1 Mir 88

SMIRONOV, ANDREI
99/0 Mir 198

SMIT, RICHARD
97/8 Louisiana Ice Gators

SMIT, SANDY
90/1 ProCards 373

SMITAL, LUKAS
96/7 Johnstown Chiefs

SMITH, ADAM
91/2 Avant Garde BCJHL 32
00/1 Kudos 148
93/4 Upper Deck E1
96/7 Binghampton Rangers
97/8 Hartford Wolf Pack
98/9 Hartford Wolf Pack
01/2 Sheffield Steelers GS
92/3 Tacoma Rockets
93/4 Tacoma Rockets

SMITH, AL
70/1 Eddie Sargent 161
71/2 Eddie Sargent 61
70/1 Esso Power Player
72/3 Post 19
70/1 O-Pee-Chee 87
71/2 O-Pee-Chee 27
76/7 O-Pee-Chee 152
79/0 O-Pee-Chee 300
80/1 O-Pee-Chee 252
77/8 OPC WHA 49
73/4 OPC WHA Poster 1
73/4 Quaker Oats 2
70/1 Topps 87
71/2 Topps 27
76/7 Topps 152
80/1 Topps 252
71/2 Toronto Sun Photo
69/0 TORO
72/3 New England Whalers

SMITH, ALEX (BOOTS)
25-27 Anonymous 22 [No Border]
25-27 Anonymous 22
33/4 Anonymous 47
33/4 Canadian Gum
36-39 Diamond Match TT1

SMITH, ALF
83 HHOF Postcard J15
83&87 HHOF 194

SMITH, B.
89/0 ProCards AHL 158

SMITH, BARRY
87/8 BUFF / Won. Bread
88/9 BUFF / Won. Bread
79/0 COLR
94/5 Erie Panthers
00/1 Kansas City Blades 24
93/4 Knoxville Cherokees
94/5 Knoxville Cherokees
96/7 Knoxville Cherokees

SMITH, BILL*
91/2 7th...Sketch OHL 96

SMITH, BILLY J.
93/4 Action Packed 3
01/2 BT Pipes 117, ✄ TW, ✄ VM, ✄ HSHSJers.
77/8 Coke
88/9 Esso All-Star
01/2 Fleer Greats 17, ✍ Aut.
01/2 Fleer Legacy 23, ✄ ITC
02/3 Fleer Throwbacks 54, 9SO, ✄ 9SO, ✍ Aut.
96/7 FLOR / Winn-Dixie
97/8 FLOR / Winn-Dixie
83/4 Funmate Puffy 19 [w/]
93/4 Hockey Wit 95
74/5 Loblaws
82/3 McDonald's Les Étoiles 4
82/3 McDonald's Les Étoiles 16
79/0 NYIS
83/4 NYIS
83/4 NYIS / News 23
83/4 NYIS / News 36
84/5 NYIS / News 27
84/5 NYIS / News 34
93/4 NYIS / Bank
99/0 NYIS / UD NY2
73/4 O-Pee-Chee 142
74/5 O-Pee-Chee 82
75/6 O-Pee-Chee 372
76/7 O-Pee-Chee 46
77/8 O-Pee-Chee 229
78/9 O-Pee-Chee 62
79/0 O-Pee-Chee 242
80/1 O-Pee-Chee 5
80/1 O-Pee-Chee 60
80/1 O-Pee-Chee 264
81/2 O-Pee-Chee 207
82/3 O-Pee-Chee 211
83/4 O-Pee-Chee 17
84/5 O-Pee-Chee 135
86/7 O-Pee-Chee 228
88/9 OPC/Topps 17
81/2 OPC Sticker 161
82/3 OPC/Topps Sticker 10
82/3 OPC/Topps Sticker 60
82/3 OPC/Topps Sticker 61
82/3 OPC/Topps Sticker 251
83/4 OPC/Topps Sticker 16
83/4 OPC/Topps Sticker 18
83/4 OPC/Topps Sticker 19
83/4 OPC/Topps Sticker 20
83/4 OPC/Topps Sticker 21
83/4 OPC/Topps Sticker 86
83/4 OPC/Topps Sticker 316
84/5 OPC Sticker 91
85/6 OPC Sticker 76-209
86/7 OPC Sticker 213-85
87/8 Panini Sticker 89
82/3 Post [NYIs.]
00/1 Premier Plus ✍ CS
83/4 Souhaits Keychain [Islanders]
97/8 SP Authentic ✍ M2, ✍ T2
73/4 Topps 162
74/5 Topps 82
76/7 Topps 46
77/8 Topps 229
78/9 Topps 62
79/0 Topps 242
80/1 Topps 5
80/1 Topps 60
80/1 Topps 264
81/2 Topps 93 [East]
84/5 Topps 101
01/2 To. Chrome -CA1, ✍ CA1
00/1 To. Stars 99, P4, P5, P6, ✍ CAI
01/2 T/O Archives 20, -Jers.
01/2 Ultimate Mem. ✄ RN, ✄ SCD, ✄ SCW
02/3 Ultimate Memorabilia ✄ CSTW, ✄ FS, ✄ Num, ✄ SCD
02/3 UD Foundations ✍ SG
01/2 UD Legends 45, 87, ✄ PoH, ✄ TT, ✄ TTC
01/2 UD Vintage ✄ GG, ✄ NL, ✄ SC

SMITH, BOBBY
90/1 Bowman 51
91/2 Bowman 117
92/3 Bowman 54
01/2 Fleer Greats 50, ✍ Aut.
92/3 Fleer Ultra 97
83/4 Funmate Puffy 14 [w/]
89/0 Kraft 26
90/1 Kraft 53
91/2 Kraft 82
86/7 Kraft Sports 39
79/0 O-Pee-Chee 206
80/1 O-Pee-Chee 17
81/2 O-Pee-Chee 157
81/2 O-Pee-Chee 170
81/2 O-Pee-Chee 174
82/3 O-Pee-Chee 175
82/3 O-Pee-Chee 176
83/4 O-Pee-Chee 181
84/5 O-Pee-Chee 273
85/6 O-Pee-Chee 181
86/7 OPC/Topps 188
87/8 OPC/Topps 48
88/9 OPC/Topps 88
88/9 OPC/Topps Box D
90/1 OPC/Topps 287
91/2 O-Pee-Chee 398
92/3 O-Pee-Chee 396
89/0 OPC/Topps 188
90/1 OPC Premier 109
81/2 OPC Sticker 88
82/3 OPC/Topps Sticker 188
83/4 OPC/Topps Sticker 116
84/5 OPC Sticker 151
84/5 OPC Sticker 152
85/6 OPC Sticker 132-252
86/7 OPC Sticker 13
87/8 OPC Sticker 10
88/9 OPC Sticker 46
89/0 opcSticker 47
87/8 Panini Sticker 62
88/9 Panini Sticker 261
89/0 Panini Sticker 236
90/1 Panini Sticker 52
91/2 Panini Sticker 113
92/3 Panini Sticker 96
91/2 Parkhurst 83
91/2 Parkhurst 217
91/2 Pinnacle 210
92/3 Pinnacle 142
81/2 Post 5
82/3 Post [Minn.]
90/1 Pro Set 160, 463
91/2 Pro Set 115
91/2 Pro Set 289
92/3 Pro Set 81
92/3 Pro Set 259
91/2 Pro Set Platinum PC13
90/1 Score 61, 75T
91/2 Score 32
91/2 Score CAN 32
92/3 Score 205
92/3 Score 446
83/4 Souhaits Keychain [North Stars]
79/0 Topps 206
80/1 Topps 17
81/2 Topps 37
81/2 Topps 55
81/2 Topps 131 [West]
84/5 Topps 83
92/3 Topps 388
91/2 To. Stadium 25
92/3 To. Stadium 427
01/2 T/O Archives 77, -Jers., -Seat
90/1 Upper Deck 72, 406
91/2 Upper Deck 293
02/3 UD Piece / Giveaway
83/4 Vachon 56-76
83/4 Vachon 56-86
78/9 MINS / Cloverleaf 5
79/0 MINS
80/1 MINS
81/2 MINS
82/3 MINS
83/4 MONT
84/5 MONT
85/6 MONT
85/6 MONT / Provigo
86/7 MONT
87/8 MONT
87/8 MONT / Kodak Poster
87/8 MONT / Vachon 26
87/8 MONT / Vachon 28
87/8 MONT / Vachon 30
87/8 MONT / Vachon 32
87/8 MONT / Vachon 41
87/8 MONT / Vachon 85
87/8 MONT / Vachon 86
88/9 MONT
89/0 MONT
89/0 MONT / Kraft

SMITH, BRAD*
81/2 O-Pee-Chee 103
87/8 Panini Sticker 335
80/1 Pepsi Bottle Cap
90/1 7th..Sketch OHL 200
80/1 CALG
86/7 TORO
86/7 TORO
87/8 TORO / 5x8
87/8 TORO / P.L.A.Y. 22
89/0 Windsor Spitfires

SMITH, BRANDON
90/1 7th..Sketch WHL 314
91/2 7th...Sketch WHL 27
00/1 SPx 93
00/1 Upper Deck 219
00/1 UD MVP 187
00/1 Victory 262
95/6 Adirondack Red Wings
01/2 Cleveland Barons
94/5 Dayton Bombers 17
98/9 Providence Bruins
99/0 Providence Bruins
00/1 Providence Bruins
89/0 Portland Winter Hawks
93/4 Portland Winter Hawks

SMITH, BRENT
89/0 Halifax Citadels

SMITH, BRIAN S.
60/1 Parkhurst 27

SMITH, BRIAN*
68/9 Bauer Photo

SMITH, CHRIS
83/4 Moncton Alpines
80/1 Oshawa Generals
81/2 Oshawa Generals
93/4 Michigan State

SMITH, CLINT (SNUFFY)
34-43 BeeHive-1 [NYRa.]
95/6 Legends of Hockey 59
39/0 O-Pee-Chee 35
91/2 Pro Set HHOF 6

SMITH, D.J.
00/1 Pacific 398
99/0 St. John's Maple Leafs
00/1 St. John's Maple Leafs
01/2 St. John's Maple Leafs
01/2 St. John's / Clarenville

SMITH, DALLAS
70/1 Eddie Sargent 16
71/2 Eddie Sargent 11
72/3 Eddie Sargent 19
70/1 Esso Power Player
72/3 Post 5
74/5 Loblaws
68/9 O-Pee-Chee 136
69/0 O-Pee-Chee 25
70/1 O-Pee-Chee 137
71/2 O-Pee-Chee 170
72/3 O-Pee-Chee 21
72/3 O-Pee-Chee 135
73/4 O-Pee-Chee 167
74/5 O-Pee-Chee 146
75/6 O-Pee-Chee 118
76/7 O-Pee-Chee 105
60/1 Shirriff 116
61/2 Shirriff 2
68/9 Shirriff / Bost. 13
61/2 Topps 4
61/2 Topps - Stamp
62/3 Topps 9
66/7 Topps 101
66/7 Topps / Test 3
67/8 Topps 41
69/0 Topps 25
72/3 Topps 45
73/4 Topps 42
74/5 Topps 146
75/6 Topps 118
76/7 Topps 105
71/2 Toronto Sun Photo
70/1 BOST
71/2 BOST
98/9 BOST / Alumni 20

SMITH, DAMIAN
94 Semic 319
96/7 Guildford Flames 13

SMITH, DAN
99/0 BAP Mem. 279
98/9 Hershey Bears
00/1 Hershey Bears
95/6 Tri-City Americans 17

SMITH, DARCY
97/8 Peoria Rivermen
98/9 Peoria Rivermen
96/7 Kamloops Blazers
93/4 Seattle Thunderbirds

SMITH, DARIN
88/9 ProCards / Peoria
89/0 ProCards IHL 9
90/1 ProCards 591
91/2 ProCards 248
95/6 Fort Wayne Komets
90/1 Kansas City Blades
85/6 London Knights

SMITH, DAVE
94/5 Binghampton Rangers
92/3 Fort Wayne Komets 24
93/4 Fort Wayne Komets 19
94/5 Fort Wayne Komets 23

SMITH, DEAN
94/5 Sheffield Steelers 4

SMITH, DENIS (D.J.)
97 Bowman 37
95/6 Classic 36, 98
95/6 Cla. 5 Sport 155
97/8 Donruss 206
97/8 Do. Canadian 142
97/8 Limited 37
94/5 Slapshot / Windsor 7
95/6 Slapshot 410
97/8 Upper Deck 194
97/8 St. John's Maple Leafs

SMITH, DENIS**
52/3 Bas du Fleuve 6
52/3 Laval Dairy Update 12
52/3 St. Lawrence 42

SMITH, DENNIS*
88/9 ProCards / Adirondack
89/0 ProCards AHL 96
91/2 ProCards 54
96/7 Michigan K-Wings
81/2 Kingston Canadians
82/3 Kingston Canadians
83/4 Kingston Canadians

SMITH, DEREK
78/9 O-Pee-Chee 222
79/0 O-Pee-Chee 89
80/1 O-Pee-Chee 199
81/2 O-Pee-Chee 25
82/3 O-Pee-Chee 95
81/2 OPC Sticker 59
82/3 Post [Detr.]
78/9 Topps 222
79/0 Topps 89
80/1 Topps 199
81/2 Topps 79 [East]
80/1 BUFF / Wendt's 2
98/9 Huntington Blizzard

SMITH, DERRICK
91/2 Bowman 245
95/6 Edge Ice 142
90/1 O-Pee-Chee 463
91/2 O-Pee-Chee 486
92/3 O-Pee-Chee 363
87/8 Panini Sticker 135
89/0 Panini Sticker 304
91/2 Panini Sticker 232
90/1 Pro Set 503
91/2 Pro Set 174
91/2 Score CAN 444
86/7 PHIL
89/0 PHIL
90/1 PHIL
96/7 Michigan K-Wings

SMITH, DES
34-43 BeeHive-1 [Maroons]
35-40 Canada Starch
37/8 O-Pee-Chee 148
39/0 O-Pee-Chee 77

SMITH, DON A.
91 C55 Reprint 19
10/1 Imperial
11/2 Imperial 19
12/3 Imperial 12

SMITH, DON2
01/2 Florida Everblades

SMITH, DOUG
82/3 O-Pee-Chee 160
84/5 O-Pee-Chee 91
86/7 O-Pee-Chee 202
90/1 OPC/Topps 326
82/3 Post [LosA.]
86/7 BUFF / Blue Shield
87/8 BUFF / Blue Shield
87/8 BUFF / Won. Bread
88/9 EDMO / Action 69
84/5 LOSA / Smokey 15
89/0 VANC / Mohawk
97/8 Central Texas
91/2 Ferris State Bulldogs

SMITH, ED
84/5 Sudbury Wolves

SMITH, FIONA
97/8 UD Coll. Choice 293

SMITH, FLOYD
45-64 BeeHive-2 [Detr.]
64-67 BeeHive-3 [Detr.]
64-67 BeeHive-3 [Detr.]
64-67 BeeHive-3 [Detr.]
64/5 Coke/Sprite [Detr.]
65/6 Coca-Cola
70/1 Dad's Cookies
70/1 Eddie Sargent 30
70/1 Esso Power Player
62/3 Cowan Tile
68/9 O-Pee-Chee 130
69/0 O-Pee-Chee 49
70/1 O-Pee-Chee 140
71/2 O-Pee-Chee 158
74/5 O-Pee-Chee 176
63/4 Parkhurst 57
95/6 Parkie 66-67 52
94/5 Parkie Tall 45
68/9 Post Marble
68/9 Shirriff / Toro. 12
64/5 Topps 42
65/6 Topps 109
66/7 Topps 106
67/8 Topps 52
68/9 Topps 130
69/0 Topps 49
74/5 Topps 176
64/5 Toronto Star Action
63/4 York 42
68/9 TORO
69/0 TORO
79/0 TORO

SMITH, FRANK D.
83 HHOF Postcard G13
83&87 HHOF 103

SMITH, GAIRIN
89/0 7th..Sketch OHL 65
90/1 7th..Sketch OHL 217
91/2 7th...Sketch OHL 100
96/7 Carolina Monarchs
93/4 Roanoke Express
94/5 Wheeling Thund'birds

SMITH, GARY (SUITCASE)
70/1 Colgate 90
70/1 Eddie Sargent 129
71/2 Eddie Sargent 43
72/3 Eddie Sargent 61
70/1 Esso Power Player
74/5 Lipton Soup 15
74/5 Loblaws
68/9 O-Pee-Chee 176
69/0 O-Pee-Chee 78
70/1 O-Pee-Chee 69
71/2 O-Pee-Chee Book. 22
72/3 O-Pee-Chee 117
72/3 O-Pee-Chee 155
73/4 O-Pee-Chee 126
74/5 O-Pee-Chee 22
75/6 O-Pee-Chee 115
76/7 O-Pee-Chee 317
77/8 O-Pee-Chee 184
79/0 O-Pee-Chee 103
72 Semic Sticker 171
68/9 Shirriff / Oakl. 6
69/0 Topps 78
70/1 Topps 69
71/2 Topps 124
72/3 Topps 114
72/3 Topps 173
73/4 Topps 126
74/5 Topps 22
75/6 Topps 115
77/8 Topps 184
79/0 Topps 103
71/2 Toronto Sun Photo
73/4 VANC / Royal Bank
74/5 VANC / Royal Bank
75/6 VANC / Royal Bank
79/0 WINN

SMITH, GEOFF
90/1 Bowman 192
91/2 Bowman 112
92/3 Bowman 95
93/4 Donruss 112
93/4 Donruss 435
93/4 Leaf 302
94/5 Leaf 366
90/1 OPC/Topps 33
91/2 O-Pee-Chee 301
92/3 O-Pee-Chee 338
90/1 Panini/EDM 21
94/5 Parkhurst 82
91/2 Pinnacle 283
92/3 Pinnacle 192
93/4 Pinnacle 416
94/5 Pinnacle 354
90/1 Pro Set 446
91/2 Pro Set 384
90/1 Score 326, 373
91/2 Score 87
91/2 Score CAN 87
92/3 Score 192
93/4 Score 306
93/4 Score 646
92/3 Topps 275
91/2 To. Stadium 42
92/3 To. Stadium 84
90/1 Upper Deck 326
94/5 Upper Deck 109
93/4 EDMO / Sheet
90/1 EDMO / IGA
91/2 EDMO / IGA
92/3 EDMO
92/3 EDMO / IGA 021
96/7 Carolina Monarchs
98/9 Cincinnati Cyclones
97/8 Hartford Wolf Pack

SMITH, GORD
76/7 O-Pee-Chee 303
77/8 O-Pee-Chee 387
78/9 O-Pee-Chee 347
79/0 O-Pee-Chee 285
74/5 WASH
78/9 WASH
79/0 WINN

SMITH, GORD
82/3 Brandon Wheat Kings

SMITH, GREG
77/8 O-Pee-Chee 269
78/9 O-Pee-Chee 303
79/0 O-Pee-Chee 11
81/2 O-Pee-Chee 168
82/3 O-Pee-Chee 96
83/4 O-Pee-Chee 130
84/5 O-Pee-Chee 64
83/4 OPC/Topps Sticker 140
87/8 Panini Sticker 172
82/3 Post [Detr.]
83/4 Souhaits Keychain [Red Wings]
79/0 Topps 11
81/2 Topps 112 [West]
84/5 DETR / Little Caesars
85/6 DETR / Little Caesars
78/9 MINS / Cloverleaf 3
80/1 MINS
86/7 WASH / Kodak
86/7 WASH / Police
87/8 WASH
87/8 WASH / Kodak
97/8 Central Texas
98/9 Wichita Thunder

SMITH, J. STEVE
90/1 Bowman 200
91/2 Bowman 106
92/3 Bowman 24
91 Canada Cup
93/4 Donruss 68
94/5 Donruss 183
95/6 Donruss 179
93/4 EA Sports 26
94/5 Flair 37
94/5 Fleer 46
02/3 Fleer Throwbacks 14
92/3 Fleer Ultra 42
93/4 Fleer Ultra 231
94/5 Fleer Ultra 45
95 Globe 78
89/0 Kraft 17
91/2 Kraft 85
93/4 Leaf 95
94/5 Leaf 257
95/6 Leaf 194
88/9 O-Pee-Chee 252
90/1 OPC/Topps 368
91/2 O-Pee-Chee 21
92/3 O-Pee-Chee 108
89/0 O-Pee-Chee 228
91/2 OPC Premier 136
88/9 OPC Sticker 225-99
89/0 opcSticker 223-82
97/8 Pa. Dynagon BKS-22
99/0 Pa. Paramount 42
87/8 Panini Sticker 259
88/9 Panini Sticker 55
89/0 Panini Sticker 83
90/1 Panini Sticker 226
90/1 Panini/EDM 22
91/2 Panini Sticker 121
92/3 Panini Sticker 12
93/4 Panini Sticker 154
99/0 Panini Sticker 188
91/2 Parkhurst 31
92/3 Parkhurst 32
92/3 Parkhurst 444
93/4 Parkhurst 310
95/6 Parkhurst 43
91/2 Pinnacle 18
92/3 Pinnacle 57
93/4 Pinnacle 70
94/5 Pinnacle 211
95/6 Pinnacle 191
94/5 POG 74
93/4 Power Play 55
93/4 Premier 39
94/5 Premier 133
90/1 Pro Set 96
91/2 Pro Set 73
91/2 Pro Set 284
91/2 Pro Set 370
92/3 Pro Set 37
91/2 Pro Set Platinum 27
90/1 Score 129
91/2 Score 11
91/2 Score 73T
91/2 Score CAN 11
91/2 Score CAN 623
92/3 Score 48
93/4 Score 192
94/5 Score 121
95/6 Score 27
94 Semic 85
95 Semic 81
92 Semic Sticker 79
92/3 Topps 315
95/6 Topps 205
99/0 Topps 62
99/0 To. Chrome 62
94/5 Topps Finest RL-12
91/2 To. Stadium 230
92/3 To. Stadium 383
93/4 To. Stadium 218
90/1 Upper Deck 148
91/2 Upper Deck 350
94/5 UD BAP R62
95/6 UD BAP 123, ✍ S123
91/2 CHIC / Coke
93/4 CHIC / Coke
85/6 EDMO / Red Rooster
86/7 EDMO
86/7 EDMO / Red Rooster
87/8 EDMO
88/9 EDMO
88/9 EDMO / Action 121
90/1 EDMO / IGA
83/4 Moncton Alpines
84/5 Nova Scotia Oilers
88/9 Salt Lake G'Eagles

SMITH, JARRETT
97 Bowman 122, BB15, ✍ Aut.
01/2 Cincinnati Mighty Ducks

SMITH, JASON
98/9 Be A Player 139, ✍ Aut. 139
92/3 Classic 10
92/3 Classic Four Sport 159
93/4 Cla. Prospects 135
93/4 Donruss 182
94/5 Donruss 256
95/6 Donruss 279
02/3 Exclusive 72
02/3 First Ed. 280
93/4 Fleer Ultra 363
93/4 Fleer Ultra WotF 17
94/5 Fleer Ultra 322
93/4 Leaf 389
94/5 Leaf 245
01/2 O-Pee-Chee 182
02/3 O-Pee-Chee 75
98/9 Pacific 421
01/2 Pacific 165
02/3 Pacific Complete 281
97/8 Pa. Invincible R-196
93/4 Parkhurst 379
94/5 Parkhurst 130
02/3 Parkhurst 168
93/4 Pinnacle 433
94/5 Pinnacle 417
97/8 Pi. Be A Player 191, ✍ Aut. 191
93/4 Power Play 381
94/5 Premier 344
93/4 Score 613
90/1 7th..Sketch WHL 62
91/2 7th...Sketch WHL 226
91/2 7th...Sketch WHL 309
02/3 Sports Vault 228
00/1 Topps 258
01/2 Topps 182
02/3 Topps 75
01/2 To. Chrome 121
02/3 To. Limited 75
94/5 To. Stadium 83
02/3 To. Total 247
93/4 Upper Deck 252
02/3 Upper Deck 319
02/3 UD Honor 82
99/0 WGretzky 70
96/7 NJER / Sharp
94/5 Erie Panthers
96/7 Saint John Flames

SMITH, JEFF1
83/4 Springfield Indians 17

SMITH, JEFF2
90/1 7th..Sketch OHL 218
91/2 7th...Sketch OHL 290
99/0 San Angelo Outlaws

SMITH, JEFF3
00/1 Red Deer Rebels

SMITH, JEFF4
02/3 Hull Olympiques

SMITH, JERAD
97/8 Portland Winter Hawks

SMITH, JIM
92/3 Wheeling Thund'birds 20
87/8 Sudbury Wolves
88/9 Sudbury Wolves

SMITH, JOEL
82/3 North Bay Centennials

SMITH, JOHN*
51/2 Laval Dairy 44

SMITH, JON
88/9 ProCards / Binghampton
89/0 ProCards AHL 296

SMITH, KEN
45-64 BeeHive-2 [Bost.]

SMITH, KENTON
98/9 Calgary Hitmen 4
99/0 Calgary Hitmen

SMITH, MARCUS
01/2 Kitchener Rangers

SMITH, MARK
00/1 BAP Mem. 425
98 Bowman 70
98 Bowman Chrome 70
00/1 PS Titanium Draft 173
00/1 SP Authentic 122
00/1 SP GU 81
00/1 SPx 171
00/1 UD Reserve 112
00/1 Upper Deck 419
00/1 UD Ice 121
00/1 UD Pros&Prosp. 122
98/9 Kentucky Tho'blades
99/0 Kentucky Tho'blades
00/1 Kentucky Tho'blades
99/0 Odessa Jackalopes
95/6 Lethbridge Hurricanes

SMITH, MARTIN
91/2 Air Canada SJHL 4
91/2 Air Canada SJHL B29
92/3 Richmond Renegades

SMITH, MATT
00/1 Cardset 153
91/2 7th...Sketch WHL 63
99/0 Peoria Rivermen

SMITH, MIKE1
93/4 Classic 82
93/4 Cla. Prospects 244
93/4 Roanoke Express
94/5 Roanoke Express
95/6 Roanoke Express
96/7 Roanoke Express 4
91/2 L. Superior State Lakers

SMITH, MIKE2
99/0 Kingston Frontenacs
01/2 Kingston Frontenacs 17
00/1 Sudbury Wolves 23

SMITH, NATHAN
00/1 UD Prospects 68, FL8
02/3 Manitoba Moose

SMITH, NEIL
01/2 Belleville Bulls Update

SMITH, NEIL**
92/3 W. Michigan Broncos

SMITH, NICK
01/2 BAP Mem. 359
02/3 Pacific 159
01/2 UD Honor Roll 74
01/2 UD Ice 138
99/0 Louisville Panthers
98/9 Barrie Colts

SMITH, NORMAN E.
34-43 BeeHive-1 [Detr.]
37/8 World Wide Gum 74

SMITH, RANDY
92 COA Winter Olympics 193
90/1 Canada Nationals 18
91/2 Canada Nationals
88/9 ProCards / Kalamazoo
89/0 ProCards IHL 87
92/3 Score COH 4
93/4 Las Vegas Thunder
83/4 Saskatoon Blades

SMITH, REG (HOOLEY)
35/6 Amalgamated Press
25-27 Anonymous 21
34-43 BeeHive-1 [Maroons]
24/5 Champ's Cigarettes
25 Dominion Chocolates 69 [Error: Hooly]
83 HHOF Postcard C14
83&87 HHOF 43
29/0 La Presse
95/6 Legends of Hockey 62
33/4 O-Pee-Chee 69
35/6 O-Pee-Chee 76
36/7 O-Pee-Chee 132
39/0 O-Pee-Chee 17
34/5 Sweet Caporal
23 Willards Chocolates 47
24/5 William Paterson 5
33/4 WWGum Premium 6
33/4 WWGum 31
37/8 World Wide Gum 20

SMITH, RICK
70/1 Eddie Sargent 11
71/2 Eddie Sargent 5
70/1 Esso Power Player
70/1 O-Pee-Chee 135
71/2 O-Pee-Chee 174
72/3 O-Pee-Chee 23
72/3 O-Pee-Chee 284
76/7 O-Pee-Chee 269
77/8 O-Pee-Chee 104
78/9 O-Pee-Chee 164
79/0 O-Pee-Chee 59
75/6 OPC WHA 41
72/3 Topps 34
77/8 Topps 104
78/9 Topps 164
79/0 Topps 59
71/2 Toronto Sun Photo
70/1 BOST
71/2 BOST
80/1 WASH
74/5 Minn. Fight. Saints
83/4 Saskatoon Blades

SMITH, ROB
01/2 Calgary Hitmen

SMITH, RON
91/2 ProCards 212
95/6 Cincinnati Cyclones
96/7 Cincinnati Cyclones
97/8 Cincinnati Cyclones
98/9 Cincinnati Cyclones
99/0 Cincinnati Cyclones
00/1 Cincinnati Cyclones

SMITH, RUSSELL
96/7 Rimouski Océanic

SMITH, RYAN*
91/2 Air Canada SJHL C11
90/1 7th..Sketch WHL 131
91/2 7th...Sketch WHL 205
92/3 Brandon Wheat Kings
93/4 Lethbridge Hurricanes

SMITH, SANDY
99/0 Eishockey 60
91/2 ProCards 299
92/3 Cleveland Lumberjacks
95/6 Minnesota Moose

SMITH, SCOTT
99/0 Sudbury Wolves 22
93/4 N. Michigan Wildcats

SMITH, SHAWN
99/0 Rockford IceHogs
00/1 Rockford IceHogs

SMITH, SID
45-64 BeeHive-2 [Toro.]
48-52 Exhibits [Maple Leafs]
51/2 Parkhurst 84
52/3 Parkhurst 45
53/4 Parkhurst 2
54/5 Parkhurst 22
55/6 Parkhurst 2
55/6 Parkhurst 75
57/8 Parkhurst [Toro.] 10
93/4 Parkie 56-57 109
45-54 Quaker Oats
57/8 Toronto Star Photo
91/2 Ultimate Original Six 43, ✍ Aut. 43
59/60 Whitby Dunlops

SMITH, SIMON
97/8 Guildford Flames
98/9 Guildford Flames

SMITH, STEVE*
88/9 ProCards / Rochester
89/0 ProCards AHL 272
90/1 ProCards 287

SMITH, STEVE**
90 7th..Sketch Mem.Cup 37
90/1 7th..Sketch OHL 199, 240

SMITH, STEVE2
83/4 Springfield Indians 22
80/1 Soo Greyhounds
81/2 Soo Greyhounds
82/3 Soo Greyhounds

SMITH, STEVE3
91/2 7th...Sketch OHL 187
89/0 Kitchener Rangers
90/1 Kitchener Rangers

SMITH, STU G.
82/3 HART / Jr. Whalers

SMITH, TODD
82/3 Oshawa Generals

SMITH, TOMMY
83 HHOF Postcard H14
83&87 HHOF 237
85/6 U. of Arizona Ice Cats

SMITH, TRAVIS
91/2 Air Canada SJHL C48
92/3 MPS SJHL 152

SMITH, TREVOR
87/8 Kingston Canadians

SMITH, TROY
95/6 Slapshot 60

SMITH, VERN
88/9 ProCards / Springfield
89/0 ProCards AHL 293
90/1 ProCards 533
91/2 ProCards 387
84/5 Springfield Indians 7

SMITH, WAYNE
85/6 Minnesota-Duluth 6

SMITH, WYATT
95/6 Do. Elite WJ 41
00/1 Pacific 323
00/1 Pr. Stock 138, PSR-17
94/5 Select 156
00/1 Vanguard 140

SMITHSON, JERRED
02/3 BAP Mem. 303
02/3 Pacific Complete 597
02/3 Ultimate Mem. 90
02/3 UD Artistic 118
02/3 UD Honor 132
02/3 UD Premier 88
01/2 Manchester Monarchs
98/9 Calgary Hitmen 19
99/0 Calgary Hitmen

SMITHURST, MICHAEL
92/3 Semic Nordisk 155

SMOLEJ, ROMAN
79 Panini Sticker 397

SMOLIK, JAROSLAV
95/6 APS 218, 343
99/0 Score 136

SMOLINSKI, BRYAN
01/2 Adrenaline 90
98/9 Aurora 120
98/9 Be A Player 233, ✍ Aut. 233
00/1 BAP Mem. 69
01/2 BAP Mem. 152
99/0 Crown Royale 68
02/3 Crown Royale ✄ GWDP 12
93/4 Donruss 30
94/5 Donruss 21
95/6 Donruss 138, 327
96/7 Donruss 99
98/9 Dynagon Ice 119
02/3 Exclusive 83, ✄ GWJ 12
96/7 Flair 58
94/5 Fleer 17
96/7 Fleer 89
95/6 Fleer Metal 120
96/7 Fl. Picks 132
93/4 Fleer Ultra 232
93/4 Fleer Ultra ARS 8
94/5 Fleer Ultra 16, ARS-9
95/6 Fleer Ultra 14, 294
02/3 Heads Up ✄ GWQ 13
95/6 Hoyle / East. 7-Club
93/4 Leaf 204
94/5 Leaf 130, GLR-14
95/6 Leaf 239
94/5 L. Limited 57
98/9 NHL Power Play
01/2 O-Pee-Chee 163
02/3 O-Pee-Chee 231
98/9 OPC Chrome 38
97/8 Omega 143
99/0 Omega 112
98/9 Pacific 289
99/0 Pacific 265
00/1 Pacific 202
01/2 Pacific 188
02/3 Pacific 175
02/3 Pacific Complete 133
97/8 Pacific CC 196
97/8 Pa. Crown Roy. 82
97/8 Pa. Dynagon 76, T-68
97/8 Pa. Invincible 84
97/8 Pa. Paramount 112
98/9 Pa. Paramount 149
00/1 Pa. Paramount 115
94/5 Panini Sticker A
95/6 Panini Sticker 60
96/7 Panini Sticker 62
97/8 Panini Sticker 81
98/9 Panini Sticker 74
99/0 Panini Sticker 255
92/3 Parkhurst 481
93/4 Parkhurst 259
94/5 Parkhurst 12, 276
95/6 Parkhurst 168
00/1 Parkhurst P-199
01/2 Parkhurst 162
94/5 Parkie SE seV26
93/4 Pinnacle 217
94/5 Pinnacle 13, 470
96/7 Pinnacle 125
96/7 Pi. Be A Player 132, ✍ Aut. 132
97/8 Pi. Certified 108
97/8 Pi. Inside 178
95/6 Pi. Summit 156
97/8 Pi. Totally 108
95/6 Playoff 188
96/7 Playoff 389
94/5 POG 38
95/6 POG 213
93/4 Power Play 291
93/4 Power Play RooS 14
93/4 Premier 466
94/5 Premier 196, 479, OF-2
02/3 Pr. Stock Reserve 47
00/1 PS Titanium ✄ GUG 24
01/2 PS Titanium ✄ DSJ 18
95/6 Pro Magnet 91
93/4 Score 472
95/6 Score 43
96/7 Score 88
97/8 Score 241

94/5 Select 132
01/2 Signature 134, ✍ Aut. 134
95/6 SBx Emotion 142
95/6 SBx Impact 135
96/7 SBx Impact 104
94/5 SP 11
02/3 Sports Vault 235
00/1 Stadium 177
98/9 Topps 38
00/1 Topps 110
01/2 Topps 163
02/3 Topps 231
00/1 To. Chrome 86
02/3 To. Limited 231
93/4 To. Stadium 274
94/5 To. Stadium 103
95/6 To. Stadium 210
02/3 To. Total 284
98/9 UD Choice 127
93/4 Upper Deck 242, SP-12
94/5 Upper Deck 399, SP-96
95/6 Upper Deck 494
96/7 Upper Deck 322
97/8 Upper Deck 310
98/9 Upper Deck 128
99/0 Upper Deck 236
00/1 Upper Deck 311
01/2 Upper Deck 82
02/3 Upper Deck 328
94/5 UD BAP ✍ 47
96/7 UD Black Diam. 120
95/6 UD CC 178
96/7 UD CC 218
97/8 UD Coll. Choice 152
98/9 UD G. Reserve 128
99/0 UD G. Reserve 236
96/7 UD Ice 39
00/1 UD MVP 84
01/2 UD MVP 88
02/3 UD MVP 87
99/0 UD MVP Cup 86
00/1 UD Vintage 166
02/3 UD Vintage 120
99/0 Victory 140
00/1 Victory 115
01/2 Victory 162
96/7 NYIS
95/6 PITT / Foodland 24
93/4 Michigan State

SMOLKA, LUKAS
99/0 OFS 232
00/1 OFS 241
01/2 OFS 39, -CL 8, -H 6

SMREK, PETER
01/2 BAP Mem. 200
01/2 O-Pee-Chee 269
01/2 Pr. Stock 132
93 Québec Pee Wee 1706
01/2 SP Authentic 161
01/2 SP GU 89
01/2 SPx 143, -RT
01/2 Stadium 122
01/2 Topps 269
01/2 To. Heritage 149
01/2 To. Reserve 118
01/2 Upper Deck 199
01/2 UD MVP 208
01/2 UD Vintage 289
01/2 Victory 381
01/2 Hartford Wolf Pack
00/1 Worcester IceCats

SMRKE, JOHN
79/0 O-Pee-Chee 340
78/9 SLOU

SMRKE, LOU
51/2 Laval Dairy 24
52/3 St. Lawrence 94

SMRKE, STAN
51/2 Laval Dairy 23
52/3 St. Lawrence 97

SMYL, STAN
83/4 Esso Stars
83/4 Funmate Puffy 2 [w/]
84/5 Kellogg's 9
84/5 Kelowna Wings &...
86/7 Kraft Sports 69
80/1 O-Pee-Chee 128
80/1 O-Pee-Chee 208
81/2 O-Pee-Chee 328
82/3 O-Pee-Chee 356
83/4 O-Pee-Chee 359
84/5 O-Pee-Chee 330
85/6 OPC/Topps 68
86/7 OPC/Topps 50
87/8 OPC/Topps 4
88/9 O-Pee-Chee 253
89/0 O-Pee-Chee 283
82/3 OPC/Topps Sticker 242
83/4 OPC/Topps Sticker 274
84/5 OPC Sticker 281
85/6 OPC Sticker 247
86/7 OPC Sticker 96
87/8 OPC Sticker 198
88/9 OPC Sticker 60
89/0 opcSticker 68-208
87/8 Panini Sticker 337
87/8 Panini Sticker 349
88/9 Panini Sticker 141
89/0 Panini Sticker 159
90/1 Panini Sticker 292
90/1 Panini/VAN 23
80/1 Pepsi Bottle Cap
81/2 Post 25
82/3 Post [Vanc.]
90/1 Pro Set 548
90/1 Score 374
84/5 7-Eleven
85/6 7-Eleven Superstars 19
83/4 Souhaits Keychain [Canucks]
80/1 Topps 128
80/1 Topps 208
81/2 Topps 38
84/5 Topps 140
90/1 Upper Deck 299
83/4 Vachon 116-36
78/9 VANC / Royal Bank
79/0 VANC / Royal Bank
80/1 VANC
80/1 VANC / Silverwood
81/2 VANC
81/2 VANC / Silverwood
82/3 VANC
83/4 VANC
84/5 VANC
85/6 VANC
86/7 VANC
87/8 VANC / Shell
88/9 VANC / Mohawk
89/0 VANC / Mohawk
90/1 VANC / Mohawk
00/1 Kansas City Blades 23

SMYL, STAN
02/3 Fleer Throwbacks 21

SMYTH, ADAM
00/1 Ottawa 67's 8
01/2 Ottawa 67's 8

SMYTH, BRAD
98/9 Be A Player 75, ✍ Aut. 75
95/6 Future Legends 20
97/8 Pa. Invincible R-99
96/7 Pi. Zenith 150
96/7 Select CE 113
90/1 7th..Sketch OHL 143
02/3 OTTA
94/5 Birmingham Bulls
93/4 Cincinnati Cyclones
97/8 Hartford Wolf Pack
99/0 Hartford Wolf Pack
00/1 Hartford Wolf Pack
01/2 Hartford Wolf Pack

SMYTH, GREG
93/4 Premier 306
91/2 Pro Set 465
89/0 ProCards AHL 177
90/1 ProCards 453
92/3 CALG / IGA 007
88/9 QUÉB
88/9 QUÉB / Gene. Foods
91/2 QUÉB / Petro-Canada
89/0 Halifax Citadels
90/1 Halifax Citadels
96/7 St. John's Maple Leafs
97/8 St. John's Maple Leafs

SMYTH, JARED
97/8 Spokane Chiefs

SMYTH, KEVIN
92/3 Classic 24
94/5 Classic 47, T30
92/3 Classic Four Sport 173
93/4 Cla. Prospects 225
93/4 Donruss 444
94/5 Donruss 59
95/6 Fleer Ultra 71
94/5 Leaf 320
95/6 Panini Sticker 30
94/5 Parkhurst 99
94/5 Premier 68
94/5 Score 225
90/1 7th..Sketch WHL 155
91/2 7th...Sketch WHL 279
95/6 Upper Deck 181
95/6 HART / Kids Club

SMYTH, MATTHEW
85/6 London Knights

SMYTH, RYAN
01/2 Adrenaline 78
01/2 Atomic 43, TN 7
02/3 Atomic 44, -SC 7, ✂ GWJ 10
98/9 Aurora 76
99/0 Aurora 59
00/1 Aurora 58
99/0 BAP Mem. 219
00/1 BAP Mem. 113
01/2 BAP Mem. 94
02/3 BAP Mem. 135
97/8 Bicycle 3-Spade
01/2 Bowman 64
02/3 Bowman 18
98/9 Bowman's Best 69
94/5 Classic 6, C8
94/5 Classic 4 Sport 120
94/5 Cla. Images 4 Sport 99
99/0 Crown Royale 57
00/1 Crown Royale 43
01/2 Crown Royale 62, JotC 13
02/3 Crown Royale 41, ✂ GWDP 10
95/6 Donruss 321, 3TWC-22
96/7 Donruss 223
97/8 Donruss 158, L2L-22, RA-2
96/7 Do. Canadian 89
97/8 Do. Canadian 52, NP-10, SCS-17
96/7 Do. Elite 124
97/8 Do. Elite 70, 140, C-21
97/8 Do. Preferred 119, 189, LT-1A
97/8 Do. Priority 24, 201, DD-5, OD-18, Post-19, Stamp-19
97/8 Do. Studio 16, HH-8, S-21, P-16, ✍ Aut.
98/9 Dynagon Ice 76, -TC 10
99/0 Dynagon Ice 85
02/3 Exclusive 73
02/3 First Ed. 195, 412R
96/7 Flair 35
01/2 Heads Up 42
02/3 Heads Up 51, ✂ GWQ 5
95/6 Leaf 196
96/7 Leaf 171
97/8 Leaf 49, 184, BS-10, FOI-9
94/5 L. Limited CAN 9
96/7 L. Preferred 72
97/8 Limited 26, 65, 99, FG-50
01/2 McDonald's 17
02/3 McDonald's 16, -SLG 4
01/2 O-Pee-Chee 235
02/3 O-Pee-Chee 67
98/9 OPC Chrome 40
97/8 Omega 95, GF-9, TL-10
98/9 Omega 96
99/0 Omega 95
98/9 Pacific 94, -TC 10
99/0 Pacific 166
00/1 Pacific 174
01/2 Pacific 166, 411, 430
02/3 Pacific 149
02/3 Pacific Complete 32
97/8 Pacific CC 9, GCDC-12
97/8 Pa. Crown Roy. 54, BOS-11, HT-9
98/9 Pa. Crown Roy. 54, -PP 11
97/8 Pa. Dynagon 51, T-47, BKS-39
97/8 Pa. Invincible 58, R-83
97/8 Pa. Paramount 77, CG-8
98/9 Pa. Paramount 92, -TC 10
99/0 Pa. Paramount 96
00/1 Pa. Paramount 100
97/8 Pa. Revolution 56, TC-10
98/9 Pa. Revolution 57
98/9 Panini Photocard
97/8 Panini Sticker 212
99/0 Panini Sticker 244
00/1 Panini Sticker 162
00/1 Parkhurst P-68
01/2 Parkhurst 49
02/3 Parkhurst 80
02/3 Parkhurst Retro 39
94/5 Pinnacle 535
95/6 Pinnacle 204
96/7 Pi. Be A Player 198, ✍ Aut. 198
97/8 Pi. Certified 79
95/6 Pi. Summit 176
97/8 Pi. Totally 79
95/6 Pi. Zenith 137
96/7 Pi. Zenith 104
99/0 Prism 58
00/1 Pr. Stock 40
01/2 Pr. Stock 41, -PS 32, ✂ GUG 48
02/3 Pr. Stock Reserve 39
00/1 PS Titanium 37
01/2 PS Titanium 58
02/3 PS Titanium 44, ✂ GWJ 30
00/1 PS Titanium Draft ✂ 44
02/3 Quest for the Cup 40
99/0 Revolution 60
00/1 Revolution 59
95/6 Score 304
97/8 Score 120, CI-8
95/6 Select CE 121
94/5 Sig. Rookies 31, ✍ 31
94/5 SR Auto-Phonex B3, ✍ B3
94/5 SR Gold Standard 92, GS18
95/6 SR Tetrad Autobilia 99
00/1 Signature 153, ✍ Aut. 27
01/2 Signature 115, ✍ Aut. 115
02/3 Signature 46, GS-81, ✍ 46
95/6 SBx Impact 198
94/5 SP 142
96/7 SP 56
97/8 SP Authentic 61
98/9 SP Authentic ✍ SotT
00/1 SP Authentic 36
01/2 SP Authentic 33
02/3 Sports Vault 225
00/1 Stadium 45
01/2 Stadium 86
02/3 Stadium 22
96/7 Team Out!
95/6 Topps 8CJ
98/9 Topps 40
99/0 Topps 32
00/1 Topps 112
01/2 Topps 235
02/3 Topps 67, HHC3
99/0 To. Chrome 32
01/2 To. Chrome 43
02/3 T. Chrome 45
94/5 Topps Finest 165
98/9 T. Gold Label 32
01/2 To. Heritage 95
02/3 To. Heritage 47
02/3 To. Limited 67
00/1 To. Stars 73
02/3 To. Total 268
98/9 UD Choice 82
00/1 UD Heroes 49
01/2 UD PlayMakers Ltd 41
00/1 UD Reserve 33
94/5 Upper Deck 443, SP-118
96/7 Upper Deck 258
97/8 Upper Deck 274
98/9 Upper Deck 272
00/1 Upper Deck 68
01/2 Upper Deck 71
02/3 Upper Deck 72
01/2 UD Challenge 33
02/3 UD Classic 41
97/8 UD Coll. Choice 92
98/9 UD G. Reserve 272
97/8 UD Ice 6, L5A
01/2 UD Mask 37
98/9 UD MVP 82
00/1 UD MVP 76
01/2 UD MVP 72
02/3 UD MVP 70
99/0 UD MVP Cup 74
02/3 UD Piece 40
00/1 UD Pros&Prosp. 33
02/3 UD Top Shelf 33
00/1 UD Vintage 143
01/2 UD Vintage 102, 104, 105
02/3 UD Vintage 100, 272, GB 100
00/1 Vanguard ✂ DGJ 7
01/2 Vanguard 41
02/3 Vanguard ✂ GWJ 21
00/1 Victory 98
01/2 Victory 137
02/3 Victory 83
99/0 WGretzky 69
97/8 Zenith 71, Z16
96/7 EDMO
97/8 EDMO

SMYTHE, CONN
83 HHOF Postcard B13
83&87 HHOF 27
92/3 Legends 2
32/3 Maple Leafs O'Keefe
01/2 UD Legends 63
37/8 World Wide Gum 95

SMYTHE, STAFFORD
59/0 Parkhurst 36

SNEDDEN, DENNIS
91/2 ProCards 615
93/4 Toledo Storm 13

SNEDDON, BOB
70/1 Esso Power Player

SNELL, CHRIS
93/4 Cla. Prospects 93
98/9 DEL 133
95/6 Edge Ice 185
99/0 Eishockey 97
91/2 ProCards 7
92 7th...Sketch Awards 4
91 7th..Sketch Mem.Cup 21
89/0 7th..Sketch OHL 51
90/1 7th..Sketch OHL 95
90/1 Upper Deck 468
00/1 UD DEL 100
01/2 UD DEL 88
94/5 Phoenix Roadrunners
95/6 Phoenix Roadrunners
91/2 Rochester Americans DD
91/2 Rochester Americans GL
91/2 Rochester Americans WPC
92/3 Rochester Americans DD
92/3 Rochester Americans WPC
93/4 St. John's Maple Leafs
00/1 St. John's Maple Leafs
93/4 Minnesota-Duluth

SNELL, TED
74/5 Loblaws
74/5 Loblaws Update

SNEPSTS, HAROLD
83/4 Esso Stars
02/3 Fleer Throwbacks 15
84/5 Kelowna Wings &...
75/6 O-Pee-Chee 396
76/7 O-Pee-Chee 366
76/7 OPC 395
77/8 O-Pee-Chee 295
78/9 O-Pee-Chee 380
79/0 O-Pee-Chee 186
80/1 O-Pee-Chee 312
81/2 O-Pee-Chee 344
82/3 O-Pee-Chee 357
83/4 O-Pee-Chee 360
84/5 O-Pee-Chee 108
85/6 O-Pee-Chee 232
89/0 O-Pee-Chee 286
81/2 OPC Sticker 250
82/3 OPC/Topps Sticker 243
85/6 OPC Sticker 44-175
87/8 OPC Sticker 110-243
87/8 Panini Sticker 241
80/1 Pepsi Bottle Cap
82/3 Post [Vanc.]
90/1 Pro Set 527
91/2 ProCards 35
90/1 Score 61T
84/5 7-Eleven
83/4 Souhaits Keychain [Canucks]
79/0 Topps 186
02/3 UD Foundations 94, ✂ CH, ✂ DF, ✂ PS
83/4 Vachon 117-37
85/6 DETR / Little Caesars
86/7 DETR / Little Caesars
84/5 MINS
90/1 SLOU / Kodak
75/6 VANC / Royal Bank
76/7 VANC / Royal Bank
77/8 VANC / Royal Bank
78/9 VANC / Royal Bank
79/0 VANC / Royal Bank
80/1 VANC
80/1 VANC / Silverwood
81/2 VANC / Silverwood
82/3 VANC
83/4 VANC
88/9 VANC / Mohawk
89/0 VANC / Mohawk
93/4 San Diego Gulls

SNESAR, SHAWN
91/2 Hampton Roads
92/3 Hampton Roads
93/4 Hampton Roads
98/9 Hampton Roads
94/5 Richmond Renegades
89/0 Saskatoon Blades

SNIDER, SHAWN
00/1 Owen Sound Attack 8

SNITA, MARCIN
95/6 Slapshot 353

SNITZER, ROB
88/9 ProCards / Moncton
89/0 ProCards AHL 50
90/1 Moncton Hawks
91/2 Moncton Hawks

SNOPEK, JAN
99/0 DS 20
00/1 DS 114
98/9 OFS 86
99/0 OFS 144
00/1 OFS 88
01/2 OFS 278
93/4 Slapshot / Oshawa 4
95/6 Slapshot 248

SNOW, GARTH
98/9 Aurora 192
99/0 Aurora 145
98/9 Be A Player 144, ✍ Aut. 144
01/2 BT Pipes 68
02/3 Between the Pipes 57
98/9 Bicycle.. 6-S
93/4 Classic 58
94/5 Classic 84, R17, W35
94/5 Classic 4 Sport 143
93/4 Cla. Images 4 Sport 21
93/4 Cla. Prospects 35
99/0 Crown Royale 140
93/4 Donruss 481
96/7 Donruss 207
97/8 Donruss 11, BTP-7
97/8 Do. Canadian 38, SCS-10
97/8 Do. Preferred 111
97/8 Do. Priority 138,PG-16
98/9 Dynagon Ice 192
95/6 Fleer Ultra 287
94/5 Leaf 180
96/7 Leaf 97
97/8 Limited 170
99/0 Millenium ✂ G-4
01/2 O-Pee-Chee 179
98/9 OPC Chrome 122
97/8 Omega 170
98/9 Omega 241
98/9 Pacific 434
99/0 Pacific 433
00/1 Pacific 416
01/2 Pacific 317
02/3 Pacific 243
02/3 Pacific Complete 477
97/8 Pacific CC 147, ITC-15
97/8 Pa. Crown Roy. FO-14
98/9 Pa. Crown Roy. 139
97/8 Pa. Dynagon 93, S-16, T-54
97/8 Pa. Paramount 137, GSL-15
98/9 Pa. Paramount 240
99/0 Pa. Paramount 240
98/9 Pa. Revolution 145
98/9 Panini Photocard
99/0 Panini Sticker 316
95/6 Parkhurst 425
97/8 Pinnacle 63, M-8, / Tin 9
97/8 Pi. Be A Player 77, STP-12, ✍ Aut. 77
97/8 Pi. Certified 28
97/8 Pi. Inside 68, SU-4, S-17, / LargeCan
97/8 Pi. Totally 28
97/8 Pi. Uncut 7
93/4 Power Play 425
00/1 PS Titanium 78
99/0 Revolution 146
93/4 Score 628
96/7 Score 204
97/8 Score 3, NW-8
97/8 Score Phil. 2
95/6 SBx Impact 215
98/9 SPx Finite 86
98/9 Topps 122
99/0 Topps 116
01/2 Topps 179
99/0 To. Chrome 116
98/9 UD Choice 207
95/6 Upper Deck 289
98/9 Upper Deck 198
99/0 Upper Deck 295
95/6 UD BAP 57, ✍ S57
98/9 UD G. Reserve 198
99/0 UD G. Reserve 295
02/3 UD Mask 52, 53
96/7 PHIL / Ocean Spray
92/3 Maine Black Bears
92/3 Maine Black Bears

SNOW, JASON
90/1 7th..Sketch OHL 96
89/0 Windsor Spitfires

SNUGGERUD, DAVE
90/1 Bowman 249
91/2 Bowman 29
92/3 Bowman 309
90/1 OPC/Topps 340
91/2 O-Pee-Chee 441
90/1 Panini Sticker 19
91/2 Panini Sticker 308
91/2 Pinnacle 223
92/3 Pinnacle 183
90/1 Pro Set 30
91/2 Pro Set 18
90/1 Score 48T
91/2 Score 206
91/2 Score CAN 206
92/3 Score 182
91/2 To. Stadium 320
90/1 Upper Deck 189
91/2 Upper Deck 194
89/0 BUFF / Blue Shield
89/0 BUFF / Campbell's
90/1 BUFF / Blue Shield
90/1 BUFF / Campbell's
91/2 BUFF / Blue Shield
91/2 BUFF / Campbell's
91/2 BUFF / Pepsi
94/5 Minnesota Moose

SNYDER, DAN
01/2 BAP Mem. 413
99 Bowman 152
02/3 Calder 53
02/3 Pacific Complete 519
95 Québec Pee Wee 949
95/6 Slapshot 294
01/2 SPx 134, -RT
01/2 Upper Deck 181
01/2 UD MVP 190
01/2 UD Top Shelf 47
01/2 Victory 362
01/2 Chicago Wolves

SOBCHUK, DENNIS
74/5 OPC WHA 56
75/6 OPC WHA 115
76/7 OPC WHA 29
77/8 OPC WHA 53
75/6 Cincinnati Stingers
86/7 Regina Pats
87/8 Regina Pats

SOBCHUK, GENE
75/6 Cincinnati Stingers

SOBEK, JEANINE
94/5 Classic W35

SOBERLAK, PETER
89/0 ProCards AHL 134
90/1 ProCards 226
91/2 ProCards 229
85/6 Kamloops Blazers

SOCCIO, LEN
96/7 DEL 218
98/9 DEL 181
99/0 Eishockey 227
00/1 UD DEL 229, ✂ GJ
01/2 UD DEL 102, GA6

SOCHOR, JAN
97/8 APS 169
00/1 DS 21
98/9 OFS 256
99/0 OFS 54
00/1 OFS 337

SOCHOREC, ALES
97/8 APS 310
99/0 Score 20

SÖDERBERG, AKE
72 Semic Sticker 70

SÖDERBERG, ANDERS
94/5 Leaf Elit Set 220
95/6 Leaf Elit Set 103, G-10
94/5 Parkie SE234
91/2 Semic Elitserien 333
94/5 SP 169
94/5 Upper Deck 521
95/6 UD Elitserien 161, 221
97/8 UD Elitserien 158
98/9 UD Elitserien 181
99/0 UD Elitserien 183
00/1 UD Elitserien 158

SÖDERGREN, HAKAN
89/0 Semic Elitserien 60
90/1 Semic Elitserien 290
89 Semic Sticker 23

SODERHOLM, PATRIK
89/0 Semic Elitserien 190

SODERLUND, KENNETH
89/0 Semic Elitserien 140
90/1 Semic Elitserien 215
91/2 Semic Elitserien 143
92/3 Semic Elitserien 172

SÖDERSTRÖM, DAN
72 Semic Sticker 68
74 Semic Sticker 10
73/4 Williams Finnish 38

SÖDERSTRÖM, MATHIAS
02/3 Coventry Blaze

SÖDERSTRÖM, TOMMY
93/4 Classic 125
92/3 Classic Prospects 91
92/3 Classic Prospects BC8
93/4 Donruss 253
96/7 Donruss 72
93/4 EA Sports 102
92/3 Fleer Ultra 160, -UI 23
93/4 Fleer Ultra 217
94/5 Fleer Ultra 160
95/6 Fleer Ultra 100
95 Globe 1
95/6 Kraft / PS
93/4 Leaf 37
93/4 Leaf GLR 12
94/5 Leaf 184
96/7 Leaf 51
94 Panini Olympics 294
93/4 Panini Sticker 55
92/3 Parkhurst 367
92/3 Parkhurst 448
93/4 Parkhurst 150
95/6 Parkhurst 127, 240
93/4 Pinnacle 19
94/5 Pinnacle 309
95/6 Pinnacle 90, GG-15
95/6 Pi. Summit 46
93/4 Power Play 185
93/4 Power Play SYS 11
93/4 Power Play Netm. 8
93/4 Premier 122
93/4 Premier 55
93/4 Score 336
93/4 Score IS 5
95/6 Score 215
96/7 Score 82
94 Semic 334
94 Semic 52
95 Semic 54, 212
89/0 Semic Elitserien 51
90/1 Semic Elitserien 273
91/2 Semic Elitserien 54
91/2 Semic Elitserien 316
91/2 Semic Elitserien 338
92/3 Semic Elitserien 343
91 Semic Sticker 29
92 Semic Sticker 51
93 Semic Sticker 19
95/6 Topps 334
93/4 To. Stadium 340
93/4 To. Stadium 430
94/5 To. Stadium 24
92/3 Upper Deck 377
92/3 Upper Deck 475
93/4 Upper Deck 182
94/5 Upper Deck 474
95/6 Upper Deck 313, SE-140
95/6 UD CC 28
95/6 UD Elitserien 238
97/8 UD Elitserien 33, 199
98/9 UD Elitserien 49, DL3
99/0 UD Elitserien 35, 219, S4, ✍ Aut.
96 Wien 38, SG4
92/3 PHIL / UD Sheet
93/4 PHIL / Sheet
93/4 PHIL / J.C. Penney

SÖDERSTRÖM, ULF
99/0 UD Elitserien 127, H9, ✍ Aut.
00/1 UD Elitserien 84

SODERVIK, JUHANI
66/7 Champion 144
70/1 Kuvajulkaisut 267

SODKE, SONNY
82/3 Brandon Wheat Kings

SOETAERT, DOUG
80/1 O-Pee-Chee 324
82/3 O-Pee-Chee 389
83/4 O-Pee-Chee 391
84/5 O-Pee-Chee 347
82/3 OPC/Topps Sticker 211
83/4 OPC/Topps Sticker 288
85/6 OPC Sticker 136-8
86/7 OPC Sticker 16-159
83/4 Vachon 137-17
84/5 MONT
85/6 MONT
85/6 MONT / Provigo
81/2 WINN
82/3 WINN
83/4 WINN
89/0 New Haven Nighthawks

SOFIKITAS,
91/2 Avant Garde BCJHL 163

SÖGAARD, KIM
92 Semic Sticker 31
93 Semic Sticker 236
92/3 Semic Nordisk 74

SOHLMAN, RAULI
80/1 Mallasjuoma 45
78/9 SM-Liiga 88

SÖILYNOJA, KEIJO
92 Semic Sticker 23

SOIN, SERGEI
00/1 Mir 54
02/3 Russian Future Stars 18

SOINI, VOITTO
66/7 Champion 70
70/1 Kuvajulkaisut 150
71/2 Williams Finnish 201

SOKE, CARLOS
99/0 Rockford IceHogs

SOKKA, MIKKO
98/9 Cardset 254
96/7 Sisu 139

SOKKANEN, JUHA
80/1 Mallasjuoma 144

SOKOLOV, ANDREI
98/9 Mir 9
99/0 Mir 8
00/1 Metallurg 47

SOKOLOV, DENIS
00/1 Mir 216

SOKOLOV, MAXIM
99/0 Mir 247
00/1 Mir 376
00/1 Mir Fetisov 9

SOKOLSKY, JAMIE
97 Bowman 38
95/6 Slapshot 37
98/9 Huntington Blizzard
99/0 Huntington Blizzard

SOLARI, KELVIN
93/4 Slapshot / Peterborough 23

SOLBACH, CARSTEN
94/5 DEL 429
95/6 DEL 385
96/7 DEL 292

SOLBERG, LARS ERIK
92/3 Semic Nordisk 156

SOLDERER, ERICH
94 Semic 238
93 Semic Sticker 275

SOLEWAY, JAY
80/1 CALG

SOLF, PATRIK
94/5 DEL 50
95/6 DEL 33

SOLHEIM, KEN
83/4 O-Pee-Chee 131
88/9 EDMO / Action 8
82/3 MINS
84/5 MINS
85/6 Nova Scotia Oilers

SOLING, JONAS
98/9 EBK ECHL All-Star
96/7 Sudbury Wolves

SOLINGER, BOB
45-64 BeeHive-2 [Toro.]
51/2 Parkhurst 88
52/3 Parkhurst 50
53/4 Parkhurst 16
45-54 Quaker Oats

SOLINSKI, JASEK
89 Semic Sticker 144

SOLLY, JIM
94/5 Huntington Blizzard
92/3 Oklahoma City Blazers

SOLNIK, ADAM
00/1 Mississauga IceDogs

SOLOBIEV, MAXIM
00/1 Mir 134

SOLODUKHIN, VYACHESLAV
91/2 Future Trends C72 28
72/3 Williams Finnish 36

SOMERS, ART
33-35 Diamond Match Silv.
36-39 Diamond Match TT2
24/5 Holland Creameries 3
33/4 O-Pee-Chee 17
28/9 Paulins Candy 49

SOMERS, CHRIS
86/7 London Knights

SOMERVILLE, ROSS
25 Dominion Chocolates 113

SOMERVUORI, EERO
98/9 Cardset 113
99/0 Cardset 64
00/1 Cardset 149
02/3 Cardset 271
95/6 Sisu 256
98/9 UD Choice 281
97/8 UD Black Diam. 139

SOMIK, RADOVAN
02/3 Atomic 129
02/3 BAP All-Star 123
02/3 BAP Mem. 306
02/3 Bowman 121
02/3 Calder 136
02/3 Crown Royale 131
02/3 In The G-U 90, ✂ C18
00/1 OFS 370
01/2 OFS 87
02/3 Pacific Complete 550
02/3 Parkhurst 233
02/3 Pr. Stock Reserve 177
02/3 PS Titanium 129
02/3 Quest for the Cup 136
02/3 Signature ✂ AR6
02/3 SP Authentic 154
02/3 SPx 172
02/3 T. Chrome 159
02/3 To. Heritage 153
02/3 To. Total 423
02/3 Ultimate Mem. 33
02/3 Upper Deck 446
02/3 UD Honor 162
02/3 UD Mask 120
02/3 UD Top Shelf 100
02/3 Vanguard 128

SOMMER, ROY
88/9 EDMO / Action 110
01/2 Cleveland Barons
98/9 Kentucky Tho'blades
00/1 Kentucky Tho'blades
92/3 Richmond Renegades
93/4 Richmond Renegades
94/5 Richmond Renegades
95/6 Richmond Renegades

SOMMERS, ART
30/1 La Presse

SOMMERS, DARB
23/4 Paulins Candy 58

SONGIN, TON
98/9 BOST / Alumni 29

SONIER, GRANT
98/9 Fort Wayne Komets

SONMEZ, JIM
90/1 7th..Sketch OHL 19
88/9 Sudbury Wolves
89/0 Sudbury Wolves

SONMOR, GLEN
79/0 MINS
80/1 MINS
81/2 MINS
72/3 Minn. Fight. Saints

SONNENBERG, ERIC
99/0 Lethbridge Hurricanes
01/2 Regina Pats

SONNENBERG, MARTIN
98 Bowman 69
98 Bowman Chrome 69
99/0 Millenium 200, ✍ Aut. 200
99/0 UD G. Reserve 347
99/0 UD MVP Cup 149
00/1 WBS Penguins
01/2 WBS Penguins

SOPEL, BRENT
00/1 BAP Mem. 34
01/2 O-Pee-Chee 260
02/3 Pacific 386
02/3 Pacific Complete 457
00/1 Signature 262, ✍ Aut. 15
00/1 SP Authentic 165
01/2 SP Authentic ✍ SotT
00/1 Topps 302
01/2 Topps 260
00/1 To. Chrome 197
02/3 To. Total 28
00/1 Upper Deck 195
00/1 UD MVP 208
00/1 UD Vintage 393
00/1 Victory 271
02/3 Victory 206
95/6 Swift Current Broncos

SORACREPPA, MARTINO
92 Semic Sticker 264

SORENSEN, ANDERS
99/0 Mobile Mysticks

SØRENSEN, BJØRNAR
92/3 Semic Nordisk 235

SORENSON, KELLY
92/3 Hampton Roads
93/4 Hampton Roads
94/5 Hampton Roads
98/9 Hampton Roads

SØRLI, ØYVIND
92/3 Semic Nordisk 122

SORMUNEN, PASI
99/0 Eishockey 42
97/8 Hockey-Box
92/3 Jyvas Hyva 13
93/4 Jyvas Hyva 21
94 Semic 11
95 Semic 6
93 Semic Sticker 60
93/4 Sisu 89
94/5 Sisu 238
95/6 Sisu 45
96/7 Sisu 44, SH-3

SOROCHAN, JASON
90/1 7th..Sketch WHL 135
91/2 7th...Sketch WHL 350

SOROCHAN, LEE
00/1 Cardset 281
95/6 Donruss C3TWC 9
94/5 Pinnacle 528
91/2 7th...Sketch WHL 338
94/5 SP 147
95/6 Topps 9CJ
94/5 Topps Finest 153
01/2 UD DEL 44
95/6 Binghampton Rangers
96/7 Binghampton Rangers
98/9 Fort Wayne Komets
97/8 Hartford Wolf Pack
98/9 Hartford Wolf Pack
93/4 Lethbridge Hurricanes

SOROKIN, SERGEI
93/4 Classic 93
95/6 DEL 85
96/7 DEL 274
91/2 O-Pee-Chee 44R
94 Panini Olympics 282
94 Semic 144
93 Semic Sticker 134
92/3 Upper Deck 343
00/1 UD DEL 50

SORRELL, JOHN
34-43 BeeHive-1 [Detr.]
33/4 Canadian Gum
33/4 O-Pee-Chee 42
39/0 O-Pee-Chee 60
37/8 World Wide Gum 25

SOSKIN, BARRY
92/3 Toledo Storm WIOT
92/3 Toledo Storm
93/4 Toledo Storm 3
94/5 Toledo Storm
95/6 Toledo Storm
96/7 Toledo Storm
97/8 Toledo Storm 27

SOTROPA, J.
92/3 MPS SJHL 139

SOTROPA, J. STEVE
91/2 Air Canada SJHL D37

SOUCHOTTE, KURTISE
91/2 Air Canada SJHL B49
92/3 MPS SJHL 72

SOUCY, ALFRED
52/3 Anonymous 42

SOUCY, CHRISTIAN
93/4 Cla. Prospects 75
94/5 Fleer Ultra 276
94/5 Parkie SE33
94/5 Upper Deck 223
93/4 Indianapolis Ice
94/5 Indianapolis Ice
95/6 Indianapolis Ice

SOUCY, JEAN-FRANÇOIS
01 UD Prospects GU 12, ✂ TPJ

SOUCY, JEAN-PHILIPPE
00/1 WBS Penguins

SOUDEK, KAREL
95/6 APS 58
96/7 APS 242
97/8 APS 269
97/8 DS 29
99/0 DS 187
00/1 DS 102
96/7 DS Sticker 76
97/8 DS Sticker 69
99/0 OFS 470, 526
00/1 OFS 193
01/2 OFS 104

SOUKOROFF, PHIL
93/4 Johnstown Chiefs 9

SOULE, RUSS
83/4 Belleville Bulls

SOULES, JASON
91/2 ProCards 219
90/1 7th..Sketch OHL 219
90/1 Upper Deck 75
88/9 Niagara Falls Thunder

SOULES, NATE
85/6 U. of Arizona Ice Cats

SOULLIERE, STEPHANE
93/4 Slapshot / Oshawa 11
94/5 Slapshot / Sarnia 11
97/8 Charlotte Checkers
96/7 Knoxville Cherokees
92/3 Oshawa Generals

SOURAY, SHELDON
99/0 NHL Power Play
98/9 Pacific 271
00/1 Pacific 214
98/9 Pa. Paramount 138
94/5 Sig. Rookies 27, ✍ 27
01/2 Signature 92, ✍ Aut. 92
00/1 Topps 262
98/9 Upper Deck 122
02/3 Upper Deck 337
98/9 UD G. Reserve 122
99/0 WGretzky 97
00/1 MONT
01/2 MONT
02/3 MONT
96/7 Albany River Rats

SOUTHERN, B
88/9 WINN / Safety Tips

SOUTUKORVA, OSMO
89/0 Semic Elitserien 150
90/1 Semic Elitserien 231
91/2 Semic Elitserien 208
97/8 UD Elitserien 121
98/9 UD Elitserien 135
99/0 UD Elitserien 137
00/1 UD Elitserien 123

SOUTUYO,
98/9 Portland Pirates
99/0 Portland Pirates

SOUZA, MIKE
01/2 Norfolk Admirals

SOVA, TOMMI
98/9 Cardset 192
99/0 Cardset 112
97/8 Hockey-Box
00/1 Kudos 123
94/5 Parkie SE224
95/6 Sisu 49
94/5 Topps Finest 138

SOZINOV, VADIM
00/1 Ottawa 67's 16

SPACEK, JAROSLAV
94/5 APS 148
95/6 APS 249, 435
96/7 APS 294, 403
97/8 APS 352
99/0 BAP Mem. 352
00/1 BAP Mem. 276
98 Bonaparte 3B
98 Bonaparte Pexeso 9
99/0 DS NS5, P8
96/7 DS Sticker 211
02/3 First Ed. 249
98/9 OFS 236, -OW 13
99/0 OFS 36
00/1 OFS 404
99/0 Pacific 181
02/3 Pacific Complete 255
99/0 Panini Sticker 57
00/1 Panini Sticker 34
99/0 Score JT4
00/1 Signature 244, ✍ Aut. 187
00/1 Stadium 175
00/1 Topps 258
99/0 Ult. Victory 39
98/9 Upper Deck 281
01/2 Upper Deck 269
97/8 UD Elitserien 55
98/9 UD G. Reserve 281
98/9 UD MVP 86
01/2 UD MVP 39
02/3 UD MVP 52
01/2 UD Vintage 55
01/2 Victory 77

SPADAFORA, PAUL
01/2 Florida Everblades
99/0 Hull Olympiques BN
99/0 Hull Olympiques 17

SPANG, DAN
97 Québec Pee Wee 1247

SPANGLER, KEN
89/0 ProCards IHL 118
91/2 ProCards 446
93/4 Flint Generals
94/5 Flint Generals
96/7 Flint Generals
88/9 Flint Spirits

SPANHEL, MARTIN
97/8 APS 71
01/2 BAP Mem. 253
01/2 Crown Royale 155
99/0 DS 91
01/2 O-Pee-Chee 296
98/9 OFS 48
99/0 OFS 372, 482, 509
01/2 Pacific 117
01/2 Parkhurst 312
01/2 PS Titanium Draft 122
01/2 SPx 136, -RT
01/2 SPx Rookie RR9
01/2 Topps 296
01/2 Upper Deck 186
01/2 UD Challenge 103
01/2 UD Honor Roll 91
01/2 UD Ice 51
01/2 UD MVP 196
01/2 UD Premier 57
01/2 UD Top Shelf 52
01/2 Victory 371
00/1 Syracuse Crunch
01/2 Syracuse Crunch

SPARKES, BRAD
85/6 Kitchener Rangers

SPARKS, ANDREW
94/5 Guildford Flames 10
95/6 Guildford Flames 21

SPARKS, TODD
90/1 7th..Sketch LHJMQ 131
91/2 7th...Sketch LHJMQ 215
96/7 Fredericton Canadiens
95/6 Richmond Renegades

SPARLING, HARRY E.
85/6 London Knights
86/7 London Knights

SPARROW, SPUNK
23/4 Paulins Candy 49

SPECK, FRED
71/2 Eddie Sargent 220
72/3 O-Pee-Chee 331
71/2 Toronto Sun Photo
72/3 Minn. Fight. Saints

SPEER, MIKE
93/4 Cla. Prospects 168
91/2 ProCards 487
90/1 7th..Sketch OHL 185, 294
94/5 Slapshot / Brantford 20
92/3 Indianapolis Ice
93/4 Indianapolis Ice

SPEIRS, PETE
23/4 Paulins Candy 2
28/9 Paulins Candy 76
23/4 Selkirks Crescent 3
24/5 Selkirks Crescent 12

SPELDA, JAROSLAV
94/5 APS 28
99/0 OFS 373
00/1 OFS 63

SPENCE, MARK
00/1 Charlotte Checkers
99/0 Huntington Blizzard
98/9 Phoenix Mustangs 5

SPENCE, WALLY
92/3 MPS SJHL 21

SPENCER, BRIAN
72/3 Eddie Sargent 132
74/5 Loblaws
71/2 O-Pee-Chee 198
72/3 O-Pee-Chee 61
73/4 O-Pee-Chee 83
74/5 O-Pee-Chee 328
75/6 O-Pee-Chee 384
76/7 O-Pee-Chee 191
77/8 O-Pee-Chee 9
78/9 O-Pee-Chee 137
72/3 Topps 53
73/4 Topps 83
76/7 Topps 191
77/8 Topps 9
78/9 Topps 137
71/2 Toronto Sun Photo
74/5 BUFF
71/2 TORO

SPENCER, IRV
62/3 Cowan Tile
60/1 Shirriff 88
61/2 Shirriff 86
61/2 Topps 47
62/3 Topps 17
73/4 Vancouver Blazers

SPENCER, SEAN
90/1 7th..Sketch OHL 97
91/2 7th...Sketch OHL 295
92/3 Ottawa 67's

SPENRATH, GREG
91/2 ProCards 145
93/4 Las Vegas Thunder

SPERGER, ZDENEK
94/5 APS 107
95/6 APS 74

SPERO, KEVIN
91/2 7th...Sketch OHL 168
91/2 Oshawa Generals
91/2 Oshawa Generals
92/3 Oshawa Generals

SPEYERS, CHRIS
24/5 Champ's Cigarettes
33-35 Diamond Match Silv.

SPEZZA, JASON
02/3 Atomic 128
02/3 BAP All-Star 138
02/3 BAP Draft Florida 2
02/3 BAP Mem. 295
99 Bowman 153, SC11
02/3 Bowman 126
02/3 Calder 133, -CR 18, ✂ GWJ 16
02/3 Choice Prospects 39
02/3 Crown Royale 127, -RR 17, -RP 8
02/3 eTopps 47
02/3 Exclusive 179
02/3 First Ed. 435R
02/3 In The G-U 200, ✂ C1, ✂ E40
02/3 O-Pee-Chee 335
02/3 Pacific Complete 577
02/3 PTC/ ASG 9
02/3 PTC/ Collections 8
02/3 PTC/ Spring Expo 7
02/3 Parkhurst 247, ✂ GJ52
02/3 Parkhurst Retro 247, ✂ RJ13, ✂ RSJ9, ✂ RM15
02/3 Pr. Stock Reserve 173
02/3 PS Titanium 126, -ROT 17
02/3 Quest for the Cup 133, -CC 10, ✂ GWJ 14
02/3 Signature ✂ SGJ54, ✂ TQ20
02/3 SP Authentic ✍ 191, ✍ SotT, ✍ SotTD, ✍ SotTT, ✍✂ Patch
02/3 SP GU 82, ✍ Sig
02/3 Sports Vault 94
02/3 SPx ✍ 175
02/3 Stadium 133
02/3 Topps 335
02/3 T. Chrome 151
02/3 To. Heritage 147
02/3 To. Total 411
02/3 Ultimate Mem. 47, ✂ CC, ✂ GUJ, ✂ NP
02/3 Upper Deck 443
02/3 UD Artistic 97, R91, CG3
02/3 UD Classic 126
02/3 UD Foundations 164
02/3 UD Honor 160, -SG22, ✍ SC
02/3 UD Mask 171
02/3 UD Piece / Giveaway
02/3 UD Premier ✍✂ 83, ✂ JD, ✍ Sig
99/0 UD Prospects 2, 81, C1,

DS1, ✄ GJ, ✍ Sig.
00/1 UD Prospects 11, 89, 99, CC3, CS1, D1, FL1, GD1, ✄ GJ (x2), ✄ GJC (x6), ✄✍ GJS (x2), ✍ Sig
01 UD Prospects GU 1, 41-44, ✄ TPJ (x3), ✄ TPJS (x3), ✄ JC (x10), ✍ SoT
02/3 UD Rookie ✍ 163, ✍ TD
02/3 UD Top Shelf 133
02/3 Vanguard 124, -IF 8, -PP 18
02/3 OTTA
01/2 Belleville Bulls Update [x3]
99/0 Brampton Batallion 27
00/1 Mississauga IceDogs

SPICER, CODY
01/2 Peterborough Petes

SPILA, TOMAS
01/2 Québec Remparts 11

SPILER, ROMAN
99/0 Score 49

SPILLER, MATTHEW
00/1 UD Prospects 63
01 UD Prospects GU 5, ✄ TPJ

SPILMAN, MIKE
93/4 Cincinnati Cyclones

SPINA, STEVE
93/4 Slapshot / S.S.Marie 27

SPINK, LONNIE
85/6 Kamloops Blazers

SPIRIDONOV, MAXIM
98/9 EBK IHL All-Star
98/9 Grand Rapids Griffins
00/1 Hamilton Bulldogs
00/1 Hamilton Bulldogs/ Staz

SPITZER, ZBYNEK
99/0 OFS 449
00/1 OFS 330

SPITZIG, TIM
91/2 7th...Sketch OHL 79
93/4 Slapshot / Kitchener 9
94/5 Slapshot / Kitchener 10

SPLETT, JAMIE
90/1 7th..Sketch WHL 178
88/9 Regina Pats
89/0 Regina Pats

SPOJCAR, PETR
99/0 Score 67

SPOLTORE, FRED
95/6 Louisiana Ice Gators

SPOLTORE, JOHN
89/0 7th..Sketch OHL 149
90/1 7th..Sketch OHL 317
91/2 7th...Sketch OHL 66
95/6 Louisiana Ice Gators-2
97/8 Louisiana Ice Gators
98/9 Louisiana Ice Gators
99/0 Louisiana Ice Gators
00/1 Louisiana Ice Gators

SPOONER, DOUG
94/5 Anchorage Aces 18

SPOTT, STEVE
01/2 Kitchener Rangers

SPRATT, LEN
84/5 Kingston Canadians

SPREGNER, JIM
85/6 Minnesota-Duluth 22

SPRING, COREY
00/1 Kudos 105
95/6 Atlanta Knights
98/9 Cleveland Lumberjacks

SPRING, DON
81/2 O-Pee-Chee 375
82/3 O-Pee-Chee 392
83/4 O-Pee-Chee 392
80/1 Pepsi Bottle Cap
82/3 Post [Winn.]
83/4 Souhaits Keychain [Jets]
80/1 WINN
81/2 WINN
82/3 WINN

SPRING, FRANK
75/6 O-Pee-Chee 341

SPRING, JESSE
24/5 Champ's Cigarettes
23/4 William Paterson 36
24/5 William Paterson 20

SPROTT, JIM
90/1 ProCards 464
91/2 ProCards 377
90/1 Halifax Citadels
86/7 London Knights

SPROXTON, DENNIS
90/1 7th..Sketch WHL 70

SPRUCE, ANDY
78/9 O-Pee-Chee 378
76/7 VANC / Royal Bank
84/5 Sudbury Wolves

SPRY, BRAD
90/1 7th..Sketch OHL 98

SPRY, EARL
94/5 DEL 227
95/6 DEL 224
96/7 DEL 75

SPURR, CHAD
96/7 Soo Greyhounds

SRDINKO, JAN
94/5 APS 237
95/6 APS 7
96/7 APS 220
97/8 APS 49
98/9 DS 78
99/0 DS 129
00/1 DS 15
96/7 DS Sticker 22
97/8 DS Sticker 169
98/9 OFS 102, 425, 474
99/0 OFS 269, 444, 527
00/1 OFS 323
01/2 OFS 31, -UHI 28

SREK, PAVEL
94/5 APS 80
95/6 APS 274
97/8 APS 178
97/8 DS Sticker 154
98/9 OFS 135
99/0 OFS 112
00/1 OFS 297
01/2 OFS 29

SROMUNEN, PASI
98/9 Cardset 13

SRSEN, TOMAS
95/6 APS 17, 368, 403
96/7 APS 228, 420
97/8 APS 38
97/8 DS 60
98/9 DS 83
00/1 DS 150
96/7 DS Sticker 34
97/8 DS Sticker 176
99/0 Eishockey 363
94/5 Leaf Elit Set 45, TG-1
98/9 OFS 343
00/1 OFS 273, -Star 31
90/1 ProCards 237
91/2 ProCards 234
95 Semic 156
92/3 Semic Elitserien 166

SRYUBKO, ANDREI
99/0 Grand Rapids Griffins
98/9 Las Vegas Thunder
00/1 Syracuse Crunch
01/2 Syracuse Crunch
97/8 Toledo Storm 6

ST-AMOUR, MARTIN
90/1 ProCards 70
91/2 Cincinnati Cyclones

ST-AMOUR, STEPHANE
91/2 7th...Sketch LHJMQ 161
93/4 Slapshot / Drummondville 12

ST-AUBIN, JOEY
90 7th..Sketch Mem.Cup 47
90/1 7th..Sketch OHL 241
88/9 Kitchener Rangers
89/0 Kitchener Rangers
90/1 Kitchener Rangers

ST-CROIX, RICK
81/2 O-Pee-Chee 252
82/3 O-Pee-Chee 258
83/4 O-Pee-Chee 340
84/5 O-Pee-Chee 310
83/4 OPC/Topps Sticker 36
85/6 OPC Sticker 8-136
83/4 Vachon 98-126
82/3 TORO
83/4 TORO
88/9 WINN / Safety Tips

ST-CYR, GERRY
90/1 7th..Sketch WHL 249
91/2 7th...Sketch WHL 64
95/6 Flint Generals
93/4 Thunder Bay Senators
94/5 Toledo Storm

ST-CYR, RAYMOND
52/3 Anonymous 44

ST-GERMAIN, DAVID
00/1 Baie-Comeau 19

ST-GERMAIN, FRANÇOIS
88/9 Richelieu Riverains

ST-GERMAIN, MATT
91/2 7th...Sketch OHL 137
93/4 Slapshot / Peterborough 12
91/2 Peterborough Petes

ST-HILAIRE, IRENE
52/3 Bas du Fleuve 19
52/3 Laval Dairy Update 55
52/3 St. Lawrence 87

ST-JACQUES, BRUNO
01/2 BAP Mem. 318
02/3 O-Pee-Chee 292
01/2 PS Titanium 175
01/2 PS Titanium Draft 157
02/3 SPx 119
02/3 Topps 292
02/3 To. Limited 292
01/2 UD PlayMakers Ltd 133
02/3 Upper Deck 218
01/2 UD Honor Roll 84
01/2 UD Premier 75
02/3 Philadelphia Phantoms

ST-JACQUES, KEVIN
92/3 Classic Prospects 136
90/1 7th..Sketch WHL 134
91/2 7th...Sketch WHL 352
92/3 Indianapolis Ice
93/4 Indianapolis Ice
89/0 Lethbridge Hurricanes

ST-JACQUES, MICHEL
90/1 7th..Sketch LHJMQ 33
91/2 7th...Sketch LHJMQ 82
91 7th..Sketch Mem.Cup 30

ST-JEAN, JACQUES
79/0 Montréal Jrs. Colour

ST-JEAN, MAURICE
52/3 Bas du Fleuve 24
51/2 Lac St-Jean 25

ST-LAURENT, ANDRÉ
75/6 O-Pee-Chee 387
76/7 O-Pee-Chee 29
77/8 O-Pee-Chee 171
78/9 O-Pee-Chee 32
79/0 O-Pee-Chee 73
80/1 O-Pee-Chee 316
83/4 O-Pee-Chee 286
83/4 Souhaits Keychain [Penguins]
76/7 Topps 29
77/8 Topps 171
78/9 Topps 32
79/0 Topps 73
83/4 PITT / Heinz

ST-LAURENT, DOLLARD
01/2 BAP Mem. ✄ RM6
45-64 BeeHive-2 [Mont.]
45-64 BeeHive-2 [Chic.]
48-52 Exhibits [Canadiens]
51/2 La Patrie
52/3 Parkhurst 52
53/4 Parkhurst 23
55/6 Parkhurst 48
57/8 Parkhurst [Mont.] 10
93/4 Parkhurst PR68
01/2 Parkhurst PR20, PR52, PR68, PR114, ✍ PA15
93/4 Parkie 56-57 69
45-54 Quaker Oats
60/1 Shirriff 74
61/2 Shirriff 35
01/2 Signature ✍ VA23
58/9 Topps 5
59/0 Topps 43
61/2 Topps 31
61/2 Topps 44
62/3 Topps 30
91/2 Ultimate Original Six 15, ✍ Aut. 15

ST-LAURENT, SAM
88/9 ProCards / Adirondack
89/0 ProCards AHL 315
90/1 ProCards 9
91/2 ProCards 193
86/7 DETR / Little Caesars

ST-LOUIS, FRANCE
94/5 Classic W2
97/8 Game of Her Life
97/8 UD Coll. Choice 284

ST-LOUIS, JONATHAN
99/0 Halifax Mooseheads
97/8 Rimouski Océanic

ST-LOUIS, JOSH
95/6 Swift Current Broncos

ST-LOUIS, MARTIN
01/2 Adrenaline 177
02/3 Bowman 100
99/0 Choice 8
01/2 Crown Royale 130
02/3 Crown Royale 89
98/9 Dynagon Ice 28
02/3 eTopps 55
02/3 O-Pee-Chee 37
98/9 Omega 38
01/2 Pacific 358
02/3 Pacific 355
02/3 Pacific Complete 393
98/9 Pa. Crown Roy. 20
02/3 Parkhurst 134
02/3 Parkhurst Retro 193
00/1 Premier Plus 85
01/2 PS Titanium 128
02/3 PS Titanium 91
02/3 Quest for the Cup 90, ✄ GWJ 20
01/2 Signature 49, ✍ Aut. 49
02/3 Sports Vault 127
02/3 Topps 37
02/3 To. Limited 37
02/3 To. Total 132
98/9 Upper Deck 234
01/2 Upper Deck 158
98/9 UD G. Reserve 234
02/3 UD MVP 167
02/3 UD Rookie 89
01/2 UD Vintage 231
02/3 UD Vintage 231
01/2 Vanguard 91
02/3 Vanguard 90
01/2 Victory 322
97/8 Cleveland Lumberjacks
97/8 Cleveland Lumberjacks

ST-LOUIS, TODD
95/6 Slapshot 175
97/8 Fort Worth Brahmas

ST-MARSEILLE, DERRICK
77/8 Nova Scotia Voyageurs

ST-MARSEILLE, FRANK
70/1 Colgate 22
70/1 Dad's Cookies
70/1 Eddie Sargent 180
71/2 Eddie Sargent 184
72/3 Eddie Sargent 188
70/1 Esso Power Player
74/5 Loblaws
69/0 O-Pee-Chee 177
70/1 O-Pee-Chee 214
70/1 O-Pee-Chee DE 26
71/2 O-Pee-Chee 38
71/2 O-Pee-Chee Book. 15
72/3 O-Pee-Chee 65
73/4 O-Pee-Chee 262
74/5 O-Pee-Chee 98
74/5 O-Pee-Chee 374
75/6 O-Pee-Chee 15
76/7 O-Pee-Chee 276
71/2 Topps 38
72/3 Topps 71
74/5 Topps 98
75/6 Topps 15
71/2 Toronto Sun Photo
71/2 SLOU
92/3 SLOU / McDon. 19
77/8 Nova Scotia Voyageurs

ST-ONGE, DAVID
96/7 Rimouski Océanic
97/8 Rimouski Océanic

ST-PIERRE, DAVID
92/3 Classic Prospects 108
90/1 7th..Sketch LHJMQ 236
91/2 7th...Sketch LHJMQ 145
91/2 Upper Deck WJC 49
95/6 Hampton Roads
92/3 Salt Lake G'Eagles

ST-PIERRE, KARL
99/0 UD Prospects 87
00/1 Chicoutimi Saguenéens
02/3 Québec Remparts

ST-PIERRE, KIM
01/2 Blizzak

ST-PIERRE, MARCEL
51/2 Bas du Fleuve 35

ST-PIERRE, MARTIN
01/2 Guelph Storm
01/2 Guelph Storm M-Cup

ST-PIERRE, SAMUEL
99 Bowman 75
99/0 Detroit Vipers

ST-PIERRE, SIMON
00/1 Victoriaville Tigres 6

ST-PIERRE, YAN
91/2 7th...Sketch LHJMQ 243
93/4 Slapshot / Drummond. 8

ST-SAUVEUR, CLAUDE
76/7 OPC 379
74/5 OPC WHA 62
75/6 OPC WHA 124
76/7 OPC WHA 90
77/8 OPC WHA 7
73/4 OPC WHA Poster 18
73/4 Vancouver Blazers

ST. CROIX, CHRIS
99 Bowman 120
01/2 Hartford Wolf Pack
96/7 Kamloops Blazers
97/8 Kamloops Blazers
98/9 Kamloops Blazers

ST. HILAIRE, ALAIN
99/0 Missouri RiverOtters

ST. JACQUES, CHRIS
99/0 Medicine Hat Tigers
00/1 Medicine Hat Tigers

ST. JAMES, TOM
82/3 Kitchener Rangers

ST. JOHN, MIKE
89/0 7th..Sketch OHL 143

STAAL, ERIC
01/2 Peterborough Petes

STAAL, KIM
99/0 UD Elitserien 158, 212
00/1 UD Elitserien 148

STABL, LUKAS
99/0 Score 37

STACCHI, MIKE
95/6 Roanoke Express

STACEY, BRIAN
91/2 7th...Sketch OHL 373
95/6 Slapshot 372
96/7 Kansas City Blades

STACEY, MICHAEL
01/2 Victoriaville Tigres 13

STACKHOUSE, RON
71/2 Eddie Sargent 64
72/3 Eddie Sargent 77
70/1 Esso Power Player
74/5 Loblaws
71/2 O-Pee-Chee 83
72/3 O-Pee-Chee 287
73/4 O-Pee-Chee 236
74/5 O-Pee-Chee 188
75/6 O-Pee-Chee 111
76/7 O-Pee-Chee 72
77/8 O-Pee-Chee 157
78/9 O-Pee-Chee 72
79/0 O-Pee-Chee 154
80/1 O-Pee-Chee 228
81/2 O-Pee-Chee 266
82/3 O-Pee-Chee 275
81/2 OPC Sticker 188
82/3 Post [Pitt.]
74/5 Topps 188
75/6 Topps 111
76/7 Topps 72
77/8 Topps 157
78/9 Topps 72
79/0 Topps 154
80/1 Topps 228
71/2 Toronto Sun Photo
74/5 PITT
77/8 PITT / McDonald's

STADLER, WAITER
72 Semic Sticker 95

STAFFORD, B
88/9 EDMO / Action 80
90/1 EDMO / IGA

STAFFORD, BEN
02/3 Philadelphia Phantoms

STAGG, BRIAN
91/2 7th...Sketch OHL 232

STAHAN, BUTCH
51/2 Laval Dairy 105
52/3 St. Lawrence 72

STAHL, CRAIG
95/6 Tri-City Americans 21

STAHL, MIKAEL
89/0 Semic Elitserien 185
90/1 Semic Elitserien 20

STAIOS, STEVE
91/2 Arena 20
91/2 Classic 24
91/2 Classic Four Sport 24
93/4 Cla. Prospects 149
96/7 Leaf 223
02/3 Pacific Complete 451
99/0 Pa. Paramount 15
96/7 Pinnacle 231
97/8 Pi. Be A Player 161, ✍ Aut. 161
91 7th..Sketch Mem.Cup 107
90/1 7th..Sketch OHL 266, 271
91/2 7th...Sketch OHL 219
91/2 Star Pics 51
00/1 To. Heritage 199
91/2 Ultimate Draft Pick 22, ✍ Aut.
96/7 Upper Deck 218
00/1 Upper Deck 241
01/2 Victory 18
93/4 Peoria Rivermen
94/5 Peoria Rivermen
92/3 Sudbury Wolves

STAIT, BILL
92/3 MPS SJHL 54

STAJAN, MATTHEW
01/2 Belleville Bulls

STAJDUHAR, NICK
93/4 Classic 28
94/5 Classic 83
93/4 Cla. 4 Sport 199
93/4 Donruss CAN19
93/4 Parkhurst 507
93/4 Pinnacle 463
90/1 7th..Sketch OHL 144
91/2 7th...Sketch OHL 380
93/4 Upper Deck 543
96/7 Upper Deck 194
94/5 Cape Breton Oilers
96/7 Pensacola Ice Pilots
97/8 Pensacola Ice Pilots

STAKOWSKI, HARTLEY
67/8 Columbus Checkers

STAMBERT, ORVAR
89/0 Semic Elitserien 54
90/1 Semic Elitserien 279
91/2 Semic Elitserien 60

STAMLER, LORNE
78/9 O-Pee-Chee 301
78/9 TORO
79/0 WINN
81/2 Indianapolis Checkers
82/3 Indianapolis Checkers

STAMP, ERIC
91/2 7th...Sketch OHL 195

STANDBERG, THOMAS
94/5 Leaf Elit Set 48

STANDING, DAVID
94/5 Humberside Hawks 15

STANDISH, BOBBY
91/2 Air Canada SJHL D3

STANDISH, MARTY
99 Bowman 114
99/0 Missouri RiverOtters
97/8 Portland Winter Hawks

STANFIELD, FRED
64-67 BeeHive-3 [Chic.]
64-67 BeeHive-3 [Chic.]
64/5 Coke/Sprite [Chic.]
65/6 Coca-Cola
70/1 Dad's Cookies
70/1 Eddie Sargent 12
71/2 Eddie Sargent 1
72/3 Eddie Sargent 15
70/1 Esso Power Player
74/5 Loblaws
74/5 Loblaws Update
68/9 O-Pee-Chee 10
69/0 O-Pee-Chee 32
70/1 O-Pee-Chee 5
70/1 O-Pee-Chee DE 7
71/2 O-Pee-Chee 7
72/3 O-Pee-Chee 150
74/5 O-Pee-Chee 31
75/6 O-Pee-Chee 332
76/7 O-Pee-Chee 58
77/8 O-Pee-Chee 161
78/9 O-Pee-Chee 352
95/6 Parkie 66-67 25
94/5 Parkie Tall 37
68/9 Shirriff / Bost. 9
65/6 Topps 63
66/7 Topps 56
67/8 Topps 36
68/9 Topps 10
69/0 Topps 32
70/1 Topps 5
71/2 Topps 7
72/3 Topps 135
74/5 Topps 31
76/7 Topps 58
77/8 Topps 161
71/2 Toronto Sun Photo
91/2 Ultimate Original Six 54, ✍ Aut. 54
70/1 BOST
71/2 BOST
98/9 BOST / Alumni 17
75/6 BUFF / Linnett
73/4 MINS

STANFIELD, JIM
71/2 Eddie Sargent 78
72/3 Eddie Sargent 86

STANFIELD, ROB
95/6 Slapshot 134
98/9 Huntington Blizzard

STANGBY, SHANE
90/1 7th..Sketch WHL 252

STANGLE, FRANK
37/8 World Wide Gum 110

STANIFORTH, KENT
90/1 7th..Sketch WHL 144
91/2 7th...Sketch WHL 272

STANIOWSKI, ED
76/7 O-Pee-Chee 104
77/8 O-Pee-Chee 54
79/0 O-Pee-Chee 327
80/1 O-Pee-Chee 328
82/3 O-Pee-Chee 393
82/3 OPC/Topps Sticker 210
82/3 Post [Winn.]
83/4 Souhaits Keychain [Jets]
76/7 Topps 104
77/8 Topps 54
78/9 SLOU
81/2 WINN
82/3 WINN

STANKIEWICZ, BRIAN
94 Semic 232
93 Semic Sticker 269

STANLEY, ALLAN
45-64 BeeHive-2 [NYRa.]
45-64 BeeHive-2 [Toro.]
45-64 BeeHive-2 [Toro.]
64-67 BeeHive-3 [Toro.]
63-65 Chex
64/5 Coke/Sprite [Toro.]
65/6 Coca-Cola
62/3 Cowan Tile
83 HHOF Postcard G14
83&87 HHOF 238
95/6 Legends of Hockey 66
68/9 O-Pee-Chee 183
68/9 O-Pee-Chee PS 16
51/2 Parkhurst 94
52/3 Parkhurst 21
53/4 Parkhurst 64
58/9 Parkhurst 23
59/0 Parkhurst 44
60/1 Parkhurst 16
61/2 Parkhurst 16
62/3 Parkhurst 9
63/4 Parkhurst 1
63/4 Parkhurst 61
92/3 Parkhurst PR-11
02/3 Parkie - Reprint 166, 184, 229, 250, 263, 274, 283, 293
93/4 Parkie 56-57 20
95/6 Parkie 66-67 110, 122
94/5 Parkie Tall 115
60/1 Shirriff 6
61/2 Shirriff 42
62/3 Shirriff 2
68/9 Shirriff / Toro. 3
54/5 Topps 41
57/8 Topps 15
64/5 Topps 104
66/7 Topps 16
66/7 Topps 128
66/7 Topps / Test 16
67/8 Topps 13
60/1 Toronto Star Photo
63/4 Toronto Star Action
63/4 Toronto Star Photo
64/5 Toronto Star Action
61/2 Toronto Star Weekend
66/7 Toronto Star Weekend
91/2 Ultimate Original Six 44, 75, ✍ Aut. 44
60/1 York Glass [Toro.]
60/1 York
61/2 York 9
63/4 York 14
67/8 York 26
67/8 York
64/5 TORO
68/9 TORO
69/0 TORO

STANLEY, CHRIS
99 Bowman 131

STANLEY, DARYL
86/7 PHIL
87/8 VANC / Shell
89/0 VANC / Mohawk
83/4 Springfield Indians 23
81/2 Saskatoon Blades

STANLEY, GRAHAM
89/0 ProCards AHL 18
90/1 ProCards 353

STANLEY, LORD
01/2 SP GU ✍ Sig
01/2 Upper Deck ✍ Cut

STANLEY, RUSSELL (BARNEY)
83 HHOF Postcard A13
83&87 HHOF 12
23/4 Paulins Candy 30
19 Vancouver Millionaires
19 Vancouver Millionaires

STANLEY OF PRESTON, LORD
83 HHOF Postcard A14
83&87 HHOF 13
92/3 Legends 18

STANOWSKI, WALLY
34-43 BeeHive-1 [Toro.]
45-64 BeeHive-2 [Toro.]
45-64 BeeHive-2 [NYRa.]
39/0 O-Pee-Chee 11
40/1 O-Pee-Chee 103
45-54 Quaker Oats

STANSFIELD, SEAN
88/9 Sudbury Wolves

STANTIEN, ROMAN
94/5 APS 242
95/6 APS 22
96/7 APS 229
97/8 APS 50
98/9 DS 86
99/0 DS 137
98/9 OFS 112
99/0 OFS 64
00/1 OFS 336
01/2 OFS -UHI 27

STANTON, PAUL
91/2 Bowman 91
92/3 Bowman 284
95/6 DEL 267
96/7 DEL 161
98/9 DEL 229
99/0 Eishockey 3
92/3 Fleer Ultra 381
91/2 O-Pee-Chee 339
92/3 O-Pee-Chee 361
90/1 OPC Premier 110
91/2 Panini Sticker 274
93/4 Parkhurst 288
92/3 Pinnacle 308
93/4 Pinnacle 330
93/4 Premier 5
90/1 Pro Set 633
91/2 Pro Set 457
89/0 ProCards IHL 156
90/1 Score 27T
91/2 Score 366
91/2 Score CAN 406
92/3 Score 135
93/4 Score 321
93/4 Score 510
92/3 Topps 460
91/2 To. Stadium 380
92/3 To. Stadium 52
93/4 To. Stadium 52
90/1 Upper Deck 404
91/2 Upper Deck 203
92/3 Upper Deck 100
00/1 UD DEL 197, S8
01/2 UD DEL SS11
91/2 PITT / Elby's
91/2 PITT / Foodland 13
92/3 PITT / Coke-Clark
92/3 PITT / Foodland 13

STAPLES, JEFF
94/5 Slapshot Memorial 28
98/9 Milwaukee Admirals
92/3 Brandon Wheat Kings

STAPLETON, MIKE
02/3 Cardset 120
94/5 Leaf 147
99/0 Pacific 327
00/1 Pacific 22
97/8 Pa. Invincible R-155
94/5 Pinnacle 228
96/7 Pi. Be A Player 92, ✍ Aut. 92
88/9 ProCards / Saginaw
90/1 ProCards 402
93/4 Score 638
86/7 CHIC / Coke
87/8 CHIC / Coke
91/2 CHIC / Coke
93/4 EDMO / Sheet
96/7 PHOE / Coca-Cola
97/8 PHOE / Coca-Cola
98/9 PHOE / Coca-Cola
92/3 PITT / Coke-Clark
93/4 PITT / Foodland 21
95/6 WINN

STAPLETON, PAT
45-64 BeeHive-2 [Bost.]
45-64 BeeHive-2 [Bost.]
64-67 BeeHive-3 [Bost.]
64-67 BeeHive-3 [Chic.]
70/1 Colgate 77
70/1 Dad's Cookies
70/1 Eddie Sargent 44
71/2 Eddie Sargent 45
72/3 Eddie Sargent 69
70/1 Esso Power Player
91/2 Future Trends C72 9, ✍ 9
62/3 Cowan Tile
91/2 Kraft 69
72/3 Post 13
73/4 Mac's Milk
68/9 O-Pee-Chee 15
69/0 O-Pee-Chee 69
69/0 O-Pee-Chee 4in1
70/1 O-Pee-Chee 17
71/2 O-Pee-Chee 25
71/2 O-Pee-Chee 258
72/3 O-Pee-Chee 4
72/3 O-Pee-Chee 249
72/3 O-Pee-Chee TC
74/5 OPC WHA 35
73/4 OPC WHA Poster 4
95/6 Parkie 66-67 38, 123
95/6 Playoff 39
61/2 Shirriff 13
68/9 Shirriff / Chic. 2
61/2 Topps 18
62/3 Topps 8
65/6 Topps 120
66/7 Topps 57
66/7 Topps 129
66/7 Topps / Test 57
67/8 Topps 61
68/9 Topps 15
69/0 Topps 69
70/1 Topps 17
71/2 Topps 25
72/3 Topps 70
72/3 Topps 129
66/7 Toronto Star Weekend
71/2 Toronto Sun Photo
68/9 CHIC

STARIBACHER, SILVESTER
79 Panini Sticker 305

STARIKOV, SERGEI
90/1 ProCards 557
91/2 ProCards 327
82 Semic Sticker 59
83/4 Soviet Stars
87/8 Soviet Stars
89/0 NJER
89/0 NJER / Caretta
92/3 San Diego Gulls

STARK, JAY
86/7 Portland Winter Hawks

STARKE, JOE
36-39 Diamond Match TT1

STARLING, CHAD
01/2 Peoria Rivermen
98/9 Kamloops Blazers
99/0 Kamloops Blazers
99/0 Kamloops Blazers
00/1 Sudbury Wolves 13

STARNYSKI, AARON
94/5 Slapshot / Sudbury 22

STAROSTENKO, DMITRI
93/4 Cla. Prospects 118
00/1 Mir 269
92/3 Red Ace Blue 25
92/3 Red Ace Violet 31
94/5 Binghampton Rangers
95/6 Binghampton Rangers

STARR, AARON
00/1 Saskatoon Blades

STARR, HAROLD
36-39 Diamond Match TT2
36-39 Diamond Match TT3

STARSHINOV, VYACHESLAV
91/2 Future Trends C72 38
70/1 Kuvajulkaisut 17
69/0 Mästar Serien 35
72 Panda MM-Toronto
72 Semic Sticker 8
74 Semic Sticker 44
69/0 Soviet Stars
70/1 Soviet Stars
71/2 Soviet Stars
71/2 Williams Finnish 16

STARTUP, JAMES
91/2 7th...Sketch WHL 106
91/2 Saskatoon Blades

STAS, SERGEI
98/9 DEL 252
99/0 Eishockey 306
00/1 UD DEL 21
01/2 UD DEL 164
94/5 Erie Panthers
95/6 Fort Wayne Komets

STASCHE, JOACHIM
74 Hellas MM-Jenkki 102
79 Panini Sticker 255

STASIUK, JEREMY
95/6 Dayton Bombers

STASIUK, VIC
45-64 BeeHive-2 [Detr.]
45-64 BeeHive-2 [Detr.]
45-64 BeeHive-2 [Detr.]
45-64 BeeHive-2 [Bost.]
62/3 Cowan Tile
51/2 Parkhurst 62
52/3 Parkhurst 90
53/4 Parkhurst 39
61/2 Parkhurst 32
62/3 Parkhurst 22
63/4 Parkhurst 58
93/4 Parkhurst PR64
93/4 Parkie 56-57 169
93/4 Parkie 56-57 9
60/1 Shirriff 103
61/2 Shirriff 63
57/8 Topps 11
58/9 Topps 9
59/0 Topps 14
60/1 Topps 66
58/9 Toronto Star Weekend
62/3 York Transfer 30
57-58 BOST
70/1 PHIL

STASTNY, ANTON
81/2 Dernière Heure
83/4 Funmate Puffy 14 [w/]
86/7 Kraft Sports 50
81/2 O-Pee-Chee 282
82/3 O-Pee-Chee 294
83/4 O-Pee-Chee 302
84/5 O-Pee-Chee 291
85/6 OPC/Topps 78
86/7 OPC/Topps 125
87/8 OPC/Topps 185
88/9 OPC/Topps 98
81/2 OPC Sticker 70
82/3 OPC/Topps Sticker 24
83/4 OPC/Topps Sticker 252
84/5 OPC Sticker 178
85/6 OPC Sticker 147
86/7 OPC Sticker 27
87/8 OPC Sticker 228
88/9 OPC Sticker 194
87/8 Panini Sticker 166
88/9 Panini Sticker 357
80/1 Pepsi Bottle Cap
82/3 Post [Québ.]
94 Semic 202
83/4 Souhaits Keychain [Nordiques]
02/3 UD Foundations 76
83/4 Vachon 75-55
80/1 QUÉB
81/2 QUÉB
82/3 QUÉB
83/4 QUÉB
84/5 QUÉB
85/6 QUÉB
85/6 QUÉB / Gene. Foods
85/6 QUÉB / McDonald's
85/6 QUÉB / Provigo
86/7 QUÉB
86/7 QUÉB / Gene. Foods
86/7 QUÉB / McDonald's
86/7 QUÉB / Yum Yum
87/8 QUÉB / Gene. Foods
87/8 QUÉB / Yum Yum
88/9 QUÉB
88/9 QUÉB / Gene. Foods

STASTNY, BOHUSLAV
72 Hellas MM-Jenkki 91
74 Hellas MM-Jenkki 82
72 Panda MM-Toronto
72 Semic Sticker 32
74 Semic Sticker 64
71/2 Williams Finnish 38
72/3 Williams Finnish 19
73/4 Williams Finnish 61

STASTNY, MARIAN
81/2 Dernière Heure
83/4 Funmate Puffy 16 [w/]
82/3 McDonald's Les Étoiles 10
82/3 O-Pee-Chee 295
83/4 O-Pee-Chee 303
84/5 O-Pee-Chee 292
82/3 OPC/Topps Sticker 20
83/4 OPC/Topps Sticker 168
83/4 OPC/Topps Sticker 251
84/5 OPC Sticker 177
86/7 OPC Sticker 144-252
79 Panini Sticker 90
82/3 Post [Québ.]
83/4 Souhaits Keychain [Nordiques]
83/4 Vachon 76-56
81/2 QUÉB
82/3 QUÉB
83/4 QUÉB
84/5 QUÉB
85/6 TORO

STASTNY, MICHAL
99/0 Missouri RiverOtters

STASTNY, PETER
90/1 Bowman 86
91/2 Bowman 287
92/3 Bowman 249
81/2 Dernière Heure
93/4 Donruss 487
94/5 Donruss 191
94/5 Flair 159
01/2 Fleer Greats 11, -RC 6, -BC 2, ✍ Aut.
92/3 Fleer Ultra 118, -UI 24
94/5 Fleer Ultra 190
88/9 Frito Lay
83/4 Funmate Puffy 13 [w/]
92/3 Future Trends C76 131
93/4 Hockey Wit 70
84/5 Kellogg's 22
89/0 Kraft 33
90/1 Kraft 54
91/2 Kraft 83
86/7 Kraft Sports 51
82/3 McDonald's Les Étoiles 24
81/2 O-Pee-Chee 269
81/2 O-Pee-Chee 286
81/2 O-Pee-Chee 287
81/2 O-Pee-Chee 395
82/3 O-Pee-Chee 276
82/3 O-Pee-Chee 292
82/3 O-Pee-Chee 293
83/4 O-Pee-Chee 304
84/5 O-Pee-Chee 293
85/6 OPC/Topps 31
86/7 OPC/Topps 20
87/8 OPC/Topps 21
88/9 OPC/Topps 22
90/1 OPC/Topps 334
91/2 O-Pee-Chee 275
92/3 O-Pee-Chee 216
89/0 OPC/Topps 143
88/9 OPC Stars 37
81/2 OPC Sticker 69
81/2 OPC Sticker 263
82/3 OPC/Topps Sticker 15
82/3 OPC/Topps Sticker 18
82/3 OPC/Topps Sticker 19
82/3 OPC/Topps Sticker 167
83/4 OPC/Topps Sticker 167
83/4 OPC/Topps Sticker 253
84/5 OPC Sticker 141
84/5 OPC Sticker 164
84/5 OPC Sticker 165
85/6 OPC Sticker 156
86/7 OPC Sticker 26
87/8 OPC Sticker 222
88/9 OPC Sticker 189
89/0 opcSticker 182
98/9 OFS Leg. 3
79 Panini Sticker 84
87/8 Panini Sticker 164
88/0 Panini Sticker 358
89/0 Panini Sticker 324
90/1 Panini Sticker 70
91/2 Panini Sticker 220
92/3 Panini Sticker 174
93/4 Panini Sticker 41
91/2 Parkhurst 103
91/2 Parkhurst 209
94/5 Parkhurst 203
80/1 Pepsi Bottle Cap
91/2 Pinnacle 266
92/3 Pinnacle 359
94/5 Pinnacle 134
94/5 POG 208
82/3 Post [Québ.]
94/5 Premier 182
90/1 Pro Set 175, 176
91/2 Pro Set 143
92/3 Pro Set 100
91/2 Pro Set Platinum 194
87/8 Pro Sport CW12
91/2 Puck / Pro Set 16
90/1 Score 96
90/1 Sco. Hot Cards 48
91/2 Score 66
91/2 Score CAN 66
92/3 Score 291
93/4 Score 22
94 Semic 200
84/5 7-Eleven
85/6 7-Eleven Superstars 16
83/4 Souhaits Keychain [Nordiques]
81/2 Topps 39
81/2 Topps 61
84/5 Topps 130
92/3 Topps 469
91/2 To. Stadium 263
92/3 To. Stadium 140
01/2 T/O Archives 21 , ✍ CAI
90/1 Upper Deck 163
91/2 Upper Deck 113
94/5 Upper Deck 60
99/0 UD C. Legends 36
02/3 UD Foundations ✍ SG
00/1 UD Legends 109
01/2 UD Legends 76
02/3 UD Piece ✄ HH, ✍ MD
83/4 Vachon 77-57
83/4 Vachon 77-90
96 Wien 227
90/1 NJER
80/1 QUÉB
81/2 QUÉB
82/3 QUÉB
83/4 QUÉB
84/5 QUÉB
85/6 QUÉB
85/6 QUÉB / Gene. Foods
85/6 QUÉB / McDonald's
85/6 QUÉB / Provigo
86/7 QUÉB
86/7 QUÉB / Gene. Foods
86/7 QUÉB / McDonald's
86/7 QUÉB / Yum Yum
87/8 QUÉB / Gene. Foods
87/8 QUÉB / Yum Yum
88/9 QUÉB
88/9 QUÉB / Gene. Foods
89/0 QUÉB
89/0 QUÉB / Gene. Foods
89/0 QUÉB / Police
90/1 QUÉB

STASZAK, RAY
85/6 DETR / Little Caesars

STATHOPULOS, MIKE
00/1 London Knights
01/2 London Knights

STATHOS, DAVE
02/3 Cardset 272, 297

STATKUS, JOE
01/2 Rockford IceHogs

STAUBER, PETE
91/2 ProCards 129

STAUBER, ROBB
92/3 Fleer Ultra 311
93/4 Fleer Ultra 347
90/1 OPC/Topps 181
92/3 OPC Premier 115
92/3 Parkhurst 303
94/5 Parkhurst 109
95/6 Parkhurst 25
93/4 Pinnacle 338
93/4 Pinnacle Mask 3
93/4 Power Play 363
93/4 Premier 109
94/5 Premier 248
90/1 ProCards 418
93/4 Score 346
93/4 To. Stadium 327
90/1 Upper Deck 165
92/3 Upper Deck 495
94/5 UD BAP R59
97/8 Hartford Wolf Pack
96/7 Portland Pirates Hershey
96/7 Portland Pirates
95/6 Rochester Americans

STAVENSKY, STANISLAV
00/1 OFS 152
99/0 Score 33

STAVJANA, ANTONIN
94/5 APS 230
95/6 APS 8, 357, 389, 401
96/7 APS 216, 354
97/8 APS 31, 373
97/8 DS 57
96/7 DS Sticker 6, 19
97/8 DS Sticker 10, 168
95 Globe 150
91/2 Jyvas Hyva 41
98/9 OFS 273, -Leg. 17
99/0 OFS 206
00/1 OFS 347, 406
95 Panini Worlds 194
94 Semic 173
92/3 Semic Elitserien 127
89 Semic Sticker 181
91 Semic Sticker 111
96 Wien 105

STAVJANA, MIROSLAV
94/5 APS 240
97/8 DS Sticker 123

STE-MARIE, ROGER
51/2 Bas du Fleuve 28
52/3 Bas du Fleuve 62

STEADMAN, RICK
01/2 London Knights

STEARNS, CAL
60/1 Cleveland Barons

STEBLECKI, ROMAN
89 Semic Sticker 145

STEBLYK, BRENT
82/3 Medicine Hat Tigers
83/4 Medicine Hat Tigers

STEBNICKI, MAREK
95/6 DEL 235
98/9 DEL 26
99/0 Eishockey 137
00/1 UD DEL 206, S3

STECHER, DINO
91 Semic Sticker 179

STEEGE, BRANDON
91/2 Minnesota G'Gophers
92/3 Minnesota G'Gophers
93/4 Minnesota G'Gophers
94/5 Minnesota G'Gophers

STEEL, ANDY
93/4 Humberside Hawks 14

STEEL, GREG
78/9 Saginaw Gears

STEEN, ANDERS
80/1 Pepsi Bottle Cap
80/1 WINN

STEEN, THOMAS
90/1 Bowman 133
91/2 Bowman 200
92/3 Bowman 312
96/7 DEL 33
98/9 DEL 162
93/4 Donruss 389
94/5 Donruss 154
93/4 EA Sports 148
92/3 Fleer Ultra 247
93/4 Fleer Ultra 69
94/5 Fleer Ultra 396
95 Globe 40
90/1 Kraft 55
86/7 Kraft Sports 80
93/4 Leaf 165
94/5 Leaf 376
82/3 O-Pee-Chee 391
83/4 O-Pee-Chee 393
84/5 O-Pee-Chee 348
85/6 O-Pee-Chee 206
86/7 O-Pee-Chee 257
87/8 O-Pee-Chee 221
88/9 O-Pee-Chee 254
90/1 OPC/Topps 283
91/2 O-Pee-Chee 218
92/3 O-Pee-Chee 385
89/0 O-Pee-Chee 290
83/4 OPC/Topps Sticker 289
84/5 OPC Sticker 292
85/6 OPC Sticker 253-133
86/7 OPC Sticker 110-243
88/9 OPC Sticker 138-9
89/0 opcSticker 144
87/8 Panini Sticker 365
88/9 Panini Sticker 159
89/0 Panini Sticker 163
90/1 Panini Sticker 316
90/1 Panini/WPG 22
91/2 Panini Sticker 68
92/3 Panini Sticker 53
93/4 Panini Sticker 191
95 Panini Worlds 291
92/3 Parkhurst 214
93/4 Parkhurst 502
94/5 Parkhurst 263
91/2 Pinnacle 275
92/3 Pinnacle 29
93/4 Pinnacle 159
94/5 Pinnacle 171
94/5 POG 255
93/4 Power Play 275
93/4 Power Play 476
93/4 Premier 11
94/5 Premier 471
90/1 Pro Set 565
91/2 Pro Set 271
92/3 Pro Set 217
91/2 Pro Set Platinum 138
90/1 Score 14
90/1 Sco. Hot Cards 8
91/2 Score 198
91/2 Score CAN 198
92/3 Score 80
93/4 Score 71
94/5 Score 65
82 Semic Sticker 150
89 Semic Sticker 15
91 Semic Sticker 209
92 Semic Sticker 70
93 Semic Sticker 36
92/3 Topps 141
91/2 To. Stadium 207
93/4 To. Stadium 282
94/5 To. Stadium 176
90/1 Upper Deck 94, 313
91/2 Upper Deck 181
92/3 Upper Deck 154
93/4 Upper Deck 166
94/5 Upper Deck 192
94/5 UD BAP ✍ 159
83/4 Vachon 138-18
81/2 WINN
82/3 WINN
83/4 WINN
84/5 WINN / Safety Tips
85/6 WINN
85/6 WINN / Safety Tips
86/7 WINN
87/8 WINN
88/9 WINN / Safety Tips
89/0 WINN / Safeway
90/1 WINN / IGA
91/2 WINN / IGA
93/4 WINN / Ruffles
93/4 WINN Readers

STEENBERGEN, LYLE
98/9 Calgary Hitmen 15

STEER, JAMIE
93/4 Cla. Prospects 240
94/5 Dayton Bombers 8
94/5 Dayton Bombers 22
92/3 Greensboro Monarchs 16
90/1 Michigan Tech Huskies
91/2 Michigan Tech Huskies
91/2 Michigan Tech Huskies
91/2 Michigan Tech Huskies

STEFAN, COACH
99/0 Eishockey 412

STEFAN, GREG
84/5 O-Pee-Chee 65
85/6 OPC/Topps 157
86/7 OPC/Topps 51
87/8 OPC/Topps 186
88/9 OPC/Topps 68
89/0 OPC/Topps 23
88/9 OPC Stars 38
84/5 OPC Sticker 41
85/6 OPC Sticker 31-161
86/7 OPC Sticker 165
88/9 OPC Sticker 252-122
89/0 opcSticker 248-109
87/8 Panini Sticker 237
88/9 Panini Sticker 37
89/0 Panini Sticker 59
84/5 Topps 48
85/6 DETR / Little Caesars
86/7 DETR / Little Caesars
87/8 DETR / Little Caesars
88/9 DETR / Little Caesars
89/0 DETR / Little Caesars
80/1 Oshawa Generals

STEFAN, JOE
90/1 ProCards 519

STEFAN, LEO
94/5 DEL 206
95/6 DEL 208
96/7 DEL 290
98/9 DEL 324
95 Globe 223
95 Panini Worlds 75
94 Semic 290
00/1 UD DEL 54, ✂ GJ
01/2 UD DEL 57
96 Wien 200
STEFAN, PATRIK
01/2 Adrenaline 11
97/8 APS 20
01/2 Atomic 4, PP 2
00/1 Aurora 8, Pins. 8, SR-3
99/0 BAP Mem. 1
00/1 BAP Mem. 268
01/2 BAP Mem. 69
02/3 BAP Mem. 143
02/3 Calder ✂ GWJ 2
99/0 Crown Royale 9, -CS 3, -C21 2, -IG 2
00/1 Crown Royale 7, JotC-3
01/2 Crown Royale 8
97/8 DS 87
97/8 DS Sticker 222
99/0 Dynagon Ice 6, -CM 18, -LL 3
02/3 Exclusive 9
02/3 First Ed. 65, ✂ Jers.
01/2 Heads Up 5, BTI 2
02/3 Heads Up ✂ GWQ 2
99/0 HoloGrFX 3, ✍ Aut.
00/1 McDonald's 3, GCDC-1
99/0 Millenium 12, C-7, ✍ Aut. 12
99/0 NHL Power Play [x3]
01/2 O-Pee-Chee 75
02/3 O-Pee-Chee 138
99/0 Omega 13, -5ST 1, -EOP 3, -Gen.10
00/1 Pacific 23
01/2 Pacific 25, TDP 2
02/3 Pacific 21
02/3 Pacific Complete 466
99/0 Pa. Paramount 251
00/1 Pa. Paramount 15
99/0 Panini Sticker 15
00/1 Panini Sticker 5
00/1 Parkhurst P-70
01/2 Parkhurst 2, ✂ PJ17, ✂ PS17
02/3 Parkhurst 17, ✂ TT9
02/3 Parkhurst Retro 185
00/1 Premier Plus 3
99/0 Prism 9, -IP 1
00/1 Pr. Stock 6, Res. 3, PSNW 1
01/2 Pr. Stock 4
02/3 Pr. Stock Reserve 5
01/2 PS Titanium 6
01/2 PS Titanium Draft ✂ 8
02/3 PS Titanium ✂ GWJ 4
00/1 Revolution 8, HD-3
00/1 Signature 214, F-2, ✍ Aut. 137, ✂ HSHSJers
01/2 Signature 2, ✍ Aut. 2, ✂ TM2
02/3 Signature 61, ✍ 61, ✂ YP5, ✂ TQ12
99/0 SP Authentic 91, -TH1, ✍ SotT
00/1 SP Authentic 4
01/2 SP Authentic 121, ✍ SotT
00/1 SP GU 3
01/2 SP GU ✂ Patch, ✂ PatchSig., ✂ PatchT
02/3 SP Game-Used ✂ PC
02/3 Sports Vault 5
99/0 SPx 163, X8
00/1 SPx 3, HH2
01/2 SPx 2
00/1 Stadion 91
99/0 Stadium 181, -Chrome 43, Big 18
00/1 Stadium 117, CA13
00/1 Topps 14, NHLD5
01/2 Topps 75
02/3 Topps 138
99/0 To. Chrome 29
00/1 To. Chrome 14
99/0 To. Gold Label 97, FG6
00/1 To. Gold Label 19, NG12
00/1 To. Heritage 11
02/3 To. Limited 138
99/0 To. Prmr. Plus 101, PR5, TNO7, ✍ SB
01/2 To. Reserve 17
00/1 To. Stars 13, P2
02/3 To. Total 46
00/1 UD Heroes 5
00/1 UD Reserve 5
00/1 Ultimate Mem. ✍ U-35, ✂ Jers. 30, ✂ J-34, ✂ S-34
02/3 Ultimate Mem. ✂ FO
99/0 Ult. Victory 91, -FF6, sg8
99/0 Upper Deck 161, 181, AS20, IG8, SB15, SS7
00/1 Upper Deck 12, P1
01/2 Upper Deck 9, ✂ NG
02/3 Upper Deck 10, ✂ BF
99/0 UD Black Diam. 5, D2, M1
00/1 UD Black Diam. 3
99/0 UD G. Reserve 161, 181, ✍ UDA
00/1 UD Ice 3, ✍ CCA
01/2 UD Ice ✂ FJ
00/1 UD Legends 4, 5, ✍ ES
00/1 UD MVP 12, ME8, ✍ PS, ✍ ME
01/2 UD MVP 7, ✂ S
02/3 UD MVP 11
99/0 UD MVP Cup 13, CC1, -GC, ✍ PS
99/0 UD Ovation 3, 90, LP9, APOH, ✍ APOH
99/0 UD PowerDeck 3
00/1 UD Pros&Prosp. 6
02/3 UD Rookie 7
01/2 UD Top Shelf 2, ✂ J, ✂✍ SJ
00/1 UD Vintage 13, 23, 24, NH3
01/2 UD Vintage 10, 17
02/3 UD Vintage 9, 262
00/1 Vanguard 6
02/3 Vanguard ✂ GWJ 4
99/0 Victory 357
00/1 Victory 9, 11, 283
01/2 Victory 13
99/0 WGretzky 8, GH8, ✂ SG
98/9 Long Beach Ice Dogs
STEFANKA, FILIP
97/8 APS 324
99/0 OFS 304
STEFANKA, JURAJ
01/2 OFS 211
STEFANSKI, SEAN
01/2 Kingston Frontenacs 18
01/2 Owen Sound Attack
STEFENELLI, PHIL
01/2 UD DEL 165
STEFFAN, JEFF
81/2 Oshawa Generals
82/3 Oshawa Generals
83/4 Oshawa Generals
STEFFAN, TODD
82/3 Kitchener Rangers
STEFISHEN, ADAM
00/1 Prince George Cougars
STEIGER, EWALD
94/5 DEL 310
STEIGER, HELMUT
94/5 DEL 267
96/7 DEL 148
82 Semic Sticker 119
89 Semic Sticker 116
91 Semic Sticker 174
STEIGER, HOLGER
95/6 DEL 260
STEIN, PHIL
34-43 BeeHive-1 [Toro.]
STEINBOCK, STEFAN
94/5 DEL 325
95/6 DEL 301
96/7 DEL 328
STEINBURG, TREVOR
89/0 ProCards AHL 154
STEINECKER, STEFAN
94/5 DEL 47
95/6 DEL 52
92 Semic Sticker 178
STEINEGGER, MARTIN
95 Panini Worlds 123
STEINER, ONDREJ
94/5 APS 158
95/6 APS 255
97/8 APS 231
99/0 Cardset 345
92/3 Classic 37
98/9 DS 27
97/8 DS Sticker 38
98/9 OFS 91
01/2 OFS 208
92/3 Upper Deck 604
STELCICH, MARTIN
94/5 APS 213
STELLJES, MATT
92/3 Minnesota G'Gophers
STELMAK, JAMIE
91/2 Air Canada SJHL B36
92/3 MPS SJHL 137
STELNOV, IGOR
91/2 O-Pee-Chee 26R
92/3 Semic Elitserien 260
89 Semic Sticker 85
87/8 Soviet Stars
STEMKOWSKI, PETE
64-67 BeeHive-3 [Toro.]
65/6 Coca-Cola
70/1 Eddie Sargent 50
71/2 Eddie Sargent 115
72/3 Eddie Sargent 143
70/1 Esso Power Player
74/5 Lipton Soup 42
74/5 Loblaws
68/9 O-Pee-Chee 33
69/0 O-Pee-Chee 65
70/1 O-Pee-Chee 25
70/1 O-Pee-Chee 182
71/2 O-Pee-Chee 217
72/3 O-Pee-Chee 78
73/4 O-Pee-Chee 217
74/5 O-Pee-Chee 77
75/6 O-Pee-Chee 303
76/7 O-Pee-Chee 166
77/8 O-Pee-Chee 272
78/9 O-Pee-Chee 290
95/6 Parkie 66-67 112
94/5 Parkie Tall 113
67/8 Post Tips 10
68/9 Shirriff / Detr. 10
77-79 Sportscaster 64-16
77-79 Sports. FIN 68-1623
65/6 Topps 84
66/7 Topps 54
66/7 Topps / Test 15
67/8 Topps 12
68/9 Topps 33
69/0 Topps 65
70/1 Topps 25
74/5 Topps 77
75/6 Topps 303
76/7 Topps 166
71/2 Toronto Sun Photo
67/8 York 14
67/8 York
67/8 York
92/3 SANJ / Pacific Bell
STEMPFLE, RYAN
00/1 Saskatoon Blades
STEN, MARKO
92/3 Jyvas Hyva 191
93/4 Sisu 210
STENFORS, PEKKA
78/9 SM-Liiga 231
STENLUND, OLA
89/0 Semic Elitserien 197
STENVALL, HEIKKO
66/7 Champion 12
65/6 Hellas 19
70/1 Kuvajulkaisut 239
STEPAN, BRAD
87/8 Soo Greyhounds 25
STEPANEK, MARTIN
94/5 APS 65
95/6 APS 85
96/7 APS 173, 399
97/8 APS 84
99/0 Cardset 284
00/1 Cardset 256
97/8 DS 44
98/9 DS 44
00/1 DS NT3, -WCH4
97/8 DS Sticker 5, 38
97/8 DS Sticker 14, 91
98/9 OFS 5, 424, 454
99/0 OFS 270
99/0 Score N 16
STEPANISHEV, ANITOLI
98/9 Mir 118
STEPANOV, ALEXANDER
00/1 Mir 326
00/1 Dynamo 23
STEPANOV, ALEXEI
98/9 Mir 132
99/0 Mir 6
00/1 Metallurg 50
STEPANOV, IGOR
98/9 Mir 111
99/0 Mir 75
STEPANOV, MAXIM
99/0 Mir 28
STEPHAN, GREG
95/6 Slapshot 79
STEPHAN, JOE
89/0 ProCards IHL 127
STEPHANSON, KEN
72/3 Ottawa Nationals
STEPHENS, CHARLIE
99 Bowman 31, ✍ BA10
02/3 Choice Prospects 40
97/8 Pi. BeeHive 72, ✍ Aut. 72
98/9 SP Authentic 132, ✍ SotT
98/9 Upper Deck 409
98/9 UD G. Reserve 409
02/3 Hershey Bears
99/0 Guelph Storm
01/2 London Knights
STEPHENS, TROY
89/0 7th...Sketch OHL 98
90/1 7th...Sketch OHL 372
STEPHENSON, BOB
79/0 O-Pee-Chee 391
79/0 TORO
STEPHENSON, SCOTT
98/9 Guildford Flames
STEPHENSON, SHAY
00/1 Red Deer Rebels
STEPHENSON, SLADE
91/2 7th...Sketch WHL 356
STEPHENSON, WAYNE
51/2 Bas du Fleuve 10
72/3 Eddie Sargent 191
72/3 O-Pee-Chee 275
73/4 O-Pee-Chee 31
74/5 O-Pee-Chee 218
75/6 O-Pee-Chee 355
76/7 O-Pee-Chee 190
77/8 O-Pee-Chee 142
78/9 O-Pee-Chee 223
79/0 O-Pee-Chee 38
80/1 O-Pee-Chee 121
73/4 Topps 31
74/5 Topps 218
76/7 Topps 190
77/8 Topps 142
78/9 Topps 223
79/0 Topps 38
80/1 Topps 121
72/3 SLOU
73/4 SLOU
79/0 WASH
80/1 WASH
STEPP, JOEL
01 UD Prospects GU 28, ✂ TPJ
00/1 Red Deer Rebels
STERBAK, JAN
99/0 OFS 417
STERFLINGER, ROBERT
94/5 DEL 99
95/6 DEL 86
96/7 DEL 275
STERFLINGER, THOMAS
94/5 DEL 336
95/6 DEL 294
96/7 DEL 323
STERN, MIKE
81/2 Oshawa Generals
82/3 Oshawa Generals
83/4 Oshawa Generals
STERN, RONNIE
93/4 Durivage 28
92/3 Fleer Ultra 271
93/4 Leaf 261
94/5 Leaf 399
95/6 Leaf 204
99/0 Pacific 382
97/8 Pacific CC 346
90/1 Panini/VAN 24
95/6 Panini Sticker 238
92/3 Parkhurst 265
93/4 Parkhurst 303
92/3 Pinnacle 217
95/6 Playoff 131
94/5 POG / Western 6
95/6 POG 69
93/4 Power Play 43
93/4 Premier 341
94/5 Premier 71
90/1 Pro Set 549
91/2 Pro Set 362
89/0 ProCards IHL 179
91/2 Score CAN 408
92/3 Score 237
93/4 Score 409
95/6 Topps 181
93/4 To. Stadium 68
94/5 Upper Deck 27
95/6 Upper Deck 368
96/7 Upper Deck 28
94/5 UD BAP R122
95/6 UD BAP 79, ✍ S79
91/2 CALG / IGA
92/3 CALG / IGA 025
88/9 VANC / Mohawk
90/1 VANC / Mohawk
87/8 Flint Spirits
STERN, RONNIE
02/3 Fleer Throwbacks 60
STERNER, ULF
00/1 Alfabilder
95 Globe 69
74 Hellas MM-Jenkki 35
70/1 Kuvajulkaisut 38
69/0 Mästär Serien 41
69/0 Mästär Serien 48
72 Panda MM-Toronto
72 Semic Sticker 56
91 Semic Sticker 234
98/9 UD Elitserien 200
71/2 Williams Finnish 58
73/4 Williams Finnish 36
STETCICH, MARTIN
99/0 Score 34
STEVENS, JOHN
88/9 ProCards / Hershey
89/0 ProCards AHL 346
90/1 ProCards 189
91/2 ProCards 108
02/3 Philadelphia Phantoms
83/4 Oshawa Generals
STEVENS, KEVIN
01/2 Atomic ✂ GWJ 46
98/9 Aurora 127
98/9 Be A Player 88, ✍ Aut. 88
99/0 BAP Mem. 294
90/1 Bowman 208
91/2 Bowman 92
92/3 Bowman 241
92/3 Bowman 366
95/6 Bowman 59
92/3 Classic Prospects 31
93/4 Donruss 265
94/5 Donruss 229
95/6 Donruss 221
95/6 Do. Elite 95
97/8 Do. Priority 42
93/4 EA Sports 106
95/6 Edge Ice L10
94/5 Flair 140
94/5 Fleer 170
95/6 Fleer Metal 11, IW-11
92/3 Fleer Ultra 171, -AS 5
93/4 Fleer Ultra 229
93/4 Fleer Ultra AS 6
94/5 Fleer Ultra 170, RLS-10
95/6 Fleer Ultra 127, 207, CC-18
95 Globe 122
01/2 Heads Up ✂ JQ 15
93/4 Hockey Wit 20
95/6 Hoyle / East. 8-Club
92/3 Humpty Dumpty
93/4 Leaf 69
93/4 Leaf GLAS 4
93/4 Leaf HTA 9
94/5 Leaf 356
95/6 Leaf 216
94/5 L. Limited 46
95/6 L. Limited 96
96/7 Maggers 78
91/2 McDonald's Mc-03
92/3 McDonald's McH-03
93/4 McDonald's McD-25
90/1 OPC/Topps 360
91/2 O-Pee-Chee 267
91/2 O-Pee-Chee 421
92/3 O-Pee-Chee 29
90/1 OPC Premier 111
91/2 OPC Premier 26
97/8 Omega 149
98/9 Pacific 301
99/0 Pacific 281
01/2 Pacific 318
97/8 Pacific CC 115
97/8 Pa. Paramount 121
98/9 Pa. Paramount 158
99/0 Pa. Paramount 157
97/8 Pa. Revolution 91
89/0 Panini Sticker 321
90/1 Panini Sticker 131
91/2 Panini Sticker 269
92/3 Panini Sticker 221, 281
93/4 Panini Sticker 79
94/5 Panini Sticker 78
95/6 Panini Sticker 7
97/8 Panini Sticker 225
99/0 Panini Sticker 103
91/2 Parkhurst 135
91/2 Parkhurst 473
92/3 Parkhurst 138
92/3 Parkhurst 466
93/4 Parkhurst 158
94/5 Parkhurst 177
95/6 Parkhurst 10, 370
94/5 Parkie SE seV9
91/2 Pinnacle 191
91/2 Pinnacle B-4
92/3 Pinnacle 288
92/3 Pinnacle TP 4
93/4 Pinnacle 149
93/4 Pinnacle NF 9
93/4 Pinnacle TP 4
94/5 Pinnacle 299, TP7
97/8 Pinnacle 143
95/6 Pi. FANtasy 28
97/8 Pi. Inside 153
95/6 Pi. Summit 67
95/6 Pi. Zenith 52, GG-2
95/6 Playoff 10,123
96/7 Playoff 333
94/5 POG 189
95/6 POG 33
93/4 Power Play 195
93/4 Power Play PL 17
93/4 Premier 170
93/4 Premier 370
94/5 Premier 290, TF-17
01/2 Pr. Stock ✂ GUG 84
00/1 PS Titanium ✂ GUG 141
00/1 PS Titanium Draft ✂ 87
95/6 Pro Magnet 15
90/1 Pro Set 240
91/2 Pro Set 185
91/2 Pro Set 314
92/3 Pro Set 140
91/2 Pro Set PotM P2
91/2 Pro Set Platinum 93
90/1 Score 53
91/2 Score 248
91/2 Score CAN 468
92/3 Score 25
92/3 Score 492
92/3 Score 518
92/3 Score USAG 10
93/4 Score 325
93/4 Score DT 23
93/4 Score/CAN DD8
93/4 Score PiAS 15
94/5 Score 182, CI-4
95/6 Score 44
97/8 Score 159
97/8 Score NYRa. 6
90/1 Sco. Young Stars 17
92/3 Seasons 66
93/4 Seasons 19
94/5 Select 106
95/6 Select CE 46
91 Semic Sticker 145
93 Semic Sticker 179
01/2 Signature 143, ✍ Aut. 143
95/6 SBx Emotion 12, NP-8
95/6 SBx Impact 13
96/7 SP 73
95/6 Super Sticker 9
96/7 Team Out!
92/3 Topps 259
92/3 Topps 343
92/3 Topps 429
95/6 Topps 282, 11HG, 5PL
94/5 Topps Finest 80, RL-13
98/9 To. Finest 56
96/7 To. Picks 81
91/2 To. Stadium 234
92/3 To. Stadium 110
92/3 T. Stad. Club 257
93/4 To. Stadium 457
93/4 To. Stadium - AS
95/6 To. Stadium 50, F6
95/6 To. Super Skills 61
90/1 Upper Deck 14
91/2 Upper Deck 164
91/2 Upper Deck 613
92/3 Upper Deck 275
92/3 Upper Deck 454
92/3 Upper Deck 630
92/3 Upper Deck G4
93/4 Upper Deck 126, 230, HT19, SP-124
94/5 Upper Deck 390, SP-62
95/6 Upper Deck 96, SE-96
96/7 Upper Deck 78, X34
98/9 Upper Deck 130
01/2 Upper Deck 141
94/5 UD BAP R82
95/6 UD BAP 12, ✍ S12
95/6 UD CC 219
96/7 UD CC 124
98/9 UD G. Reserve 130
92/3 UD Locker 14
01/2 UD Vintage 206
99/0 Victory 198
98/9 NYRA
89/0 PITT / Elby's
89/0 PITT / Foodland 7
90/1 PITT / Foodland 9
91/2 PITT / Elby's
91/2 PITT / Foodland 8
91/2 PITT / Foodl. Stickers
92/3 PITT / Coke-Clark
92/3 PITT / Foodland 15
92/3 PITT / Food. Stickers
93/4 PITT / Foodland 17
94/5 PITT / Foodland 19
96/7 PITT / Tribune
STEVENS, MIKE
98/9 DEL 236
95/6 Edge Ice 118
99/0 Eishockey 15
88/9 ProCards / Springfield
89/0 ProCards AHL 240
90/1 ProCards 146
91/2 ProCards 345
01/2 UD DEL 177
92/3 Binghampton Rangers
94/5 Cincinnati Cyclones
95/6 Cleveland Lumberjacks
85/6 Fredericton Express
86/7 Fredericton Express
90/1 Newmarket Saints
83/4 Kitchener Rangers
84/5 Kitchener Rangers
STEVENS, P.C.
23/4 Paulins Candy 33
STEVENS, R
91/2 Michigan Tech Huskies
STEVENS, RANDY
95/6 Classic 80, ✍ Aut.
STEVENS, ROD
91/2 7th...Sketch WHL 82
96/7 Syracuse Crunch
01/2 Belfast Giants
93/4 Kamloops Blazers
STEVENS, SCOTT
01/2 Adrenaline 117
98/9 Aurora 113
00/1 Aurora 85
02/3 BAP All-Star 87, ✂ ASJ
99/0 BAP Mem. 52, ✂ TM-31
00/1 BAP Mem. 59, ✂ J-2, ✂ H-21, ✂ TM-21, ✂ TM-31
01/2 BAP Mem. 26, ✂ AST, ✂ SCP
02/3 BAP Mem. 171, / Cup
95/6 Bicycle Sports Aces 2-Club
91/2 Bowman 369
92/3 Bowman 160
92/3 Bowman 242
95/6 Bowman 50, BB4
01/2 Bowman 96
02/3 Bowman 33
91 Canada Cup
01/2 Crown Royale 87
93/4 Donruss 192
94/5 Donruss 262, D-2
95/6 Donruss 163
96/7 Donruss 57, HL-9
97/8 Donruss 194
96/7 Do. Canadian 103
97/8 Do. Canadian 114
95/6 Do. Elite 70
96/7 Do. Elite 30
96/7 Duracell DC16,JB16
98/9 Dynagon Ice 112
93/4 EA Sports 73
02/3 First Ed. 12, 329, ✂ Jers.
94/5 Flair 100
96/7 Flair 54
94/5 Fleer 119
96/7 Fleer 61
95/6 Fleer Metal 85, IW-12
92/3 Fleer Ultra 119
93/4 Fleer Ultra 189
93/4 Fleer Ultra 123
95/6 Fleer Ultra 91, 196, 197
96/7 Fl. Ultra 95
88/9 Frito Lay
95 Globe 81
01/2 Heads Up 58
02/3 Heads Up ✂ GWQ 17
93/4 Hockey Wit 65
95/6 Hoyle / East. 9-Club
92/3 Humpty Dumpty
90/1 Kraft 56
91/2 Kraft 53
93/4 Kraft / PB
94/5 Kraft / PB
95/6 Kraft / IP
96/7 Kraft / PB
97/8 Kraft / PB
99/0 Kraft / KD
00/1 Kraft 4
93/4 Leaf 60
94/5 Leaf 363, GLS-12
95/6 Leaf 124
96/7 Leaf 175
94/5 L. Limited 85
96/7 L. Limited 23
96/7 L. Preferred 38
97/8 Limited 176
96/7 Maggers 92
91/2 McDonald's Mc-24
92/3 McDonald's McD-27
93/4 McDonald's McD-26
94/5 McDonald's McD-7
99/0 McDonald's ✂ GJ
00/1 McDonald's 22
96/7 Metal Univ. 88
00/1 Mir Fetisov 24
98/9 NHL Power Play
83/4 O-Pee-Chee 376
84/5 O-Pee-Chee 206
85/6 OPC/Topps 62
86/7 OPC/Topps 126
87/8 OPC/Topps 25
88/9 OPC/Topps 60
90/1 OPC/Topps 211, 394
91/2 O-Pee-Chee 481
92/3 O-Pee-Chee 251
92/3 O-Pee-Chee 336
92/3 OPC - Anniv. 16
01/2 O-Pee-Chee 41
02/3 O-Pee-Chee 83
89/0 OPC/Topps 93
98/9 OPC Chrome 23, B12
90/1 OPC Premier 120
91/2 OPC Premier 84
88/9 OPC Stars 39
83/4 OPC/Topps Sticker 188
85/6 OPC Sticker 107-239
86/7 OPC Sticker 254-146
87/8 OPC Sticker 233-99
88/9 OPC Sticker 68
89/0 opcSticker 76-215
97/8 Omega 134
98/9 Omega 143
98/9 Pacific 272
99/0 Pacific 250
00/1 Pacific 243
01/2 Pacific 238
02/3 Pacific 229
02/3 Pacific Complete 467
97/8 Pacific CC 273
97/8 Pa. Crown Roy. 77
98/9 Pa. Paramount 139
00/1 Pa. Paramount 149
87/8 Panini Sticker 177
88/9 Panini Sticker 368
89/0 Panini Sticker 341
90/1 Panini Sticker 155
91/2 Panini Sticker 26
92/3 Panini Sticker 181
93/4 Panini Sticker 43
94/5 Panini Sticker 34
95/6 Panini Sticker 89
96/7 Panini Sticker 80
99/0 Panini Sticker 76
91/2 Parkhurst 102
92/3 Parkhurst 92
92/3 Parkhurst CP18
93/4 Parkhurst 114
94/5 Parkhurst V41, YCTG-13
95/6 Parkhurst 121, AS-4
00/1 Parkhurst P-144
01/2 Parkhurst 165, ✂ PJ28, ✂ PS28, ✂ M13, ✂ H12, ✂ T14
02/3 Parkhurst 15, ✂ TT5
02/3 Parkhurst Retro 125
94/5 Parkie SE97
91/2 Pinnacle 81
92/3 Pinnacle 280
93/4 Pinnacle 25, CA13, TP3
94/5 Pinnacle 310, TP5
95/6 Pinnacle 86, FC-2
96/7 Pinnacle 4
97/8 Pinnacle 158
97/8 Pi. Certified 115
97/8 Pi. Inside 154
95/6 Pi. Summit 134, GMC-8
96/7 Pi. Summit 9
97/8 Pi. Totally 115
95/6 Pi. Zenith 89
96/7 Pi. Zenith 73
95/6 Playoff 61, 167
94/5 POG 152, 262, 345
95/6 POG 165
93/4 Power Play 143
93/4 Premier 80
94/5 Premier 126, 153, 370, 451, 494
00/1 Premier Plus 71, WP5
01/2 PS Titanium 85, ✂ DSJ21
01/2 PS Titanium Draft ✂ 55
02/3 PS Titanium ✂ GWJ 40
95/6 Pro Magnet 35
90/1 Pro Set 321, 528
91/2 Pro Set 216
91/2 Pro Set 292
91/2 Pro Set 423
92/3 Pro Set 95
91/2 Pro Set Platinum 72
00/1 Revolution 88
90/1 Score 188, 341, 40T
90/1 Sco. Hot Cards 82
91/2 Score 40
91/2 Score 303
91/2 Score CAN 40
91/2 Score CAN 307
91/2 Score CAN 595
92/3 Score 75
92/3 Score 429
93/4 Score 111
93/4 Score DT 5
93/4 Score PiAS 4
94/5 Score TF 11
94/5 Score 193, CI-2, DT-5, TF-13
95/6 Score 160
96/7 Score 138
97/8 Score 224
97/8 Score NJer. 8
92/3 Seasons 50
94/5 Select 82, FL-8
95/6 Select CE 66, DS-18
96/7 Select CE 54
94 Semic 83
89 Semic Sticker 58
91 Semic Sticker 56
92 Semic Sticker 78
93 Semic Sticker 196
00/1 Signature 115, ✍ Aut. 152, ✂ DD-6, ✂ J-17
01/2 Signature C-43, ✍ Aut., ✂ GJ33, ✂ GSJ33, ✂ TM18
02/3 Signature 147, GS-84, ✍ 147, ✂ DW6, ✂ TQ7
95/6 SBx Emotion 102
95/6 SBx Impact 97
96/7 SBx Impact 71
02/3 Slam Card
94/5 SP 66
95/6 SP 81, FX13
96/7 SP 89
97/8 SP Authentic 85, I35
98/9 SP Authentic 49
01/2 SP Authentic 50, ✂ NN
01/2 SP GU ✂ AF
02/3 Sports Vault 68
96/7 SPx 24
97/8 SPx 26
99/0 SPx 84
00/1 SPx 40, 73
00/1 Stadion 95
99/0 Stadium 132
00/1 Stadium 33, SF1
00/1 Stadium G9, HS6
02/3 Stadium 53
95/6 SLU
95/6 Super Sticker 68, 72
96/7 Team Out!
84/5 Topps 149
88/9 OPC/Topps - Stick. 4
92/3 Topps 156
92/3 Topps 269
95/6 Topps 275, M17, PF13, 6RL
98/9 Topps 23, B12
99/0 Topps 167
00/1 Topps 28
01/2 Topps 41
02/3 Topps 27
99/0 To. Chrome 167
00/1 To. Chrome 26, 161
01/2 To. Chrome 41
02/3 T. Chrome 51
94/5 Topps Finest 18, DF-7
95/6 To. Finest 33, 152
98/9 To. Finest 132
98/9 T. Gold Label 100
99/0 To. Gold Label 72
00/1 To. Gold Label 40
00/1 To. Heritage 59, 228, 239, HH9
01/2 To. Heritage 91, 118
02/3 To. Heritage 66
02/3 To. Limited 82
96/7 To. Picks 115, ID-4
99/0 To. Prmr. Plus 46
91/2 To. Stadium 265
92/3 To. Stadium 151
93/4 To. Stadium 383
93/4 To. Stadium - AS
94/5 To. Stadium 4
95/6 To. Stadium 45, F4, N1
93/4 TSC Members Only 30
94/5 TSC Members Only 10
95/6 TSC Members Only 27
00/1 To. Stars 48, P7
95/6 To. Super Skills 7
02/3 To. Total 53
98/9 UD Choice 113, 239
00/1 UD Heroes 73
00/1 Ultimate Mem. ✍ U-36, ✂ J-39, ✂ S-39
01/2 Ultimate Mem. ✂ A8, ✍ Aut.
02/3 Ultimate Mem. ✂ CSTW, ✂ FS, ✂ Num, ✂ SCD
99/0 Ult. Victory 51
90/1 Upper Deck 236, 436, 482
91/2 Upper Deck 132
91/2 Upper Deck 539
92/3 Upper Deck 297
93/4 Upper Deck 119, SP-89
94/5 Upper Deck 73, C30, IG5, R48, SP-45
95/6 Upper Deck 482, AS-2, H-35, SE-49
96/7 Upper Deck 286, X36, P9, SS9B
97/8 Upper Deck 95, 396, T11C
98/9 Upper Deck 121
99/0 Upper Deck 250
00/1 Upper Deck 108
01/2 Upper Deck 106, LP7, ✂ PoaND, ✂ SCFJers., ✂ SCFJerseyD
02/3 Upper Deck 102, ✂ LN
95/6 UD ASG MVP27
93/4 Upper Deck Be A Player 36
94/5 UD BAP R146
95/6 UD BAP 219, ✍ S219
96/7 UD Black Diam. 124
97/8 UD Black Diam. 17
98/9 UD Black Diam. 49
00/1 UD Black Diam. 35
95/6 UD CC 223
96/7 UD CC 148, 305, 322, UD36
97/8 UD Coll. Choice 140, W17
98/9 UD G. Reserve 121
99/0 UD G. Reserve 250
01/2 UD Honor Roll 23, 53, TC3, -DPuck, ✂ PPM
02/3 UD Honor 88
00/1 UD Legends 78, 79
92/3 UD Locker 15
98/9 UD MVP 118
99/0 UD MVP 114
00/1 UD MVP 109
01/2 UD MVP 111
02/3 UD MVP 109
99/0 UD MVP Cup 105
95/6 UD Post 12
96/7 UD Post
00/1 UD Pros&Prosp. 51, CR5
99/0 UD Retro 46
02/3 UD Rookie ✍ 151c, ✂ 161b
01/2 UD SCup Champs 69
02/3 UD Top Shelf ✂ AS, ✂ ST
00/1 UD Vintage 210, 221
01/2 UD Vintage 155, 157, 265
02/3 UD Vintage 148, 278
97/8 Valu-net, ✍ Aut.
99/0 Victory 170
00/1 Victory 139
01/2 Victory 206, 434
02/3 Victory 124
99/0 WGretzky 96
96 Wien 80
96/7 NJER / Sharp
90/1 SLOU / Kodak
92/3 SLOU / McDon. 20
82/3 WASH
84/5 WASH / Pizza Hut
85/6 WASH / Pizza Hut
86/7 WASH / Kodak
86/7 WASH / Police
87/8 WASH
87/8 WASH / Kodak
88/9 WASH
88/9 WASH / Smokey
89/0 WASH
89/0 WASH / Kodak
STEVENS, TROY
96/7 Dayton Ice Bandits
STEVENSON, JASON
91/2 7th...Sketch OHL 90
STEVENSON, JEREMY
90/1 7th...Sketch OHL 22, 48
91/2 7th...Sketch OHL 8
93/4 Slapshot / S.S.Marie 25
97/8 Pacific 171
00/1 Victory 272
98/9 Cincinnati M'Ducks 17
99/0 Cincinnati M'Ducks
94/5 Greensboro Monarchs
00/1 Milwaukee Admirals
01/2 Milwaukee Admirals
91/2 Cornwall Royals
STEVENSON, SHAYNE
00/1 Kudos 106
91/2 O-Pee-Chee 121
90/1 ProCards 123
90/1 Score 405
90 7th..Sketch Mem.Cup 49
89/0 7th...Sketch OHL 182
91/2 Upper Deck 332
92/3 Atlanta Knights
93/4 Fort Wayne Komets 20
88/9 Kitchener Rangers
89/0 Kitchener Rangers
86/7 London Knights
STEVENSON, TURNER
98/9 Be A Player 71, ✍ Aut. 71
00/1 BAP Mem. 462
95/6 Donruss 218
94/5 Fleer 110
94/5 Fleer Ultra 317
94/5 Leaf 492
95/6 Leaf 285
99/0 Pacific 211
97/8 Pa. Invincible R-106
95/6 Parkhurst 385
95/6 Pinnacle 115
97/8 Pi. Be A Player 181, ✍ Aut. 181
94/5 Premier 392
90/1 Score 426
90/1 7th...Sketch WHL 9
91/2 7th...Sketch WHL 125
91/2 7th...Sketch WHL 273
95/6 Topps 34
91/2 Upper Deck 691
93/4 Upper Deck 236, 248
94/5 Upper Deck 221, SP-132
95/6 Upper Deck 202
96/7 Upper Deck 85
97/8 Upper Deck 297
94/5 UD Canada Junior 6
95/6 UD CC 167
91/2 Upper Deck WJC 65
94/5 MONT
95/6 MONT
95/6 MONT / Export
96/7 MONT
96/7 MONT
96/7 MONT / Export
97/8 MONT
92/3 Fredericton Canadiens
93/4 Fredericton Canadiens
94/5 Fredericton Canadiens
STEWART, ALLAN
90/1 OPC Premier 113
90/1 Pro Set 480
88/9 ProCards / Utica
90/1 NJER
STEWART, ANTHONY
01/2 Kingston Frontenacs 19
STEWART, BILL*
52/3 Anonymous 94
36-39 Diamond Match BH TT
36-39 Diamond Match BH BT
37/8 World Wide Gum 135
STEWART, BILL**
95 Globe 230
79/0 O-Pee-Chee 313
93 Semic Sticker 213
83/4 TORO
97/8 Saint John Flames
STEWART, BLACK
02/3 Ultimate Mem. ✍ Cut
STEWART, BLAIR
78/9 O-Pee-Chee 355
79/0 O-Pee-Chee 332
STEWART, BOB
77/8 Coke
72/3 Eddie Sargent 56
74/5 Loblaws
73/4 O-Pee-Chee 188
74/5 O-Pee-Chee 92
75/6 O-Pee-Chee 47
76/7 O-Pee-Chee 291
77/8 O-Pee-Chee 299
78/9 O-Pee-Chee 46
79/0 O-Pee-Chee 297
73/4 Topps 159
74/5 Topps 92
75/6 Topps 47
78/9 Topps 46
78/9 SLOU
STEWART, BOBBY
99/0 Mobile Mysticks
STEWART, BRETT
95/6 DEL 353
STEWART, BRIAN
95/6 Slapshot 376
96/7 Soo Greyhounds
STEWART, CAM
94/5 Classic ✍ Aut.
93/4 Cla. Prospects 36
93/4 Donruss 20
94/5 Donruss 316
98/9 EBK IHL All-Star
93/4 Fleer Ultra 270
93/4 Leaf 337
94/5 Leaf 281
93/4 Parkhurst 284
93/4 Pinnacle 434
93/4 Power Play 292
94/5 Premier 111
93/4 Score 588
00/1 Signature 140, ✍ Aut. 151
00/1 Stadium 202
93/4 To. Stadium 440
93/4 Upper Deck 464
94/5 Upper Deck 487
00/1 UD Vintage 182
STEWART, CHARLES
25-27 Anonymous 39
STEWART, DANY
01/2 Rimouski Océanic 3
STEWART, DAVE
90/1 7th...Sketch OHL 71
91/2 7th...Sketch OHL 236
92/3 Phoenix Roadrunners
93/4 Phoenix Roadrunners
94/5 Roanoke Express
95/6 Roanoke Express
96/7 Roanoke Express 2
STEWART, DOUG
91/2 Avant Garde BCJHL 63
83/4 Brantford Alexanders
81/2 Ottawa 67's
82/3 Ottawa 67's
STEWART, GARY
88/9 ProCards / Indianapolis
STEWART, GAYE (BOX CAR)
34-43 BeeHive-1 [Toro.]
34-43 BeeHive-1 [Toro.]
45-64 BeeHive-2 [Chic.]
45-64 BeeHive-2 [Detr.]
43-47 Parade Sportive
51/2 Parkhurst 99
52/3 Parkhurst 25
54/5 Parkhurst 92
02/3 Parkie - Reprint 168
45-54 Quaker Oats
91/2 Ultimate Original Six 45, ✍ Aut. 45
STEWART, GLENN
94/5 Greensboro Monarchs
97/8 Quad City Mallards
98/9 Quad City Mallards
99/0 Quad City Mallards
STEWART, JACK (BLACK JACK)
34-43 BeeHive-1 [Detr.]
45-64 BeeHive-2 [Detr.]
45-64 BeeHive-2 [Chic.]
51 Berk Ross
83 HHOF Postcard N15
83&87 HHOF 210
40/1 O-Pee-Chee 124
51/2 Parkhurst 53
02/3 Parkie - Reprint 158
76 DETR
STEWART, JOHN A.
74/5 O-Pee-Chee 175
74/5 Topps 175
72/3 ATLF
STEWART, JON
91/2 Rayside-Balfour
STEWART, JUSTIN
00/1 Québec Remparts 9
STEWART, KARL
02/3 Plymouth Whalers
STEWART, MICHAEL
92/3 Classic 71
92/3 Classic Four Sport 197
94/5 Classic 4 Sport 147
92/3 Binghampton Rangers
94/5 Binghampton Rangers
97/8 Manitoba Moose
98/9 Manitoba Moose
99/0 Manitoba Moose
STEWART, NELS
25-27 Anonymous 92
25-27 Anonymous 97
34-43 BeeHive-1 [NYAm.]
39/0 Bruins Magazine
33/4 Canadian Gum
33-35 Diamond Match Silv.
36-39 Diamond Match TT1
36-39 Diamond Match TT2
36-39 Diamond Match TT3
83 HHOF Postcard F12
83&87 HHOF 86
28/9 La Presse
33/4 O-Pee-Chee 6
34/5 Sweet Caporal
60/1 Topps 5
61/2 Topps - Stamp
02/3 Ultimate Mem. ✂ BOS
33/4 WWGum 12
STEWART, PAUL
90/1 Pro Set 699
STEWART, RALPH
74/5 Loblaws
74/5 O-Pee-Chee 158
75/6 O-Pee-Chee 233
75/6 O-Pee-Chee 182
76/7 O-Pee-Chee 229
77/8 O-Pee-Chee 386
74/5 Topps 158
74/5 Topps 233
75/6 Topps 182
76/7 Topps 229
76/7 VANC / Royal Bank
STEWART, ROB
01/2 Belfast Giants
STEWART, RON
45-64 BeeHive-2 [Toro.]
64-67 BeeHive-3 [Bost.]
64-67 BeeHive-3 [Toro.]
64-67 BeeHive-3 [Toro.]
63-65 Chex
64/5 Coke/Sprite [Toro.]
65/6 Coca-Cola
70/1 Eddie Sargent 120
70/1 Esso Power Player
62/3 Cowan Tile
68/9 O-Pee-Chee 168
69/0 O-Pee-Chee 41
70/1 O-Pee-Chee 64
71/2 O-Pee-Chee 236
52/3 Parkhurst 94
53/4 Parkhurst 9
54/5 Parkhurst 23
55/6 Parkhurst 5
57/8 Parkhurst [Toro.] 7
58/9 Parkhurst 14
59/0 Parkhurst 26
60/1 Parkhurst 6
61/2 Parkhurst 6
62/3 Parkhurst 6
63/4 Parkhurst 14
63/4 Parkhurst 74
02/3 Parkie - Reprint 177, 190, 200, 220, 240, 246, 258, 296
93/4 Parkie 56-57 110
95/6 Parkie 66-67 2
94/5 Parkie Tall 128
45-54 Quaker Oats
60/1 Shirriff 10
62/3 Shirriff 21
68/9 Shirriff / NYRa. 16
64/5 Topps 99
65/6 Topps 103
66/7 Topps 94
69/0 Topps 41
70/1 Topps 64
57/8 Toronto Star Photo
58/9 Toronto Star Photo
62/3 Toronto Star Photo
63/4 Toronto Star Action
64/5 Toronto Star Action
60/1 Toronto Star Weekend
60/1 York
61/2 York 20
63/4 York 3
64/5 TORO
STEWART, RYAN
87/8 Moncton Hawks
02/3 Manchester Storm
STEWART, RYAN*
84/5 Kamloops Blazers
STEWART, RYAN**
93/4 Slapshot / Windsor 19
STEWART, SCOTT
91/2 Air Canada SJHL B24
STEWART, TOM
99/0 Indianapolis Ice
98/9 Topeka Scarecrows
STICKLE, LEON
90/1 Pro Set 700
STICKNEY, BRENT
93/4 Flint Generals
STIEG, LEE
98/9 Dayton Bombers
STIENBURG, TREVOR
90/1 ProCards 462
91/2 ProCards 372
88/9 QUEB
88/9 QUEB / Gene. Foods
86/7 Fredericton Express
89/0 Halifax Citadels
90/1 Halifax Citadels
STILES, TONY
84/5 Moncton G'Flames
85/6 Moncton G'Flames
STILL, ALASTAIR
90/1 7th...Sketch OHL 395
91/2 7th...Sketch OHL 230
88/9 Sudbury Wolves
89/0 Sudbury Wolves
90/1 Sudbury Wolves
STILLMAN, CORY
01/2 Adrenaline 162, ✂ GWJ 40
98/9 Aurora 29
99/0 Aurora 24
99/0 BAP Mem. 57
00/1 BAP Mem. 167
01/2 BAP Mem. 243
95/6 Bowman 131
95/6 Bowman BB27
92/3 CSC 7
92/3 Classic 5
92/3 Classic 8
92/3 Classic LP5
93/4 Classic 29
94/5 Classic 45, T11
92/3 Classic Four Sport 155
94/5 Classic 4 Sport 144
94/5 Cla. Images 38
93/4 Cla. Prospects 190
01/2 Crown Royale ✂ TT 19
95/6 Donruss 152,RR-12
96/7 Donruss 221
96/7 Do. Elite 106
97/8 Do. Priority 88
99/0 Dynagon Ice 39
95/6 Edge Ice 74
02/3 First Ed. 252
95/6 Fleer Ultra 214
98/9 Kraft / KD

95/6 Leaf 5
96/7 Leaf 138
96/7 L. Preferred 15
99/0 Millenium 43, ✍ Aut. 43
01/2 O-Pee-Chee 241
02/3 O-Pee-Chee 145
98/9 OPC Chrome 191
97/8 Omega 35
98/9 Omega 35
99/0 Omega 41
98/9 Pacific 125
99/0 Pacific 62
00/1 Pacific 75
01/2 Pacific 331, ✂ GWJ 32
02/3 Pacific 328
02/3 Pacific Complete 320
97/8 Pacific CC 211
97/8 Pa. Crown Roy. 21
98/9 Pa. Paramount 32
99/0 Pa. Paramount 43
00/1 Pa. Paramount 39
97/8 Pa. Revolution 20
98/9 Pa. Revolution 22
98/9 Panini Photocard
96/7 Panini Sticker 238
98/9 Panini Sticker 180
99/0 Panini Sticker 191
95/6 Parkhurst 299
00/1 Parkhurst P-231
94/5 Parkie SE29
94/5 Pinnacle 494
95/6 Pinnacle 212
97/8 Pi. Be A Player 24, ✍ Aut. 24
97/8 Pi. Inside 164
95/6 Pi. Zenith 123, RRC-16
96/7 Pi. Zenith 113
95/6 POG 51
94/5 Premier 515
99/0 Prism 26
01/2 Pr. Stock ✂ GUG 88
00/1 PS Titanium ✂ GUG 71
02/3 PS Titanium 84
00/1 PS Titanium Draft ✂ 90
02/3 Quest for the Cup 83
99/0 Revolution 26
95/6 Score 300
96/7 Score 243
97/8 Score 225
95/6 Select CE 128
96/7 Select CE 58
92 7th...Sketch Awards 5
90/1 7th..Sketch OHL 192
91/2 7th...Sketch OHL 175
01/2 Signature 123, ✍ Aut. 123
02/3 Signature 117, ✍ 117
96/7 SBx Impact 172
02/3 Slam Card
95/6 SP 17
97/8 SP Authentic 19
02/3 Sports Vault 274
99/0 Stadium 97
95/6 Topps 332
98/9 Topps 191
99/0 Topps 57
00/1 Topps 253
01/2 Topps 241
02/3 Topps 145
99/0 To. Chrome 57
95/6 To. Finest 61
02/3 To. Limited 145
96/7 To. Picks 145, RS-9
95/6 To. Super Skills SR4
02/3 To. Total 93
98/9 UD Choice 33
00/1 UD Heroes 19
99/0 Ult. Victory 15
94/5 Upper Deck 268
95/6 Upper Deck 283
96/7 Upper Deck 229
98/9 Upper Deck 54
00/1 Upper Deck 256
01/2 Upper Deck 154
02/3 Upper Deck 155
95/6 UD BAP 132, ✍ S132
95/6 UD CC 111
96/7 UD CC 40
98/9 UD G. Reserve 54
01/2 UD MVP 168
99/0 UD MVP Cup 31
00/1 UD Vintage 57
01/2 UD Vintage 222
02/3 UD Vintage 222
00/1 Vanguard ✂ DGJ 10
01/2 Vanguard ✂ DGM 6
02/3 Vanguard 83
00/1 Victory 40
01/2 Victory 304
02/3 Victory 190
99/0 WGretzky 32
97/8 Zenith 52
94/5 Saint John Flames
92/3 Windsor Spitfires

STILLMAN, CORY2
00/1 UD Prospects 8
01 UD Prospects GU 30, ✂ TPJ, ✂ TPJS, ✂ JC, ✍ SoT
99/0 Kingston Frontenacs
00/1 Kingston Frontenacs 20
01/2 Kingston Frontenacs 20

STILLMAN, FREDRIK
95/6 DEL 55
99/0 Eishockey 268
95 Globe 17
94/5 Leaf Elit Set 216, GC-6, SS-5
95 Panini Worlds 140
94 Semic 57
95 Semic 56
89/0 Semic Elitserien 101
90/1 Semic Elitserien 103
91/2 Semic Elitserien 108
91/2 Semic Elitserien 345
92/3 Semic Elitserien 135
91 Semic Sticker 34
93 Semic Sticker 6
97/8 UD Elitserien 89, S5
98/9 UD Elitserien 104
00/1 UD Elitserien 95

STIOS, JOHN
90/1 7th..Sketch OHL 119

STIRLING, STEVE
99/0 Lowell Lock Monsters
00/1 Lowell Lock Monsters

STITT, MARK
95/6 Toledo Storm

STIVER, DAN
93/4 Cla. Prospects 99
93/4 St. John's Maple Leafs

STOCCO, REGAN
93/4 Slapshot / Guelph 7
94/5 Slapshot / Guelph 8
95/6 Slapshot 81
95/6 Guelph Storm

STOCK, COREY
90/1 7th..Sketch WHL 309
91/2 7th...Sketch WHL 162
92/3 Tacoma Rockets
93/4 Tacoma Rockets

STOCK, DAN (BEAK)
98/9 Hershey Bears

STOCK, DEAN
97/8 Halifax Moosehead
97/8 Halifax Moosehead

STOCK, P.J.
01/2 BAP Update ✂ TC14, ✂ TC36
02/3 First Ed. 224
02/3 Pacific 33
02/3 Pacific Complete 397
01/2 Parkhurst 370
01/2 Signature 175, ✂ -Aut. 175
02/3 To. Total 70
98/9 Upper Deck 131
98/9 UD G. Reserve 131
01/2 UD Mask 10
02/3 UD Vintage 18
02/3 Victory 17
98/9 NYRA
97/8 Hartford Wolf Pack
98/9 Hartford Wolf Pack
99/0 Hartford Wolf Pack

STOCKHAM, DARYL
94/5 Slapshot Memorial 46
95/6 Brandon Wheat Kings

STODDARD, JACK
52/3 Parkhurst 97
53/4 Parkhurst 60

STOILOV, LUBOMIR
79 Panini Sticker 351

STOJANOV, ALEK
91/2 Arena 5
95/6 Bowman 141
91/2 Classic 6
91/2 Classic Four Sport 6
95/6 Donruss 329
95/6 Leaf 297
96/7 Pi. Be A Player 80, ✍ Aut. 80
91 7th..Sketch Mem.Cup 110
90/1 7th..Sketch OHL 220
91/2 Star Pics 46
95/6 Topps 368
91/2 Ultimate Draft Pick 6, 62, ✍ Aut.
95/6 Upper Deck 195
99/0 Detroit Vipers

STOKES, RYAN
02/3 Mississauga IceDogs

STOLK, DARREN
89/0 ProCards IHL 157
90/1 ProCards 384
91/2 ProCards 579
92/3 Salt Lake G'Eagles

STOLL, JARRET
02/3 BAP Mem. 305
02/3 SP Authentic 216
02/3 SPx 184
02/3 Ultimate Mem. 72
02/3 UD Premier 72
99/0 UD Prospects 35, 78
02/3 UD Rookie ✂ 160
02/3 Hamilton Bulldogs

STOLP, JEFF
93/4 Dayton Bombers
94/5 Dayton Bombers 18
94/5 Dayton Bombers 24
91/2 Minnesota G'Gophers

STOLTZ, ROLAND
00/1 Alfabilder
98/9 UD Elitserien 198, 208

STOMPF, LADISLAV
94/5 DEL 110
95/6 DEL 105

STONE, B.J.
99/0 Peoria Rivermen

STONE, JASON
00/1 Kelowna Rockets

STONE, MATT
90/1 7th..Sketch OHL 99
91/2 7th...Sketch OHL 311

STONE, MIKE
94/5 Huntington Blizzard

STONE, SHAWN
91/2 7th...Sketch WHL 31

STONIER, TROY
95/6 Slapshot 271
00/1 Austin Ice Bats

STOPAR, ROB
89/0 7th..Sketch OHL 94
90/1 7th..Sketch OHL 242
90/1 Kitchener Rangers

STOREY, BEN
00/1 Hershey Bears

STOREY, RED
83 HHOF Postcard B14
83&87 HHOF 28
94/5 Legends 37

STORF, FLORIAN
94/5 DEL 106
95/6 DEL 104
96/7 DEL 49

STORK, DEAN
92/3 BCJHL 12
99/0 Hampton Roads

STORM, JIM
94/5 Classic ✍ Aut.
93/4 Cla. Prospects 37
93/4 Donruss 445
94/5 Donruss 280
94/5 Leaf 213
93/4 Parkhurst 354
94/5 Pinnacle 237
93/4 Power Play 356
93/4 Premier - USA Hockey 22
93/4 Score 610
93/4 Topps Stadium Club - Team U.S.A. 23
94/5 To. Stadium 26
93/4 HART / Coke
96/7 Michigan K-Wings
90/1 Michigan Tech Huskies
91/2 Michigan Tech Huskies
91/2 Michigan Tech Huskies

STORMQVIST, JAN-ERIK
89/0 Semic Elitserien 34
90/1 Semic Elitserien 182

STORR, JAMIE
98/9 Aurora 89
99/0 Aurora 71
00/1 Aurora 69
99/0 BAP Mem. 95
00/1 BAP Mem. 76
01/2 BT Pipes 60
02/3 Between the Pipes 24, ✂ GUJ43, ✂ T10
98/9 Bicycle.. 4-C
95/6 Bowman 128
98/9 Bowman's Best F20
94/5 Classic 7, C9, R18, T33
94/5 Classic 4 Sport 121
94/5 Cla. Images 75
94/5 Cla. Images 4 Sport 100
00/1 Crown Royale 51
93/4 Donruss CAN20
95/6 Donruss 67, C3TWC-1, PP-15
97/8 Donruss 31
97/8 Do. Preferred 27
97/8 Do. Priority 153
02/3 First Ed. 127, ✂ Jers.
94/5 Fleer 99, RS-9
96/7 Fleer 133, CC-8
95/6 Fleer Metal 192
94/5 Fleer Ultra P-8
95/6 Fleer Ultra 77, 356
96/7 Fl. Ultra 82, UR-18
95/6 Future Legends 42, PC-8
94/5 Leaf P-1
95/6 Leaf 12, SR-13
97/8 Leaf 138
94/5 L. Limited CAN 10
95/6 L. Limited 101
97/8 Limited 76
96/7 Metal Univ. 192
99/0 Millenium 123, ✍ Aut. 123
99/0 NHL Power Play
98/9 OPC Chrome 24
97/8 Omega 113
98/9 Omega 113
99/0 Omega 113
98/9 Pacific 245
99/0 Pacific 198
00/1 Pacific 203
01/2 Pacific 189
02/3 Pacific 176
02/3 Pacific Complete 99
98/9 Pa. Paramount 108
99/0 Pa. Paramount 112
00/1 Pa. Paramount 116
96/7 Panini Sticker 302
93/4 Parkhurst 508
95/6 Parkhurst 104
00/1 Parkhurst P-249
02/3 Parkhurst 164
94/5 Parkie SE80
93/4 Pinnacle 458
94/5 Pinnacle 254, 475, 521, RTP1
97/8 Pinnacle 82
95/6 Playoff 52
94/5 Premier 437
00/1 PS Titanium 44
95/6 Pro Magnet 64
99/0 Revolution 72
00/1 Revolution 70
94/5 Score 201,TR-5
97/8 Score 46
94/5 Select 170, YE-1
95/6 Select CE 136
91/2 7th...Sketch OHL 270
00/1 Signature 40, ✍ Aut. 155
02/3 Signature 33, ✍ 33
95/6 SBx Emotion 84, GN-14
95/6 SBx Impact 204
96/7 SBx Impact 159
94/5 Slapshot / Windsor 2
94/5 SP 137
95/6 Topps 363, 2CJ
98/9 Topps 24
99/0 Topps 102
99/0 To. Chrome 102
94/5 Topps Finest 12, 146, BBR-7
00/1 To. Heritage 119
00/1 UD Reserve 41
98/9 UD3 6, 66, 126
00/1 Ultimate Mem. ✂ G-14
93/4 Upper Deck 538
94/5 Upper Deck 236, 531, 568, SP-128
95/6 Upper Deck 47
97/8 Upper Deck 287
98/9 Upper Deck 107
00/1 Upper Deck 312
02/3 Upper Deck 327
94/5 UD BAP R157
94/5 UD Canada Junior 15
95/6 UD CC 213
98/9 UD G. Reserve 107
97/8 UD Ice 34
02/3 UD Mask 39, 40
00/1 UD Vintage 169, 172
99/0 Victory 141
95/6 Phoenix Roadrunners
93/4 Owen Sound Platers
93/4 Owen Sound Platers
93/4 Owen Sound Platers
93/4 Owen Sound Platers

STOS, JASON
90/1 7th..Sketch OHL 193
91/2 7th...Sketch OHL 183
92/3 Toledo Storm WIOT
89/0 Windsor Spitfires

STOS, JON
91/2 Rayside-Balfour
89/0 Windsor Spitfires

STOTHERS, MIKE
88/9 ProCards / Hershey
89/0 ProCards AHL 343
90/1 ProCards 39
91/2 ProCards 270
94/5 Hershey Bears
81/2 Kingston Canadians

STOUGHTON, BLAINE (STASH)
83/4 Funmate Puffy 15 [w/]
74/5 O-Pee-Chee 348
75/6 O-Pee-Chee 265
79/0 O-Pee-Chee 356
80/1 O-Pee-Chee 30
80/1 O-Pee-Chee 59
80/1 O-Pee-Chee 161
80/1 O-Pee-Chee 167
81/2 O-Pee-Chee 132
82/3 O-Pee-Chee 122
82/3 O-Pee-Chee 130
82/3 O-Pee-Chee 131
83/4 O-Pee-Chee 135
83/4 O-Pee-Chee 136
83/4 O-Pee-Chee 147
84/5 O-Pee-Chee 154
81/2 OPC Sticker 63
82/3 OPC/Topps Sticker 126
83/4 OPC/Topps Sticker 258
83/4 OPC/Topps Sticker 259
77/8 OPC WHA 6
82/3 Post [Hart.]
83/4 Souhaits Keychain [Whalers]
75/6 Topps 265
80/1 Topps 30
80/1 Topps 59
80/1 Topps 161
80/1 Topps 167
81/2 Topps 86 [East]
82/3 HART / Jr. Whalers
83/4 HART / Jr. Whalers
74/5 TORO
75/6 TORO
91/2 Cincinnati Cyclones
92/3 Cincinnati Cyclones

STOWE, MARK
90/1 7th..Sketch WHL 263
90/1 Prince Albert Raiders

STOYANOVICH, DAVE
83/4 Nova Scotia Voyageurs

STOYANOVICH, STEVE
83/4 HART / Jr. Whalers
81/2 Indianapolis Checkers
82/3 Indianapolis Checkers

STRACHAN, AL
93/4 Action Packed 10

STRACHAN, RICK
00/1 Kudos 58
01/2 Cardiff Devils

STRACHAN, WAYNE
99/0 Rockford IceHogs
91/2 L. Superior State Lakers

STRAIN, RYAN
90/1 7th..Sketch WHL 90
91/2 7th...Sketch WHL 163
90/1 Saskatoon Blades

STRAKA, JOSEF
95/6 APS 165
96/7 APS 186
97/8 APS 95
98/9 DS 49
99/0 DS 69
96/7 DS Sticker 54
98/9 OFS 12
99/0 OFS 159, 379
00/1 OFS 72
01/2 OFS 229

STRAKA, MARTIN
01/2 Adrenaline 156
94/5 APS 155
96/7 APS 361
01/2 Atomic 80, Stat. 19
98/9 Aurora 157
99/0 Aurora 118
00/1 Aurora 118
98/9 Be A Player 115, ✍ Aut. 115
99/0 BAP Mem. 177
00/1 BAP Mem. 261, ✂ TM-20
01/2 BAP Mem. 164, ✂ SCP
02/3 BAP Mem. 147
98 Bonaparte 7B
98 Bonaparte Pexeso 23
95/6 Bowman 72
92/3 Classic 33
92/3 Classic Four Sport 180
00/1 Crown Royale 88, ✂ GWJ-23
01/2 Crown Royale ✂ TT 17, ✂ TT 20
93/4 Donruss 266
94/5 Donruss 224
99/0 DS NS14
00/1 DS JT5
01/2 DS 39, -IH5
98/9 Dynagon Ice 154
99/0 Dynagon Ice 163
02/3 Exclusive 140
02/3 First Ed. 59, ✂ Jers.
94/5 Flair 141
94/5 Fleer 171
95/6 Fleer Metal 107
92/3 Fleer Ultra 382
93/4 Fleer Ultra 244
94/5 Fleer Ultra 171
95/6 Fleer Ultra 282
01/2 Heads Up ✂ JQ 18, ✂ JQ 28
93/4 Leaf 220
94/5 Leaf 36
95/6 Leaf 253
94/5 L. Limited 62
99/0 Millenium 198, ✍ Aut. 198
98/9 NHL Power Play
01/2 O-Pee-Chee 60
02/3 O-Pee-Chee 70
98/9 OPC Chrome 45
92/3 OPC Premier 21
98/9 OFS 246, -OW 20
99/0 OFS 37
00/1 OFS 393
98/9 Omega 199
99/0 Omega 191
98/9 Pacific 82
99/0 Pacific 347
00/1 Pacific 337
01/2 Pacific 319, ✂ GWJ 31
02/3 Pacific 318
02/3 Pacific Complete 29
97/8 Pacific CC 139
98/9 Pa. Paramount 197
99/0 Pa. Paramount 192
00/1 Pa. Paramount 202
97/8 Pa. Revolution 115
98/9 Pa. Revolution 120
96/7 Panini Sticker 76
97/8 Panini Sticker 57
98/9 Panini Sticker 52
99/0 Panini Sticker 138
00/1 Panini Sticker 82
95 Panini Worlds 207
92/3 Parkhurst 140
93/4 Parkhurst 156
94/5 Parkhurst V16
95/6 Parkhurst 145, 397
00/1 Parkhurst P-140
01/2 Parkhurst 63PJ41
02/3 Parkhurst 151
02/3 Parkhurst Retro 88
94/5 Parkie SE134
93/4 Pinnacle 204
94/5 Pinnacle 352
95/6 Playoff 289
96/7 Playoff 410
94/5 POG 190
95/6 POG 193
93/4 Power Play 415
93/4 Power Play RisS 7
93/4 Premier 155
94/5 Premier 164
99/0 Prism 116
00/1 Pr. Stock 81, PS-48
01/2 Pr. Stock 79, ✂ GUG 85
00/1 PS Titanium 79, ✂ GUG-142, ✂ GUG-155
01/2 PS Titanium ✂ DSJ 34
00/1 PS Titanium Draft ✂ 88
95/6 Pro Magnet 114
99/0 Revolution 120
00/1 Revolution 120
93/4 Score 375
94/5 Score 82
95/6 Score 132
99/0 Score JT17
94/5 Select 36
95 Semic 160
00/1 Signature 199
01/2 Signature ✂ GU89
02/3 Signature 28, ✍ 28, ✂ TQ8
95/6 SBx Emotion 127
95/6 SBx Impact 121
97/8 SP Authentic 129
98/9 SP Authentic 69
99/0 SP Authentic 70
99/0 SPx 121
00/1 Stadion 77
99/0 Stadium 62
01/2 Stadium 71
95/6 Topps 246
98/9 Topps 45
99/0 Topps 91, PP2
00/1 Topps 165
01/2 Topps 60 , -OTG6
02/3 Topps 70
99/0 To. Chrome 91
00/1 To. Chrome 114
01/2 To. Chrome 60
02/3 T. Chrome 47
95/6 To. Finest 92
00/1 To. Heritage 155
01/2 To. Heritage 99, ✂ GWJ
02/3 To. Limited 70
01/2 To. Reserve 64, ✂ TR
93/4 To. Stadium 415
94/5 To. Stadium 34
95/6 To. Stadium 87
02/3 To. Total 196
00/1 UD Heroes 97
99/0 Ult. Victory 70
92/3 Upper Deck 559
92/3 Upper Deck ER19
93/4 Upper Deck 40, SP-125
94/5 Upper Deck 289, SP-153
95/6 Upper Deck 427, SE-146
96/7 Upper Deck 65
98/9 Upper Deck 349
99/0 Upper Deck 276
00/1 Upper Deck 367
01/2 Upper Deck 368
02/3 Upper Deck 139
95/6 UD BAP 106, ✍ S106
99/0 UD Black Diam. 69
00/1 UD Black Diam. 48
01/2 UD Challenge 70
91/2 Upper Deck WJC 99
98/9 UD G. Reserve 349
99/0 UD G. Reserve 276
96/7 UD Ice 24
98/9 UD MVP 168
99/0 UD MVP 166
00/1 UD MVP 145
01/2 UD MVP 155
02/3 UD MVP 149
x99/0 UD MVP Cup GC
99/0 UD Retro 65
02/3 UD Rookie 80
00/1 UD Vintage 294
01/2 UD Vintage 204, 208, 262
02/3 UD Vintage 201, GB 201
00/1 Vanguard 81
01/2 Vanguard ✂ DGM 23, ✂ DGM 27
99/0 Victory 239
00/1 Victory 188
01/2 Victory 283, 436
02/3 Victory 171
99/0 WGretzky 137
96/7 FLOR / Winn-Dixie
95/6 OTTA
92/3 PITT / Coke-Clark
92/3 PITT / Foodland 17
93/4 PITT / Foodland 8
94/5 PITT / Foodland 25

STRAKA, MICHAL
94/5 APS 156
95/6 APS 254
96/7 APS 303
97/8 APS 184
98/9 DS 61
99/0 DS 92
00/1 DS 34
96/7 DS Sticker 222
97/8 DS Sticker 160
98/9 OFS 44
99/0 OFS 374
00/1 OFS 70
01/2 OFS 227

STRAKHOV, ALEXEI
99/0 Mir 114

STRAKHOV, ANDREJ
01/2 UD DEL 264

STRAKHOV, YURI
90/1 O-Pee-Chee 484

STRAMKOWSKI, JENS
98/9 DEL 217
99/0 Eishockey 202
00/1 UD DEL 215

STRANDBERG, TOMAS
95/6 Leaf Elit Set 156, FTF-1
89/0 Semic Elitserien 254
90/1 Semic Elitserien 167
91/2 Semic Elitserien 17
92/3 Semic Elitserien 39
95/6 UD Elitserien 13
97/8 UD Elitserien 7

STRANDER, ARI-PEKKA
80/1 Mallasjuoma 116
78/9 SM-Liiga 174

STRANKA, G
95/6 DEL 334

STRANSKY, VLADIMIR
95/6 APS 291

STRATTON, ART
63/4 York 44

STRAUB, BRIAN
91/2 ProCards 323
94/5 Atlanta Knights 18
95/6 Fort Wayne Komets

STRAUB, CHRIS
95/6 DEL 284

STRAUB, JOSEF
94/5 APS 199
95/6 APS 39
96/7 APS 62, 428
97/8 APS 333
97/8 DS 116
98/9 DS 113
99/0 DS 9
00/1 DS 167
96/7 DS Sticker 244
97/8 DS Sticker 278
98/9 OFS 27
99/0 OFS 455
00/1 OFS 253, -Star. 28
01/2 OFS 41

STRAUBE, CHRIS
98/9 DEL 258
99/0 Eishockey 22
00/1 UD DEL 12

STRAUSSE, CHRIS
94/5 DEL 319

STRBA, MARTIN
95/6 APS 73
97/8 APS 284
99/0 DS 40
98/9 OFS 204
99/0 OFS 285
00/1 OFS 22
01/2 OFS 147

STRBAK, MARTIN
00/1 DS 17
99/0 OFS 160
00/1 OFS 325
01/2 OFS 76

STREBNICKI, MAREK
94/5 DEL 241
96/7 DEL 86

STREET, KEITH
89/0 ProCards IHL 171
94/5 Anchorage Aces 21
98/9 Anchorage Aces
99/0 Anchorage Aces

STREIT, MARTIN
97/8 APS 233
99/0 DS 26
96/7 DS Sticker 177
97/8 DS Sticker 40
99/0 OFS 145, 436
00/1 OFS 284
01/2 OFS 72

STRELOW, WARREN
90/1 NJER

STREU, CRAIG
96/7 DEL 15

STRIDA, FLORIAN
95/6 APS 315

STRIEMITZER, KLAUS
94/5 DEL 354

STRINGER, REJEAN
91/2 Air Canada SJHL A9
92/3 MPS SJHL 122

STROBEL, ERIC
80 Olympic USA
94/5 SR Miracle 35,36, ✍ 35,36

STROBEL, MARK
96/7 Albany River Rats

STROHACK, MARK
90/1 7th..Sketch OHL 295
97/8 Fort Worth Brahmas
98/9 Fort Worth Brahmas

STROHMAIER, HERBERT
79 Panini Sticker 391

STROKA, RAFAL
92 Semic Sticker 274

STROM, DENNIS
90/1 Semic Elitserien 119
91/2 Semic Elitserien 122
92/3 Semic Elitserien 144

STROM, INGEMAR
89/0 Semic Elitserien 187
90/1 Semic Elitserien 21
91/2 Semic Elitserien 220

STRÖM, PETER
94/5 Leaf Elit Set 233, ND-8
95/6 Leaf Elit Set 148, G-4
94/5 Parkie SE242
95/6 UD Elitserien 212
97/8 UD Elitserien 83
98/9 UD Elitserien 79, 83
99/0 UD Elitserien 83
00/1 UD Elitserien 72

STROMBACK, DOUG
93/4 Huntington Blizzard
84/5 Kitchener Rangers

STRÖMBERG, MIKA
98/9 Cardset 104, -Leij. 16
02/3 Cardset 273
95 Hartwall Karjala
97/8 Hockey-Box
91/2 Jyvas Hyva 23
92/3 Jyvas Hyva 55
93/4 Jyvas Hyva 111
95 Panini Worlds 163
94 Semic 14
95 Semic 26
93 Semic Sticker 61
94/5 SR Tetrad CXV, ✍ Aut.
93/4 Sisu 9
94/5 Sisu 313, J-9
95/6 Sisu 47, 168, DT-2, G-10
96/7 Sisu 42, 183, ATG-6
95/6 Sisu Limited 12
95 Suomen Beckett Card 7
96 Wien 18

STROMQVIST, HAKAN
89/0 Semic Elitserien 172

STRÖMVALL, JOHAN
94/5 Leaf Elit Set 30, SS-7
95/6 Leaf Elit Set 249
89/0 Semic Elitserien 156
90/1 Semic Elitserien 234
91/2 Semic Elitserien 163
92/3 Semic Elitserien 187
95/6 UD Elitserien 125

STRONG, KEN
95 Globe 183

STROT, BRETT
93/4 Flint Generals

STROZYNSKI, SEBASTIEN
00/1 Rouyn-Noranda 5

STRUCH, DAVID
00/1 Kudos 139
90/1 7th..Sketch WHL 78
94/5 Saint John Flames
95/6 Saint John Flames
92/3 Salt Lake G'Eagles
00/1 Nottingham Panthers
89/0 Saskatoon Blades
90/1 Saskatoon Blades
91/2 Saskatoon Blades

STRUDWICK, JASON
00/1 BAP Mem. 321
95/6 Edge Ice 96
01/2 Signature 66, ✍ Aut. 66
94/5 Slapshot Memorial 21
99/0 Upper Deck 296
99/0 UD G. Reserve 296
98/9 UD MVP 202
01/2 VANC / Coke
96/7 Kentucky Tho'blades
97/8 Kentucky Tho'blades
93/4 Kamloops Blazers

STRUEBY, TODD
90/1 Canada Nationals 19
91/2 ProCards 585
88/9 EDMO / Action 132
83/4 Moncton Alpines
84/5 Nova Scotia Oilers
81/2 Saskatoon Blades

STRUMM, BOB
93/4 Las Vegas Thunder
94/5 Las Vegas Thunder
95/6 Las Vegas Thunder
96/7 Las Vegas Thunder
97/8 Las Vegas Thunder 11
98/9 Las Vegas Thunder

STRUNK, STEVE
93/4 Milwaukee Admirals
96/7 Milwaukee Admirals

STUART, BILLY
23/4 William Paterson 22
24/5 William Paterson 31

STUART, BRAD
99/0 BAP Mem. 242
00/1 BAP Mem. 19
01/2 BAP Mem. 22
99 Bowman 99, SC15
98 Bowman 66, 138, -SC8, ✍ A22
98 Bowman Chrome 66, 138
98/9 Bowman's Best 137
02/3 Calder 6
99/0 Dynagon Ice 176
02/3 First Ed. 204
99/0 HoloGrFX 50
99/0 Millenium 214, C-41, ✍ Aut. 214
99/0 NHL Power Play [x3]
01/2 O-Pee-Chee 118
98/9 OPC Chrome 228
99/0 Omega 212
00/1 Pacific 366
01/2 Pacific 345
02/3 Pacific 341
02/3 Pacific Complete 145
00/1 Pa. Paramount 218
99/0 Panini Sticker 304
00/1 Parkhurst P-81
01/2 Parkhurst 131
02/3 Parkhurst 90
00/1 Premier Plus 47, ✍ PS
99/0 Prism 128, -IP 7
00/1 Signature 8, ✍ Aut. 84
01/2 Signature 76, ✍ Aut. 76
02/3 Signature ✂ YP6
99/0 SP Authentic 71, ✍ SotT
01/2 SP Authentic 125
00/1 SPx 58
99/0 Stadium 195
00/1 Stadium 155, ✍ LS10
98/9 Topps 228
00/1 Topps 237, OTG27
01/2 Topps 118
99/0 To. Chrome 288
00/1 To. Chrome 147
98/9 To. Finest F4
99/0 To. Gold Label 89
00/1 To. Gold Label NG6
00/1 To. Heritage 108
99/0 To. Prmr. Plus 125, PR2
00/1 To. Stars 30, P8, ✍ CAI
02/3 To. Total 225
00/1 UD Heroes 100
00/1 Ultimate Mem. ✍ U-49
99/0 Upper Deck 167, 281
00/1 Upper Deck 147
01/2 Upper Deck 376
99/0 UD G. Reserve 167, 281
01/2 UD Honor Roll 29, 59
00/1 UD MVP 147
01/2 UD MVP 158
99/0 UD Ovation 51
00/1 UD Vintage 301
01/2 UD Vintage 215, 217
02/3 UD Vintage 216
99/0 Victory 365
00/1 Victory 194
01/2 Victory 294
02/3 Victory 180
99/0 WGretzky 154
96/7 Regina Pats
97/8 Regina Pats

STUART, BRUCE
91 C55 Reprint 15
83 HHOF Postcard O15
83&87 HHOF 224
10/1 Imperial
10/1 Imperial 17
11/2 Imperial 15

STUART, HOD
83 HHOF Postcard F13
83&87 HHOF 87

STUART, IRA
28/9 Paulins Candy 61

STUART, RED
25-27 Anonymous 40

STUBEL, CHRIS
01/2 Vancouver Giants

STUCK, DAN
88/9 ProCards / Hershey
89/0 ProCards AHL 358
94/5 Hershey Bears

STUCKEY, MARK
94/5 DEL 248

STUCKY, JIM
97/8 Indianapolis Ice 3

STÜMPEL, JOZEF
01/2 Adrenaline 16
98/9 Aurora 90
99/0 Aurora 72
00/1 Aurora 70, Pins. 70
98/9 Be A Player 63, ✍ Aut. 63
99/0 BAP Mem. 241
00/1 BAP Mem. 168
01/2 BAP Mem. 110, 469
02/3 BAP Mem. 163
98/9 Bowman's Best 91
91/2 Classic 34
91/2 Classic Four Sport 34
92/3 Classic Prospects 83
92/3 Classic Prospects BC16
95/6 DEL 448
93/4 Donruss 23
94/5 Donruss 322
95/6 Donruss 195
97/8 Donruss 134
97/8 Do. Canadian 43
97/8 Do. Elite 26
97/8 Do. Preferred 55
97/8 Do. Priority 60
98/9 Dynagon Ice 91
99/0 Dynagon Ice 99
96/7 Flair 7
93/4 Fleer Ultra 212
93/4 Fleer Ultra ARS 9
94/5 Fleer Ultra 261
97/8 Kraft / KD
93/4 Leaf 404
94/5 Leaf 143
95/6 Leaf 223
96/7 Leaf 116
97/8 Leaf 40
97/8 Limited 96
98/9 NHL Power Play
01/2 O-Pee-Chee 207
02/3 O-Pee-Chee 201
98/9 OPC Chrome 132, SB24
97/8 Omega 114
98/9 Omega 114
98/9 Pacific 246, -TC 12
99/0 Pacific 199
00/1 Pacific 204
01/2 Pacific 190
02/3 Pacific 34
02/3 Pacific Complete 218
97/8 Pacific CC 71
97/8 Pa. Crown Roy. 66
98/9 Pa. Crown Roy. 66
97/8 Pa. Dynagon 9, T-31
97/8 Pa. Invincible 10
97/8 Pa. Paramount 92
98/9 Pa. Paramount 109
99/0 Pa. Paramount 113
00/1 Pa. Paramount 117
97/8 Pa. Revolution 67, TC-12
98/9 Pa. Revolution 70
96/7 Panini Sticker 9
97/8 Panini Sticker 3
98/9 Panini Sticker 201
99/0 Panini Sticker 259
00/1 Panini Sticker 168
91/2 Parkhurst 231
93/4 Parkhurst 15
94/5 Parkhurst 19, 293
95/6 Parkhurst 13
00/1 Parkhurst P-15
01/2 Parkhurst 198, 369
02/3 Parkhurst Retro 78
92/3 Pinnacle 412
94/5 Pinnacle 418
97/8 Pinnacle 138
97/8 Pi. Certified 97
97/8 Pi. Inside 127
97/8 Pi. Totally 97
93/4 Power Play 293
93/4 Premier 416
94/5 Premier 214
00/1 PS Titanium ✂ GUG 25
96/7 Score 187
97/8 Score 122
00/1 Signature 174
01/2 Signature 116, ✍ Aut. 116
97/8 SP Authentic 71
98/9 SP Authentic ✍ SotT
99/0 SP Authentic ✍ SotT
02/3 Sports Vault 18
01/2 SPx 157
98/9 SPx Finite 41
99/0 Stadium 37
00/1 Stadium 112
98/9 Topps 132, SB24
99/0 Topps 41
00/1 Topps 177
01/2 Topps 207
02/3 Topps 201
99/0 To. Chrome 41
00/1 To. Chrome 118
98/9 To. Finest 67
99/0 To. Gold Label 83
02/3 To. Limited 201
93/4 To. Stadium 488
02/3 To. Total 153
98/9 UD Choice 100
92/3 Upper Deck 485
93/4 Upper Deck 379
94/5 Upper Deck 155
95/6 Upper Deck 157
96/7 Upper Deck 12
98/9 Upper Deck 103
99/0 Upper Deck 237
00/1 Upper Deck 83
01/2 Upper Deck 83, 248
02/3 Upper Deck 260
95/6 UD BAP 208, ✍ S208
96/7 UD Black Diam. 60
95/6 UD CC 308
97/8 UD Coll. Choice 18, SQ17
98/9 UD G. Reserve 103
99/0 UD G. Reserve 237
01/2 UD Ice 87
99/0 UD MVP 97
00/1 UD MVP 86
01/2 UD MVP 85
02/3 UD MVP 18
99/0 UD MVP Cup ✍ PS
01/2 UD Vintage 120, 122
02/3 UD Vintage 21
99/0 Victory 136
00/1 Victory 112
01/2 Victory 161
02/3 Victory 15
99/0 WGretzky 82
96 Wien 230
97/8 Zenith 28, Z23

STUMPF, JURI
94/5 DEL 35
95/6 DEL 28

STURGEON, ADAM
01/2 Belleville Bulls
01/2 Mississauga IceDogs

STURGEON, MIKE
82/3 Brandon Wheat Kings

STURGEON, PETER
75/6 O-Pee-Chee 393

STURM, MARCO
01/2 Adrenaline 171
98/9 Aurora 171
98/9 Be A Player 119, ✍ Aut. 119
99/0 BAP Mem. 248
00/1 BAP Mem. 16
01/2 Bowman 109
02/3 Bowman 75
98/9 Bowman's Best 83
95/6 DEL 261
96/7 DEL 149
97/8 Do. Priority 168
98/9 Dynagon Ice 169
98/9 NHL Power Play
99/0 NHL Power Play
01/2 O-Pee-Chee 97
02/3 O-Pee-Chee 253
98/9 OPC Chrome 17, SB12
97/8 Omega 206
98/9 Omega 215
98/9 Pacific 392
99/0 Pacific 383
00/1 Pacific 367
01/2 Pacific 346
02/3 Pacific 342
97/8 Pa. Crown Roy. 122
98/9 Pa. Crown Roy. 121
98/9 Pa. Paramount 215
99/0 Pa. Paramount 210
97/8 Pa. Revolution 127
98/9 Pa. Revolution 129
98/9 Panini Sticker 214
99/0 Panini Sticker 302
97/8 Pi. Be A Player 243, OT-19, ✍ Aut. 243
97/8 Pi. BeeHive BHT 25
97/8 SP Authentic 192, I40
02/3 Sports Vault 288
99/0 SPx 130
98/9 SPx Finite 72, 150
02/3 Stadium 83, ✂ NHLP17
98/9 Topps 17, -IA 12, -SB 12
99/0 Topps 114, TW20
01/2 Topps 97
02/3 Topps 253
99/0 To. Chrome 114
01/2 To. Chrome 97
02/3 T. Chrome 136
98/9 To. Finest 147
98/9 T. Gold Label 71
02/3 To. Heritage ✂ GS, ✂ GSB
02/3 To. Limited 253
02/3 To. Total 108
98/9 UD Choice 181
98/9 UD3 27, 87, 147
97/8 Upper Deck 355
98/9 Upper Deck 169
99/0 Upper Deck 279
00/1 Upper Deck 377
02/3 Upper Deck 148
97/8 UD Black Diam. 71, PC12
98/9 UD G. Reserve 169
99/0 UD G. Reserve 279
97/8 UD Ice 52
98/9 UD MVP 172
99/0 UD MVP 177
00/1 UD Vintage 302
02/3 UD Vintage 214
99/0 Victory 253
01/2 Victory 299
02/3 Victory - NP29
99/0 WGretzky 153
97/8 Zenith 87, RR-9, ZT-15, Z68

SUBBOTIN, ANDREI
98/9 Mir 40

SUBBOTIN, DMITRI
00/1 Mir 320

SUBR, BO
99/0 Guelph Storm

SUCHAN, GREG
89/0 7th..Sketch OHL 133
89/0 Niagara Falls Thunder

SUCHAN, JAROSLAV
98/9 OFS 50

SUCHANEK, KAMIL
99/0 OFS 246

SUCHANEK, KAREL
95/6 APS 220
96/7 APS 96

SUCHANEK, PETR
97/8 APS 111
98/9 OFS 318
99/0 OFS 245
00/1 OFS 272

SUCHANEK, RUDOLF
94/5 APS 103
95/6 APS 55
96/7 APS 241
97/8 APS 268
97/8 DS 28
98/9 DS 33
99/0 DS 33
00/1 DS 76
96/7 DS Sticker 81
97/8 DS Sticker 68
98/9 OFS 195
99/0 OFS 189
00/1 OFS 9, -Star
01/2 OFS 132, -RE9D, UHI 18

SUCHANEK, PAVEL
91/2 Avant Garde BCJHL 30
92/3 BCJHL 68

SUCHY, JAN
70/1 Kuvajulkaisut 59
69/0 Mästär Serien 12
72 Semic Sticker 36
74 Semic Sticker 67
91 Semic Sticker 247
96 Wien HL17
71/2 Williams Finnish 39

SUCHY, PETR
98/9 OFS 347
99/0 OFS 65
00/1 OFS 144
99/0 Score 149

SUCHY, RADOSLAV
99/0 BAP Mem. 315
97 Bowman 64
02/3 First Ed. 291
01/2 Heads Up ✂ JQ 26
99/0 NHL Power Play
99/0 Omega 186
00/1 Panini Sticker 191
00/1 Pr. Stock ✂ GUG 88
00/1 PS Titanium Draft ✂ 79
00/1 Upper Deck 364
97/8 Las Vegas Thunder 23

SUDA, JUSTIN
01/2 Kingston Frontenacs 21

SUDERMAN, JOE
98/9 Kelowna Rockets
00/1 Kelowna Rockets

SUDERMAN, MATT
00/1 Saskatoon Blades

SUGDEN, BRANDON
95/6 Slapshot 160
98/9 Dayton Bombers

SUHONEN, ALPO
66/7 Champion 44
93/4 Jyvas Hyva 103
70/1 Kuvajulkaisut 187
93/4 Sisu 2
89/0 WINN / Safeway

SUHRADA, JIRI
95/6 APS 217

SUHY, ANDY
92/3 Toledo Storm WIOT
92/3 Toledo Storm
93/4 Toledo Storm 8

SUIKKANEN, KAI
80/1 Mallasjuoma 105
78/9 SM-Liiga 148

SUK, JOE
87/8 Hull Olympiques

SUK, STEVE
93/4 Michigan State

SUKOVIC, MIL
91/2 7th...Sketch LHJMQ 8

SULANDER, ARI
98/9 Cardset 4, DT 2
99/0 Cardset 179
00/1 Cardset 231
02/3 Cardset 121
95 Hartwall Karjala
97/8 Hockey-Box
93/4 Jyvas Hyva 104
93/4 Sisu 3
94/5 Sisu 41, 388, N-3, SS-8
95/6 Sisu 43, 167, GG-3, G-3
96/7 Sisu 41, 175, ATG-8, KG-1, MA-4
95/6 Sisu Limited 10
96 Wien 10

SULC, JAN
01/2 OFS 163

SULKOVSKY, DAVID
99/0 Eishockey 238

SULKU, SEBASTIAN
98/9 Cardset 146
99/0 Cardset 236
00/1 Cardset 25
02/3 Cardset 122
93/4 Sisu 7
94/5 Sisu 275
95/6 Sisu 137

SULLAMAA, PETRI
92/3 Jyvas Hyva 51

SULLIMAN, DOUG
90/1 Bowman 110
80/1 O-Pee-Chee 306
82/3 O-Pee-Chee 132
83/4 O-Pee-Chee 148
85/6 O-Pee-Chee 234
86/7 OPC/Topps 121
87/8 OPC/Topps 116
88/9 OPC/Topps 172
90/1 O-Pee-Chee 473
82/3 OPC/Topps Sticker 128
83/4 OPC/Topps Sticker 256
87/8 OPC Sticker 59-200
87/8 Panini Sticker 82
82/3 Post [Hart.]
83/4 Souhaits Keychain [Whalers]
82/3 HART / Jr. Whalers
83/4 HART / Jr. Whalers
84/5 NJER
86/7 NJER / S.O.B.E.R.
90/1 NJER
89/0 PHIL

SULLIVAN, ANDY
93/4 St. John's Maple Leafs

SULLIVAN, BOB
83/4 O-Pee-Chee 149
83/4 OPC/Topps Sticker 189

83/4 Souhaits Keychain [Whalers]
82/3 HART / Jr. Whalers

SULLIVAN, BRIAN

92/3 Classic Prospects 77
91/2 ProCards 412
97/8 Grand Rapids Griffins

SULLIVAN, CHRIS

96/7 Dayton Bombers
93/4 Michigan State

SULLIVAN, DALE

00/1 Hull Olympiques 19
01/2 Hull Olympiques 20
02/3 Hull Olympiques

SULLIVAN, DAN

00/1 Mississauga IceDogs
00/1 Owen Sound Attack 22
01/2 Owen Sound Attack

SULLIVAN, GEORGE (RED)

45-64 BeeHive-2 [Bost.]
45-64 BeeHive-2 [NYRa.]
51/2 Parkhurst 27
52/3 Parkhurst 79
93/4 Parkie 56-57 170
93/4 Parkie 56-57 86
94/5 Parkie Tall 108
60/1 Shirriff 82
61/2 Shirriff 91
54/5 Topps 42
57/8 Topps 56
58/9 Topps 48
59/0 Topps 59
60/1 Topps 18
61/2 Topps 48
63/4 Topps 44
64/5 Topps 29
65/6 Topps 87
59/0 Toronto Star Photo
59/0 Toronto Star Weekend
91/2 Ultimate Original Six 29, ✍ Aut. 29

SULLIVAN, JEFFREY

96/7 Halifax Moosehead
96/7 Halifax Moosehead
97/8 Halifax Moosehead
97/8 Halifax Moosehead
98/9 Halifax Moosehead

SULLIVAN, JERRY

65/6 Hellas 137

SULLIVAN, KEVIN

90/1 ProCards 595
90/1 Kansas City Blades

SULLIVAN, MICHAEL

90/1 Rayside-Balfour

SULLIVAN, MIKE

92/3 Bowman 116
95/6 Donruss 211
99/0 Eishockey 296
95/6 Leaf 167
92/3 O-Pee-Chee 144
97/8 Pa. Invincible R-32
99/0 Pa. Paramount 183
93/4 Panini Sticker 262
91/2 Parkhurst 383
92/3 Parkhurst 395
93/4 Parkhurst 454
95/6 Parkhurst 300
93/4 Pinnacle 287
97/8 Pi. Be A Player 179, ✍ Aut. 179
93/4 Premier 21
90/1 ProCards 307
92/3 Score 533
93/4 Score 390
92/3 Topps 282
92/3 To. Stadium 262
93/4 To. Stadium 139
92/3 Upper Deck 46
00/1 Upper Deck 137
94/5 UD BAP ✍ 75
98/9 PHOE / Coca-Cola
92/3 SANJ / Pacific Bell
97/8 Pensacola Ice Pilots
96/7 Toledo Storm

SULLIVAN, PETER (SILKY)

79/0 O-Pee-Chee 378
80/1 O-Pee-Chee 29
76/7 OPC WHA 42
77/8 OPC WHA 27
80/1 Pepsi Bottle Cap
80/1 Topps 29
79/0 WINN
80/1 WINN
78/9 Winnipeg Jets

SULLIVAN, STEVE

01/2 Adrenaline 41
01/2 Atomic 20
00/1 Aurora 33
98/9 Be A Player 286, ✍ Aut. 286
00/1 BAP Mem. 57
01/2 BAP Mem. 277
02/3 BAP Mem. 138
01/2 Bowman 85
02/3 Bowman 54
99/0 Challenger 4
01/2 Crown Royale 33
02/3 Cr. Royale ✂ GWDP 4
96/7 Donruss 229
97/8 Donruss 39
97/8 Do. Canadian 94
97/8 Do. Preferred 131
97/8 Do. Priority 92
95/6 Edge Ice 10
02/3 First Ed. 112, ✂ Jers.
95/6 Future Legends 21, PC-4
01/2 Heads Up 19, ✂ JQ 7
02/3 Heads Up ✂ GWQ 7
96/7 Leaf GLR-10
97/8 Leaf 84
96/7 L. Preferred 143
97/8 Limited 46, 116
01/2 O-Pee-Chee 72
02/3 O-Pee-Chee 179
99/0 Omega 55
98/9 Pacific 422
99/0 Pacific 415
00/1 Pacific 102
01/2 Pacific 92, 407
02/3 Pacific 82, ✂ GWJ 8
02/3 Pacific Complete 211
97/8 Pacific CC 283
97/8 Pa. Dynagon 123, T-52
97/8 Pa. Invincible 138
99/0 Pa. Paramount 229
00/1 Pa. Paramount 53
97/8 Panini Sticker 175
00/1 Panini Sticker 128
00/1 Parkhurst P-172
01/2 Parkhurst 151
02/3 Parkhurst 83
02/3 Parkhurst Retro 59
96/7 Pinnacle 226
97/8 Pinnacle 134
96/7 Pi. Be A Player 209, ✍ Aut. 209
97/8 Pi. Certified 83
97/8 Pi. Inside 102
96/7 Pi. Summit 180
97/8 Pi. Totally 83
96/7 Pi. Zenith 140
01/2 Pr. Stock 18, ✂ GUG 25
00/1 PS Titanium 17
01/2 PS Titanium ✂ DSJ 10, ✂ DSJ 73
01/2 PS Titanium Draft ✂ 24
02/3 PS Titanium ✂ GWJ 15
00/1 PS Titanium Draft ✂ 20
91/2 ProCards 443
00/1 Revolution 31
97/8 Score 185
97/8 Score Toro. 7
00/1 Signature 160, ✍ Aut. 98
01/2 Signature 83, ✍ Aut. 83
02/3 Signature 100, ✍ 100
96/7 SBx Impact 160
02/3 Slam Card
93/4 Slapshot / S.S.Marie 24
97/8 SP Authentic 154
00/1 SP Authentic 19
01/2 SP Authentic 15
00/1 SP GU 12
02/3 SP GU ✂ AF
02/3 Sports Vault 174
01/2 SPx 12, ✂ DT, ✂ TT
02/3 SPx ✂ SS
00/1 Stadium 143
01/2 Stadium 55
02/3 Stadium 48
00/1 Topps 232
01/2 Topps 72
02/3 Topps 179
01/2 To. Chrome 72
02/3 T. Chrome 104
00/1 To. Heritage 192
01/2 To. Heritage 53
02/3 To. Limited 179
01/2 To. Reserve 97
02/3 To. Total 17
00/1 UD Heroes 27
01/2 UD PlayMakers Ltd 20
00/1 UD Reserve 18
99/0 Ult. Victory 20
96/7 Upper Deck 185
97/8 Upper Deck 160
00/1 Upper Deck 38
01/2 Upper Deck 37
02/3 Upper Deck 40, ✂ CG, ✂ SD
01/2 UD Challenge 15
97/8 UD Coll. Choice 248, SQ4
01/2 UD Mask 19, ✂ GJ, ✂ JP, ✂ DP
00/1 UD MVP 45
01/2 UD MVP 37
02/3 UD MVP 40
02/3 UD Piece 19, ✂ PH
00/1 UD Pros&Prosp. 19
01/2 UD Top Shelf 84
02/3 UD Top Shelf ✂ CP, ✂ GO, ✂ R, ✂ SH, ✂ ST, ✂ SW, ✂ TS
00/1 UD Vintage 76
01/2 UD Vintage 58, 60, 61
02/3 UD Vintage 53, GB 53
01/2 Vanguard ✂ DGM 8
00/1 Victory 52
01/2 Victory 72, 435
02/3 Victory 46
96/7 NJER / Sharp
96/7 Albany River Rats
93/4 Soo Greyhounds 16

SULLIVAN, TOM

90/1 7th..Sketch OHL 120
91/2 7th...Sketch OHL 186

SUMMANEN, ARTO

72/3 Williams Finnish 186

SUMMANEN, RAIMO

98/9 Cardset Leij. 42
99/0 Cardset AH 8-pata
02/3 Cardset 274
95 Hartwall Karjala
91/2 Jyvas Hyva 16
92/3 Jyvas Hyva 182
89 Semic Sticker 40
91 Semic Sticker 20
92 Semic Sticker 16
93/4 Sisu 377
94/5 Sisu 252, H-15
95/6 Sisu Gold 22
95/6 Sisu Limited 7
96 Wien 7
83/4 EDMO / McDonald's
85/6 EDMO / Red Rooster
86/7 EDMO
86/7 EDMO / Red Rooster
88/9 EDMO / Action 3
84/5 Nova Scotia Oilers

SUMMERHILL, BILL

34-43 BeeHive-1 [Mont.]

SUMMERS, JOHN

95/6 Tallahasee Tiger Sharks

SUMNER, ROB

89/0 Victoria Cougars

SUMNER, S.

89/0 ProCards AHL 310

SUMNER, STEVE

99/0 Houston Aeros

SUNDBERG, REINO

89/0 Semic Elitserien 217
90/1 Semic Elitserien 51
91/2 Semic Elitserien 226

SUNDBLAD,

97/8 Hockey-Box

SUNDBLAD, NIKLAS

91/2 Arena 15
91/2 Classic 16
91/2 Classic Four Sport 16
93/4 Cla. Prospects 143
96/7 Leaf 234
96/7 Pinnacle 230
96/7 Pi. Summit 176
90/1 Semic Elitserien 96
91/2 Semic Elitserien 23
92/3 Semic Elitserien 46
91/2 Star Pics 8
91/2 Ultimate Draft Pick 16, 72, 85, ✍ Aut.
92/3 Upper Deck 227
00/1 UD DEL 49
01/2 UD DEL 149
98/9 UD Elitserien 164
99/0 UD Elitserien 166
94/5 Saint John Flames
95/6 Saint John Flames

SUNDELIN, ERKKI

71/2 Williams Finnish 257
73/4 Williams Finnish 321

SUNDERLAND, MATHIEU

95/6 Classic 23
93/4 Slapshot / Drummondville 23
96/7 Rimouski Océanic

SUNDIN, MATS

01/2 Adrenaline 185, WB 19, ✂ GWJ 47
01/2 ASG History
01/2 Atomic 93, PP 32, TN 13, ✂ GWJ 48
02/3 Atomic 94, -CF 22
98/9 Aurora 185, -ALC 17, -CF 46, -MACF 17, -Cube
99/0 Aurora 138, -Stripe 138, -CF 20, -ST 19
00/1 Aurora 140, Pins. 140, SR-20, TPS-10B
02/3 BAP All-Star 88-89, ✂ ASJ, ✂ HSHSJers
98/9 Be A Player 136, P-20, ✍ Aut. 136, ✂ G-2, ✂ AS-5, ✂ S-5, ✂✍ G-2
99/0 BAP Mem. 233, H-21, ✂ J-5, ✂ D-6, ✂ H-21, ✂ TM-25, ✂ TM-30, ✂ TM-41
00/1 BAP Mem. 296, ✂ J-2, ✂ H-4, ✂ PP-4, ✂ TM-24
01/2 BAP Mem. 298, ✂ ASD, ✂ AST, HSHS, ✂ PP, ✂ SCP
02/3 BAP Mem. 198, 228, ✂ ASJ54, ✂ ASE23, ✂ ASN23, ✂ ASTJ20, ✂ AST8, ✂ AST16, ✂ FP28, ✂ HSHSJers 26, ✂ TM8
01/2 BAP Update ✂ H10, ✂ PTT6
02/3 Between the Pipes ✂ GN10
96/7 Bic.Sports Aces 8-D
97/8 Bicycle 9-Club
95/6 Bicycle Sports Aces 10-Diamond
91/2 Bowman 137
92/3 Bowman 344
95/6 Bowman 49
01/2 Bowman 5
02/3 Bowman 12
98/9 Bowman's Best 39
02/3 Calder 50, ✂ GWJ 22
99/0 Crown Royale 135, -CS 19, -IG 25, -TC 9
00/1 Crown Royale 102, ✂ GWJ-24, JotC-25, NP-18
01/2 Crown Royale 134, ASH 20, JotC 29, ✂ TT 12
02/3 Crown Royale 93, -LOR 19
93/4 Donruss 283
93/4 Donruss S
95/6 Donruss 176
96/7 Donruss 30
97/8 Donruss 139, RA-9
96/7 Do. Canadian 12
97/8 Do. Canadian 40
95/6 Do. Elite 72, CE-11
96/7 Do. Elite 55
97/8 Do. Elite 58
97/8 Do. Preferred 38
97/8 Do. Priority 56
97/8 Do. Studio 67, HH-24
96/7 Duracell JB13
98/9 Dynagon Ice 184, -FT 18, -TC 25
99/0 Dynagon Ice 190, -ASP 19, -CM 30
93/4 EA Sports 111
97/8 Esso 42
01/2 eTopps 20
02/3 eTopps 4, -Intro
02/3 Exclusive 163, -MO 18, ✂ GWJ 24
02/3 First Ed. 137, 305, 368, 372, 378, 402R, ✂ Jers., ✂ DGJ 4, ✂ HSHSJers 3, ✂ TSL 18
94/5 Flair 186
96/7 Flair 92, CIS-9
94/5 Fleer 220
96/7 Fleer 110
95/6 Fleer Metal 147, IS-20
92/3 Fleer Ultra 180, -UI 25
93/4 Fleer Ultra 137
94/5 Fleer Ultra 220, 379
95/6 Fleer Ultra 164, EA-19, PP-9
96/7 Fl. Ultra 166, MM-9
00 Gatorade Sticker
95 Globe 13
x95 Globe 252-255,270
01/2 Heads Up 92, ASGN 5, HD 9, SM 19
02/3 Heads Up 118, -EIT 14, -ITN 21, -PSP 10, -SM 13, ✂ GWQ 31, / Bobble
93/4 Hockey Wit 51
99/0 HoloGrFX 55
95/6 Hoyle / West. 7-Club
92/3 Humpty Dumpty
02/3 In The G-U 72, 172, ✂ E16, ✂ F28, ✂ IE3, ✂ GUJ16, ✂ SJ16, ✂ T12, ✂ TM3
90/1 Kraft 42
91/2 Kraft 4
94/5 Kraft / HH
95/6 Kraft / KD
96/7 Kraft / KD
97/8 Kraft / JTP, KD, Casecard
98/9 Kraft / KD
99/0 Kraft / KD, / OML, / PB
00/1 Kraft 27
96/7 Kraft Magnet
93/4 Leaf 136
94/5 Leaf 530
95/6 Leaf 244, FOI-8
96/7 Leaf 53
97/8 Leaf 142, BS-19
94/5 Leaf Elit Set 232, GS-1
94/5 L. Limited 42
95/6 L. Limited 120, SG-9
96/7 L. Limited 28
96/7 L. Preferred 14, LS-33
97/8 Limited 9, 13, 128, FG-16, FG-26
96/7 Maggers 151
95/6 McDonald's McD-18
97/8 McDonald's McD-13, F10
98/9 McDonald's McD12
99/0 McDonald's McD-9
00/1 McDonald's 33, CL-7, DAS-6, GWJ-10
01/2 McDonald's 39, -CF 6, ✂ Jpatch 19
02/3 McDonald's 38, -A 5, -CC 6
96/7 Metal Univ. 154
99/0 Millenium 226, ✍ Aut. 226, ✂ J-15, ✂✍ J-15, ✂ JS-15
98/9 NHL Power Play
91/2 O-Pee-Chee 12
91/2 O-Pee-Chee 219
92/3 O-Pee-Chee 110
01/2 O-Pee-Chee 19
02/3 O-Pee-Chee 29, 329
98/9 OPC Chrome 71
90/1 OPC Premier 114
97/8 Omega 225, SHLC-18
98/9 Omega 231, -EOP 19, -FTF 8, -Onl. 33, -PI 11, -Prism 19
99/0 Omega 228, -5ST 24, -EOP 19, -WAS 9, ✂ GWJ 10
98/9 Pacific 13, -GCDC 32, -TC 25, -Time. 18
99/0 Pacific 416, -Cl 19, -GC 35
00/1 Pacific 399, 448, IO-20, CCA-10, ES-9, GCDC-33, PR-19
01/2 Pacific 373, 423, 442, IZ 19, TDP 7, WAS 10, ✂ GWJ 35
02/3 Pacific 370, -CCA 10, -L 12, -MA 18, -MI 16
02/3 Pacific Complete 304
97/8 Pacific CC 205, SS-10B
97/8 Pa. Crown Roy. 132, HT-17
98/9 Pa. Crown Roy. 132, -MP 18, -PotG 23, -PP 22
97/8 Pa. Dynagon 124, 144, T-16, T-27, BKS-93
97/8 Pa. Invincible 139, FP-34
97/8 Pa. Paramount 185
98/9 Pa. Paramount 231, -SD 17, -TC 25
99/0 Pa. Paramount 230, IAd-19, PB-35
00/1 Pa. Paramount 233, ES-19, FF-34, SZ-10
97/8 Pa. Revolution 137, TC-24
98/9 Pa. Revolution 140, -ASG 28, -CTLC 18, -Show. 34
94 Panini Olympics 292
98/9 Panini Photocard [x2]
90/1 Panini/QUE 20, H
91/2 Panini Sticker 255
92/3 Panini Sticker 212
92/3 Panini Sticker 302
93/4 Panini Sticker 68
94/5 Panini Sticker 55
95/6 Panini Sticker 201
96/7 Panini Sticker 218
97/8 Panini Sticker 179
98/9 Panini Sticker 164
99/0 Panini Sticker 153
00/1 Panini Sticker 95
95 Panini Worlds 292
91/2 Parkhurst 144
92/3 Parkhurst 148
92/3 Parkhurst 221
93/4 Parkhurst 435
93/4 Parkhurst F5
94/5 Parkhurst 185
95/6 Parkhurst 201, 247, CCP-8, IAS-6
00/1 Parkhurst P-126
01/2 Parkhurst 20, ✂ PJ4, ✂ PS4, ✂ PSJ3, ✂ HSHSJers, ✂ M33, ✂ T7, ✂ T26
02/3 Parkhurst 92, -HHP9, -HHR9, ✂ FP28, ✂ GJ47, ✂ SJ47, ✂ HSHSJers, ✂ MM7, ✂ MS8, ✂ NH8, ✂ PP2, ✂ TT3
02/3 Parkhurst Retro 23, ✂ RF28, ✂ RJ21, ✂ RSJ14, ✂ HSHSJers, ✂ RM24, ✂ RR3
94/5 Parkie SE175, ES2, seV37
91/2 Pinnacle 10
91/2 Pinnacle 389
92/3 Pinnacle 90
92/3 Pinnacle T2K 7
93/4 Pinnacle 2
93/4 Pinnacle T2K1 15
94/5 Pinnacle 386, NL10
95/6 Pinnacle 19, GG-3, R20-7
96/7 Pinnacle 144
97/8 Pinnacle 50, P-16
96/7 Pi. Be A Player BB-12
97/8 Pi. BeeHive 39
97/8 Pi. Certified 53, CT-15
97/8 Pi. Inside 21, IT-23, / Can 23
96/7 Pi. Mint 17
97/8 Pi. Mint 10
95/6 Pi. Summit 9
96/7 Pi. Summit 51
97/8 Pi. Totally 53
95/6 Pi. Zenith 19
96/7 Pi. Zenith 64
95/6 Playoff 99
94/5 POG 237
95/6 POG 259
93/4 Power Play 205
93/4 Power Play GG 8
93/4 Power Play PL 18
93/4 Premier 460
93/4 Prmr. - BG-OPC 6
93/4 Premier - Finest 5
94/5 Premier 160, 345, 412
00/1 Premier Plus 74
99/0 Prism 139, -CA 20
00/1 Pr. Stock 94, PS-56, PSS-25, ✂ GUG-99
01/2 Pr. Stock 92, Res. 19, -PS 71, ✂ GUG 97
02/3 Pr. Stock Reserve ✂ 146
00/1 PS Titanium 93, 3SS-20, WAS-9
01/2 PS Titanium 132, SK 20, TSS 19, TAS 19, ✂ DSJ 30, ✂ DSJ 42
01/2 PS Titanium Draft ✂ 90
02/3 PS Titanium 94, -SK 9
00/1 PS Titanium Draft ✂ 97
95/6 Pro Magnet 75
90/1 Pro Set 636
91/2 Pro Set 197
92/3 Pro Set 149
91/2 Pro Set Platinum 99
02/3 Quest for the Cup 93, -CTC 17
99/0 Revolution 140, -NI 19, -Orn. 19, -Show. 34, -TotL 19, / CSC 140
00/1 Revolution 140, HD-34, NI-19, SM-29
90/1 Score 398, 100T
91/2 Score 130
91/2 Score CAN 130
92/3 Score 153
93/4 Score 9
93/4 Score/CAN DD5
93/4 Score IS 10
94/5 Score 89
95/6 Score 56, BB-15, GB-16
96/7 Score 160, S-3
97/8 Score 95
97/8 Score Toro. 4
90/1 Sco. Young Stars 7
91/2 Score Young Stars 3
92/3 Score Young Stars 3
94/5 Select 21
95/6 Select CE 7
96/7 Select CE 85
94 Semic 74
95 Semic 62
89/0 Semic Elitserien 72
91/2 Semic Elitserien 323
91/2 Semic Elitserien 357
92/3 Semic Elitserien 348
91 Semic Sticker 211
92 Semic Sticker 72
93 Semic Sticker 33
00/1 Signature 34, HSHS, ✍ Aut. 93, ✂ J-15, ✂ HSHSJers
01/2 Signature C-29, ✂ FP28, ✂ GUE40, ✂ GJ62, ✂ GSJ62, ✂ HSHSJers, ✂ ITN40, ✂ TM28
02/3 Signature 119, GS-54, ✍ 119, ✂ FJ28, ✂ SGJ16, ✂ TQ2, ✂ TM2
95/6 SBx Emotion 175
95/6 SBx Impact 165
96/7 SBx Impact 130
02/3 Slam Card
94/5 SP 116
95/6 SP 141, E26
96/7 SP 151, CW-12, HC-20
97/8 SP Authentic 150, I33, ✍ SotT
98/9 SP Authentic 83, ✍ SotT, SS23
99/0 SP Authentic 81
00/1 SP Authentic 82
01/2 SP Authentic 83
02/3 SP Authentic 84, ✂ SP
00/1 SP GU 56, ✂ TotG, ✂ C, ✂ P
01/2 SP GU 55, ✂ Patch, ✂ PatchC,
02/3 SP GU 46, ✂ AF (x2), ✂ PC, ✂ PH (x2), ✂ TG
02/3 Sports Vault 133
96/7 SPx 43
97/8 SPx 46, D-SPX17
99/0 SPx 143, XT13
00/1 SPx 66, X14, ✂ WM
01/2 SPx 65, ✂ DT, ✂ TT
02/3 SPx 70, 99, 140, ✂ SS, ✂ X
98/9 SPx Finite 82, 118, 162
98/9 SPx Prospects 55, H27, L8, PS13, -✂ WM
00/1 Stadion 81
99/0 Stadium 2, -Chrome 2, -Big 2, -CA17, EG8, ✍ CS4, ✍ CS7, ✍ CS8, ✍ LS3, ✂ SCS
00/1 Stadium 150, SF10
01/2 Stadium 50, G3, NHLP3
02/3 Stadium 14, -WS-19, ✂ NHLP4
91/2 Star Pics 50
96/7 SLU
02/3 Starz
95/6 Super Sticker 118
96/7 Team Out!
92/3 Topps 415
95/6 Topps 19, 150, 10CG
98/9 Topps 71, L2
99/0 Topps 15, IM6, TW5, ✍ TA5
00/1 Topps 4, NHLD6
01/2 Topps 19
02/3 Topps 29, 329, CC4, HHC5, OTG4, OTG7, ✂ CC5, ✂ CC6, ✂ CC11, ✂ FRF, ✂✍ FRF
99/0 To. Chrome 15, IM6
00/1 To. Chrome 4
01/2 To. Chrome 19
02/3 T. Chrome 29, ✂ FRF
94/5 Topps Finest 110
95/6 To. Finest 177
98/9 To. Finest 106, R19
95 Topps Finest Bronze 11
98/9 T. Gold Label 53
99/0 To. Gold Label 56, QC10
00/1 To. Gold Label 24, B6
00/1 To. Heritage 13, OSA, ✂ OSS
01/2 To. Heritage 6
02/3 To. Heritage 13, 108, 109, 124, -Light 13
02/3 To. Limited 29, 329
96/7 To. Picks 43, TS-13
99/0 To. Prmr. Plus 54, PT5
01/2 To. Reserve 43
91/2 To. Stadium 300
92/3 To. Stadium 478
93/4 To. Stadium 370
93/4 To. Stadium 425
94/5 To. Stadium 90
95/6 To. Stadium 75, MP
94/5 TSC Members Only 26
95/6 TSC Members Only 18
00/1 To. Stars 10
95/6 To. Super Skills 32
02/3 To. Total 280, TTC28, TP3, TT6
98/9 UD Choice 203, BH17, SQ19
00/1 UD Heroes 111, TS6, ✂ GT, ✂ GC
01/2 UD PlayMakers Ltd 93
00/1 UD Reserve 81, GS9
02/3 UD Superstars 244, ✂ CAS
98/9 UD3 48, 108, 168
00/1 Ultimate Mem. ✍ U-15, ✂ J-15, ✂ Jers. 13, ✂ JJ-5, ✂ S-15, ✂ TM-12, ✂ TM-14, ✂ TM-34, ✂ TM-38, ✂ UC-3
01/2 Ultimate Mem. ✂ A8, ✂ ASGH, ✂ CP, ✂ Corn., ✂ DD, ✂ Emb., ✂ Jers., ✂ S&J, ✂ GA), ✂ ITN, ✂ JE, ✂ JJ, ✂ NP, ✂ UC, ✂ WTF
02/3 Ultimate Mem. ✂ CP, ✂ Cor, ✂ DD, ✂ Emb, ✂ FO, ✂ GUJ, ✂ GUSJ, ✂ GAO, ✂ HT, ✂ ITN, ✂ UC
99/0 Ult. Victory 82
90/1 Upper Deck 365
91/2 Upper Deck 31
91/2 Upper Deck 93
91/2 Upper Deck 134
91/2 Upper Deck E13
92/3 Upper Deck 121
92/3 Upper Deck 374
92/3 Upper Deck E18
92/3 Upper Deck WG17
93/4 Upper Deck 220, 228, 302, 419, HT20, SP-132
94/5 Upper Deck 51, 548, SP-170
95/6 Upper Deck 147, 219, AS-18, SE-169
96/7 Upper Deck 160, X38, LS19, P28, SS23A, ✂ GJ13
97/8 Upper Deck 369, SS13, SG13, S13, T14B
98/9 Upper Deck 370, FF14, LS24, P28, ✂ GJ19
99/0 Upper Deck 121, AS9, CT13, MA8, SS17
00/1 Upper Deck 391, FF11, P9, SS19, TT3, ✂ GJ, ✂ DGJ
01/2 Upper Deck 164, FC15, LP15, ✂ ASJ, ✂ PoaN, ✂ PoaND, ✂ PotL
02/3 Upper Deck 164, 244, -SS13, ✂ DM, ✂ GO, ✂ LN, ✂ PL, ✂ PW, ✂ UDPL
96/7 UD All-Star YCTG AR7
02/3 UD Artistic 82, R82, CG12, ✂ AT, / Art
94/5 UD BAP R76
95/6 UD BAP 203, ✍ S203
96/7 UD Black Diam. 163, RC13
97/8 UD Black Diam. 77, PC30
98/9 UD Black Diam. 84, WF27
99/0 UD Black Diam. 82, D15, DM8
00/1 UD Black Diam. 56
99/0 UD C. Legends 66
01/2 UD Challenge 84, CR9, ✂ UC
02/3 UD Classic 91, ET15, ✂ HR, ✂ SC
95/6 UD CC 90, C30
96/7 UD CC 255, 332, UD44, C29, CR29
97/8 UD Coll. Choice 245, 320, SQ83, S17, C23, CR23, / 5x7 5
97/8 UD Diam. Vision 17
95/6 UD Elitserien 236
02/3 UD Foundations 89
98/9 UD G. Reserve 370
99/0 UD G. Reserve 121
99/0 UD Gretzky Excl. 78
01/2 UD Honor Roll SG6, -DPuck, ✂ GAJ, ✂ PPM
02/3 UD Honor 65, 98, -SG29, -TW14, ✂ GA
97/8 UD Ice 73,IC13, L4C
00/1 UD Ice 38
01/2 UD Ice 122
00/1 UD Legends 125, ✂ LGJ
92/3 UD Locker 59
01/2 UD Mask 92, ✂ GJ, ✂ JP, ✂ DP
02/3 UD Mask 84, ✂ IO, ✂ PG
98/9 UD MVP 195, PG8
99/0 UD MVP 196
00/1 UD MVP 167, ✂ CG
01/2 UD MVP 173, ✂ S
02/3 UD MVP 175
99/0 UD MVP Cup 173, SS11, SC18, -GC
99/0 UD Ovation 56
02/3 UD Piece 83, ✂ PH, ✂ SS
01/2 UD Premier 48, ✂ B
02/3 UD Premier 50, ✂ Jers, ✂ Patch, ✂ NHLP
00/1 UD Pros&Prosp. 81
99/0 UD Retro 74
02/3 UD Rookie 92, 113, ✂ DJ
01/2 UD Top Shelf 42
02/3 UD Top Shelf 83, ✂ AS, ✂ CP, ✂ GO, ✂ SH, ✂ SW
00/1 UD Vintage 334, 345, 346, NH20
01/2 UD Vintage 236, 242, 243
02/3 UD Vintage 237, 288, 306, T60, ✂ OS
00/1 Vanguard 94, HV-33, IF-18, ✂ DGJ-2
01/2 Vanguard 94, EMW 9, IF 9, VT 19, ✂ DGM 34, ✂ DGM 44
02/3 Vanguard 93, -EMW 6
99/0 Victory 280, 281
00/1 Victory 216, 217, 326
01/2 Victory 426
02/3 Victory 200, -NP49
01/2 Waving the Flag 17
99/0 WGretzky 160, ✂ TG, W9
96 Wien 56, NS3
97/8 Zenith 48, Z52
90/1 QUÉB / Petro-Canada
91/2 QUÉB / Petro-Canada
92/3 QUÉB / Petro-Canada
99/0 TORO / Pizza Pizza 20

SUNDIN, RONNIE

94/5 Leaf Elit Set 24
95/6 Leaf Elit Set 141
92/3 Semic Elitserien 308
95/6 UD Elitserien 207
98/9 UD Elitserien 70
99/0 UD Elitserien 72
00/1 UD Elitserien 64
97/8 Hartford Wolf Pack

SUNDLÖV, MICHAEL

94/5 Leaf Elit Set 126, CS-2, GC-15
95/6 Leaf Elit Set 15, C-12, LM-1, S-2
89/0 Semic Elitserien 28
90/1 Semic Elitserien 175
91/2 Semic Elitserien 28
92/3 Semic Elitserien 51
95/6 UD Elitserien 19
97/8 UD Elitserien 17, 216

SUNDQVIST, CARL

72 Hellas MM-Jenkki 28
72/3 Williams Finnish 58

SUNDQVIST, KARL-JOHAN

74 Hellas MM-Jenkki 36
74 Semic Sticker 7
73/4 Williams Finnish 37

SUNDSTRÖM, NIKLAS

98/9 Be A Player 240, ✍ Aut. 240
99/0 BAP Mem. 112
00/1 BAP Mem. 256
95/6 Bowman 113, BB21
93/4 Classic 8
93/4 Classic - Top Ten DP8
94/5 Classic 79, T44
93/4 Cla. 4 Sport 192
95/6 Donruss 382, RR-13
96/7 Donruss 237
97/8 Donruss 178
95/6 Do. Elite 60, R-14
96/7 Do. Elite 47
97/8 Do. Priority 67
99/0 Dynagon Ice 177
02/3 First Ed. 77, ✂ Jers.
96/7 Fleer 72
95/6 Fleer Metal 193, IS-21
95/6 Fleer Ultra 357, EA-18
96/7 Fl. Ultra 112
95 Globe 60
99/0 HoloGrFX 48
96/7 Leaf 172
97/8 Leaf 36
94/5 Leaf Elit Set 284
95/6 L. Limited 104, RP-4
97/8 Limited 64
96/7 Metal Univ. 102
99/0 Millenium 212, ✍ Aut. 212
01/2 O-Pee-Chee 232
02/3 O-Pee-Chee 114
98/9 OPC Chrome 197
97/8 Omega 150
98/9 Pacific 302
99/0 Pacific 282
00/1 Pacific 447
01/2 Pacific 347
02/3 Pacific Complete 137
97/8 Pacific CC 86
97/8 Pa. Crown Roy. 88
98/9 Pa. Paramount 159
96/7 Panini Sticker 108
97/8 Panini Sticker 89
98/9 Panini Sticker 86
99/0 Panini Sticker 297
00/1 Panini Sticker 201
93/4 Parkhurst 506
95/6 Parkhurst 261, 514
01/2 Parkhurst 185
94/5 Parkie SE237
97/8 Pi. Inside 155
95/6 Pi. Summit 187
95/6 Pi. Zenith 128, RRC-14
96/7 Score 269
97/8 Score 194
97/8 Score NYRa. 5
95/6 Select CE 135
91/2 Semic Elitserien 331
92/3 Semic Elitserien 244
95/6 SBx Impact 213, F-16
96/7 SBx Impact 85
94/5 SP 168
95/6 SP 96
96/7 SP HC-26
97/8 SP Authentic 104
99/0 Stadium 152
00/1 SLU 19
95/6 Topps 341
98/9 Topps 197
00/1 Topps 34
01/2 Topps 232
02/3 Topps 114
95/6 To. Finest 59
98/9 To. Finest 121
02/3 To. Limited 114
96/7 To. Picks RS18
95/6 To. Stadium ER205
95/6 To. Super Skills SR14
02/3 To. Total 181
98/9 UD Choice 132
92/3 Upper Deck 597
95/6 Upper Deck 261, H-28
96/7 Upper Deck 107, X24
97/8 Upper Deck 106, T7B
98/9 Upper Deck 136, -GN26
99/0 Upper Deck 280
00/1 Upper Deck 376
95/6 UD BAP 177, ✍ S177
95/6 UD CC 408
97/8 UD Coll. Choice 165, SQ41
98/9 UD G. Reserve 136
99/0 UD G. Reserve 280
98/9 UD MVP 137
00/1 UD Vintage 297
99/0 Victory 279
02/3 MONT
98/9 NYRA

SUNDSTRÖM, OLIE

89/0 Semic Elitserien 122
90/1 Semic Elitserien 199
91/2 Semic Elitserien 129
93/4 Cleveland Lumberjacks
96/7 Johnstown Chiefs

SUNDSTRÖM, PATRIK

90/1 Bowman 89
91/2 Bowman 279
86/7 Kraft Sports 70
83/4 O-Pee-Chee 361
84/5 O-Pee-Chee 331
85/6 OPC/Topps 115
86/7 OPC/Topps 156
87/8 OPC/Topps 34
88/9 OPC/Topps 67
90/1 OPC/Topps 306
91/2 O-Pee-Chee 451
89/0 OPC/Topps 56
83/4 OPC/Topps Sticker 152
84/5 OPC Sticker 279
85/6 OPC Sticker 241-108
86/7 OPC Sticker 101-230
87/8 OPC Sticker 201
89/0 opcSticker 82-223
87/8 Panini Sticker 348
88/9 Panini Sticker 277
89/0 Panini Sticker 250
90/1 Panini Sticker 65
91/2 Panini Sticker 217
91/2 Pinnacle 290
90/1 Pro Set 176, 176
91/2 Pro Set 141
91/2 Pro Set Platinum 71
90/1 Score 19
90/1 Sco. Hot Cards 10
91/2 Score 117
91/2 Score CAN 117
82 Semic Sticker 15
89 Semic Sticker 21
85/6 7-Eleven Superstars 19
91/2 To. Stadium 229
90/1 Upper Deck 288
91/2 Upper Deck 369
83/4 Vachon 118-38
88/9 NJER / Caretta
89/0 NJER
89/0 NJER / Caretta
90/1 NJER
82/3 VANC
83/4 VANC
84/5 VANC
85/6 VANC
86/7 VANC

SUNDSTRÖM, PETER

94/5 Leaf Elit Set 127
84/5 O-Pee-Chee 155
90/1 Semic Elitserien 136
91/2 Semic Elitserien 191
92/3 Semic Elitserien 219
82 Semic Sticker 16
84/5 Topps 116
89/0 NJER
89/0 NJER / Caretta
87/8 WASH
87/8 WASH / Kodak
88/9 WASH
88/9 WASH / Smokey

SUNDT, ROBERT

92/3 Semic Nordisk 62

SUNI, ERKKI

70/1 Kuvajulkaisut 288
71/2 Williams Finnish 160
72/3 Williams Finnish 187

SUNOHARA, VICKY

97/8 Game of Her Life
97/8 General Mills
97/8 UD Coll. Choice 280

SUOKAS, JARI

70/1 Kuvajulkaisut 321

SUOKKO, ERKKI

65/6 Hellas 110

SUOKKO, JORMA

66/7 Champion 184
65/6 Hellas 109

SUOKNUUTI, SIMO

70/1 Kuvajulkaisut 305
71/2 Williams Finnish 258

SUOMALAINEN, JUKKA

94/5 Sisu 280
95/6 Sisu 138

SUOMINEN, TAPANI

66/7 Champion 31
65/6 Hellas 77

SUOMINEN, VEIKKO

70/1 Kuvajulkaisut 306
72 Panda MM-Toronto
78/9 SM-Liiga 62
71/2 Williams Finnish 187
72/3 Williams Finnish 136
73/4 Williams Finnish 192

SUONIEMI, RAIMO

74 Hellas MM-Jenkki 17
74 Semic Sticker 90
71/2 Williams Finnish 146
72/3 Williams Finnish 206
73/4 Williams Finnish 170

SUONIEMI, TOMI

00/1 Cardset 145

SUORANIEMI, KARI

94/5 Leaf Elit Set 116
80/1 Mallasjuoma 92
89/0 Semic Elitserien 194
92/3 Semic Elitserien 255
89 Semic Sticker 37
94/5 Sisu 372

SUORANIEMI, SEPPO

72 Hellas MM-Jenkki 22
74 Hellas MM-Jenkki 18
80/1 Mallasjuoma 179
74 Semic Sticker 81
82 Semic Sticker 32
94/5 Sisu 399
82 Skopbank
78/9 SM-Liiga 202
77-79 Sports. FIN 85-2017
71/2 Williams Finnish 161
72/3 Williams Finnish 113
73/4 Williams Finnish 120

SUORSA, JARI

96/7 Sisu 38

SUP, MICHAL

94/5 APS 88
95/6 APS 139
96/7 APS 23
97/8 APS 163
91/2 Avant Garde BCJHL 16
98/9 DS 74
99/0 DS 121
97/8 DS Sticker 200
98/9 OFS 219
99/0 OFS 55, 510
00/1 OFS 99, 413
01/2 OFS 277
91/2 7th...Sketch WHL 90

SUPLER, JULIUS

98/9 OFS 129
97/8 Portland Winter Hawks

SURA, TAPANI

72/3 Williams Finnish 238
73/4 Williams Finnish 273

SURETTE, BRIAN

95/6 Halifax Moosehead

SURMA, DAMIAN

95 Québec Pee Wee 764
00/1 SP Authentic 127
00/1 SP GU 90
00/1 SPx ✂ 128
00/1 Upper Deck 439
00/1 UD Pros&Prosp. 132

SUROVY, TOMAS

02/3 BAP Mem. 387
02/3 Calder 140
02/3 Pacific Complete 522
02/3 Quest for the Cup 140
02/3 SP Authentic 205
02/3 Ultimate Mem. 64
02/3 UD Rookie 134
01/2 WBS Penguins
02/3 WBS Penguins

SUSHINSKY, MAXIM

00/1 BAP Mem. 412
98/9 Mir 23
99/0 Mir 169
00/1 Parkhurst P-185
93/4 Pinnacle 510
00/1 Pr. Stock 127
00/1 Signature 273, ✍ Aut. 235
00/1 To. Gold Label 33
00/1 To. Heritage 131
00/1 UD Heroes 61

SUSI, TIMO

80/1 Mallasjuoma 162
82 Semic Sticker 48
82 Skopbank
78/9 SM-Liiga 185
77-79 Sports. FIN 90-2169

SUTER, BOB

80 Olympic USA
94/5 SR Miracle 33,34, ✍ 33,34

SUTER, CURTIS

97/8 Spokane Chiefs

SUTER, GARY

99/0 BAP Mem. 33
00/1 BAP Mem. 294
90/1 Bowman 101
91/2 Bowman 254
92/3 Bowman 55
93/4 Donruss 415
93/4 Donruss 53
94/5 Donruss 217
95/6 Donruss 99
96/7 Donruss 130
95/6 Do. Elite 11
93/4 EA Sports 19
94/5 Flair 38
94/5 Fleer 47
96/7 Fleer 19
95/6 Fleer Metal 29
92/3 Fleer Ultra 30
93/4 Fleer Ultra 226
94/5 Fleer Ultra 46
95/6 Fleer Ultra 36
96/7 Fl. Ultra 33
95 Globe 104
93/4 Hockey Wit 41
89/0 Kraft 61
91/2 Kraft 72
86/7 Kraft Sports 8
93/4 Leaf 140
94/5 Leaf 317
95/6 Leaf 219
96/7 Leaf 32
96/7 Maggers 31
96/7 Metal Univ. 28
86/7 OPC/Topps 189
87/8 OPC/Topps 176
88/9 OPC/Topps 43
90/1 OPC/Topps 205
91/2 O-Pee-Chee 151
92/3 O-Pee-Chee 278
01/2 O-Pee-Chee 146
89/0 OPC/Topps 108
98/9 OPC Chrome 26
88/9 OPC Stars 40
86/7 OPC Sticker 134-120
86/7 OPC Sticker 192-54
87/8 OPC Sticker 49
88/9 OPC Sticker 89
88/9 OPC Sticker 113-243
89/0 opcSticker 100
99/0 Omega 211
98/9 Pacific 152
00/1 Pacific 368
02/3 Pacific 343
97/8 Pacific CC 212
87/8 Panini Sticker 207
88/9 Panini Sticker 7
89/0 Panini Sticker 30
90/1 Panini Sticker 177
90/1 Panini/CGY 21, H
91/2 Panini Sticker 57
92/3 Panini Sticker 48
93/4 Panini Sticker 186
94/5 Panini Sticker 133
95/6 Panini Sticker 165
96/7 Panini Sticker 163
98/9 Panini Sticker 116
99/0 Panini Sticker 299
95 Panini Worlds 219
91/2 Parkhurst 25
92/3 Parkhurst 23
93/4 Parkhurst 299
94/5 Parkhurst 47, V74
95/6 Parkhurst 39, PP-26
91/2 Pinnacle 11
91/2 Pinnacle 392
92/3 Pinnacle 195
93/4 Pinnacle 14
94/5 Pinnacle 137
95/6 Pinnacle 68
96/7 Pinnacle 195
96/7 Pi. Be A Player 180, ✍ Aut. 180
95/6 Pi. Summit 59
95/6 Pi. Zenith 73
95/6 Playoff 238
94/5 POG 75
95/6 POG 69
93/4 Power Play 44
93/4 Premier 178
93/4 Prmr. - BG-Top. 10
94/5 Premier 168
90/1 Pro Set 46
91/2 Pro Set 32
91/2 Pro Set 276
92/3 Pro Set 27
91/2 Pro Set Platinum 20
90/1 Score 88
91/2 Score 244
91/2 Score CAN 464
92/3 Score 17
93/4 Score 13
94/5 Score 44
95/6 Score 82
96/7 Score 182
94 Semic 121
89 Semic Sticker 155
91 Semic Sticker 132
92 Semic Sticker 152
93 Semic Sticker 176
95/6 SBx Emotion 34
95/6 SBx Impact 34
96/7 SBx Impact 20
95/6 SP 25
96/7 SP 29
96/7 Team Out!
88/9 OPC/Topps - Stick. 11
92/3 Topps 308
95/6 Topps 156, 9HG
98/9 Topps 26
01/2 Topps 146
95/6 To. Finest 126
96/7 To. Picks 41
91/2 To. Stadium 143
92/3 To. Stadium 423
93/4 To. Stadium 228
95/6 To. Stadium 124
98/9 UD Choice 47
90/1 Upper Deck 273
91/2 Upper Deck 341
91/2 Upper Deck 510
92/3 Upper Deck 249
93/4 Upper Deck 357
94/5 Upper Deck 74, SP-107
95/6 Upper Deck 284, AS-8, SE-107
96/7 Upper Deck 235, X37
94/5 UD BAP R94, ✍ 112
95/6 UD CC 8
96/7 UD CC 52
97/8 UD Coll. Choice 45
99/0 UD MVP 179
99/0 Victory 254
96 Wien 162
85/6 CALG / Red Rooster
86/7 CALG / Red Rooster
87/8 CALG / Red Rooster
90/1 CALG / McGavin's
91/2 CALG / IGA
92/3 CALG / IGA 008

SUTHERBY, BRIAN

01/2 Adrenaline 225, RR 20
01/2 Atomic 125
01/2 BAP Mem. 307
01/2 Bowman 123
02/3 Bowman 130, ✂ FFDS, ✂ FFJ, ✂ FFP, ✂ FFR, ✂ FFRP, ✂ FFS, ✂ FFTS, ✂ YSMVP, ✍ YSA, / ✍ Puck
02/3 Calder 100
01/2 Crown Royale 180
01/2 Heads Up 120
01/2 O-Pee-Chee 345
02/3 O-Pee-Chee 291
02/3 Pacific Complete 559
01/2 Parkhurst 262
01/2 Pr. Stock 140, -PS 92
01/2 PS Titanium 184
01/2 PS Titanium Draft 172
01/2 Signature 223, ✍ Aut. 223
01/2 SP GU 100
01/2 SPx 132
01/2 SPx Rookie RR30
01/2 Stadium 138
01/2 Topps 345
02/3 Topps 291
01/2 To. Chrome 163
01/2 To. Heritage 140
02/3 To. Limited 291
01/2 To. Reserve 103
01/2 UD PlayMakers Ltd 145
01/2 Upper Deck 231
02/3 Upper Deck 424
01/2 UD Challenge 134
01/2 UD Ice 72
01/2 UD Mask 170
01/2 UD MVP 232
01/2 UD Premier 108
01/2 UD Top Shelf 76
01/2 UD Vintage 300

01/2 Vanguard 130
01/2 Victory 452
02/3 Victory 217
01/2 Moose Jaw Warriors 10

SUTHERLAND, BILL
60/1 Cleveland Barons
71/2 Eddie Sargent 188
68/9 O-Pee-Chee 196
69/0 O-Pee-Chee 172
70/1 O-Pee-Chee 83
71/2 O-Pee-Chee 141
89/0 ProCards AHL 75
63/4 Québec Aces
65/6 Québec Aces
70/1 Topps 83
71/2 Toronto Sun Photo
68/9 TORO
79/0 WINN
81/2 WINN
82/3 WINN
84/5 WINN / Safety Tips
85/6 WINN
85/6 WINN / Safety Tips
86/7 WINN
88/9 WINN / Safety Tips

SUTHERLAND, JAMES T.
83 HHOF Postcard C15
83&87 HHOF 44

SUTHERLAND, ROBBIE
00/1 Halifax Moosehead
99/0 Halifax Mooseheads

SUTHERLAND, STEVE
76/7 OPC WHA 127
72/3 Los Angeles Sharks
76/7 Québec Nordiques
76/7 Québ. / Antoinette

SUTINEN, TIMO
96/7 DEL 134
74 Hellas MM-Jenkki 19
74 Semic Sticker 91
71/2 Williams Finnish 108
72/3 Williams Finnish 152
73/4 Williams Finnish 79
73/4 Williams Finnish 121

SUTTER, BRENT
90/1 Bowman 126
91/2 Bowman 226
92/3 Bowman 147
91 Canada Cup
93/4 Donruss 69
94/5 Donruss 290
01/2 Fleer Legacy 54
92/3 Fleer Ultra 43
93/4 Fleer Ultra 206
94/5 Fleer Ultra 47
84/5 Kelowna Wings &...
90/1 Kraft 57
91/2 Kraft 43
93/4 Leaf 142
94/5 Leaf 30
82/3 O-Pee-Chee 216
83/4 O-Pee-Chee 18
84/5 O-Pee-Chee 136
85/6 OPC/Topps 107
86/7 OPC/Topps 117
87/8 OPC/Topps 27
88/9 OPC/Topps 7
90/1 OPC/Topps 258
91/2 O-Pee-Chee 165
92/3 O-Pee-Chee 60
89/0 OPC/Topps 14
90/1 OPC Premier 115
91/2 OPC Premier 156
82/3 OPC/Topps Sticker 56
84/5 OPC Sticker 88
85/6 OPC Sticker 71
85/6 OPC Sticker 117
86/7 OPC Sticker 211
87/8 OPC Sticker 241-107
88/9 OPC Sticker 105-235
89/0 opcSticker 115-252
97/8 Pacific CC 186
87/8 Panini Sticker 99
88/9 Panini Sticker 292
89/0 Panini Sticker 266
90/1 Panini Sticker 90
91/2 Panini Sticker 246
93/4 Panini Sticker 151
96/7 Panini Sticker 165
91/2 Parkhurst 35
92/3 Parkhurst 33
92/3 Parkhurst CP3
93/4 Parkhurst 308
91/2 Pinnacle 79
92/3 Pinnacle 39
93/4 Pinnacle 91
94/5 Pinnacle 117
94/5 POG 72
93/4 Power Play 56
93/4 Premier 147
90/1 Pro Set 191
91/2 Pro Set 154
91/2 Pro Set 374
92/3 Pro Set 36
91/2 Pro Set Platinum 74
91/2 Pro Set Platinum 164
90/1 Score 39
90/1 Sco. Hot Cards 19
91/2 Score 243
91/2 Score 103T
91/2 Score CAN 463
92/3 Score 112
93/4 Score 44
94/5 Score 32
95/6 Score 272
94 Semic 91
92 Semic Sticker 92
83/4 Souhaits Keychain [Islanders]
84/5 Topps 102
92/3 Topps 75
91/2 To. Stadium 180
92/3 To. Stadium 428
93/4 To. Stadium 211
94/5 To. Stadium 218
90/1 Upper Deck 249
91/2 Upper Deck 140
91/2 Upper Deck 645
92/3 Upper Deck 199
95/6 UD BAP 140, ✍ S140
01/2 UD Legends ✂ M
00/1 UD Vintage ✂ D-POH
91/2 CHIC / Coke
93/4 CHIC / Coke
83/4 NYIS
83/4 NYIS / News 12
84/5 NYIS / News 13
89/0 NYIS

SUTTER, BRIAN
01/2 Fleer Greats 69, ✍ Aut.
83/4 Funmate Puffy 17 [w/]
78/9 O-Pee-Chee 319
79/0 O-Pee-Chee 84
80/1 O-Pee-Chee 244
81/2 O-Pee-Chee 297
82/3 O-Pee-Chee 298
82/3 O-Pee-Chee 311
83/4 O-Pee-Chee 308
83/4 O-Pee-Chee 320
84/5 O-Pee-Chee 192
85/6 OPC/Topps 135
85/6 OPC/Topps Box N
86/7 OPC/Topps 72
86/7 OPC/Topps Box O
81/2 OPC Sticker 133
82/3 OPC/Topps Sticker 198
83/4 OPC/Topps Sticker 127
83/4 OPC/Topps Sticker 128
84/5 OPC Sticker 56
85/6 OPC Sticker 46
86/7 OPC Sticker 175-38
88/9 OPC Sticker 15-142
87/8 Panini Sticker 303
88/9 Panini Sticker 111
82/3 Post [SLou.]
90/1 Pro Set 676
91/2 Score 378
91/2 Score CAN 268
85/6 7-Eleven Superstars 17
79/0 Topps 84
80/1 Topps 244
81/2 Topps 122 [West]
84/5 Topps 135
91/2 Upper Deck 645
78/9 SLOU
87/8 SLOU
87/8 SLOU / Kodak
88/9 SLOU
89/0 SLOU / Kodak
90/1 SLOU / Kodak
92/3 SLOU / McDon. 25

SUTTER, DARRYL
81/2 O-Pee-Chee 65
82/3 O-Pee-Chee 76
83/4 O-Pee-Chee 113
84/5 O-Pee-Chee 47
85/6 OPC/Topps 100
86/7 OPC/Topps 49
83/4 OPC/Topps Sticker 105
84/5 OPC Sticker 30
85/6 OPC Sticker 23-152
86/7 OPC Sticker 151-6
87/8 Panini Sticker 234
88/9 ProCards / Saginaw
89/0 ProCards IHL 58
83/4 Souhaits Keychain [Blackhawks]
81/2 Topps 77 [West]
84/5 Topps 36
91/2 Upper Deck 645
80/1 CHIC / Colour
80/1 CHIC / Brown
81/2 CHIC
82/3 CHIC
86/7 CHIC / Coke
87/8 CHIC / Coke
90/1 CHIC / Coke
91/2 CHIC / Coke
93/4 CHIC / Coke

SUTTER, DUANE
90/1 Bowman 12
84/5 Kelowna Wings &...
81/2 O-Pee-Chee 211
82/3 O-Pee-Chee 212
83/4 O-Pee-Chee 19
84/5 O-Pee-Chee 137
85/6 O-Pee-Chee 227
86/7 OPC/Topps 39
87/8 OPC/Topps 43
90/1 O-Pee-Chee 466
89/0 O-Pee-Chee 221
82/3 OPC/Topps Sticker 52
85/6 OPC Sticker 72-199
86/7 OPC Sticker 210
87/8 Panini Sticker 102
90/1 Pro Set 61
91/2 Upper Deck 645
87/8 CHIC / Coke
89/0 CHIC / Coke
96/7 FLOR / Winn-Dixie
97/8 FLOR / Winn-Dixie
83/4 NYIS
83/4 NYIS / News 13
84/5 NYIS / News 14
93/4 Indianapolis Ice
94/5 Indianapolis Ice

SUTTER, RICH
91/2 Bowman 370
92/3 Bowman 256
92/3 Fleer Ultra 398
93/4 Fleer Ultra 293
84/5 Kelowna Wings &...
84/5 O-Pee-Chee 169
85/6 O-Pee-Chee 208
86/7 OPC/Topps 29
87/8 O-Pee-Chee 258
88/9 O-Pee-Chee 255
90/1 O-Pee-Chee 405
91/2 O-Pee-Chee 143
89/0 O-Pee-Chee 282
84/5 OPC Sticker 111
86/7 OPC Sticker 242-109
87/8 OPC Sticker 193-52
88/9 OPC Sticker 57-190
89/0 opcSticker 62-204
87/8 Panini Sticker 350
88/9 Panini Sticker 142
89/0 Panini Sticker 157
91/2 Panini Sticker 33
92/3 Panini Sticker 19
93/4 Panini Sticker 160
91/2 Parkhurst 372
91/2 Pinnacle 268
93/4 Pinnacle 108
94/5 Pinnacle 235
93/4 Power Play 317
90/1 Pro Set 272
91/2 Pro Set 217
91/2 Pro Set Platinum 108
90/1 Score 281
91/2 Score 63
91/2 Score 378
91/2 Score CAN 63
91/2 Score CAN 268
92/3 Score 327
93/4 Score 323
93/4 Score 498
92/3 Topps 434
91/2 To. Stadium 192
92/3 To. Stadium 389
93/4 To. Stadium 488
93/4 To. Stadium 46
90/1 Upper Deck 328
91/2 Upper Deck 317
91/2 Upper Deck 645
92/3 Upper Deck 143
93/4 CHIC / Coke
83/4 PHIL / J.C. Penney
83/4 PITT / Heinz
90/1 SLOU / Kodak
91/2 SLOU
96/7 VANC
87/8 VANC / Shell
88/9 VANC / Mohawk
89/0 VANC / Mohawk

SUTTER, RON
91/2 Bowman 238
92/3 Bowman 175
93/4 Donruss 288
93/4 Donruss 482
92/3 Fleer Ultra 190
84/5 Kelowna Wings &...
93/4 Leaf 275
94/5 Leaf 351
99/0 Millenium 208, ✍ Aut. 208
84/5 O-Pee-Chee 170
85/6 OPC/Topps 6
86/7 OPC/Topps 109
87/8 OPC/Topps 113
88/9 OPC/Topps 126
90/1 OPC/Topps 45
91/2 O-Pee-Chee 232
92/3 O-Pee-Chee 362
01/2 O-Pee-Chee 249
89/0 OPC/Topps 173
91/2 OPC Premier 95
84/5 OPC Sticker 107
86/7 OPC Sticker 243-110
87/8 OPC Sticker 102-235
89/0 opcSticker 107-246
97/8 Pa. Invincible R-181
99/0 Pa. Paramount 211
87/8 Panini Sticker 137
89/0 Panini Sticker 299
90/1 Panini Sticker 109
91/2 Panini Sticker 233
92/3 Panini Sticker 20
93/4 Panini Sticker 161
91/2 Parkhurst 158
92/3 Parkhurst 389
94/5 Parkhurst 192
91/2 Pinnacle 95
93/4 Pinnacle 95
94/5 Pinnacle 383
97/8 Pi. Be A Player 106, ✍ Aut. 106
93/4 Premier 103
94/5 Premier 428
90/1 Pro Set 224
91/2 Pro Set 178
91/2 Pro Set 476
92/3 Pro Set 162
91/2 Pro Set Platinum 222
90/1 Score 153
91/2 Score 298
91/2 Score 378
91/2 Score 69T
91/2 Score CAN 268
91/2 Score CAN 619
92/3 Score 86
93/4 Score 39
93/4 Score 640
94/5 Score 177
95/6 Score 113
84/5 Topps 122
92/3 Topps 371
01/2 Topps 249
91/2 To. Stadium 49
92/3 To. Stadium 36
92/3 To. Stadium 488
93/4 To. Stadium 86
90/1 Upper Deck 68
91/2 Upper Deck 309
91/2 Upper Deck 645
92/3 Upper Deck 184
93/4 Upper Deck 33
83/4 PHIL / J.C. Penney
86/7 PHIL
89/0 PHIL
90/1 PHIL
91/2 SLOU

SUTTER, SHAUN
00/1 Calgary Hitmen
99/0 Medicine Hat Tigers

SUTTON, ANDY
98/9 Be A Player 268, ✍ Aut. 268
01/2 O-Pee-Chee 116
02/3 Pacific Complete 276
01/2 Topps 116
00/1 Upper Deck 89
99/0 UD MVP 181
01/2 Victory 181

SUTTON, BOYD
91/2 Greensboro Monarchs
92/3 Oklahoma City Blazers

SUTTON, DAVE
91/2 Rayside-Balfour

SUTTON, KEN
92/3 Bowman 422
92/3 Fleer Ultra 20
93/4 Leaf 295
94/5 Leaf 498
92/3 O-Pee-Chee 165
91/2 Parkhurst 239
92/3 Parkhurst 254
91/2 Pinnacle 325
92/3 Pinnacle 216
93/4 Pinnacle 336
94/5 Pinnacle 437
93/4 Premier 89
89/0 ProCards AHL 260
90/1 ProCards 271
91/2 Score 393
91/2 Score CAN 283
92/3 Score 292
93/4 Score 410
92/3 Topps 59
01/2 To. Heritage 186
92/3 To. Stadium 292
93/4 To. Stadium 219
91/2 Upper Deck 458
00/1 UD Vintage 219
91/2 BUFF / Blue Shield
91/2 BUFF / Campbell's
91/2 BUFF / Pepsi
92/3 BUFF / Blue Shield
92/3 BUFF / Jubilee
97/8 Albany River Rats
98/9 Albany River Rats
99/0 Albany River Rats
00/1 Albany River Rats
02/3 Albany River Rats
89/0 Saskatoon Blades

SUTTON, PAT
02/3 Owen Sound Attack

SUTTON, SCOTT
89/0 Rayside-Balfour
91/2 Rayside-Balfour

SUTVLA, KEN
67/8 Columbus Checkers

SUURSOO,
97/8 Hockey-Box

SUURSOO, TOIVO
98/9 UD Elitserien 165
99/0 UD Elitserien 167

SUVANTO, ESA
70/1 Kuvajulkaisut 342

SUVANTO, HARRI
99/0 Cardset 85
92/3 Jyvas Hyva 124
93/4 Sisu 192
94/5 Sisu 100
95/6 Sisu 134

SUZOR, MARK
78/9 O-Pee-Chee 307
78/9 Saginaw Gears

SVANBERG, BO
94/5 Leaf Elit Set 79
95/6 Leaf Elit Set 95
90/1 Semic Elitserien 145
91/2 Semic Elitserien 197
92/3 Semic Elitserien 213
95/6 UD Elitserien 145

SVANGSTU, LEE
00/1 Asheville Smoke

SVARTVADET, PER
99/0 BAP Mem. 334
99/0 Dynagon Ice 19
94/5 Leaf Elit Set 245
95/6 Leaf Elit Set 107
99/0 Millenium C-45
00/1 Pacific 24
02/3 Pacific Complete 367
99/0 Panini Sticker 16
94/5 Parkie SE235
99/0 To. Chrome 295
99/0 To. Prmr. Plus 123
99/0 Upper Deck 177
00/1 Upper Deck 238
95/6 UD Elitserien 166
97/8 UD Elitserien 162, 204, 215
98/9 UD Elitserien 176
99/0 UD G. Reserve 177

SVEC, DAVID
99/0 Score 127

SVEDBERG,
97/8 Hockey-Box

SVEDBERG, LENNART (LILL-STRIMMA)
95 Globe 66
70/1 Kuvajulkaisut 39
69/0 Mästar Serien 46
69/0 Mästar Serien 50
72 Panda MM-Toronto
72 Semic Sticker 46
91 Semic Sticker 232
98/9 UD Elitserien 207, 210
71/2 Williams Finnish 59

SVEDBERG, MATHIAS
94/5 Leaf Elit Set 111
90/1 Semic Elitserien 107
91/2 Semic Elitserien 113
92/3 Semic Elitserien 132
98/9 UD Elitserien 3
99/0 UD Elitserien 3

SVEHLA, ROBERT
01/2 Adrenaline ✂ GWJ 19
98/9 BAP 59, ✍ Aut. 59
99/0 BAP Mem. 8
00/1 BAP Mem. 208
02/3 BAP Mem. 244
99/0 Challenger 2
95/6 Donruss 370
96/7 Donruss 77
02/3 First Ed. 290, 381
96/7 Flair 39
96/7 Fleer 43
95/6 Fleer Metal 194
96/7 Fl. Picks 42
95/6 Fleer Ultra 358, HS-18
96/7 Fl. Ultra 69
98/9 Kraft / PB
95/6 Leaf 230
96/7 Leaf 77
94/5 Leaf Elit Set 43, TG-6
96/7 Metal Univ. 63
97/8 Omega 101
99/0 Omega 101
98/9 Pacific 228
99/0 Pacific 182
00/1 Pacific 187
01/2 Pacific 177
02/3 Pacific 160
02/3 Pacific Complete 83
97/8 Pacific CC 243
97/8 Pa. Dynagon 56, T-51
98/9 Pa. Paramount 100
00/1 Pa. Paramount 106
96/7 Panini Sticker 74
97/8 Panini Sticker 55
98/9 Panini Sticker 57
99/0 Panini Sticker 55
00/1 Panini Sticker 36
95/6 Parkhurst 84
00/1 Parkhurst P-179
02/3 Parkhurst Retro 184
96/7 Pinnacle 38
97/8 Pinnacle 141
97/8 Pi. Inside 159
95/6 Pi. Summit 196
96/7 Pi. Summit 52
95/6 Pi. Zenith 148
01/2 Pr. Stock ✂ GUG 50
00/1 PS Titanium ✂ GUG 99
00/1 PS Titanium Draft ✂ 47
96/7 Score 83
97/8 Score 189
95/6 Select CC 115
92/3 Semic Elitserien 207
93 Semic Sticker 102
01/2 Signature 158, ✍ Aut. 158
96/7 SBx Impact 49
96/7 SP 63
98/9 SPx Finite 38
00/1 Stadium 196
96/7 Team Out!
95/6 Topps 257
99/0 Topps 154
00/1 Topps 47
99/0 To. Chrome 154
95/6 To. Finest 183
98/9 To. Finest 77
95/6 To. Stadium 216
00/1 To. Stars 62
98/9 UD Choice 88
95/6 Upper Deck 172
96/7 Upper Deck 67
97/8 Upper Deck 73
98/9 Upper Deck 278
00/1 Upper Deck 306
01/2 Upper Deck 78
02/3 Upper Deck 409
95/6 UD BAP 169, ✍ S169
96/7 UD CC 104
97/8 UD Coll. Choice 104, SQ2
98/9 UD G. Reserve 278
98/9 UD MVP 88
99/0 UD MVP W20
00/1 UD Vintage 157
99/0 Victory 128
01/2 Victory 150
96 Wien 221
96/7 FLOR / Winn-Dixie
97/8 FLOR / Winn-Dixie

SVEJKOVSKY, JAROSLAV
95/6 Bowman P32
97/8 Donruss 220, RR-9
97/8 Do. Canadian 143
97/8 Do. Elite 22, 141, C-5
97/8 Do. Preferred 146, 167, LT-8B
97/8 Do. Priority 167, 219, DD-19
97/8 Do. Studio 47, P-32
98/9 Dynagon Ice 199
96/7 Flair 125
97/8 Leaf 67, 167
97/8 Limited 33, 96, 143, FG-32
97/8 McDonald's McD-35
98/9 Pacific 447
99/0 Pacific 447
97/8 Pa. Crown Roy. 143
97/8 Pa. Paramount 200
00/1 Panini Sticker 90
97/8 Pinnacle 25
97/8 Pi. Be A Player 242, ✍ Aut. 242
97/8 Pi. Inside 125
97/8 Pi. Mint 25
96/7 Portland Pirates Hershey
96/7 Portland Pirates
97/8 Score 53
97/8 SP Authentic ✍ SofT
99/0 SPx 157
99/0 Topps 161
99/0 To. Chrome 161
95/6 Tri-City Americans 16
97/8 Upper Deck 195, SG52
98/9 Upper Deck 384
99/0 Upper Deck 130
97/8 UD Coll. Choice 272
98/9 UD G. Reserve 384
99/0 UD G. Reserve 130
97/8 UD Ice 40
98/9 UD MVP 217
99/0 UD MVP 213
99/0 Victory 307

SVENDSBERGET,
92/3 Semic Nordisk 210 [Rookie]

SVENDSBERGET, GEIR
92/3 Semic Nordisk 170

SVENSSON, ANDERS
90/1 Semic Elitserien 132
91/2 Semic Elitserien 184
92/3 Semic Elitserien 202

SVENSSON, LEIF
79/0 O-Pee-Chee 374
78/9 WASH
79/0 WASH

SVENSSON, MAGNUS
95/6 Donruss 166
95 Globe 12
95/6 Leaf 10
94/5 Leaf Elit Set GC 13
95/6 Panini Sticker 78
95 Panini Worlds 138
95/6 Parkhurst 83
94 Semic 58
95 Semic 55, 203
89/0 Semic Elitserien 125
91/2 Semic Elitserien 133
92/3 Semic Elitserien 158
95/6 SBx Emotion 71
95/6 SBx Impact 69
95/6 UD Elitserien 243
97/8 UD Elitserien 97, 104, C11
98/9 UD Elitserien 123
00/1 UD Elitserien 107, ✍ Sig.
96 Wien 46

SVENSSON, NILS-GUNNAR
89/0 Semic Elitserien 103

SVENSSON, PELLE
96/7 DEL 40
98/9 DEL 173
99/0 Eishockey 327
92/3 Semic Elitserien 265
95/6 UD Elitserien 182

SVENSSON, PER-JOHAN
94/5 Leaf Elit Set 57
95/6 Leaf Elit Set 120

SVERZTOV, ALEXANDER
91/2 Upper Deck WJC 8

SVETLIK, MARTIN
99/0 Score 15
90/1 7th..Sketch WHL 101

SVETLOV, SERGEI
82 Semic Sticker 59

SVIK, JAN
01/2 OFS 225

SVITOV, ALEXANDER
02/3 Atomic 124
02/3 BAP All-Star 136
02/3 BAP Draft Florida 3
02/3 BAP Mem. 299
02/3 Bowman 115, ✂ FFDS, ✂ FFJ, ✂ FFP, ✂ FFR, ✂ FFRP, ✂ FFS, ✂ FFTS, ✍ YSA, ✍ Puck
02/3 Calder 146
02/3 Crown Royale 137, -RR 20
02/3 eTopps 48
02/3 Exclusive 200, ✍ 200
02/3 First Ed. 436H
02/3 Heads Up 136
02/3 In The G-U 195, ✂ C7
99/0 Mir 176
00/1 Mir 229, 309
02/3 O-Pee-Chee 334
02/3 Pacific 126
02/3 Pacific Complete 563
02/3 PTC/ ASG 10
02/3 Parkhurst 229, -HHC 3
02/3 Parkhurst Retro 229
02/3 Pr. Stock Reserve 182, -MIT 8
02/3 PS Titanium 137
02/3 Quest for the Cup 147
02/3 SP Authentic ✍ 194, ✍ ✂ Patch
02/3 SP GU 93
02/3 SPx ✍ 159
02/3 Stadium 122
02/3 Topps 334
02/3 T. Chrome 179
02/3 To. Heritage 136
02/3 To. Total 435
02/3 Ultimate Mem. 29, ✂ CC, ✍ RAut
02/3 Upper Deck 245
02/3 UD Artistic 122, R100, CG16
02/3 UD Classic 128
02/3 UD Foundations 162
02/3 UD Honor 164, ✍ SC
02/3 UD Mask 163
02/3 UD Piece 147
02/3 UD Premier ✍ ✂ 84, ✂ Jers, ✍ Sig
02/3 UD Rookie ✍ 149
02/3 UD Top Shelf 135
02/3 Vanguard 134

SVOBODA, ADAM
96/7 APS 382
97/8 APS 245
99/0 DS 72
00/1 DS 86, G8
97/8 DS Sticker 128
98/9 OFS 146
99/0 OFS 548
00/1 OFS 32, Star-11
01/2 OFS 228, H13

SVOBODA, DALIMIL
99/0 Score 13

SVOBODA, JAROSLAV
02/3 BAP Mem. 113
02/3 Bowman 139
02/3 Calder 62
02/3 Exclusive 32
02/3 Pacific Complete 37
94 Québec Pee Wee 1759
02/3 Signature GS-40
02/3 SP Authentic 111
02/3 SPx 105
02/3 Stadium 114
00/1 Upper Deck 204
02/3 Upper Deck 31
00/1 UD Black Diam. 69
00/1 UD Ice 49
02/3 UD Vintage 325
00/1 Victory 279
00/1 Cincinnati Cyclones

SVOBODA, KAREL
86/7 Sherb. Canadiens 25

SVOBODA, LADISLAV
95/6 APS 146
96/7 APS 87
97/8 APS 208
97/8 DS 94
98/9 DS 98
99/0 DS 162
00/1 DS 139
96/7 DS Sticker 145
97/8 DS Sticker 240
98/9 OFS 169
99/0 OFS 173
00/1 OFS 120
01/2 OFS 168, -UHI 20

SVOBODA, OLDRICH
95/6 APS 53, 423
96/7 APS 239, 392
97/8 APS 266
97/8 DS 27
98/9 DS 13
00/1 DS 97, G9
96/7 DS Sticker 75
97/8 DS Sticker 67
99/0 Eishockey 341
93/4 Jyvas Hyva 254
98/9 OFS 410
00/1 OFS 187, -Star. 33
01/2 OFS 110, G7, -UHI 3
94 Semic 164
92 Semic Sticker 123
93/4 Sisu 280

SVOBODA, PETR
94/5 APS 205
98/9 Be A Player 104, ✍ Aut. 104
00/1 BAP Mem. 39
98 Bonaparte 5D, 6A
98 Bonaparte Pexeso 19
90/1 Bowman 46
91/2 Bowman 341
92/3 Bowman 47
92/3 BUFF / Blue Shield
92/3 BUFF / Jubilee
93/4 Donruss 41
95/6 Donruss 306
99/0 DS NS8
93/4 EA Sports 14
92/3 Fleer Ultra 263
89/0 Kraft 27
86/7 Kraft Sports 40
93/4 Leaf 131
94/5 Leaf 393
95/6 Leaf 180
84/5 MONT
85/6 MONT
85/6 MONT / Provigo
86/7 MONT
87/8 MONT
87/8 MONT / Vachon 75
87/8 MONT / Vachon 77
88/9 MONT
89/0 MONT
89/0 MONT / Kraft
90/1 MONT
91/2 MONT
88/9 O-Pee-Chee 256
90/1 OPC/Topps 246
91/2 O-Pee-Chee 76
92/3 O-Pee-Chee 109
89/0 O-Pee-Chee 238
91/2 OPC Premier 168
88/9 OPC Stars 41
85/6 OPC Sticker 139-11
86/7 OPC Sticker 17-160
87/8 OPC Sticker 18-158
88/9 OPC Sticker 44-177
89/0 opcSticker 54-198
97/8 OFS 231, -OW 10
99/0 Pacific 397
00/1 Pacific 381
97/8 Pacific CC 277
00/1 Pa. Paramount 224
88/9 Panini Sticker 255
89/0 Panini Sticker 244
90/1 Panini Sticker 50
90/1 Panini/MTL 23
91/2 Panini Sticker 185
96/7 Panini Sticker 120
97/8 Panini Sticker 97
98/9 Panini Sticker 89
99/0 Panini Sticker 144
00/1 Panini Sticker 93
91/2 Parkhurst 237
95/6 Parkhurst 427
94/5 Parkie SE21
94/5 PHIL / Sheet
96/7 PHIL / Ocean Spray
91/2 Pinnacle 197
92/3 Pinnacle 117
93/4 Pinnacle 32
94/5 Pinnacle 424
95/6 Pinnacle 168, GG-21
96/7 Pi. Be A Player 56, ✍ Aut. 56
95/6 POG 208
93/4 Premier 308
93/4 Premier 324
00/1 Pr. Stock ✍ GUG 94
01/2 PS Titanium ✍ DSJ 40
90/1 Pro Set 161
91/2 Pro Set 123
92/3 Pro Set 16
91/2 Pro Set Platinum 65
00/1 Revolution ✍ GWJ 10
90/1 Score 191
91/2 Score 95
91/2 Score CAN 95
92/3 Score 114
93/4 Score 110
95/6 Score 287
97/8 Score Phil. 17
96/7 SP 111
00/1 Stadion 76
92/3 Topps 312
99/0 Topps 208
00/1 Topps 162
99/0 To. Chrome 208
91/2 To. Stadium 127
92/3 To. Stadium 227
93/4 To. Stadium 132
90/1 Upper Deck 193
91/2 Upper Deck 285
93/4 Upper Deck 465
95/6 Upper Deck 76
95/6 UD CC 93
00/1 UD MVP 164
99/0 UD MVP Cup 172, -GC
00/1 UD Vintage 331, 332

SVOBODA, PETR2
00/1 BAP Mem. 456
01/2 O-Pee-Chee 292
98/9 OFS 54
99/0 OFS 202
00/1 Premier Plus 131
00/1 Pr. Stock 147
00/1 Signature 266, ✍ Aut, ✂ 228
00/1 SP Authentic 164
00/1 Stadium 242
01/2 Topps 292
00/1 To. Heritage 84
00/1 To. Stars 120
00/1 Vanguard 148
01/2 St. John's Maple Leafs
01/2 St. John's / Clarenville

SVOBODA, RADEK
96/7 APS 280
97/8 APS 235
96/7 DS Sticker 182
97/8 DS Sticker 42
98/9 OFS 337
99/0 OFS 127

SVOBODA, VALERY
95/6 Slapshot 424

SVOZIL, LADISLAV
95/6 APS 292
96/7 APS 190
97/8 APS 124
98/9 OFS 113

SWAIN, BRAD
92/3 BCJHL 19

SWAIN, GARRY
76/7 OPC WHA 91

SWAN, JIM
86/7 Portland Winter Hawks

SWANSON, BRAD
93/4 Portland Winter Hawks

SWANSON, BRIAN
00/1 BAP Mem. 470
95/6 Do. Elite WJ 42
00/1 Premier Plus 105
00/1 Pr. Stock 119
00/1 SP Authentic 143
00/1 SPx 178
00/1 Upper Deck 422
00/1 UD Ice 112
00/1 UD Pros&Prosp. 104
00/1 Vanguard 120
99/0 Hamilton Bulldogs
00/1 Hamilton Bulldogs
01/2 Hamilton Bulldogs
01/2 Hamilton Bulldogs/ Staz

SWANSON, KEVIN
98/9 Kelowna Rockets
00/1 Kelowna Rockets

SWANSON, SCOTT
99/0 Houston Aeros

SWARBRICK, GEORGE
68/9 O-Pee-Chee 174
70/1 O-Pee-Chee 82
68/9 Shirriff / Oakl. 5
70/1 Topps 82
70/1 PHIL

SWÄRDH, MAGNUS
94/5 Leaf Elit Set 89
95/6 Leaf Elit Set 113, S-11
95/6 UD Elitserien 170

SWARTZ, TIM
95/6 Slapshot 383
96/7 Sudbury Wolves

SWEENEY, BOB
90/1 Bowman 28
91/2 Bowman 357
92/3 Bowman 5
92/3 Fleer Ultra 264
93/4 Fleer Ultra 278
94/5 Leaf 417
88/9 OPC/Topps 134
90/1 OPC/Topps 99
91/2 O-Pee-Chee 99
92/3 O-Pee-Chee 21
89/0 OPC/Topps 92
92/3 OPC Premier 110
88/9 OPC Sticker 130-266
89/0 OPC Sticker 28-168
88/9 OPC Sticker 68
88/9 Panini Sticker 214
90/1 Panini Sticker 15
91/2 Panini Sticker 177
93/4 Panini Sticker 104
92/3 Parkhurst 251
93/4 Parkhurst 290
94/5 Parkie SE17
91/2 Pinnacle 222
93/4 Pinnacle 118
94/5 Pinnacle 411
95/6 Playoff 232
93/4 Power Play 34
93/4 Premier 431
90/1 Pro Set 15
91/2 Pro Set 6
90/1 Score 235
91/2 Score 176
91/2 Score CAN 176
92/3 Score 317
93/4 Score 146
92/3 Topps 111
91/2 To. Stadium 75
92/3 To. Stadium 455
93/4 To. Stadium 63
90/1 Upper Deck 138
91/2 Upper Deck 391
92/3 Upper Deck 47
92/3 Upper Deck 449
93/4 Upper Deck 312
94/5 Upper Deck 445
95/6 Upper Deck 443
95/6 UD BAP 26, ✍ S26
96/7 UD CC 37
00/1 UD DEL S7
88/9 BOST / Sports Action
89/0 BOST / Sports Action
90/1 BOST / Sports Action
91/2 BOST / Sports Action
92/3 BUFF / Blue Shield
92/3 BUFF / Jubilee
86/7 Moncton G'Flames

SWEENEY, DON
91/2 Bowman 365
92/3 Bowman 402
93/4 Donruss 21
94/5 Donruss 281
95/6 Donruss 101
93/4 EA Sports 8
02/3 First Ed. 163
94/5 Flair 14
94/5 Fleer 18
92/3 Fleer Ultra 257
93/4 Fleer Ultra 271
94/5 Fleer Ultra 17
95/6 Fleer Ultra 208
01/2 Heads Up ✂ JQ 3
02/3 Heads Up ✂ GWQ 3
93/4 Leaf 281
94/5 Leaf 518
95/6 Leaf 191
01/2 McDonald's -HP 3
91/2 O-Pee-Chee 319
92/3 O-Pee-Chee 40
98/9 OPC Chrome 141
01/2 Pacific 39
97/8 Pa. Invincible R-17
00/1 Pa. Paramount 22
91/2 Panini Sticker 180
93/4 Panini Sticker 11
95/6 Panini Sticker 11
97/8 Panini Sticker 7
91/2 Parkhurst 228
92/3 Parkhurst 244
93/4 Parkhurst 13
95/6 Parkhurst 283
94/5 Parkie SE15
91/2 Pinnacle 419
92/3 Pinnacle 179
93/4 Pinnacle 269
94/5 Pinnacle 91
95/6 Pinnacle 141
96/7 Pi. Be A Player 97, ✍ Aut. 97
94/5 POG 40
95/6 POG 35
93/4 Power Play 24
93/4 Premier 334
94/5 Premier 262
00/1 PS Titanium Draft ✂ 7
90/1 Pro Set 412
91/2 Pro Set Platinum 153
89/0 ProCards AHL 58
90/1 Score 51
91/2 Score 146
91/2 Score CAN 146
92/3 Score 186
93/4 Score 169
94/5 Score 101
95/6 Score 163
97/8 Score Bost. 20
95/6 SBx Emotion 13
02/3 Slam Card
95/6 SP 11
96/7 SP 10
92/3 Topps 417
95/6 Topps 127
98/9 Topps 141
91/2 To. Stadium 370
92/3 To. Stadium 337
93/4 To. Stadium 117
95/6 To. Stadium 146
95/6 To. Super Skills 26
91/2 Upper Deck 338
92/3 Upper Deck 391
93/4 Upper Deck 101
94/5 Upper Deck 446
95/6 Upper Deck 35
96/7 Upper Deck 217
97/8 Upper Deck 14
98/9 Upper Deck 40
94/5 UD BAP ✍ 60
95/6 UD CC 91
96/7 UD CC 14
98/9 UD G. Reserve 40
00/1 UD Vintage 35
00/1 Vanguard ✂ DGJ 14
01/2 Vanguard ✂ DGM 3
99/0 Victory 31
89/0 BOST / Sports Action
90/1 BOST / Sports Action
91/2 BOST / Sports Action
92/3 BOST / Postcard

SWEENEY, TIM
91/2 Bowman 261
93/4 Donruss 11
94/5 Donruss 214
94/5 Flair 6
93/4 Fleer Ultra 262
94/5 Fleer Ultra 8
94/5 Leaf 21
90/1 OPC Premier 116
97/8 Omega 151
98/9 Pacific 303
97/8 Pacific CC 183
90/1 Panini/CGY 22
95 Panini Worlds 226
93/4 Parkhurst 7
94/5 Parkhurst 9
94/5 Pinnacle 93
97/8 Pi. Be A Player 156, ✍ Aut. 156
94/5 POG 34
93/4 Power Play 12
93/4 Premier 426
94/5 Premier 147
90/1 Pro Set 597
91/2 Pro Set 364
89/0 ProCards IHL 203
90/1 Score 13T
95 Semic 108
91/2 To. Stadium 394
93/4 To. Stadium 473
90/1 Upper Deck 531
91/2 Upper Deck 375
92/3 Upper Deck 95
93/4 Upper Deck 385
94/5 Upper Deck 38
93/4 ANAH / Cap 1
90/1 CALG / McGavin's
91/2 CALG / IGA
97/8 Hartford Wolf Pack
96/7 Providence Bruins

SWEET, TROY
90/1 7th..Sketch OHL 347
91/2 7th..Sketch OHL 159
90/1 Oshawa Generals
91/2 Oshawa Generals

SWEITZER, JASON
95/6 Cla. Vis. Signings 70, ✍ Aut.
95/6 Slapshot 252

SWENSON, BARKLEY
91/2 7th...Sketch WHL 257
91/2 Prince Albert Raiders
92/3 Tacoma Rockets

SWIATE, ANDRZEI
89 Semic Sticker 136

SWIBENKO, MARCO
94/5 DEL 41
95/6 DEL 38

SWINSON, WES
93/4 Slapshot / Kitchener 20
94/5 Slapshot / Kitchener 22
95/6 Slapshot 127
99/0 Greensboro Generals

SWITZER, DEREK
89/0 7th..Sketch OHL 150
90/1 7th..Sketch OHL 318

SWITZER, JASON
91/2 Avant Garde BCJHL 23
92/3 BCJHL 199

SYCHRA, MARTIN
97/8 DS Sticker 61
99/0 Eishockey 347
93/4 Slapshot / Kingston 14
00/1 UD DEL 156
01/2 UD DEL 69
98/9 Charlotte Checkers
94/5 Fredericton Canadiens

SYCHRA, MICHAL
97/8 APS 118

SYDOR, DARRYL
98/9 Aurora 60
02/3 BAP All-Star 90, ✂ ASJ
98/9 Be A Player 191, ✍ 191
99/0 BAP Mem. 271, ✂ TM-29
00/1 BAP Mem. 112, ✂ J-19, ✂ TM-14
01/2 BAP Mem. 176
02/3 BAP Mem. 21
92/3 Bowman 321
93/4 Donruss 164
94/5 Donruss 70
95/6 Donruss 73
02/3 First Ed. 111, ✂ Jers.
92/3 Fleer Ultra 312
93/4 Fleer Ultra 60
94/5 Fleer Ultra 308
95/6 Fleer Ultra 78
01/2 Heads Up ✂ JQ 10
98/9 Kraft / PB
93/4 Leaf 206
93/4 Leaf GLR 15
94/5 Leaf 136
95/6 Leaf 199
97/8 Limited 6
99/0 McDonald's ✂ GJ
99/0 Millenium 85, ✍ Aut. 85
92/3 O-Pee-Chee 11
91/2 OPC Premier 90
92/3 OPC Premier 16
97/8 Omega 75
98/9 Omega 75
98/9 Pacific 183
99/0 Pacific 129
00/1 Pacific 141, ✂ GWJ-6
01/2 Pacific 135
02/3 Pacific 118
02/3 Pacific Complete 340
97/8 Pacific CC 48
98/9 Pa. Crown Roy. 43
97/8 Pa. Dynagon 39, T-34
97/8 Pa. Paramount 62
98/9 Pa. Paramount 70
99/0 Pa. Paramount 77
00/1 Pa. Paramount ✂ J&P 5
98/9 Pa. Revolution 46
92/3 Panini Sticker F
95/6 Panini Sticker 275
97/8 Panini Sticker 140
98/9 Panini Sticker 125
99/0 Panini Sticker 223
95 Panini Worlds 6
92/3 Parkhurst 69
93/4 Parkhurst 96
95/6 Parkhurst 371
00/1 Parkhurst P-64
01/2 Parkhurst 145, ✂ T12
94/5 Parkie SE82
91/2 Pinnacle 321
93/4 Pinnacle 113
94/5 Pinnacle 328
95/6 Pinnacle 96
97/8 Pinnacle 139
96/7 Pi. Be A Player 176, ✍ Aut. 176
96/7 Pi. Summit 33
95/6 Playoff 160
96/7 Playoff 375
95/6 POG 141
93/4 Power Play 122
93/4 Premier 226
94/5 Premier 86
00/1 Pr. Stock ✂ GUG 40-41
01/2 Pr. Stock ✂ GUG 39
00/1 PS Titanium ✂ GUG 92
00/1 PS Titanium Draft ✂ 35
91/2 Pro Set 542
92/3 Pro Set 228
90/1 Score 425
91/2 Score 81T
91/2 Score CAN 631
92/3 Score 410
93/4 Score 311
94/5 Score 97
95/6 Score 26
97/8 Score 238
92 7th...Sketch Awards 14
90 7th..Sketch Mem.Cup 12
90/1 7th..Sketch WHL 307
00/1 Signature 223
01/2 Signature 182, ✍ Aut. 182
02/3 Signature 161, ✍ 161
95/6 SBx Emotion 85
95/6 SBx Impact 82
02/3 Sports Vault 209
99/0 SPx 49
92/3 Topps 39
99/0 Topps 240
00/1 Topps 256
99/0 To. Chrome 240
98/9 To. Finest 148
92/3 To. Stadium 72
93/4 To. Stadium 225
94/5 To. Stadium 164
02/3 To. Total 253
98/9 UD Choice 67
00/1 Ultimate Mem. ✂ TM-28
90/1 Upper Deck 358
91/2 Upper Deck 549
92/3 Upper Deck 63
93/4 Upper Deck 83, SP-74
94/5 Upper Deck 104
95/6 Upper Deck 5
97/8 Upper Deck 54
98/9 Upper Deck 79, ✂ GJ20
99/0 Upper Deck 217
00/1 Upper Deck 58
01/2 Upper Deck 287
94/5 UD BAP ✍ 26
98/9 UD Black Diam. 28
95/6 UD CC 83
97/8 UD Coll. Choice 72
98/9 UD G. Reserve 79
99/0 UD G. Reserve 217
98/9 UD MVP 62
99/0 UD MVP 61
01/2 UD SCup Champs 55
00/1 UD Vintage 120
01/2 Vanguard ✂ DGM 12
99/0 Victory 94
01/2 Victory 120
96/7 DALL / Southwest
97/8 DALL / Score 238
00/1 DALL / Southwest
01/2 DALL / Southwest
02/3 DALL / Southwest
88/9 Kamloops Blazers
89/0 Kamloops Blazers

SYKES, PHIL
91/2 Bowman 194
86/7 O-Pee-Chee 216
91/2 O-Pee-Chee 189
87/8 Panini Sticker 285
90/1 Panini/WPG 23
88/9 ProCards / New Haven
89/0 ProCards AHL 4
91/2 Score CAN 534
91/2 To. Stadium 271
84/5 LOSA / Smokey 22
87/8 LOSA
90/1 WINN / IGA
91/2 WINN / IGA

SYKORA, MAREK
94/5 APS 279
96/7 APS 1
97/8 APS 170
98/9 OFS 285, 445
99/0 OFS 116
00/1 OFS 56

SYKORA, MICHAL
96/7 APS 345
93/4 Classic 30
93/4 Cla. Prospects 38
93/4 Donruss 307
94/5 Donruss 204
99/0 DS 145, 401, 506
00/1 DS VP3, WCH6
01/2 DS 10, BB3
97/8 DS Sticker 129
94/5 Fleer 201
94/5 Fleer Ultra 369
93/4 Leaf 431
94/5 Leaf 122
98/9 OFS 373
99/0 OFS 401, 506
01/2 OFS 248, RE11D
97/8 Pa. Invincible R-47
95/6 Panini Sticker 286
96/7 Panini Sticker 285
97/8 Panini Sticker 132
93/4 Parkhurst 257
95/6 Parkhurst 181
93/4 Pinnacle 452
96/7 Pi. Be A Player 113, ✍ Aut. 113
95/6 POG 230
94/5 Premier 362
93/4 Score 600
91/2 7th...Sketch WHL 164
95/6 Topps 105
93/4 Upper Deck 489
94/5 Upper Deck 195
96/7 Upper Deck 151
92/3 SANJ / Pacific Bell
97/8 Indianapolis Ice 23
94/5 Kansas City Blades 3
92/3 Tacoma Rockets
92/3 Tacoma Rockets
93/4 Tacoma Rockets

SYKORA, OTTO
94/5 DEL 341
95/6 DEL 307
96/7 DEL 334

SYKORA, PETR
01/2 Adrenaline ✂ GWJ 26
96/7 APS 362
94/5 Assets 60, 85
99/0 Aurora 88
00/1 Aurora 86, ✂ GWJ-6
99/0 BAP Mem. 281, SL-13
00/1 BAP Mem. 128, ✂ TM-1, ✂ TM-27
01/2 BAP Mem. 79
02/3 BAP Mem. 269 [w/ Tverdovsky]
95/6 Bowman 116
01/2 Bowman 93
02/3 Bowman 66
94/5 Classic DP10
95/6 Classic 18, BK16, ✍ Aut.
95/6 Cla. Assets 45
95/6 Cla. Clear Assets 57, Phone
95/6 Cla. 5 Sport 137,FT14, SFF-7
94/5 Cla. Images 81, CE11, PD4, ✍ Aut.
94/5 Cla. Images 4 Sport 117
95/6 Cla. Visions 91
95/6 Cla. Vis. Signings 76, A-6, ✍ Aut.
99/0 Crown Royale 83
01/2 Crown Royale 88
95/6 Donruss RR 16
96/7 Donruss RR-2
96/7 Do. Canadian 72
96/7 Do. Elite 122, A-3
99/0 DS NS23
99/0 Dynagon Ice 120
95/6 Edge Ice 11
02/3 Exclusive 4
02/3 First Edition 129, ✂ Jers.
02/3 First Edition 415 [Hobby]
96/7 Fleer RS-9
96/7 Fl. Picks 74
96/7 Fl. Ultra 96
95/6 Future Legends 22
02/3 In The GU 3, 103
96/7 Leaf 206
96/7 L. Limited 54
96/7 L. Preferred 21, LS-12
96/7 Metal Univ. 89
99/0 Millenium 145, ✍ Aut. 145
96/7 NJER / Sharp
99/0 NHL Power Play
01/2 O-Pee-Chee 109
02/3 O-Pee-Chee 164, Update 164
98/9 OPC Chrome 2
97/8 Omega 135
98/9 Omega 144
99/0 Omega 138
98/9 Pacific 273
99/0 Pacific 248
00/1 Pacific 244
01/2 Pacific 239
02/3 Pacific 230
02/3 Pacific Complete 313
99/0 Pa. Paramount 139
00/1 Pa. Paramount 150
96/7 Panini Sticker 81
97/8 Panini Sticker 68
98/9 Panini Sticker 64
99/0 Panini Sticker 78
00/1 Panini Sticker 47
95/6 Parkhurst 512, 523, PP-43
00/1 Parkhurst P-180
01/2 Parkhurst 48
02/3 Parkhurst Retro 100
97/8 Pi. Be A Player 134, ✍ Aut. 134
96/7 Pi. Summit 170
96/7 Pi. Zenith 56
99/0 Prism 84
00/1 Pr. Stock 60, EA-12, ✂ GUG-65, PS-34
02/3 Pr. Stock Reserve 3
02/3 Pr. Stock Titanium 3
99/0 Revolution 89
00/1 Revolution 89
96/7 Score 237
97/8 Score NJer. 14
95/6 Select CE 144
00/1 Signature 233, ✍ Aut. 75
01/2 Signature 138, ✍ Aut. 138, ✂ GU74
02/3 Signature Series 121, GS-73, ✍ 121
96/7 SBx Impact 72, 171, F-19
95/6 SP 83
96/7 SP 88
97/8 SP Authentic 90
00/1 SP Authentic ✍ SotT, ✍ SotTD
01/2 SP Authentic ✍ SotTT
02/3 Sports Vault 157
96/7 SPx 23
99/0 Stadium 63
00/1 Stadium 170
01/2 Stadium 72, NHLP12
02/3 Stadium 105
98/9 Topps 2
99/0 Topps 100, NS5
00/1 Topps 156
01/2 Topps 109
02/3 Topps 164, Update 164
99/0 To. Chrome 100
00/1 To. Chrome 110
01/2 To. Chrome 109
02/3 T. Chrome 98
95/6 To. Finest 134
99/0 To. Gold Label 51, FG5
01/2 To. Heritage 60
02/3 To. Heritage 159
02/3 To. Limited 164
96/7 To. Picks RS6
99/0 To. Prmr. Plus 72
01/2 To. Reserve 23
95/6 TSC Members Only 49
02/3 To. Total 340
98/9 UD Choice 112
95/6 Upper Deck 318
96/7 Upper Deck 93, X26, SS21B
98/9 Upper Deck 310
99/0 Upper Deck 79
00/1 Upper Deck 103
01/2 Upper Deck 334
02/3 Upper Deck 248
96/7 UD CC 147, 339
98/9 UD G. Reserve 310
99/0 UD G. Reserve 79
01/2 UD Ice ✍ CCA
99/0 UD MVP 119
01/2 UD MVP 114
01/2 UD SCup Champs 74
00/1 UD Vintage 218
01/2 UD Vintage 153
99/0 Victory 171
01/2 Victory 211
02/3 Victory 123, -NP17
99/0 WGretzky 98

SYKORA, PETR2
96/7 APS 162
97/8 APS 262
98/9 Milwaukee Admirals
99/0 OFS 358
00/1 OFS 52
01/2 OFS 259

SYKORA, PETR?
00/1 DS JT3
01/2 DS 20, 49
00/1 OFS 391
01/2 OFS -UHI 38

SYKORA, TOMAS
99/0 OFS 305
00/1 OFS 283

SYKORA, VACLAV
96/7 APS 120
97/8 APS 2
93/4 Jyvas Hyva 223
98/9 OFS 272
99/0 OFS 146
00/1 OFS 133
93/4 Sisu 182
94/5 Sisu 396
95/6 Sisu 388

SYLVEGÅRD, PATRIK
94/5 Leaf Elit Set 103
95/6 Leaf Elit Set 90
92/3 Semic Elitserien 215
95/6 UD Elitserien 146
97/8 UD Elitserien 145
98/9 UD Elitserien 161

SYLVESTER, DEAN
99/0 Omega 14
00/1 Pacific 25
99/0 SP Authentic 92
00/1 Topps 251
00/1 Upper Deck 7
99/0 UD Black Diam. 6
00/1 UD MVP 10
99/0 UD MVP Cup 11
00/1 UD Vintage 18
00/1 Victory 15
96/7 Kansas City Blades
98/9 Rochester Americans

SYLVESTER, DEREK
93/4 Slapshot / Niagara Falls 21

SYLVIA, MIKE
95/6 Do. Elite WJ 43
95/6 Upper Deck 565

SYMES, BRAD
94/5 Sig. Rookies 64, ✍ 64
97/8 New Orleans Brass
93/4 Portland Winter Hawks

SYNISHIN, DOUG
89/0 7th..Sketch OHL 42

SYNOWIETZ, HEINRICH
96/7 DEL 208

SYNOWIETZ, PAUL
96/7 DEL 209

SYPOSZ, JANUSZ
92 Semic Sticker 270

SYVÄSALMI, KARI
93/4 Sisu 227
95/6 Sisu 365

SYVERSEN, ARILD
92/3 Semic Nordisk 226

SYVERSEN, LASSE
92/3 Semic Nordisk 73

SYVERSEN, PETTER
92/3 Semic Nordisk 174

SZABO, DAVE
91/2 7th...Sketch OHL 64

SZABO, TONY
93/4 Roanoke Express

SZATMARY, ROB
92/3 BCJHL 82

SZEJA, JAN
73/4 Williams Finnish 100

SZERYK, JEFF
90/1 Kitchener Rangers
89/0 Soo Greyhounds

SZODINSKI, ROBERT
89 Semic Sticker 134

SZOKE, MARK
91 7th..Sketch Mem.Cup 81
90/1 7th..Sketch WHL 213
91/2 7th...Sketch WHL 6
93/4 Lethbridge Hurricanes

SZOPINSKI, ROBERT
92 Semic Sticker 271

SZTURM, PAT
94/5 Thunder Bay Senators
95/6 Thunder Bay Senators

SZUMLAK, STANLEY
87/8 Regina Pats

SZUPER, LEVENTE
02/3 BAP All-Star 107
02/3 BAP Mem. 392
02/3 Between the Pipes 102
02/3 In The G-U 99
02/3 Parkhurst 246
02/3 Parkhurst Retro 227
02/3 SP Authentic 167
02/3 SP GU 98
02/3 Ultimate Mem. 74
02/3 Upper Deck 431
02/3 UD Artistic 107, CG5
02/3 UD Honor 107
02/3 UD Mask 141
02/3 UD Premier 49
99/0 Ottawa 67's

SZURA, JOE
68/9 O-Pee-Chee 175
70/1 O-Pee-Chee 73
72/3 O-Pee-Chee 313
70/1 Topps 73
72/3 Los Angeles Sharks

SZWEZ, JEFF
01/2 Kitchener Rangers

SZYSKY, CHRIS
99/0 Grand Rapids Griffins
00/1 Grand Rapids Griffins
01/2 Grand Rapids Griffins
95/6 Swift Current Broncos

T

TABARA, ZDISLAV
94/5 APS 298
95/6 APS 2
96/7 APS 213
97/8 APS 27
98/9 OFS 97, 468
99/0 OFS 56
00/1 OFS 318

TABARACCI, RICK
98/9 Bicycle.. 8-H
91/2 Bowman 207
92/3 Bowman 324
93/4 Donruss 363
94/5 Donruss 49
95/6 Donruss 214
96/7 Donruss 10
97/8 Do. Priority 105
94/5 Flair 204
92/3 Fleer Ultra 445
94/5 Fleer Ultra 239
93/4 Leaf 241
96/7 Leaf 149
91/2 O-Pee-Chee 375
98/9 OPC Chrome 77
97/8 Omega 36
98/9 Pacific 126
99/0 Pacific 448
97/8 Pacific CC 256
97/8 Pa. Paramount 31
98/9 Pa. Paramount 33
97/8 Pa. Revolution 21
90/1 Panini/WPG 24
98/9 Panini Sticker 179
94/5 Parkhurst 255
95/6 Parkhurst 32
93/4 Pinnacle 299
94/5 Pinnacle 444, MA5
96/7 Pinnacle 66
96/7 Pi. Be A Player 164, ✍ Aut. 164
94/5 POG 299
93/4 Power Play 267
93/4 Premier 239
94/5 Premier 367
90/1 Pro Set 649
89/0 ProCards AHL 45
90/1 ProCards 343
91/2 ProCards 185
91/2 Score CAN 244
92/3 Score 529
93/4 Score 403
96/7 Score 23
97/8 Score 28
92/3 Topps 453
98/9 Topps 77
91/2 To. Stadium 395
92/3 To. Stadium 135
93/4 To. Stadium 378
93/4 To. Stadium - Master Photo-2 7
94/5 To. Stadium 74
95/6 To. Stadium 119
90/1 Upper Deck 520
91/2 Upper Deck 339
92/3 Upper Deck 58
92/3 Upper Deck 358
94/5 Upper Deck 187
95/6 Upper Deck 196, SE-103
97/8 Upper Deck 236
90/1 WINN / IGA
91/2 WINN / IGA
90/1 Moncton Hawks
91/2 Moncton Hawks
00/1 Utah Grizzlies

TABARIN, DIMITRI
94/5 Sig. Rookies 32, ✍ 32
94/5 SR Gold Standard 93

TABOBONDUNG, BARRY
80/1 Oshawa Generals

TABOR, JAN
94/5 DEL 404
95/6 DEL 423

TABORSKY, MARTIN
98/9 OFS 399
99/0 OFS 333
00/1 OFS 118

TABORSKY, PAVEL
94/5 APS 78
95/6 APS 9
98/9 OFS 165

TAFFE, JEFF
02/3 Atomic 130
02/3 BAP All-Star 131
02/3 BAP Mem. 279
02/3 Calder 138
02/3 Choice Prospects 41
02/3 Crown Royale 132
02/3 First Edition 435 [Hobby]
02/3 In The GU 190
02/3 Pacific Complete 578
02/3 Parkhurst 231
02/3 Parkhurst Retro 231
02/3 Pr. Stock Reserve 178
02/3 Pr. Stock Titanium 130
02/3 Quest for the Cup 138
02/3 SP Authentic ✍ 192
02/3 SP GU Edition 89
02/3 SPx ✍ 157
02/3 T. Chrome 171
02/3 To. Total 428
02/3 Ultimate Memorabilia 31
02/3 Upper Deck 448
02/3 UD Artistic 119, CG20
02/3 UD Classic 125
02/3 UD Foundations 161
02/3 UD Honor 123
02/3 UD Mask 174
02/3 UD Premier ✍ 76, ✍ Sig
02/3 UD Rookie ✂ 153
02/3 UD Top Shelf 134
02/3 Vanguard 129

TAGLIANETTI, PETER
94/5 Donruss 89
92/3 Fleer Ultra 204
93/4 Fleer Ultra 397
88/9 O-Pee-Chee 257
90/1 O-Pee-Chee 435
89/0 O-Pee-Chee 297
90/1 OPC Premier 117
89/0 opcSticker 146-265
88/9 Panini Sticker 152
89/0 Panini Sticker 174
93/4 Parkhurst 430
94/5 Parkie SE141
92/3 Pinnacle 383
94/5 Pinnacle 505
93/4 Premier 248
90/1 Pro Set 505
90/1 Score 16T
91/2 Score CAN 448
93/4 Score 295
93/4 To. Stadium 243
93/4 Upper Deck 100
91/2 PITT / Elby's
91/2 PITT / Foodland 14
93/4 PITT / Foodland 22
94/5 PITT / Foodland 18
87/8 WINN
88/9 WINN / Safety Tips
89/0 WINN / Safeway
86/7 Sherb. Canadiens 26

TÄHTINEN, MARKKU
99/0 Cardset 346
00/1 Cardset 349
02/3 Cardset 132

TÄHTISALO, PETRI
99/0 Cardset 331

TAILLEFER, PETE
52/3 Laval Dairy Update 26

TAILLEFER, TERRY
88/9 ProCards / Maine

TAILLENS, RETO
72 Semic Sticker 162

TAIMIO, TOMI
78/9 SM-Liiga 41

TAIT, ASHLEY
00/1 Kudos 140
02/3 Coventry Blaze
00/1 Nottingham Panthers
01/2 Nottingham Panthers

TAIT, TERRY
84/5 Springfield Indians 11
80/1 Soo Greyhounds
81/2 Soo Greyhounds
82/3 Soo Greyhounds
87/8 Soo Greyhounds 33

TAJCNAR, RUDOLF
72 Hellas MM-Jenkki 85
74 Hellas MM-Jenkki 83
72 Panda MM-Toronto
72 Semic Sticker 25
74 Semic Sticker 69
72/3 Williams Finnish 20

TAKAC, ROMAN
99/0 Prince George Cougars

TAKALA, MARKKU
93/4 Sisu 276

TAKHAR, DALJIT
92/3 BCJHL 218

TAKKO, KARI
98/9 Cardset Top. 12
99/0 Cardset AH A-pata
02/3 Cardset 123
91/2 Jyvas Hyva 67
92/3 Jyvas Hyva 189
93/4 Jyvas Hyva 344
80/1 Mallasjuoma 220
87/8 Panini Sticker 288
88/9 Panini Sticker 85
89/0 Panini Sticker 102, 106
89 Pelimiehen Passi
90/1 ProCards 106
93/4 Sisu 208
93/4 Sisu 354
94/5 Sisu 27, 151, N-2, SS-6
95/6 Sisu 149, GG-4
96/7 Sisu 149, MA-1, Super
95/6 Sisu Limited 19, LG-6
90/1 Upper Deck 543
97/8 UD Elitserien 84
98/9 UD Elitserien 100
99/0 UD Elitserien 86, L5
90/1 EDMO / IGA
87/8 MINS
88/9 MINS / ADA

TALA, HANNU
00/1 Cardset 110

TALAFOUS, DEAN
75/6 O-Pee-Chee 197
76/7 O-Pee-Chee 103
77/8 O-Pee-Chee 49
78/9 O-Pee-Chee 149
79/0 O-Pee-Chee 54
80/1 O-Pee-Chee 132
81/2 O-Pee-Chee 235
75/6 Topps 197
76/7 Topps 103
77/8 Topps 49
78/9 Topps 149
79/0 Topps 54
80/1 Topps 132

TALAKOWKI, RON
93/4 Thunder Bay Senators

TALBOT, JEAN-GUY
01/2 BAP Mem. ✂ RM10
45-64 BeeHive-2 [Mont.]
64-67 BeeHive-3 [Mont.]
63-65 Chex
64/5 Coke/Sprite [Mont.]
65/6 Coca-Cola
77/8 Dernière Heure
70/1 Eddie Sargent 189
62/3 Cowan Tile
51/2 La Patrie
68/9 O-Pee-Chee 179
69/0 O-Pee-Chee 15
70/1 O-Pee-Chee 100
55/6 Parkhurst 53
57/8 Parkhurst [Mont.] 9
58/9 Parkhurst 41
59/0 Parkhurst 49
60/1 Parkhurst 52
61/2 Parkhurst 48
62/3 Parkhurst 51
63/4 Parkhurst 22
63/4 Parkhurst 81
93/4 Parkhurst PR52
01/2 Parkhurst PR11, PR44, PR111, PR129, ✍ PA17
93/4 Parkie 56-57 80
95/6 Parkie 66-67 68
94/5 Parkie Tall 76
60/1 Shirriff 35
61/2 Shirriff 109
62/3 Shirriff 39
62/3 Shirriff 44
01/2 Signature ✍ VA25
64/5 Topps 52
65/6 Topps 4
66/7 Topps 3
67/8 Topps 104
69/0 Topps 15
70/1 Topps 100
58/9 Toronto Star Photo
63/4 Toronto Star Action
61/2 Toronto Star Weekend
91/2 Ultimate Original Six 16
60/1 York
61/2 York 12
62/3 York Transfer 4
63/4 York 23
67/8 MONT
92/3 MONT / OPC 53
72/3 SLOU
73/4 SLOU

TALBOT, JOE
99/0 Ottawa 67's
00/1 Ottawa 67's 1

TALBOT, MAXIME
00/1 Hull Olympiques 16
01/2 Hull Olympiques 18
02/3 Hull Olympiques
00/1 Rouyn-Noranda 7

TALIERCIO, CHRIS
02/3 Louisiana Ice Gators

TALLAIRE, GERALD
91/2 Air Canada SJHL 35
91/2 Air Canada SJHL B19
92/3 MPS SJHL 3

TALLAIRE, SEAN
91/2 Air Canada SJHL C18
01/2 UD DEL 120
97/8 Grand Rapids Griffins
00/1 Kansas City Blades 5
99/0 Utah Grizzlies
91/2 L. Superior State Lakers

TALLAS, ROBBIE
91/2 Avant Garde BCJHL 106
91/2 Avant Garde BCJHL 119
98/9 Be A Player 158, ✍ Aut. 158
98/9 Bicycle.. 2-D
98/9 Omega 18
98/9 Pacific 100
99/0 Pacific 29
97/8 Score Bost. 3
91/2 7th...Sketch WHL 126
97/8 Upper Deck 223
96/7 Providence Bruins
97/8 Providence Bruins
01/2 WBS Penguins
02/3 WBS Penguins
93/4 Seattle Thunderbirds

TALLBERG, THOMAS
94/5 Leaf Elit Set 1
95/6 Leaf Elit Set 22
91/2 Semic Elitserien 44
92/3 Semic Elitserien 62

TALLINDER, HENRIK
02/3 Bowman 107, ✂ FFDS, ✂ FFJ, ✂ FFP, ✂ FFR, ✂ FFRP, ✂ FFS, ✂ FFTS, ✍ YSA, / ✍ Puck
02/3 Calder 59
00/1 Cardset 216
02/3 Cardset 275
02/3 Pacific Complete 562
01/2 Parkhurst 322
02/3 SPx 104
02/3 Upper Deck 198
98/9 UD Elitserien 7
99/0 UD Elitserien 7, 201
02/3 UD Foundations 124
02/3 UD MVP 196
02/3 UD Piece 123
02/3 UD Vintage 323

TALLON, DALE
71/2 Colgate Head
70/1 Colgate 81
70/1 Dad's Cookies
70/1 Eddie Sargent 215
71/2 Eddie Sargent 209
72/3 Eddie Sargent 211
70/1 Esso Power Player
91/2 Future Trends C72 22, ✍ 22
72/3 Post 20
74/5 Lipton Soup 22
74/5 Loblaws
73/4 Mac's Milk
70/1 O-Pee-Chee 225
71/2 O-Pee-Chee 234
71/2 O-Pee-Chee Book. 3
72/3 O-Pee-Chee 121
72/3 O-Pee-Chee Crest 21
73/4 O-Pee-Chee 211
74/5 O-Pee-Chee 360
75/6 O-Pee-Chee 351
76/7 O-Pee-Chee 89
76/7 OPC 382
77/8 O-Pee-Chee 124
78/9 O-Pee-Chee 146
71/2 O-Pee-Chee Poster 5
70/1 Post Shooters
91/2 Pro Set 595
72 Semic Sticker 222
71/2 Topps 95
72/3 Topps 15
73/4 Topps 129
76/7 Topps 89
77/8 Topps 124
78/9 Topps 146
71/2 Toronto Sun Photo
70/1 VANC / Royal Bank
71/2 VANC / Royal Bank 10
72/3 VANC / Royal Bank

TAMBELLINI, STEVE
83/4 Funmate Puffy 4 [w/]
80/1 O-Pee-Chee 365
81/2 O-Pee-Chee 81
82/3 O-Pee-Chee 134
82/3 O-Pee-Chee 147
83/4 O-Pee-Chee 93
83/4 O-Pee-Chee 223
84/5 O-Pee-Chee 237
87/8 O-Pee-Chee 259
88/9 O-Pee-Chee 258
82/3 OPC/Topps Sticker 226
83/4 OPC/Topps Sticker 219
84/5 OPC Sticker 239
88/9 OPC Sticker 62-197
87/8 Panini Sticker 351
82/3 Post [Colo.]
83/4 Souhaits Keychain [Devils]
81/2 Topps 86 [West]
83/4 Vachon 19-139
81/2 COLR
79/0 NYIS
85/6 VANC
86/7 VANC
87/8 VANC / Shell

TAMBIJEVS, LEONIDS
98/9 Cardset 179
99/0 Cardset 91, 165

TAMBURRO, MIKE
96/7 Cleveland Lumberjacks
97/8 Cleveland Lumberjacks

TAMER, CHRIS
93/4 Classic 83
94/5 Classic 94, ✍ Aut.
93/4 Cla. Prospects 119
95/6 Edge Ice 119
94/5 Leaf 513
98/9 Pacific 359
97/8 Pa. Invincible R-165
95/6 Parkhurst 436
94/5 Pinnacle 259, RTP4
96/7 Pi. Be A Player 182, ✍ Aut. 182
94/5 Premier 224
00/1 Stadium 174
95/6 Topps 169
94/5 Upper Deck 318
97/8 Upper Deck 345
01/2 UD Vintage 12
98/9 NYRA
94/5 PITT / Foodland 12
95/6 PITT / Foodland 18
93/4 Cleveland Lumberjacks

TAMER, JOHN
84/5 Belleville Bulls

TAMMELIN, RAULI
70/1 Kuvajulkaisut 169
80/1 Mallasjuoma 186
78/9 SM-Liiga 213
71/2 Williams Finnish 240
72/3 Williams Finnish 224
73/4 Williams Finnish 301

TAMMI, JUHANI*
65/6 Hellas 102

TAMMI, JUKKA
98/9 Cardset Top. 4, -Leij. 3
96/7 DEL 47
98/9 DEL 132
95 Hartwall Karjala
91/2 Jyvas Hyva 13
92/3 Jyvas Hyva 36
93/4 Jyvas Hyva 74
95 Panini Worlds 162
94 Semic 3
95 Semic 30, 216
89 Semic Sticker 28
91 Semic Sticker 4
93/4 Sisu 109
94/5 Sisu 38, MN-10
95/6 Sisu 339, GG-8, G-4
95/6 Sisu Limited 91
96 Wien 12

TAMMI, VELI-MATTI
70/1 Kuvajulkaisut 356

TAMMINEN, JOE
93/4 Minnesota-Duluth

TAMMINEN, JUHA*
70/1 Kuvajulkaisut 357

TAMMINEN, JUHANI
72 Hellas MM-Jenkki 16
74 Hellas MM-Jenkki 20
70/1 Kuvajulkaisut 77
70/1 Kuvajulkaisut 170
80/1 Mallasjuoma 190
79 Panini Sticker 176
72 Semic Sticker 88
74 Semic Sticker 92
82 Semic Sticker 50
92 Semic Sticker 194
96/7 Sisu 198
82 Skopbank
78/9 SM-Liiga 16
78/9 SM-Liiga 208
77-79 Sports. FIN 46-1084
71/2 Williams Finnish 76
71/2 Williams Finnish 162
72/3 Williams Finnish 75
72/3 Williams Finnish 114
73/4 Williams Finnish 80
73/4 Williams Finnish 144
76/7 Phoenix Roadrunners

TAMMINEN, KAUKO
71/2 Williams Finnish 335

TAMMINEN, MIKKO
98/9 Cardset 209

TAMMINEN, TEEMU
93/4 Sisu 252

TAMMINEN, TINY
51/2 Lac St-Jean 37

TANABE, DAVID
99/0 BAP Mem. 359
00/1 BAP Mem. 47
01/2 BAP Mem. 48
01/2 Bowman 133, ✂ FFJ, ✂ FFS, ✂ FFDS, ✂ FFR, ✍ YSA
99/0 Dynagon Ice 44
99/0 Millenium C-5
99/0 NHL Power Play [x3]
01/2 O-Pee-Chee 196
02/3 O-Pee-Chee 119
99/0 Omega 50
00/1 Pacific 90
02/3 Pacific 70
02/3 Pacific Complete 82
00/1 Pa. Paramount 46
00/1 Parkhurst P-223
01/2 Parkhurst 51
00/1 Signature 116, ✍ Aut. 162
01/2 Signature 113, ✍ Aut. 113
99/0 SP Authentic ✍ SotT
99/0 SPx 178
98/9 SPx Prospects 90
99/0 Stadium 178
02/3 Stadium ✂ YSS13
00/1 Topps 279
01/2 Topps 196
02/3 Topps 119
00/1 To. Chrome 174
99/0 To. Gold Label 93
02/3 To. Limited 119
99/0 To. Prmr. Plus 124
02/3 To. Total 242
00/1 Upper Deck 35
01/2 Upper Deck 34
98/9 UD Black Diam. 120
99/0 UD Black Diam. 18
00/1 UD MVP 36
01/2 UD MVP 36
99/0 UD Ovation 12
00/1 UD Vintage 70
01/2 UD Vintage 47
02/3 UD Vintage 51
00/1 Victory 274
01/2 Victory 66
99/0 WGretzky 36

TANAKA, YASUSHIN
79 Panini Sticker 288

TANBERG, T.J.
99/0 Greensboro Generals

TANCILL, CHRIS
92/3 Classic Prospects 20
93/4 Donruss 84
93/4 Parkhurst 318
96/7 Pinnacle 71
93/4 Premier 429
91/2 Pro Set 539
90/1 ProCards 179
91/2 ProCards 104
91/2 Upper Deck 455
94/5 Kansas City Blades 6
95/6 Kansas City Blades
96/7 Kentucky Tho'blades

TANEL, MATT
01/2 Mississauga IceDogs

TANEVSKI, DAN
90/1 7th..Sketch OHL 221
93/4 Soo Greyhounds 2

TANG, SHAO
79 Panini Sticker 356

TANGUAY, ALEX
01/2 Adrenaline 51
01/2 Atomic 28
00/1 Aurora 42, Pins. 42, ✍ Aut. 42
00/1 BAP All-Star AS-7
99/0 BAP Mem. 79
00/1 BAP Mem. 25
01/2 BAP Mem. 13, ✂ SCC
02/3 BAP Mem. 17, ✂ FG17
01/2 BAP Update ✂ HSHSJers 37
99 Bowman 55, SC18
01/2 Bowman 113
98 Bowman 108, 152, SC15, ✍ A35
98 Bowman Chrome 108, 152
98/9 Collection Souvenir 10
99/0 Crown Royale 41, CS 8
01/2 Crown Royale 41
99/0 Dynagon Ice 62
02/3 Exclusive 47
02/3 First Edition 87, 420H, ✂ Jers.
01/2 Heads Up BTI 7
02/3 Heads Up ✂ GWQ 8
02/3 In The GU 12, 112
00/1 McDonald's GCDC 2
99/0 Millenium 73, C-1, ✍ Aut. 73
99/0 NHL Power Play [x3]
01/2 O-Pee-Chee 12
02/3 O-Pee-Chee 95
98/9 OPC Chrome 237
99/0 Omega 67, 5ST-2
00/1 Pacific 123, ✍ Aut. 123
01/2 Pacific 108
02/3 Pacific 97
02/3 Pacific Complete 279
00/1 Pa. Paramount 65, ✂ GUS-7
99/0 Panini Sticker 216, 355
00/1 Parkhurst P-38
01/2 Parkhurst 68, ✂ PJ54, ✂ PS37, ✂ HSHSJers
02/3 Parkhurst 45, ✂ GJ27, ✂ SJ27
02/3 Parkhurst Retro 98
99/0 Prism 42, CA 6, -IP 3
00/1 Pr. Stock PS-14, ✂ GUG 32
01/2 Pr. Stock 25
02/3 Pr. Stock Reserve 28
00/1 PS Titanium 24
01/2 PS Titanium ✂ DSJ 12, ✂ DSJ 14
01/2 PS Titanium Draft ✂ 28
92 Québec Pee Wee 1252
93 Québec Pee Wee 523
00/1 Revolution 40
00/1 Signature 137, ✍ Aut. 120
01/2 Signature 103, ✍ Aut. 103, ✂ GJ14, ✂ GSJ14
02/3 Signature Series 41, GS-4, ✍ 41, ✂ YP7
02/3 Slam Card
99/0 SP Authentic ✍ SotT
01/2 SP Authentic 116
02/3 SP GU ✂ AF (x2), ✂ PC, ✂ FF, ✂ PH (x2)
02/3 Sports Vault 186
99/0 SPx 41, X13
01/2 SPx 167, ✂ TT
99/0 Stadium 194, -Chrome 46
00/1 Stadium 161
01/2 Stadium 68
02/3 Stadium ✂ FC3, ✂ PC3
98/9 Topps 237
00/1 Topps 229, OTG22
01/2 Topps 12
02/3 Topps 95
99/0 To. Chrome 287
00/1 To. Chrome 144
01/2 To. Chrome 12
02/3 T. Chrome 60
98/9 To. Finest F10
99/0 To. Gold Label 91, FG9
00/1 To. Gold Label NG4
00/1 To. Heritage 139, 229
01/2 To. Heritage 56
02/3 To. Heritage ✂ GS, ✂ GSB
02/3 To. Limited 95
99/0 To. Prmr. Plus 133, PR1, ✍ SB5
01/2 To. Reserve 98
02/3 To. Total 215
98/9 UD Choice 257
00/1 UD Heroes 30
98/9 Upper Deck ✂ GJ13
99/0 Upper Deck 212
00/1 Upper Deck 275, P3
01/2 Upper Deck 44, ✂ SCFJersD
02/3 Upper Deck 286, ✂ CG, ✂ PA, ✂ UDPL
00/1 UD ASG CA4
97/8 UD Black Diam. 105
02/3 UD Classic ✂ HR (x2), ✂ SC
99/0 UD G. Reserve 212
01/2 UD Honor Roll ✂ PPM
01/2 UD Mask 24, ✂ GJ, ✂ JP, ✂ DP
00/1 UD MVP 54
01/2 UD MVP 50
02/3 UD MVP -SD, ST, Souv.
99/0 UD MVP Cup ✍ PS
99/0 UD Ovation 16
02/3 UD Piece 28
01/2 UD SCup Champs 33
01/2 UD Top Shelf 87
02/3 UD Top Shelf ✂ GO, ✂ SH, ✂ SW, ✂ TS
00/1 UD Vintage 95
02/3 UD Vintage 70, GB 70, T19
01/2 Vanguard 28, QTH 16
99/0 Victory 364
00/1 Victory 67
01/2 Victory 87
02/3 Victory 55
99/0 WGretzky 52
97/8 Zenith 99, Z79
96/7 Halifax Moosehead
96/7 Halifax Moosehead
97/8 Halifax Moosehead
97/8 Halifax Moosehead
97/8 Halifax Moosehead
98/9 Halifax Moosehead

TANGUAY, CHRISTIAN
82/3 Fredericton Express
83/4 Fredericton Express

TANGUAY, MARTIN
93/4 Cla. Prospects 132
91/2 7th...Sketch LHJMQ 135
93/4 Atlanta Knights
93/4 Knoxville Cherokees
96/7 Knoxville Cherokees
88/9 Richelieu Riverains

TANNAHILL, DON
72/3 O-Pee-Chee 238
73/4 O-Pee-Chee 69
74/5 OPC 117
73/4 Topps 69
74/5 Topps 117
72/3 VANC / Royal Bank
73/4 VANC / Royal Bank

TANNER, JOHN
90/1 OPC Premier 118
90/1 Panini/QUE 21
90/1 Pro Set 637
91/2 ProCards 366
92/3 Score 452
89/0 7th..Sketch OHL 38
90/1 7th..Sketch OHL 145, 377
91/2 Upper Deck 119
90/1 QUÉB / Petro-Canada
92/3 QUÉB / Petro-Canada

TANSOWNY, STEVE
92/3 MPS SJHL 53

TANTI, TONY
90/1 Bowman 213
91/2 Bowman 34
92/3 Bowman 172
83 Canada Juniors
94/5 DEL 54
95/6 DEL 59
96/7 DEL 256
88/9 Frito Lay
89/0 Kraft 45
86/7 Kraft Sports 71
83/4 O-Pee-Chee 362
84/5 O-Pee-Chee 332
84/5 O-Pee-Chee 369
85/6 OPC/Topps 153
86/7 OPC/Topps 120
87/8 OPC/Topps 97
88/9 OPC/Topps 82
90/1 OPC/Topps 157
91/2 O-Pee-Chee 133
92/3 O-Pee-Chee 34
89/0 O-Pee-Chee 280
84/5 OPC Sticker 274
84/5 OPC Sticker 275
85/6 OPC Sticker 245-127
86/7 OPC Sticker 99
87/8 OPC Sticker 195
88/9 OPC Sticker 59
89/0 opcSticker 71
87/8 Panini Sticker 345
88/9 Panini Sticker 143
89/0 Panini Sticker 149, 151
90/1 Panini Sticker 124
91/2 Parkhurst 236
90/1 Pro Set 241
87/8 Pro Sport CW15
90/1 Score 137
91/2 Score 49
91/2 Score CAN 49
92/3 Score 116
84/5 7-Eleven
84/5 Topps 141
92/3 Topps 235
91/2 To. Stadium 285
92/3 To. Stadium 312
90/1 Upper Deck 197
92/3 Upper Deck 182
02/3 UD Foundations 96
01/2 UD Legends 65
83/4 Vachon 119-39
83/4 Vachon 119-93
91/2 BUFF / Blue Shield
91/2 BUFF / Campbell's
91/2 BUFF / Pepsi
81/2 CHIC
90/1 PITT / Foodland 14
83/4 VANC
84/5 VANC
85/6 VANC
86/7 VANC
87/8 VANC / Shell
88/9 VANC / Mohawk
89/0 VANC / Mohawk
80/1 Oshawa Generals
81/2 Oshawa Generals
82/3 Oshawa Generals

TAPPER, BRAD
00/1 BAP Mem. 437
01/2 BAP Mem. 221
01/2 O-Pee-Chee 302
02/3 Pacific Complete 429
00/1 Premier Plus 113
00/1 PS Titanium 104
00/1 PS Titanium Draft 104
92 Québec Pee Wee 491
01/2 Signature 217, ✍ Aut. 217
00/1 SP Authentic 93
00/1 Stadium 247
01/2 Topps 302
00/1 To. Heritage 83
00/1 UD Ice 105
01/2 Chicago Wolves

TARASENKO, ANDREI
00/1 Mir 160

TARASOV, ANATOLI V.
91/2 Future Trends C72 4
83 HHOF Postcard D15
83&87 HHOF 239
69/0 Soviet Stars
70/1 Soviet Stars
71/2 Soviet Stars

TARASOV, DMITRI
99/0 Mir 166
00/1 Mir 11

TARASOV, EVGENY
98/9 Mir 42
96 Wien 131

TARASOV, VADIM
98/9 Mir 103
99/0 Mir 197
00/1 Mir 173, 300
01/2 Québec Citadelles

TARASOV, VLADIMIR
98/9 Mir 137
99/0 Mir 184

TARASUK, ALLAN
82/3 Brandon Wheat Kings
83/4 Brandon Wheat Kings

TARASUK, RICK
91/2 7th...Sketch OHL 269

TARASYENKO, ANDREI
95 Panini Worlds 40

TARATUKHIN, ANDREI
02/3 Russian Future Stars 10

TARDIF, CHRISTIAN
90/1 7th..Sketch LHJMQ 71
91/2 7th...Sketch LHJMQ 33

TARDIF, JAMIE
01/2 Peterborough Petes

TARDIF, MARC
93/4 Cla. Prospects 223
70/1 Colgate 17
72/3 Dernière Heure
81/2 Dernière Heure
71/2 Eddie Sargent 112
72/3 Eddie Sargent 118
70/1 Esso Power Player
83/4 Esso Stars
70/1 O-Pee-Chee 179
71/2 O-Pee-Chee 29
72/3 O-Pee-Chee 11
79/0 O-Pee-Chee 108
80/1 O-Pee-Chee 256
81/2 O-Pee-Chee 283
82/3 O-Pee-Chee 296
83/4 O-Pee-Chee 305
81/2 OPC Sticker 76
82/3 OPC/Topps Sticker 21
83/4 OPC/Topps Sticker 247
80/1 O-Pee-Chee Super 17
74/5 OPC WHA 43
75/6 OPC WHA 30
75/6 OPC WHA 71
76/7 OPC WHA 1
76/7 OPC WHA 2
76/7 OPC WHA 3
76/7 O-Pee-Chee WHA 5
76/7 OPC WHA 118
77/8 OPC WHA 20
73/4 OPC WHA Poster 20
80/1 Pepsi Bottle Cap
82/3 Post [Québ.]
90/1 7th..Sketch LHJMQ 109
91/2 7th...Sketch LHJMQ 73
71/2 Topps 29
72/3 Topps 105
79/0 Topps 108
80/1 Topps 256
71/2 Toronto Sun Photo
69/0 MONT / Pro Star
70/1 MONT
71/2 MONT / Pro Star
72/3 MONT / Pro Star
80/1 QUÉB
81/2 QUÉB
82/3 QUÉB
83/4 QUÉB
76/7 Québec Nordiques
76/7 Québ. / Antoinette
93/4 Atlanta Knights

TARDIF, PATRICE
94/5 Classic T60
94/5 Cla. Images 27, CE14
95/6 Donruss 87
95/6 Edge Ice 97
94/5 Fleer 192
95/6 Leaf 22
95/6 Score 88
95/6 Topps 172
94/5 Upper Deck 470
00/1 UD DEL 121
96/7 Detroit Vipers
98/9 Manitoba Moose
99/0 Manitoba Moose
94/5 Peoria Rivermen
99/0 Québec Citadelles 12
97/8 Rochester Americans
92/3 Maine Black Bears
93/4 Maine Black Bears

TARDIF, STEVE
93/4 Slapshot / Drummondville 22
98/9 Florida Everblades
99/0 Florida Everblades
97/8 Indianapolis Ice 24

TARDIFF, MARC
78/9 Dernière Heure

TARKIAINEN, JUHANI
66/7 Champion 211

TARKO, KARI-PEKKA
72/3 Williams Finnish 354

TARNOWSKI, CHRIS
85/6 Kamloops Blazers
86/7 Kamloops Blazers
86/7 Regina Pats
84/5 Victoria Cougars

TARNSTRÖM, DICK
02/3 Atomic 123
02/3 Crown Royale 133
02/3 Pacific Complete 599
02/3 Pr. Stock Reserve 179
02/3 Pr. Stock Titanium 133
02/3 Quest for the Cup 141
02/3 SP Authentic 180
02/3 Sports Vault 119
02/3 Ultimate Memorabilia 36
02/3 UD Artistic 98
02/3 UD Honor 124
02/3 UD Mask 138
02/3 UD Premier 70
02/3 Vanguard 130

TÄRNSTRÖM, DICK
02/3 BAP All-Star 122
02/3 BAP Mem. 334
02/3 In The GU 95
94/5 Leaf Elit Set 211, ND-10
95/6 Leaf Elit Set 9
02/3 Parkhurst 234
02/3 Parkhurst Retro 250
94/5 Parkie SE239
92/3 Semic Elitserien 31
95/6 UD Elitserien 3, NA2
97/8 UD Elitserien 5
98/9 UD Elitserien 4
99/0 UD Elitserien 4
00/1 UD Elitserien 3

TARRANT, JERRY
89/0 ProCards IHL 27
91/2 ProCards 373

TARTARI, STÉPHANE
90/1 7th..Sketch LHJMQ 115

TARVAINEN, JUSSI
98/9 Cardset 134
99/0 Cardset 177, 323
00/1 Cardset 88
02/3 Cardset 124
97/8 Hockey-Box
94/5 Parkie SE225
93/4 Sisu 180
94/5 Sisu 71, J-8, ND-3
95/6 Sisu 75
96/7 Sisu 81
94/5 Topps Finest 142

TASALA, LASSE
80/1 Mallasjuoma 33

TASKER, MICHAEL
02/3 Coventry Blaze

TASKULA, KEIJO
80/1 Mallasjuoma 135

TASSONE, JOE
97/8 Central Texas

TATARINOV, MIKHAIL
91/2 Bowman 298
92/3 Bowman 395
92/3 Fleer Ultra 181
91 Ivan Fiodorov 10
93/4 Leaf 342
91/2 O-Pee-Chee 465
92/3 O-Pee-Chee 253
91/2 OPC Premier 62
91/2 Panini Sticker 210
92/3 Panini Sticker 208
91/2 Parkhurst 145
91/2 Pinnacle 97
92/3 Pinnacle 35
90/1 Pro Set 647
91/2 Pro Set 462
91/2 Pro Set Platinum 218
91/2 Red Ace
90/1 Score 53T
91/2 Score 37
91/2 Score 12T

91/2 Score CAN 37
91/2 Score CAN 562
92/3 Score 107
93/4 Score 328
94 Semic 336
91 Semic Sticker 215
92 Semic Sticker 102
92/3 Topps 180
91/2 To. Stadium 390
92/3 To. Stadium 47
90/1 Upper Deck 401
92/3 Upper Deck 183
93/4 Upper Deck 386
91/2 QUÉB / Petro-Canada
92/3 QUÉB / Petro-Canada
90/1 WASH / Kodak
90/1 WASH / Smokey

TATARINTSEV, KONSTANTIN
99/0 Mir 91

TATARYN, JOSH
99/0 Ottawa 67's

TATTNER, MICHAEL
94/5 DEL 373

TAUBERT, KRISTIAN
00/1 Cardset 178
92/3 Jyvas Hyva 47
94/5 Sisu 353
02/3 Nottingham Panthers

TAUGHER, JOHNNY
37/8 World Wide Gum 116

TAURIAINEN, JARMO
70/1 Kuvajulkaisut 380
80/1 Mallasjuoma 109

TAVESKI, DAN
91/2 7th...Sketch OHL 347

TAVI, MIKKO
93/4 Jyvas Hyva 176
93/4 Sisu 165
94/5 Sisu 113
92/3 Clarkson G'Knights

TAYLOR, ANDREW
94/5 Sig. Rookies 65, ✍ 65
93/4 Slapshot / Kitchener 18
93/4 Slapshot / Kitchener 29
94/5 Slapshot / Detroit Jr. 13
94/5 Slapshot / Kitchener 20
95/6 Slapshot 70
94/5 Slapshot Memorial 87
98/9 Florida Everblades

TAYLOR, BART
91/2 Avant Garde BCJHL 121
92/3 BCJHL 172

TAYLOR, BILLY J.
34-43 BeeHive-1 [Toro.]
39/0 O-Pee-Chee 15
40/1 O-Pee-Chee 107
45-54 Quaker Oats

TAYLOR, BOBBY
73/4 O-Pee-Chee 238
92/3 Parkhurst 475

TAYLOR, CHRIS
92/3 Classic Prospects 113
95/6 Score 303
89/0 7th..Sketch OHL 26
90/1 7th..Sketch OHL 146
91/2 7th...Sketch OHL 370
91/2 Upper Deck 454
00/1 Rochester Americans
02/3 Rochester Americans

TAYLOR, DAVE
90/1 Bowman 149, -HT 22
91/2 Bowman 186
92/3 Bowman 37
01/2 Fleer Greats 61, ✍ Aut.
92/3 Fleer Ultra 313
93/4 Fleer Ultra 348
83/4 Funmate Puffy 12 [w/]
93/4 Hockey Wit 21
93/4 Leaf 374
78/9 O-Pee-Chee 353
79/0 O-Pee-Chee 232
80/1 O-Pee-Chee 137
81/2 O-Pee-Chee 143
81/2 O-Pee-Chee 152
81/2 O-Pee-Chee 391
82/3 O-Pee-Chee 161
83/4 O-Pee-Chee 163
84/5 O-Pee-Chee 92
85/6 O-Pee-Chee 214
86/7 OPC/Topps 63
87/8 OPC/Topps 118
88/9 OPC/Topps 46
90/1 OPC/Topps 314
91/2 O-Pee-Chee 138
89/0 OPC/Topps 58
81/2 OPC Sticker 149
81/2 OPC Sticker 237
81/2 OPC Sticker 268
82/3 OPC/Topps Sticker 164
82/3 OPC/Topps Sticker 231
84/5 OPC Sticker 267
85/6 OPC Sticker 238-106
86/7 OPC Sticker 90-220
87/8 OPC Sticker 215-83
88/9 OPC Sticker 155-26
89/0 opcSticker 151-11
87/8 Panini Sticker 280
88/9 Panini Sticker 79
89/0 Panini Sticker 98
90/1 Panini Sticker 236
91/2 Panini Sticker 89
93/4 Panini Sticker 206
91/2 Parkhurst 67
91/2 Parkhurst 214
92/3 Parkhurst 307
93/4 Parkhurst 367
91/2 Pinnacle 249
91/2 Pinnacle 373
92/3 Pinnacle 367
93/4 Pinnacle 412
82/3 Post [LosA.]
93/4 Power Play 364
90/1 Pro Set 128
91/2 Pro Set 103
91/2 Pro Set 325
92/3 Pro Set 258
91 Pro Set Awards AC16
90/1 Score 166
91/2 Score 214
91/2 Score 374
91/2 Score 435
91/2 Score CAN 214
91/2 Score CAN 264
91/2 Score CAN 325
92/3 Score 49
93/4 Score 389
84/5 7-Eleven
85/6 7-Eleven Superstars 8
79/0 Topps 232
80/1 Topps 137
81/2 Topps 40
81/2 Topps 132 [West]
92/3 Topps 446
91/2 To. Stadium 232
92/3 To. Stadium 234
93/4 TSC Members Only 14
90/1 Upper Deck 214
91/2 Upper Deck 270
80/1 LOSA 12
84/5 LOSA / Smokey 16
87/8 LOSA
88/9 LOSA / Smokey
89/0 LOSA / Smokey 6
90/1 LOSA / Smokey 8

TAYLOR, DAVE*
95/6 Lethbridge Hurricanes

TAYLOR, DYLAN
95/6 Slapshot 124

TAYLOR, ERIC
79/0 Montréal Juniors B&W

TAYLOR, FRED (CYCLONE)
91 C55 Reprint 20
83 HHOF Postcard A15
83&87 HHOF 14
10/1 Imperial
10/1 Imperial 15
11/2 Imperial 20
12/3 Imperial 43
60/1 Topps 46
61/2 Topps - Stamp
19 Vancouver Millionaires
19 Vancouver Millionaires

TAYLOR, GARY
90/1 7th..Sketch OHL 222

TAYLOR, GREG
91/2 Air Canada SJHL D28

TAYLOR, HARRY
45-64 BeeHive-2 [Toro.]
45-54 Quaker Oats

TAYLOR, JACK
51/2 Laval Dairy 67

TAYLOR, JASON
00/1 Utah Grizzlies

TAYLOR, JASON*
97/8 Central Texas

TAYLOR, JUSTIN
99/0 Medicine Hat Tigers

TAYLOR, KARL
89/0 7th..Sketch OHL 45
90/1 7th..Sketch OHL 319

TAYLOR, MARK
83/4 O-Pee-Chee 273
84/5 O-Pee-Chee 180
83/4 OPC/Topps Sticker 190
84/5 OPC Sticker 121
84/5 Topps 127
83/4 PITT / Coke Is It!
84/5 PITT / Heinz

TAYLOR, MATT
84/5 Belleville Bulls

TAYLOR, MIKE
94/5 Richmond Renegades
95/6 Richmond Renegades
96/7 Richmond Renegades

TAYLOR, PAUL
91/2 Avant Garde BCJHL 49
91/2 Avant Garde BCJHL 158
94/5 Dayton Bombers 2
95/6 Peoria Rivermen
93/4 N. Michigan Wildcats

TAYLOR, RANDY
88/9 ProCards / Indianapolis
89/0 ProCards IHL 151

TAYLOR, ROD
92/3 Hampton Roads
93/4 Hampton Roads
94/5 Hampton Roads
95/6 Hampton Roads
96/7 Hampton Roads
97/8 Hampton Roads
98/9 Hampton Roads
98/9 Hampton Roads
99/0 Hampton Roads

TAYLOR, RYAN
95/6 Slapshot 184

TAYLOR, SCOTT
85/6 Kitchener Rangers
86/7 Kitchener Rangers

TAYLOR, TED
71/2 Eddie Sargent 223
72/3 O-Pee-Chee 312
73/4 Quaker Oats 28
65/6 Topps 95
70/1 VANC / Royal Bank
71/2 VANC / Royal Bank 16
75/6 Houston Aeros

TAYLOR, TIM
95/6 Donruss 349
02/3 First Edition 167
94/5 Fleer Ultra 286
98/9 Pacific 101
97/8 Pa. Dynagon BKS-35
97/8 Pi. Be A Player 114, ✍ Aut. 114
89/0 ProCards AHL 80
90/1 ProCards 211
91/2 ProCards 563
92 Semic Sticker 146
94/5 SR Tetrad CXVI, ✍ Aut.
97/8 SP Authentic 9
95/6 Topps 132
99/0 Ult. Victory 58
94/5 Upper Deck 325
95/6 Upper Deck 295
98/9 Upper Deck 37
95/6 UD Be A Player 101, ✍ S101
98/9 UD G. Reserve 37
00/1 UD Vintage 245
91/2 Baltimore Skipjacks

TEAL, GORDON
28/9 Paulins Candy 65

TEAL, JEFF
83/4 Nova Scotia Voyageurs

TEBBUTT, GREG
83/4 PITT / Coke Is It!

TEEVENS, MARK
94/5 DEL 69
95/6 DEL 70
96/7 DEL 265
88/9 ProCards / Indianapolis

TEICHMANN, BRAD
90/1 7th..Sketch OHL 20
91/2 7th...Sketch OHL 46

TEIJONMAA, OLLI
71/2 Williams Finnish 336

TEIMONEN, MIIKKA
95/6 Sisu 288

TEJKL, PETR
94/5 APS 4
95/6 APS 105
96/7 APS 101, 427
96/7 DS Sticker 269
99/0 OFS 247

TELJUKIN, ANDREI
01/2 UD DEL 223

TELLQVIST, MIKAEL
02/3 BAP All-Star 114
02/3 BAP Mem. 280
02/3 Between the Pipes 77
02/3 Bowman 146
02/3 Calder 148
02/3 In The GU 191
02/3 Pacific Complete 594
02/3 Parkhurst 232
02/3 Parkhurst Retro 232
02/3 Pr. Stock Titanium 139
02/3 Quest for the Cup 149
02/3 SP Authentic ✍ 195
02/3 SP GU Edition 102
02/3 SPx ✍ 158
02/3 T. Chrome 157
02/3 To. Total 421
02/3 Ultimate Memorabilia 32
02/3 Upper Deck 455
02/3 UD Artistic 115
00/1 UD Elitserien 44, 186, M2, ✍ Sig., T3
02/3 UD Honor 165
02/3 UD Mask 82, 179
02/3 UD Premier ✍ 77, ✍ Sig
02/3 UD Rookie ✍ 171, ✍ TD
02/3 UD Top Shelf 103
01/2 St. John's Maple Leafs
02/3 St. John's Maple Leafs

TEMPLE, JEFF
95/6 Brandon Wheat Kings

TEMPLETON, BERT
89/0 7th..Sketch OHL 173
90/1 7th..Sketch OHL 323
91/2 7th...Sketch OHL 72
93/4 Slapshot / North Bay 23
95/6 Slapshot 6
98/9 Barrie Colts
82/3 North Bay Centennials
83/4 North Bay Centennials
99/0 Sudbury Wolves 2
00/1 Sudbury Wolves 2

TENHUNEN, SEPPO
80/1 Mallasjuoma 97
78/9 SM-Liiga 139

TENISI, GUIDO
82 Semic Sticker 124

TENKRAT, PETR
96/7 APS 93
97/8 APS 211
00/1 BAP Mem. 507
01/2 BAP Mem. 412
99/0 Cardset 243
00/1 Cardset MB 3
02/3 Cardset 276
01/2 DS 35, IH10
97/8 DS Sticker 243
98/9 OFS 171, 459
99/0 OFS 271
00/1 Parkhurst P-157
01/2 Parkhurst 365
00/1 PS Titanium Draft 153
00/1 SP Authentic 91
00/1 UD Black Diam. 112
00/1 UD Ice 104
01/2 Victory 8

TENNANT, KEN
52/3 Anonymous 126

TENNANT, NATHAN
99/0 Kingston Frontenacs
00/1 Kingston Frontenacs 21
01/2 Kingston Frontenacs 22

TEPLYAKOV, DMITRI
99/0 Mir 190
00/1 Mir 67

TEPPER, STEPHEN
93/4 Roanoke Express

TERBENCHE, PAUL
70/1 O-Pee-Chee 123
73/4 O-Pee-Chee 229
75/6 OPC WHA 112
67/8 Topps 58
70/1 Topps 123
72/3 BUFF
73/4 BUFF
78/9 Winnipeg Jets

TEREKHOV, ALEXANDER
95/6 APS 323
98/9 Mir 25

TEREKHOV, VLADIMIR
00/1 Mir 282

TERESHENKO, ALEXEI
00/1 Dynamo 1

TERNAVSKI, ARTEM
00/1 Sherbrooke Castors 13

TERRERI, CHRIS
01/2 Atomic ✂ GWJ 39
98/9 Bicycle.. 5-C
91/2 Bowman 283
92/3 Bowman 386
01/2 Crown Royale ✂ TT 13
93/4 Donruss 194
94/5 Donruss 285
96/7 Donruss 38
93/4 EA Sports 78
96/7 Fleer 102
92/3 Fleer Ultra 120
93/4 Fleer Ultra 209
94/5 Fleer Ultra 323
95/6 Fleer Ultra 306
91/2 Gillette 38
93/4 Hockey Wit 31
92/3 Humpty Dumpty
92/3 Kraft / PB
93/4 Leaf 430
94/5 Leaf 134
96/7 Leaf 94
96/7 Maggers 129
90/1 OPC/Topps 284, 375
91/2 O-Pee-Chee 422
92/3 O-Pee-Chee 282
91/2 OPC Premier 197
98/9 Pacific 40
99/0 Pacific 249
00/1 Pacific 245
01/2 Pacific 254, ✂ GWJ 20
97/8 Pa. Crown Roy. 31
97/8 Pa. Invincible R-48
90/1 Panini Sticker 68
91/2 Panini Sticker 221
92/3 Panini Sticker 171
93/4 Panini Sticker D
94/5 Panini Sticker 36
96/7 Panini Sticker 280
91/2 Parkhurst 98
92/3 Parkhurst 93
93/4 Parkhurst 112
95/6 Parkhurst 451
94/5 Parkie SE94
91/2 Pinnacle 247
92/3 Pinnacle 274
93/4 Pinnacle 267
94/5 Pinnacle 335
96/7 Pinnacle 103
97/8 Pi. Be A Player 30, ✍ Aut. 30
96/7 Pi. Summit 89
94/5 POG 285
93/4 Power Play 144
93/4 Premier 213
94/5 Premier 13, 83
00/1 Pr. Stock ✂ GUG 66
00/1 PS Titanium ✂ GUG 107
00/1 PS Titanium Draft ✂ 64
90/1 Pro Set 481
91/2 Pro Set 137
92/3 Pro Set 97
91/2 Pro Set Platinum 68
91/2 Pro Set Platinum 288
88/9 ProCards / Utica
90/1 Score 239
91/2 Score 151
91/2 Score CAN 151
92/3 Score 270
93/4 Score 237
95/6 Score 243
96/7 Score 28
97/8 Score 48
91/2 Score Young Stars 15
92/3 Seasons 51
91 Semic Sticker 129
96/7 SBx Impact 119
95/6 SP 131
97/8 SP Authentic 33
92/3 Topps 303
95/6 To. Finest 149
91/2 To. Stadium 297
92/3 To. Stadium 74
93/4 To. Stadium 328
90/1 Upper Deck 183
91/2 Upper Deck 115
92/3 Upper Deck 43
93/4 Upper Deck 110
95/6 Upper Deck 450
96/7 Upper Deck 147
97/8 Upper Deck 40
98/9 Upper Deck 307
95/6 UD Be A Player 27, ✍ S27
96/7 UD CC 239, 330
98/9 UD G. Reserve 307
00/1 Vanguard ✂ DGJ 19
89/0 NJER
89/0 NJER / Caretta
90/1 NJER

TERRION, GREG
86/7 Kraft Sports 58
81/2 O-Pee-Chee 155
82/3 O-Pee-Chee 333
83/4 O-Pee-Chee 342
84/5 O-Pee-Chee 312
86/7 O-Pee-Chee 244
87/8 O-Pee-Chee 241
82/3 OPC/Topps Sticker 234
83/4 OPC/Topps Sticker 37
84/5 OPC Sticker 19
85/6 OPC Sticker 18-149
86/7 OPC Sticker 147-255
87/8 OPC Sticker 153-14
88/9 ProCards / Newmarket
83/4 Souhaits Keychain [Maple Leafs]
83/4 Vachon 99-122
82/3 TORO
83/4 TORO
84/5 TORO
85/6 TORO
86/7 TORO
86/7 TORO
87/8 TORO / 5x8
87/8 TORO / P.L.A.Y. 21

TERRIS, MARC
96/7 Peoria Rivermen
97/8 Peoria Rivermen

TERTYSHNY, ALEXEI
99/0 Mir 126
00/1 Mir 41

TERTYSHNY, DMITRI
99/0 BAP Mem. DT-5
98/9 Bowman's Best 118
98/9 Omega 179
98/9 Upper Deck 336
98/9 UD G. Reserve 336

TERTYSHNY, SERGEI
98/9 Mir 14
99/0 Mir 21
00/1 Mir 158
94/5 Portland Pirates
95/6 Portland Pirates
00/1 Metallurg 29

TERVO, HEIMO
65/6 Hellas 78

TERVONEN, KAI
92/3 Jyvas Hyva 14
93/4 Jyvas Hyva 25
93/4 Sisu 93

TERZO, ANTHONY
99/0 Huntington Blizzard

TESAREK, TOMAS
00/1 Prince George Cougars

TESARIK, DANIEL
96/7 APS 235

TESARIK, RADIM
94/5 APS 187
95/6 APS 36, 402
96/7 APS 31, 417
97/8 APS 30
97/8 DS 58
98/9 DS 79
99/0 DS 132
00/1 DS 18
96/7 DS Sticker 99
97/8 DS Sticker 170
98/9 OFS 101
99/0 OFS 66, 485, 528
00/1 OFS 326
01/2 OFS -UHI 4

TESKEY, DOUG
99/0 Fort Wayne Komets

TESSIER, BRIAN
86/7 Kingston Canadians

TESSIER, DAN
99 Bowman 132
00/1 Louisiana Ice Gators
99/0 Ottawa 67's

TESSIER, JASON
99/0 Rouyn-Noranda

TESSIER, ORVAL
52/3 Anonymous 104
60/1 Shirriff 114
82/3 CHIC
83/4 CHIC

TESSIER, PATRICK
91/2 7th...Sketch LHJMQ 34

TETARENKO, JOEY
01/2 BAP Update ✂ TC10
97 Bowman 86
01/2 Signature 133, ✍ Aut. 133
95/6 Upper Deck 523
99/0 Louisville Panthers
00/1 Louisville Panthers
98/9 New Haven Beast 18
97/8 Portland Winter Hawks

TETRAULT, DANIEL
97 Bowman 134, ✍ Aut.
96/7 Upper Deck 376
00/1 Austin Ice Bats
95/6 Brandon Wheat Kings
98/9 Brandon Wheat Kings
99/0 Brandon Wheat Kings

TÉTRAULT, ÉRIC
99 Québec Pee Wee 183

TETZLAFF, JEFF
95/6 Slapshot 25
98/9 Barrie Colts

TEXEIRA, CHUCK
92/3 Maine Black Bears
93/4 Maine Black Bears

TEZIKOV, ALEXEI
99/0 BAP Mem. 81
98 Bowman 118
98 Bowman Chrome 118
99/0 Millenium C-29
99/0 NHL Power Play
99/0 Omega 247
99/0 Pacific 450
99/0 Pa. Paramount 249
00/1 Topps 313
00/1 To. Chrome 208
99/0 Upper Deck 302
99/0 UD G. Reserve 302
99/0 Portland Pirates
00/1 Portland Pirates

THACKER, ROD
87/8 Soo Greyhounds 32

THALER, ALEX
95 Panini Worlds 83
94 Semic 297

THALER, CHRIS
00/1 Mississauga IceDogs

THANNER, RUDOLPH
72 Hellas MM-Jenkki 46

THEBERGE, EDOUARD
51/2 Bas du Fleuve 23

THEBERGE, GERRY
51/2 Lac St-Jean 14

THEBERGE, GREG
82/3 Post [Wash.]
81/2 WASH

THELIN, MATS
89/0 Semic Elitserien 4
90/1 Semic Elitserien 78
91/2 Semic Elitserien 6
92/3 Semic Elitserien 29
82 Semic Sticker 8
84/5 BOST

THELVEN, MICHAEL
87/8 OPC/Topps 24
87/8 Panini Sticker 9
88/9 Panini Sticker 206
88/9 BOST / Sports Action
89/0 BOST / Sports Action

THÉODORE, JOSÉ
01/2 Adrenaline 101, CL 10, PP 20
01/2 Atomic 53
02/3 Atomic 57, -D 10, -GWJ 11
00/1 Aurora 75, Pins. 75, ✍ Aut. 75
02/3 BAP All-Star 91, ✂ ASJ, Bobble
98/9 Be A Player 219, ✍ Aut. 219
00/1 BAP Mem. 287
01/2 BAP Mem. ✂ CoO, ✂ GJ, ✂ GT
02/3 BAP Mem. 93, 216, ✂ ASJ55, ✂ ASE24, ✂ ASN24, ✂ AST26, ✂ FP16, ✂ FG6, ✂ HSHSJers 15, ✂ SC6, ✂ TM12
01/2 BAP Update HSHS, ✂ HSHSJers (x2)
01/2 BT Pipes 44, HSHS, -Mask, ✂ DM, ✂ GJ, ✂ S&J, ✂ GG, ✂ GT, ✂ HSHS Jers.
02/3 Between the Pipes 2, 136, M16, ✂ ASJ10, ✂ BM11, ✂ DM5, ✂ GUE14, ✂ FW2, ✂ GUJ14, ✂ GP6, ✂ GSJ14, ✂ HSHSJers 20, ✂ ITN14, ✂ I3, ✂ T9, ✍ Aut.
98/9 Bicycle.. 9-H
01/2 Bowman 26
02/3 Bowman 72
98/9 Bowman's Best F19
02/3 Calder 43, -HH 7
99/0 Crown Royale 73
00/1 Crown Royale 58
01/2 Crown Royale 79, ✂ TT 4
02/3 Crown Royale 52, COA 5, ✂ GWJ 9
96/7 Donruss 227
97/8 Donruss 81, BTP-6
96/7 Do. Canadian LG-10
97/8 Do. Canadian LG 6, SCS-14
95/6 Do. Elite WJ 2
96/7 Do. Elite 139
97/8 Do. Preferred 102, CG-11
97/8 Do. Studio 24
02/3 eTopps 7
02/3 Exclusive 94, -EA 10
02/3 First Edition 138, 314, 356, 377, ✂ Jers., ✂ HSHSJers 25
96/7 Flair 112
96/7 Fleer 134, CC-9
00 Gatorade Sticker
01/2 Heads Up 52, HD 16, SS 11
02/3 Heads Up 66, -ITN 12, -PSP 9, -S 12, ✂ GWQ 15, / Bobble
02/3 In The GU 39, 139, ✂ E13, ✂ F16, ✂ GP1, ✂ GUJ13, ✂ SJ13, ✂ T6
96/7 Leaf GLR 3
97/8 Leaf 122, PD-9
97/8 Limited 81, 161, 162, FG-71
99/0 McDonald's McD-16, ✍ SS
01/2 McDonald's 22, -GNFS 3
02/3 McDonald's 22, -GSNF 4, ✂ JP 8
02/3 Mike's Restaurant
01/2 O-Pee-Chee 98
02/3 O-Pee-Chee 190, 319
99/0 Omega 123
99/0 Pacific 212
00/1 Pacific 215, IO-11, ✍ Aut. 215
01/2 Pacific 213, SC 10
02/3 Pacific 203, -MA 10, -MI 4, ✂ GWJ 27
02/3 Pacific Complete 412
97/8 Pa. Invincible R-107
00/1 Pa. Paramount 132, GS-11
01/2 PTC Collectors 5
02/3 PTC/ Les Gardiens 5
00/1 Parkhurst P-94
01/2 Parkhurst 74
02/3 Parkhurst 93, -HHH 5, -HHV 3, ✂ FP16, ✂ GJ2, ✂ HSHSJers, ✂ SJ2, ✂ MM10, ✂ TT7
02/3 Parkhurst Retro 135, ✂ RF16, ✂ RJ24, ✂ RSJ17, ✂ HSHSJers, ✂ RM7
96/7 Pinnacle 217
97/8 Pi. Inside 56, S-14
96/7 Pi. Summit 182
00/1 Pr. Stock 53, PS-29, PSNW-11
01/2 Pr. Stock 51, ✂ GUG 55
02/3 Pr. Stock Reserve -ICS 12, ✂ 127
00/1 PS Titanium 50
01/2 PS Titanium 76, SK 11, TAS 12, ✂ DSJ 20
02/3 Pr. Stock Titanium 57, -MM 4, -SK 5, ✂ GWJ GWJ 36
02/3 Quest for the Cup 52, -CTC 8
00/1 Revolution 79, SM-15
96/7 Score 267
97/8 Score 42
97/8 Score Mont. 3
94/5 Sig. Rookies 10, ✍ 10
94/5 SR Auto-Phonex B5, ✍ B5
00/1 Signature 44, ✍ Aut. 195
01/2 Signature ✂ FP16, ✂ GU85, ✂ TM16
02/3 Signature Series 65, ✍ 65, ✂ FJ16, ✂ SGJ13, ✂ TQ6
96/7 SBx Impact 161
94/5 Slapshot Memorial 73
96/7 SP 174
97/8 SP Authentic ✍ SotT
99/0 SP Authentic 45
00/1 SP Authentic 46, ✍ SotT
01/2 SP Authentic 43
02/3 SP Authentic 47, ✂ SP, ✂ DP
00/1 SP GU 32
01/2 SP GU 28, ✂ AF, ✂ AFD, ✂✍ ISD, ✂✍ PatchSig, ✂ TotG, ✂ TotGSig, ✂ TotGC
02/3 SP GU Edition 25, ✂ AF, ✂ CF, ✂ PH, ✂ TG
02/3 Sports Vault 60
01/2 SPx ✂ DT, ✂ TT
02/3 SPx 40, 92, ✂ WM, ✂ X
99/0 Stadium 144
00/1 Stadium ✍ LS6
01/2 Stadium 38
02/3 Stadium 1, -BT5, -PSH4, ✍ LSS
99/0 Topps 195
00/1 Topps 25, ✍ CAI
01/2 Topps 98
02/3 Topps 190, 319, HHC9
99/0 To. Chrome 195
00/1 To. Chrome 24
01/2 To. Chrome 98
02/3 T. Chrome 109
00/1 To. Heritage 162, 233
01/2 To. Heritage 41
02/3 To. Heritage 3, 105, 116, 129, -Light 3
02/3 To. Limited 190, 319
01/2 To. Reserve 76
02/3 To. Total 31, TTC16, AW4, TT4
00/1 UD Heroes 63
01/2 UD PlayMakers Ltd 53
00/1 UD Reserve 45, GG5
02/3 UD Superstars 138
01/2 Ultimate Mem. ✂ BAPL, ✂ LC
02/3 Ultimate Memorabilia ✂ GUJ, ✂ GUSJ, ✂ RAT, ✍ RAut
95/6 Upper Deck 530
96/7 Upper Deck 279
97/8 Upper Deck 85, SG60, T12C
98/9 Upper Deck 114, GN8
00/1 Upper Deck 96, RP3, ✂ DGJ
01/2 Upper Deck 320, ✂ TendThr.
02/3 Upper Deck 92, -LL7, -SA7, ✂ ASJ, ✂ ASP, ✂ DM, ✂ GT, ✂ PN, ✂ SV, ✂ FC, ✂ PW, ✂ UDPL
02/3 UD Artistic 49, R49, ✂ AT, / Art
96/7 UD Black Diam. 116
00/1 UD Black Diam. 30
02/3 UD Classic 53, ET9, ✂ CS, ✂ HH, ✂ HR
96/7 UD CC 351
97/8 UD Coll. Choice 135, / 5x7 3
98/9 UD G. Reserve 114
02/3 UD Honor 38
96/7 UD Ice 90
97/8 UD Ice 36
00/1 UD Ice 22
01/2 UD Ice 25
00/1 UD Legends 72
01/2 UD Mask 116, -GP, ✂ GJ, ✂ JP, ✂ DP, ✂ MB, ✂ StS, ✂ SuS, / Mask
02/3 UD Mask 45, 46, 47, 97, ✂ GG, ✂ MM, ✂ BM, ✂ NB, ✂ PW, ✂ SS, ✂ VC, / Mask, ✍ Mask
98/9 UD MVP ✍ PS
00/1 UD MVP 92
01/2 UD MVP 100, ✂ GS
02/3 UD MVP 96, MM3
99/0 UD MVP Cup 93
02/3 UD Piece 48, ✂ PH, ✂ TT
01/2 UD Premier 30, ✂ B, ✂ D, ✍ Sig
02/3 UD Premier 31, ✂ Jers, ✂ JD, ✂ Patch
00/1 UD Pros&Prosp. 44
02/3 UD Rookie 54, ✂ DJ
01/2 UD Top Shelf 98, ✂ GG-LP, ✂ J, ✂✍ SJ
02/3 UD Top Shelf 45, ✂ R, ✂ ST, ✂ SS, ✂ SW, ✍ Sig
00/1 UD Vintage 193, 196, 197, GG11, ✂ O6-POH
01/2 UD Vintage 134, 139
02/3 UD Vintage 134, 276, 318, 319, T35, ✂ OS
00/1 Vanguard 53
01/2 Vanguard 52, SW 10, ✂ DGM 32, ✂ DGM 43
02/3 Vanguard 57, -SW 6, -VT 4, ✂ GWJ 25
99/0 Victory 153
00/1 Victory 121
01/2 Victory 182, 186
02/3 Victory 109
00/1 MONT
01/2 MONT
02/3 MONT
96/7 Fredericton Canadiens

THÉORET, LUC
99 Bowman 100
98 Bowman 65
98 Bowman Chrome 65
96/7 Upper Deck 377
95/6 Lethbridge Hurricanes

THERIAULT, PATRICK
92/3 Clarkson G'Knights

THERIAULT, PAUL
81/2 Oshawa Generals
82/3 Oshawa Generals
83/4 Oshawa Generals

THÉRIAULT, JOEL
96/7 Hampton Roads
97/8 Hampton Roads
95/6 Halifax Moosehead

THÉRIAULT, PATRICE
00/1 Rouyn-Noranda 14

THERIEN, CHRIS
93/4 Canada Nationals
93/4 Classic 84
94/5 Cla. Images 32
93/4 Cla. Prospects IA6
93/4 Cla. Prospects LP19
95/6 Donruss 72
95/6 Edge Ice 47, C-9
02/3 First Edition 181
94/5 Flair 132
94/5 Fleer 159
95/6 Fleer Metal 114
93/4 Fleer Ultra 474
94/5 Fleer Ultra 347
95/6 Fleer Ultra 121
94/5 Leaf 480
95/6 Leaf 18
98/9 OPC Chrome 144
98/9 Pacific 332
99/0 Pacific 312
00/1 Pacific 307
02/3 Pacific Complete 62
97/8 Pa. Invincible R-148
95/6 Panini Sticker 118, 301
95/6 Parkhurst 156
94/5 Parkie SE127
94/5 Pinnacle 495
95/6 Pinnacle 165
95/6 Playoff 296
93/4 Power Play 495
93/4 Premier - Canada 9
94/5 Premier 322
94/5 Score CT19
95/6 Score 98
97/8 Score 256
97/8 Score Phil. 15
95/6 SBx Emotion 135
95/6 SBx Impact 129, F-8
98/9 SPx Finite 63
95/6 Topps 364, 12NG
98/9 Topps 144
94/5 Topps Finest 13
98/9 UD Choice 154
94/5 Upper Deck 248
95/6 Upper Deck 107
98/9 Upper Deck 338, ✂ GJ21
95/6 UD BAP 21, ✍ S21
95/6 UD CC 184, 374
96/7 UD CC 197
98/9 UD G. Reserve 338
00/1 UD Vintage 270
94/5 PHIL / Sheet
94/5 PHIL / Sheet
96/7 PHIL / Ocean Spray
01/2 PHIL

THÉRIEN, GASTON
96/7 Rimouski Océanic

THERRIEN, GASTON*
82/3 Fredericton Express

THERRIEN, MICHEL
00/1 MONT
01/2 MONT
02/3 MONT
83/4 Nova Scotia Voyageurs
80/1 Québec Remparts

THERRIEN, PIERRE-LUC
99 Bowman 62
97 Bowman 140, BB20, ✍ Aut.
96/7 Upper Deck 372

THÉRRIEN, BENOÎT
90/1 7th..Sketch LHJMQ 68
91/2 7th...Sketch LHJMQ 47

THÉRRIEN, MARIO
90/1 7th..Sketch LHJMQ 86
91/2 7th...Sketch LHJMQ 36

THIBAUDEAU, GILLES
90/1 Panini Sticker 288
90/1 Pro Set 290
87/8 MONT
88/9 MONT
89/0 NYIS
86/7 Sherb. Canadiens 27

THIBAULT, DANIEL
90/1 7th..Sketch LHJMQ 87
91/2 7th...Sketch LHJMQ 110

THIBAULT, ÉTIENNE
91/2 7th...Sketch LHJMQ 13

THIBAULT, GILLES
52/3 Anonymous 76

THIBAULT, JOCELYN
01/2 Adrenaline 42, CL 3, PP 8
01/2 Atomic 21, ✂ GWJ 10
02/3 Atomic 21, -D 4
98/9 Aurora 98
99/0 Aurora 33, -GU 5
00/1 Aurora 34
98/9 Be A Player 66, ✍ Aut. 66
99/0 BAP Mem. 293
00/1 BAP Mem. 189
01/2 BAP Mem. 12, ✂ GJ, ✂ GT
02/3 BAP Mem. 75, 232
01/2 BT Pipes 18, 102, HSHS, ✂ DM, ✂ GJ, ✂ GE, ✂ S&J, ✂ GG, ✂ GT, ✂ HSHSJers, ✂ ITN
02/3 Between the Pipes 21, 127, M7, ✂ BM10, ✂ CP8, ✂ DM13, ✂ GUE13, ✂ GB6, ✂ GUJ13, ✂ GP14, ✂ GSJ13, ✂ GT14, ✂ HSHSJers 18, ✂ ITN13, ✂ T3, ✍ Aut.
96/7 Bic.Sports Aces 6-H
98/9 Bicycle.. 8-D
01/2 Bowman 41
02/3 Bowman 23
98/9 Bowman's Best 92
93/4 Classic 10
93/4 Classic - Top Ten DP10
93/4 Cla. 4 Sport 194
94/5 Cla. Images 6, CE6, ✍ Aut.
93/4 Cla. Images 4 Sport 74
93/4 Cla. Images 4 Sport SI7
93/4 Cla. Prospects 39
99/0 Crown Royale 34
00/1 Crown Royale 24
01/2 Crown Royale 34
02/3 Crown Royale 21
93/4 Donruss 275
93/4 Donruss RR 11
94/5 Donruss 71
95/6 Donruss 97
96/7 Donruss 101, BTP-7, D-2
97/8 Donruss 35, BTP-10
96/7 Do. Canadian 2, LG-2
97/8 Do. Canadian 15, LG-7
95/6 Do. Elite 1, PW-7
96/7 Do. Elite 6, PW-5
97/8 Do. Elite 88, BF-2, ✍ BF-2
97/8 Do. Preferred 87, CG-9
97/8 Do. Priority 78, OD-21, PG-6, Post-36, Stamp-36
97/8 Do. Studio 77
93/4 Durivage 3, ✍ Aut.
98/9 Dynagon Ice 98
99/0 Dynagon Ice 52
02/3 eTopps 56
02/3 Exclusive 37
02/3 First Edition 14, 409R, ✂ Jers.
96/7 Flair 51, HG-11
96/7 Fleer 56
96/7 Fl. Picks 82
93/4 Fleer Ultra 406
93/4 Fleer Ultra WotF 18
94/5 Fleer Ultra 361
x95/6 Fleer Ultra 258, HS-19, RS-8
96/7 Fl. Ultra 90
01/2 Heads Up 20, ✂ JQ 6
02/3 Heads Up 26, -S 5
02/3 In The GU 11, 111, ✂ GP4
96/7 Kraft / TT
93/4 Leaf 428
93/4 Leaf FP 10
94/5 Leaf 231, GLR-15
95/6 Leaf 97
96/7 Leaf 182, SD-3, TBO-9
97/8 Leaf 42, PD-12
94/5 L. Limited 15
95/6 L. Limited 79
96/7 L. Limited 44
96/7 L. Preferred 73, LS-55, MM-8
97/8 Limited 44, 123, FG-62
96/7 Maggers 82
96/7 McDonald's McD-36
98/9 McDonald's McD19
96/7 Metal Univ. 83
99/0 Millenium 61, ✍ Aut. 61
99/0 NHL Power Play
01/2 O-Pee-Chee 209
02/3 O-Pee-Chee 222
98/9 OPC Chrome 217
97/8 Omega 124
98/9 Omega 55
99/0 Omega 56
98/9 Pacific 258
99/0 Pacific 97
00/1 Pacific 103
01/2 Pacific 93, SC 4
02/3 Pacific 83
02/3 Pacific Complete 411
97/8 Pacific CC 168, ITC-11
98/9 Pa. Crown Roy. 31
97/8 Pa. Dynagon 66, S-11, T-13
97/8 Pa. Invincible 74
98/9 Pa. Paramount 119
99/0 Pa. Paramount 58, -GS 5
00/1 Pa. Paramount 54, GS-6
97/8 Pa. Revolution 74
98/9 Pa. Revolution 32
02/3 PTC/ Les Gardiens 2
98/9 Panini Photocard
94/5 Panini Sticker 62
95/6 Panini Sticker 254
96/7 Panini Sticker 36
98/9 Panini Sticker 35
93/4 Parkhurst 247
93/4 Parkhurst C16
94/5 Parkhurst 189, 275, V61
95/6 Parkhurst 53, 384
00/1 Parkhurst P-147
01/2 Parkhurst 121, ✂ T9
02/3 Parkhurst 63, ✂ TT13
02/3 Parkhurst Retro 132, ✂ RF7, ✂ RJ38, ✂ RSJ30, ✂ VH6
93/4 Pinnacle 440
94/5 Pinnacle 205, GT18
95/6 Pinnacle 158, M-10
96/7 Pinnacle 142, BTN-13, M-5
97/8 Pinnacle 98
96/7 Pi. Be A Player SP-15
97/8 Pi. Be A Player 10, STP-9, ✍ Aut. 10
97/8 Pi. BeeHive 32
97/8 Pi. Certified 26
97/8 Pi. Inside 43, IT-17, SU-3, S-15, / Can 6, LargeCan
96/7 Pi. Mint 27
95/6 Pi. Summit 29, ITC-7
96/7 Pi. Summit 102, ITC-11
97/8 Pi. Totally 26
95/6 Pi. Zenith 34
96/7 Pi. Zenith 69, ZT-11
95/6 Playoff 29
96/7 Playoff 336
93/4 Power Play 426
93/4 Power Play RooS 15
93/4 Premier 393
94/5 Premier 123
00/1 Premier Plus 40
99/0 Prism 35
00/1 Pr. Stock 20, -PSNW-7
01/2 Pr. Stock 19, -PS 14, ✂ GUG 26
02/3 Pr. Stock Reserve 21, -ICS 4
00/1 PS Titanium 18
01/2 PS Titanium 32
02/3 Pr. Stock Titanium 23
00/1 PS Titanium Draft ✂ 21
02/3 Quest for the Cup 18
99/0 Revolution 35, / CSC 35
00/1 Revolution 32
93/4 Score 593
94/5 Score 250
95/6 Score 131
96/7 Score 96, NW-9, SD-8
97/8 Score 41, NW-11
97/8 Score Mont. 2
95/6 Select CE 30, CF-4
96/7 Select CE 3, F-12
91/2 7th...Sketch LHJMQ 123
00/1 Signature 189, ✍ Aut. 138
01/2 Signature ✂ GU90
02/3 Signature Series 43, ✍ 43, ✂ FJ7
95/6 SBx Emotion 43
95/6 SBx Impact 42, D-7
96/7 SBx Impact 65
02/3 Slam Card
95/6 SP 76
96/7 SP 81,HC-11
02/3 SP Authentic 19
02/3 SP GU ✂ AF, ✂ CF, ✂ PH (x2)
02/3 Sports Vault 180
99/0 SPx 36
00/1 SPx ✂ WM
01/2 SPx 164, ✂ DT (x2), ✂ TT
02/3 SPx 15
00/1 Stadion 193
99/0 Stadium 128
00/1 Stadium 22, PP4
02/3 Stadium 90
95/6 Topps 343
98/9 Topps 217
99/0 Topps 176
00/1 Topps 85
01/2 Topps 209
02/3 Topps 222
99/0 To. Chrome 176
00/1 To. Chrome 67
01/2 To. Chrome 126
02/3 T. Chrome 122
98/9 To. Finest C18
00/1 To. Gold Label 21
00/1 To. Heritage 154
02/3 To. Heritage 61
02/3 To. Limited 222
93/4 To. Stadium 479
94/5 To. Stadium 114
95/6 To. Stadium 98
00/1 To. Stars 83
02/3 To. Total 24, TTC6
00/1 UD Heroes 25
01/2 UD PlayMakers Ltd 21
00/1 Ultimate Mem. ✂ G-7, ✂ PJ-13
01/2 Ultimate Mem. ✂ BAPL, ✂ CP
93/4 Upper Deck 394, SP-133
94/5 Upper Deck 147
95/6 Upper Deck 369, SE-131
96/7 Upper Deck 83, X5, SS11B
97/8 Upper Deck 90
98/9 Upper Deck 295
99/0 Upper Deck 204
00/1 Upper Deck 267
01/2 Upper Deck 41, ✂ TendThr.
02/3 Upper Deck ✂ GT, ✂ SV
02/3 UD Artistic 19, R19, / Art
95/6 UD BAP 199, ✍ S199
96/7 UD Black Diam. 41
02/3 UD Classic 22, ✂ HR (x2)
95/6 UD CC 316
96/7 UD CC 136, 321
97/8 UD Coll. Choice 134
98/9 UD G. Reserve 295
99/0 UD G. Reserve 204
02/3 UD Honor 14
96/7 UD Ice 91, S4
00/1 UD Ice ✂ IGJ I
01/2 UD Mask 107, ✂ GJ, ✂ JP, ✂ DP, ✂ MM, ✂ MB, ✂ PM, ✂ StS
02/3 UD Mask 19, 20, 96, ✂ CW, ✂ MM, ✂ PW, ✂ VC
98/9 UD MVP 42
99/0 UD MVP 47
00/1 UD MVP 43
01/2 UD MVP MM4
02/3 UD MVP 41
02/3 UD Piece 20
01/2 UD Premier 10, ✂ D
02/3 UD Premier 12
02/3 UD Rookie 23
02/3 UD Top Shelf 18, ✂ ST, ✂ SS, ✂ SW, ✂ TS
00/1 UD Vintage 79, 85, 86
02/3 UD Vintage 58, 267, GB 58, T14
00/1 Vanguard 23
01/2 Vanguard 22, QTH 11
02/3 Vanguard 24
99/0 Victory 71
00/1 Victory 55
01/2 Victory 71, 78
02/3 Victory 44
97/8 Zenith 65, CTC-9, Z33
96-98 MONT
94/5 QUÉB / Burger King

THIBAULT, LARRY
52/3 Anonymous 102

THIBEAULT, DAVID
99 Bowman 80
97 Bowman 78
98 Bowman 96
98 Bowman Chrome 96

THIBEAULT, MARC
91/2 7th...Sketch LHJMQ 254

THIBERT, BENOÎT
99/0 Indianapolis Ice

THIBODEAU, MATHIEU
00/1 Sherbrooke Castors 17

THIEL, ROB
87/8 Kitchener Rangers
88/9 Kitchener Rangers

THIELE, GEORG
94/5 Anchorage Aces 22

THIESSEN, KELLY
90/1 7th..Sketch WHL 64
89/0 Brandon Wheat Kings

THIESSEN, TRAVIS
90/1 7th..Sketch WHL 145
91/2 7th...Sketch WHL 277
92/3 Cleveland Lumberjacks
93/4 Cleveland Lumberjacks
99/0 Colorado Gold Kings
94/5 Indianapolis Ice
95/6 Peoria Rivermen

THIETKE, MARK
84/5 Kamloops Blazers
83/4 Saskatoon Blades

THIFFAULT, CHARLES
90/1 MONT
91/2 MONT
81/2 QUÉB
82/3 QUÉB
85/6 QUÉB
85/6 QUÉB / Gene. Foods
86/7 QUÉB
86/7 QUÉB / Gene. Foods

THIFFAULT, MAURICE
51/2 Lac St-Jean 33

THINEL, MARC-ANDRÉ
99 Bowman 27, 76, 164, ✍ BA14
95 Québec Pee Wee 448
00/1 SP Authentic 128
00/1 SP GU 85
00/1 SPx ✂ 127
00/1 UD Reserve 115
00/1 Upper Deck 203
00/1 UD Black Diam. 68
00/1 UD Ice 48
00/1 UD Pros&Prosp. 127
00/1 UD Vintage 394
01/2 Québec Citadelles
00/1 Victoriaville Tigres 9

THINEL, SÉBASTIEN
01/2 Québec Remparts 23
00/1 Victoriaville Tigres 22

THIVIERGE, STÉPH.
95/6 DEL 286

THOLSON, STAFFAN
91/2 Semic Elitserien 307
92/3 Semic Nordisk 72

THOM, HENRY
95/6 DEL 311
THOMA, BRYCE
00/1 Red Deer Rebels
THOMAS, BILL
32/3 Maple Leafs O'Keefe
THOMAS, CY
45-54 Quaker Oats
THOMAS, GORD
84/5 Ottawa 67's
THOMAS, KAHLIL
98/9 Flint Generals
THOMAS, REG
76/7 OPC WHA 82
77/8 OPC WHA 29
THOMAS, RYAN
01/2 Vancouver Giants
THOMAS, SCOTT
92/3 Classic 74
92/3 Classic Four Sport 198
92/3 Classic Prospects 19
92/3 Classic Prospects 125
98/9 EBK IHL All-Star
93/4 Leaf 360
93/4 Parkhurst 25
93/4 Power Play 302
93/4 Premier 336
93/4 Score 469
90/1 7th..Sketch WHL 143
91/2 7th...Sketch WHL 165
93/4 To. Stadium 471
93/4 Upper Deck 247
95/6 Cincinnati Cyclones
96/7 Cincinnati Cyclones
97/8 Detroit Vipers
01/2 Manchester Monarchs
98/9 Manitoba Moose
00/1 Manitoba Moose
92/3 Rochester Americans DD
92/3 Rochester Americans WPC
93/4 Rochester Americans
THOMAS, STEVE
92/3 American Licorice 6
99/0 Aurora 139
00/1 Aurora 141
99/0 BAP Mem. 148
00/1 BAP Mem. 42
01/2 BAP Mem. 492
02/3 BAP Mem. 346
90/1 Bowman 4, -HT 13
91/2 Bowman 391
92/3 Bowman 117
95/6 Bowman 19
93/4 Donruss 208
94/5 Donruss 142
95/6 Donruss 32, 363
96/7 Donruss 193
95/6 Do. Elite 71
99/0 Dynagon Ice 191
93/4 EA Sports 82
94/5 Flair 108
94/5 Fleer 129, SA-10
96/7 Fleer 62
95/6 Fleer Metal 88
92/3 Fleer Ultra 131
93/4 Fleer Ultra 216
94/5 Fleer Ultra 132
95/6 Fleer Ultra 263
96/7 Fl. Ultra 97
95/6 Hoyle / East. 10-Club
92/3 Humpty Dumpty
86/7 Kraft Sports 59
93/4 Leaf 81
94/5 Leaf 67
95/6 Leaf 125
96/7 Leaf 25
94/5 L. Limited 6
95/6 L. Limited 84
99/0 McDonald's ✍ SS
01/2 McDonald's -HP 10
96/7 Metal Univ. 90
86/7 O-Pee-Chee 245
87/8 OPC/Topps 188
88/9 O-Pee-Chee 259
90/1 OPC/Topps 92
91/2 O-Pee-Chee 210
92/3 O-Pee-Chee 395
01/2 O-Pee-Chee 134
89/0 OPC/Topps 82
91/2 OPC Premier 195
86/7 OPC Sticker 135-121
86/7 OPC Sticker 140-250
87/8 OPC Sticker 154-15
89/0 opcSticker 15-157
98/9 Omega 232
99/0 Omega 229
98/9 Pacific 274
99/0 Pacific 417
00/1 Pacific 400
01/2 Pacific 374
02/3 Pacific 84
02/3 Pacific Complete 142
97/8 Pacific CC 195
99/0 Pa. Paramount 231
00/1 Pa. Paramount 234
87/8 Panini Sticker 329
88/9 Panini Sticker 30
89/0 Panini Sticker 50
91/2 Panini Sticker 14
92/3 Panini Sticker 203
93/4 Panini Sticker 57
94/5 Panini Sticker 51
95/6 Panini Sticker 95
96/7 Panini Sticker 78
99/0 Panini Sticker 154
00/1 Panini Sticker 97
95 Panini Worlds 22
91/2 Parkhurst 105
92/3 Parkhurst 338
92/3 Parkhurst 454
93/4 Parkhurst 124
94/5 Parkhurst V68
95/6 Parkhurst 390
00/1 Parkhurst P-131
01/2 Parkhurst 372
94/5 Parkie SE102
91/2 Pinnacle 116
92/3 Pinnacle 128
93/4 Pinnacle 173
94/5 Pinnacle 52, BR11
96/7 Pinnacle 53
97/8 Pi. Be A Player 71, ✍ Aut. 71
95/6 Pi. Summit 161
96/7 Pi. Summit 31
95/6 Pi. Zenith 114, GG-18
96/7 Pi. Zenith 33
95/6 Playoff 169
94/5 POG 159
95/6 POG 158
93/4 Power Play 154
93/4 Premier 300
94/5 Premier 495, TF-14
90/1 Pro Set 62
91/2 Pro Set 45
91/2 Pro Set 438
92/3 Pro Set 106
91/2 Pro Set Platinum 203
99/0 Revolution 141, / CSC 141
90/1 Score 66
90/1 Sco. Hot Cards 30
91/2 Score 94
91/2 Score 51T
91/2 Score CAN 94
92/3 Score 12
93/4 Score 141
94/5 Score 37
95/6 Score 226
96/7 Score 64
97/8 Score NJer. 10
94/5 Select 105
00/1 Signature 152, ✍ Aut. 17
95/6 SBx Impact 98
96/7 SBx Impact 73
94/5 SP 71
95/6 SP 80
92/3 Topps 222
95/6 Topps 256
99/0 Topps 115
00/1 Topps 191
01/2 Topps 134
99/0 To. Chrome 115
00/1 To. Chrome 127
94/5 Topps Finest 37
95/6 To. Finest 14
96/7 To. Picks 75
91/2 To. Stadium 109
92/3 To. Stadium 369
93/4 To. Stadium 195
94/5 To. Stadium 80
95/6 To. Stadium 16
00/1 To. Stars 89, PP4
02/3 To. Total 375
90/1 Upper Deck 221
91/2 Upper Deck 162
91/2 Upper Deck 534
92/3 Upper Deck 171
93/4 Upper Deck 122, SP-95
94/5 Upper Deck 275, SP-139
95/6 Upper Deck 472, SE-136
96/7 Upper Deck 284
98/9 Upper Deck 374
99/0 Upper Deck 124
00/1 Upper Deck 162
01/2 Upper Deck 271
94/5 UD BAP R171, ✍ 145
95/6 UD CC 248
96/7 UD CC 145, 322, C16, CR16
98/9 UD G. Reserve 374
99/0 UD G. Reserve 124
96/7 UD Ice 37
98/9 UD MVP 196
99/0 UD MVP 200
00/1 UD MVP 170
00/1 UD Vintage 337
99/0 Victory 287
00/1 Victory 223
99/0 WGretzky 161
87/8 CHIC / Coke
88/9 CHIC / Coke
89/0 CHIC / Coke
90/1 CHIC / Coke
96/7 NJER / Sharp
85/6 TORO
86/7 TORO
86/7 TORO
99/0 TORO / Pizza Pizza 10
THOMAS, TIM
02/3 BAP All-Star 116
02/3 BAP Mem. 383
02/3 Between the Pipes 63, ✂ GUJ38
02/3 Cardset 277
02/3 Crown Royale 104
02/3 Parkhurst 244
02/3 Pr. Stock Reserve 154
02/3 Pr. Stock Titanium 106
02/3 Quest for the Cup 106
02/3 SP Authentic 137
02/3 T. Chrome 162
02/3 Ultimate Memorabilia 45
02/3 Upper Deck 429
00/1 UD Elitserien 1, M1
02/3 UD Honor 104
02/3 UD Mask 143
02/3 UD Premier 45
02/3 UD Top Shelf 91
02/3 Vanguard 104
99/0 Detroit Vipers
THOMAS, WAYNE
72/3 Dernière Heure
73/4 Dernière Heure
75/6 Hockey Heroes
74/5 Loblaws Update
73/4 O-Pee-Chee 221
75/6 O-Pee-Chee 347
76/7 O-Pee-Chee 84
77/8 O-Pee-Chee 19
78/9 O-Pee-Chee 166
79/0 O-Pee-Chee 126
88/9 ProCards / Peoria
89/0 ProCards IHL 23
76/7 Topps 84
77/8 Topps 19
78/9 Topps 166
79/0 Topps 126
87/8 CHIC / Coke
73/4 MONT / Pro Star
74/5 MONT
75/6 TORO
76/7 TORO
THOMERSON, BOB
74/5 Sioux City Musketeers
THOMLINSON, DAVE
90/1 Bowman 21
88/9 ProCards / Peoria
89/0 ProCards IHL 15
90/1 ProCards 82
91/2 ProCards 53
91/2 Upper Deck 557
89/0 SLOU / Kodak
92/3 Binghampton Rangers
97/8 Manitoba Moose
94/5 Phoenix Roadrunners
95/6 Phoenix Roadrunners
83/4 Brandon Wheat Kings
84/5 Brandon Wheat Kings
85/6 Brandon Wheat Kings
THOMPSON, ADAM
81/2 Saskatoon Blades
91/2 L. Superior State Lakers
THOMPSON, BILLY
99/0 Prince George Cougars
00/1 Prince George Cougars
THOMPSON, BLAINE
93/4 Soo Greyhounds 21
THOMPSON, BRENT
93/4 Premier 406
91/2 ProCards 402
92/3 Score 455
90/1 7th..Sketch WHL 43
92/3 Topps 161
92/3 To. Stadium 92
93/4 To. Stadium 489
91/2 Upper Deck 608
97/8 Hartford Wolf Pack
98/9 Hartford Wolf Pack
01/2 Hershey Bears
02/3 Hershey Bears
99/0 Louisville Panthers
00/1 Louisville Panthers
96/7 Springfield Falcons
THOMPSON, BRETT
95/6 Slapshot 83
95/6 Guelph Storm
96/7 Guelph Storm
THOMPSON, BRIANE
91/2 7th...Sketch OHL 317
93/4 Slapshot / S.S.Marie 19
01/2 Florida Everblades
02/3 Nottingham Panthers
THOMPSON, BRYAN
01/2 London Knights
THOMPSON, CECIL (TINY)
34-43 BeeHive-1 [Bost.]
01/2 BT Pipes 129, ✂ 134, ✂ TW, ✂ VM
02/3 Between the Pipes 111, ✂ VM14
91/2 BOST / SA Legends
39/0 Bruins Magazine
33-35 Diamond Match Silv.
83 HHOF Postcard A16
83&87 HHOF 15
02/3 In The GU ✂ VM4
29/0 La Presse
33/4 O-Pee-Chee 68
39/0 O-Pee-Chee 75
02/3 Parkhurst ✂ VM13, ✂ VT19
94/5 Parkie Tall 9
34/5 Sweet Caporal
60/1 Topps 55
02/3 Ultimate Memorabilia ✂ Cor, ✂ SCD, ✍ Cut
33/4 WWGum 57
37/8 World Wide Gum 12
THOMPSON, CHAD
91/2 Knoxville Cherokees
01/2 London Knights
THOMPSON, CHARLIE
88/9 ProCards / Peoria
THOMPSON, CHRIS
95/6 Slapshot 8
98/9 Albany River Rats
THOMPSON, COREY
91/2 Air Canada SJHL B4
THOMPSON, DALLAS
99/0 Prince George Cougars
92/3 Tacoma Rockets
93/4 Tacoma Rockets
THOMPSON, DANNY
94/5 Humberside Hawks 14
THOMPSON, DEREK
87/8 Sudbury Wolves
88/9 Sudbury Wolves
THOMPSON, DEWAR
52/3 Laval Dairy Update 53
52/3 St. Lawrence 88
THOMPSON, ERROL
75/6 Hockey Heroes
74/5 Loblaws
75/6 O-Pee-Chee 114
76/7 O-Pee-Chee 259
76/7 O-Pee-Chee 394
77/8 O-Pee-Chee 293
78/9 O-Pee-Chee 57
79/0 O-Pee-Chee 106
80/1 O-Pee-Chee 234
75/6 Topps 114
76/7 Topps 259
78/9 Topps 57
79/0 Topps 106
80/1 Topps 234
79/0 DETR
80/1 DETR
72/3 TORO
73/4 TORO
74/5 TORO
76/7 TORO
77/8 TORO
THOMPSON, JAMIE
98/9 EBK ECHL All-Star
98/9 Peoria Rivermen
98/9 Peoria Rivermen
00/1 Worcester IceCats
01/2 Worcester IceCats
92/3 Maine Black Bears
THOMPSON, J-G
51/2 Lac St-Jean 54
THOMPSON, JEREMY
95/6 Tri-City Americans 19
THOMPSON, MARK
97/8 Regina Pats
THOMPSON, PAUL
33/4 Anonymous 50
34-43 BeeHive-1 [Chic.]
36-39 Diamond Match TT1
36-39 Diamond Match TT2
36-39 Diamond Match TT3
36-39 Diamond Match BH TT
36-39 Diamond Match Chic.
36-39 Diamond Match BH BT
37/8 World Wide Gum 6
02/3 Coventry Blaze
94/5 Guildford Flames 11
95/6 Guildford Flames 23
95/6 Guildford Flames 26
96/7 Guildford Flames 8
97/8 Guildford Flames
98/9 Guildford Flames
98/9 Guildford Flames
THOMPSON, RHYS
34-43 BeeHive-1 [Toro.]
THOMPSON, ROCKY
01/2 BAP Mem. 444
01/2 BAP Update ✂ TC20, ✂ TC36
01/2 Victory 373
01/2 Hershey Bears
00/1 Louisville Panthers
97/8 Saint John Flames
THOMPSON, RYAN
01/2 Guelph Storm
01/2 Guelph Storm M-Cup
THOMPSON, SCOTT
98/9 Quad City Mallards
99/0 Brampton Batallion 26
THOMPSON, SEAN
02/3 Plymouth Whalers
THOMPSON, SHAWN
91/2 Air Canada SJHL B15
97/8 Kamloops Blazers
THOMPSON, TIM
93/4 Slapshot / Niagara Falls 6
THOMPSON, WAYNE
83/4 Nova Scotia Voyageurs
THOMS, BILL
33/4 Anonymous 10
34-43 BeeHive-1 [Toro.]
33/4 Hamilton Gum 7
35/6 O-Pee-Chee 85
37/8 O-Pee-Chee 143
39/0 O-Pee-Chee 48
38/9 Quaker Oats
33/4 WWGum 50
THOMSEN, STEEN
79 Panini Sticker 366
THOMSON, BEN
99/0 Medicine Hat Tigers
00/1 Medicine Hat Tigers
THOMSON, BRUCE
82/3 Brandon Wheat Kings
THOMSON, DARRYL
99/0 Kingston Frontenacs
00/1 Kingston Frontenacs 22
THOMSON, FLOYD
74/5 Loblaws
74/5 O-Pee-Chee 298
75/6 O-Pee-Chee 149
76/7 O-Pee-Chee 356
77/8 O-Pee-Chee 358
75/6 Topps 149
71/2 SLOU
72/3 SLOU
73/4 SLOU
THOMSON, GREG
94/5 DEL 232
95/6 DEL 106
96/7 DEL 50
THOMSON, JIM R.
45-64 BeeHive-2 [Toro.]
48-52 Exhibits [Maple Leafs]
51/2 Parkhurst 82
52/3 Parkhurst 43
53/4 Parkhurst 8
54/5 Parkhurst 32
55/6 Parkhurst 11
93/4 Parkie 56-57 119
93/4 Parkie 56-57 154
45-54 Quaker Oats
57/8 Topps 23
57/8 Toronto Star Photo
55 Toronto Star Weekend
THOMSON, JIM*
89/0 ProCards AHL 225
90/1 ProCards 422
92/3 Topps 67
94/5 ANAH / Carl's Jr. 23
THOMSON, PAUL
35/6 Amalgamated Press
THOMSON, TOM
91/2 Air Canada SJHL C32
92/3 MPS SJHL 131
THÖNY, ROGER
93 Semic Sticker 126
THORBURN, CHRIS
01 UD Prospects GU 31, ✂ TPJ, ✂ TPJS, ✂ JC, ✍ SoT
02/3 Plymouth Whalers
THORESEN, JAN_ERIK
92/3 Semic Nordisk 75
THORESEN, PATRICK
02/3 Baie-Comeau
01/2 Moncton Wildcats 20
THORESEN, PETTER
95 Panini Worlds 252
94 Semic 270
92/3 Semic Nordisk 32
92 Semic Sticker 44
93 Semic Sticker 239
THORING, CLAY
01/2 Vancouver Giants
THORKILDSEN, KJELL
79 Panini Sticker 300
THORNBERG, OVE
94/5 Leaf Elit Set 76, TG-8
89/0 Semic Elitserien 109
90/1 Semic Elitserien 113
91/2 Semic Elitserien 117
92/3 Semic Elitserien 137
THORNBURN, CHRIS
00/1 UD Prospects 14
THORNBURY, TOM
84/5 Fredericton Express
THORNTON, BOB
93/4 Slapshot / North Bay 18
THORNTON, ERIN
91/2 Avant Garde BCJHL 129
92/3 BCJHL 35
90/1 7th..Sketch WHL 187
THORNTON, JOE
01/2 Adrenaline 17, PM 1
96/7 All-Sport PPF 171
01/2 Atomic 9, CP 2, PP 4, TN 1
02/3 Atomic 8, -CF 4, -SC 2
99/0 Aurora 14
00/1 Aurora 15, SR-4
96/7 Autograph Coll. 45, GB29, ✍ Aut.
97/8 Aut. Coll. 4, AE2, ✍ Aut.
02/3 BAP All-Star 92, ✂ ASJ
98/9 Be A Player 9, ✍ Aut. 9
99/0 BAP Mem. 35
00/1 BAP Mem. 127
01/2 BAP Mem. 8
02/3 BAP Mem. 122, 203, ✂ ASJ56, ✂ FP3, ✂ FG10, ✂ SC5
01/2 BAP Update HSHS, ✂ HSHSJers, ✂ PTT1
01/2 Bowman 14
02/3 Bowman 5
97 Bowman 32, 125, BB1, ✍ Aut.
98/9 Bowman's Best 84
02/3 Calder 31, -CG 1, -HS 1
02/3 Calder ✂ GWJ 4
95/6 Classic 95
99/0 Crown Royale 15, -CS 4, -IE 3
00/1 Crown Royale 12, JotC-5
01/2 Crown Royale 13, JotC 2
02/3 Crown Royale 9, -LOR 4
98/9 Donruss ES 11
97/8 Do. Elite 6,138,148, BF-1, C-24, ✍ BF-1
97/8 Do. Preferred 151, 200, LT-2B, PM-2, / Tin 16, WideTin 1
97/8 Do. Priority 173, 207, 215, DD-25, OD-28, Post-16, Stamp-16
97/8 Do. Studio 54, P-22
98/9 Dynagon Ice 15
99/0 Dynagon Ice 26
02/3 eTopps 37
02/3 Exclusive 15, -MO 4, ✂ GWJ 2
02/3 First Edition 159, 333, 343, 416R, ✂ Jers., ✂ DGJ 17, ✂ HSHSJers 15
01/2 Heads Up 10, SM 2, ✂ JQ 2
02/3 Heads Up 11, -EIT 3, -HF 4, -ITN 4, -SM 4, ✂ GWQ 3, / Bobble
02/3 In The GU 7, 107, ✂ E12, ✂ F3, ✂ GUJ12, ✂ SJ12, ✂ T3, ✂ TM1
00/1 Kraft 13
97/8 Leaf 41, 150, FOI-14
97/8 Limited 92, 187
97/8 McDonald's McD-33
00/1 McDonald's 4
01/2 McDonald's 2
02/3 McDonald's 4, -CC 1
99/0 Millenium 24, ✍ Aut. 24
98/9 NHL Power Play
99/0 NHL Power Play
01/2 O-Pee-Chee 88
02/3 O-Pee-Chee 10
98/9 OPC Chrome 112
97/8 Omega 19
98/9 Omega 19
99/0 Omega 22
98/9 Pacific 102
99/0 Pacific 30
00/1 Pacific 43, GCDC-3
01/2 Pacific 40, 426, PCC 354, GCDC 2, TDP 4
02/3 Pacific 35, -CCA 3, -IZ 3, -L 3, -MA 3, -MI 10, ✂ GWJ 3
02/3 Pacific Complete 492
97/8 Pa. Crown Roy. 11, BOS-3, CCA-3, HT-3, L-3
97/8 Pa. Dynagon Rookie
97/8 Pa. Paramount 16, P-3, CG-2, BN-3
99/0 Pa. Paramount 24
00/1 Pa. Paramount 23
97/8 Pa. Revolution 11, TC-2
01/2 PTC National 2
98/9 Panini Photocard
99/0 Panini Sticker 26
00/1 Panini Sticker 16
00/1 Parkhurst P-26
01/2 Parkhurst 79, ✂ PJ21, ✂ PS21, ✂ PSJ20, ✂ H5, ✂ T4, ✂ T19
02/3 Parkhurst 114, ✂ FP3, ✂ GJ40, ✂ SJ40, ✂ HSHSJers, ✂ NH2, ✂ PP10, ✂ TT8
02/3 Parkhurst Retro 6, ✂ RF3, ✂ RJ7, ✂ RSJ7, ✂ HH2, ✂ HSHSJers, ✂ RM3, ✂ RM19, ✂ RR7
97/8 Pinnacle 23, P-3
97/8 Pi. Be A Player 232, OT-20, ✍ Aut. 232
97/8 Pi. BeeHive 51, BHT-22, ✍ Aut. 51
97/8 Pi. Certified A
97/8 Pi. Mint 29
00/1 Premier Plus 9, PA5
99/0 Prism 15
00/1 Pr. Stock 9, AC-3, PS-4, PSNW-2
01/2 Pr. Stock 7, Res. 2, -PS 5
02/3 Pr. Stock Reserve ✂ 104
00/1 PS Titanium 7
01/2 PS Titanium 11, SK 2, TAS 1, ✂ DSJ 74
01/2 PS Titanium Draft ✂ 11
02/3 Pr. Stock Titanium 10, -S 2, ✂ GWJ 5
00/1 PS Titanium Draft ✂ 8
02/3 Quest for the Cup 8, -CTC 4, ✂ GWJ 3
99/0 Revolution 15, / CSC 15
00/1 Revolution 13, HD-4
96/7 Soo Greyhounds
96/7 Soo Greyhounds
97/8 Score 54
97/8 Score Bost. 17
00/1 Signature 36, F-3, ✍ Aut. 113
01/2 Signature C-21, ✍ Aut., ✂ GP3, ✂ GUE3, ✂ GJ3, ✂ GSJ3, ✂ HSHSJers, ✂ ITN3
02/3 Signature Series 122, ✍ 122, ✂ FJ3, ✂ SGJ12, ✂ TQ11, ✂ TM4
02/3 Slam Card
95/6 Slapshot 363
97/8 SP Authentic 171, I9, ✍ SotT, ✍ T3
98/9 SP Authentic 5, ✍ SotT
99/0 SP Authentic 6, TH2
00/1 SP Authentic 7, NPS2
01/2 SP Authentic 6, ✍ SotT, ✍ SotTD
02/3 SP Authentic 6, 92, ✍ SotT, ✍ SotTD, ✍ SotTT (x2), ✂ SP, ✂ DP, ✂ TP
00/1 SP GU 5
01/2 SP GU 3, ✂ AF, ✂ AFD, ✂✍ IS, ✂✍ ISD, ✂ Patch, ✂✍ PatchSig, ✂✍ PatchCSig, ✂ TotG, ✂ TotGSig, ✂ TotGCSig
02/3 SP GU Edition 4, ✂ AF, ✂ CF, ✂ PC, ✂ PH, ✂ TG, ✍ Sig
02/3 Sports Vault 17
99/0 SPx 11
00/1 SPx HH3, ✂ WM
01/2 SPx 4
02/3 SPx 5, 80, ✂ WM, ✂ SS, ✂ X
98/9 SPx Finite 133
98/9 SPx Prospects 5
99/0 Stadium 75, -Chrome 27
00/1 Stadium 89, BT15
01/2 Stadium 91, ✂ SCS, ✂ SCST
02/3 Stadium 74, -BT9
98/9 SLU
98/9 Topps 112, -IA I13
99/0 Topps 21, ✍ TA10
00/1 Topps 16, TC7, NHLD7
01/2 Topps 88
02/3 Topps 10, CC7, HHU18
99/0 To. Chrome 21
00/1 To. Chrome 16, TC7
01/2 To. Chrome 88
02/3 T. Chrome 10
98/9 To. Finest C17
98/9 T. Gold Label 81
99/0 To. Gold Label 40, -FG2
00/1 To. Gold Label 7, NG3
00/1 To. Heritage 12, NT5, OSA, OSJ, ✍ CAI, ✍ OSA
01/2 To. Heritage 57, ✂ GWJ
02/3 To. Heritage 5
02/3 To. Limited 10
99/0 To. Prmr. Plus 79, -TNO4
01/2 To. Reserve 49, ✂ TR
00/1 To. Stars 51
02/3 To. Total 211, TTC2, TT8
98/9 UD Choice 19
00/1 UD Heroes 10
01/2 UD PlayMakers Ltd 8
00/1 UD Reserve 8, PSJ, ✍ PSJ
98/9 UD3 15, 75, 135
00/1 Ultimate Mem. ✍ U-45
01/2 Ultimate Mem. ✂ Corn., ✂ NP
02/3 Ultimate Memorabilia ✂ Cor, ✂ DD, ✂ Emb, ✂ FO, ✂ GUJ, ✂ GUSJ, ✂ GAO, ✂ HT, ✂ ITN, ✂ NP, ✂ UC, ✍ UAut
96/7 Upper Deck 370
97/8 Upper Deck 218, SS6, SG6
98/9 Upper Deck 19, 218, GN12
99/0 Upper Deck 18, N19, ✂ GJ
00/1 Upper Deck 13, ✂ GJ, ✂ DGJ
01/2 Upper Deck 13 , T1
02/3 Upper Deck 11, 425, -NC1, -SS3, -SS2, ✂ CG, ✂ DM, ✂ PN, ✂ PA, ✂ GJ, ✂✍ SGJ, ✂ PW, ✂ UDPL
02/3 UD Artistic 6, R6, GD12, ✂ AT, / ✍ Art
96/7 UD Black Diam. 160
97/8 UD Black Diam. 112, PC17
98/9 UD Black Diam. 7
99/0 UD Black Diam. 10
00/1 UD Black Diam. 4, G-TH
99/0 UD C. Legends 78
01/2 UD Challenge 5, ✂✍ UCS
02/3 UD Classic 7, ✂ CS, ✂ HH, ✂ HR (x2)
97/8 UD Coll. Choice 296
02/3 UD Foundations 145
98/9 UD G. Reserve 19, 218
99/0 UD G. Reserve 18
99/0 UD Gretzky Excl. 85
01/2 UD Honor Roll 26, 56, ✂ GAJ
02/3 UD Honor 5, 73, -SG3, -TW1, ✂ GA
96/7 UD Ice 116
97/8 UD Ice 46, IC6, L1C
00/1 UD Ice 4, ✂ IGJ
01/2 UD Ice 2
00/1 UD Legends 11, 13, ✍ ES
01/2 UD Mask 8
02/3 UD Mask 10, ✂ IO
98/9 UD MVP 12
99/0 UD MVP 13, ✍ PS
99/0 UD MVP ✍ PS
00/1 UD MVP 17
01/2 UD MVP 12
02/3 UD MVP 14, HN2, VF3, SA, ST (x3)
99/0 UD MVP Cup 16, SS2, -GC
02/3 UD Piece 5, ✂ PH, ✂ SS, ✍ MD
01/2 UD Premier 3, ✂ S, ✂ D, ✍ SigS
02/3 UD Premier 5, ✂ Jers, ✂ JD, ✂ Patch, ✍ Sig (x2)
00/1 UD Pros&Prosp. 7
99/0 UD Retro 6
02/3 UD Rookie 9, 106, 172, ✂ DJ, ✂ S
01/2 UD Top Shelf 3, ✂ J, ✂✍ SJ.
02/3 UD Top Shelf 6, ✂ CP, ✂ GO, ✂ HT (x2), ✂ R, ✂ ST (x3), ✂ SW, ✂ TS
00/1 UD Vintage 25, 36-37
01/2 UD Vintage 23, 25, 26
02/3 UD Vintage 23, 263, T5
00/1 Vanguard 10, HV-4, VP-11, ✂ DGJ-1
01/2 Vanguard 8
02/3 Vanguard 10, -EMW 2, -VT 8, ✂ GWJ 5
99/0 Victory 23
00/1 Victory 17, 20, 285
01/2 Victory 26
02/3 Victory 18
97/8 Visions Signings 41, ✍ 41
99/0 WGretzky 16
97/8 Zenith 92, RR-2, ZT-10, Z74
THORNTON, LARRY
98/9 Dayton Bombers
96/7 Dayton Ice Bandits
THORNTON, MIKE
98/9 BC Icemen 20
98/9 BC Icemen
96/7 Dayton Ice Bandits
THORNTON, SCOTT
00/1 BAP Mem. 353
91/2 Bowman 168
95/6 Donruss 262
02/3 Exclusive 153
94/5 Leaf 431
99/0 Millenium 135, ✍ Aut. 135
00/1 Pacific 142
01/2 Pacific 348
02/3 Pacific 344
02/3 Pacific Complete 325
95/6 Panini Sticker 258
99/0 Panini Sticker 70
94/5 Parkhurst 73
95/6 Pinnacle 162
96/7 Pi. Be A Player 153, ✍ Aut. 153
95/6 POG 112
02/3 Pr. Stock Reserve 89
90/1 Pro Set 640
91/2 Score 55T
91/2 Score CAN 605
89/0 7th..Sketch OHL 83
00/1 Stadium 225
95/6 Topps 82
00/1 Topps 144
98/9 To. Finest 93
00/1 To. Heritage 182
91/2 To. Stadium 378
02/3 To. Total 295
90/1 Upper Deck 459
91/2 Upper Deck 353
91/2 Upper Deck 521
94/5 Upper Deck 426
00/1 Upper Deck 375
01/2 Upper Deck 146
02/3 Upper Deck 394
01/2 UD Vintage 213
02/3 UD Vintage 209
01/2 Victory 297
02/3 Victory 182
93/4 EDMO / Sheet
91/2 EDMO / IGA
96-98 MONT
96/7 MONT / Export
90/1 TORO
THORNTON, SHAWN
02/3 BAP All-Star 120
02/3 BAP Mem. 291
02/3 Bowman 150
02/3 In The GU 194
95/6 Slapshot 316
02/3 SP Authentic 139
02/3 T. Chrome 153
02/3 To. Heritage 142
02/3 Upper Deck 432
02/3 UD Classic 107
02/3 UD Honor 108
02/3 UD Mask 118
02/3 UD Top Shelf 108
01/2 Norfolk Admirals
97/8 St. John's Maple Leafs
99/0 St. John's Maple Leafs
00/1 St. John's Maple Leafs
THORNTON, STEVE
00/1 Kudos 67
95/6 Peoria Rivermen
01/2 Cardiff Devils
THORNTON, STEVEN
96/7 DEL 180
THORP, ERNIE
01/2 Rockford IceHogs
THORP, MATT
69 Columbus Checkers
THORPE, ROBERT
90/1 7th..Sketch OHL 122
91/2 7th...Sketch OHL 69
96/7 Toledo Storm
97/8 Toledo Storm 2
THORPE, RYAN
97/8 Kamloops Blazers
98/9 Kamloops Blazers
THRUSSELL, RYAN
97/8 Portland Winter Hawks
THUDIUM, CALVIN
91 7th..Sketch Mem.Cup 91
90/1 7th..Sketch WHL 212
88/9 Portland Winter Hawks
THUN, CHRISTER
65/6 Hellas 144
THURESSON, MARCUS
94/5 Leaf Elit Set 29
95/6 Leaf Elit Set 226
89/0 Semic Elitserien 142
90/1 Semic Elitserien 213
91/2 Semic Elitserien 140
92/3 Semic Elitserien 164
95/6 UD Elitserien 92
98/9 UD Elitserien 158, DL8
99/0 UD Elitserien 161, H11
00/1 UD Elitserien 142, 204, ✍ Sig.
THURIER, ALFRED
34-43 BeeHive-1 [NYAm.]
THURIER, FRED
51/2 Cleveland Barons
THURLOW, BILLY
98/9 Louisiana Ice Gators
THURNER, MICHAEL
99/0 Eishockey 235
THURSTON, BRENT
91 7th..Sketch Mem.Cup 78
90/1 7th..Sketch WHL 204
THURSTON, BRETT
98/9 Brandon Wheat Kings
99/0 Brandon Wheat Kings
THURSTON, ERIC
81/2 Victoria Cougars
82/3 Victoria Cougars
83/4 Victoria Cougars
THURSTON, TREVOR
91/2 Air Canada SJHL A19
THUSBERG, JORMA
70/1 Kuvajulkaisut 116
72 Panda MM-Toronto
71/2 Williams Finnish 126
72/3 Williams Finnish 97
73/4 Williams Finnish 145
THUSS, CHUCK
95/6 Louisiana Ice Gators-2
99/0 Mississippi S'Wolves
99/0 Mississippi S'Wolves
THYER, MARIO
89/0 ProCards IHL 85
90/1 ProCards 119
91/2 ProCards 160
90/1 Score 382
92/3 Cincinnati Cyclones
TIAINEN, RAIMO
66/7 Champion 9
TIAINEN, TERO
98/9 Cardset 26
99/0 Cardset 16
95/6 Sisu 289
96/7 Sisu 87
TIBBATTS, DEREK
90/1 7th..Sketch WHL 79
91/2 7th...Sketch WHL 111
90/1 Saskatoon Blades
91/2 Saskatoon Blades
93/4 Saskatoon Blades
TIBBATTS, F
93/4 Saskatoon Blades
TIBBATTS, TRENT
92/3 MPS SJHL 96
TIBBETTS, BILLY
01/2 BAP Mem. 242
01/2 Crown Royale 175
02/3 Pacific 288
01/2 PS Titanium 178
01/2 PS Titanium Draft 158
01/2 SPx 122
01/2 SPx Rookie RR24
01/2 Upper Deck 205
01/2 UD Ice 66
01/2 UD MVP 213
01/2 UD Top Shelf 63
01/2 Victory 385
00/1 WBS Penguins
TICHY, MAREK
94/5 APS 235
96/7 APS 269
96/7 DS Sticker 175
TICHY, MILAN
92/3 Classic Prospects 25
93/4 Fleer Ultra 247
93/4 Fleer Ultra ARS 10
93/4 Power Play 101
91/2 ProCards 485
93/4 Score 461
92/3 Indianapolis Ice
TIDBALL, CURTIS
02/3 Québec Remparts
TIDEY, ALEX
88/9 EDMO / Action 163
TIDSBURY, SHANE
92/3 BCJHL 175
TIE, JUSSI
95/6 UD CC 325
TIERNYCH, ALEXANDER
89 Semic Sticker 100
TIGLIANI, GIORGIO
79 Panini Sticker 387
TIILIKAINEN,
97/8 Hockey-Box
TIILIKAINEN, JARNO
00/1 Cardset 289
TIILIKAINEN, JUKKA
98/9 Cardset 114
99/0 Cardset 65
00/1 Cardset 247
93/4 Jyvas Hyva 199
95 Semic 228
93/4 Sisu 265
94/5 Sisu 227
95/6 Sisu 129
TIINUS, MARKKU
92/3 Jyvas Hyva 114
TIK,
92/3 Semic Nordisk 185 [Elitseriemester]
TIKHOMIROV, VLADIMIR
00/1 Mir 275, 297
TIKHONOV, SERGEI
99/0 Mir 233
TIKHONOV, VASILY
92/3 Jyvas Hyva 188
95/6 Kansas City Blades
TIKHONOV, VICTOR
89 Semic Sticker 77
92 Semic Sticker 98
TIKHONOV, VIKTOR
00/1 Mir Fetisov 40
90/1 O-Pee-Chee 17R
79/0 Soviet Stars 2
83/4 Soviet Stars
87/8 Soviet Stars
89/0 Soviet Stars
TIKKANEN, ESA
90/1 Bowman 194
91/2 Bowman 98
92/3 Bowman 144
98/9 Cardset 2, Leij. 43
99/0 Cardset 265, -AH K-pata
00/1 Cardset 240
02/3 Cardset 125
93/4 Donruss 215
95/6 Donruss 17
97/8 Esso 49
94/5 Flair 160
94/5 Fleer 193
95/6 Fleer Metal 87
92/3 Fleer Ultra 67
93/4 Fleer Ultra 377
94/5 Fleer Ultra 191
95/6 Fleer Ultra 143, 264
96/7 Fl. Ultra 171
91/2 Gillette 2
95 Globe 138
95/6 Hoyle / West. 8-Club
93 Koululainen
95 Koululainen
89/0 Kraft 18
93/4 Leaf 288
95/6 Leaf 319
96/7 Maggers 161
98/9 McD's T6
96/7 Metal Univ. 160
87/8 OPC/Topps 7
88/9 O-Pee-Chee 260
90/1 OPC/Topps 156
91/2 O-Pee-Chee 378
91/2 Topps - Team Leader 6
92/3 O-Pee-Chee 319
89/0 OPC/Topps 12
89/0 O-Pee-Chee 328
91/2 OPC Premier 121
87/8 OPC Sticker 83-215
88/9 OPC Sticker 220-92
89/0 opcSticker 219-78
98/9 Omega 162
98/9 Pacific 448
97/8 Pacific CC 249
97/8 Pa. Paramount 85
94 Panini Olympics 303
87/8 Panini Sticker 264
88/9 Panini Sticker 63
90/1 Panini Sticker 223
90/1 Panini/EDM 23
91/2 Panini Sticker 123
92/3 Panini Sticker 103
93/4 Panini Sticker 95
95/6 Panini Sticker 192
96/7 Panini Sticker 297
97/8 Panini Sticker 86
98/9 Panini Sticker 109
95 Panini Worlds 295
91/2 Parkhurst 55
92/3 Parkhurst 46
93/4 Parkhurst 135
95/6 Parkhurst 173, 235, 478
94/5 Parkie SE157, ES11
89 Pelimiehen Passi
91/2 Pinnacle 24
92/3 Pinnacle 336
93/4 Pinnacle 279
94/5 Pinnacle 174
95/6 Pinnacle 57, GG-10
96/7 Pinnacle 46
96/7 Pi. Be A Player 31, ✍ Aut. 31
95/6 Playoff 196
96/7 Playoff 392
94/5 POG 209
95/6 POG 239
93/4 Power Play 395
93/4 Power Play GG 9
93/4 Premier 282
94/5 Premier 504, 528
95/6 Pro Magnet 7
90/1 Pro Set 97
91/2 Pro Set 71
92/3 Pro Set 53
91 Pro Set Awards AC14
91/2 Pro Set Platinum 39
90/1 Score 13, 342
90/1 Sco. Hot Cards 6
91/2 Score 241
91/2 Score CAN 461
92/3 Score 16
93/4 Score 97
94/5 Score 136
95/6 Score 123
97/8 Score 236
94 Semic 34
94 Semic 349
95 Semic 43
91 Semic Sticker 203
92 Semic Sticker 14
93 Semic Sticker 80
94/5 Sisu 276, GS-10
95/6 Sisu Limited 40, SAS-8
95/6 SBx Emotion 153
95/6 SBx Impact 145
94/5 SP 103
95/6 SP 153
95 Suomen All-Star 5
96/7 Team Out!
92/3 Topps 476
91/2 To. Stadium 69
92/3 To. Stadium 104
93/4 To. Stadium 477
93/4 To. Stadium - Master Photo-2 1
94/5 To. Stadium 258
90/1 Upper Deck 167
91/2 Upper Deck 83
91/2 Upper Deck 182
91/2 Upper Deck E10
92/3 Upper Deck 188
93/4 Upper Deck 457, SP-104
94/5 Upper Deck 42, SP-160
95/6 Upper Deck 126, SE-70
96/7 Upper Deck 352
97/8 Upper Deck 111
95/6 UD CC 268
96/7 UD CC 273
00/1 UD DEL 170, S6
96 Wien 28, NS6
85/6 EDMO / Red Rooster
86/7 EDMO
86/7 EDMO / Red Rooster
87/8 EDMO
88/9 EDMO
88/9 EDMO / Action 29
90/1 EDMO / IGA
91/2 EDMO / IGA
92/3 EDMO / IGA 023
97/8 FLOR / Winn-Dixie
98/9 NYRA
96/7 VANC / IGA
TIKKANEN, HARRI
98/9 Cardset 186
99/0 Cardset 107
00/1 Cardset 321
02/3 Cardset 126
TILEY, BRAD
99/0 Choice 9
92/3 Classic Prospects 129
91/2 ProCards 61
91 7th..Sketch Mem.Cup 6
90/1 7th..Sketch OHL 173
02/3 Philadelphia Phantoms
92/3 Phoenix Roadrunners
93/4 Phoenix Roadrunners
97/8 Springfield Falcons
TILLEY, TOM
91/2 Bowman 377
98/9 EBK IHL All-Star
95/6 Future Legends 43
90/1 O-Pee-Chee 498
89/0 Panini Sticker 128
93/4 Parkhurst 442
90/1 ProCards 83
93/4 Upper Deck 491
87/8 SLOU
88/9 SLOU
88/9 SLOU / Kodak
89/0 SLOU / Kodak
98/9 Chicago Wolves
98/9 Chicago Wolves Champs
99/0 Chicago Wolves
00/1 Chicago Wolves
95/6 Milwaukee Admirals
96/7 Milwaukee Admirals
TILSON, MICHAEL
95/6 Slapshot 110
99/0 Fort Worth Brahmas
TILTGEN, DEAN
90/1 7th..Sketch WHL 104
91/2 7th...Sketch WHL 289
TIMAKOV, STANISLAV
00/1 Mir 204
TIMANDER, MATTIAS
96/7 Do. Canadian 138
96/7 Do. Elite 135
96/7 Flair 101
94/5 Leaf Elit Set 179
95/6 Leaf Elit Set 101, FTF-10
96/7 L. Preferred 120
97/8 Pacific CC 235
97/8 Panini Sticker 5
00/1 Panini Sticker 140
97/8 Pi. Be A Player 151, ✍ Aut. 151
96/7 Pi. Zenith 134
96/7 Select CE 99
92/3 Semic Elitserien 233
00/1 Signature 117, ✍ Aut.172
96/7 SP 170
96/7 Upper Deck 220
97/8 Upper Deck 224
02/3 Upper Deck 358
96/7 UD Black Diam. 47
95/6 UD Elitserien 153, NA19
01/2 COLU
98/9 Providence Bruins
TIMCHENKO, OLEG
98 Bowman 105
98 Bowman Chrome 105
99/0 Greensboro Generals
TIMCHENKO, VYACHESLAV
98/9 Mir 117
TIMEWELL, JASON
91/2 Avant Garde BCJHL 67
TIMGREN, RAY
45-64 BeeHive-2 [Toro.]
48-52 Exhibits [Maple Leafs]
51/2 Parkhurst 78
02/3 Parkie - Reprint 161
45-54 Quaker Oats
54/5 Topps 13
TIMMINS, SEAN
91/2 Air Canada SJHL D26
TIMMONS, K.C.
00/1 Hershey Bears
01/2 Hershey Bears
TIMMONS, KC
02/3 Hershey Bears
TIMOFEEV, DENIS
99/0 Providence Bruins
TIMONEN, JUSSI
02/3 Cardset -BFG 9, ✍ BFG
TIMONEN, KIMMO
01/2 Adrenaline ✂ GWJ 24
99/0 BAP Mem. 397
00/1 BAP Mem. 56
98/9 Cardset 5, Leij. 17
99/0 Cardset 188, -BP 3, AH 5-pata
00/1 Cardset 352
02/3 Cardset 278
98/9 EBK IHL All-Star
97/8 Hockey-Box
93/4 Jyvas Hyva 165
02/3 O-Pee-Chee 252
98/9 Omega 134
00/1 Pacific 226
02/3 Pacific 214
02/3 Pacific Complete 41
99/0 Panini Sticker 265
00/1 Panini Sticker 184
00/1 Parkhurst P-5
94/5 Parkie SE218
00/1 PS Titanium Draft ✂ 57
95 Semic 10, 233
00/1 Signature 35, ✍ Aut. 103
02/3 Signature Series 34, ✍ 34
93/4 Sisu 163
93/4 Sisu 396
94/5 Sisu 304
95/6 Sisu 123, DT-1
96/7 Sisu 182
95/6 Sisu Limited 65
94/5 SP 160
02/3 Sports Vault 259
00/1 Stadium 197
02/3 Topps 252
94/5 Topps Finest 129
02/3 To. Limited 252
00/1 To. Stars 63
02/3 To. Total 331
93/4 Upper Deck 268
94/5 Upper Deck 510
99/0 Upper Deck 74
00/1 Upper Deck 101

01/2 Upper Deck 100
02/3 Upper Deck 345
99/0 UD G. Reserve 74
99/0 UD MVP 111
01/2 UD MVP 107
02/3 UD MVP 100
00/1 UD Vintage 206
02/3 UD Vintage 143
00/1 Vanguard ✂ DGJ 12
99/0 Victory 159
00/1 Victory 131
01/2 Victory 197
02/3 Victory 120
99/0 WGretzky 93
98/9 NASH / Wendy's 20

TIMORFEYEV, BORIS
95 Panini Worlds 37

TIMOSAARI, ARI
70/1 Kuvajulkaisut 381
80/1 Mallasjuoma 108
71/2 Williams Finnish 315

TIMOSCHUK, ROLAND
94/5 DEL 186
95/6 DEL 186
96/7 DEL 125

TINORDI, MARK
91/2 Bowman 124
92/3 Bowman 218
92/3 Bowman 399
91 Canada Cup
93/4 Donruss 79
94/5 Donruss 206
95/6 Donruss 255
96/7 Donruss 153
93/4 EA Sports 31
94/5 Flair 45
94/5 Fleer 239
92/3 Fleer Ultra 98
93/4 Fleer Ultra 213
94/5 Fleer Ultra 57
95/6 Fleer Ultra 178
95 Globe 80
92/3 Humpty Dumpty
91/2 Kraft 22
93/4 Kraft / PB
93/4 Leaf 146
94/5 Leaf 91
96/7 Leaf 31
91/2 O-Pee-Chee 308
92/3 O-Pee-Chee 17
98/9 OPC Chrome 157
98/9 Pacific 449
97/8 Pacific CC 181
91/2 Panini Sticker 109
92/3 Panini Sticker 97
93/4 Panini Sticker 275
94/5 Panini Sticker 232
95/6 Panini Sticker 144
91/2 Parkhurst 304
92/3 Parkhurst 76
93/4 Parkhurst 320
94/5 Parkhurst 59
95/6 Parkhurst 224
91/2 Pinnacle 199
92/3 Pinnacle 18
92/3 Pinnacle 252
93/4 Pinnacle 16
93/4 Pinnacle CA6
94/5 Pinnacle 29
95/6 Pinnacle FC 10
95/6 Pi. Summit 93
95/6 Playoff 215
94/5 POG 85
95/6 POG 284
93/4 Power Play 66
93/4 Premier 24
94/5 Premier 24, 452
90/1 Pro Set 145
91/2 Pro Set 107
91/2 Pro Set 575
92/3 Pro Set 78
91/2 Pro Set Platinum 58
90/1 Score 304
91/2 Score 93
91/2 Score CAN 93
92/3 Score 7
93/4 Score 53
94/5 Score 68
95/6 Score 144
96/7 Score 11
91/2 Score Young Stars 18
94 Semic 82
95 Semic 84
92 Semic Sticker 83
92/3 Topps 4
95/6 Topps 198
98/9 Topps 157
94/5 Topps Finest 25
91/2 To. Stadium 392
92/3 To. Stadium 435
93/4 To. Stadium 384
95/6 To. Stadium 67
94/5 TSC Members Only 21
91/2 Upper Deck 295
92/3 Upper Deck 73
93/4 Upper Deck 89
94/5 Upper Deck 369, SP-177
95/6 Upper Deck 94
97/8 Upper Deck 385
95/6 UD BAP 220, ✍ S220
95/6 UD CC 141
96/7 UD Ice 74
94/5 DALL / Cap
95/6 WASH

TIPLER, CURTIS
95/6 Bowman P33
99/0 Rockford IceHogs
96/7 Regina Pats

TIPLER, TRAVIS
98/9 Wichita Thunder

TIPPETT, BRAD
90/1 7th...Sketch WHL 182
91/2 7th...Sketch WHL 241

TIPPETT, DAVE
98/9 EBK IHL All-Star
93/4 Leaf 349
86/7 OPC/Topps 148
87/8 OPC/Topps 86
88/9 OPC/Topps 85
90/1 OPC/Topps 183
91/2 O-Pee-Chee 384
89/0 OPC/Topps 134
90/1 OPC Premier 119
89/0 opcSticker 268-149
87/8 Panini Sticker 51
88/9 Panini Sticker 244
89/0 Panini Sticker 226
90/1 Panini Sticker 37
93/4 Panini Sticker 85
92/3 Parkhurst 372
93/4 Power Play 410
93/4 Premier 387
90/1 Pro Set 111, 555
90/1 Score 192, 29T
91/2 Score 437
91/2 Score CAN 409
93/4 Score 584
93/4 To. Stadium 124
90/1 Upper Deck 270
91/2 Upper Deck 480
84/5 HART / Jr. Whalers
85/6 HART / Jr. Whalers
86/7 HART / Jr. Whalers
87/8 HART / Jr. Whalers
88/9 HART / Jr. Whalers
89/0 HART / Jr. Whalers
93/4 PHIL / Sheet
93/4 PHIL / J.C. Penney
92/3 PITT / Coke-Clark
92/3 PITT / Foodland 16
90/1 WASH / Kodak
90/1 WASH / Smokey
91/2 WASH / Kodak
91/2 WASH / Smokey
95/6 Houston Aeros

TIRE, GINMAN
98/9 Muskegon Fury

TIRKKONEN, ANTTI
95/6 Sisu 342

TIRKKONEN, HEIKKI
70/1 Kuvajulkaisut 268

TIRKKONEN, PAAVO
66/7 Champion 128
70/1 Kuvajulkaisut 269

TIRKKONEN, PEKKA
98/9 Cardset 151
99/0 Cardset 310
00/1 Cardset 79
02/3 Cardset 279
96/7 DEL 197
91/2 Jyvas Hyva 32
92/3 Jyvas Hyva 96
93/4 Jyvas Hyva 168
94 Semic 25
93/4 Sisu 178
93/4 Sisu 338
94/5 Sisu 40, 171
95/6 Sisu 80
95/6 Sisu Limited 70

TISDALE, TIM
89/0 ProCards AHL 142
90/1 ProCards 227
94/5 Fredericton Canadiens
92/3 Wheeling Thund'birds 17
94/5 Wheeling Thund'birds

TITOV, ALEXANDER
99/0 Mir 119

TITOV, GERMAN
98/9 Be A Player 262, ✍ Aut. 262
99/0 BAP Mem. 96
00/1 BAP Mem. 407
93/4 Classic 94
93/4 Donruss 56
94/5 Donruss 228
95/6 Donruss 229
96/7 Donruss 58
95/6 Do. Elite 41
99/0 Dynagon Ice 164
94/5 Flair 29
94/5 Fleer 36
96/7 Fleer 14
96/7 Fl. Picks 106
94/5 Fleer Ultra 36
96/7 Fl. Ultra 27
95/6 Hoyle / West. 9-Club
92/3 Jyvas Hyva 185
93/4 Leaf 309
94/5 Leaf 261
95/6 Leaf 281
96/7 Maggers 24
96/7 Metal Univ. 23
97/8 Omega 37
99/0 Omega 192
98/9 Pacific 127
99/0 Pacific 348
00/1 Pacific 175
02/3 Pacific 9
97/8 Pacific CC 263
98/9 Pa. Crown Roy. 112
97/8 Pa. Dynagon 19, T-34
97/8 Pa. Invincible 21
97/8 Pa. Paramount 32
99/0 Pa. Paramount 193
94/5 Panini Sticker 158
95/6 Panini Sticker 234
96/7 Panini Sticker 235
97/8 Panini Sticker 192
98/9 Panini Sticker 178
99/0 Panini Sticker 139
00/1 Panini Sticker 159
93/4 Parkhurst 255
95/6 Parkhurst 28
94/5 Parkie SE26
94/5 Pinnacle 167
95/6 Pinnacle 52, GG-9
96/7 Pinnacle 36
96/7 Pi. Be A Player 49, ✍ Aut. 49
97/8 Pi. Certified 88
96/7 Pi. Summit 108
97/8 Pi. Totally 88
95/6 Playoff 20
96/7 Playoff 354
95/6 POG 50
93/4 Power Play 310
94/5 Premier 9
95/6 Pro Magnet 42
93/4 Score 614
94/5 Score 95
95/6 Score 71
96/7 Score 165
97/8 Score 197
93/4 Sisu 376
93/4 Sisu 352
94/5 Sisu 361, GS-11
95/6 SBx Impact 25
96/7 SBx Impact 15
94/5 SP 18
95/6 SP 18
96/7 SP 24
97/8 SP Authentic 37
98/9 SP Authentic 68
99/0 SPx 123
00/1 Topps 143
94/5 Topps Finest 75
93/4 To. Stadium 364
98/9 UD Choice 30
93/4 Upper Deck 476
94/5 Upper Deck 2
95/6 Upper Deck 207, SE-14
96/7 Upper Deck 227
98/9 Upper Deck 346
00/1 Upper Deck 233
98/9 UD Black Diam. 70
95/6 UD CC 15
96/7 UD CC 39
97/8 UD Coll. Choice 39
98/9 UD G. Reserve 346
98/9 UD MVP 169
99/0 UD MVP 167
00/1 UD Vintage 1
99/0 Victory 242
96 Wien 154

TITUS, STEPHEN
86/7 London Knights

TIURIKOV, VLADIMIR
91 Semic Sticker 85

TJÄLLDEN, MIKAEL
98/9 Cardset 170
00/1 Kudos 75
92/3 Semic Elitserien 352

TJÄRNQVIST, DANIEL
94/5 Leaf Elit Set 209, RR-6
95/6 Leaf Elit Set 116
02/3 Pacific 22
01/2 Parkhurst 300
01/2 PS Titanium Draft 109
94/5 Sig. Rookies 49, ✍ 49
01/2 Signature 202, ✍ Aut. 202
95/6 SP 186
95/6 UD Elitserien 175
97/8 UD Elitserien 40, S14, C3
98/9 UD Elitserien 53
99/0 UD Elitserien 39
00/1 UD Elitserien 49
02/3 UD Vintage 16

TJÄRNQVIST, MATHIAS
98/9 SPx Prospects 83
98/9 UD Black Diam. 113
99/0 UD Elitserien 48, 203
00/1 UD Elitserien 54

TJUMENEV, VIKTOR
87/8 Soviet Stars

TJUTIN, FEDOR
01/2 Guelph Storm
01/2 Guelph Storm M-Cup

TKACHENKO, IVAN
00/1 Mir 389

TKACHENKO, SERGEI
98/9 Anchorage Aces
96/7 Louisiana Ice Gators

TKACHUCK, PETE
51/2 Laval Dairy 34

TKACHUK, ALEXEI
98/9 Mir 100
99/0 Mir 215
00/1 Mir 261

TKACHUK, GRANT
88/9 ProCards / Rochester
89/0 ProCards IHL 105
90/1 ProCards 281
84/5 Saskatoon Blades
86/7 Saskatoon Blades

TKACHUK, KEITH
01/2 Adrenaline 163, WB 17
01/2 Atomic 83, PP 29
02/3 Atomic 84, -NPU 9, -PC 17, -SC 13
98/9 Aurora 148, -CF 38
99/0 Aurora 113, -Stripe 113, -ST 16
00/1 Aurora 113, Pins. 113
02/3 BAP All-Star 93, ✂ ASJ
98/9 Be A Player 256, ✍ Aut. 256
99/0 BAP Mem. 291
00/1 BAP Mem. 244, 499, ✂ H-10, ✂ TM-5, ✂ TM-30
01/2 BAP Mem. 140, ✂ ASJ, ✂ ASE, ✂ ASN, ✂ CoO
02/3 BAP Mem. 178, ✂ ASJ57, ✂ AST13, ✂ SC22, ✂ TM17
01/2 BAP Update ✂ H6, ✂ TP5
96/7 Bic.Sports Aces 10-H
97/8 Bicycle 8-Heart
95/6 Bicycle Sports Aces J-Spade
95/6 Bowman 69
01/2 Bowman 37
02/3 Bowman 27
98/9 Bowman's Best 6, F12
99/0 Crown Royale 110, -IG 20, -TC 6
00/1 Crown Royale 85
01/2 Crown Royale 121, JotC 26
02/3 Crown Royale 82, ✂ GWDP 18
93/4 Donruss 390
94/5 Donruss 192
95/6 Donruss 78, PP-7
96/7 Donruss 134, D-8, HL-10
97/8 Donruss 83, 227, RA-4
98/9 Donruss ES 5
96/7 Do. Canadian 22
97/8 Do. Canadian 16
95/6 Do. Elite 81
96/7 Do. Elite 61, S-2
97/8 Do. Elite 112, C-28
97/8 Do. Preferred 6, 191, LT-3B
97/8 Do. Priority 3, 202, DD-17, OD-3, Post-26, Stamp-26
97/8 Do. Studio 8, HH-7, S-18, P-8
96/7 Duracell DC18, JB18
98/9 Dynagon Ice 145, -TC 20
99/0 Dynagon Ice 155, -ASP 17, -CM 11
97/8 Esso 23
01/2 eTopps 24
02/3 Exclusive 146, ✂ GWJ 21
02/3 First Edition 69, 331, 430H, ✂ Jers., ✂ DGJ 19, ✂ HSHSJers 29
94/5 Flair 211
96/7 Flair 73
94/5 Fleer 246, FF-8
96/7 Fleer 92, 141, ART-22
95/6 Fleer Metal 166, IW-14
96/7 Fl. Picks 18, F50-44, CC-7, DL-5
92/3 Fleer Ultra 446
93/4 Fleer Ultra 111
94/5 Fleer Ultra 247, UP-10
95/6 Fleer Ultra 184, CC-20
96/7 Fl. Ultra 136, CTI-10
01/2 Heads Up 81, SM 15
02/3 Heads Up 105, ✂ GWQ 23
99/0 HoloGrFX 46
95/6 Hoyle / West. 10-Club
02/3 In The GU 69, 169, ✂ E27, ✂ GUJ27, ✂ SJ27, ✂ T8
94/5 Kraft / SS
95/6 Kraft / PB
96/7 Kraft / KD
97/8 Kraft / KD
93/4 Leaf 105
93/4 Leaf GLR 11
94/5 Leaf 94
95/6 Leaf 79
96/7 Leaf 133, LL-2, TBO-5
97/8 Leaf 73, 185, BS-14
94/5 L. Limited 108
95/6 L. Limited 57
96/7 L. Limited 3, BTB-5
96/7 L. Preferred 89, 148, VP-12
97/8 Limited 83, 133, 138, 140, FG-18
96/7 McDonald's McD-13
97/8 McDonald's McD-7
96/7 Metal Univ. 122, CS-11, LW-19
99/0 Millenium 188, ✍ Aut. 188
98/9 NHL Power Play
92/3 O-Pee-Chee 346
01/2 O-Pee-Chee 38
02/3 O-Pee-Chee 39
98/9 OPC Chrome 154, SB18
92/3 OPC Premier 43
97/8 Omega 177, 245, GF-15
98/9 Omega 188, -EOP 17, -FTF 5, -Onl. 29, -PI 18, -Prism 17
99/0 Omega 185, -5ST 10, -EOP 15
98/9 Pacific 344, -GCDC 27, -TC 20, -Time. 15
99/0 Pacific 328, -GC 30, -TL 1
00/1 Pacific 322, GCDC-26
01/2 Pacific 332, GCDC 18
02/3 Pacific 329, -MA 17
02/3 Pacific Complete 470
97/8 Pacific CC 28, CS-17, SS-7A
97/8 Pa. Crown Roy. 107, HT-14, L-16
98/9 Pa. Crown Roy. 105, -PotG 20, -PP 20
97/8 Pa. Dynagon 98, DD-12B, T-6, BKS-76
97/8 Pa. Invincible 109, OTG-16, R-156
97/8 Pa. Paramount 144, P-16, BN-16
98/9 Pa. Paramount 186, -SD 15, -TC 20
99/0 Pa. Paramount 184, -IAI 21, -PB 30
00/1 Pa. Paramount 194
97/8 Pa. Revolution 109, TC-19
98/9 Pa. Revolution 112, -ASG 29, -TPA 7, -CTLC 15, -Show. 30
98/9 Panini Photocard
93/4 Panini Sticker 193
94/5 Panini Sticker 168
95/6 Panini Sticker 214
96/7 Panini Sticker 191
97/8 Panini Sticker 123, 162
98/9 Panini Sticker 144
99/0 Panini Sticker 276
00/1 Panini Sticker 190
91/2 Parkhurst 424
92/3 Parkhurst 206
93/4 Parkhurst 228
94/5 Parkhurst 264
95/6 Parkhurst 501
00/1 Parkhurst P-130
01/2 Parkhurst 19, ✂ PS48
02/3 Parkhurst 27, -CR3, ✂ CRm3, ✂ HSHSJers
02/3 Parkhurst Retro 10
94/5 Parkie SE seV38
92/3 Pinnacle 222
93/4 Pinnacle 33
93/4 Pinnacle CA26
94/5 Pinnacle 103, GR18, NL12
x95/6 Pinnacle FC 11
97/8 Pinnacle 114
97/8 Pinnacle 40, TP-6, P-6
96/7 Pi. Be A Player BB-6
97/8 Pi. Be A Player 22, OT-2, ✍ Aut. 22
97/8 Pi. BeeHive 14, BHT-17
97/8 Pi. Certified 37, CT-11
97/8 Pi. Epix E6
97/8 Pi. Inside 5, IT-24, / Can 18
96/7 Pi. Mint 19
97/8 Pi. Mint 21
95/6 Pi. Summit 152, GMC-6
96/7 Pi. Summit 104
97/8 Pi. Totally 37
95/6 Pi. Zenith 74, GG-1
96/7 Pi. Zenith 6, ZT-12
95/6 Playoff 109, 220
96/7 Playoff 351
94/5 POG 256
95/6 POG 293, I-016
93/4 Power Play 276
93/4 Power Play RisS 8
93/4 Premier 27
93/4 Premier 502
94/5 Premier 242, 300, TF-18
00/1 Premier Plus 67, WP11
99/0 Prism 110, -SGDC 18
00/1 Pr. Stock 77, PS-45
01/2 Pr. Stock 82, Res. 16, -PS 62
02/3 Pr. Stock Reserve ✂ 140
00/1 PS Titanium 74
01/2 PS Titanium 119
02/3 PS Titanium ✂ GWJ 59
95/6 Pro Magnet 59
92/3 Pro Set 243
02/3 Quest for the Cup 84
99/0 Revolution 114, -NI 16, -Show. 29, -TotL 8, / CSC 114
00/1 Revolution 115, HD-28
92/3 Score 450
93/4 Score 195
94/5 Score CI14
95/6 Score 33, CI-11
96/7 Score 47, CI-3
97/8 Score 87, CI-4
92/3 Score Young Stars 29
94/5 Select 75
95/6 Select CE 37, DS-17
96/7 Select CE 24, C-10
00/1 Signature 21, F-23, ✂ J-40, ✂ HSHSJers
01/2 Signature ✂ GU77, ✂ HSHSJers, ✂ IS14, ✂ TM26
02/3 Signature Series 170, ✍ 170, ✂ SGJ27, ✂ TQ15
95/6 SBx Emotion 197, NP-9
95/6 SBx Impact 185, 239
96/7 SBx Impact 107, BR-22
02/3 Slam Card
94/5 SP 132
95/6 SP 164, E30
96/7 SP 118, GF-5, Ins.
97/8 SP Authentic 119, I23
98/9 SP Authentic 66, SS25, SO11, ✍ SotT
99/0 SP Authentic 66, SS10
00/1 SP Authentic 68, SF6
01/2 SP Authentic 77
02/3 SP Authentic 79, 103
00/1 SP GU 47, ✂ TotG, ✂ C, ✂ P
01/2 SP GU 48
02/3 SP GU Edition 44, ✂ CF (x2), ✂ PC, ✂ TG
02/3 Sports Vault 275
96/7 SPx 35
97/8 SPx 40, D-SPX15
99/0 SPx 115, P6, X12, XT2, S10
00/1 SPx 53, 77, 147, ✂ WM (x2), ✂ ✍ WM
01/2 SPx 59
02/3 SPx 64
98/9 SPx Finite 64
98/9 SPx Prospects 46, H23, L4, PS29
99/0 Stadium 15, -Chrome 14, -CA16
00/1 Stadium 100, SF19
01/2 Stadium 54, G19, P11
02/3 Stadium 49
97/8 SLU
95/6 Super Sticker 136
96/7 Team Out!
92/3 Topps 102
95/6 Topps 152, HGA-5, M-14, 2PL, 7PL
98/9 Topps 154, M13, SB18, ✍ CAI
99/0 Topps 4, AT9, IM17, TW11
00/1 Topps 146
01/2 Topps 38
02/3 Topps 39
99/0 To. Chrome 4, AT9, IM17
00/1 To. Chrome 106
01/2 To. Chrome 38
02/3 T. Chrome 35
94/5 Topps Finest 19, BBB-17
95/6 To. Finest 123
98/9 To. Finest 80, R17, M42, M45, M48, M50
98/9 T. Gold Label 12, GR6
99/0 To. Gold Label 6, QC2
00/1 To. Gold Label 41, B7, GG9, ✂ GLJ
00/1 To. Heritage 20, HH15
01/2 To. Heritage 9
02/3 To. Heritage 12
02/3 To. Limited 39
99/0 To. Prmr. Plus 63, CR1
01/2 To. Reserve 33
92/3 To. Stadium 116
93/4 To. Stadium 135
94/5 To. Stadium 5
95/6 To. Stadium 90, F9
94/5 TSC Members Only 39
00/1 To. Stars 43, ✂ GG
95/6 T. Super Skills 51
02/3 To. Total 279, TTC 26
98/9 UD Choice 160, BH2, SQ30
00/1 UD Heroes 92, L8
01/2 UD PlayMakers Ltd 86
00/1 UD Reserve 67
02/3 UD Superstars 235, ✂ CAST
98/9 UD3 52, 112, 172
00/1 Ultimate Mem. ✂ J-47, ✂ Jers. 39, ✂ JJ-11, ✂ S-47, ✂ TM-5, ✂ TM-33, ✂ UC-2
01/2 Ultimate Mem. ✂ DD, ✂ Emb., ✂ Jers., ✂ S&J, ✂ GSL, ✂ ITN, ✂ JE, ✂ JJ, ✂ NP, ✂ WTF, ✍ Aut.
02/3 Ultimate Memorabilia ✂ HT, ✂ Num
99/0 Ult. Victory 67, S10
91/2 Upper Deck 698
92/3 Upper Deck 364
92/3 Upper Deck 398
92/3 Upper Deck 419
92/3 Upper Deck AC2
92/3 Upper Deck CC15
92/3 Upper Deck G18
93/4 Upper Deck 195, NL5, SP-178
94/5 Upper Deck 145, SP-89
95/6 Upper Deck 243, 464, SE88
96/7 Upper Deck 313, X15, HH6, LS17, SS6A
97/8 Upper Deck 126, SS23, SG37, S15, T6C
98/9 Upper Deck 154, FF9, FT19, LS21
99/0 Upper Deck 100, 146, AS6, CT26, FF8, MA14, SS19
00/1 Upper Deck 363, A8, FF8, NC5, TT6, UDF, ✂ GJ, ✂ SG
01/2 Upper Deck 150, CT12, FF6, GA3, SS7, T9
02/3 Upper Deck 154, NC12, ✂ GO, ✂ R50
96/7 UD All-Star YCTG AR11
02/3 UD Artistic 78, R78, / Art
94/5 UD BAP R36
95/6 UD BAP 215, LL1, ✍ S215
96/7 UD Black Diam. 153
97/8 UD Black Diam. 110, PC14
98/9 UD Black Diam. 66, M4, WF23
99/0 UD Black Diam. 66, D13, DM6, ✂ APOH
00/1 UD Black Diam. 46
99/0 UD C. Legends 64, E8
01/2 UD Challenge 78
02/3 UD Classic 87, ✂ SC
95/6 UD CC 168, 356, 382
96/7 UD CC 201, 295, 327, UD16, C26, CR26
97/8 UD Coll. Choice 194, SQ87, C27, CR27
91/2 Upper Deck WJC 85
97/8 UD Diam. Vision 18
98/9 UD G. Reserve 154
99/0 UD G. Reserve 100, 146
99/0 UD Gretzky Excl. 80
01/2 UD Honor Roll ✂ PPM
02/3 UD Honor 61, -SG27
96/7 UD Ice 100, S8
97/8 UD Ice 70, IC15, L3A
00/1 UD Ice 72, ✂ IGJ
01/2 UD Ice 38
00/1 UD Legends 103, 104, ✂ LGJ, ✍ ES
01/2 UD Mask 83, GG
98/9 UD MVP 156, OT12, PG2
99/0 UD MVP 158, GU10, ✂ GU24
00/1 UD MVP 135, TD9, ✂ GS
01/2 UD MVP 163, ✂ S
02/3 UD MVP 160
99/0 UD MVP Cup 139, SS9, SC16, -GC
99/0 UD Ovation 44, LP7
02/3 UD Piece 77, / Giveaway
95/6 UD Post 23
01/2 UD Premier 44
02/3 UD Premier 47
00/1 UD Pros&Prosp. 67, ✂ GJS
99/0 UD Retro 61, G2C
02/3 UD Rookie 84, ✂ 160b
01/2 UD Top Shelf 39, ✂ S
02/3 UD Top Shelf 77, ✂ AS, ✂ CP, ✂ SW
00/1 UD Vintage 276, 283-84
01/2 UD Vintage 219, 226
02/3 UD Vintage 220, T56
00/1 Vanguard 77, HV-28
01/2 Vanguard 83
02/3 Vanguard ✂ GWJ 39
99/0 Victory 222, 224
00/1 Victory 177, 316
01/2 Victory 303, 406
02/3 Victory 188, -NP59
01/2 Waving the Flag 28
99/0 WGretzky 129, EG12
96 Wien 168
97/8 Zenith 7, Z18
96/7 PHOE / Coca-Cola
96/7 PHOE / Coca-Cola
97/8 PHOE / Coca-Cola
98/9 PHOE / Coca-Cola
98/9 PHOE / Coca-Cola
93/4 WINN / Ruffles
93/4 WINN Readers
95/6 WINN
95/6 WINN Readers

TKACS, WOJCIECH
92 Semic Sticker 287

TKACZUK, DANIEL
01/2 BAP Mem. 208
97/8 Bell
99 Bowman 133, SC14
97 Bowman 8, 152, BB4, ✍ Aut.
98 Bowman 34, SC3
98 Bowman Chrome 34
98/9 Bowman's Best 146
98/9 Collection Souvenir 09
01/2 O-Pee-Chee 287
98/9 OPC Chrome 227
01/2 Pacific 66
00/1 Parkhurst P-203
97/8 Pi. BeeHive 65, ✍ Aut. 65
00/1 Premier Plus 96
92 Québec Pee Wee 495
93 Québec Pee Wee 562
00/1 Signature 298
95/6 Slapshot 17
98/9 SPx Prospects 65
98/9 Topps 227
99/0 Topps 249
01/2 Topps 287
99/0 To. Chrome 249
98/9 UD Choice 254
96/7 Upper Deck 387
98/9 Upper Deck ✂ GJ10
96/7 UD Black Diam. 38
97/8 UD Black Diam. 55
98/9 UD Black Diam. 93
00/1 UD Black Diam. 93
97/8 UD Coll. Choice 298
01/2 Worcester IceCats
98/9 Barrie Colts

TKACZUK, WALT
71/2 Bazooka Panel
71/2 Colgate Head
70/1 Dad's Cookies
70/1 Eddie Sargent 117
71/2 Eddie Sargent 120
72/3 Eddie Sargent 149
70/1 Esso Power Player
72/3 Post 4
74/5 Lipton Soup 12
74/5 Loblaws
69/0 O-Pee-Chee 43
70/1 O-Pee-Chee 180
70/1 O-Pee-Chee DE 41
71/2 O-Pee-Chee 75
72/3 O-Pee-Chee 110
72/3 O-Pee-Chee Crest 14
73/4 O-Pee-Chee 25
74/5 O-Pee-Chee 119
75/6 O-Pee-Chee 128
76/7 O-Pee-Chee 220
77/8 O-Pee-Chee 90
78/9 O-Pee-Chee 235
79/0 O-Pee-Chee 15
80/1 O-Pee-Chee 211
72 Semic Sticker 212
69/0 Topps 43
71/2 Topps 75
72/3 Topps 14
73/4 Topps 25
74/5 Topps 119
75/6 Topps 128
76/7 Topps 220
77/8 Topps 90
78/9 Topps 235
79/0 Topps 15
80/1 Topps 211
71/2 Toronto Sun Photo

TKATCH, STAS
97/8 Quad City Mallards

TLACIL, JAN
00/1 OFS 4

TOAL, MIKE
88/9 EDMO / Action 111

TOBIN, JIM
94/5 Anchorage Aces 9

TOBIN, MIKE
00/1 Rockford IceHogs

TOBLER, RYAN
01/2 BAP Mem. 445
01/2 SP Authentic 173
01/2 SP GU 97
01/2 Upper Deck 440
01/2 UD Challenge 132
01/2 UD Ice 83
02/3 Chicago Wolves
99/0 Milwaukee Admirals
00/1 Milwaukee Admirals

TOCCHET, RICK
98/9 Aurora 149
99/0 Aurora 112
98/9 Be A Player 105, ✍ Aut. 105
99/0 BAP Mem. 276, 329
00/1 BAP Mem. 370
90/1 Bowman 108, -HT 14
91/2 Bowman 230
92/3 Bowman 159
95/6 Bowman 36
98/9 Bowman's Best 38
91 Canada Cup
93/4 Donruss 267
95/6 Donruss 41
96/7 Donruss 122
97/8 Donruss 45
97/8 Do. Priority 148
96/7 Duracell DC14
98/9 Dynagon Ice 146
99/0 Dynagon Ice 156
94/5 Flair 83
94/5 Fleer 100
96/7 Fleer 8
95/6 Fleer Metal 74, IW-15
92/3 Fleer Ultra 172
93/4 Fleer Ultra 225
94/5 Fleer Ultra 309
95/6 Fleer Ultra 79, CC-19
96/7 Fl. Ultra 12
95 Globe 92
93/4 Hockey Wit 58
95/6 Hoyle / West. J-Club
91/2 Kellogg's / Score 2
89/0 Kraft 57
90/1 Kraft 58
91/2 Kraft 45
98/9 Kraft / Post 4
89/0 Kraft Stickers 2
93/4 Leaf 109
94/5 Leaf 100, 474
95/6 Leaf 29
96/7 Leaf 90
94/5 L. Limited 117
95/6 L. Limited 112
97/8 Limited 83
96/7 Maggers 14
91/2 McDonald's Mc-02
96/7 Metal Univ. 11
98/9 NHL Power Play
87/8 OPC/Topps 2
88/9 OPC/Topps 177
90/1 OPC/Topps 26
90/1 Topps-TL 9
91/2 O-Pee-Chee 160
91/2 Topps - Team Leader 13
92/3 O-Pee-Chee 148
01/2 O-Pee-Chee 176
89/0 OPC/Topps 80
98/9 OPC Chrome 34
90/1 OPC Premier 120
91/2 OPC Premier 63
88/9 OPC Sticker 99-225
89/0 opcSticker 108-247
97/8 Omega 178
98/9 Omega 189
98/9 Pacific 92
99/0 Pacific 329
00/1 Pacific 308
01/2 Pacific 295
97/8 Pacific CC 311
98/9 Pa. Crown Roy. 106
97/8 Pa. Paramount 145
98/9 Pa. Paramount 187
99/0 Pa. Paramount 185
00/1 Pa. Paramount 186
98/9 Pa. Revolution 113
87/8 Panini Sticker 134
88/9 Panini Sticker 326
89/0 Panini Sticker 295
90/1 Panini Sticker 121
91/2 Panini Sticker 229
91/2 Panini Sticker 331
92/3 Panini Sticker 226
93/4 Panini Sticker 80
94/5 Panini Sticker 77
95/6 Panini Sticker 271
96/7 Panini Sticker 6
98/9 Panini Sticker 282
91/2 Parkhurst 129
91/2 Parkhurst 354
92/3 Parkhurst 139
92/3 Parkhurst CP12
93/4 Parkhurst 428
94/5 Parkhurst V25
95/6 Parkhurst 287
00/1 Parkhurst P-161
94/5 Parkie SE79
91/2 Pinnacle 20
92/3 Pinnacle 282
93/4 Pinnacle 174
94/5 Pinnacle 371, BR18, GR12
96/7 Pinnacle 23
97/8 Pi. Be A Player 127, ✍ Aut. 127
97/8 Pi. Inside 174
95/6 Pi. Summit 103
95/6 Pi. Zenith 118, GG-5
95/6 Playoff 161
96/7 Playoff 376
95/6 POG 137
93/4 Power Play 196
93/4 Premier 72
94/5 Premier 281, 346
99/0 Prism 111
00/1 Pr. Stock ✂ GUG 86
95/6 Pro Magnet 65
90/1 Pro Set 225, 374
91/2 Pro Set 177
91/2 Pro Set 311
91/2 Pro Set 580
92/3 Pro Set 138
91/2 Pro Set Platinum 88
99/0 Revolution 115
90/1 Score 80
90/1 Sco. Hot Cards 40
91/2 Score 9
91/2 Score 302
91/2 Score 334
91/2 Score CAN 9
91/2 Score CAN 306
91/2 Score CAN 364
92/3 Score 245
93/4 Score 340
93/4 Score PIAS 14
94/5 Score CI11
95/6 Score 37
96/7 Score 92
97/8 Score 246
92/3 Seasons 37
94/5 Select 2
95/6 Select CE 98
94 Semic 358
94 Semic 95
95 Semic 98
92 Semic Sticker 96
93 Semic Sticker 200
01/2 Signature 141, ✍ Aut. 141
95/6 SBx Emotion 86, NP-10
95/6 SBx Impact 83, 247
96/7 SBx Impact 9
94/5 SP 55
96/7 SP 12
97/8 SP Authentic 121
01/2 SP Authentic ✂ NN
99/0 SPx 116
00/1 SPx 50
00/1 Stadion 198
99/0 Stadium 94
95/6 Super Sticker 59
96/7 Team Out!
92/3 Topps 70
95/6 Topps 264, 15HG
98/9 Topps 34
99/0 Topps 117
00/1 Topps 220
01/2 Topps 176
99/0 To. Chrome 117
94/5 Topps Finest 52
95/6 To. Finest 133
98/9 T. Gold Label 48
00/1 To. Heritage 163
96/7 To. Picks 111
91/2 To. Stadium 35
92/3 To. Stadium 76
93/4 To. Stadium 329
93/4 To. Stadium - AS
94/5 To. Stadium 160
95/6 To. Stadium 32, F5
95/6 T. Super Skills 64
90/1 Upper Deck 263, 488
91/2 Upper Deck 91
92/3 Upper Deck 122
91/2 Upper Deck 503
92/3 Upper Deck 238
92/3 Upper Deck 454
93/4 Upper Deck 179, 233, HT12, SP-126
94/5 Upper Deck 224, SP-129
95/6 Upper Deck 274, SE-40
96/7 Upper Deck 10, X32
97/8 Upper Deck 339
98/9 Upper Deck 341
00/1 Upper Deck 131
94/5 UD BAP G18
95/6 UD BAP 82, ✍ S82
96/7 UD Black Diam. 55
95/6 UD CC 254
96/7 UD CC 18
98/9 UD G. Reserve 341
96/7 UD Ice 4
92/3 UD Locker 16
98/9 UD MVP 162
99/0 UD MVP 159
00/1 UD Vintage 261, 271
99/0 Victory 231
96 Wien 89
86/7 PHIL
89/0 PHIL
90/1 PHIL
91/2 PHIL / J.C. Penney
01/2 PHIL
97/8 PHOE / Coca-Cola
98/9 PHOE / Coca-Cola
91/2 PITT / Elby's
91/2 PITT / Foodland 5
92/3 PITT / Coke-Clark
92/3 PITT / Foodland 4
92/3 PITT / Food. Stickers
93/4 PITT / Foodland 4
81/2 Soo Greyhounds
82/3 Soo Greyhounds
83/4 Soo Greyhounds
87/8 Soo Greyhounds 26

TOCHER, RYAN
91/2 7th...Sketch OHL 204
95/6 Slapshot 235

TODD, BRODY
00/1 Kingston Frontenacs 23

TODD, DICK
89/0 7th...Sketch OHL 123
90/1 7th...Sketch OHL 376
91/2 7th...Sketch OHL 123
91/2 Peterborough Petes

TODD, KEVIN
92/3 Bowman 21
92/3 Fleer Ultra 121, -UR 8
93/4 Fleer Ultra 294
91/2 Gillette 40
93/4 Leaf 15
94/5 Leaf 350
91/2 O-Pee-Chee 400
92/3 O-Pee-Chee 1
91/2 OPC Premier 22
97/8 Pacific CC 182
92/3 Panini Sticker 275
92/3 Panini Sticker O
96/7 Panini Sticker 271
91/2 Parkhurst 97
91/2 Parkhurst 444
92/3 Parkhurst 94
92/3 Parkhurst 238
92/3 Parkhurst 285
93/4 Parkhurst 37
94/5 Parkhurst 108
95/6 Parkhurst 374
91/2 Pinnacle 308
92/3 Pinnacle 272
92/3 Pinnacle T2K 22
93/4 Pinnacle 270
96/7 Pi. Be A Player 101, ✍ Aut. 101
93/4 Power Play 318
91/2 Pro Set 548
92/3 Pro Set 94
92/3 Pro Set RGL 7
91/2 Pro Set Platinum 260
88/9 ProCards / Utica
89/0 ProCards AHL 205
90/1 ProCards 570
91/2 Score 397
91/2 Score CAN 287
92/3 Score 162
93/4 Score 338
93/4 Score 507
97/8 Score Anah. 6
92/3 Score Young Stars 19
92/3 Topps 15
92/3 Topps 228
92/3 To. Stadium 465
93/4 To. Stadium 8
91/2 Upper Deck 401
92/3 Upper Deck 11
92/3 Upper Deck 303
92/3 Upper Deck 365
92/3 Upper Deck AR3
93/4 Upper Deck 88, 440, SP-33
94/5 Upper Deck 120
95/6 Upper Deck 364
97/8 Upper Deck 3
94/5 UD BAP ✍ 74
96/7 UD CC 127
97/8 UD Coll. Choice 11
96/7 UD Ice 1
96/7 ANAH / Up Front 4
93/4 CHIC / Coke
92/3 EDMO

TODOROV, ATANAS
79 Panini Sticker 351

TOEWS, LORNE
90/1 7th...Sketch WHL 36
91/2 7th...Sketch WHL 316

TOFFEY, JOHN
96 Québec Pee Wee 1112

TOFFOLO, MARK
78/9 Saginaw Gears

TOIVANEN, HARRI
80/1 Mallasjuoma 76

TOIVOLA, MARKO
94/5 Sisu 303
95/6 Sisu 119

TOIVOLA, TERO
93/4 Sisu 75

TOIVONEN, EMARKO
98/9 Cardset 168

TOIVONEN, HANNU
02/3 Cardset 280, -BFG 10, ✍ BFG

TOIVONEN, HARRI
78/9 SM-Liiga 121

TOIVONEN, KALEVI
66/7 Champion 179

TOIVONEN, KARI-PEKKA
70/1 Kuvajulkaisut 204
72 Panda MM-Toronto

TOIVONEN, MARKO
99/0 Cardset 285
00/1 Cardset 64

TOIVONEN, TIMO
72/3 Williams Finnish 355

TOK, CHRIS
95/6 Fort Wayne Komets
99/0 Missouri RiverOtters

TOKARCZYK, TREVOR
95/6 Slapshot 367
96/7 Soo Greyhounds

TOKARZ, LESZEK
74 Hellas MM-Jenkki 88
79 Panini Sticker 135
73/4 Williams Finnish 101

TOKARZ, WIESLAV
74 Hellas MM-Jenkki 89
73/4 Williams Finnish 102

TOLJANICH, MARK
91/2 7th...Sketch WHL 300
93/4 Red Deer Rebels

TOLKUNOV, DMITRI
99 Bowman 48
98 Bowman 117
98 Bowman Chrome 117
99/0 Cleveland Lumberjacks
01/2 Norfolk Admirals
98/9 Québec Remparts

TOLL, STEVEN
99/0 Indianapolis Ice

TOLSA, JARI
00/1 UD Elitserien 70

TOLVANEN, ISMO
71/2 Williams Finnish 337

TOLVANEN, J
95/6 DEL 168

TOMAJKO, JAN
95/6 APS 122
96/7 APS 277
97/8 APS 48
97/8 DS 64
98/9 DS 82
99/0 DS 135
01/2 DS 21
96/7 DS Sticker 185
97/8 DS Sticker 181
98/9 OFS 111
99/0 OFS 67, 272
00/1 OFS 335
01/2 OFS 25
95/6 Upper Deck 544

TOMAN, ILMAR
94/5 DEL 419

TOMANEK, ROBERT
01/2 OFS 24

TOMASEK, ALES
94/5 APS 6
95/6 APS 301, 413
96/7 APS 194
97/8 APS 224
97/8 DS 15
98/9 DS 102
99/0 DS 48
96/7 DS Sticker 195
97/8 DS Sticker 30
98/9 OFS 68, 358, 476
99/0 OFS 295
00/1 OFS 271

TOMASEK, MARTIN
97/8 APS 144
99/0 DS 181
99/0 OFS 430
00/1 OFS 257

TOMASONI, DICK
72 Semic Sticker 137

TOMASSONI, DAVE
82 Semic Sticker 128

TOMBERLIN, JUSTIN
92/3 Maine Black Bears
93/4 Maine Black Bears

TOMEK, MICHAL
94/5 APS 245
95/6 APS 23
96/7 APS 225
97/8 APS 113
97/8 DS 25
99/0 DS 11
97/8 DS Sticker 56
98/9 OFS 26
99/0 OFS 217

TOMICA, MAREK
99/0 OFS 393
00/1 OFS 104
01/2 OFS 281

TOMIK, ROBERT
00/1 DS 131
00/1 OFS 176
01/2 OFS -UHI 37

TOMILIN, VITALI
92/3 Classic 53
92/3 Classic Four Sport 191
93/4 Upper Deck 278

TOMLAK, MIKE
91/2 Bowman 14
90/1 OPC/Topps 95
91/2 O-Pee-Chee 410
90/1 Panini Sticker 46
91/2 Panini Sticker 319
90/1 Pro Set 452
90/1 ProCards 176
91/2 ProCards 114
91/2 Score CAN 538
91/2 To. Stadium 266
90/1 Upper Deck 343
91/2 Upper Deck 310
89/0 HART / Jr. Whalers
90/1 HART / Jr. Whalers
94/5 Milwaukee Admirals
95/6 Milwaukee Admirals
96/7 Milwaukee Admirals
97/8 Milwaukee Admirals

TOMLINSON, DAVE
92/3 Classic Prospects 12
96/7 DEL 170
98/9 DEL 227
95/6 Edge Ice 114
99/0 Eishockey 7
94/5 Panini Sticker S
91/2 ProCards 346
00/1 UD DEL 2, S9
01/2 UD DEL 178
94/5 Cincinnati Cyclones
95/6 Cincinnati Cyclones
93/4 Phoenix Roadrunners
92/3 St. John's Maple Leafs

TOMLINSON, JUSTIN
94/5 Raleigh Icecaps

TOMLINSON, KIRK
88/9 ProCards / Kalamazoo
91/2 ProCards 122
99/0 Colorado Gold Kings
93/4 Las Vegas Thunder
94/5 Peoria Rivermen
95/6 Peoria Rivermen
88/9 Kitchener Rangers

TOMLINSON, MIKE
89/0 7th...Sketch OHL 108
90/1 7th...Sketch OHL 373
91/2 7th...Sketch OHL 126
91/2 Peterborough Petes

TOMLINSON, SHAYNE
93/4 N. Michigan Wildcats

TOMMILA, ESA
92/3 Jyvas Hyva 46
93/4 Jyvas Hyva 89
93/4 Sisu 126
94/5 Sisu 285
95/6 Sisu 188

TOMMILA, TERO
71/2 Williams Finnish 375

TOMPKINS, DAN
99/0 Missouri RiverOtters

TOMS, C.
10/1 Imperial 29

TOMS, JEFF
97/8 Pacific CC 342
91/2 7th...Sketch OHL 334
93/4 Slapshot / S.S.Marie 23

00/1 To. Gold Label 98
94/5 Atlanta Knights 19
95/6 Atlanta Knights
98/9 Portland Pirates
93/4 Soo Greyhounds 25

TON, ANDY
95 Panini Worlds 133
91 Semic Sticker 190
92 Semic Sticker 207
93 Semic Sticker 118

TON, PETR
94/5 APS 62
95/6 APS 95
96/7 APS 89
97/8 APS 206
98/9 Cardset 21
99/0 Cardset 279
00/1 Cardset 51
02/3 Cardset 127
97/8 DS 11
96/7 DS Sticker 148
97/8 DS Sticker 237

TONELLI, JOHN
90/1 Bowman 148
91/2 Bowman 175
88/9 Esso All-Star
83/4 Funmate Puffy 21 [w/]
79/0 O-Pee-Chee 146
80/1 O-Pee-Chee 305
81/2 O-Pee-Chee 218
82/3 O-Pee-Chee 213
83/4 O-Pee-Chee 20
84/5 O-Pee-Chee 138
85/6 OPC/Topps 41
85/6 OPC/Topps Box O
86/7 OPC/Topps 132
87/8 OPC/Topps 84
90/1 OPC/Topps 281
91/2 O-Pee-Chee 161
89/0 OPC/Topps 8
91/2 OPC Premier 37
91/2 OPC Premier 159
82/3 OPC/Topps Sticker 49
83/4 OPC/Topps Sticker 74
83/4 OPC/Topps Sticker 75
84/5 OPC Sticker 80
84/5 OPC Sticker 81
85/6 OPC Sticker 80
85/6 OPC Sticker 116
86/7 OPC Sticker 81-207
87/8 OPC Sticker 47-186
88/9 OPC Sticker 87-217
89/0 Panini Sticker 90
90/1 Panini Sticker 235
91/2 Panini Sticker 90
91/2 Pinnacle 284
82/3 Post [NYIs.]
90/1 Pro Set 129
91/2 Pro Set 373
92/3 Pro Set 263
91/2 Pro Set Platinum 22
90/1 Score 89
91/2 Score 172
91/2 Score 17T
91/2 Score CAN 172
91/2 Score CAN 567
92/3 Score 342
83/4 Souhaits Keychain [Islanders]
79/0 Topps 146
84/5 Topps 103
85/6 OPC/Topps-Stick. 7
92/3 Topps 119
91/2 To. Stadium 189
92/3 To. Stadium 159
90/1 Upper Deck 95
86/7 CALG / Red Rooster
87/8 CALG / Red Rooster
91/2 CHIC / Coke
88/9 LOSA / Smokey
89/0 LOSA / Smokey 13
90/1 LOSA / Smokey 14
79/0 NYIS
83/4 NYIS
83/4 NYIS / News 14
84/5 NYIS / News 15
93/4 NYIS / Bank
99/0 NYIS / UD NY11
75/6 Houston Aeros

TONINATO, JIM
85/6 Minnesota-Duluth 12

TONOZAKI, KAZUMA
79 Panini Sticker 286

TOOKEY, TIM
93/4 Cla. Prospects 84
88/9 ProCards / New Haven
89/0 ProCards AHL 353
90/1 ProCards 51
91/2 ProCards 281
82/3 Fredericton Express
98/9 Hershey Bears

TOOMEY, DICK
72 Semic Sticker 134

TOOMEY, SEAN
85/6 Minnesota-Duluth 24

TOOR, GARRY
99/0 Prince George Cougars

TOOR, GARY
95/6 Tri-City Americans 15

TOOTOO, JORDIN
00/1 UD Prospects 45
01 UD Prospects GU 34, ✂- TPJ, ✂- JC
99/0 Brandon Wheat Kings

TOPATIGH, LUCIO
95 Panini Worlds 88
95 Semic 175
92 Semic Sticker 261
93 Semic Sticker 221

TOPOLINSKY, CRAIG
94/5 DEL 147

TOPOLL, DEL
53/4 La Patrie

TOPOROWSKI, BRAD
91/2 7th...Sketch WHL 14
97/8 Louisiana Ice Gators

TOPOROWSKI, KERRY
91/2 ProCards 499
91 7th..Sketch Mem.Cup 85
90/1 7th..Sketch WHL 206
91/2 Ultimate Draft Pick 48, 48, ✍ Aut.
95/6 Adirondack Red Wings
92/3 Indianapolis Ice
93/4 Indianapolis Ice
93/4 Las Vegas Thunder
94/5 Las Vegas Thunder
97/8 Quad City Mallards
00/1 Quad City Mallards
89/0 Spokane Chiefs

TOPOROWSKI, SHAYNE
00/1 Cardset 252
97/8 Donruss 224
95/6 Edge Ice 84
95/6 St. John's Maple Leafs
96/7 St. John's Maple Leafs
01/2 Belfast Giants
93/4 Prince Albert Raiders

TOPPAZZINI, JERRY
45-64 BeeHive-2 [Bost.]
62/3 Cowan Tile
53/4 Parkhurst 98
92/3 Parkhurst PR-27
93/4 Parkie 56-57 1
60/1 Shirriff 110
61/2 Shirriff 9
54/5 Topps 21
57/8 Topps 5
58/9 Topps 45
59/0 Topps 38
60/1 Topps 28
61/2 Topps 9
62/3 Topps 13
62/3 Topps Dollar
63/4 Topps 18
60/1 Toronto Star Weekend
91/2 Ultimate Original Six 55
57-58 BOST

TOPPAZZINI, TED
52/3 Anonymous 145

TOPPAZZINI, ZELLIO
45-64 BeeHive-2 [Bost.]
52/3 Parkhurst 73

TORCHIA, MIKE
92/3 Classic Prospects 119
95/6 Donruss 143
95/6 Fleer Ultra 43
95/6 Leaf 213
95/6 Score 311
92 7th...Sketch Awards 6
90 7th..Sketch Mem.Cup 31
89/0 7th..Sketch OHL 191, 192
90/1 7th..Sketch OHL 244
91/2 7th...Sketch OHL 75
91/2 Star Pics 26
91/2 Ultimate Draft Pick 50, 57, ✍ Aut.
97/8 Milwaukee Admirals
01/2 Manchester Storm
01/2 Manchester Storm
02/3 Manchester Storm
02/3 Manchester Storm
01/2 Sheffield Steelers GS
88/9 Kitchener Rangers
89/0 Kitchener Rangers
90/1 Kitchener Rangers

TOREN, JOHAN
79 Panini Sticker 279

TORGAJEV, PAVEL
95/6 Fleer Ultra 215
00/1 Mir 199
95/6 Parkhurst 302
93/4 Sisu 46
94/5 Sisu 309

TORKKEL, KARI
66/7 Champion 62
70/1 Kuvajulkaisut 151
71/2 Williams Finnish 202
72/3 Williams Finnish 239
73/4 Williams Finnish 274

TORKKELI, JORMA
80/1 Mallasjuoma 106
78/9 SM-Liiga 151

TORKKELI, VEIKKO
80/1 Mallasjuoma 103
78/9 SM-Liiga 143

TORKKI, JARI
96/7 DEL 194
91/2 Jyvas Hyva 45
92/3 Jyvas Hyva 130
93/4 Jyvas Hyva 239
88/9 ProCards / Saginaw
89/0 ProCards IHL 55
91 Semic Sticker 22
93/4 Sisu 194
94/5 Sisu 13, FOI-15
95/6 Sisu 104, 189
96/7 Sisu 107
95/6 Sisu Limited 34

TORKKI, SAMI
00/1 Cardset 67
01/2 Cardset 133
02/3 Cardset 281

TORMA, HANNU
66/7 Champion 3
65/6 Hellas 29

TÖRMÄNEN, ANTTI
95/6 Bowman 117
98/9 Cardset Leij. 45
99/0 Cardset 200, -AH 9-hertta
00/1 Cardset 163
02/3 Cardset 133
95/6 Donruss 347, RR-15
95/6 Fleer Metal 196
95/6 Fleer Ultra 360
95 Hartwall Karjala
97/8 Hockey-Box
95 Leaf Latkaliiga 2
96/7 Panini Sticker 53
95/6 Parkhurst 415, 522
95/6 Pi. Summit 174
96/7 Pi. Summit 118
95/6 Pi. Zenith 135, RC-4
96/7 Pi. Zenith 78
96/7 Score 265
95/6 Select CE 111
94 Semic 28
95 Semic 49
93/4 Sisu 16
94/5 Sisu 63, MN-7, ND-8
95/6 Sisu Gold-23
95/6 Sisu Limited 17
95/6 SP 105
95/6 To. Finest 118
95/6 To. Stadium 156
95/6 T. Super Skills SR13
95/6 Upper Deck 347
96/7 Upper Deck 114
96/7 UD CC 184
98/9 UD Elitserien 110
99/0 UD Elitserien 96
96 Wien 15
95/6 OTTA

TORNBERG, JOHAN
94/5 Leaf Elit Set 212
95/6 Leaf Elit Set 294
95/6 UD Elitserien 190
97/8 UD Elitserien 186
98/9 UD Elitserien 154
99/0 UD Elitserien 152, ✍ Aut.
00/1 UD Elitserien 140

TORNQUIST, MICHAEL
98/9 Odessa Jackalopes
99/0 Odessa Jackalopes

TOROPCHENKO, LEONID
93/4 Cla. 4 Sport 250
92/3 Classic Prospects 95
93/4 Cla. Prospects 212
00/1 Mir 203
93/4 Cleveland Lumberjacks

TORREL, DOUG
92/3 Hamilton Canucks

TORRES, RAFFI
01/2 BAP Mem. 350
01/2 Bowman 146
02/3 Calder 70
01/2 Crown Royale 170
02/3 First Edition 258
02/3 Heads Up -HF 9
02/3 O-Pee-Chee 308
02/3 Pacific 244
02/3 Pacific Complete 54
01/2 PTC Draft 7
01/2 PTC Collectibles 7
01/2 PTC Rookie 8
01/2 Parkhurst 329
01/2 PS Titanium 170, TSS 29, TRT 9
01/2 PS Titanium Draft 151
01/2 SP Authentic ✍ 180
02/3 SP Authentic 123
01/2 SP GU 86
02/3 SP GU ✂- PC
01/2 SPx 210, -RT
01/2 SPx Rookie RR19
01/2 Topps 360
02/3 Topps 308
01/2 To. Chrome 179
02/3 To. Limited 308
01/2 UD PlayMakers Ltd 128
01/2 Upper Deck 436
01/2 UD Challenge 124
01/2 UD Honor Roll 94
01/2 UD Ice 61, 143
01/2 UD Mask 154
01/2 UD MVP 228
01/2 UD Premier 112, ✍ Sig
99/0 UD Prospects 23
00/1 UD Prospects 34, CS3, FL2, GD4, ✂- GJ, ✂- GJC, ✂- ✍ GJS, ✍ Sig.
01 UD Prospects GU ✂- SoT
01/2 UD Top Shelf 133
02/3 UD Top Shelf ✂- Sig
02/3 UD Vintage 156, GB 156
01/2 Vanguard 121
01/2 Victory 448
02/3 Victory 133
99/0 Brampton Batallion 11

TORRETTI, DOMINIC
99/0 Des Moines Buc's

TORREY, BILL
83/4 NYIS / News 28
84/5 NYIS / News 28

TORREY, JEFF
92/3 Richmond Renegades

TORTI, SLOAN
86/7 Kingston Canadians

TORTORELLA, JOHN
88/9 ProCards / New Haven
89/0 BUFF / Campbell's
90/1 BUFF / Campbell's
97/8 PHOE / Coca-Cola
95/6 Rochester Americans
96/7 Rochester Americans

TORTUNOV, BORIS
98/9 Mir 18
99/0 Mir 19
00/1 Mir 219
00/1 Metallurg 33

TORY, JEFF
91/2 Avant Garde BCJHL 18
91/2 Avant Garde BCJHL 159
92/3 BCJHL 138
88/9 EBK IHL All-Star
01/2 UD DEL 135

TOSIO, RENATO
95 Globe 209
95 Panini Worlds 117
95 Semic 189
91 Semic Sticker 177
92 Semic Sticker 195
93 Semic Sticker 109

TOSKALA, VESA
01/2 BT Pipes 86
02/3 Between the Pipes 100
02/3 Calder 95
98/9 Cardset 74, MM 4
99/0 Cardset 180, -PA 10
00/1 Cardset 111
02/3 Cardset 128
97/8 Hockey-Box
02/3 Pacific Complete 598
01/2 PS Titanium Draft 166
95/6 Sisu 230, DD-7
96/7 Sisu 27, MA-6
95/6 Sisu Limited 100
95/6 UD CC 335
99/0 UD Elitserien 52
02/3 UD Mask 73
01/2 Cleveland Barons
00/1 Kentucky Tho'blades

TOSKALO, VESA
96/7 Sisu RE 8

TOTH, RADEK
97/8 DS Sticker 227
99/0 Eishockey 353
00/1 UD DEL 113

TOTH, TONY
92/3 MPS SJHL 164

TÓTH, RADEK
94/5 APS 251
95/6 APS 126
97/8 APS 195
97/8 DS 89

TOTTLE, SCOTT
85/6 Fredericton Express

TOUCHETTE, JEAN-FRANÇOIS
99/0 Québec Remparts 10

TOUGAS, VINCENT
01/2 Victoriaville Tigres 16

TOUHEY, BILL
33/4 Canadian Gum
33/4 O-Pee-Chee 26

TOUJIKOV, ROUSLAN
94/5 Roanoke Express

TOUJNIK, EVGENI
98 Québec Pee Wee 1023

TOUPAL, KAMIL
94/5 APS 31
95/6 APS 61
96/7 APS 244
97/8 APS 271
96/7 DS Sticker 77
97/8 DS Sticker 73
98/9 OFS 197

TOUPAL, RADEK
95/6 APS 65, 443
96/7 APS 250, 406
97/8 APS 276
94/5 DEL 377
97/8 DS 31
98/9 DS 34
99/0 DS 38
96/7 DS Sticker 86
97/8 DS Sticker 74
92/3 Jyvas Hyva 28
98/9 OFS 201, 466
99/0 OFS 190
95 Panini Worlds 209
95 Semic 149
91 Semic Sticker 117

TOUPIN, SIMON
90/1 7th..Sketch LHJMQ 129
91/2 7th...Sketch LHJMQ 177

TOUSIGANT, DAN
85/6 Minnesota-Duluth 23

TOUZIMSKY, ZDENEK
94/5 APS 73
95/6 APS 182
96/7 APS 316
96/7 DS Sticker 155
99/0 Eishockey 344
98/9 OFS 363
00/1 OFS 64

TOVELL, TREVOR
91 7th..Sketch Mem.Cup 86
90/1 7th..Sketch WHL 192
89/0 Spokane Chiefs

TOWER, GEORGE
92/3 Semic Nordisk 180

TOWNSEND, SCOTT
90/1 7th..Sketch WHL 37
91/2 7th...Sketch WHL 325
93/4 Lethbridge Hurricanes

TOWNSHEND, GRAEME
89/0 ProCards AHL 70
90/1 ProCards 133
91/2 ProCards 456
89/0 BOST / Sports Action
93/4 OTTA
95/6 Houston Aeros

TOYE, RANDY
91/2 7th...Sketch WHL 20

TRACHTA, DAVID
94/5 APS 161
95/6 APS 262

TRACHTA, KAREL
94/5 APS 289
95/6 APS 242
97/8 APS 219
98/9 OFS 81

TRACHTA, TOMAS
96/7 APS 83
97/8 APS 213
99/0 Score 18

TRACY, JOE
91/2 Semic Elitserien 247

TRACY, TRIPP
96/7 Richmond Renegades

TRACZE, STEVE
95/6 Slapshot 42

TRADER, LARRY
83 Canada Juniors
88/9 ProCards / Binghampton
84/5 DETR / Little Caesars
87/8 MONT
87/8 MONT / Vachon 44

TRAINER, CHRIS
83/4 Kitchener Rangers

TRAINERS, PHOENIX
95/6 Phoenix Roadrunners

TRAKHANOV, PAVEL
00/1 Mir 331

TRAMPUH, ROBBIE
92/3 BCJHL 131

TRAPP, BARRY
82/3 Regina Pats
83/4 Regina Pats

TRAPP, BOB
23/4 Paulins Candy 42

TRAPP, DOUG
82/3 Regina Pats
83/4 Regina Pats

TRATTNER, JÜRGEN
98/9 DEL 197

TRAUB, PUSS
23/4 Paulins Candy 23

TRAVERSE, PATRICK
98/9 Omega 171
91/2 7th...Sketch LHJMQ 63
01/2 Signature 79, ✍ Aut. 79
00/1 To. Heritage 206
01/2 MONT
02/3 MONT
98/9 OTTA
99/0 OTTA

TRAVIS, SHANNON
89/0 ProCards IHL 174

TRAVNICEK, MIKHAIL
99/0 DS 70
98/9 OFS 16
99/0 OFS 340
00/1 St. John's Maple Leafs
01/2 St. John's Maple Leafs

TRAVNICEK, ZDENEK
94/5 DEL 300
95/6 DEL 389
96/7 DEL 72

TRAYNOR, PAUL
97 Bowman 39
94/5 Slapshot / Kitchener 8
95/6 Slapshot 159
97/8 Albany River Rats
00/1 Rochester Americans

TRBOYEVICH, DEAN
94/5 Anchorage Aces 25
98/9 Anchorage Aces
97/8 Grand Rapids Griffins

TREBIL, DAN
99/0 Choice 10
97/8 Donruss 105
98/9 Cincinnati M'Ducks 18
99/0 Cincinnati M'Ducks
92/3 Minnesota G'Gophers
93/4 Minnesota G'Gophers
94/5 Minnesota G'Gophers

TREEN, ALF
59/60 Whitby Dunlops

TREFILOV, ANDREI
93/4 Classic 95
93/4 Cla. 4 Sport 248
92/3 Classic Prospects 30
92/3 Classic Prospects BC2
93/4 Cla. Prospects 181
93/4 Donruss 409
94/5 Donruss 244
95/6 Donruss 273
94/5 Fleer Ultra 271
95 Globe 163
94/5 Leaf 87
00/1 Mir 394
91/2 O-Pee-Chee 45R
93/4 Parkhurst 29
94/5 Parkhurst 36
95/6 Parkhurst 296
93/4 Power Play 311
94/5 Premier 166
92/3 Red Ace Blue 4
93/4 Score 599
94 Semic 136
92 Semic Sticker 99
91/2 Star Pics 49
92/3 Upper Deck 345
93/4 Upper Deck 514
95/6 Upper Deck 277
96/7 Upper Deck 225
00/1 UD DEL 58, P11
01/2 UD DEL 58
01/2 UD DEL G3, ✂- GJ
99/0 Chicago Wolves
98/9 Indianapolis Ice
94/5 Saint John Flames
92/3 Salt Lake G'Eagles

TREMBECKY, JEFF
98/9 Peoria Rivermen

TREMBLAY, ALEXANDRE
99 Bowman 77
99/0 Rimouski Océanic 7

TREMBLAY, CLÉMENT
51/2 Bas du Fleuve 4
52/3 Bas du Fleuve 32

TREMBLAY, DAVE
90/1 7th..Sketch LHJMQ 29
91/2 7th...Sketch LHJMQ 80

TREMBLAY, DAVID
02/3 Hull Olympiques

TREMBLAY, DENIS
79/0 Montréal Juniors B&W

TREMBLAY, DIDIER
99 Bowman 68
98 Bowman 84
98 Bowman Chrome 84
00/1 Peoria Rivermen
95/6 Halifax Moosehead
96/7 Halifax Moosehead
96/7 Halifax Moosehead
97/8 Halifax Moosehead

TREMBLAY, ÉRIC
99 Bowman 46

TREMBLAY, FRANK
85/6 London Knights

TREMBLAY, GILLES
45-64 BeeHive-2 [Mont.]
45-64 BeeHive-2 [Mont.]
64-67 BeeHive-3 [Mont.]
64-67 BeeHive-3 [Mont.]
63-65 Chex
64/5 Coke/Sprite [Mont.]
65/6 Coca-Cola
62/3 Cowan Tile
68/9 O-Pee-Chee 66
69/0 O-Pee-Chee 168
62/3 Parkhurst 46
63/4 Parkhurst 21
63/4 Parkhurst 80
95/6 Parkie 66-67 71
94/5 Parkie Tall 74
66/7 Post Cereal Box
68/9 Post Marble
67/8 Post Tips 3
67/8 Post Tips 9
61/2 Shirriff 112
62/3 Shirriff 24
68/9 Shirriff / Mont. 7
64/5 Topps 2
66/7 Topps 4
66/7 Topps / Test 4
67/8 Topps 5
68/9 Topps 66
63/4 Toronto Star Action
62/3 Toronto Star Weekend
60/1 York Glass [Mont.]
60/1 York
61/2 York 4
62/3 York Transfer 34
63/4 York 21
66/7 MONT / IGA Stamp
67/8 MONT
67/8 MONT / IGA Card
68/9 MONT / IGA Card
69/0 MONT / Pro Star
80/1 Québec Remparts

TREMBLAY, J.F.
96/7 Roanoke Express 8

TREMBLAY, JACQUES
87/8 Kingston Canadians

TREMBLAY, JEAN-CLAUDE
45-64 BeeHive-2 [Mont.]
45-64 BeeHive-2 [Mont.]
64-67 BeeHive-3 [Mont.]
63-65 Chex
64/5 Coke/Sprite [Mont.]
65/6 Coca-Cola
70/1 Colgate 64
70/1 Dad's Cookies
76/7 Dernière Heure
78/9 Dernière Heure
70/1 Eddie Sargent 99
71/2 Eddie Sargent 97
70/1 Esso Power Player
71/2 Frito Lay
62/3 Cowan Tile
66/7 MONT / IGA Stamp
67/8 MONT
67/8 MONT / IGA Card
68/9 MONT / IGA Card
69/0 MONT / Pro Star
70/1 MONT
71/2 MONT / Pro Star
68/9 O-Pee-Chee 59
69/0 O-Pee-Chee 206
69/0 O-Pee-Chee 5
70/1 O-Pee-Chee 178
71/2 O-Pee-Chee 130
71/2 O-Pee-Chee 252
72/3 O-Pee-Chee 293
74/5 OPC WHA 18
75/6 OPC WHA 62
75/6 OPC WHA 130
76/7 O-Pee-Chee WHA 2
76/7 OPC WHA 30
76/7 OPC WHA 62
77/8 OPC WHA 44
73/4 OPC WHA Poster 2
62/3 Parkhurst 54
63/4 Parkhurst 31
63/4 Parkhurst 90
92/3 Parkie - Reprint 282, 288, 297
95/6 Parkie 66-67 67
94/5 Parkie Tall 74
66/7 Post Cereal Box
66/7 Post [Small]
68/9 Post Marble
67/8 Post Tips 10
67/8 Post Shooters
73/4 Quaker Oats 30
72/3 Québec Nordiques
73/4 Québec Nordiques
76/7 Québec Nordiques
76/7 Québ. / Antoinette
60/1 Shirriff 36
61/2 Shirriff 118
62/3 Shirriff 30
68/9 Shirriff / Mont. 5
81/2 TCMA 3
64/5 Topps 88
65/6 Topps 69
66/7 Topps 5
66/7 Topps / Test 5
67/8 Topps 73
68/9 Topps 59
69/0 Topps 5
71/2 Topps 130
63/4 Toronto Star Action
64/5 Toronto Star Action
65/6 Toronto Star Photo
71/2 Toronto Sun Photo
61/2 York 34
62/3 York Transfer 6
63/4 York 24
67/8 York 13
67/8 York 19
67/8 York 24
67/8 York
67/8 York

TREMBLAY, JÉRÔME
99 Bowman 74
97 Bowman 75
99/0 Rouyn-Noranda
99/0 Rouyn-Noranda

TREMBLAY, JULES
51/2 Lac St-Jean 42

TREMBLAY, LUDGER
51/2 Laval Dairy 11
52/3 St. Lawrence 49

TREMBLAY, LUIS
00/1 Baie-Comeau 8
01/2 Baie-Comeau 7
02/3 Baie-Comeau

TREMBLAY, MARC-AURÈLE
51/2 Lac St-Jean 34

TREMBLAY, MARIO
80/1 Dernière Heure
83/4 Dernière Heure
83/4 Esso Stars
83/4 Funmate Puffy 5 [w/]
84/5 Kellogg's 2
75/6 O-Pee-Chee 223
76/7 O-Pee-Chee 97
77/8 O-Pee-Chee 163
78/9 O-Pee-Chee 376
79/0 O-Pee-Chee 123
80/1 O-Pee-Chee 297
81/2 O-Pee-Chee 192
82/3 O-Pee-Chee 193
83/4 O-Pee-Chee 199
84/5 O-Pee-Chee 274
85/6 O-Pee-Chee 245
86/7 O-Pee-Chee 223
82/3 OPC/Topps Sticker 30
83/4 OPC/Topps Sticker 69
84/5 OPC Sticker 161
85/6 OPC Sticker 134-254
86/7 OPC Sticker 9-154
80/1 Pepsi Bottle Cap
81/2 Post 21
82/3 Post [Mont.]
83/4 Souhaits Keychain [Canadiens]
75/6 Topps 223
76/7 Topps 97
77/8 Topps 163
79/0 Topps 123
83/4 Vachon 57-77
83/4 Vachon 57-87
74/5 MONT
75/6 MONT
76/7 MONT
77/8 MONT
78/9 MONT
79/0 MONT
80/1 MONT
81/2 MONT
82/3 MONT
82/3 MONT / Steinberg
83/4 MONT
84/5 MONT
85/6 MONT
85/6 MONT / Provigo
95/6 MONT
96/7 MONT

TREMBLAY, MICHEL
98 Bowman 93
98 Bowman Chrome 93

TREMBLAY, NELSON
67/8 Columbus Checkers

TREMBLAY, NILS
52/3 Bas du Fleuve 31
51/2 Laval Dairy 51
51/2 Laval Dairy Update 51
52/3 St. Lawrence 80

TREMBLAY, PAUL
51/2 Lac St-Jean 29

TREMBLAY, REGIS
90 7th..Sketch Mem.Cup 65

TREMBLAY, RÉMY
02/3 Québec Remparts
01/2 Val d'Or Foreurs 4

TREMBLAY, SÉBASTIEN*
91/2 7th...Sketch LHJMQ 269

TREMBLAY, SÉBASTIEN**
90/1 7th..Sketch LHJMQ 246

TREMBLAY, SIMON
99 Bowman 45
98/9 Québec Remparts
00/1 Sherbrooke Castors 3

TREMBLAY, TREVOR
90/1 Rayside-Balfour
91/2 Rayside-Balfour

TREMBLAY, VINCENT
82/3 O-Pee-Chee 334
82/3 OPC/Topps Sticker 70
93/4 Slapshot / Drummondville 13
81/2 TORO
82/3 TORO

TREMBLAY, YANNICK
97/8 Omega 226
98/9 Pacific 423
00/1 Pacific 26
02/3 Pacific Complete 193
99/0 Panini Sticker 19
01/2 Signature 149, ✍ Aut. 149
02/3 Sports Vault 7
00/1 Stadium 60
00/1 Topps 251
02/3 To. Total 189
98/9 Upper Deck 190
01/2 Upper Deck 238
98/9 UD G. Reserve 190
99/0 UD MVP Cup 12
00/1 UD Vintage 16
96/7 St. John's Maple Leafs
97/8 Rimouski Océanic

TRÉPANIER, PASCAL
98/9 Bowman's Best 128
99/0 Omega 7
91/2 7th...Sketch LHJMQ 107
01/2 Signature 87, ✍ Aut. 87

TRESL, LADISLAV
92/3 APS 208
88/9 ProCards / Halifax
89/0 ProCards AHL 175
90/1 ProCards 433
91/2 ProCards 614
89/0 Halifax Citadels
93/4 Milwaukee Admirals

TRETIAK, DOUG
92/3 Hamilton Canucks
97/8 Las Vegas Thunder 13

TRETIAK, VLADISLAV
00/1 BAP Mem. ✂- G-7, ✂- G-16, ✂- G-22
01/2 BT Pipes 133, ✂- VM10
02/3 Between the Pipes ✂- GT1, ✂- I6, ✂- VM18, ✍ Aut.
90/1 Canada Nationals 20
92/3 Canada Nationals
82/3 Dernière Heure
91/2 Future Trends C72 5, 11, 31, 71, ✍ 11
92/3 Future Trends C76 103
92/3 Future Trends C76 163
92/3 Future Trends C76 / Promo
95 Globe 235
72 Hellas MM-Jenkki 79
74 Hellas MM-Jenkki 57
91 Ivan Fiodorov 11
70/1 Kuvajulkaisut 18
80 Olympic USSR
72 Panda MM-Toronto
79 Panini Sticker 140
012 Parkhurst ✂- H11
02/3 Parkhurst ✂- VM17, ✂- VT15
72 Semic Sticker 20
74 Semic Sticker 26
82 Semic Sticker 51
91 Semic Sticker 241
00/1 Signature ✂- GLS-4
70/1 Soviet Stars
71/2 Soviet Stars
73/4 Soviet Stars 2
74/5 Soviet Stars 2
79/0 Soviet Stars 4
83/4 Soviet Stars
77-79 Sports. FIN 78-1861
00/1 Ultimate Mem. ✂- UG-2, ✂-GM-17
02/3 Ultimate Memorabilia ✂- Num, ✂- VGJ
99/0 UD Retro 102, DR15, ✍ Ink.
71/2 Williams Finnish 17
72/3 Williams Finnish 37
73/4 Williams Finnish 17
90/1 CHIC / Coke

TRETOWICZ, DAVE
92/3 Classic 112
92/3 Classic Four Sport 218
93/4 Fort Wayne Komets 21
92/3 Phoenix Roadrunners

TRETTENES, STEFFEN
92/3 Semic Nordisk 143

TREVISANI, CARTER
01/2 Ottawa 67's 4

TRIBUNTSOVS, ATVARS
98/9 Cardset 165

TRIFONOV, LEV
00/1 Mir 356

TRIHEY, HARRY
83 HHOF Postcard F14
83&87 HHOF 88

TRIM, LEE
84/5 Brandon Wheat Kings
85/6 Brandon Wheat Kings

TRIMPER, TIM
80/1 O-Pee-Chee 357
81/2 O-Pee-Chee 376
82/3 O-Pee-Chee 394
80/1 CHIC / Colour
80/1 CHIC / Brown
80/1 WINN
81/2 WINN
84/5 Springfield Indians 12

TRINEER, NEAIL
81/2 Kingston Canadians

TRIPP, JOHN
02/3 BAP Mem. 336
97 Bowman 9
95/6 Classic 55, 91
95/6 Slapshot 238
02/3 Ultimate Memorabilia 84
02/3 UD Rookie 131
01/2 Hartford Wolf Pack
97/8 Saint John Flames

TRIULZI, ROBERTO
95 Panini Worlds 134
95 Semic 194

TRLICIK, MOJMIR
99/0 OFS 418
00/1 OFS 238

TRNKA, PAVEL
94/5 APS 49
99/0 Millenium 7, ✍ Aut. 7
97/8 Omega 9
02/3 Pacific Complete 396
99/0 Panini Sticker 184
97/8 SP Authentic 170
00/1 Stadium 181
02/3 To. Total 195
98/9 Upper Deck 35
00/1 Upper Deck 235
98/9 UD G. Reserve 35
99/0 Cincinnati M'Ducks

TROFIMENKOFF, DAVE
02/3 London Knights

TROFIMENKOFF, DAVID
00/1 Kudos 90
91/2 7th...Sketch WHL 353
93/4 Lethbridge Hurricanes

TROFIMOV, ALEXANDER
98/9 Mir 56
99/0 Mir 78

TROINI, JASON
96/7 Halifax Moosehead
96/7 Halifax Moosehead
97/8 Halifax Moosehead
97/8 Halifax Moosehead
98/9 Halifax Moosehead

TROJAN, RICHARD
94/5 DEL 418
95/6 DEL 390
96/7 DEL 298

TROJOVSKY, MATEJ
01/2 Regina Pats

TROMBLEY, RHETT
91/2 7th...Sketch WHL 99
93/4 Slapshot / S.S.Marie 16
95/6 Las Vegas Thunder
96/7 Las Vegas Thunder
94/5 Toledo Storm
91/2 Saskatoon Blades

TRONRUD, ØYSTEIN
92/3 Semic Nordisk 94

TROPPER, MARC
98/9 EBK ECHL All-Star
99/0 Charlotte Checkers
99/0 Charlotte Checkers
99/0 Charlotte Checkers
00/1 Charlotte Checkers

TROSCHINSKY, ANDREI
00/1 Worcester IceCats
01/2 Worcester IceCats

TROSHINSKI, ALEXEI
98/9 Mir 155
00/1 Mir 123
91/2 Upper Deck WJC 6
00/1 Dynamo 9

TROTTA, JOE
99/0 Indianapolis Ice
00/1 Peoria Rivermen

TROTTIER, BRYAN
01/2 ASG History
01/2 BAP Mem. ✂- 500GS
02/3 BAP Mem. / Cup
91/2 Bowman 93
92/3 Bowman 152
92/3 Bowman 243
82/3 Dernière Heure
93/4 Donruss 268
88/9 Esso All-Star
01/2 Fleer Greats 29, -RC 9, ✍ Aut.
01/2 Fleer Legacy 7, 52, ✂- HK
94/5 Fleer Ultra 398
88/9 Frito Lay
83/4 Funmate Puffy 21 [w/]
75/6 Hockey Heroes
93/4 Hockey Wit 44
84/5 Islander News Trottier 1-33
84/5 Kelowna Wings &...
93/4 Leaf 318
82/3 McDonald's Les Étoiles 25
76/7 O-Pee-Chee 67
76/7 O-Pee-Chee 115
76/7 O-Pee-Chee 216
77/8 O-Pee-Chee 105
78/9 O-Pee-Chee 10
78/9 O-Pee-Chee 64
78/9 O-Pee-Chee 65
78/9 O-Pee-Chee 333
79/0 OPC 2
79/0 O-Pee-Chee 3
79/0 OPC 7
79/0 O-Pee-Chee 100
79/0 O-Pee-Chee 165
80/1 O-Pee-Chee 40
81/2 O-Pee-Chee 200
81/2 O-Pee-Chee 210
82/3 O-Pee-Chee 5
82/3 O-Pee-Chee 214
83/4 O-Pee-Chee 21
84/5 O-Pee-Chee 139
84/5 O-Pee-Chee 214
85/6 OPC/Topps 60
86/7 OPC/Topps 155
86/7 OPC/Topps Box P
87/8 OPC/Topps 60
87/8 OPC/Topps Box O
88/9 OPC/Topps 97
90/1 OPC/Topps 6, 291
91/2 O-Pee-Chee 472
92/3 O-Pee-Chee 107
92/3 O-Pee-Chee 130
92/3 OPC - Anniv. 9
89/0 OPC/Topps 149
87/8 OPC Leaders 41
90/1 OPC Premier 121
81/2 OPC Sticker 7
81/2 OPC Sticker 9
81/2 OPC Sticker 152
81/2 OPC Sticker 160
82/3 OPC/Topps Sticker 47
82/3 OPC/Topps Sticker 48
83/4 OPC/Topps Sticker 76
83/4 OPC/Topps Sticker 77
84/5 OPC Sticker 86
84/5 OPC Sticker 87
85/6 OPC Sticker 65
86/7 OPC Sticker 216
87/8 OPC Sticker 240-106
88/9 OPC Sticker 112
89/0 opcSticker 118
87/8 Panini Sticker 96
88/9 Panini Sticker 293
89/0 Panini Sticker 269, 382
90/1 Panini Sticker 83
92/3 Panini Sticker 227
91/2 Parkhurst 208
91/2 Parkhurst 360
91/2 Parkhurst 431
93/4 Parkhurst 431
01/2 Parkhurst ✂- 500GS, ✂- PA30
02/3 Parkhurst ✂- NH4, ✂- VT10
91/2 Pinnacle 241
93/4 Pinnacle 411
82/3 Post [NYIs.]
93/4 Power Play 416
93/4 Premier 296
90/1 Pro Set 192, 511
91/2 Pro Set 192
91/2 Pro Set Platinum 216
91/2 Pro Set Platinum PC19
90/1 Score 270, 106T
91/2 Score 229
91/2 Score CAN 229
92/3 Score 157
92/3 Score 518
93/4 Score 567
84/5 7-Eleven
85/6 7-Eleven Superstars 12
01/2 Signature ✂- 500GS, ✍ VA34
83/4 Souhaits Keychain [Islanders]
97/8 SP Authentic ✍ M4, ✍ T4
77-79 Sportscaster 46-21
77-79 Sports. FIN 49-1197
76/7 Topps 67
76/7 Topps 115
76/7 Topps 216
76/7 Topps NS 15
77/8 Topps 105
78/9 Topps 10
78/9 Topps 64
78/9 Topps 65
79/0 Topps 2
79/0 Topps 3
79/0 Topps 7
79/0 Topps 100
79/0 Topps 165
80/1 Topps 40
81/2 Topps 41
81/2 Topps 132 [East]
84/5 Topps 104
84/5 Topps 160
92/3 Topps 416
00/1 Topps SCH, ✍ SCHA
91/2 To. Stadium 91
92/3 To. Stadium 26
01/2 T/O Archives 12, -Seat, ✍ CAI
00/1 UD Heroes 131, ✍ SG
01/2 Ultimate Mem. ✂- 500GS, ✂- ASGH, ✂- CT, ✂- EA, ✂- RT, ✂- SCD, ✂- SCW
02/3 Ultimate Memorabilia ✂- CSTW, ✂- Cor, ✂- FS, ✂- SL, ✂- Num, ✂- PS (x2), ✂- RAT, ✂- VGJ
90/1 Upper Deck 137, 425
91/2 Upper Deck 329
00 ✂- UD APOH 500, ✂- ✍ 500
99/0 UD C. Legends 30
02/3 UD Foundations ✂- 1000Jers, ✂- 1000Stick, ✂- CTW, ✂- CH, ✂- MS, ✂- PP
00/1 UD Legends 82, 88, PH11, ✍ ES, ✂- LGJ
01/2 UD Legends 43, FC, ✂- M, ✂- PoH, ✂- TT, ✂- TTC, ✍ ES
92/3 UD Locker 50
02/3 UD Piece ✂- HS, ✍ MD
01/2 UD SCup Champs 22, ✂- S, ✂- G
00/1 UD Vintage ✂- D-POH
01/2 UD Vintage ✂- SC
96 Wien HL9
79/0 NYIS
83/4 NYIS
83/4 NYIS / News 15
83/4 NYIS / News 37
84/5 NYIS / News 16
84/5 NYIS / News 35
89/0 NYIS
99/0 NYIS / UD NY1
90/1 PITT / Foodland 15
91/2 PITT / Elby's
91/2 PITT / Foodland 12
91/2 PITT / Food. Stickers
93/4 PITT / Foodland 12
96/7 PITT / Tribune
97/8 Portland Pirates

TROTTIER, DAVE
34-43 BeeHive-1 [Maroons]
35-40 Canada Starch
33/4 Canadian Gum
33/4 O-Pee-Chee 62
36/7 O-Pee-Chee 126
37/8 O-Pee-Chee 168
34/5 Sweet Caporal
37/8 World Wide Gum 70

TROTTIER, GUY
71/2 Bazooka Panel
70/1 Esso Power Player
71/2 O-Pee-Chee 5
72/3 O-Pee-Chee 326
73/4 Quaker Oats 40
71/2 Toronto Sun Photo
70/1 TORO
71/2 TORO
72/3 Ottawa Nationals

TROTTIER, JOEL
97 Bowman 10
98 Bowman 40
98 Bowman Chrome 40
95/6 Slapshot 273
98/9 Providence Bruins

TROTTIER, MONTY
81/2 Indianapolis Checkers
82/3 Indianapolis Checkers
84/5 Springfield Indians 19

TROTTIER, ROCKY
89/0 ProCards AHL 356
82/3 Medicine Hat Tigers
83/4 Medicine Hat Tigers

TROTZ, BARRY
90/1 ProCards 218
91/2 ProCards 572
93/4 Portland Pirates
95/6 Portland Pirates
96/7 Portland Pirates
81/2 Regina Pats

TRUBACHEV, YURI
00/1 Mir 16
02/3 Russian Future Stars 9

TRUDEL, FRANCIS
00/1 Sherbrooke Castors 7
01/2 Sherbrooke Castors 10

TRUDEL, JEAN-GUY
00/1 BAP Mem. 260
91/2 7th...Sketch LHJMQ 190
94/5 Slapshot Memorial 64
00/1 SP Authentic 158
00/1 SPx 107
00/1 Upper Deck 224
00/1 UD Black Diam. 83
00/1 UD Ice 99
98/9 Kansas City Blades 14
96/7 Peoria Rivermen
97/8 Peoria Rivermen

TRUDEL, LOUIS
34-43 BeeHive-1 [Chic.]
34-43 BeeHive-1 [Mont.]
35-40 Canada Starch
33-35 Diamond Match Silv.
36-39 Diamond Match TT1
36-39 Diamond Match TT2
36-39 Diamond Match TT3
36-39 Diamond Match BH TT
36-39 Diamond Match Chic.
36-39 Diamond Match BH BT
37/8 World Wide Gum 71

TRUDEL, MARTIN
90/1 7th..Sketch LHJMQ 65
91/2 7th...Sketch LHJMQ 11

TRUDELLE, JEAN-SÉBASTIEN
99/0 Shawinigan 9

TRUE, MADS
92/3 MPS SJHL 5

TRUE, SOREN
89/0 ProCards IHL 47
90/1 ProCards 530
91/2 ProCards 311

TRUKHNO, LEONID
91/2 O-Pee-Chee 61R

TRUMBLEY, ROB
00/1 Kudos 107

TRUNCHION, WAYNE
94/5 Guildford Flames 4
95/6 Guildford Flames 24

TRUNTSCHKA, BERND
94/5 DEL 95
95/6 DEL 96
96/7 DEL 285
89 Semic Sticker 120
91 Semic Sticker 164
93 Semic Sticker 162

TRUNTSCHKA, GERD
94 Panini Olympics 328
89 Semic Sticker 115
91 Semic Sticker 163
93 Semic Sticker 157

TRVAJ, JIRI
99/0 DS 170
00/1 DS 158
98/9 OFS 114
99/0 OFS 543
00/1 OFS 240
01/2 OFS 42, H7

TRZCINSKI, JASON
91/2 L. Superior State Lakers

TSAREV, ANDREI
99/0 Mir 137

TSCHUMI, RICK
95 Globe 216
91 Semic Sticker 181
92 Semic Sticker 197
93 Semic Sticker 114

TSCHUPP, CHRIS
94/5 Erie Panthers

TSELIOS, NIKOS
97 Bowman 138, ✍ Aut.
93 Québec Pee Wee 704
98/9 UD Choice 304
97/8 UD Black Diam. 91
99/0 Victory 373
99/0 Cincinnati Cyclones
00/1 Cincinnati Cyclones

TSEPLIS, GATIS
97/8 Fort Worth Brahmas
99/0 Fort Worth Brahmas

TSHERVJAKOV,
97/8 Hockey-Box

TSIRKOUNOV, OLEG
95/6 Slapshot 287
99/0 Topeka Scarecrows

TSUJIURA, STEVE
88/9 ProCards / Maine
83/4 Springfield Indians 6

TSULYGIN, NIKOLAI
93/4 Classic 46
94/5 Classic 78, T2
93/4 Cla. 4 Sport 206
95/6 Edge Ice 16
99/0 Mir 125
00/1 Mir 250
95 Panini Worlds 28
93/4 Parkhurst 526
93/4 Pinnacle 507
94/5 Sig. Rookies 33, ✍ 33
94/5 SR Gold Standard 94
92/3 Upper Deck 614
96/7 ANAH / Up Front 14

TSVETKOV, ALEXEI
00/1 Mir 78

TSYBUK, EVGENY
98/9 Michigan K-Wings
99/0 Michigan K-Wings

TSYCANKOV, GENNADY
91/2 Future Trends C72 67
72 Hellas MM-Jenkki 67
74 Hellas MM-Jenkki 58
00/1 Mir Fetisov 16
79 Panini Sticker 145
72 Semic Sticker 7
74 Semic Sticker 29
71/2 Soviet Stars
73/4 Soviet Stars 11
74/5 Soviet Stars 8
79/0 Soviet Stars 8
71/2 Williams Finnish 18
72/3 Williams Finnish 38
73/4 Williams Finnish 18

TSYGUROV, DENIS
96/7 APS 106
94/5 Donruss 200
96/7 DS Sticker 266
94/5 Flair 23
94/5 Fleer Ultra 267
94/5 Leaf 161
99/0 Mir 104
94/5 Pinnacle 258, RTP3
94/5 Premier 29

TSYPLAKOV, ALEXANDER
96/7 APS 151
97/8 DS Sticker 134

TSYPLAKOV, VLADIMIR
98/9 Aurora 91
98/9 Be A Player 213, ✍ Aut. 213
00/1 BAP Mem. 31
93/4 Cla. Prospects 103
98/9 Dynagon Ice 92
98/9 OPC Chrome 14
97/8 Omega 115
98/9 Omega 115
98/9 Pacific 247
99/0 Pacific 200
00/1 Pacific 58
97/8 Pacific CC 82
97/8 Pa. Dynagon 61, T-43
97/8 Pa. Invincible 69
98/9 Pa. Paramount 110
97/8 Pa. Revolution 68
97/8 Panini Sticker 218
98/9 Panini Sticker 204
95/6 Parkhurst 377
97/8 Pi. Be A Player 197, ✍ Aut. 197
97/8 SP Authentic 74
98/9 SPx Finite 40
98/9 Topps 14
00/1 Topps 253
98/9 UD Choice 101
97/8 Upper Deck 289
98/9 Upper Deck 287
99/0 Upper Deck 65
96/7 UD Black Diam. 8
97/8 UD Coll. Choice 122
98/9 UD G. Reserve 287
99/0 UD G. Reserve 65
99/0 UD MVP 98
99/0 Victory 135
93/4 Fort Wayne Komets 22
94/5 Fort Wayne Komets 5
95/6 Las Vegas Thunder

TSYPLAKOV, YURI
95 Panini Worlds 47

TUCEK, PETR
99/0 OFS 550
00/1 OFS 351
01/2 OFS 84, H9
99/0 Score 121

TUCKER, BRIAN
99/0 Muskegon Fury

TUCKER, CHRIS
91/2 Upper Deck WJC 67
94/5 Richmond Renegades

TUCKER, DARCY
01/2 Adrenaline 186
02/3 Atomic ✂ GWJ 23
99/0 Aurora 133
99/0 BAP Mem. 58
00/1 BAP Mem. 134
02/3 BAP Mem. 188
01/2 Crown Royale 135
02/3 Crown Royale ✂ GWDP 21
95/6 Donruss C3TWC 13
97/8 Donruss 182
96/7 Do. Canadian 143
97/8 Do. Canadian 111
97/8 Do. Preferred 28
99/0 Dynagon Ice 183
95/6 Edge Ice 42
02/3 Exclusive 164
02/3 First Edition 11, ✂ Jers.
96/7 Fl. Picks 148
95/6 Future Legends 23, PC-5
02/3 Heads Up ✂ GWQ 26
96/7 Leaf GLR-8
97/8 Leaf 77
96/7 L. Preferred 134
97/8 Limited 34, 53
98/9 NHL Power Play
01/2 O-Pee-Chee 145
02/3 O-Pee-Chee 171
98/9 OPC Chrome 183
98/9 Omega 222
98/9 Pacific 407
99/0 Pacific 398
00/1 Pacific 401
01/2 Pacific 375
02/3 Pacific 371, ✂ GWJ 48
02/3 Pacific Complete 405
97/8 Pacific CC 83
99/0 Pa. Paramount 220
00/1 Pa. Paramount 235
99/0 Panini Sticker 151
00/1 Panini Sticker 96
02/3 Parkhurst 53
02/3 Parkhurst Retro 91
94/5 Pinnacle 537
97/8 Pinnacle 140
97/8 Pi. Be A Player 119, ✍ Aut. 119
96/7 Pi. Zenith 130
99/0 Prism 133
02/3 Pr. Stock Reserve 94
01/2 PS Titanium 133
02/3 PS Titanium ✂ GWJ 68
99/0 Revolution 134
00/1 Revolution 141
97/8 Score 202
97/8 Score Mont. 13
91/2 7th...Sketch WHL 88
01/2 Signature 102, ✍ Aut. 102
02/3 Signature Series 64, ✍ 64
02/3 Slam Card
94/5 Slapshot Memorial 12
02/3 Sports Vault 135
99/0 Stadium 87
00/1 Stadium 193
02/3 Stadium 60
95/6 Topps 16CJ
98/9 Topps 183
99/0 Topps 239
00/1 Topps 235
01/2 Topps 145
02/3 Topps 171, HHC19
99/0 To. Chrome 239
00/1 To. Chrome 145
01/2 To. Chrome 115
94/5 Topps Finest 164
02/3 To. Limited 171
02/3 To. Total 311
94/5 Upper Deck 503
96/7 Upper Deck 281
97/8 Upper Deck 88
99/0 Upper Deck 288
00/1 Upper Deck 163
01/2 Upper Deck 165
99/0 UD G. Reserve 288
96/7 UD Ice 33
01/2 UD Mask 90
99/0 UD MVP 192
00/1 UD MVP 166
01/2 UD MVP 177
02/3 UD MVP 173
00/1 UD Vintage 341
01/2 UD Vintage 238, 243
02/3 UD Vintage 239
02/3 Vanguard ✂ GWJ 45
99/0 Victory 276
00/1 Victory 218
01/2 Victory 332
02/3 Victory 204
99/0 WGretzky 155
96/7 MONT
99/0 TORO / Pizza Pizza 17
95/6 Fredericton Canadiens
93/4 Kamloops Blazers

TUCKER, GIB
90 7th..Sketch Mem.Cup 43
90/1 7th..Sketch OHL 245
91/2 7th...Sketch OHL 85
89/0 Kitchener Rangers
90/1 Kitchener Rangers

TUCKER, JOHN
93/4 Donruss 328
94/5 Donruss 87
95/6 Donruss 311
92/3 Fleer Ultra 414
93/4 Fleer Ultra 211
94/5 Fleer Ultra 210
93/4 Leaf 21
94/5 Leaf 38
95/6 Leaf 269
86/7 OPC/Topps 67
87/8 OPC/Topps 154
88/9 OPC/Topps 74
90/1 OPC/Topps 374
89/0 OPC/Topps 37
90/1 OPC Premier 122
85/6 OPC Sticker 184-58
86/7 OPC Sticker 48-189
87/8 OPC Sticker 145-254
87/8 Panini Sticker 30
88/9 Panini Sticker 229
89/0 Panini Sticker 212
90/1 Panini Sticker 157
93/4 Panini Sticker 212
95/6 Panini Sticker 125
92/3 Parkhurst 405
93/4 Parkhurst 462
95/6 Parkhurst 192
94/5 Parkie SE170
93/4 Pinnacle 144
93/4 Pinnacle CA22
94/5 Pinnacle 226
95/6 Playoff 312
94/5 POG 226
95/6 POG 249
93/4 Power Play 235
93/4 Premier 473
94/5 Premier 132
90/1 Pro Set 322, 420
93/4 Score 354
94/5 Score 23
95/6 Score 191
91/2 To. Stadium 335
93/4 To. Stadium 38
90/1 Upper Deck 387
92/3 Upper Deck 548
93/4 Upper Deck 409
95/6 Upper Deck 78
95/6 UD BAP 120, ✍ S120
95/6 UD CC 104
84/5 BUFF / Blue Shield
85/6 BUFF / Blue Shield
86/7 BUFF / Blue Shield
87/8 BUFF / Blue Shield
87/8 BUFF / Won. Bread
88/9 BUFF / Blue Shield
88/9 BUFF / Won. Bread
90/1 BUFF / Blue Shield
90/1 BUFF / Campbell's
92/3 TAMP / Sheraton Inn
94/5 TAMP / Sky Box
95/6 TAMP / Sky Box
89/0 WASH / Kodak
82/3 Kitchener Rangers
83/4 Kitchener Rangers

TUCKER, KEVIN
01/2 Peoria Rivermen

TUCKER, TRAVIS
97/8 Quad City Mallards

TUCKWELL, HARRY
23/4 Paulins Candy 51

TUDIN, DAN
95/6 Slapshot 266

TUER, AL
88/9 ProCards / Binghampton
89/0 ProCards AHL 289
90/1 ProCards 313
91/2 ProCards 367
92/3 Cincinnati Cyclones
81/2 Regina Pats
82/3 Regina Pats
83/4 Regina Pats

TUGNUTT, RON
01/2 Adrenaline 56, PP 11
99/0 Aurora 101, -GU 14
02/3 BAP All-Star 94, ✂ ASJ
98/9 Be A Player 244, ✍ Aut. 244
99/0 BAP Mem. 84, 351
00/1 BAP Mem. 169, 489
01/2 BAP Mem. 35
01/2 BT Pipes 3, ✂ GJ, ✂ S&J, ✂ HSHSJers.
02/3 Between the Pipes 59, ✂ GUJ45, ✂ T19
98/9 Bicycle.. 7-C
91/2 Bowman 151
99/0 Crown Royale 99
00/1 Crown Royale 33
01/2 Crown Royale 45
93/4 Donruss 12
93/4 Donruss 453
93/4 Donruss A
94/5 Donruss 69
97/8 Donruss 103
97/8 Do. Canadian 63
97/8 Do. Priority 76
99/0 Dynagon Ice 141
95/6 Edge Ice 57
02/3 First Edition 107, ✂ Jers.
92/3 Fleer Ultra 298
93/4 Fleer Ultra 263
00 Gatorade Sticker
02/3 Heads Up ✂ GWQ 10
99/0 Kraft / JELL-O
00/1 Kraft 29
93/4 Leaf 277
94/5 Leaf 46
99/0 Millenium 172, ✍ Aut. 172
90/1 OPC/Topps 367
91/2 O-Pee-Chee 181
92/3 O-Pee-Chee 211
01/2 O-Pee-Chee 166
02/3 O-Pee-Chee 216
89/0 O-Pee-Chee 263
97/8 Omega 158
98/9 Omega 169
99/0 Omega 163
98/9 Pacific 316
99/0 Pacific 296, -ITCNF 13
00/1 Pacific 338
01/2 Pacific 118
02/3 Pacific 107, ✂ GWJ 13
02/3 Pacific Complete 410
97/8 Pacific CC 87
97/8 Pa. Crown Roy. 93
97/8 Pa. Invincible 96
98/9 Pa. Paramount 167
99/0 Pa. Paramount 166, -GS 14
00/1 Pa. Paramount 72
97/8 Pa. Revolution 95
89/0 Panini Sticker 332
90/1 Panini Sticker 142
90/1 Panini/QUE 22
91/2 Panini Sticker 267
99/0 Panini Sticker 117, 348
00/1 Panini Sticker 138
91/2 Parkhurst 149
91/2 Parkhurst 277
92/3 Parkhurst 290
00/1 Parkhurst P-113
01/2 Parkhurst 105
02/3 Parkhurst 143
91/2 Pinnacle 124
92/3 Pinnacle 366
93/4 Pinnacle 187
94/5 Pinnacle 172
97/8 Pinnacle 99
97/8 Pi. Be A Player 36, ✍ Aut. 36
97/8 Pi. Certified 29
97/8 Pi. Inside 82
97/8 Pi. Totally 29
93/4 Power Play 13
93/4 Premier 286
94/5 Premier 523
00/1 Premier Plus 25
99/0 Prism 98
01/2 Pr. Stock 27
00/1 PS Titanium 26, ✂ GUG-13
01/2 PS Titanium 41
01/2 PS Titanium Draft ✂ 31
02/3 PS Titanium ✂ GWJ 21
90/1 Pro Set 258
91/2 Pro Set 202
91/2 Pro Set Platinum 98
88/9 ProCards / Halifax
99/0 Revolution 104, / CSC 104
90/1 Score 126
91/2 Score 41
91/2 Score CAN 41
92/3 Score 387
93/4 Score 368
93/4 Score 504
94/5 Score 21
95/6 Score 70
97/8 Score 49
91/2 Score Young Stars 33
00/1 Signature 177, F-9, ✍ Aut. 16
02/3 Signature Series 103, ✍ 103
00/1 SP Authentic 26, ✍ SotT
01/2 SP Authentic 21
00/1 SP GU 17
01/2 SP GU 13
99/0 SPx 104
00/1 SPx 18
01/2 SPx 18
99/0 Stadium 91, -GC6
00/1 Stadium 210
01/2 Stadium 21
00/1 SLU 18
99/0 Topps 129
00/1 Topps 248
01/2 Topps 166
02/3 Topps 216
99/0 To. Chrome 129
00/1 To. Chrome 221
99/0 To. Gold Label 41
00/1 To. Gold Label 50
00/1 To. Heritage 106
02/3 To. Heritage 180
02/3 To. Limited 216
99/0 To. Prmr. Plus 27
01/2 To. Reserve 29
91/2 To. Stadium 115
93/4 To. Stadium 325
00/1 To. Stars 97, ✂ GG
02/3 To. Total 276
00/1 UD Heroes 34
01/2 UD PlayMakers Ltd ✂ PCJ
00/1 UD Reserve 25
99/0 Ult. Victory 62
90/1 Upper Deck 27
91/2 Upper Deck 277
93/4 Upper Deck 426, SP-5
94/5 Upper Deck 321
97/8 Upper Deck 113
99/0 Upper Deck 263
00/1 Upper Deck 54, 278
01/2 Upper Deck 49
02/3 Upper Deck 300, ✂ CG, ✂ SV
02/3 UD Classic ✂ HR
97/8 UD Coll. Choice 181
99/0 UD G. Reserve 263
01/2 UD Ice 11
01/2 UD Mask 109, ✂ GJ, ✂ JP, ✂ DP, ✂ MM, ✂ StS
02/3 UD Mask 26, 27, ✂ CW
99/0 UD MVP 142, ✍ PS
01/2 UD MVP 55
02/3 UD MVP -SD, ST, Souv.
99/0 UD MVP Cup 127
02/3 UD Piece ✂ PH
02/3 UD Top Shelf ✂ ST, ✂ SS
00/1 UD Vintage 102, 111
01/2 UD Vintage 71, 78
02/3 UD Vintage ✂ EE
00/1 Vanguard 32
01/2 Vanguard 30
99/0 Victory 207
00/1 Victory 189
01/2 Victory 96, 100
02/3 Victory 62
99/0 WGretzky 120
01/2 COLU
01/2 COLU
02/3 DALL / Southwest
92/3 EDMO / IGA 024
94/5 MONT / Export
94/5 MONT
96/7 OTTA
97/8 OTTA
98/9 OTTA
99/0 OTTA
87/8 QUÉB / Gene. Foods
89/0 QUÉB
89/0 QUÉB / Gene. Foods
89/0 QUÉB / Police
90/1 QUÉB
90/1 QUÉB / Petro-Canada
91/2 QUÉB / Petro-Canada
95/6 Portland Pirates

TUKIO, ARTO
99/0 Cardset 245
00/1 Cardset 31, NG-6
02/3 Cardset 129

TULEY, BRAD
89/0 Soo Greyhounds

TULI, JUKKA
70/1 Kuvajulkaisut 343

TULI, RAIMO
66/7 Champion 22

TULLEY, BRENT
00/1 UD DEL 115

TULLY, BRENT
93/4 Classic 31
98/9 DEL 184
93/4 Donruss CAN21
99/0 Eishockey 184
93/4 Pinnacle 464
90/1 7th..Sketch OHL 374
91/2 7th...Sketch OHL 130
93/4 Slapshot / Peterborough 9
92/3 Upper Deck 592
93/4 Upper Deck 530
94/5 UD Canada Junior 9
01/2 UD DEL 89
96/7 Syracuse Crunch
91/2 Peterborough Petes

TUMA, ZBYNEK
01/2 OFS 275

TUMBA, SVEN
91 Semic Sticker 233

TUMBACH, TROY
94/5 DEL 144
95/6 DEL 41

TUNIKOV, VADIM
92/3 Semic Nordisk 85

TUOHIMAA, HARRI
91/2 Jyvas Hyva 4
80/1 Mallasjuoma 128
78/9 SM-Liiga 171
71/2 Williams Finnish 376

TUOHIMAA, JUHA
91/2 Jyvas Hyva 35
92/3 Jyvas Hyva 94
80/1 Mallasjuoma 94
78/9 SM-Liiga 136

TUOHIMAA, PASI
80/1 Mallasjuoma 118
71/2 Williams Finnish 377

TUOKKO, MARCO
98/9 Cardset 240
99/0 Cardset 143
00/1 Cardset 218
02/3 Cardset 282

TUOMAINEN, MARKO
98/9 Cardset 50, -Leij. 44
99/0 Cardset 199, -BP 6, -PA 7, AH J-pata
00/1 Cardset 118
02/3 Cardset 283
95/6 Donruss 56
95/6 Edge Ice 36
97/8 Hockey-Box
95/6 Leaf 171
99/0 Omega 114
95/6 Topps 189
91/2 Upper Deck 675
95/6 Upper Deck 12
95/6 UD CC 121
91/2 Upper Deck WJC 38
99/0 UD MVP Cup 89
00/1 Lowell Lock Monsters
92/3 Clarkson G'Knights

TUOMAINEN, TEEMU*
98/9 Cardset 148

TUOMAINEN, TIMO
66/7 Champion 132
70/1 Kuvajulkaisut 270

TUOMENOKSA, ANTTI
92/3 Jyvas Hyva 98
93/4 Jyvas Hyva 170
93/4 Sisu 167
94/5 Sisu 89, H-3
95/6 Sisu 190

TUOMI, RISTO
80/1 Mallasjuoma 204

TUOMINEN, AKI
99/0 Cardset 227
00/1 Cardset 133

TUOMINEN, JOUNI
94/5 Sisu 331
95/6 Sisu 144

TUOMINEN, OLLI
80/1 Mallasjuoma 119
78/9 SM-Liiga 165

TUOMINEN, PASI
98/9 Cardset 215
99/0 Cardset 320
00/1 Cardset 206
95/6 Sisu 364
96/7 Sisu 158

TUOMISTO, MARTTI
80/1 Mallasjuoma 46

TUOMISTO, PEKKA
91/2 Jyvas Hyva 3
92/3 Jyvas Hyva 12
93/4 Jyvas Hyva 24
70/1 Kuvajulkaisut 382
80/1 Mallasjuoma 101
93 Semic Sticker 81
93/4 Sisu 102
94/5 Sisu 18
95/6 Sisu 214

TUPA, MARTIN
95/6 APS 185
96/7 APS 317
97/8 APS 295
97/8 DS Sticker 111
98/9 OFS 51
00/1 OFS 142
01/2 OFS 155
99/0 Score 32

TURBIDE, PATRICK
01/2 Victoriaville Tigres 2

TURCO, MARTY
01/2 Adrenaline 61, PP 13
02/3 Atomic 34, -D 6
02/3 BAP All-Star 104
00/1 BAP Mem. 440
01/2 BAP Mem. 151
02/3 BAP Mem. 104
01/2 BAP Update ✂ HSHSJers
01/2 BT Pipes 26, ✂ GJ, ✂ GG, ✂ GT, ✂ -HSHSJers.
02/3 Between the Pipes 23, 130, M10, ✂ BM1, ✂ CP5, ✂ DM9, ✂ GUE19, ✂ FW10, ✂ GB7, ✂ GUJ19, ✂ GP3, ✂ GSJ19, ✂ GT15, ✂ HSHSJers 4, ✂ ITN19, ✂ T19, ✍ Aut.
02/3 Calder 36, -CS 5, -HS 5, ✂ GWJ 9
00/1 Crown Royale 122, 21CR-9
02/3 Crown Royale 31, -COA 2, ✂ GWJ 5
00/1 Crown Royale G-1
98/9 EBK IHL All-Star
02/3 eTopps 35
02/3 Exclusive 58, -EA 6
02/3 First Edition 68, 376, 377, ✂ Jers.
01/2 Heads Up BTI 9
02/3 Heads Up 40, -S 7, ✂ GWQ 11
02/3 In The GU 20, 210, ✂ GP11, ✂ T13
02/3 O-Pee-Chee 85
01/2 Pacific 136, 446
02/3 Pacific 119
02/3 Pacific Complete 7
00/1 Parkhurst P-210
01/2 Parkhurst ✂ T21
02/3 Parkhurst 26
02/3 Parkhurst Retro 82, ✂ RJ11, ✂ RSJ8, ✂ HH4, ✂ HSHSJers, ✂ RM12, ✂ VH2
00/1 Premier Plus 126, ✂ GP, ✍ PS
00/1 Pr. Stock 117, PSR-8
01/2 Pr. Stock -PS 24
02/3 Pr. Stock Reserve 33, -ICS 7
00/1 PS Titanium 116
01/2 PS Titanium ✂ DSJ 53, ✂ DSJ 57
02/3 Pr. Stock Titanium 33, -MM 2, ✂ GWJ 22
00/1 PS Titanium Draft 116
02/3 Quest for the Cup 30, -CTC 5, ✂ GWJ 8
00/1 Signature 288, ✍ Aut. 250
02/3 Signature Series 165, ✍ 165, ✂ DW5, ✂ SGJ68, ✂ TQ16
00/1 SP Authentic 102, ✍ SotT
02/3 SP Authentic 29
00/1 SP GU 67
02/3 SP GU ✂ FF
02/3 Sports Vault 210
00/1 SPx 159
01/2 SPx ✂✍ HTSig
02/3 SPx 24, ✂ X
00/1 Stadium 259
01/2 Stadium NR1, ✍ NR, ✂ SCS, ✂ SCSD
02/3 Stadium 66, -PSH7
02/3 Topps 85
00/1 To. Chrome 243
02/3 T. Chrome 53
00/1 To. Gold Label 105, ✍ GLA
00/1 To. Heritage 75
01/2 To. Heritage 78, 129
02/3 To. Heritage 72, ✂ CP, ✂ CPB
02/3 To. Limited 85
01/2 To. Reserve ✂ TR
00/1 To. Stars 112, 147, P5
02/3 To. Total 204
00/1 UD Reserve 93
02/3 Ultimate Memorabilia ✂ GUJ, ✂ GUSJ, ✂ Num
00/1 Upper Deck 428
01/2 Upper Deck ✂ GoalJ, ✂ NG
02/3 Upper Deck 58, -SA5, ✂ GT, ✂ SV, ✂ PW, ✂ UDPL
02/3 UD Artistic 28, R28, / Art
00/1 UD Black Diam. 117
02/3 UD Classic 31
02/3 UD Honor 22
00/1 UD Ice 69
01/2 UD Mask ✂ GJ, ✂ JP, ✂ DP, ✂ MM, ✂ VC
02/3 UD Mask 26, 27, 28, 29, 95, ✂ GG, ✂ MM, ✂ BM, ✂ NB, ✂ PW, ✂ VC
02/3 UD MVP 57, SD (x2), Souv.
02/3 UD Piece 30, ✂ PH
02/3 UD Premier 20
00/1 UD Pros&Prosp. 102
02/3 UD Rookie 33
01/2 UD Top Shelf ✂ J, ✂✍ SJ.
02/3 UD Top Shelf 28
02/3 UD Vintage 82, 270, 317, GB 82, ✂ EE
00/1 Vanguard 117
02/3 Vanguard 34, -EMW 10, -SW 2, -VT 2
01/2 Victory 118
02/3 Victory 66
00/1 DALL / Southwest
01/2 DALL / Southwest
02/3 DALL / Southwest
98/9 Michigan K-Wings
99/0 Michigan K-Wings

TURCOT, ALEX
00/1 Val d'Or Foreurs 11

TURCOTTE, ALAIN
99/0 Rouyn-Noranda

TURCOTTE, ALEX
00/1 Chicoutimi Saguenéens 2

TURCOTTE, ALFIE
94/5 DEL 440
84/5 Kelowna Wings &...
89/0 ProCards AHL 81
90/1 ProCards 200
83/4 MONT
84/5 MONT
97/8 Indianapolis Ice 25

TURCOTTE, DARREN
98/9 Aurora 105
98/9 Be A Player 74, ✍ Aut. 74
99/0 BAP Mem. 272
90/1 Bowman 216
91/2 Bowman 62
92/3 Bowman 156
93/4 Donruss 224
94/5 Donruss 286
95/6 Donruss 43, 295, PP-10
96/7 Donruss 59
97/8 Donruss 176
98/9 Dynagon Ice 105
94/5 Flair 75
94/5 Fleer 90
95/6 Fleer Metal 167
92/3 Fleer Ultra 143
93/4 Fleer Ultra 341
94/5 Fleer Ultra 94
95/6 Fleer Ultra 72, 328
96/7 Fl. Ultra 154
95 Globe 123
93/4 Hockey Wit 30
95/6 Hoyle / East. J-Club
93/4 Leaf 45
94/5 Leaf 210
95/6 Leaf 173
96/7 Leaf 184
97/8 Limited 191
91/2 McDonald's Mc-07
96/7 Metal Univ. 141
90/1 OPC/Topps 48
91/2 O-Pee-Chee 71
92/3 O-Pee-Chee 387
90/1 OPC/Topps K
90/1 OPC Premier 123
98/9 Pacific 373
97/8 Pacific CC 229
98/9 Pa. Paramount 128
90/1 Panini Sticker 107
91/2 Panini Sticker 285
92/3 Panini Sticker 235
93/4 Panini Sticker 94
95/6 Panini Sticker 27
96/7 Panini Sticker 281
98/9 Panini Sticker 139
91/2 Parkhurst 118
92/3 Parkhurst 345
93/4 Parkhurst 356
95/6 Parkhurst 93, 498
94/5 Parkie SE75
91/2 Pinnacle 47
92/3 Pinnacle 33
93/4 Pinnacle 386
94/5 Pinnacle 161
95/6 Pinnacle 20
96/7 Pinnacle 165
96/7 Pi. Be A Player 70, ✍ Aut. 70
95/6 Pi. Summit 22
96/7 Pi. Summit 54
95/6 Playoff 267
96/7 Playoff 413
94/5 POG 119
93/4 Power Play 166
93/4 Power Play 357
93/4 Premier 246
94/5 Premier 2
95/6 Pro Magnet 128
90/1 Pro Set 208, 400
91/2 Pro Set 160
91/2 Pro Set 310
92/3 Pro Set 114
90/1 Score 241
91/2 Score 196
91/2 Score CAN 196
92/3 Score 224
93/4 Score 24
93/4 Score 570
94/5 Score 169
95/6 Score 224
96/7 Score 219
97/8 Score 251
97/8 Score SLou. 8
90/1 Sco. Young Stars 16
91/2 Score Young Stars 28
91 Semic Sticker 139
95/6 SBx Emotion 79
95/6 SBx Impact 186
94/5 SP 49
96/7 SP 142
92/3 Topps 203
95/6 Topps 251, HGA7
91/2 To. Stadium 346
92/3 To. Stadium 360
93/4 To. Stadium 476
94/5 To. Stadium 201
95/6 To. Stadium 27
90/1 Upper Deck 274, 475
91/2 Upper Deck 90
91/2 Upper Deck 155
91/2 Upper Deck 513
92/3 Upper Deck 169
93/4 Upper Deck - SP 66
94/5 Upper Deck 84, SP-123
95/6 Upper Deck 481, SE-37, SE-180
96/7 Upper Deck 333
98/9 Upper Deck 297
94/5 UD BAP R14, R124, ✍ 35
95/6 UD CC 24
96/7 UD CC 235, 330
97/8 UD Coll. Choice 219
98/9 UD G. Reserve 297
93/4 HART / Coke
98/9 NASH / Wendy's 21
89/0 NYRA / Marine
95/6 WINN

TURCOTTE, YAN
01/2 Québec Remparts 3

TUREANU, DORU
79 Panini Sticker 316

TUREK, FILIP
94/5 APS 109
95/6 APS 68
96/7 APS 253
97/8 APS 280
98/9 DS 35
99/0 DS 36
00/1 DS 79
96/7 DS Sticker 89
97/8 DS Sticker 77
98/9 OFS 202
99/0 OFS 286
00/1 OFS 16

TUREK, JOSEF
99/0 Score 23

TUREK, MATT
91/2 7th...Sketch OHL 341
96/7 Knoxville Cherokees

TUREK, ROMAN
01/2 Adrenaline 29, PP 6, ✂ GWJ 6
94/5 APS 93
95/6 APS 354
96/7 APS 338
01/2 Atomic 15, TN 2
02/3 Atomic 14, -D 2, ✂ GWJ 2
00/1 Aurora 124, Pins. 124
02/3 BAP All-Star 95, ✂ ASJ
98/9 Be A Player 41, ✍ Aut. 41
99/0 BAP Mem. 161, SL-18
00/1 BAP Mem. 152
01/2 BAP Mem. 5, 392, ✂ ASJ, ✂ ASE, ✂ ASN, ✂ AST, ✂ GJ, ✂ SCP
02/3 BAP Mem. 183, 256, ✂ TM20
01/2 BAP Update ✂ H24, ✂ TP3
01/2 BT Pipes 65, HSHS, -Mask, ✂ ASJ, ✂ DM, ✂ GJ, ✂ JE, ✂ S&J, ✂ GG, ✂ GT, ✂ ITN, ✂ -HSHSJers.
02/3 Between the Pipes 34, 125, M5, ✂ ASJ12, ✂ DM10, ✂ GUE28, ✂ GB14, ✂ GUJ28, ✂ GSJ28, ✂ HSHSJers 11, ✂ ITN28, ✍ Aut.
98/9 Bicycle.. 4-S
01/2 Bowman 42
02/3 Bowman 82
99/0 Crown Royale 120
00/1 Crown Royale 90
01/2 Crown Royale 24, ASH 2, JotC 4, ✂ TT 2, ✂ TT 12
02/3 Crown Royale 15
95/6 DEL 289
97/8 Donruss 64
97/8 Do. Priority 29
99/0 DS P2
00/1 DS JT1
99/0 Dynagon Ice 168
02/3 Exclusive 24, -EA 2
02/3 First Edition 28, ✂ Jers.
96/7 Flair 106
01/2 Heads Up 14, HD 11, SS 3
02/3 Heads Up 18, -S3, ✂ GWQ 5
02/3 In The GU ✂ GP9, ✂ IE25
97/8 Leaf 56
97/8 Limited 42, 113
00/1 McDonald's 29
02/3 McDonald's 7
01/2 O-Pee-Chee 105, Update 105
02/3 O-Pee-Chee 98
00/1 OFS 378
98/9 Omega 76
99/0 Omega 201, -WAS 8
98/9 Pacific 184
99/0 Pacific 130
00/1 Pacific 352, ES-8, GCDC-30, ✍ Aut. 352
01/2 Pacific 333, SC 17
02/3 Pacific 60, -MA 1, ✂ GWJ 5
02/3 Pacific Complete 12
97/8 Pa. Invincible R-66
98/9 Pa. Paramount 71
00/1 Pa. Paramount 209, FF-31, GS-16
99/0 Panini Sticker 285
00/1 Panini Sticker 196
95 Panini Worlds 187
00/1 Parkhurst P-27
01/2 Parkhurst 221, ✂ PS56
02/3 Parkhurst 129
02/3 Parkhurst Retro 166
97/8 Pi. Be A Player 35, ✍ Aut. 35
97/8 Pi. Inside 79, S-9
00/1 Premier Plus 55, MB17
99/0 Prism 121
00/1 Pr. Stock 85, PSNW-20
01/2 Pr. Stock 13, ✂ GUG 17
02/3 Pr. Stock Reserve -ICS 2, ✂ 107
00/1 PS Titanium 82, 3SS-7, ✂ GUG-45
01/2 PS Titanium 22, TSS 1, ✂ DSJ 5, ✂ DSJ 6
01/2 PS Titanium Draft ✂ 17
02/3 Pr. Stock Titanium 16, ✂ GWJ 12
02/3 Quest for the Cup 13
00/1 Revolution 125, HD-30, SM-18
97/8 Score 36
99/0 Score JT26
95 Semic 142
93 Semic Sticker 90
00/1 Signature 6, ✍ Aut. 63
01/2 Signature C-37, ✍ Aut., ✂ GU92, ✂ TM5
02/3 Signature Series 123, GS-79, ✍ 123
96/7 SP 175
99/0 SP Authentic 76
00/1 SP Authentic 78, SS5
01/2 SP Authentic 12
02/3 SP Authentic 13
00/1 SP GU 52
01/2 SP GU 6
02/3 SP GU ✂ PH
02/3 Sports Vault 170
00/1 SPx 61, X12
01/2 SPx 160
02/3 SPx 9, ✂ X
00/1 Stadion 13, 109
00/1 Stadium 47, GS6
02/3 Stadium 86
00/1 Topps 100, OTG12, ✍ CAI
01/2 Topps 105, Update 105
02/3 Topps 98, HHC12
00/1 To. Chrome 78
01/2 To. Chrome 105
02/3 T. Chrome 62
00/1 To. Gold Label 44, BTM6, B5
00/1 To. Heritage 35, 227, 231, 237, 241
01/2 To. Heritage 168
02/3 To. Heritage 90, 115
02/3 To. Limited 98
01/2 To. Reserve 60
00/1 To. Stars 82
02/3 To. Total 7
00/1 UD Heroes 104, PI6, ✍ SG
01/2 UD PlayMakers Ltd 15
00/1 UD Reserve 76, GG9
00/1 Ultimate Mem. ✍ U-32, ✂ G-25, ✂ PJ-11, ✂ J-4, ✂ Jers. 3, ✂ S-4, ✂ GM-13
01/2 Ultimate Mem. ✂ JE
02/3 Ultimate Memorabilia ✂ NO, ✂ Num
99/0 Ult. Victory 77, -NW 6
96/7 Upper Deck X28
97/8 Upper Deck 53
99/0 Upper Deck 283, -UD6
00/1 Upper Deck 154, RP7, TT10
01/2 Upper Deck 256
02/3 Upper Deck 24, -SA2, ✂ DM, ✂ GT, ✂ SV
02/3 UD Artistic 12, / Art
96/7 UD Black Diam. 1
00/1 UD Black Diam. 52, ✂ GG
01/2 UD Challenge 10, BB1
02/3 UD Classic 13, ✂ HR
96/7 UD CC 358
99/0 UD G. Reserve 283
97/8 UD Ice 35
00/1 UD Ice 35, ✍ CCA
01/2 UD Ice 89
00/1 UD Legends 116
01/2 UD Mask 105, 173
02/3 UD Mask 13, 14, 15, 16, ✂ CW, ✂ GG, ✂ MM, ✂ PW, ✂ SS, ✂ VC
00/1 UD MVP 158, MM8, ME6, ✍ PS, ✍ ME
02/3 UD MVP 26
99/0 UD MVP Cup 162
02/3 UD Piece 15
00/1 UD Pros&Prosp. 75
02/3 UD Rookie 18, ✂ DJ
01/2 UD Top Shelf 82
02/3 UD Top Shelf 13
00/1 UD Vintage 315, 320, 321, GG16
02/3 UD Vintage 36, 265, GB 36, T9
00/1 Vanguard 84
01/2 Vanguard 14, SW 4, VT 1, ✂ DGM 5, ✂ DGM 41
02/3 Vanguard 16
99/0 Victory 268
00/1 Victory 205, 258, 324
01/2 Victory 302, 313
02/3 Victory 30
99/0 WGretzky 144
96 Wien 102, SG6, AS1
99/0 SLOU / Taco Bell 18
96/7 Michigan K-Wings

TURGEON, PIERRE
01/2 Adrenaline 62, ✂ GWJ 14
01/2 Atomic 34
98/9 Aurora 164, -CF 42
99/0 Aurora 128
00/1 Aurora 125
98/9 Be A Player 275, ✍ Aut. 275
99/0 BAP Mem. 158
00/1 BAP Mem. 108
01/2 BAP Mem. 296, 353
02/3 BAP Mem. 175
96/7 Bic.Sports Aces 10-C
97/8 Bicycle 6-Club
95/6 Bicycle Sports Aces 8-Heart
90/1 Bowman 241
91/2 Bowman 27
92/3 Bowman 23
95/6 Bowman 6
01/2 Bowman 60
98/9 Bowman's Best 86
99/0 Crown Royale 121
00/1 Crown Royale 91
01/2 Crown Royale 50, ✂ TT 8, ✂ TT 19
02/3 Crown Royale ✂ GWDP 8
93/4 Donruss 209
93/4 Donruss N
94/5 Donruss 23
95/6 Donruss 61, I-4
96/7 Donruss 17, D-6
97/8 Donruss 28
96/7 Do. Canadian 110
97/8 Do. Canadian 24, NP-24
95/6 Do. Elite 90, CE-10
96/7 Do. Elite 112
97/8 Do. Elite 105
97/8 Do. Preferred 117
97/8 Do. Priority 41
97/8 Do. Studio 64
96/7 Duracell JB14
92/3 Durivage 11
93/4 Durivage 30
98/9 Dynagon Ice 163
99/0 Dynagon Ice 169
93/4 EA Sports 81
02/3 Exclusive 59, ✂ GWJ 6
02/3 First Edition 58, 428R, ✂ Jers.
94/5 Flair 109
94/5 Fleer 130
96/7 Fleer 57, ART-23
95/6 Fleer Metal 80
96/7 Fl. Picks 32, F50-45
92/3 Fleer Ultra 132
93/4 Fleer Ultra 197
93/4 Fleer Ultra AS 3
93/4 Fleer Ultra PP 9
93/4 Fleer Ultra SK 5
94/5 Fleer Ultra 133
95/6 Fleer Ultra 85
96/7 Fl. Ultra 148
91/2 Gillette 35
01/2 Heads Up 33
02/3 Heads Up ✂ GWQ 11
93/4 Hockey Wit 27
02/3 In The GU ✂ GUJ50, ✂ SJ50
91/2 Kellogg's / Score 6
90/1 Kraft 59, 91
93/4 Kraft / KD
95/6 Kraft / IP
99/0 Kraft / PB
93/4 Leaf 25
93/4 Leaf 340
93/4 Leaf HTA 5
94/5 Leaf 367, LL-14
95/6 Leaf 90, FF-2
96/7 Leaf 186, LL-18
97/8 Leaf 43
94/5 L. Limited 52
95/6 L. Limited 102
96/7 L. Limited 38
96/7 L. Preferred 70, LS-26
97/8 Limited 158, 172
96/7 Maggers 85
93/4 McDonald's McD-27
94/5 McDonald's McD-26
95/6 McDonald's McD-13
96/7 McDonald's McD-19
96/7 Metal Univ. 84
99/0 Millenium 205, ✍ Aut. 205
88/9 OPC/Topps 194
90/1 OPC/Topps 66
90/1 Topps-TL 20
91/2 O-Pee-Chee 416
92/3 O-Pee-Chee 47
01/2 O-Pee-Chee 79, Update 79
02/3 O-Pee-Chee 113
89/0 OPC/Topps 25, / Box P
90/1 OPC/Topps M
98/9 OPC Chrome 208
90/1 OPC Premier 124
91/2 OPC Premier 59
88/9 OPC Sticker 133-269
88/9 OPC Sticker 69-198
89/0 opcSticker 262
97/8 Omega 199
98/9 Omega 206
99/0 Omega 202
98/9 Pacific 374
99/0 Pacific 364
00/1 Pacific 353
01/2 Pacific 334, 420, 440, TDP 9
02/3 Pacific 120
02/3 Pacific Complete 449
97/8 Pacific CC 32, SS-9B
97/8 Pa. Crown Roy. 118
98/9 Pa. Crown Roy. 117
97/8 Pa. Dynagon 108, T-59, BKS-83
97/8 Pa. Invincible 122, R-173
97/8 Pa. Paramount 161
98/9 Pa. Paramount 207
99/0 Pa. Paramount 201, -IAI 23
00/1 Pa. Paramount 210
97/8 Pa. Revolution 122
98/9 Pa. Revolution 125
98/9 Panini Photocard
88/9 Panini Sticker 230
89/0 Panini Sticker 204
90/1 Panini Sticker 28
91/2 Panini Sticker 303
92/3 Panini Sticker 196
93/4 Panini Sticker F
94/5 Panini Sticker 48
95/6 Panini Sticker 37
96/7 Panini Sticker 40
97/8 Panini Sticker 164
98/9 Panini Sticker 154
99/0 Panini Sticker 292
00/1 Panini Sticker 194
91/2 Parkhurst 106
92/3 Parkhurst 103
93/4 Parkhurst 389
93/4 Parkhurst F7
93/4 Parkhurst E10
94/5 Parkhurst 135, YCTG-14
95/6 Parkhurst 109, PP-50
00/1 Parkhurst P-74
01/2 Parkhurst 62, ✂ PS55
02/3 Parkhurst 14
02/3 Parkhurst Retro 81
94/5 Parkie SE seV31
91/2 Pinnacle 30
92/3 Pinnacle 165
92/3 Pinnacle T2K 17
93/4 Pinnacle 160
93/4 Pinnacle 225
93/4 Pinnacle NF 7
93/4 Pinnacle T2K1 13
94/5 Pinnacle 78
95/6 Pinnacle 34, CS-14, R20-20
96/7 Pinnacle 22
97/8 Pinnacle 75
97/8 Pi. Be A Player TN14
97/8 Pi. Certified 62
97/8 Pi. Inside 122
95/6 Pi. Summit 43
96/7 Pi. Summit 90
97/8 Pi. Totally 62
95/6 Pi. Zenith 38
96/7 Pi. Zenith 39, A-12
95/6 Playoff 56
94/5 POG 160
95/6 POG 145
93/4 Power Play 155
93/4 Power Play PL 19
93/4 Premier 190
93/4 Prmr. - BG-Top. 20
93/4 Premier - Finest 7
94/5 Premier 115
00/1 Premier Plus 24
99/0 Prism 122
00/1 Pr. Stock 86, PS-53, PSS-23
01/2 Pr. Stock 31, ✂ GUG 40
02/3 Pr. Stock Reserve 34
00/1 PS Titanium 83
01/2 PS Titanium 47, ✂ DSJ 52, ✂ DSJ 65
01/2 PS Titanium Draft ✂ 35
02/3 Pr. Stock Titanium 34
95/6 Pro Magnet 18
90/1 Pro Set 31, 366
91/2 Pro Set 15
91/2 Pro Set 433
92/3 Pro Set 104
91/2 Pro Set Platinum 10
02/3 Quest for the Cup 31
99/0 Revolution 125
00/1 Revolution 126
90/1 Score 110
90/1 Sco. Hot Cards 53
91/2 Score 4
91/2 Score 377
91/2 Score 416
91/2 Score 101T
91/2 Score CAN 4
91/2 Score CAN 267
91/2 Score CAN 332
92/3 Score 325
92/3 Score 430
92/3 Score SS 25
93/4 Score 6
93/4 Score DT 15
93/4 Score/CAN DD9
93/4 Score PiAS 5
93/4 Score TF 12
93/4 Score / Promo 6
94/5 Score 166, NP-14, TF-14
95/6 Score 90, BB-1, L-6
96/7 Score 71, SD-1
97/8 Score 118
97/8 Score SLou. 2
90/1 Sco. Young Stars 1
92/3 Score Young Stars 27
92/3 Seasons 53
94/5 Select 46
95/6 Select CE 49
96/7 Select CE 82
91 Semic Sticker 66
96/7 SB 7-Eleven Phonecard
00/1 Signature 181, ✍ Aut. 56
01/2 Signature C-34, ✍ Aut., ✂ GJ11, ✂ GSJ11
02/3 Signature Series 154, ✍ 154

95/6 SBx Emotion 93
95/6 SBx Impact 89
96/7 SBx Impact 66, BR-23
94/5 SP 61
95/6 SP 71, E15
96/7 SP 137
97/8 SP Authentic 141
98/9 SP Authentic 73
99/0 SP Authentic 77
00/1 SP Authentic 76
01/2 SP Authentic 25
01/2 SP GU 16
02/3 Sports Vault 206
96/7 SPx 22
99/0 SPx 134
01/2 SPx 21
02/3 SPx 134
98/9 SPx Finite 74
99/0 Stadium 112
00/1 Stadium 56
01/2 Stadium 106
95/6 SLU
95/6 Super Sticker 63, DC-1
96/7 Team Out!
92/3 Topps 289
95/6 Topps 21, 224, 7CG, HGC3, 9PL
98/9 Topps 208
99/0 Topps 223
00/1 Topps 205, PC-14
01/2 Topps 79, Update 79
02/3 Topps 113
99/0 To. Chrome 223
00/1 To. Chrome 135, PC-14
01/2 To. Chrome 79
02/3 T. Chrome 73
94/5 Topps Finest 78, BBB-9
95/6 To. Finest 46, 182
98/9 To. Finest 125
98/9 T. Gold Label 30
99/0 To. Gold Label 65
00/1 To. Gold Label 35
00/1 To. Heritage 48
01/2 To. Heritage 163
02/3 To. Limited 113
99/0 To. Prmr. Plus 20
01/2 To. Reserve 61
91/2 To. Stadium 77
92/3 To. Stadium 276
93/4 To. Stadium 145
93/4 To. Stadium 380
93/4 To. Stadium - Master Photo-2 8
93/4 To. Stadium - AS
95/6 To. Stadium EC175, EN7, PS1
93/4 TSC Members Only 38
94/5 TSC Members Only 20
95/6 TSC Members Only 39
00/1 To. Stars 31
95/6 T. Super Skills 9
02/3 To. Total 187
98/9 UD Choice 184
00/1 UD Heroes 105
01/2 UD PlayMakers Ltd 32
00/1 Ultimate Mem. ✍ U-48
90/1 Upper Deck 43, 318
91/2 Upper Deck 176
91/2 Upper Deck 554
92/3 Upper Deck 175
93/4 Upper Deck 224, 297, 347, AW7, HT11, H7, SP-96
94/5 Upper Deck 77, SP-48
95/6 Upper Deck 389, AS-15, SE-44
97/8 Upper Deck 353
98/9 Upper Deck 172
99/0 Upper Deck 287
00/1 Upper Deck 379
01/2 Upper Deck 57
02/3 Upper Deck 302
93/4 Upper Deck Be A Player 37
94/5 UD BAP R80
95/6 UD BAP 152, ✍ S152
96/7 UD Black Diam. 135
97/8 UD Black Diam. 100
01/2 UD Challenge 23
95/6 UD CC 131, C15
96/7 UD CC 133, 321, S19
97/8 UD Coll. Choice 226, SQ56
98/9 UD G. Reserve 172
99/0 UD G. Reserve 287
96/7 UD Ice 61
01/2 UD Ice 94
92/3 UD Locker 17
01/2 UD Mask 28
98/9 UD MVP 181
99/0 UD MVP 184
00/1 UD MVP 157
01/2 UD MVP 63
99/0 UD MVP Cup 161
00/1 UD Pros&Prosp. 76
00/1 UD Vintage 319
01/2 UD Vintage 81
02/3 UD Vintage 80, 270, GB 80
00/1 Vanguard 85, HV-30, VP-10
01/2 Vanguard 33, ✄ DGM 30
02/3 Vanguard ✄ GWJ 17
99/0 Victory 266
00/1 Victory 207
01/2 Victory 310, 412
02/3 Victory 71
99/0 WGretzky 143
97/8 Zenith 23, Z61
87/8 BUFF / Blue Shield
87/8 BUFF / Won. Bread
88/9 BUFF / Blue Shield
88/9 BUFF / Won. Bread
89/0 BUFF / Blue Shield
89/0 BUFF / Campbell's
90/1 BUFF / Blue Shield
90/1 BUFF / Campbell's
01/2 DALL / Southwest
02/3 DALL / Southwest
95/6 MONT
95/6 MONT / Export
99/0 SLOU / Taco Bell 4

TURGEON, SYLVAIN
90/1 Bowman 81
92/3 Bowman 167
83 Canada Juniors
93/4 Donruss 235
94/5 Donruss 105
92/3 Durivage 29
93/4 Durivage 36
93/4 EA Sports 94
99/0 Eishockey 187
94/5 Fleer 148
92/3 Fleer Ultra 149
93/4 Fleer Ultra 190
94/5 Fleer Ultra 341
93/4 Leaf 74
94/5 Leaf 191
95/6 Leaf 33
84/5 O-Pee-Chee 79
84/5 O-Pee-Chee 372
85/6 OPC/Topps 43
86/7 OPC/Topps 103
87/8 OPC/Topps 70
88/9 OPC/Topps 24
90/1 OPC/Topps 73
91/2 O-Pee-Chee 231
92/3 O-Pee-Chee 315
91/2 OPC Premier 184
92/3 OPC Premier 116
84/5 OPC Sticker 191
84/5 OPC Sticker 192
85/6 OPC Sticker 165
86/7 OPC Sticker 53
87/8 OPC Sticker 203-61
87/8 Panini Sticker 36
87/8 Panini Sticker 50
88/9 Panini Sticker 245
90/1 Panini Sticker 71
93/4 Panini Sticker K
94/5 Panini Sticker 105
95/6 Panini Sticker 52
91/2 Parkhurst 91
92/3 Parkhurst 121
93/4 Parkhurst 136
94/5 Parkhurst 153, V51
95/6 Parkhurst 146
91/2 Pinnacle 226
92/3 Pinnacle 373
93/4 Pinnacle 64
94/5 Pinnacle 288
95/6 Playoff 290
94/5 POG 173
93/4 Power Play 176
93/4 Premier 97
94/5 Premier 23
90/1 Pro Set 177, 474
91/2 Pro Set 416
92/3 Pro Set 123
90/1 Score 116, 108T
91/2 Score 208
91/2 Score 377
91/2 Score CAN 208
91/2 Score CAN 267
92/3 Score 367
92/3 Score 516
93/4 Score 46
84/5 7-Eleven
84/5 Topps 62
92/3 Topps 375
92/3 To. Stadium 59
93/4 To. Stadium 482
90/1 Upper Deck 70
91/2 Upper Deck 579
92/3 Upper Deck 107
93/4 Upper Deck 44
94/5 Upper Deck 336, SP-146
95/6 Upper Deck 177
94/5 UD BAP R60
00/1 UD DEL 127, A10
83/4 HART / Jr. Whalers
84/5 HART / Jr. Whalers
85/6 HART / Jr. Whalers
86/7 HART / Jr. Whalers
87/8 HART / Jr. Whalers
88/9 HART / Jr. Whalers
90/1 MONT
91/2 MONT
89/0 NJER
89/0 NJER / Caretta
92/3 OTTA
93/4 OTTA
94/5 OTTA
95/6 Houston Aeros

TURGEON, YAN
00/1 Rockford IceHogs

TURKIEWICZ, JIM
76/7 OPC WHA 18

TURKOVSKI, VASILI
00/1 Mir 258

TURKULAINEN, RAIMO
66/7 Champion 127
70/1 Kuvajulkaisut 271

TURLER, MICHEL
72 Semic Sticker 161

TURMEL, GUY
00/1 Baie-Comeau 16

TURMEL, NICOLAS
91/2 7th...Sketch LHJMQ 114

TURMEL, RICHARD
83/4 Fredericton Express

TURNBULL, DALE
87/8 Soo Greyhounds 9
89/0 Soo Greyhounds

TURNBULL, IAN
74/5 Loblaws
74/5 O-Pee-Chee 289
75/6 O-Pee-Chee 41
76/7 O-Pee-Chee 39
77/8 O-Pee-Chee 186
77/8 O-Pee-Chee 215
78/9 O-Pee-Chee 127
79/0 O-Pee-Chee 228
80/1 O-Pee-Chee 133
81/2 O-Pee-Chee 309
81/2 OPC Sticker 100
80/1 O-Pee-Chee Super 21
80/1 Pepsi Bottle Cap
75/6 Topps 41
76/7 Topps 39
77/8 Topps 186
77/8 Topps 215
78/9 Topps 127
79/0 Topps 228
80/1 Topps 133
81/2 Topps 42
73/4 TORO
74/5 TORO
75/6 TORO
75/6 TORO
76/7 TORO
77/8 TORO
78/9 TORO
79/0 TORO
80/1 TORO

TURNBULL, PERRY
86/7 Kraft Sports 81
80/1 O-Pee-Chee 169
81/2 O-Pee-Chee 298
82/3 O-Pee-Chee 312
83/4 O-Pee-Chee 321
84/5 O-Pee-Chee 349
85/6 O-Pee-Chee 254
86/7 OPC/Topps 170
82/3 OPC/Topps Sticker 203
83/4 OPC/Topps Sticker 124
88/9 Panini Sticker 196
82/3 Post [SLou.]
80/1 Topps 169
81/2 Topps 123 [West]
83/4 MONT
87/8 SLOU / Kodak
92/3 SLOU / McDon. 26
84/5 WINN / Safety Tips
85/6 WINN
85/6 WINN / Safety Tips
86/7 WINN

TURNER, BART
93/4 Michigan State

TURNER, BOB
45-64 BeeHive-2 [Mont.]
45-64 BeeHive-2 [Chic.]
45-64 BeeHive-2 [Chic.]
64-67 BeeHive-3 [Chic.]
62/3 Cowan Tile
55/6 Parkhurst 54
57/8 Parkhurst [Mont.] 13
58/9 Parkhurst 40
59/0 Parkhurst 43
60/1 Parkhurst 43
61/2 Parkhurst 41
93/4 Parkie 56-57 81
60/1 Shirriff 37
61/2 Shirriff 37
61/2 Topps 41
62/3 Topps 29
63/4 Topps 32
58/9 Toronto Star Photo
60/1 York
01/2 Mississauga IceDogs

TURNER, BOBBY
00/1 London Knights

TURNER, BRAD
93/4 Fleer Ultra 475
93/4 Premier - Canada 10
91/2 ProCards 381
94/5 Sisu 302

TURNER, DAN
82/3 Medicine Hat Tigers
83/4 Medicine Hat Tigers

TURNER, IAN
00/1 London Knights
01/2 London Knights

TURNER, JACK
67/8 Columbus Checkers
69 Columbus Checkers

TURNER, LLOYD
83 HHOF Postcard B15
83&87 HHOF 29

TURNER, MARK
91/2 ProCards 245
99/0 Mobile Mysticks
93/4 Muskegon Fury
95/6 Muskegon Fury
87/8 Kingston Canadians
85/6 Sudbury Wolves
86/7 Sudbury Wolves
88/9 Sudbury Wolves

TURNER, SCOTT
91/2 7th...Sketch OHL 124
91/2 Peterborough Petes

TURPEINEN, UNTO
71/2 Williams Finnish 274

TURTIAINEN, KIMMO
72/3 Williams Finnish 297

TURUNEN, JYRKI
66/7 Champion 131
70/1 Kuvajulkaisut 272

TURUNEN, KIMMO
70/1 Kuvajulkaisut 322

TURUNEN, MARTTI
70/1 Kuvajulkaisut 273

TURUNEN, OLLI-PEKKA
71/2 Williams Finnish 354
72/3 Williams Finnish 338

TURUNEN, TIMO
72 Hellas MM-Jenkki 17
70/1 Kuvajulkaisut 188
71/2 Williams Finnish 109
72/3 Williams Finnish 76
72/3 Williams Finnish 153
73/4 Williams Finnish 81
73/4 Williams Finnish 122

TURUNEN, TOMMI
98/9 Cardset 135
99/0 Cardset 300
00/1 Cardset 74
02/3 Cardset 130
95/6 Sisu 305
96/7 Sisu 103

TURVEY, WARD
23/4 Selkirks Crescent 10

TUSTIAN, ROB
91/2 ProCards 42
90/1 Michigan Tech Huskies

TUSTIN, NORMAN
34-43 BeeHive-1 [NYRa.]

TUTEN, AUDLEY
34-43 BeeHive-1 [Chic.]

TUTL, CLYDE
93/4 Sheffield Steelers 20

TUTT,
92/3 Semic Nordisk 190 [Mest Utvist]
92/3 Semic Nordisk 192 [Arets Lag]

TUTT, BRIAN
96/7 DEL 297
98/9 DEL 245
99/0 Eishockey 239
89/0 ProCards AHL 91
93/4 Sisu 363
94/5 Sisu 318

TUTT, W. THAYER
83 HHOF Postcard I15
83&87 HHOF 134

TUTTLE, STEVE
92/3 Fleer Ultra 205
90/1 OPC/Topps 278
89/0 OPC/Topps 157
89/0 Panini Sticker 126
90/1 Pro Set 273
90/1 ProCards 84
91/2 ProCards 41
90/1 Upper Deck 195
87/8 SLOU
88/9 SLOU
88/9 SLOU / Kodak
89/0 SLOU / Kodak
90/1 SLOU / Kodak
93/4 Milwaukee Admirals
94/5 Milwaukee Admirals
95/6 Milwaukee Admirals
96/7 Milwaukee Admirals
97/8 Milwaukee Admirals
94/5 Peoria Rivermen

TUULOLA,
93/4 Sisu 358

TUULOLA, MARKO
02/3 Cardset 131
92/3 Jyvas Hyva 26
93/4 Jyvas Hyva 235
94 Semic 7
95 Semic 25
93/4 Sisu 187
94/5 Sisu 6
95/6 Sisu 248
96/7 Sisu 43
98/9 UD Elitserien 35
99/0 UD Elitserien 20
00/1 UD Elitserien 34

TUYL, CLYDE
94/5 Sheffield Steelers 23
95/6 Sheffield Steelers
97/8 Sheffield Steelers

TUZZOLINO, TONY
01/2 BAP Mem. 453
01/2 UD PlayMakers Ltd 106
01/2 UD Ice 129
98/9 Cincinnati M'Ducks 24
99/0 Hartford Wolf Pack
00/1 Hartford Wolf Pack
97/8 Kentucky Tho'blades
02/3 Louisiana Ice Gators
01/2 Providence Bruins
93/4 Michigan State

TVERDOVSKY, OLEG
01/2 Adrenaline 6, ✄ GWJ 1
02/3 Atomic ✄ GWJ 13
98/9 Aurora 150
98/9 Be A Player 258, ✍ Aut. 258
99/0 BAP Mem. 140
00/1 BAP Mem. 135
01/2 BAP Mem. 87
02/3 BAP Mem. 126, 269
95/6 Bowman 88
93/4 Classic 111
94/5 Classic 2, CP12, R19, T3
94/5 Classic 4 Sport 116,HV8
94/5 Cla. Images 4 Sport 95
93/4 Cla. Prospects 208
01/2 Crown Royale ✄ TT 1
95/6 Donruss 3, RT-6
96/7 Donruss 105
97/8 Donruss 54, L2L-6
97/8 Do. Canadian 62
95/6 Do. Elite 6
97/8 Do. Elite 109
97/8 Do. Preferred 137
97/8 Do. Priority 53
97/8 Do. Studio 38
98/9 Dynagon Ice 147
99/0 Dynagon Ice 13
02/3 First Edition 48, ✄ Jers.
96/7 Flair 74
94/5 Fleer 8, RS-10
96/7 Fleer 93
95/6 Fleer Metal 5
94/5 Fleer Ultra UP-9
95/6 Fleer Ultra 6
96/7 Fl. Ultra 137
02/3 Heads Up ✄ GWQ 1
94/5 Leaf P-6
95/6 Leaf 28, SR-6
96/7 Leaf 3
97/8 Leaf 92
94/5 L. Limited 24
95/6 L. Limited 46
96/7 L. Preferred 71
97/8 Limited 93
95/6 McDonald's McD-35
96/7 Metal Univ. 123
99/0 Millenium 3, ✍ Aut. 3
00/1 Mir Fetisov 13
99/0 NHL Power Play
01/2 O-Pee-Chee 111
02/3 O-Pee-Chee 207
97/8 Omega 179
98/9 Omega 190
98/9 Pacific 345
99/0 Pacific 330
00/1 Pacific 12
01/2 Pacific 12
02/3 Pacific 10
02/3 Pacific Complete 147
97/8 Pacific CC 252
98/9 Pa. Crown Roy. 107
97/8 Pa. Dynagon 99, T-66
97/8 Pa. Invincible 110
97/8 Pa. Paramount 146
98/9 Pa. Paramount 188
00/1 Pa. Paramount 8
98/9 Panini Photocard
95/6 Panini Sticker 231
96/7 Panini Sticker 192
97/8 Panini Sticker 163
98/9 Panini Sticker 146
99/0 Panini Sticker 183
00/1 Panini Sticker 114
93/4 Parkhurst 531
95/6 Parkhurst 9, 496
00/1 Parkhurst P-83
01/2 Parkhurst 106
02/3 Parkhurst 156
02/3 Parkhurst Retro 170
93/4 Pinnacle 506
94/5 Pinnacle 261, RTP2
95/6 Pinnacle 60, GG-11
96/7 Pinnacle 145
97/8 Pinnacle 166
97/8 Pi. Certified 103
97/8 Pi. Inside 132
95/6 Pi. Summit 37
96/7 Pi. Summit 129
97/8 Pi. Totally 103
95/6 Pi. Zenith 71
96/7 Pi. Zenith 70
95/6 Playoff 4
96/7 Playoff 332
95/6 POG 24
94/5 Premier 464
01/2 Pr. Stock ✄ GUG 5
01/2 PS Titanium ✄ DSJ 2
01/2 PS Titanium Draft ✄ 3
95/6 Pro Magnet 37
94/5 Score 214, TR-4
95/6 Score 16
96/7 Score 89
97/8 Score 195
94/5 Select 169, YE-2
95/6 Select CE 79, CF-9
00/1 Signature 96
01/2 Signature 148, ✍ Aut. 148, ✄ DD4, ✄ IB5
02/3 Signature Series 93, ✍ 93
95/6 SBx Emotion 4
95/6 SBx Impact 5, 236
96/7 SBx Impact 109
02/3 Slam Card
94/5 SP 2, P-5
95/6 SP 166
96/7 SP 121
00/1 SP Authentic 3
99/0 SPx 7
99/0 Stadium 156
00/1 Stadium 137
95/6 Super Sticker 1, 4
95/6 Topps 365, 4NG, YS7
00/1 Topps 86
01/2 Topps 111
02/3 Topps 207
00/1 To. Chrome 68
01/2 To. Chrome 111
94/5 Topps Finest 2, BBM-4, BBR-2
98/9 To. Finest 104
02/3 To. Heritage 179
02/3 To. Limited 207
96/7 To. Picks 97
95/6 To. Stadium 113
95/6 T. Super Skills 12
98/9 UD Choice 159
00/1 UD Heroes 3
94/5 Upper Deck 243, 540, C14, SP-93
95/6 Upper Deck 408, SE-2
96/7 Upper Deck 129, SS25A
97/8 Upper Deck 335, SG42
98/9 Upper Deck 153
99/0 Upper Deck 102, 173
00/1 Upper Deck 3
01/2 Upper Deck 232
02/3 Upper Deck 347
94/5 UD BAP R160
95/6 UD BAP 61, ✍ S61
96/7 UD Black Diam. 102
95/6 UD CC 81
96/7 UD CC 199, 327
97/8 UD Coll. Choice 198, SQ28
98/9 UD G. Reserve 153
99/0 UD G. Reserve 102, 173
96/7 UD Ice 99
98/9 UD MVP 161, ✍ PS
99/0 UD MVP 9
00/1 UD MVP 3
01/2 UD MVP 4
99/0 UD MVP Cup 4
00/1 UD Vintage 4
01/2 UD Vintage 4, 9
01/2 Vanguard ✄ DGM 1
99/0 Victory 6
00/1 Victory 5
01/2 Victory 3
02/3 Victory 5
99/0 WGretzky 5
94/5 ANAH / Carl's Jr. 24
96/7 PHOE / Coca-Cola
98/9 PHOE / Coca-Cola

TVETEN, ERIK
95 Panini Worlds 254
92/3 Semic Nordisk 3

TVRDIK, MICHAL
00/1 DS 96
98/9 OFS 381
99/0 OFS 99
00/1 OFS 48
01/2 OFS 258

TVRZNIK, MARTIN
00/1 OFS 155

TWIST, TONY
98/9 Aurora 165
01/2 Fleer Legacy 51, ✄ ITC
94/5 Leaf 13, 454
98/9 Omega 207
98/9 Pacific 375
99/0 Pacific 365
97/8 Pacific CC 254
97/8 Pa. Paramount 162
98/9 Pa. Paramount 208
98/9 Pa. Revolution TPA 8
96/7 Panini Sticker 210
88/9 ProCards / Peoria
90/1 ProCards 85
91/2 Score CAN 396
93/4 Score 400
96/7 Score 207
97/8 Score 157
97/8 Score SLou. 10
95/6 Topps 203
97/8 Upper Deck 201
98/9 Upper Deck 177
95/6 UD BAP 214, ✍ S214
96/7 UD CC 231
97/8 UD Coll. Choice 230
02/3 UD Foundations 86, ✄ CH, ✄ PS
98/9 UD G. Reserve 177
98/9 UD MVP 184
91/2 QUÉB / Petro-Canada
92/3 QUÉB / Petro-Canada
89/0 SLOU / Kodak
96/7 SLOU / Dispatch 4
86/7 Saskatoon Blades

TWIST, TONY
02/3 Fleer Throwbacks 68, 7SO, ✄ 3DTG, ✄ 7SC, ✄ 7SCTD, ✄ 7SO, ✍ Aut.

TWOHEY, JEFF
89/0 7th..Sketch OHL 118
91/2 Peterborough Petes

TWOMEY, CHRISTIAN
92/3 BCJHL 209

TWORDIK, BRAD
99 Bowman 94
98/9 Brandon Wheat Kings
99/0 Brandon Wheat Kings

TYBURSKI, ED
88/9 ProCards / Springfield
89/0 ProCards AHL 249

TYCHKIN, ALEXANDER
00/1 Mir 5

TYERS, SHAWN
85/6 Kitchener Rangers

TYJNYCH, ALEXANDER
89/0 ProCards AHL 144
90/1 ProCards 236

TYMCHAK, JOSH
99/0 Asheville Smoke
99/0 Asheville Smoke

TYMCHUK, GREG
95/6 Slapshot 200

TYMCHYSHYN, DARREN
91/2 Avant Garde BCJHL 40
92/3 BCJHL 56

TYNKKYNEN, MATTI
80/1 Mallasjuoma 123
78/9 SM-Liiga 168

TYULYAPKIN, DENIS
00/1 Mir 200

TYURIKOV, VLADIMIR
99/0 Mir 30
00/1 Mir 18

TYURIN, DENIS
00/1 Mir 191

TYUTIN, FEDOR
00/1 Mir 77
02/3 Russian Future Stars 5

U

UBRIACO, GENE
69/0 O-Pee-Chee 149
92 Semic Sticker 242
92/3 Atlanta Knights
93/4 Atlanta Knights

UCHAIKIN, DMITRI
00/1 Mir 19

UCHEVATOV, VICTOR
01/2 Albany River Rats
02/3 Albany River Rats

UDLE, CLARK
96/7 Halifax Moosehead

UDVARI, FRANK
83 HHOF Postcard N16
83&87 HHOF 240

UDVARI, STEVE
89/0 7th..Sketch OHL 138
89/0 Niagara Falls Thunder
87/8 Soo Greyhounds 12

UDYANSKI, STANISLAV
00/1 Mir 207

UENS, JIM
81/2 Oshawa Generals

UGOLNIKOV, OLEG
99/0 Mir 175

UHER, ZDENEK
95/6 APS 352
96/7 APS 336

UHLBÄCK, JAAKKO
98/9 Cardset 160
99/0 Cardset 325
00/1 Cardset 90
97/8 Hockey-Box

UITUS, PEKKA
66/7 Champion 175
70/1 Kuvajulkaisut 256
71/2 Williams Finnish 221
72/3 Williams Finnish 169
73/4 Williams Finnish 237

UJCIK, VIKTOR
94/5 APS 175
95/6 APS 136, 378, 444
96/7 APS 19, 347, 370, 391
97/8 APS 159, 360
97/8 DS 12
98/9 DS 8
99/0 DS NS9
00/1 DS 68
01/2 DS 22, 55
96/7 DS Sticker 14, 129
97/8 DS Sticker 19, 196
98/9 OFS 184, 428
99/0 OFS 203, 273, 529
00/1 OFS 224, 412, -Star 25
01/2 OFS 12, RE1D

UJCIK, VIKTOR
91/2 Upper Deck WJC 92

UJVARY, LUBOMIR
70/1 Kuvajulkaisut 60

UKKOLA, TIMO
80/1 Mallasjuoma 18

UKKONEN, VEIKKO
66/7 Champion 16
65/6 Hellas 123

UKSILA, C.
19 Vancouver Millionaires
19 Vancouver Millionaires

ULANDER, MATS
82 Semic Sticker 18

ULANOV, IGOR
92/3 Bowman 392
94/5 Fleer Ultra 397
94/5 Leaf 416
91/2 O-Pee-Chee 62R
92/3 O-Pee-Chee 229
99/0 Pa. Paramount 121
97/8 Panini Sticker 106
91/2 Parkhurst 421
92/3 Parkhurst 440
97/8 Pi. Be A Player 209, ✍ Aut. 209
93/4 Power Play 477
94/5 Premier 179
92/3 Pro Set 216
92/3 Score 467
95 Semic 129
92/3 Topps 468
92/3 To. Stadium 366
91/2 Upper Deck 590
92/3 Upper Deck 300
92/3 Upper Deck E15
00/1 Upper Deck 69
94/5 UD BAP ✍ 70
96/7 UD CC 252
97/8 UD Coll. Choice 239
97/8 MONT
93/4 WINN / Ruffles
93/4 WINN Readers
01/2 Hartford Wolf Pack

ÚLEHLA, PETR
99/0 OFS 128

ULIN, PATRIK
92/3 Semic Elitserien 297

ULION, GRETZHEN
94/5 Classic W29

ULLMAN, NORM
71/2 Bazooka Panel
99/0 BAP Mem. R-10, ✍ R-10
45-64 BeeHive-2 [Detr.]
64-67 BeeHive-3 [Detr.]
63-65 Chex
64/5 Coke/Sprite [Detr.]
65/6 Coca-Cola
71/2 Colgate Head
71/2 Colgate Head
70/1 Colgate 12
70/1 Dad's Cookies
70/1 Eddie Sargent 204
71/2 Eddie Sargent 193
72/3 Eddie Sargent 197
70/1 Esso Power Player
88/9 Esso All-Star
01/2 Fleer Greats 43, ✍ Aut.
71/2 Frito Lay
62/3 Cowan Tile
83 HHOF Postcard G15
83&87 HHOF 104
92/3 Legends 17
72/3 Post 17
74/5 Lipton Soup 1
74/5 Loblaws
73/4 Mac's Milk
68/9 O-Pee-Chee 131
69/0 O-Pee-Chee 54
69/0 O-Pee-Chee Stamp
70/1 O-Pee-Chee 110
70/1 O-Pee-Chee DE 48
71/2 O-Pee-Chee 30
72/3 O-Pee-Chee 147
73/4 O-Pee-Chee 27
74/5 O-Pee-Chee 219
74/5 O-Pee-Chee 236
71/2 O-Pee-Chee Poster 11
76/7 OPC WHA 126
60/1 Parkhurst 26
61/2 Parkhurst 26
62/3 Parkhurst 21
63/4 Parkhurst 52
92/3 Parkhurst PR-25
02/3 Parkie - Reprint 253, 266, 277
93/4 Parkie 56-57 45
95/6 Parkie 66-67 45, SL3
94/5 Parkie Tall 58, AS4, SL3
66/7 Post Cereal Box
68/9 Post Marble
72 Semic Sticker 163
60/1 Shirriff 45
61/2 Shirriff 76
68/9 Shirriff / Toro. 10
81/2 TCMA 1
57/8 Topps 46
58/9 Topps 65
59/0 Topps 45
64/5 Topps 15
65/6 Topps 49
66/7 Topps 52
66/7 Topps / Test 52
67/8 Topps 101
67/8 Topps 132
68/9 Topps 131
69/0 Topps 54
70/1 Topps 110
71/2 Topps 30
72/3 Topps 168
73/4 Topps 148
74/5 Topps 219
74/5 Topps 236
01/2 To. Heritage S6, ✍ CAI
01/2 T/O Archives 11, -Seat., ✍ CAI
58/9 Toronto Star Photo
63/4 Toronto Star Action
64/5 Toronto Star Action
64/5 Toronto Star Photo
65/6 Toronto Star Photo
59/0 Toronto Star Weekend
71/2 Toronto Sun Photo
91/2 Ultimate Original Six 72, 78, ✍ Aut. 72
62/3 York Transfer 29
63/4 York 47
94/5 Zellers, ✍ Aut.
69/0 TORO
71/2 TORO
72/3 TORO
73/4 TORO
74/5 TORO

ULLMANN, DAVID
00/1 Medicine Hat Tigers

ULLRYCH, TOMAS
99/0 OFS 174

ULMER, JASON
00/1 Quad City Mallards

ULMER, JEFF
01/2 BAP Mem. 184
00/1 PS Titanium Draft 167
00/1 SPx 183
00/1 UD Ice 116
01/2 Victory 381
01/2 Grand Rapids Griffins
00/1 Hartford Wolf Pack

ULRICH, MARTIN
96/7 DEL 166
99/0 Eishockey 288
95 Globe 184
95 Panini Worlds 259
94 Semic 237
93 Semic Sticker 273
00/1 UD DEL 42
01/2 UD DEL 59

ULRICH, NORM
99/0 Peoria Rivermen

ULRICH, SHAWN
99/0 Asheville Smoke
00/1 Asheville Smoke

ULVIRA, EDUARD
82 Semic Sticker 86

ULYANOV, ANTON
99/0 Mir 48

UMUNNA, GEORGE
99/0 Odessa Jackalopes

UNDERHILL, JASON
90/1 7th..Sketch LHJMQ 206

UNGER, GARRY
71/2 Bazooka Panel
71/2 Colgate Head
70/1 Colgate 7
70/1 Dad's Cookies
70/1 Eddie Sargent 61
71/2 Eddie Sargent 178
72/3 Eddie Sargent 184
70/1 Esso Power Player
72/3 Post 6
74/5 Lipton Soup 5
74/5 Loblaws
73/4 Nabisco s 14
68/9 O-Pee-Chee 142
69/0 O-Pee-Chee 159
70/1 O-Pee-Chee 26
70/1 O-Pee-Chee DE 16
71/2 O-Pee-Chee 26
71/2 O-Pee-Chee Book. 14
72/3 O-Pee-Chee 120
73/4 O-Pee-Chee 15
74/5 O-Pee-Chee 197
74/5 O-Pee-Chee 237
75/6 O-Pee-Chee 40
75/6 O-Pee-Chee 327
76/7 O-Pee-Chee 68
76/7 O-Pee-Chee 260
76/7 O-Pee-Chee 393
77/8 O-Pee-Chee 35
78/9 O-Pee-Chee 5
78/9 O-Pee-Chee 110
79/0 O-Pee-Chee 33
80/1 O-Pee-Chee 273
81/2 O-Pee-Chee 123
82/3 O-Pee-Chee 120
71/2 O-Pee-Chee Poster 20
89/0 ProCards IHL 112
90/1 ProCards 368
72 Semic Sticker 191
68/9 Shirriff / Detr. 9
77-79 Sportscaster 18-23
77-79 Sports. FIN 52-1232
70/1 Topps 26
71/2 Topps 26
72/3 Topps 35
73/4 Topps 15
74/5 Topps 197
74/5 Topps 237
75/6 Topps 40
75/6 Topps 327
76/7 Topps 68
76/7 Topps 260
77/8 Topps 35
78/9 Topps 5
78/9 Topps 110
79/0 Topps 33
02/3 Topps - Reprint 13, ✍ Reprint 13
01/2 T/O Archives 56
71/2 Toronto Sun Photo
79/0 ATLF / B&W
79/0 ATLF / Colour
70/1 DETR / Marathon Oil
81/2 EDMO / Red Rooster
82/3 EDMO / Red Rooster
88/9 EDMO / Action 1
80/1 LOSA 13
71/2 SLOU
72/3 SLOU
73/4 SLOU
73/4 SLOU
78/9 SLOU
92/3 SLOU / McDon. 27
97/8 New Mexico Scorpions

UNIAC, JOHN
90 7th..Sketch Mem.Cup 36
90/1 7th..Sketch OHL 246
95/6 Tallahasee Tiger Sharks
92/3 Wheeling Thund'birds 18
88/9 Kitchener Rangers
89/0 Kitchener Rangers
90/1 Kitchener Rangers
87/8 Sudbury Wolves

UNIACKE, RICHARD
93/4 Slapshot / S.S.Marie 10
95/6 Slapshot 361
96/7 Soo Greyhounds

UNKILA, MAURI
72/3 Williams Finnish 339

UNSER, CORY
98/9 Brandon Wheat Kings
99/0 Brandon Wheat Kings

UNSINN, XAVER
89 Semic Sticker 102

UNTERLUGGAUER, GERHARD
95 Panini Worlds 263
01/2 UD DEL 239
95/6 Brandon Wheat Kings

UOTILA, ILMO
80/1 Mallasjuoma 61
78/9 SM-Liiga 68

UOTILA, PENTTI
66/7 Champion 199
65/6 Hellas 116

UPSHALL, RANDY
00/1 Halifax Moosehead

UPSHALL, SCOTTIE
02/3 Atomic 117
02/3 BAP All-Star 149
02/3 BAP Draft Toronto 3
02/3 BAP Mem. 298
02/3 Bowman 162
02/3 Calder 130
02/3 Crown Royale 124, -RR 14
02/3 Exclusive 183
02/3 First Edition 439 [Retail]
02/3 Heads Up 126
02/3 In The GU 96
02/3 Pacific Complete 572
02/3 Parkhurst 219, ✄ GJ58
02/3 Parkhurst Retro 219
02/3 Pr. Stock Reserve 170
02/3 Pr. Stock Titanium 125, -ROT 14
97 Québec Pee Wee 0290
02/3 Quest for the Cup 130
02/3 Signature Series 188, ✍ 188, ✄ SGJ61
02/3 SP Authentic ✍ 199, ✍ ✄ Patch
02/3 SP GU Edition 85
02/3 SPx ✍ 155
02/3 T. Chrome 168
02/3 To. Heritage 151
02/3 To. Total 403
02/3 UD Superstars 276
02/3 Ultimate Memorabilia 19, ✍ RAut
02/3 Upper Deck 440
02/3 UD Artistic 117, CG17
02/3 UD Classic 121
02/3 UD Honor 158
02/3 UD Mask 176
02/3 UD Premier ✍ 75, ✍ Sig
02/3 UD Rookie ✍ 169
02/3 UD Top Shelf 132
02/3 Vanguard 123, -PP 15
00/1 Kamloops Blazers
01/2 Kamloops Blazers
02/3 Kamloops Blazers

URAKIN, ALEXANDER
00/1 Mir 119

URAM, MAREK
99/0 OFS 462
00/1 OFS 199, -Star 34
01/2 OFS 119, RE16D, -UHI 7

URICK, BRIAN
00/1 Hamilton Bulldogs

URPALAINEN, SEPPO
80/1 Mallasjuoma 151
72/3 Williams Finnish 188

URQUHART, CORY
00/1 Québec Remparts 23
01/2 Québec Remparts 24

URVIKKO, JOUKO
80/1 Mallasjuoma 27
78/9 SM-Liiga 47

USKI, JANI
92/3 Jyvas Hyva 153
93/4 Jyvas Hyva 269
93/4 Sisu 298

USTORF, PETER
96/7 DEL 246

USTORF, STEFAN
95/6 Bowman 147
92/3 Classic 29
92/3 Classic Four Sport 178
95/6 Donruss 294
95/6 Edge Ice 55
95 Globe 224
96/7 Panini Sticker 143
95/6 Parkhurst 520, 538
93 Semic Sticker 159
94/5 Sig. Rookies 28, ✍ 28
94/5 SR Gold Standard 95
95/6 SP 161
92/3 Upper Deck 371
95/6 Upper Deck 502
96/7 UD CC 284
01/2 UD DEL 180, -GA9
95/6 WASH
99/0 Cincinnati Cyclones
00/1 Cincinnati Cyclones
98/9 Las Vegas Thunder
94/5 Portland Pirates
95/6 Portland Pirates

USTRNUL, LIBOR
99/0 UD Prospects 13
00/1 UD Prospects 22
02/3 Chicago Wolves

USTYUGOV, ANATOLI
98/9 Mir 73
99/0 Mir 92
00/1 Mir 12

UUSIKARTANO, AKI
99/0 Cardset 228
00/1 Cardset 17
02/3 Cardset 284

UUSIKARTANO, JARI
72/3 Williams Finnish 319

UUSIMAA, VELI-MATTI
71/2 Williams Finnish 355
72/3 Williams Finnish 356

UVAJEV, VYACH.
91 Semic Sticker 86

UVIRA, EDUARD
94/5 DEL 251
95/6 DEL 245

V

VAAHTOLUOTO, TIMO
71/2 Williams Finnish 338

VÄÄNÄNEN, AUVO
80/1 Mallasjuoma 30
78/9 SM-Liiga 97

VÄÄNÄNEN, JARKKO
98/9 Cardset 115
99/0 Cardset 61
00/1 Cardset 229

VÄÄNÄNEN, OSSI
00/1 BAP Mem. 484
01/2 BAP Mem. 102
02/3 Bowman 112, ✄ FFDS, ✄ FFJ, ✄ FFP, ✄ FFR, ✄ FFRP, ✄ FFS, ✄ FFTS, ✍ YSA, / ✍ Puck
98/9 Cardset 105
99/0 Cardset 259
00/1 Cardset 39
02/3 Cardset 295, -SGSP 3
02/3 Pacific Complete 185
01/2 Parkhurst 142
00/1 Premier Plus 116
00/1 Pr. Stock 139, PSR-18
00/1 PS Titanium Draft 171
00/1 Signature 258, ✍ Aut. 249
01/2 Signature 105, ✍ Aut. 105
00/1 SP Authentic 159
00/1 SPx 184
00/1 Stadium 252
00/1 Upper Deck 425
00/1 UD Ice 119
00/1 Vanguard 141

VAATAMOINEN, ANTERO
70/1 Kuvajulkaisut 275
80/1 Mallasjuoma 145

VAATAMOINEN, MATTI
72/3 Williams Finnish 189

VAATAMOINEN, TIMO
66/7 Champion 91
65/6 Hellas 91
72/3 Williams Finnish 190

VACATKO, VLADIMIR
82 Semic Sticker 115

VACHON, MARC
93/4 Flint Generals
89/0 Johnstown Chiefs

VACHON, NICHOLAS
93/4 Knoxville Cherokees
97/8 Long Beach Ice Dogs
94/5 Phoenix Roadrunners
95/6 Phoenix Roadrunners

VACHON, PAT
85/6 London Knights
86/7 London Knights

VACHON, ROGATIEN
01/2 BT Pipes ✄ VM
02/3 Between the Pipes ✍ Aut.
77/8 Coke
70/1 Colgate 85
70/1 Dad's Cookies
76/7 Dernière Heure
70/1 Eddie Sargent 100
71/2 Eddie Sargent 68
72/3 Eddie Sargent 87
70/1 Esso Power Player
01/2 Fleer Greats 68, ✍ Aut.
92/3 Future Trends C76 154, 184, 195, ✍ Aut.
93/4 Hockey Wit 24
72/3 Post 1
74/5 Lipton Soup 7
74/5 Loblaws
68/9 O-Pee-Chee 164
68/9 O-Pee-Chee 212
69/0 O-Pee-Chee 165
70/1 O-Pee-Chee 49
70/1 O-Pee-Chee DE 22
71/2 O-Pee-Chee 156
72/3 O-Pee-Chee 100
73/4 O-Pee-Chee 64
74/5 O-Pee-Chee 235
75/6 O-Pee-Chee 160
75/6 O-Pee-Chee 213
75/6 O-Pee-Chee 297
76/7 O-Pee-Chee 40
77/8 OPC 8
77/8 O-Pee-Chee 160
77/8 O-Pee-Chee NS 21
78/9 O-Pee-Chee 20
79/0 OPC 8
79/0 O-Pee-Chee 235
80/1 O-Pee-Chee 110
80/1 O-Pee-Chee 168
81/2 O-Pee-Chee 10
82/3 O-Pee-Chee 23
81/2 OPC Sticker 47
95/6 Parkie 66-67 75
94/5 Parkie Tall FS-5
91/2 Pinnacle 387
68/9 Post Marble
82/3 Post [Bost.]
67/8 Post Tips 2
72 Semic Sticker 232
68/9 Shirriff / Mont. 2
77-79 Sportscaster 43-06
77-79 Sports. FIN 50-1197
67/8 Topps 75
70/1 Topps 49
72/3 Topps 51
73/4 Topps 64
74/5 Topps 235
75/6 Topps 160
75/6 Topps 213
75/6 Topps 297
76/7 Topps 40
77/8 Topps 8
77/8 Topps 160
77/8 ToppsNS 21
78/9 Topps 20
79/0 Topps 8
79/0 Topps 235
80/1 Topps 110
80/1 Topps 168
81/2 Topps 74 [East]
71/2 Toronto Sun Photo
02/3 Ultimate Memorabilia ✄ SF
01/2 UD Legends 29
01/2 UD Vintage ✄ GG
67/8 York 15
67/8 York 31
67/8 York 32
67/8 York
67/8 York
67/8 York
67/8 York
79/0 DETR
91/2 LOSA / GW Forum
67/8 MONT
67/8 MONT / IGA Card
68/9 MONT / IGA Card
69/0 MONT / Pro Star
70/1 MONT
71/2 MONT / Pro Star
71/2 MONT / Pro Star

VACHULKA, JOSEF
99/0 Score 110

VADNAIS, CAROL
70/1 Colgate 86
70/1 Dad's Cookies
79/0 Dernière Heure
82/3 Dernière Heure
70/1 Eddie Sargent 130
71/2 Eddie Sargent 137
72/3 Eddie Sargent 25
70/1 Esso Power Player
74/5 Loblaws
68/9 O-Pee-Chee 81
69/0 O-Pee-Chee 82
69/0 O-Pee-Chee 4in1
69/0 O-Pee-Chee Stamp
70/1 O-Pee-Chee 70
70/1 O-Pee-Chee DE 36
71/2 O-Pee-Chee 46
72/3 O-Pee-Chee 39
73/4 O-Pee-Chee 58
74/5 O-Pee-Chee 165
75/6 O-Pee-Chee 27
76/7 O-Pee-Chee 257
76/7 OPC 390
77/8 O-Pee-Chee 154

78/9 O-Pee-Chee 85
79/0 O-Pee-Chee 145
80/1 O-Pee-Chee 57
81/2 O-Pee-Chee 236
82/3 O-Pee-Chee 148
83/4 OPC/Topps Sticker 224
72 Semic Sticker 181
68/9 Shirriff / Oakl. 5
67/8 Topps 9
68/9 Topps 81
69/0 Topps 82
70/1 Topps 70
71/2 Topps 46
72/3 Topps 85
73/4 Topps 58
74/5 Topps 165
75/6 Topps 27
76/7 Topps 257
77/8 Topps 154
78/9 Topps 85
79/0 Topps 145
80/1 Topps 57
71/2 Toronto Sun Photo
67/8 MONT
67/8 MONT / IGA Card

VAGNER, MARTIN
01/2 Hull Olympiques 13
02/3 Hull Olympiques

VÄHÄ-RUOHOLA, KIMMO
00/1 Cardset 155

VAHALAHTI, VILLE
99/0 Cardset 142
00/1 Cardset 341
02/3 Cardset 134

VÄHÄNEN, KIM
93/4 Sisu 238

VÄHÄNEN, TIMO
70/1 Kuvajulkaisut 383

VAIC, LUBOMIR
02/3 Cardset 285
97/8 Pa. Paramount 191
00/1 UD DEL 68

VAIHINEN, KARI
80/1 Mallasjuoma 181

VAIHINEN, RISTO
70/1 Kuvajulkaisut 358

VAIL, ERIC
74/5 Loblaws
74/5 O-Pee-Chee 391
75/6 O-Pee-Chee 135
75/6 O-Pee-Chee 313
76/7 O-Pee-Chee 51
77/8 O-Pee-Chee 168
78/9 O-Pee-Chee 129
79/0 O-Pee-Chee 188
80/1 O-Pee-Chee 15
81/2 O-Pee-Chee 38
82/3 O-Pee-Chee 97
81/2 OPC Sticker 230
80/1 Pepsi Bottle Cap
75/6 Topps 135
75/6 Topps 313
76/7 Topps 51
77/8 Topps 168
78/9 Topps 129
79/0 Topps 188
80/1 Topps 15
81/2 Topps 43
74/5 ATLF
77/8 ATLF
78/9 ATLF / Colour
79/0 ATLF / B&W
79/0 ATLF / Colour
80/1 CALG

VAILLANCOURT, MIKE
99/0 Sudbury Wolves 24
00/1 Sudbury Wolves 9

VAINIO, RISTO
66/7 Champion 66
70/1 Kuvajulkaisut 152
71/2 Williams Finnish 203
72/3 Williams Finnish 240
73/4 Williams Finnish 275

VAINIO, SEPPO
65/6 Hellas 21

VAIR, STEVE
91 C55 Reprint 18
10/1 Imperial
11/2 Imperial 18
12/3 Imperial 10

VAISANEN, MATTI
70/1 Kuvajulkaisut 117
72 Panda MM-Toronto
71/2 Williams Finnish 127
72/3 Williams Finnish 99
73/4 Williams Finnish 147

VAISANEN, PERTTI
70/1 Kuvajulkaisut 345

VAIVE, JEFF
81/2 Ottawa 67's
82/3 Ottawa 67's

VAIVE, RICK
90/1 Bowman 250
91/2 Bowman 39
83/4 Esso Stars
83/4 Funmate Puffy 2 [w/]
84/5 Kellogg's 31
86/7 Kraft Sports 60
80/1 O-Pee-Chee 242
81/2 O-Pee-Chee 310
82/3 O-Pee-Chee 314
82/3 O-Pee-Chee 335
82/3 O-Pee-Chee 336
83/4 O-Pee-Chee 323
83/4 O-Pee-Chee 324
83/4 O-Pee-Chee 343
84/5 O-Pee-Chee 313
84/5 O-Pee-Chee 368
85/6 OPC/Topps 106
86/7 OPC/Topps 191
87/8 OPC/Topps 155
88/9 OPC/Topps 77
90/1 OPC/Topps 148
91/2 O-Pee-Chee 457
89/0 OPC/Topps 125
81/2 OPC Sticker 101
82/3 OPC/Topps Sticker 62
82/3 OPC/Topps Sticker 63
83/4 OPC/Topps Sticker 25
83/4 OPC/Topps Sticker 26
84/5 OPC Sticker 11
84/5 OPC Sticker 12
84/5 OPC Sticker 139
85/6 OPC Sticker 6
86/7 OPC Sticker 138
87/8 OPC Sticker 155
88/9 OPC Sticker 9-138
89/0 opcSticker 256-117
87/8 Panini Sticker 328
88/9 Panini Sticker 31
89/0 Panini Sticker 206
90/1 Panini Sticker 23
91/2 Panini Sticker 297
80/1 Pepsi Bottle Cap
82/3 Post [Toro.]
90/1 Pro Set 32
91/2 Pro Set 26
87/8 Pro Sport CW9
90/1 Score 103
91/2 Score 26
91/2 Score CAN 26
84/5 7-Eleven
85/6 7-Eleven Superstars 18
83/4 Souhaits Keychain [Maple Leafs]
80/1 Topps 242
81/2 Topps 44
84/5 Topps 138
91/2 To. Stadium 13
90/1 Upper Deck 376
91/2 Upper Deck 179
02/3 UD Foundations ✂ CH, ✂ PS
01/2 UD Legends 61
83/4 Vachon 100-125
88/9 BUFF / Blue Shield
89/0 BUFF / Blue Shield
89/0 BUFF / Campbell's
90/1 BUFF / Blue Shield
90/1 BUFF / Campbell's
91/2 BUFF / Blue Shield
91/2 BUFF / Campbell's
91/2 BUFF / Pepsi
87/8 CHIC / Coke
88/9 CHIC / Coke
80/1 TORO
81/2 TORO
82/3 TORO
83/4 TORO
84/5 TORO
85/6 TORO
86/7 TORO
79/0 VANC / Royal Bank
92/3 Hamilton Canucks
00/1 Mississauga IceDogs

VAK, TOMAS
98/9 OFS 382
99/0 OFS 100
01/2 OFS 257

VAKHRUSHEV, ALEXEI
99/0 Mir 103

VAKIPARTA, ERKKI
70/1 Kuvajulkaisut 207
80/1 Mallasjuoma 203
72 Panda MM-Toronto
78/9 SM-Liiga 234
71/2 Williams Finnish 95
72/3 Williams Finnish 260
73/4 Williams Finnish 258

VALA, ALES
99/0 Score 74

VALA, PETR
99/0 DS 14
00/1 DS 58
98/9 OFS 32
99/0 OFS 218
00/1 OFS 363
01/2 OFS 243

VALAITIS, PAUL
99/0 Prince George Cougars

VALASEK, HORST
94/5 APS 297
95/6 APS 1, 422
96/7 APS 25, 431

VALDEK, OLDRICH
92/3 Semic Nordisk 67

VALEEV, IGOR
01/2 Worcester IceCats
02/3 Worcester IceCats

VALEK,
92/3 Semic Nordisk 196 [Årets Lag]

VALEK, OLDRICH
94/5 APS 179
89 Semic Sticker 197
93/4 Sisu 289

VALENGA,
92/3 Semic Nordisk 184 [Norgesmester]

VALENTA, PETER
90/1 7th..Sketch LHJMQ 6
91/2 7th...Sketch LHJMQ 224

VALENTI, MAREN
98/9 DEL 157

VALENTI, SVEN
94/5 DEL 294
95/6 DEL 285
98/9 DEL 262

VALENTINE, CHRIS
94/5 DEL 82
95/6 DEL 88
98/9 DEL 86
99/0 Eishockey 24
82/3 O-Pee-Chee 373
82/3 OPC/Topps Sticker 155
82/3 Post [Wash.]
81/2 WASH
82/3 WASH

VALESANO, M
85/6 Minnesota-Duluth 34

VALICEVIC, CHRIS
98/9 EBK ECHL All-Star
93/4 Greensboro Monarchs
95/6 Louisiana Ice Gators
95/6 Louisiana Ice Gators-2
96/7 Louisiana Ice Gators
98/9 Louisiana Ice Gators
99/0 Louisiana Ice Gators
01/2 Louisiana Ice Gators

VALICEVIC, ROBERT
98/9 EBK IHL All-Star
00/1 Pa. Paramount 138
99/0 Prism 78
99/0 SP Authentic 48
99/0 To. Prmr. Plus 85
99/0 Ult. Victory 49
00/1 Upper Deck 98
99/0 UD Black Diam. 50
99/0 UD MVP Cup 99
95/6 Louisiana Ice Gators
95/6 Louisiana Ice Gators-2
01/2 Manchester Monarchs
91/2 L. Superior State Lakers

VALIHARJU, SAKARI
70/1 Kuvajulkaisut 384

VALIKANGAS, MATTI
66/7 Champion 220

VÄLILÄ, MIKA
92/3 Jyvas Hyva 129
93/4 Jyvas Hyva 238
95 Semic 34
93/4 Sisu 197
94/5 Sisu 317

VALIMAKI, JYRKI
70/1 Kuvajulkaisut 364

VALIMAKI, TEPPO
72/3 Williams Finnish 359

VALIMONT, CARL
89/0 ProCards IHL 184
90/1 ProCards 325
91/2 ProCards 603
95/6 Houston Aeros
93/4 Milwaukee Admirals

VALIOJA, ESA
80/1 Mallasjuoma 165

VALIOTS, JAAK
91/2 Rayside-Balfour

VALIQUETTE, JACK
76/7 O-Pee-Chee 294
77/8 O-Pee-Chee 64
78/9 O-Pee-Chee 391
79/0 O-Pee-Chee 229
80/1 O-Pee-Chee 108
77/8 Topps 64
79/0 Topps 229
80/1 Topps 108
79/0 COLR
76/7 TORO
77/8 TORO

VALIQUETTE, STEPHEN
00/1 BAP Mem. 5
02/3 Between the Pipes 107
00/1 Pacific 256
00/1 Pa. Paramount 158
00/1 Revolution 93
95/6 Slapshot 382
00/1 SPx 102
00/1 Topps 321
00/1 To. Chrome 216
00/1 Upper Deck 191
00/1 UD Black Diam. 81
00/1 UD Ice 60
00/1 UD MVP 199
00/1 UD Vintage 386
00/1 Victory 266
98/9 Hampton Roads
99/0 Lowell Lock Monsters
96/7 Sudbury Wolves

VALIVAARA, JYRKI
98/9 Cardset 125
99/0 Cardset 69
00/1 Cardset 48
02/3 Cardset 294

VALK, GARRY
91/2 Bowman 314
93/4 Donruss 401
94/5 Donruss 198
94/5 Flair 7
94/5 Fleer Ultra 253
94/5 Leaf 206
91/2 O-Pee-Chee 117
99/0 Pacific 418
93/4 Parkhurst 4
94/5 Parkhurst V19
95/6 Parkhurst 5
94/5 Parkie SE7
91/2 Pinnacle 291
93/4 Pinnacle 181
94/5 Pinnacle 119
96/7 Pi. Be A Player 155, ✍ Aut. 155
94/5 POG 370
93/4 Power Play 286
93/4 Premier 354
94/5 Premier 372
95/6 Pro Magnet 40
91/2 Pro Set 499
90/1 ProCards 322
91/2 Score 195
91/2 Score CAN 195
92/3 Score 355
93/4 Score 641
97/8 Score Pitt. 12
92/3 Topps 383
00/1 To. Gold Label 100
01/2 To. Reserve 84
91/2 To. Stadium 318
92/3 To. Stadium 493
93/4 To. Stadium 407
94/5 To. Stadium 89
90/1 Upper Deck 530
91/2 Upper Deck 152
92/3 Upper Deck 114
93/4 Upper Deck 515
94/5 Upper Deck 282, IG12, SP-3
94/5 UD BAP R116, ✍ 118
94/5 ANAH / Carl's Jr. 8
95/6 ANAH / Photo
99/0 TORO / Pizza Pizza 4
90/1 VANC / Mohawk
92/3 VANC / Road Trip

VALK, PHIL
91/2 Avant Garde BCJHL 92
92/3 BCJHL 115

VALKEAPÄÄ, PERTTI
72 Hellas MM-Jenkki 18
74 Hellas MM-Jenkki 21
80/1 Mallasjuoma 158
74 Semic Sticker 95
78/9 SM-Liiga 4
78/9 SM-Liiga 180
72/3 Williams Finnish 77
72/3 Williams Finnish 207
73/4 Williams Finnish 171

VALKO, LUKAS
01/2 OFS 70

VALKO, PAVOL
99/0 OFS 219, 461
00/1 OFS 194

VALKONEN, PERTTI
66/7 Champion 108

VALLEE, SEBASTIEN
94/5 Sig. Rookies 55, ✍ 55

VALLEY, MIKE
00/1 Louisiana Ice Gators

VALLIERE, MICHEL
96/7 DEL 316
98/9 DEL 263
95 Globe 200
95 Panini Worlds 97
94 Semic 211
93 Semic Sticker 250
96 Wien 184

VALLIERES, DAVID
00/1 Kudos 84
00/1 Florida Everblades
98/9 Kansas City Blades 21
99/0 Kansas City Blades
97/8 Peoria Rivermen

VALLIN, ARI
98/9 Cardset 56
99/0 Cardset 316
00/1 Cardset 141
02/3 Cardset 135

VALLIS, LINDSAY
92/3 Classic Prospects 41
91/2 ProCards 82
90/1 7th..Sketch WHL 10
99/0 Asheville Smoke
92/3 Fredericton Canadiens
93/4 Fredericton Canadiens

VALOIS, RICHARD
88/9 Richelieu Riverains

VALOIS, STEPHANE
88/9 Richelieu Riverains

VALTONEN, JORMA
65/6 Hellas 16
72 Hellas MM-Jenkki 19
70/1 Kuvajulkaisut 78
70/1 Kuvajulkaisut 205
72 Panda MM-Toronto
72 Semic Sticker 90
74 Semic Sticker 76
78/9 SM-Liiga 198
77-79 Sports. FIN 107-2559
77-79 Sports. FIN 16-364
71/2 Williams Finnish 77
71/2 Williams Finnish 93
72/3 Williams Finnish 78
72/3 Williams Finnish 258
73/4 Williams Finnish 82
73/4 Williams Finnish 123

VALTONEN, TOMEK
99/0 Cardset 264
00/1 Cardset 282
02/3 Cardset 286

VALUI, VITALI
99/0 Mir 200

VAMPOLA, PETR
00/1 OFS 345
01/2 OFS 69

VAN ALLEN, SHAUN
98/9 Be A Player 245, ✍ Aut. 245
01/2 BAP Mem. 500
92/3 Classic Prospects 64
92/3 Classic Prospects 150
93/4 Donruss 14
95/6 Donruss 26
96/7 Donruss 86
92/3 Fleer Ultra 299
93/4 Fleer Ultra 264
95/6 Fleer Ultra 7
94/5 Leaf 338
95/6 Leaf 248
91/2 O-Pee-Chee 414
99/0 Omega 164
98/9 Pacific 317
02/3 Pacific Complete 373
97/8 Pa. Invincible R-138
95/6 Panini Sticker 223
96/7 Panini Sticker 231
92/3 Parkhurst 288
93/4 Parkhurst 278
95/6 Parkhurst 8
95/6 Pinnacle 102
96/7 Pi. Be A Player 163, ✍ Aut. 163
95/6 Playoff 115
94/5 POG 31
95/6 POG 23
93/4 Power Play 15
93/4 Premier 396
94/5 Premier 432
88/9 ProCards / Cape Breton
89/0 ProCards AHL 151
90/1 ProCards 223
91/2 ProCards 221
95/6 Score 166
96/7 Score 227
95/6 SBx Emotion 5
95/6 SBx Impact 6
95/6 Topps 297
93/4 To. Stadium 361
94/5 To. Stadium 207
91/2 Upper Deck 52
93/4 Upper Deck 506
94/5 Upper Deck 312
95/6 Upper Deck 488
95/6 UD CC 173
96/7 UD CC 6
96/7 UD MVP Cup 130
00/1 UD Vintage 117
94/5 ANAH / Carl's Jr. 7
00/1 DALL / Southwest
92/3 EDMO / IGA 025
01/2 MONT
96/7 OTTA
97/8 OTTA
98/9 OTTA
99/0 OTTA
02/3 OTTA
86/7 Saskatoon Blades

VAN BILSEN, HARRY
79 Panini Sticker 276

VAN BOXMEER, JOHN
83/4 Funmate Puffy 9 [w/]
76/7 O-Pee-Chee 330
77/8 O-Pee-Chee 315
78/9 O-Pee-Chee 224
79/0 O-Pee-Chee 96
80/1 O-Pee-Chee 183
81/2 O-Pee-Chee 26
82/3 O-Pee-Chee 36
82/3 O-Pee-Chee 37
83/4 O-Pee-Chee 73
81/2 OPC Sticker 58
82/3 OPC/Topps Sticker 121
83/4 OPC/Topps Sticker 244
82/3 Post [Buff.]
88/9 ProCards / Rochester
89/0 ProCards AHL 266
91/2 ProCards 20
83/4 Souhaits Keychain [Sabres]
78/9 Topps 224
79/0 Topps 96
80/1 Topps 183
81/2 Topps 80 [East]
83/4 Vachon 78-58
79/0 BUFF / Bells Market
80/1 BUFF / Wendt's 2
81/2 BUFF / Wendt's 2
82/3 BUFF / Wendt's 4
90/1 BUFF / Campbell's
74/5 MONT
98/9 Long Beach Ice Dogs
92/3 Rochester Americans WPC
93/4 Rochester Americans

VAN DEN BROEK, KLAAS
79 Panini Sticker 278

VAN DEN THILLART, LEO
98/9 DEL 36

VAN DER GRIENDT, JOHN
79 Panini Sticker 281

VAN DER HORST, JAMIE
97/8 Sheffield Steelers

VAN DORP, WAYNE
90/1 O-Pee-Chee 527
88/9 ProCards / Rochester
89/0 CHIC / Coke
88/9 EDMO / Action 164
87/8 PITT / Kodak
91/2 QUEB / Petro-Canada
92/3 QUEB / Petro-Canada

VAN DRUNEN, DAVE
02/3 Grand Rapids Griffins

VAN DRUNEN, DAVID
99/0 Grand Rapids Griffins
01/2 Grand Rapids Griffins
99/0 Mobile Mysticks
95/6 Prince Albert Raiders

VAN DYK, CHRIS
95/6 Cla. 5 Sport 150
94/5 Slapshot / Windsor 6
95/6 Slapshot 409

VAN HELLEMOND, ANDY
90/1 Pro Set 701
01/2 UD Legends 52, ✂ TT

VAN HERPT, ED
01/2 Kingston Frontenacs 23

VAN HERPT, NICK
01/2 Kingston Frontenacs 24

VAN HERZELE, LARRY
83/4 Brantford Alexanders

VAN HOOF, JEREMY
99/0 Ottawa 67's
00/1 Ottawa 67's 3

VAN HORLICK, QUINTEN
01/2 Rockford IceHogs

VAN IMPE, DARREN
98/9 Be A Player 159, ✍ Aut. 159
95/6 Edge Ice 12
96/7 Fl. Ultra 7
95/6 Leaf 138
96/7 Metal Univ. 193
00/1 Pacific 44
97/8 Pacific CC 286
97/8 Pa. Invincible 5
96/7 Panini Sticker 229
97/8 Panini Sticker 185
97/8 Score Anah. 9
91 7th..Sketch Mem.Cup 117
90/1 7th..Sketch WHL 268
91/2 7th...Sketch WHL 258
96/7 SP 4
99/0 Ult. Victory 9
96/7 Upper Deck 213
97/8 Upper Deck 4
97/8 UD Coll. Choice 4
96/7 ANAH / Up Front 16
90/1 Prince Albert Raiders
91/2 Prince Albert Raiders
93/4 Red Deer Rebels

VAN IMPE, ED
71/2 Bazooka Panel
64-67 BeeHive-3 [Chic.]
70/1 Colgate 78
70/1 Dad's Cookies
70/1 Eddie Sargent 159
71/2 Eddie Sargent 150
72/3 Eddie Sargent 160
70/1 Esso Power Player
72/3 Post 11
74/5 Loblaws
68/9 O-Pee-Chee 91
69/0 O-Pee-Chee 92
69/0 O-Pee-Chee 4in1
70/1 O-Pee-Chee 80
70/1 O-Pee-Chee DE 34
71/2 O-Pee-Chee 126
72/3 O-Pee-Chee 33
73/4 O-Pee-Chee 206
74/5 O-Pee-Chee 85
75/6 O-Pee-Chee 38
76/7 O-Pee-Chee 157
92/3 Parkhurst 479
95/6 Parkie 66-67 36
63/4 Topps 30
68/9 Topps 91
69/0 Topps 92
70/1 Topps 80
71/2 Topps 126
72/3 Topps 9
74/5 Topps 85
75/6 Topps 38
76/7 Topps 157
71/2 Toronto Sun Photo
72/3 PHIL / Milk

VAN KESSEL, JOHN
98/9 DEL 28

VAN KESSEL, JOHN
89/0 ProCards AHL 26
90/1 ProCards 348
89/0 7th..Sketch OHL 162

VAN KESSEL, JOHN
94/5 Cape Breton Oilers

VAN LEUSEN, AARON
99/0 Brampton Batallion 20

VAN LEYEN, THORSTEN
94/5 DEL 90

VAN OENE, DARREN
95/6 Bowman P34
94/5 Slapshot Memorial 44
95/6 Upper Deck 511
98/9 Rochester Americans
00/1 Rochester Americans
95/6 Brandon Wheat Kings

VAN ONLANGS, ROBERT
79 Panini Sticker 280

VAN ROOYEN, KEITH
85/6 Sudbury Wolves

VAN RYN, MIKE
02/3 O-Pee-Chee 302
02/3 Pacific Complete 172
00/1 Pr. Stock 142
01/2 SP Authentic 115
98/9 SPx Prospects 63
02/3 Topps 302
02/3 To. Limited 302
98/9 UD Choice 266
96/7 Upper Deck 378
99/0 Upper Deck 352
98/9 UD Black Diam. 95
99/0 UD G. Reserve 332
99/0 UD Prospects 20, ✍ Sig.
01/2 Victory 387
00/1 Worcester IceCats
01/2 Worcester IceCats

VAN SLOOTEN, MIKE
86/7 Regina Pats
87/8 Regina Pats

VAN SOLDT, FRANK
79 Panini Sticker 277

VAN VOLSEN, JOE
93/4 Slapshot / S.S.Marie 17
95/6 Slapshot 51
93/4 Soo Greyhounds 26

VAN VOLSEN, MIKE
95/6 Slapshot 33

VAN WIEREN, LARRY
79 Panini Sticker 279

VANBIESBROUCK, JOHN
94/5 Action Packed
98/9 Aurora 142
99/0 Aurora 108, -Stripe 108, -GU 15
00/1 Aurora 91
98/9 Be A Player 252, H-11, ✍ Aut. 252
99/0 BAP Mem. 44, H-4
00/1 BAP Mem. 101, 413, ✂ V-14
01/2 BT Pipes 153, -Mask
96/7 Bic.Sports Aces Q-C
97/8 Bicycle Q-Diamond
98/9 Bicycls.. K-D
95/6 Bicycle Sports Aces 7-Spade
90/1 Bowman 222
91/2 Bowman 68
92/3 Bowman 132
95/6 Bowman 30
98/9 Bowman's Best 82
99/0 Crown Royale 106, -CS 17, -IG 19
00/1 Crown Royale 68
93/4 Donruss 132
94/5 Donruss 176, D3, IM-10, MM-10
95/6 Donruss 106
96/7 Donruss 187, BTP-4, D-1
97/8 Donruss 58, BTP-3, ES-8
96/7 Do. Canadian 84
97/8 Do. Canadian 7, SCS-16
95/6 Do. Elite 83, PW-6
96/7 Do. Elite 74, PW-4
97/8 Do. Elite 3, 126, C-1, PN-8
97/8 Do. Preferred 9, 182, CG-4, PM-13, / Tin 6, WideTin 8
97/8 Do. Priority 5, 193, OD-5, PG-2, Post-11, Stamp-11
97/8 Do. Studio 17, S-16, P-17
98/9 Dynagon Ice 140, -IW 7
99/0 Dynagon Ice 150, -GM 4,9
93/4 EA Sports 54
97/8 Esso 34
94/5 Flair 69
96/7 Flair 40, HG-12
94/5 Fleer 83, N-10
96/7 Fleer 44, VT-10
01/2 Fleer Legacy 64, ✂ HK
95/6 Fleer Metal 62
96/7 Fl. Picks 88, F50-46, DL-8
92/3 Fleer Ultra 144
93/4 Fleer Ultra 333
94/5 Fleer Ultra 86
95/6 Fleer Ultra 64, 378, PPM-11
96/7 Fl. Ultra 70
95 Globe 101
93/4 High Liner 5
95/6 Hoyle / East. Q-Club
94/5 Incomnet Phonecard
90/1 Kraft 60
92/3 Kraft / PB
93/4 Kraft / KD
94/5 Kraft / KD
95/6 Kraft / PS
96/7 Kraft / KD
94/5 Kraft Mask
93/4 Leaf 371
94/5 Leaf PW 8
94/5 Leaf 70, CP-5, GLS-13, LL-9
95/6 Leaf 172
96/7 Leaf 193, SD-2, S-4
97/8 Leaf 5, 172, PD-2
94/5 L. Limited 72
95/6 L. Limited 47, SS-6
96/7 L. Limited 30
96/7 L. Preferred 41, MM-3, VP-2
97/8 Limited 5, 62, 113, FG-7
96/7 Maggers 68
96/7 McDonald's McD-35
97/8 McDonald's McD-24
96/7 Metal Univ. 64, AP-12, CS-12
99/0 Millenium 185, ✍ Aut. 185
98/9 NHL Power Play
86/7 OPC/Topps 9
87/8 OPC/Topps 36
88/9 OPC/Topps 102
90/1 OPC/Topps 75
91/2 O-Pee-Chee 153
92/3 O-Pee-Chee 275
89/0 OPC/Topps 114
98/9 OPC Chrome 215
88/9 OPC Stars 42
85/6 OPC Sticker 88-221
86/7 OPC Sticker 218
86/7 OPC Sticker 114-128
86/7 OPC Sticker 190-51
87/8 OPC Sticker 33-178
88/9 OPC Sticker 241-109
89/0 opcSticker 246-107
97/8 Omega 102, NSZ-5
98/9 Omega 180, -Onl. 27, -PI 12
99/0 Omega 176, -5ST 29, -EOP 14, ✂ GWJ 8
98/9 Pacific 34, -TC 11
99/0 Pacific 313, -GC 28, -ITCNF 14, -PAP 18
00/1 Pacific 309
01/2 Pacific 240
02/3 Pacific 231
97/8 Pacific CC 34, CS-9, GCDC-13, ITC-10, TC-11
97/8 Pa. Crown Roy. 60, FO-9
98/9 Pa. Crown Roy. 101, -PotG 19, -PP 19
97/8 Pa. Dynagon 57, KN-5, S-10, T-13,BKS-43
97/8 Pa. Invincible 64, FP-17, R-89
97/8 Pa. Paramount 86, P-11, GSL-9, BN-11
98/9 Pa. Paramount 178
99/0 Pa. Paramount 176, -GS 15, -PB 28, -JAP 7
00/1 Pa. Paramount ✂ J&P 7
97/8 Pa. Revolution 62, RTS-9, TC-11
98/9 Pa. Revolution 107, -TPA 17, -Show. 27
98/9 Panini Photocard
87/8 Panini Sticker 106
88/9 Panini Sticker 300
89/0 Panini Sticker 282
90/1 Panini Sticker 108
91/2 Panini Sticker 282
92/3 Panini Sticker 232
93/4 Panini Sticker 98
94/5 Panini Sticker 72
95/6 Panini Sticker 79
96/7 Panini Sticker 70
98/9 Panini Sticker 60
99/0 Panini Sticker 128, 337
91/2 Parkhurst 338
92/3 Parkhurst 349
93/4 Parkhurst 73
94/5 Parkhurst V13, YCTG-9
95/6 Parkhurst 85, CCP-12, GP-7, PP-5, PP-29
00/1 Parkhurst P-189
01/2 Parkhurst 387
95 Parkhurst Phonecard
94/5 Parkie SE67
91/2 Pinnacle 121
91/2 Pinnacle 367
92/3 Pinnacle 186
93/4 Pinnacle 148
93/4 Pinnacle Expa. 1
93/4 Pinnacle Mask 9
94/5 Pinnacle 100, GT3, MA2
96/7 Pinnacle 203, M-3, TP-8
97/8 Pinnacle 37, M-1, TP-10, P-13, / Tin 10
96/7 Pi. Be A Player LTH10B, SP-4, ✍ Aut. LTH10B
97/8 Pi. Be A Player STP 8, TN-6
97/8 Pi. BeeHive 27, BHT-5
97/8 Pi. Certified 6, CT-3
97/8 Pi. Epix E2
95/6 Pi. FANtasy 16
96/7 Pi. FANtasy 9
97/8 Pi. Inside 19, IT-7, SU-2, S-2, / Can 3, LargeCan
96/7 Pi. Mint 26
97/8 Pi. Mint 4
95/6 Pi. Summit 130, ITC-15
96/7 Pi. Summit 66, ITC-10
97/8 Pi. Totally 6
97/8 Pi. Uncut 6
95/6 Pi. Zenith 36
96/7 Pi. Zenith 91, ZT-17
95/6 Playoff 44
96/7 Playoff 425
94/5 POG 261, 280
95/6 POG 123
93/4 Power Play 102
93/4 Premier 160
93/4 Premier 314
94/5 Premier 82, 360
00/1 Premier Plus ✍ CS, ✂ GP
99/0 Prism 105, -SGDC 17
00/1 Pr. Stock 63, ✂ GUG-72
00/1 PS Titanium 59
95/6 Pro Magnet 90
90/1 Pro Set 209
91/2 Pro Set 447
91/2 Pro Set Platinum PC1
99/0 Revolution 110, -NI 15, SS-27, / CSC 110
90/1 Score 175
90/1 Sco. Hot Cards 76
91/2 Score 10
91/2 Score CAN 10
92/3 Score 160
92/3 Score USAG 7
93/4 Score 162
93/4 Score 445
93/4 Score 492
93/4 Score 501
94/5 Score TF9
95/6 Score 241, 322
96/7 Score 63, NW-8, SD-7, / Promo 63
97/8 Score 34, NW-15
94/5 Select 7
95/6 Select CE 85
96/7 Select CE 59, F-4
95 Semic 102, 217
89 Semic Sticker 154
91 Semic Sticker 147
92 Semic Sticker 147
00/1 Signature 168, ✍ Aut. 180
95/6 SBx Emotion 72
95/6 SBx Impact 70, D-6
96/7 SBx Impact 50, ZH-10
94/5 SP 44
95/6 SP 56
96/7 SP 61, CW-9, GF-8
97/8 SP Authentic 69, I1
98/9 SP Authentic 62, SS16, SO10
97/8 SP GU 39
97/8 SPx 20, -DV
99/0 SPx 109
98/9 SPx Prospects 45, H20, L2, PS10, ✂ WM
99/0 Stadium 126
00/1 Stadium 227
97/8 SLU
98/9 SLU
00/1 SLU 8
95 Starting Lineup Collector Club
95/6 Super Sticker 46, 47
96/7 Team Out!
86/7 OPC/Topps - Stick. 1
92/3 Topps 169
95/6 Topps 252, HGA8, PF9
98/9 Topps 215
99/0 Topps 201
00/1 Topps 265
99/0 To. Chrome 201
00/1 To. Chrome 159
94/5 Topps Finest 40, BBB-8
95/6 To. Finest 20, 188
98/9 To. Finest 3
98/9 T. Gold Label 59
00/1 To. Heritage 103
96/7 To. Picks ID12
99/0 To. Prmr. Plus IG6
91/2 To. Stadium 323
92/3 To. Stadium 58
93/4 To. Stadium 85
93/4 To. Stadium 330
93/4 To. Stadium - Master Photo-1 10
94/5 To. Stadium 95
95/6 To. Stadium 35
93/4 TSC Members Only 40
94/5 TSC Members Only 7
95/6 TSC Members Only 34
00/1 To. Stars 94
95/6 T. Super Skills 78
98/9 UD Choice 89, 247, BH10
00/1 UD Heroes 77
00/1 UD Reserve 55, GG8
98/9 UD3 54, 114, 174
00/1 Ultimate Mem. ✂ A8-5, ✂ G-19, ✂ GM-15
02/3 Ultimate Memorabilia ✂ SCD
90/1 Upper Deck 279
91/2 Upper Deck 324
92/3 Upper Deck 44
93/4 Upper Deck 8, SP-SP60
94/5 Upper Deck 46, C20, H32, SP-31
95/6 Upper Deck 321, AS-19, H-19, SE-122
96/7 Upper Deck 63, X7, HH6, SS2B, ✂ GJ7
97/8 Upper Deck 72, SG54, S7, T2C
98/9 Upper Deck 148, P7
99/0 Upper Deck 268
00/1 Upper Deck 339
94/5 UD BAP R20, R135, ✍ 20
93/4 UD BAP Roots 27
96/7 UD Black Diam. 165, RC6
97/8 UD Black Diam. 42
98/9 UD Black Diam. 64, M2
00/1 UD Black Diam. ✂ GG
95/6 UD CC 253, 368
96/7 UD CC 101, 318, UD12
97/8 UD Coll. Choice 102, 317, SQ84, S2
97/8 UD Diam. Vision 7
98/9 UD G. Reserve 148
99/0 UD G. Reserve 268
96/7 UD Ice 110, S3
97/8 UD Ice 74, IC17
00/1 UD Legends 57
98/9 UD MVP 149
99/0 UD MVP 155, LL7
96/7 UD Post
01/2 UD Top Shelf ✂ GG-LP
00/1 UD Vintage 230, 233, 234
00/1 Vanguard 63, ✂ DGJ-9
99/0 Victory 219, 385
99/0 WGretzky 128
96 Wien 156
97/8 Zenith 9, Z4
94/5 FLOR
94/5 FLOR / Health Plan
94/5 FLOR / Winn-Dixie
96/7 FLOR / Winn-Dixie
97/8 FLOR / Winn-Dixie
89/0 NYRA / Marine
80/1 Soo Greyhounds
81/2 Soo Greyhounds
82/3 Soo Greyhounds
87/8 Soo Greyhounds 16

VANCLIEF, CHRIS
89/0 Oshawa Generals

VANDAL, JEAN-PAUL
51/2 Bas du Fleuve 15

VANDAL, STEEVE
99/0 Rouyn-Noranda
99/0 Rouyn-Noranda

VANDALE, DUANE
92/3 MPS SJHL 94

VANDENBERGHE, MIKE
90/1 7th..Sketch WHL 225
91/2 7th...Sketch WHL 334
94/5 Dayton Bombers 19
96/7 Knoxville Cherokees
99/0 Odessa Jackalopes
88/9 Brandon Wheat Kings
89/0 Brandon Wheat Kings
90/1 Brandon Wheat Kings

VANDENBUSSCHE, RYAN
00/1 BAP Mem. 98, ✂ T-20
01/2 BAP Update ✂ TC21, ✂ TC35
00/1 Pacific 104
97/8 Pi. Be A Player 223, ✍ Aut. 223
90/1 7th..Sketch OHL 49
91/2 7th...Sketch OHL 22
02/3 UD Vintage 54
01/2 Victory 82
95/6 Binghamton Rangers
96/7 Binghamton Rangers
97/8 Hartford Wolf Pack
98/9 Indianapolis Ice
93/4 St. John's Maple Leafs
94/5 St. John's Maple Leafs
91/2 Cornwall Royals

VANDER WAL, WES
95/6 Slapshot 148

VANDERKLOK, BEN
98/9 Barrie Colts

VANDERKRACHT, BRAM
91 7th..Sketch Mem.Cup 88
90/1 7th..Sketch WHL 211
91/2 7th...Sketch WHL 194
89/0 Spokane Chiefs

VANDERMEER, DAN
97/8 Spokane Chiefs

VANDERMEER, JIM
02/3 BAP Mem. 329
02/3 Calder 137
02/3 Pacific Complete 543
02/3 Parkhurst Retro 242
02/3 Quest for the Cup 137
02/3 Ultimate Memorabilia 66
02/3 UD Artistic 133
02/3 UD Honor 138
02/3 UD Mask 157
02/3 UD Premier 89
02/3 Philadelphia Phantoms
00/1 Red Deer Rebels

VANDERMEER, PETE
97/8 BC Icemen 2
98/9 BC Icemen
00/1 Providence Bruins
93/4 Red Deer Rebels
95/6 Red Deer Rebels

VANDERMEER, PETER
02/3 Philadelphia Phantoms

VANDERSLOT, ADRIAN
88/9 Niagara Falls Thunder

VANDERYDT, ROB
91/2 Richmond Renegades

VANECEK, FILIP
96/7 APS 319
97/8 APS 274
01/2 OFS 133

VANHERZELE, LARRY
84/5 Belleville Bulls

VANI, CARMINE
94 Semic 310
93 Semic Sticker 222
81/2 Kingston Canadians
82/3 Kingston Canadians
83/4 Kitchener Rangers

VANIK, MILOS
94/5 DEL 142
95/6 DEL 140
96/7 DEL 335

VANKKA, LEO
66/7 Champion 115

VANNE, ANTTI
70/1 Kuvajulkaisut 359

VANNE, ARI
70/1 Kuvajulkaisut 360

VANSTAALDUINEN, BART
91/2 Air Canada SJHL 22
91/2 Air Canada SJHL B37
93/4 Michigan State

VANTIGHEM, TRAVIS
91/2 Air Canada SJHL D12
92/3 MPS SJHL 78

VANYASOV, DMITRI
98/9 Mir 77

VAPOLA, ARI
00/1 Cardset 223

VARADA, VACLAV
99/0 Challenger 21
97/8 Donruss 217
97/8 Do. Canadian 141
97/8 Do. Preferred 159
00/1 DS JT16
01/2 DS 48
98/9 Dynagon Ice 22
96/7 Flair 102
97/8 Leaf 48, 166
97/8 Limited 23, 178
99/0 Millenium 34, ✍ Aut. 34
99/0 OFS 38, 233
00/1 OFS 392
98/9 Pacific 111
99/0 Pacific 47
00/1 Pacific 59
02/3 Pacific Complete 266
98/9 Pa. Paramount 23
99/0 Panini Sticker 41
00/1 Panini Sticker 21
99/0 Score JT14
94/5 Sig. Rookies 1, ✍ 1
01/2 Signature 54, ✍ Aut. 54
96/7 SP 171
97/8 UD Choice 20
98/9 UD3 24, 84, 144
96/7 Upper Deck 224
97/8 Upper Deck 229
98/9 Upper Deck 48
00/1 Upper Deck 253
01/2 Upper Deck 23
98/9 UD G. Reserve 48
96/7 Rochester Americans
97/8 Rochester Americans

VARCOE, F
93/4 Soo Greyhounds 32

VARDALE, DUANE
91/2 Air Canada SJHL D38

VARGA, CHRIS
90/1 7th..Sketch OHL 3, 21
91/2 7th...Sketch OHL 38

VARGA, JOHN
93/4 Donruss USA21
98/9 EBK ECHL All-Star
93/4 Pinnacle 500
91/2 7th...Sketch WHL 150
93/4 Upper Deck 559
99/0 Florida Everblades
97/8 Louisiana Ice Gators
98/9 Louisiana Ice Gators
92/3 Tacoma Rockets
93/4 Tacoma Rockets

VARGAS, ERNIE
89/0 ProCards IHL 170
86/7 Sherb. Canadiens 28

VARGO, JAMIE
89/0 Windsor Spitfires

VARHOLIK, JAN
94 Semic 194

VARICKIJ, IGOR
98/9 OFS 126

VARIS, PETRI
99/0 Cardset 268, -AH 9-pasta
00/1 Cardset 43
02/3 Cardset 136
98/9 DEL 92
92/3 Jyvas Hyva 199
93/4 Jyvas Hyva 180
95 Panini Worlds 180
94 Semic 46
95 Semic 28
93 Semic Sticker 82
93/4 Sisu 23
93/4 Sisu 393
94/5 Sisu 248, 376
95/6 Sisu 259, P-7, SS-1
96/7 Sisu 47, 180, ATG-1
95/6 Sisu Limited 18
97/8 Indianapolis Ice 26

VARITSKIN, IGOR
99/0 Mir 185
00/1 Mir 370

VARITSKY, IGOR
95/6 DEL 162
95 Panini Worlds 43

VARJAMO, RIKU
99/0 Cardset 9
00/1 Cardset 171

VARJANEN, KARI
66/7 Champion 82
70/1 Kuvajulkaisut 171

VARJANOV, NIKOLAI
90/1 O-Pee-Chee 504

VARJARNO, RIKU
98/9 Cardset 6

VARJONEN, TOMMI
92/3 Jyvas Hyva 29
93/4 Jyvas Hyva 52
93/4 Sisu 251
94/5 Sisu 74

VARLAMOV, EVGENI
98/9 Mir 50
99/0 Mir 74
00/1 Mir 42

VARLAMOV, SERGEI
00/1 BAP Mem. 70
97 Bowman 120
98 Bowman 79, SC9
98 Bowman Chrome 79
98/9 Bowman's Best 142
02/3 Crown Royale ✂ GWJ 19
02/3 Heads Up ✂ GWQ 23
02/3 O-Pee-Chee 270
98/9 OPC Chrome 231
98/9 Pacific 58
00/1 Pacific 77
02/3 Pacific Complete 67
97/8 Pi. BeeHive 73, ✍ Aut. 73
01/2 PS Titanium Draft 163
02/3 PS Titanium ✂ GWJ 60
98/9 Topps 231
00/1 Topps 286
02/3 Topps 270
00/1 To. Chrome 181
02/3 To. Limited 270
02/3 Worcester IceCats
95/6 Swift Current Broncos

VARNAKOV, MICHAEL
87/8 Soviet Stars

VARPELA, MATTI
66/7 Champion 45

VARTIAINEN, EERO
78/9 SM-Liiga 146

VARTIAINEN, MATTI
66/7 Champion 123

VARTIAINEN, SEPPO
72/3 Williams Finnish 130
73/4 Williams Finnish 124

VARTY, BRENT
00/1 London Knights

VARVIO,
97/8 Hockey-Box

VARVIO, JARKKO
98/9 Cardset Leij. 46
99/0 Cardset AH 10-hertta
00/1 Cardset 220
92/3 Classic 30
92/3 Classic Four Sport 179
93/4 Cla. Prospects 125
93/4 Donruss 90
93/4 Donruss RR 6
94/5 Donruss 129
93/4 Fleer Ultra 302
93/4 Fleer Ultra WotF 19
94/5 Fleer Ultra 281
92/3 Jyvas Hyva 24
93/4 Leaf 383
93/4 Leaf FP 8
94/5 Leaf 199
94/5 Panini Sticker Z
93/4 Parkhurst 252
93/4 Parkhurst C8
94/5 Parkie SE40
93/4 Pinnacle 430
93/4 Score 620
94 Semic 44
95 Semic 44
93 Semic Sticker 83
93/4 Sisu 371
94/5 Sisu 349, GS-12

95/6 Sisu 306
96/7 Sisu 108
95/6 Sisu Limited 89
91/2 Upper Deck 676
93/4 Upper Deck 422, SP-40
94/5 Upper Deck 429
91/2 Upper Deck WJC 39
98/9 UD Elitserien 115
99/0 UD Elitserien 12

VARY, JOHN
89/0 7th..Sketch OHL 155
90/1 7th..Sketch OHL 75, 320
91/2 7th...Sketch OHL 237
95/6 Louisiana Ice Gators
95/6 Louisiana Ice Gators-2
98/9 Muskegon Fury
99/0 Topeka Scarecrows

VARY, MARC-OLIVIER
01/2 Cape Breton Eagles 10

VASICEK, JOSEF
00/1 BAP Mem. 429
01/2 BAP Mem. 172
02/3 BAP Mem. 134
00/1 Crown Royale 115
02/3 Exclusive 33
01/2 O-Pee-Chee 227
02/3 O-Pee-Chee 146
02/3 Pacific 71
02/3 Pacific Complete 337
01/2 Parkhurst 244
00/1 Premier Plus 106, PR6
00/1 Pr. Stock 108, PSR-5
00/1 PS Titanium 109
00/1 PS Titanium Draft 109
00/1 Signature 264, ✍ Aut. 226
02/3 Signature Series GS-45
00/1 SP Authentic 96
00/1 SP GU 64
00/1 SPx 155
00/1 Stadium 254
01/2 Topps 227
02/3 Topps 146
01/2 To. Chrome 76
00/1 To. Gold Label 108
00/1 To. Heritage 86
01/2 To. Heritage 77
02/3 To. Limited 146
00/1 To. Stars 114
02/3 To. Total 267
00/1 UD Reserve 90
00/1 Upper Deck 205
01/2 Upper Deck 35
02/3 Upper Deck 29
00/1 UD Black Diam. 70
00/1 UD Ice 50, 66
00/1 UD MVP 212
00/1 UD Pros&Prosp. 97
02/3 UD Vintage 48
00/1 Vanguard 108
01/2 Victory 68

VASICEK, MICHAL
98/9 OFS 289

VASICEK, TOMAS
94/5 APS 116
96/7 APS 192

VASILEV, IVAN
95/6 APS 336

VASILEVSKI, ALEX
94/5 Cla. Images 11
95/6 Edge Ice 98
94/5 Slapshot Memorial 49
99/0 Muskegon Fury

VASILEVSKI, ANDREI
00/1 Mir 147

VASILIEV, ALEXEI
00/1 BAP Mem. 304
98/9 Hartford Wolf Pack
99/0 Hartford Wolf Pack
00/1 Milwaukee Admirals

VASILIEV, ANDREI
95/6 Parkhurst 513
95/6 Upper Deck 412
01/2 UD DEL 19
98/9 Grand Rapids Griffins
97/8 Long Beach Ice Dogs

VASILJEVS, HERBERT
01/2 BAP Mem. 268
94/5 DEL 230
00/1 Pacific 28
95/6 Slapshot 94
00/1 SPx 91
00/1 Upper Deck 216
96/7 Carolina Monarchs
98/9 Kentucky Tho'blades
02/3 Manitoba Moose
95/6 Guelph Storm

VASILYEV, ALEXEI
95/6 SR Tetrad Autobilia 53
95/6 Upper Deck 555

VASILYEV, ANDREI
99/0 Eishockey 88

VASILYEV, MIKHAIL
83/4 Soviet Stars

VASILYEV, VALERI
91/2 Future Trends C72 68
92/3 Future Trends C76 132
72 Hellas MM-Jenkki 68
74 Hellas MM-Jenkki 59
70/1 Kuvajulkaisut 19
80 Olympic USSR
79 Panini Sticker 144
82 Semic Sticker 56
70/1 Soviet Stars
73/4 Soviet Stars 5
74/5 Soviet Stars 5
79/0 Soviet Stars 7
96 Wien HL4
72/3 Williams Finnish 39
73/4 Williams Finnish 19

VASKE, DENNIS
94/5 Fleer Ultra 134
95/6 Fleer Ultra 272
91/2 O-Pee-Chee 230
97/8 Pa. Invincible R-122
95/6 Panini Sticker 100
92/3 Parkhurst 335
94/5 Parkhurst 141
94/5 Pinnacle 456
97/8 Pi. BAP 120, ✍ Aut. 120
95/6 Playoff 170
93/4 Power Play 387
93/4 Premier 438
90/1 ProCards 508
91/2 ProCards 460
91/2 Score 310
91/2 Score CAN 340
95/6 SBx Emotion 110
95/6 SBx Impact 106
92/3 Topps 87
92/3 To. Stadium 362
93/4 To. Stadium 358
91/2 Upper Deck 49
92/3 Upper Deck 50
92/3 Upper Deck 383
96/7 NYIS

VASKO, ELMER
45-64 BeeHive-2 [Chic.]
64-67 BeeHive-3 [Chic.]
63-65 Chex
64/5 Coke/Sprite [Chic.]
65/6 Coca-Cola
62/3 Cowan Tile
68/9 O-Pee-Chee 147
68/9 O-Pee-Chee PS 8
93/4 Parkie 56-57 31
94/5 Parkie Tall 30, 141
60/1 Shirriff 73
61/2 Shirriff 26
57/8 Topps 27
58/9 Topps 12
59/0 Topps 3
60/1 Topps 23
61/2 Topps 25
61/2 Topps - Stamp
62/3 Topps 27
62/3 Topps Dollar
63/4 Topps 26
64/5 Topps 5
65/6 Topps 114
60/1 Toronto Star Photo
61/2 Toronto Star Photo
63/4 Toronto Star Action
64/5 Toronto Star Action
61/2 Toronto Star Weekend
91/2 Ultimate Original Six 64, ✍ Aut. 64

VASKO, RICK
80/1 DETR

VASSIE, VALERIE
96/7 Guildford Flames 28

VASSIEUX, JEAN
79 Panini Sticker 382

VASSILIEV, VLADIMIR
94/5 DEL 198

VASYUCHKOV, MAXIM
99/0 Mir 131

VATER, MATTHIAS
98/9 DEL 216

VAUCLAIR, JULIEN
01/2 Grand Rapids Griffins

VAUGHAN, DOUG
52/3 Anonymous 117

VAUGHAN, KEVIN
93/4 Slapshot / Oshawa 17

VAUGHAN, LYLE
91/2 Air Canada SJHL C40

VAUGHN, DR. R.L.
89/0 7th..Sketch OHL 97
83/4 Belleville Bulls
84/5 Belleville Bulls

VAUHKONEA, JONNI
96/7 Sisu 105

VAUHKONEN, JONNI
98/9 Cardset 173
99/0 Cardset 86
00/1 Cardset 190
92/3 Jyvas Hyva 146
93/4 Jyvas Hyva 262
93/4 Parkhurst 525
95 Semic 234
93/4 Sisu 296
93/4 Sisu 392
94/5 Sisu 174
92/3 Upper Deck 619

VAUTOUR, YVON
81/2 O-Pee-Chee 84
81/2 COLR
84/5 Fredericton Express

VAVRECKA, JAN
94/5 APS 8
95/6 APS 31

VAVROCH, ROBERT
99/0 Score 54

VEALE, BRIAN
91/2 Avant Garde BCJHL 105
91/2 Avant Garde BCJHL 147
92/3 BCJHL 113

VEBER, JIRI
95/6 APS 10, 417
96/7 APS 218, 340,411
97/8 APS 32, 348
98/9 DS 77
99/0 DS 131
96/7 DS Sticker 2, 23
98/9 OFS 100, 422, 472
99/0 OFS 445
95 Panini Worlds 196
95 Semic 147
94/5 Sisu 337

VEBER, ROMAN
96/7 APS 268
96/7 DS Sticker 176

VECCHIARELLI, JOHN
94 Semic 303
93 Semic Sticker 219

VECCIA, RON
84/5 Soo Greyhounds

VEDOVA, SCOTT DELLA
00/1 Québec Remparts 17

VEHANEN, PETRI
99/0 Cardset 79
00/1 Cardset 300
02/3 Cardset 149, 287

VEHMANEN, HANNU
70/1 Kuvajulkaisut 361

VEHMANEN, JORMA
66/7 Champion 14
70/1 Kuvajulkaisut 79
70/1 Kuvajulkaisut 240
80/1 Mallasjuoma 117
72 Semic Sticker 89
96/7 Sisu 194
78/9 SM-Liiga 164
71/2 Williams Finnish 78
71/2 Williams Finnish 163
72/3 Williams Finnish 115
73/4 Williams Finnish 83
73/4 Williams Finnish 213

VEIJALAINEN, ARI
71/2 Williams Finnish 378

VEILLEUX, ERIC
93/4 Cla. Prospects 67
91/2 7th...Sketch LHJMQ 245

VEILLEUX, ÉRIC
98/9 Kentucky Tho'blades
00/1 Lowell Lock Monsters
99/0 Manitoba Moose

VEILLEUX, STÉPHANE
02/3 Atomic 127
02/3 BAP All-Star 129
02/3 BAP Mem. 352
02/3 Calder 125
02/3 Crown Royale 119
02/3 In The GU 189
02/3 Pacific Complete 533
02/3 Parkhurst 240
02/3 Pr. Stock Reserve 166
02/3 Pr. Stock Titanium 120
02/3 Quest for the Cup 125
02/3 Signature Series 187, ✍ 187
02/3 SP Authentic 148
02/3 SP GU Edition 100
02/3 To. Total 437
02/3 Ultimate Memorabilia 40, ✍ RAut
02/3 Upper Deck 439
02/3 UD Honor 116
02/3 UD Mask 124
02/3 UD Premier 57
02/3 UD Top Shelf 115
02/3 Vanguard 119
00/1 Val d'Or Foreurs 23

VEILLEUX, STEVE
89/0 ProCards IHL 167
90/1 ProCards 332
91/2 ProCards 79
92/3 Fredericton Canadiens

VEINONEN, JUSSI
93/4 Sisu 22

VEISOR, MIKE
75/6 O-Pee-Chee 385
77/8 O-Pee-Chee 393
80/1 O-Pee-Chee 361
79/0 CHIC
82/3 HART / Jr. Whalers
83/4 HART / Jr. Whalers

VEITCH, DARREN
95/6 Edge Ice 180
87/8 OPC/Topps 114
87/8 Panini Sticker 239
88/9 Panini Sticker 39
82/3 Post [Wash.]
89/0 ProCards AHL 123
90/1 ProCards 155
86/7 DETR / Little Caesars
87/8 DETR / Little Caesars
88/9 TORO / P.L.A.Y. 22
80/1 WASH
81/2 WASH
82/3 WASH
85/6 WASH / Pizza Hut
91/2 Moncton Hawks
90/1 Newmarket Saints
92/3 Peoria Rivermen
93/4 Peoria Rivermen
94/5 Peoria Rivermen
98/9 Phoenix Mustangs 21

VEJVODA, MARTIN
99/0 OFS 175

VEJVODA, OTAKAR
94/5 APS 59
95/6 APS 96, 372, 426
96/7 APS 351
98/9 OFS 408
99/0 OFS 161
00/1 OFS 134
97/8 UD Elitserien 15
96 Wien 115

VELEBNY, LUBOS
01/2 Belleville Bulls Update

VELIKOV, MAXIM
00/1 Mir 221

VELISCHEK, RANDY
91/2 Bowman 152
92/3 Bowman 131
92/3 Durivage 45
90/1 O-Pee-Chee 453
91/2 O-Pee-Chee 377
92/3 O-Pee-Chee 288
89/0 O-Pee-Chee 245
90/1 OPC Premier 125
89/0 Panini Sticker 259
90/1 Panini/QUE 23
91/2 Panini Sticker 265
90/1 Pro Set 518
91/2 Pro Set 206
90/1 Score 64T
91/2 Score 257
91/2 Score CAN 477
92/3 Topps 430
91/2 To. Stadium 27
92/3 To. Stadium 460
90/1 Upper Deck 392
91/2 Upper Deck 484
83/4 MINS
85/6 NJER 10
86/7 NJER / S.O.B.E.R.
88/9 NJER / Caretta
89/0 NJER
89/0 NJER / Caretta
91/2 QUÉB / Petro-Canada
93/4 Milwaukee Admirals
94/5 Milwaukee Admirals
84/5 Springfield Indians 4

VELLAN,
92/3 Semic Nordisk 206 [Rookie]

VELLAN, PER K
92/3 Semic Nordisk 124

VELLINGA, MIKE
95/6 Slapshot 92
95/6 Guelph Storm
96/7 Guelph Storm

VELLUCCI, MIKE
88/9 ProCards / Binghampton
83/4 Belleville Bulls

VENÄLÄINEN, SAMI
00/1 Cardset 332

VENASKY, VIC
74/5 O-Pee-Chee 389
75/6 O-Pee-Chee 312
76/7 O-Pee-Chee 211
77/8 O-Pee-Chee 187
78/9 O-Pee-Chee 321
79/0 O-Pee-Chee 269
80/1 O-Pee-Chee 290
75/6 Topps 312
76/7 Topps 211
77/8 Topps 187

VENEDAM, SEAN
97 Bowman 11
93/4 Slapshot / Sudbury 11
94/5 Slapshot / Sudbury 10
95/6 Slapshot 393
97/8 Toledo Storm 7
93/4 Sudbury Wolves

VENERA, ZDENEK
98/9 OFS 17
00/1 OFS 348

VENERUZZO, GARY
68/9 O-Pee-Chee 119
70/1 O-Pee-Chee 101
72/3 O-Pee-Chee 330
74/5 OPC WHA 55
76/7 OPC WHA 21
73/4 Quaker Oats 32
68/9 Topps 119
70/1 Topps 101
75/6 Cincinnati Stingers
72/3 Los Angeles Sharks
76/7 San Diego Mariners

VENKRBEC, MIROSLAV
96/7 APS 264
98/9 OFS 98
99/0 OFS 437
00/1 OFS 319

VENTO, JOUNI
96/7 DEL 231
92/3 Jyvas Hyva 195
93/4 Jyvas Hyva 355
93/4 Sisu 214
93/4 Sisu 311
94/5 Sisu 53, 177
95/6 Sisu 354

VERAVAINEN, HEIKKI
66/7 Champion 18
65/6 Hellas 67

VERBEEK, BRIAN
84/5 Kingston Canadians
85/6 Kingston Canadians

VERBEEK, PAT
00/1 Aurora 53
00/1 BAP Mem. 302
01/2 BAP Mem. ✂ 500GS
90/1 Bowman 257
91/2 Bowman 12
92/3 Bowman 112
83 Canada Juniors
93/4 Donruss 148
94/5 Donruss 299
95/6 Donruss 29
96/7 Donruss 200
97/8 Donruss 23
96/7 Do. Canadian 48
97/8 Do. Canadian 27
95/6 Do. Elite 76
96/7 Do. Elite 42
97/8 Do. Preferred 57
93/4 EA Sports 59
02/3 First Edition 202
94/5 Flair 76
96/7 Flair 25
94/5 Fleer 91
95/6 Fleer Metal 101
96/7 F. Picks DL 10
92/3 Fleer Ultra 305
93/4 Fleer Ultra 175
94/5 Fleer Ultra 95
95/6 Fleer Ultra 107
96/7 Fl. Ultra 47
91/2 Gillette 24
92/3 Humpty Dumpty
91/2 Kraft 23
93/4 Kraft / PB
93/4 Leaf 144
94/5 Leaf 172
95/6 Leaf 16
96/7 Leaf 59
97/8 Leaf 78
94/5 L. Limited 27
96/7 L. Limited 33
96/7 L. Preferred 8, LS-14
97/8 Limited 75
96/7 Maggers 105
96/7 Metal Univ. 43
84/5 O-Pee-Chee 121
85/6 OPC/Topps 56
86/7 OPC/Topps 46
87/8 OPC/Topps 6
88/9 OPC/Topps 29
90/1 OPC/Topps 112
91/2 O-Pee-Chee 499
91/2 Topps - Team Leader 1
92/3 O-Pee-Chee 197
01/2 O-Pee-Chee 126
89/0 OPC/Topps 32
98/9 OPC Chrome 120
91/2 OPC Premier 5
88/9 OPC Stars 43
84/5 OPC Sticker 73
86/7 OPC Sticker 202-75
87/8 OPC Sticker 58-199
88/9 OPC Sticker 81-210
97/8 Omega 76
99/0 Omega 86
98/9 Pacific 185
99/0 Pacific 131
00/1 Pacific 159
01/2 Pacific 150
02/3 Pacific 121
97/8 Pacific CC 162
97/8 Pa. Crown Roy. 43
97/8 Pa. Invincible 44
97/8 Pa. Paramount 63
00/1 Pa. Paramount 90
87/8 Panini Sticker 81
88/9 Panini Sticker 278
90/1 Panini Sticker 36
91/2 Panini Sticker 313
92/3 Panini Sticker 256
93/4 Panini Sticker 124
94/5 Panini Sticker 112
95/6 Panini Sticker 108
97/8 Panini Sticker 137
98/9 Panini Sticker 126
95 Panini Worlds 17
91/2 Parkhurst 64
92/3 Parkhurst 58
93/4 Parkhurst 353
94/5 Parkhurst 92
95/6 Parkhurst 407
00/1 Parkhurst P-238
01/2 Parkhurst ✂ 500GS
94/5 Parkie SE seV7
91/2 Pinnacle 43
92/3 Pinnacle 348
93/4 Pinnacle 243
93/4 Pinnacle CA10
94/5 Pinnacle 37
95/6 Pinnacle 111
96/7 Pinnacle 68
97/8 Pinnacle 173
96/7 Pi. Be A Player 38, ✍ Aut. 38
97/8 Pi. Certified 111
97/8 Pi. Inside 157
95/6 Pi. Summit 107
96/7 Pi. Summit 5
97/8 Pi. Totally 111
95/6 Pi. Zenith 82
96/7 Pi. Zenith 93
95/6 Playoff 70
96/7 Playoff 359
94/5 POG 120
95/6 POG 182
93/4 Power Play 110
93/4 Premier 47
94/5 Premier 390
01/2 Pr. Stock -PS 25
90/1 Pro Set 112
91/2 Pro Set 86
91/2 Pro Set 303
92/3 Pro Set 58
91/2 Pro Set Platinum 44
91/2 Puck / Pro Set 10
91/2 Puck / Pro Set Prototype
90/1 Score 35
90/1 Sco. Hot Cards 18
91/2 Score 70
91/2 Score CAN 70
92/3 Score 282
93/4 Score 10
94/5 Score CI18
95/6 Score 122
96/7 Score 94
97/8 Score 124, CI-18
92/3 Seasons 44
94/5 Select 76
95/6 Select CE 108
96/7 Select CE 49
01/2 Signature 155, ✍ Aut. 155, ✂ 500GS
02/3 Signature Series GS-67
95/6 SBx Emotion 120
95/6 SBx Impact 115
94/5 SP 72
95/6 SP 93
96/7 SP 41
84/5 Topps 90
92/3 Topps 493
95/6 Topps 37, 3PL
98/9 Topps 120
00/1 Topps 218, PC-16, PP5
01/2 Topps 126
00/1 To. Chrome 140, PC-16
95/6 To. Finest 131
98/9 To. Finest 69
00/1 To. Heritage 187
96/7 To. Picks 69
91/2 To. Stadium 102
92/3 To. Stadium 197
93/4 To. Stadium 36
94/5 To. Stadium 120
95/6 To. Stadium 17
95/6 TSC Members Only 35
95/6 T. Super Skills 43
00/1 UD Heroes 45
01/2 Ultimate Mem. ✂ 500GS
90/1 Upper Deck 172
91/2 Upper Deck 193
92/3 Upper Deck 7
92/3 Upper Deck 204
93/4 Upper Deck 331, SP-67
94/5 Upper Deck 278, SP-124
95/6 Upper Deck 98, AS-13
96/7 Upper Deck 249
97/8 Upper Deck 262
98/9 Upper Deck 257
00 ✂ UD APOH 500, ✂✍ 500
93/4 Upper Deck Be A Player 38
94/5 UD BAP R61, ✍ 71
96/7 UD Black Diam. 136
95/6 UD CC 55
97/8 UD Coll. Choice 66, SQ16
98/9 UD G. Reserve 257
96/7 UD Ice 17
00/1 UD Legends ✍ ES
00/1 UD MVP 68, ME5, ✍ ME
99/0 UD MVP Cup 69
02/3 UD Top Shelf ✂ M
00/1 Victory 87, 250
96/7 DALL / Southwest
97/8 DALL / Score 124
01/2 DALL / Southwest
89/0 HART / Jr. Whalers
90/1 HART / Jr. Whalers
91/2 HART / Jr. Whalers
92/3 HART / Dairymart
93/4 HART / Coke
83/4 NJER
84/5 NJER
86/7 NJER / S.O.B.E.R.
88/9 NJER / Caretta

VERBEEK, TIM
98/9 Barrie Colts

VERCHOTA, PHIL
80 Olympic USA
94/5 SR Miracle 37,38, ✍ 37,38

VERDULE, JIMMY
99/0 Rouyn-Noranda

VERENIKIN, SERGEI
00/1 Mir 190

VERMETTE, ANTOINE
96 Québec Pee Wee 992
99/0 UD Prospects 57, 79
00/1 UD Prospects 83
98/9 Québec Remparts
00/1 Victoriaville Tigres 8

VERMETTE, MARK
89/0 ProCards AHL 163
90/1 ProCards 450
91/2 Upper Deck 470
88/9 QUÉB
88/9 QUÉB / Gene. Foods
91/2 QUÉB / Petro-Canada
92/3 QUÉB / Petro-Canada
89/0 Halifax Citadels
90/1 Halifax Citadels
93/4 Las Vegas Thunder

VERMEULEN, PHILIPPE
79 Panini Sticker 342

VERNARSKY, KRIS
02/3 BAP Mem. 371
02/3 Calder 105
02/3 Pacific Complete 558
02/3 Parkhurst Retro 244
96 Québec Pee Wee 680
02/3 Ultimate Memorabilia 77
02/3 UD Mask 156
02/3 UD Premier 94
00/1 UD Prospects 24

VERNELLI, NICK
02/3 Plymouth Whalers

VERNER, ANDREW
91/2 Arena 25
91/2 Classic 30
91/2 Classic Four Sport 30
92/3 Classic Prospects 84
99/0 Eishockey 118
89/0 7th..Sketch OHL 121
90/1 7th..Sketch OHL 375
91/2 7th...Sketch OHL 143
91/2 Star Pics 21
91/2 Star Pics 36
91/2 Ultimate Draft Pick 26, 57, ✍ Aut.
91/2 Upper Deck 74
00/1 UD DEL 128
01/2 UD DEL 103, G4, ✂ GJ
97/8 UD Elitserien 134
98/9 UD Elitserien 149
91/2 Peterborough Petes

VERNER, BRANDON
00/1 Owen Sound Attack 6

VERNON, MIKE
01/2 Adrenaline 30
98/9 Aurora 172, -CF 44
99/0 Aurora 123
99/0 BAP Mem. 251, 323
00/1 BAP Mem. 458
01/2 BAP Mem. ✂ GJ-3
01/2 BT Pipes 54, ✂ DM, ✂ GJ, ✂ S&J, ✂ GG, ✂ GT
97/8 Bicycle 2-Heart
98/9 Bicycle.. 8-C
90/1 Bowman 94
91/2 Bowman 253
92/3 Bowman 86
98/9 Bowman's Best 17
83 Canada Juniors
99/0 Crown Royale 63
93/4 Donruss 54
95/6 Donruss BTP 3
96/7 Donruss 52
97/8 Donruss 73
96/7 Do. Canadian 94
97/8 Do. Canadian 118, NP-28, ✍ SCS-31
96/7 Do. Elite 86
97/8 Do. Preferred 82, CG-12
97/8 Do. Priority 159, PG-11
97/8 Do. Studio 69
98/9 Dynagon Ice 170, -TC 23
99/0 Dynagon Ice 178
93/4 EA Sports 24
95/6 Edge Ice L8
94/5 Flair 53
94/5 Fleer 66
96/7 Fleer 144
92/3 Fleer Ultra 31
93/4 Fleer Ultra 207
94/5 Fleer Ultra 287
95/6 Fleer Ultra 50, PPM-12
93/4 Hockey Wit 45
89/0 Kraft 62
90/1 Kraft 61, 76
91/2 Kraft 19
92/3 Kraft / PB
93/4 Kraft / JELL-O
94/5 Kraft / KD
95/6 Kraft / PS
96/7 Kraft / TT
98/9 Kraft / Post 17
99/0 Kraft / JELL-O
86/7 Kraft Sports 9
89/0 Kraft Stickers 4
93/4 Leaf 83
93/4 Leaf PW 7
94/5 Leaf 464
95/6 Leaf 8
96/7 Leaf 147
97/8 Leaf 94
96/7 L. Preferred LS-57
97/8 Limited 188, FG-17
96/7 Maggers 60
91/2 McDonald's Mc-20
87/8 O-Pee-Chee 215
88/9 O-Pee-Chee 261
90/1 OPC/Topps 351
91/2 O-Pee-Chee 107
91/2 O-Pee-Chee 247
92/3 O-Pee-Chee 247
01/2 O-Pee-Chee 152
89/0 OPC/Topps 163
89/0 Topps - Sticker 12
90/1 OPC/Topps L
98/9 OPC Chrome 86
90/1 OPC Premier 126
91/2 OPC Premier 9
88/9 OPC Stars 44
87/8 OPC Sticker 41-182
88/9 OPC Sticker 86-216
89/0 opcSticker 94, 167-29, / AS 34
97/8 Omega 207
98/9 Omega 216
99/0 Omega 102
98/9 Pacific 393
99/0 Pacific 384, -ITCNF 18, -TL 24
00/1 Pacific 188, ITC-4
01/2 Pacific 67
02/3 Pacific 61
97/8 Pacific CC 24, ITC-8
97/8 Pa. Crown Roy. 123, FO-18
98/9 Pa. Crown Roy. 122
97/8 Pa. Dynagon 45, S-8, T-44
97/8 Pa. Invincible 52, FP-15
97/8 Pa. Paramount 170, GSL-19
98/9 Pa. Paramount 216, -GS 18
99/0 Pa. Paramount 212
97/8 Pa. Revolution 128, RTS-18, TC-22
98/9 Pa. Revolution 130
98/9 Panini Photocard
87/8 Panini Sticker 203
88/9 Panini Sticker 4
89/0 Panini Sticker 34, 178
90/1 Panini Sticker 175, 329
90/1 Panini/CGY 23
91/2 Panini Sticker 55
91/2 Panini Sticker 328
92/3 Panini Sticker 39
93/4 Panini Sticker 188
94/5 Panini Sticker 162
95/6 Panini Sticker 188
98/9 Panini Sticker 211
99/0 Panini Sticker 305
91/2 Parkhurst 27
92/3 Parkhurst 24
93/4 Parkhurst 301
95/6 Parkhurst 334
00/1 Parkhurst P-168
94/5 Parkie SE52
91/2 Pinnacle 132
92/3 Pinnacle 318
93/4 Pinnacle 231
93/4 Pinnacle Mask 2
94/5 Pinnacle 377, GT10
x95/6 Pinnacle Mask 6
96/7 Pinnacle 16,T-6
97/8 Pinnacle 36
97/8 Pi. Certified 8
97/8 Pi. Inside 84, SU-1, S-11, / Can 8
95/6 Pi. Summit 114
96/7 Pi. Summit 101
97/8 Pi. Totally 8
95/6 Pi. Zenith 60
95/6 Playoff 255
94/5 POG 278
95/6 POG 104
93/4 Power Play 45
93/4 Premier 15
93/4 Prmr. - BG-OPC 5
94/5 Premier 302, 348
00/1 PS Titanium 13
95/6 Pro Magnet IC5
90/1 Pro Set 47, 338
91/2 Pro Set 35, 277
92/3 Pro Set 25
91/2 Pro Set Platinum 21
99/0 Revolution 130, / CSC 130
90/1 Score 52
90/1 Sco. Hot Cards 23
91/2 Score 80
91/2 Score CAN 80
92/3 Score 60
93/4 Score 43
93/4 Score PIAS 40
95/6 Score 219, 319
96/7 Score 164, NW-14
97/8 Score 4
92/3 Seasons 61
94/5 Select 54
95/6 Select CE 42
00/1 Signature 125
01/2 Signature C-56, ✂ GUE9, ✂ ITN9
95/6 SBx Emotion 59
97/8 SP Authentic 133
99/0 SPx 131
00/1 Stadium 214
92/3 Topps 20
95/6 Topps 11, 160
98/9 Topps 86
99/0 Topps 159
00/1 Topps 65
01/2 Topps 152
99/0 To. Chrome 159
94/5 Topps Finest 36
98/9 To. Finest 135
91/2 To. Stadium 269
92/3 To. Stadium 345
93/4 To. Stadium 319
93/4 To. Stadium - AS
94/5 To. Stadium 79, 189
95/6 To. Stadium 12
95/6 T. Super Skills 84
98/9 UD Choice 177
00/1 Ultimate Mem. ✂ A8-5, ✂ D-20, ✂ G-5, ✂ TM-31, ✂ GM-3
01/2 Ultimate Mem. ✂ A8
02/3 Ultimate Memorabilia ✂ CSTW, ✂ SCD (x3), ✂ SCDE, ✂ SCDGJ, ✂ SCDN
90/1 Upper Deck 254, 495
91/2 Upper Deck 163
92/3 Upper Deck 112
93/4 Upper Deck 177
94/5 Upper Deck 141, SP-115
95/6 Upper Deck 4
97/8 Upper Deck 60, 356
98/9 Upper Deck 167
00/1 Upper Deck 257
98/9 UD Black Diam. 74
95/6 UD CC 100
97/8 UD Coll. Choice 77, SQ53
98/9 UD G. Reserve 167
98/9 UD MVP 176
99/0 UD MVP Cup 79
00/1 UD Pros&Prosp. 15
01/2 UD SCup Champs 27
00/1 UD Vintage 52
99/0 Victory 257
85/6 CALG / Red Rooster
86/7 CALG / Red Rooster
87/8 CALG / Red Rooster
90/1 CALG / McGavin's
91/2 CALG / IGA
92/3 CALG / IGA 010
84/5 Moncton G'Flames

VEROT, DARCY
00/1 WBS Penguins
01/2 WBS Penguins

VERSCHRAEGEN, BOB
79 Panini Sticker 343

VERSHININ, DMITRI
99/0 Mir 33

VERTALA, TIMO
98/9 Cardset 136
99/0 Cardset 324
00/1 Cardset 213
02/3 Cardset 137
98/9 UD Choice 277
97/8 UD Black Diam. 25
01/2 Québec Citadelles

VERVERGAERT, DENNIS
74/5 Loblaws
74/5 OPC 117
74/5 O-Pee-Chee 207
75/6 O-Pee-Chee 42
76/7 O-Pee-Chee 175
76/7 OPC 395
77/8 O-Pee-Chee 56
78/9 O-Pee-Chee 52
79/0 O-Pee-Chee 214
80/1 O-Pee-Chee 99
81/2 O-Pee-Chee 356
74/5 Topps 117
74/5 Topps 207
75/6 Topps 42
76/7 Topps 175
77/8 Topps 56
78/9 Topps 52
79/0 Topps 214
80/1 Topps 99
73/4 VANC / Royal Bank
74/5 VANC / Royal Bank
75/6 VANC / Royal Bank
76/7 VANC / Royal Bank
77/8 VANC / Royal Bank
78/9 VANC / Royal Bank
80/1 WASH

VERVILLE, DAVE
00/1 Chicoutimi Saguenéens 19
99/0 Shawinigan 13

VERWEY, ROLAND
99/0 Eishockey 352

VERZHININ, DMITRI
98/9 Mir 133

VESA, KIMMO
98/9 Cardset 162
99/0 Cardset 257
93/4 Sisu 184
94/5 Sisu 245

VESALA, HEIKKI
94/5 Sisu 391

VESCIO, KEVIN
82/3 North Bay Centennials
83/4 North Bay Centennials

VESELOVSKY, PETER
94/5 APS 149
94 Semic 201

VESELY, ONDREJ
99/0 DS 13
00/1 DS 24
98/9 OFS 280
99/0 OFS 456
00/1 OFS 341

VESEY, JIM
88/9 ProCards / Peoria
89/0 ProCards IHL 16
91/2 BOST / Sports Action
93/4 Phoenix Roadrunners
94/5 Phoenix Roadrunners

VESSLIN, ESA
66/7 Champion 32

VESTERGAARD, CHAD
91/2 Avant Garde BCJHL 115
92/3 BCJHL 177

VETCHY, ONDREJ
01/2 OFS 68

VETTRAINO, SCOTT
96/7 Dayton Ice Bandits
90/1 Michigan Tech Huskies
91/2 Michigan Tech Huskies

VEVCHERENKO, OLEG
98/9 Mir 108
99/0 Mir 116
00/1 Mir 22

VÉZINA, GEORGES
25-27 Anonymous 3
00/1 BAP Mem. ✂ V-1 to ✂ V-16
01/2 BT Pipes 132, ✂ VM
02/3 Between the Pipes 115
91 C55 Reprint 38
24/5 Champ's Cigarettes
25 Dominion Chocolates 120
83 HHOF Postcard B16
83&87 HHOF 30
10/1 Imperial
11/2 Imperial 38
12/3 Imperial 1
27/8 La Patrie
27/8 La Presse
93/4 Legends of Hockey 26
24/5 Maple Crispette [V130] 13
55/6 Parkhurst 56
01/2 Parkhurst PR43
93/4 Parkie 56-57 P-3
91/2 Pro Set 333
60/1 Topps 19
61/2 Topps - Stamp
00/1 Ultimate Mem. ✂ GM-20
02/3 Ultimate Memorabilia ✂ BOS, ✂ SF
23/4 William Paterson 19
24/5 William Paterson 43
92/3 MONT / OPC 28

VÉZINA, J. JACQUES
79/0 Montréal Juniors B&W
79/0 Montréal Jrs. Colour

VÉZINA, STEVE
99/0 Colorado Gold Kings

VIAL, DENNIS
00/1 Kudos 149
93/4 Parkhurst 406
90/1 Pro Set 628
89/0 ProCards IHL 32
91/2 Score CAN 428
95/6 UD BAP 131, ✍ S131
91/2 DETR / Little Caesars
93/4 OTTA
94/5 OTTA
95/6 OTTA
96/7 OTTA
97/8 OTTA
98/9 Chicago Wolves
98/9 Chicago Wolves Champs
01/2 Sheffield Steelers GS
88/9 Niagara Falls Thunder

VICEK, LADISLAV
00/1 DS 143

VICHOREK, MARK
90/1 ProCards 590
88/9 Flint Spirits

VICKERS, CHRIS
84/5 Ottawa 67's

VICKERS, STEVE
74/5 Lipton Soup 34
74/5 Loblaws
72/3 O-Pee-Chee 254
73/4 O-Pee-Chee 57
74/5 O-Pee-Chee 29
75/6 O-Pee-Chee 19
75/6 O-Pee-Chee 295
75/6 O-Pee-Chee 324
76/7 O-Pee-Chee 75
76/7 OPC 390
77/8 O-Pee-Chee 136
78/9 O-Pee-Chee 55
79/0 O-Pee-Chee 195
80/1 O-Pee-Chee 23
82/3 Post [NYRa.]
73/4 Topps 57
74/5 Topps 29
75/6 Topps 19
75/6 Topps 295
75/6 Topps 324
76/7 Topps 75
77/8 Topps 136
78/9 Topps 55
79/0 Topps 195
80/1 Topps 23

VIENONEN, JUSSI
99/0 Cardset 104

VIENS, STEPHAN
91/2 7th...Sketch LHJMQ 121

VIERIMAA, HANNU
80/1 Mallasjuoma 129

VIG, MITCH
99/0 Mobile Mysticks

VIGIER, JEAN-PIERRE
01/2 Pacific 26
01/2 Parkhurst 353
00/1 UD Ice 107
01/2 Victory 362
01/2 Chicago Wolves
02/3 Chicago Wolves

VIGIER, JP
02/3 Choice Prospects 42

VIGILANTE, JOHN
02/3 Plymouth Whalers

VIGLASI, RON
84/5 Kelowna Wings &...
82/3 Victoria Cougars

VIGNEAULT, ALAIN
91/2 7th...Sketch LHJMQ 222
97/8 MONT
87/8 Hull Olympiques

VIGNOLA, RÉJEAN
83/4 Fredericton Express

VIHANTO, PENTTI
66/7 Champion 53
70/1 Kuvajulkaisut 153
71/2 Williams Finnish 204
72/3 Williams Finnish 241
73/4 Williams Finnish 276

VIHKO, JOONAS
00/1 Cardset 263
02/3 Cardset 138, -Nimik.

VIILMA, OLLI
70/1 Kuvajulkaisut 291
71/2 Williams Finnish 165

VIINANEN, MIKA
02/3 Cardset 139

VIINIKAINEN, JUHA
98/9 Cardset 130
99/0 Cardset 72
96/7 Sisu 66
95/6 UD CC 329

VIITA, MAURI
71/2 Williams Finnish 356

VIITAKOSKI, MATTI
96/7 Sisu 109

VIITAKOSKI, VESA
98/9 Cardset 91
99/0 Cardset 55
00/1 Cardset 159
02/3 Cardset 140
93/4 Classic 47
94/5 Classic 45, T12
93/4 Cla. Prospects 42
93/4 Donruss 60
94/5 Donruss 295
94/5 Fleer Ultra 272
97/8 Hockey-Box
91/2 Jyvas Hyva 58
93/4 Leaf 433
94/5 Leaf 34
94 Panini Olympics 302
93/4 Parkhurst 263
93/4 Parkhurst C20
93/4 Pinnacle 444
94/5 Premier 472
93/4 Score 622
94 Semic 22
95 Semic 45
93 Semic Sticker 84
93/4 Upper Deck 344, SP-26
94/5 Saint John Flames
95/6 Saint John Flames

VIITALA, JARI
70/1 Kuvajulkaisut 323
80/1 Mallasjuoma 38
78/9 SM-Liiga 61

VIITALAHTI, KARI
78/9 SM-Liiga 95
71/2 Williams Finnish 275
73/4 Williams Finnish 238

VIITANEN, PENTTI
71/2 Williams Finnish 296
73/4 Williams Finnish 214

VIK, PETR
97/8 DS Sticker 115

VIKINGSTAD, TORE
01/2 UD DEL 50
99/0 UD Elitserien 65
00/1 UD Elitserien 117

VIKSTROM, SEPPO
66/7 Champion 63

VIKTORSSON, JAN
95/6 Leaf Elit Set 191, C-15
89/0 Semic Elitserien 63
90/1 Semic Elitserien 285
91/2 Semic Elitserien 67
91/2 Semic Elitserien 352
92/3 Semic Elitserien 99
91 Semic Sticker 41
95/6 UD Elitserien 55
97/8 UD Elitserien 48
98/9 UD Elitserien 62

VIKULOV, VLADIMIR
91/2 Future Trends C72 12
91/2 Future Trends C72 47
92/3 Future Trends C76 164
72 Hellas MM-Jenkki 77
74 Hellas MM-Jenkki 60
70/1 Kuvajulkaisut 20
72 Semic Sticker 18
74 Semic Sticker 49
69/0 Soviet Stars
70/1 Soviet Stars
71/2 Soviet Stars
71/2 Williams Finnish 19
72/3 Williams Finnish 40
73/4 Williams Finnish 20

VILANDER, JUKKA
91/2 Jyvas Hyva 63
92/3 Jyvas Hyva 186
93/4 Jyvas Hyva 317
89 Semic Sticker 47
93/4 Sisu 42
93/4 Sisu 332

VILASEK, DANIEL
97/8 APS 143
99/0 OFS 296
99/0 Score 99

VILEN, JORMA
66/7 Champion 180
70/1 Kuvajulkaisut 257
71/2 Williams Finnish 222
72/3 Williams Finnish 170
73/4 Williams Finnish 239

VILEN, PETRI
93/4 Sisu 235

VILGRAIN, CLAUDE
92/3 Bowman 191
98/9 DEL 204
92/3 O-Pee-Chee 133
91/2 Parkhurst 321
91/2 Pro Set 425
91/2 Pro Set Platinum 195
89/0 ProCards AHL 211
90/1 ProCards 558
92/3 Score 326
92/3 Score SS 14
92/3 Topps 187
92/3 To. Stadium 422
90/1 Upper Deck 250

VILJANEN, RISTO
72/3 Williams Finnish 357

VILJANEN, TIMO
78/9 SM-Liiga 209

VILLA, ISMO
80/1 Mallasjuoma 121
78/9 SM-Liiga 167
77-79 Sports. FIN 90-2165
73/4 Williams Finnish 322

VILLE, CHRISTOPHE
95 Globe 203
94 Semic 225
95 Semic 199
92 Semic Sticker 238
93 Semic Sticker 267

VILLEMURE, G
71/2 Pro Star Promotions

VILLEMURE, GILLES
71/2 Bazooka Panel
70/1 Colgate 89
71/2 Eddie Sargent 127
70/1 Esso Power Player
74/5 Loblaws
70/1 O-Pee-Chee 183
71/2 O-Pee-Chee 18
71/2 O-Pee-Chee 248
72/3 O-Pee-Chee 132
72/3 O-Pee-Chee 286
73/4 O-Pee-Chee 119
74/5 O-Pee-Chee 179
75/6 O-Pee-Chee 379
76/7 O-Pee-Chee 61
63/4 Topps 46
64/5 Topps 74
67/8 Topps 86
71/2 Topps 18
72/3 Topps 64
72/3 Topps 137
73/4 Topps 153
74/5 Topps 179
76/7 Topps 61
71/2 Toronto Sun Photo

VILLENEUVE, ANDRE
86/7 Sherb. Canadiens 29

VILLENEUVE, BRUNO
90/1 7th..Sketch LHJMQ 145
91/2 Knoxville Cherokees
93/4 Knoxville Cherokees

VILLENEUVE, JONATHAN
01/2 Shawinigan 8
02/3 Shawinigan Cataractes

VILLENEUVE, MARTIN
97/8 New Orleans Brass
99/0 Quad City Mallards
00/1 Quad City Mallards
99/0 Rouyn-Noranda

VILLENEUVE, SAMUEL
01/2 Drummondville

VILLENEUVE, STEVE
01/2 Cape Breton Eagles 1

VILNEFF, MARK
90/1 7th..Sketch OHL 296
94/5 Muskegon Fury
95/6 Muskegon Fury
98/9 Muskegon Fury
99/0 Muskegon Fury

VILONEN, MIKKO
70/1 Kuvajulkaisut 324
80/1 Mallasjuoma 156

VINARD, ALAIN
79 Panini Sticker 384

VINCE, BILL
82/3 Brandon Wheat Kings

VINCELETTE, DAN
90/1 OPC Premier 87
89/0 ProCards IHL 59
91/2 ProCards 480

87/8 CHIC / Coke
88/9 CHIC / Coke
90/1 QUÉB / Petro-Canada
92/3 Atlanta Knights

VINCENT, ANDRÉ
01/2 Drummondville
01/2 Victoriaville Tigres 8

VINCENT, PASCAL
90/1 7th...Sketch LHJMQ 70
91/2 7th...Sketch LHJMQ 246

VINCENT, PAUL
93/4 Cla. 4 Sport 226
95/6 Edge Ice 85
94/5 Sig. Rookies 34, ✍ 34
94/5 SR Gold Standard 96
99/0 Odessa Jackalopes
96/7 Peoria Rivermen
95/6 St. John's Maple Leafs
93/4 Seattle Thunderbirds

VINCENT, ROBERT
51/2 Lac St-Jean 30

VINCENT, SHAWN
83/4 Kelowna Wings

VINES, MARK
90/1 Pro Set 702

VINET, CLAUDE
52/3 Anonymous 137

VINNEAU, JUSTIN
02/3 Shawinigan Cataractes

VINOGRADOV, ALEX.
00/1 Mir 392
95 Panini Worlds 46

VINOKUROV, DENIS
91/2 Upper Deck WJC 4

VIPOND, KELLY
91/2 7th...Sketch OHL 142
91/2 Peterborough Petes
92/3 Windsor Spitfires

VIRAG, DUSTIN
94/5 Slapshot / North Bay 16
95/6 Slapshot 222

VIRHIMO, TAPIO
70/1 Kuvajulkaisut 258
80/1 Mallasjuoma 44
78/9 SM-Liiga 43
71/2 Williams Finnish 223
72/3 Williams Finnish 171
73/4 Williams Finnish 193

VIRKGUNEN, TOMMY
91/2 Avant Garde BCJHL 170

VIRKKU, KALEVI
65/6 Hellas 18

VIRKKUNEN, TEEMU
00/1 Cardset 128
98/9 SPx Prospects 69
98/9 UD Black Diam. 101

VIRMANEN, MATTI
80/1 Mallasjuoma 56

VIROLAINEN, MIKKO
93/4 Sisu 55

VIRTA, HANNU
98/9 Cardset Leij. 18
99/0 Cardset AH 2-hertta
02/3 Cardset 289
95 Globe 132
95 Hartwall Karjala
91/2 Jyvas Hyva 66
92/3 Jyvas Hyva 183
93/4 Jyvas Hyva 315
95/6 Kellogg's Pop-Ups 3
95 Panini Worlds 168
95 Semic 23
89 Semic Sticker 34
91 Semic Sticker 6
93/4 Sisu 37
95/6 Sisu Gold 11
95/6 Sisu Limited 2, LG-7
96 Wien 23
82/3 BUFF / Wendt's 16
84/5 BUFF / Blue Shield
85/6 BUFF / Blue Shield

VIRTA, HEIKKI
70/1 Kuvajulkaisut 362

VIRTA, PASI
80/1 Mallasjuoma 180
78/9 SM-Liiga 118

VIRTA, PEKKA
97/8 Hockey-Box
94/5 Sisu 212, MN-6
95/6 Sisu 146, 360
96/7 Sisu 157

VIRTA, SEPPO
80/1 Mallasjuoma 172

VIRTA, TONI
92/3 Jyvas Hyva 33
93/4 Jyvas Hyva 53
93/4 Sisu 243
94/5 Sisu 46
95/6 Sisu 224

VIRTA, TONY
01/2 BAP Mem. 454
98/9 Cardset 237
99/0 Cardset 137, 172
00/1 Cardset 98, 239
02/3 Cardset 141
96/7 DEL 56
01/2 Parkhurst 319
02/3 SPx 113
01/2 UD Mask 149
02/3 UD MVP 206
02/3 Victory 108

VIRTANEN, ANTO
66/7 Champion 38
65/6 Hellas 33
70/1 Kuvajulkaisut 206
72 Panda MM-Toronto
71/2 Williams Finnish 94
72/3 Williams Finnish 259
73/4 Williams Finnish 257

VIRTANEN, ANTTI
98/9 Cardset 70
99/0 Cardset 36
00/1 Cardset 177
02/3 Cardset 290
66/7 Champion 165
65/6 Hellas 147
97/8 Hockey-Box

VIRTANEN, HANNU
70/1 Kuvajulkaisut 363

VIRTANEN, JAAKKO
70/1 Kuvajulkaisut 325

VIRTANEN, JANI
00/1 Cardset 143

VIRTANEN, JANNE
91/2 Jyvas Hyva 68
92/3 Jyvas Hyva 193
93/4 Jyvas Hyva 348
93/4 Sisu 219
93/4 Sisu 311
94/5 Sisu 67
95/6 Sisu 157, 281

VIRTANEN, JARI
93/4 Sisu 133
94/5 Sisu 72
95/6 Sisu 39
78/9 SM-Liiga 141

VIRTANEN, JORMA
72 Panda MM-Toronto
78/9 SM-Liiga 111
72/3 Williams Finnish 98
73/4 Williams Finnish 146

VIRTANEN, JUHA
98/9 Cardset 62
99/0 Cardset 35
00/1 Cardset 164
94/5 Sisu 264
95/6 Sisu 142
95/6 Sisu Limited 98

VIRTANEN, JUKKA
92/3 Jyvas Hyva 184
70/1 Kuvajulkaisut 344
80/1 Mallasjuoma 203
93/4 Sisu 385

VIRTANEN, MARKO
98/9 Cardset 139
99/0 Cardset 77
92/3 Jyvas Hyva 75
93/4 Jyvas Hyva 148
94 Semic 49
93 Semic Sticker 85
93/4 Sisu 150
93/4 Sisu 348
94/5 Sisu 249, H-18
95/6 Sisu 67, P-8
95/6 Sisu Limited 53
97/8 UD Elitserien 172

VIRTANEN, TIMO
71/2 Williams Finnish 357
72/3 Williams Finnish 358

VIRTUE, TERRY
90/1 7th...Sketch WHL 107, 329
99/0 Hartford Wolf Pack
00/1 Hartford Wolf Pack
01/2 Hartford Wolf Pack
98/9 Providence Bruins
93/4 Wheeling Thund'birds
02/3 Worcester IceCats

VISCOVICH, PETER
84/5 Kingston Canadians
85/6 Kingston Canadians

VISHEAU, MARK
93/4 Cla. Prospects 101
98/9 Omega 116
90/1 7th...Sketch OHL 147, 149
91/2 7th...Sketch OHL 378
97/8 Milwaukee Admirals

VISHNEVSKI, VITALY
99/0 BAP Mem. 330
00/1 BAP Mem. 243
01/2 BAP Mem. 55
00/1 Mir Fetisov 18
99/0 Omega 8
00/1 Pacific 13
00/1 Panini Sticker 113
00/1 Parkhurst P-16
01/2 Parkhurst 116
00/1 Signature 141, ✍ Aut. 161
01/2 Signature 126, ✍ Aut. 126
00/1 Topps 309
00/1 To. Chrome 204
02/3 To. Total 179
98/9 UD Choice 285
00/1 Upper Deck 234
01/2 Upper Deck 236
02/3 Upper Deck 1
97/8 UD Black Diam. 93
00/1 UD MVP 184
02/3 UD Vintage 1
00/1 Victory 3
01/2 Victory 5
02/3 Victory 1
99/0 Cincinnati M'Ducks

VISHNEVSKY, VITALI
02/3 UD Vintage 261

VISKARI, ESA
66/7 Champion 137

VISKARI, TIMO
66/7 Champion 126
70/1 Kuvajulkaisut 274

VISKOVICH, PETER
86/7 Kingston Canadians

VISNOVSKY, LUBOMIR
00/1 BAP Mem. 451
01/2 BAP Mem. 51
01/2 O-Pee-Chee 149
01/2 Pacific 191
00/1 Parkhurst P-228
01/2 Parkhurst 140
00/1 Premier Plus 139
00/1 Pr. Stock 123
00/1 PS Titanium 125
00/1 PS Titanium Draft 125
01/2 Signature 107, ✍ Aut. 107
00/1 SP Authentic 109
02/3 Sports Vault 239
01/2 Stadium 62
01/2 Topps 149, OTG14
00/1 To. Heritage 87
01/2 To. Heritage 108
02/3 To. Total 305
00/1 Upper Deck 430
01/2 Upper Deck 311
00/1 UD Black Diam. 120
01/2 UD MVP 90
00/1 Vanguard 125

VIT, PAVEL
95/6 DEL 425
96/7 DEL 62

VITALE, PHIL
52/3 Laval Dairy Update 72
52/3 St. Lawrence 28

VITEK, JIRI
95/6 APS 214

VITELI, JARMO
70/1 Kuvajulkaisut 326
71/2 Williams Finnish 358
72/3 Williams Finnish 340

VITELI, PETRI
71/2 Williams Finnish 359

VITOLINSH, HARIJS
93/4 Cla. Prospects 197
95/6 Leaf Elit Set 285
90/1 O-Pee-Chee 521
93/4 Parkhurst 496
93/4 Upper Deck 428
95/6 UD Elitserien 183

VITUCCI, NICK
96/7 Charlotte Checkers
91/2 Greensboro Monarchs
92/3 Hampton Roads
93/4 Peoria Rivermen
93/4 Toledo Storm 7
94/5 Toledo Storm
97/8 Toledo Storm 13

VIUHKOLA, JARI
00/1 Cardset 61
02/3 Cardset 291

VIVEIROS, EMANUEL
96/7 DEL 314
88/9 ProCards / Kalamazoo
90/1 ProCards 183
84/5 Prince Albert Raiders

VIZZUTTI, CHAD
92/3 BCJHL 159

VLACEK, IVAN
96/7 DS Sticker 212

VLACH, ROSTISLAV
94/5 APS 246
95/6 APS 18, 390, 411
96/7 APS 224
97/8 APS 36, 365
97/8 DS 66
96/7 DS Sticker 29
97/8 DS Sticker 174
91/2 Jyvas Hyva 38
98/9 OFS 329
01/2 OFS 67, -RE15D
89 Semic Sticker 194

VLASAK, TOMAS
94/5 APS 218
95/6 APS 169
96/7 APS 183, 363, 401
97/8 APS 87
00/1 BAP Mem. 441
98/9 Cardset 72
99/0 Cardset 6, 42, 160
00/1 Cardset 268
02/3 Cardset 142
97/8 DS 45
00/1 DS JT15, NT9, WCH9
96/7 DS Sticker 52
97/8 DS Sticker 95
99/0 OFS 274
00/1 OFS 396
00/1 Signature 196, ✍ Aut. 210

VLASÁK, TOMÁS
93/4 Parkhurst 515

VLASANEK, PETR
99/0 OFS 248

VLASOV, IGOR
95/6 UD Elitserien DS2

VLASSENKOV, DMITRI
98/9 UD Choice 287
97/8 UD Black Diam. 124

VLCEK, IVAN
94/5 APS 147
96/7 APS 290
97/8 APS 175
97/8 DS 51
99/0 DS 88
00/1 DS 29
97/8 DS Sticker 150
98/9 OFS 287, 453
99/0 OFS 129
00/1 OFS 61, -Star 18
01/2 OFS 206, -UHI 39

VLCEK, LADISLAV
99/0 OFS 334
00/1 OFS 125
01/2 OFS 268

VLK, PETR
95/6 APS 187
96/7 APS 322, 425
97/8 APS 301
97/8 DS 36
98/9 DS 38
96/7 DS Sticker 163
98/9 OFS 56
89 Semic Sticker 189
91 Semic Sticker 123

VLK, VLADIMIR
00/1 DS 65
99/0 OFS 415
00/1 OFS 215

VLZEK, IVAN
95/6 Sisu 276, 384, DT-7
96/7 Sisu 72

VODAK, JIRI
96/7 APS 26

VODILA, JAN
89 Semic Sticker 192

VODRAZKA, JAN
95/6 Slapshot 72
99/0 Kansas City Blades
00/1 Kansas City Blades 2

VOEVODIN, NIKOLAI
00/1 Mir 92

VOGEL, ANTHONY
94/5 DEL 303
95/6 DEL 183
92 Semic Sticker 192

VOGEL, THOMAS
95/6 DEL 250

VOGEL, TONY
81/2 Regina Pats
82/3 Regina Pats
83/4 Regina Pats

VOGELTANZ, PETR
96/7 APS 94

VOHRALIK, KAREL
74 Hellas MM-Jenkki 84
73/4 Williams Finnish 62

VOIGT, BENJAMIN
01/2 UD DEL 259

VOISARD, GAETAN
91/2 Upper Deck 664
91/2 Upper Deck WJC 25

VOJTEK, MARTIN
01/2 OFS 130, -CL 9, -H4
99/0 Score 97

VOJTYNEK, HENRYK
74 Hellas MM-Jenkki 90
73/4 Williams Finnish 103

VOKES, JEREMY
01/2 Rockford IceHogs

VOKOUN, TOMÁN
01/2 DS 26

VOKOUN, TOMAS
01/2 Adrenaline 108
94/5 APS 48
00/1 BAP Mem. 394
01/2 BT Pipes 15, ✂ GSJ
02/3 Between the Pipes 36, 137, ✂ T11
02/3 Bowman 19
02/3 Calder ✂ GWJ 13
97/8 Donruss 209, RR-1
97/8 Do. Canadian 138
01/2 DS IH1
02/3 In The GU ✂ GP14
97/8 Leaf 157
99/0 Millenium 139, ✍ Aut. 139
99/0 NHL Power Play
98/9 Omega 133
99/0 Omega 129
99/0 Pacific 232
00/1 Pacific 227
01/2 Pacific 222
02/3 Pacific 215
02/3 Pacific Complete 332
00/1 Pa. Paramount 139
98/9 Pa. Revolution 81
02/3 Parkhurst Retro 191
97/8 Pi. Inside 72
02/3 Pr. Stock Titanium 61
02/3 Quest for the Cup 55
02/3 SP Authentic 50
02/3 Sports Vault 260
00/1 Stadium 122
99/0 Topps 72
99/0 To. Chrome 72
00/1 To. Heritage 212
01/2 To. Reserve ✂ TR
02/3 To. Total 370
00/1 UD Reserve 49
99/0 Upper Deck 245
00/1 Upper Deck 329
01/2 Upper Deck 329
02/3 Upper Deck 98
02/3 UD Artistic 51, R51, / Art
99/0 UD G. Reserve 245
02/3 UD Honor 43
02/3 UD Mask 48, 49
02/3 UD Rookie 57
99/0 Victory 163
01/2 Victory 204
98/9 NASH / Wendy's 22
96/7 Fredericton Canadiens

VOLAK, MILAN
94/5 APS 151
95/6 APS 258
96/7 APS 298
97/8 APS 185
97/8 DS 56
98/9 DS 63
97/8 DS 98
00/1 DS 33
96/7 DS Sticker 215
97/8 DS Sticker 159
98/9 OFS 45
00/1 OFS 69

VOLAK, MILANB
01/2 OFS 222

VOLCAN, MICKEY
83/4 O-Pee-Chee 94
90/1 ProCards 365
83/4 Souhaits Keychain [Whalers]
83/4 Vachon 20-140
82/3 HART / Jr. Whalers
84/5 Moncton G'Flames
85/6 Nova Scotia Oilers

VOLCHENKOV, ANTON
02/3 Atomic 120
02/3 BAP All-Star 140
02/3 BAP Mem. 296
02/3 Bowman 122, ✂ FFDS, ✂ FFJ, ✂ FFP, ✂ FFR, ✂ FFRP, ✂ FFS, ✂ FFTS, ✍ YSA, / ✍ Puck
02/3 Calder 134
02/3 Crown Royale 128
02/3 Exclusive 186
02/3 First Edition 434 [Retail]
02/3 Heads Up 126
02/3 In The GU 94, ✂ C17
00/1 Mir 47
00/1 Mir 302
02/3 Pacific Complete 574
02/3 Parkhurst 226
02/3 Parkhurst Retro 226
02/3 Pr. Stock Reserve 174
02/3 Pr. Stock Titanium 127
02/3 Quest for the Cup 134
02/3 Signature Series 198, ✍ 198
02/3 SP Authentic 162
02/3 SP GU Edition 86
02/3 SPx 163
02/3 T. Chrome 167
02/3 To. Heritage 154
02/3 To. Total 404
02/3 Ultimate Memorabilia 26, ✂ CC, ✍ RAut
02/3 Upper Deck 444
02/3 UD Artistic 103
02/3 UD Classic 122
02/3 UD Foundations 160
02/3 UD Honor 161
02/3 UD Mask 166
02/3 UD Piece 142
02/3 UD Premier 61, ✂ Jers
02/3 UD Rookie ✂ 161
02/3 UD Top Shelf 98
02/3 Vanguard 125
02/3 OTTA

VOLCHKOV, ALEXANDER (SR.)
91/2 Future Trends C72 59
74 Hellas MM-Jenkki 61
73/4 Soviet Stars 13
77-79 Sportscaster 103-08
73/4 Williams Finnish 21

VOLCHKOV, ALEXANDRE (JR.)
96/7 All-Sport PPF 73
96/7 Autograph Coll. 48, GB30
97 Bowman 12
99/0 Choice 11
95/6 Cla. Vis. Signings 62, ✍ Aut.
99/0 Dynagon Ice 205
95/6 Future Legends ✍ SSD-1
99/0 Omega 247
97/8 Portland Pirates
99/0 Portland Pirates
95/6 Slapshot 16, 431
99/0 SP Authentic 121
99/0 Upper Deck 303
99/0 UD Black Diam. 90
99/0 UD G. Reserve 303
99/0 WGretzky 178

VOLEK, DAVID
95/6 APS 270
90/1 Bowman 127
91/2 Bowman 223
92/3 Bowman 196
00/1 DS JT10
92/3 Fleer Ultra 350
90/1 OPC/Topps 300
91/2 O-Pee-Chee 488
92/3 O-Pee-Chee 3
89/0 OPC/Topps 72
89/0 opcSticker 113-250, 43-189, / FS 9
99/0 OFS 39
00/1 OFS 395
89/0 Panini Sticker 267
91/2 Panini Sticker 241
92/3 Panini Sticker 200
91/2 Parkhurst 104
92/3 Parkhurst 340
93/4 Parkhurst 395
94/5 Parkhurst 139
91/2 Pinnacle 198
92/3 Pinnacle 188
93/4 Pinnacle 423
93/4 Power Play 388
93/4 Premier 371
90/1 Pro Set 193
91/2 Pro Set 147
91/2 Pro Set Platinum 75
90/1 Score 12
91/2 Score 88
91/2 Score CAN 88
92/3 Score 166
93/4 Score 495
99/0 Score JT18
91 Semic Sticker 221
93 Semic Sticker 108
92/3 Topps 204
91/2 To. Stadium 204
92/3 To. Stadium 319
93/4 To. Stadium 324
90/1 Upper Deck 1
91/2 Upper Deck 89
92/3 Upper Deck 173
92/3 Upper Deck 313
93/4 Upper Deck 370
89/0 NYIS

VOLEK, MILAN
99/0 OFS 375

VÖLK, JOSEF
72 Hellas MM-Jenkki 45
72 Semic Sticker 96

VOLKOV, ALEXEI
99 Bowman 42
02/3 Russian Future Stars 16
99/0 UD Sobey's 1
98/9 SPx Prospects 78
99/0 Upper Deck 328
98/9 UD Black Diam. 104
99/0 UD Black Diam. 104
99/0 UD G. Reserve 328
99/0 UD Ovation 74
99/0 UD Prospects 58, IN4, ✍ Sig.
98/9 Halifax Moosehead [x2]
99/0 Halifax Mooseheads

VOLKOV, MIKHAIL
93/4 Cla. Prospects 104
00/1 Mir 262
91/2 Upper Deck WJC 5
93/4 Rochester Americans
95/6 Rochester Americans

VOLKOV, OLEG
00/1 Mir 360

VOLLAND, ANDREAS
94/5 DEL 188
95/6 DEL 188

VOLLHOFFER, TROY
88/9 ProCards / Muskegon
88/9 Flint Spirits
84/5 Saskatoon Blades

VOLLMER, JOCHEN
99/0 Eishockey 355

VOLMAR, DOUG
73/4 O-Pee-Chee 215

VOLOGJANINOV, IVAN
94/5 Slapshot Memorial 6
93/4 Lethbridge Hurricanes

VOLPE, MIKE
85/6 Kitchener Rangers

VOLSTAD, CRAIG
91/2 Air Canada SJHL C17

VOLTERA, ROB
02/3 Hershey Bears

VON ARX, RETO
00/1 BAP Mem. 459
01/2 BAP Mem. 215
00/1 Premier Plus 107
00/1 Signature 269, ✍ Aut. 231
00/1 SP Authentic 97
00/1 To. Heritage 79
00/1 Upper Deck 413
00/1 UD Prospects 79
00/1 UD Vintage 376

VON STEFENELLI, PHIL
98/9 DEL 145
99/0 Eishockey 142

VON STEFENELLI, PHIL
91/2 ProCards 604
96/7 Detroit Vipers
92/3 Hamilton Canucks

VON TRZCINSKI, CHRISTIAN
95/6 DEL 198

VONDRKA, MICHAL
00/1 OFS 27
01/2 OFS 142

VOPAT, JAN
94/5 APS 211
95/6 APS 362
95/6 Edge Ice 186
96/7 Fl. Ultra 83
96/7 Leaf 222
99/0 OFS 40
97/8 Pacific CC 271
98/9 Panini Sticker 137
95 Panini Worlds 193
96/7 Pinnacle 214
99/0 Score JT3
95 Semic 143
97/8 Upper Deck 79
98/9 Upper Deck 299
97/8 UD Coll. Choice 126
98/9 UD G. Reserve 299
99/0 Victory 164
96 Wien 108
98/9 NASH / Wendy's 23
95/6 Phoenix Roadrunners

VOPAT, JAN
92/3 Classic 36
94 Semic 171
92/3 Upper Deck 601
91/2 Upper Deck WJC 95

VOPAT, ROMAN
95/6 Bowman 139
00/1 Cardset 196
02/3 Cardset 292
95/6 Donruss 307
96/7 Donruss 216
97/8 Donruss 117
96/7 Fleer 135, CC-10
97/8 Leaf 69
97/8 Limited 129, 180
96/7 Metal Univ. 194
95/6 Parkhurst 447
97/8 Pi. Be A Player 103, ✍ Aut. 103
96/7 Score 252
94/5 Sig. Rookies 2, ✍ 2
94/5 SR Gold Standard 97
95/6 SBx Impact 219
96/7 SBx Impact 162
99/0 Stadium 39
95/6 Upper Deck 440
97/8 Upper Deck 78
97/8 UD Coll. Choice 124
95/6 Prince Albert Raiders

VORDERBRUGGEN, REINER
94/5 DEL 335

VOREL, MAREK
95/6 APS 346
97/8 APS 73
99/0 DS 193
98/9 OFS 173
99/0 OFS 85
00/1 OFS 205
01/2 OFS 264

VORLICEK, FRANTISEK
94/5 APS 295
95/6 APS 174
96/7 APS 309

VOROBIEV, ALEXEI
00/1 Mir 99

VOROBIEV, ILJA
94/5 DEL 109
96/7 DEL 57
98/9 DEL 136
00/1 UD DEL 147

VOROBIEV, ILYA
99/0 Eishockey 129

VOROBIEV, PAVEL
00/1 Mir 295

VOROBIEV, PIOTR
94/5 DEL 103
95/6 DEL 100

VOROBIEV, VLADIMIR
97/8 Donruss 210
97/8 Do. Canadian 139
97/8 Limited 97, 121, 197
00/1 Mir 235
98/9 Pacific 304
97/8 Pinnacle 188
97/8 Pi. Inside 123
97/8 Score 75
97/8 Score NYRa. 13
97/8 UD Coll. Choice 164
96/7 Binghampton Rangers
99/0 Hamilton Bulldogs
97/8 Hartford Wolf Pack
98/9 Hartford Wolf Pack

VORONOV, SERGEI
98/9 Mir 142
00/1 Mir 105, 278
95/6 Hampton Roads

VOROSHNIN, PAVEL
02/3 Mississauga IceDogs

VOS, RALPH
96/7 DEL 222

VOSHELL, TOD
83/4 Kelowna Wings

VOSKAR, JOZEF
00/1 DS 144
00/1 OFS 126

VOSKERTIAN, CHRISTIAN
79 Panini Sticker 342

VOSS, CARL
34-43 BeeHive-1 [Detr.]
35-40 Canada Starch
36-39 Diamond Match TT1
36-39 Diamond Match TT2
36-39 Diamond Match TT3
83 HHOF Postcard O16
83&87 HHOF 225
37/8 O-Pee-Chee 175
37/8 World Wide Gum 66

VOSSEN, DALE
91/2 7th...Sketch WHL 236

VOSSEN, JAMIE
95/6 Slapshot 211

VOSTA, ONDREJ
94/5 APS 108
95/6 APS 69
96/7 APS 256
97/8 APS 281
97/8 DS Sticker 79

VOSTRAK, PAVEL
96/7 APS 308
97/8 APS 186
02/3 Cardset 143
98/9 DS 60
99/0 DS 94
00/1 DS 31
01/2 DS 23
96/7 DS Sticker 224
98/9 OFS 46
99/0 OFS 130
00/1 OFS 67
01/2 OFS 221, -UHI 40

VOSTRAKA, PAVEL
97/8 DS Sticker 163

VOSTRIKOV, SERGEI
99/0 Eishockey 152
91/2 O-Pee-Chee 27R
00/1 UD DEL 16, A4
01/2 UD DEL 15, GA1

VOTH, BRAD
01/2 Peoria Rivermen
02/3 Peoria Rivermen
01/2 Worcester IceCats
99/0 Medicine Hat Tigers
00/1 Medicine Hat Tigers

VOUTILAINEN, JUKKA
02/3 Cardset 293, -DD 5, -Nimik.

VOZAR, PATRICK
94/5 DEL 122
95/6 DEL 122

VOZDECKY, MARTIN
99/0 OFS 68

VOZKA, TOMAS
99/0 Score 76

VRABEC, THOMAS
91 Semic Sticker 200
92 Semic Sticker 215

VRATARIC, RICH
95/6 Slapshot 196

VRBATA, DAVID
00/1 Calgary Hitmen

VRBATA, RADIM
01/2 BAP Mem. 338
02/3 BAP Mem. 193, 379
99 Bowman 21, ✍ BA20
01/2 Bowman 137
02/3 Bowman 130
02/3 Exclusive 48, -GE 5
02/3 First Edition 212
02/3 O-Pee-Chee 83
02/3 Pacific 98, -SM 4
02/3 Pacific Complete 375
01/2 PTC Collectibles 4
01/2 PTC Rookie 4
01/2 Parkhurst 351
02/3 Parkhurst 162
02/3 Parkhurst Retro 194
02/3 Pr. Stock Reserve 29
01/2 PS Titanium 38, TSS 25, TRT 5
01/2 PS Titanium Draft 117
02/3 Signature Series 60, ✍ 60
02/3 SP Authentic 113
01/2 SPx 170
99/0 Topps 256
02/3 Topps 83, Aut- SF
99/0 To. Chrome 256
02/3 T. Chrome 52, ✍ Graph
02/3 To. Heritage 78
02/3 To. Limited 83
02/3 To. Total 61, ✍ Sig
02/3 Upper Deck 44
01/2 UD Ice 91
00/1 UD Prospects 86, FL9
02/3 Victory 51
01/2 Hershey Bears
99/0 Hull Olympiques BN
99/0 Hull Olympiques 12
00/1 Shawinigan 10

VRIES, GREG
02/3 To. Total 244

VRLA, DANIEL
94/5 APS 232
95/6 APS 11

VUJTEK, VLADIMIR
02/3 Cardset 144

VUJTEK, VLADIMIR (JR.)
94/5 APS 131
95/6 APS 303, 409
96/7 APS 431
97/8 APS 362
98/9 DS 5
00/1 DS 7, NT4
93/4 EDMO / Sheet
92/3 EDMO
92/3 EDMO / IGA 022
93/4 Fleer Ultra 319
94/5 Fleer Ultra 293
98/9 OFS 119, 349, 430
99/0 OFS 402, 492
00/1 OFS 210, 302
01/2 OFS -UHI 41
93/4 Parkhurst 339
92/3 Pinnacle 396
97/8 Pi. Be A Player 113, ✍ Aut. 113
93/4 Power Play 343
93/4 Premier 459
94/5 Premier 503
93/4 Score 465
91/2 7th...Sketch WHL 303
93/4 To. Stadium 278
92/3 Upper Deck 417
92/3 Upper Deck 496
93/4 Upper Deck 168

VUJTEK, VLADIMIR (SR.)
94/5 APS 293
95/6 APS 27, 422
96/7 APS 189
97/8 APS 123
99/0 OFS 221

VUKONICH, MIKE
92/3 Classic 110
92/3 Classic Four Sport 219
91/2 ProCards 391
98/9 Indianapolis Ice
92/3 Phoenix Roadrunners

VUKOTA, MICK
84/5 Kelowna Wings &...
90/1 OPC/Topps 10
91/2 O-Pee-Chee 25
98/9 Pacific 259
94/5 Parkie SE101
97/8 Pi. Be A Player 56, ✍ Aut. 56
90/1 Pro Set 488
91/2 Score CAN 387
92/3 Score 549
91/2 To. Stadium 309
90/1 Upper Deck 39
91/2 Upper Deck 135
95/6 Upper Deck 380
97/8 MONT
89/0 NYIS
96/7 NYIS
99/0 Utah Grizzlies
99/0 Utah Grizzlies

VUKOTA, MICK
02/3 Fleer Throwbacks 83

VUKOUKAL, JIRI
96 Wien 107

VUKOVIC, NICK
00/1 Owen Sound Attack 20

VUORELA, JANNE
98/9 Cardset 213
99/0 Cardset 121
00/1 Cardset 329

VUORI, ARI
92/3 Jyvas Hyva 187
93/4 Jyvas Hyva 319
89 Semic Sticker 49
93/4 Sisu 51
93/4 Sisu 357
93/4 Sisu 358
94/5 Sisu 109
95/6 Sisu 191

VUORINEN, JARMO
80/1 Mallasjuoma 22

VUORINEN, JUKKA-PEKKA
78/9 SM-Liiga 108

VUORINEN, TEEMU
94/5 Sisu 222
95/6 Sisu 234
96/7 Sisu 28

VUORIO, JARI
80/1 Mallasjuoma 67

VUORIO, MATTI
93/4 Sisu 282

VUORIVIRTA, JUHA
98/9 Cardset 218
97/8 Hockey-Box
94/5 Sig. Rookies 29, ✍ 29
94/5 Sisu 290
95/6 Sisu 120, DD-10
94/5 Topps Finest 141

VUOTI, ARTO
94/5 Sisu 204

VYAZMIKIN, IGOR
98/9 Mir 151

VYBORNY, DAVID
95/6 APS 280
96/7 APS 135, 358
97/8 APS 361
00/1 BAP Mem. 410
01/2 BAP Mem. 108
02/3 BAP Mem. 79
93/4 Classic 48
94/5 Classic 77
00/1 Crown Royale 121
98/9 DS 11
99/0 DS 147, NS21
00/1 DS WCH10
01/2 DS 43, -IH9
96/7 DS Sticker 11, 71
01/2 O-Pee-Chee 195
02/3 O-Pee-Chee 221
98/9 OFS 137, 427, 456
99/0 OFS 113, 275, 493
01/2 Pacific 119
02/3 Pacific 108
02/3 Pacific Complete 186
01/2 Parkhurst 154
00/1 Pr. Stock 114, PSR-7
00/1 PS Titanium 115
00/1 PS Titanium Draft 115
94 Semic 185
95 Semic 148
01/2 Signature 131, ✍ Aut. 131
01/2 Topps 195, OTG20
02/3 Topps 221
00/1 To. Chrome 230
01/2 To. Heritage 105
02/3 To. Limited 221
02/3 To. Total 23
00/1 UD Heroes 36
92/3 Upper Deck 600
01/2 Upper Deck 280
00/1 UD Black Diam. 95
97/8 UD Elitserien 165
02/3 UD Vintage 72
00/1 Vanguard 115
01/2 Victory 99
01/2 COLU
94/5 Cape Breton Oilers

VYBORNY, FRANTISEK
94/5 APS 283
95/6 APS 267
98/9 OFS 361
99/0 OFS 394
00/1 OFS 288

VYBORNY, MARTIN
01/2 OFS 210
99/0 Score 75

VYDARENY, RENÉ
02/3 Manitoba Moose
99/0 Rimouski Océanic 13

VYHLIDAL, MICHAEL
94/5 APS 189
95/6 APS 179
96/7 APS 315
97/8 APS 293
97/8 DS 35
98/9 DS 66
99/0 DS 45
00/1 DS 147
96/7 DS Sticker 153
97/8 DS Sticker 109
98/9 OFS 316
99/0 OFS 249
00/1 OFS 266
01/2 OFS 247, -UHI 8

VYKOUKAL, JIRI
95/6 APS 271, 360, 424
96/7 APS 123, 346, 387
97/8 APS 24, 347
98/9 Cardset 10
99/0 Cardset 8
00/1 Cardset 7
02/3 Cardset 145
97/8 DS 6
96/7 DS Sticker 3, 61
97/8 DS Sticker 12, 209
95 Globe 152
94/5 Leaf Elit Set 279, FA-6
98/9 OFS 421
99/0 OFS 276
95 Panini Worlds 195
99/0 Score N 5

VYKOUKAL, JIRÍ
90/1 ProCards 214
91/2 ProCards 562

VYMAZAL, MARTIN
00/1 Red Deer Rebels
00/1 Saskatoon Blades

VYSHEDKEVICH, SERGEI
00/1 BAP Mem. 252
00/1 Mir Fetisov 12
00/1 Pacific 28
00/1 Signature 274, ✍ Aut. 150
00/1 SPx 112
00/1 Topps 298
00/1 To. Chrome 193
00/1 Upper Deck 217
96/7 Albany River Rats
97/8 Albany River Rats
98/9 Albany River Rats

VYSKOCIL, TOMAS
99/0 Score 71

VYTISK, JAN
99/0 OFS 234
00/1 OFS 249
01/2 OFS 43

VYUKHIN, ALEXANDER
98/9 Mir 126
99/0 Mir 258
00/1 Mir 223

W

WADDELL, DON
91/2 ProCards 332
87/8 Flint Spirits
88/9 Flint Spirits

WADE, RYAN
98/9 Kelowna Rockets

WADEL, JASON
91/2 7th...Sketch OHL 238

WAGAR, BLAIR
91/2 Air Canada SJHL A41

WAGER, ROMAN
91 Semic Sticker 193
93 Semic Sticker 123

WAGHORN, GRAHAM
94 Semic 317

WAGHORNE, FRED C.
83 HHOF Postcard H15
83&87 HHOF 119

WAGNER, BERND
94/5 DEL 250
91 Semic Sticker 161

WAGNER, THOMAS
94/5 DEL 403
95/6 DEL 422

WAHL, GREG
91/2 Air Canada SJHL C33
92/3 MPS SJHL 138

WAHL, HENRIK
70/1 Kuvajulkaisut 289

WAHLBERG, MIKAEL
98/9 DEL 171
99/0 Eishockey 58
94/5 Leaf Elit Set 163
95/6 Leaf Elit Set 21
92/3 Semic Elitserien 65
95/6 UD Elitserien 30

WAHLSTEN,
97/8 Hockey-Box

WAHLSTEN, JALI
92/3 Jyvas Hyva 67
93/4 Jyvas Hyva 118
93 Semic Sticker 86
93/4 Sisu 19

WAHLSTEN, JUHANI
66/7 Champion 78
65/6 Hellas 8

WAHLSTEN, SAMI
94 Semic 45
93 Semic Sticker 87
94/5 Sisu 308

WAHLSTEN, VEIJO
73/4 Williams Finnish 302

WAIBEL, HARALD
94/5 DEL 308
95/6 DEL 145

WAINIO, PATRIK
78/9 SM-Liiga 66

WAITE, JIMMY
98/9 Be A Player 260, ✍ Aut. 260
91/2 Bowman 396
92/3 Bowman 120
93/4 Donruss 302
93/4 Durivage 49
93/4 EA Sports 200
93/4 Fleer Ultra 419
93/4 Leaf 324
94/5 Leaf 405
90/1 OPC/Topps 214
91/2 O-Pee-Chee 127
98/9 Omega 191
98/9 Pacific 346
98/9 Pa. Revolution 114
92/3 Parkhurst 270
93/4 Parkhurst 181
94/5 Parkhurst 214
91/2 Pinnacle 316
93/4 Pinnacle 371
94/5 Pinnacle MA9
93/4 Power Play 438
93/4 Premier 388
94/5 Premier 496
91/2 Pro Set 530
89/0 ProCards IHL 73
90/1 ProCards 401
90/1 Score 407
91/2 Score 82T
91/2 Score CAN 632
93/4 Score 365
94/5 Score 539
92/3 Topps 100
92/3 To. Stadium 35
91/2 Upper Deck 443
92/3 Upper Deck 67
93/4 Upper Deck 501
94/5 UD BAP ✍ 126
01/2 UD DEL 74, ✂ GJ
88/9 CHIC / Coke
91/2 CHIC / Coke
97/8 PHOE / Coca-Cola
98/9 PHOE / Coca-Cola
92/3 SANJ / Pacific Bell
95/6 Indianapolis Ice
99/0 St. John's Maple Leafs
00/1 St. John's Maple Leafs

WAKALUK, DARCY
91/2 Bowman 33
92/3 Bowman 148
94/5 Cla. Images PL9
93/4 Donruss 420
94/5 Donruss 17
92/3 Fleer Ultra 99
94/5 Fleer Ultra 282
95/6 Fleer Ultra 231
84/5 Kelowna Wings &...
94/5 Leaf 152
92/3 O-Pee-Chee 63
94/5 Panini Sticker 234
91/2 Parkhurst 306
92/3 Parkhurst 315
95/6 Parkhurst 331
94/5 Parkie SE44
94/5 Pinnacle 157
93/4 Power Play 327
93/4 Premier 399
94/5 Premier 81, 424
88/9 ProCards / Rochester
89/0 ProCards AHL 258
90/1 ProCards 288
91/2 Score CAN 653
92/3 Score 313
93/4 Score 432
95/6 Score 197
96/7 Score 210
92/3 Topps 108
95/6 Topps 313
95/6 To. Finest 156
92/3 To. Stadium 153
93/4 To. Stadium 276
94/5 To. Stadium 187
94/5 Upper Deck 459
95/6 UD BAP 90, ✍ S90
94/5 DALL / Southwest
94/5 DALL / Cap
96/7 PHOE / Coca-Cola
97/8 PHOE / Coca-Cola
83/4 Kelowna Wings

WAKEFIELD, LANCE
91/2 Air Canada SJHL D50

WAKELY, ERNIE
70/1 Colgate 92
70/1 Eddie Sargent 181
70/1 Esso Power Player
70/1 O-Pee-Chee 97
71/2 O-Pee-Chee 81
75/6 OPC WHA 132
76/7 OPC WHA 92
73/4 Quaker Oats 41
70/1 Topps 97
71/2 Topps 81
71/2 Toronto Sun Photo
71/2 SLOU
76/7 San Diego Mariners

WAKLEY, ERNIE
71/2 Eddie Sargent 185
72/3 Post 12

WALBERG, TORE
79 Panini Sticker 294

WALBY, STEFFON
92/3 BCJHL 61
92/3 BCJHL 246
93/4 Cla. Prospects 97
97/8 Fort Wayne Komets
00/1 Hershey Bears
98/9 Rochester Americans
93/4 St. John's Maple Leafs
94/5 St. John's Maple Leafs
95/6 St. John's Maple Leafs

WALBYE,
92/3 Semic Nordisk 198 [Draften Av NHL]

WALBYE, KNUT
92/3 Semic Nordisk 40

WALBYE, PER O
92/3 Semic Nordisk 45

WALCH, SHAWN
93/4 Classic 59

WALCOT, BRAD
82/3 Kingston Canadians
83/4 Oshawa Generals
85/6 Sudbury Wolves

WALCOTT, RICHIE
91/2 ProCards 564
99/0 Asheville Smoke
98/9 Fort Worth Brahmas
93/4 Hampton Roads

WALDER, RAYMOND
91 Semic Sticker 191
92 Semic Sticker 205

WALITALO, GÖTE
82 Semic Sticker 2

WALKER, CHAD
83/4 Kelowna Wings

WALKER, DARBY
00/1 Kudos 85
91/2 7th...Sketch WHL 312

WALKER, GORD
84/5 Kamloops Blazers

WALKER, GORDIE
88/9 ProCards / New Haven
89/0 ProCards AHL 22

WALKER, HOWARD
82/3 O-Pee-Chee 59
80/1 WASH
81/2 WASH

WALKER, JACK
83 HHOF Postcard E16
83&87 HHOF 75
94/5 Legends 47

WALKER, JEFF
89/0 7th..Sketch OHL 148
90/1 7th..Sketch OHL 272
91/2 7th...Sketch OHL 133
89/0 Niagara Falls Thunder
91/2 Peterborough Petes

WALKER, JOHNNY
94/5 DEL 242
95/6 DEL 236
96/7 DEL 87
98/9 DEL 23
99/0 Eishockey 138
88/9 ProCards / Utica
00/1 UD DEL 78
01/2 UD DEL 90

WALKER, JORDAN
99/0 Kamloops Blazers
99/0 Kamloops Blazers

WALKER, KELLY
85/6 U. of Arizona Ice Cats

WALKER, KURT
78/9 O-Pee-Chee 282
76/7 TORO
77/8 TORO

WALKER, MATT
02/3 BAP Mem. 311
02/3 Calder 142
02/3 Pacific Complete 565
02/3 Parkhurst Retro 212
02/3 Quest for the Cup 143
02/3 SP Authentic 165
02/3 Ultimate Memorabilia 60
02/3 UD Honor 142
00/1 Worcester IceCats
01/2 Worcester IceCats
02/3 Worcester IceCats
97/8 Portland Winter Hawks

WALKER, SCOTT
01/2 Adrenaline 109
01/2 Atomic ✂ GWJ 36
99/0 Aurora 82
98/9 Be A Player 224, ✍ Aut. 224
01/2 BAP Mem. 113
95/6 Bowman 143
93/4 Cla. Prospects 165
01/2 Crown Royale 83, ✂ TT 16
95/6 Donruss 303
99/0 Dynagon Ice 112
95/6 Edge Ice 90
01/2 Heads Up ✂ JQ 13
02/3 Heads Up ✂ GWQ 16
95/6 Leaf 108
98/9 Pacific 435
99/0 Pacific 233
00/1 Pacific 228
01/2 Pacific 223
02/3 Pacific 216
02/3 Pacific Complete 140
97/8 Pa. Invincible R-205
98/9 Pa. Paramount 129
99/0 Pa. Paramount 129
98/9 Panini Sticker 142
99/0 Panini Sticker 266
95/6 Parkhurst 484
00/1 Parkhurst P-174
01/2 Parkhurst 127
97/8 Pi. Be A Player 33, ✍ Aut. 33
02/3 PS Titanium ✂ GWJ 38
00/1 PS Titanium Draft ✂ 58
99/0 Revolution 82
91/2 7th...Sketch OHL 274
00/1 Signature 4, ✍ Aut. 43
01/2 Signature 64, ✍ Aut. 64
02/3 Signature Series 37, GS-85, ✍ 37
00/1 To. Heritage 194
02/3 To. Total 218
95/6 Upper Deck 418
96/7 Upper Deck 351
01/2 Upper Deck 326
01/2 UD Challenge 49
01/2 UD MVP 108
00/1 UD Vintage 205
01/2 UD Vintage 142, 148
02/3 Vanguard ✂ GWJ 26
01/2 Victory 196
98/9 NASH / Wendy's 24
96/7 VANC / IGA
93/4 Owen Sound Platers

WALKER, STEVE
98/9 EBK IHL All-Star
00/1 UD DEL 67
01/2 UD DEL 45
96/7 Detroit Vipers
97/8 Detroit Vipers
98/9 Detroit Vipers
99/0 Detroit Vipers
94/5 Muskegon Fury
95/6 Muskegon Fury

WALKER, TODD
91/2 7th...Sketch OHL 9
91/2 Cornwall Royals

WALKER, WILDMAN
92/3 Cincinnati Cyclones
93/4 Cincinnati Cyclones

WALKINGTON, TROY
00/1 Kudos 50

WALL, BOB
64-67 BeeHive-3 [Detr.]
70/1 Dad's Cookies
70/1 Eddie Sargent 191
71/2 Eddie Sargent 50
70/1 Esso Power Player
68/9 O-Pee-Chee 145
69/0 O-Pee-Chee 140, 4in1
70/1 O-Pee-Chee 98
72/3 O-Pee-Chee 323
68/9 Shirriff / LosA. 3
66/7 Topps 49
70/1 Topps 98

WALL, KYOSTI
65/6 Hellas 62

WALLACE, BRUCE
52/3 Anonymous 58

WALLACE, GREG
85/6 Kamloops Blazers

WALLACE, SPIKE
96/7 Kamloops Blazers

WALLENBERG, PATRIK
98/9 Cardset 181
95/6 Upper Deck 563
95/6 UD CC 352
95/6 UD Elitserien 70
97/8 UD Elitserien 66
00/1 UD Elitserien 162

WALLENBURG, PATRICK
01/2 Nottingham Panthers

WALLENIUS, JUHANI
80/1 Mallasjuoma 131
78/9 SM-Liiga 173

WALLIN, C-G
91/2 Semic Elitserien 311

WALLIN, DANIEL
99/0 UD Elitserien 101

WALLIN, ESA
80/1 Mallasjuoma 122

WALLIN, JESSE
01/2 BAP Mem. 228
95/6 Bowman P35
97 Bowman 104
02/3 Calder 67
01/2 Pacific 160
02/3 Pacific Complete 552
00/1 Pa. Paramount 91
98/9 UD Choice 262
96/7 UD Ice 128
99/0 Cincinnati M'Ducks
95/6 Red Deer Rebels

WALLIN, JUSTIN
00/1 Red Deer Rebels
00/1 Saskatoon Blades

WALLIN, MAGNUS
89/0 Semic Elitserien 257

WALLIN, MATS
89/0 Semic Elitserien 57
90/1 Semic Elitserien 85

WALLIN, NICLAS
00/1 BAP Mem. 419
01/2 BAP Mem. 280
02/3 Pacific Complete 484
00/1 Premier Plus 132
00/1 PS Titanium Draft 156
00/1 Stadium 243
00/1 To. Stars 103
00/1 Upper Deck 421
02/3 Upper Deck 30
97/8 UD Elitserien 25
98/9 UD Elitserien 39
99/0 UD Elitserien 23
01/2 UD MVP 192
02/3 UD Vintage 47

WALLIN, PER
94/5 Leaf Elit Set 21
95/6 Leaf Elit Set 118
90/1 Semic Elitserien 24
91/2 Semic Elitserien 218
92/3 Semic Elitserien 270

WALLIN, PETER
95/6 Leaf Elit Set 161, R-1
89/0 Semic Elitserien 129
94/5 SR Auto-Phonex 40, ✍ 40
95/6 SR Tetrad Autobilia 54
95/6 UD CC 354
95/6 UD Elitserien 177

WALLIN, RICKARD
02/3 BAP Mem. 338
02/3 Parkhurst 228
02/3 Parkhurst Retro 220
02/3 SP Authentic 164
02/3 Ultimate Memorabilia 69
02/3 UD Artistic 113
02/3 UD Honor 143
02/3 UD Premier 58

WALLINHEIMO, SINUHE
98/9 Cardset 163, MM 8, OD 8
00/1 UD DEL 210
01/2 UD DEL 224, G10, ✂ GJ

WALLWORK, BOBBY
91/2 Cincinnati Cyclones
95/6 Muskegon Fury

WALSER, DERRICK
02/3 Bowman 164
97 Bowman 68
98 Bowman 119
98 Bowman Chrome 119
98/9 Bowman's Best 144
98/9 OPC Chrome 229
98/9 Topps 229
01/2 Syracuse Crunch
96/7 Rimouski Océanic
97/8 Rimouski Océanic

WALSH,
91/2 Avant Garde BCJHL 160

WALSH, FLAT
29/0 La Presse

WALSH, GORD
95/6 Classic 86
93/4 Slapshot / Kingston 7
95/6 Slapshot 112

WALSH, JONATHAN
00/1 Baie-Comeau 1

WALSH, KURT
95/6 Bowman P36
95/6 Slapshot 249, 304, 437

WALSH, MARTY
91 C55 Reprint 11
83 HHOF Postcard F15
83&87 HHOF 89
10/1 Imperial
10/1 Imperial 7
11/2 Imperial 11
12/3 Imperial 49

WALSH, MICHAEL
96 Québec Pee Wee 1113

WALSH, MIKE
88/9 ProCards / Springfield
89/0 ProCards AHL 230
91/2 ProCards 52

WALSH, RYAN
00/1 Toronto St. Mike's

WALSH, TREVOR
90/1 7th..Sketch OHL 194
89/0 Windsor Spitfires

WALTER, JAROSLAV
95/6 APS 198

WALTER, RYAN
83/4 Funmate Puffy 3 [w/]
84/5 Kelowna Wings &...
86/7 Kraft Sports 41
79/0 O-Pee-Chee 236
80/1 O-Pee-Chee 154
81/2 O-Pee-Chee 352
82/3 O-Pee-Chee 194
83/4 O-Pee-Chee 200
84/5 O-Pee-Chee 275
86/7 O-Pee-Chee 224
87/8 O-Pee-Chee 231
88/9 O-Pee-Chee 262
90/1 OPC/Topps 296
89/0 O-Pee-Chee 240
81/2 OPC Sticker 192
82/3 OPC/Topps Sticker 152
83/4 OPC/Topps Sticker 62
83/4 OPC/Topps Sticker 63
84/5 OPC Sticker 159
87/8 OPC Sticker 17-157
88/9 OPC Sticker 40-171
88/9 Panini Sticker 262
89/0 Panini Sticker 15
90/1 Panini/MTL 24
91/2 Parkhurst 401
92/3 Pinnacle 255
82/3 Post [Wash.]
90/1 Pro Set 475
91/2 Pro Set 504
91/2 Score 41T
91/2 Score CAN 591
79/0 Topps 236
80/1 Topps 154
81/2 Topps 122 [East]
93/4 To. Stadium 185
02/3 UD Foundations 56
83/4 Vachon 58-78
82/3 MONT
82/3 MONT / Steinberg
83/4 MONT
84/5 MONT
85/6 MONT
85/6 MONT / Provigo
86/7 MONT
87/8 MONT
87/8 MONT / Vachon 24, 25
88/9 MONT
89/0 MONT
89/0 MONT / Kraft
90/1 MONT
91/2 VANC
91/2 VANC / Photo
92/3 VANC / Road Trip
78/9 WASH
79/0 WASH
80/1 WASH
81/2 WASH

WALTERS, GREG
90/1 ProCards 147
91/2 ProCards 349
89/0 7th..Sketch OHL 50
99/0 Houston Aeros
90/1 Newmarket Saints
96/7 Rochester Americans
97/8 Rochester Americans
98/9 Rochester Americans

WALTERS, RON
72/3 O-Pee-Chee 301

WALTERS, S.
28/9 Paulins Candy 69

WALTERSON, IAN
99/0 Greensboro Generals

WALTIN, MATS
79 Panini Sticker 188
74 Semic Sticker 18
82 Semic Sticker 6

WALTON, JOHN
98/9 Cincinnati M'Ducks 4

WALTON, MIKE
64-67 BeeHive-3 [Toro.]
65/6 Coca-Cola
70/1 Colgate 3
70/1 Dad's Cookies
70/1 Eddie Sargent 206
71/2 Eddie Sargent 12
72/3 Eddie Sargent 24
70/1 Esso Power Player
68/9 O-Pee-Chee 132
69/0 O-Pee-Chee 50
69/0 O-Pee-Chee 4in1
70/1 O-Pee-Chee 109
71/2 O-Pee-Chee 171
72/3 O-Pee-Chee 94
76/7 O-Pee-Chee 23
77/8 O-Pee-Chee 350
78/9 O-Pee-Chee 38
74/5 OPC WHA 10
75/6 OPC WHA 26
73/4 OPC WHA Poster 15
95/6 Parkie 66-67 101
68/9 Post Marble
68/9 Shirriff / Toro. 5
65/6 Topps 86
66/7 Topps 14
66/7 Topps / Test 14
67/8 Topps 15
68/9 Topps 132
69/0 Topps 50
70/1 Topps 109
76/7 Topps 23
78/9 Topps 38
71/2 Toronto Sun Photo
67/8 York 13
67/8 York 23
67/8 York
67/8 York
67/8 York
71/2 BOST
69/0 TORO
70/1 TORO
76/7 VANC / Royal Bank
77/8 VANC / Royal Bank
74/5 Minn. Fight. Saints

WALTZE, KRIS
99/0 San Angelo Outlaws
97/8 Spokane Chiefs

WALZ, WES
01/2 Adrenaline 95
01/2 BAP Mem. 156
91/2 Bowman 353
93/4 Donruss 57
94/5 Donruss 319
93/4 Fleer Ultra 287
94/5 Fleer Ultra 37
93/4 Leaf 393
94/5 Leaf 154
91/2 O-Pee-Chee 134
90/1 OPC Premier 127
01/2 Pacific 201
02/3 Pacific 188
02/3 Pacific Complete 79
93/4 Parkhurst 305
94/5 Parkhurst 38
01/2 Parkhurst 108
94/5 POG 62
94/5 Premier 137
90/1 Pro Set 589
91/2 ProCards 48
90/1 Score 418
91/2 Score CAN 430
01/2 Signature 78, ✍ Aut. 78
00/1 To. Gold Label 95
91/2 To. Stadium 325
02/3 To. Total 98
90/1 Upper Deck 527
91/2 Upper Deck 123
93/4 Upper Deck 431
94/5 Upper Deck 350
01/2 Upper Deck 315
02/3 Upper Deck 86
01/2 UD MVP 93
02/3 UD MVP 92
01/2 UD Vintage 127, 130
01/2 Victory 173
02/3 Victory 105
90/1 BOST / Sports Action
01/2 MINW
95/6 Adirondack Red Wings
88/9 Lethbridge Hurricanes
89/0 Lethbridge Hurricanes

WAMSLEY, RICK
90/1 Bowman 98
91/2 Bowman 268
92/3 Bowman 97
83/4 Dernière Heure
82/3 McDonald's Les Étoiles 5
82/3 O-Pee-Chee 195
83/4 O-Pee-Chee 201
86/7 O-Pee-Chee 240
87/8 OPC/Topps 65
90/1 O-Pee-Chee 409
91/2 O-Pee-Chee 459
92/3 O-Pee-Chee 310
89/0 O-Pee-Chee 204
82/3 OPC/Topps Sticker 37
82/3 OPC/Topps Sticker 252
83/4 OPC/Topps Sticker 72
84/5 OPC Sticker 157
86/7 OPC Sticker 179-43
87/8 OPC Sticker 22-163
89/0 opcSticker 93-232
87/8 Panini Sticker 305
90/1 Panini Sticker 186
90/1 Panini/CGY 24
91/2 Parkhurst 394
90/1 Pro Set 48
91/2 Pro Set 367
91/2 Score CAN 232
92/3 Topps 425
91/2 To. Stadium 294
92/3 To. Stadium 53
90/1 Upper Deck 10
91/2 Upper Deck 120
83/4 Vachon 58-78
90/1 CALG / McGavin's
91/2 CALG / IGA
81/2 MONT
82/3 MONT
82/3 MONT / Steinberg
83/4 MONT
87/8 SLOU / Kodak

WANCHUK, MIKE
77/8 Kalamazoo Wings

WANDLER, BRYCE
00/1 Charlotte Checkers

WANDLER, DION
99/0 San Angelo Outlaws

WANHAINEN, ROLF
92/3 Upper Deck 223

WANNSTROM, JORGEN
89/0 Semic Elitserien 212

WANSBOROUGH, SHAWN
98/9 Las Vegas Thunder
98/9 Orlando Solar Bears

WANVIG, KYLE
99 Bowman 7, ✂ BA27
02/3 Calder 74
02/3 Choice Prospects 43
02/3 Crown Royale 120
02/3 Pacific Complete 591
02/3 Pr. Stock Titanium 121
98/9 SP Authentic 133
98/9 Upper Deck 410
98/9 UD G. Reserve 410
00/1 Red Deer Rebels

WARD, AARON
93/4 Classic 85
94/5 Classic ✍ Aut.
94/5 Cla. Images 98, ✍ Aut.
93/4 Cla. Prospects 120
93/4 Donruss 93
95/6 Edge Ice 5
93/4 Leaf 359
94/5 Leaf 312
99/0 Millenium 92, ✍ Aut. 92
99/0 Pacific 150
01/2 Pacific 151
02/3 Pacific Complete 458
97/8 Pa. Invincible R-74
93/4 Parkhurst 262
95/6 Parkhurst 71
93/4 Pinnacle 432
97/8 Pi. BAP 200, ✍ 200
93/4 Premier 484
94/5 Score 229
93/4 To. Stadium 423
93/4 Upper Deck 479
94/5 Upper Deck 293
95/6 Upper Deck 552
97/8 Upper Deck 270
95/6 Adirondack Red Wings

WARD, BLAKE
99/0 UD Prospects 48, 89

WARD, CALEB
94/5 Slapshot / Windsor 23
95/6 Slapshot 26

WARD, COLIN
00/1 Kudos 27
01/2 Belfast Giants
92/3 W. Michigan Broncos
93/4 W. Michigan Broncos

WARD, DIXON
98/9 Aurora 21
98/9 Be A Player 16, ✍ Aut. 16
92/3 Classic 84
93/4 Donruss 449
92/3 Fleer Ultra 431
93/4 Fleer Ultra 102
93/4 Leaf 97
99/0 Millenium 36, ✍ Aut. 36
01/2 O-Pee-Chee 256
92/3 OPC Premier 67
98/9 Omega 29
98/9 Pacific 112
99/0 Pacific 42
97/8 Pa. Invincible R-24
98/9 Pa. Paramount 24
99/0 Pa. Paramount 32
98/9 Pa. Revolution 17
92/3 Parkhurst 194
93/4 Parkhurst 209
94/5 Parkhurst 192
93/4 Pinnacle 176
94/5 Pinnacle 239
96/7 Pi. Be A Player 130, ✍ Aut. 130
93/4 Power Play 257
93/4 Power Play 365
93/4 Premier 127
93/4 Premier 58
94/5 Premier 112
99/0 Revolution 21
93/4 Score 210
93/4 Score 654
97/8 Score Buff. 3
99/0 Stadium 57
01/2 Topps 256
93/4 To. Stadium 454
92/3 Upper Deck 580
92/3 Upper Deck CC1
94/5 Upper Deck 62, SP-167
97/8 Upper Deck 21
99/0 Upper Deck 25
99/0 UD G. Reserve 25
99/0 UD MVP 27
99/0 Victory 36
92/3 VANC / Road Trip
95/6 Rochester Americans

WARD, ED
95/6 Bowman 105
93/4 Cla. Prospects 196
01/2 Pacific 241
97/8 Pa. Invincible R-33
95/6 Parkhurst 305
97/8 Pi. Be A Player 172, ✍ Aut. 172
98/9 UD MVP 31
99/0 UD MVP Cup 9
00/1 Albany River Rats

WARD, GEOFF
94/5 Slapshot / Kitchener 27
95/6 Slapshot 155
01/2 Hamilton Bulldogs
01/2 Hamilton Bulldogs/ Staz

WARD, JASON
99 Bowman 154
97 Bowman 129, BB5, ✍ Aut.
98 Bowman 9
98 Bowman Chrome 9
99/0 Omega 125
00/1 Signature 77, ✍ Aut. 20
95/6 Slapshot 186
98/9 UD Choice 272
96/7 Upper Deck 388
97/8 UD Coll. Choice 303
02/3 Hamilton Bulldogs
99/0 Québec Citadelles 8
00/1 Québec Citadelles
01/2 Québec Citadelles

WARD, JIMMY
34-43 BeeHive-1 [Maroons]
35-40 Canada Starch
35-40 Canada Starch
33/4 Canadian Gum
28/9 La Presse
33/4 O-Pee-Chee 56
37/8 O-Pee-Chee 170
38/9 Quaker Oats
34/5 Sweet Caporal
33/4 WWGum 37
37/8 World Wide Gum 2

WARD, JOEL
00/1 Owen Sound Attack 17

WARD, LANCE
95/6 Bowman P37
00/1 SP Authentic 145
00/1 SPx 139
99/0 Louisville Panthers
98/9 New Haven Beast 18
95/6 Red Deer Rebels

WARD, RON
72/3 O-Pee-Chee 332
74/5 OPC WHA 21
75/6 OPC WHA 73
76/7 OPC WHA 35
73/4 Quaker Oats 34
71/2 Toronto Sun Photo
69/0 TORO
71/2 VANC / Royal Bank 8

WARD, SPENCER
92/3 BCJHL 192

WARD, WES
94/5 Slapshot / Windsor 13
95/6 Slapshot 417

WARDE, MICHAEL
94/5 Anchorage Aces 11

WARDEN, JIM
79 Panini Sticker 207

WARDEN, TOM
93/4 Thunder Bay Senators

WARE, JEFF
95/6 Classic 15, 91, BK14
94/5 Cla. Images 86
97/8 Do. Canadian 129
94/5 Parkie SE257
94/5 Select 163
95/6 Slapshot 246
94/5 SP 188
97/8 Upper Deck 370
96/7 UD Ice 131
99/0 Louisville Panthers
97/8 St. John's Maple Leafs
00/1 Syracuse Crunch
01/2 Syracuse Crunch

WARE, MIKE
98/9 DEL 196
00/1 Kudos 68
88/9 ProCards / Cape Breton
90/1 ProCards 232
88/9 EDMO / Action 151
95/6 St. John's Maple Leafs
01/2 Cardiff Devils
97/8 Sheffield Steelers
93/4 Michigan State

WARES, EDDIE
34-43 BeeHive-1 [Detr.]
39/0 O-Pee-Chee 73

WARKUS, T.J.
00/1 Sudbury Wolves 4

WARNER, JIM
79/0 O-Pee-Chee 384
79 Panini Sticker 221

WARR, ANDREW
97/8 Halifax Moosehead

WARR, STEVE
72/3 Ottawa Nationals

WARREN, MORGAN
00/1 St. John's Maple Leafs
01/2 St. John's Maple Leafs
02/3 St. John's / Clarenville

WARRENER, RHETT
95/6 Bowman 108
95/6 Donruss 358
95/6 Do. Elite WJ 9
02/3 First Edition 166
99/0 Omega 102
96/7 Pi. Be A Player 138, ✍ Aut. 138
94/5 Sig. Rookies 35, ✍ 35
94/5 SR Gold Standard 98
95/6 Topps 272
95/6 To. Stadium 140
95/6 Upper Deck 528
96/7 Upper Deck 266
02/3 Upper Deck 266
00/1 UD Vintage 46
01/2 UD Vintage 31
99/0 Victory 41
96/7 FLOR / Winn-Dixie
97/8 FLOR / Winn-Dixie
93/4 Saskatoon Blades

WARRENER, TREVOR
91/2 Air Canada SJHL B7
92/3 MPS SJHL 129

WARRINER, MIKE
92/3 BCJHL 146

WARRINER, TODD
95/6 Bowman 106
93/4 Canada Nationals
94/5 Classic 109
94/5 Cla. Prospects IA7
93/4 Cla. Prospects LP20
95/6 Donruss 85
97/8 Donruss 91
93/4 Fleer Ultra 476
95/6 Leaf 101
97/8 Limited 162
99/0 Millenium 225, ✍ Aut. 225
97/8 Pacific CC 257
00/1 Pa. Paramount 225
97/8 Panini Sticker 177
95/6 Parkhurst 472
95/6 Pinnacle 219
96/7 Pi. Be A Player 122, ✍ Aut. 122
97/8 Pi. Inside 166
93/4 Power Play 496
93/4 Premier - Canada 19
94/5 Score CT3
95/6 Score 296
97/8 Score 207
97/8 Score Toro. 9
90/1 7th..Sketch OHL 174, 195
91/2 7th...Sketch OHL 173
93/4 Slapshot / Kitchener 15
99/0 Stadium 30
95/6 Topps 45
96/7 Upper Deck 163
97/8 Upper Deck 163
00/1 Upper Deck 157
94/5 UD BAP R163
96/7 UD Black Diam. 93
97/8 UD Coll. Choice 254
99/0 UD MVP Cup 170
00/1 UD Vintage 330
01/2 Victory 321
94/5 St. John's Maple Leafs
95/6 St. John's Maple Leafs
92/3 Windsor Spitfires [x2]

WARRING, JEREMY
90/1 7th..Sketch WHL 102
91/2 7th...Sketch WHL 22

WARSET, JON
92/3 Semic Nordisk 224

WARUS, MIKE
88/9 ProCards / Moncton

WARWICK, GRANT (KNOBBY)
34-43 BeeHive-1 [NYRa.]
45-64 BeeHive-2 [NYRa.]
45-64 BeeHive-2 [Mont.]
48-52 Exhibits [Canadiens]
45-54 Quaker Oats

WASAMA, JARMO
65/6 Hellas 124
96/7 Sisu 190

WASCHUK, DANIEL
01/2 Regina Pats

WASELKO, BRIAN
98/9 BC Icemen 19

WASHBURN, STEVE
95/6 Classic 92
94/5 Cla. Images 36, ✍ Aut.
97/8 Donruss 115
95/6 Edge Ice 25
96/7 Fl. Ultra 71
96/7 Leaf 237
96/7 L. Preferred 138
98/9 OPC Chrome 158
97/8 Omega 103
98/9 Pacific 229
97/8 Pa. Invincible R-90
96/7 Pinnacle 232
97/8 Pi. Be A Player 139, ✍ Aut. 139
91/2 7th...Sketch OHL 308
98/9 Topps 158
97/8 UD Coll. Choice 107
97/8 FLOR / Winn-Dixie
96/7 Carolina Monarchs
92/3 Ottawa 67's

WASHKURAK, JOE
01/2 Mississauga IceDogs

WASHKURAK, JOEL
90/1 7th..Sketch OHL 72

WASKE, RON
83/4 NYIS / News 30

WASLEY, CHARLIE
92/3 Minnesota G'Gophers
93/4 Minnesota G'Gophers
94/5 Minnesota G'Gophers

WASNIE, NICK
33/4 Canadian Gum
33/4 Hamilton Gum 1
33/4 O-Pee-Chee 47
28/9 Paulins Candy 64

WASSBERGER, JOAKIN
96/7 Mississippi S'Wolves

WASSERMANN, SEPP
94/5 DEL 339
95/6 DEL 306

WASYLKO, STEVE
95/6 Bowman P38
95/6 Slapshot 71

WASYLUK, TREVOR
95/6 Bowman P39
95/6 Cla. Vis. Signings 63, ✍ Aut.
95/6 Upper Deck 512

WATCHORN, JEFF
90 7th..Sketch Mem.Cup 13
90/1 7th..Sketch WHL 292
91/2 7th...Sketch WHL 92
89/0 Kamloops Blazers

WATHEN, TREVOR
91/2 Air Canada SJHL A16
92/3 MPS SJHL 61

WATHIER, FRANCIS
01/2 Hull Olympiques 6
02/3 Hull Olympiques

WATHIER, MATHIEU
01/2 Sherbrooke Castors 13
00/1 Victoriaville Tigres 10

WATKINS, JOE
00/1 Kudos 32

WATKINS, LANNY
90/1 7th..Sketch WHL 258
91/2 7th...Sketch WHL 320

WATKINS, TOM
02/3 Coventry Blaze

WATSON, BILL
86/7 OPC/Topps 151
87/8 Panini Sticker 232
88/9 ProCards / Saginaw
86/7 CHIC / Coke
87/8 CHIC / Coke

WATSON, BLAKE
24/5 Falcons Crescent 14

WATSON, BRENT
90/1 7th..Sketch OHL 223
91/2 7th...Sketch OHL 351

WATSON, BRUCE
99/0 Asheville Smoke [x2]

WATSON, BRYAN
70/1 Dad's Cookies
70/1 Eddie Sargent 164
71/2 Eddie Sargent 164
72/3 Eddie Sargent 172
70/1 Esso Power Player
74/5 Loblaws
68/9 O-Pee-Chee 173
69/0 O-Pee-Chee 112
70/1 O-Pee-Chee 204
71/2 O-Pee-Chee 132
72/3 O-Pee-Chee 90
72/3 O-Pee-Chee 268
73/4 O-Pee-Chee 14
74/5 O-Pee-Chee 5
74/5 O-Pee-Chee 259
75/6 O-Pee-Chee 31
76/7 O-Pee-Chee 4
76/7 O-Pee-Chee 228
76/7 OPC 385
77/8 O-Pee-Chee 342
78/9 O-Pee-Chee 316
72 Semic Sticker 217
65/6 Topps 45
66/7 Topps 48
69/0 Topps 112
72/3 Topps 65
72/3 Topps 116
73/4 Topps 144
74/5 Topps 5
74/5 Topps 259
75/6 Topps 31
76/7 Topps 4
76/7 Topps 228
71/2 Toronto Sun Photo
80/1 EDMO / Zellers
88/9 EDMO / Action 124
67/8 MONT
71/2 PITT / Sportcolor

WATSON, BRYAN
02/3 Fleer Throwbacks 72

WATSON, DAN
99 Bowman 160
00/1 Syracuse Crunch
01/2 Syracuse Crunch
01/2 Syracuse Crunch
02/3 Syracuse Crunch

WATSON, GREG
00/1 UD Prospects 59, 98
01 UD Prospects GU 35, ✂ TPJ, ✂ TPJS, ✂ JC, ✍ SoT

WATSON, HARRY P.
34-43 BeeHive-1 [NYAm.]
45-64 BeeHive-2 [Toro.]
83 HHOF Postcard G16
83&87 HHOF 105
96/7 Legends 79
51/2 Parkhurst 70
52/3 Parkhurst 46
53/4 Parkhurst 12
54/5 Parkhurst 17
93/4 Parkhurst DPR-11
93/4 Parkie 56-57 36
45-54 Quaker Oats
55 Toronto Star Weekend
91/2 Ultimate Original Six 46, ✍ Aut. 46

WATSON, HARRY*
25 Dominion Chocolates 114
23 Willards Chocolates 43

WATSON, JIM A. (WATTY)
70/1 Eddie Sargent 32
71/2 Eddie Sargent 21
70/1 Esso Power Player
70/1 O-Pee-Chee 144
71/2 O-Pee-Chee 165
68/9 Shirriff / Detr. 15
67/8 Topps 107
71/2 Toronto Sun Photo
72/3 Los Angeles Sharks

WATSON, JIMMY*
77/8 Coke
74/5 Loblaws
74/5 O-Pee-Chee 303
75/6 O-Pee-Chee 202
76/7 O-Pee-Chee 247
77/8 O-Pee-Chee 43
78/9 O-Pee-Chee 247
79/0 O-Pee-Chee 26
80/1 O-Pee-Chee 224
81/2 O-Pee-Chee 259
82/3 Post [Phil.]
75/6 Topps 202
76/7 Topps 247
77/8 Topps 43
78/9 Topps 247
79/0 Topps 26
80/1 Topps 224
90/1 Upper Deck 514

WATSON, JOE
77/8 Coke
70/1 Dad's Cookies
70/1 Eddie Sargent 156
71/2 Eddie Sargent 158
72/3 Eddie Sargent 159
70/1 Esso Power Player
74/5 Loblaws
68/9 O-Pee-Chee 90
69/0 O-Pee-Chee 93
70/1 O-Pee-Chee 79
72/3 O-Pee-Chee 62
73/4 O-Pee-Chee 91
74/5 O-Pee-Chee 217
75/6 O-Pee-Chee 281
76/7 O-Pee-Chee 45
77/8 O-Pee-Chee 247
78/9 O-Pee-Chee 43
92/3 Parkhurst 474
01/2 Parkhurst ✍ PA41
95/6 Parkie 66-67 3
66/7 Topps 33
68/9 Topps 90
69/0 Topps 93
70/1 Topps 79
72/3 Topps 156
73/4 Topps 91
74/5 Topps 217
75/6 Topps 281
76/7 Topps 45
77/8 Topps 247
78/9 Topps 43
71/2 Toronto Sun Photo
01/2 Ultimate Mem. ✂ SCD
01/2 Ultimate Mem. ✂ SCD

WATSON, PHIL
52/3 Anonymous 80
34-43 BeeHive-1 [NYRa.]
39/0 O-Pee-Chee 83
43-47 Parade Sportive
93/4 Parkie 56-57 108
61/2 Shirriff 19
61/2 Topps 1
62/3 Topps 1
37/8 World Wide Gum 80

WATSON, ROSS
52/3 Anonymous 159

WATT, MIKE
99/0 Aurora 92
98/9 Bowman's Best F11
95/6 Do. Elite WJ 21
98/9 NHL Power Play
98/9 Omega 153
99/0 Pacific 266
99/0 Pa. Paramount 147
98/9 Pa. Revolution 91
99/0 Revolution 94
98/9 SP Authentic 103
99/0 SPx 90
98/9 SPx Finite 138
95/6 Upper Deck 536
98/9 Upper Deck 14, 316, -GN 15
98/9 UD G. Reserve 14, 316
98/9 UD MVP 128
99/0 UD MVP 125
99/0 Victory 185
97/8 EDMO
00/1 Milwaukee Admirals

WATT, SYLVAIN
00/1 Chicoutimi Saguenéens 8

WATT, TOM
90/1 Pro Set 677
91/2 TORO / P.L.A.Y. 5
81/2 WINN
82/3 WINN
95/6 St. John's Maple Leafs

WATTERS, TIM
82/3 O-Pee-Chee 395
83/4 O-Pee-Chee 394
84/5 O-Pee-Chee 350
87/8 O-Pee-Chee 219
90/1 O-Pee-Chee 461
89/0 O-Pee-Chee 212
82/3 Post [Winn.]
93/4 Premier 298
90/1 Pro Set 458
90/1 Score 204
91/2 Score CAN 523
83/4 Stater Mint H13
90/1 Upper Deck 117
91/2 Upper Deck 471
83/4 Vachon 139-19
88/9 LOSA / Smokey
89/0 LOSA / Smokey 2
90/1 LOSA / Smokey 4
81/2 WINN
82/3 WINN
83/4 WINN
84/5 WINN / Safety Tips
85/6 WINN
85/6 WINN / Safety Tips
86/7 WINN
87/8 WINN
92/3 Phoenix Roadrunners
94/5 Phoenix Roadrunners
90/1 Michigan Tech Huskies

WATTS, MORGAN
85/6 London Knights

WAVER, JEFF
88/9 ProCards / Muskegon
90/1 ProCards 523
84/5 Brandon Wheat Kings
85/6 Brandon Wheat Kings

WAY, JIM
86/7 Sudbury Wolves

WAY, SHAWN
89/0 7th..Sketch OHL 84

WAYLETT, STAN
59/60 Whitby Dunlops

WEAVER, DAVE
92/3 W. Michigan Broncos

WEAVER, JASON
00/1 Kudos 159
90/1 7th..Sketch OHL 348
91/2 7th...Sketch OHL 160
97/8 Grand Rapids Griffins
01/2 Sheffield Steelers GS
90/1 Oshawa Generals
91/2 Oshawa Generals
91/2 Oshawa Generals

WEAVER, JONATHAN
00/1 Kudos 20
99/0 Mississippi S'Wolves

WEAVER, MIKE
01/2 BAP Mem. 400
01/2 UD PlayMakers Ltd 103
01/2 UD Honor Roll 62
02/3 UD MVP 192
01/2 Chicago Wolves

WEAVER, SCOTT
91/2 Air Canada SJHL D23

WEBB, STEVE
02/3 BAP Mem. 161
97/8 Pacific CC 248
00/1 Signature 180, ✍ Aut. 46
99/0 Topps 73
99/0 To. Chrome 73
97/8 Upper Deck 308
02/3 Upper Deck 110
02/3 UD MVP 118
96/7 Kentucky Tho'blades
97/8 Kentucky Tho'blades
95/6 Muskegon Fury
92/3 Windsor Spitfires

WEBBER, MIKE
83/4 North Bay Centennials

WEBER, CHRISTIAN
95 Globe 212
91 Semic Sticker 196
92 Semic Sticker 212
93 Semic Sticker 125

WEBER, JEFF
02/3 Plymouth Whalers

WEBER, MARC
91/2 Upper Deck 666
91/2 Upper Deck WJC 27

WEBER, MATT
98/9 Des Moines Buc's

WEBER, PATRIK
94/5 APS 42
95/6 APS 329
99/0 Score 19

WEBER, RANDALL
00/1 Kudos 141
00/1 Nottingham Panthers
01/2 Nottingham Panthers

WEBSTER, CHRIS
87/8 Brockville Braves
88/9 Brockville Braves

WEBSTER, DAVE
82/3 Kitchener Rangers

WEBSTER, GLEN
90/1 7th..Sketch WHL 230
89/0 Brandon Wheat Kings
90/1 Brandon Wheat Kings

WEBSTER, TOM
70/1 Dad's Cookies
70/1 Eddie Sargent 57
71/2 Eddie Sargent 135
70/1 Esso Power Player
70/1 O-Pee-Chee 155
71/2 O-Pee-Chee 78
74/5 OPC WHA 8
75/6 OPC WHA 95
76/7 OPC WHA 14
77/8 OPC WHA 55
90/1 Pro Set 667
71/2 Topps 78
97/8 CARO / Sprint
70/1 DETR / Marathon Oil
94/5 PHIL / Sheet
72/3 New England Whalers

WECKSTROM, KARI
80/1 Mallasjuoma 150

WEDDERBURN, TIM
02/3 Hershey Bears
99/0 Prince George Cougars
00/1 Prince George Cougars

WEDER, MATT
96/7 Flint Generals

WEDL, ALEXANDER
94/5 DEL 107
95/6 DEL 152
96/7 DEL 230
98/9 DEL 54

WEEKES, KEVIN
01/2 Adrenaline 178
00/1 Aurora 135
99/0 BAP Mem. 196
01/2 BAP Mem. 471
02/3 BAP Mem. 158
01/2 BT Pipes 40
02/3 Between the Pipes 19, M6
02/3 Bowman 60
00/1 Crown Royale 98
97/8 Do. Priority 177
99/0 Dynagon Ice 198
95/6 Edge Ice 26
02/3 First Edition 248
01/2 O-Pee-Chee 20
97/8 Omega 104
99/0 Omega 145
98/9 Pacific 230
99/0 Pacific 434
00/1 Pacific 257
01/2 Pacific 359
02/3 Pacific 72
02/3 Pacific Complete 143
97/8 Pa. Crown Roy. 61
02/3 Parkhurst 41
02/3 Parkhurst Retro 102
02/3 Pr. Stock Titanium 20
01/2 Signature 170, ✍ Aut. 170
97/8 SP Authentic 183
02/3 Sports Vault 40
00/1 Stadium CA14
00/1 Topps 29
01/2 Topps 20
00/1 To. Heritage 118
02/3 To. Heritage 40
02/3 To. Total 287
98/9 Upper Deck 100
99/0 Upper Deck 128
02/3 Upper Deck 274
98/9 UD G. Reserve 100
99/0 UD G. Reserve 128
02/3 UD Mask 17, 18
99/0 UD MVP 208
00/1 UD Pros&Prosp. 77
02/3 Vanguard 20
99/0 Victory 297
01/2 Victory 314, 319
99/0 WGretzky 169
97/8 FLOR / Winn-Dixie
96/7 Carolina Monarchs
98/9 Detroit Vipers
97/8 Fort Wayne Komets
93/4 Owen Sound Platers
93/4 Owen Sound Platers
93/4 Owen Sound Platers

WEEKLEY, DAVE
93/4 Huntington Blizzard

WEEKS, STEVE
92/3 Bowman 274
82/3 O-Pee-Chee 234
90/1 O-Pee-Chee 407
89/0 O-Pee-Chee 285
82/3 OPC/Topps Sticker 141
87/8 Panini Sticker 39
89/0 Panini Sticker 150
92/3 Pinnacle 380
82/3 Post [NYRa.]
90/1 ProCards 331
92/3 Score 547
92/3 Topps 461
92/3 To. Stadium 273
90/1 Upper Deck 107
84/5 HART / Jr. Whalers
85/6 HART / Jr. Whalers
86/7 HART / Jr. Whalers
87/8 HART / Jr. Whalers
92/3 OTTA
88/9 VANC / Mohawk
89/0 VANC / Mohawk

WEENK, HEATH
90/1 7th..Sketch WHL 185
91/2 7th...Sketch WHL 220

WEGLEITNER, MIKE
84/5 Kelowna Wings &...

WEHRSTEDT, MIKE
00/1 Mississauga IceDogs
01/2 Mississauga IceDogs

WEIDENBACH, ANDY
90/1 7th..Sketch OHL 124
96/7 Hampton Roads

WEIDENBACH, JOHN
93/4 Michigan State

WEIGHT, DOUG
01/2 Adrenaline 164, ✂ GWJ 41
01/2 Atomic 84
98/9 Aurora 77, -CF 21
99/0 Aurora 60, -Stripe 60
00/1 Aurora 59
02/3 BAP All-Star 96, ✂ ASJ
99/0 BAP Mem. 204
00/1 BAP Mem. 73
01/2 BAP Mem. 282, 371, ✂ ASJ, ✂ ASE, ✂ ASN, ✂ AST, ✂ CoO
02/3 BAP Mem. 103, ✂ ASJ58, ✂ TM17
01/2 BAP Update ✂ TP12
96/7 Bic.Sports Aces 10-D
97/8 Bicycle 8-Spade
92/3 Bowman 36
95/6 Bowman 68
01/2 Bowman 30
02/3 Bowman 10
98/9 Bowman's Best 46
02/3 Calder ✂ GWJ 20
99/0 Crown Royale 58
00/1 Crown Royale 44, JotC-15
01/2 Crown Royale 122, ASH 18
02/3 Crown Royale 83
95/6 DEL 449
93/4 Donruss 118
94/5 Donruss 3
95/6 Donruss 25
96/7 Donruss 85, ES-3, HL-5
97/8 Donruss 32
96/7 Do. Canadian 14
97/8 Do. Canadian 86
95/6 Do. Elite 5
96/7 Do. Elite 25, S-4
97/8 Do. Elite 103
97/8 Do. Preferred 74, 181
97/8 Do. Priority 161
97/8 Do. Studio 95
98/9 Dynagon Ice 77
99/0 Dynagon Ice 86
93/4 EA Sports 45
97/8 Esso 26
01/2 eTopps 35
02/3 Exclusive 147
02/3 First Edition 26, ✂ Jers.
94/5 Flair 62
96/7 Flair 36
96/7 Fleer 38, ART-24
95/6 Fleer Metal 57
96/7 Fl. Picks F50-47, JE-4
92/3 Fleer Ultra 358
93/4 Fleer Ultra 195
94/5 Fleer Ultra 77
95/6 Fleer Ultra 58
96/7 Fl. Ultra 63
00 Gatorade Sticker
95 Globe 125
01/2 Heads Up 82, ASGN 3, ✂ JQ 22
02/3 Heads Up 106
99/0 HoloGrFX 24
95/6 Hoyle / West. Q-Club
02/3 In The GU 68, 168, ✂ GUJ43, ✂ SJ43, ✂ TM14
95/6 Kraft / KD
96/7 Kraft / KD
97/8 Kraft / KD, Casecard

98/9 Kraft / KD
99/0 Kraft / JELL-O
00/1 Kraft 6
96/7 Kraft Magnet
93/4 Leaf 184
94/5 Leaf 40
95/6 Leaf 145
96/7 Leaf 136, FOI-6, TBO-7
97/8 Leaf 131
94/5 L. Limited 53
95/6 L. Limited 110
96/7 L. Limited 71
96/7 L. Preferred 54, LS-49
97/8 Limited 173, 191
96/7 McDonald's McD-16
97/8 McDonald's McD-18
99/0 McDonald's McD-11
00/1 McDonald's 16, CL-2
01/2 McDonald's 34, -CF 1
96/7 Metal Univ. 56, LW-20
99/0 Millenium 96, ✍ Aut. 96
98/9 NHL Power Play
92/3 O-Pee-Chee 114
01/2 O-Pee-Chee 24 , Update 24
02/3 O-Pee-Chee 257
98/9 OPC Chrome 8
91/2 OPC Premier 32
91/2 OPC Premier 139
97/8 Omega 96
98/9 Omega 97
99/0 Omega 96
98/9 Pacific 217
99/0 Pacific 167, CI 12
00/1 Pacific 176
01/2 Pacific 167, 430, NAAS 7, ✄ GWJ 15
02/3 Pacific 330
02/3 Pacific Complete 34
97/8 Pacific CC 138
97/8 Pa. Crown Roy. 55
98/9 Pa. Crown Roy. 55
97/8 Pa. Dynagon 52, T-46
97/8 Pa. Invincible 59
97/8 Pa. Paramount 78
98/9 Pa. Paramount 93
99/0 Pa. Paramount 97, -IAdv. 11
00/1 Pa. Paramount 101, FF-17, ✄ GUS-11
97/8 Pa. Revolution 57
98/9 Pa. Revolution 58
98/9 Panini Photocard
92/3 Panini Sticker 236
93/4 Panini Sticker 235
94/5 Panini Sticker 199
95/6 Panini Sticker 259
96/7 Panini Sticker 257
97/8 Panini Sticker 215
98/9 Panini Sticker 197
99/0 Panini Sticker 243
00/1 Panini Sticker 158
95 Panini Worlds 231
91/2 Parkhurst 116
92/3 Parkhurst 115
92/3 Parkhurst 229
93/4 Parkhurst 69
94/5 Parkhurst 74
95/6 Parkhurst 346
00/1 Parkhurst P-133
01/2 Parkhurst 233, ✄ PS57, ✄ HSHSJers
02/3 Parkhurst 126, -CR 11, ✄ CRM11, ✄ GJ26, ✄ SJ26, ✄ TT16
02/3 Parkhurst Retro 47
94/5 Parkie SE seV23
91/2 Pinnacle 310
91/2 Pinnacle 383
92/3 Pinnacle 189
93/4 Pinnacle 17
94/5 Pinnacle 18
96/7 Pinnacle 158, BTN-5, TP-4
97/8 Pinnacle 54
96/7 Pi. Be A Player 174, ✍ Aut. 174
97/8 Pi. BeeHive 34
97/8 Pi. Certified 66
97/8 Pi. Inside 48
95/6 Pi. Summit 110
96/7 Pi. Summit 92, U-11
97/8 Pi. Totally 66
96/7 Pi. Zenith 12
95/6 Playoff 259
96/7 Playoff 434
94/5 POG 101
94/5 POG / Western 22
95/6 POG 105
93/4 Power Play 87
93/4 Premier 136
94/5 Premier 8
00/1 Premier Plus 39
99/0 Prism 59
00/1 Pr. Stock 41, ✄ GUG-50, PS-24
01/2 Pr. Stock 83, -PS 63, ✄ GUG 89
02/3 Pr. Stock Reserve 85
00/1 PS Titanium 38
01/2 PS Titanium 120
02/3 Pr. Stock Titanium 85
00/1 PS Titanium Draft ✄ 45
95/6 Pro Magnet 83
91/2 Pro Set 549
91/2 Pro Set Platinum 263
02/3 Quest for the Cup 85, ✄ GWJ 19
99/0 Revolution 61, SS-18, / CSC 61
00/1 Revolution 60
91/2 Score 396
91/2 Score CAN 286
92/3 Score 314
93/4 Score 253
94/5 Score 58
95/6 Score 263
96/7 Score 170, CI-14, S-2
97/8 Score 100
94/5 Select 27
95/6 Select CE 109
96/7 Select CE 50
96/7 SB 7-Eleven Phonecard
00/1 Signature 209, F-12, ✍ Aut. 86
01/2 Signature C-12, ✍ Aut., ✄ FP26, ✄ GUE25, ✄ GJ56, ✄ GSJ56, ✄ HSHSJers, ✄ ITN25, ✄ IS4, ✄ TM26
02/3 Signature Series 163, ✍ 163, ✄ SGJ43, ✄ TQ15
95/6 SBx Emotion 67
95/6 SBx Impact 65
96/7 SBx Impact 43, BR-24
02/3 Slam Card
94/5 SP 39
95/6 SP 50, FX9
96/7 SP 57, CW-10, HC-24
97/8 SP Authentic 58, I32, ✍ SotT
98/9 SP Authentic 33, SO5, ✍ SotT
99/0 SP Authentic 34
00/1 SP Authentic 35
01/2 SP Authentic 76, ✍ SotT, ✍ SotTD, ✍ SotTT
02/3 SP Authentic 77
00/1 SP GU 25
01/2 SP GU 51, ✄✍ ISD
02/3 SP GU ✄ CF
02/3 Sports Vault 276
96/7 SPx 17
97/8 SPx 17, -DV, ✍ DVS
99/0 SPx 62
00/1 SPx 26
01/2 SPx 60, ✍ Sig.
98/9 SPx Finite 34, 113
98/9 SPx Prospects 27, PS28
99/0 Stadium 81, -Chrome 29
00/1 Stadium 4
01/2 Stadium 107
02/3 Stadium 79
95/6 Super Sticker 43
92/3 Topps 477
95/6 Topps 158
98/9 Topps 8
99/0 Topps 104
00/1 Topps 81
01/2 Topps 24, OTG8, Update 24
02/3 Topps 257, HHU16
99/0 To. Chrome 104
00/1 To. Chrome 64
01/2 To. Chrome 24
02/3 T. Chrome 140
95/6 To. Finest 104
98/9 To. Finest 133
98/9 T. Gold Label 18
99/0 To. Gold Label 28
00/1 To. Heritage 22
01/2 To. Heritage 161
02/3 To. Heritage 38
02/3 To. Limited 257
96/7 To. Picks 23
99/0 To. Prmr. Plus 18, ✄ GP
01/2 To. Reserve 100
92/3 To. Stadium 380
93/4 To. Stadium 382
95/6 To. Stadium 74
95/6 TSC Members Only 12
00/1 To. Stars 18
02/3 To. Total 131
98/9 UD Choice 85
00/1 UD Heroes 47
01/2 UD PlayMakers Ltd 87, / PM
00/1 UD Reserve 35
00/1 Ultimate Mem. ✍ U-38
01/2 Ultimate Mem. ✄ DD, ✄ Emb., ✄ Jers., ✄ S&J, ✄ GAO, ✄ ITN, ✄ NP, ✄ WTF
02/3 Ultimate Memorabilia ✄ HT
99/0 Ult. Victory 35
91/2 Upper Deck 440
91/2 Upper Deck 444
92/3 Upper Deck 279
93/4 Upper Deck 291, 442, SP-53
94/5 Upper Deck 44, 549, SP-28
95/6 Upper Deck 280, AS-16, SE-31
96/7 Upper Deck 58, X13, SS17A
97/8 Upper Deck 65, SS10, SG20, T13B, ✄ GJ12
98/9 Upper Deck 90, FF21, LS22, P22
99/0 Upper Deck 229
00/1 Upper Deck 296
01/2 Upper Deck 155, LP13, ✄ JPatch, ✄ PoaN, ✄ PoaNT, ✄✍ JersSig.
02/3 Upper Deck 151
02/3 UD Artistic 77, R77, / Art
93/4 Upper Deck Be A Player 39
94/5 UD BAP R118, ✍ 117
96/7 UD Black Diam. 172
97/8 UD Black Diam. 84
98/9 UD Black Diam. 34
99/0 UD Black Diam. 40
00/1 UD Black Diam. 24
01/2 UD Challenge 74, ✄ FP, ✄✍ FPS
02/3 UD Classic 86, ✄ HR
95/6 UD CC 172
96/7 UD CC 91, 317, UD9, C9, CR9
97/8 UD Coll. Choice 87, 319, SQ68, C3, CR3
97/8 UD Diam. Vision 15
98/9 UD G. Reserve 90
99/0 UD G. Reserve 229, / Backup 162
01/2 UD Honor Roll ✄ GAJ
96/7 UD Ice 87, S9
97/8 UD Ice 9
00/1 UD Ice 19
01/2 UD Ice 119, ✄ GJ
00/1 UD Legends 53, 54
01/2 UD Mask 85
98/9 UD MVP 77, ✍ PS
99/0 UD MVP 79
00/1 UD MVP 74
01/2 UD MVP 166
02/3 UD MVP 159
99/0 UD MVP Cup 72
99/0 UD Ovation 25
01/2 UD Premier ✍ SigS
00/1 UD Pros&Prosp. 35
99/0 UD Retro 31, ✍ Ink.
02/3 UD Rookie 83
01/2 UD Top Shelf 117, ✄ J, ✄✍ SJ.
02/3 UD Top Shelf ✄ CP, ✍ Sig
00/1 UD Vintage 138, 148, 149
01/2 UD Vintage 220
02/3 UD Vintage 221, GB 221
00/1 Vanguard 44, HV-15, ✄ DGJ-7
01/2 Vanguard 84, QTH 9, ✄ DGM 47
02/3 Vanguard 84
99/0 Victory 108, 113
00/1 Victory 92, 97, 303
01/2 Victory 139, 422
02/3 Victory 187, -NP60
01/2 Waving the Flag 22
99/0 WGretzky 67, ✄ TG
96 Wien 172
97/8 Zenith 62, Z50
93/4 EDMO / Sheet
92/3 EDMO
96/7 EDMO
97/8 EDMO

WEILAND, COONEY
33/4 Anonymous 24
34-43 BeeHive-1 [Bost.]
83 HHOF Postcard H16
83&87 HHOF 120
33/4 O-Pee-Chee 27
39/0 O-Pee-Chee 92
33/4 WWGum 65
37/8 World Wide Gum 69
91/2 BOST / SA Legends
91/2 BOST / SA Legends

WEILAND, MARKUS
99/0 Eishockey 16

WEILAND, RALPH
34/5 Sweet Caporal

WEILLEUX, ERIC
98/9 Cardset 203

WEINFURTER, MICHAEL
94/5 DEL 338
95/6 DEL 295

WEINGARTNER, ROB
96/7 Louisiana Ice Gators
98/9 Louisiana Ice Gators

WEINHANDL, MATTIAS
02/3 Bowman 156, ✄ FFDS, ✄ FFJ, ✄ FFP, ✄ FFR, ✄ FFRP, ✄ FFS, ✄ FFTS, ✍ YSA, / ✍ Puck
02/3 Calder 83
02/3 Crown Royale 126
02/3 Pacific Complete 520
02/3 Pr. Stock Reserve 172
98/9 SPx Prospects 82
99/0 Upper Deck 327
98/9 UD Black Diam. 112
99/0 UD Black Diam. 118
99/0 UD Elitserien 178, 214, S13
00/1 UD Elitserien 160, 207, 219, S5, T10, P8, ✍ Sig.
99/0 UD G. Reserve 327
99/0 UD Ovation 80

WEINRICH, ERIC
98/9 Be A Player 30, ✍ Aut. 30
00/1 BAP Mem. 320
90/1 Bowman 90
91/2 Bowman 278
92/3 Bowman 343
93/4 Donruss 136
93/4 Donruss 416
94/5 Donruss 302
93/4 EA Sports 56
92/3 Fleer Ultra 76, 306
93/4 Fleer Ultra 295
95 Globe 108
93/4 Leaf 271
94/5 Leaf 221
90/1 O-Pee-Chee 416
91/2 O-Pee-Chee 10
91/2 O-Pee-Chee 92
92/3 O-Pee-Chee 95
92/3 OPC Premier 63
98/9 Pacific 153
99/0 Pacific 213
00/1 Pacific 216
01/2 Pacific 41, ✄ GWJ 2
02/3 Pacific 289
02/3 Pacific Complete 192
97/8 Pa. Invincible R-49
98/9 Pa. Paramount 50
91/2 Panini Sticker 223
93/4 Panini Sticker 130
97/8 Panini Sticker 134
98/9 Panini Sticker 117
99/0 Panini Sticker 74
91/2 Parkhurst 318
92/3 Parkhurst 56
93/4 Parkhurst 311
94/5 Parkhurst 43, V83
95/6 Parkhurst 310
01/2 Parkhurst 249
91/2 Pinnacle 89
92/3 Pinnacle 297
93/4 Pinnacle 281
94/5 Pinnacle 186
95/6 Pinnacle 182
96/7 Pi. Be A Player 71, ✍ Aut. 71
93/4 Power Play 111
93/4 Power Play 319
93/4 Premier 195
94/5 Premier 106
00/1 Pr. Stock ✄ GUG 60
00/1 PS Titanium ✄ GUG 29, ✄ GUG-101
00/1 PS Titanium Draft ✄ 9
90/1 Pro Set 622
91/2 Pro Set 133
91/2 Pro Set Platinum PC10
88/9 ProCards / Utica
89/0 ProCards AHL 222
90/1 Score 389
91/2 Score 131
91/2 Score 350
91/2 Score CAN 131
91/2 Score CAN 380
92/3 Score 308
93/4 Score 227
93/4 Score 573
91/2 Score Young Stars 26
94 Semic 112
92 Semic Sticker 154
01/2 Signature 120, ✍ Aut. 120
92/3 Topps 399
95/6 Topps 289
01/2 To. Heritage 181
91/2 To. Stadium 339
92/3 To. Stadium 165
02/3 To. Total 343
90/1 Upper Deck 245
91/2 Upper Deck 44
91/2 Upper Deck 344
91/2 Upper Deck 509
92/3 Upper Deck 195
92/3 Upper Deck 553
93/4 Upper Deck 497
94/5 Upper Deck 119
95/6 Upper Deck 45
96/7 Upper Deck 34, X4
97/8 Upper Deck 246
98/9 Upper Deck 67
99/0 Upper Deck 68
00/1 Upper Deck 322
02/3 Upper Deck 128
94/5 UD BAP R19, ✍ 139
95/6 UD CC 63
96/7 UD CC 51
97/8 UD Coll. Choice 52
98/9 UD G. Reserve 67
99/0 UD G. Reserve 68
96/7 UD Ice 12
00/1 UD Legends 70
98/9 UD MVP 107
99/0 UD MVP 103
00/1 UD Vintage 187
02/3 UD Vintage 190
01/2 Vanguard ✄ DGM 21
99/0 Victory 147
00/1 Victory 120
01/2 Victory 32
99/0 WGretzky 89
93/4 CHIC / Coke
92/3 HART / Dairymart
00/1 MONT
89/0 NJER
89/0 NJER / Caretta
90/1 NJER
01/2 PHIL

WEINRICH, JASON
94/5 Huntington Blizzard
92/3 Maine Black Bears
93/4 Maine Black Bears

WEINSTOCK, ULF
79 Panini Sticker 187

WEIR, BERT
84/5 Ottawa 67's

WEIR, BILL
98/9 Quad City Mallards

WEIR, JOHN
83/4 Brantford Alexanders

WEIR, MATT
01/2 London Knights

WEIR, NOLAN
91/2 Air Canada SJHL C38
92/3 MPS SJHL 16

WEIR, STAN
74/5 Loblaws
74/5 O-Pee-Chee 355
75/6 O-Pee-Chee 132
75/6 O-Pee-Chee 316
76/7 O-Pee-Chee 270
77/8 O-Pee-Chee 356
79/0 O-Pee-Chee 331
80/1 O-Pee-Chee 153
81/2 O-Pee-Chee 124
80/1 Pepsi Bottle Cap
75/6 Topps 132
75/6 Topps 316
80/1 Topps 153
79/0 EDMO
80/1 EDMO / Zellers
81/2 EDMO / Red Rooster
81/2 EDMO / West Mall
88/9 EDMO / Action 66
75/6 TORO
76/7 TORO

WEIR, WALLY
78/9 Dernière Heure
81/2 Dernière Heure
79/0 O-Pee-Chee 388
81/2 O-Pee-Chee 284
82/3 O-Pee-Chee 297
83/4 O-Pee-Chee 306
80/1 Pepsi Bottle Cap
82/3 Post [Québ.]
83/4 Vachon 79-59
80/1 QUÉB
81/2 QUÉB
82/3 QUÉB
83/4 QUÉB
76/7 Québec Nordiques
76/7 Québ. / Antoinette

WEISBROD, JOHN
92/3 Kansas City Blades

WEISENBACH, HEINZ
72 Semic Sticker 106

WEISHAAR, TOBY
91/2 7th...Sketch WHL 166
92/3 Tacoma Rockets

WEISHAUPT, ERICH
79 Panini Sticker 96
82 Semic Sticker 101

WEISMANN, PAUL
99/0 Eishockey 260

WEISS, DAVE
87/8 Kingston Canadians
84/5 Kitchener Rangers
85/6 Kitchener Rangers
86/7 Kitchener Rangers

WEISS, DOUG
88/9 ProCards / Springfield
89/0 Johnstown Chiefs

WEISS, KEN
93/4 Richmond Renegades

WEISS, STEPHEN
02/3 Atomic 47
01/2 BAP Draft Florida 4
01/2 BAP Mem. 448
02/3 BAP Mem. 139
02/3 Bowman 157, ✄ FFDS, ✄ FFJ, ✄ FFP, ✄ FFR, ✄ FFRP, ✄ FFS, ✄ FFTS, ✍ YSA, / ✍ Puck
02/3 Calder 72, -CR 12
02/3 Crown Royale -RR 12
02/3 Exclusive 78, -DFG 8, -GE 9
02/3 First Edition 282, 424R
02/3 Heads Up 54, -HF 5
02/3 In The GU ✄ C4
02/3 O-Pee-Chee 305
02/3 Pacific 161, -SM 7
02/3 Pacific Complete 238
01/2 Parkhurst 318
02/3 Parkhurst 169, -HHC9, ✄ GJ53, ✄ NH12
02/3 Parkhurst Retro 183
02/3 Pr. Stock Reserve 43, -CA 9, -MIT 4
01/2 PS Titanium Draft 133
02/3 Pr. Stock Titanium -ROT 10
02/3 Signature Series 156, ✍ 156, ✄ AR4, ✄ TQ5
02/3 Sports Vault 46
02/3 SPx 111
02/3 Stadium 115, ✍ LSS
02/3 Topps 305
02/3 T. Chrome 147, ✍ Graph
02/3 To. Heritage 55, ✍ Aut.
02/3 To. Limited 305
02/3 To. Total 128, ✍ Sig
02/3 Ultimate Memorabilia ✄ CC
02/3 Upper Deck 205
02/3 UD Foundations 130
01/2 UD Mask 145
02/3 UD MVP 202
02/3 UD Piece 131
01/2 UD Premier 63
02/3 UD Premier 26
00/1 UD Prospects 21, 92, FL4
01 UD Prospects GU 27, ✄ TPJ, ✄ TPJS, ✄ JC (x4), ✍ SoT
02/3 UD Vintage 273, 333, T31
02/3 Vanguard -PP 12
02/3 Victory 89

WEISSMAN, MIKA
72/3 Williams Finnish 321

WEISSMANN, ONDREJ
94/5 APS 296
97/8 APS 75
98/9 OFS 1
00/1 OFS 82

WELCH, JASON
91/2 L. Superior State Lakers
93/4 N. Michigan Wildcats

WELKER,
91/2 Avant Garde BCJHL 163

WELLING, JESSE
00/1 Cardset 274
99/0 Rockford IceHogs

WELLS, BRAD
83/4 Brandon Wheat Kings

WELLS, BRIAN
83/4 Brandon Wheat Kings

WELLS, BRYAN
93/4 Thunder Bay Senators
98/9 Wichita Thunder

WELLS, CHRIS
95/6 Bowman 136
94/5 Classic 20, T54
94/5 Classic 4 Sport 137, T5
94/5 Cla. Images 19
94/5 Cla. Images 4 Sport 111
97/8 Pa. Invincible R-91
97/8 Pi. Be A Player 62, ✍ Aut. 62
91/2 7th...Sketch WHL 141
94/5 Sig. Rookies 15, ✍ 15
96/7 FLOR / Winn-Dixie
97/8 FLOR / Winn-Dixie
95/6 PITT / Foodland 3
99/0 Louisville Panthers
00/1 Utah Grizzlies
93/4 Seattle Thunderbirds

WELLS, JAY
91/2 Bowman 35
85/6 O-Pee-Chee 178
86/7 O-Pee-Chee 217
87/8 OPC/Topps 151
86/7 OPC Sticker 92-223
87/8 OPC Sticker 212-79
97/8 Pa. Invincible R-189
87/8 Panini Sticker 274
88/9 Panini Sticker 72
94/5 Pinnacle 507
82/3 Post [LosA.]
94/5 Premier 249
92/3 Score 548
93/4 Score 416
95/6 UD BAP 29, ✍ S29
90/1 BUFF / Blue Shield
90/1 BUFF / Campbell's
91/2 BUFF / Blue Shield
91/2 BUFF / Campbell's
91/2 BUFF / Pepsi
80/1 LOSA 14
84/5 LOSA / Smokey 17
87/8 LOSA
89/0 PHIL
98/9 Hershey Bears
97/8 Portland Pirates

WELLS, JAY
02/3 Fleer Throwbacks 40, ✄ 7SW

WELLS, JEFF
95/6 Birmingham Bulls
95/6 Cincinnati Cyclones
96/7 Cincinnati Cyclones
97/8 Cincinnati Cyclones
98/9 Cincinnati Cyclones
99/0 Providence Bruins

WELLS, MARC
94/5 SR Miracle 39,40, ✍ 39,40

WELLS, MARTY
96/7 Dayton Ice Bandits

WELLWOOD, KYLE
00/1 UD Prospects 33
01/2 Belleville Bulls

WELSH, KEITH
94/5 Slapshot / Kitchener 17
95/6 Slapshot 150

WELSING, ROCKY
99/0 Charlotte Checkers
98/9 Kansas City Blades 13

WELTE, WADE
91/2 Air Canada SJHL D14
92/3 MPS SJHL 80

WELTER, JOSH
92/3 MPS SJHL 92

WELZ, MARKUS
96/7 DEL 332

WEN, CHEN SHENG
79 Panini Sticker 360

WEN, TSUI TING
79 Panini Sticker 355

WENAAS, JEFF
89/0 ProCards IHL 194
88/9 Salt Lake G'Eagles
84/5 Medicine Hat Tigers

WENAAS, STUART
83/4 Kelowna Wings

WENBLOM, MAGNUS
94/5 Leaf Elit Set 68

WENNBERG, PETER
92/3 Semic Elitserien 269

WENSINK, JOHN
78/9 O-Pee-Chee 133
79/0 O-Pee-Chee 182
80/1 O-Pee-Chee 390
80/1 Pepsi Bottle Cap
82/3 Post [Colo.]
78/9 Topps 133
79/0 Topps 182
81/2 COLR
80/1 QUEB

WENSINK, JOHN
02/3 Fleer Throwbacks 38

WENSLEY, CLINT
01/2 Rockford IceHogs

WENTWORTH, CY
34-43 BeeHive-1 [Maroons]
34-43 BeeHive-1 [Mont.]
35-40 Canada Starch
35-40 Canada Starch
33/4 O-Pee-Chee 61
36/7 O-Pee-Chee 116
37/8 O-Pee-Chee 163
39/0 O-Pee-Chee 30
38/9 Quaker Oats
34/5 Sweet Caporal
33/4 WWGum 43
37/8 World Wide Gum 19

WENTZELL, JAMIE
95/6 Slapshot 161

WERENKA, BRAD
98/9 Be A Player 264, ✍ Aut. 264
92/3 Classic 99
92/3 Classic Four Sport 212
99/0 Pacific 349
92/3 Parkhurst 289
93/4 Parkhurst 68
97/8 Pi. Be A Player 41, ✍ Aut. 41
93/4 Score 438
94/5 Score CT21
93/4 Upper Deck 41, SP-54
00/1 Upper Deck 259, S5, ✍ SG
93/4 EDMO / Sheet
92/3 EDMO
95/6 Indianapolis Ice
94/5 Milwaukee Admirals

WERENKA, DARCY
91/2 Arena 28
00/1 Cardset 266
91/2 Classic 33
91/2 Classic Four Sport 33
93/4 Cla. Prospects 96
91 7th..Sketch Mem.Cup 101
90/1 7th..Sketch WHL 122
91/2 7th...Sketch WHL 351
91/2 Star Pics 54
91/2 Ultimate Draft Pick 29, ✍ Aut.
92/3 Upper Deck 594
01/2 UD DEL 240
94/5 Binghampton Rangers
99/0 Utah Grizzlies
92/3 Brandon Wheat Kings
89/0 Lethbridge Hurricanes

WERENKA, NIGEL
91/2 Air Canada SJHL D25
92/3 MPS SJHL 162

WERNBLOM, MAGNUS
95/6 Leaf Elit Set 110
91/2 Semic Elitserien 215
92/3 Semic Elitserien 235
95/6 UD Elitserien 160, NA20
97/8 UD Elitserien 157, UDS14
98/9 UD Elitserien 174
99/0 UD Elitserien 176, S12
00/1 UD Elitserien 157, 206

WERNER, THOMAS
94/5 DEL 133
95/6 DEL 134
91 Semic Sticker 172

WESELRO, BRIAN
98/9 BC Icemen

WESENBERG, BRIAN
97 Bowman 33
95/6 Classic 26, 85
94/5 Slapshot / Guelph 16
95/6 Slapshot 96
99/0 UD MVP 154
99/0 Victory 220
95/6 Guelph Storm
96/7 Guelph Storm

WESLEY, BLAKE
82/3 O-Pee-Chee 133
83/4 O-Pee-Chee 307
84/5 O-Pee-Chee 294
82/3 Post [Hart.]
83/4 Souhaits Keychain [Nordiques]
83/4 Vachon 80-60
82/3 HART / Jr. Whalers
83/4 QUÉB
85/6 TORO
84/5 Fredericton Express

WESLEY, GLEN
98/9 Be A Player 26, ✍ Aut. 26
99/0 BAP Mem. 230
91/2 Bowman 350
92/3 Bowman 15
93/4 Donruss 19
94/5 Donruss 232
95/6 Donruss 186
94/5 Fleer 92
95/6 Fleer Metal 68
92/3 Fleer Ultra 11
93/4 Fleer Ultra 272
94/5 Fleer Ultra 18, 303
95/6 Fleer Ultra 248
93/4 Leaf 268
94/5 Leaf 6, 460
95/6 Leaf 231
94/5 L. Limited 13
88/9 OPC/Topps 166
90/1 OPC/Topps 379
91/2 O-Pee-Chee 452
92/3 O-Pee-Chee 150
89/0 OPC/Topps 51
88/9 OPC Sticker 85-215
89/0 opcSticker 27-165
98/9 Pacific 141
99/0 Pacific 82
02/3 Pacific Complete 328
97/8 Pacific CC 244
00/1 Pa. Paramount 47
88/9 Panini Sticker 207
89/0 Panini Sticker 200
90/1 Panini Sticker 6
91/2 Panini Sticker 182
92/3 Panini Sticker 145
93/4 Panini Sticker 6
94/5 Panini Sticker 6
99/0 Panini Sticker 48
91/2 Parkhurst 5
92/3 Parkhurst 6
93/4 Parkhurst 17
94/5 Parkhurst 17
95/6 Parkhurst 98
91/2 Pinnacle 112
92/3 Pinnacle 326
93/4 Pinnacle 383
94/5 Pinnacle 388
95/6 Pinnacle 80
97/8 Pinnacle 132
95/6 Pi. Summit 73
95/6 Playoff 158
95/6 POG 130
93/4 Power Play 25
93/4 Premier 114
94/5 Premier 357
90/1 Pro Set 16
91/2 Pro Set 1
92/3 Pro Set 10
91/2 Pro Set Platinum 7
90/1 Score 97
90/1 Sco. Hot Cards 57
91/2 Score 273
91/2 Score CAN 493
92/3 Score 230
93/4 Score 243
95/6 Score 194
90/1 Sco. Young Stars 8
94/5 Select 81
95/6 SBx Impact 77
97/8 SP Authentic 23
00/1 Stadium 158
96/7 Team Out!
92/3 Topps 346
95/6 Topps 213
99/0 Topps 27
99/0 To. Chrome 27
94/5 Topps Finest 60
96/7 To. Picks 155
91/2 To. Stadium 190
92/3 To. Stadium 279
93/4 To. Stadium 222
94/5 To. Stadium 210
95/6 To. Stadium 4
95/6 T. Super Skills 39
02/3 To. Total 273
98/9 UD Choice 41
90/1 Upper Deck 377
91/2 Upper Deck 370
92/3 Upper Deck 244
93/4 Upper Deck 208
94/5 Upper Deck 89, SP-125
95/6 Upper Deck 137
97/8 Upper Deck 244
98/9 Upper Deck 59
95/6 UD BAP 116, ✍ S116
95/6 UD CC 315
97/8 UD Coll. Choice 114
98/9 UD G. Reserve 59
00/1 UD Vintage 72
99/0 Victory 63
88/9 BOST / Sports Action
89/0 BOST / Sports Action
90/1 BOST / Sports Action
91/2 BOST / Sports Action
92/3 BOST / Postcard
97/8 CARO / Sprint
98/9 CARO / Highwoods
95/6 HART / Kids Club
96/7 HART / Kids Club
86/7 Portland Winter Hawks

WESSLIN, SAMU
99/0 Cardset 340
00/1 Cardset 109
02/3 Cardset 288

WEST, DAN
93/4 Slapshot / Windsor 21

WEST, JOSEPH
96/7 DEL 213
98/9 DEL 183
99/0 Eishockey 223

WEST, MARC
83/4 Brantford Alexanders

WEST, RUSS
90/1 7th..Sketch WHL 142
91/2 7th...Sketch WHL 282

WEST, STEVE
78/9 Winnipeg Jets

WESTCOTT, DUVIE
01/2 BAP Mem. 417
02/3 Choice Prospects 44
01/2 UD Premier 60
01/2 Syracuse Crunch

WESTERBY, BOB
94/5 Slapshot Memorial 20
95/6 Rochester Americans
93/4 Kamloops Blazers

WESTFALL, ED
64-67 BeeHive-3 [Bost.]
64/5 Coke/Sprite [Bost.]
65/6 Coca-Cola
77/8 Coke
70/1 Eddie Sargent 7
71/2 Eddie Sargent 2
72/3 Eddie Sargent 127
70/1 Esso Power Player
75/6 Hockey Heroes
74/5 Lipton Soup 47
74/5 Loblaws
68/9 O-Pee-Chee 135
69/0 O-Pee-Chee 29
70/1 O-Pee-Chee 139
71/2 O-Pee-Chee 169
72/3 O-Pee-Chee 104
72/3 O-Pee-Chee Crest 13
73/4 O-Pee-Chee 67
74/5 O-Pee-Chee 32
75/6 O-Pee-Chee 302
76/7 O-Pee-Chee 11
77/8 O-Pee-Chee 153
78/9 O-Pee-Chee 232
95/6 Parkie 66-67 4
94/5 Parkie Tall 6
68/9 Shirriff / Bost. 2
63/4 Topps 8
64/5 Topps 51
65/6 Topps 37
66/7 Topps 32
66/7 Topps / Test 32
67/8 Topps 95
69/0 Topps 29
72/3 Topps 159
73/4 Topps 67
74/5 Topps 32
75/6 Topps 302
76/7 Topps 11
77/8 Topps 153
78/9 Topps 232
01/2 T/O Archives 51, ✄ Jers, ✍ CAI
71/2 Toronto Sun Photo
91/2 Ultimate O-Six 56, ✍ 56
70/1 BOST
71/2 BOST
91/2 BOST / SA Legends
93/4 NYIS / Bank

WESTIN, ZACK
94/5 Anchorage Aces 3

WESTLUND, TODD
91/2 Minnesota G'Gophers
92/3 Minnesota G'Gophers

WESTLUND, TOMMY
99/0 BAP Mem. 345
00/1 BAP Mem. 371
99/0 Dynagon Ice 45
99/0 Omega 50
00/1 Pacific 91
99/0 Panini Sticker 51
01/2 Signature 56, ✍ Aut. 56
00/1 Topps 234
00/1 Upper Deck 262
97/8 UD Elitserien 23
99/0 UD MVP Cup 42
01/2 Victory 69
98/9 New Haven Beast 20

WESTNER, DAVE
78/9 Saginaw Gears

WESTON, ANNE
95/6 Sheffield Steelers

WESTRUM, PATRICK
79 Panini Sticker 211

WESTWICK, HARRY
83 HHOF Postcard I16
83&87 HHOF 135

WETHERILL, DARREN
97/8 Cleveland Lumberjacks
94/5 Richmond Renegades
95/6 Richmond Renegades
91/2 L. Superior State Lakers

WETZEL, CARL
72 Semic Sticker 117
72/3 Minn. Fight. Saints

WETZEL, TODD
98/9 DEL 8
90/1 7th..Sketch OHL 273
91/2 7th...Sketch OHL 213
95/6 Toledo Storm

WETZELL, STIG
70/1 Kuvajulkaisut 290
80/1 Mallasjuoma 1
78/9 SM-Liiga 21
71/2 Williams Finnish 164
72/3 Williams Finnish 79
72/3 Williams Finnish 116
73/4 Williams Finnish 148

WEVERS, MIKE
92/3 MPS SJHL 132

WHARRAM, KEN
52/3 Anonymous 176
45-64 BeeHive-2 [Chic.]
64-67 BeeHive-3 [Chic.]
63-65 Chex
64/5 Coke/Sprite [Chic.]
65/6 Coca-Cola
62/3 Cowan Tile
68/9 O-Pee-Chee 22
69/0 O-Pee-Chee 74
95/6 Parkie 66-67 29, AS6
94/5 Parkie Tall 23, 137, 150
60/1 Shirriff 70
61/2 Shirriff 32
68/9 Shirriff / Chic. 5
58/9 Topps 14
61/2 Topps 30
61/2 Topps 43
62/3 Topps 39
63/4 Topps 38
64/5 Topps 28
64/5 Topps 108
65/6 Topps 61
66/7 Topps 117
66/7 Topps / Test 44
67/8 Topps 117
67/8 Topps 125
68/9 Topps 22
69/0 Topps 74
58/9 Toronto Star Photo
62/3 Toronto Star Photo
63/4 Toronto Star Action
63/4 Toronto Star Photo
64/5 Toronto Star Photo
63/4 Toronto Star Weekend
66/7 Toronto Star Weekend
68/9 CHIC

WHEATCROFT, JIM
88/9 Lethbridge Hurricanes

WHEATON, JOHN
01/2 Owen Sound Attack
02/3 Owen Sound Attack

WHEELDON, SIMON
99/0 Eishockey 321
89/0 ProCards IHL 39
90/1 ProCards 246
91/2 ProCards 553
00/1 UD DEL 174, ✄ GJ
01/2 UD DEL 195
90/1 WINN / IGA
91/2 Baltimore Skipjacks
90/1 Moncton Hawks
83/4 Victoria Cougars

WHEELER, SHAWN
93/4 Cla. Prospects 235
96/7 Charlotte Checkers
97/8 Charlotte Checkers
98/9 Charlotte Checkers
91/2 Greensboro Monarchs
93/4 Hampton Roads
92/3 Peoria Rivermen

WHELAN, SHANE
86/7 London Knights

WHIDDEN, BOB
72/3 Cleveland Crusaders
72/3 Clev. WHA / Linnett

WHISTLE, BILL
88/9 Brandon Wheat Kings

WHISTLE, DAVE
00/1 Kudos 22
01/2 Belfast Giants

WHISTLE, ROB
88/9 ProCards / Baltimore

WHITAKER, GORD
87/8 Moncton Hawks

WHITCROFT, FRED
83 HHOF Postcard C16
83&87 HHOF 45

WHITE, AL
67/8 Columbus Checkers
69 Columbus Checkers

WHITE, ALEX
01/2 Belleville Bulls
01/2 London Knights

WHITE, ALTON
72/3 Los Angeles Sharks

WHITE, ALVIN
77/8 Kalamazoo Wings

WHITE, BILL
71/2 Eddie Sargent 47
72/3 Eddie Sargent 62
70/1 Esso Power Player
91/2 Future Trends C72 15, ✍ 15
74/5 Loblaws
73/4 Mac's Milk
68/9 O-Pee-Chee 37
69/0 O-Pee-Chee 101
71/2 O-Pee-Chee 11
72/3 O-Pee-Chee 158
72/3 O-Pee-Chee 248
72/3 O-Pee-Chee Crest 6
72/3 O-Pee-Chee TC
73/4 O-Pee-Chee 78
74/5 O-Pee-Chee 90
74/5 O-Pee-Chee 136
75/6 O-Pee-Chee 157
76/7 O-Pee-Chee 235
68/9 Shirriff / LosA. 4
68/9 Topps 37
69/0 Topps 101
71/2 Topps 11
72/3 Topps 40
72/3 Topps 128
73/4 Topps 180
74/5 Topps 90
74/5 Topps 136
75/6 Topps 157
76/7 Topps 235
71/2 Toronto Sun Photo
70/1 CHIC
85/6 Sudbury Wolves
86/7 Sudbury Wolves

WHITE, BRIAN
01/2 Cincinnati Mighty Ducks
98/9 Hershey Bears
00/1 Hershey Bears

WHITE, CAM
94/5 Slapshot / North Bay 6

WHITE, CLUCKER
23/4 Paulins Candy 55

WHITE, COLIN
01/2 BAP Mem. 226
00/1 Crown Royale 131, 21CR-14
01/2 McDonald's -HP 9
01/2 O-Pee-Chee 214
00/1 Pacific 246
01/2 Pacific 414
02/3 Pacific Complete 490
00/1 Pa. Paramount 151
00/1 Premier Plus 134
00/1 Pr. Stock 130, PSR-13
00/1 Signature 270, ✍ Aut. 117
94/5 Slapshot Memorial 67
00/1 SPx 99
00/1 Topps 288
01/2 Topps 214
00/1 To. Chrome 183
00/1 To. Heritage 92
02/3 To. Total 399
00/1 UD Heroes 169
00/1 Upper Deck 189
02/3 Upper Deck 352
00/1 UD Black Diam. 80
00/1 UD Ice 59
00/1 UD MVP 196
00/1 UD Pros&Prosp. 112
00/1 UD Vintage 385
00/1 Vanguard 132
97/8 Albany River Rats
98/9 Albany River Rats
99/0 Albany River Rats

WHITE, GEOFF
92/3 BCJHL 187

WHITE, GEORGE
84/5 Moncton G'Flames
85/6 Moncton G'Flames

WHITE, JASON
91/2 Avant Garde BCJHL 143
91/2 Avant Garde BCJHL 156
90/1 7th..Sketch WHL 157, 234
90/1 Brandon Wheat Kings

WHITE, JIM
74/5 Sioux City Musketeers

WHITE, K.J.
89/0 Windsor Spitfires

WHITE, KAM
94/5 Slapshot / Sarnia 4
95/6 Slapshot 208
96/7 Johnstown Chiefs

WHITE, KEVIN
90/1 7th..Sketch OHL 321

WHITE, MIKE
95/6 Slapshot 27

WHITE, PETER
93/4 Donruss 431
95/6 Edge Ice 37
95/6 Fleer Ultra 240
93/4 Power Play 344
93/4 Score 629
01/2 Signature 46, ✍ Aut. 46
00/1 To. Gold Label 94
93/4 EDMO / Sheet
02/3 OTTA
94/5 Cape Breton Oilers
01/2 Norfolk Admirals
02/3 Philadelphia Phantoms

WHITE, ROBERT
52/3 Anonymous 106

WHITE, RYAN
00/1 Halifax Moosehead

WHITE, SCOTT
92/3 Classic Prospects 56
91/2 Greensboro Monarchs
90/1 Kansas City Blades

WHITE, SHERMAN
53/4 La Patrie
51/2 Laval Dairy 35

WHITE, TODD
01/2 Crown Royale 103
02/3 First Edition 206
02/3 O-Pee-Chee 204
98/9 Omega 57
98/9 Pacific 154
02/3 Pacific 274
02/3 Pacific Complete 229
01/2 PS Titanium 102
02/3 Signature Series GS-96
02/3 Topps 204
02/3 To. Limited 204
02/3 To. Total 144
01/2 Upper Deck 355
02/3 Upper Deck 120
02/3 Victory 153
01/2 OTTA
99/0 Cleveland Lumberjacks
00/1 Grand Rapids Griffins
97/8 Indianapolis Ice 27

WHITE, TONY
76/7 O-Pee-Chee 279
76/7 OPC 396
77/8 O-Pee-Chee 314

WHITFIELD, TRENT
97 Bowman 89
98 Bowman 50
98 Bowman Chrome 50
00/1 PS Titanium 150
00/1 PS Titanium Draft 150
96/7 UD Ice 127
98/9 Portland Pirates
99/0 Portland Pirates
95/6 Spokane Chiefs 9
97/8 Spokane Chiefs

WHITLEY, BRIAN
94/5 Slapshot / North Bay 15
95/6 Slapshot 221

WHITLOCK, BOB
74/5 OPC WHA 12
75/6 OPC WHA 93

WHITMORE, KAY
91/2 Bowman 3
92/3 Bowman 155
93/4 Donruss 359
93/4 Fleer Ultra 443
94/5 Leaf 524
90/1 OPC/Topps 232
91/2 OPC Premier 182
92/3 OPC Premier 87
92/3 Panini Sticker 255
91/2 Parkhurst 58
92/3 Parkhurst 423
93/4 Parkhurst 478
91/2 Pinnacle 22
93/4 Pinnacle 138
94/5 Pinnacle 438
93/4 Power Play 462
93/4 Premier 514
94/5 Premier 85, 134
90/1 Pro Set 610
91/2 Pro Set Platinum 178
88/9 ProCards / Binghampton
89/0 ProCards AHL 303
90/1 Score 402
91/2 Score 75T
91/2 Score CAN 625
92/3 Score 304
93/4 Score 360
92/3 Topps 381
00/1 To. Heritage 200
92/3 To. Stadium 459
93/4 To. Stadium 60
91/2 Upper Deck 291
92/3 Upper Deck 76
91/2 HART / Jr. Whalers
92/3 VANC / Road Trip
94/5 VANC
95/6 VANC / Abalene 2
98/9 Hartford Wolf Pack
97/8 Long Beach Ice Dogs
98/9 Milwaukee Admirals
99/0 Providence Bruins
00/1 Providence Bruins

WHITMORE, KEITH
90/1 7th..Sketch OHL 297
93/4 Flint Generals
94/5 Flint Generals
91/2 Hampton Roads

WHITNEY, DEAN
93/4 Prince Albert Raiders

WHITNEY, MIKE
95/6 Red Deer Rebels

WHITNEY, RAY
02/3 Atomic 30
98/9 Aurora 84
99/0 Aurora 66
00/1 Aurora 64
98/9 Be A Player 56, ✍ Aut. 56
99/0 BAP Mem. 20
00/1 BAP Mem. 93
02/3 BAP Mem. 45
02/3 Bowman 103
91/2 Classic 20
92/3 Classic 119
92/3 Classic / Promo

91/2 Classic Four Sport 20
92/3 Classic Four Sport 223
99/0 Crown Royale 62
00/1 Crown Royale 47
94/5 Donruss 117
95/6 Donruss 308
99/0 Dynagon Ice 93
02/3 Exclusive 53
02/3 First Edition 217
94/5 Fleer 202
93/4 Fleer Ultra 420
95/6 Fleer Ultra 150
02/3 Heads Up 36
94/5 Leaf 448
95/6 Leaf 208, RTTC-1
99/0 Millenium 112, ✍ Aut. 112
02/3 O-Pee-Chee 191
97/8 Omega 105
98/9 Omega 107
99/0 Omega 103
98/9 Pacific 231
99/0 Pacific 183
00/1 Pacific 189
01/2 Pacific 120
02/3 Pacific 109
02/3 Pacific Complete 209
98/9 Pa. Paramount 101
99/0 Pa. Paramount 106
00/1 Pa. Paramount 109
97/8 Pa. Revolution 63
95/6 Panini Sticker 280
96/7 Panini Sticker 286
98/9 Panini Sticker 58
00/1 Panini Sticker 35
91/2 Parkhurst 454
92/3 Parkhurst 160
93/4 Parkhurst 182
95/6 Parkhurst 183
00/1 Parkhurst P-78
02/3 Parkhurst 198
02/3 Parkhurst Retro 28
94/5 Parkie SE163
92/3 Pinnacle 227
94/5 Pinnacle 316
96/7 Pinnacle 20
97/8 Pi. Be A Player 105, ✍ Aut. 105
96/7 Pi. Summit 83
95/6 Playoff 304
95/6 POG 225
93/4 Power Play 439
94/5 Premier 33
99/0 Prism 64
02/3 Pr. Stock Reserve 32
01/2 PS Titanium 42
92/3 Pro Set 241
02/3 Quest for the Cup 26
99/0 Revolution 66
00/1 Revolution 65
92/3 Score 475
93/4 Score 324
95/6 Score 84
92 7th...Sketch Awards 20
91 7th..Sketch Mem.Cup 82
90/1 7th..Sketch WHL 201
00/1 Signature 29, ✍ Aut. 42
02/3 Signature Series 45, ✍ 45
95/6 SBx Emotion 161
94/5 SP 106
97/8 SP Authentic 66
00/1 SP Authentic 39
02/3 SP Authentic 25
02/3 SP GU ✂ AF
02/3 Sports Vault 196
98/9 SPx Finite 37
99/0 Stadium 71
00/1 Stadium 123
92/3 Topps 205
95/6 Topps 68
99/0 Topps 83
00/1 Topps 88
02/3 Topps 191
99/0 To. Chrome 83
00/1 To. Chrome 70
98/9 To. Finest 138
98/9 T. Gold Label 26
00/1 To. Heritage 185
02/3 To. Limited 191
92/3 To. Stadium 490
94/5 To. Stadium 149
95/6 To. Stadium 86
00/1 To. Stars 76
02/3 To. Total 397
98/9 UD Choice 87
00/1 UD Heroes 51
01/2 UD PlayMakers Ltd 29
00/1 UD Reserve 37
92/3 Upper Deck 407
93/4 Upper Deck 4
94/5 Upper Deck 149, SP-163
95/6 Upper Deck 62
96/7 Upper Deck 150
98/9 Upper Deck 97
00/1 Upper Deck 75
01/2 Upper Deck 50
02/3 Upper Deck 52, ✂ HS
95/6 UD BAP 125, ✍ S125
01/2 UD Challenge 22
95/6 UD CC 225
96/7 UD CC 240
98/9 UD G. Reserve 97
02/3 UD Honor 19, 79
01/2 UD Mask 26, ✂ GJ, ✂ JP, ✂ DP
98/9 UD MVP 89
99/0 UD MVP 87
00/1 UD MVP 80
01/2 UD MVP 53
02/3 UD MVP 54, ST
99/0 UD MVP Cup 81
00/1 UD Pros&Prosp. 37
02/3 UD Top Shelf ✂ ST
00/1 UD Vintage 151
02/3 UD Vintage 75
00/1 Vanguard 47

00/1 Victory 106
02/3 Victory 58
01/2 COLU
97/8 FLOR / Winn-Dixie
92/3 SANJ / Pacific Bell
92/3 SANJ / Pacific Bell
89/0 Spokane Chiefs

WHITNEY, RYAN
97 Québec Pee Wee 1165

WHITTEN, ERIN
94/5 Classic W40
93/4 Cla. Prospects 249, ✍ Aut.
95/6 Flint Generals
93/4 Toledo Storm 27

WHITTEN, WADE
91 7th..Sketch Mem.Cup 8
90/1 7th..Sketch OHL 175
91/2 7th...Sketch OHL 347
89/0 Soo Greyhounds

WHITTLE, JEFF
91/2 7th...Sketch WHL 167
98/9 Detroit Vipers
94/5 Flint Generals
95/6 Flint Generals
96/7 Flint Generals
98/9 Flint Generals

WHITTOM, DAVE*
91/2 7th...Sketch LHJMQ 283
91 7th..Sketch Mem.Cup 58

WHITTON, MIKE
95/6 Toledo Storm
96/7 Toledo Storm
92/3 W. Michigan Broncos
93/4 W. Michigan Broncos

WHITWELL, DAVID
02/3 Peterborough Phantoms

WHITWORTH, DAVID
92/3 BCJHL 129
99/0 Greensboro Generals

WHYNOT, CRAIG
95/6 Slapshot 258

WHYTE, DARRYL
93/4 Slapshot / Kitchener 3
94/5 Slapshot / Kitchener 3

WHYTE, DEAN
84/5 Belleville Bulls

WHYTE, GEORGE
52/3 Anonymous 63

WHYTE, SANDRA
94/5 Classic W30

WHYTE, SEAN
92/3 Classic Prospects 101
90/1 ProCards 346
91/2 ProCards 401
98/9 Phoenix Mustangs 22
92/3 Phoenix Roadrunners

WIBNER, CHRISTIAN
98/9 Odessa Jackalopes

WICKBERG, HÅKAN
72 Hellas MM-Jenkki 41
74 Hellas MM-Jenkki 37
70/1 Kuvajulkaisut 40
72 Panda MM-Toronto
72 Semic Sticker 52
74 Semic Sticker 9
71/2 Williams Finnish 60
72/3 Williams Finnish 59
73/4 Williams Finnish 39

WICKENHEISER, CHRIS
98/9 EBK ECHL All-Star
93/4 Red Deer Rebels
95/6 Red Deer Rebels

WICKENHEISER, DOUG
82/3 McDonald's Les Étoiles 26
81/2 O-Pee-Chee 193
82/3 O-Pee-Chee 196
83/4 O-Pee-Chee 202
84/5 O-Pee-Chee 193
85/6 O-Pee-Chee 229
87/8 OPC/Topps 193
88/9 O-Pee-Chee 263
83/4 OPC/Topps Sticker 67
84/5 OPC Sticker 58
85/6 OPC Sticker 52-183
88/9 OPC Sticker 56-187
87/8 Panini Sticker 318
80/1 Pepsi Bottle Cap
83/4 Souhaits Keychain [Canadiens]
83/4 Vachon 60-80
80/1 MONT
81/2 MONT
82/3 MONT
82/3 MONT / Steinberg
83/4 MONT
87/8 VANC / Shell
89/0 WASH
93/4 Fort Wayne Komets 23
92/3 Peoria Rivermen

WICKENHEISER, HAYLEY
94/5 Classic W13
97/8 Esso 58, ✍ Aut.
97/8 Game of Her Life
97/8 UD Coll. Choice 279

WICKENHEISER, KURT
82/3 Regina Pats
83/4 Regina Pats

WICKS, RON
91/2 Ultimate Original Six 87

WICKSTROM, KJELL-ARNE
74 Hellas MM-Jenkki 38
73/4 Williams Finnish 40

WICKWARE, RANDY
81/2 Victoria Cougars

WIDEMAN, DENNIS
01/2 London Knights
99/0 Sudbury Wolves 7
00/1 Sudbury Wolves 8

WIDING, DANIEL
00/1 UD Elitserien 114

WIDING, JUHA
70/1 Colgate 11
70/1 Dad's Cookies
70/1 Eddie Sargent 76
71/2 Eddie Sargent 65
72/3 Eddie Sargent 93
70/1 Esso Power Player
74/5 Loblaws
71/2 O-Pee-Chee 86
71/2 O-Pee-Chee Book. 19
72/3 O-Pee-Chee 46
73/4 O-Pee-Chee 159
74/5 O-Pee-Chee 258
75/6 O-Pee-Chee 142
75/6 O-Pee-Chee 320
76/7 O-Pee-Chee 354
77/8 OPC WHA 33
71/2 Topps 86
72/3 Topps 108
73/4 Topps 156
74/5 Topps 258
75/6 Topps 142
75/6 Topps 320
71/2 Toronto Sun Photo

WIDMER, JASON
95/6 Leaf 287
91 7th..Sketch Mem.Cup 129
90/1 7th..Sketch WHL 136
91/2 7th...Sketch WHL 357
96/7 Kentucky Tho'blades
97/8 Kentucky Tho'blades
93/4 Lethbridge Hurricanes

WIEBE, ART
34-43 BeeHive-1 [Chic.]
36-39 Diamond Match TT1
36-39 Diamond Match TT2
36-39 Diamond Match TT3
36-39 Diamond Match BH TT
36-39 Diamond Match Chic.
36-39 Diamond Match BH BT
36/7 O-Pee-Chee 113
39/0 O-Pee-Chee 49
37/8 World Wide Gum 124

WIEBE, DAN
92/3 Toledo Storm

WIECKOWSKI, KRZYSTOF
98/9 SP Authentic 134
98/9 Upper Deck 411
98/9 UD G. Reserve 411

WIECZOREK, DARIUSZ
89 Semic Sticker 130

WIEGAND, CHUCK
93/4 Johnstown Chiefs 13

WIEGAND, JOHN
93/4 Michigan State

WIELAND, MARKUS
94/5 DEL 370
95/6 DEL 362
96/7 DEL 137
98/9 DEL 78

WIELE, SVEN
99/0 Eishockey 328

WIELOCH, SLAWOMIR
92 Semic Sticker 284

WIEMER, JASON
98/9 Be A Player 21, ✍ Aut. 21
94/5 Classic 8, T66
94/5 Classic 4 Sport 122
94/5 Cla. Images 4 Sport 101
95/6 Donruss 11
94/5 Flair 176
94/5 Fleer 211
94/5 Fleer Ultra 374, P-10
95/6 Fleer Ultra 156
94/5 Leaf 489, P-4
95/6 Leaf 23, SR-19
94/5 L. Limited 119
98/9 Omega 36
98/9 Pacific 128
99/0 Pacific 63
00/1 Pacific 76
01/2 Pacific 68, 405
02/3 Pacific 162
02/3 Pacific Complete 349
97/8 Pa. Dynagon BKS-90
95/6 Parkhurst 193
01/2 Parkhurst 216
94/5 Parkie SE172
94/5 Pinnacle 484
95/6 Pinnacle 77
96/7 Pi. Be A Player 26, ✍ Aut. 26
94/5 Premier 463
95/6 Score 149
94/5 Select 171
00/1 Topps 254
94/5 Topps Finest BBM-5, BBR-16
93/4 Upper Deck E3
94/5 Upper Deck 262, SP-166
95/6 Upper Deck 391
96/7 Upper Deck 157
01/2 Upper Deck 306
00/1 UD Vintage 61
01/2 FLOR
95/6 TAMP / Sky Box
93/4 Portland Winter Hawks

WIEMER, JIM
91/2 Bowman 363
90/1 O-Pee-Chee 439
91/2 O-Pee-Chee 475
90/1 Pro Set 413
88/9 ProCards / Cape Breton
91/2 Score CAN 535
91/2 To. Stadium 16

89/0 BOST / Sports Action
91/2 BOST / Sports Action
88/9 EDMO / Action 25
89/0 New Haven Nighthawks

WIENKE, STEVE
86/7 Kamloops Blazers

WIESEL, ADAM
95/6 Classic 81, ✍ Aut.
95/6 Cla. 5 Sport 152
95/6 Fredericton Canadiens
96/7 Fredericton Canadiens

WIEST, RICH
86/7 Kamloops Blazers

WIGHT, DAVID
96/7 Soo Greyhounds

WIGLE, DENNIS
84/5 Ottawa 67's

WIITA, MARTIN
91/2 Semic Elitserien 148
92/3 Semic Nordisk 107
98/9 UD Elitserien 28
02/3 Dundee Texol Stars

WIKLANDER, LARS-GÖRAN
95/6 Leaf Elit Set 203, R-4
95/6 UD Elitserien 217
97/8 UD Elitserien 67
98/9 UD Elitserien 60
99/0 UD Elitserien 45

WIKLANDER, MIKAEL
94/5 Leaf Elit Set 191
95/6 Leaf Elit Set 179
95/6 UD Elitserien 22

WIKMAN, JUHA
72/3 Williams Finnish 298

WIKSTRÖM, JÖRGEN
98/9 UD Elitserien 17

WIKSTRÖM, SAMI
92/3 Jyvas Hyva 143
93/4 Jyvas Hyva 264
93/4 Sisu 295

WIKSTRÖM, SEPPO
70/1 Kuvajulkaisut 307
71/2 Williams Finnish 205
72/3 Williams Finnish 242

WIKSTRØM, TERJE
92/3 Semic Nordisk 176

WIKULOW, SERGEI
94/5 DEL 168

WILCOX, ARCHIE
33/4 O-Pee-Chee 57
33/4 WWGum 9

WILCOX, GEORGE
98/9 Anchorage Aces
99/0 Anchorage Aces
87/8 Hull Olympiques

WILD, LEONARD
00/1 UD DEL 167
01/2 UD DEL 247

WILD, MARTIN
79 Panini Sticker 104

WILDE, MARTIN
01/2 Providence Bruins

WILDER, ARCHIE
34-43 BeeHive-1 [Detr.]
40/1 O-Pee-Chee 145

WILDGOOSE, LYLE
93/4 Cla. Prospects 242
93/4 Raleigh Icecaps
94/5 Raleigh Icecaps

WILENIUS, BENGT
66/7 Champion 110
78/9 SM-Liiga 211
71/2 Williams Finnish 241
72/3 Williams Finnish 225
73/4 Williams Finnish 303

WILEY, JIM
74/5 Loblaws
74/5 VANC / Royal Bank
76/7 VANC / Royal Bank
96/7 Kentucky Tho'blades
97/8 Kentucky Tho'blades

WILFORD, MARTY
97 Bowman 18
95/6 Slapshot 233
99/0 Houston Aeros
97/8 Indianapolis Ice 28
98/9 Indianapolis Ice
01/2 St. John's Maple Leafs
01/2 St. John's / Clarenville

WILHELMY, JONATHAN
98/9 Québec Remparts

WILKIE, BOB
95/6 DEL 11
94/5 Parkhurst 171
89/0 ProCards AHL 307
90/1 ProCards 477
91/2 Score 328
91/2 Score CAN 358
99/0 Anchorage Aces
95/6 Cincinnati Cyclones
92/3 Fort Wayne Komets 25
94/5 Hershey Bears

WILKIE, BRIAN
86/7 Regina Pats

WILKIE, DAVID
92/3 Classic 11
92/3 Classic LP7
92/3 Classic Four Sport 160
93/4 Donruss USA22
95/6 Edge Ice 43
96/7 Flair 113
96/7 Fl. Ultra 91, UR-19
96/7 Got-Um
94/5 Leaf 458
95/6 Leaf 259
96/7 Metal Univ. 195
97/8 Pacific CC 54
93/4 Pinnacle 487
96/7 Pi. Be A Player 108, ✍ Aut. 108

94/5 Premier 481
90/1 7th..Sketch WHL 11
91/2 7th...Sketch WHL 95
96/7 SP 82
96/7 To. Picks 173
93/4 Upper Deck 558
96/7 Upper Deck 282
96/7 MONT / Export
96/7 MONT
94/5 Fredericton Canadiens
99/0 Houston Aeros
93/4 Kamloops Blazers

WILKINS, BARRY
71/2 Eddie Sargent 221
72/3 Eddie Sargent 217
70/1 Esso Power Player
74/5 Loblaws
74/5 Loblaws Update
71/2 O-Pee-Chee 230
72/3 O-Pee-Chee 109
74/5 O-Pee-Chee 182
75/6 O-Pee-Chee 148
72/3 Topps 102
74/5 Topps 182
75/6 Topps 148
76/7 Topps 102
71/2 Toronto Sun Photo
70/1 VANC / Royal Bank
71/2 VANC / Royal Bank 13
72/3 VANC / Nalley's
72/3 VANC / Royal Bank
73/4 VANC / Royal Bank

WILKINSON, BILL
92/3 W. Michigan Broncos
93/4 W. Michigan Broncos

WILKINSON, DEREK
97/8 Donruss 213
95/6 Edge Ice 103
95/6 Future Legends 44
91/2 7th...Sketch OHL 48
94/5 Atlanta Knights 23
95/6 Atlanta Knights
99/0 Charlotte Checkers
96/7 Cleveland Lumberjacks
97/8 Cleveland Lumberjacks
98/9 Cleveland Lumberjacks
01/2 Belfast Giants

WILKINSON, NEIL
90/1 Bowman 184
93/4 Donruss 62
93/4 EA Sports 116
92/3 Fleer Ultra 198
92/3 Humpty Dumpty
93/4 Leaf 357
90/1 O-Pee-Chee 443
91/2 O-Pee-Chee 348
91/2 OPC Premier 110
92/3 Panini Sticker 128
91/2 Parkhurst 382
92/3 Parkhurst 165
93/4 Parkhurst 315
95/6 Parkhurst 439
91/2 Pinnacle 108
92/3 Pinnacle 27
93/4 Pinnacle 354
90/1 Pro Set 465
91/2 Pro Set 328
91/2 Pro Set 483
92/3 Pro Set 168
91/2 Pro Set Platinum 229
88/9 ProCards / Kalamazoo
89/0 ProCards IHL 91
91/2 Score 369
91/2 Score 8T
91/2 Score CAN 328
91/2 Score CAN 558
92/3 Score 235
93/4 Score 138
93/4 Score 523
92/3 Topps 76
91/2 To. Stadium 293
92/3 To. Stadium 219
90/1 Upper Deck 547
91/2 Upper Deck 55
91/2 Upper Deck 95
92/3 Upper Deck 30
93/4 Upper Deck 378
94/5 Upper Deck 392
97/8 Upper Deck 347
94/5 UD BAP R70, ✍ 44
93/4 CHIC / Coke
91/2 SANJ / Sports Action

WILKINSON, PETER
92/3 W. Michigan Broncos
93/4 W. Michigan Broncos

WILKS, BRIAN
88/9 ProCards / New Haven
89/0 ProCards AHL 148
82/3 Kitchener Rangers
83/4 Kitchener Rangers
84/5 Kitchener Rangers

WILLARD, CRAIG
98/9 Oklahoma City Blazers

WILLARD, ROD
83/4 Springfield Indians 18

WILLBERG, ESA
70/1 Kuvajulkaisut 292

WILLETT, PAUL
91/2 ProCards 368
92/3 Fort Wayne Komets 26
94/5 Fort Wayne Komets 12
95/6 Fort Wayne Komets
98/9 Muskegon Fury

WILLIAMS, BARRY
74/5 PITT

WILLIAMS, BRIAN
86/7 Sherb. Canadiens 30

WILLIAMS, DAN
89/0 Johnstown Chiefs

WILLIAMS, DARRYL
88/9 ProCards / New Haven
89/0 ProCards AHL 25
90/1 ProCards 416
91/2 ProCards 369

97/8 Long Beach Ice Dogs
98/9 Long Beach Ice Dogs
92/3 Phoenix Roadrunners
93/4 Phoenix Roadrunners

WILLIAMS, DAVE (TIGER)
01/2 BAP Update ✂ TC1
84/5 DETR / Little Caesars
01/2 Fleer Greats 39, ✍ Aut.
83/4 Funmate Puffy 4 [w/]
75/6 Hockey Heroes
87/8 LOSA
76/7 O-Pee-Chee 373
76/7 O-Pee-Chee 394
77/8 O-Pee-Chee 4
77/8 O-Pee-Chee 5
77/8 O-Pee-Chee 383
78/9 O-Pee-Chee 66
78/9 O-Pee-Chee 359
79/0 O-Pee-Chee 4
79/0 O-Pee-Chee 97
80/1 O-Pee-Chee 105
80/1 O-Pee-Chee 164
81/2 O-Pee-Chee 345
81/2 O-Pee-Chee 385
82/3 O-Pee-Chee 358
83/4 O-Pee-Chee 363
86/7 OPC/Topps 6
81/2 OPC Sticker 247
86/7 OPC Sticker 94-225
87/8 Panini Sticker 283
01/2 Parkhurst ✍ PA44
02/3 Parkhurst ✂ VT20
80/1 Pepsi Bottle Cap
81/2 Post 10
82/3 Post [Vanc.]
84/5 7-Eleven
02/3 Signature Series ✂ FS1
83/4 Souhaits Keychain [Canucks]
77/8 Topps 4
77/8 Topps 5
78/9 Topps 66
79/0 Topps 4
79/0 Topps 97
80/1 Topps 105
80/1 Topps 164
74/5 TORO
75/6 TORO
76/7 TORO
77/8 TORO
78/9 TORO
02/3 Ultimate Memorabilia ✂ RT
83/4 Vachon 120-40
80/1 VANC
80/1 VANC / Silverwood
81/2 VANC
81/2 VANC / Silverwood
82/3 VANC
83/4 VANC

WILLIAMS, DAVE*
00/1 Rochester Americans

WILLIAMS, DAVID*
92/3 Bowman 377
94/5 Leaf 538
92/3 O-Pee-Chee 250
92/3 Pro Set 172
92/3 Score 539
92/3 Topps 372
92/3 To. Stadium 461
92/3 Upper Deck 51
94/5 ANAH / Carl's Jr. 25
97/8 Cincinnati Cyclones
92/3 Kansas City Blades

WILLIAMS, DOUG
59/60 Whitby Dunlops

WILLIAMS, ERNIE
26 Dominion Chocolates 18

WILLIAMS, GORDIE
83/4 Springfield Indians 7

WILLIAMS, JACK
90 7th..Sketch Mem.Cup 48
90/1 7th..Sketch OHL 247
91/2 7th...Sketch OHL 57
96/7 Louisiana Ice Gators
97/8 Louisiana Ice Gators
89/0 Kitchener Rangers
90/1 Kitchener Rangers

WILLIAMS, JASON
00/1 BAP Mem. 510
01/2 BAP Mem. 25
02/3 BAP Mem. ✂ SCC12
02/3 Heads Up ✂ GWQ 12
01/2 O-Pee-Chee 307
02/3 Pacific 136, ✂ GWJ 18
02/3 Pacific Complete 163
01/2 Parkhurst 299
01/2 Pr. Stock 104, -PS 81
02/3 PS Titanium ✂ GWJ 27
94 Québec Pee Wee 1418
01/2 Signature 211, ✍ Aut. 211
00/1 SP Authentic 104
01/2 Stadium 119
01/2 Topps 307
00/1 UD Black Diam. 118
01/2 Victory 369
01/2 Cincinnati Mighty Ducks

WILLIAMS, JEFF
93/4 Slapshot / Guelph 17
94/5 Slapshot / Guelph 18
95/6 Slapshot 98
97/8 Albany River Rats
98/9 Albany River Rats
99/0 Albany River Rats
00/1 Syracuse Crunch
95/6 Guelph Storm

WILLIAMS, JOHN
85/6 London Knights

WILLIAMS, JUSTIN
01/2 Adrenaline 144
00/1 BAP Mem. 444
01/2 BAP Mem. 101
02/3 BAP Mem. 156, ✂ FG20
01/2 Bowman 155, ✂ FFJ, ✂ FFS, ✂ FFDS, ✂ FFR, ✍ YSA
00/1 Crown Royale 136, 21CR-19
01/2 O-Pee-Chee 33
02/3 O-Pee-Chee 184
01/2 Pacific 296
02/3 Pacific 290
02/3 Pacific Complete 131
00/1 Parkhurst P-226
02/3 Parkhurst Retro 156
00/1 Premier Plus 128, PR5
00/1 Pr. Stock 136, PSR-16
00/1 PS Titanium 138
00/1 PS Titanium Draft 138
95 Québec Pee Wee 692
00/1 Signature 260, ✍ Aut. 222
00/1 SP Authentic 118
01/2 SP Authentic 114
02/3 SP Authentic ✍ SotT, ✍ SotTD
00/1 SP GU 79
02/3 SP GU ✂ AF, ✂ PC, ✍ Sig
00/1 SPx 120
01/2 SPx ✂ DT
00/1 Stadium 245
02/3 Stadium ✂ YSS11, ✂ YSD5
01/2 Topps 33
02/3 Topps 184
00/1 To. Chrome 241
00/1 To. Gold Label 106, ✍ GLA
00/1 To. Heritage 97
01/2 To. Heritage ✍ CAI
02/3 To. Limited 184
00/1 To. Stars 109
02/3 To. Total 185
00/1 UD Heroes 174
00/1 UD Reserve 109
00/1 Upper Deck 214
01/2 Upper Deck 129, ✂ GN, ✂ NG
02/3 Upper Deck 131, ✂ UDPL
02/3 UD Artistic ✂ RT
00/1 UD Black Diam. 129
00/1 UD Ice 97
01/2 UD Mask ✂ GJ, ✂ JP, ✂ DP
01/2 UD MVP 139
02/3 UD MVP 137,SD (x2), Souv.
02/3 UD Premier ✍ Sig.
00/1 UD Pros&Prosp. 119, NA6
01/2 UD Top Shelf ✂ J
02/3 UD Top Shelf ✂ R
00/1 UD Vintage 389
02/3 UD Vintage 187, GB 187, ✂ HS
00/1 Vanguard 138
01/2 Victory 257
02/3 Victory 160
01/2 PHIL

WILLIAMS, MARTIN
98/9 DEL 146

WILLIAMS, MIKE
93/4 Slapshot / Peterborough 18
95/6 Slapshot 322
98/9 Oklahoma City Blazers
92/3 Toledo Storm WIOT

WILLIAMS, PAUL
98/9 Anchorage Aces
99/0 Anchorage Aces

WILLIAMS, ROD
84/5 Kelowna Wings &...
85/6 Brandon Wheat Kings
86/7 Regina Pats

WILLIAMS, SEAN
88/9 ProCards / Saginaw
89/0 ProCards IHL 50
90/1 ProCards 393
91/2 ProCards 488
92/3 Indianapolis Ice
94/5 Minnesota Moose
95/6 Minnesota Moose

WILLIAMS, STEVE*
91/2 Avant Garde BCJHL 95
92/3 BCJHL 130

WILLIAMS, TOM
70/1 MINS / Colour

WILLIAMS, TOM C.
74/5 Loblaws
74/5 O-Pee-Chee 394
75/6 O-Pee-Chee 179
76/7 O-Pee-Chee 319
77/8 O-Pee-Chee 44
78/9 O-Pee-Chee 314
75/6 Topps 179
77/8 Topps 44
72/3 New England Whalers

WILLIAMS, TOM M.
45-64 BeeHive-2 [Bost.]
64-67 BeeHive-3 [Bost.]
51/2 Cleveland Barons
60/1 Cleveland Barons
64/5 Coke/Sprite [Bost.]
65/6 Coca-Cola
70/1 Colgate 5
70/1 Dad's Cookies
70/1 Eddie Sargent 83
71/2 Eddie Sargent 130
70/1 Esso Power Player
62/3 Cowan Tile
68/9 O-Pee-Chee 11
69/0 O-Pee-Chee 128
70/1 O-Pee-Chee 169
71/2 O-Pee-Chee 31
75/6 O-Pee-Chee 79

75/6 O-Pee-Chee 330
95/6 Parkie 66-67 11
94/5 Parkie Tall 4
61/2 Shirriff 17
68/9 Shirriff / Bost. 16
62/3 Topps 21
63/4 Topps 12
64/5 Topps 58
65/6 Topps 35
66/7 Topps 38
66/7 Topps / Test 38
67/8 Topps 40
68/9 Topps 11
69/0 Topps 128
71/2 Topps 31
75/6 Topps 79
75/6 Topps 330
63/4 Toronto Star Weekend
71/2 Toronto Sun Photo

WILLIAMS, VINCE
01/2 Florida Everblades

WILLIAMS, WARREN (BUTCH)
75/6 O-Pee-Chee 217
75/6 Topps 217

WILLIAMSON, ANDREW
98/9 EBK ECHL All-Star
95/6 Slapshot 55, 199
97/8 Toledo Storm 23

WILLIAMSON, BRAD
99/0 Houston Aeros

WILLIAMSON, GLEN
91/2 WINN / IGA

WILLIAMSON, MIKE
91/2 7th...Sketch WHL 28
93/4 Portland Winter Hawks
97/8 Portland Winter Hawks

WILLIS, JORDAN
95/6 Edge Ice 143
96/7 Dayton Bombers
00/1 Nottingham Panthers

WILLIS, RALPH
52/3 Anonymous 98

WILLIS, RICK
95/6 Binghampton Rangers
96/7 Binghampton Rangers

WILLIS, SHANE
01/2 Adrenaline 37
99/0 BAP Mem. 28
01/2 BAP Mem. 11, 489
02/3 BAP Mem. 100
97 Bowman 113
98 Bowman 75
98 Bowman Chrome 75
95/6 Classic 48
00/1 Crown Royale 116, 21CR-5
02/3 Exclusive 158
01/2 Heads Up BTI 4
01/2 O-Pee-Chee 165
01/2 Pacific 81
02/3 Pacific 356
02/3 Pacific Complete 30
99/0 Pa. Paramount 51
00/1 Parkhurst P-152
01/2 Parkhurst 66
00/1 Premier Plus PA8
00/1 Pr. Stock 109
00/1 PS Titanium 110, 3SS-21
00/1 PS Titanium Draft 110
00/1 Signature 265, ✍ Aut. 72
01/2 Signature 6, ✍ Aut. 6
02/3 Signature Series 151, ✍ 151
00/1 SPx 134
01/2 Stadium 64
99/0 Topps 163
00/1 Topps 308
01/2 Topps 165, OTG 12
99/0 To. Chrome 163
00/1 To. Chrome 203
00/1 To. Heritage 120
01/2 To. Heritage 101
01/2 Upper Deck 33
02/3 Upper Deck 405
96/7 UD Black Diam. 26
97/8 UD Coll. Choice 300
96/7 UD Ice 126
00/1 UD Ice 65
99/0 UD MVP 41
01/2 UD MVP 31
02/3 UD MVP 170
01/2 UD Vintage 46
02/3 UD Vintage 228
00/1 Vanguard 109
01/2 Victory 67
99/0 Cincinnati Cyclones
98/9 New Haven Beast 7
95/6 Prince Albert Raiders

WILLIS, TYLER
92/3 BCJHL 71
97 Bowman 87
00/1 Peoria Rivermen
00/1 Worcester IceCats
95/6 Swift Current Broncos

WILLMAN, JAY
99/0 San Angelo Outlaws

WILLMAN, TIMO
98/9 Cardset 76
99/0 Cardset 338
00/1 Cardset 104, 245

WILLMANN, DIETER
94/5 DEL 287

WILLMANN, PETER
99/0 Eishockey 229

WILLNER, BRAD
91/2 L. Superior State Lakers

WILLSIE, BRIAN
99/0 BAP Mem. 388
98 Bowman 8
98 Bowman Chrome 8

01/2 Crown Royale RR 6
99/0 Omega 69
02/3 Pacific Complete 173
01/2 PS Titanium Draft 118
95/6 Slapshot 100
00/1 Topps 322
00/1 To. Chrome 217
98/9 UD Choice 273
98/9 Hershey Bears
02/3 Hershey Bears
95/6 Guelph Storm
96/7 Guelph Storm

WILM, CLARKE
98/9 Bowman's Best 129
98/9 Omega 37
99/0 Pacific 64
02/3 Pacific Complete 365
00/1 Pa. Paramount 40
00/1 Signature 14, ✍ Aut. 145
99/0 Stadium 51, PP6
00/1 Upper Deck 29
01/2 Upper Deck 258
00/1 UD Vintage 54
01/2 Victory 57
96/7 Saint John Flames
97/8 Saint John Flames
93/4 Saskatoon Blades
93/4 Saskatoon Blades

WILMOT, LEFTY
30s A&BC Chewing Gum 41

WILSON, BEHN
83/4 Funmate Puffy 12 [w/]
79/0 O-Pee-Chee 111
80/1 O-Pee-Chee 145
81/2 O-Pee-Chee 239
82/3 O-Pee-Chee 260
81/2 OPC Sticker 175
82/3 Post [Phil.]
79/0 Topps 111
80/1 Topps 145
81/2 Topps 45
86/7 CHIC / Coke
87/8 CHIC / Coke

WILSON, BEHN
02/3 Fleer Throwbacks 86

WILSON, BERT
74/5 O-Pee-Chee 384
75/6 O-Pee-Chee 338
76/7 O-Pee-Chee 378
78/9 O-Pee-Chee 369
80/1 Pepsi Bottle Cap
80/1 CALG

WILSON, BOB
52/3 Anonymous 171

WILSON, CAREY
90/1 Bowman 214
91/2 Bowman 265
92/3 Fleer Ultra 272
86/7 Kraft Sports 10
85/6 O-Pee-Chee 191
86/7 OPC/Topps 166
87/8 O-Pee-Chee 211
88/9 OPC/Topps 75
90/1 OPC/Topps 54
91/2 O-Pee-Chee 85
89/0 OPC/Topps 66
90/1 OPC/Topps N
90/1 OPC Premier 128
88/9 OPC Stars 45
85/6 OPC Sticker 213-82
87/8 OPC Sticker 45-185
88/9 OPC Sticker 266-130
89/0 opcSticker 239-102
87/8 Panini Sticker 211
88/9 Panini Sticker 246
89/0 Panini Sticker 280
90/1 Panini Sticker 105
91/2 Panini Sticker 56
91/2 Pinnacle 364
92/3 Pinnacle 369
90/1 Pro Set 210, 453
91/2 Pro Set 36
90/1 Score 254, 42T
91/2 Score 227
91/2 Score CAN 227
92/3 Score 127
91/2 To. Stadium 301
91/2 Upper Deck 538
85/6 CALG / Red Rooster
86/7 CALG / Red Rooster
91/2 CALG / IGA
92/3 CALG / IGA 011
88/9 HART / Jr. Whalers
90/1 HART / Jr. Whalers
89/0 NYRA / Marine

WILSON, CHAD
92/3 BCJHL 151

WILSON, COLIN
91/2 7th...Sketch OHL 125
91/2 Peterborough Petes
92/3 Windsor Spitfires

WILSON, CRAIG
89/0 7th..Sketch OHL 69

WILSON, CULLY
23/4 Paulins Candy 67

WILSON, DEVIN
99/0 Prince George Cougars
00/1 Prince George Cougars

WILSON, DOUG
90/1 Bowman 2
91/2 Bowman 400
92/3 Bowman 75
92/3 Bowman 219
93/4 EA Sports 115
92/3 Fleer Ultra 199
93/4 Fleer Ultra 230
83/4 Funmate Puffy 14 [w/]
84/5 Kellogg's 34
91/2 Kellogg's / Score 19
90/1 Kraft 62, 77
91/2 Kraft 34
82/3 McDonald's Les Étoiles 36
78/9 O-Pee-Chee 168

80/1 O-Pee-Chee 12
81/2 O-Pee-Chee 66
82/3 O-Pee-Chee 77
82/3 O-Pee-Chee 78
83/4 O-Pee-Chee 114
84/5 O-Pee-Chee 48
85/6 OPC/Topps 45
85/6 OPC/Topps Box P
86/7 OPC/Topps 106
87/8 OPC/Topps 14
88/9 OPC/Topps 89
90/1 OPC/Topps 111, 203
91/2 O-Pee-Chee 49
92/3 O-Pee-Chee 281
89/0 OPC/Topps 112
90/1 OPC Premier 129
91/2 OPC Premier 6
82/3 OPC/Topps Sticker 163
82/3 OPC/Topps Sticker 172
82/3 OPC/Topps Sticker 254
83/4 OPC/Topps Sticker 112
83/4 OPC/Topps Sticker 165
84/5 OPC Sticker 27
85/6 OPC Sticker 25
85/6 OPC Sticker 122
86/7 OPC Sticker 153
87/8 OPC Sticker 77-211
88/9 OPC Sticker 6-135
89/0 opcSticker 14-156
87/8 Panini Sticker 222
88/9 Panini Sticker 24
89/0 Panini Sticker 45
90/1 Panini Sticker 189
91/2 Panini Sticker 18
92/3 Panini Sticker 129
93/4 Panini Sticker 264
91/2 Parkhurst 168
92/3 Parkhurst 167
91/2 Pinnacle 13
91/2 Pinnacle 369
92/3 Pinnacle 52
82/3 Post [Chic.]
93/4 Premier 77
90/1 Pro Set 63, 346
91/2 Pro Set 52
91/2 Pro Set 478
91/2 Pro Set 584
92/3 Pro Set 165
91/2 Pro Set Platinum 107
90/1 Score 280, 320
90/1 Sco. Hot Cards 68
91/2 Score 35
91/2 Score 1T
91/2 Score CAN 35
91/2 Score CAN 551
92/3 Score 15
93/4 Score 115
92/3 Seasons 63
85/6 7-Eleven Superstars 4
83/4 Souhaits Keychain [Blackhawks]
78/9 Topps 168
80/1 Topps 12
81/2 Topps 78 [West]
84/5 Topps 37
85/6 OPC/Topps-Stick. 11
92/3 Topps 482
91/2 To. Stadium 131
92/3 To. Stadium 470
01/2 T/O Archives 68, -Seat
90/1 Upper Deck 223
92/3 Upper Deck 150
79/0 CHIC
80/1 CHIC / Brown
81/2 CHIC
82/3 CHIC
86/7 CHIC / Coke
87/8 CHIC / Coke
88/9 CHIC / Coke
89/0 CHIC / Coke
90/1 CHIC / Coke
91/2 SANJ / Sports Action
00/1 Ottawa 67's 28

WILSON, DUNC
71/2 Eddie Sargent 222
72/3 Eddie Sargent 213
70/1 Esso Power Player
72/3 Post 20
74/5 Loblaws
71/2 O-Pee-Chee 24
72/3 O-Pee-Chee 18
73/4 O-Pee-Chee 257
74/5 O-Pee-Chee 327
76/7 O-Pee-Chee 102
77/8 OPC 8
77/8 O-Pee-Chee 224
72/3 Topps 91
77/8 Topps 8
77/8 Topps 224
71/2 Toronto Sun Photo
77/8 PITT / McDonald's
73/4 TORO
74/5 TORO
70/1 VANC / Royal Bank
71/2 VANC / Royal Bank 14
72/3 VANC / Royal Bank

WILSON, GORD (PHAT)
83 HHOF Postcard J16
83&87 HHOF 195
23/4 Paulins Candy 16

WILSON, JEFF
90/1 7th..Sketch OHL 196
87/8 Kingston Canadians

WILSON, JESSE
90/1 7th..Sketch WHL 12
91/2 7th...Sketch WHL 132

WILSON, JOHNNY
45-64 BeeHive-2 [Detr.]
45-64 BeeHive-2 [Toro.]
52/3 Parkhurst 89
53/4 Parkhurst 51
54/5 Parkhurst 44
59/0 Parkhurst 13
60/1 Parkhurst 14
60/1 Shirriff 15
61/2 Shirriff 100
54/5 Topps 4
57/8 Topps 47
58/9 Topps 22
91/2 Ultimate Original Six 65, ✍ Aut. 65
77/8 PITT / McDonald's

WILSON, LANDON
99/0 BAP Mem. 143
95/6 Bowman 95
97/8 Donruss 87
95/6 Edge Ice 30
96/7 Fl. Ultra 41, UR-20
95/6 Future Legends 24
96/7 Leaf 215
97/8 Leaf 147
97/8 Limited 52
96/7 Metal Univ. 196
99/0 Pacific 31
01/2 Pacific 309
02/3 Pacific Complete 394
97/8 Pacific CC 105
95/6 Parkhurst 526
96/7 Pi. Be A Player 106, ✍ Aut. 106
96/7 Pi. Summit 188
96/7 Pi. Zenith 142
96/7 Score 257
95/6 Select CE 134
01/2 Signature 34, ✍ Aut. 34
95/6 Upper Deck 424
96/7 Upper Deck 242
97/8 Upper Deck 10
01/2 UD MVP 146
01/2 UD Vintage 197
01/2 Victory 269
97/8 Providence Bruins
98/9 Providence Bruins

WILSON, LARRY
45-64 BeeHive-2 [Chic.]
52/3 Parkhurst 92
53/4 Parkhurst 74
54/5 Parkhurst 85
54/5 Topps 40

WILSON, MIKE
00/1 BAP Mem. 232
95/6 Bowman 94
93/4 Classic 32
95/6 Edge Ice 66
95/6 Future Legends 45
97/8 Pa. Invincible R-25
95/6 Parkhurst 534
96/7 Pi. Be A Player 23, ✍ Aut. 23
97/8 Score Buff. 20
93/4 Slapshot / Sudbury 6
94/5 Slapshot / Sudbury 4
00/1 Upper Deck 78
98/9 Las Vegas Thunder
95/6 Rochester Americans
01/2 WBS Penguins
02/3 WBS Penguins
92/3 Sudbury Wolves
93/4 Sudbury Wolves

WILSON, MITCH
88/9 ProCards / Muskegon
89/0 ProCards IHL 149
90/1 ProCards 376

WILSON, MURRAY
72/3 Dernière Heure
73/4 Dernière Heure
74/5 Loblaws
74/5 O-Pee-Chee 359
75/6 O-Pee-Chee 162
76/7 O-Pee-Chee 254
77/8 O-Pee-Chee 69
75/6 Topps 162
76/7 Topps 254
77/8 Topps 69
72/3 MONT / Pro Star
73/4 MONT / Pro Star
74/5 MONT
75/6 MONT
76/7 MONT
77/8 MONT

WILSON, RICK
74/5 Loblaws
74/5 O-Pee-Chee 284
75/6 O-Pee-Chee 356
76/7 O-Pee-Chee 293
77/8 O-Pee-Chee 57
77/8 Topps 57
94/5 DALL / Cap
81/2 Kingston Canadians

WILSON, ROB
00/1 Kudos 116
01/2 Manchester Storm
02/3 Manchester Storm
01/2 Sheffield Steelers
94/5 Sheffield Steelers 21
97/8 Sheffield Steelers
86/7 Sudbury Wolves
87/8 Sudbury Wolves

WILSON, RON
77/8 Kalamazoo Wings
77/8 Nova Scotia Voyageurs

WILSON, RON L.
91/2 Bowman 382
92/3 Bowman 364
93/4 Fleer Ultra 356
93/4 Leaf 316
80/1 O-Pee-Chee 243
81/2 O-Pee-Chee 377
87/8 O-Pee-Chee 224
91/2 O-Pee-Chee 120
81/2 OPC Sticker 140
87/8 Panini Sticker 291
91/2 Panini Sticker 34
92/3 Panini Sticker 18
93/4 Panini Sticker 162
80/1 Pepsi Bottle Cap
93/4 Power Play 373
93/4 Premier 194
90/1 Pro Set 529
91/2 Pro Set 220

88/9 ProCards / Moncton
89/0 ProCards AHL 51
91/2 Score CAN 533
92/3 Score 365
93/4 Score 431
80/1 Topps 243
92/3 Topps 78
91/2 To. Stadium 347
92/3 To. Stadium 429
93/4 MONT
90/1 SLOU / Kodak
91/2 SLOU
79/0 WINN
80/1 WINN
83/4 WINN
84/5 WINN / Safety Tips
85/6 WINN
85/6 WINN / Safety Tips
86/7 WINN
87/8 WINN

WILSON, RON*
89/0 ProCards IHL 188
96/7 ANAH / Up Front 27
87/8 MINS
78/9 TORO
79/0 TORO
97/8 Springfield Falcons
85/6 Sudbury Wolves

WILSON, ROSS**
89/0 ProCards AHL 17
90/1 ProCards 437
91/2 ProCards 389
96/7 Flint Generals
98/9 Flint Generals

WILSON, RUSS
80/1 DETR

WILSON, STACY
94/5 Classic W9
97/8 Esso 60, ✍ Aut.
97/8 UD Coll. Choice 287

WILSON, STEVE
98/9 DEL 101
99/0 Eishockey 102
01/2 UD DEL 104
92/3 Dayton Bombers
93/4 Dayton Bombers
94/5 Dayton Bombers 3
94/5 Dayton Bombers 23
92/3 Fort Wayne Komets 27
95/6 Peoria Rivermen
95/6 Phoenix Roadrunners

WINCH, JASON
91/2 ProCards 14
89/0 7th..Sketch OHL 135
90/1 7th..Sketch OHL 274
91/2 Rochester Americans WPC
92/3 Rochester Americans WPC
89/0 Niagara Falls Thunder

WINCHES, HERB
95/6 Birmingham Bulls

WINDLER, HARALD
94/5 DEL 68

WING, JOHNNY
37/8 World Wide Gum 102

WINGERTER, MARK
84/5 Kelowna Wings &...

WINGFIELD, BRAD
92/3 BCJHL 8
00/1 Kudos 48
97/8 New Mexico Scorpions

WINKLER, CHRIS
92/3 MPS SJHL 127

WINLKER, HAL
23/4 Paulins Candy 46

WINNES, CHRIS
91/2 Pinnacle 351
91/2 Pro Set 522
91/2 Upper Deck 514
92/3 Upper Deck 380
91/2 BOST / Sports Action
97/8 Hartford Wolf Pack
98/9 Hartford Wolf Pack
94/5 Hershey Bears

WINSTANLEY, JEFF
96/7 DEL 119

WINTER, JEFF
98/9 Cincinnati M'Ducks 22

WIRLL, MIKE
99/0 UD Prospects 30
99/0 UD Prospects 80
98/9 Brandon Wheat Kings
99/0 Brandon Wheat Kings

WIRTZ, ARTHUR
83 HHOF Postcard F16
83&87 HHOF 90

WIRTZ, BILL
70/1 CHIC
83 HHOF Postcard M15
83&87 HHOF 179

WIRZENIUS, OLLI
65/6 Hellas 115

WISE, TONY
24/5 Falcons Crescent 10

WISEMAN, BRIAN
94/5 Classic 63
98/9 EBK IHL All-Star
99/0 Houston Aeros
96/7 St. John's Maple Leafs

WISEMAN, CARL
91/2 7th...Sketch LHJMQ 100

WISEMAN, CHAD
02/3 BAP Mem. 335
02/3 Ultimate Memorabilia 62
00/1 UD Prospects 12
02/3 UD Rookie 135
01/2 Cleveland Barons
00/1 Mississauga IceDogs

WISEMAN, EDDIE
34-43 BeeHive-1 [NYAm.]
40/1 O-Pee-Chee 149

WISEMAN, LYALL
51/2 Laval Dairy 63
52/3 Laval Dairy Update 121
52/3 St. Lawrence 100

WISKE, RON
84/5 NYIS / News 31

WISMER, CHRIS
95/6 Slapshot 302
98/9 Dayton Bombers
98/9 Roanoke Express

WISNIEWSKI, JAMES
02/3 Plymouth Whalers

WISOCKI, TODD
98/9 Florida Everblades
00/1 Florida Everblades

WISSMAN, STEVE
93/4 Las Vegas Thunder

WISTE, JIM
70/1 Dad's Cookies
70/1 Eddie Sargent 223
74/5 OPC WHA 34
73/4 Quaker Oats 1
70/1 VANC / Royal Bank
72/3 Clev. WHA / Linnett

WITEHALL, JOHAN
00/1 Pacific 271
90/1 Semic Elitserien 48
00/1 SPx 105
00/1 Upper Deck 222
97/8 UD Elitserien 110
00/1 MONT
98/9 Hartford Wolf Pack
99/0 Hartford Wolf Pack

WITKOWSKI, BYRON
92/3 W. Michigan Broncos

WITT, BRENDAN
99/0 BAP Mem. 210
95/6 Bowman 127
94/5 Classic 90, C10, T75
93/4 Donruss CAN22
95/6 Donruss 361, PP-18
96/7 Do. Elite 83
96/7 Fleer 120
95/6 Fleer Metal 197
95/6 Fleer Ultra 361, HS-20
95/6 L. Limited 117
96/7 L. Preferred 74
96/7 Metal Univ. 168
99/0 Millenium 247, ✍ Aut. 247
02/3 O-Pee-Chee 104
98/9 Pacific 450
02/3 Pacific Complete 471
97/8 Pa. Invincible R-214
96/7 Panini Sticker 136
95/6 Parkhurst 258
02/3 Parkhurst 184
93/4 Pinnacle 465
97/8 Pi. Be A Player 162, ✍ Aut. 162
95/6 Pi. Summit 189
96/7 Pi. Summit 162
95/6 Pi. Zenith 124, RRC-3
96/7 Pi. Zenith 50
95/6 Pro Magnet 27
94/5 Score 205
96/7 Score 270
95/6 Select CE 119
91/2 7th...Sketch WHL 129
02/3 Signature Series ✂ DW9
95/6 SBx Emotion gN 6
95/6 SBx Impact 225
96/7 SBx Impact 143
95/6 SP 162
95/6 Topps 346
02/3 Topps 104
95/6 To. Finest 106
02/3 To. Limited 104
95/6 To. Stadium ER193
02/3 To. Total 332
93/4 Upper Deck 544
95/6 Upper Deck 265
96/7 Upper Deck 177
97/8 Upper Deck 384
95/6 UD CC 400
96/7 UD CC 283, 345
00/1 UD Vintage 368
02/3 UD Vintage 252
95/6 WASH
93/4 Seattle Thunderbirds

WITT, JARED
92/3 MPS SJHL 136

WITTBROCK, MARC
94/5 DEL 145
95/6 DEL 132

WITTENBERG, TOM
92/3 BCJHL 1

WITTLIFF, PHIL
94/5 Milwaukee Admirals
95/6 Milwaukee Admirals
96/7 Milwaukee Admirals

WITTMAN, DON
97/8 Pi. CBC Sports 13

WITTMAN, THEO
95 Panini Worlds 135

WITTWER, BRUNO
72 Semic Sticker 141

WLASOW, LEO
93/4 Maine Black Bears
93/4 Maine Black Bears

WOCHY, STEVE
51/2 Cleveland Barons

WOHL, PAVEL
89 Semic Sticker 177

WOHLERS, NICK
92/3 St. John's Maple Leafs

WOIT, BENNY
45-64 BeeHive-2 [Detr.]
51/2 Parkhurst 58
52/3 Parkhurst 62
53/4 Parkhurst 45
54/5 Parkhurst 38
93/4 Parkie 56-57 40
54/5 Topps 9

WOJCIK, ADAM
00/1 Victoriaville Tigres 15

WOJTYNEK, HENRYK
79 Panini Sticker 118

WOLAK, MIKE
89/0 ProCards IHL 13
85/6 Kitchener Rangers

WOLANIN, CHRIS
91/2 Greensboro Monarchs
92/3 Greensboro Monarchs 2

WOLANIN, CRAIG
90/1 Bowman 166
91/2 Bowman 138
92/3 Bowman 41
95 Globe 110
90/1 OPC/Topps 40
91/2 O-Pee-Chee 199
86/7 OPC Sticker 58
97/8 Pa. Dynagon BKS-94
97/8 Pa. Invincible R-197
87/8 Panini Sticker 77
88/9 Panini Sticker 270
90/1 Panini/QUE 24
91/2 Panini Sticker 264
95 Panini Worlds 218
91/2 Parkhurst 369
91/2 Pinnacle 217
92/3 Pinnacle 107
94/5 Pinnacle 445
94/5 Premier 228
90/1 Pro Set 519
91/2 Pro Set 203
91/2 Pro Set / Prototype
90/1 Score 167
91/2 Score 74
91/2 Score CAN 74
92/3 Score 21
93/4 Score 406
94 Semic 109
95 Semic 103
92/3 Topps 487
91/2 To. Stadium 4
92/3 To. Stadium 317
91/2 Upper Deck 486
97/8 Upper Deck 373
95/6 UD BAP 59, ✍ S59
85/6 NJER 7
86/7 NJER / S.O.B.E.R.
88/9 NJER / Caretta
89/0 NJER
89/0 NJER / Caretta
90/1 QUÉB / Petro-Canada
91/2 QUÉB / Petro-Canada
92/3 QUÉB / Petro-Canada
94/5 QUÉB / Burger King
84/5 Kitchener Rangers

WOLANSKI, PAUL
89/0 7th..Sketch OHL 136
90/1 7th..Sketch OHL 275
91/2 7th...Sketch OHL 383
88/9 Niagara Falls Thunder
89/0 Niagara Falls Thunder

WOLD, VIDAR
92/3 Semic Nordisk 153

WOLF, MANFRED
82 Semic Sticker 116
89 Semic Sticker 121

WOLF, RUDOLF
94/5 APS 119
95/6 APS 296

WOLFE, BERNIE
76/7 O-Pee-Chee 227
77/8 O-Pee-Chee 138
78/9 O-Pee-Chee 81
76/7 Topps 227
77/8 Topps 138
78/9 Topps 81
78/9 WASH

WOLFE, DWIGHT
97/8 Halifax Moosehead
97/8 Halifax Moosehead

WOLFE, HARRY
81/2 Soo Greyhounds
82/3 Soo Greyhounds
83/4 Soo Greyhounds
84/5 Soo Greyhounds
87/8 Soo Greyhounds 31

WOLFE, JOHN
96/7 Guildford Flames 2

WOLITSKI, SHELDON
91/2 Avant Garde BCJHL 4
91/2 Avant Garde BCJHL 155

WOLKOWSKI, CHAD
00/1 Calgary Hitmen
01/2 Calgary Hitmen

WONG, RANDY
00/1 Medicine Hat Tigers

WOO, LARRY
90/1 7th..Sketch WHL 250
89/0 Victoria Cougars

WOOD, DAN
84/5 Fredericton Express
81/2 Kingston Canadians

WOOD, DEREK
98/9 Fort Wayne Komets
93/4 Lethbridge Hurricanes

WOOD, DODY
95/6 Bowman 161
91/2 Classic 38
91/2 Classic Four Sport 38
93/4 Cla. 4 Sport 251
97/8 Pa. Dynagon BKS-87
93/4 Parkhurst 186
90/1 7th..Sketch WHL 13
91/2 7th...Sketch WHL 134
91/2 Star Pics 12
91/2 Ultimate Draft Pick 33, ✍ Aut.
93/4 Upper Deck 238
95/6 Upper Deck 415
92/3 SANJ / Pacific Bell
92/3 Kansas City Blades
93/4 Kansas City Blades
94/5 Kansas City Blades 11
98/9 Kansas City Blades 11
99/0 Kansas City Blades Moment
99/0 Kansas City Blades
00/1 Kansas City Blades 8
02/3 Nottingham Panthers

WOOD, DUSTIN
01/2 Peterborough Petes

WOOD, FRASER
81/2 Ottawa 67's

WOOD, GORD
87/8 Kingston Canadians

WOOD, IAN
95/6 DEL 310
96/7 DEL 93
84/5 Nova Scotia Oilers

WOOD, JASON
92/3 BCJHL 109

WOOD, MARTY
81/2 Regina Pats

WOOD, PRYCE
88/9 Brandon Wheat Kings
89/0 Brandon Wheat Kings

WOOD, RANDY
90/1 Bowman 121
91/2 Bowman 227
92/3 Bowman 246
95/6 Donruss 154
92/3 Fleer Ultra 265
93/4 Fleer Ultra 279
93/4 Leaf 226
94/5 Leaf 544
95/6 Leaf 168
88/9 OPC/Topps 140
90/1 OPC/Topps 97
91/2 O-Pee-Chee 205
89/0 OPC/Topps 35
88/9 OPC Sticker 107-237
88/9 OPC Sticker 202
88/9 Panini Sticker 294
90/1 Panini Sticker 79
91/2 Panini Sticker 244
92/3 Panini Sticker 251
93/4 Panini Sticker 105
91/2 Parkhurst 13
93/4 Parkhurst 297
94/5 Parkhurst 25
91/2 Pinnacle 104
92/3 Pinnacle 133
92/3 Pinnacle 234
93/4 Pinnacle 177
94/5 Pinnacle 218
95/6 Pinnacle 164
95/6 Playoff 205
96/7 Playoff 395
94/5 POG 51
95/6 POG 262
93/4 Power Play 35
93/4 Premier 119
94/5 Premier 61
90/1 Pro Set 194
91/2 Pro Set 151
91/2 Pro Set 359
91/2 Pro Set / Prototype
92/3 Pro Set 20
91/2 Pro Set Platinum 160
90/1 Score 119
91/2 Score 281
91/2 Score 42T
91/2 Score CAN 501
92/3 Score 73
93/4 Score 55
95/6 Score 63
92 Semic Sticker 168
92/3 Topps 170
91/2 To. Stadium 221
92/3 To. Stadium 206
93/4 To. Stadium 89
90/1 Upper Deck 16
91/2 Upper Deck 289
92/3 Upper Deck 245
93/4 Upper Deck 22
95/6 UD BAP 35, ✍ S35
95/6 UD CC 74
91/2 BUFF / Blue Shield
91/2 BUFF / Campbell's
91/2 BUFF / Pepsi
92/3 BUFF / Blue Shield
92/3 BUFF / Jubilee
89/0 NYIS
96/7 NYIS

WOOD, WAYNE
76/7 OPC WHA 31
77/8 OPC WHA 42

WOODALL, FRANK
24/5 Holland Creameries 4
23/4 Selkirks Crescent 12

WOODBURN, STEVEN
95 Panini Worlds 104
92 Semic Sticker 226

WOODBURN, TIM
93/4 Birmingham Bulls

WOODCOCK, TOM
71/2 SLOU

WOODCROFT, CRAIG
93/4 Canada Nationals
98/9 DEL 99
99/0 Eishockey 192
93/4 Fleer Ultra 477
93/4 Power Play 497
93/4 Premier - Canada 5
91/2 ProCards 492
94 Semic 103
01/2 UD DEL 75
92/3 Indianapolis Ice

WOODGATE, PETER
82/3 North Bay Centennials
83/4 North Bay Centennials

WOODLEY, DAN
89/0 ProCards AHL 190
90/1 ProCards 64, 528
87/8 Flint Spirits
93/4 Muskegon Fury
86/7 Portland Winter Hawks

WOODLEY, DARRELL
95/6 Slapshot 19
97/8 Louisiana Ice Gators

WOODS, BOB
89/0 ProCards AHL 218
90/1 ProCards 560
95/6 Hampton Roads
93/4 Johnstown Chiefs 4
99/0 Mississippi S'Wolves
99/0 Mississippi S'Wolves
88/9 Brandon Wheat Kings

WOODS, BRAD
99/0 Brampton Batallion 10
88/9 Brandon Wheat Kings

WOODS, BROCK
90/1 7th..Sketch OHL 73
91/2 7th...Sketch OHL 279
92/3 Greensboro Monarchs 4
93/4 Wheeling Thund'birds
94/5 Wheeling Thund'birds

WOODS, MARTIN
91/2 7th...Sketch LHJMQ 255
96/7 Johnstown Chiefs
97/8 New Orleans Brass

WOODS, PAUL
78/9 O-Pee-Chee 159
79/0 O-Pee-Chee 48
80/1 O-Pee-Chee 148
81/2 O-Pee-Chee 104
82/3 O-Pee-Chee 98
83/4 O-Pee-Chee 133
84/5 O-Pee-Chee 66
82/3 OPC/Topps Sticker 187
82/3 Post [Detr.]
78/9 Topps 159
79/0 Topps 48
80/1 Topps 148
79/0 DETR
80/1 DETR

WOODS, PETER
00/1 Nottingham Panthers

WOODS, ROB
00/1 Saskatoon Blades

WOODS, STEVE
90/1 7th..Sketch OHL 224

WOOG, DAN
92/3 Minnesota G'Gophers
93/4 Minnesota G'Gophers
94/5 Minnesota G'Gophers

WOOG, DOUG
92/3 Minnesota G'Gophers
93/4 Minnesota G'Gophers
94/5 Minnesota G'Gophers

WOOG, STEVE
93/4 N. Michigan Wildcats

WOOLF, MARK
91 7th..Sketch Mem.Cup 92
90/1 7th..Sketch WHL 200
94/5 Huntington Blizzard

WOOLLARD, CHAD
96/7 Soo Greyhounds

WOOLLEY, JASON
98/9 Be A Player 13, ✍ Aut. 13
99/0 BAP Mem. 125
00/1 BAP Mem. 109
01/2 BAP Mem. 126
92 C.O.A. Winter Olympics 194
91/2 Canada Nationals
92/3 Classic 97
94/5 Cla. Images 90
93/4 Donruss 364
95/6 Donruss 260
96/7 Fl. Picks 62
95/6 Fleer Ultra 244
93/4 Leaf 273
95/6 Leaf 307
98/9 OPC Chrome 9
92/3 OPC Premier 98
98/9 Pacific 113
99/0 Pacific 49
00/1 Pacific 60
02/3 Pacific Complete 158
97/8 Pacific CC 279
99/0 Pa. Paramount 33
99/0 Panini Sticker 36
92/3 Parkhurst 429
95/6 Parkhurst 89
92/3 Pinnacle 415
96/7 Pi. Be A Player 58, ✍ Aut. 58
92/3 Score COH 7
93/4 Score 435
97/8 Score Buff. 17
99/0 Stadium 104
98/9 Topps 9
99/0 Topps 122
00/1 Topps 139
99/0 To. Chrome 122
02/3 To. Total 40
92/3 Upper Deck 422
93/4 Upper Deck 462
95/6 Upper Deck 335, SE-124
97/8 Upper Deck 138
97/8 UD Coll. Choice 203
99/0 UD MVP Cup 26
92/3 WASH / Kodak
93/4 Portland Pirates

WORDEN, SCOTT
93/4 Michigan State

WORLSEY, GUMP
00/1 To. Heritage OSA

WORLTON, JEFF
02/3 Louisiana Ice Gators

WORMALD, BRENT
92/3 BCJHL 226

WORRELL, PETER
00/1 BAP Mem. 355, ✂ T-10
01/2 BAP Update m> TC4, ✂ TC12
97 Bowman 56
02/3 First Edition 375
99/0 NHL Power Play
01/2 O-Pee-Chee 167
02/3 O-Pee-Chee 241
98/9 Omega 108
98/9 Pacific 232
99/0 Pacific 184
00/1 Pacific 190
01/2 Pacific 178, 412
02/3 Pacific 163
02/3 Pacific Complete 45
01/2 Signature 61, ✍ Aut. 61, ✂ VA
02/3 Signature Series ✂ FS4
94/5 Slapshot Memorial 71
01/2 Topps 167
02/3 Topps 241
02/3 To. Heritage 96, 114
02/3 To. Limited 241
98/9 Upper Deck 99
98/9 UD G. Reserve 99
98/9 UD MVP 90
00/1 UD Vintage 160
01/2 UD Vintage 266
02/3 UD Vintage 112, 273, 313
99/0 Victory 129
01/2 Victory 156

WORSLEY, GUMP
02/3 BAP Mem. 234, / Cup
45-64 BeeHive-2 [NYRa.]
45-64 BeeHive-2 [Mont.]
64-67 BeeHive-3 [Mont.]
01/2 BT Pipes 120, 131, ✂ DM, ✂ VM
02/3 Between the Pipes ✍ Aut.
63-65 Chex
65/6 Coca-Cola
70/1 Dad's Cookies
70/1 Eddie Sargent 84
71/2 Eddie Sargent 96
72/3 Eddie Sargent 105
70/1 Esso Power Player
88/9 Esso All-Star
01/2 Fleer Greats 88, ✍ Aut.
62/3 Cowan Tile
83 HHOF Postcard M16
83&87 HHOF 180
93/4 Hockey Wit 14
93/4 Legends of Hockey 30
72/3 Post 4
70/1 MINS / Colour
73/4 MINS
66/7 MONT / IGA Stamp
67/8 MONT
67/8 MONT / IGA Card
68/9 MONT / IGA Card
92/3 MONT / OPC 64
68/9 O-Pee-Chee 56
68/9 O-Pee-Chee 199
68/9 O-Pee-Chee PS 6
69/0 O-Pee-Chee 1
69/0 O-Pee-Chee 4in1
70/1 O-Pee-Chee 40
71/2 O-Pee-Chee 241
72/3 O-Pee-Chee 28
72/3 O-Pee-Chee 189
72/3 O-Pee-Chee 286
73/4 O-Pee-Chee 230
71/2 O-Pee-Chee Poster 23
53/4 Parkhurst 53
63/4 Parkhurst 39
63/4 Parkhurst 98
92/3 Parkhurst PR-4
93/4 Parkhurst PR41
01/2 Parkhurst PR116, PR132, PR143, ✍ PA38
93/4 Parkie 56-57 92,165, 175, ✍ A-4
02/3 Parkhurst Retro ✂ NN9
95/6 Parkie 66-67 76, 121, 131
94/5 Parkie Tall 81
66/7 Post Cereal Box
66/7 Post [Small]
68/9 Post Marble
67/8 Post Tips 1
63/4 Québec Aces
72 Semic Sticker 201
61/2 Shirriff 85
68/9 Shirriff / Mont. 1
01/2 Signature ✍ VA18
77-79 Sportscaster 06-07
81/2 TCMA 2
54/5 Topps 10
57/8 Topps 53
58/9 Topps 39
59/0 Topps 15
59/0 Topps 54
60/1 Topps 36
61/2 Topps 50
61/2 Topps 64
61/2 Topps 65
61/2 Topps - Stamp
62/3 Topps 45
62/3 Topps Dollar
65/6 Topps 2
66/7 Topps 2
66/7 Topps 65
66/7 Topps 130
66/7 Topps / Test 2
67/8 Topps 1
68/9 Topps 56
69/0 Topps 1
70/1 Topps 40
72/3 Topps 55
72/3 Topps 64
02/3 Topps - Reprint 5, ✍ Reprint 5
00/1 To. Heritage ✍ CAI, ✍ OSA
01/2 T/O Archives 59
57/8 Toronto Star Photo
60/1 Toronto Star Photo
61/2 Toronto Star Photo
61/2 Toronto Star Weekend
71/2 Toronto Sun Photo
02/3 Ultimate Memorabilia ✂ SCD, ✂ SF
91/2 Ultimate Original Six 17, ✍ Aut. 17
63/4 York 22
67/8 York 17
67/8 York 18
67/8 York 22
67/8 York 24
67/8 York 35
67/8 York
93/4 Zellers, ✍ Aut.

WORSTER, WIL
92/3 Toledo Storm WIOT

WORTERS, ROY
35/6 Amalgamated Press
25-27 Anonymous 47
34-43 BeeHive-1 [NYAm.]
01/2 BT Pipes 150
02/3 Between the Pipes 120, ✂ HSHSJers 22, ✂ VM13
35-40 Canada Starch
33-35 Diamond Match Silv.
36-39 Diamond Match TT1
36-39 Diamond Match TT2
36-39 Diamond Match TT3
83 HHOF Postcard D16
83&87 HHOF 60
02/3 In The GU ✂ VM3
33/4 O-Pee-Chee 45
02/3 Parkhurst Retro ✂ NN15
02/3 Ultimate Memorabilia ✂ EA, ✂ VGJ
33/4 WWGum 11
37/8 World Wide Gum 7

WORTMAN, KEVIN
98/9 Cardset 123
92/3 Classic 116
92/3 Classic Four Sport 220
99/0 Eishockey 196
97/8 Hockey-Box
91/2 ProCards 578
00/1 UD DEL 165
95/6 Fort Wayne Komets
94/5 Kansas City Blades 4
92/3 Salt Lake G'Eagles

WOTTON, MARK
95/6 Leaf 296
90/1 7th..Sketch WHL 86
91/2 7th...Sketch WHL 115
96/7 VANC / IGA
99/0 Michigan K-Wings
96/7 Syracuse Crunch
01/2 Utah Grizzlies
90/1 Saskatoon Blades
91/2 Saskatoon Blades
93/4 Saskatoon Blades

WOTTON, SCOTT
91/2 Air Canada SJHL A48

WOYTOWICH, BOB
68/9 Bauer Photo
65/6 Coca-Cola
70/1 Dad's Cookies
70/1 Eddie Sargent 163
71/2 Eddie Sargent 165
70/1 Esso Power Player
72/3 Post 7
68/9 O-Pee-Chee 49
68/9 O-Pee-Chee 192
69/0 O-Pee-Chee 151
69/0 O-Pee-Chee 4in1
70/1 O-Pee-Chee 88
70/1 O-Pee-Chee DE 8
71/2 O-Pee-Chee 28
72/3 O-Pee-Chee 325
75/6 OPC WHA 123
95/6 Parkie 66-67 8
94/5 Parkie Tall 13
68/9 Shirriff / Minn. 2
65/6 Topps 100
66/7 Topps 34
68/9 Topps 49
69/0 Topps 113
70/1 Topps 88
71/2 Topps 28
71/2 Toronto Sun Photo
71/2 PITT / Sportcolor

WOYWITKA, JEFF
00/1 UD Prospects 54
01 UD Prospects GU 4, ✂ TPJ, ✂ JC
00/1 Red Deer Rebels

WRAY, DICK
51/2 Laval Dairy 28
52/3 Laval Dairy Update 118

WRAY, SCOTT
00/1 Charlotte Checkers

WREGGET, KEN
98/9 Be A Player 169, ✍ Aut. 169
99/0 BAP Mem. 114
98/9 Bicycle.. 2-C
91/2 Bowman 231
92/3 Bowman 182
95/6 Donruss 182
96/7 Donruss 136
97/8 Donruss 27
97/8 Do. Canadian 76
97/8 Do. Preferred 118
98/9 Dynagon Ice 29
94/5 Fleer 172
92/3 Fleer Ultra 383
93/4 Fleer Ultra 399
94/5 Fleer Ultra 353
95/6 Fleer Ultra 128
84/5 Kelowna Wings &...
86/7 Kraft Sports 61
94/5 Leaf 76
95/6 Leaf 19
96/7 Leaf 40
97/8 Leaf 82
97/8 Limited 188
87/8 O-Pee-Chee 242
88/9 O-Pee-Chee 264
90/1 O-Pee-Chee 415
91/2 O-Pee-Chee 136
89/0 O-Pee-Chee 255
87/8 OPC Sticker 164-23
88/9 OPC Sticker 177-44
99/0 Omega 87
98/9 Pacific 360
99/0 Pacific 65
00/1 Pacific 161
97/8 Pacific CC 201
98/9 Pa. Crown Roy. 21
00/1 Pa. Paramount 92
87/8 Panini Sticker 322
88/9 Panini Sticker 117
90/1 Panini Sticker 112
90/1 Panini/TOR G
91/2 Panini Sticker 236
95/6 Panini Sticker 68
91/2 Parkhurst 357
92/3 Parkhurst 371
95/6 Parkhurst 167
94/5 Parkie SE139
92/3 Pinnacle 356
93/4 Pinnacle 325
94/5 Pinnacle 230
95/6 Pinnacle 107
97/8 Pinnacle 96
97/8 Pi. Certified 17
97/8 Pi. Inside 32
95/6 Pi. Summit 112
96/7 Pi. Summit 60
97/8 Pi. Totally 17
95/6 Playoff 80
95/6 POG 220
93/4 Power Play 417
93/4 Premier 277
94/5 Premier 84, 328
90/1 Pro Set 226
91/2 Pro Set 450
91/2 Pro Set Platinum 210
90/1 Score 263
91/2 Score 141
91/2 Score CAN 141
92/3 Score 399
93/4 Score 329
95/6 Score 126
96/7 Score 183
97/8 Score 32
97/8 Score Pitt. 2
95/6 SBx Emotion 143
95/6 SBx Impact 136
94/5 SP 88
92/3 Topps 494
95/6 Topps 190
91/2 To. Stadium 8
92/3 To. Stadium 130
94/5 To. Stadium 133
90/1 Upper Deck 89
91/2 Upper Deck 206
94/5 Upper Deck 362
95/6 Upper Deck 108
96/7 Upper Deck 135
97/8 Upper Deck 344
98/9 Upper Deck 230
95/6 UD BAP 67, ✍ S67
95/6 UD CC 314
96/7 UD CC 220
97/8 UD Coll. Choice 210
98/9 UD G. Reserve 230
89/0 PHIL
90/1 PHIL
91/2 PHIL / J.C. Penney
92/3 PITT / Coke-Clark
93/4 PITT / Foodland 10
94/5 PITT / Foodland 16
95/6 PITT / Foodland 9
84/5 TORO
85/6 TORO
86/7 TORO
86/7 TORO
87/8 TORO / 5x8
87/8 TORO / P.L.A.Y. 29
88/9 TORO / P.L.A.Y. 29
00/1 Manitoba Moose

WREN, BOB
01/2 BAP Mem. 406
99/0 Choice 12
93/4 Classic 33
93/4 Cla. 4 Sport 216
01/2 Pacific 13
91/2 7th...Sketch OHL 37
93/4 Slapshot / Detroit 25
01/2 SP Authentic 174
01/2 SPx 129
01/2 SPx Rookie RR28
01/2 UD Ice 70
01/2 UD Vintage 299
98/9 Cincinnati M'Ducks 19
99/0 Cincinnati M'Ducks
01/2 St. John's Maple Leafs

WRENA, BLAIR
78/9 Saginaw Gears

WRIGHT, BILLY
90/1 7th..Sketch OHL 322
91/2 7th...Sketch OHL 63

WRIGHT, DARREN
97/8 New Mexico Scorpions
99/0 San Angelo Outlaws
96/7 Kamloops Blazers
84/5 Kingston Canadians
85/6 Kingston Canadians
82/3 Kitchener Rangers
83/4 Kitchener Rangers
93/4 Prince Albert Raiders
95/6 Prince Albert Raiders

WRIGHT, JAMIE
98/9 Bowman's Best 121, F12
95/6 Do. Elite WJ 22
98/9 Omega 78
98/9 Pacific 186
93/4 Slapshot / Guelph 11
94/5 Slapshot / Guelph 12
95/6 Slapshot 93
95/6 Upper Deck 535
98/9 Upper Deck 253
02/3 Upper Deck 273
98/9 UD G. Reserve 253
96/7 Michigan K-Wings
99/0 Michigan K-Wings
95/6 Guelph Storm

WRIGHT, JASON
96/7 Richmond Renegades
01/2 Belfast Giants

WRIGHT, JOHN
74/5 Loblaws
74/5 O-Pee-Chee 156
74/5 Topps 156
72/3 VANC / Royal Bank
73/4 VANC / Royal Bank

WRIGHT, KORY
94/5 Anchorage Aces 4

WRIGHT, LARRY
74/5 Loblaws
78/9 O-Pee-Chee 360

WRIGHT, MARK
93/4 Sheffield Steelers 11
94/5 Sheffield Steelers 18
95/6 Sheffield Steelers

WRIGHT, PETER
51/2 Laval Dairy 41
52/3 St. Lawrence 85

WRIGHT, SHAYNE
95/6 Edge Ice 67
99/0 Eishockey 132
00/1 UD DEL 148
01/2 UD DEL 134
95/6 Rochester Americans
96/7 Rochester Americans
97/8 Rochester Americans
93/4 Owen Sound Platers

WRIGHT, TYLER
91/2 Arena 9
00/1 BAP Mem. 130
91/2 Classic 10
91/2 Classic Four Sport 10
93/4 Cla. Prospects 140
93/4 Fleer Ultra 240
93/4 Fleer Ultra Pros. 10
93/4 Leaf 347
92/3 OPC Premier 32
99/0 Omega 193
01/2 Pacific 121
02/3 Pacific Complete 357
93/4 Parkhurst 340
00/1 Parkhurst P-108
93/4 Pinnacle 214
97/8 Pi. Be A Player 64, ✍ Aut. 64
93/4 Score 463
91 7th..Sketch Mem.Cup 112
90/1 7th..Sketch WHL 56
91/2 7th...Sketch WHL 191
00/1 Signature 45, ✍ Aut. 206
95/6 SBx Impact 199
00/1 Stadium 211
91/2 Star Pics 16
91/2 Star Pics 36
00/1 To. Chrome 228
02/3 To. Total 232
00/1 UD Heroes 35
91/2 Ultimate Draft Pick 10, 66, ✍ Aut.
91/2 Upper Deck 67
91/2 Upper Deck 686
92/3 Upper Deck 558
92/3 Upper Deck 584
93/4 Upper Deck 256
95/6 Upper Deck 327
01/2 Upper Deck 281
02/3 Upper Deck 298
94/5 UD Canada Junior 8
91/2 Upper Deck WJC 60
01/2 UD MVP 56
00/1 UD Pros&Prosp. 26
01/2 UD Vintage 74
01/2 Victory 102
01/2 COLU
93/4 EDMO / Sheet
94/5 Cape Breton Oilers

WUNSCH, ALEXANDER
94/5 DEL 112
95/6 DEL 314

WYCHERLY, RALPH
34-43 BeeHive-1 [NYAm.]
34-43 BeeHive-1 [xN.Larson's card]

WYKOFF, S.
88/9 ProCards / Maine

WYNIA, SJON
91/2 Avant Garde BCJHL 50
92/3 BCJHL 93
91/2 Nanaimo Clippers

WYNNE, DEREK
91/2 Air Canada SJHL B44
92/3 MPS SJHL 62

WYNNE, JOHN
90/1 7th..Sketch OHL 121
91/2 7th...Sketch OHL 28

WYNNE, TEEDER
00/1 Kudos 21
02/3 Dundee Texol Stars

WYROZUB, RANDY
70/1 Eddie Sargent 31
70/1 O-Pee-Chee 141
72/3 BUFF

WYWROT, PETE
52/3 Laval Dairy Update 46
52/3 St. Lawrence 76

WYZANSKY, BEN
94/5 Johnstown Chiefs 19
92/3 Richmond Renegades

Y

YABLONSKI, JEREMY
02/3 Peoria Rivermen

YACBOSKI, DARRYL
01/2 Regina Pats

YACHANOV, DMITRI
99/0 Mir 70
00/1 Mir 34

YACHIMEL, BERT
83/4 Moncton Alpines

YACHMENEV, VITALI
00/1 BAP Mem. 368
95/6 Bowman 115, BB20
94/5 Classic CP5
95/6 Classic 90
00/1 Crown Royale 61
01/2 Crown Royale ✂ TT 10
95/6 Donruss 318, RR-9
96/7 Donruss 233
96/7 Do. Canadian 80
95/6 Do. Elite 52, R-2
96/7 Do. Elite 94
96/7 Fleer 51, RS-10
95/6 Fleer Metal 198,IS-22
96/7 Fl. Picks 142
95/6 Fleer Ultra 362
96/7 Fl. Ultra 84
96/7 Leaf 157
95/6 L. Limited 115, RP-5
96/7 L. Limited 34
96/7 L. Preferred 99, LS-41
96/7 Metal Univ. 78
01/2 Pacific 224
02/3 Pacific 217
02/3 Pacific Complete 169
97/8 Pacific CC 167
00/1 Pa. Paramount 140
96/7 Panini Sticker 266
97/8 Panini Sticker 222
99/0 Panini Sticker 272
00/1 Panini Sticker 179
95/6 Parkhurst 266, 506, PP-37
94/5 Parkie SE229
96/7 Pinnacle 206
97/8 Pi. Inside 144
95/6 Pi. Summit 180
96/7 Pi. Summit 171
95/6 Pi. Zenith 131, RRC-11
96/7 Pi. Zenith 52
96/7 Score 241
97/8 Score 212
95/6 Select CE 130
94/5 SR Gold Standard 99
94/5 SR Tetrad CXVII, ✍ Aut.
95/6 SBx Impact 205
96/7 SBx Impact 59, 173, F-20
93/4 Slapshot / North Bay 22
93/4 Slapshot / North Bay 25
94/5 Slapshot / North Bay 24
94/5 SP 167
95/6 SP 68, FX11
96/7 SP 78
96/7 SPx 20, GF-1
00/1 Stadium 180
95/6 Topps 351
99/0 Topps 139
99/0 To. Chrome 139
95/6 To. Finest 157
96/7 To. Picks RS3
95/6 To. Stadium ER190
95/6 TSC Members Only 48
95/6 T. Super Skills SR15
02/3 To. Total 254
94/5 Upper Deck 513
95/6 Upper Deck 263, H21
96/7 Upper Deck 77, X20, SS24A
97/8 Upper Deck 291, SG43
00/1 Upper Deck 328
01/2 Upper Deck 330
95/6 UD BAP 181, ✍ S181
96/7 UD Black Diam. 43
95/6 UD CC 409
96/7 UD CC 125, 320, UD32, C8, CR8
97/8 UD Coll. Choice 123, SQ43
00/1 UD MVP 100
01/2 UD Vintage 146
00/1 Vanguard ✂ DGJ 11
01/2 Vanguard ✂ DGM 16
01/2 Victory 195
98/9 NASH / Wendy's 25

YAGANISKI, JASON
91/2 Air Canada SJHL C19

YAGER, CAM
91/2 Air Canada SJHL A37

YAKABUSKI, MARK
92/3 Ottawa 67's

YAKE, TERRY
91/2 Bowman 4
92/3 Classic Prospects 148
93/4 Donruss 4
94/5 Donruss 124
93/4 EA Sports 3
93/4 Fleer Ultra 221, 265
94/5 Fleer Ultra 9
95/6 Future Legends 49
93/4 Leaf 406
94/5 Leaf 88
91/2 O-Pee-Chee 169
98/9 Pacific 376
93/4 Panini Sticker 125
94/5 Panini Sticker 121
92/3 Parkhurst 293
93/4 Parkhurst 271
94/5 Parkhurst V10
93/4 Pinnacle 340
93/4 Pinnacle Expa. 5
94/5 Pinnacle 282
97/8 Pi. Be A Player 190, ✍ Aut. 190
93/4 Power Play 14
93/4 Premier 432
88/9 ProCards / Binghampton
89/0 ProCards AHL 304
90/1 ProCards 186
90/1 Score 419
93/4 Score 259
93/4 Score 511
94/5 Score 93
92/3 Topps 432
91/2 To. Stadium 374
92/3 To. Stadium 496
93/4 To. Stadium 490
94/5 To. Stadium 226
91/2 Upper Deck 323
92/3 Upper Deck 512
93/4 Upper Deck 311, SP-6
98/9 Upper Deck 360
93/4 Upper Deck Be A Player 40
98/9 UD G. Reserve 360
99/0 UD MVP Cup 193
93/4 ANAH / Cap 4
92/3 HART / Dairymart
95/6 Milwaukee Admirals
96/7 Rochester Americans
85/6 Brandon Wheat Kings

YAKHAILOV, ALEXANDER
72 Hellas MM-Jenkki 74

YAKHANOV, ANDREI
00/1 Mir 245
95 Panini Worlds 34
97/8 Providence Bruins

YAKIMISHYN, SHAWN
90/1 7th..Sketch WHL 80
91/2 7th...Sketch WHL 119
90/1 Saskatoon Blades
91/2 Saskatoon Blades

YAKIMOVICH, SERGEI
00/1 Mir 74

YAKIWCHUK, DALE
81/2 Milwaukee Admirals

YAKOVENKO, ANDREI
91/2 O-Pee-Chee 63R

YAKUBOV, MIKHAIL
00/1 Mir 197, 293

YAKUBOV, RAFIK
98/9 Mir 52
99/0 Mir 61
00/1 Mir 387

YAKUBOV, RAVIL
98/9 Mir 37
99/0 Mir 145
00/1 Mir 136, 333
91/2 O-Pee-Chee 46R
95 Panini Worlds 44
92/3 Red Ace Blue 29
92/3 Red Ace Violet 32
92/3 Upper Deck 349
97/8 UD Elitserien 164
96/7 Saint John Flames

YAKUSHEV, ALEXANDER
91/2 Future Trends C72 70
91/2 Future Trends C72 97
92/3 Future Trends C76 106
74 Hellas MM-Jenkki 46
70/1 Kuvajulkaisut 4
74 Semic Sticker 38
69/0 Soviet Stars
70/1 Soviet Stars
73/4 Soviet Stars 19
74/5 Soviet Stars 16
77-79 Sports. FIN 71-1686
77-79 Sports. FIN 84-2015
72/3 Williams Finnish 25
73/4 Williams Finnish 5

YAKUSHIN, DMITRY
99/0 BAP Mem. 390
99/0 Omega 230
00/1 Topps 277
00/1 To. Chrome 172
99/0 St. John's Maple Leafs
00/1 St. John's Maple Leafs

YARDLEY, SHAUN
02/3 Peterborough Phantoms

YAREMA, BRENDAN
00/1 Kudos 86
94/5 Slapshot / Sarnia 16
95/6 Slapshot 344
98/9 Kansas City Blades 8
99/0 Kansas City Blades
97/8 Kentucky Tho'blades

YAREMCHUK, GARY
81/2 TORO

YAREMCHUK, KEN
88/9 ProCards / Newmarket

YAREMKO, CHAD
99/0 Lethbridge Hurricanes

YARI, J.D.
81/2 Soo Greyhounds

YAROSH, TROY
98/9 Wichita Thunder

YASAKOV, SERGEI
98/9 Mir 71
99/0 Mir 94
00/1 Mir 3

YASHIN, ALEXEI
01/2 Adrenaline 123, WB 11
01/2 Atomic 62, AB 7, CP 11, PP 21, Stat 16, TN 9
02/3 Atomic 65, -PC 12, ✂ GWJ 14
98/9 Aurora 134, -CF 34
99/0 Aurora 102, -Stripe 20, -ST 13
02/3 BAP All-Star 97, ✂ ASJ, ✂ HSHSJers
98/9 Be A Player 246, P-23, ✍ Aut. 246, ✂ G-24, ✂✍ G-24
99/0 BAP Mem. 244, ✂ J-17

01/2 BAP Mem. 291, 394, ✂ ASJ, ✂ ASE, ✂ ASN, ✂ ASD, ✂ AST, ✂ CoO
02/3 BAP Mem. 56, 219, ✂ ASJ59, ✂ AST15, ✂ FP19, ✂ SC4
01/2 BAP Update HSHS, ✂ HSHSJers, ✂ TP9
96/7 Bic.Sports Aces 2-D
97/8 Bicycle 8-Club
95/6 Bicycle Sports Aces 8-Spade
01/2 Bowman 67
02/3 Bowman 15
98/9 Bowman's Best 37
02/3 Calder 44
99/0 Challenger 5
92/3 Classic 2
92/3 Classic 60
92/3 Classic LP2
93/4 Classic 34
93/4 Classic 96
94/5 Classic AR3
92/3 Classic Four Sport 152
92/3 Classic Four Sport LP25
93/4 Cla. Images 4 Sport 125
93/4 Cla. Images 4 Sport 130
93/4 Cla. Images 4 Sport CC13
93/4 Cla. Prospects 40, LP25, ✍ Aut.
99/0 Crown Royale 100
00/1 Crown Royale 77, ✂ GWJ-18
01/2 Crown Royale 93, ASH 14, JotC 20
02/3 Crown Royale 62, ✂ GWDP 15
93/4 Donruss 238
93/4 Donruss ES U5
93/4 Donruss RR 7
94/5 Donruss 63
95/6 Donruss 107
96/7 Donruss 124
97/8 Donruss 19
96/7 Do. Canadian 61
97/8 Do. Canadian 127, SCS-11
95/6 Do. Elite 79
96/7 Do. Elite 41
97/8 Do. Elite 27
97/8 Do. Preferred 42
97/8 Do. Priority 147, 213
97/8 Do. Studio 31
98/9 Dynagon Ice 132, -TC 18
99/0 Dynagon Ice 142
97/8 Esso 37
02/3 eTopps 28
02/3 Exclusive 111, -MO 13
02/3 First Edition 146, 334, 359, 407R, ✂ Jers., ✂ TSL 11
94/5 Flair 124, SP-10
96/7 Flair 65
94/5 Fleer 149, FF-9
96/7 Fleer 77
96/7 Fl. Picks 48, F50-48, JE-5
93/4 Fleer Ultra 384
93/4 Fleer Ultra WotF 20
94/5 Fleer Ultra 152, ARS-10, GG-10
95/6 Fleer Ultra 114, RS-9
96/7 Fl. Ultra 120
95 Globe 172
01/2 Heads Up 62
02/3 Heads Up 76, -ITN 14, ✂ GWQ 18, ✂ GWQ 30, / Bobble
95/6 Hoyle / East. JOKER
02/3 In The GU 44, 144, ✂ E18, ✂ F19, ✂ IE13, ✂ GUJ18, ✂ SJ18, ✂ TM15
94/5 Kraft / SS
96/7 Kraft / KD
97/8 Kraft / KD, Casecard
98/9 Kraft / KD
99/0 Kraft / KD, / OML
96/7 Kraft Magnet
93/4 Leaf 386
93/4 Leaf FP 9
94/5 Leaf 19, GLR-3, GLS-5, LL-16
95/6 Leaf 153
96/7 Leaf 101
97/8 Leaf 59
94/5 L. Limited 80
95/6 L. Limited 50
96/7 L. Limited 31
96/7 L. Preferred 17, LS-16
97/8 Limited 69, 71, 189
96/7 Maggers 109
94/5 McDonald's McD-3
98/9 McDonald's McD09
99/0 McDonald's ✍ SS
02/3 McDonald's 25
96/7 Metal Univ. 108
00/1 Mir Fetisov 11
98/9 NHL Power Play
01/2 O-Pee-Chee 14, Update 14
02/3 O-Pee-Chee 233
98/9 OPC Chrome 5
97/8 Omega 159
98/9 Omega 170, -Onl. 24, -Pl 6, -Prism 14
99/0 Omega 165
98/9 Pacific 318, -TC 18
99/0 Pacific 297, -Cl 15, -GC 24, -TL 19
00/1 Pacific 288
01/2 Pacific 281, 436
02/3 Pacific 245, -L 8, -MA 12, ✂ GWJ 33
02/3 Pacific Complete 246
97/8 Pacific CC 120
97/8 Pa. Crown Roy. 94
98/9 Pa. Crown Roy. 96, -PP 17
97/8 Pa. Dynagon 87, T-70
97/8 Pa. Invincible 97
97/8 Pa. Paramount 129
98/9 Pa. Paramount 168, -IG 8, -TC 18
99/0 Pa. Paramount 167, IAI-19, -PB 24
97/8 Pa. Revolution 96
98/9 Pa. Revolution 102, -ASG 30, -CTLC 12, -Show. 24
98/9 Panini Photocard
94/5 Panini Sticker L
95/6 Panini Sticker 48
96/7 Panini Sticker 48
97/8 Panini Sticker 43
98/9 Panini Sticker 43
99/0 Panini Sticker 322
93/4 Parkhurst 254
93/4 Parkhurst C10
93/4 Parkhurst E7
94/5 Parkhurst 273, YCTG-16
95/6 Parkhurst 151, 242
00/1 Parkhurst P-155
01/2 Parkhurst 35, ✂ WCJ8, ✂ WCE8, ✂ WCN8
02/3 Parkhurst 101, -FP19, ✂ GJ48, ✂ SJ48
02/3 Parkhurst Retro 17
94/5 Parkie SE123, seV21
93/4 Pinnacle 455
93/4 Pinnacle SR5
94/5 Pinnacle 28, 465, NL7, WE17
96/7 Pinnacle 121
97/8 Pinnacle 126
96/7 Pi. Be A Player 48, ✍ Aut. 48
97/8 Pi. BeeHive 21
97/8 Pi. Certified 78
97/8 Pi. Epix E4
97/8 Pi. Inside 57
95/6 Pi. Summit 101, MH-12
96/7 Pi. Summit 34
97/8 Pi. Totally 78
96/7 Pi. Zenith 23, A-1
95/6 Playoff 74
94/5 POG 174
95/6 POG 191
94/5 Post
97/8 Pi. Post 23
93/4 Power Play 403
93/4 Power Play GG 10
93/4 Power Play RooS 16
93/4 Premier 317
94/5 Premier 192, 365, OF-15
00/1 Premier Plus 84
99/0 Prism 99
01/2 Pr. Stock 60, Res. 10, -PS 46, ✂ GUG 65
02/3 Pr. Stock Reserve ✂ 132
00/1 PS Titanium 67, ✂ GUG-120
01/2 PS Titanium 91, TAS 14
02/3 Pr. Stock Titanium 67, ✂ GWJ 42
00/1 PS Titanium Draft ✂ 71
02/3 Quest for the Cup 62, -CTC 9
92/3 Red Ace Blue 27
92/3 Red Ace Violet 33
99/0 Revolution 105, SS-25, TL-17
93/4 Score 603
93/4 Score/CAN DD3
94/5 Score 253
95/6 Score 230, GB-7
96/7 Score 181
97/8 Score 116
94/5 Select 135
95/6 Select CE 36
96/7 Select CE 83
94 Semic 147
95 Semic 136
93 Semic Sticker 136
00/1 Signature 20, ✍ Aut. 207, ✂ HSHSJers
01/2 Signature 139, ✍ Aut. 139, ✂ FP20, ✂ GUE42, ✂ GJ43, ✂ GSJ43, ✂ HSHSJers, ✂ ITN42, ✂ IB4, ✂ TM20
02/3 Signature Series 26, GS-6, ✍ 26, ✂ SGJ18
95/6 SBx Emotion 128, Xce-5, Xci-7
95/6 SBx Impact 122
96/7 SBx Impact 91
94/5 SP 79
95/6 SP 101
96/7 SP 108, HC-13
97/8 SP Authentic 105
98/9 SP Authentic 59
00/1 SP Authentic 61
01/2 SP Authentic 52
02/3 SP Authentic 56
00/1 SP GU 43
01/2 SP GU 33
02/3 SP GU 31, ✂ AF, ✂ PC, ✂ PH
02/3 Sports Vault 77
96/7 SPx 31
97/8 SPx 35
99/0 SPx 102
00/1 SPx 142
01/2 SPx 181
02/3 SPx 46, ✂ WM
98/9 SPx Finite 57, 98
98/9 SPx Prospects 42
00/1 Stadion 72
99/0 Stadium 28, ✍ CS5, ✍ CS7, ✍ CS9, ✍ LSS 2
01/2 Stadium 102
02/3 Stadium 76, -WS11
98/9 SLU
96/7 Team Out!
95/6 Topps 170, 2CG, YS5
98/9 Topps 5
99/0 Topps 2, IM14, FF4, TW 7, ✍ TA4
01/2 Topps 14, -SM16, -Update 14
02/3 Topps 233
99/0 To. Chrome 2, -IM14, -FF 4
01/2 To. Chrome 14
02/3 T. Chrome 127
94/5 Topps Finest 56
95/6 To. Finest 151
98/9 To. Finest 96, C5, R12
98/9 T. Gold Label 11
00/1 To. Gold Label 76
00/1 To. Heritage 6
01/2 To. Heritage 170
02/3 To. Heritage 30
02/3 To. Limited 233
01/2 To. Reserve 68
93/4 To. Stadium 359
94/5 To. Stadium 116, 175
95/6 To. Stadium EC182, MP
93/4 TSC Members Only 42
94/5 TSC Members Only 14
02/3 To. Total 224
98/9 UD Choice 141, SQ10
00/1 UD Heroes 82, L6
01/2 UD PlayMakers Ltd 61
00/1 UD Reserve 61
02/3 UD Superstars ✂ LLT
98/9 UD3 49, 109, 169
00/1 Ultimate Mem. ✂ J-49, ✂ Jers. 40, ✂ S-49
01/2 Ultimate Mem. ✂ DD, ✂ Emb., ✂ Jers., ✂ S&J, ✂ GAO, ✂ ITN, ✂ JE, ✂ JJ, ✂ WTF, ✍ Aut.
02/3 Ultimate Memorabilia ✂ Cor, ✂ HT
91/2 Upper Deck 651
92/3 Upper Deck 334
93/4 Upper Deck 277, 349, H8, SP-112
94/5 Upper Deck 129, 554, SP-55
95/6 Upper Deck 15, SE-59
96/7 Upper Deck 110
97/8 Upper Deck 321, SG23
98/9 Upper Deck 139, FF18
99/0 Upper Deck 90, 147, CT12, FF7, MA7
01/2 Upper Deck 338, CT8, SS11
02/3 Upper Deck 111, 237
02/3 UD Artistic 55, R55, / Art
93/4 Upper Deck Be A Player 17
94/5 UD BAP R92, R172, ✍ 150
93/4 UD BAP Roots 14
96/7 UD Black Diam. 159
97/8 UD Black Diam. 111
98/9 UD Black Diam. 59, WF20
00/1 UD Black Diam. 104, ✂ GG
99/0 UD C. Legends 68
01/2 UD Challenge 54
02/3 UD Classic 61
95/6 UD CC 189, C18
96/7 UD CC 179, 324
97/8 UD Coll. Choice 173, SQ72, C15, CR15
91/2 Upper Deck WJC 12
98/9 UD G. Reserve 139
99/0 UD G. Reserve 90, 147
99/0 UD Gretzky Excl. 81
02/3 UD Honor 44, -SG19
96/7 UD Ice 96
97/8 UD Ice 28
00/1 UD Ice 74
01/2 UD Ice 104
01/2 UD Mask 61
02/3 UD Mask ✂ IO
98/9 UD MVP 139
99/0 UD MVP 138, -GU13, ✂ GU26
02/3 UD MVP 115
02/3 UD Piece 55
96/7 UD Post
01/2 UD Premier 33
00/1 UD Pros&Prosp. 60, GS6
99/0 UD Retro 54
02/3 UD Rookie 61, ✂ 150a, ✂ 159b, ✂ DJ
01/2 UD Top Shelf 101, ✂ J
02/3 UD Top Shelf 54
00/1 UD Vintage 258
02/3 UD Vintage 163, 279, 309
00/1 Vanguard 70, VP-16
01/2 Vanguard 62, EMW 5
02/3 Vanguard 65
99/0 Victory 199, 201, 329
01/2 Victory 413
02/3 Victory 134, -NP36
01/2 Waving the Flag 29
96 Wien 148
97/8 Zenith 72
93/4 OTTA
94/5 OTTA
95/6 OTTA
96/7 OTTA
97/8 OTTA
98/9 OTTA
00/1 OTTA

YASHIN, OLEG
91/2 O-Pee-Chee 64R
95/6 Fort Wayne Komets
93/4 Roanoke Express
94/5 Roanoke Express

YASHIN, SERGEI
90/1 O-Pee-Chee 482
89 Semic Sticker 88
87/8 Soviet Stars
89/0 Soviet Stars

YATES, JOEL
91/2 7th...Sketch OHL 239
93/4 Slapshot / Niagara Falls

YATES, ROSS
94/5 DEL 151
96/7 DEL 157
00/1 Syracuse Crunch

YAWNEY, TRENT
91/2 Bowman 393
90/1 OPC/Topps 297
91/2 O-Pee-Chee 255
89/0 O-Pee-Chee 222
97/8 Pa. Dynagon BKS-84
89/0 Panini Sticker 53
90/1 Panini Sticker 187
91/2 Parkhurst 245
92/3 Parkhurst 262
92/3 Pinnacle 174
93/4 Pinnacle 123
94/5 Pinnacle 245
90/1 Pro Set 64
91/2 ProCards 491
90/1 Score 292
91/2 Score CAN 439
92/3 Score 216
93/4 Score 332
91/2 To. Stadium 205
93/4 To. Stadium 472
94/5 To. Stadium 44
90/1 Upper Deck 82
95/6 UD BAP 146, ✍ S146
92/3 CALG / IGA 012
88/9 CHIC / Coke
89/0 CHIC / Coke
90/1 CHIC / Coke
01/2 Norfolk Admirals
83/4 Saskatoon Blades
84/5 Saskatoon Blades

YDERSTRÖM, DICK
74 Hellas MM-Jenkki 39
74 Semic Sticker 13
73/4 Williams Finnish 41

YEATMAN, D.
28/9 Paulins Candy 67

YEGOROV, ALEXEI
96/7 Fl. Picks 174
96/7 Leaf 216
96/7 Pi. Summit 195
96/7 SBx Impact 163
96/7 Upper Deck 192
00/1 UD DEL 219
95/6 Kansas City Blades
96/7 Kentucky Tho'blades
97/8 Kentucky Tho'blades

YELLE, STÉPHANE
95/6 Bowman 124
95/6 Donruss 350
96/7 Donruss 220
96/7 Do. Canadian 45
02/3 First Edition 60, ✂ Jers.
95/6 Fleer Ultra 363
96/7 Leaf 150
98/9 Pacific 170
99/0 Pacific 116
00/1 Pacific 124
02/3 Pacific Complete 443
97/8 Pacific CC 344
00/1 Panini Sticker 133
95/6 Parkhurst 539
96/7 Pi. Be A Player 15, ✍ Aut. 15
96/7 Pi. Summit 156
00/1 PS Titanium ✂ GUG 10
97/8 Score Colo. 19
91/2 7th...Sketch OHL 161
93/4 Slapshot / Oshawa 10
02/3 Sports Vault 167
02/3 To. Total 345
96/7 Upper Deck 40
97/8 Upper Deck 49
00/1 Upper Deck 277
02/3 Upper Deck 41, 272
00/1 UD ASG CA6
96/7 UD CC 61
02/3 UD Vintage 62
99/0 COLO / Kid Smart
91/2 Oshawa Generals [x2]
92/3 Oshawa Generals

YELLOWAGA, KEVIN
89/0 Saskatoon Blades

YEO, MICHAEL
90/1 7th..Sketch OHL 396
91/2 7th...Sketch OHL 253
93/4 Slapshot / Sudbury 22
95/6 Houston Aeros
00/1 WBS Penguins
01/2 WBS Penguins
02/3 WBS Penguins
90/1 Sudbury Wolves
91/2 Sudbury Wolves
92/3 Sudbury Wolves
93/4 Sudbury Wolves

YEOMAN, JUSTIN
98/9 Brandon Wheat Kings

YEREMEYEV, VITALI
01/2 BAP Mem. 281
01/2 BT Pipes 77
00/1 SP Authentic 153
00/1 UD Black Diam. 126
01/2 Victory 381
00/1 Charlotte Checkers
00/1 Hartford Wolf Pack

YERKOVICH, SERGEI
99/0 Hamilton Bulldogs
99/0 Hamilton Bulldogs/ Staz
96/7 Las Vegas Thunder
97/8 Las Vegas Thunder 10

YEWCHUK, MARTY
95/6 Louisiana Ice Gators

YINGST, DOUG
88/9 ProCards / Hershey

YINGST, MATT
94/5 Johnstown Chiefs 20

YLAJA, MIKKO
73/4 Williams Finnish 323

YLI-MAENPAA, KARI
89/0 Semic Elitserien 196

YLI-MAENPAA, MIKA
95/6 Sisu 98

YLI-MÄENPÄÄ, MIKA
93/4 Sisu 185
94/5 Sisu 45

YLI-TORKKO, JONI
00/1 Cardset 205

YLITIE, PÄIVI
99/0 Cardset AH Q-risti

YLÖNEN, JUHA
01/2 BAP Mem. 470
98/9 Cardset Leij. 47
99/0 Cardset AH 6-hertta
02/3 Cardset 296
95 Hartwall Karjala
92/3 Jyvas Hyva 23
93/4 Jyvas Hyva 114
97/8 Omega 180
98/9 Pacific 347
99/0 Pacific 331
99/0 Panini Sticker 275
97/8 Pi. Be A Player 240, ✍ Aut. 240
93/4 Sisu 21
94/5 Sisu 220
95/6 Sisu 254, G-24
96/7 Sisu 53
99/0 Topps 177
99/0 To. Chrome 177
98/9 UD Choice 164
91/2 Upper Deck 673
97/8 Upper Deck 192
98/9 Upper Deck 151
91/2 Upper Deck WJC 36
98/9 UD G. Reserve 151
96 Wien 21
97/8 PHOE / Coca-Cola
98/9 PHOE / Coca-Cola
96/7 Springfield Falcons

YLÖNEN, PETRI
95 Globe 199
95 Panini Worlds 96
94 Semic 212
95 Semic 195
92 Semic Sticker 220
93 Semic Sticker 249
96 Wien 183

YLÖNEN, URPO
66/7 Champion 71
70/1 Kuvajulkaisut 80
70/1 Kuvajulkaisut 154
69/0 Mästär Serien 14
72 Panda MM-Toronto
79 Panini Sticker 162
72 Semic Sticker 71
91 Semic Sticker 226
96/7 Sisu 192
78/9 SM-Liiga 197
71/2 Williams Finnish 79
71/2 Williams Finnish 206
72/3 Williams Finnish 243
73/4 Williams Finnish 277

YLÖNEN, VEIJO
73/4 Williams Finnish 324

YODER, JAMI
98/9 Hampton Roads

YONKMAN, NOLAN
01/2 BAP Mem. 401
99 Bowman 3, ✍ BA23
99/0 Topps 267
99/0 To. Chrome 267
98/9 Kelowna Rockets

YORK, HARRY
97/8 Donruss 138
96/7 Do. Elite 130
97/8 Do. Preferred 50
97/8 Do. Priority 156
96/7 Flair 122
96/7 Fl. Ultra 149
97/8 Leaf 133
97/8 Limited 1, 158
97/8 Pacific CC 176
97/8 Pa. Dynagon 109, T-61
97/8 Pinnacle 161
96/7 Pi. Be A Player LTH2A, ✍ Aut. LTH2A
96/7 Pi. Zenith 131
97/8 Score 192
97/8 Score SLou. 5
96/7 Select CE 96
96/7 SP 134
99/0 Stadium 64
99/0 Ult. Victory 86
96/7 Upper Deck 329
97/8 Upper Deck 140
97/8 UD Coll. Choice 229

YORK, JASON
98/9 Be A Player 247, ✍ Aut. 247
94/5 Donruss 115
94/5 Flair 54
94/5 Fleer Ultra 288
94/5 Leaf 275
99/0 Millenium 175, ✍ Aut. 175
98/9 Pacific 319
99/0 Pacific 298
00/1 Pacific 289
02/3 Pacific 11
02/3 Pacific Complete 175
97/8 Pa. Dynagon BKS-67
94/5 Parkie SE56
97/8 Pi. Be A Player 95, ✍ Aut. 95
91/2 ProCards 139
90 7th..Sketch Mem.Cup 32
90/1 7th..Sketch OHL 197
00/1 Signature 190, ✍ Aut. 148
95/6 Upper Deck 306
96/7 Upper Deck 5
00/1 Upper Deck 351
01/2 Upper Deck 235
02/3 UD MVP 5
99/0 UD MVP Cup 129
00/1 UD Vintage 250
96/7 OTTA
97/8 OTTA
98/9 OTTA
99/0 OTTA
00/1 OTTA

YORK, MIKE
01/2 Atomic ✂ GWJ 41
99/0 BAP Mem. 327
00/1 BAP Mem. 96
01/2 BAP Mem. 18, 477
02/3 BAP Mem. 151
01/2 Bowman 58
99/0 Crown Royale 93
95/6 Do. Elite WJ 44
99/0 Dynagon Ice 135
02/3 Exclusive 74
02/3 First Edition 246
01/2 Heads Up ✂ JQ 25
99/0 Millenium 167, C-11, ✍ Aut. 167
99/0 NHL Power Play [x3]
01/2 O-Pee-Chee 92
02/3 O-Pee-Chee 259
99/0 Omega 154
00/1 Pacific 272, ✍ Aut. 272
01/2 Pacific 268
02/3 Pacific 150
02/3 Pacific Complete 223
00/1 Pa. Paramount 168
00/1 Parkhurst P-9
01/2 Parkhurst 159, 377
02/3 Parkhurst 160
02/3 Parkhurst Retro 60
99/0 Prism 93
02/3 Pr. Stock Reserve 40
01/2 PS Titanium 97, TSS 17, ✂ DSJ 28
00/1 PS Titanium Draft ✂ 69
92 Québec Pee Wee 1576
00/1 Revolution 100
00/1 Signature 5, ✍ Aut. 53
02/3 Signature Series 21, ✍ 21
99/0 SP Authentic 57
00/1 SP Authentic ✍ SotT, ✍ SotTD
01/2 SP GU ✂ AF
02/3 SP GU ✂ PH
02/3 Sports Vault 226
00/1 SPx 44
01/2 SPx 174, ✂ DT
00/1 Stadium 44, ✍ CO4, ✍ LS9
00/1 Topps 61, OTG23
01/2 Topps 92, ✂ GWJ, ✍ CA
02/3 Topps 259, HHC4
00/1 To. Chrome 49
01/2 To. Chrome 92
02/3 T. Chrome 142
00/1 To. Gold Label ✍ GLA
00/1 To. Heritage 142
02/3 To. Limited 259
99/0 To. Prmr. Plus 126
01/2 To. Reserve ✂ TR
00/1 To. Stars ✍ CAI
02/3 To. Total 297
00/1 UD Heroes 79, ✍ SG, TM7
99/0 Upper Deck 262
00/1 Upper Deck 116, P7, ✍ SG, ✂ GJ, ✂ DGJ
01/2 Upper Deck 345, ✂ GN, ✂ NG
02/3 Upper Deck 318, ✂ BF
99/0 UD G. Reserve 262
96/7 UD Ice 147
00/1 UD Ice 27, ✍ CCA
01/2 UD Mask ✂ GJ, ✂ JP, ✂ DP
00/1 UD MVP 118, ME9, ✍ PS, ✍ ME
99/0 UD MVP Cup 119
02/3 UD Rookie ✂ 153b
02/3 UD Top Shelf ✂ GO, ✂ SH, ✂ ST
00/1 UD Vintage 241, ✂ O6-POH
02/3 UD Vintage 101, GB 101
01/2 Vanguard ✂ DGM 20
00/1 Victory 157
01/2 Victory 231
02/3 Victory 87

YORK, SHAWN
91/2 Avant Garde BCJHL 59
92/3 BCJHL 100
91/2 Nanaimo Clippers

YOUNG,
98/9 Portland Pirates
99/0 Portland Pirates

YOUNG, ADAM
93/4 Slapshot / Windsor 10
94/5 Slapshot / Windsor 12
95/6 Slapshot 414
92/3 Windsor Spitfires

YOUNG, ALAN
94/5 DEL 420
95/6 DEL 394
96/7 DEL 302

YOUNG, ANDREW
92/3 BCJHL 162

YOUNG, B.J.
97 Bowman 112
99/0 Cincinnati M'Ducks
95/6 Red Deer Rebels

YOUNG, BARRY
90/1 7th..Sketch OHL 397
91/2 7th...Sketch OHL 248
89/0 Sudbury Wolves
90/1 Sudbury Wolves
91/2 Sudbury Wolves

YOUNG, BILL
72/3 Los Angeles Sharks
72/3 Minn. Fight. Saints

YOUNG, C.J.
93/4 Fleer Ultra 248
92/3 Parkhurst 246
93/4 Premier 347
90/1 ProCards 617
93/4 To. Stadium 316
92/3 Upper Deck 395

YOUNG, CLAYTON
90 7th..Sketch Mem.Cup 19
89/0 Kamloops Blazers

YOUNG, DON
82/3 North Bay Centennials

YOUNG, DOUG
34-43 BeeHive-1 [Detr.]
34-43 BeeHive-1 [Mont.]
35-40 Canada Starch
26 Dominion Chocolates 23
39/0 O-Pee-Chee 58
37/8 World Wide Gum 49

YOUNG, GEORDIE
91/2 Avant Garde BCJHL 45
91/2 Nanaimo Clippers

YOUNG, HOWIE
45-64 BeeHive-2 [Detr.]
45-64 BeeHive-2 [Chic.]
62/3 Cowan Tile
68/9 O-Pee-Chee 82
68/9 O-Pee-Chee 151
61/2 Shirriff 74
68/9 Shirriff / Oakl. 12
63/4 Topps 29
67/8 Topps 49
68/9 Topps 82
62/3 York Transfer 35

YOUNG, IAN
94/5 DEL 324
95/6 DEL 300
91/2 Oshawa Generals

YOUNG, JASON
91/2 Classic 45
91/2 Classic Four Sport 45
93/4 Cla. Prospects 226
98/9 DEL 234
99/0 Eishockey 116
90/1 7th..Sketch OHL 398
91/2 7th...Sketch OHL 251
91/2 Star Pics 65
91/2 Ultimate Draft Pick 40, ✍ Aut.
00/1 UD DEL 134
01/2 UD DEL 150
92/3 Rochester Americans DD
92/3 Rochester Americans WPC
93/4 Rochester Americans
91/2 Rayside-Balfour
89/0 Sudbury Wolves
90/1 Sudbury Wolves
91/2 Sudbury Wolves

YOUNG, JOEY
91/2 7th...Sketch WHL 151

YOUNG, JOHN
93/4 Greensboro Monarchs
94/5 Minnesota Moose
90/1 Michigan Tech Huskies
90/1 Michigan Tech Huskies
91/2 Michigan Tech Huskies

YOUNG, KEVIN
96/7 Dayton Ice Bandits

YOUNG, MATT
91/2 7th...Sketch WHL 182

YOUNG, SCOTT
02/3 Victory 189

YOUNG, SCOTT A.
01/2 Adrenaline ✂ GWJ 42
98/9 Be A Player 278, ✍ Aut. 278
01/2 BAP Mem. 187
90/1 Bowman 253
91/2 Bowman 86
00/1 Crown Royale 92
01/2 Crown Royale ✂ TT 18
95/6 DEL 450
93/4 Donruss 284
94/5 Donruss 310
95/6 Donruss 36
96/7 Donruss 129
96/7 Do. Canadian 30
99/0 Dynagon Ice 170
92/3 Fleer Ultra 391
94/5 Fleer Ultra 181
95/6 Fleer Ultra 226
95 Globe 124
93/4 Leaf 108
94/5 Leaf 108
95/6 Leaf 317
96/7 Leaf 181
96/7 L. Preferred 98
90/1 OPC/Topps 84
91/2 O-Pee-Chee 235
01/2 O-Pee-Chee 125
02/3 O-Pee-Chee 248
89/0 O-Pee-Chee 209
89/0 opcSticker 264-143, 44-190, / FS 7
98/9 Pacific 48
99/0 Pacific 366
00/1 Pacific 352
01/2 Pacific 335
97/8 Pacific CC 187
97/8 Pa. Paramount 8
99/0 Pa. Paramount 202
00/1 Pa. Paramount 211
89/0 Panini Sticker 224
90/1 Panini Sticker 34
91/2 Panini Sticker 273
93/4 Panini Sticker 73
94/5 Panini Sticker 59
95/6 Panini Sticker 250
96/7 Panini Sticker 253
99/0 Panini Sticker 288
95 Panini Worlds 227
92/3 Parkhurst 383
95/6 Parkhurst 322
00/1 Parkhurst P-235
01/2 Parkhurst 132
93/4 Pinnacle 129
94/5 Pinnacle 361
96/7 Pinnacle 197
97/8 Pi. Be A Player 143, ✍ Aut. 143
96/7 Pi. Summit 78
96/7 Pi. Zenith 115
94/5 POG 200
95/6 POG 78
93/4 Power Play 206
94/5 Premier 519
01/2 Pr. Stock ✂ GUG 90
01/2 PS Titanium ✂ DSJ 38
90/1 Pro Set 113
91/2 Pro Set 195
90/1 Score 21
90/1 Sco. Hot Cards 12
91/2 Score 287
91/2 Score CAN 507
93/4 Score 56
95/6 Score 278
96/7 Score 140
97/8 Score Anah. 10
90/1 Sco. Young Stars 14
95 Semic 110
01/2 Signature 111, ✍ Aut. 111
99/0 Stadium 86
02/3 Stadium 106
00/1 Topps 189
01/2 Topps 125
02/3 Topps 248
02/3 T. Chrome 135
00/1 To. Gold Label 57
00/1 To. Heritage 143
01/2 To. Heritage 84
02/3 To. Limited 248
96/7 To. Picks 113
91/2 To. Stadium 74
93/4 To. Stadium 261
94/5 To. Stadium 153
95/6 To. Stadium 47
00/1 UD Reserve 75
90/1 Upper Deck 87
92/3 Upper Deck 397
96/7 Upper Deck 42
00/1 Upper Deck 152
01/2 Upper Deck 153
02/3 Upper Deck 301
95/6 UD BAP 107, ✍ S107
96/7 UD Black Diam. 48
95/6 UD CC 271
01/2 UD MVP 164
99/0 UD MVP Cup 166
01/2 UD Vintage 225
01/2 Vanguard ✂ DGM 31
01/2 Victory 306
96 Wien 173
89/0 HART / Jr. Whalers
90/1 HART / Jr. Whalers
92/3 QUÉB / Petro-Canada
94/5 QUÉB / Burger King
99/0 SLOU / Taco Bell 5

YOUNG, SCOTT*
89/0 ProCards AHL 13
90/1 ProCards 438

YOUNG, SCOTT2
00/1 Kudos 11
94/5 Humberside Hawks 3
02/3 Dundee Texol Stars

YOUNG, SCOTT_A
02/3 Atomic ✂ GWJ 5
02/3 BAP Mem. 159
02/3 Pacific 331
02/3 Pacific Complete 225
02/3 Signature Series 168, ✍ 168
02/3 Sports Vault 207
02/3 To. Heritage 162
02/3 To. Total 44
02/3 DALL / Southwest

YOUNG, STEVE
89/0 Portland Winter Hawks

YOUNG, TIM
76/7 O-Pee-Chee 158
76/7 OPC 387
77/8 OPC 2
77/8 O-Pee-Chee 223
77/8 O-Pee-Chee NS 22
78/9 O-Pee-Chee 138
79/0 O-Pee-Chee 36
80/1 O-Pee-Chee 174
81/2 O-Pee-Chee 169
82/3 O-Pee-Chee 177
83/4 O-Pee-Chee 395
84/5 O-Pee-Chee 351
81/2 OPC Sticker 94
82/3 Post [Minn.]
76/7 Topps 158
77/8 Topps 2
77/8 Topps 223
77/8 ToppsNS 22
78/9 Topps 138
79/0 Topps 36
80/1 Topps 174
81/2 Topps 113 [West]
83/4 Vachon 140-20
78/9 MINS / Cloverleaf 8
79/0 MINS
80/1 MINS
81/2 MINS
82/3 MINS
83/4 WINN

YOUNG, WARREN
85/6 OPC/Topps 152
86/7 O-Pee-Chee 209
85/6 OPC Sticker 100
85/6 DETR / Little Caesars
86/7 PITT / Kodak

YOUNG, WENDELL
90/1 Bowman 203
93/4 EA Sports 132
95/6 Edge Ice 109, TW-6
92/3 Fleer Ultra 206
92/3 Kraft / PB
90/1 OPC/Topps 309
92/3 OPC Premier 76
90/1 Panini Sticker 127
93/4 Panini Sticker 221
92/3 Parkhurst 170
92/3 Pinnacle 381
93/4 Pinnacle Mask 7
93/4 Premier 166
90/1 Pro Set 512
90/1 Score 298
92/3 Score 511
93/4 Score 341
94/5 SR Tetrad CXVIII, ✍ Aut.
90/1 Upper Deck 102
89/0 PITT / Foodland 14
91/2 PITT / Elby's
92/3 TAMP / Sheraton Inn
93/4 TAMP / Kash N' Karry
94/5 TAMP / Sky Box
86/7 VANC
98/9 Chicago Wolves
98/9 Chicago Wolves Champs
99/0 Chicago Wolves
00/1 Chicago Wolves
84/5 Fredericton Express
85/6 Fredericton Express
82/3 Kitchener Rangers

YOUNGHANS, TOM
78/9 O-Pee-Chee 295
79/0 O-Pee-Chee 177
80/1 O-Pee-Chee 343
81/2 O-Pee-Chee 173
79 Panini Sticker 218
79/0 Topps 177
78/9 MINS / Cloverleaf 9
79/0 MINS
80/1 MINS

YRJOLA, JUHA
72/3 Williams Finnish 360

YSEBAERT, PAUL
98/9 Aurora 177
91/2 Bowman 53
92/3 Bowman 376
93/4 Donruss 376
93/4 Donruss 417
94/5 Donruss 2
95/6 Donruss 258
98/9 Dynagon Ice 175
92/3 Fleer Ultra 54
93/4 Fleer Ultra 457
94/5 Fleer Ultra 277
95/6 Fleer Ultra 157
91/2 Kraft 46
96/7 Kraft / PB
93/4 Leaf 388
94/5 Leaf 202
95/6 Leaf 185
90/1 OPC/Topps 49
91/2 O-Pee-Chee 248
92/3 O-Pee-Chee 46
97/8 Omega 215
98/9 Pacific 408
97/8 Pacific CC 178
97/8 Pa. Crown Roy. 127
97/8 Pa. Invincible 134
97/8 Pa. Paramount 177
98/9 Pa. Paramount 222
97/8 Pa. Revolution 131
92/3 Panini Sticker 118
93/4 Panini Sticker 248
94/5 Panini Sticker 132
95/6 Panini Sticker 129
98/9 Panini Sticker 101
91/2 Parkhurst 42
91/2 Parkhurst 435
92/3 Parkhurst 43
93/4 Parkhurst 504
94/5 Parkhurst 48
95/6 Parkhurst 191
91/2 Pinnacle 36
92/3 Pinnacle 93
93/4 Pinnacle 348
94/5 Pinnacle 301
95/6 Pinnacle 17
97/8 Pi. Be A Player 163, ✍ Aut. 163
95/6 Playoff 313
95/6 POG 250
93/4 Power Play 277
94/5 Premier 368
95/6 Pro Magnet 69
90/1 Pro Set 607
91/2 Pro Set 59
91/2 Pro Set 608
92/3 Pro Set 41
92/3 Pro Set 248
92/3 Pro Set PV1
91/2 Pro Set Platinum 167
88/9 ProCards / Utica
89/0 ProCards AHL 209
90/1 Score 406
91/2 Score 166
91/2 Score CAN 166
92/3 Score 95
92/3 Score 414
93/4 Score 239
93/4 Score 517
95/6 Score 116
92/3 Score Young Stars 35
95/6 SBx Emotion 167
92/3 Topps 58
92/3 Topps 314
95/6 Topps 320
98/9 To. Finest 73
91/2 To. Stadium 171
92/3 To. Stadium 378
93/4 To. Stadium 360
98/9 UD Choice 194
90/1 Upper Deck 375
91/2 Upper Deck 278
92/3 Upper Deck 176
93/4 Upper Deck 365, SP-179
94/5 Upper Deck 491
95/6 Upper Deck 109, SE-165
96/7 Upper Deck 159
97/8 Upper Deck 159
95/6 UD BAP 139, ✍ S139
95/6 UD CC 27
96/7 UD CC 251
91/2 DETR / Little Caesars
95/6 TAMP / Sky Box
93/4 WINN / Ruffles
93/4 WINN Readers

YTFELDT, DAVID
99/0 UD Elitserien 107, 208

YTFELDT, FREDRIK
98/9 DEL 123
99/0 Eishockey 269

YTTER, MATS
94/5 Leaf Elit Set 134
95/6 Leaf Elit Set 126, S-12
89/0 Semic Elitserien 240
90/1 Semic Elitserien 150
91/2 Semic Elitserien 252
92/3 Semic Elitserien 274
95/6 UD Elitserien 186

YUBIN, ILDAR
00/1 Mir 46
96/7 Dayton Bombers

YUDIN, ALEXANDER
99/0 Mir 239, 252, 264
00/1 Mir 125, 161
91/2 O-Pee-Chee 47R
92/3 Upper Deck 336

YULE, STEVE
90 7th..Sketch Mem.Cup 22
90/1 7th..Sketch WHL 286
91/2 7th...Sketch WHL 78
88/9 Kamloops Blazers
89/0 Kamloops Blazers

YULE, STEVEN
96/7 Mississippi S'Wolves

YURESKO, YURI
97/8 Hampton Roads

YURSINOV, VLADIMIR
92/3 Jyvas Hyva 171
93/4 Jyvas Hyva 313
90/1 O-Pee-Chee 494
93/4 Sisu 28
93/4 Sisu 373
94/5 Sisu 152, 398
95/6 Sisu 385, 396
69/0 Soviet Stars
79/0 Soviet Stars 3
83/4 Soviet Stars
87/8 Soviet Stars
73/4 Williams Finnish 217

YUSHKEVICH, DMITRY
01/2 Adrenaline ✂ GWJ 48
01/2 Atomic ✂ GWJ 49
99/0 BAP Mem. 6
00/1 BAP Mem. 87
02/3 BAP Mem. 244 [w/ Svehla]
93/4 Classic 97
93/4 Donruss 254
94/5 Donruss 308
95/6 Donruss 387
93/4 EA Sports 98
02/3 First Edition 33, ✂ Jers.
94/5 Fleer 160
92/3 Fleer Ultra 161
93/4 Fleer Ultra 198
94/5 Fleer Ultra 161
95 Globe 171
93/4 Leaf 82
94/5 Leaf 37
95/6 Leaf 291
92/3 OPC Premier 65
00/1 Pacific 402
02/3 Pacific 372
02/3 Pacific Complete 422
97/8 Pacific CC 153
95/6 Panini Sticker 121
97/8 Panini Sticker 173
98/9 Panini Sticker 161
92/3 Parkhurst 133
93/4 Parkhurst 145
94/5 Parkhurst 163
95/6 Parkhurst 469
92/3 Pinnacle 394
93/4 Pinnacle 146
94/5 Pinnacle 227
93/4 Power Play 186
93/4 Premier 18
94/5 Premier 468
00/1 PS Titanium ✂ GUG 148
01/2 PS Titanium Draft ✂ 91
92/3 Red Ace Blue 35
92/3 Red Ace Violet 34
93/4 Score 216
97/8 Score Toro. 16
95 Semic 126
93 Semic Sticker 144
00/1 Signature 241, ✍ Aut. 157, ✂ DD-18
00/1 Stadium 11
95/6 Topps 192
98/9 To. Finest 115
01/2 To. Reserve ✂ TR
93/4 To. Stadium 492
94/5 To. Stadium 78
02/3 To. Total 41
92/3 Upper Deck 350
92/3 Upper Deck 570
92/3 Upper Deck CC20
92/3 Upper Deck ER12
93/4 Upper Deck 127, SP-119
94/5 Upper Deck 349
95/6 Upper Deck 81, 376
96/7 Upper Deck 164
00/1 Upper Deck 166
02/3 Upper Deck 321
95/6 UD BAP 7, ✍ S7
95/6 UD CC 249
96/7 UD CC 263
00/1 UD MVP 171
00/1 UD Vintage 340
01/2 Victory 336
96 Wien 137
92/3 PHIL / UD Sheet
92/3 PHIL / J.C. Penney
93/4 PHIL / Sheet [x2]
93/4 PHIL / J.C. Penney
94/5 PHIL / Sheet
99/0 TORO / Pizza Pizza 15

YZERMAN, STEVE
94/5 Action Packed
89/0 Action Packed 3
01/2 Adrenaline 70, BR 5, WB 6, ✂ GWJ 16
01/2 ASG History
01/2 Atomic 40, AB 4, CP 5, PP 14, TN 6, ✂ GWJ 26
02/3 Atomic 41, -CF 12, -NPC 7
98/9 Aurora 69, -ALC 11, -CF 20, -FL 5, -MACF 10, -NC 6, -Cube 10
99/0 Aurora 55, -Stripe 55, -CC 6, -CF 13, -CP 7, -ST 10
00/1 Aurora 54, Pins. 54, CC-5, CF-12, ✂ GWJ-4, ✂ GWJ-13, TPS-6B
02/3 BAP All-Star 98-99, ✂ ASJ, ✂ HSHSJers, Bobble
98/9 Be A Player 46, P-5, H-7, M4, M10, ✍ Aut. 46, ✂ G-15, ✂ AS-9, ✂ S-9, ✂✍ G-15
99/0 BAP Mem. 141, ✂ TM-14, ✂ TM-37, ✂ TM-39, ✂ TM-40
00/1 BAP Mem. 124, ✂ J-29, ✂ PP-2, ✂ TM-13, ✂ TM-29
01/2 BAP Mem. 15, ✂ 500GS, ✂ ASJ, ✂ ASE, ✂ ASN, ✂ ASD, ✂ AST, ✂ CoO, HSHS, ✂ PP
02/3 BAP Mem. 1, 211, ✂ ASJ60, ✂ ASE25, ✂ ASN25, ✂ AST7, ✂ AST17, ✂ FP11, ✂ HSHSJers 1, ✂ SCC5, ✂ SC14, ✂ SC31, ✂ TM1, / Cup
01/2 BAP Update ✂ PTT3
02/3 Between the Pipes ✂ GN4
96/7 Bic.Sports Aces 7-H
95/6 Bicycle Sports Aces 3-Spade
90/1 Bowman 233, -HT 5
91/2 Bowman 41, 42
92/3 Bowman 103, 220
95/6 Bowman 21
01/2 Bowman 35
02/3 Bowman 47
98/9 Bowman's Best 1, SB7
02/3 Calder 29, -HH 6
83 Canada Juniors
99/0 Challenger 18
99/0 Crown Royale 53, -CS 11, -CCA 6, -GC 4, -IE 12, -TC 4
00/1 Crown Royale 41, JotC-14, Land.-5, NP-8
01/2 Crown Royale 57, ASH 10, CA 15, JotC 12, LH 4, ✂ TT 11
02/3 Crown Royale 37, -LOR 10, -RP 6
93/4 Donruss 95, G
94/5 Donruss 1
95/6 Donruss 96, I-8
96/7 Donruss 171, 240
97/8 Donruss 2, ES-6, L2L-5
98/9 Donruss ES 15
96/7 Do. Canadian 39
97/8 Do. Canadian 4, NP-4, SCS-9
95/6 Do. Elite 99
96/7 Do. Elite 38, P-3
97/8 Do. Elite 15, 122, BF-8, C-16, PN-10, ✍ BF-8
97/8 Do. Preferred 41, 179, LT-6B, PM-14, / Tin 13, Wide Tin 6
97/8 Do. Priority 4, 209, DD-2, OD-4, Post-3, Stamp-3
97/8 Do. Studio 10, 106, HH-10, S-10, P-10
96/7 Duracell DC15
98/9 Dynagon Ice 69, -AR 7, -FT 11, -PP 6, -TC 9
99/0 Dynagon Ice 79, -ASP 8, -CM 22, -LL 5, -LotR 7
93/4 EA Sports 39
01/2 EASports
01/2 eTopps 16
02/3 eTopps 21
02/3 Exclusive 68, -EIS 6, -MO 10
02/3 First Edition 151, 315, 351, 426H, ✂ Jers., ✂ DGJ 10, ✂ HSHSJers 7
94/5 Flair 55, HN-10
96/7 Flair 31, CIS-10
94/5 Fleer 67
96/7 Fleer 35, ART-25
95/6 Fleer Metal 51

96/7 Fl. Picks F50-49, CC2
92/3 Fleer Ultra 55
93/4 Fleer Ultra 201, -AS 12, -PP 10, -SK 6
94/5 Fleer Ultra 67, -PP 10, -SK 7
95/6 Fleer Ultra 51, -EA 20
96/7 Fl. Ultra 56, MM-10
88/9 Frito Lay
95 Globe 89
96/7 Got-Um
01/2 Heads Up 39, HD 5, RI 6, SM 7, / Bobble
02/3 Heads Up 48, -EIT 10, -PSP 8, -SM 9
93/4 Hockey Wit 108
99/0 HoloGrFX 21
95/6 Hoyle / West. JOKER
92/3 Humpty Dumpty
02/3 In The GU 30, 130, ✄ E2, ✄ F11, ✄ IE4, ✄ GUJ2, ✄ SJ2, ✄ T5, ✄ TM17
91/2 Kellogg's / Score 14
89/0 Kraft 63
90/1 Kraft 63, 78
91/2 Kraft 68
92/3 Kraft / Kraft Singles
93/4 Kraft / PB
94/5 Kraft / HH
96/7 Kraft / PB
97/8 Kraft / KD, PB
98/9 Kraft / Post 9
99/0 Kraft / JELL-O, / KD, / PB
00/1 Kraft 12
89/0 Kraft Stickers 3
93/4 Leaf 162, -HTA 10, -SSS 5
94/5 Leaf 148
95/6 Leaf 60
96/7 Leaf 13, 239, FOI-12
97/8 Leaf 4, 171, BS-5, FOI-4
94/5 L. Limited 120
95/6 L. Limited 105
96/7 L. Limited 40, S-14
96/7 L. Preferred 102, VP-4
97/8 Limited 41, 115, 165, FG-49, FG-70
96/7 Maggers 55
91/2 McDonald's Mc-19
92/3 McDonald's McD-14
93/4 McDonald's McD-13
96/7 McDonald's McD-17
97/8 McDonald's McD-19, F3
98/9 McDonald's McD06
99/0 McDonald's McD-4, ✍ SS
00/1 McDonald's 15, DAS-2, GWJ-5
01/2 McDonald's 15, -HG 5, -Jers.
02/3 McDonald's 13, -A 4, -SLG 5
96/7 Metal Univ. 51
99/0 Millenium 88, P-8, D-10, ✍ Aut. 88, ✍ P-8, ✍ D-10, ✄ J-30, ✄✍ J-30, ✄ JS-30
98/9 NHL Power Play
84/5 O-Pee-Chee 67
84/5 O-Pee-Chee 385
85/6 OPC/Topps 29
86/7 OPC/Topps 11
87/8 OPC/Topps 56
87/8 OPC/Topps Box C
88/9 OPC/Topps 196
88/9 OPC/Topps Box L
90/1 OPC/Topps 133, 222, Box J, Topps-TL 19
91/2 O-Pee-Chee 424, Topps-TL 3
92/3 O-Pee-Chee 61, 321, -Ann. 17
01/2 O-Pee-Chee 2
02/3 O-Pee-Chee 4
89/0 OPC/Topps 83, / Box L
98/9 OPC Chrome 175
90/1 OPC Premier 130
91/2 OPC Premier 73, 142
84/5 OPC Sticker 37
85/6 OPC Sticker 30
86/7 OPC Sticker 161-20
87/8 OPC Sticker 111
88/9 OPC Sticker 253
89/0 opcSticker 254
97/8 Omega 88, GF-8, S-6, SHLC-9, TL-9
98/9 Omega 88, -CS 4, -EOP 11, -FTF 6, -Onl. 16, -PI 24, -Prism 10
99/0 Omega 88, -5ST 21, -CC 10, -EOP 9, -Gen. 6, -NAAS 6, ✄ GWJ 3
98/9 Pacific 19, -DI 10, -GCDC 16, -TC 9, -Time. 8, -TW 10
99/0 Pacific 151, -CL 11, -CCA 7, -GC 18, -HAA 7,17, -PAP 13, -TL 10
00/1 Pacific 162, IO-9, CCA-5, GCDC-15, NAS-6, PR-10, ✄ GWJ-8
01/2 Pacific 152, 410, CCA 5, GCDC 10
02/3 Pacific 137, -CCA 7, -L 7, -MA 7, -MI 13
02/3 Pacific Complete 500
97/8 Pacific CC 19, CS-8, CCA-6, GCDC-11, SS-3C, TL-9
97/8 Pa. Crown Roy. 51, BOS-10, CCA-6, HT-8, L-9
98/9 Pa. Crown Roy. 49, -CCA 6, -LL 6, -MP 11, -PotG 14
97/8 Pa. Dynagon 46, 139, DD-8B, T-7, T-26, BKS-36
97/8 Pa. Invincible 53, AZ-11, FP-16, OTG-9, -R-75
97/8 Pa. Paramount 71, BN-10, CG-7, P-10
98/9 Pa. Paramount 83, -HOFB 5, -IG 5, -SD 9, -TC 9
99/0 Pa. Paramount 88, -HOFB 6, -IAdv. 10, -IAll. 10, -PB 18
00/1 Pa. Paramount 93, ES-11, FF-16, HOFB-6, SZ-5
97/8 Pa. Revolution 52, I-5, TC-9
98/9 Pa. Revolution 53, -TPA 26, -CTLC 10, -NI 6, -Show. 18
01/2 PTC National 6
98/9 Panini Photocard [x2]
87/8 Panini Sticker 243
88/9 Panini Sticker 47
88/9 Panini Sticker 187
89/0 Panini Sticker 57
90/1 Panini Sticker 208
91/2 Panini Sticker 134
92/3 Panini Sticker 112
93/4 Panini Sticker V
94/5 Panini Sticker 209
95/6 Panini Sticker 179
96/7 Panini Sticker 181
97/8 Panini Sticker 149
98/9 Panini Sticker 135
99/0 Panini Sticker 231
00/1 Panini Sticker 156
95 Panini Worlds 280
91/2 Parkhurst 44, 434
92/3 Parkhurst 44, 456
93/4 Parkhurst 326, W5
94/5 Parkhurst 299, V57
95/6 Parkhurst 70
00/1 Parkhurst P-146
01/2 Parkhurst 31, ✄ 500GS, ✄ PJ18, ✄ PS18, ✄ PSJ1, ✄ HSHSJers, ✄ M14, ✄ M17, ✄ M26, ✄ M37, ✄ H2, ✄ T1, ✄ T23, ✄ T28, ✄ WCJ1, ✄ WCE1, ✄ WCN1
02/3 Parkhurst 100, ✄ FP11, ✄ GJ5, ✄ SJ5, ✄ HSHSJers, ✄ MM2, ✄ NH2, ✄ NH4, ✄ NH10, ✄ PP2, ✄ TT4
02/3 Parkhurst Retro 22, ✄ RF11, ✄ RJ22, ✄ RSJ15, ✄ HSHSJers, ✄ NN22, ✄ RM14
94/5 Parkie SE55
91/2 Pinnacle 75, 383
92/3 Pinnacle 241, 258, 350
93/4 Pinnacle 175, CA7, -NF 8
94/5 Pinnacle 271
96/7 Pinnacle 25
97/8 Pinnacle 71, TP-9, P-18
96/7 Pi. Be A Player LTH9B, BB-13, ✍ Aut. LTH9B
97/8 Pi. BeeHive 11, BHT-16
97/8 Pi. Certified 38, -CT 13
97/8 Pi. Epix E9
97/8 Pi. Inside 24, IT-9, / Can 14
96/7 Pi. Mint 12
97/8 Pi. Mint 5
95/6 Pi. Summit 154
96/7 Pi. Summit 76
97/8 Pi. Totally 38
95/6 Pi. Zenith 93
96/7 Pi. Zenith 5, ZT-6
95/6 Playoff 147
96/7 Playoff 366
94/5 POG 92
95/6 POG 96
97/8 Pi. Post 10
93/4 Power Play 77, -Game. 10, -PL 20
93/4 Premier 280, BG/OPC 23, BG/Top. 16
94/5 Premier 235, GTG 12
00/1 Premier Plus 58, TT9, WP14
99/0 Prism 54, -CA 9, -DAS 7, SGDC-11
00/1 Pr. Stock 38, AC-12, EA-9, Res. 10, PS-23, PSS-13
01/2 Pr. Stock 38, Res. 5, -PS 29, ✄ GUG 45
02/3 Pr. Stock Reserve -RE 4, ✄ 121
00/1 PS Titanium 35, ✄ GUG-17, ✄ GUG-98
01/2 PS Titanium 54, SK 7, TSS 15
02/3 Pr. Stock Titanium 40, -SK 4, -S 5
00/1 PS Titanium Draft ✄ 42
95/6 Pro Magnet 105
90/1 Pro Set 79, 347
91/2 Pro Set 62, 281, 571
92/3 Pro Set 39, 247, -TL 3
91/2 Pro Set Platinum 32
91/2 Puck / Pro Set 8
02/3 Quest for the Cup 37, -RTC 8
99/0 Revolution 56, -IS 5, -NI 11, -Orn. 11, -TotL 14, / CSC 56
00/1 Revolution 55, II-11, NI-12, SM-26, ✄ GUG-6
90/1 Score 3, 339
90/1 Sco. Hot Cards 49
91/2 Score 190, 419, Shows 7
91/2 Score CAN 190, 335
92/3 Score 400, 423
93/4 Score 310, 448, -DT 16, DD9, -PLAS 36, -TF 6
94/5 Score 150, DT20
95/6 Score 240, -GB 12
96/7 Score 60, SD-2
97/8 Score 86, 263
97/8 Score Detr. 2
92/3 Seasons 6
93/4 Seasons 20
94/5 Select 35
95/6 Select CE 94
96/7 Select CE 41, C-14
89 Semic Sticker 72
91 Semic Sticker 65
92 Semic Sticker 87
93 Semic Sticker 203
84/5 7-Eleven
85/6 7-Eleven Superstars 5
96/7 SB 7-Eleven Phonecard
00/1 Signature 11, HSHS, F-11, ✍ Aut. 114, ✄ J-30, ✄ HSHSJers
01/2 Signature C-44, ✍ Aut., ✄ 500GS, ✄ FP11, ✄ GUE22, ✄ GJ23, ✄ GSJ23, ✄ HSHSJers, ✄ ITN22, ✄ IG8, ✄ TM11
02/3 Signature Series 112, GS-90, ✍ 112, ✄ CJ3, ✄ FJ11, ✄ SGJ2, ✄ TQ13, ✄ TM3
95/6 SBx Emotion 60
95/6 SBx Impact 58
96/7 SBx Impact 40, BR-25
92/3 Slam Card
94/5 SP 34
95/6 SP 46, -E14, -FX7
96/7 SP 47, CW-15, -Ins.
97/8 SP Authentic 52, I21, ✍ SotT
98/9 SP Authentic 31, SS3, ✍ SotT, SO23-25, -Trade
99/0 SP Authentic 30, HR3, SF4, ✍ SotT
00/1 SP Authentic ST3, ✍ SotT, ✍ SotTD, ✍ SotTT
01/2 SP Authentic 28, 97, ✄ NN, ✍ SotT, ✍ SotTD, ✍ SotTT
02/3 SP Authentic 36, 96, ✍ SotT, ✍ SotTD (x2), ✄ SP, ✄ DP, ✄ TP
00/1 SP GU 21, ✄ TotG, ✄ C, ✄ P, ✄✍ A
01/2 SP GU 18, ✄ AF, ✄ AFD, ✄ AFT, ✄ AFQ, ✄✍ IS, ✄✍ IS2, ✄✍ ISD, ✄ Patch, ✄✍ PatchSig, ✄ PatchC, ✄ PatchT, ✄ TotG, ✄ TotGSig, ✄ TotGCSig
02/3 SP GU 17, ✄ AF, ✄ CF, ✄ PC, ✄ PH, ✄ Sig
02/3 Sports Vault 216
96/7 SPx 14, HH3
97/8 SPx 14, -DV
99/0 SPx 55, P9, X4, ✄ WM
00/1 SPx 25, 86, P4, ✄ WM, ✄✍ WM
01/2 SPx 22, 75, 85, ✄ HT, ✄✍ HTSig, ✄✍ SY1-19, ✄ SY20-26
02/3 SPx 26, 90, 128, ✄ WM, ✄ M, ✄ SS, ✄ X
98/9 SPx Finite 30, 93, 156, 175
98/9 SPx Prospects 21, H14, L19, PS26
00/1 Stadion 85
99/0 Stadium 145, CA25, -Chrome 40, -Big 16
00/1 Stadium 24, BT4, SF6
01/2 Stadium 24, G37, HS3, NHLP20, P8
02/3 Stadium 38, -BT-1
93/4 SLU [x2]
94/5 Starting Lineup
98/9 SLU
99/0 SLU 85
00/1 SLU 17
02/3 Starz
95/6 Super Sticker 37, -DC 25
96/7 Team Out!
84/5 Topps 49
92/3 Topps 207
95/6 Topps 237, -HGC 16
98/9 Topps 175
99/0 Topps 14, 286, AT12, IM15, -SCH7
00/1 Topps 22, 329, PC-2, TC9, HM10, OTG10
01/2 Topps 2, SM6
02/3 Topps 4, HHU4
99/0 To. Chrome 14, 286, AT12, IM15
00/1 To. Chrome 21, PC-2, TC9, HM10
01/2 To. Chrome 2
02/3 T. Chrome 4
94/5 Topps Finest 84
95/6 To. Finest 162
98/9 To. Finest 72, M31, M35-37, R7, Big 5
98/9 T. Gold Label 31
99/0 To. Gold Label 4, QC1
00/1 To. Gold Label 79, B3, GG5
00/1 To. Heritage 10, 216, 238, HH3, OSA, ✄ OSS
01/2 To. Heritage 32
02/3 To. Heritage 32, -Light 32
02/3 To. Limited 4
96/7 To. Picks 31, FC-7, TS-15
99/0 To. Prmr. Plus 4, CR4, FP3, PT7
01/2 To. Reserve 6
91/2 To. Stadium 81
92/3 To. Stadium 19, 254
93/4 To. Stadium 70, _AS
95/6 To. Stadium 20
00/1 To. Stars 4, 139, AS8, P3, WF7
95/6 T. Super Skills 10
02/3 To. Total 289, TTC10, TT11
98/9 UD Choice 73, 310, BH27, RW1, SQ18
00/1 UD Heroes 146, L4, SS5, ✄ GT, ✄ GC, ✍ SG
01/2 UD PlayMakers Ltd 38, / PM
00/1 UD Reserve 32, PP3, BT4
02/3 UD Superstars 82, K9, ✄ CAST, ✄ LL, ✄ LLT
98/9 UD3 60, 120, 180
00/1 Ultimate Mem. ✄ U-30, ✄ A8-1, ✄ A8-2, ✄ D-13, ✄ J-30, ✄ Jers. 26, ✄ MO-1, ✄ RA-5, ✄ S-30, ✄ TM-1, ✄ TM-3, ✄ TM-4, ✄ TM-31, ✄ UC-1
01/2 Ultimate Mem. ✄ 500GS, ✄ A8, ✄ ASGH, ✄ Com., ✄ DD, ✄ Emb., ✄ Jers., ✄ S&J, ✄ ITN, ✄ NP, ✄ PP, ✄ RA, ✄ UC, ✄ WTF, ✍ Aut.
02/3 Ultimate Memorabilia ✄ A8 (x4), ✄ CSTW, ✄ Cor, ✄ DD, ✄ Emb, ✄ FS (x2), ✄ GUJ, ✄ GUSJ, ✄ GD, ✄ HT, ✄ ITN, ✄ LA, ✄ MO, ✄ NP, ✄ Num, ✄ PS (x3), ✄ RAT, ✄ SCDE, ✄ SCDJ, ✄ SCDN, ✄ UC
99/0 Ult. Victory 31, FF10, TV3, UV7
90/1 Upper Deck 56, 303, 477, Sticker
91/2 Upper Deck 146, 626
92/3 Upper Deck 155, G10, WG7
93/4 Upper Deck 227, 290, 388, HT6, NL3, E14, R6, SP 47
94/5 Upper Deck 300, 550, H22, R24, R43, -IG1, -SP-25
95/6 Upper Deck 113, 218, R15, R58, SE30
96/7 Upper Deck 50, X13, HH19, SS16B, ✄ GJ1
97/8 Upper Deck 57, SS20, SG19, S19, T3B
98/9 Upper Deck 85, 209, 389, FF20, FT1, GN4-6, LS14, P3
99/0 Upper Deck 49, 140, 304, AS10, CT2, FF14, HOF4, MA9, SB3, SS8, PD4, ✄ GJ, ✄✍ GJS
00/1 Upper Deck 179, 293, 409, D5, EC3, FF5, FT4, GA6, L4, TT5, ✄ GJ, ✄ DGJ
01/2 Upper Deck 61, 179, 216, CT6, FC10, GA12, LP5, SS15, T3, ✄ CJers., ✄ JPatch, ✄ PatchL, ✄ PatchN, ✄ PatchNu, ✄ PoaN, ✄ PoaND, ✄ PoaNT, ✄ SCFJers., ✄ SCFJersD, ✄ SCFJersT, ✄ SupSwe, ✄✍ JerSig, ✄✍ SigJer
02/3 Upper Deck 61, 180, 186, -GG8, -SS7, ✄ CG, ✄ DM, ✄ LN, ✄ PN, ✄ R50, ✄ FC, ✄ GJ, ✄✍ SGJ, ✄ PW, ✄ UDPL
00 ✄ UD APOH 500, ✄✍ 500
95/6 UD ASG MVP15
96/7 UD All-Star YCTG AR5
02/3 UD Artistic 31, R31, CG19, GD8, ✄ SS, / ✍ Art
93/4 Upper Deck Be A Player 18
94/5 UD BAP R29, R115, UC-5, G19, ✍ 115
93/4 UD BAP Roots 4
96/7 UD Black Diam. 162, RC9
97/8 UD Black Diam. 123, PC7
98/9 UD Black Diam. 30, M19, WF11
99/0 UD Black Diam. 36, D19, M7, ✄ APOH
00/1 UD Black Diam. 23, 87, IC3
99/0 UD C. Legends 56
01/2 UD Challenge 28, CM3, CR5, FF5, ✄ FP, ✄ UC, ✄✍ FPS
02/3 UD Classic 34, ET5, GG4, ✄ HH, ✄ HR, ✄ SC
95/6 UD CC 266, C26
96/7 UD CC 79, 292, UD14, S22, C10, CR10
97/8 UD Coll. Choice 78, 313, SQ67, S29, W3, C19
01/2 UD Collectors
97/8 UD Diam. Vision 4, DM3
02/3 UD Foundations 28, 113, ✄ 1000Jers, ✄ 1000Stick, ✄ CH, ✄ MS, ✄ PP
98/9 UD G. Reserve 85, 209, 389, ✍ Aut., ✄ Stick
99/0 UD G. Reserve 49, 140, 304, ✄ GR, ✍ UDA
99/0 UD Gretzky Excl. 71
01/2 UD Honor Roll 20, 50, DF3, SG4
02/3 UD Honor 24, 81, -SG13, ✄ GA, ✍ SC
96/7 UD Ice 109, S2
97/8 UD Ice 89, IC19, L5B
00/1 UD Ice 18, IC3, FP5, ✍ CCA
01/2 UD Ice 15, ✍ CCA, ✄ JC, ✄ FJ
00/1 UD Legends 46, 47, 135, EG8, PH2, SM5, ✄ LGJ, ✍ ES
01/2 UD Legends ✄ M
92/3 UD Locker 36
01/2 UD Mask 33, ✄ GJ, ✄ JP, ✄ DP, ✄ PM
02/3 UD Mask 32, ✄ IO, ✄ PG
98/9 UD MVP 69, OT1, S11, F7, Souv.
99/0 UD MVP 69, S7, H10, MVP6, W5, GU11, ✄ GU28, ✍ PS
00/1 UD MVP 70, 220, ME5, TP5, VC5, ✄ GS, ✍ ME
01/2 UD MVP 64, 219, MT6, VC1, ✄ S
02/3 UD MVP 67, 189, VF9
99/0 UD MVP Cup 65, CP4, GM5, GC, ✄ GU, ✍ PS
99/0 UD Ovation 24, 87, LP14
02/3 UD Piece 32, 95, AC12, HB3, SB4, ✄ PH, ✄ SS, ✍ MD
99/0 UD PowerDeck 11, T7
01/2 UD Premier 21, ✄ G, ✄ D, ✍ SigS
02/3 UD Premier 21, ✄ Jers, ✄ JD, ✄ Patch, ✄ NHLP, ✍ Sig
00/1 UD ProsProsp. 32, 90, CR3, NP3, ✄✍ GJS
99/0 UD Retro 27, DR5, TC5, ✍ Ink.
02/3 UD Rookie 34, 108, ✄ DJ, ✄ S, ✍ TD
01/2 UD SCup Champs 57, ✄ S, ✄ G, ✄ T
01/2 UD Top Shelf 15, ✄ P, ✄ J, ✄✍ SJ, ✄ S
02/3 UD Top Shelf 29, ✄ CP, ✄ GO, ✄ HH (x2), ✄ M (x4), ✄ R, ✄ SH, ✄ ST, ✄ SW, ✄ TS, ✍ Sig
00/1 UD Vintage 125, 136, 137, UD7, NH11, S3A, ✄ D-POH
01/2 UD Vintage 88, 96, ✄ NL, ✄ SC
02/3 UD Vintage 88, 271, 295, T24, ✄ FS, ✄ OS
97/8 Valu-net, ✍ Aut.
00/1 Vanguard 41, CF-5, HV-14, IF-9, VP-7
01/2 Vanguard 38, EMW 7, IF 5, QTH 4, VT 14, ✄ DGM 13
02/3 Vanguard 40, -EMW 3, -IF 6, -VT 10
99/0 Victory 96, 98, 320
00/1 Victory 81, 83, 249, 300
01/2 Victory 123, 403
02/3 Victory 77, -NP6
01/2 Waving the Flag 3
99/0 WGretzky 60, GH6, W2
96 Wien 101
97/8 Zenith 5, CTC-15, Z21
84/5 DETR / Little Caesars
85/6 DETR / Little Caesars
86/7 DETR / Little Caesars
87/8 DETR / Little Caesars
88/9 DETR / Little Caesars
88/9 DETR / S.A.M.
89/0 DETR / Little Caesars
90/1 DETR / Little Caesars
91/2 DETR / Little Caesars
99/0 DETR / News 1

ZABAWA, ANDRZEJ
79 Panini Sticker 132

ZABEL, NORBERT
94/5 DEL 182

ZABKA, BORIS
00/1 OFS 359

ZABRANSKY, LIBOR
94/5 APS 104
95/6 APS 60, 436
96/7 APS 371
99/0 DS 130
00/1 DS 3
01/2 DS 11
98/9 OFS 348
99/0 OFS 446, 486, 530
00/1 OFS 293
01/2 OFS 99
97/8 Score SLou. 17
97/8 Upper Deck 144

Z

ZABRODSKY, VLADIMIR
01/2 DS L5

ZACH, HANS
94/5 DEL 77
95/6 DEL 146
98/9 DEL 64, 339
99/0 Eishockey 194, 392

ZACH, JOHANN
79 Panini Sticker 112

ZACHA, ALES
01/2 OFS 86

ZACHARIE, CARL
01/2 Victoriaville Tigres 19

ZACHARY, TRAVIS
98/9 Québec Remparts

ZADELENKO, SERGEI
00/1 Mir 213

ZADINA, MAREK
94/5 APS 38
95/6 APS 235
96/7 APS 65
97/8 APS 326
97/8 DS 118
99/0 DS 106
00/1 DS 63
96/7 DS Sticker 240
97/8 DS Sticker 281
98/9 OFS 277, 487
99/0 OFS 204
00/1 OFS 228
01/2 OFS 56

ZADRAZIL, JIRI
95/6 APS 24
96/7 APS 110

ZAICHKOWSKI, JASON
92/3 BCJHL 143

ZAINE, ROD
71/2 Toronto Sun Photo

ZAINULLIN, RUSLAN
00/1 Mir 268

ZAITSEV, SERGEI
90/1 O-Pee-Chee 487

ZAJANKALA, GEORGE
99/0 Eishockey 112
91/2 7th...Sketch WHL 124
92/3 Cleveland Lumberjacks
95/6 Dayton Bombers
94/5 Knoxville Cherokees

ZAJGLA, PETR
99/0 OFS 69
00/1 OFS 343

ZAJIC, JOSEF
94/5 APS 35
95/6 APS 97
96/7 APS 85
97/8 APS 141
97/8 APS 204
97/8 DS 92
96/7 DS Sticker 143
97/8 DS Sticker 235
99/0 Eishockey 354
00/1 UD DEL 205
01/2 UD DEL 205

ZAJIC, VLADIMIR
98/9 OFS 39

ZAJICEK, JAN
79 Panini Sticker 81

ZAJONC, PETR
95/6 APS 232
96/7 APS 63
97/8 APS 141
96/7 DS Sticker 245
97/8 DS Sticker 263

ZAK, ROMAN
00/1 DS 126
00/1 OFS 168
99/0 Score 112

ZAK, ZDENEK
00/1 OFS 154

ZAKALL, BRIAN
91/2 Avant Garde BCJHL 74

ZAKHAROV, EVGENI
98/9 Mir 78
99/0 Mir 128

ZALAPSKI, ZARLEY
90/1 Bowman 207
91/2 Bowman 15
92/3 Bowman 173
93/4 Donruss 149
93/4 Donruss 410
94/5 Donruss 248
95/6 Donruss 177
96/7 Donruss 4
93/4 EA Sports 55
94/5 Flair 30
92/3 Fleer Ultra 77
93/4 Fleer Ultra 234
94/5 Fleer Ultra 38
95/6 Fleer Ultra 29
92/3 Humpty Dumpty
93/4 Leaf 8
94/5 Leaf 294
95/6 Leaf 225
96/7 Leaf 95
90/1 OPC/Topps 78
91/2 O-Pee-Chee 344
92/3 O-Pee-Chee 248
89/0 OPC/Topps 168
98/9 OPC Chrome 196
89/0 opcSticker 232-93, 45-191, / FS 14
97/8 Pa. Dynagon BKS-15
89/0 Panini Sticker 318
90/1 Panini Sticker 126
91/2 Panini Sticker 322
92/3 Panini Sticker 263
93/4 Panini Sticker 129
95/6 Panini Sticker 242
96/7 Panini Sticker 243
91/2 Parkhurst 61
92/3 Parkhurst 89
93/4 Parkhurst 88
94/5 Parkhurst 31
95/6 Parkhurst 31
91/2 Pinnacle 110
92/3 Pinnacle 271
93/4 Pinnacle 257
94/5 Pinnacle 342
96/7 Pinnacle 119
97/8 Pi. Be A Player 68, ✍ Aut. 68
95/6 Playoff 132
94/5 POG 64
94/5 POG / Western 20
95/6 POG 58
93/4 Power Play 112
93/4 Premier 70
94/5 Premier 379
90/1 Pro Set 242
91/2 Pro Set 91
92/3 Pro Set 59
91/2 Pro Set Platinum 47
90/1 Score 218
91/2 Score 111
91/2 Score CAN 111
92/3 Score 238
93/4 Score 104
93/4 Score PIAS 2
95/6 Score 69
96/7 Score 205
94/5 Select 140
89 Semic Sticker 60
91 Semic Sticker 60
95/6 SBx Emotion 26
95/6 SBx Impact 26
96/7 SP 25
95/6 Super Sticker 19
96/7 Team Out!
92/3 Topps 82
95/6 Topps 263
98/9 Topps 196
91/2 To. Stadium 228
92/3 To. Stadium 25
93/4 To. Stadium 102
93/4 To. Stadium - AS
94/5 To. Stadium 141
95/6 To. Stadium 56
90/1 Upper Deck 33
91/2 Upper Deck 231
92/3 Upper Deck 316
93/4 Upper Deck 213
94/5 Upper Deck 110
95/6 Upper Deck 480
96/7 Upper Deck 24
98/9 Upper Deck 321
95/6 UD BAP 108, ✍ S108
95/6 UD CC 123
96/7 UD CC 41
98/9 UD G. Reserve 321
92/3 UD Locker 18
91/2 HART / Jr. Whalers
92/3 HART / Dairymart
93/4 HART / Coke
97/8 MONT
89/0 PITT / Elby's
89/0 PITT / Foodland 3
90/1 PITT / Foodland 12
99/0 Utah Grizzlies

ZALASKY, LEE
01/2 Moose Jaw Warriors 13

ZALBA, BILL
00/1 Owen Sound Attack 18

ZALESAK, MIROSLAV
02/3 BAP Mem. 330
02/3 Ultimate Memorabilia 57
02/3 UD Rookie 145
01/2 Cleveland Barons
00/1 Kentucky Tho'blades

ZALYUKHNY, ALEXEI
00/1 Dynamo 22

ZAMBITO, MISTY
93/4 Huntington Blizzard

ZAMBON, MIKE
91/2 Avant Garde BCJHL 34
91/2 Avant Garde BCJHL 158

ZAMOJSKI, JACEK
89 Semic Sticker 131
92 Semic Sticker 273

ZAMUNER, ROB
98/9 Aurora 178, -CF 45
98/9 Be A Player 132, ✍ Aut. 132
92/3 Classic 98
92/3 Classic Four Sport 211
93/4 Donruss 329
91/2 Do. Priority 112
98/9 Dynagon Ice 176
99/0 Dynagon Ice 143
92/3 Fleer Ultra 415
93/4 Fleer Ultra 199
97/8 Kraft / PB
98/9 Kraft / Post 21
93/4 Leaf 173
94/5 Leaf 427
97/8 Limited 88
99/0 Millenium 177, ✍ Aut. 177
98/9 NHL Power Play
98/9 OPC Chrome 43
92/3 OPC Premier 69
97/8 Omega 216
98/9 Omega 223
98/9 Pacific 409, -TC 24
99/0 Pacific 399
00/1 Pacific 290
01/2 Pacific 282
02/3 Pacific Complete 95
97/8 Pacific CC 204
97/8 Pa. Crown Roy. 127
98/9 Pa. Paramount 223, -TC 24
97/8 Pa. Revolution 132, TC-23
98/9 Pa. Revolution 135
93/4 Panini Sticker 214
96/7 Panini Sticker 131
97/8 Panini Sticker 108
98/9 Panini Sticker 99
99/0 Panini Sticker 111
92/3 Parkhurst 171
93/4 Parkhurst 194
94/5 Parkhurst 224
01/2 Parkhurst 203
92/3 Pinnacle 414
93/4 Pinnacle 121
96/7 Pi. Be A Player 114, ✍ Aut. 114
95/6 Playoff 200
93/4 Power Play 236
93/4 Premier 19
95/6 Pro Magnet 68
89/0 ProCards IHL 40
90/1 ProCards 1
91/2 ProCards 204
93/4 Score 291
97/8 Score 200
02/3 Slam Card
92/3 Topps 426
98/9 Topps 43
98/9 To. Finest 20
92/3 To. Stadium 439
93/4 To. Stadium 376
94/5 To. Stadium 48
98/9 UD Choice 196
92/3 Upper Deck 583
92/3 Upper Deck CC4
93/4 Upper Deck 202, SP-154
94/5 Upper Deck 468
96/7 Upper Deck 158
97/8 Upper Deck 364
00/1 Upper Deck 354
01/2 Upper Deck 247
94/5 UD BAP R175, ✍ 147
96/7 UD CC 248
97/8 UD Coll. Choice 238
98/9 UD MVP 191
99/0 UD MVP Cup 128
97/8 Valu-net, ✍ Aut.
99/0 OTTA
00/1 OTTA
92/3 TAMP / Sheraton Inn
94/5 TAMP / Sky Box
95/6 TAMP / Sky Box

ZANIER, MARK
83/4 Moncton Alpines

ZANIER, MIKE
92 Semic Sticker 244
88/9 EDMO / Action 4
84/5 Nova Scotia Oilers

ZANKOVETS, EDUARD
00/1 Rockford IceHogs

ZANOSKI, TOM
01/2 Owen Sound Attack
02/3 Owen Sound Attack

ZANUSSI, JOE
76/7 O-Pee-Chee 324

ZANUSSI, RON
78/9 O-Pee-Chee 252
79/0 O-Pee-Chee 22
80/1 O-Pee-Chee 192
81/2 O-Pee-Chee 325
78/9 Topps 252
79/0 Topps 22
80/1 Topps 192
78/9 MINS / Cloverleaf 9
79/0 MINS
80/1 MINS
81/2 TORO

ZANUTTO, MIKE
95/6 Slapshot 245
97/8 Rochester Americans

ZAPLETAL, TOMAS
98/9 OFS 330
99/0 OFS 250

ZAPORZAN, TERRY
84/5 Kelowna Wings &...
83/4 Kelowna Wings

ZAPOTOCNY, DANIEL
97/8 APS 299
98/9 OFS 297
01/2 OFS 44
99/0 Score 47

ZAPT, BILL
92/3 BCJHL 240

ZARILLO, BRUNO
94 Semic 308
93 Semic Sticker 225

ZARIPOV, DANIS
99/0 Mir 260

ZAROWNY, AARON
93/4 Lethbridge Hurricanes

ZARRILLO, BRUNO
96/7 DEL 352
98/9 DEL 89
99/0 Eishockey 109
95 Globe 231
95 Panini Worlds 90
92 Semic Sticker 254
00/1 UD DEL 129, ✄ GJ
01/2 UD DEL 210

ZATONSKI, DMITRI
98/9 Mir 38
99/0 Mir 174
00/1 Mir 227

ZATOPEK, LIBOR
95/6 APS 239

ZATOPEK, LUKAS
98/9 OFS 354
99/0 OFS 235
00/1 OFS 247

ZAVALNYUK, VYACHESLAV
98/9 Mir 88
99/0 Mir 250
00/1 Mir 53

ZAVARUKHIN, NIKOLAI
93/4 Classic 49
00/1 Mir 162
93/4 Parkhurst 530
94/5 Parkie SE230
94/5 SP 163
94/5 Upper Deck 516

ZAVARYKHIN, NIKOLAI
99/0 Mir 127

ZAVEDIUK, TOM
95/6 Tri-City Americans 11

ZAVISHA, BRAD
90/1 7th...Sketch WHL 14
91/2 7th...Sketch WHL 358
93/4 EDMO / Sheet
94/5 Cape Breton Oilers

ZAVYAKOV, VLADIMIR
99/0 Mir 109

ZAVYALOV, ALEXANDER
98/9 Mir 107
99/0 Mir 76
00/1 Mir 39

ZAVYALOV, VLADIMIR
00/1 Mir 64

ZAWATSKY, ED
91/2 Rochester Americans GL

ZAYONCE, DEAN
00/1 7th...Sketch WHL 118
96/7 Carolina Monarchs
98/9 Charlotte Checkers
99/0 Greensboro Generals
91/2 Greensboro Monarchs
93/4 Greensboro Monarchs
94/5 Greensboro Monarchs

ZBONTAR, MARJAN
79 Panini Sticker 395

ZBYNEK, MICHALEK
00/1 Shawinigan 2

ZDRAHAL, PAVEL
95/6 APS 307
99/0 DS 54
98/9 OFS 78
99/0 OFS 302
00/1 OFS 280
01/2 OFS 244, RE13D, -UHI 10

ZDUNEK, PIOTR
89 Semic Sticker 138
92 Semic Sticker 279

ZEDNIK, RICHARD
01/2 Adrenaline 102
98/9 Aurora 200
00/1 BAP Mem. 331
01/2 BAP Mem. 261
02/3 BAP Mem. 127
99/0 Challenger 3
02/3 Crown Royale 53
96/7 Do. Canadian 125
98/9 Dynagon Ice 200
99/0 Dynagon Ice 206
02/3 Exclusive 95
02/3 First Edition 259
96/7 L. Preferred 133
96/7 Metal Univ. 197
99/0 NHL Power Play
01/2 O-Pee-Chee 168
02/3 O-Pee-Chee 194
98/9 OPC Chrome 92
97/8 Omega 244
98/9 Omega 250
98/9 Pacific 451
99/0 Pacific 449
00/1 Pacific 430
01/2 Pacific 214
02/3 Pacific 204
02/3 Pacific Complete 215
97/8 Pa. Crown Roy. 144
98/9 Pa. Paramount 250
99/0 Pa. Paramount 250
00/1 Pa. Paramount 250
98/9 Pa. Revolution 150
99/0 Panini Sticker 172
00/1 Panini Sticker 170
01/2 Parkhurst 170
02/3 Parkhurst 161
02/3 Parkhurst Retro 199
97/8 Pi. Be A Player OT 17
96/7 Pi. Zenith 132
02/3 Pr. Stock Reserve 55
02/3 Pr. Stock Titanium 58
02/3 Quest for the Cup 53
96/7 Select CE 110
00/1 Signature 156, ✍ Aut. 57
01/2 Signature 108, ✍ Aut. 108
02/3 Signature Series 25, ✍ 25
97/8 SP Authentic 197
02/3 Sports Vault 54
99/0 SPx 156
98/9 SPx Finite 135
00/1 Stadium 189
02/3 Stadium 85
98/9 Topps 92
99/0 Topps 93
00/1 Topps 200
01/2 Topps 168
02/3 Topps 194
99/0 To. Chrome 93
02/3 To. Limited 194
02/3 To. Total 377
98/9 UD Choice 218
98/9 UD3 7, 67, 127
96/7 Upper Deck 356
97/8 Upper Deck 388
98/9 Upper Deck 206, GN23
00/1 Upper Deck 175
01/2 Upper Deck 91
02/3 Upper Deck 94
97/8 UD Black Diam. 51
98/9 UD Black Diam. 90
98/9 UD G. Reserve 206
97/8 UD Ice 55
99/0 UD MVP 215
99/0 UD MVP 212
01/2 UD MVP 101
02/3 UD MVP 95
01/2 UD Top Shelf 47
00/1 UD Vintage 380
01/2 UD Vintage 137
02/3 UD Vintage 133
99/0 Victory 310
01/2 Victory 183
97/8 Zenith 83, RR-15, ZT-17, Z72
01/2 MONT
02/3 MONT
96/7 Portland Pirates

ZEHNDER, ANDREAS
95 Panini Worlds 124

ZEHR, JEFF
99/0 BAP Mem. 380
97 Bowman 149, ✍ Aut.
95/6 Slapshot 416

ZEIDEL, LARRY
45-64 BeeHive-2 [Detr.]
68/9 O-Pee-Chee 92
52/3 Parkhurst 91
53/4 Parkhurst 73
68/9 Topps 92

ZELENCHEV, IGOR
98/9 Mir 92
99/0 Mir 207
00/1 Mir 174

ZELENKA, JIRI
94/5 APS 83
95/6 APS 279
96/7 APS 133
97/8 APS 11
97/8 DS 84
98/9 DS 94
99/0 DS 153
97/8 DS Sticker 16, 215
98/9 OFS 136, 458
99/0 OFS 114
00/1 OFS 309, Star. 8
01/2 OFS RE5D

ZELENKO, BORIS
98/9 Mir 164
98/9 Hampton Roads
00/1 Dynamo 24

ZELEPUKIN, VALERI
98/9 Be A Player 254, ✍ Aut. 254
92/3 Bowman 430
93/4 Donruss 193
94/5 Donruss 291
95/6 Donruss 320
94/5 Flair 101
92/3 Fleer Ultra 122
93/4 Fleer Ultra 222
94/5 Fleer Ultra 124
93/4 Kraft / KD
93/4 Leaf 104
94/5 Leaf 17
95/6 Leaf 260
91/2 O-Pee-Chee 65R
98/9 OPC Chrome 187
98/9 Pacific 218
99/0 Pacific 314
00/1 Pacific 310
97/8 Pacific CC 299
92/3 Panini Sticker 177
93/4 Panini Sticker 38
94/5 Panini Sticker 33
96/7 Panini Sticker 87
97/8 Panini Sticker 67
99/0 Panini Sticker 123
00/1 Panini Sticker 79
91/2 Parkhurst 324
92/3 Parkhurst 228
93/4 Parkhurst 327
93/4 Parkhurst 383
94/5 Parkhurst 124
95/6 Parkhurst 391
91/2 Pinnacle 354
92/3 Pinnacle 286
93/4 Pinnacle 94
94/5 Pinnacle 49
95/6 Pinnacle 194, GG-25
95/6 Playoff 168
94/5 POG 149
93/4 Power Play 145
94/5 Premier 58
92/3 Pro Set RGL 10
91/2 Pro Set Platinum 261
91/2 ProCards 427
92/3 Red Ace Blue 7
92/3 Score 206
93/4 Score 278
94/5 Score 49
95/6 Score 179
97/8 Score NJer. 9
92/3 Topps 462
98/9 Topps 187
00/1 Topps 209
92/3 To. Stadium 99
93/4 To. Stadium 314
94/5 To. Stadium 225
91/2 Tri Globe From... 15-16
91/2 Upper Deck 589
92/3 Upper Deck 295
92/3 Upper Deck E12
93/4 Upper Deck 369
94/5 Upper Deck 143
97/8 Upper Deck 303
00/1 Upper Deck 271
95/6 UD BAP 207, ✍ S207
96/7 UD Ice 38
00/1 UD Vintage 81
96/7 NJER / Sharp
01/2 Norfolk Admirals

ZELEZNY, OTTO
95/6 APS 199

ZEMCHENOK, SERGEI
98/9 Mir 2
99/0 Mir 20
00/1 Metallurg 34

ZEMLAK, RICHARD
94/5 Classic PR1
89/0 ProCards IHL 154
90/1 ProCards 623
91/2 ProCards 590
87/8 MINS
85/6 QUEB
85/6 QUEB / Gene. Foods
86/7 QUEB
86/7 QUEB / Gene. Foods
93/4 Milwaukee Admirals

ZEMLICKA, RICHARD
95/6 APS 290, 366
96/7 APS 132
97/8 APS 12, 367, 372
94/5 DEL 47
97/8 DS 83
98/9 DS 92
99/0 DS 152
00/1 DS 12
96/7 DS Sticker 67
97/8 DS Sticker 214
95 Globe 154
98/9 OFS 367
99/0 OFS 115
00/1 OFS 308, Star-9
01/2 OFS 118
95 Panini Worlds 198
94 Semic 180
95 Semic 151
91 Semic Sticker 125
92 Semic Sticker 134
93 Semic Sticker 95
96 Wien 120

ZEMLYANOI, IGOR
98/9 Mir 13
00/1 Metallurg 30

ZEMLYANOL, IGOR
99/0 Mir 2

ZENHAUSERN, ALDO
79 Panini Sticker 259

ZENT, JASON
94/5 Classic 117
94/5 Cla. Images 54, ✍ Aut.
95/6 Edge Ice 50
96/7 OTTA

ZEPP, ROB
00/1 UD Prospects 23, CC5, CS4, ✄ GJ, ✄ GJC (x3), ✄✍ GJS, ✄✍ Sig

ZERWESZ, RAINER
94/5 DEL 101
95/6 DEL 212
96/7 DEL 356
98/9 DEL 102
99/0 Eishockey 13
01/2 UD DEL 60

ZETEK, ONDREJ
94/5 APS 212
95/6 APS 154
96/7 APS 59
97/8 APS 179
99/0 DS 111
96/7 DS Sticker 232
99/0 OFS 410, 420
00/1 OFS 219

ZETTEL, MICHAEL
94/5 DEL 223

ZETTERBERG, HENRIK
02/3 Atomic 107
02/3 BAP All-Star 139
02/3 BAP Mem. 286
02/3 Bowman 137
02/3 Calder 116, -CR 9
02/3 Crown Royale 111, -RR 9
02/3 eTopps 41
02/3 Exclusive 197, ✍ 197
02/3 Heads Up 126
02/3 In The GU 198
02/3 O-Pee-Chee 331
02/3 Pacific 126
02/3 Pacific Complete 521
02/3 PTC/ ASG 5
02/3 PTC/ Collections 4
02/3 PTC/ Spring Expo 4
02/3 Parkhurst 216, -HHC 2
02/3 Parkhurst Retro 216
02/3 Pr. Stock Reserve 160, -CA 7
02/3 Pr. Stock Titanium 114, -ROT 7
02/3 Quest for the Cup 117, -CC 7
02/3 Signature Series 190, ✍ 190
02/3 SP Authentic ✍ 186, ✍ SotT, ✍ SotTD (x2), ✍ SotTT, ✍✄ Patch
02/3 SP GU 75
02/3 SPx ✍ 151
02/3 Stadium 127
02/3 Topps 331
02/3 T. Chrome 182
02/3 To. Heritage 131
02/3 To. Total 426
02/3 UD Superstars 268
02/3 Ultimate Memorabilia 16, ✄ CC, ✍ RAut
02/3 Upper Deck 234, ✄ GJ, ✄✍ SGJ
02/3 UD Artistic 92, CG12, CG21
02/3 UD Classic 111
00/1 UD Elitserien 175, 208, ✍ Sig.
02/3 UD Foundations 151
02/3 UD Honor 151, ✍ SC
02/3 UD Mask 162
02/3 UD Piece 128
02/3 UD Premier ✍ 81, ✍ Sig
02/3 UD Rookie ✍ 168, ✍ TD
02/3 UD Top Shelf 127
02/3 Vanguard 113, -PP 9

ZETTERBERG, PATRIK
94/5 Leaf Elit Set 254
95/6 Leaf Elit Set 292
00/1 UD DEL 101
01/2 UD DEL 105
98/9 UD Elitserien 90
99/0 UD Elitserien 194

ZETTERSTROM, LARS
79 Panini Sticker 190
78/9 VANC / Royal Bank

ZETTLER, ROB
92/3 Bowman 84
90/1 OPC/Topps 289
91/2 O-Pee-Chee 272
92/3 O-Pee-Chee 366
91/2 OPC Premier 21
97/8 Pacific CC 101
92/3 Panini Sticker 127
94/5 Parkhurst 164
91/2 Pinnacle 213
92/3 Pinnacle 89
96/7 Pi. Be A Player 64, ✍ Aut. 64
91/2 Pro Set 330
88/9 ProCards / Kalamazoo
89/0 ProCards IHL 81
91/2 Score 370
91/2 Score 93T
91/2 Score CAN 643
92/3 Score 191
93/4 Score 413
92/3 Topps 227
91/2 To. Stadium 194
92/3 To. Stadium 225
94/5 To. Stadium 109
91/2 Upper Deck 61
94/5 Upper Deck 454
93/4 PHIL / Sheet
94/5 PHIL / Sheet
91/2 SANJ / Sports Action
92/3 SANJ / Pacific Bell
99/0 Portland Pirates
00/1 Portland Pirates
87/8 Soo Greyhounds 14

ZEVAKHIN, ALEXANDER
99/0 Mir 123
98/9 SPx Prospects 77
98/9 UD Black Diam. 106
00/1 WBS Penguins
01/2 WBS Penguins
02/3 WBS Penguins

ZEZEL, PETER
98/9 Be A Player 294, ✍ Aut. 294
90/1 Bowman 19
91/2 Bowman 164
92/3 Bowman 263
93/4 Donruss 338
92/3 Fleer Ultra 216
93/4 Fleer Ultra 436
93/4 Leaf 107
94/5 Leaf 533
85/6 OPC/Topps 24
86/7 OPC/Topps 190
87/8 OPC/Topps 71
88/9 OPC/Topps 146
90/1 OPC/Topps 15
91/2 O-Pee-Chee 445
92/3 O-Pee-Chee 337
89/0 OPC/Topps 27
98/9 OPC Chrome 56
90/1 OPC Premier 131
85/6 OPC Sticker 94-227
86/7 OPC Sticker 245-137
87/8 OPC Sticker 96-229
88/9 OPC Sticker 102-234
89/0 opcSticker 23
98/9 Pacific 436
87/8 Panini Sticker 129
89/0 Panini Sticker 118
90/1 Panini Sticker 264
91/2 Panini Sticker 103
92/3 Panini Sticker 81
91/2 Parkhurst 174
92/3 Parkhurst 410
93/4 Parkhurst 206
91/2 Pinnacle 174
91/2 Pinnacle 414
92/3 Pinnacle 283
93/4 Pinnacle 297
94/5 Pinnacle 109
96/7 Pi. Be A Player 94, ✍ Aut. 94
93/4 Power Play 455
93/4 Premier 454
94/5 Premier 22
90/1 Pro Set 274, 556
91/2 Pro Set 227
92/3 Pro Set 187
91/2 Pro Set Platinum 232
90/1 Score 24, 6T
91/2 Score 269
91/2 Score CAN 489
92/3 Score 174
93/4 Score 31
92/3 Topps 319
98/9 Topps 56
91/2 To. Stadium 104
92/3 To. Stadium 433
93/4 To. Stadium 116
90/1 Upper Deck 17
91/2 Upper Deck 241
92/3 Upper Deck 389
93/4 Upper Deck 199
94/5 Upper Deck 140
95/6 Upper Deck 377
94/5 UD BAP ✍ 100
96/7 UD CC 222
94/5 DALL / Southwest
86/7 PHIL
88/9 SLOU / Kodak
89/0 SLOU / Kodak
91/2 TORO / P.L.A.Y. 19
92/3 TORO / Kodak
93/4 TORO / Abalene
93/4 TORO / Black's 4
97/8 Albany River Rats

ZHAMNOV, ALEXEI
01/2 Adrenaline 43, ✂ GWJ 8
98/9 Aurora 44
99/0 Aurora 34
00/1 Aurora 35
02/3 BAP All-Star 100, ✂ ASJ
98/9 Be A Player 29, ✍ Aut. 29
99/0 BAP Mem. 118
00/1 BAP Mem. 236
02/3 BAP Mem. 15, 252
95/6 Bicycle Sports Aces K-Heart
95/6 Bowman 60
02/3 Bowman 32
02/3 Calder ✂ GWJ 6
99/0 Challenger 30
00/1 Crown Royale 25
02/3 Crown Royale 22, ✂ GWDP 4
93/4 Donruss 380
94/5 Donruss 73
95/6 Donruss 155, E-1, I-6
96/7 Donruss 89
97/8 Donruss 96
96/7 Do. Canadian 88
97/8 Do. Canadian 91
95/6 Do. Elite 29
96/7 Do. Elite 65
97/8 Do. Priority 62
99/0 Dynagon Ice 53
93/4 EA Sports 147
02/3 Exclusive 38
02/3 First Edition 21, ✂ Jers.
94/5 Flair 212
96/7 Flair 17
94/5 Fleer 247
96/7 Fleer 94
95/6 Fleer Metal 168, IS-23, MW-9
96/7 Fl. Picks 56, F50-50, JE-14
92/3 Fleer Ultra 447
93/4 Fleer Ultra 128
94/5 Fleer Ultra 398
95/6 Fleer Ultra 185, 398, PP-10, RLS-10, UV-10
95 Globe 173
01/2 Heads Up ✂ JQ 7
02/3 Heads Up 27
95/6 Hoyle / West. JOKER
95/6 Kraft / KD, PB
93/4 Leaf 84
93/4 Leaf GLR 5
94/5 Leaf 97
95/6 Leaf 104, FOI-3, FF-5, GLS-4
96/7 Leaf 107
94/5 L. Limited 113
95/6 L. Limited 116
96/7 L. Preferred 95
94/5 McDonald's McD-27
95/6 McDonald's McD-3
96/7 Metal Univ. 29
91/2 O-Pee-Chee 48R
01/2 O-Pee-Chee 186
02/3 O-Pee-Chee 121
98/9 OPC Chrome 135
92/3 OPC Premier 13
97/8 Omega 53
98/9 Omega 56
99/0 Omega 57
98/9 Pacific 155
99/0 Pacific 98
00/1 Pacific 105
01/2 Pacific 94, ✂ GWJ 7
97/8 Pacific CC 316
97/8 Pa. Invincible 32
97/8 Pa. Paramount 47
98/9 Pa. Paramount 51
99/0 Pa. Paramount 59
00/1 Pa. Paramount 55
93/4 Panini Sticker 190
94/5 Panini Sticker 163
95/6 Panini Sticker 212
96/7 Panini Sticker 196
97/8 Panini Sticker 128
98/9 Panini Sticker 112
99/0 Panini Sticker 200
00/1 Panini Sticker 125
92/3 Parkhurst 210
93/4 Parkhurst 243
93/4 Parkhurst 503
94/5 Parkhurst 260
95/6 Parkhurst 226, 241
00/1 Parkhurst P-92
01/2 Parkhurst 191, ✂ PJ32
02/3 Parkhurst 87, ✂ TT13
02/3 Parkhurst Retro 30
94/5 Parkie SE seV45
92/3 Pinnacle 416
93/4 Pinnacle 56
94/5 Pinnacle 147
95/6 Pinnacle 23, R20-11
96/7 Pinnacle 13
97/8 Pinnacle 123
96/7 Pi. Be A Player 11
97/8 Pi. Be A Player 99, ✍ Aut. 99
97/8 Pi. Certified 101
97/8 Pi. Inside 107
95/6 Pi. Summit 3, MH-5
96/7 Pi. Summit 37
97/8 Pi. Totally 101
95/6 Pi. Zenith 26
96/7 Pi. Zenith 108
95/6 Playoff 110, 330
94/5 POG 375
95/6 POG 289, I-015
93/4 Power Play 278
93/4 Power Play SYS 12
93/4 Power Play RisS 9
93/4 Premier 128
93/4 Premier 420
93/4 Prmr. - BG-Top. 8
94/5 Premier 217
99/0 Prism 36
00/1 Pr. Stock 21, ✂ GUG-17
01/2 Pr. Stock ✂ GUG 27
00/1 PS Titanium ✂ GUG 6, ✂ GUG-73
01/2 PS Titanium 33, ✂ DSJ 10
00/1 PS Titanium Draft ✂ 22
95/6 Pro Magnet 60
02/3 Quest for the Cup 19
92/3 Red Ace Blue 2
92/3 Red Ace Violet 35
99/0 Revolution 36, / CSC 36
00/1 Revolution 33
93/4 Score 256
93/4 Score/CAN DD2
94/5 Score 154
95/6 Score 85, BB-12, L-10
96/7 Score 128
97/8 Score 175
94/5 Select 51
95/6 Select CE 6, DS-20
94 Semic 150
94 Semic 356
91 Semic Sticker 95
92 Semic Sticker 110
00/1 Signature 138, ✍ Aut. 130
02/3 Signature Series 2, ✍ 2
95/6 SBx Emotion 198, Xce-10, Xci-17
95/6 SBx Impact 187, IQ-12
96/7 SBx Impact 21
02/3 Slam Card
94/5 SP 133
95/6 SP 167
96/7 SP 30
97/8 SP Authentic 32
02/3 SP Authentic 17
02/3 SP GU ✂ PH
02/3 Sports Vault 175
96/7 SPx 36
99/0 Stadium 107
00/1 Stadium 113
01/2 Stadium ✂ SCS
95/6 Super Sticker 135
95/6 Topps 22, 331, 2PL
98/9 Topps 135
99/0 Topps 247
00/1 Topps 50
01/2 Topps 186
02/3 Topps 121
99/0 To. Chrome 247
02/3 T. Chrome 77
94/5 Topps Finest 102
95/6 To. Finest 78
98/9 To. Finest 134
00/1 To. Heritage 160, OSJ
02/3 To. Heritage 97
02/3 To. Limited 121
01/2 To. Reserve ✂ TR
93/4 To. Stadium 56
95/6 To. Stadium 95
95/6 T. Super Skills 70
02/3 To. Total 91
91/2 Tri Globe From... 7-8
98/9 UD Choice 48
00/1 UD Heroes 26
00/1 UD Reserve 19
91/2 Upper Deck 2
92/3 Upper Deck 578
92/3 Upper Deck ER8
93/4 Upper Deck 162, SP-180
94/5 Upper Deck 7, SP-90
95/6 Upper Deck 64, 234, F13, R28
96/7 Upper Deck 125, 233, SS24B
97/8 Upper Deck 42, T19C
98/9 Upper Deck 245, ✂ GJ2
99/0 Upper Deck 208
00/1 Upper Deck 42
01/2 Upper Deck 270
02/3 Upper Deck 36, ✂ S
02/3 UD Artistic 17, R17, / Art
94/5 UD BAP ✍ 21
96/7 UD Black Diam. 106
97/8 UD Black Diam. 56
02/3 UD Classic 20, ✂ HR
02/3 UD Classic ✂ HH
95/6 UD CC 49, 383, C8
96/7 UD CC 203, 327, C11, CR11
97/8 UD Coll. Choice SQ46
98/9 UD G. Reserve 245
99/0 UD G. Reserve 208
02/3 UD Honor 77
92/3 UD Locker 60
99/0 UD MVP 50
00/1 UD MVP 41
01/2 UD MVP 42
02/3 UD MVP 38
99/0 UD MVP Cup 46
00/1 UD Pros&Prosp. 20
02/3 UD Top Shelf 20
00/1 UD Vintage 82
01/2 UD Vintage 54, 61
02/3 UD Vintage 60, 267
00/1 Vanguard 24, ✂ DGJ-10
02/3 Vanguard ✂ GWJ 12
99/0 Victory 72
00/1 Victory 56
01/2 Victory 76
02/3 Victory 43, -NP33
99/0 WGretzky 44
96 Wien 143
93/4 WINN / Ruffles
93/4 WINN Readers
95/6 WINN
95/6 WINN Readers
95/6 WINN Readers

ZHAMNOV, ALEXEI
02/3 Pacific 85
02/3 Pacific Complete 219
02/3 Pr. Stock Reserve 22

ZHDAN, ALEXANDER
99/0 Mir 43
00/1 Mir 36, 311
93/4 Richmond Renegades

ZHEREBTSOV, SERGEI
00/1 Mir 184

ZHITNIK, ALEXEI
98/9 Aurora 22
98/9 Be A Player 166, ✍ Aut. 166
99/0 BAP Mem. 122
00/1 BAP Mem. 8
98/9 Bowman's Best 88
01/2 Crown Royale ✂ TT 5
93/4 Donruss 165
94/5 Donruss 279
95/6 Donruss 50
96/7 Donruss 11
96/7 Do. Elite 115
96/7 Flair 10
95/6 Fleer Metal 17
96/7 Fl. Picks 152
92/3 Fleer Ultra 314
93/4 Fleer Ultra 87
94/5 Fleer Ultra 104
95/6 Fleer Ultra 22, RS-10
95 Globe 169
01/2 Heads Up ✂ JQ 23
98/9 Kraft / PB
93/4 Leaf 123
93/4 Leaf GLR 8
94/5 Leaf 8
95/6 Leaf 4
96/7 Leaf 155
94/5 L. Limited 111
98/9 OPC Chrome 192
92/3 OPC Premier 125
98/9 Pacific 114
99/0 Pacific 50
01/2 Pacific 55
02/3 Pacific 49
02/3 Pacific Complete 423
97/8 Pacific CC 236
98/9 Pa. Paramount 25
99/0 Pa. Paramount 34
94/5 Panini Sticker 179
95/6 Panini Sticker 20
96/7 Panini Sticker 17
97/8 Panini Sticker 11
98/9 Panini Sticker 22
99/0 Panini Sticker 35
00/1 Panini Sticker 22
92/3 Parkhurst 71
93/4 Parkhurst 92
94/5 Parkhurst 101
95/6 Parkhurst 19, IAS-3
00/1 Parkhurst P-217
01/2 Parkhurst ✂ T11
92/3 Pinnacle 392
93/4 Pinnacle 23
94/5 Pinnacle 87
95/6 Pinnacle 64
96/7 Pinnacle 180
96/7 Pi. Summit 69
95/6 Playoff 14
94/5 POG 131
95/6 POG 47
93/4 Power Play 123
93/4 Premier 2
94/5 Premier 57
00/1 PS Titanium ✂ GUG 63
01/2 PS Titanium ✂ DSJ 4
95/6 Pro Magnet 107
92/3 Red Ace Violet 36
93/4 Score 148
94/5 Score 171
95/6 Score 47
96/7 Score 70
97/8 Score Buff. 18
96/7 Select CE 45
95 Semic 128
95/6 SBx Emotion 19
95/6 SBx Impact 19
94/5 SP 16
95/6 SP 15
96/7 SP 19
97/8 SP Authentic 17
99/0 SPx 16
91/2 Star Pics 38
95/6 Super Sticker 13
96/7 Team Out!
95/6 Topps 49
98/9 Topps 192
99/0 Topps 232
99/0 To. Chrome 232
98/9 To. Finest 33
99/0 To. Prmr. Plus 39
93/4 To. Stadium 221
95/6 To. Stadium 143
02/3 To. Total 257
98/9 UD Choice 26
91/2 Upper Deck 660
92/3 Upper Deck 566
92/3 Upper Deck CC7
92/3 Upper Deck ER13
93/4 Upper Deck 161, SP-75
94/5 Upper Deck - SP-38
95/6 Upper Deck 187, SE-11
96/7 Upper Deck 17
98/9 Upper Deck 226
99/0 Upper Deck 191
00/1 Upper Deck 251
01/2 Upper Deck 255
95/6 UD BAP 28, ✍ S28
97/8 UD Black Diam. 1
95/6 UD CC 303
96/7 UD CC 26, 311
97/8 UD Coll. Choice 29
91/2 Upper Deck WJC 21
98/9 UD G. Reserve 226
99/0 UD G. Reserve 191
00/1 UD Vintage 45
02/3 UD Vintage 35
99/0 Victory 42
01/2 Victory 44
99/0 WGretzky 23
96 Wien 134

ZHLUKTOV, VIKTOR
92/3 Future Trends C76 138
79 Panini Sticker 149

ZHOLTOK, SERGEI
01/2 Atomic ✂ GWJ 30
00/1 BAP Mem. 359
92/3 Classic 50
93/4 Cla. Prospects 227
98/9 Dynagon Ice 99
01/2 Heads Up ✂ JQ 12
93/4 Leaf 376
94/5 Leaf 508
02/3 O-Pee-Chee 165
98/9 Pacific 320
99/0 Pacific 214
00/1 Pacific 217
02/3 Pacific 189
02/3 Pacific Complete 231
97/8 Pacific CC 328
97/8 Panini Sticker 39
00/1 Panini Sticker 42
92/3 Parkhurst 482
93/4 Parkhurst 281
01/2 Parkhurst 380
94/5 Parkie SE10
97/8 Pi. Be A Player 192, ✍ Aut. 192
93/4 Power Play 294
00/1 PS Titanium ✂ GUG 102
00/1 PS Titanium Draft ✂ 51
93/4 Score 475
00/1 Signature 113, ✍ Aut. 131
02/3 Sports Vault 246
00/1 Stadium 96
00/1 Topps 159
02/3 Topps 165
02/3 To. Limited 165
94/5 To. Stadium 254
02/3 To. Total 191
91/2 Upper Deck 659
93/4 Upper Deck 244
94/5 Upper Deck 419
97/8 Upper Deck 116
00/1 Upper Deck 320
01/2 Upper Deck 318
97/8 UD Coll. Choice 177
91/2 Upper Deck WJC 20
00/1 UD MVP 95
99/0 UD MVP Cup 95
00/1 UD Vintage 188
00/1 Victory 119
01/2 MINW / Crime 21
96/7 OTTA
97/8 OTTA
95/6 Las Vegas Thunder
96/7 Las Vegas Thunder

ZHURIK, ALEXANDER
98/9 Mir 161
00/1 Mir 129
93/4 Slapshot / Kingston 10
99/0 Hamilton Bulldogs
99/0 Hamilton Bulldogs/ Staz

ZIB, LUKAS
95/6 APS 57
96/7 APS 246
97/8 APS 272
98/9 OFS 411
99/0 OFS 281
00/1 OFS 358

ZIBIN, ALEXANDER
99/0 Mir 67

ZIDLICKY, MAREK
94/5 APS 56
95/6 APS 86
96/7 APS 80
97/8 APS 198
99/0 Cardset 221
00/1 Cardset 14
02/3 Cardset 146
98/9 DS 97
96/7 DS Sticker 137
97/8 DS Sticker 230
98/9 OFS 163

ZIEGLER, JOHN
83&87 HHOF 257

ZIEGLER, THOMAS
01/2 BAP Mem. 450
01/2 Pacific 360
01/2 SPx 127
01/2 Upper Deck 208
01/2 UD MVP 217
01/2 UD Top Shelf 64
01/2 UD Vintage 298
01/2 Victory 388

ZIESCHE, JOACHIM
70/1 Kuvajulkaisut 100

ZIESCHE, STEFFAN
91/2 Upper Deck 679

ZIESCHE, STEFFEN
95/6 DEL 111
91/2 Upper Deck WJC 42
01/2 UD DEL 154

ZIETARA, WALENTY
74 Hellas MM-Jenkki 91
79 Panini Sticker 129
73/4 Williams Finnish 104

ZIGOMANIS, MICHAEL
99 Bowman 36, 134, ✍ BA5
98/9 SP Authentic 135, ✍ SotT
98/9 Upper Deck 412
99/0 Upper Deck 334
99/0 UD Black Diam. 94
98/9 UD G. Reserve 412
99/0 UD G. Reserve 334
99/0 UD MVP Cup 215
99/0 UD Prospects 8
00/1 UD Prospects 10, CC2, FL5
99/0 Kingston Frontenacs
00/1 Kingston Frontenacs 24

ZILIOTTO, MARK
89/0 ProCards AHL 64

ZILKA, KEN
91/2 7th...Sketch WHL 195

ZILUKTOV, VIKTOR
82 Semic Sticker 64
83/4 Soviet Stars

ZIMA, ALES
94/5 APS 19
95/6 APS 116, 383
96/7 APS 39
97/8 APS 63
97/8 DS 105
98/9 DS 123
99/0 DS 51
96/7 DS Sticker 108
97/8 DS Sticker 296
98/9 OFS 188
99/0 OFS 303

ZIMAKOV, SERGEI
99/0 Mir 160
00/1 Mir 256
95/6 Upper Deck 558

ZIMIN, EVGENY
91/2 Future Trends C72 14
72 Panda MM-Toronto
72 Semic Sticker 9
74 Semic Sticker 47
69/0 Soviet Stars
71/2 Soviet Stars
71/2 Williams Finnish 20

ZIMMER, BRAD
91 7th..Sketch Mem.Cup 127
90/1 7th..Sketch WHL 125
91/2 7th...Sketch WHL 349
89/0 Lethbridge Hurricanes
93/4 Red Deer Rebels

ZIMMER, DEVIN
91/2 Air Canada SJHL D8

ZIMMERMAN, JASON
92/3 MPS SJHL 34

ZIMMERMAN, SHAWN
92/3 MPS SJHL 38
93/4 W. Michigan Broncos

ZINCK, GARY
00/1 Halifax Moosehead
99/0 Halifax Mooseheads

ZINEVYCH, ALEX
00/1 Albany River Rats

ZINGER, DARRIN
95/6 Guildford Flames 25
96/7 Guildford Flames 17
97/8 Guildford Flames

ZINGER, DWAYNE
01/2 Cincinnati Mighty Ducks

ZINGER, VIKTOR
69/0 Mästär Serien 27
69/0 Mästär Serien 29
69/0 Soviet Stars

ZININE, DIMITRI
93/4 Jyvas Hyva 169
93/4 Sisu 172

ZINOVIEV, SERGEI
99/0 Mir 224
02/3 Russian Future Stars 17

ZINOVJEV, DIMITRI
90/1 O-Pee-Chee 478

ZION, JON
98/9 SP Authentic 122
98/9 Upper Deck 399
98/9 UD G. Reserve 399
00/1 UD Prospects 17
99/0 Ottawa 67's
00/1 Ottawa 67's 4
01/2 Ottawa 67's 5

ZISKA, JAKUB
99/0 Score 16

ZIVNY, MARTIN
94/5 APS 154
95/6 APS 257
99/0 Score 93

ZIZKA, TOMAS
97/8 APS 74
02/3 BAP Mem. 386
02/3 Choice Prospects 45
99/0 DS 6
00/1 DS 51
98/9 OFS 24
99/0 OFS 220
00/1 OFS 352
02/3 Ultimate Memorabilia 71
02/3 UD Premier 92
01/2 Manchester Monarchs

ZLOV, YURI
00/1 Mir 366

ZLUKTOV, VIKTOR
79/0 Soviet Stars 19

ZMOLEK, DOUG
92/3 Classic 88
92/3 Classic Four Sport 207
93/4 Donruss 313
92/3 Fleer Ultra 405
93/4 Leaf 112
94/5 Leaf 453
91/2 O-Pee-Chee 9S
92/3 OPC Premier 18
97/8 Pacific CC 297
93/4 Panini Sticker 263
92/3 Parkhurst 393
93/4 Parkhurst 457
93/4 Pinnacle 117
96/7 Pi. Be A Player 151, ✍ Aut. 151
93/4 Premier 143
93/4 Score 327
99/0 Topps 85
99/0 To. Chrome 85
93/4 To. Stadium 171
92/3 Upper Deck 509
93/4 Upper Deck 193
94/5 DALL / Southwest
92/3 SANJ / Pacific Bell
91/2 Minnesota G'Gophers

ZMRHAL, PAVEL
94/5 APS 166

ZNAROK, OLEG
91/2 Jyvas Hyva 70
90/1 O-Pee-Chee 477

ZNOJEMSKY, MARTIN
98/9 OFS 263

ZOHIL, JASON
90/1 7th..Sketch OHL 198, 243
91/2 7th...Sketch OHL 268
91/2 Sudbury Wolves
89/0 Windsor Spitfires

ZOL, DIANO
92/3 BCJHL 53

ZOLOTOV, ROMAN
92/3 Classic 55
00/1 Dynamo 5

ZOLOTOV, SERGEI
98/9 Mir 75
99/0 Mir 45
00/1 Mir 30, 299

ZOMBO, MIKE
85/6 London Knights

ZOMBO, RICK
91/2 Bowman 54
92/3 Bowman 87
90/1 OPC/Topps 21
91/2 O-Pee-Chee 454
92/3 O-Pee-Chee 97
89/0 Panini Sticker 64
90/1 Panini Sticker 206
91/2 Panini Sticker 137
91/2 Parkhurst 380
91/2 Pinnacle 259
91/2 Pinnacle 393
91/2 Pinnacle 410
92/3 Pinnacle 129
93/4 Pinnacle 306
94/5 Pinnacle 447
90/1 Pro Set 80
91/2 Pro Set 64
91/2 Pro Set 474
90/1 Score 101
90/1 Sco. Hot Cards 49
91/2 Score 177
91/2 Score 60T
91/2 Score CAN 177
92/3 Score 154
93/4 Score 211
94/5 Score 75
92/3 Topps 288
91/2 To. Stadium 32
92/3 To. Stadium 100
90/1 Upper Deck 115
91/2 Upper Deck 395
95/6 Upper Deck 319
95/6 UD BAP 136, ✍ S136
86/7 DETR / Little Caesars
87/8 DETR / Little Caesars
88/9 DETR / Little Caesars
88/9 DETR / S.A.M.
89/0 DETR / Little Caesars
90/1 DETR / Little Caesars
91/2 SLOU

ZORICA, JOE
52/3 Anonymous 2

ZORKIN, VLADIMIR
98/9 Mir 26
99/0 Mir 106

ZORN, JEFF
99/0 Prince George Cougars

ZORYK, STEVE
93/4 Slapshot / S.S.Marie 11
95/6 Slapshot 269

ZUBICEK, PAVEL
95/6 APS 205
97/8 APS 42
99/0 DS 140
97/8 DS Sticker 173
98/9 OFS 104
99/0 OFS 70
00/1 OFS 327
01/2 OFS 134

ZUBKOV, ANDREI
99/0 Mir 261

ZUBKOV, VLADIMIR
82 Semic Sticker 72
83/4 Soviet Stars

ZUBOV, SERGEI
01/2 Atomic ✂ GWJ 20
98/9 Aurora 61
98/9 Be A Player 43, ✍ Aut. 43
99/0 BAP Mem. 24
00/1 BAP Mem. 32
01/2 BAP Mem. 74
02/3 BAP Mem. 246
92/3 Classic Prospects 70
92/3 Classic Prospects 74
92/3 Classic Prospects BC6
93/4 Cla. Prospects 115
01/2 Crown Royale ✂ TT 3
93/4 Donruss 225
94/5 Donruss 219
95/6 Donruss 130, 357, D-3
96/7 Donruss 91
95/6 Do. Elite 37
96/7 Do. Elite 111
97/8 Do. Preferred 91
97/8 Do. Priority 51
98/9 Dynagon Ice 61
95/6 Edge Ice C16
02/3 First Edition 62, ✂ Jers.
94/5 Flair 118
94/5 Fleer 140, FF-10
96/7 Fleer 28
95/6 Fleer Metal 121, IS-24, MW-8
96/7 Fl. Picks 26
92/3 Fleer Ultra 359
93/4 Fleer Ultra 243
94/5 Fleer Ultra 144
95/6 Fleer Ultra 108, 295
96/7 Fl. Ultra 48
95 Globe 165
95/6 Hoyle / East. JOKER
93/4 Leaf 164
94/5 Leaf 111
95/6 Leaf 126
96/7 Leaf 130
94/5 L. Limited 65
95/6 L. Limited 74
96/7 L. Preferred 63
97/8 Limited 93
96/7 Metal Univ. 44
91/2 O-Pee-Chee 28R
91/2 O-Pee-Chee 30R
01/2 O-Pee-Chee 17
02/3 O-Pee-Chee 225
98/9 OPC Chrome 176, B7
97/8 Omega 77
98/9 Omega 77
99/0 Omega 77
98/9 Pacific 56
99/0 Pacific 132
00/1 Pacific 142
01/2 Pacific 137, ✂ GWJ 12
02/3 Pacific 122
02/3 Pacific Complete 124
97/8 Pacific CC 76
97/8 Pa. Crown Roy. 44
97/8 Pa. Dynagon 40, T-44
97/8 Pa. Invincible 45
98/9 Pa. Paramount 72
99/0 Pa. Paramount 78
00/1 Pa. Paramount 82
97/8 Pa. Revolution 45
94/5 Panini Sticker 89
95/6 Panini Sticker 111
96/7 Panini Sticker 64
97/8 Panini Sticker 138
98/9 Panini Sticker 124
99/0 Panini Sticker 221
00/1 Panini Sticker 146
92/3 Parkhurst 351
93/4 Parkhurst 133
94/5 Parkhurst 144
95/6 Parkhurst 434, IAS-3, PP-27
00/1 Parkhurst P-46
01/2 Parkhurst 139
02/3 Parkhurst 152
02/3 Parkhurst Retro 158, ✂ NH5
93/4 Pinnacle 156
94/5 Pinnacle 36
96/7 Pinnacle 122
95/6 Pi. Summit 74
96/7 Pi. Summit 119
95/6 Pi. Zenith 66
96/7 Pi. Zenith 38
95/6 Playoff 187
96/7 Playoff 383
94/5 POG 172
95/6 POG 217
93/4 Power Play 167
93/4 Power Play RisS 10
93/4 Premier 217
94/5 Premier 221, 382, 493
00/1 Premier Plus WP4
00/1 Pr. Stock ✂ GUG 42,93
01/2 Pr. Stock ✂ GUG 41
01/2 PS Titanium Draft ✂ 36
95/6 Pro Magnet 94
93/4 Score 313
95/6 Score 188
96/7 Score 171
94/5 Select 14
95/6 Select CE 67
94 Semic 140
00/1 Signature 7, ✍ Aut. 74, ✂ DD-11
02/3 Signature Series ✂ DW5
95/6 SBx Emotion 144
95/6 SBx Impact 137
96/7 SBx Impact 32
94/5 SP 78
95/6 SP 117
96/7 SP 43
97/8 SP Authentic 46
02/3 Sports Vault 208
02/3 Stadium ✂ FC9, ✂ PC9
95/6 Super Sticker 99
95/6 Topps 333
98/9 Topps 176, B7
00/1 Topps 128
01/2 Topps 17
02/3 Topps 225, ✂ CC3
00/1 To. Chrome 97
01/2 To. Chrome 17
95/6 To. Finest 171
00/1 To. Heritage 193
01/2 To. Heritage 104
02/3 To. Limited 225
01/2 To. Reserve ✂ TR
93/4 To. Stadium 312
95/6 To. Stadium 92
00/1 To. Stars ✂ GG
02/3 To. Total 346
98/9 UD Choice 66
00/1 UD Heroes 40
00/1 Ultimate Mem. ✂ TM-27
92/3 Upper Deck 516
93/4 Upper Deck 181
94/5 Upper Deck 100, SP-142
95/6 Upper Deck 474, H37, SE-155
96/7 Upper Deck 246, X39
97/8 Upper Deck 263
98/9 Upper Deck 254
99/0 Upper Deck 218
00/1 Upper Deck 285
01/2 Upper Deck 284
02/3 Upper Deck 57
96/7 UD Black Diam. 56
01/2 UD Challenge 26
95/6 UD CC 10
96/7 UD CC 214
98/9 UD G. Reserve 254
99/0 UD G. Reserve 218
96/7 UD Ice 16
01/2 UD Mask 31
98/9 UD MVP 65
00/1 UD MVP 62
01/2 UD MVP 59
01/2 UD SCup Champs 49
00/1 UD Vintage 115
01/2 UD Vintage 83, 87
99/0 Victory 95
00/1 Victory 73
01/2 Victory 113
02/3 Victory 68
96 Wien 136
96/7 DALL / Southwest
00/1 DALL / Southwest
01/2 DALL / Southwest
95/6 PITT / Foodland 12
92/3 Binghampton Rangers

ZUBRUS, DAINIUS
96/7 All-Sport PPF 98, 170
98/9 Aurora 143, -CF 37
96/7 Auto. Coll. ✍ Aut.
98/9 Be A Player 102, ✍ Aut. 102
00/1 BAP Mem. 78
98/9 Collection Souvenir 07
97/8 Donruss 75
96/7 Do. Canadian 147
96/7 Do. Elite 141, A-15
97/8 Do. Elite 50, 135
97/8 Do. Preferred 59, 190, LT-8C
97/8 Do. Priority 23, DD-29, Post-34, Stamp-34
97/8 Do. Studio 26, HH-5, P-27
98/9 Dynagon Ice 141
02/3 Exclusive 175
02/3 First Edition 223
96/7 Flair 119
96/7 Fl. Ultra 129
01/2 Heads Up ✂ JQ 12
97/8 Leaf 124, 186, BS-22, FOI-13
96/7 L. Limited LR-6
96/7 L. Preferred 128
97/8 Limited 109, 195, FG-3
96/7 Metal Univ. 198
98/9 OPC Chrome SB30
97/8 Omega 171, GF-14
98/9 Omega 181
98/9 Pacific 333, -GCDC 26
99/0 Pacific 215
00/1 Pacific 218
01/2 Pacific 400, ✂ GWJ 36
02/3 Pacific 400
02/3 Pacific Complete 312
97/8 Pacific CC 303
97/8 Pa. Crown Roy. 101, L-15
98/9 Pa. Crown Roy. 102
97/8 Pa. Dynagon 94, DD-11B, T-9
97/8 Pa. Invincible 105, OTG-15
97/8 Pa. Paramount 138
98/9 Pa. Paramount 179
99/0 Pa. Paramount 122
00/1 Pa. Paramount 133
97/8 Pa. Revolution 104
98/9 Pa. Revolution 108
97/8 Panini Sticker 95, 249
98/9 Panini Sticker 92
99/0 Panini Sticker 73
00/1 Panini Sticker 44
00/1 Parkhurst P-60
01/2 Parkhurst 192
97/8 Pinnacle 105
97/8 Pi. Be A Player 26, ✍ Aut. 26
97/8 Pi. Certified 116
97/8 Pi. Inside 33, IT-30
97/8 Pi. Totally 116
96/7 Pi. Zenith 123
00/1 Pr. Stock ✂ GUG 61
02/3 Pr. Stock Reserve 100
01/2 PS Titanium ✂ DSJ 43
00/1 PS Titanium Draft ✂ 100
92 Québec Pee Wee 1464
97/8 Score 249
97/8 Score Phil. 12
96/7 Select CE 120
00/1 Signature 127, ✍ Aut. 18
96/7 SP 117
97/8 SP Authentic 117, ✍ SotT
02/3 Sports Vault 148
98/9 Topps SB30
00/1 Topps 201
98/9 To. Finest 14, 150
02/3 To. Total 325
96/7 Upper Deck 309
97/8 Upper Deck 122, SG59, T15B
98/9 Upper Deck 145
00/1 Upper Deck 92
01/2 Upper Deck 409
02/3 Upper Deck 178
96/7 UD Black Diam. 68
97/8 UD Black Diam. 8
97/8 UD Coll. Choice 187
98/9 UD G. Reserve 145
97/8 UD Ice 49
98/9 UD MVP 102
00/1 UD MVP 91
99/0 UD MVP Cup 92
00/1 UD Vintage 189
00/1 Victory 125
01/2 Victory 359
02/3 Victory 216
97/8 Visions Signings 40, A20, ✍ 40, ✍ A20
00/1 MONT
96/7 PHIL / Ocean Spray

ZUBYCK, JOHN
96/7 Guelph Storm

ZUEV, YURI
98/9 Mir 89

ZUK, GREG
84/5 Kelowna Wings &...
83/4 Kelowna Wings

ZUKE, MIKE*
80/1 O-Pee-Chee 209
81/2 O-Pee-Chee 299
82/3 O-Pee-Chee 313
83/4 O-Pee-Chee 322
84/5 O-Pee-Chee 80
85/6 OPC/Topps 19
81/2 OPC Sticker 132
84/5 OPC Sticker 195
82/3 Post [SLou.]
80/1 Topps 209
81/2 Topps 124 [West]
84/5 Topps 63
83/4 HART / Jr. Whalers
84/5 HART / Jr. Whalers
85/6 HART / Jr. Whalers

ZUKE, MIKE**
93/4 Slapshot / S.S.Marie 30
89/0 Soo Greyhounds
93/4 Soo Greyhounds 32
96/7 Soo Greyhounds

ZUKIWSKY, JARRET
90/1 7th..Sketch WHL 247
91/2 7th...Sketch WHL 284
89/0 Victoria Cougars

ZUKIWSKY, JONATHAN
95/6 Bowman P40
95/6 Cla. Vis. Signings 66, ✍ Aut.
93/4 Red Deer Rebels
95/6 Red Deer Rebels

ZULTEK, MATT
97 Bowman 132, ✍ Aut.
93 Québec Pee Wee 1441
00/1 Upper Deck 199
00/1 UD Black Diam. 64
00/1 UD Ice 44
00/1 UD MVP 213
99/0 Ottawa 67's

ZULYNIAK, SHANE
90/1 7th..Sketch WHL 278
91/2 7th...Sketch WHL 264
90/1 Prince Albert Raiders
91/2 Prince Albert Raiders
93/4 Prince Albert Raiders

ZUPANCIC, NIK
99/0 Cardset 275
00/1 UD Elitserien 172

ZURBA, PETER
91/2 Avant Garde BCJHL 13
92/3 BCJHL 189
97/8 Central Texas

ZUREK, JAN
96/7 DS Sticker 282

ZUREK, JIRI
97/8 APS 117
98/9 OFS 77
99/0 OFS 205
00/1 OFS 78

ZVACHKIN, LEONID
01/2 Guelph Storm
01/2 Guelph Storm M-Cup

ZVYAGIN, SERGEI
97/8 Quad City Mallards
98/9 Quad City Mallards

ZWAKMAN, GREG
92/3 Minnesota G'Gophers
93/4 Minnesota G'Gophers
94/5 Minnesota G'Gophers

ZWIJACK, TIM
80/1 Soo Greyhounds

ZWIKEL, ALAIN
79 Panini Sticker 340

ZWYER, DAVE
92/3 MPS SJHL 148

ZYEV, YURI
00/1 Mir 176

ZYTYNSKY, TARAS
83/4 Springfield Indians 24
79/0 Montréal Juniors B&W
79/0 Montréal Jrs. Colour

ZYUZIN, ANDREI
96/7 All-Sport PPF 77, 197
96/7 Autograph Coll. 50, ✍ Aut.
98/9 Be A Player 116, ✍ Aut. 116
99/0 BAP Mem. 214, SL-16
00/1 BAP Mem. 279
95/6 Classic 69, ✍ Aut.
95/6 Future Legends ✍ SSD-8
99/0 NHL Power Play
97/8 Omega 208
98/9 Pacific 394
98/9 Panini Sticker 213
99/0 Panini Sticker 149
92 Québec Pee Wee 1462
00/1 Signature 38, ✍ Aut. 134
99/0 SPx 140
98/9 SPx Finite 134
98/9 UD Choice 179
98/9 UD3 18, 78, 138
98/9 Upper Deck 168
99/0 Upper Deck 289
00/1 Upper Deck 389
98/9 UD Black Diam. 73
98/9 UD G. Reserve 168
99/0 UD G. Reserve 289
98/9 UD MVP 171
99/0 WGretzky 157
97/8 Kentucky Tho'blades
98/9 Kentucky Tho'blades

ZYWITZA, SVEN
94/5 DEL 13
95/6 DEL 14
96/7 DEL 14